SCOTT

# 2023 STANDARD POSTAGE STAMP CATALOGUE

ONE HUNDRED AND SEVENTY-NINTH EDITION IN SIX VOLUMES

## Volume 5B

### PIT-SAM


| | |
|---|---|
| EDITOR-IN-CHIEF | Jay Bigalke |
| EDITOR-AT-LARGE | Donna Houseman |
| CONTRIBUTING EDITOR | Charles Snee |
| EDITOR EMERITUS | James E. Kloetzel |
| SENIOR EDITOR /NEW ISSUES AND VALUING | Martin J. Frankevicz |
| ADMINISTRATIVE ASSISTANT/CATALOGUE LAYOUT | Eric Wiessinger |
| PRINTING AND IMAGE COORDINATOR | Stacey Mahan |
| SENIOR GRAPHIC DESIGNER | Cinda McAlexander |
| SALES DIRECTOR | David Pistello |
| SALES DIRECTOR | Eric Roth |
| SALES DIRECTOR | Brenda Wyen |
| SALES REPRESENTATIVE | Julie Dahlstrom |

Released August 2022

Includes New Stamp Listings through the June 2022 *Linn's Stamp News Monthly* Catalogue Update




AMOS MEDIA

1660 Campbell Road, Suite A, Sidney, OH 45365

Publishers of *Linn's Stamp News, Linn's Stamp News Monthly, Coin World* and *Coin World Monthly.*

# Table of contents



See the following volumes for other country listings:
Volume 1A: United States, United Nations, Abu Dhabi-Australia; Volume 1B: Austria-B
Volume 2A: C-Cur; Volume 2B: Cyp-F
Volume 3A: G; Volume 3B: H-I
Volume 4A: J-L; Volume 4B: M
Volume 5A: N-Phil
Volume 6A: San-Tete; Volume 6B: Thai-Z

**Scott Catalogue Mission Statement**

The Scott Catalogue Team exists to serve the recreational, educational and commercial hobby needs of stamp collectors and dealers.
We strive to set the industry standard for philatelic information and products by developing and providing goods that help collectors identify, value, organize and present their collections.
Quality customer service is, and will continue to be, our highest priority.
We aspire toward achieving total customer satisfaction.



ISBN 978-0-89487-661-5

Library of Congress Card No. 2-3301

# What's new for 2023 Scott Standard Volu

Another catalog season is upon us as we continue the journey of the 154-year history of the Scott catalogs. The 2023 volumes are the 179th edition of the Scott *Standard Postage Stamp Catalogue*. Volume 5A includes listings for the countries of the world Namibia through Philippines.

Listings for Pitcairn Islands through Samoa can be found in Volume 5B.

This year's covers feature the New Caledonia 1989 58-franc French Revolution Bicentennial stamp (Scott 614) from a set of three with the themes of liberty, equality and fraternity on the Vol. 5A catalog and the Poland 1986 15-zloty Greco-Roman Wrestling stamp (Scott 2753) from a set of six victories of Polish athletes at the 1985 World Championships on Vol. 5B.

The time period in which we were working on this year's catalog continued to be interrupted by the COVID-19 pandemic. In regard to new issues, stamps from some locations proved harder than usual to obtain because of transportation issues worldwide.

However, the Scott catalog editors worked tirelessly to stay up to date as best as possible.

The stamps of Nepal were reviewed with approximately 750 value changes made reflecting a mix of increases and decreases. One of the notable increases was for the 1-anna Sripech and Crossed Khurkis stamp (Scott 7) which moved from $50 in unused and used conditions to $90 and $120, respectively. One modern increase was for the 2013 Nepal Red Cross Society 50th anniversary stamp (908) that went from $2.25 to $2.75 in unused condition.

Namibia was reviewed with nearly 200 value changes made. One standout increase was a 1992 Views of Swakopmund souvenir sheet of four (Scott 717a) which went from 95¢ in unused condition and 70¢ used to $3.25 and $2.50, respectively. Some relatively recent stamp issues also showed slight increases, but slight decreases also were noted in between 1992 to 2003.

The stamps of Nigeria were looked at closely with approximately 100 value changes made that showed both increases and decreases. The 1986 set of 14 stamps (Scott 488-500) moved from $5.85 in unused condition to $7.10. This set of stamps features many different themes including an image of a Volkswagen Automobile Assembly Factory, to telephone operators, and a stamp showing coconut harvesting.

Pitcairn Islands was reviewed with slightly more than 300 value changes made, nearly a third of which were increases. Among the increases was for the first set of 10 stamps from 1940-51 (Scott 1-8 that includes two lettered major numbers) that went from $66.75 to $84.75 in unused condition and in used condition from $29.60 to $41.05.

The stamps of Rwanda were looked at closely and nearly 600 value changes were made, mostly slight decreases.

**The first set of 1940-51 Pitcairn Islands stamps (Scott 1-8) increased in value in unused condition from $66.75 to $84.75 for Vol. 5 of the Scott *Standard Postage Stamp Catalog*. Shown here are the low and high denomination stamps from the set.**

One exceptio for the Cogwhee souvenir sheets, valued at $4.50 each in unused and used condition, that were bumped up slightly to $4.75 each, respectively.

A look at the stamps Philippines netted approximately 100 value changes. Editorially, a few sheets received status upgrades to a minor letter listing status. Those are listed in the Number Additions page in this volume.

The countries of New Caledonia and French New Hebrides were also reviewed with a handful of value changes made across both.

Many other countries received reviews that are not noted in this letter. We encourage you to pay special attention to the Number Additions, Deletions and Changes listing in this volume. We also suggest reading the catalog introduction, which includes an abundance of useful information.

Lastly, the Scott *Stamp Illustrated Identifier,* formerly included as the Illustrated Identifier in each Scott Standard catalog volume, continues to be offered as a separate publication.

The softcover 6-inch-by-9-inch booklet makes it easier to identify stamps while consulting listings in the Scott catalog without having to flip back and forth. To purchase, visit online at www.amosadvantage.com.

A digital subscription is also available for the Scott catalogs, and information about the subscription can be found online at www.amosadvantage.com.

Best wishes in your collecting pursuits!

Jay Bigalke, Scott catalog editor-in-chief

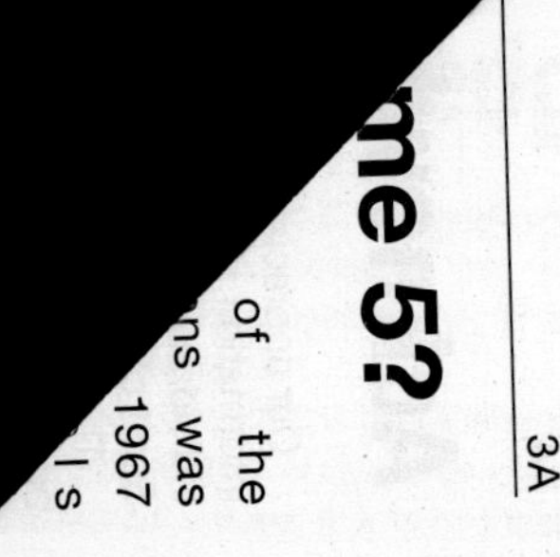

# ...ents

...o the following individuals who have assisted us in preparing ...Scott catalogues. Some helpers prefer anonymity. These ...eir stamp knowledge with others through the medium of the

...ion that is in addition to the hundreds of dealer price lists and ...catalogues and realizations that were used in producing the ...d here that we have been able to obtain information on items ...d advertisements. Support from these people goes beyond ...hey also are key to editorial changes.

> A special acknowledgment to Liane and Sergio Sismondo of The Classic Collector for their assistance and knowledge sharing that have aided in the preparation of this year's Standard and Classic Specialized Catalogues.

Clifford J. Alexander
(Carriers and Locals Society)
Roland Austin
Michael & Cecilia Ball (A To Z Stamps)
Jim Bardo (Bardo Stamps)
John Birkinbine II
Brian M. Bleckwenn
(The Philatelic Foundation)
Les Bootman
Roger S. Brody
Tom Brougham
(Canal Zone Study Group)
Paul and Josh Buchsbayew
(Cherrystone Auctions, Inc.)
Timothy Bryan Burgess
Tina and John Carlson (JET Stamps)
Jay T. Carrigan
Carlson Chambliss
Bob Coale
Tony L. Crumbley
(Carolina Coin and Stamp, Inc.)
Christopher Dahle
Charles Deaton
Bob and Rita Dumaine
(Sam Houston Duck Co.)
Charles Epting (H.R. Harmer)
Mike Farrell
David Feldman International Auctioneers
Robert A. Fisher
Jeffrey M. Forster
Robert S. Freeman
Henry L. Gitner
(Henry Gitner Philatelists, Inc.)
Stan Goldfarb

Marc E. Gonzales
Daniel E. Grau
Bruce Hecht (Bruce L. Hecht Co.)
Eric Jackson
Michael Jaffe (Michael Jaffe Stamps, Inc.)
William A. (Bill) Jones
Allan Katz (Ventura Stamp Co.)
Patricia A. Kaufmann
(Civil War Philatelic Society)
Jon Kawaguchi
(Ryukyu Philatelic Specialist Society)
Han Ki Kim
Ingert Kuzych
Ulf Lindahl (Ethiopian Philatelic Society)
Ignacio Llach (Filatelia Llach, S.L.)
William K. McDaniel
Pat McElroy
Brian Metz
Mark S. Miller (India Study Circle)
Gary Morris (Pacific Midwest Co.)
Peter Mosiondz Jr.
Bruce M. Moyer
(Moyer Stamps & Collectables)
Scott Murphy
Dr. Tiong Tak Ngo
Nik & Lisa Oquist
Don Peterson
(International Philippine Philatelic Society)
Stanley M. Piller
(Stanley M. Piller & Associates)
Todor Drumev Popov
Dr. Charles Posner
Peter W. W. Powell

Ed Reiser (Century Stamp Co.)
Ghassan D. Riachi
Robert G. Rufe
Theodosios D. Sampson Ph.D.
Dennis W. Schmidt
Joyce & Chuck Schmidt
Guy Shaw
(Mexico-Elmhurst Philatelic Society International)
J. Randall Shoemaker
(Philatelic Stamp Authentication and Grading, Inc.)
Sergio and Liane Sismondo
(The Classic Collector)
Jay Smith
Telah Smith
Mark Stelmacovich
Scott R. Trepel
(Siegel Auction Galleries, Inc.)
Dan Undersander
Steven Unkrich
Herbert R. Volin
Philip T. Wall
Val Zabijaka (Zabijaka Auctions)

# Addresses, telephone numbers, web sites, email addresses of general and specialized philatelic societies

Collectors can contact the following groups for information about the philately of the areas within the scope of these societies, or inquire about membership in these groups. Aside from the general societies, we limit this list to groups that specialize in particular fields of philately, particular areas covered by the Scott *Standard Postage Stamp Catalogue*, and topical groups. Many more specialized philatelic society exist than those listed below. These addresses are updated yearly, and they are, to the best of our knowledge, correct and current. Groups should inform the editors of address changes whenever they occur. The editors also want to hear from other such specialized groups not listed.

Unless otherwise noted all website addresses begin with http://

## General Societies

**American Philatelic Society,** 100 Match Factory Place, Bellefonte, PA 16823-1367; (814) 933-3803; https://stamps.org; apsinfo@stamps.org

**International Society of Worldwide Stamp Collectors,** Joanne Murphy, M.D., P.O. Box 19006, Sacramento, CA 95819; www.iswsc.org; executivedirector@iswsc.org

**Royal Philatelic Society of Canada,** P.O. Box 69080, St. Clair Post Office, Toronto, ON M4T 3A1 Canada; (888) 285-4143; www.rpsc.org; info@rpsc.org

**Royal Philatelic Society London,** 15 Abchurch Lane, London EX4N 7BW, United Kingdom; +44 (0) 20 7486 1044; www.rpsl.org.uk; secretary@rpsl.org.uk

## Libraries, Museums, and Research Groups

**American Philatelic Research Library,** 100 Match Factory Place, Bellefonte, PA 16823; (814) 933-3803; www.stamplibrary.org; library@stamps.org.

**V. G. Greene Philatelic Research Foundation,** P.O. Box 69100, St. Clair Post Office, Toronto, ON M4T 3A1, Canada; (416) 921-2073; info@greenefoundation.ca

### Aero/Astro Philately

**American Air Mail Society,** Stephen Reinhard, P.O. Box 110, Mineola, NY 11501; www.americanairmailsociety.org; sreinhard1@optonline.net

## Postal History

**Auxiliary Markings Club,** Jerry Johnson, 6621 W. Victoria Ave., Kennewick, WA 99336; www.postal-markings.org; membership-2010@postal-markings.org

**Postage Due Mail Study Group,** Bob Medland, Camway Cottage, Nanny Hurn's Lane, Cameley, Bristol BS39 5AJ, United Kingdom; 01761 45959; www.postageduemail.org.uk; secretary.pdmsg@gmail.com

**Postal History Society,** Yamil Kouri, 405 Waltham St. #347, Lexington, MA 02421; www.postalhistorysociety.org; yhkouri@massmed.org

**Post Mark Collectors Club,** Bob Milligan, 7014 Woodland Oaks Drive, Magnolia, TX 77354; (281) 259-2735; www.postmarks.org; bob.milligan0@gmail.com

**U.S. Cancellation Club,** Roger Curran, 18 Tressler Blvd., Lewisburg, PA 17837; rdcnrc@ptd.net

### Revenues and Cinderellas

**American Revenue Association,** Lyman Hensley, 473 E. Elm St., Sycamore, IL 60178-1934; www.revenuer.org; ilrno2@netzero.net

**Christmas Seal and Charity Stamp Society,** John Denune Jr., 234 E. Broadway, Granville, OH 43023; (740) 814-6031; www.seal-society.org

**National Duck Stamp Collectors Society,** Anthony J. Monico, P.O. Box 43, Harleysville, PA 19438-0043; www.ndscs.org; ndscs@ndscs.org

**State Revenue Society,** Kent Gray, P.O. Box 67842, Albuquerque, NM 87193; www.staterevenue.org; srssecretary@comcast.net

## Thematic Philately

**Americana Unit,** Dennis Dengel, 17 Peckham Road, Poughkeepsie, NY 12603-2018; www.americanaunit.org; ddengel@americanaunit.org

**American Topical Association,** Jennifer Miller, P.O. Box 2143, Greer, SC 29652-2143; (618) 985-5100; americantopical.org; ata@americantopical.org

**Astronomy Study Unit,** Leonard Zehr, 1411 Chateau Ave., Windsor, ON N8P 1M2, Canada; (416) 833-9317; www.astronomystudyunit.net; lenzehr@gmail.com

**Bicycle Stamps Club,** Corey Hjalseth, 1102 Broadway, Suite 200, Tacoma, WA 98402; (253) 318-6222; www.bicyclestampsclub.org; coreyh@evergreenhomeloans.com

**Biology Unit,** Chris Dahle, 1401 Linmar Drive NE, Cedar Rapids, IA 52402-3724; www.biophilately.org; chris-dahle@biophilately.org

**Bird Stamp Society,** Mr. S. A. H. (Tony) Statham, Ashlyns Lodge, Chesham Road, Berkhamsted, Herts HP4 2ST United Kingdom; www.bird-stamps.org/bss; tony.statham@sky.com

**Captain Cook Society,** Jerry Yucht, 8427 Leale Ave., Stockton, CA 95212, www.captaincooksociety.com; us@captaincooksociety.com

**The CartoPhilatelic Society,** Marybeth Sulkowski, 2885 Sanford Ave., SW, #32361, Grandville, MI 49418-1342; www.mapsonstamps.org; secretary@mapsonstamps.org

**Casey Jones Railroad Unit,** Jeff Lough, 2612 Redbud Land, Apt. C, Lawrence, KS 66046; www.uqp.de/cjr; jeffydplaugh@gmail.com

**Cats on Stamps Study Unit,** Robert D. Jarvis, 2731 Teton Lane, Fairfield, CA 94533; www.catstamps.info; catmews1@yahoo.com

**Chemistry and Physics on Stamps Study Unit,** Dr. Roland Hirsch, 13830 Metcalf Ave., Apt. 15218, Overland Park, KS 66223-8017; (301) 792-6296; www.cpossu.org; rfhirsch@cpossu.org

**Chess on Stamps Study Unit,** Barry Keith, 511 First St. N., Apt. 106; Charlottesville, VA 22902; www.chessonstamps.org; keithfam@embarqmail.com

**Cricket Philatelic Society,** A. Melville-Brown, 11 Weppons, Ravens Road, Shorham-by-Sea, West Sussex BN43 5AW, United Kingdom; www.cricketstamp.net; mel.cricket.100@googlemail.com

**Earth's Physical Features Study Group,** Fred Klein, 515 Magdalena Ave., Los Altos, CA 94024; http://epfsu.jeffhayward.com; epfsu@jeffhayward.com

**Ebony Society of Philatelic Events and Reflections (ESPER),** Don Neal, P.O. Box 5245, Somerset, NJ 08875-5245; www.esperstamps.org; esperdon@verizon.net

**Europa Study Unit,** Tonny E. Van Loij, 3002 S. Xanthia St.; Denver, CO 80231-4237; (303) 752-0189; www.europastudyunit.org; tvanloij@gmail.com

**Fire Service in Philately,** John Zaranek, 81 Hillpine Road, Cheektowaga, NY 14227-2259; (716) 668-3352; jczaranek@roadrunner.com

**Gastronomy on Stamps Study Unit,** David Wolfersburger, 5062 NW 35th Lane Road, Ocala, FL 34482; (314) 494-3795; www.gastronomystamps.org

**Gay and Lesbian History on Stamps Club,** Joe Petronie, P.O. Box 190842, Dallas, TX 75219-0842; www.glhsonline.org; glhsc@aol.com

**Gems, Minerals and Jewelry Study Unit,** Fred Haynes, 10 Country Club Drive, Rochester, NY 14618-3720; fredmhaynes55@gmail.com

**Graphics Philately Association,** Larry Rosenblum. 1030 E. El Camino Real, PMB 107, Sunnyvale, CA 94087-3759; www.graphics-stamps.org; larry@graphics-stamps.org

**Journalists, Authors and Poets on Stamps,** Christopher D. Cook, 7222 Hollywood Road, Berrien Springs, MI 49103; cdcook2@gmail.com

**Lighthouse Stamp Society,** www.lighthousestampsociety.org; dalene@lighthousestampsociety.org

**Lions International Stamp Club,** David McKirdy, s-Gravenwetering 248, 3062 SJ Rotterdam, Netherlands; 31(0) 10 212 0313; www.lisc.nl; davidmckirdy@aol.com

**Masonic Study Unit,** Gene Fricks, 25 Murray Way, Blackwood, NJ 08012-4400; genefricks@comcast.net

**Medical Subjects Unit,** Dr. Frederick C. Skvara, P.O. Box 6228, Bridgewater, NJ 08807; fcskvara@optonline.net

**Napoleonic Age Philatelists,** Ken Berry, 4117 NW 146th St., Oklahoma City, OK 73134-1746; (405) 748-8646; www.nap-stamps.org; krb4117@att.net

**Old World Archaeological Study Unit,** Caroline Scannell, 14 Dawn Drive, Smithtown, NY 11787-176; www.owasu.org; editor@owasu.org

**Petroleum Philatelic Society International,** Feitze Papa, 922 Meander Drive, Walnut Creek, CA 94598-4239; www.ppsi.org.uk; oildad@astound.net

**Rotary on Stamps Fellowship,** Gerald L. Fitzsimmons, 105 Calle Ricardo, Victoria, TX 77904; www.rotaryonstamps.org; glfitz@suddenlink.net

**Scouts on Stamps Society International,** Woodrow (Woody) Brooks, 498 Baldwin Road, Akron, OH 44312; (330) 612-1294; www.sossi.org; secretary@sossi.org

**Ships on Stamps Unit,** Erik Th. Matzinger, Voorste Havervelden 30, 4822 AL Breda, Netherlands; www.shipsonstamps.org; erikships@gmail.com

**Space Topic Study Unit,** David Blog, P.O. Box 174, Bergenfield, NJ 07621; www.space-unit.com; davidblognj@gmail.com

**Stamps on Stamps Collectors Club,** Michael Merritt, 73 Mountainside Road, Mendham, NJ 07945; www.stampsonstamps.org; michael@mischu.me

**Windmill Study Unit,** Walter J. Hallien, 607 N. Porter St., Watkins Glenn, NY 14891-1345; (607) 229-3541; www.windmillworld.com

**Wine On Stamps Study Unit,** David Wolfersburger, 5062 NW 35th Lane Road, Ocala, FL 34482; (314) 494-3795; www.wine-on-stamps.org;

## United States

**American Air Mail Society,** Stephen Reinhard, P.O. Box 110, Mineola, NY 11501; www.americanairmailsociety.org; sreinhard1@optonline.net

**American First Day Cover Society,** P.O. Box 246, Colonial Beach VA 22443-0246; (520) 321-0880; www.afdcs.org; afdcs@afdcs.org

**Auxiliary Markings Club,** Jerry Johnson, 6621 W. Victoria Ave., Kennewick, WA 99336; www.postal-markings.org; membership-2010@postal-markings.org

**American Plate Number Single Society,** Rick Burdsall, APNSS Secretary, P.O. BOX 1023, Palatine, IL 60078-1023; www.apnss.org; apnss.sec@gmail.com

**American Revenue Association,** Lyman Hensley, 473 E. Elm St., Sycamore, IL 60178-1934; www.revenuer.org; ilrno2@netzero.net

**American Society for Philatelic Pages and Panels,** Ron Walenciak, P.O. Box 1042, Washington Township, NJ 07676; www.asppp.org; ron.walenciak@asppp.org

**Canal Zone Study Group,** Mike Drabik, P.O. Box 281, Bolton, MA 01740, www.canalzonestudygroup.com; czsgsecretary@gmail.com

**Carriers and Locals Society,** John Bowman, 14409 Pentridge Drive, Corpus Christi, TX 78410; (361) 933-0757; www.pennypost.org; jbowman@stx.rr.com

**Christmas Seal & Charity Stamp Society,** John Denune Jr., 234 E. Broadway, Granville, OH 43023; (740) 814-6031; www.seal-society.org; john@christmasseals.net

**Civil War Philatelic Society,** Patricia A. Kaufmann, 10194 N. Old State Road, Lincoln, DE 19960-3644; (302) 422-2656; www.civilwarphilatelicsociety.org; trishkauf@comcast.net

**Error, Freaks, and Oddities Collectors Club,** Scott Shaulis, P.O. Box 549, Murrysville, PA 15668-0549; (724) 733-4134; www.efocc.org; scott@shaulisstamps.com

**National Duck Stamp Collectors Society,** Anthony J. Monico, P.O. Box 43, Harleysville, PA 19438-0043; www.ndscs.org; ndscs@ndscs.org

**Plate Number Coil Collectors Club (PNC3),** Gene Trinks, 16415 W. Desert Wren Court, Surprise, AZ 85374; (623) 322-4619; www.pnc3.org; gctrinks@cox.net

**Post Mark Collectors Club,** Bob Milligan, 7014 Woodland Oaks Drive, Magnolia, TX 77354; (281) 259-2735; www.postmarks.org; bob.milligan0@gmail.com

**Souvenir Card Collectors Society,** William V. Kriebel, www.souvenircards.org; kriebewv@drexel.edu

**United Postal Stationery Society,** Dave Kandziolka, 404 Sundown Drive, Knoxville, TN 37934; www.upss.org; membership@upss.org

**U.S. Cancellation Club,** Roger Curran, 18 Tressler Blvd., Lewisburg, PA 17837; rdcnrc@ptd.net

**U.S. Philatelic Classics Society,** Rob Lund, 2913 Fulton St., Everett, WA 98201-3733; www.uspcs.org; membershipchairman@uspcs.org

**US Possessions Philatelic Society,** Daniel F. Ring, P.O. Box 113, Woodstock, IL 60098; http://uspps.tripod.com; danielfring@hotmail.com

**United States Stamp Society,** Rod Juell, P.O. Box 3508, Joliet, IL 60434-3508; www.usstamps.org; execsecretary@usstamps.org

## Africa

**Bechuanalands and Botswana Society,** Otto Peetoom, Roos, East Yorkshire HU12 0LD, United Kingdom; 44(0)1964 670239; www.bechuanalandphilately.com; info@bechuanalandphilately.com

**Egypt Study Circle,** Mike Murphy, 11 Waterbank Road, Bellingham, London SE6 3DJ United Kingdom; (44) 0203 6737051; www.egyptstudycircle.org.uk; secretary@egyptstudycircle.org.uk

**Ethiopian Philatelic Society,** Ulf Lindahl, 21 Westview Place, Riverside, CT 06878; (203) 722-0769; https://ethiopianphilatelicsociety.weebly.com; ulindahl@optonline.net

**Liberian Philatelic Society,** P.O. Box 1570, Parker, CO 80134; www.liberiastamps.org; liberiastamps@comcast.net

**Orange Free State Study Circle,** J. R. Stroud, RDPSA, 24 Hooper Close, Burnham-on-sea, Somerset TA8 1JQ United Kingdom; 44 1278 782235; www.orangefreestatephilately.org.uk; richard@richardstroud.plus.com

**Philatelic Society for Greater Southern Africa,** David McNamee, 15 Woodland Drive, Alamo, CA 94507; www.psgsa.org; alan.hanks@sympatico.ca

**Rhodesian Study Circle,** William R. Wallace, P.O. Box 16381, San Francisco, CA 94116; (415) 564-6069; www.rhodesianstudycircle.org.uk; bwall8rscr@earthlink.net

**Society for Moroccan and Tunisian Philately,** S.P.L.M., 206, Bld Pereire, 75017 Paris, France; http://splm-philatelie.org; splm206@aol.com

**South Sudan Philatelic Society,** William Barclay, 1370 Spring Hill Road, South Londonderry, VT 05155; barclayphilatelics@gmail.com

**Sudan Study Group,** Andy Neal, Bank House, Coedway, Shrewsbury SY5 9AR United Kingdom; www.sudanstamps.org; andywneal@gmail.com

**Transvaal Study Circle,** c/o 9 Meadow Road, Gravesend, Kent DA11 7LR United Kingdom; www.transvaalstamps.org.uk; transvaalstudycircle@aol.co.uk

**West Africa Study Circle,** Martin Bratzel, 1233 Virginia Ave., Windsor, ON N8S 2Z1 Canada; www.wasc.org.uk; marty_bratzel@yahoo.ca

## Asia

**Aden & Somaliland Study Group,** Malcom Lacey, 108 Dalestorth Road, Sutton-in-Ashfield, Nottinghamshire NG17 3AA, United Kingdom; www.stampdomain.com/aden; neil53williams@yahoo.co.uk

**Burma (Myanmar) Philatelic Study Circle,** Michael Whittaker, 1, Ecton Leys, Hillside, Rugby, Warwickshire CV22 5SL United Kingdom; https://burmamyanmarphilately.wordpress.com/burma-myanmar-philatelic-study-circle; manningham8@mypostoffice.co.uk

**Ceylon Study Circle,** Rodney W. P. Frost, 42 Lonsdale Road, Cannington, Bridgwater, Somerset TA5 2JS United Kingdom; 01278 652592; www.ceylonsc.org; rodney.frost@tiscali.co.uk

**China Stamp Society,** H. James Maxwell, 1050 W. Blue Ridge Blvd., Kansas City, MO 64145-1216; www.chinastampsociety.org; president@chinastampsociety.org

**Hong Kong Philatelic Society,** John Tang, G.P.O. Box 446, Hong Kong; www.hkpsociety.com; hkpsociety@outlook.com

**Hong Kong Study Circle,** Robert Newton, www.hongkongstudycircle.com/index.html; newtons100@gmail.com

**India Study Circle,** John Warren, P.O. Box 7326, Washington, DC 20044; (202) 488-7443; https://indiastudycircle.org; jw-kbw@earthlink.net

**International Philippine Philatelic Society,** James R. Larot, Jr., 4990 Bayleaf Court, Martinez, CA 94553; (925) 260-5425; www.theipps.info; jlarot@ccwater.com

**International Society for Japanese Philately,** P.O. Box 1283, Haddonfield NJ 08033; www.isjp.org; secretary@isjp.org

**Iran Philatelic Study Circle,** Nigel Gooch, Marchwood, 56, Wickham Ave., Bexhill-on-Sea, East Sussex TN39 3ER United Kingdom; www.iranphilately.org; nigelmgooch@gmail.com

**Korea Stamp Society,** Peter Corson, 1109 Gunnison Place, Raleigh, NC 27609; (919) 787-7611; koreastampsociety.org; pbcorson@aol.com

**Nepal & Tibet Philatelic Study Circle,** Colin Hepper, 12 Charnwood Close, Peterborough, Cambs PE2 9BZ United Kingdom; http://fuchs-online.com/ntpsc; ntpsc@fuchs-online.com

**Pakistan Philatelic Study Circle,** Jeff Siddiqui, P.O. Box 7002, Lynnwood, WA 98046; jeffsiddiqui@msn.com

**Society of Indo-China Philatelists,** Ron Bentley, 2600 N. 24th St., Arlington, VA 22207; (703) 524-1652; www.sicp-online.org; ron.bentley@verizon.net

**Society of Israel Philatelists, Inc.,** Sarah Berezenko, 100 Match Factory Place, Bellefonte, PA 16823-1367; (814) 933-3803 ext. 212; www.israelstamps.com; israelstamps@gmail.com

## Australasia and Oceania

**Australian States Study Circle of the Royal Sydney Philatelic Club,** Ben Palmer, G.P.O. 1751, Sydney, NSW 2001 Australia; http://club.philas.org.au/states

**Fellowship of Samoa Specialists,** Trevor Shimell, 18 Aspen Drive, Newton Abbot, Devon TQ12 4TN United Kingdom; www.samoaexpress.org; trevor.shimell@gmail.com

**Malaya Study Group,** Michael Waugh, 151 Roker Lane, Pudsey, Leeds LS28 9ND United Kingdom; http://malayastudygroup.com; mawpud43@gmail.com

**New Zealand Society of Great Britain,** Michael Wilkinson, 121 London Road, Sevenoaks, Kent TN13 1BH United Kingdom; 01732 456997; www.nzsgb.org.uk; mwilkin799@aol.com

**Pacific Islands Study Circle,** John Ray, 24 Woodvale Ave., London SE25 4AE United Kingdom; www.pisc.org.uk; secretary@pisc.org.uk

**Papuan Philatelic Society,** Steven Zirinsky, P.O. Box 49, Ansonia Station, New York, NY 10023; (718) 706-0616; www.papuanphilatelicsociety.com; szirinsky@cs.com

**Pitcairn Islands Study Group,** Dr. Everett L. Parker, 207 Corinth Road, Hudson, ME 04449-3057; (207) 573-1686; www.pisg.net; eparker@hughes.net

**Ryukyu Philatelic Specialist Society,** Laura Edmonds, P.O. Box 240177, Charlotte, NC 28224-0177; (336) 509-3739; www.ryukyustamps.org; secretary@ryukyustamps.org

**Society of Australasian Specialists / Oceania,** Steve Zirinsky, P.O. Box 230049, New York, NY 10023-0049; www.sasoceania.org; president@sosoceania.org

**Sarawak Specialists' Society,** Stephen Schumann, 2417 Cabrallo Drive, Hayward, CA 94545; (510) 785-4794; www.britborneostamps.org.uk; vpnam@s-s-s.org.uk

**Western Australia Study Group,** Brian Pope, P.O. Box 423, Claremont, WA 6910 Australia; (61) 419 843 943; www.wastudygroup.com; wastudygroup@hotmail.com

## Europe

**American Helvetia Philatelic Society,** Richard T. Hall, P.O. Box 15053, Asheville, NC 28813-0053; www.swiss-stamps.org; secretary2@swiss-stamps.org

**American Society for Netherlands Philately,** Hans Kremer, 50 Rockport Court, Danville, CA 94526; (925) 820-5841; www.asnp1975.com; hkremer@usa.net

**Andorran Philatelic Study Circle,** David Hope, 17 Hawthorn Drive, Stalybridge, Cheshire SK15 1UE United Kingdom; www.andorranpsc.org.uk; andorranpsc@btinternet.com

**Austria Philatelic Society,** Ralph Schneider, P.O. Box 978, Iowa Park, TX 76376; (940) 213-5004; www.austriaphilatelicsociety.com; rschneiderstamps@gmail.com

**Channel Islands Specialists Society,** Richard Flemming, Burbage, 64 Falconers Green, Hinckley, Leicestershire, LE102SX, United Kingdom; www.ciss.uk; secretary@ciss.uk

**Cyprus Study Circle,** Rob Wheeler, 47 Drayton Ave., London W13 0LE United Kingdom; www.cyprusstudycircle.org; robwheeler47@aol.com

**Danish West Indies Study Unit of Scandinavian Collectors Club,** Arnold Sorensen, 7666 Edgedale Drive, Newburgh, IN 47630; (812) 480-6532; www.scc-online.org; valbydwi@hotmail.com

**Eire Philatelic Association,** John B. Sharkey, 1559 Grouse Lane, Mountainside, NJ 07092-1340; www.eirephilatelicassoc.org; jsharkeyepa@me.com

**Faroe Islands Study Circle,** Norman Hudson, 40 Queen's Road, Vicar's Cross, Chester CH3 5HB United Kingdom; www.faroeislandssc.org; jntropics@hotmail.com

**France & Colonies Philatelic Society,** Edward Grabowski, 111 Prospect St., 4C, Westfield, NJ 07090; (908) 233-9318; www.franceandcolsps.org; edjjg@alum.mit.edu

**Germany Philatelic Society,** P.O. Box 6547, Chesterfield, MO 63006-6547; www.germanyphilatelicusa.org; info@germanyphilatelicsocietyusa.org

**Gibraltar Study Circle,** Susan Dare, 22, Byways Park, Strode Road, Clevedon, North Somerset BS21 6UR United Kingdom; www.gibraltarstudycircle.wordpress.com; smldare@yahoo.co.uk

**International Society for Portuguese Philately,** Clyde Homen, 1491 Bonnie View Road, Hollister, CA 95023-5117; www.portugalstamps.com; ispp1962@sbcglobal.net

**Italy and Colonies Study Circle,** Richard Harlow, 7 Duncombe House, 8 Manor Road, Teddington, Middlesex TW118BE United Kingdom; 44 208 977 8737; www.icsc-uk.com; richardharlow@outlook.com

**Liechtenstudy USA,** Paul Tremaine, 410 SW Ninth St., Dundee, OR 97115-9731; (503) 538-4500; www.liechtenstudy.org; tremaine@liechtenstudy.org

**Lithuania Philatelic Society,** Audrius Brazdeikis, 9915 Murray Landing, Missouri City, TX 77459; (281) 450-6224; www.lithuanianphilately.com/lps; audrius@lithuanianphilately.com

**Luxembourg Collectors Club,** Gary B. Little, 7319 Beau Road, Sechelt, BC V0N 3A8 Canada; (604) 885-7241; http://lcc.luxcentral.com; gary@luxcentral.com

**Plebiscite-Memel-Saar Study Group of the German Philatelic Society,** Clayton Wallace, 100 Lark Court, Alamo, CA 94507; claytonwallace@comcast.net

**Polonus Polish Philatelic Society,** Daniel Lubelski, P.O. Box 2212, Benicia, CA 94510; (419) 410-9115; www.polonus.org; info@polonus.org

**Rossica Society of Russian Philately,** Alexander Kolchinsky, 1506 Country Lake Drive, Champaign, IL 61821-6428; www.rossica.org; alexander.kolchinsky@rossica.org

**Scandinavian Collectors Club,** Alan Warren, Scandinavian Collectors Club, P.O. Box 39, Exton PA 19341-0039; (612) 810-8640; www.scc-online.org; alanwar@att.net

**Society for Czechoslovak Philately,** Tom Cossaboom, P.O. Box 4124, Prescott, AZ 86302; (928) 771-9097; www.csphilately.org; klfck1@aol.com

**Society for Hungarian Philately,** Alan Bauer, P.O. Box 4028, Vineyard Haven, MA 02568; (617) 645-4045; www.hungarianphilately.org; alan@hungarianstamps.com

**Spanish Study Circle,** Edith Knight, www.spaincircle.wixsite.com/spainstudycircle; spaincircle@gmail.com

**Ukrainian Philatelic & Numismatic Society,** Martin B. Tatuch, 5117 8th Road N., Arlington, VA 22205-1201; www.upns.org; treasurer@upns.org

**Vatican Philatelic Society,** Dennis Brady, 4897 Ledyard Drive, Manlius NY 13104-1514; www.vaticanphilately.org; dbrady7534@gmail.com

**Yugoslavia Study Group,** Michael Chant, 1514 N. Third Ave., Wausau, WI 54401; 208-748-9919; www.yugosg.org; membership@yugosg.org

## Interregional Societies

**American Society of Polar Philatelists,** Alan Warren, P.O. Box 39, Exton, PA 19341-0039; (610) 321-0740; www.polarphilatelists.org; alanwar@att.net

**First Issues Collector's Club,** Kurt Streepy, 3128 E. Mattatha Drive, Bloomington, IN 47401; www.firstissues.org; secretary@firstissues.org

**Former French Colonies Specialist Society,** Col.fra, BP 628, 75367 Paris, France; www.colfra.org; postmaster@colfra.org

**France & Colonies Philatelic Society,** Edward Grabowski, 111 Prospect St., 4C, Westfield, NJ 07090; (908) 233-9318, www.franceandcolsps.org; edjjg@alum.mit.edu

**Joint Stamp Issues Society,** Richard Zimmermann, 29A, Rue Des Eviats, 67220 Lalaye, France; www.philarz.net; richard.zimmermann@club-internet.fr

**The King George VI Collectors Society,** Brian Livingstone, 21 York Mansions, Prince of Wales Drive, London SW11 4DL United Kingdom; www.kg6.info; livingstone484@btinternet.com

**International Society of Reply Coupon Collectors,** Peter Robin, P.O. Box 353, Bala Cynwyd, PA 19004; peterrobin@verizon.net

**Italy and Colonies Study Circle,** Richard Harlow, 7 Duncombe House, 8 Manor Road, Teddington, Middlesex TW118BE United Kingdom; 44 208 977 8737; www.icsc-uk.com; richardharlow@outlook.com

**St. Helena, Ascension & Tristan Da Cunha Philatelic Society,** Dr. Everett L. Parker, 207 Corinth Road, Hudson, ME 04449-3057; (207) 573-1686; www.shatps.org; eparker@hughes.net

**United Nations Philatelists,** Blanton Clement, Jr., P.O. Box 146, Morrisville, PA 19067-0146; www.unpi.com; bclemjunior@gmail.com

## Latin America

**Asociación Filatélica de Panamá,** Edward D. Vianna B. ASOFILPA, 0819-03400, El Dorado, Panama; http://asociacionfilatelicadepanama.blogspot.com; asofilpa@gmail.com

**Asociacion Mexicana de Filatelia (AMEXFIL),** Alejandro Grossmann, Jose Maria Rico, 129, Col. Del Valle, 3100 Mexico City, DF Mexico; www.amexfil.mx; amexfil@gmail.com

**Associated Collectors of El Salvador,** Pierre Cahen, Vipsal 1342, P.O. Box 02-5364, Miami FL 33102; www.elsalvadorphilately.org; sfes-aces@elsalvadorphilately.org

**Association Filatelic de Costa Rica,** Giana Wayman (McCarty), #SJO 4935, P.O. Box 025723, Miami, FL 33102-5723; 011-506-2-228-1947; scotland@racsa.co.cr

**Brazil Philatelic Association,** William V. Kriebel, www.brazilphilatelic.org, info@brazilphilatelic.org

**Canal Zone Study Group,** Mike Drabik, P.O. Box 281, Bolton, MA 01740; www.canalzonestudygroup.com; czsgsecretary@gmail.com

**Colombia-Panama Philatelic Study Group,** Allan Harris, 26997 Hemmingway Ct, Hayward CA 94542-2349; www.copaphil.org; copaphilusa@aol.com

**Falkland Islands Philatelic Study Groups,** Morva White, 42 Colton Road, Shrivenham, Swindon SN6 8AZ United Kingdom; 44(0) 1793 783245; www.fipsg.org.uk; morawhite@supanet.com

**Federacion Filatelica de la Republica de Honduras,** Mauricio Mejia, Apartado Postal 1465, Tegucigalpa, D.C. Honduras; 504 3399-7227; www.facebook.com/filateliadehonduras; ffrh@hotmail.com

**International Cuban Philatelic Society (ICPS),** Ernesto Cuesta, P.O. Box 34434, Bethesda, MD 20827; (301) 564-3099; www.cubafil.org; ecuesta@philat.com

**International Society of Guatemala Collectors,** Jaime Marckwordt, 449 St. Francis Blvd., Daly City, CA 94015-2136; (415) 997-0295; www.guatemalastamps.com; president@guatamalastamps.com

**Mexico-Elmhurst Philatelic Society International,** Eric Stovner, P.O. Box 10097, Santa Ana, CA 92711-0097; www.mepsi.org; treasurer@mepsi.org

**Nicaragua Study Group,** Erick Rodriguez, 11817 S. W. 11th St., Miami, FL 33184-2501; nsgsec@yahoo.com

## North America (excluding United States)

**British Caribbean Philatelic Study Group,** Bob Stewart, 7 West Dune Lane, Long Beach Township, NJ 08008; (941) 379-4108; www.bcpsg.com; bcpsg@comcast.net

**British North America Philatelic Society,** Andy Ellwood, 10 Doris Ave., Gloucester, ON K1T 3W8 Canada; www.bnaps.org; secretary@bnaps.org

**British West Indies Study Circle,** Steve Jarvis, 5 Redbridge Drive, Andover, Hants SP10 2LF United Kingdom; 01264 358065; www.bwisc.org; info@bwisc.org

**Bermuda Collectors Society,** John Pare, 405 Perimeter St., Mount Horeb, WI 53572; (608) 852-7358; www.bermudacollectorssociety.com; pare16@mhtc.net

**Haiti Philatelic Society,** Ubaldo Del Toro, 5709 Marble Archway, Alexandria, VA 22315; www.haitiphilately.org; u007ubi@aol.com

**Hawaiian Philatelic Society,** Gannon Sugimura, P.O. Box 10115, Honolulu, HI 96816-0115, www.hpshawaii.com; hiphilsoc@gmail.com

## Stamp Dealer Associations

**American Stamp Dealers Association, Inc.,** P.O. Box 513, Centre Hall PA 16828; (800) 369-8207; www.americanstampdealer.com; asda@americanstampdealer.com

**National Stamp Dealers Association,** Sheldon Ruckens, President, 3643 Private Road 18, Pinckneyville, IL 62274-3426; (618) 357-5497; www.nsdainc.org; nsda@nsdainc.org

## Youth Philately

**Young Stamp Collectors of America,** 100 Match Factory Place, Bellefonte, PA 16823; (814) 933-3803; https://stamps.org/learn/youth-in-philately; ysca@stamps.org

# Expertizing services

The following organizations will, for a fee, provide expert opinions about stamps submitted to them. Collectors should contact these organizations to find out about their fees and requirements before submitting philatelic material to them. The listing of these groups here is not intended as an endorsement by Amos Media Co.

## General Expertizing Services

**American Philatelic Expertizing Service (a service of the American Philatelic Society)**
100 Match Factory Place
Bellefonte PA 16823-1367
(814) 237-3803
www.stamps.org/stamp-authentication
apex@stamps.org
Areas of Expertise: Worldwide

**BPA Expertising, Ltd.**
P.O. Box 1141
Guildford, Surrey, GU5 0WR
United Kingdom
www.bpaexpertising.com
sec@bpaexpertising.org
Areas of Expertise: British Commonwealth, Great Britain, Classics of Europe, South America and the Far East

**Philatelic Foundation**
22 E. 35th St., 4th Floor
New York NY 10016
(212) 221-6555
www.philatelicfoundation.org
philatelicfoundation@verizon.net
Areas of Expertise: U.S. & Worldwide

**Philatelic Stamp Authentication and Grading, Inc.**
P.O. Box 41-0880
Melbourne FL 32941-0880
(305) 345-9864
www.psaginc.com
info@psaginc.com
Areas of Expertise: U.S., Canal Zone, Hawaii, Philippines, Canada & Provinces

**Professional Stamp Experts**
P.O. Box 539309
Henderson NV 89053-9309
(702) 776-6522
www.gradingmatters.com
www.psestamp.com
info@gradingmatters.com
Areas of Expertise: Stamps and Covers of U.S., U.S. Possessions, British Commonwealth

**Royal Philatelic Society London Expert Committee**
15 Abchurch Lane
London, EX4N 7BW
United Kingdom
www.rpsl.limited/experts.aspx
experts@rpsl.limited
Areas of Expertise: Worldwide

## Expertizing Services Covering Specific Fields or Countries

**China Stamp Society Expertizing Service**
1050 W. Blue Ridge Blvd.
Kansas City MO 64145
(816) 942-6300
hjmesq@aol.com
Areas of Expertise: China

**Civil War Philatelic Society Authentication Service**
C/O Stefan T. Jaronski
P.O. Box 232
Sidney, MT 59270-0232
www.civilwarphilatelicsociety.org/authentication/
authentication@civilwarphilatelicsociety.org
Areas of Expertise: Confederate stamps and postal history

**Errors, Freaks and Oddities Collectors Club Expertizing Service**
138 East Lakemont Drive
Kingsland GA 31548
(912) 729-1573
Areas of Expertise: U.S. errors, freaks and oddities

**Hawaiian Philatelic Society Expertizing Service**
P.O. Box 10115
Honolulu HI 96816-0115
www.stampshows.com/hps.html
hiphilsoc@gmail.com
Areas of Expertise: Hawaii

**Hong Kong Stamp Society Expertizing Service**
P.O. Box 206
Glenside PA 19038
Areas of Expertise: Hong Kong

**International Association of Philatelic Experts United States Associate members:**

Paul Buchsbayew
119 W. 57th St.
New York NY 10019
(212) 977-7734
Areas of Expertise: Russia, Soviet Union

William T. Crowe
P.O. Box 2090
Danbury CT 06813-2090
wtcrowe@aol.com
Areas of Expertise: United States

John Lievsay
(see American Philatelic Expertizing Service and Philatelic Foundation)
Areas of Expertise: France

Robert W. Lyman
P.O. Box 348
Irvington on Hudson NY 10533
(914) 591-6937
Areas of Expertise: British North America, New Zealand

Robert Odenweller
P.O. Box 401
Bernardsville NJ 07924-0401
(908) 766-5460
Areas of Expertise: New Zealand, Samoa to 1900

Sergio Sismondo
The Regency Tower, Suite 1109
770 James St.
Syracuse NY 13203
(315) 422-2331
Areas of Expertise: British East Africa, Cameroons, Cape of Good Hope, Canada, British North America

**International Society for Japanese Philately Expertizing Committee**
132 North Pine Terrace
Staten Island NY 10312-4052
(718) 227-5229
Areas of Expertise: Japan and related areas, except WWII Japanese Occupation issues

**International Society for Portuguese Philately Expertizing Service**
P.O. Box 43146
Philadelphia PA 19129-3146
(215) 843-2106
s.s.washburne@worldnet.att.net
Areas of Expertise: Portugal and Colonies

**Mexico-Elmhurst Philatelic Society International Expert Committee**
Expert Committee Administrator
Marc E. Gonzales
P.O. Box 29040
Denver CO 80229-0040
www.mepsi.org/expert_committeee.htm
expertizations@mepsi.org
Areas of Expertise: Mexico

**Ukrainian Philatelic & Numismatic Society Expertizing Service**
30552 Dell Lane
Warren MI 48092-1862
Areas of Expertise: Ukraine, Western Ukraine

**V. G. Greene Philatelic Research Foundation**
P.O. Box 69100
St. Clair Post Office
Toronto, ON M4T 3A1
Canada
(416) 921-2073
www.greenefoundation.ca
info@greenefoundation.ca
Areas of Expertise: British North America

# Information on catalogue values, grade and condition

## Catalogue value

The Scott Catalogue value is a retail value; that is, an amount you could expect to pay for a stamp in the grade of Very Fine with no faults. Any exceptions to the grade valued will be noted in the text. The general introduction on the following pages and the individual section introductions further explain the type of material that is valued. The value listed for any given stamp is a reference that reflects recent actual dealer selling prices for that item.

Dealer retail price lists, public auction results, published prices in advertising and individual solicitation of retail prices from dealers, collectors and specialty organizations have been used in establishing the values found in this catalogue. Amos Media Co. values stamps, but Amos Media is not a company engaged in the business of buying and selling stamps as a dealer.

Use this catalogue as a guide for buying and selling. The actual price you pay for a stamp may be higher or lower than the catalogue value because of many different factors, including the amount of personal service a dealer offers, or increased or decreased interest in the country or topic represented by a stamp or set. An item may occasionally be offered at a lower price as a "loss leader," or as part of a special sale. You also may obtain an item inexpensively at public auction because of little interest at that time or as part of a large lot.

Stamps that are of a lesser grade than Very Fine, or those with condition problems, generally trade at lower prices than those given in this catalogue. Stamps of exceptional quality in both grade and condition often command higher prices than those listed.

Values for pre-1900 unused issues are for stamps with approximately half or more of their original gum. Stamps with most or all of their original gum may be expected to sell for more, and stamps with less than half of their original gum may be expected to sell for somewhat less than the values listed. On rarer stamps, it may be expected that the original gum will be somewhat more disturbed than it will be on more common issues. Post-1900 unused issues are assumed to have full original gum. From breakpoints in most countries' listings, stamps are valued as never hinged, due to the wide availability of stamps in that condition. These notations are prominently placed in the listings and in the country information preceding the listings. Some countries also feature listings with dual values for hinged and never-hinged stamps.

## Grade

A stamp's grade and condition are crucial to its value. The accompanying illustrations show examples of Very Fine stamps from different time periods, along with examples of stamps in Fine to Very Fine and Extremely Fine grades as points of reference. When a stamp seller offers a stamp in any grade from fine to superb without further qualifying statements, that stamp should not only have the centering grade as defined, but it also should be free of faults or other condition problems.

**FINE** stamps (illustrations not shown) have designs that are quite off center, with the perforations on one or two sides very close to the design but not quite touching it. There is white space between the perforations and the design that is minimal but evident to the unaided eye. Imperforate stamps may have small margins, and earlier issues may show the design just touching one edge of the stamp design. Very early perforated issues normally will have the perforations slightly cutting into the design. Used stamps may have heavier than usual cancellations.

**FINE-VERY FINE** stamps will be somewhat off center on one side, or slightly off center on two sides. Imperforate stamps will have two margins of at least normal size, and the design will not touch any edge. For perforated stamps, the perfs are well clear of the design, but are still noticeably off center. *However, early issues of a country may be printed in such a way that the design naturally is very close to the edges. In these cases, the perforations may cut into the design very slightly.* Used stamps will not have a cancellation that detracts from the design.

**VERY FINE** stamps will be just slightly off center on one or two sides, but the design will be well clear of the edge. The stamp will present a nice, balanced appearance. Imperforate stamps will be well centered within normal-sized margins. *However, early issues of many countries may be printed in such a way that the perforations may touch the design on one or more sides. Where this is the case, a boxed note will be found defining the centering and margins of the stamps being valued.* Used stamps will have light or otherwise neat cancellations. This is the grade used to establish Scott Catalogue values.

**EXTREMELY FINE** stamps are close to being perfectly centered. Imperforate stamps will have even margins that are slightly larger than normal. Even the earliest perforated issues will have perforations clear of the design on all sides.

**Amos Media Co. recognizes that there is no formally enforced grading scheme for postage stamps, and that the final price you pay or obtain for a stamp will be determined by individual agreement at the time of transaction.**

## Condition

*Grade addresses* only centering and (for used stamps) cancellation. *Condition* refers to factors other than grade that affect a stamp's desirability.

Factors that can increase the value of a stamp include exceptionally wide margins, particularly fresh color, the presence of selvage, and plate or die varieties. Unusual cancels on used stamps (particularly those of the 19th century) can greatly enhance their value as well.

Factors other than faults that decrease the value of a stamp include loss of original gum, regumming, a hinge remnant or foreign object adhering to the gum, natural inclusions, straight edges, and markings or notations applied by collectors or dealers.

Faults include missing pieces, tears, pin or other holes, surface scuffs, thin spots, creases, toning, short or pulled perforations, clipped perforations, oxidation or other forms of color changelings, soiling, stains, and such man-made changes as reperforations or the chemical removal or lightening of a cancellation.

## Grading illustrations

On the following two pages are illustrations of various stamps from countries appearing in this volume. These stamps are arranged by country, and they represent early or important issues that are often found in widely different grades in the marketplace. The editors believe the illustrations will prove useful in showing the margin size and centering that will be seen on the various issues.

In addition to the matters of margin size and centering, collectors are reminded that the very fine stamps valued in the Scott catalogues also will possess fresh color and intact perforations, and they will be free from defects.

Examples shown are computer-manipulated images made from single digitized master illustrations.

## Stamp illustrations used in the catalogue

It is important to note that the stamp images used for identification purposes in this catalogue may not be indicative of the grade of stamp being valued. Refer to the written discussion of grades on this page and to the grading illustrations on the following two pages for grading information.

Fine-Very Fine →

SCOTT CATALOGUES VALUE STAMPS IN THIS GRADE

Very Fine →

Extremely Fine →

Fine-Very Fine →

SCOTT CATALOGUES VALUE STAMPS IN THIS GRADE

Very Fine →

Extremely Fine →

**Fine-Very Fine** →

**SCOTT CATALOGUES VALUE STAMPS IN THIS GRADE**

**Very Fine** →

**Extremely Fine** →

**Fine-Very Fine** →

**SCOTT CATALOGUES VALUE STAMPS IN THIS GRADE**

**Very Fine** →

**Extremely Fine** →

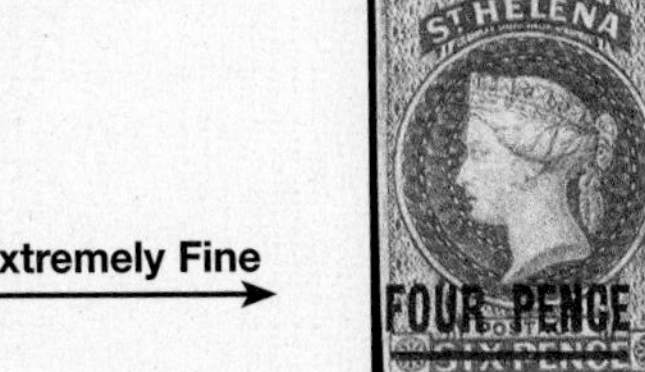

## Gum Conditions

For purposes of helping to determine the gum condition and value of an unused stamp, Scott presents the following chart which details different gum conditions and indicates how the conditions correlate with the Scott values for unused stamps. Used together, the Illustrated Grading Chart on the previous pages and this Illustrated Gum Chart should allow catalogue users to better understand the grade and gum condition of stamps valued in the Scott catalogues.

**Never Hinged (NH; ★★):** A never-hinged stamp will have full original gum that will have no hinge mark or disturbance. The presence of an expertizer's mark does not disqualify a stamp from this designation.

**Original Gum (OG; ★):** Pre-1900 stamps should have approximately half or more of their original gum. On rarer stamps, it may be expected that the original gum will be somewhat more disturbed than it will be on more common issues. Post-1900 stamps should have full original gum. Original gum will show some disturbance caused by a previous hinge(s) which may be present or entirely removed. The actual value of a post-1900 stamp will be affected by the degree of hinging of the full original gum.

**Disturbed Original Gum:** Gum showing noticeable effects of humidity, climate or hinging over more than half of the gum. The significance of gum disturbance in valuing a stamp in any of the Original Gum categories depends on the degree of disturbance, the rarity and normal gum condition of the issue and other variables affecting quality.

**Regummed (RG; (★))**: A regummed stamp is a stamp without gum that has had some type of gum privately applied at a time after it was issued. This normally is done to deceive collectors and/or dealers into thinking that the stamp has original gum and therefore has a higher value. A regummed stamp is considered the same as a stamp with none of its original gum for purposes of grading.

| Gum Categories: | MINT N.H. | ORIGINAL GUM (O.G.) | | | | NO GUM |
|---|---|---|---|---|---|---|
| |  **Mint Never Hinged** *Free from any disturbance* |  **Lightly Hinged** *Faint impression of a removed hinge over a small area* |  **Hinge Mark or Remnant** *Prominent hinged spot with part or all of the hinge remaining* |  **Large part o.g.** *Approximately half or more of the gum intact* |  **Small part o.g.** Approximately less than half of the gum intact | **No gum** *Only if issued with gum* |
| **Commonly Used Symbol:** | ★★ | ★ | ★ | ★ | ★ | (★) |
| Pre-1900 Issues (Pre-1881 for U.S.) | *Very fine pre-1900 stamps in these categories trade at a premium over Scott value* | | | Scott Value for "Unused" | | Scott "No Gum" listings for selected unused classic stamps |
| From 1900 to breakpoints for listings of never-hinged stamps | Scott "Never Hinged" listings for selected unused stamps | Scott Value for "Unused" (Actual value will be affected by the degree of hinging of the full o.g.) | | | | |
| *From breakpoints noted for many countries* | Scott Value for "Unused" | | | | | |

# Catalogue listing policy

It is the intent of Amos Media Co. to list all postage stamps of the world in the Scott *Standard Postage Stamp Catalogue*. The only strict criteria for listing is that stamps be decreed legal for postage by the issuing country and that the issuing country actually have an operating postal system. Whether the primary intent of issuing a given stamp or set was for sale to postal patrons or to stamp collectors is not part of our listing criteria. Scott's role is to provide basic comprehensive postage stamp information. It is up to each stamp collector to choose which items to include in a collection.

It is Scott's objective to seek reasons why a stamp should be listed, rather than why it should not. Nevertheless, there are certain types of items that will not be listed. These include the following:

1. Unissued items that are not officially distributed or released by the issuing postal authority. If such items are officially issued at a later date by the country, they will be listed. Unissued items consist of those that have been printed and then held from sale for reasons such as change in government, errors found on stamps or something deemed objectionable about a stamp subject or design.

2. Stamps "issued" by non-existent postal entities or fantasy countries, such as Nagaland, Occusi-Ambeno, Staffa, Sedang, Torres Straits and others. Also, stamps "issued" in the names of legitimate, stamp-issuing countries that are not authorized by those countries.

3. Semi-official or unofficial items not required for postage. Examples include items issued by private agencies for their own express services. When such items are required for delivery, or are valid as prepayment of postage, they are listed.

4. Local stamps issued for local use only. Postage stamps issued by governments specifically for "domestic" use, such as Haiti Scott 219-228, or the United States nondenominated stamps, are not considered to be locals, since they are valid for postage throughout the country of origin.

5. Items not valid for postal use. For example, a few countries have issued souvenir sheets that are not valid for postage. This area also includes a number of worldwide charity labels (some denominated) that do not pay postage.

6. Egregiously exploitative issues such as stamps sold for far more than face value, stamps purposefully issued in artificially small quantities or only against advance orders, stamps awarded only to a selected audience such as a philatelic bureau's standing order customers, or stamps sold only in conjunction with other products. All of these kinds of items are usually controlled issues and/or are intended for speculation. These items normally will be included in a footnote.

7. Items distributed by the issuing government only to a limited group, club, philatelic exhibition or a single stamp dealer or other private company. These items normally will be included in a footnote.

8. Stamps not available to collectors. These generally are rare items, all of which are held by public institutions such as museums. The existence of such items often will be cited in footnotes.

The fact that a stamp has been used successfully as postage, even on international mail, is not in itself sufficient proof that it was legitimately issued. Numerous examples of so-called stamps from non-existent countries are known to have been used to post letters that have successfully passed through the international mail system.

There are certain items that are subject to interpretation. When a stamp falls outside our specifications, it may be listed along with a cautionary footnote.

A number of factors are considered in our approach to analyzing how a stamp is listed. The following list of factors is presented to share with you, the catalogue user, the complexity of the listing process.

**Additional printings** — "Additional printings" of a previously issued stamp may range from an item that is totally different to cases where it is impossible to differentiate from the original. At least a minor number (a small-letter suffix) is assigned if there is a distinct change in stamp shade, noticeably redrawn design, or a significantly different perforation measurement. A major number (numeral or numeral and capital-letter combination) is assigned if the editors feel the "additional printing" is sufficiently different from the original that it constitutes a different issue.

**Commemoratives** — Where practical, commemoratives with the same theme are placed in a set. For example, the U.S. Civil War Centennial set of 1961-65 and the Constitution Bicentennial series of 1989-90 appear as sets. Countries such as Japan and Korea issue such material on a regular basis, with an announced, or at least predictable, number of stamps known in advance. Occasionally, however, stamp sets that were released over a period of years have been separated. Appropriately placed footnotes will guide you to each set's continuation.

**Definitive sets** — Blocks of numbers generally have been reserved for definitive sets, based on previous experience with any given country. If a few more stamps were issued in a set than originally expected, they often have been inserted into the original set with a capital-letter suffix, such as U.S. Scott 1059A. If it appears that many more stamps than the originally allotted block will be released before the set is completed, a new block of numbers will be reserved, with the original one being closed off. In some cases, such as the U.S. Transportation and Great Americans series, several blocks of numbers exist. Appropriately placed footnotes will guide you to each set's continuation.

**New country** — Membership in the Universal Postal Union is not a consideration for listing status or order of placement within the catalogue. The index will tell you in what volume or page number the listings begin.

**"No release date" items** — The amount of information available for any given stamp issue varies greatly from country to country and even from time to time. Extremely comprehensive information about new stamps is available from some countries well before the stamps are released. By contrast some countries do not provide information about stamps or release dates. Most countries, however, fall between these extremes. A country may provide denominations or subjects of stamps from upcoming issues that are not issued as planned. Sometimes, philatelic agencies, those private firms hired to represent countries, add these later-issued items to sets well after the formal release date. This time period can range from weeks to years. If these items were officially released by the country, they will be added to the appropriate spot in the set. In many cases, the specific release date of a stamp or set of stamps may never be known.

**Overprints** — The color of an overprint is always noted if it is other than black. Where more than one color of ink has been used on overprints of a single set, the color used is noted. Early overprint and surcharge illustrations were altered to prevent their use by forgers.

**Personalized Stamps** — Since 1999, the special service of personalizing stamp vignettes, or labels attached to stamps, has been offered to customers by postal administrations of many countries. Sheets of these stamps are sold, singly or in quantity, only through special orders made by mail, in person, or through a sale on a computer website with the postal administrations or their agents for which an extra fee is charged, though some countries offer to collectors at face value personalized stamps having generic images in the vignettes or on the attached labels. It is impossible for any catalogue to know what images have been chosen by customers. Images can be 1) owned or created by the customer, 2) a generic image, or 3) an image pulled from a library of stock images on the stamp creation website. It is also impossible to know the quantity printed for any stamp having a particular image. So from a valuing standpoint, any image is equivalent to any other image for any personalized stamp having the same catalogue number. Illustrations of personalized stamps in the catalogue are not always those of stamps having generic images.

Personalized items are listed with some exceptions. These include:

1. Stamps or sheets that have attached labels that the customer cannot personalize, but which are nonetheless marketed as "personalized," and are sold for far more than the franking value.

2. Stamps or sheets that can be personalized by the customer, but where a portion of the print run must be ceded to the issuing country for sale to other customers.

3. Stamps or sheets that are created exclusively for a particular commercial client, or clients, including stamps that differ from any similar stamp that has been made available to the public.

4. Stamps or sheets that are deliberately conceived by the issuing authority that have been, or are likely to be, created with an excessive number of different face values, sizes, or other features that are changeable.

5. Stamps or sheets that are created by postal administrations using the same system of stamp personalization that has been put in place for use by the public that are printed in limited quantities and sold above face value.

6. Stamps or sheets that are created by licensees not directly affiliated or controlled by a postal administration.

Excluded items may or may not be footnoted.

**Se-tenants** — Connected stamps of differing features (se-tenants) will be listed in the format most commonly collected. This includes pairs, blocks or larger multiples. Se-tenant units are not always symmetrical. An example is Australia Scott 508, which is a block of seven stamps. If the stamps are primarily collected as a unit, the major number may be assigned to the multiple, with minors going to each component stamp. In cases where continuous-design or other unit se-tenants will receive significant postal use, each stamp is given a major Scott number listing. This includes issues from the United States, Canada, Germany and Great Britain, for example.

# Understanding the listings

On the opposite page is an enlarged "typical" listing from this catalogue. Below are detailed explanations of each of the highlighted parts of the listing.

**1 Scott number** — Scott catalogue numbers are used to identify specific items when buying, selling or trading stamps. Each listed postage stamp from every country has a unique Scott catalogue number. Therefore, Germany Scott 99, for example, can only refer to a single stamp. Although the Scott catalogue usually lists stamps in chronological order by date of issue, there are exceptions. When a country has issued a set of stamps over a period of time, those stamps within the set are kept together without regard to date of issue. This follows the normal collecting approach of keeping stamps in their natural sets.

When a country issues a set of stamps over a period of time, a group of consecutive catalogue numbers is reserved for the stamps in that set, as issued. If that group of numbers proves to be too few, capital-letter suffixes, such as "A" or "B," may be added to existing numbers to create enough catalogue numbers to cover all items in the set. A capital-letter suffix indicates a major Scott catalogue number listing. Scott generally uses a suffix letter only once. Therefore, a catalogue number listing with a capital-letter suffix will seldom be found with the same letter (lower case) used as a minor-letter listing. If there is a Scott 16A in a set, for example, there will seldom be a Scott 16a. However, a minor-letter "a" listing may be added to a major number containing an "A" suffix (Scott 16Aa, for example).

Suffix letters are cumulative. A minor "b" variety of Scott 16A would be Scott 16Ab, not Scott 16b.

There are times when a reserved block of Scott catalogue numbers is too large for a set, leaving some numbers unused. Such gaps in the numbering sequence also occur when the catalogue editors move an item's listing elsewhere or have removed it entirely from the catalogue. Scott does not attempt to account for every possible number, but rather attempts to assure that each stamp is assigned its own number.

Scott numbers designating regular postage normally are only numerals. Scott numbers for other types of stamps, such as air post, semi-postal, postal tax, postage due, occupation and others have a prefix consisting of one or more capital letters or a combination of numerals and capital letters.

**2 Illustration number** — Illustration or design-type numbers are used to identify each catalogue illustration. For most sets, the lowest face-value stamp is shown. It then serves as an example of the basic design approach for other stamps not illustrated. Where more than one stamp use the same illustration number, but have differences in design, the design paragraph or the description line clearly indicates the design on each stamp not illustrated. Where there are both vertical and horizontal designs in a set, a single illustration may be used, with the exceptions noted in the design paragraph or description line.

When an illustration is followed by a lower-case letter in parentheses, such as "A2(b)," the trailing letter indicates which overprint or surcharge illustration applies.

Illustrations normally are 70 percent of the original size of the stamp. Oversized stamps, blocks and souvenir sheets are reduced even more. Overprints and surcharges are shown at 100 percent of their original size if shown alone, but are 70 percent of original size if shown on stamps. In some cases, the illustration will be placed above the set, between listings or omitted completely. Overprint and surcharge illustrations are not placed in this catalogue for purposes of expertizing stamps.

**3 Paper color** — The color of a stamp's paper is noted in italic type when the paper used is not white.

**4 Listing styles** — There are two principal types of catalogue listings: major and minor.

Major listings are in a larger type style than minor listings. The catalogue number is a numeral that can be found with or without a capital-letter suffix, and with or without a prefix.

Minor listings are in a smaller type style and have a small-letter suffix or (if the listing immediately follows that of the major number) may show only the letter. These listings identify a variety of the major item. Examples include perforation and shade differences, multiples (some souvenir sheets, booklet panes and se-tenant combinations), and singles of multiples.

Examples of major number listings include 16, 28A, B97, C13A, 10N5, and 10N6A. Examples of minor numbers are 16a and C13Ab.

**5 Basic information about a stamp or set** — Introducing each stamp issue is a small section (usually a line listing) of basic information about a stamp or set. This section normally includes the date of issue, method of printing, perforation, watermark and, sometimes, some additional information of note. *Printing method, perforation and watermark apply to the following sets until a change is noted.* Stamps created by overprinting or surcharging previous issues are assumed to have the same perforation, watermark, printing method and other production characteristics as the original. Dates of issue are as precise as Scott is able to confirm and often reflect the dates on first-day covers, rather than the actual date of release.

**6 Denomination** — This normally refers to the face value of the stamp; that is, the cost of the unused stamp at the post office at the time of issue. When a denomination is shown in parentheses, it does not appear on the stamp. This includes the nondenominated stamps of the United States, Brazil and Great Britain, for example.

**7 Color or other description** — This area provides information to solidify identification of a stamp. In many recent cases, a description of the stamp design appears in this space, rather than a listing of colors.

**8 Year of issue** — In stamp sets that have been released in a period that spans more than a year, the number shown in parentheses is the year that stamp first appeared. Stamps without a date appeared during the first year of the issue. Dates are not always given for minor varieties.

**9 Value unused and Value used** — The Scott catalogue values are based on stamps that are in a grade of Very Fine unless stated otherwise. Unused values refer to items that have not seen postal, revenue or any other duty for which they were intended. Pre-1900 unused stamps that were issued with gum must have at least most of their original gum. Later issues are assumed to have full original gum. From breakpoints specified in most countries' listings, stamps are valued as never hinged. Stamps issued without gum are noted. Modern issues with PVA or other synthetic adhesives may appear ungummed. Unused self-adhesive stamps are valued as appearing undisturbed on their original backing paper. Values for used self-adhesive stamps are for examples either on piece or off piece. For a more detailed explanation of these values, please see the "Catalogue Value," "Condition" and "Understanding Valuing Notations" sections elsewhere in this introduction.

In some cases, where used stamps are more valuable than unused stamps, the value is for an example with a contemporaneous cancel, rather than a modern cancel or a smudge or other unclear marking. For those stamps that were released for postal and fiscal purposes, the used value represents a postally used stamp. Stamps with revenue cancels generally sell for less.

Stamps separated from a complete se-tenant multiple usually will be worth less than a pro-rated portion of the se-tenant multiple, and stamps lacking the attached labels that are noted in the listings will be worth less than the values shown.

**10 Changes in basic set information** — Bold type is used to show any changes in the basic data given for a set of stamps. These basic data categories include perforation gauge measurement, paper type, printing method and watermark.

**11 Total value of a set** — The total value of sets of three or more stamps issued after 1900 are shown. The set line also notes the range of Scott numbers and total number of stamps included in the grouping. The actual value of a set consisting predominantly of stamps having the minimum value of 25 cents may be less than the total value shown. Similarly, the actual value or catalogue value of se-tenant pairs or of blocks consisting of stamps having the minimum value of 25 cents may be less than the catalogue values of the component parts.

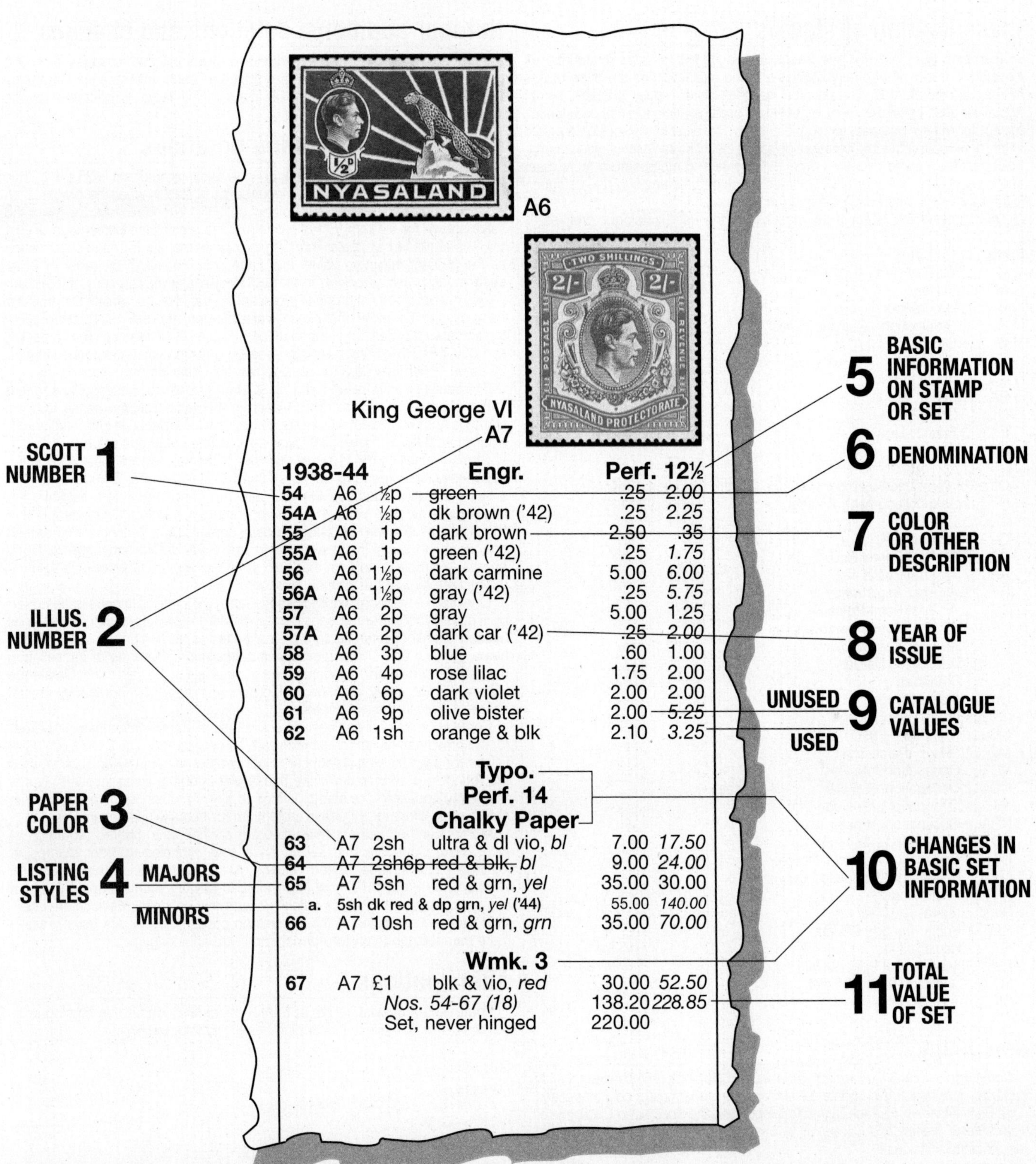
NYASALAND
A6
TWO SHILLINGS
2/- 2/-
POSTAGE
REVENUE
NYASALAND PROTECTORATE
King George VI
A7
1938-44 Engr. Perf. 12½
54 A6 ½p green .25 2.00
54A A6 ½p dk brown ('42) .25 2.25
55 A6 1p dark brown 2.50 .35
55A A6 1p green ('42) .25 1.75
56 A6 1½p dark carmine 5.00 6.00
56A A6 1½p gray ('42) .25 5.75
57 A6 2p gray 5.00 1.25
57A A6 2p dark car ('42) .25 2.00
58 A6 3p blue .60 1.00
59 A6 4p rose lilac 1.75 2.00
60 A6 6p dark violet 2.00 2.00
61 A6 9p olive bister 2.00 5.25
62 A6 1sh orange & blk 2.10 3.25
Typo.
Perf. 14
Chalky Paper
63 A7 2sh ultra & dl vio, bl 7.00 17.50
64 A7 2sh6p red & blk, bl 9.00 24.00
65 A7 5sh red & grn, yel 35.00 30.00
a. 5sh dk red & dp grn, yel ('44) 55.00 140.00
66 A7 10sh red & grn, grn 35.00 70.00
Wmk. 3
67 A7 £1 blk & vio, red 30.00 52.50
Nos. 54-67 (18) 138.20 228.85
Set, never hinged 220.00
SCOTT NUMBER 1
ILLUS. NUMBER 2
PAPER COLOR 3
LISTING STYLES 4 MAJORS
MINORS
5 BASIC INFORMATION ON STAMP OR SET
6 DENOMINATION
7 COLOR OR OTHER DESCRIPTION
8 YEAR OF ISSUE
UNUSED
9 CATALOGUE VALUES
USED
10 CHANGES IN BASIC SET INFORMATION
11 TOTAL VALUE OF SET

# Special notices

## Classification of stamps

The Scott Standard Postage Stamp Catalogue lists stamps by country of issue. The next level of organization is a listing by section on the basis of the function of the stamps. The principal sections cover regular postage, semi-postal, air post, special delivery, registration, postage due and other categories. Except for regular postage, catalogue numbers for all sections include a prefix letter (or number-letter combination) denoting the class to which a given stamp belongs. When some countries issue sets containing stamps from more than one category, the catalogue will at times list all of the stamps in one category (such as air post stamps listed as part of a postage set).

The following is a listing of the most commonly used catalogue prefixes.

**Prefix.......Category**
C..........Air Post
M.........Military
P..........Newspaper
N..........Occupation - Regular Issues
O..........Official
Q..........Parcel Post
J ..........Postage Due
RA .......Postal Tax
B..........Semi-Postal
E..........Special Delivery
MR.......War Tax

Other prefixes used by more than one country include the following:
H..........Acknowledgment of Receipt
I ...........Late Fee
CO .......Air Post Official
CQ.......Air Post Parcel Post
RAC.....Air Post Postal Tax
CF........Air Post Registration
CB .......Air Post Semi-Postal
CBO ....Air Post Semi-Postal Official
CE .......Air Post Special Delivery
EY........Authorized Delivery
S..........Franchise
G..........Insured Letter
GY .......Marine Insurance
MC.......Military Air Post
MQ .......Military Parcel Post
NC .......Occupation - Air Post
NO .......Occupation - Official
NJ........Occupation - Postage Due
NRA.....Occupation - Postal Tax
NB .......Occupation - Semi-Postal
NE .......Occupation - Special Delivery
QY .......Parcel Post Authorized Delivery
AR .......Postal-fiscal
RAJ......Postal Tax Due
RAB .....Postal Tax Semi-Postal
F ..........Registration
EB........Semi-Postal Special Delivery
EO .......Special Delivery Official
QE .......Special Handling

## New issue listings

Updates to this catalogue appear each month in the *Linn's Stamp News* monthly magazine. Included in this update are additions to the listings of countries found in the Scott *Standard Postage Stamp Catalogue* and the *Specialized Catalogue of United States Stamps and Covers,* as well as corrections and updates to current editions of this catalogue.

From time to time there will be changes in the final listings of stamps from the *Linn's Stamp News* magazine to the next edition of the catalogue. This occurs as more information about certain stamps or sets becomes available.

The catalogue update section of the *Linn's Stamp News* magazine is the most timely presentation of this material available. Annual subscriptions to *Linn's Stamp News* are available from Linn's Stamp News, Box 4129, Sidney, OH 45365-4129.

## Number additions, deletions and changes

A listing of catalogue number additions, deletions and changes from the previous edition of the catalogue appears in each volume. See Catalogue Number Additions, Deletions & Changes in the table of contents for the location of this list.

## Understanding valuing notations

The *minimum catalogue value* of an individual stamp or set is 25 cents. This represents a portion of the cost incurred by a dealer when he prepares an individual stamp for resale. As a point of philatelic-economic fact, the lower the value shown for an item in this catalogue, the greater the percentage of that value is attributed to dealer mark up and profit margin. In many cases, such as the 25-cent minimum value, that price does not cover the labor or other costs involved with stocking it as an individual stamp. The sum of minimum values in a set does not properly represent the value of a complete set primarily composed of a number of minimum-value stamps, nor does the sum represent the actual value of a packet made up of minimum-value stamps. Thus a packet of 1,000 different common stamps — each of which has a catalogue value of 25 cents — normally sells for considerably less than $250!

The *absence of a retail value* for a stamp does not necessarily suggest that a stamp is scarce or rare. A dash in the value column means that the stamp is known in a stated form or variety, but information is either lacking or insufficient for purposes of establishing a usable catalogue value.

Stamp values in *italics* generally refer to items that are difficult to value accurately. For expensive items, such as those priced at $1,000 or higher, a value in italics indicates that the affected item trades very seldom. For inexpensive items, a value in italics represents a warning. One example is a "blocked" issue where the issuing postal administration may have controlled one stamp in a set in an attempt to make the whole set more valuable. Another example is an item that sold at an extreme multiple of face value in the marketplace at the time of its issue.

One type of warning to collectors that appears in the catalogue is illustrated by a stamp that is valued considerably higher in used condition than it is as unused. In this case, collectors are cautioned to be certain the used version has a genuine and contemporaneous cancellation. The type of cancellation on a stamp can be an important factor in determining its sale price. Catalogue values do not apply to fiscal, telegraph or non-contemporaneous postal cancels, unless otherwise noted.

Some countries have released back issues of stamps in canceled-to-order form, sometimes covering as much as a 10-year period. The Scott Catalogue values for used stamps reflect canceled-to-order material when such stamps are found to predominate in the marketplace for the issue involved. Notes frequently appear in the stamp listings to specify which items are valued as canceled-to-order, or if there is a premium for postally used examples.

Many countries sell canceled-to-order stamps at a marked reduction of face value. Countries that sell or have sold canceled-to-order stamps at *full* face value include United Nations, Australia, Netherlands, France and Switzerland. It may be almost impossible to identify such stamps if the gum has been removed, because official government canceling devices are used. Postally used examples of these items on cover, however, are usually worth more than the canceled-to-order stamps with original gum.

## Abbreviations

Scott uses a consistent set of abbreviations throughout this catalogue to conserve space, while still providing necessary information.

**Color Abbreviations**

| | | |
|---|---|---|
| amb.......... amber | crim.........crimson | ol................. olive |
| anil........... aniline | cr.............. cream | olvn........... olivine |
| ap...............apple | dk................ dark | org .......... orange |
| aqua..aquamarine | dl...................dull | pck.........peacock |
| az...............azure | dp ............. deep | pnksh pinkish |
| bis............. bister | db .............. drab | Prus .......Prussian |
| bl..................blue | emer....... emerald | pur ........... purple |
| bld............. blood | gldn.......... golden | redsh........reddish |
| blk..............black | grysh........grayish | res............reseda |
| bril...........brilliant | grn ............ green | ros.............rosine |
| brn ........... brown | grnsh......greenish | ryl................royal |
| brnsh ....brownish | hel....... heliotrope | sal ...........salmon |
| brnz.......... bronze | hn..............henna | saph.......sapphire |
| brt............. bright | ind.............indigo | scar..........scarlet |
| brnt............burnt | int............intense | sep.............sepia |
| car..........carmine | lav .........lavender | sien ..........sienna |
| cer.............cerise | lem............lemon | sil ............... silver |
| chlky ......... chalky | lil .................. lilac | sl ...............slate |
| cham......chamois | lt...................light | stl ...............steel |
| chnt........chestnut | mag....... magenta | turq ...... turquoise |
| choc.....chocolate | man..........manila | ultra... ultramarine |
| chr.......... chrome | mar ......... maroon | Ven.........Venetian |
| cit.............. citron | mv............mauve | ver......... vermilion |
| cl................claret | multi..multicolored | vio..............violet |
| cob........... cobalt | mlky........... milky | yel............ yellow |
| cop.......... copper | myr............myrtle | yelsh .....yellowish |

When no color is given for an overprint or surcharge, black is the color used. Abbreviations for colors used for overprints and surcharges include: "(B)" or "(Blk)," black; "(Bl)," blue; "(R)," red; and "(G)," green.

Additional abbreviations in this catalogue are shown below:

Adm. ............Administration
AFL ..............American Federation of Labor
Anniv. ...........Anniversary
APS...............American Philatelic Society
Assoc............Association
ASSR. ...........Autonomous Soviet Socialist Republic
b....................Born
BEP...............Bureau of Engraving and Printing
Bicent. ..........Bicentennial
Bklt. ..............Booklet
Brit. ...............British
btwn.............Between
Bur. ...............Bureau
c. or ca. ........Circa
Cat. ...............Catalogue
Cent. .............Centennial, century, centenary
CIO ...............Congress of Industrial Organizations
Conf. .............Conference
Cong. ............Congress
Cpl. ...............Corporal
CTO .............Canceled to order
d....................Died
Dbl. ...............Double
EDU .............Earliest documented use
Engr..............Engraved
Exhib............Exhibition
Expo. ............Exposition
Fed................Federation
GB ................Great Britain
Gen. ..............General
GPO .............General post office
Horiz. ............Horizontal
Imperf. ..........Imperforate
Impt. .............Imprint
Intl.................International
Invtd.............Inverted
L....................Left
Lieut., lt.........Lieutenant
Litho.............Lithographed
LL..................Lower left
LR .................Lower right
mm ...............Millimeter
Ms.................Manuscript
Natl. .............National
No. ................Number
NY.................New York
NYC .............New York City
Ovpt. .............Overprint
Ovptd............Overprinted
P ...................Plate number
Perf. ..............Perforated, perforation
Phil................Philatelic
Photo. ...........Photogravure
PO.................Post office
Pr. .................Pair
P.R. ...............Puerto Rico
Prec. .............Precancel, precanceled
Pres. .............President
PTT ...............Post, Telephone and Telegraph
R ...................Right
Rio ................Rio de Janeiro
Sgt. ...............Sergeant
Soc. ..............Society
Souv..............Souvenir
SSR...............Soviet Socialist Republic, see ASSR
St. .................Saint, street
Surch. ...........Surcharge
Typo. .............Typographed
UL .................Upper left
Unwmkd. ......Unwatermarked
UPU ..............Universal Postal Union
UR.................Upper Right
US.................United States
USPOD .........United States Post Office Department
USSR............Union of Soviet Socialist Republics
Vert. ..............Vertical
VP .................Vice president
Wmk. ............Watermark
Wmkd. ..........Watermarked
WWI .............World War I
WWII .............World War II

## Examination

Amos Media Co. will not comment upon the genuineness, grade or condition of stamps, because of the time and responsibility involved. Rather, there are several expertizing groups that undertake this work for both collectors and dealers. Neither will Amos Media Co. appraise or identify philatelic material. The company cannot take responsibility for unsolicited stamps or covers sent by individuals.

All letters, emails, etc. are read attentively, but they are not always answered because of time considerations.

## How to order from your dealer

When ordering stamps from a dealer, it is not necessary to write the full description of a stamp as listed in this catalogue. All you need is the name of the country, the Scott catalogue number and whether the desired item is unused or used. For example, "Japan Scott 422 unused" is sufficient to identify the unused stamp of Japan listed as "422 A206 5y brown."

# Basic stamp information

A stamp collector's knowledge of the combined elements that make a given stamp issue unique determines his or her ability to identify stamps. These elements include paper, watermark, method of separation, printing, design and gum. On the following pages each of these important areas is briefly described.

## Paper

Paper is an organic material composed of a compacted weave of cellulose fibers and generally formed into sheets. Paper used to print stamps may be manufactured in sheets, or it may have been part of a large roll (called a web) before being cut to size. The fibers most often used to create paper on which stamps are printed include bark, wood, straw and certain grasses. In many cases, linen or cotton rags have been added for greater strength and durability. Grinding, bleaching, cooking and rinsing these raw fibers reduces them to a slushy pulp, referred to by paper makers as "stuff." Sizing and, sometimes, coloring matter is added to the pulp to make different types of finished paper.

After the stuff is prepared, it is poured onto sieve-like frames that allow the water to run off, while retaining the matted pulp. As fibers fall onto the screen and are held by gravity, they form a natural weave that will later hold the paper together. If the screen has metal bits that are formed into letters or images attached, it leaves slightly thinned areas on the paper. These are called watermarks.

When the stuff is almost dry, it is passed under pressure through smooth or engraved rollers — dandy rolls — or placed between cloth in a press to be flattened and dried.

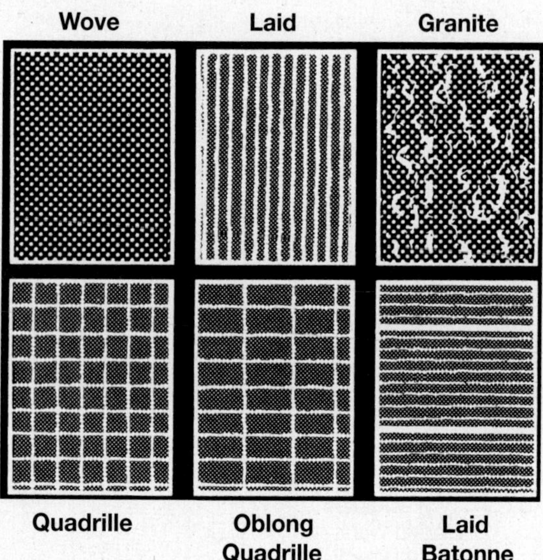


Stamp paper falls broadly into two types: wove and laid. The nature of the surface of the frame onto which the pulp is first deposited causes the differences in appearance between the two. If the surface is smooth and even, the paper will be of fairly uniform texture throughout. This is known as wove paper. Early papermaking machines poured the pulp onto a continuously circulating web of felt, but modern machines feed the pulp onto a cloth-like screen made of closely interwoven fine wires. This paper, when held to a light, will show little dots or points very close together. The proper name for this is "wire wove," but the type is still considered wove. Any U.S. or British stamp printed after 1880 will serve as an example of wire wove paper.

Closely spaced parallel wires, with cross wires at wider intervals, make up the frames used for what is known as laid paper. A greater thickness of the pulp will settle between the wires. The paper, when held to a light, will show alternate light and dark lines. The spacing and the thickness of the lines may vary, but on any one sheet of paper they are all alike. See Russia Scott 31-38 for examples of laid paper.

**Batonne,** from the French word meaning "a staff," is a term used if the lines in the paper are spaced quite far apart, like the printed ruling on a writing tablet. Batonne paper may be either wove or laid. If laid, fine laid lines can be seen between the batons.

**Quadrille** is the term used when the lines in the paper form little squares. Oblong quadrille is the term used when rectangles, rather than squares, are formed. Grid patterns vary from distinct to extremely faint. See Mexico-Guadalajara Scott 35-37 for examples of oblong quadrille paper.

Paper also is classified as thick or thin, hard or soft, and by color. Such colors may include yellowish, greenish, bluish and reddish.

Brief explanations of other types of paper used for printing stamps, as well as examples, follow.

**Colored** — Colored paper is created by the addition of dye in the paper-making process. Such colors may include shades of yellow, green, blue and red. Surface-colored papers, most commonly used for British colonial issues in 1913-14, are created when coloring is added only to the surface during the finishing process. Stamps printed on surface-colored paper have white or uncolored backs, while true colored papers are colored through. See Jamaica Scott 71-73.

**Pelure** — Pelure paper is a very thin, hard and often brittle paper that is sometimes bluish or grayish in appearance. See Serbia Scott 169-170.

**Native** — This is a term applied to handmade papers used to produce some of the early stamps of the Indian states. Stamps printed on native paper may be expected to display various natural inclusions that are normal and do not negatively affect value. Japanese paper, originally made of mulberry fibers and rice flour, is part of this group. See Japan Scott 1-18.

**Manila** — This type of paper is often used to make stamped envelopes and wrappers. It is a coarse-textured stock, usually smooth on one side and rough on the other. A variety of colors of manila paper exist, but the most common range is yellowish-brown.

**Silk** — Introduced by the British in 1847 as a safeguard against counterfeiting, silk paper contains bits of colored silk thread scattered throughout. The density of these fibers varies greatly and can include as few as one fiber per stamp or hundreds. U.S. revenue Scott R152 is a good example of an easy-to-identify silk paper stamp.

Silk-thread paper has uninterrupted threads of colored silk arranged so that one or more threads run through the stamp or postal stationery. See Great Britain Scott 5-6 and Switzerland Scott 14-19.

**Granite** — Filled with minute cloth or colored paper fibers of various colors and lengths, granite paper should not be confused with either type of silk paper. Austria Scott 172-175 and a number of Swiss stamps are examples of granite paper.

**Chalky** — A chalk-like substance coats the surface of chalky paper to discourage the cleaning and reuse of canceled stamps, as well as to provide a smoother, more acceptable printing surface. Because the designs of stamps printed on chalky paper are imprinted on what is often a water-soluble coating, any attempt to remove a cancellation will destroy the stamp. Do not soak these stamps in any fluid. To remove a stamp printed on chalky paper from an envelope, wet the paper from underneath the stamp until the gum dissolves enough to release the stamp from the paper. See St. Kitts-Nevis Scott 89-90 for examples of stamps printed on this type of chalky paper.

**India** — Another name for this paper, originally introduced from China about 1750, is "China Paper." It is a thin, opaque paper often used for plate and die proofs by many countries.

**Double** — In philately, the term double paper has two distinct meanings. The first is a two-ply paper, usually a combination of a thick and a thin sheet, joined during manufacture. This type was used experimentally as a means to discourage the reuse of stamps.

The design is printed on the thin paper. Any attempt to remove a cancellation would destroy the design. U.S. Scott 158 and other Banknote-era stamps exist on this form of double paper.

The second type of double paper occurs on a rotary press, when the end of one paper roll, or web, is affixed to the next roll to save time feeding the paper through the press. Stamp designs are printed over the joined paper and, if overlooked by inspectors, may get into post office stocks.

**Goldbeater's Skin** — This type of paper was used for the 1866 issue of Prussia, and was a tough, translucent paper. The design was printed in reverse on the back of the stamp, and the gum applied over the printing. It is impossible to remove stamps printed on this type of paper from the paper to which they are affixed without destroying the design.

**Ribbed** — Ribbed paper has an uneven, corrugated surface made by passing the paper through ridged rollers. This type exists on some copies of U.S. Scott 156-165.

Various other substances, or substrates, have been used for stamp manufacture, including wood, aluminum, copper, silver and gold foil, plastic, and silk and cotton fabrics.

## Watermarks

Watermarks are an integral part of some papers. They are formed in the process of paper manufacture. Watermarks consist of small designs, formed of wire or cut from metal and soldered to the surface of the mold or, sometimes, on the dandy roll. The designs may be in the form of crowns, stars, anchors, letters or other characters or symbols. These pieces of metal — known in the paper-making industry as "bits" — impress a design into the paper. The design sometimes may be seen by holding the stamp to the light. Some are more easily seen with a watermark detector. This important tool is a small black tray into which a stamp is placed face down and dampened with a fast-evaporating watermark detection fluid that brings up the watermark image in the form of dark lines against a lighter background. These dark lines are the thinner areas of the paper known as the watermark. Some watermarks are extremely difficult to locate, due to either a faint impression, watermark location or the color of the stamp. There also are electric watermark detectors that come with plastic filter disks of various colors. The disks neutralize the color of the stamp, permitting the watermark to be seen more easily.

**Multiple watermarks of Crown Agents and Burma**

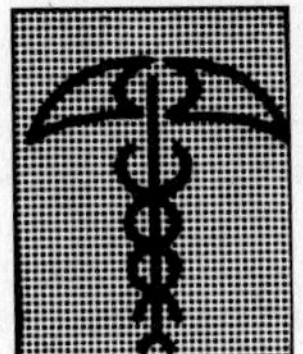

**Watermarks of Uruguay, Vatican City and Jamaica**

**WARNING: Some inks used in the photogravure process dissolve in watermark fluids (Please see the section on Soluble Printing Inks).** Also, see "chalky paper."

Watermarks may be found normal, reversed, inverted, reversed and inverted, sideways or diagonal, as seen from the back of the stamp. The relationship of watermark to stamp design depends on the position of the printing plates or how paper is fed through the press. On machine-made paper, watermarks normally are read from right to left. The design is repeated closely throughout the sheet in a "multiple-watermark design." In a "sheet watermark," the design appears only once on the sheet, but extends over many stamps. Individual stamps may carry only a small fraction or none of the watermark.

"Marginal watermarks" occur in the margins of sheets or panes of stamps. They occur on the outside border of paper (ostensibly outside the area where stamps are to be printed). A large row of letters may spell the name of the country or the manufacturer of the paper, or a border of lines may appear. Careless press feeding may cause parts of these letters and/or lines to show on stamps of the outer row of a pane.

## Soluble printing inks

**WARNING:** Most stamp colors are permanent; that is, they are not seriously affected by short-term exposure to light or water. Many colors, especially of modern inks, fade from excessive exposure to light. There are stamps printed with inks that dissolve easily in water or in fluids used to detect watermarks. Use of these inks was intentional to prevent the removal of cancellations. Water affects all aniline inks, those on so-called safety paper and some photogravure printings - all such inks are known as fugitive colors. Removal from paper of such stamps requires care and alternatives to traditional soaking.

## Separation

"Separation" is the general term used to describe methods used to separate stamps. The three standard forms currently in use are perforating, rouletting and die-cutting. These methods are done during the stamp production process, after printing. Sometimes these methods are done on-press or sometimes as a separate step. The earliest issues, such as the 1840 Penny Black of Great Britain (Scott 1), did not have any means provided for separation. It was expected the stamps would be cut apart with scissors or folded and torn. These are examples of imperforate stamps. Many stamps were first issued in imperforate formats and were later issued with perforations. Therefore, care must be observed in buying single imperforate stamps to be certain they were issued imperforate and are not perforated copies that have been altered by having the perforations trimmed away. Stamps issued imperforate usually are valued as singles. However, imperforate varieties of normally perforated stamps should be collected in pairs or larger pieces as indisputable evidence of their imperforate character.

### PERFORATION

The chief style of separation of stamps, and the one that is in almost universal use today, is perforating. By this process, paper between the stamps is cut away in a line of holes, usually round, leaving little bridges of paper between the stamps to hold them together. Some types of perforation, such as hyphen-hole perfs, can be confused with roulettes, but a close visual inspection reveals that paper has been removed. The little perforation bridges, which project from the stamp when it is torn from the pane, are called the teeth of the perforation.

As the size of the perforation is sometimes the only way to differentiate between two otherwise identical stamps, it is necessary to be able to accurately measure and describe them. This is done with a perforation gauge, usually a ruler-like device that has dots or graduated lines to show how many perforations may be counted in the space of two centimeters. Two centimeters is the space universally adopted in which to measure perforations.

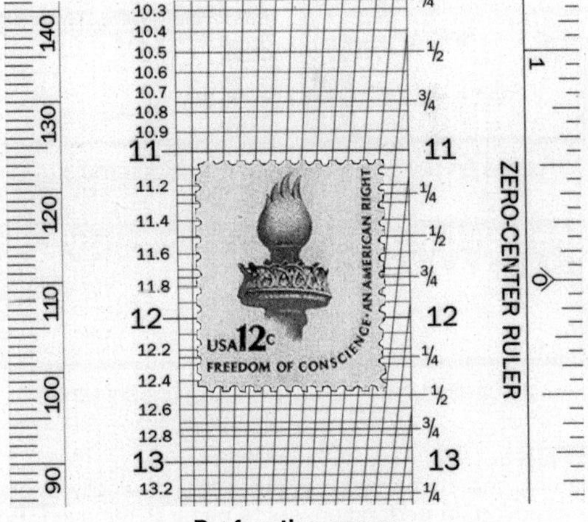


**Perforation gauge**

To measure a stamp, run it along the gauge until the dots on it fit exactly into the perforations of the stamp. If you are using a graduated-line perforation gauge, simply slide the stamp along the surface until the lines on the gauge perfectly project from the center of the bridges or holes. The number to the side of the line of dots or lines that fit the stamp's perforation is the measurement. For example, an "11" means that 11 perforations fit between two centimeters. The description of the stamp therefore is "perf. 11." If the gauge of the perforations on the top and bottom of a stamp differs from that on the sides, the result is what is known as compound perforations. In measuring compound perforations, the gauge at top and bottom is always given first, then the sides. Thus, a stamp that measures 11 at top and bottom and 10½ at the sides is "perf. 11 x 10½." See U.S. Scott 632-642 for examples of compound perforations.

Stamps also are known with perforations different on three or all four sides. Descriptions of such items are clockwise, beginning with the top of the stamp.

A perforation with small holes and teeth close together is a "fine perforation." One with large holes and teeth far apart is a "coarse perforation." Holes that are jagged, rather than clean-cut, are "rough perforations." *Blind perforations* are the slight impressions left by the perforating pins if they fail to puncture the paper. Multiples of stamps showing blind perforations may command a slight premium over normally perforated stamps.

The term *syncopated perfs* describes intentional irregularities in the perforations. The earliest form was used by the Netherlands from 1925-33, where holes were omitted to create distinctive patterns. Beginning in 1992, Great Britain has used an oval perforation to help prevent counterfeiting. Several other countries have started using the oval perfs or other syncopated perf patterns.

A new type of perforation, still primarily used for postal stationery, is known as microperfs. Microperfs are tiny perforations (in some cases hundreds of holes per two centimeters) that allows items to be intentionally separated very easily, while not accidentally breaking apart as easily as standard perforations. These are not currently measured or differentiated by size, as are standard perforations.

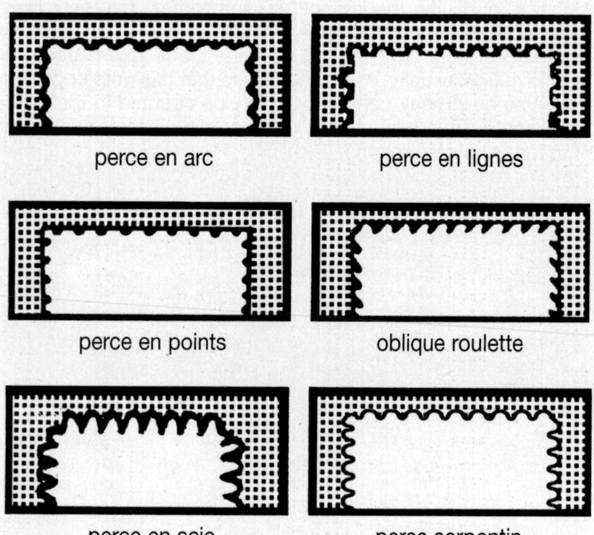


**ROULETTING**

In rouletting, the stamp paper is cut partly or wholly through, with no paper removed. In perforating, some paper is removed. Rouletting derives its name from the French roulette, a spur-like wheel. As the wheel is rolled over the paper, each point makes a small cut. The number of cuts made in a two-centimeter space determines the gauge of the roulette, just as the number of perforations in two centimeters determines the gauge of the perforation.

The shape and arrangement of the teeth on the wheels varies. Various roulette types generally carry French names:

*Perce en lignes* — rouletted in lines. The paper receives short, straight cuts in lines. This is the most common type of rouletting. See Mexico Scott 500.

*Perce en points* — pin-rouletted or pin-perfed. This differs from a small perforation because no paper is removed, although round, equidistant holes are pricked through the paper. See Mexico Scott 242-256.

*Perce en arc and perce en scie* — pierced in an arc or saw-toothed designs, forming half circles or small triangles. See Hanover (German States) Scott 25-29.

*Perce en serpentin* — serpentine roulettes. The cuts form a serpentine or wavy line. See Brunswick (German States) Scott 13-18.

Once again, no paper is removed by these processes, leaving the stamps easily separated, but closely attached.

**DIE-CUTTING**

The third major form of stamp separation is die-cutting. This is a method where a die in the pattern of separation is created that later cuts the stamp paper in a stroke motion. Although some standard stamps bear die-cut perforations, this process is primarily used for self-adhesive postage stamps. Die-cutting can appear in straight lines, such as U.S. Scott 2522, shapes, such as U.S. Scott 1551, or imitating the appearance of perforations, such as New Zealand Scott 935A and 935B.

## Printing processes

**ENGRAVING (Intaglio, Line-engraving, Etching)**

**Master die** — The initial operation in the process of line engraving is making the master die. The die is a small, flat block of softened steel upon which the stamp design is recess engraved in reverse.

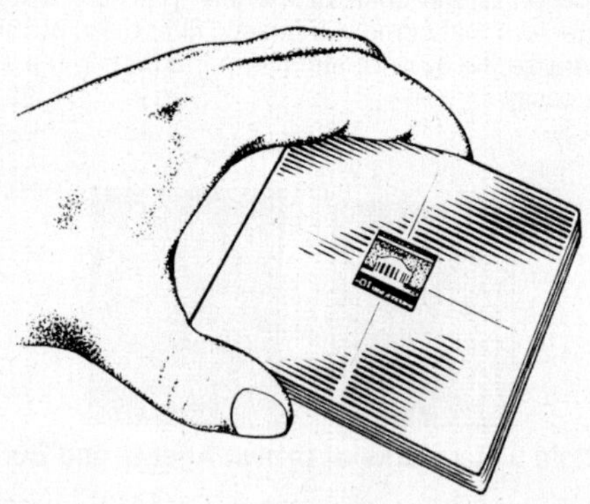

Photographic reduction of the original art is made to the appropriate size. It then serves as a tracing guide for the initial outline of the design. The engraver lightly traces the design on the steel with his graver, then slowly works the design until it is completed. At various points during the engraving process, the engraver hand-inks the die and makes an impression to check his progress. These are known as progressive die proofs. After completion of the engraving, the die is hardened to withstand the stress and pressures of later transfer operations.

**Transfer roll**

**Transfer roll** — Next is production of the transfer roll that, as the name implies, is the medium used to transfer the subject from the master die to the printing plate. A blank roll of soft steel, mounted on a mandrel, is placed under the bearers of the transfer press to allow it to roll freely on its axis. The hardened die is placed on the bed of the press and the face of the transfer roll is applied to the die, under pressure. The bed or the roll is then rocked back and forth under increasing pressure, until the soft steel of the roll is forced into every engraved line of the die. The resulting impression on the roll is known as a "relief" or a "relief transfer." The engraved image is now positive in appearance and stands out from the steel. After the required number of reliefs are "rocked in," the soft steel transfer roll is hardened.

Different flaws may occur during the relief process. A defective relief may occur during the rocking in process because of a minute piece of foreign material lodging on the die, or some other cause. Imperfections in the steel of the transfer roll may result in a breaking away of parts of the design. This is known as a relief break, which will show up on finished stamps as small, unprinted areas. If a damaged relief remains in use, it will transfer a repeating defect to the plate. Deliberate alterations of reliefs sometimes occur. "Altered reliefs" designate these changed conditions.

**Plate** — The final step in pre-printing production is the making of the printing plate. A flat piece of soft steel replaces the die on the bed of the transfer press. One of the reliefs on the transfer roll is positioned over this soft steel. Position, or layout, dots determine the correct position on the plate. The dots have been lightly marked on the plate in advance. After the correct position of the relief is determined, the design is rocked in by following the same method used in making the transfer roll. The difference is that this time the image is being transferred from the transfer roll, rather than to it. Once the design is entered on the plate, it appears in reverse and is recessed. There are as many transfers entered on the plate as there are subjects printed on the sheet of stamps. It is during this process that double and shifted transfers occur, as well as re-entries. These are the result of improperly entered images that have not been properly burnished out prior to rocking in a new image.

Modern siderography processes, such as those used by the U.S. Bureau of Engraving and Printing, involve an automated form of rocking designs in on preformed cylindrical printing sleeves. The same process also allows for easier removal and re-entry of worn images right on the sleeve.

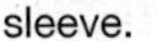

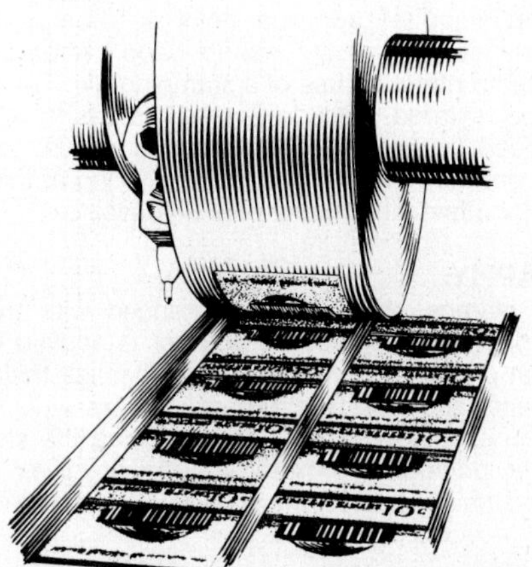

**Transferring the design to the plate**

Following the entering of the required transfers on the plate, the position dots, layout dots and lines, scratches and other markings generally are burnished out. Added at this time by the siderographer are any required guide lines, plate numbers or other marginal markings. The plate is then hand-inked and a proof impression is taken. This is known as a plate proof. If the impression is approved, the plate is machined for fitting onto the press, is hardened and sent to the plate vault ready for use.

On press, the plate is inked and the surface is automatically wiped clean, leaving ink only in the recessed lines. Paper is then forced under pressure into the engraved recessed lines, thereby receiving the ink. Thus, the ink lines on engraved stamps are slightly raised, and slight depressions (debossing) occur on the back of the stamp. Prior to the advent of modern high-speed presses and more advanced ink formulations, paper had to be dampened before receiving the ink. This sometimes led to uneven shrinkage by the time the stamps were perforated, resulting in improperly perforated stamps, or misperfs. Newer presses use drier paper, thus both *wet and dry printings* exist on some stamps.

**Rotary Press** — Until 1914, only flat plates were used to print engraved stamps. Rotary press printing was introduced in 1914, and slowly spread. Some countries still use flat-plate printing.

After approval of the plate proof, older rotary press plates require additional machining. They are curved to fit the press cylinder. "Gripper slots" are cut into the back of each plate to receive the "grippers," which hold the plate securely on the press. The plate is then hardened. Stamps printed from these bent rotary press plates are longer or wider than the same stamps printed from flat-plate presses. The stretching of the plate during the curving process is what causes this distortion.

**Re-entry** — To execute a re-entry on a flat plate, the transfer roll is re-applied to the plate, often at some time after its first use on the press. Worn-out designs can be resharpened by carefully burnishing out the original image and re-entering it from the transfer roll. If the original impression has not been sufficiently removed and the transfer roll is not precisely in line with the remaining impression, the resulting double transfer will make the re-entry obvious. If the registration is true, a re-entry may be difficult or impossible to distinguish. Sometimes a stamp printed from a successful re-entry is identified by having a much sharper and clearer impression than its neighbors. With the advent of rotary presses, post-press re-entries were not possible. After a plate was curved for the rotary press, it was impossible to make a re-entry. This is because the plate had already been bent once (with the design distorted).

However, with the introduction of the previously mentioned modern-style siderography machines, entries are made to the preformed cylindrical printing sleeve. Such sleeves are dechromed and softened. This allows individual images to be burnished out and re-entered on the curved sleeve. The sleeve is then rechromed, resulting in longer press life.

**Double Transfer** — This is a description of the condition of a transfer on a plate that shows evidence of a duplication of all, or a portion of the design. It usually is the result of the changing of the registration between the transfer roll and the plate during the rocking in of the original entry. Double transfers also occur when only a portion of the design has been rocked in and improper positioning is noted. If the worker elected not to burnish out the partial or completed design, a strong double transfer will occur for part or all of the design.

It sometimes is necessary to remove the original transfer from a plate and repeat the process a second time. If the finished re-worked image shows traces of the original impression, attributable to incomplete burnishing, the result is a partial double transfer.

With the modern automatic machines mentioned previously, double transfers are all but impossible to create. Those partially doubled images on stamps printed from such sleeves are more than likely re-entries, rather than true double transfers.

**Re-engraved** — Alterations to a stamp design are sometimes necessary after some stamps have been printed. In some cases, either the original die or the actual printing plate may have its "temper" drawn (softened), and the design will be re-cut. The resulting impressions from such a re-engraved die or plate may differ slightly from the original issue, and are known as "re-engraved." If the alteration was made to the master die, all future printings will be consistently different from the original. If alterations were made to the printing plate, each altered stamp on the plate will be slightly different from each other, allowing specialists to reconstruct a complete printing plate.

**Dropped Transfers** — If an impression from the transfer roll has not been properly placed, a dropped transfer may occur. The final stamp image will appear obviously out of line with its neighbors.

**Short Transfer** — Sometimes a transfer roll is not rocked its entire length when entering a transfer onto a plate. As a result, the finished transfer on the plate fails to show the complete design, and the finished stamp will have an incomplete design printed. This is known as a "short transfer." U.S. Scott No. 8 is a good example of a short transfer.

## TYPOGRAPHY (Letterpress, Surface Printing, Flexography, Dry Offset, High Etch)

Although the word "Typography" is obsolete as a term describing a printing method, it was the accepted term throughout the first century of postage stamps. Therefore, appropriate Scott listings in this catalogue refer to typographed stamps. The current term for this form of printing, however, is "letterpress."

As it relates to the production of postage stamps, letterpress printing is the reverse of engraving. Rather than having recessed areas trap the ink and deposit it on paper, only the raised areas of the design are inked. This is comparable to the type of printing seen by inking and using an ordinary rubber stamp. Letterpress includes all printing where the design is above the surface area, whether it is wood, metal or, in some instances, hardened rubber or polymer plastic.

For most letterpress-printed stamps, the engraved master is made in much the same manner as for engraved stamps. In this instance, however, an additional step is needed. The design is transferred to another surface before being transferred to the transfer roll. In this way, the transfer roll has a recessed stamp design, rather than one done in relief. This makes the printing areas on the final plate raised, or relief areas.

For less-detailed stamps of the 19th century, the area on the die not used as a printing surface was cut away, leaving the surface area raised. The original die was then reproduced by stereotyping or electrotyping. The resulting electrotypes were assembled in the required number and format of the desired sheet of stamps. The plate used in printing the stamps was an electroplate of these assembled electrotypes.

Once the final letterpress plates are created, ink is applied to the raised surface and the pressure of the press transfers the ink impression to the paper. In contrast to engraving, the fine lines of letterpress are impressed on the surface of the stamp, leaving a debossed surface. When viewed from the back (as on a typewritten page), the corresponding line work on the stamp will be raised slightly (embossed) above the surface.

## PHOTOGRAVURE (Gravure, Rotogravure, Heliogravure)

In this process, the basic principles of photography are applied to a chemically sensitized metal plate, rather than photographic paper. The design is transferred photographically to the plate through a halftone, or dot-matrix screen, breaking the reproduction into tiny dots. The plate is treated chemically and the dots form depressions, called cells, of varying depths and diameters, depending on the degrees of shade in the design. Then, like engraving, ink is applied to the plate and the surface is wiped clean. This leaves ink in the tiny cells that is lifted out and deposited on the paper when it is pressed against the plate.

Gravure is most often used for multicolored stamps, generally using the three primary colors (red, yellow and blue) and black. By varying the dot matrix pattern and density of these colors, virtually any color can be reproduced. A typical full-color gravure stamp will be created from four printing cylinders (one for each color). The original multicolored image will have been photographically separated into its component colors.

Modern gravure printing may use computer-generated dot-matrix screens, and modern plates may be of various types including metal-coated plastic. The catalogue designation of Photogravure (or "Photo") covers any of these older and more modern gravure methods of printing.

For examples of the first photogravure stamps printed (1914), see Bavaria Scott 94-114.

## LITHOGRAPHY (Offset Lithography, Stone Lithography, Dilitho, Planography, Collotype)

The principle that oil and water do not mix is the basis for lithography. The stamp design is drawn by hand or transferred from engraving to the surface of a lithographic stone or metal plate in a greasy (oily) substance. This oily substance holds the ink, which will later be transferred to the paper. The stone (or plate) is wet with an acid fluid, causing it to repel the printing ink in all areas not covered by the greasy substance.

Transfer paper is used to transfer the design from the original stone or plate. A series of duplicate transfers are grouped and, in turn, transferred to the final printing plate.

**Photolithography** — The application of photographic processes to lithography. This process allows greater flexibility of design, related to use of halftone screens combined with line work. Unlike photogravure or engraving, this process can allow large, solid areas to be printed.

**Offset** — A refinement of the lithographic process. A rubber-covered blanket cylinder takes the impression from the inked lithographic plate. From the "blanket" the impression is offset or transferred to the paper. Greater flexibility and speed are the principal reasons offset printing has largely displaced lithography. The term "lithography" covers both processes, and results are almost identical.

### EMBOSSED (Relief) Printing

Embossing, not considered one of the four main printing types, is a method in which the design first is sunk into the metal of the die. Printing is done against a yielding platen, such as leather or linoleum. The platen is forced into the depression of the die, thus forming the design on the paper in relief. This process is often used for metallic inks.

Embossing may be done without color (see Sardinia Scott 4-6); with color printed around the embossed area (see Great Britain Scott 5 and most U.S. envelopes); and with color in exact registration with the embossed subject (see Canada Scott 656-657).

## HOLOGRAMS

For objects to appear as holograms on stamps, a model exactly the same size as it is to appear on the hologram must be created. Rather than using photographic film to capture the image, holography records an image on a photoresist material. In processing, chemicals eat away at certain exposed areas, leaving a pattern of constructive and destructive interference. When the photoresist is developed, the result is a pattern of uneven ridges that acts as a mold. This mold is then coated with metal, and the resulting form is used to press copies in much the same way phonograph records are produced.

A typical reflective hologram used for stamps consists of a reproduction of the uneven patterns on a plastic film that is applied to a reflective background, usually a silver or gold foil. Light is reflected off the background through the film, making the pattern present on the film visible. Because of the uneven pattern of the film, the viewer will perceive the objects in their proper three-dimensional relationships with appropriate brightness. The first hologram on a stamp was produced by Austria in 1988 (Scott 1441).

## FOIL APPLICATION

A modern technique of applying color to stamps involves the application of metallic foil to the stamp paper. A pattern of foil is applied to the stamp paper by use of a stamping die. The foil usually is flat, but it may be textured. Canada Scott 1735 has three different foil applications in pearl, bronze and gold. The gold foil was textured using a chemical-etch copper embossing die. The printing of this stamp also involved two-color offset lithography plus embossing.

## THERMOGRAPHY

In the 1990s stamps began to be enhanced with thermographic printing. In this process, a powdered polymer is applied over a sheet that has just been printed. The powder adheres to ink that lacks drying or hardening agents and does not adhere to areas where the ink has these agents. The excess powder is removed and the sheet is briefly heated to melt the powder. The melted powder solidifies after cooling, producing a raised, shiny effect on the stamps. See Scott New Caledonia C239-C240.

## COMBINATION PRINTINGS

Sometimes two or even three printing methods are combined in producing stamps. In these cases, such as Austria Scott 933 or Canada 1735 (described in the preceding paragraph), the multiple-printing technique can be determined by studying the individual characteristics of each printing type. A few stamps, such as Singapore Scott 684-684A, combine as many as three of the four major printing types (lithography, engraving and typography). When this is done it often indicates the incorporation of security devices against counterfeiting.

## INK COLORS

Inks or colored papers used in stamp printing often are of mineral origin, although there are numerous examples of organic-based pigments. As a general rule, organic-based pigments are far more subject to varieties and change than those of mineral-based origin.

The appearance of any given color on a stamp may be affected by many aspects, including printing variations, light, color of paper, aging and chemical alterations.

Numerous printing variations may be observed. Heavier pressure or inking will cause a more intense color, while slight interruptions in the ink feed or lighter impressions will cause a lighter appearance. Stamps printed in the same color by water-based and solvent-based inks can differ significantly in appearance. This affects several stamps in the U.S. Prominent Americans series. Hand-mixed ink formulas (primarily from the 19th century) produced under different conditions (humidity and temperature) account for notable color variations in early printings of the same stamp (see U.S. Scott 248-250, 279B, for example). Different sources of pigment can also result in significant differences in color.

Light exposure and aging are closely related in the way they affect stamp color. Both eventually break down the ink and fade colors, so that a carefully kept stamp may differ significantly in color from an identical copy that has been exposed to light. If stamps are exposed to light either intentionally or accidentally, their colors can be faded or completely changed in some cases.

Papers of different quality and consistency used for the same stamp printing may affect color appearance. Most pelure papers, for example, show a richer color when compared with wove or laid papers. See Russia Scott 181a, for an example of this effect.

The very nature of the printing processes can cause a variety of differences in shades or hues of the same stamp. Some of these shades are scarcer than others, and are of particular interest to the advanced collector.

## Luminescence

All forms of tagged stamps fall under the general category of luminescence. Within this broad category is fluorescence, dealing with forms of tagging visible under longwave ultraviolet light, and phosphorescence, which deals with tagging visible only under shortwave light. Phosphorescence leaves an afterglow and fluorescence does not. These treated stamps show up in a range of different colors when exposed to UV light. The differing wavelengths of the light activates the tagging material, making it glow in various colors that usually serve different mail processing purposes.

Intentional tagging is a post-World War II phenomenon, brought about by the increased literacy rate and rapidly growing mail volume. It was one of several answers to the problem of the need for more automated mail processes. Early tagged stamps served the purpose of triggering machines to separate different types of mail. A natural outgrowth was to also use the signal to trigger machines that faced all envelopes the same way and canceled them.

Tagged stamps come in many different forms. Some tagged stamps have luminescent shapes or images imprinted on them as a form of security device. Others have blocks (United States), stripes, frames (South Africa and Canada), overall coatings (United States), bars (Great Britain and Canada) and many other types. Some types of tagging are even mixed in with the pigmented printing ink (Australia Scott 366, Netherlands Scott 478 and U.S. Scott 1359 and 2443).

The means of applying taggant to stamps differs as much as the intended purposes for the stamps. The most common form of tagging is a coating applied to the surface of the printed stamp. Since the taggant ink is frequently invisible except under UV light, it does not interfere with the appearance of the stamp. Another common application is the use of phosphored papers. In this case the paper itself either has a coating of taggant applied before the stamp is printed, has taggant applied during the papermaking process (incorporating it into the fibers), or has the taggant mixed into the coating of the paper. The latter method, among others, is currently in use in the United States.

Many countries now use tagging in various forms to either expedite mail handling or to serve as a printing security device against counterfeiting. Following the introduction of tagged stamps for public use in 1959 by Great Britain, other countries have steadily joined the parade. Among those are Germany (1961); Canada and Denmark (1962); United States, Australia, France and Switzerland (1963); Belgium and Japan (1966); Sweden and Norway (1967); Italy (1968); and Russia (1969). Since then, many other countries have begun using forms of tagging, including Brazil, China, Czechoslovakia, Hong Kong, Guatemala, Indonesia, Israel, Lithuania, Luxembourg, Netherlands, Penrhyn Islands, Portugal, St. Vincent, Singapore, South Africa, Spain and Sweden to name a few.

In some cases, including United States, Canada, Great Britain and Switzerland, stamps were released both with and without tagging. Many of these were released during each country's experimental period. Tagged and untagged versions are listed for the aforementioned countries and are noted in some other countries' listings. For at least a few stamps, the experimentally tagged version is worth far more than its untagged counterpart, such as the 1963 experimental tagged version of France Scott 1024.

In some cases, luminescent varieties of stamps were inadvertently created. Several Russian stamps, for example, sport highly fluorescent ink that was not intended as a form of tagging. Older stamps, such as early U.S. postage dues, can be positively identified by the use of UV light, since the organic ink used has become slightly fluorescent over time. Other stamps, such as Austria Scott 70a-82a (varnish bars) and Obock Scott 46-64 (printed quadrille lines), have become fluorescent over time.

Various fluorescent substances have been added to paper to make it appear brighter. These optical brightners, as they are known, greatly affect the appearance of the stamp under UV light. The brightest of these is known as Hi-Brite paper. These paper varieties are beyond the scope of the Scott Catalogue.

Shortwave UV light also is used extensively in expertizing, since each form of paper has its own fluorescent characteristics that are impossible to perfectly match. It is therefore a simple matter to detect filled thins, added perforation teeth and other alterations that involve the addition of paper. UV light also is used to examine stamps that have had cancels chemically removed and for other purposes as well.

## Gum

The Illustrated Gum Chart in the first part of this introduction shows and defines various types of gum condition. Because gum condition has an important impact on the value of unused stamps, we recommend studying this chart and the accompanying text carefully.

The gum on the back of a stamp may be shiny, dull, smooth, rough, dark, white, colored or tinted. Most stamp gumming adhesives use gum arabic or dextrine as a base. Certain polymers such as polyvinyl alcohol (PVA) have been used extensively since World War II.

The *Scott Standard Postage Stamp Catalogue* does not list items by types of gum. The *Scott Specialized Catalogue of United States Stamps and Covers* does differentiate among some types of gum for certain issues.

Reprints of stamps may have gum differing from the original issues. In addition, some countries have used different gum formulas for different seasons. These adhesives have different properties that may become more apparent over time.

Many stamps have been issued without gum, and the catalogue will note this fact. See, for example, United States Scott 40-47. Sometimes, gum may have been removed to preserve the stamp. Germany Scott B68, for example, has a highly acidic gum that eventually destroys the stamps. This item is valued in the catalogue with gum removed.

## Reprints and reissues

These are impressions of stamps (usually obsolete) made from the original plates or stones. If they are valid for postage and reproduce obsolete issues (such as U.S. Scott 102-111), the stamps are reissues. If they are from current issues, they are designated as *second, third,* etc., *printing*. If designated for a particular purpose, they are called *special printings*.

When special printings are not valid for postage, but are made from original dies and plates by authorized persons, they are *official reprints*. *Private reprints* are made from the original plates and dies by private hands. An example of a private reprint is that of the 1871-1932 reprints made from the original die of the 1845 New Haven, Conn., postmaster's provisional. *Official reproductions* or imitations are made from new dies and plates by government authorization. Scott will list those reissues that are valid for postage if they differ significantly from the original printing.

The U.S. government made special printings of its first postage stamps in 1875. Produced were official imitations of the first two stamps (listed as Scott 3-4), reprints of the demonetized pre-1861 issues (Scott 40-47) and reissues of the 1861 stamps, the 1869 stamps and the then-current 1875 denominations. Even though the official imitations and the reprints were not valid for postage, Scott lists all of these U.S. special printings.

Most reprints or reissues differ slightly from the original stamp in some characteristic, such as gum, paper, perforation, color or watermark. Sometimes the details are followed so meticulously that only a student of that specific stamp is able to distinguish the reprint or reissue from the original.

## Remainders and canceled to order

Some countries sell their stock of old stamps when a new issue replaces them. To avoid postal use, the remainders usually are canceled with a punch hole, a heavy line or bar, or a more-or-less regular-looking cancellation. The most famous merchant of remainders was Nicholas F. Seebeck. In the 1880s and 1890s, he arranged printing contracts between the Hamilton Bank Note Co., of which he was a director, and several Central and South American countries. The contracts provided that the plates and all remainders of the yearly issues became the property of Hamilton. Seebeck saw to it that ample stock remained. The "Seebecks," both remainders and reprints, were standard packet fillers for decades.

Some countries also issue stamps *canceled-to-order (CTO)*, either in sheets with original gum or stuck onto pieces of paper or envelopes and canceled. Such CTO items generally are worth less than postally used stamps. In cases where the CTO material is far more prevalent in the marketplace than postally used examples, the catalogue value relates to the CTO examples, with postally used examples noted as premium items. Most CTOs can be detected by the presence of gum. However, as the CTO practice goes back at least to 1885, the gum inevitably has been soaked off some stamps so they could pass as postally used. The normally applied postmarks usually differ slightly from standard postmarks, and specialists are able to tell the difference. When applied individually to envelopes by philatelically minded persons, CTO material is known as *favor canceled* and generally sells at large discounts.

## Cinderellas and facsimiles

*Cinderella* is a catch-all term used by stamp collectors to describe phantoms, fantasies, bogus items, municipal issues, exhibition seals, local revenues, transportation stamps, labels, poster stamps and many other types of items. Some cinderella collectors include in their collections local postage issues, telegraph stamps, essays and proofs, forgeries and counterfeits.

A *fantasy* is an adhesive created for a nonexistent stamp-issuing authority. Fantasy items range from imaginary countries (Occusi-Ambeno, Kingdom of Sedang, Principality of Trinidad or Torres Straits), to non-existent locals (Winans City Post), or nonexistent transportation lines (McRobish & Co.'s Acapulco-San Francisco Line).

On the other hand, if the entity exists and could have issued stamps (but did not) or was known to have issued other stamps, the items are considered bogus stamps. These would include the Mormon postage stamps of Utah, S. Allan Taylor's Guatemala and Paraguay inventions, the propaganda issues for the South Moluccas and the adhesives of the Page & Keyes local post of Boston.

*Phantoms* is another term for both fantasy and bogus issues.

*Facsimiles* are copies or imitations made to represent original stamps, but which do not pretend to be originals. A catalogue illustration is such a facsimile. Illustrations from the Moens catalogue of the last century were occasionally colored and passed off as stamps. Since the beginning of stamp collecting, facsimiles have been made for collectors as space fillers or for reference. They often carry the word "facsimile," "falsch" (German), "sanko" or "mozo" (Japanese), or "faux" (French) overprinted on the face or stamped on the back. Unfortunately, over the years a number of these items have had fake cancels applied over the facsimile notation and have been passed off as genuine.

## Forgeries and counterfeits

Forgeries and counterfeits have been with philately virtually from the beginning of stamp production. Over time, the terminology for the two has been used interchangeably. Although both forgeries and counterfeits are reproductions of stamps, the purposes behind their creation differ considerably.

Among specialists there is an increasing movement to more specifically define such items. Although there is no universally accepted terminology, we feel the following definitions most closely mirror the items and their purposes as they are currently defined.

Forgeries (also often referred to as Counterfeits) are reproductions of genuine stamps that have been created to defraud collectors. Such spurious items first appeared on the market around 1860, and most old-time collections contain one or more. Many are crude and easily spotted, but some can deceive experts.

An important supplier of these early philatelic forgeries was the Hamburg printer Gebruder Spiro. Many others with reputations in this craft included S. Allan Taylor, George Hussey, James Chute, George Forune, Benjamin & Sarpy, Julius Goldner, E. Oneglia and L.H. Mercier. Among the noted 20th-century forgers were Francois Fournier, Jean Sperati and the prolific Raoul DeThuin.

Forgeries may be complete replications, or they may be genuine stamps altered to resemble a scarcer (and more valuable) type. Most forgeries, particularly those of rare stamps, are worth only a small fraction of the value of a genuine example, but a few types, created by some of the most notable forgers, such as Sperati, can be worth as much or more than the genuine. Fraudulently produced copies are known of most classic rarities and many medium-priced stamps.

In addition to rare stamps, large numbers of common 19th- and early 20th-century stamps were forged to supply stamps to the early packet trade. Many can still be easily found. Few new philatelic forgeries have appeared in recent decades. Successful imitation of well-engraved work is virtually impossible. It has proven far easier to produce a fake by altering a genuine stamp than to duplicate a stamp completely.

Counterfeit (also often referred to as Postal Counterfeit or Postal Forgery) is the term generally applied to reproductions of stamps that have been created to defraud the government of revenue. Such items usually are created at the time a stamp is current and, in some cases, are hard to detect. Because most counterfeits are seized when the perpetrator is captured, postal counterfeits, particularly used on cover, are usually worth much more than a genuine example to specialists. The first postal counterfeit was of Spain's 4-cuarto carmine of 1854 (the real one is Scott 25). Apparently, the counterfeiters were not satisfied with their first version, which is now very scarce, and they soon created an engraved counterfeit, which is common. Postal counterfeits quickly followed in Austria, Naples, Sardinia and the Roman States. They have since been created in many other countries as well, including the United States.

An infamous counterfeit to defraud the government is the 1-shilling Great Britain "Stock Exchange" forgery of 1872, used on telegraph forms at the exchange that year. The stamp escaped detection until a stamp dealer noticed it in 1898.

## Fakes

*Fakes* are genuine stamps altered in some way to make them more desirable. One student of this part of stamp collecting has estimated that by the 1950s more than 30,000 varieties of fakes were known. That number has grown greatly since then. The widespread existence of fakes makes it important for stamp collectors to study their philatelic holdings and use relevant literature. Likewise, collectors should buy from reputable dealers who guarantee their stamps and make full and prompt refunds should a purchased item be declared faked or altered by some mutually agreed-upon authority. Because fakes always have some genuine characteristics, it is not always possible to obtain unanimous agreement among experts regarding specific items. These students may change their opinions as philatelic knowledge increases. More than 80 percent of all fakes on the philatelic market today are regummed, reperforated (or perforated for the first time), or bear forged overprints, surcharges or cancellations.

Stamps can be chemically treated to alter or eliminate colors. For example, a pale rose stamp can be re-colored to resemble a blue shade of high market value. In other cases, treated stamps can be made to resemble missing color varieties. Designs may be changed by painting, or a stroke or a dot added or bleached out to turn an ordinary variety into a seemingly scarcer stamp. Part of a stamp can be bleached and reprinted in a different version, achieving an inverted center or frame. Margins can be added or repairs done so deceptively that the stamps move from the "repaired" into the "fake" category.

Fakers have not left the backs of the stamps untouched either. They may create false watermarks, add fake grills or press out genuine grills. A thin India paper proof may be glued onto a thicker backing to create the appearance an issued stamp, or a proof printed on cardboard may be shaved down and perforated to resemble a stamp. Silk threads are impressed into paper and stamps have been split so that a rare paper variety is added to an otherwise inexpensive stamp. The most common treatment to the back of a stamp, however, is regumming.

Some in the business of faking stamps have openly advertised fool-proof application of "original gum" to stamps that lack it, although most publications now ban such ads from their pages. It is believed that very few early stamps have survived without being hinged. The large number of never-hinged examples of such earlier material offered for sale thus suggests the widespread extent of regumming activity. Regumming also may be used to hide repairs or thin spots. Dipping the stamp into watermark fluid, or examining it under longwave ultraviolet light often will reveal these flaws.

Fakers also tamper with separations. Ingenious ways to add margins are known. Perforated wide-margin stamps may be falsely represented as imperforate when trimmed. Reperforating is commonly done to create scarce coil or perforation varieties, and to eliminate the naturally occurring straight-edge stamps found in sheet margin positions of many earlier issues. Custom has made straight-edged stamps less desirable. Fakers have obliged by perforating straight-edged stamps so that many are now uncommon, if not rare.

Another fertile field for the faker is that of overprints, surcharges and cancellations. The forging of rare surcharges or overprints began in the 1880s or 1890s. These forgeries are sometimes difficult to detect, but experts have identified almost all. Occasionally, overprints or cancellations are removed to create non-overprinted stamps or seemingly unused items. This is most commonly done by removing a manuscript cancel to make a stamp resemble an unused example. "SPECIMEN" overprints may be removed by scraping and repainting to create non-overprinted varieties. Fakers use inexpensive revenues or pen-canceled stamps to generate unused stamps for further faking by adding other markings. The quartz lamp or UV lamp and a high-powered magnifying glass help to easily detect removed cancellations.

The bigger problem, however, is the addition of overprints, surcharges or cancellations — many with such precision that they are very difficult to ascertain. Plating of the stamps or the overprint can be an important method of detection.

Fake postmarks may range from many spurious fancy cancellations to a host of markings applied to transatlantic covers, to adding normally appearing postmarks to definitives of some countries with stamps that are valued far higher used than unused. With the increased popularity of cover collecting, and the widespread interest in postal history, a fertile new field for fakers has come about. Some have tried to create entire covers. Others specialize in adding stamps, tied by fake cancellations, to genuine stampless covers, or replacing less expensive or damaged stamps with more valuable ones. Detailed study of postal rates in effect at the time a cover in question was mailed, including the analysis of each handstamp used during the period, ink analysis and similar techniques, usually will unmask the fraud.

## Restoration and repairs

Scott bases its catalogue values on stamps that are free of defects and otherwise meet the standards set forth earlier in this introduction. Most stamp collectors desire to have the finest copy of an item possible. Even within given grading categories there are variances. This leads to a controversial practice that is not defined in any universal manner: stamp *restoration*.

There are broad differences of opinion about what is permissible when it comes to restoration. Carefully applying a soft eraser to a stamp or cover to remove light soiling is one form of restoration, as is washing a stamp in mild soap and water to clean it. These are fairly accepted forms of restoration. More severe forms of restoration include pressing out creases or removing stains caused by tape. To what degree each of these is acceptable is dependent upon the individual situation. Further along the spectrum is the freshening of a stamp's color by removing oxide build-up or the effects of wax paper left next to stamps shipped to the tropics.

At some point in this spectrum the concept of *repair* replaces that of restoration. Repairs include filling thin spots, mending tears by reweaving or adding a missing perforation tooth. Regumming stamps may have been acceptable as a restoration or repair technique many decades ago, but today it is considered a form of fakery.

Restored stamps may or may not sell at a discount, and it is possible that the value of individual restored items may be enhanced over that of their pre-restoration state. Specific situations dictate the resultant value of such an item. Repaired stamps sell at substantial discounts from the value of sound stamps.

# Terminology

**Booklets** — Many countries have issued stamps in small booklets for the convenience of users. This idea continues to become increasingly popular in many countries. Booklets have been issued in many sizes and forms, often with advertising on the covers, the panes of stamps or on the interleaving.

The panes used in booklets may be printed from special plates or made from regular sheets. All panes from booklets issued by the United States and many from those of other countries contain stamps that are straight edged on the sides, but perforated between. Others are distinguished by orientation of watermark or other identifying features. Any stamp-like unit in the pane, either printed or blank, that is not a postage stamp, is considered to be a *label* in the catalogue listings.

Scott lists and values booklet panes. Modern complete booklets also are listed and valued. Individual booklet panes are listed only when they are not fashioned from existing sheet stamps and, therefore, are identifiable from their sheet stamp counterparts.

Panes usually do not have a used value assigned to them because there is little market activity for used booklet panes, even though many exist used and there is some demand for them.

**Cancellations** — The marks or obliterations put on stamps by postal authorities to show that they have performed service and to prevent their reuse are known as cancellations. If the marking is made with a pen, it is considered a "pen cancel." When the location of the post office appears in the marking, it is a "town cancellation." A "postmark" is technically any postal marking, but in practice the term generally is applied to a town cancellation with a date. When calling attention to a cause or celebration, the marking is known as a "slogan cancellation." Many other types and styles of cancellations exist, such as duplex, numerals, targets, fancy and others. See also "precancels," below.

**Coil Stamps** — These are stamps that are issued in rolls for use in dispensers, affixing and vending machines. Those coils of the United States, Canada, Sweden and some other countries are perforated horizontally or vertically only, with the outer edges imperforate. Coil stamps of some countries, such as Great Britain and Germany, are perforated on all four sides and may in some cases be distinguished from their sheet stamp counterparts by watermarks, counting numbers on the reverse or other means.

**Covers** — Entire envelopes, with or without adhesive postage stamps, that have passed through the mail and bear postal or other markings of philatelic interest are known as covers. Before the introduction of envelopes in about 1840, people folded letters and wrote the address on the outside. Some people covered their letters with an extra sheet of paper on the outside for the address, producing the term "cover." Used airletter sheets, stamped envelopes and other items of postal stationery also are considered covers.

**Errors** — Stamps that have some major, consistent, unintentional deviation from the normal are considered errors. Errors include, but are not limited to, missing or wrong colors, wrong paper, wrong watermarks, inverted centers or frames on multicolor printing, inverted or missing surcharges or overprints, double impressions, missing perforations, unintentionally omitted tagging and others. Factually wrong or misspelled information, if it appears on all examples of a stamp, are not considered errors in the true sense of the word. They are errors of design. Inconsistent or randomly appearing items, such as misperfs or color shifts, are classified as freaks.

**Color-Omitted Errors** — This term refers to stamps where a missing color is caused by the complete failure of the printing plate to deliver ink to the stamp paper or any other paper. Generally, this is caused by the printing plate not being engaged on the press or the ink station running dry of ink during printing.

**Color-Missing Errors** — This term refers to stamps where a color or colors were printed somewhere but do not appear on the finished stamp. There are four different classes of color-missing errors, and the catalog indicates with a two-letter code appended to each such listing what caused the color to be missing. These codes are used only for the United States' color-missing error listings.

**FO** = A *foldover* of the stamp sheet during printing may block ink from appearing on the face of a stamp. Instead, the color will appear on the back of the foldover (where it might fall on the back of the selvage or perhaps a bit on the back of the stamp or on the back of another stamp. FO also will be used in the case of foldunders, where the paper may fold underneath the other stamp paper and the color will print on the platen.

**EP** = When the extraneous paper is removed, an unprinted area of stamp paper remains and may show a color or colors to be totally missing on the finished stamp.

**CM** = A misregistration of the printing plates during printing will result in a *color misregistration*, and such a misregistraion may result in a color not appearing on the finished stamp.

**PS** = *A perforation shift* after printing may remove a color from the finished stamp. Normally, this will occur on a row of stamps at the edge of the stamp pane.

**Measurements** – When measurements are given in the Scott catalogues for stamp size, grill size or any other reason, the first measurement given is always for the top and bottom dimension, while the second measurement will be for the sides (just as perforation gauges are measured). Thus, a stamp size of 15mm x 21mm will indicate a vertically oriented stamp 15mm wide at top and bottom, and 21mm tall at the sides. The same principle holds for measuring or counting items such as U.S. grills. A grill count of 22x18 points (B grill) indicates that there are 22 grill points across by 18 grill points down.

**Overprints and Surcharges** — Overprinting involves applying wording or design elements over an already existing stamp. Overprints can be used to alter the place of use (such as "Canal Zone" on U.S. stamps), to adapt them for a special purpose ("Porto" on Denmark's 1913-20 regular issues for use as postage due stamps, Scott J1-J7) or to commemorate a special occasion (United States Scott 647-648).

A *surcharge* is a form of overprint that changes or restates the face value of a stamp or piece of postal stationery.

Surcharges and overprints may be handstamped, typeset or, occasionally, lithographed or engraved. A few hand-written overprints and surcharges are known.

**Personalized Stamps** — In 1999, Australia issued stamps with se-tenant labels that could be personalized with pictures of the customer's choice. Other countries quickly followed suit, with some offering to print the selected picture on the stamp itself within a frame that was used exclusively for personalized issues. As the picture used on these stamps or labels vary, listings for such stamps are for any picture within the common frame (or any picture on a se-tenant label), be it a "generic" image or one produced especially for a customer, almost invariably at a premium price.

**Precancels** — Stamps that are canceled before they are placed in the mail are known as precancels. Precanceling usually is done to expedite the handling of large mailings and generally allow the affected mail pieces to skip certain phases of mail handling.

In the United States, precancellations generally identified the point of origin; that is, the city and state. This information appeared across the face of the stamp, usually centered between parallel lines. More recently, bureau precancels retained the parallel lines, but the city and state designations were dropped. Recent coils have a service inscription that is present on the original printing plate. These show the mail service paid for by the stamp. Since these stamps are not intended to receive further cancellations when used as intended, they are considered precancels. Such items often do not have parallel lines as part of the precancellation.

In France, the abbreviation *Affranchts* in a semicircle together with the word *Postes* is the general form of precancel in use. Belgian precancellations usually appear in a box in which the name of the city appears. Netherlands precancels have the name of the city enclosed between concentric circles, sometimes called a "lifesaver." Precancellations of other countries usually follow these patterns, but may be any arrangement of bars, boxes and city names.

Precancels are listed in the Scott catalogues only if the precancel changes the denomination (Belgium Scott 477-478); if the precanceled stamp is different from the non-precanceled version (such as untagged U.S. precancels); or if the stamp exists only precanceled (France Scott 1096-1099, U.S. Scott 2265).

**Proofs and Essays** — Proofs are impressions taken from an approved die, plate or stone in which the design and color are the same as the stamp issued to the public. Trial color proofs are impressions taken from approved dies, plates or stones in colors that vary from the final version. An essay is the impression of a design that differs in some way from the issued stamp. "Progressive die proofs" generally are considered to be essays.

**Provisionals** — These are stamps that are issued on short notice and intended for temporary use pending the arrival of regular issues. They usually are issued to meet such contingencies as changes in government or currency, shortage of necessary postage values or military occupation.

During the 1840s, postmasters in certain American cities issued stamps that were valid only at specific post offices. In 1861, postmasters of the Confederate States also issued stamps with limited validity. Both of these examples are known as "postmaster's provisionals."

**Se-tenant** — This term refers to an unsevered pair, strip or block of stamps that differ in design, denomination or overprint.

Unless the se-tenant item has a continuous design (see U.S. Scott 1451a, 1694a) the stamps do not have to be in the same order as shown in the catalogue (see U.S. Scott 2158a).

**Specimens** — The Universal Postal Union required member nations to send samples of all stamps they released into service to the International Bureau in Switzerland. Member nations of the UPU received these specimens as samples of what stamps were valid for postage. Many are overprinted, handstamped or initial-perforated "Specimen," "Canceled" or "Muestra." Some are marked with bars across the denominations (China-Taiwan), punched holes (Czechoslovakia) or back inscriptions (Mongolia).

Stamps distributed to government officials or for publicity purposes, and stamps submitted by private security printers for official approval, also may receive such defacements.

The previously described defacement markings prevent postal use, and all such items generally are known as "specimens."

**Tete-Beche** — This term describes a pair of stamps in which one is upside down in relation to the other. Some of these are the result of intentional sheet arrangements, such as Morocco Scott B10-B11. Others occurred when one or more electrotypes accidentally were placed upside down on the plate, such as Colombia Scott 57a. Separation of the tete-beche stamps, of course, destroys the tete beche variety.

# Pronunciation Symbols

ə .... banana, collide, abut

ˈə, ˌə .... humdrum, abut

ə .... immediately preceding \l\, \n\, \m\, \ŋ\, as in battle, mitten, eaten, and sometimes open \ˈō-pəm\, lock and key \-ᵊŋ-\; immediately following \l\, \m\, \r\, as often in French table, prisme, titre

ər .... further, merger, bird

ˈər- / ˈə-r .... as in two different pronunciations of hurry \ˈhər-ē, ˈhə-rē\

a .... mat, map, mad, gag, snap, patch

ā .... day, fade, date, aorta, drape, cape

ä .... bother, cot, and, with most American speakers, father, cart

ȧ .... father as pronounced by speakers who do not rhyme it with *bother*; French patte

au̇ .... now, loud, out

b .... baby, rib

ch .... chin, nature \ˈnā-chər\

d .... did, adder

e .... bet, bed, peck

ˈē, ˌē .... beat, nosebleed, evenly, easy

ē .... easy, mealy

f .... fifty, cuff

g .... go, big, gift

h .... hat, ahead

hw .... whale as pronounced by those who do not have the same pronunciation for both *whale* and *wail*

i .... tip, banish, active

ī .... site, side, buy, tripe

j .... job, gem, edge, join, judge

k .... kin, cook, ache

k̲ .... German ich, Buch; one pronunciation of loch

l .... lily, pool

m .... murmur, dim, nymph

n .... no, own

ⁿ .... indicates that a preceding vowel or diphthong is pronounced with the nasal passages open, as in French *un bon vin blanc* \œⁿ-bōⁿ-vaⁿ-bläⁿ\

ŋ .... sing \ˈsiŋ\, singer \ˈsiŋ-ər\, finger \ˈfiŋ-gər\, ink \ˈiŋk\

ō .... bone, know, beau

ȯ .... saw, all, gnaw, caught

œ .... French boeuf, German Hölle

œ̄ .... French feu, German Höhle

ȯi .... coin, destroy

p .... pepper, lip

r .... red, car, rarity

s .... source, less

sh .... as in shy, mission, machine, special (actually, this is a single sound, not two); with a hyphen between, two sounds as in *grasshopper* \ˈgras-ˌhä-pər\

t .... tie, attack, late, later, latter

th .... as in thin, ether (actually, this is a single sound, not two); with a hyphen between, two sounds as in *knighthood* \ˈnīt-ˌhu̇d\

th̲ .... then, either, this (actually, this is a single sound, not two)

ü .... rule, youth, union \ˈyün-yən\, few \ˈfyü\

u̇ .... pull, wood, book, curable \ˈkyu̇r-ə-bəl\, fury \ˈfyu̇r-ē\

ue .... German füllen, hübsch

ue̅ .... French rue, German fühlen

v .... vivid, give

w .... we, away

y .... yard, young, cue \ˈkyü\, mute \ˈmyüt\, union \ˈyün-yən\

ʸ .... indicates that during the articulation of the sound represented by the preceding character the front of the tongue has substantially the position it has for the articulation of the first sound of *yard*, as in French *digne* \dēnʸ\

z .... zone, raise

zh .... as in vision, azure \ˈa-zhər\ (actually, this is a single sound, not two); with a hyphen between, two sounds as in *hogshead* \ˈhȯgz-ˌhed, ˈhägz-\

\ .... slant line used in pairs to mark the beginning and end of a transcription: \ˈpen\

ˈ .... mark preceding a syllable with primary (strongest) stress: \ˈpen-mən-ˌship\

ˌ .... mark preceding a syllable with secondary (medium) stress: \ˈpen-mən-ˌship\

\- .... mark of syllable division

( ) .... indicate that what is symbolized between is present in some utterances but not in others: *factory* \ˈfak-t(ə-)rē\

÷ .... indicates that many regard as unacceptable the pronunciation variant immediately following: *cupola* \ˈkyü-pə-lə, ÷-ˌlō\

# Vols. 5A-5B number additions, deletions and changes

| Number in 2022 Catalogue | Number in 2023 Catalogue |
|---|---|
| **New Zealand** | |
| 130d | 130D |
| 131d | 131D |
| 130e | 130E |
| 131e | 131E |
| 133e | 133E |
| 137e | 137E |
| **Nyasaland Protectorate** | |
| new | 16a |
| new | 17a |
| **Philippines** | |
| new | 2a |
| new | 2914a |
| new | 2934a |
| new | 3058a |
| new | 3556a |

## PITCAIRN ISLANDS

ˈpit-ˌkarn ˈī-ləndsˌ

LOCATION — South Pacific Ocean, nearly equidistant from Australia and South America

GOVT. — British colony under the British High Commissioner in New Zealand

AREA — 18 sq. mi. (includes all islands)

POP. — 43 (2007 est.)

The district of Pitcairn also includes the uninhabited islands of Ducie, Henderson and Oeno.

Postal affairs are administered by New Zealand.

12 Pence = 1 Shilling
100 Cents = 1 Dollar (1967)

**Catalogue values for all unused stamps in this country are for Never Hinged items.**

**Watermarks**

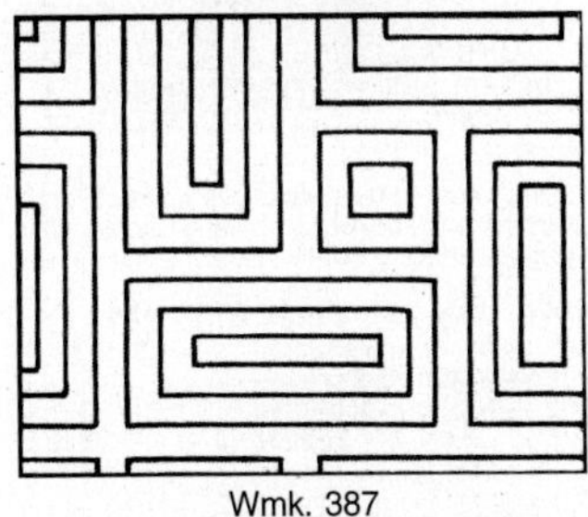

Wmk. 387

Cluster of Oranges A1

Fletcher Christian with Crew and View of Pitcairn Island — A2

John Adams and His House A3

William Bligh and H. M. Armed Vessel "Bounty" A4

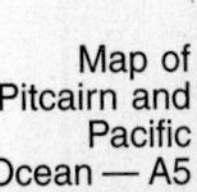

Map of Pitcairn and Pacific Ocean — A5

Bounty Bible — A6

H.M. Armed Vessel "Bounty" A7

Pitcairn School, 1949 — A8

Fletcher Christian and View of Pitcairn Island — A9

Fletcher Christian with Crew and Coast of Pitcairn A10

***Perf. 12½, 11½x11***

**1940-51 Engr. Wmk. 4**

| No. | Type | Description | Unused | Used |
|---|---|---|---|---|
| 1 | A1 | ½p blue grn & org | 1.25 | *1.25* |
| 2 | A2 | 1p red lil & rose vio | 1.50 | .80 |
| 3 | A3 | 1½p rose car & blk | 1.50 | .50 |
| 4 | A4 | 2p dk brn & brt grn | 2.50 | 1.50 |
| 5 | A5 | 3p dk blue & yel grn | 1.25 | 1.50 |
| 5A | A6 | 4p dk blue grn & blk | 22.50 | 15.00 |
| 6 | A7 | 6p sl grn & dp brn | 7.00 | 1.50 |
| 6A | A8 | 8p lil rose & grn | 22.50 | 11.00 |
| 7 | A9 | 1sh slate & vio | 6.75 | 3.75 |
| 8 | A10 | 2sh6p red brn & bl grn | 18.00 | 4.25 |
| | | *Nos. 1-8 (10)* | 84.75 | 41.05 |

Nos. 1-5, 6 and 7-8 exist in a booklet of eight panes of one. Value $3,000.

Issued: 4p, 8p, 9/1/51; others, 10/15/40.

Common Design Types pictured following the introduction.

**Peace Issue**
Common Design Type

**1946, Dec. 2** ***Perf. 13½x14***

| No. | Type | Description | Unused | Used |
|---|---|---|---|---|
| 9 | CD303 | 2p brown | .65 | .30 |
| 10 | CD303 | 3p deep blue | .75 | .30 |

**Silver Wedding Issue**
Common Design Types

**1949, Aug. 1 Photo.** ***Perf. 14x14½***

| No. | Type | Description | Unused | Used |
|---|---|---|---|---|
| 11 | CD304 | 1½p scarlet | 1.50 | 1.50 |

***Perf. 11½x11***

**Engraved; Name Typographed**

| No. | Type | Description | Unused | Used |
|---|---|---|---|---|
| 12 | CD305 | 10sh purple | 43.00 | *52.50* |

**UPU Issue**
Common Design Types

**Engr.; Name Typo. on 3p & 6p**

**1949, Oct. 10** ***Perf. 13½, 11x11½***

| No. | Type | Description | Unused | Used |
|---|---|---|---|---|
| 13 | CD306 | 2½p red brown | 1.80 | 3.25 |
| 14 | CD307 | 3p indigo | 6.50 | 3.75 |
| 15 | CD308 | 6p green | 3.25 | 3.75 |
| 16 | CD309 | 1sh rose violet | 3.50 | *3.50* |
| | | *Nos. 13-16 (4)* | 15.05 | 14.25 |

**Coronation Issue**
Common Design Type

**1953, June 2** ***Perf. 13½x13***

| No. | Type | Description | Unused | Used |
|---|---|---|---|---|
| 19 | CD312 | 4p dk green & blk | 2.00 | 3.50 |

Ti Plant — A11

Map — A12

Designs: 2p, John Adams and Bounty Bible. 2½p, Handicraft (Carving). 3p, Bounty Bay. 4p, School (actually Schoolteacher's House). 6p, Fiji-Pitcairn connection (Map). 8p, Inland scene. 1sh, Handicraft (Ship model). 2sh, Wheelbarrow. 2sh6p, Whaleboat.

***Perf. 13x12½, 12½x13***

**1957, July 2 Engr. Wmk. 4**

| No. | Type | Description | Unused | Used |
|---|---|---|---|---|
| 20 | A11 | ½p lilac & green | 1.25 | *1.50* |
| 21 | A12 | 1p olive grn & blk | 4.50 | 2.25 |
| 22 | A12 | 2p blue & brown | 2.25 | .50 |
| 23 | A11 | 2½p orange & brn | .75 | .40 |
| 24 | A11 | 3p ultra & emer | .80 | .40 |
| 25 | A11 | 4p ultra & rose red *(Pitcairn School)* | .90 | .40 |
| 26 | A11 | 6p indigo & buff | 3.50 | .50 |
| 27 | A11 | 8p magenta & grn | .75 | *.40* |
| 28 | A11 | 1sh brown & blk | 2.25 | .40 |
| 29 | A12 | 2sh dp org & grn | 11.00 | 10.00 |
| 30 | A11 | 2sh6p mag & ultra | 25.00 | 14.00 |
| | | *Nos. 20-30 (11)* | 52.95 | 30.75 |

See Nos. 31, 38.

**Type of 1957 Corrected**

**1958, Nov. 5** ***Perf. 13x12½***

| No. | Type | Description | Unused | Used |
|---|---|---|---|---|
| 31 | A11 | 4p ultra & rose red *(School-teacher's House)* | 4.00 | 1.50 |

Simon Young and Pitcairn A13

Designs: 6p, Maps of Norfolk and Pitcairn Islands. 1sh, Schooner Mary Ann.

***Perf. 14½x13½***

**1961, Nov. 15 Photo. Wmk. 314**

| No. | Type | Description | Unused | Used |
|---|---|---|---|---|
| 32 | A13 | 3p yellow & black | .50 | .50 |
| 33 | A13 | 6p blue & red brown | 1.10 | .75 |
| 34 | A13 | 1sh brt green & dp org | 1.10 | .75 |
| | | *Nos. 32-34 (3)* | 2.70 | 2.00 |

Pitcairn Islanders return from Norfolk Island.

**Freedom from Hunger Issue**
Common Design Type

**1963, June 4** ***Perf. 14x14½***

| No. | Type | Description | Unused | Used |
|---|---|---|---|---|
| 35 | CD314 | 2sh6p ultra | 3.50 | 1.50 |

**Red Cross Centenary Issue**
Common Design Type

**1963, Dec. 9 Litho.** ***Perf. 13***

| No. | Type | Description | Unused | Used |
|---|---|---|---|---|
| 36 | CD315 | 2p black & red | 1.00 | 1.00 |
| 37 | CD315 | 2sh6p ultra & red | 1.50 | 3.00 |

**Type of 1957**

***Perf. 13x12½***

**1963, Dec. 4 Engr. Wmk. 314**

| No. | Type | Description | Unused | Used |
|---|---|---|---|---|
| 38 | A11 | ½p lilac & green | .65 | .60 |

Pitcairn Longboat A14

Queen Elizabeth II — A15

1p, H.M. Armed Vessel Bounty. 2p, Oarsmen rowing longboat. 3p, Great frigate bird. 4p, Fairy tern 6p, Pitcairn reed warbler. 8p, Red-footed booby. 10p, Red-tailed tropic birds. 1sh, Henderson Island flightless rail. 1sh6p, Henderson Island lory. 2sh6p, Murphy's petrel. 4sh, Henderson Island fruit pigeon.

**1964-65 Photo.** ***Perf. 14x14½***

| No. | Type | Description | Unused | Used |
|---|---|---|---|---|
| 39 | A14 | ½p multicolored | .30 | *.30* |
| *a.* | | Blue omitted | 800.00 | |
| 40 | A14 | 1p multicolored | 1.00 | .30 |
| 41 | A14 | 2p multicolored | .30 | .30 |
| 42 | A14 | 3p multicolored | .75 | .30 |
| 43 | A14 | 4p multicolored | .75 | .30 |
| 44 | A14 | 6p multicolored | .75 | .30 |
| 45 | A14 | 8p multicolored | .75 | .30 |
| *a.* | | Gray (beak) omitted | 600.00 | |
| 46 | A14 | 10p multicolored | .60 | .30 |
| 47 | A14 | 1sh multicolored | .60 | .30 |
| 48 | A14 | 1sh6p multicolored | 1.50 | 1.25 |
| 49 | A14 | 2sh6p multicolored | 1.50 | 1.50 |
| 50 | A14 | 4sh multicolored | 1.50 | 1.50 |
| 51 | A15 | 8sh multicolored | 1.25 | 2.00 |
| | | *Nos. 39-51 (13)* | 11.55 | 8.95 |

Issued: ½p-4sh, 8/5/64; 8sh, 4/5/65.

For surcharges see Nos. 72-84.

**ITU Issue**
Common Design Type

**1965, May 17 Litho.** ***Perf. 11x11½***

| No. | Type | Description | Unused | Used |
|---|---|---|---|---|
| 52 | CD317 | 1p red lilac & org brn | .40 | .40 |
| 53 | CD317 | 2sh6p grnsh blue & ultra | 1.25 | 1.50 |

**Intl. Cooperation Year Issue**
Common Design Type

**1965, Oct. 25** ***Perf. 14½***

| No. | Type | Description | Unused | Used |
|---|---|---|---|---|
| 54 | CD318 | 1p bl grn & cl | .35 | .35 |
| 55 | CD318 | 1sh6p lt vio & grn | 1.25 | 1.50 |

**Churchill Memorial Issue**
Common Design Type

**1966, Jan. 24 Photo.** ***Perf. 14***

**Design in Black, Gold and Carmine Rose**

| No. | Type | Description | Unused | Used |
|---|---|---|---|---|
| 56 | CD319 | 2p brt blue | .70 | .85 |
| 57 | CD319 | 3p green | 1.25 | 1.00 |
| 58 | CD319 | 6p brown | 1.25 | 1.75 |
| 59 | CD319 | 1sh violet | 1.25 | 2.50 |
| | | *Nos. 56-59 (4)* | 4.45 | 6.10 |

**World Cup Soccer Issue**
Common Design Type

**1966, Aug. 1 Litho.** ***Perf. 14***

| No. | Type | Description | Unused | Used |
|---|---|---|---|---|
| 60 | CD321 | 4p multi | .75 | 1.00 |
| 61 | CD321 | 2sh6p multi | 1.25 | 1.00 |

**WHO Headquarters Issue**
Common Design Type

**1966, Sept. 20 Litho.** ***Perf. 14***

| No. | Type | Description | Unused | Used |
|---|---|---|---|---|
| 62 | CD322 | 8p multi | 2.00 | 3.25 |
| 63 | CD322 | 1sh6p multi | 3.50 | 3.75 |

**UNESCO Anniversary Issue**
Common Design Type

**1966, Dec. 1 Litho.** ***Perf. 14***

| No. | Type | Description | Unused | Used |
|---|---|---|---|---|
| 64 | CD323 | ½p "Education" | .30 | *1.00* |
| 65 | CD323 | 10p "Science" | 1.25 | .75 |
| 66 | CD323 | 2sh "Culture" | 2.50 | 2.25 |
| | | *Nos. 64-66 (3)* | 4.05 | 4.00 |

Mangarevan Canoe, c. 1325, and Pitcairn Island — A16

Designs: 1p, Pedro Fernandez de Quiros and galleon, 1606. 8p, "San Pedro," 17th century Spanish brigantine, 1606. 1sh, Capt. Philip Carteret and H.M.S. Swallow. 1sh6p, "Hercules," 1819.

**Wmk. 314**

**1967, Mar. 1 Photo.** ***Perf. 14½***

| No. | Type | Description | Unused | Used |
|---|---|---|---|---|
| 67 | A16 | ½p multicolored | .30 | .25 |
| 68 | A16 | 1p multicolored | .30 | .25 |
| 69 | A16 | 8p multicolored | .30 | .25 |
| 70 | A16 | 1sh multicolored | .30 | .25 |
| 71 | A16 | 1sh6p multicolored | .30 | .25 |
| | | *Nos. 67-71 (5)* | 1.50 | 1.25 |

Bicentenary of the discovery of Pitcairn Islands by Capt. Philip Carteret.

Nos. 39-51 Surcharged in Gold

**1967, July 10** ***Perf. 14x14½***

| | | | | |
|---|---|---|---|---|
| **72** | A14 | ½c on ½p | .30 | .25 |
| *a.* | | Brown omitted | 1,500. | |
| **73** | A14 | 1c on 1p | .50 | *1.25* |
| **74** | A14 | 2c on 2p | .30 | *1.25* |
| **75** | A14 | 2½c on 3p | .30 | *1.25* |
| **76** | A14 | 3c on 4p | .30 | .25 |
| **77** | A14 | 5c on 6p | .30 | 1.25 |
| **78** | A14 | 10c on 8p | .50 | .30 |
| *a.* | | "10c" omitted | *2,000.* | |
| *b.* | | Pale blue (beak) omitted | *900.00* | |
| **79** | A14 | 15c on 10p | 1.50 | .40 |
| **80** | A14 | 20c on 1sh | 1.50 | .55 |
| **81** | A14 | 25c on 1sh6p | 1.50 | 1.25 |
| **82** | A14 | 30c on 2sh6p | 1.50 | 1.25 |
| **83** | A14 | 40c on 4sh | 1.75 | 1.25 |
| **84** | A15 | 45c on 8sh | 1.50 | 1.50 |
| | | *Nos. 72-84 (13)* | 11.75 | 12.00 |

Size of gold rectangle and anchor varies. The anchor symbol is designed after the anchor of H.M.S. Bounty.

Admiral Bligh and Bounty's Launch — A17

Designs: 8c, Bligh and his followers adrift in a boat. 20c, Bligh's tomb, St. Mary's Cemetery, Lambeth, London.

**Unwmk.**

**1967, Dec. 7** **Litho.** ***Perf. 13***

| | | | | |
|---|---|---|---|---|
| **85** | A17 | 1c ultra, lt blue & blk | .30 | .25 |
| **86** | A17 | 8c brt rose, yel & blk | .50 | .50 |
| **87** | A17 | 20c brown, yel & blk | 1.00 | 1.00 |
| | | *Nos. 85-87 (3)* | 1.80 | 1.75 |

150th anniv. of the death of Admiral William Bligh (1754-1817), capt. of the Bounty.

Human Rights Flame A18

***Perf. 13½x13***

**1968, Mar. 4** **Litho.** **Wmk. 314**

| | | | | |
|---|---|---|---|---|
| **88** | A18 | 1c rose & multi | .30 | .25 |
| **89** | A18 | 2c ocher & multi | .30 | .25 |
| **90** | A18 | 25c multicolored | .50 | .35 |
| | | *Nos. 88-90 (3)* | 1.10 | .85 |

International Human Rights Year.

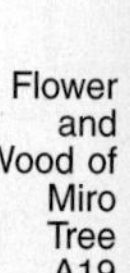
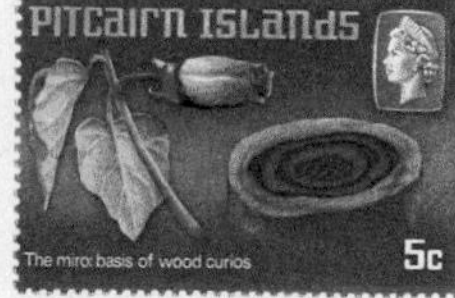


Flower and Wood of Miro Tree A19

Pitcairn Handicraft: 10c, Carved flying fish. 15c, Two "hand" vases, vert. 20c, Old and new woven baskets, vert.

***Perf. 14½x14, 14x14½***

**1968, Aug. 19** **Photo.** **Wmk. 314**

| | | | | |
|---|---|---|---|---|
| **91** | A19 | 5c chocolate & multi | .30 | .30 |
| **92** | A19 | 10c dp green & multi | .30 | .40 |
| **93** | A19 | 15c brt violet & multi | .30 | .40 |
| **94** | A19 | 20c black & multi | .30 | .45 |
| | | *Nos. 91-94 (4)* | 1.20 | 1.55 |

See Nos. 194-197.

Microscope, Cell, Germs and WHO Emblem — A20

20c, Hypodermic and jars containing pills.

**1968, Nov. 25** **Litho.** ***Perf. 14***

| | | | | |
|---|---|---|---|---|
| **95** | A20 | 2c vio blue, grnsh bl & blk | .30 | .25 |
| **96** | A20 | 20c black, magenta & org | .40 | .50 |

20th anniv. of WHO.

Capt. Bligh and his Larcum-Kendall Chronometer — A21

1c, Pitcairn Island. 3c, Bounty's anchor, vert. 4c, Plan of the Bounty, drawn 1787. 5c, Breadfruit and method of transporting young plants. 6c, Bounty Bay. 8c, Pitcairn longboat. 10c, Ship Landing Point and palms. 15c, Fletcher Christian's Cave. 20c, Thursday October Christian's house. 25c, "Flying Fox" cable system (for hauling cargo), vert. 30c, Radio Station at Taro Ground. 40c, Bounty Bible.

***Perf. 13x12½, 12½x13***

**1969, Sept. 17** **Litho.** **Wmk. 314**

| | | | | |
|---|---|---|---|---|
| **97** | A21 | 1c brn, yel & gold | 1.25 | *1.50* |
| **98** | A21 | 2c brn, blk & gold | .30 | .25 |
| **99** | A21 | 3c red, blk & gold | .30 | .25 |
| **100** | A21 | 4c buff, brn & gold | 2.00 | .25 |
| **101** | A21 | 5c gold & multi | .80 | .25 |
| **102** | A21 | 6c gold & multi | .30 | .30 |
| **103** | A21 | 8c gold & multi | 2.00 | .30 |
| **104** | A21 | 10c gold & multi | 1.50 | .80 |
| **105** | A21 | 15c gold & multi | 2.25 | 1.75 |
| *a.* | | Gold (Queen's head) omitted | *1,100.* | |
| **106** | A21 | 20c gold & multi | .70 | .45 |
| **107** | A21 | 25c gold & multi | .80 | .45 |
| **108** | A21 | 30c gold & multi | .55 | .45 |
| **109** | A21 | 40c red lil, blk & gold | .75 | .60 |
| | | *Nos. 97-109 (13)* | 13.50 | 7.60 |

For overprint see No. 118.

Lantana — A22

Pitcairn Flowers: 2c, Indian shot (canna indica). 5c, Pulau (hibiscus tiliaceus). 25c, Wild gladioli.

**1970, Mar. 23** **Litho.** ***Perf. 14***

| | | | | |
|---|---|---|---|---|
| **110** | A22 | 1c black & multi | .30 | .50 |
| **111** | A22 | 2c black & multi | .30 | .60 |
| **112** | A22 | 5c black & multi | .30 | .70 |
| **113** | A22 | 25c black & multi | .65 | 1.00 |
| | | *Nos. 110-113 (4)* | 1.55 | 2.80 |

Rudderfish (Dream Fish) — A23

Fish: 5c, Groupers (Auntie and Ann). 15c, Wrasse (Elwyn's trousers). 20c, Wrasse (Whistling daughter).

***Perf. 14½x14***

**1970, Oct. 12** **Photo.** **Wmk. 314**

| | | | | |
|---|---|---|---|---|
| **114** | A23 | 5c black & multi | 1.25 | 1.25 |
| **115** | A23 | 10c grnsh bl & blk | 1.25 | 1.25 |
| **116** | A23 | 15c multicolored | 1.25 | 1.50 |
| **117** | A23 | 20c multicolored | 1.75 | 1.50 |
| | | *Nos. 114-117 (4)* | 5.50 | 5.50 |

**No. 104 Overprinted in Silver: "ROYAL VISIT 1971"**

**1971, Feb. 22** **Litho.** ***Perf. 13x12½***

| | | | | |
|---|---|---|---|---|
| **118** | A21 | 10c gold & multi | 2.40 | 2.40 |

Polynesian Artifacts — A24

Polynesian Art on Pitcairn: 5c, Rock carvings, vert. 15c, Making of stone fishhook. 20c, Seated deity, vert.

**1971, May 3** **Litho.** ***Perf. 13½***

**Queen's Head in Gold**

| | | | | |
|---|---|---|---|---|
| **119** | A24 | 5c dk brown & bis | 1.00 | 1.00 |
| **120** | A24 | 10c ol green & blk | 1.10 | 1.10 |
| **121** | A24 | 15c black & lt vio | 1.25 | 1.25 |
| **122** | A24 | 20c black & rose red | 1.60 | 1.60 |
| | | *Nos. 119-122 (4)* | 4.95 | 4.95 |

Health Care A25

4c, South Pacific Commission flag & Southern Cross, vert. 18c, Education (elementary school). 20c, Economy (country store).

**1972, Apr. 4** **Litho.** ***Perf. 14x14½***

| | | | | |
|---|---|---|---|---|
| **123** | A25 | 4c vio bl, yel & ultra | .65 | .65 |
| **124** | A25 | 8c brown & multi | .75 | .75 |
| **125** | A25 | 18c yellow grn & multi | .85 | .85 |
| **126** | A25 | 20c orange & multi | 1.25 | 1.25 |
| | | *Nos. 123-126 (4)* | 3.50 | 3.50 |

So. Pacific Commission, 25th anniv.

**Silver Wedding Issue, 1972**

Common Design Type

Design: Queen Elizabeth II, Prince Philip, skuas and longboat.

**1972, Nov. 20** **Photo.** **Wmk. 314**

| | | | | |
|---|---|---|---|---|
| **127** | CD324 | 4c slate grn & multi | .30 | .25 |
| **128** | CD324 | 20c ultra & multi | .60 | .60 |

Pitcairn Coat of Arms A26

**1973, Jan. 2** **Litho.** ***Perf. 14½x14***

| | | | | |
|---|---|---|---|---|
| **129** | A26 | 50c multicolored | 3.00 | *10.00* |

Rose Apple — A27

**1973, June 25** ***Perf. 14***

| | | | | |
|---|---|---|---|---|
| **130** | A27 | 4c shown | .85 | .85 |
| **131** | A27 | 8c Mountain apple | .95 | .95 |
| **132** | A27 | 15c Lata (myrtle) | 1.25 | 1.25 |
| **133** | A27 | 20c Cassia | 1.40 | 1.40 |
| **134** | A27 | 35c Guava | 2.00 | 2.00 |
| | | *Nos. 130-134 (5)* | 6.45 | 6.45 |

**Princess Anne's Wedding Issue**

Common Design Type

**1973, Nov. 14** **Litho.** ***Perf. 14***

| | | | | |
|---|---|---|---|---|
| **135** | CD325 | 10c lilac & multi | .30 | .25 |
| **136** | CD325 | 25c gray grn & multi | .40 | .35 |

Miter and Horn Shells A28

**1974, Apr. 15**

| | | | | |
|---|---|---|---|---|
| **137** | A28 | 4c shown | .70 | .70 |
| **138** | A28 | 10c Dove shells | .95 | .95 |
| **139** | A28 | 18c Limpets and false limpet | 1.10 | 1.10 |
| **140** | A28 | 50c Lucine shells | 2.00 | 2.00 |
| *a.* | | Souvenir sheet of 4, #137-140 | 5.50 | 5.50 |
| | | *Nos. 137-140 (4)* | 4.75 | 4.75 |

Pitcairn Post Office, UPU Emblem A29

UPU, cent.: 20c, Stampless cover, "Posted at Pitcairn Island No Stamps Available." 35c, Longboat leaving Bounty Bay for ship offshore.

**1974, July 22** **Wmk. 314** ***Perf. 14½***

| | | | | |
|---|---|---|---|---|
| **141** | A29 | 4c multicolored | .30 | .30 |
| **142** | A29 | 20c multicolored | .45 | .45 |
| **143** | A29 | 35c multicolored | .50 | .45 |
| | | *Nos. 141-143 (3)* | 1.25 | 1.20 |

Churchill: "Lift up your hearts . . ." — A30

Design: 35c, Churchill and "Give us the tools and we will finish the job."

**1974, Nov. 30** **Litho.** **Wmk. 373**

| | | | | |
|---|---|---|---|---|
| **144** | A30 | 20c black & citron | .40 | .40 |
| **145** | A30 | 35c black & yellow | .75 | .75 |

Sir Winston Churchill (1874-1965).

Queen Elizabeth II — A31

**1975, Apr. 21** **Wmk. 314** ***Perf. 14½***

| | | | | |
|---|---|---|---|---|
| **146** | A31 | $1 multicolored | 7.00 | *15.00* |

Mailboats — A32

**1975, July 22** **Litho.** ***Perf. 14½***

| | | | | |
|---|---|---|---|---|
| **147** | A32 | 4c Seringapatam, 1830 | .50 | .50 |
| **148** | A32 | 10c Pitcairn, 1890 | .60 | .60 |
| **149** | A32 | 18c Athenic, 1901 | .90 | .90 |
| **150** | A32 | 50c Gothic, 1948 | 1.25 | 1.25 |
| *a.* | | Souvenir sheet of 4, #147-150, perf. 14 | 10.00 | 10.00 |
| | | *Nos. 147-150 (4)* | 3.25 | 3.25 |

Pitcairn Wasp A33

Insects: 6c, Grasshopper. 10c, Pitcairn moths. 15c, Dragonfly. 20c, Banana moth.

**Wmk. 314**

**1975, Nov. 9 Litho. *Perf. 14½***

**151** A33 4c blue grn & multi .45 .45
**152** A33 6c carmine & multi .55 .55
**153** A33 10c purple & multi .75 .75
**154** A33 15c black & multi .85 .85
**155** A33 20c multicolored 1.00 1.00
*Nos. 151-155 (5)* 3.60 3.60

Fletcher Christian — A34 H.M.S. Bounty — A35

American Bicentennial: 30c, George Washington. 50c, Mayflower.

**1976, July 4 Wmk. 373 *Perf. 13½***

**156** A34 5c multicolored .30 .30
**157** A35 10c multicolored .55 .55
**158** A34 30c multicolored .70 .70
*a.* Pair, #156, 158 1.40 1.40
**159** A35 50c multicolored .85 .85
*a.* Pair, #157, 159 1.75 1.75
*Nos. 156-159 (4)* 2.40 2.40

Prince Philip's Arrival, 1971 Visit — A36

20c, Chair of homage. 50c, The enthronement.

**1977, Feb. 6 *Perf. 13***

**160** A36 8c silver & multi .30 .25
**161** A36 20c silver & multi .30 .30
**162** A36 50c silver & multi .55 .55
*Nos. 160-162 (3)* 1.15 1.10

25th anniv. of the reign of Elizabeth II.

Building Longboat — A37

Designs: 1c, Man ringing Island Bell, vert. 5c, Landing cargo. 6c, Sorting supplies. 9c, Cleaning wahoo (fish), vert. 10c, Farming. 15c, Sugar mill. 20c, Women grating coconuts and bananas. 35c, Island church. 50c, Gathering miro logs, Henderson Island. 70c, Burning obsolete stamps, vert. $1, Prince Philip and "Britannia." $2, Elizabeth II, vert.

**1977-81 Litho. *Perf. 14½***

**163** A37 1c multicolored .30 *.45*
**164** A37 2c multicolored .30 *.45*
**165** A37 5c multicolored .30 *.45*
**166** A37 6c multicolored .30 *.45*
**167** A37 9c multicolored .30 *.45*
**168** A37 10c multicolored .30 *.45*
**168A** A37 15c multicolored 1.10 *2.25*
**169** A37 20c multicolored .30 *.50*
**170** A37 35c multicolored .30 *.65*
**171** A37 50c multicolored .35 *.75*
**171A** A37 70c multicolored 1.10 *2.50*
**172** A37 $1 multicolored .50 *.90*
**173** A37 $2 multicolored .70 *1.00*
*Nos. 163-173 (13)* 6.15 *11.25*

Issued: #168A, 171A, 10/1/81; others, 9/12/77.

Building "Bounty" Model A38

Bounty Day: 20c, Bounty model afloat. 35c, Burning Bounty.

**1978, Jan. 9 *Perf. 14½***

**174** A38 6c yellow & multi .40 .40
**175** A38 20c yellow & multi .55 .55
**176** A38 35c yellow & multi .70 .70
*a.* Souvenir sheet of 3, #174-176 6.50 6.50
*Nos. 174-176 (3)* 1.65 1.65

Souvenir Sheet

Elizabeth II in Coronation Regalia — A39

**Wmk. 373**

**1978, Sept. Litho. *Perf. 12***

**177** A39 $1.20 silver & multi 1.10 1.10

25th anniv. of coronation of Elizabeth II.

Unloading "Sir Geraint" A40

Designs: 15c, Harbor before development. 30c, Work on the jetty. 35c, Harbor after development.

**Wmk. 373**

**1978, Dec. 18 Litho. *Perf. 13½***

**178** A40 15c multicolored .30 .30
**179** A40 20c multicolored .40 .40
**180** A40 30c multicolored .55 .55
**181** A40 35c multicolored .70 .70
*Nos. 178-181 (4)* 1.95 1.95

Development of new harbor on Pitcairn.

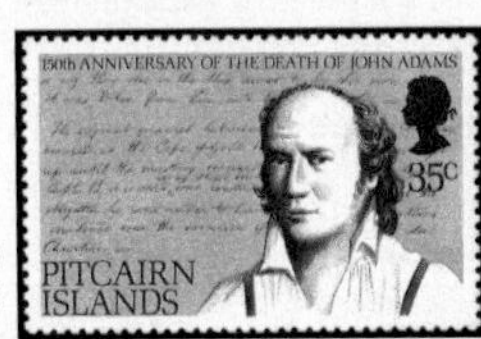

John Adams A41

Design: 70c, John Adams' grave.

**1979, Mar. 5 Litho. *Perf. 14½***

**182** A41 35c multicolored .45 .45
**183** A41 70c multicolored .75 .75

John Adams (1760-1829), founder of Pitcairn Colony, 150th death anniversary.

Pitcairn Island Seen from "Amphitrite" — A42

Engravings (c. 1850): 9c, Bounty Bay and Pitcairn Village, 20c, Lookout Ridge. 70c, Church and schoolhouse.

**1979, Sept. 12 Litho. *Perf. 14***

**184** A42 6c multicolored .30 .25
**185** A42 9c multicolored .30 .25
**186** A42 20c multicolored .30 .25
**187** A42 70c multicolored .40 .40
*Nos. 184-187 (4)* 1.30 1.15

Taking Presents to the Square, IYC Emblem — A43

IYC Emblem and Children's Drawings: 9c, Decorating trees with presents. 20c, Distributing presents. 35c, Carrying the presents home.

**Wmk. 373**

**1979, Nov. 28 Litho. *Perf. 13½***

**188** A43 6c multicolored .30 .25
**189** A43 9c multicolored .30 .25
**190** A43 20c multicolored .30 .25
**191** A43 35c multicolored .35 .35
*a.* Souvenir sheet of 4, #188-191 1.40 1.40
*Nos. 188-191 (4)* 1.25 1.10

Christmas and IYC.

Souvenir Sheet

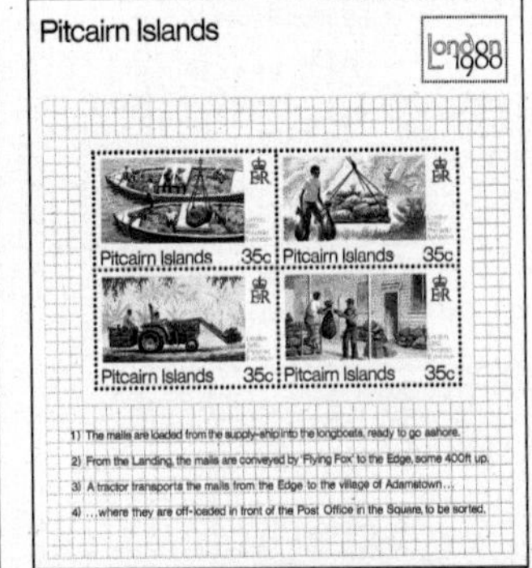

London 80 Intl. Phil. Exhibition — A44

**Wmk. 373**

**1980, May 6 Litho. *Perf. 14½***

**192** A44 Sheet of 4 1.25 1.25
*a.* 35c Mail Transport by Longboat .30 .30
*b.* 35c Mail crane lift .30 .30
*c.* 35c Tractor transport .30 .30
*d.* 35c Arrival at post office .30 .30

London 80 Intl. Phil. Exhib., May 6-14.

**Queen Mother Elizabeth Birthday Issue**

Common Design Type

**Wmk. 373**

**1980, Aug. 4 Litho. *Perf. 14***

**193** CD330 50c multicolored .60 .60

**Handicraft Type of 1968**

***Perf. 14½x14, 14x14½***

**1980, Sept. 29 Litho. Wmk. 373**

**194** A19 9c Turtles .30 .25
**195** A19 20c Wheelbarrow .30 .25
**196** A19 35c Gannet, vert. .30 .25
**197** A19 40c Bonnet and fan, vert. .30 .30
*Nos. 194-197 (4)* 1.20 1.05

Big George — A45

**Wmk. 373**

**1981, Jan. 22 Litho. *Perf. 14***

**198** A45 6c View of Adamstown .30 .25
**199** A45 9c shown .30 .25
**200** A45 20c Christian's Cave, Gannet's Ridge .30 .25
**201** A45 35c Pawala Valley Ridge .30 .25
**202** A45 70c Tatrimoa .35 .35
*Nos. 198-202 (5)* 1.55 1.35

Citizens Departing for Norfolk Island — A46

**1981, May 3 Photo. *Perf. 13x14½***

**203** A46 9c shown .30 .25
**204** A46 35c Norfolk Isld. from Morayshire .35 .35
**205** A46 70c Morayshire .65 .65
*Nos. 203-205 (3)* 1.30 1.25

Migration to Norfolk Is., 125th anniv.

**Royal Wedding Issue**

Common Design Type

**Wmk. 373**

**1981, July 22 Litho. *Perf. 14***

**206** CD331 20c Bouquet .30 .25
**207** CD331 35c Charles .30 .25
**208** CD331 $1.20 Couple .60 .60
*Nos. 206-208 (3)* 1.20 1.10

Lemon A47

**1982, Feb. 23 Litho. *Perf. 14½***

**209** A47 9c shown .30 .25
**210** A47 20c Pomegranate .30 .30
**211** A47 35c Avocado .35 .35
**212** A47 70c Pawpaw .50 .50
*Nos. 209-212 (4)* 1.45 1.40

**Princess Diana Issue**

Common Design Type

**1982, July 1 Litho. *Perf. 14½x14***

**213** CD333 6c Arms .30 .25
**214** CD333 9c Diana .35 .35
**215** CD333 70c Wedding .45 .45
**216** CD333 $1.20 Portrait .80 .80
*Nos. 213-216 (4)* 1.90 1.85

Christmas — A48

Designs: Various paintings of angels by Raphael. 50c, $1 vert.

**1982, Oct. 19 Litho. *Perf. 14***

**217** A48 15c multicolored .30 .30
**218** A48 20c multicolored .30 .30
**219** A48 50c multicolored .40 .40
**220** A48 $1 multicolored .60 .60
*Nos. 217-220 (4)* 1.60 1.60

A48a

**1983, Mar. 14**

**221** A48a 6c Radio operator .30 .25
**222** A48a 9c Postal clerk .30 .25
**223** A48a 70c Fisherman .40 .40
**224** A48a $1.20 Artist .75 .75
*Nos. 221-224 (4)* 1.75 1.65

Commonwealth Day.

175th Anniv. of Capt. Folger's Discovery of the Settlers A49

6c, Topaz off Pitcairn Isld. 20c, Topaz, islanders. 70c, John Adams welcoming Folger. $1.20, Presentation of Chronometer.

**Wmk. 373**

**1983, June 14 Litho. *Perf. 14***

**225** A49 6c multicolored .30 .30
**226** A49 20c multicolored .45 .45
**227** A49 70c multicolored .70 .70
**228** A49 $1.20 multicolored 1.10 1.10
*Nos. 225-228 (4)* 2.55 2.55

Local Trees A50

**1983, Oct. 6 Litho. *Perf. 13½***

**229** Pair 1.00 1.00
*a.* A50 35c Hattie .40 .40
*b.* A50 35c Branch, wood painting .40 .40
**230** Pair 1.75 1.75
*a.* A50 70c Pandanus .70 .70
*b.* A50 70c Branch, basket weaving .70 .70

See Nos. 289-290.

Pseudojuloides Atavai — A51

4c, Halichoeres melasmapomus. 6c, Scarus longipinnis. 9c, Variola louti. 10c, Centropyge hotumatua. 15c, Stegastes emeryi. 20c, Chaetodon smithi. 35c, Xanthichthys mento. 50c, Chrysiptera galba. 70c, Genicanthus spinus. $1, Myripristis tiki. $1.20, Anthias ventralis. $2, Pseudocaranx dentex.

**Wmk. 373**

**1984, Jan. 11 Litho. *Perf. 14½***

**231** A51 1c multicolored .30 .40
**232** A51 4c multicolored .40 .30
**233** A51 6c multicolored .40 .30
**234** A51 9c multicolored .40 .30
**235** A51 10c multicolored .40 .35
**236** A51 15c multicolored .40 .35
**237** A51 20c multicolored .50 *.50*
**238** A51 35c multicolored .70 *.75*
**239** A51 50c multicolored .70 *1.00*
**240** A51 70c multicolored 1.00 *1.25*
**241** A51 $1 multicolored 1.00 *1.50*
**242** A51 $1.20 multicolored 1.20 *1.75*
**243** A51 $2 multicolored 1.60 *2.00*
*Nos. 231-243 (13)* 9.00 10.75

See Nos. 295-296.

Constellations — A52

**1984, May 14 Wmk. 373**

**244** A52 15c Crux Australis .30 .25
**245** A52 20c Piscis Australis .30 .30
**246** A52 70c Canis Minor .50 .50
**247** A52 $1 Virgo .85 .85
*Nos. 244-247 (4)* 1.95 1.90

Souvenir Sheet

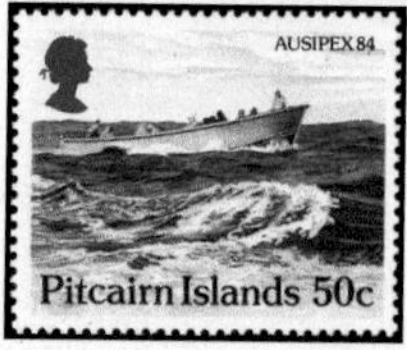


AUSIPEX '84 — A53

Longboats.

**1984, Sept. 21 Litho. Wmk. 373**

**248** Sheet of 2 2.50 2.50
*a.* A53 50c multicolored .50 .50
*b.* A53 $2 multicolored 1.75 1.75

HMS Portland off Bounty Bay, by J. Linton Palmer, 1853 — A54

Paintings by J. Linton Palmer, 1853, and William Smyth, 1825: 9c, Christian's Look Out at Pitcairn Island. 35c, The Golden Age. $2, View of Village, by Smyth.

**Wmk. 373**

**1985, Jan. 16 Litho. *Perf. 14***

**249** A54 6c multicolored .35 .35
**250** A54 9c multicolored .35 .35
**251** A54 35c multicolored .70 .70

**Size: 48x32mm**

**252** A54 $2 multicolored 1.60 1.60
*Nos. 249-252 (4)* 3.00 3.00

Examples of No. 252 with "1835" date were not issued. Value, $65.

See Nos. 291-294.

**Queen Mother 85th Birthday**

Common Design Type

6c, In Dundee, 1964. 35c, At 80th birthday celebration. 70c, Queen Mother. $1.20, Holding Prince Henry.

$2, In coach at the Races, Ascot.

***Perf. 14½x14***

**1985, June 7 Litho. Wmk. 384**

**253** CD336 6c multi .30 *.30*
**254** CD336 35c multi .35 *.55*
**255** CD336 70c multi .65 *.85*
**256** CD336 $1.20 multi 1.25 *1.50*
*Nos. 253-256 (4)* 2.55 *3.20*

**Souvenir Sheet**

**257** CD336 $2 multi 2.75 2.75

Act 6 — A55

Essi Gina A56

**1985, Aug. 28 *Perf. 14½x14***

**258** A55 50c shown 1.00 1.00
**259** A55 50c Columbus Louisiana 1.00 1.00

***Perf. 14***

**260** A56 50c shown 1.00 1.00
**261** A56 50c Stolt Spirit 1.00 1.00
*Nos. 258-261 (4)* 4.00 4.00

See Nos. 281-284.

Christmas A57

Madonna & child paintings: 6c, by Raphael. 9c, by Krause. 35c, by Andreas Mayer. $2, by an unknown Austrian master.

**1985, Nov. 26 *Perf. 14***

**262** A57 6c multicolored .65 .65
**263** A57 9c multicolored .65 .65
**264** A57 35c multicolored 1.10 1.10
**265** A57 $2 multicolored 3.50 3.50
*Nos. 262-265 (4)* 5.90 5.90

Turtles A58

Designs: 9c, 20c, Chelonia mydas. 70c, $1.20, Eretmochelys imbricata.

**Wmk. 384**

**1986, Feb. 12 Litho. *Perf. 14½***

**266** A58 9c multicolored 1.00 1.00
**267** A58 20c multi, diff. 1.50 1.50
**268** A58 70c multicolored 2.40 2.40
**269** A58 $1.20 multi, diff. 3.00 3.00
*Nos. 266-269 (4)* 7.90 7.90

**Queen Elizabeth II 60th Birthday**

Common Design Type

Designs: 6c, In Royal Lodge garden, Windsor, 1946. 9c, Wedding of Princess Anne and Capt. Mark Philips, 1973. 20c, Wearing mantle and robes of Order of St. Paul's Cathedral, 1961. $1.20, Concert, Royal Festival Hall, London, 1971. $2, Visting Crown Agents' offices, 1983.

**1986, Apr. 21 Litho. *Perf. 14½***

**270** CD337 6c multi .30 .25
**271** CD337 9c multi .30 .25
**272** CD337 20c multi .35 .35
**273** CD337 $1.20 multi .75 .75
**274** CD337 $2 multi 1.10 1.10
*Nos. 270-274 (5)* 2.80 2.70

**Royal Wedding Issue, 1986**

Common Design Type

Designs: 20c, Informal portrait. $1.20, Andrew aboard royal navy vessel.

**Wmk. 384**

**1986, July 23 Litho. *Perf. 14***

**275** CD338 20c multi .40 .40
**276** CD338 $1.20 multi 2.00 2.00

7th Day Adventist Church, Cent. — A59

Designs: 6c, First church, 1886, and John I. Tay, missionary. 20c, Second church, 1907, and mission ship Pitcairn, 1890. 35c, Third church, 1945, baptism and Down Isaac. $2, Church, 1954, and sailing ship.

**1986, Oct. 18**

**277** A59 6c multicolored .50 .50
**278** A59 20c multicolored 1.25 1.25
**279** A59 35c multicolored 1.50 1.50
**280** A59 $2 multicolored 4.25 4.25
*Nos. 277-280 (4)* 7.50 7.50

**Ship Type of 1985**

**1987, Jan. 20 *Perf. 14x14½***

**281** A55 50c Brussel 1.40 1.40
**282** A55 50c Samoan Reefer 1.40 1.40

***Perf. 14***

**283** A56 50c Australian Exporter 1.40 1.40
**284** A56 50c Taupo 1.40 1.40
*Nos. 281-284 (4)* 5.60 5.60

Island Houses — A60

**1987, May 21 Wmk. 373 *Perf. 14***

**285** A60 70c lt greenish blue, bluish grn & blk .65 .65
**286** A60 70c cream, yel bister & blk .65 .65
**287** A60 70c lt blue, brt blue & blk .65 .65
**288** A60 70c lt lil, brt vio & blk .65 .65
*Nos. 285-288 (4)* 2.60 2.60

**Tree Type of 1983**

**1987, Aug. 10 Wmk. 384 *Perf. 14½***

**289** Pair 1.75 1.75
*a.* A50 40c Leaves, blossoms .80 .80
*b.* A50 40c Monkey puzzle tree .80 .80
**290** Pair 6.00 6.00
*a.* A50 $1.80 Leaves, blossoms, nuts 2.50 2.50
*b.* A50 $1.80 Duduinut tree 2.50 2.50

**Art Type of 1985**

Paintings by Lt. Conway Shipley, 1848: 20c, House and Tomb of John Adams. 40c, Bounty Bay, with H.M.S. Calypso. 90c, School House and Chapel. $1.80, Pitcairn Island with H.M.S. Calypso.

**1987, Dec. 7 Litho. *Perf. 14***

**291** A54 20c multi .65 .65
**292** A54 40c multi 1.00 1.00
**293** A54 90c multi 2.00 2.00

**Size: 48x32mm**

**294** A54 $1.80 multi 3.00 3.00
*Nos. 291-294 (4)* 6.65 6.65

**Fish Type of 1984**

**Wmk. 384**

**1988, Jan. 14 Litho. *Perf. 14½***

**295** A51 90c Variola louti 3.50 3.50
**296** A51 $3 Gymnothorax eurostus 5.00 5.00

Souvenir Sheet

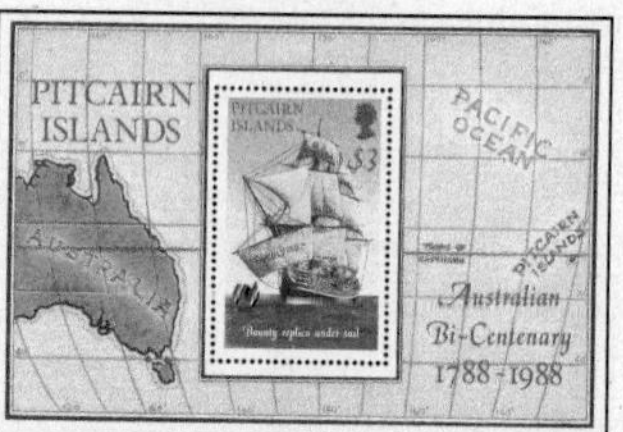


Australia Bicentennial — A61

**1988, May 9 Wmk. 384 *Perf. 14***

**297** A61 $3 HMS Bounty replica under sail 7.00 7.00

Visiting Ships A62

5c, HMS Swallow, 1767. 10c, HMS Pandora, 1791. 15c, HMS Briton and HMS Tagus, 1814. 20c, HMS Blossom, 1825. 30c, S.V. Lucy Anne, 1831. 35c, S.V. Charles Doggett, 1831. 40c, HMS Fly, 1838. 60c, LMS Camden, 1840. 90c, HMS Virago, 1853. $1.20, S.S. Rakaia, 1867. $1.80, HMS Sappho, 1882. $5, HMS Champion, 1893.

**Wmk. 373**

**1988, Aug. 14 Litho. *Perf. 13½***

**298** A62 5c multicolored .50 *.60*
**299** A62 10c multicolored .50 *.60*
**300** A62 15c multicolored .50 *.60*
**301** A62 20c multicolored .60 *.70*
*a.* Wmk. 384 1.75 *2.00*
*b.* Booklet pane of 4, #301a 7.00
**302** A62 30c multicolored .70 *.80*
**303** A62 35c multicolored .70 *.80*
**304** A62 40c multicolored .80 .80
**305** A62 60c multicolored 1.00 *1.25*
**306** A62 90c multicolored 1.10 *4.00*
*a.* Wmk. 384 3.75 *4.25*
*b.* Booklet pane of 4, #306a 15.00
**307** A62 $1.20 multicolored 1.10 *1.50*
**308** A62 $1.80 multicolored 1.50 *2.00*
**309** A62 $5 multicolored 3.50 *5.00*
*Nos. 298-309 (12)* 12.50 *18.65*

Inscribed "1988" below design. Nos. 301a and 366a are inscribed "1990."

Issued: #301a-301b, 306a-306b, 5/3/90.

Constitution, 150th Anniv. — A63

Text and: 20c, Raising the Union Jack. 40c, Signing of the constitution aboard the H.M.S. "Fly," 1838. $1.05, Suffrage. $1.80, Equal education.

**1988, Nov. 30 Wmk. 373 *Perf. 14***

| | | | | | |
|---|---|---|---|---|---|
| **315** | A63 | 20c | multicolored | .40 | .40 |
| **316** | A63 | 40c | multicolored | .60 | .60 |
| **317** | A63 | $1.05 | multicolored | .95 | .95 |
| **318** | A63 | $1.80 | multicolored | 1.40 | 1.40 |
| | | | *Nos. 315-318 (4)* | 3.35 | 3.35 |

Christmas A64

a, Angel, animals in stable. b, Holy Family. c, Two Magi. d, Magus and shepherd boy.

**1988, Nov. 30 Wmk. 384 *Perf. 14***

| | | | |
|---|---|---|---|
| **319** | Strip of 4 | 3.50 | 3.50 |
| *a.-d.* | A64 90c any single | .80 | .80 |

Miniature Sheets

Pitcairn Isls., Bicent. — A65

No. 320 (*Bounty* sets sail for the South Seas, Dec. 23, 1787): a, Fitting out the *Bounty* at Deptford. b, *Bounty* leaving Spithead. c, *Bounty* trying to round Cape Horn. d, Anchored in Adventure Bay, Tasmania. e, Ship's mates collecting breadfruit. f, Breadfruit in great cabin.

No. 321 (the mutiny, Apr. 28, 1789): a, *Bounty* leaving Matavai Bay. b, Mutineers waking Capt. Bligh. c, Confrontation between Fletcher Christian and Bligh. d, Bligh and crew members set adrift in an open boat. e, Castaways. f, Throwing breadfruit overboard.

No. 322: a, like No. 321e. b, Isle of Man #393. c, Norfolk Is. #453.

**1989 Litho. Wmk. 373**

| | | | |
|---|---|---|---|
| **320** | A65 Sheet of 6 | 6.00 | 6.00 |
| *a.-f.* | 20c any single | .75 | .75 |
| **321** | A65 Sheet of 6 | 12.50 | 12.50 |
| *a.-f.* | 90c any single | 2.00 | 2.25 |

**Souvenir Sheet**

**Wmk. 384**

| | | | |
|---|---|---|---|
| **322** | Sheet of 3 + label | 5.25 | 5.25 |
| *a.-c.* | A65 90c any single | 1.50 | 1.50 |

See #331, Isle of Man #389-394 and Norfolk Is. #452-456.

Issued: #320, Feb. 22; #321-322, Apr. 28.

Difference between #. 321e and 322a is inscription at bottom of #322a: "C. Abbott 1989 BOT."

Aircraft A66

20c, RNZAF Orion. 80c, Beechcraft Queen Air. $1.05, Navy helicopter, USS *Breton*. $1.30, RNZAF Hercules.

**Wmk. 384**

**1989, July 25 Litho. *Perf. 14½***

| | | | | | |
|---|---|---|---|---|---|
| **323** | A66 | 20c | multicolored | 1.00 | 1.00 |
| **324** | A66 | 80c | multicolored | 2.25 | 2.25 |
| **325** | A66 | $1.05 | multicolored | 2.50 | 2.50 |
| **326** | A66 | $1.30 | multicolored | 2.75 | 2.75 |
| | | | *Nos. 323-326 (4)* | 8.50 | 8.50 |

Second mail drop on Pitcairn, Mar. 21, 1985 (20c); photo mission from Tahiti, Jan. 14, 1983 (80c); diesel fuel delivery by the navy, Feb. 12, 1969 ($1.05); and parachute delivery of a bulldozer, May 31, 1983 ($1.30).

The Islands A67

**Wmk. 373**

**1989, Oct. 23 Litho. *Perf. 14***

| | | | | | |
|---|---|---|---|---|---|
| **327** | A67 | 15c | Ducie Is. | .50 | .50 |
| **328** | A67 | 90c | Henderson Is. | 1.50 | 1.50 |
| **329** | A67 | $1.05 | Oeno Is. | 2.00 | 2.00 |
| **330** | A67 | $1.30 | Pitcairn Is. | 2.25 | 2.25 |
| | | | *Nos. 327-330 (4)* | 6.25 | 6.25 |

**Bicentennial Type of 1989**

Miniature Sheet

Designs: a, Mutineers aboard *Bounty* anticipating landing on Pitcairn. b, Landing. c, Exploration of the island. d, Carrying goods ashore. e, Burning the *Bounty.* f, Settlement.

**1990, Jan. 15 Wmk. 384 *Perf. 14***

| | | | |
|---|---|---|---|
| **331** | Sheet of 6 + 3 labels | 10.00 | 10.00 |
| *a.-f.* | A65 40c any single | 1.10 | 1.10 |

Stamp World London '90 — A68

Links with the UK: 80c, Peter Heywood and Ennerdale, Cumbria. 90c, John Adams and The Tower of St. Augustine, Hackney. $1.05, William Bligh and The Citadel Gateway, Plymouth. $1.30, Fletcher Christian and birthplace, Cockermouth.

**1990, May 3 Wmk. 373 *Perf. 14***

| | | | | | |
|---|---|---|---|---|---|
| **332** | A68 | 80c | multicolored | 1.00 | 1.00 |
| **333** | A68 | 90c | multicolored | 1.10 | 1.10 |
| **334** | A68 | $1.05 | multicolored | 1.25 | 1.25 |
| **335** | A68 | $1.30 | multicolored | 1.75 | 1.75 |
| | | | *Nos. 332-335 (4)* | 5.10 | 5.10 |

**Queen Mother 90th Birthday**

Common Design Types

**1990, Aug. 4 Wmk. 384 *Perf. 14x15***

| | | | | |
|---|---|---|---|---|
| **336** | CD343 | 40c Portrait, 1937 | .75 | .75 |

***Perf. 14½***

| | | | | |
|---|---|---|---|---|
| **337** | CD344 | $3 King, Queen in carriage | 3.50 | 3.50 |

First Pitcairn Island Postage Stamps, 50th Anniv — A69

Historical items and Pitcairn Islands stamps — 20c, Chronometer, #2. 80c, Bounty's Bible, #31. 90c, Bounty's Bell, #108. $1.05, Bounty, #172. $1.30, Penny Black, #300.

***Perf. 13½x14***

**1990, Oct. 15 Wmk. 373**

| | | | | | |
|---|---|---|---|---|---|
| **338** | A69 | 20c | multicolored | .80 | .80 |
| **339** | A69 | 80c | multicolored | 1.60 | 1.60 |
| **340** | A69 | 90c | multicolored | 1.75 | 1.75 |
| **341** | A69 | $1.05 | multicolored | 2.00 | 2.00 |
| **342** | A69 | $1.30 | multicolored | 2.25 | 2.25 |
| | | | *Nos. 338-342 (5)* | 8.40 | 8.40 |

Birds — A70

**1990, Dec. 5 Wmk. 373 *Perf. 14***

| | | | | | |
|---|---|---|---|---|---|
| **343** | A70 | 20c | Redbreast | 1.00 | 1.00 |
| **344** | A70 | 90c | Wood pigeon | 1.75 | 1.75 |
| **345** | A70 | $1.30 | Sparrow | 2.00 | 2.00 |
| **346** | A70 | $1.80 | Flightless chicken | 2.25 | 2.25 |
| | | | *Nos. 343-346 (4)* | 7.00 | 7.00 |

Birdpex '90, 20th Intl. Ornithological Congress, New Zealand.

Miniature Sheet

Pitcairn Islands, Bicent. — A71

Bicentennial celebrations: a, Re-enacting the landing. b, Commemorative plaque. c, Memorial church service. d, Cricket match. e, Bounty model burning. f, Fireworks.

**Wmk. 384**

**1991, Mar. 24 Litho. *Perf. 14½***

| | | | | |
|---|---|---|---|---|
| **347** | A71 | 80c Sheet of 6, #a.-f. | 12.00 | 12.00 |

**Elizabeth & Philip, Birthdays**

Common Design Types

**Wmk. 384**

**1991, July 12 Litho. *Perf. 14½***

| | | | | | |
|---|---|---|---|---|---|
| **348** | CD346 | 20c | multicolored | .50 | .50 |
| **349** | CD345 | $1.30 | multicolored | 2.00 | 2.00 |
| *a.* | | | Pair, #348-349 + label | 3.25 | 3.25 |

Cruise Ships A72

15c, Europa. 80c, Royal Viking Star. $1.30, World Discoverer. $1.80, Sagafjord.

**1991, June 17**

| | | | | | |
|---|---|---|---|---|---|
| **350** | A72 | 15c | multicolored | 1.25 | 1.25 |
| **351** | A72 | 80c | multicolored | 2.25 | 2.25 |
| **352** | A72 | $1.30 | multicolored | 2.75 | 2.75 |
| **353** | A72 | $1.80 | multicolored | 3.25 | 3.25 |
| | | | *Nos. 350-353 (4)* | 9.50 | 9.50 |

Island Vehicles A73

**1991, Sept. 25 Wmk. 373 *Perf. 14***

| | | | | | |
|---|---|---|---|---|---|
| **354** | A73 | 20c | Bulldozer | .60 | .60 |
| **355** | A73 | 80c | Motorcycle | 1.50 | 1.50 |
| **356** | A73 | $1.30 | Tractor | 1.75 | 1.75 |
| **357** | A73 | $1.80 | All-terrain vehicle | 2.50 | 2.50 |
| | | | *Nos. 354-357 (4)* | 6.35 | 6.35 |

Christmas — A74

**1991, Nov. 18 *Perf. 14x14½***

| | | | | | |
|---|---|---|---|---|---|
| **358** | A74 | 20c | The Annunciation | .50 | .50 |
| **359** | A74 | 80c | Shepherds | 1.25 | 1.25 |
| **360** | A74 | $1.30 | Nativity scene | 1.50 | 1.50 |
| **361** | A74 | $1.80 | Three wise men | 2.10 | 2.10 |
| | | | *Nos. 358-361 (4)* | 5.35 | 5.35 |

**Queen Elizabeth II's Accession to the Throne, 40th Anniv.**

Common Design Type

**Wmk. 384**

**1992, Feb. 6 Litho. *Perf. 14***

| | | | | | |
|---|---|---|---|---|---|
| **362** | CD349 | 20c | multicolored | .50 | .50 |
| **363** | CD349 | 60c | multicolored | .85 | .85 |
| **364** | CD349 | 90c | multicolored | 1.10 | 1.10 |
| **365** | CD349 | $1 | multicolored | 1.15 | 1.15 |

**Wmk. 373**

| | | | | | |
|---|---|---|---|---|---|
| **366** | CD349 | $1.80 | multicolored | 1.75 | 1.75 |
| | | | *Nos. 362-366 (5)* | 5.35 | 5.35 |

Sharks — A75

Designs: 20c, Carcharhinus galapagensis. $1, Eugomphodus taurus. $1.50, Carcharhinus melanopterus. $1.80, Carcharhinus amblyrhynchos.

***Perf. 15x14½***

**1992, June 30 Litho. Wmk. 373**

| | | | | | |
|---|---|---|---|---|---|
| **367** | A75 | 20c | multicolored | .75 | .75 |
| **368** | A75 | $1 | multicolored | 2.25 | 2.25 |
| **369** | A75 | $1.50 | multicolored | 2.50 | 2.50 |
| **370** | A75 | $1.80 | multicolored | 3.00 | 3.00 |
| | | | *Nos. 367-370 (4)* | 8.50 | 8.50 |

Sir Peter Scott Commemorative Expedition to Pitcairn Islands, 1991-92 — A76

Designs: 20c, Montastrea, acropora coral sticks. $1, Henderson sandalwood. $1.50, Murphy's petrel. $1.80, Henderson hawkmoth.

***Perf. 14x15***

**1992, Sept. 11 Litho. Wmk. 373**

| | | | | | |
|---|---|---|---|---|---|
| **371** | A76 | 20c | multicolored | .80 | .80 |
| **372** | A76 | $1 | multicolored | 1.75 | 1.75 |
| **373** | A76 | $1.50 | multicolored | 3.00 | 3.00 |
| **374** | A76 | $1.80 | multicolored | 3.50 | 3.50 |
| | | | *Nos. 371-374 (4)* | 9.05 | 9.05 |

Captain William Bligh, 175th Anniv. of Death A77

20c, Bligh's birthplace, St. Tudy, Cornwall, HMS Resolution. $1, On deck of HMAV Bounty, breadfruit plant. $1.50, Voyage in open boat, Bligh's answers at court martial. $1.80, Portrait by Rachel H. Combe, Battle of Camperdown, 1797.

**Wmk. 373**

**1992, Dec. 7 Litho.** ***Perf. 14½***

**375** A77 20c multicolored .60 .60
**376** A77 $1 multicolored 1.75 1.75
**377** A77 $1.50 multicolored 2.25 2.25
**378** A77 $1.80 multicolored 2.75 2.75
*Nos. 375-378 (4)* 7.35 7.35

Royal Naval Vessels A78

**Wmk. 384**

**1993, Mar. 10 Litho.** ***Perf. 14***

**379** A78 15c HMS Chichester .85 .85
**380** A78 20c HMS Jaguar 1.00 1.00
**381** A78 $1.80 HMS Andrew 4.25 4.25
**382** A78 $3 HMS Warrior 6.75 6.75
*Nos. 379-382 (4)* 12.85 12.85

Coronation of Queen Elizabeth II, 40th Anniv. A79

**Wmk. 373**

**1993, June 17 Litho.** ***Perf. 13***

**383** A79 $5 multicolored 7.00 7.00

Scenic Views A80

10c, Pawala Valley Ridge. 90c, St. Pauls. $1.20, Matt's Rocks from Water Valley. $1.50, Ridge Rope to St. Paul's Pool. $1.80, Ship Landing Point.

**Wmk. 373**

**1993, Sept. 8 Litho.** ***Perf. 14***

**384** A80 10c multicolored .40 .40
**385** A80 90c multicolored 1.10 1.10
**386** A80 $1.20 multicolored 1.50 1.50
**387** A80 $1.50 multicolored 1.60 1.60
**388** A80 $1.80 multicolored 2.50 2.50
*Nos. 384-388 (5)* 7.10 7.10

Lizards A81

Designs: 20c, Indopacific tree gecko. No. 390, Stump-toed gecko. No. 391, Mourning gecko. $1, Moth skink No. 393, Snake-eyed skink. No. 394, White-bellied skink.

***Perf. 13x13½***

**1993, Dec. 14 Litho. Wmk. 373**

**389** A81 20c multicolored .95 .95
**390** A81 45c multicolored 1.00 1.00
**391** A81 45c multicolored 1.00 1.00
*a.* Pair, #390-391 2.50 2.50
**392** A81 $1 multicolored 2.00 2.00
**393** A81 $1.50 multicolored 2.50 2.50
**394** A81 $1.50 multicolored 2.50 2.50
*a.* Pair, #393-394 7.00 7.00
*Nos. 389-394 (6)* 9.95 9.95

**Nos. 390-391, 393-394 Ovptd. with Hong Kong '94 Emblem**

***Perf. 13x13½***

**1994, Feb. 18 Litho. Wmk. 373**

**395** A81 45c on #390 .80 .80
**396** A81 45c on #391 .80 .80
*a.* Pair, #395-396 2.00 2.00
**397** A81 $1.50 on #393 2.25 2.25
**398** A81 $1.50 on #394 2.25 2.25
*a.* Pair, #397-398 6.00 6.00
*Nos. 395-398 (4)* 6.10 6.10

Early Pitcairners — A82

Designs: 5c, Friday October Christian. 20c, Moses Young. $1.80, James Russell McCoy. $3, Rosalind Amelia Young.

**1994, Mar. 7** ***Perf. 14***

**399** A82 5c multicolored .30 .30
**400** A82 20c multicolored .60 .60
**401** A82 $1.80 multicolored 2.50 2.50
**402** A82 $3 multicolored 4.00 4.00
*Nos. 399-402 (4)* 7.40 7.40

Shipwrecks A83

20c, Wildwave, Oeno Island, 1858. 90c, Cornwallis, Pitcairn Island, 1875. $1.80, Acadia, Ducie Island, 1881. $3, Oregon, Oeno Island, 1883.

**Wmk. 373**

**1994, June 22 Litho.** ***Perf. 14***

**403** A83 20c multicolored .75 .75
**404** A83 90c multicolored 2.00 2.00
**405** A83 $1.80 multicolored 3.25 3.25
**406** A83 $3 multicolored 4.75 4.75
*Nos. 403-406 (4)* 10.75 10.75

Corals A84

Designs: 20c, Fire coral, vert. 90c, Cauliflower coral, arc-eye hawkfish. $1, Snubnose chub, lobe coral, vert.
$3, Coral garden, butterflyfish, vert.

**Wmk. 373**

**1994, Sept. 15 Litho.** ***Perf. 14***

**407** A84 20c multicolored .90 .90
**408** A84 90c multicolored 2.00 2.00
**409** A84 $1 multicolored 2.50 2.50
*Nos. 407-409 (3)* 5.40 5.40

**Souvenir Sheet**

**410** A84 $3 multicolored 5.50 5.50

Christmas A85

Flowers: 20c, Morning glory. 90c, Hibiscus, vert. $1, Frangipani. $3, Ginsey, vert.

**Wmk. 373**

**1994, Nov. 24 Litho.** ***Perf. 14***

**411** A85 20c multicolored .45 .45
**412** A85 90c multicolored 1.50 1.50
**413** A85 $1 multicolored 1.75 1.75
**414** A85 $3 multicolored 3.50 3.50
*Nos. 411-414 (4)* 7.20 7.20

Birds A86

Designs: 5c, Fairy tern. 10c, Red-tailed tropicbird chick, vert. 15c, Henderson rail. 20c, Red-footed booby, vert. 45c, Blue-gray noddy. 50c, Henderson reed warbler. 90c, Common noddy. $1, Masked booby, chick, vert. $1.80, Henderson fruit dove. $2, Murphy's petrel. $3, Christmas shearwater. $5, Red-tailed tropicbird juvenile.

**1995, Mar. 8** ***Perf. 13½***

**415** A86 5c multicolored .60 .60
**416** A86 10c multicolored .60 .60
**417** A86 15c multicolored .75 .75
**418** A86 20c multicolored .75 .75
**419** A86 45c multicolored 1.00 1.00
**420** A86 50c multicolored 1.25 1.25
**421** A86 90c multicolored 1.50 1.50
**422** A86 $1 multicolored 1.75 1.75
**423** A86 $1.80 multicolored 2.50 2.50
**424** A86 $2 multicolored 2.75 2.75
**425** A86 $3 multicolored 3.00 3.00
**426** A86 $5 multicolored 4.25 4.25
*Nos. 415-426 (12)* 20.70 20.70

Oeno Island Vacation — A87

Designs: 20c, Boating. 90c, Volleyball on the beach. $1.80, Picnic. $3, Sing-a-long.

**1995, June 26** ***Perf. 14x15***

**427** A87 20c multicolored .50 .50
**428** A87 90c multicolored 1.25 1.25
**429** A87 $1.80 multicolored 2.25 2.25
**430** A87 $3 multicolored 3.75 3.75
*Nos. 427-430 (4)* 7.75 7.75

**Souvenir Sheet**

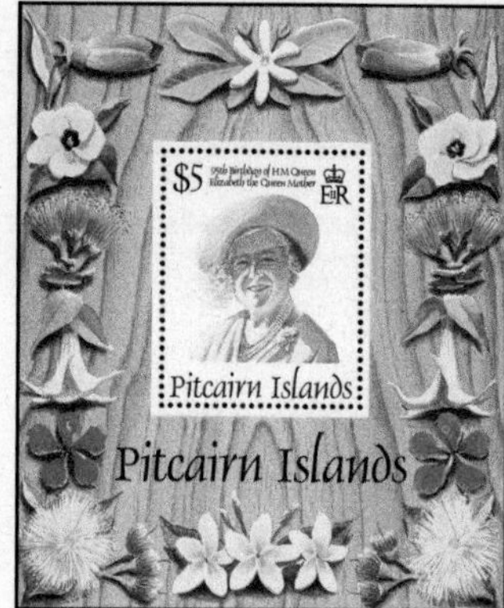


Queen Mother, 95th Birthday — A88

**1995, Aug. 4** ***Perf. 14½***

**431** A88 $5 multicolored 7.50 7.50

Radio, Cent. — A89

Designs: 20c, Guglielmo Marconi, radio equipment, 1901. $1, Man, Pitcairn radio, 1938. $1.50, Woman, satellite earth station equipment, 1994. $3, Satellite in orbit, 1992.

**1995, Sept. 5** ***Perf. 13***

**432** A89 20c multicolored .45 .45
**433** A89 $1 multicolored 1.25 1.25
**434** A89 $1.50 multicolored 2.00 2.00
**435** A89 $3 multicolored 4.00 4.00
*Nos. 432-435 (4)* 7.70 7.70

**UN, 50th Anniv.**

Common Design Type

Designs: 20c, Lord Mayor's Show. $1, RFA Brambleleaf. $1.50, UN ambulance. $3, Royal Air Force Tristar.

**Wmk. 373**

**1995, Oct. 24 Litho.** ***Perf. 14***

**436** CD353 20c multicolored .40 .40
**437** CD353 $1 multicolored 1.75 1.75
**438** CD353 $1.50 multicolored 2.25 2.25
**439** CD353 $3 multicolored 3.75 3.75
*Nos. 436-439 (4)* 8.15 8.15

Supply Ship Day — A90

**1996, Jan. 30** ***Perf. 14x14½***

**440** A90 20c Early morning .35 .35
**441** A90 40c Meeting ship .50 .50
**442** A90 90c Unloading supplies 1.25 1.25
**443** A90 $1 Landing work 1.40 1.40
**444** A90 $1.50 Supply sorting 1.75 1.75
**445** A90 $1.80 Last load 2.25 2.25
*Nos. 440-445 (6)* 7.50 7.50

**Queen Elizabeth II, 70th Birthday**

Common Design Type

Various portraits of Queen, scenes from Pitcairn Islands: 20c, Bounty Bay. 90c, Jetty, Landing Point, Bounty Bay. $1.80, Matt's Rocks. $3, St. Paul's.

**1996, Apr. 21** ***Perf. 13½x14***

**446** CD354 20c multicolored .60 .60
**447** CD354 90c multicolored 1.75 1.75
**448** CD354 $1.80 multicolored 2.50 2.50
**449** CD354 $3 multicolored 3.75 3.75
*Nos. 446-449 (4)* 8.60 8.60

CHINA '96, 9th Asian Intl. Philatelic Exhibition — A91

#450, Chinese junk. #451, HMAV Bounty. No. 452: a, Chinese rat. b, Polynesian rat.

**1996, May 17** ***Perf. 14***

**450** A91 $1.80 multicolored 2.75 2.75
**451** A91 $1.80 multicolored 2.75 2.75

**Souvenir Sheet**

**452** A91 90c Sheet of 2, #a.-b. 3.00 3.00

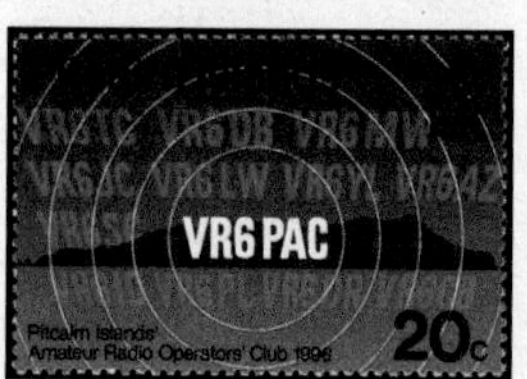


Amateur Radio — A92

Designs: 20c, Call signs of members in Amateur Radio Operator's Club, 1996. No. 454, VR6 1M calling for medical assistance. No. 455, Operator receiving transmission, physician standing by. $2.50, Andrew Young, Pitcairn's first operator, 1938.

**1996, Sept. 4 Wmk. 384** ***Perf. 14***

**453** A92 20c multicolored .65 .65
**454** A92 $1.50 multicolored 2.50 2.50
**455** A92 $1.50 multicolored 2.50 2.50
*a.* Pair, #454-455 6.00 6.00
**456** A92 $2.50 multicolored 3.25 3.25
*Nos. 453-456 (4)* 8.90 8.90

Birds A93

World Wildlife Fund: 5c, Henderson Island reed-warbler, vert. 10c, Stephen's lorikeet, vert. 20c, Henderson Island rail, vert. 90c, Henderson Island fruit-dove, vert. No. 461, Masked booby. No. 462, Common fairy-tern.

**1996, Nov. 20** **Wmk. 373**

| | | | | |
|---|---|---|---|---|
| **457** | A93 5c multicolored | | .65 | .65 |
| **458** | A93 10c multicolored | | .65 | .65 |
| **459** | A93 20c multicolored | | 1.25 | 1.25 |
| **460** | A93 90c multicolored | | 1.50 | 1.50 |
| **461** | A93 $2 multicolored | | 2.00 | 2.00 |
| **462** | A93 $2 multicolored | | 2.00 | 2.00 |
| | *Nos. 457-462 (6)* | | 8.05 | 8.05 |

Nos. 461 and 462 do not include WWF emblem.

Souvenir Sheet

Coat of Arms — A94

**1997, Feb. 12** ***Perf. 14½x14***

| | | | |
|---|---|---|---|
| **463** | A94 $5 multicolored | 7.25 | 7.25 |

Hong Kong '97.

South Pacific Commission, 50th Anniv. — A95

a, MV David Baker. b, MV McLachlan.

***Perf. 13½x14***

**1997, May 26** **Litho.** **Wmk. 373**

| | | | |
|---|---|---|---|
| **464** | A95 $2.50 Sheet of 2, #a.-b. | 8.00 | 8.00 |

Health Care A96

Designs: 20c, New Health Center. $1, Resident nurse treating patient. $1.70, Dental officer treating patient. $3, Patient being taken aboard ship.

**Wmk. 373**

**1997, Sept. 12** **Litho.** ***Perf. 14***

| | | | |
|---|---|---|---|
| **465** | A96 20c multicolored | .50 | .50 |
| **466** | A96 $1 multicolored | 1.25 | 1.25 |
| **467** | A96 $1.70 multicolored | 2.00 | 2.00 |
| **468** | A96 $3 multicolored | 4.50 | 4.50 |
| | *Nos. 465-468 (4)* | 8.25 | 8.25 |

Queen Elizabeth II and Prince Philip, 50th Wedding Anniv. — A97

Designs: No. 469, Prince driving team of horses. No. 470, Queen wearing wide-brimmed hat. No. 471, Prince in formal riding attire. No. 472, Queen, horse. No. 473, Queen and Prince standing behind flowers. No. 474, Prince Charles riding horse.

**Wmk. 373**

**1997, Nov. 20** **Litho.** ***Perf. 13***

| | | | |
|---|---|---|---|
| **469** | 20c multicolored | .40 | .40 |
| **470** | 20c multicolored | .40 | .40 |
| *a.* | A97 Pair, #469-470 | 1.00 | 1.00 |
| **471** | $1 multicolored | 1.25 | 1.25 |
| **472** | $1 multicolored | 1.25 | 1.25 |
| *a.* | A97 Pair, #471-472 | 3.00 | 3.00 |
| **473** | $1.70 multicolored | 1.75 | 1.75 |
| **474** | $1.70 multicolored | 1.75 | 1.75 |
| *a.* | A97 Pair, #473-474 | 4.25 | 4.25 |
| | *Nos. 469-474 (6)* | 6.80 | 6.80 |

Christmas A98

Flower, picture: 20c, Gardenia taitensis, view of Island at night. 80c, Bauhinia variegata, ringing public bell. $1.20, Metrosideros collina, children's baskets hanging on line. $3, Hibiscus tiliaceus, Pitcairn Church, Square at Adamstown.

**Wmk. 373**

**1997, Dec. 1** **Litho.** ***Perf. 13½***

| | | | |
|---|---|---|---|
| **475** | A98 20c multicolored | .50 | .50 |
| **476** | A98 80c multicolored | 1.50 | 1.50 |
| **477** | A98 $1.20 multicolored | 1.75 | 1.75 |
| **478** | A98 $3 multicolored | 3.25 | 3.25 |
| | *Nos. 475-478 (4)* | 7.00 | 7.00 |

Views of Christian's Cave — A99

5c, Dorcas Apple, looking across Adamstown. 20c, Rocks near Betty's Edge looking past Tatinanny. 35c, Cave mouth. $5, Cave from road near where Fletcher Christian built home.

**Wmk. 384**

**1998, Feb. 9** **Litho.** ***Perf. 13½***

| | | | |
|---|---|---|---|
| **479** | A99 5c multi | .35 | .35 |
| **480** | A99 20c multi | .65 | .65 |
| **481** | A99 35c multi, vert. | .85 | .85 |
| **482** | A99 $5 multi, vert. | 5.00 | 5.00 |
| | *Nos. 479-482 (4)* | 6.85 | 6.85 |

Sailing Ships A100

Designs: 20c, HMS Bounty, 1790. 90c, HMS Swallow, 1767. $1.80, HMS Briton & HMS Tagus, 1814. $3, HMS Fly, 1838.

***Perf. 14½x14***

**1998, May 28** **Litho.** **Wmk. 373**

| | | | |
|---|---|---|---|
| **483** | A100 20c multicolored | .90 | .90 |
| **484** | A100 90c multicolored | 1.50 | 1.50 |
| **485** | A100 $1.80 multicolored | 2.25 | 2.25 |
| **486** | A100 $3 multicolored | 3.25 | 3.25 |
| | *Nos. 483-486 (4)* | 7.90 | 7.90 |

**Diana, Princess of Wales (1961-97)**

Common Design Type

a, In evening dress. b, Wearing white hat, pearls. c, In houndstooth top. d, Wearing white hat, top.

***Perf. 14½x14***

**1998, Aug. 31** **Litho.** **Wmk. 373**

| | | | |
|---|---|---|---|
| **487** | CD355 90c Sheet of 4, #a.-d. | 4.75 | 4.75 |

No. 487 sold for $3.60 + 40c with surtax being donated to the Princess Diana Memorial Fund.

Flowers A101

20c, Bidens mathewsii. 90c, Hibiscus. $1.80, Osteomeles anthyllidifolia. $3, Ipomoea littoralis.

**Wmk. 373**

**1998, Oct. 20** **Litho.** ***Perf. 14***

| | | | |
|---|---|---|---|
| **488** | A101 20c multicolored | 1.25 | 1.25 |
| **489** | A101 90c multicolored | 2.00 | 2.00 |
| **490** | A101 $1.80 multicolored | 3.50 | 3.50 |
| **491** | A101 $3 multicolored | 4.00 | 4.00 |
| | *Nos. 488-491 (4)* | 10.75 | 10.75 |

Flowers are below inscriptions on Nos. 489, 491.

Intl. Year of the Ocean A102

Designs: 20c, Fishing. 90c, Divers, vert. $1.80, Reef fish. $3, Murphy's petrel, vert.

**Unwmk.**

**1998, Dec. 16** **Litho.** ***Perf. 14***

| | | | |
|---|---|---|---|
| **492** | A102 20c multicolored | 1.40 | 1.40 |
| **493** | A102 90c multicolored | 2.50 | 2.50 |
| **494** | A102 $1.80 multicolored | 4.00 | 4.00 |
| **495** | A102 $3 multicolored | 5.75 | 5.75 |
| *a.* | Souv. sheet of 4, #492-495 + label | 16.00 | 16.00 |
| | *Nos. 492-495 (4)* | 13.65 | 13.65 |

Government Education on Pitcairn, 50th Anniv. — A103

Scenes on pages of books: 20c, Schoolmaster George Hunn Nobbs, students, 1828. 90c, Schoolmaster Simon Young, daughter Rosalind, teacher Hattie Andre, 1893. $1.80, Teacher Roy Clark, 1932. $3, Modern school at Palau, 1999.

**Unwmk.**

**1999, Feb. 15** **Litho.** ***Perf. 14***

| | | | |
|---|---|---|---|
| **496** | A103 20c multicolored | 1.05 | 1.05 |
| **497** | A103 90c multicolored | 1.60 | 1.60 |
| **498** | A103 $1.80 multicolored | 3.25 | 3.25 |
| **499** | A103 $3 multicolored | 5.25 | 5.25 |
| | *Nos. 496-499 (4)* | 11.15 | 11.15 |

Archaeological Expedition to Survey Wreck of the Bounty — A104

Scenes of ship during last voyage and: a, 50c, Anchor. b, $1, Cannon. c, $1.50, Chronometer. d, $2, Copper caldron.

**1999, Mar. 19**

| | | | |
|---|---|---|---|
| **500** | A104 Sheet of 4, #a.-d. | 13.00 | 13.00 |

19th Cent. Pitcairn Island A105

Designs: 20c, John Adams (d. 1829), Bounty Bay. 90c, Topaz, 1808. $1.80, George Hunn Nobbs, Norfolk Island. $3, HMS Champion, 1893.

***Perf. 14½x14***

**1999, May 25** **Litho.** **Wmk. 373**

| | | | |
|---|---|---|---|
| **501** | A105 20c multicolored | 1.00 | 1.00 |
| **502** | A105 90c multicolored | 2.40 | 2.40 |
| **503** | A105 $1.80 multicolored | 3.00 | 3.00 |
| **504** | A105 $3 multicolored | 5.50 | 5.50 |
| | *Nos. 501-504 (4)* | 11.90 | 11.90 |

**Wedding of Prince Edward and Sophie Rhys-Jones**

Common Design Type

***Perf. 13¾x14***

**1999, June 18** **Litho.** **Wmk. 384**

| | | | |
|---|---|---|---|
| **505** | CD356 $2.50 Separate portraits | 3.50 | 3.50 |
| **506** | CD356 $2.50 Couple | 3.50 | 3.50 |

Honey Bees A106

Designs: 20c, Beekeepers, hives. $1, Bee, white and purple flower. $1.80, Bees, honeycomb. $3, Bee on flower, honey jar.

***Die Cut Perf. 9***

**1999, Sept. 12** **Litho.**

**Self-Adhesive**

| | | | |
|---|---|---|---|
| **507** | A106 20c multicolored | 1.25 | 1.25 |
| **508** | A106 $1 multicolored | 2.50 | 2.50 |
| *a.* | Souvenir sheet of 1 | 6.00 | 6.00 |
| **509** | A106 $1.80 multicolored | 4.00 | 4.00 |
| **510** | A106 $3 multicolored | 5.75 | 5.75 |
| | *Nos. 507-510 (4)* | 13.50 | 13.50 |

China 1999 World Philatelic Exhibition, No. 508a. Issued 8/21.

Protection of Galapagos Tortoise "Mr. Turpen" A107

Designs: a, 5c, Arrival of the ship Yankee, 1937. b, 20c, Off-loading Mr. Turpen to a long-boat. c, 35c, Mr. Turpen. d, $5, Close-up of tortoise's head.

*Perf. 14¼*

**2000, Jan. 14 Litho. Unwmk.**

**511** A107 Strip of 4 + label 9.50 9.50

Flowers A108

Designs: 10c, Guettarda speciosa. 15c, Hibiscus tiliaceus. 20c, Selenicereus grandiflorus. 30c, Metrosideros collina. 50c, Alpinia zerumbet. $1, Syzygium jambos. $1.50, Commelina diffusa. $1.80, Canna indica. $2, Allamanda cathartica. $3, Calophyllum inophyllum. $5, Ipomea indica. $10, Bauhinia monandra (40x40mm).

**Litho., Litho. with Foil Application ($10)**

*Perf. 13¾x13¼, 13¼x13¾ ($10)*

**2000, May 22 Unwmk.**

**512-523** A108 Set of 12 26.50 26.50

*520a* Souvenir sheet, #518, 520 8.25 8.25

The Stamp Show 2000, London (No. 520a).

Millennium — A109

Old and modern pictures: 20c, Longboat at sea. 90c, Landing and longboat house. $1.80, Transportation of crops. $3, Communications.

**Wmk. 373**

**2000, June 28 Litho.** *Perf. 13¾*

**524-527** A109 Set of 4 12.00 12.00

Souvenir Sheets

Satellite Recovery Mission — A110

No. 528: a, Surveryor, helicopter. b, Military personnel, boat, ship, helicopter.

**2000, July 7 Unwmk.** *Perf. 14¼*

**528** A110 $2.50 Sheet of 2, #a-b 15.00 15.00

World Stamp Expo 2000, Anaheim.

Illustration shows lower half of the entire sheet. The upper half, which has descriptive text, and is printed on the reverse, is the same size as the lower half. The entire sheet is folded where the halves meet.

Queen Mother, 100th Birthday — A111

No. 529: a, $2, Blue hat. b, $3, Maroon hat.

**2000, Aug. 4** *Perf. 14*

**529** A111 Sheet of 2, #a-b 7.00 7.00

Christmas A112

*Perf. 14½*

**2000, Nov. 22 Litho. Unwmk.**

**530** Strip of 4 11.00 11.00

*a.* A112 20c Woman .75 .75

*b.* A112 80c Man, boy 2.00 2.00

*c.* A112 $1.50 Woman, child 3.00 3.00

*d.* A112 $3 Three children 4.00 4.00

Cruise Ships A113

Designs: No. 531, $1.50, Bremen. No. 532, $1.50, MV Europa. No. 533, $1.50, MS Rotterdam. No. 534, $1.50, Saga Rose.

*Perf. 14¾*

**2001, Feb. 1 Litho. Unwmk.**

**531-534** A113 Set of 4 13.00 13.00

Values are for stamps with surrounding selvage.

Tropical Fruit — A114

Designs: 20c, Cocos nucifera. 80c, Punica granatum. $1, Passiflora edulis. $3, Ananas comosus.

**2001, Apr. 6 Litho.** *Perf. 13½x13¼*

**535-538** A114 Set of 4 7.50 7.50

*538a* Souvenir sheet, #536, 538 5.25 5.25

Allocation of ".pn" Internet Domain Suffix — A115

CD and: 20c, Computer keyboard. 50c, Circuit board. $1, Integrated circuit. $5, Mouse.

**2001, June 11** *Serpentine Die Cut*

**Self-Adhesive**

**539-542** A115 Set of 4 11.00 11.00

Tropical Fish — A116

Designs: 20c, Chaetodon ornatissimus. 80c, Chaetodon reticulatus. $1.50, Chaetodon lunula. $2, Henochus chrysostomus.

*Perf. 13x13¼*

**2001, Sept. 4 Litho. Unwmk.**

**543-546** A116 Set of 4 9.50 9.50

*546a* Souvenir sheet, #543, 546 3.25 3.25

Wood Carving — A117

No. 547: a, 20c, Miro flower, man on beach carrying log. b, 50c, Toa flower, artisans carving fish. c, $1.50, Pulau flower, man using machine, woman looking at carved objects. d, $3, Ship, boat, carved objects.

**2001, Oct. 11**

**547** A117 Horiz. strip of 4, #a-d, + central label 8.50 8.50

Cowrie Shells A118

Designs: 20c, Cypraea argus. 80c, Cypraea isabella. $1, Cypraea mappa. $3, Cypraea mauritana.

**2001, Dec. 6** *Perf. 13¼x13*

**548-551** A118 Set of 4 7.75 7.75

**Reign Of Queen Elizabeth II, 50th Anniv. Issue**

Common Design Type

Souvenir Sheet

No. 552: a, 50c, With Queen Mother and Princess Margaret. b, $1, Wearing tiara. c, $1.20, Without hat. d, $1.50, Wearing hat. e, $2, 1955 portrait by Annigoni (38x50mm).

*Perf. 14¼x14½, 13¾ (#552e)*

**2002, Feb. 6 Litho. Wmk. 373**

**552** CD360 Sheet of 5, #a-e 8.50 8.50

Famous Men — A119

Designs: No. 553, $1.50, Gerald DeLeo Bliss (1882-1957), Panamanian postmaster who expedited Pitcairn mail. No. 554, $1.50, Capt. Arthur C. Jones (1898-1987), shipper of trees to Pitcairn. No. 555, $1.50, James Russell McCoy (1845-1924), missionary. No. 556, $1.50, Adm. Sir Fairfax Moresby (1786-1877), philanthropist.

*Perf. 14¼x14¾*

**2002, Apr. 5 Litho. Unwmk.**

**553-556** A119 Set of 4 12.00 12.00

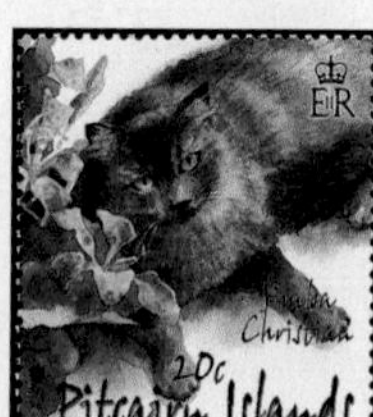

Cats — A120

Local cats: 20c, Simba Christian. $1, Miti Christian. $1.50, Nala Brown. $3, Alicat Pulau.

*Perf. 13¼x13*

**2002, June 28 Litho. Unwmk.**

**557-560** A120 Set of 4 8.25 8.25

*a.* Souvenir sheet of 2, #557, 560 5.00 5.00

**Queen Mother Elizabeth (1900-2002)**

Common Design Type

Designs: 40c, As child, c. 1910 (black and white photograph). Nos. 562, 565a, $1, As young woman, without hat. $1.50, Wearing flowered hat. Nos. 564, 565b, $2, Wearing light blue hat.

**Wmk. 373**

**2002, Aug. 5 Litho.** *Perf. 14¼*

**With Purple Frames**

**561** CD361 40c multicolored 1.25 1.25

**562** CD361 $1 multicolored 2.00 2.00

**563** CD361 $1.50 multicolored 2.50 2.50

**564** CD361 $2 multicolored 3.00 3.00

*Nos. 561-564 (4)* 8.75 8.75

**Souvenir Sheet**

**Without Purple Frames**

*Perf. 14½x14¼*

**565** CD361 Sheet of 2, #a-b 6.50 6.50

Weaving — A121

No. 566: a, 40c, Woman cutting thatch. b, 80c, Woman dyeing thatch. c, $1.50, Millie Christian weaving. d, $2.50, Thelma Brown with finished products.

*Perf. 13¼x12¾*

**2002, Oct. 18 Litho. Unwmk.**

**566** A121 Horiz. strip of 4, #a-d + central label 12.00 12.00

Trees A122

Designs: 40c, Dudwi nut. $1, Toa. $1.50, Miro. $3, Hulianda.

*Perf. 13¼*

**2002, Dec. 1 Litho. Unwmk.**

**567-570** A122 Set of 4 9.50 9.50

Souvenir Sheet

Blue Star Line Ships — A123

**2003, Jan. 8 Litho.** *Perf. 14x13¼*

**571** A123 $5 multi 11.00 11.00

Cone Shells A124

Designs: 40c, Conus geographus. 80c, Conus textile. $1, Conus striatus. $1.20, Conus marmoreus. $3, Conus litoglyphus.

*Perf. 13½x13¾*

**2003, Mar. 14 Litho. Unwmk.**

**572-576** A124 Set of 5 10.00 10.00

**Coronation of Queen Elizabeth II, 50th Anniv.**

Common Design Type

Designs: Nos. 577, 581a, 40c, Queen wearing tiara. No. 578, 80c, Carriage in procession. No. 579, $1.50, Queen wearing tiara, diff. Nos. 580, 581b, $3, Queen in procession at coronation.

*Perf. 14¼x14½*

**2003, June 2 Litho. Wmk. 373**

**Vignettes Framed, Red Background**

**577** CD363 40c multicolored .90 .90
**578** CD363 80c multicolored 1.50 1.50
**579** CD363 $1.50 multicolored 2.25 2.25
**580** CD363 $3 multicolored 4.00 4.00
*Nos. 577-580 (4)* 8.65 8.65

**Souvenir Sheet**

**Vignettes Without Frame, Purple Panel**

**581** CD363 Sheet of 2, #a-b 5.75 5.75

Painted Leaves — A125

No. 582: a, 40c, Women putting leaves in earthenware jar. b, 80c, Washing leaves. c, $1.50, Leaf painter. d, $3, Leaf painter, diff.

*Perf. 13¼*

**2003, Aug. 18 Litho. Unwmk.**

**582** A125 Horiz. strip of 4, #a-d, + central label 12.00 12.00

Squirrelfish A126

Designs: 40c, Sargocentron diadema. 80c, Sargocentron spiniferum. $1.50, Sargocentron caudimaculatum. $3, Neoniphon sammara.

*Perf. 13¼*

**2003, Oct. 8 Litho. Unwmk.**

**583-586** A126 Set of 4 9.00 9.00
*586a* Souvenir sheet of 1 8.00 8.00

Christmas A127

Morning glory and: 40c, Holy Virgin in a Wreath of Flowers, by Peter Paul Rubens and Jan Brueghel. $1, Madonna della Rosa, by Raphael. $1.50, Stuppacher Madonna, by Matthias Grünewald. $3, Madonna with Cherries, by Titian.

**Litho. with Foil Application**

**2003, Nov. 17** ***Perf. 13¾***

**587-590** A127 Set of 4 9.00 9.00

Shells A128

Designs: 40c, Terebra maculata. 80c, Terebra subulata. $1.20, Terebra crenulata. $3, Terebra dimidata.

*Perf. 14x14½*

**2004, Jan. 21 Litho. Unwmk.**

**591-594** A128 Set of 4 9.00 9.00

Scenery A129

Designs: 50c, Anchor, Bounty Bay and Hill of Difficulty, vert. $1, Flower, Christian's Cave on Rock Face. $1.50, Shells, St. Paul's Pool, vert. $2.50, Bird, Ridge Rope towards St. Paul's Point.

*Perf. 13¼*

**2004, Apr. 28 Litho. Unwmk.**

**595-598** A129 Set of 4 12.50 12.50

**Souvenir Sheet**

Commissioning of HMS Pitcairn, 60th Anniv. — A130

*Perf. 13¼*

**2004, July 7 Litho. Unwmk.**

**599** A130 $5.50 multi 12.00 12.00

HMAV Bounty Replica, Sydney A131

Replica and: 60c, Sail and mast. 80c, Stern. $1, Figurehead. $3.50, Rigging.

**2004, Sept. 8** ***Perf. 14¼x14***

**600-603** A131 Set of 4 12.00 12.00
*603a* Souvenir sheet of 1 12.00 12.00

Murphy's Petrel A132

Designs: 40c, Three in flight. 50c, Adult and chicks. $1, Adult nesting, flower, vert. $2, Head of adult, vert. $2.50, In flight.

**2004, Nov. 17 Litho.** ***Perf. 14½***

**604-608** A132 Set of 5 9.50 9.50
*608a* Souvenir sheet, #604-608 10.00 10.00

Views of Ducie and Oeno Islands A133

Designs: 50c, Beach, Ducie Island, lizards. 60c, Rocks off Ducie Island, starfish. 80c, Sun on horizon, Ducie Island, birds. $1, Boat off Oeno Island, palm tree. $1.50, Beach and palm trees, Oeno Island, shells. $2.50, Boat with fishermen off Oeno Island, fish.

**2005, Feb. 10 Litho.** ***Perf. 13¼***

**609-614** A133 Set of 6 12.50 12.50

**Souvenir Sheet**

Blue Moon Butterfly — A134

No. 615: a, $1.50, Male. b, $4, Female.

**2005, Apr. 8 Litho.** ***Perf. 14½***

**615** A134 Sheet of 2, #a-b 16.00 16.00

**Souvenir Sheet**

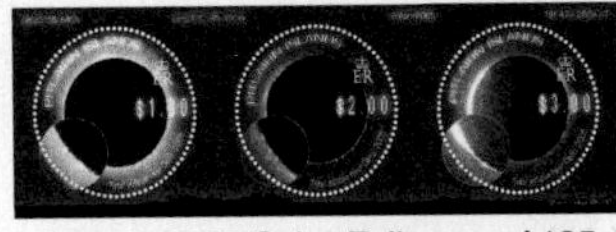

Apr. 8, 2005 Solar Eclipse — A135

No. 616 — Eclipse and various solar prominences: a, $1. b, $2. c, $3.

**2005, Apr. 8** ***Perf.***

**616** A135 Sheet of 3, #a-c 12.00 12.00

No. 616 contains three 38mm diameter stamps.

Wedding of Prince Charles and Camilla Parker Bowles A136

**Litho. With Foil Application**

**2005, Apr. 9** ***Perf. 14x14½***

**617** A136 $5 multi 17.50 17.50

HMS Bounty Replica, US A137

Replica, map, emblem for Bounty Post and: 40c, Ship's wheel. $1, Lantern. $1.20, Bell. $3, Rigging.

**2005, June 21 Litho.** ***Perf. 14¼x14***

**618-621** A137 Set of 4 15.00 15.00
*621a* Souvenir sheet of 1 9.50 9.50

Bristle-thighed Curlew — A138

Designs: 60c, Curlews on rock. $1, Head of curlew. $1.50, Curlew with open beak, vert. $1.80, Head of curlew, two curlews in flight, vert. $2, Curlew on driftwood.

**2005, Sept. 14 Litho.** ***Perf. 14½***

**622-626** A138 Set of 5 15.00 15.00
*626a* Souvenir sheet, #622-626 15.00 15.00

Christmas A139

Christmas ornament with: 40c, Hibiscus flower. 80c, Seabird. $1.80, Coat of arms. $2.50, HMS Bounty.

**Litho. with Foil Application**

**2005, Nov. 23** ***Perf. 13¼***

**627-630** A139 Set of 4 14.00 14.00

Henderson Island — A140

Various scenes of Henderson Island and: 50c, Insects. 60c, Parrots. $1, Sea birds. $1.20, Lobsters. $1.50, Octopi. $2, Turtles.

**2006, Feb. 15 Litho.** ***Perf. 13¼***

**631-636** A140 Set of 6 13.00 13.00

**Souvenir Sheet**

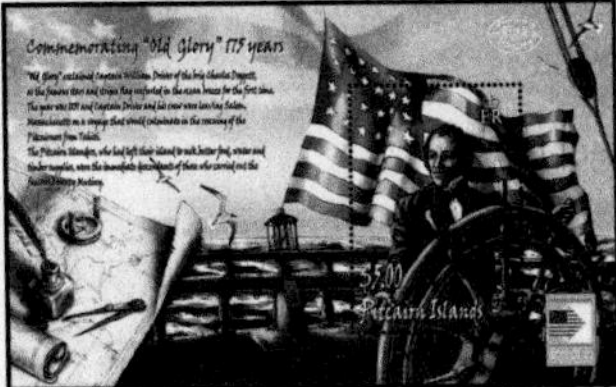

Washington 2006 World Philatelic Exhibition — A141

**2006, Apr. 21 Litho.** ***Perf. 14½x14¾***

**637** A141 $5 multi 10.00 10.00

Queen Elizabeth II, 80th Birthday A142

Queen: 40c, As young woman. 80c, Wearing tiara. No. 640, $1.80, Wearing yellow dress. No. 641, $3.50, Wearing red hat and jacket.

No. 642: a, $1.80, Wearing tiara. b, $3.50, Wearing yellow dress.

**2006, Apr. 21** ***Perf. 14¼***

**Stamps With White Frames**

**638-641** A142 Set of 4 10.00 10.00

**Souvenir Sheet**

**Stamps Without White Frames**

**642** A142 Sheet of 2, #a-b 9.00 9.00

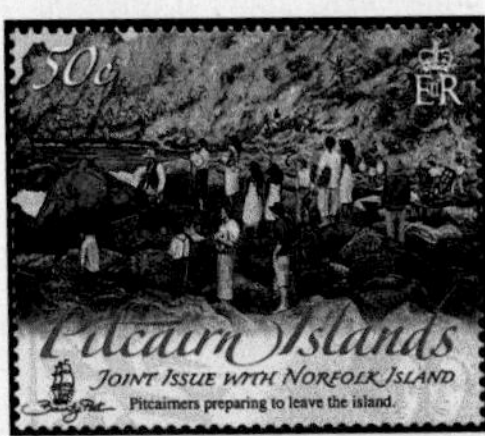

Journey to Norfolk Island A143

No. 643: a, Pitcairners preparing to leave Pitcairn Island. b, Ship, Morayshire, departing Pitcairn Island. c, Morayshire at anchor in Kingston Bay, Norfolk Island. d, Pitcairn settlers arrive in Kingston, Norfolk Island.

**2006, June 7** ***Perf. 14½***

**643** Horiz. strip of 4 + central label 11.00 11.00
*a.* A143 50c multi 1.25 1.25
*b.* A143 $1 multi 1.75 1.75
*c.* A143 $1.50 multi 2.75 2.75
*d.* A143 $3 multi 5.00 5.00

See Norfolk Island Nos. 875-879.

**Souvenir Sheet**

Cave Dwellers of Henderson Island — A144

No. 644: a, 60c, Man carrying caught fish. b, $1.20, Child, bird, boat, horiz. c, $2, Man sitting on beach, horiz. d, $2.50, Two women.

**2006, Aug. 30** ***Perf. 13¼***
**644** A144 Sheet of 4, #a-d 10.50 10.50

Humpback Whales A145

Designs: $1.50, Whales underwater. $3.50, Tail of whale above water.

**2006, Nov. 22** ***Perf. 14½***
**645-646** A145 Set of 2 10.50 10.50
*646a* Souvenir sheet, #645-646 10.50 10.50

Worldwide Fund for Nature (WWF) A146

**2007, Feb. 28 Litho.** ***Perf. 14¼***
**647** Horiz. strip of 4 9.00 9.00
*a.* A146 50c Sooty tern .70 .70
*b.* A146 60c Blue-gray ternlet .80 .80
*c.* A146 $2 Brown noddies 2.75 2.75
*d.* A146 $3 Black noddy 4.25 4.25
*e.* Miniature sheet, 2 each #647a-647d 18.00 18.00

Raising of the Anchor of the Bounty, 50th Anniv. — A147

No. 648: a, Diver approaching anchor. b, Two divers at anchor. c, Pulling anchor onto ship. d, Anchor on shore.

**2007, Apr. 20 Litho.** ***Perf. 13¼***
**648** Horiz. strip of 4 + central label 12.00 12.00
*a.* A147 60c multi 1.50 1.50
*b.* A147 $1 multi 2.50 2.50
*c.* A147 $1.20 multi 2.75 2.75
*d.* A147 $2.50 multi 5.00 5.00

Souvenir Sheet

Rock Carvers of Pitcairn Island — A148

No. 649: a, 60c, Man carving on rock face. b, $1.20, Two men pounding rock, horiz. c, $2, Man near fire, horiz. d, $2.50, Man making stone ax.

**2007, June 13**
**649** A148 Sheet of 4, #a-d 12.50 12.50

Utetheisa Pulchelloides A149

Design: $2, Moth on branch. $4, Moth in flight.

**2007, Aug. 27 Litho.** ***Perf. 14½***
**650-651** A149 Set of 2 12.00 12.00
*651a* Souvenir sheet, #650-651 12.00 12.00

HMS Bounty Replica, United States A150

Designs: 10c, Crow's nest. 20c, Ropes and pulleys. 40c, Cannon. 50c, Compass. 80c, Captain's wheel. $1, Figurehead. $1.50, Mast. $2, Sails. $3.50, Sextant. $4, Lamp and transom. $5, Bell. $10, Chronometer.

**2007, Oct. 17 Litho.** ***Perf. 14½***
**652** A150 10c multi .30 .25
**653** A150 20c multi .40 .40
**654** A150 40c multi .75 .75
**655** A150 50c multi .85 .85
**656** A150 80c multi 1.00 1.00
**657** A150 $1 multi 1.25 1.25
**658** A150 $1.50 multi 1.75 1.75
**659** A150 $2 multi 2.25 2.25
**660** A150 $3.50 multi 4.00 4.00
*a.* Souvenir sheet of 3, #656, 657, 660 9.50 9.50
**661** A150 $4 multi 3.75 3.75
**662** A150 $5 multi 4.25 4.25
**663** A150 $10 multi 9.00 9.00
*Nos. 652-663 (12)* 29.55 29.50

Issued: No. 660a, 5/8/10. London 2010 Festival of Stamps (No. 660a).

Fish — A151

No. 664: a, Dog tooth tuna. b, Wahoo. c, Dorado-Mahimahi. d, Yellowfin tuna. e, Giant trevally. f, Bonito.

**2007, Dec. 12 Litho.** ***Perf. 14½***
**664** A151 $1 Block of 6, #a-f 12.50 12.50

Pictures of Islands Taken By DigitalGlobe QuickBird Satellite A152

Islands: 60c, Oeno. $1, Pitcairn. $2, Henderson. $2.50, Ducie.

***Serpentine Die Cut***
**2008, Feb. 27 Litho.**
**Self-Adhesive**
**665-668** A152 Set of 4 12.00 12.00

Longboat History — A153

No. 669 — Inscriptions: a, From 1880 Timber framed longboat. b, 1983, Last wooden longboat launched. c, 1995, Diesel powered aluminum. d, Oeno sunsets brought within reach.

**2008, Apr. 24 Litho.** ***Perf. 14x14¼***
**669** Horiz. strip of 4 + central label 12.00 12.00
*a.* A153 50c multi 1.25 1.25
*b.* A153 $1 multi 1.75 1.75
*c.* A153 $1.50 multi 2.75 2.75
*d.* A153 $3.50 multi 5.00 5.00

Bees and Flowers A154

Apis mellifera ligustica and: $1, Yellow guava. $1.20, Portulaca. $1.50, Sunflower. $3, Mountain chestnut.

**2008, June 25** ***Perf. 13¼***
**670-673** A154 Set of 4 11.00 11.00
*673a* Souvenir sheet, #672-673 9.00 9.00

Sunsets — A155

Sun and various photographs of sunsets: 50c, 60c, 80c, $1, $2, $2.50.

**2008, Aug. 20 Litho.** ***Perf. 14¾***
**674-679** A155 Set of 6 12.50 12.50

Souvenir Sheet

Discovery of Bounty Mutineer Community on Pitcairn by Capt. Mayhew Folger, Bicent. — A156

**2008, Oct. 22 Litho.** ***Perf. 13¼***
**680** A156 $5 multi 7.75 7.75

Miniature Sheet

Green Turtles of Henderson Island — A157

No. 681: a, 60c, Head of turtle, vert. b, $1, Turtle swimming. c, $2, Turtle coming ashore. d, $2.50, Hatchlings heading toward ocean, vert.

**2008, Dec. 3 Litho.** ***Perf. 14***
**681** A157 Sheet of 4, #a-d 9.00 9.00

Coconut Crab — A158

Crab: $2.80, Top view. $4, Side view.

**2009, Feb. 17** ***Perf. 14½***
**682-683** A158 Set of 2 11.00 11.00
*683a* Souvenir sheet of 2, #682-683 11.00 11.00

Return of Pitcairn Islanders to Pitcairn Island, 150th Anniv. — A159

No. 684: a, Pitcairn islanders leave Kingston Jetty on Norfolk Island. b, Passengers approach the Mary Ann. c, Pitcairn Islanders on board the Mary Ann approach Pitcairn Island. d, Arrival of Pitcairn Islanders on Pitcairn Island.

**2009, Apr. 22 Litho.** ***Perf. 14¾x13½***
**684** Horiz. strip of 4 + central label 10.00 10.00
*a.* A159 60c multi 1.00 1.00
*b.* A159 $1 multi 1.75 1.75
*c.* A159 $2 multi 2.50 2.50
*d.* A159 $3.50 multi 3.75 3.75

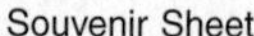
Souvenir Sheet

Hong Kong 2009 Intl. Stamp Exhibition — A160

**2009, May 14** ***Perf. 13½***
**685** A160 Sheet of 2, Pitcairn Islands #685a, Vanuatu #976a 10.00 10.00
*a.* $2.50 One panda 5.00 5.00

Joint issue between Pitcairn Islands and Vanuatu.

No. 685 sold for $5 and 310 Vanuatu vatus, and is identical to Vanuatu No. 976.

Charles Darwin (1809-82), Naturalist A161

Darwin and: 50c, Ship "Beagle" and fossil. $1.50, Tortoise and iguana. $2, Birds. $3.50, Darwin's book "On the Origin of Species by Means of Natural Selection" and ape.

**2009, June 24** ***Perf. 14½***
**686-689** A161 Set of 4 12.00 12.00

Wandering Glider Dragonfly A162

Dragonfly: $2.50, At flower's anthers. $4, On flower's petal.

**2009, Aug. 26**
**690-691** A162 Set of 2 11.00 11.00
*691a* Souvenir sheet, #690-691 11.00 11.00

Aircraft Flying Over Pitcairn Island A163

Designs: $1, Walrus amphibious biplane. $1.50, Alouette III helicopter. $1.80, Dassault VP-BMS Falcon 900. $2.50, Piper Comanche 260C.

**2009, Oct. 21**
**692-695** A163 Set of 4 13.00 13.00

Miniature Sheet

Visiting Royal Navy Ships — A164

No. 696: a, 80c, HMS Actaeon, 1837. b, 80c, HMS Calypso, 1860. c, 80c, HMS Juno, 1855. d, $2, HMS Sutlej, 1864. e, $2, HMS Shah, 1878. f, $2, HMS Pelican, 1886.

**2009, Dec. 9 Litho. *Perf. 14***
**696** A164 Sheet of 6, #a-f 15.00 15.00

See No. 711.

Children's Art A165

Island sites and children's drawings of them: 50c, Flatland, by Bradley Christian. 60c, Tedside, by Torika Warren-Peu. $1, St. Pauls, by Jayden Warren-Peu. $1.80, Isaac's Valley, by Kimiora Warren-Peu. $2, Garnets Ridge, by Ralph Warren-Peu. $2.50, Ship Landing Point, by Ariel Brown.

**2010, Feb. 24 Litho. *Perf. 14¼***
**697-702** A165 Set of 6 12.00 12.00

ANZAC Day — A166

No. 703 — Poppy and: a, 50c, Tank. b, $1, Airplanes.
No. 704 — Poppy and: a, $1.80, Transport ship. b, $4, Gunboat.

**2010, Apr. 23 *Perf. 14½x14***
**Horiz. Pairs, #a-b**
**703-704** A166 Set of 2 11.00 11.00

Worldwide Fund for Nature (WWF) A167

No. 705 — Fish: a, Centropyge flavissima. b, Chaetodon smithi. c, Centropyge loricula. d, Chaetodon lineolatus.

**2010, June 23 *Perf. 14¼***

| | | | |
|---|---|---|---|
| **705** | Strip or block of 4 | 8.75 | 8.75 |
| *a.* | A167 60c multi | .90 | .90 |
| *b.* | A167 $1 multi | 1.20 | 1.20 |
| *c.* | A167 $2 multi | 1.80 | 1.80 |
| *d.* | A167 $2.50 multi | 2.20 | 2.20 |
| *e.* | Sheet of 8, 2 each #705a-705d | 17.50 | 17.50 |

Exploration of Volcanic Hotspots A168

No. 706: a, Research Vessel L'Atalante. b, Submersible Nautile. c, Photographing lava tube. d, Approaching Adams Volcano.

**2010, Aug. 18 *Perf. 14***

| | | | |
|---|---|---|---|
| **706** | Horiz. strip of 4 + central label | 10.00 | 10.00 |
| *a.* | A168 80c multi | 1.45 | 1.45 |
| *b.* | A168 $1.20 multi | 1.75 | 1.75 |
| *c.* | A168 $1.50 multi | 2.20 | 2.20 |
| *d.* | A168 $3 multi | 3.25 | 3.25 |

Snails A169

Designs: 80c, Orobophana solidula. $1, Philonesia filiceti. $1.80, Orobophana solidula, diff. $2.50, Philonesia filiceti, diff.

**2010, Oct. 20 *Serpentine Die Cut***
**Self-Adhesive**
**707-710** A169 Set of 4 9.00 9.00

**Visiting Royal Navy Ships Type of 2009**

Miniature Sheet

No. 711: a, $1, HMS Royalist, 1898. b, $1, HMS Cambrian, HMS Flora, 1906. c, $1, HMS Algerine, 1911. d, $1.80, HMS Leander, 1937. e, $1.80, HMS Monmouth, 1995. f, $1.80, HMS Sutherland, 2001.

**2010, Dec. 9 *Perf. 14***
**711** A164 Sheet of 6, #a-f 13.00 13.00

Yellow Fauta Flower A170

Designs: $2.50, Flower and bud. $3, Flower and three buds.

**2011, Feb. 12 Litho.**

| | | | |
|---|---|---|---|
| **712** | A170 $2.50 multi | 4.50 | 4.50 |
| **713** | A170 $3 multi | 5.50 | 5.50 |
| *a.* | Souvenir sheet of 1 | 5.75 | 5.75 |

Indipex 2011 World Philatelic Exhibition, New Delhi (No. 713a).

Peonies — A171

No. 714 — Peonies with denomination color of: a, White. b, Pink.

**2011, Apr. 21**
**714** A171 $1 Horiz. pair, #a-b 4.50 4.50

Printed in sheets containing 3 pairs.

Paper Wasp A172

Wasp on nest facing: $2.50, Right. $4, Left.

**2011, Apr. 21**

| | | | |
|---|---|---|---|
| **715-716** | A172 Set of 2 | 12.00 | 12.00 |
| *716a* | Souvenr sheet of 2, #715-716 | 13.00 | 13.00 |

Wedding of Prince William and Catherine Middleton A173

**Litho. With Foil Application**
**2011, May 25 *Perf. 14½x14¾***

| | | | |
|---|---|---|---|
| **717** | Horiz. pair + central label | 13.00 | 13.00 |
| *a.* | A173 $2.80 Couple | 5.00 | 5.00 |
| *b.* | A173 $6 Couple at wedding | 6.50 | 6.50 |

Supply Ships A174

Designs: $1, Southern Salvor. $1.80, Claymore II. $2.10, Braveheart. $3, Taporo VIII.

**2011, Aug. 31 Litho. *Perf. 14¼x14***
**718-721** A174 Set of 4 12.50 12.50

Parkin Christian (1883-1971) A175

**2011, Oct. 26 *Perf. 14½***

| | | | |
|---|---|---|---|
| **722** | Horiz. strip of 4 + central label | 12.00 | 12.00 |
| *a.* | A175 $1.50 Navigator | 2.00 | 2.00 |
| *b.* | A175 $1.80 Goodwill ambassador | 2.25 | 2.25 |
| *c.* | A175 $2.10 Magistrate | 2.50 | 2.50 |
| *d.* | A175 $2.40 Religious leader | 2.75 | 2.75 |

Christmas — A176

Designs: $1, Magus and camel. $1.50, Magus and camel, diff. $2.10, Magus and camel, diff. $3, Holy Family.

**2011, Dec. 7 *Perf. 14¼***
**723-726** A176 Set of 4 12.00 12.00

Henderson Island Birds — A177

Designs: 20c, Henderson crakes. 40c, Henderson fruit doves. $1.50, Henderson petrels. $2.10, Henderson reed warblers. $4.40, Henderson lorikeets.

**2011, July 20 *Perf. 14¼x14***
**727-731** A177 Set of 5 17.00 17.00

Souvenir Sheet

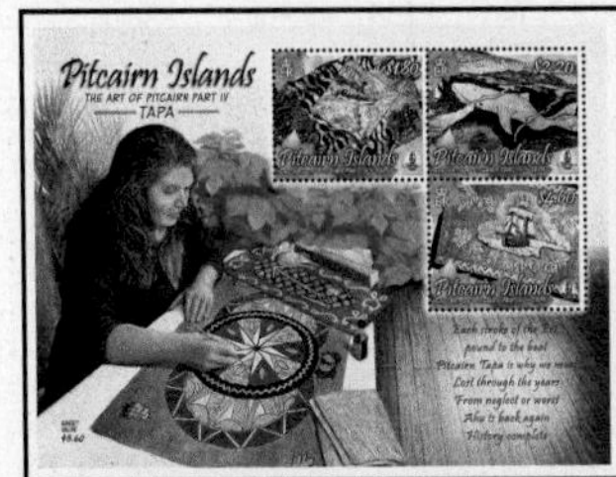


Tapa Cloth Designs — A178

No. 732: a, $1.80, Lognboat. b, $2.20, Whale. c, $4.60, HMS Bounty.

**2012, Feb. 21 *Perf. 13¾x13½***
**732** A178 Sheet of 3, #a-c 14.00 14.00

Dolphins A179

Designs: $1, Fraser's dolphin. $1.50, Spinner dolphin. $2.10, Spotted dolphin. $3, Bottlenose dolphin.

**2012, Apr. 26 *Perf. 14¼***

| | | | |
|---|---|---|---|
| **733-736** | A179 Set of 4 | 12.00 | 12.00 |
| *736a* | Souvenir sheet of 2, #734, 736 | 7.25 | 7.25 |

Reign of Queen Elizabeth II, 60th Anniv. A180

No. 737: a, Queen in uniform. b, Queen wearing blue green hat and dress.

**2012, June 1 *Perf. 14¼x14½***

| | | | |
|---|---|---|---|
| **737** | Horiz. pair + central label | 14.00 | 14.00 |
| *a.* | A180 $2.80 multi | 5.00 | 5.00 |
| *b.* | A180 $4.40 multi | 6.50 | 6.50 |

Photographs of Bounty Replicas — A181

Various photographs: 20c, $1, $2.10, $4.60

**2012, July 31**

| | | | |
|---|---|---|---|
| **738-741** | A181 Set of 4 | 13.00 | 13.00 |
| *741a* | Souvenir sheet of 1 #741 | 7.50 | 7.50 |

Roy P. Clark (1893-1980) A182

**2012, Sept. 26 *Perf. 14½***

| | | | |
|---|---|---|---|
| **742** | Horiz. strip of 4 + central label | 14.50 | 14.50 |
| *a.* | A182 $1 Teacher | 2.50 | 2.50 |
| *b.* | A182 $1.50 Postmaster | 3.25 | 3.25 |
| *c.* | A182 $2.20 Writer | 3.50 | 3.50 |
| *d.* | A182 $2.80 Community and church elder | 4.00 | 4.00 |

Worldwide Fund for Nature (WWF) A183

Various depictions of Fluted giant clam.

**2012, Oct. 31** ***Perf. 14¼x14½***

| | | | |
|---|---|---|---|
| **743** | Strip of 4 | 11.50 | 11.50 |
| *a.* | A183 20c multi | .80 | .80 |
| *b.* | A183 $1 multi | 2.00 | 2.00 |
| *c.* | A183 $2.10 multi | 2.75 | 2.75 |
| *d.* | A183 $3 multi | 3.25 | 3.25 |
| *e.* | Souvenir sheet of 8, 2 each #743a-743d | 20.00 | 20.00 |

Charles Dickens (1812-70), Writer A184

Various photographs of Dickens and characters from his novels: $1, $1.80, $2.10, $3.

**2012, Dec. 5** ***Perf. 14¾x14½***
**744-747** A184 Set of 4 13.00 13.00

Books in the Bounty Trilogy, by Charles Bernard Nordhoff and James Norman Hall — A185

Designs: $1, Mutiny on the Bounty. $2.10, Men Against the Sea. $3, Pitcairn's Island.

**2013, Feb. 27** ***Perf. 14½x14¾***

| | | | |
|---|---|---|---|
| **748-750** | A185 Set of 3 | 9.50 | 9.50 |
| *750a* | Souvenir sheet of 3, #748-750, perf. 14¾ | 9.50 | 9.50 |

Cruise Ships — A186

Designs: No. 751, $2, MV Marina. No. 752, $2, Pacific Princess. No. 753, $2, Costa Neo Romantica. No. 754, $2, Arcadia.

**2013, Apr. 24** ***Perf. 14½x14***
**751-754** A186 Set of 4 13.50 13.50

Souvenir Sheet

Lobsters — A187

No. 755: a, $1, Easter Island spiny lobster. b, $2, Aesop slipper lobster. c, $3.40, Pronghorn spiny lobster.

**2013, May 29** ***Perf. 14***
**755** A187 Sheet of 3, #a-c 10.50 10.50

Coronation of Queen Elizabeth II, 60th Anniv. — A188

**Litho. & Embossed**

**2013, July 11** ***Perf. 14½x14***
**756** A188 $6 blue 9.50 9.50

No. 756 was printed in sheets of 2 stamps.

Souvenir Sheet

Birth of Prince George of Cambridge — A189

No. 757: a, $3.40, Duke, Duchess of Cambridge, Prince George. b, $4.40, Duke of Cambridge, Pricne George.

**2013, Aug. 16** **Litho.** ***Perf. 14½***
**757** A189 Sheet of 2, #a-b 13.00 13.00

Lily Warren (1878-1969), Midwife A190

Varios photographs of Warren.

**2013, Sept. 25**

| | | | |
|---|---|---|---|
| **758** | Horiz. strip of 4 + central label | 13.00 | 13.00 |
| *a.* | A190 $1 multi | 1.75 | 1.75 |
| *b.* | A190 $1.50 multi | 2.50 | 2.50 |
| *c.* | A190 $2.20 multi | 3.75 | 3.75 |
| *d.* | A190 $2.80 multi | 4.75 | 4.75 |

Pres. John F. Kennedy (1917-63) A191

Headlines for events in Kennedy's presidency: $1, Inaugural address, Jan. 20, 1961. $1.80, Announcement of plans to put a man on the Moon, May 25, 1961. $2.10, Announcement of naval blockade of Cuba, Oct. 22, 1962. $3, "Ich bin ein Berliner" speech, June 26, 1963.

**2013, Nov. 22** **Litho.** ***Perf. 14½***
**759-762** A191 Set of 4 13.00 13.00

The April 18, 1962 date shown on the $2.10 stamp is incorrect for the headline. Kennedy announced plans for a nuclear disarmament treaty on April 18, 1962.

Ship Landing Point and Bounty Bay A192

Designs: 40c, Ship Landing Point as seen from Bounty Bay. No. 764, $1, Palm trees and Ship Landing Point. No. 765, $1, Bounty Bay framed by cliffs. No. 766, $2, Clouds above Ship Landing Point. No. 767, $2, Bounty Bay and rock promontory. $2.10, Aerial view of Bounty Bay.

**2013, Dec. 18** **Litho.** ***Perf. 14***
**763-768** A192 Set of 6 14.00 14.00

Souvenir Sheet

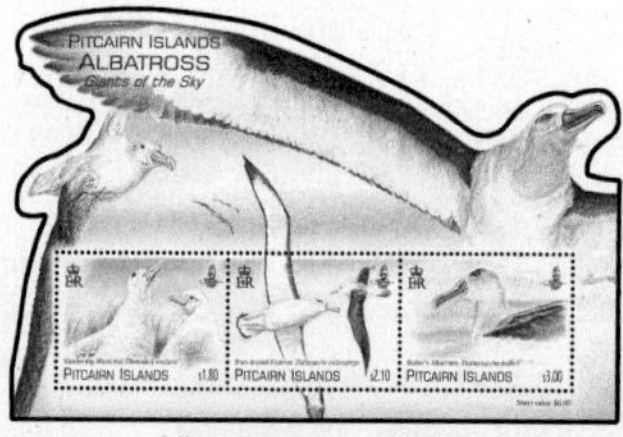


Albatrosses — A193

No. 769: a, $1.80, Wandering albatrosses. b, $2.10, Black-browed albatrosses. c, $3, Butler's albatross.

**2014, Feb. 27** **Litho.** ***Perf. 13½***
**769** A193 Sheet of 3, #a-c 11.50 11.50

Mutiny on the Bounty, 225th Anniv. A194

Designs: $1, Mutiny. $2, Captain Bligh and loyal crew set adrift in small boat. $2.10, Bounty leaving small boat with Captain Blight. $3, Bounty approaching Pitcairn Island.

**2014, Apr. 28** **Litho.** ***Perf. 14½***
**770-773** A194 Set of 4 14.00 14.00

Flora — A195

Designs: 20c, Cerbera manghas. $1, Portulaca lutea. $1.80, Canna sp. $2, Chamaesyce sparrmannii. $2.10, Coprosma benefica. $3, Pandanus tectorius.

**2014, June 12** **Litho.** ***Perf. 14x14¼***
**774-779** A195 Set of 6 18.00 18.00

Souvenir Sheet

World War I, Cent. — A196

No. 780 — Poppies and: a, $1, Ten soldiers hiking. b, $2.20, Three soldiers. c, $2.80, Bugler and five soldiers at attention.

**2014, July 28** **Litho.** ***Perf. 14***
**780** A196 Sheet of 3, #a-c 10.50 10.50

Actors Depicting Fletcher Christian in Movies — A197

Christian and actor portraying him: 20c, Wilton Power, 1916. $1, Errol Flynn, 1933. $2.10, Clark Gable, 1935. $2.80, Marlon Brando, 1962. $3, Mel Gibson, 1984.

**2014, Sept. 25** **Litho.** ***Perf. 14***
**781-785** A197 Set of 5 14.50 14.50

Fletcher Christian (1764-93), mutiny leader.

Nelson Mandela (1918-2013), President of South Africa — A198

Various photographs of Mandela and quote beginning with: $1, "What counts in life. . ." $1.80, "A good head. . .", vert. $2.10, "For to be free. . . .", vert. $3, "Education is the most powerful weapon. . ."

***Perf. 14¼x14, 14x14¼***

**2014, Nov. 3** **Litho.**
**786-789** A198 Set of 4 12.50 12.50

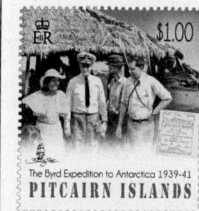

Visit to Pitcairn Islands of Richard E. Byrd Antarctic Expedition, 75th Anniv. A199

No. 790: a, Expedition members on Pitcairn, envelope cachet. b, USMS North Star, stamped cover to Philadelphia. c, USMS North Star, Snow Cruiser. d, Snow Cruiser, Admiral Byrd in parka.

**Wmk. 387**

**2014, Dec. 11** **Litho.** ***Perf. 14½***

| | | | |
|---|---|---|---|
| **790** | Horiz. strip of 4 + central label | 12.00 | 12.00 |
| *a.* | A199 $1 multi | 1.50 | 1.50 |
| *b.* | A199 $1.80 multi | 2.75 | 2.75 |
| *c.* | A199 $2 multi | 3.25 | 3.25 |
| *d.* | A199 $2.80 multi | 4.50 | 4.50 |

Souvenir Sheet

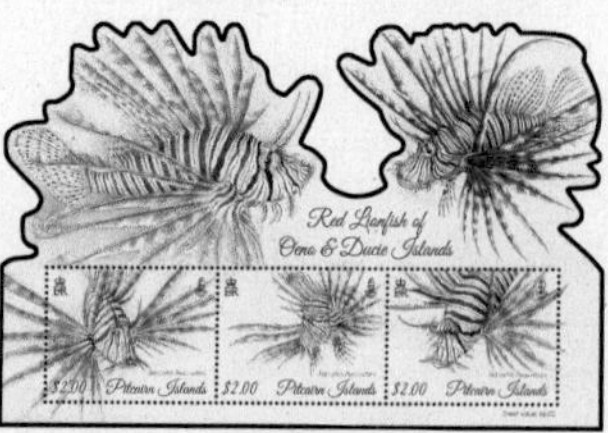

Red Lionfish — A200

No. 791: a, Denomination over fins. b, Fins above denomination. c, Fins touching "R" at UL.

**Unwmk.**

**2015, Feb. 26** **Litho.** ***Perf. 14***
**791** A200 $2 Sheet of 3, #a-c 9.25 9.25

Paintings — A201

Designs: $1, Interior of Pitcairn, 1830, by F. W. Beechey. $2, Pitcairn Island, c. 1808, by E. Low. $2.10, Christian's House, Pitcairn Island, c. 1824, by Conway Shipley. $3, Landing in Bounty Bay, 1830, by Beechey.

**2015, Apr. 29 Litho.** ***Perf. 14¾x14¼***
**792-795** A201 Set of 4 12.50 12.50

Ben Christian (1921-92), Island Secretary A202

No. 796 — Christian: a, On telephone. b, Carving wood. c, Holding caught fish. d, With medal.

**2015, June 24 Litho.** ***Perf. 14½***
**796** Horiz. strip of 4 + central label 10.50 10.50
*a.* A202 $1 multi 1.40 1.40
*b.* A202 $1.50 multi 2.00 2.00
*c.* A202 $2.10 multi 3.00 3.00
*d.* A202 $2.80 multi 3.75 3.75

Souvenir Sheet

Breadfruit — A203

No. 797: a, $1, Flower. b, $2, Breadfruit half. c, $3, Mature breadfruit.

**2015, Aug. 26 Litho.** ***Perf. 13½***
**797** A203 Sheet of 3, #a-c 7.75 7.75

First Pitcairn Islands Postage Stamps, 75th Anniv. A204

King George VI and: 10c, Cluster of oranges. 40c, Fletcher Christian with crew and view of Pitcairn Island. 60c, John Adams and his house. 80c, Map of Pitcairn and Pacific Ocean. $1, Bounty Bible. $2, H.M. Armed Vessel "Bounty." $4, William Bligh and H.M. Armed Vessel "Bounty." $5, Pitcairn School, 1949. $6, Fletcher Christian and view of Pitcairn Island. $10, Fletcher Christian with crew and coast of Pitcairn Island

**2015, Oct. 15 Litho.** ***Perf. 14x14¼***
**798** A204 10c multi .25 .25
**799** A204 40c multi .55 .55
**800** A204 60c multi .80 .80
**801** A204 80c multi 1.10 1.10
**802** A204 $1 multi 1.40 1.40
**803** A204 $2 multi 2.75 2.75
**804** A204 $4 multi 5.50 5.50
**805** A204 $5 multi 6.75 6.75
**806** A204 $6 multi 8.25 8.25
**807** A204 $10 multi 13.50 13.50
*Nos. 798-807 (10)* 40.85 40.85

Christmas A205

Carols: $1, Hark! The Herald Angels Sing. $2, Once in Royal David's City. $2.10, Away in a Manger. $3, Silent Night.

**2015, Dec. 9 Litho.** ***Perf. 14¼***
**808-811** A205 Set of 4 11.00 11.00

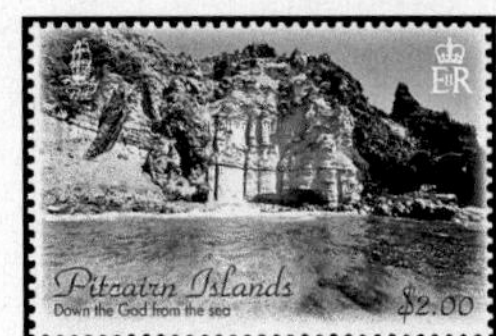


Landscapes — A206

No. 812 — Inscriptions: a, Down the God from the sea. b, Rainbow over St. Paul's Pool. c, Sunset over Ship Landing Point. d, Cliff view towards Bounty Bay. e, Adamstown from inside Christian's cave. f, Tautama toward Aute Valley and Break Em Hip.

**2016, Jan. 13 Litho.** ***Perf. 14¼x14***
**812** Block of 6 16.00 16.00
*a.-f.* A206 $2 Any single 2.60 2.60
Complete booklet, #812a-812f 16.00

Scenes from Plays by William Shakespeare (1564-1616) A207

No. 813: a, Macbeth. b, Hamlet. c, A Midsummer Night's Dream. d, Romeo and Juliet.

**2016, Mar. 9 Litho.** ***Perf. 14¼x14½***
**813** Horiz. strip of 4 + central label 9.75 9.75
*a.* A207 $1 multi 1.40 1.40
*b.* A207 $1.80 multi 2.50 2.50
*c.* A207 $2 multi 2.75 2.75
*d.* A207 $2.20 multi 3.00 3.00

Queen Elizabeth II, 90th Birthday — A208

Queen Elizabeth II wearing: No. 814, $1.80, Gray lilac hat. No. 815, $1.80, Light blue hat. No. 816, $2.10, Gray brown and white hat with ribbon. No. 817, $2.10, Light yellow hat with black edge.

**2016, Apr. 19 Litho.** ***Perf. 14x14¼***
**814-817** A208 Set of 4 11.00 11.00

Worldwide Fund for Nature (WWF) — A209

No. 818 — Phoenix petrel: a, Bird in nest. b, Two birds in nest. c, Two birds in flight. d, One bird in flight.

**2016, July 6 Litho.** ***Perf. 14¼***
**818** Strip of 4 9.00 9.00
*a.* A209 20c multi .30 .30
*b.* A209 $1 multi 1.40 1.40
*c.* A209 $2.10 multi 3.00 3.00
*d.* A209 $3 multi 4.25 4.25
*e.* Souvenir sheet of 8, 2 each #818a-818d 18.00 18.00

Adamstown — A210

**2016, Aug. 24 Litho.** ***Perf. 14½x14***
**819** Horiz. pair 1.75 1.75
*a.* A210 20c Store .30 .30
*b.* A210 $1 Museum 1.40 1.40
**820** Horiz. pair 9.75 9.75
*a.* A210 $2 Church 3.00 3.00
*b.* A210 $4.60 School 6.75 6.75

Ferns — A211

Designs: 20c, Dicranopteris linearis. $1, Loxoscaphe gibberosum. $3, Ctenitis cumingii. $3.40, Angiopteris chauliodonta.

**2016, Oct. 19 Litho.** ***Perf. 14x14½***
**821-824** A211 Set of 4 11.00 11.00
*824a* Souvenir sheet of 2, #823-824 9.25 9.25

Miniature Sheet

Pitcairn Language — A212

No. 825 — Pitcairn and English words for: a, 20c, Sea urchin. b, 20c, Goat. c, $1, Weaving strand. d, $1, Seedling. e, $1, Loader. f, $2, Melon. g, $2, Swimming. h, $2, Orange.

**2016, Dec. 7 Litho.** ***Perf. 14x14¼***
**825** A212 Sheet of 8, #a-h 13.00 13.00

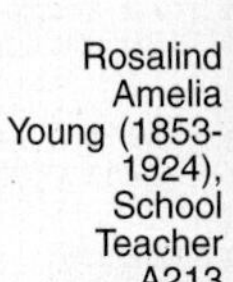

Rosalind Amelia Young (1853-1924), School Teacher A213

No. 826 — Young and: a, Blackboard. b, Her poetry, and husband, David. c, School children. d, Her book, *Story of Pitcairn Island.*

**2017, Feb. 22 Litho.** ***Perf. 14½***
**826** Horiz. strip of 4 + central label 10.50 10.50
*a.* A213 $1 multi 1.40 1.40
*b.* A213 $1.50 multi 2.10 2.10
*c.* A213 $2.10 multi 3.00 3.00
*d.* A213 $2.80 multi 4.00 4.00

Souvenir Sheet

Women of the Bounty — A214

No. 827: a, $1.80, Polynesian women on board the Bounty. b, $2.20, Women watching the burning of the Bounty. c, $2.80, Women and men starting life on Pitcairn Island.

***Perf. 13¼x13½***
**2017, Mar. 30 Litho.**
**827** A214 Sheet of 3, #a-c 9.50 9.50

See French Polynesia No. 1186.

Maps of Pitcairn Islands — A215

Map by: 20c, John Bayly, 1773. $1, Capt. Frederick Beechey, 1825. $2.10, Fred Christian, 1961. $4.40, David Evans, 2005.

**2017, May 17 Litho.** ***Perf. 14½***
**828-831** A215 Set of 4 11.00 11.00

Miniature Sheet

Pitcairn Islands Marine Reserve — A216

No. 832: a, $1, Titan triggerfish. b, $1, Pitcairn angelfish. c, $1, Whitetip reef shark. d, $1, Multibar goatfish. e, $2, Whitemouth moray. f, $2, Lyretail hogfish. g, $2, Yellow-edged lyretail. h, $2, Peacock grouper.

**2017, July 26 Litho.** ***Perf. 13x13¼***
**832** A216 Sheet of 8, #a-h 18.00 18.00

First Sighting of Pitcairn Islands, by Robert Pitcairn (1752-70?), 250th Anniv. — A217

No. 833 — Pitcairn: a, Pointing to island. b, Holding telescope.

**2017, Sept. 13 Litho.** ***Perf. 14¼***
**833** A217 $3 Horiz. pair, #a-b, + central label 8.75 8.75

Transverse Ladybird A218

Ladybird on: $2.10, Green foliage. $3, Brown foliage.

No. 836: a, $1, Ladybird with elytra open and wings up. b, $4.60, Ladybird with elytra partially open.

**2017, Oct. 25 Litho. *Perf. 14¼x14***
**834-835** A218 Set of 2 7.00 7.00

**Souvenir Sheet**

**836** A218 Sheet of 2, #a-b 7.75 7.75

William Bligh (1754-1817), Captain of HMAV Bounty — A219

Maps and paintings of Bligh and: $1, Capt. James Cook. $2.10, Mutiny on the Bounty. $2.80, Vice Admiral Horatio Nelson. $3, Statue of Bligh, Sydney, Australia.

**2017, Dec. 7 Litho. *Perf. 13¾x13¼***
**837-840** A219 Set of 4 13.00 13.00

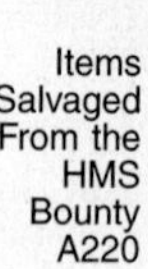

Items Salvaged From the HMS Bounty A220

Designs: $1, Copper fragment. $1.80, Bronze bell strike. $2.10, Copper hull sheathing. $3, Large cannon ball.

***Perf. 13½x13¼***
**2018, Feb. 27 Litho.**
**841-844** A220 Set of 4 11.50 11.50

Drafters of the Pitcairn Islands Constitution — A221

No. 845: a, Captain Russell Eliott (1802-81). b, George Hunn Nobbs (1799-1884).

**2018, Apr. 5 Litho. *Perf. 14¼***
**845** A221 $3 Horiz. pair, #a-b, + central label 8.50 8.50

Wedding of Prince Harry and Meghan Markle — A222

No. 846: a, $3, Engagement photograph. b, $5, Wedding photograph.

**Litho. With Foil Application**
**2018, May 30 *Perf. 14¼***
**846** A222 Horiz. pair, #a-b, + central label 11.50 11.50

**Miniature Sheet**

Flowers — A223

No. 847: a, $1, Hibiscus rosa-sinensis. b, $1, Strelitzia reginae. c, $1, Heliconia rostrata. d, $2, Anthurium andraeanum. e, $2, Alpinia purpurata. f, $2, Allamanda blanchetii.

**2018, July 18 Litho. *Perf. 14¼***
**847** A223 Sheet of 6, #a-f 12.50 12.50

**Souvenir Sheet**

Big Blue Octopus — A224

No. 848 — Various depictions of Octopus cyanea: a, $1. b, $2.80. c, $3.

***Perf. 13¼x13½***
**2018, Sept. 19 Litho.**
**848** A224 Sheet of 3, #a-c 9.00 9.00

**Miniature Sheet**

End of World War I, Cent. — A225

No. 849: a, $1, Armistice signing between Allies and Germany. b, $1, Soldiers celebrating end of World War I. c, $2, Crowd of people celebrating end of World War I, equestrian statue in background. d, $2, British people in automobile celebrating end of World War I, Big Ben in background. e, $3, People on double-decker bus celebrating end of World War I. f, $3, Poppy.

**2018, Nov. 11 Litho. *Perf. 14***
**849** A225 Sheet of 6, #a-f 17.00 17.00

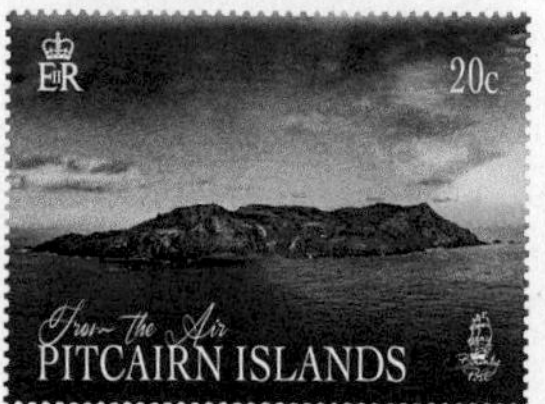


Aerial Views of Pitcairn Island — A226

Various aerial photographs: 20c, $1, $3, $4.60.

**2018, Dec. 12 Litho. *Perf. 14½***
**850-853** A226 Set of 4 12.00 12.00

Paintings of the HMAV Bounty — A227

Painting by: $1, John Charles Alcott. $2.10, Roger Morris. $2.80, John Hagan. $3, Alfred Memelink.

**2019, Feb. 27 Litho. *Perf. 14½x14***
**854-857** A227 Set of 4 12.50 12.50

**Miniature Sheet**

Flowers — A228

No. 858: a, $1, Lilium longiflorum. b, $1.80, Brugmansia suaveolens. c, $2.80, Epiphyllum oxypetalum. d, $3, Cestrum nocturnum.

**2019, Apr. 30 Litho. *Perf. 14½***
**858** A228 Sheet of 4, #a-d 11.50 11.50

Pitcairn Reed Warbler A229

No. 859: a, Bird's head. b, Two birds. c, One bird.

**2019, June 14 Litho. *Perf. 14¼x14***

| | | | |
|---|---|---|---|
| **859** | Horiz. strip of 3 | 9.75 | 9.75 |
| *a.* | A229 $1.80 multi | 2.50 | 2.50 |
| *b.* | A229 $2.10 multi | 2.75 | 2.75 |
| *c.* | A229 $3.40 multi | 4.50 | 4.50 |

First Man on the Moon, 50th Anniv. A230

Designs: $1, Crew of Apollo 11. $2.20, Crew of Apollo 11 wearing space helmets. $3, Launch of Apollo 11. $3.40, Astronaut on ladder of Lunar Module.

**2019, July 19 Litho. *Perf. 14½***
**860-863** A230 Set of 4 12.50 12.50

**Miniature Sheet**

Mata ke Ti Randi Dark Sky Sanctuary — A231

No. 864 — Various views of Mata ki te Rangi at night: a, 20c. b, $2. c, $2.10. d, $3.

**2019, Sept. 4 Litho. *Perf. 14***
**864** A231 Sheet of 4, #a-d 9.25 9.25

Echinoderms — A232

Designs: 20c, Heterocentrotus mamillatus. $1, Brissus latecarinatus. $3, Neoferdina cumingi. $4.60, Macrophiothrix demessa.

**2019, Oct. 23 Litho. *Perf. 14½x14***
**865-868** A232 Set of 4 11.50 11.50

Christmas — A233

No. 869 — Angel over part of Pitcairn Island: a, $1.80. b, $2.20. c, $2.80.

**2019, Dec. 4 Litho. *Perf. 13¼x13½***
**869** A233 Horiz. strip of 3, #a-c 9.25 9.25

# POLAND

'pō-lənd

LOCATION — Europe between Russia and Germany
GOVT. — Republic
AREA — 120,628 sq. mi.
POP. — 38,608,929 (1999 est.)
CAPITAL — Warsaw

100 Kopecks = 1 Ruble
100 Fenigi = 1 Marka (1918)
100 Halerzy = 1 Korona (1918)
100 Groszy = 1 Zloty (1924)

**Catalogue values for unused stamps in this country are for Never Hinged items, beginning with Scott 534 in the regular postage section, Scott B63 in the semi-postal section, Scott C28 in the airpost section, Scott CB1 in the airpost semi-postal section, and Scott J146 in the postage due section.**

### Watermarks

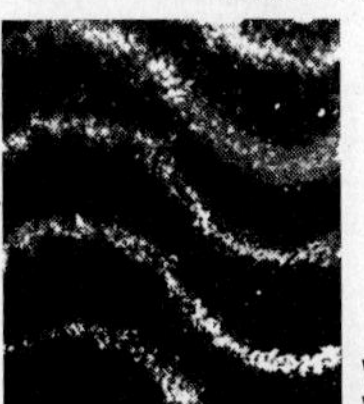

Wmk. 145 — Wavy Lines

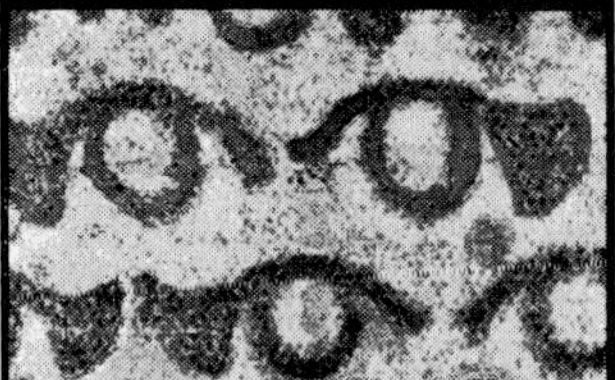

Wmk. 234 — Multiple Post Horns

Wmk. 326 — Multiple Post Horns

### Issued under Russian Dominion

Coat of Arms — A1

*Perf. 11½ to 12½*

**1860 Typo. Unwmk.**

| | | | | |
|---|---|---|---|---|
| 1 | A1 10k blue & rose | | 2,400. | 300. |
| | *a.* | 10k blue & carmine | 2,600. | 375. |
| | *b.* | 10k dark blue & rose | 3,000. | 425. |
| | *c.* | Added blue frame for inner oval | 10,000. | 1,400. |
| | *d.* | Imperf. | — | 7,500. |

Used for letters within the Polish territory and to Russia. Postage on all foreign letters was paid in cash.

These stamps were superseded by those of Russia in 1865.

Counterfeits exist.

### Issues of the Republic

Local issues were made in various Polish cities during the German occupation.

In the early months of the Republic many issues were made by overprinting the German occupation stamps with the words "Poczta Polska" and an eagle or bars often with the name of the city.

These issues were not authorized by the Government but were made by the local authorities and restricted to local use. In 1914 two stamps were issued for the Polish Legion and in 1918 the Polish Expeditionary Force used surcharged Russian stamps. The regularity of these issues is questioned.

Numerous counterfeits of these issues abound.

### Warsaw Issues

Stamps of the Warsaw Local Post Surcharged

Statue of Sigismund III — A2

Coat of Arms of Warsaw — A3

Polish Eagle A4

Sobieski Monument A5

**1918, Nov. 17 Wmk. 145** ***Perf. 11½***

| | | | | |
|---|---|---|---|---|
| 11 | A2 | 5f on 2gr brn & buff | 1.40 | .90 |
| | *a.* | Inverted surcharge | 200.00 | 200.00 |
| 12 | A3 | 10f on 6gr grn & buff | .70 | .65 |
| | *a.* | Inverted surcharge | 15.00 | 15.00 |
| 13 | A4 | 25f on 10gr rose & buff | 7.00 | 3.25 |
| | *a.* | Inverted surcharge | 27.50 | 27.50 |
| 14 | A5 | 50f on 20gr bl & buff | 8.50 | 6.25 |
| | *a.* | Inverted surcharge | 350.00 | 350.00 |
| | | *Nos. 11-14 (4)* | 17.60 | 11.05 |

Counterfeits exist.

### Occupation Stamps Nos. N6-N16 Overprinted or Surcharged

a

b

**1918-19 Wmk. 125** ***Perf. 14, 14½***

| | | | | |
|---|---|---|---|---|
| 15 | A16 | 3pf brown ('19) | 35.00 | 27.50 |
| 16 | A22 | 5pf on 2½pf gray | 1.40 | .70 |
| 17 | A16 | 5pf on 3pf brown | 5.00 | 3.50 |
| 18 | A16 | 5pf green | 1.75 | .70 |
| 19 | A16 | 10pf carmine | 1.40 | .50 |
| 20 | A22 | 15pf dark violet | 1.00 | .50 |
| 21 | A16 | 20pf blue | 1.40 | .50 |
| | *a.* | 20pf ultramarine | *775.00* | *2,250.* |
| 23 | A22 | 25pf on 7½pf org | 1.00 | .50 |
| 24 | A16 | 30pf org & blk, *buff* | 1.00 | .50 |
| 25 | A16 | 40pf brt car & black | 1.75 | 1.25 |
| 26 | A16 | 60pf magenta | 1.40 | .50 |
| | | *Nos. 15-26 (11)* | 52.10 | 36.65 |

There are two settings of this overprint. The first printing, issued Dec. 5, 1918, has space of 3½mm between the middle two bars. The second printing, issued Jan. 15, 1919, has space of 4mm. No. 15 comes only in the second setting; all others in both. The German overprint on No. 21a is very glossy.

Varieties of this overprint and surcharge are numerous: double; inverted; misspellings (Pocata, Poczto, Pelska); letters omitted, inverted or wrong font; 3 bars instead of 4, etc.

No. 21a requires competent expertization. A number of shades of the blue No. 21 exist. Counterfeits exist.

### Lublin Issue

Austrian Military Semi-Postal Stamps of 1918 Overprinted

**1918, Dec. 5 Unwmk.** ***Perf. 12½x13***

| | | | | |
|---|---|---|---|---|
| 27 | MSP7 | 10h gray green | 8.50 | 7.50 |
| | *a.* | Inverted overprint | 80.00 | 80.00 |
| | *b.* | Double overprint | 1,750. | 700.00 |
| | *c.* | Double ovpt., one inverted | 2,100. | 850.00 |
| 28 | MSP8 | 20h magenta | 6.50 | 7.50 |
| | *a.* | Inverted overprint | 50.00 | 50.00 |
| | *b.* | Double ovpt., one inverted | 1,750. | 500.00 |
| 29 | MSP7 | 45h blue | 6.50 | 7.50 |
| | *a.* | Inverted overprint | 50.00 | 50.00 |
| | *b.* | Double ovpt., one inverted | 1,750. | 500.00 |
| | | *Nos. 27-29 (3)* | 21.50 | 22.50 |

Austrian Military Stamps of 1917 Surcharged

**1918-19** ***Perf. 12½***

| | | | | |
|---|---|---|---|---|
| 30 | M3 | 3hal on 3h ol gray | 27.50 | 20.00 |
| | *a.* | Inverted surcharge | *3,900.* | *3,900.* |
| | *b.* | Perf. 11½ | 50.00 | 27.50 |
| | *c.* | Perf. 11½x12½ | 30.00 | 27.50 |
| 31 | M3 | 3hal on 15h brt rose | 7.00 | 7.00 |
| | *a.* | Inverted surcharge | 25.00 | 30.00 |

Surcharged in Black

| | | | | |
|---|---|---|---|---|
| 32 | M3 | 10hal on 30h sl grn | 7.00 | 7.00 |
| | *a.* | Inverted surcharge | 25.00 | 30.00 |
| | *b.* | Brown surcharge (error) | 75.00 | 65.00 |
| 34 | M3 | 25hal on 40h ol bis | 15.00 | 12.00 |
| | *a.* | Inverted surcharge | 37.50 | 42.50 |
| | *b.* | Perf. 11½ | 52.50 | 27.50 |
| | *c.* | As "b," inverted surcharge | 175.00 | 175.00 |
| 35 | M3 | 45hal on 60h rose | 7.00 | 7.00 |
| | *a.* | Inverted surcharge | 30.00 | 27.50 |
| 36 | M3 | 45hal on 80h dl blue | 8.50 | 8.50 |
| | *a.* | Inverted surcharge | 35.00 | 35.00 |
| 37 | M3 | 50hal on 60h rose | 18.00 | 14.00 |
| | *a.* | Inverted surcharge | 52.50 | 35.00 |

**Similar surcharge with bars instead of stars over original value**

| | | | | |
|---|---|---|---|---|
| 38 | M3 | 45hal on 80h dl blue | 12.00 | 10.00 |
| | *a.* | Inverted surcharge | 40.00 | 35.00 |
| | *b.* | Double srch., one inverted | 1,350. | — |

Overprinted

| | | | | |
|---|---|---|---|---|
| 39 | M3 | 50h deep green | 27.50 | 27.50 |
| | *a.* | Inverted overprint | 100.00 | 100.00 |
| 40 | M3 | 90h dark violet | 7.00 | 7.00 |
| | *a.* | Inverted overprint | 140.00 | 100.00 |
| | | *Nos. 30-40 (10)* | 136.50 | 120.00 |

### Counterfeits

**All Cracow issues, Nos. 41-60, J1-J12 and P1-P5, have been extensively counterfeited. Competent expertization is necessary. Prices apply only for authenticated stamps with identified plating position. Cost of certificate is not included in the catalogue value.**

### Cracow Issues

Austrian Stamps of 1916-18 Overprinted

POCZTA
POLSKA

**1919, Jan. 17 Typo.**

| | | | | |
|---|---|---|---|---|
| 41 | A37 | 3h brt violet | 500.00 | 500.00 |
| 42 | A37 | 5h lt green | 550.00 | 550.00 |
| 43 | A37 | 6h deep orange | 70.00 | 65.00 |
| | *a.* | Inverted overprint | *50,000.* | |
| 44 | A37 | 10h magenta | 500.00 | 500.00 |
| 45 | A37 | 12h lt blue | 75.00 | 75.00 |
| 46 | A39 | 40h olive green | 30.00 | 25.00 |
| | *a.* | Inverted overprint | 550.00 | — |
| | *b.* | Double overprint | *2,500.* | |
| 47 | A39 | 50h blue green | 15.00 | 15.00 |
| | *a.* | Inverted overprint | | *35,000.* |
| 48 | A39 | 60h deep blue | 10.00 | 10.00 |
| | *a.* | Inverted overprint | *375.00* | — |
| 49 | A39 | 80h orange brown | 14.00 | 14.00 |
| | *a.* | Inverted overprint | *325.00* | *250.00* |
| | *b.* | Double overprint | *1,750.* | — |
| 50 | A39 | 90h red violet | 1,500. | 1,400. |
| 51 | A39 | 1k carmine, *yel* | 25.00 | 25.00 |

**Engr.**

| | | | | |
|---|---|---|---|---|
| 52 | A40 | 2k blue | 12.00 | 14.00 |
| 53 | A40 | 3k carmine rose | 190.00 | 175.00 |
| 54 | A40 | 4k yellow green | 200.00 | 175.00 |
| 55 | A40 | 10k deep violet | *14,000.* | *13,000.* |

The 3k is on granite paper.

The overprint on Nos. 52-55 is litho. and slightly larger than illustration with different ornament between lines of type.

### Same Overprint on Nos. 168-171

**1919** **Typo.**

| No. | Type | Description | Unused | Used |
|---|---|---|---|---|
| 56 | A42 | 15h dull red | 70.00 | 65.00 |
| 57 | A42 | 20h dark green | 300.00 | 160.00 |
| 58 | A42 | 25h blue | 2,000. | 1,600. |
| 59 | A42 | 30h dull violet | 600.00 | 400.00 |

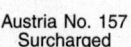

Austria No. 157 Surcharged

**1919, Jan. 24**

| No. | Type | Description | Unused | Used |
|---|---|---|---|---|
| 60 | A39 | 25h on 80h org brn | 8.00 | 8.00 |
| a. | | Inverted surcharge | 225.00 | 140.00 |

Excellent counterfeits of Nos. 27 to 60 exist.

Polish Eagle — A9

**1919, Feb. 25** **Litho.** ***Imperf.***

### Without gum

### Yellowish Paper

| No. | Type | Description | Unused | Used |
|---|---|---|---|---|
| 61 | A9 | 2h gray | 1.75 | 1.40 |
| 62 | A9 | 3h dull violet | 1.00 | 1.00 |
| 63 | A9 | 5h green | 1.00 | .70 |
| 64 | A9 | 6h orange | 17.50 | 20.00 |
| 65 | A9 | 10h lake | 1.00 | .70 |
| 66 | A9 | 15h brown | 1.00 | .70 |
| 67 | A9 | 20h olive green | 1.00 | 1.00 |

### Bluish Paper

| No. | Type | Description | Unused | Used |
|---|---|---|---|---|
| 68 | A9 | 25h carmine | .70 | .70 |
| 69 | A9 | 50h indigo | 1.00 | 1.00 |
| 70 | A9 | 70h deep blue | 1.75 | 1.40 |
| 71 | A9 | 1k ol gray & car | 1.75 | 1.75 |
| | | *Nos. 61-71 (11)* | 29.45 | 30.35 |

Nos. 61-71 exist with privately applied perforations.

Counterfeits exist.

For surcharges see Nos. J35-J39.

### Posen (Poznan) Issue

Germany Nos. 84-85, 87, 96, 98 Overprinted in Black

***Perf. 14, 14½***

**1919, Aug. 5** **Wmk. 125**

| No. | Type | Description | Unused | Used |
|---|---|---|---|---|
| 72 | A22 | 5pf on 2pf gray | 30.00 | 18.00 |
| 73 | A22 | 5pf on 7½pf org | 2.00 | 1.40 |
| a. | | Double surcharge | 1,550. | 1,300. |
| 74 | A16 | 5pf on 20pf bl vio | 2.00 | 1.25 |
| 75 | A16 | 10pf on 25pf org & blk, *yel* | 6.00 | 3.50 |
| 76 | A16 | 10pf on 40pf lake & blk | 3.50 | 1.40 |
| | | *Nos. 72-76 (5)* | 43.50 | 25.55 |

Counterfeits exist.

### Germany Nos. 96 and 98 Surcharged in Red or Green

a

b

**1919, Sept. 15**

| No. | Type | Description | Unused | Used |
|---|---|---|---|---|
| 77 | A22 | 5pf on 2pf (R) | 250.00 | 190.00 |
| a. | | Inverted surcharge | *25,000.* | |
| 78 | A22 | 10pf on 7½pf (G) | 350.00 | 140.00 |

Nos. 77-78 are a provisional issue for use in Gniezno. Counterfeit surcharges abound.

Eagle and Fasces, Symbolical of United Poland
A10 A11

"Agriculture" A12

"Peace" — A13

Polish Cavalryman A14

### For Northern Poland

Denominations as "F" or "M"

**1919, Jan. 27** ***Imperf.***

### Wove or Ribbed Paper

| No. | Type | Description | Unused | Used |
|---|---|---|---|---|
| 81 | A10 | 3f bister brn | .25 | .35 |
| 82 | A10 | 5f green | .25 | .35 |
| 83 | A10 | 10f red violet | .25 | .35 |
| 84 | A10 | 15f deep rose | .25 | .25 |
| 85 | A11 | 20f deep blue | .25 | .50 |
| 86 | A11 | 25f olive green | .25 | .50 |
| 87 | A11 | 50f blue green | .25 | .50 |
| 88 | A12 | 1m violet | 2.50 | 3.75 |
| 89 | A12 | 1.50m deep green | 4.25 | 7.00 |
| 90 | A12 | 2m dark brown | 4.25 | 8.50 |
| 91 | A13 | 2.50m orange brn | 8.50 | 22.50 |
| 92 | A14 | 5m red violet | 17.50 | 40.00 |
| | | *Nos. 81-92 (12)* | 38.75 | 84.55 |

***Perf. 10, 11, 11½, 10x11½, 11½x10***

**1919-20**

| No. | Type | Description | Unused | Used |
|---|---|---|---|---|
| 93 | A10 | 3f bister brn | .25 | .25 |
| 94 | A10 | 5f green | .25 | .25 |
| 95 | A10 | 10f red violet | .25 | .25 |
| 96 | A10 | 10f brown ('20) | .25 | .25 |
| 97 | A10 | 15f deep rose | .25 | .25 |
| 98 | A10 | 15f vermilion ('20) | .25 | .25 |
| 99 | A11 | 20f deep blue | .25 | .25 |
| 100 | A11 | 25f olive green | .25 | .25 |
| 101 | A11 | 40f brt violet ('20) | .25 | .25 |
| 102 | A11 | 50f blue green | .25 | .25 |
| 103 | A12 | 1m violet | .70 | .25 |
| 105 | A12 | 1.50m deep green | .70 | .35 |
| 106 | A12 | 2m dark brown | 1.75 | .50 |
| 107 | A13 | 2.50m orange brn | 1.00 | .70 |
| 108 | A14 | 5m red violet | 2.00 | 1.50 |
| | | *Nos. 93-108 (15)* | 8.65 | 5.80 |

No. 108 exists in various shades of brown and violet.

Several denominations among Nos. 81-132 are found with double impression or in pairs imperf. between. See Nos. 109-132, 140-152C, 170-175. For surcharges & overprints, see Nos. 153, 199-200, B1-B14, 2K1-2K12, Eastern Silesia 41-50.

### For Southern Poland

Denominations as "H" or "K"

**1919, Jan. 27** ***Imperf.***

| No. | Type | Description | Unused | Used |
|---|---|---|---|---|
| 109 | A10 | 3h red brown | .35 | .35 |
| 110 | A10 | 5h emerald | .35 | .25 |
| 111 | A10 | 10h orange | .35 | .25 |
| 112 | A10 | 15h vermilion | .35 | .25 |
| 113 | A11 | 20h gray brown | .35 | .25 |
| 114 | A11 | 25h light blue | .35 | .25 |
| 115 | A11 | 50h orange brn | .35 | .70 |
| 116 | A12 | 1k dark green | .35 | 1.40 |
| 117 | A12 | 1.50k red brown | 4.75 | 4.00 |
| 118 | A12 | 2k dark blue | 2.00 | 3.50 |
| 119 | A13 | 2.50k dark violet | 12.50 | 8.00 |
| 120 | A14 | 5k slate blue | 15.00 | 12.00 |
| | | *Nos. 109-120 (12)* | 37.05 | 31.20 |

***Perf. 10, 11½, 10x11½, 11½x10***

| No. | Type | Description | Unused | Used |
|---|---|---|---|---|
| 121 | A10 | 3h red brown | .25 | .25 |
| 122 | A10 | 5h emerald | .25 | .25 |
| 123 | A10 | 10h orange | .25 | .25 |
| 124 | A10 | 15h vermilion | .25 | .25 |
| 125 | A11 | 20h gray brown | .25 | .25 |
| 126 | A11 | 25h light blue | .25 | .25 |
| 127 | A11 | 50h orange brn | .25 | .25 |
| 128 | A12 | 1k dark green | .25 | .25 |
| 129 | A12 | 1.50k red brown | .50 | .25 |
| 130 | A12 | 2k dark blue | .80 | .25 |
| 131 | A13 | 2.50k dark violet | 2.00 | .80 |
| 132 | A14 | 5k slate blue | 2.00 | 1.40 |
| | | *Nos. 121-132 (12)* | 7.30 | 4.70 |

### National Assembly Issue

A20

Ignacy Jan Paderewski — A21

Adalbert Trampczynski — A22

Eagle Watching Ship — A24

25f, Gen. Josef Pilsudski. 1m, Griffin.

**1919-20** ***Perf. 11½***

### Wove or Ribbed Paper

| No. | Type | Description | Unused | Used |
|---|---|---|---|---|
| 133 | A20 | 10f red violet | .40 | .25 |
| 134 | A21 | 15f brown red | .40 | .25 |
| a. | | Imperf., pair | 25.00 | |
| 135 | A22 | 20f dp brown (21x25mm) | .40 | .25 |
| 136 | A22 | 20f dp brown (17x20mm) ('20) | 1.75 | *2.25* |
| 137 | A21 | 25f olive green | .40 | .25 |
| 138 | A24 | 50f Prus blue | .40 | .25 |
| 139 | A24 | 1m purple | 1.25 | .40 |
| | | *Nos. 133-139 (7)* | 5.00 | 3.90 |

First National Assembly of Poland.

### General Issue

**1919** ***Perf. 9 to 14½ and Compound***

### Thin Laid Paper

| No. | Type | Description | Unused | Used |
|---|---|---|---|---|
| 140 | A11 | 25f olive green | .25 | .25 |
| 141 | A11 | 50f blue green | .25 | .25 |
| 142 | A12 | 1m dark gray | .25 | .25 |
| 143 | A12 | 2m bister brn | .25 | .25 |
| 144 | A13 | 3m red brown | 2.00 | .35 |
| a. | | Pair, imperf. vert. | 8.00 | 8.00 |
| 145 | A14 | 5m red violet | 1.25 | .25 |
| 146 | A14 | 6m deep rose | 1.40 | .25 |
| a. | | Pair, imperf. vert. | 8.00 | 8.00 |
| 147 | A14 | 10m brown red | .50 | .30 |
| a. | | Horizontal pair, imperf. | 8.00 | 8.00 |
| 148 | A14 | 20m gray green | 1.40 | .50 |
| | | *Nos. 140-148 (9)* | 7.55 | 2.65 |

### Type of 1919 Redrawn

***Perf. 9 to 14½ and Compound***

**1920-22** **Thin Laid or Wove Paper**

| No. | Type | Description | Unused | Used |
|---|---|---|---|---|
| 149 | A10 | 1m red | .25 | .25 |
| 150 | A10 | 2m gray green | .25 | .25 |
| 151 | A10 | 3m light blue | .50 | .35 |
| 152 | A10 | 4m rose red | .25 | .25 |
| 152A | A10 | 5m dark violet | .25 | .25 |
| b. | | Horiz. pair, imperf. vert. | 8.00 | 8.00 |
| 152C | A10 | 8m gray brown ('22) | .50 | .50 |
| | | *Nos. 149-152C (6)* | 2.00 | 1.85 |

The word "POCZTA" is in smaller letters and the numerals have been enlarged.

The color of No. 152A varies from dark violet to red brown.

No. 101 Surcharged

***Perf. 10, 11½, 10x11½, 11½x10***

**1921, Jan. 25** **Thick Wove Paper**

| No. | Type | Description | Unused | Used |
|---|---|---|---|---|
| 153 | A11 | 3m on 40f brt vio | .40 | .25 |
| a. | | Double surcharge | 25.00 | 25.00 |
| b. | | Inverted surcharge | — | — |

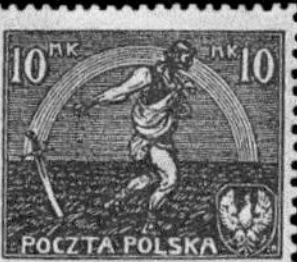

Sower and Rainbow of Hope — A27

### Thin Laid or Wove Paper

***Perf. 9 to 14½ and Compound***

**1921** **Size: 28x22mm** **Litho.**

| No. | Type | Description | Unused | Used |
|---|---|---|---|---|
| 154 | A27 | 10m grnsh blue | 1.00 | .30 |
| 155 | A27 | 15m light brown | .65 | .30 |
| 155A | A27 | 20m red | 1.50 | .30 |
| | | *Nos. 154-155A (3)* | 3.15 | .90 |

Signing of peace treaty with Russia.

Nos. 154-155A exist imperf. Value, unused, each $6.

See No. 191. For surcharges see Nos. 196-198.

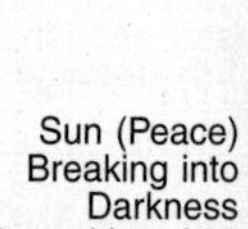

Sun (Peace) Breaking into Darkness (Despair) — A28

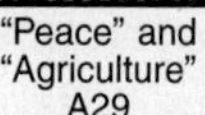

"Peace" and "Agriculture" A29

"Peace" A30

***Perf. 11, 11½, 12, 12½, 13 and Compound***

**1921, May 2**

| No. | Type | Description | Unused | Used |
|---|---|---|---|---|
| 156 | A28 | 2m green | .70 | 9.50 |
| 157 | A28 | 3m blue | 2.50 | 10.00 |
| 158 | A28 | 4m red | .60 | .70 |
| a. | | 4m carmine rose (error) | *600.00* | |
| 159 | A29 | 6m carmine rose | .60 | 1.50 |
| 160 | A29 | 10m slate blue | 2.10 | .80 |
| 161 | A30 | 25m dk violet | 3.50 | .70 |
| 162 | A30 | 50m slate bl & buff | 2.10 | .70 |
| | | *Nos. 156-162 (7)* | 12.10 | 23.90 |

Issued to commemorate the Constitution.

Polish Eagle — A31

***Perf. 9 to 14½ and Compound***

**1921-23**

| No. | Type | Description | Unused | Used |
|---|---|---|---|---|
| 163 | A31 | 25m violet & buff | .80 | .30 |
| 164 | A31 | 50m carmine & buff | .80 | .30 |
| a. | | Vert. pair, imperf. horiz. | | |
| 165 | A31 | 100m blk brn & org | .80 | .30 |
| 166 | A31 | 200m black & rose ('23) | .80 | .30 |
| 167 | A31 | 300m olive grn ('23) | .40 | .30 |
| 168 | A31 | 400m brown ('23) | .55 | .30 |
| 169 | A31 | 500m brn vio ('23) | .70 | .30 |
| 169A | A31 | 1000m orange ('23) | 1.25 | .30 |
| 169B | A31 | 2000m dull blue ('23) | .35 | .30 |
| | | *Nos. 163-169B (9)* | 6.45 | 2.70 |

For surcharge see No. 195.

### Type of 1919 and

Miner — A32

***Perf. 9 to 14½ and Compound***

**1922-23**

| No. | Type | Description | Unused | Used |
|---|---|---|---|---|
| 170 | A10 | 5f blue | .25 | .75 |
| 171 | A10 | 10f lt violet | .25 | .75 |
| 172 | A11 | 20f pale red | .25 | 1.50 |
| 173 | A11 | 40f violet brn | .25 | 1.50 |
| 174 | A11 | 50f orange | .25 | 1.50 |

**175** A11 75f blue green .25 2.25
**176** A32 1m black .25 1.50
**177** A32 1.25m dark green .25 3.25
**178** A32 2m deep rose .25 1.50
**179** A32 3m emerald .25 1.50
**180** A32 4m deep ultra .25 3.00
**181** A32 5m yellow brn .25 1.50
**182** A32 6m red orange .25 6.50
**183** A32 10m lilac brn .25 2.50
**184** A32 20m deep violet .25 3.00
**185** A32 50m olive green .25 2.50
**187** A32 80m vermilion ('23) 1.00 20.00
**188** A32 100m violet ('23) .60 13.00
**189** A32 200m orange ('23) 2.50 30.00
**190** A32 300m pale blue ('23) 6.00 45.00
*Nos. 170-190 (20)* 14.10 143.00

Union of Upper Silesia with Poland.

There were 2 printings of Nos. 176 to 190, the 1st being from flat plates, the 2nd from rotary press on thin paper, perf. 12½.

Nos. 173 and 175 are printed from new plates showing larger value numerals and a single "f."

### Sower Type Redrawn

Size: 25x21mm

**1922 Thick or Thin Wove Paper**

**191** A27 20m carmine 1.25 .50

In this stamp the design has been strengthened and made more distinct, especially the ground and the numerals in the upper corners.

Nicolaus Copernicus A33

Father Stanislaus Konarski — A34

**1923** ***Perf. 10 to 12½***

**192** A33 1000m indigo .60 .30
**193** A34 3000m brown .50 .60
*a.* "Konapski" 18.00 17.00
**194** A33 5000m rose .90 .30
*Nos. 192-194 (3)* 2.00 1.20

Nicolaus Copernicus (1473-1543), astronomer (Nos. 192, 194); Stanislaus Konarski (1700-1773), educator, and the creation by the Polish Parliament of the Commission of Public Instruction (No. 193).

No. 163 Surcharged

**1923** ***Perf. 9 to 14½ and Compound***

**195** A31 10000m on 25m 5.00 .25
*a.* Double surcharge 100.00
*b.* Inverted surcharge 75.00

Stamps of 1921 Surcharged

**196** A27 25000m on 20m red 3.50 1.75
*a.* Double surcharge 100.00 —
*b.* Inverted surcharge 75.00
**197** A27 50000m on 10m grnsh bl 1.60 .25
*a.* Double surcharge 100.00 —
*b.* Inverted surcharge 75.00 —

No. 191 Surcharged

**198** A27 25000m on 20m car 2.00 .25
*a.* Double surcharge 100.00 —
*b.* Inverted surcharge 75.00

### No. 150 Surcharged with New Value

**1924**

**199** A10 20000m on 2m gray grn 1.50 .25
*a.* Inverted surcharge 75.00 —
*b.* Double surcharge 100.00 —

### Type of 1919 Issue Surcharged with New Value

**200** A10 100000m on 5m red brn 1.60 .25
*a.* Double surcharge 100.00 —
*b.* Inverted surcharge 75.00 —
*Nos. 195-200 (6)* 15.20 3.00

Arms of Poland — A35

***Perf. 10 to 14½ and Compound***

**1924 Thin Paper Litho.**

**205** A35 10,000m lilac brn 2.00 .40
**206** A35 20,000m ol grn 1.20 .25
**207** A35 30,000m scarlet 1.60 .25
**208** A35 50,000m apple grn 4.75 .25
**209** A35 100,000m brn org 1.60 .25
**210** A35 200,000m lt blue 1.60 .25
**211** A35 300,000m red vio 4.00 .65
**212** A35 500,000m brn 4.00 .75
**213** A35 1,000,000m ple rose .40 *26.00*
**214** A35 2,000,000m dk grn .80 *175.00*
*Nos. 205-214 (10)* 21.95 204.05
Set, never hinged 65.00

Arms of Poland A36

President Stanislaus Wojciechowski A37

***Perf. 10 to 13½ and Compound***

**1924**

**215** A36 1g orange brown .60 .50
**216** A36 2g dark brown .60 .25
**217** A36 3g orange .60 .25
**218** A36 5g olive green .60 .25
**219** A36 10g blue green 1.75 .25
**220** A36 15g red 2.50 .25
**221** A36 20g blue 9.50 .25
**222** A36 25g red brown 17.00 .25
*a.* 25g indigo *12,000.* *6,000.*
**223** A36 30g deep violet 22.00 .25
*a.* 30g gray blue *250.00* *125.00*
**224** A36 40g indigo 8.00 .70
**225** A36 50g magenta 1.50 .25

***Perf. 11½, 12***

**226** A37 1z scarlet 22.50 1.60
*Nos. 215-226 (12)* 87.15 5.05
Set, never hinged 300.00

For overprints see Nos. 1K1-1K11.

Holy Gate of Wilno (Vilnius) — A38

Poznan Town Hall — A39

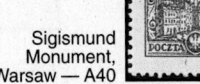

Sigismund Monument, Warsaw — A40

Wawel Castle at Cracow — A41

Sobieski Statue at Lwow — A42

Ship of State — A43

**1925-27** ***Perf. 10 to 13***

**227** A38 1g bister brown .55 .25
**228** A42 2g brown olive .65 .50
**229** A40 3g blue 2.00 .25
**230** A39 5g yellow green 2.75 .25
**231** A40 10g violet 2.00 .25
**232** A41 15g rose red 3.00 .25
**233** A43 20g dull red 13.00 .25
**234** A38 24g gray blue 5.50 .75
**235** A42 30g dark blue 1.60 .25
**236** A41 40g lt blue ('27) 1.60 .25
**237** A43 45g dark violet 11.00 .25
*Nos. 227-237 (11)* 43.65 3.50
Set, never hinged 110.00

For overprints see Nos. 1K11A-1K17.

**1926-27 Redrawn**

**238** A40 3g blue 2.00 .25
**239** A39 5g yellow green 2.50 .25
**240** A40 10g violet 2.00 .25
**241** A41 15g rose red 2.50 .25
*Nos. 238-241 (4)* 9.00 1.00
Set, never hinged 25.00

On Nos. 229-232 the lines representing clouds touch the numerals. On the redrawn stamps the numerals have white outlines, separating them from the cloud lines.

Marshal Pilsudski — A44

Frederic Chopin — A45

**1927 Typo.** ***Perf. 12½, 11½***

**242** A44 20g red brown 3.25 .50
**243** A45 40g deep ultra 10.00 2.00
Set, never hinged 35.00

See No. 250. For overprint see No. 1K18.

President Ignacy Moscicki — A46

**1927, May 4** ***Perf. 11½***

**245** A46 20g red 4.00 1.00
Never hinged 10.50

Dr. Karol Kaczkowski — A47

**1927, May 27** ***Perf. 11½, 12½***

**246** A47 10g gray green 4.50 4.00
**247** A47 25g carmine 6.50 4.00
**248** A47 40g dark blue 9.00 2.00
*Nos. 246-248 (3)* 20.00 10.00
Set, never hinged 60.00

4th Intl. Congress of Military Medicine and Pharmacy, Warsaw, May 30-June 4.

Juliusz Slowacki — A48

**1927, June 28** ***Perf. 12½***

**249** A48 20g rose 4.00 1.10
Never hinged 12.00

Transfer from Paris to Cracow of the remains of Julius Slowacki, poet.

### Pilsudski Type of 1927

Design Redrawn

**1928** ***Perf. 11½, 12x11½, 12½x13***

**250** A44 25g yellow brown 3.00 .40
Never hinged 10.00

Souvenir Sheet

A49

**1928, May 3 Engr.** ***Perf. 12½***

**251** A49 Sheet of 2 250.00 325.00
Never hinged 475.00
*a.* 50g black brown 25.00 85.00
*b.* 1z black brown 25.00 85.00

1st Natl. Phil. Exhib., Warsaw, May 3-13.

Sold to each purchaser of a 1.50z ticket to the Warsaw Philatelic Exhibition.

Counterfeits exist.

Marshal Pilsudski — A49a

***Perf. 10½ to 14 and Compound***

**1928-31 Wove Paper**

**253** A49a 50g bluish slate 6.50 .25
**254** A49a 50g blue grn ('31) 22.50 .40
Set, never hinged 82.50

See No. 315.

Pres. Moscicki — A50

***Perf. 12x12½, 11½ to 13½ and Compound***

**1928 Laid Paper**

**255** A50 1z black, *cream* 15.00 .70
Never hinged 50.00
*a.* Horizontally laid paper ('30) 40.00 2.25
Never hinged 120.00

See Nos. 305, 316. For surcharges and overprints see Nos. J92-J94, 1K19, 1K24.

General Josef Bem — A51

**Wove Paper**

**1928, May** **Typo.** ***Perf. 12½***

| | | | |
|---|---|---|---|
| **256** A51 25g rose red | 3.75 | .50 |
| Never hinged | 8.50 | |

Return from Syria to Poland of the ashes of General Josef Bem.

Henryk Sienkiewicz — A52

**1928, Oct.**

| | | |
|---|---|---|
| **257** A52 15g ultra | 2.00 | .40 |
| Never hinged | 4.00 | |

For overprint see No. 1K23.

Eagle Arms — A53

**1928-29** ***Perf. 12x12½***

| | | |
|---|---|---|
| **258** A53 5g dark violet | .40 | .25 |
| **259** A53 10g green | .60 | .25 |
| **260** A53 25g red brown | .80 | .30 |
| *Nos. 258-260 (3)* | 1.80 | .80 |
| Set, never hinged | 4.25 | |

See design A58. For overprints see Nos. 1K20-1K22.

"Swiatowid," Ancient Slav God — A54

**1928, Dec. 15** ***Perf. 12½x12***

| | | |
|---|---|---|
| **261** A54 25g brown | 2.00 | .40 |
| Never hinged | 5.00 | |

Poznan Agricultural Exhibition.

King John III Sobieski — A55

**1930, July** ***Perf. 12x12½***

| | | |
|---|---|---|
| **262** A55 75g claret | 2.25 | .40 |
| Never hinged | 7.00 | |

Stylized Soldiers — A56

**1930, Nov. 1** ***Perf. 12½***

| | | |
|---|---|---|
| **263** A56 5g violet brown | .40 | .25 |
| **264** A56 15g dark blue | 3.00 | .45 |
| **265** A56 25g red brown | .60 | .25 |
| **266** A56 30g dull red | 6.50 | 4.00 |
| *Nos. 263-266 (4)* | 10.50 | 4.95 |
| Set, never hinged | 30.00 | |

Centenary of insurrection of 1830.

Kosciuszko, Washington, Pulaski — A57

**Laid Paper**

**1932, May 3** ***Perf. 11½***

| | | |
|---|---|---|
| **267** A57 30g brown | 2.00 | .45 |
| Never hinged | 4.00 | |

200th birth anniv. of George Washington.

A58

***Perf. 12x12½***

**1932-33** **Typo.** **Wmk. 234**

| | | |
|---|---|---|
| **268** A58 5g dull vio ('33) | .40 | .25 |
| **269** A58 10g green | .60 | .25 |
| **270** A58 15g red brown ('33) | .40 | .25 |
| **271** A58 20g gray | .65 | .25 |
| **272** A58 25g buff | .75 | .25 |
| **273** A58 30g deep rose | 1.50 | .25 |
| **274** A58 60g blue | 5.00 | .50 |
| *Nos. 268-274 (7)* | 9.30 | 2.00 |
| Set, never hinged | 32.50 | |

For overprints and surcharge see Nos. 280-281, 284, 292, 1K25-1K27.

Torun City Hall — A59

**1933, Jan. 2** **Engr.** ***Perf. 11½***

| | | |
|---|---|---|
| **275** A59 60g blue | 35.00 | 1.00 |
| Never hinged | 92.50 | |

700th anniversary of the founding of the City of Torun by the Grand Master of the Knights of the Teutonic Order.
See No. B28.

Altar Panel of St. Mary's Church, Cracow — A60

***Perf. 11½-12½ & Compound***

**1933, July 10** **Laid Paper** **Unwmk.**

| | | |
|---|---|---|
| **277** A60 80g red brown | 14.00 | 1.25 |
| Never hinged | 35.00 | |

400th death anniv. of Veit Stoss, sculptor and woodcarver.
For surcharge see No. 285.

John III Sobieski and Allies before Vienna, painted by Jan Matejko — A61

**1933, Sept. 12** **Laid Paper**

| | | |
|---|---|---|
| **278** A61 1.20z indigo | 24.00 | 6.50 |
| Never hinged | 70.00 | |

250th anniv. of the deliverance of Vienna by the Polish and allied forces under command of John III Sobieski, King of Poland, when besieged by the Turks in 1683.
For surcharge see No. 286.

Cross of Independence A62

**Wmk. 234**

**1933, Nov. 11** **Typo.** ***Perf. 12½***

| | | |
|---|---|---|
| **279** A62 30g scarlet | 3.00 | .50 |
| Never hinged | 8.00 | |

15th anniversary of independence.

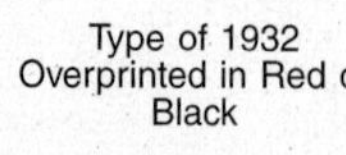

Type of 1932 Overprinted in Red or Black

**1934, May 5** ***Perf. 12***

| | | |
|---|---|---|
| **280** A58 20g gray (R) | 22.50 | 40.00 |
| **281** A58 30g deep rose | 32.50 | 45.00 |
| Set, never hinged | 175.00 | |

Katowice Philatelic Exhibition. Counterfeits exist.

Josef Pilsudski — A63

***Perf. 11½ to 12½ and Compound***

**1934, Aug. 6** **Engr.** **Unwmk.**

| | | |
|---|---|---|
| **282** A63 25g gray blue | 3.00 | .70 |
| **283** A63 30g black brown | 3.50 | .70 |
| Set, never hinged | 19.00 | |

Polish Legion, 20th anniversary.
For overprint see No. 293.

**Nos. 274, 277-278 Surcharged in Black or Red**

**1934** **Wmk. 234** ***Perf. 12x12½***

| | | |
|---|---|---|
| **284** A58 55g on 60g blue | 3.75 | .45 |

***Perf. 11½-12½ & Compound***

**Unwmk.**

| | | |
|---|---|---|
| **285** A60 25g on 80g red brn | 5.00 | .65 |
| **286** A61 1z on 1.20z ind (R) | 17.00 | 4.25 |
| *a.* Figure "1" in surcharge 5mm high instead of 4½mm | 17.00 | 4.25 |
| Never hinged | 50.00 | |
| *Nos. 284-286 (3)* | 25.75 | 5.35 |
| Set, never hinged | 77.50 | |

Surcharge of No. 286 includes bars.

Marshal Pilsudski — A64

**1935** ***Perf. 11 to 13 and Compound***

| | | |
|---|---|---|
| **287** A64 5g black | .50 | .25 |
| **288** A64 15g black | .50 | .35 |
| **289** A64 25g black | .70 | .25 |
| **290** A64 45g black | 3.25 | .50 |
| **291** A64 1z black | 6.00 | 3.50 |
| *Nos. 287-291 (5)* | 10.95 | 4.85 |
| Set, never hinged | 32.50 | |

Pilsudski mourning issue.
Nos. 287-288 are typo., Nos. 290-291 litho. No. 289 exists both typo. and litho.
See No. B35b.

Nos. 270, 282 Overprinted in Blue or Red

**1935** **Wmk. 234** ***Perf. 12x12½***

| | | |
|---|---|---|
| **292** A58 15g red brown | .90 | .25 |

***Perf. 11½, 11½x12½***

**Unwmk.**

| | | |
|---|---|---|
| **293** A63 25g gray blue (R) | 2.75 | .85 |
| Set, never hinged | 12.00 | |

Issued in connection with the proposed memorial to Marshal Pilsudski, the stamps were sold at Cracow exclusively.

"The Dog Cliff" — A65

President Ignacy Moscicki — A75

Designs: 10g, "Eye of the Sea." 15g, M. S. "Pilsudski." 20g, View of Pieniny. 25g, Belvedere Palace. 30g, Castle in Mira. 45g, Castle at Podhorce. 50g, Cloth Hall, Cracow. 55g, Raczynski Library, Poznan. 1z, Cathedral, Wilno.

**1935-36** **Typo.** ***Perf. 12½x13***

| | | |
|---|---|---|
| **294** A65 5g violet blue | .30 | .25 |
| **295** A65 10g yellow green | .50 | .25 |
| **296** A65 15g Prus green | 3.00 | .25 |
| **297** A65 20g violet black | 2.50 | .25 |

**Engr.**

| | | |
|---|---|---|
| **298** A65 25g myrtle green | .30 | .30 |
| **299** A65 30g rose red | 1.00 | .25 |
| **300** A65 45g plum ('36) | .30 | .25 |
| **301** A65 50g black ('36) | .25 | .25 |
| **302** A65 55g blue ('36) | 1.50 | .25 |
| **303** A65 1z brown ('36) | 5.00 | 3.00 |
| **304** A75 3z black brown | 1.25 | 4.00 |
| *Nos. 294-304 (11)* | 15.90 | 9.30 |
| Set, never hinged | 42.50 | |

See Nos. 308-311. For overprints see Nos. 306-307, 1K28-1K32.

**Type of 1928 inscribed "1926. 3. VI. 1936" on Bottom Margin**

**1936, June 3**

| | | |
|---|---|---|
| **305** A50 1z ultra | 3.00 | 5.00 |
| Never hinged | 8.00 | |

Presidency of Ignacy Moscicki, 10th anniv.

Nos. 299, 302 Overprinted in Blue or Red

**1936, Aug. 15**

| | | |
|---|---|---|
| **306** A65 30g rose red | 4.00 | 3.50 |
| **307** A65 55g blue (R) | 7.00 | 2.25 |
| Set, never hinged | 30.00 | |

Gordon-Bennett Intl. Balloon Race. Counterfeits exist.

**Scenic Type of 1935-36**

Designs: 5g, Church at Czestochowa. 10g, Maritime Terminal, Gdynia. 15g, University, Lwow. 20g, Municipal Building, Katowice.

**1937** **Engr.** ***Perf. 12½***

| | | |
|---|---|---|
| **308** A65 5g violet blue | .30 | .25 |
| **309** A65 10g green | .50 | .25 |
| **310** A65 15g red brown | .45 | .25 |
| **311** A65 20g orange brown | .45 | .25 |
| *Nos. 308-311 (4)* | 1.70 | 1.00 |
| Set, never hinged | 5.00 | |

For overprints see Nos. 1K31-1K32.

Marshal Smigly-Rydz — A80

**1937** ***Perf. 12½x13***

| | | |
|---|---|---|
| **312** A80 25g slate green | .30 | .25 |
| **313** A80 55g blue | .30 | .25 |
| Set, never hinged | 2.25 | |

For surcharges see Nos. N30, N32.

### Types of 1928-37

**1937** **Souvenir Sheets**

**314** Sheet of 4 14.00 20.00
*a.* A80 25g, dark brown 1.75 2.75
**315** Sheet of 4 14.00 20.00
*a.* A49a 50g, deep blue 1.75 2.75
**316** Sheet of 4 12.50 20.00
*a.* A50 1z, gray black 1.75 2.75
Set, never hinged 120.00

Visit of King Carol of Romania to Poland, June 26-July 1.
See No. B35c.

President Moscicki — A81

**1938, Feb. 1** ***Perf. 12½***

**317** A81 15g green blue .70 .25
**318** A81 30g rose violet .35 .25
Set, never hinged 3.00

71st birthday of President Moscicki.
For surcharge see No. N31.

Kosciuszko, Paine and Washington and View of New York City — A82

**1938, Mar. 17** ***Perf. 12x12½***

**319** A82 1z gray blue 1.40 1.00
Never hinged 5.00

150th anniv. of the US Constitution.

Boleslaus I and Emperor Otto III at Gnesen — A83

Marshal Pilsudski — A95

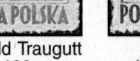

Designs: 10g, King Casimir III. 15g, King Ladislas II Jagello and Queen Hedwig. 20g, King Casimir IV. 25g, Treaty of Lublin. 30g, King Stephen Bathory commending Wielock, the peasant. 45g, Stanislas Zolkiewski and Jan Chodkiewicz. 50g, John III Sobieski entering Vienna. 55g, Union of nobles, commoners and peasants. 75g, Dabrowski, Kosciuszko and Poniatowski. 1z, Polish soldiers. 2z, Romuald Traugutt.

**1938, Nov. 11** **Engr.** ***Perf. 12½***

**320** A83 5g red orange .25 .25
**321** A83 10g green .25 .25
**322** A83 15g fawn .25 .25
**323** A83 20g peacock blue .25 .25
**324** A83 25g dull violet .40 .25
**325** A83 30g rose red .40 .25
**326** A83 45g black .50 .25
**327** A83 50g brt red vio .40 .25
**328** A83 55g ultra .40 .25
**329** A83 75g dull green 2.60 1.00
**330** A83 1z orange 3.25 1.75
**331** A83 2z carmine rose 8.50 15.00
**332** A95 3z gray black 5.00 10.00
*Nos. 320-332 (13)* 22.45 30.00
Set, never hinged 62.50

20th anniv. of Poland's independence. See No. 339. For surcharges see Nos. N33-N47.

Souvenir Sheet

Marshal Pilsudski, Gabriel Narutowicz, President Moscicki, Marshal Smigly-Rydz — A96

**1938, Nov. 11** ***Perf. 12½***

**333** A96 Sheet of 4 13.00 20.00
Never hinged 35.00
*a.* 25g dull violet (Pilsudski) 1.40 1.90
*b.* 25g dull violet (Narutowicz) 1.40 1.90
*c.* 25g dull violet (Moscicki) 1.40 1.90
*d.* 25g dull violet (Smigly-Rydz) 1.40 1.90

20th anniv. of Poland's independence.

Poland Welcoming Teschen People — A97

**1938, Nov. 11**

**334** A97 25g dull violet 1.75 .60
Never hinged 5.00

Restoration of the Teschen territory ceded by Czechoslovakia.

Skier — A98

**1939, Feb. 6**

**335** A98 15g orange brown .60 *.80*
**336** A98 25g dull violet .90 1.50
**337** A98 30g rose red 2.00 1.50
**338** A98 55g brt ultra 4.50 3.75
*Nos. 335-338 (4)* 8.00 7.55
Set, never hinged 23.00

Intl. Ski Meet, Zakopane, Feb. 11-19.

### Type of 1938

15g, King Ladislas II Jagello, Queen Hedwig.

### Re-engraved

**1939, Mar. 2** ***Perf. 12½***

**339** A83 15g redsh brown .45 .35
Never hinged .85

No. 322 with crossed swords and helmet at lower left. No. 339, swords and helmet have been removed.

Marshal Pilsudski Reviewing Troops — A99

**1939, Aug. 1** **Engr.**

**340** A99 25g dull rose violet .40 *.50*
Never hinged 1.10

Polish Legion, 25th anniv. See No. B35a.

## Polish Peoples Republic

Romuald Traugutt A100

Tadeusz Kosciuszko A101

Design: 1z, Jan Henryk Dabrowski.

***Perf. 11½***

**1944, Sept. 7** **Litho.** **Unwmk.**
**Without Gum**

**341** A100 25g crimson rose 37.50 *55.00*
**342** A101 50g deep green 35.00 *45.00*
**343** A101 1z deep ultra 35.00 *50.00*
*Nos. 341-343 (3)* 107.50 *150.00*

Counterfeits exist.
For surcharges see Nos. 362-363.

Polish Eagle — A103

Grunwald Monument, Cracow — A104

**1944, Sept. 13** **Photo.** ***Perf. 12½***

**344** A103 25g deep red .60 .45
*a.* 25g dull red, typo. 1.00
Never hinged 2.75
**345** A104 50g dk slate green .45 .30
Set, never hinged 2.75

No. 344a was not put on sale without surcharge. See Nos. 346, 349a. For surcharges see Nos. 345A-356, 364, B54, C19-C20.

### No. 344 Surcharged in Black

a

b

c

**1944-45**

**345A** A103 1z on 25g 1.25 5.25
**345B** A103 2z on 25g ('45) 1.25 6.50
**345C** A103 3z on 25g ('45) 1.00 5.25
*Nos. 345A-345C (3)* 3.50 17.00
Set, never hinged 7.00

Issued to honor Polish government agencies. K. R. N. — Krajowa Rada Narodowa (Polish National Council), P. K. W. N. — Polski Komitet Wyzwolenia Narodu (Polish National Liberation Committee) and R. T. R. P. — Rzad Tymczasowy Rzeczypospolitej Polskiej (Temporary Administration of the Polish Republic).
Counterfeits exist.

No. 344a Surcharged in Brown

**1945, Sept. 1**

**346** A103 1.50z on 25g dull red .45 .25
Never hinged 1.50
*a.* 1.50z on 25g deep red, #344 650.00 400.00

Counterfeits of No. 346a exist.

No. 344 Surcharged in Blue

**1945, Feb. 12**

**347** A103 3z on 25g 1.75 5.75
**348** A103 3z on 25g *(Radom, 16. I. 1945)* 1.75 5.75
**349** A103 3z on 25g *(Warszawa, 17. I. 1945)* 10.00 21.00
*a.* 3z on 25g dull red, #344a 125.00 150.00
**350** A103 3z on 25g *(Czestochowa, 17. I. 1945)* 1.75 5.75
**351** A103 3z on 25g *(Krakow, 19. I. 1945)* 1.75 5.75
**352** A103 3z on 25g *(Lodz, 19. I. 1945)* 1.75 5.75
**353** A103 3z on 25g *(Gniezno, 22. I. 1945)* 1.75 5.75
**354** A103 3z on 25g *(Bydgoszcz, 23. I. 1945)* 2.00 5.75
**355** A103 3z on 25g *(Kalisz, 24. I. 1945)* 1.75 5.75
**356** A103 3z on 25g *(Zakopane, 29. I. 1945)* 2.50 5.75
*Nos. 347-356 (10)* 26.75 72.75
Set, never hinged 57.50

Dates overprinted are those of liberation for each city.
Counterfeits exist.

Grunwald Monument, Cracow — A105

Kosciuszko Statue, Cracow — A106

Cloth Hall, Cracow A107

Copernicus Memorial — A108

Wawel Castle — A109

**1945, Apr. 10 Photo. *Perf. 10½, 11***

| | | | |
|---|---|---|---|
| **357** A105 50g dk violet brn | .25 | .25 |
| *a.* 50g dark brown | .50 | .50 |
| Never hinged | 1.00 | |
| **358** A106 1z henna brown | .35 | .25 |
| **359** A107 2z sapphire | .50 | .35 |
| **360** A108 3z dp red violet | .85 | .30 |
| **361** A109 5z blue green | 2.00 | 7.25 |
| *Nos. 357-361 (5)* | 3.95 | 8.40 |
| Set, never hinged | 8.00 | |

Liberation of Cracow Jan. 19, 1945.

Nos. 357-361 exist imperf. Value, set: unused $24; never hinged $55.

No. 357a is a coarser printing from a new plate showing designer's name (J. Wilczyk) in lower left margin. No. 357 does not show his name.

**Nos. 341-342 Surcharged in Black or Red**

d

e

**1945 *Perf. 11½***

| | | |
|---|---|---|
| **362** A100(d) 5z on 25g | 30.00 | *60.00* |
| **363** A101(e) 5z on 50g (R) | 5.00 | *40.00* |
| Never hinged | 15.00 | |

No. 362 was issued without gum.

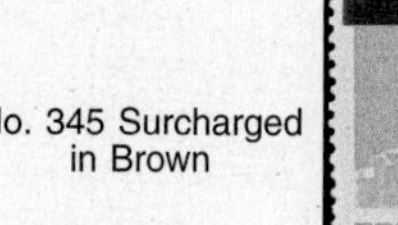

No. 345 Surcharged in Brown

**1945, Sept. 10 *Perf. 12½***

| | | |
|---|---|---|
| **364** A104 1z on 50g dk sl grn | .40 | .25 |
| Never hinged | 1.40 | |

Lodz Skyline A110

Kosciuszko Monument, Lodz A111

Flag Bearer Carrying Wounded Comrade — A112

**1945, Mar. 9 Litho. *Perf. 11, 9 (3z)***

| | | |
|---|---|---|
| **365** A110 1z deep ultra | .55 | .25 |
| **366** A111 3z dull red violet | 1.25 | .25 |
| **367** A112 5z deep carmine | 1.50 | 1.90 |
| *Nos. 365-367 (3)* | 3.30 | 2.40 |
| Set, never hinged | 5.00 | |

Nos. 365 and 367 commemorate the liberation of Lodz and Warsaw.

Grunwald Battle Scene — A113

**1945, July 16**

| | | |
|---|---|---|
| **368** A113 5z deep blue | 3.00 | *15.00* |
| Never hinged | 8.00 | |

Battle of Grunwald (Tannenberg), July 15, 1410.

Eagle Breaking Fetters and Manifesto of Freedom — A114

**1945, July 22**

| | | |
|---|---|---|
| **369** A114 3z rose carmine | 6.00 | *20.00* |
| Never hinged | 12.00 | |

1st anniv. of the liberation of Poland.

Crane Tower, Gdansk — A115

Stock Tower, Gdansk — A116

Ancient High Gate, Gdansk A117

**1945, Sept. 15 Photo. Unwmk.**

| | | |
|---|---|---|
| **370** A115 1z olive | .25 | .25 |
| **371** A116 2z sapphire | .25 | .25 |
| **372** A117 3z dark violet | .80 | .50 |
| *Nos. 370-372 (3)* | 1.30 | 1.00 |
| Set, never hinged | 2.75 | |

Recovery of Poland's access to the sea at Gdansk (Danzig).

Nos. 370-372 exist imperf. Value, set $25.

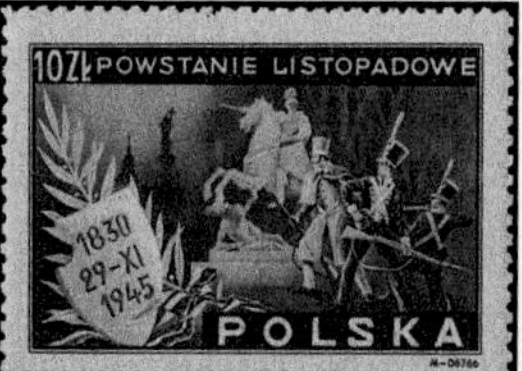

Civilian and Soldiers in Rebellion — A118

**1945, Nov. 29**

| | | |
|---|---|---|
| **373** A118 10z black | 4.25 | *20.00* |
| Never hinged | 8.50 | |

115th anniv. of the "November Uprising" against the Russians, Nov. 29, 1830.

Holy Cross Church — A119

Views of Warsaw, 1939 and 1945: 1.50z, Warsaw Castle, 1939 and 1945. 3z, Cathedral of St. John. 3.50z, City Hall. 6z, Post Office. 8z, Army General Staff Headquarters.

**1945-46 Unwmk. *Imperf.***

| | | |
|---|---|---|
| **374** A119 1.50z crimson | .25 | .25 |
| **375** A119 3z dark blue | .25 | .25 |
| **376** A119 3.50z lt blue grn | .50 | .50 |
| **377** A119 6z gray black ('46) | .50 | .25 |
| **378** A119 8z brown ('46) | 1.00 | .50 |
| **379** A119 10z dark violet ('46) | .80 | .25 |
| *Nos. 374-379 (6)* | 3.30 | 2.00 |
| Set, never hinged | 7.75 | |

Nos. 374-379 exist with private produced rouletting.

**Nos. 374-379 Overprinted in Black**

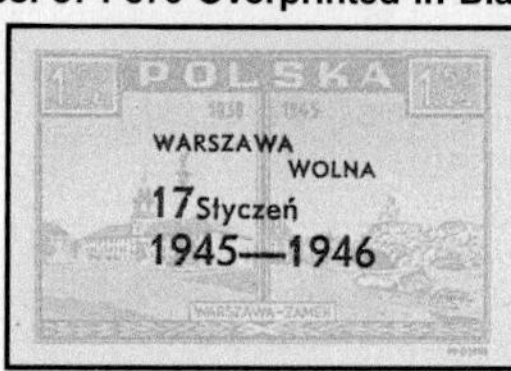


**1946, Jan. 17**

| | | |
|---|---|---|
| **383** A119 1.50z crimson | 1.00 | *3.00* |
| **384** A119 3z dark blue | 1.00 | *3.00* |
| **385** A119 3.50z lt blue grn | 1.00 | *3.00* |
| **386** A119 6z gray black | 1.00 | *3.00* |
| **387** A119 8z brown | 1.00 | *3.00* |
| **388** A119 10z dark violet | 1.00 | *3.00* |
| *Nos. 383-388 (6)* | 6.00 | *18.00* |
| Set, never hinged | 14.00 | |

Liberation of Warsaw, 1/17/45, 1st anniv. Counterfeits exist.

Polish Revolutionist A125

**1946, Jan. 22 *Perf. 11***

| | | |
|---|---|---|
| **389** A125 6z slate blue | 4.00 | *14.00* |
| Never hinged | 8.00 | |

Revolt of Jan. 22, 1863.

Infantry Advancing — A126

**1946, May 9**

| | | |
|---|---|---|
| **390** A126 3z brown | .30 | .25 |
| Never hinged | .60 | |

Polish freedom, first anniversary.

Premier Edward Osubka-Morawski Pres. Boleslaw Bierut and Marshal Michael Rola-Zymierski — A127

***Perf. 11x10½***

**1946, July 22 Unwmk.**

| | | |
|---|---|---|
| **391** A127 3z purple | .80 | *17.00* |
| Never hinged | 2.10 | |

For surcharge see No. B53.

No. 391 exists imperf. Value $55.

Bedzin Castle — A128

Duke Henry IV of Silesia, from Tomb at Wroclaw — A129

Lanckrona Castle A130

**1946, Sept. 1 Photo. *Imperf.***

| | | |
|---|---|---|
| **392** A128 5z olive gray | .35 | .25 |
| **393** A128 5z brown | .25 | .25 |
| ***Perf. 10½*** | | |
| **394** A129 6z gray black | .35 | .35 |
| ***Imperf*** | | |
| **395** A130 10z deep blue | 1.00 | .25 |
| *Nos. 392-395 (4)* | 1.95 | 1.10 |
| Set, never hinged | 3.50 | |

Perforated examples of Nos. 392, 393 and 395 have been privately made. No. 394 exists imperf. Value, $175.

For surcharge see No. 404.

Jan Matejko, Jacek Malczewski, Josef Chelmonski — A131

Adam Chmielowski (Brother Albert) — A132

Designs: 3z, Chopin. 5z, Wojciech Boguslawski, Helena Modjeska and Stefan Jaracz. 6z, Alexander Swietochowski, Stephen Zeromski and Boleslaw Prus. 10z, Marie Sklodowska Curie. 15z, Stanislaw Wyspianski, Juliusz Slowacki and Jan Kasprowicz. 20z, Adam Mickiewicz.

**1947 *Perf. 11***

| | | |
|---|---|---|
| **396** A131 1z blue | .35 | .25 |
| **397** A132 2z brown | .35 | .25 |
| **398** A132 3z Prus green | .35 | .25 |
| **399** A131 5z olive green | .35 | .25 |
| **400** A131 6z gray green | .75 | .35 |
| **401** A132 10z gray brown | .50 | .25 |
| **402** A131 15z sepia | 1.40 | .35 |
| **403** A132 20z gray black | 1.00 | .25 |
| *Nos. 396-403 (8)* | 5.05 | 2.20 |
| Set, never hinged | 13.00 | |
| ***Imperf*** | | |
| **403A** A131 1z blue | .30 | .25 |
| **403B** A132 2z brown | .40 | .25 |
| **403C** A132 3z Prus green | .40 | .25 |
| **403D** A131 5z olive green | .40 | .25 |
| **403E** A131 6z gray green | .60 | .35 |
| **403F** A132 10z gray brown | 1.00 | .25 |
| **403G** A131 15z sepia | 1.60 | .35 |
| **403H** A132 20z gray black | 1.75 | .25 |
| *Nos. 403A-403H (8)* | 6.45 | 2.20 |

No. 394 Surcharged in Red

**1947, Feb. 25** ***Perf. 10½***

**404** A129 5z on 6z gray blk .50 .25
Never hinged 1.00

Exists imperf. Value $20.

### Types of 1947

| **1947** | **Photo.** | ***Perf. 11*** | |
|---|---|---|---|
| **405** A131 | 1z slate gray | .25 | .25 |
| **406** A132 | 2z orange | .25 | .25 |
| **407** A132 | 3z olive green | .25 | .35 |
| **408** A131 | 5z olive brown | .35 | .25 |
| **409** A131 | 6z carmine rose | .35 | .25 |
| **410** A132 | 10z blue | 1.25 | .30 |
| **411** A131 | 15z chestnut brn | .70 | .35 |
| **412** A132 | 20z dark violet | 1.40 | .35 |
| *a.* | Souv. sheet of 8, #405-412 | *100.00* | *300.00* |
| | Never hinged | *190.00* | |
| | *Nos. 405-412 (8)* | 4.80 | 2.35 |
| | Set, never hinged | 11.00 | |

No. 412a sold for 500z.

***Imperf***

| | | | |
|---|---|---|---|
| **412B** A131 | 1z slate gray | .75 | .25 |
| **412C** A132 | 2z orange | .75 | .25 |
| **412D** A132 | 3z olive green | 1.00 | .25 |
| **412E** A131 | 5z olive brown | 2.40 | .25 |
| **412F** A131 | 6z carmine rose | .75 | .25 |
| **412G** A132 | 10z blue | 1.60 | .25 |
| **412H** A131 | 15z chestnut brn | 3.00 | .25 |
| **412I** A132 | 20z dark violet | 4.00 | .25 |
| | *Nos. 412B-412I (8)* | 14.25 | 2.00 |

Laborer — A139

Farmer — A140

Fisherman A141

Miner A142

| **1947, Aug. 20** | **Engr.** | ***Perf. 13*** | |
|---|---|---|---|
| **413** A139 | 5z rose brown | .60 | .25 |
| **414** A140 | 10z brt blue green | .40 | .25 |
| **415** A141 | 15z dark blue | 1.75 | .25 |
| **416** A142 | 20z brown black | .40 | .25 |
| | *Nos. 413-416 (4)* | 3.15 | 1.00 |
| | Set, never hinged | 6.75 | |

Allegory of the Revolution — A143

**1948, Mar. 15** **Photo.** ***Perf. 11***

**417** A143 15z brown .25 .25
Never hinged .60

Revolution of 1848. See Nos. 430-432.

Insurgents — A144

**1948, Apr. 19**

**418** A144 15z gray black .65 *5.75*
Never hinged 2.00

Ghetto uprising, Warsaw, 5th anniv. Exists imperf., value $1,700.

Decorated Bicycle Wheel A145

**1948, May 1**

**419** A145 15z brt rose & blue 2.00 1.00
Never hinged 2.75

1st Intl. Bicycle Peace Race, Warsaw-Prague-Warsaw.

Launching Ship — A146

Loading Freighter A147

35z, Racing yacht "Gen. Mariusz Zaruski."

| **1948, June 22** | | | |
|---|---|---|---|
| **420** A146 | 6z violet | .85 | *6.75* |
| **421** A147 | 15z brown car | .85 | *2.75* |
| **422** A147 | 35z slate gray | .85 | *4.50* |
| | *Nos. 420-422 (3)* | 2.55 | 14.00 |
| | Set, never hinged | 6.00 | |

Polish Merchant Marine.

Cyclists A148

| **1948, June 22** | | | |
|---|---|---|---|
| **423** A148 | 3z gray | 1.00 | *4.00* |
| **424** A148 | 6z brown | 1.00 | *4.00* |
| **425** A148 | 15z green | 1.00 | *5.50* |
| | *Nos. 423-425 (3)* | 3.00 | 13.50 |
| | Set, never hinged | 7.00 | |

Poland Bicycle Race, 7th Circuit, 6/22-7/4.

A149

| **1948, July 15** | | | |
|---|---|---|---|
| **426** A149 | 6z blue | .50 | .25 |
| **427** A149 | 15z red | 1.00 | .25 |
| **428** A149 | 18z rose brown | .25 | .25 |
| **429** A149 | 35z dark brown | .50 | .25 |
| | *Nos. 426-429 (4)* | 2.25 | 1.00 |
| | Set, never hinged | 5.75 | |

Exhibition to commemorate the recovery of Polish territories, Wroclaw, 1948.

Gen. Henryk Dembinski and Gen. Josef Bem — A150

Designs: 35z, S. Worcell, P. Sciegienny and E. Dembowski. 60z, Friedrich Engels and Karl Marx.

| **1948, July 15** | | | |
|---|---|---|---|
| **430** A150 | 30z dark brown | .80 | .40 |
| **431** A150 | 35z olive green | 1.50 | .55 |
| **432** A150 | 60z bright rose | 1.25 | .80 |
| | *Nos. 430-432 (3)* | 3.55 | 1.75 |
| | Set, never hinged | 8.00 | |

Revolution of 1848, cent. See No. 417.

Symbolical of United Youth — A151

**1948, Aug. 8**

**433** A151 15z blue .50 .35
Never hinged 1.00

Intl. Congress of Democratic Youth, Warsaw, Aug.

Stagecoach Leaving Torun Gate — A152

**1948, Sept. 4**

**434** A152 15z brown .70 .45
Never hinged 1.40

Philatelic Exhibition, Torun, Sept.

Clock Dial and Locomotive A153

**1948, Oct. 6** ***Perf. 11½***

**435** A153 18z blue 2.75 *16.00*
Never hinged 6.00

European Railroad Schedule Conference, Cracow.

Pres. Boleslaw Bierut — A154

| **1948-49** | **Unwmk.** | ***Perf. 11, 11½*** | |
|---|---|---|---|
| **436** A154 | 2z orange ('49) | .25 | .25 |
| **437** A154 | 3z blue grn ('49) | .25 | .25 |
| **438** A154 | 5z brown | .25 | .25 |
| **439** A154 | 6z slate | .90 | .35 |
| **440** A154 | 10z violet ('49) | .25 | .25 |
| **441** A154 | 15z dp carmine | .25 | .25 |
| **442** A154 | 18z gray green | 1.20 | .25 |
| **443** A154 | 30z blue | 1.20 | .25 |
| **444** A154 | 35z violet brown | 2.50 | .35 |
| | *Nos. 436-444 (9)* | 7.05 | 2.45 |
| | Set, never hinged | 15.00 | |

Workers Carrying Flag A155

Designs: 15z, Marx, Engels, Lenin and Stalin. 25z, Ludwig Warynski.

**Inscribed: "Kongres Jednosci Klasy Robotniczej 8. XII. 1948."**

| **1948, Dec. 8** | | ***Perf. 11*** | |
|---|---|---|---|
| **445** A155 | 5z crimson | .65 | .25 |
| **446** A155 | 15z dull violet | .50 | .65 |
| **447** A155 | 25z brown | 1.00 | .60 |
| | *Nos. 445-447 (3)* | 2.15 | 1.50 |
| | Set, never hinged | 5.75 | |

**Redrawn**
**Dated: "XII. 1948"**

Designs as before.

| **1948, Dec. 15** | | ***Perf. 11½*** | |
|---|---|---|---|
| **448** A155 | 5z brown carmine | .50 | .70 |
| **449** A155 | 15z bright blue | 1.00 | 1.40 |
| **450** A155 | 25z dark green | 1.90 | 4.00 |
| | *Nos. 448-450 (3)* | 3.40 | 6.10 |
| | Set, never hinged | 8.25 | |

Congress of the Union of the Working Class, Warsaw, Dec. 1948.

"Socialism" A156

Designs: 5z, "Labor." 15z, "Peace."

***Perf. 11½***

| **1949, May 31** | **Unwmk.** | **Photo.** | |
|---|---|---|---|
| **451** A156 | 3z carmine rose | .60 | .25 |
| **452** A156 | 5z deep blue | .60 | .25 |
| **453** A156 | 15z deep green | .80 | *2.75* |
| | *Nos. 451-453 (3)* | 2.00 | 3.25 |
| | Set, never hinged | 5.00 | |

8th Trade Union Congress, June 5, 1949.

Warsaw Scene — A157

Pres. Boleslaw Bierut — A158

Radio Station — A159

***Perf. 13x12½, 12½x13***

| **1949, July 22** | | **Litho.** | |
|---|---|---|---|
| **454** A157 | 10z gray black | 1.40 | 2.00 |
| **455** A158 | 15z lilac rose | 1.20 | 2.00 |
| **456** A159 | 35z gray blue | 1.40 | 2.00 |
| | *Nos. 454-456 (3)* | 4.00 | 6.00 |
| | Set, never hinged | 9.25 | |

5th anniv. of "People's Poland."

A160

UPU, 75th Anniv.: 6z, Stagecoach and world map. 30z, Ship and map. 80z, Plane and map.

| **1949, Oct. 10** | **Engr.** | ***Perf. 13x12½*** | |
|---|---|---|---|
| **457** A160 | 6z gray purple | .30 | *.35* |
| **458** A160 | 30z blue | .85 | *1.90* |
| **459** A160 | 80z dull green | 2.10 | *5.75* |
| | *Nos. 457-459 (3)* | 3.25 | 8.00 |
| | Set, never hinged | 7.25 | |

A161

Symbolical of United Poland.

**1949** ***Perf. 13½x13***

**460** A161 5z brown red 1.00 .25
**461** A161 10z rose red .25 .25
**462** A161 15z green .25 .25
**463** A161 35z dark brown 2.00 1.00
*Nos. 460-463 (4)* 3.50 1.75
Set, never hinged 7.00

Congress of the People's Movement for Unity.

Adam Mickiewicz A162

Frederic Chopin A163

Design: 35z, Juliusz Slowacki.

**1949, Dec. 5** ***Perf. 12½***

**464** A162 10z brown violet .70 1.00
**465** A163 15z brown rose 1.00 1.75
**466** A162 35z deep blue 2.50 6.50
*Nos. 464-466 (3)* 4.20 9.25
Set, never hinged 9.50

Mail Delivery — A164

**1950, Jan. 21**

**467** A164 15z red violet 1.50 *4.25*
Never hinged 3.25

3rd Congress of PTT Trade Unions, Jan. 21-23, 1950.

Adam Mickiewicz and Pushkin — A165

**1949, Dec. 15**

**468** A165 15z lilac 1.00 *4.75*
Never hinged 3.25

Polish-Soviet friendship.

Pres. Boleslaw Bierut — A166

**1950, Feb. 25 Engr.** ***Perf. 12x12½***

**469** A166 15z red .75 .25
Never hinged 1.60

See Nos. 478-484, 490-496. For surcharge see No. 522.

Julian Marchlewski — A167

**1950, Mar. 23 Photo.** ***Perf. 11x10½***

**470** A167 15z gray black .65 .40
Never hinged 1.50

25th death anniv. of Julian Marchlewski, author and political leader.

Reconstruction, Warsaw — A168

***Perf. 11, 12 and Compounds of 13***

**1950, Apr. 15**

**471** A168 5z dark brown .25 .25
Never hinged .45

See No. 497.

Worker Holding Hammer, Flag and Olive Branch — A169

Workers of Three Races with Flag — A170

**1950, Apr. 26** ***Perf. 11½***

**472** A169 10z deep lilac rose .80 .70
**473** A170 15z brown olive 1.00 .85
Set, never hinged 4.75

60th anniversary of Labor Day.

Freedom Monument, Poznan — A171

**1950, Apr. 27**

**474** A171 15z chocolate .35 .25
Never hinged .50

Poznan Fair, Apr. 29-May 14, 1950.

Dove on Globe — A172

**1950, May 15** **Unwmk.**

**475** A172 10z dark green .75 .30
**476** A172 15z dark brown .40 .25
Set, never hinged 2.40

Day of Intl. Action for World Peace.

Polish Workers — A173

**1950, July 20** ***Perf. 12½x13***

**477** A173 15z violet blue .25 .25
Never hinged .55

Poland's 6-year plan. See Nos. 507A-510, 539.

**Bierut Type of 1950, No Frame**

**1950 Engr.** ***Perf. 12x12½***

**478** A166 5z dull green .25 .25
**479** A166 10z dull red .25 .25
**480** A166 15z deep blue 1.50 .25
**481** A166 20z violet brown .25 .25
**482** A166 25z yellow brown .25 .25
**482A** A166 30z rose brown .75 .25
**483** A166 40z brown .40 .25
**484** A166 50z olive 1.50 .35
*Nos. 478-484 (8)* 5.15 2.10
Set, never hinged 11.50

Hibner, Kniewski and Rutkowski A174

**1950, Aug. 18 Photo.** ***Perf. 11***

**485** A174 15z gray black 1.50 1.00
Never hinged 3.50

25th anniv. of the execution of three Polish revolutionists, Wladyslaw Hibner, Wladyslaw Kniewski and Henryk Rutkowski.

Worker and Dove — A175

**1950, Aug. 31 Engr.** ***Perf. 12½***

**486** A175 15z gray green .35 .25
Never hinged .70

Polish Peace Congress, Warsaw, 1950.

---

"GROSZY"

To provide denominations needed as a result of the currency revaluation of Oct. 28, 1950, each post office was authorized to surcharge stamps of its current stock with the word "Groszy." Many types and sizes of this surcharge exist. The surcharge was applied to most of Poland's 1946-1950 issues. All stamps of that period could receive the surcharge upon request of anyone. Counterfeits exist.

---

Dove by Picasso — A176

**1950, Nov. 13**

**487** A176 40g blue 1.00 .25
**488** A176 45g brown red .50 .45
Set, never hinged 3.00

2nd World Peace Congress.
For Type A176 surcharged, see No. 500.

Josef Bem and Battle Scene — A177

**1950, Dec. 10**

**489** A177 45g blue .85 *1.75*
Never hinged 2.40

Death centenary of Gen. Josef Bem.

**Type of 1950 with Frame Omitted**

***Perf. 12x12½***

**1950, Dec. 16 Engr. Unwmk.**

**490** A166 5g brown violet .25 .25
**491** A166 10g bluish green .25 .25
**492** A166 15g dp yellow grn .25 .25
**493** A166 25g dark red .35 .25
**493A** A166 30g red .35 .25
**494** A166 40g vermilion .60 .25
**495** A166 45g deep blue 1.25 .50
**496** A166 75g brown 1.00 .25
*Nos. 490-496 (8)* 4.30 2.25
Set, never hinged 10.00

**Reconstruction Type of 1950**

***Perf. 11, 11x11½, 13x11***

**1950 Photo.**

**497** A168 15g green .25 .25
Never hinged .40

Woman and Doves — A178

**1951, Mar. 2 Engr.** ***Perf. 12½***

**498** A178 45g dark red .25 .25
Never hinged .50

Congress of Women, Mar. 3-4, 1951.

Gen. Jaroslaw Dabrowski — A179

**1951, Mar. 24** ***Perf. 12x12½***

**499** A179 45g dark green .35 .25
Never hinged .70

80th anniv. of the Insurrection of Paris and the death of Gen. Jaroslaw Dabrowski.

**Dove Type of 1950 Surcharged**

**1951, Apr. 20** ***Perf. 12½***

**500** A176 45g on 15z brn red .60 .35
Never hinged 1.20

Worker and Flag — A180

**1951, Apr. 25 Photo.** ***Perf. 14x11***

**501** A180 45g scarlet .50 .25
Never hinged 1.00

Labor Day, May 1.

Steel Mill, Nowa Huta — A181

**1951 Engr. *Perf. 12½***
**502** A181 40g dark blue .25 .25
**503** A181 45g black .35 .25
**504** A181 60g brown .25 .25
**505** A181 90g dark carmine 1.00 .25
*Nos. 502-505 (4)* 1.85 1.00
Set, never hinged 4.00

Pioneer Saluting A182

Boy and Girl Pioneers A183

**1951, Apr. 1 Photo.**
**506** A182 30g olive brown 1.00 .90
**507** A183 45g brt grnsh blue 2.25 1.50
Set, never hinged 8.50

Issued to publicize Children's Day, June 1, 1951.

**Workers Type of 1950**

**1951 Unwmk. Engr. *Perf. 12½x13***
**507A** A173 45g violet blue .25 .25
**508** A173 75g black brown .25 .25
**509** A173 1.15z dark green .85 .25
**510** A173 1.20z dark red .35 .25
*Nos. 507A-510 (4)* 1.70 1.00
Set, never hinged 4.00

Issued to publicize Poland's 6-year plan.

Stanislaw Staszik — A184

Congress Emblem — A186

Z. F. von Wroblewski and Karol S. Olszewski — A185

Portraits: 40g, Marie Sklodowska Curie. 60g, Marceli Nencki. 1.15z, Nicolaus Copernicus.

***Perf. 12½, 14x11***
**1951, Apr. 25 Photo.**
**511** A184 25g carmine rose 1.75 *3.00*
**512** A184 40g ultra .35 .25
**513** A185 45g purple 2.25 1.75
**514** A184 60g green .45 .25
**515** A184 1.15z claret .45 .25
**516** A186 1.20z gray .90 .70
*Nos. 511-516 (6)* 6.15 6.20
Set, never hinged 17.00

1st Congress of Polish Science.

Feliks E. Dzerzhinski — A187

**1951, July 5 Engr. *Perf. 12x12½***
**517** A187 45g chestnut brown .25 .25
Never hinged .50

25th death anniv. of Feliks E. Dzerzhinski, Polish revolutionary, organizer of Russian secret police.

Pres. Boleslaw Bierut — A188

**1951, July 22 *Perf. 12½***
**518** A188 45g dark carmine 1.20 .35
**519** A188 60g deep green 7.00 9.50
**520** A188 90g deep blue 2.25 1.00
*Nos. 518-520 (3)* 10.45 10.85
Set, never hinged 26.00

7th anniv. of the formation of the Polish People's Republic.

Flag and Sports Emblem — A189

**1951, Sept. 8 Photo. *Perf. 11x14***
**521** A189 45g green .80 .50
Never hinged 1.75

National Sports Festival, 1951.
No. 521 exists perf. 12½. Values: unused, $1.75; never hinged, $4.

**Type of 1950 with Frame Omitted Surcharged with New Value in Black**

**1951, Sept. 1 Engr. *Perf. 12½x11½***
**522** A166 45g on 35z org red .45 .35
Never hinged .90

Youths Encircling Globe — A190

**1951, Aug. 5 Photo. *Perf. 12½x11***
**523** A190 40g deep ultra .80 .35
Never hinged 1.75

3rd World Youth Festival, Berlin, Aug. 5-19.

Joseph V. Stalin — A191

**1951, Oct. 30 Engr. *Perf. 12½***
**524** A191 45g lake .30 .25
**525** A191 90g gray black .50 .45
Set, never hinged 1.75

Month of Polish-Soviet friendship, Nov. 1951.

Frederic Chopin and Stanislaw Moniuszko A192

**1951, Nov. 15 Unwmk.**
**526** A192 45g gray .25 .25
**527** A192 90g brownish red .80 .80
Set, never hinged 1.90

Festival of Polish Music, 1951.

Apartment House Construction A193

Coal Mining A194

Design: Nos. 529-530, Electrical installation.

**1951-52 Inscribed: "Plan 6," etc.**
**528** A193 30g dull green .25 .25
**529** A193 30g gray black ('52) .25 .25
**530** A193 45g red ('52) .25 .25
**531** A194 90g chocolate .25 .25
**532** A193 1.15z violet brn ('52) .25 .25
**533** A194 1.20z deep blue ('52) .25 .25
*Nos. 528-533,B68-B69A (9)* 3.95 2.25
Set, never hinged 4.50

Poland's 6-year plan.

**Catalogue values for unused stamps in this section, from this point to the end of the section, are for Never Hinged items.**

Pawel Finder — A195

Portrait: 1.15z, Malgorzata Fornalska.

**1952, Jan. 18**
**534** A195 90g chocolate .50 .25
**535** A195 1.15z red orange .30 .25
*Nos. 534-535,B63 (3)* 1.05 .75

Polish Workers Party, 10th anniv. See No. B63.

Flag, Two Women — A196

**1952, Mar. 8 *Perf. 12½x12***
**536** A196 1.20z deep carmine .55 .25

Intl. Women's Day. See No. B64.

Gen. Karol Swierczewski-Walter A197

**1952, Mar. 28 *Perf. 12½***
**537** A197 90g blue gray 1.40 .25

Gen. Karol Swierczewski-Walter (1896-1947). See No. B65.

Pres. Boleslaw Bierut — A198

**1952, Apr. 18**
**538** A198 90g dull green 1.60 .70
*Nos. 538,B66-B67 (3)* 3.00 1.20

60th birth anniv. of Pres. Boleslaw Bierut.

**Souvenir Sheet**

A199

**1951, Nov. 15**
**539** A199 Sheet of 4 40.00 15.00
*a.* 45g red brown (A173) 2.75 2.10
*b.* 75g red brown (A173) 2.75 2.10
*c.* 1.15z red brown (A173) 2.75 2.10
*d.* 1.20z red brown (A173) 2.75 2.10

Polish Philatelic Association Congress, Warsaw, 1951. Sold for 5 zloty.

Workers with Flag — A200

**1952, May 1 Unwmk. *Perf. 12½***
**540** A200 75g deep green .90 .25

Labor Day, May 1, 1952. See No. B70.

J. I. Kraszewski — A201

1z, Hugo Kollataj. 1.15z, Maria Konopnicka.

**1952, May Various Frames**
**541** A201 25g brown violet 1.00 .35
**542** A201 1z yellow green .70 .25
**543** A201 1.15z red brown .95 .25
*Nos. 541-543,B71-B72 (5)* 3.50 1.85

Nikolai Gogol — A202

**1952, June 5**

**544** A202 25g deep green 1.10 .70

100th death anniv. of Nikolai V. Gogol, writer.

Gymnast — A203

**1952, June 21 Photo. *Perf. 13***

**545** A203 1.15z Runners 4.50 3.50
**546** A203 1.20z shown .50 .25
*Nos. 545-546,B75-B76 (4)* 10.00 5.00

Racing Cyclists — A204

**1952, Apr. 25 *Perf. 13½***

**547** A204 40g blue 1.75 .85

5th Intl. Peace Bicycle Race, Warsaw-Berlin-Prague.

Shipyard Worker and Collier — A205

**1952, June 28 Engr. *Perf. 12½***

**548** A205 90g violet brown .90 1.75
*Nos. 548,B77-B78 (3)* 7.40 3.50

Shipbuilders' Day, 1952.

Concrete Works, Wierzbica — A206

**1952, June 17**

**549** A206 3z gray 1.75 .30
**550** A206 10z brown red 4.00 1.10

Bugler — A207

**1952, July 17 *Perf. 12½x12***

**551** A207 90g brown 1.00 .40

Youth Festival, 1952. See Nos. B79-B80.

Celebrating New Constitution A208

**1952, July 22 Photo. *Perf. 12½***

**552** A208 3z vio & dk brn .90 .75

Proclamation of a new constitution. See No. B81.

Power Plant, Jaworzno A209

**1952, Aug. 7 Engr.**

**553** A209 1z black 3.00 .25
**554** A209 1.50z deep green .75 .25
*Nos. 553-554,B82 (3)* 4.50 .75

Grywald — A210

**1952, Aug. 18**

**555** A210 60g dark green 1.75 1.50
**556** A210 1z red ("Niedzica") 4.75 .25
*a.* 1z red ("Niedziga") 12.00 .75
*Nos. 555-556,B85 (3)* 8.10 2.95

Parachute Descent — A211

**1952, Aug. 23**

**557** A211 90g deep blue 1.50 .35
*Nos. 557,B86-B87 (3)* 7.00 1.70

Aviation Day, Aug. 23.

Avicenna — A212

Portrait: 90g, Victor Hugo.

**1952, Sept. 1**

**558** A212 75g red brown .60 .35
**559** A212 90g sepia .80 .35

Anniversaries of the births of Avicenna (1000th) and Victor Hugo (150th).

Shipbuilding — A213

**1952, Sept. 10**

**560** A213 5g deep green .30 .25
**561** A213 15g red brown .60 .25

Reconstruction of Gdansk shipyards.

Assault on the Winter Palace, 1917 A214

**1952, Nov. 7 *Perf. 12x12½***

**562** A214 60g dark brown .90 .25

Russian Revolution, 35th anniv. See No. B92.

Nos. 562, B92 exist imperf. Values, set: never hinged $27.50; used $32.50.

Auto Assembly Plant, Zeran — A215

**1952, Dec. 12 *Perf. 12½***

**563** A215 1.15z brown .75 .60

See No. B99.

Dove — A216

**1952, Dec. 12 Photo.**

**564** A216 30g green .40 .30
**565** A216 60g ultra 2.10 .80

Congress of Nations for Peace, Vienna, Dec. 12-19, 1952.

Soldier with Flag — A217

**1953, Feb. 2 Unwmk. *Perf. 11***
**Flag in Carmine**

**566** A217 60g olive gray 5.50 3.00
**567** A217 80g blue gray 3.00 .70

10th anniv. of the Battle of Stalingrad.

Karl Marx — A218

**1953, Mar. 14 *Perf. 12½***

**568** A218 60g dull blue 25.00 17.00
**569** A218 80g dark brown 1.25 .25

70th death anniv. of Karl Marx.

Cyclists and Arms of Warsaw — A219

Arms: No. 571, Berlin. No. 572, Prague.

**1953, Apr. 30**

**570** A219 80g dark brown .80 .25
**571** A219 80g dark green 1.00 .25
**572** A219 80g red 24.00 13.50
*Nos. 570-572 (3)* 25.80 14.00

6th Intl. Peace Bicycle Race, Warsaw-Berlin-Prague.

Flag and Globe — A220

**1953, Apr. 28**

**573** A220 60g vermilion *15.00 3.75*
**574** A220 80g carmine .40 .40

Labor Day, May 1, 1953.

Boxer — A221

Design: 95g, Boxing match.

**1953, May 17**

**575** A221 40g red brown .85 .25
**576** A221 80g orange 21.00 12.00
**577** A221 95g violet brown .85 .25
*Nos. 575-577 (3)* 22.70 12.50

European Championship Boxing Matches, Warsaw, May 17-24, 1953.

Copernicus Watching Heavens, by Jan Matejko — A222

Nicolaus Copernicus — A223

***Perf. 12x12½, 12½x12***

**1953, May 22 Engr.**

**578** A222 20g brown .80 .25
**579** A223 80g deep blue 18.00 8.50

480th birth anniv. of Nicolaus Copernicus, astronomer.

Fishing Boat — A224

Design: 1.35z, Freighter "Czech."

**1953, July 15 *Perf. 12½***

**580** A224 80g dark green 1.50 .25
**581** A224 1.35z deep blue 3.50 1.50

Issued for Merchant Marine Day.

Old Part of Warsaw — A225

**1953, July 15** **Photo.**
**582** A225 20g red brown .25 .25
**583** A225 2.35z blue 3.75 1.75

36th anniv. of the proclamation of "People's Poland."

Students of Two Races — A226 Schoolgirl and Dove — A227

1.35z, Congress badge (similar to AP7).

**1953, Aug. 24**
**584** A226 40g dark brown .35 .25
**585** A227 1.35z green .50 .25
**586** A227 1.50z blue 6.00 4.00
*Nos. 584-586,C32-C33 (5)* 11.60 6.25

3rd World Congress of Students, Warsaw, 1953.

Nurse Feeding Baby — A228

Design: 1.75z, Nurse instructing mother.

**1953, Nov. 21**
**587** A228 80g rose carmine 8.25 7.25
**588** A228 1.75z deep green .25 .25

Poland's Social Health Service.

Mieczylaw Kalinowski A229 Battle Scene, Polish and Soviet Flags A230

Portrait: 1.75z, Roman Pazinski.

**1953, Oct. 10**
**589** A229 45g brown 4.75 2.25
**590** A230 80g brown lake .50 .25
**591** A229 1.75z olive gray .50 .25
*Nos. 589-591 (3)* 5.75 2.75

10th anniv. of Poland's People's Army.

Jan Kochanowski A231 Courtyard, Wawel Castle A232

Portrait: 1.35z, Mikolaj Rej.

**1953, Nov. 10** **Engr.**
**592** A231 20g red brown .50 .25
**593** A232 80g deep plum .80 .25
**594** A231 1.35z gray black 2.75 1.00
*Nos. 592-594 (3)* 4.05 1.50

Issued for the "Renaissance Year."

For surcharges see Nos. 733-736.

Palace of Culture, Warsaw A233

Designs: 1.75z, Constitution Square. 2z, Old Section, Warsaw.

**1953, Nov. 30** ***Perf. 12x12½***
**595** A233 80g vermilion 11.00 .50
**596** A233 1.75z deep blue 1.00 .25
**597** A233 2z violet brown 8.00 4.25
*Nos. 595-597 (3)* 20.00 5.00

Issued for the reconstruction of Warsaw.

Ice Dancer — A236 Skier — A237

Design: 2.85z, Ice hockey player.

**1953, Dec. 31** **Litho.** ***Perf. 12½***
**602** A236 80g blue 1.60 .25
**603** A237 95g blue green 1.60 .25
**604** A236 2.85z dark red 4.75 2.25
*Nos. 602-604 (3)* 7.95 2.75

---

Canceled to Order

The government stamp agency began late in 1951 to sell canceled sets of new issues. Until 1990, at least, values in the second ("used") column are for these canceled-to-order stamps. Postally used stamps are worth more.

---

Children at Play — A238

Designs: 80g, Girls on the way to school. 1.50z, Two students in class.

**1953, Dec. 31** **Photo.**
**605** A238 10g violet .25 .25
**606** A238 80g red brown .75 .25
**607** A238 1.50z dark green 6.50 2.60
*Nos. 605-607 (3)* 7.50 3.10

Krynica Spa A239 Dunajec Canyon, Pieniny Mountains A240

Designs: 80g, Morskie Oko, Tatra Mts. 2z, Windmill and framework, Ciechocinek.

**1953, Dec. 16**
**608** A239 20g blue & rose brn .40 .25
**609** A240 80g bl grn & dk vio 5.50 2.50
**610** A240 1.75z ol bis & dk grn 1.20 .25
**611** A239 2z brick red & blk 1.20 .25
*Nos. 608-611 (4)* 8.30 3.25

Electric Passenger Train — A241

Design: 80g, Electric locomotive and cars.

**1954, Jan. 26** **Engr.**
**612** A241 60g deep blue 6.00 3.00
**613** A241 80g red brown .55 .25

Spinning Mill, Worker — A242

Designs: 40g, Woman letter carrier. 80g, Woman tractor driver.

**1954, Mar. 24** **Photo.**
**614** A242 20g deep green 2.25 1.00
**615** A242 40g deep blue .50 .25
**616** A242 80g dark brown .55 .25
*Nos. 614-616 (3)* 3.30 1.50

Flags and May Flowers — A243

**1954, Apr. 28**
**617** A243 40g chocolate .60 .25
**618** A243 60g deep blue 1.00 .25
**619** A243 80g carmine rose .60 .25
*Nos. 617-619 (3)* 2.20 .75

Labor Day, May 1, 1954.

"Peace" Uniting Three Capitals — A244

No. 621, Dove, olive branch and wheel.

**1954, Apr. 29** ***Perf. 12½x12***
**620** A244 80g red brown .60 .25
**621** A244 80g deep blue .70 .45

7th Intl. Bicycle Tour, May 2-17, 1954.

A245

**1954, Apr. 30** **Engr.** ***Perf. 11½***
**622** A245 25g gray 1.50 .50
**623** A245 80g brown carmine .35 .25

3rd Trade Union Congress, Warsaw 1954.

Glider and Framed Clouds — A246

60g, Glider, flags. 1.35z, Glider, large cloud.

**1954, May 31** **Photo.** ***Perf. 12½***
**624** A246 45g dark green .65 .25
**625** A246 60g purple 3.75 2.50
**626** A246 60g brown 1.25 .25
**627** A246 1.35z blue 2.40 .25
*Nos. 624-627 (4)* 8.05 3.25

Intl. Glider Championships, Leszno.

Fencing — A247 Handstand on Horizontal Bars — A248

Design: 1z, Relay racers.

**1954, July 17**
**628** A247 25g violet brown 2.10 .25
**629** A248 60g Prus blue 1.60 .30
**630** A247 1z violet blue 4.25 1.75
*Nos. 628-630 (3)* 7.95 2.30

Javelin Throwers A249

**1954, July 17** ***Perf. 12***
**631** A249 60g rose brn & dk red brn 1.00 .70
**632** A249 1.55z gray & black 2.50 .70

Nos. 628-632 were issued to publicize the second Summer Spartacist Games, 1954.

Studzianki Battle Scene — A250

Design: 1z, Soldier and flag bearer.

**1954, Aug. 24** ***Perf. 12½***
**633** A250 60g dark green 2.00 .30
**634** A250 1z violet blue 6.50 2.75

10th anniversary, Battle of Studzianki.

Railway Signal — A251

Design: 60g, Modern train.

**1954, Sept. 9**
**635** A251 40g dull blue 7.25 .25
**636** A251 60g black 4.00 1.90

Issued to publicize Railwaymen's Day.

Ivan Michurin, Horticulturalist A252

**1954, Sept. 15**
**637** A252 40g violet 2.00 1.60
**638** A252 60g black .25 .25

Month of Polish-Soviet friendship.

View of Elblag A253

Cities: 45g, Gdansk. 60g, Torun. 1.40z, Malbork. 1.55z, Olsztyn.

**1954, Oct. 16 Engr. *Perf. 12x12½***

**639** A253 20g dk car, *bl* 5.20 1.50
**640** A253 45g brown, *yel* .40 .25
**641** A253 60g dk green, *cit* .40 .25
**642** A253 1.40z dk blue, *pink* .65 .25
**643** A253 1.55z dk vio brn, *cr* .65 .25
*Nos. 639-643 (5)* 7.30 2.50

Pomerania's return to Poland, 500th anniv.
For overprint see No. 866.

Chopin and Piano — A254

**1954, Nov. 8 Photo. *Perf. 12½***

**644** A254 45g dark brown .30 .25
**645** A254 60g dark green .30 .25
**646** A254 1z dark blue 3.25 1.60
*Nos. 644-646 (3)* 3.85 2.10

5th Intl. Competition of Chopin's Music.

Coal Mine — A255

Designs: 20g, Soldier, flag and map. 25g, Steel mill. 40g, Relaxing worker in deck chair. 45g, Building construction. 60g, Tractor in field. 1.15z, Lublin Castle. 1.40z, Books and publications. 1.55z, Loading ship. 2.10z, Attacking tank.

**Photo.; Center Engr.**

**1954-55 *Perf. 12½x12***

**647** A255 10g red brn & choc .80 .25
**648** A255 20g rose & grnsh blk .80 .25
**649** A255 25g bister & blk 2.25 .25
**650** A255 40g yel org & choc .80 .25
**651** A255 45g claret & vio brn 1.25 .25
**652** A255 60g emerald & red brn .55 .25
**653** A255 1.15z brt bl grn & sep 2.00 .25
**654** A255 1.40z orange & choc 17.00 3.50
**655** A255 1.55z blue & indigo 7.00 .35
**656** A255 2.10z ultra & indigo 6.50 1.75
*Nos. 647-656 (10)* 38.95 7.35

10th anniversary of "People's Poland."
Issued: 25g, 60g, 1955; others, 12/23/54.

**Photo.; Center Litho.**

**1954, Oct. 30**

**656A** A255 25g bister & blk 12.00 1.75
**656B** A255 60g emer & red brn 3.00 .70

Insurgents Attacking Russians — A256

60g, Gen. Tadeusz Kosciuszko and insurgents. 1.40z, Kosciuszko leading attack in Cracow.

**1954, Nov. 30 Engr. *Perf. 12½***

**657** A256 40g grnsh black .60 .25
**658** A256 60g violet brown .80 .25
**659** A256 1.40z dark gray 2.75 1.40
*Nos. 657-659 (3)* 4.15 1.90

160th anniv. of the Insurrection of 1794.
No. 658 exists in a trial color proof in black blue.

Bison — A257

60g, European elk. 1.90z, Chamois. 3z, Beaver.

**Engr.; Background Photo.**

**1954, Dec. 22**

**660** A257 45g yel grn & blk brn .30 .25
**661** A257 60g emerald & dk brn .30 .25
**662** A257 1.90z blue & blk brn .60 .25
**663** A257 3z bl grn & dk brn 3.00 1.50
*Nos. 660-663 (4)* 4.20 2.25

Exist imperf. Value, set: mint, $7, used $2.40.

Liberators Entering Warsaw — A258

60g, Allegory of freedom (Warsaw Mermaid).

**1955, Jan. 17 Photo.**

**664** A258 40g red brown 1.75 1.40
**665** A258 60g dull blue 1.75 .25

Liberation of Warsaw, 10th anniversary.

Frederic Chopin — A259

**1955, Feb. 22 Engr.**

**666** A259 40g dark brown .25 .25
**667** A259 60g indigo 2.10 1.00

5th Intl. Competition of Chopin's Music, Feb. 22-Mar. 21.

Nicolaus Copernicus A260

Sigismund III A261

Warsaw monuments: 5g, Mermaid. 10g, Feliks E. Dzerzhinski. 20g, Brothers in Arms Monument. 45g, Marie Sklodowska Curie. 60g, Adam Mickiewicz. 1.55z, Jan Kilinski.

**1955, May 3 Unwmk. *Perf. 12½***

**668** A260 5g dk grn, *grnsh* .25 .25
**669** A260 10g vio brn, *yel* .25 .25
**670** A261 15g blk brn, *bluish* .25 .25
**671** A260 20g dk bl, *pink* .25 .25
**672** A260 40g vio, *vio* .25 .25
**673** A261 45g vio brn, *cr* 1.50 .25
**674** A260 60g dk bl, *gray* .35 .25
**675** A261 1.55z sl bl, *grysh* 3.00 1.10
*Nos. 668-675 (8)* 6.10 2.85

See Nos. 737-739.

Palace of Culture and Flags of Poland and USSR — A262

Design: 60g, Monument.

***Perf. 12½x12, 11***

**1955, Apr. 21 Photo.**

**676** A262 40g rose red .85 .30
**677** A262 40g lt brown .25 .25
**678** A262 60g Prus blue .25 .25
**679** A262 60g dk olive brn .25 .25
*Nos. 676-679 (4)* 1.60 1.05

Polish-USSR treaty of friendship, 10th anniv.

Arms and Bicycle Wheels — A263

Design: 60g, Three doves above road.

**1955, Apr. 25 *Perf. 12***

**680** A263 40g chocolate .80 .25
**681** A263 60g ultra .25 .25

8th Intl. Peace Bicycle Race, Prague-Berlin-Warsaw.

Poznan Town Hall and Fair Emblem — A264

**1955, June 10 Photo. *Perf. 12½***

**682** A264 40g brt ultra .45 .25
**683** A264 60g dull red .25 .25

24th Intl. Fair at Poznan, July 3-24, 1955.

"Laikonik" Carnival Costume A265

A265a

**1955, June 16 Typo. *Perf. 12***

**Multicolored Centers**

**684** A265 20g emerald & henna 2.00 .70
**685** A265a 40g brt org & lil .25 .25
**686** A265 60g blue & carmine .30 .25
*Nos. 684-686 (3)* 2.55 1.20

Cracow Celebration Days.

Pansies — A266

40g, 60g, (#690), Dove & Tower of Palace of Science & Culture. 45g, Pansies. 60g, (#691), 1z, "Peace" (POKOJ) & Warsaw Mermaid.

**1955, July 13 Litho. *Perf. 12***

**687** A266 25g vio brn, org & car .25 .25
**688** A266 40g gray bl & gray blk .25 .25
**689** A266 45g brn lake, yel & car .85 .25
**690** A266 60g sepia & orange .30 .25
**691** A266 60g ultra & lt blue .30 .25
**692** A266 1z purple & lt blue 1.00 .65
*Nos. 687-692 (6)* 2.95 1.90

5th World Festival of Youth, Warsaw, July 31-Aug. 14, 1955.
Exist imperf. Value, set: mint, $5.50, used $3.50.

Motorcyclists A267

**1955, July 20 Photo. *Perf. 12½***

**693** A267 40g chocolate .80 .25
**694** A267 60g dark green .30 .25

13th Intl. Motorcycle Race in the Tatra Mountains, Aug. 7-9, 1955.

Stalin Palace of Culture and Science, Warsaw — A268

**1955, July 21**

**695** A268 60g ultra .25 .25
**696** A268 60g gray .25 .25
**697** A268 75g blue green .40 .30
**698** A268 75g brown .40 .30
*Nos. 695-698 (4)* 1.30 1.10

Polish National Day, July 22, 1955. Sheets contain alternating stamps of the 60g values or the 75g values respectively.

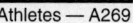

Athletes — A269

Stadium — A270

Designs: 40g, Hammer throwing. 1z, Basketball. 1.35z, Sculling. 1.55z, Swimming.

**1955, July 27 Unwmk. *Perf. 12½***

**699** A269 20g chocolate .25 .25
**700** A269 40g plum .25 .25
**701** A270 60g dull blue .30 .25
**702** A269 1z orange ver .45 .25
**703** A269 1.35z dull violet .60 .25
**704** A269 1.55z peacock green 1.75 .65
*Nos. 699-704 (6)* 3.60 1.90

2nd International Youth Games, 1955. Exist imperf. Values, set: mint, $5; used, $4.

Town Hall, Szczecin (Stettin) — A271

Designs: 40g, Cathedral, Wroclaw (Breslau) 60g, Town Hall, Zielona Gora (Grunberg). 95g, Town Hall, Opole (Oppeln).

**1955, Sept. 22 Engr. *Perf. 11½***
**705** A271 25g dull green .25 .25
**706** A271 40g red brown .25 .25
**707** A271 60g violet blue .45 .25
**708** A271 95g dark gray 1.40 .80
*Nos. 705-708 (4)* 2.35 1.55

10th anniv. of the acquisition of Western Polish Territories.

Rebels with Flag — A272

**1955, Sept. 30 Photo. *Perf. 12x12½***
**709** A272 40g dark brown 1.00 .30
**710** A272 60g dk carmine rose .25 .25

Revolution of 1905, 50th anniversary.

Adam Mickiewicz — A273

Mickiewicz Monument, Paris — A274

60g, Death mask. 95g, Statue, Warsaw.

**1955, Oct. 10 *Perf. 12x12½, 12½***
**711** A273 20g dark brown .25 .25
**712** A274 40g brn org & dk brn .25 .25
**713** A274 60g green & brown .25 .25
**714** A274 95g brn red & blk 1.75 1.20
*Nos. 711-714 (4)* 2.50 1.95

Death cent. of Adam Mickiewicz, poet, and to publicize the celebration of Mickiewicz year.

Teacher and Child — A275

Design: 60g, Flame and open book.

***Perf. 12½x13***

**1955, Oct. 21 Unwmk.**
**715** A275 40g brown 2.00 .25
**716** A275 60g ultra 2.00 .85

Polish Teachers' Trade Union, 50th anniv.

Rook and Hands — A276

Design: 60g, Chess knight and hands.

**1956, Feb. 9 *Perf. 12½***
**717** A276 40g dark red 2.50 .25
**718** A276 60g blue 1.50 2.40

First World Chess Championship of the Deaf and Dumb, Feb. 9-23.

Captain and S. S. Kilinski A277

10g, Sailor and barges. 20g, Dock worker and S. S. Pokoj. 45g, Shipyard and worker. 60g, Fisherman, S. S. Chopin and trawlers.

**1956, Mar. 16 Engr. *Perf. 12x12½***
**719** A277 5g green .25 .25
**720** A277 10g carmine lake .25 .25
**721** A277 20g deep ultra .40 .25
**722** A277 45g rose brown 2.10 .80
**723** A277 60g violet blue 4.00 .25
*Nos. 719-723 (5)* 7.00 1.80

Snowflake and Ice Skates — A278

Designs: 40g, Snowflake and Ice Hockey sticks. 60g, Snowflake and Skis.

**1956, Mar. 7 Photo. *Perf. 12½***
**724** A278 20g brt ultra & blk 6.50 3.00
**725** A278 40g brt grn & vio bl .80 .25
**726** A278 60g lilac & lake .45 .25
*Nos. 724-726 (3)* 7.75 3.50

XI World Students Winter Sport Championship, Mar. 7-13.

Cyclist — A279

**1956, Apr. 25**
**727** A279 40g dark blue 1.25 .60
**728** A279 60g dark green .25 .25

9th Intl. Peace Bicycle Race, Warsaw-Berlin-Prague, May 1-15.

Zakopane Mountains and Shelter — A280

40g, Map, compass & knapsack. 60g, Map of Poland & canoe. 1.15z, Skis & mountains.

**1956, May 25**
**729** A280 30g dark green .40 .25
**730** A280 40g lt red brown .40 .25
**731** A280 60g blue 2.60 .90
**732** A280 1.15z dull purple .40 .25
*Nos. 729-732 (4)* 3.80 1.65

Polish Tourist industry.

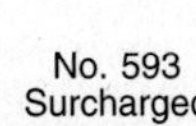

No. 593 Surcharged

**1956, July 6 Engr. *Perf. 12½***
**733** A232 10g on 80g dp plum 1.50 .45
**734** A232 40g on 80g dp plum .25 .25
**735** A232 60g on 80g dp plum .25 .25
**736** A232 1.35z on 80g dp plum 2.25 1.10
*Nos. 733-736 (4)* 4.25 2.05

The size and type of surcharge and obliteration of old value differ for each denomination.

### Type of 1955

Warsaw Monuments: 30g, Ghetto Monument. 40g, John III Sobieski. 1.55z, Prince Joseph Poniatowski.

**1956, July 10**
**737** A260 30g black .25 .25
**738** A260 40g red brn, *grnsh* 1.25 .25
**739** A260 1.55z vio brn, *pnksh* .25 .25
*Nos. 737-739 (3)* 1.75 .75

No. 737 measures 22½x28mm, instead of 21x27mm.

A281

Polish-Soviet Friendship Month — A281a

Designs: 40g, Polish and Russian dancers. 60g, Open book and cogwheels.

**1956, Sept. 14 Litho. *Perf. 12***
**740** A281 40g brn red & brn 1.00 .40
**741** A281a 60g bister & red .25 .25

Ludwika Wawrzynska and Children — A282

**1956, Sept. 17 Photo. *Perf. 12½***
**742** A282 40g dull red brown 1.40 .40
**743** A282 60g blue .25 .25

Issued in honor of a heroic school teacher who saved three children from a burning house.

Bee on Clover and Beehive — A283

Design: 60g, Father Jan Dzierzon.

**1956, Oct. 30 Litho. Unwmk.**
**744** A283 40g org yel & brn 1.10 .45
**745** A283 60g yel org & brn .25 .25

50th death anniv. of Father Jan Dzierzon, the inventor of the modernized beehive.

"Lady with the Ermine" by Leonardo da Vinci A284

40g, Niobe. 60g, Madonna by Veit Stoss.

**1956 Engr. *Perf. 11½x11***
**746** A284 40g dark green 3.00 1.40
**747** A284 60g dark violet .60 .25
**748** A284 1.55z chocolate 1.75 .30
*Nos. 746-748 (3)* 5.35 1.95

Intl. Museum Week (UNESCO), Oct. 8-14.

Fencer A285

Designs: 20g, Boxer. 25g, Sculling. 40g, Steeplechase racer. 60g, Javelin thrower. No. 755, Woman gymnast. No. 756, Woman broad jumper.

**1956 Engr. *Perf. 11½***
**750** A285 10g slate & chnt .25 .25
**751** A285 20g lt brn & dl vio .35 .25
*a.* Center inverted 17,500.
**752** A285 25g lt blue & blk 1.20 .25
**753** A285 40g brt bl grn & redsh brn .25 .25
**754** A285 60g rose car & ol brn .25 .25
**755** A285 1.55z lt vio & sepia 2.50 .65
**756** A285 1.55z orange & chnt 1.25 .40
*Nos. 750-756 (7)* 6.05 2.30

16th Olympic Games, Melbourne, 11/22-12/8.

15th Century Mailman — A286

### Lithographed and Engraved

**1956, Nov. 30 Unwmk. *Perf. 12½***
**757** A286 60g lt blue & blk 2.75 1.00

Reopening of the Postal Museum in Wroclaw.

Skier and Snowflake A287

Ski Jumper and Snowflake — A288

Design: 1z, Skier in right corner.

**1957, Jan. 18 Photo. *Perf. 12½***
**758** A287 40g blue .25 .25
**759** A288 60g dark green .25 .25
**760** A287 1z purple .70 .55
*Nos. 758-760 (3)* 1.20 1.05

50 years of skiing in Poland.

Globe and Tree A289

UN Emblem — A290

UN Building, NY — A291

**1957, Feb. 26 Photo. *Perf. 12***

**761** A289 5g mag & brt grnsh bl .25 .25
**762** A290 15g blue & gray .55 .25
**763** A291 40g brt bl grn & gray .50 .45
*Nos. 761-763 (3)* 1.30 .95

Issued in honor of the United Nations.

Exist imperf. Value, set: mint $4, used $3.50.

An imperf. souvenir sheet exists, containing a 1.50z stamp in a redrawn design similar to A291. The stamp is blue and bright bluish green. Value, $25 unused, $14 canceled.

Skier — A292

**1957, Mar. 22 *Perf. 12½***

**764** A292 60g blue 1.25 .30
**765** A292 60g brown .25 .25

12th anniv. of the death of the skiers Bronislaw Czech and Hanna Marusarzowna.

Sword, Foil and Saber on World Map — A293

Designs: No. 767, Fencer facing right. No. 768, Fencer facing left.

**1957, Apr. 20 Unwmk. *Perf. 12½***

**766** A293 40g deep plum .55 .30
**767** A293 60g carmine .25 .25
**768** A293 60g ultra .25 .25
*a.* Pair, #767-768 .75 .50

World Youth Fencing Championships, Warsaw.

No. 768a has continuous design.

Dr. Sebastian Petrycy — A294

Doctors' Portraits: 20g Wojciech Oczko. 40g, Jedrzej Sniadecki. 60g, Tytus Chalubinski. 1z, Wladyslaw Bieganski. 1.35z, Jozef Dietl. 2.50z, Benedykt Dybowski. 3z, Henryk Jordan.

**Portraits Engr., Inscriptions Typo.**

**1957 *Perf. 11½***

**769** A294 10g sepia & ultra .25 .25
**770** A294 20g emerald & claret .25 .25
**771** A294 40g gray & org red .25 .25
**772** A294 60g blue & pale brn 1.10 .45
**773** A294 1z org & dk blue .25 .25
**774** A294 1.35z gray brn & grn .25 .25
**775** A294 2.50z dull vio & lil rose .25 .25
**776** A294 3z violet & ol brn .25 .25
*Nos. 769-776 (8)* 2.85 2.20

Bicycle Wheel and Carnation — A295

**1957, May 4 Photo. *Perf. 12½***

**777** A295 60g shown .50 .25
**778** A295 1.50z Cyclist .40 .35

10th Intl. Peace Bicycle Race, Warsaw-Berlin-Prague.

Poznan Fair Emblem — A296

**1957, June 8 Litho. Unwmk.**

**779** A296 60g ultramarine .25 .25
**780** A296 2.50z lt blue green .35 .25

Issued to publicize the 26th Fair at Poznan.

Turk's Cap — A297

Flowers: No. 782, Carline Thistle. No. 783, Sea Holly. No. 784, Edelweiss. No. 785, Lady's-slipper.

**1957, Aug. 12 Photo. *Perf. 12***

**781** A297 60g bl grn & claret .40 .25
**782** A297 60g gray, grn & yel .50 .25
**783** A297 60g lt blue & grn .50 .25
**784** A297 60g gray & yel grn 1.60 .25
**785** A297 60g lt grn, mar & yel .70 .25
*Nos. 781-785 (5)* 3.70 1.25

Fire Fighter — A298

60g, Child & flames. 2.50z, Grain & flames.

**1957, Sept. 11 *Perf. 12***

**786** A298 40g black & red .25 .25
**787** A298 60g dk grn & org red .25 .25
**788** A298 2.50z violet & red .65 .30
*Nos. 786-788 (3)* 1.15 .80

Intl. Fire Brigade Conf., Warsaw.

Town Hall, Leipzig and Congress Emblem — A299

**1957, Sept. 25 Photo. *Perf. 12½***

**789** A299 60g violet .25 .25

4th Intl. Trade Union Cong., Leipzig, Oct. 4-15.

"Girl Writing Letter" by Fragonard A300

**1957, Oct. 9 *Perf. 12***

**790** A300 2.50z dark blue green .65 .25

Issued for Stamp Day, Oct. 9.

Karol Libelt — A301

**1957, Nov. 15 Photo. *Perf. 12½***

**791** A301 60g carmine lake .35 .25

Centenary of the Poznan Scientific Society and to honor Karol Libelt, politician and philosopher.

Broken Chain and Flag — A302

Design: 2.50z, Lenin Statue, Poronin.

**1957, Nov. 7**

**792** A302 60g brt blue & red .25 .25
**793** A302 2.50z black & red brn .40 .25

40th anniv. of the Russian Revolution.

Jan A. Komensky (Comenius) A303

**1957, Dec. 11 *Perf. 12***

**794** A303 2.50z brt carmine .40 .25

300th anniv. of the publication of "Didactica Opera Omnia."

Henri Wieniawski — A304

**1957, Dec. 2 *Perf. 12½***

**795** A304 2.50z blue .55 .25

3rd Wieniawski Violin Competition in Poznan.

Andrzej Strug — A305

**1957, Dec. 16 Unwmk. *Perf. 12½***

**796** A305 2.50z brown .35 .25

20th death anniv. of Andrzej Strug, novelist.

Joseph Conrad and "Torrens" A306

**1957, Dec. 30 Engr. *Perf. 12x12½***

**797** A306 60g brown, *grnsh* .25 .25
**798** A306 2.50z dk blue, *pink* .75 .40

Birth cent. of Joseph Conrad, Polish-born English writer.

Postilion and Stylized Plane — A307

Designs: 40g, Tomb of Prosper Prowana, globe with plane and satellite. 60g, St. Mary's Church, Cracow, mail coach and plane. 95g, Mail coach and postal bus. 2.10z, Medieval postman and train. 3.40z, Medieval galleon and modern ships.

**1958 Litho. *Perf. 12½***

**799** A307 40g lt blue & vio brn .30 .25
**800** A307 60g pale vio & blk .25 .25
**801** A307 95g lemon & violet .25 .25
**802** A307 2.10z gray & ultra .40 .25
**803** A307 2.50z brt blue & blk .40 .25
**804** A307 3.40z aqua & maroon .50 .25
*Nos. 799-804 (6)* 2.10 1.50

400th anniversary of the Polish posts. Imperfs. exist of all but No. 803.

Town Hall at Biecz — A308

Town Halls: 40g, Wroclaw. 60g, Tarnow, horiz. 2.10z, Danzig. 2.50z, Zamosc.

**1958, Mar. 29 Engr. *Perf. 12½***

**805** A308 20g green .25 .25
**806** A308 40g brown .25 .25
**807** A308 60g dark blue .35 .25
**808** A308 2.10z rose lake .50 .25
**809** A308 2.50z violet .65 .35
*Nos. 805-809 (5)* 2.00 1.35

Giant Pike Perch A309

Fishes: 60g, Salmon, vert. 2.10z, Pike, vert. 2.50z, Trout, vert. 6.40z, Grayling.

**1958, Apr. 22 Photo. *Perf. 12***

**810** A309 40g bl, blk, grn & yel .75 .30
**811** A309 60g yel grn, dk grn & bl .75 .25
**812** A309 2.10z dk bl, grn & yel .75 .25
**813** A309 2.50z pur, blk & yel grn 2.40 .35
**814** A309 6.40z bl grn, brn & red .75 .35
*Nos. 810-814 (5)* 5.40 1.50

Casimir Palace, Warsaw University — A310

**1958, May 14 Unwmk. *Perf. 12½***

**815** A310 2.50z violet blue .35 .25

140th anniv. of the University of Warsaw.

Stylized Glider and Cloud — A311

Design: 2.50z, Design reversed.

**1958, June 14 Litho.**

**816** A311 60g gray blue & blk .25 .25
**817** A311 2.50z gray & blk .40 .25

7th Intl. Glider Competitions.

Fair Emblem — A312

**1958, June 9**

| | | | | |
|---|---|---|---|---|
| 818 | A312 | 2.50z black & rose | .40 | .25 |

27th Fair at Poznan.

Armed Postman and Mail Box — A313

**1958, Sept. 1 Engr. *Perf. 11***

| | | | | |
|---|---|---|---|---|
| 819 | A313 | 60g dark blue | .35 | .25 |

19th anniv. of the defense of the Polish post office at Danzig (Gdansk). Inscribed: "You were the first."

Letter, Quill and Postmark — A314

**1958, Oct. 9 Litho.**

| | | | | |
|---|---|---|---|---|
| 820 | A314 | 60g blk, bl grn & ver | .60 | .25 |

Issued for Stamp Day. Exists imperf., value $250.

Polar Bear — A315

Design: 2.50z, Rocket and Sputnik.

**1958, Sept. 30 Photo. *Perf. 12½x12***

| | | | | |
|---|---|---|---|---|
| 821 | A315 | 60g gray & black | .25 | .25 |
| 822 | A315 | 2.50z blue & dark blue | .60 | .25 |

Intl. Geophysical Year.

Partisan's Cross — A316

Designs: 60g, Virtuti Militari Cross. 2.50z, Grunwald Cross.

**1958, Oct. 10 *Perf. 11***

| | | | | |
|---|---|---|---|---|
| 823 | A316 | 40g black, grn & ocher | .25 | .25 |
| 824 | A316 | 60g black, blue & yel | .25 | .25 |
| 825 | A316 | 2.50z multicolored | 1.25 | .30 |
| | | *Nos. 823-825 (3)* | 1.75 | .80 |

Polish People's Army, 15th anniv.

17th Century Ship — A317

Design: 2.50z, Polish immigrants.

**1958, Oct. 29 *Perf. 11***

| | | | | |
|---|---|---|---|---|
| 826 | A317 | 60g dk slate grn | .25 | .25 |
| 827 | A317 | 2.50z dk carmine rose | .85 | .25 |

350th anniversary of the arrival of the first Polish immigrants in America.

UNESCO Building, Paris — A318

**1958, Nov. 3 Unwmk.**

| | | | | |
|---|---|---|---|---|
| 828 | A318 | 2.50z yellow grn & blk | .60 | .25 |

UNESCO Headquarters in Paris, opening, Nov. 3.

Stagecoach — A319

**Wmk. 326**

**1958, Oct. 26 Engr. *Perf. 12½***

| | | | | |
|---|---|---|---|---|
| 829 | A319 | 2.50z slate, *buff* | 1.25 | .35 |
| *a.* | | Souvenir sheet of 6 | 11.00 | 11.00 |

Philatelic exhibition in honor of the 400th anniv. of the Polish post, Warsaw, Oct. 25-Nov. 10.

**Souvenir Sheet**

**1958, Dec. 12 Unwmk. *Imperf.***
**Printed on Silk**

| | | | | |
|---|---|---|---|---|
| 830 | A319 | 50z dark blue | *135.00* | *52.50* |

400th anniversary of the Polish posts.

Stanislaw Wyspianski — A320

Portrait: 2.50z, Stanislaw Moniuszko.

**1958, Nov. 25 Engr. *Perf. 12½***

| | | | | |
|---|---|---|---|---|
| 831 | A320 | 60g dark violet | .25 | .25 |
| 832 | A320 | 2.50z dk slate grn | .40 | .25 |

Stanislaw Wyspianski, painter and poet, and Stanislaw Moniuszko, composer.

Kneeling Figure — A321

**1958, Dec. 10 Litho.**

| | | | | |
|---|---|---|---|---|
| 833 | A321 | 2.50z lt brn & red brn | .50 | .25 |

Signing of the Universal Declaration of Human Rights, 10th anniv.

Red Flag — A322

**1958, Dec. 16 Photo.**

| | | | | |
|---|---|---|---|---|
| 834 | A322 | 60g plum & red | .30 | .25 |

Communist Party of Poland, 40th anniv.

Sailing — A323

Sports: 60g, Girl archer. 95g, Soccer. 2z, Horsemanship.

**1959, Jan. 3**

| | | | | |
|---|---|---|---|---|
| 835 | A323 | 40g lt bl & vio bl | .25 | .25 |
| 836 | A323 | 60g salmon & brn vio | .25 | .25 |
| 837 | A323 | 95g green & brn vio | .70 | .25 |
| 838 | A323 | 2z dp bl & lt grn | .35 | .25 |
| | | *Nos. 835-838 (4)* | 1.55 | 1.00 |

Hand at Wheel — A324

Wheat, Hammer and Flag — A325

**1959, Mar. 10 Wmk. 326 *Perf. 12½***

| | | | | |
|---|---|---|---|---|
| 839 | A324 | 40gr shown | .25 | .25 |
| 840 | A325 | 60gr shown | .25 | .25 |
| 841 | A324 | 1.55z Factory | .40 | .25 |
| | | *Nos. 839-841 (3)* | .90 | .75 |

3rd Workers Congress.

Amanita Phalloides — A326

Designs: Various mushrooms.

**1959, May 8 Photo. *Perf. 11½***

| | | | | |
|---|---|---|---|---|
| 842 | A326 | 20g yel, grn & brn | 4.00 | 2.10 |
| 843 | A326 | 30g multicolored | 1.40 | .50 |
| 844 | A326 | 40g multicolored | .75 | .25 |
| 845 | A326 | 60g yel grn, brn & ocher | .75 | .25 |
| 846 | A326 | 1z multicolored | .75 | .25 |
| 847 | A326 | 2.50z blue, grn & brn | 1.10 | .35 |
| 848 | A326 | 3.40z multicolored | 2.00 | .40 |
| 849 | A326 | 5.60z dl yel, brn & grn | 4.75 | 2.10 |
| | | *Nos. 842-849 (8)* | 15.50 | 6.20 |

"Storks," by Jozef Chelmonski A327

Paintings by Polish Artists: 60g, Mother and Child, Stanislaw Wyspianski, vert. 1z, Mme. de Romanet, Henryk Rodakowski, vert. 1.50z, Old Man and Death, Jacek Malczewski, vert. 6.40z, River Scene, Aleksander Gierymski.

**1959 Engr. *Perf. 12, 12½x12***

| | | | | |
|---|---|---|---|---|
| 850 | A327 | 40g gray green | .25 | .25 |
| 851 | A327 | 60g dull purple | .25 | .25 |
| 852 | A327 | 1z intense black | .35 | .25 |
| 853 | A327 | 1.50z brown | .65 | .25 |
| 854 | A327 | 6.40z blue | 3.00 | .50 |
| | | *Nos. 850-854 (5)* | 4.50 | 1.50 |

Nos. 850 and 854 measure 36x28mm; Nos. 851 and 853, 28x36mm; No. 852, 28x37mm.

Miner and Globe — A328

**1959, July 1 Litho.**

| | | | | |
|---|---|---|---|---|
| 855 | A328 | 2.50z multicolored | 1.00 | .25 |

3rd Miners' Conf., Katowice, July 1959.

Symbol of Industry — A329

Map of Poland and: 40g, Map of Poland and Symbol of Agriculture. 1.50z, Symbol of art and science.

***Perf. 12x12½***

**1959, July 21 Wmk. 326**

| | | | | |
|---|---|---|---|---|
| 856 | A329 | 40g black, bl & grn | .25 | .25 |
| 857 | A329 | 60g black & ver | .25 | .25 |
| 858 | A329 | 1.50z black & blue | .30 | .25 |
| | | *Nos. 856-858 (3)* | .80 | .75 |

15 years of the Peoples' Republic of Poland.

Lazarus Ludwig Zamenhof — A330

Design: 1.50z, Star, globe and flag.

**1959, July 24 *Perf. 12½***

| | | | | |
|---|---|---|---|---|
| 859 | A330 | 60g blk & grn, *ol* | .25 | .25 |
| 860 | A330 | 1.50z ultra, grn & red, *gray* | 2.50 | .40 |

Centenary of the birth of Lazarus Ludwig Zamenhof, author of Esperanto, and in conjunction with the Esperanto Congress in Warsaw.

Map of Austria and Flower — A331

**1959, July 27 Litho.**

| | | | | |
|---|---|---|---|---|
| 861 | A331 | 60g sep, red & grn, *yel* | .25 | .25 |
| 862 | A331 | 2.50z bl, red, & grn, *gray* | .75 | .25 |

7th World Youth Festival, Vienna, July 26-Aug. 14.

Symbolic Plane — A332

**1959, Aug. 24 Wmk. 326 *Perf. 12½***

| | | | | |
|---|---|---|---|---|
| 863 | A332 | 60g vio bl, grnsh bl & blk | .30 | .25 |

30th anniv. of LOT, the Polish airline.

Sejm (Parliament) Building — A333

**1959, Aug. 27 Photo. *Perf. 12x12½***
**864** A333 60g lt grn, blk & red .25 .25
**865** A333 2.50z vio gray, blk & red .75 .25

48th Interparliamentary Conf., Warsaw.

**No. 640 Overprinted in Blue: "BALPEX I — GDANSK 1959"**

**1959, Aug. 30 Engr. Unwmk.**
**866** A253 45g brown, *yel* .75 .50

Intl. Phil. Exhib. of Baltic States at Gdansk.

Stylized Dove and Globe — A334

**Wmk. 326**

**1959, Sept. 1 Photo. *Perf. 12½***
**867** A334 60g blue & gray .30 .25

World Peace Movement, 10th anniv.

Red Cross Nurse — A335

Designs: 60g, Nurse. 2.50z, Henri Dunant.

**Size: 21x26mm**

**1959, Sept. 21 Litho. *Perf. 12½***
**868** A335 40g red, lt grn & blk .25 .25
**869** A335 60g bis brn, brn & red .25 .25

***Perf. 11***

**Size: 23x23mm**

**870** A335 2.50z red, pink & blk 1.00 .35
*Nos. 868-870 (3)* 1.50 .85

Polish Red Cross, 40th anniv.; Red Cross, cent.

Polish-Chinese Friendship Society Emblem — A336

**Wmk. 326**

**1959, Sept. 28 Litho. *Perf. 11***
**871** A336 60g multicolored 1.20 .60
**872** A336 2.50z multicolored .50 .25

Polish-Chinese friendship.

Flower Made of Stamps — A337

**1959, Oct. 9 *Perf. 12½***
**873** A337 60g lt grnsh bl, grn & red .25 .25
**874** A337 2.50z red, grn & vio .40 .25

Issued for Stamp Day, 1959.

Sputnik 3 — A338

60g, Luna I, sun. 2.50z, Earth, moon, Sputnik 2.

**1959, Nov. 7 Photo. Wmk. 326**
**875** A338 40g Prus blue & gray .25 .25
**876** A338 60g maroon & black .30 .25
**877** A338 2.50z green & dk blue .90 .50
*Nos. 875-877 (3)* 1.45 1.00

42nd anniv. of the Russian Revolution and the landing of the Soviet moon rocket.

Exist imperf. Value, set: mint $2.75, used $2.

Child Doing Homework — A339

Design: 60g, Three children leaving school.

**Lithographed and Engraved**

**1959, Nov. 14 *Perf. 11½***
**878** A339 40g green & dk brn .25 .25
**879** A339 60g blue & red .25 .25

"1,000 Schools" campaign for the 1,000th anniversary of Poland.

Charles Darwin — A340

Scientists: 40g, Dmitri I. Mendeleev. 60g, Albert Einstein. 1.50z, Louis Pasteur. 1.55z, Isaac Newton. 2.50z, Nicolaus Copernicus.

**1959, Dec. 10 Engr. *Perf. 11***
**880** A340 20g dark blue .25 .25
**881** A340 40g olive gray .25 .25
**882** A340 60g claret .35 .25
**883** A340 1.50z dk violet brn .35 .25
**884** A340 1.55z dark green .35 .25
**885** A340 2.50z violet 1.25 .50
*Nos. 880-885 (6)* 2.80 1.75

Man from Rzeszow A341

Woman from Rzeszow A342

Regional Costumes: 40g, Cracow. 60g, Kurpiow. 1z, Silesia. 2z, Lowicz. 2.50z, Mountain people. 3.10z, Kujawy. 3.40z, Lublin. 5.60z, Szamotuli. 6.50z, Lubuski.

**Engraved and Photogravure**

**1959-60 Wmk. 326 *Perf. 12, Imperf.***
**886** A341 20g slate grn & blk .25 .25
**887** A342 20g slate grn & blk .25 .25
*a.* Pair, #886-887 .25 .25
**888** A341 40g lt bl & rose car ('60) .25 .25
**889** A342 40g rose car & bl ('60) .25 .25
*a.* Pair, #888-889 .25 .25
**890** A341 60g black & pink .25 .25
**891** A342 60g black & pink .25 .25
*a.* Pair, #890-891 .25 .25
**892** A341 1z grnsh red & dk red .25 .25
**893** A342 1z grnsh bl & dk red .25 .25
*a.* Pair, #892-893 .25 .25
**894** A341 2z yel & ultra ('60) .25 .25
**895** A342 2z yel & ultra ('60) .25 .25
*a.* Pair, #894-895 .40 .25
**896** A341 2.50z green & rose lil .75 .25
**897** A342 2.50z green & rose lil .75 .25
*a.* Pair, #896-897 1.50 .50
**898** A341 3.10z yel grn & sl grn ('60) .25 .25
**899** A342 3.10z yel grn & sl grn ('60) .25 .25
*a.* Pair, #898-899 .50 .50
**900** A341 3.40z gray grn & brn ('60) .25 .25
**901** A342 3.40z gray grn & brn ('60) .25 .25
*a.* Pair, #900-901 .50 .50
**902** A341 5.60z yel grn & gray bl .75 .25
**903** A342 5.60z yel grn & gray bl .75 .25
*a.* Pair, #902-903 1.50 .50
**904** A341 6.50z vio & gray grn ('60) 1.50 .60
**905** A342 6.50z vio & gray grn ('60) 1.50 .60
*a.* Pair, #904-905 3.00 1.20
*Nos. 886-905 (20)* 9.50 5.70

Nos. 886-905 exist imperf. Value, same as perf.

Piano — A343

Frederic Chopin — A344

Design: 1.50z, Musical note and manuscript.

**1960, Feb. 22 Litho. *Perf. 12***
**906** A343 60g brt violet & blk .40 .25
**907** A343 1.50z black, gray & red .60 .25

***Perf. 12½x12***

**Engr.**

**908** A344 2.50z black 2.50 1.00
*Nos. 906-908 (3)* 3.50 1.50

150th anniversary of the birth of Frederic Chopin and to publicize the Chopin music competition.

Stamp of 1860 A345

Designs: 60g, Ski meet stamp of 1939. 1.35z, Design from 1860 issue. 1.55z, 1945 liberation stamp. 2.50z, 1957 stamp day stamp.

**Litho. (40g, 1.35z); Litho. and Photo.**
***Perf. 11½x11***

**1960, Mar. 21 Wmk. 326**
**909** A345 40g multicolored .25 .25
**910** A345 60g violet, ultra & blk .25 .25
**911** A345 1.35z gray, red & bl .55 .25
**912** A345 1.55z green, car & blk .80 .25
**913** A345 2.50z ap grn, dk grn & blk 1.40 .40
*Nos. 909-913 (5)* 3.25 1.40

Centenary of Polish stamps. Nos. 909-913 were also issued in sheets of 4. Values, set of 4 sheets: $625 mint, $675 used.

For overprint see No. 934.

Discus Thrower, Amsterdam 1928 — A346

Polish Olympic Victories: No. 915, Runner. No. 916, Bicyclist. No. 917, Steeplechase. No. 918, Trumpeters. No. 919, Boxers. No. 920, Olympic flame. No. 921 Woman jumper.

**Lithographed and Embossed**
***Perf. 12x12½***

**1960, June 15 Unwmk.**
**914** A346 60g blue & blk .25 .25
**915** A346 60g car rose & blk .25 .25
**916** A346 60g violet & blk .25 .25
**917** A346 60g blue grn & blk .25 .25
*a.* Block of 4, #914-917 1.50 .75
**918** A346 2.50z ultra & blk .55 .25
**919** A346 2.50z chestnut & blk .55 .25
**920** A346 2.50z red & blk .55 .25
**921** A346 2.50z emerald & blk .55 .25
*a.* Block of 4, #918-921 4.25 2.00
*Nos. 914-921 (8)* 3.20 2.00

17th Olympic Games, Rome, 8/25-9/11.

Nos. 917a and 921a have continuous design forming the stadium oval.

Nos. 914-921 exist imperf. Value, same as perf.

Tomb of King Wladyslaw II Jagiello — A347

Battle of Grunwald by Jan Matejko — A348

90g, Detail from Grunwald monument.

***Perf. 11x11½***

**1960 Wmk. 326 Engr.**
**922** A347 60g violet brown .35 .25
**923** A347 90g olive gray .70 .35

**Size: 78x37mm**

**924** A348 2.50z dark gray 2.50 1.00
*Nos. 922-924 (3)* 3.55 1.60

550th anniversary, Battle of Grunwald.

The Annunciation — A349

Carvings by Veit Stoss, St. Mary's Church, Cracow: 30g, Nativity. 40g, Adoration of the Kings. 60g, The Resurrection. 2.50z, The Ascension. 5.60z, Descent of the Holy Ghost. 10z, The Assumption of the Virgin, vert.

**1960 Wmk. 326 Engr. *Perf. 12***
**925** A349 20g Prus blue .25 .25
**926** A349 30g lt red brown .25 .25
**927** A349 40g violet .25 .25
**928** A349 60g dull green .25 .25
**929** A349 2.50z rose lake 1.25 .25
**930** A349 5.60z dark brown 8.00 3.25
*Nos. 925-930 (6)* 10.25 4.50

### Miniature Sheet
*Imperf*

**931** A349 10z black 8.00 5.50

No. 931 contains one vertical stamp which measures 72x95mm.

A350

**1960, Sept. 26** *Perf. 12½*

**932** A350 2.50z black .35 .25

Birth cent. of Ignacy Jan Paderewski, statesman and musician.

A351

Lukasiewicz and kerosene lamp.

**Engr. & Photo.**

**1960, Sept. 14** *Perf. 11*

**933** A351 60g citron & black .35 .25

5th Pharmaceutical Congress; Ignacy Lukasiewicz, chemist-pharmacist.

**No. 909 Overprinted: "DZIEN ZNACZKA 1960"**

**1960 Litho.** *Perf. 11½x11*

**934** A345 40g multicolored 1.00 .45

Issued for Stamp Day, 1960.

Great Bustard A352

Birds: 20g, Raven. 30g, Great cormorant. 40g, Black stork. 50g, Eagle owl. 60g, White-tailed sea eagle. 75g, Golden eagle. 90g, Short-toed eagle. 2.50z, Rock thrush. 4z, European kingfisher. 5.60z, Wall creeper. 6.50z, European roller.

**1960 Unwmk. Photo.** *Perf. 11½*

**Birds in Natural Colors**

**935** A352 10g gray & blk .25 .25
**936** A352 20g gray & blk .25 .25
**937** A352 30g gray & blk .25 .25
**938** A352 40g gray & blk .25 .25
**939** A352 50g pale grn & blk .30 .25
**940** A352 60g pale grn & blk .40 .25
**941** A352 75g pale grn & blk .40 .25
**942** A352 90g pale grn & blk .65 .25
**943** A352 2.50z pale ol gray & blk 6.75 3.00
**944** A352 4z pale ol gray & blk 2.75 1.00
**945** A352 5.60z pale ol gray & blk 4.50 1.00
**946** A352 6.50z pale ol gray & blk 5.50 2.00
*Nos. 935-946 (12)* 22.25 9.00

Gniezno — A353

Historic Towns: 10g, Cracow. 20g, Warsaw. 40g, Poznan. 50g, Plock. 60g, Kalisz. No. 952A, Tczew. 80g, Frombork. 90g, Torun. 95g, Puck (ships). 1z, Slupsk. 1.15z, Gdansk (Danzig). 1.35z, Wroclaw. 1.50z, Szczecin. 1.55z, Opole. 2z, Kolobrzeg. 2.10z, Legnica. 2.50z, Katowice. 3.10z, Lodz. 5.60z, Walbrzych.

**1960-61 Engr.** *Perf. 11½, 13x12½*

**947** A353 5g red brown .25 .25
**948** A353 10g green .25 .25
**949** A353 20g dark brown .25 .25
**950** A353 40g vermilion .25 .25
**951** A353 50g violet .25 .25
**952** A353 60g rose claret .25 .25
**952A** A353 60g lt ultra ('61) .50 .25
**953** A353 80g blue .25 .25
**954** A353 90g brown ('61) 1.20 .25
**955** A353 95g olive gray .35 .25

**Engraved and Lithographed**

**956** A353 1z orange & gray .25 .25
**957** A353 1.15z slate grn & sal .25 .25
**958** A353 1.35z lil rose & lt grn .25 .25
**959** A353 1.50z sep & pale grn .35 .25
**960** A353 1.55z car lake & buff .25 .25
**961** A353 2z dk blue & pink .25 .25
**962** A353 2.10z sepia & yel .35 .25
**963** A353 2.50z dl vio & pale grn .35 .25
**964** A353 3.10z ver & gray 1.50 .75
**965** A353 5.60z sl grn & lt grn 5.00 1.75
*Nos. 947-965 (20)* 12.60 7.00

Front Page of "Merkuriusz" A354

Newspapers: 60g, "Proletaryat," first issue, Sept. 15, 1883. 2.50z, "Rzeczpospolita," first issue, July 23, 1944.

**Lithographed and Embossed**

**1961 Wmk. 326** *Perf. 12*

**966** A354 40g black, ultra & emer .35 .25
**967** A354 60g black, org brn & yel .35 .25
**968** A354 2.50z black, violet & bl 2.75 2.00
*Nos. 966-968 (3)* 3.45 2.50

300th anniv. of the Polish newspaper Merkuriusz.

Ice Hockey — A355

60g, Ski jump. 1z, Soldiers on skis. 1.50z, Slalom.

**1961, Feb. 1 Litho. Wmk. 326**

**969** A355 40g lt violet, blk & yel .30 .25
**970** A355 60g lt ultra, blk & car .30 .25
**971** A355 1z lt blue, ol & red 5.50 2.00
**972** A355 1.50z grnsh bl, blk & yel .30 .25
*Nos. 969-972 (4)* 6.40 2.75

1st Winter Spartacist Games of Friendly Armies.

Part of Cogwheel — A356

**1961, Feb. 11** *Perf. 12½*

**973** A356 60g red & black .25 .25

Fourth Congress of Polish Engineers.

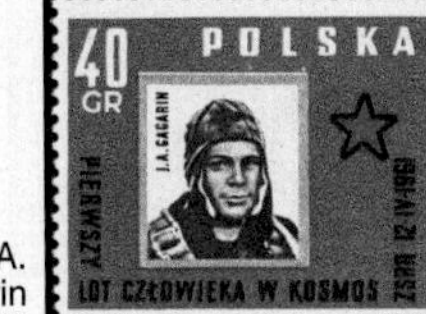
Maj. Yuri A. Gagarin A357

Design: 60g, Globe and path of rocket.

**1961, Apr. 27 Photo.** *Perf. 12*

**974** A357 40g dark red & black .50 .25
**975** A357 60g ultra, black & car .50 .25

1st man in space, Yuri A. Gagarin, Apr. 12, 1961.

Emblem of Poznan Fair — A358

**1961, May 25 Litho.** *Perf. 12½x12*

**977** A358 40g brt bl, blk & red org .25 .25
**978** A358 1.50z red org, blk & brt bl .35 .25
*a.* Souvenir sheet of 2 4.00 2.75

30th Intl. Fair at Poznan.

No. 978a contains two of No. 978 with simulated perforation and blue marginal inscriptions. Sold for 4.50z. Issued July 29, 1961.

Famous Poles A359

No. 979, Mieszko I. No. 980, Casimir Wielki. No. 981, Casimir Jagiello. No. 982, Nicolaus Copernicus. No. 983, Andrzej Frycz-Modrzewski. No. 984, Tadeusz Kosciuszko.

**Photogravure and Engraved**

**1961, June 15** *Perf. 11x11½*

**Black Inscriptions and Designs**

**979** A359 60g chalky blue .25 .25
**980** A359 60g deep rose .25 .25
**981** A359 60g slate .25 .25
**982** A359 60g dull violet .35 .25
**983** A359 60g lt brown .25 .25
**984** A359 60g olive sepia .60 .25
*Nos. 979-984 (6)* 1.95 1.50

See Nos. 1059-1064, 1152-1155.

Trawler — A360

Designs: Various Polish Cargo Ships.

**Unwmk.**

**1961, June 24 Litho.** *Perf. 11*

**985** A360 60g multicolored .25 .25
**986** A360 1.55z multicolored .35 .25
**987** A360 2.50z multicolored .50 .25
**988** A360 3.40z multicolored .65 .30
**989** A360 4z multicolored 1.25 .60
**990** A360 5.60z multicolored 3.50 1.50
*Nos. 985-990 (6)* 6.50 3.15

Polish ship industry. Sizes (width): 60g, 2.50z, 54mm; 1.55z, 3.40z, 4z, 80mm; 5.60z, 108mm.

Post Horn and Telephone Dial — A361

Post horn and: 60g, Radar screen. 2.50z, Conference emblem, globe.

**1961, June 26**

**991** A361 40g sl, gray & red org .25 .25
**992** A361 60g gray, yel & vio .25 .25
**993** A361 2.50z ol bis, brt bl & vio bl .35 .25
*a.* Souvenir sheet of 3, #991-993 4.75 2.00
*Nos. 991-993 (3)* .85 .75

Conference of Communications Ministers of Communist Countries, Warsaw.

No. 993a sold for 5z.

Seal of Opole, 13th Century — A362

Cement Works, Opole A363

Designs: No. 996, Tombstone of Henry IV and seal, Wroclaw. No. 997, Apartment houses, Wroclaw. No. 998, Seal of Conrad II and Silesian eagle. No. 999, Textile mill, Gorzow. No. 1000, Seal of Prince Barnim I. No. 1001, Seaport, Szczecin. No. 1002, Seal of Princess Elizabeth. No. 1003, Factory, Szczecinek. No. 1004, Seal of Unislaw. No. 1005, Shipyard, Gdansk. No. 1005A, Copernicus Tower, Frombork. No. 1005B, Agricultural College, Kortow.

**1961-62 Wmk. 326 Engr.** *Perf. 11*

**Western Territories**

**994** A362 40g brown, *grysh* .25 .25
**995** A363 40g brown, *grysh* .25 .25
*a.* "Block," #994-995 + label .25 .25
**996** A362 60g violet, *pink* .25 .25
**997** A363 60g violet, *pink* .25 .25
*a.* "Block," #996-997 + label .25 .25
**998** A362 95g green, *bluish* .50 .25
**999** A363 95g green, *bluish* .50 .25
*a.* "Block," #998-999 + label 1.00 .25
**1000** A362 2.50z ol grn, *grnsh* .50 .25
**1001** A363 2.50z ol grn, *grnsh* .50 .25
*a.* "Block," #1000-1001 + label 1.00 .40

**Northern Territories**

**1002** A362 60g vio bl, *bluish* .25 .25
**1003** A363 60g vio bl, *bluish* .25 .25
*a.* "Block," #1002-1003 + label .25 .25
**1004** A362 1.55z brown, *buff* .25 .25
**1005** A363 1.55z brown, *buff* .25 .25
*c.* "Block," #1004-1005 + label .50 .35
**1005A** A362 2.50z slate bl, *grysh* .75 .25
**1005B** A363 2.50z slate bl, *grysh* .75 .25
*d.* "Block," #1005A-1005B + label 1.50 .40
*Nos. 994-1005B (14)* 5.50 3.50

Issued: #994-997, 1000-1001, 7/21; 95g, 2/23/62; #1002-1005B, 7/21/62.

Kayak Race Start and "E" — A364

Designs: 60g, Four-man canoes and "E." 2.50z, Paddle, Polish flag and "E," vert.

**Wmk. 326**

**1961, Aug. 18 Litho.** *Perf. 12½*

**1006** A364 40g bl grn, yel & red .25 .25
**1007** A364 60g multicolored .25 .25
**1008** A364 2.50z multicolored .90 .25
*Nos. 1006-1008 (3)* 1.40 .75

6th European Canoe Championships, Poznan, Aug. 18-20. Exist imperf. Value, set: mint $2.25, used $2.

Maj. Gherman Titov, Star, Globe, Orbit
A365

Dove and Earth
A366

***Perf. 12x12½***

**1961, Aug. 24 Photo. Unwmk.**

**1009** A365 40g pink, blk & red .40 .25
**1010** A366 60g blue & black .40 .25

Manned space flight of Vostok 2, Aug. 6-7, in which Russian Maj. Gherman Titov orbited the earth 17 times.

Insurgents' Monument, St. Ann's Mountain
A367

Design: 1.55z, Cross of Silesian Insurgents.

**Wmk. 326**

**1961, Sept. 15 Litho. *Perf. 12***

**1011** A367 60g gray & emerald .25 .25
**1012** A367 1.55z gray & blue .25 .25

40th anniv. of the third Silesian uprising.

"PKO," Initials of Polish Savings Bank
A368

Initials and: #1014, Bee and clover. #1015, Ant. #1016, Squirrel. 2.50z, Savings bankbook.

**1961, Oct. 2 Wmk. 326 *Perf. 12***

**1013** A368 40g ver, blk & org .25 .25
**1014** A368 60g blue, blk & brt pink .25 .25
**1015** A368 60g bis brn, blk & ocher .25 .25
**1016** A368 60g brt grn, blk & dl red .50 .25
**1017** A368 2.50z car rose, gray & blk 1.50 .50
*Nos. 1013-1017 (5)* 2.75 1.50

Issued to publicize Savings Month.

Mail Cart, by Jan Chelminski — A369

**1961, Oct. 9 Engr. *Perf. 12x12½***

**1018** A369 60g deep green .25 .25
**1019** A369 60g violet brown .25 .25

Polish Postal Museum, 40th anniv; Stamp Day.

Congress Emblem
A370

**1961, Nov. 20 Wmk. 326 *Perf. 12***

**1020** A370 60g black .25 .25

Issued to publicize the Fifth World Congress of Trade Unions, Moscow, Dec. 4-16.

Seal of Kopasyni Family, 1284 — A371

60g, Seal of Bytom, 14th century. 2.50z, Emblem of International Miners Congress, 1958.

**1961, Dec. 4 Litho. *Perf. 11x11½***

**1021** A371 40g multicolored .25 .25
**1022** A371 60g bl, gray bl & vio bl .25 .25
**1023** A371 2.50z yel grn, grn & blk .50 .25
*Nos. 1021-1023 (3)* 1.00 .75

1,000 years of the Polish mining industry.

Child and Syringe — A372

Designs: 60g, Children of three races, horiz. 2.50z, Mother, child and milk bottle.

**1961, Dec. 11 *Perf. 12½x12, 12x12½***

**1024** A372 40g lt blue & blk .25 .25
**1025** A372 60g orange & blk .25 .25
**1026** A372 2.50z brt bl grn & blk .50 .25
*Nos. 1024-1026 (3)* 1.00 .75

15th anniversary of UNICEF.

Emblem
A373

Design: 60g, Map with oil pipe line from Siberia to Central Europe.

**1961, Dec. 12 Wmk. 326 *Perf. 12***

**1027** A373 40g dk red, yel & vio bl .25 .25
**1028** A373 60g vio bl, bl & red .25 .25

15th session of the Council of Mutual Economic Assistance of the Communist States.

Ground Beetle — A374

Black Apollo Butterfly
A375

Insects: 30g, Violet runner. 40g, Alpine longicorn beetle. 50g, Great oak capricorn beetle. 60g, Gold runner. 80g, Stag-horned beetle. 1.35z, Death's-head moth. 1.50z, Tiger-striped swallowtail butterfly. 1.55z, Apollo butterfly. 2.50z, Red ant. 5.60z, Bumble bee.

***Perf. 12½x12***

**1961, Dec. 30 Photo. Unwmk.**

**Insects in Natural Colors**

**1029** A374 20g bister brown .35 .25
**1030** A374 30g pale gray grn .35 .25
**1031** A374 40g pale yellow grn .35 .25
**1032** A374 50g blue green .35 .25
**1033** A374 60g dull rose lilac .35 .25
**1034** A374 80g pale green .70 .25

***Perf. 11½***

**1035** A375 1.15z ultra .70 .25
**1036** A375 1.35z sapphire .70 .25
**1037** A375 1.50z bluish green .70 .25
**1038** A375 1.55z brt purple 1.00 .25
**1039** A375 2.50z brt green 1.75 .85
**1040** A375 5.60z orange brown 8.00 3.50
*Nos. 1029-1040 (12)* 15.30 6.85

Worker with Gun — A376

#1042, Worker with trowel and gun. #1043, Worker with hammer. #1044, Worker at helm. #1045, Worker with dove and banner.

***Perf. 12½x12***

**1962, Jan. 5 Litho. Unwmk.**

**1041** A376 60g red, blk & green .25 .25
**1042** A376 60g red, blk & slate .25 .25
**1043** A376 60g blk & vio bl, *red* .25 .25
**1044** A376 60g blk & bis, *red* .25 .25
**1045** A376 60g blk & gray, *red* .25 .25
*Nos. 1041-1045 (5)* 1.25 1.25

Polish Workers' Party, 20th anniversary.

Women Skiers
A377

Designs: 60g, Long distance skier. 1.50z, Ski jump, vert. 10z, FIS emblem, vert.

**Lithographed and Embossed**

**1962, Feb. 14 *Perf. 12***

**1046** A377 40g gray, red & gray bl .25 .25
*a.* 40g sepia, red & dull blue .35 .25
**1047** A377 60g gray, red & gray bl .25 .25
*a.* 60g sepia, red & dull blue .45 .25
**1048** A377 1.50z gray, red & gray bl .35 .25
*a.* 1.50z gray, lilac & red 1.40 .70
*Nos. 1046-1048 (3)* .85 .75

**Souvenir Sheet**

***Imperf***

**1049** A377 10z gray, red & gray bl 3.25 .85

World Ski Championships at Zakopane (FIS).

No. 1049 contains one stamp with simulated perforation. The sheet sold for 15z.

Each of Nos. 1046-1048 exists in a souvenir sheet of four. Value, set of 3, $200.

Broken Flower and Prison Cloth (Auschwitz) — A378

Majdanek Concentration Camp — A379

Design: 1.50z, Proposed memorial, Treblinka concentration camp.

**Wmk. 326**

**1962, Apr. 3 Engr. *Perf. 11½***

**1050** A378 40g slate blue .25 .25
**1051** A379 60g dark gray .25 .25
**1052** A378 1.50z dark violet .40 .25
*Nos. 1050-1052 (3)* .90 .75

International Resistance Movement Month to commemorate the millions who died in concentration camps, 1940-45.

Bicyclist
A380

2.50z, Cyclists in race. 3.40z, Wheel & arms of Berlin, Prague & Warsaw.

**Unwmk.**

**1962, Apr. 27 Litho. *Perf. 12***

**1053** A380 60g blue & blk .25 .25
**1054** A380 2.50z yellow & blk .35 .25
**1055** A380 3.40z lilac & blk .50 .25
*Nos. 1053-1055 (3)* 1.10 .75

15th Intl. Peace Bicycle Race, Warsaw-Berlin-Prague.

Size of No. 1053, 1055: 36x22mm, No. 1054: 74x22mm.

Lenin in Bialy Dunajec — A381

Designs: 60g, Lenin. 2.50z, Lenin and Cloth Hall, Cathedral, Cracow.

**Engraved and Photogravure**

***Perf. 11x11½***

**1962, May 25 Wmk. 326**

**1056** A381 40g pale grn & Prus grn .25 .25
**1057** A381 60g pink & dp claret .25 .25
**1058** A381 2.50z yellow & dk brn .50 .25
*Nos. 1056-1058 (3)* 1.00 .75

50th anniv. of Lenin's arrival in Poland.

**Famous Poles Type of 1961**

Famous Poles: No. 1059, Adam Mickiewicz. No. 1060, Juliusz Slowacki. No. 1061, Frederic Chopin. No. 1062, Romuald Traugutt. No. 1063, Jaroslaw Dabrowski. No. 1064, Maria Konopnicka.

**1962, June 20 Engr. & Photo.**

**Black Inscriptions and Designs**

**1059** A359 60g dull green .25 .25
**1060** A359 60g brown orange .25 .25

***Perf. 12x12½***

**Litho.**

**1061** A359 60g dull blue .25 .25
**1062** A359 60g brown olive .25 .25
**1063** A359 60g rose lilac .25 .25
**1064** A359 60g blue green .25 .25
*Nos. 1059-1064 (6)* 1.50 1.50

Karol Swierczewski-Walter — A382

*Perf. 11x11½*

**1962, July 14 Engr. Unwmk.**

**1065** A382 60g black .25 .25

15th death anniv. of General Karol Swierczewski-Walter, organizer of the new Polish army.

Crocus — A383

Flowers: No. 1067, Orchid. No. 1068, Monkshood. No. 1069, Gas plant. No. 1070, Water lily. No. 1071, Gentian. No. 1072, Daphne mezereum. No. 1073, Cowbell. No. 1074, Anemone. No. 1075, Globeflower. No. 1076, Snowdrop. No. 1077, Adonis vernalis.

**Unwmk.**

**1962, Aug. 8 Photo.** ***Perf. 12***

**Flowers in Natural Colors**

**1066** A383 60g dull yel & red .75 .25
**1067** A383 60g redsh brn & vio .25 .25
**1068** A383 60g pink & lilac .25 .25
**1069** A383 90g olive & green .25 .25
**1070** A383 90g yel grn & red .25 .25
**1071** A383 90g lt ol grn & red .25 .25
**1072** A383 1.50z gray bl & bl .35 .25
**1073** A383 1.50z yel grn & dk grn .35 .25
**1074** A383 1.50z Prus grn & dk bl .35 .25
**1075** A383 2.50z gray grn & dk bl .65 .35
**1076** A383 2.50z dk bl grn & dk bl .90 .35
**1077** A383 2.50z gray bl & grn 1.75 1.25
*Nos. 1066-1077 (12)* 6.35 4.20

The Poisoned Well by Jacek Malczewski — A384

**1962, Aug. 15 Engr. Wmk. 326**

**1078** A384 60g black, *buff* .50 .25

Issued in sheets of 40 with alternating label for FIP Day (Federation Internationale de Philatelie), Sept. 1. Also issued in miniature sheet of 4. Value: mint $30, used $22.50.

Pole Vault — A385

Designs: 60g, Relay race. 90g, Javelin. 1z, Hurdles. 1.50z, High jump. 1.55z, Discus. 2.50z, 100m. dash. 3.40z, Hammer throw.

**Unwmk.**

**1962, Sept. 12 Litho.** ***Perf. 11***

**1079** A385 40g multicolored .25 .25
**1080** A385 60g multicolored .25 .25
**1081** A385 90g multicolored .25 .25
**1082** A385 1z multicolored .25 .25
**1083** A385 1.50z multicolored .25 .25
**1084** A385 1.55z multicolored .25 .25
**1085** A385 2.50z multicolored .45 .25
**1086** A385 3.40z multicolored .75 .25
*Nos. 1079-1086 (8)* 2.70 2.00

7th European Athletic Championships, Belgrade, Sept. 12-16.
Exist imperf. Value, set: mint $3.50, used $2.25.

Anopheles Mosquito A386

Designs: 1.50z, Malaria blood cells. 2.50z, Cinchona flowers. 3z, Anopheles mosquito.

**1962, Oct. 1 Wmk. 326** ***Perf. 13x12***

**1087** A386 60g ol blk, dk brn & bl grn .25 .25
**1088** A386 1.50z red, gray & brt vio .25 .25
**1089** A386 2.50z multicolored .90 .30
*Nos. 1087-1089 (3)* 1.40 .80

**Miniature Sheet**

***Imperf***

**1090** A386 3z multicolored 1.25 .70

WHO drive to eradicate malaria.

Pavel R. Popovich and Andrian G. Nikolayev — A387

Design: 2.50z, Two stars in orbit around earth. 10z, Two stars in orbit.

**1962, Oct. 6** ***Perf. 12½x12***

**1091** A387 60g violet, blk & citron .30 .25
**1092** A387 2.50z Prus bl, blk & red .30 .25

**Souvenir Sheet**

***Perf. 12x11***

**1093** A387 10z sl bl, blk & red 2.40 1.40

1st Russian group space flight, Vostoks III and IV, Aug. 11-15, 1962.

Woman Mailing Letter Warsaw — A388

**1962, Oct. 9 Engr.** ***Perf. 12½x12***

**1094** A388 60g black .25 .25
**1095** A388 2.50z red brown .45 .25

Stamp Day. The design is from the painting "A Moment of Decision," by Aleksander Kaminski.

Mazovian Princes' Mansion, A389

**1962, Oct. 13 Litho.**

**1096** A389 60g red & black .25 .25

25th anniversary of the founding of the Polish Democratic Party.

Cruiser "Aurora" — A390

**Photo. & Engr.**

**1962, Nov. 3** ***Perf. 11***

**1097** A390 60g red & dk blue .25 .25

Russian October revolution, 45th anniv.

Janusz Korczak by K. Dunikowski A391

King on Horseback A392

Illustrations from King Matthew books: 90g, King giving watch to Island girl. 1z, King handcuffed and soldier with sword. 2.50z, King with dead bird. 5.60z, King ice skating in moonlight.

***Perf. 13x12***

**1962, Nov. 12 Unwmk. Litho.**

**1098** A391 40g brn, bis & sep .25 .25
**1099** A392 60g multicolored .25 .25
**1100** A392 90g multicolored .40 .25
**1101** A392 1z multicolored .40 .25
**1102** A392 2.50z brn, yel & brt grn .70 .45
**1103** A392 5.60z brn, dk bl & grn 1.75 .75
*Nos. 1098-1103 (6)* 3.75 2.20

20th anniversary of the death of Dr. Janusz Korczak (Henryk Goldszmit), physician, pedagogue and writer, in the Treblinka concentration camp, Aug. 5, 1942.

View of Old Warsaw — A393

**1962, Nov. 26 Wmk. 326** ***Perf. 11***

**1104** A393 3.40z multicolored .55 .30
*a.* Sheet of 4 5.00 3.00

5th Trade Union Cong., Warsaw, 11/26-12/1.

Orphan Mary and the Dwarf — A394

Various Scenes from "Orphan Mary and the Dwarfs" by Maria Konopnicka.

***Perf. 13x12***

**1962, Dec. 31 Unwmk. Litho.**

**1105** A394 40g multicolored .35 .25
**1106** A394 60g multicolored 2.00 .35
**1107** A394 1.50z multicolored .75 .25
**1108** A394 1.55z multicolored .75 .25
**1109** A394 2.50z multicolored .75 .30
**1110** A394 3.40z multicolored 2.75 1.40
*Nos. 1105-1110 (6)* 7.35 2.80

120th anniversary of the birth of Maria Konopnicka, poet and fairy tale writer.

Romuald Traugutt A395

***Perf. 11½x11***

**1963, Jan. 31 Wmk. 326**

**1111** A395 60g aqua, blk & pale pink .25 .25

Centenary of the 1863 insurrection and to honor its leader, Romuald Traugutt.

Tractor and Wheat A396

Designs: 60g, Man reaping and millet. 2.50z, Combine and rice.

***Perf. 12x12½***

**1963, Feb. 25 Litho. Wmk. 326**

**1112** A396 40g gray, bl, blk & ocher .25 .25
**1113** A396 60g brn red, blk, brn & grn .50 .25
**1114** A396 2.50z yel, buff, blk & grn .70 .25
*Nos. 1112-1114 (3)* 1.45 .75

FAO "Freedom from Hunger" campaign.

Cocker Spaniel — A397

30g, Polish sheep dog. 40g, Boxer. 50g, Airedale terrier, vert. 60g, French bulldog, vert. 1z, Poodle, vert. 2.50z, Hunting dog. 3.40z, Sheep dog, vert. 6.50z, Great Dane.

**1963, Mar. 25 Unwmk.** ***Perf. 12½***

**1115** A397 20g lil, blk & org brn .25 .25
**1116** A397 30g rose car & blk .25 .25
**1117** A397 40g lil, blk & yel grn .25 .25
**1118** A397 50g multicolored .25 .25
**1119** A397 60g lt blue & blk .30 .25
**1120** A397 1z yel grn & blk .50 .25
**1121** A397 2.50z org, blk & brn 1.00 .35
**1122** A397 3.40z red org & blk 2.75 1.00
**1123** A397 6.50z brt yel & blk 6.50 2.40
*Nos. 1115-1123 (9)* 12.05 5.25

Egyptian Ship — A398

Ancient Ships: 10g, Phoenician merchant ship. 20g, Greek trireme. 30g, 3rd century merchantman. 40g, Scandinavian "Gokstad." 60g, Frisian "Kogge." 1z. 14th century "Holk." 1.15z, 15th century "Caraca."

**Photo. (Background) & Engr.**

**1963, Apr. 5** ***Perf. 11½***

**1124** A398 5g brown, *tan* .25 .25
**1125** A398 10g green, *gray grn* .25 .25
**1126** A398 20g ultra, *gray* .25 .25
**1127** A398 30g black, *gray ol* .25 .25
**1128** A398 40g lt bl, *bluish* .25 .25
**1129** A398 60g claret, *gray* .25 .25
**1130** A398 1z black, *bl* .25 .25
**1131** A398 1.15z grn, *pale rose* .25 .25
*Nos. 1124-1131 (8)* 2.00 2.00

See Nos. 1206-1213, 1299-1306.

Fighter and Ruins of Warsaw Ghetto — A399

***Perf. 11½x11***

**1963, Apr. 19** **Wmk. 326**

**1132** A399 2.50z gray brn & gray .50 .25

Warsaw Ghetto Uprising, 20th anniv.

Centenary Emblem — A400

***Perf. 12½x12***

**1963, May 8** **Litho.** **Unwmk.**

**1133** A400 2.50z blue, yel & red .75 .25

Intl. Red Cross, cent. Every other stamp in sheet inverted.

Sand Lizard A401

40g, Smooth snake. 50g, European pond turtle. 60g, Grass snake. 90g, Slow worm. 1.15z, European tree frog. 1.35z, Alpine newt. 1.50z, Crested newt. 1.55z, Green toad. 2.50z, Firebellied toad. 3z, Fire salamander. 3.40z, Natterjack.

***Perf. 11½***

**1963, June 1** **Unwmk.** **Photo.**

**Reptiles and Amphibians in Natural Colors**

**1134** A401 30g grnsh gray & blk .25 .25
**1135** A401 40g gray ol & blk .25 .25
**1136** A401 50g bis brn & blk .25 .25
**1137** A401 60g tan & blk .25 .25
**1138** A401 90g gray grn & blk .25 .25
**1139** A401 1.15z gray & blk .25 .25
**1140** A401 1.35z gray bl & dk bl .35 .25
**1141** A401 1.50z bluish grn & blk .50 .25
**1142** A401 1.55z bluish gray & blk .50 .25
**1143** A401 2.50z gray vio & blk .50 .25
**1144** A401 3z gray grn & blk .85 .35
**1145** A401 3.40z gray & blk 2.40 1.25
*Nos. 1134-1145 (12)* 6.60 4.10

Foil, Saber, Sword and Helmet A402

Designs: 40g, Fencers and knights in armor. 60g, Fencers and dragoons. 1.15z, Contemporary and 18th cent. fencers. 1.55z, Fencers and old houses, Gdansk. 6.50z, Arms of Gdansk, vert.

***Perf. 12x12½, 12½x12***

**1963, June 29** **Litho.** **Unwmk.**

**1146** A402 20g brown & orange .25 .25
**1147** A402 40g dk blue & blue .25 .25
**1148** A402 60g red & dp org .25 .25
**1149** A402 1.15z green & emer .25 .25
**1150** A402 1.55z violet & lilac .35 .25
**1151** A402 6.50z yel brn, mar & yel 1.10 .40
*Nos. 1146-1151 (6)* 2.45 1.65

28th World Fencing Championships, Gdansk, July 15-28. A souvenir sheet exists containing one each of Nos. 1147-1150. Value: mint $40, used $32.50.

**Famous Poles Type of 1961**

No. 1152, Ludwik Warynski. No. 1153, Ludwik Krzywicki. No. 1154, Marie Sklodowska Curie. No. 1155, Karol Swierczewski-Walter.

***Perf. 12x12½***

**1963, July 20** **Wmk. 326**

**Black Inscriptions and Designs**

**1152** A359 60g red brown .25 .25
**1153** A359 60g gray brown .25 .25
**1154** A359 60g blue .30 .25
**1155** A359 60g green .25 .25
*Nos. 1152-1155 (4)* 1.05 1.00

Valeri Bykovski — A403

Designs: 60g, Valentina Tereshkova. 6.50z, Rockets "Falcon" and "Mew" and globe.

**Unwmk.**

**1963, Aug. 26** **Litho.** ***Perf. 11***

**1156** A403 40g ultra, emer & blk .25 .25
**1157** A403 60g green, ultra & blk .25 .25
**1158** A403 6.50z multicolored .85 .35
*Nos. 1156-1158 (3)* 1.35 .85

Space flights of Valeri Bykovski June 14-19, and Valentina Tereshkova, first woman cosmonaut, June 16-19, 1963.

For overprints see Nos. 1175-1177.

Basketball A404

Designs: Various positions of ball, hands and players. 10z, Town Hall, People's Hall and Arms of Wroclaw.

**1963, Sept. 16** **Unwmk.** ***Perf. 11½***

**1159** A404 40g multicolored .25 .25
**1160** A404 50g fawn, grn & blk .25 .25
**1161** A404 60g red, lt grn & blk .25 .25
**1162** A404 90g multicolored .25 .25
**1163** A404 2.50z multicolored .25 .25
**1164** A404 5.60z multicolored 1.00 .25
*Nos. 1159-1164 (6)* 2.25 1.50

**Souvenir Sheet**

***Imperf***

**1165** A404 10z multicolored 2.00 1.10

13th European Men's Basketball Championship, Wroclaw, Oct. 4-13. No. 1165 contains one stamp; inscription on margin also commemorates the simultaneous European Sports Stamp Exhibition. Sheet sold for 15z.

Eagle and Ground-to-Air Missile — A405

Eagle and: 40g, Destroyer. 60g, Jet fighter plane. 1.15z, Radar. 1.35z, Tank. 1.55z, Self-propelled rocket launcher. 2.50z, Amphibious troop carrier. 3z, Swords and medieval and modern soldiers.

**1963, Oct. 1** ***Perf. 12x12½***

**1166** A405 20g multicolored .25 .25
**1167** A405 40g violet, grn & red .25 .25
**1168** A405 60g multicolored .25 .25
**1169** A405 1.15z multicolored .25 .25
**1170** A405 1.35z multicolored .25 .25
**1171** A405 1.55z multicolored .25 .25
**1172** A405 2.50z multicolored .35 .25
**1173** A405 3z multicolored .80 .35
*Nos. 1166-1173 (8)* 2.65 2.10

Polish People's Army, 20th anniversary.

"Love Letter" by Wladyslaw Czachórski — A406

***Perf. 11½***

**1963, Oct. 9** **Unwmk.** **Engr.**

**1174** A406 60g dark red brown .40 .25

Issued for Stamp Day.

**Nos. 1156-1158 Overprinted "23-28 X. 1963" and name of astronaut in Red or Black**

**1963** **Litho.** ***Perf. 11***

**1175** A403 40g multi (R) .40 .25
**1176** A403 60g multi (Blk) .40 .25
**1177** A403 6.50z multi (Blk) 2.00 .50
*Nos. 1175-1177 (3)* 2.80 1.00

Visit of Valentina Tereshkova and Valeri Bykovski to Poland, Oct. 23-28. The overprints are: 40g, W. F. Bykowski / w Polsce; 60g, W. W. Tierieszkowa / w Polsce; 6.50z, W. F. BYKOWSKI I W. W. TIERIESZKOWA W POLSCE.

Konstantin E. Tsiolkovsky's Rocket and Rocket Speed Formula — A407

American and Russian Spacecrafts: 40g, Sputnik 1. 50g, Explorer 1. 60g, Lunik 2. 1z, Lunik 3. 1.50z, Vostok 1. 1.55z, Friendship 7. 2.50z, Vostoks 3 & 4. 5.60z, Mariner 2. 6.50z, Mars 1.

***Perf. 12½x12***

**1963, Nov. 11** **Litho.** **Unwmk.**

**Black Inscriptions**

**1178** A407 30g dull bl grn & gray .25 .25
**1179** A407 40g lt ol grn & gray .25 .25
**1180** A407 50g violet bl & gray .25 .25
**1181** A407 60g brn org & gray .25 .25
**1182** A407 1z brt grn & gray .25 .25
**1183** A407 1.50z org red & gray .25 .25
**1184** A407 1.55z blue & gray .25 .25
**1185** A407 2.50z lilac & gray .25 .25
**1186** A407 5.60z brt yel grn & gray .40 .25
**1187** A407 6.50z grnsh bl & gray .80 .25
*Nos. 1178-1187 (10)* 3.20 2.50

Conquest of space. A souvenir sheet containing 2 each of Nos. 1186-1187 exists with top and bottom perfs, value: mint $60, used $40; and with bottom perfs only, value: mint $125, used $75.

Arab Stallion "Comet" — A408

Horses from Mazury Region — A409

Horses: 30g, Tarpans (wild horses). 40g, Horse from Sokolka. 50g, Arab mares and foals, horiz. 90g, Steeplechasers, horiz. 1.55z, Arab stallion "Witez II." 2.50z, Head of Arab horse, facing right. 4z, Mixed breeds, horiz. 6.50z, Head of Arab horse, facing left.

***Perf. 11½x11 (A408); 12½x12, 12***

**1963, Dec. 30** **Photo.**

**1188** A408 20g black, yel & car .25 .25
**1189** A408 30g multicolored .25 .25
**1190** A408 40g multicolored .25 .25

**Sizes: 75x26mm (50g, 90g, 4z); 28x38mm (60g, 1.55z, 2.50z, 6.50z)**

**1191** A409 50g multicolored .25 .25
**1192** A409 60g multicolored .25 .25
**1193** A409 90g multicolored .35 .25
**1194** A409 1.55z multicolored .45 .25
**1195** A409 2.50z multicolored .95 .30
**1196** A409 4z multicolored 2.10 .75
**1197** A409 6.50z yel, dl bl & blk 3.25 1.50
*Nos. 1188-1197 (10)* 8.35 4.30

Issued to publicize Polish horse breeding.

Ice Hockey A410

Sports: 30g, Slalom. 40g, Skiing. 60g, Speed skating. 1z, Ski jump. 2.50z, Tobogganing. 5.60z, Cross-country skiing. 6.50z, Figure skating pair.

**1964, Jan. 25** **Litho.** ***Perf. 12x12½***

**1198** A410 20g multicolored .25 .25
**1199** A410 30g multicolored .25 .25
**1200** A410 40g multicolored .25 .25
**1201** A410 60g multicolored .25 .25
**1202** A410 1z multicolored .35 .25
**1203** A410 2.50z multicolored .35 .25
**1204** A410 5.60z multicolored .65 .25
**1205** A410 6.50z multicolored 1.25 .60
*Nos. 1198-1205 (8)* 3.60 2.35

9th Winter Olympic Games, Innsbruck, Jan. 29-Feb. 9. A souvenir sheet contains 2 each of Nos. 1203, 1205. Value $35.

**Ship Type of 1963**

Sailing Ships: 1.35z, Caravel of Columbus, vert. 1.50z, Galleon. 1.55z, Polish warship, 1627, vert. 2z, Dutch merchant ship, vert. 2.10z, Line ship. 2.50z, Frigate. 3z, 19th century merchantman. 3.40z, "Dar Pomorza," 20th century school ship, vert.

**1964, Mar. 19** **Engr.** ***Perf. 12½***

**1206** A398 1.35z ultra .25 .25
**1207** A398 1.50z claret .25 .25
**1208** A398 1.55z black .25 .25
**1209** A398 2z violet .25 .25
**1210** A398 2.10z green .25 .25
**1211** A398 2.50z carmine rose .25 .25

**1212** A398 3z olive green .40 .25
**1213** A398 3.40z brown .60 .25
*Nos. 1206-1213 (8)* 2.50 2.00

European Cat — A411

40g, 60g, 1.55z, 2.50z, 6.50z, Various European cats. 50g, Siamese cat. 90g, 1.35z, 3.40z, Various Persian cats. 60g, 90g, 1.35z, 1.55z horiz.

**1964, Apr. 30 Litho. *Perf. 12½***
**Cats in Natural Colors; Black Inscriptions**

**1216** A411 30g yellow .25 .25
**1217** A411 40g orange .25 .25
**1218** A411 50g yellow .25 .25
**1219** A411 60g brt green .25 .25
**1220** A411 90g lt brown .35 .25
**1221** A411 1.35z emerald .40 .25
**1222** A411 1.55z violet blue .40 .25
**1223** A411 2.50z lilac .50 .25
**1224** A411 3.40z rose 2.25 .60
**1225** A411 6.50z violet 3.50 1.75
*Nos. 1216-1225 (10)* 8.40 4.35

King Casimir III, the Great — A412

Designs: No. 1227, Hugo Kollataj. No. 1228, Jan Dlugosz. No. 1229, Nicolaus Copernicus. 2.50z, King Wladyslaw II Jagiello and Queen Jadwiga.

**1964, May 5 Engr. *Perf. 11x11½***
**Size: 22x35mm**

**1226** A412 40g dull claret .25 .25
**1227** A412 40g green .25 .25
**1228** A412 60g violet .25 .25
**1229** A412 60g dark blue .50 .25

**Size: 35½x37mm**

**1230** A412 2.50z gray brown .50 .25
*Nos. 1226-1230 (5)* 1.75 1.25

Jagiellonian University, Cracow, 600th anniv.

Lapwing A413

Waterfowl: 40g, White-spotted bluethroat. 50g, Black-tailed godwit. 60g, Osprey. 90g, Gray heron. 1.35z, Little gull. 1.55z, Shoveler. 5.60z, Arctic loon. 6.50z, Great crested grebe.

***Perf. 11½***
**1964, June 5 Unwmk. Photo.**
**Birds in Natural Colors; Black Inscriptions**
**Size: 34x34mm**

**1231** A413 30g chalky blue .25 .25
**1232** A413 40g bister .25 .25
**1233** A413 50g brt yellow grn .25 .25

***Perf. 11½x11***
**Size: 34x48mm**

**1234** A413 60g blue .25 .25
**1235** A413 90g lemon .25 .25
**1236** A413 1.35z green .35 .25

***Perf. 11½***
**Size: 34x34mm**

**1237** A413 1.55z olive .35 .25
**1238** A413 5.60z blue green .85 .25
**1239** A413 6.50z brt green 1.40 .60
*Nos. 1231-1239 (9)* 4.20 2.60

Hands Holding Red Flag — A414

Designs: No. 1241, Red and white ribbon around hammer. No. 1242, Hammer and rye. No. 1243, Brick wall under construction and red flag.

**1964, June 15 Litho. *Perf. 11***

**1240** A414 60g ol bis, red, blk & pink .25 .25
**1241** A414 60g red, gray & black .25 .25
**1242** A414 60g magenta, blk & yel .25 .25
**1243** A414 60g gray, red, sal & blk .25 .25
*Nos. 1240-1243 (4)* 1.00 1.00

4th congress of the Polish United Workers Party.

Symbols of Peasant-Worker Alliance — A415

Atom Symbol and Book — A416

Shipyard, Gdansk — A417

Designs: No. 1245, Stylized oak. No. 1247, Factory and cogwheel. No. 1248, Tractor and grain. No. 1249, Pen, brush, mask and ornament. No. 1251, Lenin Metal Works, Nowa Huta. No. 1252, Cement factory, Chelm. No. 1253, Power Station, Turoszow. No. 1254, Oil refinery, Plock. No. 1255, Sulphur mine, Tarnobrzeg.

**1964 Litho. *Perf. 12x12½***

**1244** A415 60g red, org & blk .25 .25
**1245** A415 60g grn, red, ocher, bl & blk .25 .25

**Photo.**
***Perf. 11***

**1246** A416 60g gray & dp vio bl .25 .25
**1247** A416 60g brt blue & blk .25 .25
**1248** A416 60g emerald & blk .25 .25
**1249** A416 60g orange & red .25 .25

**Photogravure and Engraved**

**1250** A417 60g dl bl grn & ultra .25 .25
**1251** A417 60g brt pink & pur .25 .25
**1252** A417 60g gray & gray brn .25 .25
**1253** A417 60g grn & slate grn .25 .25
**1254** A417 60g salmon & claret .25 .25
**1255** A417 60g citron & sepia .25 .25
*Nos. 1244-1255 (12)* 3.00 3.00

Polish People's Republic, 20 anniv.

Warsaw Fighters, 1944 — A418

**1964, Aug. 1 Litho. *Perf. 12½x12***

**1256** A418 60g multicolored .25 .25

20th anniv. of the Warsaw insurrection against German occupation.

Long Jump — A419

Women's High Jump — A420

Olympic Sports — A421

Sport: 40g, Rowing (single). 60g, Weight lifting. 90g, Relay race (square). 1z, Boxing (square). 2.50z, Soccer (square). 6.50z, Diving.

**Unwmk.**
**1964, Aug. 17 Litho. *Perf. 11***

**1257** A419 20g multicolored .25 .25
**1258** A419 40g grnsh bl, bl & yel .25 .25
**1259** A419 60g vio bl, red & rose lil .25 .25
**1260** A419 90g dk brown, red & yel .25 .25
**1261** A419 1z dk violet, lil & gray .25 .25
**1262** A419 2.50z multicolored .30 .25
**1263** A420 5.60z multicolored .75 .30
**1264** A420 6.50z multicolored 1.50 .50
*Nos. 1257-1264 (8)* 3.80 2.30

**Souvenir Sheet**
***Imperf***

**1265** A421 Sheet of 4 3.00 1.60
*a.* 2.50z Sharpshooting .40 .25
*b.* 2.50z Canoeing .40 .25
*c.* 5z Fencing .40 .25
*d.* 5z Basketball .40 .25

18th Olympic Games, Tokyo, Oct. 10-25. Size of stamps in No. 1265: 24x24mm. A souvenir sheet containing 2 each of Nos. 1263-1264 with black marginal inscription exists. Value: mint $42.50, used $32.50.

Warsaw Mermaid and Stars — A422

**1964, Sept. 7 *Perf. 12½x12***

**1266** A422 2.50z violet & black .55 .25

15th Astronautical Congress, Warsaw, Sept. 7-12.

Stefan Zeromski by Monika Zeromska — A423

**1964, Sept. 21 Photo. *Perf. 12½***

**1267** A423 60g olive gray .25 .25

Stefan Zeromski (1864-1925), writer.

Gun and Hand Holding Hammer — A424

**1964, Sept. 21 Litho. *Perf. 11***

**1268** A424 60g brt grn, blk & red .35 .25

Union of Fighters for Freedom and Democracy Congress, Warsaw, 9/24-26.

Globe and Red Flag — A425

**1964, Sept. 28 Photo. *Perf. 12½***

**1269** A425 60g black & red org .35 .25

First Socialist International, centenary.



Stagecoach by Jozef Brodowski — A426

**1964, Oct. 9 Engr. *Perf. 11½***

| | | | | |
|---|---|---|---|---|
| **1270** | A426 | 60g green | .25 | .25 |
| **1271** | A426 | 60g lt brown | .25 | .25 |

Issued for Stamp Day.

Eleanor Roosevelt (1884-1962) — A427

**1964, Oct. 10 *Perf. 12½***

| | | | | |
|---|---|---|---|---|
| **1272** | A427 | 2.50z black | .45 | .25 |

Proposed Monument for Defenders of Westerplatte, 1939 — A428

Polish Soldiers Crossing Oder River, 1945 A429

Designs: No. 1274, Virtuti Military Cross. No. 1275, Nike, proposed monument for the martyrs of Bydgoszcz (woman with sword and torch). No. 1277, Battle of Studzianki, 1944.

***Perf. 12x11, 11x12***

**1964, Nov. 16 Engr. Unwmk.**

| | | | | |
|---|---|---|---|---|
| **1273** | A428 | 40g gray violet | .25 | .25 |
| **1274** | A428 | 40g slate | .25 | .25 |
| **1275** | A428 | 60g dark blue | .25 | .25 |
| **1276** | A429 | 60g dark blue grn | .25 | .25 |
| **1277** | A429 | 60g grnsh black | .25 | .25 |
| | | *Nos. 1273-1277 (5)* | 1.25 | 1.25 |

Struggle and martyrdom of the Polish people, 1939-45. The vertical stamps are printed in sheets of 56 stamps (8x7) with 7 labels in each outside vertical row. The horizontal stamps are printed in sheets of 50 stamps (5x10) with 10 labels in each outside vertical row. See Nos. 1366-1368.

Souvenir Sheet

Col. Vladimir M. Komarov, Boris B. Yegorov and Dr. Konstantin Feoktistov — A430

**1964, Nov. 21 Litho. *Perf. 11½x11***

| | | | | |
|---|---|---|---|---|
| **1278** | A430 | Sheet of 3 | 1.40 | .85 |
| *a.* | | 60g red & black (Komarov) | .25 | .25 |
| *b.* | | 60g brt grn & blk (Feoktistov) | .25 | .25 |
| *c.* | | 60g ultra & blk (Yegorov) | .25 | .25 |

Russian three-manned space flight in space ship Voskhod, Oct. 12-13, 1964. Size of stamps: 27x36mm.

Cyclamen A431

Garden Flowers: 30g, Freesia. 40g, Monique rose. 50g, Peony. 60g, Royal lily. 90g, Oriental poppy. 1.35z, Tulip. 1.50z, Narcissus. 1.55z, Begonia. 2.50z, Carnation. 3.40z, Iris. 5.60z, Camellia.

**1964, Nov. 30 Photo. *Perf. 11***

**Size: 35½x35½mm**

**Flowers in Natural Colors**

| | | | | |
|---|---|---|---|---|
| **1279** | A431 | 20g violet | .25 | .25 |
| **1280** | A431 | 30g deep lilac | .25 | .25 |
| **1281** | A431 | 40g blue | .25 | .25 |
| **1282** | A431 | 50g violet blue | .25 | .25 |
| **1283** | A431 | 60g lilac | .25 | .25 |
| **1284** | A431 | 90g deep green | .25 | .25 |

**Size: 26x37½mm**

| | | | | |
|---|---|---|---|---|
| **1285** | A431 | 1.35z dark blue | .25 | .25 |
| **1286** | A431 | 1.50z deep carmine | .50 | .30 |
| **1287** | A431 | 1.55z green | .25 | .25 |
| **1288** | A431 | 2.50z ultra | .45 | .25 |
| **1289** | A431 | 3.40z redsh brown | .85 | .35 |
| **1290** | A431 | 5.60z olive gray | 2.00 | .90 |
| | | *Nos. 1279-1290 (12)* | 5.80 | 3.80 |

Future Interplanetary Spacecraft A432

Designs: 30g, Launching of Russian rocket. 40g, Dog Laika and launching tower. 60g, Lunik 3 photographing far side of the Moon. 1.55z, Satellite exploring the ionosphere. 2.50z, Satellite "Elektron 2" exploring radiation belt. 5.60z, "Mars 1" between Mars and Earth.

***Perf. 12½x12***

**1964, Dec. 30 Litho. Unwmk.**

| | | | | |
|---|---|---|---|---|
| **1291** | A432 | 20g multicolored | .25 | .25 |
| **1292** | A432 | 30g multicolored | .25 | .25 |
| **1293** | A432 | 40g ol grn, blk & bl | .25 | .25 |
| **1294** | A432 | 60g dk bl, blk & dk red | .25 | .25 |
| **1295** | A432 | 1.55z gray & multi | .25 | .25 |
| **1296** | A432 | 2.50z multicolored | .35 | .25 |
| **1297** | A432 | 5.60z multicolored | .75 | .35 |
| | | *Nos. 1291-1297,B108 (8)* | 3.60 | 2.30 |

Issued to publicize space research.

Warsaw Mermaid, Ruins and New Buildings A433

**1965, Jan. 15 Engr. *Perf. 11x11½***

| | | | | |
|---|---|---|---|---|
| **1298** | A433 | 60g slate green | .25 | .25 |

Liberation of Warsaw, 20th anniversary.

**Ship Type of 1963**

Designs as before.

**1965, Jan. 25 Engr. *Perf. 12½***

| | | | | |
|---|---|---|---|---|
| **1299** | A398 | 5g dark brown | .25 | .25 |
| **1300** | A398 | 10g slate green | .25 | .25 |
| **1301** | A398 | 20g slate blue | .25 | .25 |
| **1302** | A398 | 30g gray olive | .25 | .25 |
| **1303** | A398 | 40g dark blue | .25 | .25 |
| **1304** | A398 | 60g claret | .25 | .25 |
| **1305** | A398 | 1z red brown | .25 | .25 |
| **1306** | A398 | 1.15z dk red brown | .30 | .25 |
| | | *Nos. 1299-1306 (8)* | 2.05 | 2.00 |

Edaphosaurus — A434

Dinosaurs: 30g, Cryptocleidus, vert. 40g, Brontosaurus. 60g, Mesosaurus, vert. 90g, Stegosaurus. 1.15z, Brachiosaurus, vert. 1.35z, Styracosaurus. 3.40z, Corythosaurus, vert. 5.60z, Rhamphorhynchus, vert. 6.50z, Tyrannosaurus.

**1965, Mar. 5 Litho. *Perf. 12½***

| | | | | |
|---|---|---|---|---|
| **1307** | A434 | 20g multicolored | .25 | .25 |
| **1308** | A434 | 30g multicolored | .25 | .25 |
| **1309** | A434 | 40g multicolored | .25 | .25 |
| **1310** | A434 | 60g multicolored | .25 | .25 |
| **1311** | A434 | 90g multicolored | .25 | .25 |
| **1312** | A434 | 1.15z multicolored | .75 | .25 |
| **1313** | A434 | 1.35z multicolored | .75 | .25 |
| **1314** | A434 | 3.40z multicolored | .75 | .25 |
| **1315** | A434 | 5.60z multicolored | 1.60 | .70 |
| **1316** | A434 | 6.50z multicolored | 2.50 | 1.40 |
| | | *Nos. 1307-1316 (10)* | 7.60 | 4.10 |

See Nos. 1395-1403.

Symbolic Wax Seal — A435

Russian and Polish Flags, Oil Refinery-Chemical Plant, Plock — A436

**1965, Apr. 21 *Perf. 12½x12, 12½***

| | | | | |
|---|---|---|---|---|
| **1317** | A435 | 60g multicolored | .25 | .25 |
| **1318** | A436 | 60g multicolored | .25 | .25 |

20th anniversary of the signing of the Polish-Soviet treaty of friendship, mutual assistance and postwar cooperation.

Polish Eagle and Town Coats of Arms A437

**1965, May 8 Engr. *Perf. 11½***

| | | | | |
|---|---|---|---|---|
| **1319** | A437 | 60g carmine rose | .35 | .25 |

20th anniversary of regaining the Western and Northern Territories.

Dove A438

**1965, May 8 Litho. *Perf. 12x12½***

| | | | | |
|---|---|---|---|---|
| **1320** | A438 | 60g red & black | .35 | .25 |

Victory over Fascism, 20th anniversary.

ITU Emblem — A439

***Perf. 12½x12***

**1965, May 17 Litho. Unwmk.**

| | | | | |
|---|---|---|---|---|
| **1321** | A439 | 2.50z brt bl, lil, yel & blk | .65 | .25 |

ITU, cent.

"The People's Friend" and Clover — A440

Factory and Rye A441

**1965, June 5 *Perf. 11***

| | | | | |
|---|---|---|---|---|
| **1322** | A440 | 40g multicolored | .25 | .25 |
| **1323** | A441 | 60g multicolored | .25 | .25 |

"Popular Movement" in Poland, 70th anniv.

Finn Class Yachts — A442

Yachts: 30g, Dragon class. 40g, 5.5-m. class. 50g, Group of Finn class. 60g, V-class. 1.35z, Group of Cadet class. 4z, Group of Star class. 5.60z, Two Flying Dutchmen. 6.50z, Two Amethyst class. 15z, Finn class race. (30g, 40g, 60g, 5.60z vertical.)

**1965, June 14 Litho. *Perf. 12½***

| | | | | |
|---|---|---|---|---|
| **1324** | A442 | 30g multicolored | .25 | .25 |
| **1325** | A442 | 40g multicolored | .25 | .25 |
| **1326** | A442 | 50g multicolored | .25 | .25 |
| **1327** | A442 | 60g multicolored | .25 | .25 |
| **1328** | A442 | 1.35z multicolored | .25 | .25 |
| **1329** | A442 | 4z multicolored | .45 | .25 |
| **1330** | A442 | 5.60z multicolored | .85 | .35 |
| **1331** | A442 | 6.50z multicolored | 1.40 | .30 |
| | | *Nos. 1324-1331 (8)* | 3.95 | 2.15 |

**Miniature Sheet**

***Perf. 11***

| | | | | |
|---|---|---|---|---|
| **1332** | A442 | 15z multicolored | 1.75 | .85 |

World Championships of Finn Class Yachts, Gdynia, July 22-29. No. 1332 contains one stamp 48x22mm.

Marx and Lenin — A443

**Photogravure and Engraved**

**1965, June 14 *Perf. 11½x11***

| | | | | |
|---|---|---|---|---|
| **1333** | A443 | 60g black, *ver* | .35 | .25 |

6th Conference of Ministers of Post of Communist Countries, Peking, June 21-July 15.

Warsaw's Coat of Arms, 17th Cent. — A444

Old Town Hall, 18th Cent. — A445

Designs: 10g, Artifacts, 13th century. 20g, Tombstone of last Duke of Mazovia. 60g, Barbican, Gothic-Renaissance castle. 1.50z,

Arsenal, 19th century. 1.55z, National Theater. 2.50z, Staszic Palace. 3.40z, Woman with sword from Heroes' Memorial and Warsaw Mermaid seal.

***Perf. 11x11½, 11½x11, 12x12½, 12½x12***

**1965, July 21 Engr. Unwmk.**

**1334** A444 5g carmine rose .25 .25
**1335** A444 10g green .25 .25
**1336** A445 20g violet blue .25 .25
**1337** A445 40g brown .25 .25
**1338** A445 60g orange .25 .25
**1339** A445 1.50z black .25 .25
**1340** A445 1.55z gray blue .25 .25
**1341** A445 2.50z lilac .25 .25

***Perf. 11½***

**Photogravure and Engraved**

**1342** A444 3.40z citron & blk 1.10 .50
*Nos. 1334-1342 (9)* 3.10 2.50

700th anniversary of Warsaw.

No. 1342 is perforated all around, with lower right quarter perforated to form a 21x26mm stamp within a stamp. It was issued in sheets of 25 (5x5).

For surcharges see Nos. 1919-1926.

IQSY Emblem A446

Designs: 2.50z, Radio telescope dish, Torun. 3.40z, Solar system.

**1965, Aug. 9 Litho.**

**1343** A446 60g vio, ver, brt grn & blk .25 .25
*a.* 60g ultra, org, yel, bl & blk .25 .25
**1344** A446 2.50z red, yel, pur & blk .40 .25
*a.* 2.50z red brn, yel, gray & blk .40 .25
**1345** A446 3.40z orange & multi .65 .25
*a.* 3.40z ol gray & multi .65 .25
*Nos. 1343-1345 (3)* 1.30 .75
*Nos. 1343a-1345a (3)* 1.30 .75

International Quiet Sun Year, 1964-65.

Odontoglossum Grande — A447

Orchids: 30g, Cypripedium hibridum. 40g, Lycaste skinneri. 50g, Cattleya. 60g, Vanda sanderiana. 1.35z, Cypripedium hibridum. 4z, Sobralia. 5.60z, Disa grandiflora. 6.50z, Cattleya labiata.

**1965, Sept. 6 Photo. *Perf. 12½x12***

**1346** A447 20g multicolored .25 .25
**1347** A447 30g multicolored .25 .25
**1348** A447 40g multicolored .25 .25
**1349** A447 50g multicolored .25 .25
**1350** A447 60g multicolored .25 .25
**1351** A447 1.35z multicolored .25 .25
**1352** A447 4z multicolored .50 .25
**1353** A447 5.60z multicolored .95 .30
**1354** A447 6.50z multicolored 1.60 .75
*Nos. 1346-1354 (9)* 4.55 2.80

Weight Lifting — A448

Sport: 40g, Boxing. 50g, Relay race, men. 60g, Fencing. 90g, Women's 80-meter hurdles. 3.40z, Relay race, women. 6.50z, Hop, step and jump. 7.10z, Volleyball, women.

**1965, Oct. 8 Photo. Unwmk.**

**1355** A448 30g gold & multi .25 .25
**1356** A448 40g gold & multi .25 .25
**1357** A448 50g silver & multi .25 .25
**1358** A448 60g gold & multi .25 .25
**1359** A448 90g silver & multi .25 .25
**1360** A448 3.40z gold & multi .35 .25
**1361** A448 6.50z gold & multi .65 .25
**1362** A448 7.10z bronze & multi 1.00 .35
*Nos. 1355-1362 (8)* 3.25 2.10

Victories won by the Polish team in 1964 Olympic Games. Each denomination printed in sheets of eight stamps and two center labels showing medals.

Mail Coach, by Piotr Michalowski — A449

Design: 2.50z, Departure of Coach, by Piotr Michalowski.

**1965, Oct. 9 Engr. *Perf. 11x11½***

**1363** A449 60g brown .25 .25
**1364** A449 2.50z slate green .40 .25

Issued for Stamp Day, 1965. Sheets of 50 with labels se-tenant inscribed "Dzien Znaczka 1965 R."

UN Emblem — A450

**1965, Oct. 24 Litho. *Perf. 12½x12***

**1365** A450 2.50z ultra .40 .25

20th anniversary of United Nations.

Memorial, Plaszow — A451

No. 1367, Kielce Memorial. No. 1368, Chelm Memorial.

***Perf. 12x11, 11x12***

**1965, Nov. 29 Engr.**

**1366** A451 60g grnsh gray .25 .25
**1367** A451 60g chocolate .25 .25
**1368** A451 60g black, horiz. .25 .25
*Nos. 1366-1368 (3)* .75 .75

Note after #1277 applies also to #1366-1368.

Wolf A452

**1965, Nov. 30 Photo. *Perf. 11½***

**1369** A452 20g shown .25 .25
**1370** A452 30g Lynx .25 .25
**1371** A452 40g Red fox .25 .25
**1372** A452 50g Badger .25 .25
**1373** A452 60g Brown bear .25 .25
**1374** A452 1.50z Wild Boar .35 .25
**1375** A452 2.50z Red deer .35 .25
**1376** A452 5.60z European bison 1.00 .45
**1377** A452 7.10z Moose 1.25 .75
*Nos. 1369-1377 (9)* 4.20 2.95

Gig — A453

Horse-drawn carriages, Lancut Museum: 40g, Coupé. 50g, Lady's basket. 60g, Vis-a-vis. 90g, Cab. 1.15z, Berlinka. 2.50z, Hunting break. 6.50z, Caleche à la Daumont. 7.10z, English break.

**1965, Dec. 30 Litho. *Perf. 11***

**Size: 50x23mm**

**1378** A453 20g multicolored .25 .25
**1379** A453 40g lilac & multi .25 .25
**1380** A453 50g orange & multi .25 .25
**1381** A453 60g fawn & multi .25 .25
**1382** A453 90g yellow & multi .25 .25

**Size: 76x23mm**

**1383** A453 1.15z multicolored .25 .25
**1384** A453 2.50z olive & multi .35 .25
**1385** A453 6.50z multicolored 1.00 .35

**Size: 103x23mm**

**1386** A453 7.10z blue & multi 1.40 .60
*Nos. 1378-1386 (9)* 4.25 2.70

Cargo Ship (No. 1389) — A454

No. 1387, Supervising Technical Organization (NOT) emblem, symbols of industry. No. 1388, Pit head & miners' badge, vert. No. 1390, Chemical plant, Plock. No. 1391, Combine. No. 1392, Railroad train. No. 1393, Building crane, vert. No. 1394, Pavilion & emblem of 35th Intl. Poznan Fair.

**1966 Litho. *Perf. 11***

**1387** A454 60g multicolored .25 .25
**1388** A454 60g multicolored .25 .25
**1389** A454 60g multicolored .25 .25
**1390** A454 60g multicolored .25 .25
**1391** A454 60g multicolored .25 .25
**1392** A454 60g multicolored .25 .25
**1393** A454 60g multicolored .25 .25
**1394** A454 60g multicolored .25 .25
*Nos. 1387-1394 (8)* 2.00 2.00

20th anniversary of the nationalization of Polish industry. No. 1394 also commemorates the 35th International Poznan Fair. Nos. 1387-1388 issued in connection with the 5th Congress of Polish Technicians, Katowice. Printed in sheets of 20 stamps and 20 labels with commemorative inscription within cogwheel on each label.

Issued: #1387-1388, 2/10; others, 5/21.

**Dinosaur Type of 1965**

Prehistoric Vertebrates: 20g, Dinichthys. 30g, Eusthenopteron. 40g, Ichthyostega. 50g, Mastodonsaurus. 60g, Cynognathus. 2.50z, Archaeopteryx, vert. 3.40z, Brontotherium. 6.50z, Machairodus. 7.10z, Mammoth.

**1966, Mar. 5 Litho. *Perf. 12½***

**1395** A434 20g multicolored .25 .25
**1396** A434 30g multicolored .25 .25
**1397** A434 40g multicolored .25 .25
**1398** A434 50g multicolored .25 .25
**1399** A434 60g multicolored .25 .25
**1400** A434 2.50z multicolored .35 .25
**1401** A434 3.40z multicolored .50 .25
**1402** A434 6.50z multicolored 1.25 .40
**1403** A434 7.10z multicolored 2.00 1.75
*Nos. 1395-1403 (9)* 5.35 3.90

Henryk Sienkiewicz A455

**Photogravure and Engraved**

**1966, Mar. 30 *Perf. 11½***

**1404** A455 60g black, *dl yel* .35 .25

Henryk Sienkiewicz (1846-1916), author and winner of 1905 Nobel Prize.

Soccer Game — A456

Designs: Various phases of soccer. Each stamp inscribed with the place and the result of final game in various preceding soccer championships.

**1966, May 6 *Perf. 13x12***

**1405** A456 20g multicolored .25 .25
**1406** A456 40g multicolored .25 .25
**1407** A456 60g multicolored .25 .25
**1408** A456 90g multicolored .25 .25
**1409** A456 1.50z multicolored .45 .25
**1410** A456 3.40z multicolored .65 .25
**1411** A456 6.50z multicolored 1.25 .40
**1412** A456 7.10z multicolored 1.75 .75
*Nos. 1405-1412 (8)* 5.10 2.65

World Cup Soccer Championship, Wembley, England, July 11-30. Each denomination printed in sheets of 10 (5x2).

See No. B109.

Peace Dove and War Memorial — A457

**Typo. & Engr.**

**1966, May 9 *Perf. 11½***

**1413** A457 60g silver & multi .35 .25

21st anniversary of victory over Fascism.

Women's Relay Race A458

20g, Start of men's short distance race. 60g, Javelin. 90g, Women's 80-meter hurdles. 1.35z, Discus. 3.40z, Finish of men's medium distance race. 6.50z, Hammer throw. 7.10z, High jump.

5z, Long distance race.

***Perf. 11½x11, 11x11½***

**1966, June 18 Litho.**

**1414** A458 20g multi, vert. .25 .25
**1415** A458 40g multi .25 .25
**1416** A458 60g multi, vert. .25 .25
**1417** A458 90g multi .25 .25
**1418** A458 1.35z multi, vert. .25 .25
**1419** A458 3.40z multi .40 .25
**1420** A458 6.50z multi, vert. .65 .25
**1421** A458 7.10z multi .65 .30
*Nos. 1414-1421 (8)* 2.95 2.05

**Souvenir Sheet**

***Imperf***

**1422** A458 5z multicolored 1.75 1.10

European Athletic Championships, Budapest, August, 1966. No. 1422 contains one 57x27mm stamp.

Polish Eagle — A459

Designs: Nos. 1424, 1426, Flag of Poland. No. 1425, Polish Eagle.

**Photogravure and Embossed**
*Perf. 12½x12*

| **1966, July 21** | | | **Unwmk.** | |
|---|---|---|---|---|
| **1423** | A459 | 60g gold, red & blk | .25 | .25 |
| **1424** | A459 | 60g gold, red & blk | .25 | .25 |
| **1425** | A459 | 2.50z gold, red & blk | .25 | .25 |
| **1426** | A459 | 2.50z gold, red & blk | .25 | .25 |
| | | *Nos. 1423-1426 (4)* | 1.00 | 1.00 |

1000th anniversary of Poland. Nos. 1423-1424 and 1425-1426 printed in 2 sheets of 10 (5x2); top row in each sheet in eagle design, bottom row in flag design.

Flowers and Farm Produce — A460

Designs: 60g, Woman holding loaf of bread. 3.40z, Farm girls holding harvest wreath.

| **1966, Aug. 15** | | **Photo.** | ***Perf. 11*** | |
|---|---|---|---|---|
| | | **Size: 22x50mm** | | |
| **1427** | A460 | 40g gold & multi | .40 | .25 |
| **1428** | A460 | 60g gold & multi | .40 | .25 |
| | | **Size: 48x50mm** | | |
| **1429** | A460 | 3.40z violet bl & multi | .65 | .45 |
| | | *Nos. 1427-1429 (3)* | 1.45 | .95 |

Issued to publicize the harvest festival.

Chrysanthemum — A461

Flowers: 20g, Poinsettia. 30g, Centaury. 40g, Rose. 60g, Zinnias. 90g, Nasturtium. 5.60z, Dahlia. 6.50z, Sunflower. 7.10z, Magnolia.

| **1966, Sept. 1** | | | ***Perf. 11½*** | |
|---|---|---|---|---|
| | | **Flowers in Natural Colors** | | |
| **1430** | A461 | 10g gold & black | .25 | .25 |
| **1431** | A461 | 20g gold & black | .25 | .25 |
| **1432** | A461 | 30g gold & black | .25 | .25 |
| **1433** | A461 | 40g gold & black | .25 | .25 |
| **1434** | A461 | 60g gold & black | .25 | .25 |
| **1435** | A461 | 90g gold & black | .25 | .25 |
| **1436** | A461 | 5.60z gold & black | .75 | .25 |
| **1437** | A461 | 6.50z gold & black | 1.00 | .30 |
| **1438** | A461 | 7.10z gold & black | 1.75 | .50 |
| | | *Nos. 1430-1438 (9)* | 5.00 | 2.55 |

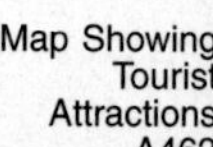
Map Showing Tourist Attractions A462

Designs: 20g, Lighthouse, Hel. 40g, Amethyst yacht on Masurian Lake. No. 1442, Poniatowski Bridge, Warsaw, and sailboat. No. 1443, Mining Academy, Kielce. 1.15z, Dunajec Gorge. 1.35z, Old oaks, Rogalin. 1.55z, Planetarium, Katowice. 2z, M.S. Batory and globe.

*Perf. 12½x12, 11½x12*

| **1966, Sept. 15** | | | **Engr.** | |
|---|---|---|---|---|
| **1439** | A462 | 10g carmine rose | .25 | .25 |
| **1440** | A462 | 20g olive gray | .25 | .25 |
| **1441** | A462 | 40g grysh blue | .25 | .25 |
| **1442** | A462 | 60g redsh brown | .25 | .25 |
| **1443** | A462 | 60g black | .25 | .25 |
| **1444** | A462 | 1.15z green | .25 | .25 |
| **1445** | A462 | 1.35z vermilion | .25 | .25 |
| **1446** | A462 | 1.55z violet | .25 | .25 |
| **1447** | A462 | 2z dark gray | .25 | .25 |
| | | *Nos. 1439-1447 (9)* | 2.25 | 2.25 |

Stableman with Percherons, by Piotr Michalowski — A463

2.50z, "Horses and Dogs" by Michalowski.

| **1966, Sept. 8** | | | ***Perf. 11x11½*** | |
|---|---|---|---|---|
| **1448** | A463 | 60g gray brown | .25 | .25 |
| **1449** | A463 | 2.50z green | .40 | .25 |

Issued for Stamp Day, 1966.

Capital of Romanesque Column from Tyniec and Polish Flag — A464

**Engraved and Photogravure**

| **1966, Oct. 7** | | | ***Perf. 11½*** | |
|---|---|---|---|---|
| **1450** | A464 | 60g dark brn & rose | .35 | .25 |

Polish Cultural Congress.

Soldier A465

| **1966, Oct. 20** | | **Litho.** | ***Perf. 11x11½*** | |
|---|---|---|---|---|
| **1451** | A465 | 60g blk, ol grn, & dl red | .40 | .25 |

Participation of the Polish Jaroslaw Dabrowski Brigade in the Spanish Civil War.

Green Woodpecker — A466

Forest Birds: 10g, The eight birds of the set combined. 30g, Eurasian jay. 40g, European golden oriole. 60g, Hoopoe. 2.50z, European redstart. 4z, Siskin (finch). 6.50z, Chaffinch. 7.10z, Great tit.

| **1966, Nov. 17** | | **Photo.** | ***Perf. 11½*** | |
|---|---|---|---|---|
| | | **Birds in Natural Colors; Black Inscription** | | |
| **1452** | A466 | 10g lt green | .25 | .25 |
| **1453** | A466 | 20g dull violet bl | .25 | .25 |
| **1454** | A466 | 30g dull green | .35 | .25 |
| **1455** | A466 | 40g gray | .35 | .25 |
| **1456** | A466 | 60g gray green | .35 | .25 |
| **1457** | A466 | 2.50z lt olive grn | .50 | .25 |
| **1458** | A466 | 4z dull violet | 1.25 | .25 |
| **1459** | A466 | 6.50z green | 1.00 | .35 |
| **1460** | A466 | 7.10z gray blue | 1.75 | .75 |
| | | *Nos. 1452-1460 (9)* | 6.05 | 2.85 |

Ceramic Ram, c. 4000 B.C. — A467

Designs: No. 1462, Bronze weapons and ornaments, c. 3500 B.C., horiz. No. 1463, Biskupin, settlement plan, 2500 B.C.

| **1966, Dec. 10** | | **Engr.** | ***Perf. 11x11½*** | |
|---|---|---|---|---|
| **1461** | A467 | 60g dull violet blue | .25 | .25 |
| **1462** | A467 | 60g brown | .25 | .25 |
| **1463** | A467 | 60g green | .25 | .25 |
| | | *Nos. 1461-1463 (3)* | .75 | .75 |

Polish Eagle, Hammer and Grain — A468

Designs: 60g, Eagle and map of Poland.

| **1966, Dec. 20** | | **Litho.** | ***Perf. 11*** | |
|---|---|---|---|---|
| **1464** | A468 | 40g brn, red & bluish lil | .25 | .25 |
| **1465** | A468 | 60g brn, red & ol grn | .25 | .25 |

Millenium of Poland.

Vostok (USSR) — A469

Spacecraft: 40g, Gemini, American Spacecraft. 60g, Ariel 2 (Great Britain). 1.35z, Proton 1 (USSR). 1.50z, FR 1 (France). 3.40z, Alouette (Canada). 6.50z, San Marco 1 (Italy). 7.10z, Luna 9 (USSR).

| **1966, Dec. 20** | | | ***Perf. 11½x11*** | |
|---|---|---|---|---|
| **1466** | A469 | 20g tan & multi | .25 | .25 |
| **1467** | A469 | 40g brown & multi | .25 | .25 |
| **1468** | A469 | 60g gray & multi | .25 | .25 |
| **1469** | A469 | 1.35z multicolored | .25 | .25 |
| **1470** | A469 | 1.50z multicolored | .25 | .25 |
| **1471** | A469 | 3.40z multicolored | .25 | .25 |
| **1472** | A469 | 6.50z multicolored | .90 | .25 |
| **1473** | A469 | 7.10z multicolored | 1.25 | .35 |
| | | *Nos. 1466-1473 (8)* | 3.65 | 2.10 |

Dressage — A470

Horses: 20g, Horse race. 40g, Jump. 60g, Steeplechase. 90g, Trotting. 5.90z, Polo. 6.60z, Stallion "Ofir." 7z, Stallion "Skowronek."

| **1967, Feb. 25** | | **Photo.** | ***Perf. 12½*** | |
|---|---|---|---|---|
| **1474** | A470 | 10g ultra & multi | .25 | .25 |
| **1475** | A470 | 20g orange & multi | .25 | .25 |
| **1476** | A470 | 40g ver & multi | .25 | .25 |
| **1477** | A470 | 60g multicolored | .25 | .25 |
| **1478** | A470 | 90g green & multi | .25 | .25 |
| **1479** | A470 | 5.90z multicolored | .80 | .25 |
| **1480** | A470 | 6.60z multicolored | 1.50 | .50 |
| **1481** | A470 | 7z violet & multi | 2.10 | .50 |
| | | *Nos. 1474-1481 (8)* | 5.65 | 2.50 |

Janov Podlaski stud farm, 150th anniv.

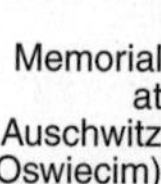
Memorial at Auschwitz (Oswiecim) A471

Emblem of Memorials Administration A472

Memorials at: No. 1484, Oswiecim-Monowice. No. 1485, Westerplatte (Walcz). No. 1486, Lodz-Radugoszcz. No. 1487, Stutthof. No. 1488, Lambinowice-Jencom. No. 1489, Zagan.

| **1967** | | **Engr.** | ***Perf. 11½x11, 11x11½*** | |
|---|---|---|---|---|
| **1482** | A471 | 40g brown olive | .25 | .25 |
| **1483** | A472 | 40g dull violet | .25 | .25 |
| **1484** | A472 | 40g black | .25 | .25 |
| **1485** | A472 | 40g green | .25 | .25 |
| **1486** | A472 | 40g black | .25 | .25 |
| **1487** | A471 | 40g ultra | .25 | .25 |
| **1488** | A471 | 40g brown | .25 | .25 |
| **1489** | A472 | 40g deep plum | .25 | .25 |
| | | *Nos. 1482-1489 (8)* | 2.00 | 2.00 |

Issued to commemorate the martyrdom and fight of the Polish people, 1939-45.

Issue dates: Nos. 1482-1484, Apr. 10. Nos. 1485-1487, Oct. 9. Nos. 1488-1489, Dec. 28.

See Nos. 1620-1624.

Striped Butterflyfish — A473

Tropical fish: 10g, Imperial angelfish. 40g, Barred butterflyfish. 60g, Spotted triggerfish. 90g, Undulate triggerfish. 1.50z, Striped triggerfish. 4.50z, Black-eye butterflyfish. 6.60z, Blue angelfish. 7z, Saddleback butterflyfish.

| **1967, Apr. 1** | | **Litho.** | ***Perf. 11x11½*** | |
|---|---|---|---|---|
| **1492** | A473 | 5g multicolored | .25 | .25 |
| **1493** | A473 | 10g multicolored | .25 | .25 |
| **1494** | A473 | 40g multicolored | .25 | .25 |
| **1495** | A473 | 60g multicolored | .25 | .25 |
| **1496** | A473 | 90g multicolored | .25 | .25 |
| **1497** | A473 | 1.50z multicolored | .25 | .25 |
| **1498** | A473 | 4.50z multicolored | .65 | .25 |
| **1499** | A473 | 6.60z multicolored | 1.00 | .75 |
| **1500** | A473 | 7z multicolored | 1.25 | .25 |
| | | *Nos. 1492-1500 (9)* | 4.40 | 2.75 |

Bicyclists — A474

| **1967, May 5** | | **Litho.** | ***Perf. 11*** | |
|---|---|---|---|---|
| **1501** | A474 | 60g multicolored | .25 | .25 |

20th Warsaw-Berlin-Prague Bicycle Race.

Men's 100-meter Race — A475

Sports and Olympic Rings: 40g, Steeplechase. 60g, Women's relay race. 90g, Weight lifter. 1.35z, Hurdler. 3.40z, Gymnast on vaulting horse. 6.60z, High jump. 7z, Boxing.

**1967, May 24 Litho. *Perf. 11***

| No. | Type | Value | Description | Unused | Used |
|---|---|---|---|---|---|
| **1502** | A475 | 20g | multicolored | .25 | .25 |
| **1503** | A475 | 40g | multicolored | .25 | .25 |
| **1504** | A475 | 60g | multicolored | .25 | .25 |
| **1505** | A475 | 90g | multicolored | .25 | .25 |
| **1506** | A475 | 1.35z | multicolored | .25 | .25 |
| **1507** | A475 | 3.40z | multicolored | .25 | .25 |
| **1508** | A475 | 6.60z | multicolored | .75 | .25 |
| **1509** | A475 | 7z | multicolored | .75 | .25 |
| | | | *Nos. 1502-1509 (8)* | 3.00 | 2.00 |

19th Olympic Games, Mexico City, 1968. Nos. 1502-1509 printed in sheets of 8, (2x4) with label showing emblem of Polish Olympic Committee between each two horizontal stamps. See No. B110.

Badge of Socialist Working Brigade A476

**1967, June 2**

| No. | Type | Value | Description | Unused | Used |
|---|---|---|---|---|---|
| **1510** | A476 | 60g | multicolored | .25 | .25 |

6th Congress of Polish Trade Unions. Printed in sheets of 20 stamps and 20 labels and in miniature sheets of 4 stamps and 4 labels.

Mountain Arnica — A477

Medicinal Plants: 60g, Columbine. 3.40z, Gentian. 4.50z, Ground pine. 5z, Iris sibirica. 10z, Azalea pontica.

**1967, June 14 *Perf. 11½x11***

**Flowers in Natural Colors**

| No. | Type | Value | Description | Unused | Used |
|---|---|---|---|---|---|
| **1511** | A477 | 40g | black & brn org | .25 | .25 |
| **1512** | A477 | 60g | black & lt blue | .25 | .25 |
| **1513** | A477 | 3.40z | black & dp org | .35 | .25 |
| **1514** | A477 | 4.50z | black & lt vio | .25 | .25 |
| **1515** | A477 | 5z | black & maroon | .45 | .25 |
| **1516** | A477 | 10z | black & bister | .85 | .25 |
| | | | *Nos. 1511-1516 (6)* | 2.40 | 1.50 |

Monument for Silesian Insurgents A478

**1967, July 21 Litho. *Perf. 11½***

| No. | Type | Value | Description | Unused | Used |
|---|---|---|---|---|---|
| **1517** | A478 | 60g | multicolored | .25 | .25 |

Unveiling of the monument for the Silesian Insurgents of 1919-21 at Katowice, July, 1967.

Marie Curie — A479

Designs: No. 1519, Curie statue, Warsaw. No. 1520, Nobel Prize diploma.

**1967, Aug. 1 Engr. *Perf. 11½x11***

| No. | Type | Value | Description | Unused | Used |
|---|---|---|---|---|---|
| **1518** | A479 | 60g | dk carmine rose | .25 | .25 |
| **1519** | A479 | 60g | violet | .25 | .25 |
| **1520** | A479 | 60g | sepia | .25 | .25 |
| | | | *Nos. 1518-1520 (3)* | .75 | .75 |

Marie Sklodowska Curie (1867-1934), discoverer of radium and polonium.

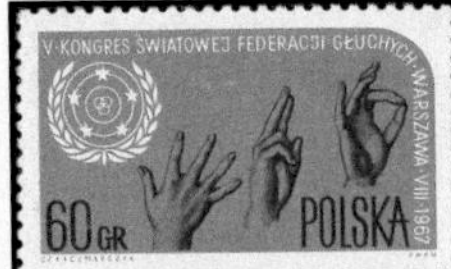


Sign Language and Emblem A480

**1967, Aug. 1 Litho. *Perf. 11x11½***

| No. | Type | Value | Description | Unused | Used |
|---|---|---|---|---|---|
| **1521** | A480 | 60g | brt blue & blk | .25 | .25 |

5th Congress of the World Federation of the Deaf, Warsaw, Aug. 10-17.

Flowers of the Meadows A481

Flowers: 40g, Poppy. 60g, Morning glory. 90g, Pansy. 1.15z, Common pansy. 2.50z, Corn cockle. 3.40z, Wild aster. 4.50z, Common pimpernel. 7.90z, Chicory.

**1967, Sept. 5 Photo. *Perf. 11½***

| No. | Type | Value | Description | Unused | Used |
|---|---|---|---|---|---|
| **1522** | A481 | 20g | multicolored | .25 | .25 |
| **1523** | A481 | 40g | multicolored | .25 | .25 |
| **1524** | A481 | 60g | multicolored | .25 | .25 |
| **1525** | A481 | 90g | multicolored | .25 | .25 |
| **1526** | A481 | 1.15z | multicolored | .25 | .25 |
| **1527** | A481 | 2.50z | multicolored | .30 | .25 |
| **1528** | A481 | 3.40z | multicolored | .45 | .25 |
| **1529** | A481 | 4.50z | multicolored | .80 | .25 |
| **1530** | A481 | 7.90z | multicolored | 1.70 | .35 |
| | | | *Nos. 1522-1530 (9)* | 4.50 | 2.35 |

Wilanow Palace, by Wincenty Kasprzycki — A482

**Engraved and Photogravure**

**1967, Oct. 9 *Perf. 11½***

| No. | Type | Value | Description | Unused | Used |
|---|---|---|---|---|---|
| **1531** | A482 | 60g | olive blk & lt bl | .25 | .25 |

Issued for Stamp Day, 1967.

Cruiser Aurora — A483

Designs: No. 1533, Lenin and library. No. 1534, Luna 10, earth and moon.

**1967, Oct. 9 Litho. *Perf. 11***

| No. | Type | Value | Description | Unused | Used |
|---|---|---|---|---|---|
| **1532** | A483 | 60g | gray, red & blk | .25 | .25 |
| **1533** | A483 | 60g | gray, dull red & blk | .25 | .25 |
| **1534** | A483 | 60g | gray, red & blk | .25 | .25 |
| | | | *Nos. 1532-1534 (3)* | .75 | .75 |

Russian Revolution, 50th anniv.

Tadeusz Kosciusko — A485

**Engraved and Photogravure**

**1967, Oct. 14 *Perf. 12x11***

| No. | Type | Value | Description | Unused | Used |
|---|---|---|---|---|---|
| **1540** | A485 | 60g | choc & ocher | .25 | .25 |
| **1541** | A485 | 2.50z | sl grn & rose car | .25 | .25 |

Tadeusz Kosciusko (1746-1817), Polish patriot and general in the American Revolution.

Vanessa Butterfly A486

Designs: Various Butterflies.

**1967, Oct. 14 Litho. *Perf. 11½***

**Butterflies in Natural Colors**

| No. | Type | Value | Description | Unused | Used |
|---|---|---|---|---|---|
| **1542** | A486 | 10g | green | .25 | .25 |
| **1543** | A486 | 20g | lt violet bl | .25 | .25 |
| **1544** | A486 | 40g | yellow green | .25 | .25 |
| **1545** | A486 | 60g | gray | .25 | .25 |
| **1546** | A486 | 2z | lemon | .30 | .25 |
| **1547** | A486 | 2.50z | Prus green | .35 | .25 |
| **1548** | A486 | 3.40z | blue | .55 | .35 |
| **1549** | A486 | 4.50z | rose lilac | 1.25 | .50 |
| **1550** | A486 | 7.90z | bister | 1.75 | .70 |
| | | | *Nos. 1542-1550 (9)* | 5.20 | 3.05 |

Polish Woman, by Antoine Watteau A487

Paintings from Polish Museums: 20g, Lady with the Ermine, by Leonardo da Vinci. 60g, Dog Fighting Heron, by Abraham Hondius. 2z, Guitarist after the Hunt, by J. Baptiste Greuze. 2.50z, Tax Collectors, by Marinus van Reymerswaele. 3.40z, Portrait of Daria Flodorowna, by Fyodor Rokotov. 4.50z, Still Life with Lobster, by Jean de Heem, horiz. 6.60z, Landscape (from the Good Samaritan), by Rembrandt, horiz.

***Perf. 11½x11, 11x11½***

**1967, Nov. 15 Photo.**

| No. | Type | Value | Description | Unused | Used |
|---|---|---|---|---|---|
| **1551** | A487 | 20g | gold & multi | .25 | .25 |
| **1552** | A487 | 40g | gold & multi | .25 | .25 |
| **1553** | A487 | 60g | gold & multi | .25 | .25 |
| **1554** | A487 | 2z | gold & multi | .25 | .25 |
| **1555** | A487 | 2.50z | gold & multi | .25 | .25 |
| **1556** | A487 | 3.40z | gold & multi | .25 | .25 |
| **1557** | A487 | 4.50z | gold & multi | .70 | .25 |
| **1558** | A487 | 6.60z | gold & multi | .95 | .35 |
| | | | *Nos. 1551-1558 (8)* | 3.15 | 2.10 |

Printed in sheets of 5 + label. Pairs, stamp and label, set: mint $6, used $2.50.

Ossolinski Medal, Book and Flags — A488

**1967, Dec. 12 Litho. *Perf. 11***

| No. | Type | Value | Description | Unused | Used |
|---|---|---|---|---|---|
| **1559** | A488 | 60g | lt bl, red & lt brn | .25 | .25 |

150th anniversary of the founding of the Ossolineum, a center for scientific and cultural activities, by Count Josef Maximilian Ossolinski.

Wladyslaw S. Reymont (1867-1924), Writer, Nobel Prize Winner — A489

**1967, Dec. 12**

| No. | Type | Value | Description | Unused | Used |
|---|---|---|---|---|---|
| **1560** | A489 | 60g | dk brn, ocher & red | .25 | .25 |

Ice Hockey A490

Designs: 60g, Skiing. 90g, Slalom. 1.35z, Speed skating. 1.55z, Long-distance skiing. 2z, Sledding. 7z, Biathlon. 7.90z, Ski jump.

**1968, Jan. 10**

| No. | Type | Value | Description | Unused | Used |
|---|---|---|---|---|---|
| **1561** | A490 | 40g | multicolored | .25 | .25 |
| **1562** | A490 | 60g | multicolored | .25 | .25 |
| **1563** | A490 | 90g | multicolored | .25 | .25 |
| **1564** | A490 | 1.35z | multicolored | .25 | .25 |
| **1565** | A490 | 1.55z | multicolored | .25 | .25 |
| **1566** | A490 | 2z | multicolored | .25 | .25 |
| **1567** | A490 | 7z | multicolored | .35 | .25 |
| **1568** | A490 | 7.90z | multicolored | .70 | .30 |
| | | | *Nos. 1561-1568 (8)* | 2.55 | 2.05 |

10th Winter Olympic Games, Grenoble, France, Feb. 6-18, 1968.

Puss in Boots — A491

Fairy Tales: 40g, The Fox and the Raven. 60g, Mr. Twardowski (man flying on a cock). 2z, The Fisherman and the Fish. 2.50z, Little Red Riding Hood. 3.40z, Cinderella. 5.50z, Thumbelina. 7z, Snow White.

**1968, Mar. 15 Litho. *Perf. 12½***

| No. | Type | Value | Description | Unused | Used |
|---|---|---|---|---|---|
| **1569** | A491 | 20g | multicolored | .25 | .25 |
| **1570** | A491 | 40g | lt violet & multi | .25 | .25 |
| **1571** | A491 | 60g | multicolored | .25 | .25 |
| **1572** | A491 | 2z | olive & multi | .25 | .25 |
| **1573** | A491 | 2.50z | ver & multi | .30 | .25 |
| **1574** | A491 | 3.40z | multicolored | .45 | .25 |
| **1575** | A491 | 5.50z | multicolored | .75 | .35 |
| **1576** | A491 | 7z | multicolored | 1.10 | .35 |
| | | | *Nos. 1569-1576 (8)* | 3.60 | 2.20 |

Bird-of-Paradise Flower — A492

Exotic Flowers: 10g, Clianthus dampieri. 20g, Passiflora quadrangularis. 40g, Coryphanta vivipara. 60g, Odontonia. 90g, Protea cynaroides.

**1968, May 15 Litho. *Perf. 11½***

| No. | Type | Value | Description | Unused | Used |
|---|---|---|---|---|---|
| **1577** | A492 | 10g | sepia & multi | .25 | .25 |
| **1578** | A492 | 20g | multicolored | .25 | .25 |
| **1579** | A492 | 30g | brown & multi | .25 | .25 |
| **1580** | A492 | 40g | ultra & multi | .25 | .25 |
| **1581** | A492 | 60g | multicolored | .25 | .25 |
| **1582** | A492 | 90g | multicolored | .25 | .25 |
| | | | *Nos. 1577-1582,B111-B112 (8)* | 3.75 | 2.20 |

"Peace" by Henryk Tomaszewski A493

2.50z, Poster for Gounod's Faust, by Jan Lenica.

**1968, May 29 Litho. *Perf. 11½x11***

**1583** A493 60g gray & multi .25 .25
**1584** A493 2.50z gray & multi .25 .25

2nd Intl. Poster Biennial Exhibition, Warsaw.

Zephyr Glider — A494

Polish Gliders: 90g, Storks. 1.50z, Swallow. 3.40z, Flies. 4z, Seal. 5.50z, Pirate.

**1968, May 29 *Perf. 12½***

**1585** A494 60g multicolored .25 .25
**1586** A494 90g multicolored .25 .25
**1587** A494 1.50z multicolored .25 .25
**1588** A494 3.40z multicolored .45 .25
**1589** A494 4z multicolored .55 .25
**1590** A494 5.50z multicolored .80 .35
*Nos. 1585-1590 (6)* 2.55 1.60

11th Intl. Glider Championships, Leszno.

Child Holding Symbolic Stamp — A495

No. 1592, Balloon over Poznan Town Hall.

**1968, July 2 Litho. *Perf. 11½x11***

**1591** A495 60g multicolored .25 .25
**1592** A495 60g multicolored .25 .25

75 years of Polish philately; "Tematica 1968" stamp exhibition in Poznan. Printed in sheets of 12 (4x3) se-tenant, arranged checkerwise.

Sosnowiec Memorial — A496

**Photogravure and Engraved**

**1968, July 20 *Perf. 11x11½***

**1593** A496 60g brt rose lilac & blk .25 .25

The monument by Helena and Roman Husarski and Witold Ceckiewicz was unveiled Sept. 16, 1967, to honor the revolutionary deeds of Silesian workers and miners.

Relay Race and Sculptured Head A497

Sports and Sculptures: 40g, Boxing. 60g. Basketball. 90g, Long jump. 2.50z, Women's javelin. 3.40z, Athlete on parallel bars. 4z, Bicycling. 7.90z, Fencing.

**1968, Sept. 2 Litho. *Perf. 11x11½***
**Size: 35x26mm**

**1594** A497 30g sepia & multi .25 .25
**1595** A497 40g brn org, brn & blk .25 .25
**1596** A497 60g gray & multi .25 .25
**1597** A497 90g violet & multi .25 .25
**1598** A497 2.50z multicolored .25 .25
**1599** A497 3.40z brt grn, blk & lt ultra .30 .25
**1600** A497 4z multicolored .30 .35
**1601** A497 7.90z multicolored .50 .30
*Nos. 1594-1601,B113 (9)* 3.85 2.55

19th Olympic Games, Mexico City, 10/12-27.

Jewish Woman with Lemons, by Aleksander Gierymski A498

Polish Paintings: 40g, Knight on Bay Horse, by Piotr Michalowski. 60g, Fisherman, by Leon Wyczolkowski. 1.35z, Eliza Parenska, by Stanislaw Wyspianski. 1.50z, "Manifest," by Wojciech Weiss. 4.50z, Stancyk (Jester), by Jan Matejko, horiz. 5z, Children's Band, by Tadeusz Makowski, horiz. 7z, Feast II, by Zygmunt Waliszewski, horiz.

***Perf. 11½x11, 11x11½***

**1968, Oct. 10 Litho.**

**1602** A498 40g gray & multi .25 .25
**1603** A498 60g gray & multi .25 .25
**1604** A498 1.15z gray & multi .25 .25
**1605** A498 1.35z gray & multi .25 .25
**1606** A498 1.50z gray & multi .35 .25
**1607** A498 4.50z gray & multi .40 .25
**1608** A498 5z gray & multi .65 .25
**1609** A498 7z gray & multi .85 .25
*Nos. 1602-1609 (8)* 3.25 2.00

Issued in sheets of 4 stamps and 2 labels inscribed with painter's name. Pair with label, set: mint $3.50, used $2.25.

"September, 1939" by M. Bylina — A499

Paintings: No. 1611, Partisans, by L. Maciag. No. 1612, Tank in Battle, by M. Bylina. No. 1613, Monte Cassino, by A. Boratynski. No. 1614, Tanks Approaching Warsaw, by S. Garwatowski. No. 1615, Battle on the Neisse, by M. Bylina. No. 1616, On the Oder, by K. Mackiewicz. No. 1617, "In Berlin," by M. Bylina. No. 1618, Warship "Blyskawica" by M. Mokwa. No. 1619, "Pursuit" (fighter planes), by T. Kulisiewicz.

**Litho., Typo. & Engr.**

**1968, Oct. 12 *Perf. 11½***

**1610** A499 40g pale yel, ol & vio .25 .25
**1611** A499 40g lil, red lil & ind .25 .25
**1612** A499 40g gray, dk bl & ol .25 .25
**1613** A499 40g pale sal, org brn & blk .25 .25
**1614** A499 40g pale grn, dk grn & plum .25 .25
**1615** A499 60g gray, vio bl & blk .25 .25
**1616** A499 60g pale grn, ol grn & vio brn .25 .25
**1617** A499 60g pink, car & grnsh blk .25 .25
**1618** A499 60g pink, brn & grn .25 .25
**1619** A499 60g lt bl, grnsh bl & blk .25 .25
*Nos. 1610-1619 (10)* 2.50 2.50

Polish People's Army, 25th anniversary.

**Memorial Types of 1967**

Designs: No. 1620, Tomb of the Unknown Soldier, Warsaw. No. 1621, Nazi War Crimes Memorial, Zamosc. No. 1622, Guerrilla Memorial, Plichno. No. 1623, Guerrilla Memorial, Kartuzy. No. 1624, Polish Insurgents' Memorial, Poznan.

***Perf. 11½x11, 11x11½***

**1968, Nov. 15 Engr.**

**1620** A471 40g slate .25 .25
**1621** A472 40g dull red .25 .25
**1622** A472 40g dark blue .25 .25
**1623** A471 40g sepia .25 .25
**1624** A472 40g sepia .25 .25
*Nos. 1620-1624 (5)* 1.25 1.25

Martyrdom & fight of the Polish people, 1939-45.

Strikers, S. Lentz A500

No. 1626, "Manifesto," by Wojciech Weiss. No. 1627, Party members, by F. Kowarski, horiz.

***Perf. 11½x11, 11x11½***

**1968, Nov. 11 Litho.**

**1625** A500 60g dark red & multi .25 .25
**1626** A500 60g dark red & multi .25 .25
**1627** A500 60g dark red & multi .25 .25
*Nos. 1625-1627 (3)* .75 .75

5th Cong. of the Polish United Workers' Party.

Departure for the Hunt, by Wojciech Kossak — A501

Hunt Paintings: 40g, Hunting with Falcon, by Juliusz Kossak. 60g, Wolves' Raid, by A. Wierusz-Kowalski. 1.50z, Bear Hunt, by Julian Falat. 2.50z, Fox Hunt, by T. Sutherland. 3.40z, Boar Hunt, by Frans Snyders. 4.50z, Hunters' Rest, by W. G. Perov. 8.50z, Lion Hunt in Morocco, by Delacroix.

**1968, Nov. 20 *Perf. 11***

**1628** A501 20g multicolored .25 .25
**1629** A501 40g multicolored .25 .25
**1630** A501 60g multicolored .25 .25
**1631** A501 1.50z multicolored .25 .25
**1632** A501 2.50z multicolored .25 .25
**1633** A501 3.40z multicolored .30 .25
**1634** A501 4.50z multicolored .60 .25
**1635** A501 8.50z multicolored 1.00 .45
*Nos. 1628-1635 (8)* 3.15 2.20

Afghan Greyhound A502

Dogs: 20g, Maltese. 40g, Rough-haired fox terrier, vert. 1.50z, Schnauzer. 2.50z, English setter. 3.40z, Pekinese. 4.50z, German shepherd. 8.50z, Pointer.

**1969, Feb. 2 *Perf. 11x11½, 11½x11***
**Dogs in Natural Colors**

**1636** A502 20g gray & brt grn .25 .25
**1637** A502 40g gray & orange .40 .25
**1638** A502 60g gray & lilac .40 .25
**1639** A502 1.50z gray & black .40 .25
**1640** A502 2.50z gray & brt pink .50 .25
**1641** A502 3.40z gray & dk grn .60 .25
**1642** A502 4.50z gray & ver 1.10 .40
**1643** A502 8.50z gray & violet 2.25 .75
*Nos. 1636-1643 (8)* 5.90 2.65

General Assembly of the Intl. Kennel Federation, Warsaw, May 1969.

Eagle-on-Shield House Sign — A503

**1969, Feb. 23 Litho. *Perf. 11½x11***

**1644** A503 60g gray, red & blk .25 .25

9th Congress of Democratic Movement.

Sheaf of Wheat A504

**1969, Mar. 29 Litho. *Perf. 11½x11***

**1645** A504 60g multicolored .25 .25

5th Congress of the United Peasant Party, Warsaw, March 29-31.

Runner — A505

Olympic Rings and: 20g, Woman gymnast. 40g, Weight lifting. 60g, Women's javelin.

**1969, Apr. 25 Litho. *Perf. 11½x11***

**1646** A505 10g orange & multi .25 .25
**1647** A505 20g ultra & multi .25 .25
**1648** A505 40g yellow & multi .25 .25
**1649** A505 60g red & multi .25 .25
*Nos. 1646-1649,B114-B117 (8)* 3.00 2.10

50th anniv. of the Polish Olympic Committee, and the 75th anniv. of the Intl. Olympic Committee.



Sailboat and Lighthouse, Kolobrzeg Harbor — A506

40g, Tourist map of Swietokrzyski National Park. 60g, Ruins of 16th cent. castle, Niedzica, vert. 1.50z, Castle of the Dukes of Pomerania & ship, Szczecin. 2.50z, View of Torun & Vistula. 3.40z, View of Klodzko, vert. 4z, View of Sulejow. 4.50z, Market Place, Kazimierz Dolny, vert.

**1969, May 20 Litho. *Perf. 11***

**1650** A506 40g multicolored .25 .25
**1651** A506 60g multicolored .25 .25
**1652** A506 1.35z multicolored .25 .25
**1653** A506 1.50z multicolored .25 .25

| | | | | | |
|---|---|---|---|---|---|
| **1654** | A506 | 2.50z | multicolored | .25 | .25 |
| **1655** | A506 | 3.40z | multicolored | .25 | .25 |
| **1656** | A506 | 4z | multicolored | .40 | .25 |
| **1657** | A506 | 4.50z | multicolored | .45 | .25 |
| | | | *Nos. 1650-1657 (8)* | 2.35 | 2.00 |

Issued for tourist publicity. Printed in sheets of 15 stamps and 15 labels. Domestic plants on labels of 40g, 60g and 1.35z, coats of arms on others.

See Nos. 1731-1735.

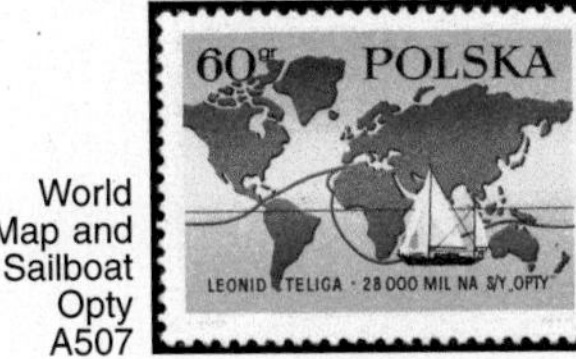


World Map and Sailboat Opty A507

**1969, June 21 Litho. *Perf. 11x11½***

| | | | | |
|---|---|---|---|---|
| **1658** | A507 | 60g multicolored | .25 | .25 |

Leonid Teliga's one-man voyage around the world, Casablanca, Jan. 21, 1967, to Las Palmas, Apr. 16, 1969.

Nicolaus Copernicus, Woodcut by Tobias Stimer — A508

Designs: 60g, Copernicus, by Jeremias Falck, 15th century globe and map of constellations. 2.50z, Copernicus, painting by Jan Matejko and map of heliocentric system.

**Photo., Engr. & Litho.**

**1969, June 26 *Perf. 11½***

| | | | | | |
|---|---|---|---|---|---|
| **1659** | A508 | 40g | dl yel, sep & dp car | .25 | .25 |
| **1660** | A508 | 60g | grnsh gray, blk & dp car | .25 | .25 |
| **1661** | A508 | 2.50z | lt vio brn, ol & dp car | .30 | .25 |
| | | | *Nos. 1659-1661 (3)* | .80 | .75 |

"Memory" Pathfinders' Cross and Protectors' Badge — A509

#1663, "Defense," military eagle and Pathfinders' cross. #1664, "Labor," map of Poland and Pathfinders' cross.

**Photo., Engr. & Litho.**

**1969, July 19 *Perf. 11x11½***

| | | | | |
|---|---|---|---|---|
| **1662** | A509 | 60g ultra, blk & red | .25 | .25 |
| **1663** | A509 | 60g green, blk & red | .25 | .25 |
| **1664** | A509 | 60g carmine, blk & grn | .25 | .25 |
| | | *Nos. 1662-1664 (3)* | .75 | .75 |

5th Natl. Alert of Polish Pathfinders' Union.

Frontier Guard and Embossed Arms of Poland — A510

Coal Miner — A511

Designs: No. 1666, Oil refinery-chemical plant, Plock. No. 1667, Combine harvester. No. 1668, Rebuilt Grand Theater, Warsaw. No. 1669, Marie Sklodowska-Curie Monument and University, Lublin. No. 1671, Chemical industry (sulphur) worker. No. 1672, Steelworker. No. 1673, Ship builder and ship.

**1969, July 21 Litho. & Embossed**

| | | | | |
|---|---|---|---|---|
| **1665** | A510 | 60g red & multi | .25 | .25 |
| **1666** | A510 | 60g red & multi | .25 | .25 |
| **1667** | A510 | 60g red & multi | .25 | .25 |
| **1668** | A510 | 60g red & multi | .25 | .25 |
| **1669** | A510 | 60g red & multi | .25 | .25 |
| *a.* | | Strip of 5, #1665-1669 | .40 | .40 |

***Perf. 11½x11***

**Litho.**

| | | | | |
|---|---|---|---|---|
| **1670** | A511 | 60g gray & multi | .25 | .25 |
| **1671** | A511 | 60g gray & multi | .25 | .25 |
| **1672** | A511 | 60g gray & multi | .25 | .25 |
| **1673** | A511 | 60g gray & multi | .25 | .25 |
| *a.* | | Strip of 4, #1670-1673 | .35 | .35 |
| | | *Nos. 1669a,1673a (2)* | .75 | .75 |

25th anniv. of the Polish People's Republic.

Landing Module on Moon, and Earth A512

**1969, Aug. 21 Litho. *Perf. 12x12½***

| | | | | |
|---|---|---|---|---|
| **1674** | A512 | 2.50z multicolored | .90 | .35 |

Man's first landing on the moon, July 20, 1969. US astronauts Neil A. Armstrong and Col. Edwin E. Aldrin, Jr., with Lieut. Col. Michael Collins piloting Apollo 11. Issued in sheets of 8 stamps and 2 tabs, with decorative border. One tab shows Apollo 11 with lunar landing module, the other shows module's take-off from moon. Value, sheet: mint, $22.50, used $16.

"Hamlet," by Jacek Malczewski — A513

Polish Paintings: 20g, Motherhood, by Stanislaw Wyspianski. 60g, Indian Summer (sleeping woman), by Jozef Chelmonski. 2z, Two Girls, by Olga Boznanska, vert. 2.50z, "The Sun of May" (Breakfast on the Terrace), by Jozef Mehoffer, vert. 3.40z, Woman Combing her Hair, by Wladyslaw Slewinski. 5.50z, Still Life, by Jozef Pankiewicz. 7z, The Abduction of the King's Daughter, by Witold Wojtkiewicz.

***Perf. 11x11½, 11½x11***

**1969, Sept. 4 Photo.**

| | | | | | |
|---|---|---|---|---|---|
| **1675** | A513 | 20g | gold & multi | .25 | .25 |
| **1676** | A513 | 40g | gold & multi | .25 | .25 |
| **1677** | A513 | 60g | gold & multi | .25 | .25 |
| **1678** | A513 | 2z | gold & multi | .25 | .25 |
| **1679** | A513 | 2.50z | gold & multi | .25 | .25 |
| **1680** | A513 | 3.40z | gold & multi | .25 | .25 |
| **1681** | A513 | 5.50z | gold & multi | .55 | .30 |
| **1682** | A513 | 7z | gold & multi | 1.00 | .35 |
| | | | *Nos. 1675-1682 (8)* | 3.05 | 2.15 |

Issued in sheets of 4 stamps and 2 labels inscribed with painter's name. Pairs, with label, set: mint $3.50, used $2.50.

Nike — A514

**1969, Sept. 19 Litho. *Perf. 11½x11***

| | | | | |
|---|---|---|---|---|
| **1683** | A514 | 60g gray, red & bister | .25 | .25 |

4th Congress of the Union of Fighters for Freedom and Democracy.

Details from Memorial, Majdanek Concentration Camp — A515

**1969, Sept. 20 *Perf. 11***

| | | | | |
|---|---|---|---|---|
| **1684** | A515 | 40g brt lil, gray & blk | .25 | .25 |

Unveiling of a monument to the victims of the Majdanek concentration camp. The monument was designed by the sculptor Wiktor Tolkin.

Costumes from Krczonow, Lublin — A516

Regional Costumes: 60g, Lowicz, Lodz. 1.15z, Rozbark, Katowice. 1.35z, Lower Silesia, Wroclaw. 1.50z, Opoczno, Lodz. 4.50z, Sacz, Cracow. 5z, Highlanders, Cracow. 7z, Kurpiow, Warsaw.

**1969, Sept. 30 Litho. *Perf. 11½x11***

| | | | | | |
|---|---|---|---|---|---|
| **1685** | A516 | 40g | multicolored | .25 | .25 |
| **1686** | A516 | 60g | multicolored | .25 | .25 |
| **1687** | A516 | 1.15z | multicolored | .25 | .25 |
| **1688** | A516 | 1.35z | multicolored | .25 | .25 |
| **1689** | A516 | 1.50z | multicolored | .25 | .25 |
| **1690** | A516 | 4.50z | multicolored | .40 | .25 |
| **1691** | A516 | 5z | multicolored | .55 | .25 |
| **1692** | A516 | 7z | multicolored | .55 | .35 |
| | | | *Nos. 1685-1692 (8)* | 2.75 | 2.10 |

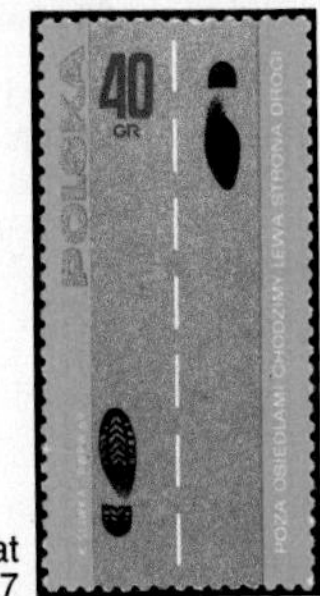


"Walk at Left" — A517

Traffic safety: 60g, "Drive Carefully" (horses on road). 2.50z, "Lower your Lights" (automobile on road).

**1969, Oct. 4 *Perf. 11***

| | | | | | |
|---|---|---|---|---|---|
| **1693** | A517 | 40g | multicolored | .25 | .25 |
| **1694** | A517 | 60g | multicolored | .25 | .25 |
| **1695** | A517 | 2.50z | multicolored | .25 | .25 |
| | | | *Nos. 1693-1695 (3)* | .75 | .75 |

ILO Emblem and Welder's Mask — A518

**1969, Oct. 20 *Perf. 11x11½***

| | | | | |
|---|---|---|---|---|
| **1696** | A518 | 2.50z violet bl & ol | .25 | .25 |

ILO, 50th anniversary.

Bell Foundry A519

Miniatures from Behem's Code, completed 1505: 60g, Painter's studio. 1.35z, Wood carvers. 1.55z, Shoemaker. 2.50z, Cooper. 3.40z, Bakery. 4.50z, Tailor. 7z, Bowyer's shop.

**1969, Nov. 12 Litho. *Perf. 12½***

| | | | | | |
|---|---|---|---|---|---|
| **1697** | A519 | 40g | gray & multi | .25 | .25 |
| **1698** | A519 | 60g | gray & multi | .25 | .25 |
| **1699** | A519 | 1.35z | gray & multi | .25 | .25 |
| **1700** | A519 | 1.55z | gray & multi | .25 | .25 |
| **1701** | A519 | 2.50z | gray & multi | .25 | .25 |
| **1702** | A519 | 3.40z | gray & multi | .35 | .25 |
| **1703** | A519 | 4.50z | gray & multi | .35 | .25 |
| **1704** | A519 | 7z | gray & multi | .65 | .35 |
| | | | *Nos. 1697-1704 (8)* | 2.60 | 2.10 |

Angel — A520

Folk Art (Sculptures): 40g, Sorrowful Christ (head). 60g, Sorrowful Christ (seated figure). 2z, Crying woman. 2.50z, Adam and Eve. 3.40z, Woman with birds.

**1969, Dec. 19 Litho. *Perf. 12½***

**Size: 21x36mm**

| | | | | | |
|---|---|---|---|---|---|
| **1705** | A520 | 20g | lt blue & multi | .25 | .25 |
| **1706** | A520 | 40g | lilac & multi | .25 | .25 |
| **1707** | A520 | 60g | multicolored | .25 | .25 |
| **1708** | A520 | 2z | multicolored | .25 | .25 |
| **1709** | A520 | 2.50z | multicolored | .25 | .25 |
| **1710** | A520 | 3.40z | multicolored | .25 | .25 |
| | | | *Nos. 1705-1710,B118-B119 (8)* | 2.65 | 2.00 |

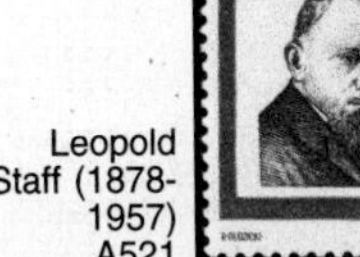

Leopold Staff (1878-1957) A521

Polish Writers: 60g, Wladyslaw Broniewski (1897-1962). 1.35z, Leon Kruczkowski (1900-1962). 1.50z, Julian Tuwim (1894-1953). 1.55z, Konstanty Ildefons Galczynski (1905-1953). 2.50z, Maria Dabrowska (1889-1965). 3.40z, Zofia Nalkowska (1885-1954).

**Litho., Typo. & Engr.**

**1969, Dec. 30 *Perf. 11x11½***

| | | | | | |
|---|---|---|---|---|---|
| **1711** | A521 | 40g | ol grn & blk, *grnsh* | .25 | .25 |
| **1712** | A521 | 60g | dp car & blk, *pink* | .25 | .25 |
| **1713** | A521 | 1.35z | vio bl & blk, *grysh* | .25 | .25 |
| **1714** | A521 | 1.50z | pur & blk, *pink* | .25 | .25 |
| **1715** | A521 | 1.55z | dp grn & blk, *grnsh* | .25 | .25 |

**1716** A521 2.50z ultra & blk, *gray* .25 .25
**1717** A521 3.40z red brn & blk, *pink* .25 .25
*Nos. 1711-1717 (7)* 1.75 1.75

Statue of Nike and Polish Colors A522

**1970, Jan. 17 Photo. *Perf. 11½***
**1718** A522 60g sil, gold, red & blk .25 .25

Warsaw liberation, 25th anniversary.

Medieval Print Shop and Modern Color Proofs — A523

**1970, Jan. 20 Litho. *Perf. 11½x11***
**1719** A523 60g multicolored .25 .25

Centenary of Polish printers' trade union.

Ringnecked Pheasant — A524

Game Birds: 40g, Mallard drake. 1.15z, Woodcock. 1.35z, Ruffs (males). 1.50z, Wood pigeon. 3.40z, Black grouse. 7z, Gray partridges (cock and hen). 8.50z, Capercaillie cock giving mating call.

**1970, Feb. 28 Litho. *Perf. 11½***
**1720** A524 40g multicolored .25 .25
**1721** A524 60g multicolored .30 .25
**1722** A524 1.15z multicolored .45 .25
**1723** A524 1.35z multicolored .45 .25
**1724** A524 1.50z multicolored .45 .25
**1725** A524 3.40z multicolored .95 .25
**1726** A524 7z multicolored 1.25 .50
**1727** A524 8.50z multicolored 2.50 .65
*Nos. 1720-1727 (8)* 6.60 2.65

Lenin in his Kremlin Study, Oct. 1918, and Polish Lenin Steel Mill — A525

Designs: 60g, Lenin addressing 3rd International Congress in Leningrad, 1920, and Luna 13. 2.50z, Lenin with delegates to 10th Russian Communist Party Congress, Moscow, 1921, dove and globe.

**Engr. & Typo.**

**1970, Apr. 22 *Perf. 11***
**1728** A525 40g grnsh blk & dl red .25 .25
**1729** A525 60g sep & dp lil rose .25 .25
*a.* Souvenir sheet of 4 2.50 1.10
**1730** A525 2.50z bluish blk & ver .25 .25
*Nos. 1728-1730 (3)* .75 .75

Lenin (1870-1924), Russian communist leader.

No. 1729a commemorates the Cracow Intl. Phil. Exhib.

**Tourist Type of 1969**

No. 1731, Townhall, Wroclaw, vert. No. 1732, Cathedral, Piast Castle tower and church towers, Opole. No. 1733, Castle, Legnica. No. 1734, Castle Tower, Bolkow. No. 1735, Town Hall, Brzeg.

**1970, May 9 Litho. *Perf. 11***
**1731** A506 60g Wroclaw .25 .25
**1732** A506 60g Opole .25 .25
**1733** A506 60g Legnica .25 .25
**1734** A506 60g Bolkow .25 .25
**1735** A506 60g Brzeg .25 .25
*Nos. 1731-1735 (5)* 1.25 1.25

Issued for tourist publicity. Printed in sheets of 15 stamps and 15 labels, showing coats of arms.

Polish and Russian Soldiers before Brandenburg Gate — A526

Flower, Eagle and Arms of 7 Cities — A527

**Lithographed and Engraved**

**1970, May 9 *Perf. 11***
**1736** A526 60g tan & multi .25 .25

***Perf. 11½***
**1737** A527 60g sil, red & sl grn .25 .25

25th anniv. of victory over Germany and of Polish administration of the Oder-Neisse border area.

Peasant Movement Flag A528

**1970, May 15 Litho. *Perf. 11½***
**1738** A528 60g olive & multi .25 .25

Polish peasant movement, 75th anniv.

A529

**1970, May 20**
**1739** A529 2.50z blue & vio bl .25 .25

Inauguration of new UPU headquarters, Bern.

A530

**1970, May 30 *Perf. 11½x11***
**1740** A530 60g multicolored .25 .25

European Soccer Cup Finals. Printed in sheets of 15 stamps and 15 se-tenant labels inscribed with the scores of the games.

Lamp of Learning A531

**1970, June 3 *Perf. 11½***
**1741** A531 60g black, bis & red .25 .25

Plock Scientific Society, 150th anniversary.

Cross-country Race — A532

No. 1743, Runners from ancient Greek vase. No. 1744, Archer, drawing by W. Skoczylas.

**1970, June 16 Photo. *Perf. 11x11½***
**1742** A532 60g yellow & multi .25 .25
**1743** A532 60g black & multi .25 .25
**1744** A532 60g dark blue & multi .25 .25
*Nos. 1742-1744 (3)* .75 .75

10th session of the Intl. Olympic Academy. See No. B120.

Copernicus, by Bacciarelli and View of Bologna — A533

Designs: 60g, Copernicus, by W. Lesseur and view of Padua. 2.50z, Copernicus, by Zinck Nora and view of Ferrara.

**Photo., Engr. & Typo.**

**1970, June 26 *Perf. 11½***
**1745** A533 40g orange & multi .25 .25
**1746** A533 60g olive & multi .25 .25
**1747** A533 2.50z multicolored .35 .25
*Nos. 1745-1747 (3)* .85 .75

Aleksander Orlowski (1777-1832), Self-portrait — A534

Miniatures: 40g, Jan Matejko (1838-1893), self-portrait. 60g, King Stefan Batory (1533-1586), anonymous painter. 2z, Maria Leszczynska (1703-1768), anonymous French painter. 2.50z, Maria Walewska (1789-1817), by Marie-Victoire Jaquotot. 3.40z, Tadeusz Kosciuszko (1746-1817), by Jan Rustem. 5.50z, Samuel Bogumil Linde (1771-1847), by G. Landolfi. 7z, Michal Oginski (1728-1800), by Nanette Rosenzweig-Windisch.

**Litho. & Photo.**

**1970, Aug. 27 *Perf. 11½***
**1748** A534 20g gold & multi .25 .25
**1749** A534 40g gold & multi .25 .25
**1750** A534 60g gold & multi .25 .25
**1751** A534 2z gold & multi .25 .25
**1752** A534 2.50z gold & multi .25 .25
**1753** A534 3.40z gold & multi .25 .25
**1754** A534 5.50z gold & multi .45 .25
**1755** A534 7z gold & multi .85 .25
*Nos. 1748-1755 (8)* 2.80 2.00

Nos. 1748-1755 printed in sheets of 4 stamps and 2 labels. Pairs, with label, set: mint $3.50, used $2.50. The miniatures show famous Poles and are from collections in the National Museums in Warsaw and Cracow.

Poster for Chopin Competition A535

**Photogravure and Engraved**

**1970, Sept. 8 *Perf. 11x11½***
**1756** A535 2.50z black & vio .25 .25

8th Intl. Chopin Piano Competition, Warsaw, Oct. 7-25.

UN Emblem A536

**1970, Sept. 8 Photo. *Perf. 11½***
**1757** A536 2.50z multicolored .25 .25

United Nations, 25th anniversary.

Poles — A537

Design: 60g, Family, home and Polish flag.

**1970, Sept. 15 Litho. *Perf. 11½x11***
**1758** A537 40g gray & multi .25 .25
**1759** A537 60g multicolored .25 .25

National Census, Dec. 8, 1970.

Grunwald Cross and Warship Piorun (Thunderbolt) — A538

Grunwald Cross and Warship: 60g, Orzel (Eagle). 2.50z, Garland.

**1970, Sept. 25 Engr. *Perf. 11½x11***

**1760** A538 40g sepia .25 .25
**1761** A538 60g black .25 .25
**1762** A538 2.50z deep brown .45 .25
*Nos. 1760-1762 (3)* .95 .75

Polish Navy during World War II.

Cellist, by Jerzy Nowosielski A539

Paintings: 40g, View of Lodz, by Benon Liberski. 60g, Studio Concert, by Waclaw Taranczewski. 1.50z, Still Life, by Zbigniew Pronaszko. 2z, Woman Hanging up Laundry, by Andrzej Wroblewski. 3.40z, "Expressions," by Maria Jarema, horiz. 4z, Canal in the Forest, by Piotr Potworowski, horiz. 8.50z, "The Sun," by Wladyslaw Strzeminski, horiz.

**1970, Oct. 9 Photo. *Perf. 11½***

**1763** A539 20g multicolored .25 .25
**1764** A539 40g multicolored .25 .25
**1765** A539 60g multicolored .25 .25
**1766** A539 1.50z multicolored .25 .25
**1767** A539 2z multicolored .25 .25
**1768** A539 3.40z multicolored .25 .25
**1769** A539 4z multicolored .35 .25
**1770** A539 8.50z multicolored .85 .25
*Nos. 1763-1770 (8)* 2.70 2.00

Issued for Stamp Day.

Luna 16 Landing on Moon — A540

**1970, Nov. 20 Litho. *Perf. 11½x11***

**1771** A540 2.50z multicolored .35 .25

Luna 16 Russian unmanned, automatic moon mission, Sept. 12-24. Issued in sheets of 8 stamps and 2 tabs. One tab shows rocket launching; the other, parachute landing of capsule. Value, sheet: mint $8.50, used $4.75.

Stag — A541

16th Cent. Tapestries in Wawel Castle: 1.15z, Stork. 1.35z, Leopard fighting dragon. 2z, Man's head. 2.50z, Child holding bird. 4z, God, Adam & Eve. 4.50z, Panel with monogram of King Sigismund Augustus. 5.50z, Poland's coat of arms.

**1970, Dec. 23 Photo. *Perf. 11½x12***

**1772** A541 60g multicolored .25 .25
**1773** A541 1.15z purple & multi .25 .25
**1774** A541 1.35z multicolored .25 .25
**1775** A541 2z sepia & multi .30 .25
**1776** A541 2.50z dk blue & multi .30 .25
**1777** A541 4z green & multi .50 .25
**1778** A541 4.50z multicolored .80 .35
*Nos. 1772-1778 (7)* 2.65 1.85

**Souvenir Sheet**

***Imperf***

**1779** A541 5.50z black & multi 1.25 1.00

No. 1779 contains one 48x57mm stamp. See No. B121.

School Sailing Ship Dar Pomorza — A542

Polish Ships: 60g, Transatlantic Liner Stefan Batory. 1.15z, Ice breaker Perkun. 1.35z, Rescue ship R-1. 1.50z, Freighter Ziemia Szczecinska. 2.50z, Tanker Beskidy. 5z, Express freighter Hel. 8.50z, Ferry Gryf.

**1971, Jan. 30 Photo. *Perf. 11***

**1780** A542 40g ver & multi .25 .25
**1781** A542 60g multicolored .25 .25
**1782** A542 1.15z blue & multi .25 .25
**1783** A542 1.35z yellow & multi .25 .25
**1784** A542 1.50z multicolored .25 .25
**1785** A542 2.50z violet & multi .25 .25
**1786** A542 5z multicolored .40 .25
**1787** A542 8.50z blue & multi .65 .30
*Nos. 1780-1787 (8)* 2.55 2.05

Checiny Castle A543

Polish Castles: 40g, Wisnicz. 60g, Bedzin. 2z, Ogrodzieniec. 2.50z, Niedzica. 3.40z, Kwidzyn. 4z, Pieskowa Skala. 8.50z, Lidzbark Warminski.

**1971, Mar. 5 Litho. *Perf. 11***

**1788** A543 20g multicolored .25 .25
**1789** A543 40g multicolored .25 .25
**1790** A543 60g multicolored .25 .25
**1791** A543 2z multicolored .25 .25
**1792** A543 2.50z multicolored .25 .25
**1793** A543 3.40z multicolored .25 .25
**1794** A543 4z multicolored .30 .25
**1795** A543 8.50z multicolored .65 .35
*Nos. 1788-1795 (8)* 2.45 2.10

Fighting in Pouilly Castle, Jaroslaw Dabrowski and Walery Wroblewski — A544

**1971, Mar. 3 *Perf. 12½x12½***

**1796** A544 60g vio bl, brn & red .25 .25

Centenary of the Paris Commune.

Seedlings A545

**1971, Mar. 30 Photo. *Perf. 11½x11***

**Sizes: 26x34mm (40g, 1.50z); 26x47mm (60g)**

**1797** A545 40g shown .25 .25
**1798** A545 60g Forest .25 .25
**1799** A545 1.50z Clearing .25 .25
*Nos. 1797-1799 (3)* .75 .75

Proper forest management.

Bishop Marianos A546

Frescoes from Faras Cathedral, Nubia, 8th-12th centuries: 60g, St. Anne. 1.15z, 1.50z, 7z, Archangel Michael (diff. frescoes). 1.35z, Hermit Anamon of Tuna el Gabel. 4.50z, Cross with symbols of four Evangelists. 5z, Christ protecting Nubian dignitary.

**1971, Apr. 20**

**1800** A546 40g gold & multi .25 .25
**1801** A546 60g gold & multi .25 .25
**1802** A546 1.15z gold & multi .25 .25
**1803** A546 1.35z gold & multi .25 .25
**1804** A546 1.50z gold & multi .25 .25
**1805** A546 4.50z gold & multi .35 .25
**1806** A546 5z gold & multi .35 .25
**1807** A546 7z gold & multi .50 .25
*Nos. 1800-1807 (8)* 2.45 2.00

Polish archaeological excavations in Nubia.

Silesian Insurrectionists — A547

**1971, May 3 Photo. *Perf. 11***

**1808** A547 60g dk red brn & gold .25 .25
*a.* Souv. sheet of 3+3 labels 1.00 .50

50th anniversary of the 3rd Silesian uprising. Printed in sheets of 15 stamps and 15 labels showing Silesian Insurrectionists monument in Katowice.

Peacock on the Lawn, by Dorota, 4 years old — A548

Children's Drawings and UNICEF Emblem: 40g, Our Army, horiz. 60g, Spring. 2z, Cat with Ball, horiz. 2.50z, Flowers in Vase. 3.40z, Friendship, horiz. 5.50z, Clown. 7z, The Unknown Planet, horiz.

**1971, May 20 *Perf. 11½x11, 11x11½***

**1809** A548 20g multicolored .25 .25
**1810** A548 40g multicolored .25 .25
**1811** A548 60g multicolored .25 .25
**1812** A548 2z multicolored .25 .25
**1813** A548 2.50z multicolored .25 .25
**1814** A548 3.40z multicolored .25 .25
**1815** A548 5.50z multicolored .35 .25
**1816** A548 7z multicolored .55 .25
*Nos. 1809-1816 (8)* 2.40 2.00

25th anniversary of UNICEF.

Fair Emblem — A549

**1971, June 1 Photo. *Perf. 11½x11***

**1817** A549 60g ultra, blk & dk car .25 .25

40th International Poznan Fair, June 13-22.

Collegium Maius, Cracow — A550

40g, Copernicus House, Torun, vert. 2.50z, Olsztyn Castle. 4z, Frombork Cathedral, vert.

**1971, June Litho. *Perf. 11***

**1818** A550 40g multicolored .25 .25
**1819** A550 60g blk, red brn & sep .25 .25
**1820** A550 2.50z multicolored .35 .25
**1821** A550 4z multicolored .50 .25
*Nos. 1818-1821 (4)* 1.35 1.00

Nicolaus Copernicus (1473-1543), astronomer. Printed in sheets of 15 with labels showing portrait of Copernicus, page from "Euclid's Geometry," astrolabe or drawing of heliocentric system, respectively.

Paper Cut-out — A551

Designs: Various paper cut-outs (folk art).

**Photo., Engr. & Typo.**

**1971, July 12 *Perf. 12x11½***

**1822** A551 20g blk & brt grn, *bluish* .25 .25
**1823** A551 40g sl grn & dk ol, *lt gray* .25 .25
**1824** A551 60g brn & bl, *gray* .25 .25
**1825** A551 1.15z plum & brn, *buff* .25 .25
**1826** A551 1.35z dk grn & ver, *yel grn* .25 .25
*Nos. 1822-1826 (5)* 1.25 1.25

Worker, by Xawery Dunikowski A552

Sculptures: No. 1828, Founder, by Xawery Dunikowski. No. 1829, Miners, by Magdalena Wiecek. No. 1830, Woman harvester, by Stanislaw Horno-Poplawski.

**1971, July 21 Photo. *Perf. 11½x12***

**1827** A552 40g silver & multi .25 .25
**1828** A552 40g silver & multi .25 .25
**1829** A552 60g silver & multi .25 .25
**1830** A552 60g silver & multi .25 .25
*a.* Souv. sheet of 4, #1827-1830 2.50 .85
*Nos. 1827-1830 (4)* 1.00 1.00

Punched Tape and Cogwheel — A553

**1971, Sept. 2 Litho. *Perf. 11x11½***

**1831** A553 60g purple & red .25 .25

6th Congress of Polish Technicians, held at Poznan, February, 1971.

Angel, by Jozef Mehoffer, 1901 — A554

Water Lilies, by Wyspianski A555

Stained Glass Windows: 60g, Detail from "The Elements" by Stanislaw Wyspianski. 1.35z, Apollo, by Wyspianski, 1904. 1.55z, Two Kings, 14th century. 3.40z, Flight into Egypt, 14th century. 5.50z, St. Jacob the Elder, 14th century.

**1971, Sept. 15 Photo. *Perf. 11½x11***

**1832** A554 20g gold & multi .25 .25
**1833** A555 40g gold & multi .25 .25
**1834** A555 60g gold & multi .25 .25
**1835** A555 1.35z gold & multi .25 .25
**1836** A554 1.55z gold & multi .25 .25
**1837** A554 3.40z gold & multi .25 .25
**1838** A554 5.50z gold & multi .35 .25
*Nos. 1832-1838,B122 (8)* 2.60 2.10

Mrs. Fedorowicz, by Witold Pruszkowski (1846-1896) — A556

Paintings of Women: 50g, Woman with Book, by Tytus Czyzewski (1885-1945). 60g, Girl with Chrysanthemums, by Olga Boznanska (1865-1940). 2.50z, Girl in Red Dress, by Jozef Pankiewicz (1866-1940), horiz. 3.40z, Nude, by Leon Chwistek (1884-1944), horiz. 4.50z, Strange Garden (woman), by Jozef Mehoffer (1869-1946). 5z, Artist's Wife with White Hat, by Zbiginew Pronaszko (1885-1958).

***Perf. 11½x11, 11x11½***

**1971, Oct. 9 Litho.**

**1839** A556 40g gray & multi .25 .25
**1840** A556 50g gray & multi .25 .25
**1841** A556 60g gray & multi .25 .25
**1842** A556 2.50z gray & multi .25 .25
**1843** A556 3.40z gray & multi .25 .25
**1844** A556 4.50z gray & multi .35 .25
**1845** A556 5z gray & multi .75 .30
*Nos. 1839-1845,B123 (8)* 3.20 2.40

Stamp Day, 1971. Printed in sheets of 4 stamps and 2 labels inscribed "Women in Polish Paintings." Pairs, with label, set: mint $5, used $2.75.

Royal Castle, Warsaw A557

**1971, Oct. 14 Photo. *Perf. 11x11½***

**1846** A557 60g gold, blk & brt red .25 .25

P-11C Dive Bombers A558

Planes and Polish Air Force Emblem: 1.50z, PZL 23-A Karas fighters. 3.40z, PZL Los bomber.

**1971, Oct. 14**

**1847** A558 90g multicolored .25 .25
**1848** A558 1.50z blue, red & blk .25 .25
**1849** A558 3.40z multicolored .30 .25
*Nos. 1847-1849 (3)* .80 .75

Martyrs of the Polish Air Force, 1939.

Lunokhod 1 on Moon — A559

No. 1850, Lunar Rover and Astronauts.

***Perf. 11x11½, 11½x11***

**1971, Nov. 17**

**1850** A559 2.50z multicolored .65 .25
**1851** A559 2.50z multicolored .65 .25

Apollo 15 US moon exploration mission, July 26-Aug. 7 (No. 1850); Luna 17 unmanned automated USSR moon mission, Nov. 10-17 (No. 1851). Printed in sheets of 6 stamps and 2 labels, with marginal inscriptions.

Worker at Helm — A560

Shipbuilding A561

No. 1853, Worker. No. 1855, Apartment houses under construction. No. 1856, "Bison" combine harvester. No. 1857, Polish Fiat 125. No. 1858, Mining tower. No. 1859, Chemical plant.

**1971, Dec. 8 *Perf. 11½x11***

**1852** A560 60g gray, ultra & red .25 .25
**1853** A560 60g red & gray .25 .25
*a.* Pair, #1852-1853 + label .25 .25

***Perf. 11x11½***

**1854** A561 60g red, gold & blk .25 .25
**1855** A561 60g red, gold & blk .25 .25
**1856** A561 60g red, gold & blk .25 .25
**1857** A561 60g red, gold & blk .25 .25
**1858** A561 60g red, gold & blk .25 .25
**1859** A561 60g red, gold & blk .25 .25
*a.* Souv. sheet of 6, #1854-1859 .90 .50
*b.* Block of 6, #1854-1859 .60 .50
*Nos. 1853a,1859b (2)* .85 .75

6th Congress of the Polish United Worker's Party. Nos. 11859a and 859b have outline of map of Poland extending over the block.

Cherry Blossoms — A562

Blossoms: 20g, Niedzwiecki's apple. 40g, Pear. 60g, Peach. 1.15z, Japanese magnolia. 1.35z, Red hawthorne. 2.50z, Apple. 3.40z, Red chestnut. 5z, Acacia robinia. 8.50z, Cherry.

**1971, Dec. 28 Litho. *Perf. 12½***

**Blossoms in Natural Colors**

**1860** A562 10g dull blue & blk .25 .25
**1861** A562 20g grnsh blue & blk .25 .25
**1862** A562 40g lt violet & blk .25 .25
**1863** A562 60g green & blk .25 .25
**1864** A562 1.15z Prus bl & blk .25 .25
**1865** A562 1.35z ocher & blk .25 .25
**1866** A562 2.50z green & blk .25 .25
**1867** A562 3.40z ocher & blk .35 .25
**1868** A562 5z tan & blk .85 .25
**1869** A562 8.50z bister & blk 1.40 .65
*Nos. 1860-1869 (10)* 4.35 2.90

Fighting Worker, by J. Jarnuszkiewicz — A563

**Photogravure and Engraved**

**1972, Jan. 5 *Perf. 11½***

**1870** A563 60g red & black .25 .25

Polish Workers' Party, 30th anniversary.

Luge and Sapporo '72 Emblem — A564

Sapporo '72 Emblem and: 60g, Women's slalom, vert. 1.65z, Biathlon, vert. 2.50z, Ski jump.

**1972, Jan. 12 Photo. *Perf. 11***

**1871** A564 40g silver & multi .25 .25
**1872** A564 60g silver & multi .25 .25
**1873** A564 1.65z silver & multi .25 .25
**1874** A564 2.50z silver & multi .40 .25
*Nos. 1871-1874 (4)* 1.15 1.00

11th Winter Olympic Games, Sapporo, Japan, Feb. 3-13. See No. B124.

Heart and Electro-cardiogram — A565

**1972, Mar. 28 Photo. *Perf. 11½x11***

**1875** A565 2.50z blue, red & blk .25 .25

"Your heart is your health," World Health Day.

Bicyclists Racing — A566

**1972, May 2 *Perf. 11***

**1876** A566 60g silver & multi .25 .25

25th Warsaw-Berlin-Prague Bicycle Race.

Berlin Monument A567

**1972, May 9 Engr. *Perf. 11½x11***

**1877** A567 60g grnsh black .25 .25

Unveiling of monument for Polish soldiers and German anti-Fascists in Berlin, May 14.

Olympic Runner — A568

Olympic Rings and "Motion" Symbol and: 30g, Archery. 40g, Boxing. 60g, Fencing. 2.50z, Wrestling. 3.40z, Weight lifting. 5z, Bicycling. 8.50z, Sharpshooting.

**1972, May 20 *Perf. 11½x11***

**1878** A568 20g multicolored .25 .25
**1879** A568 30g multicolored .25 .25
**1880** A568 40g multicolored .25 .25
**1881** A568 60g gray & multi .25 .25
**1882** A568 2.50z multicolored .25 .25
**1883** A568 3.40z multicolored .25 .25
**1884** A568 5z blue & multi .25 .25
**1885** A568 8.50z multicolored .70 .25
*Nos. 1878-1885 (8)* 2.45 2.00

20th Olympic Games, Munich, Aug. 26-Sept. 10. See No. B125.

Vistula and Cracow — A569

**1972, May 28 Photo. *Perf. 11½x11***

**1886** A569 60g red, grn & ocher .25 .25

50th anniversary of Polish Immigrants Society in Germany (Rodlo).

Knight of King Mieszko I — A570

**1972, June 12**
**1887** A570 60g gold, red brn, yel & blk .25 .25

Millennium of the Battle of Cedynia (Cidyny).

Zoo Animals — A571

**1972, Aug. 20 Litho. *Perf. 12½***
**1888** A571 20g Cheetah .25 .25
**1889** A571 40g Giraffe, vert .25 .25
**1890** A571 60g Toco toucan .25 .25
**1891** A571 1.35z Chimpanzee .35 .25
**1892** A571 1.65z Gibbon .35 .25
**1893** A571 3.40z Crocodile .35 .25
**1894** A571 4z Kangaroo 1.25 .25
**1895** A571 4.50z Tiger, vert 1.75 .85
**1896** A571 7z Zebra 4.00 1.50
*Nos. 1888-1896 (9)* 8.80 4.10

Ludwik Warynski — A572

**1972, Sept. 1 Photo. *Perf. 11***
**1897** A572 60g multicolored .25 .25

90th anniversary of Proletariat Party, founded by Ludwik Warynski. Printed in sheets of 25 stamps each se-tenant with label showing masthead of party newspaper "Proletariat."

Feliks Dzerzhinski A573

**1972, Sept. 11 Litho. *Perf. 11x11½***
**1898** A573 60g red & black .25 .25

Feliks Dzerzhinski (1877-1926), Russian politician of Polish descent.

Congress Emblem — A574

**1972, Sept. 15 Photo. *Perf. 11½x11***
**1899** A574 60g multicolored .25 .25

25th Congress of the International Cooperative Union, Warsaw, Sept. 1972.

"In the Barracks," by Moniuszko A575

Scenes from Operas or Ballets by Moniuszko: 20g, The Countess. 40g, The Frightful Castle. 60g, Halka. 1.15z, A New Don Quixote. 1.35z, Verbum Nobile. 1.55z, Ideal. 2.50z, Paria.

**Photogravure and Engraved**

**1972, Sept. 15 *Perf. 11½***
**1900** A575 10g gold & violet .25 .25
**1901** A575 20g gold & dk brn .25 .25
**1902** A575 40g gold & slate grn .25 .25
**1903** A575 60g gold & indigo .25 .25
**1904** A575 1.15z gold & dk blue .25 .25
**1905** A575 1.35z gold & dk blue .25 .25
**1906** A575 1.55z gold & grnsh blk .25 .25
**1907** A575 2.50z gold & dk brn .30 .25
*Nos. 1900-1907 (8)* 2.05 2.00

Stanislaw Moniuszko (1819-72), composer.

"Amazon," by Piotr Michalowski — A576

Paintings: 40g, Ostafi Daszkiewicz, by Jan Matejko. 60g, "Summer Rain" (dancing woman), by Wojciech Gerson. 2z, Woman from Naples, by Aleksander Kotsis. 2.50z, Girl Taking Bath, by Pantaleon Szyndler. 3.40z, Count of Thun (child), by Artur Grottger. 4z, Rhapsodist (old man), by Stanislaw Wyspianski. 60g and 2.50z inscribed "DZIEN ZNACZKA 1972."

**1972, Sept. 28 Photo. *Perf. 10½x11***
**1908** A576 30g gold & multi .25 .25
**1909** A576 40g gold & multi .25 .25
**1910** A576 60g gold & multi .25 .25
**1911** A576 2z gold & multi .25 .25
**1912** A576 2.50z gold & multi .25 .25
**1913** A576 3.40z gold & multi .35 .25
**1914** A576 4z gold & multi .85 .25
*Nos. 1908-1914,B126 (8)* 3.85 2.30

Stamp Day.

Copernicus, by Jacob van Meurs, 1654, Heliocentric System — A577

Portraits of Copernicus: 60g, 16th century etching and Prussian coin, 1530. 2.50z, by Jeremiah Falck, 1645, and coat of arms of King of Prussia, 1520. 3.40z, Copernicus with lily of the valley, and page from Theophilactus Simocatta's "Letters on Customs."

**1972, Sept. 28 Litho. *Perf. 11x11½***
**1915** A577 40g brt blue & blk .25 .25
**1916** A577 60g ocher & blk .25 .25
**1917** A577 2.50z red & blk .25 .25
**1918** A577 3.40z yellow grn & blk .40 .25
*Nos. 1915-1918 (4)* 1.15 1.00

See No. B127.

**Nos. 1337-1338 Surcharged in Red or Black**

a

b

**1972 Engr. *Perf. 11½x11***
**1919** A445(a) 50g on 40g (R) .25 .25
**1920** A445(a) 90g on 40g (R) .25 .25
**1921** A445(a) 1z on 40g (R) .25 .25
**1922** A445(b) 1.50z on 60g .25 .25
**1923** A445(a) 2.70z on 40g (R) .25 .25
**1924** A445(b) 4z on 60g .25 .25
**1925** A445(b) 4.50z on 60g .25 .25
**1926** A445(b) 4.90z on 60g .35 .25
*Nos. 1919-1926 (8)* 2.10 2.00

Issued: #1919-1920, 11/17; others, 10/2.

The Little Soldier, by E. Piwowarski A578

**1972, Oct. 16 Litho. *Perf. 11½***
**1927** A578 60g rose & black .25 .25

Children's health center (Centrum Zdrowia Dzieck), to be built as memorial to children killed during Nazi regime.

Warsaw Royal Castle, 1656, by Erik J. Dahlbergh — A579

**1972, Oct. 16 Photo. *Perf. 11x11½***
**1928** A579 60g violet, bl & blk .25 .25

Rebuilding of Warsaw Castle, destroyed during World War II.

Ribbons with Symbols of Trade Union Activities — A580

**1972, Nov. 13 *Perf. 11½x11***
**1929** A580 60g multicolored .25 .25

7th and 13th Polish Trade Union congresses, Nov. 13-15.

Mountain Lodge, Chocholowska Valley — A581

Mountain Lodges in Tatra National Park: 60g, Hala Ornak, West Tatra, horiz. 1.55z, Hala Gasienicowa. 1.65z, Pieciu Stawow Valley, horiz. 2.50z, Morskie Oko, Rybiego Potoku Valley

**1972, Nov. 13 *Perf. 11***
**1930** A581 40g multicolored .25 .25
**1931** A581 60g multicolored .25 .25
**1932** A581 1.55z multicolored .25 .25
**1933** A581 1.65z multicolored .25 .25
**1934** A581 2.50z multicolored .35 .25
*Nos. 1930-1934 (5)* 1.35 1.25

Japanese Azalea — A582

Flowering Shrubs: 50g, Alpine rose. 60g, Pomeranian honeysuckle. 1.65z, Chinese quince. 2.50z, Viburnum. 3.40z, Rhododendron. 4z, Mock orange. 8.50z, Lilac.

**1972, Dec. 15 Litho. *Perf. 12½***
**1935** A582 40g gray & multi .25 .25
**1936** A582 50g blue & multi .25 .25
**1937** A582 60g multicolored .25 .25
**1938** A582 1.65z ultra & multi .25 .25
**1939** A582 2.50z ocher & multi .35 .25
**1940** A582 3.40z multicolored .35 .25
**1941** A582 4z multicolored .70 .25
**1942** A582 8.50z multicolored 1.00 .45
*Nos. 1935-1942 (8)* 3.40 2.20

Emblem — A583

**1972, Dec. 15 Photo. *Perf. 11½***
**1943** A583 60g red & multi .25 .25

5th Congress of Socialist Youth Union.

Copernicus — A584

**Coil Stamps**

**1972, Dec. 28 Photo. *Perf. 14***
**1944** A584 1z deep claret .25 .25
**1945** A584 1.50z yellow brown .25 .25

Nicolaus Copernicus (1473-1543), astronomer. Black control number on back of every 5th stamp.

Piast Knight, 10th Century A585

Polish Cavalry: 40g, Knight, 13th century. 60g, Knight of Ladislas Jagello, 15th century, horiz. 1.35z, Hussar, 17th century. 4z, National Guard Uhlan, 18th century. 4.50z, Congress Kingdom Period, 1831. 5z, Light cavalry, 1939, horiz. 7z, Light cavalry, People's Army, 1945.

**1972, Dec. 28** *Perf. 11*

| | | | | |
|---|---|---|---|---|
| **1946** | A585 | 20g violet & multi | .25 | .25 |
| **1947** | A585 | 40g multicolored | .25 | .25 |
| **1948** | A585 | 60g orange & multi | .25 | .25 |
| **1949** | A585 | 1.35z orange & multi | .25 | .25 |
| **1950** | A585 | 4z orange & multi | .25 | .25 |
| **1951** | A585 | 4.50z orange & multi | .35 | .25 |
| **1952** | A585 | 5z brown & multi | .70 | .25 |
| **1953** | A585 | 7z multicolored | 1.20 | .75 |
| | | *Nos. 1946-1953 (8)* | 3.50 | 2.50 |

Man and Woman, Sculpture by Wiera Muchina — A586

Design: 60g, Globe with Red Star.

**1972, Dec. 30**

| | | | | |
|---|---|---|---|---|
| **1954** | A586 | 40g gray & multi | .25 | .25 |
| **1955** | A586 | 60g blk, red & vio bl | .25 | .25 |

50th anniversary of the Soviet Union.

Nicolaus Copernicus, by M. Bacciarelli A587

Portraits of Copernicus: 1.50z, painted in Torun, 16th century. 2.70z, by Zinck Nor. 4z, from Strasbourg clock. 4.90z, Copernicus in his Observatory, by Jan Matejko, horiz.

*Perf. 11½x11, 11x11½*

**1973, Feb. 18** **Photo.**

| | | | | |
|---|---|---|---|---|
| **1956** | A587 | 1z brown & multi | .25 | .25 |
| **1957** | A587 | 1.50z multicolored | .25 | .25 |
| **1958** | A587 | 2.70z multicolored | .25 | .25 |
| **1959** | A587 | 4z multicolored | .35 | .25 |
| **1960** | A587 | 4.90z multicolored | .45 | .25 |
| | | *Nos. 1956-1960 (5)* | 1.55 | 1.25 |

Piast Coronation Sword, 12th Century — A588

Polish Art: No. 1962, Kruzlowa Madonna, c. 1410. No. 1963, Hussar's armor, 17th century. No. 1964, Wawel head, wood, 16th century. No. 1965, Cock, sign of Rifle Fraternity, 16th century. 2.70z, Cover of Queen Anna Jagiellonka's prayer book (eagle), 1582. 4.90z, Skarbimierz Madonna, wood, c. 1340. 8.50z, The Nobleman Tenczynski, portrait by unknown artist, 17th century.

**1973, Mar. 28** **Photo.** *Perf. 11½x11*

| | | | | |
|---|---|---|---|---|
| **1961** | A588 | 50g violet & multi | .25 | .25 |
| **1962** | A588 | 1z lt blue & multi | .25 | .25 |
| **1963** | A588 | 1z ultra & multi | .25 | .25 |
| **1964** | A588 | 1.50z blue & multi | .25 | .25 |
| **1965** | A588 | 1.50z green & multi | .25 | .25 |
| **1966** | A588 | 2.70z multicolored | .25 | .25 |
| **1967** | A588 | 4.90z multicolored | .45 | .25 |
| **1968** | A588 | 8.50z black & multi | .75 | .25 |
| | | *Nos. 1961-1968 (8)* | 2.70 | 2.00 |

Lenin Monument, Nowa Huta — A589

**1973, Apr. 28** **Litho.** *Perf. 11x11½*

| | | | | |
|---|---|---|---|---|
| **1969** | A589 | 1z multicolored | .25 | .25 |

Unveiling of Lenin Monument at Nowa Huta.

Envelope Showing Postal Code A590

**1973, May 5** *Perf. 11x11½*

| | | | | |
|---|---|---|---|---|
| **1970** | A590 | 1.50z multicolored | .25 | .25 |

Introduction of postal code system in Poland.

Wolf — A591

**1973, May 21** **Photo.** *Perf. 11*

| | | | | |
|---|---|---|---|---|
| **1971** | A591 | 50g shown | .25 | .25 |
| **1972** | A591 | 1z Mouflon | .25 | .25 |
| **1973** | A591 | 1.50z Moose | .25 | .25 |
| **1974** | A591 | 2.70z Capercaillie | .35 | .25 |
| **1975** | A591 | 3z Deer | .70 | .25 |
| **1976** | A591 | 4.50z Lynx | 1.20 | .25 |
| **1977** | A591 | 4.90z European hart | 2.00 | .85 |
| **1978** | A591 | 5z Wild boar | 2.00 | 1.00 |
| | | *Nos. 1971-1978 (8)* | 7.00 | 3.35 |

Intl. Hunting Committee Congress and 50th anniv. of Polish Hunting Assoc.

US Satellite "Copernicus" over Earth — A592

No. 1980, USSR satellite Salyut over earth.

**1973, June 20**

| | | | | |
|---|---|---|---|---|
| **1979** | A592 | 4.90z multicolored | .35 | .25 |
| **1980** | A592 | 4.90z multicolored | .35 | .25 |

American and Russian astronomical observatories in space. No. 1979 and No. 1980 issued in sheets of 6 stamps and 2 labels. Value: mint $14, used $7.

Flame Rising from Book — A593

**1973, June 26** **Litho.**

| | | | | |
|---|---|---|---|---|
| **1981** | A593 | 1.50z blue & multi | .25 | .25 |

2nd Polish Science Cong., Warsaw, June 26-29.

Arms of Poznan on 14th Century Seal — A594

Polska '73 Emblem and: 1.50z, Tombstone of Nicolas Tomicki, 1524. 2.70z, Kalisz paten, 12th century. 4z, Lion knocker from bronze gate, Gniezno, 12th century, horiz.

*Perf. 11½x11, 11x11½*

**1973, June 30**

| | | | | |
|---|---|---|---|---|
| **1982** | A594 | 1z pink & multi | .25 | .25 |
| **1983** | A594 | 1.50z orange & multi | .25 | .25 |
| **1984** | A594 | 2.70z buff & multi | .25 | .25 |
| **1985** | A594 | 4z yellow & multi | .30 | .25 |
| | | *Nos. 1982-1985 (4)* | 1.05 | 1.00 |

POLSKA '73 Intl. Phil. Exhib., Poznan, Aug. 19-Sept. 2. See No. B128.

Marceli Nowotko — A595

**1973, Aug. 8** **Litho.** *Perf. 11½x11*

| | | | | |
|---|---|---|---|---|
| **1986** | A595 | 1.50z red & black | .25 | .25 |

Marceli Nowotko (1893-1942), labor leader, member of Central Committee of Communist Party of Poland.

Emblem and Orchard — A596

Human Environment Emblem and: 90g, Grazing cows. 1z, Stork's nest. 1.50z, Pond with fish and water lilies. 2.70z, Flowers on meadow. 4.90z, Underwater fauna and flora. 5z, Forest scene. 6.50z, Still life.

**1973, Aug. 30** **Photo.** *Perf. 11*

| | | | | |
|---|---|---|---|---|
| **1987** | A596 | 50g black & multi | .25 | .25 |
| **1988** | A596 | 90g black & multi | .25 | .25 |
| **1989** | A596 | 1z black & multi | .25 | .25 |
| **1990** | A596 | 1.50z black & multi | .25 | .25 |
| **1991** | A596 | 2.70z black & multi | .25 | .25 |
| **1992** | A596 | 4.90z black & multi | .45 | .25 |
| **1993** | A596 | 5z black & multi | 1.00 | .40 |
| **1994** | A596 | 6.50z black & multi | 1.50 | .70 |
| | | *Nos. 1987-1994 (8)* | 4.20 | 2.60 |

Protection of the environment.

Motorcyclist — A597

**1973, Sept. 2** *Perf. 11½*

| | | | | |
|---|---|---|---|---|
| **1995** | A597 | 1.50z silver & multi | .25 | .25 |

Finals in individual world championship motorcycle race on cinder track, Chorzów, Sept. 2.

Tank — A598

**1973, Oct. 12** **Litho.** *Perf. 12½*

| | | | | |
|---|---|---|---|---|
| **1996** | A598 | 1z shown | .25 | .25 |
| **1997** | A598 | 1z Fighter plane | .25 | .25 |
| **1998** | A598 | 1.50z Missile | .50 | .25 |
| **1999** | A598 | 1.50z Warship | .35 | .25 |
| | | *Nos. 1996-1999 (4)* | 1.35 | 1.00 |

Polish People's Army, 30th anniversary.

Grzegorz Piramowicz — A599

Design: 1.50z, J. Sniadecki, Hugo Kollataj and Julian Ursyn Niemcewicz.

**Photogravure and Engraved**

**1973, Oct. 13** *Perf. 11½x11*

| | | | | |
|---|---|---|---|---|
| **2000** | A599 | 1z buff & dk brn | .25 | .25 |
| **2001** | A599 | 1.50z gray & sl grn | .25 | .25 |

Natl. Education Commission, bicent.

Henryk Arctowski, and Penguins A600

Polish Scientists: No. 2003, Pawel Edmund Strzelecki and Kangaroo. No. 2004, Benedykt Tadeusz Dybowski and Lake Baikal. No. 2005, Stefan Rogozinski, sailing ship "Lucja-Malgorzata." 2z, Bronislaw Malinowski, Trobriand Island drummers. 2.70z, Stefan Drzewiecki and submarine. 3z, Edward Adolf Strasburger and plants. 8z, Ignacy Domeyko, geological strata.

**1973, Nov. 30** **Photo.** *Perf. 10½x11*

| | | | | |
|---|---|---|---|---|
| **2002** | A600 | 1z gold & multi | .25 | .25 |
| **2003** | A600 | 1z gold & multi | .25 | .25 |
| **2004** | A600 | 1.50z gold & multi | .25 | .25 |
| **2005** | A600 | 1.50z gold & multi | .25 | .25 |
| **2006** | A600 | 2z gold & multi | .25 | .25 |
| **2007** | A600 | 2.70z gold & multi | .25 | .25 |
| **2008** | A600 | 3z gold & multi | .40 | .30 |
| **2009** | A600 | 8z gold & multi | .85 | .50 |
| | | *Nos. 2002-2009 (8)* | 2.75 | 2.30 |

Polish Flag — A601

**1973, Dec. 15 Photo.** ***Perf. 11½x11***
**2010** A601 1.50z dp ultra, red & gold .25 .25

Polish United Workers' Party, 25th anniv.

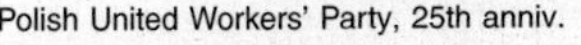

Jelcz-Berliet Bus — A602

Designs: Polish automotives.

**1973, Dec. 28 Photo.** ***Perf. 11x11½***
**2011** A602 50g shown .25 .25
**2012** A602 90g Jelcz 316 .35 .25
**2013** A602 1z Polski Fiat 126p .25 .25
**2014** A602 1.50z Polski Fiat 125p .25 .25
**2015** A602 4z Nysa M-521 bus .35 .25
**2016** A602 4.50z Star 660 truck .50 .25
*Nos. 2011-2016 (6)* 1.95 1.50

Iris — A603

Flowers: 1z, Dandelion. 1.50z, Rose. 3z, Thistle. 4z, Cornflowers. 4.50z, Clover. (Paintings by Stanislaw Wyspianski.)

**1974, Jan. 22 Engr.** ***Perf. 12x11½***
**2017** A603 50g lilac .25 .25
**2018** A603 1z green .25 .25
**2019** A603 1.50z red orange .25 .25
**2020** A603 3z deep violet .25 .25
**2021** A603 4z violet blue .30 .25
**2022** A603 4.50z emerald .35 .25
*Nos. 2017-2022 (6)* 1.65 1.50

Cottage, Kurpie A604

Designs: 1.50z, Church, Sekowa. 4z, Town Hall, Sulmierzyce. 4.50z, Church, Lachowice. 4.90z, Windmill, Sobienie-Jeziory. 5z, Orthodox Church, Ulucz.

**1974, Mar. 5 Photo.** ***Perf. 11x11½***
**2023** A604 1z multicolored .25 .25
**2024** A604 1.50z yellow & multi .25 .25
**2025** A604 4z pink & multi .25 .25
**2026** A604 4.50z lt blue & multi .25 .25
**2027** A604 4.90z multicolored .35 .25
**2028** A604 5z pink & multi .70 .25
*Nos. 2023-2028 (6)* 2.05 1.50

Mail Coach and UPU Emblem — A605

**1974, Mar. 30** ***Perf. 11½x12***
**2029** A605 1.50z multicolored .25 .25

Centenary of Universal Postal Union.

Embroidery from Cracow — A606

Embroideries from: 1.50z, Lowicz. 4z, Slask.

**1974, May 7 Photo.** ***Perf. 11½x11***
**2030** A606 50g multicolored .25 .25
**2031** A606 1.50z multicolored .25 .25
**2032** A606 4z multicolored .30 .25
*a.* Souvenir sheet of 3 #2032, imperf. 1.25 1.00
*b.* As "a," perf. 11½x11 5.00 5.00
*Nos. 2030-2032 (3)* .80 .75

SOCPHILEX IV International Philatelic Exhibition, Katowice, May 18-June 2.
No. 2032a sold for 17z.
No. 2032b sold for 17z plus 15z for 4 envelopes.

Association Emblem — A607

**1974, May 8 Litho.** ***Perf. 12x11½***
**2033** A607 1.50z gray & red .25 .25

5th Congress of the Assoc. of Combatants for Liberty & Democracy, Warsaw, May 8-9.

Soldier and Dove — A608

**1974, May 9** ***Perf. 11½x11***
**2034** A608 1.50z org, lt bl & blk .25 .25

29th anniversary of victory over Fascism.

Comecon Building, Moscow A609

**1974, May 15** ***Perf. 11x11½***
**2035** A609 1.50z gray bl, bis & red .25 .25

25th anniv. of the Council of Mutual Economic Assistance.

Soccer Ball and Games' Emblem A610

Design: No. 2037, Soccer players, Olympic rings and 1972 medal.

**1974, June 15 Photo.** ***Perf. 11x11½***
**2036** A610 4.90z olive & multi .50 .25
*a.* Souv. sheet of 4 + 2 labels 4.50 2.00
**2037** A610 4.90z olive & multi .50 .25
*a.* Souv. sheet, 2 each #2036-2037 12.00 7.00

World Cup Soccer Championship, Munich, June 13-July 7.

No. 2036a issued to commemorate Poland's silver medal in 1974 Championship.

Sailing Ship, 16th Century — A611

Polish Sailing Ships: 1.50z, "Dal," 1934. 2.70z, "Opty," sailed around the world, 1969. 4z, "Dar Pomorza," winner "Operation Sail," 1972. 4.90z, "Polonez," sailed around the world, 1973.

**1974, June 29 Litho.** ***Perf. 11½x11***
**2038** A611 1z multicolored .25 .25
**2039** A611 1.50z multicolored .25 .25
**2040** A611 2.70z multicolored .25 .25
**2041** A611 4z green & multi .35 .25
**2042** A611 4.90z dp blue & multi .70 .25
*Nos. 2038-2042 (5)* 1.80 1.25

Chess, by Jan Kochanowski A612

Design: 1.50z, "Education," etching by Daniel Chodowiecki.

**1974, July 15 Litho.** ***Perf. 11½x11***
**2043** A612 1z multicolored .25 .25
**2044** A612 1.50z multicolored .30 .25

10th International Chess Festival, Lublin.

Man and Map of Poland — A613

Polish Eagle — A614

**1974, July 21 Photo.** ***Perf. 11½x11***
**2045** A613 1.50z black, gold & red .25 .25
**2046** A614 1.50z silver & multi .25 .25
**2047** A614 1.50z red & multi .25 .25
*Nos. 2045-2047 (3)* .75 .75

People's Republic of Poland, 30th anniv.

Lazienkowska Bridge Road — A615

**1974, July 21** ***Perf. 11x11½***
**2048** A615 1.50z multicolored .25 .25

Opening of Lazienkowska Bridge over Vistula south of Warsaw.

Strawberries and Congress Emblem — A616

**1974, Sept. 10 Photo.** ***Perf. 11½***
**2049** A616 50g shown .25 .25
**2050** A616 90g Black currants .25 .25
**2051** A616 1z Apples .25 .25
**2052** A616 1.50z Cucumbers .35 .25
**2053** A616 2.70z Tomatoes .35 .25
**2054** A616 4.50z Peas .35 .25
**2055** A616 4.90z Pansies .70 .35
**2056** A616 5z Nasturtiums 1.25 .75
*Nos. 2049-2056 (8)* 3.75 2.60

19th Intl. Horticultural Cong., Warsaw, Sept.

Civic Militia and Security Service Badge — A617

**1974, Oct. 3 Photo.** ***Perf. 11½x11***
**2057** A617 1.50g multicolored .25 .25

30th anniv. of the Civic Militia and the Security Service.

Polish Child, by Lukasz Orlowski — A618

Polish paintings of Children: 90g, Girl with Pigeon, Anonymous artist, 19th century. 1z, Girl, by Stanislaw Wyspianski. 1.50z, The Orphan from Poronin, by Wladyslaw Slewinski. 3z, Peasant Boy, by Kazimierz Sichulski. 4.50z, Florentine Page, by Aleksander Gierymski. 4.90z, The Artist's Son Tadeusz, by Piotr Michalowski. 6.50z, Boy with Doe, by Aleksander Kotsis.

**1974, Oct. 9**
**2058** A618 50g multicolored .25 .25
**2059** A618 90g multicolored .25 .25
**2060** A618 1z multicolored .25 .25
**2061** A618 1.50z multicolored .25 .25
**2062** A618 3z multicolored .25 .25
**2063** A618 4.50z multicolored .30 .25
**2064** A618 4.90z multicolored .50 .25
**2065** A618 6.50z multicolored .50 .30
*Nos. 2058-2065 (8)* 2.55 2.05

Children's Day. The 1z and 1.50z are inscribed "Dzien Znaczka (Stamp Day) 1974."

Cracow Manger — A619

King Sigismund Vasa — A620

Masterpieces of Polish art: 1.50z, Flight into Egypt, 1465. 4z, King Jan Olbracht.

**1974, Dec. 2 Litho. *Perf. 11½x11***

| | | | | | |
|---|---|---|---|---|---|
| **2066** | A619 | 1z | multicolored | .25 | .25 |
| **2067** | A620 | 1.50z | multicolored | .25 | .25 |
| **2068** | A620 | 2z | multicolored | .25 | .25 |
| **2069** | A619 | 4z | multicolored | .45 | .25 |
| | | | *Nos. 2066-2069 (4)* | 1.20 | 1.00 |

Angler — A621

Designs: 1.50z, Hunter with bow and arrow. 4z, Boy snaring geese. 4.50z, Beekeeper. Designs from 16th century woodcuts.

**1974-77 Engr. *Perf. 11½x11***

| | | | | | |
|---|---|---|---|---|---|
| **2070** | A621 | 1z | black | .25 | .25 |
| **2071** | A621 | 1.50z | indigo | .25 | .25 |
| **2071A** | A621 | 4z | slate green | .25 | .25 |
| **2071B** | A621 | 4.50z | dark brown | .25 | .25 |
| | | | *Nos. 2070-2071B (4)* | 1.00 | 1.00 |

Issued: 1z-1.50z, 12/30; 4z-4.50z, 12/12/77.

Pablo Neruda, by Osvaldo Guayasamin A622

**1974, Dec. 31 Litho. *Perf. 11½x11***

| | | | | | |
|---|---|---|---|---|---|
| **2072** | A622 | 1.50z | multicolored | .25 | .25 |

Pablo Neruda (1904-1973), Chilean poet.

Nike Monument and Opera House, Warsaw — A623

**1975, Jan. 17 Photo. *Perf. 11***

| | | | | | |
|---|---|---|---|---|---|
| **2073** | A623 | 1.50z | multicolored | .25 | .25 |

30th anniversary of the liberation of Warsaw.

Hobby Falcon — A624

No. 2074, Lesser kestrel, male. No. 2075, Lesser kestrel, female. No. 2076, Red-footed falcon, male. No. 2077, Red-footed falcon, female. No. 2079, Kestrel. No. 2080, Merlin. No. 2081, Peregrine.

**1975, Jan. 23 *Perf. 11½x12***

| | | | | | |
|---|---|---|---|---|---|
| **2074** | A624 | 1z | multi | .25 | .25 |
| **2075** | A624 | 1z | multi | .25 | .25 |
| *a.* | | | Pair, #2074-2075 | .35 | .25 |
| **2076** | A624 | 1.50z | multi | .50 | .25 |
| **2077** | A624 | 1.50z | multi | .50 | .25 |
| *a.* | | | Pair, #2076-2077 | 1.00 | .25 |
| **2078** | A624 | 2z | shown | .50 | .25 |
| **2079** | A624 | 3z | multi | .65 | .35 |
| **2080** | A624 | 4z | multi | 2.00 | 1.20 |
| **2081** | A624 | 8z | multi | 3.00 | 1.40 |
| | | | *Nos. 2074-2081 (8)* | 7.65 | 4.20 |

Falcons.

"Auschwitz" A625

**Photogravure and Engraved**

**1975, Jan. 27 *Perf. 11½x11***

| | | | | | |
|---|---|---|---|---|---|
| **2082** | A625 | 1.50z | red & black | .40 | .25 |

30th anniversary of the liberation of Auschwitz (Oswiecim) concentration camp.

Women's Hurdle Race A626

Designs: 1.50z, Pole vault. 4z, Hop, step and jump. 4.90z, Sprinting.

**1975, Mar. 8 Litho. *Perf. 11x11½***

| | | | | | |
|---|---|---|---|---|---|
| **2083** | A626 | 1z | multicolored | .25 | .25 |
| **2084** | A626 | 1.50z | olive & multi | .25 | .25 |
| **2085** | A626 | 4z | multicolored | .35 | .25 |
| **2086** | A626 | 4.90z | green & multi | .45 | .25 |
| | | | *Nos. 2083-2086 (4)* | 1.30 | 1.00 |

6th European Indoor Athletic Championships, Katowice, Mar. 1975.

St. Anne, by Veit Stoss, Arphila Emblem A627

**1975, Apr. 15 Photo. *Perf. 11x11½***

| | | | | | |
|---|---|---|---|---|---|
| **2087** | A627 | 1.50z | multicolored | .25 | .25 |

ARPHILA 75, International Philatelic Exhibition, Paris, June 6-10.

Amateur Radio Union Emblem, Globe A628

**1975, Apr. 15 Litho. *Perf. 11½***

| | | | | | |
|---|---|---|---|---|---|
| **2088** | A628 | 1.50z | multicolored | .25 | .25 |

International Amateur Radio Union Conference, Warsaw, Apr. 1975.

Mountain Guides' Badge and Sudetic Mountains — A629

No. 2089, Pine, badge and Tatra Mountains, vert. No. 2090, Gentian and Tatra Mountains, vert. No. 2092, Yew branch with berries, and Sudetic Mountains. No. 2093, River, Beskids Mountains and badge, vert. No. 2094, Arnica and Beskids Mountains, vert.

**1975, Apr. 30 Photo. *Perf. 11***

| | | | | | |
|---|---|---|---|---|---|
| **2089** | A629 | 1z | multicolored | .25 | .25 |
| **2090** | A629 | 1z | multicolored | .25 | .25 |
| *a.* | | | Pair, #2089-2090 | .25 | .25 |
| **2091** | A629 | 1.50z | multicolored | .25 | .25 |
| **2092** | A629 | 1.50z | multicolored | .25 | .25 |
| *a.* | | | Pair, #2091-2092 | .30 | .25 |
| **2093** | A629 | 4z | multicolored | .25 | .25 |
| **2094** | A629 | 4z | multicolored | .25 | .25 |
| *a.* | | | Pair, #2093-2094 | .60 | .25 |
| | | | *Nos. 2090a,2092a,2094a (3)* | 1.15 | .75 |

Centenary of Polish Mountain Guides Organizations. Pairs have continuous design.

Hands Holding Tulips and Rifle — A630

**1975, May 9 *Perf. 11½x11***

| | | | | | |
|---|---|---|---|---|---|
| **2095** | A630 | 1.50z | blue & multi | .25 | .25 |

End of WWII, 30th anniv.; victory over Fascism.

Warsaw Treaty Members' Flags — A631

**1975, May 14**

| | | | | | |
|---|---|---|---|---|---|
| **2096** | A631 | 1.50z | blue & multi | .25 | .25 |

20th anniversary of the signing of the Warsaw Treaty (Bulgaria, Czechoslovakia, German Democratic Rep., Hungary, Poland, Romania, USSR).

Cock and Hen, Congress Emblem — A632

**1975, June 23 Photo. *Perf. 12x11½***

| | | | | | |
|---|---|---|---|---|---|
| **2097** | A632 | 50g | shown | .25 | .25 |
| **2098** | A632 | 1z | Geese | .25 | .25 |
| **2099** | A632 | 1.50z | Cattle | .25 | .25 |
| **2100** | A632 | 2z | Cow | .25 | .25 |
| **2101** | A632 | 3z | Arabian stallion | .30 | .25 |
| **2102** | A632 | 4z | Wielkopolska horses | .50 | .25 |
| **2103** | A632 | 4.50z | Pigs | 1.25 | .50 |
| **2104** | A632 | 5z | Sheep | 1.75 | 1.40 |
| | | | *Nos. 2097-2104 (8)* | 4.80 | 3.40 |

20th Congress of the European Zootechnical Federation, Warsaw.

Apollo and Soyuz Linked in Space A633

**1975, July 15 *Perf. 11x11½***

| | | | | | |
|---|---|---|---|---|---|
| **2105** | A633 | 1.50z | shown | .25 | .25 |
| **2106** | A633 | 4.90z | Apollo | .35 | .25 |
| **2107** | A633 | 4.90z | Soyuz | .35 | .25 |
| *a.* | | | Souv. sheet, 2 each #2105-2107 + 2 labels | 5.25 | 2.25 |
| *b.* | | | Pair, #2106-2107 | .75 | .35 |
| | | | *Nos. 2105-2107 (3)* | .95 | .75 |

Apollo Soyuz space test project (Russo-American cooperation), launching July 15; link-up, July 17.

Health Fund Emblem — A634

**1975, July 12 *Perf. 11½x11***

| | | | | | |
|---|---|---|---|---|---|
| **2108** | A634 | 1.50z | silver, blk & bl | .25 | .25 |

National Fund for Health Protection.

"E" and Polish Flag A635

**1975, July 30 Litho. *Perf. 11x11½***

| | | | | | |
|---|---|---|---|---|---|
| **2109** | A635 | 4z | lt blue, red & blk | .40 | .25 |

European Security and Cooperation Conference, Helsinki, July 30-Aug. 1.

UN Emblem and Sunburst A636

**1975, July 25**

| | | | | | |
|---|---|---|---|---|---|
| **2110** | A636 | 4z | blue & multi | .45 | .25 |

30th anniversary of the United Nations.

Bolek and Lolek A637

Cartoon Characters and Children's Health Center Emblem: 1z, Jacek and Agatka. 1.50z, Reksio, the dog. 4z, Telesfor, the dragon.

**1975, Aug. 30 Photo. *Perf. 11x11½***

| | | | | | |
|---|---|---|---|---|---|
| **2111** | A637 | 50g | violet bl & multi | .25 | .25 |
| **2112** | A637 | 1z | multicolored | .25 | .25 |
| **2113** | A637 | 1.50z | multicolored | .25 | .25 |
| **2114** | A637 | 4z | multicolored | .35 | .25 |
| | | | *Nos. 2111-2114 (4)* | 1.10 | 1.00 |

Children's television programs.

Circular Bar Graph and Institute's Emblem — A638

**1975, Sept. 1 Litho. *Perf. 11½x11***

**2115** A638 1.50z multicolored .25 .25

International Institute of Statistics, 40th session, Warsaw, Sept. 1975.

IWY Emblem, White, Yellow and Brown Women — A639

**1975, Sept. 8 Photo.**

**2116** A639 1.50z multicolored .25 .25

International Women's Year.

A640

George Washington A641

Designs: 1z, First Poles Arriving on "Mary and Margaret" 1608. 1.50z, Polish glass blower and glass works, Jamestown, 1608. 2.70z, Helena Modrzejewska (1840-1909), Polish actress, came to US in 1877. 4z, Casimir Pulaski (1747-1779), and 6.40z, Tadeusz Kosciusko (1748-1817), heroes of American War of Independence.

**1975, Sept. 24 Litho. *Perf. 11x11½***

| | | | | | |
|---|---|---|---|---|---|
| **2117** | A640 | 1z | black & multi | .25 | .25 |
| **2118** | A640 | 1.50z | black & multi | .25 | .25 |
| **2119** | A640 | 2.70z | black & multi | .25 | .25 |
| **2120** | A640 | 4z | black & multi | .40 | .25 |
| **2121** | A640 | 6.40z | black & multi | .60 | .30 |
| | | | *Nos. 2117-2121 (5)* | 1.75 | 1.30 |

**Souvenir Sheet**

***Perf. 12***

| | | | |
|---|---|---|---|
| **2122** | Sheet of 3+3 labels | 1.75 | .85 |
| *a.* | A641 4.90z shown | .40 | .25 |
| *b.* | A641 4.90z Kosciusko | .40 | .25 |
| *c.* | A641 4.90z Pulaski | .40 | .25 |

American Revolution, bicentenary.

Albatross Biplane, 1918-1925 A642

Design: 4.90z, IL 62 jet, 1975.

**1975, Sept. 25 *Perf. 11x11½***

| | | | | | |
|---|---|---|---|---|---|
| **2123** | A642 | 2.40z | buff & multi | .25 | .25 |
| **2124** | A642 | 4.90z | gray & multi | .30 | .25 |

50th anniversary of Polish air post stamps.

Frederic Chopin — A643

**1975, Oct. 7 Photo.**

**2125** A643 1.50z gold, lt vio & blk .25 .25

9th International Chopin Piano Competition, Warsaw, Oct. 7-28.

Printed in sheets of 50 stamps with alternating labels with commemorative inscription.

Dunikowski, Self-portrait A644

Sculptures: 1z, "Breath." 1.50z, "Maternity."

**1975, Oct. 9 *Perf. 11½x11***

| | | | | | |
|---|---|---|---|---|---|
| **2126** | A644 | 50g | silver & multi | .25 | .25 |
| **2127** | A644 | 1z | silver & multi | .25 | .25 |
| **2128** | A644 | 1.50z | silver & multi | .25 | .25 |
| | | | *Nos. 2126-2128 (3)* | .75 | .75 |

Stamp Day. Xawery Dunikowski (1875-1964), sculptor. See No. B131.

Town Hall, Zamosc — A645

1z, Arcades, Kazimierz Dolny, horiz.

**Coil Stamps**

**1975, Nov. 11 Photo. *Perf. 14***

| | | | | | |
|---|---|---|---|---|---|
| **2129** | A645 | 1z | olive green | .25 | .25 |
| **2130** | A645 | 1.50z | rose brown | .25 | .25 |

European Architectural Heritage Year. Black control number on back of every fifth stamp of Nos. 2129-2130.

Lodz, by Wladyslaw Strzeminski A646

**1975, Nov. 22 Litho. *Perf. 12½***

| | | | | | |
|---|---|---|---|---|---|
| **2131** | A646 | 4.50z | multicolored | .35 | .25 |
| *a.* | | | Souvenir sheet | .80 | .40 |

Lodz 75, 12th Polish Philatelic Exhibition, for 25th anniv. of Polish Philatelists Union.

Piast Family Eagle A647

1.50z, Seal of Prince Boleslaw of Legnica. 4z, Coin of Prince Jerzy Wilhelm (1660-1675).

**1975, Nov. 29 Engr. *Perf. 11x11½***

| | | | | | |
|---|---|---|---|---|---|
| **2132** | A647 | 1z | green | .25 | .25 |
| **2133** | A647 | 1.50z | brown | .25 | .25 |
| **2134** | A647 | 4z | dull violet | .25 | .25 |
| | | | *Nos. 2132-2134 (3)* | .75 | .75 |

Piast dynasty's influence on the development of Silesia.

"7" Inscribed "ZJAZD" and "PZPR" — A648

"VII ZJAZD PZPR" — A649

**1975, Dec. 8 Photo. *Perf. 11½x11***

| | | | | | |
|---|---|---|---|---|---|
| **2135** | A648 | 1z | lt blue & multi | .25 | .25 |
| **2136** | A649 | 1.50z | silver, red & ultra | .25 | .25 |

7th Cong. of Polish United Workers' Party.

Ski Jump A650

Designs (Winter Olympic Games Emblem and): 1z, Ice hockey. 1.50z, Slalom. 2z, Speed skating. 4z, Luge. 6.40z, Biathlon.

**1976, Jan. 10 *Perf. 11x11½***

| | | | | | |
|---|---|---|---|---|---|
| **2137** | A650 | 50g | silver & multi | .25 | .25 |
| **2138** | A650 | 1z | silver & multi | .25 | .25 |
| **2139** | A650 | 1.50z | silver & multi | .25 | .25 |
| **2140** | A650 | 2z | silver & multi | .25 | .25 |
| **2141** | A650 | 4z | silver & multi | .30 | .25 |
| **2142** | A650 | 6.40z | silver & multi | .70 | .35 |
| | | | *Nos. 2137-2142 (6)* | 2.00 | 1.60 |

12th Winter Olympic Games, Innsbruck, Austria, Feb. 4-15.

Engine by Richard Trevithick, 1803 — A651

Locomotives by: 1z, M. Murray and J. Blenkinsop, 1810. No. 2145, George Stephenson's Rocket, 1829. No. 2146, Polish electric locomotive, 1969. 2.70z, Stephenson, 1837. 3z, Joseph Harrison, 1840. 4.50z, Thomas Rogers, 1855. 4.90z, Chrzanow (Polish), 1922.

**1976, Feb. 13 Photo. *Perf. 11½x12***

| | | | | | |
|---|---|---|---|---|---|
| **2143** | A651 | 50g | multicolored | .25 | .25 |
| **2144** | A651 | 1z | multicolored | .25 | .25 |
| **2145** | A651 | 1.50z | multicolored | .25 | .25 |
| **2146** | A651 | 1.50z | multicolored | .25 | .25 |
| **2147** | A651 | 2.70z | multicolored | .25 | .25 |
| **2148** | A651 | 3z | multicolored | .35 | .25 |
| **2149** | A651 | 4.50z | multicolored | .55 | .25 |
| **2150** | A651 | 4.90z | multicolored | .85 | .35 |
| | | | *Nos. 2143-2150 (8)* | 3.00 | 2.10 |

History of the locomotive.

Telephone, Radar and Satellites, ITU Emblem — A652

**1976, Mar. 10 *Perf. 11***

**2151** A652 1.50z multicolored .25 .25

Centenary of first telephone call by Alexander Graham Bell, Mar. 10, 1876.

Atom Symbol and Flags of Communist Countries A653

**1976, Mar. 10 Litho. *Perf. 11½***

**2152** A653 1.50z multicolored .25 .25

Joint Institute of Nuclear Research, Dubna, USSR, 20th anniversary.

Ice Hockey — A654

Design: 1.50z, like 1z, reversed.

**1976, Apr. 8 Photo. *Perf. 11½x11***

| | | | | | |
|---|---|---|---|---|---|
| **2153** | A654 | 1z | multicolored | .25 | .25 |
| **2154** | A654 | 1.50z | multicolored | .25 | .25 |

Ice Hockey World Championship 1976, Katowice.

Soldier and Map of Sinai A655

**1976, Apr. 30 Photo. *Perf. 11x11½***

| | | | | |
|---|---|---|---|---|
| **2155** | A655 | 1.50z multicolored | .25 | .25 |

Polish specialist troops serving with UN Forces in Sinai Peninsula.

No. 2155 printed se-tenant with label with commemorative inscription.

Sappers' Monument, by Stanislaw Kulow, Warsaw — A656

Design: No. 2157, First Polish Army Monument, by Bronislaw Koniuszy, Warsaw.

**1976, May 8 *Perf. 11½***

| | | | | |
|---|---|---|---|---|
| **2156** | A656 | 1z gold & multi | .25 | .25 |
| **2157** | A656 | 1z silver & multi | .25 | .25 |

Memorials unveiled on 30th anniv. of WWII victory.

Interphil 76, Philadelphia A657

**1976, May 20 Litho. *Perf. 11½x11***

| | | | | |
|---|---|---|---|---|
| **2158** | A657 | 8.40z gray & multi | .45 | .25 |

Interphil 76, Intl. Phil. Exhib., Philadelphia, May 29-June 6.

Wielkopolski Park and Owl — A658

National Parks: 1z, Wolinski Park and eagle. 1.50z, Slowinski Park and sea gull. 4.50z, Bieszczadzki Park and lynx. 5z, Ojcowski Park and bat. 6z, Kampinoski Park and elk.

**1976, May 22 Photo. *Perf. 12x11½***

| | | | | |
|---|---|---|---|---|
| **2159** | A658 | 90g multicolored | .25 | .25 |
| **2160** | A658 | 1z multicolored | .25 | .25 |
| **2161** | A658 | 1.50z multicolored | .25 | .25 |
| **2162** | A658 | 4.50z multicolored | .30 | .25 |
| **2163** | A658 | 5z multicolored | .60 | .25 |
| **2164** | A658 | 6z multicolored | .75 | .25 |
| | | *Nos. 2159-2164 (6)* | 2.40 | 1.50 |

UN Headquarters, Dove-shaped Globe — A659

**1976, June 29 Litho. *Perf. 11x11½***

| | | | | |
|---|---|---|---|---|
| **2165** | A659 | 8.40z multicolored | .45 | .25 |

UN postage stamps, 25th anniversary.

Fencing and Olympic Rings A660

**1976, June 30 Photo.**

| | | | | |
|---|---|---|---|---|
| **2166** | A660 | 50g shown | .25 | .25 |
| **2167** | A660 | 1z Bicycling | .25 | .25 |
| **2168** | A660 | 1.50z Soccer | .25 | .25 |
| **2169** | A660 | 4.20z Boxing | .30 | .25 |
| **2170** | A660 | 6.90z Weight lifting | .40 | .25 |
| **2171** | A660 | 8.40z Running | .55 | .25 |
| | | *Nos. 2166-2171 (6)* | 2.00 | 1.50 |

21st Olympic Games, Montreal, Canada, July 17-Aug. 1. See No. B132.

Polish Theater, Poznan — A662

**1976, July 12 Litho. *Perf. 11x11½***

| | | | | |
|---|---|---|---|---|
| **2173** | A662 | 1.50z gray olive & org | .25 | .25 |

Polish Theater in Poznan, centenary.

Czekanowski, Lake Baikal — A663

**1976, Sept. 3 Photo. *Perf. 11x11½***

| | | | | |
|---|---|---|---|---|
| **2174** | A663 | 1.50z silver & multi | .25 | .25 |

Aleksander Czekanowski (1833-1876), geologist, death centenary.

Siren A664

Designs: 1z, Sphinx, vert. 2z, Lion. 4.20z, Bull. 4.50z, Goat. Designs from Corinthian vases, 7th century B.C.

***Perf. 11x11½, 11½x11***

**1976, Oct. 30 Photo.**

| | | | | |
|---|---|---|---|---|
| **2175** | A664 | 1z gold & multi | .25 | .25 |
| **2176** | A664 | 1.50z gold & multi | .25 | .25 |
| **2177** | A664 | 2z gold & multi | .25 | .25 |
| **2178** | A664 | 4.20z gold & multi | .25 | .25 |
| **2179** | A664 | 4.50z gold & multi | .25 | .25 |
| | | *Nos. 2175-2179,B133 (6)* | 2.05 | 1.55 |

Stamp Day.

Warszawa M20 — A665

Automobiles: 1.50z, Warszawa 223. 2z, Syrena 104. 4.90z, Polski Fiat 125.

**1976, Nov. 6 Photo. *Perf. 11***

| | | | | |
|---|---|---|---|---|
| **2180** | A665 | 1z multicolored | .25 | .25 |
| **2181** | A665 | 1.50z multicolored | .25 | .25 |
| **2182** | A665 | 2z multicolored | .25 | .25 |
| **2183** | A665 | 4.90z multicolored | .30 | .25 |
| *a.* | | Souvenir sheet of 4, #2180-2183 + 2 labels | 1.50 | 1.00 |
| | | *Nos. 2180-2183 (4)* | 1.05 | 1.00 |

Zeran Automobile Factory, Warsaw, 25th anniv.

Pouring Ladle — A666

**1976, Nov. 26 Litho. *Perf. 11***

| | | | | |
|---|---|---|---|---|
| **2184** | A666 | 1.50z multicolored | .25 | .25 |

First steel production at Katowice Foundry.

Virgin and Child, Epitaph, 1425 — A667

6z, The Beautiful Madonna, sculpture, c. 1410.

**1976, Dec. 15**

| | | | | |
|---|---|---|---|---|
| **2185** | A667 | 1z multicolored | .25 | .25 |
| **2186** | A667 | 6z multicolored | .30 | .25 |

Polish Trade Union Emblem — A668

**1976, Dec. 29**

| | | | | |
|---|---|---|---|---|
| **2187** | A668 | 1.50z multicolored | .25 | .25 |

8th Polish Trade Union Congress.

Tanker Zawrat Unloading, Gdansk — A669

Polish Ports: No. 2189, Ferry "Gryf" and cars at pier, Gdansk. No. 2190, Loading containers, Gdynia. No. 2191, "Stefan Batory" and "People of the Sea" monument, Gdynia. 2z, Barge and cargoship "Ziemia Szczecinska", Szczecin. 4.20z, Coal loading installations, Swinoujscie. 6.90z, Liner, hydrofoil and lighthouse, Kolobrzeg. 8.40z, Map of Polish Coast with ports, ships and emblem of Union of Polish Ports.

**1976, Dec. 29 Photo. *Perf. 11***

| | | | | |
|---|---|---|---|---|
| **2188** | A669 | 1z multicolored | .25 | .25 |
| **2189** | A669 | 1z multicolored | .25 | .25 |
| **2190** | A669 | 1.50z multicolored | .25 | .25 |
| **2191** | A669 | 1.50z multicolored | .25 | .25 |
| **2192** | A669 | 2z multicolored | .25 | .25 |
| **2193** | A669 | 4.20z multicolored | .25 | .25 |
| **2194** | A669 | 6.90z multicolored | .45 | .25 |
| **2195** | A669 | 8.40z multicolored | .50 | .30 |
| | | *Nos. 2188-2195 (8)* | 2.45 | 2.05 |

Nurse Helping Old Woman — A670

**1977, Jan. 24 Litho. *Perf. 11½x11***

| | | | | |
|---|---|---|---|---|
| **2196** | A670 | 1.50z multicolored | .25 | .25 |

Polish Red Cross.

Civilian Defense Medal — A671

**1977, Feb. 26 Litho. *Perf. 11***

| | | | | |
|---|---|---|---|---|
| **2197** | A671 | 1.50z multicolored | .25 | .25 |

Civilian Defense.

Ball on the Road — A672

**1977, Mar. 12 Photo.**

| | | | | |
|---|---|---|---|---|
| **2198** | A672 | 1.50z olive & multi | .25 | .25 |

Social Action Committee (founded 1966), "Stop, Child on the Road!"

Forest Fruits — A673

**1977, Mar. 17 *Perf. 11½x11***

| | | | | |
|---|---|---|---|---|
| **2199** | A673 | 50g Dewberry | .25 | .25 |
| **2200** | A673 | 90g Cranberry | .25 | .25 |
| **2201** | A673 | 1z Wild strawberry | .25 | .25 |
| **2202** | A673 | 1.50z Bilberry | .25 | .25 |
| **2203** | A673 | 2z Raspberry | .25 | .25 |
| **2204** | A673 | 4.50z Blueberry | .30 | .25 |
| **2205** | A673 | 6z Dog rose | .35 | .25 |
| **2206** | A673 | 6.90z Hazelnut | .75 | .25 |
| | | *Nos. 2199-2206 (8)* | 2.65 | 2.00 |

Flags of USSR and Poland as Computer Tape — A674

**1977, Apr. 4 Litho. *Perf. 11½x11***

| | | | | |
|---|---|---|---|---|
| **2207** | A674 | 1.50z red & multi | .25 | .25 |

Scientific and technical cooperation between Poland and USSR, 30th anniversary.

Emblem and Graph — A675

**1977, Apr. 22**
**2208** A675 1.50z red & multi .25 .25

7th Congress of Polish Engineers.

Venus, by Rubens A676

Paintings by Flemish painter Peter Paul Rubens (1577-1640): 1.50z, Bathsheba. 5z, Helene Fourment. 6z, Self-portrait.

**1977, Apr. 30** ***Perf. 11½***
**Frame in Gray Brown**

| | | | | | |
|---|---|---|---|---|---|
| **2209** | A676 | 1z | multicolored | .25 | .25 |
| **2210** | A676 | 1.50z | multicolored | .25 | .25 |
| **2211** | A676 | 5z | multicolored | .55 | .25 |
| **2212** | A676 | 6z | multicolored | .70 | .25 |
| | | | *Nos. 2209-2212 (4)* | 1.75 | 1.00 |

See No. B134.

Peace Dove A677

**1977, May 6** ***Perf. 11x11½***
**2213** A677 1.50z black, ultra & yel .25 .25

Congress of World Council of Peace, Warsaw, May 6-11.

Bicyclist A678

**1977, May 6** **Photo.**
**2214** A678 1.50z gray & multi .25 .25

30th International Peace Bicycling Race, Warsaw-Berlin-Prague.

Wolf — A679

Wildlife Fund Emblem and: No. 2216, Great bustard. No. 2217, Kestrel. 6z, Otter.

**1977, May 12** **Photo.** ***Perf. 11½x11***

| | | | | | |
|---|---|---|---|---|---|
| **2215** | A679 | 1z | silver & multi | .35 | .25 |
| **2216** | A679 | 1.50z | silver & multi | .40 | .25 |
| **2217** | A679 | 1.50z | silver & multi | .40 | .25 |
| **2218** | A679 | 6z | silver & multi | .90 | .50 |
| | | | *Nos. 2215-2218 (4)* | 2.05 | 1.25 |

Wildlife protection.

Violinist, by Jacob Toorenvliet A680

**1977, May 16**
**2219** A680 6z gold & multi .45 .25

AMPHILEX '77 Intl. Phil. Exhib., Amsterdam, May 26-June 5. No. 2219 issued in sheets of 6.

Midsummer Bonfire — A681

Folk Customs: 1z, Easter cock. 1.50z, Dousing the women on Easter Monday. 3z, Harvest festival. 6z, Christmas procession with crèche. 8.40z, Wedding dance. 1z, 1.50z, 3z, 6z vertical.

***Perf. 11x11½, 11½x11***
**1977, June 13** **Photo.**

| | | | | | |
|---|---|---|---|---|---|
| **2220** | A681 | 90g | multicolored | .25 | .25 |
| **2221** | A681 | 1z | multicolored | .25 | .25 |
| **2222** | A681 | 1.50z | multicolored | .25 | .25 |
| **2223** | A681 | 3z | multicolored | .25 | .25 |
| **2224** | A681 | 6z | multicolored | .45 | .25 |
| **2225** | A681 | 8.40z | multicolored | .55 | .25 |
| | | | *Nos. 2220-2225 (6)* | 2.00 | 1.50 |

Henryk Wieniawski and Musical Symbol — A682

**1977, June 30** **Litho.** ***Perf. 11½x11***
**2226** A682 1.50z gold, blk & red .30 .25

Wieniawski Music Festivals, Poznan: 5th Intl. Lute Competition, June 30-July 10, and 7th Intl. Violin Competition, Nov. 13-27.

Parnassius Apollo — A683

Butterflies: No. 2228, Nymphalis polychloros. No. 2229, Papilio machaon. No. 2230, Nymphalis antiopa. 5z, Fabriciana adippe. 6.90z, Argynnis paphia.

**1977, Aug. 22** **Photo.** ***Perf. 11***

| | | | | | |
|---|---|---|---|---|---|
| **2227** | A683 | 1z | multicolored | .25 | .25 |
| **2228** | A683 | 1z | multicolored | .25 | .25 |
| **2229** | A683 | 1.50z | multicolored | .35 | .25 |
| **2230** | A683 | 1.50z | multicolored | .35 | .25 |
| **2231** | A683 | 5z | multicolored | .90 | .35 |
| **2232** | A683 | 6.90z | multicolored | 2.10 | 1.00 |
| | | | *Nos. 2227-2232 (6)* | 4.20 | 2.35 |

Arms of Slupsk, Keyboard — A684

**1977, Sept. 3** ***Perf. 11½***
**2233** A684 1.50z multicolored .25 .25

Slupsk Piano Festival.

Feliks Dzerzhinski A685

**1977, Sept. 10** **Litho.** ***Perf. 11½x11***
**2234** A685 1.50z olive bis & sepia .25 .25

Feliks E. Dzerzhinski (1877-1926), organizer and head of Russian Secret Police (Cheka).

Earth and Sputnik A686

**1977, Oct. 1** **Litho.** ***Perf. 11x11½***
**2235** A686 1.50z ultra & car .25 .25
*a.* Souvenir sheet of 3+3 labels .90 .35

60th anniv. of the Russian Revolution and 20th anniv. of Sputnik space flight. Printed in sheets of 15 stamps and 15 carmine labels showing Winter Palace, Leningrad.

Boleslaw Chrobry's Denarius, 11th Century — A687

Silver Coins: 1z, King Kazimierz Wielki's Cracow groszy, 14th century. 1.50z, Legniza-Brzeg-Wolow thaler, 17th century. 4.20z, King Augustus III guilder, Gdansk, 18th century. 4.50z, 5z (ship), 1936. 6z, 100z, Poland's millenium, 1966.

**1977, Oct. 9** **Photo.** ***Perf. 11½x11***

| | | | | | |
|---|---|---|---|---|---|
| **2236** | A687 | 50g | silver & multi | .25 | .25 |
| **2237** | A687 | 1z | silver & multi | .25 | .25 |
| **2238** | A687 | 1.50z | silver & multi | .25 | .25 |
| **2239** | A687 | 4.20z | silver & multi | .25 | .25 |
| **2240** | A687 | 4.50z | silver & multi | .35 | .25 |
| **2241** | A687 | 6z | silver & multi | .50 | .25 |
| | | | *Nos. 2236-2241 (6)* | 1.85 | 1.50 |

Stamp Day.

Monastery, Przasnysz — A688

Architectural landmarks: No. 2242, Wolin Gate, vert. No. 2243, Church, Debno, vert. No. 2245, Cathedral, Plock. 6z, Castle, Kornik. 6.90z, Palace and Garden, Wilanow.

***Perf. 11½x11, 11x11½***
**1977, Nov. 21** **Photo.**

| | | | | | |
|---|---|---|---|---|---|
| **2242** | A688 | 1z | multicolored | .25 | .25 |
| **2243** | A688 | 1z | multicolored | .25 | .25 |
| **2244** | A688 | 1.50z | multicolored | .25 | .25 |
| **2245** | A688 | 1.50z | multicolored | .25 | .25 |
| **2246** | A688 | 6z | multicolored | .45 | .25 |
| **2247** | A688 | 6.90z | multicolored | .50 | .30 |
| | | | *Nos. 2242-2247 (6)* | 1.95 | 1.55 |

Vostok (USSR) and Mercury (USA) A689

**1977, Dec. 28** **Photo.** ***Perf. 11x11½***
**2248** A689 6.90z ultra & multi .50 .30
*a.* Souvenir sheet of 6 4.75 2.40

20 years of space conquest. No. 2248a contains 6 No. 2248 (2 tete-beche pairs) and 2 labels, one showing Sputnik 1 and "4.X.1957," the other Explorer 1 and "31.1.1958."

DN Class Iceboats — A690

Design: No. 2250, One iceboat.

**1978, Feb. 6** **Litho.** ***Perf. 11***
**2249** A690 1.50z lt ultra & blk .25 .25
**2250** A690 1.50z lt ultra & blk .25 .25
*a.* Pair, #2249-2250 + label .50 .25

6th World Iceboating Championships, Feb. 6-11.

Electric Locomotive, Katowice Station, 1957 — A691

Locomotives in Poland: No. 2252, Narrow-gauge engine and Gothic Tower, Znin. No. 2253, Pm36 and Ceglelski factory, Poznan, 1936. No. 2254, Electric train and Otwock Station, 1936. No. 2255, Marki Train and Warsaw Stalow Station, 1907. 4.50z, Ty51 coal train and Gdynia Station, 1933. 5z, Tr21 and Chrzanow factory, 1920. 6z, "Cockerill" and Vienna Station, 1848.

**1978, Feb. 28** **Photo.** ***Perf. 12x11½***

| | | | | | |
|---|---|---|---|---|---|
| **2251** | A691 | 50g | multicolored | .25 | .25 |
| **2252** | A691 | 1z | multicolored | .25 | .25 |
| **2253** | A691 | 1z | multicolored | .25 | .25 |
| **2254** | A691 | 1.50z | multicolored | .25 | .25 |
| **2255** | A691 | 1.50z | multicolored | .25 | .25 |
| **2256** | A691 | 4.50z | multicolored | .35 | .25 |
| **2257** | A691 | 5z | multicolored | .40 | .25 |
| **2258** | A691 | 6z | multicolored | .85 | .45 |
| | | | *Nos. 2251-2258 (8)* | 2.85 | 2.20 |

Pierwsze Wzloty, 1896, and Czeslaw Tanski A692

Polish Aviation: 1z, Zwyciezcy-Challenge, 1932, F. Zwirko and S. Wigura, vert. 1.50z, RWD-5 bis over South Atlantic, 1933, and S. Skarzynski, vert. 4.20z, MI-2 helicopter over mountains, Pezetel emblem, vert. 6.90z, PZL-104 Wilga 35, Pezetel emblem. 8.40z, Motoszybowiec SZD-45 Ogar.

**1978, Apr. 15** ***Perf. 11x11½, 11½x11***

| | | | | | |
|---|---|---|---|---|---|
| **2259** | A692 | 50g | multicolored | .25 | .25 |
| **2260** | A692 | 1z | multicolored | .25 | .25 |
| **2261** | A692 | 1.50z | multicolored | .25 | .25 |
| **2262** | A692 | 4.20z | multicolored | .30 | .25 |

**2263** A692 6.90z multicolored .65 .40
**2264** A692 8.40z multicolored .50 .40
*Nos. 2259-2264 (6)* 2.20 1.80

Soccer — A693

Design: 6.90z, Soccer ball, horiz.

***Perf. 11½x11, 11x11½***

**1978, May 12** **Litho.**

**2265** A693 1.50z multicolored .25 .25
**2266** A693 6.90z multicolored .50 .25

11th World Cup Soccer Championships, Argentina, June 1-25.

Poster — A694

**1978, June 1** ***Perf. 12x11½***

**2267** A694 1.50z multicolored .25 .25

7th International Poster Biennale, Warsaw.

Fair Emblem — A695

**1978, June 10** ***Perf. 11***

**2268** A695 1.50z multicolored .25 .25

50th International Poznan Fair.

Polonez Passenger Car — A696

**1978, June 10** **Photo.** ***Perf. 11***

**2269** A696 1.50z multicolored .25 .25

Maj. Miroslaw Hermaszewski A697

6.90z, Hermaszewski, globe & trajectory.

***Perf. 11½x11, 11x11½***

**1978, June 27** **Photo.**

**2270** A697 1.50z multi .25 .25
*a.* Without date .25 .25
**2271** A697 6.90z multi, horiz. .35 .25
*a.* Without date .65 .65

1st Polish cosmonaut on Russian space mission. Nos. 2270a, 2271a printed in sheets of 6 stamps and 2 labels.

Stamps and sheets showing Zenon Jankowski were prepared but not issued.

Youth Festival Emblem A698

**1978, July 12** **Litho.** ***Perf. 11½***

**2272** A698 1.50z multicolored .25 .25

11th Youth Festival, Havana, July 28-Aug. 5.

Souvenir Sheet

Flowers — A699

**1978, July 20** ***Perf. 11½x11***

**2273** A699 1.50z gold & multi .45 .25

30th anniv. of Polish Youth Movement.

Anopheles Mosquito and Blood Cells — A700

Design: 6z, Tsetse fly and blood cells.

**1978, Aug. 19** **Litho.** ***Perf. 11½x11***

**2274** A700 1.50z multicolored .25 .25
**2275** A700 6z multicolored .45 .25

4th International Parasitological Congress.

Norway Maple, Environment Emblem — A701

Emblem and: 1z, English oak. 1.50z, White poplar. 4.20z, Scotch pine. 4.50z, White willow. 6z, Birch.

**1978, Sept. 6** **Photo.** ***Perf. 14***

**2276** A701 50g gold & multi .25 .25
**2277** A701 1z gold & multi .25 .25
**2278** A701 1.50z gold & multi .25 .25
**2279** A701 4.20z gold & multi .30 .25
**2280** A701 4.50z gold & multi .35 .25
**2281** A701 6z gold & multi .50 .30
*Nos. 2276-2281 (6)* 1.90 1.55

Protection of the environment.

Souvenir Sheet

Jan Zizka, Battle of Grunwald, by Jan Matejko — A702

**1978, Sept. 8** ***Perf. 11½x11***

**2282** A702 6z gold & multi 1.10 .60

PRAGA '78 Intl. Phil. Exhib., Prague, Sept. 8-17.

Letter, Telephone and Satellite — A703

**1978, Sept. 20** **Litho.** ***Perf. 11***

**2283** A703 1.50z multicolored .25 .25

20th anniversary of the Organization of Ministers of Posts and Telecommunications of Warsaw Pact countries.

Peace, by Andre le Brun — A704

**1978-79** **Litho.** ***Perf. 11½ (1z), 12½***

**2284** A704 1z violet .25 .25
**2285** A704 1.50z steel blue .25 .25
**2286** A704 2z brown .25 .25
**2287** A704 2.50z ultra .25 .25
*Nos. 2284-2287 (4)* 1.00 1.00

Issued: 1z, 9/30; 1.50z, 4/28/79; 2z, 11/30/79; 2.50z, 11/5/79.

Polish Unit, UN Middle East Emergency Force — A706

Designs: No. 2289, Color Guard, Kosziusko Division (4 soldiers). No. 2290, Color Guard, field training (3 soldiers).

**1978, Oct. 6** **Photo.** ***Perf. 12x11½***

**2289** A706 1.50z multicolored .25 .25
**2290** A706 1.50z multicolored .25 .25
**2291** A706 1.50z multicolored .25 .25
*Nos. 2289-2291 (3)* .75 .75

35th anniversary of People's Army.

Young Man, by Raphael A707

**1978, Oct. 9** ***Perf. 11***

**2292** A707 6z multicolored .30 .25

Stamp Day.

Dr. Korczak and Children — A708

**1978, Oct. 11** **Litho.** ***Perf. 11½x11***

**2293** A708 1.50z multicolored .25 .25

Dr. Janusz Korczak, physician, educator, writer, birth centenary.

Wojciech Boguslawski (1757-1829) — A709

Polish dramatists: 1z, Aleksander Fredro (1793-1878). 1.50z, Juliusz Slowacki (1809-1849). 2z, Adam Mickiewicz (1798-1855). 4.50z, Stanislaw Wyspianski (1869-1907). 6z, Gabriela Zapolska (1857-1921).

**1978, Nov. 11** **Litho.** ***Perf. 11½***

**2294** A709 50g multicolored .25 .25
**2295** A709 1z multicolored .25 .25
**2296** A709 1.50z multicolored .25 .25
**2297** A709 2z multicolored .25 .25
**2298** A709 4.50z multicolored .30 .25
**2299** A709 6z multicolored .40 .25
*Nos. 2294-2299 (6)* 1.70 1.50

Polish Combatants Monument, and Eiffel Tower, Paris — A710

**1978, Nov. 2** **Photo.** ***Perf. 11x11½***

**2300** A710 1.50z brown, red & bl .25 .25

Przewalski Mare and Colt — A711

Animals: 1z, Polar bears. 1.50z, Indian elephants. 2z, Jaguars. 4.20z, Gray seals. 4.50z, Hartebeests. 6z, Mandrills.

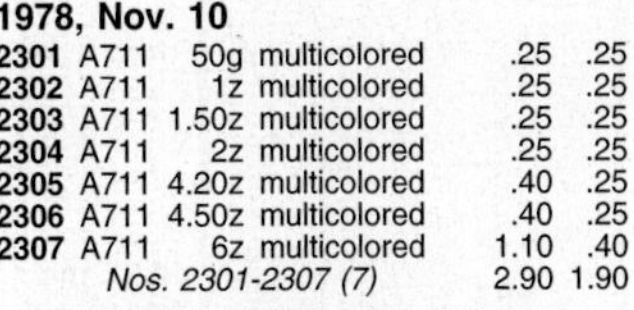

**1978, Nov. 10**

| No. | Type | Value | Color | Unused | Used |
|---|---|---|---|---|---|
| 2301 | A711 | 50g | multicolored | .25 | .25 |
| 2302 | A711 | 1z | multicolored | .25 | .25 |
| 2303 | A711 | 1.50z | multicolored | .25 | .25 |
| 2304 | A711 | 2z | multicolored | .25 | .25 |
| 2305 | A711 | 4.20z | multicolored | .40 | .25 |
| 2306 | A711 | 4.50z | multicolored | .40 | .25 |
| 2307 | A711 | 6z | multicolored | 1.10 | .40 |
| | | | *Nos. 2301-2307 (7)* | 2.90 | 1.90 |

Warsaw Zoological Gardens, 50th anniv.

Adolf Warski (1868-1937) A712

Party Emblem A713

#2309, Julian Lenski (1889-1937). #2310, Aleksander Zawadzki (1899-1964). #2311, Stanislaw Dubois (1901-1942).

*Perf. 11½x11, 11x11½*

**1978, Dec. 15** **Photo.**

| No. | Type | Value | Color | Unused | Used |
|---|---|---|---|---|---|
| 2308 | A712 | 1.50z | red & brown | .25 | .25 |
| 2309 | A712 | 1.50z | red & black | .25 | .25 |
| 2310 | A712 | 1.50z | red & dk vio | .25 | .25 |
| 2311 | A712 | 1.50z | red & dk blue | .25 | .25 |
| 2312 | A713 | 1.50z | black, red & gold | .25 | .25 |
| | | | *Nos. 2308-2312 (5)* | 1.25 | 1.25 |

Polish United Workers' Party, 30th anniv.

LOT Planes, 1929 and 1979 A714

**1979, Jan. 2** **Photo.** ***Perf. 11x11½***

| No. | Type | Value | Color | Unused | Used |
|---|---|---|---|---|---|
| 2313 | A714 | 6.90z | gold & multi | .35 | .25 |

LOT, Polish airline, 50th anniversary.

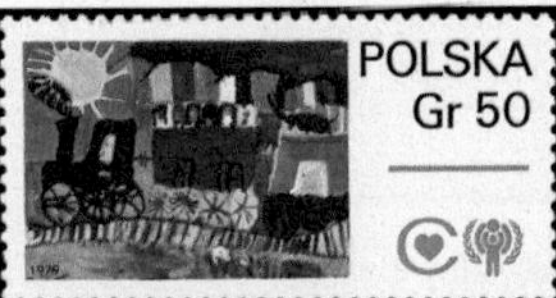


Train and IYC Emblem — A715

Children's Paintings: 1z, Children with toys. 1.50z, Children in meadow. 6z, Family.

**1979, Jan. 13** ***Perf. 11***

| No. | Type | Value | Color | Unused | Used |
|---|---|---|---|---|---|
| 2314 | A715 | 50g | multicolored | .25 | .25 |
| 2315 | A715 | 1z | multicolored | .25 | .25 |
| 2316 | A715 | 1.50z | multicolored | .25 | .25 |
| 2317 | A715 | 6z | multicolored | .35 | .25 |
| | | | *Nos. 2314-2317 (4)* | 1.10 | 1.00 |

International Year of the Child.

Artist's Wife, by Karol Mondral — A716

Modern Polish Graphic Arts: 50g, "Lightning," by Edmund Bartlomiejczyk, horiz. 1.50z, Musicians, by Tadeusz Kulisiewicz. 4.50z, Portrait of a Brave Man, by Wladyslaw Skoczylas.

*Perf. 11½x12, 12x11½*

**1979, Mar. 5** **Engr.**

| No. | Type | Value | Color | Unused | Used |
|---|---|---|---|---|---|
| 2318 | A716 | 50g | brt violet | .25 | .25 |
| 2319 | A716 | 1z | slate green | .25 | .25 |
| 2320 | A716 | 1.50z | blue gray | .25 | .25 |
| 2321 | A716 | 4.50z | violet brown | .30 | .25 |
| | | | *Nos. 2318-2321 (4)* | 1.05 | 1.00 |

Andrzej Frycz-Modrzewski, Stefan Batory, Jan Zamoyski — A717

**Photogravure and Engraved**

**1979, Mar. 12** ***Perf. 12x11½***

| No. | Type | Value | Color | Unused | Used |
|---|---|---|---|---|---|
| 2322 | A717 | 1.50z | cream & sepia | .25 | .25 |

Royal Tribunal in Piotrkow Trybunalski, 400th anniversary.

Pole Vault and Olympic Emblem — A718

Olympic Emblem and: 1.50z, High jump. 6z, Cross-country skiing. 8.40z, Equestrian.

**1979, Mar. 26** **Photo.** ***Perf. 12x11½***

| No. | Type | Value | Color | Unused | Used |
|---|---|---|---|---|---|
| 2323 | A718 | 1z | multicolored | .25 | .25 |
| 2324 | A718 | 1.50z | multicolored | .25 | .25 |
| 2325 | A718 | 6z | multicolored | .30 | .25 |
| 2326 | A718 | 8.40z | multicolored | .45 | .25 |
| | | | *Nos. 2323-2326 (4)* | 1.25 | 1.00 |

1980 Olympic Games.

Flounder — A720

Fish and Emblem: 90g, Perch. 1z, Grayling. 1.50z, Salmon. 2z, Trout. 4.50z, Pike. 5z, Carp. 6z, Catfish and frog.

**1979, Apr. 26** **Photo.** ***Perf. 11½x11***

| No. | Type | Value | Color | Unused | Used |
|---|---|---|---|---|---|
| 2327 | A720 | 50g | multicolored | .25 | .25 |
| 2328 | A720 | 90g | multicolored | .25 | .25 |
| 2329 | A720 | 1z | multicolored | .25 | .25 |
| 2330 | A720 | 1.50z | multicolored | .25 | .25 |
| 2331 | A720 | 2z | multicolored | .25 | .25 |
| 2332 | A720 | 4.50z | multicolored | .25 | .25 |
| 2333 | A720 | 5z | multicolored | .55 | .25 |
| 2334 | A720 | 6z | multicolored | .85 | .40 |
| | | | *Nos. 2327-2334 (8)* | 2.90 | 2.15 |

Polish angling, centenary, and protection of the environment.

A721

**1979, Apr. 30** **Litho.** ***Perf. 11x11½***

| No. | Type | Value | Color | Unused | Used |
|---|---|---|---|---|---|
| 2335 | A721 | 1.50z | multicolored | .25 | .25 |

Council for Mutual Economic Aid of Socialist Countries, 30th anniversary.

Faces and Emblem — A722

**1979, May 7** ***Perf. 11***

| No. | Type | Value | Color | Unused | Used |
|---|---|---|---|---|---|
| 2336 | A722 | 1.50z | red & black | .25 | .25 |

6th Congress of Association of Fighters for Liberty and Democracy, Warsaw, May 7-8.

St. George's Church, Sofia A722a

**1979, May 15** **Photo.** ***Perf. 11x11½***

| No. | Type | Value | Color | Unused | Used |
|---|---|---|---|---|---|
| 2337 | A722a | 1.50z | multicolored | .25 | .25 |

Philaserdica '79 Phil. Exhib., Sofia, Bulgaria, May 18-27.

Pope John Paul II, Cracow Cathedral A723

Designs: 8.40z, Pope John Paul II, Auschwitz-Birkenau Memorial. 50z, Pope John Paul II.

**1979, June 2** **Photo.** ***Perf. 11x11½***

| No. | Type | Value | Color | Unused | Used |
|---|---|---|---|---|---|
| 2338 | A723 | 1.50z | multicolored | .25 | .25 |
| 2339 | A723 | 8.40z | multicolored | .60 | .25 |

**Souvenir Sheet**

***Perf. 11½x11***

| No. | Type | Value | Color | Unused | Used |
|---|---|---|---|---|---|
| 2340 | A723 | 50z | multicolored & gold | 5.50 | 3.50 |

Visit of Pope John Paul II to Poland, June 2-11. No. 2340 contains one 26x35mm stamp.

A variety of No. 2340 with silver margin exists. Values, unused $25, used $17.50.

Paddle Steamer Prince Ksawery and Old Warsaw — A724

Designs: 1.50z, Steamer Gen. Swierczewski and Gdansk, 1914. 4.50z, Tug Aurochs and Plock, 1960. 6z, Motor ship Mermaid and modern Warsaw, 1959.

**1979, June 15** **Litho.** ***Perf. 11***

| No. | Type | Value | Color | Unused | Used |
|---|---|---|---|---|---|
| 2341 | A724 | 1z | multicolored | .25 | .25 |
| 2342 | A724 | 1.50z | multicolored | .25 | .25 |
| 2343 | A724 | 4.50z | multicolored | .25 | .25 |
| 2344 | A724 | 6z | multicolored | .40 | .25 |
| | | | *Nos. 2341-2344 (4)* | 1.15 | 1.00 |

Vistula River navigation, 150th anniversary.

Kosciuszko Monument, Philadelphia A725

**1979, July 1** **Photo.** ***Perf. 11½***

| No. | Type | Value | Color | Unused | Used |
|---|---|---|---|---|---|
| 2345 | A725 | 8.40z | multicolored | .50 | .30 |

Gen. Tadeusz Kosziuszko (1746-1807), Polish soldier and statesman who served in American Revolution.

Mining Machinery — A726

Design: 1.50z, Salt crystals.

**1979, July 14** **Photo.** ***Perf. 14***

| No. | Type | Value | Color | Unused | Used |
|---|---|---|---|---|---|
| 2346 | A726 | 1z | lt brown & blk | .25 | .25 |
| 2347 | A726 | 1.50z | blue grn & blk | .25 | .25 |

Wieliczka ancient rock-salt mines.

Eagle and People — A727

No. 2349, Man with raised hand and flag.

**1979, July 21** ***Perf. 11½x11***

| No. | Type | Value | Color | Unused | Used |
|---|---|---|---|---|---|
| 2348 | A727 | 1.50z | red, blue & gray | .25 | .25 |
| 2349 | A727 | 1.50z | silver, red & blk | .25 | .25 |

35 years of Polish People's Republic.

**Souvenir Sheet**

**1979, Sept. 2** **Photo.** ***Perf. 11½x11***

| No. | Type | Description | Unused | Used |
|---|---|---|---|---|
| 2350 | A727 | Sheet of 2, #2348-2349 + label | .55 | .30 |

13th National Philatelic Exhibition.

Poland No. 1, Rowland Hill (1795-1879), Originator of Penny Postage — A728

**1979, Aug. 16** **Litho.** ***Perf. 11½x11***

| No. | Type | Value | Color | Unused | Used |
|---|---|---|---|---|---|
| 2351 | A728 | 6z | multicolored | .30 | .25 |

Souvenir Sheet

The Rape of Europa, by Bernardo Strozzi — A729

**1979, Aug. 20 Photo. *Perf. 11x11½***

| | | | | |
|---|---|---|---|---|
| **2352** | A729 10z multicolored | | .75 | .35 |

Europhil '79, Intl. Phil. Exhib.

Wojciech Jastrzebowski A730

**1979, Aug. 27 *Perf. 11½x11***

| | | | | |
|---|---|---|---|---|
| **2353** | A730 1.50z multicolored | | .25 | .25 |

International Ergonomics Society Congress.

Postal Workers' Monument A731

**1979, Sept. 1 *Perf. 11x11½***

| | | | | |
|---|---|---|---|---|
| **2354** | A731 1.50z multicolored | | .25 | .25 |

40th anniversary of Polish postal workers' resistance to Nazi invaders. See No. B137.

ITU Emblem, Radio Antenna A732

**1979, Sept. 24 *Perf. 11x11½***

| | | | | |
|---|---|---|---|---|
| **2355** | A732 1.50z multicolored | | .25 | .25 |

Intl. Radio Consultative Committee (CCIR) of the ITU, 50th anniv.

Violin A733

**1979, Sept. 25 Litho.**

| | | | | |
|---|---|---|---|---|
| **2356** | A733 1.50z dk blue, org, grn | | .25 | .25 |

Henryk Wieniawski Young Violinists' Competition, Lublin.

Pulaski Monument, Buffalo — A734

**1979, Oct. 1 Photo. *Perf. 11½x12***

| | | | | |
|---|---|---|---|---|
| **2357** | A734 8.40z multicolored | | .35 | .25 |

Gen. Casimir Pulaski (1748-1779), Polish nobleman who served in American Revolutionary War.

Gen. Franciszek Jozwiak — A735

**1979, Oct. 3 *Perf. 11½x11***

| | | | | |
|---|---|---|---|---|
| **2358** | A735 1.50z gray blue, dk blue & gold | | .25 | .25 |

35th anniv. of Civil and Military Security Service, founded by Gen. Franciszek Jozwiak (1895-1966).

Drive-in Post Office — A736

Designs: 1.50z, Parcel sorting. 4.50z, Loading mail train. 6z, Mobile post office.

**1979, Oct. 9 *Perf. 11½***

| | | | | |
|---|---|---|---|---|
| **2359** | A736 | 1z multicolored | .25 | .25 |
| **2360** | A736 | 1.50z multicolored | .25 | .25 |
| **2361** | A736 | 4.50z multicolored | .30 | .25 |
| **2362** | A736 | 6z multicolored | .40 | .25 |
| | | *Nos. 2359-2362 (4)* | 1.20 | 1.00 |

Stamp Day.

Christmas A737

Designs: 2z, Holy Family. 6.90z, Nativity, horiz.

***Perf. 11½x11, 11x11½***

**1979, Dec. 4 Photo.**

| | | | | |
|---|---|---|---|---|
| **2363** | A737 | 2z multicolored | .25 | .25 |
| **2364** | A737 | 6.90z multicolored | .35 | .25 |

A738

Space Achievements: 1z, Soyuz 30 and Salyut 6. 1.50z, Kopernik 500 and Copernicus satellite. 2z, Lunik 2 and Ranger 7. 4.50z, Yuri Gagarin and Vostok. 6.90z, Neil Armstrong and Apollo 11.

**1979, Dec. 28 Photo. *Perf. 11½x11***

| | | | | |
|---|---|---|---|---|
| **2365** | A738 | 1z multi | .25 | .25 |
| **2366** | A738 | 1.50z multi | .25 | .25 |
| **2367** | A738 | 2z multi | .25 | .25 |
| **2368** | A738 | 4.50z multi | .25 | .25 |
| **2369** | A738 | 6.90z multi | .30 | .25 |
| *a.* | | Souvenir sheet of 5 | 1.50 | 1.00 |
| | | *Nos. 2365-2369 (5)* | 1.30 | 1.25 |

No. 2369a contains Nos. 2365-2369, tete beche plus label.

A739

Designs: Horse Paintings.

**1980, Jan. 31 Photo. *Perf. 11½x12***

| | | | | |
|---|---|---|---|---|
| **2370** | A739 | 1z Stagecoach | .25 | .25 |
| **2371** | A739 | 2z Horse, trainer | .25 | .25 |
| **2372** | A739 | 2.50z Trotters | .25 | .25 |
| **2373** | A739 | 3z Fox hunt | .25 | .25 |
| **2374** | A739 | 4z Sled | .25 | .25 |
| **2375** | A739 | 6z Hay cart | .35 | .25 |
| **2376** | A739 | 6.50z Pairs | .40 | .25 |
| **2377** | A739 | 6.90z Hurdles | .60 | .35 |
| | | *Nos. 2370-2377 (8)* | 2.60 | 2.10 |

Sierakov horse stud farm, 150th anniv.

Party Slogan on Map of Poland — A740

Worker, by Janusz Stanny — A741

**1980, Feb. 11 Photo. *Perf. 11½x11***

| | | | | |
|---|---|---|---|---|
| **2378** | A740 | 2.50z multi | .25 | .25 |
| **2379** | A741 | 2.50z multi | .25 | .25 |

Polish United Workers' Party, 8th Congress.

Equestrian, Olympic Rings — A742

**1980, Mar. 31 *Perf. 12x11½***

| | | | | |
|---|---|---|---|---|
| **2380** | A742 | 2z shown | .25 | .25 |
| **2381** | A742 | 2.50z Archery | .25 | .25 |
| **2382** | A742 | 6.50z Biathlon | .35 | .25 |
| **2383** | A742 | 8.40z Volleyball | .60 | .25 |
| | | *Nos. 2380-2383 (4)* | 1.45 | 1.00 |

13th Winter Olympic Games, Lake Placid, NY, Feb. 12-24 (6.50z); 22nd Summer Olympic Games, Moscow, July 19-Aug. 3. See No. B138.

Map and Old Town Hall, 1591, Zamosc A743

**1980, Apr. 3 Litho. *Perf. 11½***

| | | | | |
|---|---|---|---|---|
| **2384** | A743 2.50z multi | | .25 | .25 |

Zamosc, 400th anniversary.

Arms of Poland and Russia A744

**1980, Apr. 21 Litho. *Perf. 11½***

| | | | | |
|---|---|---|---|---|
| **2385** | A744 2.50z multi | | .25 | .25 |

Treaty of Friendship, Cooperation and Mutual Assistance between Poland and USSR, 35th anniversary.

Lenin, 110th Birth Anniversary — A745

**1980, Apr. 22 Photo. *Perf. 11***

| | | | | |
|---|---|---|---|---|
| **2386** | A745 2.50z multi | | .25 | .25 |

Workers Marching A746

**1980, May 1 *Perf. 11½x11***

| | | | | |
|---|---|---|---|---|
| **2387** | A746 2.50z multi | | .25 | .25 |

Revolution of 1905, 75th anniversary.

Dove Over Liberation Date — A747

**1980, May 9 *Perf. 11½x12***

| | | | | |
|---|---|---|---|---|
| **2388** | A747 2.50z multi | | .25 | .25 |

Victory over fascism, 35th anniversary.

Arms of Treaty-signing Countries A748

**1980, May 14 Litho. *Perf. 11½x11***
**2389** A748 2z red & blk .25 .25

Signing of Warsaw Pact (Bulgaria, Czechoslovakia, German Democratic Rep., Hungary, Poland, Romania, USSR), 25th anniversary.

A749

No. 2390, Caverns, (1961 Expedition) Map of Cuba. No. 2391, Seals, Antarctica, 1959. No. 2392, Ethnology, Mongolia, 1963. No. 2393, Archaeology, Syria, 1959. No. 2394, Mountain climbing, Nepal, 1978. No. 2395, Paleontology, Mongolia, 1963.

**1980, May 22 Photo. *Perf. 14***
**2390** A749 2z multi .25 .25
**2391** A749 2z multi .25 .25
**2392** A749 2.50z multi .25 .25
**2393** A749 2.50z multi .25 .25
**2394** A749 6.50z multi .35 .25
**2395** A749 8.40z multi .85 .35
*Nos. 2390-2395 (6)* 2.20 1.60

Malachowski Lyceum Arms — A750

**1980, June 7 Photo. *Perf. 11x12***
**2396** A750 2z blk & dl grn .25 .25

Malachowski Lyceum (oldest school in Plock), 800th anniversary.

A751

No. 2397, Xerocomus Parasiticus. No. 2398, Clathrus ruber. No. 2399, Phallus hadriani. No. 2400, Strobilomyces floccopus. No. 2401, Sparassis crispa. No. 2402, Langermannia gigantea.

**1980, June 30 *Perf. 11½x11***
**2397** A751 2z multi .25 .25
**2398** A751 2z multi .25 .25
**2399** A751 2.50z multi .25 .25
**2400** A751 2.50z multi .25 .25
**2401** A751 8z multi .60 .25
**2402** A751 10.50z multi .70 .30
*Nos. 2397-2402 (6)* 2.30 1.55

Sandomierz Millennium — A752

**1980, July 12 Photo. *Perf. 11x11½***
**2403** A752 2.50z dk brown .25 .25

"Lwow," T. Ziolkowski — A753

Ships and Teachers: 2.50z, Antoni Garnuszewski, A. Garnuszewski. 6z, Zenit, A. Ledochowski. 6.50z, Jan Turlejski, K. Porebski. 6.90z, Horyzon, G. Kanski. 8.40z, Dar Pomorza, K. Maciejewicz.

**1980, July 21 Litho. *Perf. 11***
**2404** A753 2z multi .25 .25
**2405** A753 2.50z multi .25 .25
**2406** A753 6z multi .35 .25
**2407** A753 6.50z multi .45 .25
**2408** A753 6.90z multi .45 .25
**2409** A753 8.40z multi .55 .25
*Nos. 2404-2409 (6)* 2.30 1.50

Training ships and teachers.

A754

Designs: Medicinal plants — No. 2410, Atropa belladonna. No. 2411, Datura innoxia. No. 2412, Valeriana. No. 2413, Mentha piperita. No. 2414, Calendula. No. 2415, Salvia officinalis.

**1980, Aug. 15 Litho. *Perf. 11½x11***
**2410** A754 2z multicolored .25 .25
**2411** A754 2.50z multicolored .25 .25
**2412** A754 3.40z multicolored .25 .25
**2413** A754 5z multicolored .35 .25
**2414** A754 6.50z multicolored .45 .25
**2415** A754 8z multicolored .35 .30
*Nos. 2410-2415 (6)* 1.90 1.55

A755

**1980, Aug. 20 *Perf. 11***
**2416** A755 2.50z multi .25 .25

Jan Kochanowski (1530-1584), poet.

United Nations, 35th Anniversary — A756

**1980, Sept. 19 Photo. *Perf. 11x11½***
**2417** A756 8.40z multi .50 .25

Chopin Piano Competition — A757

**1980, Oct. 2 Litho. *Perf. 11½***
**2418** A757 6.90z blk & tan .45 .25

Mail Pick-up — A758

**1980, Oct. 9 Photo. *Perf. 12x11½***
**2419** A758 2z shown .25 .25
**2420** A758 2.50z Letter sorting .25 .25
**2421** A758 6z Loading mail plane .40 .25
**2422** A758 6.50z Mail boxes .40 .25
*a.* Souvenir sheet of 4, #2419-2422 3.25 2.75
*Nos. 2419-2422 (4)* 1.30 1.00

Stamp Day.

Girl Embracing Dove, UN Emblem A759

**1980, Nov. 21 Litho. *Perf. 11x11½***
**2423** A759 8.40z multicolored .50 .25

UN Declaration on the Preparation of Societies for Life in Peace.

Battle of Olzynska Grochowska, by W. Kossak — A760

**1980, Nov. 29 Photo. *Perf. 11***
**2424** A760 2.50z multicolored .25 .25

Battle of Olzynska Grochowska, 1830.

Horse-drawn Fire Engine — A761

Designs: Horse-drawn vehicles.

**1980, Dec. 16**
**2425** A761 2z shown .25 .25
**2426** A761 2.50z Passenger coach .25 .25
**2427** A761 3z Beer wagon .25 .25
**2428** A761 5z Sled .35 .25
**2429** A761 6z Bus .40 .25
**2430** A761 6.50z Two-seater .65 .30
*Nos. 2425-2430 (6)* 2.15 1.55

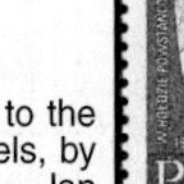

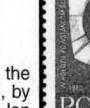

Honor to the Silesian Rebels, by Jan Borowczak — A762

**1981, Jan. 22 Engr. *Perf. 11½***
**2431** A762 2.50z gray grn .25 .25

Silesian uprising, 60th anniversary.

Pablo Picasso — A763

**1981, Mar. 10 Photo. *Perf. 11½x11***
**2432** A763 8.40z multi .40 .25
*a.* Miniature sheet of 2 + 2 labels 1.90 1.00

Pablo Picasso (1881-1973), artist, birth centenary. No. 2432 se-tenant with label showing A Crying Woman. Sold for 20.80z.

Balloon Flown by Pilatre de Rozier, 1783 — A764

Gordon Bennett Cup (Balloons): No. 2434, J. Blanchard, J. Jeffries, 1875. 2.50z, F. Godard, 1850. 3z, F. Hynek, Z. Burzynski, 1933. 6z, Z. Burzynski, N. Wysocki, 1935. 6.50z, B. Abruzzo, M. Anderson, L. Newman, 1978. 10.50z, Winners' names, 1933-1935, 1938.

**1981, Mar. 25 Photo. *Perf. 11½x12***
**2433** A764 2z multi .25 .25
**2434** A764 2z multi .25 .25
**2435** A764 2.50z multi .25 .25
**2436** A764 3z multi .25 .25
**2437** A764 6z multi .45 .25
**2438** A764 6.50z multi .50 .25
*Nos. 2433-2438 (6)* 1.95 1.50

**Souvenir Sheet**

***Imperf***

**2439** A764 10.50z multi .85 .60

Iphigenia, by Franz Anton Maulbertsch (1724-1796), WIPA '81 Emblem — A765

**1981, May 11 Litho. *Perf. 11½***
**2440** A765 10.50z multi .95 .25

WIPA '81 Intl. Phil. Exhib., Vienna, 5/22-31.

Wroclaw, 1493 — A766

**1981, May 15 Photo. *Perf. 14***

| | | | | |
|---|---|---|---|---|
| **2441** | A766 | 6.50z brown | .35 | .25 |

See Nos. 2456-2459. For surcharge see No. 2526.

Gen. Wladyslaw Sikorski (1881-1943) A767

**1981, May 20 *Perf. 11½x11***

| | | | | |
|---|---|---|---|---|
| **2442** | A767 | 6.50z multi | .30 | .25 |

Kwan Vase, 18th Cent. — A768

2z, Cup, saucer, 1820. 2.50z, Jug, 1820. 5z, Portrait plate, 1880. 6.50z, Vase, 1900. 8.40z, Basket, 1840.

**1981, June 15**

| | | | | |
|---|---|---|---|---|
| **2443** | A768 | 1z shown | .25 | .25 |
| **2444** | A768 | 2z multi | .25 | .25 |
| **2445** | A768 | 2.50z multi | .25 | .25 |
| **2446** | A768 | 5z multi | .35 | .25 |
| **2447** | A768 | 6.50z multi | .45 | .25 |
| **2448** | A768 | 8.40z multi | .60 | .25 |
| | | *Nos. 2443-2448 (6)* | 2.15 | 1.50 |

See Nos. 2502-2507.

Intl. Architects Union, 14th Congress, Warsaw — A769

**1981, July 15 Litho.**

| | | | | |
|---|---|---|---|---|
| **2449** | A769 | 2.50z multi | .25 | .25 |

Moose, Rifle and Pouch — A770

**1981, July 30**

| | | | | |
|---|---|---|---|---|
| **2450** | A770 | 2z shown | .25 | .25 |
| **2451** | A770 | 2z Boar | .25 | .25 |
| **2452** | A770 | 2.50z Fox | .30 | .25 |
| **2453** | A770 | 2.50z Elk | .30 | .25 |
| **2454** | A770 | 6.50z Greylag goose, horiz. | .80 | .25 |
| **2455** | A770 | 6.50z Fen duck | .85 | .25 |
| | | *Nos. 2450-2455 (6)* | 2.75 | 1.50 |

**City Type of 1981**

4z, Gdansk, 1652, vert. 5z, Krakow, 1493, vert. 6z, Legnica, 1744. 8z, Warsaw, 1618.

***Perf. 11x11½, 11½x13***

**1981, July 28 Photo.**

| | | | | |
|---|---|---|---|---|
| **2456** | A766 | 4z dark violet | .35 | .25 |
| **2457** | A766 | 5z blue green | .40 | .25 |
| **2458** | A766 | 6z orange | .50 | .25 |
| **2459** | A766 | 8z dark blue | .60 | .30 |
| | | *Nos. 2456-2459 (4)* | 1.85 | 1.05 |

For surcharge see #2939.

A770a

**1982, Nov. 2 Photo. *Perf. 11½***

| | | | | |
|---|---|---|---|---|
| **2461** | A770a | 12z Vistula River | .25 | .25 |
| **2463** | A770a | 17z Kasimierz Dolny | .25 | .25 |
| **2466** | A770a | 25z Gdansk | .35 | .25 |
| | | *Nos. 2461-2466 (3)* | .85 | .75 |

Wild Bison — A771

No. 2471 — Bison bonasus: a, Adult looking forward in center, adult grazing at right, tree without leaves at UR. b. Adult grazing at left, adult at center, hindquarters of juvenile at right, tree with leaves at UL. c, Adults and juvenile, inscribed "Karat-2000" at bottom. d, Juvenile suckling female. e, Two adults facing right.

**1981, Aug. 27 *Perf. 11½x11***

| | | | | |
|---|---|---|---|---|
| **2471** | | Horiz. strip of 5 | 3.00 | 1.25 |
| ***a.-e.*** | | A771 6.50z Any single | .50 | .25 |

60th Anniv. of Polish Tennis Federation — A772

**1981, Sept. 17 Photo. *Perf. 11x11½***

| | | | | |
|---|---|---|---|---|
| **2472** | A772 | 6.50z multi | .75 | .25 |

Model Airplane — A773

**1981, Sept. 24 *Perf. 14***

| | | | | |
|---|---|---|---|---|
| **2473** | A773 | 1z shown | .25 | .25 |
| **2474** | A773 | 2z Boats | .25 | .25 |
| **2475** | A773 | 2.50z Racing cars | .25 | .25 |
| **2476** | A773 | 4.20z Gliders | .35 | .25 |
| **2477** | A773 | 6.50z Radio-controlled racing cars | .40 | .25 |
| **2478** | A773 | 8z Yachts | .60 | .30 |
| | | *Nos. 2473-2478 (6)* | 2.10 | 1.55 |

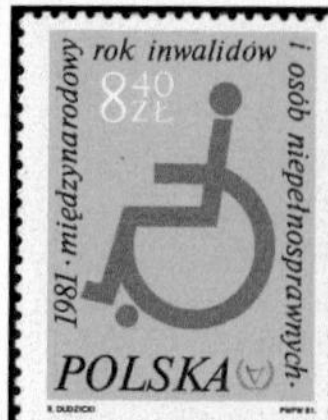


Intl. Year of the Disabled — A774

**1981, Sept. 25 Litho. *Perf. 11½x11***

| | | | | |
|---|---|---|---|---|
| **2479** | A774 | 8.40z multi | .60 | .25 |

Stamp Day — A775

2.50z, Pistol, 18th cent., horiz. 8.40z, Sword, 18th cent.

**1981, Oct. 9 Photo. *Perf. 14***

| | | | | |
|---|---|---|---|---|
| **2480** | A775 | 2.50z multi | .25 | .25 |
| **2481** | A775 | 8.40z multi | .50 | .25 |

A776

**1981, Oct. 10 *Perf. 11½x12***

| | | | | |
|---|---|---|---|---|
| **2482** | A776 | 2.50z multi | .25 | .25 |

Henryk Wieniawski (1835-1880), violinist and composer.

A777

Working Movement Leaders: 50g, Bronislaw Wesolowski (1870-1919). 2z, Malgorzata Fornalska (1902-1944). 2.50z, Maria Koszutska (1876-1939). 6.50z, Marcin Kasprzak (1860-1905).

**1981, Oct. 15 Litho.**

| | | | | |
|---|---|---|---|---|
| **2483** | A777 | 50g grn & blk | .25 | .25 |
| **2484** | A777 | 2z bl & blk | .25 | .25 |
| **2485** | A777 | 2.50z brn & blk | .25 | .25 |
| **2486** | A777 | 6.50z lil rose & blk | .35 | .25 |
| | | *Nos. 2483-2486 (4)* | 1.10 | 1.00 |

World Food Day — A778

**1981, Oct. 16 *Perf. 11½x11***

| | | | | |
|---|---|---|---|---|
| **2487** | A778 | 6.90z multi | .45 | .25 |

Old Theater, Cracow, 200th Anniv. — A779

Theater Emblem and: 2z, Helena Modrzejewska (1840-1909), actress. 2.50z, Stanislaw Kozmian (1836-1922), theater director, 1865-1885, founder of Cracow School. 6.50z, Konrad Swinarski (1929-1975), stage manager.

**Photo. & Engr.**

**1981, Oct. 17 *Perf. 12x11½***

| | | | | |
|---|---|---|---|---|
| **2488** | A779 | 2z multi | .25 | .25 |
| **2489** | A779 | 2.50z multi | .45 | .25 |
| **2490** | A779 | 6.50z multi | .45 | .25 |
| **2491** | A779 | 8z multi | .45 | .25 |
| | | *Nos. 2488-2491 (4)* | 1.60 | 1.00 |

Souvenir Sheet

Vistula River Project — A780

**1981, Dec. 20 Litho. *Perf. 11½x12***

| | | | | |
|---|---|---|---|---|
| **2492** | A780 | 10.50z multi | 1.25 | .75 |

Flowering Succulent Plants A781

No. 2493, Epiphyllopsis gaertneri. No. 2494, Cereus tonduzii. No. 2495, Cylindropuntia leptocaulis. No. 2496, Cylindroppuntia fulgida. No. 2497, Caralluma lugardi. No. 2498, Nopalea cochenillifera. No. 2499, Lithopsps helmutii. No. 2500, Cylindropuntia spinosior.

**1981, Dec. 22 Photo. *Perf. 13***

| | | | | |
|---|---|---|---|---|
| **2493** | A781 | 90g multicolored | .25 | .25 |
| **2494** | A781 | 1z multicolored | .25 | .25 |
| **2495** | A781 | 2z multicolored | .25 | .25 |
| **2496** | A781 | 2.50z multicolored | .25 | .25 |
| **2497** | A781 | 2.50z multicolored | .25 | .25 |
| **2498** | A781 | 6.50z multicolored | .40 | .25 |
| **2499** | A781 | 6.50z multicolored | .40 | .25 |
| **2500** | A781 | 10.50z multicolored | 1.00 | .45 |
| | | *Nos. 2493-2500 (8)* | 3.05 | 2.20 |

Polish Workers' Party, 40th Anniv. — A782

**1982, Jan. 5 Photo. *Perf. 11½x11***

| | | | | |
|---|---|---|---|---|
| **2501** | A782 | 2.50z multi | .25 | .25 |

Stoneware Plate, 1890 — A783

Porcelain or Stoneware: 2z, Plate, mug, 1790. 2.50z, Soup tureen, gravy dish, 1830. 6z, Salt and pepper dish, 1844, 8z, Stoneware jug, 1840. 10.50z, Stoneware figurine, 1740.

**1982, Jan. 20**

**2502** A783 1z multi .25 .25
**2503** A783 2z multi .25 .25
**2504** A783 2.50z multi .25 .25
**2505** A783 6z multi .40 .25
**2506** A783 8z multi .50 .25
**2507** A783 10.50z multi .75 .30
*Nos. 2502-2507 (6)* 2.40 1.55

Ignacy Lukasiewicz (1822-1882), Oil Lamp Inventor — A784

Designs: Various oil lamps.

**1982, Mar. 22 Photo. *Perf. 11½x11***

**2508** A784 1z multi .25 .25
**2509** A784 2z multi .25 .25
**2510** A784 2.50z multi .25 .25
**2511** A784 3.50z multi .25 .25
**2512** A784 9z multi .50 .25
**2513** A784 10z multi .55 .25
*Nos. 2508-2513 (6)* 2.05 1.50

Karol Szymanowski (1882-1937), Composer A785

**1982, Apr. 8**

**2514** A785 2.50z dk brn & gold .25 .25

Victory in Challenge Trophy Flights A786

**1982, May 5 Photo. *Perf. 11x11½***

**2515** A786 27z RWD-6 monoplane .75 .25
**2516** A786 31z RWD-9 1.25 .25
*a.* Souv. sheet of 2, #2515-2516 2.25 1.25

Henryk Sienkiewicz (1846-1916), Writer — A787

Polish Nobel Prize Winners: 15z, Wladyslaw Reymont (1867-1925), writer, 1924. 25z, Marie Curie (1867-1934), physicist 1903, 1911. 31z, Czeslaw Milosz (b. 1911), poet, 1980.

**1982, May 10 Litho. *Perf. 11½x11***

**2517** A787 3z black & dk grn .25 .25
**2518** A787 15z black & brown .40 .25
**2519** A787 25z black .50 .25
**2520** A787 31z black & gray .90 .25
*Nos. 2517-2520 (4)* 2.05 1.00

1982 World Cup — A788

***Perf. 11½x11, 11x11½***

**1982, May 28 Photo.**

**2521** A788 25z Ball .75 .25
**2522** A788 27z Bull, ball, horiz. .75 .25

**Souvenir Sheet**

Maria Kaziera Sobieska — A789

**1982, June 11 Photo. *Perf. 11½x11***

**2523** A789 65z multi 2.50 1.50

PHILEXFRANCE '82 Intl. Stamp Exhibition, Paris, June 11-21.

Assoc. Presidents Stanislaw Sierakowski and Boleslaw Domanski — A790

**1982, July 20 Litho.**

**2524** A790 4.50z multi .35 .25

Assoc. of Poles in Germany, 60th anniv.

2nd UN Conference on Peaceful Uses of Outer Space, Vienna, Aug. 9-21 — A791

**1982, Aug. 9 Photo.**

**2525** A791 31z Globe .75 .25

No. 2441 Surcharged

**1982, Aug. 20**

**2526** A766 10z on 6.50z brn .30 .25

Black Madonna of Jasna Gora, 600th Anniv. A792

2.50z, Father Augustin Kordecki (1603-1673). 25z, Siege of Jasna Gora by Swedes, 1655, horiz.

**1982, Aug. 26 *Perf. 11***

**2527** A792 2.50z multi .25 .25
**2528** A792 25z multi .40 .25
**2529** A792 65z multi 1.20 .35
*Nos. 2527-2529 (3)* 1.85 .85

A souvenir sheet of 2 No. 2529 exists. Value: mint $10, used $9.

Workers' Movement A793

**1982, Sept. 3 *Perf. 11½x11***

**2530** A793 6z multicolored .30 .25

Norbert Barlicki (1880-1941) — A794

Workers' Activists: 6z, Pawel Finder (1904-1944). 15z, Marian Buczek (1896-1939). 20z, Cezaryna Wojnarowska (1861-1911). 29z, Ignacy Daszynski (1866-1936).

**1982, Sept. 10 *Perf. 12x11½***

**2531** A794 5z multi .25 .25
**2532** A794 6z multi .25 .25
**2533** A794 15z multi .25 .25
**2534** A794 20z multi .25 .25
**2535** A794 29z multi .25 .25
*Nos. 2531-2535 (5)* 1.25 1.25

Carved Head, Wawel Castle — A795

**1982, Sept. 25**

**2536** A795 60z Woman's head .75 .25
**2537** A795 100z Man's head .75 .25

TB Bacillus Centenary A796

10z, Koch. 25z, Oko Bujwid (1857-1942), bacteriologist.

**1982, Sept. 22 *Perf. 11½x11***

**2538** A796 10z multicolored .30 .25
**2539** A796 25z multicolored .50 .25

St. Maximilian Kolbe (1894-1941) A797

**1982, Oct.**

**2540** A797 27z multi .65 .25

50th Anniv. of Polar Research A798

**1982, Oct. 25 Litho. *Perf. 11½***

**2541** A798 27z multi .65 .25

Stanislaw Zaremba (1863-1942), Mathematician — A799

Mathematicians: 6z, Waclaw Sierpinski (1882-1969). 12z, Zygmunt Janiszewski (1888-1920). 15z, Stefan Banach (1892-1945).

**1982, Nov. 23 Photo. *Perf. 11x11½***

**2542** A799 5z multicolored .25 .25
**2543** A799 6z multicolored .25 .25
**2544** A799 12z multicolored .30 .25
**2545** A799 15z multicolored .40 .25
*Nos. 2542-2545 (4)* 1.20 1.00

First Anniv. of Military Rule — A800

**1982, Dec. 13 *Perf. 12x11½***

**2546** A800 2.50z Medal obverse and reverse .25 .25

Cracow Monuments Restoration A801

**1982, Dec. 20 Litho. *Perf. 11½x11***

**2547** A801 15z Deanery portal .35 .25
**2548** A801 25z Law College portal .50 .25

**Souvenir Sheet**

**Lithographed and Engraved**

***Imperf***

**2549** A801 65z City map 1.00 .75

No. 2549 contains one stamp 22x27mm.

See Nos. 2593-2594, 2656-2657, 2717-2718, 2809, 2847.

Map of Poland, by Bernard Wapowski, 1526
A802

Maps: 6z, Warsaw, Polish Kingdom Quartermaster, 1839. 8z, Poland, Romer's Atlas, 1908. 25z, Krakow, by A. Buchowiecki, 1703, astrolabe, 17th cent.

**1982, Dec. 28 Litho. *Perf. 11½***

**2550** A802 5z multicolored .25 .25
**2551** A802 6z multicolored .25 .25
**2552** A802 8z multicolored .25 .25
**2553** A802 25z multicolored .65 .25
*Nos. 2550-2553 (4)* 1.40 1.00

120th Anniv. of 1863 Uprising — A803

**1983, Jan. 22 Photo. *Perf. 12x11½***

**2554** A803 6z The Battle, by Arthur Grottger (1837-67) .25 .25

Warsaw Theater Sesquicentennial — A804

**1983, Feb. 24 Photo. *Perf. 11***

**2555** A804 6z multicolored .25 .25

10th Anniv. of UN Conference on Human Environment, Stockholm — A805

**1983, Mar. 24 Litho. *Perf. 11½***

**2556** A805 5z Wild flowers .25 .25
**2557** A805 6z Swan, carp, eel .25 .25
**2558** A805 17z Hoopoe .40 .25
**2559** A805 30z Fish .50 .50
**2560** A805 31z Deer, fawn, buffalo .50 .50
**2561** A805 38z Fruit .75 .30
*Nos. 2556-2561 (6)* 2.65 2.05

Karol Kurpinski (1785-1857), Composer
A806

Famous People: 6z, Maria Jasnorzewska Pawlikowska (1891-1945), poet. 17z, Stanislaw Szober (1879-1938), linguist. 25z, Tadeusz Banachiewicz (1882-1954), astronomer. 27z, Jaroslaw Iwaszkiewicz (1894-1980), writer. 31z, Wladyslaw Tatarkiewicz (1886-1980), philosopher, art historian.

**1983, Mar. 25 Photo. *Perf. 11½x11***

**2562** A806 5z tan & brn .25 .25
**2563** A806 6z pink & vio .25 .25
**2564** A806 17z dk grn & lt grn .35 .25
**2565** A806 25z bister & brn .60 .25
**2566** A806 27z lt bl & dk bl .60 .25
**2567** A806 31z violet & pur .75 .25
*Nos. 2562-2567 (6)* 2.80 1.50

Polish Medalists in 22nd Olympic Games, 1980
A807

**1983, Apr. 5 *Perf. 11x11½***

**2568** A807 5z Steeplechase .25 .25
**2569** A807 6z Equestrian .25 .25
**2570** A807 15z Soccer, 1982 World Cup .35 .25
**2571** A807 27z + 5z Pole vault .70 .25
*Nos. 2568-2571 (4)* 1.55 1.00

Warsaw Ghetto Uprising, 40th Anniv. — A808

Heroes' Monument, by Natan Rappaport.

**1983, Apr. 19 Photo. *Perf. 11½x11***

**2572** A808 6z multicolored .25 .25

Se-tenant with label showing anniversary medal.

Customs Cooperation Council, 30th Anniv. — A809

**1983, Apr. 28**

**2573** A809 5z multicolored .25 .25

Second Visit of Pope John Paul II — A810

Portraits of Pope. 31z vert.

**1983, June 16 Photo. *Perf. 11***

**2574** A810 31z multicolored .80 .25
**2575** A810 65z multicolored 1.50 .75
*a.* Souvenir sheet 1.75 1.25

Army of King John III Sobieski — A811

No. 2576, Dragoons. No. 2577, Knight in armor. No. 2578, Non-commissioned infantry officers. No. 2579, Light cavalryman. No. 2580, Hussars.

**1983, July 5 *Perf. 11½x11***

**2576** A811 5z multi .25 .25
**2577** A811 5z multi .25 .25
**2578** A811 6z multi .25 .25
**2579** A811 15z multi .35 .25
**2580** A811 27z multi .70 .25
*Nos. 2576-2580 (5)* 1.80 1.25

750th Anniv. of Torun Municipality — A812

**1983, Aug. 25 Photo. *Perf. 11***

**2581** A812 6z multicolored .25 .25
*a.* Souvenir sheet of 4 3.00 5.50

No. 2581a had limited distribution.

60th Anniv. of Polish Boxing Union
A813

**1983, Nov. 4 Litho. *Perf. 11½x11***

**2582** A813 6z multicolored .25 .25

Enigma Decoding Machine, 50th Anniv. — A813a

**1983, Aug. 16 Litho. *Perf. 11½x11***

**2582A** A813a 5z multicolored .25 .25

Girl Near House — A813b

**1983 Photo. *Perf. 11½x12***

**2582B** A813b 6z multicolored .25 .25

Public courtesy campaign.

Portrait of King John III Sobieski
A814

King's Portraits by: #2584, Unknown court painter. #2585, Sobieski on Horseback, by Francesco Trevisani (1656-1746). 25z, Jerzy Eleuter Szymonowicz-Siemiginowski (1660-1711). 65z+10z, Sobieski at Vienna, by Jan Matejko (1838-1893).

**1983, Sept. 12 *Perf. 11***

**2583** A814 5z multicolored .25 .25
**2584** A814 6z multicolored .25 .25
**2585** A814 6z multicolored .25 .25
**2586** A814 25z multicolored .60 .25
*Nos. 2583-2586 (4)* 1.35 1.00

**Souvenir Sheet**

***Imperf***

**2587** A814 65z + 10z multi 1.50 1.25

Victory over the Turks in Vienna, 300th anniv.

Polish Peoples' Army, 40th Anniv. — A815

#2588, General Zygmunt Berling (1896-1980). #2589, Wanda Wasilewska (1905-64). #2591, Troop formation.

**1983, Oct. 12 Photo. *Perf. 11***

**2588** A815 5z multicolored .25 .25
**2589** A815 5z multicolored .25 .25
**2590** A815 6z multicolored .25 .25
**2591** A815 6z multi, horiz. .25 .25
*Nos. 2588-2591 (4)* 1.00 1.00

World Communications Year — A816

**1983, Oct. 18 Photo. *Perf. 11***

**2592** A816 15z multicolored .35 .25

**Cracow Restoration Type of 1982**

**1983, Nov. 25 Litho. *Perf. 11***

**2593** A801 5z Cloth Hall, horiz. .25 .25
**2594** A801 6z Town Hall Tower .30 .25

Traditional Hats — A818

**1983, Dec. 16 Photo. *Perf. 11½x11***

**2595** A818 5z Biskupianski .25 .25
**2596** A818 5z Rozbarski .25 .25
**2597** A818 6z Warminsko-Mazurski .25 .25
**2598** A818 6z Cieszynski .25 .25

2599 A818 25z Kurpiowski .45 .25
2600 A818 38z Lubuski .75 .25
*Nos. 2595-2600 (6)* 2.20 1.50

Natl. People's Council, 40th Anniv. — A819

Hand holding sword (poster).

**1983, Dec. 31**
2601 A819 6z multicolored .25 .25

People's Army, 40th Anniv. — A820

**1984, Jan. 1 Litho. *Perf. 11½x11***
2602 A820 5z Gen. Bem Brigade badge .25 .25

Musical Instruments A821

**1984, Feb. 10 Photo.**
2603 A821 5z Dulcimer .25 .25
2604 A821 6z Drum, tambourine .25 .25
2605 A821 10z Accordion .25 .25
2606 A821 15z Double bass .30 .25
2607 A821 17z Bagpipes .45 .25
2608 A821 29z Figurines by Tadeusz Zak .60 .25
*Nos. 2603-2608 (6)* 2.10 1.50

See Nos. 2682-2687.

Wincenty Witos (1874-1945), Prime Minister — A822

**1984, Mar. 2 Litho. *Perf. 11½x11***
2609 A822 6z green & sepia .25 .25

Local Flowers (Clematis Varieties) A823

**1984, Mar. 26 Photo. *Perf. 11x11½***
2610 A823 5z Lanuginosa .25 .25
2611 A823 6z Tangutica .25 .25
2612 A823 10z Texensis .25 .25
2613 A823 17z Alpina .40 .25
2614 A823 25z Vitalba .60 .35
2615 A823 27z Montana .75 .50
*Nos. 2610-2615 (6)* 2.50 1.85

The Ecstasy of St. Francis, by El Greco A824

**1984, Apr. 21 *Perf. 11***
2616 A824 27z multicolored 1.10 .50

1984 Olympics A825

**1984, Apr. 25 Litho. *Perf. 11x11½***
2617 A825 5z Handball .25 .25
2618 A825 6z Fencing .25 .25
2619 A825 15z Bicycling .35 .25
2620 A825 16z Running .40 .25
2621 A825 17z Running, diff. .45 .25
*a.* Souv. sheet of 2, #2620-2621 1.25 1.00
2622 A825 31z Skiing .75 .30
*Nos. 2617-2622 (6)* 2.45 1.55

No. 2621a sold for 43z.

Battle of Monte Cassino, 40th Anniv. — A826

**1984, May 18 Photo. *Perf. 11½x11***
2623 A826 15z Memorial Cross .40 .25

View of Warsaw from the Praga Bank, by Bernardo Belotto Canaletto — A827

Paintings of Vistula River views: 6z, Trumpet Festivity, by Aleksander Gierymski. 25z, The Vistula near the Bielany District, by Jozef Rapacki. 27z, Steamship Harbor in the Powisle District, by Franciszek Kostrzewski.

**1984, June 20 Photo. *Perf. 11***
2624 A827 5z multicolored .25 .25
2625 A827 6z multicolored .25 .25
2626 A827 25z multicolored .60 .25
2627 A827 27z multicolored .60 .25
*Nos. 2624-2627 (4)* 1.70 1.00

Eastern Ruler — A828

Sculptures: 3.50z, Eastern ruler. No. 2628A, Woman wearing wreath. 10z, Man wearing hat. No. 2629, Warrior's Head, Wawel Castle.

**1984-85 Photo. *Perf. 11½x12***
2628 A828 3.50z brown .25 .25
2628A A828 5z dark claret .25 .25
2628B A828 10z brt ultra .25 .25
*Nos. 2628-2628B (3)* .75 .75

**Coil Stamp**
***Perf. 13½x14***
2629 A828 5z dk blue grn .25 .25

Issued: 3.50z, 1/24/85; No. 2628A, 10z, 7/8/85; No. 2629, 7/10/84.
No. 2629 has black control number on back of every fifth stamp.
See Nos. 2738-2744.

Order of Grunwald Cross — A829

Designs: 6z, Order of Revival of Poland. 10z, Order of the Banner of Labor, First Class. 16z, Order of Builders of People's Poland.

**1984, July 21 Photo. *Perf. 11½***
2630 A829 5z multicolored .25 .25
2631 A829 6z multicolored .25 .25
2632 A829 10z multicolored .25 .25
2633 A829 16z multicolored .25 .25
*a.* Sheet of 4, #2630-2633, perf. 11½x12 2.40 2.25
*Nos. 2630-2633 (4)* 1.00 1.00

40th anniversary of July Manifesto (Origin of Polish People's Republic).

Warsaw Uprising, 40th Anniv. A830

**1984, Aug. 1**
2634 A830 4z multicolored .25 .25
2635 A830 5z multicolored .25 .25
2636 A830 6z multicolored .25 .25
2637 A830 25z multicolored .75 .25
*Nos. 2634-2637 (4)* 1.50 1.00

Broken Heart Monument, Lodz — A831

**1984, Aug. 31**
2638 A831 16z multicolored .40 .25

Defense of Oksywie Holm, Col. S. Dabek — A832

6z, Bzura River battle, Gen. T. Kutrzeba.

**1984, Sept. 1**
2639 A832 5z shown .25 .25
2640 A832 6z multicolored .25 .25

Invasion of Poland, 45th anniversary.
See Nos. 2692-2693, 2757, 2824-2826, 2864-2866, 2922-2925.

Polish Militia, 40th Anniv. A833

6z, Militiaman at Control Center.

**1984, Sept. 29 Photo. *Perf. 11½***
2641 A833 5z shown .25 .25
2642 A833 6z multicolored .25 .25

Polish Aviation A834

No. 2643, Balloon ascent, 1784. No. 2644, Powered flight, 1911. No. 2645, Balloon Polonez, 1983. No. 2646 Modern gliders. No. 2647, Wilga, 1983. No. 2648, Farman, 1914. No. 2649, Los and PZL P-7.

**1984, Nov. 6 Photo. *Perf. 11x11½***
2643 A834 5z multi .25 .25
2644 A834 5z multi .25 .25
2645 A834 6z multi .25 .25
2646 A834 10z multi .25 .25
2647 A834 16z multi .35 .25
2648 A834 27z multi .60 .25
2649 A834 31z multi .65 .25
*Nos. 2643-2649 (7)* 2.60 1.75

Protected Animals A835

**1984, Dec. 4 Photo. *Perf. 11x11½***
2650 A835 4z Mustela nivalis .25 .25
2651 A835 5z Martes foina .25 .25
2652 A835 5z Mustela erminea .25 .25

***Perf. 11½x11***
2653 A835 10z Castor fiber, vert. .25 .25
2654 A835 10z Lutra lutra, vert. .25 .25
2655 A835 65z Marmota marmota, vert. 1.50 .75
*Nos. 2650-2655 (6)* 2.75 2.00

**Cracow Restoration Type of 1982**

5z, Royal Cathedral, Wawel. 15z, Royal Castle, Wawel, horiz.

***Perf. 11½x11, 11x11½***
**1984, Dec. 10 Litho.**
2656 A801 5z multi .25 .25
2657 A801 15z multi .30 .25

Religious Buildings A837

5z, Protestant Church, Warsaw. 10z, Saint Andrew Church, Cracow. 15z, Greek Orthodox Church, Rychwald. 20z, Orthodox Church, Warsaw. 25z, Tykocin Synagogue, horiz. 31z, Tartar Mosque, Kruszyniany, horiz.

***Perf. 11½x12, 12x11½***
**1984, Dec. 28 Photo.**
2658 A837 5z multicolored .25 .25
2659 A837 10z multicolored .25 .25
2660 A837 15z multicolored .25 .25
2661 A837 20z multicolored .25 .25
2662 A837 25z multicolored .25 .25
2663 A837 31z multicolored .45 .25
*Nos. 2658-2663 (6)* 1.70 1.50

Classic and Contemporary Fire Engines — A838

Designs: 4z, Horse-drawn fire pump, 19th cent. 10z, Polski Fiat, c. 1930. 12z, Jelcz 315, 1970s. 15z, Horse-drawn hand pump, 1899. 20z, Jelcz engine, Magirus power ladder, 1970s. 30z, Hand pump, 18th cent.

**1985, Feb. 25 Photo.** ***Perf. 11x11½***

**2664** A838 4z multicolored .25 .25
**2665** A838 10z multicolored .25 .25
**2666** A838 12z multicolored .25 .25
**2667** A838 15z multicolored .25 .25
**2668** A838 20z multicolored .25 .25
**2669** A838 30z multicolored .85 .25
*Nos. 2664-2669 (6)* 2.10 1.50

Battle of Raclawice, April, 1794, by Jan Styka, 1894 — A839

**1985, Apr. 4** ***Perf. 11***

**2670** A839 27z multicolored .50 .25

Kosciuszko Insurrection cent.

A840

**1985, Apr. 11 Litho.** ***Perf. 11½***

**2671** A840 10z sal rose & dk vio bl .25 .25

Wincenty Rzymowski (1883-1950),Democratic Party founder.

Blue Jeans, Badge — A841

**1985, Apr. 25 Photo.** ***Perf. 11½x11***

**2672** A841 15z multicolored .25 .25

Intl. Youth Year.

Prince Boleslaw Krzywousty (1085-1138) — A842

Regional maps and: 10z, Wladyslaw Gomulka (1905-82), sec.-gen. of the Polish Workers Party, prime minister 1945-49. 20z, Piotr Zaremba (b. 1910), president of Gdansk Province 1945-50.

**1985, May 8 Litho.** ***Perf. 11½***

**2673** A842 5z multicolored .25 .25
**2674** A842 10z multicolored .25 .25
**2675** A842 20z multicolored .35 .25
*Nos. 2673-2675 (3)* .85 .75

Restoration of the Western & Northern Territories to Polish control, 40th anniv.

Victory Berlin 1945, by Jozef Mlynarski (b. 1925) — A843

Painting: Polish and Soviet soldiers at Brandenburg Gate, May 9, 1945.

**1985, May 9 Photo.** ***Perf. 12x11½***

**2676** A843 5z multicolored .25 .25

Liberation from German occupation, 40th anniv.

Warsaw Treaty Org., 30th Anniv. — A844

**1985, May 14 Litho.** ***Perf. 11½x11***

**2677** A844 5z Emblem, member flags .25 .25

World Wildlife Fund A845

Endangered Wildlife: Canis lupus — No. 2678, Wolves, winter landscape. No. 2679, Female, cubs. No. 2680, Wolf. No. 2681, Wolves, summer landscape.

**1985, May 25 Photo.** ***Perf. 11x11½***

**2678** A845 5z multicolored .25 .25
**2679** A845 10z multicolored .35 .25
**2680** A845 10z multicolored .35 .25
**2681** A845 20z multicolored 2.50 .75
*Nos. 2678-2681 (4)* 3.45 1.50

A846

Folk instruments.

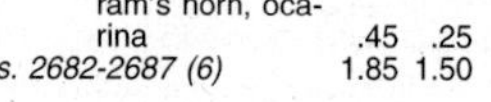

**1985, June 25** ***Perf. 11½x11***

**2682** A846 5z Wooden rattle .25 .25
**2683** A846 10z Jingle .25 .25
**2684** A846 12z Clay whistles .25 .25
**2685** A846 20z Wooden fiddles .30 .25
**2686** A846 25z Tuned bells .35 .25
**2687** A846 31z Shepherd's flutes, ram's horn, ocarina .45 .25
*Nos. 2682-2687 (6)* 1.85 1.50

A847

Design: O.R.P. Iskra and emblem.

**Photogravure and Engraved**

**1985, June 29**

**2688** A847 5z bluish blk & yel .25 .25

Polish Navy, 40th anniv.

Tomasz Nocznicki (1862-1944) — A848

Polish Labor Movement founders: 20z, Maciej Rataj (1884-1940).

**1985, July 26 Engr.** ***Perf. 11x11½***

**2689** A848 10z grnsh black .25 .25
**2690** A848 20z brown black .25 .25

Natl. labor movement, 90th anniv.

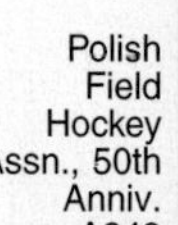

Polish Field Hockey Assn., 50th Anniv. A849

**1985, Aug. 22 Litho.** ***Perf. 11½x11***

**2691** A849 5z multicolored .25 .25

**World War II Battles Type of 1984**

Designs: 5z, Defense of Wizny, Capt. Wladyslaw Raginis. 10z, Attack on Mlawa, Col. Wilhelm Andrzej Liszka-Lawicz.

**1985, Sept. 1 Photo.** ***Perf. 12x11½***

**2692** A832 5z multicolored .25 .25
**2693** A832 10z multicolored .25 .25

Pafawag Railway Rolling Stock Co. A850

**1985, Sept. 18 Litho.** ***Perf. 11½***

**2694** A850 5z Box car .25 .25
**2695** A850 10z 201 E locomotive .25 .25
**2696** A850 17z Two-axle coal car .25 .25
**2697** A850 20z Passenger car .50 .25
*Nos. 2694-2697 (4)* 1.25 1.00

Wild Ducks A851

No. 2698, Anas crecca. No. 2699, Anas querquedula. No. 2700, Aythya fuligula. No. 2701, Bucephala clangula. No. 2702, Somateria mollissima. No. 2703, Netta rufina.

**1985, Oct. 21 Photo.** ***Perf. 11x11½***

**2698** A851 5z multicolored .25 .25
**2699** A851 5z multicolored .25 .25
**2700** A851 10z multicolored .30 .25
**2701** A851 15z multicolored .35 .25
**2702** A851 25z multicolored .50 .25
**2703** A851 29z multicolored .65 .35
*Nos. 2698-2703 (6)* 2.30 1.60

UN, 40th Anniv. A852

**1985, Oct. 24 Litho.** ***Perf. 11½x11***

**2704** A852 27z multicolored .50 .25

Polish Ballet, 200th Anniv. — A853

**1985, Dec. 4**

**2705** A853 5z Prima ballerina .25 .25
**2706** A853 15z Male dancer .25 .25

Paintings by Stanislaw Ignacy Witkiewicz (1885-1939) — A854

5z, Marysia and Burek in Ceylon. No. 2708, Woman with a Fox. No. 2709, Self-portrait, 1931. 20z, Compositions, 1917. 25z, Portrait of Nena Stachurska, 1929. Nos. 2707, 2709-2711 vert.

***Perf. 11½x11, 11x11½***

**1985, Dec. 6 Photo.**

**2707** A854 5z multicolored .25 .25
**2708** A854 10z multicolored .25 .25
**2709** A854 10z multicolored .25 .25
**2710** A854 20z multicolored .25 .25
**2711** A854 25z multicolored .50 .25
*Nos. 2707-2711 (5)* 1.50 1.25

Souvenir Sheet

Johann Sebastian Bach — A855

**1985, Dec. 30** ***Perf. 11½x11***

**2712** A855 65z multicolored 1.25 .45
*a.* With inscription 6.00 6.00

No. 2712a inscribed "300 Rocznica Urodzin Jana Sebastiana Bacha." Distribution was limited.

Profile, Emblem, Sigismond III Column, Royal Castle Tower — A856

**1986, Jan. 16** *Perf. 11½x11*
**2713** A856 10z lt ultra, brt ultra & ultra .25 .25

Congress of Intellectuals for World Peace, Warsaw.

Halley's Comet A857

Designs: No. 2714, Michal Kamienski (1879-1973), astronomer, orbit diagram. No. 2715, Comet, Vega, Giotto, Planet-A, ICE-3 space probes.

**1986, Feb. 7** **Photo.** *Perf. 11½*
**2714** A857 25z multicolored .40 .25
**2715** A857 25z multicolored .40 .25
*a.* Pair, #2714-2715 .90 .50

Intl. Peace Year — A858

**1986, Mar. 20** **Photo.** *Perf. 11½x11*
**2716** A858 25z turq bl, yel & ultra .35 .25

### Cracow Restoration Type of 1982

Designs: 5z, Collegium Maius, Jagiellonian Museum. 10z, Town Hall, Kazimierz.

**1986, Mar. 20** **Litho.** *Perf. 11½*
**2717** A801 5z multicolored .25 .25
**2718** A801 10z multicolored .25 .25

Wildlife A859

No. 2719, Perdix perdix. No. 2720, Oryctolagus cuniculus. No. 2721, Dama dama. No. 2722, Phasianus colchicus. No. 2723, Lepus europaeus. No. 2724, Ovis ammon.

**1986, Apr. 15** **Photo.** *Perf. 11½x11*
**2719** A859 5z multicolored .25 .25
**2720** A859 5z multicolored .25 .25
**2721** A859 10z multicolored .25 .25
**2722** A859 10z multicolored .25 .25
**2723** A859 20z multicolored .35 .25
**2724** A859 40z multicolored .75 .50
*Nos. 2719-2724 (6)* 2.10 1.75

Nos. 2719-2720, 2723-2724 vert.

Stanislaw Kulczynski (1895-1975), Scientist, Party Leader — A860

### Photogravure and Engraved

**1986, May 3** *Perf. 11½x11*
**2725** A860 10z buff & choc .25 .25

Warsaw Fire Brigade, 150th Anniv. — A861

Painting detail: The Fire Brigade on the Cracow Outskirts on Their Way to a Fire, 1871, by Josef Brodowski (1828-1900).

**1986, May 16** *Perf. 11*
**2726** A861 10z dl brn & dk brn .25 .25

Paderewski A862

**1986, May 22** *Perf. 11½x11*
**2727** A862 65z multicolored 1.00 .25

AMERIPEX'86.

1986 World Cup Soccer Championships, Mexico — A863

**1986, May 26** *Perf. 11½*
**2728** A863 25z multicolored .35 .25

Ferryboats — A864

**1986, June 18** **Photo.** *Perf. 11*
**2729** A864 10z Wilanow .25 .25
**2730** A864 10z Wawel .25 .25
*a.* Souv. sheet of 2, #2729-2730 1.25 .75
**2731** A864 15z Pomerania .30 .25
**2732** A864 25z Rogalin .35 .25
*a.* Souv. sheet of 2, #2731-2732 2.50 2.50
*Nos. 2729-2732 (4)* 1.15 1.00

Nos. 2729-2732 printed se-tenant with labels picturing historic sites from the names of cities serviced. No. 2730a sold for 30z; No. 2732a for 55z. Surtax for the Natl. Assoc. of Philatelists.

Antarctic Agreement, 25th Anniv. — A865

Map of Antarctica and: 5z, A. B. Dobrowolski, Kopernik research ship. 40z, H. Arctowski, Professor Siedlecki research ship.

**1986, June 23** **Litho.** *Perf. 11½x11*
**2733** A865 5z ver, pale grn & blk .25 .25
**2734** A865 40z org, pale vio & dk vio .75 .40

Polish United Workers' Party, 10th Congress A866

**1986, July 29** **Photo.** *Perf. 11x11½*
**2735** A866 10z red & dk gray bl .25 .25

### Wawel Heads Type of 1984-85

Designs: 15z, Woman wearing a wreath (like No. 2628A). No. 2739, Thinker. No. 2740, Eastern ruler. 40z, Youth wearing beret. 60z, Warrior. 200z, Man's head.

***Perf. 11½x12, 14 (15z, No. 2740, 60z)***
**Engr., Photo. (15z, No. 2740, 60z)**

**1986-89**
**2738** A828 15z rose brown .25 .25
**2739** A828 20z green .25 .25
**2740** A828 20z peacock blue .25 .25
**2742** A828 40z gray .25 .35
**2743** A828 60z dark green .25 .25
**2744** A828 200z dark gray .25 .25
*Nos. 2738-2744 (6)* 1.50 1.60

Issued: 15z, 9/22/88; #2739, 2742, 7/30/86; #2740, 3/31/89; 60z, 12/15/89; #2744, 11/11/86.

No. 2740 and 60z are coil stamps, have black control number on back of every 5th stamp.

For surcharge see No. 2954.

Jasna Gora Monastery Collection A867

Designs: No. 2746, The Paulinite Church on Skalka in Cracow, oil painting detail, circa 1627. No. 2747, Jesse's Tree, oil on wood, 17th cent. No. 2748, Gilded chalice, 18th cent. No. 2749, Virgin Mary embroidery, 15th cent.

**1986, Aug. 15** **Photo.** *Perf. 11½x11*
**2746** A867 5z multicolored .25 .25
**2747** A867 5z multicolored .25 .25
**2748** A867 20z multicolored .35 .25
**2749** A867 40z multicolored .50 .25
*Nos. 2746-2749 (4)* 1.35 1.00

Victories of Polish Athletes at 1985 World Championships — A868

Designs: No. 2750, Precision Flying, Kissimmee, Florida, won by Waclaw Nycz. No. 2751, Wind Sailing, Tallinn, USSR, won by Malgorzata Palasz-Piasecka. No. 2752, Glider Acrobatics, Vienna, won by Jerzy Makula. No. 2753, Greco-Roman Wrestling (82kg), Kolboten, Norway, won by Bogdan Daras. No. 2754, Road Cycling, Giavera del Montello, Italy, won by Lech Piasecki. No. 2755, Women's Modern Pentathlon, Montreal, won by Barbara Kotowska.

**1986, Aug. 21** *Perf. 11½*
**2750** A868 5z multicolored .25 .25
**2751** A868 10z multicolored .25 .25
**2752** A868 10z multicolored .25 .25
**2753** A868 15z multicolored .25 .25
**2754** A868 20z multicolored .25 .25
**2755** A868 30z multicolored .50 .25
*Nos. 2750-2755 (6)* 1.75 1.50

STOCKHOLMIA '86 — A869

**1986, Aug. 28** *Perf. 11x11½*
**2756** A869 65z multicolored 1.00 .35
*a.* Souvenir sheet 1.00 .50

### World War II Battles Type of 1984

Design: Battle of Jordanow, Col. Stanislaw Maczek, motorized cavalry 10th brigade commander-in-chief.

**1986, Sept. 1** *Perf. 12x11½*
**2757** A832 10z multicolored .25 .25

Albert Schweitzer — A870

### Photogravure and Engraved

**1986, Sept. 26** *Perf. 12x11½*
**2758** A870 5z pale bl vio, sep & buff .25 .25

World Post Day — A871

**1986, Oct. 9** **Litho.** *Perf. 11x11½*
**2759** A871 40z org, ultra & sep .50 .25
*a.* Souvenir sheet of 2 8.50 8.50

No. 2759a sold for 120z.

Folk and Fairy Tale Legends A872

Designs: No. 2760, Basilisk. No. 2761, Duke Popiel, vert. No. 2762, Golden Duck. No. 2763, Boruta, the Devil, vert. No. 2764, Janosik the Thief, vert. No. 2765, Lajkonik, conqueror of the Tartars, 13th cent., vert.

**1986, Oct. 28** **Photo.** *Perf. 11½x11*
**2760** A872 5z multicolored .25 .25
**2761** A872 5z multicolored .25 .25
**2762** A872 10z multicolored .25 .25
**2763** A872 10z multicolored .25 .25
**2764** A872 20z multicolored .30 .25
**2765** A872 50z multicolored .80 .35
*Nos. 2760-2765 (6)* 2.10 1.60

Prof. Tadeusz Kotarbinski (1886-1981) — A873

**1986, Nov. 19** **Litho.** *Perf. 11½*
**2766** A873 10z sepia, buff & brn blk .25 .25

17th-20th Cent. Architecture — A874

Designs: No. 2767, Church, Baczal Dolny. No. 2768, Windmill, Zygmuntow. 10z, Oravian cottage, Zubrzyca Gorna. 15z, Kashubian Arcade cottage, Wazydze. 25z, Barn, Grzawa. 30z, Water mill, Molkowice Stare.

***Perf. 11x11½, 11½x11***

**1986, Nov. 26** **Photo.**

| | | | | |
|---|---|---|---|---|
| **2767** | A874 | 5z multicolored | .25 | .25 |
| **2768** | A874 | 5z multi, vert. | .25 | .25 |
| **2769** | A874 | 10z multicolored | .25 | .25 |
| **2770** | A874 | 15z multicolored | .25 | .25 |
| **2771** | A874 | 25z multicolored | .35 | .25 |
| **2772** | A874 | 30z multicolored | .65 | .40 |
| | | *Nos. 2767-2772 (6)* | 2.00 | 1.65 |

Royalty A875

**Photogravure and Engraved**

**1986, Dec. 4** ***Perf. 11***

| | | | | |
|---|---|---|---|---|
| **2773** | A875 | 10z Mieszko I | .40 | .25 |
| **2774** | A875 | 25z Dobrava | .50 | .40 |

See Nos. 2838-2839, 2884-2885, 2932-2933, 3033-3034, 3068-3069, 3141-3144, 3191-3192, 3222-3225, 3309-3312, 3366-3369, 3394-3397, 3479-3482, 3553-3556.

For surcharges see Nos. 3016-3017.

New Year 1987 A876

**1986, Dec. 12** **Photo.** ***Perf. 11x11½***

| | | | | |
|---|---|---|---|---|
| **2775** | A876 | 25z multicolored | .35 | .25 |

Warsaw Cyclists Soc., Cent. A877

No. 2776, First trip to Bielany, uniformed escort, 1887. No. 2777, Jan Stanislaw Skrodzki (1867-1957), 1895 record-holder. No. 2778, Dynasy Society building, 1892-1937. No. 2779, Mieczyslaw Baranski, champion, 1896. No. 2780, Karolina Kociecka (b. 1875), female competitor. No. 2781, Henryk Weiss (d. 1912), Dynasy champion, 1904-1908.

***Perf. 13x12½, 12½x13***

**1986, Dec. 19** **Litho.**

| | | | | |
|---|---|---|---|---|
| **2776** | A877 | 5z multi | .25 | .25 |
| **2777** | A877 | 5z multi, vert. | .25 | .25 |
| **2778** | A877 | 10z multi, vert. | .25 | .25 |
| **2779** | A877 | 10z multi, vert. | .25 | .25 |
| **2780** | A877 | 30z multi, vert. | .35 | .25 |
| **2781** | A877 | 50z multi, vert. | .65 | .25 |
| | | *Nos. 2776-2781 (6)* | 2.00 | 1.50 |

Henryk Arctowski Antarctic Station, King George Island, 10th Anniv. A878

Wildlife and ships: No. 2782, Euphausia superba, training freighter Antoni Garnuszewski. No. 2783, Notothenia rossi, Dissostichus mawsoni, Zulawy transoceanic ship. No. 2784, Fulmarus glacialoides, yacht Pogoria. No. 2785, Pigoscelis adeliae, yacht Gedania. 30z, Arctocephalus, research boat Dziunia. 40z, Hydrurga leptonyx, ship Kapitan Ledochowski.

**1987, Feb. 13** **Litho.** ***Perf. 11½***

| | | | | |
|---|---|---|---|---|
| **2782** | A878 | 5z multicolored | .25 | .25 |
| **2783** | A878 | 5z multicolored | .25 | .25 |
| **2784** | A878 | 10z multicolored | .25 | .25 |
| **2785** | A878 | 10z multicolored | .25 | .25 |
| **2786** | A878 | 30z multicolored | .45 | .30 |
| **2787** | A878 | 40z multicolored | .65 | .35 |
| | | *Nos. 2782-2787 (6)* | 2.10 | 1.65 |

Paintings by Leon Wyczolkowski (1852-1936) — A879

No. 2788, Cineraria Flowers, 1924. No. 2789, Portrait of a Woman, 1883. No. 2790, Wood Church, 1910. No. 2791, Harvesting Beetroot, 1910. No. 2792, Wading Fishermen, 1891. No. 2793, Self-portrait, 1912.

**1987, Mar. 20** **Photo.** ***Perf. 11***

| | | | | |
|---|---|---|---|---|
| **2788** | A879 | 5z multicolored | .25 | .25 |
| **2789** | A879 | 10z multicolored | .25 | .25 |
| **2790** | A879 | 10z multicolored | .25 | .25 |
| **2791** | A879 | 25z multicolored | .35 | .25 |
| **2792** | A879 | 30z multicolored | .45 | .30 |
| **2793** | A879 | 40z multicolored | .75 | .40 |
| | | *Nos. 2788-2793 (6)* | 2.30 | 1.70 |

Nos. 2789 and 2791 vert.

The Ravage, 1866, by Artur Grottger (1837-1867) — A880

**1987, Mar. 26** **Photo.** ***Perf. 11***

| | | | | |
|---|---|---|---|---|
| **2794** | A880 | 15z dk brown & buff | .25 | .25 |

Gen. Karol Swierczewski-Walter (1897-1947) — A881

**1987, Mar. 27** **Engr.** ***Perf. 11½x12***

| | | | | |
|---|---|---|---|---|
| **2795** | A881 | 15z olive green | .25 | .25 |

Pawel Edmund Strzelecki (1797-1873), Explorer — A882

**1987, Apr. 23** **Photo.** ***Perf. 11½x11***

| | | | | |
|---|---|---|---|---|
| **2796** | A882 | 65z olive black | .80 | .30 |

Colonization of Australia, bicentennial.

2nd PRON Congress A883

**1987, May 8** **Litho.** ***Perf. 11½***

| | | | | |
|---|---|---|---|---|
| **2797** | A883 | 10z pale gray, brn, red & brt ultra | .25 | .25 |

Patriotic Movement of the National Renaissance Congress.

Motor Vehicles — A884

No. 2798, 1936 Saurer-Zawrat. No. 2799, 1928 CWS T-1. No. 2800, 1928 Ursus-A. No. 2801, 1936 Lux-Sport. No. 2802, 1939 Podkowa 100. No. 2803, 1935 Sokol 600 RT.

**1987, May 19** **Photo.** ***Perf. 12x11½***

| | | | | |
|---|---|---|---|---|
| **2798** | A884 | 10z multicolored | .25 | .25 |
| **2799** | A884 | 10z multicolored | .25 | .25 |
| **2800** | A884 | 15z multicolored | .25 | .25 |
| **2801** | A884 | 15z multicolored | .25 | .25 |
| **2802** | A884 | 25z multicolored | .35 | .25 |
| **2803** | A884 | 45z multicolored | .60 | .35 |
| | | *Nos. 2798-2803 (6)* | 1.95 | 1.60 |

Royal Castle, Warsaw — A885

**1987, June 5**

| | | | | |
|---|---|---|---|---|
| **2804** | A885 | 50z multicolored | .60 | .25 |

A souvenir sheet of 1 exists. Value $50.

A886

State Visit of Pope John Paul II — A887

**1987, June 8** ***Perf. 11***

| | | | | |
|---|---|---|---|---|
| **2805** | A886 | 15z shown | .25 | .25 |
| **2806** | A886 | 45z Portrait, diff. | .50 | .30 |
| *a.* | | Pair, #2805-2806 | .75 | .50 |

**Souvenir Sheet**

***Perf. 12x11½***

| | | | | |
|---|---|---|---|---|
| **2807** | A887 | 50z shown | 1.00 | 1.00 |

No. 2806a has continuous design.

**Cracow Restoration Type of 1982**

**1987, July 6** **Litho.** ***Perf. 11½***

| | | | | |
|---|---|---|---|---|
| **2809** | A801 | 10z Barbican Gate, Wawel, horiz. | .25 | .25 |

Esperanto Language, Cent. — A890

**1987, July 25** **Litho.** ***Perf. 11½***

| | | | | |
|---|---|---|---|---|
| **2811** | A890 | 45z Ludwig L. Zamenhof | .40 | .25 |

A891

Poznan and Town Hall, by Stanislaw Wyspianski.

**1987, Aug. 3**

| | | | | |
|---|---|---|---|---|
| **2812** | A891 | 15z blk & pale salmon | .25 | .25 |

POZNAN '87, Aug. 8-16.

A892

No. 2813, Queen. No. 2814, Worker. No. 2815, Drone. No. 2816, Box hive, orchard. No. 2817, Bee collecting pollen. No. 2818, Beekeeper collecting honey.

**1987, Aug. 20** **Photo.** ***Perf. 11½x11***

| | | | | |
|---|---|---|---|---|
| **2813** | A892 | 10z multicolored | .25 | .25 |
| **2814** | A892 | 10z multicolored | .25 | .25 |
| **2815** | A892 | 15z multicolored | .25 | .25 |
| **2816** | A892 | 15z multicolored | .25 | .25 |
| **2817** | A892 | 40z multicolored | .25 | .50 |
| **2818** | A892 | 50z multicolored | .70 | .25 |
| | | *Nos. 2813-2818 (6)* | 1.95 | 1.75 |

31st World Apiculture Congress, Warsaw.

Success of Polish Athletes at World Championship Events — A894

10z, Acrobatics, France. 15z, Kayak, Canada. 20z, Marksmanship, E. Germany. 25z, Wrestling, Hungary.

**1987, Sept. 24 Litho. *Perf. 14***

| | | | | |
|---|---|---|---|---|
| **2820** | A894 10z multicolored | .25 | .25 |
| **2821** | A894 15z multicolored | .25 | .25 |
| **2822** | A894 20z multicolored | .25 | .25 |
| **2823** | A894 25z multicolored | .25 | .25 |
| | *Nos. 2820-2823 (4)* | 1.00 | 1.00 |

### World War II Battles Type of 1984

Designs: No. 2824, Battle of Mokra, Julian Filipowicz. No. 2825, Battle scene near Oleszycami, Brig.-Gen. Josef Rudolf Kustron. 15z, Air battles over Warsaw, pilot Stefan Pawlikowski.

**1987, Sept. 1 Photo. *Perf. 12x11½***

| | | | |
|---|---|---|---|
| **2824** | A832 10z multicolored | .25 | .25 |
| **2825** | A832 10z multicolored | .25 | .25 |
| **2826** | A832 15z multicolored | .35 | .25 |
| | *Nos. 2824-2826 (3)* | .85 | .75 |

Jan Hevelius (1611-1687), Astronomer, and Constellations — A895

**1987, Sept. 15 Litho. *Perf. 11½***

| | | | |
|---|---|---|---|
| **2827** | A895 15z Hevelius, sextant, vert. | .25 | .25 |
| **2828** | A895 40z shown | .40 | .30 |

Souvenir Sheet

1st Artificial Satellite, Sputnik, 30th Anniv. — A896

**1987, Oct. 2 Photo. *Perf. 11½x11***

| | | | |
|---|---|---|---|
| **2829** | A896 40z Stacionar 4 satellite | .90 | .75 |

World Post Day A897

Design: Ignacy Franciszek Przebendowski (1730-1791), postmaster general, and post office building, 19th cent., Krakowskie Przedmiescie, Warsaw.

**1987, Oct. 9 Litho.**

| | | | |
|---|---|---|---|
| **2830** | A897 15z lt olive grn & rose claret | .25 | .25 |

Col. Stanislaw Wieckowski — A898

**Photo. & Engr.**

**1987, Oct. 16 *Perf. 12x11½***

| | | | |
|---|---|---|---|
| **2831** | A898 15z deep blue & blk | .25 | .25 |

Col. Wieckowski (1884-1942), physician and social reformer executed by the Nazis at Auschwitz.

HAFNIA '87 — A899

Fairy tales by Hans Christian Andersen (1805-1875): No. 2832, The Little Mermaid. No. 2833, The Nightingale. No. 2834, The Wild Swan. No. 2835, The Match Girl. 30z, The Snow Queen. 40z, The Brave Toy Soldier.

**1987, Oct. 16 Photo. *Perf. 11x11½***

| | | | |
|---|---|---|---|
| **2832** | A899 10z multicolored | .25 | .25 |
| **2833** | A899 10z multicolored | .25 | .25 |
| **2834** | A899 20z multicolored | .35 | .25 |
| **2835** | A899 20z multicolored | .35 | .25 |
| **2836** | A899 30z multicolored | .35 | .30 |
| **2837** | A899 40z multicolored | .50 | .30 |
| | *Nos. 2832-2837 (6)* | 2.05 | 1.60 |

### Royalty Type of 1986

**Photo. & Engr.**

**1987, Dec. 4 *Perf. 11***

| | | | |
|---|---|---|---|
| **2838** | A875 10z Boleslaw I Chrobry | .35 | .25 |
| **2839** | A875 15z Mieszko II | .75 | .25 |

No. 2838 exists with label. Value: mint $4, used $6.25.

New Year 1988 A900

**1987, Dec. 14 Photo. *Perf. 11x11½***

| | | | |
|---|---|---|---|
| **2840** | A900 15z multicolored | .25 | .25 |

Dragonflies — A901

No. 2841, Anax imperator. No. 2842, Libellula quadrimaculata, vert. No. 2843, Calopteryx splendens. No. 2844, Cordulegaster annulatus, vert. No. 2845, Sympetrum pedemontanum. No. 2846, Aeschna viridis, vert.

***Perf. 11x11½, 11½x11***

**1988, Feb. 23 Photo.**

| | | | |
|---|---|---|---|
| **2841** | A901 10z multicolored | .25 | .25 |
| **2842** | A901 15z multicolored | .25 | .25 |
| **2843** | A901 15z multicolored | .25 | .25 |
| **2844** | A901 20z multicolored | .25 | .25 |
| **2845** | A901 30z multicolored | .35 | .25 |
| **2846** | A901 50z multicolored | .75 | .40 |
| | *Nos. 2841-2846 (6)* | 2.10 | 1.65 |

### Cracow Restoration Type of 1982

**1988, Mar. 8 Litho. *Perf. 11½x11***

| | | | |
|---|---|---|---|
| **2847** | A801 15z Florianska Gate, 1300 | .25 | .25 |

Intl. Year of Graphic Design A903

**1988, Apr. 28 Photo. *Perf. 11x11½***

| | | | |
|---|---|---|---|
| **2848** | A903 40z multicolored | .35 | .25 |

Antique Clocks — A904

Clocks in the Museum of Artistic and Precision Handicrafts, Warsaw, and clockworks: No. 2849, Frisian wall clock, 17th cent., vert. No. 2850, Anniversary clock and rotary pendulum, 20th cent. No. 2851, Carriage clock, 18th cent., vert. No. 2852, Louis XV rococo bracket clock, 18th cent., vert. 20z, Pocket watch, 19th cent. 40z, Gdansk six-sided clock signed by Benjamin Zoll, 17th cent.

***Perf. 11½x12, 12x11½***

**1988, May 19 Photo.**

| | | | |
|---|---|---|---|
| **2849** | A904 10z lt green & multi | .25 | .25 |
| **2850** | A904 10z purple & multi | .25 | .25 |
| **2851** | A904 15z dull org & multi | .25 | .25 |
| **2852** | A904 15z brown & multi | .25 | .25 |
| **2853** | A904 20z multicolored | .35 | .25 |
| **2854** | A904 40z multicolored | .50 | .25 |
| | *Nos. 2849-2854 (6)* | 1.85 | 1.50 |

1988 Summer Olympics, Seoul A905

**1988, June 27 Photo. *Perf. 11x11½***

| | | | |
|---|---|---|---|
| **2855** | A905 15z Triple jump | .25 | .25 |
| **2856** | A905 20z Wrestling | .25 | .25 |
| **2857** | A905 20z Two-man kayak | .25 | .25 |
| **2858** | A905 25z Judo | .25 | .25 |
| **2859** | A905 40z Shooting | .40 | .25 |
| **2860** | A905 55z Swimming | .50 | .30 |
| | *Nos. 2855-2860 (6)* | 1.90 | 1.55 |

See No. B148.

Natl. Industry A906

**1988, Aug. 23 Photo. *Perf. 11x11½***

**Size: 35x27mm**

| | | | |
|---|---|---|---|
| **2861** | A906 45z Los "Elk" aircraft | .30 | .25 |

State Aircraft Works, 60th anniv.
See Nos. 2867, 2871, 2881-2883.

16th European Regional FAO Conference, Cracow — A907

15z, Computers and agricultural growth. 40z, Balance between industry and nature.

**1988, Aug. 22 *Perf. 11½x11***

| | | | |
|---|---|---|---|
| **2862** | A907 15z multicolored | .25 | .25 |
| **2863** | A907 40z multicolored | .40 | .25 |

### World War II Battles Type of 1984

Battle scenes and commanders: 15z, Modlin, Brig.-Gen. Wiktor Thommee. No. 2865, Warsaw, Brig.-Gen. Walerian Czuma. No. 2866, Tomaszow Lubelski, Brig.-Gen. Antoni Szylling.

**1988, Sept. 1 Photo. *Perf. 12x11½***

| | | | |
|---|---|---|---|
| **2864** | A832 15z multicolored | .25 | .25 |
| **2865** | A832 20z multicolored | .25 | .25 |
| **2866** | A832 20z multicolored | .25 | .25 |
| | *Nos. 2864-2866 (3)* | .75 | .75 |

### Natl. Industries Type of 1988

Design: Stalowa Wola Ironworks, 50th anniv.

**1988, Sept. 5 *Perf. 11x11½***

**Size: 35x27mm**

| | | | |
|---|---|---|---|
| **2867** | A906 15z multicolored | .25 | .25 |

World Post Day A909

Design: Postmaster Tomasz Arciszewski (1877-1955), Post and Telegraph Administration emblem used from 1919 to 1927.

**1988, Oct. 9 Litho. *Perf. 11½x11***

| | | | |
|---|---|---|---|
| **2868** | A909 20z multicolored | .25 | .25 |

Also printed in sheet of 12 plus 12 labels.

World War II Combat Medals — A910

No. 2869, Battle of Lenino Cross. No. 2870, On the Field of Glory Medal.

**1988, Oct. 12 Photo.**

| | | | |
|---|---|---|---|
| **2869** | A910 20z multicolored | .25 | .25 |
| **2870** | A910 20z multicolored | .25 | .25 |

See Nos. 2930-2931.

### Natl. Industries Type of 1988

Air Force Medical Institute, 60th anniv.

**1988, Oct. 12 *Perf. 11x11½***

**Size: 38x27mm**

| | | | |
|---|---|---|---|
| **2871** | A906 20z multicolored | .25 | .25 |

Stanislaw Malachowski, Kazimierz Nestor Sapieha — A912

**1988, Oct. 16 *Perf. 11***

| | | | |
|---|---|---|---|
| **2872** | A912 20z multicolored | .25 | .25 |

Four Years' Sejm (Parliament) (1788-1792), bicent.

National Leaders — A913

No. 2873, Wincenty Witos. No. 2874, Ignacy Daszynski. No. 2875, Wojciech Korfanty. No. 2876, Stanislaw Wojciechowski. No. 2877,

Julian Marchlewski. No. 2878, Ignacy Paderewski. No. 2879, Jozef Pilsudski. No. 2880, Gabriel Narutowicz.

**1988, Nov. 11** *Perf. 12x11½*

**2873** A913 15z multicolored .25 .25
**2874** A913 15z multicolored .25 .25
**2875** A913 20z multicolored .25 .25
**2876** A913 20z multicolored .25 .25
**2877** A913 20z multicolored .25 .25
**2878** A913 200z multicolored .25 .25
**2879** A913 200z multicolored .25 .25
**2880** A913 200z multicolored .25 .25
*a.* Souvenir sheet of 3, #2878-2880 25.00 25.00
*Nos. 2873-2880 (8)* 2.00 2.00

Natl. independence, 70th anniv.

### Natl. Industries Type of 1988

15z, Wharf, Gdynia. 20z, Industrialist Hipolit Cegielski, 1883 steam locomotive. 40z, Poznan fair grounds, Upper Silesia Tower.

**1988** **Photo.** *Perf. 11x11½*

**Size: 39x27mm**

**2881** A906 15z multicolored .25 .25
**2882** A906 20z multicolored .25 .25

**Size: 35x27mm**

**2883** A906 40z multicolored .25 .25
*Nos. 2881-2883 (3)* .75 .75

70th anniv. of Polish independence. Gdynia Port, 65th anniv (15z); Metal Works in Poznan, 142nd anniv. (20z); and Poznan Intl. Fair 60th anniv. (40z).

Issued: 15z, 12/12; 20z, 11/28; 40z, 12/21.

### Royalty Type of 1986

10z, Rycheza. 15z, Kazimierz I Odnowiciel.

**Photo. & Engr.**

**1988, Dec. 4** *Perf. 11*

**2884** A875 10z multicolored .35 .25
**2885** A875 15z multicolored .55 .25

New Year 1989 A914

**1988, Dec. 9** **Photo.** *Perf. 11x11½*

**2886** A914 20z multicolored .25 .25

Unification of Polish Workers' Unions, 40th Anniv. — A915

**1988, Dec. 15** *Perf. 11½x12*

**2887** A915 20z black & ver .25 .25

Fire Boats — A916

**1988, Dec. 29** **Litho.** *Perf. 14*

**2888** A916 10z Blysk .25 .25
**2889** A916 15z Zar .25 .25
**2890** A916 15z Plomien .25 .25
**2891** A916 20z Strazak 4 .25 .25
**2892** A916 20z Strazak 11 .25 .25
**2893** A916 45z Strazak 25 .45 .40
*Nos. 2888-2893 (6)* 1.70 1.65

Horses — A917

**1989, Mar. 6** **Photo.** *Perf. 11*

**2894** A917 15z Lippizaner .25 .25
**2895** A917 15z Arden, vert. .25 .25
**2896** A917 20z English .25 .25
**2897** A917 20z Arabian, vert. .25 .25
**2898** A917 30z Wielkopolski .35 .25
**2899** A917 70z Polish, vert. .75 .25
*Nos. 2894-2899 (6)* 2.10 1.50

Dogs — A918

No. 2900, Wire-haired dachshund. No. 2901, Cocker spaniel. No. 2902, Czech fousek pointer. No. 2903, Welsh terrier. No. 2904, English setter. No. 2905, Pointer.

**1989, May 3** **Photo.** *Perf. 11½x11*

**2900** A918 15z multicolored .25 .25
**2901** A918 15z multicolored .25 .25
**2902** A918 20z multicolored .25 .25
**2903** A918 20z multicolored .25 .25
**2904** A918 25z multicolored .35 .25
**2905** A918 45z multicolored .85 .60
*Nos. 2900-2905 (6)* 2.20 1.85

Battle of Monte Cassino, 45th Anniv. — A919

Design: 80z, Gen. W. Anders. 165z, Battle of Falaise, General Stanislaw Maczek, horiz. 210z, Battle of Arnhem, Gen. Stanislaw Sosabowski, vert.

**1989, May 18** *Perf. 11½x12*

**2906** A919 80z multicolored .25 .25
**2907** A919 165z multicolored .50 .25
**2907A** A919 210z multicolored .60 .25
*Nos. 2906-2907A (3)* 1.35 .75

1st Armored Division at the Battle of Falaise, 45th anniv. Battle of Arnhem, 45th anniv.

See No. 2968.

A 50z stamp for Gen. Grzegorz Korczynski was prepared but not released. Value: mint $25, cto $35.

Woman Wearing a Phrygian Cap — A920

**1989, July 3** **Litho.** *Perf. 11½x11*

**2908** A920 100z blk, dark red & dark ultra .25 .25
*a.* Souv. sheet of 2+2 labels 1.00 .75

French revolution bicent., PHILEXFRANCE '89. No. 2908 printed se-tenant with inscribed label picturing exhibition emblem. No. 2908a sold for 270z. Surcharge benefited the Polish Philatelic Union.

Polonia House, Pultusk — A921

**1989, July 16** **Photo.** *Perf. 11½*

**2909** A921 100z multicolored .35 .25

First Moon Landing, 20th Anniv. A922

**1989, July 21** *Perf. 11x11½*

**2910** A922 100z multicolored .35 .25
*a.* Souvenir sheet of 1 1.25 .50

No. 2910a exists imperf. Value $20.

Polish People's Republic, 45th Anniv. — A923

Winners of the Order of the Builders of People's Poland: No. 2911, Ksawery Dunikowski (1875-1964), artist. No. 2912, Stanislaw Mazur (1897-1964), agriculturist. No. 2913, Natalia Gasiorowska (1881-1964), historian. No. 2914, Wincenty Pstrowski (1904-1948), coal miner.

**1989, July 21** *Perf. 11½x11*

**2911** A923 35z multicolored .25 .25
**2912** A923 35z multicolored .25 .25
**2913** A923 35z multicolored .25 .25
**2914** A923 35z multicolored .25 .25
*Nos. 2911-2914 (4)* 1.00 1.00

Security Service and Militia, 45th Anniv. A924

**1989, July 21** *Perf. 11x11½*

**2915** A924 35z dull brn & slate blue .25 .25

World Fire Fighting Congress, July 25-30, Warsaw — A925

**1989, July 25** *Perf. 11½x11*

**2916** A925 80z multicolored .35 .25

Daisy — A926

Designs: 60z, Juniper. 150z, Daisy. 500z, Wild rose. 1000z, Blue corn flower.

**1989** **Photo.** *Perf. 11x12*

**2917** A926 40z slate green .25 .25
**2918** A926 60z violet blue .25 .25
**2919** A926 150z rose lake .25 .25
**2920** A926 500z bright violet .25 .25
**2921** A926 1000z bright blue .25 .25
*Nos. 2917-2921 (5)* 1.25 1.25

Issue dates: 40z, 60z, Aug. 25. 150z, Dec. 4; 500z, 1000z, Dec. 19.

See Nos. 2978-2979, 3026. For surcharge see No. 2970.

### World War II Battles Type of 1984

Battle scenes and commanders: No. 2922, Westerplatte, Capt. Franciszek Dabrowski. No. 2923, Hel, Artillery Capt. B. Przybyszewski. No. 2924, Kock, Brig.-Gen. Franciszek Kleeberg. No. 2925, Lwow, Brig.-Gen. Wladyslaw Langner.

**1989, Sept. 1** *Perf. 12x11½*

**2922** A832 25z multicolored .25 .25
**2923** A832 25z multicolored .25 .25
**2924** A832 35z multicolored .25 .25
**2925** A832 35z multicolored .25 .25
*Nos. 2922-2925 (4)* 1.00 1.00

Nazi invasion of Poland, 50th anniv.

Caricature Museum — A927

**1989, Sept. 15** **Photo.** *Perf. 11½x11*

**2926** A927 40z multicolored .25 .25

Teaching Surgery at Polish Universities, Bicent., and Surgeon's Soc. Cent. — A928

Surgeons: 40z, Rafal Jozef Czerwiakowski (1743-1813), 1st professor of surgery and founder of the 1st surgical department, Jagellonian University, Cracow. 60z, Ludwik Rydygier (1850-1920), founder of the Polish Surgeons Society.

**1989, Sept. 18** *Perf. 11½x12*

**2927** A928 40z black & brt ultra .25 .25
**2928** A928 60z black & brt green .25 .25

World Post Day — A929

Design: Emil Kalinski (1890-1973), minister of the Post and Telegraph from 1933-1939.

**1989, Oct. 9** *Perf. 12x11½*

**2929** A929 60z multicolored .35 .25

Printed se-tenant with label picturing postal emblem of the second republic.

### WWII Decorations Type of 1988

Medals: No. 2930, Participation in the Struggle for Control of the Nation. No. 2931, Defense of Warsaw, 1939-45.

**1989, Oct. 12** **Photo.** *Perf. 11½x11*

**2930** A910 60z multicolored .25 .25
**2931** A910 60z multicolored .25 .25

### Royalty Type of 1986

20z, Boleslaw II Szczodry. 30z, Wladyslaw I Herman.

**Photo. & Engr.**

**1989, Oct. 18** *Perf. 11*

**2932** A875 20z multicolored .50 .30
**2933** A875 30z multicolored .60 .50

World Stamp Expo '89, Washington, DC, Nov. 17-Dec.3 — A930

**1989, Nov. 14 Photo.** ***Perf. 11x11½***
**2934** A930 500z multicolored .90 .35

Exists imperf. Value: mint $1.50, used $1.40.

Polish Red Cross Soc., 70th Anniv. — A931

**1989, Nov. 17** ***Perf. 11½x11***
**2935** A931 200z blk, brt yel grn & scar .35 .25

Treaty of Versailles, 70th Anniv. A932

Design: State arms and representatives of Poland who signed the treaty, including Ignacy Jan Paderewski (1860-1941), pianist, composer, statesman, and Roman Dmowski (1864-1939), statesman.

**1989, Nov. 21** ***Perf. 11x11½***
**2936** A932 350z multicolored .65 .25

Camera Shutter as the Iris of the Eye — A933

Designs: 40z, Photographer in silhouette, Maksymilian Strasz (1804-1870), pioneer of photography in Poland.

***Perf. 11½x12, 12x11½***
**1989, Nov. 27**
**2937** A933 40z multicolored .25 .25
**2938** A933 60z shown .25 .25

Photography, 150th anniv.

**No. 2456 Surcharged**

**1989, Nov. 30 Photo.** ***Perf. 11x11½***
**2939** A766 500z on 4z dark violet .25 .25

Flowers, Still-life Paintings in the National Museum, Warsaw A934

25z, Jan Ciaglinski. 30z, Wojciech Weiss. 35z, Antoni Kolasinski. 50z, Stefan Nacht-Samborski. 60z, Jozef Pankiewicz. 85z, Henryka Beyer. 110z, Wladyslaw Slewinski. 190z, Czeslaw Wdowiszewski.

**1989, Dec. 18** ***Perf. 13***
**2940** A934 25z multicolored .25 .25
**2941** A934 30z multicolored .25 .25
**2942** A934 35z multicolored .25 .25
**2943** A934 50z multicolored .25 .25
**2944** A934 60z multicolored .25 .25
**2945** A934 85z multicolored .25 .25
**2946** A934 110z multicolored .25 .25
**2947** A934 190z multicolored .50 .30
*Nos. 2940-2947 (8)* 2.25 2.05

Religious Art — A935

50z, Jesus, shroud. 60z, Two saints. 90z, Three saints. 150z, Jesus, Mary, Joseph. 200z, Madonna and Child Enthroned. 350z, Holy Family with angels.

**1989, Dec. 21** ***Perf. 11½x11***
**2948** A935 50z multicolored .25 .25
**2949** A935 60z multicolored .25 .25
**2950** A935 90z multicolored .25 .25

***Perf. 11x11½***
**2951** A935 150z multicolored .25 .25
**2952** A935 200z multicolored .30 .25
**2953** A935 350z multicolored .50 .30
*Nos. 2948-2953 (6)* 1.80 1.55

Nos. 2951-2953 vert.

**Republic of Poland**
No. 2738 Surcharged

**1990, Jan. 31 Photo.** ***Perf. 11½x12***
**2954** A828 350z on 15z rose brn .25 .25

Opera Singers — A936

Portraits: 100z, Krystyna Jamroz (1923-1986). 150z, Wanda Werminska (1900-1988). 350z, Ada Sari (1882-1968). 500z, Jan Kiepura (1902-1966).

**1990, Feb. 9** ***Perf. 12x11½***
**2955** A936 100z multicolored .25 .25
**2956** A936 150z multicolored .25 .25
**2957** A936 350z multicolored .25 .25
**2958** A936 500z multicolored .35 .25
*Nos. 2955-2958 (4)* 1.10 1.00

Yachting A937

**1990, Mar. 29** ***Perf. 11x11½***
**2959** A937 100z shown .25 .25
**2960** A937 200z Rugby .25 .25
**2961** A937 400z High jump .25 .25
**2962** A937 500z Figure skating .25 .25
**2963** A937 500z Diving .25 .25
**2964** A937 1000z Rhythmic gymnastics .55 .25
*Nos. 2959-2964 (6)* 1.80 1.50

Roman Kozlowski (1889-1977), Paleontologist — A938

**1990, Apr. 17 Photo.** ***Perf. 11x11½***
**2965** A938 500z red & olive bis .30 .25

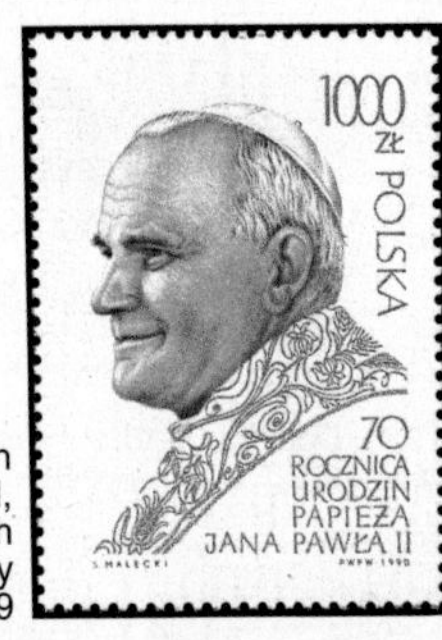

Pope John Paul II, 70th Birthday A939

**1990, May 18** ***Perf. 11***
**2966** A939 1000z multicolored .55 .30

Souvenir Sheet

First Polish Postage Stamp, 130th Anniv. — A940

Design includes No. 1 separated by simulated perforations from 1000z commemorative version at right.

**1990, May 25** ***Perf. 11½***
**2967** A940 1000z multicolored .90 .60

**World War II Battle Type of 1989**

Design: Battle of Narvik, 1940, General Z. Bohusz-Szyszko.

**1990, May 28** ***Perf. 11½x12***
**2968** A919 1500z multicolored .45 .25

World Cup Soccer Championships, Italy — A941

**1990, June 8** ***Perf. 11½x11***
**2969** A941 1000z multicolored .35 .30

No. 2918 Surcharged in Vermilion

**1990, June 18 Photo.** ***Perf. 11x12***
**2970** A926 700z on 60z vio bl .25 .25

Memorial to Victims of June 1956 Uprising, Poznan — A942

**1990, June 28 Photo.** ***Perf. 12x11½***
**2971** A942 1500z multicolored .30 .25

Social Insurance Institution, 70th Anniv. — A943

**1990, July 5** ***Perf. 11x11½***
**2972** A943 1500z multicolored .30 .25

Shells — A944

#2973, Mussel. #2974, Fresh water snail.

**1990, July 16** ***11½, 14 (#2974)***
**2973** A944 B (500z) dk pur .65 .25
**2974** A944 A (700z) olive grn .65 .25

Katyn Forest Massacre, 50th Anniv. — A945

**1990, July 20**
**2975** A945 1500z gray, red & blk .30 .25

Polish Meteorological Service — A946

**1990, July 27** ***Perf. 11x11½***
**2976** A946 500z shown .25 .25
**2977** A946 700z Water depth gauge .35 .25

**Flower Type of 1989**

2000z, Nuphar. 5000z, German iris.

**1990, Aug. 13** ***Die Cut***
**Self Adhesive**
**2978** A926 2000z olive grn .35 .25
**2979** A926 5000z violet .50 .25

World Kayaking Championships, Poznan — A947

Design: 1000z, One-man kayak.

**1990, Aug. 22 Photo.** ***Perf. 11x11½***
**2980** A947 700z multicolored .25 .25
**2981** A947 1000z multicolored .30 .25
*a.* Souv. sheet of 1 + label 2.50 2.50

A948

**1990, Aug. 31** *Perf. 11½x11*

**2982** A948 1500z blk, red & gray .50 .25

Solidarity, 10th anniv.

A949

Flowers — No. 2983, Polemonium coeruleum. No. 2984, Nymphoides peltata. No. 2985, Dracocephalum ruyschiana. No. 2986, Helleborus purpurascens. No. 2987, Daphne cneorum. No. 2988, Dianthus superbus.

**1990, Sept. 24 Photo.** *Perf. 11½x11*

**2983** A949 200z multi .25 .25
**2984** A949 700z multi .25 .25
**2985** A949 700z multi .25 .25
**2986** A949 1000z multi .25 .25
**2987** A949 1500z multi .50 .35
**2988** A949 1700z multi .65 .35
*Nos. 2983-2988 (6)* 2.15 1.70

Cmielow Porcelain Works, Bicentennial — A950

Designs: 700z, Platter, 1870-1887. 800z, Plate, 1887-1890, vert. No. 2991, Figurine, 1941-1944, vert. No. 2992, Cup, saucer, c. 1887. 1500z, Candy box, 1930-1990. 2000z, Vase, 1979, vert.

**1990, Oct. 31 Photo.** *Perf. 11*

**2989** A950 700z multicolored .25 .25
**2990** A950 800z multicolored .25 .25
**2991** A950 1000z multicolored .25 .25
**2992** A950 1000z multicolored .25 .25
**2993** A950 1500z multicolored .30 .25
**2994** A950 2000z multicolored .65 .25
*Nos. 2989-2994 (6)* 1.95 1.50

Owls — A951

**1990, Nov. 6 Litho.** *Perf. 14*

**2995** A951 200z Athene noctua .25 .25
**2996** A951 500z shown .35 .25
**2997** A951 500z Strix aluco, winter .25 .25
**2998** A951 1000z Asio flammeus .30 .25
**2999** A951 1500z Asio otus .40 .40
**3000** A951 2000z Tyto alba 1.25 .75
*Nos. 2995-3000 (6)* 2.80 2.15

Pres. Lech Walesa, 1983 Nobel Peace Prize Winner A952

**1990, Dec. 12 Litho.** *Perf. 11x11½*

**3001** A952 1700z multicolored .60 .25

A953

**1990, Dec. 21 Photo.** *Perf. 11½x11*

**3002** A953 1500z multicolored .40 .25

Polish participation in Battle of Britain, 50th anniv.

A954

Architecture: 700z, Collegiate Church, 12th cent., Leczyca. 800z, Castle, 14th cent., Reszel. 1500z, Town Hall, 16th cent., Chelmno. 1700z, Church of the Nuns of the Visitation, 18th cent., Warsaw.

**1990, Dec. 28 Litho.** *Perf. 11½*

**3003** A954 700z multicolored .25 .25
**3004** A954 800z multicolored .25 .25
**3005** A954 1500z multicolored .50 .25
**3006** A954 1700z multicolored .50 .25
*Nos. 3003-3006 (4)* 1.50 1.00

No. 3006 printed with se-tenant label for World Philatelic Exhibition, Poland '93.

Art Treasures of the Natl. Gallery, Warsaw A955

Paintings: 500z, King Sigismund Augustus. 700z, The Adoration of the Magi, Pultusk Codex. 1000z, St. Matthew, Pultusk Codex. 1500z, Christ Removing the Moneychangers by Mikolaj Haberschrack. 1700z, The Annunciation. 2000z, The Three Marys by Haberschrack.

**1991, Jan. 11 Photo.** *Perf. 11*

**3007** A955 500z multicolored .25 .25
**3008** A955 700z multicolored .25 .25
**3009** A955 1000z multicolored .25 .25
**3010** A955 1500z multicolored .30 .30
**3011** A955 1700z multicolored .40 .25
**3012** A955 2000z multicolored .60 .35
*Nos. 3007-3012 (6)* 2.05 1.65

Pinecones — A956

**1991, Feb. 22** *Perf. 12x11½*

**3013** A956 700z Abies alba .40 .25
**3014** A956 1500z Pinus strobus .40 .25

See Nos. 3163-3164, 3231-3232.

Radziwill Palace A957

**1991, Mar. 3 Photo.** *Perf. 11x12*

**3015** A957 1500z multicolored 1.00 .50

Admission to CEPT.

**Royalty Type of 1986 Srchd. in Red**

Designs: 1000z, Boleslaw III Krzywousty. 1500z, Wladyslaw II Wygnaniec.

**Photo. & Engr.**

**1991, Mar. 25** *Perf. 11*

**3016** A875 1000z on 40z, grn & blk .60 .25
**3017** A875 1500z on 50z, red vio & gray blk .80 .40

Not issued without surcharge.

Brother Albert (Adam Chmielowski, 1845-1916) — A958

**1991, Mar. 29 Photo.** *Perf. 12x11½*

**3018** A958 2000z multicolored .55 .30

Battle of Legnica, 750th Anniv. A959

**Photo. & Engr.**

**1991, Apr. 9** *Perf. 14½x14*

**3019** A959 1500z multicolored .65 .35

See Germany No. 1635.

Polish Icons A960

Designs: 500z, 1000z, 1500z, Various paintings of Madonna and Child. 700z, 2000z, 2200z, Various paintings of Jesus.

**1991, Apr. 22 Photo.** *Perf. 11*

**3020** A960 500z multicolored .25 .25
**3021** A960 700z multicolored .25 .25
**3022** A960 1000z multicolored .25 .25
**3023** A960 1500z multicolored .25 .25
**3024** A960 2000z multicolored .45 .25
**3025** A960 2200z multicolored .75 .40
*Nos. 3020-3025 (6)* 2.20 1.65

**Flower Type of 1989**

Design: 700z, Lily of the Valley.

**1991, Apr. 26 Litho.** *Perf. 14*

**3026** A926 700z dk blue green .25 .25

**Royalty Type of 1986**

Designs: 1000z, Boleslaw IV Kedzierzawy. 1500z, Mieszko III Stary.

**Photo. & Engr.**

**1991, Apr. 30** *Perf. 11x11½*

**3033** A875 1000z brn red & black .75 .25
**3034** A875 1500z brt bl & bluish blk 1.00 .45

A961

2000z, Title page of act. 2500z, Debate in the Sejm. 3000z, Adoption of Constitution, May 3, 1791, by Jan Matejko (1838-1893).

**1991, May 2 Litho.** *Perf. 11½*

**3035** A961 2000z brown & ver .35 .25
**3036** A961 2500z brown & ver .50 .35

**Souvenir Sheet**

**3037** A961 3000z multicolored .85 .50

May 3, 1791 Polish constitution, bicent.

A962

**1991, May 6 Litho.** *Perf. 11½x11*

**3038** A962 1000z multicolored *1.60* .75

Europa.

European Conference for Protection of Cultural Heritage, Cracow — A963

**1991, May 27 Litho.** *Perf. 11½*

**3039** A963 2000z blue & lake .55 .30

Sinking of the Bismarck, 50th Anniv. — A964

**1991, May 27**

| | | | | |
|---|---|---|---|---|
| **3040** | A964 | 2000z multicolored | .60 | .25 |

A965

Designs: 1000z, Pope John Paul II. 2000z, Pope wearing white.

**1991, June 1 Litho. *Perf. 11½x11***

| | | | | |
|---|---|---|---|---|
| **3041** | A965 | 1000z multicolored | .40 | .30 |
| **3042** | A965 | 2000z multicolored | .65 | .40 |

A966

**1991, June 21 Litho. *Perf. 11½***

| | | | | |
|---|---|---|---|---|
| **3043** | A966 | 2000z multicolored | .50 | .25 |

Antarctic Treaty, 30th anniv.

Polish Paper Industry, 500th Anniv. A967

**1991, July 8**

| | | | | |
|---|---|---|---|---|
| **3044** | A967 | 2500z lake & gray | .40 | .25 |

Victims of Stalin — A968

**1991, July 29 Litho. *Perf. 11½x12***

| | | | | |
|---|---|---|---|---|
| **3045** | A968 | 2500z black & red | .40 | .25 |

Souvenir Sheet

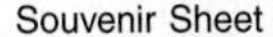

Pope John Paul II — A969

**1991, Aug. 15 Photo. *Perf. 11½x11***

| | | | | |
|---|---|---|---|---|
| **3046** | A969 | 3500z multicolored | .95 | .50 |

Basketball, Cent. — A970

**1991, Aug. 19 Litho. *Perf. 11x11½***

| | | | | |
|---|---|---|---|---|
| **3047** | A970 | 2500z multicolored | .45 | .25 |

Leon Wyczolkowski (1852-1936), painter — A971

**1991, Sept. 7 Photo. *Perf. 11½x12***

| | | | | |
|---|---|---|---|---|
| **3048** | A971 | 3000z olive brown | .40 | .25 |
| *a.* | | Sheet of 4 | 2.25 | *3.00* |

16th Polish Philatelic Exhibition, Bydgoszcz '91.

Kazimierz Twardowski (1866-1938) — A972

**1991, Oct. 10 *Perf. 11x11½***

| | | | | |
|---|---|---|---|---|
| **3049** | A972 | 2500z sepia & blk | .50 | .25 |

Butterflies — A973

No. 3050, Papilio machaon. No. 3051, Mormonia sponsa. No. 3052, Vanessa cardui. No. 3053, Iphiclides podalirius. No. 3054, Panaxia dominula. No. 3055, Nymphalis io. No. 3056, Aporia crataegi.

**1991, Nov. 16 Litho. *Perf. 12½***

| | | | | |
|---|---|---|---|---|
| **3050** | A973 | 1000z multi | .25 | .25 |
| **3051** | A973 | 1000z multi | .25 | .25 |
| **3052** | A973 | 1500z multi | .25 | .25 |
| **3053** | A973 | 1500z multi | .25 | .25 |
| **3054** | A973 | 2500z multi | .50 | .30 |
| **3055** | A973 | 2500z multi | .50 | .30 |
| *a.* | | Block of 6, #3050-3055 | 2.25 | 1.60 |

**Souvenir Sheet**

| | | | | |
|---|---|---|---|---|
| **3056** | A973 | 15,000z multi | 2.00 | 2.00 |

No. 3056 has a holographic image on the stamp and comes se-tenant with a Phila Nippon '91 label. The image may be affected by soaking in water. Varieties such as missing hologram, double and shifted images, and imperfs exist.

On Jan. 15, 1994, the Polish postal administration demonetized No. 3056.

Nativity Scene, by Francesco Solimena A974

**1991, Nov. 25 Photo. *Perf. 11***

| | | | | |
|---|---|---|---|---|
| **3057** | A974 | 1000z multicolored | .50 | .25 |

Polish Armed Forces at Tobruk, 50th Anniv. — A975

**1991, Dec. 10 Photo. *Perf. 11½***

| | | | | |
|---|---|---|---|---|
| **3058** | A975 | 2000z Gen. Stanislaw Kopanski | .65 | .25 |

A976

World War II Commanders: 2000z, Brig. Gen. Michal Tokarzewski-Karaszewicz (1893-1964). 2500z, Gen. Kazimierz Sosukowski (1885-1969). 3000z, Gen. Stefan Rowecki (1895-1944). 5000z, Gen. Tadeusz Komorowski (1895-1966). 6500z, Brig. Gen. Leopold Okulicki (1898-1946).

**1991, Dec. 20 Litho.**

| | | | | |
|---|---|---|---|---|
| **3059** | A976 | 2000z vermilion & blk | .35 | .25 |
| **3060** | A976 | 2500z violet bl & lake | .45 | .25 |
| **3061** | A976 | 3000z mag & dk bl | .55 | .25 |
| **3062** | A976 | 5000z olive & brn | 1.00 | .30 |
| **3063** | A976 | 6500z brn org & brn | 1.25 | .35 |
| | | *Nos. 3059-3063 (5)* | 3.60 | 1.40 |

A977

Boy Scouts in Poland, 80th anniv.: 1500z, Lord Robert Baden-Powell, founder of Boy Scouts. 2000z, Andrzej Malkowski (1889-1919), founder of Boy Scouts in Poland. 2500z, Scout standing guard, 1920. 3500z, Soldier scout, 1944.

**1991, Dec. 30 Photo. *Perf. 12x11½***

| | | | | |
|---|---|---|---|---|
| **3064** | A977 | 1500z multicolored | .35 | .25 |
| **3065** | A977 | 2000z multicolored | .35 | .25 |
| **3066** | A977 | 2500z multicolored | .40 | .25 |
| **3067** | A977 | 3500z multicolored | .85 | .40 |
| | | *Nos. 3064-3067 (4)* | 1.95 | 1.15 |

**Royalty Type of 1986**

Designs: 1500z, Kazimierz II Sprawiedliwy. 2000z, Leszek Bialy.

**Photo. & Engr.**

**1992, Jan. 15 *Perf. 11***

| | | | | |
|---|---|---|---|---|
| **3068** | A875 | 1500z olive green & brn | .45 | .25 |
| **3069** | A875 | 2000z gray blue & blk | 1.00 | .35 |

Paintings A978

Paintings (self-portraits except for 2200z) by: 700z, Sebastien Bourdon. 1000z, Sir Joshua Reynolds. 1500z, Sir Gottfried Kneller. 2000z, Murillo. 2200z, Rubens. 3000z, Diego de Silva y Velazquez.

**1992, Jan. 16 Photo.**

| | | | | |
|---|---|---|---|---|
| **3070** | A978 | 700z multicolored | .25 | .25 |
| **3071** | A978 | 1000z multicolored | .25 | .25 |
| **3072** | A978 | 1500z multicolored | .25 | .25 |
| **3073** | A978 | 2000z multicolored | .25 | .25 |
| **3074** | A978 | 2200z multicolored | .55 | .25 |
| **3075** | A978 | 3000z multicolored | .60 | .50 |
| | | *Nos. 3070-3075 (6)* | 2.15 | 1.75 |

1992 Winter Olympics, Albertville A979

**1992, Feb. 8 Litho. *Perf. 11x11½***

| | | | | |
|---|---|---|---|---|
| **3076** | A979 | 1500z Skiing | .35 | .25 |
| **3077** | A979 | 2500z Hockey | .60 | .35 |

See Nos. 3095-3098.

Tadeusz Manteuffel (1902-1970), Historian A980

**1992, Mar. 5 Photo. *Perf. 11½x11***

| | | | | |
|---|---|---|---|---|
| **3078** | A980 | 2500z brown | .45 | .25 |

Famous Poles A981

Designs: 1500z, Nicolaus Copernicus, astronomer. 2000z, Frederic Chopin, composer. 2500z, Henryk Sienkiewicz, novelist. 3500z, Marie Sklodowska Curie, scientist. 5000z, Casimir Funk, biochemist.

**1992, Mar. 5 Litho.** ***Perf. 11x11½***
**3079** A981 1500z multicolored .25 .25
**3080** A981 2000z multicolored .40 .25
**3081** A981 2500z multicolored .65 .25
**3082** A981 3500z multicolored 1.00 .50
*Nos. 3079-3082 (4)* 2.30 1.25

**Souvenir Sheet**

**3083** A981 5000z multicolored 2.75 .75

Expo '92, Seville (No. 3083).

Discovery of America, 500th Anniv. — A982

No. 3084, Columbus, chart. No. 3085, Chart, Santa Maria.

**1992, May 5**
**3084** A982 1500z multicolored .30 .25
**3085** A982 3000z multicolored .45 .25
*a.* Pair, #3084-3085 1.50 1.10

Europa.

Waterfalls A983

2000z, Pstrag (trout). 2500z, Zimorodek (kingfisher). 3000z, Jelec (whiting). 3500z, Pluszcz.

**1992, June 1 Litho.** ***Perf. 11½***
**3086** A983 2000z multicolored .25 .25
**3087** A983 2500z multicolored .50 .25
**3088** A983 3000z multicolored .80 .35
**3089** A983 3500z multicolored .95 .35
*Nos. 3086-3089 (4)* 2.50 1.20

Order of Virtuti Militari, Bicent. A984

Designs: 1500z, Prince Jozef Poniatowski (1763-1813). 3000z, Marshal Jozef Pilsudski (1867-1935). No. 3092, Black Madonna of Czestochowa.

**1992, June 18** ***Perf. 11***
**3090** A984 1500z multi .40 .25
**3091** A984 3000z multi .55 .25

**Souvenir Sheet**

***Imperf***

**3092** A984 20,000z multi 3.50 2.50

No. 3092 contains one 39x60mm stamp.

Children's Drawings of Love — A985

1500z, Heart between woman and man. 3000z, Butterfly, animals with sun and rain.

**1992, June 26 Litho.** ***Perf. 11½x11***
**3093** A985 1500z multicolored .25 .25
**3094** A985 3000z multicolored .40 .25
*a.* Pair, #3093-3094 .55 .50

**Olympics Type of 1992**

**1992, July 25 Litho.** ***Perf. 11x11½***
**3095** A979 1500z Fencing .50 .25
**3096** A979 2000z Boxing .25 .25
**3097** A979 2500z Sprinting .35 .30
**3098** A979 3000z Cycling .50 .35
*Nos. 3095-3098 (4)* 1.60 1.15

1992 Summer Olympics, Barcelona.

**Souvenir Sheet**

OLYMPHILEX '92, Barcelona — A986

**1992, July 29**
**3099** A986 20,000z Runners 3.00 3.00

Exists imperf. Value: mint $6, used $7.

Janusz Korczak (1879-1942), Physician, Concentration Camp Victim — A987

**1992, Aug. 5 Photo.** ***Perf. 11x11½***
**3100** A987 1500z multicolored .35 .25

Polish Emigrants Assoc. World Meeting — A988

**1992, Aug. 19** ***Perf. 12x11½***
**3101** A988 3000z multicolored .65 .30

World War II Combatants World Meeting — A989

**1992, Aug. 14** ***Perf. 11½x11***
**3102** A989 3000z multicolored .50 .30

Stefan Cardinal Wyszynski (1901-1981) — A990

3000z, Pope John Paul II embracing person.

**1992, Aug. 15** **Litho.**
**3103** A990 1500z multicolored .45 .25
**3104** A990 3000z multicolored .65 .50
*a.* Block of 2, #3103-3104 + 2 labels 1.60 1.10

6th World Youth Cong., Czestochowa (#3104).

Adampol, Polish Village in Turkey, 150th Anniv. A991

**1992, Sept. 15 Photo.** ***Perf. 11x11½***
**3105** A991 3500z multicolored .60 .35

World Post Day — A992

**1992, Oct. 9** ***Perf. 11½x11***
**3106** A992 3500z multicolored .65 .35

Bruno Schulz (1892-1942), Author — A993

**1992, Oct. 26 Litho.** ***Perf. 11x11½***
**3107** A993 3000z multicolored .55 .30

Polish Sculptures, Natl. Museum, Warsaw A994

Designs: 2000z, Seated Girl, by Henryk Wicinski. 2500z, Portrait of Tytus Czyzewski, by Zbigniew Pronaszko. 3000z, Polish Nike, by Edward Wittig. 3500z, The Nude, by August Zamoyski.

**1992, Oct. 29** ***Perf. 11½***
**3108** A994 2000z multicolored .35 .25
**3109** A994 2500z multicolored .35 .25
**3110** A994 3000z multicolored .40 .25
**3111** A994 3500z multicolored .40 .25
*a.* Souvenir sheet of 4, #3108-3111 1.50 .75
*Nos. 3108-3111 (4)* 1.50 1.00

Polska '93 (No. 3111a).

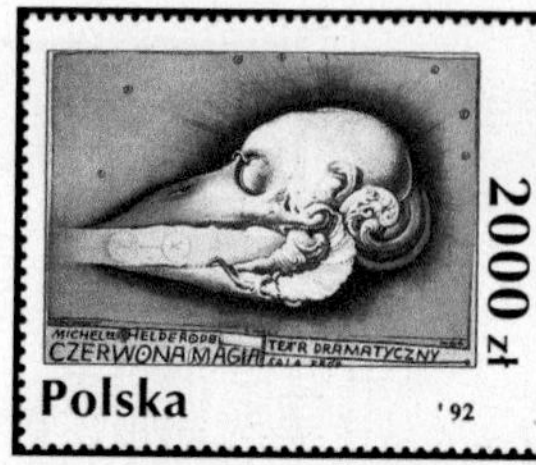

Posters — A995

Designs: 1500z, 10th Theatrical Summer in Zamosc, by Jan Mlodozeniec, vert. 2000z, Red Magic, by Franciszek Starowieyski. 2500z, Circus, by Waldemar Swierzy, vert. 3500z, Mannequins, by Henryk Tomaszewski.

**1992, Oct. 30** ***Perf. 13½***
**3112** A995 1500z multicolored .25 .25
**3113** A995 2000z multicolored .40 .25
**3114** A995 2500z multicolored .50 .30
**3115** A995 3500z multicolored .65 .40
*Nos. 3112-3115 (4)* 1.80 1.20

Illustrations by Edward Lutczyn A996

Designs: 1500z, Girl using snake as jump rope. 2000z, Boy on rocking horse with rockers reversed. 2500z, Boy using bird as arrow. 3500z, Girl with ladder, wind-up giraffe with keys on back.

**1992, Nov. 16 Photo.** ***Perf. 11***
**3116** A996 1500z multicolored .25 .25
**3117** A996 2000z multicolored .40 .25
**3118** A996 2500z multicolored .55 .25
**3119** A996 3500z multicolored .85 .40
*Nos. 3116-3119 (4)* 2.05 1.15

Polska '93.

Home Army A997

**1992, Nov. 20 Litho.** ***Perf. 13½***
**3120** A997 1500z shown .30 .25
**3121** A997 3500z Soldiers, diff. .60 .25
*a.* Pair, #3120-3121 1.00 .75

**Souvenir Sheet**

**3122** A997 20,000z +500z "WP AK," vert. 2.50 2.00

Christmas A998

**1992, Nov. 25 Photo.** ***Perf. 11½***
**3123** A998 1000z multicolored .25 .25

A999

**1992, Dec. 5 Photo. *Perf. 11½x11***
**3124** A999 1500z Wheat stalks .25 .25
**3125** A999 3500z Food products .40 .30

Intl. Conference on Nutrition, Rome.

A1000

**1992, Dec. 10 Litho.**
**3126** A1000 3000z multicolored .55 .30

Postal Agreement with the Sovereign Military Order of Malta, Aug. 1, 1991.

Natl. Arms — A1001

**1992, Dec. 14 Photo. *Perf. 12x11½***
**3127** A1001 2000z 1295 .30 .25
**3128** A1001 2500z 15th cent. .30 .25
**3129** A1001 3000z 18th cent. .35 .25
**3130** A1001 3500z 1919 .35 .25
**3131** A1001 5000z 1990 .70 .25
*Nos. 3127-3131 (5)* 2.00 1.25

Polish Philatelic Society, Cent. A1002

**1993, Jan. 6 Photo. *Perf. 11½***
**3132** A1002 1500z multicolored .35 .25

A1003

**1993, Feb. 5 *Perf. 11½x11***
**3133** A1003 3000z multicolored .55 .30

1993 Winter University Games, Zakopane.

A1004

Design: I Love You.

**1993, Feb. 14**
**3134** A1004 1500z shown .30 .25
**3135** A1004 3000z Heart on envelope .45 .30

Amber — A1005

Various pieces of amber.
20,000z, Necklace, map, horiz.

**1993, Jan. 29 Litho. *Perf. 13½***
**3136** A1005 1500z multicolored .30 .25
**3137** A1005 2000z multicolored .40 .25
**3138** A1005 2500z multicolored .45 .30
**3139** A1005 3000z multicolored .85 .40
*Nos. 3136-3139 (4)* 2.00 1.20

**Souvenir Sheet**

**3140** A1005 20,000z multi 2.25 1.40

Polska '93 (No. 3140).

**Royalty Type of 1986**

Designs: 1500z, Wladyslaw Laskonogi. 2000z, Henryk I Brodaty (1201-38). 2500z, Konrad I Mazowiecki. 3000z, Boleslaw V Wstydliwy.

**Photo. & Engr.**

**1993, Mar. 25 *Perf. 11***
**3141** A875 1500z yel grn & brn .25 .25
**3142** A875 2000z red vio & ind .25 .25
**3143** A875 2500z gray & black .50 .25
**3144** A875 3000z yel brn & brn 2.00 .50
*Nos. 3141-3144 (4)* 3.00 1.25

No. 3144 printed with se-tenant label for Polska '93. Value, without label $1.25.

Battle of the Arsenal, 50th Anniv. — A1006

**1993, Mar. 26 Photo. *Perf. 11½***
**3145** A1006 1500z multicolored .40 .25

Intl. Medieval Knights' Tournament, Golub-Dobrzyn — A1007

Various knights on horseback.

**1993, Mar. 29 *Perf. 11x11½***
**3146** A1007 1500z multicolored .25 .25
**3147** A1007 2000z multicolored .35 .25
**3148** A1007 2500z multicolored .40 .30
**3149** A1007 3500z multicolored .75 .25
*Nos. 3146-3149 (4)* 1.75 1.05

City of Szczecin, 750th Anniv. A1008

**1993, Apr. 3 Litho. *Perf. 11½x11***
**3150** A1008 1500z multicolored .40 .25

Warsaw Ghetto Uprising, 50th Anniv. — A1009

**1993, Apr. 19 Litho. *Perf. 14***
**3151** A1009 4000z gray, blk & yel .65 .30

See Israel No. 1163.

Europa — A1010

Contemporary art by: No. 3152, A. Szapocznikow and J. Lebenstein. No. 3153, S. Gierowski and B. Linke.

**1993, Apr. 30 Photo. *Perf. 11x11½***
**3152** A1010 1500z multicolored .40 .25
**3153** A1010 4000z multicolored .70 .35
*a.* Pair, #3152-3153 1.10 .50

Polish Parliament (Sejm), 500th Anniv. — A1011

**1993, May 2 Photo. *Perf. 11***
**3154** A1011 2000z multicolored .40 .25

Death of Francesco Nullo, 130th Anniv. — A1012

**1993, May 5 Litho. *Perf. 11x11½***
**3155** A1012 2500z multicolored .45 .30

**Souvenir Sheet**

Legend of the White Eagle — A1013

**1993, May 7 Engr. *Perf. 13½***
**3156** A1013 50,000z dark brn 6.25 6.25

Polska '93.

No. 3156 exists imperf., value: mint $10.50, used $12.

Cadets of Second Polish Republic — A1014

**1993, May 21 Litho. *Perf. 11x11½***
**3157** A1014 2000z multicolored .35 .25

Nicolaus Copernicus (1473-1543) — A1015

**1993, May 24**
**3158** A1015 2000z multicolored .70 .35

Kornel Makuszymski, 40th Death Anniv. — A1016

Illustrations: 1500z, Lion, monkey. 2000z, Goat walking. 3000z, Monkey. 5000z, Goat riding bird.

**1993, June 1**
**3159** A1016 1500z multicolored .25 .25
**3160** A1016 2000z multicolored .40 .25
**3161** A1016 3000z multicolored .80 .30
**3162** A1016 5000z multicolored 1.15 .70
*Nos. 3159-3162 (4)* 2.60 1.50

**Pine Cone Type of 1991**

10,000z, Pinus cembra. 20,000z, Pinus sylvestris.

**1993, June 30 Photo. *Perf. 12x11½***
**3163** A956 10,000z multi 1.50 .50
**3164** A956 20,000z multi 2.75 .75

Birds — A1017

No. 3165, Passer montanus. No. 3166, Motacilla alba. No. 3167, Dendrocopos syriacus. No. 3168, Carduelis carduelis. No. 3169, Sturnus vulgaris. No. 3170, Pyrrhula pyrrhula.

**1993, July 15 Litho. *Perf. 11½***

| | | | | |
|---|---|---|---|---|
| **3165** A1017 1500z multi | | | .25 | .25 |
| **3166** A1017 2000z multi | | | .35 | .25 |
| **3167** A1017 3000z multi | | | .40 | .25 |
| **3168** A1017 4000z multi | | | .65 | .30 |
| **3169** A1017 5000z multi | | | 1.90 | .80 |
| **3170** A1017 6000z multi | | | 1.60 | 1.00 |
| *Nos. 3165-3170 (6)* | | | 5.15 | 2.85 |

Polish Natl. Anthem, Bicent. A1018

**1993, July 20 Photo. *Perf. 11x11½***
**3171** A1018 1500z multicolored .35 .25

See No. 3206.

Madonna and Child A1019

Designs: 1500z, Stone carving from Basilica, Lesna Podlaska. 2000z, Statue, Swieta Lipska.

***Perf. 11x11½ Syncopated***
**1993, Aug. 15**
**3172** A1019 1500z multicolored .50 .30
**3173** A1019 2000z multicolored .85 .30

World Post Day — A1020

**Photo. & Engr.**
**1993, Oct. 9 *Perf. 11½x11***
**3174** A1020 2500z multicolored .55 .30

Polish Parachute Brigade A1021

***Perf. 11x11½, Syncopated***
**1993, Sept. 25 Photo.**
**3175** A1021 1500z multicolored .45 .25

Death of St. Hedwig (Jadwiga), 750th Anniv. — A1022

**1993, Oct. 14 Litho. *Perf. 14***
**3176** A1022 2500z multicolored .75 .40

See Germany No. 1816.

35th Intl. Jazz Jamboree — A1023

***Perf. 11½ Syncopated***
**1993, Sept. 27 Litho.**
**3177** A1023 2000z multicolored .50 .30

Souvenir Sheet

Election of Pope John Paul II, 15th Anniv. — A1024

**1993, Oct. 16**
**3178** A1024 20,000z multicolored 2.60 2.00

A1025

**1993, Nov. 11**
**3179** A1025 4000z Eagle, crown 1.00 .60

**Souvenir Sheet**
**3180** A1025 20,000z Dove 2.50 1.75

Independence, 75th anniv. No. 3180 has a continuous design.

A1026

**1993, Nov. 25**
**3181** A1026 1500z multicolored .45 .25

Christmas.

Posters A1027

Designs: 2000z, "Come and see Polish mountains." 5000z, Alban Berg Wozzeck.

**1993, Dec. 10**
**3182** A1027 2000z multicolored .50 .35
**3183** A1027 5000z multicolored .80 .50

See Nos. 3203-3204, 3259-3260.

"I Love You" — A1028

***Perf. 11½x11 Syncopated***
**1994, Jan. 14 Litho.**
**3184** A1028 1500z multicolored .55 .35

A1029

2500z, Cross-country skiing. 5000z, Ski jumping.
10,000z, Downhill skiing.

**1994, Feb. 12 Photo. *Perf. 11½x11***
**3185** A1029 2500z multi .70 .35
**3186** A1029 5000z multi 1.10 .70

**Souvenir Sheet**
**3187** A1029 10,000z multi 1.90 1.40

1994 Winter Olympics, Lillehammer. Intl. Olympic Committee, cent. (No. 2187).

Kosciuszko Insurrection, Bicent. — A1030

***Perf. 11½x11 Syncopated***
**1994, Mar. 24 Photo.**
**3188** A1030 2000z multicolored .55 .30

Zamosc Academy, 400th Anniv. — A1031

**1994, Mar. 15**
**3189** A1031 5000z brn, blk & gray .95 .50

Gen. Jozef Bem (1794-1850) — A1032

***Perf. 11½ Syncopated***
**1994, Mar. 14**
**3190** A1032 5000z multicolored .95 .50

**Royalty Type of 1986 with Denomination at Bottom**

**Photo. & Engr.**

**1994, Apr. 15 *Perf. 11***
**3191** A875 2500z Leszek Czarny .75 .75
**3192** A875 5000z Przemysl II 1.75 .75

Inventions A1033

Europa: 2500z, Petroleum lamp, invented by I. Lukasiewicz (1822-82). 6000z, Astronomical sighting device, with profile of Copernicus (1473-1543).

***Perf. 11½x11 Syncopated***
**1994, Apr. 30 Litho.**
**3193** A1033 2500z multicolored .50 .35
**3194** A1033 6000z multicolored 1.10 .70

St. Mary's Sanctuary A1034

4000z, Our Lady of Kalwaria Zebrzydowska.

***Perf. 11½x11 Syncopated***
**1994, May 16 Litho.**
**3195** A1034 4000z multicolored 1.00 .60

Battle of Monte Cassino, 50th Anniv. A1035

***Perf. 11x11½ Syncopated***
**1994, May 18**
**3196** A1035 6000z multicolored .80 .40

Traditional Dances A1036

**1994, May 25 *Perf. 11½ Syncopated***

| | | |
|---|---|---|
| **3197** A1036 3000z Mazurka | .50 | .35 |
| **3198** A1036 4000z Goralski | .85 | .50 |
| **3199** A1036 9000z Krakowiak | 1.10 | .50 |
| *Nos. 3197-3199 (3)* | 2.45 | 1.35 |

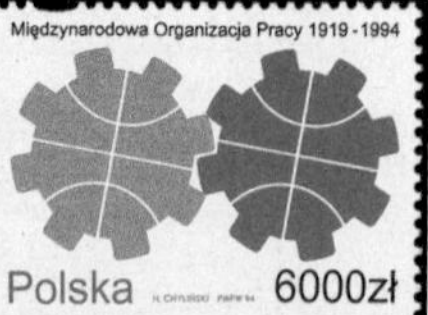


ILO, 75th Anniv. A1037

***Perf. 11½x11 Syncopated***
**1994, June 7 Litho.**
**3200** A1037 6000z multicolored .65 .35

Polish Electricians Assoc., 75th Anniv.
A1038

***Perf. 11x11½ Syncopated***

**1994, June 10**

**3201** A1038 4000z multicolored .75 .35

1994 World Soccer Cup Championships, U.S. — A1039

***Perf. 11½x11 Syncopated***

**1994, June 17**

**3202** A1039 6000z multicolored .90 .50

**Poster Art Type of 1993**

4000z, Mr. Fabre, by Wiktor Gorka. 6000z, VIII OISTAT Congress, by Hubert Hilscher, horiz.

***Perf. 11x11½, 11½x11 Syncopated***

**1994, July 4** **Litho.**

**3203** A1027 4000z multicolored .55 .35
**3204** A1027 6000z multicolored .75 .50

Florian Znaniecki (1882-1958), Sociologist
A1040

***Perf. 11½ Syncopated***

**1994, July 15** **Litho.**

**3205** A1040 9000z multicolored .75 .45

**Polish Natl. Anthem Type of 1993**

Design: 2500z, Battle of Raclawice, 1794.

**1994, July 20** **Photo.** ***Perf. 11x11½***

**3206** A1018 2500z multicolored .40 .25

A1042

***Perf. 11½x11 Syncopated***

**1994, Aug. 1** **Litho.**

**3207** A1042 2500z Natl. arms .55 .25

Warsaw Uprising, 50th anniv.

PHILAKOREA '94 — A1043

**1994, Aug. 16**

**3208** A1043 4000z multicolored .70 .35

Stamp Day.

Basilica of St. Brigida, Gdansk
A1044

**1994, Aug. 28**

**3209** A1044 4000z multicolored .85 .55

Modern Olympic Games, Cent.
A1045

***Perf. 11x11½ Syncopated***

**1994, Sept. 5**

**3210** A1045 4000z multicolored .75 .60

Krzysztof Komeda (1931-69), Jazz Muscian — A1046

***Perf. 11½ Syncopated***

**1994, Sept. 22** **Litho.**

**3211** A1046 6000z multicolored .85 .50

Aquarium Fish — A1047

Designs: No. 3212a, Ancistrus dolichopterus. b, Pterophyllum scalare. c, Xiphophorus helleri, paracheirodon innesi. d, Poecilia reticulata.

***Perf. 11½x11 Syncopated***

**1994, Sept. 28** **Litho.**

**3212** Strip of 4 2.40 1.75
*a.-d.* A1047 4000z any single .50 .40

World Post Day — A1048

**1994, Oct. 9**

**3213** A1048 4000z Postal Arms, 1858 .80 .50

St. Maximilian Kolbe (1894-1941), Concentration Camp Victim — A1049

**1994, Oct. 24** **Photo.** ***Perf. 11x11½***

**3214** A1049 2500z multicolored .65 .35

Pigeons
A1050

a, Mewka polska. b, Krymka biatostacka. c, Srebrniak polski. d, Sokot gdanski. 10,000z, Polski golab pocztowy.

***Perf. 11x11½ Syncopated***

**1994, Oct. 28** **Litho.**

**3215** Block of 4 2.50 1.60
*a.-b.* A1050 4000z any single .50 .35
*c.-d.* A1050 6000z any single .50 .35

**Souvenir Sheet**

**3216** A1050 10,000z multicolored 1.60 1.00

Christmas
A1051

***Perf. 11x11½ Syncopated***

**1994, Nov. 25** **Litho.**

**3217** A1051 2500z multicolored .80 .40

European Union
A1052

**1994, Dec. 15**

**3218** A1052 6000z multicolored 1.20 .70

Love Stamp — A1053

***Perf. 11½x11 Syncopated***

**1995, Jan. 31** **Litho.**

**3219** A1053 35g dk bl & rose car .80 .40

Hydro-Meteorological Service, 75th Anniv. — A1054

***Perf. 11x11½ Syncopated***

**1995, Jan. 31**

**3220** A1054 60g multicolored .80 .40

Poland's Renewed Access to the Sea, 75th Anniv.
A1055

**1995, Feb. 10**

**3221** A1055 45g multicolored .50 .30

**Royalty Type of 1986 with Denomination at Bottom**

35g, Waclaw II. 45g, Wladyslaw I Lotiek. 60g, Kazimierz III, the Great. 80g, Ludwik Wegierski.

**Photo. & Engr.**

**1995, Feb. 28** ***Perf. 11***

**3222** A875 35g multicolored .35 .25
**3223** A875 45g multicolored .45 .25
**3224** A875 60g multicolored .60 .35
**3225** A875 80g multicolored 1.10 .50
*Nos. 3222-3225 (4)* 2.50 1.35

St. John of God (1495-1550), Initiator of Order — A1056

***Perf. 12x11½ Syncopated***

**1995, Mar. 8** **Litho.**

**3226** A1056 60g multicolored .50 .30

Easter Eggs
A1057

Each stamp showing various designs on 3 eggs.

***Perf. 11½ Syncopated***

**1995, Mar. 16** **Background Color**

**3227** A1057 35g dull red .35 .25
**3228** A1057 35g violet .35 .25
**3229** A1057 45g bright blue .45 .35
**3230** A1057 45g blue green .45 .35
*Nos. 3227-3230 (4)* 1.60 1.20

**Pine Cone Type of 1991**

**1995, Mar. 27** **Photo.** ***Perf. 11½***

**3231** A956 45g Larix decidua .30 .25
**3232** A956 80g Pinus mugo .45 .25

Katyn Forest Massacre, 55th Anniv.
A1058

***Perf. 11½ Syncopated***

**1995, Apr. 13** **Litho.**

**3233** A1058 80g multicolored .60 .40

Europa
A1060

*Perf. 11x11½ Syncopated*

**1995, Apr. 28** **Litho.**

**3234** A1060 35g shown .40 .30
**3235** A1060 80g Flowers in helmet .70 .40

Ruturn of Western Polish Territories, 50th Anniv. — A1061

*Perf. 11½ Syncopated*

**1995, May 6** **Litho.**

**3236** A1061 45g multicolored .50 .25

Pope John Paul II, 75th Birthday A1062

*Perf. 11½ Syncopated*

**1995, May 18** **Litho.**

**3237** A1062 80g multicolored .90 .60

Groteska Theatre of Fairy Tales, 50th Anniv. — A1063

Designs: No. 3238, Two performing. No. 3239, Stage scene. No. 3240, Puppet leaning on barrel, vert. No. 3241, Character holding flower, vert.

**1995, May 25**

**3238** 35g multicolored .35 .30
**3239** 35g multicolored .35 .30
*a.* A1063 Pair, #3238-3239 1.10 .75
**3240** 45g multicolored .45 .30
**3241** 45g multicolored .45 .30
*a.* A1063 Pair, #3240-3241 .90 .65
*Nos. 3238-3241 (4)* 1.60 1.20

Polish Railways, 150th Anniv. A1064

Designs: 35g, Warsaw-Vienna steam train, 1945. 60g, Combustion fuel powered train, 1927. 80g, Electric train, 1936. 1z, Euro City Sobieski, Warsaw-Vienna, 1992.

**1995, June 9**

**3242** 35g multicolored .35 .25
**3243** 60g multicolored .35 .25
*a.* A1064 Pair, #3242-3243 .75 .50
**3244** 80g multicolored .50 .35
**3245** 1z multicolored .85 .55
*a.* A1064 Pair, #3244-3245 1.50 1.00
*Nos. 3242-3245 (4)* 2.05 1.40

UN, 50th Anniv. A1065

*Perf. 11½ Syncopated*

**1995, June 26** **Litho.**

**3246** A1065 80g multicolored .75 .35

Handlowy Bank, Warsaw, 125th Anniv. — A1066

**1995, June 30**

**3247** A1066 45g multicolored .55 .25

Polish Peasants' Movement, Cent. A1067

*Perf. 11½ Syncopated*

**1995, July 13** **Litho.**

**3248** A1067 45g multicolored .45 .25

Polish Natl. Anthem, Bicent. A1068

**1995, July 20** **Photo.** *Perf. 11x11½*

**3249** A1068 35g multicolored .40 .25

Deciduous Trees — A1069

**1995, July 31** *Perf. 12x11½*

**3250** A1069 B Quercus petraea .85 .25
**3251** A1069 A Sorbus aucuparia .85 .25

On day of issue, No. 3250 was valued at 35g; No. 3551 at 45g.

St. Mary of Consolation, Holy Trinity and All Saints Basilica, Lezajsk A1070

*Perf. 11½ Syncopated*

**1995, Aug. 2** **Litho.**

**3252** A1070 45g multicolored .35 .25

Battle of Warsaw, 75th Anniv. A1071

Design: 45g, Józef Pilsudski (1867-1935).

**1995, Aug. 14**

**3253** A1071 45g multicolored .45 .25

Horse-Equipage Driving World Championships, Poznan — A1072

Designs: 60g, Horses pulling carriage, men in formal attire. 80g, Marathon race through water, around pylons.

*Perf. 11½ Syncopated*

**1995, Aug. 23** **Litho.**

**3254** A1072 60g multicolored .70 .35
**3255** A1072 80g multicolored .70 .50
*a.* Pair, #3254-3255 1.50 .95

18th All Polish Philatelic Exhibition, Warsaw A1073

Designs: 35g, Warsaw Technical University, School of Architecture. 1z, Warsaw Castle Place, Old Town, horiz.

*Perf. 11½ Syncopated*

**1995, Aug. 30** **Litho.**

**3256** A1073 35g multicolored .35 .25

**Souvenir Sheet**

**3257** A1073 1z multicolored 1.25 1.00

11th World Congress of Space Flight Participants, Warsaw A1074

*Perf. 11½ Syncopated*

**1995, Sept. 10** **Litho.**

**3258** A1074 80g multicolored .65 .45

**Poster Art Type of 1993**

35g, The Crazy Locomotive, by Jan Sawka. 45g, The Wedding, by Eugeniusz Get Stankiewicz.

*Perf. 11½ Syncopated*

**1995, Sept. 27** **Litho.**

**3259** A1027 35g multicolored .45 .25
**3260** A1027 45g multicolored .55 .30

13th Intl. Chopin Piano Festival A1076

*Perf. 11½ Syncopated*

**1995, Oct. 1** **Litho.**

**3261** A1076 80g Polonaise score .65 .45

A1077

World Post Day 45g, Postman in uniform, Polish Kingdom. 80g, Feather, wax seal of Stanislaw II Poniatowski.

**1995, Oct. 9**

**3262** A1077 45g multicolored .35 .25
**3263** A1077 80g multicolored .50 .45

A1078

**1995, Oct. 26**

**3264** A1078 45g multicolored .35 .25

Acrobatic Sports World Championships, Wroclaw.

Janusz Groszkowski (1898-1984), Physicist — A1079

*Perf. 11½ Syncopated*

**1995, Nov. 10** **Litho.**

**3265** A1079 45g multicolored .35 .25

Christmas — A1080

**1995, Nov. 27**

**3266** 35g Nativity .35 .25
**3267** 45g Magi, tree .45 .25
*a.* A1080 Pair, Nos. 3266-3267 .90 .50

No. 3267a is a continuous design.

Songbird Chicks — A1081

Designs: a, 35g, Parus caeruleus. b, 45g, Aegithalos caudatus. c, 60g, Lanius excubitor. d, 80g, Coccothraustes.

**1995, Dec. 15**

**3268** A1081 Block of 4, #a.-d. 2.00 1.10

See No. 3377.

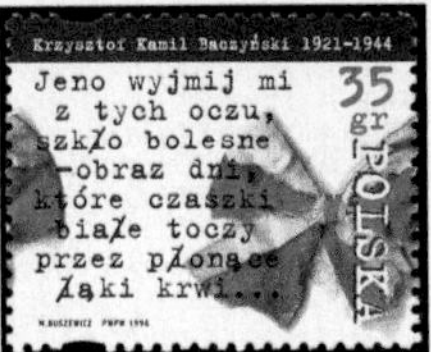

Krzysztof Kamil Baczynski (1921-44), Poet A1082

***Perf. 11½ Syncopated***

**1996, Jan. 22** **Litho.**
**3269** A1082 35g multicolored .40 .25

Love — A1083

**1996, Jan. 31**
**3270** A1083 40g Cherries .40 .25

Architecture A1084

40g, Romanesque style church, Inowlodz, 11-12th cent. 55g, Gothic syle, St. Virgin Mary's Church, Cracow, 14th cent. 70g, Renaissance period, St. Sigismundus Chapel of Cracow, Wawel Castle, 1519-33. 1z, Order of Holy Sacrament Nuns Baroque Church, Warsaw, 1688-92.

***Perf. 11½ Syncopated***

**1996, Feb. 27** **Litho.**
**3271** A1084 40g multicolored .35 .25
**3272** A1084 55g multicolored .50 .25
**3273** A1084 70g multicolored .65 .30
**3274** A1084 1z multicolored 1.00 .60
*Nos. 3271-3274 (4)* 2.50 1.40

Polish Sailing Ships — A1085

Designs: a, 40g, Topmast schooner, "Oceania," 1985. b, 55g, Staysail schooner, "Zawisza Czarny," 1961. c, 70g, Schooner, "General Zaruski," 1939. d, 75g, Brig, "Fryderyk Chopin," 1992.

**1996, Mar. 11**
**3275** A1085 Strip of 4, #a.-d. 2.25 1.40

Warsaw, Capital of Poland, 400th Anniv. A1086

**1996, Mar. 18**
**3276** A1086 55g multicolored .50 .25

Signs of the Zodiac — A1087

**1996** **Photo.** ***Perf. 12x11½***
**3277** A1087 5g Aquarius .25 .25
**3278** A1087 10g Pisces .25 .25
**3279** A1087 20g Taurus .25 .25
**3280** A1087 25g Gemini .25 .25
**3281** A1087 30g Cancer .25 .25
**3282** A1087 40g Virgo .25 .25
**3283** A1087 50g Leo .35 .25
**3284** A1087 55g Libra .40 .25
**3285** A1087 70g Aries .50 .25
**3286** A1087 1z Scorpio .70 .25
**3287** A1087 2z Sagittarius 1.40 .25
**3288** A1087 5z Capricorn 3.50 .30
*Nos. 3277-3288 (12)* 8.35 3.05

Design will dissolve when soaked on at least three denominations, 5g, 20g and 25g, from the second printing which is on fluorescent paper.

Issued: 70g, 3/21; 20g, 4/21; 25g, 5/10; 30g, 5/20; 40g, 50g, 5/31; 55g, 6/10; 1z, 6/20; 2z, 6/28; 5z, 7/10; 5g, 7/19; 10g, 7/31.

Famous Women A1088

Europa: 40g, Hanka Ordonówa (1902-50), singer. 1z, Pola Negri (1896-1987), actress.

***Perf. 11½ Syncopated***

**1996, Apr. 30** **Litho.**
**3289** A1088 40g multicolored .35 .30
**3290** A1088 1z multicolored .90 .60

3rd Silesian Uprising, 75th Anniv. A1089

***Perf. 11 ½ Syncopated***

**1996, May 2** **Litho.**
**3291** A1089 55g multicolored .50 .25

UNICEF, 50th Anniv. — A1090

Illustrations from tales of Jan Brzechwa: No. 3292, Cat and mouse. No. 3293. Man at table, waiters. No. 3294, People with "onion heads." No. 3295, Chef, duck, vegetables at table. No. 3296, Man talking to bird with human head. No. 3297, Fox standing in front of bears.

**1996, May 31**
**3292** A1090 40g multicolored .30 .25
**3293** A1090 40g multicolored .30 .25
**3294** A1090 55g multicolored .40 .25
**3295** A1090 55g multicolored .40 .25
**3296** A1090 70g multicolored .50 .35
**3297** A1090 70g multicolored .50 .35
*Nos. 3292-3297 (6)* 2.40 1.70

Drawings by Stanislaw Noakowski (1867-1928) A1091

Designs: 40g, Renaissance building. 55g, Renaissance bedroom. 70g, Gothic village church. 1z, Stanislaw August Library, 18th cent.

**1996, June 28**
**3298** A1091 40g multicolored .35 .25
**3299** A1091 55g multicolored .35 .25
**3300** A1091 70g multicolored .50 .25
**3301** A1091 1z multicolored .90 .90
*Nos. 3298-3301 (4)* 2.10 1.65

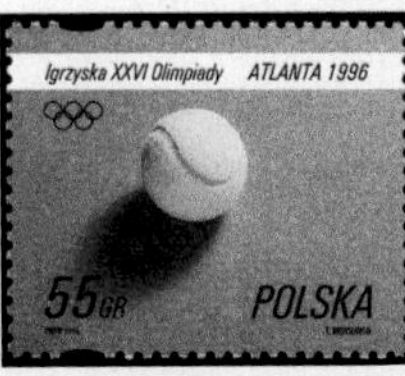

1996 Summer Olympic Games, Atlanta A1092

40g, Discus as medallion, vert. 55g, Tennis ball. 70g, Polish flag, Olympic rings. 1z, Tire & wheel of mountain bicycle, vert.

**1996, July 5**
**3302** A1092 40g multicolored .30 .25
**3303** A1092 55g multicolored .35 .25
**3304** A1092 70g multicolored .55 .35
**3305** A1092 1z multicolored .90 .35
*Nos. 3302-3305 (4)* 2.10 1.20

OLYMPHILEX '96, Atlanta — A1093

**1996, July 5**
**3306** A1093 1z multicolored .70 .40

National Anthem, Bicent. A1094

**1996, July 20** **Photo.** ***Perf. 11x11½***
**3307** A1094 40g multicolored .35 .25

Madonna and Child, St. Mary's Ascension Church, Przeczyce A1095

***Perf. 11½x11 Syncopated***

**1996, Aug. 2** **Litho.**
**3308** A1095 40g multicolored .45 .25

**Royalty Type of 1986**

Designs: 40g, Jadwiga. 55g, Wladyslaw II Jagiello. 70g, Wladyslaw II Warnenczyk. 1z, Kazimierz Jagiellonczyk.

**1996, Aug. 29** **Engr.** ***Perf. 11***
**3309** A875 40g olive brown & brown .40 .25
**3310** A875 55g red violet & violet .50 .25
**3311** A875 70g gray & black .70 .35
**3312** A875 1z yellow green & green 1.25 .60
*Nos. 3309-3312 (4)* 2.85 1.45

Mountain Scenes, Tatra Natl. Park A1096

***Perf. 11½ Syncopated***

**1996, Sept. 5** **Litho.**
**3313** A1096 40g Giewont .30 .25
**3314** A1096 40g Krzesanica .30 .25
**3315** A1096 55g Swinica .40 .25
**3316** A1096 55g Koscielec .40 .25
**3317** A1096 70g Rysy .65 .35
**3318** A1096 70g Miguszowieckie Szczyty .65 .35
*Nos. 3313-3318 (6)* 2.70 1.70

Zbigniew Seifert (1946-79), Jazz Musician A1097

***Perf. 11½ Syncopated***

**1996, Sept. 25** **Litho.**
**3319** A1097 70g multicolored .65 .35

Post and Telecommunications Museum, Wroclaw, 75th Anniv. — A1098

Paintings: 40g, Horse Exchange and Post Station, by M. Watorski. 1z+20g, Stagecoach in Jagniatkowo, by Prof. Täger.

**1996, Oct. 9** **Photo.** ***Perf. 12x11½***
**3320** A1098 40g multicolored .35 .25

**Souvenir Sheet**

***Perf. 11x11½***

**3321** A1098 1z +20g multi 1.40 1.00

Nos. 3321 contains one 43x31mm stamp.

Christmas A1099

***Perf. 11½ Syncopated***

**1996, Nov. 27** **Litho.**
**3322** A1099 40g Santa in sleigh .30 .25
**3323** A1099 55g Carolers .40 .30

Bison Bonasus A1100

**1996, Dec. 4**
**3324** A1100 55g shown .35 .25
**3325** A1100 55g Facing .35 .25
**3326** A1100 55g Two animals .35 .25
**3327** A1100 55g Adult male .35 .25
*a.* Strip of 4, #3324-3327 2.00 1.40

Wislawa Szymborska, 1996 Nobel Laureate in Literature A1101

**1996, Dec. 10**
**3328** A1101 1z multicolored .70 .45

Queen of Hearts A1102

***Perf. 11x11½ Syncopated***
**1997, Jan. 14 Litho.**
**3329** A1102 B King of Hearts .75 .25
**3330** A1102 A Queen of Hearts .75 .35
*a.* Pair, #3329-3330 1.60 .65
Complete booklet, 4 #3330a 6.50

Nos. 3329-3330 sold for 40g and 55g, respectively, on day of issue.

Easter Traditions A1103

50g, Man, woman in traditional costumes holding palms. 60g, Decorating eggs. 80g, Blessing the Easter meal. 1.10z, Man pouring water on woman.

***Perf. 11x11½ Syncopated***
**1997, Mar. 14 Litho.**
**3331** A1103 50g multicolored .30 .25
**3332** A1103 60g multicolored .40 .25
**3333** A1103 80g multicolored .55 .30
**3334** A1103 1.10z multicolored .70 .35
*Nos. 3331-3334 (4)* 1.95 1.15

A1104

St. Adalbert (956-97) A1105

50g, St. Adalbert among heathen, horiz.

**1997 Engr. *Perf. 11x11½, 11½x11***
**3335** A1104 50g brown .30 .25
**3336** A1104 60g slate .40 .25
**3337** A1105 1.10z purple .75 .50
*Nos. 3335-3337 (3)* 1.45 1.00

See Czech Republic No. 3012, Germany No. 1964, Hungary No. 3569, Vatican City No. 1040.

Issued: Nos. 3335-3336, 4/19; No. 3337, 4/23.

Stories and Legends A1106

Europa: 50g, shown. 1.10z, Mermaid.

**1997, May 5 *Perf. 11½ Syncopated***
**3338** A1106 50g multicolored .40 .25
**3339** A1106 1.10z multicolored .85 .50

46th Eucharistic Congress — A1107

**1997, May 6**
**3340** A1107 50g multicolored .50 .30

Souvenir Sheet

Pope John Paul II — A1108

***Perf. 11x11½ Syncopated***
**1997, May 28**
**3341** A1108 1.10z multicolored 1.75 1.25

City of Gdansk, 1000th Anniv. — A1109

Design: 1.10z, View of city, horiz.

***Perf. 11½x11, 11x11½***
**1997, Apr. 18 Engr.**
**3342** A1109 50g multicolored .35 .25

**Souvenir Sheet**
**3343** A1109 1.10z multicolored 1.50 1.40

No. 3343 exists imperf., value $12.

Polish Country Estates — A1110

**1997 Photo. *Perf. 11½x12***
**3344** A1110 50g Lopusznej .35 .25
**3345** A1110 60g Zyrzyna .45 .25
**3346** A1110 1.10z Ozarowie .80 .40
**3347** A1110 1.70z Tulowicach 1.20 .50
**3348** A1110 2.20z Kuznocinie 1.60 .60
**3349** A1110 10z Koszutach 6.50 2.25
*Nos. 3344-3349 (6)* 10.90 4.25

Issued: 50g, 60g, 4/26/97; 1.10z, 1.70z, 2.20z, 10z, 5/23/97.

See Nos. 3385-3390, 3463-3467, 3511-3514, 3571-3574

PACIFIC 97 — A1111

Design: San Francisco-Oakland Bay Bridge.

***Perf. 11½ Syncopated***
**1997, May 20 Litho.**
**3350** A1111 1.30z multicolored .85 .45

Bats A1113

50g, Plecotus auritus. 60g, Nyctalus noctula. 80g, Myotis myotis. 1.30z, Vespertilio murinus.

**1997, May 30**
**3352** A1113 50g multicolored .35 .25
**3353** A1113 60g multicolored .45 .25
**3354** A1113 80g multicolored .55 .30
**3355** A1113 1.30z multicolored .95 .65
*Nos. 3352-3355 (4)* 2.30 1.45

Jagiellon University School of Theology, 600th Anniv. A1114

Painting by Jan Matejko.

**1997, June 6 *Perf. 11***
**3356** A1114 80g multicolored .60 .30

Polish Settlement in Argentina, Cent. — A1115

**1997, June 6 *Perf. 11½ Syncopated***
**3357** A1115 1.40z multicolored 1.00 .45

Paintings, by Juliusz Kossak (1824-99) — A1116

Designs: 50g, Man on horse, woman, child. 60g, Men on galloping horses, carriage. 80g, Feeding horses in stable. 1.10z, Man with horses.

**1997, July 4 Photo. *Perf. 11***
**3358** A1116 50g multicolored .35 .25
**3359** A1116 60g multicolored .45 .25
**3360** A1116 80g multicolored .65 .30
**3361** A1116 1.10z multicolored .80 .50
*Nos. 3358-3361 (4)* 2.25 1.30

Polish Natl. Anthem, Bicent. A1117

Designs: 50g, People in city waving hats at Gen. Jan Henryk Dabrowski.
1.10z, Words to Natl. Anthem, Dabrowski.

**1997, July 18 *Perf. 11x11½***
**3362** A1117 50g multicolored .35 .25

**Souvenir Sheet**
**3363** A1117 1.10z multicolored 1.10 .80

Pawel Edmund Strzelecki (1797-1873), Geographer — A1118

***Perf. 11½ Syncopated***
**1997, July 20 Litho.**
**3364** A1118 1.50z multicolored 1.10 .50

Virgin of Consolation, Church of the Virgin of Consolation and St. Michael Archangel, Gorka Duchowna A1119

***Perf. 11½x11 Syncopated***
**1997, Aug. 28**
**3365** A1119 50g multicolored .50 .25

**Royalty Type of 1986**

Kings: 50g, Jan I Olbracht (1459-1501). 60g, Aleksander (1461-1506). 80g, Sigismundus I Stary (1467-48). 1.10z, Sigismundus II Augustus (1520-72).

**1997, Sept. 22 Engr. *Perf. 11***
**3366** A875 50g brn & dk brn .40 .25
**3367** A875 60g blue & dp brn .50 .25
**3368** A875 80g grn & dk slate .65 .30
**3369** A875 1.10z mag & dk mag .85 .55
*Nos. 3366-3369 (4)* 2.40 1.35

Mieczyslaw Kosz (1944-73), Jazz Musician — A1120

***Perf. 11½ Syncopated***
**1997, Oct. 3 Litho.**
**3370** A1120 80g multicolored .55 .40

World Post Day — A1121

**1997, Oct. 9**
**3371** A1121 50g multicolored .50 .25

Moscow '97 Intl. Philatelic Exhibition A1122

**1997, Oct. 13** ***Perf. 11½ Syncopated***
**3372** A1122 80g multicolored .70 .35

Theater Poster Art — A1123

#3373, "Sam Pierze Radion," black cat becoming white cat, by T. Gronowski, 1926. #3374, "Szewcy" (Bootmakers), by R. Cieslewicz, 1971. #3375, "Goya," by W. Sadowski, 1983. #3376, "Maz i zona," by A. Pagowski, 1977.

***Perf. 11x11½, 11½x11 Syncopated***
**1997, Nov. 14** **Litho.**
**3373** A1123 50g multi .30 .25
**3374** A1123 50g multi, vert. .30 .25
**3375** A1123 60g multi, vert. .40 .25
**3376** A1123 60g multi, vert. .40 .25
*Nos. 3373-3376 (4)* 1.40 1.00

**Chick Type of 1995**

Designs: a, Tadorna tadorna. b, Mergus merganser. c, Gallinago gallinago. d, Gallinula chloropus.

**1997, Dec. 5** ***Perf. 11½ Syncopated***
**3377** A1081 50g Block of 4, #a.-d. 2.00 1.20

Christmas A1124

50g, Nativity. 60g, Food, candles. 80g, Outdoor winter scene, star, church. 1.10z, Carolers.

***Perf. 11½x11, 11x11½ Syncopated***
**1997, Nov. 27**
**3378** A1124 50g multi, vert. .35 .25
**3379** A1124 60g multi .45 .25
**3380** A1124 80g multi .55 .35
**3381** A1124 1.10z multi, vert. .75 .40
*Nos. 3378-3381 (4)* 2.10 1.25

A1125

***Perf. 11½ Syncopated***
**1998, Jan. 5** **Litho.**
**3382** A1125 1.40z multicolored .95 .50

1998 Winter Olympic Games, Nagano.

A1126

Love Stamps: B, Face of dog, cat on shirt. A, Face of cat, dog on shirt.

***Perf. 12x11½ Syncopated***
**1998, Jan. 14**
**3383** A1126 B multicolored .65 .35
**3384** A1126 A multicolored .65 .35

Nos. 3383-3384 were valued at 55g and 65g, respectively, on day of issue.

**Polish Country Estates Type of 1997**

Designs: B, Gluchach. 55g, Oblegorku. A, Czarnolesie. 65g, Bronowicach. 90g, Oborach. 1.20z, Romanowie.

**1998** **Photo.** ***Perf. 11½x12***
**3385** A1110 B multicolored .70 .35
**3386** A1110 55g multicolored .40 .25
**3387** A1110 A multicolored .70 .25
**3388** A1110 65g multicolored .45 .25
**3389** A1110 90g multicolored .65 .25
**3390** A1110 1.20z multicolored .85 .30
*Nos. 3385-3390 (6)* 3.75 1.65

No. 3385 was valued at 55g, and No. 3387 was valued at 65g on day of issue.
Issued: B, A, 1/15; 55g, 65g, 90g, 1.20z, 3/3.

Easter — A1127

***Perf. 11½ Syncopated***
**1998, Mar. 12** **Litho.**
**3391** A1127 55g shown .40 .25
**3392** A1127 65g Image of Christ .45 .30

European Revolutionary Movements of 1848, 150th Anniv. — A1128

**1998, Mar. 20** **Engr.** ***Perf. 11x11½***
**3393** A1128 55g gray violet .80 .25

**Royalty Type of 1986**

Designs: 55g, Henryk Walezy. 65g, Anna Jagiellonka. 80g, Stefan Batory. 90g, Zygmunt III.

**1998, Mar. 31** ***Perf. 11***
**3394** A875 55g multicolored .40 .25
**3395** A875 65g multicolored .45 .25
**3396** A875 80g multicolored .55 .25
**3397** A875 90g multicolored .65 .30
*Nos. 3394-3397 (4)* 2.05 1.05

Protection of the Baltic Sea — A1129

Marine life: #3398, Halichoerus grypus. #3399, Pomatoschistus microps. #3400, Alosa fallax, syngnathus typhle. #3401, Acipenser sturio. #3402, Salmo salar. #3403, Phocoena phocoena.
1.20z, Halichoerus grypus.

***Perf. 11½ Syncopated***
**1998, Apr. 28** **Litho.**
**3398** A1129 65g multicolored .45 .25
**3399** A1129 65g multicolored .45 .25
**3400** A1129 65g multicolored .45 .25
**3401** A1129 65g multicolored .45 .25
**3402** A1129 65g multicolored .45 .25
**3403** A1129 65g multicolored .45 .25
*a.* Strip of 6, #3398-3403 2.75 1.75

**Souvenir Sheet**

**3404** A1129 1.20z multicolored 1.00 .75

Israel '98 World Philatelic Exhibition, Tel Aviv — A1130

**1998, Apr. 30** ***Perf. 11½ Syncopated***
**3405** A1130 90g Israel No. 8, logo .70 .45

Natl. Holidays and Festivals A1131

Europa: 55g, Logo of Warwaw Autumn, Intl. Festival of Contemporary Music. 1.20z, First bars of song, "Welcome the May Dawn," 3rd of May Constitution Day.

**1998, May 5**
**3406** A1131 55g multicolored .40 .25
**3407** A1131 1.20z multicolored .85 .40
*a.* Pair, #3406-3407 1.40 .85

Coronation of Longing Holy Mother — A1132

***Perf. 11½x12 Syncopated***
**1998, June 28** **Litho.**
**3408** A1132 55g multicolored .45 .30

Nikifor (Epifan Drowniak) (1895-1968), Artist — A1133

Paintings: 55g, "Triple Self-portrait." 65g, "Cracow Office." 1.20z, "Orthodox Church." 2.35z, "Ucrybów Station."

***Perf. 11½ Syncopated***
**1998, July 10** **Litho.**
**3409** A1133 55g multicolored .40 .25
**3410** A1133 65g multicolored .40 .25
**3411** A1133 1.20z multicolored .85 .30
**3412** A1133 2.35z multicolored 1.60 .55
*Nos. 3409-3412 (4)* 3.25 1.35

Main Board of Statistics, 80th Anniv. A1134

***Perf. 11x11½ Syncopated***
**1998, July 13**
**3413** A1134 55g multicolored .45 .30

15th Cent. Statue of Madonna and Child, Sejny Basilica A1135

***Perf. 11½ Syncopated***
**1998, Aug. 14**
**3414** A1135 55g multicolored .45 .30

Warsaw Diocese, Bicent. A1136

**1998, Aug. 28**
**3415** A1136 65g multicolored .45 .30

**Souvenir Sheet**

17th Polish Philatelic Exhibition, Szczecin — A1137

View of city, 1624: a, People on raft, pier. b, Sailing ships, pier.

**1998, Sept. 18** **Engr.** ***Perf. 11x11½***
**3416** A1137 65g Sheet of 2, #a.-b. 1.15 1.00

No. 3416 exists imperf. Value, $14.

Discovery of Radium and Polonium, Cent. A1138

***Perf. 11½ Syncopated***
**1998, Sept. 18** **Litho.**
**3417** A1138 1.20z Pierre, Marie Curie .85 .50

Mazowsze Song and Dance Ensemble, 50th Anniv. — A1139

Couple dancing, denomination at: No. 3418, LL. No. 3419, LR.

**1998, Sept. 22**
**3418** 65g multicolored .40 .25
**3419** 65g multicolored .40 .25
*a.* A1139 Pair, #3418-3419 .90 .60

Mniszech Palace (Belgian Embassy), Warsaw, Bicent. A1140

**Photo. & Engr.**

**1998, Sept. 28** ***Perf. 11½***
**3420** A1140 1.20z multicolored .85 .50

See Belgium No. 1706.

Sigismund III Vasa (1566-1632), King of Sweden and Poland — A1141

**1998, Oct. 3** **Engr.** ***Perf. 11½x11***
**3421** A1141 1.20z deep claret .85 .55

See Sweden No. 2312.

World Stamp Day — A1142

***Perf. 11½x11 Syncopated***
**1998, Oct. 9** **Litho.**
**3422** A1142 65g multicolored .45 .30

Pontificate of John Paul II, 20th Anniv. — A1143

***Perf. 11½x12 Syncopated***
**1998, Oct. 16**
**3423** A1143 65g multicolored .70 .40

Independence, 80th Anniv. — A1144

***Perf. 12x11½ Syncopated***
**1998, Nov. 11**
**3424** A1144 65g multicolored .45 .30

Christmas A1145

Paintings: 55g, Nativity scene. 65g, Adoration of the Magi.

**1998, Nov. 27** **Photo.** ***Perf. 11½x11***
**3425** A1145 55g multicolored .35 .25
**3426** A1145 65g multicolored .45 .25

Universal Declaration of Human Rights, 50th Anniv. A1146

***Perf. 11x11½ Syncopated***
**1998, Dec. 10** **Litho.**
**3427** A1146 1.20z blue & dark blue .90 .45

Adam Mickiewicz (1798-1855), Poet — A1147

Scenes, quotations from poems: 55g, Maryla Wereszczakówna, flower, night landscape. 65g, Cranes flying over tomb of Maria Potocka. 90g, Burning candles, cross. 1.20z, Nobleman's house, flowers, uhlan's cap.
2.45z, Bust of Mickiewicz, by Jean David d'Angers.

***Perf. 12x11½ Syncopated***
**1998, Dec. 24**
**3428** A1147 55g multicolored .40 .25
**3429** A1147 65g multicolored .45 .25
**3430** A1147 90g multicolored .65 .25
**3431** A1147 1.20z multicolored .85 .40
*Nos. 3428-3431 (4)* 2.35 1.15

**Souvenir Sheet**

**3432** A1147 2.45z multicolored 1.75 1.25

No. 3432 contains one 27x35mm stamp.

Polish Navy, 80th Anniv. (in 1998) A1148

No. 3433, Destroyer ORP Piorun, 1942-46. No. 3434, Frigate ORP Piorun, 1994.

***Perf. 11¼x11½ Syncopated***
**1999, Jan. 4** **Litho.**
**3433** A1148 55g multicolored .40 .25
**3434** A1148 55g multicolored .40 .25
*a.* Pair, #3433-3434 1.00 .50

Love Stamps A1149

***Perf. 11½x11¼ Syncopated***
**1999, Feb. 5**
**3435** A1149 B Dominoes .75 .30
**3436** A1149 A Dominoes, diff. .75 .35

Nos. 3535-3436 were valued at 55g and 65g, respectively, on day of issue.

Famous Polish Men A1150

Designs: 1z, Ernest Malinowski (1818-99), constructor of Central Trans-Andean Railway, Peru. 1.60z, Rudolf Modrzejewski (Ralph Modjeski) (1861-1940), bridge builder.

***Perf. 11½ Syncopated***
**1999, Feb. 12**
**3437** A1150 1z multicolored .55 .30
**3438** A1150 1.60z multicolored .90 .40

Easter — A1151

Scenes from Srudziadz Polyptych: 60g, Prayer in Ogrójec. 65g, Carrying cross. 1.40z, Resurrection.
1z, Tubadzin Pieta, 15th cent.

**1999, Mar. 5** ***Perf. 11½x11¼***
**3439** A1151 60g multicolored .35 .25
**3440** A1151 65g multicolored .35 .25
**3441** A1151 1z multicolored .60 .30
**3442** A1151 1.40z multicolored .85 .40
*Nos. 3439-3442 (4)* 2.15 1.20

**Souvenir Sheet**

China 1999, World Philatelic Exhibition — A1152

***Perf. 11½x11¼ Syncopated***
**1999, Mar. 31**
**3443** A1152 1.70z Ideogram, dragon 1.60 1.00

Virgin Mary, Patron Saint of Soldiers A1153

***Perf. 11½x11¾ Syncopated***
**1999, Apr. 2** **Litho.**
**3444** A1153 60g shown .40 .25
**3445** A1153 70g Katyn .50 .25

Characters from Works by Henryk Sienkiewicz — A1154

No. 3446, Jan Skrzetuski. No. 3447, Onufry Zagloba. No. 3448, Longin Podbipieta. No. 3449, Bohun. No. 3450, Andrzej Kmicic. No. 3451, Michal Jerzy Wolodyjowski.

***Perf. 11¾x11½ Syncopated***
**1999, Apr. 6** **Litho.**
**3446** A1154 70g multicolored .50 .30
**3447** A1154 70g multicolored .50 .30
**3448** A1154 70g multicolored .50 .30
**3449** A1154 70g multicolored .50 .30
**3450** A1154 70g multicolored .50 .30
**3451** A1154 70g multicolored .50 .30
*a.* Block of 6, # 3446-3451 3.50 2.10

Poland's Admission to NATO — A1155

***Perf. 11½ Syncopated***
**1999, Apr. 22** **Litho.**
**3452** A1155 70g multicolored .50 .30

Council of Europe, 50th Anniv. — A1156

***Perf. 11½x11 Syncopated***
**1999, May 5** **Litho.**
**3453** A1156 1z multicolored .70 .30

Europa A1157

***Perf. 11½ Syncopated***
**1999, May 5** **Litho.**
**3454** A1157 1.40z multicolored 1.00 .70

Sports A1158

***Perf. 11½ Syncopated***
**1999, June 1** **Litho.**
**3455** A1158 60g Cycling .40 .25
**3456** A1158 70g Snowboarding .40 .25
**3457** A1158 1z Skateboarding .65 .30
**3458** A1158 1.40z Roller blading .90 .35
*Nos. 3455-3458 (4)* 2.35 1.15

Visit of Pope John Paul II — A1159

Pope and: 60g, Church of the Virgin Mary, Cracow, crowd with Solidarity banners. 70g, Crowd with crosses. 1z, Crowd with flags. 1.40z, Eiffel Tower, Monument to Christ the Redeemer, Rio, Shrine of Our Lady of Fatima.

***Perf. 11¾x11½ Syncopated***
**1999, June 5** **Litho.**
**3459** A1159 60g multicolored .40 .25
Complete booklet, 10 #3459 4.00
**3460** A1159 70g multicolored .50 .25
Complete booklet, 10 #3460 5.00
**3461** A1159 1z multicolored .70 .35
**3462** A1159 1.40z multicolored 1.00 .45
*Nos. 3459-3462 (4)* 2.60 1.30

### Country Estates Type of 1997

*Perf. 11½x11¾*

**1999, June 15** **Photo.**

**3463** A1110 70g Modlnicy .50 .30
**3464** A1110 1z Krzeslawicach .70 .35
**3465** A1110 1.40z Winnej Górze 1.00 .35
**3466** A1110 1.60z Potoku Zlotym 1.10 .40
**3467** A1110 1.85z Kasnej Dolnej 1.25 .45
*Nos. 3463-3467 (5)* 4.55 1.85

Versailles Treaty, 80th Anniv. A1159a

*Perf. 11¼x11½ Syncopated*

**1999, June 29** **Litho.**

**3467A** A1159a 1.40z multi 1.00 .50

Depictions of the Virgin Mary — A1160

Designs: 60g, Painting from church in Rokitno. 70g, Crowned statue.

*Perf. 11½x11¼ Syncopated*

**1999, July 9** **Litho.**

**3468** A1160 60g multi .40 .30
**3469** A1160 70g multi .50 .30

Insects — A1161

Designs: No. 3470, Corixa punctata. No. 3471, Dytiscus marginalis. No. 3472, Perla marginata. No. 3473, Limnophilus. No. 3474, Anax imperator. No. 3475, Ephemera vulgata.

*Perf. 11½x11¾ Syncopated*

**1999, July 16** **Litho.**

**3470** A1161 60g multi .45 .30
**3471** A1161 60g multi .45 .30
**3472** A1161 70g multi .50 .30
**3473** A1161 70g multi .50 .30
**3474** A1161 1.40z multi .90 .50
**3475** A1161 1.40z multi .90 .50
*Nos. 3470-3475 (6)* 3.70 2.20

Souvenir Sheet

Ksiaz Castle — A1162

**Engr. (Margin Photo.)**

**1999, Aug. 14** ***Perf. 11¼x11***

**3476** A1162 1z blue 1.10 .85

Natl. Philatelic Exhibition, Walbrzych, Czeslaw Slania's 1001st stamp design.

No. 3476 exists imperf., value $12.

Polish-Ukrainian Cooperation in Nature Conservation — A1163

Designs: No. 3477, Cervus elaphus. No. 3478, Felis silvestris.

*Perf. 11x11½ Syncopated*

**1999, Sept. 22** **Litho.**

**3477** A1163 1.40z multi .90 .60
**3478** A1163 1.40z multi .90 .60
*a.* Pair, #3477-3478 2.00 1.50

See Ukraine No. 354.

### Royalty Type of 1986 with Denomination at Bottom

Designs: 60g, Wladyslaw IV. 70g, Jan II Kazimierz. 1z, Michal Korybut Wisniowiecki. 1.40z, Jan III Sobieski.

**Photo. & Engr.**

**1999, Sept. 25** ***Perf. 10¾x11***

**3479** A875 60g olive & black .40 .25
**3480** A875 70g brn & dk brn .50 .25
**3481** A875 1z blue & black .70 .35
**3482** A875 1.40z lilac & claret .90 .40
*Nos. 3479-3482 (4)* 2.50 1.25

UPU, 125th Anniv., World Post Day A1164

*Perf. 11¾x11½ Syncopated*

**1999, Oct. 9** **Litho.**

**3483** A1164 1.40z multi 1.00 .50

Frédéric Chopin (1810-49), Composer — A1165

**1999, Oct. 17** **Engr.** ***Perf. 11x11½***

**3484** A1165 1.40z dark green 1.10 .55

See France No. 2744.

Jerzy Popieluszko (1947-84), Priest Murdered by Secret Police — A1166

*Perf. 11½x11¼ Syncopated*

**1999, Oct. 19** **Litho.**

**3485** A1166 70g multi .55 .30

Souvenir Sheet

Memorial to Heroes of World War II — A1167

**1999, Oct. 21**

**3486** A1167 1z multi 1.10 .85

Christmas A1168

Various angels.

*Perf. 11¼x11½ Syncopated*

**1999, Nov. 26** **Litho.**

**Panel Color**

**3487** A1168 60g orange .45 .25
**3488** A1168 70g blue .50 .25
**3489** A1168 1z red .70 .30
**3490** A1168 1.40z olive green 1.00 .45
*Nos. 3487-3490 (4)* 2.65 1.25

Polish Cultural Buildings in Foreign Countries A1169

Designs: 1z, Polish Museum, Rapperswil, Switzerland. 1.40z, Marian Fathers' Museum at Fawley Court Historic House, United Kingdom. 1.60z, Polish History and Literary Society Library, Paris. 1.80z, Polish Institute and Sikorski Museum, London.

*Perf. 11½x11¾ Syncopated*

**1999, Dec. 6** **Litho.**

**3491** A1169 1z multi .70 .35
**3492** A1169 1.40z multi 1.00 .45
**3493** A1169 1.60z multi 1.10 .50
**3494** A1169 1.80z multi 1.25 .60
*Nos. 3491-3494 (4)* 4.05 1.90

New Year 2000 — A1170

*Perf. 11½x11¾ Syncopated*

**2000, Jan. 2** **Litho.**

**3495** A1170 A multi 1.00 .25

No. 3495 sold for 70g on day of issue.

Famous Poles A1171

Designs: 1.55z, Bronislaw Malinowski (1884-1942), ethnologist. 1.95z, Józef Zwierzycki (1888-1961), geologist.

*Perf. 11¼x11½ Syncopated*

**2000, Feb. 22**

**3496** A1171 1.55z multi 1.10 .40
**3497** A1171 1.95z multi 1.40 .55

Gniezno Summit, 1000th Anniv. — A1172

Designs: 70g, Holy Roman Emperor Otto III granting crown to Boleslaw Chrobry. 80g, Four bishops.

1.55z, Sclaunia, Germania, Gallia, Roma and Otto III, horiz.

*Perf. 11½x11¼*

**2000, Mar. 12** **Photo.**

**3498** A1172 70g multi .50 .25
**3499** A1172 80g multi .55 .25

**Souvenir Sheet**

***Perf. 11¼x11½***

**3500** A1172 1.55z multi 1.40 .85

Organization of Roman Catholic Church in Poland, 1000th anniv.

Easter A1173

Designs: 70g, Christ in tomb. 80g, Resurrected Christ.

*Perf. 11¼x11½ Syncopated*

**2000, Mar. 24** **Litho.**

**3501** A1173 70g multi .50 .25
**3502** A1173 80g multi .55 .25

Dinosaurs — A1174

No. 3503, Saurolophus. No. 3504, Gallimimus. No. 3505, Saichania. No. 3506, Protoceratops. No. 3507, Prenocephale. No. 3508, Velociraptor.

*Perf. 11¾x11½ Syncopated*

**2000, Mar. 24** **Litho.**

**3503** A1174 70g multi .50 .25
**3504** A1174 70g multi .50 .25
**3505** A1174 80g multi .55 .25
**3506** A1174 80g multi .55 .25
**3507** A1174 1.55z multi .90 .40
**3508** A1174 1.55z multi .90 .40
*a.* Souvenir sheet, #3503-3508 *5.50 3.25*
*Nos. 3503-3508 (6)* 3.90 1.80

Awarding of Honorary Academy Award to Director Andrzej Wajda A1175

**2000, Mar. 26**

**3509** A1175 1.10z blk & gray .75 .25
*a.* Tete beche pair 1.75 .85

Holy Year 2000 — A1176

***Perf. 11½x11¼ Syncopated***

**2000, Apr. 7**

**3510** A1176 80g multi .50 .35

**Country Estates Type of 1997**

80g, Grabonóg. 1.55z, Zelazowa Wola. 1.65z, Sucha, Wegrów. 2.65z, Liwia, Wegrów.

***Perf. 11½x11¾***

**2000, Apr. 14** **Photo.**

**3511** A1110 80g multicolored .55 .25
**3512** A1110 1.55z multicolored 1.10 .40
**3513** A1110 1.65z multicolored 1.20 .45
**3514** A1110 2.65z multicolored 1.75 .75
*Nos. 3511-3514 (4)* 4.60 1.85

Cracow, 2000 European City of Culture — A1177

70g, Jan Matejko, Franciszek Joseph, Stanislaw Wyspianski, Konstanty Ildefons Galczynski, Stanislaw Lem, Slawomir Mrozek, Piotr Skrzynecki and Cloth Hall. 1.55z, Queen Jadwiga, Józef Dietl, Krzystof Penderecki, Casimir the Great, Pope John Paul II, Jerzy Turowicz, Brother Albert, Copernicus, Collegium Maius and St. Mary's Church.
1.75z, Panorama of Cracow from 1493 wood engraving.

***Perf. 11½x11¼ Syncopated***

**2000, Apr. 26** **Litho.**

**3515** A1177 70g multi .50 .30
**3516** A1177 1.55z multi 1.10 .45

**Souvenir Sheet**

**Engr.**

***Perf. 11¼x11½ Syncopated***

**3517** A1177 1.75z blue 1.50 1.10

No. 3517 contains one 39x31mm stamp.
No. 3517 exists imperf. Value $11.

Fight Against Drug Addiction A1178

***Perf. 11¼x11½ Syncopated***

**2000, Apr. 28** **Litho.**

**3518** A1178 70g multi .50 .25

**Europa, 2000**

Common Design Type

***Perf. 11½x11¾ Syncopated***

**2000, May 9**

**3519** CD17 1.55z multi 1.25 .75

Pope John Paul II, 80th Birthday A1179

Designs: 80g, Pope. 1.10z, Black Madonna of Jasna Gora. 1.55z, Pope's silver cross.

**Engr., Litho. & Engr. (1.10z)**

**2000, May 9** ***Perf. 12¾***

**3520** A1179 80g purple .55 .25
**3521** A1179 1.10z multi .75 .35
**3522** A1179 1.55z green 1.10 .50
*Nos. 3520-3522 (3)* 2.40 1.10

See Vatican City Nos. 1153-1155.

España 2000 Intl. Philatelic Exhibition A1180

***Perf. 11½x11¼ Syncopated***

**2000, May 26** **Litho.**

**3523** A1180 1.55z multi 1.10 .50

Parenthood A1181

***Perf. 11½x11¼ Syncopated***

**2000, May 31**

**3524** A1181 70g multi .50 .25

Souvenir Sheet

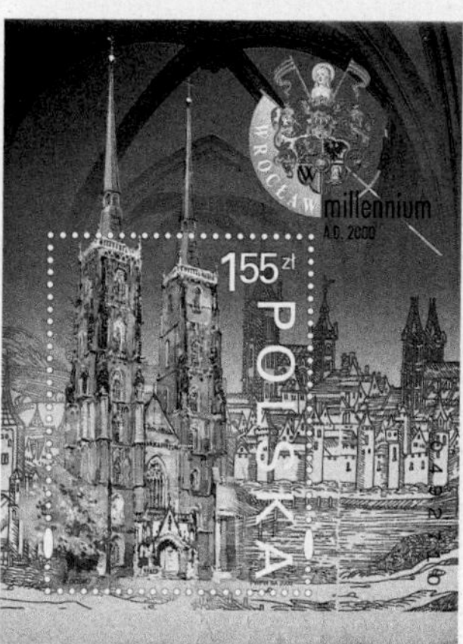

Wroclaw, 1000th Anniv. — A1182

***Perf. 11¼x11½ Syncopated***

**2000, June 15**

**3525** A1182 1.55z multi 1.25 .70

Social Activists A1183

70g, Karol Marcinkowski (1800-46), philantropist. 80g, Blessed Josemaría Escrivá de Balaguer, (1902-75), founder of Opus Dei.

***Perf. 11¼x11½ Suncopated***

**2000, June 23**

**3526-3527** A1183 Set of 2 1.00 .50

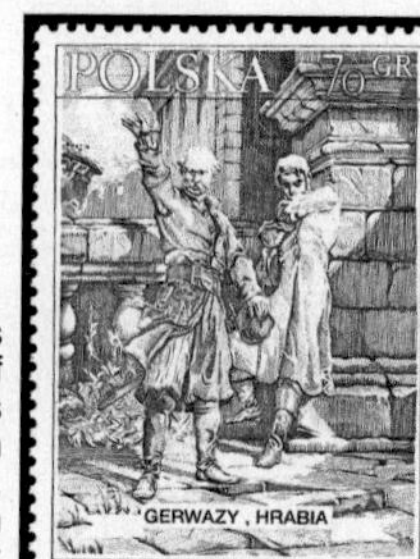

Illustrations of Characters from Pan Tadeusz, by Adam Mickiewicz A1184

No. 3528, 70g, Gerwazy & Count. No. 3529, 70g, Telimena & Judge. No. 3530, 80g, Father Robak, Judge & Gerwazy. No. 3531, 80g, Wojski. No. 3532, 1.10z, Jankiel. No. 3533, 1.10z, Zofia & Tadeusz.

**2000, June 30** **Engr.** ***Perf. 11x11¼***

**3528-3533** A1184 Set of 6 3.50 1.90

National Pilgrimage to Rome — A1185

Designs: 80g, Pope John Paul II, St. Peter's Basilica. 1.55z, Cross, Colosseum.

***Perf. 11½x11¾ Syncopated***

**2000, July 1** **Litho.**

**3534-3535** A1185 Set of 2 1.60 .70

Piotr Michalowski (1800-55), Artist — A1186

70g, Self-portrait, vert. 80g, Portrait of Boy in a Hat, vert. 1.10z, Stableboy Bridling Percherons. 1.55z, Horses & a Horse Cart.

***Perf. 11½x11¼ (no syncopation), 11¾x11½ Syncopated***

**2000, July 2**

**3536-3539** A1186 Set of 4 2.75 1.00

Depictions of the Virgin Mary — A1187

Designs: 70g, Rózanostok. 1.55z, Lichen.

***Perf. 11½x11¼ Syncopated***

**2000, Aug. 14**

**3540-3541** A1187 Set of 2 1.60 .65

St. John Bosco and Adolescents A1188

***Perf. 11¼x11½ Syncopated***

**2000, Aug. 25**

**3542** A1188 80g multi .55 .25

Educational work of Salesian order.

Souvenir Sheet

Solidarity Labor Union, 20th Anniv. — A1189

***Perf. 11½x11¼ Syncopated***

**2000, Aug. 31**

**3543** A1189 1.65z multi 1.40 .75

2000 Summer Olympics, Sydney A1190

Designs: 70g, Runners. 80g, Diving, sailing, rowing. 1.10z, High jump, weight lifting, fencing. 1.55z, Basketball, judo, runner.

***Perf. 11¾x11½ Syncopated***

**2000, Sept. 1**

**3544-3547** A1190 Set of 4 2.75 1.25

World Post Day — A1191

Children's art by: 70g, Tomasz Wistuba, vert. 80g, Katarzyna Chrzanowska. 1.10z, Joanna Zbik. 1.55z, Katarzyna Lonak.

***Perf. 11½x11¼, 11¼x11½ Syncopated***

**2000, Oct. 9** **Litho.**

**3548-3551** A1191 Set of 4 2.75 1.10

Souvenir Sheet

Polish Philatelic Union, 50th Anniv. — A1192

***Perf. 11¼x11½ Syncopated***

**2000, Oct. 12**

**3552** A1192 1.55z multi 1.25 .75

**Royalty Type of 1986 With Denominations at Bottom**

Designs: 70g, August II. 80g, Stanislaw Leszczynski. 1.10z, August III. 1.55z, Stanislaw August Poniatowski.

**2000, Oct. 23 Engr. *Perf. 10¾x11***

**3553-3556** A875 Set of 4 3.00 1.25

Katyn Massacre, 60th Anniv. — A1193

Designs: 70g, Priest and cross. 80g, Pope John Paul II at monument in Warsaw.

***Perf. 11½x11¾ Syncopated***

**2000, Nov. 15 Litho.**

**3557-3558** A1193 Set of 2 1.10 .50

Christmas A1194

Scenes from the life of Jesus: 70g, Nativity. 80g, Wedding at Cana. 1.10g, Last Supper. 1.55z, Ascension.

***Perf. 11½ Syncopated***

**2000, Nov. 27**

**3559-3562** A1194 Set of 4 2.75 1.25

Zacheta Art Museum, Warsaw, Cent. — A1195

***Perf. 11½x11¼ Syncopated***

**2000, Dec. 4**

**3563** A1195 70g multi .50 .25

Underground Post During Martial Law — A1196

***Perf. 11½x11¼ Syncopated***

**2000, Dec. 13**

**3564** A1196 80g multi + label .85 .35

*a.* Tete beche block of 2 stamps + 2 labels 2.25 1.10

End of Holy Year 2000 — A1197

***Perf. 11¾x11½ Syncopated***

**2001, Jan. 6 Litho.**

**3565** A1197 A multi .85 .35

Sold for 1z on day of issue.

20th Winter Universiade, Zakopane — A1198

***Perf. 11¼x11½ Syncopated***

**2001, Feb. 7**

**3566** A1198 1z multi .65 .30

Internet A1199

***Perf. 11¼x11½ Syncopated***

**2001, Feb. 22**

**3567** A1199 1z multi .65 .30

World Ski Championships, Lahti, Finland — A1200

***Perf. 11½ Syncopated***

**2001, Feb. 23**

**3568** A1200 1z shown .70 .30

**With Inscription "Adam Malysz" in Black**

**3569** A1200 1z multi .70 .30

**As #3569, With Inscription "Mistrzem Swiata" in Red**

**3570** A1200 1z multi .70 .30

*Nos. 3568-3570 (3)* 2.10 .90

**Country Estates Type of 1997**

***Perf. 11½x11¾***

**2001, Feb. 28 Photo.**

**3571** A1110 10g Lipków .25 .25

**3572** A1110 1.50z Sulejówek 1.10 .35

**3573** A1110 1.90z Petrykozy 1.40 .45

**3574** A1110 3z Janowiec 2.10 .75

*Nos. 3571-3574 (4)* 4.85 1.80

Issued: 1.90z, 3z, 2/28. 10g, 1.50z, 6/20.

Easter A1201

Designs: 1z, Women at empty tomb. 1.90z, Resurrected Christ with apostles.

***Perf. 11½ Syncopated***

**2001, Mar. 16 Litho.**

**3575-3576** A1201 Set of 2 2.00 .70

12th Salesian Youth World Championships — A1202

***Perf. 11¾x11½ Syncopated***

**2001, Apr. 28**

**3577** A1202 1z multi .65 .30

Europa — A1203

***Perf. 11½x11¼ Syncopated***

**2001, May 5**

**3578** A1203 1.90z multi 1.25 .75

Greetings A1204

Designs: No. 3579, 1z, All the best (couple in field of flowers). No. 3580, 1z, Vacation greetings (merman and mermaid at beach).

***Perf. 11½x11¾ Syncopated***

**2001, May 10 Litho.**

**3579-3580** A1204 Set of 2 1.40 .50

Wrzesnia Children's Strike Against German Language, Cent. — A1205

***Perf. 11½x11¾ Syncopated***

**2001, May 20**

**3581** A1205 1z multi .70 .30

Polish Cultural Buildings in North America A1206

Designs: 1z, Poland Scientific Institute and Wanda Stachiewicz Polish Library, Montreal. 1.90z, Josef Pilsudski Institute, New York. 2.10z, Polonia Archives, Library and Museum, Orchard Lake, Mich. 2.20z, Polish Museum, Chicago.

***Perf. 11½ Syncopated***

**2001, June 29**

**3582** A1206 1z multi .80 .30

*a.* Tete beche pair 1.60 .70

**3583** A1206 1.90z multi 1.50 .50

*a.* Tete beche pair 3.00 1.40

**3584** A1206 2.10z multi 1.60 .55

*a.* Tete beche pair 3.25 1.60

**3585** A1206 2.20z multi 1.60 .60

*a.* Tete beche pair 3.25 1.75

*Nos. 3582-3585 (4)* 5.50 1.95

Endangered Flora and Fauna — A1207

Convention on Intl. Trade in Endangered Species emblem and: No. 3586, 1z, Parnassius apollo, Orchis sambucina. No. 3587, 1z, Bubo bubo, Adonis vernalis. No. 3588, 1z, Galanthus nivalis, Lynx lynx. No. 3589, 1.90z, Orchis latifolia, Lutra lutra. No. 3590, 1.90z, Falco peregrinus, Orchis pallens. No. 3591, 1.90z, Cypripedium calceolus, Ursus arctos. 2z, World map.

**2001, July 10 *Perf. 11½ Syncopated***

**3586-3591** A1207 Set of 6 6.00 2.25

**Souvenir Sheet**

***Perf. 11¼x11½ Syncopated***

**3592** A1207 2z multi 1.50 .95

No. 3592 contains one 39x30mm stamp.

Stefan Cardinal Wyszynski (1901-81) A1208

***Perf. 11¾x11½ Syncopated***

**2001, Aug. 3**

**3593** A1208 1z multi .70 .35

St. Maximilian Kolbe (1894-1941) — A1209

***Perf. 11¾x11½ Syncopated***

**2001, Aug. 14**

**3594** A1209 1z multi .70 .35

Depictions of the Virgin Mary — A1210

Designs: No. 3595, 1z, Pieknej Milosci, Bydgoszcz. No. 3596, 1z, Królowa Podhala, Ludzmierz. 1.90z, Mariampol, Wroclaw.

***Perf. 11½x11¼ Syncopated***

**2001, Aug. 14**

**3595-3597** A1210 Set of 3 2.75 1.10

See Nos. 3650-3652, 3694-3696.

Extension of God's Mercy Sanctuary, Cracow — A1211

**2001, Aug. 31**

**3598** A1211 1z multi .70 .35

Euro Cuprum 2001 Philatelic Exhibition, Lubin — A1212

Designs: 1z, Copper smelter. 1.90z, Copper engravers at work. 2z, Copying with a copper engraving press.

3z, Engraver's burin, view of Lubin, 18th cent.

***Perf. 11½x11¼ Syncopated***

**2001, Sept. 1** **Litho. & Engr.**

**3599-3601** A1212 Set of 3 3.50 1.40

**Souvenir Sheet**

**Litho.**

**3602** A1212 3z multi 2.25 1.10

No. 3602 exists imperf. Value: mint $4, used $11.

Premiere of Movie "Quo Vadis," Directed by Jerzy Kawalerowicz — A1213

No. 3603: a, Ligia, Vinicius, Petrinius (red and light yellow inscriptions). b, Nero singing (blue and red inscriptions). c, Apostle Peter in catacombs, baptism of Chilon Chilonides (orange and yellow inscriptions). d, Chilon Chilonides, fire in Rome (white and yellow inscriptions). e, Ligia tied to back of aurochs, Ursus holding Ligia (red and white inscriptions). f, Apostle Peter blessing Vinicius and Ligia, close-up of Peter (purple and pink inscriptions).

***Perf. 11¾x11½ Syncopated***

**2001, Sept. 1** **Litho.**

**3603** A1213 1z Sheet of 6, #a-f 4.25 2.75

A1214

Design: Exhibition on Christian Traditions in Military at Polish Army Museum.

***Perf. 11¾x11½ Syncopated***

**2001, Sept. 10** **Litho.**

**3604** A1214 1z multi .70 .35

Polish State Railways, 75th Anniv. — A1215

**2001, Sept. 24**

**3605** A1215 1z multi .70 .35

Children's Stamp Design Contest Winners A1216

Art by: 1z, Marcin Kuron. 1.90z, Agata Grzyb, vert. 2z, Joanna Sadrakula.

***Perf. 11½ Syncopated***

**2001, Sept. 28**

**3606-3608** A1216 Set of 3 3.25 1.40

Poland's Advancement to 2002 World Cup Soccer Championships A1217

***Perf. 11½x11¾ Syncopated***

**2001, Oct. 6**

**3609** A1217 1z multi .70 .35

Year of Dialogue Among Civilizations A1218

**2001, Oct. 9**

**3610** A1218 1.90z multi *3.00* .65
*a.* Tete beche pair *6.50* 1.60

12th Intl. Henryk Wieniawski Violin Competition — A1219

***Perf. 11¾x11½ Syncopated***

**2001, Oct. 13**

**3611** A1219 1z multi .70 .35

Papal Day — A1220

***Perf. 11½x11¾ Syncopated***

**2001, Oct. 14**

**3612** A1220 1z multi .85 .40

Warsaw Philharmonic, Cent. — A1221

***Perf. 11½x11¼ Syncopated***

**2001, Nov. 5**

**3613** A1221 1z multi .70 .35
*a.* Tete beche pair 1.75 .90

Millennium — A1222

No. 3614: a, Pope John Paul II, Gniezno Doors. b, Pres. Lech Walesa taking oath, cover of May 1791 Constitution. c, Covers of three magazines. d, Playwright Wojciech Boguslawski and Director Jerzy Grotowski, manuscript by Adam Mickiewicz. e, Marshal Józef Pilsudski, Solidarity posters. f, NATO emblem, Gen. Casimir Pulaski. g, Astronomers Nicolaus Copernicus and Aleksander Wolszczan, text from De Revolutionibus Orbium Coelestium, by Copernicus. h, Woodcut of mathematician Jan of Glogow, physicist Tadeusz Kotarbinski. i, Detail from 1920 poster and painting, Battle of Grunwald, by Jan Matejko. j, Four members of the Belvedere Group, masthead of Warsaw Walczy newspaper, soldiers at Warsaw Uprising of 1944, seal of Marian Langiewicz. k, Head of John the Apostle, by Veit Stoss, and self-sculpture, by Magdalena Abakanowicz. l, Composers Krzysztof Penderecki and Frederic Chopin, Mazurka No. 10, Opus 50, by Karol Szymanowski. m, Engraving of Cracow and Royal Castle, Warsaw. n, Portrait of Jan III Sobieski, flag of European Union. o, Writers Wislawa Szymborska and Mikolaj Rej. p, Runners Janusz Kusocinski and Robert Korzeniowski.

***Perf. 11¼x11½ Syncopated***

**2001, Nov. 11**

**3614** A1222 1z Sheet of 16, #a-p 12.00 6.00

Christmas A1223

Creches from Lower Silesia: 1z, 1.90z.

**2001, Nov. 27**

**3615-3616** A1223 Set of 2 2.00 .85

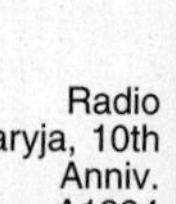

Radio Maryja, 10th Anniv. A1224

Designs: No. 3617, 1z, Head of Virgin Mary statue, building.

No. 3618: a, 1z, Statue of Virgin Mary praying, crowd with flag. b, 1z, Statue of crowned Virgin Mary, crowd with flag.

**2001, Dec. 7**

**3617** A1224 1z multi .70 .35

**Souvenir Sheet**

**3618** A1224 1z Sheet, #a-b, 3617 2.10 1.10

Love A1225

***Perf. 11¾x11½ Syncopated***

**2002, Feb. 4** **Litho.**

**3619** A1225 1.10z multi .75 .35

2002 Winter Olympics, Salt Lake City — A1226

***Perf. 11½x11¼ Syncopated***

**2002, Feb. 8**

**3620** A1226 1.10z multi .75 .35
*a.* Stamp + label .85 .50

No. 3620a was issued 2/22, and lists medals won by Adam Malysz.

Famous Poles A1227

Designs: No. 3621, 2z, Jan Czerski (1845-92), geologist. No. 3622, 2z, Bronislaw Pilsudski (1866-1918), linguist.

***Perf. 11¾x11½ Syncopated***

**2002, Feb. 22**

**3621-3622** A1227 Set of 2 2.75 1.25

City Landmarks — A1228

Designs: 2z, Cathedral, St. Adalbert's coffin, Gniezno. 2.10z, Wawel Cathedral, St. Mary's Church, Lajkonik, Cracow. 3.20z, Mermaid monument, Royal Palace, Warsaw.

**2002, Mar. 1** **Photo.** ***Perf. 11¾x11½***

| | | | | |
|---|---|---|---|---|
| **3623** | A1228 | 2z multi | 1.25 | .50 |
| **3624** | A1228 | 2.10z multi | 1.35 | .55 |
| **3625** | A1228 | 3.20z multi | 2.00 | .90 |
| | | *Nos. 3623-3625 (3)* | 4.60 | 1.95 |

See Nos. 3643-3644, 3665-3666, 3709-3712, 3763.

Easter — A1229

Designs: 1.10z, Flowers. 2z, Chicks.

***Perf. 11½x11¾ Syncopated***

**2002, Mar. 8** **Litho.**
**3626-3627** A1229 Set of 2 2.10 .85

Mammals and Their Young — A1230

No. 3628: a, Dog (purple denomination). b, Cat (brown denomination). c, Wolf (red denomination). d, Lynx (blue denomination).

***Perf. 11¾x11½ Syncopated***

**2002, Mar. 25**
**3628** Horiz. strip of 4 3.00 1.75
***a.-d.*** A1230 1.10z Any single .75 .35

Evacuation of Gen. Wladyslaw Anders' Army from USSR, 60th Anniv. A1231

***Perf. 11½ Syncopated***

**2002, Mar. 26**
**3629** A1231 1.10z multi .75 .35

Paintings by Disabled Artists A1232

Unnamed works by: No. 3630, 1.10z, Henryk Paraszczuk, vert. No. 3631, 1.10z, Amanda Zejmis, vert. 2z, Lucjan Matula. 3.20z, Józefa Laciak.

***Perf. 11½x11¼ Sync., 11¼x11½ Sync.***

**2002, Apr. 17** **Litho.**
**3630-3633** A1232 Set of 4 5.00 2.50

Census A1233

**2002, Apr. 30** ***Perf. 11¼x11½ Sync.***
**3634** A1233 1.10z multi .75 .35

Radio Free Europe, 50th Anniv. — A1234

**2002, May 2** ***Perf. 11¾x11½ Sync.***
**3635** A1234 2z multi 1.40 .60

State Fire Brigade, 10th Anniv. A1235

**2002, May 4** ***Perf. 11¼x11½ Sync.***
**3636** A1235 1.10z multi .75 .50

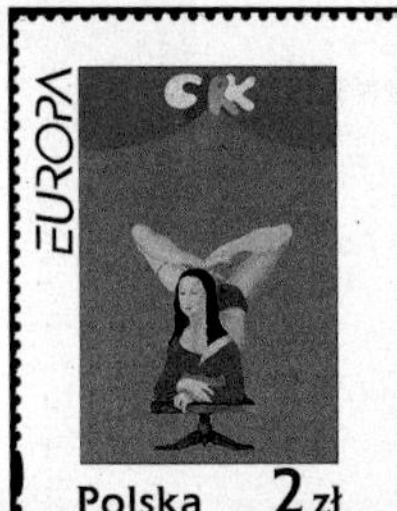

Europa A1236

**2002, May 5**
**3637** A1236 2z multi 1.20 .70

Madonna With Child, St. John the Baptist and Angel, by Sandro Botticelli A1237

**2002, May 18** ***Perf. 11½ Sync.***
**3638** A1237 1.10z multi .75 .35

National Gallery, Warsaw, 140th anniv.

Maria Konopnicka (1842-1910), Poet — A1238

**Photo. & Engr.**

**2002, May 23** ***Perf. 11½x11¼***
**3639** A1238 1.10z multi .75 .35

Children's Activities — A1239

No. 3640: a, Child playing badminton. b, Child flying kite. c, Child riding scooter.

***Perf. 11½x11¼ Syncopated***

**2002, May 31** **Litho.**
**3640** A1239 1.10z Horiz. strip of 3, #a-c 2.25 1.10

2002 World Cup Soccer Championships, Japan and Korea — A1240

Soccer ball and: 1.10z, Map. 2z, Players.

**2002, June 1**
**3641-3642** A1240 Set of 2 2.00 1.00
*3642a* Souvenir sheet, 2 each #3641-3642 4.50 3.50

**City Landmarks Type of 2002**

Designs: 1.80z, Roman paten, St. Joseph's Sanctuary, Kalisz. 2.60z, Castle, reliquary of St. Sigismund, Plock, horiz.

***Perf. 11¾x11½, 11½x11¾***

**2002, July 1** **Photo.**
**3643** A1228 1.80z multi 1.25 .70
**3644** A1228 2.60z multi 1.90 1.10

Ignacy Domeyko (1802-89), Mineralogist — A1241

***Perf. 11¾x11½ Syncopated***

**2002, July 3** **Litho.**
**3645** A1241 2.60z multi 1.75 .90

See Chile No. 1389.

Philakorea 2002 and Anphilex 2002 Stamp Exhibitions — A1242

**2002, July 12**
**3646** A1242 2z multi 1.40 .60

Seventh Visit of Pope John Paul II A1243

Pope at: 1.10z, Kalwaria Zebrzydowska. 1.80z, Lagiewniki, Cracow. 3.20z, Wawel Castle, Cracow.

***Perf. 11¾x11½ Syncopated***

**2002** **Litho.**
**3647-3648** A1243 Set of 2 2.00 .80

**Souvenir Sheet**

**Engr.**

***Perf. 11x11½***

**3649** A1243 3.20z blue 2.25 1.25

Issued: 1.10z, 1.80z, 8/5; 3.20z, 8/16.

**Depictions of the Virgin Mary Type of 2001**

Designs: No. 3650, 1.10z, Holy Lady of Incessant Assistance (Matka Boza Nieustajacej Pomocy), Jaworzno. No. 3651, 1.10z, Holy Lady of Opole. 2z, Holy Lady of Trabki, Trabki Wielkie.

***Perf. 11½x11¼ Syncopated***

**2002, Aug. 14** **Litho.**
**3650-3652** A1210 Set of 3 3.00 1.00

Souvenir Sheet

23rd Polish Philatelic Association Convention, Ciechocinek — A1244

**Engr. (Margin Photo. & Engr.)**

**2002, Sept. 1** ***Perf. 11x10¾***
**3653** A1244 3.20z brown 2.50 1.50

Exists imperf. Value $7.50.

Premiere of Film "Zemsta," Directed by Andrzej Wajda — A1245

No. 3654: a, Czesnik and Dyndalski reading letter. b, Klara and Waclaw kissing. c, Papkin with mandolin. d, Rejent and Papkin, in chair. e, Rejent and Czesnik shaking hands. f, Attendant and Klara.

***Perf. 11¾x11½ Syncopated***

**2002, Sept. 12** **Litho.**
**3654** A1245 1.10z Sheet of 6, #a-f 8.50 4.75

Steam Locomotives — A1246

Designs: No. 3655, 1.10z, Ok1-359. No. 3656, 1.10z, Ol49-7. No. 3657, 2z, TKi3-87. No. 3658, 2z, Pm36-2.

***Perf. 11¾x11½ Syncopated***

**2002, Sept. 21** **Litho.**
**3655-3658** A1246 Set of 4 4.25 1.50
***a.*** Horiz. strip of 4, #3655-3658 4.50 1.75

World Post Day A1247

***Perf. 11¼x11½ Syncopated***

**2002, Oct. 9**
**3659** A1247 2z multi 1.40 .65

Fight Against Cancer A1248

*Perf. 11¾x11½ Syncopated*

**2002, Oct. 25**

**3660** A1248 1.10z multi .75 .35

Polish Television, 50th Anniv. — A1249

No. 3661 — Programs: a, Wiadomosci (News, red background). b, Teatru Televizji (Television theater, green background). c, Pegaz (Cultural program). d, Teleranek (children's program).

*Perf. 11¼x11½ Syncopated*

**2002, Oct. 25**

**3661** A1249 1.10z Sheet of 4, #a-d 3.00 1.50

Saints — A1250

No. 3662: a, St. Stanislaw of Szczepanow (1030-79). b, St. Kazimierz (1458-84). c, St. Faustyna Kowalska (1905-38). d, St. Benedict (480-547). e, Sts. Cyril (826-869) and Methodius (815-85). f, St. Catherine of Siena (1347-80).

*Perf. 11½x11¼ Syncopated*

**2002, Nov. 8**

**3662** A1250 1.10z Sheet of 6, #a-f 4.50 2.25

Christmas A1251

Ornaments: 1.10z, 2z.

*Perf. 11¼x11½ Syncopated*

**2002, Nov. 27**

**3663-3664** A1251 Set of 2 2.10 .80
Booklet, 10 #3663 7.50

**City Landmarks Type of 2002**

Designs: 1.20z, Towers of Old City Hall, Statue of Nicolaus Copernicus, Torun, horiz. 3.40z, Church and well, Kazimierz Dolny, horiz.

**2003 Photo.** *Perf. 11½x11¾*

**3665** A1228 1.20z multi .70 .35
**3666** A1228 3.40z multi 2.00 1.00

Issued: 1.20z, 1/31; 3.40z, 4/10.

1998-2002 Negotiations to Join European Union A1252

**2003, Feb. 18** *Perf. 11x11½*

**3667** A1252 1.20z multi .85 .45

A1253

Pontificate of John Paul II, 25th Anniv. — A1254

No. 3668: a, Election as Pope, 1978. b, In Poland, 1979. c, In France, 1980. d, Assassination attempt, 1981. e, At Fatima, Portugal, 1982. f, Extraordinary Holy Year, 1983. g, At Quirinale Palace, Rome, 1984. h, World Youth Day, 1985. i, At synagogue, Rome, 1986. j, Pentecost vigil, 1987. k, At European Parliament, Strasbourg, France, 1988. l, Meeting with Mikhail Gorbachev, 1989. m, At Guinea-Bissau leper colony, 1990. n, At European Bishops' Synod, 1991. o, Publication of Catechism of the Catholic Church, 1992. p, Praying for the Balkans in Assisi, 1993. q, At Sistine Chapel, 1994. r, At UN Headquarters for 50th anniv. celebrations, 1995. s, In Germany, 1996. t, In Sarajevo, Bosnia & Herzcgovina, 1997. u, In Cuba, 1998. v, Opening Holy Doors, 1999. w, World Youth Day, 2000. x, Closing Holy Doors, 2001. y, Addressing Italian Parliament, 2002.

**2003, Mar. 20 Litho.** *Perf. 13x13¼*

**3668** Sheet of 25 22.50 12.50
*a.-y.* A1253 1.20z Any single .85 .35

**Etched on Silver Foil**

***Die Cut Perf. 12½x13***

**Self-Adhesive**

**3669** A1254 10z Pope John Paul II 8.00 *12.00*

Cancels can be easily removed from No. 3669. See Vatican City Nos. 1236-1237.

Andrzej Frycz-Modrzewski (1503-72), Writer — A1255

**2003, Mar. 28 Engr.** *Perf. 11½x11*

**3670** A1255 1.20z brown .85 .35

Easter — A1256

Folk representations: 1.20z, Jesus seated. 2.10z, Jesus standing.

**2003, Mar. 28 Photo.** *Perf. 11½x11*

**3671-3672** A1256 Set of 2 2.00 .90

Granting of Municipal Rights to Poznan, 750th Anniv. — A1257

Designs: 1.20z, Old and modern skylines of Poznan. 3.40z, View of Poznan, 1626.

*Perf. 11¾x11½*

**2003, Apr. 15 Photo.**

**3673** A1257 1.20z multi .75 .35

**Souvenir Sheet**

**Photo. & Engr.**

***Perf. 11¼x11½***

**3674** A1257 3.40z brown & lt brown 2.10 .90

No. 3674 contains one 39x31mm stamp.

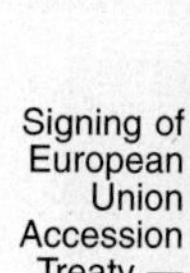

Signing of European Union Accession Treaty — A1257a

**2003, Apr. 16 Photo.** *Perf. 11x11½*

**3674A** A1257a 1.20z multi .85 .45

Europa A1258

**2003, May 5 Photo.** *Perf. 11*

**3675** A1258 2.10z multi 1.25 .85

European Union Referendum — A1258a

**2003, May 26 Photo.** *Perf. 11x11½*

**3675A** A1258a 1.20z multi .85 .45

Lazienkowski Park Landmarks, Warsaw — A1259

Designs: 1.20z, Palac Na Wyspie. 1.80z, Palac Na Wyspie, diff. 2.10z, Palac Myslewicki. 2.60z, Amphitheater.

*Perf. 11¼x11½*

**2003, May 30 Photo.**

**3676-3679** A1259 Set of 4 5.25 2.25

Children's Dream Vacations — A1260

Children's art by: 1.20z, Anna Golebiewska. 1.80z, Marlena Krejpcio, vert. 2.10z, Michal Korzen. 2.60z, Ewa Zajdler.

**2003, June 20** *Perf. 11*

**3680-3683** A1260 Set of 4 5.25 2.25

Fairy Tales A1261

Designs: 1.20z, Krak, traditional tale. 1.80z, Stupid Mateo, by Jozef Ignacy Kraszewski. 2.10z, The Princess Enchanted Into a Frog, by Antoni Jozef Glinski. 2.60z, The Crock of Gold, by Kraszewski.

**2003, June 30**

**3684-3687** A1261 Set of 4 5.25 2.25

**Souvenir Sheet**

19th National Philatelic Exhibition, Katowice — A1262

**Photo. & Engr.**

**2003, Aug. 18** *Perf. 11½x11¼*

**3688** A1262 3.40z multi 2.40 1.10

No. 3688 exists imperf. Value: mint $6, used $9.

Paintings of Julian Falat (1853-1929) — A1263

Designs: 1.20z, Self-portrait, vert. 1.80z, Spearsmen, vert. 2.10z, Winter Landscape with River and Bird. 2.60z, On the Ship — Merchants at Ceylon.

*Perf. 11½x11¼, 11¼x11½*

**2003, Sept. 30 Photo.**

**3689-3692** A1263 Set of 4 5.25 2.10

World Post Day — A1264

**2003, Oct. 9** ***Perf. 11½x11¼***

**3693** A1264 2.10z multi 1.25 .60

### Depictions of the Virgin Mary Type of 2001

Designs: 1.20z, Mother of the Redeemer. 1.80z, Holy Mother Benevolent, Krzeszowice. 2.10z, Holy Mother, Zieleniec.

**2003, Oct. 14**

**3694-3696** A1210 Set of 3 3.50 2.00

Motorcycle Racing in Poland, Cent. — A1265

No. 3697 — Motorcycles of various eras with text in: a, Yellow. b, Green. c, Pink.

**2003, Oct. 20** ***Perf. 11¼x11½***

**3697** Horiz. strip of 3 2.25 1.15

***a.-c.*** A1265 1.20z Any single .80 .35

Silesian Folk Ensemble — A1266

No. 3698: a, Denomination at left. b, Denomination at right.

**2003, Oct. 29** ***Perf. 11½x11¼***

**3698** A1266 1.20z Horiz. pair, #a-b 1.75 .70

Cranes and Polish Government Internet Address — A1267

**2003, Oct. 31** ***Perf. 11¼x11½***

**3699** A1267 2.10z multi 1.50 .60

Worldwide Fund for Nature (WWF) — A1268

No. 3700 — Pandion haliaetus: a, On branch holding fish. b, Adult and young at nest. c, Adult hunting for prey. d, Adult flying with fish in talons.

**2003, Oct. 31** ***Perf. 11½x11¼***

**3700** Horiz. strip of 4 3.25 1.75

***a.-d.*** A1268 1.20z Any single .80 .35

Christmas — A1269

Designs: 1.20z, Nativity. 1.80z, The Magi. 2.10z, The Annunciation, vert. 2.60z, Holy Family, vert.

***Perf. 11½ Syncopated***

**2003, Nov. 27** **Litho.**

**3701-3704** A1269 Set of 4 4.75 2.25

Foreign Stamps Depicting Polish Subjects A1270

Designs: 1.20z, Sweden No. 2399a (Wislawa Szymborska), vert. 1.80z, France No. 1195 (Marie Curie). 2.10z, Sweden No. 1598 (Czeslaw Milosz), vert. 2.60z, Vatican City No. 437 (Black Madonna of Czestochowa).

**2003, Dec. 12**

**3705-3708** A1270 Set of 4 4.75 2.25

### City Landmarks Type of 2002

Designs: 5g, Town Hall, church archway, Sandomierz, horiz. 1.25z, Town Hall, Neptune Fountain, Gdansk. 1.90z, Church of the Descent of the Holy Ghost, Israel Poznanski House, Lódz, horiz. 3.45z, Union Monument, Lublin Castle, Lublin, horiz.

***Perf. 11½x11¾, 11¾x11½***

**2004** **Photo.**

**3709** A1228 5g multi .25 .25

**3710** A1228 1.25z multi .85 .35

**3711** A1228 1.90z multi 1.25 .60

**3712** A1228 3.45z multi 2.40 1.00

*Nos. 3709-3712 (4)* 4.75 2.20

Issued: 5g, 1/1; 1.25z, 1/9; 1.90z, 5/14; 3.45z, 2/23. Sheet margins of No. 3711 served as etiquettes.

12th Concert of the Great Holiday Help Orchestra — A1271

**2004, Jan. 5** ***Perf. 11x11½***

**3713** A1271 1.25z multi .85 .35

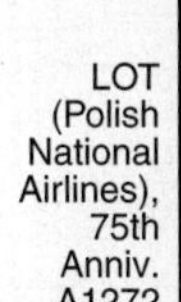

LOT (Polish National Airlines), 75th Anniv. A1272

**2004, Jan. 21**

**3714** A1272 1.25z multi .85 .35

Love A1273

**2004, Feb. 2**

**3715** A1273 1.25z multi .85 .35

Famous Poles A1274

Designs: No. 3716, 2.10z, Helena Paderewska (1856-1934), chairwoman of Polish White Cross. No. 3717, 2.10z, Father Lucjan Bójnowski (1868-1960), Polish Army recruiter in US.

**2004, Feb. 27**

**3716-3717** A1274 Set of 2 3.00 1.00

Easter — A1275

Designs: 1.25z, Rabbit. 2.10z, Lamb.

**2004, Mar. 12** ***Perf. 11½x11¾***

**3718-3719** A1275 Set of 2 2.25 .90

Flora and Fauna in Reservoirs — A1276

No. 3720: a, Beaver, frog, flowers. b, Kingfisher holding fish, crawfish holding fish, snail, beetle and water lilies. c, Grayling, leech, mussel, snail. d, Pike chasing smaller fish, grebe, snail.

***Perf. 11¾x11½ Syncopated***

**2004, Mar. 30** **Litho.**

**3720** Horiz. strip of 4 3.50 1.50

***a.-d.*** A1276 1.25z Any single .85 .35

Admission to European Union — A1277

***Perf. 11½x11¾ Syncopated***

**2004, May 1**

**3721** A1277 2.10z multi + label 1.50 .80

Europa A1278

**2004, May 5**

**3722** A1278 2.10z multi 1.50 .70

Tenth Government Postage Stamp Printers' Conference, Krakow A1279

**Photo. & Engr.**

**2004, May 7** ***Perf. 11½x11¾***

**3723** A1279 3.45z multi + label 2.25 .90

A1280

Visits to Poland by Pope John Paul II — A1281

No. 3724: a, Wearing red stole, hand on chin. b, Wearing red stole, praying. c, Holding crucifix with rays. d, Holding crucifix.

No. 3725: a, Wearing gold stole, holding crucifix. b, With arm raised. c, Wearing white vestments, seated. d, Wearing red stole, seated.

**Litho. (Embossed Labels)**

**2004, June 2** ***Perf. 13¼x13***

**Country Name in Blue**

**3724** A1280 1.25z Sheet of 4, #a-d, + 8 labels 3.50 2.00

**Country Name in Red**

**3725** A1281 1.25z Sheet of 4, #a-d, + 8 labels 3.50 2.00

See Vatican City Nos. 1264-1265.

Birds — A1282

No. 3726: a, Platycercus elegans, Platycercus eximius. b, Nymphicus hollandicus. c, Melopsittacus undulatus. d, Chloebia gouldiae, Poephila guttata, Padda oryzivora.

***Perf. 11½x11¾ Syncopated***

**2004, June 30** **Litho.**

**3726** A1282 1.25z Block of 4, #a-d 3.50 1.25

Paintings by Jacek Malczewski (1854-1929) — A1283

Designs: 1.20z, Self-portrait, vert. 1.90z, Ellenai, vert. 2.10z, Tobias and Harpy. 2.60z, The Unknown Note.

***Perf. 11½x11¼, 11¼x11½***

**2004, July 15** **Photo.**

**3727-3730** A1283 Set of 4 5.50 2.00

Souvenir Sheet

Singapore World Stamp Championship 2004 — A1284

***Perf. 11¼x11½ Syncopated***

**2004, July 30** **Litho.**

**3731** A1284 3.45z multi 2.50 1.00

*a.* Imperf. *9.50 11.00*

Miniature Sheet

2004 Summer Olympics, Athens — A1285

No. 3732: a, Boxing. b, Women's track. c, Equestrian. d, Wrestling.

***Perf. 11¾x11½ Syncopated***

**2004, Aug. 2**

**3732** A1285 1.25z Sheet of 4, #a-d 3.25 1.50

Witold Gombrowicz (1904-69), Writer — A1286

***Perf. 11½x11¼ Syncopated***

**2004, Aug. 4**

**3733** A1286 1.25z blue .85 .35

Depictions of the Virgin Mary — A1287

Inscriptions: No. 3734, 1.25z, Matka Boza Dzikowska. No. 3735, 1.25z, Matka Boza Fatimska. No. 3736, 1.25z, Matka Boza Jasnagórska. No. 3737, 1.25z, Matka Boza Laskawa. No. 3738, 1.25z, Matka Boza Lomzynska. No. 3739, 1.25z, Matka Boza Miedzenska. No. 3740, 1.25z, Matka Boza Nieustajacej Pomocy. No. 3741, 1.25z, Matka Boza Bolesna Oborska. No. 3742, 1.25z, Matka Boza Piekarska. No. 3743, 1.25z, Matka Boza Placzaca. No. 3744, 1.25z, Matka Boza Pokorna Rudzka. No. 3745, 1.25z, Matka Boza Rychwaldzka. No. 3746, 1.25z, Matka Boza Rywaldzka. No. 3747, 1.25z, Matka Boza Rzeszowska. No. 3748, 1.25z, Matka Boza Sianowska. No. 3749, 1.25z, Bolesna Matka Boza Skrzatuska. No. 3750, 1.25z, Matka Boza Swietorodzinna.

***Perf. 11½x11¼ Syncopated***

**2004, Aug. 14** **Litho.**

**3734-3750** A1287 Set of 17 14.00 6.25

Czeslaw Niemen (1939-2004), Musician — A1288

***Perf. 11¾x11½ Syncopated***

**2004, Aug. 30** **Litho.**

**3751** A1288 1.25z black & gray .85 .35

Dunajec River Raftsmen — A1289

**2004, Sept. 3**

**3752** A1289 2.10z multi 1.40 .75

See Slovakia No. 463.

Motor Sports A1290

No. 3753: a, Cinder track motorcycle racing (four motorcycles). b, Auto racing. c, Go-kart racing. d, Motorcycle racing (one motorcycle).

***Perf. 11¼x11½ Syncopated***

**2004, Sept. 11**

**3753** Horiz. strip of 4 3.50 1.50

*a.-d.* A1290 1.25z Any single .85 .30

World Post Day A1291

***Perf. 11¼x11½ Syncopated***

**2004, Oct. 9** **Litho.**

**3754** A1291 2.10z multi 1.40 .60

UNESCO World Heritage Sites — A1292

Designs: No. 3755, 1.25z, Castle of the Teutonic Order, Malbork. No. 3756, 1.25z, Historic Center of Warsaw. No. 3757, 1.25z, Historic Center of Cracow, vert. No. 3758, 1.25z, Medieval Town of Torun, vert. No. 3759, 1.25z, Old City of Zamosc.

**2004, Oct. 20** ***Perf. 11½ Syncopated***

**3755-3759** A1292 Set of 5 4.25 1.60

Christmas A1293

Designs: 1.25z, Worshippers at shrine. 2.10z, Window, ornaments, candle, poinsettia.

**2004, Nov. 5** **Photo.** ***Perf. 11½x11¾***

**3760-3761** A1293 Set of 2 2.25 .85

History of the Earth — A1294

No. 3762: a, Birth (narodziny). b, Infancy (dziecinstwo). c, Youth (mlodosc). d, Maturity (dojrzalosc).

***Perf. 11½ Syncopated***

**2004, Dec. 3** **Litho.**

**3762** A1294 1.25z Block of 4, #a-d 3.50 1.25

**City Landmarks Type of 2002**

Design: Monument of Hygea, Raczynski Library, Poznan.

**2005, Jan. 3** **Photo.** ***Perf. 11½x11¾***

**3763** A1228 1.30z multi .80 .35

13th Concert of the Great Holiday Help Orchestra — A1295

**2005, Jan. 6** ***Perf. 11¼x11½***

**3764** A1295 1.30z multi .90 .40

Konstanty Ildefons Galczynski (1905-53), Poet — A1296

**2005, Jan. 14** ***Perf. 11½x11¼***

**3765** A1296 1.30z multi .90 .40

Mikolaj Rej (1505-69), Writer A1297

**2005, Jan. 26** ***Perf. 11¼x11½***

**3766** A1297 1.30z black & red .90 .40

Love A1298

**2005, Feb. 1** **Photo.** ***Perf. 11¼x11½***

**3767** A1298 1.30z multi .90 .40

Easter — A1299

Flowers and: 1.30z, Rabbit. 2.20z, Chick.

**2005, Mar. 1** ***Perf. 11¾x11½***

**3768-3769** A1299 Set of 2 2.10 1.00

Hans Christian Andersen (1805-75), Author — A1300

Designs: No. 3770, 1.30z, The Little Mermaid (Mala Syrenka), No. 3771, 1.30z, The Snow Queen (Królowa Sniegu).

***Perf. 11½x11¾ Syncopated***

**2005, Mar. 15** **Litho.**

**3770-3771** A1300 Set of 2 1.60 .70

Pope John Paul II (1920-2005) A1301

***Perf. 11½x11¾ Syncopated***

**2005, Apr. 8** **Litho.**

**3772** A1301 1.30z multi .90 .40

Extreme Sports — A1302

No. 3773: a, Parachuting. b, Bungee jumping. c, Rock climbing. d, White water rafting.

***Perf. 11¾x11½ Syncopated***

**2005, Apr. 15** **Litho.**

**3773** A1302 1.30z Block of 4, #a-d 3.50 1.50

Souvenir Sheet

Pacific Explorer 2005 World Stamp Expo, Sydney — A1303

***Perf. 11¼x11½ Syncopated***

**2005, Apr. 21**

**3774** A1303 3.50z multi 2.40 1.00

No. 3774 exists imperf., value: mint $7.50, used $9.

Souvenir Sheet

Pope John Paul II (1920-2005) — A1304

***Perf. 11½x11¼ Syncopated***

**2005, Apr. 22**

**3775** A1304 3.50z multi 2.25 1.10

All Saints Collegiate Church, Sieradz — A1305

Buildings, Katowice A1306

Baltic Shore, Sopot — A1307

Buildings, Szczecin A1308

St. John the Baptist Cathedral, Przemysl A1309

***Perf. 11¾x11½, 11½x11¾***

**2005** **Photo.**

**3776** A1305 20g multi .25 .25

**3777** A1306 30g multi .25 .25

**3778** A1307 2.20z multi 1.25 .65

**3779** A1308 2.80z multi 1.60 .80

**3780** A1309 3.50z multi 2.00 .90

*Nos. 3776-3780 (5)* 5.35 2.85

Issued: 20g, 7/29; 2.20z, 6/15; 2.80z, 5/30; 30g, 10/5; 3.50z, 4/30.

Europa A1310

***Perf. 11¼x11½ Syncopated***

**2005, May 5** **Litho. & Embossed**

**3781** A1310 2.20z multi 1.50 .85

End of World War II, 60th Anniv. — A1311

***Perf. 11¾x11½ Syncopated***

**2005, May 6** **Litho.**

**3782** A1311 1.30z multi .85 .40

Souvenir Sheet

Youth Literature — A1312

No. 3783: a, 1.30z, *Hour of the Crimson Rose,* by Maria Krüger. b, 2z, *The Little Prince,* by Antoine de Saint-Exupery. c, 2.20z, *20,000 Leagues Under the Sea,* by Jules Verne. d, 2.80z, *In Desert and Wilderness,* by Henryk Sienkiewicz.

***Perf. 11½ Syncopated***

**2005, June 1** **Litho.**

**3783** A1312 Sheet of 4, #a-d 5.75 2.75

Souvenir Sheet

Items in the Wilanow Museum — A1313

No. 3784: a, 1.30z, Portrait of Stanislaw Kostka Potocki, by Jacques Louis David, 1781. b, 2z, Nautilus wine cup, 17th cent. c, 2.20z, Porcelain figurine of flower girl, 18th cent. d, 2.80z, Decorative clock, 19th cent.

***Perf. 11½x11¼***

**2005, June 21** **Photo.**

**3784** A1313 Sheet of 4, #a-d 5.75 2.50

Embroidered Roses — A1314

Embroidered roses from: 1.30z, Podhale region. 2z, Lowicz region. 2.20z, Lowicz region, diff. 2.80z, Lowicz region, diff.

***Perf. 11½x11¼ Syncopated***

**2005, July 15** **Litho.**

**3785-3788** A1314 Set of 4 5.00 2.25

Souvenir Sheet

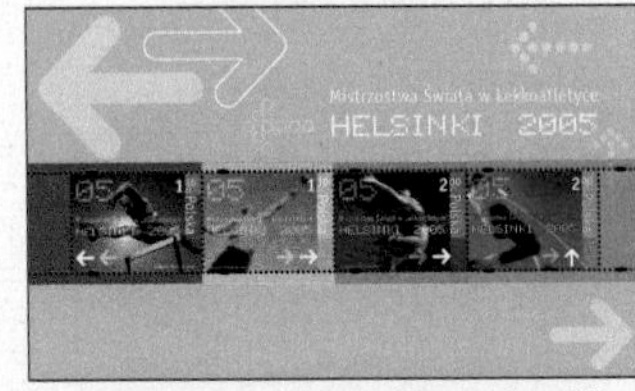

World Track and Field Championships, Helsinki — A1315

No. 3789: a, 1.30z, Hurdles. b, 1.30z, Shot put. c, 2z, Long jump. d, 2z, Pole vault.

***Perf. 11¾x11½ Syncopated***

**2005, Aug. 8**

**3789** A1315 Sheet of 4, #a-d 4.50 1.75

Souvenir Sheet

Polish Eagle and Józef Pilsudski — A1316

***Perf. 11¼x11½***

**2005, Aug. 12** **Photo.**

**3790** A1316 3.50z multi 2.40 1.00

"Miracle on the Vistula," repulse of Red Army counter-offensive, 85th anniv.

Lech Walesa and Solidarity Emblem A1317

***Perf. 11½x11¼ Syncopated***

**2005, Aug. 17** **Litho.**

**3791** A1317 2.20z red & gray 1.50 .65

Solidarity Trade Union, 25th anniv.

Polish Radio, 80th Anniv. — A1318

***Perf. 11½x11¾ Syncopated***

**2005, Sept. 1** **Photo.**

**3792** A1318 1.30z multi .90 .40

15th Frederic Chopin Piano Competition A1319

***Perf. 11¼x11½ Syncopated***

**2005, Sept. 16** **Litho.**

**3793** A1319 2.20z multi 1.50 .65
*a.* Souvenir sheet of 4 7.50 7.50

Zoo Animals A1320

Designs: 1.30z, Lemuridae, Opole Zoo. 2z, Panthera tigris altaica, Wroclaw Zoo. 2.20z, Ceratotherium simum, Poznan Zoo. 2.80z, Myrmecophagidae, Warsaw Zoo.

***Perf. 11½x11¾ Syncopated***

**2005, Sept. 30**

**3794-3797** A1320 Set of 4 5.00 2.50

Main Post Office, Cracow A1321

***Perf. 11¾x11½ Syncopated***

**2005, Oct. 7**

**3798** A1321 1.30z multi .90 .40

World Post Day.

United Nations, 60th Anniv. A1322

***Perf. 11¼x11½ Syncopated***

**2005, Oct. 14**

**3799** A1322 2.20z multi 1.40 .70

Landmarks in European Union Capitals A1323

Designs: No. 3800, 1.30z, Vilnius Cathedral, Vilnius, Lithuania. No. 3801, 1.30z, St. Matthias's Church, Statue of St. Stephen, Budapest, Hungary. No. 3802, 2.20z, Government building, Dublin, Ireland. No. 3803, 2.20z, Monument, Lisbon, Portugal. 2.80z, Arc de Triomphe, Paris, France.

***Perf. 11¼x11½ Syncopated***

**2005, Oct. 24**

**3800-3804** A1323 Set of 5 6.25 2.75

See Nos. 3838-3842, 3875-3879, 3914-3918, 3957-3961, 4095.

Souvenir Sheet

Paintings by Polish Impressionists — A1324

No. 3805: a, 1.30z, Plowing in the Ukraine, by L. J. Wyczolkowski. b, 1.30z, Still Life, by J. Pankiewicz. c, 2z, Flower Sellers, by O. Boznanska. d, 2z, Gooseberry Bushes, by W. Podkowinski.

**2005, Nov. 3** **Photo.**

**3805** A1324 Sheet of 4, #a-d, + 2 labels 4.50 3.00

Polish Doctors' Association, Bicent. — A1325

***Perf. 11½x11¼ Syncopated***

**2005, Nov. 24** **Litho.**

**3806** A1325 1.30z multi .90 .40

Christmas — A1326

Christmas trees and angel in: 1.30z, Blue. 2.20z, Rose pink.

***Perf. 11¾x11½***

**2005, Nov. 28** **Photo.**

**3807-3808** A1326 Set of 2 2.25 .90

2006 Winter Olympics, Turin — A1327

***Perf. 11¾x11½ Syncopated***

**2006, Feb. 7** **Litho.**

**3809** A1327 2.40z multi + label 1.60 .75

Love — A1328

***Perf. 11½x11¼***

**2006, Feb. 10** **Photo.**

**3810** A1328 1.30z multi .90 .50

Wolfgang Amadeus Mozart (1756-91), Composer — A1329

***Perf. 11¾x11½ Syncopated***

**2006, Feb. 15** **Litho.**

**3811** A1329 2.40z multi 1.50 .75

Independent Students Association, 25th Anniv. — A1330

**2006, Feb. 17**

**3812** A1330 1.30z multi .90 .50

Museum of Industry, Warsaw, and Zygmunt Gloger (1845-1910), First President of Polish Touring Society — A1331

**2006, Feb. 20**

**3813** A1331 1.30z multi .90 .50

Polish Touring Society, cent.

Endangered Flora — A1332

Designs: 1.30z, Pedicularis sudetica. 2.40z, Trapa natans.

**2006, Mar. 14**

**3814-3815** A1332 Set of 2 2.50 1.00

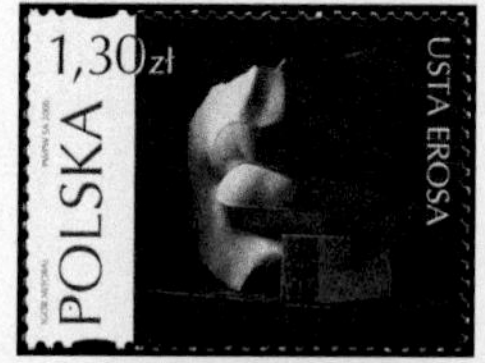
A1333

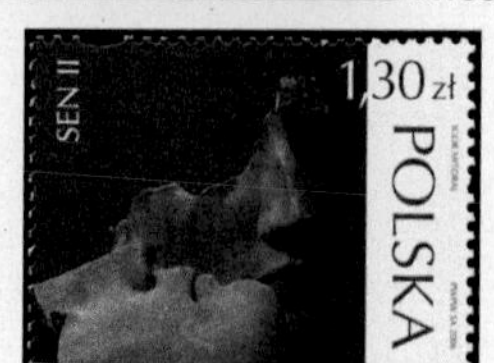
Sculptures by Igor Mitoraj — A1334

**2006, Mar. 27**

**3816** A1333 1.30z Lips of Eros .90 .40
**3817** A1334 1.30z Dream II .90 .40
*a.* Souvenir sheet, 2 each #3816-3817 3.50 *4.00*

Easter — A1335

Traditional customs: 1.30z, Women holding paper flower palms. 2.40z, Man dousing woman with water.

**2006, Apr. 3** ***Perf. 11½x11¾***

**3818-3819** A1335 Set of 2 2.00 1.10

Convent of Jasna Gora, Czestochowa A1336

**2006, Apr. 24** **Photo.**

**3820** A1336 2.40z multi 1.30 .70

Europa — A1337

***Perf. 11½x11¾ Syncopated***

**2006, May 5** **Litho.**

**3821** A1337 2.40z multi 1.60 .70

Souvenir Sheet

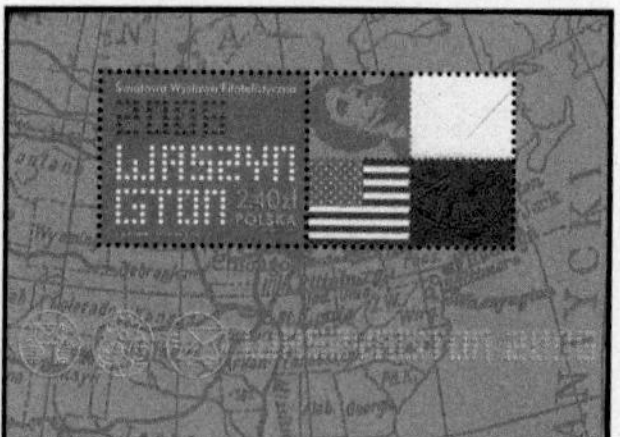
Washington 2006 World Philatelic Exhibition — A1338

***Perf. 11¼x11½***

**2006, May 19** **Photo.**

**3822** A1338 2.40z multi + label 1.60 .70

Visit of Pope Benedict XVI — A1339

***Perf. 11½x11¼ Syncopated***

**2006, May 25** **Litho.**

**3823** A1339 1.30z multi .80 .45

Souvenir Sheet

Lighthouses — A1340

No. 3824: a, Stilo. b, Krynica Morska. c, Gaski. d, Niechorze.

*Perf. 11½x11¼*

**2006, May 29** **Photo.**
**3824** A1340 2.40z Sheet of 4, #a-d 6.25 2.75

Toys — A1341

Designs: No. 3825, 1.30z, Pinwheel. No. 3826, 1.30z, Top.

*Perf. 11 Syncopated*

**2006, June 1** **Litho.**
**3825-3826** A1341 Set of 2 1.75 .80

See Nos. 3896-3897.

Souvenir Sheets

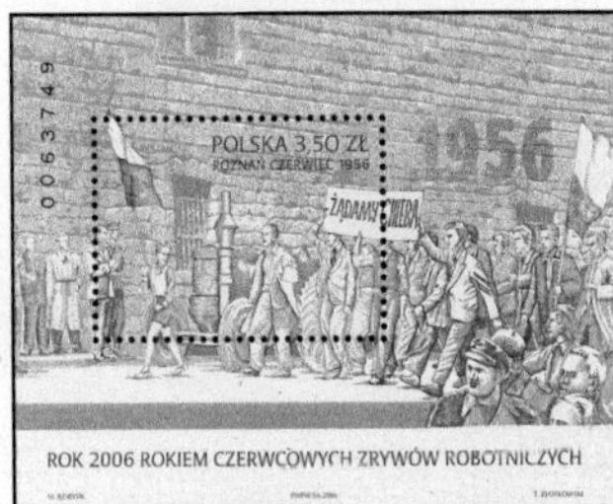

Worker Uprisings — A1342

**Photo. & Engr.**

**2006** ***Perf. 11¼x11½***
**3827** A1342 3.50z Poznan, 1956 2.00 1.00
**3828** A1342 3.50z Radom, 1976 2.00 1.00

Issued: No. 3827, 6/25; No. 3828, 6/28.

Silver and Gold Objects — A1343

No. 3829: a, Tankard with Biblical designs, by Peter Rohde, Poland. b, Jeweled Qing Dynasty cup, China.

*Perf. 11½x11¼*

**2006, June 20** **Photo.**
**3829** A1343 1.30z Horiz. pair, #a-b 1.25 .75

See People's Republic of China Nos. 3506-3507.

Jerzy Giedroyc (1906-2000), Literary Magazine Editor — A1344

**2006, July 27** **Engr.**
**3830** A1344 1.30z black .80 .40

Polish Society of Internal Medicine, Cent. — A1345

Doctors: No. 3831, 1.30z, Witold Eugeniusz Orlowski (1874-1966). No. 3832, 1.30z, Edward Szczeklik (1898-1985). 3z, Antoni Wladyslaw Gluzinski (1856-1935).

*Perf. 11¾x11½ Syncopated*

**2006, Sept. 8** **Litho.**
**3831-3833** A1345 Set of 3 3.00 1.50

Souvenir Sheet

19th Polish Philatelic Congress, Lubin — A1346

**Photo. & Engr.**

**2006, Sept. 20** ***Perf. 11¼x11½***
**3834** A1346 3.50z multi 2.00 1.00

No. 3834 exists imperf. Value, $6.50.

Miniature Sheets

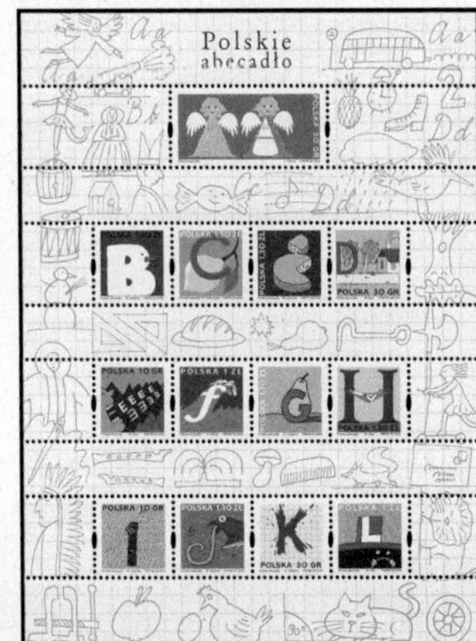

Polish Alphabet — A1347

No. 3835 — Depictions of Polish words starting with letters of the alphabet: a, 10gr, Man shouting "E". b, 10gr, Indian. c, 30gr, Angels. d, 30gr, House. e, 30gr, Ink-splattered "K." f, 1z, Wave. g, 1z, Driver and "L." h, 1.30z, Snowman. i, 1.30z, Lemon. j, 1.30z, Cake. k, 1.30z, Pear. l, 1.30z, Hammock. m, 1.30z, Lizard's tongue.

No. 3836: a, 10gr, Musical notes. b, 10gr, Child. c, 30gr, Carrots. d, 30gr, Eagle. e, 30gr, Zebra. f, 1z, Peacock. g, 1z, Strawberry. h, 1.30z, Patch on "L." i, 1.30z, Lobster. j, 1.30z, Elephant. k, 1.30z, Snail. l, 1.30z, Face with large lips. m, 1.30z, Wolf.

**2006** **Litho.** ***Perf. 11½ Syncopated***
**Sheets of 13, #a-m**
**3835-3836** A1347 Set of 2 14.00 7.00

Issued: No. 3835, 9/29; No. 3836, 11/7. Nos. 3835c and 3836e are 41x19mm; other stamps are 18x19mm.

World Post Day A1348

**2006, Oct. 9** **Photo.** ***Perf. 11¼x11½***
**3837** A1348 2.40z multi 1.40 .60

**Landmarks in European Capitals Type of 2005**

Designs: No. 3838, 2.40z, Brandenburg Gate, Berlin, Germany. No. 3839, 2.40z, Colosseum, Rome, Italy. No. 3840, 2.40z, Royal Dramatic Theater, Stockholm, Sweden. No. 3841, 2.40z, St. Alexander Nevski Cathedral, Tallinn, Estonia. No. 3842, 2.40z, St. Paul's Cathedral, Valletta, Malta.

*Perf. 11¼x11½ Syncopated*

**2006, Oct. 24** **Litho.**
**3838-3842** A1323 Set of 5 6.75 3.25

Dogs A1349

No. 3843: a, Ogar polski (Polish bloodhound). b, Gonczy polski (Polish hound). c, Polski owczarek nizinny (Polish Lowland sheepdog). d, Chart polski (Polish greyhound). e, Polski owczarek podhalanski (Polish Podhale sheepdog).

**2006, Nov. 6**
**3843** Horiz. strip of 5 4.50 3.00
***a.-e.*** A1349 1.30z Any single .80 .45

Christmas A1350

Designs: 1.30z, Nativity. 2.40z, Angel, "Christmas" in Polish, Italian, English, French and German.

*Perf. 11½x11¾*

**2006, Nov. 30** **Photo.**
**3844-3845** A1350 Set of 2 2.10 .90

Wujek Coal Mine Massacre, 25th Anniv. — A1351

*Perf. 11¾ Syncopated*

**2006, Dec. 16** **Litho.**
**3846** A1351 1.30z multi .80 .40

15th Concert of the Great Holiday Help Orchestra — A1352

**2007, Jan. 4** **Photo.** ***Perf. 11¼x11½***
**3847** A1352 1.35z multi .85 .40

Cathedral of the Assumption, Pauksch Fountain, Gorzów Wielkopolski A1353

**2007, Jan. 19** ***Perf. 11¾x11½***
**3848** A1353 1.35z multi .85 .40

2007 European Figure Skating Championships, Warsaw — A1354

*Perf. 11¾x11½ Syncopated*

**2007, Jan. 22** **Litho.**
**3849** A1354 2.40z multi 1.50 .70

Love — A1355

*Perf. 11½x11¾ Syncopated*

**2007, Feb. 8** **Litho.**
**3850** A1355 1.35z multi .85 .40

No. 3850 exists in a sheet of eight with eight labels that could be personalized. Value, $50.

Easter A1356

Folk art: 1.35z, Lamb made of straw. 2.40z, Chicken made from wooden eggs.

**2007, Mar. 8** **Photo.** ***Perf. 11¼x11½***
**3851-3852** A1356 Set of 2 2.40 1.10

Treaty of Rome, 50th Anniv. — A1357

*Perf. 11½x11¾ Syncopated*

**2007, Mar. 20** **Litho.**
**3853** A1357 3.55z multi 2.25 1.00

Greetings for Special Days — A1358

Designs: No. 3854, 1.35z, Birthday cake and confetti. No. 3855, 1.35z, Grapes, chalice, bread, monogram of Jesus. No. 3856, 1.35z, Wedding rings, rose.

*Perf. 11½ Syncopated*

**2007, Mar. 30** **Litho.**

**3854-3856** A1358 Set of 3 2.50 1.25

Earth Day A1359

*Perf. 11¾x11½ Syncopated*

**2007, Apr. 22** **Litho.**

**3857** A1359 1.35z multi .95 .40

Railway Cars A1360

No. 3858: a, Type 5G postal car, 1956. b, Type Cd21b passenger car, 1924. c, Type C3Pr07 passenger car, 1909. d, Type Ci29 passenger car, 1929.

**2007, Apr. 28**

**3858** Horiz. strip of 4 5.00 2.25
*a.-b.* A1360 1.35z Either single .90 .40
*c.-d.* A1360 2.40z Either single 1.60 .70

Europa A1361

**2007, May 5**

**3859** A1361 3z multi 2.25 1.00

Scouting, cent.

Little Helen with a Vase of Flowers, by Stanislaw Wyspianski — A1362

**2007, May 18**

**3860** A1362 1.35z multi .90 .40

Stanislaw Wyspianski Year.

Karol Szymanowski (1882-1937), Composer A1363

**2007, May 26** *Perf. 11½x11¼*

**3861** A1363 1.35z multi .90 .40

Karol Szymanowski Year.

Granting of Municipal Rights to Cracow, 750th Anniv. — A1364

**Photo. & Engr.**

**2007, May 29** *Perf. 11¾x11½*

**3862** A1364 2.40z multi 1.75 .80

Souvenir Sheet

St. Petersburg Intl. Philatelic Exhibition — A1365

**2007, June 12** *Perf. 11¼x11*

**3863** A1365 3z multi 2.25 .90

Nicolaus Copernicus Planetarium, Chorzów A1366

*Perf. 11½x11¾*

**2007, June 15** **Photo.**

**3864** A1366 3.55z multi 2.40 1.10

Souvenir Sheet

Lighthouses — A1367

No. 3865: a, 1.35z, Gdansk Lighthouse. b, 2.40z. Rozewie Lighthouse. c, 3z, Kolobrzeg Lighthouse. d, 3.55z, Hel Lighthouse.

**2007, June 15** *Perf. 11½x11¼*

**3865** A1367 Sheet of 4, #a-d 7.50 3.00

Holy Virgin of Lesniów A1368

*Perf. 11½x11¼ Syncopated*

**2007, July 2** **Litho.**

**3866** A1368 1.35z multi .90 .40

Lesniów Jubilee Year.

Arabian Horses — A1369

No. 3867 — Color of horse: a, Brown. b, White. c, Brown, diff. d, White, diff.

*Perf. 11½x11¾ Syncopated*

**2007, Aug. 31**

**3867** Horiz. strip of 4 8.00 4.00
*a.* A1369 1.35z multi .95 .40
*b.* A1369 3z multi 2.10 1.00
*c.-d.* A1369 3.55z Either single 2.40 1.25

Animals in Polish Zoos — A1370

Designs: 1.35z, Saguinus imperator, Plock Zoo. 2.40z, Ciconia nigra, Lódz Zoo. 3z, Loxodonta africana, Gdansk Zoo. 3.55z, Uncia uncia, Cracow Zoo.

*Perf. 11½x11¾ Syncopated*

**2007, Sept. 11** **Litho.**

**3868-3871** A1370 Set of 4 7.75 3.50

50th Warsaw Autumn Intl. Contemporary Music Festival — A1371

*Perf. 11¼x11½ Syncopated*

**2007, Sept. 21**

**3872** A1371 3z multi 2.10 .90

Theater in Katowice, Cent. A1372

*Perf. 11x11½ Syncopated*

**2007, Oct. 5** **Litho.**

**3873** A1372 1.35z multi 1.10 .55

World Post Day A1373

*Perf. 11¾x11½ Syncopated*

**2007, Oct. 9** **Litho.**

**3874** A1373 1.35z multi 1.10 .55

**Landmarks in European Union Capitals Type of 2005**

Designs: No. 3875, 1.35z, Statue of St. Roland and House of Blackheads, Riga, Latvia. No. 3876, 1.35z, Dragon's Bridge, Ljubljana, Slovenia. No. 3877, 3z, Plaza de Cibeles, Madrid. No. 3878, 3z, Luxembourg Philharmonic Building, Luxembourg. 3.55z, Tower Bridge, London.

*Perf. 11¼x11½ Syncopated*

**2007, Oct. 24** **Litho.**

**3875-3879** A1323 Set of 5 9.75 3.25

Pope John Paul II Foundation, 25th Anniv. A1374

**2007, Oct. 30**

**3880** A1374 1.35z multi 1.10 .55

Self-portrait, by Jerzy Duda-Gracz (1941-2004) — A1375

**2007, Nov. 5**

**3881** A1375 1.35z multi 1.10 .55

Teddy Bear and Christmas Tree — A1376

Adoration of the Magi, by Mikolaj Haberschrack A1377

*Perf. 11½x11¼*

**2007, Nov. 27** **Photo.**

**3882** A1376 1.35z multi .95 .40
**3883** A1377 3z multi 2.00 .75

Joseph Conrad (1857-1924), Writer — A1378

**2007, Dec. 3 Engr.** *Perf. 11¼x11½*
3884 A1378 3z black 2.00 .90

Souvenir Sheet

PostEurop Plenary Assembly, Cracow — A1379

*Perf. 11½x11¼ Syncopated*
**2008, Jan. 15 Litho.**
3885 A1379 3z multi 2.00 .90

Love A1380

*Perf. 11¾x11½ Syncopated*
**2008, Feb. 7 Litho.**
3886 A1380 1.35z multi .95 .40

Easter — A1381

Designs: 1.35z, Easter eggs. 2.40z, Easter eggs, diff.

*Perf. 11½x11¼*
**2008, Feb. 29 Photo.**
3887-3888 A1381 Set of 2 2.25 1.00

Photography by Karol Beyer (1818-77) A1382

No. 3889: a, Self-portrait, 1858. b, Peasants from Wilanów, 1866. c, Holy Cross Church, Warsaw, 1858, d, Russian Army in Castle Square, Warsaw, 1861.

*Perf. 11½x11¾ Syncopated*
**2008, Feb. 29 Litho.**
3889 Horiz. strip of 4 3.75 1.75
*a.-d.* A1382 1.35z Any single .90 .35

Border Guards, 80th Anniv. — A1383

*Perf. 11½x11¼ Syncopated*
**2008, Mar. 22 Litho.**
3890 A1383 2.10z multi 1.50 .70

Military Aircraft — A1384

No. 3891: a, 3z, TS-11 Iskra (Spark). b, 3.55z, F-16 Jastrzab (Falcon).

*Perf. 11½x11¾ Syncopated*
**2008, Mar. 31**
3891 A1384 Horiz. pair, #a-b 4.50 2.25

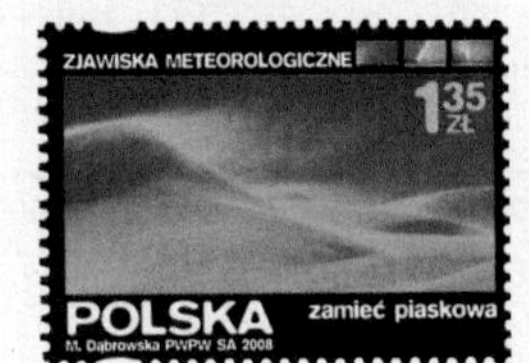

Meteorological Phenomena — A1385

No. 3892: a, Sandstorm. b, Lightning. c, Rainbow. d, Tornado.

*Perf. 11¾x11½ Syncopated*
**2008, Apr. 25**
3892 Horiz. strip of 4 6.00 3.00
*a.-b.* A1385 1.35z Either single 1.10 .40
*c.-d.* A1385 2.40z Either single 1.90 1.00

Europa A1386

**2008, May 5**
3893 A1386 3z multi 2.00 .90

European Organization of Supreme Audit Institutions Congress, Cracow A1387

*Perf. 11½x11¾ Syncopated*
**2008, May 30**
3894 A1387 3.55z multi 2.40 1.00

UEFA Euro 2008 Soccer Championships, Austria and Switzerland A1388

*Perf. 11½x11¼ Syncopated*
**2008, May 30 Photo.**
3895 A1388 1.35z multi .90 .40

**Toys Type of 2006**

Designs: 1.35z, Wooden train. 3z, Xylophone.

*Perf. 11 Syncopated*
**2008, June 1 Litho.**
3896-3897 A1341 Set of 2 3.00 1.00

Boy and Iranian Rug — A1389

*Perf. 11½x11¼ Syncopated*
**2008, June 10**
3898 A1389 2.40z multi 1.60 .65

Esfahan, Iran, city of Polish exiled orphan children.

Souvenir Sheet

EFIRO 2008 Philatelic Exhibition, Bucharest, Romania — A1390

**Photo. & Engr.**
**2008, June 20** *Perf. 11x11½*
3899 A1390 3z multi 2.00 1.00

No. 3899 exists imperf. Value: mint $7, used $8.

Coronation of St. Mary of the Snow Icon, 25th Anniv. — A1391

*Perf. 11½x11¼ Syncopated*
**2008, June 21 Litho.**
3900 A1391 1.35z multi .90 .40

Towns — A1392

Designs: 1.45z, Tower and column, Racibórz. 3.65z, Town Hall and Neptune Fountain, Jelenia Góra.

**2008 Photo.** *Perf. 11¾x11½*
3901 A1392 1.45z multi 1.00 .40
3902 A1392 3.65z multi 2.50 .90

Issued: 1.45z, 7/1. 3.65z, 8/1.

2008 Summer Olympics, Beijing — A1393

No. 3903: a, Swimming. b, Women's volleyball. c, Women's pole vault. d, Fencing.

*Perf. 11½ Syncopated*
**2008, Aug. 8 Litho.**
3903 Horiz. strip of 4 2.00 1.25
*a.-b.* A1393 10g Either single .25 .25
*c.-d.* A1393 1.45z Either single 1.00 .60
*e.* Souvenir sheet, #3903 3.00 3.00

Bridges A1394

No. 3904: a, Siekierkowski Bridge, Warsaw. b, Poniatowski Bridge, Warsaw. c, Welded bridge over Sludwia River, Maurzyce. d, Ernest Malinowski Bridge, Torun.

*Perf. 11¾x11½ Syncopated*
**2008, Aug. 29 Litho. & Embossed**
3904 Horiz. strip of 4 6.00 3.25
*a.-b.* A1394 1.45z Either single 1.00 .55
*c.-d.* A1394 3z Either single 2.00 1.00

Souvenir Sheet

Polish Post, 450th Anniv. — A1395

No. 3905: a, Prosper Provana, first supervisor of Krakow to Venice postal service. b, King Sigismund II August and grant to Provana (50x30mm). c, Sebastian Montelupi, administrator of royal postal service in 1564.

**Photo. & Engr.**
**2008, Sept. 15** *Perf. 11¾x11½*
3905 A1395 1.45z Sheet of 3, #a-c 3.25 1.50

Sheet margin of No. 3905 is embossed.

Miniature Sheet

Presidents of the Republic of Poland in Exile — A1396

No. 3906: a, Wladyslaw Raczkiewicz (1885-1947), 1939-47 President. b, August Zaleeski (1883-1972), 1947-72 President. c, Stanislaw Ostrowski (1892-1982), 1972-79 President. d, Edward Raczynski (1891-1993), 1979-86 President. e, Kazimierz Sabbat (1913-89), 1986-89 President. f, Ryszard Kaczorowski, 1989-90 President.

***Perf. 11¾x11½ Syncopated***

**2008, Sept. 24 Litho.**

**3906** A1396 1.45z Sheet of 6, #a-f 6.50 2.75

Lódz Sports Club, Cent. A1397

***Perf. 11¼x11½***

**2008, Sept. 30 Photo.**

**3907** A1397 1.45z red & silver 1.25 .60

Arrival of Poles in America, 400th Anniv. A1398

***Perf. 11¾x11½ Syncopated***

**2008, Sept. 30 Litho.**

**3908** A1398 3z multi 2.00 1.00

World Post Day A1399

***Perf. 11¾x11½ Syncopated***

**2008, Oct. 9 Litho.**

**3909** A1399 2.10z multi 1.40 .60

Composers A1400

Designs: No. 3910, 1.45z, Henryk Mikolaj Górecki. No. 3911, 1.45z, Mieczylaw Karlowicz (1876-1909). No. 3912, 1.45z, Wojciech Kilar. No. 3913, 1.45z, Witold Lutoslawski (1913-94).

***Perf. 11½x11¾ Syncopated***

**2008, Oct. 18 Litho.**

**3910-3913** A1400 Set of 4 4.50 1.75

**Landmarks in European Union Capitals Type of 2005**

Designs: No. 3914, 1.45z, Rijksmuseum, Amsterdam, Netherlands. No. 3915, 1.45z, Royal Library, Copenhagen, Denmark. No. 3916, 3z, Acropolis, Athens, Greece. No. 3917, 3z, Charles Bridge, Prague, Czech Republic. 3.65z, Parliament, Vienna, Austria.

***Perf. 11¼x11½ Syncopated***

**2008, Oct. 24**

**3914-3918** A1323 Set of 5 8.00 3.50

Jeremi Przybora (1915-2004) and Jerzy Wasowski (1913-84), Television Performers — A1401

***Perf. 11¾x11½ Syncopated***

**2008, Oct. 30**

**3919** A1401 1.45z multi 1.10 .45

Television show, Kabaret Starszych Panów (Senior Men's Cabaret), 50th anniv.

The Oath, Poem by Maria Konopnicka, Cent. — A1402

**2008, Nov. 7**

**3920** A1402 3.65z multi + label 2.40 1.00

Independence, 90th Anniv. — A1403

**2008, Nov. 11 Engr. *Perf. 11x11¼***

**3921** A1403 1.45z carmine lake 1.00 .40

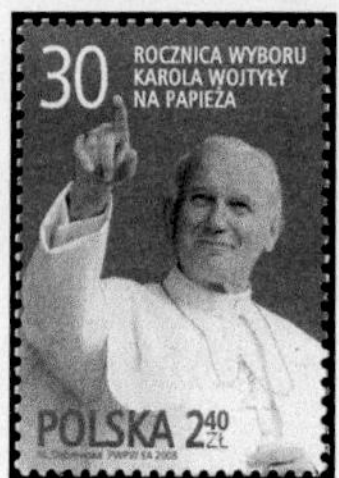

Election of Karol Woytyla as Pope John Paul II, 30th Anniv. — A1404

***Perf. 11½x11¼***

**2008, Nov. 27 Photo.**

**3922** A1404 2.40z multi 1.75 .85

Christmas A1405

Stars and snowflakes with background color of: 1.45z, Blue. 3z, Red violet.

***Perf. 11½x11¼***

**2008, Nov. 27 Photo.**

**3923-3924** A1405 Set of 2 3.00 1.25

Zbigniew Herbert (1924-98), Writer — A1406

***Perf. 11½x11¼ Syncopated***

**2008, Dec. 1 Litho.**

**3925** A1406 2.10z multi 1.40 .60

United Nations Conference on Climate Change, Poznan A1407

**2008, Dec. 1 Photo. *Perf. 11½x11¼***

**3926** A1407 2.40z multi 1.60 .70

**Souvenir Sheet**

Polish Post, 450th Anniv. — A1408

**Printed On Silk**

**Self-Adhesive**

**Silk-screened**

**2008, Dec. 19 *Imperf.***

**3927** A1408 20z multi 14.00 11.00

Louis Braille (1809-52), Educator of the Blind — A1409

***Perf. 11¾x11½ Syncopated***

**2009, Jan. 4 Litho.**

**3928** A1409 1.45z multi + label 1.00 .45

Concentration Camp Survivors A1410

No. 3929: a, Witold Pilecki (1901-48), organizer of resistance movement at Auschwitz. b, Józef Wladyslaw Wolski (1910-2008), historian. c, Bishop Ignacy Ludwik Jez (1914-2007). d, Stanislawa Maria Sawicka (1895-1982), art and music historian.

***Perf. 11½x11¼ Syncopated***

**2009, Jan. 30 Litho.**

**3929** Horiz. strip of 4 5.75 2.25
- *a.* A1410 1.45z multi .95 .40
- *b.* A1410 2.10z multi 1.40 .40
- *c.* A1410 2.40z multi 1.40 .65
- *d.* A1410 3z multi 2.00 .80

No. 3929 was initially issued with the name "Jozef" missing on No. 3929b. It was quickly withdrawn from sale. Value, $30.

Love — A1411

***Perf. 11½x11¾ Syncopated***

**2009, Feb. 6**

**3930** A1411 1.45z multi 1.00 .45

Sculpture and Fabric Art by Wladyslaw Hasior (1928-99) A1412

Designs: No. 3930A, 1.45z, Zwiastowanie (The Herald). No. 3930B, 1.45z, Mucha (The Fly). No. 3930C, 2.10z, Sztandar Zielonej Poetki (Banner of the Green Poet). No. 3930D, 2.40z, Sztandar Rozbieranie do snu (The Night Undressing Banner).

***Perf. 11½x11¾ Syncopated***

**2009, Mar. 6 Litho.**

**3930A-3930D** A1412 Set of 4 5.25 3.75

*3930De* Sheet of 4, #3930A-3930D 5.25 3.50

Easter — A1413

Paintings by Szymon Czechowicz (1689-1775): 1.55z, Chrystus Zmartwychwstaly (Christ Resurrected). 3z, Zlozenie do Grobu (Entombment), vert.

***Perf. 11½x11¾, 11¾x11½***

**2009, Apr. 1 Photo.**

**3932-3933** A1413 Set of 2 3.00 1.10

**Souvenir Sheet**

China 2009 World Philatelic Exhibition, Luoyang — A1414

***Perf. 11½x11¼ Syncopated***

**2009, Apr. 16 Litho.**

**3934** A1414 3z multi 2.00 1.00

**Souvenir Sheet**

Berek Joselewicz, A Jewish Fighter for Polish Freedom's Last Battle, Kock, by Juliusz Kossak — A1415

*Perf. 11¼x11½ Syncopated*

**2009, Apr. 22**

**3935** A1415 3z multi 2.00 1.00

See Israel No. 1772.

Miniature Sheet

Photographs of African Animals by Tomasz Gudzowaty — A1416

No. 3936: a, 1.55z, First Lesson of Killing (cheetahs and antelope). b, 1.95z, Zebras at Waterhole. c, 2.40z, Paradise Crossing (crocodile and gnus in water). d, 3z, Elephants.

*Perf. 11¾x11½ Syncopated*

**2009, Apr. 30**

**3936** A1416 Sheet of 4, #a-d 6.50 3.00

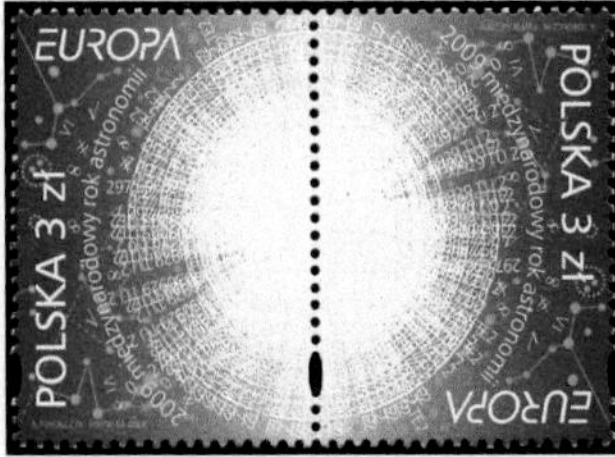

Europa — A1417

No. 3937 — Star map drawings and overlapping text with: a, Syncopation near "O" in Polska. b, Syncopation near "Europa."

*Perf. 11½x11¾ Syncopated*

**2009, May 5**

**3937** A1417 3z Horiz. pair, #a-b 4.00 1.75

Intl. Year of Astronomy.

Grazyna Bacewicz (1909-69), Composer A1418

**2009, May 28**

**3938** A1418 1.55z multi .95 .50

Tytus, Romek, and A'Tomek, Comic Book Characters by Papcio Chmiel — A1419

No. 3939: a, Tytus (ape). b, Romek (boy in boots). c, A'Tomek (man in suit).

**2009, May 29**

**3939** A1419 1.55z Horiz. strip of 3, #a-c 3.00 1.50

Souvenir Sheet

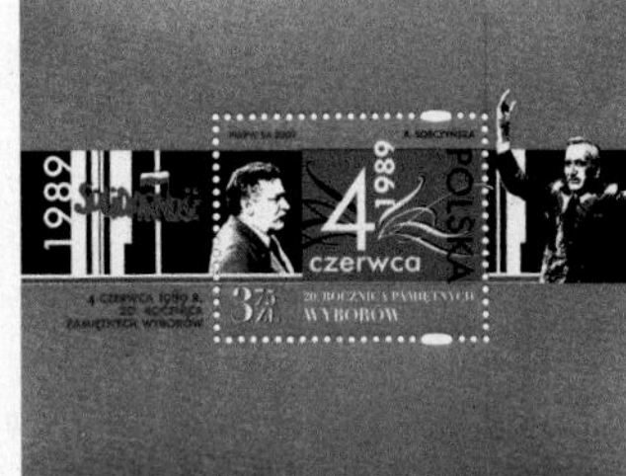

Lech Walesa — A1420

*Perf. 11¼x11½ Syncopated*

**2009, May 30**

**3940** A1420 3.75z multi 2.50 1.10

Victories of Solidarity candidates in June 4, 1989 parliamentary elections, 20th anniv.

St. Bruno of Querfurt (c. 974-1009) A1421

*Perf. 11½x11¼*

**2009, June 19** **Photo.**

**3941** A1421 3z multi 2.00 1.10

Souvenir Sheet

Ship "Dar Mlodzilzy" — A1422

**Photo. & Engr.**

**2009, June 30** ***Perf. 11¼x11***

**3942** A1422 3.75z multi 2.40 1.00

2009 Tall Ships Race, Gdynia.

Baltic Sea Mammals A1423

No. 3943: a, Phocoena phocoena. b, Halichoerus grypus. c, Phoca vitulina. d, Phoca hispida.

*Perf. 11½x11¾ Syncopated*

**2009, July 31** **Litho.**

**3943** Horiz. strip of 4 4.50 2.00

*a.-b.* A1423 1.55z Either single .60 .40

*c.-d.* A1423 1.95z Either single .75 .60

Souvenir Sheet

Warsaw Uprising, 65th Anniv. — A1424

**Photo. & Engr.**

**2009, Aug. 1** ***Perf. 11½x11¼***

**3944** A1424 3.75z multi 2.60 1.00

Fruit and Flowers A1425

Designs: 1.95z, Cerasus avium. 3.75z, Calendula officinalis.

*Perf. 11½x11¾*

**2009, Aug. 10** **Photo.**

**3945-3946** A1425 Set of 2 3.50 1.00

See Nos. 3986, 4029, 4178-4180, 4205-4207, 4234-4236, 4255, 4331-4332.

Famous Polish Emigrés A1426

Designs: No. 3947, 1.55z, Jan Czochralski (1885-1953), metallurgist. No. 3948, 1.55z, Antoni Patek (1812-77), watchmaker. No. 3949, 1.95z, Ludwik Hirszfeld (1884-1954), serologist. No. 3950, 1.95z, Jerzy Rózycki (1909-42), Marian Rejewski (1905-80) and Henryk Zygalski (1907-78), cryptologists who broke the Enigma code.

*Perf. 11½x11¾ Syncopated*

**2009, Aug. 28** **Litho.**

**3947-3950** A1426 Set of 4 4.50 2.00

Juliusz Slowacki (1809-49), Writer — A1427

*Perf. 11¼x11½*

**2009, Aug. 31** **Photo.**

**3951** A1427 1.55z multi 1.10 .50

Start of World War II, 70th Anniv. A1428

Battles of: 1.55z, Wegierska Górka. 2.40z, Wielun.

**2009, Sept. 1**

**3952-3953** A1428 Set of 2 2.60 1.25

European Men's Basketball Championships, Poland — A1429

*Perf. 11½x11¾ Syncopated*

**2009, Sept. 7** **Litho.**

**3954** A1429 3z multi 2.25 .75

Selection of Tadeusz Mazowiecki as Prime Minister, 20th Anniv. — A1430

*Perf. 11¾x11½ Syncopated*

**2009, Sept. 11** **Litho. & Embossed**

**3955** A1430 1.55z multi 1.00 .40

European Women's Volleyball Championships, Poland — A1431

*Perf. 11¾x11½ Syncopated*

**2009, Sept. 25** **Litho.**

**3956** A1431 3z multi 2.25 .80

**Landmarks in European Capitals Type of 2005**

Designs: No. 3957, 1.55z, Castle, Bratislava, Slovakia. No. 3958, 1.55z, Famagusta Gate, Nicosia, Cyprus. No. 3959, 3z, Grand Place, Brussels, Belgium. No. 3960, 3z, Plac Zamkowy (Castle Square), Warsaw. 3.75z, National Museum, Helsinki, Finland.

*Perf. 11¼x11½ Syncopated*

**2009, Oct. 6** **Litho.**

**3957-3961** A1323 Set of 5 9.00 4.00

World Post Day — A1432

**Photo. & Engr.**

**2009, Oct. 9** ***Perf. 11½x11¼***

**3962** A1432 3z multi 2.10 .80

Father Jerzy Popieluszko (1947-84), Murdered Supporter of Solidarity Movement — A1433

*Perf. 11¾x11½ Syncopated*

**2009, Oct. 19** **Litho.**

**3963** A1433 1.55z multi 1.00 .45

Tatra Mountain Volunteer Rescue Corps, Cent. — A1434

***Perf. 11½x11¾ Syncopated***

**2009, Oct. 24 Litho.**

**3964** A1434 1.55z multi 1.10 .40

Pawel Jasienica (1909-70), Writer — A1435

***Perf. 11½x11¼ Syncopated***

**2009, Nov. 10 Photo.**

**3965** A1435 1.55z blk & silver 1.10 .45

Jerzy Franciszek Kulczycki (1640-94), Hero of Battle of Vienna and Viennese Café Proprietor — A1436

**2009, Nov. 16 Litho.**

**3966** A1436 1.55z multi + label 1.00 .50

Lost Artworks — A1437

No. 3967: a, Exlibris Willibald Pirckheimer, by Albrecht Dürer. b, Christ Falling Under the Cross, by Peter Paul Rubens. c, Joseph's Dream, by Rembrandt.

***Perf. 11½x11¼***

**2009, Nov. 20 Photo.**

**3967** A1437 1.55z Horiz. strip of 3, #a-c 3.00 1.50

Christmas
A1438 A1439

**2009, Nov. 27** ***Perf. 11¾x11½***

**3968** A1438 1.55z multi 1.00 .30
**3969** A1439 2.40z multi 1.60 .60

Souvenir Sheet

First Polish Postage Stamp, 150th Anniv. — A1440

***Perf. 11½x11¼ Syncopated***

**2010, Jan. 15 Litho.**

**3970** A1440 4.15z multi 2.75 1.40

No. 3970 exists with an overprint celebrating the 60th anniversary of the Polish Philatelic Union. Five hundred sheets were issued thus.

2010 Winter Olympics, Vancouver — A1441

***Perf. 11¾x11½ Syncopated***

**2010, Jan. 27**

**3971** A1441 3z multi 1.90 .85

Miniature Sheet

Cats — A1442

No. 3972 — Breeds: a, 1.55z, Brytyjski krótkowlosy (British shorthair). b, 1.55z, Tajski (Siamese). c, 1.95z, Somalijski (Somali). d, 1.95z, Maine Coon. e, 3z, Pers (Persian). f, 3z, Egzotyk (Exotic).

***Perf. 11½x11¾ Syncopated***

**2010, Feb. 17 Litho.**

**3972** A1442 Sheet of 6, #a-f 9.00 5.00

Souvenir Sheet

Frédéric Chopin (1810-49), Composer — A1443

***Perf. 11¼x11½ Syncopated***

**2010, Feb. 22**

**3973** A1443 4.15z multi 3.00 1.50

No. 3973 exists imperf. Value, *$20.*

Easter — A1444

Designs: 1.55z, Lamb and banner. 2.40z, Eggs in basket.

**2010, Mar. 5 Photo.** ***Perf. 11¾x11½***

**3974-3975** A1444 Set of 2 2.75 1.10

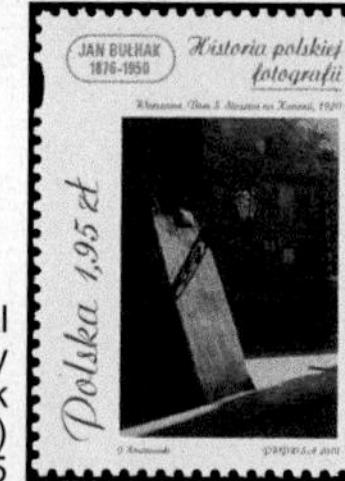
Historical Photographs by Jan Bulhak (1876-1950) A1445

No. 3976: a, House of Stanislaw Stazic, Warsaw, 1920 (shown). b, 16 Poselska Street, Cracow, 1921. c, Vestibule of house in Old Town, Warsaw, 1920. d, Chapel of St. Casimir's Cathedral, Vilnius, 1912.

***Perf. 11½x11¾ Syncopated***

**2010, Mar. 31 Litho.**

**3976** Horiz. strip of 4 5.75 2.50
*a.-d.* A1445 1.95z Any single 1.40 .55

Special Services of the Republic of Poland, 20th Anniv. — A1446

**2010, Apr. 6**

**3977** A1446 1.55z multi 1.10 .55

Souvenir Sheet

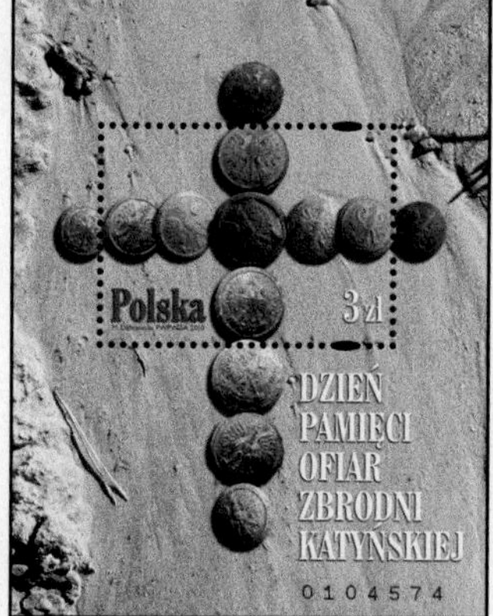
Katyn Massacre Remembrance Day — A1447

***Perf. 11¾x11½ Syncopated***

**2010, Apr. 7**

**3978** A1447 3z multi 2.10 1.10

Souvenir Sheet

Portugal 2010 Intl. Philatelic Exhibition, Lisbon — A1448

***Perf. 11½x11¾ Syncopated***

**2010, Apr. 30**

**3979** A1448 3z multi 2.10 1.10

Europa — A1449

**2010, May 5**

**3980** A1449 3z multi 1.90 .95

Pope John Paul II (1920-2005) and St. Peter Apostle Church, Wadowice — A1450

***Perf. 11¾x11½ Syncopated***

**2010, May 18 Litho. & Embossed**

**3981** A1450 1.95z multi + label 1.40 .70

Tczew Bridge — A1451

***Perf. 11½x11¼***

**2010, May 27 Photo.**

**3982** A1451 1.55z multi 1.00 .45

Tczew, 750th anniv.

Beatification of Father Jerzy Popieluszko (1947-84) — A1452

***Perf. 11¾x11½ Syncopated***

**2010, June 6 Litho.**

**3983** A1452 1.95z multi 1.40 .50

Dominican Convent of Ursuline Sisters, Sieradz, 750th Anniv. — A1453

*Perf. 11¼x11½*

**2010, June 24** **Photo.**
**3984** A1453 1.55z multi 1.00 .45

Souvenir Sheet

Battle of Grunwald, 600th Anniv. — A1454

**2010, July 15** *Perf. 11x11¼*
**3985** A1454 8.30z multi 5.50 2.75

### Fruit and Flowers Type of 2009

Design: 4.15z, Myosotis arvensis.

*Perf. 11½x11¾*

**2010, Aug. 10** **Photo.**
**3986** A1425 4.15z multi 3.00 1.50

Scouting in Poland, Cent. — A1455

**2010, Aug. 17** *Perf. 11½x11¼*
**3987** A1455 1.95z multi 1.40 .70

Lech Walesa and Gdansk Shipyard A1456

*Perf. 11¾x11½ Syncopated*

**2010, Aug. 31** **Litho. & Embossed**
**3988** A1456 3.75z multi 2.75 1.00

Government cessions after settlement of Solidarity-led strikes, 30th anniv.

Minerals A1457

*Perf. 11¾x11½ Syncopated*

**2010, Sept. 3** **Litho.**

| | | |
|---|---|---|
| **3989** | Vert. strip of 4 | 7.00 3.00 |
| *a.* | A1457 1.55z Sphalerite | 1.15 .40 |
| *b.* | A1457 1.95z Gypsum | 1.50 .55 |
| *c.* | A1457 2.40z Agate | 1.90 .70 |
| *d.* | A1457 3z Chrysoprase | 2.25 .80 |

World Post Day — A1458

**2010, Oct. 9** **Photo.** *Perf. 11½x11¼*
**3990** A1458 1.95z multi 1.40 .70
*a.* Tete-beche pair 2.80 1.40

### Landmarks in European Capitals Type of 2005

Designs: 1.95z, Alexander Nevsky Cathedral, Sofia, Bulgaria. 3z, Romanian Atheneaum, Bucharest, Romania.

*Perf. 11¼x11½ Syncopated*

**2010, Oct. 24** **Litho.**
**3991-3992** A1323 Set of 2 3.75 1.90

Personalized Stamp — A1459

*Perf. 11½x11¾ Syncopated*

**2010, Oct. 29** **Litho.**
**3993** A1459 A multi + label 5.75 5.75

No. 3993 had a franking value of 1.55z on day of issue and was printed in sheets of 8 stamps + 8 labels that could be personalized for 56z.

Widzew Lódz Soccer Team, Cent. A1460

**2010, Nov. 5** **Photo.** *Perf. 11¼x11½*
**3994** A1460 1.55z multi 1.00 .50

Ignacy Jan Paderewski (1860-1941), Pianist, Prime Minister A1461

*Perf. 11½x11¾ Syncopated*

**2010, Nov. 18** **Litho.**
**3995** A1461 3z multi 2.10 1.10

Christmas A1462

Star of Bethlehem, text in Polish and: 1.55z, Christmas tree. 2.40z, Night sky.

*Perf. 11½x11¾*

**2010, Nov. 27** **Photo.**
**3996-3997** A1462 Set of 2 2.75 1.40

Love — A1463

*Perf. 11½x11¾*

**2010, Dec. 30** **Photo.**
**3998** A1463 A multi 1.10 .55

No. 3998 sold for 1.55z on day of issue.

Johannes Hevelius (1611-87), Astronomer — A1464

*Perf. 11¾x11½ Syncopated*

**2011, Jan. 28** **Litho.**
**3999** A1464 3z multi + label 2.10 1.10

No. 3999 was printed in sheets of 6 + 6 labels.

Field Hockey A1465

**2011, Feb. 4**
**4000** A1465 2.40z multi 1.75 .85

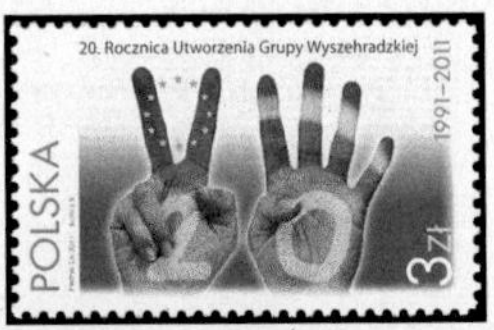

Visegrád Group, 20th Anniv. — A1466

**2011, Feb. 11** *Perf. 12*
**4001** A1466 3z multi 3.00 1.50

See Czech Republic No. 3490, Hungary No. 4183, Slovakia No. 611.

Governmental Registration of Lódz Independent Student's Union, 30th Anniv. — A1467

*Perf. 11¼x11½ Syncopated*

**2011, Feb. 17**
**4002** A1467 1.95z multi 1.40 .70

Cystic Fibrosis Week — A1468

*Perf. 11½x11¼*

**2011, Feb. 28** **Photo.**
**4003** A1468 1.55z multi 1.10 .55

Stefan Kisielewski (1911-91), Composer and Writer — A1469

*Perf. 11¾x11½ Syncopated*

**2011, Mar. 7** **Litho.**
**4004** A1469 1.95z multi 1.40 .70
*a.* Tete beche pair 2.80 1.40

Easter — A1470

Flowers and: 1.55z, Chick. 2.40z, Rabbit.

*Perf. 11¾x11½*

**2011, Mar. 25** **Photo.**
**4005-4006** A1470 Set of 2 3.00 1.50

Adam Cardinal Kozlowiecki (1911-2007) — A1471

**2011, Mar. 31** **Photo.** *Perf. 11x11½*
**4007** A1471 1.95z multi 1.50 .75

Miniature Sheet

Photographs of People by Elzbieta Dzikowska — A1472

No. 4008: a, 1.95z, Monk from Myanmar (red panel). b, 1.95z, Hamer girl from Ethiopia (purple panel). c, 2.40z, Girl from Myanmar (yellow green panel). d, 2.40z, man from Palestine and camel (yellow orange panel). e, 3z, Woman from Nepal (blue panel). f, 3z, Indian woman from Peru (red violet panel).

*Perf. 11½x11¾ Syncopated*

**2011, Apr. 18** **Litho.**
**4008** A1472 Sheet of 6, #a-f 11.00 5.50

Souvenir Sheet

Beatification of Pope John Paul II — A1473

***Perf. 11½x11¼ Syncopated***

**2011, Apr. 28**

**4009** A1473 8.30z multi 6.00 3.00

See Vatican City No. 1471.

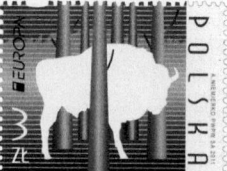

Europa A1474

***Perf. 11¾x11½ Syncopated***

**2011, May 5**

**4010** A1474 3z multi 2.25 1.10

Intl. Year of Forests.

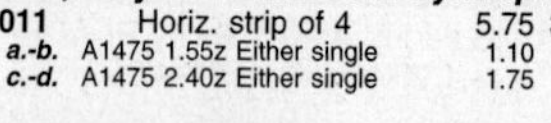


Cartoon Characters by Bohdan Butenko A1475

No. 4011: a, Cezar (blue dog). b, Gucio (brown hippopotamus). c, Kwapiszon (boy with white hat). d, Gapiszon (boy with striped stocking hat).

**2011, May 27** ***Perf. 11½ Syncopated***

**4011** Horiz. strip of 4 5.75 3.00
***a.-b.*** A1475 1.55z Either single 1.10 .55
***c.-d.*** A1475 2.40z Either single 1.75 .85

Polish Presidency of European Union Council — A1476

***Perf. 11¾x11½ Syncopated***

**2011, June 30** **Litho.**

**4012** A1476 3z multi + label 2.25 1.10

Souvenir Sheet

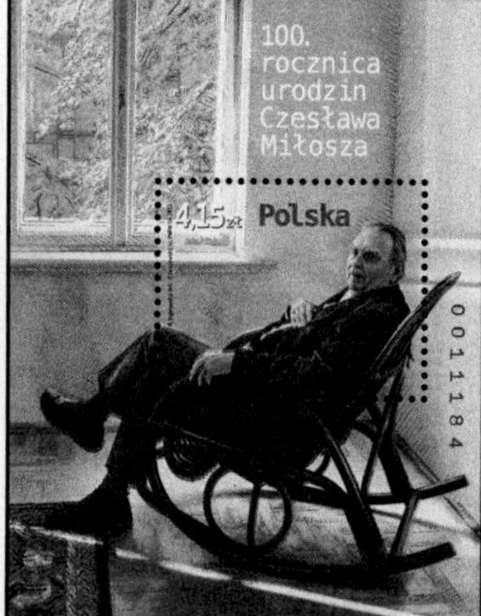


Czeslaw Milosz (1911-2004), 1980 Nobel Laureate in Literature — A1477

**Photo. & Engr.**

**2011, June 30** ***Perf. 11x11½***

**4013** A1477 4.15z multi 3.00 1.50

St. Maximilian Kolbe (1894-1941) A1478

***Perf. 11½x11¾ Syncopated***

**2011, Aug. 12** **Litho.**

**4014** A1478 1.95z multi 1.40 .70

Famous Poles A1479

Designs: 1.55z, Michal Sedziwój (1566-1636), chemist. 1.95z. Jan Szczepanik (1872-1926), inventor. No. 4017, 3z, Jan Józef Baranowski (1805-88), inventor. No. 4018, 3z, Rudolf Stefan Weigl (1883-1957), biologist.

***Perf. 11¾x11½ Syncopated***

**2011, Aug. 29**

**4015-4018** A1479 Set of 4 7.00 3.50

Father Jan Dzierzon (1811-1906), Apiarist A1480

***Perf. 11½x11¾ Syncopated***

**2011, Sept. 2**

**4019** A1480 1.55z multi 1.00 .50

Church of the Assumption of the Virgin Mary, Niegowic, First Pastoral Assignment of Pope John Paul II — A1481

***Perf. 11¾x11½ Syncopated***

**2011, Sept. 22**

**4020** A1481 1.95z multi + label 1.50 .75

Souvenir Sheet

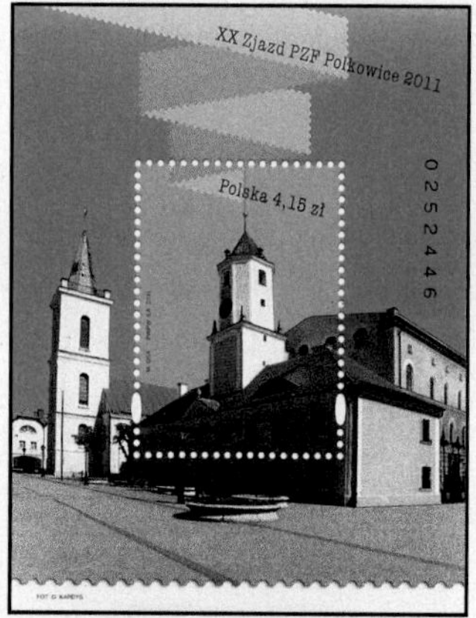


20th Congress of Polish Association of Philatelists, Polkowice — A1482

***Perf. 11½x11¾ Syncopated***

**2011, Sept. 30**

**4021** A1482 4.15z multi 2.75 1.40

Lost Works of Art A1483

No. 4022: a, Double Portrait of Eliza Parenska, by Stanislaw Wyspianski. b, Scene from the Legends of Theophilus of Adana, by Veit Stoss. c, Woman Looking Backwards, by Jean-Antoine Watteau.

**2011, Oct. 21** ***Perf. 11¼x11½***

**4022** Horiz. strip of 3 4.75 2.40
***a.*** A1483 1.95z multi 1.25 .60
***b.*** A1483 2.40z multi 1.60 .80
***c.*** A1483 3z multi 1.90 .95

Souvenir Sheet

First Polish Scientific Satellite — A1484

***Perf. 11¾x11½ Syncopated***

**2011, Nov. 4**

**4023** A1484 4.15z multi 2.60 1.40

Souvenir Sheet

Intl. Year of Chemistry — A1485

No. 4024: a, 3z, Nobel medal and radium (36x28mm). b, Marie Curie (1867-1934), 1911 Nobel laureate for Chemistry (40x55mm).

***Perf. 12¾ (#4024a), 13x12¾ (#4024b)***

**2011, Nov. 17** **Litho. & Engr.**

**4024** A1485 Sheet of 2, #a-b 7.75 3.75

See Sweden No. 2672.

Christmas A1486

Designs: 1.55z, Santa Claus, reindeer and sleigh. 2.40z, Nativity.

***Perf. 11½x11¾***

**2011, Nov. 25** **Photo.**

**4025** A1486 1.55z multi .95 .45

**Self-Adhesive**

**Litho.**

***Die Cut Perf. 11½x11¾***

**4026** A1486 2.40z multi 1.50 .75

Souvenir Sheet

Military Suppression of Warsaw Fire Academy Strike, 30th Anniv. — A1487

***Perf. 11½x11¾ Syncopated***

**2011, Dec. 2**

**4027** A1487 4.15z multi 2.60 1.30

Independence of Kazakhstan, 20th Anniv. — A1488

**2011, Dec. 8 Photo. *Perf. 11¼x11½***
**4028** A1488 2.40z multi 1.50 .75

**Fruit and Flowers Type of 2009**
***Perf. 11½x11¾***

**2011, Dec. 16 Photo.**
**4029** A1425 1.55z Rubus idaeus 1.00 .50

Souvenir Sheet

20th Concert of the Great Holiday Help Orchestra — A1489

**Litho. (With Foil Application in Sheet Margin)**
***Perf. 11¾x11½ Syncopated***

**2012, Jan. 8**
**4030** A1489 1.95z multi 1.25 .60

National Army, 70th Anniv. — A1490

***Perf. 11½x11¼***

**2012, Feb. 14 Photo.**
**4031** A1490 1.55z multi 1.00 .50

Souvenir Sheet

Zygmunt Krasinski (1812-59), Poet — A1491

***Perf. 11½x11¾ Syncopated***

**2012, Feb. 19 Litho.**
**4032** A1491 4.15z multi 2.75 1.40

Easter — A1492

Stylized flowers and: 1.55z, Lamb. 1.95z, Easter egg. 3z, Rabbit.

**2012, Mar. 9 *Perf. 11¾x11½***
**4033-4035** A1492 Set of 3 4.25 2.10

Leopold Kronenberg (1812-78), Banker and Leader of January 1863 Uprising A1493

**2012, Mar. 20 Photo. *Perf. 11½x11***
**4036** A1493 2.40z multi 1.50 .75

Photographs of Warsaw by Konrad Brandel (1838-1920) — A1494

No. 4037: a, Dworzec Wiedenski (Vienna Station), c. 1890. b, Krakowskie Przedmiescie, c. 1880. c, Plac Trzech Krzyzy (Three Crosses Square), c. 1875. d, Wiadukt Pancera (Pancera Viaduct), c. 1890.

***Perf. 11¾x11½ Syncopated***

**2012, Mar. 28 Litho.**
**4037** Vert. strip of 4 5.50 2.75
*a.-b.* A1494 1.95z Either single 1.25 .60
*c.-d.* A1494 2.40z Either single 1.50 .75

Suwalki, 300th Anniv. A1495

**2012, Mar. 30 Photo. *Perf. 11x11½***
**4038** A1495 1.95z multi 1.25 .60

Miniature Sheet

First Polish Discoveries in Egypt, 150th Anniv. — A1496

No. 4039: a, 1.,55z, Porcelain statue. b, 1.95z, Porcelain statue, diff. c, 2.40z. Nefertem amulet. d, 3z, Michal Tyszkiewicz (1828-97), Egyptologist.

**2012, Apr. 30 *Perf. 11½x11***
**4039** A1496 Sheet of 4, #a-d 5.75 3.00

Souvenir Sheet

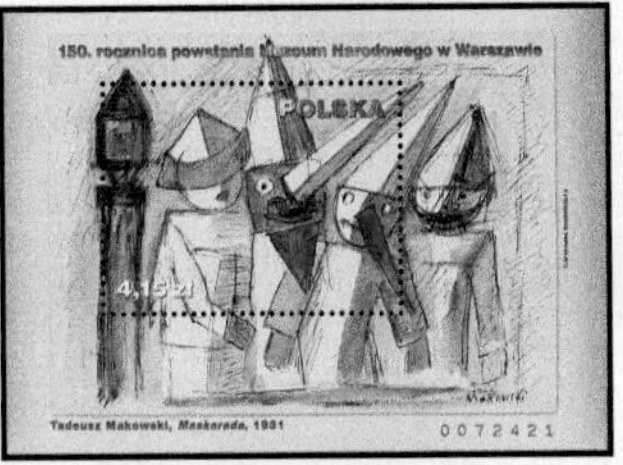

Masquerade, by Tadeusz Makowski — A1497

**2012, May 17 *Perf. 11¼x10¾***
**4040** A1497 4.15z multi 2.40 1.25

National Museum, Warsaw, 150th anniv.

Europa A1498

***Perf. 11½ Syncopated***

**2012, May 22 Litho.**
**4041** A1498 3z multi 1.75 .85

Heart, by Michal Batory — A1499

Piano, by Michal Batory A1500

**2012, May 25**
**4042** A1499 1.95z multi 1.10 .55
**4043** A1500 3z multi 1.75 .85

Souvenir Sheet

Animated Film *Parauszek the Rabbit* — A1501

**2012, May 30**
**4044** A1501 4.15z multi 2.40 1.25

2012 European Soccer Championships, Poland and Ukraine — A1502

Tournament stadiums in Poland: 1.55z, Municipal Stadium, Poznan. 1.95z, National Stadium, Warsaw. 2.40z, PGE Arena, Gdansk. 3z, Municipal Stadium, Wroclaw.

**2012, June 8**
**4045-4048** A1502 Set of 4 5.25 2.60
*4048a* Souvenir sheet of 4, #4045-4048 5.25 2.60

Nos. 4045-4048 each were printed in sheets of 8 + central label.

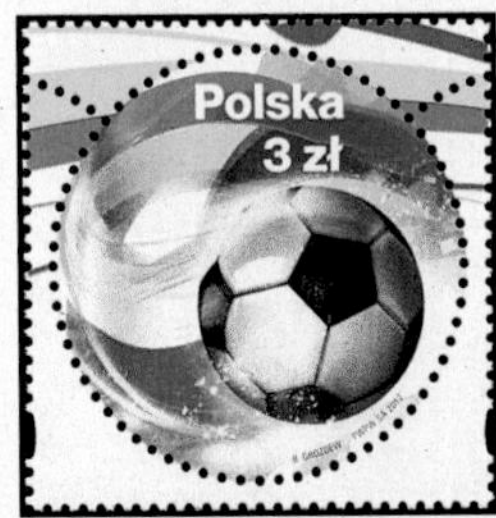

Soccer Ball, Flags of Ukraine and Poland A1503

**2012, June 15**
**4049** A1503 3z multi 1.75 .85

2012 European Soccer Championships, Poland and Ukraine. No. 4049 was printed in sheets of 6. Selvage surrounding each stamp on the sheet differs. Values are for stamps with surrounding selvage.

Muzakowski Park UNESCO World Heritage Site, Poland and Germany — A1504

***Perf. 11¾x11½ Syncopated***

**2012, July 12**
**4050** A1504 3z multi 1.90 .95

See Germany No. 2683.

Miniature Sheet

2012 Summer Olympics, London — A1505

No. 4051: a, 1.55z, Rowing. b, 1.95z, Volleyball. c, 2.40z, Weight lifting. d, 3z, Shot put.

**2012, July 27**
**4051** A1505 Sheet of 4, #a-d 5.50 2.75

Józef Ignacy Kraszewski (1812-87), Writer — A1506

*Perf. 11½x11¼*

**2012, July 28** **Photo.**

**4052** A1506 4.15z multi + label 2.60 1.25

Miniature Sheet

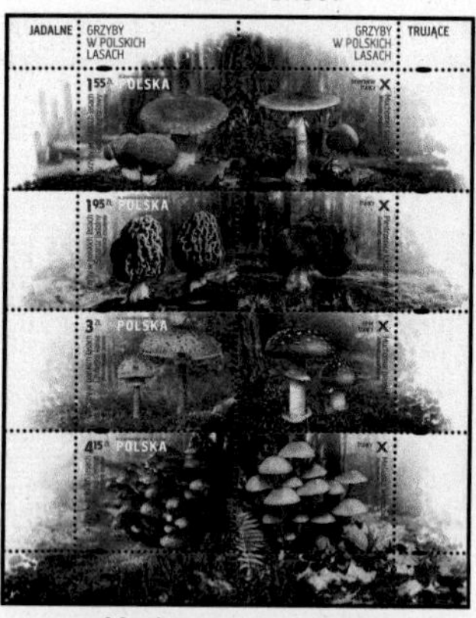

Mushrooms — A1507

No. 4053: a, 1.55z, Russula virescens. b, 1.95z, Morchella esculenta. c, 3z, Macrolepiota procera. d, 4.15z, Armillaria ostoyae.

*Perf. 11¾x11½ Syncopated*

**2012, Aug. 31** **Litho.**

**4053** A1507 Sheet of 4, #a-d, + 4 labels 6.75 3.50

2012 Polish-German Philatelic Exhibition, Kargowa A1508

*Perf. 11½x11¾ Syncopated*

**2012, Sept. 6**

**4054** A1508 2.40z multi 1.50 .75

Piotr Skarga (1536-1612), Counter-reformation Preacher — A1509

*Perf. 11¼x11½*

**2012, July 27** **Photo.**

**4055** A1509 1.55z multi 1.00 .55

Piotr Kwit (1929-2002), Painter — A1510

**2012, Oct. 10** *Perf. 11½x11¼*

**4056** A1510 1.55z multi .95 .50

Pope John Paul II and Wawel Cathedral — A1511

*Perf. 11¾x11½ Syncopated*

**2012, Oct. 13** **Litho.**

**4057** A1511 1.95z multi + label 1.50 .75

Stage and Film Stars — A1512

Designs: 1.55z, Jadwiga Smosarska (1898-1971). 1.95z, Aleksander Zabczynski (1900-58). 3z, Eugeniusz Bodo (1899-1943).

*Perf. 11½x11¾ Syncopated*

**2012, Oct. 31**

**4058-4060** A1512 Set of 3 4.00 2.00

*4060a* Souvenir sheet of 3, #4058-4060 4.00 2.00

See Nos. 4098-4100, 4149-4151, 4194-4196, 4258-4260, 4306-4308, 4371-4373, 4456-4458.

Souvenir Sheet

Turczynek Villa, Milanówek — A1513

*Perf. 11¾x11½ Syncopated*

**2012, Oct. 31**

**4061** A1513 4.15z multi 2.60 1.25

Christmas — A1514

Designs: A, Angels. 2.40z, Children with gifts, horiz.

*Perf. 11¾x11½, 11½x11¾*

**2012, Nov. 30** **Photo.**

**4062-4063** A1514 Set of 2 2.50 1.25

No. 4062 sold for 1.55z on day of issue.

Jerzy Turowicz (1912-99), Journalist A1515

*Perf. 11½x11¾ Syncopated*

**2012, Dec. 10** **Litho.**

**4064** A1515 1.55z multi 1.00 .50

21st Concert of the Great Holiday Help Orchestra A1516

**2013, Jan. 13** *Die Cut Perf.*

**Self-Adhesive**

**4065** A1516 A multi 1.10 .55

No. 4065 sold for 1.60z on day of issue and was printed in sheets of 6. Unused values are for stamps with surrounding selvage.

A1517

A1518

A1519

A1520

**2013, Mar. 8** **Photo.** *Perf. 11¾x11½*

**4066** A1517 (1.60z) multi 1.00 .50

**4067** A1518 (2.35z) multi 1.50 .75

**4068** A1519 (3.75z) multi 2.40 1.25

**4069** A1520 (5.10z) multi 3.25 1.60

*Nos. 4066-4069 (4)* 8.15 4.10

A1521

A1522

A1523

A1524

**2013, Mar. 29**

**4070** A1521 (3.70z) multi 2.25 1.10

**4071** A1522 (4.50z) multi 2.75 1.40

**4072** A1523 (4.75z) multi 3.00 1.50

**4073** A1524 (7.10z) multi 4.50 2.25

*Nos. 4070-4073 (4)* 12.50 6.25

Souvenir Sheet

Alcedo Atthis — A1525

*Perf. 11½ Syncopated*

**2013, Apr. 12** **Litho.**

**4074** A1525 4.55z multi 3.00 1.50

Wieslaw Chrzanowski (1923-2012), Marshal of the Sejm — A1526

**2013, Apr. 16**

**4075** A1526 3.80z multi 2.40 1.25

Warsaw Ghetto Uprising, 70th Anniv. — A1527

**2013, Apr. 19** **Photo.** *Perf. 11½x11*

**4076** A1527 3.80z multi 2.40 1.25

Flag Day A1528

*Perf. 11½ Syncopated*

**2013, May 2** **Litho.**

**4077** A1528 1.60z multi 1.00 .50

Europa A1529

**2013, May 6**

**4078** A1529 4.60z multi 3.00 1.50

Souvenir Sheet

Disney Cartoon Characters — A1530

**2013, June 1**
**4079** A1530 4.60z multi 3.00 1.50

Miniature Sheet

Lighthouses — A1531

No. 4080: a, 1.60z, Darlowo Lighthouse. b, 2.35z, Jaroslawiec Lighthouse. c, 3.75z, Ustka Lighthouse. d, 3.80z, Czolpino Lighthouse.

**2013, June 14 Photo. *Perf. 11½x11***
**4080** A1531 Sheet of 4, #a-d 7.25 3.75

A1532

A1533

A1534

A1535

***Perf. 11¾x11½***

| | | | |
|---|---|---|---|
| **2013, June 20** | **Photo.** | | |
| **4081** A1532 | (6.30z) multi | 4.00 | 2.00 |
| **4082** A1533 | (7.30z) multi | 4.50 | 2.25 |
| **4083** A1534 | (8.80z) multi | 5.50 | 2.75 |
| **4084** A1535 | (10.90z) multi | 6.75 | 3.50 |
| *Nos. 4081-4084 (4)* | | 20.75 | 10.50 |

Souvenir Sheet

Prince Boleslaw III the Wrymouthed (1086-1138) — A1536

**Photo. & Engr.**

**2013, June 28 *Perf. 11½x11¼***
**4085** A1536 8.50z red & brn blk 5.25 2.60

Deeds of the Princes of the Poles, chronicle of Polish history by Gallus Anonymus, 900th anniv. of publication.

Strawberry — A1537

**2013, July 18 Litho. *Perf. 11¼x11½***
**4086** A1537 4.60z multi 3.00 1.50

Tour de Pologne Bicycle Race — A1538

No. 4087: a, One cyclist. b, Two cyclists.

***Perf. 11½ Syncopated***

| | | | |
|---|---|---|---|
| **2013, July 30** | **Litho.** | | |
| **4087** A1538 | Horiz. pair | 4.00 | 2.00 |
| *a.* | 1.60z multi | 1.00 | .50 |
| *b.* | 4.60z multi | 3.00 | 1.50 |

Souvenir Sheet

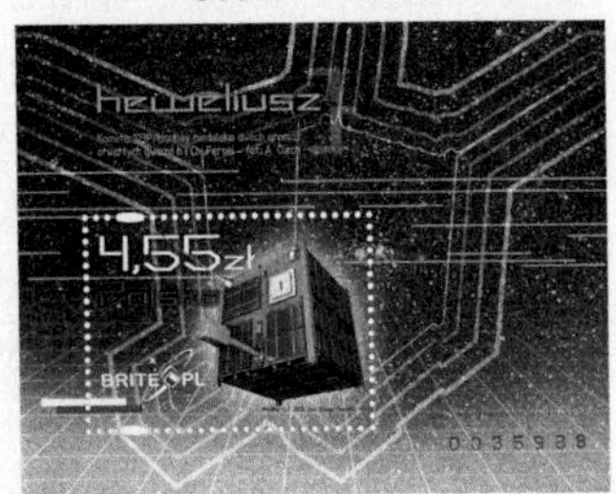

Heweliusz Satellite — A1539

***Perf. 11¾x11½ Syncopated***

**2013, July 31 Litho.**
**4088** A1539 4.55z multi 3.00 1.50

Woodstock Festival Poland, Kostrzyn nad Odra A1540

***Die Cut Perf. 11½***

**2013, Aug. 1 Litho.**

**Self-Adhesive**

**4089** A1540 2.35z multi 1.50 .75

Souvenir Sheet

Szczecin 2013 Tall Ships Regatta — A1541

**Photo. & Engr.**

**2013, Aug. 3 *Perf. 11¼x11***
**4090** A1541 8.50z black & blue 5.50 2.75

Modernization of Polish Armed Forces — A1542

No. 4091: a, General Dynamics F-16 Block 52+ jets. b, Rosomak armored vehicle. c, ORP Kontradmiral Xawery Czernicki support ship.

***Perf. 11¾x11½ Syncopated***

**2013, Aug. 14 Litho.**
**4091** A1542 1.60z Vert. strip of 3, #a-c 3.00 1.50

Souvenir Sheet

Traditional Costumes of Poland and Romania — A1543

***Perf. 11½x11¾ Syncopated***

**2013, Sept. 11 Litho.**
**4092** A1543 4.60z multi 3.00 1.50

See Romania No. 5483.

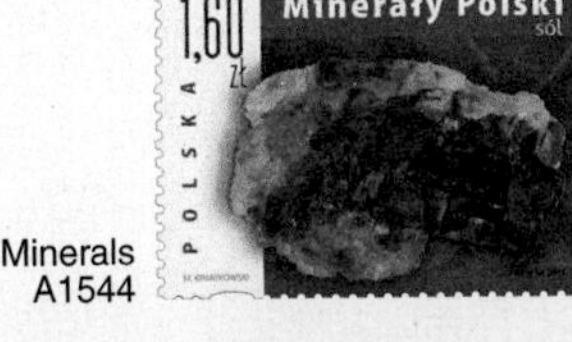

Minerals A1544

No. 4093: a, Salt (gray violet panel). b, Malachite and azurite (blue panel). c, Marcasite (blue green panel). d, Gypsum (red panel).

***Perf. 11¾x11½ Syncopated***

**Litho. & Silk-screened**

| | | | |
|---|---|---|---|
| **2013, Sept. 20** | | | |
| **4093** | Vert. strip of 4 | 5.50 | 2.75 |
| *a.-b.* | A1544 1.60z Either single | 1.10 | .55 |
| *c.-d.* | A1544 2.35z Either single | 1.60 | .80 |

Pres. Lech Walesa, 70th Birthday A1545

***Perf. 11½x11¼ Syncopated***

**2013, Sept. 29 Litho.**
**4094** A1545 3.80z multi 2.50 1.25

**Landmarks in European Capitals Type of 2005**

Design: St. Mark's Church, Zagreb, Croatia.

***Perf. 11¼x11½ Syncopated***

**2013, Oct. 11 Litho.**
**4095** A1323 4.60z multi 3.00 1.50

World Post Day A1546

***Perf. 11¼x11½***

**2013, Oct. 18 Photo.**
**4096** A1546 4.60z multi 3.00 1.50

Polish postal services, 455th anniv.

Lost Works of Art A1547

No. 4097 — Pastel drawings by Stanislaw Wyspianski of the actor Ludwik Solski in costume in plays: a, Treasure, by Leopold Staff. b, The Twelfth Night, by William Shakespeare. c, Varsovian Anthem, by Wyspianski.

***Perf. 11¼x11½***

| | | | |
|---|---|---|---|
| **2013, Oct. 21** | **Photo.** | | |
| **4097** | Horiz. strip of 3 | 5.00 | 2.50 |
| *a.* | A1547 1.60z multi | 1.00 | .50 |
| *b.* | A1547 2.35z multi | 1.50 | .75 |
| *c.* | A1547 3.80z multi | 2.50 | 1.25 |

**Stage and Film Stars Type of 2012**

Designs: 1.60z, Helena Grossówna (1904-94). 2.35z, Adolf Dymsza (1900-75). 3.80z, Mieczyslawa Cwiklinska (1879-1972).

***Perf. 11½x11¾ Syncopated***

| | | | |
|---|---|---|---|
| **2013, Oct. 31** | **Litho.** | | |
| **4098** A1512 | 1.60z multi | 1.00 | .50 |
| **4099** A1512 | 2.35z multi | 1.50 | .75 |
| **4100** A1512 | 3.80z multi | 2.50 | 1.25 |
| *a.* | Souvenir sheet of 3, #4098-4100 | 5.00 | 2.50 |

Krzystof Penderecki, Composer, 80th Birthday A1548

***Perf. 11½x11¼***

**2013, Nov. 23 Photo.**
**4101** A1548 3.80z multi 2.50 1.25

Spiders A1549

Designs: 1.60z, Argiope bruennichi. 2.35z, Atypus muralis. 3.80z, Eresus kollari. 4.55z, Philaeus chrysops.

***Perf. 11¾x11½ Syncopated***
**Litho. & Silk-screened**

**2013, Nov. 29**
**4102-4105** A1549 Set of 4 8.25 4.25

Nos. 4102-4105 were each printed in sheets of 8 + label.

2014 Winter Olympics, Sochi, Russia A1550

No. 4106: a, Ski jumping. b, Cross-country skiing.

***Perf. 11¾x11½ Syncopated***
**2014, Feb. 7 Litho. & Embossed**
**4106** A1550 Vert. pair 4.50 2.25
*a.* 1.75z multi 1.25 .60
*b.* 5z multi 3.25 1.60

No. 4106 was printed in sheets containing two pairs.

Oskar Kolberg (1814-90), Ethnologist and Composer A1551

**2014, Feb. 22 Photo. *Perf. 11½x11***
**4107** A1551 4.20z multi 2.75 1.40

World Indoors Track and Field Championships, Sopot — A1552

***Perf. 11¼x11½ Syncopated***
**Litho. & Silk-Screened**

**2014, Mar. 7**
**4108** A1552 5z multi 3.00 1.75

No. 4108 was printed in sheets of 4.

Easter — A1553

Color of egg: 1.75z, Green. 5z, Purple.

***Perf. 11¾x11½***
**2014, Mar. 26 Photo.**
**4109-4110** A1553 Set of 2 4.25 2.25

See Nos. 4162-4163.

Souvenir Sheet

Consecration of Wawel Cathedral, 650th Anniv. — A1554

No. 4111: a, 4.20z, Wawel Cathedral spires, 14th-15th cent.. b, 8.30z, Wawel Cathedral, Sigismund Bell.

**Photo. & Engr.**
**2014, Mar. 28 *Perf. 11***
**4111** A1554 Sheet of 2, #a-b 7.50 4.25

Souvenir Sheet

Canonization of Popes John Paul II and John XXIII — A1555

No. 4112: a, Pope John Paul II. b, Pope John XXIII.

***Perf. 11½x11¼ Syncopated***
**2014, Apr. 2 Litho.**
**4112** A1555 5z Sheet of 2, #a-b 6.25 3.25

See Vatican City No. 1558.

A1556

Canonization of Pope John Paul II — A1557

***Perf. 11½x11¾ Syncopated***
**2014, Apr. 2 Litho.**
**4113** A1556 2.35z multi 1.40 .80

**Souvenir Sheets**

***Perf. 11¼x11½ Syncopated***
**4114** A1557 5z multi 3.25 1.75

**Engr.**
**4115** A1557 8.50z brown 5.25 2.75

See Vatican City Nos. 1559-1561.

Souvenir Sheet

Polish Gold Medalists at 2014 Winter Olympics — A1558

No. 4116: a, Kamil Stoch, ski jumping. b, Justyna Kowalczyk, cross-country skiing. c, Zbigniew Bródka, speed skating.

***Perf. 11¾x11½ Syncopated***
**2014, Apr. 11 Litho.**
**4116** A1558 4.20z Sheet of 3, #a-c 7.50 4.25

Jan Karski (1914-2000), World War II Resistance Fighter — A1559

***Perf. 11½x11¼***
**2014, Apr. 24 Photo.**
**4117** A1559 4.20z multi 2.50 1.40
*a.* Tete-beche pair 5.50 3.00

Admission to the European Union, 10th Anniv. A1560

***Perf. 11¼x11½ Syncopated***
**2014, May 1 Litho.**
**4118** A1560 5.20z multi 3.00 1.75

Bagpipes A1561

***Perf. 11½x11¾ Syncopated***
**2014, May 5 Litho.**
**4119** A1561 5.20z multi 3.00 1.75

Europa.

International Year of the Family — A1562

***Perf. 11¼x11½***
**2014, May 15 Photo.**
**4120** A1562 2.35z multi 1.50 .80

Battle of Monte Cassino, 70th Anniv. — A1563

***Perf. 11½x11¾ Syncopated***
**2014, May 18 Litho.**
**4121** A1563 1.75z multi 1.10 .60

Freedom Festival — A1564

***Perf. 11½x11¼***
**2014, May 28 Photo.**
**4122** A1564 2.35z multi 1.40 .80

Elections of June 4, 1989, 25th anniv.

Souvenir Sheet

Premiere of Animated Film *The Pirate Fairy* — A1565

***Perf. 11¾x11½ Syncopated***
**2014, June 1 Litho.**
**4123** A1565 5.20z multi 3.00 1.75

Miniature Sheet

Coaches — A1566

No. 4124: a, Kazimierz Górski (1921-2006), soccer coach. b, Hubert Wagner (1941-2002), volleyball coach. c, Feliks Stamm (1901-76), boxing coach. d, Henryk Lasak (1932-73), cycling coach.

*Perf. 11¼x11½*

**2014, June 27** **Photo.**

4124 A1566 2.35z Sheet of 4, #a-d 5.75 3.25

Historic Photographs by Henryk Poddebski (1890-1945) — A1567

No. 4125: a, Zinc smelter, Szopienice. b, Machinery at Kleofas colliery. c, Smokestacks and buildings, Krolewska Huta. d, Coal transport at Gdynia Harbor.

*Perf. 11¾x11½ Syncopated*

**2014, July 11** **Litho.**

| | | | |
|---|---|---|---|
| 4125 | Vert. strip of 4 | 7.00 | 4.00 |
| *a.* | A1567 1.75z multi | 1.00 | .55 |
| *b.* | A1567 2.35z multi | 1.25 | .75 |
| *c.* | A1567 3.75z multi | 2.25 | 1.25 |
| *d.* | A1567 4.20z multi | 2.50 | 1.40 |

Apple A1568

*Perf. 11¼x11½*

**2014, July 18** **Photo.**

4126 A1568 5z multi 3.00 1.60

Souvenir Sheet

Merops Apiaster — A1569

*Perf. 11½x11¾ Syncopated*

**2014, July 31** **Litho.**

4127 A1569 5.50z multi 3.25 1.75

Souvenir Sheet

Warsaw Uprising, 70th Anniv. — A1570

*Perf. 11½x11¾ Syncopated*

**2014, Aug. 1** **Litho.**

4128 A1570 5.20z multi 3.00 1.75

Souvenir Sheet

Józef Pilsudski (1867-1935), Prime Minister, and Members of Polish Legion — A1571

**Photo. & Engr.**

**2014, Aug. 6** *Perf. 11¼*

4129 A1571 8.50z multi 5.00 2.60

Icons A1572

Designs: 1.75z, Our Lady of Drohobycz. 4.20z. Our Lady of Kochawinskiej.

**2014, Aug. 14** **Photo.** *Perf. 10¾x11*

4130-4131 A1572 Set of 2 3.50 1.90

Miniature Sheet

Mushrooms — A1573

No. 4132: a, 1.75z, Cantharellus cibarius. b, 2.35z, Agaricus campestris. c, 3.75z, Russula vesca. d, 4.20z, Boletus edulis.

*Perf. 11¾x11½ Syncopated*

**2014, Aug. 29** **Litho.**

4132 A1573 Sheet of 4, #a-d, + 4 labels 7.25 3.75

Miniature Sheet

2014 Men's World Volleyball Championships, Poland — A1574

No. 4133 — Color of player's shirt: a, 1.75z, White. b, 1.75z, Dark blue. c, 2.35z, Green. d, 5z, Red. e, 5.10z, White. f, 5.50z, Yellow.

*Perf. 11½x11¾ Syncopated*

**2014, Aug. 30** **Litho.**

4133 A1574 Sheet of 6, #a-f 15.00 7.50

Dr. Clown Charitable Foundation — A1575

*Perf. 11½x11¼*

**2014, Sept. 5** **Photo.**

4134 A1575 1.75z multi 1.10 .55

Souvenir Sheet

Mural by Natalia Rak — A1576

*Perf. 11¾x11½ Syncopated*

**2014, Sept. 26** **Litho.**

4135 A1576 4.20z multi 2.50 1.25

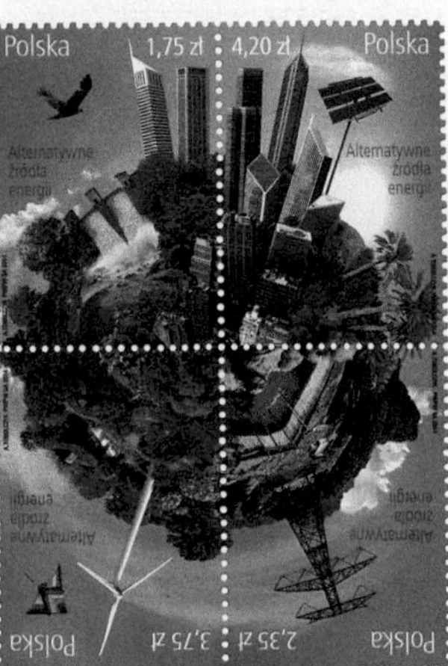


Alternative Energy Sources — A1577

No. 4136: a, Hydroelectric dam. b, Geothermal energy. c, Wind generator. d, Solar panel.

*Perf. 11½x11¼*

**2014, Sept. 29** **Photo.**

| | | | |
|---|---|---|---|
| 4136 A1577 | Block of 4 | 7.00 | 3.75 |
| *a.* | 1.75z multi | 1.00 | .55 |
| *b.* | 2.35z multi | 1.40 | .75 |
| *c.* | 3.75z multi | 2.10 | 1.10 |
| *d.* | 4.20z multi | 2.40 | 1.25 |

Meteorological Phenomena — A1578

No. 4137: a, Aurora. b, Sun dog. c, Smoke. d, Frost.

*Perf. 11¾x11½ Syncopated*

**Litho. & Silk-Screened**

**2014, Sept. 30**

| | | | |
|---|---|---|---|
| 4137 | Horiz. strip of 4 | 8.00 | 4.50 |
| *a.* | A1578 1.75z multi | 1.00 | .55 |
| *b.* | A1578 2.35z multi | 1.25 | .75 |
| *c.* | A1578 4.20z multi | 2.40 | 1.25 |
| *d.* | A1578 5.50z multi | 3.25 | 1.75 |

Jan Nowak-Jezioranski (1914-2005), Head of Polish Section for Radio Free Europe — A1579

**2014, Oct. 2** **Photo.** *Perf. 11½x11¼*

4138 A1579 4.20z multi 2.40 1.25

Fish — A1580

Designs: 35g, Acanthurus sohal. 45g, Chaetodon capistratus. 55g, Rhinomuraena quaesita. 65g, Hippocampus sp. 1.10z, Balistoides conspicillum. 1.20z, Pomacanthus xanthometopon. 1.30z, Chelmon rostratus. 1.40z, Amphiprion ocellaris.

*Perf. 11½x11¼*

**2014, Oct. 10** **Photo.**

4139-4146 A1580 Set of 8 4.50 2.25

*4146a* Souvenir sheet of 8, #4139-4146 + 4 labels *52.50 32.50*

2014 National Philatelic Exhibition, Warsaw.

Nos. 4139-4146 each were printed in sheets of 12 + 4 labels. Value, set of eight sheets $45.

Stefan Zeromski (1864-1925), Writer — A1581

*Perf. 11½x11¼ Syncopated*

**2014, Oct. 14** **Litho.**

4147 A1581 4.20z multi 2.50 1.25

Miniature Sheet

Victory of Polish Men's Volleyball Team and 2014 World Championships — A1582

No. 4148: a, Stéphan Antiga. b, Piotr Nowakowski. c, Michal Winiarski. d, Dawid Konarski. e, Rafal Buszek. f, Pawel Zagumny. g, Karol Klos. h, Andrzej Wrona. i, Mariusz Wlazly. j, Fabian Drzyzga. k, Michal Kubiak. l, Krzysztof Ignaczak. m, Pawel Zatorski. n, Marcin Mozdzonek. o, Mateusz Mika. p, Philippe Blain.

*Perf. 11¾x11½ Syncopated*

**2014, Oct. 18** **Litho.**

**4148** A1582 1z Sheet of 16, #a-p, + 4 labels 9.00 4.75

**Stage and Film Stars Type of 2012**

Designs: 1.75z, Tola Mankiewiczówna (1900-85). 2.35z, Antoni Fertner (1874-1959). 4.20z, Loda Halama (1911-96).

*Perf. 11½x11¾ Syncopated*

**2014, Oct. 31** **Litho.**

**4149-4151** A1512 Set of 3 4.75 2.50

*4151a* Souvenir sheet of 3, #4149-4151 4.75 2.50

Christmas — A1583

Stained-glass windows depicting: 2.35z, Holy Family. 5.20z, Adoration of the Magi.

**2014, Nov. 14** **Photo.** ***Perf. 11¼***

**4152-4153** A1583 Set of 2 4.25 2.25

William Shakespeare (1564-1616), Writer — A1584

*Perf. 11½x11¾*

**2014, Nov. 21** **Photo.**

**4154** A1584 4.20z multi 2.50 1.25

Souvenir Sheet

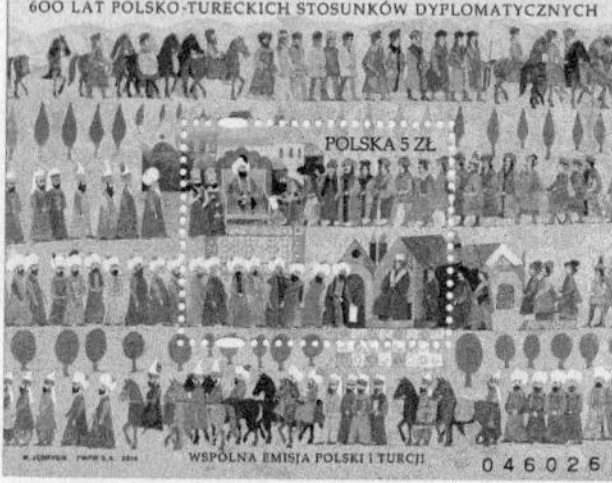

Diplomatic Relations Between Poland and Turkey, 600th Anniv. — A1585

*Perf. 11¼x11½ Syncopated*

**2014, Nov. 28** **Litho.**

**4155** A1585 5z multi 2.75 1.50

See Turkey No. 3416.

Ring of Youths A1586

Main Square, Cracow A1587

*Perf. 11¼ Syncopated*

**2014, Dec. 19** **Litho.**

**4156** A1586 1.75z multi 1.00 .50

*Perf. 11½ Syncopated*

**4157** A1587 5z multi 2.75 1.50

Selection of Cracow as host city of 2016 World Youth Day.

23rd Concert of the Great Holiday Help Orchestra A1588

*Perf. 11½x11¾ Syncopated*

**2015, Jan. 7** **Litho.**

**4158** A1588 2.35z multi 1.25 .65

Love A1589

**Litho. & Silk-Screened**

**2015, Feb. 6** ***Perf. 11½ Syncopated***

**4159** A1589 2.35z multi 1.25 .65

Values are for stamps with surrounding selvage.

Kazimierz Przerwa-Tetmajer (1865-1940), Poet — A1590

*Perf. 11½x11¼ Syncopated*

**2015, Feb. 12** **Litho.**

**4160** A1590 1.75z multi .90 .45

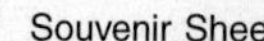

Souvenir Sheet

Witkacy (1885-1939), Writer and Painter — A1591

*Perf. 11½x11¾ Syncopated*

**2015, Feb. 24** **Litho.**

**4161** A1591 5.20z multi 2.75 1.40

**Easter Type of 2014**

Color of egg: 2.35z, Purplish black. 5.20z, Red.

**2015, Mar. 6** **Photo.** ***Perf. 11¾x11½***

**4162-4163** A1553 Set of 2 4.00 2.10

Organ Transplantation — A1592

**2015, Mar. 20** **Photo.** ***Perf. 11x11½***

**4164** A1592 1.75z multi .95 .45

Awarding of Best Foreign Film Academy Award to Polish Movie "Ida" A1593

*Perf. 11½ Syncopated*

**2015, Mar. 31** **Litho.**

**4165** A1593 2.35z multi 1.25 .65

No. 4165 was printed in sheets of 8 + central label.

Tadeusz Kantor (1915-90), Theater Director — A1594

*Perf. 11½x11¾ Syncopated*

**2015, Apr. 3** **Photo.**

**4166** A1594 1.75z multi .95 .45

Katyn Massacre, 75th Anniv. — A1595

*Perf. 11½x11¼ Syncopated*

**2015, Apr. 7** **Litho.**

**4167** A1595 1.75z multi 1.00 .50

2016 World Youth Day, Cracow — A1596

Emblem and: 1.75z, St. John Paul II. 5z, Map of Poland, signature of St. John Paul II.

*Perf. 11½x11¼*

**2015, Apr. 27** **Photo.**

**4168-4169** A1596 Set of 2 3.50 1.90

Toy Made of Nuts A1597

*Perf. 11¾x11½ Syncopated*

**2015, May 5** **Litho.**

**4170** A1597 5z multi 2.50 1.50

Europa.

Souvenir Sheet

End of World War II, 70th Anniv. — A1598

**2015, May 8** **Photo.** ***Perf. 11½x11¼***

**4171** A1598 2.35z multi 1.25 .65

Souvenir Sheet

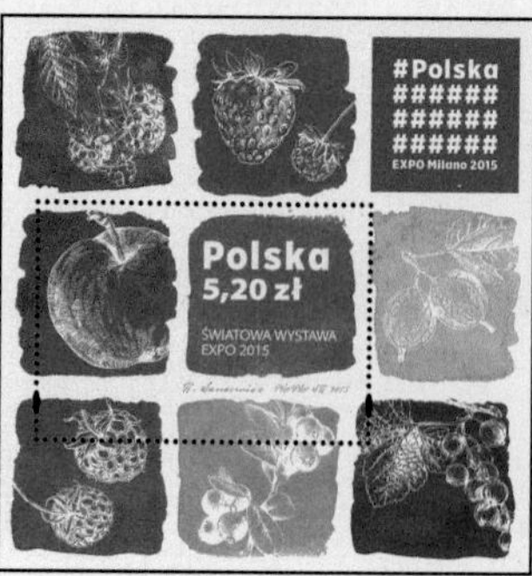

Expo 2015, Milan — A1599

*Perf. 11½x11¾ Syncopated*

**2015, May 28** **Litho.**

**4172** A1599 5.20z multi 2.50 1.50

Father Jan Twardowski (1915-2006), Poet — A1600

***Perf. 11½x11¾ Syncopated***

**2015, May 29** **Litho.**

**4173** A1600 1.75z multi .95 .45

Souvenir Sheet

Characters From Animated Film *Frozen* — A1601

No. 4174: a, Anna, denomination at UL. b, Elsa, denomination at UR.

***Perf. 11½ Syncopated***

**2015, June 1** **Litho.**

**4174** A1601 2.35z Sheet of 2, #a-b 2.60 1.25

World Blood Donor Day — A1602

***Perf. 11½x11¼***

**2015, June 14** **Photo.**

**4175** A1602 1.75z multi .95 .45

Miniature Sheet

Lighthouses — A1603

No. 4176: a, Rozewie II Lighthouse. b, Kikut Lighthouse. c, Swinoujscie Lighthouse. d, Jastarnia Lighthouse. e, Gdansk North Port Lighthouse.

***Perf. 11½x11¼***

**2015, June 19** **Photo.**

**4176** A1603 2.35z Sheet of 5, #a-e, + label 5.75 3.25

Count Jan Potocki (1761-1815), Writer — A1604

***Perf. 11½x11¼ Syncopated***

**2015, June 25** **Litho.**

**4177** A1604 5z multi 2.50 1.40

**Fruit and Flowers Type of 2009**

**2015** **Photo.** ***Perf. 11½x11¾***

**4178** A1425 10g Nymphaea .25 .25
**4179** A1425 1z Helianthus .50 .25
**4180** A1425 5z Rose 2.40 1.40
*Nos. 4178-4180 (3)* 3.15 1.90

Issued: 1z, 6/26, 10g, 5z, 9/15.

Polish Presidency of Council of Baltic Sea States for 2015-16 A1605

***Perf. 11½x11¼ Syncopated***

**2015, July 1** **Litho.**

**4181** A1605 5z multi 2.50 1.40

Cows and Korycinski Cheese — A1606

***Perf. 11¾x11½ Syncopated***

**2015, July 17** **Litho. & Embossed**

**4182** A1606 5z multi 2.50 1.40

Souvenir Sheet

Pipe Organ, Cistercian Monastery Church, Jedrzejów — A1607

No. 4183: a, 4.20z, Organ pipes and balcony railing. b, 8.30z, Organ pipes and ceiling.

***Perf. 11½x11¼ Syncopated***

**2015, July 30** **Litho. & Engr.**

**4183** A1607 Sheet of 2, #a-b 6.00 3.50

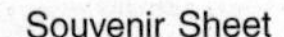

Souvenir Sheet

St. John Bosco (1815-88) — A1608

**Photo. & Engr.**

**2015, Aug. 16** ***Perf. 11x11¼***

**4184** A1608 5.20z multi 2.50 1.40

2015 Radom Air Show — A1609

No. 4185: a, Helicopter. b, Airplane.

***Perf. 11¼x11½ Syncopated***

**2015, Aug. 22** **Litho.**

**4185** A1609 2.35z Pair, #a-b 2.25 1.25

Optimist Class Sailboat World Championships — A1610

***Perf. 11¾x11½ Syncopated***

**2015, Aug. 26** **Litho.**

**4186** A1610 1.75z multi .95 .45

Miniature Sheet

Metal Crystals — A1611

No. 4187: a, 1.75fr, Cast iron (green, yellow, pink & black). b, 1.75z, Bronze (blue violet, red and orange). c, 2.35z, Iron (large crystals at top, small crystals at bottom). d, 2.35z, Iron (large round crystal).

**Litho. & Silk-Screened**
***Perf. 11½ Syncopated***

**2015, Sept. 11**

**4187** A1611 Sheet of 4, #a-d 4.00 2.25

Warsaw Post Office, Cent. — A1612

***Perf. 11½x11¾ Syncopated***

**2015, Sept. 23** **Litho.**

**4188** A1612 2.35z multi 1.25 .60

Depictions of Quotations from Polish Literature — A1613

Designs: No. 4189, 2.35z, Woman, man holding crocodile balloon (quotation from Revenge, by Aleksander Fredro). No. 4190, 2.35z, Dogs (quotation from Ashes, by Stefan Zeromski).

***Perf. 11¾x11½ Syncopated***

**2015, Sept. 23** **Litho.**

**4189-4190** A1613 Set of 2 2.50 1.25

17th Chopin Intl. Piano Competition A1614

***Perf. 11½x11¼ Syncopated***

**2015, Oct. 1** **Litho.**

**4191** A1614 1.75z multi .95 .45

Letter of Reconciliation from Polish Bishops to German Bishops, 50th Anniv. — A1615

***Perf. 11½x11¼***

**2015, Oct. 23** **Photo.**

**4192** A1615 1.75z multi .90 .45

Miniature Sheet

Owls — A1616

No. 4193: a, Bubo bubo. b, Aegolius funereus. c, Tyto alba. d, Strix nebulosa.

*Perf. 11¾x11½ Syncopated*

**2015, Oct. 23 Litho. & Embossed**

**4193** A1616 2.35z Sheet of 4, #a-d, + 4 labels 5.00 2.50

**Stage and Film Stars Type of 2012**

Designs: 1.75z, Jerzy Pichelski (1903-63). 2.35z, Hanka Bielicka (1915-2006). 4.20z, Aleksander Zelwerowicz (1877-1955).

*Perf. 11½x11¾ Syncopated*

**2015, Oct. 30 Litho.**

**4194-4196** A1512 Set of 3 4.50 2.25
*4196a* Souvenir sheet of 3, #4194-4196 4.50 2.25

Christmas — A1617

Designs: 1.75z, Holy Family and animals. 2.35z, Annunciation. 5.20z, Adoration of the Magi.

*Perf. 11¾x11½*

**2015, Nov. 16 Photo.**

**4197-4199** A1617 Set of 3 4.75 2.40

Wojciech Boguslawski (1757-1829), Director of National Theater, Warsaw A1618

*Perf. 11½x11¼*

**2015, Nov. 19 Photo.**

**4200** A1618 1.75z gold & multi .90 .45

National Theater, 250th anniv.

National Day of Rights of the Child — A1619

*Perf. 11½x11¼*

**2015, Nov. 20 Photo.**

**4201** A1619 1.75z multi .90 .45

Wladyslaw Bartoszewski (1922-2015), Minister of Foreign Affairs — A1620

*Perf. 11¾x11½ Syncopated*

**2015, Nov. 25 Litho.**

**4202** A1620 1.75z gold & multi .90 .45

City of Cracow and Jan Dlugosz (1415-80), Diplomat and Chronicler of Polish History A1621

*Perf. 11¼x11½*

**2015, Nov. 30 Photo.**

**4203** A1621 1.75z gold & multi .90 .45

Beatification of Fathers Michal Tomaszek (1960-91), and Zbigniew Strzalkowski (1958-91), Murdered Missionaries to Peru — A1622

*Perf. 11½x11¾ Syncopated*

**2015, Dec. 5 Litho.**

**4204** A1622 1.75z gold & multi .90 .45

**Fruit and Flowers Type of 2009**

**2015-16 Photo.** ***Perf. 11½x11¾***

**4205** A1425 5g Lilacs .25 .25
**4206** A1425 50g Coneflower .25 .25
**4207** A1425 10z Poppy 5.25 2.60
*Nos. 4205-4207 (3)* 5.75 3.10

Issued: 5g, 12/7; 50g, 1/20/16; 10z, 4/22/16.

St. Paraskevi Church, Kwiaton, Poland and St. George's Church, Drohobych, Ukraine — A1623

**Photo. & Engr.**

**2015, Dec. 18** ***Perf. 11x10¾***

**4208** A1623 5z multi 2.60 1.25

Wooden Churches of the Carpathian Region of Poland and Ukraine UNESCO World Heritage Site. See Ukraine No. 1045

European Men's Handball Championships, Poland — A1625

No. 4210 — Handball and: a, Player. b, Hand.

*Perf. 11½ Syncopated*

**2016, Jan. 15 Litho.**

**4210** Vert. pair 3.75 1.90
*a.* A1625 2.35z multi 1.25 .60
*b.* A1625 5z multi 2.50 1.25

Printed in sheets containing 3 each Nos. 4210a and 4210b, with each stamp in the sheet having a different selvage surrounding the stamp, and a different orientation within that selvage.

Souvenir Sheet

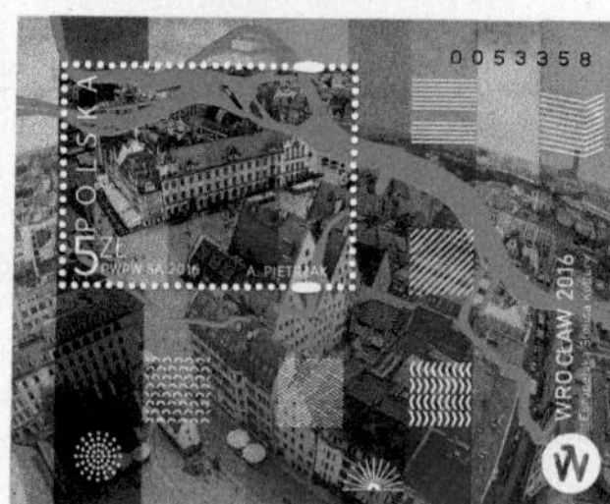

Wroclaw, 2016 European Capital of Culture — A1626

*Perf. 11¾x11½ Syncopated*

**2016, Jan. 15 Litho.**

**4211** A1626 5z multi 2.50 1.25

Warsaw Mint, 250th Anniv. — A1627

*Perf. 11½x11¾ Syncopated*

**2016, Jan. 21 Litho.**

**4212** A1627 2.35z brnz & dark brn 1.25 .60

First Successful Kidney Transplant in Poland, 50th Anniv. A1628

*Perf. 11¼x11½*

**2016, Jan. 22 Photo.**

**4213** A1628 1.75z multi .90 .45

National Day of Remembrance A1629

*Perf. 11½x11¾*

**2016, Feb. 28 Photo.**

**4214** A1629 A multi 1.00 .50

No. 4214 sold for 2z on day of issue.

Easter — A1630

Easter eggs: 2z, Pisanka huculska. 2.50z, Pisanka lemkowska. 6z, Pisanka lubelska.

**2016, Mar. 3 Photo.** ***Perf. 11¾x11½***

**4215-4217** A1630 Set of 3 5.75 2.75

Historic Photographs — A1631

No. 4218: a, Summer in Warsaw, by Jan Kosidowski, 1966. b, Construction of the Turow Power Plant, by Wieslaw Prazuch, 1961. c, Aleja Jerozolimskie Near Kruczej, Warsaw, by Kosidowski, 1963. d, May 1 Procession, Warsaw, by Prazuch, 1953.

*Perf. 11¾x11½ Syncopated*

**2016, Mar. 23 Litho.**

**4218** Vert. strip of 4 5.00 2.50
*a.-b.* A1631 2z Either single 1.10 .55
*c.-d.* A1631 2.50z Either single 1.40 .70

Souvenir Sheet

Bringing Christianity, by Jan Matejko — A1632

**Photo. & Engr.**

**2016, Mar. 30** ***Perf. 11½x11¼***

**4219** A1632 6z multi 3.25 1.60

Adoption of Christianity in Poland, 1050th anniv.

Extraordinary Jubilee Year of Mercy — A1633

**2016, Apr. 2 Photo.** ***Perf. 11½x11¾***

**4220** A1633 2.50z multi 1.40 .70

Souvenir Sheet

Legia Warszawa Soccer Team, Cent. — A1634

***Perf. 11½x11¼ Syncopated***

**2016, Apr. 20** **Litho.**
**4221** A1634 6z blk & gold 3.25 1.60

Europa A1635

**2016, May 9 Litho.** ***Perf. 11¾x11½***
**4222** A1635 5z multi 2.60 1.40

Think Green Issue.

World Youth Day, Cracow A1636

Designs: 2.50z, Pope Francis and youths. 6z, Pope Francis.

***Perf. 11¼x11½***

**2016, May 10** **Photo.**
**4223** A1636 2.50z multi 1.25 .65

**Souvenir Sheet**

**Photo. & Engr.**

***Perf. 11¼x11***

**4224** A1636 6z multi 3.00 1.50

No. 4224 contains one 54x41mm stamp. See Vatican City Nos. 1626-1627.

Souvenir Sheet

University of Warsaw, 200th Anniv. — A1637

***Perf. 11½ Syncopated***

**2016, May 13** **Litho.**
**4225** A1637 5z multi 2.60 1.40

Characters From "Reksio" Animated Films — A1638

No. 4226 — Chickens and: a, Reksio painting bird house. b, Reksio picking up eggs.

***Perf. 11¼x10¾***

**2016, May 20** **Photo.**
**4226** A1638 Pair 2.25 1.10
*a.* 2z multi 1.00 .50
*b.* 2.50z multi 1.25 .60

No. 4226 was printed in sheets containing two pairs.

Souvenir Sheet

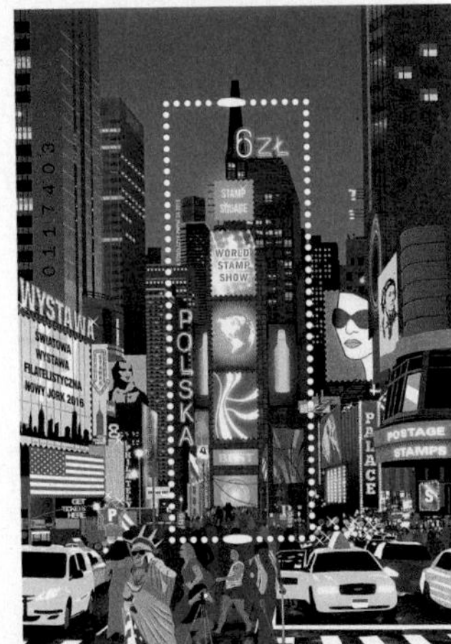

World Stamp Show 2016, New York — A1639

**Litho. & Silk-screened**

**2016, May 28** ***Perf. 11½ Syncopated***
**4227** A1639 6z multi 3.25 1.60

Family with Cat and Dog A1640

***Perf. 11¾x11½ Syncopated***

**2016, June 1** **Litho.**
**4228** A1640 3.70z multi 1.90 .95

Polish-German Youth Office, 25th Anniv. — A1641

***Perf. 11¾x11½ Syncopated***

**2016, June 2** **Litho.**
**4229** A1641 2.50z multi 1.25 .60

See Germany No. 2927.

Canonization of St. Stanislaus Papczynski (1631-1701) A1642

***Perf. 11½x11¼ Syncopated***

**2016, June 5** **Photo.**
**4230** A1642 3.70z multi 1.90 .95

Miniature Sheet

Clouds — A1643

No. 4231: a, Cumulonimbus capillatus praecipitatio arcus. b, Cirrus uncinus. c, Cumulonimbus mamma. d, Cumulonimbus capillatus.

***Perf. 11½x11¼ Syncopated***

**2016, June 15** **Litho.**
**4231** A1643 Sheet of 4 4.50 2.25
*a.-b.* 2z Either stamp 1.00 .50
*c.-d.* 2.50z Either stamp 1.25 .60

Jan Jessenius (1566-1621), Physician and Professor of Anatomy — A1644

**Photo. & Engr.**

**2016, June 22** ***Perf. 11***
**4232** A1644 6z multi + label 3.00 1.50

See Czech Republic No. 3677, Hungary No. 4393, Slovakia No. 743.

NATO Summit, Warsaw A1645

***Perf. 11¼x11½ Syncopated***

**2016, June 24** **Litho.**
**4233** A1645 5z multi 2.50 1.25

**Fruit and Flowers Type of 2009**

Design: 20g, Saffron crocus. 2z, Iris. 6z, Lily.

**2016** **Photo.** ***Perf. 11½x11¾***
**4234** A1425 20g multi .25 .25
**4235** A1425 2z multi 1.10 .55
**4236** A1425 6z multi 3.25 1.60

Issued: 20g, 7/6; 2z, 7/22; 6z, 7/15.

Miniature Sheet

2016 Summer Olympics, Rio de Janeiro — A1646

No. 4237: a, Sailboarding. b, Cycling. c, Discus. d, Women's tennis.

**2016, July 8 Photo.** ***Perf. 11¼x11½***
**4237** A1646 2z Sheet of 4, #a-d 4.25 2.10

Postcrossing — A1647

***Perf. 11½ Syncopated***

**2016, July 14** **Photo.**
**4238** A1647 5z multi 2.60 1.40

Bees and Jar of Honey A1648

***Perf. 11½ Syncopated***

**2016, July 18** **Litho. & Embossed**
**4239** A1648 5z multi 2.60 1.40

Gen. Wladyslaw Anders (1892-1970), and Soldiers in Anders' Army — A1649

***Perf. 11¼x11½ Syncopated***

**2016, July 21** **Litho.**
**4240** A1649 2.50z multi 1.40 .70

Depictions of the Virgin Mary A1650

Designs: 2.50z, Our Lady of Fraga. 3.70z, Our Lady of Zólkiewska. No. 4243, 6z, Our Lady of Bialokamienska. No. 4244, 6z, Our Lady, Queen of the Polish Crown (with flags).

**2016, Aug. 30 Photo.** ***Perf. 11x11¼***
**4241-4244** A1650 Set of 4 9.25 4.75

Endangered Fish — A1651

Designs: 2z, Rhodeus sericeus. 2.50z, Carassius carassius. 3.70z, Eupallasella percnurus. 6z, Acipenser oxyrinchus.

***Perf. 11½x11¼ Syncopated***

**2016, Aug. 31** **Litho.**

**4245-4248** A1651 Set of 4 7.25 3.75

Year of the Cichociemni (World War II Paratroopers) — A1652

**2016, Sept. 1** **Photo.** ***Perf. 11***

**4249** A1652 3.70z multi 1.90 .95

21st Assembly of Polish Philatelic Union, Ilawa A1653

***Perf. 11¼x11½ Syncopated***

**2016, Sept. 8** **Litho.**

**4250** A1653 2.50z multi 1.40 .70

No. 4250 was printed in sheets of 12 + 4 labels. Exists imperf.

Beatification of Father Wladyslaw Bukowinski (1904-74), Prisoner in Soviet Gulag — A1654

***Perf. 11½x11¾ Syncopated***

**2016, Sept. 11** **Litho.**

**4251** A1654 6z multi 3.25 1.60

No. 4251 was printed in sheets of 4.

Souvenir Sheet

Geralt of Rivia, Fictional Character From *The Witcher,* by Andrzej Sapkowski — A1655

***Perf. 11½x11¼***

**2016, Sept. 16** **Photo.**

**4252** A1655 6z multi 3.25 1.60

Polish Bible Society, 200th Anniv. — A1656

**2016, Oct. 3** **Photo.** ***Perf. 11½x11¼***

**4253** A1656 2.50z multi 1.40 .70

Our Lady of Perpetual Help — A1657

**2016, Oct. 5** **Photo.** ***Perf. 11½x11¼***

**4254** A1657 3.70z multi 1.90 .95

**Fruit and Flowers Type of 2009**

***Perf. 11½x11¾***

**2016, Oct. 20** **Photo.**

**4255** A1425 15g Vaccinium oxycoccus .25 .25

Lost Works of Art — A1658

No. 4256: a, Shepherd with a Whip in a Meadow, by Józef Chelmonski, 1892. b, Self-portrait, by Aleksander Gierymski, 1899 or 1900. c, Portrait of Wife, Olga, by Leon Chwistek, before 1933.

***Perf. 11½x11¼***

**2016, Oct. 24** **Photo.**

**4256** Vert. strip of 3 3.00 1.50

*a.-c.* A1658 2z Any single 1.00 .50

Miniature Sheet

Historians and Scientists — A1659

No. 4257: a, Aleksander Gieysztor (1916-99), medieval historian, and Royal Castle, Warsaw. b, Witold Kula (1916-88), historian, and balance. c, Gerard Labuda (1916-2010), medieval historian, and Ostrów Lednicki Church. d, Edmund Faustyn Biernacki (1866-1911), physician, and measuring tube, blood drop. e, Hilary Koprowski (1916-2013), virologist, and polio virus. f, Wladyslaw Kunicki-Goldfinger (1916-95), microbiologist, and bacteria.

**2016, Oct. 29** **Photo.** ***Perf. 11***

**4257** A1659 2.50z Sheet of 6, #a-f 7.75 4.00

**Stage and Film Stars Type of 2012**

Designs: 2z, Franciszek Brodniewicz (1892-1944). 2.50z, Elzbieta Barszczewska (1913-87). 6z, Tadeusz Fijewski (1911-78).

***Perf. 11½x11¾ Syncopated***

**2016, Oct. 31** **Litho.**

**4258-4260** A1512 Set of 3 5.50 2.75

*4260a* Souvenir sheet of 3, #4258-4260 5.50 2.75

Christmas — A1660

Icons: 2z, Annunciation. 6z, Holy Family.

***Perf. 11¾x11½***

**2016, Nov. 16** **Photo.**

**4261-4262** A1660 Set of 2 4.00 2.00

Radio Maryja, 25th Anniv. A1661

***Perf. 11¼x11½***

**2016, Nov. 25** **Photo.**

**4263** A1661 A multi .95 .50

No. 4263 sold for 2z on day of issue.

Polish Gold Medalists at 2016 Summer Olympics, Rio de Janeiro A1662

Designs: No. 4264, 2.50z, Anita Wlodarczyk, women's hammer throw. No. 4265, 2.50z, Natalia Madaj and Magdalena Fularczyk-Kozlowska, women's double sculls.

**2016, Nov. 28** **Photo.** ***Perf. 10¾x11***

**4264-4265** A1662 Set of 2 2.40 1.25

Rafal Wilk, 2016 Paralympics Handcycling Gold Medalist — A1663

**2016, Dec. 3** **Photo.** ***Perf. 11x10¾***

**4266** A1663 B multi 1.25 .60

No. 4266 sold for 2.50z on day of issue.

Vive Kielce, 2016 European Handball Federation Champions A1664

**2016, Dec. 9** **Photo.** ***Perf. 10¾x11***

**4267** A1664 3.70z multi 1.75 .90

Souvenir Sheet

1960 Syrena Sport Prototype Automobile — A1665

***Perf. 11¼x11½ Syncopated***

**2016, Dec. 30** **Litho.**

**4268** A1665 6z multi 3.00 1.50

Erwin Axer (1917-2012), Theater Director — A1666

***Perf. 11½x11 Syncopated***

**2017, Jan. 2** **Litho.**

**4269** A1666 2.50z multi 1.25 .60

Adoration of the Magi, by Santi di Tito — A1667

**2017, Jan. 6** **Photo.** ***Perf. 11½x11***

**4270** A1667 B multi 1.25 .60

Epiphany. No. 4270 sold for 2.50z on day of issue.

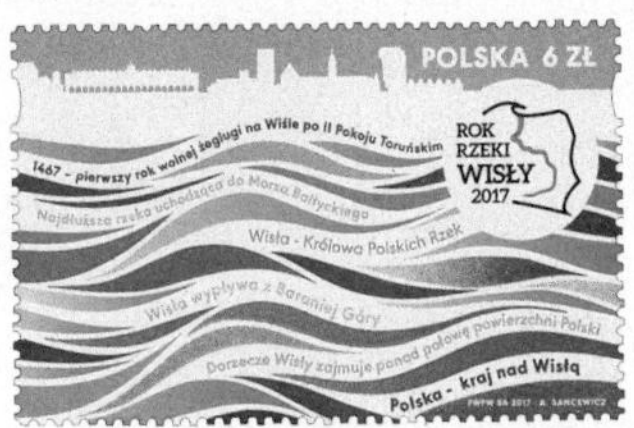
Year of the Vistula River — A1668

***Perf. 11½x11¼ Syncopated***
**Photo. & Silk-Screened**
**2017, Jan. 30**
**4271** A1668 6z multi 3.00 1.50

General Mariusz Zaruski (1867-1941), Yachtsman A1669

***Perf. 11½x11¾ Syncopated***
**2017, Jan. 31** **Litho.**
**4272** A1669 B multi 1.25 .60

No. 4272 sold for 2.50z on day of issue.

Tadeusz Kosciuszko (1746-1817), General — A1670

***Perf. 11¾x11½ Syncopated***
**2017, Feb. 4** **Litho.**
**4273** A1670 3.20z multi 1.60 .80

World Day of the Sick A1671

**2017, Feb. 11 Photo.** ***Perf. 11x11½***
**4274** A1671 5z multi 2.50 1.25

Protestant Reformation, 500th Anniv. — A1672

**2017, Feb. 28 Photo.** ***Perf. 11½x11***
**4275** A1672 3.20z multi 1.60 .80

Souvenir Sheet

Soldier's Gorgets — A1673

No. 4276 — Gorget depicting: a, Black Madonna above eagle, belonging to Franciszek Majewski. b, Black Madonna on eagle with motto, belonging to Mieczyslaw Dziemieszkiewicz.

***Perf. 11¼ Syncopated***
**2017, Mar. 1 Litho. & Embossed**
**4276** A1673 6z Sheet of 2, #a-b, + 2 labels 6.00 3.00

Souvenir Sheet

Apparition of the Virgin Mary at Fatima, Portugal, Cent. — A1674

***Perf. 11½x12 Syncopated***
**2017, Mar. 12** **Litho.**
**4277** A1674 6.80z multi 3.50 1.75

See Luxembourg No. 1461, Portugal No. 3888, Slovakia No. 759.

Easter — A1675

Background color of egg: A, White. 6z, Black.

***Perf. 11¾x11½***
**2017, Mar. 15** **Photo.**
**4278-4279** A1675 Set of 2 4.50 2.25

No. 4278 sold for 2.60z on day of issue.

Lublin, 700th Anniv. A1676

***Perf. 11¼x11½***
**2017, Mar. 15** **Photo.**
**4280** A1676 2.60z multi 1.40 .70

Souvenir Sheet

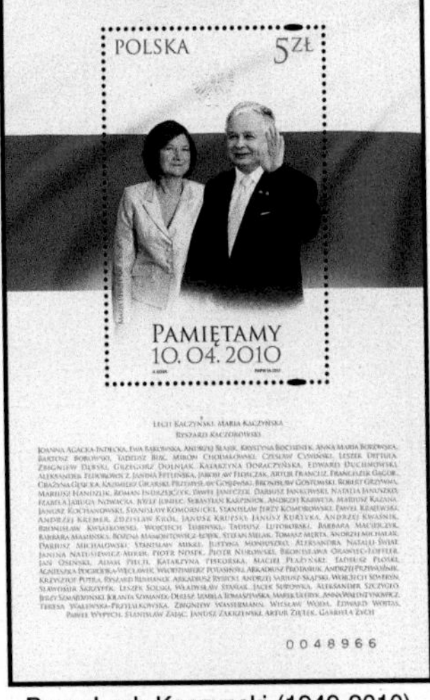
Pres. Lech Kaczynski (1949-2010), and Wife, Maria (1942-2010) — A1677

***Perf. 11¼ Syncopated***
**2017, Apr. 10 Litho. & Embossed**
**4281** A1677 5z multi 2.60 1.40

Europa A1678

***Perf. 11½x11¼ Syncopated***
**2017, May 5** **Litho.**
**4282** A1678 5z multi 2.75 1.40

Wladyslaw Reymont (1867-1925), Writer — A1679

**2017, May 7 Photo.** ***Perf. 11¼x11½***
**4283** A1679 2.60z multi 1.40 .70

Souvenir Sheet

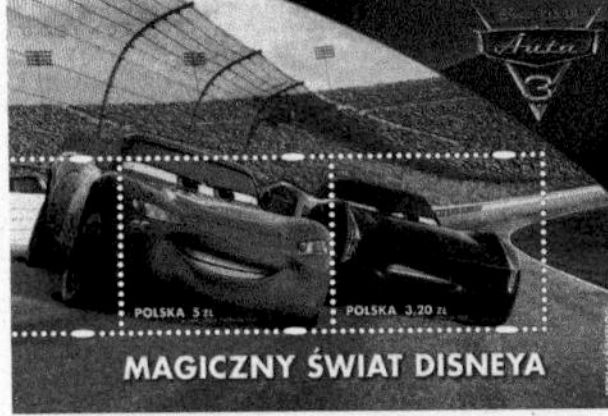
Characters from *Cars 3* Animated Film — A1680

No. 4284: a, 3.20z, Jackson Storm. b, 5z, Lightning McQueen.

***Perf. 11x11½ Syncopated***
**Litho. & Silk-Screened**
**2017, May 30**
**4284** A1680 Sheet of 2 4.50 2.25
*a.* 3.20z multi 1.75 .85
*b.* 5z multi 2.75 1.40

Lieutenant General Józef Haller (1873-1960), Creator of Blue Army — A1681

***Perf. 11½x11¾ Syncopated***
**2017, May 31** **Litho.**
**4285** A1681 2.60z multi 1.40 .70

Blue Army, cent.

Franciszek Stefczyk (1861-1924), Founder of Savings and Loan Cooperatives A1682

**2017, June 8 Photo.** ***Perf. 11½x11***
**4286** A1682 2.60z multi 1.40 .70

10th World Games, Wroclaw A1683

***Perf. 11x11½ Syncopated***
**2017, June 9** **Litho.**
**4287** A1683 5z multi 2.75 1.40

Expo 2017, Astana, Kazakhstan A1684

***Perf. 11½x11¼ Syncopated***
**2017, June 16** **Litho.**
**4288** A1684 2.60z multi 1.40 .70

No. 4288 was printed in sheets of 12 + 4 central labels.

St. Albert Chmielowski (1845-1916), Founder of Servants of the Poor — A1685

***Perf. 11½ Syncopated***
**2017, June 17** **Litho.**
**4289** A1685 2.60z multi 1.40 .70

St. Albert Chmielowski Year. Values are for stamps with surrounding selvage.

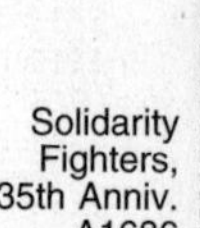
Solidarity Fighters, 35th Anniv. A1686

***Perf. 11x11½ Syncopated***

**2017, June 20** **Litho.**

**4290** A1686 2.60z multi 1.40 .70

Souvenir Sheet

Rysy and Nearby Mountain Peaks — A1687

***Perf. 11¾x11½***

**2017, June 30** **Photo.**

**4291** A1687 6z multi 3.25 1.60

Arabian Horses Bred at Janów Podlaski Stud Farm — A1688

No. 4292: a, Algeria. b, Etruria. c, Pogrom. d, Pilarka. e, Pinga. f, Ecaho. g, Bandos. h, Pianissima. i, Bandola.

***Perf. 11¾x11½ Syncopated***

**2017, July 31** **Litho.**

| | | | |
|---|---|---|---|
| **4292** | Sheet of 9 | 13.50 | 6.75 |
| ***a.-i*** | A1688 2.60z Any single | 1.50 | .75 |

Souvenir Sheet

2017 Tall Ships Race, Szczecin — A1689

**2017, Aug. 5** **Photo.** ***Perf. 11¼x11½***

**4293** A1689 6z multi 3.50 1.75

A1690

A1691

A1692

2017 European Men's Volleyball Championships, Poland — A1693

***Perf. 11½ Syncopated***

**2017, Aug. 10** **Litho.**

| | | | |
|---|---|---|---|
| **4294** | Horiz. strip of 4 | 6.00 | 3.00 |
| ***a.*** | A1690 2.60z multi | 1.50 | .75 |
| ***b.*** | A1691 2.60z multi | 1.50 | .75 |
| ***c.*** | A1692 2.60z multi | 1.50 | .75 |
| ***d.*** | A1693 2.60z multi | 1.50 | .75 |

Printed in sheets containing two strips.

Coronation of Icon of Our Lady of Lichen, 50th Anniv. — A1694

***Perf. 11½x11¾***

**2017, Aug. 12** **Photo.**

**4295** A1694 2.60z multi 1.50 .75

Coronation of Icon of Our Lady of Czestochowa, 300th Anniv. — A1695

***Perf. 11½x11¾***

**2017, Aug. 26** **Photo.**

**4296** A1695 2.60z multi 1.50 .75

Miniature Sheet

Herbs — A1696

No. 4297: a, Centaurea cyanus. b, Matricaria chamomilla. c, Achillea millefolium. d, Thymus serpyllum.

***Perf. 11¼ Syncopated***

**2017, Aug. 31** **Litho.**

**4297** A1696 2.60z Sheet of 4, #a-d 5.75 3.00

Ecstascy of Saint Francis, by El Greco — A1697

***Perf. 11½x11¼ Syncopated***

**2017, Sept. 2** **Photo.**

**4298** A1697 2.60z multi 1.50 .75

No. 4298 was printed in sheets of 8 + central label.

Souvenir Sheet

Organ, Cathedral Basilica of the Assumption, Pelplin — A1698

***Perf. 11½x11¼ Syncopated***

**2017, Sept. 16** **Litho. & Engr.**

**4299** A1698 11z multi 6.00 3.00

Knotted Rope — A1699

***Perf. 11¾x11½***

**2017, Sept. 29** **Photo.**

**4300** A1699 A multi 1.50 .75

1937-38 purge and execution of Poles by Soviet NKVD. No. 4300 sold for 2.60z on day of issue.

Our Lady of Piekary — A1700

***Perf. 11½x11¾***

**2017, Oct. 13** **Photo.**

**4301** A1700 5z multi 2.75 1.40

Knights of the Immaculata, Cent. — A1701

***Perf. 11½x11¼***

**2017, Oct. 14** **Photo.**

**4302** A1701 5z multi + label 2.75 1.40

Feliks Selmanowicz (1904-46), Anti-Communist Soldier Executed by Communists A1702

***Perf. 11½ Syncopated***

**2017, Oct. 18** **Litho.**

**4303** A1702 3.20z multi 1.75 .90

Souvenir Sheet

Children's Art on Theme of Health — A1703

No. 4304: a, Girl and horse, by Ariadna Kruszy. b, Girl and bird, by Kamila Rylska. c, Clock and bicycle, by Sandra Marwitz.

***Perf. 11½x11¼ Syncopated***

**2017, Oct. 25** **Litho.**

**4304** A1703 2.60z Sheet of 3, #a-c 4.50 2.25

Miniature Sheet

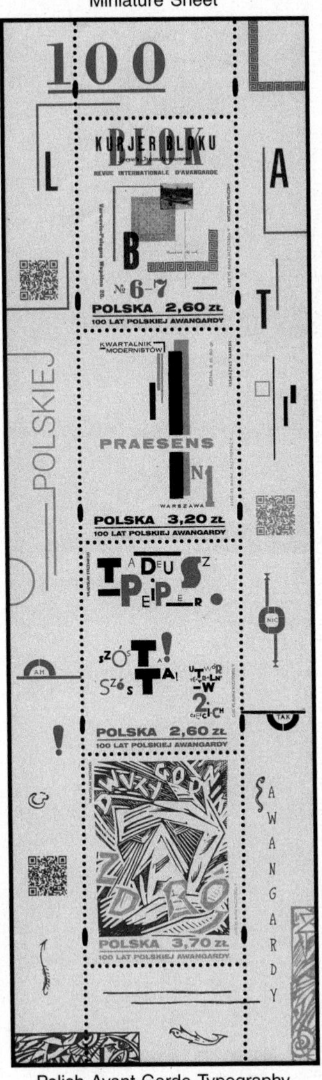

Polish Avant-Garde Typography, Cent. — A1704

No. 4305: a, Cover of *Kurier Blok* magazine, by Mieczyslaw Szczuka. b, Cover of sheet music for song *Szósta! Szósta!* by Wladyslaw Strzeminski. c, Cover of *Praesens* journal, by Henryk Stazewski. d, Cover of *Zdrój* magazine, by Wladyslaw Skotarek.

***Perf. 11¼x11½ Syncopated***

**2017, Oct. 27** **Litho.**

**4305** A1704 Sheet of 4 6.75 3.50
*a.-b.* 2.60z Either single 1.50 .75
*c.* 3.20z multi 1.75 .90
*d.* 3.70z multi 2.00 1.00

**Stage and Film Stars Type of 2012**

Designs: 2.60z, Mieczyslaw Cybulski (1903-84). 3.20z, Ina Benita (1912-44). 3.70z, Kazimierz Junosza-Stepowski (1880-1943).

***Perf. 11½x11¾ Syncopated***

**2017, Oct. 30** **Litho.**

**4306-4308** A1512 Set of 3 5.25 2.60
*4308a* Souvenir sheet of 3, #4306-4308 5.25 2.60

Badge of 22nd Artillery Supply Company of the Second Polish Corps Depicting Wojtek the Bear — A1705

***Perf. 11½x11¼***

**2017, Oct. 31** **Photo.**

**4309** A1705 A multi 1.50 .75

No. 4309 sold for 2.60z on day of issue.

Croissant, Walnuts and Poppies — A1706

***Perf. 11½ Syncopated***

**2017, Nov. 3** **Litho. & Embossed**

**4310** A1706 5z multi 3.00 1.50

Marie Sklodowska-Curie (1867-1934), 1903 Nobel Laureate in Physics and 1911 Nobel Laureate in Chemistry A1707

***Perf. 11½x11¾ Syncopated***

**2017, Nov. 7** **Litho.**

**4311** A1707 6z multi 3.50 1.75

No. 4311 was printed in sheets of 8 + central label.

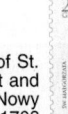

Statue of St. Margaret and Town Hall, Nowy Sacz — A1708

**2017, Nov. 8** **Photo.** ***Perf. 11½x11¼***

**4312** A1708 20g multi .25 .25

Christmas — A1709

Illustrations from the Olbracht Missal: A, Madonna and Child. B, Adoration of the Magi. 6z, Annunciation.

***Perf. 11¾x11½***

**2017, Nov. 16** **Photo.**

**4313-4315** A1709 Set of 3 6.75 3.50

On day of issue, No. 4313 sold for 2.60z, and No. 4314 sold for 3.20z.

Snowflake A1710

***Perf. 11½x11¾ Syncopated***

**2017, Nov. 18** **Litho.**

**4316** A1710 2.60z multi 1.50 .75

Gold medal by ski jumping team of Maciej Kot, Dawid Kubacki, Kamil Stoch and Piotr Zyla at 2017 Nordic World Skiing Championships, Lahti, Finland.

Jarek Smietana (1951-2013), Jazz Guitarist and Composer — A1711

***Perf. 11¾x11½ Syncopated***

**2017, Nov. 27** **Litho.**

**4317** A1711 2.60z multi 1.50 .75

Miniature Sheet

Owls — A1712

No. 4318 — Face of: a, Bubo scandiacus. b, Athene noctua. c, Surnia ulula. d, Asio otus.

***Perf. 11¾x11½ Syncopated***

**2017, Nov. 30** **Litho. & Embossed**

**4318** A1712 5z Sheet of 4, #a-d, + 4 labels 11.50 5.75

Souvenir Sheet

1516 Bookplate — A1713

***Perf. 11½x11¼ Syncopated***

**2017, Dec. 3** **Litho.**

**4319** A1713 6z multi 3.50 1.75

Marshal Józef Pilsudski (1867-1935) — A1714

**Photo. & Engr.**

**2017, Dec. 5** ***Perf. 10¾x11***

**4320** A1714 10z gold & multi 5.75 3.00

Gen. Wladylaw Anders (1892-1970), and His Soldiers in Kazakhstan — A1715

***Perf. 11¼x11½ Syncopated***

**2017, Dec. 6** **Litho.**

**4321** A1715 5z multi 3.00 1.50

See Kazakhstan No. 839.

Nine Coal Miners Massacred in 1981 Wujek Mine Strike — A1716

***Perf. 11¾x11½***

**2017, Dec. 16** **Photo.**

**4322** A1716 2.60z multi 1.50 .75

Supreme Court, Cent. — A1717

***Perf. 11½x11¼***

**2017, Dec. 29** **Photo.**

**4323** A1717 3.70z multi 2.25 1.10

Poland's 2018-19 Term on United Nations Security Council A1718

***Perf. 11¼x11½***

**2017, Dec. 29** **Photo.**

**4324** A1718 3.70z multi 2.25 1.10

Sign at Entrance to Auschwitz Concentration Camp — A1719

***Perf. 11¼x11½ Syncopated***

**2018, Jan. 27** **Litho.**

**4325** A1719 2.60z black & red 1.60 .80

2018 Winter Olympics, PyeongChang, South Korea — A1720

*Perf. 11½x11 Syncopated*

**2018, Feb. 1** **Litho.**
**4326** A1720 5.20z multi 3.25 1.60

Perforate and imperforate souvenir sheets of 1 of No. 4326 with the denomination obliterated were given to members of the Polish Philatelic Union.

Virgin Mary, Teacher of Youth — A1721

*Perf. 11½ Syncopated*

**2018, Feb. 24** **Litho.**
**4327** A1721 2.60z multi 1.50 .75

2018 Winter Paralympics, PyeongChang, South Korea — A1722

**2018, Mar. 1** **Photo.** ***Perf. 11x10¾***
**4328** A1722 5.20z multi 3.00 1.50

Souvenir Sheet

Soldier's Gorgets — A1723

No. 4329 — Gorget depicing: a, Black Madonna and eagle, belonging to Witold Pilecki. b, Black Madonna and eagle on banner with red cross, belonging to 5th Vilnius Brigade.

*Perf. 11¼ Syncopated*

**2018, Mar. 1** **Litho. & Embossed**
**4329** A1723 6z Sheet of 2, #a-b, + 2 labels 7.00 3.50

Easter — A1724

**2018, Mar. 6** **Photo.** ***Perf. 11¾x11½***
**4330** A1724 B multi 1.90 .95

No. 4330 sold for 3.20z on day of issue.

**Fruit and Flowers Type of 2009**

Designs: 25g, Narcissus jonquilla. 6.80z, Lily of the valley.

**2018** **Photo.** ***Perf. 11½x11¾***
**4331** A1425 25g multi .25 .25
**4332** A1425 6.80z multi 3.75 1.90

Issued: 25g, 3/9. 6.80z, 5/11.

Irena Sendler (1910-2008), Resistance Leader in World War II — A1725

**2018, Mar. 24** **Photo.** ***Perf. 11x11½***
**4333** A1725 2.60z multi 1.60 .80

Bar Confederation Soldier, Madonna and Child — A1726

*Perf. 11¾x11½*

**2018, Mar. 31** **Photo.**
**4334** A1726 1z multi .60 .30

Bar Confederation, 250th anniv.

Kamil Stoch, 2018 Winter Olympics Gold Medalist Ski Jumper — A1727

*Perf. 11½x11¾*

**2018, Apr. 14** **Photo.**
**4335** A1727 3.70z multi 2.10 1.10

Photographs by Ignacy Krieger (1817-89) A1728

No. 4336 — Photograph of: a, Krieger. b, Man from Szaflary holding boots. c, Boy carrying bagels. d, Chimney sweeps.

*Perf. 11½ Syncopated*

**2018, Apr. 24** **Litho.**
**4336** Block or horiz. strip of 4 6.00 3.00
*a.-d.* A1728 2.60z Any single 1.50 .75

Map of Poland in Ribbon — A1729

**2018, May 2** **Photo.** ***Perf. 11¾x11½***
**4337** A1729 A multi 1.40 .70

No. 4337 sold for 2.60z on day of issue.

Tczew Bridge — A1730

*Perf. 11½x11 Syncopated*

**2018, May 2** **Litho.**
**4338** A1730 5z multi 2.75 1.40

Europa.

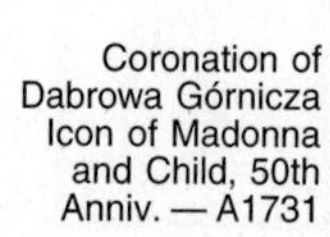


Coronation of Dabrowa Górnicza Icon of Madonna and Child, 50th Anniv. — A1731

*Perf. 11¾x11½*

**2018, May 19** **Photo.**
**4339** A1731 B multi 1.75 .85

No. 4339 sold for 3.20z on day of issue.

Souvenir Sheet

*Prosze Slonia* (Please, Elephant) Animated Film Series, 50th Anniv. — A1732

No. 4340: a, 2.60z, Boy on elephant. b, 3.20z, Boy, parents and sofa on elephant.

*Perf. 11½ Syncopated*

**2018, May 30** **Litho.**
**4340** A1732 Sheet of 2, #a-b 3.25 1.60

Souvenir Sheet

Pipe Organ, St. Mary's Church, Gdansk — A1733

*Perf. 11½x11 Syncopated*

**2018, June 3** **Litho. & Embossed**
**4341** A1733 6.80z multi 3.75 1.90

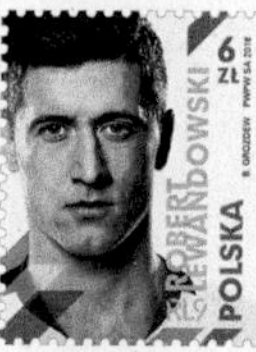


Robert Lewandowski, Captain of 2018 Polish National Soccer Team — A1734

*Perf. 11¾x11½*

**2018, June 14** **Photo.**
**4342** A1734 6z multi 3.25 1.60

St. Pio of Pietrelcina (1887-1968) A1735

**2018, June 16** **Photo.** ***Perf. 11½x11***
**4343** A1735 2.60z multi 1.40 .70

Bishop Jordan, First Bishop of Poland, and Poznan Cathedral A1736

**2018, June 22** **Photo.** ***Perf. 10¾x11***
**4344** A1736 A multi 1.40 .70

Poznan Bishopric, 1050th anniv. No. 4344 sold for 2.60z on day of issue.

Statue and Zywiec Castle, Zywiec — A1737

*Perf. 11½x11¾*

**2018, June 22** **Photo.**
**4345** A1737 10z multi 5.25 2.60

St. Dorothea of Montau (1347-94) A1738

**2018, Juno 24** **Photo.** ***Perf. 11½x11***
**4346** A1738 2.60z multi 1.40 .70

Polish-Lithuanian Commonwealth, 550th Anniv. — A1739

*Perf. 11½ Syncopated*

**2018, June 27** **Litho.**
**4347** A1739 3.20z multi 1.75 .85

Tourist Attractions — A1740

No. 4348: a, 2.60z, Weimar Chamber, Wieliczka Salt Mines. b, 5.20z, Baltic Sea coast.

*Perf. 11¼ Syncopated*

**2018, July 23** **Litho.**
**4348** A1740 Pair, #a-b 4.25 2.10

Coronation of Our Lady of Trakai, 300th Anniv. — A1741

**2018, July 27 Photo.** ***Perf. 11x11¼***
**4349** A1741 3.20z multi + label 1.75 .85

No. 4349 was printed in sheets of 2 + 2 labels.

Gen. Wladyslaw Sikorski (1881-1943) A1742

***Perf. 11¼x11¾ Syncopated***
**2018, July 28 Litho.**
**4350** A1742 2.60z multi 1.50 .75

Lisiecka Sausage A1743

***Perf. 11¾x11½ Syncopated***
**2018, July 30 Litho. & Embossed**
**4351** A1743 6z multi 3.25 1.60

Coronation of Our Lady of Swieta Lipka, 50th Anniv. — A1744

***Perf. 11½x11¼***
**2018, Aug. 11 Photo.**
**4352** A1744 2.60z gold & multi 1.40 .70

St. Stanislaw Kostka (1550-68) A1745

***Perf. 11¼x11½***
**2018, Aug. 19 Photo.**
**4353** A1745 2.60z gold & multi 1.40 .70

Icons A1746

Designs: No. 4354, 2.60z, Our Lady of Zbaraski icon (black panels). No. 4355, 2.60z, Our Lady Queen of the Polish Crown from Kalusz (blue panels). No. 4356, 2.60z, Our Lady of Lutsk (gray panels). No. 4357, 2.60z, Our Lady, Queen of the Polish Crown from Porchowa, Ukraine (red panels).

**2018, Aug. 23 Photo.** ***Perf. 11***
**4354-4357** A1746 Set of 4 5.75 2.75

Roundhouse, Kedzierzyn-Kozle, Cent. — A1747

No. 4358: a, 2.60z, TKt48 locomotive. b, 3.20z, Ty42 locomotive.

***Perf. 11¾x11½ Syncopated***
**2018, Aug. 31 Litho.**
**4358** A1747 Horiz. pair, #a-b 3.25 1.60

Botanical Garden of the University of Warsaw, 200th Anniv. — A1748

***Perf. 11¼x11 Syncopated***
**2018, Sept. 10 Litho.**
**4359** A1748 3.20z multi 1.75 .85

No. 4359 was printed in sheets of 8 + central label.

World Congress of the Polish Diaspora and Poles Abroad, Warsaw A1749

***Perf. 11¼x11½ Syncopated***
**2018, Sept. 20 Litho.**
**4360** A1749 2.60z multi 1.40 .70

Waclaw Sieroszewski (1858-1945), Writer Exiled to Siberia — A1750

**2018, Sept. 24 Photo.** ***Perf. 11x11½***
**4361** A1750 5.20z multi 3.00 1.50

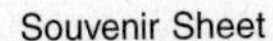

Souvenir Sheet

Children's Art — A1751

No. 4362 — Winning designs in children's art contest on theme of saving the climate: a, Necessary Changes, by Oliwia Gola (green denomination). b, To Rescue our Planet, by Benjamin Czajkowski (red denomination). c, Fight Against Smog, by Natalia Gaska (blue denomination).

***Perf. 11¼ Syncopated***
**2018, Sept. 26 Litho.**
**4362** A1751 2.60z Sheet of 3, #a-c 4.25 2.10

Beetles — A1752

Designs: No. 4363, 3.20z, Oryctes nasicornis. No. 4364, 3.20z, Cucujus cinnaberinus.

***Perf. 11¼ Syncopated***
**2018, Sept. 28 Litho.**
**4363-4364** A1752 Set of 2 3.50 1.75

Nos. 4363-4364 were each printed in sheets of 8 + label.

Father Idzi Radziszewski (1871-1922), Founder of Catholic University of Lublin — A1753

**2018, Oct. 1 Photo.** ***Perf. 11½x11¼***
**4365** A1753 2.60z multi 1.40 .70

Catholic University of Lublin, cent.

Planned Via Carpathia Highway — A1754

**2018, Oct. 3 Photo.** ***Perf. 11¾x11½***
**4366** A1754 20g multi .25 .25

Town Hall Clock, Poznan — A1755

***Perf. 11½ Syncopated***
**2018, Oct. 3 Litho.**
**4367** A1755 2.60z gold & multi 1.40 .70

National Philatelic Exhibition, Poznan. No. 4367 was printed in sheets of 12 + 4 labels.

Election of Cardinal Karol Wojtyla as Pope, 40th Anniv. — A1756

***Perf. 11½x11¼ Syncopated***
**2018, Oct. 16 Litho.**
**4368** A1756 3.20z gold & multi 1.75 .85

Souvenir Sheet

Polish Postal Service, 460th Anniv. — A1757

***Perf. 11½x11 Syncopated***
**2018, Oct. 18 Engr.**
**4369** A1757 10z gold & multi 5.25 2.60

Cardinal August Hlond (1881-1948) A1758

***Perf. 11¾x11½***
**2018, Oct. 22 Photo.**
**4370** A1758 5z multi 2.75 1.40

**Stage and Film Stars Type of 2012**

Designs: No. 4371, 2.60z, Stefan Jaracz (1883-1945). No. 4372, 2.60z, Adam Brodzisz (1906-86). 3.20z, Maria Bogda (1909-81).

***Perf. 11½x11¾ Syncopated***
**2018, Oct. 31 Photo.**
**4371-4373** A1512 Set of 3 4.50 2.25
*4373a* Souvenir sheet of 3, #4371-4373 4.50 2.25

Lost Works of Art A1759

No. 4374: a, 2.60z, View of Zamosc, by Marcin Zaleski. b, 2.60z, Solec Harbor, by Aleksander Gierymski. c, 3.20z, View of Kraków, by Julian Falat.

***Perf. 11¼x11½***

**2018, Oct. 31** **Photo.**

**4374** A1759 Vert. strip of 3, #a-c 4.50 2.25

Brühl Palace, Warsaw A1760

***Perf. 11¼x11½***

**2018, Oct. 31** **Photo.**

**4375** A1760 2.60z multi 1.40 .70

Polish Foreign Service, cent.

Fireworks and Flags of Israel and Poland A1761

**2018, Nov. 5** **Litho.** ***Perf. 13x13¼***

**4376** A1761 2.60z multi 1.40 .70

Independence of Israel, 70th anniv.; and of Poland, cent. See Israel No. 2201.

End of World War I, Cent. A1762

***Perf. 11¼ Syncopated***

**2018, Nov. 11** **Litho.**

**4377** A1762 2.60z multi 1.40 .70

Miniature Sheet

First Days of Polish Independence — A1763

No. 4378: a, Nine Silesian insurgents. b, Marshal Edward Rydz-Smigly (1886-1941), vert. c, Major General Franciszek Ksawery Latinik (1864-1949), vert. d, Officers of the First Polish Guard Czeslaw Zajaczkowski, Wilhelm Stec and Jan Gawron in Kraków, vert. e, Seven soldiers guarding Lwów.

***Die Cut Perf. 11½x11¾, 11¾x11½***

**2018, Nov. 11** **Litho.**

**Self-Adhesive**

**4378** A1763 2.60z Sheet of 5, #a-e 7.00 3.50

Miniature Sheet

Independence, Cent. — A1764

No. 4379: a, Ignacy Jan Paderewski (1860-1941), prime minister and pianist. b, Marshal Józef Pilsudski (1867-1935), prime minister and military leader. c, Roman Dmowski (1864-1939), politician. d, Order of the Rebirth of Poland. e, Mother of God, Hetman of the Polish Soldier icon. f, Wincenty Witos (1874-1945), prime minister. g, Ignacy Daszynski (1866-1936), prime minister. h, Wojciech Korfanty (1873-1939), deputy prime minister.

**Litho., Litho. With Hologram Affixed on Central Label**

***Perf. 11½ Syncopated***

**2018, Nov. 11**

**4379** A1764 2.60z Sheet of 8, #a-h, + central label 11.00 5.50

Miniature Sheet

Armed Forces of Re-established Republic of Poland, Cent. — A1765

No. 4380 — Members of: a, Army (54x27mm). b, Horse cavalry (54x27mm). c, Navy (54x27mm). d, Air Force (54x27mm). e, Modern armed forces (108x27mm)

**2018, Nov. 11** **Photo.** ***Perf. 11x11¼***

**4380** A1765 2.60z Sheet of 5, #a-e 7.00 3.50

Miniature Sheet

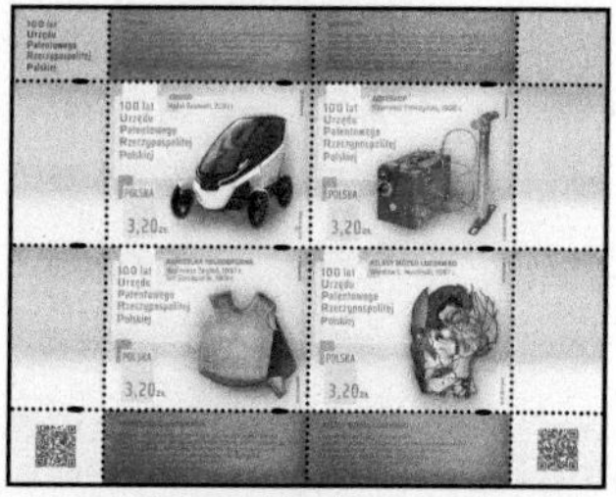

Items Patented by Patent Office of Republic of Poland — A1766

No. 4381: a, Triggo electric vehicle. b, Aeroscope compressed air camera. c, Bulletproof vest. d, Atlas of the human brain.

***Perf. 11½x11 Syncopated***

**2018, Nov. 26** **Litho.**

**4381** A1766 3.20z Sheet of 4, #a-d 7.00 3.50

Patent Office of the Republic of Poland, cent.

Jedrzej Sniadecki (1768-1838), Chemist and Writer — A1767

***Perf. 11¼x11½***

**2018, Nov. 30** **Photo.**

**4382** A1767 2.60z gold & multi 1.40 .70

Ernest Malinowski (1818-99), Constructor of Peruvian Railroad A1768

***Perf. 11½x11¾ Syncopated***

**2018, Dec. 10** **Litho.**

**4383** A1768 5.20z multi 2.75 1.40

Polish Industrial Design — A1769

No. 4384: a, Figurine of sitting girl, by Henryk Jedrasiak. b, RM58 chair, by Roman Modzelewski.

***Perf. 11¼ Syncopated***

**2018, Dec. 21** **Litho.**

**4384** A1769 2.60z Pair, #a-b 2.75 1.40

Printed in sheets of 4 containing two each of Nos. 4384a-4384b.

Greater Poland Uprising, Cent. — A1770

***Perf. 11½x11¾ Syncopated***

**2018, Dec. 27** **Litho.**

**4385** A1770 2.60z gold & multi 1.40 .70

Printed in sheets of 8 + central label.

Adult and Juvenile Animals A1771

Designs: No. 4386, 1.30z, Rhinocerso unicornis. No. 4387, 1.30z, Pan troglodytes. No. 4388, 3z, Choloepus didactylus. No. 4389, 3z, Giraffa camelopardalis.

***Perf. 11½x11¾ Syncopated***

**Litho. & Silk-Screened**

**2018, Dec. 28**

**4386-4389** A1771 Set of 4 4.50 2.25

Nos. 4386-4389 were each printed in sheets of 12 + 4 labels.

Miniature Sheet

2018 World Champion Polish Men's Volleyball Team — A1772

No. 4390: a, Piotr Nowakowski. b, Dawid Konarski. c, Bartosz Kurek. d, Artur Szalpuk. e, Damian Schulz. f, Damian Wojtaszek. g, Fabian Drzyzga. h, Grzegorz Lomacz. i, Michal Kubiak. j. Aleksander Sliwka. k, Jakub Kochanowski. l, Pawel Zatorski. m, Bartosz Kwolek. n, Mateusz Bieniek. o, Vital Heynen, trainer. p, Trophy and gold medal.

***Perf. 11½x11¾ Syncopated***

**2018, Dec. 28** **Litho.**

**4390** A1772 1z Sheet of 16, #a-p, + 4 labels 8.50 4.25

Self-portrait of Stanislaw Wyspianski (1869-1907), Painter and Poet — A1773

**2019, Jan. 15** **Photo.** ***Perf. 11½x11***

**4391** A1773 3.20z gold & multi 1.75 .85

Polish Red Cross, Cent. — A1774

*Perf. 11½x11¼ Syncopated*

**2019, Jan. 18** **Litho.**
**4392** A1774 3.20z multi 1.75 .85

Souvenir Sheet

Pres. Ignacy Jan Paderewski (1860-1941) — A1775

*Perf. 11¼x11½ Syncopated*

**2019, Jan. 25** **Litho. & Engr.**
**4393** A1775 14.50z multi 7.75 4.00

Polish Security Printing Works, cent.

LOT Polish Airlines, 90th Anniv. — A1776

*Perf. 11½x11¾ Syncopated*

**2019, Jan. 31** **Litho.**
**4394** A1776 5.20z multi 2.75 1.40

Archbishop Achille Ratti (Later Pope Pius XI, 1857-1939) and Archbishop Stanislaw Galla (1865-1942) — A1777

**2019, Feb. 5** **Photo.** ***Perf. 11x11½***
**4395** A1777 2.60z gold & multi 1.40 .70

Military Ordinariate of Poland, cent.

PKO Bank Polski, Cent. — A1778

**2019, Feb. 7** **Photo.** ***Perf. 11½x11***
**4396** A1778 3.20z sil & multi 1.75 .85

State Archives Network, Cent. — A1779

**2019, Feb. 7** **Photo.** ***Perf. 11½x11***
**4397** A1779 3.20z sil & multi 1.75 .85

Supreme Audit Office, Cent. A1780

*Perf. 11½ Syncopated*

**2019, Feb. 7** **Litho.**
**4398** A1780 5z sil & multi 2.60 1.40

No. 4398 was printed in sheets of 8 + central label.

Polish Prison Service, Cent. A1781

**2019, Feb. 8** **Photo.** ***Perf. 11x11½***
**4399** A1781 2.60z gold & multi 1.40 .70

Wojciech Trampczynski (1860-1953), First Marshal of Sejm — A1782

*Perf. 11½x11 Syncopated*

**2019, Feb. 8** **Litho.**
**4400** A1782 5z multi 2.60 1.40

Sejm, cent.

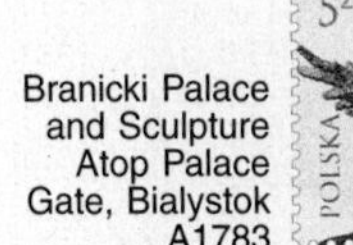

Branicki Palace and Sculpture Atop Palace Gate, Bialystok A1783

*Perf. 11½x11¾*

**2019, Feb. 19** **Photo.**
**4401** A1783 5z multi 2.60 1.40

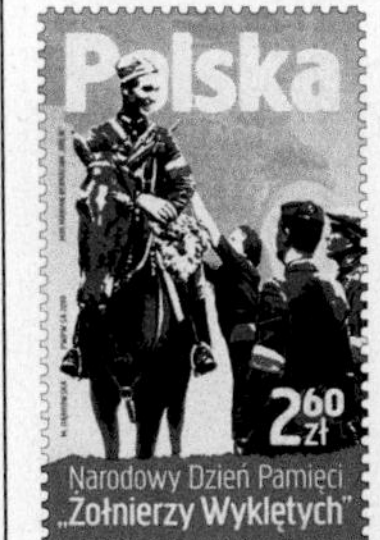

Major Marian Bernaciak (1917-46), Leader of Polish Anti-Communist Forces, and People of Ryki — A1784

**2019, Mar. 1** **Photo.** ***Perf. 11½x11¾***
**4402** A1784 2.60z sil & multi 1.40 .70

Remembrance of the "Cursed Soldiers" (anti-Communist forces).

2019 Summer Special Olympics, Abu Dhabi A1785

*Perf. 11½ Syncopated*

**2019, Mar. 7** **Litho.**
**4403** A1785 2.60z multi 1.40 .70

Easter

A1786 A1787

*Perf. 11¾x11½*

**2019, Mar. 18** **Photo.**
**4404** A1786 A gold & multi 1.75 .85
**4405** A1787 6z gold & multi 3.25 1.60

No. 4404 sold for 3.20z on day of issue.

Nazi Execution of Family of Józef (1900-44) and Wiktoria Ulma (1912-44) for Hiding Jews, 75th Anniv. A1788

*Perf. 11x11½ Syncopated*

**2019, Mar. 24** **Litho.**
**4406** A1788 3.30z multi 1.75 .85

No. 4406 was printed in sheets of 8 + central label.

End of Independence Cruise of the Dar Mlodziedzy — A1789

*Perf. 11¼ Syncopated*

**2019, Mar. 28** **Litho.**
**4407** A1789 3.30z multi 1.75 .85

Marshal Józef Pilsudski (1867-1935) and Pope Benedict XV (1854-1922) A1790

*Perf. 11x11½ Syncopated*

**2019, Mar. 29** **Litho.**
**4408** A1790 5z gold & multi 2.60 1.40

Diplomatic relations between Poland and Vatican City, cent. See Vatican City No. 1715.

Souvenir Sheet

Diplomatic Relations Between Poland and France, Cent. — A1791

No. 4409: a, Charles de Gaulle (1890-1970), French army captain, later president of France. b, Józef Haller (1873-1960), Polish lieutenant general.

*Perf. 11½ Syncopated*

**2019, Apr. 2** **Litho.**
**4409** A1791 5z Sheet of 2, #a-b 5.25 2.60

See France No. 5638.

Sokol Gymnastic Society, Cent. — A1792

**2019, Apr. 17** **Photo.** ***Perf. 11½x11***
**4410** A1792 3.30z gold & multi 1.75 .85

Fringilla Coelebs A1793

*Perf. 11¼x11½ Syncopated*

**2019, Apr. 24** **Litho.**
**4411** A1793 5z multi 2.60 1.40

Europa.

St. Adalbert of Prague (956-97), Patron Saint of Poland A1794

**2019, Apr. 27** **Photo.** ***Perf. 11x11½***
**4412** A1794 3.30z multi 1.75 .85

Diplomatic Relations Between Poland and Greece, Cent. A1795

*Perf. 11x11½ Syncopated*

**2019, Apr. 30** **Litho.**
**4413** A1795 3.30z multi 1.75 .85

Miniature Sheet

Polish Landscapes — A1796

No. 4414: a, Fields and forests, Central Poland. b, Islands in Warta River Delta. c, Meadow near Tatra Mountains. d, Snow-covered forest in Bieszczady Mountains.

***Perf. 11x11½ Syncopated***

**2019, Apr. 30** **Litho.**

**4414** A1796 3.30z Sheet of 4, #a-d 7.00 3.50

Poland's Admission to the European Union, 15th Anniv. — A1797

***Perf. 11½x11 Syncopated***

**2019, May 1** **Litho.**

**4415** A1797 3.30z multi 1.75 .85

Stanislaw Moniuszko (1819-72), Composer A1798

**2019, May 5** **Photo.** ***Perf. 11½x11***

**4416** A1798 3.30z multi 1.75 .85

Sluzewiec Racetrack, Warsaw, 80th Anniv. A1799

***Perf. 11½ Syncopated***

**2019, May 5** **Litho.**

**4417** A1799 3.30z multi 1.75 .85

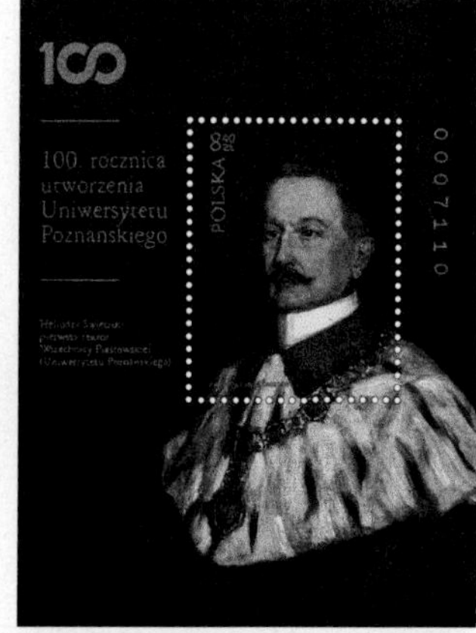

Heliodor Swiecicki (1854-1923), First Rector of Poznan University — A1800

**2019, May 7** **Photo.** ***Perf. 11½x11***

**4418** A1800 8.40z multi 4.50 2.25

Poznan University, cent.

Polish Olympic Committee, Cent. A1801

***Perf. 11x11½ Syncopated***

**2019, May 16** **Litho.**

**4419** A1801 4.10z multi 2.25 1.10

Royal Castle, Warsaw, 400th Anniv. — A1802

***Perf. 11¾x11½ Syncopated***

**2019, May 29** **Litho.**

**4420** A1802 3.30z multi 1.75 .85

Miniature Sheet

Buildings in Baku, Azerbaijan Designed by Polish Architects — A1803

No. 4421: a, Junior High School for Boys, by Konstanty Borysoglebski. b, City Council Building (with spire), by Józef Goslawski. c, Taghiyev School for Girls (with balcony), by Goslawski. d, House of Tigran Melikov (on street corner), by Goslawski. e, Haji Sultan Ali Mosque, by Józef Ploszko. f, Mukhtarov Palace, by Ploszko. g, House of Agabala Guliyev, by Eugeniusz Skibinski. h, Rothschild Office Building, by Kazimierz Skorewicz.

***Perf. 11¼x11½ Syncopated***

**2019, May 31** **Litho.**

**4421** A1803 3.30z Sheet of 8, #a-h 14.00 7.00

See Azerbaijan No. 1226.

Souvenir Sheet

First Pilgrimage to Poland by Pope John Paul II, 40th Anniv. — A1804

***Perf. 11½ Syncopated***

**2019, June 2** **Litho.**

**4422** A1804 8.40z multi 4.50 2.25

Marshal's Staff of Polish Senate — A1805

***Perf. 11½x11¾ Syncopated***

**2019, June 4** **Litho.**

**4423** A1805 5z multi 2.60 1.40

Re-establishment of the Polish Senate, and free elections, 30th anniv.

Beatification of 108 Polish Martyrs of World War II, 20th Anniv. — A1806

**2019, June 15** **Photo.** ***Perf. 10¾x11***

**4424** A1806 3.30z multi 1.75 .90

Painted Wooden Bird — A1807

***Perf. 11¾x11½***

**2019, June 19** **Photo.**

**4425** A1807 4.10z multi 2.25 1.10

Beskid Culture Week.

Souvenir Sheet

Organ From St. John the Baptist and St. John the Evangelist Cathedral, Torun — A1808

***Perf. 11½x11 Syncopated***

**2019, June 21** **Litho.**

**4426** A1808 6.60z multi 3.50 1.75

Anna Walentynowicz (1929-2010), Co-Founder of Solidarity Labor Union — A1809

***Perf. 11¾x11½***

**2019, June 24** **Photo.**

**4427** A1809 8.70z multi 4.75 2.40

Miniature Sheet

Clematis Varieties — A1810

No. 4428 — Clematis variety: a, General Sikorski (purple flowers). b, Cardinal Wyszynski (two magenta flowers). c, Solidarity (three red flowers). d, Marie Sklodowska-Curie (white flowers).

***Perf. 11½x11¾ Syncopated***

**2019, June 25** **Litho.**

**4428** A1810 3.30z Sheet of 4, #a-d 7.00 3.50

1877 Apparitions of the Virgin Mary in Gietrzwald
A1811

**2019, June 27 Photo.** ***Perf. 11½x11***
**4429** A1811 3.30z multi 1.75 .90

Teczynski Family Arms — A1812

**2019, June 28 Photo.** ***Perf. 11½x11***
**4430** A1812 3.30z multi 1.75 .90

Garlic
A1813

***Perf. 11½ Syncopated***
**2019, June 28 Litho. & Embossed**
**4431** A1813 6z multi 3.25 1.60

Souvenir Sheet

Union of Lublin, by Jan Matejko (1838-93) — A1814

**2019, July 1 Photo.** ***Perf. 11½x11***
**4432** A1814 8.40z multi 4.50 2.25

Union of Lublin, 450th anniv.

Souvenir Sheet

First Man on the Moon, 50th Anniv. — A1815

***Perf. 11½ Syncopated***
**2019, July 20 Litho.**
**4433** A1815 8.40z multi 4.50 2.25

Polish State Police, Cent. — A1816

**2019, July 24 Photo.** ***Perf. 11½x11***
**4434** A1816 3.30z multi 1.75 .85

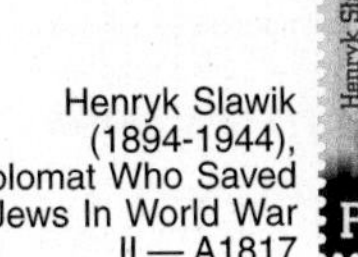

Henryk Slawik (1894-1944), Diplomat Who Saved Jews In World War II — A1817

***Perf. 11¾x11½***
**2019, July 26 Photo.**
**4435** A1817 4z multi 2.10 1.10

Polish Soccer Association, Cent. — A1818

***Perf. 11½ Syncopated***
**2019, July 30 Litho.**
**4436** A1818 4z multi 2.10 1.10

Souvenir Sheet

Zbigniew Scibor-Rylski (1917-2018), Brigadier General, and Warsaw Uprising Memorial Wall — A1819

***Perf. 11½ Syncopated***
**2019, Aug. 1 Litho.**
**4437** A1819 7.30z multi 3.75 1.90

Warsaw Uprising, 75th anniv.

Racers in Solidarity Street Run, Kolobrzeg Lighthouse — A1820

**2019, Aug. 2 Photo.** ***Perf. 11¾x11½***
**4438** A1820 30g multi .25 .25

Blessed Stefan Wincenty Frelichowski (1913-45), Priest Who Died at Dachau Concentration Camp — A1821

**2019, Aug. 8 Photo.** ***Perf. 11¾x11½***
**4439** A1821 6.30z multi 3.25 1.60

Kazimierz Deyna (1947-89), Soccer Player — A1822

***Perf. 11¾x11½***
**2019, Aug. 12 Photo.**
**4440** A1822 5.90z multi 3.00 1.50

Striking Coal Miners, Map of Silesia, and Alfons Zgrzebniok (1891-1937), Leader of Polish Forces in Silesian Uprisings A1823

***Perf. 11½ Syncopated***
**2019, Aug. 16 Litho.**
**4441** A1823 3.30z multi 1.75 .85

Central Road Administration, 200th Anniv. — A1824

***Perf. 11¼x11½***
**2019, Aug. 28 Photo.**
**4442** A1824 3.30z multi 1.75 .85

Jerzy Milian (1935-2018), Jazz Musician and Composer A1825

***Perf. 11½x11 Syncopated***
**2019, Aug. 30 Litho.**
**4443** A1825 3.30z multi 1.75 .85

Start of World War II, 80th Anniv. — A1826

**2019, Sept. 1 Photo.** ***Perf. 11x10¾***
**4444** A1826 3.30z multi 1.75 .85

Defense of the Gdansk Post Office, 80th Anniv. — A1827

***Perf. 11½ Syncopated***
**2019, Sept. 1 Litho.**
**4445** A1827 3.30z multi 1.75 .85

Confederation of Independent Poland Political Party, 40th Anniv. — A1828

***Perf. 11¼x11½***
**2019, Sept. 1 Photo.**
**4446** A1828 3.30z multi 1.75 .85

Zegrze Military Communications Training Center, Cent. — A1829

***Perf. 11½x11¾***
**2019, Sept. 12 Photo.**
**4447** A1829 3.30z multi 1.75 .85

Souvenir Sheet

Finance of Poland Anniversaries — A1830

No. 4448: a, Public financing, cent. ("100" from banknote). b, Budget, 250th anniv. (arms of King Stanislaw II Augustus). c, National Treasury Administration, cent. (emblem).

***Perf. 11x11½ Syncopated***
**2019, Sept. 20 Litho.**
**4448** A1830 3.30z Sheet of 3, #a-c 5.25 2.60

Polish Underground State, 80th Anniv. — A1831

***Perf. 11¼x11½***
**2019, Sept. 27 Photo.**
**4449** A1831 3.30z multi 1.75 .85

Souvenir Sheet

Children's Art — A1832

No. 4450: a, Ruddy Orchard, by Paulina Malarz. b, Beauty of the Orchard, by Karolina Rupik. c, Bee's Paradise, by Patryk Zielanski.

***Perf. 11½x11 Syncopated***

**2019, Sept. 27** **Litho.**

**4450** A1832 3.30z Sheet of 3, #a-c 5.25 2.60

Origami Stork on Japan Flag — A1833

***Perf. 11½x11 Syncopated***

**2019, Sept. 30** **Litho.**

**4451** A1833 3.30z multi 1.75 .85

Assistance for Polish orphans from Eastern Siberia by Fukudenkai Orphanage in Japan, cent.

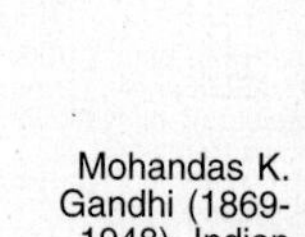

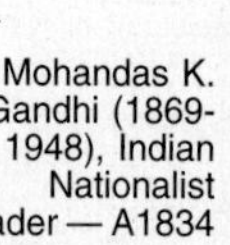

Mohandas K. Gandhi (1869-1948), Indian Nationalist Leader — A1834

***Perf. 11½x11¼***

**2019, Sept. 30** **Photo.**

**4452** A1834 3.30z multi 1.75 .85

Memorial to Victims of Piasnica Massacre — A1835

**2019, Oct. 3** **Photo.** ***Perf. 11¾x11½***

**4453** A1835 2.60z multi 1.40 .70

Mass murder committed by Nazis in Piasnica, 80th anniv.

Souvenir Sheet

Organ, Basilica of St. Andrew the Apostle, Olkusz. — A1836

***Perf. 11½x11 Syncopated***

**2019, Oct. 5** **Litho.**

**4454** A1836 6.60z multi 3.50 1.75

Settlement of Poznan by Bambergs, 300th Anniv. — A1837

***Perf. 11½ Syncopated***

**2019, Oct. 19** **Litho.**

**4455** A1837 3.30z multi 1.75 .85

**Stage and Film Stars Type of 2012**

Designs: No. 4456, 3.30z, Michal Znicz (1888-1943). No. 4457, 3.30z, Jadwiga Andrzejewska (1915-77). No. 4458, 3.30z, Józef Wegrzyn (1884-1952).

***Perf. 11½ Syncopated***

**2019, Oct. 25** **Litho.**

**4456-4458** A1512 Set of 3 5.25 2.60

*4458a* Souvenir sheet of 3, #4456-4458 5.25 2.60

Liberation of Breda, Netherlands by Polish Troops of Gen. Stanislaw Maczek, 75th Anniv. — A1838

**2019, Oct. 26** **Photo.** ***Perf. 11½x11***

**4459** A1838 3.30z multi 1.75 .85

Sermon of St. John the Baptist, by Pieter Brueghel the Younger (1564-1638) — A1839

***Perf. 11½x11 Syncopated***

**2019, Oct. 28** **Litho.**

**4460** A1839 6z multi 3.25 1.60

No. 4460 was printed in sheets of 5 + label.

Souvenir Sheet

Birds of Singapore and Poland — A1840

No. 4461: a, Anthracoceros albirostris. b, Falco peregrinus.

***Perf. 11½x11 Syncopated***

**2019, Oct. 30** **Litho.**

**4461** A1840 3.30z Sheet of 2, #a-b 3.50 1.75

See Singapore Nos. 1997-1998.

Miniature Sheet

First Days of Polish Independence — A1841

No. 4462: a, Lieutenant General Józef Haller (1873-1960). b, Parade of Polish cavalry, Sejny, horiz. c, Seizure of Vilnius, horiz. d, Lieutenant General Józef Dowbor-Musnicki (1867-1937). e, Government ministers of Prime Minister Jedrzej Moraczewski (1870-1944), horiz. f, Soldiers parading in Bialystok, horiz.

***Die Cut Perf. 11¾x11½ (vert. stamps), 11½x11¾ (horiz. stamps)***

**2019, Nov. 11** **Litho.**

**Self-Adhesive**

**4462** A1841 3.30z Sheet of 6, #a-f 10.50 5.25

Gabriela Balicka (1871-1962), Botanist and Politician A1842

***Perf. 11½x11 Syncopated***

**2019, Nov. 28** **Litho.**

**4463** A1842 3.30z multi 1.75 .85

Woman suffrage in Poland, 101st anniv.

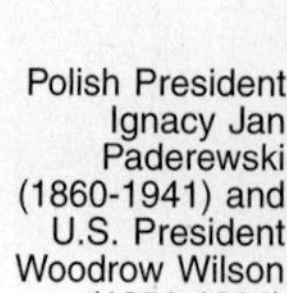

Polish President Ignacy Jan Paderewski (1860-1941) and U.S. President Woodrow Wilson (1856-1924) A1843

***Perf. 11½ Syncopated***

**2019, Dec. 20** **Litho.**

**4464** A1843 3.30z multi 1.75 .85

Diplomatic relations between Poland and the United States, cent.

Monument to Insurgents and Town Hall, Leszno — A1844

***Perf. 11¾x11½***

**2020, Jan. 17** **Photo.**

**4465** A1844 3.30z multi 1.75 1.75

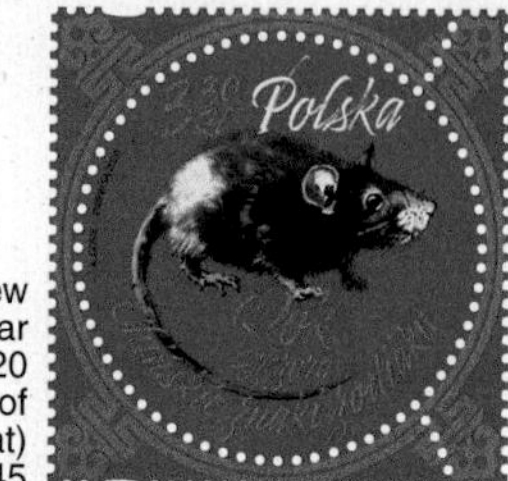

New Year 2020 (Year of the Rat) A1845

***Perf. 11½ Syncopated***

**2020, Jan. 27** **Litho.**

**4466** A1845 3.30z multi 1.75 1.75

Value are for stamps with surrounding selvage.

Liberation of Auschwitz Concentration Camp, 75th Anniv. — A1846

***Perf. 11½x11¾***

**2020, Jan. 27** **Photo.**

**4467** A1846 3.30z multi 1.75 1.75

First Polish Postage Stamp, 160th Anniv. — A1847

***Perf. 11½x11 Syncopated***

**2020, Jan. 31** **Litho.**

**4468** A1847 3.30z multi 1.75 1.75

No. 4468 was printed in sheets of 8 + label.

The Marriage of Poland and the Baltic Sea, by Wojciech Kossak (1856-1942) A1848

***Perf. 11x11½ Syncopated***

**2020, Feb. 10** **Litho.**

**4469** A1848 3.30z multi 1.75 1.75

Recovery of Pomerania by troops of Gen. Józef Haller, cent.

Love A1849

***Perf. 11x11½ Syncopated***

**2020, Feb. 14** **Litho.**

**4470** A1849 3.30z multi 1.75 1.75

Fatala Khan Khojski (1875-1920), Azerbaijan Foreign Affairs Minister, and Stanislaw Patek (1866-1944), Polish Foreign Affairs Minister — A1850

**Perf. 11½ Syncopated**

**2020, Feb. 20** **Litho.**
**4471** A1850 3.30z multi 1.75 1.75

Diplomatic relations between Poland and Azerbaijan, cent.

Miniature Sheet

Soldier's Gorgets — A1851

No. 4472 — Gorget depicting: a, Madonna and child above eagle, belonging to Wladyslaw Gurgacz. b, Madonna and child on breast of eagle, belonging to Henryk Jastrzebski.

**Perf. 11¼ Syncopated**

**2020, Mar. 1** **Litho.**
**4472** A1851 6z Sheet of 2, #a-b, + 2 labels 6.25 6.25

Miniature Sheet

Road to Freedom — A1852

No. 4473: a, Conductors on strike in Poznan, 1956. b, Polish Catholicism Millennium celebrations at Jasna Góra Monastery, Czestochowa, 1966. c, Student demonstrations in Warsaw, 1968. d, December Revoltin Gdynia, 1970. e, Workers' strike, 1976. f, First pilgrimage of Pope John Paul II to Poland, 1979. g, Gdansk Shipyard strike, 1980. h, Massacre of strikers at Wujek Coal Mine, 1981. i, Street demonstrations in Lubin, 1982.

**Perf. 11½ Syncopated**

**2020, Mar. 8** **Litho.**
**4473** A1852 3.30z Sheet of 9, #a-i 14.00 14.00

Edward Raczynski (1891-1993), President of Poland — A1853

**2020, Mar. 24** **Photo.** ***Perf. 11½x11***
**4474** A1853 3.30z gold & multi 1.60 1.60

Raczynski wrote one of the first accounts of mass extermination of Jews by Nazis in World War II while Minister of Foreign Affairs for the Republic of Poland in Exile.

Katyn Massacre, 80th Anniv. — A1854

**Perf. 11½ Syncopated**

**2020, Apr. 4** **Litho.**
**4475** A1854 3.30z multi 1.60 1.60

Pres. Lech Kaczynski (1949-2010), Flags of Poland and Georgia — A1855

**Perf. 11½ Syncopated**

**2020, Apr. 10** **Litho.**
**4476** A1855 3.30z sil & multi 1.60 1.60

See Georgia No. 571.

Ruch Chorzów Sports Club, Cent. A1856

**Perf. 11¼ Syncopated**

**2020, Apr. 20** **Litho.**
**4477** A1856 3.30z multi 1.60 1.60

Map of 16th Century Polish Postal Routes — A1857

**Perf. 11x11¾ Syncopated**

**2020, Apr. 29** **Litho.**
**4478** A1857 5z multi 2.40 2.40

Europa.

**Fruit and Flowers Type of 2009**

**2020, May 7** **Photo.** ***Perf. 11½x11¾***
**4479** A1425 8.40z Chamomile 4.25 4.25

St. John Paul II (1920-2005) — A1858

**Perf. 11½ Syncopated**

**2020, May 13** **Litho.**
**4480** A1858 5z multi + label 2.50 2.50

Joint issue between Poland and Slovakia. See Slovakia No. 848.

Leopold Tyrmand (1920-85), Writer — A1859

**Perf. 11½ Syncopated**

**2020, May 16** **Litho.**
**4481** A1859 3.30z sil, gold & multi 1.75 1.75

St. Andrzej Bobola (1591-1651), Missionary — A1860

**2020, May 16** **Photo.** ***Perf. 11x11½***
**4482** A1860 3.30z gold & multi 1.75 1.75

Railroad Crossing Gate and Tracks — A1861

**Perf. 11½x11¾**

**2020, May 30** **Photo.**
**4483** A1861 30g sil & multi .25 .25

Jagiellonia Bialystok Soccer Team, Cent. A1862

**Perf. 11¼ Syncopated**

**2020, May 30** **Litho.**
**4484** A1862 3.30z multi 1.75 1.75

No. 4484 was printed in sheets of 5 + label.

Rzeczpospolita Newspaper, Cent. — A1863

**Perf. 11½ Syncopated**

**2020, June 15** **Litho.**
**4485** A1863 3.30z multi 1.75 1.75

Adult and Juvenile Animals — A1864

Designs: No. 4486, 3.30z, Acinonyx jubatus. No. 4487, 3.30z, Macropus rufus. No. 4488, 3.30z, Camelus bactrianus. No. 4489, 3.30z, Lemur catta.

**Perf. 11½ Syncopated**

**2020, June 15** **Litho.**
**4486-4489** A1864 Set of 4 6.75 6.75

Nos. 4486-4489 were each printed in sheets of 12 + 4 labels.

Aerial Views of Parks — A1865

No. 4490 — QR code and aerial view of: a, Muzakowski Park UNESCO World Heritage Site (denomination at UR). b, Biebrza National Park (denomination at UL).

**Perf. 11½x11 Syncopated**

**2020, June 29** **Litho.**
**4490** A1865 3.30z Pair, #a-b 3.50 3.50

Lieutenant Colonel Jan Kowalewski (1892-1965), Head of Polish Cipher Bureau — A1866

**Perf. 11¾x11½**

**2020, June 30** **Photo.**
**4491** A1866 1.80z gold & multi .90 .90

Abai Kunanbayev (1845-1904), Poet — A1867

**Perf. 11½x11 Syncopated**

**2020, June 30** **Litho.**
**4492** A1867 3.30z multi 1.75 1.75

Sigismund II Augustus and Barbara at the Radziwill Court in Vilnius, by Jan Matejko — A1868

**2020, Aug. 1** **Photo.** ***Perf. 11x10¾***
**4493** A1868 3.30z multi 1.75 1.75

See Lithuania No. 1168.

Soldiers, Airplane and Our Lady of Warsaw A1869

Gen. Józef Pilsudski (1867-1935) on Horseback — A1870

Female Soldier A1871

Polish Soldier Attacking Russian Flagbearer A1872

Father Ignacy Skorupa (1893-1920) — A1873

***Perf. 11x11½ Syncopated***

**2020, Aug. 15** **Litho.**

**4494** A1869 3.30z sil & multi 1.90 1.90
**4495** A1870 3.30z sil & multi 1.90 1.90
**4496** A1871 3.30z sil & multi 1.90 1.90
**4497** A1872 3.30z sil & multi 1.90 1.90
*Nos. 4494-4497 (4)* 7.60 7.60

**Souvenir Sheet**

***Perf. 11½ Syncopated***

**4498** A1873 6.60z sil & multi 3.75 3.75

Details of painting, *Miracle on the Vistula,* by Jerzy Kossak (1886-1955). Battle of Warsaw, cent.

Dr. Andrzej Mielecki (1864-1920), Upper Silesian Political Activist and Map of Upper Silesia — A1874

***Perf. 11½ Syncopated***

**2020, Aug. 20** **Litho.**

**4499** A1874 3.30z multi 1.90 1.90

Silesian Uprising, cent.

Father Józef Maria Bochenski (1902-95), Logician and Philosopher — A1875

***Perf. 11½ Syncopated***

**2020, Aug. 30** **Litho.**

**4500** A1875 3.30z multi 1.90 1.90

Solidarity Trade Union, 40th Anniv. — A1876

***Perf. 11¾x11½***

**2020, Aug. 31** **Photo.**

**4501** A1876 4.70z multi 2.60 2.60

**Souvenir Sheet**

The Battle of Cecora, Painting by Witold Piwnicki (1851-1932) — A1877

**2020, Sept. 18 Photo.** ***Perf. 11x10¾***

**4502** A1877 8.70z gold & multi 4.50 4.50

Battle of Cecora, 200th anniv.

Blessed Eusebius of Esztergom (c. 1200-70), Founder of Pauline Fathers — A1878

**2020, Sept. 21 Photo.** ***Perf. 11½x11***

**4503** A1878 3.30z gold & multi 1.75 1.75

Statue of Duchess Salome of Greater Poland and Collegiate Church, Glogów, 900th Anniv. — A1879

***Perf. 11½x11¾***

**2020, Sept. 25** **Photo.**

**4504** A1879 1z gold & multi .55 .55

**Souvenir Sheet**

Children's Art — A1880

No. 4505: a, Volunteer Umbrella, by Robert Koldras (denomination in red). b, Better Together, by Anna Pietron (denomination in gray green). c, Together We Can Do Everything, by Klaudia Peterko (denomination in violet).

**2020, Sept. 28 Litho.** ***Perf. 11½x11***

**4505** A1880 3.30z Sheet of 3, #a-c 5.25 5.25

**Miniature Sheet**

Medicinal Plants — A1881

No. 4506: a, Hypericum perforatum. b, Utrica dioica. c, Equisetum arvense. d, Valeriana officinalis.

***Perf. 11¼ Syncopated***

**2020, Sept. 30** **Litho.**

**4506** A1881 3.30z Sheet of 4, #a-d 7.00 7.00

St. Mary's Collegiate Church, Stargard — A1882

**2020, Oct. 7 Photo.** ***Perf. 11¾x11½***

**4507** A1882 4z gold & multi 2.10 2.10

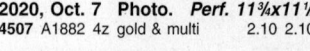

Butterflies — A1883

No. 4508: a, Morpho helene. b, Morpho portis. c, Danaus plexippus. d, Agrias narcissus.

***Perf. 11½ Syncopated***

**2020, Oct. 8** **Litho.**

**4508** A1883 3.30z Block or horiz. strip of 4, #a-d 6.75 6.75

Statue of the Queen of Peace, Chapel of Perpetual Adoration, Niepokalanów A1884

***Perf. 11½ Syncopated***

**2020, Oct. 13** **Litho.**

**4509** A1884 3.30z gold & multi 1.75 1.75

St. John Paul II (1920-2005) — A1885

***Perf. 11½ Syncopated***

**2020, Oct. 16** **Litho.**

**4510** A1885 5z multi + label 2.60 2.60

No. 4510 was printed in sheets of 6 + 6 labels. See Vatican City No. 1749.

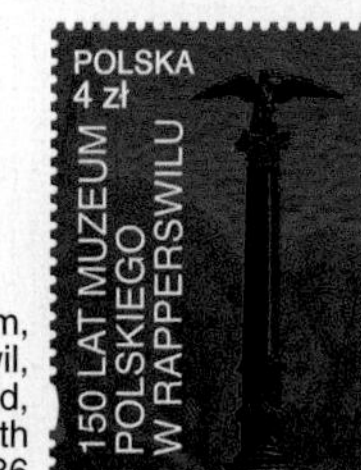

Polish Museum, Rapperswil, Switzerland, 150th Anniv. — A1886

***Perf. 11½ Syncopated***

**2020, Oct. 23** **Litho.**

**4511** A1886 4z multi 2.10 2.10

United Nations, 75th Anniv. — A1887

**2020, Oct. 24 Photo.** ***Perf. 11½x11***

**4512** A1887 3.30z multi 1.75 1.75

Soldiers and Gen. Wladyslaw Anders (1892-1970) A1888

***Perf. 11x11½ Syncopated***

**2020, Oct. 28** **Litho.**

**4513** A1888 4z multi 2.10 2.10
*a.* Tete-beche pair 4.25 4.25

**Souvenir Sheet**

Battle of Britain, 80th Anniv. — A1889

***Perf. 11½ Syncopated***

**2020, Oct. 28** **Litho.**

**4514** A1889 8.70z multi 4.50 4.50

Independent Students' Association, 80th Anniv. — A1890

*Perf. 11½x11¾*

**2020, Oct. 30** **Photo.**
**4515** A1890 4.70z multi 2.40 2.40

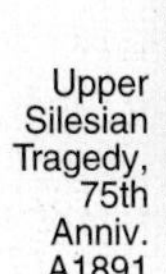

Upper Silesian Tragedy, 75th Anniv. A1891

**2020, Nov. 6** **Photo.** ***Perf. 11x11½***
**4516** A1891 3.30z multi 1.75 1.75

Deportation of Polish miners to Russia, 70th anniv.

Miniature Sheet

Marshals of the Sejm of the Second Polish Republic — A1892

No. 4517: a, Maciej Rataj (1884-1940). b, Ignacy Daszynski (1866-1936). c, Kazimierz Switalski (1886-1962). d, Stanislaw Car (1882-1938). e, Walery Slawek (1879-1939). f, Waclaw Makowski (1880-1942).

***Perf. 11½x11¾ Syncopated***

**2020, Nov. 11** **Litho.**
**4517** A1892 3.30z Sheet of 6, #a-f, + 3 labels 11.00 11.00

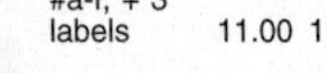

Christmas — A1893

*Perf. 11¾x11½*

**2020, Nov. 16** **Photo.**
**4518** A1893 8z gold & multi 4.25 4.25

Diplomatic Relations Between Poland and Brazil, Cent. A1894

***Perf. 11x11½ Syncopated***

**2020, Nov. 19** **Litho.**
**4519** A1894 4z multi 2.25 2.25

Dinosaurs — A1895

No. 4520: a, Coelophysis (celofyz). b, Dilophopsaurus (dilofozaur). c, Scelidosaurus (scelidozaur).

***Perf. 11¾x11½ Syncopated***

**2020, Nov. 25** **Litho.**
**4520** A1895 3.30z Vert. strip of 3, #a-c 5.50 5.50

Main Post Office and Monument to King Casimir III the Great, Bydgoszcz A1896

*Perf. 11½x11¾*

**2020, Nov. 30** **Photo.**
**4521** A1896 95g multi .55 .55

Miniature Sheet

Birds — A1897

No. 4522: a, Ciconia ciconia. b, Ciconia nigra. c, Ardea alba. d, Ardea cinerea.

***Perf. 11½ Syncopated***

**2020, Nov. 30** **Litho.**
**4522** A1897 3.30z Sheet of 4, #a-d, + 4 labels 7.25 7.25

Postal Gift Foundation, 10th Anniv. — A1898

**2020, Dec. 4** **Photo.** ***Perf. 11¾x11½***
**4523** A1898 4.10z gold & multi 2.25 2.25

Ludwig van Beethoven (1770-1827), Composer — A1899

***Perf. 11¼ Syncopated***

**2020, Dec. 15** **Litho.**
**4524** A1899 3.30z gold & multi 1.75 1.75

No. 4524 was printed in sheets of 5 + label.

Tile Stove, Potocki Castle, Lancut — A1900

Tile Stove, Górków Castle, Szamotuly A1901

Tile Stove, Radziwill Castle, Nieborów A1902

Tile Stove, Potocki Castle, Lancut — A1903

***Perf. 11½x11¾ Syncopated***

**2020, Dec. 21** **Litho.**
**4525** Block or horiz. strip of 4 7.00 7.00
*a.* A1900 3.30z multi 1.75 1.75
*b.* A1901 3.30z multi 1.75 1.75
*c.* A1902 3.30z multi 1.75 1.75
*d.* A1903 3.30z multi 1.75 1.75

Krzystof Kamil Baczynski (1921-44), Poet and Soldier — A1904

*Perf. 11¾x11½*

**2021, Jan. 22** **Photo.**
**4526** A1904 4.10z gold & multi 2.25 2.25

Territorial Defence Forces — A1905

*Perf. 11½x11¾*

**2021, Feb. 14** **Photo.**
**4527** A1905 1.40z multi .75 .75

Visegrad Group, 30th Anniv. A1906

***Perf. 11¾x11½ Syncopated***

**2021, Feb. 15** **Litho.**
**4528** A1906 8z multi 4.25 4.25

See Czech Republic No. 3860, Hungary No. 4582, Slovakia No. 870.

Easter — A1907

*Perf. 11¾x11½*

**2021, Feb. 19** **Photo.**
**4529** A1907 8z gold & multi 4.25 4.25

Souvenir Sheet

St. Maria Faustina (1905-38) and St. John Paul II (1920-2005) — A1908

**2021, Feb. 22** **Photo.** ***Perf. 10¾x11***
**4530** A1908 11.50z multi + 2 labels 6.25 6.25

New Year 2021 (Year of the Ox) A1909

**2021, Feb. 26** **Litho.** ***Perf. 11½***
**4531** A1909 3.30z multi 1.75 1.75

Values are for stamps with surrounding selvage.

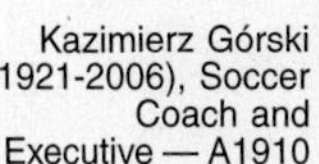

Kazimierz Górski (1921-2006), Soccer Coach and Executive — A1910

*Perf. 11¾x11½*

**2021, Feb. 26** **Photo.**

**4532** A1910 4z gold & multi 2.25 2.25

Lukasz Cieplinski (1913-51), Resistance Fighter Against Nazis and Communists A1911

**2021, Mar. 1** **Photo.** ***Perf. 11½x11¾***

**4533** A1911 3.30z sil & multi 1.75 1.75

National Day of Remembrance of the Cursed Soldiers.

Treaty of Riga, Cent. A1912

*Perf. 11½ Syncopated*

**2021, Mar. 18** **Litho.**

**4534** A1912 3.30z multi 1.75 1.75

Unveiling of Monument to Poles and Jews Murdered by Nazis, Popardowa A1913

*Perf. 11¼x11½*

**2021, Mar. 24** **Photo.**

**4535** A1913 3.30z multi 1.75 1.75

Day of remembrance for Poles who saved Jews from the Holocaust.

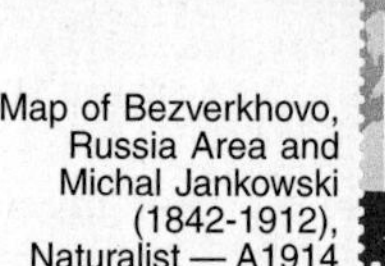


Map of Bezverkhovo, Russia Area and Michal Jankowski (1842-1912), Naturalist — A1914

*Perf. 11¾x11½*

**2021, Mar. 25** **Photo.**

**4536** A1914 1z gold & multi .55 .55

Jerzy Iwanow-Szajnowicz (1911-43), Water Polo Player and Executed Resistance Fighter — A1915

*Perf. 11½x11¾*

**2021, Mar. 25** **Photo.**

**4537** A1915 8z sil & multi 4.25 4.25

Miniature Sheet

European Year of Rail — A1916

No. 4538 — Trains: a, Pendolino. b, Dart. c, Impuls. d, Pt31 64. e, FLIRT. f, Elf II.

*Perf. 11¾x11½ Syncopated*

**2021, Mar. 31** **Litho.**

**4538** A1916 3.30z Sheet of 6, #a-f 10.50 10.50

Warsaw Stock Exchange, 30th Anniv. — A1917

*Perf. 11½x11 Syncopated*

**2021, Apr. 16** **Litho.**

**4539** A1917 3.30z multi 1.75 1.75

*a.* Tete-beche pair 3.50 3.50

Lynx Lynx — A1918

*Perf. 11¼x11 Syncopated*

**2021, Apr. 21** **Litho.**

**4540** A1918 3.30z multi 1.75 1.75

Europa.

Red Bumblebee A1919

Honeybee A1920

Halictid Bee A1921

Blood Bee A1922

Metallic Bee A1923

Pantaloon Bee A1924

*Perf. 11¼ Syncopated*

**2021, Apr. 30** **Litho.**

| | | | | |
|---|---|---|---|---|
| **4541** | A1919 3.30z multi | | 1.75 | 1.75 |
| **4542** | A1920 3.30z multi | | 1.75 | 1.75 |
| **4543** | A1921 3.30z multi | | 1.75 | 1.75 |
| **4544** | A1922 3.30z multi | | 1.75 | 1.75 |
| **4545** | A1923 3.30z multi | | 1.75 | 1.75 |
| **4546** | A1924 3.30z multi | | 1.75 | 1.75 |
| | *Nos. 4541-4546 (6)* | | 10.50 | 10.50 |

Nos. 4541-4546 were each printed in sheets of 5 + label.

St. Joseph Holding Infant Jesus — A1925

**2021, May 1** **Photo.** ***Perf. 11¾***

**4547** A1925 3.30z gold & multi 1.75 1.75

Wojciech Korfanty (1873-1939), Organizer of Silesian Uprisings, and Map of Uprising Sites — A1926

*Perf. 11½ Syncopated*

**2021, May 2** **Litho.**

**4548** A1926 3.30z multi 1.75 1.75

Kornel Morawiecki (1941-2019), Physicist and Politician A1927

**2021, May 3** **Photo.** ***Perf. 11½x11***

**4549** A1927 3.30z gold & multi 1.75 1.75

May 3rd, 1791 Constitution, Painting by Jan Matejko (1838-93) — A1928

*Perf. 11½ Syncopated*

**2021, May 3** **Litho.**

**4550** A1928 3.30z brnz & multi 1.75 1.75

Adoption of May 3rd Constitution, 230th anniv.

St. Stanislaw of Szczepanów (1030-79) — A1929

**2021, May 8** **Photo.** ***Perf. 11x11½***

**4551** A1929 3.30z gold & multi 1.90 1.90

Creation of Rural Solidarity, 40th Anniv. — A1930

*Perf. 11¾x11½*

**2021, May 12** **Photo.**

**4552** A1930 5g multi .25 .25

Anita Wlodarczyk and Pawel Fajdek, Hammer Throwers, and Silesian Stadium, Chorzów — A1931

*Perf. 11½ Syncopated*

**2021, May 28** **Litho.**

**4553** A1931 4z multi 2.25 2.25

2021 European Track and Field Team Championships, Chorzów. Values are for stamps with surrounding selvage.

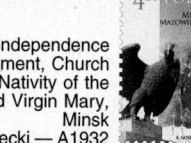

Independence Monument, Church of the Nativity of the Blessed Virgin Mary, Minsk Mazowiecki — A1932

*Perf. 11¾x11½*

**2021, May 29** **Photo.**

**4554** A1932 4z multi 2.25 2.25

Our Lady of Bolszowce, Ukraine A1933

Our Lady of Mariajampole, Lithuania — A1934

Our Lady of Consolation, Lviv, Ukraine — A1935

Our Lady of Tarnopol, Ukraine A1936

**2021, May 31 Photo.** ***Perf. 11x11¼***

**4555** A1933 4z gold & multi 2.25 2.25
**4556** A1934 4z gold & multi 2.25 2.25
**4557** A1935 4z gold & multi 2.25 2.25
**4558** A1936 4z gold & multi 2.25 2.25
*Nos. 4555-4558 (4)* 9.00 9.00

Icons of the Virgin Mary now in Polish churches.

Post and Telecommunications Museum, Warsaw, Cent. — A1937

***Perf. 11½x11¾ Syncopated***

**2021, June 12** **Litho.**

**4559** A1937 3.30z multi + label 1.90 1.90

No. 4559 was printed in sheets of 6 + 6 different labels depicting items in the museum.

Henryk Arctowski (1871-1958), Meteorologist and Antarctic Explorer — A1938

***Perf. 11¼ Syncopated***

**2021, July 15** **Litho.**

**4560** A1938 3.30z multi 1.75 1.75

No. 4560 was printed in sheets of 5 + label.

2020 Summer Olympics, Tokyo A1939

***Perf. 11x11½ Syncopated***

**2021, July 15** **Litho.**

**4561** A1939 4z multi 2.10 2.10

The 2020 Summer Olympics were postponed until 2021 because of the COVID-19 pandemic.

2020 Summer Paralympics, Tokyo — A1940

***Perf. 11½ Syncopated***

**2021, July 15** **Litho.**

**4562** A1940 4z multi 2.10 2.10

The 2020 Summer Paralympics were postponed until 2021 because of the COVID-19 pandemic.

COVID-19 Vaccination Campaign A1941

***Perf. 11½x11¾***

**2021, July 15** **Photo.**

**4563** A1941 4.70z multi 2.50 2.50

Ocean Liners — A1942

No. 4564: a, S.S. Kosciuszko. b, S.S. Pulaski. c, S.S. Polonia.

***Perf. 11¾x11½ Syncopated***

**2021, July 23** **Litho.**

**4564** Vert. strip of 3 5.25 5.25
*a.-c.* A1942 3.30z Any single 1.75 1.75

Pilgrim on Way of St. James, Spain — A1943

***Perf. 11¾x11½***

**2021, July 25** **Photo.**

**4565** A1943 4.10z multi 2.25 2.25

Year of St. James the Apostle.

Sept. 1, 1939, Defenders of the Gdansk Post Office — A1944

***Perf. 11½ Syncopated***

**2021, Sept. 1** **Litho.**

**4566** A1944 3.30z sil & multi 1.75 1.75

Battle of Chocim, by Józef Brandt (1841-1915) — A1945

***Perf. 11x11½ Syncopated***

**2021, Sept. 2** **Litho.**

**4567** A1945 8z multi 4.00 4.00

Battle of Chocim, 400th anniv. See Lithuania No. 1190; Ukraine No. 1313.

Krzystof Krawczyk (1946-2021). Singer and Guitarist A1946

**2021, Sept. 3 Litho.** ***Perf. 11x11½***

**4568** A1946 4z gold & multi 2.10 2.10

2021 European Amputee Soccer Championships, Cracow — A1947

***Perf. 11½ Syncopated***

**2021, Sept. 12** **Litho.**

**4569** A1947 4z multi 2.10 2.10

Stanislaw Lem (1921-2006), Science Fiction Writer — A1948

***Perf. 11½x11 Syncopated***

**2021, Sept. 12** **Litho.**

**4570** A1948 4z multi 2.10 2.10
*a.* Tete-beche pair 4.25 4.25

Beatification of Mother Elzbieta Róza Czacka (1876-1961), Founder of Society for the Care of the Blind — A1949

**Litho., Label Litho. & Embossed**
***Perf. 11½ Syncopated***

**2021, Sept. 12**

**4571** A1949 4z multi + label 2.10 2.10

Beatification of Cardinal Stefan Wyszynski (1901-81) — A1950

***Perf. 11½ Syncopated***

**2021, Sept. 12** **Litho.**

**4572** A1950 4z sil & multi 2.10 2.10

Cyprian Kamil Norwid (1821-83), Writer, Painter and Sculptor A1951

**2021, Sept. 24 Photo.** ***Perf. 11½x11***

**4573** A1951 3.30z multi 1.75 1.75

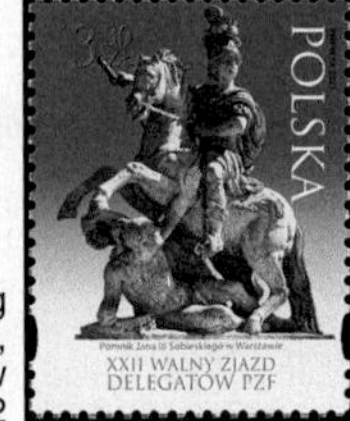


Statue of King Jan III Sobieski, Warsaw A1952

***Perf. 11½x11 Syncopated***

**2021, Sept. 30** **Litho.**

**4574** A1952 3.30z multi 1.75 1.75

22nd General Assembly of the Polish Philatelic Association. No. 4574 was printed in sheets of 12 + 4 labels. Imperforate examples of No. 4574 were distributed exclusively to members of the Polish Philatelic Association.

Souvenir Sheet

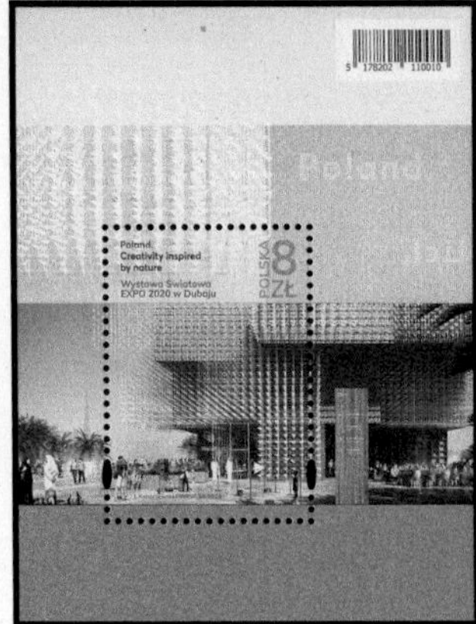


Polish Pavilion, Expo 2020, Dubai — A1953

***Perf. 11½ Syncopated***

**2021, Oct. 1** **Litho.**

**4575** A1953 8z gold & multi 4.00 4.00

Caritas Polska Charity, 30th Anniv. — A1954

**2021, Oct. 6 Photo.** ***Perf. 12x11½***

**4576** A1954 10z dark red 5.00 5.00

Polish Membership in Organization for Economic Co-operation and Development, 25th Anniv. — A1955

**2021, Oct. 16 Photo.** ***Perf. 11x11¼***
**4577** A1955 3.30z multi 1.75 1.75

Souvenir Sheet

Czeslaw Slania (1921-2005), Engraver of Postage Stamps — A1956

**Engr., Sheet Margin Litho.**
***Perf. 11x11½ Syncopated***
**2021, Oct. 22**
**4578** A1956 15.30z multi 7.75 7.75

See Sweden No. 2879.

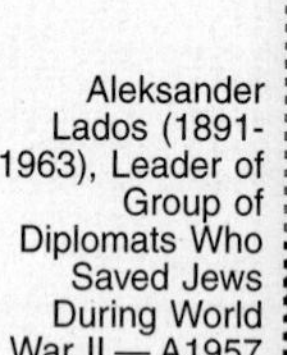

Aleksander Lados (1891-1963), Leader of Group of Diplomats Who Saved Jews During World War II — A1957

***Perf. 11½ Syncopated***
**2021, Oct. 23 Litho.**
**4579** A1957 4z multi 2.00 2.00

Gen. Wlsdyslaw Anders (1892-1970), and His Soldiers Climbing Hill — A1958

***Perf. 11x11½ Syncopated***
**2021, Nov. 17 Litho.**
**4580** A1958 4z multi 2.00 2.00
*a.* Tete-beche pair 4.00 4.00

Polonia Warszawa Soccer Team, 110th Anniv. A1959

***Perf. 11½ Syncopated***
**2021, Nov. 19 Litho.**
**4581** A1959 3.30z multi 1.60 1.60

No. 4581 was printed in sheets of 5 + label.

Beatification of Jan Franciszek Macha (1914-42), Priest Executed by Nazis — A1960

***Perf. 11½ Syncopated***
**2021, Nov. 20 Litho.**
**4582** A1960 4z multi 2.00 2.00

Salt Crystals and Their Sources — A1961

No. 4583: a, Ston Saltworks, Croatia. b, Bochnia Salt Mine, Poland.

***Perf. 11½x11 Syncopated***
**2021, Dec. 2 Litho.**
**4583** A1961 4z Pair, #a-b 4.00 4.00

Joint issue between Poland and Croatia. See Croatia No.

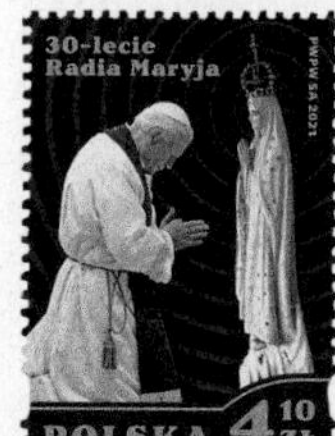


St. John Paul II (1920-2005) and Statue of Our Lady of Fatima — A1962

***Perf. 11½ Syncopated***
**2021, Dec. 4 Litho.**
**4584** A1962 4.10z cop & multi 2.10 2.10

Radio Maryja, 30th anniv.

Our Lady of Election, Painting by Unknown Artist, 1621 — A1963

***Perf. 11½ Syncopated***
**2021, Dec. 8 Litho.**
**4585** A1963 4.10z multi 2.10 2.10

Marek Edelman (c. 1919-2009), Cardiologist and Last Surviving Leader Of Warsaw Ghetto Uprising — A1964

**2022, Jan. 2 Photo.** ***Perf. 11¾x11½***
**4586** A1964 (4.50z) multi 2.25 2.25

2022 Winter Olympics, Beijing — A1965

***Perf. 11½x11¾ Syncopated***
**2022, Jan. 24 Litho.**
**4587** A1965 4z gold & multi 2.00 2.00

2022 Winter Paralympics, Beijing — A1966

***Perf. 11¾x11½ Syncopated***
**2022, Jan. 24 Litho.**
**4588** A1966 4z sil & multi 2.00 2.00

Patches of Polish Army, Border Guard and Police — A1967

***Perf. 11½x11¾***
**2022, Jan. 27 Photo.**
**4589** A1967 (3.60z) multi 1.75 1.75

City Council Building, Baku, Azerbaijan, Designed by Józef Goslawski (1865-1904) — A1968

**2022, Jan. 31 Photo.** ***Perf. 11¼x11***
**4590** A1968 4z gold & multi 2.00 2.00

New Year 2022 (Year of the Tiger) A1969

**2022, Feb. 1 Litho.** ***Perf. 11½***
**4591** A1969 4z multi 2.00 2.00

Values are for stamps with surrounding selvage.

Iwona Kruglowska, Postal Worker and Member of the Home Army — A1970

***Perf. 11½ Syncopated***
**2022, Feb. 14 Litho.**
**4592** A1970 3.60z multi 1.75 1.75

Home Army, 80th anniv. No. 4592 was printed in sheets of 5 + label.

Polish Civil Service, Cent. A1971

***Perf. 11¼x11½***
**2022, Feb. 17 Photo.**
**4593** A1971 3.60z multi 1.75 1.75

Polish Embassy in Ankara, Turkey A1972

***Perf. 11¾x11½ Syncopated***
**2022, Feb. 28 Litho.**
**4594** A1972 4z gold & multi 1.90 1.90

Józef Franczak (1918-63), Last of the Anti-Communist "Cursed Soldiers" A1973

**2022, Mar. 1 Photo.** ***Perf. 11½x11¾***
**4595** A1973 4.50z multi 2.10 2.10

Louis Pasteur (1822-95), Microbiologist A1974

**2022, Mar. 7 Photo.** ***Perf. 11½x11¾***
**4596** A1974 30g gold & multi .30 .30

Souvenir Sheet

Ignacy Lukasiewicz (1822-82), Inventor of Kerosene Lamp — A1975

*Perf. 11½x11¾ Syncopated*

**2022, Mar. 8** **Litho.**

| | | | | |
|---|---|---|---|---|
| **4597** | A1975 | 11.50z multi + 2 labels | 5.50 | 5.50 |

Easter — A1976

*Perf. 11½x11¾*

**2022, Mar. 17** **Photo.**

| | | | | |
|---|---|---|---|---|
| **4598** | A1976 | (4.50z) multi | 2.25 | 2.25 |

1922-23 Lech Poznan Soccer Team A1977

*Perf. 11¼ Syncopated*

**2022, Mar. 19** **Litho.**

| | | | | |
|---|---|---|---|---|
| **4599** | A1977 | 4.50z multi | 2.25 | 2.25 |

Lech Poznan soccer team, cent.

Family of Adam and Bronislawa Kowalski, Burned by Nazis for Hiding Jews in 1942 — A1978

*Perf. 11½x11¼*

**2022, Mar. 24** **Photo.**

| | | | | |
|---|---|---|---|---|
| **4600** | A1978 | 3.60z multi | 1.75 | 1.75 |

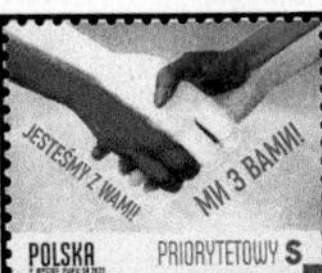

Polish Solidarity With Ukraine A1979

*Perf. 11½x11¾*

**2022, Mar. 25** **Photo.**

| | | | | |
|---|---|---|---|---|
| **4601** | A1979 | (4.50z) multi | 2.25 | 2.25 |

## SEMI-POSTAL STAMPS

### Regular Issue of 1919 Surcharged in Violet

a

b

**1919, May 3** **Unwmk.** ***Imperf.***

| | | | | |
|---|---|---|---|---|
| **B1** | A10(a) | 5f + 5f grn | .40 | .40 |
| **B2** | A10(a) | 10f + 5f red vio | .40 | .55 |
| **B3** | A10(a) | 15f + 5f dp red | .40 | .55 |
| **B4** | A11(b) | 25f + 5f ol grn | .40 | .40 |
| **B5** | A11(b) | 50f + 5f bl grn | .40 | .75 |

*Perf. 11½*

| | | | | |
|---|---|---|---|---|
| **B6** | A10(a) | 5f + 5f grn | .30 | .30 |
| **B7** | A10(a) | 10f + 5f red vio | .55 | .55 |
| **B8** | A10(a) | 15f + 5f dp red | .30 | .30 |
| **B9** | A11(b) | 25f + 5f ol grn | .30 | .30 |
| **B10** | A11(b) | 50f + 5f bl grn | .40 | .40 |
| | | *Nos. B1-B10 (10)* | 3.85 | 4.50 |
| | | Set, never hinged | 18.00 | |

First Polish Philatelic Exhibition. The surtax benefited the Polish White Cross Society.

Regular Issue of 1920 Surcharged in Red and Carmine

**1921, Mar. 5** ***Perf. 9***

**Thin Laid Paper**

| | | | | |
|---|---|---|---|---|
| **B11** | A14 | 5m + 30m red vio | 1.50 | *8.50* |
| **B12** | A14 | 6m + 30m dp rose | 1.50 | *8.50* |
| **B13** | A14 | 10m + 30m lt red | 3.00 | *8.50* |
| **B14** | A14 | 20m + 30m gray grn | 65.00 | *120.00* |
| | | *Nos. B11-B14 (4)* | 71.00 | 145.50 |
| | | Set, never hinged | 150.00 | |

Counterfeits, differently perforated, exist of Nos. B11-B14.

SP1

**1925, Jan. 1** **Typo.** ***Perf. 12½***

| | | | | |
|---|---|---|---|---|
| **B15** | SP1 | 1g orange brn | 4.50 | 26.00 |
| **B16** | SP1 | 2g dk brown | 4.50 | 26.00 |
| **B17** | SP1 | 3g orange | 4.50 | 26.00 |
| **B18** | SP1 | 5g olive grn | 4.50 | 26.00 |
| **B19** | SP1 | 10g blue grn | 4.50 | 26.00 |
| **B20** | SP1 | 15g red | 4.50 | 26.00 |
| **B21** | SP1 | 20g blue | 4.50 | 26.00 |
| **B22** | SP1 | 25g red brown | 4.50 | 26.00 |
| **B23** | SP1 | 30g dp violet | 4.50 | 26.00 |
| **B24** | SP1 | 40g indigo | 110.00 | 26.00 |
| **B25** | SP1 | 50g magenta | 4.50 | 26.00 |
| | | *Nos. B15-B25 (11)* | 155.00 | 286.00 |
| | | Set, never hinged | 325.00 | |

"Na Skarb" means "National Funds." These stamps were sold at a premium of 50 groszy each, for charity.

Light of Knowledge — SP2

**1927, May 3** ***Perf. 11½***

| | | | | |
|---|---|---|---|---|
| **B26** | SP2 | 10g + 5g choc & grn | 6.25 | 7.00 |
| **B27** | SP2 | 20g + 5g dk bl & buff | 7.50 | 12.00 |
| | | Set, never hinged | 40.00 | |

"NA OSWIATE" means "For Public Instruction." The surtax aided an Association of Educational Societies.

### Torun Type of 1933

**1933, May 21** **Engr.**

| | | | | |
|---|---|---|---|---|
| **B28** | A59 | 60g (+40g) red brn, *buff* | 11.00 | 21.00 |
| | | Never hinged | 30.00 | |

Philatelic Exhibition at Torun, May 21-28, 1933, and sold at a premium of 40g to aid the exhibition funds.

Souvenir Sheet

Stagecoach and Wayside Inn — SP3

**1938, May 3** **Engr.** ***Imperf.***

| | | | | |
|---|---|---|---|---|
| **B29** | SP3 | Sheet of 4 | 52.50 | 125.00 |
| | | Never hinged | 125.00 | |
| *a.* | | 45g green | 5.25 | 8.75 |
| *b.* | | 55g blue | 5.25 | 8.75 |

*Perf. 12*

| | | | | |
|---|---|---|---|---|
| **B29C** | SP3 | Sheet of 4 | 67.50 | 145.00 |
| | | Never hinged | 150.00 | |
| *d.* | | 45g green | 6.50 | 10.00 |
| *e.* | | 55g blue | 6.50 | 10.00 |

5th Phil. Exhib., Warsaw, May 3-8. The sheets each contain two 45g and two 55g stamps. Sold for 3z.

Souvenir Sheet

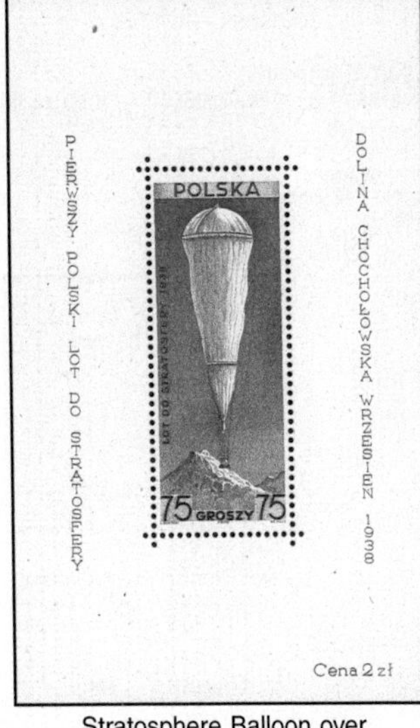

Stratosphere Balloon over Mountains — SP4

**1938, Sept. 15** ***Perf. 12½***

| | | | | |
|---|---|---|---|---|
| **B31** | SP4 | 75g dp vio, sheet | 40.00 | 65.00 |
| | | Never hinged | 120.00 | |

Issued in advance of a proposed Polish stratosphere flight. Sold for 2z.

### Winterhelp Issue

SP5

**1938-39**

| | | | | |
|---|---|---|---|---|
| **B32** | SP5 | 5g + 5g red org | .45 | *.25* |
| **B33** | SP5 | 25g + 10g dk vio ('39) | .90 | *.25* |
| **B34** | SP5 | 55g + 15g brt ultra ('39) | 1.10 | *3.75* |
| | | *Nos. B32-B34 (3)* | 2.45 | *4.25* |
| | | Set, never hinged | 9.50 | |

For surcharges see Nos. N48-N50.

Souvenir Sheet

SP6

**1939, Aug. 1**

| | | | | |
|---|---|---|---|---|
| **B35** | SP6 | Sheet of 3, dark blue gray | 15.00 | 26.00 |
| | | Never hinged | 40.00 | |
| *a.* | | 25g Marshal Pilsudski Reviewing Troops | 3.50 | 3.00 |
| *b.* | | 25g Marshal Pilsudski | 3.50 | 3.00 |
| *c.* | | 25g Marshal Smigly-Rydz | 3.50 | 3.00 |

25th anniv. of the founding of the Polish Legion. The sheets sold for 1.75z, the surtax going to the National Defense fund.

See types A64, A80, A99.

### Polish People's Republic

Polish Warship SP7

Sailing Vessel — SP8

Polish Naval Ensign and Merchant Flag — SP9

Crane and Crane Tower, Gdansk SP10

**1945, Apr. 24** **Typo.** ***Perf. 11***

| | | | | |
|---|---|---|---|---|
| **B36** | SP7 | 50g + 2z red | 2.50 | 19.00 |
| **B37** | SP8 | 1z + 3z dp bl | 1.75 | 10.00 |
| **B38** | SP9 | 2z + 4z dk car | 1.50 | 10.00 |
| **B39** | SP10 | 3z + 5z ol grn | 1.50 | 13.00 |
| | | *Nos. B36-B39 (4)* | 7.25 | 52.00 |
| | | Set, never hinged | 20.00 | |

Polish Maritime League, 25th anniv.

City Hall, Poznan — SP11

**1945, June 16** **Photo.**

| | | | | |
|---|---|---|---|---|
| **B40** | SP11 | 1z + 5z green | 8.50 | 30.00 |
| | | Never hinged | 20.00 | |

Postal Workers' Convention, Poznan, June 16, 1945. Exists imperf. Value, never hinged *$90.*

Last Stand at Westerplatte — SP12

**1945, Sept. 1**

| | | | | |
|---|---|---|---|---|
| **B41** | SP12 | 1z + 9z steel blue | 7.00 | 27.50 |
| | | Never hinged | 29.00 | |

Polish army's last stand at Westerplatte, Sept. 1, 1939. Exists imperf. Value, never hinged *$100.*

"United Industry" — SP13

**1945, Nov. 18 Unwmk. *Perf. 11***

**B42** SP13 1.50z + 8.50z sl blk 2.00 10.00
Never hinged 7.25

Trade Unions Congress, Warsaw, Nov. 18.
No. B42 exists imperf. Value, never hinged *$2,500.*

Polish Volunteers in Spain — SP14

**1946, Mar. 10**

**B43** SP14 3z + 5z red 1.50 15.00
Never hinged 3.50

Participation of the Jaroslaw Dabrowski Brigade in the Spanish Civil War.

14th Century Piast Eagle and Soldiers — SP15

**1946, May 2**

**B44** SP15 3z + 7z brn .40 3.50
Never hinged 1.10

Silesian uprisings of 1919-21, 1939-45.

"Death" Spreading Poison Gas over Majdanek Prison Camp — SP16

**1946, Apr. 29**

**B45** SP16 3z + 5z Prus grn 4.25 *16.00*
Never hinged 9.25

Issued to recall Majdanek, a concentration camp of World War II near Lublin.

Bydgoszcz (Bromberg) Canal — SP17

**1946, Apr. 19 Unwmk. *Perf. 11***

**B46** SP17 3z + 2z ol blk 1.50 13.00
Never hinged 3.25

600th anniv. of Bydgoszcz (Bromberg).

Map of Polish Coast and Baltic Sea — SP18

**1946, July 21**

**B47** SP18 3z + 7z dp bl .70 11.00
Never hinged 2.00

Maritime Holiday of 1946. The surtax was for the Polish Maritime League.

Salute to P.T.T. Casualty and Views of Gdansk — SP19

**1946, Sept. 14**

**B48** SP19 3z + 12z slate 1.00 14.00
Never hinged 2.25

Polish postal employees killed in the German attack on Danzig (Gdansk), Sept. 1939.
No. B48 exists imperf. Value, never hinged $160.

School Children — SP20

Designs: 6z+24z, Courtyard of Jagiellon University, Cracow. 11z+19z, Gregor Piramowicz (1735-1801), founder of Education Commission.

**1946, Oct. 10 Unwmk. *Perf. 11½***

**B49** SP20 3z + 22z dk red 16.50 65.00
**B49A** SP20 6z + 24z dk bl 16.50 65.00
**B49B** SP20 11z + 19z dk grn 16.50 65.00
*c.* Souv. sheet of 3, #B49-B49B 210.00 575.00
Never hinged 425.00
*Nos. B49-B49B (3)* 49.50 195.00
Never hinged 95.00

Polish educational work. Surtax was for International Bureau of Education.
No. B49Bc sold for 100z.

Stanislaw Stojalowski, Jakob Bojko, Jan Stapinski and Wincenty Witos — SP21

**1946, Dec. 1**

**B50** SP21 5z + 10z bl grn .45 12.00
**B51** SP21 5z + 10z dull blue .50 12.00
**B52** SP21 5z + 10z dk olive .45 12.00
*Nos. B50-B52 (3)* 1.40 36.00
Set, never hinged 3.25

50th anniv. of the Peasant Movement. The surtax was for education and cultural improvement among the Polish peasantry.

**No. 391 Surcharged in Red**

**1947, Feb. 4 *Perf. 11x10½***

**B53** A127 3z + 7z purple 3.50 22.50
Never hinged 7.00

Opening of the Polish Parliament, 1/19/47.

No. 344 Surcharged in Blue

**1947, Feb. 21 *Perf. 12½***

**B54** A103 5z + 15z on 25g 1.50 8.50
Never hinged 3.25

Ski Championship Meet, Zakopane. Counterfeits exist.

Emil Zegadlowicz — SP22

**1947, Mar. 1 Photo. *Perf. 11***

**B55** SP22 5z + 15z dl gray grn 1.00 12.00
Never hinged 2.25

Nurse and War Victims — SP23

**1947, June 1 *Perf. 10½***

**B56** SP23 5z + 5z ol blk & red 1.75 10.00
Never hinged 4.00

The surtax was for the Red Cross.

Adam Chmielowski SP24

**1947, Dec. 21 *Perf. 11***

**B57** SP24 2z + 18z dk vio .45 9.50
Never hinged 1.10

Zamkowy Square and Proposed Highway SP25

**1948, Nov. 1**

**B58** SP25 15z + 5z green .40 1.10

The surtax was to aid in the reconstruction of Warsaw.

Infant and TB Crosses — SP26

Various Portraits of Children

**1948, Dec. 16 *Perf. 11½***

**B59** SP26 3z + 2z dl grn 1.75 5.00
**B60** SP26 5z + 5z brn 1.40 3.50
**B61** SP26 6z + 4z vio .85 2.40
**B62** SP26 15z + 10z car lake .35 1.00
*Nos. B59-B62 (4)* 4.35 11.90
Set, never hinged 8.50

Alternate vertical rows of stamps was ten different labels. The surtax was for anti-tuberculosis work among children.

**Catalogue values for unused stamps in this section, from this point to the end of the section, are for Never Hinged items.**

**Workers Party Type of 1952**

***Perf. 12½***

**1952, Jan. 18 Engr. Unwmk.**

**B63** A195 45g + 15g Marceli Nowotko .25 .25

**Women's Day Type of 1952**

**1952, Mar. 8 *Perf. 12½x12***

**B64** A196 45g + 15g chocolate .35 .35

**Swierczewski-Walter Type of 1952**

**1952, Mar. 28 *Perf. 12½***

**B65** A197 45g + 15g chocolate .65 .30

**Bierut Type of 1952**

**1952, Apr. 18**

**B66** A198 45g + 15g red .70 .25
**B67** A198 1.20z + 15g ultra .70 .25

**Type of Regular Issue of 1951-52 Inscribed "Plan 6," etc.**

Design: 45g+15g, Electrical installation.

**1952**

**B68** A193 30g + 15g brn red .75 .25
**B69** A193 45g + 15g chocolate 1.15 .25
**B69A** A194 1.20z + 15g red org .55 .25
*Nos. B68-B69A (3)* 2.45 .75

**Labor Day Type of Regular Issue of 1952**

**1952, May 1**

**B70** A200 45g + 15g car rose .50 .25

**Similar to Regular Issue of 1952**

No. B71, Maria Konopnicka. No. B72, Hugo Kollataj.

**1952, May Different Frames**

**B71** A201 30g + 15g blue green .50 .60
**B72** A201 45g + 15g brown .35 .40

Issued: No. B71, May 10. No. B72, May 20.

Leonardo da Vinci — SP28

**1952, June 1**

**B73** SP28 30g + 15g ultra 1.10 .65

500th birth anniv. of Leonardo da Vinci.

Pres. Bierut and Children — SP29

**1952, June 1 Photo. *Perf. 13½x14***

**B74** SP29 45g + 15g blue 2.50 1.20

Intl. Children's Day, June 1.

**Sports Type**

**1952, June 21 *Perf. 13***

45g+15g, Soccer players and trophy.

**B75** A203 30g + 15g blue 3.75 1.00
**B76** A203 45g + 15g purple 1.25 .25

Yachts SP31 — "Dar Pomorza" SP32

**1952, June 28 Engr. *Perf. 12½***

| | | | |
|---|---|---|---|
| **B77** SP31 | 30g + 15g dp bl grn | 4.25 | 1.40 |
| **B78** SP32 | 45g + 15g dp ultra | 2.25 | .35 |

Shipbuilders' Day, 1952.

Workers on Holiday — SP33

Students SP34

**1952, July 17 *Perf. 12½x12, 12x12½***

| | | | |
|---|---|---|---|
| **B79** SP33 | 30g + 15g dp grn | .50 | .25 |
| **B80** SP34 | 45g + 15g red | .50 | .25 |

Issued to publicize the Youth Festival, 1952.

### Constitution Type of Regular Issue

**1952, July 22 Photo. *Perf. 11***

| | | | |
|---|---|---|---|
| **B81** A208 | 45g + 15g lt bl grn & dk brn | 2.75 | .25 |

### Power Plant Type of Regular Issue

**1952, Aug. 7 Engr. *Perf. 12½***

| | | | |
|---|---|---|---|
| **B82** A209 | 45g + 15g red | .75 | .25 |

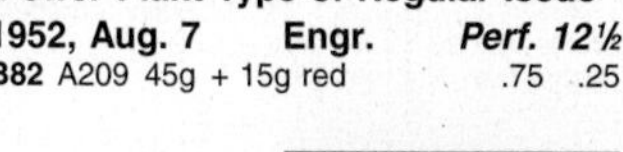

Ludwik Warynski SP36

**1952, July 31**

| | | | |
|---|---|---|---|
| **B83** SP36 | 30g + 15g dk red | .45 | .25 |
| **B84** SP36 | 45g + 15g blk brn | 1.15 | .40 |

70th birth anniv. of Ludwik Warynski, political organizer.

Church of Frydman — SP37

**1952, Aug. 18**

| | | | |
|---|---|---|---|
| **B85** SP37 | 45g + 15g vio brn | 1.60 | 1.20 |

Aviator Watching Glider — SP38

Design: 45g+15g, Pilot entering plane.

**1952, Aug. 23**

| | | | |
|---|---|---|---|
| **B86** SP38 | 30g + 15g grn | 1.75 | .85 |
| **B87** SP38 | 45g + 15g brn red | 3.75 | .50 |

Aviation Day, Aug. 23.

Henryk Sienkiewicz — SP39

**1952, Oct. 25**

| | | | |
|---|---|---|---|
| **B88** SP39 | 45g + 15g vio brn | 1.00 | .40 |

Henryk Sienkiewicz (1846-1916), author of "Quo Vadis" and other novels, Nobel prizewinner (literature, 1905).

### Revolution Type of Regular Issue

**1952, Nov. 7 *Perf. 12x12½***

| | | | |
|---|---|---|---|
| **B92** A214 | 45g + 15g red brn | 1.50 | .25 |

Exists imperforate. See No. 562.

Lenin — SP42

**1952, Nov. 7 *Perf. 12½***

| | | | |
|---|---|---|---|
| **B93** SP42 | 30g + 15g vio brn | .70 | .60 |
| **B94** SP42 | 45g + 15g brn | 1.10 | .25 |
| *a.* | "LENIN" omitted | | 32.50 |

Month of Polish-Soviet friendship, Nov. 1952.

Miner — SP43

**1952, Dec. 4**

| | | | |
|---|---|---|---|
| **B95** SP43 | 45g + 15g blk brn | .80 | .25 |
| **B96** SP43 | 1.20z + 15g brn | 1.20 | .60 |

Miners' Day, Dec. 4.

Henryk Wieniawski and Violin — SP44

**1952, Dec. 5 Photo.**

| | | | |
|---|---|---|---|
| **B97** SP44 | 30g + 15g dk grn | 1.50 | .85 |
| **B98** SP44 | 45g + 15g purple | 1.50 | .40 |

Henryk Wieniawski; 2nd Intl. Violin Competition.

### Type of Regular Issue of 1952

**1952, Dec. 12 Engr.**

| | | | |
|---|---|---|---|
| **B99** A215 | 45g + 15g dp grn | .35 | .25 |

Truck Factory, Lublin — SP45

**1953, Feb. 20**

| | | | |
|---|---|---|---|
| **B100** SP45 | 30g + 15g dp bl | 1.40 | .60 |
| **B101** SP45 | 60g + 20g vio brn | .35 | .25 |

Souvenir Sheet

Town Hall in Poznan — SP46

**Photo. & Litho.**

**1955, July 7 *Imperf.***

| | | | |
|---|---|---|---|
| **B102** SP46 | 2z pck grn & ol grn | 1.75 | 1.40 |
| **B103** SP46 | 3z car rose & ol blk | 24.00 | 14.00 |

6th Polish Philatelic Exhibition in Poznan. Sheets sold for 3z and 4.50z respectively.

Souvenir Sheet

"Peace" (POKOJ) and Warsaw Mermaid — SP47

Design: 1z, Pansies (A266) and inscription on map of Europe, Africa and Asia.

**1955, Aug. 3**

| | | | |
|---|---|---|---|
| **B104** SP47 | 1z bis, rose vio & yel | 1.75 | .75 |
| **B105** SP47 | 2z ol gray, ultra & lt bl | 20.00 | 9.50 |

Intl. Phil. Exhib., Warsaw, Aug. 1-14, 1955. Sheets sold for 2z and 3z respectively.

Souvenir Sheet

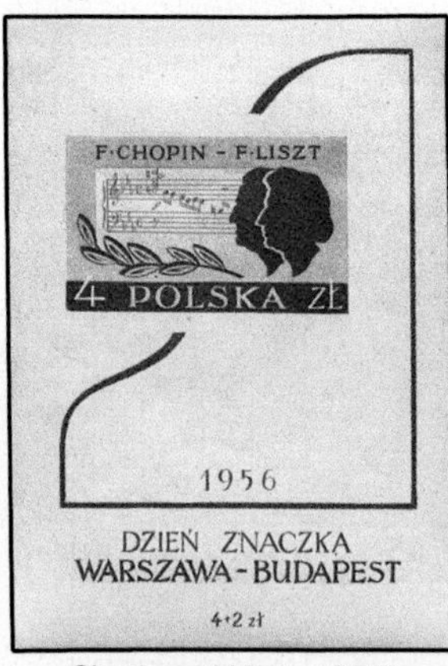


Chopin and Liszt — SP48

**1956, Oct. 25 Photo. *Imperf.***

| | | | |
|---|---|---|---|
| **B106** SP48 | 4z dk blue grn | 27.50 | 16.00 |

Day of the Stamp; Polish-Hungarian friendship. The sheet sold for 6z.

Souvenir Sheet

Stamp of 1860 — SP49

**Wmk. 326**

**1960, Sept. 4 Litho. *Perf. 11***

| | | | |
|---|---|---|---|
| **B107** SP49 | Sheet of 4 | 50.00 | 42.50 |
| *a.* | 10z + 10z blue, red & black | 9.00 | 9.00 |

Intl. Phil. Exhib. "POLSKA 60," Warsaw, 9/3-11.
Sold only with 5z ticket to exhibition.

### Type of Space Issue, 1964

Design: Yuri A. Gagarin in space capsule.

***Perf. 12½x12***

**1964, Dec. 30 Unwmk.**

| | | | |
|---|---|---|---|
| **B108** A432 | 6.50z + 2z Prus grn & multi | 1.25 | .45 |

Souvenir Sheet

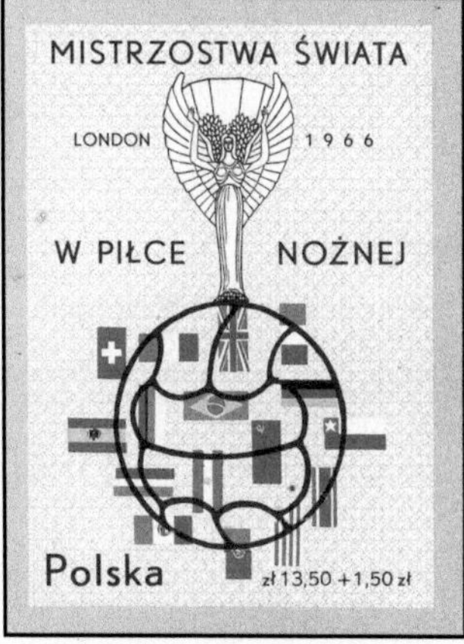


Jules Rimet Cup and Flags of Participating Countries — SP50

**1966, May 9 Litho. *Imperf.***

| | | | |
|---|---|---|---|
| **B109** SP50 | 13.50z + 1.50z multi | 2.00 | 1.00 |

World Cup Soccer Championship, Wembley, England, July 11-30.

Souvenir Sheet

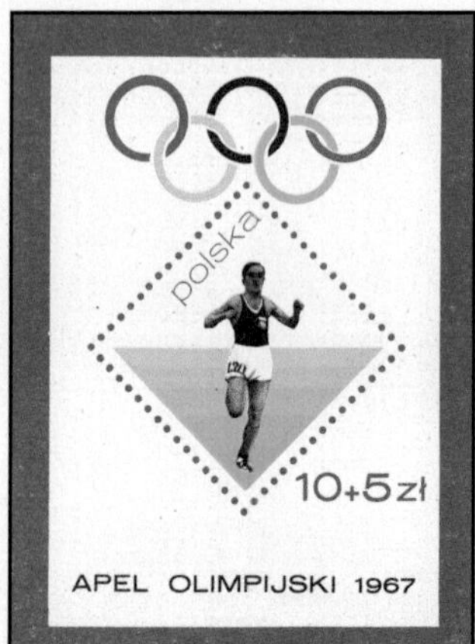


J. Kusocinski, Olympic Winner 10,000-Meter Race, 1932 — SP51

**1967, May 24 Litho. *Imperf.***
**B110** SP51 10z + 5z multi 1.50 .80

19th Olympic Games, Mexico City, 1968. Simulated perforations.

### Flower Type of Regular Issue

Flowers: 4z+2z, Abutilon. 8z+4z, Rosa polyantha hybr.

**1968, May 15 Litho. *Perf. 11½***
**B111** A492 4z + 2z vio & multi .85 .30
**B112** A492 8z + 4z lt vio & multi 1.40 .40

### Olympic Type of Regular Issue, 1968

Design: 10z+5z, Runner with Olympic torch and Chin cultic carved stone disc showing Mayan ball player and game's scoreboard.

**1968, Sept. 2 Litho. *Perf. 11½***
**Size: 56x45mm**
**B113** A497 10z + 5z multi 1.50 .40

19th Olympic Games, Mexico City, Oct. 12-27. The surtax was for the Polish Olympic Committee.

### Olympic Type of Regular Issue, 1969

Olympic Rings and: 2.50z+50g, Women's discus. 3.40z+1z, Running. 4z+1.50z, Boxing. 7z+2z, Fencing.

**1969, Apr. 25 Litho. *Perf. 11½x11***
**B114** A505 2.50z + 50g multi .25 .25
**B115** A505 3.40z + 1z multi .25 .25
**B116** A505 4z + 1.50z multi .50 .25
**B117** A505 7z + 2z multi 1.00 .35
*Nos. B114-B117 (4)* 2.00 1.10

### Folk Art Type of Regular Issue

5.50z+1.50z, Choir. 7z+1.50z, Organ grinder.

**1969, Dec. 19 Litho. *Perf. 11½x11***
**Size: 24x36mm**
**B118** A520 5.50z + 1.50z multi .50 .25
**B119** A520 7z + 1.50z multi .65 .25

### Sports Type of Regular Issue
Souvenir Sheet

Design: "Horse of Glory," by Z. Kaminski.

**1970, June 16 Photo. *Imperf.***
**B120** A532 10z + 5z multi 1.50 .75

The surtax was for the Polish Olympic Committee. No. B120 contains one imperf. stamp with simulated perforations.

### Tapestry Type of Regular Issue
Souvenir Sheet

Design: 7z+3z, Satyrs holding monogram of King Sigismund Augustus.

**1970, Dec. 23 Photo. *Imperf.***
**B121** A541 7z + 3z multi 1.40 .75

### Type of Regular Issue

Design: 8.50z+4z, Virgin Mary, 15th century stained glass window.

**1971, Sept. 15 *Perf. 11½x11***
**B122** A555 8.50z + 4z multi .75 .35

### Painting Type of Regular Issue

7z+1z, Nude, by Wojciech Weiss (1875-1950).

**1971, Oct. 9 Litho.**
**B123** A556 7z + 1z multi .85 .60

### Winter Olympic Type of Regular Issue
Souvenir Sheet

Slalom and Sapporo '72 emblem, vert.

**1972, Jan. 12 Photo. *Imperf.***
**B124** A564 10z + 5z multi 2.25 1.00

No. B124 contains one stamp with simulated perforations, 27x52mm.

### Summer Olympic Type of Regular Issue
Souvenir Sheet

Design: 10z+5z, Archery (like 30g).

**1972, May 20 Photo. *Perf. 11½x11***
**B125** A568 10z + 5z multi 1.50 .75

### Painting Type of Regular Issue, 1972

Design: 8.50z+4z, Portrait of a Young Lady, by Jacek Malczewski, horiz.

**1972, Sept. 28 Photo. *Perf. 11x10½***
**B126** A576 8.50z + 4z multi 1.40 .55

Souvenir Sheet

Copernicus — SP52

### Engraved and Photogravure

**1972, Sept. 28 *Perf. 11½***
**B127** SP52 10z + 5z vio bl, gray & car 1.75 .80

Nicolaus Copernicus (1473-1543), astronomer. No. B127 shows the Ptolemaic and Copernican concepts of solar system from L'Harmonica Microcosmica, by Cellarius, 1660.

Souvenir Sheet

Poznan, 1740, by F. B. Werner — SP53

**1973, Aug. 19 *Imperf.***
**B128** SP53 10z + 5z ol & dk brn 1.00 .60
*a.* 10z + 5z pale lilac & dk brn 5.00 5.25

POLSKA 73 Intl. Phil. Exhib., Poznan, Aug. 19-Sept. 2. No. B128 contains one stamp with simulated perforations.

No. B128a was sold only in combination with an entrance ticket.

Copernicus, by Marcello Bacciarelli — SP54

**1973, Sept. 27 Photo. *Perf. 11x11½***
**B129** SP54 4z + 2z multi .40 .25

Stamp Day. The surtax was for the reconstruction of the Royal Castle in Warsaw.

Souvenir Sheet

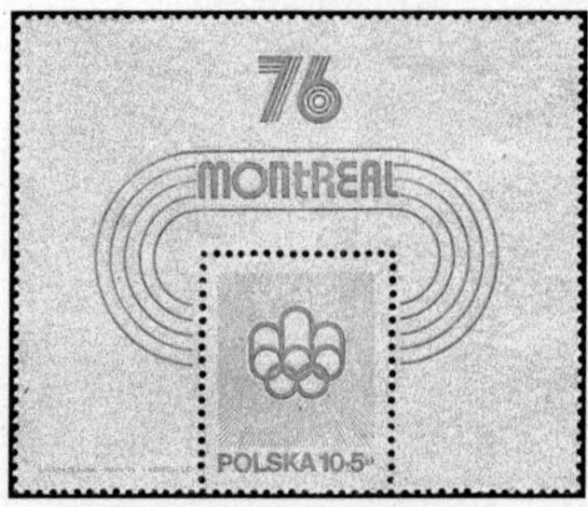


Montreal Olympic Games Emblem — SP55

### Photo. & Engr.

**1975, Mar. 8 *Perf. 12***
**B130** SP55 10z + 5z sil & grn 1.75 .65

21st Olympic Games, Montreal, July 17-Aug. 8, 1976.
Outer edge of souvenir sheet is perforated.

### Dunikowski Type of 1975

Design: 8z+4z, Mother and Child, from Silesian Insurrectionist Monument, by Dunikowski.

**1975, Oct. 9 Photo. *Perf. 11½x11***
**B131** A644 8z + 4z multi .50 .25

Souvenir Sheet

Volleyball — SP56

### Engraved and Photogravure

**1976, June 30 *Perf. 11½***
**B132** SP56 10z + 5z blk & car 1.50 .75

21st Olympic Games, Montreal, Canada, July 17-Aug. 1. No. B132 contains one perf. 11½ stamp and is perf. 11½ all around.

### Corinthian Art Type 1976

Design: 8z+4z, Winged Sphinx, vert.

**1976, Oct. 30 Photo. *Perf. 11½x11***
**B133** A664 8z + 4z multi .80 .30

Souvenir Sheet

Stoning of St. Stephen, by Rubens — SP57

**1977, Apr. 30 Engr. *Perf. 12x11½***
**B134** SP57 8z + 4z sepia 1.00 .40

Peter Paul Rubens (1577-1640), Flemish painter.
Outer edge of souvenir sheet is perforated.

Souvenir Sheet

Kazimierz Gzowski — SP58

**1978, June 6 Photo. *Perf. 11½x11***
**B135** SP58 8.40z + 4z multi 1.10 .60

CAPEX, '78 Canadian Intl. Phil. Exhib., Toronto, June 9-18.
K. S. Gzowski (1813-1898), Polish engineer and lawyer living in Canada, built International Bridge over Niagara River.

Souvenir Sheet

Olympic Rings — SP59

**1979, May 19 Engr. *Imperf.***
**B136** SP59 10z + 5z black .90 .65

1980 Olympic Games.

### Monument Type of 1979
Souvenir Sheet

**1979, Sept. 1 Photo. *Imperf.***
**B137** A731 10z + 5z multi 1.00 .60

Surtax was for monument.

### Summer Olympic Type of 1980
Souvenir Sheet

**1980, Mar. 31 Photo. *Perf. 11x11½***
**B138** A742 10.50z + 5z Kayak 1.00 .60

No. B138 contains one stamp 42x30mm.

Souvenir Sheet

Intercosmos Cooperative Space Program — SP60

**1980, Apr. 12** ***Perf. 11½x11***
**B139** SP60 6.90z + 3z multi .80 .60

SP61

1970 Uprising Memorial: 2.50z + 1z, Triple Crucifix, Gdansk (27x46mm). 6.50z + 1z, Monument, Gdynia.

**1981, Dec. 16** **Photo.** ***Perf. 11½x12***
**B140** SP61 2.50 + 1z blk & red .35 .25
**B141** SP61 6.50 + 1z blk & lil .40 .25

SP62

Portrait of a German Princess, by Lucas Cranach.

**1984, May 15** **Photo.** ***Perf. 11½x12***
**B142** SP62 27z + 10z multi 1.25 1.00

1984 UPU Congress, Hamburg. No. B142 issued se-tenant with multicolored label showing UPU emblem and text.

Souvenir Sheet

Madonna with Child, St. John and the Angel, by Sandro Botticelli (1445-1510), Natl. Museum, Warsaw — SP63

**1985, Sept. 25** **Photo.** ***Perf. 11***
**B143** SP63 65z + 15z multi 2.25 1.25
*a.* Inscribed: 35 LAT POLSKIEGO . . . 5.00 5.00

ITALIA '85. Surtax for Polish Association of Philatelists.

No. B143a was for the 35th anniv. of the Polish Philatelic Union. Distribution was limited.

Joachim Lelewel (1786-1861), Historian — SP64

**1986, Dec. 22** **Photo.** ***Perf. 11½x12***
**B144** SP64 10z + 5z multi .40 .25

Surtax for the Natl. Committee for School Aid.

Polish Immigrant Settling in Kasubia, Ontario — SP65

**1987, June 13** **Photo.** ***Perf. 12x11½***
**B145** SP65 50z + 20z multi .75 .30

CAPEX '87, Toronto, Canada. Surtaxed for the Polish Philatelists' Union.

Souvenir Sheet

OLYMPHILEX '87, Rome — SP66

**1987, Aug. 28** **Litho.** ***Perf. 14***
**B146** SP66 45z + 10z like #2617 1.10 1.10

FINLANDIA '88 — SP67

**1988, June 1** **Photo.** ***Perf. 12x11½***
**B147** SP67 45z +20z Salmon, reindeer .75 .30

Souvenir Sheet

Jerzy Kukuczka, Mountain Climber Awarded Medal by the Intl. Olympic Committee for Climbing the Himalayas — SP68

**1988, Aug. 17** **Photo.** ***Perf. 11x11½***
**B148** SP68 70z +10z multi 1.00 .65

Surtax for the Polish Olympic Fund.

Aid for Victims of 1997 Oder River Flood — SP69

**1997, Aug. 18** **Photo.** ***Perf. 11½x12***
**B149** SP69 60g +30g multi .65 .40

Souvenir Sheet

Museum of Posts and Telecommunications, 80th Anniv. — SP70

**2001, Oct. 9** **Photo.** ***Perf. 11¼x11½***
**B150** SP70 3z +75g multi 2.40 1.25

---

**AIR POST STAMPS**

Biplane — AP1

***Perf. 12½***
**1925, Sept. 10** **Typo.** **Unwmk.**
**C1** AP1 1g lt blue .65 9.00
**C2** AP1 2g orange .65 9.00
**C3** AP1 3g yellow brn .65 9.00
**C4** AP1 5g dk brown .65 .80
**C5** AP1 10g dk green .65 .80
**C6** AP1 15g red violet 3.25 .80
**C7** AP1 20g olive grn 7.50 4.00
**C8** AP1 30g dull rose 7.50 2.25
**C9** AP1 45g dk violet 8.50 3.75
*Nos. C1-C9 (9)* 30.00 39.40
Set, never hinged 95.00

Counterfeits exist.

Nos. C1-C9 exist imperf. Value, set $125.

For overprint see No. C11.

Capt. Franciszek Zwirko and Stanislaus Wigura — AP2

***Perf. 11½ to 12½ and Compound***
**1933, Apr. 15** **Engr.** **Wmk. 234**
**C10** AP2 30g gray green 16.50 1.40
Never hinged 47.50

Winning of the circuit of Europe flight by two Polish aviators in 1932. The stamp was available for both air mail and ordinary postage.

For overprint see No. C12.

Nos. C7 and C10 Ovptd. in Red

**1934, Aug. 28** **Unwmk.** ***Perf. 12½***
**C11** AP1 20g olive green 7.75 7.00

**Wmk. 234**
***Perf. 11½***
**C12** AP2 30g gray green 8.75 2.00
Set, never hinged 45.00

**Polish People's Republic**

Douglas Plane over Ruins of Warsaw — AP3

**Unwmk.**
**1946, Mar. 5** **Photo.** ***Perf. 11***
**C13** AP3 5z grnsh blk .35 .25
*a.* Without control number 5.75 1.20
Never hinged 11.00
**C14** AP3 10z dk purple .35 .25
**C15** AP3 15z blue 1.15 .25
**C16** AP3 20z rose brn .70 .25
**C17** AP3 25z dk bl grn 1.50 .40
**C18** AP3 30z red 2.25 .55
*Nos. C13-C18 (6)* 6.30 1.95
Set, never hinged 13.50

The 10z, 20z and 30z were issued only with control number in lower right stamp margin. The 15z and 25z exist only without number. The 5z comes both ways.

Nos. C13-C18 exist imperforate. Value, set $125.

**Nos. 345, 344 and 344a Surcharged in Red or Black**

a

b

**1947, Sept. 10** ***Perf. 12½***
**C19** A104(a) 40z on 50g (R) 1.75 1.50
**C20** A103(b) 50z on 25g dl red 2.25 2.50
*a.* 50z on 25g deep red 3.00 2.75
Never hinged, #C20a 4.50 2.25
Set, never hinged 9.00

Counterfeits exist.

Centaur
AP4

**1948** *Perf. 11*

| | | | | |
|---|---|---|---|---|
| **C21** | AP4 | 15z dk violet | 1.50 | .25 |
| **C22** | AP4 | 25z deep blue | .80 | .25 |
| **C23** | AP4 | 30z brown | .65 | .25 |
| **C24** | AP4 | 50z dk green | 1.25 | .25 |
| **C25** | AP4 | 75z gray black | 1.50 | .25 |
| **C26** | AP4 | 100z red orange | 1.50 | .25 |
| | | *Nos. C21-C26 (6)* | 7.20 | 1.50 |
| | | Set, never hinged | 15.00 | |

Nos. C21-C26 exist imperf.

Pres. F. D. Roosevelt
AP5

100z, Casimir Pulaski. 120z, Tadeusz Kosciusko.

**1948, Dec. 30 Photo.** *Perf. 11½*

**Granite Paper**

| | | | | |
|---|---|---|---|---|
| **C26A** | AP5 | 80z blue blk | 13.00 | *27.00* |
| **C26B** | AP5 | 100z purple | 14.00 | *27.00* |
| **C26C** | AP5 | 120z deep blue | 14.00 | *27.00* |
| *d.* | | Souvenir sheet of 3 | 210.00 | *300.00* |
| | | Never hinged | 325.00 | |
| | | *Nos. C26A-C26C (3)* | 41.00 | *81.00* |
| | | Set, never hinged | 67.50 | |

Nos. C26A-C26C were issued in panes containing 16 stamps and 4 labels. Value, never hinged set of three with labels $140.

No. C26Cd contains stamps similar to Nos. C26A-C26C with colors changed: 80z ultramarine, 100z carmine rose, 120z dark green. Sold for 500z.

Airplane Mechanic and Propeller — AP5a

**1950, Feb. 6 Engr.** *Perf. 12½*

| | | | | |
|---|---|---|---|---|
| **C27** | AP5a | 500z rose lake | 3.75 | 6.50 |
| | | Never hinged | 6.00 | |

**Catalogue values for unused stamps in this section, from this point to the end of the section, are for Never Hinged items.**

Seaport
AP6

Designs: 90g, Mechanized farm. 1.40z, Warsaw. 5z, Steel mill.

**1952, Apr. 10** *Perf. 12x12½*

| | | | | |
|---|---|---|---|---|
| **C28** | AP6 | 55g intense blue | 1.00 | .25 |
| **C29** | AP6 | 90g dull green | 1.25 | .35 |
| **C30** | AP6 | 1.40z violet brn | 1.10 | .25 |
| **C31** | AP6 | 5z gray black | 1.25 | .35 |
| | | *Nos. C28-C31 (4)* | 4.60 | 1.20 |

Nos. C28-C31 exist imperf. Value $29.

Congress
Badge — AP7

**1953, Aug. 24 Photo.** *Imperf.*

| | | | | |
|---|---|---|---|---|
| **C32** | AP7 | 55g brown lilac | 1.75 | .35 |
| **C33** | AP7 | 75g brown org | 3.00 | 1.40 |

3rd World Congress of Students, Warsaw 1953.

Souvenir Sheet

AP8

**1954, May 23 Engr.** *Perf. 12x12½*

| | | | | |
|---|---|---|---|---|
| **C34** | AP8 | 5z gray green | 40.00 | 25.00 |

3rd congress of the Polish Phil. Assoc., Warsaw, 1954. Sold for 7.50 zlotys. A similar sheet, imperf. and in dark blue, was issued but had no postal validity. Value: mint $275; cto $275.

Paczkow Castle, Luban — AP9

80g, Kazimierz Dolny. 1.15z, Wawel castle, Cracow. 1.50z, City Hall, Wroclaw. 1.55z, Lazienki Park, Warsaw. 1.95z, Cracow gate, Lublin.

**1954, July 13** *Perf. 12½*

| | | | | |
|---|---|---|---|---|
| **C35** | AP9 | 60g dk gray grn | .60 | .25 |
| **C36** | AP9 | 80g red | .60 | .25 |
| **C37** | AP9 | 1.15z black | 3.75 | 1.25 |
| **C38** | AP9 | 1.50z rose lake | .60 | .25 |
| **C39** | AP9 | 1.55z dp gray bl | .60 | .25 |
| **C40** | AP9 | 1.95z chocolate | 1.75 | .85 |
| | | *Nos. C35-C40 (6)* | 7.90 | 3.10 |

Plane over "Peace" Steelworks — AP10

Plane over: 1.50z, Castle Square, Warsaw. 3.40z, Old Market, Cracow. 3.90z, King Boleslaw Chrobry Wall, Szczecin. 4z, Karkonosze mountains. 5z, Gdansk. 10z, Ruins of Liwa Castle. 15z, Old City, Lublin. 20z, Kasprowy Wierch Peak and cable car. 30z, Porabka dam. 50z, M. S. Batory and Gdynia harbor.

**Wmk. 326 ('58 Values); Unwmkd.**

**1957-58 Engr. & Photo.** *Perf. 12½*

| | | | | |
|---|---|---|---|---|
| **C41** | AP10 | 90g black & pink | .35 | .25 |
| **C42** | AP10 | 1.50z brn & salmon | .35 | .25 |
| **C43** | AP10 | 3.40z sep & buff | .35 | .25 |
| **C44** | AP10 | 3.90z dk brn & cit | .35 | .25 |
| **C45** | AP10 | 4z ind & lt grn | .35 | .25 |
| **C46** | AP10 | 5z maroon & gray | .75 | .25 |
| **C47** | AP10 | 10z sepia & grn | 1.40 | .25 |
| **C48** | AP10 | 15z vio bl & pale bl | 1.40 | .70 |
| **C49** | AP10 | 20z vio blk & lem | 1.50 | .70 |
| **C50** | AP10 | 30z ol gray & bis | 4.25 | 3.25 |
| **C51** | AP10 | 50z dk bl & gray | 10.00 | 4.50 |
| | | *Nos. C41-C51 (11)* | 21.05 | 10.90 |

Issue dates: 5z, 10z, 20z, 30z, 50z, Dec. 15, 1958. Others, Dec. 6, 1957.

**1959, May 23 Litho. Wmk. 326**

| | | | | |
|---|---|---|---|---|
| **C52** | AP10 | 10z sepia | 2.00 | 1.75 |
| *a.* | | With 5z label | 3.50 | 3.50 |

65th anniv. of the Polish Philatelic Society. Sheet of 6 stamps and 2 each of 3 different labels. Each label carries an added charge of 5z for a fund to build a Society clubhouse in Warsaw.

Jantar
Glider — AP11

Contemporary aviation: 10z, Mi6 transport helicopter. 20z, PZL-106 Kruk, crop spraying plane. 50z, Plane over Warsaw Castle.

**1976-78 Unwmk. Engr.** *Perf. 11½*

| | | | | |
|---|---|---|---|---|
| **C53** | AP11 | 5z dk blue grn | .45 | .30 |
| **C54** | AP11 | 10z dk brown | .95 | .60 |
| **C55** | AP11 | 20z grnsh black | 1.60 | .30 |
| **C56** | AP11 | 50z claret | 2.75 | .65 |
| | | *Nos. C53-C56 (4)* | 5.75 | 1.85 |

Issued: 5z, 10z, 3/27/76; 20z, 2/15/77; 50z, 2/2/78.

## AIR POST SEMI-POSTAL STAMP

**Catalogue values for unused stamps in this section are for Never Hinged items.**

### Polish People's Republic

Wing of Jet Plane and Letter — SPAP1

*Perf. 11½*

**1957, Mar. 28 Unwmk. Photo.**

| | | | | |
|---|---|---|---|---|
| **CB1** | SPAP1 | 4z + 2z blue | 2.75 | 2.75 |
| *a.* | | Souv. sheet of 1, ultra, imperf. | 10.00 | 5.00 |

7th Polish National Philatelic Exhibition, Warsaw. Sheet of 12 with 4 diagonally arranged gray labels.

## REGISTRATION STAMPS

Insects — R1

Designs: (3.80z), Polyommatus semiargus. (5.90z), Rosalia alpina. (6.70z), Gerris paludum. (9.30z), Sympetrum flaveolum.

*Perf. 11¾x11½*

**2013, Aug. 16 Photo.**

| | | | | |
|---|---|---|---|---|
| **F1** | R1 | (3.80z) multi | 2.40 | 2.40 |
| **F2** | R1 | (5.90z) multi | 3.75 | 3.75 |
| **F3** | R1 | (6.70z) multi | 4.25 | 4.25 |
| **F4** | R1 | (9.30z) multi | 6.00 | 6.00 |
| | | *Nos. F1-F4 (4)* | 16.40 | 16.40 |

Insects — R2

Designs: (5.90z), Coccinella septempunctata. (6.70z), Chorthippus parallelus. (6.95z), Inachis io. (9.30z), Formica rufa.

*Perf. 11¾x11½*

**2013, Sept. 30 Photo.**

| | | | | |
|---|---|---|---|---|
| **F5** | R2 | (5.90z) multi | 4.00 | 4.00 |
| **F6** | R2 | (6.70z) multi | 4.50 | 4.50 |
| **F7** | R2 | (6.95z) multi | 4.50 | 4.50 |
| **F8** | R2 | (9.30z) multi | 6.00 | 6.00 |
| | | *Nos. F5-F8 (4)* | 19.00 | 19.00 |

Insects — R3

Designs: (8.50z), Arctia caja. (9.50z), Papilio machaon caterpillar. (11z), Apis mellifera. (13.10z), Lucanus cervus.

*Perf. 11¾x11½*

**2013, Oct. 18 Photo.**

| | | | | |
|---|---|---|---|---|
| **F9** | R3 | (8.50z) multi | 5.50 | 5.50 |
| **F10** | R3 | (9.50z) multi | 6.00 | 6.00 |
| **F11** | R3 | (11z) multi | 7.00 | 7.00 |
| **F12** | R3 | (13.10z) multi | 8.50 | 8.50 |
| | | *Nos. F9-F12 (4)* | 27.00 | 27.00 |

## POSTAGE DUE STAMPS

### Cracow Issues

Postage Due Stamps of Austria, 1916, Overprinted in Black or Red

**1919, Jan. 10 Unwmk.** *Perf. 12½*

| | | | | |
|---|---|---|---|---|
| **J1** | D4 | 5h rose red | 15.50 | 15.50 |
| **J2** | D4 | 10h rose red | *4,000.* | *6,500.* |
| **J3** | D4 | 15h rose red | 10.50 | 9.00 |
| *a.* | | Inverted overprint | 7,750. | *2,250.* |
| **J4** | D4 | 20h rose red | 650.00 | *525.00* |
| **J5** | D4 | 25h rose red | 32.50 | *35.00* |
| **J6** | D4 | 30h rose red | *1,600.* | *1,200.* |
| **J7** | D4 | 40h rose red | *300.00* | *300.00* |
| **J8** | D5 | 1k ultra (R) | *4,250.* | *4,750.* |
| **J9** | D5 | 5k ultra (R) | *4,250.* | *4,750.* |
| **J10** | D5 | 10k ultra (R) | *17,000.* | *20,000.* |
| *a.* | | Black overprint | *65,000.* | *77,500.* |

Overprint on Nos. J1-J7, J10a is type. Overprint on Nos. J8-J10 is slightly larger than illustration, has a different ornament between lines of type and is litho.

Austria Nos. J61 and J63 Surcharged in Black

**1919, Jan. 10**

| | | | | |
|---|---|---|---|---|
| **J11** | A38 | 15h on 36h vio | *525.00* | 325.00 |
| **J12** | A38 | 50h on 42h choc | 65.00 | *37.50* |
| *a.* | | Double surcharge | 2,750. | *4,250.* |

**See note above No. 41. Counterfeits exist of Nos. J1-J12.**

### Regular Issues

Numerals of Value — D7

**1919** **Typo.** ***Perf. 11½***

**For Northern Poland**

| | | | | |
|---|---|---|---|---|
| **J13** | D7 | 2f red orange | .25 | .25 |
| **J14** | D7 | 4f red orange | .25 | .25 |
| **J15** | D7 | 5f red orange | .25 | .25 |
| **J16** | D7 | 10f red orange | .25 | .25 |
| **J17** | D7 | 20f red orange | .25 | .25 |
| **J18** | D7 | 30f red orange | .25 | .25 |
| **J19** | D7 | 50f red orange | .25 | .25 |
| **J20** | D7 | 100f red orange | .50 | .35 |
| **J21** | D7 | 500f red orange | 2.50 | 2.40 |

**For Southern Poland**

| | | | | |
|---|---|---|---|---|
| **J22** | D7 | 2h dark blue | .25 | .25 |
| **J23** | D7 | 4h dark blue | .25 | .25 |
| **J24** | D7 | 5h dark blue | .25 | .25 |
| **J25** | D7 | 10h dark blue | .25 | .25 |
| **J26** | D7 | 20h dark blue | .25 | .25 |
| **J27** | D7 | 30h dark blue | .25 | .25 |
| **J28** | D7 | 50h dark blue | .35 | .25 |
| **J29** | D7 | 100h dark blue | .45 | .80 |
| **J30** | D7 | 500h dark blue | 1.40 | 1.60 |
| | | *Nos. J13-J30 (18)* | 8.45 | 8.65 |
| | | Set, never hinged | 33.00 | |

Counterfeits exist.

**1920** ***Perf. 9, 10, 11½***

**Thin Laid Paper**

| | | | | |
|---|---|---|---|---|
| **J31** | D7 | 20f dark blue | .25 | .25 |
| **J32** | D7 | 100f dark blue | .25 | .25 |
| **J33** | D7 | 200f dark blue | .35 | .25 |
| **J34** | D7 | 500f dark blue | .35 | .25 |
| | | *Nos. J31-J34 (4)* | 1.20 | 1.00 |
| | | Set, never hinged | 4.25 | |

Regular Issue of 1919 Surcharged

**1921, Jan. 25** ***Imperf.***

**Wove Paper**

| | | | | |
|---|---|---|---|---|
| **J35** | A9 | 6m on 15h brown | .75 | .75 |
| **J36** | A9 | 6m on 25h car | .75 | .75 |
| **J37** | A9 | 20m on 10h lake | 5.00 | 7.00 |
| **J38** | A9 | 20m on 50h indigo | 4.00 | 5.25 |
| **J39** | A9 | 35m on 70h dp bl | 7.00 | 9.25 |
| | | *Nos. J35-J39 (5)* | 17.50 | 23.00 |
| | | Set, never hinged | 21.00 | |

Counterfeits exist.

Numerals of Value — D8

**Thin Laid or Wove Paper**

**Size: 17x22mm**

***Perf. 9 to 14½ and Compound***

**1921-22** **Typo.**

| | | | | |
|---|---|---|---|---|
| **J40** | D8 | 1m indigo | .25 | .25 |
| **J41** | D8 | 2m indigo | .25 | .25 |
| **J42** | D8 | 4m indigo | .25 | .25 |
| **J43** | D8 | 6m indigo | .45 | .25 |
| **J44** | D8 | 8m indigo | .45 | .25 |
| **J45** | D8 | 20m indigo | .45 | .25 |
| **J46** | D8 | 50m indigo | .45 | .25 |
| **J47** | D8 | 100m indigo | .70 | .35 |
| | | *Nos. J40-J47 (8)* | 3.25 | 2.10 |
| | | Set, never hinged | 13.00 | |

**Nos. J44-J45, J41 Surcharged**

***Perf. 9 to 14½ and Compound***

**1923, Nov.**

| | | | | |
|---|---|---|---|---|
| **J48** | D8 | 10,000(m) on 8m indigo | .35 | .25 |
| **J49** | D8 | 20,000(m) on 20m indigo | .35 | .25 |
| **J50** | D8 | 50,000(m) on 2m indigo | .45 | .45 |
| | | *Nos. J48-J50 (3)* | 1.15 | .95 |
| | | Set, never hinged | 5.75 | |

**Type of 1921-22 Issue**

**Size: 19x24mm**

**1923** **Typo.** ***Perf. 12½***

| | | | | |
|---|---|---|---|---|
| **J51** | D8 | 50m indigo | .25 | .25 |
| **J52** | D8 | 100m indigo | .25 | .25 |
| **J53** | D8 | 200m indigo | .25 | .25 |
| **J54** | D8 | 500m indigo | .60 | .25 |
| **J55** | D8 | 1000m indigo | .35 | .25 |
| **J56** | D8 | 2000m indigo | .40 | .30 |
| **J57** | D8 | 10,000m indigo | .25 | .25 |
| **J58** | D8 | 20,000m indigo | .35 | .25 |
| **J59** | D8 | 30,000m indigo | .35 | .25 |
| **J60** | D8 | 50,000m indigo | .35 | .25 |
| **J61** | D8 | 100,000m indigo | .40 | .25 |
| **J62** | D8 | 200,000m indigo | .40 | .25 |
| **J63** | D8 | 300,000m indigo | 5.00 | .35 |
| **J64** | D8 | 500,000m indigo | 1.75 | .25 |
| **J65** | D8 | 1,000,000m indigo | 1.00 | .30 |
| **J66** | D8 | 2,000,000m indigo | 1.75 | .35 |
| **J67** | D8 | 3,000,000m indigo | 3.00 | 1.40 |
| | | *Nos. J51-J67 (17)* | 16.70 | 5.70 |
| | | Set, never hinged | 67.50 | |

D9

***Perf. 10 to 13½ and Compound***

**1924** **Size: 20x25½mm**

| | | | | |
|---|---|---|---|---|
| **J68** | D9 | 1g brown | .25 | .25 |
| **J69** | D9 | 2g brown | .25 | .25 |
| **J70** | D9 | 4g brown | .30 | .25 |
| **J71** | D9 | 6g brown | .30 | .25 |
| **J72** | D9 | 10g brown | 1.25 | .25 |
| **J73** | D9 | 15g brown | 4.50 | .25 |
| **J74** | D9 | 20g brown | 3.25 | .25 |
| **J75** | D9 | 25g brown | 6.25 | .25 |
| **J76** | D9 | 30g brown | .75 | .25 |
| **J77** | D9 | 40g brown | 1.00 | .25 |
| **J78** | D9 | 50g brown | 1.00 | .25 |
| **J79** | D9 | 1z brown | .45 | .25 |
| **J80** | D9 | 2z brown | .45 | .25 |
| **J81** | D9 | 3z brown | .75 | 1.50 |
| **J82** | D9 | 5z brown | .40 | .60 |
| | | *Nos. J68-J82 (15)* | 21.15 | 5.35 |
| | | Set, never hinged | 92.50 | |

Nos. J68-J69 and J72-J75 exist measuring 19½x24½mm.

For surcharges see Nos. J84-J91.

D10

**1930, July** ***Perf. 12½***

| | | | | |
|---|---|---|---|---|
| **J83** | D10 | 5g olive brown | .70 | .25 |
| | | Never hinged | 1.00 | |

Postage Due Stamps of 1924 Surcharged

***Perf. 10 to 13½ and Compound***

**1934-38**

| | | | | |
|---|---|---|---|---|
| **J84** | D9 | 10g on 2z brown ('38) | .25 | .25 |
| **J85** | D9 | 15g on 2z brown | .25 | .25 |
| **J86** | D9 | 20g on 1z brown | .40 | .25 |
| **J87** | D9 | 20g on 5z brown | 6.00 | .25 |
| **J88** | D9 | 25g on 40g brown | .85 | .25 |
| **J89** | D9 | 30g on 40g brown | 1.40 | .25 |
| **J90** | D9 | 50g on 40g brown | 1.40 | .50 |
| **J91** | D9 | 50g on 3z brown ('35) | .85 | .35 |
| | | *Nos. J84-J91 (8)* | 11.40 | 2.35 |
| | | Set, never hinged | 52.50 | |

No. 255a Surcharged in Red or Indigo

**1934-36** **Laid Paper**

| | | | | |
|---|---|---|---|---|
| **J92** | A50 | 10g on 1z (R) ('36) | .80 | .25 |
| | *a.* | Vertically laid paper (No. 255) | 25.00 | 18.00 |
| **J93** | A50 | 20g on 1z (R) ('36) | 2.50 | .80 |
| **J94** | A50 | 25g on 1z (I) | .80 | .30 |
| | *a.* | Vertically laid paper (No. 255) | 30.00 | 18.00 |
| | | *Nos. J92-J94 (3)* | 4.10 | 1.35 |
| | | Set, never hinged | 13.00 | |

D11

**1938-39** **Typo.** ***Perf. 12½x12***

| | | | | |
|---|---|---|---|---|
| **J95** | D11 | 5g dark blue green | .25 | .25 |
| **J96** | D11 | 10g dark blue green | .25 | .25 |
| **J97** | D11 | 15g dark blue green | .25 | .25 |
| **J98** | D11 | 20g dark blue green | .35 | .25 |
| **J99** | D11 | 25g dark blue green | .35 | .25 |
| **J100** | D11 | 30g dark blue green | .60 | .25 |
| **J101** | D11 | 50g dark blue green | .95 | .25 |
| **J102** | D11 | 1z dark blue green | 5.00 | 1.65 |
| | | *Nos. J95-J102 (8)* | 8.00 | 3.40 |
| | | Set, never hinged | 14.00 | |

For surcharges see Nos. N51-N55.

**Polish People's Republic**

Post Horn with Thunderbolts D12

**Size: 26½x19½mm**

***Perf. 11x10½***

**1945, May 20** **Litho.** **Unwmk.**

| | | | | |
|---|---|---|---|---|
| **J103** | D12 | 1z orange brown | .25 | .25 |
| **J104** | D12 | 2z orange brown | .25 | .25 |
| **J105** | D12 | 3z orange brown | .25 | .25 |
| **J106** | D12 | 5z orange brown | .35 | .30 |
| | | *Nos. J103-J106 (4)* | 1.10 | 1.05 |
| | | Set, never hinged | 3.25 | |

Nos. J103-J106 exist imperf. Value, set $40.

**Type of 1945**

***Perf. 11, 11½ (P) or Imperf. (I)***

**1946-49** **Size: 29x21½mm** **Photo.**

| | | | | |
|---|---|---|---|---|
| **J106A** | D12 | 1z org brn (P) ('49) | .25 | .25 |
| **J107** | D12 | 2z org brn (P,I) | .25 | .25 |
| **J108** | D12 | 3z org brn (P,I) | .25 | .25 |
| **J109** | D12 | 5z org brn (I) | .25 | .25 |
| **J110** | D12 | 6z org brn (I) | .25 | .25 |
| **J111** | D12 | 10z org brn (I) | .25 | .25 |
| **J112** | D12 | 15z org brn (P,I) | .55 | .30 |
| **J113** | D12 | 25z org brn (P,I) | .75 | .60 |
| **J114** | D12 | 100z brn (P) ('49) | 1.50 | .90 |
| **J115** | D12 | 150z brn (P) ('49) | 2.00 | 1.00 |
| | | *Nos. J106A-J115 (10)* | 6.30 | 4.30 |
| | | Set, never hinged | 8.00 | |

Polish Eagle — D13

**1950** **Engr.** ***Perf. 12x12½***

| | | | | |
|---|---|---|---|---|
| **J116** | D13 | 5z red brown | .25 | .25 |
| **J117** | D13 | 10z red brown | .25 | .25 |
| **J118** | D13 | 15z red brown | .25 | .25 |
| **J119** | D13 | 20z red brown | .25 | .25 |
| **J120** | D13 | 25z red brown | .25 | .25 |
| **J121** | D13 | 50z red brown | .50 | .30 |
| **J122** | D13 | 100z red brown | .50 | .35 |
| | | *Nos. J116-J122 (7)* | 2.25 | 1.90 |
| | | Set, never hinged | 3.00 | |

**1951-52**

| | | | | |
|---|---|---|---|---|
| **J123** | D13 | 5g red brown | .25 | .25 |
| **J124** | D13 | 10g red brown | .25 | .25 |
| **J125** | D13 | 15g red brown | .25 | .25 |
| **J126** | D13 | 20g red brown | .25 | .25 |
| **J127** | D13 | 25g red brown | .25 | .25 |
| **J128** | D13 | 30g red brown | .25 | .25 |
| **J129** | D13 | 50g red brown | .25 | .25 |
| **J130** | D13 | 60g red brown | .25 | .25 |
| **J131** | D13 | 90g red brown | .50 | .45 |
| **J132** | D13 | 1z red brown | .25 | .25 |
| **J133** | D13 | 2z red brown | .25 | .25 |
| **J134** | D13 | 5z brown violet | .60 | .60 |
| | | *Nos. J123-J134 (12)* | 3.60 | 3.55 |
| | | Set, never hinged | 4.00 | |

**Without imprint**

**1953, Apr.** **Photo.**

| | | | | |
|---|---|---|---|---|
| **J135** | D13 | 5g red brown | .25 | .25 |
| **J136** | D13 | 10g red brown | .25 | .25 |
| **J137** | D13 | 15g red brown | .25 | .25 |
| **J138** | D13 | 20g red brown | .25 | .25 |
| **J139** | D13 | 25g red brown | .25 | .25 |
| **J140** | D13 | 30g red brown | .25 | .25 |
| **J141** | D13 | 50g red brown | .25 | .25 |
| **J142** | D13 | 60g red brown | .35 | .25 |
| **J143** | D13 | 90g red brown | .30 | .25 |
| **J144** | D13 | 1z red brown | .25 | .25 |
| **J145** | D13 | 2z red brown | .55 | .55 |
| | | *Nos. J135-J145 (11)* | 3.20 | 3.05 |
| | | Set, never hinged | 3.50 | |

**Catalogue values for unused stamps in this section, from this point to the end of the section, are for Never Hinged items.**

**1980, Sept. 2** **Litho.** ***Perf. 12½***

| | | | | |
|---|---|---|---|---|
| **J146** | D13 | 1z lt red brown | .25 | .25 |
| **J147** | D13 | 2z gray olive | .25 | .25 |
| **J148** | D13 | 3z dull violet | .25 | .25 |
| **J149** | D13 | 5z brown | .40 | .25 |
| | | *Nos. J146-J149 (4)* | 1.15 | 1.00 |

D14

**1998, June 18** **Litho.** ***Perf. 14***

| | | | | |
|---|---|---|---|---|
| **J150** | D14 | 5g lilac, blk & yel | .25 | .25 |
| **J151** | D14 | 10g green blue, blk & yel | .25 | .25 |
| **J152** | D14 | 20g green, blk & yel | .25 | .25 |
| **J153** | D14 | 50g yellow & black | .30 | .30 |
| **J154** | D14 | 80g orange, blk & yel | .40 | .45 |
| **J155** | D14 | 1z red, blk & yel | .60 | .70 |
| | | *Nos. J150-J155 (6)* | 2.05 | 2.20 |

## OFFICIAL STAMPS

O1

***Perf. 10, 11½, 10x11½, 11½x10***

**1920, Feb. 1** **Litho.** **Unwmk.**

| | | | | |
|---|---|---|---|---|
| **O1** | O1 | 3f vermilion | .25 | .25 |
| **O2** | O1 | 5f vermilion | .25 | .25 |
| **O3** | O1 | 10f vermilion | .25 | .25 |
| **O4** | O1 | 15f vermilion | .25 | .25 |
| **O5** | O1 | 25f vermilion | .25 | .25 |
| **O6** | O1 | 50f vermilion | .25 | .25 |
| **O7** | O1 | 100f vermilion | .25 | .25 |
| **O8** | O1 | 150f vermilion | .25 | .25 |
| **O9** | O1 | 200f vermilion | .65 | .45 |
| **O10** | O1 | 300f vermilion | .75 | .50 |
| **O11** | O1 | 600f vermilion | 1.40 | 1.75 |
| | | *Nos. O1-O11 (11)* | 4.80 | 4.70 |
| | | Set, never hinged | 14.00 | |

The stars on either side of the denomination do not appear on Nos. O7-O11. Nos. O7-O11 exist imperf. Value, set $27.50.

**Numerals Larger**

**Stars inclined outward**

**1920, Nov. 20** ***Perf. 11½***

**Thin Laid Paper**

| | | | | |
|---|---|---|---|---|
| **O12** | O1 | 5f red | .25 | .25 |
| **O13** | O1 | 10f red | .25 | .25 |
| **O14** | O1 | 15f red | .25 | .25 |
| **O15** | O1 | 25f red | .60 | .25 |
| **O16** | O1 | 50f red | .35 | .25 |
| | | *Nos. O12-O16 (5)* | 1.70 | 1.25 |
| | | Set, never hinged | 6.50 | |

Polish Eagle — O3

***Perf. 12x12½***

**1933, Aug. 1** **Typo.** **Wmk. 234**

| | | | | |
|---|---|---|---|---|
| **O17** | O3 | (30g) vio (Zwyczajna) | .35 | .25 |
| **O18** | O3 | (80g) red (Polecona) | .35 | .25 |
| | | Set, never hinged | 3.00 | |

Polish Eagle — O4

**1935, Apr. 1**
**O19** O4 (25g) bl vio (Zwyczajna) .25 .25
**O20** O4 (55g) car (Polecona) .25 .25
Set, never hinged 1.40

Stamps inscribed "Zwyczajna" or "Zwykla" were for ordinary official mail. Those with "Polecona" were for registered official mail.

### Polish People's Republic

Polish Eagle — O5

*Perf. 11, 14*
**1945, July 1 Photo. Unwmk.**
**O21** O5 (5z) bl vio (Zwykla) .25 .25
*a.* Imperf. 3.50 3.50
**O22** O5 (10z) red (Polecona) .25 .25
*a.* Imperf. 7.00 7.00
Set, never hinged, #O21, O22 1.40
Set, never hinged, #O21a, O22a 10.00

Control number at bottom right: M-01705 on No. O21; M-01706 on No. O22.

### Type of 1945 Redrawn

**1946, July 31**
**O23** O5 (5z) dl bl vio (Zwykla) .25 .25
**O24** O5 (10z) dl rose red (Polecona) .25 .25
Set, never hinged 1.50

The redrawn stamps appear blurred and the eagle contains fewer lines of shading.
Control number at bottom right: M-01709 on Nos. O23-O26.

### Redrawn Type of 1946

**1946, July 31** *Imperf.*
**O25** O5 (60g) dl bl vio (Zwykla) .25 .25
**O26** O5 (1.55z) dl rose red (Polecona) .25 .25
Set, never hinged 1.50

### Type of 1945, 2nd Redrawing

No Control Number at Lower Right
*Perf. 11, 11½, 11x12½*
**1950-53 Unwmk.**
**O27** O5 (60g) blue (Zwykla) .25 .25
**O28** O5 (1.55z) red (Polecona) ('53) .25 .25
Set, never hinged 1.50

### Redrawn Type of 1952

**1954** *Perf. 13x11, 11½, 14*
**O29** O5 (60g) slate gray (Zwykla) 3.00 1.00
Never hinged 5.00

O6

*Perf. 11x11½, 12x12½*
**1954, Aug. 15 Engr.**
**O30** O6 (60g) dark blue (Zwykla) .25 .25
**O31** O6 (1.55z) red (Polecona) .30 .25
Set, never hinged 2.00

Polish People's Republic, 10th anniversary.

## NEWSPAPER STAMPS

Austrian Newspaper Stamps of 1916 Overprinted

**1919, Jan. 10 Unwmk.** *Imperf.*
**P1** N9 2h brown 19.00 *19.00*
**P2** N9 4h green 18.00 *15.00*
**P3** N9 6h dark blue 15.00 *14.00*
**P4** N9 10h orange 240.00 175.00
**P5** N9 30h claret 19.00 17.00
*Nos. P1-P5 (5)* 311.00 240.00

**See note above No. 41. Counterfeits exist of Nos. P1-P5.**

## OCCUPATION STAMPS

### Issued under German Occupation

German Stamps of 1905 Overprinted

*Perf. 14, 14½*
**1915, May 12 Wmk. 125**
**N1** A16 3pf brown .65 .85
**N2** A16 5pf green 1.40 .85
**N3** A16 10pf carmine 1.40 .85
**N4** A16 20pf ultra 2.75 1.25
**N5** A16 40pf lake & blk 8.25 6.25
*Nos. N1-N5 (5)* 14.45 10.05
Set, never hinged 45.00

German Stamps of 1905-17 Overprinted

**1916-17**
**N6** A22 2½pf gray 1.50 *2.50*
**N7** A16 3pf brown 1.50 *2.50*
**N8** A16 5pf green 1.50 *2.50*
**N9** A22 7½pf orange 1.50 *2.50*
**N10** A16 10pf carmine 1.50 *2.50*
**N11** A22 15pf yel brn 4.25 3.50
**N12** A22 15pf dk vio ('17) 1.50 *2.50*
**N13** A16 20pf ultra 2.10 *2.50*
**N14** A16 30pf org & blk, *buff* 8.50 *15.00*
**N15** A16 40pf lake & blk 3.00 2.50
**N16** A16 60pf magenta 3.50 *3.50*
*Nos. N6-N16 (11)* 30.35 42.00
Set, never hinged 95.00

For overprints and surcharges see #15-26.

German Stamps of 1934 Surcharged in Black

**1939, Dec. 1 Wmk. 237** *Perf. 14*
**N17** A64 6g on 3pf bister .25 *.40*
**N18** A64 8g on 4pf dl bl .25 *.40*
**N19** A64 12g on 6pf dk grn .25 *.40*
**N20** A64 16g on 8pf vermilion .50 1.25
**N21** A64 20g on 10pf choc .25 .40
**N22** A64 24g on 12pf dp car .25 .25
**N23** A64 30g on 15pf maroon .50 1.25
**N24** A64 40g on 20pf brt bl .50 .40
**N25** A64 50g on 25pf ultra .50 .80
**N26** A64 60g on 30pf ol grn .50 .40
**N27** A64 80g on 40pf red vio .55 .80
**N28** A64 1z on 50pf dk grn & blk 1.10 1.60
**N29** A64 2z on 100(pf) org & blk 2.25 *3.00*
*Nos. N17-N29 (13)* 7.65 11.35
Set, never hinged 27.50

Stamps of Poland 1937, Surcharged in Black or Brown

**1940 Unwmk.** *Perf. 12½, 12½x13*
**N30** A80 24g on 25g sl grn 1.25 *3.25*
**N31** A81 40g on 30g rose vio .40 1.25
**N32** A80 50g on 55g blue .30 *.80*

### Similar Surcharge on Stamps of 1938-39

**N33** A83 2g on 5g red org .25 *.40*
**N34** A83 4(g) on 5g red org .25 *.40*
**N35** A83 6(g) on 10g grn .25 *.40*
**N36** A83 8(g) on 10g grn (Br) .25 *.40*
**N37** A83 10(g) on 10g grn .25 *.40*
**N38** A83 12(g) on 15g redsh brn (#339) .25 *.40*
**N39** A83 16(g) on 15g redsh brn (#339) .25 *.40*
**N40** A83 24g on 25g dl vio .25 *.40*
**N41** A83 30(g) on 30g rose red .25 *.40*
**N42** A83 50(g) on 50g brt red vio .25 *.65*
**N43** A83 60(g) on 55g ultra 6.00 *17.00*
**N44** A83 80(g) on 75g dl grn 6.00 *17.00*
**N45** A83 1z on 1z org 6.25 *17.00*
**N46** A83 2z on 2z car rose 3.00 *7.50*
**N47** A95 3z on 3z gray blk 4.00 *10.00*

### Similar Surcharge on Nos. B32-B34

**N48** SP5 30g on 5g+5g .25 .65
**N49** SP5 40g on 25g+10g .25 .65
**N50** SP5 1z on 55g+15g 4.00 *10.00*

### Similar Surcharge on Nos. J98-J102

*Perf. 12½x12*
**N51** D11 50(g) on 20g 1.25 *3.25*
**N52** D11 50(g) on 25g 6.00 *17.50*
**N53** D11 50(g) on 30g 14.00 *37.50*
**N54** D11 50(g) on 50g .75 *2.40*
**N55** D11 50(g) on 1z 1.75 *4.75*
*Nos. N30-N55 (26)* 57.95 *154.75*
Set, never hinged 160.00

The surcharge on Nos. N30 to N55 is arranged to fit the shape of the stamp and obliterate the original denomination. On some values, "General Gouvernement" appears at the bottom. Counterfeits exist.

St. Florian's Gate, Cracow — OS1

Palace, Warsaw — OS13

Designs: 8g, Watch Tower, Cracow. 10g, Cracow Gate, Lublin. 12g, Courtyard and statue of Copernicus. 20g, Dominican Church, Cracow. 24g, Wawel Castle, Cracow. 30g, Church, Lublin. 40g, Arcade, Cloth Hall, Cracow. 48g, City Hall, Sandomierz. 50g, Court House, Cracow. 60g, Courtyard, Cracow. 80g, St. Mary's Church, Cracow.

**1940-41 Unwmk. Photo.** *Perf. 14*
**N56** OS1 6g brown .25 *.75*
**N57** OS1 8g brn org .25 *.75*
**N58** OS1 8g bl blk ('41) .45 *.50*
**N59** OS1 10g emerald .25 *.25*
**N60** OS1 12g dk grn 2.00 .70
**N61** OS1 12g dp vio ('41) .30 *.25*
**N62** OS1 20g dk ol brn .25 .25
**N63** OS1 24g henna brn .25 .25
**N64** OS1 30g purple .25 .25
**N65** OS1 30g vio brn ('41) .30 *.25*
**N66** OS1 40g slate blk .25 .25
**N67** OS1 48g chnt brn ('41) .60 *1.50*
**N68** OS1 50g brt bl .25 .25
**N69** OS1 60g slate grn .25 *.25*
**N70** OS1 80g dull pur .25 *.50*
**N71** OS13 1z rose lake 2.00 1.25
**N72** OS13 1z Prus grn ('41) .55 *1.00*
*Nos. N56-N72 (17)* 8.70 9.20
Set, never hinged 22.50

For surcharges see Nos. NB1-NB4.

Cracow Castle and City, 15th Century OS14

**1941, Apr. 20 Engr.** *Perf. 14½*
**N73** OS14 10z red & ol blk 1.10 *2.75*
Never hinged 2.50

Printed in sheets of 8.

Rondel and Florian's Gate, Cracow OS15

Design: 4z, Tyniec Monastery, Vistula River.

**1941** *Perf. 13½x14*
**N74** OS15 2z dk ultra .90 *1.00*
**N75** OS15 4z slate grn .90 *1.75*
Set, never hinged 3.50

Adolf Hitler — OS17

**1941-43 Unwmk. Photo.** *Perf. 14*
**N76** OS17 2g gray blk .25 .25
**N77** OS17 6g golden brn .25 .25
**N78** OS17 8g slate blue .25 .25
**N79** OS17 10g green .25 .25
**N80** OS17 12g purple .25 .25
**N81** OS17 16g org red 1.60 *2.00*
**N82** OS17 20g blk brn .25 .25
**N83** OS17 24g henna .25 .25
**N84** OS17 30g rose vio .25 .25
**N85** OS17 32g dk bl grn .50 *.50*
**N86** OS17 40g brt blue .25 .25
**N87** OS17 48g chestnut 1.40 *.80*
**N88** OS17 50g vio bl ('43) .30 .50
**N89** OS17 60g dk olive ('43) .30 .50
**N90** OS17 80g dk vio ('43) .30 .50
*Nos. N76-N90 (15)* 6.65 7.05
Set, never hinged 12.00

A 20g black brown exists with head of Hans Frank substituted for that of Hitler. It was printed and used by Resistance movements.
Nos. N76-N90 exist imperf. Value, set unused $300.

**1942-44 Engr.** *Perf. 12½*
**N91** OS17 50g vio bl .50 *1.00*
**N92** OS17 60g dk ol .50 *1.00*
**N93** OS17 80g dk red vio .50 *1.00*
**N94** OS17 1z slate grn .50 *1.00*
*a.* Perf. 14 ('44) 1.00 *12.00*
**N95** OS17 1.20z dk brn .80 *1.60*
*a.* Perf. 14 ('44) 2.00 *16.00*
**N96** OS17 1.60z bl vio .80 *1.60*
*a.* Perf. 14 ('44) 2.00 *20.00*
*Nos. N91-N96 (6)* 3.60 *7.20*
Set, never hinged 7.25
Set, #N94a, N95a, N96a, never hinged 9.50

Nos. N91-N96 exist imperf. Value, set unused *$1,250.*

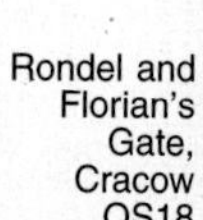

Rondel and Florian's Gate, Cracow OS18

Designs: 4z, Tyniec Monastery, Vistula River. 6z, View of Lwow. 10z, Cracow Castle and City, 15th Century.

**1943-44** *Perf. 13½x14*
**N100** OS18 2z slate grn .40 .80
**N101** OS18 4z dk gray vio 1.20 *2.40*
**N102** OS18 6z sepia ('44) .60 *1.20*
**N103** OS18 10z org brn & gray blk .60 *1.60*
*Nos. N100-N103 (4)* 2.80 *6.00*
Set, never hinged 5.50

## OCCUPATION SEMI-POSTAL STAMPS

### Issued under German Occupation

Types of 1940 Occupation Postage Stamps Surcharged in Red

**Unwmk.**

**1940, Aug. 17 Photo. *Perf. 14***

| | | | | |
|---|---|---|---|---|
| **NB1** | OS1 | 12g + 8g olive gray | 2.00 | *3.50* |
| **NB2** | OS1 | 24g + 16g olive gray | 2.00 | *3.50* |
| **NB3** | OS1 | 50g + 50g olive gray | 2.00 | *4.50* |
| **NB4** | OS1 | 80g + 80g olive gray | 2.00 | *6.00* |
| | | *Nos. NB1-NB4 (4)* | 8.00 | *17.50* |
| | | Set, never hinged | 16.00 | |

German Peasant Girl in Poland OSP1

Designs: 24g+26g, Woman wearing scarf. 30g+20g, Similar to type OSP4.

**1940, Oct. 26 Engr. *Perf. 14½***

**Thick Paper**

| | | | | |
|---|---|---|---|---|
| **NB5** | OSP1 | 12g + 38g dk sl grn | 1.20 | 2.75 |
| **NB6** | OSP1 | 24g + 26g cop red | 1.20 | 2.75 |
| **NB7** | OSP1 | 30g + 20g dk pur | 2.00 | *5.00* |
| | | *Nos. NB5-NB7 (3)* | 4.40 | 10.50 |
| | | Set, never hinged | 8.75 | |

1st anniversary of the General Government.

German Peasant OSP4

**1940, Dec. 1 *Perf. 12***

| | | | | |
|---|---|---|---|---|
| **NB8** | OSP4 | 12g + 8g dk grn | .80 | *1.60* |
| **NB9** | OSP4 | 24g + 16g rose red | .80 | *2.00* |
| **NB10** | OSP4 | 30g + 30g vio brn | 1.40 | *2.50* |
| **NB11** | OSP4 | 50g + 50g ultra | 1.40 | *3.00* |
| | | *Nos. NB8-NB11 (4)* | 4.40 | *9.10* |
| | | Set, never hinged | 8.75 | |

The surtax was for war relief.

Adolf Hitler — OSP5

**Unwmk.**

**1942, Apr. 20 Engr. *Perf. 11***

**Thick Cream Paper**

| | | | | |
|---|---|---|---|---|
| **NB12** | OSP5 | 30g + 1z brn car | .60 | *1.60* |
| **NB13** | OSP5 | 50g + 1z dk ultra | .60 | *1.60* |
| **NB14** | OSP5 | 1.20z + 1z brown | .60 | *1.60* |
| | | *Nos. NB12-NB14 (3)* | 1.80 | *4.80* |
| | | Set, never hinged | 3.50 | |

To commemorate Hitler's 53rd birthday. Printed in sheets of 25.

Ancient Lublin — OSP6

Designs: 24g+6g, 1z+1z, Modern Lublin.

**1942, Aug. 15 Photo. *Perf. 12½***

| | | | | |
|---|---|---|---|---|
| **NB15** | OSP6 | 12g + 8g rose vio | .30 | *.65* |
| **NB16** | OSP6 | 24g + 6g henna | .30 | *.65* |
| **NB17** | OSP6 | 50g + 50g dp bl | .30 | *1.20* |
| **NB18** | OSP6 | 1z + 1z dp grn | .65 | *1.60* |
| | | *Nos. NB15-NB18 (4)* | 1.55 | *4.10* |
| | | Set, never hinged | 3.25 | |

600th anniversary of Lublin.

Veit Stoss — OSP8

Designs: 24g+26g, Hans Durer. 30g+30g, Johann Schuch. 50g+50g, Joseph Elsner. 1z+1z, Nicolaus Copernicus.

**1942, Nov. 20 Engr. *Perf. 13½x14***

| | | | | |
|---|---|---|---|---|
| **NB19** | OSP8 | 12g + 18g dl pur | .25 | *.40* |
| **NB20** | OSP8 | 24g + 26g dl henna | .25 | *.40* |
| **NB21** | OSP8 | 30g + 30g dl rose vio | .25 | *.40* |
| **NB22** | OSP8 | 50g + 50g dl bl vio | .25 | *.65* |
| **NB23** | OSP8 | 1z + 1z dl myr grn | .25 | *.80* |
| | | *Nos. NB19-NB23 (5)* | 1.25 | 2.65 |
| | | Set, never hinged | 1.60 | |

For overprint see No. NB27.

Adolf Hitler — OSP13

**1943, Apr. 20**

| | | | | |
|---|---|---|---|---|
| **NB24** | OSP13 | 12g + 1z purple | .60 | *1.35* |
| **NB25** | OSP13 | 24g + 1z rose car | .60 | *1.35* |
| **NB26** | OSP13 | 84g + 1z myrtle grn | .60 | *1.35* |
| | | *Nos. NB24-NB26 (3)* | 1.80 | 4.05 |
| | | Set, never hinged | 3.50 | |

To commemorate Hitler's 54th birthday.

Type of 1942 Overprinted in Black

**1943, May 24**

| | | | | |
|---|---|---|---|---|
| **NB27** | OSP8 | 1z + 1z rose lake | .55 | *1.60* |
| | | Never hinged | .90 | |

Nicolaus Copernicus. Printed in sheets of 10, with marginal inscription.

Cracow Gate, Lublin — OSP14

Designs: 24g+76g, Cloth Hall, Cracow. 30g+70g, New Government Building, Radom. 50g+1z, Bruhl Palace, Warsaw. 1z+2z, Town Hall, Lwow.

The center of the designs is embossed with the emblem of the National Socialist Party.

**1943 Photogravure, Embossed**

| | | | | |
|---|---|---|---|---|
| **NB28** | OSP14 | 12g + 38g dk grn | .30 | *.95* |
| **NB29** | OSP14 | 24g + 76g red | .30 | *.95* |
| **NB30** | OSP14 | 30g + 70g rose vio | .30 | *.95* |
| **NB31** | OSP14 | 50g + 1z brt bl | .30 | *.95* |
| **NB32** | OSP14 | 1z + 2z bl blk | .30 | *.95* |
| | | *Nos. NB28-NB32 (5)* | 1.50 | 4.75 |
| | | Set, never hinged | 3.25 | |

3rd anniversary of the National Socialist Party in Poland.

Adolf Hitler — OSP19

**1944, Apr. 20 Photo. *Perf. 14x13½***

| | | | | |
|---|---|---|---|---|
| **NB33** | OSP19 | 12g + 1z green | .25 | *.95* |
| **NB34** | OSP19 | 24g + 1z brn red | .25 | *.95* |
| **NB35** | OSP19 | 84g + 1z dk vio | .25 | *.95* |
| | | *Nos. NB33-NB35 (3)* | .75 | 2.85 |
| | | Set, never hinged | 1.25 | |

To commemorate Hitler's 55th birthday. Printed in sheets of 25.

Conrad Celtis — OSP20

Designs: 24g+26g, Andreas Schluter. 30g+30g, Hans Boner. 50g+50g, Augustus II. 1z+1z, Georg Gottlieb Pusch.

**1944, July 15 Engr. *Perf. 13½x14***

| | | | | |
|---|---|---|---|---|
| **NB36** | OSP20 | 12g + 18g dk grn | .25 | *1.20* |
| **NB37** | OSP20 | 24g + 26g dk red | .25 | *1.20* |
| **NB38** | OSP20 | 30g + 30g rose vio | .25 | *1.60* |
| **NB39** | OSP20 | 50g + 50g ultra | .25 | *2.00* |
| **NB40** | OSP20 | 1z + 1z dl red brn | .25 | *2.00* |
| | | *Nos. NB36-NB40 (5)* | 1.25 | 8.00 |
| | | Set, never hinged | 1.60 | |

Cracow Castle OSP25

**1944, Oct. 26 *Perf. 14½***

| | | | | |
|---|---|---|---|---|
| **NB41** | OSP25 | 10z + 10z red & blk | 7.50 | *40.00* |
| | | Never hinged | 15.00 | |
| | *a.* | Imperf. | 12.00 | |
| | | Never hinged | 24.00 | |
| | *b.* | 10z + 10z car & greenish blk | 12.50 | 25.00 |
| | | Never hinged | 25.00 | |
| | *c.* | Horiz. pair, imperf. btwn. | *65.00* | |
| | | Never hinged | *90.00* | |

5th anniv. of the General Government, Oct. 26, 1944. Printed in sheets of 8.

## OCCUPATION RURAL DELIVERY STAMPS

### Issued under German Occupation

OSD1

***Perf. 13½***

**1940, Dec. 1 Photo. Unwmk.**

| | | | | |
|---|---|---|---|---|
| **NL1** | OSD1 | 10g red orange | .60 | *1.20* |
| **NL2** | OSD1 | 20g red orange | .60 | *1.25* |
| **NL3** | OSD1 | 30g red orange | .60 | *1.25* |
| **NL4** | OSD1 | 50g red orange | 1.40 | *3.00* |
| | | *Nos. NL1-NL4 (4)* | 3.20 | *6.70* |
| | | Set, never hinged | 6.50 | |

## OCCUPATION OFFICIAL STAMPS

### Issued under German Occupation

Eagle and Swastika OOS1

***Perf. 12, 13½x14***

**1940, Apr. Photo. Unwmk.**

**Size: 31x23mm**

| | | | | |
|---|---|---|---|---|
| **NO1** | OOS1 | 6g lt brown | .80 | *2.40* |
| **NO2** | OOS1 | 8g gray | .80 | *2.40* |
| **NO3** | OOS1 | 10g green | .80 | *2.40* |
| **NO4** | OOS1 | 12g dk green | .80 | *1.75* |
| **NO5** | OOS1 | 20g dk brown | .80 | *2.75* |
| **NO6** | OOS1 | 24g henna brn | 10.00 | 1.75 |
| **NO7** | OOS1 | 30g rose lake | .80 | *2.60* |
| **NO8** | OOS1 | 40g dl violet | .80 | *5.00* |
| **NO9** | OOS1 | 48g dl olive | 3.25 | *5.00* |
| **NO10** | OOS1 | 50g royal bl | .80 | 2.60 |
| **NO11** | OOS1 | 60g dk ol grn | .60 | *2.40* |
| **NO12** | OOS1 | 80g rose vio | .60 | *2.40* |

**Size: 35x26mm**

| | | | | |
|---|---|---|---|---|
| **NO13** | OOS1 | 1z gray blk & brn vio | 1.50 | *4.75* |
| **NO14** | OOS1 | 3z gray blk & chnt | 1.50 | *4.75* |
| **NO15** | OOS1 | 5z gray blk & org brn | 2.50 | *6.50* |
| | | *Nos. NO1-NO15 (15)* | 26.35 | 49.45 |
| | | Set, never hinged | 75.00 | |

**1940 Size: 21¼x16¼mm *Perf. 12***

| | | | | |
|---|---|---|---|---|
| **NO16** | OOS1 | 6g brown | .65 | *1.20* |
| **NO17** | OOS1 | 8g slate | .65 | *1.40* |
| **NO18** | OOS1 | 10g dp grn | 1.00 | *2.00* |
| **NO19** | OOS1 | 12g slate grn | .65 | *1.40* |
| **NO20** | OOS1 | 20g blk brn | .65 | *1.20* |
| **NO21** | OOS1 | 24g cop brn | 1.00 | *1.20* |
| **NO22** | OOS1 | 30g rose lake | .80 | *1.60* |
| **NO23** | OOS1 | 40g dl pur | .80 | *2.00* |
| **NO24** | OOS1 | 50g royal blue | .80 | *2.00* |
| | | *Nos. NO16-NO24 (9)* | 7.00 | *14.00* |
| | | Set, never hinged | 25.00 | |

Nazi Emblem and Cracow Castle — OOS2

**1943 Photo. *Perf. 14***

| | | | | |
|---|---|---|---|---|
| **NO25** | OOS2 | 6g brown | .30 | *.80* |
| **NO26** | OOS2 | 8g slate blue | .30 | *.80* |
| **NO27** | OOS2 | 10g green | .30 | *.80* |
| **NO28** | OOS2 | 12g dk vio | .30 | .80 |
| **NO29** | OOS2 | 16g red org | .40 | *.80* |
| **NO30** | OOS2 | 20g dk brn | .30 | .80 |
| **NO31** | OOS2 | 24g dk red | .30 | .80 |
| **NO32** | OOS2 | 30g rose vio | .30 | .80 |
| **NO33** | OOS2 | 40g blue | .30 | .80 |
| **NO34** | OOS2 | 60g olive grn | .30 | .80 |
| **NO35** | OOS2 | 80g dull claret | .30 | .80 |
| **NO36** | OOS2 | 100g slate blk | .60 | *1.60* |
| | | *Nos. NO25-NO36 (12)* | 4.00 | 10.40 |
| | | Set, never hinged | 18.00 | |

## POLISH OFFICES ABROAD

### OFFICES IN DANZIG

Poland Nos. 215-225 Overprinted

**1925, Jan. 5 Unwmk. *Perf. 11½x12***

| | | | | |
|---|---|---|---|---|
| **1K1** | A36 | 1g orange brn | .55 | 2.50 |
| **1K2** | A36 | 2g dk brown | .55 | 5.25 |
| **1K3** | A36 | 3g orange | .55 | 1.60 |
| **1K4** | A36 | 5g olive grn | 18.00 | 7.50 |
| **1K5** | A36 | 10g blue grn | 5.50 | 3.00 |
| **1K6** | A36 | 15g red | 30.00 | 7.50 |
| **1K7** | A36 | 20g blue | 1.60 | 1.50 |
| **1K8** | A36 | 25g red brown | 2.10 | 1.50 |
| **1K9** | A36 | 30g dp violet | 2.10 | 1.50 |
| **1K10** | A36 | 40g indigo | 2.10 | 1.50 |
| **1K11** | A36 | 50g magenta | 2.60 | 2.25 |
| | | *Nos. 1K1-1K11 (11)* | 65.65 | 35.60 |
| | | Set, never hinged | 375.00 | |

**Same Ovpt. on Poland Nos. 230-231**

**1926** ***Perf. 11½, 12***

| | | | | |
|---|---|---|---|---|
| **1K11A** | A39 | 5g yellow grn | 60.00 | 40.00 |
| **1K12** | A40 | 10g violet | 16.00 | 16.00 |
| | | Set, never hinged | 160.00 | |

Counterfeit overprints are known on Nos. 1K1-1K32.

No. 232 Overprinted

**1926-27**

| | | | | |
|---|---|---|---|---|
| **1K13** | A41 | 15g rose red | 50.00 | 55.00 |
| | | Never hinged | 200.00 | |

**Same Overprint on Redrawn Stamps of 1926-27**

***Perf. 13***

| | | | | |
|---|---|---|---|---|
| **1K14** | A39 | 5g yellow grn | 1.60 | 2.00 |
| **1K15** | A40 | 10g violet | 2.75 | 2.25 |
| **1K16** | A41 | 15g rose red | 5.00 | 4.00 |
| **1K17** | A43 | 20g dull red | 3.25 | 2.25 |
| | | *Nos. 1K14-1K17 (4)* | 12.60 | 10.50 |
| | | Set, never hinged | 40.00 | |

**Same Ovpt. on Poland Nos. 250, 255a**

**1928-30** ***Perf. 12½***

| | | | | |
|---|---|---|---|---|
| **1K18** | A44 | 25g yellow brn | 5.00 | 3.25 |
| | | Never hinged | 20.00 | |

**Laid Paper**

***Perf. 11½x12, 12½x11½***

| | | | | |
|---|---|---|---|---|
| **1K19** | A50 | 1z blk, *cr* ('30) | 20.00 | 32.50 |
| | | Never hinged | 55.00 | |

Poland Nos. 258-260 Overprinted

**1929-30** ***Perf. 12x12½***

| | | | | |
|---|---|---|---|---|
| **1K20** | A53 | 5g dk violet | 4.00 | 2.00 |
| **1K21** | A53 | 10g green ('30) | 4.00 | 2.00 |
| **1K22** | A53 | 25g red brown | 8.00 | 2.00 |
| | | *Nos. 1K20-1K22 (3)* | 16.00 | 6.00 |
| | | Set, never hinged | 32.50 | |

**Same Overprint on Poland No. 257**

**1931, Jan. 5** ***Perf. 12½***

| | | | | |
|---|---|---|---|---|
| **1K23** | A52 | 15g ultra | 8.50 | *6.00* |
| | | Never hinged | 20.00 | |

Poland No. 255 Overprinted in Dark Blue

**1933, July 1 Laid Paper** ***Perf. 11½***

| | | | | |
|---|---|---|---|---|
| **1K24** | A50 | 1z black, *cream* | 70.00 | *140.00* |
| | | Never hinged | 140.00 | |

Poland Nos. 268-270 Overprinted in Black

**1934-36 Wmk. 234** ***Perf. 12x12½***

| | | | | |
|---|---|---|---|---|
| **1K25** | A58 | 5g dl violet | 3.75 | 6.50 |
| **1K26** | A58 | 10g green ('36) | 32.50 | *100.00* |
| **1K27** | A58 | 15g red brown | 3.75 | 6.50 |
| | | *Nos. 1K25-1K27 (3)* | 40.00 | *113.00* |
| | | Set, never hinged | 110.00 | |

Poland Nos. 294, 296, 298 Overprinted in Black in one or two lines

**1935-36 Unwmk.** ***Perf. 12½x13***

| | | | | |
|---|---|---|---|---|
| **1K28** | A65 | 5g violet blue | 3.00 | *12.00* |
| **1K29** | A65 | 15g Prus green | 3.00 | *18.00* |
| **1K30** | A65 | 25g myrtle green | 4.00 | *9.00* |
| | | *Nos. 1K28-1K30 (3)* | 10.00 | *39.00* |
| | | Set, never hinged | 35.00 | |

**Same Overprint in Black on Poland Nos. 308, 310**

**1937, June 5**

| | | | | |
|---|---|---|---|---|
| **1K31** | A65 | 5g violet blue | 1.75 | *6.00* |
| **1K32** | A65 | 15g red brown | 1.75 | *6.00* |
| | | Set, never hinged | 11.00 | |

Polish Merchants Selling Wheat in Danzig, 16th Century — A2

**1938, Nov. 11 Engr.** ***Perf. 12½***

| | | | | |
|---|---|---|---|---|
| **1K33** | A2 | 5g red orange | .40 | *12.00* |
| **1K34** | A2 | 15g red brown | .40 | *12.00* |
| **1K35** | A2 | 25g dull violet | 1.00 | *12.00* |
| **1K36** | A2 | 55g brt ultra | 1.50 | *12.00* |
| | | *Nos. 1K33-1K36 (4)* | 3.30 | *48.00* |
| | | Set, never hinged | 14.00 | |

## OFFICES IN THE TURKISH EMPIRE

Stamps of Poland 1919, Overprinted in Carmine

**1919, May Unwmk.** ***Perf. 11½***

**Wove Paper**

| | | | | |
|---|---|---|---|---|
| **2K1** | A10 | 3f bister brn | 60.00 | 110.00 |
| **2K2** | A10 | 5f green | 60.00 | 110.00 |
| **2K3** | A10 | 10f red vio | 60.00 | 110.00 |
| **2K4** | A10 | 15f red | 60.00 | 110.00 |
| **2K5** | A11 | 20f dp blue | 60.00 | 110.00 |
| **2K6** | A11 | 25f olive grn | 60.00 | 110.00 |
| **2K7** | A11 | 50f blue grn | 60.00 | 110.00 |

Overprinted

| | | | | |
|---|---|---|---|---|
| **2K8** | A12 | 1m violet | 150.00 | 130.00 |
| **2K9** | A12 | 1.50m dp green | 150.00 | 130.00 |
| **2K10** | A12 | 2m dk brown | 150.00 | 150.00 |
| **2K11** | A13 | 2.50m orange brn | 150.00 | 130.00 |
| **2K12** | A14 | 5m red violet | 150.00 | 150.00 |
| | | *Nos. 2K1-2K12 (12)* | 1,170. | 1,460. |

Counterfeit cancellations are plentiful.

Counterfeits exist of Nos. 2K1-2K12.

*Reissues are lighter, shiny red. Value, set $25.*

Polish stamps with "P.P.C." overprint (Poste Polonaise Constantinople) were used on consular mail for a time.

Seven stamps with these overprints were not issued. Value, set: unused $15, never hinged $35.

## EXILE GOVERNMENT IN GREAT BRITAIN

These stamps were issued by the Polish government in exile for letters posted from Polish merchant ships and warships.

United States Embassy Ruins, Warsaw — A1

Polish Ministry of Finance Ruins, Warsaw — A2

Destruction of Mickiewicz Monument, Cracow — A3

Polish Submarine "Orzel" — A8

Ruins of Warsaw A4

Polish Machine Gunners A5

Armored Tank A6

Polish Planes in Great Britain A7

***Perf. 12½, 11½x12***

**1941, Dec. 15 Engr. Unwmk.**

| | | | | |
|---|---|---|---|---|
| **3K1** | A1 | 5g rose violet | .60 | *1.25* |
| **3K2** | A2 | 10g dk bl grn | .80 | *1.60* |
| **3K3** | A3 | 25g black | 1.25 | *2.00* |
| **3K4** | A4 | 55g dark blue | 1.60 | *2.75* |
| **3K5** | A5 | 75g olive grn | 3.50 | *7.25* |
| **3K6** | A6 | 80g dk car rose | 3.50 | *7.25* |
| **3K7** | A7 | 1z slate blue | 3.50 | *7.25* |
| **3K8** | A8 | 1.50z copper brn | 3.50 | *7.25* |
| | | *Nos. 3K1-3K8 (8)* | 18.25 | *36.60* |
| | | Set, never hinged | 35.00 | |

These stamps were used for correspondence carried on Polish ships and, on certain days, in Polish Military camps in Great Britain.

For surcharges see Nos. 3K17-3K20.

Polish Air Force in Battle of the Atlantic — A9

Polish Army in France, 1939-40 — A11

Polish Merchant Navy A10

Polish Army in Narvik, Norway, 1940 — A12

The Homeland Fights On — A15

Polish Army in Libya, 1941-42 A13

General Sikorsky and Polish Soldiers in the Middle East, 1943 A14

The Secret Press in Poland A16

**1943, Nov. 1**

| | | | | |
|---|---|---|---|---|
| **3K9** | A9 | 5g rose lake | .50 | *1.20* |
| **3K10** | A10 | 10g dk bl grn | .75 | *1.50* |
| **3K11** | A11 | 25g dk vio | .75 | *1.50* |
| **3K12** | A12 | 55g sapphire | 1.25 | *2.00* |
| **3K13** | A13 | 75g brn car | 2.00 | *3.50* |
| **3K14** | A14 | 80g rose car | 2.50 | *5.25* |
| **3K15** | A15 | 1z olive blk | 2.50 | *5.00* |
| **3K16** | A16 | 1.50z black | 3.25 | *7.50* |
| | | *Nos. 3K9-3K16 (8)* | 13.50 | *27.45* |
| | | Set, never hinged | 22.50 | |

**Nos. 3K5 to 3K8 Surcharged in Blue**

***Perf. 12½, 11½x12***

**1944, June 27 Unwmk.**

| | | | | |
|---|---|---|---|---|
| **3K17** | A5 | 45g on 75g | 7.50 | *22.50* |
| **3K18** | A6 | 55g on 80g | 7.50 | *22.50* |
| **3K19** | A7 | 80g on 1z | 7.50 | *22.50* |
| **3K20** | A8 | 1.20z on 1.50z | 7.50 | *22.50* |
| | | *Nos. 3K17-3K20 (4)* | 30.00 | *90.00* |
| | | Set, never hinged | 80.00 | |

Capture of Monte Cassino by the Poles, May 18, 1944.

## EXILE GOVERNMENT IN GREAT BRITAIN SEMI-POSTAL STAMP

Heroic Defenders of Warsaw — SP1

***Perf. 11½***

**1945, Feb. 3 Unwmk. Engr.**

| | | | | |
|---|---|---|---|---|
| **3KB1** | SP1 | 1z + 2z slate green | 4.75 | *12.00* |
| | | Never hinged | 9.50 | |

Warsaw uprising, Aug. 1-Oct. 3, 1944.

## PONTA DELGADA

ˌpän-tə del-ˈgä-də

LOCATION — Administrative district of the Azores comprising the islands of Sao Miguel and Santa Maria
GOVT. — A district of Portugal
AREA — 342 sq. mi.
POP. — 124,000 (approx.)
CAPITAL — Ponta Delgada

1000 Reis = 1 Milreis

King Carlos — A1

**1892-93 Typo. Unwmk.**
***Perf. 12½, 11½ (25r), 13½ (75r, 150r)***

| No. | Type | Description | Unused | Used |
|---|---|---|---|---|
| 1 | A1 | 5r yellow | 3.75 | 1.40 |
| c. | | Diagonal half used as 2½r on piece | | 18.00 |
| 2 | A1 | 10r reddish vio | 4.25 | 2.40 |
| 3 | A1 | 15r chocolate | 5.50 | 3.00 |
| 4 | A1 | 20r lavender | 5.50 | 3.00 |
| a. | | Perf. 13½ | 9.25 | 3.00 |
| 5d | A1 | 25r green | 10.25 | 1.75 |
| 6 | A1 | 50r ultra | 11.00 | 4.25 |
| 7 | A1 | 75r carmine | 10.50 | 7.25 |
| 8 | A1 | 80r yellow grn | 16.00 | 12.00 |
| 9 | A1 | 100r brn, *yel* | 16.00 | 7.25 |
| 10 | A1 | 150r car, *rose* | 75.00 | 52.50 |
| 11 | A1 | 200r dk bl, *bl* | 75.00 | 52.50 |
| 12 | A1 | 300r dk bl, *salmon* | 80.00 | 55.00 |
| | | *Nos. 1-12 (12)* | 312.75 | 202.30 |

*Nos. 1, 4 and 9-12 were reprinted in 1900 (perf. 11½). Value, each $50. All values were reprinted in 1905 (perf. 13½). Value, each $25. The reprints are on paper slightly thinner than that of the originals, and unsurfaced. They have white gum and clean-cut perfs.*

*See the Scott Classic Specialized Catalogue for listings by perforation.*

King Carlos — A2

**Name and Value in Black except Nos. 25 and 34**

**1897-1905** ***Perf. 11½***

| No. | Type | Description | Unused | Used |
|---|---|---|---|---|
| 13 | A2 | 2½r gray | .60 | .35 |
| 14 | A2 | 5r orange | .60 | .35 |
| 15 | A2 | 10r lt green | .60 | .35 |
| 16 | A2 | 15r brown | 9.00 | 7.25 |
| 17 | A2 | 15r gray grn ('99) | 2.40 | 1.75 |
| 18 | A2 | 20r dull violet | 2.40 | 1.40 |
| 19 | A2 | 25r sea green | 3.75 | 1.40 |
| 20 | A2 | 25r rose red ('99) | 2.40 | .60 |
| 21 | A2 | 50r blue | 3.75 | 1.40 |
| 22 | A2 | 50r ultra ('05) | 22.50 | 13.00 |
| 23 | A2 | 65r slate blue ('98) | 1.40 | .60 |
| 24 | A2 | 75r rose | 8.00 | 1.40 |
| 25 | A2 | 75r brn & car, *yel* ('05) | 17.00 | 8.50 |
| 26 | A2 | 80r violet | 2.40 | 1.40 |
| 27 | A2 | 100r dk bl, *bl* | 5.00 | 1.00 |
| 28 | A2 | 115r org brn, *rose* ('98) | 4.25 | 1.75 |
| 29 | A2 | 130r gray brn, *buff* ('98) | 3.00 | 1.75 |
| 30 | A2 | 150r lt brn, *buff* | 3.00 | 2.10 |
| 31 | A2 | 180r sl, *pnksh* ('98) | 3.00 | 2.10 |
| 32 | A2 | 200r red vio, *pnksh* | 8.50 | 6.00 |
| 33 | A2 | 300r blue, *rose* | 10.00 | 5.50 |
| a. | | Perf. 12½ | 57.50 | 35.00 |
| 34 | A2 | 500r blk & red, *bl* | 21.00 | 13.00 |
| a. | | Perf. 12½ | 32.00 | 18.00 |
| | | *Nos. 13-34 (21)* | 133.95 | 72.60 |

Imperfs are proofs.

The stamps of Ponta Delgada were superseded by those of the Azores, which in 1931 were replaced by those of Portugal.

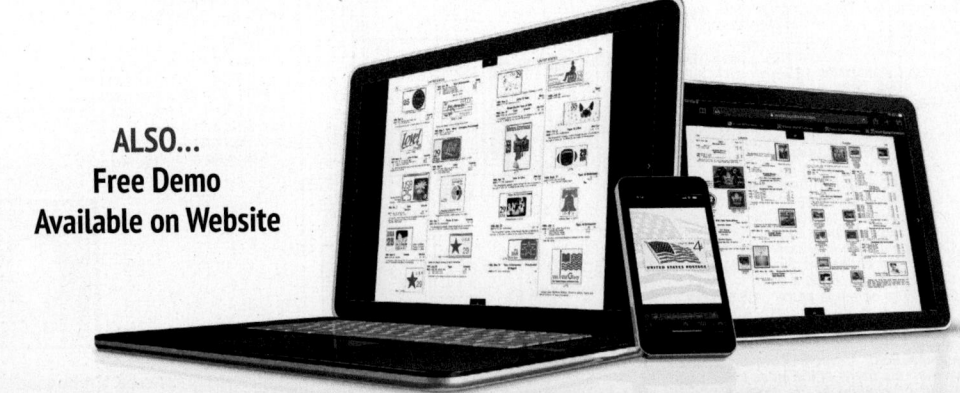

# PORTUGAL

'pōr-chi-gəl

LOCATION — Southern Europe, on the western coast of the Iberian Peninsula
GOVT. — Republic
AREA — 35,516 sq. mi.
POP. — 9,918,040 (1999 est.)
CAPITAL — Lisbon

Figures for area and population include the Azores and Madeira, which are integral parts of the republic. The republic was established in 1910. See Azores, Funchal, Madeira.

1000 Reis = 1 Milreis
10 Reis = 1 Centimo
100 Centavos = 1 Escudo (1912)
100 Cents = 1 Euro (2002)

**Catalogue values for unused stamps in this country are for Never Hinged items, beginning with Scott 662 in the regular postage section, Scott C11 in the air-post section, Scott J65 in the postage due section, and Scott O2 in the officials section.**

Queen Maria II
A1 A2

A3 A4

### Typo. & Embossed

**1853** **Unwmk.** ***Imperf.***

| | | | | |
|---|---|---|---|---|
| **1** | A1 | 5r reddish brown | 2,850. | 850.00 |
| *b.* | | Double impression | | *4,250.* |
| **2** | A2 | 25r blue | 925. | 19.00 |
| *b.* | | Double impression | *4,750.* | *1,500.* |
| **3** | A3 | 50r dp yellow grn | 3,400. | 875.00 |
| *a.* | | 50r blue green | 6,750. | 1,650. |
| *c.* | | Double impression | *14,000.* | *6,000.* |
| **4** | A4 | 100r lilac | 31,000. | 1,900. |

*The stamps of the 1853 issue were reprinted in 1864, 1885, 1905 and 1953. Many stamps of subsequent issues were reprinted in 1885 and 1905. The reprints of 1864 are on thin white paper with white gum. The originals have brownish gum which often stains the paper. The reprints of 1885 are on a stout, very white paper. They are usually ungummed, but occasionally have a white gum with yellowish spots. The reprints of 1905 are on creamy white paper of ordinary quality with shiny white gum.*

*When perforated the reprints of 1885 have a rather rough perforation 13½ with small holes; those of 1905 have a clean-cut perforation 13½ with large holes making sharp pointed teeth.*

*The colors of the reprints usually differ from those of the originals, but actual comparison is necessary.*

*The reprints are often from new dies which differ slightly from those used for the originals.*

*5 reis: There is a defect in the neck which makes the Adam's apple appear very large in the first reprint. The later ones can be distinguished by the paper and the shades and by the absence of the pendant curl.*

*25 reis: The burelage of the ground work in the original is sharp and clear, while in the 1864 reprints it is blurred in several places; the upper and lower right hand corners are very thick and blurred. The central oval is less than ½mm from the frame at the sides in the originals and fully ¾mm in the 1885 and 1905 reprints.*

*50 reis: In the reprints of 1864 and 1885 there is a small break in the upper right hand diagonal line of the frame, and the initials of the engraver (F. B. F.), which in the originals are plainly discernible in the lower part of the bust, do not show. The reprints of 1905 have not the break in the frame and the initials are distinct.*

*100 reis: The small vertical lines at top and bottom at each side of the frame are heavier in the reprints of 1864 than in the originals. The reprints of 1885 and 1905 can be distinguished only by the paper, gum and shades.*

*Reprints of 1953 have thick paper, no gum and dates "1853/1953" on back. Value $55 each.*

*Values of lowest-cost earlier reprints (1905) of Nos. 1, $100; No. 2, $120; Nos. 3, 4, $150.*

King Pedro V
A5 A6

A7 A8

**1855** **With Straight Hair**

TWENTY-FIVE REIS:
Type I — Pearls mostly touch each other and oval outer line.
Type II — Pearls are separate from each other and oval outer line.

| | | | | |
|---|---|---|---|---|
| **5** | A5 | 5r red brown | 8,250. | 900.00 |
| **6** | A6 | 25r blue, type II | 950.00 | 25.00 |
| *a.* | | 25r blue, type I | 1,150. | 30.00 |
| **7** | A7 | 50r green | 600.00 | 70.00 |
| *b.* | | Double impression | 1,900. | 725.00 |
| **8** | A8 | 100r lilac | 800.00 | 90.00 |

**1856** **With Curled Hair**

TWENTY-FIVE REIS:
Type I — The network is fine (single lines).
Type II — The network is coarse (double lines).

| | | | | |
|---|---|---|---|---|
| **9** | A5 | 5r brown | 500.00 | 70.00 |
| *g.* | | Double impression | 1,400. | 375.00 |
| **10** | A6 | 25r blue, type II | 400.00 | 13.50 |
| *a.* | | 25r blue, type I | *9,500.* | 55.00 |

**1858**

| | | | | |
|---|---|---|---|---|
| **11** | A6 | 25r rose, type II | 275.00 | 6.50 |
| *a.* | | Double impression | 525.00 | *275.00* |

*The 5r dark brown, formerly listed and sold at about $1, is now believed by the best authorities to be a reprint made before 1866. It is printed on thin yellowish white paper with yellowish white gum and is known only unused. The same remarks will apply to a 25r blue which is common unused but not known used. It is printed from a die which was not used for the issued stamps but the differences are slight and can only be told by expert comparison.*

*Nos. 9 and 10, also 10a in rose, were reprinted in 1885 and Nos. 9, 10, 10a and 11 in 1905. Value of lowest-cost reprints, $40 each.*

*See note after No. 4.*

King Luiz
A9 A10

A11 A12

A13

FIVE REIS:
Type I — The distance between "5" and "reis" is 3mm.
Type II — The distance between "5" and "reis" is 2mm.

**1862-64**

| | | | | |
|---|---|---|---|---|
| **12** | A9 | 5r brown, type I | 125.00 | 10.00 |
| *a.* | | 5r brown, type II | 160.00 | 25.00 |
| *b.* | | Double impression, type II | 650.00 | 350.00 |
| *d.* | | Double embossing, type I | — | 275.00 |
| **13** | A10 | 10r orange | 125.00 | 40.00 |
| **14** | A11 | 25r rose | 100.00 | 4.75 |
| *a.* | | Double impression | 1,350. | 375.00 |
| *b.* | | Double embossing, type I | 1,350. | 375.00 |
| **15** | A12 | 50r yellow green | 725.00 | 77.50 |
| **16** | A13 | 100r lilac ('64) | 900.00 | 90.00 |
| | | *Nos. 12-16 (5)* | 1,975. | 222.25 |

*All values were reprinted in 1885 and all except the 25r in 1905. Value of lowest-cost reprints, $10 each.*

*See note after No. 4.*

King Luiz — A14

**1866-67** ***Imperf.***

| | | | | |
|---|---|---|---|---|
| **17** | A14 | 5r black | 100.00 | 10.00 |
| *a.* | | Double impression | 275.00 | 190.00 |
| **18** | A14 | 10r yellow | 225.00 | 140.00 |
| **19** | A14 | 20r bister | 175.00 | 67.50 |
| **20** | A14 | 25r rose ('67) | 200.00 | 6.00 |
| *a.* | | Double impression | | 225.00 |
| **21** | A14 | 50r green | 250.00 | 50.00 |
| **22** | A14 | 80r orange | 250.00 | 50.00 |
| **23** | A14 | 100r dk lilac ('67) | 300.00 | 75.00 |
| **24** | A14 | 120r blue | 325.00 | 70.00 |
| *a.* | | Double impression | 725.00 | 450.00 |
| | | *Nos. 17-24 (8)* | 1,825. | 468.50 |

All values were reprinted in 1885 and all except the 25r in 1905. Value of lowest-cost reprints, $10 each. Some values with unofficial percé en croix (diamond) perforation were used in Madeira.

*All values were reprinted in 1885 and 1905. Value: Nos. 17-23, each $30-$40; No. 24, $100.*

*See note after No. 4.*

### Typographed & Embossed

**1867-70** ***Perf. 12½***

| | | | | |
|---|---|---|---|---|
| **25** | A14 | 5r black | 125.00 | 42.50 |
| *a.* | | Double impression | 225.00 | 110.00 |
| **26** | A14 | 10r yellow | 250.00 | 110.00 |
| **27** | A14 | 20r bister ('69) | 300.00 | 110.00 |
| **28** | A14 | 25r rose | 65.00 | 5.00 |
| *a.* | | Double impression | 550.00 | 200.00 |
| **29** | A14 | 50r green ('68) | 250.00 | 100.00 |
| **30** | A14 | 80r orange ('69) | 350.00 | 100.00 |
| **31** | A14 | 100r lilac ('69) | 250.00 | 100.00 |
| **32** | A14 | 120r blue | 300.00 | 67.50 |
| *a.* | | Double impression | 625.00 | 160.00 |
| **33** | A14 | 240r pale violet ('70) | 1,000. | 475.00 |
| | | *Nos. 25-33 (9)* | 2,890. | 1,110. |

Nos. 25-33 frequently were separated with scissors. Slightly blunted perfs on one or two sides are to be expected for stamps of this issue.

Two types each of 5r and 100r differ in the position of the "5" at upper right and the "100" at lower right in relation to the end of the label.

*Nos. 25-33 were reprinted in 1885 and 1905. Some of the 1885 reprints were perforated 12½ as well as 13½. Value of the lowest-cost reprints, $40 each.*

*See note after No. 4.*

King Luiz — A15

### Typographed & Embossed

**1870-84** ***Perf. 12½, 13½***

| | | | | |
|---|---|---|---|---|
| **34** | A15 | 5r black | 55.00 | 5.00 |
| *a.* | | Imperf | 550.00 | |
| *f.* | | Double impression | 275.00 | 67.50 |

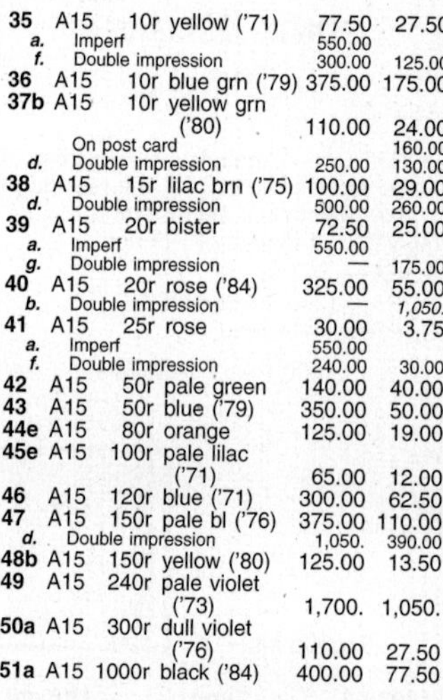

| | | | | |
|---|---|---|---|---|
| **35** | A15 | 10r yellow ('71) | 77.50 | 27.50 |
| *a.* | | Imperf | 550.00 | |
| *f.* | | Double impression | 300.00 | 125.00 |
| **36** | A15 | 10r blue grn ('79) | 375.00 | 175.00 |
| **37b** | A15 | 10r yellow grn ('80) | 110.00 | 24.00 |
| | | On post card | | 160.00 |
| *d.* | | Double impression | 250.00 | 130.00 |
| **38** | A15 | 15r lilac brn ('75) | 100.00 | 29.00 |
| *d.* | | Double impression | 500.00 | 260.00 |
| **39** | A15 | 20r bister | 72.50 | 25.00 |
| *a.* | | Imperf | 550.00 | |
| *g.* | | Double impression | — | 175.00 |
| **40** | A15 | 20r rose ('84) | 325.00 | 55.00 |
| *b.* | | Double impression | — | *1,050.* |
| **41** | A15 | 25r rose | 30.00 | 3.75 |
| *a.* | | Imperf | 550.00 | |
| *f.* | | Double impression | 240.00 | 30.00 |
| **42** | A15 | 50r pale green | 140.00 | 40.00 |
| **43** | A15 | 50r blue ('79) | 350.00 | 50.00 |
| **44e** | A15 | 80r orange | 125.00 | 19.00 |
| **45e** | A15 | 100r pale lilac ('71) | 65.00 | 12.00 |
| **46** | A15 | 120r blue ('71) | 300.00 | 62.50 |
| **47** | A15 | 150r pale bl ('76) | 375.00 | 110.00 |
| *d.* | | Double impression | 1,050. | 390.00 |
| **48b** | A15 | 150r yellow ('80) | 125.00 | 13.50 |
| **49** | A15 | 240r pale violet ('73) | 1,700. | 1,050. |
| **50a** | A15 | 300r dull violet ('76) | 110.00 | 27.50 |
| **51a** | A15 | 1000r black ('84) | 400.00 | 77.50 |

Nos. 34-51 were printed on three types of paper, plain, ribbed and enamel surfaced, and with perfs gauging 11, 12½, 13½, or 14¼. Values are for the least expensive varieties. For detailed listings, see the *Scott Classic Specialized Catalogue.*

Two types each of 15r, 20r and 80r differ in the distance between the figures of value.

Imperfs probably are proofs.

For overprints and surcharges see Nos. 86-87, 94-96.

*All values of the issues of 1870-84 were reprinted in 1885 and 1905. Value of the lowest-cost reprints, $10 each.*

*See note after No. 4.*

King Luiz
A16 A17

A18 A19

**1880-81** **Typo.** ***Perf. 12½, 13½***

| | | | | |
|---|---|---|---|---|
| **52** | A16 | 5r black | 40.00 | 4.00 |
| **53** | A17 | 25r bluish gray | 300.00 | 29.00 |
| **54** | A18 | 25r gray | 45.00 | 3.50 |
| **55** | A18 | 25r brown vio ('81) | 45.00 | 3.50 |
| **56** | A19 | 50r blue ('81) | 300.00 | 15.00 |
| | | *Nos. 52-56 (5)* | 730.00 | 55.00 |

*All values were reprinted in 1885 and 1905. Value of the lowest-cost reprints, $15 each.*

*See note after No. 4.*

A20 A21

King Luiz
A22 A23

A24

A24a

**1882-87** *Perf. 11½, 12½, 13½*

| No. | Type | Description | Unused | Used |
|---|---|---|---|---|
| 57 | A20 | 2r black ('84) | 20.00 | 15.00 |
| 58 | A21 | 5r black ('84) | 32.50 | 3.50 |
| 59 | A22 | 10r green ('84) | 35.00 | 4.00 |
| 60c | A23 | 25r brown | 32.50 | 2.60 |
| 61 | A24 | 50r blue | 45.00 | 3.00 |
| 62 | A24a | 500r black ('84) | 600.00 | 300.00 |
| 63 | A24a | 500r violet ('87) | 300.00 | 52.50 |
| | | *Nos. 57-63 (7)* | 1,065. | 380.60 |

Nos. 57-63 were printed on both plain and enamel surfaced papers, with one or more perf varieties for each value. Values are for the least expensive varieties. For a detailed listing, see the *Scott Classic Specialized Catalogue.*

For overprints see Nos. 79-82, 85, 88-89, 93.

*The stamps of the 1882-87 issues were reprinted in 1885, 1893 and 1905. Value of the lowest-cost reprints, $5 each.*

*See note after No. 4.*

A25

A26

**1887** *Perf. 11½*

| No. | Type | Description | Unused | Used |
|---|---|---|---|---|
| 64 | A25 | 20r rose | 50.00 | 17.00 |
| 65 | A26 | 25r violet | 40.00 | 3.00 |
| 66 | A26 | 25r lilac rose | 30.00 | 3.00 |
| | | *Nos. 64-66 (3)* | 120.00 | 23.00 |

For overprints see Nos. 83-84, 90-92.

*Nos. 64-66 were reprinted in 1905. Value $22.50 each. See note after No. 4.*

King Carlos — A27

**1892-93** *Perf. 11½, 12½, 13½*

| No. | Type | Description | Unused | Used |
|---|---|---|---|---|
| 67 | A27 | 5r orange | 11.00 | 2.00 |
| 68 | A27 | 10r redsh violet | 30.00 | 4.00 |
| 69b | A27 | 15r chocolate | 27.50 | 5.00 |
| 70 | A27 | 20r lavender | 35.00 | 9.25 |
| 71a | A27 | 25r dark green | 27.50 | 2.00 |
| 72 | A27 | 50r blue | 35.00 | 9.25 |
| 73 | A27 | 75r carmine ('93) | 67.50 | 8.00 |
| 74a | A27 | 80r yellow green | 85.00 | 42.50 |
| 75 | A27 | 100r brn, *buff* ('93) | 65.00 | 6.25 |
| 76 | A27 | 150r car, *rose* ('93) | 160.00 | 42.50 |
| 77 | A27 | 200r dk bl, *bl* ('93) | 160.00 | 35.00 |
| 78 | A27 | 300r dk bl, *sal* ('93) | 175.00 | 57.50 |
| | | *Nos. 67-78 (12)* | 878.50 | 223.25 |

Nos. 67-78 were issued on two types of paper: enamel surfaced, which is white, with a uniform low gloss; and chalky, which bears a low-gloss application in a pattern of tiny lozenges, producing a somewhat duller appearance.

*Nos. 76-78 were reprinted in 1900 (perf. 11½). Value, each $100. All values were reprinted in 1905 (perf. 13½). Value, each $50.*

*See note after No. 4.*

### Stamps and Types of Previous Issues Overprinted in Black or Red

a

b

c

**1892**

| No. | Type | Description | Unused | Used |
|---|---|---|---|---|
| 79 | A21 (a) | 5r gray blk | 16.00 | 8.75 |
| *a.* | | Double overprint | 650.00 | 450.00 |
| 80 | A22 (b) | 10r green | 16.00 | 8.75 |
| *a.* | | Inverted overprint | — | — |
| *b.* | | Double overprint | 650.00 | 450.00 |

**1892-93**

| No. | Type | Description | Unused | Used |
|---|---|---|---|---|
| 81 | A21 (c) | 5r gray blk (R) | 13.50 | 6.75 |
| 82 | A22 (c) | 10r green (R) | 16.00 | 9.25 |
| *a.* | | Inverted overprint | 160.00 | 160.00 |
| 83 | A25 (c) | 20r rose | 42.50 | 22.50 |
| *a.* | | Inverted overprint | 225.00 | 225.00 |
| 84 | A26 (c) | 25r rose lilac, perf. 11½ | 14.50 | 5.25 |
| *a.* | | Perf. 12½ | 475.00 | 70.00 |
| 85 | A24 (c) | 50r blue (R) ('93) | 77.50 | 62.50 |
| | | *Nos. 81-85 (5)* | 164.00 | 106.25 |

**1893**

| No. | Type | Description | Unused | Used |
|---|---|---|---|---|
| 86 | A15 (c) | 15r bister brn (R) | 20.00 | 12.00 |
| 87 | A15 (c) | 80r yellow | 110.00 | 87.50 |

Nos. 86-87 are found in two types each. See note below No. 51.

*Some of Nos. 79-87 were reprinted in 1900 and all values in 1905. Value of lowest-cost reprint, $10.*

*See note after No. 4.*

### Stamps and Types of Previous Issues Overprinted or Surcharged in Black or Red

d

e

**1893** *Perf. 11½, 12½*

| No. | Type | Description | Unused | Used |
|---|---|---|---|---|
| 88 | A21 (d) | 5r gray blk (R) | 30.00 | 22.50 |
| 89 | A22 (d) | 10r grn, perf. 11½ (R) | 24.00 | 20.00 |
| *a.* | | "1938" | 300.00 | 300.00 |
| *b.* | | "1863" | 300.00 | 300.00 |
| *c.* | | "1836" | 300.00 | 300.00 |
| *d.* | | Perf. 12½ | 1,650. | 1,100. |
| 90 | A25 (d) | 20r rose | 45.00 | 32.50 |
| *a.* | | Inverted overprint | 125.00 | 100.00 |
| *b.* | | "1938" | 300.00 | 300.00 |
| 91 | A26 (e) | 20r on 25r lil rose | 60.00 | 47.50 |
| 92 | A26 (d) | 25r lilac rose | 110.00 | 100.00 |
| *a.* | | Inverted overprint | 275.00 | 275.00 |
| 93 | A24 (d) | 50r blue (R) | 125.00 | 110.00 |

*Perf. 12½*

| No. | Type | Description | Unused | Used |
|---|---|---|---|---|
| 94 | A15 (e) | 50r on 80r yel | 150.00 | 100.00 |
| 95 | A15 (e) | 75r on 80r yel | 100.00 | 72.50 |
| *a.* | | "1893" and "50rs" double | 350.00 | 200.00 |
| 96 | A15 (d) | 80r yellow | 150.00 | 95.00 |
| *a.* | | "1893" double | 450.00 | 450.00 |
| | | *Nos. 88-96 (9)* | 794.00 | 600.00 |

Nos. 94-96 are found in two types each. See note below No. 51.

*Some of Nos. 88-96 were reprinted in 1900 and all values in 1905. Value of lowest-cost reprint, $45 each.*

*See note after No. 4.*

Prince Henry on his Ship — A46

Prince Henry Directing Fleet Maneuvers A47

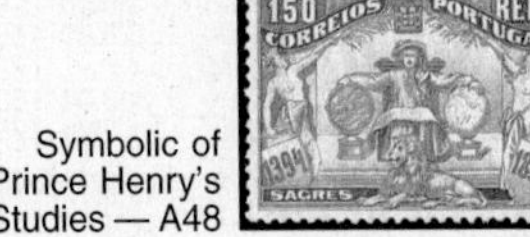
Symbolic of Prince Henry's Studies — A48

**1894** **Litho.** *Perf. 14*

| No. | Type | Description | Unused | Used |
|---|---|---|---|---|
| 97 | A46 | 5r orange | 3.25 | .50 |
| 98 | A46 | 10r magenta | 3.25 | .50 |
| 99 | A46 | 15r red brown | 10.00 | 3.00 |
| 100 | A46 | 20r dull violet | 10.00 | 3.50 |
| 101 | A47 | 25r gray green | 9.50 | 1.00 |
| 102 | A47 | 50r blue | 25.00 | 5.50 |
| 103 | A47 | 75r car rose | 47.50 | 10.50 |
| 104 | A47 | 80r yellow grn | 47.50 | 12.50 |
| 105 | A47 | 100r lt brn, *pale buff* | 37.50 | 9.50 |

**Engr.**

| No. | Type | Description | Unused | Used |
|---|---|---|---|---|
| 106 | A48 | 150r lt car, *pale rose* | 125.00 | 32.50 |
| 107 | A48 | 300r dk bl, *sal buff* | 140.00 | 37.50 |
| 108 | A48 | 500r dp vio, *pale lil* | 300.00 | 75.00 |
| 109 | A48 | 1000r gray blk, *grysh* | 550.00 | 110.00 |
| | | *Nos. 97-109 (13)* | 1,309. | 301.50 |

5th centenary of the birth of Prince Henry the Navigator.

King Carlos — A49

**1895-1905** **Typo.** *Perf. 11½*

**Value in Black or Red (#122, 500r)**

| No. | Type | Description | Unused | Used |
|---|---|---|---|---|
| 110 | A49 | 2½r gray | .25 | .25 |
| 111 | A49 | 5r orange | .25 | .25 |
| 112 | A49 | 10r lt green | .50 | .25 |
| 113 | A49 | 15r brown | 80.00 | 3.25 |
| 114 | A49 | 15r gray grn ('99) | 42.50 | 2.25 |
| 115 | A49 | 20r gray violet | 1.00 | .30 |
| 116 | A49 | 25r sea green | 55.00 | .25 |
| 117 | A49 | 25r car rose ('99) | .50 | .25 |
| 118 | A49 | 50r blue | 75.00 | .35 |
| 119 | A49 | 50r ultra ('05) | .50 | .25 |
| 120 | A49 | 65r slate bl ('98) | .50 | .25 |
| 121 | A49 | 75r rose | 110.00 | 4.00 |
| 122 | A49 | 75r brn, *yel* ('05) | 2.00 | .75 |
| 123 | A49 | 80r violet | 2.00 | 1.00 |
| 124 | A49 | 100r dk bl, *bl* | 1.00 | .35 |
| 125 | A49 | 115r org brn, *pink* ('98) | 4.50 | 3.25 |
| 126 | A49 | 130r gray brn, *straw* ('98) | 3.50 | 1.40 |
| 127 | A49 | 150r lt brn, *straw* | 130.00 | 21.00 |
| 128 | A49 | 180r sl, *pnksh* ('98) | 16.00 | 9.50 |
| 129 | A49 | 200r red lil, *pnksh* | 4.00 | 1.00 |
| 130 | A49 | 300r blue, *rose* | 3.50 | 1.75 |
| 131 | A49 | 500r blk, *bl* ('96) | 10.00 | 4.00 |
| *a.* | | Perf. 12½ | 110.00 | 25.00 |
| | | *Nos. 110-131 (22)* | 542.50 | 55.90 |

Several values of the above type exist without figures of value, also with figures inverted or otherwise misplaced but they were not regularly issued.

St. Anthony and his Vision — A50

St. Anthony Preaching to Fishes — A51

St. Anthony Ascends to Heaven — A52

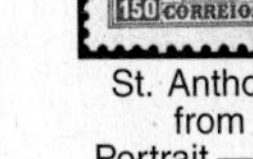
St. Anthony, from Portrait — A53

***Perf. 11½, 12½ and Compound***

**1895** **Typo.**

| No. | Type | Description | Unused | Used |
|---|---|---|---|---|
| 132 | A50 | 2½r black | 4.00 | 1.00 |

**Litho.**

| No. | Type | Description | Unused | Used |
|---|---|---|---|---|
| 133 | A51 | 5r brown org | 4.00 | 1.00 |
| 134 | A51 | 10r red lilac | 12.50 | 7.50 |
| 135 | A51 | 15r chocolate | 13.50 | 7.50 |
| 136 | A51 | 20r gray violet | 13.50 | 8.00 |
| 137 | A51 | 25r grn & vio | 12.50 | 1.00 |
| 138 | A52 | 50r blue & brn | 30.00 | 20.00 |
| 139 | A52 | 75r rose & brn | 45.00 | 35.00 |
| 140 | A52 | 80r lt grn & brn | 60.00 | 55.00 |
| 141 | A52 | 100r choc & blk | 50.00 | 27.50 |
| 142 | A53 | 150r car & bis | 150.00 | 90.00 |
| 143 | A53 | 200r blue & bis | 150.00 | 110.00 |
| 144 | A53 | 300r slate & bis | 210.00 | 140.00 |
| 145 | A53 | 500r vio brn & grn | 375.00 | 275.00 |
| 146 | A53 | 1000r vio & grn | 600.00 | 375.00 |
| | | *Nos. 132-146 (15)* | 1,730. | 1,154. |

7th centenary of the birth of Saint Anthony of Padua. Stamps have eulogy in Latin printed on the back.

Common Design Types pictured following the introduction.

### Vasco da Gama Issue

Common Design Types

**1898** **Engr.** *Perf. 12½ to 16*

| No. | Type | Description | Unused | Used |
|---|---|---|---|---|
| 147 | CD20 | 2½r blue green | 1.50 | .25 |
| 148 | CD21 | 5r red | 1.50 | .25 |
| 149 | CD22 | 10r red violet | 7.50 | 1.50 |
| 150 | CD23 | 25r yel grn | 4.50 | .50 |
| 151 | CD24 | 50r dark blue | 10.00 | 2.75 |
| 152 | CD25 | 75r violet brown | 40.00 | 9.50 |
| 153 | CD26 | 100r bister brown | 27.50 | 9.50 |
| 154 | CD27 | 150r bister | 62.50 | 26.00 |
| | | *Nos. 147-154 (8)* | 155.00 | 50.25 |

For overprints and surcharges see Nos. 185-192, 199-206.

King Manuel II
A62 A63

| 1910 | Typo. | | *Perf. 14½x15* | |
|---|---|---|---|---|
| **156** | A62 | 2½r violet | .25 | .25 |
| **157** | A62 | 5r black | .25 | .25 |
| **158** | A62 | 10r gray green | .25 | .25 |
| **159** | A62 | 15r lilac brown | 2.50 | 2.50 |
| **160** | A62 | 20r carmine | .75 | .60 |
| **161** | A62 | 25r violet brn | .55 | .25 |
| **162** | A62 | 50r dark blue | 1.40 | .60 |
| **163** | A62 | 75r bister brn | 8.50 | 4.50 |
| **164** | A62 | 80r slate | 2.40 | 2.00 |
| **165** | A62 | 100r brn, *lt grn* | 9.00 | 2.75 |
| **166** | A62 | 200r dk grn, *sal* | 5.50 | 3.75 |
| **167** | A62 | 300r blk, *azure* | 6.00 | 4.50 |
| **168** | A63 | 500r ol grn & vio brn | 13.00 | 11.50 |
| **169** | A63 | 1000r dk bl & blk | 30.00 | 23.00 |
| | | *Nos. 156-169 (14)* | 80.35 | 56.70 |

For overprint see No. RA1.

Preceding Issue Overprinted in Carmine or Green

| 1910 | | | | |
|---|---|---|---|---|
| **170** | A62 | 2½r violet | [illegible] | [illegible] |
| **171** | A62 | 5r black | .25 | .25 |
| **172** | A62 | 10r gray green | 3.25 | 1.10 |
| **173** | A62 | 15r lilac brn | 1.00 | .80 |
| **174** | A62 | 20r carmine (G) | 4.00 | 1.50 |
| **175** | A62 | 25r violet brn | .70 | .25 |
| **176** | A62 | 50r dk blue | 5.50 | 2.00 |
| **177** | A62 | 75r bister brn | 8.50 | 4.00 |
| **178** | A62 | 80r slate | 3.00 | 2.25 |
| **179** | A62 | 100r brn, *lt grn* | 2.00 | .75 |
| **180** | A62 | 200r dk grn, *sal* | 2.50 | 1.60 |
| **181** | A62 | 300r blk, *azure* | 3.50 | 3.00 |
| **182** | A63 | 500r ol grn & vio brn | 9.00 | 8.00 |
| **183** | A63 | 1000r dk bl & blk | 22.50 | 20.00 |
| | | *Nos. 170-183 (14)* | 65.95 | 45.75 |

The numerous inverted and double overprints on this issue were unofficially and fraudulently made.

The 50r with blue overprint is a fraud.

**Vasco da Gama Issue Overprinted or Surcharged**

a

b

c

| 1911 | | | *Perf. 12½ to 16* | |
|---|---|---|---|---|
| **185** | CD20(a) | 2½r blue grn | .50 | .25 |
| *a.* | | Inverted overprint | 15.00 | 13.00 |
| **186** | CD21(b) | 15r on 5r red | 1.00 | .50 |
| *a.* | | Inverted surcharge | 10.00 | 9.50 |
| **187** | CD23(a) | 25r yel grn | .50 | .25 |
| *a.* | | Inverted overprint | 12.50 | 11.00 |
| *b.* | | Double overprint | 17.50 | 16.00 |
| **188** | CD24(a) | 50r dk blue | 3.00 | 2.10 |
| *a.* | | Inverted overprint | 27.50 | 24.00 |
| **189** | CD25(a) | 75r vio brn | 37.50 | 32.50 |
| **190** | CD27(b) | 80r on 150r bis | 6.00 | 5.00 |
| **191** | CD26(a) | 100r bis brn | 6.00 | 4.50 |
| *a.* | | Inverted overprint | 30.00 | 24.00 |
| **192** | CD22(c) | 1000r on 10r red vio | 55.00 | 40.00 |
| *a.* | | Inverted overprint | 150.00 | 140.00 |
| | | *Nos. 185-192 (8)* | 109.50 | 85.10 |

**Postage Due Stamps of 1898 Overprinted or Surcharged for Regular Postage**

d

e

| 1911 | | | *Perf. 12* | |
|---|---|---|---|---|
| **193** | D1(d) | 5r black | 1.00 | .50 |
| *a.* | | Inverted overprint | 15.00 | 11.00 |
| *b.* | | Double overprint | 15.00 | 11.00 |
| *c.* | | Double ovpt., one inverted | 15.00 | 11.00 |
| **194** | D1(d) | 10r magenta | 1.50 | .75 |
| *a.* | | Double ovpt., one inverted | 15.00 | 11.00 |
| **195** | D1(d) | 20r orange | 5.00 | 3.00 |
| *a.* | | Inverted overprint | 22.50 | 17.50 |
| *b.* | | Double overprint | 22.50 | 17.50 |
| **196** | D1(d) | 200r brn, *buff* | 110.00 | 62.50 |
| **197** | D1(e) | 300r on 50r slate | 80.00 | 40.00 |
| **198** | D1(e) | 500r on 100r car, *pink* | 45.00 | 24.00 |
| *a.* | | Inverted surcharge | 110.00 | 87.50 |
| *b.* | | Double surcharge | 110.00 | 87.50 |
| | | *Nos. 193-198 (6)* | 242.50 | 130.75 |

**Vasco da Gama Issue of Madeira [illegible] or Srchd. Types "a," "b" and "c"**

| 1911 | | | *Perf. 12½ to 16* | |
|---|---|---|---|---|
| **199** | CD20(a) | 2½r blue grn | 11.00 | 8.00 |
| **200** | CD21(b) | 15r on 5r red | 3.00 | 2.50 |
| *a.* | | Inverted surcharge | 12.00 | 11.00 |
| **201** | CD23(a) | 25r yellow grn | 5.00 | 4.50 |
| **202** | CD24(a) | 50r dk blue | 10.00 | 7.50 |
| **203** | CD25(a) | 75r violet brn | 10.00 | 5.00 |
| *a.* | | Inverted overprint | 35.00 | 30.00 |
| *b.* | | Double overprint | 45.00 | 35.00 |
| **204** | CD27(b) | 80r on 150r bis | 11.00 | 10.50 |
| *a.* | | Inverted surcharge | 45.00 | 42.50 |
| **205** | CD26(a) | 100r bister brn | 35.00 | 8.00 |
| *a.* | | Inverted overprint | 120.00 | 100.00 |
| *b.* | | Double overprint | 120.00 | 100.00 |
| **206** | CD22(c) | 1000r on 10r red vio | 35.00 | 25.00 |
| | | *Nos. 199-206 (8)* | 120.00 | 71.00 |

Ceres — A64

**Chalky Paper With Imprint**

| 1912-20 | Typo. | | *Perf. 15x14* | |
|---|---|---|---|---|
| **207** | A64 | ¼c dark olive | 8.00 | 5.00 |
| **208** | A64 | ½c black | 8.00 | 5.00 |
| **209** | A64 | 1c deep green | 6.50 | 2.50 |
| **210** | A64 | 1½c chocolate | 20.00 | 9.00 |
| **211** | A64 | 2c carmine | 20.00 | 9.00 |
| **212** | A64 | 2½c violet | 9.50 | 9.50 |
| **213** | A64 | 5c dp blue | 5.50 | .55 |
| **214** | A64 | 7½c yellow brn | 65.00 | 13.50 |
| **215** | A64 | 8c slate | 3.00 | 3.00 |
| **216** | A64 | 10c org brn | 45.00 | 25.00 |
| **217** | A64 | 15c plum | 300.00 | 75.00 |
| **218** | A64 | 20c vio brn, *grn* | 13.00 | 1.50 |
| **219** | A64 | 20c brn, *buff* ('20) | 15.00 | 3.50 |
| **220** | A64 | 30c brn, *pink* | 100.00 | 9.50 |
| **221** | A64 | 30c lt brn, *yel* ('17) | 8.75 | 1.60 |
| **222** | A64 | 50c org, *sal* ('18) | 12.00 | 1.10 |
| **223** | A64 | 1e dp grn, *bl* | 19.00 | 1.40 |
| | | *Nos. 207-223 (17)* | 658.25 | 175.65 |

| 1920 | Typo. | | *Perf. 12x11½* | |
|---|---|---|---|---|
| **224** | A64 | 14c dk bl, *yel* | 3.25 | 1.25 |
| **225** | A64 | 20c choc, *buff* | 800.00 | 200.00 |
| **226** | A64 | 50c org, *salmon* | 225.00 | 30.00 |
| | | *Nos. 224-226 (3)* | 1,028. | 231.25 |

**1917-21 Typo. *Perf. 15x14***

**Ordinary Paper**

| No. | Type | Description | Unused | Used |
|---|---|---|---|---|
| **227** | A64 | ¼c dk ol ('18) | .65 | .25 |
| **228** | A64 | ½c black ('18) | .40 | .25 |
| **229** | A64 | 1c deep green | .65 | .25 |
| **230** | A64 | 1c chocolate | .25 | .25 |
| **231** | A64 | 1½c chocolate | 5.50 | 2.50 |
| **232** | A64 | 1½c dp grn ('18) | .30 | .25 |
| **233** | A64 | 2c carmine | 5.50 | 2.50 |
| **234** | A64 | 2c orange ('18) | .25 | .25 |
| **235** | A64 | 2½c violet | .25 | .25 |
| **236** | A64 | 3c car rose | .25 | .25 |
| **237** | A64 | 3c ultra ('21) | 200.00 | 80.00 |
| **238** | A64 | 3½c lt grn ('18) | .25 | .25 |
| **239** | A64 | 4c lt grn ('19) | .40 | .30 |
| **240** | A64 | 5c yel brn | .50 | .30 |
| **240A** | A64 | 5c deep blue | 2.40 | .25 |
| **241** | A64 | 6c pale rose ('20) | .25 | .25 |
| **242** | A64 | 7½c dp blue | .50 | .45 |
| **243** | A64 | 7½c yellow brn | 12.00 | 2.50 |
| **244** | A64 | 8c slate | 5.50 | .75 |
| **245** | A64 | 10c org brn | 25.00 | 1.50 |
| **246** | A64 | 12c bl gray ('20) | 1.25 | .65 |
| **247** | A64 | 15c plum | 3.25 | .85 |
| **248** | A64 | 20c choc ('20) | 60.00 | 5.00 |
| **249** | A64 | 30c gray brown | 120.00 | 21.00 |
| **250** | A64 | 36c red ('21) | 4.50 | 1.25 |
| **251** | A64 | 60c blue ('21) | 4.00 | 1.90 |
| **252** | A64 | 80c brn rose ('21) | 1.40 | 1.10 |
| **253** | A64 | 90c blue ('21) | 5.50 | 4.75 |
| **254** | A64 | 1e violet ('21) | 185.00 | 65.00 |
| | | *Nos. 227-254 (29)* | 645.70 | 195.05 |

**1919-26 *Perf. 12x11½***

**Ordinary Paper**

| No. | Type | Description | Unused | Used |
|---|---|---|---|---|
| **255** | A64 | ¼c dark olive | .40 | .25 |
| **256** | A64 | ½c black | .40 | .25 |
| **257** | A64 | 1c chocolate | .25 | .25 |
| **258** | A64 | 1½c dp grn | .25 | .25 |
| **259** | A64 | 2c orange | .70 | .40 |
| **260** | A64 | 2c yellow | .55 | .25 |
| **261** | A64 | 2c choc ('26) | 1.40 | *8.00* |
| **262** | A64 | 2½c violet | 4.00 | 2.25 |
| **263** | A64 | 3c car rose | .30 | .30 |
| **264** | A64 | 3c ultra ('21) | .50 | .25 |
| **265** | A64 | 4c lt grn ('19) | .25 | .25 |
| **266** | A64 | 4c org ('26) | 1.40 | 1.60 |
| **267** | A64 | 5c yel brn | 1.00 | .40 |
| **268** | A64 | 5c ol brn ('23) | .25 | .25 |
| **269** | A64 | 6c pale rose | .40 | .40 |
| **270** | A64 | 6c brown ('24) | .55 | .25 |
| **271** | A64 | 7½c dp blue | .25 | .25 |
| **272** | A64 | 8c slate | .25 | .25 |
| **273** | A64 | [illegible] bl [illegible] | .45 | .25 |
| **274** | A64 | 8c org ('24) | .45 | .40 |
| **275** | A64 | 10c org brn | .45 | .25 |
| **276** | A64 | 12c dp grn ('21) | .45 | .40 |
| **277** | A64 | 13½c chlky bl | 1.40 | .45 |
| **278** | A64 | 14c brt vio ('21) | 1.10 | .55 |
| **279** | A64 | 15c black ('23) | .40 | .25 |
| **280** | A64 | 16c brt ultra ('24) | .90 | .65 |
| **281** | A64 | 20c dk brn | .50 | .25 |
| **282** | A64 | 20c dp grn ('23) | .45 | .25 |
| **283** | A64 | 20c gray ('24) | .25 | .25 |
| **284** | A64 | 24c grnsh bl ('21) | .45 | .25 |
| **285** | A64 | 25c sal pink ('23) | .45 | .25 |
| **286** | A64 | 25c lt gray ('26) | .45 | .25 |
| **287** | A64 | 30c gray brn ('21) | .50 | .25 |
| **288** | A64 | 30c dk brn ('24) | 20.00 | 4.00 |
| **289** | A64 | 32c dp grn ('24) | 1.10 | .40 |
| **290** | A64 | 36c red ('21) | 1.75 | .45 |
| **291** | A64 | 40c dk bl ('23) | .90 | .55 |
| **292** | A64 | 40c choc ('24) | .45 | .45 |
| **293** | A64 | 40c green ('26) | .25 | .25 |
| **294** | A64 | 48c rose ('24) | 7.50 | 4.00 |
| **295** | A64 | 50c yellow ('21) | 1.90 | .70 |
| **296** | A64 | 60c blue ('21) | 1.40 | .60 |
| **297** | A64 | 64c pale ultra ('24) | 9.50 | 5.50 |
| **298** | A64 | 75c dull rose ('23) | 15.00 | 7.50 |
| **298A** | A64 | 80c brn rose ('21) | 32.50 | 9.50 |
| **298B** | A64 | 80c violet ('24) | 1.00 | .55 |
| **298C** | A64 | 90c chalky bl ('21) | 1.60 | .85 |
| **298D** | A64 | 96c dp rose ('26) | 42.50 | 35.00 |
| **298E** | A64 | 1e violet ('21) | 4.50 | 1.90 |
| **298F** | A64 | 1.10e yel brn ('21) | 4.50 | 1.60 |
| **298G** | A64 | 1.20e yel grn ('21) | 2.50 | 1.40 |
| **298H** | A64 | 2e sl grn ('21) | 45.00 | 5.50 |
| | | *Nos. 255-298H (52)* | 215.60 | 101.80 |

**1923-26 *Perf. 12x11½***

**Glazed Paper**

| No. | Type | Description | Unused | Used |
|---|---|---|---|---|
| **298I** | A64 | 1e dk blue | 5.00 | 2.25 |
| **298J** | A64 | 1e gray vio ('24) | 1.50 | 1.10 |
| **298K** | A64 | 1.20e buff ('24) | 50.00 | 32.50 |
| **298L** | A64 | 1.50e blk vio | 17.50 | 3.25 |
| **298M** | A64 | 1.50e lilac ('24) | 30.00 | 5.00 |
| **298N** | A64 | 1.60e dp bl ('24) | 19.00 | 5.00 |
| **298O** | A64 | 2e sl grn ('24) | 37.50 | 5.50 |
| **298P** | A64 | 2.40e ap grn ('26) | 160.00 | 110.00 |
| **298Q** | A64 | 3e pink ('26) | 160.00 | 100.00 |
| **298R** | A64 | 3.20e gray grn ('24) | 32.50 | 12.00 |
| **298S** | A64 | 5e emer ('24) | 35.00 | 9.00 |
| **298T** | A64 | 10e pink ('24) | 175.00 | 50.00 |
| **298U** | A64 | 20e pale turq ('24) | 300.00 | 160.00 |
| | | *Nos. 298I-298U (13)* | 1,023. | 495.60 |

See design A85. For surcharges & overprints see Nos. 453-495, RA2.

See 496A-496R.

Presidents of Portugal and Brazil and Aviators Cabral and Coutinho A65

| 1923 | Litho. | | *Perf. 14* | |
|---|---|---|---|---|
| **299** | A65 | 1c brown | .25 | *.75* |
| **300** | A65 | 2c orange | .25 | *.75* |
| **301** | A65 | 3c ultra | .25 | *.75* |
| **302** | A65 | 4c yellow grn | .25 | *.75* |
| **303** | A65 | 5c bister brn | .25 | *.75* |
| **304** | A65 | 10c brown org | .25 | *.75* |
| **305** | A65 | 15c black | .25 | *.75* |
| **306** | A65 | 20c blue grn | .25 | *.75* |
| **307** | A65 | 25c rose | .25 | *.75* |
| **308** | A65 | 30c olive brn | .60 | *2.00* |
| **309** | A65 | 40c chocolate | .25 | *.75* |
| **310** | A65 | 50c yellow | .30 | *.90* |
| **311** | A65 | 75c violet | .30 | *1.10* |
| **312** | A65 | 1e dp blue | .30 | *2.00* |
| **313** | A65 | 1.50e olive grn | .65 | *2.50* |
| **314** | A65 | 2e myrtle grn | .65 | *6.50* |
| | | *Nos. 299-314 (16)* | 5.30 | *22.50* |

Flight of Sacadura Cabral and Gago Coutinho from Portugal to Brazil.

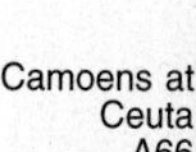

Camoens at Ceuta A66

Camoens Saving the Lusiads — A67

Luis de Camoens — A68

First Edition of the Lusiads — A69

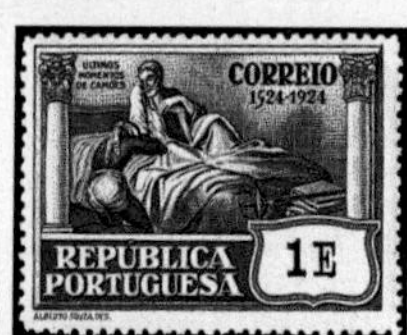

Camoens Dying — A70

Tomb of Camoens A71

Monument to Camoens — A72

**Engr.; Values Typo. in Black**

| 1924, Nov. 11 | | | *Perf. 14, 14½* | |
|---|---|---|---|---|
| **315** | A66 | 2c lt blue | .25 | .25 |
| **316** | A66 | 3c orange | .25 | .25 |
| **317** | A66 | 4c dk gray | .25 | .25 |
| **318** | A66 | 5c yellow grn | .25 | .25 |
| **319** | A66 | 6c lake | .25 | .25 |

**320** A67 8c orange brn .25 .25
**321** A67 10c gray vio .25 .25
**322** A67 15c olive grn .25 .25
**323** A67 16c violet brn .25 .25
**324** A67 20c dp orange .30 .40
**325** A68 25c lilac .30 .40
**326** A68 30c dk brown .30 .40
**327** A68 32c dk green .90 1.25
**328** A68 40c ultra .25 .35
**329** A68 48c red brown 1.10 1.50
**330** A69 50c red orange 1.25 1.60
**331** A69 64c green 1.25 1.60
**332** A69 75c dk violet 1.40 .90
**333** A69 80c bister 1.00 1.25
**334** A69 96c lake 1.00 1.25
**335** A70 1e slate 1.00 1.25
**336** A70 1.20e lt brown 6.00 4.75
**337** A70 1.50e red 1.10 1.75
**338** A70 1.60e dk blue 1.10 1.75
**339** A70 2e apple grn 5.00 6.00
**340** A71 2.40e green, *grn* 3.25 4.00
**341** A71 3e dk bl, *bl* 1.40 2.00
*a.* Value double 125.00 125.00
**342** A71 3.20e blk, *green* 1.40 2.00
**343** A71 4.50e blk, *orange* 3.75 5.00
**344** A71 10e dk brn, *pnksh* 8.50 11.00
**345** A72 20e dk vio, *lil* 8.50 11.00
*Nos. 315-345 (31)* 52.30 63.65

Birth of Luis de Camoens, poet, 400th anniv.
For overprints see Nos. 1S6-1S71.

Castello-Branco's House at Sao Miguel de Seide — A73

Castello-Branco's Study — A74

Camillo Castello-Branco A75

Teresa de Albuquerque A76

Mariana and Joao de Cruz — A77

Simao de Botelho — A78

**1925, Mar. 26** *Perf. 12½*

**346** A73 2c orange .25 .25
**347** A73 3c green .25 .25
**348** A73 4c ultra .25 .25
**349** A73 5c scarlet .25 .25
**350** A73 6c brown vio .25 .25
*a.* "6" and "C" omitted
**351** A73 8c black brn .25 .25
**352** A74 10c pale blue .25 .25
**353** A75 15c olive grn .25 .25
**354** A74 16c red orange .30 .30
**355** A74 20c dk violet .30 .30
**356** A75 25c car rose .30 .30
**357** A74 30c bister brn .30 .30
**358** A74 32c green 1.75 1.75
**359** A75 40c green & blk .65 .65
**360** A74 48c red brn 3.50 3.50
**361** A76 50c blue green .65 .65
**362** A76 64c orange brn 3.50 3.50
**363** A76 75c gray blk .60 .60
**364** A75 80c brown .60 .60
**365** A76 96c car rose 2.00 2.00
**366** A76 1e gray vio 1.50 1.50
**367** A76 1.20e yellow grn 1.50 1.50
**368** A77 1.50e dk bl, *bl* 25.00 15.00
**369** A75 1.60e indigo 4.75 3.75
**370** A77 2e dk grn, *grn* 6.25 4.75
**371** A77 2.40e red, *org* 52.50 32.50
**372** A77 3e lake, *bl* 65.00 42.50
**373** A77 3.20e *green* 30.00 30.00
**374** A75 4.50e red & blk 11.00 4.00
**375** A77 10e brn, *yel* 11.50 4.00
**376** A78 20e *orange* 12.50 5.00
*Nos. 346-376 (31)* 237.95 160.95
Set, never hinged 400.00

Centenary of the birth of Camillo Castello-Branco, novelist.

### First Independence Issue

Alfonso the Conqueror, First King of Portugal — A79

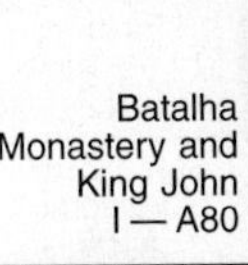

Batalha Monastery and King John I — A80

Battle of Aljubarrota A81

Filipa de Vilhena Arming her Sons A82

King John IV (The Duke of Braganza) A83

Independence Monument, Lisbon — A84

### Center in Black

**1926, Aug. 13** *Perf. 14, 14½*

**377** A79 2c orange .25 .25
**378** A80 3c ultra .25 .25
**379** A79 4c yellow grn .25 .25
**380** A80 5c black brn .25 .25
**381** A79 6c ocher .25 .25
**382** A80 15c dk green .25 .25
**383** A79 16c dp blue .65 1.20
**384** A81 20c dull violet .65 1.20
**385** A82 25c scarlet .65 1.20
**386** A81 32c dp green .80 2.00
**387** A82 40c yellow brn .80 2.00
**388** A80 46c carmine 3.00 4.00
**389** A82 50c olive bis 3.00 4.00
**390** A83 64c blue green 4.50 6.00
**391** A82 75c brown red 4.50 6.00
**392** A84 96c dull red 6.75 7.50
**393** A83 1e black vio 6.75 8.50
**394** A81 1.60e myrtle grn 8.50 11.00
**395** A84 3e plum 25.00 29.00
**396** A84 4.50e olive grn 32.50 35.00
**397** A81 10e carmine 50.00 55.00
*Nos. 377-397 (21)* 149.55 175.10
Set, never hinged 250.00

The use of these stamps instead of the regular issue was obligatory on Aug. 13th and 14th, Nov. 30th and Dec. 1st, 1926.

### Stamps of 1926 Surcharged in Black

No. 397A

No. 397D

No. 397K

**1926 Center in Black** *Perf. 13½x14*

**397A** A80 2c on 5c blk brn 1.10 1.40
**397B** A80 2c on 46c car 1.10 1.40
**397C** A83 2c on 64c bl grn 1.50 2.00
**397D** A82 3c on 75c brn red 1.50 2.00
**397E** A84 3c on 96c dull red 2.00 2.50
**397F** A83 3c on 1e blk vio 1.75 2.25
**397G** A81 4c on 1.60e myr grn 11.00 12.50
**397H** A84 4c on 3e plum 3.75 4.25
**397J** A84 6c on 4.50e ol grn 3.75 4.25
**397K** A81 6c on 10e carmine 4.25 5.00
*Nos. 397A-397K (10)* 31.70 37.55
Set, never hinged 60.00

There are two styles of the ornaments in these surcharges.

Ceres — A85

### Without Imprint

**1926, Dec. 2 Typo.** *Perf. 13½x14*

**398** A85 2c chocolate .25 .25
**399** A85 3c brt blue .25 .25
**400** A85 4c dp orange .25 .25
**401** A85 5c dp brown .25 .25
**402** A85 6c orange brn .25 .25
**403** A85 10c orange red .25 .25
**404** A85 15c black .25 .25
**405** A85 16c ultra .25 .25
**406** A85 25c gray .25 .25
**407** A85 32c dp green .55 .35
**408** A85 40c blue green .35 .25
**409** A85 48c rose 1.10 .90
**410** A85 50c ocher 1.75 1.60
**411** A85 64c deep blue 1.75 1.60
**412** A85 80c violet 3.50 .55
**413** A85 96c car rose 2.00 1.00
**414** A85 1e red brown 9.00 1.00
**415** A85 1.20e yellow brn 9.00 1.00
**416** A85 1.60e dark blue 2.25 .55
**417** A85 2e green 13.00 1.00
**418** A85 3.20e olive grn 5.00 1.00
**419** A85 4.50e yellow 5.00 1.00
**420** A85 5e brown olive 65.00 3.75
**421** A85 10e red 8.00 2.00
*Nos. 398-421 (24)* 129.50 19.80
Set, never hinged 290.00

See design A64.

### Second Independence Issue

Gonçalo Mendes da Maia — A86

Dr. Joao das Regras — A88

Guimaraes Castle — A87

Battle of Montijo — A89

Brites de Almeida — A90

Joao Pinto Ribeiro — A91

### Center in Black

**1927, Nov. 29 Engr.** *Perf. 14*

**422** A86 2c brown .25 .25
**423** A87 3c ultra .25 .25
**424** A86 4c orange .25 .25
**425** A88 5c olive brn .25 .25
**426** A89 6c orange brn .25 .25
**427** A87 15c black brn .45 1.00
**428** A88 16c deep blue 1.00 1.75
**429** A86 25c gray 1.25 1.75
**430** A89 32c blue grn 2.25 3.00
**431** A90 40c yellow grn .60 1.00
**432** A86 48c brown red 10.00 12.50
**433** A87 80c dk violet 7.50 9.00
**434** A90 96c dull red 13.00 15.00
**435** A88 1.60e myrtle grn 14.00 15.00
**436** A91 4.50e bister 20.00 22.50
*Nos. 422-436 (15)* 71.30 83.75
Set, never hinged 125.00

The use of these stamps instead of the regular issue was compulsory on Nov. 29-30, Dec. 1-2, 1927. The money derived from their sale was used for the purchase of a palace for a war museum, the organization of an international exposition in Lisbon, in 1940, and for fêtes to be held in that year in commemoration of the 8th cent. of the founding of Portugal and the 3rd cent. of its restoration.

### Third Independence Issue

Gualdim Paes — A93

The Siege of Santarem — A94

Battle of Rolica — A95

Battle of Atoleiros A96

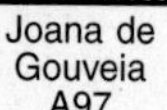

Joana de Gouveia A97

Matias de Albuquerque A98

| 1928, Nov. 28 | | Center in Black | | |
|---|---|---|---|---|
| 437 | A93 | 2c lt blue | .25 | .25 |
| 438 | A94 | 3c lt green | .25 | .25 |
| 439 | A95 | 4c lake | .25 | .25 |
| 440 | A96 | 5c olive grn | .25 | .25 |
| 441 | A97 | 6c orange brn | .25 | .25 |
| 442 | A94 | 15c slate | .65 | .85 |
| 443 | A95 | 16c dk violet | .65 | .85 |
| 444 | A93 | 25c ultra | .65 | 1.00 |
| 445 | A97 | 32c dk green | 3.50 | 4.00 |
| 446 | A96 | 40c olive brn | .65 | 1.00 |
| 447 | A95 | 50c red orange | 8.50 | 10.00 |
| 448 | A94 | 80c lt gray | 9.00 | 10.00 |
| 449 | A97 | 96c carmine | 15.00 | 18.00 |
| 450 | A96 | 1e claret | 25.00 | 29.00 |
| 451 | A93 | 1.60e dk blue | 11.50 | 13.50 |
| 452 | A98 | 4.50e yellow | 12.50 | 15.00 |
| | | *Nos. 437-452 (16)* | 88.85 | 104.45 |
| | | Set, never hinged | 150.00 | |

Obligatory Nov. 27-30. See note after No. 436.

Type and Stamps of 1912-28 Surcharged in Black

| 1928-29 | | *Perf. 12x11½, 15x14* | | |
|---|---|---|---|---|
| 453 | A64 | 4c on 8c orange | .35 | .30 |
| 454 | A64 | 4c on 30c dk brn | .35 | .30 |
| 455 | A64 | 10c on ¼c dk ol | .35 | .30 |
| *a.* | | Inverted surcharge | 100.00 | 90.00 |
| 456 | A64 | 10c on ½c blk (R) | .50 | .40 |
| *a.* | | Perf. 15x14 | 17.50 | 14.00 |
| 457 | A64 | 10c on 1c choc | .50 | .40 |
| *a.* | | Perf. 15x14 | *65.00* | *50.00* |
| 458 | A64 | 10c on 4c grn | .40 | .35 |
| *a.* | | Perf. 15x14 | *75.00* | *60.00* |
| 459 | A64 | 10c on 4c orange | .40 | .35 |
| 460 | A64 | 10c on 5c ol brn | .40 | .35 |
| 461 | A64 | 15c on 16c blue | 1.00 | .75 |
| 462 | A64 | 15c on 16c ultra | 1.00 | .75 |
| 463 | A64 | 15c on 20c brown | 32.50 | 30.00 |
| 464 | A64 | 15c on 20c gray | .35 | .30 |
| 465 | A64 | 15c on 24c grnsh bl | 2.10 | 1.60 |
| 466 | A64 | 15c on 25c gray | .35 | .30 |
| 467 | A64 | 15c on 25c sal pink | .35 | .30 |
| 468 | A64 | 16c on 32c dp grn | .75 | .70 |
| 469 | A64 | 40c on 2c orange | .35 | .30 |
| 470 | A64 | 40c on 2c yellow | 4.00 | 3.00 |
| 471 | A64 | 40c on 2c choc | .35 | .30 |
| 472 | A64 | 40c on 3c ultra | .40 | .35 |
| 473 | A64 | 40c on 50c yellow | .35 | .30 |
| 474 | A64 | 40c on 60c blue | .75 | .65 |
| *a.* | | Perf. 15x14 | 9.00 | 7.50 |
| 475 | A64 | 40c on 64c pale ultra | .75 | .70 |
| 476 | A64 | 40c on 75c dl rose | .85 | .80 |
| 477 | A64 | 40c on 80c violet | .60 | .50 |
| 478 | A64 | 40c on 90c chlky bl | 4.00 | 3.00 |
| *a.* | | Perf. 15x14 | 10.00 | 8.50 |
| 479 | A64 | 40c on 1e gray vio | .75 | .70 |
| 480 | A64 | 40c on 1.10e yel brn | .75 | .70 |
| 481 | A64 | 80c on 6c pale rose | .75 | .70 |
| 482 | A64 | 80c on 6c choc | .75 | .70 |
| 483 | A64 | 80c on 48c rose | 1.10 | 1.00 |
| 484 | A64 | 80c on 1.50e lilac | 1.75 | 1.25 |
| 485 | A64 | 96c on 1.20e yel grn | 3.50 | 2.50 |
| 486 | A64 | 96c on 1.20e buff | 4.50 | 3.50 |
| 487 | A64 | 1.60e on 2e slate grn | 40.00 | 27.50 |
| 487A | A64 | 1.60e on 2e sl grn, *glazed paper* | 32.50 | 27.50 |
| 488 | A64 | 1.60e on 3.20e gray grn | 9.00 | 7.00 |
| 489 | A64 | 1.60e on 20e pale turq | 12.00 | 10.00 |
| | | *Nos. 453-489 (37)* | 128.90 | 102.90 |
| | | Set, never hinged | 275.00 | .30 |

Stamps of 1912-26 Overprinted in Black or Red

| 1929 | | *Perf. 12x11½* | | |
|---|---|---|---|---|
| 490 | A64 | 10c orange brn | .40 | |
| *a.* | | Perf. 15x14 | 275.00 | 275.00 |
| 491 | A64 | 15c black (R) | .40 | .30 |
| 492 | A64 | 40c lt green | .60 | .50 |
| 493 | A64 | 40c chocolate | .60 | .40 |
| 494 | A64 | 96c dp rose | 5.00 | 4.50 |
| 495 | A64 | 1.60e brt blue | 22.50 | 16.00 |
| *a.* | | Double overprint | 110.00 | 100.00 |
| | | *Nos. 490-495 (6)* | 29.50 | 21.70 |
| | | Set, never hinged | 45.00 | |

Liberty — A100

| 1929, May | | *Perf. 12x11½* | | |
|---|---|---|---|---|
| 496 | A100 | 1.60e on 5c red brn | 13.00 | 10.00 |

**Types of 1912-20 Issues**
With Imprint

| 1930-31 | | Typo. *Perf. 12x11½* | | |
|---|---|---|---|---|
| 496A | A64 | 4c orange | .30 | .25 |
| 496B | A64 | 5c blk brn ('31) | .30 | .25 |
| 496C | A64 | 6c red brn | .30 | .25 |
| 496D | A64 | 10c red ('31) | .30 | .25 |
| 496E | A64 | 15c black | 1.75 | .30 |
| 496F | A64 | 25c lt gray | .45 | .25 |
| 496G | A64 | 25c blue grn | .45 | .25 |
| 496H | A85 | 32c dp green | .45 | .25 |
| 496I | A64 | 40c green | 3.50 | .55 |
| 496J | A64 | 50c bister | 1.75 | .80 |
| 496K | A64 | 50c red brn ('30) | 1.75 | .80 |
| 496L | A64 | 75c car rose | 1.75 | .85 |
| 496M | A64 | 80c dk grn | 1.75 | .85 |
| 496N | A64 | 1e brn lake | 3.50 | .85 |
| 496O | A64 | 1.20e pur brn ('31) | 3.00 | 1.00 |
| 496P | A64 | 1.25e dk bl ('31) | 2.50 | 1.00 |
| 496Q | A64 | 2e red vio ('31) | 17.50 | 6.50 |
| 496R | A64 | 4.50e org ('31) | 45.00 | 40.00 |
| | | *Nos. 496A-496R (18)* | 86.30 | 55.25 |
| | | Set, never hinged | 160.00 | |

Nos. 496A-496R were printed at the Lisbon Mint from new plates produced from the original dies. The paper is whiter than the paper used for earlier Ceres stamps. The gum is white.

"Portugal" Holding Volume of "Lusiads" — A101

| 1931-38 | | Typo. *Perf. 14* | | |
|---|---|---|---|---|
| 497 | A101 | 4c bister brn | .25 | .25 |
| 498 | A101 | 5c olive gray | .25 | .25 |
| 499 | A101 | 6c lt gray | .25 | .25 |
| 500 | A101 | 10c dk violet | .25 | .25 |
| 501 | A101 | 15c gray blk | .25 | .25 |
| 502 | A101 | 16c brt blue | 1.10 | .75 |
| 503 | A101 | 25c deep green | 3.00 | .35 |
| 504 | A101 | 25c brt bl ('33) | 3.25 | .40 |
| 505 | A101 | 30c dk grn ('33) | 1.75 | .40 |
| 506 | A101 | 40c orange red | 5.50 | .25 |
| 507 | A101 | 48c fawn | 1.10 | .95 |
| 508 | A101 | 50c lt brown | .30 | .25 |
| 509 | A101 | 75c car rose | 4.50 | 1.10 |
| 510 | A101 | 80c emerald | .35 | .25 |
| 511 | A101 | 95c car rose ('33) | 15.00 | 6.50 |
| 512 | A101 | 1e claret | 27.50 | .25 |
| 513 | A101 | 1.20e olive grn | 2.00 | 1.10 |
| 514 | A101 | 1.25e dk blue | 1.75 | .25 |
| 515 | A101 | 1.60e dk blue ('33) | 30.00 | 4.00 |
| 516 | A101 | 1.75e dk blue ('38) | .65 | .25 |
| 517 | A101 | 2e dull violet | .65 | .25 |
| 518 | A101 | 4.50e orange | 1.50 | .30 |
| 519 | A101 | 5e yellow grn | 1.50 | .30 |
| | | *Nos. 497-519 (23)* | 102.65 | 19.15 |
| | | Set, never hinged | 200.00 | |

Birthplace of St. Anthony A102

Font where St. Anthony was Baptized A103

Lisbon Cathedral A104

St. Anthony with Infant Jesus A105

Santa Cruz Cathedral A106

St. Anthony's Tomb at Padua A107

| 1931, June | | Typo. *Perf. 12* | | |
|---|---|---|---|---|
| 528 | A102 | 15c plum | .65 | .25 |
| | | **Litho.** | | |
| 529 | A103 | 25c gray & pale grn | 1.00 | .25 |
| 530 | A104 | 40c gray brn & buff | .65 | .25 |
| 531 | A105 | 75c dl rose & pale rose | 21.00 | 14.00 |
| 532 | A106 | 1.25e gray & pale bl | 47.50 | 27.50 |
| 533 | A107 | 4.50e gray vio & lil | 23.00 | 3.50 |
| | | *Nos. 528-533 (6)* | 93.80 | 45.75 |
| | | Set, never hinged | 210.00 | |

7th centenary of the death of St. Anthony of Padua and Lisbon.

For surcharges see Nos. 543-548.

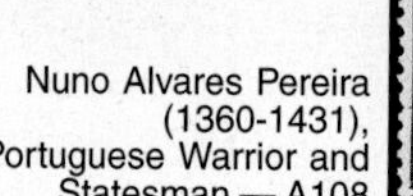

Nuno Alvares Pereira (1360-1431), Portuguese Warrior and Statesman — A108

| 1931, Nov. 1 | | Typo. *Perf. 12x11½* | | |
|---|---|---|---|---|
| 534 | A108 | 15c black | 1.10 | 1.10 |
| 535 | A108 | 25c gray grn & blk | 1.75 | 1.10 |
| 536 | A108 | 40c orange | 2.75 | .50 |
| *a.* | | Value omitted | 150.00 | 150.00 |
| 537 | A108 | 75c car rose | 32.50 | 27.50 |
| 538 | A108 | 1.25e dk bl & pale bl | 26.00 | 21.00 |
| 539 | A108 | 4.50e choc & lt grn | 120.00 | 52.50 |
| *a.* | | Value omitted | 350.00 | 350.00 |
| | | *Nos. 534-539 (6)* | 184.10 | 103.70 |
| | | Set, never hinged | 350.00 | |

For surcharges see Nos. 549-554.

Nos. 528-533 Surcharged

| 1933 | | *Perf. 12* | | |
|---|---|---|---|---|
| 543 | A104 | 15c on 40c | .75 | .35 |
| 544 | A102 | 40c on 15c | 2.50 | 1.25 |
| 545 | A103 | 40c on 25c | 2.00 | .35 |
| 546 | A105 | 40c on 75c | 8.00 | 5.25 |
| 547 | A106 | 40c on 1.25e | 8.00 | 5.25 |
| 548 | A107 | 40c on 4.50e | 8.00 | 5.25 |
| | | *Nos. 543-548 (6)* | 29.25 | 17.70 |
| | | Set, never hinged | 52.50 | |

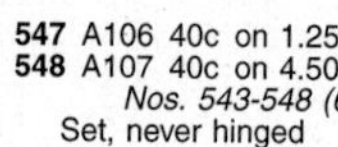

Nos. 534-539 Surcharged

| 1933 | | *Perf. 12x11½* | | |
|---|---|---|---|---|
| 549 | A108 | 15c on 40c | .90 | .35 |
| 550 | A108 | 40c on 15c | 3.75 | 2.75 |
| 551 | A108 | 40c on 25c | 1.10 | .90 |
| 552 | A108 | 40c on 75c | 8.00 | 6.50 |
| 553 | A108 | 40c on 1.25e | 8.00 | 4.00 |
| 554 | A108 | 40c on 4.50e | 8.00 | 4.00 |
| | | *Nos. 549-554 (6)* | 29.75 | 18.50 |
| | | Set, never hinged | 55.00 | |

President Carmona — A109

| 1934, May 28 | | Typo. *Perf. 11½* | | |
|---|---|---|---|---|
| 556 | A109 | 40c brt violet | 17.50 | .35 |
| | | Never hinged | 32.50 | |

Head of a Colonial — A110

| 1934, July | | *Perf. 11½x12* | | |
|---|---|---|---|---|
| 558 | A110 | 25c dk brown | 3.00 | 1.75 |
| 559 | A110 | 40c scarlet | 19.00 | .40 |
| 560 | A110 | 1.60e dk blue | 29.00 | 13.00 |
| | | *Nos. 558-560 (3)* | 51.00 | 15.15 |
| | | Set, never hinged | 125.00 | |

Colonial Exposition.

Roman Temple, Evora A111

Prince Henry the Navigator A112

"All for the Nation" A113

Coimbra Cathedral A114

| 1935-41 | | *Perf. 11½x12* | | |
|---|---|---|---|---|
| 561 | A111 | 4c black | .40 | .25 |
| 562 | A111 | 5c blue | .45 | .25 |
| 563 | A111 | 6c choc ('36) | .75 | .30 |
| | | ***Perf. 11½, 12x11½ (1.75e)*** | | |
| 564 | A112 | 10c turq grn | .65 | .25 |
| 565 | A112 | 15c red brown | .25 | .25 |
| *a.* | | Booklet pane of 4 | | |
| 566 | A113 | 25c dp blue | 5.25 | .40 |
| *a.* | | Booklet pane of 4 | | |
| 567 | A113 | 40c brown | 1.75 | .25 |
| *a.* | | Booklet pane of 4 | | |
| 568 | A113 | 1e rose red | 8.50 | .45 |
| 568A | A114 | 1.75e blue | 70.00 | 1.25 |
| 568B | A113 | 10e gray blk ('41) | 20.00 | 3.00 |

**569** A113 20e turq grn ('41) 26.00 2.00
*Nos. 561-569 (11)* 134.00 8.65
Set, never hinged 240.00

For overprint see No. O1.

Queen Maria — A115

**Typographed, Head Embossed**

**1935, June 1** *Perf. 11½*
**570** A115 40c scarlet 1.25 .25
Never hinged 2.00

First Portuguese Philatelic Exhibition.

Rod and Bowl of Aesculapius — A116

**1937, July 24 Typo.** *Perf. 11½x12*
**571** A116 25c blue 9.50 .90
Never hinged 15.00

Centenary of the establishment of the School of Medicine in Lisbon and Oporto.

Gil Vicente — A117

**1937**
**572** A117 40c dark brown 17.00 .25
**573** A117 1e rose red 2.00 .25
Set, never hinged 32.50

400th anniversary of the death of Gil Vicente (1465-1536), Portuguese playwright. Design shows him in cowherd role in his play, "Auto do Vaqueiro."

Grapes — A118

**1938** *Perf. 11½*
**575** A118 15c brt purple 1.25 .50
**576** A118 25c brown 3.00 1.60
**577** A118 40c dp red lilac 9.00 .30
**578** A118 1.75e dp blue 26.00 24.00
*Nos. 575-578 (4)* 39.25 26.40
Set, never hinged 65.00

International Vineyard and Wine Congress.

Emblem of Portuguese Legion — A119

**1940, Jan. 27 Unwmk.** *Perf. 11½*
**579** A119 5c dull yellow .30 .25
**580** A119 10c violet .30 .25
**581** A119 15c brt blue .30 .25
**582** A119 25c brown 20.00 1.10
**583** A119 40c dk green 32.50 .40
**584** A119 80c yellow grn 2.10 .60
**585** A119 1e brt red 50.00 3.50
**586** A119 1.75e dark blue 7.00 2.60
*a.* Souv. sheet of 8, #579-586 290.00 290.00
Never hinged 600.00
*Nos. 579-586 (8)* 112.50 8.95
Set, never hinged 190.00

Issued in honor of the Portuguese Legion. No. 586a sold for 5.50e, the proceeds going to various charities.

Portuguese World Exhibition A120

King John IV — A121

Discoveries Monument, Belém — A122

King Alfonso I — A123

**1940 Engr.** *Perf. 12x11½, 11½x12*
**587** A120 10c brown violet .25 .25
**588** A121 15c dk grnsh bl .25 .25
**589** A122 25c dk slate grn 1.20 .25
**590** A121 35c yellow green 1.10 .35
**591** A123 40c olive bister 2.50 .25
**592** A120 80c dk violet 5.00 .35
**593** A122 1e dark red 11.00 1.60
**594** A123 1.75e ultra 6.50 2.60
*a.* Souv. sheet of 8, #587-594 ('41) 150.00 110.00
Never hinged 300.00
*Nos. 587-594 (8)* 27.80 5.90
Set, never hinged 47.50

Portuguese Intl. Exhibition, Lisbon (10c, 80c); restoration of the monarchy, 300th anniv (15c, 35c); Portuguese independence, 800th anniv (40c, 1.75e).

No. 594a sold for 10e.

Sir Rowland Hill — A124

**1940, Aug. 12 Typo.** *Perf. 11½x12*
**595** A124 15c dk violet brn .25 .25
**596** A124 25c dp org brn .25 .25
**597** A124 35c green .30 .25
**598** A124 40c brown violet .45 .25
**599** A124 50c turq green 17.00 3.25
**600** A124 80c lt blue 2.00 1.10
**601** A124 1e crimson 20.00 3.50
**602** A124 1.75e dk blue 6.00 3.50
*a.* Souv. sheet of 8, #595-602 ('41) 75.00 75.00
Never hinged 120.00
*Nos. 595-602 (8)* 46.25 12.35
Set, never hinged 75.00

Postage stamp centenary. No. 602a sold for 10e.

Fisherwoman of Nazare A126

Native of Coimbra A127

Native of Saloio — A128

Fisherwoman of Lisbon — A129

Native of Olhao — A130

Native of Aveiro — A131

Native of Madeira A132

Native of Viana do Castelo A133

Rancher of Ribatejo A134

Peasant of Alentejo A135

**1941, Apr. 4 Typo.** *Perf. 11½*
**605** A126 4c sage green .25 .25
**606** A127 5c orange brn .25 .25
**607** A128 10c red violet 3.25 1.25
**608** A129 15c lt yel grn .25 .25
**609** A130 25c rose violet 2.25 .70
**610** A131 40c yellow grn .25 .25
**611** A132 80c lt blue 3.25 2.10
**612** A133 1e rose red 9.50 1.60
**613** A134 1.75e dull blue 10.50 4.75
**614** A135 2e red orange 40.00 22.50
*a.* Sheet of 10, #605-614 125.00 125.00
Never hinged 225.00
*Nos. 605-614 (10)* 69.75 33.90
Set, never hinged 120.00

No. 614a sold for 10e.

Ancient Sailing Vessel — A136

**1943** *Perf. 14*
**615** A136 5c black .25 .25
**616** A136 10c fawn .25 .25
**617** A136 15c lilac gray .25 .25
**618** A136 20c dull violet .25 .25
**619** A136 30c brown violet .25 .25
**620** A136 35c dk blue grn .25 .25
**621** A136 50c plum .25 .25
**622** A136 1e deep rose 6.75 .25
**623** A136 1.75e indigo 21.00 .25

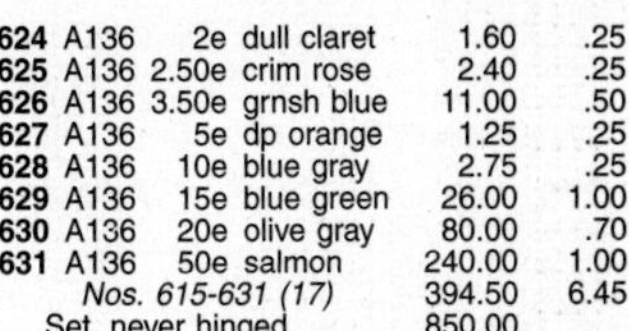

**624** A136 2e dull claret 1.60 .25
**625** A136 2.50e crim rose 2.40 .25
**626** A136 3.50e grnsh blue 11.00 .50
**627** A136 5e dp orange 1.25 .25
**628** A136 10e blue gray 2.75 .25
**629** A136 15e blue green 26.00 1.00
**630** A136 20e olive gray 80.00 .70
**631** A136 50e salmon 240.00 1.00
*Nos. 615-631 (17)* 394.50 6.45
Set, never hinged 850.00

See Nos. 702-710.

Farmer — A137

**1943, Oct.** *Perf. 11½*
**632** A137 10c dull blue .75 .25
**633** A137 50c red 1.25 .35
Set, never hinged 3.00

Congress of Agricultural Science.

Postrider — A138

**1944, May** **Unwmk.**
**634** A138 10c dk violet brn .25 .25
**635** A138 50c purple .25 .25
**636** A138 1e cerise 3.25 .65
**637** A138 1.75e brt blue 3.25 1.75
*a.* Sheet of 4, #634-637 32.50 35.00
Never hinged 52.50
*Nos. 634-637 (4)* 7.00 2.90
Set, never hinged 10.50

3rd Philatelic Exhibition, Lisbon. No. 637a sold for 7.50e.

Portrait of Avellar Brotero — A139

Statue of Brotero — A140

**1944, Nov. 23 Typo.** *Perf. 11½x12*
**638** A139 10c chocolate .25 .25
**639** A140 50c dull green 1.20 .25
**640** A140 1e carmine 7.00 1.60
**641** A139 1.75e dark blue 6.25 2.60
*a.* Sheet of 4,#638-641 ('45) 32.50 32.50
Never hinged 62.50
*Nos. 638-641 (4)* 14.70 4.70
Set, never hinged 21.00

Avellar Brotero, botanist, 200th birth anniv. No. 641a sold for 7.50e.

Gil Eannes — A141

Designs: 30c, Joao Goncalves Zarco. 35c, Bartolomeu Dias. 50c, Vasco da Gama. 1e, Pedro Alvares Cabral. 1.75e, Fernando Magellan. 2e, Goncalo Velho. 3.50e, Diogo Cao.

**1945, July 29 Engr. *Perf. 13½***

**642** A141 10c violet brn .25 .25
**643** A141 30c yellow brn .25 .25
**644** A141 35c blue green .35 .25
**645** A141 50c dk olive grn 1.25 .25
**646** A141 1e vermilion 3.00 .65
**647** A141 1.75e slate blue 3.50 2.10
**648** A141 2e black 4.50 2.40
**649** A141 3.50e carmine rose 8.00 4.25
*a.* Sheet of 8, #642-649 32.50 40.00
Never hinged 50.00
*Nos. 642-649 (8)* 21.10 10.40
Set, never hinged 32.50

Portuguese navigators of 15th and 16th centuries.
No. 649a sold for 15e.

Pres. Antonio Oscar de Fragoso Carmona — A149

***Perf. 11½***

**1945, Nov. 12 Photo. Unwmk.**

**650** A149 10c bright violet .25 .25
**651** A149 30c copper brn .25 .25
**652** A149 35c dark green .25 .25
**653** A149 50c dark olive .35 .25
**654** A149 1e dark red 9.50 1.25
**655** A149 1.75e dark blue 7.50 3.75
**656** A149 2e deep claret 42.50 5.00
**657** A149 3.50e slate black 30.00 7.50
*a.* Sheet of 8, #650-657 110.00 110.00
Never hinged 210.00
*Nos. 650-657 (8)* 90.60 18.50
Set, never hinged 150.00

No. 657a sold for 15e.

Astrolabe — A150

**1945, Dec. 27 Litho.**

**658** A150 10c light brown .25 .25
**659** A150 50c gray green .25 .25
**660** A150 1e brown red 3.00 .75
**661** A150 1.75e dull chalky bl 3.25 2.60
*a.* Sheet of 4, #658-661 ('46) 26.00 27.50
Never hinged 42.50
*Nos. 658-661 (4)* 6.75 3.85
Set, never hinged 10.50

Centenary of the Portuguese Naval School.
No. 661a, issued Apr. 29, sold for 7.50e.

**Catalogue values for unused stamps in this section, from this point to the end of the section, are for Never Hinged items.**

Silves Castle A151

Almourol Castle A152

Castles: 30c, Leiria. 35c, Feira. 50c, Guimaraes. 1.75e, Lisbon. 2e, Braganca. 3.50e, Ourem.

**1946, June 1 Engr.**

**662** A151 10c brown vio .25 .25
**663** A151 30c brown red .25 .25
**664** A151 35c olive grn .25 .25
**665** A151 50c gray blk .75 .25
**666** A152 1e brt carmine 30.00 1.00
**667** A152 1.75e dk blue 16.50 2.40
*a.* Sheet of 4 175.00 100.00
Hinged 95.00
**668** A152 2e dk gray grn 60.00 4.50
**669** A152 3.50e orange brn 26.00 5.50
*Nos. 662-669 (8)* 134.00 14.40

No. 667a printed on buff granite paper, size 135x102mm, sold for 12.50e.

Figure with Tablet and Arms — A153

**1946, Nov. 19 *Perf. 12x11½***

**670** A153 50c dark blue 1.00 .25
*a.* Sheet of 4 155.00 120.00
Hinged 80.00

Establishment of the Bank of Portugal, cent.
No. 670a measures 155x143½mm and sold for 7.50e.

Madonna and Child — A154

**1946, Dec. 8 Unwmk. *Perf. 13½***

**671** A154 30c gray black .30 .25
**672** A154 50c deep green .30 .25
**673** A154 1e rose car 3.25 1.10
**674** A154 1.75e brt blue 5.25 2.25
*a.* Sheet of 4, #671-674 ('47) 67.50 52.50
Hinged 37.50
*Nos. 671-674 (4)* 9.10 3.85

300th anniv. of the proclamation making the Virgin Mary patroness of Portugal.
No. 674a sold for 7.50e.

Shepherdess, Caramullo — A155

30c, Timbrel player, Malpique. 35c, Flute player, Monsanto. 50c, Woman of Avintes. 1e, Field laborer, Maia. 1.75e, Woman of Algarve. 2e, Bastonet player, Miranda. 3.50e, Woman of the Azores.

**1947, Mar. 1 Photo. *Perf. 11½***

**675** A155 10c rose violet .25 .25
**676** A155 30c dark red .25 .25
**677** A155 35c dk olive grn .35 .25
**678** A155 50c dark brown .60 .25
**679** A155 1e red 19.00 .55
**680** A155 1.75e slate blue 20.00 4.00
**681** A155 2e peacock bl 65.00 4.50
**682** A155 3.50e slate blk 50.00 7.50
*a.* Sheet of 8, #675-682 260.00 260.00
Hinged 145.00
*Nos. 675-682 (8)* 155.45 17.55

No. 682a sold for 15e.

Surrender of the Moors, 1147 — A163

**1947, Oct. 13 Engr. *Perf. 12½***

**683** A163 5c blue green .25 .25
**684** A163 20c dk carmine .25 .25
**685** A163 50c violet .30 .25
**686** A163 1.75e dark blue 7.25 5.00
**687** A163 2.50e chocolate 11.00 6.50
**688** A163 3.50e slate black 19.00 10.50
*Nos. 683-688 (6)* 38.05 22.75

Conquest of Lisbon from the Moors, 800th anniv.

St. John de Britto
A164 A165

**1948, May 28 *Perf. 11½x12***

**689** A164 30c green .25 .25
**690** A165 50c dark brown .25 .25
**691** A164 1e rose carmine 10.50 1.60
**692** A165 1.75e blue 13.00 2.75
*Nos. 689-692 (4)* 24.00 4.85

Birth of St. John de Britto, 300th anniv.

Architecture and Engineering A166

**1948, May 28 *Perf. 13x12½***

**693** A166 50c violet brn .65 .25

Exposition of public Works and Natl. Congress of Engineering and Architecture, 1948.

King John I — A167

Designs: 30c, Philippa of Lancaster. 35c, Prince Ferdinand. 50c, Prince Henry the Navigator. 1e, Nuno Alvarez Pereira. 1.75e, John das Regras. 2e, Fernao Lopes. 3.50e, Affonso Domingues.

***Perf. 11½***

**1949, May 6 Unwmk. Photo.**

**694** A167 10c brn vio & cr .25 .25
**695** A167 30c dk bl grn & cr .25 .25
**696** A167 35c dk ol grn & cr .50 .25
**697** A167 50c dp blue & cr 1.50 .25
**698** A167 1e dk red & cr 1.50 .25
**699** A167 1.75e dk gray & cr 27.00 15.00
**700** A167 2e dk gray bl & cr 16.00 2.00
**701** A167 3.50e dk brn & gray 55.00 17.00
*a.* Sheet of 8, #694-701 80.00 80.00
*Nos. 694-701 (8)* 102.00 35.25

No. 701a sold for 15e. Stamps from No. 701a differ from Nos. 694-701 in that they do not have "P. GUEDES" and "COURVOISIER S.A." below the design. Each stamp from the sheet of 8 has the same retail value.

**Ship Type of 1942**

**1948-49 Typo. *Perf. 14***

**702** A136 80c dp green 4.75 .45
**703** A136 1e dp claret ('48) 3.25 .25
**704** A136 1.20e dp carmine 5.00 .25
**705** A136 1.50e olive 55.00 .40
**706** A136 1.80e yellow org 50.00 3.00
**707** A136 2e deep blue 7.50 .50
**708** A136 4e orange 75.00 2.75
**709** A136 6e yellow grn 145.00 4.00
**710** A136 7.50e grnsh gray 45.00 3.50
*Nos. 702-710 (9)* 390.50 15.10
Set, hinged 230.00

Angel, Coimbra Museum — A168

**1949, Dec. 20 Engr. *Perf. 13x14***

**711** A168 1e red brown 11.50 .25
**712** A168 5e olive brown 3.00 .25

16th Intl. Congress of History and Art.

Symbols of the UPU — A169

**1949, Dec. 29**

**713** A169 1e brown violet .35 .25
**714** A169 2e deep blue 1.10 .25
**715** A169 2.50e deep green 5.75 1.25
**716** A169 4e brown red 16.00 3.50
*Nos. 713-716 (4)* 23.20 5.25

75th anniv. of the UPU.

Madonna of Fatima — A170

**1950, May 13 *Perf. 11½x12***

**717** A170 50c dark green .65 .25
**718** A170 1e dark brown 3.25 .25
**719** A170 2e blue 8.50 1.60
**720** A170 5e lilac 100.00 29.00
*Nos. 717-720 (4)* 112.40 31.10

Holy Year, 1950, and to honor "Our Lady of the Rosary" at Fatima.

St. John of God Helping Ill Man — A171

**1950, Oct. 30 Engr. Unwmk.**

**721** A171 20c gray violet .35 .25
**722** A171 50c cerise .50 .25
**723** A171 1e olive grn 2.00 .45
**724** A171 1.50e deep orange 17.00 3.00
**725** A171 2e blue 14.50 2.25
**726** A171 4e chocolate 60.00 8.50
*Nos. 721-726 (6)* 94.35 14.70

400th anniv. of the death of St. John of God.

Guerra Junqueiro A172

**1951, Mar. 2 Litho. *Perf. 13½***

**727** A172 50c dark brown 8.50 .35
**728** A172 1e dk slate gray 2.00 .30

Birth centenary of Guerra Junqueiro, poet.

Fisherman and Catch — A173

**1951, Mar. 9**

**729** A173 50c gray grn, *buff* 5.00 .50
**730** A173 1e rose lake, *buff* 1.00 .25

3rd National Congress of Fisheries.

Dove — A174

Pope Pius XII — A175

**1951, Oct. 11**

731 A174 20c dk brn & buff .40 .25
732 A174 90c dk ol grn & cr 9.00 1.75
733 A175 1e dp cl & pink 9.00 .25
734 A175 2.30e dk bl grn & bl 12.00 2.10
*Nos. 731-734 (4)* 30.40 4.35

End of the Holy Year.

15th Century Colonists, Terceira A176

**1951, Oct. 24** ***Perf. 13x13½***

735 A176 50c dk bl, *salmon* 3.75 .45
736 A176 1e dk brn, *cream* 1.25 .35

500th anniversary (in 1950) of the colonizing of the island of Terceira.

Student, Soldiers and Workers A177

**1951, Nov. 22** ***Perf. 13½x13***

737 A177 1e violet brown 10.00 .25
738 A177 2.30e dark blue 7.50 1.40

25th anniversary of the national revolution.

16th Century Coach A178

Designs: Various coaches.

***Perf. 13x13½***

**1952, Jan. 8** **Engr.** **Unwmk.**

739 A178 10c purple .25 .25
740 A178 20c olive gray .25 .25
741 A178 50c steel blue 1.00 .25
742 A178 90c green 3.50 1.50
743 A178 1e red orange 1.50 .25
744 A178 1.40e rose pink 8.00 4.50
745 A178 1.50e rose brown 7.50 2.25
746 A178 2.30e deep ultra 5.50 2.00
*Nos. 739-746 (8)* 27.50 11.25

National Museum of Coaches.

Symbolical of NATO — A179

**1952, Apr. 4** **Litho.** ***Perf. 12½***

747 A179 1e green & blk 7.50 .25
748 A179 3.50e gray & vio bl 290.00 15.00
Set, hinged 140.00

North Atlantic Treaty signing, 3rd anniv.

Hockey Players on Roller Skates A180

**1952, June 28** ***Perf. 13x13½***

749 A180 1e dk blue & gray 5.00 .25
750 A180 3.50e dk red brown 7.50 2.25

Issued to publicize the 8th World Championship Hockey-on-Skates matches.

Francisco Gomes Teixeira — A181

**1952, Nov. 25** ***Perf. 14x14½***

751 A181 1e cerise 1.25 .25
752 A181 2.30e deep blue 8.00 4.25

Centenary of the birth of Francisco Gomes Teixeira (1851-1932), mathematician.

St. Francis and Two Boys — A182

**1952, Dec. 23** ***Perf. 13½***

753 A182 1e dark green 1.25 .25
754 A182 2e dp claret 2.50 .35
755 A182 3.50e chalky blue 26.00 11.00
756 A182 5e dark purple 50.00 3.75
*Nos. 753-756 (4)* 79.75 15.35

400th anniv. of the death of St. Francis Xavier.

Marshal Carmona Bridge A183

Designs: 1.40e, "28th of May" Stadium. 2e, University City, Coimbra. 3.50e, Salazar Dam.

**1952, Dec. 10** **Unwmk.** ***Perf. 12½***

**Buff Paper**

757 A183 1e red brown 1.00 .25
758 A183 1.40e dull purple 14.00 5.00
759 A183 2e dark green 7.50 2.50
760 A183 3.50e dark blue 11.50 4.00
*Nos. 757-760 (4)* 34.00 11.75

Centenary of the foundation of the Ministry of Public Works.

Equestrian Seal of King Diniz — A184

**1953-56** **Litho.**

761 A184 5c green, *citron* .25 .25
762 A184 10c ind, *salmon* .25 .25
763 A184 20c org red, *citron* .25 .25
763A A184 30c rose lil, *cr* ('56) .25 .25
764 A184 50c gray .25 .25
765 A184 90c dk grn, *cit* 17.50 1.00
766 A184 1e vio brn, *rose* .45 .25
767 A184 1.40e rose red 18.00 1.10
768 A184 1.50e red, *cream* .65 .25
769 A184 2e gray 1.25 .25
770 A184 2.30e blue 24.00 .85
771 A184 2.50e gray blk, *sal* 1.60 .25
772 A184 5e rose vio, *cr* 1.60 .25
773 A184 10e blue, *citron* 10.00 .25
774 A184 20e bis brn, *cit* 20.00 .30
775 A184 50e rose violet 6.00 .45
*Nos. 761-775 (16)* 102.30 6.45

St. Martin of Braga — A185

***Perf. 13x13½***

**1953, Feb. 26** **Unwmk.**

776 A185 1e gray blk & gray 1.60 .25
777 A185 3.50e dk brn & yel 14.00 4.00

14th centenary of the arrival of St. Martin of Dume on the Iberian peninsula.

Guilherme Gomes Fernandes — A186

**1953, Mar. 28** ***Perf. 13***

778 A186 1e red violet 1.10 .25
779 A186 2.30e deep blue 11.00 5.50

Birth of Guilherme Gomes Fernandes, General Inspector of the Firemen of Porto.

Emblems of Automobile Club — A187

**1953, Apr. 15** ***Perf. 12½***

780 A187 1e dk grn & yel grn .80 .25
781 A187 3.50e dk brn & buff 13.50 5.00

Portuguese Automobile Club, 50th anniv.

Princess St. Joanna — A188

***Perf. 14½x14***

**1953, May 14** **Litho.** **Unwmk.**

782 A188 1e blk & gray grn 2.00 .25
783 A188 3.50e dk blue & blue 13.50 6.00

Birth of Princess St. Joanna, 500th anniv.

Queen Maria II — A189

**1953, Oct. 3** **Photo.** ***Perf. 13½***

**Background of Lower Panel in Gold**

784 A189 50c red brown .25 .25
785 A189 1e claret brn .25 .25
786 A189 1.40e dk violet 2.10 .65
787 A189 2.30e dp blue 5.00 2.00
788 A189 3.50e violet blue 5.00 2.10
789 A189 4.50e dk blue grn 3.50 1.50
790 A189 5e dk ol grn 8.00 1.50
791 A189 20e red violet 72.50 8.00
*Nos. 784-791 (8)* 96.60 16.25

Centenary of Portugal's first postage stamp.

Allegory A190

**1954, Sept. 22** ***Perf. 13***

792 A190 1e bl & dk grnsh bl .60 .25
793 A190 1.50e buff & dk brn 3.50 .65

150th anniversary of the founding of the State Secretariat for Financial Affairs.

Open Textbook A191

**1954, Oct. 15** **Litho.**

794 A191 50c blue .40 .25
795 A191 1e red .40 .25
796 A191 2e dk green 35.00 1.40
797 A191 2.50e orange brn 29.00 1.25
*Nos. 794-797 (4)* 64.80 3.15

National literacy campaign.

Cadet and College Arms — A192

**1954, Nov. 17**

798 A192 1e choc & lt grn 1.60 .25
799 A192 3.50e dk bl & gray grn 6.50 2.50

150th anniversary of the Military College.

Manuel da Nobrega and Crucifix — A193

**1954, Dec. 17** **Engr.** ***Perf. 14x13***

800 A193 1e brown .80 .25
801 A193 2.30e deep blue 60.00 22.50
802 A193 3.50e gray green 17.00 3.25
803 A193 5e green 50.00 4.75
*Nos. 800-803 (4)* 127.80 30.75

Founding of Sao Paulo, Brazil, 400th anniv.

King Alfonso I — A194

Kings: 20c, Sancho I. 50c, Alfonso II. 90c, Sancho II. 1e, Alfonso III. 1.40e, Diniz. 1.50e, Alfonso IV. 2e, Pedro I. 2.30e, Ferdinand I.

**1955, Mar. 17** ***Perf. 13½x13***

804 A194 10c rose violet .25 .25
805 A194 20c dk olive grn .25 .25
806 A194 50c dk blue grn .35 .25
807 A194 90c green 3.25 1.40
808 A194 1e red brown 1.40 .25
809 A194 1.40e carmine rose 9.00 3.00
810 A194 1.50e olive brn 4.00 1.10
811 A194 2e deep orange 11.00 3.00
812 A194 2.30e violet blue 10.00 2.50
*Nos. 804-812 (9)* 39.50 12.00

Telegraph Pole — A195

**1955, Sept. 16 Litho. *Perf. 13½***

**813** A195 1e ocher & hn brn .75 .25
**814** A195 2.30e gray grn & Prus bl 27.50 3.50
**815** A195 3.50e lemon & dp grn 25.00 3.25
*Nos. 813-815 (3)* 53.25 7.00

Centenary of the telegraph system in Portugal.

A. J. Ferreira da Silva — A196

**1956, May 8 Photo. Unwmk.**

**816** A196 1e blue & dk blue .50 .25
**817** A196 2.30e grn & dk grn 16.00 5.00

Centenary of the birth of Prof. Antonio Joaquim Ferreira da Silva, chemist.

Steam Locomotive, 1856 — A197

Design: 1.50e, 2e, Electric train, 1956.

**1956, Oct. 28 Litho. *Perf. 13***

**818** A197 1e lt & dk ol grn 1.00 .25
**819** A197 1.50e Prus bl & lt grnsh bl 4.75 .35
**820** A197 2e dk org brn & bis 35.00 1.40
**821** A197 2.50e choc & brn 47.50 2.25
*Nos. 818-821 (4)* 88.25 4.25

Centenary of the Portuguese railways.

Madonna, 15th Century — A198

**1956, Dec. 8 Photo.**

**822** A198 1e dp grn & lt ol grn 1.25 .25
**823** A198 1.50e dk red brn & ol bis 2.50 .30

Mothers' Day, Dec. 8.

J. B. Almeida Garrett A199

**1957, Mar. 7 Engr. *Perf. 13½x14***

**824** A199 1e sepia .75 .25
**825** A199 2.30e lt purple 45.00 11.00
**826** A199 3.50e dull green 10.00 1.10
**827** A199 5e rose carmine 85.00 10.50
*Nos. 824-827 (4)* 140.75 22.85

Issued in honor of Joao Baptista da Silva Leitao de Almeida Garrett, poet.

Cesarío Verde — A200

**1957, Dec. 12 Litho. *Perf. 13½***

**828** A200 1e citron & brown .40 .25
**829** A200 3.30e gray grn, yel grn & dk ol 1.90 1.10

Jose Joaquim de Cesario Verde (1855-86), poet.

Exhibition Emblems — A201

**1958, Apr. 7**

**830** A201 1e multicolored .35 .25
**831** A201 3.30e multicolored 1.60 1.40

Universal & Intl. Exposition at Brussels.

Queen St. Isabel — A202

Design: 2e, 5e, St. Teotonio.

***Perf. 14½x14***

**1958, July 10 Photo. Unwmk.**

**832** A202 1e rose brn & buff .25 .25
**833** A202 2e dk green & buff .65 .35
**834** A202 2.50e purple & buff 5.50 .85
**835** A202 5e brown & buff 7.00 1.00
*Nos. 832-835 (4)* 13.40 2.45

Institute for Tropical Medicine A203

**1958, Sept. 4 Litho. *Perf. 13***

**836** A203 1e dk grn & lt gray 2.50 .25
**837** A203 2.50e bl & pale bl 7.75 1.50

6th Intl. Cong. for Tropical Medicine and Malaria, Lisbon, Sept. 1958, and opening of the new Tropical Medicine Institute.

Cargo Ship and Loading Crane — A204

**1958, Nov. 27 Unwmk. *Perf. 13***

**838** A204 1e brn & dk brn 6.50 .25
**839** A204 4.50e vio bl & dk bl 5.00 2.25

2nd Natl. Cong. of the Merchant Marine, Porto.

Queen Leonor A205

**1958, Dec. 17**

**840** A205 1e multi .25 .25
**841** A205 1.50e bis, blk, bl & dk bis brn 4.00 .70
*a.* Dark bister brown omitted
**842** A205 2.30e multi 3.75 1.10
**843** A205 4.10e multi 3.75 1.60
*Nos. 840-843 (4)* 11.75 3.65

500th anniv. of the birth of Queen Leonor.

Arms of Aveiro — A206

**1959, Aug. 30 Litho. *Perf. 13***

**844** A206 1e ol bis, brn, gold & sil 1.75 .25
**845** A206 5e grnsh gray, gold & sil 13.00 1.90

Millennium of Aveiro.

Symbols of Hope and Peace — A207

**1960, Mar. 2 *Perf. 12½***

**846** A207 1e lt violet & blk .35 .25
**847** A207 3.50e gray & dk grn 3.25 1.75

10th anniversary (in 1959) of NATO.

Open Door to "Peace" and WRY Emblem — A208

**1960, Apr. 7 Unwmk. *Perf. 13***

**848** A208 20c multi .25 .25
**849** A208 1e multi .50 .25
**850** A208 1.80e yel grn, org & blk 1.10 .95
*Nos. 848-850 (3)* 1.85 1.45

World Refugee Year, 7/1/59-6/30/60.

Glider — A209

Designs: 1.50e, Plane. 2e, Plane and parachutes. 2.50e, Model plane.

**1960, May 2**

**851** A209 1e yel, gray & bl .25 .25
**852** A209 1.50e multicolored .65 .25
**853** A209 2e bl grn, yel & blk 1.25 .60
**854** A209 2.50e grnsh bl, ocher & red 2.50 1.10
*Nos. 851-854 (4)* 4.65 2.20

Aero Club of Portugal, 50th anniv. (in 1959).

Father Cruz — A210

**1960, July 18 Unwmk. *Perf. 13***

**855** A210 1e deep brown .25 .25
**856** A210 4.30e Prus blue & blk 8.75 6.25

Father Cruz, "father of the poor."

University of Evora Seal — A211

**1960, July 18 Litho.**

**857** A211 50c violet blue .25 .25
**858** A211 1e red brn & yel .40 .25
**859** A211 1.40e rose cl & rose 2.75 1.50
*Nos. 857-859 (3)* 3.40 2.00

Founding of the University of Evora, 400th anniv.

Arms of Prince Henry — A212

Designs: 2.50e, Caravel. 3.50e, Prince Henry. 5e, Prince Henry's motto. 8e, Prince Henry's sloop. 10e, Old chart of Sagres region of Portugal.

**1960, Aug. 4 Photo. *Perf. 12x12½***

**860** A212 1e gold & multi .35 .25
**861** A212 2.50e gold & multi 3.50 .35
**862** A212 3.50e gold & multi 5.00 1.40
**863** A212 5e gold & multi 8.00 .80
**864** A212 8e gold & multi 2.00 .75
**865** A212 10e gold & multi 14.00 2.00
*Nos. 860-865 (6)* 32.85 5.55

500th anniversary of the death of Prince Henry the Navigator.

**Europa Issue, 1960**

Common Design Type

**1960, Sept. 16 Litho. *Perf. 13***

**Size: 31x21mm**

**866** CD3 1e ultra & gray blue .25 .25
**867** CD3 3.50e brn red & rose red *2.75 1.50*
*Nos. 866-867 (2)* 3.00 1.75

Arms of Lisbon and Symbolic Ship — A213

**1960, Nov. 17 *Perf. 13***

**868** A213 1e gray ol, blk & vio bl .40 .25
**869** A213 3.30e bl, blk & ultra 5.25 3.25

5th Natl. Philatelic Exhibition, Lisbon, part of the Prince Henry the Navigator festivities. (The ship in the design is in honor of Prince Henry).

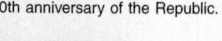

Flag and Laurel — A214

**1960, Dec. 20 Litho. *Perf. 13***

**870** A214 1e multicolored .30 .25

50th anniversary of the Republic.

King Pedro V A215

**1961, Aug. 3 Engr. *Perf. 13***
**871** A215 1e gray brn & dk grn .30 .25
**872** A215 6.50e dk blue & blk 3.50 .65

Centenary of the founding of the Faculty of Letters, Lisbon University.

Setubal Sea Gate and Ships A216

**1961, Aug. 24 Litho. *Perf. 12x11½***
**873** A216 1e gold & multi .35 .25
**874** A216 4.30e gold & multi 16.00 5.00

Centenary of the city of Setubal.

**Europa Issue**

Clasped Hands and CEPT Emblem — A217

**1961, Sept. 18 *Perf. 13½x13***
**875** A217 1e blue & lt blue .25 .25
**876** A217 1.50e green & brt green 1.25 .75
**877** A217 3.50e brown, pink & red 1.50 1.00
*Nos. 875-877 (3)* 3.00 2.00

Tomar Castle and River Nabao — A218

**1962, Jan. 26 *Perf. 11½x12***
**878** A218 1e gold & multi .25 .25
**879** A218 3.50e gold & multi 1.40 .85

800th anniversary of the city of Tomar.

National Guardsman — A219

**1962, Feb. 20 Unwmk. *Perf. 13½***
**880** A219 1e multi .25 .25
**881** A219 2e multi 2.00 .60
**882** A219 2.50e multi 2.00 .50
*Nos. 880-882 (3)* 4.25 1.35

Republican National Guard, 50th anniv.

Archangel Gabriel — A220

**1962, Mar. 24 Litho. *Perf. 13***
**883** A220 1e ol, pink & red brn .70 .25
**884** A220 3.50e ol, pink & dk grn .50 .40

Issued for St. Gabriel's Day. St. Gabriel is patron of telecommunications.

Tents and Scout Emblem A221

**1962, June 11 Unwmk. *Perf. 13***
**885** A221 20c gray, bis, yel & blk .25 .25
*a.* Double impression of gray frame lettering
**886** A221 50c multi .25 .25
**887** A221 1e multi .60 .25
**888** A221 2.50e multi 4.00 .50
**889** A221 3.50e multi .90 .50
**890** A221 6.50e multi 1.25 .65
*Nos. 885-890 (6)* 7.25 2.40

50th anniv. of the Portuguese Boy Scouts and the 18th Boy Scout World Conf., Sept. 19-24, 1961.

Children Reading A222

Designs: 1e, Vaccination. 2.80e, Children playing ball. 3.50e, Guarding sleeping infant.

**1962, Sept. 10 Litho. *Perf. 13½***
**891** A222 50c bluish grn, yel & blk .25 .25
**892** A222 1e pale bl, yel & blk .90 .25
**893** A222 2.80e dp org yel & blk 2.50 .90
**894** A222 3.50e dl rose, yel & blk 5.00 1.40
*Nos. 891-894 (4)* 8.65 2.80

10th Intl. Cong. of Pediatrics, Lisbon, Sept. 9-15.

19-Cell Honeycomb A223

**1962, Sept. 17**
**895** A223 1e bl, dk bl & gold .25 .25
**896** A223 1.50e lt & dk grn & gold 1.00 .55
**897** A223 3.50e dp rose, mar & gold 1.40 1.00
*Nos. 895-897 (3)* 2.65 1.80

Europa. The 19 cells represent the 19 original members of the Conference of European Postal and Telecommunications Administrations, C.E.P.T.

St. Zenon, the Courier — A224

**1962, Dec. 1 Unwmk. *Perf. 13½***
**898** A224 1e multi .25 .25
**899** A224 2e multi .95 .70
**900** A224 2.80e multi 1.90 1.50
*Nos. 898-900 (3)* 3.10 2.45

Issued for Stamp Day.

European Soccer Cup and Emblem — A225

**1963, Feb. 5 *Perf. 13½***
**901** A225 1e multi .80 .25
**902** A225 4.30e multi 1.10 .90

Victories of the Benfica Club of Lisbon in the 1961 and 1962 European Soccer Championships.

Wheat Emblem A226

**1963, Mar. 21 Litho.**
**903** A226 1e multi .25 .25
**904** A226 3.30e multi 1.40 .80
**905** A226 3.50e multi 1.25 .75
*Nos. 903-905 (3)* 2.90 1.80

FAO "Freedom from Hunger" campaign.

Stagecoach — A227

**1963, May 7 *Perf. 12x11½***
**906** A227 1e gray, lt & dk bl .25 .25
**907** A227 1.50e bis, dk brn & lil rose 1.75 .40
**908** A227 5e org brn, dk brn & rose lil .60 .30
*Nos. 906-908 (3)* 2.60 .95

1st Intl. Postal Conference, Paris, 1863.

St. Vincent de Paul by Monsaraz — A228

**1963, July 10 Photo. *Perf. 13½x14***
**Gold Inscription**
**909** A228 20c lt blue & ultra .25 .25
*a.* Gold inscription omitted 60.00
**910** A228 1e gray & slate .35 .25
**911** A228 2.80e green & slate 3.50 1.40
*a.* Gold inscription omitted 70.00
**912** A228 5e dp rose car & sl 2.50 1.00
*Nos. 909-912 (4)* 6.60 2.90

Tercentenary of the death of St. Vincent de Paul.

Emblem of Order and Knight A229

**1963, Aug. 13 Litho. *Perf. 11½***
**913** A229 1e multi .25 .25
**914** A229 1.50e multi .55 .25
**915** A229 2.50e multi 1.40 .70
*Nos. 913-915 (3)* 2.20 1.20

800th anniv. of the Military Order of Avis.

**Europa Issue**

Stylized Bird — A230

**1963, Sept. 16 *Perf. 13½***
**916** A230 1e lt bl, gray & blk .25 .25
**917** A230 1.50e grn, gray & blk 2.00 .60
**918** A230 3.50e red, gray & blk 3.50 .90
*Nos. 916-918 (3)* 5.75 1.75

Jet Plane — A231

**1963, Dec. 1 Unwmk. *Perf. 13½***
**919** A231 1e dk bl & lt bl .25 .25
**920** A231 2.50e dk grn & yel grn 1.25 .50
**921** A231 3.50e org brn & org 1.60 .85
*Nos. 919-921 (3)* 3.10 1.60

Transportes Aéreos Portugueses, TAP, 10th anniv.

Apothecary Jar — A232

**1964, Apr. 9 Litho.**
**922** A232 50c brn ol, dk brn & blk .30 .25
**923** A232 1e rose brn, dp cl & blk .30 .25
**924** A232 4.30e dk gray, sl & blk 3.75 2.75
*Nos. 922-924 (3)* 4.35 3.25

4th centenary of the publication (in Goa, Apr. 10, 1563) of "Coloquios Dos Simples e Drogas" (Herbs and Drugs in India) by Garcia D'Orta.

Emblem of National Overseas Bank — A233

**1964, May 19 Unwmk. *Perf. 13½***
**925** A233 1e bister, yel & dk bl .25 .25
**926** A233 2.50e ocher, yel & grn 2.50 .75
**927** A233 3.50e bister, yel & brn 2.00 .90
*Nos. 925-927 (3)* 4.75 1.90

Centenary of National Overseas Bank.

Mt. Sameiro Church — A234

**1964, June 5 Litho.**
**928** A234 1e red brn, bis & dl brn .25 .25
**929** A234 2e brn, bis & dl brn 1.75 .60
**930** A234 5e dk vio bl, bis & gray 2.25 .80
*Nos. 928-930 (3)* 4.25 1.65

Centenary of the Shrine of Our Lady of Mt. Sameiro, Braga.

**Europa Issue**
Common Design Type

**1964, Sept. 14 Unwmk. *Perf. 13½***
**Size: 19x32mm.**
**931** CD7 1e bl, lt bl & dk bl *1.00 .25*
**932** CD7 3.50e rose brn, buff & dk brn *4.00 .50*
**933** CD7 4.30e grn, yel grn & dk grn *5.00 1.25*
*Nos. 931-933 (3) 10.00 2.00*

Partial Eclipse of Sun — A235

**1964**
**934** A235 1e multicolored .25 .25
**935** A235 8e multicolored 1.50 1.00

International Quiet Sun Year, 1964-65.

Olympic Rings, Emblems of Portugal and Japan — A236

**Black Inscriptions; Olympic Rings in Pale Yellow**

**1964, Dec. 1 Unwmk. *Perf. 13½***

**936** A236 20c tan, red & vio bl .25 .25
**937** A236 1e ultra, red & vio bl .25 .25
**938** A236 1.50e yel grn, red & vio bl 1.75 1.00
**939** A236 6.50e rose lil, red & vio bl 2.90 1.90
*Nos. 936-939 (4)* 5.15 3.40

18th Olympic Games, Tokyo, Oct. 10-25.

Eduardo Coelho — A237

**1964, Dec. 28 Litho. *Perf. 13½***

**940** A237 1e multicolored .45 .25
**941** A237 5e multicolored 6.50 1.00

Centenary of the founding of Portugal's first newspaper, "Diario de Noticias," and to honor the founder, Eduardo Coelho, journalist.

Traffic Signs and Signals A238

**1965, Feb. 15 Litho.**

**942** A238 1e yellow, red & emer .25 .25
**943** A238 3.30e multicolored 5.75 3.00
**944** A238 3.50e red, yellow & emer 3.50 1.10
*Nos. 942-944 (3)* 9.50 4.35

1st National Traffic Cong., Lisbon, 2/15-19.

Ferdinand I, Duke of Braganza — A239

**1965, Mar. 16 Unwmk. *Perf. 13½***

**945** A239 1e rose brown & blk .25 .25
**946** A239 10e Prus green & blk 2.40 .65

500th anniv. of the city of Braganza (in 1964).

Coimbra Gate, Angel with Censer and Sword — A240

**1965, Apr. 27 *Perf. 11½x12***

**947** A240 1e blue & multi .25 .25
**948** A240 2.50e multi 2.10 1.10
**949** A240 5e multi 2.10 1.40
*Nos. 947-949 (3)* 4.45 2.75

9th centenary (in 1964) of the capture of the city of Coimbra from the Moors.

ITU Emblem — A241

**1965, May 17 *Perf. 13½***

**950** A241 1e bis brn, ol grn & ol .25 .25
**951** A241 3.50e ol, rose cl & dp cl 1.60 1.00
**952** A241 6.50e yel grn, dl bl & sl bl 1.40 .90
*Nos. 950-952 (3)* 3.25 2.15

International Telecommunication Union, cent.

Calouste Gulbenkian A242

**1965, July 20 Litho. *Perf. 13½***

**953** A242 1e multicolored .60 .25
**954** A242 8e multicolored .55 .40

Gulbenkian (1869-1955), oil industry pioneer and sponsor of the Gulbenkian Foundation.

Red Cross — A243

**1965, Aug. 17 Unwmk. *Perf. 13½***

**955** A243 1e grn, red & blk .50 .25
**956** A243 4e ol, red & blk 2.25 .90
**957** A243 4.30e lt rose brn, red & blk 10.00 5.00
*Nos. 955-957 (3)* 12.75 6.15

Centenary of the Portuguese Red Cross.

**Europa Issue**

Common Design Type

**1965, Sept. 27 Litho. *Perf. 13***

**Size: 31x24mm**

**958** CD8 1e saph, grnsh bl & dk bl *2.00 .25*
**959** CD8 3.50e rose brn, sal & brn *3.00 .50*
**960** CD8 4.30e grn, yel grn & dk grn *5.00 2.00*
*Nos. 958-960 (3) 10.00 2.75*

Military Plane — A244

**1965, Oct. 20 *Perf. 13½***

**961** A244 1e ol grn, red & dk grn .25 .25
**962** A244 2e sepia, red & dk grn 1.25 .55
**963** A244 5e chlky bl, red & dk grn 2.25 1.10
*Nos. 961-963 (3)* 3.75 1.90

Portuguese Air Force founding, 50th anniv.

Woman — A245

Designs: Characters from Gil Vicente Plays.

**1965, Dec. 1 Litho. *Perf. 13½***

**964** A245 20c ol, pale yel & blk .25 .25
**965** A245 1e brn, pale yel & blk .30 .25
**966** A245 2.50e dk red, buff & blk 2.90 .45
**967** A245 6.50e blue, gray & blk 1.00 .55
*Nos. 964-967 (4)* 4.45 1.50

Gil Vicente (1465?-1536?).

Chrismon with Alpha and Omega A246

**1966, Mar. 28 Litho. *Perf. 13½***

**968** A246 1e ol bis, gold & blk .25 .25
**969** A246 3.30e gray, gold & blk 5.00 2.75
**970** A246 5e rose cl, gold & blk 4.00 .90
*Nos. 968-970 (3)* 9.25 3.90

Congress of the International Committee for the Defense of Christian Civilization, Lisbon.

Symbols of Peace and Labor — A247

**1966, May 28 Litho. *Perf. 13½***

**971** A247 1e dk bl, sl bl & lt sl bl .25 .25
**972** A247 3.50e ol, ol brn, & lt ol 2.40 1.10
**973** A247 4e dk brn, brn car & dl rose 2.50 .85
*Nos. 971-973 (3)* 5.15 2.20

40th anniversary of National Revolution.

Knight Giraldo on Horseback A248

**1966, June 8**

**974** A248 1e multicolored .30 .25
**975** A248 8e multicolored 1.10 .55

Conquest of Evora from the Moors, 800th anniv.

Salazar Bridge — A249

Designs: 2.80e, 4.30e, View of bridge, vert.

**1966, Aug. 6 Litho. *Perf. 13½***

**976** A249 1e gold & red .25 .25
**977** A249 2.50e gold & ultra 1.25 .50
**978** A249 2.80e silver & dp ultra 2.00 1.10
**979** A249 4.30e silver & dk grn 2.25 1.25
*Nos. 976-979 (4)* 5.75 3.10

Issued to commemorate the opening of the Salazar Bridge over the Tejo River, Lisbon.

**Europa Issue**

Common Design Type

**1966, Sept. 26 Litho. *Perf. 11½x12***

**Size: 26x32mm**

**980** CD9 1e blue & blk *1.00* .25
**981** CD9 3.50e red brn & blk *3.75 .75*
**982** CD9 4.30e yel grn & blk *5.00 1.25*
*Nos. 980-982 (3) 9.75* 2.25

Pestana — A250

Portraits: 20c, Camara Pestana (1863-1899), bacteriologist. 50c, Egas Moniz (1874-1955), neurologist. 1e, Antonio Pereira Coutinho (1851-1939), botanist. 1.50e, José Corrêa da Serra (1750-1823), botanist. 2e, Ricardo Jórge (1858-1938), hygienist and anthropologist. 2.50e, J. Liete de Vasconcelos (1858-1941), ethnologist. 2.80e, Maximiano Lemos (1860-1923), medical historian. 4.30e, José Antonio Serrano, anatomist.

**Portrait and Inscription in Dark Brown and Bister**

**1966, Dec. 1 Litho. *Perf. 13½***

**983** A250 20c gray green .25 .25
**984** A250 50c orange .25 .25
**985** A250 1e lemon .25 .25
**986** A250 1.50e bister brn .30 .25
**987** A250 2e brown org 1.50 .25
**988** A250 2.50e pale green 1.60 .40
**989** A250 2.80e salmon 1.90 1.25
**990** A250 4.30e Prus blue 3.25 2.10
*Nos. 983-990 (8)* 9.30 5.00

Issued to honor Portuguese scientists.

Bocage — A251

**1966, Dec. 28 Litho. *Perf. 11½x12***

**991** A251 1e bis, grnsh gray & blk .25 .25
**992** A251 2e brn org, grnsh gray & blk .75 .35
**993** A251 6e gray, grnsh gray & blk 1.20 .65
*Nos. 991-993 (3)* 2.20 1.25

200th anniversary of the birth of Manuel Maria Barbosa du Bocage (1765-1805), poet.

**Europa Issue**

Common Design Type

**1967, May 2 Litho. *Perf. 13***

**Size: 21½x31mm**

**994** CD10 1e lt bl, Prus bl & blk *1.00* .25
**995** CD10 3.50e sal, brn red & blk *3.50 .60*
**996** CD10 4.30e yel grn, ol grn & blk *5.00 1.00*
*Nos. 994-996 (3) 9.50* 1.85

Apparition of Our Lady of Fatima — A252

Designs: 2.80e, Church and Golden Rose. 3.50e, Statue of the Pilgrim Virgin, with lilies and doves. 4e, Doves holding crown over Chapel of the Apparition.

**1967, May 13 *Perf. 11½x12***

**997** A252 1e multicolored .25 .25
**998** A252 2.80e multicolored .55 .40
**999** A252 3.50e multicolored .35 .25
**1000** A252 4e multicolored .50 .25
*Nos. 997-1000 (4)* 1.65 1.15

50th anniversary of the apparition of the Virgin Mary to 3 shepherd children at Fatima.

Statues of Roman Senators — A253

**1967, June 1 Litho. *Perf. 13***

**1001** A253 1e gold & rose claret .25 .25
**1002** A253 2.50e gold & dull blue 1.90 1.00

| | | | | |
|---|---|---|---|---|
| 1003 | A253 | 4.30e gold & gray green | 1.40 | 1.00 |
| | | *Nos. 1001-1003 (3)* | 3.55 | 2.25 |

Introduction of a new civil law code.

Shipyard, Margueira, Lisbon — A254

Design: 2.80e, 4.30e, Ship's hull and map showing location of harbor.

**1967, June 23**

| | | | | |
|---|---|---|---|---|
| 1004 | A254 | 1e aqua & multi | .25 | .25 |
| 1005 | A254 | 2.80e multicolored | 2.10 | 1.00 |
| 1006 | A254 | 3.50e multicolored | 1.40 | .85 |
| 1007 | A254 | 4.30e multicolored | 2.10 | .95 |
| | | *Nos. 1004-1007 (4)* | 5.85 | 3.05 |

Issued to commemorate the inauguration of the Lisnave Shipyard at Margueira, Lisbon.

Symbols of Healing — A255

**1967, Oct. 8 Litho. *Perf. 13½***

| | | | | |
|---|---|---|---|---|
| 1008 | A255 | 1e multicolored | .25 | .25 |
| 1009 | A255 | 2e multicolored | 1.00 | .50 |
| 1010 | A255 | 5e multicolored | 1.50 | .95 |
| | | *Nos. 1008-1010 (3)* | 2.75 | 1.70 |

Issued to publicize the 6th European Congress of Rheumatology, Lisbon, Oct. 8-13.

Flags of EFTA Nations — A256

**1967, Oct. 24 Litho. *Perf. 13½***

| | | | | |
|---|---|---|---|---|
| 1011 | A256 | 1e bister & multi | .25 | .25 |
| 1012 | A256 | 3.50e buff & multi | 1.10 | 1.00 |
| 1013 | A256 | 4.30e gray & multi | 3.00 | 2.50 |
| | | *Nos. 1011-1013 (3)* | 4.35 | 3.75 |

Issued to publicize the European Free Trade Association. See note after Norway No. 501.

Tables of the Law — A257

**1967, Dec. 27 Litho. *Perf. 13½***

| | | | | |
|---|---|---|---|---|
| 1014 | A257 | 1e olive | .25 | .25 |
| 1015 | A257 | 2e red brown | 1.25 | .65 |
| 1016 | A257 | 5e green | 2.10 | 1.25 |
| | | *Nos. 1014-1016 (3)* | 3.60 | 2.15 |

Centenary of abolition of death penalty.

Bento de Goes — A258

***Perf. 13½ (#1017), 12x11½ (#1018)***

**1968, Feb. 14 Engr.**

| | | | | |
|---|---|---|---|---|
| 1017 | A258 | 1e olive, indigo & dk brn | .75 | .25 |
| 1018 | A258 | 8e org brn, dl pur & ol grn | 1.25 | .50 |

360th anniversary (in 1967) of the death of Bento de Goes (1562-1607), Jesuit explorer of the route to China.

**Europa Issue**

Common Design Type

**1968, Apr. 29 Litho. *Perf. 13***

**Size: 31x21mm**

| | | | | |
|---|---|---|---|---|
| 1019 | CD11 | 1e multicolored | 1.00 | .25 |
| 1020 | CD11 | 3.50e multicolored | *3.75* | *.60* |
| 1021 | CD11 | 4.30e multicolored | *5.00* | *1.25* |
| | | *Nos. 1019-1021 (3)* | *9.75* | 2.10 |

Mother's and Child's Hands — A259

**1968, May 26 Litho. *Perf. 13½***

| | | | | |
|---|---|---|---|---|
| 1022 | A259 | 1e lt gray, blk & red | .25 | .25 |
| 1023 | A259 | 2e salmon, blk & red | 1.50 | .60 |
| 1024 | A259 | 5e lt bl, blk & red | 3.00 | 1.40 |
| | | *Nos. 1022-1024 (3)* | 4.75 | 2.25 |

Mothers' Organization for Natl. Education. 30th anniv.

"Victory over Disease" and WHO Emblem A260

**1968, July 10 Litho. *Perf. 12½***

| | | | | |
|---|---|---|---|---|
| 1025 | A260 | 1e multicolored | .60 | .25 |
| 1026 | A260 | 3.50e multicolored | 1.40 | .50 |
| 1027 | A260 | 4.30e tan & multi | 5.00 | 3.00 |
| | | *Nos. 1025-1027 (3)* | 7.00 | 3.75 |

20th anniv. of WHO.

Madeira Grapes and Wine A261

Joao Fernandes Vieira — A262

Designs: 1e, Fireworks on New Year's Eve. 1.50e, Mountains and valley. 3.50e, Woman doing Madeira embroidery. 4.30e, Joao Gonçalves Zarco. 20e, Muschia aurea (flower.)

***Perf. 12x11½, 11½x12***

**1968, Aug. 17 Litho.**

| | | | | |
|---|---|---|---|---|
| 1028 | A261 | 50c multi | .25 | .25 |
| 1029 | A261 | 1e multi | .25 | .25 |
| 1030 | A261 | 1.50e multi | .30 | .25 |
| 1031 | A262 | 2.80e multi | 2.25 | 1.50 |
| 1032 | A262 | 3.50e multi | 1.50 | 1.00 |
| 1033 | A262 | 4.30e multi | 8.00 | 6.00 |
| 1034 | A262 | 20e multi | 4.00 | 1.00 |
| | | *Nos. 1028-1034 (7)* | 16.55 | 10.25 |

Issued to publicize Madeira and the Lubrapex 1968 stamp exhibition.

Design descriptions in Portuguese, French and English printed on back of stamps.

Pedro Alvares Cabral A263

Cabral's Fleet A264

Design: 3.50e, Cabral's coat of arms, vert.

***Perf. 12x12½, 12½x12***

**1969, Jan. 30 Engr.**

| | | | | |
|---|---|---|---|---|
| 1035 | A263 | 1e vio bl, bl & gray bl | .25 | .25 |
| 1036 | A263 | 3.50e deep claret | 4.25 | 2.00 |

**Litho.**

| | | | | |
|---|---|---|---|---|
| 1037 | A264 | 6.50e green & multi | 2.50 | 1.75 |
| | | *Nos. 1035-1037 (3)* | 7.00 | 4.00 |

5th cent. of the birth of Pedro Alvarez Cabral (1468-1520), navigator, discoverer of Brazil. Nos. 1035-1037 have description of the designs printed on the back in Portuguese, French and English.

**Europa Issue**

Common Design Type

**1969, Apr. 28 Litho. *Perf. 13***

**Size: 31x22½mm**

| | | | | |
|---|---|---|---|---|
| 1038 | CD12 | 1e dp blue & multi | 1.00 | .25 |
| 1039 | CD12 | 3.50e multicolored | 6.75 | *.65* |
| 1040 | CD12 | 4.30e grn & multi | 10.00 | *1.50* |
| | | *Nos. 1038-1040 (3)* | 17.75 | 2.40 |

King José I and Arms of National Press — A265

**1969, May 14 Litho. *Perf. 11½x12***

| | | | | |
|---|---|---|---|---|
| 1041 | A265 | 1e multicolored | .25 | .25 |
| 1042 | A265 | 2e multicolored | 1.10 | .45 |
| 1043 | A265 | 8e multicolored | 1.00 | .60 |
| | | *Nos. 1041-1043 (3)* | 2.35 | 1.30 |

Bicentenary of the National Press.

ILO Emblem A266

**1969, May 28 *Perf. 13***

| | | | | |
|---|---|---|---|---|
| 1044 | A266 | 1e bluish grn, blk & sil | .25 | .25 |
| 1045 | A266 | 3.50e red, blk & sil | 1.40 | .65 |
| 1046 | A266 | 4.30e brt bl, blk & sil | 2.25 | 1.50 |
| | | *Nos. 1044-1046 (3)* | 3.90 | 2.40 |

50th anniversary of the ILO.

Juan Cabrillo Rodriguez A267

**1969, July 16 Litho. *Perf. 11½x12***

| | | | | |
|---|---|---|---|---|
| 1047 | A267 | 1e multi | .25 | .25 |
| 1048 | A267 | 2.50e multi | 1.60 | .45 |
| 1049 | A267 | 6.50e multi | 1.75 | .90 |
| | | *Nos. 1047-1049 (3)* | 3.60 | 1.60 |

Bicent. of San Diego, Calif., & honoring Juan Cabrillo Rodriguez, explorer of California coast.

Backs inscribed. See note below No. 1034.

Vianna da Motta, by Columbano Bordalo Pinheiro — A268

**1969, Sept. 24 Litho. *Perf. 12***

| | | | | |
|---|---|---|---|---|
| 1050 | A268 | 1e multicolored | .90 | .25 |
| 1051 | A268 | 9e gray & multi | .90 | .60 |

Centenary of the birth of Vianna da Motta (1868-1948), pianist and composer.

Gago Coutinho and 1922 Seaplane A269

Design: 2.80e, 4.30e, Adm. Coutinho and Coutinho sextant.

**1969, Oct. 22**

| | | | | |
|---|---|---|---|---|
| 1052 | A269 | 1e grnsh gray, dk & lt brn | .25 | .25 |
| 1053 | A269 | 2.80e yel bis, dk & lt brn | 2.25 | 1.00 |
| 1054 | A269 | 3.30e gray bl, dk & lt brn | 2.10 | 1.40 |
| 1055 | A269 | 4.30e lt rose brn, dk & lt brn | 2.10 | 1.50 |
| | | *Nos. 1052-1055 (4)* | 6.70 | 4.15 |

Admiral Carlos Viegas Gago Coutinho (1869-1959), explorer and aviation pioneer.

Vasco da Gama A270

Designs: 2.80e, Da Gama's coat of arms. 3.50e, Map showing route to India and compass rose, horiz. 4e, Da Gama's fleet, horiz.

***Perf. 12x11½, 11½x12***

**1969, Dec. 30 Litho.**

| | | | | |
|---|---|---|---|---|
| 1056 | A270 | 1e multi | .50 | .25 |
| 1057 | A270 | 2.80e multi | 3.00 | 1.75 |
| 1058 | A270 | 3.50e multi | 2.25 | .75 |
| 1059 | A270 | 4e multi | 2.10 | .60 |
| | | *Nos. 1056-1059 (4)* | 7.85 | 3.35 |

Vasco da Gama (1469-1525), navigator who found sea route to India.

Design descriptions in Portuguese, French and English printed on back of stamps.

**Europa Issue**

Common Design Type

**1970, May 4 Litho. *Perf. 13½***

**Size: 31x22mm**

| | | | | |
|---|---|---|---|---|
| 1060 | CD13 | 1e multicolored | *1.00* | *.25* |
| 1061 | CD13 | 3.50e multicolored | *3.75* | *.60* |
| 1062 | CD13 | 4.30e multicolored | *5.00* | *1.50* |
| | | *Nos. 1060-1062 (3)* | *9.75* | 2.35 |

Distillation Plant — A271

Design: 2.80e, 6e, Catalytic cracking tower.

**1970, June 5 Litho. *Perf. 13***

| No. | Type | Denomination & Description | Unused | Used |
|---|---|---|---|---|
| **1063** | A271 | 1e dk bl & dl bl | .25 | .25 |
| **1064** | A271 | 2.80e sl grn & pale grn | 2.25 | 1.40 |
| **1065** | A271 | 3.30e dk ol grn & ol | 1.40 | 1.00 |
| **1066** | A271 | 6e dk brn & dl ocher | 1.40 | .85 |
| | | *Nos. 1063-1066 (4)* | 5.30 | 3.50 |

Opening of the Oporto Oil Refinery.

Marshal Carmona and Oak Leaves A272

Designs: 2.50e, Carmona, Portuguese coat of arms and laurel. 7e, Carmona and ferns.

**Litho. & Engr.**

**1970, July 1 *Perf. 12x12½***

| No. | Type | Denomination & Description | Unused | Used |
|---|---|---|---|---|
| **1067** | A272 | 1e ol grn & blk | .25 | .25 |
| **1068** | A272 | 2.50e red, ultra & blk | 1.60 | .60 |
| **1069** | A272 | 7e slate bl & blk | 1.50 | .90 |
| | | *Nos. 1067-1069 (3)* | 3.35 | 1.75 |

Centenary of the birth of Marshal Antonio Oscar de Fragoso Carmona (1869-1951), President of Portugal, 1926-1951.

Emblem of Plant Research Station A273

**1970, July 29 Litho.**

| No. | Type | Denomination & Description | Unused | Used |
|---|---|---|---|---|
| **1070** | A273 | 1e multi | .25 | .25 |
| **1071** | A273 | 2.50e multi | 1.10 | .40 |
| **1072** | A273 | 5e multi | 1.60 | .60 |
| | | *Nos. 1070-1072 (3)* | 2.95 | 1.25 |

25th anniv. of the Plant Research Station at Elvas.

Compass Rose and EXPO Emblem — A274

Designs: 5e, Monogram of Christ (IHS) and EXPO emblem. 6.50e, "Portugal and Japan" as written in old manuscripts, and EXPO emblem.

**1970, Sept. 16 Litho. *Perf. 13***

| No. | Type | Denomination & Description | Unused | Used |
|---|---|---|---|---|
| **1073** | A274 | 1e gold & multi | .25 | .25 |
| **1074** | A274 | 5e silver & multi | 1.40 | .90 |
| **1075** | A274 | 6.50e multicolored | 3.00 | 2.25 |
| | | *Nos. 1073-1075,C11 (4)* | 5.35 | 3.80 |

EXPO '70 International Exhibition, Osaka, Japan, Mar. 15-Sept. 13.

Castle (from Arms of Santarem) A275

#1077, Star & wheel, from Covilha coat of arms. 2.80e, Ram & Covilha coat of arms. 4e, Knights on horseback & Santarem coat of arms.

**1970, Oct. 7 Litho. *Perf. 12x11½***

| No. | Type | Denomination & Description | Unused | Used |
|---|---|---|---|---|
| **1076** | A275 | 1e multicolored | .25 | .25 |
| **1077** | A275 | 1e ultra & multi | .25 | .25 |
| **1078** | A275 | 2.80e red & multi | 2.50 | 1.25 |
| **1079** | A275 | 4e gray & multi | 1.50 | .70 |
| | | *Nos. 1076-1079 (4)* | 4.50 | 2.45 |

City of Santarem, cent. (#1076, 1079); City of Covilha, cent. (#1077-1078).

Paddlesteamer Great Eastern Laying Cable — A276

Designs: 2.80e, 4e, Cross section of cable.

**1970, Nov. 21 Litho. *Perf. 14***

| No. | Type | Denomination & Description | Unused | Used |
|---|---|---|---|---|
| **1080** | A276 | 1e multi | .25 | .25 |
| **1081** | A276 | 2.50e multi | 1.60 | .40 |
| **1082** | A276 | 2.80e multi | 3.00 | 2.25 |
| **1083** | A276 | 4e multi | 1.40 | .70 |
| | | *Nos. 1080-1083 (4)* | 6.25 | 3.60 |

Centenary of the Portugal-Great Britain submarine telegraph cable.

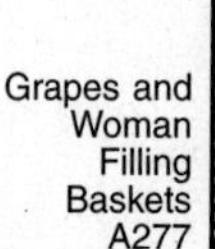

Grapes and Woman Filling Baskets A277

Designs: 1e, Worker carrying basket of grapes, and jug. 3.50e, Glass of wine, and barge with barrels on River Douro. 7e, Wine bottle and barrels.

**1970, Dec. 20 Litho. *Perf. 12x11½***

| No. | Type | Denomination & Description | Unused | Used |
|---|---|---|---|---|
| **1084** | A277 | 50c multi | .25 | .25 |
| **1085** | A277 | 1e multi | .25 | .25 |
| **1086** | A277 | 3.50e multi | 1.00 | .25 |
| **1087** | A277 | 7e multi | 1.00 | .50 |
| | | *Nos. 1084-1087 (4)* | 2.50 | 1.25 |

Publicity for port wine export.

Mountain Windmill, Bussaco Hills — A278

Windmills: 50c, Beira Litoral Province. 1e, Estremadura Province. 2e, St. Miguel, Azores. 3.30e, Porto Santo, Madeira. 5e, Pico, Azores.

**1971, Feb. 24 Litho. *Perf. 13***

| No. | Type | Denomination & Description | Unused | Used |
|---|---|---|---|---|
| **1088** | A278 | 20c multicolored | .25 | .25 |
| **1089** | A278 | 50c lt blue & multi | .25 | .25 |
| **1090** | A278 | 1e gray & multi | .25 | .25 |
| **1091** | A278 | 2e multicolored | .90 | .25 |
| **1092** | A278 | 3.30e ocher & multi | 2.00 | 1.00 |
| **1093** | A278 | 5e multicolored | 1.75 | .55 |
| | | *Nos. 1088-1093 (6)* | 5.40 | 2.55 |

Backs inscribed. See note below No. 1034.

**Europa Issue**

Common Design Type

**1971, May 3 Photo. *Perf. 14***

**Size: 32x22mm**

| No. | Type | Denomination & Description | Unused | Used |
|---|---|---|---|---|
| **1094** | CD14 | 1e dk bl, lt grn & blk | *1.00* | *.25* |
| **1095** | CD14 | 3.50e red brn, yel & blk | *3.75* | *.50* |
| **1096** | CD14 | 7.50e olive, yel & blk | *5.00* | *1.00* |
| | | *Nos. 1094-1096 (3)* | *9.75* | 1.75 |

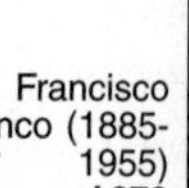
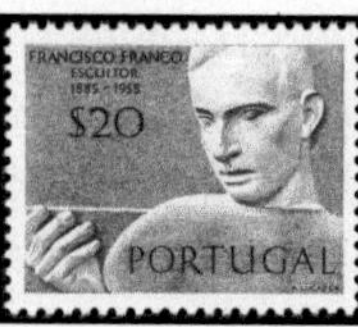


Francisco Franco (1885-1955) A279

Portuguese Sculptors: 1e, Antonio Teixeira Lopes (1866-1942). 1.50e, Antonio Augusto da Costa Mota (1862-1930). 2.50e, Rui Roque Gameiro (1906-1935). 3.50e, José Simoes de Almeida (nephew; 1880-1950). 4e, Francisco dos Santos (1878-1930).

***Perf. 11½x12½; 13½ (2.50e, 4e)***

**1971, July 7 Engr.**

| No. | Type | Denomination & Description | Unused | Used |
|---|---|---|---|---|
| **1097** | A279 | 20c black | .25 | .25 |
| *a.* | | Perf. 13½ | 2.50 | .30 |
| **1098** | A279 | 1e claret | .30 | .25 |
| **1099** | A279 | 1.50e sepia | .50 | .40 |
| **1100** | A279 | 2.50e dark blue | .90 | .30 |
| **1101** | A279 | 3.50e carmine rose | 1.40 | .45 |
| **1102** | A279 | 4e gray green | 2.40 | 1.50 |
| | | *Nos. 1097-1102 (6)* | 5.75 | 3.15 |

Pres. Antonio Salazar — A280

**1971, July 27 Engr. *Perf. 13½***

| No. | Type | Denomination & Description | Unused | Used |
|---|---|---|---|---|
| **1103** | A280 | 1e multicolored | .25 | .25 |
| *a.* | | Perf. 12½x12 | *100.00* | 2.75 |
| **1104** | A280 | 5e multicolored | 1.50 | .35 |
| **1105** | A280 | 10e multicolored | 2.50 | .95 |
| *a.* | | Perf. 12½x12 | *25.00* | 1.75 |
| | | *Nos. 1103-1105 (3)* | 4.25 | 1.55 |

Wolframite Crystals A281

Minerals: 2.50e, Arsenopyrite (gold). 3.50e, Beryllium. 6.50e, Chalcopyrite (copper).

**1971, Sept. 24 Litho. *Perf. 12***

| No. | Type | Denomination & Description | Unused | Used |
|---|---|---|---|---|
| **1106** | A281 | 1e multicolored | .25 | .25 |
| **1107** | A281 | 2.50e carmine & multi | 1.90 | .40 |
| **1108** | A281 | 3.50e green & multi | .65 | .30 |
| **1109** | A281 | 6.50e blue & multi | 1.10 | .45 |
| | | *Nos. 1106-1109 (4)* | 3.90 | 1.40 |

Spanish-Portuguese-American Economic Geology Congress.

Town Gate, Castelo Branco — A282

Designs: 3e, Memorial column. 12.50e, Arms of Castelo Branco, horiz.

**1971, Oct. 7 *Perf. 14***

| No. | Type | Denomination & Description | Unused | Used |
|---|---|---|---|---|
| **1110** | A282 | 1e multi | .25 | .25 |
| **1111** | A282 | 3e multi | 1.25 | .50 |
| **1112** | A282 | 12.50e multi | 1.00 | .50 |
| | | *Nos. 1110-1112 (3)* | 2.50 | 1.25 |

Bicentenary of Castelo Branco as a town.

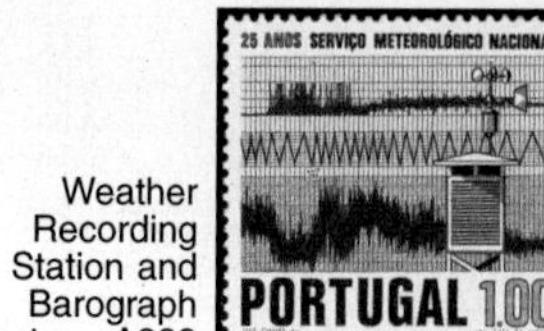


Weather Recording Station and Barograph Charts — A283

Designs: 4e, Stratospheric weather balloon and weather map of southwest Europe and North Africa. 6.50e, Satellite and aerial map of Atlantic Ocean off Portugal.

**1971, Oct. 29 *Perf. 13½***

| No. | Type | Denomination & Description | Unused | Used |
|---|---|---|---|---|
| **1113** | A283 | 1e buff & multi | .25 | .25 |
| **1114** | A283 | 4e multicolored | 2.10 | .85 |
| **1115** | A283 | 6.50e blk, dl red brn & org | 1.50 | .45 |
| | | *Nos. 1113-1115 (3)* | 3.85 | 1.55 |

25 years of Portuguese meteorological service.

Missionaries and Ship — A284

**1971, Nov. 24**

| No. | Type | Denomination & Description | Unused | Used |
|---|---|---|---|---|
| **1116** | A284 | 1e gray, ultra & blk | .25 | .25 |
| **1117** | A284 | 3.30e dp bis, lil & blk | 1.75 | 1.00 |
| **1118** | A284 | 4.80e olive, grn & blk | 1.90 | 1.10 |
| | | *Nos. 1116-1118 (3)* | 3.90 | 2.35 |

400th anniv. of the martyrdom of a group of Portuguese missionaries on the way to Brazil.

"Man" A285

Nature Conservation: 3.30e, "Earth" (animal, vegetable, mineral). 3.50e, "Air" (birds). 4.50e, "Water" (fish).

**1971, Dec. 22 Litho. *Perf. 12***

| No. | Type | Denomination & Description | Unused | Used |
|---|---|---|---|---|
| **1119** | A285 | 1e brown & multi | .25 | .25 |
| **1120** | A285 | 3.30e lt bl, yel & grn | .55 | .30 |
| **1121** | A285 | 3.50e lt bl, rose & vio | .65 | .25 |
| **1122** | A285 | 4.50e lt bl, grn & ultra | 2.25 | 1.25 |
| | | *Nos. 1119-1122 (4)* | 3.70 | 2.05 |

City Hall, Sintra — A286

Designs: 5c, Aqueduct, Lisbon. 50c, University, Coimbra. 1e, Torre dos Clerigos, Porto. 1.50e, Belem Tower, Lisbon. 2.50e, Castle, Vila da Feira. 3e, Misericordia House, Viana do Castelo. 3.50e, Window, Tomar Convent. 8e, Ducal Palace, Guimaraes. 10e, Cape Girao, Madeira. 20e, Episcopal Garden, Castelo Branco. 100e, Lakes of Seven Cities, Azores.

**1972-73 Litho. *Perf. 12½***

**Size: 22x17½mm**

| No. | Type | Denomination & Description | Unused | Used |
|---|---|---|---|---|
| **1123** | A286 | 5c gray, grn & blk, "1973" | .25 | .25 |
| **1124** | A286 | 50c gray bl, blk & org, "1972" | .25 | .25 |
| *a.* | | "1973" | .65 | .25 |
| *b.* | | "1974" | .45 | .25 |
| *c.* | | "1975" | .25 | .25 |
| *d.* | | "1976" | .25 | .25 |
| **1125** | A286 | 1e green, blk & brn, "1972" | .45 | .25 |
| *a.* | | "1973" | .90 | .25 |
| *b.* | | "1976" | .45 | .25 |
| *c.* | | "1977" | .45 | .25 |
| *d.* | | Unlettered paper, "1978" | .25 | .25 |
| **1126** | A286 | 1.50e blue, bis & blk, "1972" | .40 | .25 |
| *a.* | | "1973" | .90 | .25 |
| *b.* | | "1974" | .25 | .25 |
| *c.* | | Unlettered paper, "1981" | .25 | .25 |
| **1127** | A286 | 2.50e brn, dk brn & gray, "1973" | .80 | .25 |
| *a.* | | "1975" | 2.75 | .25 |
| *b.* | | Unlettered paper, "1978" | .25 | .25 |
| **1128** | A286 | 3e yellow, blk & brn, "1972" | .25 | .25 |
| *a.* | | "1974" | .50 | .25 |
| *b.* | | "1976" | .25 | .25 |
| **1129** | A286 | 3.50e dp org, sl & brn, "1973" | 1.40 | .25 |
| *a.* | | "1975" | 1.40 | .25 |
| *b.* | | Unlettered paper, "1978" | .25 | .25 |
| **1130** | A286 | 8e blk, ol & grn, "1973" | 1.40 | .25 |
| *a.* | | "1975" | 1.40 | .25 |
| *b.* | | Unlettered paper, "1978" | 1.10 | .25 |

***Perf. 13½***

**Size: 31x22mm**

**1131** A286 10e gray & multi, "1972" .55 .25
*a.* "1974" 1.00 .25
*b.* "1977" 1.40 .25
*c.* Unlettered paper, "1978" .45 .25
**1132** A286 20e green & multi, "1972" 5.50 .25
*a.* "1974" 3.50 .25
*b.* "1975" 3.50 .25
*c.* "1977" 7.25 .25
**1133** A286 50e gray bl, ocher & blk, "1972" 4.50 .25
*a.* "1973" 6.75 .25
*b.* "1977" 3.50 .25
*c.* Unlettered paper, "1978" 1.75 .25
**1134** A286 100e green & multi, "1972" 7.25 .55
*a.* Unlettered paper, "1978" 9.00 .60
*Nos. 1123-1134 (12)* 23.00 3.30

"CTT" and year date printed in minute gray multiple rows on back of stamps. Values are for most common dates.

Issue dates: 1e, 1.50e, 50e, 100e, Mar. 1; 50c, 3e, 10e, 20e, Dec. 6, 1972; 5c, 2.50e, 3.50e, 8e, Sept. 5, 1973.

See Nos. 1207-1214.

Tagging

Starting in 1975, phosphor (bar or L-shape) was applied to the face of most definitives and commemoratives.

Stamps issued both with and without tagging include Nos. 1124-1125, 1128, 1130-1131, 1209, 1213-1214, 1250, 1253, 1257, 1260, 1263.

Window, Pinhel Church — A287

1e, Arms of Pinhel, horiz. 7.50e, Stone lantern.

**1972, Mar. 29** ***Perf. 13½***
**1135** A287 1e blue & multi .25 .25
*a.* Perf. 11½x12½ 70.00 3.00
**1136** A287 2.50e multicolored 1.50 .30
**1137** A287 7.50e blue & multi 1.40 .50
*Nos. 1135-1137 (3)* 3.15 1.05

Bicentenary of Pinhel as a town.

Heart and Pendulum A288

Designs: 4e, Heart and spiral pattern. 9e, Heart and continuing coil pattern.

**1972, Apr. 24**
**1138** A288 1e violet & red .25 .25
**1139** A288 4e green & red 2.40 .90
**1140** A288 9e brown & red 1.20 .60
*Nos. 1138-1140 (3)* 3.85 1.75

"Your heart is your health," World Health Day.

**Europa Issue**

Common Design Type

**1972, May 1** ***Perf. 13½***

**Size: 21x31mm**

**1141** CD15 1e gray & multi *1.00* .25
**1142** CD15 3.50e salmon & multi *2.75* .35
**1143** CD15 6e grn & multi *6.00* .90
*Nos. 1141-1143 (3)* *9.75* 1.50

Trucks — A289

**1972, May 17** **Litho.** ***Perf. 13½***
**1144** A289 1e shown .25 .25
**1145** A289 4.50e Taxi 1.90 .90
**1146** A289 8e Autobus 1.50 .70
*Nos. 1144-1146 (3)* 3.65 1.85

13th Congress of International Union of Road Transport (I.R.U.), Estoril, May 15-18.

Soccer, Olympic Rings A290

1e, Running. 1.50e, Equestrian. 3.50e, Swimming, women's. 4.50e, Yachting. 5e, Gymnastics, women's.

**1972, July 26** **Litho.** ***Perf. 14***
**1147** A290 50c shown .25 .25
**1148** A290 1e multicolored .25 .25
**1149** A290 1.50e multicolored .40 .25
**1150** A290 3.50e multicolored .95 .30
**1151** A290 4.50e multicolored 1.20 .85
**1152** A290 5e multicolored 2.50 .80
*Nos. 1147-1152 (6)* 5.55 2.70

20th Olympic Games, Munich, 8/26-9/11.

Marquis of Pombal — A291

2.50e, Scientific apparatus. 8e, Seal of Univ. of Coimbra.

**1972, Aug. 28** ***Perf. 13½***
**1153** A291 1e shown .25 .25
**1154** A291 2.50e multicolored 1.50 .60
**1155** A291 8e multicolored 1.60 .95
*Nos. 1153-1155 (3)* 3.35 1.80

Bicentenary of the Pombaline reforms of University of Coimbra.

Tomé de Sousa — A292

Designs: 2.50e, José Bonifacio. 3.50e, Dom Pedro IV. 6e, Allegory of Portuguese-Brazilian Community.

**1972, Oct. 5** **Litho.** ***Perf. 13½***
**1156** A292 1e gray & multi .25 .25
**1157** A292 2.50e green & multi .65 .25
**1158** A292 3.50e multicolored .65 .30
**1159** A292 6e blue & multi 1.40 .65
*Nos. 1156-1159 (4)* 2.95 1.45

150th anniv. of Brazilian independence.

Sacadura Cabral, Gago Coutinho and Plane — A293

2.50e, 3.80e, Map of flight from Lisbon to Rio.

**1972, Nov. 15** ***Perf. 11½x12½***
**1160** A293 1e blue & multi .25 .25
*a.* Perf. 13½ 40.00 .95
**1161** A293 2.50e multi .80 .30
**1162** A293 2.80e multi 1.00 .60
**1163** A293 3.80e multi 1.60 1.00
*a.* Perf. 13½ *125.00* *37.50*
*Nos. 1160-1163 (4)* 3.65 2.15

50th anniv. of the Lisbon to Rio flight by Commander Arturo de Sacadura Cabral and Adm. Carlos Viegas Gago Coutinho, Mar. 30-June 5, 1922.

Luiz Camoens A294

Designs: 3e, Hand saving manuscript from sea. 10e, Symbolic of man's questioning and discovering the unknown.

**1972, Dec. 27** **Litho.** ***Perf. 13***
**1164** A294 1e org brn, buff & blk .25 .25
**1165** A294 3e dull bl, lt grn & blk 1.20 .50
**1166** A294 10e red brn, buff & yel 1.50 .65
*Nos. 1164-1166 (3)* 2.95 1.40

4th centenary of the publication of The Lusiads by Luiz Camoens (1524-1580).

Graphs and Sequence Count — A295

**1973, Apr. 11** **Litho.** ***Perf. 14½***
**1167** A295 1e shown .25 .25
**1168** A295 4e Odometer 1.10 .50
**1169** A295 9e Graphs 1.00 .45
*Nos. 1167-1169 (3)* 2.35 1.20

Productivity Conference '72, 1/17-22/72.

**Europa Issue**

Common Design Type

**1973, Apr. 30** ***Perf. 13***

**Size: 31x29mm**

**1170** CD16 1e multicolored *1.00* .25
**1171** CD16 4e brn red & multi *5.00* .65
**1172** CD16 6e green & multi *7.00* *1.25*
*Nos. 1170-1172 (3)* *13.00* 2.15

Gen. Medici, Arms of Brazil and Portugal A296

2.80e, 4.80e, Gen. Medici and world map.

**Lithographed and Engraved**

**1973, May 16** ***Perf. 12x11½***
**1173** A296 1e dk grn, blk & sep .25 .25
**1174** A296 2.80e olive & multi .70 .50
**1175** A296 3.50e dk bl, blk & buff .80 .45
**1176** A296 4.80e multicolored .90 .50
*Nos. 1173-1176 (4)* 2.65 1.70

Visit of Gen. Emilio Garrastazu Medici, President of Brazil, to Portugal.

Child and Birds — A297

4e, Child and flowers. 7.50e, Child.

**1973, May 28** **Litho.** ***Perf. 13***
**1177** A297 1e ultra & multi .25 .25
**1178** A297 4e multicolored 1.25 .50
**1179** A297 7.50e bister & multi 1.40 .80
*Nos. 1177-1179 (3)* 2.90 1.55

To pay renewed attention to children.

Transportation, Weather Map — A298

3.80e, Communications: telegraph, telephone, radio, satellite. 6e, Postal service: mailbox, truck, mail distribution diagram.

**1973, June 25**
**1180** A298 1e multi .25 .25
**1181** A298 3.80e multi .40 .30
**1182** A298 6e multi 1.00 .50
*Nos. 1180-1182 (3)* 1.65 1.05

Ministry of Communications, 25th anniv.

Pupil and Writing Exercise — A299

Designs: 4.50e, Illustrations from 18th century primer. 5.30e, School and children, by 9-year-old Marie de Luz, horiz. 8e, Symbolic chart of teacher-pupil link, horiz.

**1973, Oct. 24** **Litho.** ***Perf. 13***
**1183** A299 1e blue & multi .25 .25
**1184** A299 4.50e brown & multi 1.40 .40
**1185** A299 5.30e lt blue & multi 1.10 .50
**1186** A299 8e green & multi 3.00 1.10
*Nos. 1183-1186 (4)* 5.75 2.25

Primary state school education, bicent.

Oporto Streetcar, 1910 A300

Designs: 1e, Horse-drawn streetcar, 1872. 3.50e, Double-decker Leyland bus, 1972.

**1973, Nov. 7** **Size: 31½x34mm**
**1187** A300 1e brn, yel & blk .25 .25
**1188** A300 3.50e choc & multi 1.75 1.00

**Size: 37½x27mm**

***Perf. 12½***

**1189** A300 7.50e buff & multi 2.00 .90
*Nos. 1187-1189 (3)* 4.00 2.15

Cent. of public transportation in Oporto.

Servicemen's League Emblem — A301

Designs: 2.50e, Sailor, soldier and aviator. 11e, Military medals.

**1973, Nov. 28** **Litho.** ***Perf. 13***
**1190** A301 1e multi .25 .25
**1191** A301 2.50e multi 1.90 .55
**1192** A301 11e dk blue & multi 1.50 .45
*Nos. 1190-1192 (3)* 3.65 1.25

50th anniv. of the Servicemen's League.

Death of Nuño Gonzalves — A302

**1973, Dec. 19**

| | | | | |
|---|---|---|---|---|
| 1193 | A302 | 1e slate blue & org | .30 | .25 |
| 1194 | A302 | 10e violet brn & org | 1.50 | .85 |

600th anniv. of the heroism of Nuno Gonzalves, alcaide of Faria Castle.

Damiao de Gois, by Dürer (?) A303

Designs: 4.50e, Title page of Cronica de Principe D. Joao. 7.50e, Lute and score of Dodecachordon.

**1974, Apr. 5 Litho. *Perf. 12***

| | | | | |
|---|---|---|---|---|
| 1195 | A303 | 1e multi | .25 | .25 |
| 1196 | A303 | 4.50e multi | 2.10 | .45 |
| 1197 | A303 | 7.50e multi | 1.10 | .40 |
| | | *Nos. 1195-1197 (3)* | 3.45 | 1.10 |

400th anniversary of the death of Damiao de Gois (1502-1574), humanist, writer, composer.

## Europa Issue

"The Exile," by Soares dos Reis — A304

**1974, Apr. 29 Litho. *Perf. 13***

| | | | | |
|---|---|---|---|---|
| 1198 | A304 | 1e multicolored | *2.00* | .25 |
| 1199 | A304 | 4e dk red & multi | *5.00* | *.50* |
| 1200 | A304 | 6e dk grn & multi | *10.00* | *1.00* |
| | | *Nos. 1198-1200 (3)* | 17.00 | 1.75 |

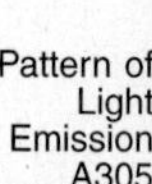

Pattern of Light Emission A305

Designs: 4.50e, Spiral wave radiation pattern. 5.30e, Satellite and earth.

**1974, June 26 Litho. *Perf. 14***

| | | | | |
|---|---|---|---|---|
| 1201 | A305 | 1.50e gray olive | .25 | .25 |
| 1202 | A305 | 4.50e dark blue | 1.25 | .50 |
| 1203 | A305 | 5.30e brt rose lilac | 2.00 | .75 |
| | | *Nos. 1201-1203 (3)* | 3.50 | 1.50 |

Establishment of satellite communications network via Intelsat among Portugal, Angola and Mozambique.

Diffusion of Hertzian Waves A306

Designs (Symbolic): 3.30e, Messages through space. 10e, Navigation help.

**1974, Sept. 4 Litho. *Perf. 12***

| | | | | |
|---|---|---|---|---|
| 1204 | A306 | 1.50e multi | .50 | .25 |
| 1205 | A306 | 3.30e multi | 2.00 | .60 |
| 1206 | A306 | 10e multi | 1.25 | .40 |
| | | *Nos. 1204-1206 (3)* | 3.75 | 1.25 |

Guglielmo Marconi (1874-1937), Italian electrical engineer and inventor.

## Buildings Type of 1972-73

Designs: 10c, Ponte do Lima (Roman bridge). 30c, Alcobaça Monastery, interior. 2e, City Hall, Bragança. 4e, New Gate, Braga. 4.50e, Dolmen of Carrazeda. 5e, Roman Temple, Evora. 6e, Leca do Balio Monastery. 7.50e, Almourol Castle.

**1974, Sept. 18 Litho. *Perf. 12½***
**Size: 22x17½mm**

| | | | | |
|---|---|---|---|---|
| 1207 | A286 | 10c multi, "1974" | .25 | .25 |
| 1208 | A286 | 30c multi, "1974" | .25 | .25 |
| 1209 | A286 | 2e multi, "1974" | 2.00 | .25 |
| *a.* | | "1975" | 2.00 | .25 |
| *b.* | | "1977" | .50 | .25 |
| *c.* | | Unlettered paper "1978" | .25 | .25 |
| 1210 | A286 | 4e multi, "1974" | .55 | .25 |
| 1211 | A286 | 4.50e multi, "1974" | .90 | .25 |
| 1212 | A286 | 5e multi, "1974" | 7.50 | .25 |
| *a.* | | "1975" | 15.00 | .25 |
| *b.* | | "1976" | 7.50 | .25 |
| 1213 | A286 | 6e multi, "1974" | 2.50 | .25 |
| *a.* | | "1975" | 25.00 | .50 |
| 1214 | A286 | 7.50e multi, "1974" | 1.00 | .25 |
| *a.* | | "1977" | 2.50 | .25 |
| | | *Nos. 1207-1214 (8)* | 14.95 | 2.00 |

"CTT" and year date printed in minute gray multiple rows on back of stamps. Values are for most common dates.

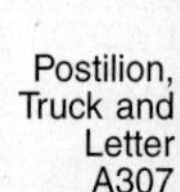

Postilion, Truck and Letter A307

Designs: 2e, Hand holding letter. 3.30e, Packet and steamship. 4.50e, Pigeon and letters. 5.30e, Hand holding sealed letter. 20e, Old and new locomotives.

**1974, Oct. 9 Litho. *Perf. 13***

| | | | | |
|---|---|---|---|---|
| 1220 | A307 | 1.50e brown & multi | .25 | .25 |
| 1221 | A307 | 2e multicolored | .65 | .25 |
| 1222 | A307 | 3.30e olive & multi | .35 | .25 |
| 1223 | A307 | 4.50e multicolored | 1.10 | .45 |
| 1224 | A307 | 5.30e multicolored | .45 | .30 |
| 1225 | A307 | 20e multicolored | 2.10 | .95 |
| *a.* | | Souvenir sheet of 6 | 6.50 | 6.50 |
| | | *Nos. 1220-1225 (6)* | 4.90 | 2.45 |

Centenary of UPU. No. 1225a contains one each of Nos. 1220-1225, arranged to show a continuous design with a globe in center. Sold for 50e.

Luisa Todi, Singer (1753-1833) A308

Marcos Portugal, Composer (1762-1838) A309

Portuguese Musicians: 2e, Joao Domingos Bomtempo (1775-1842). 2.50e, Carlos Seixas (1704-1742). 3e, Duarte Lobo (1565-1646). 5.30e, Joao de Sousa Carvalho (1745-1798).

**1974, Oct. 30 Litho. *Perf. 12***

| | | | | |
|---|---|---|---|---|
| 1226 | A308 | 1.50e brt pink | .25 | .25 |
| 1227 | A308 | 2e vermilion | 1.10 | .25 |
| 1228 | A308 | 2.50e brown | .65 | .25 |
| 1229 | A308 | 3e bluish black | 1.10 | .30 |
| 1230 | A308 | 5.30e slate green | .65 | .40 |
| 1231 | A309 | 11e rose lake | .80 | .45 |
| | | *Nos. 1226-1231 (6)* | 4.55 | 1.90 |

Coat of Arms of Beja A310

2,000th Anniv. of Beja: 3.50e, Men of Beja in costumes from Roman times to date. 7e, Moorish Arches and view across plains.

**1974, Nov. 13**

| | | | | |
|---|---|---|---|---|
| 1232 | A310 | 1.50e multi | .25 | .25 |
| 1233 | A310 | 3.50e multi | 2.00 | .80 |
| 1234 | A310 | 7e multi | 2.25 | .95 |
| | | *Nos. 1232-1234 (3)* | 4.50 | 2.00 |

Annunciation A311

Christmas: 4.50e, Adoration of the Shepherds. 10e, Flight into Egypt. Designs show Portuguese costumes from Nazare township.

**1974, Dec. 4 Litho. *Perf. 13***

| | | | | |
|---|---|---|---|---|
| 1235 | A311 | 1.50e red & multi | .25 | .25 |
| 1236 | A311 | 4.50e multicolored | 3.00 | .45 |
| 1237 | A311 | 10e blue & multi | 2.25 | .60 |
| | | *Nos. 1235-1237 (3)* | 5.50 | 1.30 |

Rainbow and Dove — A312

**1974, Dec. 18 *Perf. 12***

| | | | | |
|---|---|---|---|---|
| 1238 | A312 | 1.50e multi | .25 | .25 |
| 1239 | A312 | 3.50e multi | 2.90 | 1.40 |
| 1240 | A312 | 5e multi | 1.60 | .50 |
| | | *Nos. 1238-1240 (3)* | 4.75 | 2.15 |

Armed Forces Movement of Apr. 25, 1974.

Egas Moniz — A313

3.30e, Lobotomy probe and Nobel Prize medal, 1949. 10e, Cerebral angiograph, 1927.

**1974, Dec. 27 Engr. *Perf. 11½x12***

| | | | | |
|---|---|---|---|---|
| 1241 | A313 | 1.50e yellow & multi | .25 | .25 |
| 1242 | A313 | 3.30e brown & ocher | 1.10 | .35 |
| 1243 | A313 | 10e gray & ultra | 4.25 | .60 |
| | | *Nos. 1241-1243 (3)* | 5.60 | 1.20 |

Egas Moniz (1874-1955), brain surgeon, birth centenary.

Soldier as Farmer, Farmer as Soldier — A314

**1975, Mar. 21 Litho. *Perf. 12***

| | | | | |
|---|---|---|---|---|
| 1244 | A314 | 1.50e green & multi | .25 | .25 |
| 1245 | A314 | 3e gray & multi | 1.90 | .50 |
| 1246 | A314 | 4.50e multicolored | 2.25 | .75 |
| | | *Nos. 1244-1246 (3)* | 4.40 | 1.50 |

Cultural progress and citizens' guidance campaign.

Hands and Dove — A315

4.50e, Brown hands reaching for dove. 10e, Dove with olive branch and arms of Portugal.

**1975, Apr. 23 Litho. *Perf. 13½***

| | | | | |
|---|---|---|---|---|
| 1247 | A315 | 1.50e red & multi | .25 | .25 |
| 1248 | A315 | 4.50e brown & multi | 2.00 | .55 |
| 1249 | A315 | 10e green & multi | 2.60 | .80 |
| | | *Nos. 1247-1249 (3)* | 4.85 | 1.60 |

Movement of April 25th, first anniversary. Slogans in Portuguese, French and English printed on back of stamps.

God's Hand Reaching Down — A316

Designs: 4.50e, Jesus' hand holding up cross. 10e, Dove (Holy Spirit) descending.

**1975, May 13 Litho. *Perf. 13½***

| | | | | |
|---|---|---|---|---|
| 1250 | A316 | 1.50e multicolored | .25 | .25 |
| 1251 | A316 | 4.50e plum & multi | 2.75 | .75 |
| 1252 | A316 | 10e blue & multi | 3.25 | .80 |
| | | *Nos. 1250-1252 (3)* | 6.25 | 1.80 |

Holy Year 1975.

Horseman of the Apocalypse, 12th Century A317

Europa: 10e, The Poet Fernando Pessoa, by Almada Negreiros (1893-1970).

**1975, May 26**

| | | | | |
|---|---|---|---|---|
| 1253 | A317 | 1.50e multi | *2.00* | *.25* |
| 1254 | A317 | 10e multi | *14.00* | *1.25* |

Assembly Building A318

**1975, June 2 Litho. *Perf. 13½***

| | | | | |
|---|---|---|---|---|
| 1255 | A318 | 2e red, blk & yel | .30 | .25 |
| 1256 | A318 | 20e emer, blk & yel | 4.25 | .75 |

Opening of Constituent Assembly.

Hikers — A319

Designs: 4.50e, Campsite on lake. 5.30e, Mobile homes on the road.

**1975, Aug. 4 Litho. *Perf. 13½***

**1257** A319 2e multicolored .75 .25
**1258** A319 4.50e multicolored 2.25 .80
**1259** A319 5.30e multicolored 1.40 .75
*Nos. 1257-1259 (3)* 4.40 1.80

36th Rally of the International Federation of Camping and Caravanning, Santo Andre Lake.

People and Sapling A320

Designs (UN Emblem and): 4.50e, People and dove. 20e, People and grain.

**1975, Sept. 17 Litho. *Perf. 13½***

**1260** A320 2e green & multi .25 .25
**1261** A320 4.50e vio & multi 1.40 .40
**1262** A320 20e multicolored 3.00 1.00
*Nos. 1260-1262 (3)* 4.65 1.65

United Nations, 30th anniversary.

Icarus and Rocket — A321

Designs: 4.50e, Apollo and Soyuz in space. 5.30e, Robert H. Goddard, Robert Esnault-Pelterie, Hermann Oberth and Konstantin Tsiolkovski. 10e, Sputnik, man in space, moon landing module.

**1975, Sept. 26 Litho. *Perf. 13½***

**Size: 30½x26½mm**

**1263** A321 2e green & multi .40 .25
**1264** A321 4.50e brown & multi 2.00 .60
**1265** A321 5.30e lilac & multi .95 .60

**Size: 65x28mm**

**1266** A321 10e blue & multi 3.50 1.00
*Nos. 1263-1266 (4)* 6.85 2.45

26th Congress of International Astronautical Federation, Lisbon, Sept. 1975.

Land Survey A322

Designs: 8e, Ocean survey. 10e, People of many races and globe.

**1975, Nov. 19 Litho. *Perf. 12x12½***

**1267** A322 2e ocher & multi .25 .25
**1268** A322 8e blue & multi 1.40 .55
**1269** A322 10e dk vio & multi 3.00 .85
*Nos. 1267-1269 (3)* 4.65 1.65

Centenary of Lisbon Geographical Society.

Arch and Trees — A323

Designs: 8e, Plan, pencil and ruler. 10e, Hand, old building and brick tower.

**1975, Nov. 28 *Perf. 13½***

**1270** A323 2e dk bl & gray .25 .25
**1271** A323 8e dk car & gray 2.50 .65
**1272** A323 10e ocher & multi 3.00 .90
*Nos. 1270-1272 (3)* 5.75 1.80

European Architectural Heritage Year 1975.

Nurse and Hospital Ward — A324

Designs (IWY Emblem and): 2e, Farm workers. 3.50e, Secretary. 8e, Factory worker.

**1975, Dec. 30 Litho. *Perf. 13½***

**1273** A324 50c multicolored .25 .25
**1274** A324 2e multicolored .75 .25
**1275** A324 3.50e multicolored .85 .45
**1276** A324 8e multicolored 1.40 .90
*a.* Souvenir sheet of 4 6.00 4.00
*Nos. 1273-1276 (4)* 3.25 1.85

International Women's Year 1975. No. 1276a contains 4 stamps similar to Nos. 1273-1276 in slightly changed colors. Sold for 25e.

Pen Nib as Plowshare A325

**1976, Feb. 6 Litho. *Perf. 12***

**1277** A325 3e dk bl & red org .35 .25
**1278** A325 20e org, ultra & red 3.25 .90

Portuguese Soc. of Writers, 50th anniv.

Telephones, 1876, 1976 — A326

10.50e, Alexander Graham Bell & telephone.

**1976, Mar. 10 Litho. *Perf. 12x12½***

**1279** A326 3e yel grn, grn & blk .65 .25
**1280** A326 10.50e rose, red & blk 2.50 .65

Centenary of first telephone call by Alexander Graham Bell, March 10, 1876.

Industry and Shipping — A327

1e, Garment, food and wine industries.

**1976, Apr. 7 Litho. *Perf. 12½***

**1281** A327 50c red brown .25 .25
**1282** A327 1e slate .45 .25

Support of national production.

Carved Spoons, Olive Wood A328

Europa: 20e, Gold filigree pendant, silver box and CEPT emblem.

**1976, May 3 Litho. *Perf. 12x12½***

**1283** A328 3e olive & multi *2.00* .25
**1284** A328 20e tan & multi *15.00 1.75*

Stamp Collectors A329

Designs: 7.50e, Stamp exhibition and hand canceler. 10e, Printing and designing stamps.

**1976, May 29 Litho. *Perf. 14½***

**1285** A329 3e multicolored .25 .25
**1286** A329 7.50e multicolored 1.00 .45
**1287** A329 10e multicolored 1.40 .50
*Nos. 1285-1287 (3)* 2.65 1.20

Interphil 76, International Philatelic Exhibition, Philadelphia, Pa., May 29-June 6.

King Ferdinand I — A330

Designs: 5e, Plowshare, farmers chasing off hunters. 10e, Harvest.

**1976, July 2 Litho. *Perf. 12***

**1288** A330 3e lt bl & multi .25 .25
**1289** A330 5e yel grn & multi 1.50 .30
**1290** A330 10e multicolored 1.60 .60
*a.* Souv. sheet of 3, #1288-1290 4.25 4.25
*Nos. 1288-1290 (3)* 3.35 1.15

Agricultural reform law (compulsory cultivation of uncultivated lands), 600th anniversary. No. 1290a sold for 30e.

Torch Bearer A331

7e, Women's relay race. 10.50e, Olympic flame.

**1976, July 16 *Perf. 13½***

**1291** A331 3e red & multi .25 .25
**1292** A331 7e red & multi 1.50 .90
**1293** A331 10.50e red & multi 2.00 .80
*Nos. 1291-1293 (3)* 3.75 1.95

21st Olympic Games, Montreal, Canada, July 17-Aug. 1.

Farm A332

**1976, Sept. 15 Litho. *Perf. 12***

**1294** A332 3e shown .55 .25
**1295** A332 3e Ship .55 .25
**1296** A332 3e City .55 .25
**1297** A332 3e Factory 1.10 .25
*b.* Souv. sheet of 4, #1294-1297 12.50 12.50
*Nos. 1294-1297 (4)* 2.75 1.00

Fight against illiteracy. #1297b sold for 25e.

***Perf. 13½***

*1294a* A332 3e *24.00 .50*
*1295a* A332 3e *.80 .25*
*1296a* A332 3e *24.00 .50*
*1297a* A332 3e *.80 .25*
*Nos. 1294a-1297a (4)* 49.60 1.50

Azure-winged Magpie A333

Designs: 5e, Lynx. 7e, Portuguese laurel cherry. 10.50e, Little wild carnations.

**1976, Sept. 30 Litho. *Perf. 12***

**1298** A333 3e multi .50 .25
**1299** A333 5e multi 1.10 .25
**1300** A333 7e multi 1.25 .65
**1301** A333 10.50e multi 1.25 .85
*Nos. 1298-1301 (4)* 4.10 2.00

Portucale 77, 2nd International Thematic Exhibition, Oporto, Oct. 29-Nov. 6, 1977.

Exhibition Hall — A334

Design: 20e, Symbolic stamp and emblem.

**1976, Oct. 9 Litho. *Perf. 13½***

**1302** A334 3e bl & multi .35 .25
**1303** A334 20e ocher & multi 2.00 1.10
*a.* Souv. sheet of 2, #1302-1303 3.75 3.75

6th Luso-Brazilian Phil. Exhib., LUBRAPEX 76, Oporto, Oct. 9. #1303a sold for 30e.

Bank Emblem and Family A335

7e, Grain. 15e, Cog wheels.

**1976, Oct. 29 *Perf. 12***

**1304** A335 3e org & multi .25 .25
**1305** A335 7e grn & multi 1.75 .60
**1306** A335 15e bl & multi 2.25 .85
*Nos. 1304-1306 (3)* 4.25 1.70

Trust Fund Bank centenary.

Sheep Grazing on Marsh A336

Designs: 3e, Drainage ditches. 5e, Fish in water. 10e, Ducks flying over marsh.

**1976, Nov. 24 Litho. *Perf. 14***

**1307** A336 1e multicolored .25 .25
**1308** A336 3e multicolored .90 .25
**1309** A336 5e multicolored 1.50 .30
**1310** A336 10e multicolored 2.75 .75
*Nos. 1307-1310 (4)* 5.40 1.55

Protection of wetlands.

"Liberty" — A337

**1976, Nov. 30 Litho. *Perf. 13½***

**1311** A337 3e gray, grn & ver .65 .25

Constitution of 1976.

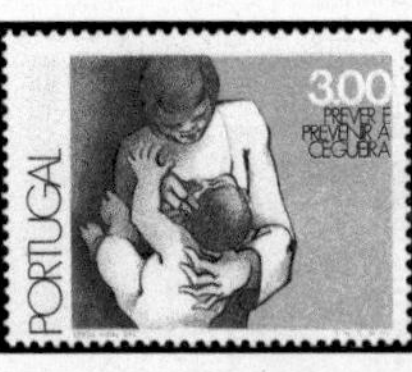

Mother Examining Child's Eyes A338

Designs: 5e, Welder with goggles. 10.50e, Blind woman reading Braille.

**1976, Dec. 13**

**1312** A338 3e multicolored .25 .25
**1313** A338 5e multicolored 1.75 .25
**1314** A338 10.50e multicolored 1.40 .80
*Nos. 1312-1314 (3)* 3.40 1.30

World Health Day and campaign against blindness.

Hydroelectric Energy — A339

Abstract Designs: 4e, Fossil fuels. 5e, Geothermal energy. 10e, Wind power. 15e, Solar energy.

**1976, Dec. 30**

| | | | | |
|---|---|---|---|---|
| **1315** | A339 | 1e multicolored | .25 | .25 |
| **1316** | A339 | 4e multicolored | .50 | .25 |
| **1317** | A339 | 5e multicolored | .65 | .25 |
| **1318** | A339 | 10e multicolored | 1.25 | .60 |
| **1319** | A339 | 15e multicolored | 2.40 | 1.10 |
| | | *Nos. 1315-1319 (5)* | 5.05 | 2.45 |

Sources of energy.

Map of Council of Europe Members A340

**1977, Jan. 28 Litho. *Perf. 12***

| | | | | |
|---|---|---|---|---|
| **1320** | A340 | 8.50e multicolored | 1.25 | .95 |
| **1321** | A340 | 10e multicolored | 1.25 | .85 |

Portugal's joining Council of Europe.

Alcoholic and Bottle — A341

Designs (Bottle and): 5e, Symbolic figure of broken life. 15e, Bars blotting out the sun.

**1977, Feb. 4 *Perf. 13***

| | | | | |
|---|---|---|---|---|
| **1322** | A341 | 3e multicolored | .25 | .25 |
| **1323** | A341 | 5e ocher & multi | .85 | .30 |
| **1324** | A341 | 15e org & multi | 2.00 | .95 |
| | | *Nos. 1322-1324 (3)* | 3.10 | 1.50 |

Anti-alcoholism Day and 10th anniversary of Portuguese Anti-alcoholism Society.

Trees Tapped for Resin — A342

Designs: 4e, Trees stripped for cork. 7e, Trees and logs. 15e, Trees at seashore as windbreakers.

**1977, Mar. 21 Litho. *Perf. 13½***

| | | | | |
|---|---|---|---|---|
| **1325** | A342 | 1e multicolored | .25 | .25 |
| **1326** | A342 | 4e multicolored | .65 | .25 |
| **1327** | A342 | 7e multicolored | 1.40 | .95 |
| **1328** | A342 | 15e multicolored | 1.50 | .95 |
| | | *Nos. 1325-1328 (4)* | 3.80 | 2.40 |

Forests, a natural resource.

"Suffering" A343

6e, Man exercising. 10e, Group exercising. All designs include emblems of WHO & Portuguese Institute for Rheumatology.

**1977, Apr. 13 Litho. *Perf. 12x12½***

| | | | | |
|---|---|---|---|---|
| **1329** | A343 | 4e blk, brn & ocher | .25 | .25 |
| **1330** | A343 | 6e blk, bl & vio | 1.10 | .75 |
| **1331** | A343 | 10e blk, pur & red | 1.00 | .50 |
| | | *Nos. 1329-1331 (3)* | 2.35 | 1.50 |

International Rheumatism Year.

Southern Plains Landscape A344

Europa: 8.50e, Northern mountain valley.

**1977, May 2**

| | | | | |
|---|---|---|---|---|
| **1332** | A344 | 4e multi | *1.00* | .25 |
| **1333** | A344 | 8.50e multi | *3.00* | *.60* |
| *a.* | | Min. sheet, 3 each #1332-1333 | *15.00* | *14.00* |

Pope John XXI Enthroned A345

Petrus Hispanus, the Physician A346

**1977, May 20 Litho. *Perf. 13½***

| | | | | |
|---|---|---|---|---|
| **1334** | A345 | 4e multicolored | .25 | .25 |
| **1335** | A346 | 15e multicolored | .60 | .35 |

Pope John XXI (Petrus Hispanus), only Pope of Portuguese descent, 7th death centenary.

Compass Rose, Camoens Quotation A347

**1977, June 8 *Perf. 12***

| | | | | |
|---|---|---|---|---|
| **1336** | A347 | 4e multi | .25 | .25 |
| **1337** | A347 | 8.50e multi | 1.10 | .80 |

Camoens Day and to honor Portuguese overseas communities.

Student, Computer and Book — A348

Designs (Book and): No. 1339, Folk dancers, flutist and boat. No. 1340, Tractor drivers. No. 1341, Atom and people.

**1977, July 20 Litho. *Perf. 12x12½***

| | | | | |
|---|---|---|---|---|
| **1338** | A348 | 4e multicolored | .40 | .25 |
| **1339** | A348 | 4e multicolored | .40 | .25 |
| **1340** | A348 | 4e multicolored | .40 | .25 |
| **1341** | A348 | 4e multicolored | .40 | .25 |
| *a.* | | Souv. sheet of 4, #1338-1341 | 4.50 | 4.50 |
| | | *Nos. 1338-1341 (4)* | 1.60 | 1.00 |

Continual education. #1341a sold for 20e.

Pyrites, Copper, Chemical Industry A349

Designs: 5e, Marble, statue, public buildings. 10e, Iron ore, girders, crane. 20e, Uranium ore, atomic diagram.

**1977, Oct. 4 Litho. *Perf. 12x11½***

| | | | | |
|---|---|---|---|---|
| **1342** | A349 | 4e multicolored | .25 | .25 |
| **1343** | A349 | 5e multicolored | .75 | .25 |
| **1344** | A349 | 10e multicolored | 1.20 | .35 |
| **1345** | A349 | 20e multicolored | 1.90 | .90 |
| | | *Nos. 1342-1345 (4)* | 4.10 | 1.75 |

Natural resources from the subsoil.

Alexandre Herculano — A350

**1977, Oct. 19 Engr. *Perf. 12x11½***

| | | | | |
|---|---|---|---|---|
| **1346** | A350 | 4e multicolored | .25 | .25 |
| **1347** | A350 | 15e multicolored | 1.60 | .50 |

Alexandre Herculano de Carvalho Araujo (1810-1877), historian, novelist, death centenary.

Maria Pia Bridge A351

4e, Arrival of first train, ceramic panel by Jorge Colaco, St. Bento railroad station.

**1977, Nov. 4 Litho. *Perf. 12x11½***

| | | | | |
|---|---|---|---|---|
| **1348** | A351 | 4e multicolored | .25 | .25 |
| **1349** | A351 | 10e multicolored | 2.25 | 1.25 |

Centenary of extension of railroad across Douro River.

Poveiro Bark A352

Coastal Fishing Boats: 3e, Do Mar bark. 4e, Nazaré bark. 7e, Algarve skiff. 10e, Xavega bark. 15e, Bateira de Buarcos.

**1977, Nov. 19 *Perf. 12***

| | | | | |
|---|---|---|---|---|
| **1350** | A352 | 2e multicolored | .40 | .25 |
| **1351** | A352 | 3e multicolored | .25 | .25 |
| **1352** | A352 | 4e multicolored | .25 | .25 |
| **1353** | A352 | 7e multicolored | .50 | .25 |
| **1354** | A352 | 10e multicolored | .80 | .40 |
| **1355** | A352 | 15e multicolored | 1.25 | .65 |
| *a.* | | Souv. sheet of 6, #1350-1355 | 4.00 | 4.00 |
| | | *Nos. 1350-1355 (6)* | 3.45 | 2.05 |

PORTUCALE 77, 2nd International Topical Exhibition. Oporto, Nov. 19-20. No. 1355a sold for 60e.

Nativity A353

Children's Drawings: 7e, Nativity. 10e, Holy Family, vert. 20e, Star and Christ Child, vert.

***Perf. 12x11½, 11½x12***

**1977, Dec. 12 Litho.**

| | | | | |
|---|---|---|---|---|
| **1356** | A353 | 4e multicolored | .25 | .25 |
| **1357** | A353 | 7e multicolored | .90 | .30 |
| **1358** | A353 | 10e multicolored | 1.00 | .45 |
| **1359** | A353 | 20e multicolored | 2.25 | .80 |
| | | *Nos. 1356-1359 (4)* | 4.40 | 1.80 |

Christmas 1977.

Old Desk and Computer — A354

Designs: Work tools, old and new — 50c, Medical. 1e, Household. 2e, Communications. 3e, Garment making. 4e, Office. 5e, Fishing craft. 5.50e, Weaving. 6e, Plows. 6.50e, Aviation. 7e, Printing. 8e, Carpentry. 8.50e, Potter's wheel. 9e, Photography. 10e, Saws. 12.50e, Compasses ('83). 16e, Mail processing ('83). 20e, Construction. 30e, Steel industry. 40e, Transportation. 50e, Chemistry. 100e, Shipbuilding. 250e, Telescopes.

**1978-83 Litho. *Perf. 12½***

**Size: 22x17mm**

| | | | | |
|---|---|---|---|---|
| **1360** | A354 | 50c multi | .25 | .25 |
| **1361** | A354 | 1e multi | .25 | .25 |
| **1362** | A354 | 2e multi | .25 | .25 |
| **1363** | A354 | 3e multi | .25 | .25 |
| **1364** | A354 | 4e multi | .25 | .25 |
| **1365** | A354 | 5e multi | .25 | .25 |
| **1366** | A354 | 5.50e multi | .25 | .25 |
| **1367** | A354 | 6e multi | .25 | .25 |
| **1368** | A354 | 6.50e multi | .25 | .25 |
| **1369** | A354 | 7e multi | .25 | .25 |
| **1370** | A354 | 8e multi | .25 | .25 |
| **1371** | A354 | 8.50e multi | .25 | .25 |
| **1372** | A354 | 9e multi | .25 | .25 |
| **1373** | A354 | 10e multi | .25 | .25 |
| **1373A** | A354 | 12.50e multi | .30 | .25 |
| **1373B** | A354 | 16e multi | .30 | .25 |

***Perf. 13½***

***Size: 31x22mm***

| | | | | |
|---|---|---|---|---|
| **1374** | A354 | 20e multi | .50 | .25 |
| **1375** | A354 | 30e multi | .60 | .30 |
| *a.* | | Incomplete arch | 1.00 | .30 |
| **1376** | A354 | 40e multi | .60 | .25 |
| **1377** | A354 | 50e multi | 1.00 | .25 |
| **1378** | A354 | 100e multi | 1.60 | .30 |
| **1379** | A354 | 250e multi | 4.25 | .60 |
| | | *Nos. 1360-1379 (22)* | 12.65 | 5.95 |

Red Mediterranean Soil — A355

Designs: 5e, Stone formation. 10e, Alluvial soil. 20e, Black soil.

**1978, Mar. 6 Litho. *Perf. 12***

| | | | | |
|---|---|---|---|---|
| **1380** | A355 | 4e multicolored | .25 | .25 |
| **1381** | A355 | 5e multicolored | .40 | .25 |
| **1382** | A355 | 10e multicolored | .80 | .45 |
| **1383** | A355 | 20e multicolored | 2.25 | .60 |
| | | *Nos. 1380-1383 (4)* | 3.70 | 1.55 |

Soil, a natural resource.

Street Crossing A356

Designs: 2e, Motorcyclist. 2.50e, Children in back seat of car. 5e, Hands holding steering wheel. 9e, Driving on country road. 12.50e, "Avoid drinking and driving."

**1978, Apr. 19 Litho. *Perf. 12***

| | | | | |
|---|---|---|---|---|
| **1384** | A356 | 1e multi | .25 | .25 |
| **1385** | A356 | 2e multi | .25 | .25 |
| **1386** | A356 | 2.50e multi | .55 | .25 |
| **1387** | A356 | 5e multi | 1.00 | .25 |
| **1388** | A356 | 9e multi | 1.90 | .50 |
| **1389** | A356 | 12.50e multi | 2.90 | 1.25 |
| | | *Nos. 1384-1389 (6)* | 6.85 | 2.75 |

Road safety campaign.

Roman Tower, Belmonte A357

Europa: 40e, Belém Monastery of Hieronymite monks (inside).

**1978, May 2**

| | | | | |
|---|---|---|---|---|
| **1390** | A357 | 10e multicolored | *1.75* | *.25* |
| **1391** | A357 | 40e multicolored | *3.75* | *.75* |
| *a.* | | Souv. sheet, 2 each #1390-1391 | *15.00* | *12.00* |

No. 1391a sold for 120e.

Trajan's Bridge — A358

Roman Tablet from Bridge — A359

**1978, June 14** **Litho.** ***Perf. 13½***

| | | | | |
|---|---|---|---|---|
| **1392** | A358 | 5e multicolored | .40 | .25 |
| **1393** | A359 | 20e multicolored | 2.50 | .80 |

1900th anniv. of Chaves (Aquae Flaviae).

Running A360

**1978, July 24** **Litho.** ***Perf. 12***

| | | | | |
|---|---|---|---|---|
| **1394** | A360 | 5e shown | .25 | .25 |
| **1395** | A360 | 10e Bicycling | .40 | .25 |
| **1396** | A360 | 12.50e Watersport | .85 | .50 |
| **1397** | A360 | 15e Soccer | .85 | .65 |
| | | *Nos. 1394-1397 (4)* | 2.35 | 1.65 |

Sport for all the people.

Pedro Nunes A361

Design: 20e, "Nonio" navigational instrument and diagram from "Tratado da Rumaçao do Globo."

**1978, Aug. 9** **Litho.** ***Perf. 12x11½***

| | | | | |
|---|---|---|---|---|
| **1398** | A361 | 5e multicolored | .25 | .25 |
| **1399** | A361 | 20e multicolored | 1.40 | .35 |

Nunes (1502-78), navigator and cosmographer.

Trawler, Frozen Fish Processing, Can of Sardines — A362

Fishing Industry: 9e, Deep-sea trawler, loading and unloading at dock. 12.50e, Trawler with radar and instruction in use of radar. 15e, Trawler with echo-sounding equipment, microscope and test tubes.

**1978, Sept. 16** **Litho.** ***Perf. 12x11½***

| | | | | |
|---|---|---|---|---|
| **1400** | A362 | 5e multi | .25 | .25 |
| **1401** | A362 | 9e multi | .65 | .25 |
| **1402** | A362 | 12.50e multi | 1.20 | .70 |
| **1403** | A362 | 15e multi | 1.75 | .90 |
| | | *Nos. 1400-1403 (4)* | 3.85 | 2.10 |

Natural resources.

Postrider A363

Designs: No. 1405, Carrier pigeon. No. 1406, Envelopes. No. 1407, Pen.

**1978, Oct. 30** **Litho.** ***Perf. 12***

| | | | | |
|---|---|---|---|---|
| **1404** | A363 | 5e yel & multi | .35 | .25 |
| **1405** | A363 | 5e bl gray & multi | .35 | .25 |
| **1406** | A363 | 5e grn & multi | .35 | .25 |
| **1407** | A363 | 5e red & multi | .35 | .25 |
| | | *Nos. 1404-1407 (4)* | 1.40 | 1.00 |

Introduction of Postal Code.

Human Figure, Flame Emblem A364

Design: 40e, Human figure pointing the way and flame emblem.

**1978, Dec. 7** **Litho.** ***Perf. 12***

| | | | | |
|---|---|---|---|---|
| **1408** | A364 | 14e multicolored | .50 | .30 |
| **1409** | A364 | 40e multicolored | 1.40 | .90 |
| *a.* | | Souv. sheet, 2 ea #1408-1409 | 5.50 | 6.25 |

Universal Declaration of Human Rights, 30th anniv. and 25th anniv. of European Declaration.

Sebastiao Magalhaes Lima — A365

**1978, Dec. 7**

| | | | | |
|---|---|---|---|---|
| **1410** | A365 | 5e multicolored | .30 | .25 |

Sebastiao Magalhaes Lima (1850-1928), lawyer, journalist, statesman.

Mail Boxes and Scale A366

Designs: 5e, Telegraph and condenser lens. 10e, Portugal Nos. 2-3 and postal card printing press, 1879. 14e, Book and bookcases, 1879, 1979.

**1978, Dec. 20**

| | | | | |
|---|---|---|---|---|
| **1411** | A366 | 4e multicolored | .25 | .25 |
| **1412** | A366 | 5e multicolored | .25 | .25 |
| **1413** | A366 | 10e multicolored | .90 | .25 |
| **1414** | A366 | 14e multicolored | 2.25 | 1.25 |
| *a.* | | Souv. sheet of 4, #1411-1414 | 5.00 | 5.00 |
| | | *Nos. 1411-1414 (4)* | 3.65 | 2.00 |

Centenary of Postal Museum and Postal Library; 125th anniversary of Portuguese stamps (10e). No. 1414a sold for 40e.

Emigrant at Railroad Station A367

Designs: 14e, Farewell at airport. 17e, Emigrant greeting child at railroad station.

**1979, Feb. 21** **Litho.** ***Perf. 12***

| | | | | |
|---|---|---|---|---|
| **1415** | A367 | 5e multicolored | .25 | .25 |
| **1416** | A367 | 14e multicolored | .70 | .35 |
| **1417** | A367 | 17e multicolored | 1.10 | .80 |
| | | *Nos. 1415-1417 (3)* | 2.05 | 1.40 |

Portuguese emigration.

Automobile Traffic — A368

Combat noise pollution: 5e, Pneumatic drill. 14e, Man with bull horn.

**1979, Mar. 14** ***Perf. 13½***

| | | | | |
|---|---|---|---|---|
| **1418** | A368 | 4e multicolored | .25 | .25 |
| **1419** | A368 | 5e multicolored | .55 | .25 |
| **1420** | A368 | 14e multicolored | 1.40 | .50 |
| | | *Nos. 1418-1420 (3)* | 2.20 | 1.00 |

NATO Emblem A369

**1979, Apr. 4** **Litho.** ***Perf. 12***

| | | | | |
|---|---|---|---|---|
| **1421** | A369 | 5e multicolored | .30 | .25 |
| **1422** | A369 | 50e multicolored | 2.50 | 1.60 |
| *a.* | | Souv. sheet, 2 ea #1421-1422 | 6.00 | 6.00 |

NATO, 30th anniv.

Mail Delivery, 16th Century A370

Europa: 40e, Mail delivery, 19th century.

**1979, Apr. 30** **Litho.** ***Perf. 12***

| | | | | |
|---|---|---|---|---|
| **1423** | A370 | 14e multicolored | *1.00* | *.30* |
| **1424** | A370 | 40e multicolored | *1.75* | *1.60* |
| *a.* | | Souv. sheet, 2 ea #1423-1424 | *8.00* | *6.00* |

Mother, Infant, Dove A371

Designs (IYC Emblem and): 5.50e, Children playing ball. 10e, Child in nursery school. 14e, Black and white boys.

**1979, June 1** **Litho.** ***Perf. 12x12½***

| | | | | |
|---|---|---|---|---|
| **1425** | A371 | 5.50e multi | .25 | .25 |
| **1426** | A371 | 6.50e multi | .30 | .25 |
| **1427** | A371 | 10e multi | .45 | .25 |
| **1428** | A371 | 14e multi | .90 | .65 |
| *a.* | | Souv. sheet of 4, #1425-1428 | 3.50 | 3.50 |
| | | *Nos. 1425-1428 (4)* | 1.90 | 1.40 |

Intl. Year of the Child. No. 1428a sold for 40e.

Salute to the Flag — A372

**1979, June 8**

| | | | | |
|---|---|---|---|---|
| **1429** | A372 | 6.50e multicolored | .35 | .25 |
| *a.* | | Souvenir sheet of 9 | 4.50 | 4.50 |

Portuguese Day.

Pregnant Woman A373

Designs: 17e, Boy sitting in a cage. 20e, Face, and hands using hammer.

**1979, June 6** **Litho.** ***Perf. 12x12½***

| | | | | |
|---|---|---|---|---|
| **1430** | A373 | 6.50e multi | .25 | .25 |
| **1431** | A373 | 17e multi | .65 | .50 |
| **1432** | A373 | 20e multi | .90 | .60 |
| | | *Nos. 1430-1432 (3)* | 1.80 | 1.35 |

Help for the mentally retarded.

Children Reading Book, UNESCO Emblem A374

17e, Teaching deaf child, and UNESCO emblem.

**1979, June 25**

| | | | | |
|---|---|---|---|---|
| **1433** | A374 | 6.50e multi | .30 | .25 |
| **1434** | A374 | 17e multi | 1.60 | .70 |

Intl. Bureau of Education, 50th anniv.

Water Cart, Brasiliana '79 Emblem A375

Brasiliana '79 Philatelic Exhibition: 5.50e, Wine sledge. 6.50e, Wine cart. 16e, Covered cart. 19e, Mogadouro cart. 20e, Sand cart.

**1979, Sept. 15** **Litho.** ***Perf. 12***

| | | | | |
|---|---|---|---|---|
| **1435** | A375 | 2.50e multi | .25 | .25 |
| **1436** | A375 | 5.50e multi | .25 | .25 |
| **1437** | A375 | 6.50e multi | .35 | .25 |
| **1438** | A375 | 16e multi | .80 | .55 |
| **1439** | A375 | 19e multi | 1.10 | .75 |
| **1440** | A375 | 20e multi | 1.20 | .30 |
| | | *Nos. 1435-1440 (6)* | 3.95 | 2.35 |

Antonio Jose de Almeida (1866-1929) A376

Republican Leaders: 6.50e, Afonso Costa (1871-1937). 10e, Teofilo Braga (1843-1924). 16e, Bernardino Machado (1851-1944). 19.50e, Joao Chagas (1863-1925). 20e, Elias Garcia (1830-1891).

**1979, Oct. 4** ***Perf. 12½x12***

| | | | | |
|---|---|---|---|---|
| **1441** | A376 | 5.50e multi | .25 | .25 |
| **1442** | A376 | 6.50e multi | .25 | .25 |
| **1443** | A376 | 10e multi | .45 | .25 |
| **1444** | A376 | 16e multi | .75 | .45 |
| **1445** | A376 | 19.50e multi | 1.25 | .80 |
| **1446** | A376 | 20e multi | 1.00 | .35 |
| | | *Nos. 1441-1446 (6)* | 3.95 | 2.35 |

See Nos. 1454-1459.

Red Cross and Family A377

20e, Doctor examining elderly man.

**1979, Oct. 26** *Perf. 12x12½*
**1447** A377 6.50e multi .30 .25
**1448** A377 20e multi 1.25 .40

National Health Service Campaign.

Holy Family, 17th Century Mosaic A378

Mosaics, Lisbon Tile Museum: 6.50e, Nativity, 16th century. 16e, Flight into Egypt, 18th century.

**1979, Dec. 5 Litho.** *Perf. 12x12½*
**1449** A378 5.50e multi .35 .25
**1450** A378 6.50e multi .35 .25
**1451** A378 16e multi .90 .70
*Nos. 1449-1451 (3)* 1.60 1.20

Christmas 1979.

Rotary International, 75th Anniversary — A379

**1980, Feb. 22** *Perf. 12x11½*
**1452** A379 16e shown 1.00 .45
**1453** A379 50e Emblem, torch 2.75 1.25

### Portrait Type of 1979

Leaders of the Republican Movement: 3.50e, Alvaro de Castro (1878-1928). 5.50e, Antonio Sergio (1883-1969). 6.50e, Norton de Matos (1867-1955). 11e, Jaime Cortesao (1884-1960). 16e, Teixeira Gomes (1860-1941). 20e, Jose Domingues dos Santos (1885-1958). Nos. 1454-1459 horizontal.

**1980, Mar. 19**
**1454** A376 3.50e multi .25 .25
**1455** A376 5.50e multi .25 .25
**1456** A376 6.50e multi .25 .25
**1457** A376 11e multi 1.40 .75
**1458** A376 16e multi .85 .50
**1459** A376 20e multi .90 .30
*Nos. 1454-1459 (6)* 3.90 2.30

### Europa Issue

Serpa Pinto (1864-1900), Explorer of Africa A380

60e, Vasco da Gama.

**1980, Apr. 14**
**1460** A380 16e shown *.70 .30*
**1461** A380 60e multicolored *2.00 1.00*
*a.* Souv. sheet, 2 each #1460-1461 *5.00 3.00*

Barn Owl A381

**1980, May 6 Litho.** *Perf. 12x11½*
**1462** A381 6.50e shown .25 .25
**1463** A381 16e Red fox .70 .30
**1464** A381 19.50e Timber wolf 1.00 .40
**1465** A381 20e Golden eagle 1.10 .35
*a.* Souv. sheet of 4, #1462-1465 3.75 3.25
*Nos. 1462-1465 (4)* 3.05 1.30

European Campaign for the Protection of Species and their Habitat (Lisbon Zoo animals); London 1980 International Stamp Exhibition, May 6-14.

Luiz Camoens (1524-80) A382

**Lithographed & Engraved**
**1980, June 9** *Perf. 11½x12*
**1466** A382 6.50e multi + label .40 .25
**1467** A382 20e multi + label .90 .75

Mendes Pinto and Chinese Men A383

**1980, June 30 Litho.** *Perf. 12x11½*
**1468** A383 6.50e shown .30 .25
**1469** A383 10e Battle at sea .90 .40

A Peregrinacao (The Peregrination,) by Fernao Mendes Pinto (1509-1583), written in 1580, published in 1614.

St. Vincent and Old Lisbon A384

Designs: 8e, Lantern Tower, Evora Cathedral. 11e, Jesus with top hat, Miranda do Douro Cathedral, and mountain. 16e, Our Lady of the Milk, Braga Cathedral, and Canicada Dam. 19.50e, Pulpit, Santa Cruz Monastery, Coimbra, and Aveiro River. 20e, Algarve chimney, and Rocha Beach.

**1980, Sept. 17 Litho.** *Perf. 12x12½*
**1470** A384 6.50e multi .30 .25
**1471** A384 8e multi .35 .25
**1472** A384 11e multi .80 .35
**1473** A384 16e multi 1.10 .55
**1474** A384 19.50e multi 1.50 .65
**1475** A384 20e multi 1.25 .40
*Nos. 1470-1475 (6)* 5.30 2.45

World Tourism Conf., Manila, Sept. 27.

Caravel, Lubrapex '80 Emblem A385

8e, Three-master Nau. 16e, Galleon. 19.50e, Paddle steam.

**1980, Oct. 18 Litho.** *Perf. 12x11½*
**1476** A385 6.50e shown .30 .25
**1477** A385 8e multicolored .60 .30
**1478** A385 16e multicolored 1.20 .45
**1479** A385 19.50e multicolored 1.75 .50
*a.* Souv. sheet of 4, #1476-1479 6.00 6.00
*Nos. 1476-1479 (4)* 3.85 1.50

Lubrapex '80 Stamp Exhib., Lisbon, Oct. 18-26.

Car Emitting Gas Fumes A386

**1980, Oct. 31**
**1480** A386 6.50e Light bulbs .25 .25
**1481** A386 16e shown 1.60 .55

Energy conservation.

Student, School and Sextant A387

**1980, Dec. 19 Litho.** *Perf. 12x11½*
**1482** A387 6.50e Founder, book, emblem .30 .25
**1483** A387 19.50e shown 1.40 .50

Lisbon Academy of Science bicentennial.

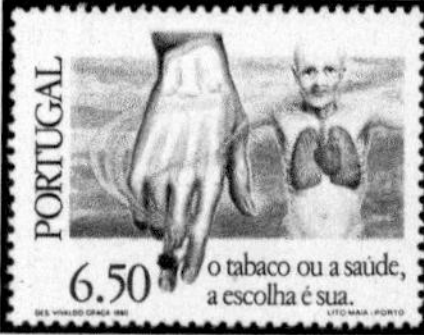

Man with Diseased Heart and Lungs, Hand Holding Cigarette A388

19.50e, Healthy man rejecting cigarette.

**1980, Dec. 19** *Perf. 13½*
**1484** A388 6.50e shown .30 .25
**1485** A388 19.50e multicolored 1.75 .80

Anti-smoking campaign.

Census Form and Houses A389

**1981, Jan. 28 Litho.** *Perf. 13½*
**1486** A389 6.50e Form, head .30 .25
**1487** A389 16e shown 1.40 .95

Fragata on Tejo River A390

8.50e, Rabelo, Douro River. 10e, Moliceiro, Aveiro River. 16e, Barco, Lima River. 19.50e, Carocho, Minho River. 20e, Varino, Tejo River.

**1981, Feb. 23 Litho.** *Perf. 12x12½*
**1488** A390 8e multicolored .25 .25
**1489** A390 8.50e multicolored .25 .25
**1490** A390 10e multicolored .45 .25
**1491** A390 16e multicolored .65 .45
**1492** A390 19.50e multicolored .75 .45
**1493** A390 20e multicolored .75 .35
*Nos. 1488-1493 (6)* 3.10 2.00

Rajola Tile, Valencia, 15th Century A391

Designs: No. 1495, Moresque tile, Coimbra 16th cent. No. 1496, Arms of Duke of Braganza, 1510. No. 1497, Pisanos design, 1595.

**1981 Litho.** *Perf. 11½x12*
**1494** A391 8.50e multi .75 .25
*a.* Miniature sheet of 6 4.50 5.00
**1495** A391 8.50e multi .75 .25
*a.* Miniature sheet of 6 4.50 4.50
**1496** A391 8.50e multi .75 .25
*a.* Miniature sheet of 6 4.50 4.50
**1497** A391 8.50e multi .75 .25
*a.* Miniature sheet of 6 4.50 4.50
*b.* Souv. sheet of 4, #1494-1497 5.00 5.00
*Nos. 1494-1497 (4)* 3.00 1.00

Issued: #1494, 3/16; #1495, 6/13; #1496, 8/28; #1497, 12/16. See #1528-1531, 1563-1566, 1593-1596, 1617-1620.

Perdigueiro A392

7e, Cao de agua. 8.50e, Serra de aires. 22e, Podengo. 22.50e, Castro laboreiro. 33.50e, Serra da estrela.

**1981, Mar. 16** *Perf. 12*
**1498** A392 7e multi .40 .25
**1499** A392 8.50e multi .40 .25
**1500** A392 15e shown 1.00 .25
**1501** A392 22e multi 1.10 .65
**1502** A392 25.50e multi 1.75 1.00
**1503** A392 33.50e multi 2.25 .65
*Nos. 1498-1503 (6)* 6.90 3.05

Portuguese Kennel Club, 50th anniversary.

Workers and Rainbow A393

25.50e, Rainbow, demonstration.

**1981, Apr. 30 Litho.** *Perf. 12x12½*
**1504** A393 8.50e shown .25 .25
**1505** A393 25.50e multi 1.25 .85

International Workers' Day.

### Europa Issue

Dancer in National Costume — A394

48e, Painted boat, horiz.

**1981, May 11** *Perf. 13½*
**1506** A394 22e shown *.80 .50*
**1507** A394 48e multi *1.60 1.25*
*a.* Souv. sheet, 2 ea #1506-1507 *6.00 4.00*

St. Anthony Writing A395

St. Anthony of Lisbon, 750th Anniversary of Death: 70e, Blessing people.

**1981, June 13** *Perf. 12x11½*
**1508** A395 8.50e multi .50 .25
**1509** A395 70e multi 3.00 1.75

500th Anniv. of King Joao II A396

27e, Joao II leading army.

**1981, Aug. 28** *Perf. 12x11½*
**1510** A396 8.50e shown .45 .25
**1511** A396 27e multi 2.00 .95

125th Anniv. of Portuguese Railroads — A397

Designs: Locomotives — 8.50e, Dom Luis, 1862. 19e, Pacific 500, 1925. 27e, ALCO 1500, 1948. 33.50e, BB 2600 ALSTHOM, '74.

**1981, Oct. 28 Litho.** *Perf. 12x11½*
**1512** A397 8.50e multi .65 .25
**1513** A397 19e multi 1.90 .90
**1514** A397 27e multi 1.90 1.00
**1515** A397 33.50e multi 2.75 .85
*Nos. 1512-1515 (4)* 7.20 3.00

Pearier Pump Fire Engine, 1856 — A398

8.50e, Ford, 1927. 27e, Renault, 1914. 33.50e, Snorkel, Ford 1978.

**1981, Nov. 18 Litho.** *Perf. 12x12½*
**1516** A398 7e shown .45 .25
**1517** A398 8.50e multi .65 .25
**1518** A398 27e multi 2.25 .95
**1519** A398 33.50e multi 2.90 .90
*Nos. 1516-1519 (4)* 6.25 2.35

A399

Christmas: Clay creches.

**1981, Dec. 16** *Perf. 12½x12*
**1520** A399 7e multi .45 .30
**1521** A399 8.50e multi .65 .25
**1522** A399 27e multi 2.10 1.40
*Nos. 1520-1522 (3)* 3.20 1.95

A400

8.50e, With animals. 27e, Building church.

**1982, Jan. 20 Litho.** *Perf. 12½x12*
**1523** A400 8.50e multi .35 .25
**1524** A400 27e multi 1.90 1.40

800th birth anniv. of St. Francis of Assisi.

Centenary of Figueira da Foz A401

10e, St. Catherine Fort. 19e, Tagus Bridge, ships.

**1982, Feb. 24 Litho.** *Perf. 13½*
**1525** A401 10e multi .45 .25
**1526** A401 19e multi 1.40 .85

25th Anniv. of European Economic Community A402

**1982, Feb. 24** *Perf. 12x11½*
**1527** A402 27e multi 1.25 .65
*a.* Souvenir sheet of 4 4.50 2.50

## Tile Type of 1981

Designs: No. 1528, Italo-Flemish pattern, 17th cent. No. 1529, Oriental fabric pattern altar frontal, 17th cent. No. 1530, Greek cross, 1630-1640. No. 1531, Blue and white design, Mother of God Convent, Lisbon, 1670.

**1982 Litho.** *Perf. 12x11½*
**1528** A391 10e multi .75 .25
*a.* Miniature sheet of 6 5.00 5.00
**1529** A391 10e multi .75 .25
*a.* Miniature sheet of 6 5.00 4.50
**1530** A391 10e multi .75 .25
*a.* Miniature sheet of 6 5.00 4.50
**1531** A391 10e red & blue .75 .25
*a.* Miniature sheet of 6 5.00 4.50
*b.* Souv. sheet of 4, #1528-1531 5.00 4.50
*Nos. 1528-1531 (4)* 3.00 1.00

Issued: No. 1528, Mar. 24; No. 1529, June 11; No. 1530, Sept. 22; No. 1531, Dec. 15.

A403

Major Sporting Events of 1982: 27e, Lisbon Sail. 33.50e, 25th Roller-hockey Championships, Lisbon and Barcelos, May 1-16. 50e, Intl. 470 Class World Championships, Cascais Bay. 75e, Espana '82 World Cup Soccer.

**1982, Mar. 24** *Perf. 12x12½*
**1532** A403 27e multi 1.25 .80
**1533** A403 33.50e multi 1.60 1.10
**1534** A403 50e multi 2.40 1.25
**1535** A403 75e multi 4.00 1.50
*Nos. 1532-1535 (4)* 9.25 4.65

A404

**1982, Apr. 14 Litho.** *Perf. 11½x12*
**1536** A404 10e Phone, 1882 .35 .25
**1537** A404 27e 1887 1.25 1.00

Telephone centenary.

Europa 1982 A405

Embassy of King Manuel to Pope Leo X, 1514.

**1982, May 3** *Perf. 12x11½*
**1538** A405 33.50e multi *1.50 .75*
*a.* Miniature sheet of 4 *6.00 4.00*

Visit of Pope John Paul II — A406

Designs: Pope John Paul and cathedrals.

**1982, May 13** *Perf. 14*
**1539** A406 10e Fatima .35 .25
**1540** A406 27e Sameiro 1.75 1.10
**1541** A406 33.50e Lisbon 1.90 1.00
*a.* Min. sheet, 2 each #1539-1541 7.50 7.50
*Nos. 1539-1541 (3)* 4.00 2.35

Tejo Estuary Nature Reserve Birds — A407

10e, Dunlin. 19e, Red-crested pochard. 27e, Greater flamingo. 33.50e, Black-winged stilt.

**1982, June 11** *Perf. 11½x12*
**1542** A407 10e multi .40 .25
**1543** A407 19e multi 1.25 .55
**1544** A407 27e multi 1.60 .80
**1545** A407 33.50e multi 1.75 .90
*Nos. 1542-1545 (4)* 5.00 2.50

PHILEXFRANCE '82 Stamp Exhibition, Paris, June 11-21.

TB Bacillus Centenary — A408

**1982, July 27** *Perf. 12x11½*
**1546** A408 27e Koch 1.25 1.00
**1547** A408 33.50e Virus, lungs 1.50 1.10

Don't Drink and Drive! — A409

**1982, Sept. 22** *Perf. 12*
**1548** A409 10e multicolored .50 .25

Boeing 747 A410

Lubrapex '82 Stamp Exhibition (Historic Flights): 10e, South Atlantic crossing, 1922. 19e, South Atlantic night crossing, 1927. 33.50e, Lisbon-Rio de Janeiro discount fare flights, 1960-1967. 50e, Portugal-Brazil service, 10th anniv.

**1982, Oct. 15** *Perf. 12x11½*
**1549** A410 10e Fairey III D MK2 .25 .25
**1550** A410 19e Dornier DO 1.00 .70
**1551** A410 33.50e DC-7C 1.50 .70
**1552** A410 50e shown 1.75 1.00
*a.* Souv. sheet of 4, #1549-1552 4.50 4.50
*Nos. 1549-1552 (4)* 4.50 2.65

Marques de Pombal, Statesman, 200th Anniv. of Death — A411

**1982, Nov. 24 Litho.** *Perf. 12x11½*
**1553** A411 10e multicolored .50 .25

75th Anniv. of Port Authority of Lisbon — A412

**1983, Jan. 5** *Perf. 12½*
**1554** A412 10e Ships .50 .25

French Alliance Centenary A413

**1983, Jan. 5** *Perf. 12x11½*
**1555** A413 27e multicolored 1.25 .70

Export Effort A414

**1983, Jan. 28**
**1556** A414 10e multicolored .50 .25

World Communications Year — A415

**1983, Feb. 23 Litho.** *Perf. 11½x12*
**1557** A415 10e blue & multi .50 .25
**1558** A415 33.50e lt brown & multi 1.60 1.00

Naval Uniforms and Ships — A416

12.50e, Midshipman, 1782, Vasco da Gama. 25e, Sailor, 1845, Estefania. 30e, Sergeant, 1900, Adamastor. 37.50e, Midshipman, 1892, Comandante Joao Belo.

**1983, Feb. 23** *Perf. 13½*
**1559** A416 12.50e multi .55 .25
**1560** A416 25e multi 1.40 .35
**1561** A416 30e multi 1.60 .50
**1562** A416 37.50e multi 2.00 .70
*a.* Bklt. pane of 4, #1559-1562 5.75
*Nos. 1559-1562 (4)* 5.55 1.80

See Nos. 1589-1592.

### Tile Type of 1981

No. 1563, Hunting scene, 1680. No. 1564, Birds, 18th cent. No. 1565, Flowers and Birds, 18th cent. No. 1566, Figurative tile, 18th cent.

**1983** ***Perf. 12x11½***
**1563** A391 12.50e multi .85 .25
*a.* Miniature sheet of 6 5.25 5.25
**1564** A391 12.50e multi .85 .25
*a.* Miniature sheet of 6 5.00 5.00
**1565** A391 12.50e multi .85 .25
*a.* Miniature sheet of 6 5.00 5.00
**1566** A391 12.50e multi .85 .25
*a.* Miniature sheet of 6 5.00 5.00
*b.* Souv. sheet of 4, #1563-1566 4.50 4.50
*Nos. 1563-1566 (4)* 3.40 1.00

Issued: No. 1563, Mar. 16; No. 1564, June 16; No. 1565, Oct. 19; No. 1566, Nov. 23.

17th European Arts and Sciences Exhibition, Lisbon — A417

Portuguese Discoveries and Renaissance Europe: 11e, Helmet, 16th cent. 12.50e, Astrolabe. 25e, Ships, Flemish tapestry. 30e, Column capital, 12th cent. 37.50e, Hour glass. 40e, Chinese panel painting.

**1983, Apr. 6**
**1567** A417 11e multi .40 .25
**1568** A417 12.50e multi .55 .25
**1569** A417 25e multi 1.25 .55
**1570** A417 30e multi 1.50 .55
**1571** A417 37.50e multi 1.60 .85
**1572** A417 40e multi 1.75 .80
*a.* Souv. sheet of 6, #1567-1572 9.00 9.00
*Nos. 1567-1572 (6)* 7.05 3.25

### Europa Issue

Antonio Egas Moniz (1874-1955), Cerebral Angiography and Pre-frontal Leucotomy Pioneer — A418

**1983, May 5** **Litho.** ***Perf. 12½***
**1573** A418 37.50e multi *1.50 .60*
*a.* Souvenir sheet of 4 *6.00 4.00*

European Conference of Ministers of Transport — A419

**1983, May 16**
**1574** A419 30e multi 2.00 .65

Endangered Sea Mammals — A420

**1983, July 29** **Litho.** ***Perf. 12x11½***
**1575** A420 12.50e Sea wolf .75 .25
**1576** A420 30e Dolphin 1.75 .45
**1577** A420 37.50e Killer whale 2.40 1.10
**1578** A420 80e Humpback whale 4.00 1.00
*a.* Souv. sheet of 4, #1575-1578 11.00 11.00
*Nos. 1575-1578 (4)* 8.90 2.80

BRASILIANA '83 Intl. Stamp Exhibition, Rio de Janeiro, July 29-Aug. 7.

600th Anniv. of Revolution of 1383 — A421

12.50e, Death of Joao Fernandes Andeiro. 30e, Rebellion.

**1983, Sept. 14** ***Perf. 13½***
**1579** A421 12.50e multi .70 .25
**1580** A421 30e multi 2.25 1.10

First Manned Balloon Flight A422

Designs: 16e, Bartolomeu Lourenco de Gusmao, Passarola flying machine. 51e, Montgolfier Balloon, first flight.

**1983, Nov. 9** **Litho.** ***Perf. 12x11½***
**1581** A422 16e multicolored .65 .25
**1582** A422 51e multicolored 1.60 .85

Christmas 1983 — A423

Stained Glass Windows, Monastery at Batalha: 12.50e, Adoration of the Magi. 30e, Flight to Egypt.

**1983, Nov. 23** ***Perf. 12½***
**1583** A423 12.50e multi .65 .25
**1584** A423 30e multi 2.00 .85

Lisbon Zoo Centenary — A424

**1984, Jan. 18** **Litho.** ***Perf. 12x11½***
**1585** A424 16e Siberian tigers 1.40 .25
**1586** A424 16e White rhinoceros 1.40 .25
**1587** A424 16e Damalisco Albifronte 1.40 .25
**1588** A424 16e Cheetahs 1.40 .25
*a.* Strip of 4, #1585-1588 6.00 2.50

### Military Type of 1983

Air Force Dress Uniforms and Planes: 16e, 1954; Hawker Hurricane II, 1943. 35e, 1960; Republic F-84G Thunderjet. 40e, Paratrooper, 1966; 2502 Nord Noratlas, 1960. 51e, 1966; Corsair II, 1982.

**1984, Feb. 5** **Litho.** ***Perf. 13½***
**1589** A416 16e multi .40 .25
**1590** A416 35e multi 1.60 .55
**1591** A416 40e multi 1.60 .60
**1592** A416 51e multi 2.10 .85
*a.* Bklt. pane of 4, #1589-1592 11.00
*Nos. 1589-1592 (4)* 5.70 2.25

### Tile Type of 1981

Design: No. 1593, Royal arms, 19th cent. No. 1594, Pombal Palace wall tile, 19th cent. No. 1595, Facade covering, 19th cent. No. 1596, Grasshoppers, by Rafael Bordallo Pinhiero, 19th cent.

**1984, Mar. 8** **Litho.** ***Perf. 12x11½***
**1593** A391 16e multi .85 .25
*a.* Miniature sheet of 6 5.00 4.00
**1594** A391 16e multi .85 .25
*a.* Miniature sheet of 6 5.00 4.00
**1595** A391 16e multi .85 .25
*a.* Miniature sheet of 6 5.00 4.00
**1596** A391 16e multi .85 .25
*a.* Miniature sheet of 6 5.00 4.00
*b.* Souv. sheet of 4, #1593-1596 6.00 4.50
*Nos. 1593-1596 (4)* 3.40 1.00

Issued: No. 1593, Mar. 8; No. 1594, July 18; No. 1595, Aug. 3; No. 1596, Oct. 17.

25th Lisbon Intl. Fair, May 9-13 A425

Events: 40e, World Food Day. 51e, 15th Rehabilitation Intl. World Congress, Lisbon, June 4-8, vert.

**1984, Apr. 3**
**1597** A425 35e multicolored 1.50 .50
**1598** A425 40e multicolored 1.60 .65
**1599** A425 51e multicolored 2.00 .85
*Nos. 1597-1599 (3)* 5.10 2.00

April 25th Revolution, 10th Anniv. — A426

**1984, Apr. 25** ***Perf. 13½***
**1600** A426 16e multicolored 1.10 .25

Europa (1959-84) A427

**1984, May 2** ***Perf. 12x11½***
**1601** A427 51e multicolored *1.50 .80*
*a.* Souvenir sheet of 4 *6.00 4.00*

LUBRAPEX '84 and Natl. Early Art Museum Centenary — A428

Paintings: 16e, Nun, 15th cent. 40e, St. John, by Master of the Retable of Santiago, 16th cent. 51e, View of Lisbon, 17th cent. 66e, Cabeca de Jovem, by Domingos Sequeira, 19th cent.

**1984, May 9** **Litho.** ***Perf. 12x11½***
**1602** A428 16e multicolored .55 .25
**1603** A428 40e multicolored 1.75 .55
**1604** A428 51e multicolored 2.50 .90
**1605** A428 66e multicolored 2.75 1.10
*a.* Souv. sheet of 4, #1602-1605 8.00 8.00
*Nos. 1602-1605 (4)* 7.55 2.80

1984 Summer Olympics A429

**1984, June 5**
**1606** A429 35e Fencing 1.25 .30
**1607** A429 40e Gymnastics 1.75 .55
**1608** A429 51e Running 2.40 .95
**1609** A429 80e Pole vault 2.60 1.00
*Nos. 1606-1609 (4)* 8.00 2.80

### Souvenir Sheet

**1610** A429 100e Hurdles 7.00 7.00

Historical Events — A430

Designs: 16e, Gil Eanes, explorer who reached west coast of Africa, 1434. 51e, King Peter I of Brazil and IV of Portugal.

**1984, Sept. 24** ***Perf. 12x11½***
**1611** A430 16e multicolored .45 .25
**1612** A430 51e multicolored 2.00 .90

See Brazil No. 1954.

Infantry Grenadier, 1740 — A431

46e, 5th Cavalry Regiment Officer, 1810. 60e, Artillery Corporal, 1892. 100e, Engineering Soldier, 1985.

**1985, Jan. 23** **Litho.** ***Perf. 13½***
**1613** A431 20e multi .45 .25
**1614** A431 46e multi 2.10 .55
**1615** A431 60e multi 2.25 .70
**1616** A431 100e multi 2.60 1.10
*a.* Bklt. pane of 4, #1613-1616 8.50
*Nos. 1613-1616 (4)* 7.40 2.60

### Tile Type of 1981

Designs: No. 1617, Tile from entrance hall of Lisbon's Faculdade de Letras, by Jorge Barradas, 20th cent.; No. 1618, Explorer and sailing ship, detail from tile panel by Maria Keil, Avenida Infante Santo, Lisbon; No. 1619, Profile and key, detail from a 20th century tile mural by Querubim Lapa; No. 1620, Geometric designs and flowers, by Manuel Cargaleiro.

**1985** **Litho.** ***Perf. 12x11½***
**1617** A391 20e multicolored .85 .25
*a.* Miniature sheet of 6 5.00 5.00
**1618** A391 20e multicolored .85 .25
*a.* Miniature sheet of 6 5.00 5.00
**1619** A391 20e multicolored .85 .25
*a.* Miniature sheet of 6 5.00 5.00
**1620** A391 20e multicolored .85 .25
*a.* Miniature sheet of 6 5.00 5.00
*b.* Souv. sheet of 4, #1617-1620 5.00 5.00
*Nos. 1617-1620 (4)* 3.40 1.00

Issued: No. 1617, Feb. 13; No. 1618, June 11; No. 1619, Aug. 20; No. 1620, Nov. 15.

Kiosks — A432

**1985, Mar. 19** **Litho.** ***Perf. 11½x12***
**1621** A432 20e Green kiosk 1.00 .25
**1622** A432 20e Red kiosk 1.00 .25
**1623** A432 20e Gray kiosk 1.00 .25
**1624** A432 20e Blue kiosk 1.00 .25
*a.* Strip of 4, #1621-1624 5.00

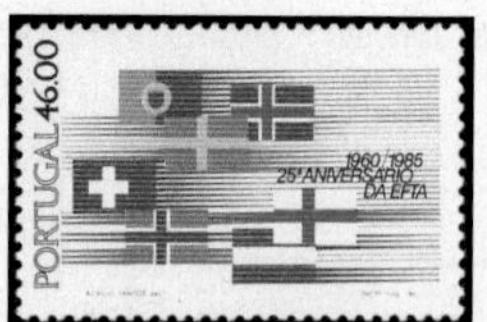


25th Anniv., European Free Trade Association — A433

**1985, Apr. 10** **Litho.** ***Perf. 12x11½***
**1625** A433 46e Flags of members 1.40 .55

Intl. Youth Year A434

60e, Heads of boy and girl.

**1985, Apr. 10** **Litho.**

**1626** A434 60e multicolored 1.25 .80

Europa 1985-Music A435

60e, Woman playing tambourine.

**1985, May 6** **Litho.** ***Perf. 11½x12***

**1627** A435 60e multicolored *1.75* *1.00*
*a.* Souvenir sheet of 4 *7.50* *4.00*

Historic Anniversaries — A436

20e, King John I at the Battle of Aljubarrota, 1385. 46e, Queen Leonor (1458-1525) founding the Caldas da Rainha Hospital. 60e, Cartographer Pedro Reinel, earliest Portuguese map, c. 1483.

**1985, July 5** **Litho.** ***Perf. 12x11½***

**1628** A436 20e multicolored .60 .25
**1629** A436 46e multicolored 1.90 .70
**1630** A436 60e multicolored 2.00 .95
*Nos. 1628-1630 (3)* 4.50 1.90

See Nos. 1678-1680.

Traditional Architecture A437

50c, Saloia, Estremadura. 1e, Beira interior. 1.50e, Ribatejo. 2.50e, Transmontanas. 10e, Minho and Douro Litoral. 20e, Farm house, Minho. 22.50e, Alentejo. 25e, African Sitio, Algarve. 27e, Beira Interior. 29e, Hill country. 30e, Algarve. 40e, Beira Interior. 50e, Private home, Beira Litoral. 55e, Tras-os-Montes. 60e, Beira Litoral. 70e, Estremadura Sul and Alentejo. 80e, Estremadura. 90e, Minho. 100e, Adobe Monte, Alentejo. 500e, Algarve.

**1985-89** **Litho.** ***Perf. 12***

**1631** A437 50c multi .25 .25
**1632** A437 1e multi .25 .25
**1633** A437 1.50e multi .25 .25
**1634** A437 2.50e multi .25 .25
**1635** A437 10e multi .25 .25
**1636** A437 20e multi .25 .25
**1637** A437 22.50e multi .25 .25
**1638** A437 25e multi .30 .25
**1639** A437 27e multi .45 .25
**1640** A437 29e multi .45 .25
**1641** A437 30e multi .45 .25
**1642** A437 40e multi .55 .25
**1643** A437 50e multi .65 .25
**1644** A437 55e multi .65 .25
**1645** A437 60e multi .85 .25
**1646** A437 70e multi .90 .25
**1647** A437 80e multi .95 .35
**1648** A437 90e multi 1.10 .35
**1649** A437 100e multi 1.40 .35
**1650** A437 500e multi 5.50 .75
*Nos. 1631-1650 (20)* 15.95 5.80

Issued: 20e, 25e, 50e, 100e, 8/20; 2.50e, 22.50e, 80e, 90e, 3/10/86; 10e, 40e, 60e, 70e, 3/6/87; 1.50e, 27e, 30e, 55e, 3/15/88; 50c, 1e, 29e, 500e, 3/8/89.

Aquilino Ribeiro (1885-1963), Author — A438

46e, Fernando Pessoa (1888-1935), poet.

**1985, Oct. 2** **Litho.** ***Perf. 12***

**1651** A438 20e multicolored .65 .25
**1652** A438 46e multicolored 1.25 .60

Natl. Parks and Reserves A439

20e, Berlenga Island. 40e, Estrela Mountain Chain. 46e, Boquilobo Marsh. 80e, Formosa Lagoon. 100e, St. Jacinto Dunes.

**1985, Oct. 25**

**1653** A439 20e multi .45 .25
**1654** A439 40e multi 1.40 .55
**1655** A439 46e multi 2.10 .80
**1656** A439 80e multi 2.40 .85
*Nos. 1653-1656 (4)* 6.35 2.45

**Souvenir Sheet**

**1657** A439 100e multi 7.00 5.00

ITALIA '85.

Christmas 1985 — A440

Illuminated codices from The Prayer Times Book, Book of King Manuel, 1517-1538.

**1985, Nov. 15** ***Perf. 11½x12***

**1658** A440 20e The Nativity .50 .25
**1659** A440 46e Adoration of the Magi 1.75 .65

Postrider A441

**1985, Dec. 13** **Litho.** ***Perf. 13½***

**1660** A441 A(22.50e) lt yel grn & dp yel grn .80 .25

See No. 1938 for another stamp with postrider inscribed "Serie A."

Flags of EEC Member Nations A442

Design: 57.50e, Map of EEC, flags.

**1986, Jan. 7** **Litho.** ***Perf. 12***

**1661** A442 20e multi .50 .25
**1662** A442 57.50e multi 2.00 .80
*a.* Souv. sheet, 2 ea #1661-1662 6.00 2.50

Admission of Portugal and Spain to the European Economic Community, Jan. 1. See Spain Nos. 2463-2466.

No. 1662a contains 2 alternating pairs of Nos. 1661-1662.

Castles A443

**1986, Feb. 18** **Litho.** ***Perf. 12***

**1663** A443 22.50e Beja .75 .25
*a.* Booklet pane of 4 3.50
**1664** A443 22.50e Feira .75 .25
*a.* Booklet pane of 4 3.50

**1986, Apr. 10**

**1665** A443 22.50e Guimaraes .75 .25
*a.* Booklet pane of 4 3.50
**1666** A443 22.50e Braganca .75 .25
*a.* Booklet pane of 4 3.50

**1986, Sept. 18**

**1667** A443 22.50e Montemor-o-Velho .75 .25
*a.* Booklet pane of 4 3.50
**1668** A443 22.50e Belmonte .75 .25
*a.* Booklet pane of 4 3.50
*Nos. 1663-1668 (6)* 4.50 1.50

See Nos. 1688-1695, 1723-1726.

Intl. Peace Year A445

**1986, Feb. 18** **Litho.** ***Perf. 12***

**1669** A445 75e multicolored 2.00 1.00

Automobile Centenary — A446

**1986, Apr. 10** **Litho.** ***Perf. 12***

**1670** 22.50e 1886 Benz .90 .25
**1671** 22.50e 1886 Daimler .90 .25
*a.* A446 Pair, #1670-1671 2.25 2.25

Europa 1986 A447

**1986, May 5** **Litho.**

**1672** A447 68.50e Shad 3.00 1.00
*a.* Souvenir sheet of 4 15.00 6.00

Horse Breeds A448

**1986, May 22** **Litho.** ***Perf. 12***

**1673** A448 22.50e Alter .55 .25
**1674** A448 47.50e Lusitano 1.75 .70
**1675** A448 52.50e Garrano 2.25 .90
**1676** A448 68.50e Sorraia 2.60 .95
*Nos. 1673-1676 (4)* 7.15 2.80

**Souvenir Sheet**

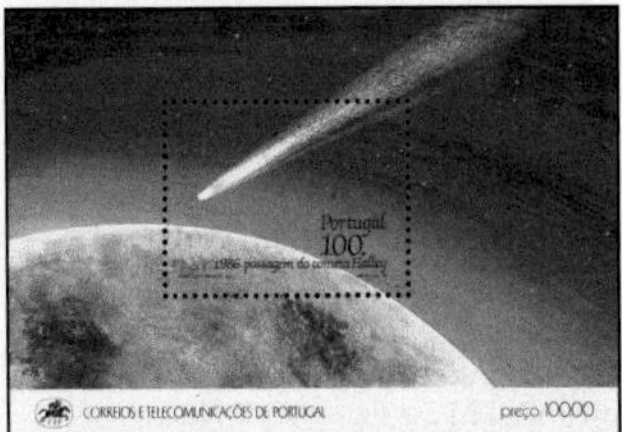


Halley's Comet — A449

**1986, June 24**

**1677** A449 100e multi 11.00 7.50

**Anniversaries Type of 1985**

Designs: 22.50e, Diogo Cao, explorer, heraldic pillar erected at Cape Lobo, 1484, 1st expedition. No. 1679, Manuel Passos, Corinthian column. No. 1680, Joao Baptista Ribeiro, painter, Oporto Academy director, c. 1836, and musicians.

**1986, Aug. 28** **Litho.**

**1678** A436 22.50e multi .50 .25
**1679** A436 52.50e multi 1.40 .70
**1680** A436 52.50e multi 1.40 .70
*Nos. 1678-1680 (3)* 3.30 1.65

Diogo Cao's voyages, 500th anniv. Academies of Fine Art, 150th anniv.

Stamp Day — A450

Natl. Guard, 75th Anniv. — A451

Order of Engineers, 50th Anniv. — A452

No. 1681, Postal card, 100th anniv.

**1986, Oct. 24** **Litho.**

**1681** A450 22.50e multi .85 .25
**1682** A451 47.50e multi 1.50 .65
**1683** A452 52.50e multi 1.50 .70
*Nos. 1681-1683 (3)* 3.85 1.60

Watermills A453

**1986, Nov. 7**

**1684** A453 22.50e Duoro .50 .25
**1685** A453 47.50e Coimbra 1.25 .85
**1686** A453 52.50e Gerez 1.75 .90
**1687** A453 90e Braga 2.75 .80
*a.* Souv. sheet of 4, #1684-1687 10.00 7.50
*Nos. 1684-1687 (4)* 6.25 2.80

LUBRAPEX '86. #1687a issued Nov. 21.

### Castle Type of 1986

**1987-88** **Litho.**

| | | | |
|---|---|---|---|
| **1688** | A443 25e Silves | .75 | .25 |
| *a.* | Booklet pane of 4 | 3.50 | |
| **1689** | A443 25e Evora Monte | .75 | .25 |
| *a.* | Booklet pane of 4 | 3.50 | |
| **1690** | A443 25e Leiria | .75 | .25 |
| *a.* | Booklet pane of 4 | 3.50 | |
| **1691** | A443 25e Trancoso | .75 | .25 |
| *a.* | Booklet pane of 4 | 3.50 | |
| **1692** | A443 25e St. George | .75 | .25 |
| *a.* | Booklet pane of 4 | 3.50 | |
| **1693** | A443 25e Marvao | .75 | .25 |
| *a.* | Booklet pane of 4 | 3.50 | |
| **1694** | A443 27e Fernando's Walls of Oporto | .75 | .25 |
| *a.* | Booklet pane of 4 | 3.50 | |
| **1695** | A443 27e Almourol | .75 | .25 |
| *a.* | Booklet pane of 4 | 3.50 | |
| | *Nos. 1688-1695 (8)* | 6.00 | 2.00 |

Issued: #1688-1689, 1/16; #1690-1691, 4/10; #1692-1693, 9/15; #1694-1695, 1/19/88.

Natl. Tourism Organization, 75th Anniv. — A454

25e, Beach houses, Tocha. 57e, Boats, Espinho. 98e, Chafariz Fountain, Arraioles.

**1987, Feb. 10** **Litho.** ***Perf. 12***

| | | | |
|---|---|---|---|
| **1696** | A454 25e multicolored | .50 | .25 |
| **1697** | A454 57e multicolored | 2.10 | .90 |
| **1698** | A454 98e multicolored | 2.75 | .85 |
| | *Nos. 1696-1698 (3)* | 5.35 | 2.00 |

European Nature Conservation Year — A455

57e, Hands, flower, map. 74.50e, Hands, star, rainbow.

**1987, Mar. 20** ***Perf. 12x12½***

| | | | |
|---|---|---|---|
| **1699** | A455 25e shown | .50 | .25 |
| **1700** | A455 57e multicolored | 1.50 | .75 |
| **1701** | A455 74.50e multicolored | 2.00 | .85 |
| | *Nos. 1699-1701 (3)* | 4.00 | 1.85 |

Europa 1987 A456

Modern architecture: Bank Borges and Irmao Agency, 1986, Vila do Conde.

**1987, May 5** **Litho.** ***Perf. 12***

| | | | |
|---|---|---|---|
| **1702** | A456 74.50e multi | *1.75* | *1.00* |
| *a.* | Souvenir sheet of 4 | *7.00* | *6.00* |

A457

Lighthouses

**1987, June 12** ***Perf. 11½x12***

| | | | |
|---|---|---|---|
| **1703** | A457 25e Aveiro | 1.00 | .25 |
| **1704** | A457 25e Berlenga | 1.00 | .25 |
| **1705** | A457 25e Cape Mondego | 1.00 | .25 |
| **1706** | A457 25e Cape St. Vincente | 1.00 | .25 |
| *a.* | Strip of 4, #1703-1706 | 5.00 | 5.00 |

A458

**1987, Aug. 27** **Litho.** ***Perf. 12***

| | | | |
|---|---|---|---|
| **1707** | A458 74.50e multi | 2.00 | .75 |

Amadeo de Souza-Cardoso (1887-1919), painter.

Portguese Royal Library, Rio de Janeiro, 150th anniv. A459

**1987, Aug. 27** ***Perf. 12x11½***

| | | | |
|---|---|---|---|
| **1708** | A459 125e multicolored | 2.25 | 1.00 |

Paper Currency of Portugal, 300th Anniv. A460

**1987, Aug. 27** ***Perf. 12x11½***

| | | | |
|---|---|---|---|
| **1709** | A460 100e multicolored | 2.00 | .75 |

Voyages of Bartolomeu Dias (d. 1499), 500th Anniv. — A461

No. 1710, Departing from Lisbon, 1487. No. 1711, Discovering the African Coast, 1488.

**1987, Aug. 27** ***Perf. 12x11½***

| | | | |
|---|---|---|---|
| **1710** | 25e multicolored | 1.00 | .25 |
| **1711** | 25e multicolored | 1.00 | .25 |
| *a.* | A461 Pair, #1710-1711 | 3.00 | 2.00 |

No. 1711a has continuous design.
See Nos. 1721-1722.

Souvenir Sheet

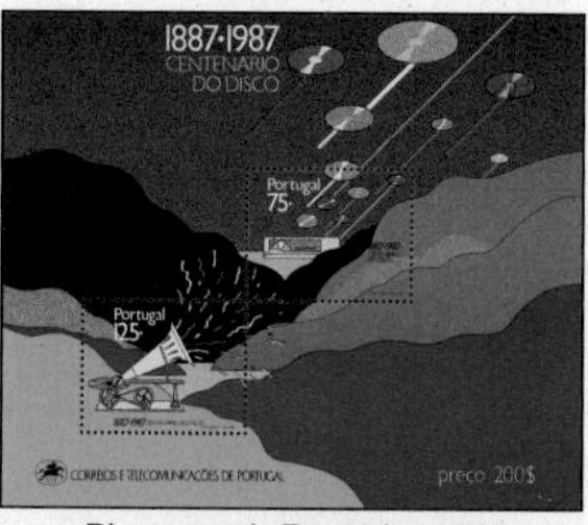


Phonograph Record, 100th Anniv. — A462

**1987, Oct. 9** **Litho.** ***Perf. 12***

| | | | |
|---|---|---|---|
| **1712** | A462 Sheet of 2 | 9.00 | 7.00 |
| *a.* | 75e Compact-disc player | 3.25 | 2.90 |
| *b.* | 125e Gramophone | 5.00 | 4.50 |

Christmas A463

Various children's drawings, Intl. Year of the Child emblem — 25e, Angels, magi, tree. 57e, Friendship circle. 74.50e, Santa riding dove.

**1987, Nov. 6**

| | | | |
|---|---|---|---|
| **1713** | A463 25e multi | .60 | .25 |
| **1714** | A463 57e multi | 1.60 | .70 |
| **1715** | A463 74.50e multi | 2.00 | 1.00 |
| *a.* | Souv. sheet of 3, #1713-1715 | 5.00 | 5.00 |
| | *Nos. 1713-1715 (3)* | 4.20 | 1.95 |

World Wildlife Fund A464

Lynx, Lynx pardina.

**1988, Feb. 3** **Litho.** ***Perf. 12***

| | | | |
|---|---|---|---|
| **1716** | A464 27e Stalking | 1.25 | .50 |
| **1717** | A464 27e Carrying prey | 1.25 | .50 |
| **1718** | A464 27e Two adults | 1.25 | .50 |
| **1719** | A464 27e Adult, young | 1.25 | .50 |
| *a.* | Strip of 4, Nos. 1716-1719 | 7.50 | 5.00 |

Printed in a continuous design.

Journey of Pero da Covilha to the East, 500th Anniv. A465

**1988, Feb. 3**

| | | | |
|---|---|---|---|
| **1720** | A465 105e multi | 2.50 | .95 |

### Bartolomeu Dias Type of 1987

Discovery of the link between the Atlantic and Indian Oceans by Dias, 500th Anniv.: No. 1721, Tidal wave, ship. No. 1722, Henricus Martelus Germanus's map (1489), picturing the African coast and linking the two oceans.

**1988, Feb. 3**

| | | | |
|---|---|---|---|
| **1721** | A461 27e multi | .85 | .25 |
| **1722** | A461 27e multi | .85 | .25 |
| *a.* | Bklt. pane of 4, Nos. 1710-1711, 1721-1722 | 6.00 | |
| *b.* | Pair, #1721-1722 | 1.75 | 1.75 |

No. 1722b has continuous design.

### Castle Type of 1986

No. 1723, Vila Nova de Cerveira. No. 1724, Palmela.

**1988, Mar. 15** **Litho.** ***Perf. 12***

| | | | |
|---|---|---|---|
| **1723** | A443 27e multicolored | .75 | .25 |
| *a.* | Bklt. pane of 4 | 3.50 | |
| **1724** | A443 27e multicolored | .75 | .25 |
| *a.* | Bklt. pane of 4 | 3.50 | |

**1988, July 1**

| | | | |
|---|---|---|---|
| **1725** | A443 27e Chaves | .75 | .25 |
| *a.* | Bklt. pane of 4 | 3.50 | |
| **1726** | A443 27e Penedono | .75 | .25 |
| *a.* | Bklt. pane of 4 | 3.50 | |
| | *Nos. 1723-1726 (4)* | 3.00 | 1.00 |

Europa 1988 A466

Transportation: Mail coach, Lisbon-Oporto route, 1855-1864.

**1988, Apr. 21** **Litho.** ***Perf. 12***

| | | | |
|---|---|---|---|
| **1735** | A466 80e multi | *2.50* | *1.00* |
| *a.* | Souv. sheet of 4 | *10.00* | *4.00* |

Jean Monnet (1888-1979), Economist — A467

**1988, May 9** **Litho.**

| | | | |
|---|---|---|---|
| **1736** | A467 60e multi | 1.25 | .55 |

Souvenir Sheet

National Heritage (Patrimony) — A468

Design: 150e, Belvedere of Cordovil House and Fountain of Porta de Moura reflected in the Garcia de Resende balcony window, Evora, 16th cent.

**1988, May 13** ***Perf. 13½x12½***

| | | | |
|---|---|---|---|
| **1737** | A468 150e multi | 7.00 | 7.00 |

No. 1737 has inscribed margin picturing LUBRAPEX '88 and UNESCO emblems.

20th Cent. Paintings by Portuguese Artists — A469

Designs: 27e, *Viola*, c. 1916, by Amadeo de Souza-Cardoso (1887-1918). 60e, *Jugglers and Tumblers Do Not Fall*, 1949, by Jose de Almada Negreiros (1893-1970). 80e, *Still-life with Guitar*, c. 1940, by Eduardo Viana (1881-1967).

**1988, Aug. 23** **Litho.** ***Perf. 11½x12***

| | | | |
|---|---|---|---|
| **1738** | A469 27e multi | .50 | .25 |
| **1739** | A469 60e multi | 1.50 | .70 |
| **1740** | A469 80e multi | 1.75 | .85 |
| *a.* | Min. sheet of 3, #1738-1740 | 5.00 | 5.00 |
| | *Nos. 1738-1740 (3)* | 3.75 | 1.80 |

See Nos. 1748-1750, 1754-1765.

1988 Summer Olympics, Seoul A470

**1988, Sept. 16** **Litho.** ***Perf. 12x11½***

| | | | |
|---|---|---|---|
| **1741** | A470 27e Archery | .45 | .25 |
| **1742** | A470 55e Weight lifting | 1.25 | .75 |
| **1743** | A470 60e Judo | 1.40 | .80 |
| **1744** | A470 80e Tennis | 2.10 | .80 |
| | *Nos. 1741-1744 (4)* | 5.20 | 2.60 |

### Souvenir Sheet

| | | | |
|---|---|---|---|
| **1745** | A470 200e Yachting | 9.00 | 7.00 |

Remains of the Roman Civilization in Portugal A471

Mozaics: 27e, "Winter Image," detail of *Mosaic of the Four Seasons,* limestone and glass, 3rd cent., House of the Waterworks, Coimbra. 80e, *Fish in Marine Water,* limestone, 3rd-4th cent., cover of a tank wall, public baths, Faro.

**1988, Oct. 18 Litho. *Perf. 12***

**1746** A471 27e multi .50 .25
**1747** A471 80e multi 1.50 .75

### 20th Cent. Art Type of 1988

Paintings by Portuguese artists: 27e, *Burial,* 1938, by Mario Eloy. 60e, *Lisbon Roofs,* c. 1936, by Carlos Botelho. 80e, *Avejao Lirico,* 1939, by Antonio Pedro.

**1988, Nov. 18 Litho. *Perf. 11½x12***

**1748** A469 27e multi .45 .25
**1749** A469 60e multi 1.40 .65
**1750** A469 80e multi 1.75 .75
*a.* Souv. sheet of 3, #1748-1750 5.00 5.00
*b.* Souv. sheet of 6, #1738-1740, 1748-1750 9.00 9.00
*Nos. 1748-1750 (3)* 3.60 1.65

Braga Cathedral, 900th Anniv. A472

**1989, Jan. 20 *Perf. 12***

**1751** A472 30e multi .80 .25

INDIA '89 — A473

55e, Caravel, Sao Jorge da Mina Fort, 1482. 60e, Navigator using astrolabe, 16th cent.

**1989, Jan. 20**

**1752** A473 55e multi 1.25 .65
**1753** A473 60e multi 1.75 .80

### 20th Cent. Art Type of 1988

Paintings by Portuguese artists: 29e, *Antithesis of Calm,* 1940, by Antonio Dacosta. 60c, *Lunch of the Unskilled Mason,* c. 1926, by Julio Pomar. 87e, *Simums,* 1949, by Vespeira.

**1989, Feb. 15 Litho. *Perf. 11½x12***

**1754** A469 29e multi .45 .25
**1755** A469 60e multi 1.20 .60
**1756** A469 87e multi 1.50 .90
*a.* Souv. sheet of 3, #1754-1756 6.00 6.00
*Nos. 1754-1756 (3)* 3.15 1.75

**1989, July 7**

Paintings by Portuguese artists: 29e, *046-72,* 1972, by Fernando Lanhas. 60e, *Les Spirales,* 1954, by Nadir Afonso. 87e, *Sim,* 1987, by Carlos Calvet.

**1757** A469 29e multi .45 .25
**1758** A469 60e multi 1.20 .55
**1759** A469 87e multi 1.50 .90
*a.* Souv. sheet of 3, #1757-1759 6.00 6.00
*b.* Souv. sheet of 6, #1754-1759 11.00 11.00
*Nos. 1757-1759 (3)* 3.15 1.70

**1990, Feb. 14**

Paintings by Portuguese artists: 32e, *Aluenda-Tordesillas* by Joaquim Rodrigo. 60e, *Pintura* by Noronha da Costa. 95e, *Pintura* by Vasco Costa (1917-1985).

**1760** A469 32e multicolored .45 .25
**1761** A469 60e multicolored 1.20 .50
**1762** A469 95e multicolored 1.50 .85
*a.* Souv. sheet of 3, #1760-1762 6.00 6.00
*Nos. 1760-1762 (3)* 3.15 1.60

**1990, Sept. 21**

Paintings by Portuguese artists: 32e, Costa Pinheiro. 60e, Paula Rego. 95e, Jose De Guimaraes.

**1763** A469 32e multicolored .45 .25
**1764** A469 60e multicolored 1.20 .55
**1765** A469 95e multicolored 1.50 .85
*a.* Min. sheet of 3, #1763-1765 6.00 6.00
*b.* Min. sheet of 6, #1760-1765 11.00 11.00
*Nos. 1763-1765 (3)* 3.15 1.65

A474

**1989, Feb. 15 Litho. *Perf. 12***

**1772** A474 29e multi .50 .25
*a.* Bklt. pane of 8 4.00
**1773** A474 60e With love 1.00 .50
*a.* Bklt. pane of 8 8.00

Special occasions.

A475

**1989, Mar. 8 Litho. *Perf. 11½x12***

**1774** A475 60e multi 1.25 .60

European Parliament elections.

Europa 1989 A476

Children's toys.

**1989, Apr. 26 Litho. *Perf. 12***

**1775** A476 80e Top *1.75 1.00*

### Souvenir Sheet

**1776** Sheet of 4, 2 each #1775, 1776a *12.50 5.00*
*a.* A476 80e Tops *2.00 1.25*

Surface Transportation, Lisbon — A477

29e, Carris Co. elevated railway, Bica Street. 65e, Carris electric tram. 87e, Carmo Elevator, Santa Justa Street. 100e, Carris doubledecker bus. 250e, Transtejo Co. riverboat *Cacilheiro,* horiz.

**1989, May 22 Litho.**

**1777** A477 29e multi .45 .25
**1778** A477 65e multi 1.40 .75
**1779** A477 87e multi 1.60 1.00
**1780** A477 100e multi 2.00 .75
*Nos. 1777-1780 (4)* 5.45 2.75

### Souvenir Sheet

**1781** A477 250e multi 7.50 6.50

Windmills A478

29e, Ansiao. 60e, Santiago do Cacem. 87e, Afife. 100e, Caldas da Rainha.

**1989, June 14 Litho.**

**1782** A478 29e multicolored .50 .25
**1783** A478 60e multicolored 1.60 .75
**1784** A478 87e multicolored 1.75 .90
**1785** A478 100e multicolored 2.00 .85
*a.* Bklt. pane of 4, #1782-1785 7.00
*Nos. 1782-1785 (4)* 5.85 2.75

Souvenir Sheet

French Revolution, 200th Anniv. — A479

**1989, July 7 Litho. *Perf. 11½x12***

**1786** A479 250e Drummer 8.50 8.50

No. 1786 has multicolored inscribed margin picturing the PHILEXFRANCE '89 emblem and the storming of the Bastille.

Natl. Palaces A480

**1989, Oct. 18 Litho. *Perf. 12***

**1787** A480 29e Ajuda, Lisbon, and King Luiz I .30 .25
**1788** A480 60e Queluz 1.20 .80

Death cent. of King Luiz.

Exhibition Emblem and Wildflowers A481

29e, Armeria pseudarmeria. 60e, Santolina impressa. 87e, Linaria lamarckii. 100e, Limonium multiforum.

**1989, Nov. 17 Litho.**

**1789** A481 29e multicolored .40 .25
**1790** A481 60e multicolored 1.10 .60
**1791** A481 87e multicolored 1.60 .85
**1792** A481 100e multicolored 2.25 1.10
*a.* Bklt. pane of 4, #1789-1792 7.00
*Nos. 1789-1792 (4)* 5.35 2.80

World Stamp Expo '89, Washington, DC.

Portuguese Faience, 17th Cent. A482

No. 1794, Nobleman (plate). No. 1795, Urn. No. 1796, Fish (pitcher). No. 1797, Crown, shield (plate). No. 1798, Lidded bowl. No. 1799, Plate.

**1990, Jan. 24 Litho. *Perf. 12x11½***

**1793** A482 33e shown .50 .25
**1794** A482 33e multicolored .50 .25
**1795** A482 35e multicolored .70 .25
**1796** A482 60e multicolored 1.25 .70
**1797** A482 60e multicolored 1.25 .70
**1798** A482 60e multicolored 1.25 .70
*Nos. 1793-1798 (6)* 5.45 2.85

### Souvenir Sheet

***Perf. 12***

**1799** A482 250e multicolored 6.00 5.00

No. 1799 contains one 52x45mm stamp. See Nos. 1829-1835, 1890-1896.

Score, Alfred Keil and Henrique Lopes de Mondonca A483

**1990, Mar. 6 *Perf. 12x11½***

**1804** A483 32e multicolored .45 .25

*A Portuguesa,* the Natl. Anthem, cent. (32e).

University Education in Portugal, 700th Anniv. — A484

**1990, Mar. 6 *Perf. 11½x12***

**1805** A484 70e multicolored 1.60 .70

Europa 1990 A485

**1990, Apr. 11 *Perf. 12x11½***

**1806** A485 80e Santo Tirso P.O. *1.25 1.00*

### Souvenir Sheet

**1807** Sheet of 4, 2 each #1806, 1807a *9.00 4.50*
*a.* A485 80e Mala Posta P.O. *1.50 1.25*

Souvenir Sheet

Gentleman Using Postage Stamp, 1840 — A486

**1990, May 3**

**1808** A486 250e multicolored 9.00 5.00

Stamp World London '90 and 150th anniv. of the Penny Black.

Greetings Issue A487

"FELICITACOES" and street scenes. No. 1809, Stairway. No. 1810, Automobile. No. 1811, Man in street. No. 1812, Street scene, girl with bouquet behind mail box.

**1990, June 5** **Litho.** ***Perf. 12***

**1809** A487 60e multi 1.00 .45
**1810** A487 60e multi 1.00 .45
**1811** A487 60e multi 1.00 .45
**1812** A487 60e multi 1.00 .45
*Nos. 1809-1812 (4)* 4.00 1.80

***Perf. 13 Vert.***

*1809a* A487 60e 1.25 1.25
*1810a* A487 60e 1.25 1.25
*1811a* A487 60e 1.25 1.25
*1812a* A487 60e 1.25 1.25
*b.* Bklt. pane of 4, #1809a-1812a 5.00

Camilo Castelo Branco (1825-1890), Writer — A488

Designs: 70e, Friar Bartolomeu dos Martires (1514-1590), theologian.

**1990, July 11** **Litho.** ***Perf. 12x11½***

**1813** A488 65e multicolored 1.00 .65
**1814** A488 70e multicolored 1.25 .70

Ships A489

**1990, Sept. 21** **Litho.** ***Perf. 12***

**1815** A489 32e Barca .40 .25
**1816** A489 60e Caravela Pescareza .95 .50
**1817** A489 70e Barinel 1.10 .75
**1818** A489 95e Caravela 1.75 1.00
*Nos. 1815-1818 (4)* 4.20 2.50

***Perf. 13½ Vert.***

*1815a* A489 32e 1.25 1.25
*1816a* A489 60e 1.25 1.25
*1817a* A489 70e 1.25 1.25
*1818a* A489 95e 1.25 1.25
*b.* Bklt. pane of 4, #1815a-1818a 5.00

National Palaces — A490

**1990, Oct. 11** ***Perf. 12***

**1819** A490 32e Pena .45 .25
**1820** A490 60e Vila 1.00 .50
**1821** A490 70e Mafra 1.20 .75
**1822** A490 120e Guimaraes 1.60 1.00
*Nos. 1819-1822 (4)* 4.25 2.50

Francisco Sa Carneiro (1934-1980), Politician — A491

**1990, Nov. 7**

**1823** A491 32e ol brn & blk .55 .25

Rossio Railway Station, Cent. A492

Various locomotives.

**1990, Nov. 7**

**1824** A492 32e Steam, 1887 .65 .25
**1825** A492 60e Steam, 1891 1.10 .50
**1826** A492 70e Steam, 1916 1.25 .75
**1827** A492 95e Electric, 1956 1.75 1.00
*Nos. 1824-1827 (4)* 4.75 2.50

**Souvenir Sheet**

**1828** A492 200e Railway station 5.00 4.00

**Ceramics Type of 1990**

**1991, Feb. 7** **Litho.** ***Perf. 12***

**1829** A482 35e Lavabo .50 .25
**1830** A482 35e Tureen and plate .50 .25
**1831** A482 35e Flower vase .50 .25
**1832** A482 60e Finger bowl 1.00 .50
**1833** A482 60e Coffee pot 1.00 .50
**1834** A482 60e Mug 1.00 .50
*Nos. 1829-1834 (6)* 4.50 2.25

**Souvenir Sheet**

**1835** A482 250e Plate 5.00 4.00

No. 1835 contains one 52x44mm stamp.

European Tourism Year A494

**1991, Mar. 6** **Litho.** ***Perf. 12***

**1836** A494 60e Flamingos 1.00 .50
**1837** A494 110e Chameleon 1.70 .85

**Souvenir Sheet**

**1838** A494 250e Deer 5.00 4.00

Portuguese Navigators A495

2e, Joao Goncalves Zarco. 3e, Pedro Lopes de Sousa. 4e, Duarte Pacheco Pereira. 5e, Tristao Vaz Teixeira. 6e, Pedro Alvares Cabral. 10e, Joao de Castro. 32e, Bartolomeu Perestrelo. 35e, Gil Eanes. 38e, Vasco da Gama. 42e, Joao de Lisboa. 45e, Joao Rodrigues Cabrillo. 60e, Nuno Tristao. 65e, Joao da Nova. 70e, Ferdinand Magellan. 75e, Pedro Fernandes de Queiros. 80e, Diogo Gomes. 100e, Diogo de Silves. 200e, Estevao Gomes. 250e, Diogo Cao. 350e, Bartolomeu Dias.

**1990-94** **Litho.** ***Perf. 12x11½***

**1839** A495 2e multi .25 .25
**1840** A495 3e multi .25 .25
**1841** A495 4e multi .25 .25
**1842** A495 5e multi .25 .25
**1843** A495 6e multi .25 .25
**1844** A495 10e multi .25 .25
**1845** A495 32e multi .40 .25
**1846** A495 35e multi .35 .25
**1847** A495 38e multi .30 .25
**1848** A495 42e multi .40 .25
**1849** A495 45e multi .35 .25
**1850** A495 60e multi .40 .30
**1851** A495 65e multi .80 .25
**1852** A495 70e multi .80 .25
**1853** A495 75e multi .70 .45
**1854** A495 80e multi 1.10 .50
**1855** A495 100e multi 1.50 .65
**1856** A495 200e multi 2.25 .60
**1857** A495 250e multi 3.50 1.25
**1858** A495 350e multi 4.25 1.50
*Nos. 1839-1858 (20)* 18.60 8.50

Issued: 2e, 5e, 32e, 100e, 3/6; 6e, 38e, 65e, 350e, 3/6/91; 35e, 60e, 80e, 250e, 3/6/92; 4e, 42e, 70e, 200e, 4/6/93; 3e, 10e, 45e, 75e, 4/29/94.

Europa A496

**1991, Apr. 11** **Litho.** ***Perf. 12***

**1859** A496 80e Eutelsat II *1.50 1.00*

**Souvenir Sheet**

**1860** Sheet, 2 ea #1859, 1860a *10.00 5.00*
*a.* A496 80e Olympus I *2.00 1.50*

Souvenir Sheet

Princess Isabel & Philip le Bon — A497

**1991, May 27** **Litho.** ***Perf. 12½***

**1861** A497 300e multicolored 7.50 4.00

Europalia '91. See Belgium No. 1402.

Discovery Ships A498

**1991, May 27** **Litho.** ***Perf. 12***

**1862** A498 35e Caravel .40 .25
**1863** A498 75e Nau 1.10 .55
**1864** A498 80e Nau, stern 1.20 .60
**1865** A498 110e Galleon 1.50 .75
*Nos. 1862-1865 (4)* 4.20 2.15

***Perf. 13½ Vert.***

*1862a* A498 35e 1.25 1.25
*1863a* A498 75e 1.25 1.25
*1864a* A498 80e 1.25 1.25
*1865a* A498 110e 1.25 1.25
*b.* Bklt. pane of 4, #1862a-1865a 5.00

Portuguese Crown Jewels — A499

Designs: 35e, Running knot, diamonds & emeralds, 18th cent. 60e, Royal scepter, 19th cent. 70e, Sash of the Grand Cross, ruby & diamonds, 18th cent. 80e, Court saber, gold & diamonds in hilt, 19th cent. 140e, Royal crown, 19th cent.

**1991, July 8** **Litho.** ***Perf. 12***

**1866** A499 35e multicolored .35 .25
**1867** A499 60e multicolored .85 .50
**1868** A499 80e multicolored .90 .60
**1869** A499 140e multicolored 1.40 .85
*Nos. 1866-1869 (4)* 3.50 2.20

***Perf. 13½ Vert.***

**1870** A499 70e multicolored 1.00 .55
*a.* Booklet pane of 5 5.00

See Nos. 1898-1902.

Antero de Quental (1842-1891), Poet — A500

First Missionaries to Congo, 500th Anniv. — A501

**1991, Aug. 2** ***Perf. 12***

**1871** A500 35e multicolored .45 .25
**1872** A501 110e multicolored 1.70 .85

Architectural Heritage — A502

Designs: 35e, School of Architecture, Oporto University, by Siza Vieira. 60e, Torre do Tombo, by Ateliers Associates of Arsenio Cordeiro. 80e, Railway Bridge over Douro River, by Edgar Cardoso. 110e, Setubal-Braga highway bridge.

**1991, Sept. 4** **Litho.** ***Perf. 12***

**1873** A502 35e multicolored .50 .25
**1874** A502 60e multicolored .80 .45
**1875** A502 80e multicolored 1.25 .60
**1876** A502 110e multicolored 1.70 .75
*Nos. 1873-1876 (4)* 4.25 2.05


1992 Summer Olympics, Barcelona A503

**1991, Oct. 9** **Litho.** ***Perf. 12***

**1877** A503 35e Equestrian .45 .25
**1878** A503 60e Fencing .85 .40
**1879** A503 80e Shooting 1.25 .60
**1880** A503 110e Sailing 1.70 .75
*Nos. 1877-1880 (4)* 4.25 2.00

History of Portuguese Communications — A504

Designs: 35e, King Manuel I appointing first Postmaster, 1520. 60e, Mailbox, telegraph, 1881. 80e, Automobile, telephone, 1911. 110e, Airplane, mail truck, 1991.

**1991, Oct. 9**

**1881** A504 35e multicolored .45 .25
**1882** A504 60e multicolored .90 .45
**1883** A504 80e multicolored 1.25 .60
*Nos. 1881-1883 (3)* 2.60 1.30

**Souvenir Sheet**

**1884** A504 110e multicolored 1.90 1.40

Automobile Museum, Caramulo A505

35e, Peugeot, 1899. 60e, Rolls Royce, 1911. 80e, Bugatti 35B, 1930. 110e, Ferrari 195 Inter, 1950.
No. 1889a, Mercedes 380K, 1934. b, Hispano-Suiza, 1924.

**1991, Nov. 15**

| | | | | |
|---|---|---|---|---|
| **1885** | A505 | 35e multi | .50 | .25 |
| **1886** | A505 | 60e multi | 1.10 | .45 |
| **1887** | A505 | 80e multi | 1.60 | .65 |
| **1888** | A505 | 110e multi | 2.00 | .70 |
| | | *Nos. 1885-1888 (4)* | 5.20 | 2.05 |

**Souvenir Sheet**

| | | | |
|---|---|---|---|
| **1889** | Sheet, 2 each #1889a-1889b | 4.50 | 4.50 |
| *a.-b.* | A505 70e any single | 1.10 | .55 |

Phila Nippon '91 (#1889). See #1903-1906A.

### Ceramics Type of 1990

No. 1890, Tureen with lid. No. 1891, Plate. No. 1892, Pitcher with lid. No. 1893, Violin. No. 1894, Bottle in form of woman. No. 1895, Man seated on barrel.
No. 1896, Political caricature.

**1992, Jan. 24 Litho. *Perf. 12***

| | | | | |
|---|---|---|---|---|
| **1890** | A482 | 40e multicolored | .60 | .30 |
| **1891** | A482 | 40e multicolored | .60 | .30 |
| **1892** | A482 | 40e multicolored | .60 | .30 |
| **1893** | A482 | 65e multicolored | .95 | .50 |
| **1894** | A482 | 65e multicolored | .95 | .50 |
| **1895** | A482 | 65e multicolored | .95 | .50 |
| | | *Nos. 1890-1895 (6)* | 4.65 | 2.40 |

**Souvenir Sheet**

| | | | | |
|---|---|---|---|---|
| **1896** | A482 | 260e multicolored | 4.75 | 3.00 |

No. 1896 contains one 51x44mm stamp.

Portuguese Presidency of the European Community Council of Ministers A506

**1992, Jan. 24**

| | | | | |
|---|---|---|---|---|
| **1897** | A506 | 65e multicolored | 1.10 | .45 |

### Crown Jewels Type of 1991

Designs: 38e, Coral flowers, 19th cent. 65e, Clock of gold, enamel, ivory and diamonds, 20th cent. 70e, Tobacco box encrusted with diamonds and emeralds, 1755. 85e, Royal scepter, 1828. 125e, Eighteen star necklace with diamonds, 1863.

**1992, Feb. 7 Litho. *Perf. 11½x12***

| | | | | |
|---|---|---|---|---|
| **1898** | A499 | 38e multicolored | .45 | .25 |
| **1899** | A499 | 70e multicolored | .85 | .40 |
| **1900** | A499 | 85e multicolored | 1.10 | .65 |
| **1901** | A499 | 125e multicolored | 1.50 | .80 |

***Perf. 13½ Vert.***

| | | | | |
|---|---|---|---|---|
| **1902** | A499 | 65e multicolored | 1.10 | .50 |
| *a.* | | Booklet pane of 5 | 5.00 | |
| | | *Nos. 1898-1902 (5)* | 5.00 | 2.60 |

### Automobile Museum Type of 1991

Designs: 38e, Citroen Torpedo, 1922. 65e, Rochet Schneider, 1914. 85e, Austin Seven, 1933. 120e, Mercedes Benz 770, 1938. No. 1906b, Renault, 1911. c, Ford Model T, 1927.

**1992, Mar. 6 Litho. *Perf. 12***

| | | | | |
|---|---|---|---|---|
| **1903** | A505 | 38e multicolored | .50 | .25 |
| **1904** | A505 | 65e multicolored | 1.25 | .50 |
| **1905** | A505 | 85e multicolored | 1.50 | .65 |
| **1906** | A505 | 120e multicolored | 1.90 | .75 |
| | | *Nos. 1903-1906 (4)* | 5.15 | 2.15 |

**Souvenir Sheet**

| | | | |
|---|---|---|---|
| **1906A** | Sheet of 2 each, #b.-c. | 4.75 | 4.50 |
| *b.-c.* | A505 70e any single | 1.10 | .55 |

Automobile Museum, Oeiras.

Portuguese Arrival in Japan, 450th Anniv. A508

Granada '92: 120e, Three men with gifts, Japanese.

**1992, Apr. 24 Litho. *Perf. 12***

| | | | | |
|---|---|---|---|---|
| **1907** | A508 | 38e shown | .45 | .25 |
| **1908** | A508 | 120e multicolored | 1.75 | .75 |

Portuguese Pavilion, Expo '92, Seville — A509

**1992, Apr. 24 Litho. *Perf. 11½x12***

| | | | | |
|---|---|---|---|---|
| **1909** | A509 | 65e multicolored | .90 | .40 |

Instruments of Navigation — A510

**1992, May 9 Litho. *Perf. 12x11½***

| | | | | |
|---|---|---|---|---|
| **1910** | A510 | 60e Cross staff | .90 | .25 |
| **1911** | A510 | 70e Quadrant | 1.10 | .50 |
| **1912** | A510 | 100e Astrolabe | 1.50 | .55 |
| **1913** | A510 | 120e Compass | 1.90 | .70 |
| *a.* | | Souv. sheet of 4, #1910-1913 | 6.00 | 6.00 |
| | | *Nos. 1910-1913 (4)* | 5.40 | 2.00 |

Lubrapex '92 (#1913a).

Royal Hospital of All Saints, 500th Anniv. A511

**1992, May 11**

| | | | | |
|---|---|---|---|---|
| **1914** | A511 | 38e multicolored | .60 | .30 |

Apparitions of Fatima, 75th Anniv. A512

**1992, May 11**

| | | | | |
|---|---|---|---|---|
| **1915** | A512 | 70e multicolored | 1.00 | .40 |

Port of Leixoes, Cent. A513

**1992, May 11**

| | | | | |
|---|---|---|---|---|
| **1916** | A513 | 120e multicolored | 1.75 | .65 |

A514

Voyages of Columbus — A515

Designs: 85e, King John II with Columbus. No. 1918, Columbus in sight of land. No. 1919, Landing of Columbus. No. 1920, Columbus soliciting aid from Queen Isabella. No. 1921, Columbus welcomed at Barcelona. No. 1922, Columbus presenting natives. No. 1923, Columbus.
Nos. 1918-1923 are similar in design to US Nos. 230-231, 234-235, 237, 245.

**1992, May 22 Litho. *Perf. 12x11½***

| | | | | |
|---|---|---|---|---|
| **1917** | A514 | 85e gold & multi | *2.50* | *.60* |

**Souvenir Sheets**

***Perf. 12***

| | | | | |
|---|---|---|---|---|
| **1918** | A515 | 260e blue | *4.50* | *4.50* |
| **1919** | A515 | 260e brown violet | *4.50* | *4.50* |
| **1920** | A515 | 260e brown | *4.50* | *4.50* |
| **1921** | A515 | 260e violet black | *4.50* | *4.50* |
| **1922** | A515 | 260e black | *4.50* | *4.50* |
| **1923** | A515 | 260e black | *4.50* | *4.50* |
| | | *Nos. 1918-1923 (6)* | *27.00* | *27.00* |

Europa.
See US Nos. 2624-2629, Italy Nos. 1883-1888, and Spain Nos. 2677-2682.

UN Conference on Environmental Development — A516

70e, Bird flying over polluted water system. 120e, Clean water system, butterfly, bird, flowers.

**1992, June 12 Litho. *Perf. 12x11½***

| | | | | |
|---|---|---|---|---|
| **1924** | | 70e multicolored | 2.00 | .55 |
| **1925** | | 120e multicolored | 3.00 | 1.00 |
| *a.* | | A516 Pair, #1924-1925 | 6.00 | 4.50 |

1992 Summer Olympics, Barcelona A517

**1992, July 29 Litho. *Perf. 11½x12***

| | | | | |
|---|---|---|---|---|
| **1926** | A517 | 38e Women's running | .55 | .30 |
| **1927** | A517 | 70e Soccer | 1.15 | .60 |
| **1928** | A517 | 85e Hurdles | 1.40 | .70 |
| **1929** | A517 | 120e Roller hockey | 1.75 | 1.00 |
| | | *Nos. 1926-1929 (4)* | 4.85 | 2.60 |

**Souvenir Sheet**

***Perf. 12***

| | | | | |
|---|---|---|---|---|
| **1930** | A517 | 250e Basketball | 9.00 | 6.00 |

Olymphilex '92 (#1930).

Campo Pequeno Bull Ring, Lisbon, Cent. A518

Various scenes of picadors.

**1992, Aug. 18 *Perf. 12x11½***

| | | | | |
|---|---|---|---|---|
| **1931** | A518 | 38e multicolored | .55 | .30 |
| **1932** | A518 | 65e multicolored | 1.00 | .55 |
| **1933** | A518 | 70e multicolored | 1.25 | .60 |
| **1934** | A518 | 155e multicolored | 2.10 | 1.25 |
| | | *Nos. 1931-1934 (4)* | 4.90 | 2.70 |

**Souvenir Sheet**

***Perf. 13½x12½***

| | | | | |
|---|---|---|---|---|
| **1935** | A518 | 250e Bull ring, vert. | 4.50 | 3.00 |

No. 1935 contains one 35x50mm stamp.

Single European Market A519

**1992, Nov. 4 Litho. *Perf. 12x11½***

| | | | | |
|---|---|---|---|---|
| **1936** | A519 | 65e multicolored | 1.10 | .50 |

European Year for Security, Hygiene and Health at Work A520

**1992, Nov. 4 *Perf. 12x11½***

| | | | | |
|---|---|---|---|---|
| **1937** | A520 | 120e multicolored | 1.60 | .90 |

Postrider A521

**1993, Mar. 9 Litho. *Perf. 12x12½***

| | | | | |
|---|---|---|---|---|
| **1938** | A521 | (A) henna brown, gray & black | .80 | .30 |

No. 1938 sold for 42e on date of issue.
See No. 2276A.

Almada Negreiros (1893-1970), Artist — A522

**1993, Mar. 9 Litho. *Perf. 11½x12***

| | | | | |
|---|---|---|---|---|
| **1939** | A522 | 40e Portrait | .60 | .30 |
| **1940** | A522 | 65e Ships | .95 | .50 |

Instruments of Navigation — A523

**1993, Apr. 6 *Perf. 12x11½***

| | | | | |
|---|---|---|---|---|
| **1941** | A523 | 42e Hourglass | .60 | .30 |
| **1942** | A523 | 70e Nocturlabe | 1.00 | .50 |
| **1943** | A523 | 90e Kamal | 1.30 | .65 |
| **1944** | A523 | 130e Backstaff | 1.90 | .95 |
| | | *Nos. 1941-1944 (4)* | 4.80 | 2.40 |

Contemporary Paintings by Jose Escada (1934-1980) — A524

Europa: No. 1945, Cathedral, 1979. No. 1946a, Abstract shapes, 1966.

**1993, May 5 Litho.** ***Perf. 12x11½***

**1945** A524 90e multicolored *1.25 .60*

**Souvenir Sheet**

**1946** Sheet, 2 each #1945, 1946a *6.00 4.00*
*a.* A524 90e multicolored *1.50 1.00*

Assoc. of Volunteer Firemen of Lisbon, 125th Anniv. A525

**1993, June 21 Litho.** ***Perf. 12x11½***

**1947** A525 70e multicolored 1.10 .45

Sao Carlos Natl. Theatre, Bicent. A526

**1993, June 21**

**1948** A526 42e Rossini .55 .25
**1949** A526 70e Verdi 1.25 .45
**1950** A526 90e Wagner 1.40 .55
**1951** A526 130e Mozart 2.10 .80
*Nos. 1948-1951 (4)* 5.30 2.05

**Souvenir Sheet**

**1952** A526 300e Theatre 5.00 4.00

Union of Portuguese Speaking Capitals — A527

**1993, July 30 Litho.** ***Perf. 11½x12***

**1953** A527 130e multicolored 1.75 .80
*a.* Miniature sheet of 4 + 2 labels 7.50 5.00

Brasiliana '93 (#1953a).

Sculpture — A528

Designs: 42e, Annunciation Angel, 12th cent. 70e, St. Mark, 16th cent., horiz. No. 1956, Virgin and Child, 17th cent. 90e, Archangel St. Michael, 18th cent. 130e, Conde de Ferreira, 19th cent. 170e, Modern sculpture, 20th cent.

No. 1960a, Head of Agrippina, the Elder, 1st cent. No. 1960b, Virgin of the Annunciation, 16th cent. No. 1960c, The Widow, 19th cent. No. 1960d, Love Ode, 20th cent.

***Perf. 11½x12, 12x11½***

**1993, Aug. 18**

**1954** A528 42e multicolored .55 .30
**1955** A528 70e multicolored .90 .45
**1956** A528 75e multicolored .95 .50
**1957** A528 90e multicolored 1.10 .60
**1958** A528 130e multicolored 1.60 .80
**1959** A528 170e multicolored 2.25 1.10
*Nos. 1954-1959 (6)* 7.35 3.75

**Souvenir Sheet**

**1960** Sheet of 4 4.50 3.50
*a.-d.* A528 75e any single .95 .95

See Nos. 2001-2007, 2067-2073.

Railway World Congress A529

90e, Cars on railway overpass, train. 130e, Traffic jam, train. 300e, Train, track skirting tree.

**1993, Sept. 6** ***Perf. 12x11½***

**1961** A529 90e multicolored .90 .55
**1962** A529 130e multicolored 2.10 .80

**Souvenir Sheet**

**1963** A529 300e multicolored 4.50 3.50

Portuguese Arrival in Japan, 450th Anniv. A530

Designs: 42e, Japanese using musket. 130e, Catholic priests. 350e, Exchanging items of trade.

**1993, Sept. 22 Litho.** ***Perf. 12***

**1964** A530 42e multicolored .55 .30
**1965** A530 130e multicolored 1.60 .85
**1966** A530 350e multicolored 4.50 2.25
*Nos. 1964-1966 (3)* 6.65 3.40

See Macao Nos. 704-706.

Trawlers A531

**1993, Oct. 1 Litho.** ***Perf. 12x11½***

**1967** A531 42e Twin-mast .55 .30
**1968** A531 70e Single-mast .90 .45
**1969** A531 90e SS Germano 3 1.10 .55
**1970** A531 130e Steam-powered 1.75 .85
*Nos. 1967-1970 (4)* 4.30 2.15

***Perf. 11½***

*1967a* A531 42e .55 .30
*1968a* A531 70e .90 .45
*1969a* A531 90e 1.10 .55
*1970a* A531 130e 1.75 .85
*b.* Booklet pane of 4, #1967a-1970a 5.00

A532

Mailboxes: 42e, Rural mail bag, 1880. 70e, Railroad wall-mounted mailbox, 19th cent. 90e, Free-standing mailbox, 19th cent. 130e, Modern mailbox, 1992. 300e, Mailbox from horse-drawn postal vehicle, 19th cent.

**1993, Oct. 9 Litho.** ***Perf. 12***

**1971** A532 42e multicolored .55 .25
**1972** A532 70e multicolored .85 .40
**1973** A532 90e multicolored 1.20 .50
**1974** A532 130e multicolored 1.60 .75
*Nos. 1971-1974 (4)* 4.20 1.90

**Souvenir Sheet**

**1975** A532 300e multicolored 4.50 3.50

No. 1975 has continuous design.

A533

Endangered birds of prey.

**1993, Oct. 9**

**1976** A533 42e Imperial eagle .50 .25
**1977** A533 70e Royal eagle owl 1.10 .40
**1978** A533 130e Peregrine falcon 1.75 .75
**1979** A533 350e Hen harrier 4.00 2.00
*Nos. 1976-1979 (4)* 7.35 3.40

Brazil-Portugal Treaty of Consultation and Friendship, 40th Anniv. — A534

**1993, Nov. 3**

**1980** A534 130e multicolored 1.60 .75

See Brazil No. 2430.

**Souvenir Sheet**

Conference of Zamora, 850th Anniv. — A535

**1993, Dec. 9**

**1981** A535 150e multicolored 3.00 2.00

West European Union, 40th Anniv. A536

**1994, Jan. 27 Litho.** ***Perf. 12***

**1982** A536 85e multicolored 1.20 .55

Intl. Olympic Committee, Cent. A537

Design: No. 1984, Olympic torch, rings.

**1994, Jan. 27**

**1983** A537 100e multicolored 1.50 .65
**1984** A537 100e multicolored 1.50 .65

Issued in sheets of 8, 4 each + label.

Oliveira Martins (1845-94), Historian A538

100e, Florbela Espanca (1894-1930), poet.

**1994, Feb. 21**

**1985** A538 45e multicolored .65 .30
**1986** A538 100e multicolored 1.50 .65

Prince Henry the Navigator (1394-1460) — A539

**1994, Mar. 4**

**1987** A539 140e multicolored 2.40 .85

See Brazil No. 2463, Cape Verde No. 664, Macao No. 719.

Transfer of Power, 20th Anniv. A540

**1994, Apr. 22 Litho.** ***Perf. 12x11½***

**1988** A540 75e multicolored 1.10 .45

Europa A541

**1994, May 5 Litho.** ***Perf. 12x11½***

**1989** A541 100e People of Ormuz *1.25 .65*

**Souvenir Sheet**

**1990** Sheet of 4, 2 each #1989, 1990a *4.50 3.50*
*a.* A541 100e Ears of corn *1.00 .50*

Intl. Year of the Family A542

**1994, May 15 Litho.** ***Perf. 12x11½***

**1991** A542 45e blk, red & brn .55 .30
**1992** A542 140e blk, red & grn 1.75 .85

Treaty of Tordesillas, 500th Anniv. — A543

**1994, June 7 Litho.** ***Perf. 12x11½***

**1993** A543 140e multicolored 1.75 .90

1994 World Cup Soccer Championships, US — A544

**1994, June 7**

**1994** A544 100e shown 1.25 .60
**1995** A544 140e Ball, 4 shoes 1.90 .95

Lisbon '94, European Capital of Culture A545

Birds and: 45e, Music. 75e, Photography. 100e, Theater and ballet. 145e, Art.

**1994, July 1**

**1996** A545 45e multicolored .55 .30
**1997** A545 75e multicolored 1.00 .50
**1998** A545 100e multicolored 1.25 .60
**1999** A545 140e multicolored 2.00 .95
*a.* Souvenir sheet of 4, #1996-1999 6.00 5.00
*Nos. 1996-1999 (4)* 4.80 2.35

Year of Road Safety — A545a

**1994, Aug. 16 Litho. *Perf. 11½x12***

**2000** A545a 45e blk, red & grn .60 .30

**Sculpture Type of 1993**

Designs: 45e, Pedra Formosa, Castreja culture. No. 2002, Carved pilaster, 7th cent., vert. 80e, Capital carved with figures, 12th cent. 100e, Laying Christ in the Tomb, 16th cent. 140e, Reliquary chapel, 17th cent. 180e, Bas relief, 20th cent.

No. 2007: a, Sarcophagus of Queen Urraca, 13th cent. b, Sarcophagus of Dom Afonso. c, Tomb of Dom Joao de Noronha and Dona Isabel de Sousa, 16th cent. d, Mausoleum of Adm. Machado Santos, 20th cent.

***Perf. 12x11½, 11½x12***

**1994, Aug. 16**

**2001** A528 45e multicolored .55 .30
**2002** A528 75e multicolored .75 .50
**2003** A528 80e multicolored 1.10 .50
**2004** A528 100e multicolored 1.40 .60
**2005** A528 140e multicolored 1.75 .85
**2006** A528 180e multicolored 2.50 1.10
*Nos. 2001-2006 (6)* 8.05 3.85

**Souvenir Sheet**

***Perf. 12x11½***

**2007** Sheet of 4 5.00 4.00
*a.-d.* A528 75e any single .95 .95

Falconry A546

Designs: 45e, Falconer, hooded bird, dog. 75e, Falcon flying after prey. 100e, Falcon, prey on ground. 140e, Three falcons on perches. 250e, Hooded falcon.

**1994, Sept. 16 Litho. *Perf. 12***

**2008** A546 45e multicolored .55 .30
**2009** A546 75e multicolored 1.10 .50
**2010** A546 100e multicolored 1.25 .60
**2011** A546 140e multicolored 1.90 .85
*Nos. 2008-2011 (4)* 4.80 2.25

**Souvenir Sheet**

**2012** A546 250e multicolored 5.00 4.00

Trawlers A547

**1994, Sept. 16 *Perf. 12x11½***

**2013** A547 45e Maria Arminda .55 .30
**2014** A547 75e Bom Pastor 1.10 .50
**2015** A547 100e With triplex haulers 1.25 .60
**2016** A547 140e Sueste 2.00 .85
*Nos. 2013-2016 (4)* 4.90 2.25

***Perf. 11½ Vert.***

*2013a* A547 45e .50 .30
*2014a* A547 75e .95 .50
*2015a* A547 100e 1.25 .60
*2016a* A547 140e 1.75 .85
*b.* Booklet pane of 4, #2013a-2016a 6.00

Modern Railway Transport — A548

45e, Sintra Railway, electric multiple car unit. 75e, 5600 series locomotives. 140e, Lisbon subway cars.

**1994, Oct. 10 Litho. *Perf. 12***

**2017** A548 45e multicolored .75 .30
**2018** A548 75e multicolored 1.00 .45
**2019** A548 140e multicolored 1.75 .90
*Nos. 2017-2019 (3)* 3.50 1.65

Vehicles of Postal Transportation — A549

45e, Horse-drawn mail coach, 19th cent. 75e, Railway postal ambulance, 1910. 100e, Mercedes station wagon, No. 222, 1950. 140e, Volkswagen van, 1952. 250e, DAF 2500 truck, 1983.

**1994, Oct. 10**

**2020** A549 45e multicolored .55 .30
**2021** A549 75e multicolored 1.00 .45
**2022** A549 100e multicolored 1.25 .65
**2023** A549 140e multicolored 1.90 .90
*Nos. 2020-2023 (4)* 4.70 2.30

**Souvenir Sheet**

**2024** A549 250e multicolored 5.00 4.00

First Savings Bank in Portugal, 150th Anniv. A550

45e, Pelican medallion. 100e, Modern coins.

**1994, Oct. 31**

**2025** A550 45e multicolored .60 .30
**2026** A550 100e multicolored 1.40 .65

World Wide Savings Day (#2026).

American Society of Travel Agents, 64th Congress, Lisbon A551

**1994, Nov. 7**

**2027** A551 140e multicolored 1.75 .90

Historical Inns A552

45e, S. Filipe Fort, Setubal. 75e, Obidos Castle. 100e, Dos Loios Convent, Evora. 140e, St. Marinha Guimaraes Monastery.

**1994, Nov. 7**

**2028** A552 45e multicolored .55 .30
**2029** A552 75e multicolored 1.00 .45
**2030** A552 100e multicolored 1.25 .60
**2031** A552 140e multicolored 1.90 .90
*Nos. 2028-2031 (4)* 4.70 2.25

Evangelization and Meeting of Cultures — A553

45e, Carving of missionary, Mozambique, 19th cent., vert. 75e, Sculpture, young Jesus ministering to the people, India, 17th cent., vert. 100e, Chalice, Macao, 17th cent., vert. 140e, Carving of native, Angola, 19th cent.

**1994, Nov. 17 Litho. *Perf. 12***

**2032** A553 45e multicolored .55 .30
**2033** A553 75e multicolored 1.00 .45
**2034** A553 100e multicolored 1.25 .60
**2035** A553 140e multicolored 1.90 .90
*Nos. 2032-2035 (4)* 4.70 2.25

Arrival of Portuguese in Senegal, 550th Anniv. A554

**1994, Nov. 17**

**2036** A554 140e multicolored 1.75 .90

See Senegal No. 1083.

Souvenir Sheet

Battle of Montijo, 350th Anniv. — A555

**1994, Dec. 1**

**2037** A555 150e multicolored 2.50 2.00

Souvenir Sheet

Christmas — A556

**1994, Dec. 8**

**2038** A556 150e Magi 2.50 1.25

Nature Conservation in Europe — A557

Designs: 42e, Otis tarda. 90e, Pandion haliaetus. 130e, Lacerta schreiberi.

**1995, Feb. 22 Litho. *Perf. 12***

**2039** A557 42e multicolored .60 .30
**2040** A557 90e multicolored 1.40 .60
**2041** A557 130e multicolored 2.00 .85
*a.* Souvenir sheet of 3, #2039-2041 5.00 4.00
*Nos. 2039-2041 (3)* 4.00 1.75

St. Joao de Deus (1495-1550), Founder of Order of Hospitalers A558

**1995, Mar. 8 Litho. *Perf. 12***

**2042** A558 45e multicolored .70 .30

Trams & Automobiles in Portugal, Cent. — A559

Designs: 90e, 1895 Electric tram, 1895. 130e, 1895 Panhard & Levassor automobile.

**1995, Mar. 8**

**2043** A559 90e multicolored 1.50 .60
**2044** A559 130e multicolored 2.00 .95

19th Century Professions A560

Designs: 1e, Baker woman. 20e, Spinning wheel and spoon vendor. 45e, Junk dealer. 50e, Fruit vendor. 75e, Whitewasher.

**1995, Apr. 20 Litho. *Perf. 12***

**2045** A560 1e multicolored .25 .25
**2046** A560 20e multicolored .25 .25
**2047** A560 45e multicolored .45 .30
Complete booklet, 10 #2047 4.50

**2048** A560 50e multicolored .65 .35
**2049** A560 75e multicolored 1.00 .50
Complete booklet, 10 #2049 10.00
*Nos. 2045-2049 (5)* 2.60 1.65

See Nos. 2088-2092, 2147-2151, 2210-2214, 2277-2281B.

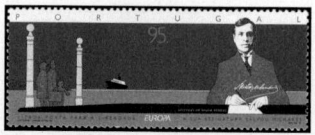

Peace & Freedom — A561

Europa: No. 2050, People awaiting ships for America, Aristides de Sousa Mendes signing entrance visas, 1940. No. 2051, Transportion of refugees from Gibraltar to Madeira, 1940.

**1995, May 5 Litho. *Perf. 12***
**2050** A561 95e multicolored *1.25 .50*
**2051** A561 95e multicolored *1.25 .50*

UN, 50th Anniv. A562

135e, like #2052, clouds in background.

**1995, May 5**
**2052** A562 75e multicolored 1.00 .50
**2053** A562 135e multicolored 1.75 .90
*a.* Souv. sheet, 2 ea #2052-2053 6.00 5.00

A563

St. Antony of Padua (1195-1231) A564

45e, *St. Anthony Holding Child Jesus.* 75e, St. Anthony with flowers. 135e, Statue of St. Antony holding child Jesus.
250e, Statue of St. Antony holding child Jesus, diff.

**1995, June 13 Litho. *Perf. 12***
**2054** A563 45e multicolored 2.00 .30
**2055** A564 75e multicolored 3.50 .50
**2056** A563 135e multicolored 6.00 .95
*Nos. 2054-2056 (3)* 11.50 1.75

**Souvenir Sheet**

**2057** A563 250e multicolored 5.00 4.00

See Italy Nos. 2040-2041, Brazil No. 2539.

Firemen in Portugal, 600th Anniv. A565

Designs: No. 2058, Carpenters with axes, women with pitchers, 1395. No. 2059, Dutch firemen, water pumper, 1701. 75e, Fireman of Lisbon, water wagon, 1780, firemen, 1782. 80e, Firemen pulling pumper, carrying water kegs, 1834. 95e, Fire chief directing firemen on Merryweather steam pumper, 1867. 135e, Firemen, hydrant, early fire truck, 1908.

**1995, July 4 Litho. *Perf. 12***
**2058** A565 45e multicolored .45 .30
**2059** A565 45e multicolored .65 .30
*a.* Miniature sheet of 4 3.00 1.25
**2060** A565 75e multicolored 1.00 .50
*a.* Miniature sheet of 4 5.00 2.00
**2061** A565 80e multicolored 1.10 .55
**2062** A565 95e multicolored 1.10 .65
**2063** A565 135e multicolored 1.50 .90
*Nos. 2058-2063 (6)* 5.80 3.20

Dom Manuel I, 500th Anniv. of Acclamation — A566

**1995, Aug. 4 Litho. *Perf. 12***
**2064** A566 45e buff, brown & red .60 .30
*a.* Miniature sheet of 4 3.00 2.50

New Electric Railway Tram — A567

**1995, Sept. 1**
**2066** A567 80e multicolored 1.10 .55
*a.* Booklet pane of 4 4.50
Complete booklet, No. 2066a 5.00

**Sculpture Type of 1993**

Designs: 45e, Warrior, Castreja culture. 75e, Two-headed fountain. 80e, Statue, "The Truth," by Texeira Lopes. 95e, Monument to the war dead. 135e, Statue of Fernão Lopes, by Martins Correia. 190e, Monument to Fernando Pessoa, by Lagoa Henriques.
Equestrian statues: No. 2073: a, Medieval cavalryman. b, D. José I. c, D. João IV. d, Vímara Peres.

**1995, Sept. 27 Litho. *Perf. 11½x12***
**2067** A528 45e multicolored .55 .30
**2068** A528 75e multicolored 1.00 .50
**2069** A528 80e multicolored 1.00 .55
**2070** A528 95e multicolored 1.10 .65
**2071** A528 135e multicolored 1.60 .90
**2072** A528 190e multicolored 2.50 1.25
*Nos. 2067-2072 (6)* 7.75 4.15

**Souvenir Sheet**

**2073** Sheet of 4 4.50 3.50
*a.-d.* A528 75e any single 1.00 1.00

Portuguese Expansion Period Art — A568

45e, Statue of the Guardian Angel of Portugal. 75e, Reliquary of Queen D. Leonor. 80e, Statue of Dom Manuel. 95e, Painting, St. Anthony, by Nuno Goncalves. 135e, Painting, Adoration of the Magi, by Vasco Fernandez. 190e, Painting, Christ on the Way to Mount Calvary, by Jorge Afonso.
200e, Altarpiece for Convent of St. Vincent, by Nuno Goncalves.

**1995, Oct. 9 Litho. *Perf. 12***
**2074** A568 45e multicolored .60 .25
**2075** A568 75e multicolored 1.00 .50
**2076** A568 80e multicolored 1.00 .50
**2077** A568 95e multicolored 1.25 .60
**2078** A568 135e multicolored 1.75 .90
**2079** A568 190e multicolored 2.50 1.25
*Nos. 2074-2079 (6)* 8.10 4.00

**Souvenir Sheet**

**2080** A568 200e multicolored 3.00 2.50

No. 2080 contains one 76x27mm stamp.

José Maria Eca de Queiroz (1845-1900), Writer — A569

**1995, Oct. 27 Litho. *Perf. 12***
**2081** A569 135e multicolored 1.75 .90

Christmas A570

**1995, Nov. 14**
**2082** A570 80e Annunciation angel 1.20 .50
*a.* "PORTUGAL" omitted 1.40 .50
*b.* Miniature sheet, 4 #2082 5.00 4.00
*c.* Miniature sheet, 4 #2082a 7.50 4.00

TAP Air Portugal, 50th Anniv. A571

**1995, Nov. 14**
**2083** A571 135e Airbus A340/300 1.75 .90

Oceanographic Voyages of King Charles I of Portugal and Prince Albert I of Monaco, Cent. — A572

95e, Ship, King Charles I holding sextant, microscope, sea life. 135e, Fish in sea, net, Prince Albert I holding binoculars, ship.

**1996, Feb. 1**
**2084** A572 95e multicolored 1.25 .60
**2085** A572 135e multicolored 2.00 .90

See Monaco Nos. 1992-1993.

Natl. Library, Bicent. A573

**1996, Feb. 29**
**2086** A573 80e multicolored 1.20 .50

Use of Portuguese as Official Language, 700th Anniv. — A574

**1996, Feb. 29**
**2087** A574 200e multicolored 2.50 1.25

**19th Cent. Professions Type**

Designs: 3e, Exchange broker. 47e, Woman selling chestnuts. 78e, Cloth seller. 100e, Black woman selling mussels. 250e, Water seller.

**1996, Mar. 20 Litho. *Perf. 11½x12***
**2088** A560 3e multicolored .25 .25
**2089** A560 47e multicolored .50 .30
*a.* Booklet pane, 10 #2089 5.00
Complete booklet, #2089a 5.00
**2090** A560 78e multicolored .90 .50
*a.* Booklet pane, 10 #2090 9.00
Complete booklet, #2090a 9.00
**2091** A560 100e multicolored 1.10 .65
**2092** A560 250e multicolored 2.75 1.60
*Nos. 2088-2092 (5)* 5.50 3.30

Joao de Deus (1830-96), Founder of New Method to Teach Reading A576

**1996, Apr. 12 *Perf. 12***
**2093** A576 78e multicolored 1.10 .50

UNICEF, 50th Anniv. — A577

**1996, Apr. 12**
**2094** A577 78e shown 1.00 .50
**2095** A577 140e Children 1.75 .90
*a.* Bklt. pane, 2 ea #2094-2095 5.50
Complete booklet, #2095a 5.50

Joao de Barros (1496-1570), Writer — A578

**1996, Apr. 12**
**2096** A578 140e multicolored 1.75 .90

Helena Vieira da Silva (1908-92), Painter — A579

**1996, May 3**
**2097** A579 98e multicolored *1.25 .60*
*a.* Souvenir sheet of 3 *3.75 3.75*

Europa.

Euro '96, European Soccer Championships, Great Britain — A580

**1996, June 7 Litho. *Perf. 12***
**2098** A580 78e Soccer players 1.00 .50
**2099** A580 140e Soccer players, diff. 1.75 .90
*a.* Souvenir sheet, #2098-2099 3.00 2.75

Joao Vaz Corte-Real, Explorer, 500th Death Anniv. — A581

**1996, June 7**

**2100** A581 140e multicolored 1.75 .90

**Souvenir Sheet**

**2101** A581 315e like #2100 4.25 4.00

No. 2101 contains one 40x31 stamp with a continuous design.

1996 Summer Olympics, Atlanta A582

**1996, June 24**

**2102** A582 47e Wrestling .60 .30
**2103** A582 78e Equestrian 1.00 .50
**2104** A582 98e Boxing 1.25 .65
**2105** A582 140e Running 1.75 .90
*Nos. 2102-2105 (4)* 4.60 2.35

**Souvenir Sheet**

**2106** A582 300e Early track event 4.00 3.00

Olymphilex '96 (#2106).

Augusto Hilário (1864-96), Singer A583

**1996, July 1 Litho. *Perf. 12x11½***

**2107** A583 80e multicolored 1.20 .50

Alphonsine Condification of Statutes, 550th Anniv. — A584

**1996, Aug. 7**

**2108** A584 350e multicolored 4.25 2.25

Motion Pictures, Cent. A585

Directors, stars of motion pictures: 47e, António Silva. 78e, Vasco Santana. 80e, Laura Alves. 98e, Aurélio Pais dos Reis. 100e, Leitao de Barros. 140e, António Lopes Ribeiro.

**1996, Aug. 7**

**2109** A585 47e multicolored .60 .30
**2110** A585 78e multicolored 1.00 .50
**2111** A585 80e multicolored 1.00 .50
*a.* Souvenir sheet, #2109-2111 2.75 2.75
**2112** A585 98e multicolored 1.25 .65
**2113** A585 100e multicolored 1.25 .65
**2114** A585 140e multicolored 1.75 .90
*a.* Souvenir sheet, #2112-2114 5.00 5.00
*b.* Souvenir sheet, #2109-2114 7.50 7.50
*Nos. 2109-2114 (6)* 6.85 3.50

Azeredo Perdigao (1896-1993), Lawyer, Chairman of Calouste Gulbenkian Foundation — A586

**1996, Sept. 19 Litho. *Perf. 12***

**2115** A586 47e multicolored .75 .30

Arms of the Districts of Portugal A587

**1996, Sept. 27**

**2116** A587 47e Aveiro .60 .30
**2117** A587 78e Beja 1.00 .50
**2118** A587 80e Braga 1.00 .50
*a.* Souvenir sheet, #2116-2118 2.75 2.75
**2119** A587 98e Branganca 1.25 .65
**2120** A587 100e Castelo Branco 1.25 .65
**2121** A587 140e Coimbra 1.75 .90
*a.* Souvenir sheet, #2119-2121 4.50 4.50
*Nos. 2116-2121 (6)* 6.85 3.50

County of Portucale, 900th Anniv. A588

**1996, Oct. 9**

**2122** A588 47e multicolored .75 .30

Home Mail Delivery, 175th Anniv. — A589

Designs: 47e, Mail carrier, 1821. 78e, Postman, 1854. 98e, Rural mail distrubutor, 1893. 100e, Postman, 1939. 140e, Postman, 1992.

**1996, Oct. 9**

**2123** A589 47e multicolored .60 .30
**2124** A589 78e multicolored 1.00 .50
**2125** A589 98e multicolored 1.25 .65
**2126** A589 100e multicolored 1.25 .65
**2127** A589 140e multicolored 1.90 .90
*Nos. 2123-2127 (5)* 6.00 3.00

Traditional Food A590

47e, Minho-style pork. 78e, Trout, Boticas. 80e, Tripe, Oporto. 98e, Baked codfish, potatoes. 100e, Eel chowder, Aveiro. 140e, Lobster, Peniche.

**1996, Oct. 9**

**2128** A590 47e multicolored .60 .30
**2129** A590 78e multicolored 1.00 .50
**2130** A590 80e multicolored 1.00 .50
**2131** A590 98e multicolored 1.25 .65
**2132** A590 100e multicolored 1.25 .65
**2133** A590 140e multicolored 2.00 .90
*Nos. 2128-2133 (6)* 7.10 3.50

See Nos. 2170-2175.

Bank of Portugal, 150th Anniv. A591

**1996, Nov. 12 Litho. *Perf. 12***

**2134** A591 78e multicolored 1.00 .50

Rights of the People of East Timor A592

**1996, Nov. 12**

**2135** A592 140e black & red 1.75 .90

Discovery of Maritime Route to India, 500th Anniv. — A593

Voyage of Vasco da Gama: 47e, Visit of D. Manuel I to shipyards. 78e, Departure from Lisbon, July 8, 1497. 98e, Trip over Atlantic Ocean. 140e, Passing Cape of Good Hope. 315e, Dream of Manuel.

**1996, Nov. 12 *Perf. 13½***

**2136** A593 47e multicolored .60 .30
**2137** A593 78e multicolored 1.00 .50
**2138** A593 98e multicolored 1.25 .60
**2139** A593 140e multicolored 1.75 .85
*Nos. 2136-2139 (4)* 4.60 2.25

**Souvenir Sheet**

**2140** A593 315e multicolored 4.00 4.00

See Nos. 2191-2195, 2265-2270.

Souvenir Sheet

1996 Organization for Security and Cooperation in Europe Summit, Lisbon — A594

**1996, Dec. 2 *Perf. 12***

**2141** A594 200e multicolored 2.50 2.50

Ships of the Indian Shipping Line A595

Designs: 49e, Portuguese galleon, 16th cent. 80e, "Principe da Beira," 1780. 100e, Bow of Frigate "D. Fernando II e Gloria," 1843. 140e, Stern of "D. Fernando II e Gloria."

**1997, Feb. 12 Litho. *Perf. 12***

**2142** A595 49e multicolored .60 .30
**2143** A595 80e multicolored 1.00 .50
**2144** A595 100e multicolored 1.25 .65
**2145** A595 140e multicolored 1.75 .90
*Nos. 2142-2145 (4)* 4.60 2.35

Project Life — A596

**1997, Feb. 20**

**2146** A596 80e multicolored 1.20 .50
*a.* Booklet pane of 5 6.00
Complete booklet, #2146a 6.00

**19th Cent. Professions Type**

Designs: 2e, Laundry woman. 5e, Broom seller. 30e, Olive oil seller. 49e, Woman with cape. 80e, Errand boy.

**1997, Mar. 12 Litho. *Perf. 11½x12***

**2147** A560 2e multicolored .25 .25
**2148** A560 5e multicolored .25 .25
**2149** A560 30e multicolored .35 .25
**2150** A560 49e multicolored .60 .30
*a.* Booklet pane of 10 6.00
Complete booklet, #2150a 6.00
**2151** A560 80e multicolored 1.00 .50
*a.* Booklet pane of 10 10.00
Complete booklet, #2151a 10.00
*Nos. 2147-2151 (5)* 2.45 1.55

Managing Institute of Public Credit, Bicent. A597

**1997, Mar. 12 Litho. *Perf. 12***

**2152** A597 49e multicolored .65 .30

World Wildlife Fund — A598

Galemys pyreanicus: No. 2153, Looking upward. No. 2154, Paws around nose. No. 2155, Eating earthworm. No. 2156, Heading downward.

**1997, Mar. 12 *Perf. 12***

**2153** 49e multicolored .65 .45
**2154** 49e multicolored .65 .45
**2155** 49e multicolored .65 .45
**2156** 49e multicolored .65 .45
*a.* A598 Strip of 4, #2153-2156 3.50 3.50

Stories and Legends — A599

Europa: Moorish girl watching over treasures.

**1997, May 5 Litho. *Perf. 12***

**2157** A599 100e multicolored *1.25 .65*
*a.* Souvenir sheet of 3 *4.50 3.25*

Sports A600

No. 2162: a, BMX bike riding. b, Hang gliding.

**1997, May 29** *Perf. 12*

| | | | | |
|---|---|---|---|---|
| **2158** | A600 | 49e Surfing | .60 | .30 |
| **2159** | A600 | 80e Skate boarding | 1.00 | .50 |
| **2160** | A600 | 100e Roller blading | 1.25 | .65 |
| **2161** | A600 | 140e Parasailing | 1.75 | .90 |
| | | *Nos. 2158-2161 (4)* | 4.60 | 2.35 |

**Souvenir Sheet**

| | | | | |
|---|---|---|---|---|
| **2162** | | Sheet of 2 | 4.00 | 3.00 |
| *a.-b.* | | A600 150e any single | 1.60 | 1.60 |

Capture of Lisbon and Santarém from the Moors, 850th Anniv. — A601

Designs: No. 2163, Soldier on horse, front of fortress of Lisbon. No. 2164, Soldiers climbing ladders into Santareém at night.

**1997, June 9** *Perf. 12*

| | | | |
|---|---|---|---|
| **2163** | 80e multicolored | 1.00 | .50 |
| **2164** | 80e multicolored | 1.00 | .50 |
| *a.* | A601 Pair, #2163-2164 | 2.00 | 2.00 |
| *b.* | Souvenir sheet, 2 #2164a | 4.25 | 4.25 |

Fr. Luís Fróis (1532-97), Missionary, Historian — A602

80e, Fróis on mission in Orient. #2166, Fróis holding hands across chest. #2167, Fróis, church.

**1997, June 9**

| | | | | |
|---|---|---|---|---|
| **2165** | A602 | 80e multi, horiz. | 1.00 | .50 |
| **2166** | A602 | 140e multi | 1.90 | .90 |
| **2167** | A602 | 140e multi | 1.90 | .90 |
| | | *Nos. 2165-2167 (3)* | 4.80 | 2.30 |

See Macao 878-879.

Fr. José de Anchieta (1534-97), Missionary in Brazil — A603

Design: No. 2169, Fr. António Vieira (1608-97), missionary in Brazil, diplomat.

**1997, June 9**

| | | | | |
|---|---|---|---|---|
| **2168** | A603 | 140e multicolored | 1.75 | .90 |
| **2169** | A603 | 350e multicolored | 4.75 | 2.25 |

See Brazil Nos. 2639-2640.

**Traditional Food Type of 1996**

10e, Roasted kid, Beira Baixa. 49e, Fried shad. 80e, Lamb stew. 100e, Fish chowder. 140e, Swordfish fillets with corn. 200e, Stewed octopus, Azores.

**1997, July 5** **Litho.** *Perf. 12*

| | | | | |
|---|---|---|---|---|
| **2170** | A590 | 10e multicolored | .25 | .25 |
| **2171** | A590 | 49e multicolored | .60 | .30 |
| **2172** | A590 | 80e multicolored | 1.00 | .50 |
| **2173** | A590 | 100e multicolored | 1.25 | .65 |
| **2174** | A590 | 140e multicolored | 1.75 | .85 |
| **2175** | A590 | 200e multicolored | 2.50 | 1.25 |
| | | *Nos. 2170-2175 (6)* | 7.35 | 3.80 |

**Souvenir Sheet**

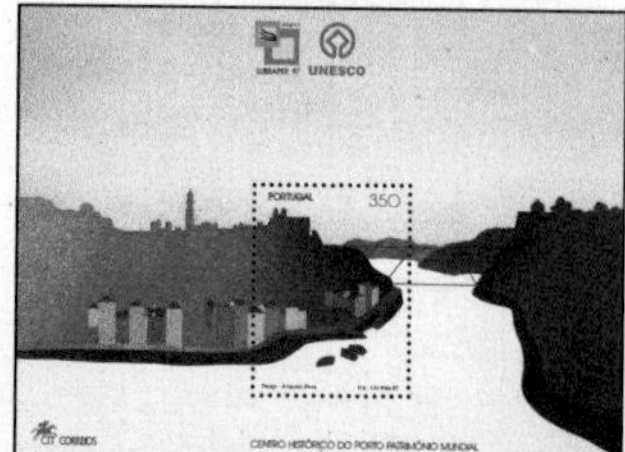

City of Oporto, UNESCO World Heritage Site — A605

**1997, July 5** **Litho.** *Perf. 12*

| | | | | |
|---|---|---|---|---|
| **2176** | A605 | 350e multicolored | 4.50 | 4.50 |

A606

**1997, July 19** **Litho.** *Perf. 12*

| | | | | |
|---|---|---|---|---|
| **2177** | A606 | 100e multicolored | 1.25 | .65 |

Brotherhood of the Yeoman of Beja, 700th anniv.

A607

**1997, Aug. 29** **Litho.** *Perf. 12*

| | | | | |
|---|---|---|---|---|
| **2178** | A607 | 50e multicolored | 1.00 | .30 |

Natl. Laboratory of Civil Engineering, 50th anniv.

Treaty of Alcanices, 700th Anniv. A608

**1997, Sept. 12**

| | | | | |
|---|---|---|---|---|
| **2179** | A608 | 80e multicolored | 1.00 | .50 |

Arms of the Districts of Portugal A609

**1997, Sept. 17**

| | | | | |
|---|---|---|---|---|
| **2180** | A609 | 10e Evora | .25 | .25 |
| **2181** | A609 | 49e Faro | .55 | .30 |
| **2182** | A609 | 80e Guarda | .85 | .50 |
| **2183** | A609 | 100e Leiria | 1.40 | .65 |
| **2184** | A609 | 140e Lisboa | 1.60 | .90 |
| *a.* | | Souv. sheet, #2180, 2182, 2184 | 3.50 | 3.00 |
| **2185** | A609 | 200e Portalegre | 2.25 | 1.25 |
| *a.* | | Souv. sheet, #2181, 2183, 2185 | 4.50 | 4.00 |
| | | *Nos. 2180-2185 (6)* | 6.90 | 3.85 |

See Nos. 2249-2254.

Incorporation of Postal Service in State Administration, Bicent. — A610

**1997, Oct. 9**

| | | | | |
|---|---|---|---|---|
| **2186** | A610 | 80e multicolored | 1.00 | .50 |

Portuguese Cartography — A611

Designs: 49e, Map from atlas of Lopo Homen-Reineis, 1519. 80e, Map from atlas of Joao Freire, 1546. 100e, Chart by Diogo Ribeiro, 1529. 140e, Anonymous map, 1630.

**1997, Oct. 9**

| | | | | |
|---|---|---|---|---|
| **2187** | A611 | 49e multicolored | .60 | .30 |
| **2188** | A611 | 80e multicolored | 1.00 | .50 |
| **2189** | A611 | 100e multicolored | 1.25 | .60 |
| **2190** | A611 | 140e multicolored | 1.75 | .90 |
| *a.* | | Souvenir sheet, #2187-2190 | 4.75 | 4.75 |
| | | *Nos. 2187-2190 (4)* | 4.60 | 2.30 |

**Discovery of Maritime Route to India Type of 1996**

Voyage of Vasco da Gama: 49e, St. Gabriel's cross, Quelimane. 80e, Stop at island off Mozambique. 100e, Arrival in Mombasa. 140e, Reception for king of Melinde. 315e, Trading with natives, Natal.

**1997, Nov. 5** *Perf. 13½*

| | | | | |
|---|---|---|---|---|
| **2191** | A593 | 49e multicolored | .60 | .30 |
| **2192** | A593 | 80e multicolored | 1.00 | .50 |
| **2193** | A593 | 100e multicolored | 1.25 | .60 |
| **2194** | A593 | 140e multicolored | 1.75 | .90 |
| | | *Nos. 2191-2194 (4)* | 4.60 | 2.30 |

**Souvenir Sheet**

| | | | | |
|---|---|---|---|---|
| **2195** | A593 | 315e multicolored | 4.25 | 4.25 |

Expo '98 — A612

Plankton: 49e, Loligo vulgaris. 80e, Scyllarus arctus. 100e, Pontellina plumata. 140e, Solea senegalensis.

No. 2200: a, Calcidiscus leptoporus. b, Tabellaria.

**1997, Nov. 5** *Perf. 12*

| | | | | |
|---|---|---|---|---|
| **2196** | A612 | 49e multicolored | .60 | .30 |
| **2197** | A612 | 80e multicolored | 1.00 | .50 |
| **2198** | A612 | 100e multicolored | 1.25 | .65 |
| **2199** | A612 | 140e multicolored | 1.75 | .90 |
| | | *Nos. 2196-2199 (4)* | 4.60 | 2.35 |

**Souvenir Sheet**

*Perf. 12½*

| | | | | |
|---|---|---|---|---|
| **2200** | | Sheet of 2 | 3.00 | 3.00 |
| *a.-b.* | | A612 100e any single | 1.50 | 1.50 |

See Nos. 2215-2219, 2226-2244.

**Souvenir Sheet**

Sintra, UNESCO World Heritage Site — A613

**1997, Dec. 5** *Perf. 12*

| | | | | |
|---|---|---|---|---|
| **2201** | A613 | 350e multicolored | 4.50 | 4.50 |

Portuguese Military Engineering, 350th Anniv. — A614

Engineering officer, map of fortress: 50e, Almeida. 80e, Miranda do Douro. 100e, Moncao. 140e, Elvas.

**1998, Jan. 28** **Litho.** *Perf. 12*

| | | | | |
|---|---|---|---|---|
| **2202** | A614 | 50e multicolored | .60 | .30 |
| **2203** | A614 | 80e multicolored | 1.00 | .50 |
| **2204** | A614 | 100e multicolored | 1.25 | .65 |
| **2205** | A614 | 140e multicolored | 1.75 | .90 |
| *a.* | | Booklet pane, #2202-2205, perf. 12 vert. | 6.00 | |
| | | Complete booklet, #2205a | 6.00 | |
| | | *Nos. 2202-2205 (4)* | 4.60 | 2.35 |

Roberto Ivens (1850-98), Naturalist A615

**1998, Jan. 28**

| | | | | |
|---|---|---|---|---|
| **2206** | A615 | 140e multicolored | 1.75 | .90 |

Misericórdias (Philanthropic Organizations), 500th Anniv. — A616

Sculptures: 80e, Madonna wearing crown surrounded by angels, people kneeling in praise, vert. 100e, People of antiquity gathered around another's bedside.

**1998, Feb. 20**

| | | | | |
|---|---|---|---|---|
| **2207** | A616 | 80e multicolored | 1.00 | .50 |
| **2208** | A616 | 100e multicolored | 1.25 | .65 |

Souvenir Sheet

Aqueduct of the Free Waters, 250th Anniv. — A617

**1998, Feb. 20**

**2209** A617 350e multicolored 4.50 2.25

### 19th Cent. Professions Type

10e, Fish seller. 40e, Collector of alms. 50e, Ceramics seller. 85e, Duck and eggs vendor. 250e, Queijadas (small cakes made of cheese) seller.

**1998, Mar. 20** ***Perf. 11½x12***

**2210** A560 10e multicolored .25 .25
**2211** A560 40e multicolored .40 .25
**2212** A560 50e multicolored .50 .30
*a.* Booklet pane of 10 5.00
Complete booklet, #2212a 5.00
**2213** A560 85e multicolored 1.00 .55
*a.* Booklet pane of 10 10.00
Complete booklet, #2213a 10.00
**2214** A560 250e multicolored 3.00 1.60
*Nos. 2210-2214 (5)* 5.15 2.95

### Expo '98 Type of 1997

Plankton: 50e, Pilumnus hirtellus. 85e, Lophius piscatorius. 100e, Sparus aurata. 140e, Cladonema radiatum.

No. 2219: a, Noctiluca miliaris. b, Dinophysis acuta.

**1998, Mar. 20** ***Perf. 12***

**2215** A612 50e multicolored .55 .30
**2216** A612 85e multicolored .90 .50
**2217** A612 100e multicolored 1.20 .65
**2218** A612 140e multicolored 1.60 .90
*Nos. 2215-2218 (4)* 4.25 2.35

**Souvenir Sheet**

**2219** A612 100e Sheet of 2, #a.-b. 2.50 2.50
*c.* Sheet of 12, #2196-2199, 2200a-2200b, 2215-2218, 2219a-2219b 15.00 15.00

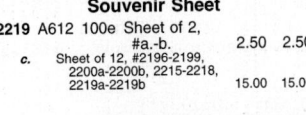

Opening of the Vasco Da Gama Bridge A618

**1998, Mar. 29** **Litho.** ***Perf. 12***

**2220** A618 200e multicolored 2.50 1.25

**Souvenir Sheet**

**2221** A618 200e like #2220 2.50 2.50

Stamp in No. 2221 is a continuous design and shows bridge cables overlapping at far left.

Oporto Industrial Assoc., 150th Anniv. A619

**1998, Apr. 30**

**2222** A619 80e multicolored 1.00 .50

Vasco da Gama Aquarium, Cent. A620

**1998, May 13**

**2223** A620 50e Seahorse .60 .30
**2224** A620 80e Fish 1.00 .50

National Festivals A621

**1998, May 21**

**2225** A621 100e People's Saints *1.25 .65*
*a.* Souvenir sheet of 3 *3.75 3.75*

Europa.

### Expo '98 Type of 1997

Designs: No. 2226, Portuguese sailing ship, face on stone cliff. No. 2227, Diver, astrolabe. No. 2228, Various fish. No. 2229, Research submersible, fish. No. 2230, Mermaid swimming. No. 2231, Children under water holding globe.

No. 2232: a, Portuguese Pavilion. b, Pavilion of the Future. c, Oceans Pavilion. d, Knowledge of the Seas Pavilion. e, Pavilion of Utopia. f, Mascot putting letter into mailbox.

No. 2233, Like #2216, inscribed "Larva de Tamboril" only. No. 2234, Like #2219a, inscribed "Protozário Broluminiscente" only. No. 2235, Like #2215, inscribed "Larvas de Caranguejos" only. No. 2236, Like #2217, inscribed "Larvas de Dourada" only. No. 2237, Like #2219b, inscribed "Dinoflagelados" only. No. 2238, Like #2218, inscribed "Medusa" only.

No. 2239, like #2227. No. 2240, like #2229. No. 2241, like #2231. No. 2242, like #2226. No. 2243, like #2228. No. 2244, like #2230.

**1998, May 21**

**2226** A612 50e multicolored .60 .30
**2227** A612 50e multicolored .60 .30
**2228** A612 85e multicolored 1.00 .50
**2229** A612 85e multicolored 1.00 .50
**2230** A612 140e multicolored 1.75 .90
**2231** A612 140e multicolored 1.75 .90
*a.* Sheet of 6, #2226-2231 6.75 6.75
**2232** Sheet of 6, #a.-f. 6.75 6.75
*a.* A612 50e multicolored .60 .30
*b.-c.* A612 85e any single 1.00 .50
*d.-e.* A612 140e any single 1.75 .90
*f.* A612 80e multicolored 1.00 .50
*g.* Souvenir sheet, #2232a-2232e 6.25 6.25

***Die Cut 11½***

**Self-Adhesive Coil Stamps**

**Size: 29x24mm**

**2233** A612 50e multicolored .60 .30
**2234** A612 50e multicolored .60 .30
**2235** A612 50e multicolored .60 .30
**2236** A612 50e multicolored .60 .30
**2237** A612 50e multicolored .60 .30
**2238** A612 50e multicolored .60 .30
*a.* Strip of 6, #2233-2238 3.75
**2239** A612 85e multicolored 1.00 .45
**2240** A612 85e multicolored 1.00 .45
**2241** A612 85e multicolored 1.00 .45
**2242** A612 85e multicolored 1.00 .45
**2243** A612 85e multicolored 1.00 .45
**2244** A612 85e multicolored 1.00 .45
*a.* Strip of 6, #2239-2244 6.00

Nos. 2233-2238 are not inscribed with Latin names.

Discovery of Radium, Cent. — A622

**1998, June 1** ***Perf. 12***

**2245** A622 140e Marie Curie 1.75 .90

Ferreira de Castro (1898-1974), Writer — A623

**1998, June 10**

**2246** A623 50e multicolored .70 .30

Bernardo Marques, Artist, Birth Cent. — A624

**1998, June 10**

**2247** A624 85e multicolored 1.10 .50

Souvenir Sheet

Universal Declaration of Human Rights, 50th Anniv. — A625

**1998, June 18**

**2248** A625 315e multicolored 4.00 2.00

### District Arms Type of 1997

**1998, June 23**

**2249** A609 50e Vila Real .65 .30
**2250** A609 85e Setubal .95 .50
**2251** A609 85e Viana do Castelo .95 .50
**2252** A609 100e Santarem 1.20 .65
**2253** A609 100e Viseu 1.20 .65
*a.* Souvenir sheet of 3, #2250, 2252-2253 4.00 4.00
**2254** A609 200e Porto 2.25 1.25
*a.* Souvenir sheet of 3, #2249, 2251, 2254 3.25 3.25
*Nos. 2249-2254 (6)* 7.20 3.85

Marinha Grande Glass Industry, 250th Anniv. A626

Designs: 50e, Blowing glass, furnace. 80e, Early worker heating glass, ornament. 100e, Factory, bottles. 140e, Modern worker heating glass, vases.

**1998, July 7**

**2255** A626 50e multicolored .55 .30
**2256** A626 80e multicolored .90 .50
**2257** A626 100e multicolored 1.10 .65
**2258** A626 140e multicolored 1.75 .90
*Nos. 2255-2258 (4)* 4.30 2.35

1998 Vasco da Gama Regatta A627

Sailing ship, country represented: 50e, Sagres, Portugal. No. 2260, Asgard II, Ireland. No. 2261, Rose, US. No. 2262, Kruzenshtern, Russia. No. 2263, Amerigo Vespucci, Italy. 140e, Creoula, Portugal.

**1998, July 31**

**2259** A627 50e multicolored .60 .30
**2260** A627 85e multicolored 1.00 .50
**2261** A627 85e multicolored 1.00 .50
**2262** A627 100e multicolored 1.25 .65
**2263** A627 100e multicolored 1.25 .65
**2264** A627 140e multicolored 1.75 .90
*Nos. 2259-2264 (6)* 6.85 3.50

### Discovery of Maritime Route to India Type of 1996

Voyage of Vasco da Gama: No. 2265, Meeting with pilot, Ibn Madjid. 80e, Storm in the Indian Ocean. 100e, Arrival in Calicut. 140e, Meeting with the Samorin of Calicut.

No. 2269: a, like #2136. b, like #2137. c, like #2138. d, like #2139. e, like #2191. f, like #2192. g, like #2193. h, like #2194. i, like #2266. j, like #2267. k, like #2268.

315e, King of Melinde listening to narration of the history of Portugal.

**1998, Sept. 4** ***Perf. 13½***

**2265** A593 50e multicolored .60 .30
**2266** A593 80e multicolored .85 .50
**2267** A593 100e multicolored 1.25 .65
**2268** A593 140e multicolored 1.60 .90
*Nos. 2265-2268 (4)* 4.30 2.35

**Sheet of 12**

**2269** A593 50e #a.-k. + #2265 7.50 7.50

**Souvenir Sheet**

**2270** A593 315e multicolored 4.00 4.00

Lisbon-Coimbra Mail Coach, Decree to Reorganize Maritime Mail to Brazil, Bicent. — A628

50e, Modern van delivering mail, postal emblm. 140e, Sailing ship, Postilhao da America, mail coach.

**1998, Oct. 9** ***Perf. 12x11½***

**2271** A628 50e multicolored 1.00 .30
**2272** A628 140e multicolored 2.00 .90

See Brazil No. 2691.

Souvenir Sheet

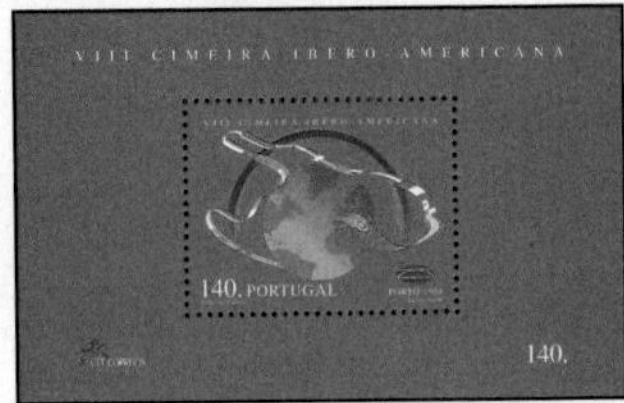

8th Iberian-American Summit, Oporto — A629

**1998, Oct. 18** ***Perf. 12½***

**2273** A629 140e multicolored 1.75 1.75

Souvenir Sheet

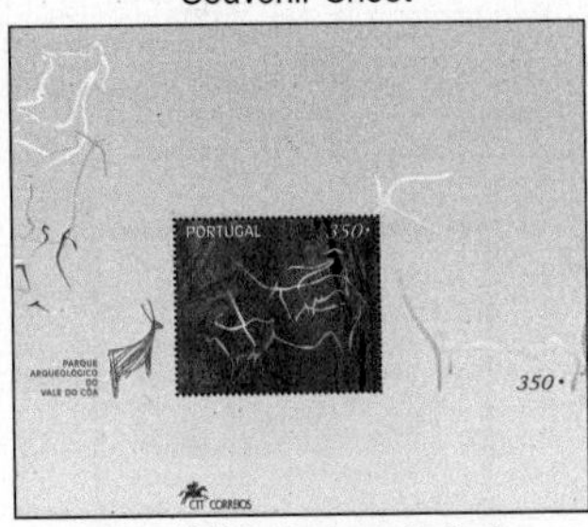

Coa Valley Archaeological Park — A630

**1998, Oct. 23** ***Perf. 13½***

**2274** A630 350e multicolored 4.25 2.25

Health in Portugal — A631

**1998, Nov. 5** ***Perf. 12***

**2275** A631 100e multicolored 1.25 .65

Souvenir Sheet

José Saramago, 1998 Nobel Prize Winner for Literature — A632

**1998, Dec. 15 Litho. *Perf. 12***

2276 A632 200e multicolored 2.50 1.25

**Postrider Type of 1993**

**1999, Jan. 11 Litho. *Perf. 13¼***

2276A A521 A brown, gray & black 1.00 .50

No. 2276A sold for 51e on date of issue. Inscription at LR reads "Imp: Lito Maia 99."

**19th Cent. Professions Type**

Designs: 51e, Knife grinder. 86e, Female bread seller. 95e, Coachman. 100e, Milkmaid. 210e, Basket seller.

**1999, Feb. 26 Litho. *Perf. 11½x12***

2277 A560 51e multicolored .45 .35
2278 A560 86e multicolored .90 .55
2279 A560 95e multicolored 1.00 .65
2280 A560 100e multicolored 1.10 .65
2281 A560 210e multicolored 2.50 1.40
*Nos. 2277-2281 (5)* 5.95 3.60

**Booklet Stamps**
**Self-Adhesive**
***Serpentine Die Cut 11¼***

2281A A560 51e like #2277 .65 .35
c. Booklet pane of 10 6.50
2281B A560 95e like #2279 1.25 .65
d. Booklet pane of 10 12.50

Nos. 2281A and 2281B were issued as coil rolls of 100 (No. 2281A) or 50 (No. 2281B) as well as in booklet form. Values the same. Used examples of each denomination are identical.

Nos. 2281Ac, 2281Bd are complete booklets. The peelable backing serves as a booklet cover.

Beginning with No. 2282 denominations are on the stamps in both escudos and euros. Listings show the value in escudos.

Introduction of the Euro — A633

**1999, Mar. 15 *Perf. 12***

2282 A633 95e multicolored 1.25 1.00

Australia '99, World Stamp Expo — A634

Portuguese in Australia: No. 2283, Sailing ship offshore, kangaroos. No. 2284, Sailing ship, natives watching.
350e, like #2283-2284.

**1999, Mar. 19**

2283 140e multicolored 1.75 .90
2284 140e multicolored 1.75 .90
a. A634 Pair, #2283-2284 3.50 3.50

**Souvenir Sheet**

2285 A634 350e multicolored 4.25 4.25

No. 2285 contains one 80x30mm stamp and is a continuous design.

Presidential Campaign of José Norton de Matos, 50th Anniv. — A635

**1999, Mar. 24**

2286 A635 80e multicolored 1.10 .50

Joao Almeida Garrett (1799-1854), Writer — A636

**1999, Mar. 24**

2287 A636 95e multicolored 1.25 .65

**Souvenir Sheet**

2288 A636 210e like #2287 2.50 1.40

Flight Between Portugal and Macao, 75th Anniv. A637

Airplanes: No. 2289, Breguet 16 Bn2, "Patria." No. 2290, DH9.

**1999, Apr. 19**

2289 A637 140e multicolored 1.75 .90
2290 A637 140e multicolored 1.75 .90
a. Souvenir sheet, #2289-2290 3.50 3.50

See Macao 979-980.

Carnation A638

Assembly building — A639

**1999, Apr. 25**

2291 A638 51e multicolored .55 .30
2292 A639 80e multicolored .95 .50
a. Souvenir sheet, #2291-2292 1.50 1.50

Revolution, 25th Anniv.

Council of Europe, 50th Anniv. A640

**1999, May 5 Litho. *Perf. 12x11¾***

2293 A640 100e multicolored 1.25 .65

Europa A641

100e, Wolf, iris, Peneda-Gerês Natl. Park.

**1999, May 5**

2294 A641 100e multicolored *1.25 .65*
a. Souvenir sheet of 3 *3.75 3.75*

Marquis de Pombal (1699-1782), Statesman — A642

No. 2295: 80e, Portrait.
No. 2296: a, 80e, Portrait and portion of statue. b, 210e, Hand, quill pen.

**1999, May 13**

2295 A642 80e multicolored 1.10 1.00

**Souvenir Sheet**

2296 A642 Sheet of 2, #a.-b. 3.50 3.50

Meeting of Portuguese and Chinese Cultures in Macao — A643

Designs: 51e, Ship, junk, bridge. 80e, Macao dancers in Portuguese outfits. 95e, Virgin Mary statue, dragon heads. 100e, Church, temple. 140e, Statues in park, horiz.

***Perf. 11¾x12, 12x11¾***

**1999, June 24 Litho.**

2297 A643 51e multicolored .50 .30
2298 A643 80e multicolored .90 .50
2299 A643 95e multicolored 1.00 .60
2300 A643 100e multicolored 1.10 .65
2301 A643 140e multicolored 1.50 .90
*Nos. 2297-2301 (5)* 5.00 2.95

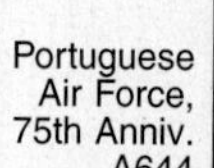

Portuguese Air Force, 75th Anniv. A644

Designs: No. 2302, De Havilland DH 82A Tiger Moth. No. 2303, Supermarine Spitfire Vb. No. 2304, Breguet Bre XIV A2. No. 2305, Spad S. VII-C1. No. 2306, Caudron G.III. No. 2307, Junkers Ju-52/3m g3e.

**1999, July 1 *Perf. 12x11¾***

2302 A644 51e multicolored .55 .30
2303 A644 51e multicolored .55 .30
2304 A644 85e multicolored .90 .55
2305 A644 85e multicolored .90 .55
2306 A644 95e multicolored 1.10 .65
2307 A644 95e multicolored 1.10 .65
a. Souv. sheet of 6, #2302-2307 5.00 5.00
*Nos. 2302-2307 (6)* 5.10 3.00

Surrealist Group of Lisbon, 50th Anniv. A645

Sections of Painting "Cadavre Exquis" by: 51e, António Pedro (1909-66). 80e, Marcellino Vespeira (b. 1926). 95e, Joao Moniz Pereira (1920-89). 100e, Fernando de Azevedo (b. 1923). 140e, António Domingues (b. 1921).

**1999, July 2 Litho. *Perf. 13¼***

2308 A645 51e multicolored .50 .30
2309 A645 80e multicolored .85 .50
2310 A645 95e multicolored 1.00 .60
2311 A645 100e multicolored 1.10 .65
2312 A645 140e multicolored 1.60 .90
a. Souv. sheet of 5, #2308-2312 5.25 5.25
*Nos. 2308-2312 (5)* 5.05 2.95

PhilexFrance 99, No. 2312a.

Inauguration of Rail Link Over 25th of April Bridge — A646

51e, No. 2315, Train, tunnel entrance. 95e, No. 2316, Train, viaduct, Tagus River.

**1999, July 29 Litho. *Perf. 12x11¾***

2313 A646 51e multicolored .60 .30
2314 A646 95e multicolored 1.25 .60

**Souvenir Sheets**

2315 A646 350e multicolored 4.25 4.25
2316 A646 350e multicolored 4.25 4.25

Nos. 2315-2316 each contain one 80x30mm stamp.

UPU, 125th Anniv. A647

Designs: 95e, Heinrich von Stephan, earth, letter. 140e, Computer, earth, letter. 315e, Von Stephan, computer, earth, letters.

**1999, Aug. 21**

2317 A647 95e multicolored 1.10 .65
2318 A647 140e multicolored 1.60 .90

**Souvenir Sheet**

2319 A647 315e multicolored 3.75 3.75

No. 2319 contains one 80x30mm stamp.

Desserts Originating in Convents A648

Designs: 51e, Trouxas de ovos. 80e, Pudim de ovos (egg pudding). 95e, Papos de anjo. 100e, Palha de Abrantes. 140e, Castanhas de Viseu. 210e, Bolo de mel (honey cake).

**1999, Aug. 30**

2320 A648 51e multicolored .60 .30
2321 A648 80e multicolored .95 .50
2322 A648 95e multicolored 1.10 .60
2323 A648 100e multicolored 1.20 .65
2324 A648 140e multicolored 1.60 .90
2325 A648 210e multicolored 2.25 1.40
*Nos. 2320-2325 (6)* 7.70 4.35

See Nos. 2366-2371.

Conquest of Algarve, 750th Anniv. A649

**1999, Sept. 3 Litho.** ***Perf. 12x11¾***

**2326** A649 100e multicolored 1.25 .65

Medical Pioneers A650

#2327, Ricardo Jorge (1858-1939), Natl. Health Inst. #2328, Camara Pestana (1863-99), microscope, Pestana Bacteriological Inst. #2329, Francisco Gentil (1878-1964), Portuguese Inst. of Oncology. #2330, Egas Moniz (1874-1955), cerebral angiogram. #2331, Reynaldo dos Santos (1880-1970), arteriogram. #2332, Joao Cid dos Santos (1907-76), performer of 1st endarterectomy.

**1999, Sept. 20**

| | | |
|---|---|---|
| **2327** A650 51e multicolored | .60 | .30 |
| **2328** A650 51e multicolored | .60 | .30 |
| **2329** A650 80e multicolored | .90 | .50 |
| **2330** A650 80e multicolored | .90 | .50 |
| **2331** A650 95e multicolored | 1.10 | .60 |
| **2332** A650 95e multicolored | 1.10 | .60 |
| *Nos. 2327-2332 (6)* | 5.20 | 2.80 |

José Diogo de Mascarenhas Neto, First Superintendent of Posts — A651

**1999, Oct. 9**

**2333** A651 80e multicolored 1.10 .50

Postal reorganization and provisional mail regulations, bicent.

Jaime Martins Barata (1899-1970), Painter, Philatelic Art Consultant — A652

**1999, Oct. 9**

**2334** A652 80e multicolored 1.10 .50

Christmas A653

Art by handicapped persons: 51e, Maria F. Gonçalves (Magi). 95e, Marta Silva. 140e, Luis F. Farinha. 210e, Gonçalves (Nativity).

**1999, Nov. 19**

| | | |
|---|---|---|
| **2335** A653 51e multicolored | .55 | .30 |
| **2336** A653 95e multicolored | 1.10 | .60 |
| **2337** A653 140e multicolored | 1.50 | .90 |
| **2338** A653 210e multicolored | 2.40 | 1.40 |
| *Nos. 2335-2338 (4)* | 5.55 | 3.20 |

Souvenir Sheet

Meeting of Portuguese and Chinese Cultures — A654

**1999, Nov. 19** ***Perf. 11¾x12***

**2339** A654 140e multicolored 2.00 1.25

See Macao No. 1009.

Souvenir Sheet

Retrospective of Macao's Portuguese History — A655

**1999, Dec. 19 Litho.** ***Perf. 12x11¾***

**2340** A655 350e multicolored 4.50 4.50

See Macao No. 1011.

Birth of Jesus Christ, 2000th Anniv. — A656

**2000, Feb. 15 Litho.** ***Perf. 11¾x12***

**2341** A656 52e multicolored .60 .30

The 20th Century A657

Designs: 86e, Astronaut and spacecraft.

No. 2343: a, Human rights. b, Fashions (60x30mm). c, Ecology (60x30mm). d, Transportation (old). e, Transportation (modern). f, Like No. 2342. g, Space shuttle.

No. 2344: a, Authors Marcel Proust, Thomas Mann, James Joyce, Franz Kafka, Fernando Pessoa, Jorge Luis Borges, Samuel Beckett (50x30mm). b, Musicians and composers Claude Debussy, Igor Stravinsky, Arnold Schoenberg, Béla Bartók, George Gershwin, Charlie Parker, Bill Evans (50x30mm). c, Stage. d, Stage, diff. (60x30mm). e, Art (50x30mm). f, Art (30x30mm). g. Cinema (50x30mm). h, Cinema and television (30x30mm). i, Architecture (denomination at LL). j, Architecture (denomination at LR). k, Architecture (denomination at center).

No. 2345: a, Philosophers Edmund Husserl, Ludwig Wittgenstein, Martin Heidegger. b, Mathematicians Jules-Henri Poincaré, Kurt Gödel, Andrei Kolmogorov. c, Physicists Max Planck, Albert Einstein, Niels Bohr (50x30mm). d, Anthropologists Franz Boas, Claude Lévi-Strauss, Margaret Mead. e, Psychoanalyst Sigmund Freud and medical researcher Sir Alexander Fleming (30x30mm). f, Transplant pioneer Dr. Christiaan Barnard. g, Economists Joseph Schumpeter, John Maynard Keynes. h, Technology. i, Technology (30x30mm). j, Computer pioneers Alan Turing, John von Neumann. k, Radio pioneer Guglielmo Marconi. l, Information and communications (30x30mm).

**2000, Feb. 18** ***Perf. 12x11¾***

**2342** A657 86e multicolored 1.20 .55

**Souvenir Sheets of 7, 11, 12**

| | | |
|---|---|---|
| **2343** A657 52e #a.-g. | 4.50 | 4.50 |
| **2344** A657 52e #a.-k. | 7.00 | 7.00 |
| **2345** A657 52e #a.-l. | 7.75 | 7.75 |

Birds — A658

Designs: 52e, Golden eagle. 85e, Great crested grebe. 90e, Flamingo. 100e, Gannet. 215e, Teal.

**2000, Mar. 2 Litho.** ***Perf. 11¾x11½***

| | | |
|---|---|---|
| **2346** A658 52e multi | .60 | .30 |
| **2347** A658 85e multi | 1.10 | .55 |
| **2348** A658 90e multi | 1.10 | .55 |
| **2349** A658 100e multi | 1.25 | .65 |
| **2350** A658 215e multi | 2.75 | 1.40 |
| *Nos. 2346-2350 (5)* | 6.80 | 3.45 |

**Booklet Stamps**

***Serpentine Die Cut 11¼***

**Self-Adhesive**

| | | |
|---|---|---|
| **2351** A658 52e Like #2346 | .60 | .30 |
| *a.* Booklet, 10 #2351 | 6.00 | |
| **2352** A658 100e Like #2349 | 1.25 | .65 |
| *a.* Booklet, 10 #2352 | 12.50 | |

See Nos. 2401-2407, 2465-2471, 2472, 2473, 2530-2535, 2537-2537A, 2621-2626, 2628.

Portuguese Presidency of Council of Europe A659

**2000, Mar. 23** ***Perf. 12x11¾***

**2353** A659 100e multi 1.40 .65

Discovery of Brazil, 500th Anniv. A660

Designs: 52e, Two sailors, three natives, parrot. 85e, sailor, ships, four natives. 100e, Sailors, natives, sails. 140e, Sailor and natives inspecting tree.

**2000, Apr. 11 Litho.** ***Perf. 12x11¾***

| | | |
|---|---|---|
| **2354** A660 52e multi | .60 | .30 |
| **2355** A660 85e multi | 1.10 | .55 |
| **2356** A660 100e multi | 1.25 | .65 |
| **2357** A660 140e multi | 1.75 | .90 |
| *a.* Souvenir sheet, #2354-2357 | 4.50 | 2.40 |
| *Nos. 2354-2357 (4)* | 4.70 | 2.40 |

Lubrapex 2000 (#2357a). See Brazil No. 2738.

**Europa, 2000**

Common Design Type

**2000, May 9** ***Perf. 11¾x12***

| | | |
|---|---|---|
| **2358** CD17 100e multi | *1.25* | *.65* |
| *a.* Souvenir sheet of 3 | *3.75* | *3.75* |

Visit of Pope John Paul II A661

**2000, May 12** ***Perf. 12x11¾***

**2359** A661 52e multi 1.00 .40

Intl. Cycling Union, Cent. and The Stamp Show 2000, London A662

Bicycles: 52e, Draisenne, 1817. 85e, Michaux, 1868. 100e, Ariel, 1871. 140e, Rover, 1888. 215e, BTX, 2000. 350e, GT, 2000.

**2000, May 22**

| | | |
|---|---|---|
| **2360** A662 52e multi | .60 | .30 |
| **2361** A662 85e multi | 1.10 | .55 |
| **2362** A662 100e multi | 1.25 | .65 |
| **2363** A662 140e multi | 1.75 | .90 |
| **2364** A662 215e multi | 2.75 | 1.40 |
| **2365** A662 350e multi | 4.50 | 2.25 |
| *a.* Souvenir sheet, #2360-2365 | 12.00 | 12.00 |
| *Nos. 2360-2365 (6)* | 11.95 | 6.05 |

**Desserts Type of 1999**

Designs: 52e, Fatias de Tomar. 85e, Dom rodrigos. 100e, Sericaia. 140e, Pao-de-ló. 215e, Pao de rala. 350e, Bolo real paraíso.

**2000, May 30**

| | | |
|---|---|---|
| **2366** A648 52e multi | .60 | .30 |
| **2367** A648 85e multi | 1.10 | .55 |
| **2368** A648 100e multi | 1.25 | .65 |
| **2369** A648 140e multi | 1.75 | .90 |
| **2370** A648 215e multi | 2.75 | 1.40 |
| **2371** A648 350e multi | 4.50 | 2.25 |
| *Nos. 2366-2371 (6)* | 11.95 | 6.05 |

Fishermen's Day — A663

**2000, May 31**

**2372** A663 52e multi .70 .35

Expo 2000, Hanover — A664

Designs: 100e, Portuguese landscapes. 350e, Portuguese pavilion.

**2000, June 1**

**2373** A664 100e multi 1.25 .65

**Souvenir Sheet**

**2374** A664 350e multi 4.25 4.25

No. 2374 contains one 40x31mm stamp.

Constituent Assembly, 25th Anniv. A665

**2000, June 2**

**2375** A665 85e multi 1.10 .55

Cod Fishing A666

Cod, various fishermen and boats.

**2000, June 24** ***Perf. 12x11¾***

**Color of Denominations**

| | | |
|---|---|---|
| **2376** A666 52e rose | .55 | .30 |
| **2377** A666 85e claret | .90 | .45 |
| **2378** A666 100e green | 1.10 | .55 |
| **2379** A666 100e red | 1.10 | .55 |

**2380** A666 140e yellow 1.50 .75
**2381** A666 215e brown 2.50 1.25
*a.* Souvenir sheet, #2376-2381 8.00 8.00
*Nos. 2376-2381 (6)* 7.65 3.85

Eça de Queiroz (1845-1900), Writer — A667

**2000, Aug. 16 Litho. *Perf. 12x11¾***
**2382** A667 85e multi 1.10 .55

2000 Summer Olympics, Sydney A668

Designs: 52e, Runner. 85e, Show jumping. 100e, Yachting. 140e, Diving.
No. 2387: a, 85e, Fencing. b, 215e, Beach volleyball.

**2000, Sept. 15**
**2383-2386** A668 Set of 4 4.25 2.10

**Souvenir Sheet**

**2387** A668 Sheet of 2, #a-b 3.75 3.75

Olymphilex 2000, Sydney (No. 2387).

Snoopy A669

Snoopy: No. 2388, 52e, At computer on dog house. No. 2389, 52e, Mailing letter. 85e, Driving mail truck. 100e, At letter sorting machine. 140e, Delivering mail. 215e, Reading letter.

**2000, Oct. 6**
**2388-2393** A669 Set of 6 7.75 3.75
*2393a* Souvenir sheet, #2288-2393 7.75 7.75

Lisbon Geographic Society, 125th Anniv. — A670

No. 2394: a, 85e, African native, geographer, theodolite, sextant. b, 100e, Sextant, society emblem, map, zebras.

**2000, Nov. 10**
**2394** A670 Horiz. pair, #a-b 2.25 1.10

Famous People — A671

No. 2395: a, Carolina Michaelis de Vasconcellos (1851-1925), teacher. b, Miguel Bombarda (1851-1910), doctor, politician. c, Bernardino Machado (1851-1944), politician. d, Tomás Alcaide (1901-67), singer. e, José Régio (1901-69), writer. f, José Rodrigues Miguéis (1901-80), writer. g, Vitorino Nemésio (1901-78), writer. h, Bento de Jesus Caraça (1901-48), mathematician.

**2001, Feb. 20 Litho. *Perf. 12x11¾***
**2395** A671 Sheet of 8 + 4 labels 8.00 8.00
*a.-h.* 85e Any single 1.00 .55

World Indoor Track and Field Championships — A672

Designs: 85e, Runners. 90e, Pole vault. 105e, Shot put. 250e, High jump.

**2001, Mar. 1**
**2396-2399** A672 Set of 4 6.00 3.00

**Souvenir Sheet**

**2400** A672 350e Hurdles 4.25 2.10

**Bird Type of 2000 and**

A672a

Designs: 53e, Sisao. No. 2402, Caimao. 105e, Perdiz-do-mar. 140e, Peneireiro cinzento. 225e, Abutre do Egipto.

**2001, Mar. 6 Litho. *Perf. 11¾x11½***
**2401** A658 53e multi .65 .35
**2402** A658 85e multi 1.10 .55
**2403** A658 105e multi 1.25 .65
**2404** A658 140e multi 1.75 .90
**2405** A658 225e multi 2.75 1.40
*Nos. 2401-2405 (5)* 7.50 3.85

***Serpentine Die Cut 11½x12***

**Self-Adhesive**

**2406** A658 53e multi .65 .35
*a.* Booklet of 10 6.50
**2406B** A672a 85e shown 1.10 .55
**2407** A658 105e multi 1.25 .65
*a.* Booklet of 10 12.50

Arab Heritage in Portugal A673

Designs: 53e, Plate with ship design, 15th cent. 90e, Tiles, 16th cent. 105e, Tombstone, 14th cent. 140e, Gold dinar, 12th cent. 225e, container, 11th cent. 350e, Ceramic jug, 12th-13th cent.

**2001, Mar. 28 Litho. *Perf. 12x11¾***
**2408-2413** A673 Set of 6 12.00 6.00

Stampin' the Future Children's Stamp Design Contest Winners A674

Art by: 85e, Angela M. Lopes. 90e, Maria G. Silva, vert. 105e, Joao A. Ferreira.

***Perf. 12x11¾, 11¾x12***

**2001, Apr. 10 Litho.**
**2414-2416** A674 Set of 3 3.50 1.75

Natl. Fine Arts Society, Cent. A675

Designs: 85e, Sculpture, building, stained glass window. 105e, Artist, painting. 350p, Hen and Chicks, by Girao.

**2001, Apr. 19 *Perf. 12x11¾***
**2417-2418** A675 Set of 2 2.40 1.25

**Souvenir Sheet**

**2419** A675 350e multi 4.25 4.25

Constitution, 25th Anniv. — A676

**2001, Apr. 25**
**2420** A676 85e multi 1.10 .55

Europa A677

**2001, May 9**
**2421** A677 105e multi 1.25 .65
*a.* Souvenir sheet of 3 3.75 3.75

Congratulations A678

Designs: No. 2422, 85e, Couple, hearts. No. 2423, 85e, Birthday cake. No. 2424, 85e, Drinks. No. 2425, 85e, Flowers.

**2001, May 16 *Perf. 11¾x12***
**2422-2425** A678 Set of 4 4.00 2.00
*2425a* Souvenir sheet, #2422-2425 4.00 4.00

Porto, European City of Culture A679

Bridge and: 53e, Open book. 85e, Globe, binary code. 105e, Piano. 140e, Stage curtain. 225e, Picture frame. 350e, Fireworks.

**2001, May 23 *Perf. 12x11¾***
**2426-2431** A679 Set of 6 11.00 5.50
*2431a* Souvenir sheet, #2426-2431 11.00 11.00

Military Museum, 150th Anniv. A680

Designs: 85e, Shell, 1773. 105e, Suit of armor, 16th cent.
No. 2434: a, 53e, Pistol of King Joseph I, 1757. b, 53e, Cannon, 1797. c, 140e, Cannon, 1533. d, 140e, Helmet, 14th-15th cent.

**2001, June 7**
**2432-2433** A680 Set of 2 2.50 1.25

**Souvenir Sheet**

**2434** A680 Sheet of 4, #a-d 5.00 5.00

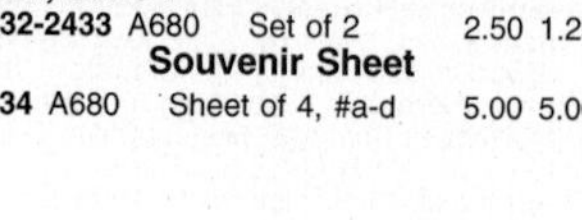

Animals at Lisbon Zoo A681

Designs: 53e, Bear. 85e, Monkey. 90e, Iguana. 105e, Penguin. 225e, Toucan. 350e, Giraffe.
No. 2441, vert.: a, 85e, Elephant. b, 85e, Zebra. c, 225e, Lion. d, 225e, Rhinoceros.

**2001, June 11 *Perf. 12x11¾***
**2435-2440** A681 Set of 6 11.00 5.50

**Souvenir Sheet**

**2441** A681 Sheet of 4, #a-d 7.50 7.50

Belgica 2001 Intl. Stamp Exhibition, Brussels (#2441).

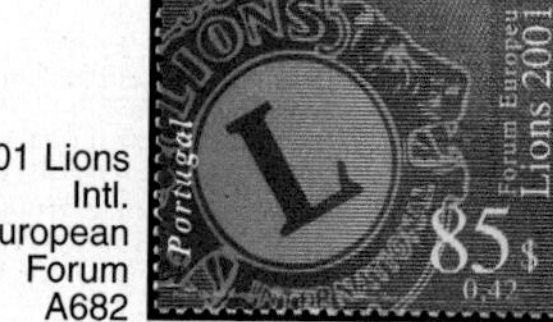


2001 Lions Intl. European Forum A682

**2001, Sept. 6 Litho. *Perf. 12x11¾***
**2442** A682 85e multi 1.10 .55

Pillars A683

No. 2443: a, Azinhoso. b, Soajo. c, Bragança. d, Linhares. e, Arcos de Valdevez. f, Vila de Rua. g, Sernancelhe. h, Frechas.

**2001, Sept. 19**
**2443** Block of 8 4.50 2.25
*a.-h.* A683 53e Any single .65 .35

Year of Dialogue Among Civilizations A684

**2001, Oct. 9**
**2444** A684 140e multi 1.60 .80

Walt Disney (1901-66) A685

Designs: No. 2445, Disney and sketches.
No. 2446 — Various tiles and: a, Huey, Dewey and Louie. b, Mickey Mouse. c, Minnie Mouse. d, Goofy. e, Pluto. f, Donald Duck. g, Scrooge McDuck. h, Daisy Duck.

**2001, Oct. 18 Litho. *Perf. 12x11¾***
**2445** A685 53e multi .70 .35

**Souvenir Sheet**

**2446** Sheet of 9, #a-h, 2445 6.25 6.25
*a.-h.* A685 53e Any single .65 .35

Security Services, 200th Anniv. A686

Designs: 53e, Royal police guards, Lisbon, 1801. 85e, Municipal guard, Lisbon, 1834.

90e, National infantry guard, 1911. 105e, National cavalry guard, 1911. 140e, Transit brigade guard, 1970. 350e, Fiscal brigade guard, 1993.
225e, National cavalry guard, 1911, diff.

**2001, Oct. 22**
**2447-2452** A686 Set of 6 10.00 5.00

**Souvenir sheet**

**2453** A686 225e multi 2.50 2.50

Sailing Ships — A687

No. 2454: a, Chinese junk, 13th cent. b, Portuguese caravel, 15th cent.

**2001, Nov. 8**
**2454** A687 53e Horiz. pair, #a-b 1.25 1.25

See People's Republic of China No. 3146.

100 Cents = 1 Euro (€)

Introduction of the Euro A688

**2002, Jan. 2 Litho.** ***Perf. 12x11¾***

| | | | | | |
|---|---|---|---|---|---|
| **2455** | A688 | 1c | 1c coin | .25 | .25 |
| **2456** | A688 | 2c | 2c coin | .25 | .25 |
| **2457** | A688 | 5c | 5c coin | .25 | .25 |
| **2458** | A688 | 10c | 10c coin | .25 | .25 |
| **2459** | A688 | 20c | 20c coin | .50 | .25 |
| **2460** | A688 | 50c | 50c coin | 1.00 | .50 |
| **2461** | A688 | €1 | €1 coin | 2.25 | 1.25 |
| **2462** | A688 | €2 | €2 coin | 4.50 | 2.25 |
| | *Nos. 2455-2462 (8)* | | | 9.25 | 5.25 |

Postrider A689

**2002, Jan. 2** ***Perf. 13¼***
**2463** A689 A multi .85 .40

No. 2463 sold for 28c on day of issue.

Damiao de Góis (1502-74), Diplomat and Historian — A690

**2002, Feb. 26** ***Perf. 12x11¾***
**2464** A690 45c multi 1.10 .55

**Bird Type of 2000 with Euro Denominations Only and**

A690a

Designs: 2c, Abelharuco. No. 2466, 28c, Andorinha do mar ana. No. 2467, 43c, Bufo real. No. 2468, 54c, Cortiçol de barriga branca. 60c, Noitibó de nuca vermelha. 70c, Cuco rabilongo. Nos. 2472A, 28c, Cuco-rabilongo. No. 2471A, 43c, Andorinha do mar ana. Nos. 2472, 2473, 54c, Bufo real.

**2002, Feb. 26** ***Perf. 11¾x11½***

| | | | | | |
|---|---|---|---|---|---|
| **2465** | A658 | 2c | multi | .25 | .25 |
| **2466** | A658 | 28c | multi | .60 | .30 |
| **2467** | A658 | 43c | multi | .90 | .45 |
| **2468** | A658 | 54c | multi | 1.20 | .60 |
| **2469** | A658 | 60c | multi | 1.40 | .70 |
| **2470** | A658 | 70c | multi | 1.60 | .80 |

**Serpentine Die Cut 11½x12, 11x11½ (#2471A)**

| | | | | | |
|---|---|---|---|---|---|
| **2471** | A658 | 28c | multi | .75 | .35 |
| **2471A** | A690a | 43c | multi | 1.00 | .50 |
| **2472** | A658 | 54c | multi | 1.40 | .70 |

**Booklet Stamps**

***Serpentine Die Cut 11¼x11***

| | | | | | |
|---|---|---|---|---|---|
| **2472A** | A658 | 28c | multi | .75 | .35 |
| *b.* | | Booklet pane of 10 | | 7.50 | |
| **2473** | A658 | 54c | multi | 1.20 | .60 |
| *a.* | | Booklet pane of 10 | | 12.00 | |
| | *Nos. 2465-2473 (11)* | | | 11.05 | 5.60 |

No. 2472A has thicker numerals than No. 2471. No. 2473 lacks dot between "bufo" and "real" found on No. 2472. No. 2472A lacks dot between "cuco" and "rebilongo" found on No. 2471.

Pedro Nunes (1502-78), Mathematician and Geographer — A691

Designs: No. 2474, 28c, Ship, Earth. No. 2475, 28c, Ship, sextant. €1.15, Nunes.

**2002, Mar. 6** ***Perf. 12x11¾***
**2474-2476** A691 Set of 3 3.50 1.75
*2476a* Souvenir sheet, #2474-2476 4.50 4.50

America Issue — Youth, Education and Literacy A692

Children and: No. 2477, 70c, Flower. No. 2478, 70c, Pencil. No. 2479, 70c, Book.

**2002, Mar. 12**
**2477-2479** A692 Set of 3 5.00 2.50

Astronomy A693

Designs: No. 2480, 28c, Nobres College, 16th cent. astrolabe, solar eclipse. No. 2481, Polytechnic Observatory, Lisbon, telescope, Jupiter. 43c, Coimbra Observatory, quadrant, stars. No. 2483, 45c, King Pedro V, telescope, sun. No. 2484, 45c, King Luis, Cassegrain telescope, comet. 54c, Ajuda Observatory, telescope, Moon. €1.15, Porto Observatory Cassegrain telescope, Saturn. €1.75 Projector of C. Gulbenkian Planetarium, planets.
No. 2488: a, 18th cent. armillary sphere. b, 19th cent. theodolite.

**2002, Apr. 23 Litho.** ***Perf. 12x11¾***
**2480-2487** A693 Set of 8 12.00 6.00

**Souvenir Sheet**

**2488** A693 70c Sheet of 2, #a-b 3.50 3.00

Grande Oriente Lusitano Masonic Organization, Bicent. — A694

**2002, May 9**
**2489** A694 43c multi 1.10 .55

Europa A695

**2002, May 9**
**2490** A695 54c multi *1.20 .70*
*a.* Souvenir sheet of 3, perf. 12½ *3.75 3.75*

Portuguese Air Force, 50th Anniv. A696

Designs: 28c, F-16. 43c, SA-300 Puma helicopter. 54c, A-Jet. 70c, C-130. €1.25, P-3P. No. 2496, €1.75, Fiat G91.
No. 2497: a, €1.15, Asas de Portugal. b, €1.75, Epsilon.

**2002, July 1 Litho.** ***Perf. 12x11¾***
**2491-2496** A696 Set of 6 12.00 6.00

**Souvenir Sheet**

**2497** A696 Sheet of 2, #a-b 7.00 7.00

Sports A697

Designs: No. 2498, 28c, Race walking. No. 2499, 28c, Gymnastics. No. 2500, 45c, Basketball. No. 2501, 45c, Handball. No. 2502, 54c, Fencing. No. 2503, 54c, Women's roller hockey. No. 2504, €1.75, Golf. No. 2505, €1.75, Soccer.
No. 2506: a, €1, Soccer players. b, €2, Soccer players, diff.

**2002, Aug. 2**
**2498-2505** A697 Set of 8 14.00 7.00

**Souvenir Sheet**

**2506** A697 Sheet of 2, #a-b 7.00 7.00

Portuguese Gymnastics Federation, 50th anniv. (#2499), World Fencing Championships (#2502), 6th Women's Roller Hockey Championships (#2503), 2002 World Cup Soccer Championships, Japan and Korea (#2505-2506), PhilaKorea 2002 World Stamp Exhibition (#2506).

13th World Economics Congress A698

**2002, Sept. 9**
**2507** A698 70c multi 1.60 .80

Ministry of Public Works, 150th Anniv. — A699

Designs: No. 2508, Anniversary emblem.
No. 2509: a, Port administration. b, Rail transportation. c, Air transportation. d, Infrastructure. e, Public buildings. f, Housing.

**2002, Sept. 30 Litho.** ***Perf. 12x12½***
**2508** A699 43c shown 1.00 .50

**Miniature Sheet**

**2509** Sheet of 6 6.50 6.50
*a.-f.* A699 43c Any single 1.00 .85

Technical Education in Portugal, 150th Anniv. A700

**2002, Oct. 9** ***Perf. 12x11¾***
**2510** A700 43c multi 1.10 .55

UNESCO World Heritage Sites — A701

Various views of: No. 2511, 28c, No. 2518, 70c, No. 2519, €1.25, Alcobaça Monastery. No. 2512, 28c, No. 2517, 70c, No. 2520, €1.25, Monastery of the Hieronymites. No. 2513, 43c, No. 2516, 54c, No. 2521, €1.25, Historic Center of Guimaraes. No. 2514, 43c, No. 2515, 54c, No. 2522, €1.25, Alto Douro Wine Region.

**2002, Nov. 7** ***Perf. 11¾x12, 12x11¾***
**2511-2518** A701 Set of 8 10.00 5.00

**Souvenir Sheets**

**2519-2522** A701 Set of 4 12.00 12.00

Size of Nos. 2515-2518: 80x30mm.

Portuguese Military College, Bicent. — A702

Military uniforms from: 20c, 1870. 30c, 1806. 43c, 1837. 55c, 1861. 70c, 1866. €2, 1912.
No. 2529: a, 1802. b, 1948.

**2003, Feb. 22 Litho.** ***Perf. 11¾x12***
**2523-2528** A702 Set of 6 10.00 4.50

**Souvenir Sheet**

**2529** A702 €1 Sheet of 2, #a-b 4.50 4.50

**Bird Type of 2000 With Euro Denominations Only and**

A703

Designs: 1c, Peto verde. 30c, Pombo das rochas. 43c, Melro azul. 55c, Toutinegra carrasqueira. 70c, Chasco ruivo.

**2003, Mar. 7** ***Perf. 11¾x11½***

| | | | | | |
|---|---|---|---|---|---|
| **2530** | A658 | 1c | multi | .25 | .25 |
| **2531** | A658 | 30c | multi | .60 | .30 |
| **2532** | A658 | 43c | multi | .85 | .45 |
| **2533** | A658 | 55c | multi | 1.10 | .60 |
| **2534** | A658 | 70c | multi | 1.50 | .75 |

**Self-Adhesive**

***Serpentine Die Cut 11¾***

**With Dots Between Words**

| | | | | | |
|---|---|---|---|---|---|
| **2535** | A658 | 30c | multi | .60 | .30 |
| **2536** | A703 | 43c | multi | .85 | .45 |
| **2537** | A658 | 55c | multi | 1.10 | .60 |
| | *Nos. 2530-2537 (8)* | | | 6.85 | 3.70 |

**Coil Stamp**

**Self-Adhesive**

**Without Dots Between Words**

**2537A** A658 30c multi 1.60 .60

Position of country name is at UL on No. 2531 but at LR on No. 2535; UR on No. 2533 but LL on No. 2537.
Nos. 2535-2537 have dots between the words in the bird's name. Two other stamps exist in this set. The editors would like to examine any examples.

European Year of Disabled People — A704

Crowd of people in design of: 30c, Person in wheelchair. 55c, Head with blue brain. 70c, Head with pink ear, eye and mouth.

**2003, Mar. 12** ***Perf. 13¼***
**2538-2540** A704 Set of 3 3.50 1.75

Portuguese Postage Stamps, 150th Anniv. A705

Designs: 30c, #1. 43c, #2. 55c, #3. 70c, #4.

**2003, Mar. 13** ***Perf. 12x11¾***
**2541-2544** A705 Set of 4 4.25 2.10

See No. 2578.

Orchids — A706

Designs: No. 2545, 46c, Aceras anthropophorum. No. 2546, 46c, Dactylorhiza maculata.

No. 2547, 30c: a, Orchis champagneuxii. b, Orchis morio. c, Serapias cordigera. d, Orchis coriophora. e, Ophrys bombyliflora. f, Ophrys vernixia. g, Ophrys speculum. h, Ophrys scolopax. i, Anacamptis pyramidalis.

No. 2548, 30c: a, Orchis italica. b, Ophrys tenthredinifera. c, Ophrys fusca fusca. d, Orchis papilionacea. e, Barlia robertiana. f, Ophrys lutea. g, Ophrys fusca. h, Ophrys apifera. i, Dactylorhiza ericetorum.

**2003, Apr. 29** **Litho.** ***Perf. 11¾x12***
**2545-2546** A706 Set of 2 2.40 1.10

**Sheets of 9, #a-i**

**2547-2548** A706 Set of 2 12.00 12.00

Europa A707

Poster art by: No. 2549, 55c, Fred Kradolfer, 1931. No. 2550, 55c, Joao Machado, 1997.

**2003, May 5** ***Perf. 12x12½***
**2549-2550** A707 Set of 2 *2.50 1.25*
*2550a* Souvenir sheet, #2549-2550 *2.50 2.00*

History of Law A708

Designs: 30c, Lawyer in black robe, lawyer in red robe, order of Portuguese lawyers. 43c, Two lawyers in black robes, national arms. 55c, Lawyer, bishop, manuscript. 70c, Lawyer in black robe, order of Portuguese lawyers, diff.

No. 2555: a, €1, Lawyer in red robe, left half of order of Portuguese lawyers. b, €2, Right half of order of Portuguese lawyers, bishop.

**2003, May 13** ***Perf. 12x11¾***
**2551-2554** A708 Set of 4 4.50 2.40

**Souvenir Sheet**

**2555** A708 Sheet of 2, #a-b 6.50 6.50

Traveling Exhibition on the 150th Anniv. of the First Portuguese Stamp A709

Exhibition stops: No. 2556, Viseu. No. 2557, Faro. No. 2558, Porto.

**2003** ***Perf. 14x13½***

**Background Color**

**2556** A709 30c yellow .75 .35
**2557** A709 30c white .75 .35
**2558** A709 30c blue .75 .35
*Nos. 2556-2558 (3)* 2.25 1.05

Issued: No. 2556, 5/23; No. 2557, 7/21.

2004 European Soccer Championships, Portugal — A710

Emblem with background color of: 30c, White. 43c, Dark blue. 47c, Brown carmine. 55c, Green. 70c, Brown orange.

No. 2564 — Emblem and quadrant of emblem with denomination at: a, LL. b, LR. c, UL. d, UR.

**2003, May 28** **Litho.** ***Perf. 14x13½***
**2559-2563** A710 Set of 5 6.00 2.75

**Souvenir Sheet**

**2564** A710 Sheet of 4 5.50 5.50
*a.-d.* 55c Any single 1.25 1.25
*e.* Souvenir sheet, #2559-2563, 2564a-2564d 12.00 12.00

Portuguese Automobile Club, Cent. A711

Emblems and: 30c, Driver in old automobile. 43c, Motorcyclist. €2, Driver in old automobile, blurred race car.

**2003, June 24** ***Perf. 12x11¾***
**2565-2567** A711 Set of 3 6.00 3.50

Ricardo do Espírito Santo Silva Foundation, 50th Anniv. — A712

Designs: No. 2568, 30c, Portrait of Ricardo do Espírito Santo Silva, by Eduardo Malta. No. 2569, 30c, Chess table, 18th cent. No. 2570, 43c, Cutlery in decorated case, c. 1720-1750. No. 2571, 43c, Salver, 15th cent. No. 2572, 55c, Chinese cutlery case, c, 1700-1722. No. 2573, 55c, Wooden tub, 18th cent.

No. 2574: a, €1, Chest with drawers, 17th cent. b, €2, Carpet, 18th cent.

**2003, July 9** ***Perf. 11¾x12***
**2568-2573** A712 Set of 6 5.50 3.00

**Souvenir Sheet**

**2574** A712 Sheet of 2, #a-b 7.00 7.00

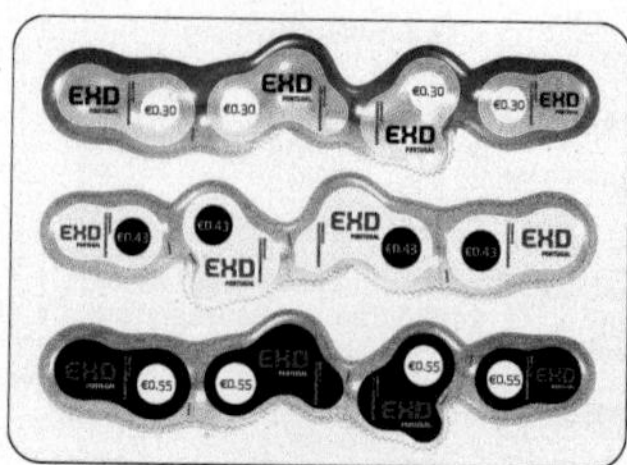


Experimental Design — A713

No. 2575: a, 2 lobes, black "EXD," white denomination circle to right. b, 3 lobes, black "EXD," white denomination circle below and to left. c, 3 lobes, black "EXD," white denomination circle above. d, 2 lobes, black "EXD," white denomination circle to left. e, 2 lobes, red "EXD," black denomination circle to right. f, 3 lobes, red "EXD," black denomination circle above. g, 3 lobes, red "EXD," black denomination circle below and to right. h, 2 lobes, red "EXD," black denomination circle to left. i, 2 lobes, red "EXD," white denomination circle to right. j, 3 lobes, red "EXD," white denomination circle below and to left. k, 3 lobes, red "EXD," white denomination circle above. l, 2 lobes, red "EXD," white denomination circle to left.

***Serpentine Die Cut***

**2003, Sept. 17** **Litho.**

**Self-Adhesive**

**2575** A713 Sheet of 12 12.00 12.00
*a.-d.* 30c Any single .65 .35
*e.-h.* 43c Any single 1.00 .50
*i.-l.* 55c Any single [illegible] [illegible]

Souvenir Sheet

Portuguese Stamps, 150th Anniv. — A714

**Litho. & Embossed**

**2003, Sept. 19** ***Perf. 12x11¾***
**2576** A714 €3 Queen Maria II, Type A2 7.00 7.00

Souvenir Sheet

Francisco de Borja Freire (1790-1869), Designer and Engraver of First Portuguese Stamp — A715

**Litho. With Hologram Applied**

**2003, Sept. 23** ***Perf. 12x12½***
**2577** A715 €2.50 multi 6.00 6.00

Souvenir Sheet

Lubrapex 2003 Philatelic Exhibition, Lisbon — A716

**2003, Sept. 25** **Litho.** ***Perf. 12x11¾***
**2578** A716 Sheet, #2578a, 4 #2541 4.00 4.00
*a.* 30c Queen Maria II 1.00 1.00

Size of No. 2578a: 40x60mm.

Fountains A717

Designs: 30c, Sao Joao Fountain, Moucós. 43c, Fountain of Virtues, Porto. 55c, Giraldo Square Fountain, Evora. 70c, Blessed Woman Fountain, Sao Marcos de Tavira. €1, Town Fountain, Castelo de Vide. €2, Santo André Fountain, Guarda.

**2003, Oct. 1** ***Perf. 12x11¾***
**2579-2584** A717 Set of 6 11.00 6.00

Glass — A718

Designs: 30c, Glass of King José I, 18th cent. 55c, Glass of Queen Maria II, 19th cent. 70c, Glass by Carmo Valente, 20th cent. €2, Glass by M. Helena Matos, 20th cent.

€1.50, Stained glass by Fernando Santos, 19th cent.

**2003, Oct. 9** ***Perf. 11¾x12***
**2585-2588** A718 Set of 4 8.00 4.25

**Souvenir Sheet**

**2589** A718 €1.50 multi 3.50 3.50

Apothecary Items A719

Designs: 30c, Persian jar, 12th-13th cent., Roman Empire medicine dropper, 1st-2nd cent. 43c, Bottle and bowl, 17th cent. 55c, Mortars and pestle, 16th and 17th cent. 70c, Alembic, 1910, and flask, 1890-1930.

**2003, Oct. 23** ***Perf. 12x11¾***
**2590-2593** A719 Set of 4 4.50 2.40

Portuguese Design A720

Designs: No. 2594, 43c, Secretary, by Daciano da Costa, 1962. No. 2595, 43c, Chair, by António Garcia, 1970, vert. No. 2596, 43c, Drawing table, by José Espinho, 1970. No. 2597, 43c, Chairs by Leonor and

António Sena da Silva, 1973. No. 2598, 43c, Telephone booth, by Pedro Silva Dias, 1998, vert. No. 2599, 43c, Cutlery, by Eduardo Afonsa Dias, 1976. No. 2600, 43c, Faucet, by Carlos Aguiar, 1998. No. 2601, 43c, Thermos bottle, by Carlos Rocha, 1982, vert. No. 2602, 43c, Tea cart, by Cruz de Carvalho, 1957.

**2003, Oct. 31** ***Perf. 12x11¾, 11¾x12***
**2594-2602** A720 Set of 9 11.00 4.50

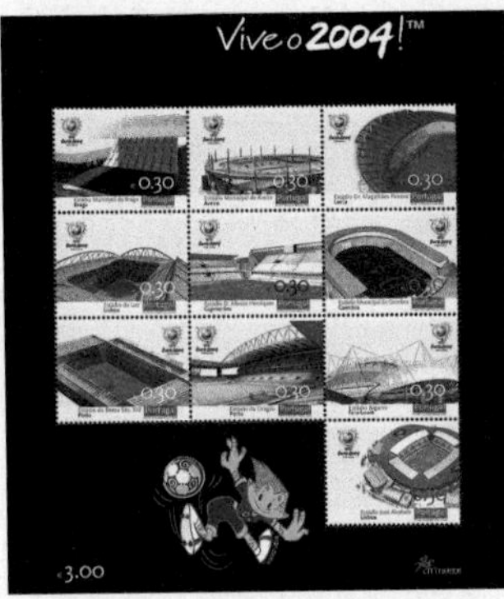

Stadiums for 2004 European Soccer Championships — A721

No. 2603: a, Braga Municipal Stadium, Braga. b, Aveiro Municpal Stadium, Aveiro. c, Dr. Magalhaes Pessoa Stadium, Leiria. d, Luz Stadium, Lisbon. e, D. Afonso Henriques Stadium, Guimaraes. f, Coimbra Municipal Stadium, Coimbra. g, Bessa 21st Century Stadium, Porto. h, Dragao Stadium, Porto. i, Algarve Stadium, Faro-Loulé. j, José Alvalade Stadium, Lisbon.

**2003, Nov. 28** **Litho.** ***Perf. 14x13½***
**2603** A721 Sheet of 10 7.00 7.00
*a.-j.* 30c Any single .65 .55

Souvenir Sheet

Coin Commemorating 150th Anniv. of First Portuguese Stamps, Bust and Portrait of Queen Maria II — A722

**2003, Dec. 12** ***Perf. 12***
**2604** A722 €1 multi 2.40 2.40

Mascot of 2004 European Soccer Championships — A723

Mascot and: 45c, CorreioAzul emblem. €1.75, Priority air mail emblem.

***Serpentine Die Cut 11½***
**2004, Mar. 16** **Litho.**
**Self-Adhesive**
**2605** A723 45c multi 1.00 .55
**2606** A723 €1.75 multi 4.00 2.10

No. 2606 is airmail.

King John IV (1604-56) — A724

No. 2607 — Vila Viçosa, birthplace and: a, 45c, Head of King. b, €1, King with sword.

**2004, Mar. 19** ***Perf. 14x13½***
**2607** A724 Horiz. pair, #a-b 3.00 1.75

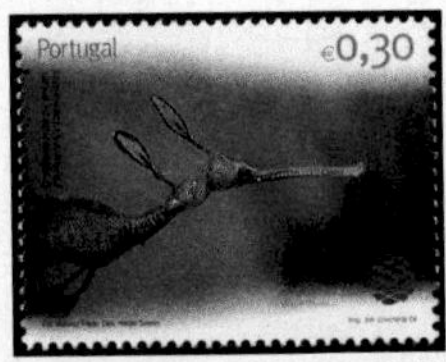

Lisbon Oceanarium — A725

Designs: 30c, Phyllopteryx taeniolatus. 45c, Spheniscus magellanicus. 56c, Hypsypops rubicundus. 72c, Enhydra lutris. €1, Carcharias taurus. €2, Fratercula arctica.
€1.50, Eudyptes chysolophus, people at Oceanarium.

**2004, Mar. 22**
**2608-2613** A725 Set of 6 11.00 6.25
**Souvenir Sheet**
**2614** A725 €1.50 multi 3.50 3.50

No. 2614 contains one 80x30mm stamp.

2004 European Soccer Championships A726

Designs: Nos. 2615a, 2616, 10c, Foot kicking soccer ball. Nos. 2615b, 2617, 20c, Soccer ball in air. Nos. 2615c, 2618, 30c, Soccer ball on chalk line. Nos. 2615d, 2619, 50c, Soccer ball, corner of goal.

**2004, Mar. 30** ***Perf.***
**Souvenir Sheet**
**2615** A726 Sheet of 4, #a-d 3.25 3.25
**Self-Adhesive**
***Serpentine Die Cut***
**2616-2619** A726 Set of 4 2.40 1.40

No. 2615 contains four 24mm diameter stamps.

Flags of Countries in 2004 European Soccer Championships and Mascot — A727

No. 2620: a, Portugal. b, France. c, Sweden. d, Czech Republic. e, Greece. f, England. g, Bulgaria. h, Latvia. i, Spain. j, Switzerland. k, Denmark. l, Germany. m, Russia. n, Croatia. o, Italy. p, Netherlands.

**2004, Apr. 6** ***Perf. 13x13¼***
**2620** A727 Sheet of 16 12.00 12.00
*a.-p.* 30c Any single .75 .40

**Bird Type of 2000 With Euro Denominations Only and**

Andorinha Daurica — A728

Designs: 30c, Cruza bico comun. No. 2622, Andorinha daurica, diff. 56c, Papa figos. 58c, Cotovia montesina. 72c, Chapim de poupa.

**2004, Apr. 15** ***Perf. 11¾x11½***
**2621** A658 30c multi .65 .35
**2622** A658 45c multi .95 .55
**2623** A658 56c multi 1.20 .65
**2624** A658 58c multi 1.25 .70
**2625** A658 72c multi 1.60 .85

**Self-Adhesive**
**Size: 26x21mm (#2626, 2628)**
***Serpentine Die Cut 11½, 11½x11¾ (#2627)***
**2626** A658 30c multi .65 .35
**2627** A728 45c multi .95 .55
**2628** A658 56c multi 1.20 .65
*Nos. 2621-2628 (8)* 8.45 4.65

Landmarks in Host Cities of 2004 European Soccer Championships and Players — A729

Host city: No. 2629, 30c, Aveiro. No. 2630, 30c, Braga. No. 2631, 30c, Coimbra. No. 2632, 30c, Faro-Loulé. No. 2633, 30c, Guimaraes. No. 2634, 30c, Leiria. No. 2635, 30c, Lisbon. No. 2636, 30c, Porto.

**2004, Apr. 20** ***Perf. 14x13¼***
**2629-2636** A729 Set of 8 5.50 3.00

Coup of Apr. 25, 1974, 30th Anniv. — A730

**2004, Apr. 25** ***Perf. 13¼x13***
**2637** A730 45c multi 1.10 .55

Stadiums for 2004 European Soccer Championships — A731

Designs: No. 2638, 30c, Aveiro Municipal Stadium, Aveiro. No. 2639, 30c, Braga Municipal Stadium, Braga. No. 2640, 30c, Coimbra Municipal Stadium, Coimbra. No. 2641, 30c, D. Afonso Henriques Stadium, Guimaraes. No. 2642, 30c, Algarve Stadium, Faro-Loulé. No. 2643, 30c, Dr. Magalhaes Pessoa Stadium, Leiria. No. 2644, 30c, José Alvalade Stadium, Lisbon. No. 2645, 30c, Luz Stadium, Lisbon. No. 2646, 30c, Bessa 21st Century Stadium, Porto. No. 2647, 30c, Dragao Stadium, Porto.

**2004, Apr. 28** ***Perf. 14x13¼***
**2638-2647** A731 Set of 10 7.00 3.50

2004 European Parliament Elections A732

**2004, May 3**
**2648** A732 30c multi .85 .35

Expansion of the European Union — A733

Designs: 56c, Flags of newly-added nations, stars. €2, Flags of newly-added nations, flags of previous members.

**2004, May 3** **Litho.**
**2649** A733 56c multi 1.40 .65
**Souvenir Sheet**
**2650** A733 €2 multi 4.50 4.50

Europa — A734

Designs: No. 2651, 56c, Woman looking at painting. No. 2652, 56c, Vacationer with gear on beach.

**2004, May 10** ***Perf. 13¼x14***
**2651-2652** A734 Set of 2 *2.50 1.40*
*2652a* Souvenir sheet, #2651-2652 *2.50 2.50*

First Telephone Line Between Lisbon and Porto, Cent. — A735

Designs: 30c, Old telephone. 45c, Telephone pole. 56c, Fiber-optic cables. 72c, Picture phone.
No. 2657: a, Old telephone, diff. b, Like 72c.

**2004, May 17**
**2653-2656** A735 Set of 4 4.50 2.50
**Souvenir Sheet**
**2657** A735 €1 Sheet of 2, #a-b 4.50 4.50

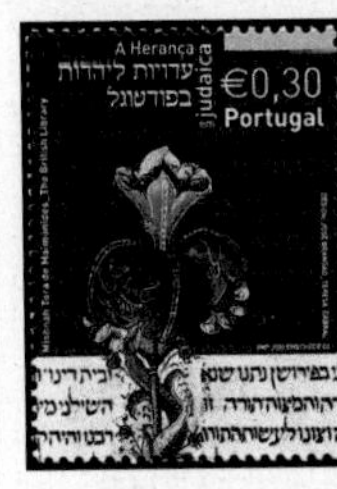

Jewish Heritage of Portugal — A736

Designs: 30c, Mishnah Torah of Maimonides, British Library. 45c, Star of David with lion, Cervera Bible, National Library. 56c, Menorah, Cervera Bible, National Library. 72c, Menorah carved on rock, Mértola Museum. €1, Abravanel Bible, Coimbra University Library. €2, Statue of prophet, Christ Convent, Tomar.
€1.50, Interior of Shaare Tikva Synagogue.

**2004, May 20**
**2658-2663** A736 Set of 6 11.00 6.00
**Souvenir Sheet**
**2664** A736 €1.50 multi 3.50 3.50

Shaare Tikva Synagogue, Cent.

Souvenir Sheet

Final Match of 2004 European Soccer Championships — A737

**2004, May 27** *Perf. 13¼x13*
**2665** A737 €1 multi 2.25 2.25

Portuguese Philatelic Federation, 50th Anniv. — A738

Designs: 30c, Anniversary emblem, #761, 2652. €1.50, Handstamp and letter.

**2004, June 18** *Perf. 14x13¼*
**2666** A738 30c multi [illegible] [illegible]

**Souvenir Sheet**

**2667** A738 €1.50 multi 3.50 3.50

Souvenir Sheet

UEFA (European Football Union), 50th Anniv. — A739

**2004, July 29 Litho.** *Perf. 13x13¼*
**2668** A739 €1 multi 2.40 2.40

2004 Summer Olympics, Athens A740

Designs: 30c, Hurdles. 45c, High jump.

**2004, Aug. 13** *Perf. 14x13¼*
**2669-2670** A740 Set of 2 1.75 .95

2004 Paralympics, Athens — A741

Designs: 30c, Swimming. 45c, Wheelchair racing. 56c, Cycling. 72c, Running.

**2004, Sept. 2** *Perf. 13¼x14*
**2671-2674** A741 Set of 4 4.50 2.50

Souvenir Sheet

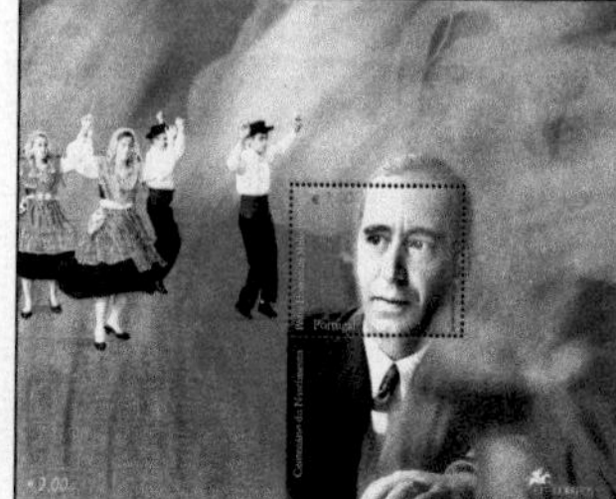

Pedro Homem de Mello (1904-84), Poet — A742

**2004, Sept. 6** *Perf. 14x13¼*
**2675** A742 €2 multi 4.50 4.50

Opening of Presidential Museum — A743

Designs: 45c, Museum exterior. €1, Museum interior.

**2004, Oct. 5**
**2676** A743 45c multi 1.10 .55

**Souvenir Sheet**

[illegible] €1 multi 2.50 2.50

Comic Strips A744

Designs: 30c, Quim e Manecas, by Stuart de Carvalhais. 45c, Guarda Abílla, by Júlio Pinto and Nuno Saraiva. 56c, Simao Infante, by Raul Correia and Eduardo Teixeira Coelho. 72c, A Pior Bando do Mundo, by José Carlos Fernandes.

No. 2682: a, O Espiao Acácio, by Relvas. b, Jim del Monaco, by Louro and Simoes. c, Tomahawk Tom, by Vitor Péon. d, Pitanga, by Arlindo Fagundes.

**2004, Oct. 8**
**2678-2681** A744 Set of 4 5.00 2.50

**Souvenir Sheet**

**2682** A744 50c Sheet of 4, #a-d 5.00 5.00

Viticulture A745

Designs: 30c, Sarcophagus depicting seasonal scenes, detail of mosaic of Autumn, 3rd cent. 45c, Detail of mosaic of Autumn, Apocalypse of Lorvao, 12th cent. 56c, Lorvao Missal illustration, 14th cent., detail of illustration from Book of Hours, by D. Fernando, 15th-16th cent. 72c, Detail of illustration from Book of Hours, detail of Group of the Lion, Columbano, 19th cent. €1, Detail of Group of the Lion, stained glass window, by Lino António, 20th cent.

No. 2688: a, Grapes, harvester. b, Harvester, wine jugs. c, Winery. d, Wine barrels, bottles and glasses.

**2004, Oct. 15**
**2683-2687** A745 Set of 5 7.50 3.75

**Souvenir Sheet**

**2688** A745 50c Sheet of 4, #a-d 5.00 5.00

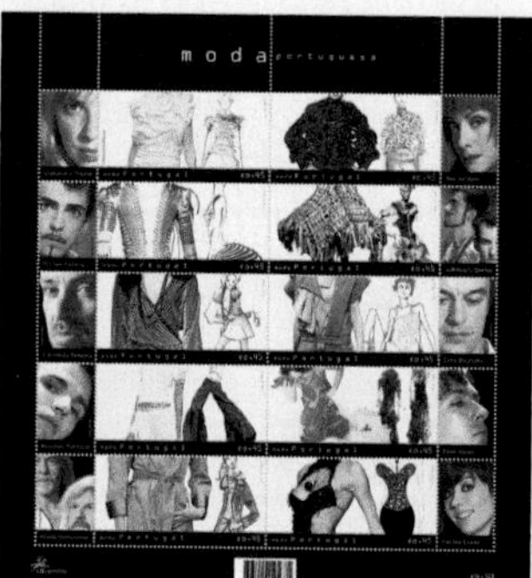

Women's Fashion — A746

No. 2689 — Clothing designed by: a, Alexandra Moura. b, Ana Salazar. c, Filipe Faisca. d, J. Branco and L. Sanchez. e, J. António Tenente. f, Luís Buchinho. g, Osvaldo Martins. h, Dino Alves. i, Alves and Gonçalves, j, Fátima Lopes. Designers names and pictures are on labels adjacent to stamps showing their clothing.

**2004, Nov. 10** *Perf. 13¾x14¼*
**2689** A746 45c Sheet of 10 + 10 labels 11.00 11.00

Christmas A747

Paintings: 30c, Adoration of the Magi, attributed to Jorge Afonso. 45c, Adoration of the Magi, by Flemish School. 56c, Flight into Egypt, by Francisco Vieira. 72c, Nativity, by Portuguese School.

€3, Nativity, by Josefa de Obidos.

**2004, Nov. 19** *Perf. 13x13¼*
**2690-2693** A747 Set of 4 4.50 2.75

**Souvenir Sheet**

***Perf. 13½x13¼***

**2694** A747 €3 multi 7.00 7.00

No. 2694 contains one 50x35mm stamp.

Masks — A748

A748a

Designs: 10c, Entrudo, Lazarim. 30c Festa dos Rapazes, Salsas. 45c, Festa dos Rapazes, Salsa, different. 57c, Cardador, Vale de Ilhavo. 74c, Festa dos Rapazes, Aveleda.

***Perf. 11¾x11½***

**2005, Feb. 17** **Litho.**

| | | | | |
|---|---|---|---|---|
| **2695** | A748 | 10c multi | .25 | .25 |
| **2696** | A748 | 30c brn red & multi | .65 | .25 |
| **2697** | A748 | 45c dk blue & multi | 1.00 | .60 |
| **2698** | A748 | 57c multi | 1.25 | .75 |
| **2699** | A748 | 74c multi | 1.75 | 1.00 |
| | | *Nos. 2695-2699 (5)* | 4.90 | 2.85 |

**Self-Adhesive**

***Serpentine Die Cut 11½, 11 (45c)***

| | | | | |
|---|---|---|---|---|
| **2699A** | A748 | 30c multi | .65 | .40 |
| **2699B** | A748a | 45c multi | 1.00 | .60 |
| **2699C** | A748 | 57c multi | 1.25 | .75 |
| | | *Nos. 2699A-2699C (3)* | 2.90 | 1.75 |

See Nos. 2797-2799, 2827-2832. No. 2696 has denomination at left; No. 2829 has denomination at right.

Public Transportation — A749

Lines of people and: 30c, Train, front of trolley. 50c, Trolley, rear of train. 57c, Ferry, rear of trolley. €1, Rear of articulated bus, front of train. €2, Front of articulated bus, rear of train.

**2005, Mar. 17** *Perf. 12x11¾*
**2700-2704** A749 Set of 5 11.50 11.50

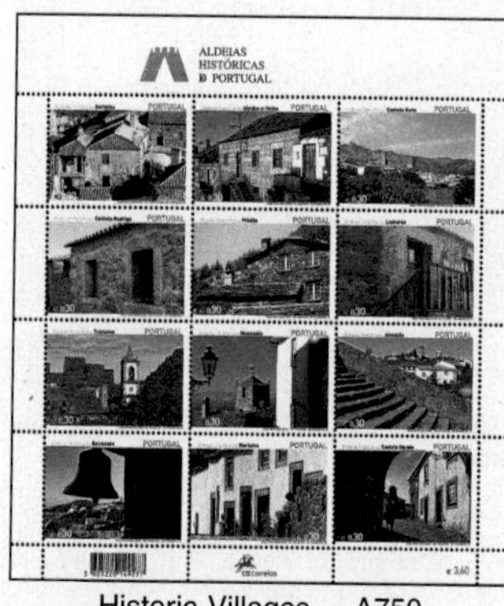

Historic Villages — A750

No. 2705: a, Sortelha. b, Idanha-a-Velha. c, Castelo Novo. d, Castelo Rodrigo. e, Piódao. f, Linhares. g, Trancoso. h, Monsanto. i, Almeida. j, Belmonte. k, Marialva. l, Castelo Mendo.

**2005, Apr. 28 Litho.** *Perf. 14x13¼*
**2705** A750 Sheet of 12 9.25 9.25
*a.-l.* 30c Any single .75 .40

Paintings by José Malhoa (1855-1933) — A751

Designs: 30c, A Beira-Mar. 45c, The Pious Offerings.

€1.77, Conversation with a Neighbor.

**2005, Apr. 28** *Perf. 12x11¾*
**2706-2707** A751 Set of 2 1.75 1.40

**Souvenir Sheet**

**2708** A751 €1.77 multi 4.00 4.00

Europa A752

Designs: No. 2709, Cozido à Portuguesa. No. 2710a, Bacalhau Assado com Batatas a Murro (dried cod and baked potatoes).

**2005, May 5** *Perf. 14x13¼*
**2709** A752 57c multi *1.50 .75*

**Souvenir Sheet**

**2710** Sheet of 2 #2710a *2.50 2.50*
*a.* A752 57c multi *1.25 1.25*

Rotary International, Cent. — A753

**2005, May 20** *Perf. 12x11¾*

2711 A753 74c Paul Harris 1.75 .95

**Souvenir Sheet**

2712 A753 €1.75 Harris, diff. 3.75 3.75

National Coach Museum, Cent. A754

Designs: No. 2713, 30c, Porto Covo carriage, 19th cent. No. 2714, 30c, Carriage, 19th cent. No. 2715, 45c, Coach of Francisca Sabóia, 17th cent. No. 2716, 45c, Sege "Das Plumas," 18th cent. 57c, Palanquin, 18th cent. 74c, Coche Dos Oceanos, 18th cent.
€1.75, Coaches and Queen Amelia.

**2005, May 23** *Perf. 14x13¼*

2713-2718 A754 Set of 6 6.00 3.00

**Souvenir Sheet**

2719 A754 €1.75 multi 3.75 3.75

Era of Kings Philip I to Philip III — A755

Arms and: 5c, Pegoes Aqueduct, Tomar. 30c, Chalice from Elvas Cathedral. 45c, Tile panel of cross from Christ Convent, Tomar. 57c, Fort St. John the Baptist, Angra.€1, Armada. €2, St. Vincent of Fora Church, Lisbon.
€1.20, Cross and reliquary from Lisbon Cathedral.

**2005, June 7** *Perf. 11¾x12*

2720-2725 A755 Set of 6 10.00 5.00

**Souvenir Sheet**

2726 A755 €1.20 multi 2.50 2.50

Miniature Sheet

Caricatures — A756

No. 2727 — Caricatures by: a, Raphael Bordallo Pinheiro. b, Sebastiao Sanhudo. c, Celso Herminio. d, Leal da Camara. e, Francisco Valença. f, Stuart Carvalhais. g, Sam. h, Joao Abel Manta. i, Augusto Cid. j, António Antunes. k, Pinheiro (Zé Povinho).

**2005, June 12** *Perf. 13¼x14*

2727 A756 Sheet of 11 + label 7.00 7.00
*a.-k.* 30c Any single .65 .35

Souvenir Sheets

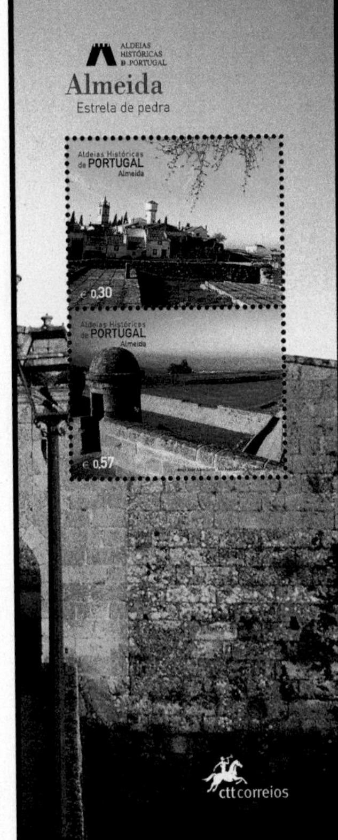


Historic Villages — A757

Various views of named villages.

**2005, June 8 Litho.** *Perf. 14x13¼*

**Sheets of 2, #a-b**

| | | | | |
|---|---|---|---|---|
| 2728 | A757 | Almeida | 2.25 | 2.25 |
| *a.* | | 30c multi | .75 | .35 |
| *b.* | | 57c multi | 1.40 | .70 |
| 2729 | A757 | Belmonte | 2.25 | 2.25 |
| *a.* | | 30c multi | .75 | .35 |
| *b.* | | 57c multi | 1.40 | .70 |
| 2730 | A757 | Castelo Mendo | 2.25 | 2.25 |
| *a.* | | 30c multi | .75 | .35 |
| *b.* | | 57c multi | 1.40 | .70 |
| 2731 | A757 | Castelo Novo | 2.25 | 2.25 |
| *a.* | | 30c multi | .75 | .35 |
| *b.* | | 57c multi | 1.40 | .70 |
| 2732 | A757 | Castelo Rodrigo | 2.25 | 2.25 |
| *a.* | | 30c multi | .75 | .35 |
| *b.* | | 57c multi | 1.40 | .70 |
| 2733 | A757 | Idanha-a-Velha | 2.25 | 2.25 |
| *a.* | | 30c multi | .75 | .35 |
| *b.* | | 57c multi | 1.40 | .70 |
| 2734 | A757 | Linhares da Beira | 2.25 | 2.25 |
| *a.* | | 30c multi | .75 | .35 |
| *b.* | | 57c multi | 1.40 | .70 |
| 2735 | A757 | Marialva | 2.25 | 2.25 |
| *a.* | | 30c multi | .75 | .35 |
| *b.* | | 57c multi | 1.40 | .70 |
| 2736 | A757 | Monsanto | 2.25 | 2.25 |
| *a.* | | 30c multi | .75 | .35 |
| *b.* | | 57c multi | 1.40 | .70 |
| 2737 | A757 | Piodao | 2.25 | 2.25 |
| *a.* | | 30c multi | .75 | .35 |
| *b.* | | 57c multi | 1.40 | .70 |
| 2738 | A757 | Sortelha | 2.25 | 2.25 |
| *a.* | | 30c multi | .75 | .35 |
| *b.* | | 57c multi | 1.40 | .70 |
| 2739 | A757 | Trancoso | 2.25 | 2.25 |
| *a.* | | 30c multi | .75 | .35 |
| *b.* | | 57c multi | 1.40 | .70 |
| | | *Nos. 2728-2739 (12)* | 27.00 | 27.00 |

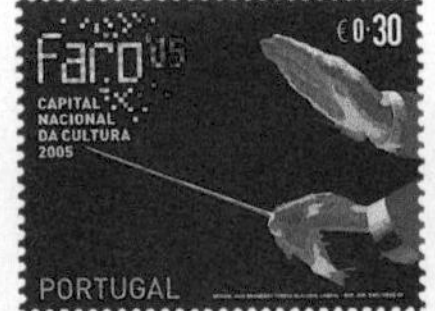


Faro, 2005 National Cultural Capital A758

Designs: 30c, Conductor's hands and baton. 45c, Broken pot. 57c, Shell. 74c, Hands applauding.

**2005, June 15**

2740-2743 A758 Set of 4 4.50 2.25

Tourism A759

Various scenes from: No. 2744, 45c, Lisbon. No. 2745, 45c, Porto e Norte. No. 2746, 48c, Lisbon, diff. No. 2747, 48c, Porto e Norte, diff. No. 2748, 57c, Lisbon, diff. No. 2749, 57c, Porto e Norte, diff.

**2005, July 8** *Perf. 12x11¾*

2744-2749 A759 Set of 6 6.50 3.25

Nature Conservation — A760

Designs: 30c, Man with hatchet inspecting tree. 45c, Forest fire prevention squad. 57c, Bird on branch, building in forest.
€2, Bird on fence, large trees.

**2005, Aug. 19** *Perf. 12x11¾*

2750-2752 A760 Set of 3 3.00 1.50

**Souvenir Sheet**

*Perf. 12x12½*

2753 A760 €2 multi 4.75 4.75

United Nations, 60th Anniv. A761

Intl. Day of Peace A762

Children at Risk A763

Intl. Year of Physics A764

**2005, Sept. 21** *Perf. 12x11¾*

| | | | | |
|---|---|---|---|---|
| 2754 | A761 | 30c multi | .70 | .35 |
| 2755 | A762 | 45c multi | 1.00 | .50 |
| 2756 | A763 | 57c multi | 1.40 | .70 |
| 2757 | A764 | 74c multi | 1.75 | .90 |
| | | *Nos. 2754-2757 (4)* | 4.85 | 2.45 |

Sundials — A765

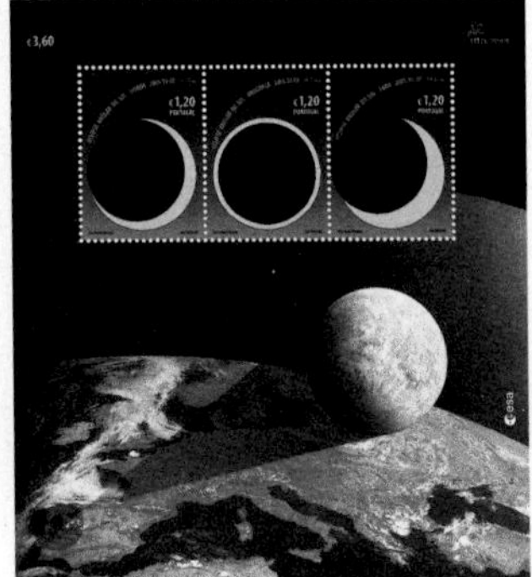

Annular Solar Eclipse, Oct. 3, 2005 — A766

Sundial from: 45c, St. John the Baptist Church, Sintra. €1, Maritime Museum, Lisbon.
No. 2760 — view of eclipsed Sun from: a, Lisbon at 9:53. b, Bragança at 9:55. c, Faro at 9:55.

**2005, Oct. 3** *Perf. 12½x12*

2758-2759 A765 Set of 2 3.25 1.60

**Souvenir Sheet**

*Perf. 12*

2760 A766 Sheet of 3 8.00 8.00
*a.-c.* €1.20 multi 2.50 1.40

A767

Communications Media — A768

Designs: 30c, Press (fountain pen). 45c, Radio (microphone). 57c, Television (portable camera). 74c, Internet (globe and "@."
No. 2765: a, Press (newspaper). b, Radio (studio).
No. 2766: a, Television (studio). b, Internet (beginning of website address).

**2005, Oct. 13** *Perf. 12x12½*

2761-2764 A767 Set of 4 4.50 1.25

**Souvenir Sheets**

| | | | | |
|---|---|---|---|---|
| 2765 | A768 | Sheet of 2 | 6.00 | 6.00 |
| *a.* | | €1.10 multi | 2.50 | 1.40 |
| *b.* | | €1.55 multi | 3.50 | 1.90 |
| 2766 | A768 | Sheet of 2 | 6.00 | 6.00 |
| *a.* | | €1.10 multi | 2.50 | 1.40 |
| *b.* | | €1.55 multi | 3.50 | 1.90 |

Fishing Villages — A769

No. 2767, 30c — Aldeia da Carrasquiera, Portugal: a, Denomination at R. b, Denomination at L.
No. 2768, 30c — Tai O, Hong Kong: a, Denomination at R. b, Denomination at L.

**2005, Oct. 18** *Perf. 13¼x13¾*

**Horiz. Pairs, #a-b**

2767-2768 A769 Set of 2 2.75 1.40

See Hong Kong Nos. 1160-1163.

Alvaro Cunhal (1913-2005), Communist Politician — A770

Designs: 30c, Cunhal in crowd. €1, Cunhal with young girl.

**2005, Nov. 10** ***Perf. 12x12½***
**2769** A770 30c multi .75 .35

**Souvenir Sheet**

**2770** A770 €1 multi 2.25 2.25

Serralves Foundation A771

Designs: No. 2771, 30c, White building. No. 2772, 45c, Silhouette of seated person. 48c, Red brown building entrance, diff. 57c, Sculpture of garden shovel. 74c, Person painting. No. 2776, €1, Walkway and hedges.

No. 2777: a, 30c, Red brown building entrance, horiz. b, 45c, Walkway and trees. c, 45c, Columns in building. d, 45c, Tower. e, 45c, Walkway and hedges, diff.

No. 2778: a, €1, White building, horiz. (80x30mm). b, €1, Art in gallery, horiz. (80x30mm). c, €1, Trees and lawn.

**2005, Nov. 15** ***Perf. 13¼x14***
**2771-2776** A771 Set of 6 7.50 3.75

**Souvenir Sheets**

**2777** Sheet of 5 4.50 4.50
*a.* A771 30c multi .65 .35
*b.-e.* A771 45c Any single .95 .50

***Perf. 14x13¼***

**2778** Sheet of 3 6.50 6.50
*a.-c.* A771 €1 Any single 2.10 1.10

Lisbon Earthquake, 250th Anniv. — A772

Designs: 45c, Fire after earthquake. €2, Victims, braced buildings.
€2.65, Victims and damaged buildings.

**2005, Nov. 25** ***Perf. 14x13¼***
**2779-2780** A772 Set of 2 5.25 2.75

**Souvenir Sheet**

**2781** A772 €2.65 multi 6.25 6.25

No. 2781 contains one 40x30mm stamp.

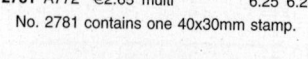

Modernization of the Navy — A773

Designs: 45c, Navpol ship. 57c, Hydrographic ship. 74c, Ocean patrol boat and helicopter. €2, Submarine.

**2005, Nov. 25** ***Perf. 12x12½***
**2782-2785** A773 Set of 4 9.00 4.50

Soccer Teams A774

Players and team emblems: No. 2786, N, Sporting Clube de Portugal. No. 2787, N, Sport Lisboa e Benfica. No. 2788, N, Futebol Clube do Porto.

No. 2789, €1, Sporting Clube de Portugal, diff. No. 2790, €1, Sport Lisboa e Benfica, diff. No. 2791, €1, Player lifting trophy, Futebol Clube do Porto.

**2005, Nov. 25** ***Perf. 12x12¼***
**2786-2788** A774 Set of 3 2.10 1.10

**Souvenir Sheets**

***Perf. 12x11¾***

**2789-2791** A774 Set of 3 6.50 6.50

Nos. 2786-2788 each sold for 30c on day of issue.

Greetings A775

Designs: No. 2792, Parabens (birthday party). No. 2793, Amote (men and women dancing and exchanging gifts, child). No. 2794, Parabens (man, woman and two children, stork with baby). No. 2795, Parabens (conductor, cocktail party). No. 2796, Parabens (man, woman, fairy, Cupid).

**2006, Feb. 7** ***Perf. 12x12½***
**2792** A775 N multi .75 .35
*a.* Perf. 12 vert. (from booklet pane) .75 .35
**2793** A775 N multi .75 .35
*a.* Perf. 12 vert. (from booklet pane) .75 .35
**2794** A775 N multi .75 .35
*a.* Perf. 12 vert. (from booklet pane) .75 .35
**2795** A775 N multi .75 .35
*a.* Perf. 12 vert. (from booklet pane) .75 .35
**2796** A775 N multi .75 .35
*a.* Perf. 12 vert. (from booklet pane) .75 .35
*b.* Booklet pane, #2792a-2796a 3.75 —
Complete booklet, #2796b 3.75
*Nos. 2792-2796 (5)* 3.75 1.75

Nos. 2792-2796 each sold for 30c on day of issue.

**Masks Type of 2005**

Designs: N, Like No. 2696. A, "Carnaval" Lazarim, Bragança. E, "Dia de Ano Novo" Mogadouro, Bragança.

***Serpentine Die Cut 11½***

**2006, Mar. 1** **Self-Adhesive**
**2797** A748 N multi .75 .35
**2798** A748 A multi 1.10 .55
**2799** A748 E multi 1.40 .70
*Nos. 2797-2799 (3)* 3.25 1.60

No. 2797 sold for 30c, No. 2798 sold for 45c, and No. 2799 sold for 57c on day of issue.

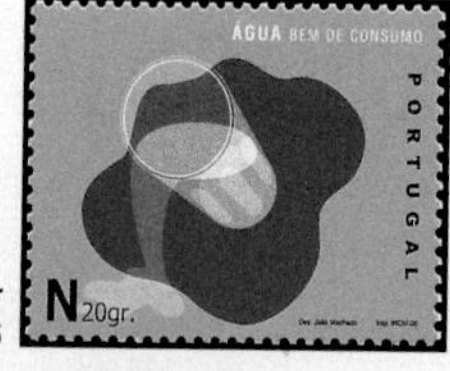

Water A776

Designs: No. 2800, N, Glass of water. No. 2801, N, Water cycle. No. 2802, A, Spigot. No. 2803, A, Turbines. No. 2804, E, Sailboat. No. 2805, E, Flower.

**2006, Mar. 22** **Litho.** ***Perf. 12x11¾***
**2800-2805** A776 Set of 6 6.00 3.00

On the day of issue Nos. 2800-2801 each sold for 30c; Nos. 2802-2803 each sold for 45c, and Nos. 2804-2805 each sold for 57c.

St. Francis Xavier (1506-52), Missionary A777

St. Francis Xavier: 45c, Baptizing man. €1, Holding cross.
€2.75, Wearing black robe.

**2006, Apr. 5**
**2806-2807** A777 Set of 2 3.00 1.50

**Souvenir Sheet**

**2808** A777 €2.75 multi 6.00 6.00

Europa A778

No. 2810 — Children's drawings: a, Child in stroller. b, Four children.

**2006, May 9** ***Perf. 12x12½***
**2809** A778 60c shown 1.60 .80

**Souvenir Sheet**

***Perf. 12x11¾***

**2810** A778 60c Sheet of 2, #a-b 2.50 2.25

Famous Men — A779

Designs, No. 2811, €1, Humberto Delgado (1906-65), founder of TAP Airlines. No. 2812, €1, Thomaz de Mello (Tom) (1906-90), artist. No. 2313, €1, Agostinho da Silva (1906-94), philosopher. No. 2814, €1, Fernando Lopes-Graça (1906-94), composer. No. 2815, €1, Rómulo de Carvalho (1906-97), poet.

**2006, May 15** ***Perf. 11¾x12***
**2811-2815** A779 Set of 5 11.00 5.50

Souvenir Sheet

UEFA Under 21 Soccer Championships, Portugal — A780

**2006, May 23** ***Perf. 12x12½***
**2816** A780 €2.75 multi 6.00 6.00

2006 World Cup Soccer Championships, Germany — A781

Silhouettes of soccer players in action: 45c, €1.
€2.40, World Cup.

**2006, June 7** ***Perf. 12x11¾***
**2817-2818** A781 Set of 2 3.75 1.90

**Souvenir Sheet**

**2819** A781 €2.40 multi 5.25 5.25

Intl. Year of Deserts and Desertification — A782

Designs: 30c, Sand dune. 60c, Dead and living trees.

**2006, June 17**
**2820-2821** A782 Set of 2 2.25 1.10

Roman Heritage A783

Designs: 30c, Mosaic of Oceanus. 40c, Roman temple, Evora. 50c, Patera. 60c, Two-headed sculpture.
€2.40, Mosaic of seahorse.

**2006, June 21**
**2822-2825** A783 Set of 4 4.00 2.00

**Souvenir Sheet**

**2826** A783 €2.40 multi 5.25 5.25

**Masks Type of 2005**

Designs: 3c, "Carnaval" Lazarim, Viseu. 5c, "Festa dos Rapazes," Baçal, Bragança. 30c, Like #2797. 45c, Like #2798. 60c, Like #2799. 75c, "Dia dos Diablos" Vinhais, Bragança.

**2006, June 29** ***Perf. 11¾x11½***
**2827** A748 3c multi .25 .25
**2828** A748 5c multi .25 .25
**2829** A748 30c dk red & multi .75 .35
**2830** A748 45c blue & multi 1.25 .60
**2831** A748 60c multi 1.50 .75
**2832** A748 75c multi 1.90 .95
*Nos. 2827-2832 (6)* 5.90 3.15

No. 2829 has denomination at right. No. 2696 has denomination at left.

Wolfgang Amadeus Mozart (1756-91), Composer. A784

Mozart and: 60c, Musical score. €2.75, Handwritten text.

**2006, July 7** ***Perf. 12x11¾***
**2833** A784 60c multi 1.25 .60

**Souvenir Sheet**

**2834** A784 €2.75 multi 6.00 6.00

Souvenir Sheet

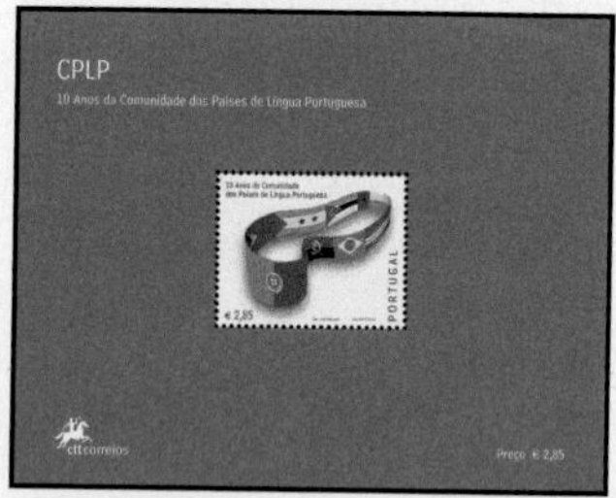

Community of Portuguese-speaking Countries, 10th Anniv. — A785

**2006, July 12** ***Perf. 12½x13***
**2835** A785 €2.85 multi 6.00 6.00

Calouste Gulbenkian Foundation, 50th Anniv. — A786

Designs: 30c, Portrait of a Young Woman by Domenico Ghirlandaio. 45c, Peacock, jewelry by René Lalique. 60c, Ceramic tile from Turkey. 75c, Flora, sculpture by Jean-Baptise Carpeaux, Roman medal. €1, Jade jar from Samarkand. €2, Portrait of Calouste Gulbenkian, by C. J. Watelet.

No. 2842, vert.: a, Sculpture and "arte." b, Bookshelf and "educaçao." c, Microscope and "ciencia." d, Painting of mother and child and "caridade."

**2006, July 18 Litho. *Perf. 12½x13***
**2836-2841** A786 Set of 6 11.00 5.50

**Souvenir Sheet**
***Perf. 13x12½***

**2842** A786 30c Sheet of 4, #a-d 2.50 2.50

Modern Architecture — A787

Designs: No. 2843, 30c, Building, Bouça neighborhood of Porto, by Alvaro Siza. No. 2844, 30c, Apartments, Lisbon, by Teotónio Pereira, Nuno Portas, Pedro Botelho, and Joao Paciencia. No. 2845, 30c, José Gomes Ferreira School, Lisbon, by Raul Hestnes Ferreira. No. 2846, 30c, Matosinhos Town Hall, by Alcino Soutinho. No. 2847, 30c, Borges & Irmao Bank, Vila do Conde, by Siza. No. 2848, 30c, Art House, Porto, by Eduardo Souto Moura. No. 2849, 30c, University of Santiago Campus, Aveiro, by Portas. No. 2850, 30c, Social Communications School, Lisbon, by Carrilho da Graça. No. 2851, 30c, Architect's Building, Lisbon, by Manuel Graça Diaz and Egas José Vieira. No. 2852, 30c, Santa Maria Church, Marco de Canaveses, by Siza.

**2006, Aug. 21 *Perf. 12½x13***
**2843-2852** A787 Set of 10 6.50 3.25

Television Broadcasting in Portugal, 50th Anniv. — A788

Men and: 30c, Camera at right. 60c, Camera at left.

**2006, Sept. 4 *Perf. 12x11¾***
**2853-2854** A788 Set of 2 2.00 1.00

Bridges Between Portugal and Spain — A789

Designs: 30c, Alcantara Bridge. 52c, Vila Real de Santo António (Ayamonte International) Bridge.

**2006, Sept. 14 Litho.**
**2855-2856** A789 Set of 2 1.75 .90

See Spain No. 3441.

**Souvenir Sheet**

Douro Demarcated Region, 250th Anniv. — A790

**2006, Sept. 14**
**2857** A790 €2.40 multi 5.25 5.25

Fish A791

Designs: 30c, Capros aper. 45c, Anthias anthias. 60c, Lepadogaster lepadogaster. 75c, Gobiusculus flavescens. €1, Coris julis. €2, Callionymus lyra.

No. 2864, 80c: a, Macroramphosus scolopax. b, Echiichthys vipera.

No. 2865, 80c: a, Thalassoma pavo. b, Blennius ocellaris.

**2006, Oct. 7 *Perf. 12¼x11¾***
**2858-2863** A791 Set of 6 11.00 5.50

**Souvenir Sheets of 2, #a-b**

**2864-2865** A791 Set of 2 7.00 7.00

España 06 Intl. Philatelic Exhibition, Malaga, Spain.

School Correspondence — A792

Various letters with denomination at: No. 2866, N, Upper left. No. 2867, N, Upper right.

**2006, Oct. 9 *Perf. 12½x13***
**2866-2867** A792 Set of 2 1.40 .70

Portuguese Railroads, 150th Anniv. — A793

Designs: 30c, Flecha de Prata. 45c, Sud-Express. 60c, Foguete. €2, Alfa Pendular. €1.60, Inaugural ceremonies, 1856.

**2006, Oct. 28 *Perf. 12x11¾***
**2868-2871** A793 Set of 4 7.50 3.75

**Souvenir Sheet**

**2872** A793 €1.60 multi 3.50 3.50

No. 2872 contains one 80x30mm stamp.

Portuguese Arrival in Ceylon, 500th Anniv. — A794

Designs: 30c, Map. 75c, Carvings. €2.40, Map, horiz.

**2006, Oct. 30 *Perf. 13x13¼***
**2873-2874** A794 Set of 2 2.50 1.25

**Souvenir Sheet**
***Perf. 12½x13***

**2875** A794 €2.40 multi 5.25 5.25

Lubrapex Intl. Philatelic Exhibition, Rio.

Islamic Influences in Lisbon A795

Designs: 30c, Ceramic tile, 16th cent. 45c, Frieze, 9th-10th cent. 52c, Sousa Leal Palace. 61c, Film Museum. 75c, Casa do Alentejo. €1, Ribeiro da Cunha Palace.

€2.95, Pitcher.

**2007, Feb. 15 Litho. *Perf. 12½x13***
**2876-2881** A795 Set of 6 7.50 7.50

**Souvenir Sheet**

**2882** A795 €2.95 multi 6.50 6.50

Miniature Sheets

Regional Garments — A796

No. 2883: a, Capote and capelo, Azores. b, Campones, Beira Litoral. c, Viloa, Madeira. d, Camponesa, Ribatejo.

No. 2884: a, Lavradeira, Minho. b, Noiva, Minho. c, Capa de honras, Trás-os-Montes. d, Pauliteiro, Trás-os-Montes. e, Camisola de pescador, Douro Litoral. f, Coroça, Beiras and Trás-os-Montes. g, Saias da Nazaré, Estremadura. h, Campino, Ribatejo. i, Camponesa, Algarve. j, Capote, Alentejo.

**2007, Feb. 28**
**2883** A796 Sheet of 4 2.75 2.75
*a.-d.* 30c Any single .65 .40
**2884** A796 Sheet of 10 6.50 6.50
*a.-j.* 30c Any single .65 .40

Art by Manuel Cargaleiro A797

Designs: 30c, Carreaux Diamants. 45c, Composizione Floreale. 61c, Decoraçao Mural.

**2007, Mar. 16**
**2885-2887** A797 Set of 3 3.00 1.50

Audit Offices in Europe, Bicent. A798

Designs: 30c, King John I Reinforces the Audit Office, by Jaime Martins Barata. 61c, Creation of Audit Tribunal, by Almada Negreiros. €2, Audit Tribunal Building.

€2.95, The Accountant, tapestry by Negreiros.

**2007, Mar. 17**
**2888-2890** A798 Set of 3 6.50 4.50

**Souvenir Sheet**

**2891** A798 €2.95 multi 7.00 7.00

Treaty of Rome, 50th Anniv. — A799

**2007, Mar. 23 *Perf. 13x12½***
**2892** A799 61c multi 1.25 .65

Historical Urban Public Transport A800

Designs: 30c, Ox-drawn carriage, 1840. 45c, Horse-drawn streetcar, 1872. 50c, Horse-drawn streetcar, 1873. 61c, Electric trolley, 1895. 75c, Electric trolley, 1901.

**2007, Mar. 30 *Perf. 11¾x11½***
**2893** A800 30c multi .60 .30
**2894** A800 45c multi .95 .50
**2895** A800 50c multi 1.00 .50
**2896** A800 61c multi 1.25 .60
**2897** A800 75c multi 1.75 .90
*Nos. 2893-2897 (5)* 5.55 2.80

A801

Dams — A802

Designs: No. 2898, Castelo do Bode Dam. No. 2899, Aguieira Dam and Reservoir. 61c, Valeira Dam and Reservoir. 75c, Alto Lindoso Dam and Reservoir. €1, Castelo do Bode Dam and Reservoir.

**2007, Apr. 19 Litho. *Perf. 12½x13***
**2898** A801 30c multi .60 .30
**2899** A802 30c multi .60 .30
**2900** A802 61c multi 1.40 .70
**2901** A802 75c multi 1.50 .55
**2902** A802 €1 multi 2.40 1.20
*Nos. 2898-2902 (5)* 6.50 3.05

Europa A803

Designs: No. 2903, Lord Robert Baden-Powell.

No. 2904: a, Compass. b, Boy Scouts looking at map.

**2007, May 9**
**2903** A803 61c multi 1.50 .75

**Souvenir Sheet**

**2904** Sheet of 2 3.00 3.00
*a.-b.* A803 61c Either single 1.50 .85

Scouting, cent.

**Historical Urban Public Transport Type of 2007**

Designs: N, Horse-drawn streetcar, 1872. A, Electric trolley, 1895. E, Electric trolley, 1901.

***Serpentine Die Cut 11½***

**2007, May 30** **Self-Adhesive**

| | | | | |
|---|---|---|---|---|
| **2905** | A800 | N red & black | .60 | .30 |
| **2906** | A800 | A blue & black | 1.00 | .50 |
| **2907** | A800 | E brown & black | 1.40 | .70 |
| | | *Nos. 2905-2907 (3)* | 3.00 | 1.50 |

Nos. 2905-2907 sold for 30c, 45c and 61c, respectively, on day of issue.

Modern Architecture — A804

Designs: No. 2908, 30c, Casa dos 24, Porto, by Fernando Távora. No. 2909, 30c, Documentation and Information Center of the President of the Republic, Lisbon, by Carrilho da Graça. No. 2910, 30c, Portugal Pavilion, Lisbon, by Alvaro Siza. No. 2911, 30c, Ilhavo Maritime Museum, Ilhavo, by ARX Portugal. No. 2912, 30c, Visual Arts Center, Coimbra, by Joao Mendes Ribeiro. No. 2913, 30c, Superior School of Art and Design, Caldas da Rainha, by Vitor Figueiredo. No. 2914, 30c, VTS Tower, Lisbon, by Gonçalo Byrne. No. 2915, 30c, Braga Municipal Stadium, Braga, by Eduardo Souto Moura. No. 2916, 30c, José Saramago Library, Loures, by Fernando Martins. No. 2917, 30c, Sines Art Center, Sines, by Aires Mateus.

€1.85, Portugal Pavilion, by Siza, diff.

**2007, May 31** ***Perf. 12½x13***

| | | | | |
|---|---|---|---|---|
| **2908-2917** | A804 | Set of 10 | 6.50 | 3.25 |

**Souvenir Sheet**

| | | | | |
|---|---|---|---|---|
| **2918** | A804 | €1.85 multi | 4.00 | 4.00 |

World Sailing Championships — A805

Designs: No. 2919, 61c, Catamarans. No. 2920, 61c, Sailboats 23 and 105. No. 2921, 75c, Sailboat 75 and other sailboat. No. 2922, 75c, Sailboats CHI 34 and POR 16.

€2.95, Like #2921.

**2007, June 12** ***Perf. 12x11¾***

| | | | | |
|---|---|---|---|---|
| **2919-2922** | A805 | Set of 4 | 6.00 | 3.00 |

**Souvenir Sheet**

| | | | | |
|---|---|---|---|---|
| **2923** | A805 | €2.95 multi | 7.00 | 7.00 |

Miniature Sheets

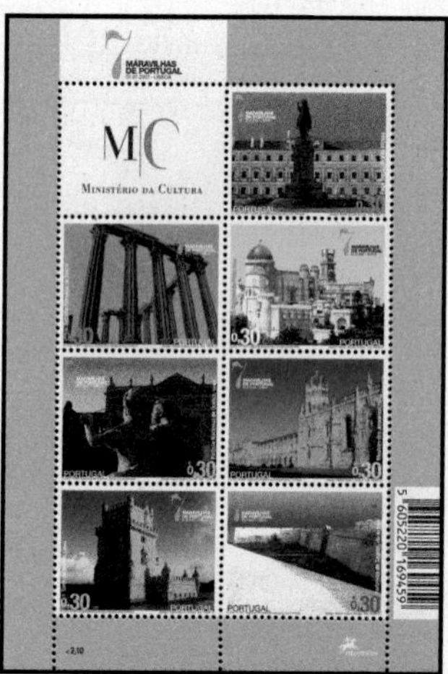

Seven Wonders of Portugal — A806

No. 2924: a, Vila Vicosa Ducal Palace. b, Roman temple, Evora. c, Pena National Palace, Sintra. d, Queluz National Palace, Sintra. e, Jéronimos Monastery, Lisbon. f, Belem Tower, Lisbon. g, Sagres Fort, Vila do Bispo.

No. 2925: a, Christ Convent, Tomar. b, Almourol Castle, Vila Nova da Barquinha. c, Alcobaça Monastery. d, Obidos Castle. e, Mafra Convent and Basilica. f, Marvao Castle. g, Monsaraz Fortifications.

No. 2926: a, Guimaraes Castle. b, Mateus Palace, Vila Real. c, Sao Francisco Church, Porto. d, Clergymen Church and Tower, Porto. e, Coimbra University Palace. f, Conimbriga Ruins, Condeixa-a-Nova. g, Batalha Monastery.

**2007, June 14** ***Perf. 12x11¾***

| | | | | |
|---|---|---|---|---|
| **2924** | A806 | Sheet of 7 + label | 6.00 | 6.00 |
| *a.-g.* | | 30c Any single | .85 | .40 |
| **2925** | A806 | Sheet of 7 + label | 6.00 | 6.00 |
| *a.-g.* | | 30c Any single | .85 | .40 |
| **2926** | A806 | Sheet of 7 + label | 6.00 | 6.00 |
| *a.-g.* | | 30c Any single | .85 | .40 |
| | | *Nos. 2924-2926 (3)* | 18.00 | 18.00 |

Art From Berardo Museum — A807

Designs: 45c, Bridge, by Amadeo de Souza Cardoso. No. 2928, 61c, Les Baigneuses, by Niki de Saint Phalle, vert. €1, Interior with Restful Paintings, by Roy Liechtenstein, vert. €2, Femme Dans un Fauteuil, by Pablo Picasso, vert.

No. 2931, 61c, vert.: a, Le Couple, by Oscar Dominguez. b, Café Man Ray, by Man Ray. c, Néctar, by Joana Vasconcelos. d, Head, by Jackson Pollock.

**2007, June 25** ***Perf. 12***

| | | | | |
|---|---|---|---|---|
| **2927-2930** | A807 | Set of 4 | 9.00 | 4.50 |

**Souvenir Sheet**

| | | | | |
|---|---|---|---|---|
| **2931** | | Sheet of 4 | 7.00 | 7.00 |
| *a.-d.* | A807 | 61c Any single | 1.75 | .85 |

Portuguese Presidency of European Union Council of Ministers — A808

Designs: 61c, Building, stars running from UL to LR. €2.45, Building, stars running from LL to UR.

***Perf. 12x11¾ Syncopated***

**2007, July 1**

| | | | | |
|---|---|---|---|---|
| **2932** | A808 | 61c multi | 1.40 | .70 |

**Souvenir Sheet**

| | | | | |
|---|---|---|---|---|
| **2933** | A808 | €2.45 multi | 6.75 | 6.75 |

Motorcycles — A809

Designs: 30c, 1935 SMC-Nacional 500cc. 52c, 1959 FAMEL Foguete. No. 2936, 61c, 1954 Vilar Cucciolo. €1, 1969, Casal Carina.

No. 2938, 61c: a, 1952 Quimera Alma. b, 1958 CINAL Pachancho. c, 1965 SIS Sachs VS. d, 1985 Casal K287.

**2007, July 4**

| | | | | |
|---|---|---|---|---|
| **2934-2937** | A809 | Set of 4 | 5.50 | 2.75 |

**Souvenir Sheet**

| | | | | |
|---|---|---|---|---|
| **2938** | | Sheet of 4 | 6.00 | 6.00 |
| *a.-d.* | A809 | 61c Any single | 1.50 | 1.50 |

Souvenir Sheet

New Seven Wonders of the World — A810

**2007, July 7** ***Perf. 12½x13¼***

| | | | | |
|---|---|---|---|---|
| **2939** | A810 | €2.95 multi | 7.00 | 7.00 |

Raul Maria Pereira, Architect, and Postal Headquarters, Lima, Peru — A811

**2007, Aug. 10** ***Perf. 12x11¾***

| | | | | |
|---|---|---|---|---|
| **2940** | A811 | 75c multi | 1.75 | .90 |

See Peru No. 1574.

Famous Men — A812

Designs: No. 2941, 45c, Miguel Torga (1907-95), writer. No. 2942, 45c, Fialho de Almeida (1857-1911), writer. No. 2943, 45c, Columbano (1857-1929), painter.

**2007, Aug. 12** ***Perf. 11¾x12***

| | | | | |
|---|---|---|---|---|
| **2941-2943** | A812 | Set of 3 | 3.00 | 1.50 |

Souvenir Sheet

Portuguese Rugby Team — A813

**2007, Aug. 22** ***Perf. 12½x13¼***

| | | | | |
|---|---|---|---|---|
| **2944** | A813 | €1.85 multi | 4.50 | 4.50 |

Art by Nadir Afonso A814

Designs: 30c, Horus. 45c, Veneza. 61c, Processao em Veneza.

**2007, Sept. 5** **Litho.** ***Perf. 12½x13***

| | | | | |
|---|---|---|---|---|
| **2945-2947** | A814 | Set of 3 | 3.00 | 1.50 |

Flora and Fauna of the Americas A815

Designs: No. 2948, 30c, Potatoes. No. 2949, 30c, Corn. No. 2950, 30c, Jacaranda. 45c, Cacao pods. 61c, Turkeys. 75c, Passion fruits.

€1.85, Hummingbird at passion fruit blossom, horiz.

**2007, Sept. 25** ***Perf. 11¾x12***

| | | | | |
|---|---|---|---|---|
| **2948-2953** | A815 | Set of 6 | 6.00 | 3.00 |

**Souvenir Sheet**

***Perf. 12x11¾***

| | | | | |
|---|---|---|---|---|
| **2954** | A815 | €1.85 multi | 4.50 | 4.50 |

Buildings — A816

Designs: 30c, Tower, Arzila, Morocco. 75c, Silves Castle, Portugal.

**2007, Sept. 26** ***Perf. 13x12½***

| | | | | |
|---|---|---|---|---|
| **2955-2956** | A816 | Set of 2 | 2.40 | 1.20 |

See No. 3623, Morocco Nos. 1043-1044.

Flags A817

Flag of: Nos. 2957, 2958a, Portugal.

No. 2958 — Flag of: b, Portuguese President. c, Portuguese Assembly. d, Azores. e, Madeira.

***Perf. 12x11¾ Syncopated***

**2007, Oct. 5**

| | | | | |
|---|---|---|---|---|
| **2957** | A817 | 30c multi | .65 | .30 |

***Perf. 13¼x13***

| | | | | |
|---|---|---|---|---|
| **2958** | | Sheet of 5 | 3.50 | 3.50 |
| *a.-e.* | A817 | 30c Any single | .65 | .30 |

No. 2958 contains five 36x28mm stamps.

Children's Art A818

Designs: No. 2959, (30c), Children and flowers, by Ines Filipa Navrat. No. 2960, (30c), Children and globe, by Sofia Fiteiro Passeira. No. 2961, (30c), Hands and globe, by Maria Correia Borges.

***Perf. 12x11¾ Syncopated***

**2007, Oct. 9**

| | | | | |
|---|---|---|---|---|
| **2959-2961** | A818 | Set of 3 | 2.10 | 1.00 |

Mafra National Reserve A819

Fauna: 30c, Cervus dama. 45c, Sus scrofa. 61c, Vulpes vulpes. 75c, Cervus elaphus. €1, Bubo bubo. €2, Hieraaetus fasciatus.
€1.25, Cervus elaphus, diff.

**2007, Oct. 16** *Perf. 12x11¾*
**2962-2967** A819 Set of 6 12.00 6.00

**Souvenir Sheet**

**2968** A819 €1.25 multi 3.25 3.25

Islamic Center, Lisbon A820

**2007, Nov. 7** *Perf. 13¼*
**2969** A820 N Ground-level view .60 .30
**2970** A820 I Aerial view 1.75 .90

Reign of Aga Khan IV, 50th anniv. On day of issue, No. 2969 sold for 30c, and No. 2970 sold for 75c.

Cork Industry A821

*Serpentine Die Cut 12½*

**2007, Nov. 28** **Litho.**

**Self-Adhesive**

**Printed on Cork Veneer**

**2971** A821 €1 multi *8.00 7.00*

Souvenir Sheet

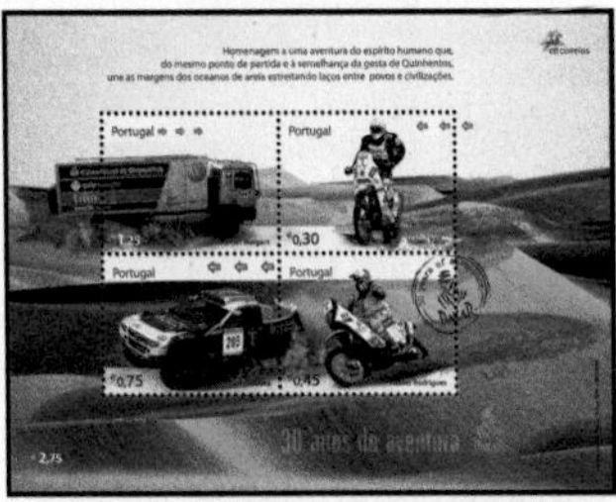

Lisbon to Dakar Rally — A822

No. 2972: a, Ruben Faria on motorcycle. b, Hélder Rodrigues on motorcycle. c, Automobile of Carlos Sousa. d, Truck of Rainer Weigart.

**2008, Jan. 5** **Litho.** *Perf. 13¼x13*
**2972** A822 Sheet of 4 6.00 6.00
*a.* 30c multi .70 .35
*b.* 45c multi 1.10 .55
*c.* 75c multi 1.75 .90
*d.* €1.25 multi 3.00 1.50

Arrival of Portuguese Royal Family in Brazil, 200th Anniv. — A823

No. 2973: a, N, Royal family and ship. b, I, King John VI and ships.

**2008, Jan. 22** *Perf. 12 Syncopated*
**2973** A823 Horiz. pair, #a-b 2.50 2.50

On day of issue, Nos. 2973a and 2973b sold for 30c and 75c, respectively.
See Brazil No. 3032.

Infertility — A824

*Perf. 11¾x12 Syncopated*

**2008, Mar. 12** **Litho.**
**2974** A824 30c multi .65 .30

Intl. Year of Planet Earth A825

Designs: 30c, Forest. 45c, Clouds. 61c, Volcano. 75c, Coral reef.

*Perf. 12x11¾ Syncopated*

**2008, Mar. 25**
**2975-2978** A825 Set of 4 4.50 4.50

2008 European Judo Championships, Lisbon — A826

Various action photos of judo opponents.

**2008, Apr. 7**
**2979** A826 30c multi .65 .35
**2980** A826 61c multi 1.40 .70

**Souvenir Sheet**

**2981** Sheet of 2 6.00 6.00
*a.* A826 45c multi 1.00 .75
*b.* A826 €2 multi 4.50 3.25

Famous People — A827

Designs: No. 2982, 30c, Maria Helena Vieira da Silva (1908-92), painter. No. 2983, 30c, Father António Vieira (1608-97), Inquisition reformer. No. 2984, 30c, Aureliano Mira Fernandes (1884-1958), mathematician. No. 2985, 30c, José Relvas (1858-1929), Prime Minister of Portugal. No. 2986, 30c, Manoel de Oliveira (b. 1908), film director. No. 2987, 30c, Ricardo Jorge (1858-1939), physician.

*Perf. 11¾x12 Syncopated*

**2008, Apr. 18**
**2982-2987** A827 Set of 6 4.00 2.00

2008 Summer Olympics, Beijing A828

Emblem of 2008 Summer Olympics and: No. 2988, 30c, Runners. No. 2989, 30c, Cyclists. 75c, Triple jump.

*Perf. 12x11¾ Syncopated*

**2008, Apr. 30**
**2988-2990** A828 Set of 3 3.00 1.50

Miniature Sheet

Olympex 2008, Beijing — A829

No. 2991 — Olympic athletes: a, Equestrian. b, Canoeing. c, Shooting. d, Rhythmic gymnastics.

*Perf. 12x11¾ Syncopated*

**2008, Apr. 30**
**2991** A829 Sheet of 4 7.00 7.00
*a.-d.* 75c Any single 1.75 1.10

European Triathlon Championships — A830

*Perf. 12x11¾ Syncopated*

**2008, May 9** **Litho.**
**2992** A830 €2 multi 4.50 2.25

Europa A831

Designs: No. 2993, Man sitting on envelope, mail truck. No. 2994a, Mail truck, bull.

**2008, May 9**
**2993** A831 61c multi 1.25 .75

**Souvenir Sheet**

**2994** Sheet of 2, #2993, 2994a 3.00 2.00
*a.* A831 61c multi 1.75 .95

Historic Public Transportation A832

Designs: N, Oldsmobile taxicab, Lisbon, 1928. A, Electric trolley, Cascais, 1926. E, Bus, Lisbon, 1944.

*Serpentine Die Cut 11½*

**2008, May 13** **Self-Adhesive**
**2995** A832 N multi .65 .35
**2996** A832 A multi 1.00 .50
**2997** A832 E multi 1.40 .70
*Nos. 2995-2997 (3)* 3.05 1.55

On day of issue, Nos. 2995-2997 sold for 30c, 45c, and 61c, respectively.
See Nos. 3026-3030.

Children's Right to Education A833

Designs: 30c, Child arriving at school. 45c, Children in classroom. 61c, Children reading and painting. 75c, Child reading with parents.
€2.95, Man hugging "4," paint brushes.

*Perf. 11¾x12 Suncopated*

**2008, June 2**
**2998-3001** A833 Set of 4 4.50 2.25

**Souvenir Sheet**

**3002** A833 €2.95 multi 7.00 4.75

UEFA Euro 2008 Soccer Championships, Austria and Switzerland. A834

Silhouettes of soccer players in: 30c, Orange and red. 61c, Blue green and lilac.
No. 3005: a, Red and lilac. b, Orange and brown.

**2008, June 5**
**3003-3004** A834 Set of 2 2.00 1.00

**Souvenir Sheet**

**3005** Sheet of 2 7.00 4.50
*a.* A834 €1.20 multi 2.75 1.90
*b.* A834 €1.66 multi 4.25 2.60

Lighthouses — A835

Designs: No. 3006, 30c, Bugio. No. 3007, 30c, Cabo de Sao Vicente. No. 3008, 30c, Cabo da Roca. No. 3009, 30c, Cabo Sardao. No. 3010, 30c, Esposende, vert. No. 3011, 30c, Santa Marta, vert. No. 3012, 30c, Cabo Espichel, vert. No. 3013, 30c, Penedo da Saudade, vert. No. 3014, 30c, Montedor, vert. No. 3015, 30c, Leça, vert.

*Perf. 12x11¾, 11¾x12 Syncopated*

**2008, June 19**
**3006-3015** A835 Set of 10 9.00 4.50

International Polar Year — A836

Designs: 30c, Calidris alba. 52c, Alca torda. 61c, Oceanites oceanicus. €1, Sterna paradisea.
€2.95, Phoca hispida, Ursus maritimus.

*Perf. 12x11¾ Syncopated*

**2008, June 23**
**3016-3019** A836 Set of 4 5.25 2.75

**Souvenir Sheet**

**3020** A836 €2.95 multi 6.50 4.75

EFIRO 2008 World Philatelic Exhibition, Bucharest, Romania (#3020). No. 3020 contains one 80x30mm stamp.

Formula 1 Racing in Portugal, 50th Anniv. A837

Race cars driven by: 31c, Stirling Moss. 67c, Jack Brabham. 80c, Mark Haywood. €2, Bobby Vernon-Roe.
€2.45, 1960 Grand Prix race at Boavista Racetrack.

*Perf. 12x11¾ Syncopated*

**2008, Sept. 11** **Litho.**

| | | | |
|---|---|---|---|
| **3021-3024** A837 | Set of 4 | 8.00 | 4.00 |

**Souvenir Sheet**

| | | | |
|---|---|---|---|
| **3025** A837 | €2.45 multi | 6.00 | 3.50 |

No. 3025 contains one 80x30mm stamp.

**Historic Public Transportation Type of 2008**

Designs: 6c, Electric trolley, Porto, 1927. 31c, Oldsmobile taxicab, Lisbon, 1928. 47c, Electric trolley, Cascais, 1926. 67c, Bus, Lisbon, 1944. 80c, Electric trolley, Coimbra, 1911.

**2008, Sept. 12** *Perf. 11¾x11½*

| | | | |
|---|---|---|---|
| **3026** A832 | 6c multi | .25 | .25 |
| **3027** A832 | 31c multi | .65 | .35 |
| **3028** A832 | 47c multi | 1.10 | .55 |
| **3029** A832 | 67c multi | 1.50 | .75 |
| **3030** A832 | 80c multi | 1.75 | .90 |
| | *Nos. 3026-3030 (5)* | 5.25 | 2.80 |

Souvenir Sheet

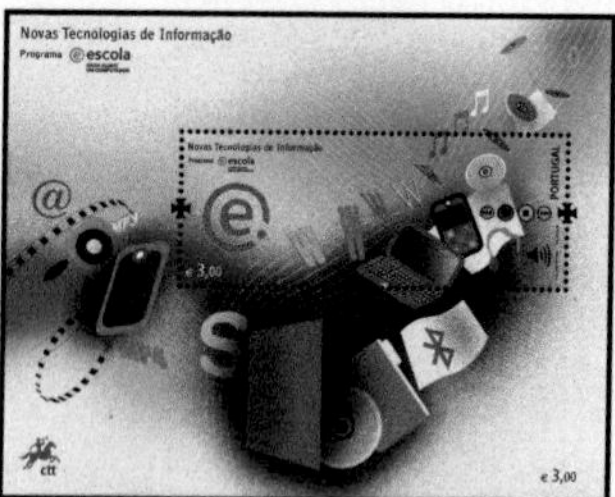

Escola School Computer Program — A838

*Perf. 12x11¾ Syncopated*

**2008, Sept. 15**

| | | | |
|---|---|---|---|
| **3031** A838 | €3 multi | 6.50 | 4.25 |

Companhia Uniao Fabril, Cent. — A839

Designs: 31c, Metalworking industry. 67c, Textile industry. €1, Naval construction industry. €2, Chemical industry.

€2.45, Alfredo da Silva, company founder, vert.

*Perf. 12x11¾ Syncopated*

**2008, Sept. 19**

| | | | |
|---|---|---|---|
| **3032-3035** A839 | Set of 4 | 9.00 | 4.50 |

*Perf. 11¾x12 Syncopated*

| | | | |
|---|---|---|---|
| **3036** A839 | €2.45 multi | 6.00 | 3.50 |

Ceramic Pharmacy Jars A840

Designs: 31c, Two jars, 17th cent. 47c, Jar, 18th cent. 67c, Three jars, 17th-18th cent. 80c, Two jars with lids, 19th cent.

€2.48, Pharmacy, 17th-18th cent.

*Perf. 12x11¾ Syncopated*

**2008, Sept. 26**

| | | | |
|---|---|---|---|
| **3037-3040** A840 | Set of 4 | 5.00 | 2.50 |

**Souvenir Sheet**

| | | | |
|---|---|---|---|
| **3041** A840 | €2.48 multi | 6.00 | 3.50 |

Demarcated Wine Regions, Cent. — A841

No. 3042, 31c: a, Colares vineyard and grapes. b, Carcavelos barrels and grapes.

No. 3043, 31c: a, Setúbal Muscatel bottles and grapes. b, Setúbal Muscatel vineyards and grapes.

No. 3044, 31c: a, Bucelas vineyard and grapes. b, Bucelas barrels and grapes.

No. 3045, 31c: a, Dao vineyard and grapes. b, Dao barrels and grapes.

No. 3046, 31c: a, Green Wine vineyard and grapes. b, Green Wine terraced vineyard.

*Perf. 12x11¾ Syncopated*

**2008, Oct. 2** **Litho.**

**Horiz. Pairs, #a-b**

| | | | |
|---|---|---|---|
| **3042-3046** A841 | Set of 5 | 6.00 | 3.00 |

Republican Ideas A842

Bust and: No. 3047, 31c, First Executive Republican Chamber. No. 3048, 31c, School and children. No. 3049, 47c, Row houses and family. No. 3050, 47c, Factory. 57c, Postal workers. No. 3052, 67c, Civil registry. No. 3053, 67c, Public health. 80c, Civic participation.

€2.95, Tagus River Railroad Bridge.

**2008, Oct. 5**

| | | | |
|---|---|---|---|
| **3047-3054** A842 | Set of 8 | 10.00 | 5.00 |

**Souvenir Sheet**

| | | | |
|---|---|---|---|
| **3055** A842 | €2.95 multi | 7.00 | 4.00 |

No. 3055 contains one 80x30mm stamp.

Olive Oil Production A843

Designs: 31c, Olive grove. 47c, Olive pickers. 57c, Olive sorters. 67c, Olive mill. 80c, Oil vats. €2, Containers of herbed olive oil.

€1.85, Hands holding olives.

**2008, Oct. 7**

| | | | |
|---|---|---|---|
| **3056-3061** A843 | Set of 6 | 11.00 | 5.50 |

**Souvenir Sheet**

| | | | |
|---|---|---|---|
| **3062** A843 | €1.85 multi | 4.50 | 2.50 |

School Correspondence — A844

Children's drawings by: 31c, Erica Bluemel Portocarrero. 47c, Eloísa O. Pereira. 67c, Joao Maria Martins Branco.

**2008, Oct. 9**

| | | | |
|---|---|---|---|
| **3063-3065** A844 | Set of 3 | 3.25 | 1.75 |

Bridges A845

Designs: 31c, April 25th Bridge, Lisbon. 47c, Arrábida Bridge, Oporto. 57c, Arade River Bridge, Portimao. 67c, Mosteiro Bridge, Cinfães. 80c, Amizade Bridge, Vila Nova de Cerveira. €1, Santa Clara Bridge, Coimbra.

No. 3072, €1.85, April 25th Bridge, Lisbon, diff. No. 3073, €1.85, Arrábida Bridge, Oporto, diff.

**2008, Oct. 16**

| | | | |
|---|---|---|---|
| **3066-3071** A845 | Set of 6 | 8.50 | 4.25 |

**Souvenir Sheets**

| | | | |
|---|---|---|---|
| **3072-3073** A845 | Set of 2 | 9.00 | 4.75 |

Nos. 3072-3073 each contain one 80x30mm stamp. See Nos. 3837, 3889.

European Year of Intercultural Dialogue — A846

Designs: 31c, Sculpture, tile design. 47c, Mask, bust. 67c, Window, feather headdress. 80c, African and Chinese masks.

**2008, Oct. 23**

| | | | |
|---|---|---|---|
| **3074-3077** A846 | Set of 4 | 5.00 | 2.50 |

Waiting for Success, Painting by Henrique Pousao (1859-84) A847

Joaquim Soeiro Pereira Gomes (1909-49), Writer A848

*Perf. 11¾x12 Syncopated*

**2009, Jan. 27** **Litho.**

| | | | |
|---|---|---|---|
| **3078** A847 | 32c multi | .70 | .35 |

*Perf. 12x11¾ Syncopated*

| | | | |
|---|---|---|---|
| **3079** A848 | 32c multi | .70 | .35 |

Creation of the Euro, 10th Anniv. A849

Euro symbols, stars and: 47c, Three stylized euro coins. €1, Two stylized euro coins.

*Perf. 12x11¾ Syncopated*

**2009, Jan. 28**

| | | | |
|---|---|---|---|
| **3080-3081** A849 | Set of 2 | 3.25 | 1.60 |

Historic Public Transportation A850

Designs: 20c, Bus, 1957. Nos. 3083, 3087, Electric train, 1957. Nos. 3084, 3088, ML7 train car, 1959. Nos. 3085, 3089, Double-decker bus, 1960. 80c, Electric trolley bus, 1961.

**2009** **Litho.** *Perf. 11¾x11½*

| | | | |
|---|---|---|---|
| **3082** A850 | 20c multi | .45 | .25 |
| **3083** A850 | 32c multi | .70 | .35 |
| **3084** A850 | 47c multi | 1.10 | .60 |
| **3085** A850 | 68c multi | 1.50 | .75 |
| **3086** A850 | 80c multi | 1.75 | .90 |
| | *Nos. 3082-3086 (5)* | 5.50 | 2.85 |

**Booklet Stamps**

**Self-Adhesive**

*Serpentine Die Cut 11½*

| | | | |
|---|---|---|---|
| **3087** A850 | N multi | .70 | .35 |
| *a.* | Booklet pane of 10 | 7.00 | |
| | Complete booklet, 10 #3087a | 70.00 | |
| **3088** A850 | A multi | 1.10 | .60 |
| *a.* | Booklet pane of 10 | 11.00 | |
| | Complete booklet, 5 #3088a | 55.00 | |
| **3089** A850 | E multi | 1.50 | .75 |
| *a.* | Booklet pane of 10 | 15.00 | |
| | Complete booklet, 5 #3089a | 75.00 | |
| | *Nos. 3087-3089 (3)* | 3.30 | 1.70 |

Issued: Nos. 3082-3086, 2/9; Nos. 3087-3089, 4/30. On day of issue, Nos. 3087-3089 sold for 32c, 47c and 68c respectively.

Charles Darwin (1809-82), Naturalist A851

Darwin and: No. 3090, 32c, Finches. No. 3091, 32c, Iguana. No. 3092, 68c, Diana monkey. No. 3093, 68c, Orchids. No. 3094, 80c, Shells and fossil skull. No. 3095, 80c, Platypus.

€2.50, Darwin and finches, vert.

*Perf. 12x11¾ Syncopated*

**2009, Feb. 12**

| | | | |
|---|---|---|---|
| **3090-3095** A851 | Set of 6 | 7.50 | 3.75 |

**Souvenir Sheet**

*Perf. 11¾x12 Syncopated*

| | | | |
|---|---|---|---|
| **3096** A851 | €2.50 multi | 6.00 | 3.25 |

African Heritage in Portugal A852

Africans as depicted in: 32c, Ceramic figurine, 19th cent. 47c, Santa Auta retable, 1522. 57c, Painting by José Conrado Roza, 1788. 68c, Ceramic tile, 19th cent. 80c, Portuguese faience, 18th cent. €2, Painted wood, 19th cent.

€2.50, Painting by Joaquim Marques, 1789.

*Perf. 12x11¾ Syncopated*

**2009, Feb. 26**

| | | | |
|---|---|---|---|
| **3097-3102** A852 | Set of 6 | 11.00 | 5.50 |

**Souvenir Sheet**

| | | | |
|---|---|---|---|
| **3103** A852 | €2.50 multi | 6.00 | 3.25 |

Molecular Models A853

Multiplication Equations — A854

**2009, Mar. 4**

| | | | |
|---|---|---|---|
| **3104** A853 | 32c multi | .70 | .35 |
| **3105** A854 | 32c multi | .70 | .35 |

Franciscan Order, 800th Anniv. A855

Designs: 32c, St. Francis of Assisi with dog.

No. 3107, vert.: a, 50c, St. Francis receiving tonsure. b, €2, Pope Innocent III.

***Perf. 12x11¾ Syncopated***

**2009, Mar. 11**

**3106** A855 32c multi .70 .35

**Souvenir Sheet**

***Perf. 11¾x12 Syncopated***

**3107** A855 Sheet of 2, #a-b 7.50 3.25

Canonization of St. Nuno de Santa Maria — A856

***Perf. 12x11¾ Syncopated***

**2009, Aug. 26**

**3108** A856 32c multi .70 .35

Europa A857

Designs: No. 3109, Three images from Mar. 3, 2007 lunar eclipse. No. 3110a, European Southern Observatory.

**2009, May 8**

**3109** A857 68c multi 1.60 .80

**Souvenir Sheet**

**3110** Sheet of 2, #3109, 3110a 4.00 2.00

*a.* A857 68c multi 1.90 .95

Intl. Year of Astronomy.

Ceramics A858

Designs: 32c, Faience mosque lamp, Turkey. 68c, Ceramic pot, Portugal.

**2009, May 12** ***Perf. 12½x13***

**3111-3112** A858 Set of 2 2.25 1.10

See Turkey Nos. 3160-3161.

Cristo Rei Sanctuary, Lisbon, 50th Anniv. — A859

Designs: 32c, Statue of Christ and base. 68c, Statue of Christ.

€2.48, Head of statue and 25 de Abril Bridge.

***Perf. 11¾x12 Syncopated***

**2009, May 17**

**3113-3114** A859 Set of 2 2.25 1.20

**Souvenir Sheet**

***Perf. 12x11¾ Syncopated***

**3115** A859 €2.48 multi 6.00 3.50

No. 3115 contains one 80x30mm stamp. See No. 3838.

Foods of Portuguese-speaking Areas — A860

Designs; No. 3116, 32c, Leitoa num ar de sarapatel, Brazil. No. 3117, 32c, Bebinca das sete colinas, India. No. 3118, 68c, Caldeirada de cabrito, Angola. No. 3119, 68c, Bacalhau, pao, vinho e aziete, Portugal. No. 3120, 80c, No caldeiro a tempura, Asia. No. 3121, 80c, Do cozido à cachupa, Cape Verde.

€1.85, Bacalhau, pao, vinho e aziete, diff., vert.

***Perf. 12x11¾ Syncopated***

**2009, June 5**

**3116-3121** A860 Set of 6 8.00 4.00

**Souvenir Sheet**

***Perf. 11¾x12 Syncopated***

**3122** A860 €1.85 multi 4.50 2.60

Lusitano Horses — A861

Designs: No. 3123, 32c, White horse with rider. No. 3124, 32c, Black horse with rider. 57c, Brown horse with rider. 68c, Brown horse rearing. 80c, Horses in team.

€2.50, Horse walking.

***Perf. 11¾x12 Syncopated***

**2009, June 11**

**3123-3127** A861 Set of 5 6.00 3.00

**Souvenir Sheet**

**3128** A861 €2.50 multi 6.00 3.50

See No. 3624.

King Afonso I (1109-85), First King of Portugal A862

Designs: 32c, Sculpture of King Afonso I €3.07, Drawing of King Afonso I on horse.

***Perf. 12x11¾ Syncopated***

**2009, June 24**

**3129** A862 32c multi .70 .35

**Souvenir Sheet**

**3130** A862 €3.07 multi 7.00 4.50

Jazz in Portugal — A863

Inscriptions: 32c, Cascais Jazz. 47c, Jazz num Dia de Verao. 57c, Fundaçao Calouste Gulbenkian Jazz em Agosto. 68c, Jazz Europeu no Porto. 80c, Guimaraes Jazz. €1, Seixal Jazz.

€3.16, Quarteto Hot Club, horiz.

***Perf. 11¾x12 Syncopated***

**2009, June 26**

**3131-3136** A863 Set of 6 9.00 4.50

**Souvenir Sheet**

***Perf. 12x11¾ Syncopated***

**3137** A863 €3.16 black 7.50 4.50

Traditional Breads A864

Designs: No. 3138, 32c, Pao de Centeio (rye bread). No. 3139, 32c, Pao de Quartos. 47c, Regueifa. No. 3141, 68c, Pao de Testa. No. 3142, 68c, Pao com Chouriço (bread with sausage). 80c, Pao de Mealhada.

No. 3144, €2, Bolo de Caco. No. 3145, €2, Pao de Milho (corn bread).

***Perf. 12x11¾ Syncopated***

**2009, July 28** **Litho.**

**3138-3143** A864 Set of 6 7.50 3.75

**Souvenir Sheets**

**3144-3145** A864 Set of 2 9.50 5.75

*3144a* Booklet pane of 1 4.50 —

*3145a* Booklet pane of 1 4.50 —

See No. 3667.

António Pedro (1909-66), Theater Founder A865

Designs: 32c, Pedro and stage art. €3.16, Pedro.

**2009, Sept. 1**

**3146** A865 32c multi .70 .35

**Souvenir Sheet**

**3147** A865 €3.16 multi 7.50 4.50

Belém Palace (Presidential Residence), Lisbon — A866

Designs: 32c, Palace exterior, 1841-42. 47c, Decorative painting. 57c, Writing desk. 68c, Bas-relief depicting satyrs. 80c, Decorative head from Gold Room. €1, Painting from Fountain Room.

€2.50, Fountain Room.

**2009, Sept. 17**

**3148-3153** A866 Set of 6 8.50 4.25

**Souvenir Sheet**

**3154** A866 €2.50 multi 6.00 3.75

Birds — A867

Designs: 32c, Pandion haliaetus. 80c, Haliaeetus albicilla.

**2009, Sept. 21** ***Perf. 13x12½***

**3155-3156** A867 Set of 2 2.50 1.25

See Iran No. 3002.

The Senses — A868

Louis Braille (1809-52), Educator of the Blind — A869

Senses: 32c, Smell (cup of coffee). 68c, Taste (ice cream bar). 80c, Sight (eyeglasses). €1, Touch (tube of paint). €2, Hearing (file)

***Perf. 11¾x12 Syncopated***

**2009, Oct. 2** **Litho.**

**3157** A868 32c multi .70 .40

**3158** A868 68c multi 1.50 .75

**Litho. with Hologram Affixed**

**3159** A868 80c multi 1.75 1.00

**Litho. & Embossed**

**3160** A868 €1 multi 2.50 1.25

**Litho.**

**3161** A868 €2 multi 5.00 2.50

*Nos. 3157-3161 (5)* 11.45 5.90

**Souvenir Sheet**

**Litho. & Embossed**

***Perf. 13¼x13½***

**3162** A869 €2.50 multi 6.00 3.75

No. 3157 is impregnated with a coffee scent. Parts of the design of No. 3161 are covered with a gritty substance.

Famous Women — A870

Designs: No. 3163, 32c, Maria Veleda (1871-1955), teacher and writer of children's books. No. 3164, 32c, Adelaide Cabete (1867-1935), doctor and feminist leader. 57c, Ana de Castro Osório (1872-1935), writer and feminist leader. 68c, Angelina Vidal (1853-1917), teacher. 80c, Carolina Beatriz Angelo (1877-1911), surgeon and feminist leader. €1, Carolina Michaelis de Vasconcelos (1851-1925), novelist.

No. 3169: a, Virginia Quaresma (1882-1973), journalist. b, Emília de Sousa Costa (1877-1959), writer and educator.

***Perf. 11¾x12 Syncopated***

**2009, Oct. 5** **Litho.**

**3163-3168** A870 Set of 6 8.00 4.00

**Souvenir Sheet**

**3169** A870 €1.15 Sheet of 2, #a-b 5.50 3.50

School Correspondence — A871

Children's art by: 32c, Martina Marques Teixeira Santos. 47c, Joel Filipe Silva Carmo. 68c, Manuel Pedro A. B. Paiva Martins.

*Perf. 12x11¾ Syncopated*

**2009, Oct. 9**

**3170-3172** A871 Set of 3 3.50 1.75

Christmas A872

Santa Claus and: 32c, Star and hearts. 47c, Door and sack of letters. 68c, Christmas tree and gift. 80c, Reindeer and gift.

No. 3177: a, 50c, Toy reindeer, "0" and "9." b, €1, Christmas stocking

*Perf. 11¾x12 Syncopated*

**2009, Oct. 21**

**3173-3176** A872 Set of 4 5.00 2.50

**Souvenir Sheet**

**3177** A872 Sheet of 2, #a-b 4.00 2.25

Abandoned Dog — A873

Viriathus (d. 138 B.C.), Lusitanian Rebel Against Roman Empire — A874

*Perf. 11¾x12 Syncopated*

**2010, Feb. 22** **Litho.**

**3178** A873 32c multi .70 .35
**3179** A874 32c multi .70 .35

Composers — A875

Designs: No. 3180, 68c, Frédéric Chopin (1810-49). No. 3181, 68c, Robert Schumann (1810-56).

No. 3182, €2, Chopin, diff. No. 3183, €2, Schumann, diff.

*Perf. 12x11¾ Syncopated*

**2010, Mar. 1**

**3180-3181** A875 Set of 2 3.00 1.50

**Souvenir Sheets**

**3182-3183** A875 Set of 2 9.50 5.50

Urban Transportation of the 1970s to 1990s — A876

Designs: 1c, Volvo articulated bus, Porto. Nos. 3185, 3189, Carris articulated tram, Lisbon. Nos. 3186, 3190, ML 79 subway train, Lisbon. Nos. 3187, 3191, Ferry boat Madragoa, Lisbon. 80c, CP electric train.

**2010, Mar. 8** **Litho.** *Perf. 11¾x11½*

**3184** A876 1c multi .25 .25
**3185** A876 32c multi .70 .35
**3186** A876 47c multi 1.10 .55
**3187** A876 68c multi 1.50 .75
**3188** A876 80c multi 1.90 .95
*Nos. 3184-3188 (5)* 5.45 2.85

**Self-Adhesive**

*Serpentine Die Cut 11½*

**3189** A876 N multi .70 .35
**3190** A876 A multi 1.10 .55
**3191** A876 E multi 1.60 .80
*Nos. 3189-3191 (3)* 3.40 1.70

On day of isse Nos. 3189-3191 sold for 32c, 47c, and 68c, respectively.

Intl. Year of Biodiversity A877

Designs: 32c, Thunnus thynnus. 47c, Centrophorus granulosus. 68c, Ailuropoda melanoleuca. 80c, Hummingbird.

€2.50, Lion tamarin.

*Perf. 12x11¾ Syncopated*

**2010, Mar. 8**

**3192-3195** A877 Set of 4 5.00 2.50

**Souvenir Sheet**

**3196** A877 €2.50 multi 6.00 3.50

Precious Stones in Sacred Art — A878

Designs: 32c, Archdiocese of Evora bouquet pin. 68c, Bodice ornament of Virgin of Carmo. €1, Processional cross of King Sancho I.

€2.50, Crown of Our Lady of Fatima sculpture.

*Perf. 12x11¾ Syncopated*

**2010, Mar. 22**

**3197-3199** A878 Set of 3 4.50 2.25

**Souvenir Sheet**

**3200** A878 €2.50 multi 5.50 3.50

Breads A879

Designs: 32c, Broa. 47c, Padas. 68c, Broa de Avintes. 80c, Alentejano bread.

No. 3205: a, 80c, Carcaça. b, €1, Mafra bread.

*Perf. 12x11¾ Syncopated*

**2010, Apr. 6**

**3201-3204** A879 Set of 4 5.00 2.50

**Souvenir Sheet**

**3205** A879 Sheet of 2, #a-b 4.00 2.50

Famous Men A880

Designs: No. 3206, 32c, Gomes Eanes de Azurara (1410-74), royal chronicler and archive keeper. No. 3207, 32c, Fernao Mendes Pinto (1510-83), travel writer. No. 3208, 32c, Alexandre Herculano (1810-77), historian. No. 3209, 32c, Francisco Keil do Amaral (1910-75), architect.

**2010, Apr. 22**

**3206-3209** A880 Set of 4 3.00 1.50

Europa — A881

Characters from children's story: No. 3210, Monkey. No. 3211a, Barber with razor.

*Perf. 11¾x12 Syncopated*

**2010, May 7**

**3210** A881 68c multi 1.50 .75

**Souvenir Sheet**

**3211** Sheet of 2, #3210, 3211a 3.00 1.75
*a.* A881 68c multi 1.50 .85

Popes A882

Designs: 68c, Pope Benedict XVI.

No. 3213, vert. — Popes who visited Portugal: a, Pope Paul VI. b, Pope John Paul II. c, Pope Benedict XVI, diff.

*Perf. 12x11¾ Syncopated*

**2010, May 10**

**3212** A882 68c multi 1.60 .80

**Souvenir Sheet**

*Perf. 11¾x12 Syncopated*

**3213** A882 80c Sheet of 3, #a-c 5.50 3.00

Visit of Pope Benedict XVI to Portugal.

Public Elevators and Funicular Railroads A883

Designs: 32c, Santa Justa Elevator, Lisbon. 47c, Glória Funicular, Lisbon. 57c Guindais Funicular, Porto. 68c, Bom Jesus Funicular, Braga. 80c, Santa Luiza Funicular, Viana do Castelo. €1, Nazaré Funicular, Nazaré.

No. 3220: a, Bica Funicular, Lisbon. b, Lavra Funicular, Lisbon.

*Perf. 11¾x12 Syncopated*

**2010, May 17**

**3214-3219** A883 Set of 6 8.50 4.25

**Souvenir Sheet**

**3220** A883 €1.25 Sheet of 2, #a-b 5.50 3.00

A884

2010 World Cup Soccer Championships, South Africa — A885

*Perf. 12x11¾ Syncopated*

**2010, May 31** **Souvenir Sheet**

**3221** A884 €2.50 multi 5.50 2.75

**Self-Adhesive**

*Serpentine Die Cut*

**3222** A885 80c multi 1.75 .95

Theater in Portugal A886

Designs: No. 3223, 32c, Estrangeiros and Vilhalpandos, by Francisco de Sá de Miranda. No. 3224, 32c, Auto da Barca do Inferno, by Gil Vicente. 57c, A Castro, by António Ferreira. No. 3226, 68c, O Fidalgo Aprendiz, by Dom Francisco Manuel de Mello. No. 3227, 68c, El-Rei Seleuco, by Luis de Camoens. 80c, Guerras de Alecrim e Manjerona, by António José da Silva.

*Perf. 12x11¾ Syncopated*

**2010, June 7**

**3223-3228** A886 Set of 6 7.50 3.75

Cheeses A887

Designs: No. 3229, 32c, Serra de Estrela. No. 3230, 32c, Rabaçal. 47c, Azeitao. 68c, Cabra Transmontano. 80c, Sao Jorge.

€2.50, Serra de Estrela, diff.

*Perf. 12x11¾ Syncopated*

**2010, June 21**

**3229-3233** A887 Set of 5 6.00 3.00

**Souvenir Sheet**

**3234** A887 €2.50 multi 5.50 3.25

Miniature Sheet

Heads of "The Republic" by Various Artists — A888

No. 3235 — Depictions by: a, 32c, Júlio Pomar. b, 32c, Francisco dos Santos. c, 32c, Costa Pinheiro. d, 32c, Bento Condado. e, 32c, Luís Maceira. f, 68c, Joao Abel Manta. g, 68c, Joao Machado. h, 80c, André Carrilho.

***Perf. 11¾x12 Syncopated***

**2010, June 24**

**3235** A888 Sheet of 8, #a-h, + central label 9.50 4.75

Portugal 2010 World Philatelic Exhibition, Lisbon.

Tiles — A889

No. 3236 — Tile from: a, 68c, Portugal, 18th cent. b, 80c, Romania, 19th cent.

**2010, June 30** **Litho.**

**3236** A889 Pair, #a-b 3.50 1.75

See Romania Nos. 5188-5189.

Jewish Culture A890

Designs: 32c, Synagogue, Tomar. 57c, Arched doorway, Rua Nova, Lamego. 68c, Jewish neighborhood, Castelo de Vide.

€2.50, Illuminated manuscript depicting Jews building structure.

***Perf. 12x11¾ Syncopated***

**2010, July 5**

**3237-3239** A890 Set of 3 3.75 2.00

**Souvenir Sheet**

**3240** A890 €2.50 multi 6.00 3.25

Rock Music Album Covers A891

Designs: 32c, Ar de Rock, by Rui Veloso. 47c, Heróis do Mar, by Heróis do Mar. 57c, Psicopátria, by GNR. 68c, A Flor da Pele, by UHF. 80c, Compacto, by Xutos & Pontapes. €1, Wolfheart, by Moonspell.

€2.50, A Lenda de El-Rei D. Sebastiao, by Quarteto 1111.

***Perf. 12x11¾ Syncopated***

**2010, July 10**

**3241-3246** A891 Set of 6 9.00 4.50

**Souvenir Sheet**

**3247** A891 €2.50 multi 6.00 3.25

Portuguese Assembly Building (St. Benedict's Palace), Lisbon A892

Designs: 32c, Sala dos Sessoes. 68c, Senate Chambers. 80c, Sala dos Passos Perdidos.

€2, Building exterior.

***Perf. 12x11¾ Syncopated***

**2010, Sept. 15**

**3247A** A892 32c multi .75 .35
**3248** A892 68c multi 1.60 .80
**3249** A892 80c multi 2.00 1.00

**Souvenir Sheet**

**3250** A892 €2 multi 4.50 2.75

Portugal 2010 World Philatelic Exhibition, Lisbon (#3250).

Peninsular War, Bicent. — A893

No. 3251: a, 32c, Battle of Vimeiro. b, 68c, Battle of Buçaco.

€2.50, Battle of Pombal.

**2010, Sept. 15**

**3251** A893 Horiz. pair, #a-b 2.50 1.25

**Souvenir Sheet**

**3252** A893 €2.50 multi 6.00 3.50

No. 3252 contains one 80x30mm stamp.

Hydrographic Institute, 50th Anniv. — A894

No. 3253: a, 32c, Lighthouse, ship's bow. b, 68c, Ship's stern, man inspecting equipment.

**2010, Sept. 22**

**3253** A894 Horiz. pair, #a-b 2.40 1.20

Circus Performers A895

Designs: 32c, Clown with broom. 47c, Clown on unicycle. 68c, Acrobat with hoops. 80c, Juggler with bowling pins.

€2.50, Trapeze artists.

***Perf. 11¾x12 Syncopated***

**2010, Sept. 29**

**3254-3257** A895 Set of 4 5.25 2.75

**Souvenir Sheet**

**3258** A895 €2.50 multi 6.00 3.50

No. 3258 contains one 30x80mm stamp.

Ceres — A896

**Litho. & Engr.**

**2010, Oct. 1** ***Perf. 14x13¼***

**3259** A896 80c multi 2.00 1.00

Republic of Portugal, cent.

History of Freedom A897

Designs: No. 3260, 32c, Liberty with Portuguese flag. No. 3261, 32c, Man with Portuguese flag, man with rifle. 47c, Soldier with cannon, man with rifle. 68c, Liberty with French flag, French man with rifle. 80c, Uncle Sam pointing at British soldiers. €1, Bishop, king and peasant.

***Perf. 12x11¾ Syncopated***

**2010, Oct. 2** **Litho.**

**3260-3265** A897 Set of 6 8.00 4.00

Portugal 2010 World Philatelic Exhibition, Lisbon

School Correspondence — A898

Children's art by: 32c, Guilherme Pereira. 47c, Diogo Gouveia. 68c, Ana Marques.

**2010, Oct. 9**

**3266-3268** A898 Set of 3 3.50 1.75

UN High Commissioner for Refugees, 60th Anniv. — A899

Designs: 80c, Refugees walking on road. €2.50, Refugee in framework for hut, vert.

***Perf. 12x11¾ Syncopated***

**2010, Oct. 18**

**3269** A899 80c multi 1.75 .90

**Souvenir Sheet**

***Perf. 11¾x12 Syncopated***

**3270** A899 €2.50 multi 5.50 3.50

Friendship Between Portugal and Japan, 150th Anniv. — A900

No. 3271 — Detail of Japanese screen painting depicting Portuguese ship's: a, 32c, Bow. b, 80c, Stern.

**2010, Oct. 22** ***Perf. 13¼x12½***

**3271** A900 Horiz. pair, #a-b 2.50 1.25

See Japan No. 3267.

Assoc. of Postal and Telecommunications Operators of Portuguese-Speaking Countries and Territories, 20th Anniv. — A901

***Perf. 12x11¾ Syncopated***

**2010, Oct. 25**

**3272** A901 80c multi 1.75 .90

Messenger on Horseback, Sculpture by Jorge Pé-Curto — A902

Designs: €1, Entire sculpture. €2.50, Head of sculpture, horiz.

***Perf. 11¾x12 Syncopated***

**2010, Nov. 2**

**3273** A902 €1 multi 2.50 1.25

**Souvenir Sheet**

***Perf. 12x11¾ Syncopated***

**3274** A902 €2.50 multi 6.00 3.50

No. 3274 contains one 80x30mm stamp.

In 2010, Portugal began issuing self-adhesive personalizable stamps as shown in the example above. These stamps, each of which were sold only in full sheets, have the inscription "Portugal CTT" at lower left, and are inscribed at the lower right with perhaps as many as 33 different denominations initially, with many more new denominations possible as postage rates change. Vignettes could be personalized or chosen from a library of stock designs.

Wind Turbines, Bridge, Buildings A903

Animals on Floating Island A904

**2011, Feb. 17** ***Perf. 13 Syncopated***

**3275** A903 32c multi .70 .35
**3276** A904 47c multi 1.10 .70

Traditional Portuguese Festivals — A905

Designs: 10c, People watching fireworks. 32c, Festa dos Tabulieros, Tomar. 47c, Festa do Sao Joao, Porto. 68c, Carneval, Loulé. 80c, Flower Festival, Madeira.

*Perf. 11¾x11½*

**2011, Feb. 21** **Litho.**

**3277** A905 10c multi .25 .25
**3278** A905 32c multi .70 .45
**3279** A905 47c multi 1.10 .70
**3280** A905 68c multi 1.50 .95
**3281** A905 80c multi 1.90 1.10
*Nos. 3277-3281 (5)* 5.45 3.45

Cheeses — A906

Designs: 32c, Serpa. 47c, Castelo Branco. 68c, Pico. 80c, Nisa. €1, Terrincho.
€2.50, Castelo Branco, diff.

**2011, Mar. 1** ***Perf. 13 Syncopated***

**3282-3286** A906 Set of 5 7.50 3.75

**Souvenir Sheet**

**3287** A906 €2.50 multi 6.00 3.50

Famous People A907

Designs: 32c, Alves Redol (1911-69), writer. 47c, Manuel da Fonseca (1911-93), writer. 57c, Trindade Coelho (1861-1908), writer. 68c, Antónia Ferreira (1811-96), businesswoman. 80c, Eugénio dos Santos (1711-60), architect.

**2011, Mar. 14**

**3288-3292** A907 Set of 5 7.00 3.50

Centenaries of Institutes of Higher Education — A908

Designs: No. 3293, 32c, University of Lisbon. No. 3294, 32c, University of Porto. No. 3295, 80c, Higher Institute of Economics and Management. No. 3296, 80c, Higher Institute of Technology.

**2011, Mar. 22**

**3293-3296** A908 Set of 4 5.00 2.50

Crédito Agrícola, Cent. A909

Hills, plants and: No. 3297, N, Tall buildings. No. 3298, E, Small buildings.

**2011, Mar. 25**

**3297-3298** A909 Set of 2 2.50 1.25

On day of issue, No. 3297 sold for 32c and No. 3298 sold for 68c.

Fish A910

Designs: 32c, Lampetra fluviatilis. 47c, Alosa alosa. 68c, Platichthys flesus. 80c, Liza ramada.
No. 3303, €1.80, Salmo salar. No. 3304, €1.80, Anguilla anguilla.

**2011, Apr. 7**

**3299-3302** A910 Set of 4 5.50 2.75

**Souvenir Sheets**

**3303-3304** A910 Set of 2 8.00 5.25

Diplomatic Relations Between Portugal and the Republic of Korea, 50th Anniv. A911

Designs: No. 3305, N, Korean turtle ship. No. 3306, I, Portuguese nau.

**2011, Apr. 15** ***Perf. 12½x13***

**3305-3306** A911 Set of 2 2.50 1.25

On day of issue, No. 3305 sold for 32c and No. 3306 sold for 80c. See South Korea No. 2355.

Republican National Guard, Cent. — A912

Designs: N, Hats. €3.60, Gloves, sword and uniform, horiz.

**2011, Apr. 21** ***Perf. 13 Syncopated***

**3307** A912 N multi .75 .40

**Souvenir Sheet**

**3308** A912 €3.60 multi 8.00 5.25

No. 3307 sold for 32c on day of issue.

Europa A913

Designs: No. 3309, Man cutting bark from cork oak, pigs. No. 3310a, Deer at edge of forest.

***Perf. 12x11¾ Syncopated***

**2011, May 9**

**3309** A913 68c multi 1.60 .80

**Souvenir Sheet**

**3310** Sheet of 2, #3309, 3310a 3.50 2.00
*a.* A913 68c multi 1.60 1.00

Intl. Year of Forests.

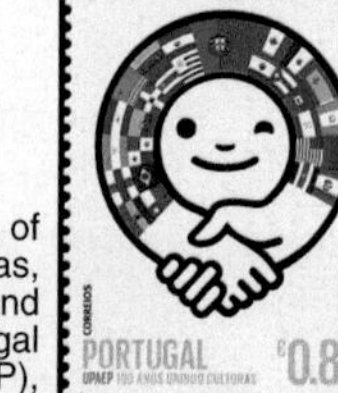


Postal Union of the Americas, Spain and Portugal ((UPAEP), Cent. — A914

**2011, May 16** ***Perf. 13 Syncopated***

**3311** A914 80c multi 1.75 1.00

Portuguese Military Academy, Cent. — A915

Designs: 32c, Shako. €1, Cadets in electronics laboratory.
€2.50, Cadet holding flag, cadet wearing shako, horiz.

**2011, May 25**

**3312-3313** A915 Set of 2 3.00 1.50

**Souvenir Sheet**

**3314** A915 €2.50 multi 5.50 3.75

Souvenir Sheet

Emblems of Portuguese Soccer Teams in 2010-11 UEFA Europa League Championship Match — A916

No. 3315 — Emblem of: a, Porto. b, Braga.

***Perf. 11¾x12 Syncopated***

**2011, May 25**

**3315** A916 €1 Sheet of 2, #a-b 5.25 3.00

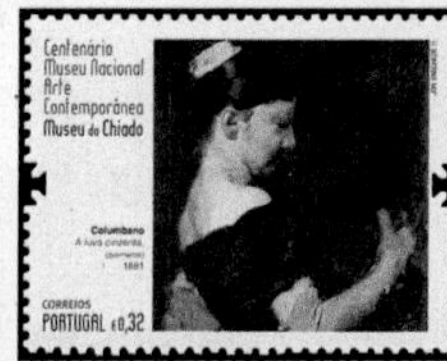


Museum of Contemporary Art, Lisbon, Cent. — A917

Designs: No. 3316, 32c, A Luva Cinzenta, by Columbano. No. 3317, 32c, Tristezas, Cabeça, by Amadeo de Souza-Cardoso. 47c, A Sesta, by Almada Negreiros. No. 3319, 68c, Cais 44, by Fernando Lanhas. No. 3320, 68c, Sombra Projectada de René Bertholo, by Lourdes Castro. 80c, A Esquiva, by Joao Maria Gusmao and Pedro Paiva.
No. 3322: a, Landscape, by Juliao Sarmento. b, Estrada da Vida, by Fernando Taborda.

**2011, May 26** ***Perf. 13 Syncopated***

**3316-3321** A917 Set of 6 8.00 4.00

**Souvenir Sheet**

**3322** A917 €1.50 Sheet of 2, #a-b 6.50 4.50

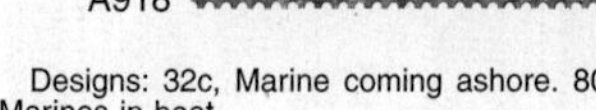

Marine Training School, 50th Anniv. A918

Designs: 32c, Marine coming ashore. 80c, Marines in boat.
€2.50, Monument.

**2011, June 3** **Litho.**

**3323-3324** A918 Set of 2 2.50 1.25

**Souvenir Sheet**

**3325** A918 €2.50 multi 6.50 3.75

Embroidery A919

Embroidery designs from: 32c, Vila Verde. 47c, Arraiolos. 57c, Castelo Branco. 68c, Viana. 80c, Madeira. €1, Azores.
No. 3332, €1.75, Guimaraes. No. 3333, €1.75, Ribatejo.

***Perf. 11¾x12 Syncopated***

**2011, June 28**

**3326-3331** A919 Set of 6 9.00 4.50
*3330a* Booklet pane of 1 2.00 —
*3331a* Booklet pane of 1 2.50 —

**Souvenir Sheets**

**3332-3333** A919 Set of 2 8.00 5.00

Nos. 3330a and 3331a are found in booklets listed under Azores and Madeira. See Nos. 3625, 3668.

A920

Diplomatic Relations Between Thailand and Portugal, 500th Anniv. — A921

No. 3334: a, 32c, Portuguese caravel, rowboats, Thai buildings and temples. b, 80c, Elephants and riders at dockside.
No. 3335: a, 32c, Portuguese caravel, Thai buildings. b, 80c, Thai boats and buildings.

**2011, July 20** ***Perf. 13x13¼***

**3334** A920 Horiz. pair, #a-b 1.50 .80
**3335** A921 Horiz. pair, #a-b 3.50 2.00

See Thailand Nos. 2617-2618.

Torre do Tombo National Archives, Cent. A922

Various historical documents and illuminations: 32c, 68c, €2.
€2.30, Torre de Tombo National Archive, document.

**2011, July 27** ***Perf. 13 Syncopated***

**3336-3338** A922 Set of 3 6.50 3.50

**Souvenir Sheet**

**3339** A922 €2.30 multi 6.50 3.50

Intl. Year of Veterinary Medicine A923

Designs: 32c, Pigs in farm trailer. 68c, Horse, DNA strands. 80c, Cat, medicines. €1, Cow, milk bottles.

€2.50, Owl in tree.

**2011, Sept. 7** **Litho.**

**3340-3343** A923 Set of 4 6.50 3.00

**Souvenir Sheet**

**3344** A923 €2.50 multi 6.00 3.50

Theater in Portugal A924

Actors and actresses: No. 3345, 32c, Laura Alves (1927-86). No. 3346, 32c, Amélia Rey Colaço (1898-1990). 47c, Raul Solnado (1929-2009). 68c, Armando Cortez (1928-2002). 80c, Eunice Muñoz. €1, Ruy de Carvalho.

No. 3351, €1: a, Scene from "Frei Luis de Sousa," by Almeida Garrett. b, Scene from "Os Velhos," by D. Joao da Câmara.

No. 3352, €1: a, Scene from "A Promessa," by Bernardo Santareno. b, Scene from "Bernilde ou a Virgem-Mâe," by José Régio.

**2011, Sept. 14**

**3345-3350** A924 Set of 6 8.00 4.00

**Souvenir Sheets of 2, #a-b**

**3351-3352** A924 Set of 2 8.50 5.50

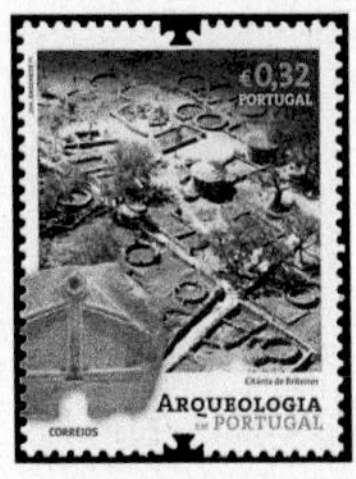

Archaeology in Portugal — A925

Artifacts from archaeological sites in: 32c, Citânia de Briteiros. 47c, Foz Côa. 68c, Conímbriga. 80c, Milreu. €1, Alcalar.

€2.50, José Leite de Vasconcelos (1858-1941), first director of National Museum of Archaeology.

**2011, Sept. 21** ***Perf. 13 Syncopated***

**3353-3357** A925 Set of 5 7.50 3.50

**Souvenir Sheet**

**3358** A925 €2.50 multi 5.50 3.50

See Nos. 3626-3627.

Protection of Water Resources and the Environment — A926

Designs: 32c, Hand holding glass under running faucet. 47c, Bandage on hose. 68c, Water bucket, filter and flowers. 80c, Recycling bins.

**2011, Sept. 30**

**3359-3362** A926 Set of 4 5.50 3.00

Fado Musicians A927

Designs: 32c, Alfredo Marceneiro (1891-1982). 47c, Carlos Ramos (1907-69). 57c, Hermínia Silva (1907-93). 68c, Maria Teresa de Noronha (1918-93). 80c, Amália Rodrigues (1920-99). €1, Carlos do Carmo.

€2.50, O Fado, painting by José Malhoa.

**2011, Oct. 3**

**3363-3368** A927 Set of 6 9.00 4.50

**Souvenir Sheet**

**3369** A927 €2.50 multi 5.50 3.50

Festival of the Trays, Tomar — A928

Festival of St. John the Baptist, Porto — A929

Loulé Carnival — A930

***Serpentine Die Cut 11½***

**2011, Oct. 3** **Self-Adhesive**

**3370** A928 N multi .75 .25

**3371** A929 A multi 1.10 .40

**3372** A930 E multi 1.50 .45

*Nos. 3370-3372 (3)* 3.35 1.10

On day of issue, No. 3370 sold for 32c; No. 3371, 47c; No. 3372, 68c.

School Correspondence — A931

Children's art: 32c, Bird and fish. 68c, Earth and sun as wheels on boy's bicycle. 80c, Three girls, duck.

**2011, Oct. 11** ***Perf. 13 Syncopated***

**3373-3375** A931 Set of 3 4.00 2.00

Portuguese Military Academy, 175th Anniv. — A932

Designs: 32c, Academy building, Marquis de Sá da Bandeira (1795-1876). 68p, Academy crest and regalia.

€2.50, Sword and regalia, vert.

**2012, Jan. 12** ***Perf. 12 Syncopated***

**3376-3377** A932 Set of 2 2.25 1.10

**Souvenir Sheet**

**3378** A932 €2.50 multi 5.50 3.25

Famous Men — A933

Designs: 32c, Marcos Portugal (1762-1830), composer. 68c, Brito Camacho (1862-1934), journalist and politician. 80c, António Vilar (1912-95), actor.

***Perf. 13¼x13 Syncopated***

**2012, Feb. 13**

**3379-3381** A933 Set of 3 4.25 2.00

Art Depicting Biblical Scenes — A934

Designs: 47c, Creation of Eve (Criaçao de Eva). 68c, Moses in the Desert (Moisés no Deserto). 80c, Adoration of the Magi (Adoraçao dos Reis Magos). €1, The Last Supper (Ultima Ceia).

No. 3386, €1.50, Crucifixion (Paixao de Cristo). No. 3387, €1.50, Pentacost (Pentecostes).

**2012, Feb. 23**

**3382-3385** A934 Set of 4 6.50 3.25

**Souvenir Sheets**

**3386-3387** A934 Set of 2 7.00 4.00

Colors and Associated Color-Blindness Shapes For Them — A935

Designs: 32c, Red (Vermelho). 47c, Blue (Azul). 68c, Yellow (Amarelo). 80c, Black (Preto). €1, White (Branco).

***Perf. 13x13¼ Syncopated***

**2012, Mar. 20**

**3388-3392** A935 Set of 5 7.50 3.75

Guimares, 2012 European Capital of Culture A936

Designs: 32c, Largo da Oliveira. 47c, Vila Flor Cultural Center. 68c, Nicolinas Festival. 80c, Santa Marinha da Costa Inn.

€3, Guimaraes Castle, sculpture by Joao Cutiliero.

***Perf. 12x11¾ Syncopated***

**2012, Apr. 10**

**3393-3396** A936 Set of 4 5.25 2.50

**Souvenir Sheet**

**3397** A936 €3 multi 6.75 4.00

No. 3397 contains one 80x30mm stamp.

Erasmus Foreign Exchange Program, 25th Anniv. A937

European landmarks and: 68c, Female student on bicycle. €3, Student on motor scooter, female student.

**2012, Apr. 17**

**3398** A937 68c multi 1.50 .75

**Souvenir Sheet**

**3399** A937 €3 multi 6.75 4.00

No. 3399 contains one 80x30mm stamp.

Europa A938

Designs: No. 3400, Steamer Principe Perfeito. No. 3401a, Lisbon waterfront.

**2012, May 9**

**3400** A938 68c multi 1.50 .75

**Souvenir Sheet**

**3401** Sheet of 2, #3400, 3401a 3.50 1.75

*a.* A938 68c multi 1.50 .75

Cathedrals A939

Cathedrals at: No. 3402, N, Braga. No. 3403, N, Faro. No. 3404, N, Guarda. No. 3405, N, Lamego. No. 3406, N, Porto. No. 3407, N, Santarém. No. 3408, N, Silves. No. 3409, N, Viana do Castelo. No. 3410, N, Vila Real. No. 3411, N, Viseu.

**2012, May 18** ***Perf. 13 Syncopated***

**3402-3411** A939 Set of 10 8.00 4.00

Nos. 3402-3411 each sold for 32c on day of issue. See No. 3890.

University of Lisbon Institute of Social Sciences, 50th Anniv. A940

Designs: N, Adérito Sedas Nunes and *Análise Social* Magazine. E, Institute of Social Sciences Building.

***Perf. 12x11¾ Syncopated***

**2012, May 31**

**3412** A940 N multi .75 .35

**3413** A940 E multi 1.60 .80

On day of issue, No. 3412 sold for 32c and No. 3413 sold for 68c.

2012 European Soccer Championships, Poland and Ukraine — A941

Design: 68c, Foosball figure and soccer ball.

€2.50, Foosball figures and soccer ball, horiz.

*Perf. 11¾x12 Syncopated*

**2012, June 4**

**3414** A941 68c multi 1.50 .75

**Souvenir Sheet**

*Perf. 12x11¾ Syncopated*

**3415** A941 €2.50 multi 5.50 3.25

2012 Summer Olympics and Paralympics, London — A942

Designs: No. 3416, N, Stylized Olympic athlete. No. 3417, N, Two stylized Paralympic athletes. No. 3418, I, Stylized Olympic fencer. No. 3419, I, Stylized athlete in wheelchair.

*Perf. 11¾x12 Syncopated*

**2012, June 19**

**3416-3419** A942 Set of 4 5.00 2.50

On day of issue, Nos. 3416-3417 each sold for 32c, and Nos. 3418-3419 each sold for 80c.

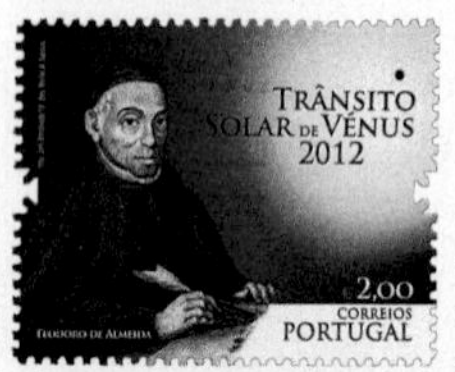


Transit of Venus A943

Designs: €2, Teodoro de Almeida (1722-1804), observer of 1761 transit, Venus and Sun. €3, Diagram showing Earth, Venus and Sun.

**2012, June 27** *Perf. 13 Syncopated*

**3420** A943 €2 multi 4.50 2.25

**Souvenir Sheet**

**3421** A943 €3 multi 6.50 3.75

Souvenir Sheet

Victory of Portuguese Team at 2012 European Soccer Championships — A944

*Perf. 11¾x12 Syncopated*

**2012, July 4**

**3422** A944 €1.50 multi 3.50 1.90

Traditional Portuguese Festivals A945

Designs: 5c, People watching fireworks. 32c, Festa de Santo António, Lisbon. 47c, Festas do Espirito Santo, Azores. 68c, Carnaval, Ilhavo. 90c, Golega Fair.

**2012, July 20** *Perf. 11¾x11½*

**3423** A945 5c multi .25 .25
**3424** A945 32c multi .80 .40
**3425** A945 47c multi 1.10 .50
**3426** A945 68c multi 1.50 .75
**3427** A945 80c multi 1.90 .80
*Nos. 3423-3427 (5)* 5.55 2.70

Compare with Types A956-A958.

Douro River A946

Designs: 32c, Riverside cliffs. 57c, Boat on river. 68c, Terraced fields and road near river. 80c, Buildings near river.

€3, Porto buildings, bridge and boats.

**2012, July 30** *Perf. 13 Syncopated*

**3428-3431** A946 Set of 4 5.50 2.75

**Souvenir Sheet**

**3432** A946 €3 multi 6.50 3.75

No. 3432 contains one 80x30mm stamp. See No. 3891.

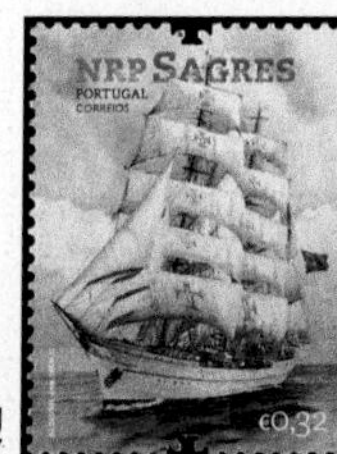


Training Ships — A947

Designs: 32c, NRP Sagres. 80c, NTM Creoula.

No. 3435, €1.75, Bell, silhouette of NRP Sagres. No. 3436, €1.75, Lifeboats, silhouette of NTM Creoula.

*Perf. 11¾x12 Syncopated, 12x11¾ Syncopated (#3436)*

**2012, Aug. 3**

**3433-3434** A947 Set of 2 2.75 1.40

**Souvenir Sheets**

**3435-3436** A947 Set of 2 8.50 4.25

See No. 3839.

Fernando Pessoa (1888-1935), Poet — A948

Joao da Cruz e Sousa (1861-98), Poet — A949

*Perf. 11¾x12 Syncopated*

**2012, Sept. 7**

**3437** A948 80c multi + label 1.90 .95
**3438** A949 80c multi + label 1.90 .95

See Brazil Nos. 3225-3226.

Sausages and Hams A950

Sausages: No. 3439, 32c, Guarda chouriço. No. 3440, 32c, Vinhais chouriça. No. 3441, 47c, Ponte de Lima onion chouriça. No. 3442, 47c, Barroso-Montalegre chouriça. 57c, Vinhais salpicao. No. 3444, 68c, Guarda morcela. No. 3445, 68c, Vila Real moura. No. 3446, 80c, Mirandela alheira.

No. 3447, 80c, vert. — Hams from: a, Melgaço. b, Vinhais. c, Barroso.

*Perf. 12x11¾ Syncopated*

**2012, Sept. 25**

**3439-3446** A950 Set of 8 10.00 5.00

**Souvenir Sheet**

*Perf. 11¾x12 Syncopated*

**3447** A950 80c Sheet of 3, #a-c 6.25 3.25

See Nos. 3483-3491.

Palaces — A951

Rooms and exterior views of: No. 3448, 32c, Pena National Palace, Sao Pedro de Penaferrim. No. 3449, 32c, Ajuda National Palace, Lisbon, Queen Consort Maria Pia of Savoy (1847-1911). No. 3450, 68c, Mafra National Palace, Mafra. No. 3451, 68c, Sintra National Palace, Sintra. No. 3452, 80c, Monserrate Palace, Sintra. No. 3453, 80c, Queluz National Palace, Queluz.

*Perf. 11¾x12 Syncopated*

**2012, Oct. 3**

**3448-3453** A951 Set of 6 8.50 4.25

School Correspondence A952

Children's art by: 32c, Martim dos Santos Onofre. 68c, Matilde Amaro Nunes. 80c, Ana Carolina Marques.

*Perf. 13¼x13 Syncopated*

**2012, Oct. 9**

**3454-3456** A952 Set of 3 4.25 2.10

Fado Musicians A953

Designs: No. 3457, 32c, Vicente da Câmara. No. 3458, 32c, Argentina Santos. 57c, Maria da Fé. 68c, Rodrigo. 80c, Camané. No. 3462, €1, Mariza. No. 3463, Caricature of Fado guitarist, neck of Fado guitar.

**2012, Oct. 11** **Litho.**

**3457-3463** A953 Set of 7 11.00 5.50

First Humorists Exhibition, Cent. — A954

Carictures and cartoon art by: No. 3464, 32c, Rafael Bordalo Pinheiro. No. 3465, 47c, Stuart Carvalhais. No. 3466, 68c, Emmerico Nunes. No. 3467, 80c, Almada Negreiros.

No. 3468: a, 32c, Francisco Valenca. b, 32c, Manuel Gustavo Bordalo Pinheiro. c, 47c, Jorge Barradas. d, 47c, Américo Amarelhe. e, 68c, Celso Herminio. f, 68c, Canto da Maya. g, 80c, Cristiano Cruz. h, 80c, Menezes Ferreira.

*Perf. 13¼x13 Syncopated*

**2012, Oct. 16**

**3464-3467** A954 Set of 4 5.00 2.50

**Souvenir Sheet**

**3468** A954 Sheet of 8, #a-h 11.50 5.75

Order of Engineers — A955

Designs: 32c, Civil, geological and mining engineering. 47c, Electrical and informational engineering. 57c, Naval and mechanical engineering. 68c, Material, chemical and biological engineering. 80c, Forestry and agronomic engineering. €1, Geographical and environmental engineering.

€3, Arch and angels.

*Perf. 13x13¼ Syncopated*

**2012, Oct. 19**

**3469-3474** A955 Set of 6 9.00 4.50

**Souvenir Sheet**

**3475** A955 €3 multi 6.50 4.00

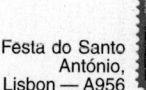

Festa do Santo António, Lisbon — A956

Festas do Espirito Santo, Azores — A957

Carnaval, Ilhavo — A958

*Serpentine Die Cut 11½*

**2012, Nov. 13** **Self-Adhesive**

**3476** A956 N multi .75 .30
**3477** A957 (47c) multi 1.10 .50
**3478** A958 E multi 1.60 .70
*Nos. 3476-3478 (3)* 3.85 1.90

Compare with type A945. On day of issue, No. 3476 sold for 32c and No. 3478 sold for 68c.

Composers A959

Designs: No. 3479, E, Giuseppe Verdi (1813-1901). No. 3480, E, Richard Wagner (1813-83).

No. 3481, €1.50, Falstaff. No. 3482, €1.50, Valkyrie.

*Perf. 11¾x12 Syncopated*

**2013, Jan. 31**

**3479-3480** A959 Set of 2 3.25 1.60

**Souvenir Sheets**

**3481-3482** A959 Set of 2 7.00 4.25

On day of issue, Nos. 3479-3480 each sold for 68c.

**Sausages and Hams Type of 2012**

Designs: No. 3483, N, Portalegre chouriço mouro. No. 3484, N, Estremoz and Borba farinheira. No. 3485, A, Estremoz and Borba chouriço. No. 3486, A, Monchique farinheira. No. 3487, E, Portalegre paio enguitado. No. 3488, E, Sao Miguel morcela. No. 3489, I, Serta maranhos. No. 3490, I, Portalegre paio ou lombo branco.

No. 3491, vert. — Hams from: a, Barrancos. b, Santana da Serra.

*Perf. 12x11¾ Syncopated*

**2013, Mar. 15**

**3483-3490** A950 Set of 8 10.00 5.00

**Souvenir Sheet**

*Perf. 11¾x12 Syncopated*

**3491** A950 €1 Sheet of 2, #a-b 4.50 2.60

On day of issue, Nos. 3483-3484 each sold for 32c, Nos. 3485-3486 each sold for 47c, Nos. 3487-3488 each sold for 68c and Nos, 3489-3490 each sold for 80c.

Falconry — A960

Designs: N, Falco peregrinus, falcon hood. A, Accipiter gentilis, pouch. E, Accipiter nisus, lure. I, Aquila chrysaetos, gauntlet.

€1.50, Royal Falconry Building, Salvaterra do Magos.

*Perf. 11¾x12 Syncopated*

**2013, Mar. 23**

| | | | | |
|---|---|---|---|---|
| **3492** | A960 | N multi | .75 | .30 |
| **3493** | A960 | A multi | 1.10 | .55 |
| **3494** | A960 | E multi | 1.60 | .70 |
| **3495** | A960 | I multi | 1.90 | .95 |
| | | *Nos. 3492-3495 (4)* | 5.35 | 2.50 |

**Souvenir Sheet**

**3496** A960 €1.50 multi 3.50 2.00

On day of issue Nos. 3492-3495 each sold for 32c, 47c, 68c and 80c, respectively.

Famous People A961

Designs: 36c, Joao Villaret (1913-61), actor. 60c, Ilse Losa (1913-2006), writer. 70c, Joao Dos Santos (1913-87), psychiatrist. 80c, Edgar Cardoso (1913-2000), civil engineer. €1, Raúl Rego (193-2002), journalist.

*Perf. 12x11¾ Syncopated*

**2013, Apr. 15**

**3497-3501** A961 Set of 5 7.50 3.75

Traditional Portuguese Festivals — A962

Designs: 3c, Icon, men in red vestments. 4c, Icon, men in blue vestments. 36c, Woman and girl, Sao Mateus Fair, Viseu. 50c, Woman, icon on boat, Feast of Our Lady of Agony, Viana do Castelo. 70c, People in costumes, Feast of Santo Estevao, Ousilhao. 80c, Men wearing hats, Feast of Our Lady of Guadalupe, Serpa. €1, Three participants, People's Festival, Campo Maior. €1.70, Man, woman and icon, Pilgrimage of Our Lady of Almortao, Idanha-a-Nova.

**2013, Apr. 30** *Perf. 11¾x11½*

| | | | | |
|---|---|---|---|---|
| **3502** | A962 | 3c multi | .25 | .25 |
| **3503** | A962 | 4c multi | .25 | .25 |
| **3504** | A962 | 36c multi | .80 | .30 |
| **3505** | A962 | 50c multi | 1.10 | .55 |
| **3506** | A962 | 70c multi | 1.50 | .75 |
| **3507** | A962 | 80c multi | 1.90 | .90 |
| **3508** | A962 | €1 multi | 2.40 | 1.20 |
| **3509** | A962 | €1.70 multi | 4.00 | 2.00 |
| | | *Nos. 3502-3509 (8)* | 12.20 | 6.20 |

Arrival of Explorer Jorge Alvares in China, 500th Anniv. — A963

Old map of Chinese coast and: 36c, Chinese compass. 80c, Compass rose.

€3, Chinese vase, old map of Chinese coast.

*Perf. 11¾x12 Syncopated*

**2013, May 8** **Litho.**

**3510-3511** A963 Set of 2 2.75 1.40

**Souvenir Sheet**

**3512** A963 €3 multi 7.00 4.00

No. 3512 contains one 30x80mm stamp.

Europa A964

Designs: No. 3513, Portuguese postal van facing left. No. 3514a, Postal worker and Portuguese postal van.

*Perf. 12x11¾ Syncopated*

**2013, May 9** **Litho.**

**3513** A964 70c multi 1.50 .75

**Souvenir Sheet**

**3514** Sheet of 2, #3513, 3514a 3.50 1.90

*a.* A964 70c multi 1.75 .80

Lay Missions in Africa, Cent. — A965

Designs: 36c, Eight missionaries to Angola. 80c, Seven missionaries to Mozambique.

€2.60, Colonial Missions Institute, Cernache do Bonjardim.

*Perf. 11¾x12 Syncopated*

**2013, May 13** **Litho.**

**3515-3516** A965 Set of 2 2.50 1.25

**Souvenir Sheet**

**3517** A965 €2.60 multi 6.25 3.50

Intl. Year of Statistics A966

Graph and: 36c, Gears. €1, People carrying streamers.

€2, Graph, trees and rain clouds.

*Perf. 12x11¾ Syncopated*

**2013, May 24** **Litho.**

**3518-3519** A966 Set of 2 3.00 1.50

**Souvenir Sheet**

**3520** A966 €2 multi 4.50 2.75

No. 3520 contains one 80x30mm stamp.

Cathedrals A967

Designs: No. 3521, 36c, Old Coimbra Cathedral (Velha). No. 3522, 36c, New Coimbra Cathedral (Nova). No. 3523, 36c, Portalegre Cathedral. No. 3524, 36c, Castelo Branco Cathedral. No. 3525, 36c, Leiria Cathedral. No. 3526, 36c, Aveiro Cathedral. No. 3527, 80c, Funchal Cathedral. No. 3528, 80c, Angra Cathedral.

*Perf. 11¾x12 Syncopated*

**2013, June 6** **Litho.**

**3521-3528** A967 Set of 8 9.00 4.50

See Madeira No. 363.

Antique Works of Jewelers A968

Designs: 36c, Bronze Age bracelet. 70c, Iron Age earring. 80c, Roman Era phiale. €1.70, Visigoth Era fibula.

€3, Iron Age necklace, vert.

*Perf. 12x11¾ Syncopated*

**2013, June 21** **Litho.**

**3529-3532** A968 Set of 4 8.00 4.00

**Souvenir Sheet**

*Perf. 11¾x12 Syncopated*

**3533** A968 €3 multi 6.50 4.00

Woman and Girl, Sao Mateus Fair, Viseu — A969

Woman, Icon on Boat, Feast of Our Lady of Agony,Viana do Castelo — A970

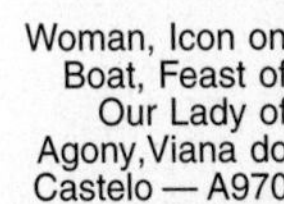

People in Costumes, Feast of Santo Estevao, Ousilhao — A971

*Die Cut Perf. 11½*

**2013, July 22** **Litho.**

**Self-Adhesive**

| | | | | |
|---|---|---|---|---|
| **3534** | A969 | N multi | .85 | .30 |
| **3535** | A970 | A multi | 1.20 | .60 |
| **3536** | A971 | E multi | 1.60 | .80 |
| | | *Nos. 3534-3536 (3)* | 3.65 | 1.70 |

On day of issue, No. 3534 sold for 36c; No. 3535, 50c; No. 3536, 70c.

Catholic Missions in Africa A972

Designs: 36c, Child at blackboard (education). 50c, Nurses and patient (health care). 70c, Children at sink (building of infrastructure). 80c, Man watering plants (agricultural development). €1, Adult education. €1.70, Priest and children (evangelization).

*Perf. 12x11¾ Syncopated*

**2013, Aug. 19** **Litho.**

**3537-3542** A972 Set of 6 11.00 5.50

Compilation of the Canon of Medicine, by Avicenna, 1000th Anniv. — A973

Designs: €1.70, Avicenna taking notes. €3.30, Avicenna examining patient, horiz.

**2013, Aug. 23** **Litho.** *Perf. 11¾x12*

**3543** A973 €1.70 multi 4.00 2.00

**Souvenir Sheet**

**3544** A973 €3.30 multi 7.00 4.50

No. 3544 contains one 61x40mm stamp.

Presentation of 12th Aga Khan Awards for Architecture — A974

Designs: 80c, Tiles. €1, Embroidery design

€3, Sao Jorge Castle, Lisbon, site of awards ceremony, vert.

**2013, Sept. 6** **Litho.** *Perf. 12x12½*

**3545-3546** A974 Set of 2 4.00 2.00

**Souvenir Sheet**

**Silk-faced Paper**

*Perf. 12½x12*

**3547** A974 €3 multi 7.00 4.00

No. 3547 contains one 30x80mm stamp.

Sculptures of Joana Vasconcelos A975

Designs: 50c, Red Independent Heart. 80c, Cinderella.

*Perf. 11¾x12 Syncopated*

**2013, Sept. 16** **Litho.**

**3548-3549** A975 Set of 2 3.00 1.50

Apiculture — A976

Designs: 36c, Bees, honeycomb, beekeeper tending hive. 50c, Bees at hive entrance and in flight. 70c, Bees in flight over field. 80c, Bees and flowers.

€1.70, Bee on flower. €1.90, Bee, beekeeper removing honey from honeycomb.

***Perf. 12x11¾ Syncopated***

**2013, Sept. 23** **Litho.**

| | | | | |
|---|---|---|---|---|
| **3550-3553** | A976 | Set of 4 | 5.00 | 2.50 |

**Souvenir Sheets**

| | | | | |
|---|---|---|---|---|
| **3554-3555** | A976 | Set of 2 | 8.00 | 5.00 |

Papal Recognition of Sovereign Military Order of Malta, 900th Anniv. — A977

Grand Masters: 36c, Afonso of Portugal (1137-1207). 70c, Luís Mendes de Vasconcelos (c. 1542-1623). 80c, António Manoel de Vilhena (1663-1736). €1, Manuel Pinto da Fonseca (1681-1773).
€1.95, Ship of Grand Master Pinto da Fonseca.

***Perf. 11¾x12 Syncopated***

**2013, Sept. 27** **Litho.**

| | | | | |
|---|---|---|---|---|
| **3556-3559** | A977 | Set of 4 | 6.50 | 3.25 |

**Souvenir Sheet**

| | | | | |
|---|---|---|---|---|
| **3560** | A977 | €1.95 multi | 4.50 | 2.60 |

No. 3560 contains one 30x80mm stamp.

School Correspondence — A978

Children's art by: N, Martim Ferreira Simao. E, David Serafim Reis. I, Francisco Maria Rasquilha.

***Perf. 12x11¾ Syncopated***

**2013, Oct. 9** **Litho.**

| | | | | |
|---|---|---|---|---|
| **3561-3563** | A978 | Set of 3 | 4.00 | 2.00 |

On day of issue, No. 3561 sold for 36c; No. 3562, 70c; No. 3563, 80c.

Christmas A979

Various creche figures: N, 50c, 60c, 70c, 80c, €1.70,

***Perf. 12x11¾ Syncopated***

**2013, Oct. 9** **Litho.**

| | | | | |
|---|---|---|---|---|
| **3564-3569** | A979 | Set of 6 | 11.00 | 5.50 |

No. 3564 sold for 36c on day of issue.

Souvenir Sheet

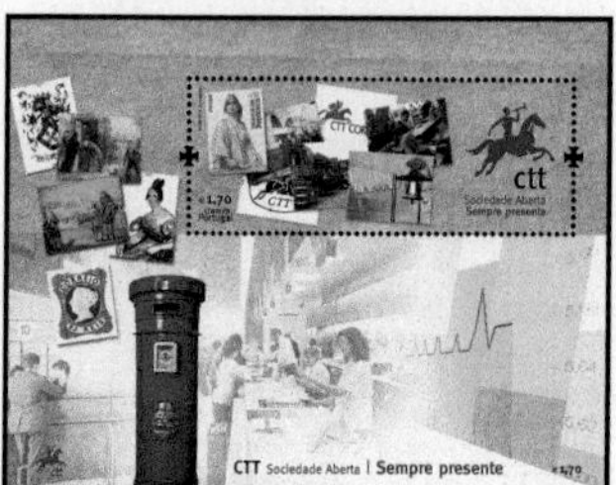


Public Trading of Shares of CTT Portugal — A980

***Perf. 12x11¾ Syncopated***

**2014, Jan. 27** **Litho.**

| | | | | |
|---|---|---|---|---|
| **3570** | A980 | €1.70 multi | 4.00 | 2.40 |

Extreme Sports — A981

Designs: 40c, Surfing. 50c, Mountain biking. 70c, Skateboarding. 80c, Kayaking. €1.70, Paragliding.

***Perf. 11¾x11½***

**2014, Feb. 10** **Litho.**

| | | | | |
|---|---|---|---|---|
| **3571** | A981 | 40c multi | .95 | .30 |
| **3572** | A981 | 50c multi | 1.20 | .60 |
| **3573** | A981 | 70c multi | 1.60 | .80 |
| **3574** | A981 | 80c multi | 1.90 | .90 |
| **3575** | A981 | €1.70 multi | 4.00 | 2.00 |
| | | *Nos. 3571-3575 (5)* | 9.65 | 4.60 |

See Nos. 3602-3604, 3669-3671, 3685-3689, 3765-3767, 3778-3782.

Publication of Peregrinaçao (Pilgrimage), Travel Writings of Fernao Mendes Pinto, 400th Anniv. — A982

Designs: €1, Front page of Peregrinaçao, ships, Buddhist deity on peacock, horseman. €3, Old map.

***Perf. 12x11¾ Syncopated***

**2014, Feb. 24** **Litho.**

| | | | | |
|---|---|---|---|---|
| **3576** | A982 | €1 multi | 2.40 | 1.20 |

**Souvenir Sheet**

| | | | | |
|---|---|---|---|---|
| **3577** | A982 | €3 multi | 7.00 | 4.25 |

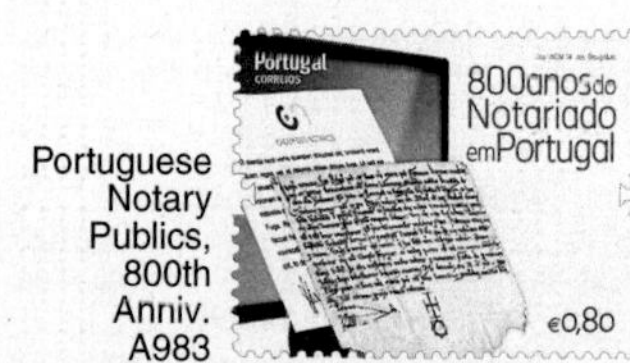


Portuguese Notary Publics, 800th Anniv. A983

Designs: 80c, Documents. €3, Notary public writing in book.

***Perf. 12x11¾ Syncopated***

**2014, Mar. 6** **Litho.**

| | | | | |
|---|---|---|---|---|
| **3578** | A983 | 80c multi | 1.90 | .95 |

**Souvenir Sheet**

| | | | | |
|---|---|---|---|---|
| **3579** | A983 | €3 multi | 7.00 | 4.25 |

No. 3579 contains one 80x30mm stamp.

Famous People — A984

Designs: 40c, Florbela Espanca (1894-1930), poet. 50c, Maria Keil (1914-2012), painter. 60c, Joaquim Namorado (1914-86), poet. 70c, Joao Hogan (1914-88), painter. 80c, António Dacosta (1914-90), painter. €1, José Sebastiao e Silva (1914-72), mathematician.

***Perf. 11¾x12 Syncopated***

**2014, Mar. 24** **Litho.**

| | | | | |
|---|---|---|---|---|
| **3580-3585** | A984 | Set of 6 | 9.00 | 4.50 |

Architects and Their Buildings — A985

Designs: No. 3586, I, Paula Rego Museum, by Eduardo Souto de Moura. No. 3587, I, Júlio Pomar Museum, by Alvaro Siza Vieira. No. 3588, I, Green Corridor of Lisbon, by Gonçalo Ribeiro Telles.

***Perf. 12x11¾ Syncopated***

**2014, Apr. 7** **Litho.**

| | | | | |
|---|---|---|---|---|
| **3586-3588** | A985 | Set of 3 | 5.50 | 2.75 |

On day of issue, Nos. 3586-3588 each sold for 80c.

Military Coup of April 25, 1974, 40th Anniv. A986

Designs: No. 3589, N, Soldiers and vehicles in Palace Square, Lisbon. No. 3590. I, Crowd surrounding soldiers in transport vehicle.
€3, Flags of Portugal, Greece and Spain.

***Perf. 12x11¾ Syncopated***

**2014, Apr. 14** **Litho.**

| | | | | |
|---|---|---|---|---|
| **3589-3590** | A986 | Set of 2 | 2.75 | 1.40 |

**Souvenir Sheet**

| | | | | |
|---|---|---|---|---|
| **3591** | A986 | €3 multi | 7.00 | 4.25 |

On day of issue, No. 3589 sold for 42c; No. 3590, for 80c. No. 3591 contains one 80x30mm stamp.

Miniature Sheet

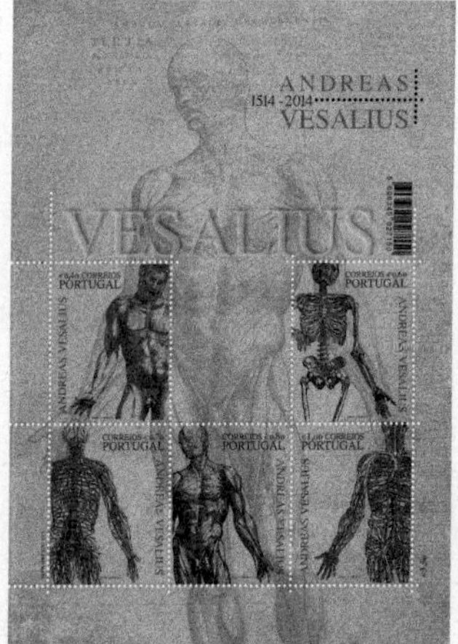


Anatomical Drawings by Andreas Vesalius (1514-64) — A987

No. 3592: a, 40c, Nude man. b, 60c, Skeleton. c, 70c, Nervous system. d, 80c, Muscular system. e, €1, Circulatory system.

**Photo. & Engr.**

**2014, Apr. 21** ***Perf. 11½***

| | | | | |
|---|---|---|---|---|
| **3592** | A987 | Sheet of 5, #a-e | 8.50 | 5.00 |

See Belgium No. 2689.

Archbishop Bartholomew of Braga (1514-90) — A988

Designs: 70c, Archbishop standing.
€3, Archbishop seated.

***Perf. 11¾x12 Syncopated***

**2014, Apr. 28** **Litho.**

| | | | | |
|---|---|---|---|---|
| **3593** | A988 | 70c multi | 1.60 | .80 |

**Souvenir Sheet**

| | | | | |
|---|---|---|---|---|
| **3594** | A988 | €3 multi | 7.00 | 4.25 |

No. 3594 contains one 30x80mm stamp.

Eusébio (1942-2014), Soccer Player — A989

Designs: No. 3595, N, Eusébio chasing soccer ball. No. 3596, E, Eusébio dribbling ball.
€2.50, Eusébio kicking ball.

***Perf. 11¾x12 Syncopated***

**2014, May 2** **Litho.**

| | | | | |
|---|---|---|---|---|
| **3595-3596** | A989 | Set of 2 | 2.75 | 1.40 |

**Souvenir Sheet**

| | | | | |
|---|---|---|---|---|
| **3597** | A989 | €2.50 multi | 6.00 | 3.50 |

On day of issue, No. 3595 sold for 42c; No. 3596, for 72c.

Portuguese Language, 800th Anniv. A990

Designs: 80c, Arms of Portugal, flags of Portuguese-speaking countries, hand with pen.
€2.50, Pen nib, green and red lines, vert.

***Perf. 12x11¾ Syncopated***

**2014, May 5** **Litho.**

| | | | | |
|---|---|---|---|---|
| **3598** | A990 | 80c multi | 1.90 | .95 |

**Souvenir Sheet**

***Perf. 11¾x12 Syncopated***

| | | | | |
|---|---|---|---|---|
| **3599** | A990 | €2.50 multi | 6.00 | 3.50 |



Europa — A991

Designs: No. 3600, Bagpiper.
No. 3601a, Bagpipes.

***Perf. 11¾x12 Syncopated***

**2014, May 9** **Litho.**

| | | | | |
|---|---|---|---|---|
| **3600** | A991 | E multi | 1.60 | .80 |

**Souvenir Sheet**

| | | | | |
|---|---|---|---|---|
| **3601** | | Sheet of 2, #3600, 3601a | 3.50 | 2.00 |
| *a.* | A991 | E multi | 1.75 | 1.00 |

On day of issue Nos. 3600 and 3601a each sold for 72c. See No. 3892.

**Extreme Sports Type of 2014**

Designs: N, Surfing. A, Mountain biking. E, Skateboarding.

***Die Cut Perf. 11½***

**2014, May 27** **Litho.**

**Self-Adhesive**

| | | | | |
|---|---|---|---|---|
| **3602** | A981 | N multi | 1.00 | .35 |
| **3603** | A981 | A multi | 1.20 | .50 |
| **3604** | A981 | E multi | 1.75 | .90 |
| | | *Nos. 3602-3604 (3)* | 3.95 | 1.75 |

On day of issue, No. 3602 sold for 42c; No. 3603, 50c; No. 3604, 72c.

Diplomatic Relations Between Portugal and Mexico, 150th Anniv. A992

Portuguese and Mexican flags with denomination color of: 42c, Gray. 80c, White.

*Perf. 12x11¾ Syncopated*

**2014, June 6 Litho.**

**3605-3606** A992 Set of 2 2.75 1.40

See Mexico Nos. 2876-2877.

2014 World Cup Soccer Championships, Brazil — A993

Designs: 42c, 2014 World Cup emblem and flag of Portugal. 72c, 2014 World Cup mascot and flag of Brazil.

€1, Silhouettes of soccer players, World Cup trophy, flag of Portugal.

*Perf. 12x11¾ Syncopated*

**2014, June 16 Litho.**

**3607-3608** A993 Set of 2 2.75 1.40

**Souvenir Sheet**

**3609** A993 €1 multi 2.50 1.40

No. 3609 contains one 80x30mm stamp.

Gardens A994

Designs: No. 3610, 42c, Chalet da Condessa D'Edla, Sintra. No. 3611, 42c, Palácio Fronteira, Lisbon. 50c, Palácio Nacional de Queluz, Sintra. 62c, Parque de Serralves, Porto. No. 3614, 72c, Mosteiro de Tibaes, Braga. No. 3615, 72c, Jardim Botânico da Universidade, Coimbra. No. 3616, 80c, Quinta do Palheiro Ferreira, Madeira. No. 3617, 80c, Parque Terra Nostra, Sao Miguel, Azores.

*Perf. 12x11¾ Syncopated*

**2014, June 26 Litho.**

**3610-3617** A994 Set of 8 12.00 6.00

See Nos. 3759, 4117, Madeira No. 364.

Garrison Border Town of Elvas and Its Fortifications UNESCO World Heritage Site — A995

Designs: 42c, Graça Fort. 50c, Amoreira Aqueduct. 72c, Santa Luzia Fort. 80c, Pelourinho.

€1.70, Olivença Gate.

*Perf. 12x11¾ Syncopated*

**2014, June 30 Litho.**

**3618-3621** A995 Set of 4 5.50 2.75

**Souvenir Sheet**

**3622** A995 €1.70 multi 4.00 2.40

See Nos. 3840, 4126.

**Types of 2007-11**

*Die Cut Perf. 10½*

**2014, July 21 Litho.**

**Self-Adhesive**

**3623** A816 E Like #2956 1.60 .80
**3624** A861 E Like #3126 1.60 .80
**3625** A919 E Like #3327 1.60 .80
**3626** A925 E Like #3356 1.60 .80
**3627** A925 E Like #3357 1.60 .80
*Nos. 3623-3627 (5)* 8.00 4.00

Nos. 3623-3627 each sold for 72c on day of issue.

Intl. Year of Crystallography — A996

Designs: 42c, Chalcopyrite. 50c, Sodium chloride. 72c, Patterson function and crystal lattice. 80c, Caffeine molecular model, coffee beans. €1, Hemoglobin.

€1.70, Snowflake, vert.

*Perf. 12x11¾ Syncopated*

**2014, July 21 Litho.**

**3628-3632** A996 Set of 5 7.50 3.75

**Souvenir Sheet**

*Perf. 11¾x12 Syncopated*

**3633** A996 €1.70 multi 4.00 2.40

King Manuel I's Diplomatic Mission to Pope Leo X, 500th Anniv. — A997

Designs: 42c, Display of Portuguese wealth before Pope Leo X. €2, Hanno, elephant gift from King Manuel I, and crowd.

*Perf. 12x11¾ Syncopated*

**2014, July 29 Litho.**

**3634-3635** A997 Set of 2 5.50 2.75

Cathedrals A998

Designs: No. 3636, 42c, Old Bragança Cathedral (antiga). No. 3637, 42c, New Bragança Cathedral (nova). No. 3638, 42c, Beja Cathedral. No. 3639, 42c, Elvas Cathedral. No. 3640, 42c, Evora Cathedral. No. 3641, 42c, Lisbon Cathedral. No. 3642, 42c, Miranda do Douro Cathedral. No. 3643, 42c, Setúbal Cathedral.

*Perf. 12x11¾ Syncopated*

**2014, Aug. 18 Litho.**

**3636-3643** A998 Set of 8 8.00 4.00

See Nos. 4118, 4127.

University of Coimbra UNESCO World Heritage Site — A999

Designs: 42c, College of Nuestra Senhora da Graça. 50c, Joanine Library. 72c, Chemistry Laboratory. 80c, Humanities Faculties Building.

€1.70, Main courtyard.

*Perf. 11¾x12 Syncopated*

**2014, Sept. 24 Litho.**

**3644-3647** A999 Set of 4 5.50 2.75

**Souvenir Sheet**

**3648** A999 €1.70 multi 4.00 2.25

See No. 3893.

Coffee — A1000

Coffee bushes and plantation workers from: 42c, Timor. 62c, Angola. 72c, Brazil. 80c, St. Thomas and Prince Islands.

€3.50, Hand holding coffee bush seedling.

*Perf. 11¾x12 Syncopated*

**2014, Sept. 29 Litho.**

**3649-3652** A1000 Set of 4 6.00 3.00

**Souvenir Sheet**

**3653** A1000 €3.50 multi 8.00 4.50

University of Coimbra Geophysical Institute, 150th Anniv. A1001

Fields of study: 42c, Seismology. 62c, Geomagnetism. 72c, Meteorology. 80c, Planetary science.

€2.80, Geophysical Institute, vert.

*Perf. 12x11¾ Syncopated*

**2014, Oct. 3 Litho.**

**3654-3657** A1001 Set of 4 6.50 3.25

**Souvenir Sheet**

*Perf. 11¾x12 Syncopated*

**3658** A1001 €2.80 multi 7.00 3.50

No. 3658 contains one 30x80mm stamp.

Modern Portuguese Tapestries A1002

Designs: No. 3659, 42c, Ambiguous Structure, by Eduardo Nery. No. 3660, 42c, Endless Purpose, by Cruzeiro Seixas. 50c, Egypte, by Vieira da Silva. 62c, Arruto, by Júlio Pomar. 72c, Racial Integration, by Almada Negreiros. 80c, Magenta, by Joana Vasconcelos.

€1.70, Weaver at loom.

*Perf. 11¾x12 Syncopated*

**2014, Oct. 9 Litho.**

**3659-3664** A1002 Set of 6 8.75 4.50

**Souvenir Sheet**

**3665** A1002 €1.70 multi 4.25 2.10

Sustainable Transportation — A1003

No. 3666: a, 42c, Train, bus, man on Segway. b, 80c, Bicycle riders, electric automobile.

*Perf. 12x11¾ Syncopated*

**2015, Jan. 27 Litho.**

**3666** A1003 Horiz. pair, #a-b 2.75 1.40

**Types of 2009-11**

*Die Cut Perf. 10½*

**2015, Jan. 19 Litho.**

**Self-Adhesive**

**3667** A864 E Like #3144 1.75 .85
**3668** A919 E Like #3330 1.75 .85

Nos. 3667-3668 each sold for 72c on day of issue.

**Extreme Sports Type of 2014**

Designs: N, Kitesurfing. A, Rock climbing. E, Rafting.

*Die Cut Perf. 10x9½*

**2015, Feb. 12 Litho.**

**Self-Adhesive**

**3669** A981 N multi .95 .45
**3670** A981 A multi 1.10 .55
**3671** A981 E multi 1.60 .80
*Nos. 3669-3671 (3)* 3.65 1.80

On day of issue, No. 3669 sold for 42c; No. 3670, 50c; No. 3671, 72c.

Orpheu Magazine, Cent. — A1004

Cover from: 42c, First edition. 72c, Second edition.

€2.50, Painting of person reading second edition.

*Perf. 11¾x12 Syncopated*

**2015, Feb. 20 Litho.**

**3672-3673** A1004 Set of 2 2.60 1.40

**Souvenir Sheet**

**3674** A1004 €2.50 multi 5.50 2.75

Music Personalities A1005

Designs: 72c, Jean Sibelius (1865-1957), composer. 80c, Elisabeth Schwarzkopf (1915-2006), opera singer.

No. 3677, €1.50, Sibelius, horiz. No. 3678, €1.50, Schwarzkopf, horiz.

*Perf. 11¾x12 Syncopated*

**2015, Mar. 26 Litho.**

**3675-3676** A1005 Set of 2 3.50 1.75

**Souvenir Sheets**

*Perf. 12x11¾ Syncopated*

**3677-3678** A1005 Set of 2 6.75 3.50

Famous People A1006

Designs: N, Francisco Vieira (1765-1805), painter. A, Manuel Maria Barbosa du Bocage (1765-1805), poet. 62c, Ramalho Ortigao (1836-1915), writer. 72c, Ruy Cinatti (1915-86), poet. 80c, Agostinho Ricca (1913-2010), architect. €1, Frederico George (1915-94), architect.

*Perf. 12x11¾ Syncopated*

**2015, Mar. 31 Litho.**

**3679-3684** A1006 Set of 6 9.25 4.75

On day of issue, No. 3679 sold for 45c; No. 3680, 55c.

**Extreme Sports Type of 2014**

Designs: 2c, Wingsuit flying. 45c, Kitesurfing. 55c, Rock climbing. 72c, Rafting. 80c, BMX cycling.

**2015, Apr. 17 Litho.** *Perf. 11¾x11½*

| | | | | |
|---|---|---|---|---|
| **3685** | A981 | 2c multi | .25 | .25 |
| **3686** | A981 | 45c multi | 1.00 | .50 |
| **3687** | A981 | 55c multi | 1.25 | .60 |
| **3688** | A981 | 72c multi | 1.75 | .85 |
| **3689** | A981 | 80c multi | 1.90 | .95 |
| | | *Nos. 3685-3689 (5)* | 6.15 | 3.15 |

Clay Figurines A1007

Figurines from: No. 3690, 45c, Barcelos. No. 3691, 45c, Vila Nova de Gaia. No. 3692, 55c, Estremoz. No. 3693, 55c, Ribolhos.

*Perf. 12x11¾ Syncopated*

**2015, Apr. 21 Litho.**

**3690-3693** A1007 Set of 4 4.50 2.25

See No. 4128, Azores No. 568, Madeira No. 338.

Intl. Association of Portuguese-Speaking Countries, 25th Anniv. — A1008

*Perf. 11¾x12 Syncopated*

**2015, Apr. 27 Litho.**

**3694** A1008 80c multi 1.75 .90

**Souvenir Sheet**

*Perf. 12x11¾ Syncopated*

**3695** A1008 €2 Emblem, horiz. 4.50 2.25

See Angola No. , Brazil No. 3300, Cape Verde No. 1004, Guinea-Bissau No. , Macao No. 1440. Mozambique No. , St. Thomas and Prince Islands No. 2954, Timor No.

Reintroduction of the Iberian Lynx to Portugal — A1009

Designs: 45c, Head of lynx. 55c, Lynx, flower. 72c, Lynx and rabbits. 80c, Lynx facing left.

€2, Pride of lynx.

*Perf. 12x11¾ Syncopated*

**2015, Apr. 30 Litho.**

**3696-3699** A1009 Set of 4 5.75 3.00

**Souvenir Sheet**

**3700** A1009 €2 multi 4.50 2.25

No. 3700 contains one 80x30mm stamp.

Europa A1010

Old toys: No. 3701, Helicopter. No. 3702a, Cabinet.

*Perf. 12x11¾ Syncopated*

**2015, May 8 Litho.**

**3701** A1010 72c multi 1.60 .80

**Souvenir Sheet**

| | | | |
|---|---|---|---|
| **3702** | Sheet of 2, #3701, 3702a | 3.25 | 1.60 |
| *a.* | A1010 72c multi | 1.60 | .80 |

Way of St. James — A1011

Inscriptions: 45c, Sao Tiago Maior. 55c, Lisboa, Santarém. 72c, Porto, San Pedro de Rates. 80c, Viseu, Chaves.

€2, Catedral de Santiago de Compostela.

*Perf. 12x11¾ Syncopated*

**2015, May 8 Litho.**

**3703-3706** A1011 Set of 4 5.75 3.00

**Souvenir Sheet**

**3707** A1011 €2 multi 4.50 2.25

International Telecommunication Union, 150th Anniv. — A1012

Designs: 80c, 150th anniv. emblem. €1, 150th anniv. emblem, world map.

**2015, May 18 Litho.** *Perf. 12x11¾*

**3708-3709** A1012 Set of 2 4.00 2.00

Belém Tower, Lisbon, 500th Anniv. A1013

Designs: 45c, Drawing of tower, king. 72c, Tower, flag and boats, rhinoceros. 80c, Photograph of tower, seaplane.

€2, Photograph of tower, diff.

*Perf. 12x11¾ Syncopated*

**2015, July 1 Litho.**

**3710-3712** A1013 Set of 3 4.50 2.25

**Souvenir Sheet**

**3713** A1013 €2 sil & multi 4.50 2.25

No. 3713 contains one 80x30mm stamp. See No. 3841.

Boats of the Mediterranean — A1014

Designs: 45c, Canoa do alto. 72c, Calao. 80c, Canoa da picada.

€1.80, Caique and Galeao.

*Perf. 12x11¾ Syncopated*

**2015, July 9 Litho.**

**3714-3716** A1014 Set of 3 4.50 2.25

**Souvenir Sheet**

**3717** A1014 €1.80 multi 4.00 2.00

No. 3717 contains one 80x30mm stamp.

Office of the Ombudsman, 40th Anniv. — A1015

Designs: 45c, Man, woman, child, building. €2, Building, birds.

*Perf. 11¾x12 Syncopated*

**2015, July 15 Litho.**

**3718** A1015 45c multi 1.00 .50

**Souvenir Sheet**

**3719** A1015 €2 multi 4.50 2.25

No. 3719 contains one 30x80mm stamp.

Mediterranean Diet — A1016

Dishes: No. 3720, 45c, Sopa de beldroegas (purslane soup). No. 3721, 45c, Carapaus de escabeche (fish in vinegar sauce). 72c, Cozido do grao com peras (bean stew with pears). 80c, Broas de batata doce (sweet potato scones).

€1.80, Caldeirada de polvo (octopus stew).

*Perf. 12x11¾ Syncopated*

**2015, July 20 Litho.**

**3720-3723** A1016 Set of 4 5.50 2.75

**Souvenir Sheet**

**3724** A1016 €1.80 multi 4.00 2.00

Rules of Heredity, 150th Anniv. — A1017

Pea plant and: 45c, Gregor Mendel (1822-84), scientist. €1, Peas on chart.

*Perf. 11¾x12 Syncopated*

**2015, Aug. 4 Litho.**

**3725-3726** A1017 Set of 2 3.25 1.60

Coimbra Question, 150th Anniv. — A1018

Designs: 45c, Antonio Feliciano de Castilho (1800-75), writer. 55c, Antero de Quental (1842-91), writer.

€2, Writers José Maria Eça de Queirós, Joaquim Pedro de Oliveira Martins, Antero de Quental, Ramalho Ortigao and Abilio Manuel Guerra Junqueiro, horiz.

*Perf. 11¾x12 Syncopated*

**2015, Aug. 12 Litho.**

**3727-3728** A1018 Set of 2 2.25 1.10

**Souvenir Sheet**

*Perf. 12x11¾ Syncopated*

**3729** A1018 €2 multi 4.50 2.25

No. 3729 contains one 80x30mm stamp.

Fruits and Nuts — A1019

Designs: No. 3730, 45c, Castanea sativa (chestnuts). No. 3731, 45c, Prunus avium (cherries). No. 3732, 55c, Pyrus communis (pears). No. 3733, 55c, Citrus spp. (oranges). 72c, Musa acuminata (bananas). 80c, Ananas comosus (pineapples).

*Perf. 11¾x12 Syncopated*

**2015, Sept. 1 Litho.**

| | | | | |
|---|---|---|---|---|
| **3730-3735** | A1019 | Set of 6 | 8.00 | 4.00 |
| *3735a* | | Souvenir sheet of 6, #3730-3735 | 8.00 | 4.00 |

See No. 4129, Madeira No. 365.

St. John Bosco (1815-88) A1020

Designs: 45c, Bosco and children. €2.50, Bosco, horiz.

*Perf. 11¾x12 Syncopated*

**2015, Sept. 3 Litho.**

**3736** A1020 45c multi 1.00 .50

**Souvenir Sheet**

*Perf. 12x11¾ Syncopated*

**3737** A1020 €2.50 gold & multi 5.75 3.00

St. Teresa of Avila (1515-82) A1021

Designs: 45c, Painting of St. Teresa. €2.50, St. Teresa, manuscript, horiz.

*Perf. 11¾x12 Syncopated*

**2015, Sept. 11 Litho.**

**3738** A1021 45c gold & multi 1.00 .50

**Souvenir Sheet**

*Perf. 12x11¾ Syncopated*

**3739** A1021 €2.50 gold & multi 5.75 3.00

No. 3739 contains one 80x30mm stamp.

Portugal's Use of the Sea A1022

Designs: 45c, Tourism. 62c, Fishing. 72c, Transportation. 80c, Energy.

€2, Science.

*Perf. 12x11¾ Syncopated*

**2015, Sept. 17** **Litho.**

**3740-3743** A1022 Set of 4 6.00 3.00

**Souvenir Sheet**

**3744** A1022 €2 multi 4.50 2.25

Portuguese Capture of Ceuta, 600th Anniv. — A1023

Designs: 55c, Map, Church of Our Lady of Africa. €1, Map, Manzanna del Revellín Cultural Center.

€2.50, Royal Walls of Ceuta, 1572 depiction of Ceuta.

*Perf. 11¾x12 Syncopated*

**2015, Sept. 28** **Litho.**

**3745-3746** A1023 Set of 2 3.50 1.75

**Souvenir Sheet**

**3747** A1023 €2.50 multi 5.75 3.00

Montepio Mutual Benefit Association, 175th Anniv. — A1024

Designs: 45c, Pelican emblem. 80c, Family and money box.

€2.50, Montepio headquarters, Lisbon, vert.

*Perf. 12x11¾ Syncopated*

**2015, Oct. 1** **Litho.**

**3748-3749** A1024 Set of 2 3.00 1.50

**Souvenir Sheet**

*Perf. 11¾x12 Syncopated*

**3750** A1024 €2.50 multi 5.75 3.00

No. 3750 contains one 30x80mm stamp.

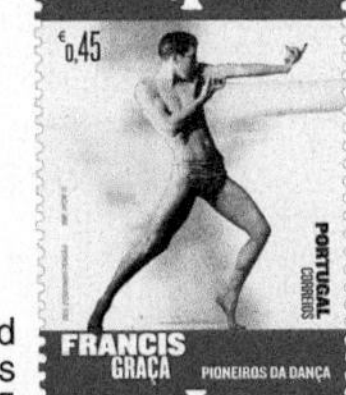


Dancers and Choreographers A1025

Designs: 45c, Francis Graça (1902-80), dancer. 55c, Margarida de Abreu (1915-2006), choreographer. 62c, Fernando Lima (1928-2005), choreographer. 72c, Agueda Sena, dancer. 80c, Isabel Santa Rosa (1931-2001), dancer. €1, Carlos Trincheiras (1937-93), dancer.

*Perf. 11¾x12 Syncopated*

**2015, Oct. 9** **Litho.**

**3751-3756** A1025 Set of 6 9.25 4.50

Intl. Year of Light — A1026

No. 3757: a, Sun, galaxy, Earth, Moon, satellite. b, Lighthouse, solar panels.

*Perf. 11¾x12 Syncopated*

**2015, Oct. 14** **Litho.**

**3757** A1026 45c Vert. pair, #a-b 2.00 1.00

Intl. Year of Soils — A1027

No. 3758: a, Earth, plant, roots, top of hourglass. b, Apple tree, apples, flowers, bottom of hourglass.

*Perf. 11¾x12 Syncopated*

**2015, Oct. 14** **Litho.**

**3758** A1027 45c Vert. pair, #a-b 2.00 1.00

**Gardens Type of 2014**

***Die Cut Perf. 10½***

**2015, Oct. 23** **Litho.**

**Self-Adhesive**

**3759** A994 E Like #3617 1.60 .80

No. 3759 sold for 72c on day of issue.

Arrival of Portuguese in Timor, 500th Anniv. — A1028

Designs: 80c, Settlement near hills, flower, woman. €1, Timorese house, Dom Aleixo Corte-Real (1886-1943), leader of revolt against Japanese occupation, Timorese sash.

€2.50, Model of Timorese house, sculpture.

*Perf. 12x11¾ Syncopated*

**2015, Oct. 28** **Litho.**

**3760-3761** A1028 Set of 2 4.00 2.00

**Souvenir Sheet**

**3762** A1028 €2.50 multi 5.50 2.25

Abade de Baçal Museum, Bragança, Cent. — A1029

Designs: 80c, Museum displays.

€2.05, Sculpture, cabinet and painting.

*Perf. 12x11¾ Syncopated*

**2016, Feb. 16** **Litho.**

**3763** A1029 80c multi 1.75 .85

**Souvenir Sheet**

**3764** A1029 €2.05 multi 4.50 2.25

**Extreme Sports Type of 2014**

Designs: N, Paddleboarding. A, Skydiving. E, Skiing.

***Die Cut Perf. 11½***

**2016, Feb. 25** **Litho.**

**Self-Adhesive**

**3765** A981 N multi 1.00 .50

**3766** A981 A multi 1.25 .65

**3767** A981 E multi 1.60 .80

*Nos. 3765-3767 (3)* 3.85 1.95

On day of issue, No. 3765 sold for 47c; No. 3766, 58c; No. 3767, 75c.

Famous Men A1030

Designs: No. 3768, N, Vergílio Ferreira (1916-96), writer. No. 3769, A, President António José de Almeida (1866-1929). No. 3770, E, Mário Dionísio (1916-93), writer and painter.

*Perf. 12x11¾ Syncopated*

**2016, Mar. 14** **Litho.**

**3768-3770** A1030 Set of 3 4.25 2.10

On day of issue, No. 3768 sold for 47c; No. 37696, 58c; No. 3770, 75c.

Grao Vasco National Museum, Viseu, Cent. — A1031

Designs: 80c, Painting and museum displays.

€2.05, Pitcher and painting.

*Perf. 12x11¾ Syncopated*

**2016, Mar. 16** **Litho.**

**3771** A1031 80c multi 1.90 .95

**Souvenir Sheet**

**3772** A1031 €2.05 multi 4.75 2.40

Jesuits A1032

Designs: 47c, St. Francis Xavier (1506-52). 58c, St. John de Britto (1647-93). 75c, Father Manuel Antunes (1918-85), educator and writer. 80c, Father Luís Archer (1926-2011), geneticist.

€2, Father António Vieira (1608-97), philosopher.

*Perf. 12x11¾ Syncopated*

**2016, Mar. 18** **Litho.**

**3773-3776** A1032 Set of 4 6.00 3.00

**Souvenir Sheet**

**3777** A1032 €2 gold & multi 4.75 2.40

No. 3777 contains one 80x30mm stamp.

**Extreme Sports Type of 2014**

Designs: 3c, Snowboarding. 47c, Paddleboarding. 58c, Skydiving. 75c, Skiing. 80c, Windsurfing.

*Perf. 11¾x11½*

**2016, Mar. 31** **Litho.**

**3778** A981 3c multi .25 .25

**3779** A981 47c multi 1.10 .55

**3780** A981 58c multi 1.40 .70

**3781** A981 75c multi 1.75 .85

**3782** A981 80c multi 1.90 .95

*Nos. 3778-3782 (5)* 6.40 3.30

Lubrapex Philatelic Exhibitions, 50th Anniv. A1033

Designs: No. 3783, 80c, Filigree heart, Portugal. No. 3784, 80c, Headdress, Brazil.

No. 3785: a, Beaded necklace, Angola. b, Beaded necklace, Cape Verde. c, Sculpture, Guinea-Bissau. d, Fan, Macao. e, Necklace, Mozambique. f, Mask, St. Thomas and Prince Islands. g, Necklace, Timor.

*Perf. 12x11¾ Syncopated*

**2016, Apr. 26** **Litho.**

**3783-3784** A1033 Set of 2 3.75 1.90

**Miniature Sheet**

**3785** A1033 47c Sheet of 7, #a-g, + label 7.75 4.00

See Brazil No. 3325.

Cante Alentejano Choral Singing — A1034

Various costumes of singers: 47c, 80c.

No. 3788: a, Singers with flowers on hats. b, Singers with miner's helmets and jackets with gray stripes.

*Perf. 11¾x12 Syncopated*

**2016, Apr. 27** **Litho.**

**3786-3787** A1034 Set of 2 3.00 1.50

**Souvenir Sheet**

**3788** A1034 €1 Sheet of 2, #a-b 4.75 2.40

Statue of Virgin Mary and Basilica, Fatima A1035

Statue and Basilica: 80c, At night.

€2, In daylight.

*Perf. 12x11¾ Syncopated*

**2016, May 2** **Litho.**

**3789** A1035 80c multi 1.90 .95

**Souvenir Sheet**

**3790** A1035 €2 multi 4.75 2.40

No. 3790 contains one 80x30mm stamp.

See No. 4119.

Europa A1036

Designs: No. 3791, Bicyclist, buildings, wind generators.

No. 3792a, Mountain climbers, castle.

*Perf. 12x11¾ Syncopated*

**2016, May 9 Litho.**

**3791** A1036 75c multi 1.75 .85

**Souvenir Sheet**

**3792** Sheet of 2, #3791, 3792a 3.50 1.75

*a.* A1036 75c multi 1.75 .85

Think Green Issue.

Art Treasures From Portuguese Museums — A1037

Details from: No. 3793, 80c, Middle left panel of St. Vincent, by Nuno Gonçalves. No. 3794, 80c, Middle rightside panel The Temptation of St. Anthony, by Hieronymus Bosch.

Details from: No. 3795, €1.80, Middle right panel of St. Vincent, by Nuno Gonçalves, diff. No. 3796, €1.80, Middle center panel The Temptation of St. Anthony, by Hieronymus Bosch, diff.

*Perf. 12x11¾ Syncopated*

**2016, May 30 Litho.**

**3793-3794** A1037 Set of 2 3.75 1.90

**Souvenir Sheets**

**3795-3796** A1037 Set of 2 8.00 4.00

Predatory Mammals A1038

Designs: No. 3797, 47c, Canis lupus. No. 3798, 47c, Vulpes vulpes. 58c, Felis silvestris. 65c, Genetta genetta. 75c, Lutra lutra. 80c, Meles meles.

*Perf. 11¾x12 Syncopated*

**2016, June 7 Litho.**

**3797-3802** A1038 Set of 6 8.25 4.25

Bilateral Trade Between Portugal and Viet Nam, 500th Anniv. A1039

Flags of Viet Nam and Portugal and: 47c, Plate, map of Lisbon. 80c, Vase, map of Hoi An, Viet Nam.

**2016, July 1 Litho.** ***Perf. 12x11¾***

**3803-3804** A1039 Set of 2 3.00 1.50

See Viet Nam Nos. 3549-3550.

Fish of the Mediterranean Sea — A1040

Designs: No. 3805, 47c, Thunnus thynnus. 58c, Katsuwonus pelamis. 75c, Sarda sarda. 80c, Scomber scombrus.

No. 3809, 47c: a, Serranus atricauda. b, Serranus scriba. c, Epinephilus marginatus. d, Serranus cabrilla.

*Perf. 12x11¾ Syncopated*

**2016, July 9 Litho.**

**3805-3808** A1040 Set of 4 5.75 3.00

**Miniature Sheet**

**3809** A1040 47c Sheet of 4, #a-d 4.25 2.10

Souvenir Sheet

Portuguese Soccer Team, 2016 European Champions — A1041

*Perf. 12x11¾ Syncopated*

**2016, July 11 Litho.**

**3810** A1041 €2 multi 4.50 2.25

First Portuguese Military Flight, Cent. A1042

Designs: 47c, Two airplanes. 80c, Airplane and pilot.

€1.50, Airplane, people around airplane near hangar.

*Perf. 12x11¾ Syncopated*

**2016, July 15 Litho.**

**3811-3812** A1042 Set of 2 3.00 1.50

**Souvenir Sheet**

**3813** A1042 €1.50 multi 3.50 1.75

No. 3813 contains one 80x30mm stamp.

Vineyards A1043

Designs: 47c, Vineyard workers and horses, grape buds. 58c, Aerial view of vineyard, white grapes. 75c, Grape harvesting, wine testing. 80c, Grape arbor, wine barrels.

€1.80, Ripe grapes on vine.

*Perf. 11¾x12 Syncopated*

**2016, July 22 Litho.**

**3814-3817** A1043 Set of 4 5.75 3.00

**Souvenir Sheet**

**3818** A1043 €1.80 multi 4.00 2.00

No. 3818 contains one 30x80mm stamp.

Decorative Walkways A1044

Location of walkway: No. 3819, 47c, Lisbon. 58c, Porto. 75c, Madeira. 80c, Azores.

No. 3823, 47c — Location of walkway: a, Macao. b, United States (E.U.A.). c, Spain. d, Brazil.

*Perf. 12x11¾ Syncopated*

**2016, July 28 Litho.**

**3819-3822** A1044 Set of 4 5.75 3.00

**Miniature Sheet**

**3823** A1044 47c Sheet of 4, #a-d 4.25 2.10

See No. 4120.

Sites in Lisbon A1045

Designs: 47c, Waterside pillars. 65c, Buildings on hillside near water. 75c, Ribiera das Naus walkway. 80c, Topiary, Edward VIII Park.

*Perf. 12x11¾ Syncopated*

**2016, Aug. 26 Litho.**

**3824-3827** A1045 Set of 4 6.00 3.00

See No. 4121.

Radio Personalities — A1046

Designs: No. 3828, 47c, Artur Agostinho (1920-2011), reporter. No. 3829, 47c, António Sala, radio show host. No. 3830, 47c, Fernando Pessa (1902-2002), reporter. 58c, Francisco Sena Santos, reporter. 75c, Herman José, comedian. 80c, Ana Galvao, radio show host.

*Perf. 12x11¾ Syncopated*

**2016, Aug. 30 Litho.**

**3828-3833** A1046 Set of 6 8.00 4.00

Publication of *Petri Nonii Salaciensis Opera (The Works of Pedro Nunes From Alcácer do Sal)*, 450th Anniv. — A1047

Nunes and: 47c, Title page. €1, Loxodrome illustration.

*Perf. 11¾x12 Syncopated*

**2016, Aug. 31 Litho.**

**3834-3835** A1047 Set of 2 3.25 1.60

Souvenir Sheet

Opening of Banco CTT — A1048

*Perf. 12x11¾ Syncopated*

**2016, Sept. 21 Litho.**

**3836** A1048 €2 multi 4.50 2.25

**Types of 2008-15**

***Die Cut Perf. 10½***

**2016, Sept. 23 Litho.**

**Self-Adhesive**

**3837** A845 E Like #3066 1.75 .85

**3838** A859 E Like #3113 1.75 .85

**3839** A947 E Like #3433 1.75 .85

**3840** A995 E Like #3621 1.75 .85

**3841** A1013 E Like #3712 1.75 .85

*Nos. 3837-3841 (5)* 8.75 4.25

Nos. 3837-3841 each sold for 75c on day of issue.

Portuguese Postal System, 500th Anniv. A1049

Designs: 47c, Messenger with large pot. 58c, Messenger delivering message. 75c, Messenger with boat. 80c, Messenger on horse.

€1.80, Messenger delivering message, diff.

*Perf. 12x11¾ Syncopated*

**2016, Oct. 10 Litho.**

**3842-3845** A1049 Set of 4 5.75 3.00

**Souvenir Sheet**

**3846** A1049 €1.80 multi 4.00 2.00

No. 3846 contains one 80x30mm stamp.

Architecture of Paris and Lisbon — A1050

Designs: 47c, Rua Augusta Arch, Lisbon. 75c, Buildings along Rue Royale, Paris.

**2016, Oct. 21 Engr.** ***Perf. 13x13¼***

**3847-3848** A1050 Set of 2 2.75 1.40

See France Nos. 5111-5112.

Army Heraldry A1051

Inscriptions at lower left: No. 3849, 47c, Exército (Army). No. 3850, 47c, Direção de História e Cultura Militar (Military History and Culture Directorate). No. 3851, 47c, Comando do Instrução e Doutrina (Training and Doctrine Command). No. 3852, 47c, Comando da Logistica (Logistics Command). No. 3853, 47c, Comando dos Forças Terrestres (Land Forces Command). No. 3854, 47c, Comando do Pessoal (Personnel Command).

*Perf. 11¾x12 Syncopated*

**2016, Oct. 21 Litho.**

**3849-3854** A1051 Set of 6 6.25 3.25

Diplomatic Relations Between Philippines and Portugal, 70th Anniv. A1052

Flags of Philippines and Portugal and: 47c, Lavandula pedunculata, national flower of Portugal. 80c, Jasminum sambac, national flower of Philippines.

**2016, Oct. 24 Litho.** ***Perf. 12x11¾***

**3855-3856** A1052 Set of 2 3.00 1.50

See Philippines No. 3691.

Historic Cafes A1053

Designs: No. 3857, 47c, Apolo Cafe, Funchal. No. 3858, 47c, Athanásio Cafe, Angra do Heroísmo. No. 3859, 47c, Arcada Cafe, Evora. No. 3860, 47c, Paraíso Cafe, Tomar. No. 3861, 47c, A Brasileira Cafe, Lisbon. No. 3862, 47c, Santa Cruz Cafe, Coimbra.
€1.50, Majestic Cafe, Porto, vert.

***Perf. 12x11¾ Syncopated***

**2016, Oct. 27** **Litho.**

**3857-3862** A1053 Set of 6 6.25 3.25

**Souvenir Sheet**

***Perf. 11¾x12 Syncopated***

**3863** A1053 €1.50 multi 3.50 1.75

No. 3863 contains one 30x80mm stamp.

Fish Canning Industry — A1054

Designs: 47c, Fishing boat, illustration of fishermen, catch and cans, two anchovies. 58c, Fishermen hauling in catch, illustration of women preparing fish, two sardines. 65c, Dock for unloading fish, illustration of boat, woman and fish in net, two mackerels. 75c, Women packing fish in cans, illustration of open cans of fish, two tunas. 80c, People working in canning factory, illustration of woman holding basket, two squids. €1, Workers at canning factory, illustration of woman holding canned fish, two eels.

***Perf. 12x11¾ Syncopated***

**2016, Oct. 31** **Litho.**

**3864** A1054 47c multi 1.10 .55
**3865** A1054 58c multi 1.25 .65
*a.* Horiz. pair, #3864-3865 2.40 —
Complete booklet, #3865a 2.40
**3866** A1054 65c multi 1.50 .75
**3867** A1054 75c multi 1.75 .85
*a.* Horiz. pair, #3866-3867 3.25 —
Complete booklet, #3867a 3.25
**3868** A1054 80c multi 1.75 .90
**3869** A1054 €1 multi 2.25 1.10
*a.* Horiz. pair, #3868-3869 4.00 —
Complete booklet, #3869a 4.00
*Nos. 3864-3869 (6)* 9.60 4.80

The three complete booklets were sold packed in a metal can similar to those in which fish are packed.

Election of António Guterres as United Nations Secretary-General — A1055

Guterres: 80c, Meeting African people. €2, Speaking at United Nations General Assembly, vert.

***Perf. 12x11¾ Syncopated***

**2017, Jan. 4** **Litho.**

**3870** A1055 80c multi 1.75 .85

**Souvenir Sheet**

***Perf. 11¾x12 Syncopated***

**3871** A1055 €2 multi 4.50 2.25

No. 3871 contains one 30x80mm stamp.

Dancers A1056

Designs: 47c, Pauliteiros dancers, Portugal. 80c, Dandiya dancers, India.

**2017, Jan. 7** **Litho.** ***Perf. 12x11¾***

**3872-3873** A1056 Set of 2 2.75 1.40
*3873a* Souvenir sheet of 2, #3872-3873 2.75 1.40

See India Nos. 2896-2897.

Lisbon, 2017 Ibero-American Capital of Culture — A1057

Designs: 47c, Machu Picchu, Peru, ceramic pot. 65c, Sao Francisco Church, Salvador da Bahia, Brazil, berimbau. No. 3876, 80c, Palace of the Argentine National Congress, Buenos Aires, Argentina, emigrants (blue panel). No. 3877, 80c, Sport City, Oaxaca, Mexico (red panel).
€2, Praça de Município, Lisbon, horiz.

***Perf. 11¾x12 Syncopated***

**2017, Jan. 7** **Litho.**

**3874-3877** A1057 Set of 4 6.00 3.00

**Souvenir Sheet**

***Perf. 12x11¾ Syncopated***

**3878** A1057 €2 multi 4.50 2.25

No. 3878 contains one 80x30mm stamp.

Dominican Order, 800th Anniv. — A1058

Designs: €1, St. Dominic (1170-1221), founder of order. €2, Pope Honorius III Accepting the Rule of St. Dominic in 1216, painting by Leandro Bassano, horiz.

***Perf. 11¾x12 Syncopated***

**2017, Jan. 9** **Litho.**

**3879** A1058 €1 multi 2.25 1.10

**Souvenir Sheet**

***Perf. 12x11¾ Syncopated***

**3880** A1058 €2 multi 4.50 2.25

No. 3880 contains one 80x30mm stamp.

Fruits — A1059

Designs: No. 3881, 47c, Ficus carica. No. 3882, 47c, Vitis vinifera. No. 3883, 58c, Prunus amygdalus. No. 3884, 58c, Malus domestica. 75c, Passiflora edulis. 80c, Annona cherimola.

***Perf. 11¾x12 Syncopated***

**2017, Feb. 22** **Litho.**

**3881-3886** A1059 Set of 6 7.75 4.00
*3886a* Souvenir sheet of 6, #3881-3886 7.75 4.00

See Azores No. 609, Madeira No. 379.

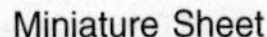

Miniature Sheet

Visit of Pope Francis to Fatima — A1060

No. 3887 — Portion of Our Lady of Fatima statue and: a, 47c, Pope Francis at base of statue, 2015. b, 58c, Lúcia Santos, Jacinta and Francisco Marto, witnesses of apparition. c, 75c, Shrine of Fatima at night. d, 80c, Pilgrims in daylight.

***Perf. 12x11¾ Syncopated***

**2017, Mar. 13** **Litho.**

**3887** A1060 Sheet of 4, #a-d 5.50 2.75

**Souvenir Sheet**

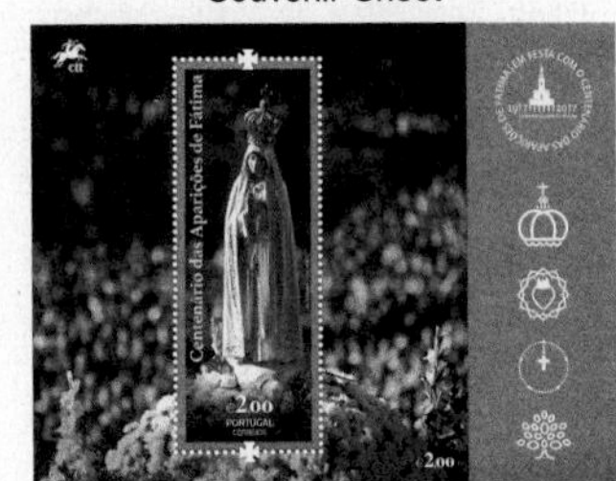


Apparition of the Virgin Mary at Fatima, Cent. — A1061

***Perf. 11¾x12 Syncopated***

**2017, Mar. 13** **Litho.**

**3888** A1061 €2 multi 4.25 2.10

See Luxembourg No. 1461, Poland No. 4277, Slovakia No. 759.

**Types of 2008-14**

***Serpentine Die Cut 11***

**2017, Mar. 24** **Litho.**

**Self-Adhesive**

**3889** A845 E Like #3067 1.75 .85
**3890** A939 E Like #3402 1.75 .85
**3891** A946 E Like #3430 1.75 .85
**3892** A991 E Like #3600 1.75 .85
**3893** A999 E Like #3646 1.75 .85
*Nos. 3889-3893 (5)* 8.75 4.25

On day of issue, Nos. 3889-3893 each sold for 80c.

Dolphin Reserarch A1062

**2017, Apr. 4** **Litho.** ***Perf. 12x12¼***

**3894** A1062 80c multi 1.75 .85

Joint issue between Portugal and Israel. See Israel No. 2139.

Famous Men — A1063

Designs: No. 3895, N, Pedro Manuel de Nóbrega (1517-70), missionary in Brazil. No. 3896, N, Raul Brandao (1867-1930), writer. No. 3897, N, Francisco da Holanda (1517-85), painter. No. 3898, A, Luís de Albuquerque (1917-92), historian and mathematician. No. 3899, A, Oscar Lopes (1917-2013), linguist. No. 3900, E, Júlio Resende (1917-2011), painter. No. 3901, I, António José Saraiva (1917-93), historian.

***Perf. 11¾x12 Syncopated***

**2017, Apr. 27** **Litho.**

**3895-3901** A1063 Set of 7 8.25 4.25

On day of issue, Nos. 3895-3897 each sold for 50c; Nos. 3898-3899, for 63c; No. 3900, for 80c; No. 3901, for 85c.

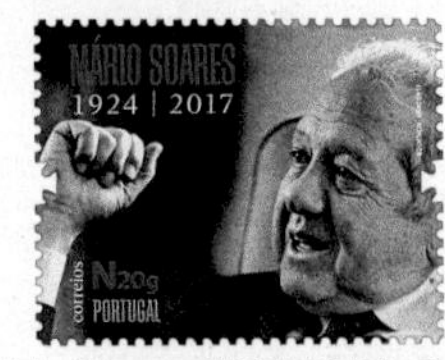


Mário Soares (1924-2017), Prime Minister — A1064

Designs: N, Photograph of Soares. €2, Drawing of Soares, vert.

***Perf. 12x11¾ Syncopated***

**2017, Apr. 28** **Litho.**

**3902** A1064 N multi 1.10 .55

**Souvenir Sheet**

***Perf. 11¾x12 Syncopated***

**3903** A1064 €2 multi 4.50 2.25

No. 3902 sold for 50c on day of issue. No. 3903 contains on 30x80mm stamp.

Lions Clubs International, Cent. — A1065

Lions Club International emblem and: 80c, Secretary-treasurer Melvin Jones (1879-1961). €2, Lions from 2017 U.S. $1 Lions Clubs International coin.

***Perf. 12x11¾ Syncopated***

**2017, Apr. 29** **Litho.**

**3904** A1065 80c multi 1.75 .85

**Souvenir Sheet**

**3905** A1065 €2 multi 4.50 2.25

No. 3905 contains on 80x30mm stamp.

Europa A1066

Designs: No. 3906, Almourol Castle. No. 3907a, Castle of Marvao.

***Perf. 12x11¾ Syncopated***

**2017, May 9** **Litho.**

**3906** A1066 80c multi 1.75 .90

**Souvenir Sheet**

**3907** Sheet of 2, #3906, 3907a 3.50 1.80
*a.* A1066 80c multi 1.75 .90

Desserts
A1067

Designs: N, Pastel de Belém. A, Ovos moles de Aveiro. E, Pastel de Tentúgal. I, Queijadas de Vila Franca do Campo.

***Serpentine Die Cut 11***

**2017, May 12 Litho.**

**Self-Adhesive**

**3908** A1067 N multi 1.10 .55
**3909** A1067 A multi 1.40 .70
**3910** A1067 E multi 1.75 .90
**3911** A1067 I multi 1.90 .95

On day of issue, No. 3908 sold for 50c; No. 3909, for 63c; No. 3910, for 80c; No. 3911, for 85c. See Nos. 3917-3922.

Rally de Portugal, 50th Anniv.
A1068

Race cars: 50c, 1967 Renault 8 Gordini. 63c, 1981 Fiat 131 Abarth. 70c, 1982 Audi Quattro S1. 80c, 1992 Lancia Delta Integrale. 85c, 2015 Volkswagen Polo WRC.

***Perf. 12x11¾ Syncopated***

**2017, May 17 Litho.**

**3912-3916** A1068 Set of 5 7.75 4.00

**Desserts Type of 2017**

Designs: 50c, Pastel de Belém. 63c, Ovos moles de Aveiro. 70c, Rebuçados de ovo de Portalegre. 80c, Pastel de Tentúgal. 85c, Queijadas de Vila Franca do Campo. €1, Tigeladas de Abrantes.

**2017, May 31 Litho.** ***Perf. 11¾x11½***

**3917** A1067 50c multi 1.10 .55
**3918** A1067 63c multi 1.40 .70
**3919** A1067 70c multi 1.60 .80
**3920** A1067 80c multi 1.75 .90
**3921** A1067 85c multi 1.90 .95
**3922** A1067 €1 multi 2.25 1.10
*Nos. 3917-3922 (6)* 10.00 5.00

Portuguese Textile Industry — A1069

Designs: 50c, Skein of yarn, fabric, woman at loom, painting of shepherd. 63c, Flower, embroidery, looms, painting of woman at loom. 80c, Silk moth on silk, fabric, women in textile factory, painting of woman, man and spinning wheel. 85c, Spools of thread, fabric, machinery at textile factory.

€2, Cotton plant, fabric, woman in textile factory, painting of woman and gear wheel.

***Perf. 12x11¾ Syncopated***

**2017, June 17 Litho.**

**3923-3926** A1069 Set of 4 6.50 3.25

**Souvenir Sheet**

**Flocked Paper**

***Perf. 12x12½***

**3927** A1069 €2 multi 4.75 2.40

World War I, Cent. — A1070

Designs: 50c, Alberto Lello Portela (1893-1949), pilot, and airplanes. 63c, Admiral Afonso Cerqueira (1872-1957), NRP Adamastor, batallion in Angola. 85c, Aníbal Milhais (1895-1970), most highly-decorated Portuguese soldier in World War I, and soldiers in France.

***Perf. 12x11¾ Syncopated***

**2017, June 30 Litho.**

**3928-3930** A1070 Set of 3 4.50 2.25

Abolition of Death Penalty in Portugal, 150th Anniv.
A1071

Designs: 50c, Augusto César Barjona de Freitas (1834-1900), Minister of Justice. €1, King Luiz (1838-89).

***Perf. 12x11¾ Syncopated***

**2017, July 1 Litho.**

**3931-3932** A1071 Set of 2 3.50 1.75

Archbishops of Braga — A1072

Designs: No. 3933, 50c, St. Martin of Braga (c. 520-80). No. 3934, 50c, St. Fructuosus of Braga (?-665). No. 3935, 50c, St. Gerald of Braga (?-1109). No. 3936, 50c, Blessed Bartholomew of Braga (1514-90), and his coat of arms. No. 3937, 50c, Rodrigo de Moura Teles (1644-1728), and his coat of arms. No. 3938, 50c, Jorge Ferreira da Costa Ortiga, current archbishop, and his coat of arms.

€1.40, Bom Jesus do Monte Sanctuary, Braga.

***Perf. 11¾x12 Syncopated***

**2017, July 7 Litho.**

**3933-3938** A1072 Set of 6 7.25 3.75

**Souvenir Sheet**

**3939** A1072 €1.40 multi 3.50 1.75

No. 3939 contains one 30x80mm stamp.

Trees of the Mediterranean Region — A1073

Euromed emblem and: 50c, Quercus suber. 63c, Pyrus bourgaeana. 80c, Arbutus unedo. 85c, Olea europaea.

***Perf. 12x11¾ Syncopated***

**2017, July 10 Litho.**

**3940-3943** A1073 Set of 4 6.75 3.25

See No. 4130.

Portuguese Public Security Police, 150th Anniv.
A1074

Designs: 50c, Emblem and shoulder patch. No. 3945: a, Policeman and policewoman, motorcycle policeman near statue. b, Policemen on motorcycle, policewomen walking.

***Perf. 12x11¾ Syncopated***

**2017, July 13 Litho.**

**3944** A1074 50c multi 1.25 .60

**Souvenir Sheet**

**3945** A1074 70c Sheet of 2, #a-b 3.50 1.75

*Star Wars* Movie Series, 40th Anniv.
A1075

Characters: No. 3946, 50c, No. 3953a, N, Luke Skywalker. No. 3947, 50c, No. 3953b, N, Princess Leia. No. 3948, 85c, No. 3953c, E, Han Solo. No. 3949, 80c, No. 3953d, E, Chewbacca. No. 3950, 85c, No. 3953e, I, Darth Vader. No. 3951, 85c, No. 3953f, I, Yoda.

No. 3952 — Movie posters for: a, *Star Wars: A New Hope.* b, *Star Wars: The Empire Strikes Back.* c, *Star Wars: The Return of the Jedi.*

***Perf. 12x11¾ Syncopated***

**2017, Aug. 25 Litho.**

**3946-3951** A1075 Set of 6 10.50 5.25

**Souvenir Sheet**

**3952** Sheet of 3 3.75 1.80
*a.-c.* A1075 50c Any single 1.25 .60

**Self-Adhesive**

***Die Cut Perf. 10½***

**3953** Booklet pane of 6 10.50
*a.-b.* A1075 N Either single 1.25 .60
*c.-d.* A1075 E Either single 1.90 .95
*e.-f.* A1075 I Either single 2.00 1.00

On day of issue, Nos. 3953a-3953b each sold for 50c; Nos. 3953c-3953d, for 80c; Nos. 3953e-3953f, for 85c.

Historic Cafes
A1076

Designs: No. 3954, 50c, Manuel Natário Cafe, Viana do Castelo. No. 3955, 50c, Aliança Cafe, Faro. No. 3956, 50c, A Brasileira Cafe, Braga. No. 3957, 50c, Milenário Cafe, Guimaraes. No. 3958, 50c, Piolho (Ancora d'Ouro) Cafe, Porto.

€1.40, Versailles Cafe, Lisbon, vert.

***Perf. 12x11¾ Syncopated***

**2017, Aug. 31 Litho.**

**3954-3958** A1076 Set of 5 6.00 3.00

**Souvenir Sheet**

***Perf. 11¾x12 Syncopated***

**3959** A1076 €1.40 multi 3.50 1.75

No. 3959 contains one 30x80mm stamp.

Cascais, 2018 European Youth Capital
A1077

Designs: 50c, Cascaes, Mural by Frederico Draw. 63c, Avarina, Mural by Add Fuel. 80c, Mermaid statue with added necklace. 85c, Terra Mar, by Alexandre Farto.

€1.40, Santa Marta Lighthouse and Casa Santa Maria.

***Perf. 12x11¾ Syncopated***

**2017, Sept. 8 Litho.**

**3960-3963** A1077 Set of 4 6.50 3.25

**Souvenir Sheet**

**3964** A1077 €1.40 multi 3.50 1.75

No. 3964 contains one 80x30mm stamp.

National Palace of Mafra — A1078

Designs: 50c, Library, statue of King John V, by Alessandro Giusti. €1, Palace exterior, statue of St. Sebastian, by Carlo Monaldi.

***Perf. 12x11¾ Syncopated***

**2017, July 18 Litho.**

**3965-3966** A1078 Set of 2 3.50 1.75

Porto
A1079

Designs: 50c, Porto Music Hall. 70c, Dom Luis I Bridge. 80c, Boat on Douro River. 85c, City skyline.

***Perf. 12x11¾ Syncopated***

**2017, Sept. 20 Litho.**

**3967-3970** A1079 Set of 4 6.75 3.50

University of Coimbra Joanina Library, 300th Anniiv. — A1080

Various library holdings: 50c, €1.

***Perf. 12x11¾ Syncopated***

**2017, Sept. 28 Litho.**

**3971-3972** A1080 Set of 2 3.50 1.75

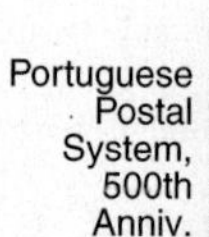

Portuguese Postal System, 500th Anniv.
A1081

Designs: No. 3973, 50c, Luís Gomes de Mata Coronel (?-1607), 5th High Courier. No. 3974, 50c, José Diogo Mascarenhas Neto (1752-c.1824), General Superintendent of the Mail and Post of the Kingdom. 63c, Guilhermino Augusto de Barros (1828-1900), 2nd Director General of the Posts. 80c, António Maria da Silva (1872-1950), 1st General Administrator of Posts and Telegraphs. 85c, Luís de Albuquerque Couto dos Santos (1896-?), General Administrator of Posts.

€1.40, Queen Maria II (1819-53), vert.

***Perf. 12x11¾ Syncopated***

**2017, Oct. 9 Litho.**

**3973-3977** A1081 Set of 5 7.75 3.75

**Souvenir Sheet**

***Perf. 11¾x12 Syncopated***

**3978** A1081 €1.40 multi 3.25 1.60

No. 3978 contains one 30x80mm stamp.

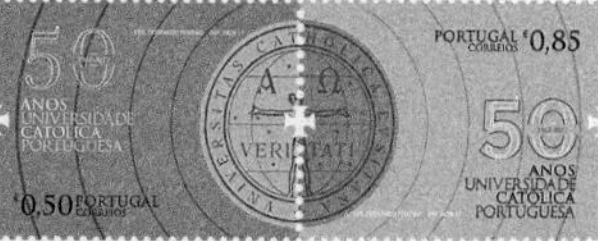

Portuguese Catholic University, 50th Anniv. — A1082

No. 3979 — Half of university emblem and: a, 50c, Denomination at LL. b, 85c, Denomination at UR.

***Perf. 12x11¾ Syncopated***

**2017, Oct. 13 Litho.**

**3979** A1082 Horiz. pair, #a-b 3.25 1.60

UNESCO Creative Cities in Portugal
A1083

Designs: No. 3980, 85c, Idanha-a-Nova. No. 3981, 85c, Obidos.

***Perf. 12x11¾ Syncopated***

**2017, Oct. 16** **Litho.**

**3980-3981** A1083 Set of 2 4.00 2.00

Desserts A1084

Designs: N, Pastel de Feijao de Torres Vedras. A, Crista de Galo de Vila Real. E, Travesseiro de Sintra. I, Queijada de Evora.

***Die Cut Perf. 11½x11¾***

**2018, Jan. 31** **Litho.**

**Self-Adhesive**

| | | | | |
|---|---|---|---|---|
| **3982** | A1084 | N multi | 1.25 | .60 |
| **3983** | A1084 | A multi | 1.60 | .80 |
| **3984** | A1084 | E multi | 2.00 | 1.00 |
| **3985** | A1084 | I multi | 2.10 | 1.10 |
| | | *Nos. 3982-3985 (4)* | 6.95 | 3.50 |

On day of issue, No. 3982 sold for 50c; No. 3983, for 63c; No. 3984, for 80c; No. 3985, for 85c.

Portuguese Breeds of Farm Animals A1085

Designs: No. 3986, 50c, Mertolenga bull. No. 3987, 50c, Barrosa cow. No. 3988, 65c, Galega Mirandesa sheep. No. 3989, 65c, Merina Preta sheep. No. 3990, 85c, Algarvia goat. No. 3991, 85c, Serrana goat.

***Perf. 12x11¾ Syncopated***

**2018, Feb. 8** **Litho.**

**3986-3991** A1085 Set of 6 9.75 5.00

*3991a* Souvenir sheet of 6, #3986-3991 9.75 5.00

Tagus River — A1086

Various views of river and: 50c, Rock carving. 70c, Horse and rider. 80c, Bird. 85c, Sailboat.

€2, Monument and Square overlooking Tagus River and drawing of ships in river.

***Perf. 11¾x12 Syncopated***

**2018, Feb. 26** **Litho.**

**3992-3995** A1086 Set of 4 7.00 3.50

**Souvenir Sheet**

**3996** A1086 €2 multi 5.00 2.50

Islamic Community of Lisbon, 50th Anniv. A1087

Designs: N, Muslim woman at mosque entrance. A, Men performing ablutions. E, Congregation listening to lecture. I, Interior of mosque.

€2, Koran in book holder, mosque floor, vert.

**2018, Mar. 16** **Litho.** ***Perf. 12x12¼***

**3997-4000** A1087 Set of 4 7.25 3.75

**Souvenir Sheet**

***Perf. 12¼x12***

**4001** A1087 €2 multi 5.00 2.50

On day of issue, No. 3997 sold for 53c; No. 3998, 65c; No. 3999, 86c; No. 4000, 91c.

Electricity in Portugal A1088

Lightbulb and: N, Wind generators. A, Hydroelectric dam. E, Solar panels. I, Geothermal station.

€2, Lightbulb, exterior and interior of power station.

***Perf. 12x11¾ Syncopated***

**2018, Mar. 19** **Litho.**

**4002-4005** A1088 Set of 4 7.25 3.75

**Souvenir Sheet**

**4006** A1088 €2 multi 5.00 2.50

On day of issue, No. 4002 sold for 53c; No. 4003, 65c; No. 4004, 86c; No. 4005, 91c. No. 4006 contains one 80x30mm stamp.

Lisbon Water Supply Company (EPAL), 150th Anniv. — A1089

No. 4007: a, Boy in brown drinking water, rural area. b, Girl in light blue green drinking water, city skyline.

€2.50, Water towers, city gate, bicyclist, vert.

***Perf. 12x11¾ Syncopated***

**2018, Apr. 2** **Litho.**

| | | | | |
|---|---|---|---|---|
| **4007** | A1089 | Horiz. pair, #a-b | 3.75 | 1.90 |
| *a.* | | N multi | 1.40 | .70 |
| *b.* | | I multi | 2.25 | 1.10 |

**Souvenir Sheet**

***Perf. 11¾x12 Syncopated***

**4008** A1089 €2.50 multi 6.25 3.25

On day of issue, No. 4007a sold for 53c; No. 4007b, 91c. No. 4008 contains one 30x80mm stamp.

Battle of the Lys, Cent. A1090

Designs: E, Soldiers and their gear.

€2, Soldiers, vert.

***Perf. 12x11¾ Syncopated***

**2018, Apr. 9** **Litho.**

**4009** A1090 E multi 2.10 1.10

**Souvenir Sheet**

***Perf. 11¾x12 Syncopated***

**4010** A1090 €2 multi 4.75 2.40

No. 4009 sold for 86c on day of issue. No. 4010 contains one 30x80mm stamp.

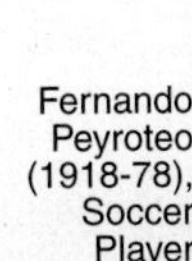

Fernando Peyroteo (1918-78), Soccer Player A1091

***Perf. 12x11¾ Syncopated***

**2018, Apr. 30** **Litho.**

**4011** A1091 N multi 1.25 .65

No. 4011 sold for 53c on day of issue.

Ajuda Botanical Gardens, 250th Anniv. A1092

Designs: N, Fountain and gardens. A, Trees. E, Path, wall and trees. I, Stairway.

€2, Fountain and King Joseph, vert.

***Perf. 12x11¾ Syncopated***

**2018, May 7** **Litho.**

**4012-4015** A1092 Set of 4 7.00 3.50

**Souvenir Sheet**

***Perf. 11¾x12 Syncopated***

**4016** A1092 €2 multi 4.75 2.40

On day of issue, No. 4012 sold for 53c; No. 4013, 65c; No. 4014, 86c; No. 4015, 91c. No. 4016 contains one 30x80mm stamp.

Orient Foundation, 30th Anniv. and Orient Museum, Lisbon, 10th Anniv. A1093

Designs: 65c, Robe. No. 4018, €1, Statue of Buddha.

No. 4019, €1: a, Pair of stirrups. b, Dragon.

***Perf. 12x11¾ Syncopated***

**2018, May 8** **Litho.**

**4017-4018** A1093 Set of 2 4.00 2.00

**Souvenir Sheet**

**4019** A1093 €1 Sheet of 2, #a-b 4.75 2.40

Europa A1094

Designs: No. 4020, Vasco da Gama Bridge, Lisbon. No. 4021a, Roman Bridge, Chaves.

***Perf. 12x11¾ Syncopated***

**2018, May 9** **Litho.**

**4020** A1094 E multi 2.00 1.00

**Souvenir Sheet**

| | | | | |
|---|---|---|---|---|
| **4021** | | Sheet of 2, #4020, 4021a | 4.00 | 2.00 |
| *a.* | A1094 | E multi | 2.00 | 1.00 |

On day of issue, Nos. 4020 and 4021a each sold for 86c.

European Cultural Heritage Year A1095

Designs: N, Ceramic figurine of devil, plate, Alcobaça Monastery. A, Pena Palace, container with ducks and duckling, pendant. E, St. Vincent with the Portuguese Royal Family, by Nuno Gonçalves, sculpture of Adam and Eve, by Ernesto Canto da Maia, chest. I, Sculpture of St. Lucia, tile, untitled painting by Joao Vieira.

No. 4026, €1: a, Praia de Maçãs, by José Malhoa, drinking glass, The Banished, sculpture by António Soares dos Reis, door, African mask. b, Tram and building, Portuguese guitar, sculpture of soldier, drawing of man, carriage of Pope Clement XI.

***Perf. 12x11¾ Syncopated***

**2018, May 9** **Litho.**

**4022-4025** A1095 Set of 4 7.00 3.50

**Souvenir Sheet**

**4026** A1095 €1 Sheet of 2, #a-b 4.75 2.40

On day of issue, No. 4022 sold for 53c; No. 4023, 65c; No. 4024, 86c; No. 4025, 91c. No. 4026 contains two 80x30mm stamps.

Famous Men A1096

Designs: No. 4027, 53c, Domingos Sequeira (1768-1837), painter. No. 4028, 53c, Bernardino António Gomes (1768-1823), botanist. No. 4029, 53c, Tomás da Annunciaçao (1818-79), painter. No. 4030, 53c, José Vianna da Motta (1868-1948), composer. No. 4031, 53c, Padre Himalaya (1868-1933), priest and inventor. No. 4032, 53c, António Champalimaud (1918-2004), industrialist. No. 4033, 53c, Vitorino Magalhaes Godinho (1918-2011), historian.

***Perf. 12x11¾ Syncopated***

**2018, June 20** **Litho.**

**4027-4033** A1096 Set of 7 8.75 4.50

Desserts A1097

Designs: 1c, Bolo de Ança. 20c, Marmelada Branca de Odivelas. 53c, Pastel de Feijao de Torres Vedras. 65c, Crista de Galo de Vila Real. 86c, Travesseiro de Sintra. 91c, Queijada de Evora. €1, Bonecas de Massa do Caniço.

**2018, July 6** **Litho.** ***Perf. 11¾x11½***

| | | | | |
|---|---|---|---|---|
| **4034** | A1097 | 1c multi | .25 | .25 |
| **4035** | A1097 | 20c multi | .45 | .25 |
| **4036** | A1097 | 53c multi | 1.25 | .60 |
| **4037** | A1097 | 65c multi | 1.50 | .75 |
| **4038** | A1097 | 86c multi | 2.00 | 1.00 |
| **4039** | A1097 | 91c multi | 2.10 | 1.10 |
| **4040** | A1097 | €1 multi | 2.40 | 1.25 |
| | | *Nos. 4034-4040 (7)* | 9.95 | 5.20 |

Houses A1098

House from: 53c, Alentejo region. 86c, Algarve region.

***Perf. 12x11¾ Syncopated***

**2018, July 9** **Litho.**

**4041-4042** A1098 Set of 2 3.25 1.60

Henrique Mendonça Palace, Lisbon — A1099

Reign of Aga Khan IV, 60th Anniv. — A1100

**2018, July 9** **Litho.** ***Perf. 12½x12***

**4043** A1099 91c sil & multi 2.10 1.10

**Souvenir Sheet**

***Perf. 13***

**4044** A1100 €2 blue green 4.75 2.40

Chocolate A1101

Designs: 53c, Opened and unopened cacao pod, cocoa beans. 65c, Colima Culture vessel for chocolate. 70c, Lady Pouring Chocolate, by Jean-Etienne Liotard, European cocoa pot. 86c, Chocolate truffle and chocolate factory.
€1.50, Chocolate bar, sculpture of Aztec carrying cacao pod, map, King John V of Portugal Being Served Chocolate by His Uncle, the Duke of Lafoes, by Alessandro Castrioto.

***Perf. 12x11¾ Syncopated***

**2018, July 13** **Litho.**
**4045-4048** A1101 Set of 4 6.50 3.25

**Souvenir Sheet**

**4049** A1101 €1.50 multi 3.50 1.75

No. 4049 contains one 80x30mm stamp.

49th International Physics Olympiad, Lisbon — A1102

Flag bearer, marchers, physics concepts, with background color of: 53c, Yellow orange. €1, Light blue lavender.

***Perf. 12x11¾ Syncopated***

**2018, July 21** **Litho.**
**4050-4051** A1102 Set of 2 3.75 1.90

Publication of *Os Maias,* by José Maria de Eça de Queiroz, 130th Anniv. — A1103

Characters: No. 4052, 53c, Carlos da Maia. No. 4053, 53c, Condessa de Gouvarinho. No. 4054, 53c, Joao da Ega. No. 4055, 53c, Dâmaso Salcede. No. 4056, 53c, Maria Eduarda. No. 4057, 53c, Afonso da Maia.
€1, José Maria de Eça de Queiroz (1845-1900), writer.

***Perf. 11¾x12 Syncopated***

**2018, July 25** **Litho.**
**4052-4057** A1103 Set of 6 7.50 3.75

**Souvenir Sheet**

**4058** A1103 €1 multi 2.40 1.25

No. 4058 contains one 30x80mm stamp.

End of World War I, Cent. — A1104

Designs: 91c, Soldier. €1.50, Soldiers and young girl, horiz.

***Perf. 11¾x12 Syncopated***

**2018, Aug. 9** **Litho.**
**4059** A1104 91c multi 2.10 1.10

**Souvenir Sheet**

***Perf. 12x11¾ Syncopated***

**4060** A1104 €1.50 multi 3.50 1.75

No. 4060 contains one 80x30mm stamp.

Manufacture of Cowbells — A1105

Manufacture of Estremoz Clay Figurines — A1106

Manufacture of Bisalhaes Black Pottery — A1107

***Perf. 12x11¾ Syncopated***

**2018, Aug. 31** **Litho.**
**4061** A1105 86c multi 2.00 1.00
**4062** A1106 86c multi 2.00 1.00
**4063** A1107 86c multi 2.00 1.00
*Nos. 4061-4063 (3)* 6.00 3.00

UNESCO Intangible Cultural Heritage.

A1108

A1109

A1110

A1111

A1112

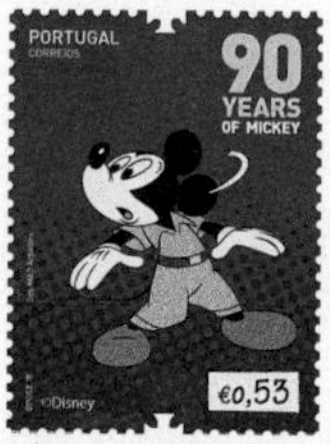

A1113

A1114

A1115

A1116

A1117

A1118

Mickey Mouse, 90th Anniv. — A1119

***Perf. 11¾x12 Syncopated***

**2018, Sept. 14** **Litho.**
**4064** A1108 53c multi 1.25 .60
**4065** A1109 91c multi 2.10 1.10

**Miniature Sheet**

**4066** Sheet of 8, #4064-4065, 4066a-4066f 12.00 5.25
*a.* A1110 53c multi 1.25 .60
*b.* A1111 53c multi 1.25 .60
*c.* A1112 53c multi 1.25 .60
*d.* A1113 53c multi 1.25 .60
*e.* A1114 53c multi 1.25 .60
*f.* A1115 53c multi 1.25 .60

**Booklet Stamps**
**Self-Adhesive**

***Die Cut Perf. 10½***

**4067** Booklet pane of 4 5.00
*a.* A1116 N multi 1.25 .60
*b.* A1117 N multi 1.25 .60
*c.* A1118 N multi 1.25 .60
*d.* A1119 N multi 1.25 .60

On day of issue, Nos. 4067a-4067d each sold for 53c.

Ships — A1120

Various ships: 53c, 70c, 86c.
€1.50, Ships, vert.

***Perf. 12x11¾ Syncopated***

**2018, Sept. 20** **Litho.**
**4068-4070** A1120 Set of 3 5.00 2.50

**Souvenir Sheet**

***Perf. 11¾x12 Syncopated***

**4071** A1120 €1.50 multi 3.50 1.75

Archaeology — A1121

Designs: 53c, Paleolithic Age carved stone, Côa River Valley. 70c, Neolithic Age container, banks of Tagus River. 75c, Megalithic Age carved schist plaque, Praia das Maças. 86c, Chalcolithic Age ivory idol, Guadiana River Valley.

***Perf. 12x11¾ Syncopated***

**2018, Oct. 2** **Litho.**
**4072-4075** A1121 Set of 4 6.50 3.25

Portuguese Postal Service, 500th Anniv. A1122

Designs: 53c, 18th century silk mail bags and royal charter of 1756. 65c, 19th century letter scale, Alentejo Mail Coach box. 86c, 1850s stagecoach, 1850s Postal Directorate plaque. 91c, Electric tricycle for mail delivery, 21st cent.
€2, Estoril Post Office, 20th cent.

***Perf. 12x11¾ Syncopated***

**2018, Oct. 9** **Litho.**
**4076-4079** A1122 Set of 4 6.75 3.50

**Souvenir Sheet**

***Perf. 12½x13 Syncopated***

**4080** A1122 €2 multi 4.75 2.40

No. 4080 contains one 54x49mm stamp.

Archbishops of Braga — A1123

Designs: No. 4081, 53c, St. Martin of Braga (c. 520-80). No. 4082, 53c, St. Fructosus of Braga (d.665). No. 4083, 53c, St. Gerald of Braga (d. 1109).

***Perf. 11¾x12 Syncopated***

**2018, Oct. 22** **Litho.**
**4081-4083** A1123 Set of 3 3.75 1.90

Portuguese Mint and Printing Office, 250th Anniv. — A1124

No. 4084: a, Printing Office Library. b, Commemorative text.

***Perf. 12x11¾ Syncopated***

**2018, Oct. 24 Litho.**

**4084** A1124 Horiz. pair 3.25 1.60
*a.* 53c sil & multi 1.25 .60
*b.* 86c gold, silver & blk 2.00 1.00

Portuguese Breeds of Farm Animals A1125

Designs: No. 4085, 53c, Serra da Estrela sheep. No. 4086, 53c, Pedrês chicken. No. 4087, 70c, Bísaro pig. No. 4088, 70c, Alentajano pig. No. 4089, 91c, Alentajana bull. No. 4090, 91c, Mirandês burro.

***Perf. 12x11¾ Syncopated***

**2019, Jan. 28 Litho.**

**4085-4090** A1125 Set of 6 10.00 5.00
*4090a* Souvenir sheet of 6, #4085-4090 10.00 5.00

Diplomatic Relations Between Portugal and People's Republic of China, 40th Anniv. A1126

Designs: 53c, Silver tea pot. 91c, Earthenware tea pot and cup.

***Perf. 12x11¾ Syncopated***

**2019, Feb. 8 Litho.**

**4091-4092** A1126 Set of 2 3.25 1.60

See People's Republic of China Nos. 4601-4602.

Famous People A1127

Designs: No. 4093, 53c, Joel Serrao (1919-2008), historian. No. 4094, 53c, Jorge de Sena (1919-78), poet. No. 4095, 53c, Gago Coutinho (1869-1959), geographer and aviation pioneer. No. 4096, 53c, Fernando Namora (1919-89), writer. No. 4097, 53c, Sophia de Mello Breyner Andresen (1919-2004), writer. No. 4098, 53c, Francisco de Lacerda (1869-1934), composer. No. 4099, 53c, Fontes Pereira de Melo (1819-87), Prime Minister.

***Perf. 12x11¾ Syncopated***

**2019, Feb. 19 Litho.**

**4093-4099** A1127 Set of 7 8.50 4.25

Queen Maria II (1819-53) A1128

Various artistic depictions of Queen Maria II: 53c, 65c, 86c, 91c.

€2, Queen Maria II and street scene, vert.

***Perf. 12x11¾ Syncopated***

**2019, Feb. 25 Litho.**

**4100-4103** A1128 Set of 4 6.75 3.50

**Souvenir Sheet**

***Perf. 11¾x12 Syncopated***

**4104** A1128 €2 multi 4.50 2.25

No. 4104 contains one 30x80mm stamp.

Abolition of Slavery in Portugal, 150th Anniv. — A1129

No. 4105 — Shackle and: a, Two slaves. b, One slave.

***Perf. 12x11¾ Syncopated***

**2019, Feb. 25 Litho.**

**4105** A1129 Horiz. pair 3.00 1.50
*a.* 53c multi 1.25 .60
*b.* 75c multi 1.75 .85

Order of Christ, 700th Anniv. A1130

Designs: 53c, King Denis (1261-1325) and 1319 bull from Pope John XXII. €1, Prince Henry the Navigator (1394-1460) and caravel. €2, Cross of the Order of Christ and angel.

***Perf. 12x11¾ Syncopated***

**2019, Mar. 14 Litho.**

**4106-4107** A1130 Set of 2 3.50 1.75

**Souvenir Sheet**

***Perf. 11¾x12 Syncopated***

**4108** A1130 €2 multi 4.50 2.25

No. 4108 contains one 30x80mm stamp.

Calouste Sarkis Gulbenkian (1869-1955), Businessman and Philanthropist — A1131

Gulbenkian and: 53c, Jeweled peacock. 91c, Ceramic bowl, 18th cent.

***Perf. 12x11¾ Syncopated***

**2019, Mar. 23 Litho.**

**4109-4110** A1131 Set of 2 3.25 1.60

See Armenia No. 1183.

Desserts A1132

Designs: N, Queijadas de Sintra. A, Fatias do Freixo. E, Cavacas das Caldas da Rainha. I, Morgados do Algarve.

***Die Cut Perf. 12½x12¼***

**2019, Mar. 29 Litho.**

**Self-Adhesive**

**4111** A1132 N multi 1.25 .65
**4112** A1132 A multi 1.50 .75
**4113** A1132 E multi 1.60 .80
**4114** A1132 I multi 2.00 1.00
*Nos. 4111-4114 (4)* 6.35 3.20

On day of issue, No. 4111 sold for 53c; No. 4112, 65c; No. 4113, 70c; No. 4114, 86c. See Nos. 4156-4160.

Souvenir Sheet

Aga Khan Music Awards — A1133

**2019, Mar. 29 Litho. *Perf. 13¼***

**4115** A1133 €2.50 multi 5.75 5.75

Museums Founded Between 1772 and 1894 A1134

No. 4116: a, University of Coimbra Museum of Science, 1772. b, Soares dos Reis National Museum, Porto, 1833. c, Military Museum, Lisbon, 1851. d, University of Lisbon National Museum of Natural History and Science, 1858. e, Geological Museum, Lisbon, c. 1860. f, Carmo Archaeological Museum, Lisbon, 1864. g, Carlos Machado Museum, Ponta Delgada, Azores, 1880. h, Lisbon Geographic Society Historical and Ethnographic Museum, 1884. i, Museum of Fine Arts, Lisbon, 1884. j, Martins Sarmento Archaeological Museum, Guimaraes, 1885. k, National Archaeological Museum, Lisbon, 1893. l, Santos Rocha Municipal Museum, Figueira da Foz, 1894. m, Faro Municipal Museum, 1894.

***Perf. 12x11¾ Syncopated***

**2019, Apr. 5 Litho.**

**4116** Vert. strip of 13 6.50 8.00
*a.-m.* A1134 N Any single 1.25 .60

On day of issue, Nos. 4116a-4116m each sold for 53c.

**Types of 2014-16**

***Die Cut Perf. 10½***

**2019, Apr. 29 Litho.**

**Self-Adhesive**

**4117** A994 I Like #3612 2.10 1.10
**4118** A998 I Like #3643 2.10 1.10
**4119** A1035 I Like #3789 2.10 1.10
**4120** A1044 I Like #3819 2.10 1.10
**4121** A1045 I Like #3827 2.10 1.10
*Nos. 4117-4121 (5)* 10.50 5.50

Nos. 4117-4121 each sold for 91c on day of issue.

International Labor Organization, Cent. — A1135

Albert Thomas (1878-1932), first Director General of International Labor Organization, and: 53c, Delegates to early assembly. 91c, Delegates to modern assembly.

***Perf. 12x11¾ Syncopated***

**2019, May 3 Litho.**

**4122-4123** A1135 Set of 2 3.25 1.60

Europa A1136

Birds: No. 4124, Erithacus rubecula. No. 4125a, Luscinia svecica.

***Perf. 12x11¾ Syncopated***

**2019, May 9 Litho.**

**4124** A1136 86c multi 2.00 1.00

**Souvenir Sheet**

**4125** Sheet of 2, #4124, 4125a 4.00 4.00
*a.* A1136 86c multi 2.00 1.00

**Types of 2014-17**

***Die Cut Perf. 10½***

**2019, May 13 Litho.**

**Self-Adhesive**

**4126** A995 I Like #3619 2.10 1.10
**4127** A998 I Like #3638 2.10 1.10
**4128** A1007 I Like #3692 2.10 1.10
**4129** A1019 I Like #3733 2.10 1.10
**4130** A1073 I Like #3942 2.10 1.10
*Nos. 4126-4139 (5)* 10.50 5.50

Nos. 4126-4130 each sold for 91c on day of issue.

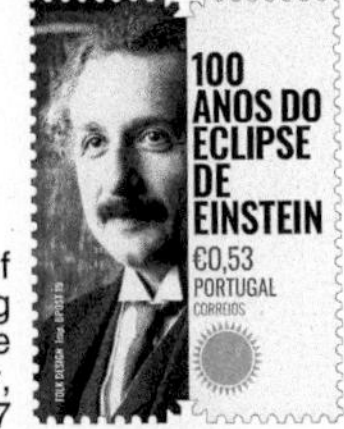


Observation of Eclipse Proving Light Waves Are Bent by Gravity, Cent. — A1137

Designs: 53c, Albert Einstein (1879-1955), physicist who theorized light waves are bent by gravity in general theory of relativity. 91c, Total solar eclipse of May 29, 1919.

€2.50, Diagram of gravity of sun bending light waves from distant star.

***Perf. 11¾x12 Syncopated***

**2019, May 16 Litho.**

**4131-4132** A1137 Set of 2 3.25 1.60

**Souvenir Sheet**

**4133** A1137 €2.50 multi 5.75 5.75

No. 4133 contains one 30x80mm stamp.

Traditional Costumes — A1138

Costumes of men and women from: 53c, Alentejo region. 86c, Algarve region.

***Perf. 12x11¾ Syncopated***

**2019, July 8 Litho.**

**4134-4135** A1138 Set of 2 3.25 1.60

Famous People — A1139

Designs: No. 4136, 86c, Clara Schumann (1819-96), composer. No. 4137, 86c, Jacques Offenbach (1819-80), composer. No. 4138, 86c, Margot Fonteyn (1919-91), ballerina.

***Perf. 11¾x12 Syncopated***

**2019, July 12 Litho.**

**4136-4138** A1139 Set of 3 5.75 3.00

International Year of the Periodic Table — A1140

Designs: N, Periodic table information for hydrogen, sun, clouds, water, plant. I, Periodic table information for mendelevium, Dmitri Mendeleev (1834-1907), formulator of periodic table of elements.
€2, Periodic table information for carbon.

***Perf. 12x11¾ Syncopated***

**2019, July 24** **Litho.**
**4139-4140** A1140 Set of 2 3.25 1.60

**Souvenir Sheet**

**4141** A1140 €2 multi 4.50 4.50

On day of issue, No. 4139 sold for 53c; No. 4140, 91c.

Artur "Pinga" de Sousa (1909-63), Soccer Player and Coach A1141

***Perf. 12x11¾ Syncopated***

**2019, Aug. 22** **Litho.**
**4142** A1141 N multi 1.25 .60

No. 4142 sold for 53c on day of issue.

Characters from *Harry Potter* Movies — A1142

Designs: 70c, Harry Potter and his owl, Hedwig. 75c, Hermione Granger and her cat, Crookshanks. 86c, Ron Weasley and his rat, Scabbers. 91c, Lord Voldemort and his snake, Nagini.
No, 4147: a, Albus Dumbledore and his phoenix, Fawkes. b, Minerva McGonagall and books. c, Severus Snape and potions. d, Rubeus Hagrid, his dragon, Norbert, and spider, Aragog.

***Perf. 11¾x12 Syncopated***

**2019, Aug. 27** **Litho.**
**4143-4146** A1142 Set of 4 7.00 3.50

**Souvenir Sheet**

**4147** A1142 50c Sheet of 4, #a-d 4.50 4.50

Souvenir Sheet

Ferdinand Magellan (c. 1480-1521), Explorer — A1143

***Perf. 11¾x12 Syncopated***

**2019, Sept. 12** **Litho.**
**4148** A1143 €3.50 multi 7.75 7.75

Magellan-Elcano Expedition around the world, 500th anniv. Joint Issue between Portugal and Spain.
See Spain No. 4378.

National Health Service, 40th Anniv. — A1144

Designs: N, Child with balloons. E, Woman with hearts. I, Man sitting on blocks.

***Perf. 11¾x12 Syncopated***

**2019, Sept. 17** **Litho.**
**4149-4151** A1144 Set of 3 5.00 2.50

On day of issue, No. 4149 sold for 53c; No. 4150, 86c; No. 4151, 91c.

Directorate General for Livestock Services, Cent. — A1145

Designs: 53c, Animal identification tags, ranchers attaching tag to animal. 65c, Instrument for disease detection, animal being milked. 86c, Inspection mark on finished cheese, cheese maker.
€1.50, Flock of sheep and bells.

***Perf. 11¾x12 Syncopated***

**2019, Sept. 27** **Litho.**
**4152-4154** A1145 Set of 3 4.50 2.25

**Souvenir Sheet**

**4155** A1145 €1.50 multi 3.75 3.75

**Desserts Type of 2019**

Designs: 10c, Cavacas de Resende. 53c, Queijadas de Sintra. 65c, Fatias de Freixo. 86c, Cavacas das Caldas da Rainha. 91c, Morgados do Algarve.

**2019, Oct. 1** **Litho.** ***Perf. 11¾x11½***
**4156** A1132 10c multi .25 .25
**4157** A1132 53c multi 1.25 .60
**4158** A1132 65c multi 1.40 .70
**4159** A1132 86c multi 1.90 .95
**4160** A1132 91c multi 2.00 1.00
*Nos. 4156-4160 (5)* 6.80 3.50

Mohandas K. Gandhi (1869-1948), Indian Nationalist Leader — A1146

Gandhi facing: 91c, Right. €3, Left.

**2019, Oct. 2** **Litho.** ***Perf. 12¼x12***
**4161** A1146 91c multi 2.00 1.00

**Souvenir Sheet**

**4162** A1146 €3 multi 6.75 6.75

No. 4162 contains one 30x80mm stamp.

Portuguese Postal System, 500th Anniv. — A1147

Designs: 53c, 1880 Postal emblem, postmen, cover of official report on postal service. 70c, 1936 Postal emblem, post office. 86c, 1953 Postal emblem, postal workers and van. 91c, 1964 Postal emblem, postman holding letter showing postal codes.
No. 4167: a, 1991 Postal emblem, CorreioAzul mail box. b, 2015 Postal emblem, BancoCTT building.

***Perf. 12½x13¼ Syncopated***

**2019, Oct. 9** **Litho.**
**4163-4166** A1147 Set of 4 6.75 3.50

**Souvenir Sheet**

**Litho., Sheet Margin Litho. & Engr.**

**4167** A1147 €1 Sheet of 2, #a-b 4.50 4.50

A1148

National Communications Authority, 30th Anniv. — A1149

***Perf. 12x11½ Syncopated***

**2019, Oct. 17** **Litho.**
**4168** A1148 53c multi 1.25 .60
**4169** A1149 53c multi 1.25 .60

Archbishops of Braga — A1150

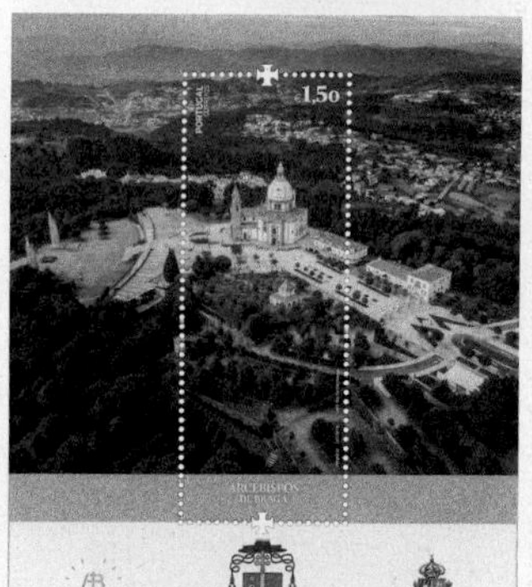


Sanctuary of Our Lady of the Immaculate Conception of Monte Sameiro — A1151

Portrait and coat of arms of: No. 4170, 53c, Archbishop Diogo de Sousa (c. 1461-1532). No. 4171, 53c, Archbishop Gaspar de Bragança (1716-89). No. 4172, 53c, Archbishop Manuel Vieira de Matos (1861-1932).

***Perf. 11¾x12 Syncopated***

**2019, Oct. 18** **Litho.**
**4170-4172** A1150 Set of 3 3.50 1.75

**Souvenir Sheet**

**4173** A1151 €1.50 gold & multi 3.50 3.50

Liberal Revolution of 1820 — A1152

Various illustrations of the Revolution: 53c, 86c.
€2, Allegrory with figures holding banners promoting constitution, vert.

***Perf. 12x11¾ Syncopated***

**2019, Oct. 21** **Litho.**
**4174-4175** A1152 Set of 2 3.25 1.60

**Souvenir Sheet**

***Perf. 11¾x12 Syncopated***

**4176** A1152 €2 multi 4.50 4.50

Christmas A1153

Designs: 53c, Magus holding chest and camel. 86c, Magus holding bottle on camel. 91c, Magus on camel.
€3.50, Nativity scene, vert.

***Perf. 12x11¾ Syncopated***

**2019, Oct. 22** **Litho.**
**4177-4179** A1153 Set of 3 5.25 2.60

**Souvenir Sheet**

***Perf. 11¾x12 Syncopated***

**4180** A1153 €3.50 multi 7.75 7.75

No. 4180 contains one 30x80mm stamp, which has an oval hole into which a small stone in a metal mount is glued to a piece of paper that is affixed to the back of the stamp.

Chronicle of 1419 — A1154

Designs: 53c, Lines and "Cronica." 91c, Lines and names of Portuguese kings.

***Perf. 12x11¾ Syncopated***

**2019, Oct. 28** **Litho.**
**4181-4182** A1154 Set of 2 3.25 1.60

Unabridged Almeida Bible, 200th Anniv. A1155

Designs: 53c, Bible, map of Europe and Africa. €1, Map of Africa and Asia.

***Perf. 12x11¾ Syncopated***

**2019, Oct. 31** **Litho.**
**4183-4184** A1155 Set of 2 3.50 1.75

Portuguese Breeds of Farm Animals A1156

Designs: No. 4185, 53c, Bravia goat. No. 4186, 53c, Churra Algarvia sheep. No. 4187, 86c, Sorraia horse. No. 4188, 86c, Garrano horse. No. 4189, 91c, Garvonês bull. No. 4190, 91c, Maronesa cow.

***Perf. 12x11¾ Syncopated***

**2020, Feb. 6** **Litho.**
**4185-4190** A1156 Set of 6 10.50 5.25
*4190a* Souvenir sheet of 6, #4185-4190 10.50 10.50

Famous Men A1157

Designs: No. 4191, 53c, António Ribiero Chiado (1520-91), poet. No. 4192, 53c, Ruben Alfredo Andresen Leitao (1920-75), writer. No. 4193, 53c, Avelino Teixeira da Mota (1920-82), cartographic historian and politician. No. 4194, 53c, Bernardo Santareno (1920-80), dramatist. No. 4195, 53c, Nadir Afonso (1920-2013), painter. No. 4196, Artur do Cruzeiros Seixas, painter, 100th birthday.

***Perf. 12x11¾ Syncopated***

**2020, Feb. 19** **Litho.**

**4191-4196** A1157 Set of 6 7.00 3.50

Ludwig van Beethoven (1770-1827), Composer A1158

Designs: 91c, Portrait of Beethoven by Joseph Karl Stieler. €2, Signature and bust of Beethoven, horiz.

***Perf. 11¾x12 Syncopated***

**2020, Feb. 26** **Litho.**

**4197** A1158 91c multi 2.10 1.10

**Souvenir Sheet**

***Perf. 12x11¾ Syncopated***

**4198** A1158 €2 multi 4.50 4.50

No. 4198 contains one 80x30mm stamp.

First Passage Through the Straits of Magellan, 500th Anniv. — A1159

No. 4199 — Map and: a, Ferdinand Magellan (c. 1480-1521), explorer. b, Ship.

€2, Ferdinand Magellan Memorial, Punta Arenas, Chile, map of Straits of Magellan, ship.

***Perf. 12x11¾ Syncopated***

**2020, Mar. 18** **Litho.**

**4199** A1159 Horiz. pair 3.25 1.60
*a.* 53c multi 1.25 .60
*b.* 91c multi 2.00 1.00

**Souvenir Sheet**

**4200** A1159 €2 multi 4.50 4.50

No. 4200 contains one 80x30mm stamp.

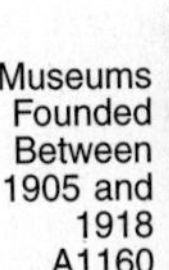

Museums Founded Between 1905 and 1918 A1160

Items in: No. 4201, N, National Museum of Coaches, Lisbon, 1905. No. 4202, N, Sao Roque Museum, Lisbon, 1905. No. 4203, N, Francisco Tavares Proença, Jr. Museum, Castelo Branco, 1910. No. 4204, N, National Museum of Contemporary Art, Lisbon, 1911. No. 4205, N, Museum of Aveiro and St. Joan of Portugal, Aveiro, 1911. No. 4206, N, Machado de Castro National Museum, Coimbra, 1911. No. 4207, N, Friar Manuel de Cenáculo National Museum, Evora, 1915. No. 4208, N, Abbot of Baçal Museum, Bragança, 1915. No. 4209, N, Grau Vasco National Museum, Viesu, 1916. No. 4210, N, Bordalo Pinheiro Museum, Lisbon, 1916. No. 4211, N, Lamego Museum, Lamego, 1917. No. 4212, N, Dom Diego de Sousa Archaeological Museum, 1918, Braga.

***Perf. 12x11¾ Syncopated***

**2020, Mar. 31** **Litho.**

**4201-4212** A1160 Set of 12 14.00 7.00

On day of issue, Nos. 4201-4212 each sold for 53c.

Archbishops of Braga — A1161

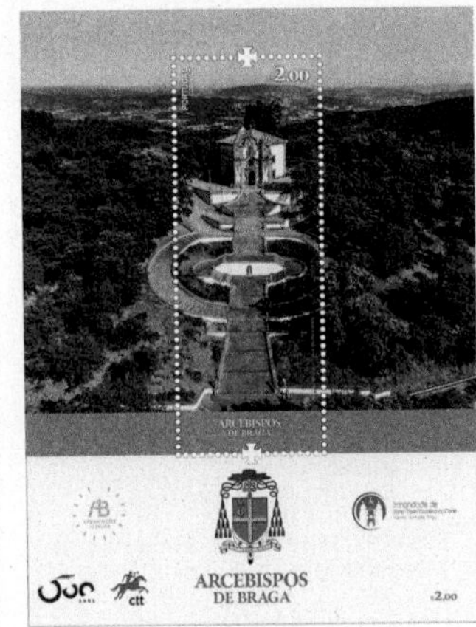

Santa Maria Madalena do Monte Sanctuary — A1162

Portrait and coat of arms of: No. 4213, 53c, Archbishop Rodrigo da Cunha (1577-1643). No. 4214, 53c, Archbishop Caetano Brandao (1740-1805). No. 4215, 53c, Archbishop Francisco Maria da Silva (1910-77).

***Perf. 11¾x12 Syncopated***

**2020, Apr. 17** **Litho.**

**4213-4215** A1161 Set of 3 3.50 1.75

**Souvenir Sheet**

**4216** A1162 €2 multi 4.50 4.50

Ancient Coins — A1163

Obverse and reverse of: N, Pre-Roman bronze coin minted in Alcácer do Sal, 2nd-1st Century B. C. A, Roman bronze dupondius minted in Evora, 27 B.C-14 A.D. E, Suevic silver siliqua minted in Braga, 448-456. I, Visigothic gold tremissis minted in Idanha-a-Velha, 710-711.

***Die Cut Perf. 12½***

**2020, Apr. 22** **Litho.**

**Self-Adhesive**

**4217** A1163 N multi 1.25 .60
**4218** A1163 A multi 1.50 .75
**4219** A1163 E multi 1.90 .95
**4220** A1163 I multi 2.00 1.00
*Nos. 4217-4220 (4)* 6.65 3.30

On day of issue, No. 4217 sold for 53c; No. 4218, 65c; No. 4219, 86c; No. 4220, 91c.

See Nos. 4291-4294. Compare with Type A1172.

---

In 2020, Portugal began issuing a wide variety of self-adhesive stamps having a value indicator of "N20g," and the inscriptions "Portugal CTT" and "meuselo". These stamps were printed by the apparatus already in place for creating personalized stamps. The sheets and booklet panes containing these stamps were produced in limited quantities and were sold at a premium above the face value that the "N20g" rate represented at the time of issuance.

---

International Association of Portuguese-Speaking Countries, 30th Anniv. — A1164

***Perf. 12x11¾ Syncopated***

**2020, May 5** **Litho.**

**4221** A1164 Horiz. pair 3.50 1.75
*a.* 65c World map 1.50 .75
*b.* 91c Emblem 2.00 1.00

See Cape Verde Nos. 1025-1026.

Europa A1165

Designs: No. 4222, Handwritten document and coat of arms. No. 4223a, Train and mail van.

***Perf. 12x11¾ Syncopated***

**2020, May 25** **Litho.**

**4222** A1165 86c multi 1.90 .95

**Souvenir Sheet**

**4223** Sheet of 2, #4222, 4223a 3.80 3.80
*a.* A1165 86c multi 1.90 .95

Ancient Postal Routes.

Religious Festivals and Pilgrimages A1166

Inscriptions: No. 4224, 53c, Festa dos Tabuleiros Festa do Espírito Santo (Festival of the Trays Festival of the Holy Spirit). No. 4225, 53c, Festas de Sao Pedro (Festival of St. Peter). No. 4226, 53c, Festas de Sao Joao Batista (Festival of St. John the Baptist). No. 4227, 53c, Festas de Santo António (Festival of St. Anthony).

No. 4228, 53c: a, Peregrinaçao a Nossa Senhora de Fátima (Pilgrimage of Our Lady of Fatima). b, Senhora do Almortao (Pilgrimage of Our Lady of Almortao). c, Festas de Nossa Senhora dos Remédios (Festival of Our Lady of Remedies). d, Mae Soberana Senhora da Piedade (Festival of the Sovereign Mother of Piety). e, Círio Romaria de Nossa Senhora do Cabo (Pilgrimage of Our Lady of the Cape). f, Festas da Senhora da Agonia (Festival of Our Lady of the Passion).

***Perf. 12x11¾ Syncopated***

**2020, May 28** **Litho.**

**4224-4227** A1166 Set of 4 5.00 2.50

**Miniature Sheet**

**4228** Sheet of 6 7.50 7.50
*a.-f.* A1166 53c Any single 1.25 .60

TAP Air Portugal, 75th Anniv. — A1167

Designs: 53c, Old and new airplanes. 91c, Flight attendants serving passengers.

€2, Crew members of old and new flights, and airplanes, vert.

***Perf. 12x11¾ Syncopated***

**2020, May 28** **Litho.**

**4229-4230** A1167 Set of 2 3.25 1.60

**Souvenir Sheet**

***Perf. 11¾x12 Syncopated***

**4231** A1167 €2 multi 4.50 4.50

Royal Academy of History, 300th Anniv. — A1168

Designs: 53c, King John V (1689-1750), and medal. €1, Medal depicting King John V. €2, Scribe, vert.

***Perf. 12x11¾ Syncopated***

**2020, June 22** **Litho.**

**4232-4233** A1168 Set of 2 3.50 1.75

**Souvenir Sheet**

***Perf. 11¾x12 Syncopated***

**4234** A1168 €2 multi 4.50 4.50

General Inquiries of King Afonso II, 800th Anniv. — A1169

Designs: 70c, Soldiers on horseback and castles. 86c, 1-morabitino coin depicting King Afonso II on horseback.

€2, King Afonso II, vert.

***Perf. 11¾x12 Syncopated***

**2020, June 29** **Litho.**

**4235-4236** A1169 Set of 2 3.50 1.75

**Souvenir Sheet**

**4237** A1169 €2 multi 4.50 4.50

No. 4237 contains one 30x80mm stamp.

Traditional Foods A1170

Designs: N, Arroz Doce à Estoiense (sweet rice pudding). E, Licor de Flor de Laranjeira (orange blossom liqueur).

***Perf. 12x11¾ Syncopated***

**2020, July 10** **Litho.**

**4238-4239** A1170 Set of 2 3.25 1.60

On day of issue, No. 4238 sold for 53c and No. 4239 sold for 86c.

Amália Rodrigues (1920-99), Fado Singer A1171

Designs: 53c, Rodrigues and dress. 86c, Rodrigues singing, and shawl.

€2, Three photographs of Rodrigues.

***Perf. 12x11¾ Syncopated***

**2020, July 23** **Litho.**

**4240-4241** A1171 Set of 2 3.25 1.60

**Souvenir Sheet**

**4242** A1171 €2 multi 4.75 4.75

No. 4242 contains one 80x30mm stamp.

Old Coins — A1172

Obverse and reverse of: 53c, 2nd-1st cent. B.C. bronze coin minted in Alcácer do Sol. 68c, Bronze dupondius minted in Evora between 27 B.C.-14 A.D. 86c, Suevic silver siliqua minted in Braga between 448-456. 91c, Visigothic gold triemissis minted in Idanha-a-Velhain 710-711. €2, Islamic gold dinar minted in Silves in 1149-1150.

**2020, Aug. 3** **Litho.** ***Perf. 12½***

**4243** A1172 53c multi 1.25 .60
**4244** A1172 68c multi 1.60 .80
**4245** A1172 86c multi 2.00 1.00
**4246** A1172 91c multi 2.25 1.10
**4247** A1172 €2 multi 4.75 2.40
*Nos. 4243-4247 (5)* 11.85 5.90

See Nos. 4313-4317. Compare with type A1163.

Archaeological Artifacts A1173

Designs: 53c, Hand axe, 400,000-10,000 B.C. 75c, Vessel with impressed decoration, 5500-3000 B.C. 86c, Decorated staff head, 3600-2000 B.C. €2, Flint halberd, 3000-1800 B.C.

***Perf. 11¾x12 Syncopated***

**2020, Aug. 20 Litho.**

**4248-4251** A1173 Set of 4 10.00 5.00

Superman A1174

Batman — A1175

Wonder Woman — A1176

Aquaman A1177

The Flash — A1178

Cyborg — A1179

Design: €2, All six characters, horiz.

***Perf. 11¾x12 Syncopated***

**2020, Aug. 24 Litho.**

**4252** A1174 91c multi 2.25 1.10
**4253** A1175 91c multi 2.25 1.10
**4254** A1176 91c multi 2.25 1.10
**4255** A1177 91c multi 2.25 1.10
**4256** A1178 91c multi 2.25 1.10
**4257** A1179 91c multi 2.25 1.10
*Nos. 4252-4257 (6)* 13.50 6.60

**Souvenir Sheet**

***Perf. 12x11¾ Syncopated***

**4258** A1179 €2 multi 4.75 4.75

Characters in *Justice League* motion picture. No. 4258 contains one 80x30mm stamp.

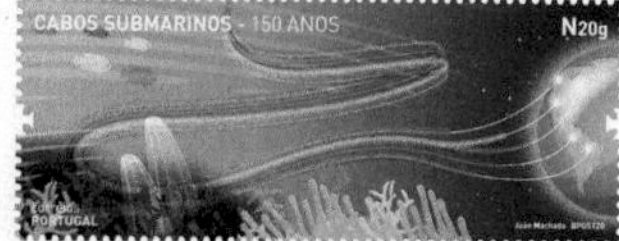
A1180

Underwater Cable Between Portugal and Great Britain, 150th Anniv. — A1181

***Perf. 12x11¾ Syncopated***

**2020, Aug. 27 Litho.**

**4259** Horiz. pair 3.50 1.75
*a.* A1180 N multi 1.25 .65
*b.* A1181 I multi 2.25 1.10

On day of issue, No. 4259a sold fo 53c and No. 4259b sold for 91c.

Motor Guarantee Fund (Insurance Fund for Victims of Traffic Accidents), 40th Anniv. A1182

***Perf. 12x11¾ Syncopated***

**2020, Sept. 25 Litho.**

**4260** A1182 53c multi 1.25 .60

United Nations, 75th Anniv. — A1183

Designs: 91c, Men on stairs. €2, Hands holding bridge.

***Perf. 11¾x12 Syncopated***

**2020, Sept. 28 Litho.**

**4261-4262** A1183 Set of 2 7.00 3.50

Portuguese Postal Service, 500th Anniv. A1184

Masked postal workers during COVID-19 pandemic: 53c, Letter exchange between postal worker and customer. 75c, Postal worker delivering mail. 86c, Postal worker removing stamps from pane. 91c, Postal worker checking paperwork for mail transport tractor trailer. €1, Postal worker scanning package label. N, Silhouette of Queen Maria II (1819-53).

***Perf. 12x11¾ Syncopated***

**2020, Oct. 9 Litho.**

**4263-4267** A1184 Set of 5 9.50 4.75

**Souvenir Sheet**
**Self-Adhesive**

***Die Cut Perf. 10½***

**4268** A1184 N multi 1.25 1.25

No. 4268 sold for 53c on day of issue.

First Piloting Course at Granja do Marqués Military Aviation School, Cent. A1185

Designs: 53c, School building. €1, Biplanes, aviators and hangars.
€2.50, Aerial view of school and airfield, vert.

***Perf. 12x11¾ Syncopated***

**2020, Oct. 12 Litho.**

**4269-4270** A1185 Set of 2 3.75 1.90

**Souvenir Sheet**

***Perf. 11¾x12 Syncopated***

**4271** A1185 €2.50 multi 6.00 6.00

No. 4271 contains one 30x80mm stamp.

Eugénio Tavares (1867-1930), Poet — A1186

***Perf. 12x11¾ Syncopated***

**2020, Oct. 18 Litho.**

**4272** A1186 €1 multi 2.40 1.25

Cape Verdean Association, 50th anniv. See Cape Verde Nos. 1027-1028.

International Year of Plant Health — A1187

Insects and the plants they damage: 53c, Daktulosphaira vitifoliae and grape vine. 86c, Monochamus galloprovincialis, Bursaphelenchus xylophilus, and pine tree. 91c, Ceratitis capitata and fruit tree. €2, Rhynchophorus ferrugineus and palm tree.

***Perf. 12x11¾ Syncopated***

**2020, Oct. 22 Litho.**

**4273-4276** A1187 Set of 4 10.00 5.00

Portuguese Naval School, Alfeite, 175th Anniv. — A1188

Designs: 53c, Sword hilts. €1, Naval officers with flag.
€3, School building, horiz.

***Perf. 11¾x12 Syncopated***

**2020, Oct. 22 Litho.**

**4277-4278** A1188 Set of 2 3.75 1.90

**Souvenir Sheet**

***Perf. 12x11¾ Syncopated***

**4279** A1188 €3 multi 7.00 7.00

No. 4279 contains one 80x30mm stamp.

**Souvenir Sheet**

Florence Nightingale (1820-1910), Nurse and Social Reformer — A1189

No. 4280 — Nightingale: a, As nurse in military hospital. b, With Diagram of the Causes of Mortality in the Army in the East.

***Perf. 12x11¾ Syncopated***

**2020, Oct. 29 Litho.**

**4280** A1189 Sheet of 2 3.50 3.50
*a.* 53c multi 1.25 .60
*b.* 91c multi 2.25 1.10

International Year of Nursing.

**Souvenir Sheet**

Portuguese Postal Service, 500th Anniv. — A1190

No. 4281: a, Stylized mailing box with arms. b, Graphene circuit.

***Serpentine Die Cut 11¼***

**2020, Nov. 6 Litho.**

**Self-Adhesive**

**4281** A1190 Sheet of 2 12.00 12.00
*a.-b.* €2.50 Either single 6.00 6.00

The graphene circuit on No. 4281b is affixed to the stamp with a piece of clear plastic with adhesive on the back. A poem that is embedded in the circuit can be accessed through a cell phone app.

Famous People — A1191

Designs: No. 4282, 53c, St. Elizabeth of Portugal (1271-1336), queen consort of King Denis. No. 4283, 53c, Princess Maria of Portugal, Duchess of Visau (1521-77), patroness of the arts. No. 4284, 53c, King John III of Portugal (1502-57). No. 4285, 53c, Afonso Costa (1871-1937), prime minister. No. 4286, 53c, Rui Grácio (1921-91), pedagogue and governmental minister. No. 4287, 53c, Carlos de Oliveira (1921-81), writer.

***Perf. 11¾x12 Syncopated***

**2021, Mar. 4 Litho.**

**4282-4287** A1191 Set of 6 7.50 3.75

Deeds of King Manuel I (1469-1521) — A1192

Designs: 53c, 1501 start of construction of Jerónimos Monastery, Lisbon. 91c, Map of Southwest Asia (continued financing of exploration).
€2.50, King Manuel I.

***Perf. 12x11¾ Syncopated***

**2021, Mar. 26** **Litho.**
**4288-4289** A1192 Set of 2 3.50 1.75

**Souvenir Sheet**

**4290** A1192 €2.50 multi 6.00 6.00

**Ancient Coins Type of 2020**

Obverse and reverse of: N, Dinheiro minted from 1143-85, in reign of King Afonso I. A, Gold morabitino minted in 1185-1211 reign of King Sancho I. E, Gold tornîs minted in 1279-1325 reign of King Denis. I, Gold justo minted in 1481-95 reign of King John II.

***Die Cut Perf. 11¾***

**2021, Mar. 30** **Litho.**

**Self-Adhesive**

**4291** A1163 N multi 1.30 .65
**4292** A1163 A multi 1.75 .85
**4293** A1163 E multi 2.10 1.10
**4294** A1163 I multi 2.25 1.10
*Nos. 4291-4294 (4)* 7.40 3.70

On day of issue, No. 4291 sold for 54c; No. 4292, 70c; No. 4293, 88c; No. 4294, 91c.

Portuguese Communist Party, Cent. — A1193

Designs: 53c, Communists carrying bundles of paper. €1, Portuguese Communist Party Congress.
€2.50, Communist rally, hammer and sickle.

***Perf. 11¾x12 Syncopated***

**2021, Mar. 31** **Litho.**
**4295-4296** A1193 Set of 2 3.75 1.90

**Souvenir Sheet**

**4297** A1193 €2.50 multi 6.00 6.00

No. 4297 contains one 30x80mm stamp.

League of Combatants, Cent. — A1194

Emblem and: 53c, Nun praying at Batalha Monastery. 91c, Victory parade of Portuguese soldiers, in Paris, 1919.

***Perf. 12x11¾ Syncopated***

**2021, Apr. 9** **Litho.**
**4298-4299** A1194 Set of 2 3.50 1.75

End of Inquisition in Portugal, 200th Anniv. — A1195

Designs: 53c, Emblem of the Portuguese Inquisition, public auto-da-fé. 88c, Inquisition headquarters, Lisbon, and Francisco Margiochi (1774-1838), mathematician and politician who proposed ending the Inquisition.

***Perf. 11¾x12 Syncopated***

**2021, Apr. 22** **Litho.**
**4300-4301** A1195 Set of 2 3.50 1.75

University Faculties of Pharmacy, Cent. A1196

Designs: 53c, University of Coimbra Pharmacy Faculty Buidling and seal. 68c, University of Porto Pharmacy Faculty Building and Aníbal Cunha (1868-1931), first director of University of Porto Pharmacy Faculty. 88c, University of Lisbon Pharmacy Faculty Building and Rui Teles Palhinha (1871-1957), director of University of Lisbon Pharmacy Faculty.

***Perf. 12x11¾ Syncopated***

**2021, Apr. 26** **Litho.**
**4302-4304** A1196 Set of 3 5.00 2.50

Miniature Sheet

2021 NATO Tiger Meet, Beja Air Base, Portugal — A1197

No. 4305 — Military aircraft: a, Fiat G91 R3 and 1987 Tiger Meet emblem. b, Fiat G91 R3 and helmet. c, Alpha Jet A and 1996 Tiger Meet emblem. d, Alpha Jet A and 2002 Tiger Meet emblem. e, F-16 AM and helmet. f, F-16 AM and 2021 Tiger Meet emblem.

***Perf. 12x11¾ Syncopated***

**2021, May 2** **Litho.**
**4305** A1197 Sheet of 6 11.50 11.50
*a.* 53c multi 1.30 .65
*b.* 68c multi 1.75 .85
*c.* 75c multi 1.90 .95
*d.* 80c multi 2.00 1.00
*e.* 88c multi 2.10 1.10
*f.* 91c multi 2.25 1.10

Europa A1198

Endangered animals: No. 4306, Anaecypris hispanica. No. 4307a, Emys orbicularis.

***Perf. 12x11¾ Syncopated***

**2021, May 7** **Litho.**
**4306** A1198 88c multi 2.25 1.10

**Souvenir Sheet**

**4307** Sheet of 2, #4306, 4307a 4.50 4.50
*a.* A1198 88c multi 2.25 1.10

Portuguese Presidency of the Council of the European Union — A1199

Designs: 54c, Squares. 88c, Vertical stripes.
€2.50, Stylized compass rose and map of Europe showing location of capital cities, vert.

***Perf. 12x11¾ Syncopated***

**2021, May 14** **Litho.**
**4308-4309** A1199 Set of 2 3.50 1.75

**Souvenir Sheet**

***Perf. 11¾x12 Syncopated***

**4310** A1199 €2.50 multi 6.25 6.25

A1200

Diplomatic Relations Between Portugal and Singapore, 40th Anniv. — A1201

***Perf. 11¾x12 Syncopated***

**2021, May 28** **Litho.**
**4311** A1200 I multi 2.25 1.10
**4312** A1201 I multi 2.25 1.10

On day of issue, Nos. 4311 and 4312 each sold for 91c. See Singapore Nos.

**Old Coins Type of 2020**

Obverse and reverse of: 5c, Gold coin minted from 1495-1521, in reign of King Manuel I. 54c, Dinheiro minted from 1143-85, in reign of King Afonso I. 70c, Gold morabitino minted in 1185-1211 reign of King Sancho I. 88c, Gold tornîs minted in 1279-1325 reign of King Denis. 91c, Gold justo minted in 1481-95 reign of King John II.

**2021, June 2** **Litho.** ***Perf. 11¾***
**4313** A1172 5c multi .30 .30
**4314** A1172 54c multi 1.30 .65
**4315** A1172 70c multi 1.75 .85
**4316** A1172 88c multi 2.10 1.10
**4317** A1172 91c multi 2.25 1.10
*Nos. 4313-4317 (5)* 7.70 4.00

Barroso Region — A1202

Designs: 68c, Barroso cattle, shepherd and sheep. 70c, Barroso Region buildings and residents.
€2.50, Farmers, cattle and farms, vert.

***Perf. 12x11¾ Syncopated***

**2021, June 9** **Litho.**
**4318-4319** A1202 Set of 2 3.25 1.60

**Souvenir Sheet**

***Perf. 11¾x12 Syncopated***

**4320** A1202 €2.50 multi 6.00 6.00

Discovery of Antarctica, 200th Anniv. (in 2020) A1203

Map and: 54c, The Vostok in Antarctic ice field, 1820, and ship's compass. 84c, Fabian Gottlieb von Bellingshausen (1778-1852), captain of the Vostok and Antarctic Expedition leader, seals on ice floe.
€2.50, Iceberg, seal, albatrosses, penguins and fish, vert.

***Perf. 12x11¾ Syncopated***

**2021, June 16** **Litho.**
**4321-4322** A1203 Set of 2 3.25 1.60

**Souvenir Sheet**

***Perf. 11¾x12 Syncopated***

**4323** A1203 €2.50 multi 6.00 6.00

No. 4323 contains one 30x80mm stamp.

Portuguese Men Who Saved Jews During the Holocaust A1204

Designs: 54c, Aristides de Sousa Mendes (1885-1954), Portuguese consul to Bordeaux, France. 70c, Carlos Sampaio Garrido (1883-1960), Portuguese ambassador to Hungary. 84c, Alberto Teixiera Branquinho (1902-73), Portuguese chargé d'affairs in Budapest, Hungary. 88c, Father Joaquim Carreira (1908-81), rector at Pontifical College, Rome. 91c, José Brito Mendes, protector of a Jewish neighbor's child in France.
€2.50, Jewish woman, front pages of Portuguese newspapers.

***Perf. 11¾x12 Syncopated***

**2021, June 17** **Litho.**
**4324-4328** A1204 Set of 5 9.25 4.50

**Souvenir Sheet**

**4329** A1204 €2.50 multi 6.00 6.00

No. 4329 contains one 30x80mm stamp.

Game Birds — A1205

Designs: No. 4330, 54c, Columba palumbus. No. 4331, 54c, Alectoris rufa. 75c, Anas platyrhynchos. 88c, Gallinago gallinago. 91c, Scolopax rusticola.

***Perf. 11¾x12 Syncopated***

**2021, June 28** **Litho.**
**4330-4334** A1205 Set of 5 8.75 4.50

Alfredo da Silva (1871-1942), Industrialist — A1206

Da Silva and: 54c, Chemical factory and smokestack. 75c, Buildings in Barreiro. 88c, Aerial view of industrial complex, pipes and industrial equipment. 91c, CUF Building and car.

€2.50, Shipyard, industrial complex, doctor treating patient, building.

***Perf. 12x11¾ Syncopated***

**2021, June 30** **Litho.**

**4335-4338** A1206 Set of 4 7.50 3.75

**Souvenir Sheet**

**4339** A1206 €2.50 multi 6.00 6.00

No. 4339 contains one 80x30mm stamp.

Protected Areas — A1207

Designs: No. 4340, 54c, Montesinho Nature Park, deer, flowers, tree. No. 4341, 54c, Serra da Estrela Nature Park, Iberian rock lizard, snowflake, stream. 84c, Serras de Aire e Candeeiros Nature Park, bat, fossil, cave. 88c, Vale do Guadiana Nature Park, falcon, bird, river rapids. 91c, Ria Formosa Nature Park, western swamphen, shoreline.

***Perf. 12x11¾ Syncopated***

**2021, July 2** **Litho.**

**4340-4344** A1207 Set of 5 9.00 4.50

Third Armada, 400th Anniv. — A1208

Designs: 54c, Soldier in dress uniform, soldiers in small boat. €1, Soldier in camouflage, row of soldiers in dress uniforms.

***Perf. 11¾x12 Syncopated***

**2021, July 6** **Litho.**

**4345-4346** A1208 Set of 2 3.75 1.90

Ancient Mediterranean Jewelry — A1209

Earring from: 54c, Mone Moliao, 5th cent. B.C. 88c, Galo, 6th cent. B.C.

***Perf. 12x11¾ Syncopated***

**2021, July 9** **Litho.**

**4347-4348** A1209 Set of 2 3.50 1.75

Freedom of the Press in Portugal, 200th Anniv. — A1210

Designs: 75c, Political cartoons, front page of 1822 publication. 84c, Censored newspaper article marked for removal, Prime Minister António de Oliveira Salazar (1889-1970), rotten apple, open newspaper.

€2.50, Rainbow painted by child wearing protective face mask holding carnation.

***Perf. 11¾x12 Syncopated***

**2021, July 12** **Litho.**

**4349-4350** A1210 Set of 2 3.75 1.90

**Souvenir Sheet**

**4351** A1210 €2.50 multi 6.00 6.00

Arrival of Ferdinand Magellan in the Philippines, 500th Anniv. — A1211

Designs: 54c, Magellan's Cross, Cebu, Philippines. €1, Holy Child of Cebu icon.

€2.50, Queen of Cebu receiving Holy Child of Cebu icon, map of the Philippines.

***Perf. 11¾x12 Syncopated***

**2021, July 19** **Litho.**

**4352-4353** A1211 Set of 2 3.75 1.90

**Souvenir Sheet**

**4354** A1211 €2.50 multi 6.00 6.00

No. 4354 contains one 30x80mm stamp.

Archbishops of Braga — A1212

Braga Cathedral — A1213

Portrait of: No. 4355, 54c, Archbishop Joao Peculiar (c. 1103-75). No. 4356, 54c, King Henry (1512-80) and his coat of arms. No. 4357, 54c, Archbishop Eurico Dias Noguiera (1923-2014) and his coat of arms.

***Perf. 11¾x12 Syncopated***

**2020, Apr. 17** **Litho.**

**4355-4357** A1212 Set of 3 4.00 2.00

**Souvenir Sheet**

**4358** A1213 €2.50 gold & multi 6.00 6.00

United Nations Decade of Ocean Sciences for Sustainable Development — A1214

Designs: 84c, Fish, coral fishing net, plastic bottles. €1, Fish and coral.

***Perf. 12x11¾ Syncopated***

**2021, Aug. 26** **Litho.**

**4359-4360** A1214 Set of 2 4.50 2.25

European Year of Rail — A1215

Designs: No. 4361, 54c, Comboios de Portugal locomotive 2246. No. 4362, 54c, Fertagus train. 88c, Medway train 4703. 91c, Takargo Rail train 6003.

€2.50, Comboios de Portugal train at station.

***Perf. 11¾x12 Syncopated***

**2021, Sept. 21** **Litho.**

**4361-4364** A1215 Set of 4 6.75 3.50

**Souvenir Sheet**

**4365** A1215 €2.50 multi 6.00 6.00

French Writers — A1216

Designs: No. 4366, 91c, Jean de La Fontaine (1621-95). No. 4367, 91c, Marcel Proust (1871-1922).

***Perf. 11¾x12 Syncopated***

**2021, Sept. 30** **Litho.**

**4366-4367** A1216 Set of 2 4.25 2.10

Joao da Nova (c. 1460-1509), Explorer — A1217

Da Nova: 70c, In boat approaching shore. 91c, On ship.

***Perf. 12x11¾ Syncopated***

**2021, Oct. 11** **Litho.**

**4368-4369** A1217 Set of 2 3.75 1.90

Seara Nova Magazine, Cent. — A1218

Designs: 54c, Censored magazine article, founders of magazine. €1, Magazine covers from 1921 and 2021.

***Perf. 11¾x12 Syncopated***

**2021, Oct. 15** **Litho.**

**4370-4371** A1218 Set of 2 3.75 1.90

## AIR POST STAMPS

Symbol of Aviation AP1

***Perf. 12x11½***

| **1936-41** | | **Unwmk.** | | **Typo.** |
|---|---|---|---|---|
| **C1** | AP1 | 1.50e dark blue | .50 | .30 |
| **C2** | AP1 | 1.75e red orange | .75 | .35 |
| **C3** | AP1 | 2.50e rose red | .75 | .35 |
| **C4** | AP1 | 3e brt blue ('41) | 12.50 | 12.00 |
| **C5** | AP1 | 4e dp yel grn ('41) | 18.00 | 18.00 |
| **C6** | AP1 | 5e car lake | 1.50 | 1.25 |
| **C7** | AP1 | 10e brown lake | 3.00 | 1.25 |
| **C8** | AP1 | 15e orange ('41) | 11.50 | 7.00 |
| **C9** | AP1 | 20e black brn | 8.00 | 2.75 |
| **C10** | AP1 | 50e brn vio ('41) | 145.00 | 75.00 |
| | | *Nos. C1-C10 (10)* | 201.50 | 118.25 |
| | | Set, never hinged | 390.00 | |

Stamps issued in 1941 have decimals "00" in the denomination.

Nos. C1-C10 exist imperf.

**Catalogue values for unused stamps in this section, from this point to the end of the section, are for Never Hinged items.**

**EXPO Type of Regular Issue**

**1970, Sept. 16** **Litho.** ***Perf. 13***

**C11** A274 3.50e silver & multi .70 .40

TAP-Airline of Portugal 35th Anniversary AP2

Design: 19e, Jet flying past sun.

**1979, Sept. 21** **Litho.** ***Perf. 12x11½***

**C12** AP2 16e multicolored 1.10 .55

**C13** AP2 19e multicolored 1.25 .80

## POSTAGE DUE STAMPS

**Vasco da Gama Issue**

The Zamorin of Calicut Receiving Vasco da Gama — D1

**Unwmk.**

**1898, May 1** **Typo.** ***Perf. 12***

**Denomination in Black**

**J1** D1 5r black 2.00 1.25

*a.* Value and "Continente" omitted 50.00 5.00

**J2** D1 10r lilac & blk 3.50 1.75
**J3** D1 20r orange & blk 6.00 2.50
**J4** D1 50r slate & blk 45.00 11.00
**J5** D1 100r car & blk, *pink* 75.00 40.00
**J6** D1 200r brn & blk, *buff* 85.00 60.00

For overprints and surcharges see Nos. 193-198.

D2

**1904** ***Perf. 11½x12***
**J7** D2 5r brown .40 .35
**J8** D2 10r orange 2.50 .90
*a.* Imperf. —
**J9** D2 20r lilac 8.00 3.75
**J10** D2 30r gray green 5.00 2.75
**J11** D2 40r gray violet 10.00 2.75
**J12** D2 50r carmine 50.00 4.50
*a.* Imperf.
**J13** D2 100r dull blue 8.75 6.50
*a.* Imperf.
*Nos. J7-J13 (7)* 84.65 21.50

Preceding Issue Overprinted in Carmine or Green

**1910**
**J14** D2 5r brown .50 .25
*a.* Inverted overprint 17.50 14.00
**J15** D2 10r orange .50 .25
*a.* Inverted overprint 17.50 14.00
**J16** D2 20r lilac 1.50 1.00
**J17** D2 30r gray green 1.50 .25
*a.* Inverted overprint 17.50 14.00
**J18** D2 40r gray violet 1.50 .25
*a.* Inverted overprint 20.00 15.00
**J19** D2 50r carmine (G) 6.00 4.50
*a.* Inverted overprint 20.00 15.00
**J20** D2 100r dull blue 7.50 5.25
*Nos. J14-J20 (7)* 19.00 11.75

See note after No. 183.

D3

**1915, Mar. 18** **Typo.**
**J21** D3 ½c brown .75 .60
**J22** D3 1c orange .75 .60
**J23** D3 2c claret .75 .60
**J24** D3 3c green .75 .60
**J25** D3 4c gray violet .75 .60
**J26** D3 5c carmine .75 .60
**J27** D3 10c dark blue .75 .60
*Nos. J21-J27 (7)* 5.25 4.20

**1921-27**
**J28** D3 ½c gray green ('22) .50 .35
**J29** D3 4c gray green ('27) .50 .35
**J30** D3 8c gray green ('23) .50 .35
**J31** D3 10c gray green ('22) .50 .35
**J32** D3 12c gray green .60 .50
**J33** D3 16c gray green ('23) .60 .50
**J34** D3 20c gray green .60 .50
**J35** D3 24c gray green .60 .50
**J36** D3 32c gray green ('23) .85 .50
**J37** D3 36c gray green 1.50 .75
**J38** D3 40c gray green ('23) 1.50 .75
**J39** D3 48c gray green ('23) .75 .65
**J40** D3 50c gray green .75 .65
**J41** D3 60c gray green .75 .65
**J42** D3 72c gray green .75 .65
**J43** D3 80c gray green ('23) 8.50 7.50
**J44** D3 1.20e gray green 3.00 3.00
*Nos. J28-J44 (17)* 22.75 18.50

D4

**1932-33**
**J45** D4 5c buff .50 .45
**J46** D4 10c lt blue .50 .45
**J47** D4 20c pink 1.25 1.00
**J48** D4 30c blue green 1.50 1.00
**J49** D4 40c lt green 1.50 1.00
*a.* Figure of value inverted —
**J50** D4 50c gray 1.60 1.00
**J51** D4 60c rose 4.25 2.00
**J52** D4 80c violet brn 10.00 4.00
**J53** D4 1.20e gray ol ('33) 13.00 12.00
*Nos. J45-J53 (9)* 34.10 22.90

D5

**1940, Feb. 1** **Unwmk.** ***Perf. 12½***
**J54** D5 5c bister, perf. 14 .50 .35
**J55** D5 10c rose lilac .30 .25
**J56** D5 20c dk car rose .30 .25
**J57** D5 30c purple .30 .25
**J58** D5 40c cerise .30 .25
**J59** D5 50c brt blue .30 .25
**J60** D5 60c yellow grn .30 .25
**J61** D5 80c scarlet .30 .25
**J62** D5 1e brown .30 .25
**J63** D5 2e dk rose vio .55 .45
**J64** D5 5e org yel, perf. 14 11.00 9.00
*a.* Perf. 12½ 175.00 125.00
*Nos. J54-J64 (11)* 14.45 11.80

Nos. J54-J64 were first issued perf. 14. In 1955 all but the 5c were reissued in perf. 12½.

**Catalogue values for unused stamps in this section, from this point to the end of the section, are for Never Hinged items.**

D6

**1967-84** **Litho.** ***Perf. 11½***
**J65** D6 10c dp org, red brn & yel .25 .25
**J66** D6 20c bis, dk brn & yel .25 .25
**J67** D6 30c org, red brn & yel .25 .25
**J68** D6 40c ol bis, dk brn & yel .25 .25
**J69** D6 50c ultra, dk bl & bl .25 .25
**J70** D6 60c grnsh bl, dk grn & lt bl .25 .25
**J71** D6 80c bl, dk bl & lt bl .25 .25
**J72** D6 1e vio bl, dk bl & lt bl .25 .25
**J73** D6 2e grn, dk grn & lt grn .25 .25
**J74** D6 3e lt grn, grn & yel ('75) .25 .25
**J75** D6 4e bl grn, dk grn & yel ('75) .25 .25
**J76** D6 5e cl, dp cl & pink .25 .25
**J77** D6 9e vio, dk vio & pink ('75) .25 .25
**J78** D6 10e lil, pur & pale vio ('75) .25 .25
**J79** D6 20e red, brn & pale vio ('75) .70 .25
**J80** D6 40e dp red lil, rose vio & bluish lil ('84) 3.00 1.25
**J81** D6 50e lil, brn & pale gray ('84) 4.50 1.50
*Nos. J65-J81 (17)* 11.70 6.50

D7

**1992-93** **Litho.** ***Perf. 12x11½***
**J82** D7 1e multicolored .25 .25
**J83** D7 2e multicolored .25 .25
**J84** D7 5e multicolored .25 .25
**J85** D7 10e multicolored .30 .25
**J86** D7 20e multicolored .50 .25
**J87** D7 50e multicolored 1.00 .25
**J88** D7 100e multicolored 2.00 .55
**J89** D7 200e multicolored 3.00 1.25
*Nos. J82-J89 (8)* 7.55 3.30

Issued: 1e, 2e, 5e, 200e, 10/7/92; 10e, 20e, 50e, 100e, 3/9/93.

**Type D7 Inscribed "CTT CORREIOS"**

**1995-96**
**J90** D7 3e multicolored .25 .25
**J91** D7 4e multicolored .25 .25
**J92** D7 5e multicolored .25 .25
**J93** D7 9e multicolored .50 .25
**J94** D7 10e multicolored .25 .25
**J95** D7 20e multicolored .25 .25
**J96** D7 40e multicolored .85 .75
**J97** D7 50e multicolored .75 .60
**J98** D7 100e multicolored 1.10 .95
*Nos. J90-J98 (9)* 4.45 3.80

Issued: 3e, 4e, 9e, 40e, 4/20/95; 50e, 5/22/95; 5e, 10e, 20e, 100e, 5/24/96.

Numerals — D8

**2002, Jan. 2** **Litho.** ***Perf. 11¾x11½***
**J99** D8 1c multi .25 .25
**J100** D8 2c multi .25 .25
**J101** D8 5c multi .25 .25
**J102** D8 10c multi .25 .25
**J103** D8 25c multi .55 .25
**J104** D8 50c multi 1.10 .35
**J105** D8 €1 multi 2.00 .70
*Nos. J99-J105 (7)* 4.65 2.30

## OFFICIAL STAMPS

No. 567 Overprinted in Black

**1938** **Unwmk.** ***Perf. 11½***
**O1** A113 40c brown .45 .25

**Catalogue values for unused stamps in this section, from this point to the end of the section, are for Never Hinged items.**

O1

**1952, Sept.** **Litho.** ***Perf. 12½***
**O2** O1 black & cream .45 .25

O2

**1975, June**
**O3** O2 black & yellow 1.00 .25

## NEWSPAPER STAMPS

N1

***Perf. 11½, 12½, 13½***
**1876** **Typo.** **Unwmk.**
**P1** N1 2½r bister 9.50 1.40
*a.* 2½r olive green 9.50 1.40

Various shades.

## PARCEL POST STAMPS

Mercury and Commerce PP1

**1920-22** **Unwmk.** **Typo.** ***Perf. 12***
**Q1** PP1 1c lilac brown .25 .25
**Q2** PP1 2c orange .25 .25
**Q3** PP1 5c lt brown .25 .25
**Q4** PP1 10c red brown .25 .25
**Q5** PP1 20c gray blue .30 .25
**Q6** PP1 40c carmine rose .35 .25
**Q7** PP1 50c black .50 .45
**Q8** PP1 60c dk blue ('21) .50 .45
**Q9** PP1 70c gray brn ('21) 3.00 2.00
**Q10** PP1 80c ultra ('21) 3.50 3.25
**Q11** PP1 90c lt vio ('21) 3.50 2.25
**Q12** PP1 1e lt green 4.00 2.25
**Q13** PP1 2e pale lilac ('22) 11.00 3.50
**Q14** PP1 3e olive ('22) 21.00 4.00
**Q15** PP1 4e ultra ('22) 42.50 7.00
**Q16** PP1 5e gray ('22) 55.00 4.75
**Q17** PP1 10e chocolate ('22) 82.50 9.25
*Nos. Q1-Q17 (17)* 228.65 40.65

Parcel Post Package PP2

**1936** ***Perf. 11½***
**Q18** PP2 50c olive brown .65 .50
**Q19** PP2 1e bister brown .65 .50
**Q20** PP2 1.50e purple .65 .50
**Q21** PP2 2e carmine lake 2.75 .60
**Q22** PP2 2.50e olive green 2.75 .60
**Q23** PP2 4.50e brown lake 5.75 .65
**Q24** PP2 5e violet 9.00 .75
**Q25** PP2 10e orange 12.00 1.75
*Nos. Q18-Q25 (8)* 34.20 5.85

## POSTAL TAX STAMPS

These stamps represent a special fee for the delivery of postal matter on certain days in each year. The money derived from their sale is applied to works of public charity.

Regular Issues Overprinted in Carmine

**1911, Oct. 4** **Unwmk.** ***Perf. 14½x15***
**RA1** A62 10r gray green 8.50 2.25

The 20r carmine of this type was for use on telegrams. Value, $8.50.

**1912, Oct. 4** ***Perf. 15x14½***
**RA2** A64 1c deep green 6.00 1.75

The 2c carmine of this type was for use on telegrams. Value, $10.

"Lisbon" — PT1

**1913, June 8** **Litho.** ***Perf. 12x11½***
**RA3** PT1 1c dark green .95 .70

The 2c dark brown of this type was for use on telegrams. Value, $5.

"Charity" — PT2

**1915, Oct. 4** **Typo.**

| | | | | |
|---|---|---|---|---|
| **RA4** | PT2 | 1c carmine | .35 | .30 |

The 2c plum of this type was for use on telegrams. Value, $5.

See No. RA6.

No. RA4 Surcharged

**1924, Oct. 4**

| | | | | |
|---|---|---|---|---|
| **RA5** | PT2 | 15c on 1c dull red | 1.25 | .70 |

The 30c on 2c claret of this type was for use on telegrams. Value, $5.

### Charity Type of 1915 Issue

**1925, Oct. 4** ***Perf. 12½***

| | | | | |
|---|---|---|---|---|
| **RA6** | PT2 | 15c carmine | .55 | .50 |

The 30c brown violet of this type was for use on telegrams. Value, $6.50.

### Comrades of the Great War Issue

Muse of History with Tablet — PT3

**1925, Apr. 8** **Litho.** ***Perf. 11***

| | | | | |
|---|---|---|---|---|
| **RA7** | PT3 | 10c brown | 1.10 | 1.10 |
| **RA8** | PT3 | 10c green | 1.10 | 1.10 |
| **RA9** | PT3 | 10c rose | 1.10 | 1.10 |
| **RA10** | PT3 | 10c ultra | 1.10 | 1.10 |
| | | *Nos. RA7-RA10 (4)* | 4.40 | 4.40 |

The use of these stamps, in addition to the regular postage, was obligatory on certain days of the year. If the tax represented by these stamps was not prepaid, it was collected by means of Postal Tax Due Stamp No. RAJ1.

### Pombal Issue

Common Design Types

### Engraved; Value and "Continente" Typographed in Black

**1925, May 8** ***Perf. 12½***

| | | | | |
|---|---|---|---|---|
| **RA11** | CD28 | 15c ultra | .65 | .40 |
| **RA12** | CD29 | 15c ultra | 1.00 | .75 |
| **RA13** | CD30 | 15c ultra | 1.00 | .75 |
| | | *Nos. RA11-RA13 (3)* | 2.65 | 1.90 |

### Olympic Games Issue

Hurdler — PT7

**1928** **Litho.** ***Perf. 12***

| | | | | |
|---|---|---|---|---|
| **RA14** | PT7 | 15c dull red & blk | 3.50 | *2.50* |

The use of this stamp, in addition to the regular postage, was obligatory on May 22-24, 1928. 10% of the money thus obtained was retained by the Postal Administration; the balance was given to a Committee in charge of Portuguese participation in the Olympic games at Amsterdam.

## POSTAL TAX DUE STAMPS

### Comrades of the Great War Issue

PTD1

**1925** **Unwmk.** **Typo.** ***Perf. 11x11½***

| | | | | |
|---|---|---|---|---|
| **RAJ1** | PTD1 | 20c brown orange | .55 | .45 |

See Note after No. RA10.

### Pombal Issue

Common Design Types

**1925** ***Perf. 12½***

| | | | | |
|---|---|---|---|---|
| **RAJ2** | CD28 | 30c ultra | 1.10 | 1.10 |
| **RAJ3** | CD29 | 30c ultra | 1.10 | 1.10 |
| **RAJ4** | CD30 | 30c ultra | 1.10 | 1.10 |
| | | *Nos. RAJ2-RAJ4 (3)* | 3.30 | 3.30 |

When the compulsory tax was not paid by the use of stamps #RA11-RA13, double the amount was collected by means of #RAJ2-RAJ4.

### Olympic Games Issue

PTD2

**1928** **Litho.** ***Perf. 11½***

| | | | | |
|---|---|---|---|---|
| **RAJ5** | PTD2 | 30c lt red & blk | 2.50 | 1.75 |

---

## FRANCHISE STAMPS

These stamps are supplied by the Government to various charitable, scientific and military organizations for franking their correspondence. This franking privilege was withdrawn in 1938.

### FOR THE RED CROSS SOCIETY

F1

***Perf. 11½***

**1889-1915** **Unwmk.** **Typo.**

| | | | | |
|---|---|---|---|---|
| **1S1** | F1 | rose & blk ('15) | .50 | .40 |
| | *a.* | Vermilion & black ('08) | 5.75 | 1.25 |
| | *b.* | Red & black, perf. 12½ | 65.00 | 6.25 |

No. 1S1 Overprinted in Green

**1917**

| | | | | |
|---|---|---|---|---|
| **1S3** | F1 | rose & black | 80.00 | 72.50 |
| | *a.* | Inverted overprint | 150.00 | 150.00 |

"Charity" Extending Hope to Invalid — F1a

**1926** **Litho.** ***Perf. 14***

**Inscribed "LISBOA"**

| | | | | |
|---|---|---|---|---|
| **1S4** | F1a | black & red | 8.00 | 8.00 |

**Inscribed "DELEGACOES"**

| | | | | |
|---|---|---|---|---|
| **1S5** | F1a | black & red | 8.00 | 8.00 |

No. 1S4 was for use in Lisbon. No. 1S5 was for the Red Cross chapters outside Lisbon.

For overprints see Nos. 1S72-1S73.

Camoens Issue of 1924 Overprinted in Black or Red

**1927**

| | | | | |
|---|---|---|---|---|
| **1S6** | A68 | 40c ultra | 1.10 | 1.00 |
| **1S7** | A68 | 48c red brown | 1.10 | 1.00 |
| **1S8** | A69 | 64c green | 1.10 | 1.00 |
| **1S9** | A69 | 75c dk violet | 1.10 | 1.00 |
| **1S10** | A71 | 4.50e blk, *org* (R) | 1.10 | 1.00 |
| **1S11** | A71 | 10e dk brn, *pnksh* | 1.10 | 1.00 |
| | | *Nos. 1S6-1S11 (6)* | 6.60 | 6.00 |

Camoens Issue of 1924 Overprinted in Red

**1928**

| | | | | |
|---|---|---|---|---|
| **1S12** | A67 | 15c olive grn | 1.10 | 1.00 |
| **1S13** | A67 | 16c violet brn | 1.10 | 1.00 |
| **1S14** | A68 | 25c lilac | 1.10 | 1.00 |
| **1S15** | A68 | 40c ultra | 1.10 | 1.00 |
| **1S16** | A70 | 1.20e lt brown | 1.10 | 1.00 |
| **1S17** | A70 | 2e apple green | 1.10 | 1.00 |
| | | *Nos. 1S12-1S17 (6)* | 6.60 | 6.00 |

Camoens Issue of 1924 Overprinted in Red

**1929**

| | | | | |
|---|---|---|---|---|
| **1S18** | A68 | 30c dk brown | 1.10 | 1.00 |
| **1S19** | A68 | 40c ultra | 1.10 | 1.00 |
| **1S20** | A69 | 80c bister | 1.10 | 1.00 |
| **1S21** | A70 | 1.50e red | 1.10 | 1.00 |
| **1S22** | A70 | 1.60e dark blue | 1.10 | 1.00 |
| **1S23** | A71 | 2.40e green, *grn* | 1.10 | 1.00 |
| | | *Nos. 1S18-1S23 (6)* | 6.60 | 6.00 |

### Same Overprint Dated "1930"

**1930**

| | | | | |
|---|---|---|---|---|
| **1S24** | A68 | 40c ultra | 1.10 | 1.00 |
| **1S25** | A69 | 50c red orange | 1.10 | 1.00 |
| **1S26** | A69 | 96c lake | 1.10 | 1.00 |
| **1S27** | A70 | 1.60e dk blue | 1.10 | 1.00 |
| **1S28** | A71 | 3e dk blue, *bl* | 1.10 | 1.00 |
| **1S29** | A72 | 20e dk violet, *lil* | 1.10 | 1.00 |
| | | *Nos. 1S24-1S29 (6)* | 6.60 | 6.00 |

Camoens Issue of 1924 Overprinted in Red

**1931**

| | | | | |
|---|---|---|---|---|
| **1S30** | A68 | 25c lilac | 1.25 | 1.10 |
| **1S31** | A68 | 32c dk green | 1.25 | 1.10 |
| **1S32** | A68 | 40c ultra | 1.25 | 1.10 |
| **1S33** | A69 | 96c lake | 1.25 | 1.10 |
| **1S34** | A70 | 1.60e dark blue | 1.25 | 1.10 |
| **1S35** | A71 | 3.20e black, *green* | 1.25 | 1.10 |
| | | *Nos. 1S30-1S35 (6)* | 7.50 | 6.60 |

### Same Overprint Dated "1932"

**1931**

| | | | | |
|---|---|---|---|---|
| **1S36** | A67 | 20c dp orange | 1.75 | 1.75 |
| **1S37** | A68 | 40c ultra | 1.75 | 1.75 |
| **1S38** | A68 | 48c red brown | 1.75 | 1.75 |
| **1S39** | A69 | 64c green | 1.75 | 1.75 |
| **1S40** | A70 | 1.60e dark blue | 1.75 | 1.75 |
| **1S41** | A71 | 10e dk brown, *pnksh* | 1.75 | 1.75 |
| | | *Nos. 1S36-1S41 (6)* | 10.50 | 10.50 |

Nos. 1S6-1S11 Overprinted in Red

**1932**

| | | | | |
|---|---|---|---|---|
| **1S42** | A68 | 40c ultra | 1.75 | 1.75 |
| **1S43** | A68 | 48c red brown | 1.75 | 1.75 |
| **1S44** | A69 | 64c green | 1.75 | 1.75 |
| **1S45** | A69 | 75c dk violet | 1.75 | 1.75 |
| **1S46** | A71 | 4.50e blk, *orange* | 1.75 | 1.75 |
| **1S47** | A71 | 10e dk brn, *pnksh* | 1.75 | 1.75 |
| | | *Nos. 1S42-1S47 (6)* | 10.50 | 10.50 |

**1933** **Dated "1934"**

| | | | | |
|---|---|---|---|---|
| **1S48** | A68 | 40c ultra | 2.25 | 2.25 |
| **1S49** | A68 | 48c red brown | 2.25 | 2.25 |
| **1S50** | A69 | 64c green | 2.25 | 2.25 |
| **1S51** | A69 | 75c dark violet | 2.25 | 2.25 |
| **1S52** | A71 | 4.50e blk, *orange* | 2.25 | 2.25 |
| **1S53** | A71 | 10e dk brown, *pnksh* | 2.25 | 2.25 |
| | | *Nos. 1S48-1S53 (6)* | 13.50 | 13.50 |

**1935** **Dated "1935"**

| | | | | |
|---|---|---|---|---|
| **1S54** | A68 | 40c ultra | 2.60 | 2.60 |
| **1S55** | A68 | 48c red brown | 2.60 | 2.60 |
| **1S56** | A69 | 64c green | 2.60 | 2.60 |
| **1S57** | A69 | 75c dk violet | 2.60 | 2.60 |
| **1S58** | A71 | 4.50e black, *orange* | 2.60 | 2.60 |
| **1S59** | A71 | 10e dk brn, *pnksh* | 2.60 | 2.60 |
| | | *Nos. 1S54-1S59 (6)* | 15.60 | 15.60 |

Camoens Issue of 1924 Overprinted in Black or Red

**1935**

| | | | | |
|---|---|---|---|---|
| **1S60** | A68 | 25c lilac | 1.10 | 1.00 |
| **1S61** | A68 | 40c ultra (R) | 1.10 | 1.00 |
| **1S62** | A69 | 50c red orange | 1.10 | 1.00 |
| **1S63** | A70 | 1e slate | 1.10 | 1.00 |
| **1S64** | A70 | 2e apple green | 1.10 | 1.00 |
| **1S65** | A72 | 20e dk violet, *lilac* | 1.10 | 1.00 |
| | | *Nos. 1S60-1S65 (6)* | 6.60 | 6.00 |

Camoens Issue of 1924 Overprinted in Red

**1936**

| | | | | |
|---|---|---|---|---|
| **1S66** | A68 | 30c dk brown | 1.10 | 1.10 |
| **1S67** | A68 | 32c dk green | 1.10 | 1.10 |
| **1S68** | A69 | 80c bister | 1.10 | 1.10 |
| **1S69** | A70 | 1.20e lt brown | 1.10 | 1.10 |
| **1S70** | A71 | 3e dk blue, *bl* | 1.10 | 1.10 |
| **1S71** | A71 | 4.50e black, *yel* | 1.10 | 1.10 |
| | | *Nos. 1S66-1S71 (6)* | 6.60 | 6.60 |

### No. 1S4 Overprinted "1935"

**1936** **Unwmk.** ***Perf. 14***

| | | | | |
|---|---|---|---|---|
| **1S72** | F1a | black & red | 10.00 | 10.00 |

### Same Stamp with Additional Overprint "Delegacoes"

**1S73** F1a black & red 10.00 10.00

After the government withdrew the franking privilege in 1938, the Portuguese Red Cross Society distributed charity labels which lacked postal validity.

### FOR CIVILIAN RIFLE CLUBS

Rifle Club Emblem — F2

*Perf. 11½x12*

**1899-1910 Typo. Unwmk.**

**2S1** F2 bl grn & car ('99) 10.00 10.00
**2S2** F2 brn & yel grn ('00) 10.00 10.00
**2S3** F2 car & buff ('01) 1.00 1.00
**2S4** F2 bl & org ('02) 1.00 1.00
**2S5** F2 grn & org ('03) 1.00 1.00
**2S6** F2 lt brn & car ('04) 1.60 1.60
**2S7** F2 mar & ultra ('05) 4.25 4.25
**2S8** F2 ultra & buff ('06) 1.00 1.00
**2S9** F2 choc & yel ('07) 1.00 1.00
**2S10** F2 car & ultra ('08) 1.60 1.60
**2S11** F2 bl & yel grn ('09) 1.00 1.00
**2S12** F2 bl grn & brn, *pink* ('10) 4.00 4.00
*Nos. 2S1-2S12 (12)* 37.45 37.45

### FOR THE GEOGRAPHICAL SOCIETY OF LISBON

Coat of Arms
F3 F4

**1903-34 Unwmk. Litho. *Perf. 11½***

**3S1** F3 blk, rose, bl & red 9.00 5.00
**3S2** F3 bl, yel, red & grn ('09) 12.00 5.00
**3S3** F4 blk, org, bl & red ('11) 5.50 4.00
**3S4** F4 blk & brn org ('22) 6.75 4.75
**3S5** F4 blk & bl ('24) 15.00 8.50
**3S6** F4 blk & rose ('26) 6.75 4.75
**3S7** F4 blk & grn ('27) 6.75 4.75
**3S8** F4 bl, yel & red ('29) 4.75 3.50
**3S9** F4 bl, red & vio ('30) 4.75 3.50
**3S10** F4 dp bl, lil & red ('31) 4.75 3.50
**3S11** F4 bis brn & red ('32) 4.75 3.50
**3S12** F4 lt grn & red ('33) 4.75 3.50
**3S13** F4 blue & red ('34) 4.75 3.50
*Nos. 3S1-3S13 (13)* 90.25 57.75

No. 3S12 with three-line overprint, "C.I.C.I. Portugal 1933," was not valid for postage and was sold only to collectors.

No. 3S2 was reprinted in 1933. Green vertical lines behind "Porte Franco" omitted. Value $7.50.

F5

**1934 Litho. *Perf. 11½***

**3S15** F5 blue & red 6.00 3.50

**1935-38 *Perf. 11***

**3S16** F5 blue 18.00 5.25
**3S17** F5 dk bl & red ('36) 4.75 4.25
**3S18** F5 lil & red ('37) 3.50 2.75
**3S19** F5 blk, grn & car ('38) 3.50 2.75
*Nos. 3S16-3S19 (4)* 29.75 15.00

The inscription in the inner circle is omitted on No. 3S16.

### FOR THE NATIONAL AID SOCIETY FOR CONSUMPTIVES

F10

*Perf. 11½x12*

**1904, July Typo. Unwmk.**

**4S1** F10 brown & green 5.00 5.00
**4S2** F10 carmine & yellow 5.00 5.00

## AZORES

Starting in 1980, stamps inscribed Azores and Madeira were valid and sold in Portugal. See Vols. 1 and 4 for prior issues.

Azores No. 2 — A33

Design: 19.50e, Azores No. 6.

**1980, Jan. 2 Litho. *Perf. 12***

**314** A33 6.50e multi .25 .25
**315** A33 19.50e multi .85 .50
*a.* Souvenir sheet of 2, #314-315 3.75 3.75

No. 315a exists overprinted for Capex 87.

Map of Azores A34

**1980, Sept. 17 Litho. *Perf. 12x11½***

**316** A34 50c shown .25 .25
**317** A34 1e Cathedral .25 .25
**318** A34 5e Windmill .40 .25
**319** A34 6.50e Local women .50 .25
**320** A34 8e Coastline .70 .25
**321** A34 30e Ponta Delgada 1.60 .45
*Nos. 316-321 (6)* 3.70 1.70

World Tourism Conf., Manila, Sept. 27.

### Europa Issue

St. Peter's Cavalcade, St. Miguel Island A35

**1981, May 11 Litho. *Perf. 12***

**322** A35 22e multicolored 1.00 .60
*a.* Souvenir sheet of 2 4.50 1.50

Bulls Attacking Spanish Soldiers A36

Battle of Salga Valley, 400th Anniv.: 33.50e, Friar Don Pedro leading citizens.

**1981, July 24 Litho. *Perf. 12x11½***

**323** A36 8.50e multi .55 .25
**324** A36 33.50e multi 2.00 .75

Tolpis Azorica — A37

Designs: Local flora — 8.50e, Ranunculus azoricus. 20e, Platanthera micranta. 50e, Laurus azorica.

**1981, Sept. 21 Litho. *Perf. 12½x12***

**325** A37 7e multicolored .25 .25
**326** A37 8.50e multicolored .35 .25
**327** A37 20e multicolored .65 .35
**328** A37 50e multicolored 1.40 .75
*a.* Booklet pane of 4, #325-328 5.00
*Nos. 325-328 (4)* 2.65 1.60

**1982, Jan. 29**

**329** A37 4e Myosotis azorica .25 .25
**330** A37 10e Lactuca watsoniana .50 .25
**331** A37 27e Vicia dennesiana 1.10 .60
**332** A37 33.50e Azorina vidalii 1.10 .75
*a.* Booklet pane of 4 5.00
*Nos. 329-332 (4)* 2.95 1.85

See Nos. 338-341.

### Europa Type of Portugal

Heroes of Mindelo embarkation, 1832.

**1982, May 3 Litho. *Perf. 12x11½***

**333** A405 33.50e multi 1.50 .65
*a.* Souvenir sheet of 3 5.00 3.00

Chapel of the Holy Ghost — A39

Various Chapels of the Holy Ghost.

**1982, Nov. 24 Litho. *Perf. 12½x12***

**334** A39 27e multi 1.25 .75
**335** A39 33.50e multi 1.75 .90

Europa 1983 A40

**1983, May 5 Litho. *Perf. 12½***

**336** A40 37.50e Geothermal energy 1.50 .55
*a.* Souvenir sheet of 3 6.00 3.50

Flag of the Autonomous Region — A41

**1983, May 23 Litho. *Perf. 12x11½***

**337** A41 12.50e multi 1.00 .25

### Flower Type of 1981

**1983, June 16 *Perf. 12½x12***

**338** A37 12.50e St. John's wort .25 .25
**339** A37 30e Prickless bramble .80 .30
**340** A37 37.50e Romania bush 1.10 .55
**341** A37 100e Common juniper 2.25 1.00
*a.* Booklet pane of 4, #338-341 6.00
*Nos. 338-341 (4)* 4.40 2.10

Woman Wearing Terceira Cloaks — A42

**1984, Mar. 8 Litho. *Perf. 13½***

**342** A42 16e Jesters costumes, 18th cent. .60 .25
**343** A42 51e shown 2.00 1.00

### Europa Type of Portugal

**1984, May 2 *Perf. 12x11½***

**344** A427 51e multicolored 1.50 .95
*a.* Souvenir sheet of 3 7.00 4.00

Megabombus Ruderatus — A44

35e, Pieris brassicae azorensis. 40e, Chrysomela banksi. 51e, Phlogophora interrupta.

**1984, Sept. 3 Litho. *Perf. 12x11½***

**345** A44 16e multicolored .30 .25
**346** A44 35e multicolored 1.00 .50
**347** A44 40e multicolored 1.40 .50
**348** A44 51e multicolored 1.60 .80
*Nos. 345-348 (4)* 4.30 2.05

***Perf. 12 Vert.***

*345a* A44 16e 1.50 1.50
*346a* A44 35e 1.50 1.50
*347a* A44 40e 1.50 1.50
*348a* A44 51e 1.50 1.50
*b.* Bklt. pane of 4, #345a-348a 7.50

**1985, Feb. 13 *Perf. 12x11½***

20e, Polyspilla polyspilla. 40e, Sphaerophoria nigra. 46e, Colias croceus. 60e, Hipparchia azorina.

**349** A44 20e multicolored .35 .25
**350** A44 40e multicolored 1.00 .40
**351** A44 46e multicolored 1.50 .60
**352** A44 60e multicolored 1.60 .65
*Nos. 349-352 (4)* 4.45 1.90

***Perf. 12 Vert.***

*349a* A44 20e 2.50 2.50
*350a* A44 40e 2.50 2.50
*351a* A44 46e 2.50 2.50
*352a* A44 60e 2.50 2.50
*b.* Bklt. pane of 4, #349a-352a 10.00

### Europa Type of Portugal

**1985, May 6 Litho. *Perf. 11½x12***

**353** A435 60e Man playing folia drum 1.75 .80
*a.* Souvenir sheet of 3 5.50 3.50

Native Boats — A46

**1985, June 19 Litho. *Perf. 12x12½***

**354** A46 40e Jeque 1.40 .70
**355** A46 60e Bote 2.00 1.00

### Europa Type of Portugal

**1986, May Litho.**

**356** A447 68.50e Pyrrhula murina 2.25 .90
*a.* Souvenir sheet of 3 7.00 4.00

Regional Architecture A48

19th Century fountains: 22.50e, Alto das Covas, Angra do Heroismo. 52.50e, Faja de Baixo, San Miguel. 68.50e, Gates of St. Peter, Terceira. 100e, Agua d'Alto, San Miguel.

**1986, Sept. 18 Litho. *Perf. 12***

**357** A48 22.50e multi .50 .25
**358** A48 52.50e multi 1.50 .70
**359** A48 68.50e multi 2.25 .90
**360** A48 100e multi 3.00 .75
*a.* Booklet pane of 4, #357-360 6.00
*Nos. 357-360 (4)* 7.25 2.60

Traditional Modes of Transportation — A49

**1986, Nov. 7 Litho.**

**361** A49 25e Isle of Santa Maria ox cart .65 .25
**362** A49 75e Ram cart 3.00 1.40

**Europa Type of Portugal**

Modern architecutre: Regional Assembly, Horta, designed by Manuel Correia Fernandes and Luis Miranda.

**1987, May 5 Litho. *Perf. 12***

**363** A456 74.50e multicolored *1.50 .90*
*a.* Souvenir sheet of 4 *6.00 4.00*

Windows and Balconies A51

51e, Santa Cruz, Graciosa. 74.50e, Ribiera Grande, San Miguel.

**1987, July 1 *Perf. 12***

**364** A51 51e multicolored 1.75 1.00
**365** A51 74.50e multicolored 2.25 .85

Aviation History A52

Seaplanes — 25e, NC-4 Curtiss Flyer, 1919. 57e, Dornier DO-X, 1932. 74.50e, Savoia-Marchetti S 55-X, 1933. 125e, Lockheed Sirius, 1933.

**1987, Oct. 9 *Perf. 12x11½***

**366** A52 25e multi .45 .25
**367** A52 57e multi 1.75 .90
**368** A52 74.50e multi 2.60 1.25
**369** A52 125e multi 3.00 1.50
*Nos. 366-369 (4)* 7.80 3.90

***Perf. 12 Vert.***

*366a* A52 25e 2.25 2.25
*367a* A52 57e 2.25 2.25
*368a* A52 74.50e 2.25 2.25
*369a* A52 125e 2.25 2.25
*b.* Bklt. pane of 4, #366a-369a 9.00

**Europa Type of Portugal**

**1988, Apr. 21 Litho. *Perf. 12***

**370** A466 80e multicolored *6.00 1.20*
*a.* Souvenir sheet of 4 *7.00 4.00*

Birds — A54

**1988, Oct. 18 Litho.**

**371** A54 27e Columba palumbus azorica .60 .25
**372** A54 60e Scolopax rusticola 1.90 1.50
**373** A54 80e Sterna dougallii 2.00 1.00
**374** A54 100e Buteo buteo 2.50 .90
*a.* Booklet pane of 4, #371-374 7.00
*Nos. 371-374 (4)* 7.00 3.65

Coats of Arms A55

**1988, Nov. 18 Litho.**

**375** A55 55e Dominion of Azores 1.25 .60
**376** A55 80e Bettencourt family 1.75 .80

Wildlife Conservation A56

Various kinglets, Regulus regulus.

**1989, Jan. 20 Litho.**

**377** A56 30e Adult on branch .75 .25
**378** A56 30e Two adults .75 .25
**379** A56 30e Adult, nest .75 .25
**380** A56 30e Bird in flight .75 .25
*a.* Strip of 4, Nos. 377-380 3.25 3.25

See Nos. 385-388.

**Europa Type of Portugal**

Children's toys.

**1989, Apr. 26 Litho.**

**381** A476 80e Tin boat *2.50 .80*

**Souvenir Sheet**

**382** Sheet, 2 each #381, 382a *10.00 4.00*
*a.* A476 80e Tin boat, diff. *2.50 1.20*

Settlement of the Azores, 550th Anniv. A58

**1989, Sept. 20 Litho.**

**383** A58 29e Friar Goncalho Velho .65 .25
**384** A58 87e Settlers farming 2.40 1.00

**Bird Type of 1989 With World Wildlife Fund Emblem**

Various Pyrrhula murina.

**1990, Feb. 14 Litho. *Perf. 12***

**385** A56 32e Adult on branch 1.00 .50
**386** A56 32e Two adults 1.00 .50
**387** A56 32e Brooding 1.00 .50
**388** A56 32e Bird in flight 1.00 .50
*a.* Strip of 4, #385-388 4.50 4.50

No. 388a has continuous design.

**Europa Type of Portugal**

**1990, Apr. 11 Litho. *Perf. 12x11½***

**389** A486 80e Vasco da Gama P.O. *1.50 .55*

**Souvenir Sheet**

**390** Sheet of 4, 2 each #389, 390a *7.50 4.50*
*a.* A486 80e Maia P.O. *1.50 1.75*

Professions A61

**1990, July 11 Litho. *Perf. 12***

**391** A61 5e Cart maker .25 .25
**392** A61 32e Potter .55 .30
**393** A61 60e Metal worker 1.50 1.00
**394** A61 100e Cooper 2.10 1.10
*Nos. 391-394 (4)* 4.40 2.65

***Perf. 13½ Vert.***

*391a* A61 5e 1.25 1.25
*392a* A61 32e 1.25 1.25
*393a* A61 60e 1.25 1.25
*394a* A61 100e 1.25 1.25
*b.* Bklt. pane of 4, #391a-394a 5.25

See Nos. 397-400, 406-409.

Europa A62

**1991, Apr. 11 Litho. *Perf. 12***

**395** A62 80e Hermes space shuttle *2.00 .75*

**Souvenir Sheet**

**396** Sheet, 2 each #395, 396a *10.00 4.00*
*a.* A62 80e Sanger *2.00 1.75*

**Professions Type of 1990**

**1991, Aug. 2 Litho. *Perf. 12x11½***

**397** A61 35e Tile makers .45 .25
**398** A61 65e Mosaic artists 1.20 .65
**399** A61 70e Quarrymen 1.25 .75
**400** A61 110e Stonemasons 2.00 1.50
*Nos. 397-400 (4)* 4.90 3.15

***Perf. 13½ Vert.***

*397a* A61 35e 1.25 1.25
*398a* A61 65e 1.25 1.25
*399a* A61 70e 1.25 1.25
*400a* A61 110e 1.25 1.25
*b.* Bklt. pane of 4, #397a-400a 5.00

Transportation in the Azores — A63

Ships and Planes: 35e, Schooner Helena, 1918. 60e, Beechcraft CS, 1947. 80e, Yacht, Cruzeiro do Canal, 1987. 110e, British Aerospace ATP, 1991.

**1991, Nov. 15 Litho. *Perf. 12x11½***

**401** A63 35e multicolored .45 .25
**402** A63 60e multicolored .90 .45
**403** A63 80e multicolored 1.25 .60
**404** A63 110e multicolored 1.60 .80
*Nos. 401-404 (4)* 4.20 2.10

See Nos. 410-413.

**Europa Type of Portugal**

85e, Columbus aboard Santa Maria.

**1992, May 22 Litho. *Perf. 12x11½***

**405** A514 85e gold & multi *4.00 .70*

**Professions Type of 1990**

**1992, June 12 Litho. *Perf. 12x11½***

**406** A61 10e Guitar maker .25 .25
**407** A61 38e Carpenter .45 .25
**408** A61 85e Basket maker 1.10 .50
**409** A61 120e Boat builders 1.40 .75
*Nos. 406-409 (4)* 3.20 1.75

***Perf. 13½ Vert.***

*406a* A61 10e 1.25 1.25
*407a* A61 38e 1.25 1.25
*408a* A61 85e 1.25 1.25
*409a* A61 120e 1.25 1.25
*b.* Bklt. pane of 4, #406a-409a 5.25

**Transportation Type of 1991**

Ships.

**1992, Oct. 7 Litho. *Perf. 12x11½***

**410** A63 38e Insulano .45 .25
**411** A63 65e Carvalho Araujo 1.00 .60
**412** A63 85e Funchal 1.20 .65
**413** A63 120e Terceirense 1.60 .80
*Nos. 410-413 (4)* 4.25 2.30

Contemporary Paintings by Antonio Dacosta (1914-90) — A64

Europa: No. 414, Two Mermaids at the Entrance to a Cave, 1980. No. 415a, Acoriana, 1986.

**1993, May 5 Litho. *Perf. 12x11½***

**414** A64 90e multicolored *1.25 .60*

**Souvenir Sheet**

**415** Sheet, 2 each #414, 415a *7.00 5.00*
*a.* A64 90e multicolored *1.25 .60*

Grinding Stones A64a

Designs: 42e, Animal-powered mill. 130e, Woman using hand-driven mill.

**1993, May 5 Litho. *Perf. 12x11***

**416** A64a 42e multicolored .50 .25
**417** A64a 130e multicolored 2.25 1.00

Architecture A65

Church of Praia da Vitoria: 42e, Main entry. 70e, South entry.

Church of Ponta Delgada: 90e, Main entry. 130e, South entry.

**1993, Nov. 3 Litho. *Perf. 12***

**418** A65 42e multicolored .45 .25
**419** A65 70e multicolored 1.00 .50
**420** A65 90e multicolored 1.20 .60
**421** A65 130e multicolored 1.60 .80
*Nos. 418-421 (4)* 4.25 2.15

Tile Used in Religious Architecture A66

Designs: 40e, Blue and white pattern, Caloura church, Sao Miguel. 70e, Blue, white and yellow pattern, Caloura church, Sao Miguel. 100e, Drawing of Adoration of the Wise Men, by Bartolomeu Antunes, Esperanca monastery, Ponta Delgada. 150e, Drawing, frontal altar, Nossa Senhora dos Anjos chapel.

**1994, Mar. 28 Litho. *Perf. 12***

**422** A66 40e multicolored .40 .25
**423** A66 70e multicolored .90 .70
**424** A66 100e multicolored 1.20 .60
**425** A66 150e multicolored 1.75 .90
*Nos. 422-425 (4)* 4.25 2.45

***Perf. 11½ Vert.***

*422a* A66 40e .45 .25
*423a* A66 70e .90 .60
*424a* A66 100e 1.20 .90
*425a* A66 150e 1.50 1.00
*b.* Bklt. pane of 4, #422a-425a 4.50

**Europa Type of Portugal**

Wildlife, country: No. 426, Monkey, Brazil. No. 427a, Armadillo, Africa.

**1994, May 5 Litho. *Perf. 12***
**426** A541 100e multicolored 1.25 .60

**Souvenir Sheet**

**427** Sheet, 2 each #426, 427a 6.00 5.00
*a.* A541 100e multicolored 1.25 .60

**Architecture Type of 1993**

45e, Church of Santa Barbara, Manueline Entry, Cedros. 140e, Railed window, Ribeira Grande.

**1994, Sept. 16 Litho. *Perf. 12***
**428** A65 45e multicolored .45 .30
**429** A65 140e multicolored 1.75 .85

Advocates of Local Autonomy A67

42e, Aristides Moreira da Motta (1855-1942). 130e, Gil Mont'Alverne de Sequeira (1859-1931).

**1995, Mar. 2 Litho. *Perf. 12***
**430** A67 42e multicolored .50 .30
**431** A67 130e multicolored 1.50 .95

19th Century Architecture A68

Designs: 45e, Santana Palace, Ponta Delgada. 80e, Our Lady of Victories Chapel, Furnas Lake. 95e, Hospital of the Santa Casa da Misericórdia, Ponta Delgada. 135e, Residence of Ernesto do Canto, Myrthes Park, Furnas Lake

**1995, Sept. 1 Litho. *Perf. 12***
**432** A68 45e multicolored .50 .30
**433** A68 80e multicolored .95 .50
**434** A68 95e multicolored 1.10 .60
**435** A68 135e multicolored 1.50 .90
*Nos. 432-435 (4)* 4.05 2.30

***Perf. 11½ Vert.***
*432a* A68 45e .60 .60
*433a* A68 80e 1.00 1.00
*434a* A68 95e 1.25 .60
*435a* A68 135e 1.75 .90
*b.* Bklt. pane, #432a-435a 4.75
Complete booklet, No. 435b 6.00

Natália Correia (1923-93), Writer A69

**1996, May 3 Litho. *Perf. 12***
**436** A69 98e multicolored 1.50 .60
*a.* Souvenir sheet of 3 6.00 5.00

Europa.

Lighthouses — A70

Designs: 47e, Contendas, Terceira Island. 78e, Molhe, Port of Ponte Delgada, San Miguel Island. 98e, Arnel, San Miguel. 140e, Santa Clara, San Miguel. 200e, Ponta da Barca, Graciosa Island.

**1996, May 3**
**437** A70 47e multicolored .55 .30
**438** A70 78e multicolored 1.10 .55
**439** A70 98e multicolored 1.25 .60
**440** A70 140e multicolored 1.90 1.00
*Nos. 437-440 (4)* 4.80 2.45

**Souvenir Sheet**

**441** A70 200e multicolored 3.00 3.00

Carved Work from Church Altar Pieces A71

49e, Leaves, berries, bird, St. Peter Church, Ponta Delgada, Sao Miguel. 80e, Cherub, Church of the Convent of St. Peter de Alcântara, Sao Roque, Pico. 100e, Cherub, All Saints Church, former Jesuits' College, Ponta Delgada. 140e, Figure holding scroll above head, St. Joseph Church, Ponta Delgada.

**1997, Apr. 16 Litho. *Perf. 12***
**442** A71 49e multicolored .55 .30
**443** A71 80e multicolored .90 .45
**444** A71 100e multicolored 1.10 .60
**445** A71 140e multicolored 1.60 .80
*Nos. 442-445 (4)* 4.15 2.15

***Perf. 11½ Vert.***
*442a* A71 49e .55 .30
*443a* A71 80e .90 .45
*444a* A71 100e 1.10 .60
*445a* A71 140e 1.60 .80
*b.* Bklt. pane, #442a-445a 5.00
Complete booklet, #445b 5.25

**Stories and Legends Type of Portugal**

Europa: Man on ship from "Legend of the Island of Seven Cities," horiz.

**1997, May 5 Litho. *Perf. 12***
**446** A599 100e multicolored 1.25 .50
*a.* Souvenir sheet of 3 4.50 3.00

**Natl. Festivals Type of Portugal**

**1998, May 21 Litho. *Perf. 12***
**447** A621 100e Holy Spirit 1.25 .55
*a.* Souvenir sheet of 3 5.00 1.75

Europa.

Ocean Creatures A72

Designs: 50e, Stenella frontalis. 140e, Physeter macrocephalus.

**1998, Aug. 4 Litho. *Perf. 12***
**448** A72 50e multicolored .60 .30

**Size: 80x30mm**

**449** A72 140e multicolored 1.75 .80

***Perf. 11½ Vert.***
*448a* A72 50e .70 .30
*449a* A72 140e 2.00 .80
*b.* Booklet pane, #448a-449a + label 3.50
Complete booklet, #449b 3.50

**Europa Type of Portugal**

100e, Flowers, Pico Mountain Natural Reserve.

**1999, May 5 Litho. *Perf. 12x11¾***
**450** A641 100e multi 1.25 .50
*a.* Souvenir sheet of 3 3.75 3.75

Paintings of the Azores A73

51e, Emigrants, by Domingos Rebelo (1891-1975). 95e, Portrait of Vitorino Nemésio, by Antonio Dacosta (1914-90), vert. 100e, Espera de Gado no Alto das Covas (1939-98), by José Van der Hagen. 140e, The Vila Franca Islands, by Duarte Maia (1867-1922).

***Perf. 12x11¾, 11¾x12***

**1999, Sept. 3 Litho.**
**451** A73 51e multi .60 .25
**452** A73 95e multi 1.10 .45
**453** A73 100e multi 1.25 .50
**454** A73 140e multi 1.75 .70

***Perf. 11¾ Vert., 11¾ Horiz. (#452a)***
*451a* A73 51e multi .60 .25
*452a* A73 95e multi 1.10 .45
*453a* A73 100e multi 1.25 .50
*454a* A73 140e multi 1.75 .70
*b.* Bklt. pane of 4, #451a-454a 4.00
Complete booklet, #454b 4.75

**Europa Issue**
**Common Design Type**

**2000, May 9 *Perf. 11¾x12***
**455** CD17 100e multi 1.25 .50
*a.* Souvenir sheet of 3 3.75 1.50

Mail Delivery Systems of the Past — A74

Designs: 85e, Buoy mail. 140e, Zeppelin mail, vert.

***Perf. 12x11¾, 11¾x12***

**2000, Oct. 9 Litho.**
**456-457** A74 Set of 2 2.75 1.10

**Europa Type of Portugal**

**2001, May 9 Litho. *Perf. 12x11¾***
**458** A677 105e Marine life 1.25 .45
*a.* Souvenir sheet of 3 3.75 3.75

Angra do Heroismo World Heritage Site — A75

View of town, sea and: 53e, Archway. 85e, Monument. 140e, Window.

**2001, June 4**
**459-461** A75 Set of 3 3.25 1.25

**Souvenir Sheet**

**462** A75 350e Map 4.00 4.00

**Europa Type of Portugal**

**2002, May 9 Litho. *Perf. 12x11¾***
**463** A695 54c Clown, diff. 1.25 .50
*a.* Souvenir sheet of 3, perf. 12½ 3.75 3.75

Flowers A76

Designs: 28c, Scabiosa nitens. 45c, Viburnum tinus. 54c, Euphorbia azorica. 70c, Lysimachia nemorum. No. 468, €1.15, Bellis azorica. No. 469, €1.75, Spergularia azorica.

No. 470: a, €1.15, Azorina vidalli. b, €1.75, Senecio malvifolius.

**2002, May 20 *Perf. 12x11¾***
**464-469** A76 Set of 6 11.50 4.50

**Souvenir Sheet**

**470** A76 Sheet of 2, #a-b 6.50 6.50

Windmills — A77

Designs: 43c, Ilha do Faial windmill, Azores. 54c, Onze-Lieve-Vrouw-Lombeek windmill, Belgium.

**2002, July 12 Litho. *Perf. 11¾x12***
**471-472** A77 Set of 2 2.10 1.20

See Belgium Nos. 1925-1926.

**Europa Type of Portugal**

Design: Poster art by Sebastiao Rodrigues, 1983.

**2003, May 5 Litho. *Perf. 12x12½***
**473** A707 55c multi 1.25 .65
*a.* Souvenir sheet of 2 2.50 2.50

Heritage of the Azores A78

Designs: 30c, Pineapple and plants. 43c, Grapes, vines. 55c, Tea leaves and plants. 70c, Tobacco leaf and plants.

No. 478: a, €1, Carnival dancers, Terceira Island. b, €2, Festival of the Holy Spirit.

**2003, June 6 *Perf. 12x11¾***
**474-477** A78 Set of 4 4.50 2.25

**Souvenir Sheet**

**478** A78 Sheet of 2, #a-b 6.25 6.25

**Europa Type of Portugal**

Design: People in flower garden.

**2004, May 10 Litho. *Perf. 13¼x14***
**479** A734 56c multi 1.20 .70
*a.* Souvenir sheet of 2 2.40 2.40

Worldwide Fund for Nature (WWF) A79

No. 480: a, Front of Makaira nigricans. b, Rear of Makira nigricans, fish in background. c, Front of Tetrapturus albidus. d, Rear of Tetrapturus albidus, fish in background.

**2004, June 28 *Perf. 13x13¼***
**480** Horiz. strip of 4 3.00 1.50
*a.-d.* A79 30c Any single .75 .40

**Europa Type of Portugal**

Designs: No. 481, Torresmos. No. 482a, Polvo Guisado (stewed octopus).

**2005, May 5 *Perf. 14x13¼***
**481** A752 57c multi 1.50 .75

**Souvenir Sheet**

**482** Sheet of 2 #482a 3.00 3.00
*a.* A752 57c multi 1.50 1.50

Tourism A80

Designs: No. 483, 30c, Cow. No. 484, 30c, Arch. No. 485, 45c, Building. No. 486, 45c, Windmill. 57c, Arm of windmill, whale, pineapple. 74c, Pineapple, volcanic lake.

No. 489: a, 30c, Statue of Jesus. b, €1.55, Embroidered dove.

**2005, May 13**
**483-488** A80 Set of 6 6.00 3.00

**Souvenir Sheet**

**489** A80 Sheet of 2, #a-b 4.50 4.50

Europa A81

No. 491 — Children's drawings: a, Child with one leg. b, People of many colors.

**2006, May 9 Litho. *Perf. 12x12½***

**490** A81 60c shown 1.40 .70
*a.* Booklet pane of 1, perf. 12x11¾ 1.40 —

**Souvenir Sheet**

***Perf. 12x11¾***

**491** A81 60c Sheet of 2, #a-b 2.75 2.75
*c.* Booklet pane of 2, #491a-491b 2.75 —

Booklet panes are separated from binding stub at left by row of rouletting.

Hydrothermal Vents — A82

Designs: 20c, Crabs and mussels. 30c, Fish and mussels. 75c, Active vent. €2, Shrimp.

**2006, July 22 *Perf. 12½x13***

**492-495** A82 Set of 4 7.00 3.50
*493a* Booklet pane of 2, #492-493 1.10 —
*495a* Souvenir sheet of 1 4.50 4.50
*495b* Booklet pane of 2, #494-495 6.50 —
*495c* Booklet pane of 1, #495 4.75 —

Lubrapex Intl. Philatelic Exhibition, Rio (#495a). Booklet panes are separated from binding stub at left by row of rouletting.

Wines of Pico Island A83

Designs: 30c, Wine barrels, vineyard, grapes. No. 497, 60c, Grapes and vineyard. No. 498, 75c, Grape harvesters, wine barrels. No. 499, €1, Wine press, workers moving wine barrel.

No. 500: a, 45c, Vineyard, small grape vines, grapes. b, 60c, Grapes, grape harvester. c, 75c, Grapes, vats, and barrels. d, €1, Barrels, men inspecting barrels.

**2006, Sept. 14**

**496-499** A83 Set of 4 5.50 2.75
*497a* Booklet pane of 2, #496-497 2.00 —
*499a* Booklet pane of 2, #498-499 3.50 —

**Souvenir Sheet**

**500** A83 Sheet of 4, #a-d 6.00 6.00
*500e* Booklet pane of 5, #500a-500d 6.00 —
Complete booklet, #490a, 491c, 493a, 495b, 495c, 497a, 499a, 500e 29.00

Booklet panes are separated from binding stub at left by row of rouletting. Complete booklet also contains a pane of four progressive proofs of No. 490. These were not valid for postage.

Europa A84

Designs: No. 501, Scout neckerchief.
No. 502: a, Knot. b, Scouts and leader at tent.

**2007, May 9 Litho. *Perf. 12½x13***

**501** A84 61c multi 1.50 .75
*a.* Booklet pane of 1 1.50 —

**Souvenir Sheet**

**502** Sheet of 2 3.00 3.00
*a.-b.* A84 61c Either single 1.50 .75
*c.* Booklet pane of 2, #502a-502b 3.00 —

Scouting, cent.
Booklet panes are separated from binding stub at left by a row of rouletting.

Windmills A85

Designs: 30c, Windmill with red domed roof. No. 504, 45c, Windmill with red conical roof. 61c, White windmill with metal roof. 75c, Blue windmill.

No. 507: a, 45c, Windmill with black conical roof. b, €2, Red striped windmill.

**2007, May 28**

**503-506** A85 Set of 4 4.50 2.50
*506a* Booklet pane of 4, #503-506 4.50 —

**Souvenir Sheet**

**507** Sheet of 2 5.50 5.50
*a.* A85 45c multi 1.00 .50
*b.* A85 €2 multi 4.50 2.25
*c.* Booklet pane of 2, #507a-507b 5.50 —

Booklet panes are separated from binding stub at left by a row of rouletting.

Sept. 27, 1957 Eruption of Capelinhos Volcano, 50th Anniv. A86

Designs: 30c, Erupting volcano, as seen from ocean. 75c, Erupting volcano and lighthouse.
€2.45, Cliff and lighthouse.

**2007, Sept. 27 Litho. *Perf. 12½x13***

**508-509** A86 Set of 2 2.50 1.25
*509a* Booklet pane of 2, #508-509 2.50 —

**Souvenir Sheet**

**510** A86 €2.45 multi 6.00 6.00
*a.* Booklet pane of 1 6.00 —
Complete booklet, #501a, 502c, 506a, 507c, 509a, 510a 23.00

No. 510 contains one 80x30mm stamp. Booklet panes are separated from binding stub at left by a row of rouletting. Complete booklet also contains a pane of four progressive proofs of No. 501. These were not valid for postage.

Europa A87

Designs: No. 511, Man in rowboat, envelope, whale. No. 512a, Windmill, envelopes.

***Perf. 12x11¾ Syncopated***

**2008, May 9 Litho.**

**511** A87 61c multi 1.25 .60
*a.* Booklet pane of 1 1.25 —

**Souvenir Sheet**

**512** Sheet of 2, #511, 512a 3.00 1.50
*a.* A87 61c multi 1.25 .60
*b.* Booklet pane of 2, #511, 512b 2.50 —

Booklet panes are separated from binding stub at left by a row of rouletting.

Pyrrhula Murina A88

Various depictions of Pyrrhula murina: 30c, 61c, 75c, €1.
€2.45, Pyrrhula murina feeding. €2.95, Pyrrhula murina with beak open.

**2008, May 28**

**513-516** A88 Set of 4 5.50 2.75
*514a* Booklet pane of 2, #513-514 2.00 —
*516a* Booklet pane of 2, #515-516 3.50 —

**Souvenir Sheets**

**517-518** A88 Set of 2 12.00 7.50
*517a* Booklet pane of 1 5.00 —
*518a* Booklet pane of 1 7.00 —

Booklet panes are separated from binding stub at left by a row of rouletting.

**Lighthouse Type of Portugal of 2008**

**2008, June 19**

**519** A835 61c Arnel Lighthouse 1.40 .70
*a.* Booklet pane of 1 1.40 —
Complete booklet, #511a, 512b, 514a, 516a, 517a, 518a, 519a 23.00

Booklet panes are separated from binding stub at left by a row of rouletting. Complete booklet also contains a pane of four progressive proofs of No. 511. These were not valid for postage.

Biodiversity of Lakes and Lagoons — A89

Designs: 32c, Galinhola (bird). 68c, Sátiro dos Açores (butterflies). 80c, Libélula (dragonflies). €2, Cedro-das-ilhas (tree).
No. 524, €2.50, Améijoa-boa, polvo-comun, moreia-pintada (clams, octopus, moray eel). No. 525, €2.50, Zarro, marrequinha, garça-real (ducks and kingfisher).

***Perf. 12x11¾ Syncopated***

**2009, Apr. 22 Litho.**

**520-523** A89 Set of 4 7.50 3.75
*521a* Booklet pane of 2, #520-521 2.00 —
*523a* Booklet pane of 2, #522-523 5.50 —

**Souvenir Sheets**

**524-525** A89 Set of 2 10.50 6.00
*524a* Booklet pane of 1 5.25 —
*525a* Booklet pane of 1 5.25 —

Nos. 524-525 each contain one 80x30mm stamp.
Booklet panes are separated from binding stub at left by a row of rouletting.

Europa A90

Designs: No. 526, Dish antenna of European Space Agency Satellite Tracking Center, Santa Maria Island. No. 527a, Ribeira Grande Astronomical Observatory, Sao Miguel Island.

**2009, May 8**

**526** A90 68c multi 1.50 .75
*a.* Booklet pane of 1 1.50 —

**Souvenir Sheet**

**527** Sheet of 2, #526, 527a 3.00 2.00
*a.* A90 68c multi 1.50 .75
*b.* Booklet pane of 2, #526, 527a 3.00 —
Complete booklet, #521a, 523a, 524a, 525a, 526a, 527b, Portugal #3145a 27.00

Intl. Year of Astronomy.
Booklet panes are separated from binding stub at left by a row of rouletting. Complete booklet also contains a pane of 4 progressive proofs of No. 526. These were not valid for postage.

Europa — A91

Characters from children's story: No. 528, Woman in green. No. 529a, King on horseback in blue.

***Perf. 11¾x12 Syncopated***

**2010, May 7 Litho.**

**528** A91 68c multi 1.50 .75
*a.* Booklet pane of 1 1.50 —

**Souvenir Sheet**

**529** Sheet of 2, #528, 529a 3.00 1.50
*a.* A91 68c multi 1.50 .75
*b.* Booklet pane of 2, #528, 529a 3.00 —

Issued: Nos. 528a, 529b, Nov.
Booklet panes are separated from binding stub at left by a row of rouletting.

Marine Invertebrates — A92

Designs: 32c, Dardanus callidus. 68c, Alicia mirabilis. 80c, Ophidiaster ophidianus. No. 533, €2, Sabella spallanzanii.
No. 534, €2, Grapsus adscencionis. No. 535, €2, Sphaerechinus granularis.

***Perf. 12x11¾ Syncopated***

**2010, July 1**

**530-533** A92 Set of 4 8.25 4.00
*531a* Booklet pane of 2, #530-531 2.25 —
*533a* Booklet pane of 2, #532-533 6.00 —

**Souvenir Sheets**

**534-535** A92 Set of 2 8.50 5.00
*534a* Booklet pane of 1 4.25 —
*535a* Booklet pane of 1 4.25 —
Complete booklet, #528a, 529b, 531a, 533a, 534a, 535a 22.00

Issued: Nos. 531a, 533a, 534a, 535a, Nov.
Booklet panes are separated from binding stub at left by a row of rouletting.

Europa A93

Designs: No. 536, Cows in pasture, bird in tree. No. 537a, Cows in pasture.

**2011, May 9**

**536** A93 68c multi 1.50 .75
*a.* Booklet pane of 1 1.50 —

**Souvenir Sheet**

**537** Sheet of 2, #536, 537a 3.00 2.00
*a.* A93 68c multi 1.50 .75
*b.* Booklet pane of 2, #536, 537a 3.00 —

Intl. Year of Forests. See No. 577.

Azores Whaling Heritage A94

Designs: 32c, Whaling boats from Azores and America. 68c, Harpooned whale, whalers. 80c, Whale hunt, whalers, whale boats. €2, Whale caught near lighthouse, whale on shore, religious statue.
No. 542, €1.75, Children, whalers and boats. No. 543, €2.30, Whalers capturing whale, whaler and boat, partially-constructed whale boat.

**2011, Aug. 26**

| | | | | |
|---|---|---|---|---|
| 538-541 | A94 | Set of 4 | 8.00 | 4.00 |
| 539a | | Booklet pane of 2, #538-539 | 2.00 | — |
| 541a | | Booklet pane of 2, #540-541 | 6.00 | — |

**Souvenir Sheets**

| | | | | |
|---|---|---|---|---|
| 542-543 | A94 | Set of 2 | 9.00 | 3.50 |
| 542a | | Booklet pane of 1 | 3.50 | — |
| 543a | | Booklet pane of 1 | 5.50 | — |
| | | Complete booklet, #536a, 537b, 539a, 541a, 542a, 543a, Portugal #3331a | 23.00 | |

Europa A95

Designs: No. 544, Steamer Funchal. No. 545a, Pico waterfront.

**2012, May 9**

| | | | | |
|---|---|---|---|---|
| 544 | A95 | 68c multi | 1.50 | .75 |
| a. | | Booklet pane of 1 | 1.50 | |

**Souvenir Sheet**

| | | | |
|---|---|---|---|
| 545 | Sheet of 2, #544, 545a | 3.00 | 1.75 |
| a. | A95 68c multi | 1.50 | .75 |
| b. | Booklet pane of 2, #544, 545a | 3.00 | — |

Issued: Nos. 544a, 545b, Nov.

Booklet panes are separated from binding stub at left by a row of rouletting. See No. 578.

Aerial Views of Towns — A96

Designs: 32c, Almas. 68c, D'Além Norte. 80c, Grande. €2, Sao Joao.

No. 550, €1.75, Caldeira de Santo Cristo. No. 551, €2.30, Cubres.

***Perf. 11¾x12 Syncopated***

**2012, June 5**

| | | | | |
|---|---|---|---|---|
| 546-549 | A96 | Set of 4 | 8.50 | 4.25 |
| 547a | | Booklet pane of 2, #546-547 | 2.25 | — |
| 549a | | Booklet pane of 2, #548-549 | 6.25 | — |

**Souvenir Sheets**

| | | | | |
|---|---|---|---|---|
| 550-551 | A96 | Set of 2 | 9.00 | 5.25 |
| 550a | | Booklet pane of 1 | 4.00 | — |
| 551a | | Booklet pane of 1 | 5.00 | — |
| | | Complete booklet, #544a, 545b, 547a, 549a, 550a, 551a | 22.50 | |

Issued: Nos. 547a, 549a, 550a, 551a, Nov.

Booklet panes are separated from binding stub at left by a row of rouletting. Complete booklet contains a pane of four imperforate progressive proofs of No. 544. These were not valid for postage. See No. 579.

Europa A97

Designs: No. 552, Portuguese postal motorcycle. No. 553a, Rider on Portuguese postal motorcycle.

***Perf. 12x11¾ Syncopated***

**2013, May 9** **Litho.**

| | | | | |
|---|---|---|---|---|
| 552 | A97 | 70c multi | 1.50 | .75 |
| a. | | Booklet pane of 1 | 1.50 | — |

**Souvenir Sheet**

| | | | |
|---|---|---|---|
| 553 | Sheet of 2, #552, 553a | 3.00 | 2.00 |
| a. | A97 70c multi | 1.50 | .75 |
| b. | Booklet pane of 2, #552, 553a | 3.00 | — |

Booklet panes are separated from binding stub at left by a row of rouletting.

Apiculture A98

Designs: 36c, Beekeepers tending hives, Sao Jorge. 70c, Beekeeper using smoker near hives, Pico. 80c, Beekeepers, bees and hives, Santa María. No. 557, €1.70, Beekeeper near hives near fruit trees, Flores.

No. 558, €1.70, Beehives on farm, Sao Miguel. €1.90, Beekeepers, hives, cattle, Terceira.

***Perf. 12x11¾ Syncopated***

**2013, Oct. 9** **Litho.**

| | | | | |
|---|---|---|---|---|
| 554-557 | A98 | Set of 4 | 8.00 | 4.00 |
| 555a | | Booklet pane of 2, #554-555 | 2.25 | — |
| 557a | | Booklet pane of 2, #556-557 | 5.75 | — |

**Souvenir Sheets**

| | | | | |
|---|---|---|---|---|
| 558-559 | A98 | Set of 2 | 8.00 | 5.00 |
| 558a | | Booklet pane of 1 | 3.75 | — |
| 559a | | Booklet pane of 1 | 4.25 | — |
| | | Complete booklet, #552a, 553b, 555a, 557a, 558a, 559a | 21.00 | |

Nos. 558-559 each contain one 80x30mm stamp. See No. 580.

Booklet panes are separated from binding stub at left by a row of rouletting. Complete booklet also contains a pane of 4 progressive proofs of No. 552. These were not valid for postage.

Europa — A99

Designs: No. 560, Viola da terra player. No. 561a, Viola da terra.

***Perf. 11¾x12 Syncopated***

**2014, May 9** **Litho.**

| | | | | |
|---|---|---|---|---|
| 560 | A99 | E multi | 1.60 | .80 |
| a. | | Booklet pane of 1 | 1.60 | — |

**Souvenir Sheet**

| | | | |
|---|---|---|---|
| 561 | Sheet of 2, #560, 561a | 3.00 | 2.00 |
| a. | A99 E multi | 1.60 | .80 |
| b. | Booklet pane of 2, #560, 561a | 3.00 | — |

On day of issue Nos. 560 and 561a each sold for 72c.

Booklet panes are separated from binding stub at left by a row of rouletting.

See No. 610.

Airplanes A100

Designs: 42c, Boeing 314 Clipper. 50c, Douglas C-47. 72c, Lockheed Constellation. 80c, Hawker-Siddeley HS-748 Avro.

€1, Boeing 314 Clipper, diff. €1.70, Lockheed Super Constellation.

***Perf. 12x11¾ Syncopated***

**2014, Sept. 4** **Litho.**

| | | | | |
|---|---|---|---|---|
| 562-565 | A100 | Set of 4 | 5.25 | 2.75 |
| 563a | | Booklet pane of 2, #562-563 | 2.00 | — |
| 565a | | Booklet pane of 2, #564-565 | 3.25 | — |

**Souvenir Sheets**

| | | | | |
|---|---|---|---|---|
| 566-567 | A100 | Set of 2 | 6.00 | 3.50 |
| 566a | | Booklet pane of 1 | 2.00 | — |
| 567a | | Booklet pane of 1 | 4.00 | — |
| | | Complete booklet, #560a, 561b, 563a, 565a, 566a, 567a | 16.00 | |

Nos. 566-567 each contain one 80x30mm stamp.

Booklet panes are separated from binding stub at left by a row of rouletting. Complete booklet also contains a pane of 4 progressive proofs of No. 560. These were not valid for postage.

**Figurines Type of Portugal of 2015**

***Perf. 12x11¾ Syncopated***

**2015, Apr. 21** **Litho.**

| | | | | |
|---|---|---|---|---|
| 568 | A1007 | 80c Azores figurines | 1.60 | .80 |
| a. | | Booklet pane of 1 | 1.60 | — |

Issued: No. 568a, 10/19.

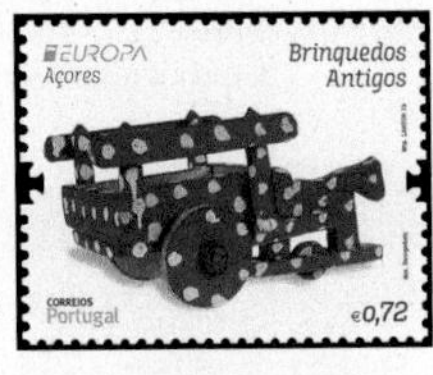


Europa A101

Old toys: No. 569, Horse-drawn cart. No. 570a, Stove.

***Perf. 12x11¾ Syncopated***

**2015, May 8** **Litho.**

| | | | | |
|---|---|---|---|---|
| 569 | A101 | 72c multi | 1.60 | .80 |
| a. | | Booklet pane of 1 | 1.60 | — |

**Souvenir Sheet**

| | | | |
|---|---|---|---|
| 570 | Sheet of 2, #569, 570a | 3.25 | 1.60 |
| a. | A101 72c multi | 1.60 | .80 |
| b. | Booklet pane of 2, #569, 570a | 3.25 | — |

Issued: No. 569a, 570b, 10/19. Booklet panes are separated from binding stub at left by a row of rouletting.

Handicrafts A102

Designs: 45c, Ceramics. 72c, Weaving. 80c, Woodworking. €1, Lace.

€1.80, Plant fiber items. €2, Embroidery.

***Perf. 11¾x12 Syncopated***

**2015, May 8** **Litho.**

| | | | | |
|---|---|---|---|---|
| 571-574 | A102 | Set of 4 | 6.50 | 3.25 |
| 572a | | Booklet pane of 2, #571-572 | 2.50 | — |
| 574a | | Booklet pane of 2, #573, 574 | 4.00 | — |

**Souvenir Sheets**

| | | | | |
|---|---|---|---|---|
| 575-576 | A102 | Set of 2 | 8.50 | 4.25 |
| 575a | | Booklet pane of 1 | 4.00 | — |
| 576a | | Booklet pane of 1 | 4.50 | — |
| | | Complete booklet, #568a, 569a, 570b, 572a, 574a, 575a, 576a | 22.00 | |

Issued: No. 572a, 574a, 575a, 576a, 10/19. Booklet panes are separated from binding stub at left by a row of rouletting. Complete booklet contains a pane of four imperforate progressive proofs of No. 569. These were not valid for postage.

See No. 611.

**Types of 2011-13**

***Die Cut Perf. 10½***

**2015, Oct. 23** **Litho.**

**Self-Adhesive**

| | | | | |
|---|---|---|---|---|
| 577 | A93 | E Like #536 | 1.60 | .80 |
| 578 | A95 | E Like #544 | 1.60 | .80 |
| 579 | A96 | E Like #547 | 1.60 | .80 |
| 580 | A98 | E Like #555 | 1.60 | .80 |
| | | *Nos. 577-580 (4)* | 6.40 | 3.20 |

Nos. 577-580 each sold for 72c on day of issue.

Europa A103

Designs: No. 581, Bicyclist, buildings, wind generators.

No. 582a, Hikers, whale, sailboats.

***Perf. 12x11¾ Syncopated***

**2016, May 9** **Litho.**

| | | | |
|---|---|---|---|
| 581 | A103 75c multi | 1.75 | .85 |

**Souvenir Sheet**

| | | | |
|---|---|---|---|
| 582 | Sheet of 2, #581, 582a | 3.50 | 1.75 |
| a. | A103 75c multi | 1.75 | .85 |

Think Green Issue.

Activities in Natural Settings A104

Designs: 47c, Bird watching. 75c, Whale watching. 80c, Canyoning. €1, Surfing.

No. 587, €1.80, Walking tours. No. 588, €1.80, Diving.

***Perf. 12x11¾ Syncopated***

**2016, May 16** **Litho.**

| | | | | |
|---|---|---|---|---|
| 583-586 | A104 | Set of 4 | 6.75 | 3.50 |

**Souvenir Sheets**

| | | | | |
|---|---|---|---|---|
| 587-588 | A104 | Set of 2 | 8.00 | 4.00 |

See No. 612.

Europa A105

Designs: No. 589, St. John the Baptist Fortress, Pico. No. 590a, Sao Brás Fort, Ponta Delgada.

***Perf. 12x11¾ Syncopated***

**2017, May 9** **Litho.**

| | | | |
|---|---|---|---|
| 589 | A105 80c multi | 1.75 | .90 |

**Souvenir Sheet**

| | | | |
|---|---|---|---|
| 590 | Sheet of 2, #589, 590a | 3.50 | 1.80 |
| a. | A105 80c multi | 1.75 | .90 |

Azores Geopark — A106

Natural feature and map of: 50c, Furnas Caldera, Sao Miguel Island. 80c, Capelinhos Volcano, Faial Island. No. 593, 85c, Mount Pico, Pico Island. No. 594, €1, Faja Grande and Fajazinha, Flores Island.

No. 595: a, 85c, Algar do Carvao, Terceira Island. b, €1, Caldera and Furna do Enxofre, Graciosa Island

***Perf. 11¾x12 Syncopated***

**2017, Sept. 7** **Litho.**

| | | | | |
|---|---|---|---|---|
| 591-594 | A106 | Set of 4 | 7.50 | 3.75 |

**Souvenir Sheet**

| | | | |
|---|---|---|---|
| 595 | Sheet of 2 | 4.50 | 2.25 |
| a. | A106 85c multi | 2.00 | 1.00 |
| b. | A106 €1 multi | 2.40 | 1.25 |

Europa A107

Designs: No. 596, Despe-te-que-suas Bridge, Nordeste. No. 597a, 8 Arches Bridge, Ribeira Grande.

***Perf. 12x11¾ Syncopated***

**2018, May 9** **Litho.**

| | | | |
|---|---|---|---|
| 596 | A107 E multi | 2.00 | 1.00 |

**Souvenir Sheet**

| | | | |
|---|---|---|---|
| 597 | Sheet of 2, #596, 597a | 4.00 | 2.00 |
| a. | A107 E multi | 2.00 | 1.00 |

On day of issue, Nos. 596 and 597a each sold for 86c.

Peter Café Sport, Horta, Cent. — A108

Designs: No. 598, 53c, Café entrance. No. 599, 53c, Café interior. 86c, Host behind counter. 91c, Café's scrimshaw museum. €1.50, Café exterior.

*Perf. 11¾x12 Syncopated*

**2018, June 18 Litho.**
598-601 A108 Set of 4 6.75 3.50

**Souvenir Sheet**

602 A108 €1.50 multi 3.50 1.75

No. 602 contains one 30x80mm stamp. Nos. 598-602 are not inscribed "Açores."
See No. 613.

Europa A109

Designs: No. 603, Regulus regulus azoricus. No. 604a, Turdus pilaris.

*Perf. 12x11¾ Syncopated*

**2019, May 9 Litho.**
603 A109 86c multi 2.00 1.00

**Souvenir Sheet**

604 Sheet of 2, #603, 604a 4.00 4.00
a. A109 86c multi 2.00 1.00

Tea Cultivation A110

Designs: 53c, Tea picker and blossom. 86c, Basket for tea leaves, machinery. 91c, Tea sorter and tea pot.
€2, Tea pickers, woman drinking tea, tea plantation.

*Perf. 12x11¾ Syncopated*

**2019, June 27 Litho.**
605-607 A110 Set of 3 5.25 2.60

**Souvenir Sheet**

608 A110 €2 multi 4.50 4.50

No. 608 contains one 80x30mm stamp.

**Fruits Type of Portugal of 2017**

*Die Cut Perf. 10½*

**2020, May 21 Litho.**

**Self-Adhesive**

609 A1059 E Like #3885 1.90 .95

No. 609 sold for 86c on day of issue.

**Types of Azores, 2014-18**

*Die Cut Perf. 10½*

**2020, May 21 Litho.**

**Self-Adhesive**

610 A99 E Like #560 1.90 .95
611 A102 E Like #571 1.90 .95
612 A104 E Like #584 1.90 .95
613 A108 E Like #598 1.90 .95
*Nos. 610-613 (4)* 7.60 3.80

No. 613 is not inscribed "Açores." Nos. 610-613 each sold for 86c on day of issue.

Europa A111

Designs: No. 614, Postcards and hand canceling devices. No. 615a, Postal workers with mail bags, ships, airplane and truck.

*Perf. 12x11¾ Syncopated*

**2020, May 25 Litho.**
614 A111 86c multi 1.90 .95

**Souvenir Sheet**

615 Sheet of 2, #614, 615a 3.80 3.80
a. A111 86c multi 1.90 .95

Ancient Postal Routes.

Divine Holy Spirit Festival A112

Designs: N, Church, distribution of bread loaves. E, Men with flag, festival marchers. I, Priest and woman near food table, soup bowls.
€2.50, Church and shrine.

*Perf. 12x11¾ Syncopated*

**2020, July 30 Litho.**
616-618 A112 Set of 3 5.50 2.75

**Souvenir Sheet**

619 A112 €2.50 multi 6.00 6.00

Europa A113

Endangered animals: No. 620, Balaenoptera musculus. No. 621a, Nyctalus azoreum.

*Perf. 12x11¾ Syncopated*

**2021, May 7 Litho.**
620 A113 88c multi 2.25 1.10

**Souvenir Sheet**

621 Sheet of 2, #620, 621a 4.50 4.50
a. A113 88c multi 2.25 1.10

Battle of Salga, 440th Anniv. A114

Designs: 54c, Battleships. 88c, Woman watching building burn. 91c, Cattle stampede.
€2.50, Ships near shore.

*Perf. 12x11¾ Syncopated*

**2021, July 25 Litho.**
622-624 A114 Set of 3 5.50 2.75

**Souvenir Sheet**

625 A114 €2.50 multi 6.00 6.00

No. 625 contains one 80x30mm stamp.

---

## MADEIRA

**Type of Azores, 1980**

6.50e, Madeira #2. 19.50e, Madeira #5.

**1980, Jan. 2 Litho. *Perf. 12***
66 A33 6.50e multi .25 .25
67 A33 19.50e multi .85 .55
a. Souvenir sheet of 2, #66-67 3.25 3.25

No. 67a exists overprinted for Capex 87.

Grapes and Wine — A7

**1980, Sept. 17 Litho. *Perf. 12x11½***
68 A7 50c Bullock cart .25 .25
69 A7 1e shown .25 .25
70 A7 5e Produce map of Madeira .40 .25
71 A7 6.50e Basket and lace .50 .25
72 A7 8e Orchid .80 .25
73 A7 30e Madeira boat 1.60 .45
*Nos. 68-73 (6)* 3.80 1.70

World Tourism Conf., Manila, Sept. 27.

**Europa Issue**

O Bailinho Folk Dance A8

**1981, May 11 Litho. *Perf. 12***
74 A8 22e multi 1.25 .65
a. Souvenir sheet of 2 3.75 1.50

Explorer Ship — A9

**1981, July 1 Litho. *Perf. 12x11½***
75 A9 8.50e shown .45 .25
76 A9 33.50e Map 1.60 .55

Discovery of Madeira anniv.

A10

Designs: Local flora.

**1981, Oct. 6 Litho. *Perf. 12½x12***
77 A10 7e Dactylorhiza foliosa .30 .25
78 A10 8.50e Echium candicans .35 .25
79 A10 20e Geranium maderense .65 .35
80 A10 50e Isoplexis sceptrum 1.40 .75
a. Booklet pane of 4, #77-80 6.00
*Nos. 77-80 (4)* 2.70 1.60

See Nos. 82-85, 90-93.

**Europa Type of Portugal**

**1982, May 3 Litho. *Perf. 12x11½***
81 A405 33.50e Sugar mills, 15th cent. 1.50 .65
a. Souvenir sheet of 3 18.00 3.00

**Type of 1981**

9e, Goodyera macrophylla. 10e, Armeria maderensis. 27e, Viola paradoxa. 33.50e, Scilla maderensis.

**1982, Aug. 31 Litho. *Perf. 12½x12***
82 A10 9e multicolored .40 .25
83 A10 10e multicolored .45 .25
84 A10 27e multicolored 1.10 .50
85 A10 33.50e multicolored 1.10 .70
a. Booklet pane of 4, #82-85 6.00
*Nos. 82-85 (4)* 3.05 1.70

A12

**1982, Dec. 15 Litho. *Perf. 13½***
86 A12 27e Brinco dancing dolls 1.25 .60
87 A12 33.50e Dancers 1.75 .80

Europa 1983 A13

**1983, May 5 Litho. *Perf. 12½***
88 A13 37.50e Levadas irrigation system 1.50 .50
a. Souvenir sheet of 3 5.00 3.00

Flag of the Autonomous Region — A14

**1983, July 1 Litho. *Perf. 12x11½***
89 A14 12.50e multi .95 .25

**Flower Type of 1981**

**1983, Oct. 19 Litho. *Perf. 12½x12***
90 A10 12.50e Matthiola maderensis .25 .25
91 A10 30e Erica maderensis .75 .35
92 A10 37.50e Cirsium latifolium 1.00 .60
93 A10 100e Clethra arborea 2.10 .90
a. Booklet pane of 4, #90-93 6.00
*Nos. 90-93 (4)* 4.10 2.10

**Europa Type of Portugal**

**1984, May 2 Litho. *Perf. 12x11½***
94 A427 51e multi 1.50 .75
a. Souvenir sheet of 3 5.00 3.00

Madeira Rally (Auto Race), 25th Anniv. — A16

Various cars.

**1984, Aug. 3 Litho. *Perf. 11½x12***
95 A16 16e multicolored .60 .25
96 A16 51e multicolored 2.00 1.25

Traditional Means of Transportation — A17

**1984, Nov. 22 *Perf. 12***
97 A17 16e Mountain sledge .35 .25
98 A17 35e Hammock .90 .50
99 A17 40e Winebag carriers' procession 1.25 .50
100 A17 51e Carreira Boat 1.60 .65
a. Booklet pane of 4, Nos. 97-100 9.00
*Nos. 97-100 (4)* 4.10 1.90

See Nos. 104-107.

**Europa Type of Portugal**

**1985, May 6 Litho. *Perf. 11½x12***
101 A435 60e Man playing guitar 1.90 .80
a. Souvenir sheet of 3 6.00 3.50

Marine Life — A19

**1985, July 5 Litho. *Perf. 12***
102 A19 40e Aphanopus carbo 1.25 .60
103 A19 60e Lampris guttatus 1.75 .90

See Nos. 108-109.

### Transportation type of 1984

**1985, Sept. 11 Litho. *Perf. 12x11½***
104 A17 20e Ox-drawn sledge .35 .25
105 A17 40e Mountain train 1.00 .50
106 A17 46e Fish vendors 1.40 .80
107 A17 60e Coastal steamer 1.60 .80
*a.* Booklet pane of 4, Nos. 104-107 5.00
*Nos. 104-107 (4)* 4.35 2.35

### Marine Life Type of 1985

**1986, Jan. 7 Litho.**
108 A19 20e Thunnus obesus .65 .25
109 A19 75e Beryx decadactylus 3.00 .90

### Europa Type of Portugal

**1986, May 5 Litho.**
110 A447 68.50e Great Shear-water *2.75 .90*
*a.* Souvenir sheet of 3 *9.00 3.50*

Forts in Funchal and Machico A21

22.50e, Sao Lourenco, 1583. 52.50e, Sao Joao do Pico, 1611. 68.50e, Sao Tiago, 1614. 100e, Sao do Amparo, 1706.

**1986, July 1 Litho. *Perf. 12***
111 A21 22.50e multi .50 .25
112 A21 52.50e multi 1.50 .70
113 A21 68.50e multi 2.25 .90
114 A21 100e multi 3.00 .75
*a.* Booklet pane of 4, #111-114 7.50
*Nos. 111-114 (4)* 7.25 2.60

A22

Indigenous birds: 25e, Regulus ignicapillus madeirensis. 57e, Columba trocaz. 74.50e, Tyto alba schmitzi. 125e, Pterodroma madeira.

**1987, Mar. 6 Litho.**
115 A22 25e multi .55 .25
116 A22 57e multi 1.60 .80
117 A22 74.50e multi 2.40 1.20
118 A22 125e multi 3.00 1.25
*a.* Booklet pane of 4, #115-118 11.00
*Nos. 115-118 (4)* 7.55 3.50

See Nos. 123-126.

### Europa Type of Portugal

Modern Architecture: Social Services Center, Funchal, designed by Raul Chorao Ramalho.

**1987, May 5 Litho. *Perf. 12***
119 A456 74.50e multicolored *1.50 .75*
*a.* Souvenir sheet of 4 *6.00 4.00*

A24

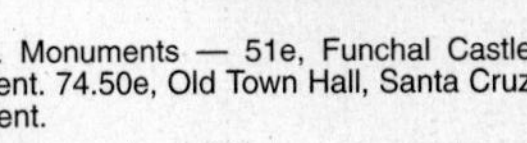
Natl. Monuments — 51e, Funchal Castle, 15th cent. 74.50e, Old Town Hall, Santa Cruz, 16th cent.

**1987, July 1 *Perf. 12x12½***
120 A24 51e multi 1.40 .70
121 A24 74.50e multi 1.75 .70

### Europa Type of Portugal

Transportation Modern mail boat PS 13 TL.

**1988, Apr. 21 Litho. *Perf. 12***
122 A466 80e multicolored *4.00 1.20*
*a.* Souvenir sheet of 4 *10.00 4.00*

### Bird Type of 1987

**1988, June 15 Litho.**
123 A22 27e Erithacus rubecula .45 .25
124 A22 60e Petronia 1.40 .75
125 A22 80e Fringilla coelebs 2.00 .80
126 A22 100e Accipiter nisus 2.25 .80
*a.* Booklet pane of 4, #123-126 6.25
*Nos. 123-126 (4)* 6.10 2.60

Portraits of Christopher Columbus and Purported Residences on Madeira A27

55e, Funchal, 1480-1481, vert. 80e, Porto Santo.

**1988, July 1 Litho.**
127 A27 55e multicolored 1.60 .80
128 A27 80e multicolored 2.00 1.00

### Europa Type of Portugal

Children's toys.

**1989, Apr. 26 Litho.**
129 A476 80e Kite *2.50 .80*

### Souvenir Sheet

130 Sheet, 2 each #129, 130a *10.00 4.50*
*a.* A476 80e Kite, diff. *2.50 1.25*

Monuments A29

Churches: 29e, Church of the Colegio (St. John the Evangelist Church). 87e, Santa Clara Church and convent.

**1989, July 28 Litho.**
131 A29 29e multi .45 .25
132 A29 87e multi 1.90 .90

Fish — A30

29e, Argyropelecus aculeatus. 60e, Pseudolepidaplois scrofa. 87e, Coris julis. 100e, Scorpaena maderensis.

**1989, Sept. 20 Litho.**
133 A30 29e multi .45 .25
134 A30 60e multi 1.25 .65
135 A30 87e multi 2.00 .85
136 A30 100e multi 2.00 1.25
*a.* Booklet pane of 4, #133-136 6.00
*Nos. 133-136 (4)* 5.70 3.00

### Europa Type of Portugal

**1990, Apr. 11 Litho. *Perf. 12x11½***
137 A486 80e Zarco P.O. *1.50 .55*

### Souvenir Sheet

138 Sheet, 2 ea #137, 138a *7.50 4.00*
*a.* A486 80e Porto da Cruz P.O. *1.50 1.40*

Subtropical Fruits and Plants — A32

**1990, June 5 Litho. *Perf. 12***
139 A32 5e Banana .25 .25
140 A32 32e Avocado .45 .25
141 A32 60e Sugar apple 1.25 .55
142 A32 100e Passion fruit 1.90 .85
*Nos. 139-142 (4)* 3.85 1.90

***Perf. 13½ Vert.***
*139a* A32 5e 1.50 1.50
*140a* A32 32e 1.50 1.50
*141a* A32 60e 1.50 1.50
*142a* A32 100e 1.50 1.50
*b.* Bklt. pane of 4, #139a-142a 6.00

See Nos. 153-160.

Boats of Madeira A33

**1990, Aug. 24 *Perf. 12***
143 A33 32e Tuna .45 .25
144 A33 60e Desert islands 1.10 .60
145 A33 70e Maneiro 1.40 .65
146 A33 95e Chavelha 2.00 1.20
*Nos. 143-146 (4)* 4.95 2.70

See Nos. 162-165.

Columba Trocaz Heineken — A34

**1991, Jan. 23 Litho. *Perf. 12***
147 35e shown .90 .40
148 35e On branch .90 .40
149 35e In flight .90 .40
150 35e On nest .90 .40
*a.* A34 Strip of 4, #147-150 4.00 4.00

Europa A35

**1991, Apr. 11 Litho. *Perf. 12***
151 A35 80e ERS-1 *1.25 .75*

### Souvenir Sheet

152 Sheet, 2 each #151, 152a *10.00 5.00*
*a.* A35 80e SPOT *2.25 1.75*

### Subtropical Fruits Type of 1990

**1991, June 7 Litho. *Perf. 12***
153 A32 35e Mango .50 .25
154 A32 65e Surinam cherry 1.10 .55
155 A32 70e Brazilian guava 1.25 .60
156 A32 110e Papaya 1.90 .95
*Nos. 153-156 (4)* 4.75 2.35

***Perf. 13½ Vert.***
*153a* A32 35e 1.10 1.10
*154a* A32 65e 1.10 1.10
*155a* A32 70e 1.10 1.10
*156a* A32 110e 1.10 1.10
*b.* Bklt. pane of 4, #153a-156a 5.00

**1992, Feb. 21 Litho. *Perf. 11½x12***
157 A32 10e Prickly pear .25 .25
158 A32 38e Tree tomato .55 .30
159 A32 85e Ceriman 1.50 .75
160 A32 125e Guava 2.00 1.00
*Nos. 157-160 (4)* 4.30 2.30

***Perf. 13½ Vert.***
*157a* A32 10e .25 .25
*158a* A32 38e .45 .25
*159a* A32 85e 1.30 .65
*160a* A32 125e 1.90 .95
*b.* Bklt. pane of 4, #157a-160a 5.00

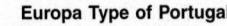

### Europa Type of Portugal

Europa: 85e, Columbus at Funchal.

**1992, May 22 Litho. *Perf. 12x11½***
161 A514 85e gold & multi *2.50 .70*

### Ships Type of 1990

**1992, Sept. 18 Litho. *Perf. 12x11½***
162 A33 38e Gaviao .50 .25
163 A33 65e Independencia 1.00 .50
164 A33 85e Madeirense 1.25 .70
165 A33 120e Funchalense 1.75 1.00
*Nos. 162-165 (4)* 4.50 2.45

Contemporary Paintings by Lourdes Castro — A36

Europa: No. 166, Shadow Projection of Christa Maar, 1968. No. 167a, Shadow Projection of a Dahlia, c. 1970.

**1993, May 5 Litho. *Perf. 11½x12***
166 A36 90e multicolored *1.25 .60*

### Souvenir Sheet

167 Sheet, 2 each #166, 167a *6.00 4.00*
*a.* A36 90e multicolored *1.25 .60*

Nature Preservation — A37

Monachus monachus: No. 168, Adult on rock. No. 169, Swimming. No. 170, Mother nursing pup. No. 171, Two on rocks.

**1993, June 30 Litho. *Perf. 12x11½***
168 42e multicolored .75 .50
169 42e multicolored .75 .50
170 42e multicolored .75 .50
171 42e multicolored .75 .50
*a.* A37 Strip of 4, #168-171 4.00 3.00

Architecture A38

Designs: 42e, Window from Sao Francisco Convent, Funchal. 130e, Window of Mercy (Old Hospital), Funchal.

**1993, July 30 *Perf. 11½x12***
172 A38 42e multicolored .60 .25
173 A38 130e multicolored 1.90 .80

### Europa Type of Portugal

Discoveries: No. 174, Native with bow and arrows. No. 175a, Palm tree.

**1994, May 5 Litho. *Perf. 12***
174 A541 100e multicolored *1.25 .60*

### Souvenir Sheet

175 Sheet, 2 each, #174-175a *6.00 4.00*
*a.* A541 100e multicolored *1.25 .60*

Native Handicrafts A39

**1994, May 5 *Perf. 12x11½***
176 A39 45e Embroidery .55 .30
177 A39 75e Tapestry .90 .45
178 A39 100e Shoes 1.25 .60
179 A39 140e Wicker work 1.60 .85
*Nos. 176-179 (4)* 4.30 2.20

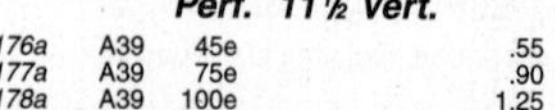

***Perf. 11½ Vert.***

| | | | | |
|---|---|---|---|---|
| *176a* | A39 | 45e | .55 | .30 |
| *177a* | A39 | 75e | .90 | .45 |
| *178a* | A39 | 100e | 1.25 | .60 |
| *179a* | A39 | 140e | 1.60 | .85 |
| *b.* | Bklt. pane of 4, #176a-179a | | 6.00 | |

Arms of Madeira Districts — A40

**1994, July 1 Litho. *Perf. 11½x12***

**180** A40 45e Funchal .55 .30
**181** A40 140e Porto Santo 1.90 .95

Traditional Arts & Crafts — A41

Designs: 45e, Chicken puppets made of flour paste. 80e, Inlaid wood furniture piece. 95e, Wicker bird cage. 135e, Knitted wool bonnet.

**1995, June 30 Litho. *Perf. 11½x12***

| | | | | |
|---|---|---|---|---|
| **182** A41 | 45e multicolored | | .55 | .30 |
| **183** A41 | 80e multicolored | | 1.00 | .50 |
| **184** A41 | 95e multicolored | | 1.10 | .65 |
| **185** A41 | 135e multicolored | | 1.50 | .95 |
| | *Nos. 182-185 (4)* | | 4.15 | 2.40 |

***Perf. 11½ Vert.***

| | | | | |
|---|---|---|---|---|
| *182a* | A41 | 45e | .55 | .30 |
| *183a* | A41 | 80e | 1.00 | .50 |
| *184a* | A41 | 95e | 1.10 | .65 |
| *185a* | A41 | 135e | 1.50 | .95 |
| *b.* | Booklet pane, #182a-185a | | 5.00 | |
| | Complete booklet, #185b | | 5.00 | |

**Famous Woman Type of Azores, 1996**

Europa: Guiomar Vilhena (1705-89), entrepeneur.

**1996, May 3 Litho. *Perf. 12***

**186** A69 98e multicolored *1.25 .60*
*a.* Souvenir sheet of 3 *3.75 1.90*

Paintings from Flemish Group, Museum of Sacred Paintings of Funchal (Madeira) A42

Designs: 47e, The Adoration of the Magi, vert. 78e, St. Mary Magdalene, vert. 98e, Annunciation. 140e, St. Peter, St. Paul and St. Andrew.

***Perf. 11½x12, 12x11½***

**1996, July 1 Litho.**

| | | | |
|---|---|---|---|
| **187** A42 | 47e multicolored | .50 | .30 |
| **188** A42 | 78e multicolored | .90 | .50 |
| **189** A42 | 98e multicolored | 1.10 | .65 |
| **190** A42 | 140e multicolored | 1.40 | .90 |
| | *Nos. 187-190 (4)* | 3.90 | 2.35 |

***Perf. 11½ on 2 Sides***

| | | | | |
|---|---|---|---|---|
| *187a* | A42 | 47e | .50 | .30 |
| *188a* | A42 | 78e | .90 | .50 |
| *189a* | A42 | 98e | 1.00 | .65 |
| *190a* | A42 | 140e | 1.40 | .90 |
| *b.* | Booklet pane, #187a-190a | | 4.50 | |
| | Complete booklet, #190b | | 5.00 | |

Moths & Butterflies A43

Designs: 49e, Eumichtis albostigmata. 80e, Menophra maderae. 100e, Vanessa indica vulcania. 140e, Pieris brassicae wollastoni.

**1997, Feb. 12 Litho. *Perf. 12***

| | | | |
|---|---|---|---|
| **191** A43 | 49e multicolored | .55 | .30 |
| **192** A43 | 80e multicolored | 1.00 | .45 |
| **193** A43 | 100e multicolored | 1.10 | .60 |
| **194** A43 | 140e multicolored | 2.40 | 1.25 |
| | *Nos. 191-194 (4)* | 5.05 | 2.60 |

***Perf. 11½ Vert.***

| | | | | |
|---|---|---|---|---|
| *191a* | A43 | 49e multicolored | .55 | .30 |
| *192a* | A43 | 80e multicolored | 1.00 | .45 |
| *193a* | A43 | 100e multicolored | 1.10 | .60 |
| *194a* | A43 | 140e multicolored | 2.40 | .80 |
| *b.* | Booklet pane, #191a-194a | | 6.00 | |
| | Complete booklet, #194b | | 6.50 | |

See Nos. 197-200.

**Stories and Legends Type of Portugal**

Europa: Man holding woman from "Legend of Machico," horiz.

**1997, May 5 Litho. *Perf. 12***

**195** A599 100e multicolored *1.25 .55*
*a.* Souvenir sheet of 3 *5.00 3.00*

**Natl. Festivals Type of Portugal**

**1998, May 21 Litho. *Perf. 12***

**196** A621 100e New Year's Eve *1.25 .55*
*a.* Souvenir sheet of 3 *5.00 3.00*

Europa.

**Moths and Butterflies Type of 1997**

Designs: 50e, Gonepteryx cleopatra. 85e, Xanthorhoe rupicola. 100e, Noctua teixeirai. 140e, Xenochlorodes nubigena.

**1998, Sept. 6 Litho. *Perf. 12***

| | | | |
|---|---|---|---|
| **197** A43 | 50e multicolored | .60 | .30 |
| **198** A43 | 85e multicolored | 1.00 | .45 |
| **199** A43 | 100e multicolored | 1.25 | .55 |
| **200** A43 | 140e multicolored | 1.60 | .80 |
| *a.* | Booklet pane, #197-200, perf. 12 vert. | 6.00 | |
| | Complete booklet, #200a | 6.00 | |
| | *Nos. 197-200 (4)* | 4.45 | 2.10 |

**Europa Type of Portugal**

100e, Flowers, Madeira Island Natural Park.

**1999, May 5 Litho. *Perf. 12x11¾***

**201** A641 100e multi *1.25 .50*
*a.* Souvenir sheet of 3 *3.75 3.75*

Glazed Tiles From Frederico de Freitas Museum, Funchal A44

Designs: 51e, Griffin, from Middle East, 13th-14th cent. 80e, Flower, from England, 19th-20th cent. 95e, Bird, from Persia, 14th cent. 100e, Geometric, from Moorish Spain, 13th cent. 140e, Ship, from Holland, 18th cent. 210e, Flowers from Syria, 13th-14th cent.

**1999, July 1**

| | | | |
|---|---|---|---|
| **202** A44 | 51e multicolored | .55 | .25 |
| **203** A44 | 80e multicolored | .85 | .40 |
| **204** A44 | 95e multicolored | 1.10 | .50 |
| **205** A44 | 100e multicolored | 1.10 | .50 |
| **206** A44 | 140e multicolored | 1.50 | .75 |
| **207** A44 | 210e multicolored | 2.10 | 1.10 |
| *a.* | Souvenir sheet of 6, #202-207 | 8.00 | 8.00 |
| | *Nos. 202-207 (6)* | 7.20 | 3.50 |

**Europa Issue**

Common Design Type

**2000, May 9 *Perf. 11¾x12***

**208** CD17 100e multi *1.25 .50*
*a.* Souvenir sheet of 3 *3.75 3.75*

Plants from Laurissilva Forest A45

52e, Purple orchid. 85e, White orchid. No. 211, 100e, Folhado. No. 212, 100e, Laurel tree. 140e, Barbusano. 350e, Visco.

**2000, July 4 Litho. *Perf. 12x11¾***

**209-214** A45 Set of 6 9.00 4.00
*214a* Souvenir sheet, #209-214 9.00 9.00

Expansion of Madeira Airport A46

**2000, Sept. 15**

**215** A46 140e multi 2.00 1.00
*a.* Souvenir sheet of 1 2.50 1.50

**Europa Type of Portugal**

**2001, May 9 Litho. *Perf. 12x11¾***

**216** A677 105e Signals *1.25 .45*
*a.* Souvenir sheet of 3 *5.00 3.75*

Scenes of Traditional Life — A47

Designs: 53e, People retruning home. 85e, On the road to the marketplace. 105e, Traditional clothes.
350e, Leisure time.

**2001, July 19 Litho. *Perf. 12x11¾***

**217-219** A47 Set of 3 3.00 1.10

**Souvenir Sheet**

**220** A47 350e multi 3.75 3.75

**Europa Type of Portugal**

**2002, May 9 Litho. *Perf. 12x11¾***

**221** A695 54c Clown, diff. *1.25 .50*
*a.* Souvenir sheet of 3, perf. 12½ *5.00 3.00*

Worldwide Fund for Nature (WWF) — A48

Streptopelia turtur: a, On nest with chicks. b, On branch, with wings extended. c, Pair on branch. d, One on branch.

**2002, Aug. 30 Litho. *Perf. 11¾x12***

**222** A48 28c Horiz. strip or block of 4, #a.-d. 4.50 2.50

**Europa Type of Portugal**

Design: Poster art by José Brandao, 1992.

**2003, May 5 Litho. *Perf. 12x12½***

**223** A707 55c multi *1.25 .65*
*a.* Souvenir sheet of 2 *2.50 2.50*

Items in Madeira Museums A49

Designs: 30c, Funchal Bay, by W. G. James. 43c, Creche, by Manuel Orlando Noronha Gois. 55c, O Largo da Fonte, by Andrew Picken. 70c, Le Depart, by Martha Teles.

No. 228: a, €1, Photograph of Vicente Gomes da Silva. b, €2, Photograph of Jorge Bettencourt.

**2003, Aug. 30 Litho. *Perf. 12x11¾***

**224-227** A49 Set of 4 4.50 2.25

**Souvenir Sheet**

**228** A49 Sheet of 2, #a-b 6.75 6.75

**Europa Type of Portugal**

Design: Hiker in flower garden.

**2004, May 10 Litho. *Perf. 13¼x14***

**229** A734 56c multi *1.40 .70*
*a.* Souvenir sheet of 2 *2.80 2.80*

Flora and Fauna of the Selvagens Islands A50

Designs: 30c, Pelagodroma marina hypoleuca. 45c, Monanthes lowei. 72c, Tarentola bischoffi.

**2004, May 24 *Perf. 13x13¼***

**230-232** A50 Set of 3 3.50 1.75
*232a* Souvenir sheet, #230-232 3.50 3.50

**Europa Type of Portugal**

Designs: No. 233, Espetada em pau de louro. No. 234a, Filete de espada (Scabbard fish filet).

**2005, May 5 *Perf. 14x13¼***

**233** A752 57c multi *1.50 .75*

**Souvenir Sheet**

**234** Sheet of 2 #234a *3.00 3.00*
*a.* A752 57c multi *1.50 1.50*

Tourism A51

Designs: No. 235, 30c, Coastal village, offshore rocks, flowers. No. 236, 30c, Flowers, bird, waterfall. No. 237, 45c, Man and woman on footpath, golf course. No. 238, 45c, Windmill on beach. 57c, Horses and riders, scuba diver. 74c, Flowers, fireworks.

No. 241: a, 30c, Wicker chair, girls with flower baskets, lace. b, €1.55, Lace, clock tower.

**2005, July 1 Litho. *Perf. 14x13¼***

**235-240** A51 Set of 6 6.75 3.50

**Souvenir Sheet**

**241** A51 Sheet of 2, #a-b 4.50 4.50

Flowers A52

Designs: 30c, Euphorbia pulcherrima. No. 243, 45c, Aloe arborescens. 57c, Senna didymobotrya. 74c, Anthurium andraeanum. €1, Strelitzia reginae. €2, Hydrangea macrophylla.

No. 248, 45c: a, Rosa cultivar. b, Leucospermum nutans. c, Paphiopedilum insigne. d, Hippeastrum vittatum.

No. 249, 45c: a, Bougainvillea cultivar. b, Cymbidium cultivar. c, Hibiscus rosa-sinensis. d, Erythrina crista-galli.

**2006, Mar. 7 Litho. *Perf. 12x11¾***

| | | | |
|---|---|---|---|
| **242-247** A52 | Set of 6 | 11.00 | 5.00 |
| *243a* | Booklet pane of 2, #242-243 | 1.50 | — |
| *245a* | Booklet pane of 2, #244-245 | 2.50 | — |
| *247a* | Booklet pane of 2, #246-247 | 7.00 | — |

**Souvenir Sheets**

| | | | |
|---|---|---|---|
| **248** | Sheet of 4 | 4.00 | 4.50 |
| *a.-d.* | A52 45c Any single | 1.00 | .55 |
| *e.* | Booklet pane of 4, #248a-248d | 4.00 | — |
| **249** | Sheet of 4 | 4.00 | 4.50 |
| *a.-d.* | A52 45c Any single | 1.00 | .55 |
| *e.* | Booklet pane of 4, #249a-249d | 4.00 | — |

Booklet panes are separated from binding stub at left by row of rouletting.

Europa
A53

No. 251 — Children's drawings: a, Children in swimming pool. b, Boy walking dog.

**2006, May 9 Litho. *Perf. 12x12½***

**250** A53 60c shown 1.50 .75
*a.* Booklet pane of 1, perf. 12x11¾ 1.50 —

**Souvenir Sheet**

***Perf. 12x11¾***

**251** A53 60c Sheet of 2, #a-b 3.25 3.25
*c.* Booklet pane of 2, #251a-251b 3.25 —

Booklet panes are separated from binding stub at left by row of rouletting.

Wines of Madeira A54

Designs: 30c, Wine bottles, terraces. 52c, Bottles, grape harvesters. No. 254, 60c, Bottles, barrels in cellar. No. 255, 75c, Bottles, barrels, wine glass.

No. 256: a, 45c, Vineyards. b, 60c, Grape harvester, grape masher. c, 75c, Bottles. d, €1, Bottles, barrels, grapes.

**2006, July 1 *Perf. 12½x13***

**252-255** A54 Set of 4 5.00 2.50
*253a* Booklet pane of 2, #252-253 1.75 —
*255a* Booklet pane of 2, #254-255 3.25 —

**Souvenir Sheet**

**256** A54 Sheet of 4, #a-d 6.00 6.00
*e.* Booklet pane of 4, #256a-256d 6.00 —
Complete booklet, #243a, 245a, 247a, 248e, 249e, 250a, 251c, 253a, 255a, 256e 35.00

Booklet panes are separated from binding stub at left by row of rouletting. Complete booklet also contains a pane of four progressive proofs of No. 250. These were not valid for postage.

Marine Creatures A55

Designs: 30c Monachus monachus. 45c, Caretta caretta. No. 259, 61c, Calonectris diomedea borealis. 75c, Aphanopus carbo.

No. 261, 61c: a, Telmatactis cricoides. b, Charonia lampas. c, Patella aspera. d, Sparisoma cretense.

**2007, Apr. 17 Litho. *Perf. 12½x13***

**257-260** A55 Set of 4 4.75 2.50
*260a* Booklet pane of 4, #257-260 4.75 —

**Souvenir Sheet**

**261** Sheet of 4 5.50 5.50
*a.-d.* A55 61c Any single 1.40 .70
*e.* Booklet pane of 4, #261a-261d 5.50 —

Booklet panes are separated from binding stub at left by a row of rouletting.

Europa A56

Designs: No. 262, Scout emblem.

No. 263: a, Lord Robert Baden-Powell. b, Scout hat.

**2007, May 9**

**262** A56 61c multi 1.50 .75
*a.* Booklet pane of 1 1.50 —

**Souvenir Sheet**

**263** Sheet of 2 3.50 3.50
*a.-b.* A56 61c Either single 1.75 .85
*c.* Booklet pane of 2, #263a-263b 3.50 —

Scouting, cent.

Booklet panes are separated from binding stub at left by a row of rouletting.

Sugar Mills A57

Designs: 30c, Man stirring syrup, man grinding cane. 75c, Oxen, man grinding cane.

€2.45, Man leading oxen, man grinding cane, man carrying cane.

**2007, July 1 *Perf. 12½x13***

**264-265** A57 Set of 2 2.50 1.25
*265a* Booklet pane of 2, #264-265 2.50 —

**Souvenir Sheet**

***Perf. 13¼x13***

**266** A57 €2.45 multi 6.00 6.00
*a.* Booklet pane of 1 6.00 —
Complete booklet, #260a, 261e, 262a, 263c, 265a, 266a 24.00

No. 266 contains one 60x40mm stamp.

Booklet panes are separated from binding stub at left by a row of rouletting. Complete booklet also contains a pane of four progressive proofs of No. 262. These were not valid for postage.

Funchal, 500th Anniv. A58

Designs: 30c, Funchal Harbor. 61c, Map. 75c, Coat of arms. €1, Boat in harbor.

No. 271, €2.45, Boat in harbor, diff. No. 272, €2.45, Man, harbor, town.

***Perf. 12x11¾ Syncopated***

**2008, Apr. 15 Litho.**

**267-270** A58 Set of 4 6.00 3.00
*268a* Booklet pane of 2, #267-268 2.00 —
*270a* Booklet pane of 2, #269-270 4.00 —

**Souvenir Sheets**

**271-272** A58 Set of 2 11.00 11.00
*271a* Booklet pane of 1 5.50 —
*272a* Booklet pane of 1 5.50 —

Booklet panes are separated from binding stub at left by a row of rouletting.

Europa A59

Designs: No. 273, Man, envelopes. No. 274a, Houses, envelopes.

***Perf. 12x11¾ Syncopated***

**2008, May 9 Litho.**

**273** A59 61c multi 1.40 .70
*a.* Booklet pane of 1 1.40 —

**Souvenir Sheet**

**274** Sheet of 2, #273, 274a 3.00 2.00
*a.* A59 61c multi 1.40 .70
*b.* Booklet pane of 2, #273, 274a 2.75 —

Booklet panes are separated from binding stub at left by a row of rouletting.

**Lighthouse Type of Portugal of 2008**

**2008, June 19**

**275** A835 61c Ponta do Pargo Lighthouse 1.40 .70
*a.* Booklet pane of 1 1.40 —
Complete booklet, #268a, 270a, 271a, 272a, 273a, 274b, 275a 23.00

Booklet panes are separated from binding stub at left by a row of rouletting. Complete booklet also contains a pane of four progressive proofs of No. 273. These were not valid for postage.

Fruits A60

Designs: 32c, Annona cherimola. 68c, Eugenia uniflora. 80c, Persea americana. €2, Psidium guajava.

No. 280, €2.50, Dwarf Cavendish bananas. No. 281, €2.50, Passiflora edulis.

***Perf. 12x11¾ Syncopated***

**2009, Apr. 27 Litho.**

**276-279** A60 Set of 4 9.00 4.50
*277a* Booklet pane of 2, #276-277 2.25 —
*279a* Booklet pane of 2, #278-279 6.75 —

**Souvenir Sheets**

**280-281** A60 Set of 2 11.00 7.50
*280a* Booklet pane of 1 5.50 —
*281a* Booklet pane of 1 5.50 —

Nos. 280-281 each contain one 80x30mm stamp. See No. 316.

Booklet panes are separated from binding stub at left by a row of rouletting.

Europa A61

Designs: No. 282, M51 galaxy. No. 283a, Telescope built by astronomy student from University of Madeira.

**2009, May 8**

**282** A61 68c multi 1.60 .80
*a.* Booklet pane of 1 1.60 —

**Souvenir Sheet**

**283** Sheet of 2, #282, 283a 3.50 2.00
*a.* A61 68c multi 1.75 .85
*b.* Booklet pane of 2, #282, 283a 3.50 —
Complete booklet, #277a, 279a, 280a, 281a, 282a, 283b, Portugal #3144a 30.00

Intl. Year of Astronomy.

Booklet panes are separated from binding stub at left by a row of rouletting. Complete booklet also contains a pane of 4 progressive proofs of No. 282. These were not valid for postage.

Botanical Gardens, 50th Anniv. A62

Designs: 32c, Musschia aurea, topiary garden. 68c, Geranium maderense, path. 80c, Ranunculus cortusifolius, path and roads. No. 287, €2, Convolvulus massonii, people in gardens.

No. 288, €2, Patterned flower gardens. No. 289, €2, Building, scientist, botanist inspecting plant, seeds.

***Perf. 12x11¾ Syncopated***

**2010, Apr. 30 Litho.**

**284-287** A62 Set of 4 8.50 4.00
*285a* Booklet pane of 2, #284-285 2.25 —
*287a* Booklet pane of 2, #286-287 6.25 —

**Souvenir Sheets**

**288-289** A62 Set of 2 9.00 5.50
*288a* Booklet pane of 1 4.50 —
*289a* Booklet pane of 1 4.50 —

Issued: Nos. 285a, 287a, 288a, 289a, Nov.

Booklet panes are separated from binding stub at left by a row of rouletting.

See Nos. 317, 349.

Europa — A63

Characters from children's story: No. 290, Woman. No. 291a, Man.

***Perf. 11¾x12 Syncopated***

**2010, May 7 Litho.**

**290** A63 68c multi 1.60 .80
*a.* Booklet pane of 1 1.60 —

**Souvenir Sheet**

**291** Sheet of 2, #290, 291a 3.50 1.75
*a.* A63 68c multi 1.75 .85
*b.* Booklet pane of 2, #290, 291a 3.50 —
Complete booklet, #285a, 287a, 288a, 289a, 290a, 291b 23.00

Issued: Nos. 290a, 291b, Nov.

Booklet panes are separated from binding stub at left by a row of rouletting.

Europa A64

Designs: No. 292, People walking on forest path, bird in tree. No. 293a, Birds in flight and on branch..

***Perf. 12x11¾ Syncopated***

**2011, May 9**

**292** A64 68c multi 1.50 .75
*a.* Booklet pane of 1 1.50 —

**Souvenir Sheet**

**293** Sheet of 2, #292, 293a 3.00 2.00
*a.* A64 68c multi 1.50 .75
*b.* Booklet pane of 2, #292, 293a 3.00 —

Intl. Year of Forests.

Country Houses A65

Designs: 32c, Quinta dos Cruzes. 68c, Quinta Jardins do Lago. 80c, Quinta Monte Palace. €2, Quinta Serra Golf.

No. 298, €1.75, Quinta do Palheiro - Casa Velha. No. 299, €2.30, Quinta Vigia.

**2011, Sept. 23**

**294-297** A65 Set of 4 8.50 4.25
*295a* Booklet pane of 2, #294-295 2.60 —
*297a* Booklet pane of 2, #296-297 6.50 —

**Souvenir Sheets**

**298-299** A65 Set of 2 8.50 5.50
*298a* Booklet pane of 1 3.50 —
*299a* Booklet pane of 1 5.00 —
Complete booklet, #292a, 293b, 295a, 297a, 298a, 299a, Portugal #3330a 24.00

Europa A66

Designs: No. 300, Steamer Santa Maria. No. 301a, Funchal waterfront.

**2012, May 9**

300 A66 68c multi 1.50 .75
a. Booklet pane of 1 1.50 —

**Souvenir Sheet**

301 Sheet of 2, #300, 301a 3.00 1.75
a. A66 68c multi 1.50 .75
b. Booklet pane of 2, #300, 301a 3.00 —

Issued: Nos. 300a, 301b, Nov.

Booklet panes are separated from binding stub at left by a row of rouletting.

Levadas A67

Irrigation canals at: 32c, Rei. 68c, Caldeirao Verde. 80c, Faja do Rodrigues. €2, 25 Fontes. €1.75. Cedros, vert. €2.30, Furado, vert.

**2012** ***Perf. 12x11¾ Syncopated***

302-305 A67 Set of 4 8.50 4.25
303a Booklet pane of 2, #302-303 2.25 —
305a Booklet pane of 2, #304-305 6.25 —

**Souvenir Sheets**

***Perf. 11¾x12 Syncopated***

306-307 A67 Set of 2 9.00 5.25
306a Booklet pane of 1 4.00 —
307a Booklet pane of 1 5.00 —
Complete booklet, #300a, 301b, 303a, 305a, 306a, 307a 24.00

Issued: Nos. 302-307, 9/21; Nos. 303a, 305a, 306a, 307a, Nov. Nos. 306-307 each contain one 30x80mm stamp.

Booklet panes are separated from binding stub at left by a row of rouletting. Complete booklet contains a pane of four imperforate progressive proofs of No. 300. These were not valid for postage.

See Nos. 318, 350, 361.

Europa A68

Designs: No. 308, Portuguese postal all-terrain vehicle. No. 309a, Rider on Portuguese all-terrain vehicle.

***Perf. 12x11¾ Syncopated***

**2013, May 9** **Litho.**

308 A68 70c multi 1.60 .80
a. Booklet pane of 1 1.60 —

**Souvenir Sheet**

309 Sheet of 2, #308, 309a 3.25 2.00
a. A68 70c multi 1.60 .85
b. Booklet pane of 2, #308, 309a 3.25 —

See No. 319.

Booklet panes are separated from binding stub at left by a row of rouletting.

Apiculture A69

Designs: 36c, Bee near water. 70c, Bee at flower. 80c, Bee at flower, diff. No. 313, €1.70, Beekeeper and bees near hives.

No. 314, €1.70, Bee approaching flower. €1.90, Hives, bee on leaf near flower.

***Perf. 12x11¾ Syncopated***

**2013, May 17** **Litho.**

310-313 A69 Set of 4 8.00 4.00
311a Booklet pane of 2, #310-311 2.50 —
313a Booklet pane of 2, #312-313 5.50 —

**Souvenir Sheets**

314-315 A69 Set of 2 9.00 5.00
314a Booklet pane of 1 4.00 —
315a Booklet pane of 1 5.00 —
Complete booklet, #308a, 309b, 311a, 313a, 314a, 315a 22.00

Nos. 314-315 each contain one 80x30mm stamp. See No. 320.

Booklet panes are separated from binding stub at left by a row of rouletting. Complete booklet also contains a pane of 4 progressive proofs of No. 308. These were not valid for postage.

**Types of 2009-13**

***Die Cut Perf. 10½***

**2014, Jan. 27** **Litho.**

**Self-Adhesive**

316 A60 E Like #277 1.60 .95
317 A62 E Like #285 1.60 .95
318 A67 E Like #303 1.60 .95
319 A68 E Like #308 1.60 .95
320 A69 E Like #311 1.60 .95
*Nos. 316-320 (5)* 8.00 4.75

On day of issue, Nos. 316-320 each sold for 70c.

Europa — A70

Designs: No. 321, Brinquinho player. No. 322a, Brinquinho.

***Perf. 11¾x12 Syncopated***

**2014, May 9** **Litho.**

321 A70 E multi 1.60 .80
a. Booklet pane of 1 1.60 —

**Souvenir Sheet**

322 Sheet of 2, #321, 322a 3.50 2.00
a. A70 E multi 1.60 .80
b. Booklet pane of 2, #321, 322a 3.50 —

On day of issue Nos. 321 and 322a each sold for 72c.

Booklet panes are separated from binding stub at left by a row of rouletting.

See Nos. 351, 380.

Diocese of Funchal, 500th Anniv. — A71

Designs: 42c, Processional cross. 50c, St. James, the Lesser. 72c, Our Lady of the Mount. 80c, Pope John Paul II.

€1, Papal bull creating Diocese of Funchal. €1.70, Funchal Cathedral.

***Perf. 11¾x12 Syncopated***

**2014, June 12** **Litho.**

323-326 A71 Set of 4 5.50 3.00
324a Booklet pane of 2, #323-324 2.00 —
326a Booklet pane of 2, #325-326 3.50 —

**Souvenir Sheets**

327-328 A71 Set of 2 6.00 3.75
327a Booklet pane of 1 2.25 —
328a Booklet pane of 1 3.75 —
Complete booklet, #321a, 322b, 324a, 326a, 327a, 328a 18.00

Booklet panes are separated from binding stub at left by a row of rouletting. Complete booklet also contains a pane of 4 progressive proofs of No. 321. These were not valid for postage.

**Types of 2011-12**

***Die Cut Perf. 10½***

**2015, Jan. 19** **Litho.**

**Self-Adhesive**

329 A64 E Like #292 1.50 .75
330 A65 E Like #296 1.50 .75
331 A66 E Like #300 1.50 .75
*Nos. 329-331 (3)* 4.50 2.25

Nos. 329-331 each sold for 72c on day of issue.

Flower Festival A72

Designs: 45c, Flower market. 72c, Street decorations. 80c, Children in costumes carrying flowers. €1, Street garden.

€1.80, Anthurium andraeanum. €2, Heliconia rostrata.

***Perf. 12x11¾ Syncopated***

**2015, Apr. 16** **Litho.**

332-335 A72 Set of 4 6.75 3.50
333a Booklet pane of 2, #332-333 2.75 —
335a Booklet pane of 2, #334-335 4.25 —

**Souvenir Sheets**

336-337 A72 Set of 2 8.75 4.25
336a Booklet pane of 1 4.25 —
337a Booklet pane of 1 4.50 —

Issued: No. 333a, 335a, 336a, 337a, 10/19.

Booklet panes are separated from binding stub at left by a row of rouletting.

See Nos. 352, 362, 381.

**Figurines Type of Portugal of 2015**

***Perf. 12x11¾ Syncopated***

**2015, Apr. 21** **Litho.**

338 A1007 72c Madeira figurines 1.60 .80
a. Booklet pane of 1 1.60 —

Issued: No. 338a, 10/19.

Europa A73

Old toys: No. 339, Sink, bucket and watering can. No. 340a, Taxi.

***Perf. 12x11¾ Syncopated***

**2015, May 8** **Litho.**

339 A73 72c multi 1.60 .80
a. Booklet pane of 1 1.60 —

**Souvenir Sheet**

340 Sheet of 2, #339, 340a 3.25 1.60
a. A73 72c multi 1.60 .80
b. Booklet pane of 2, #339, 340a 3.25 —
Complete booklet, #333a, 335a, 336a, 337a, 338a, 339a, 340b 22.50

Issued: Nos. 339a, 340b, 10/19. Booklet panes are separated from binding stub at left by a row of rouletting. Complete booklet contains a pane of four imperforate progressive proofs of No. 339. These were not valid for postage.

See No. 382.

Christmas and New Year's Day — A74

Designs: 47c, Outdoor creche. 75c, Fruit market. 80c, Christmas decoration. €1, New Year's fireworks display.

No. 345a, Infant Jesus creche figurine. No. 346a, Fireworks display near ship,

***Perf. 12x11¾ Syncopated***

**2016, Apr. 7** **Litho.**

341-344 A74 Set of 4 6.50 3.25

**Souvenir Sheets**

345 Sheet of 2, #343, 345a 4.25 2.10
a. A74 €1 multi 2.40 1.25
346 Sheet of 2, #344, 346a 4.25 2.10
a. A74 80c multi 1.90 .95

See No. 353.

Europa A75

Designs: No. 347, Bicyclist, buildings, wind generators. No. 348a, Skydiver, boats.

***Perf. 12x11¾ Syncopated***

**2016, May 9** **Litho.**

347 A75 75c multi 1.75 .85

**Souvenir Sheet**

348 Sheet of 2, #347, 348a 3.50 1.75
a. A75 75c multi 1.75 .85

Think Green Issue.

**Types of 2010-16**

***Die Cut Perf. 10½***

**2016, Aug. 8** **Litho.**

**Self-Adhesive**

349 A62 E Like #286 1.60 .80
350 A67 E Like #305 1.60 .80
351 A70 E Like #321 1.60 .80
352 A72 E Like #334 1.60 .80
353 A74 E Like #344 1.60 .80
*Nos. 349-353 (5)* 8.00 4.00

On day of issue, Nos. 349-353 each sold for 75c.

Europa A76

Designs: No. 354, St. John the Baptist Fortress, Angra do Heroísmo. No. 355a, Sao Tiago Fortress, Funchal.

***Perf. 12x11¾ Syncopated***

**2017, May 9** **Litho.**

354 A76 80c multi 1.75 .90

**Souvenir Sheet**

355 Sheet of 2, #354, 355a 3.50 1.80
a. A76 80c multi 1.75 .90

See No. 383.

Mountain Peaks — A77

Designs: 50c, Pico Ruivo. 80c, Pico do Castelo. No. 358, 85c, Pico do Veado. No. 359, €1, Pico Branco.

No. 360: a, 85c, Pico Ana Ferreira. b, €1, Pico do Arieiro.

***Perf. 11¾x12 Syncopated***

**2017, Nov. 17** **Litho.**

356-359 A77 Set of 4 7.50 3.75

**Souvenir Sheet**

360 Sheet of 2 4.50 2.40
a. A77 85c multi 2.10 1.10
b. A77 €1 multi 2.40 1.25

**Types of Madeira 2012-15**

***Die Cut Perf. 10½***

**2018, Jan. 15** **Litho.**

**Self-Adhesive**

361 A67 E Like #304 2.25 1.10
362 A72 E Like #332 2.25 1.10

On day of issue, Nos. 361-362 each sold for 86c.

**Types of Portugal 2013-15**

***Die Cut Perf. 10½***

**2018, Jan. 15** **Litho.**

**Self-Adhesive**

363 A967 E Like #3527 2.25 1.10
364 A994 E Like #3616 2.25 1.10
365 A1019 E Like #3734 2.25 1.10
*Nos. 363-365 (3)* 6.75 3.30

On day of issue, Nos. 363-365 each sold for 86c.

Europa A78

Designs: No. 366, Socorridos Bridge, Câmara de Lobos. No. 367a, Ribeira de Metade Bridge, Faial.

***Perf. 12x11¾ Syncopated***

**2018, May 9 Litho.**
**366** A78 E multi 2.00 1.00

**Souvenir Sheet**

**367** Sheet of 2, #366, 367a 4.00 2.00
*a.* A78 E multi 2.00 1.00

On day of issue, Nos. 366 and 367a each sold for 86c.

Discovery of Madeira, 600th Anniv. — A79

Porto Santo buildings and: No. 368, 53c, Cowherd and cows. No. 369, 53c, Cows, corn. 86c, Man, woman and dragon tree. 91c, Cows, sugar cane.
€1.50, Man, dragon tree, ship, horiz.

***Perf. 11¾x12 Syncopated***

**2018, June 22 Litho.**
**368-371** A79 Set of 4 6.75 3.50

**Souvenir Sheet**

***Perf. 12x11¾ Syncopated***

**372** A79 €1.50 multi 3.50 1.75

No. 372 contains one 80x30mm stamp.

Europa A80

Designs: No. 373, Serinus canaria. No. 374a, Carduelis carduelis.

***Perf. 12x11¾ Syncopated***

**2019, May 9 Litho.**
**373** A80 86c multi 2.00 1.00

**Souvenir Sheet**

**374** Sheet of 2, #373, 374a 4.00 4.00
*a.* A80 86c multi 2.00 1.00

Discovery of Madeira, 600th Anniv. A81

Designs: 53c, Woman and cat. 86c, Two men. 91c, Guitarist and ships.
€2, Statues, vert.

***Perf. 12x11¾ Syncopated***

**2019, June 7 Litho.**
**375-377** A81 Set of 3 5.25 2.60

**Souvenir Sheet**

***Perf. 11¾x12 Syncopated***

**378** A81 €2 multi 4.50 4.50

No. 378 contains one 30x80mm stamp.

**Fruits Type of Portugal of 2017**

***Die Cut Perf. 10½***

**2020, Jan. 8 Litho.**

**Self-Adhesive**

**379** A1059 E Like #3886 1.90 .95

No. 379 sold for 86c on day of issue.

**Types of Madeira, 2014-17**

***Die Cut Perf. 10½***

**2020, Jan. 8 Litho.**

**Self-Adhesive**

**380** A70 E Like #322a 1.90 .95
**381** A72 E Like #333 1.90 .95
**382** A73 E Like #340a 1.90 .95
**383** A76 E Like #354 1.90 .95
*Nos. 380-383 (4)* 7.60 3.80

Nos. 380-383 each sold for 86c on day of issue.

Europa A82

Designs: No. 384, Stamped covers and pillar box. No. 385a, Postal workers with mail bags, truck and ship.

***Perf. 12x11¾ Syncopated***

**2020, May 25 Litho.**
**384** A82 86c multi 1.90 .95

**Souvenir Sheet**

**385** Sheet of 2, #384, 385a 3.80 3.80
*a.* A82 86c multi 1.90 .95

Ancient Postal Routes.

Madeira Photographic Museum — A83

Designs: N, Old camera, photogrpah of room. E, Vicente Gomes da Silva (1827-1906), photographer, camera and museum staircase. I, Camera and museum's sign and entrance.
€2.50, Camera, photographic studio's furnishings.

***Perf. 12x11¾ Syncopated***

**2020, July 21 Litho.**
**386-388** A83 Set of 3 5.50 2.75

**Souvenir Sheet**

**389** A83 €2.50 multi 6.00 6.00

No. 389 contains one 80x30mm stamp.

Europa A84

Endangered animals: No. 390, Caretta caretta. No. 391a, Pterodroma madeira.

***Perf. 12x11¾ Syncopated***

**2021, May 7 Litho.**
**390** A84 88c multi 2.25 1.10

**Souvenir Sheet**

**391** Sheet of 2, #390, 391a 4.50 4.50
*a.* A84 88c multi 2.25 1.10

Madeira Regional Archive, 90th Anniv. A85

Designs: 54c, Books on shelves, hygrometer. 88c, Archives room, illuminated manuscript. 91c, Archivists photgraphing documents and preserving book.
€2.50, Archives Building, preserved document.

***Perf. 12x11¾ Syncopated***

**2021, June 28 Litho.**
**392-394** A85 Set of 3 5.50 2.75

**Souvenir Sheet**

**395** A85 €2.50 multi 6.00 6.00

No. 395 contains one 80x30mm stamp.

## PORTUGUESE AFRICA

'pōr-chə-‚gēz 'a-fri-kə

For use in any of the Portuguese possessions in Africa.

1000 Reis = 1 Milreis
100 Centavos = 1 Escudo

Common Design Types pictured following the introduction.

**Vasco da Gama Issue**

Common Design Types
Inscribed "Africa - Correios"

***Perf. 13½ to 15½***

**1898, Apr. 1 Engr. Unwmk.**
**1** CD20 2½r blue green 1.20 .85
**2** CD21 5r red 1.20 .85
**3** CD22 10r red violet 1.20 .85
**4** CD23 25r yellow green 1.20 .85
**5** CD24 50r dark blue 1.20 .85
**6** CD25 75r violet brown 8.50 7.25
**7** CD26 100r bister brown 8.50 6.00
**8** CD27 150r bister 12.00 6.00
*Nos. 1-8 (8)* 35.00 23.50
Set, never hinged 120.00

Vasco da Gama's voyage to India.

**POSTAGE DUE STAMPS**

D1

**1945 Unwmk. Typo.** ***Perf. 11½x12***

**Denomination in Black**

**J1** D1 10c claret .75 .50
**J2** D1 20c purple .75 .50
**J3** D1 30c deep blue .75 .50
**J4** D1 40c chocolate .75 .50
**J5** D1 50c red violet .75 .75
**J6** D1 1e orange brown 3.00 3.00
**J7** D1 2e yellow green 6.00 6.00
**J8** D1 3e bright carmine 9.00 9.00
**J9** D1 5e orange yellow 17.50 17.50
*Nos. J1-J9 (9)* 39.25 38.25
Set, never hinged 52.50

**WAR TAX STAMPS**

Liberty WT1

**Overprinted in Black, Orange or Carmine**

***Perf. 12x11½, 15x14***

**1919 Typo. Unwmk.**
**MR1** WT1 1c green (Bk) 1.50 1.50
*a.* Figures of value omitted 15.00 7.50
**MR2** WT1 4c green (O) 3.00
**MR3** WT1 5c green (C) 1.50 1.50
*Nos. MR1-MR3 (3)* 6.00 3.00

Values the same for either perf.
No. MR2 used is known only with fiscal cancelation. Some authorities consider No. MR2 a revenue stamp.

## PORTUGUESE CONGO

'pōr-chi-gēz 'käŋ-‚gō

LOCATION — The northernmost district of the Portuguese Angola Colony on the southwest coast of Africa
CAPITAL — Cabinda

Stamps of Angola replaced those of Portuguese Congo.

1000 Reis = 1 Milreis
100 Centavos = 1 Escudo (1913)

King Carlos — A1

***Perf. 12½***

**1894, Aug. 5 Typo. Unwmk.**
**1** A1 5r yellow 1.60 1.40
**2** A1 10r redsh violet 2.40 1.45
*a.* Perf. 13½ 27.50 14.50
**3** A1 15r chocolate 4.00 3.00
*a.* Perf. 11½ 8.00 4.50
**4** A1 20r lav, ordinary paper 4.25 3.00
*b.* Perf. 11½ 8.00 4.50
**5** A1 25r green 2.40 1.00
*b.* Perf. 11½ 5.50 1.20

***Perf. 13½***

**6** A1 50r light blue 4.50 2.75
*a.* Perf. 11½ 22.00 9.75

***Perf. 11½***

**7** A1 75r rose 8.00 4.50
*a.* Perf. 12½ 33.00 19.00
**8** A1 80r yellow green 11.00 7.25
*a.* Perf. 12½ 97.50 57.50
**9** A1 100r brown, *yel* 9.00 6.00
*a.* Perf. 13½ 55.00 29.00

***Perf. 12½***

**10** A1 150r carmine, *rose* 18.00 13.50
**11** A1 200r dk blue, *bl* 18.00 13.50
**12** A1 300r dk blue, *salmon* 22.00 18.00
*Nos. 1-12 (12)* 105.15 75.35

For surcharges and overprints see Nos. 36-47, 127-131.

King Carlos — A2

**Name & Value in Black except 500r**

**1898-1903** ***Perf. 11½***
**13** A2 2½r gray .50 .30
**14** A2 5r orange .50 .30
**15** A2 10r lt green .85 .30
**16** A2 15r brown 1.75 1.75
**17** A2 15r gray grn ('03) 1.50 .35
**18** A2 20r gray violet 1.50 1.00
**19** A2 25r sea green 1.75 1.00
**20** A2 25r car rose ('03) 1.50 .35
**21** A2 50r deep blue 2.60 1.60
**22** A2 50r brown ('03) 3.50 1.90
**23** A2 65r dull blue ('03) 12.00 8.25
**24** A2 75r rose 4.50 3.00
**25** A2 75r red lilac ('03) 4.50 3.75
**26** A2 80r violet 4.50 3.00
**27** A2 100r dk bl, *bl* 3.75 2.50
**28** A2 115r org brn, *pink* ('03) 10.25 7.00
**29** A2 130r brn, *straw* ('03) 20.00 11.00
**30** A2 150r brown, *buff* 5.25 3.75
**31** A2 200r red lilac, *pnksh* 7.25 4.25
**32** A2 300r dk blue, *rose* 6.50 4.00
*a.* 300r dk blue, *yel* 9.00 5.25
**33** A2 400r dl bl, *straw* ('03) 14.00 11.00
**34** A2 500r blk & red, *bl* ('01) 25.00 11.50
**35** A2 700r vio, *yelsh* ('01) 40.00 22.00
*Nos. 13-35 (23)* 173.45 103.85

For overprints and surcharges see Nos. 49-53, 60-74, 117-126, 136-138.

Surcharged in Black

***Perf. 12½, 11½ (#41, 43), 13½ (#44)***

**1902 On Issue of 1894**

**36** A1 65r on 15r choc 6.00 4.00
*a.* Perf. 11½ 27.50 14.50
**37** A1 65r on 20r lav (#4) 6.00 4.00
**38** A1 65r on 25r green (#5) 6.00 4.00
*a.* Perf. 11½ 27.50 17.00
**39** A1 65r on 300r bl, *sal* 8.00 7.25
**40** A1 115r on 10r red vio 6.00 4.00
**41** A1 115r on 50r lt bl 6.00 4.00
*a.* Perf. 13½ 6.00 4.00
**42** A1 130r on 5r yellow 6.00 4.00
*a.* Inverted surcharge 55.00 50.00
*b.* Perf. 13½ 6.00 4.50
**43** A1 130r on 75r rose 6.00 4.25
*a.* Perf. 12½ 10.50 9.00
**44** A1 130r on 100r brn, *yel* 6.00 4.50
*a.* Inverted surcharge 50.00 45.00
*b.* Perf. 11½ 33.00 19.50
**45** A1 400r on 80r yel grn 3.00 1.75
*a.* Perf. 12½ 8.00 5.25
**46** A1 400r on 150r car, *rose* 4.25 3.00
**47** A1 400r on 200r bl, *bl* 4.25 3.00

**On Newspaper Stamps of 1894**

**48** N1 115r on 2½r brn 6.00 3.75
*a.* Inverted surcharge 45.00 40.00
*b.* Perf. 13½ 6.00 3.75
*Nos. 36-48 (13)* 73.50 51.50

Nos. 16, 19, 21 and 24 Overprinted in Black

**1902** ***Perf. 11½***

**49** A2 15r brown 3.25 1.75
**50** A2 25r sea green 3.25 1.75
**51** A2 50r blue 3.25 1.75
*a.* Double overprint 67.50 55.00
**52** A2 75r rose 6.75 4.25
*a.* Double ovpt, one albino 30.00 24.00
*Nos. 49-52 (4)* 16.50 9.50

No. 23 Surcharged

**1905**

**53** A2 50r on 65r dull blue 7.00 3.75

**Angola Stamps of 1898-1903 (Port. Congo type A2) Overprinted or Surcharged**

a

b

**1911**

**54** (a) 2½r gray 2.75 1.75
**55** (a) 5r orange 3.00 2.10
*a.* "REPUBLICA" inverted 15.00 12.50
**56** (a) 10r lt green 3.00 2.10
*a.* "REPUBLICA" inverted 15.00 11.00
**57** (a) 15r gray green 3.00 2.10
*a.* "REPUBLICA" inverted 15.00 11.00
**58** (b) 25r on 200r red vio, *pnksh* 3.50 2.40
*a.* "REPUBLICA" inverted 15.00 11.00
*b.* "CONGO" double 15.00 11.00

**Thin Bar and "CONGO" as Type "b"**

**59** (a) 2½r gray 3.75 2.75
*Nos. 54-59 (6)* 19.00 13.20

Issue of 1898-1903 Overprinted in Carmine or Green — c

**1911**

**60** A2 2½r gray .35 .25
**61** A2 5r orange .35 .35
**62** A2 10r lt green .35 .35
**63** A2 15r gray grn .35 .35
**64** A2 20r gray vio .35 .35
**65** A2 25r car rose (G) .60 .50
**66** A2 50r brown .70 .45
**67** A2 75r red lilac 1.20 .75
**68** A2 100r dk bl, *bl* 1.30 .75
**69** A2 115r org brn, *pink* 2.25 1.50
*a.* 115r org brn, *yel* 3.50 2.10
**70** A2 130r brown, *straw* 2.25 1.50
**71** A2 200r red vio, *pnksh* 3.75 2.40
**72** A2 400r dull bl, *straw* 7.00 4.25
**73** A2 500r blk & red, *bl* 7.00 4.50
**74** A2 700r violet, *yelsh* 9.50 5.50
*Nos. 60-74 (15)* 37.30 23.75

Numerous inverts and doubles exist. These are printer's waste or made to order.

Common Design Types pictured following the introduction.

Vasco da Gama Issue of Various Portuguese Colonies Surcharged

**1913 On Stamps of Macao**

**75** CD20 ¼c on ½a bl grn 1.75 1.60
**76** CD21 ½c on 1a red 1.75 1.60
**77** CD22 1c on 2a red vio 1.90 1.60
**78** CD23 2½c on 4a yel grn 1.90 1.60
**79** CD24 5c on 8a dk blue 1.90 1.60
**80** CD25 7½c on 12a vio brn 4.00 2.60
**81** CD26 10c on 16a bis brn 2.50 1.75
*a.* Inverted surcharge 50.00 50.00
**82** CD27 15c on 24a bister 2.50 1.75
*Nos. 75-82 (8)* 18.20 14.10

**On Stamps of Portuguese Africa**

**83** CD20 ¼c on 2½r bl grn 1.50 1.60
**84** CD21 ½c on 5r red 1.50 1.60
**85** CD22 1c on 10r red vio 1.50 1.60
**86** CD23 2½c on 25r yel grn 1.50 1.60
**87** CD24 5c on 50r dk bl 1.75 1.60
**88** CD25 7½c on 75r vio brn 3.50 2.25
**89** CD26 10c on 100r bis brn 2.40 1.60
*a.* Inverted surcharge 42.50 42.50
**90** CD27 15c on 150r bister 2.10 1.60
*Nos. 83-90 (8)* 15.75 13.45

**On Stamps of Timor**

**91** CD20 ¼c on ½a bl grn 1.75 1.60
**92** CD21 ½c on 1a red 1.75 1.60
**93** CD22 1c on 2a red vio 1.90 1.60
**94** CD23 2½c on 4a yel grn 1.90 1.60
**95** CD24 5c on 8a dk blue 1.90 1.60
*a.* Double surcharge 42.50 42.50
**96** CD25 7½c on 12a vio brn 4.00 2.60
**97** CD26 10c on 16a bis brn 2.50 1.75
**98** CD27 15c on 24a bister 2.50 1.75
*Nos. 91-98 (8)* 18.20 14.10
*Nos. 75-98 (24)* 52.15 41.65

Ceres — A3

**Name and Value in Black**
**Chalky Paper**

**1914 Typo.** ***Perf. 15x14***

**99** A3 ¼c olive brn 1.10 *.50*
*a.* Inscriptions inverted *20.00*
**100** A3 ½c black 1.15 *.50*
**101** A3 1c blue grn 3.25 *2.10*
**102** A3 1½c lilac brn 2.25 *1.35*
**103** A3 2c carmine 2.50 *2.10*
**104** A3 2½c lt violet .80 *.65*
**105** A3 5c dp blue 1.15 *1.20*
**106** A3 7½c yellow brn 1.90 *1.50*
**107** A3 8c slate 1.90 *1.75*
**108** A3 10c orange brn 1.90 *1.75*
**109** A3 15c plum 2.50 *2.10*
**110** A3 20c yellow grn 2.50 *2.10*
**111** A3 30c brown, *grn* 5.25 *3.50*
**112** A3 40c brown, *pink* 5.25 *3.50*
**113** A3 50c orange, *salmon* 6.75 4.00
**114** A3 1e green, *blue* 8.50 5.25
*Nos. 99-114 (16)* 48.65 *33.85*

**1920 Ordinary Paper**

**115** A3 ¼c olive brn .90 *.80*
**116** A3 2c carmine 1.25 *.90*

Issue of 1898-1903 Overprinted Locally in Green or Red

**1914-18** ***Perf. 11½***

**117** A2 50r brown (G) 2.10 1.50
**118** A2 75r rose (G) *500.00*
**119** A2 75r red lilac (G) 17.50 10.25
**120** A2 100r blue, *bl* (R) 2.10 1.50
**121** A2 200r red vio, *pink* (G) 7.50 6.75
**122** A2 400r dl bl, *straw* (R) ('18) 110.00 110.00
**123** A2 500r blk & red, *bl* (R) 90.00 90.00

**Same on Nos. 51-52**

**124** A2 50r blue (R) 2.10 1.50
**125** A2 75r rose (G) 2.75 2.10

**Same on No. 53**

**126** A2 50r on 65r dl bl (R) 2.10 1.75
*Nos. 117,119-126 (9)* 236.15 225.35

No. 118 was not regularly issued.

**Provisional Issue of 1902 Overprinted Type "c" in Red**

***Perf. 11½ (#130-131), 12½ (#127), 13½ (#128-129)***

**1915**

**127** A1 115r on 10r red vio 1.20 .75
*a.* Perf. 13½ 27.00 23.00
**128** A1 115r on 50r lt bl 2.50 1.35
*a.* Perf. 11½ 2.50 1.35
**129** A1 130r on 5r yellow 1.75 1.25
*a.* Perf. 12½ 2.50 1.75
*b.* As "a," inverted surcharge 40.00 21.00
**130** A1 130r on 75r rose 2.50 1.75
*a.* Perf. 12½ 3.50 2.10
**131** A1 130r on 100r brn, *buff* 1.35 .85
*a.* Inverted surcharge 40.00 21.00
*b.* Perf. 13½ 1.35 .85
**135** N1 115r on 2½r brn 1.75 1.25
*a.* Perf. 12½ 1.75 1.25

**Nos. 49, 51 Overprinted Type "c"**

**136** A2 15r brown 1.75 1.25
*a.* Perf. 12½ 2.10 1.40
**137** A2 50r blue 1.75 1.25

**No. 53 Overprinted Type "c"**

**138** A2 50r on 65r dull blue 1.75 1.25
*Nos. 127-138 (9)* 16.30 10.95

**NEWSPAPER STAMP**

N1

***Perf. 12½***

**1894, Aug. 5 Typo. Unwmk.**

**P1** N1 2½r chocolate 1.75 1.40
*a.* Perf. 13½ 1.75 1.40

For surcharge and overprint see Nos. 48, 135.

# PORTUGUESE GUINEA

'pōr-chi-gēz 'gi-nē

LOCATION — On the west coast of Africa between Senegal and Guinea
GOVT. — Portuguese Overseas Territory
AREA — 13,944 sq. mi.
POP. — 560,000 (est. 1970)
CAPITAL — Bissau

The territory, including the Bissagos Islands, became an independent republic on Sept. 10, 1974. See Guinea-Bissau in Vol. 3.

1000 Reis = 1 Milreis
100 Centavos = 1 Escudo (1913)

**Catalogue values for unused stamps in this country are for Never Hinged items, beginning with Scott 273 in the regular postage section, Scott J40 in the postage due section, and Scott RA17 in the postal tax section.**

Nos. 1-7 are valued with small faults such as short perfs or small thins. Completely fault-free examples of any of these stamps are very scarce and are worth more than the values given.

Stamps of Cape Verde, 1877-85 Overprinted in Black

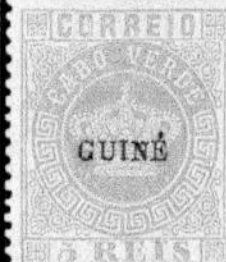

**1881 Unwmk.** ***Perf. 12½***

**Without Gum (Nos. 1-7)**

**1** A1 5r black *1,100.* *900.*
**1A** A1 10r yellow *2,000.* *975.*
**2** A1 20r bister *600.* *350.*
**3** A1 25r rose *1,600.* *975.*
**4** A1 40r blue *1,400.* *975.*
*a.* Cliché of Mozambique in Cape Verde plate *18,000.* *17,000.*
**4B** A1 50r green *2,000.* *975.*
**5** A1 100r lilac 350. 240.
**6** A1 200r orange *725.* *600.*
**7** A1 300r brown *725.* *600.*

Excellent forgeries exist of Nos. 1-7.

Overprinted in Red or Black

**1881-85** ***Perf. 12½, 13½***

**8** A1 5r black (R) 6.50 4.25
**9** A1 10r yellow 190.00 190.00
**10** A1 10r green ('85) 9.75 8.00
**11** A1 20r bister 4.50 3.75
**12** A1 20r rose ('85) 11.00 8.00
*a.* Double overprint
**13** A1 25r carmine 3.75 3.00
*a.* Perf. 13½ 97.50 45.00
**14** A1 25r violet ('85) 4.50 3.00
*a.* Double overprint
**15** A1 40r blue 240.00 150.00
*a.* Cliché of Mozambique in Cape Verde plate *1,500.* *1,100.*
**16** A1 40r yellow ('85) 3.00 2.40
*a.* Cliché of Mozambique in Cape Verde plate 67.50 50.00
*b.* Imperf.
*c.* As "a," imperf.
*g.* Double overprint
**17** A1 50r green 240.00 150.00
**18** A1 50r blue ('85) 9.00 4.25
*a.* Imperf.
*b.* Double overprint
**19** A1 100r lilac 13.00 10.00
*a.* Inverted overprint
**20** A1 200r orange 18.00 13.00
**21** A1 300r yellow brn 22.00 16.50
*a.* 300r lake brown 22.00 16.50

Varieties of this overprint may be found without accent on "E" of "GUINE," or with grave instead of acute accent.

*Stamps of the 1881-85 issues were reprinted on a smooth white chalky paper, ungummed, and on thin white paper with shiny white gum and clean-cut perforation 13½.*

*See Scott Classic Catalogue for listings by perforation.*

King Luiz — A3

**1886 Typo.** ***Perf. 12½, 13½***

**22** A3 5r gray black 9.75 8.50
*a.* Imperf.
**23** A3 10r green 11.50 6.00
*a.* Perf. 13½ 13.00 10.00
*b.* Imperf.
**24** A3 20r carmine 17.00 6.00
**25** A3 25r red lilac 17.00 7.00
*a.* Imperf.
**26** A3 40r chocolate 14.00 9.75
*a.* Perf. 12½ 120.00 90.00
**27** A3 50r blue 26.00 9.75
*a.* Imperf.
**28** A3 80r gray 24.00 16.50
*a.* Perf. 12½ 120.00 90.00
**29** A3 100r brown 24.00 16.50
*a.* Perf. 12½ 60.00 33.00

30 A3 200r gray lilac 60.00 33.00
31 A3 300r orange 72.50 50.00
a. Perf. 13½ 270.00 270.00
*Nos. 22-31 (10)* 275.75 163.00

Varieties of this overprint may be found without accent on "E" of "GUINE," or with grave instead of acute accent. For surcharges and overprints see Nos. 67-76, 180-183.

*Reprinted in 1905 on thin white paper with shiny white gum and clean-cut perforation 13½.*

King Carlos — A4

**1893-94** ***Perf. 11½***

32 A4 5r yellow 3.00 1.75
a. Perf. 12½ 4.25 2.40
33 A4 10r red violet 3.00 1.75
34 A4 15r chocolate 3.75 2.40
35 A4 20r lavender 3.75 2.40
36 A4 25r blue green 3.75 2.40
37 A4 50r lt blue 6.75 4.00
a. Perf. 12½ 25.00 18.00
38 A4 75r rose 18.00 11.00
39 A4 80r lt green 18.00 11.00
40 A4 100r brn, *buff* 18.00 11.00
41 A4 150r car, *rose* 19.00 11.00
42 A4 200r dk bl, *bl* 27.50 21.00
43 A4 300r dk bl, *sal* 30.00 21.00
*Nos. 32-43 (12)* 154.50 100.70

Almost all of Nos. 32-43 were issued with and without gum.

For surcharges and overprints see #77-88, 184-188, 203-205.

King Carlos — A5

**1898-1903** ***Perf. 11½***

**Name & Value in Black except 500r**

44 A5 2½r gray .50 .35
45 A5 5r orange .50 .35
46 A5 10r lt green .50 .35
47 A5 15r brown 4.50 3.50
48 A5 15r gray grn ('03) 2.75 1.45
49 A5 20r gray violet 2.40 1.35
50 A5 25r sea green 2.75 1.35
51 A5 25r carmine ('03) 1.50 1.00
52 A5 50r dark blue 3.75 1.75
53 A5 50r brown ('03) 3.75 2.75
54 A5 65r dl blue ('03) 14.00 9.00
55 A5 75r rose 22.50 13.00
56 A5 75r lilac ('03) 5.50 4.50
57 A5 80r brt violet 4.50 2.75
58 A5 100r dk bl, *bl* 4.50 2.75
a. Perf. 12½ 300.00 150.00
59 A5 115r org brn, *pink* ('03) 13.00 9.00
a. 115r orange brown, *yellowish* 15.00 9.00
60 A5 130r brn, *straw* ('03) 13.50 9.00
61 A5 150r lt brn, *buff* 14.00 5.75
62 A5 200r red lilac, *pnksh* 14.00 5.75
63 A5 300r blue, *rose* 13.00 7.25
64 A5 400r dl bl, *straw* ('03) 17.50 10.00
65 A5 500r blk & red, *bl* ('01) 19.50 11.00
66 A5 700r vio, *yelsh* ('01) 26.00 19.50
*Nos. 44-66 (23)* 204.40 123.45

Nos. 44-45 and 49 were issued with and without gum.

For overprints and surcharges see Nos. 90-115, 190-194, 197.

Issue of 1886 Surcharged in Black or Red

**1902, Oct. 20** ***Perf. 12½***

67 A3 65r on 10r green 10.00 5.75
a. Inverted surcharge 60.00 55.00
b. Perf. 13½ 67.50 55.00
68 A3 65r on 20r car 10.00 5.75
69 A3 65r on 25r red lilac 10.00 5.75
70 A3 115r on 40r choc 9.00 5.50
a. Perf. 13½ 21.00 9.75
71 A3 115r on 50r blue 9.00 5.50
a. Inverted surcharge 60.00 55.00
72 A3 115r on 300r orange 12.00 10.25
73 A3 130r on 80r gray 12.00 8.50
a. Perf. 13½ 21.00 9.75
74 A3 130r on 100r brown 13.00 8.50
a. Perf. 13½ 31.00 22.00
75 A3 400r on 200r gray lil 67.50 60.00
76 A3 400r on 5r gray blk (R) 23.00 13.50
*Nos. 67-76 (10)* 175.50 129.00

*Reprints of No. 76 are in black and have clean-cut perforation 13½.*

**Same Surcharge on Issue of 1893-94**

***Perf. 11½, 12½ (#80)***

77 A4 65r on 10r red vio 8.50 4.25
a. Perf. 11
78 A4 65r on 15r choc 8.50 4.25
79 A4 65r on 20r lav 8.50 4.25
80 A4 65r on 50r lt bl
a. Perf. 12½ 21.00 18.00
81 A4 115r on 5r yel 8.50 4.25
a. Inverted surcharge 60.00 55.00
b. Perf. 12½ 80.00 72.50
82 A4 115r on 25r bl grn 9.00 4.50
83 A4 130r on 150r car, *rose* 9.00 4.50
84 A4 130r on 200r dk bl, *bl* 9.75 5.25
85 A4 130r on 300r dk bl, *sal* 9.75 5.50
86 A4 400r on 75r rose 6.75 5.50
87 A4 400r on 80r lt grn 4.25 2.40
a. Inverted surcharge 60.00 55.00
88 A4 400r on 100r brn, *buff* 5.50 2.40

**Same Surcharge on No. P1**

***Perf. 13½***

89 N1 115r on 2½r brn 6.00 4.00
a. Inverted surcharge 60.00 55.00
b. Perf. 12½ 8.50 4.25
c. As "b," inverted surcharge 60.00 55.00
*Nos. 77-89 (13)* 99.00 54.80

Issue of 1898 Overprinted in Black

**1902, Oct. 20** ***Perf. 11½***

90 A5 15r brown 3.75 2.25
91 A5 25r sea green 3.75 2.25
92 A5 50r dark blue 5.00 2.60
93 A5 75r rose 9.00 7.25
*Nos. 90-93 (4)* 21.50 14.35

No. 54 Surcharged in Black

**1905**

94 A5 50r on 65r dull blue 7.25 4.25

No. 94 was issued without gum.

Issue of 1898-1903 Overprinted in Carmine or Green

**1911** ***Perf. 11½***

95 A5 2½r gray .70 .50
a. Inverted overprint 24.00 24.00
96 A5 5r orange .70 .50
97 A5 10r lt green .90 .60
98 A5 15r gray green .90 .75
99 A5 20r gray violet .90 .75
100 A5 25r carmine (G) .90 .75
a. Double overprint 21.00 18.00
101 A5 50r brown .85 .75
102 A5 75c lilac .85 .75
103 A5 100r dk bl, *bl* 2.40 .85
104 A5 115r org brn, *pink* 2.40 1.00
105 A5 130r brn, *straw* 2.40 1.00
106 A5 200r red lil, *pink* 10.25 4.50
107 A5 400r dl bl, *straw* 3.50 2.75
108 A5 500r blk & red, *bl* 3.50 2.75
109 A5 700r vio, *yelsh* 5.50 4.50
*Nos. 95-109 (15)* 36.65 22.70

Issued with and without gum: Nos. 96, 98, 99 and 103. Issued without gum: Nos. 101-102, 104-105, 107.

Issue of 1898-1903 Overprinted in Red

**1913** ***Perf. 11½***

**Without Gum (Nos. 110-115)**

110 A5 15r gray grn 21.00 14.00
111 A5 75r lilac 21.00 14.00
a. Inverted overprint 72.50 55.00
112 A5 100r bl, *bl* 11.00 8.50
a. Inverted overprint 72.50 55.00
113 A5 200r red lil, *pnksh* 52.50 40.00
a. Inverted overprint 90.00 92.50

**Same Overprint on Nos. 90, 93 in Red**

114 A5 15r brown 21.00 14.00
a. "REPUBLICA" double, one inverted 90.00 80.00
b. "REPUBLICA" inverted 72.50 55.00
115 A5 75r rose 21.00 14.00
a. "REPUBLICA" inverted 72.50 55.00
*Nos. 110-115 (6)* 147.50 104.50

Vasco da Gama Issue of Various Portuguese Colonies Surcharged

**1913** **On Stamps of Macao**

116 CD20 ¼c on ½a bl grn 2.40 2.00
117 CD21 ½c on 1a red 2.40 2.00
118 CD22 1c on 2a red vio 2.40 2.00
119 CD23 2½c on 4a yel grn 2.40 2.00
120 CD24 5c on 8a dk bl 2.40 2.00
121 CD25 7½c on 12a vio brn 5.00 3.75
122 CD26 10c on 16a bis brn 4.25 3.75
a. Inverted surcharge 42.50 42.50
123 CD27 15c on 24a bis 6.00 4.00
*Nos. 116-123 (8)* 27.25 21.50

**On Stamps of Portuguese Africa**

124 CD20 ¼c on 2½c bl grn 2.10 1.75
125 CD21 ½c on 5r red 2.10 1.75
126 CD22 1c on 10r red vio 2.10 1.75
127 CD23 2½c on 25r yel grn 2.10 1.75
128 CD24 5c on 50r dk bl 2.10 1.75
129 CD25 7½c on 75r vio brn 5.00 3.75
130 CD26 10c on 100r bis brn 2.75 1.75
131 CD27 15c on 150r bis 6.00 5.00
*Nos. 124-131 (8)* 24.25 19.25

**On Stamps of Timor**

132 CD20 ¼c on ½a bl grn 2.40 2.00
133 CD21 ½c on 1a red 2.40 2.00
134 CD22 1c on 2a red vio 2.40 2.00
135 CD23 2½c on 4a yel grn 2.40 2.00
136 CD24 5c on 8a dk blue 2.40 2.00
137 CD25 7½c on 12a vio brn 5.00 3.75
138 CD26 10c on 16a bis brn 4.25 3.75
139 CD27 15c on 24a bister 6.00 4.00
*Nos. 132-139 (8)* 27.25 21.50
*Nos. 116-139 (24)* 78.75 62.25

Ceres — A6

**Name and Value in Black**

**1914** **Chalky Paper** ***Perf. 15x14***

140 A6 ¼c olive brown .55 .40
141 A6 ½c black .55 .40
142 A6 1c blue green 1.60 .95
143 A6 1½c lilac brn 1.00 .65
144 A6 2c carmine 1.05 .70
145 A6 2½c lt violet 1.60 .50
146 A6 5c deep blue 1.05 .65
147 A6 7½c yellow brn 1.75 1.10
148 A6 8c slate 1.20 .90
149 A6 10c orange brn 1.50 1.10
150 A6 15c plum 12.00 8.50
151 A6 20c yellow grn 3.00 1.50
152 A6 30c brown, *grn* 8.00 6.00
153 A6 40c brown, *pink* 5.25 1.40
154 A6 50c orange, *salmon* 5.25 1.40
155 A6 1e green, *blue* 7.25 4.50
*Nos. 140-155 (16)* 52.60 30.65

**1919-20** **Ordinary Paper**

156 A6 ¼c olive brown 1.20 1.00
157 A6 ½c black ('20) .25 .25
158 A6 1c blue green 3.75 3.00
159 A6 2c carmine 1.50 1.10
*Nos. 156-159 (4)* 6.70 5.35

**1921-26** ***Perf. 12x11½***

160 A6 ¼c olive brown .50 .45
161 A6 ½c black .25 .25
162 A6 1c yellow green ('22) .25 .25
163 A6 1½c lilac brn .25 .25
164 A6 2c carmine .25 .25
165 A6 2c gray ('25) .25 *.60*
166 A6 2½c lt violet .25 .25
167 A6 3c orange ('22) .25 *.50*
168 A6 4c deep red ('22) .25 *.50*
169 A6 4½c gray ('22) .25 *.50*
170 A6 5c brt blue ('22) .25 .25
171 A6 6c lilac ('22) .25 *.50*
172 A6 7c ultra ('22) .75 *.50*
173 A6 7½c yellow brn .25 .25
174 A6 8c slate .25 .25
175 A6 10c orange brn .25 .25
176 A6 12c blue grn ('22) 1.50 .60
177 A6 15c brn rose ('22) .50 .35
178 A6 20c yellow grn .25 .25
179 A6 24c ultra ('25) 2.75 2.10
179A A6 25c brown ('25) 2.00 .65
179B A6 30c gray grn ('22) 1.50 .60
179C A6 40c turq bl ('22) 1.50 .70
179D A6 50c violet ('25) 2.00 1.35
179E A6 60c dk blue ('22) 2.40 1.75
179F A6 60c dp rose ('26) 3.00 1.75
179G A6 80c brt rose ('22) 3.75 2.40
179H A6 1e indigo ('26) 5.00 3.25
*Nos. 160-179H (28)* 30.90 21.55

**1922-25** **Glazed Paper**

179I A6 1e pale rose 5.00 2.00
179J A6 2e dk violet 5.00 3.00
m. Ordinary paper (error) *100.00*
179K A6 5e buff ('25) 23.00 12.50
179L A6 10e pink ('25) 42.50 16.50
179M A6 20e pale turq ('25) 87.50 47.50
*Nos. 179I-179M (5)* 163.00 81.50

For surcharges see Nos. 195-196, 211-213.

Provisional Issue of 1902 Overprinted in Carmine

**1915** ***Perf. 11½, 12½, 13½***

180 A3 115r on 40r choc 1.50 1.40
a. Perf. 13½ 10.50 8.50
181 A3 115r on 50r blue 1.50 1.40
182 A3 130r on 80r gray 5.00 3.00
a. Perf. 12½ 60.00 35.00
183 A3 130r on 100r brn 4.00 3.50
a. Perf. 13½ 15.00 11.50
184 A4 115r on 5r yellow 1.75 1.20
a. Perf. 11½ 7.25 5.75
185 A4 115r on 25r bl grn 1.75 1.50
186 A4 130r on 150r car, *rose* 1.75 1.50
187 A4 130r on 200r bl, *bl* 1.75 1.50
188 A4 130r on 300r dk bl, *sal* 1.75 1.50
189 N1 115r on 2½r brn 5.00 3.00
a. Perf. 13½ — —
b. Inverted overprint 67.50 60.00

Nos. 90, 92, 94 Overprinted

***Perf. 11½***

190 A5 15r brown 1.75 1.50
191 A5 50r dark blue 1.75 1.50
192 A5 50r on 65r dl bl 1.75 1.50
*Nos. 180-192 (13)* 31.00 24.00

Nos. 64, 66 Overprinted

**1919** **Without Gum** ***Perf. 11½***

193 A5 400r dl bl, *straw* 80.00 45.00
194 A5 700r vio, *yelsh* 26.00 18.00

### Nos. 140, 141 and 59 Surcharged

a

b

**1920, Sept.** *Perf. 15x14, 11½*

**Without Gum**

| No. | Type | Description | Unused | Used |
|---|---|---|---|---|
| 195 | A6(a) | 4c on ¼c | 6.00 | 4.50 |
| 196 | A6(a) | 6c on ½c | 6.00 | 4.50 |
| 197 | A5(b) | 12c on 115r | 15.00 | 11.00 |
| | | *Nos. 195-197 (3)* | 27.00 | 20.00 |

Nos. 86-88 Surcharged

**1925** *Perf. 11½*

| No. | Type | Description | Unused | Used |
|---|---|---|---|---|
| 203 | A4 | 40c on 400r on 75r | 1.75 | 1.50 |
| 204 | A4 | 40c on 400r on 80r | 1.75 | 1.50 |
| 205 | A4 | 40c on 400r on 100r | 1.75 | 1.50 |
| | | *Nos. 203-205 (3)* | 5.25 | 4.50 |

Nos. 179F-179G, 179J Surcharged

**1931** *Perf. 12x11½*

| No. | Type | Description | Unused | Used |
|---|---|---|---|---|
| 211 | A6 | 50c on 60c dp rose | 3.50 | 2.40 |
| 212 | A6 | 70c on 80c pink | 3.50 | 3.00 |
| 213 | A6 | 1.40e on 2e dk vio | 8.50 | 6.00 |
| | | *Nos. 211-213 (3)* | 15.50 | 11.40 |

Ceres — A7

**1933** **Wmk. 232**

| No. | Type | Description | Unused | Used |
|---|---|---|---|---|
| 214 | A7 | 1c bister | .25 | .25 |
| 215 | A7 | 5c olive brn | .25 | .25 |
| 216 | A7 | 10c violet | .25 | .25 |
| 217 | A7 | 15c black | .25 | .25 |
| 218 | A7 | 20c gray | .25 | .25 |
| 219 | A7 | 30c dk green | .25 | .25 |
| 220 | A7 | 40c red orange | 1.20 | .50 |
| 221 | A7 | 45c lt blue | 1.20 | .60 |
| 222 | A7 | 50c lt brown | 1.20 | .60 |
| 223 | A7 | 60c olive grn | 1.40 | .60 |
| 224 | A7 | 70c orange brn | 1.40 | .70 |
| 225 | A7 | 80c emerald | 2.00 | .95 |
| *a.* | | Value omitted | 35.00 | 35.00 |
| 226 | A7 | 85c deep rose | 4.00 | 1.75 |
| 227 | A7 | 1e red brown | 1.75 | 1.20 |
| 228 | A7 | 1.40e dk blue | 6.75 | 4.25 |
| 229 | A7 | 2e red violet | 3.50 | 2.10 |
| 230 | A7 | 5e apple green | 11.50 | 8.00 |
| 231 | A7 | 10e olive bister | 23.00 | 9.75 |
| 232 | A7 | 20e orange | 60.00 | 34.00 |
| | | *Nos. 214-232 (19)* | 120.40 | 66.50 |

Common Design Types pictured following the introduction.

Common Design Types

**Engr.; Name & Value Typo. in Black**

**1938** **Unwmk.** *Perf. 13½x13*

| No. | Type | Description | Unused | Used |
|---|---|---|---|---|
| 233 | CD34 | 1c gray grn | .25 | .25 |
| 234 | CD34 | 5c orange brn | .25 | .25 |
| 235 | CD34 | 10c dk carmine | .30 | .30 |
| 236 | CD34 | 15c dk vio brn | .30 | .30 |
| 237 | CD34 | 20c slate | .60 | .30 |
| 238 | CD35 | 30c rose violet | .70 | .45 |
| 239 | CD35 | 35c brt green | .70 | .45 |
| 240 | CD35 | 40c brown | .70 | .45 |
| 241 | CD35 | 50c brt red vio | .70 | .45 |
| 242 | CD36 | 60c gray black | .70 | .45 |
| 243 | CD36 | 70c brown vio | .70 | .45 |
| 244 | CD36 | 80c orange | 1.40 | .60 |
| 245 | CD36 | 1e red | 1.60 | .60 |
| 246 | CD37 | 1.75e blue | 2.10 | 1.20 |
| 247 | CD37 | 2e brown car | 5.75 | 2.00 |
| 248 | CD37 | 5e olive grn | 8.00 | 4.25 |
| 249 | CD38 | 10e blue vio | 10.25 | 5.00 |
| 250 | CD38 | 20e red brown | 34.00 | 8.00 |
| | | *Nos. 233-250 (18)* | 69.00 | 25.75 |

Fort of Cacheu A8

Nuno Tristam — A9

Ulysses S. Grant — A10

Designs: 3.50e, Teixeira Pinto. 5e, Honorio Barreto. 20e, Bissau Church.

**Unwmk.**

**1946, Jan. 12** **Litho.** *Perf. 11*

| No. | Type | Description | Unused | Used |
|---|---|---|---|---|
| 251 | A8 | 30c gray & lt gray | .95 | .50 |
| 252 | A9 | 50c black & pink | .70 | .40 |
| 253 | A9 | 50c gray grn & lt grn | .70 | .40 |
| 254 | A10 | 1.75e blue & lt blue | 2.75 | 1.40 |
| 255 | A10 | 3.50e red & pink | 5.00 | 1.75 |
| 256 | A10 | 5e lt brn & buff | 12.50 | 5.75 |
| 257 | A8 | 20e vio & lt vio | 21.00 | 9.00 |
| *a.* | | Sheet of 7, #251-257 ('47) | 110.00 | 95.00 |
| | | *Nos. 251-257 (7)* | 43.60 | 19.20 |

Discovery of Guinea, 500th anniversary. No. 257a sold for 40 escudos.

Guinea Village — A11

Designs: 10c, Crowned crane. 20c, 3.50e, Tribesman. 35c, 5e, Woman in ceremonial dress. 50c, Musician. 70c, Man. 80c, 20e, Girl. 1e, 2e, Drummer. 1.75e, Antelope.

**1948, Apr.** **Photo.** *Perf. 11½*

| No. | Type | Description | Unused | Used |
|---|---|---|---|---|
| 258 | A11 | 5c chocolate | .25 | .25 |
| 259 | A11 | 10c lt violet | 2.75 | 1.25 |
| 260 | A11 | 20c dull rose | .70 | .45 |
| 261 | A11 | 35c green | .90 | .45 |
| 262 | A11 | 50c dp orange | .45 | .25 |
| 263 | A11 | 70c dp gray bl | .70 | .40 |
| 264 | A11 | 80c dk ol grn | 1.00 | .40 |
| 265 | A11 | 1e rose red | 1.00 | .40 |
| 266 | A11 | 1.75e ultra | 13.00 | 5.00 |
| 267 | A11 | 2e blue | 15.00 | 1.50 |
| 268 | A11 | 3.50e orange brn | 3.25 | 1.25 |
| 269 | A11 | 5e slate | 5.75 | 2.50 |
| 270 | A11 | 20e violet | 24.00 | 6.50 |
| *a.* | | Sheet of 13, #258-270 + 2 labels | 130.00 | 120.00 |
| | | *Nos. 258-270 (13)* | 68.75 | 20.60 |

No. 270a sold for 40 escudos.

**Lady of Fatima Issue**

Common Design Type

**1948, Oct.** **Litho.** *Perf. 14½*

| No. | Type | Description | Unused | Used |
|---|---|---|---|---|
| 271 | CD40 | 50c deep green | 6.50 | 3.50 |

UPU Symbols — A12

**1949, Oct.** *Perf. 14*

| No. | Type | Description | Unused | Used |
|---|---|---|---|---|
| 272 | A12 | 2e dp org & cream | 4.50 | 2.50 |

Universal Postal Union, 75th anniversary.

**Catalogue values for unused stamps in this section, from this point to the end of the section, are for Never Hinged items.**

**Holy Year Issue**

Common Design Types

**1950, May** *Perf. 13x13½*

| No. | Type | Description | Unused | Used |
|---|---|---|---|---|
| 273 | CD41 | 1e brown lake | 4.75 | 1.50 |
| 274 | CD42 | 3e blue green | 6.50 | 2.00 |

**Holy Year Extension Issue**

Common Design Type

**1951, Oct.** *Perf. 14*

| No. | Type | Description | Unused | Used |
|---|---|---|---|---|
| 275 | CD43 | 1e choc & pale brn + label | 1.75 | .90 |

Stamps without label attached sell for less.

**Medical Congress Issue**

Common Design Type

Design: Physical examination.

**1952** *Perf. 13½*

| No. | Type | Description | Unused | Used |
|---|---|---|---|---|
| 276 | CD44 | 50c purple & choc | 1.00 | .45 |

Exhibition Entrance — A13

**1953, Jan.** **Litho.** *Perf. 13*

| No. | Type | Description | Unused | Used |
|---|---|---|---|---|
| 277 | A13 | 10c brn lake & ol | .25 | .25 |
| 278 | A13 | 50c dk blue & bister | 1.60 | .25 |
| 279 | A13 | 3e blk, dk brn & sal | 3.50 | 1.00 |
| | | *Nos. 277-279 (3)* | 5.35 | 1.50 |

Exhibition of Sacred Missionary Art held at Lisbon in 1951.

Stamp of Portugal and Arms of Colonies — A14

**1953** **Photo.** **Unwmk.**

| No. | Type | Description | Unused | Used |
|---|---|---|---|---|
| 280 | A14 | 50c multicolored | 1.75 | .90 |

Centenary of Portugal's first postage stamps.

Analeptes Trifasciata — A15

**1953** *Perf. 11½*

**Various Beetles in Natural Colors**

| No. | Type | Description | Unused | Used |
|---|---|---|---|---|
| 281 | A15 | 5c yellow | .40 | .25 |
| 282 | A15 | 10c blue | .40 | .25 |
| 283 | A15 | 30c org vermilion | .40 | .25 |
| 284 | A15 | 50c yellow grn | .40 | .25 |
| 285 | A15 | 70c gray brn | .60 | .25 |
| 286 | A15 | 1e orange | .60 | .25 |
| 287 | A15 | 2e pale ol grn | 1.50 | .25 |
| 288 | A15 | 3e lilac rose | 2.25 | .70 |
| 289 | A15 | 5e lt blue grn | 3.75 | 1.10 |
| 290 | A15 | 10e lilac | 6.00 | 3.00 |
| | | *Nos. 281-290 (10)* | 16.30 | 6.55 |

**Sao Paulo Issue**

Common Design Type

**1954** **Litho.** *Perf. 13½*

| No. | Type | Description | Unused | Used |
|---|---|---|---|---|
| 291 | CD46 | 1e lil rose, bl gray & blk | .35 | .25 |

Belem Tower, Lisbon, and Colonial Arms — A16

**1955, Apr. 14**

| No. | Type | Description | Unused | Used |
|---|---|---|---|---|
| 292 | A16 | 1e blue & multi | .25 | .25 |
| 293 | A16 | 2.50e gray & multi | .50 | .25 |

Visit of Pres. Francisco H. C. Lopes.

Fair Emblem, Globe and Arms — A17

**1958** **Unwmk.** *Perf. 12x11½*

| No. | Type | Description | Unused | Used |
|---|---|---|---|---|
| 294 | A17 | 2.50e multicolored | .65 | .55 |

World's Fair at Brussels.

**Tropical Medicine Congress Issue**

Common Design Type

Design: Maytenus senegalensis.

**1958** *Perf. 13½*

| No. | Type | Description | Unused | Used |
|---|---|---|---|---|
| 295 | CD47 | 5e multicolored | 3.00 | 1.10 |

Honorio Barreto — A18

**1959, Apr. 29** **Litho.** *Perf. 13½*

| No. | Type | Description | Unused | Used |
|---|---|---|---|---|
| 296 | A18 | 2.50e multicolored | .40 | .25 |

Centenary of the death of Honorio Barreto, governor of Portuguese Guinea.

Nautical Astrolabe — A19

**1960, June 25** *Perf. 13½*

| No. | Type | Description | Unused | Used |
|---|---|---|---|---|
| 297 | A19 | 2.50e multicolored | .40 | .25 |

500th anniversary of the death of Prince Henry the Navigator.

Traveling Medical Unit — A20

**1960** **Unwmk.** *Perf. 14½*

| No. | Type | Description | Unused | Used |
|---|---|---|---|---|
| 298 | A20 | 1.50e multicolored | .40 | .25 |

10th anniv. of the Commission for Technical Cooperation in Africa South of the Sahara (C.C.T.A.).

### Sports Issue
Common Design Type

**1962, Jan. 18 Litho. *Perf. 13½***

| | | | | |
|---|---|---|---|---|
| **299** | CD48 | 50c Automobile race | .50 | .25 |
| **300** | CD48 | 1e Tennis | .80 | .40 |
| **301** | CD48 | 1.50e Shot put | .50 | .25 |
| **302** | CD48 | 2.50e Wrestling | .90 | .45 |
| **303** | CD48 | 3.50e Trapshooting | .90 | .45 |
| **304** | CD48 | 15e Volleyball | 2.40 | 1.20 |
| | | *Nos. 299-304 (6)* | 6.00 | 3.00 |

### Anti-Malaria Issue
Common Design Type

Design: Anopheles gambiae.

**1962 Unwmk. *Perf. 13½***
**305** CD49 2.50e multicolored 1.25 .45

African Spitting Cobra — A21

Snakes: 35c, African rock python. 70c, Boomslang. 80c, West African mamba. 1.50e, Smythe's water snake. 2e, Common night adder, horiz. 2.50e, Green swamp snake. 3.50e, Brown house snake. 4e, Spotted wolf snake. 5e, Common puff adder. 15e, Striped beauty snake. 20e, African egg-eating snake, horiz.

**1963, Jan. 17 Litho. *Perf. 13½***

| | | | | |
|---|---|---|---|---|
| **306** | A21 | 20c multicolored | .25 | .25 |
| **307** | A21 | 35c multicolored | .25 | .25 |
| **308** | A21 | 70c multicolored | .75 | .30 |
| **309** | A21 | 80c multicolored | .75 | .25 |
| **310** | A21 | 1.50e multicolored | .75 | .25 |
| **311** | A21 | 2e multicolored | .35 | .25 |
| **312** | A21 | 2.50e multicolored | 3.25 | .35 |
| **313** | A21 | 3.50e multicolored | .50 | .25 |
| **314** | A21 | 4e multicolored | .65 | .25 |
| **315** | A21 | 5e multicolored | 1.20 | .35 |
| **316** | A21 | 15e multicolored | 2.40 | 1.25 |
| **317** | A21 | 20e multicolored | 4.00 | 2.00 |
| | | *Nos. 306-317 (12)* | 15.10 | 6.00 |

For overprints see Guinea-Bissau Nos. 696-703.

### Airline Anniversary Issue
Common Design Type

**1963 Litho. *Perf. 14½***
**318** CD50 2.50e lt brown & multi .65 .35

### National Overseas Bank Issue
Common Design Type

Design: 2.50e, Joao de Andrade Córvo.

**1964, May 16 *Perf. 13½***
**319** CD51 2.50e multicolored .65 .40

### ITU Issue
Common Design Type

**1965, May 17 Unwmk. *Perf. 14½***
**320** CD52 2.50e lt blue & multi 1.90 .75

Soldier, 1548 — A22

40c, Rifleman, 1578. 60c, Rifleman, 1640. 1e, Grenadier, 1721. 2.50e, Fusiliers captain, 1740. 4.50e, Infantryman, 1740. 7.50e, Sergeant major, 1762. 10e, Engineers' officer, 1806.

**1966, Jan. 8 Litho. *Perf. 13½***

| | | | | |
|---|---|---|---|---|
| **321** | A22 | 25c multicolored | .25 | .25 |
| **322** | A22 | 40c multicolored | .25 | .25 |
| **323** | A22 | 60c multicolored | .35 | .25 |
| **324** | A22 | 1e multicolored | .40 | .25 |
| **325** | A22 | 2.50e multicolored | .90 | .25 |
| **326** | A22 | 4.50e multicolored | 2.25 | .60 |
| **327** | A22 | 7.50e multicolored | 3.75 | 1.75 |
| **328** | A22 | 10e multicolored | 4.00 | 1.90 |
| | | *Nos. 321-328 (8)* | 12.15 | 5.50 |

### National Revolution Issue
Common Design Type

2.50e, Berta Craveiro Lopes School and Central Pavilion of Bissau Hospital.

**1966, May 28 Litho. *Perf. 11½***
**329** CD53 2.50e multicolored .55 .35

### Navy Club Issue
Common Design Type

Designs: 50c, Capt. Oliveira Muzanty and cruiser Republica. 1e, Capt. Afonso de Cerqueira and torpedo boat Guadiana.

**1967, Jan. 31 Litho. *Perf. 13***

| | | | | |
|---|---|---|---|---|
| **330** | CD54 | 50c multicolored | .40 | .25 |
| **331** | CD54 | 1e multicolored | .80 | .65 |

Sacred Heart of Jesus Monument and Chapel of the Apparition — A23

**1967, May 13 *Perf. 12½x13***
**332** A23 50c multicolored .35 .35

50th anniv. of the appearance of the Virgin Mary to three shepherd children at Fatima.

Pres. Rodrigues Thomaz — A24

**1968, Feb. 2 Litho. *Perf. 13½***
**333** A24 1e multicolored .25 .25

Issued to commemorate the 1968 visit of Pres. Americo de Deus Rodrigues Thomaz.

Cabral's Coat of Arms — A25

**1968, Apr. 22 Litho. *Perf. 14***
**334** A25 2.50e multicolored .55 .25

Pedro Alvares Cabral, navigator who took possession of Brazil for Portugal, 500th birth anniv.

### Admiral Coutinho Issue
Common Design Type

Design: 1e, Adm. Coutinho and astrolabe.

**1969, Feb. 17 Litho. *Perf. 14***
**335** CD55 1e multicolored .35 .25

### Vasco da Gama Issue

Da Gama Coat of Arms — A26

**1969, Aug. 29 Litho. *Perf. 14***
**336** A26 2.50e multicolored .35 .25

Vasco da Gama (1469-1524), navigator.

### Administration Reform Issue
Common Design Type

**1969, Sept. 25 Litho. *Perf. 14***
**337** CD56 50c multicolored .25 .25

### King Manuel I Issue

Arms of King Manuel I — A27

**1969, Dec. 1 Litho. *Perf. 14***
**338** A27 2e multicolored .35 .25

Pres. Ulysses S. Grant and View of Bolama — A28

**1970, Oct. 25 Litho. *Perf. 13½***
**339** A28 2.50e multicolored .45 .25

Centenary of Pres. Grant's arbitration in 1868 of Portuguese-English dispute concerning Bolama.

### Marshal Carmona Issue
Common Design Type

Design: 1.50e, Antonio Oscar Carmona in general's uniform.

**1970, Nov. 15 Litho. *Perf. 14***
**340** CD57 1.50e multicolored .35 .25

Luiz Camoens — A29

**1972, May 25 Litho. *Perf. 13***
**341** A29 50c brn org & multi .25 .25

4th centenary of publication of The Lusiads by Luiz Camoens (1524-1580).

### Olympic Games Issue
Common Design Type

Design: 2.50e, Weight lifting, hammer throw and Olympic emblem.

**1972, June 20 *Perf. 14x13½***
**342** CD59 2.50e multicolored .45 .25

### Lisbon-Rio de Janeiro Flight Issue
Common Design Type

1e, "Lusitania" taking off from Lisbon.

**1972, Sept. 20 Litho. *Perf. 13½***
**343** CD60 1e multicolored .25 .25

### WMO Centenary Issue
Common Design Type

**1973, Dec. 15 Litho. *Perf. 13***
**344** CD61 2e lt brown & multi .45 .35

## AIR POST STAMPS

Common Design Type
*Perf. 13½x13*

**1938, Sept. 19 Engr. Unwmk.**
**Name and Value in Black**

| | | | | |
|---|---|---|---|---|
| **C1** | CD39 | 10c red orange | 1.40 | .75 |
| **C2** | CD39 | 20c purple | 1.40 | .75 |
| **C3** | CD39 | 50c orange | 1.40 | .75 |
| **C4** | CD39 | 1e ultra | 1.50 | .75 |
| **C5** | CD39 | 2e lilac brown | 11.50 | 5.25 |
| **C6** | CD39 | 3e dark green | 5.00 | 1.60 |
| **C7** | CD39 | 5e red brown | 6.50 | 1.05 |
| **C8** | CD39 | 9e rose carmine | 12.00 | 5.75 |
| **C9** | CD39 | 10e magenta | 20.50 | 6.75 |
| | | *Nos. C1-C9 (9)* | 61.20 | 23.40 |

No. C7 exists with overprint "Exposicao Internacional de Nova York, 1939-1940" and Trylon and Perisphere. Value $300.

## POSTAGE DUE STAMPS

D1

**Without Gum**

**1904 Unwmk. Typo. *Perf. 12***

| | | | | |
|---|---|---|---|---|
| **J1** | D1 | 5r yellow green | 1.40 | .60 |
| **J2** | D1 | 10r slate | 1.40 | .60 |
| **J3** | D1 | 20r yellow brown | 1.40 | .60 |
| **J4** | D1 | 30r red orange | 2.50 | 1.75 |
| **J5** | D1 | 50r gray brown | 2.50 | 1.75 |
| **J6** | D1 | 60r red brown | 6.50 | 3.75 |
| **J7** | D1 | 100r lilac | 6.50 | 3.75 |
| **J8** | D1 | 130r dull blue | 6.50 | 3.75 |
| **J9** | D1 | 200r carmine | 10.00 | 8.00 |
| **J10** | D1 | 500r violet | 22.50 | 9.00 |
| | | *Nos. J1-J10 (10)* | 61.20 | 33.55 |

Same Overprinted in Carmine or Green

**1911 Without Gum**

| | | | | |
|---|---|---|---|---|
| **J11** | D1 | 5r yellow green | .25 | .25 |
| **J12** | D1 | 10r slate | .35 | .25 |
| **J13** | D1 | 20r yellow brown | .60 | .35 |
| **J14** | D1 | 30r red orange | .60 | .35 |
| **J15** | D1 | 50r gray brown | .70 | .40 |
| **J16** | D1 | 60r red brown | 1.75 | 1.35 |
| **J17** | D1 | 100r lilac | 4.00 | 2.40 |
| **J18** | D1 | 130r dull blue | 4.00 | 2.40 |
| **J19** | D1 | 200r carmine (G) | 4.00 | 2.40 |
| **J20** | D1 | 500r violet | 3.25 | 2.10 |
| | | *Nos. J11-J20 (10)* | 19.50 | 12.25 |

Nos. J2-J10 Overprinted

**1919 Without Gum**

| | | | | |
|---|---|---|---|---|
| **J21** | D1 | 10r slate | 7.75 | 7.00 |
| **J22** | D1 | 20r yellow brown | 9.25 | 7.75 |
| **J23** | D1 | 30r red orange | 7.00 | 4.25 |
| **J24** | D1 | 50r gray brown | 3.50 | 2.40 |
| **J25** | D1 | 60r red brown | 325.00 | |
| **J26** | D1 | 100r lilac | 3.50 | 3.00 |
| **J27** | D1 | 130r dull blue | 45.00 | 29.00 |
| **J28** | D1 | 200r carmine | 6.50 | 3.75 |
| **J29** | D1 | 500r violet | 35.00 | 24.00 |
| | | *Nos. J21-J24,J26-J29 (8)* | 117.50 | 81.15 |

No. J25 was not regularly issued but exists on genuine covers.

D2

**1921**

| | | | | |
|---|---|---|---|---|
| **J30** | D2 | ½c yellow green | .25 | .25 |
| **J31** | D2 | 1c slate | .25 | .25 |
| **J32** | D2 | 2c orange brown | .25 | .25 |
| **J33** | D2 | 3c orange | .25 | .25 |
| **J34** | D2 | 5c gray brown | .25 | .25 |
| **J35** | D2 | 6c light brown | 1.25 | 1.00 |
| **J36** | D2 | 10c red violet | 1.25 | 1.00 |
| **J37** | D2 | 13c dull blue | 1.25 | 1.00 |
| | *a.* | Double impression | 140.00 | 95.00 |

**J38** D2 20c carmine 1.25 1.00
**J39** D2 50c gray 1.25 1.00
*Nos. J30-J39 (10)* 7.50 6.25

**Catalogue values for unused stamps in this section, from this point to the end of the section, are for Never Hinged items.**

Common Design Type

**Photogravure and Typographed**

**1952 Unwmk. *Perf. 14***

**Numeral in Red, Frame Multicolored**

**J40** CD45 10c olive green .25 .25
**J41** CD45 30c purple .25 .25
**J42** CD45 50c dark green .25 .25
**J43** CD45 1e violet blue .30 .30
**J44** CD45 2e olive black .50 .50
**J45** CD45 5e brown red 1.00 1.00
*Nos. J40-J45 (6)* 2.55 2.55

## WAR TAX STAMPS

WT1

***Perf. 11½x12***

**1919, May 20 Typo. Unwmk.**

**MR1** WT1 10r brn, buff & blk *120.00 100.00*
**MR2** WT1 40r brn, buff & blk *120.00 100.00*
**MR3** WT1 50r brn, buff & blk *120.00 100.00*
*Nos. MR1-MR3 (3) 360.00 300.00*

The 40r is not overprinted "REPUBLICA."
Some authorities consider Nos. MR2-MR3 to be revenue stamps.

## NEWSPAPER STAMP

N1

**1893 Typo. Unwmk. *Perf. 12½***

**P1** N1 2½r brown 2.50 1.50
*a.* Perf. 13½ 2.50 1.50

For surcharge and overprint see Nos. 89, 189.

## POSTAL TAX STAMPS

**Pombal Issue**

Common Design Types

**1925 Unwmk. Engr. *Perf. 12½***

**RA1** CD28 15c red & black .95 .80
**RA2** CD29 15c red & black .95 .80
**RA3** CD30 15c red & black .95 .80
*Nos. RA1-RA3 (3)* 2.85 2.40

Coat of Arms — PT7

**Without Gum**

**1934, Apr. 1 Typo. *Perf. 11½***

**RA4** PT7 50c red brn & grn 17.00 8.50
*a.* Tête beche pair 200.00

Coat of Arms — PT8

**1938-40 Without Gum**

**RA5** PT8 50c ol bis & citron 15.50 8.50
**RA6** PT8 50c lt grn & ol brn ('40) 15.50 8.50
**RA6A** PT8 50c grnsh yel & yel olive ('40) 18.00 15.00
**RA6B** PT8 50c gry olive & brn ('40) 18.00 15.00

Coat of Arms — PT9

**1942 Without Gum *Perf. 11***

**RA7** PT9 50c black & yellow 4.25 3.00
**RA7A** PT9 50c black & yellow 4.25 3.00
**RA7B** PT9 50c brown & yellow 60.00 42.50

**1959, July Unwmk. Without Gum**

**RA8** PT9 30c black & green .25 .25

See Nos. RA24-RA26.

Lusignian Cross — PT10

**1967 Typo. *Perf. 11x11½***

**Without Gum**

**RA9** PT10 50c pink, red & blk 1.00 1.00
**RA10** PT10 1e grn, red & blk 1.40 .90
**RA11** PT10 5e gray, red & blk 3.00 1.75
**RA12** PT10 10e lt bl, red & blk 4.75 3.75
*Nos. RA9-RA12 (4)* 10.15 7.40

The tax was for national defense.
A 50e was used for revenue only.

Lusignian Cross — PT11

**1967, Aug. Typo. *Perf. 11***

**Without Gum**

**RA13** PT11 50c pink, blk & red .25 .25
**RA14** PT11 1e pale grn, blk & red .50 .50
**RA15** PT11 5e gray, blk & red 1.00 1.00
**RA16** PT11 10e lt bl, blk & red 3.25 2.75
*Nos. RA13-RA16 (4)* 5.00 4.50

The tax was for national defense.

**Catalogue values for unused stamps in this section, from this point to the end of the section, are for Never Hinged items.**

Carved Figurine — PT12

Art from Bissau Museum: 1e, Tree of Life, with 2 birds, horiz. No. RA19, Man wearing horned headgear ("Vaca Bruto"). 2.50e, The Magistrate. 5e, Man bearing burden on head. 10e, Stylized pelican.

**1968 Litho. *Perf. 13½***

**RA17** PT12 50c gray & multi .25 .25
*a.* Yellow paper 4.25 4.25
**RA18** PT12 1e multi .25 .25
**RA19** PT12 2e multi .25 .25
**RA21** PT12 2.50e multi .70 .45
**RA22** PT12 5e multi 1.00 .60
**RA23** PT12 10e multi 1.75 1.10
*Nos. RA17-RA19,RA21-RA23 (6)* 4.20 2.90

Obligatory on all inland mail Mar. 15-Apr. 15 and Dec. 15-Jan. 15, and all year on parcels.
A souvenir sheet containing Nos. RA17-RA23 exists. The stamps have simulated perforations. Value $30.
A 2e stamp with the design of RA19, inscribed "Tocador de Bombolon" was printed but not issued. The stamp was used for RA27-RA28. Value, unsurcharged example, $22.50.
For surcharges see Nos. RA27-RA28.

**Arms Type of 1942**

**1968 Typo. *Perf. 11***

**Without Gum**

**RA24** PT9 2.50e lt blue & blk 3.00 1.50
**RA25** PT9 5e green & blk 4.25 3.50
**RA26** PT9 10e dp blue & blk 7.00 5.50
*Nos. RA24-RA26 (3)* 14.25 10.50

PT12a

**1968 Litho. *Perf. 13½***

**RA27** PT12a 50c on 2e multi 1.00 .50

RA27 does not exist without surcharge.

**RA28** PT12a 1e on 2e multi 1.00 .50

Black and White Hands Holding Sword — PT13

**1968 Litho. *Perf. 13½***

**RA29** PT13 50c pink & multi .25 .25
**RA30** PT13 1e multicolored .25 .25
**RA31** PT13 2e yellow & multi .45 .25
**RA32** PT13 2.50e buff & multi .80 .45
**RA33** PT13 3e multicolored .95 .60
**RA34** PT13 4e gray & multi 1.20 .75
**RA35** PT13 5e multicolored 1.55 .90
**RA36** PT13 10e multicolored 5.75 3.75
*Nos. RA29-RA36 (8)* 11.20 7.20

The surtax was for national defense. Other denominations exist: 8e, 9e, 15e. Value, $4 each.

Mother and Children — PT14

**1971, June Litho. *Perf. 13½***

**RA37** PT14 50c multicolored .25 .25
**RA38** PT14 1e multicolored .25 .25
**RA39** PT14 2e multicolored .45 .40
**RA40** PT14 3e multicolored 1.25 1.00
**RA41** PT14 4e multicolored 1.50 1.15
**RA42** PT14 5e multicolored 2.50 1.75
**RA43** PT14 10e multicolored 4.25 3.25
*Nos. RA37-RA43 (7)* 10.45 8.05

A 20e exists. Value $4.

## POSTAL TAX DUE STAMPS

**Pombal Issue**

Common Design Types

**1925 Unwmk. *Perf. 12½***

**RAJ1** CD28 30c red & black .75 .75
**RAJ2** CD29 30c red & black .75 .75
**RAJ3** CD30 30c red & black .75 .75
*Nos. RAJ1-RAJ3 (3)* 2.25 2.25

# PORTUGUESE INDIA

'pōr-chi-gēz 'in-dē-ə

LOCATION — West coast of the Indian peninsula
GOVT. — Portuguese colony
AREA — 1,537 sq. mi.
POP. — 649,000 (1958)
CAPITAL — Panjim (Nova-Goa)

The colony was seized by India on Dec. 18, 1961, and annexed by that republic.

1000 Reis = 1 Milreis
12 Reis = 1 Tanga (1881-82)
(Real = singular of Reis)
16 Tangas = 1 Rupia
100 Centavos = 1 Escudo (1959)

**Catalogue values for unused stamps in this country are for Never Hinged items, beginning with Scott 490 in the regular postage section, Scott J43 in the postage due section, and Scott RA6 in the postal tax section.**

Expect Nos. 1-55, 70-112 to have rough perforations. Stamps frequently were cut apart because of the irregular and missing perforations. Scissor separations that do not remove perfs do not negatively affect value.

Numeral of Value — A1

A1: Large figures of value. "REIS" in Roman capitals. "S" and "R" of "SERVICO" smaller and "E" larger than the other letters. 33 lines in background. Side ornaments of four dashes.

A2: Large figures of value. "REIS" in block capitals. "S," "E" and "R" same size as other letters of "SERVICO." 44 lines in background. Side ornaments of five dots.

### Handstamped from a Single Die
*Perf. 14 to 18 & Compound*

**1871, Oct. 1** **Unwmk.**

**Thin Transparent Brittle Paper**

| No. | Type | Description | Unused | Used |
|---|---|---|---|---|
| 1 | A1 | 10r black | 650.00 | 325.00 |
| 2 | A1 | 20r dk carmine | 1,550. | 350.00 |
| 3 | A1 | 40r Prus blue | 525.00 | *400.00* |
| 4 | A1 | 100r yellow grn | 650.00 | 425.00 |
| 5 | A1 | 200r ocher yel | 1,025. | 550.00 |

For detailed listings, see *Scott Classic Specialized Catalogue of Stamps & Covers 1840-1940.*

**1871, Nov. 1** *13 to 16 & Compound*

**Thick Soft Wove Paper**

| No. | Type | Description | Unused | Used |
|---|---|---|---|---|
| 5A | A1 | 10r black | *1,600.* | 425.00 |
| 6 | A1 | 20r dk carmine | *1,700.* | 500.00 |
| 7 | A1 | 20r orange ver | *2,000.* | 500.00 |
| 7A | A1 | 40r Prus blue | *2,400.* | *1,350.* |
| 7B | A1 | 100r yellow grn | *2,400.* | *1,550.* |
| 8 | A1 | 200r ocher yel | *2,400.* | 1,350. |
| 9 | A1 | 300r dp red violet | | *3,000.* |

Numeral of Value — A2

*Perf. 12½ to 14½ & Compound*

**1871, Dec. 1**

| No. | Type | Description | Unused | Used |
|---|---|---|---|---|
| 10 | A2 | 10r black | 330.00 | 130.00 |
| 11 | A2 | 20r vermilion | 260.00 | 115.00 |
| 12 | A2 | 40r blue | 100.00 | 75.00 |
| 13 | A2 | 100r deep green | 80.00 | 57.50 |
| 14 | A2 | 200r yellow | 325.00 | 275.00 |
| 15 | A2 | 300r red violet | 325.00 | 275.00 |
| *a.* | | Imperf. | | |
| 16 | A2 | 600r red violet | 220.00 | 175.00 |
| 17 | A2 | 900r red violet | 260.00 | 175.00 |
| | | *Nos. 10-17 (8)* | 1,900. | 1,278. |

**1872, Apr.**

**White Laid Paper**

| No. | Type | Description | Unused | Used |
|---|---|---|---|---|
| 18 | A2 | 10r black | 52.50 | 42.50 |
| 19 | A2 | 20r vermilion | 45.00 | 40.00 |
| 20 | A2 | 40r blue | 97.50 | 75.00 |
| 21 | A2 | 100r green | 87.50 | 60.00 |
| 22 | A2 | 200r yellow | 225.00 | 200.00 |
| | | *Nos. 18-22 (5)* | 507.50 | 417.50 |

### Re-issues

**1873** **Thin Bluish Toned Paper**

| No. | Type | Description | Unused | Used |
|---|---|---|---|---|
| 23 | A2 | 20r vermilion | 250.00 | 175.00 |
| 24 | A1 | 10r black | 15.00 | 10.00 |
| 25 | A1 | 20r vermilion | 21.00 | 14.00 |
| 26 | A1 | 300r dp violet | 140.00 | 110.00 |
| 27 | A1 | 600r dp violet | 175.00 | 135.00 |
| 28 | A1 | 900r dp violet | 175.00 | 135.00 |
| | | *Nos. 23-28 (6)* | 776.00 | 579.00 |

A3

A3: Same as A1 with small figures.

**1874** **Thin Bluish Toned Paper**

| No. | Type | Description | Unused | Used |
|---|---|---|---|---|
| 29 | A3 | 10r black | 45.00 | 35.00 |
| 30 | A3 | 20r vermilion | 600.00 | 425.00 |

For surcharge see No. 84. For more detailed listings, see *Scott Classic Specialized Catalogue of Stamps & Covers 1840-1940.*

A4

A4: Same as A2 with small figures.

**1875**

| No. | Type | Description | Unused | Used |
|---|---|---|---|---|
| 31 | A4 | 10r black | 52.50 | 30.00 |
| *b.* | | "20" instead of "10" | *900.00* | |
| 32 | A4 | 15r rose | 16.00 | 12.00 |
| 33 | A4 | 20r vermilion | 97.50 | 57.50 |
| | | *Nos. 31-33 (3)* | 166.00 | 99.50 |

For surcharges see Nos. 74, 78, 85. For more detailed listings, see *Scott Classic Specialized Catalogue of Stamps & Covers 1840-1940.*

A5

A6

A5: Re-cutting of A1. Small figures. "REIS" in Roman capitals. Letters larger. "V" of "SERVICO" barred. 33 lines in background. Side ornaments of five dots.

A6: First re-cutting of A2. Small figures. "REIS" in block capitals. Letters re-cut. "V" of "SERVICO" barred. 41 lines above and 43 below "REIS." Side ornaments of five dots.

*Perf. 12½ to 13½ & Compound*

**1876**

| No. | Type | Description | Unused | Used |
|---|---|---|---|---|
| 34 | A5 | 10r black | 29.00 | 19.50 |
| 35 | A5 | 20r vermilion | 23.00 | 15.00 |
| 36 | A6 | 10r black | 8.00 | 6.00 |
| 37 | A6 | 15r rose | 550.00 | 400.00 |
| 38 | A6 | 20r vermilion | 33.00 | 24.00 |
| 39 | A6 | 40r blue | 135.00 | 110.00 |
| 40 | A6 | 100r green | 210.00 | 190.00 |
| *a.* | | Imperf. | | |
| 41 | A6 | 200r yellow | 1,000. | 825.00 |
| 42 | A6 | 300r violet | 600.00 | 500.00 |
| 43 | A6 | 600r violet | *850.00* | *700.00* |
| 44 | A6 | 900r violet | *1,200.* | *800.00* |

For surcharges see Nos. 75-76, 78C-80, 86-87, 91-92, 98, 102, 107, 111.

For more detailed listings, see *Scott Classic Specialized Catalogue of Stamps & Covers 1840-1940.*

A7

A8

A9

A7: Same as A5 with addition of a star above and a bar below the value.

A8: Second re-cutting of A2. Same as A6 but 41 lines both above and below "REIS." Star above and bar below value.

A9: Third re-cutting of A2. 41 lines above and 38 below "REIS." Star above and bar below value. White line around central oval.

**1877**

| No. | Type | Description | Unused | Used |
|---|---|---|---|---|
| 45 | A7 | 10r black | 40.00 | 30.00 |
| 46 | A8 | 10r black | 60.00 | 50.00 |
| 47 | A9 | 10r black | 40.00 | 30.00 |
| 48 | A9 | 15r rose | 42.50 | 34.00 |
| 49 | A9 | 20r vermilion | 12.00 | 11.00 |
| 50 | A9 | 40r blue | 24.00 | 21.00 |
| 51 | A9 | 100r green | 115.00 | 72.50 |
| 52 | A9 | 200r yellow | 100.00 | 90.00 |
| 53 | A9 | 300r violet | 160.00 | 100.00 |
| 54 | A9 | 600r violet | 160.00 | 100.00 |
| 55 | A9 | 900r violet | 160.00 | 100.00 |
| | | *Nos. 45-55 (11)* | 913.50 | 638.50 |

For surcharges see Nos. 77, 81, 88-90, 93, 112.

No. 47, 20r, 40r and 200r exist imperf.

For more detailed listings, see *Scott Classic Specialized Catalogue of Stamps & Covers 1840-1940.*

Portuguese Crown — A10

**1877, July 15** **Typo.** ***Perf. 12½, 13½***

| No. | Type | Description | Unused | Used |
|---|---|---|---|---|
| 56 | A10 | 5r black | 8.00 | 3.50 |
| 57 | A10 | 10r yellow | 13.50 | 11.00 |
| *a.* | | Imperf. | | |
| 58 | A10 | 20r bister | 13.00 | 11.00 |
| 59 | A10 | 25r rose | 14.50 | 11.50 |
| 60 | A10 | 40r blue | 19.50 | 13.50 |
| *a.* | | Perf. 12½ | 220.00 | 175.00 |
| 61 | A10 | 50r yellow grn | 35.00 | 25.00 |
| 62 | A10 | 100r lilac | 18.50 | 14.50 |
| 63 | A10 | 200r orange | 32.00 | 24.00 |
| 64 | A10 | 300r yel brn | 34.00 | 32.00 |
| | | *Nos. 56-64 (9)* | 188.00 | 146.00 |

**1880-81**

| No. | Type | Description | Unused | Used |
|---|---|---|---|---|
| 65a | A10 | 10r green | 14.50 | 13.50 |
| 66 | A10 | 25r slate | 60.00 | 42.50 |
| 67a | A10 | 25r violet | 42.50 | 30.00 |
| 68 | A10 | 40r yellow | 52.50 | 40.00 |
| 69a | A10 | 50r dk blue | 52.50 | 35.00 |
| | | *Nos. 65a-69a (4)* | 169.50 | 121.00 |

For surcharges see Nos. 113-161. The 1880-81 issue exists perf 12½ and 13½ on thin paper, and 13½ on medium paper. Nos. 65a-69a above are the most common varieties. For detailed listings, see the *Scott Classic Specialized Catalogue.*

*The stamps of the 1877-81 issues were reprinted in 1885, on stout very white paper, ungummed and with rough perforation 13½. They were again reprinted in 1905 on thin white paper with shiny white gum and clean-cut perforation 13½ with large holes. Value of the lowest-cost reprint, $3 each.*

Stamps of 1871-77 Surcharged with New Values

Three types of 5r surcharges exist:
Type I: Surcharge 5.5mm tall I
Type II: Surcharge 5mm tall
Type III: Surcharge 4.5mm tall

**1881** **Black Surcharge**

| No. | Type | Description | Unused | Used |
|---|---|---|---|---|
| 70 | A1 | 1½r on 20r (#2) | *450.00* | *500.00* |
| 71 | A1 | 1½r on 20r (#7) | | *400.00* |
| 72 | A2 | 1½r on 20r (#11) | | *260.00* |
| 72A | A2 | 1½r on 20r (#19) | | *250.00* |
| 73 | A1 | 1½r on 20r (#25) | *250.00* | *225.00* |
| 74 | A4 | 1½r on 20r (#33) | *160.00* | *140.00* |
| 75 | A5 | 1½r on 20r (#35) | *105.00* | *90.00* |
| 76 | A6 | 1½r on 20r (#38) | *140.00* | *120.00* |
| 77 | A9 | 1½r on 20r (#49) | *210.00* | *160.00* |
| 78 | A4 | 5r on 15r (#32) (I) | 14.00 | 14.00 |
| *a.* | | Double surcharge | — | |
| *b.* | | Inverted surcharge | — | |
| *d.* | | Type II | 14.00 | 14.00 |
| 78C | A6 | 5r on 15r (#37) (I) | 190.00 | 180.00 |
| 78E | A6 | 5r on 20r (#2) (I) | | *600.00* |
| 78F | A6 | 5r on 20r (#11) (III) | | *800.00* |
| 78G | A6 | 5r on 20r (#19) (II) | | *675.00* |
| 78H | A6 | 5r on 20r (#23) (II) | *250.00* | *250.00* |
| *k.* | | Type III | | *800.00* |
| 78I | A6 | 5r on 20r (#25) (I) | *250.00* | *250.00* |
| *m.* | | Type III | *550.00* | *425.00* |
| 78J | A6 | 5r on 20r (#33) (III) | *950.00* | *850.00* |
| 79 | A5 | 5r on 20r (#35) (I) | 5.00 | 5.00 |
| *c.* | | Type II | 5.00 | 5.00 |
| *d.* | | Type III | — | 7.25 |
| *e.* | | On #35a | *375.00* | |
| 80 | A6 | 5r on 20r (#38) (I) | 5.00 | 5.00 |
| *c.* | | Type II | 5.00 | 5.00 |
| *d.* | | Type III | — | 7.25 |
| 81 | A9 | 5r on 20r (#49) (I) | 5.75 | 5.00 |
| *c.* | | Type II | 5.00 | 5.00 |

**Red Surcharge**

| No. | Type | Description | Unused | Used |
|---|---|---|---|---|
| 82 | A2 | 5r on 10r (#10) | *400.00* | *400.00* |
| 83 | A1 | 5r on 10r (#24) | *400.00* | *400.00* |
| 84 | A3 | 5r on 10r (#29) | *1,750.* | |
| 85 | A4 | 5r on 10r (#31) | *180.00* | *180.00* |
| 86 | A5 | 5r on 10r (#34) | 13.00 | 13.00 |
| *a.* | | Double surcharge | — | |
| 87 | A6 | 5r on 10r (#36) | 10.00 | 10.00 |
| 88 | A7 | 5r on 10r (#45) | 100.00 | 42.50 |
| *a.* | | Inverted surcharge | — | |
| 89 | A8 | 5r on 10r (#46) | 85.00 | 70.00 |
| 90 | A9 | 5r on 10r (#47) | 60.00 | 50.00 |
| 90C | A2 | 1½r on 10r (#10) | *400.00* | *375.00* |
| 90D | A1 | 1½r on 10r (#24) | *400.00* | *375.00* |
| 90E | A4 | 1½r on 10r (#31) | *400.00* | — |

For more detailed listings, see *Scott Classic Specialized Catalogue of Stamps & Covers 1840-1940.*

### Similar Surcharge, Handstamped
### Black Surcharge

**1883**

| No. | Type | Description | Unused | Used |
|---|---|---|---|---|
| 91 | A5 | 1½r on 10r (#34) | 1,650. | *600.00* |
| 92 | A6 | 1½r on 10r (#36) | 1,100. | *600.00* |
| 93 | A9 | 1½r on 10r (#47) | *825.00* | *400.00* |
| 94 | A1 | 4½r on 40r (#3) | 2,000. | *775.00* |
| 95 | A2 | 4½r on 40r (#12) | 45.00 | 45.00 |
| 96 | A2 | 4½r on 40r (#20) | 45.00 | 45.00 |
| 98 | A6 | 4½r on 40r (#39) | 45.00 | 45.00 |
| 99 | A1 | 4½r on 100r (#4) | 2,000. | *775.00* |
| 100 | A2 | 4½r on 100r (#13) | 52.50 | 45.00 |
| 101 | A2 | 4½r on 100r (#21) | 52.50 | 45.00 |
| 102 | A6 | 4½r on 100r (#40) | 42.50 | 32.00 |
| 104 | A1 | 6r on 100r (#4) | 2,200. | *900.00* |
| 105 | A2 | 6r on 100r (#13) | 425.00 | *290.00* |
| 106 | A2 | 6r on 100r (#21) | *275.00* | *225.00* |
| 107 | A6 | 6r on 100r (#40) | *280.00* | *250.00* |
| 108 | A1 | 6r on 200r (#5) | *825.00* | *700.00* |
| 109 | A2 | 6r on 200r (#14) | | *600.00* |
| 110 | A2 | 6r on 200r (#22) | *275.00* | *210.00* |
| 111 | A6 | 6r on 200r (#41) | 500.00 | *525.00* |
| 112 | A9 | 6r on 200r (#52) | *575.00* | *525.00* |

For more detailed listings, see *Scott Classic Specialized Catalogue of Stamps & Covers 1840-1940.*

Stamps of 1877-81 Surcharged in Black

**1881-82** ***Perf. 12½***

| No. | Type | Description | Unused | Used |
|---|---|---|---|---|
| 113 | A10 | 1½r on 5r blk | 2.75 | 1.75 |
| *a.* | | With additional surcharge "4½" in blue | 175.00 | 125.00 |
| 114 | A10 | 1½r on 10r grn | 2.75 | 2.10 |
| *a.* | | With additional surch. "6" | 200.00 | 175.00 |
| 115 | A10 | 1½r on 20r bis | 26.00 | 19.50 |
| *a.* | | Inverted surcharge | 27.50 | |
| *b.* | | Double surcharge | 27.50 | |
| *c.* | | Pair, one without surcharge | — | |
| 116 | A10 | 1½r on 25r slate | 90.00 | 70.00 |
| 117 | A10 | 1½r on 100r lil | 115.00 | 87.50 |
| 118 | A10 | 4½r on 10r grn | 240.00 | 240.00 |
| 119 | A10 | 4½r on 20r bis | 6.00 | 5.00 |
| *a.* | | Inverted surcharge | 82.50 | 65.00 |
| 120 | A10 | 4½r on 25r vio | 24.00 | 19.50 |
| 121 | A10 | 4½r on 100r lil | 200.00 | 175.00 |
| 122 | A10 | 6r on 10r yel | 97.50 | 90.00 |

123 A10 6r on 10r grn 21.00 16.50
124 A10 6r on 20r bis 27.50 19.50
125 A10 6r on 25r slate 85.00 57.50
126 A10 6r on 25r vio 7.25 5.00
127 A10 6r on 40r blue 220.00 190.00
129 A10 6r on 50r grn 115.00 90.00
130 A10 6r on 50r blue 120.00 100.00
*Nos. 113-130 (18)* 1,490. 1,264.

### *Perf. 13½, Thin or Medium Paper*

*113b* A10 1½r on 5r blk 6.75 5.00
*c.* With additional surcharge "4½" in blue 200.00
*114b* A10 1½r on 10r grn 6.75 5.00
*115d* A10 1½r on 20r bis 26.00 19.50
*116a* A10 1½r on 25r slate 60.00 47.50
*117a* A10 1½r on 100r lil 95.00 85.00
*118a* A10 4½r on 10r grn 240.00 240.00
*119b* A10 4½r on 20r bis 8.50 6.75
*120a* A10 4½r on 25r vio 24.00 19.50
*121a* A10 4½r on 100r lil 175.00 175.00
*122a* A10 6r on 10r yel 90.00 67.50
*123a* A10 6r on 10r grn 24.00 19.00
*124a* A10 6r on 20r bis 65.00 42.50
*125a* A10 6r on 25r slate 65.00 42.50
*126a* A10 6r on 25r vio 5.00 3.75
*127a* A10 6r on 40r blue 120.00 90.00
**128** A10 6r on 40r yel 90.00 75.00
*129a* A10 6r on 50r grn 85.00 72.50
*130a* A10 6r on 50r blue 115.00 87.50

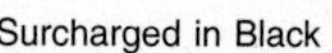

Surcharged in Black

### *Perf. 12½*

131 A10 1t on 10r grn 325.00 275.00
*a.* With additional surch. "6" 600.00 525.00
132 A10 1t on 20r bis 85.00 67.50
133 A10 1t on 25r slate 90.00 72.50
134 A10 1t on 25r vio 24.00 18.00
135 A10 1t on 40r blue 31.00 24.00
136 A10 1t on 50r grn 100.00 80.00
137 A10 1t on 50r blue 45.00 31.00
138 A10 1t on 100r lil 40.00 23.00
139 A10 1t on 200r org 67.50 57.50
140 A10 2t on 25r slate 72.50 57.50
141 A10 2t on 25r vio 24.00 17.00
142 A10 2t on 40r blue 115.00 75.00
144 A10 2t on 50r grn 45.00 35.00
*a.* Inverted surcharge *110.00 100.00*
145 A10 2t on 50r blue 145.00 120.00
146 A10 2t on 100r lil 21.00 17.00
147 A10 2t on 200r org 75.00 57.50
149 A10 4t on 10r grn 35.00 27.50
*a.* Inverted surcharge *45.00 45.00*
150 A10 4t on 50r grn 35.00 24.00
*a.* With additional surch. "2" *200.00 110.00*
151 A10 4t on 200r org 80.00 57.50
152 A10 8t on 20r bis 87.50 65.00
153 A10 8t on 25r rose 350.00 300.00
154 A10 8t on 40r blue 75.00 65.00
155 A10 8t on 100r lil 67.50 57.50
156 A10 8t on 200r org 67.50 57.50
157 A10 8t on 300r brn 67.50 52.50
*Nos. 131-157 (27)* 2,293. 1,837.

For more detailed listings, see *Scott Classic Specialized Catalogue of Stamps & Covers 1840-1940.*

### *Perf. 13½*
### Thin or Medium Paper

*131b* A10 1t on 10r grn 210.00 200.00
*132a* A10 1t on 20r bis 95.00 80.00
*133a* A10 1t on 25r slate 57.50 45.00
*134a* A10 1t on 25r vio 24.00 19.00
*135a* A10 1t on 40r blue 75.00 72.50
*136a* A10 1t on 50r grn 97.50 87.50
*137b* A10 1t on 50r blue 85.00 72.50
*138a* A10 1t on 100r lilac 85.00 72.50
*139a* A10 1t on 200r org 80.00 67.50
*140b* A10 2t on 25r slate 65.00 50.00
*141a* A10 2t on 25r vio 42.50 35.00
*142a* A10 2t on 40r blue 57.50 47.50
**143** A10 2t on 40r yel 57.50 45.00
*144b* A10 2t on 50r grn 34.00 27.00
*145a* A10 2t on 50r blue 150.00 120.00
*147a* A10 2t on 200r org 67.50 50.00
**148** A10 2t on 300r brn 65.00 57.50
*149b* A10 4t on 10r grn 19.00 16.00
*150b* A10 4t on 50r grn 19.00 16.00
*c.* With additional surch. "2" 525.00 425.00
*151a* A10 4t on 200r org 80.00 57.50
*152a* A10 8t on 20r bis 75.00 57.50
*153a* A10 8t on 25r rose 325.00 280.00
*154a* A10 8t on 40r blue 85.00 75.00
*155a* A10 8t on 100r lil 67.50 57.50
*156a* A10 8t on 200r org 57.50 50.00
**157** A10 8t on 300r brn 67.50 52.50

For more detailed listings, see *Scott Classic Specialized Catalogue of Stamps & Covers 1840-1940.*

**1882**

### *Perf. 12½*
### Blue Surcharge

158 A10 4½r on 5r black 13.00 13.00
*a.* Perf. 13½ 13.00 13.00

### Similar Surcharge, Handstamped

**1883**

159 A10 1½r on 5r black 35.00 30.00
160 A10 1½r on 10r grn 30.00 25.00
161 A10 4½r on 100r lil *400.00 325.00*

The "2" in "½" is 3mm high, instead of 2mm as on Nos. 113, 114 and 121.

The handstamp is known double on #159-161.

A12

First Printing — Type 1

Third Printing — Type 2

There were three printings of the 1882-83 issue.

The first had "REIS" in thick letters with acute accent on the "E."

The second had "REIS" in thin letters with accent on the "E."

The third had the "E" without accent. In the first printing the "E" sometimes had a grave or circumflex accent.

The third printing may be divided into two sets, with or without a small circle in the cross of the crown.

Nos. 162-168 exist with two types of crosses on the top of the crown.

Type I: Closed narrow cross.

Type II: Open cross with dot in the center

### With or Without Accent on "E" of "REIS"

**1882-83** **Typo.**

### Type I
### *Perf. 12½, Thin to Medium Paper*

162 A12 1½r black 1.00 .85
163 A12 4½r olive bister 1.10 .60
164 A12 6r green 1.25 1.00
165 A12 1t rose 1.25 1.00
166 A12 2t blue 1.25 1.00
167 A12 4t lilac 6.00 3.50
168 A12 8t orange 6.00 5.00
*Nos. 162-168 (7)* 17.85 12.95

### *Perf. 13½, Thin or Medium Paper*

*162b* A12 1½r black 1.50 1.05
*163a* A12 4½r olive bister 1.50 1.05
*164a* A12 6r green 1.50 1.05
*165a* A12 1t rose 1.50 1.05
*166a* A12 2t blue 1.50 1.05
*167a* A12 4t lilac 30.00 24.00
*168a* A12 8t orange 8.00 5.50

### *Perf. 12½, Medium Paper*
### Type II

*162c* A12 1½r black 1.50 1.20
*163b* A12 4½r olive bister 1.50 1.20
*164b* A12 6r green 1.50 1.20
*165b* A12 1t rose 19.50 15.00

### *Perf. 13½, Medium Paper*

*162d* A12 1½r black 1.50 1.05
*163c* A12 4½r olive bister 16.00 13.50
*164c* A12 6r green 16.00 13.50
*165c* A12 1t rose 19.50 15.00
*166b* A12 2t blue 16.00 13.50
*167b* A12 4t lilac 30.00 24.00
*168b* A12 8t orange 30.00 24.00

"REIS" no serifs — A13

"REIS" with serifs — A14

**1883** **Litho.** ***Imperf.***

169 A13 1½r black 2.40 1.75
*a.* Tête bêche pair *3,500.*
170 A13 4½r olive grn 24.00 17.00
171 A13 6r green 21.00 14.50
*a.* Tête bêche pair *1,800.*
172 A14 1½r black 240.00 67.50
173 A14 6r green 90.00 55.00
*Nos. 169-173 (5)* 377.40 155.75

King Luiz — A15

**1886, Apr. 29** **Embossed** ***Perf. 12½***

174 A15 1½r black 3.75 1.75
175 A15 4½r bister 4.25 2.10
176 A15 6r dp green 5.75 2.75
177 A15 1t brt rose 7.25 4.25
178 A15 2t deep blue 14.00 6.75
179 A15 4t gray vio 14.00 6.75
180 A15 8t orange 14.00 6.75
*Nos. 174-180 (7)* 63.00 31.10

For surcharges and overprints see Nos. 224-230, 277-278, 282, 317-323, 354, 397.

*Nos. 178-179 were reprinted. Originals have yellow gum. Reprints have white gum and clean-cut perforation 13½. Value, $4 each.*

### *Perf. 13½*

*174a* A3 1½r black 1,800. 1,500.
*175a* A3 4½r bister 97.50 42.50
*176a* A3 6r dp green 97.50 42.50
*177a* A3 1t brt rose 24.00 13.50
*178a* A3 2t deep blue 24.00 13.50
*179a* A3 4t gray vio 24.00 11.00
*180a* A3 8t orange 19.50 11.00

King Carlos — A16

**1895-96** **Typo.** ***Perf. 12½***

181 A16 1½r black 2.60 .85
182 A16 4½r pale orange 2.10 .85
*183a* A16 6r green 5.50 2.00
184 A16 9r gray lilac ('96) 7.50 4.50
*185a* A16 1t lt blue 8.00 3.75
*186a* A16 2t rose 24.00 13.50
*187a* A16 4t dk blue 6.75 4.00
188 A16 8t brt violet ('96) 5.50 3.75
*Nos. 181-188 (8)* 28.70 15.05

For surcharges and overprints see Nos. 231-238,275-276, 279-281, 324-331, 352.

*No. 184 was reprinted. Reprints have white gum, and clean-cut perforation 13½. Value $10.*

### *Perf. 11½*

*181a* A3 1½r black 2.40 1.25
*182b* A3 4½r pale orange 1.75 1.25
**185** A16 1t lt blue 3.00 1.75
**186** A16 2t rose 2.40 1.00
**187** A16 4t dk blue 3.50 1.50

### *Perf. 13½*

*181b* A16 1½r black 1.75 1.00
*182a* A16 4½r pale orange 11.00
**183** A16 6r green 2.10 .85
*184b* A16 9r gray lilac ('96) 7.25 5,50

---

Common Design Types pictured following the introduction.

---

### Vasco da Gama Issue
Common Design Types

**1898, May 1** **Engr.** ***Perf. 14 to 15***

189 CD20 1½r blue green 1.25 .70
190 CD21 4½r red 1.25 .70
191 CD22 6r red violet 1.25 .90
192 CD23 9r yellow green 2.00 1.00
193 CD24 1t dk blue 3.50 2.10
194 CD25 2t violet brn 4.25 2.10

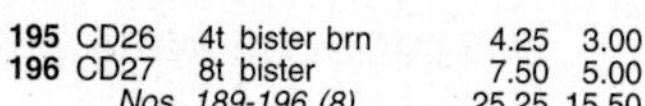
195 CD26 4t bister brn 4.25 3.00
196 CD27 8t bister 7.50 5.00
*Nos. 189-196 (8)* 25.25 15.50

For overprints and surcharges see Nos. 290-297, 384-389.

King Carlos — A17

### Name and Value in Black except No. 219

**1898-1903** **Typo.** ***Perf. 11½***

197 A17 1r gray ('02) .35 .25
198 A17 1½r orange .35 .25
199 A17 1½r slate ('02) .45 .25
200 A17 2r orange ('02) .35 .25
201 A17 2½r yel brn ('02) .45 .25
202 A17 3r dp blue ('02) .45 .25
203 A17 4½r lt green 1.25 .55
204 A17 6r brown 1.25 .55
205 A17 6r gray grn ('02) .45 .25
206 A17 9r dull vio 1.25 .55
*a.* 9r gray lilac 1.75 1.00
208 A17 1t sea green 1.50 .60
209 A17 1t car rose ('02) .75 .25
210 A17 2t blue 1.75 .60
*a.* Perf. 13½ 55.00 21.00
211 A17 2t brown ('02) 3.50 1.60
212 A17 2½t dull bl ('02) 13.50 6.50
213 A17 4t blue, *blue* 3.75 2.50
*a.* 4t blue, *yelsh* 4.25 2.40
214 A17 5t brn, *straw* ('02) 4.25 2.50
215 A17 8t red lil, *pnksh* 4.25 2.10
216 A17 8t red vio, *pink* ('02) 7.25 3.50
217 A17 12t blue, *pink* ('00) 6.50 3.50
218 A17 12t grn, *pink* ('02) 8.50 3.50
219 A17 1rp blk & red, *bl* ('00) 13.00 5.25
220 A17 1rp dl bl, *straw* ('02) 17.00 14.50
221 A17 2rp vio, *yelsh* ('00) 17.00 8.50
222 A17 2rp gray blk, *straw* ('03) 29.00 27.50
*Nos. 197-222 (25)* 138.10 86.30

No. 210 Surcharged in Black

**1900**

223 A17 1½r on 2t blue 4.25 2.40
*a.* Inverted surcharge *240.00 240.00*
*b.* Perf. 13½ 180.00 150.00

For more detailed listings, see *Scott Classic Specialized Catalogue of Stamps & Covers 1840-1940.*

Stamps of 1885-96 Surcharged in Black or Red

### On Stamps of 1886

**1902** ***Perf. 12½, 13½ (#224, 229-230)***

224 A15 1r on 2t blue 1.20 .50
*a.* Perf. 12½ 1.50 .90
225 A15 2r on 4½r bis .65 .50
*a.* Inverted surcharge *22.50 22.50*
*b.* Double surcharge
226 A15 2½r on 6r green .55 .25
227 A15 3r on 1t rose .55 .25
228 A15 2½t on 1½r blk (R) 3.00 2.10
229 A15 2½t on 4t gray vio 3.00 2.10
*a.* Perf. 12½ 20.00 14.50
230 A15 5t on 8t orange 1.75 1.00
*a.* Perf. 12½ 35.00 21.00

### On Stamps of 1895-96
### *Perf. 11½ (#235-238), 12½*

231 A16 1r on 6r green .50 .25
*a.* Perf. 13½ 210.00 160.00
232 A16 2r on 8t brt vio .35 .25
233 A16 2½r on 9r gray vio .35 .35
234 A16 3r on 4½r yel 2.25 1.40
*a.* Inverted surcharge 28.00 28.00
*b.* Perf. 11½ — 7.25
235 A16 3r on 1t lt bl 2.10 1.50
236 A16 2½t on 1½r blk (R) 2.60 1.50
*a.* Perf. 12½ 5.25 3.75
*b.* Perf. 13½ 3.00 1,75
237 A16 5t on 2t rose 2.60 1.50
*a.* Perf. 12½ 210.00 160.00

238 A16 5t on 4t dk bl 2.60 1.50
a. Perf. 12½ 210.00 160.00
*Nos. 224-238 (15)* 24.05 14.95

*Nos. 224, 229, 231, 233, 234, 235 and 238 were reprinted in 1905. They have whiter gum than the originals and very clean-cut perf. 13½. Value $2.50 each.*

Nos. 204, 208, 210 Overprinted

**1902** ***Perf. 11½***
239 A17 6r brown 3.25 1.50
a. Inverted overprint
240 A17 1t sea green 3.25 1.50
241 A17 2t blue 3.25 1.50
a. Perf. 13½ 725.00 500.00
*Nos. 239-241 (3)* 9.75 4.50

No. 212 Surcharged in Black

**1905**
243 A17 2t on 2½t dull blue 3.50 2.75

Stamps of 1898-1903 Overprinted in Lisbon in Carmine or Green

**1911**
244 A17 1r gray .25 .25
a. Inverted overprint 11.00 11.00
245 A17 1½r slate .25 .25
a. Double overprint 11.00 11.00
246 A17 2r orange .25 .25
a. Double overprint 15.00 15.00
b. Inverted overprint 11.00 11.00
247 A17 2½r yellow brn .40 .25
248 A17 3r deep blue .40 .25
249 A17 4½r light green .40 .25
250 A17 6r gray green .35 .25
251 A17 9r gray lilac .40 .25
252 A17 1t car rose (G) .60 .25
253 A17 2t brown .60 .25
254 A17 4t blue, *blue* 1.50 1.25
255 A17 5t brn, *straw* 2.40 1.25
256 A17 8t vio, *pink* 6.75 3.75
257 A17 12t grn, *pink* 7.25 4.00
a. 12t grn, *yellow* 9.00 5.00
258 A17 1rp dl bl, *straw* 11.50 9.50
259 A17 2rp gray blk, *straw* 14.50 10.00
*Nos. 244-259 (16)* 47.80 32.25

A18

Values are for pairs, both halves.

**1911** **Perforated Diagonally**
260 A18 1r on 2r orange 1.00 .85
a. Without diagonal perf. 42.50 34.00
b. Cut diagonally instead of perf. 21.00 17.00

## Stamps of Preceding Issues Perforated Vertically through the Middle and Each Half Surcharged

a

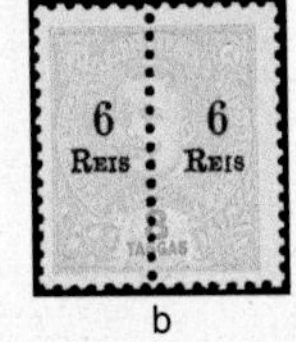

b

Four types of 1½r surcharge exist differing in numerals in the fraction.
Type I: top end of "2" points downward.
Type II: top serif on "1" in horizonal, top end of "2" points upward.
Type III: cursive "2."
Type IV: top serif on "1" pointing downward, top end of "2" points upward.
Values are for pairs, both halves of the stamp.

**1912-13** **On Issue of 1898-1903**
260C A17(a) 1r on 2r org 1.00 .75
261 A17(a) 1r on 1t car 1.00 .75
262 A17(a) 1r on 5t brn, *straw* 140.00 85.00
263 A17(b) 1r on 5t brn, *straw* 6.50 5.00
264 A17(a) 1½r on 2½r yel brn (II) 2.40 1.75
a. Type I 4.25 3.75
d. Type IV 4.25 3.75
264B A17(b) 1½r on 2½r yel brn (II) 42.50 35.00
h. Type I 67.50 50.00
i. Type IV 67.50 50.00
264C A17(a) 1½r on 4½r lt grn (I) 21.00 12.00
j. Type II 45.00 30.00
k. Type IV 30.00 21.00
265 A17(a) 1½r on 9r gray lil (III) 1.50 1.25
a. Type I 3.50 2.40
b. Type IV 3.50 2.40
266 A17(a) 1½r on 4t bl, *bl* (II) 3.25 2.00
a. Type IV 3.50 2.40
b. Type IV 3.50 2.40
267 A17(a) 2r on 2½r yel brn 1.50 1.25
268 A17(a) 2r on 4t bl, *bl* 2.25 1.75
269 A17(a) 3r on 2½r yel brn 1.50 1.25
270 A17(a) 3r on 2t brown 2.00 1.50
271 A17(a) 6r on 4½r lt grn 1.75 1.50
272 A17(a) 6r on 9r gray lil 1.75 1.50
273 A17(b) 6r on 9r dull vio 300.00 240.00
a. A17(a) 6r on 9r dull vio 2.50 2.10
274 A17(b) 6r on 8t red vio, *pink* 3.00 2.50

**On Nos. 237-238, 230, 226, 233**
***Perf. 11½, 12½ (#278-279), 13½ (#277, 282)***
275 A16(b) 1r on 5t on 2t 24.00 17.00
276 A16(b) 1r on 5t on 4t 14.00 10.00
a. Perf. 12½ 50.00 —
277 A15(b) 1r on 5t on 8t 5.00 3.25
a. Perf. 12½ 100.00 100.00
278 A15(a) 2r on 2½r on 6r 5.00 3.25
279 A16(a) 2r on 2½r on 9r 45.00 37.50
280 A16(b) 3r on 5t on 2t 22.50 17.50
b. Perf. 12½ 42.50
281 A16(b) 3r on 5t on 4t 14.00 10.00
b. Perf. 12½ 67.50 55.00
282 A15(b) 3r on 5t on 8t 2.75 2.00
d. Perf. 12½ 21.00 17.00

**On Issue of 1911**
283 A17(a) 1r on 1r gray .50 .45
283B A17(a) 1r on 2r org .50 .45
284 A17(a) 1r on 1t car .50 .45
285 A17(a) 1r on 5t brn, *straw* .50 .45
285A A17(b) 1r on 5t brn, *straw* 1,150. 975.00
285B A17(a) 1½r on 4½r lt grn 1.25 1.00
286 A17(a) 3r on 2t brn 21.00 16.50
289 A17(a) 6r on 9r gray lil 1.25 1.00

There are several settings of these surcharges and many minor varieties of the letters and figures, notably a small "6." Nos. 260-289 were issued mostly without gum.

More than half of Nos. 260C-289 exist with inverted or double surcharge, or with bisecting perforation omitted. The legitimacy of these varieties is questioned. Price of inverted surcharges, $3-$15; double surcharges, $1-$4; perf. omitted, $1.50-$15.

Similar surcharges made without official authorization on stamps of type A17 are: 2r on 2½r, 3r on 2½r, 3r on 5t, and 6r on 4½r.

Vasco da Gama Issue Overprinted

**1913**
290 CD20 1½r blue green .35 .25
291 CD21 4½r red .35 .25
a. Double overprint 22.50
292 CD22 6r red violet .45 .40
a. Double overprint 22.50
293 CD23 9r yellow grn .50 .45
294 CD24 1t dark blue 1.40 .60
295 CD25 2t violet brown 2.40 2.10
296 CD26 4t orange brn 1.75 .60
297 CD27 8t bister 3.00 1.50
*Nos. 290-297 (8)* 10.20 6.15

Issues of 1898-1913 Overprinted Locally in Red

**1913-15** **On Issues of 1898-1903**
300 A17 2r orange 30.00 24.00
301 A17 2½r yellow brn 7.50 6.00
302 A17 3r dp blue 19.00
303 A17 4½r lt green 12.00 8.50
304 A17 6r gray grn 25.00
305 A17 9r gray lilac 18.00 15.00
306 A17 1t sea green 45.00
307 A17 2t blue 50.00
309 A17 4t blue, *blue* 60.00 55.00
310 A17 5t brn, *straw* 55.00
311 A17 8t red vio, *pink* 65.00
312 A17 12t grn, *pink* 24.00 18.00
313 A17 1rp blk & red, *bl* 100.00
314 A17 1rp dl bl, *straw* 57.50 50.00
315 A17 2rp gray blk, *straw* 85.00 72.50
316 A17 2rp vio, *yelsh* 85.00 72.50
*Nos. 300-316 (16)* 738.00 321.50

Inverted or double overprints exist on 2½r, 4½r, 9r, 1rp and 2rp.

Nos. 300-316 were issued without gum except 4½r and 9r.

Nos. 302, 304, 306, 307, 310, 311 and 313 were not regularly issued. Nor were the 1½r, 2t brown and 12t blue on pink with preceding overprint.

**Same Overprint in Red or Green on Provisional Issue of 1902**
317 A15 1r on 2t blue 45.00
a. "REPUBLICA" inverted 140.00
318 A15 2r on 4½r bis 45.00
a. "REPUBLICA" inverted 140.00
319 A15 2½r on 6r grn 9.00 7.25
a. "REPUBLICA" inverted 19.00
320 A15 3r on 1t rose (R) 11.00
321 A15 2½t on 4t gray vio 110.00
323 A15 5t on 8t org (G) 17.50 12.00
a. Red overprint 50.00 40.00
b. Perf. 12½ 60.00 50.00
324 A16 1r on 6r grn 35.00 22.50
325 A16 2r on 8t vio 50.00 42.50
a. Inverted surcharge 110.00
327 A16 3r on 4½r yel 82.50
328 A16 3r on 1t lt bl 82.50
329 A16 5t on 2t rose (G) 24.00 18.00
330 A16 5t on 4t bl (G) 15.00 11.00
331 A16 5t on 4t bl (R) 33.00 27.00
a. "REPUBLICA" inverted 55.00
b. "REPUBLICA" double 55.00
c. Perf. 12½ 42.50 35.00
*Nos. 317-331 (13)* 559.50 140.25

The 2½r on 1½r of types A15 and A16, the 3r on 1t (A15) and 2½r on 9r (A16) were clandestinely printed.

Some authorities question the status of No. 317-318, 320-321, 324, 327-328.

**Same Overprint on Nos. 240-241**
**1913-15**
334 A17 1t sea green 72.50 60.00
335 A17 2t blue 72.50 60.00

This overprint was applied to No. 239 without official authorization. Value $35.

**On Issue of 1912-13 Perforated through the Middle**

Values are for pairs, both halves of the stamp.

336 A17(a) 1r on 2r org 135.00 12.00
340 A17(a) 1½r on 4½r lt grn 17.50 13.50
a. Type II 21.00 17.00
b. Type III 18.00 15.00
341 A17(a) 1½r on 9r gray lil 20.00
342 A17(a) 1½r on 4t bl, *bl* 27.50
343 A17(a) 2r on 2½r yel brn 20.00
344 A17(a) 2r on 4t bl, *bl* 27.50
345 A17(a) 3r on 2½r yel brn 22.50
346 A17(a) 3r on 2t brn 13.00 7.25
347 A17(a) 6r on 4½r lt grn 6.75 5.25
a. Large "E" 12.00 8.50
b. Large "I" 18.00 12.00
c. Large "S" 18.00 12.00
d. "S" sans-serif 18.00 12.00
348 A17(a) 6r on 9r gray lil 9.75 7.25
350 A17(b) 6r on 8t red vio, *pink* 9.75 8.50
352 A16(b) 1r on 5t on 4t bl 110.00
354 A15(a) 2r on 2½r on 6r grn 13.00
*Nos. 334-354 (15)* 577.25

Ceres — A21

**Name and Value in Black**
**Chalky Paper**

**1914** **Typo.** ***Perf. 15x14***
357 A21 1r olive brn .75 *.70*
358 A21 1½r yellow grn .75 *.70*
359 A21 2r black 1.10 *.70*
360 A21 2½r olive grn 1.10 *.70*
361 A21 3r lilac 1.20 *.70*
362 A21 4½r orange brn 1.20 *.70*
363 A21 5r blue green 1.20 *.70*
364 A21 6r lilac brown .90 *.70*
365 A21 9r ultra 1.20 *.70*
366 A21 10r carmine 1.50 .85
367 A21 1t lt violet 2.40 .85
368 A21 2t deep blue 3.00 1.20
369 A21 3t yellow brown 3.75 1.50
370 A21 4t slate 2.40 1.75
371 A21 8t plum 7.25 6.00
372 A21 12t brown, *green* 6.75 5.50
373 A21 1rp brown, *pink* 35.00 *21.00*
374 A21 2rp org, *salmon* 21.00 *17.00*
375 A21 3rp green, *blue* 28.00 42.50
*Nos. 357-375 (19)* 120.45 104.45

**Glazed Paper**

**1915, Jan.**
*357a* A21 1r olive brn 1.50 1.50
*359a* A21 2r black 1.50 1.50
*360a* A21 2½r olive grn 1.50 1.50
*361a* A21 3r lilac 1.50 1.50
*362a* A21 4½r orange brn 1.50 1.50
*363a* A21 5r blue green 1.50 1.50
*364a* A21 6r lilac brown 1.50 1.50
*366a* A21 10r carmine 1.50 1.50
*367a* A21 1t lt violet 1.75 1.50
*369a* A21 3t yel brown 1.75 1.50

**1916-20** **Ordinary Paper**
375A A21 1r olive brn 2.75 *2.50*
375B A21 1½r yellow grn 2.75 *2.50*
b. Imperf.
375C A21 2r black ('19) 5.25 *5.00*
375D A21 2½r olive grn ('19) 2.75 *2.50*
375E A21 3r lilac ('16) 2.75 *2.50*
375F A21 4½r orange brn ('19) 2.75 *2.50*
375G A21 6r lilac brown ('16) 2.75 *2.50*
375H A21 1t lt violet ('16) 2.75 *2.50*
375I A21 2t deep blue ('16) 5.25 *3.00*
*Nos. 375A-375I (9)* 29.75 25.50

**1921-23** ***Perf. 12x11½***
375J A21 1r olive brn 2.75 *2.40*
375K A21 1½r yellow grn 2.75 *2.40*
375L A21 2r black 3.75 *3.00*
375M A21 3r lilac ('22) 2.75 *2.40*
375N A21 4r blue ('22) 2.10 1.75
375O A21 4½r orange brn 11.00 9.00
375P A21 5r blue green 14.50 12.00
375Q A21 6r lilac brown 2.10 1.75
375R A21 9r ultra 6.75 5.00
375S A21 10r carmine 30.00 21.00
375T A21 1t lt violet 9.75 6.00
375U A21 1½t gray green ('22) 2.10 1.20
375V A21 2t deep blue 9.75 7.25
375W A21 2½t turquoise blue ('22) 2.40 1.75
375X A21 3t4r yellow brown ('23) 6.75 4.25
375Y A21 4t slate 9.75 7.25
375Z A21 8t plum 16.00 13.00
*Nos. 375J-375Z (17)* 134.95 101.40

The 1, 2, 2½, 3, 4½r, 1, 2, and 4t exist with the black inscriptions inverted and the 2½r with them double, one inverted, but it is not known that any of these were regularly issued.

For surcharges see Nos. 400, 400A, 420, 421, 423.

Nos. 249, 251-253, 256-259 Surcharged in Black

**1914**
376 A17 1½r on 4½r grn 1.35 1.00
a. Type II 5.50 4.00
b. Type III 2.75 2.10
c. Inverted surcharge 15.00 12.00
d. "REPUBLICA" omitted 18.00 14.50
377 A17 1½r on 9r gray lil 1.35 1.00
a. Type II 5.50 4.00
b. Type III 2.75 2.10
c. Inverted surcharge 15.00 12.00
378 A17 1½r on 12t grn, *pink* 2.10 1.75
a. Type II 8.00 6.00
b. Type III 4.25 3.00
379 A17 3r on 1t car rose 1.50 1.25
b. Inverted surcharge 15.00 12.00
c. "REPUBLICA" omitted 18.00 14.50
380 A17 3r on 2t brn 8.00 6.75
b. Inverted surcharge 27.00 21.00
381 A17 3r on 8t red vio, *pink* 10.00 8.00
382 A17 3r on 1rp dl bl, *straw* 2.10 1.35
383 A17 3r on 2rp gray blk, *straw* 2.75 1.75

Vasco da Gama Issue Surcharged in Black

384 CD21 1½r on 4½r red 1.00 .60
a. Inverted surcharge 13.50
385 CD23 1½r on 9r yel grn 1.00 .60
a. Inverted surcharge 13.50
386 CD24 3r on 1t dk bl 1.10 .60
a. Inverted surcharge 13.50
387 CD25 3r on 2t vio brn 4.25 3.50
388 CD26 3r on 4t org brn 1.10 .60
389 CD27 3r on 8t bister 3.75 2.75
a. Inverted surcharge 21.00
*Nos. 376-389 (14)* 41.35 31.50

For more detailed listings, see *Scott Classic Specialized Catalogue of Stamps & Covers 1840-1940.*

Nos. 303, 305, 312 and 315 Surcharged in Black

**1915**

390 A17 1½r on 4½r grn 45.00 22.50
a. "REPUBLICA" omitted *77.50 47.50*
b. "REPUBLICA" inverted 82.50
391 A17 1½r on 9r gray lil 14.00 8.25
a. "REPUBLICA" omitted 35.00
392 A17 1½r on 12t grn, *pink* 6.00 4.25
a. Type II 13.50 11.00
b. Type III 9.00 7.25
396 A17 3r on 2rp gray blk, *straw* 15.50 13.00
*Nos. 390-396 (4)* 80.50 48.00

Nos. 390, 390a, 390b, 391, and 391a were not regularly issued. The 3r on 2½r (A17) was surcharged without official authorization.

Preceding Issues Overprinted in Carmine

**1915** **On No. 230**

397 A15 5t on 8t org 3.25 1.75

**On Nos. 241, 243**

398 A17 2t blue 2.50 1.75
399 A17 2t on 2½t dl bl 3.00 1.75
*Nos. 397-399 (3)* 8.75 5.25

Nos. 375C, 359 Surcharged in Carmine

**1922**

400 A21 1½r on 2r black (ordinary paper) 2.10 1.20
400A A21 1½r on 2r black (chalky paper) 1.20 .75
b. Glazed paper 3.75 1.75

**Ceres Type of 1913-23**
**Name and Value in Black**

**1922** **Typo.** ***Perf. 12x11½***
**Glazed Paper**

407 A21 1rp gray brn 24.00 20.00
408 A21 2rp yellow 28.00 *28.00*
409 A21 3rp bluish grn 42.50 *42.50*
410 A21 5rp carmine rose 50.00 *50.00*
*Nos. 407-410 (4)* 144.50 140.50

Vasco da Gama and Flagship
A22

**1925, Jan. 30** **Litho.**
**Without Gum**

411 A22 6r brown 6.75 6.00
412 A22 1t red violet 9.00 7.25

400th anniv. of the death of Vasco da Gama (1469?-1524), Portuguese navigator.

Monument to St. Francis — A23

Image of St. Francis — A25

Autograph of St. Francis
A24

Image of St. Francis — A26

Tomb of St. Francis — A28

Church of Bom Jesus at Goa — A27

**1931, Dec. 3** ***Perf. 14***

414 A23 1r gray green 1.00 .80
415 A24 2r brown 1.00 .80
416 A25 6r red violet 2.00 1.00
417 A26 1½t yellow brn 7.75 5.00
418 A27 2t deep blue 11.50 7.25
419 A28 2½t light red 16.50 8.00
*Nos. 414-419 (6)* 39.75 22.85

Exposition of St. Francis Xavier at Goa, in December, 1931.

Nos. 371 and 375X Surcharged

**1931-32** ***Perf. 15x14***
**Chalky Paper**

420 A21 1½r on 8t plum ('32) 5.50 3.00

**Ordinary Paper**
***Perf. 12x11½***

421 A21 1½r on 8t plum ('32) 3.75 2.40
423 A21 2½t on 3t4r yel brn 77.50 57.50

"Portugal" and Vasco da Gama's Flagship "San Gabriel" — A29

***Perf. 11½x12***

**1933** **Typo.** **Wmk. 232**

424 A29 1r bister .25 .25
425 A29 2r olive brn .25 .25
426 A29 4r violet .25 .25
427 A29 6r dk green .25 .25
428 A29 8r black .30 .25
429 A29 1t gray .30 .25
430 A29 1½t dp rose .30 .25
431 A29 2t brown .30 .25
432 A29 2½t dk blue 1.60 .50
433 A29 3t brt blue 1.75 .50
434 A29 5t red orange 1.75 .50
435 A29 1rp olive grn 7.75 3.25
436 A29 2rp maroon 19.50 7.50
437 A29 3rp orange 28.00 8.75
438 A29 5rp apple grn 40.00 25.00
*Nos. 424-438 (15)* 102.55 48.00

For surcharges see Nos. 454-463, 472-474, J34-J36.

**Common Design Types**
***Perf. 13½x13***

**1938, Sept. 1** **Engr.** **Unwmk.**
**Name and Value in Black**

439 CD34 1r gray grn .25 .25
440 CD34 2r orange brn .25 .25
441 CD34 3r dk vio brn .25 .25
442 CD34 6r brt green .25 .25
443 CD35 10r dk carmine .40 .25
444 CD35 1t brt red vio .40 .25
445 CD35 1½t red .40 .25
446 CD37 2t orange .40 .25
447 CD37 2½t blue .40 .25
448 CD37 3t slate 1.00 .35
449 CD36 5t rose vio 1.75 .40
450 CD36 1rp brown car 4.50 1.00
451 CD36 2rp olive grn 7.00 2.75
452 CD38 3rp blue vio 13.00 6.00
453 CD38 5rp red brown 27.00 8.50
*Nos. 439-453 (15)* 57.25 21.25

For surcharges see Nos. 492-495, 504-505.

Stamps of 1933 Surcharged in Black

**1941, June** **Wmk. 232** ***Perf. 11½x12***

454 A29 1t on 1½t dp rose 2.50 2.00
455 A29 1t on 1rp olive grn 2.50 2.00
456 A29 1t on 2rp maroon 2.50 2.00
457 A29 1t on 5rp apple grn 2.50 2.00
*Nos. 454-457 (4)* 10.00 8.00

Nos. 430-431 Surcharged

**1943**

458 A29 3r on 1½t dp rose 1.25 .80
459 A29 1t on 2t brown 2.75 2.25

**Nos. 434, 428, 437 and 432 Surcharged in Dark Blue or Carmine**

a

b

**1945-46** **Wmk. 232** ***Perf. 11½x12***

460 A29(a) 1r on 5t red org (DB) .90 .80
461 A29(b) 2r on 8r blk (C) .90 .80
462 A29(b) 3r on 3rp org (DB) ('46) 2.25 1.75
463 A29(b) 6r on 2½t dk bl (C) 2.25 1.75
*Nos. 460-463 (4)* 6.30 5.10

St. Francis Xavier
A30

Luis de Camoens
A31

Garcia de Orta — A32

St. John de Britto — A33

Arch of the Viceroy
A34

Affonso de Albuquerque
A35

Vasco da Gama — A36

Francisco de Almeida — A37

***Perf. 11½***

**1946, May 28** **Litho.** **Unwmk.**

464 A30 1r black & gray blk .50 .25
465 A31 2r rose brn & pale rose brn .50 .25
466 A32 6r ocher & dl yel .50 .25
467 A33 7r vio & pale vio 3.00 3.00
468 A34 9r sepia & buff 3.00 1.40
469 A35 1t dk sl grn & sl grn 2.25 1.40
470 A36 3½t ultra & pale ultra 2.25 2.10
471 A37 1rp choc & bis brn 6.25 2.75
a. Miniature sheet of 8, #464-471 35.00 30.00
*Nos. 464-471 (8)* 18.25 11.40

No. 471a sold for 1½ rupias.

See #476. For surcharges see #595, J43-J46.

No. 428, 431 and 433 Surcharged in Carmine or Black

**1946** **Wmk. 232** ***Perf. 11½x12***

472 A29 (c) 1r on 8r blk (C) .80 .80
473 A29 (b) 3r on 2t brn .80 .80
474 A29 (b) 6r on 3t brt bl 2.25 1.90
*Nos. 472-474 (3)* 3.85 3.50

**Type of 1946 and**

Joao de Castro — A38

José Vaz — A39

Luis de Ataide — A40

Duarte Pacheco Pereira — A41

**1948 Unwmk. Litho. *Perf. 11½***

| | | | | |
|---|---|---|---|---|
| **475** | A38 | 3r brt ultra & lt bl | 1.10 | .55 |
| **476** | A30 | 1t dk grn & yel grn | 1.10 | .65 |
| **477** | A39 | 1½t dk pur & dl vio | 2.25 | 1.25 |
| **478** | A40 | 2½t brt ver | 3.00 | 1.60 |
| **479** | A41 | 7½t dk brn & org brn | 4.75 | 2.60 |
| *a.* | | Miniature sheet of 5 | 35.00 | 27.50 |
| | | *Nos. 475-479 (5)* | 12.20 | 6.65 |

No. 476 measures 21x31mm.

No. 479a measures 106x146mm. and contains one each of Nos. 475-479. Marginal inscriptions in gray. The sheet sold for 16 tangas (1 rupia).

For surcharge see No. 591.

### Lady of Fatima Issue

Common Design Type

**1948 *Perf. 14½***

| | | | | |
|---|---|---|---|---|
| **480** | CD40 | 1t dk blue green | 4.50 | 3.00 |

A souvenir sheet of nine, including Nos. 480 and 485 and stamps from seven Portuguese colonies, exists. Value, $100. For additional information, see note following Common Design No. 40 listings in the Common Design Types section of the catalog.

Our Lady of Fatima — A42

**1949 Litho. *Perf. 14***

| | | | | |
|---|---|---|---|---|
| **481** | A42 | 1r blue | 1.00 | .75 |
| **482** | A42 | 3r orange yel | 1.00 | .75 |
| **483** | A42 | 9r dk car rose | 1.50 | 1.00 |
| **484** | A42 | 2t green | 5.00 | 1.90 |
| **485** | A42 | 9t orange red | 4.50 | 2.50 |
| **486** | A42 | 2rp dk vio brn | 8.25 | 3.00 |
| **487** | A42 | 5rp olive grn | 16.50 | 7.25 |
| **488** | A42 | 8rp violet blue | 34.00 | 13.50 |
| | | *Nos. 481-488 (8)* | 71.75 | 30.65 |

Our Lady of the Rosary at Fatima, Portugal.

UPU Symbols — A42a

**1949, Oct.**

| | | | | |
|---|---|---|---|---|
| **489** | A42a | 2½t scarlet & pink | 4.25 | 2.25 |

UPU, 75th anniversary.

**Catalogue values for unused stamps in this section, from this point to the end of the section, are for Never Hinged items.**

### Holy Year Issue

Common Design Types

**1950, May *Perf. 13x13½***

| | | | | |
|---|---|---|---|---|
| **490** | CD41 | 1r olive bister | 1.25 | .45 |
| **491** | CD42 | 2t dk gray green | 1.75 | .60 |

See Nos. 496-503.

A souvenir sheet of eight, including No. 490 and stamps from seven Portuguese colonies, exists. Value, $100. For additional information, see note following Common Designs No. 41 and 42 listings in the Common Design Types section of the catalog.

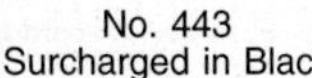

No. 443 Surcharged in Black

**1950 *Perf. 13½x13***

| | | | | |
|---|---|---|---|---|
| **492** | CD35 | 1r on 10r dk car | .75 | .40 |
| **493** | CD35 | 2r on 10r dk car | .75 | .40 |

### Similar Surcharge on No. 447 in Black or Red

| | | | | |
|---|---|---|---|---|
| **494** | CD37 | 1r on 2½t blue | .75 | .40 |
| **495** | CD37 | 3r on 2½t blue (R) | .75 | .40 |
| | | *Nos. 492-495 (4)* | 3.00 | 1.60 |

Letters with serifs, small (lower case) "r" in "real" and "réis."

### Holy Year Issue

Common Design Types

**1951 Litho. *Perf. 13½***

| | | | | |
|---|---|---|---|---|
| **496** | CD41 | 1r dp car rose | .60 | .30 |
| **497** | CD41 | 2r emerald | .60 | .30 |
| **498** | CD42 | 3r red brown | .60 | .30 |
| **499** | CD41 | 6r gray | .60 | .40 |
| **500** | CD42 | 9r brt pink | 1.25 | .60 |
| **501** | CD41 | 1t blue violet | 1.25 | .60 |
| **502** | CD42 | 2t yellow | 1.25 | .70 |
| **503** | CD41 | 4t violet brown | 1.25 | .70 |
| | | *Nos. 496-503 (8)* | 7.40 | 3.90 |

### No. 447 with Surcharge Similar to Nos. 492-493 in Red

**1951 *Perf. 13½x13***

| | | | | |
|---|---|---|---|---|
| **504** | CD37 | 6r on 2½t blue | .75 | .40 |
| **505** | CD37 | 1t on 2½t blue | .75 | .40 |

Letters with serifs, small (lower case) "r" in "réis."

### Holy Year Extension Issue

Common Design Type

**1951 Litho. *Perf. 14***

| | | | | |
|---|---|---|---|---|
| **506** | CD43 | 1rp bl vio & pale vio + label | 2.50 | 1.00 |

Stamp without label sells for less.

José Vaz — A43

Ruins of Sancoale Church — A44

Design: 12t, Altar.

### Dated: "1651-1951"

**1951 Litho. *Perf. 14½***

| | | | | |
|---|---|---|---|---|
| **507** | A43 | 1r Prus bl & pale bl | .25 | .25 |
| **508** | A44 | 2r ver & red brn | .25 | .25 |
| **509** | A43 | 3r gray blk & gray | .70 | .25 |
| **510** | A44 | 1t vio bl & ind | .40 | .25 |
| **511** | A43 | 2t dp cl & cl | .40 | .25 |
| **512** | A44 | 3t ol grn & blk | .60 | .25 |
| **513** | A43 | 9t indigo & ultra | .60 | .45 |
| **514** | A44 | 10t lilac & vio | 1.40 | .65 |
| **515** | A44 | 12t blk brn & brn | 2.00 | .95 |
| | | *Nos. 507-515 (9)* | 6.60 | 3.55 |

300th anniversary of the birth of José Vaz.

### Medical Congress Issue

Common Design Type

Design: Medical School, Goa.

**1952 Unwmk. *Perf. 13½***

| | | | | |
|---|---|---|---|---|
| **516** | CD44 | 4½t blk & lt blue | 5.50 | 2.00 |

### St. Francis Xavier Issue

Statue of Saint Francis Xavier — A44a

A45

St. Francis Xavier and his Tomb, Goa — A46

Designs: 2t, Miraculous Arm of St. Francis. 4t, 5t, Tomb of St. Francis.

**1952, Oct. 25 Litho. *Perf. 14***

| | | | | |
|---|---|---|---|---|
| **517** | A44a | 6r aqua & multi | .45 | .25 |
| **518** | A44a | 2t cream & multi | 2.25 | .60 |
| **519** | A44a | 5t pink & silver | 4.25 | 1.40 |
| | | *Nos. 517-519 (3)* | 6.95 | 2.25 |

### Souvenir Sheets

***Perf. 13***

| | | | | |
|---|---|---|---|---|
| **520** | A45 | 9t brn & dk brn | 14.50 | 11.00 |
| **521** | A46 | 12t Sheet of 2 | 14.50 | 11.00 |
| *a.* | | 4t orange buff & black | 3.25 | 3.25 |
| *b.* | | 8t slate & black | 3.25 | 3.25 |

400th anniv. of the death of St. Francis Xavier.

Numeral A47

St. Francis Xavier A48

**1952, Dec. 4 Litho. *Perf. 13½***

| | | | | |
|---|---|---|---|---|
| **522** | A47 | 3t black | 9.50 | 8.50 |
| **523** | A48 | 5t dk violet & blk | 9.50 | 8.50 |
| *a.* | | Strip of 2 + label | 25.00 | 21.00 |

Issued to publicize Portuguese India's first stamp exhibition, Goa, 1952.

No. 523a consists of a tête bêche pair of Nos. 522-523 separated by a label publicizing the exhibition.

Statue of Virgin Mary — A49

**1953, Jan.**

| | | | | |
|---|---|---|---|---|
| **524** | A49 | 6r dk & lt blue | .25 | .25 |
| **525** | A49 | 1t brown & buff | 1.25 | .70 |
| **526** | A49 | 3t dk pur & pale ol | 2.75 | 1.25 |
| | | *Nos. 524-526 (3)* | 4.25 | 2.20 |

Exhibition of Sacred Missionary Art held at Lisbon in 1951.

For surcharge see No. 594.

### Stamp Centenary Issue

Stamp of Portugal and Arms of Colonies — A49a

**1953 *Typo.***

| | | | | |
|---|---|---|---|---|
| **527** | A49a | 1t multicolored | 2.00 | .95 |

Centenary of Portugal's first postage stamps.

Claudio da Gama Pinto, Ophthalmologist and Author, Birth Cent. — A50

**1954, Apr. 10 Litho. *Perf. 11½***

| | | | | |
|---|---|---|---|---|
| **528** | A50 | 3r gray & ol grn | .40 | .25 |
| **529** | A50 | 2t black & gray blk | .80 | .30 |

### Sao Paulo Issue

Common Design Type

**1954, Oct. 2 Unwmk. *Perf. 13½***

| | | | | |
|---|---|---|---|---|
| **530** | CD46 | 2t dk Prus bl, bl & blk | .80 | .40 |

For surcharge see No. 593.

Affonso de Albuquerque School — A51

**1955, Feb. 26**

| | | | | |
|---|---|---|---|---|
| **531** | A51 | 9t multicolored | 1.75 | .55 |

Centenary (in 1954) of the founding of the Affonso de Albuquerque National School.

Msgr. Sebastiao Rodolfo Dalgado — A52

**1955, Nov. 15 Unwmk. *Perf. 13½***

| | | | | |
|---|---|---|---|---|
| **532** | A52 | 1r multicolored | .25 | .25 |
| **533** | A52 | 1t multicolored | .75 | .25 |

Birth cent. of Msgr. Sebastiao Rodolfo Dalgado.

Francisco de Almeida — A53

Manuel Antonio de Sousa — A54

Map of Bassein by Pedro Barreto de Resendo, 1635 — A55

Portraits: 9r, Affonso de Albuquerque. 1t, Vasco da Gama. 1½t, Filipe Nery Xavier. 3t, Nuno da Cunha. 4t, Agostinho Vicente

Lourenco. 8t, Jose Vaz. 9t, Manuel Godinho de Heredia. 10t, Joao de Castro. 2rp, Antonio Caetano Pacheco. 3rp, Constantino de Braganca.

Maps of ancient forts, drawn in 1635: 2½t, Mombaim (Bombay). 3½t, Damao (Daman). 5t, Diu. 12t, Cochin. 1rp, Goa.

### Inscribed: "450 Aniversario da Fundacao do Estado da India 1505-1955."

***Perf. 11½x12 (A53), 14½ (A54), 12½ (A55)***

**1956, Mar. 24** **Unwmk.**

| No. | Type | Value | Color | Unused | Used |
|---|---|---|---|---|---|
| **534** | A53 | 3r | multicolored | .25 | .25 |
| **535** | A54 | 6r | multicolored | .25 | .25 |
| **536** | A53 | 9r | multicolored | .25 | .25 |
| **537** | A53 | 1t | multicolored | .35 | .25 |
| **538** | A54 | 1½t | multicolored | .25 | .25 |
| **539** | A55 | 2t | multicolored | 3.50 | 1.90 |
| **540** | A55 | 2½t | multicolored | 1.50 | 1.00 |
| **541** | A53 | 3t | multicolored | .65 | .35 |
| **542** | A55 | 3½t | multicolored | 1.50 | 1.00 |
| **543** | A54 | 4t | multicolored | .30 | .25 |
| **544** | A55 | 5t | multicolored | .80 | .40 |
| **545** | A54 | 8t | multicolored | .85 | .35 |
| **546** | A54 | 9t | multicolored | .85 | .35 |
| **547** | A53 | 10t | multicolored | 1.00 | .35 |
| **548** | A55 | 12t | multicolored | 1.25 | .75 |
| **549** | A55 | 1rp | multicolored | 3.00 | 1.50 |
| **550** | A54 | 2rp | multicolored | 3.50 | 1.75 |
| **551** | A53 | 3rp | multicolored | 4.50 | 1.90 |
| | | | *Nos. 534-551 (18)* | 24.55 | 13.10 |

Portuguese settlements in India, 450th anniv.

For surcharges see Nos. 575-577, 579-581, 592.

Map of Damao and Nagar Aveli — A56

### Map and Inscriptions in Black, Red, Ocher and Blue

**1957** **Litho.** ***Perf. 11½***

| No. | Type | Value | Color | Unused | Used |
|---|---|---|---|---|---|
| **552** | A56 | 3r | gray & buff | .25 | .25 |
| **553** | A56 | 6r | bl grn & pale lem | .30 | .25 |
| **554** | A56 | 3t | pink & lt gray | .35 | .25 |
| **555** | A56 | 6t | blue | .35 | .25 |
| **556** | A56 | 11t | ol bis & lt vio gray | 1.00 | .45 |
| **557** | A56 | 2rp | lt vio & pale gray | 2.00 | .90 |
| **558** | A56 | 3rp | citron & pink | 2.75 | 1.75 |
| **559** | A56 | 5rp | magenta & pink | 4.50 | 2.40 |
| | | | *Nos. 552-559 (8)* | 11.50 | 6.50 |

For surcharges see Nos. 571, 578, 584-585, 588-590.

Arms of Vasco da Gama — A57

Arms of: 6r, Lopo Soares de Albergaria. 9r, Francisco de Almeida. 1t, Garcia de Noronha. 4t, Alfonso de Albuquerque. 5t, Joao de Castro. 11t, Luis de Ataide. 1rp, Nuno da Cunha.

### Arms in Original Colors Inscriptions in Black and Red

**1958, Apr. 3** **Unwmk.** ***Perf. 13x13½***

| No. | Type | Value | Color | Unused | Used |
|---|---|---|---|---|---|
| **560** | A57 | 2r | buff & ocher | .30 | .25 |
| **561** | A57 | 6r | gray & ocher | .30 | .25 |
| **562** | A57 | 9r | pale blue & emer | .30 | .25 |
| **563** | A57 | 1t | pale citron & brn | .40 | .25 |
| **564** | A57 | 4t | pale bl grn & lil | .45 | .25 |
| **565** | A57 | 5t | buff & blue | .55 | .35 |
| **566** | A57 | 11t | pink & lt brn | 1.00 | .75 |
| **567** | A57 | 1rp | pale grn & maroon | 1.40 | .90 |
| | | | *Nos. 560-567 (8)* | 4.70 | 3.25 |

For surcharges see Nos. 570, 572-574, 582-583, 586-587.

Exhibition Emblem and View — A58

**1958, Dec. 15** **Litho.** ***Perf. 14½***

| No. | Type | Value | Color | Unused | Used |
|---|---|---|---|---|---|
| **568** | A58 | 1rp | multicolored | .95 | .50 |

World's Fair, Brussels, Apr. 17-Oct. 19.
For surcharge see No. 597.

### Tropical Medicine Congress Issue

Common Design Type

Design: Holarrhena antidysenterica.

**1958, Dec. 15** ***Perf. 13½***

| No. | Type | Value | Color | Unused | Used |
|---|---|---|---|---|---|
| **569** | CD47 | 5t | gray, brn, grn & red | 1.75 | .75 |

For surcharge see No. 596.

### Stamps of 1955-58 Surcharged with New Values and Bars

**1959, Jan. 1** **Litho.** **Unwmk.**

| No. | Type | Value | Description | Unused | Used |
|---|---|---|---|---|---|
| **570** | A57 | 5c | on 2r (#560) | .30 | .25 |
| **571** | A56 | 10c | on 3r (#552) | .30 | .25 |
| **572** | A57 | 15c | on 6r (#561) | .30 | .25 |
| **573** | A57 | 20c | on 9r (#562) | .30 | .25 |
| **574** | A57 | 30c | on 1t (#563) | .30 | .25 |
| **575** | A55 | 40c | on 2t (#539) | .65 | .30 |
| **576** | A55 | 40c | on 2½t (#540) | .80 | .35 |
| **577** | A55 | 40c | on 3½t (#542) | .40 | .25 |
| **578** | A56 | 50c | on 3t (#554) | .40 | .25 |
| **579** | A53 | 80c | on 3t (#541) | .40 | .25 |
| **580** | A53 | 80c | on 10t (#547) | 1.10 | .80 |
| **581** | A53 | 80c | on 3rp (#551) | 1.60 | .95 |
| **582** | A57 | 1e | on 4t (#564) | .40 | .25 |
| **583** | A57 | 1.50e | on 5t (#565) | .40 | .25 |
| **584** | A56 | 2e | on 6t (#555) | .65 | .35 |
| **585** | A56 | 2.50e | on 11t (#556) | .95 | .25 |
| **586** | A57 | 4e | on 11t (#566) | 1.10 | .55 |
| **587** | A57 | 4.50e | on 1rp (#567) | 1.10 | .55 |
| **588** | A56 | 5e | on 2rp (#557) | 1.20 | .55 |
| **589** | A56 | 10e | on 3rp (#558) | 2.25 | 1.60 |
| **590** | A56 | 30e | on 5rp (#559) | 5.00 | 2.25 |
| | | | *Nos. 570-590 (21)* | 19.90 | 11.00 |

### Types of 1946-1958 Surcharged with New Values, Old Values Obliterated

**1959** **Litho.** **Unwmk.**

| No. | Type | Value | Description | Unused | Used |
|---|---|---|---|---|---|
| **591** | A39 | 40c | on 1½t dl pur | .65 | .25 |
| **592** | A54 | 40c | on 1½t multi | .65 | .25 |
| **593** | CD46 | 40c | on 2t bl & gray | 1.10 | .80 |
| **594** | A49 | 80c | on 3t blk & pale cit | .65 | .25 |
| **595** | A36 | 80c | on 3½t dk bl | .80 | .25 |
| **596** | CD47 | 80c | on 5t gray, brn, grn & red | .80 | .45 |
| **597** | A58 | 80c | on 1rp multi | 2.25 | .65 |
| | | | *Nos. 591-597 (7)* | 6.90 | 2.90 |

Coin, Manuel I — A59

Various Coins from the Reign of Manuel I (1495-1521) to the Republic.

### Inscriptions in Black and Red

***Perf. 13½x13***

**1959, Dec. 1** **Litho.** **Unwmk.**

| No. | Type | Value | Color | Unused | Used |
|---|---|---|---|---|---|
| **598** | A59 | 5c | lt bl & gold | .30 | .25 |
| **599** | A59 | 10c | pale brn & gold | .30 | .25 |
| **600** | A59 | 15c | pale grn & gray | .30 | .25 |
| **601** | A59 | 30c | salmon & gray | .30 | .25 |
| **602** | A59 | 40c | pale yel & gray | .30 | .25 |
| **603** | A59 | 50c | lilac & gray | .30 | .25 |
| **604** | A59 | 60c | pale yel grn & gray | .30 | .25 |
| **605** | A59 | 80c | lt bl & gray | .30 | .25 |
| **606** | A59 | 1e | ocher & gray | .30 | .25 |
| **607** | A59 | 1.50e | blue & gray | .30 | .25 |
| **608** | A59 | 2e | pale bl & gold | .30 | .25 |
| **609** | A59 | 2.50e | pale gray & gold | .35 | .25 |
| **610** | A59 | 3e | citron & gray | .35 | .25 |
| **611** | A59 | 4e | pink & gray | .75 | .25 |
| **612** | A59 | 4.40e | pale bis & vio brn | .90 | .35 |
| **613** | A59 | 5e | pale dl vio & gray | 1.00 | .45 |
| **614** | A59 | 10e | brt yel & gray | 2.00 | .80 |
| **615** | A59 | 20e | beige & gray | 4.00 | 2.25 |
| **616** | A59 | 30e | brt yel grn & lt cop brn | 5.00 | 3.00 |
| **617** | A59 | 50e | lt gray & gray | 10.00 | 5.00 |
| | | | *Nos. 598-617 (20)* | 27.65 | 15.35 |

Arms of Prince Henry — A60

**1960, June 25** ***Perf. 13½***

| No. | Type | Value | Color | Unused | Used |
|---|---|---|---|---|---|
| **618** | A60 | 3e | multicolored | 2.75 | .60 |

500th anniversary of the death of Prince Henry the Navigator.

Portugal continued to print special-issue stamps for its lost colony after its annexation by India Dec. 18, 1961: Sports, six stamps issued Dec. 1961, value (set) $3; Anti-Malaria, one stamp issued April, 1962, value 75c.

Stamps of India were first used on Dec. 29. Stamps of Portuguese India remained valid until Jan. 5, 1962.

## AIR POST STAMPS

Common Design Type

***Perf. 13½x13***

**1938, Sept. 1** **Engr.** **Unwmk.**

### Name and Value in Black

| No. | Type | Value | Color | Unused | Used |
|---|---|---|---|---|---|
| **C1** | CD39 | 1t | red orange | 1.50 | .75 |
| **C2** | CD39 | 2½t | purple | 1.50 | .75 |
| **C3** | CD39 | 3½t | orange | 1.50 | .75 |
| **C4** | CD39 | 4½t | ultra | 1.50 | .75 |
| **C5** | CD39 | 7t | lilac brown | 2.25 | .85 |
| **C6** | CD39 | 7½t | dark green | 2.25 | .85 |
| **C7** | CD39 | 9t | red brown | 7.00 | 2.50 |
| **C8** | CD39 | 11t | magenta | 8.00 | 2.50 |
| | | | *Nos. C1-C8 (8)* | 25.50 | 9.70 |

No. C4 exists with overprint "Exposicao Internacional de Nova York, 1939-1940" and Trylon and Perisphere. Value, unused $90, never hinged $125.

Counterfeits exist.

## POSTAGE DUE STAMPS

D1

**1904** **Unwmk.** **Typo.** ***Perf. 11½***

### Name and Value in Black

| No. | Type | Value | Color | Unused | Used |
|---|---|---|---|---|---|
| **J1** | D1 | 2r | gray green | .60 | .45 |
| **J2** | D1 | 3r | yellow grn | .60 | .45 |
| **J3** | D1 | 4r | orange | .60 | .50 |
| **J4** | D1 | 5r | slate | .60 | .50 |
| **J5** | D1 | 6r | gray | .60 | .50 |
| **J6** | D1 | 9r | yellow brn | 1.00 | 1.00 |
| **J7** | D1 | 1t | red orange | 1.25 | 1.10 |
| **J8** | D1 | 2t | gray brown | 2.10 | 1.40 |
| **J9** | D1 | 5t | dull blue | 4.75 | 3.50 |
| **J10** | D1 | 10t | carmine | 5.00 | 4.00 |
| **J11** | D1 | 1rp | dull vio | 19.00 | 8.50 |
| | | | *Nos. J1-J11 (11)* | 36.10 | 21.90 |

Nos. J1-J11 Overprinted in Carmine or Green

**1911**

| No. | Type | Value | Color | Unused | Used |
|---|---|---|---|---|---|
| **J12** | D1 | 2r | gray grn | .25 | .25 |
| **J13** | D1 | 3r | yellow grn | .25 | .25 |
| **J14** | D1 | 4r | orange | .25 | .25 |
| **J15** | D1 | 5r | slate | .25 | .25 |
| **J16** | D1 | 6r | gray | .50 | .25 |
| **J17** | D1 | 9r | yellow brn | .60 | .45 |
| **J18** | D1 | 1t | red org | .70 | .45 |
| **J19** | D1 | 2t | gray brn | 1.10 | .70 |
| **J20** | D1 | 5t | dull blue | 2.50 | 1.75 |
| **J21** | D1 | 10t | carmine (G) | 6.00 | 4.00 |
| **J22** | D1 | 1rp | dull violet | 7.00 | 4.00 |
| | | | *Nos. J12-J22 (11)* | 19.40 | 12.60 |

Nos. J1-J11 Overprinted

**1914**

| No. | Type | Value | Color | Unused | Used |
|---|---|---|---|---|---|
| **J23** | D1 | 2r | gray grn | 1.00 | .90 |
| **J24** | D1 | 3r | yellow grn | 1.00 | .90 |
| **J25** | D1 | 4r | orange | 1.00 | .90 |
| **J26** | D1 | 5r | slate | 1.00 | .90 |
| **J27** | D1 | 6r | gray | 1.00 | .90 |
| **J28** | D1 | 9r | yellow brn | 1.00 | .90 |
| **J29** | D1 | 1t | red org | 1.00 | .90 |
| **J30** | D1 | 2t | gray brn | 7.75 | 1.00 |
| **J31** | D1 | 5t | dull blue | 8.25 | 5.25 |
| **J32** | D1 | 10t | carmine | 13.00 | 6.50 |
| **J33** | D1 | 1rp | dull violet | 21.00 | 11.00 |
| | | | *Nos. J23-J33 (11)* | 57.00 | 30.05 |

Nos. 432, 433 and 434 Surcharged In Red or Black

**1943** **Wmk. 232** ***Perf. 11½x12***

| No. | Type | Description | Unused | Used |
|---|---|---|---|---|
| **J34** | A29 | 3r on 2½t dk bl (R) | .60 | .50 |
| **J35** | A29 | 6r on 3t brt bl (R) | 1.20 | .75 |
| **J36** | A29 | 1t on 5t red org (Bk) | 2.10 | 2.10 |
| | | *Nos. J34-J36 (3)* | 3.90 | 3.35 |

D2

**1945** **Typo.** **Unwmk.**

### Country Name and Denomination in Black

| No. | Type | Value | Color | Unused | Used |
|---|---|---|---|---|---|
| **J37** | D2 | 2r | brt carmine | 1.00 | .85 |
| **J38** | D2 | 3r | blue | 1.00 | .85 |
| **J39** | D2 | 4r | orange yel | 1.00 | .85 |
| **J40** | D2 | 6r | yellow grn | 1.00 | .85 |
| **J41** | D2 | 1t | bister brn | 1.25 | 1.10 |
| **J42** | D2 | 2t | chocolate | 1.40 | 1.25 |
| | | | *Nos. J37-J42 (6)* | 6.65 | 5.75 |

**Catalogue values for unused stamps in this section, from this point to the end of the section, are for Never Hinged items.**

Nos. 467 and 471 Surcharged in Carmine or Black

**1951, Jan. 1** ***Perf. 11½***

| No. | Type | Description | Unused | Used |
|---|---|---|---|---|
| **J43** | A33 | 2r on 7r vio & pale vio (C) | 1.25 | .60 |
| **J44** | A33 | 3r on 7r vio & pale vio (C) | 1.25 | .60 |
| **J45** | A37 | 1t on 1rp choc & bis brn | 1.25 | .60 |
| **J46** | A37 | 2t on 1rp choc & bis brn | 1.25 | .60 |
| | | *Nos. J43-J46 (4)* | 5.00 | 2.40 |

### Common Design Type

### Photogravure and Typographed

**1952** ***Perf. 14***

### Numeral in Red; Frame Multicolored

| No. | Type | Value | Color | Unused | Used |
|---|---|---|---|---|---|
| **J47** | CD45 | 2r | olive | .25 | .25 |
| **J48** | CD45 | 3r | black | .40 | .40 |
| **J49** | CD45 | 6r | dark blue | .55 | .55 |
| **J50** | CD45 | 1t | dk carmine | .80 | .80 |
| **J51** | CD45 | 2t | orange | 1.10 | 1.10 |
| **J52** | CD45 | 10t | violet blue | 3.00 | 3.00 |
| | | | *Nos. J47-J52 (6)* | 6.10 | 6.10 |

**Nos. J47-J49 and J51-J52 Surcharged with New Value and Bars**

**1959, Jan.**

**Numeral in Red; Frame Multicolored**

| | | | | |
|---|---|---|---|---|
| **J53** | CD45 | 5c on 2r olive | .25 | .25 |
| **J54** | CD45 | 10c on 3r black | .35 | .45 |
| **J55** | CD45 | 15c on 6r dk blue | .65 | .80 |
| **J56** | CD45 | 60c on 2t orange | 1.00 | 1.40 |
| **J57** | CD45 | 60c on 10t vio blue | 2.25 | 2.25 |
| | | *Nos. J53-J57 (5)* | 4.50 | 5.15 |

### WAR TAX STAMPS

**Overprinted in Black or Carmine**

WT1

**Denomination in Black**

*Perf. 15x14*

**1919, Apr. 15 Typo. Unwmk.**

| | | | | |
|---|---|---|---|---|
| **MR1** | WT1 | 0:00:05,48rp grn | 3.50 | 2.75 |
| **MR2** | WT1 | 0:01:09,94rp grn | 6.75 | 4.50 |
| **MR3** | WT1 | 0:02:03,43rp grn (C) | 6.75 | 4.50 |
| | | *Nos. MR1-MR3 (3)* | 17.00 | 11.75 |

Some authorities consider No. MR2 a revenue stamp.

### POSTAL TAX STAMPS

**Pombal Issue**

Common Design Types

**1925 Unwmk. *Perf. 12½***

| | | | | |
|---|---|---|---|---|
| **RA1** | CD28 | 6r rose & black | .50 | .50 |
| **RA2** | CD29 | 6r rose & black | .50 | .50 |
| **RA3** | CD30 | 6r rose & black | .50 | .50 |
| | | *Nos. RA1-RA3 (3)* | 1.50 | 1.50 |

Mother and Child — PT1

**1948 Litho. *Perf. 11***

| | | | | |
|---|---|---|---|---|
| **RA4** | PT1 | 6r yellow green | 4.00 | 3.00 |
| **RA5** | PT1 | 1t carmine | 4.00 | 3.00 |

See Nos. RA7-RA7A, RA9, RA12. For surcharge and overprint see Nos. RA6, RA8.

**Catalogue values for unused stamps in this section, from this point to the end of the section, are for Never Hinged items.**

**Type of 1948 Surcharged with New Value and Bar in Black**

**1951**

| | | | | |
|---|---|---|---|---|
| **RA6** | PT1 | 1t on 6r carmine | 4.00 | 2.25 |

**Type of 1948**

**1952-53**

| | | | | |
|---|---|---|---|---|
| **RA7** | PT1 | 1t gray | 5.00 | 2.50 |
| **RA7A** | PT1 | 1t red orange ('53) | 4.00 | 2.10 |

No. RA5 Overprinted in Black

**1953**

| | | | | |
|---|---|---|---|---|
| **RA8** | PT1 | 1t carmine | 11.00 | 6.50 |

**Type of 1948**

**1954 Typo.**

| | | | | |
|---|---|---|---|---|
| **RA9** | PT1 | 6r pale bister | 4.50 | 3.25 |

Mother and Child — PT2

**Surcharged in Black**

**1956 Typo. *Perf. 11***

| | | | | |
|---|---|---|---|---|
| **RA10** | PT2 | 1t on 4t lt blue | 13.50 | 11.00 |

Mother and Child — PT3

**1956 Litho. *Perf. 13***

| | | | | |
|---|---|---|---|---|
| **RA11** | PT3 | 1t blk, pale grn & red | 1.40 | 1.00 |

See No. RA14. For surcharges see Nos. RA13, RA15-RA16.

**Type of 1948 Redrawn**

**1956 *Perf. 11***

**Without Gum**

| | | | | |
|---|---|---|---|---|
| **RA12** | PT1 | 1t bluish green | 6.50 | 3.25 |

Denomination in white oval at left.

**No. RA11 Surcharged with New Value and Bars in Red**

**1957 *Perf. 13½***

| | | | | |
|---|---|---|---|---|
| **RA13** | PT3 | 6r on 1t | 1.50 | 1.10 |

**Type of 1956**

**1958 Unwmk. *Perf. 13***

| | | | | |
|---|---|---|---|---|
| **RA14** | PT3 | 1t dk bl, sal & grn | 1.00 | .75 |

**No. RA14 Surcharged with New Values and Four Bars**

**1959, Jan. Litho. *Perf. 13***

| | | | | |
|---|---|---|---|---|
| **RA15** | PT3 | 20c on 1t | .75 | .60 |
| **RA16** | PT3 | 40c on 1t | .75 | .60 |

Arms and People Seeking Help — PT4

**1960 *Perf. 13½***

| | | | | |
|---|---|---|---|---|
| **RA17** | PT4 | 20c brown & red | .75 | .50 |

### POSTAL TAX DUE STAMPS

**Pombal Issue**

Common Design Types

**1925 Unwmk. *Perf. 12½***

| | | | | |
|---|---|---|---|---|
| **RAJ1** | CD28 | 1t rose & black | .65 | .65 |
| **RAJ2** | CD29 | 1t rose & black | .65 | .65 |
| **RAJ3** | CD30 | 1t rose & black | .65 | .65 |
| | | *Nos. RAJ1-RAJ3 (3)* | 1.95 | 1.95 |

See note after Portugal No. RAJ4.

## PUERTO RICO

ˌpwer-tə-ˈrē-ˌkō

(Porto Rico)

LOCATION — A large island in the West Indies, east of Hispaniola
GOVT. — Former Spanish Colony
AREA — 3,435 sq. mi.
POP. — 953,243 (1899)
CAPITAL — San Juan

The island was ceded to the United States by the Treaty of 1898.

100 Centimes = 1 Peseta
1000 Milesimas = 100 Centavos = 1 Peso (1881)
100 Cents = 1 Dollar (1898)

Puerto Rican stamps of 1855-73, a part of the Spanish colonial period, were also used in Cuba. They are listed as Cuba Nos. 1-4, 9-14, 18-21, 31-34, 39-41, 47-49, 51-53, 55-57.

**Issued under Spanish Dominion**

Values for unused stamps are for examples with original gum as defined in the catalogue introduction. Very fine examples of Nos. 1-170, MR1-MR13 will have perforations clear of the design but will be noticeably poorly centered. Extremely fine examples will be well centered; these are scarce and command substantial premiums.

**Stamps of Cuba Overprinted in Black**

a

b

c

d

**1873 Unwmk. *Perf. 14***

| | | | | |
|---|---|---|---|---|
| 1 | A10 (a) | 25c gray | 62.50 | 2.10 |
| 2 | A10 (a) | 50c brown | 140.00 | 6.25 |
| 3 | A10 (a) | 1p red brown | 600.00 | 21.00 |
| | | *Nos. 1-3 (3)* | 802.50 | 29.35 |

**1874**

| | | | | |
|---|---|---|---|---|
| 4 | A11 (b) | 25c ultra | 47.50 | 10.00 |
| *a.* | | Double overprint | 275.00 | |
| *b.* | | Inverted overprint | 275.00 | |

**1875**

| | | | | |
|---|---|---|---|---|
| 5 | A12 (b) | 25c ultra | 37.50 | 3.25 |
| *a.* | | Inverted overprint | 95.00 | 55.00 |
| 6 | A12 (b) | 50c green | 45.00 | 3.50 |
| *a.* | | Inverted overprint | *210.00* | *105.00* |
| 7 | A12 (b) | 1p brown | 160.00 | 17.50 |
| | | *Nos. 5-7 (3)* | 242.50 | 24.25 |

**1876**

| | | | | |
|---|---|---|---|---|
| 8 | A13 (c) | 25c pale violet | 4.25 | 1.90 |
| *a.* | | 25c bluish gray | 5.50 | 2.75 |
| 9 | A13 (c) | 50c ultra | 10.50 | 3.25 |
| 10 | A13 (c) | 1p black | 75.00 | 12.00 |
| 11 | A13 (d) | 25c pale violet | 35.00 | 1.40 |
| 12 | A13 (d) | 1p black | 75.00 | 11.00 |
| | | *Nos. 8-12 (5)* | 199.75 | 29.55 |

Varieties of overprint on Nos. 8-11 include: inverted, double, partly omitted and sideways. Counterfeit overprints exist.

King Alfonso XII — A5

**1877 Typo.**

| | | | | |
|---|---|---|---|---|
| 13 | A5 | 5c yellow brown | 13.00 | 2.75 |
| *a.* | | 5c carmine (error) | 300.00 | — |
| 14 | A5 | 10c carmine | 45.00 | 7.50 |
| *a.* | | 10c brown (error) | 300.00 | — |
| 15 | A5 | 15c deep green | 65.00 | 15.50 |
| 16 | A5 | 25c ultra | 25.00 | 2.60 |
| 17 | A5 | 50c bister | 45.00 | 6.50 |
| | | *Nos. 13-17 (5)* | 193.00 | 34.85 |

Imperf. examples of Nos. 13-17 are from proof or trial sheets. Value, set $400.

**1878 Dated "1878"**

| | | | | |
|---|---|---|---|---|
| 18 | A5 | 5c ol bister | 22.00 | 22.00 |
| 19 | A5 | 10c red brown | 350.00 | 120.00 |
| 20 | A5 | 25c deep green | 2.75 | 1.75 |
| 21 | A5 | 50c ultra | 9.00 | 3.50 |
| 22 | A5 | 1p bister | 18.00 | 8.50 |
| | | *Nos. 18-22 (5)* | 401.75 | 155.75 |

Imperf. examples of Nos. 18-22 are from proof or trial sheets. Value, set $600.

**1879 Dated "1879"**

| | | | | |
|---|---|---|---|---|
| 23 | A5 | 5c lake | 20.00 | 6.50 |
| 24 | A5 | 10c dark brown | 20.00 | 6.50 |
| 25 | A5 | 15c dk olive grn | 20.00 | 6.50 |
| 26 | A5 | 25c blue | 5.00 | 2.25 |
| 27 | A5 | 50c dark green | 20.00 | 6.50 |
| 28 | A5 | 1p gray | 110.00 | 30.00 |
| | | *Nos. 23-28 (6)* | 195.00 | 58.25 |

Imperf, examples of Nos. 23-28 are from proof or trial sheets.

King Alfonso XII — A6

**1880**

| | | | | |
|---|---|---|---|---|
| 29 | A6 | ¼c deep green | 37.50 | 25.00 |
| 30 | A6 | ½c brt rose | 9.00 | 3.25 |
| 31 | A6 | 1c brown lilac | 16.50 | 13.00 |
| 32 | A6 | 2c gray lilac | 8.50 | 5.50 |
| 33 | A6 | 3c buff | 9.50 | 6.00 |
| 34 | A6 | 4c black | 9.50 | 6.00 |
| 35 | A6 | 5c gray green | 4.75 | 2.50 |
| 36 | A6 | 10c rose | 5.25 | 3.00 |
| 37 | A6 | 15c yellow brn | 9.50 | 4.50 |
| 38 | A6 | 25c gray blue | 4.75 | 2.10 |
| 39 | A6 | 40c gray | 18.00 | 22.00 |
| 40 | A6 | 50c dark brown | 40.00 | 20.00 |
| 41 | A6 | 1p olive bister | 150.00 | 26.50 |
| | | *Nos. 29-41 (13)* | 322.75 | 139.35 |

**1881 Dated "1881"**

| | | | | |
|---|---|---|---|---|
| 42 | A6 | ½m lake | .55 | .50 |
| 43 | A6 | 1m violet | .55 | .30 |
| 44 | A6 | 2m pale rose | .75 | .50 |
| 45 | A6 | 4m brt yellowish green | 1.30 | .30 |
| 46 | A6 | 6m brown lilac | 1.30 | .70 |
| 47 | A6 | 8m ultra | 3.25 | 1.75 |
| 48 | A6 | 1c gray green | 4.25 | 1.50 |
| 49 | A6 | 2c lake | 5.75 | 4.75 |
| 50 | A6 | 3c dark brown | 12.50 | 7.75 |
| 51 | A6 | 5c grayish ultra | 4.75 | .55 |
| 52 | A6 | 8c brown | 4.75 | 2.25 |
| 53 | A6 | 10c slate | 75.00 | 11.50 |
| 54 | A6 | 20c olive bister | 90.00 | 21.00 |
| | | *Nos. 42-54 (13)* | 204.70 | 53.35 |

Alfonso XII — A7

**1882-86**

| | | | | |
|---|---|---|---|---|
| 55 | A7 | ½m rose | .30 | .25 |
| *a.* | | ½m salmon rose | .55 | .35 |
| 56 | A7 | ½m lake ('84) | .90 | .40 |
| 57 | A7 | 1m pale lake | .90 | 1.10 |
| 58 | A7 | 1m brt rose ('84) | .30 | .25 |
| 59 | A7 | 2m violet | .30 | .25 |

**60** A7 4m brown lilac .30 .25
**61** A7 6m brown .45 .25
**62** A7 8m yellow green .45 .25
**63** A7 1c gray green .30 .25
**64** A7 2c rose 1.15 .25
**65** A7 3c yellow 4.25 2.25
*a.* Cliché of 8c in plate of 3c 120.00
**66** A7 3c yellow brn ('84) 4.25 .90
*a.* Cliché of 8c in plate of 3c 25.00
**67** A7 5c gray blue 15.00 1.25
**68** A7 5c gray bl, 1st retouch ('84) 15.00 3.00
**69** A7 5c gray bl, 2nd retouch ('86) 115.00 5.75
**70** A7 8c gray brown 3.75 .25
**71** A7 10c dark green 3.75 .30
**72** A7 20c gray lilac 5.50 .30
*a.* 20c olive brown (error) *120.00*
**73** A7 40c blue 65.00 15.00
**74** A7 80c olive bister 70.00 21.00
*Nos. 55-74 (20)* 306.85 53.50

For differences between the original and the retouched stamps see note on the 1883-86 issue of Cuba.

Alfonso XIII — A8

**1890-97**

**75** A8 ½m black .30 .25
**76** A8 ½m olive gray ('92) .25 .25
**77** A8 ½m red brn ('94) .25 .25
**78** A8 ½m dull vio ('96) .25 .25
**79** A8 1m emerald .25 .25
**80** A8 1m dk violet ('92) .25 .25
**81** A8 1m ultra ('94) .25 .25
**82** A8 1m dp brown ('96) .25 .25
**83** A8 2m lilac rose .25 .25
**84** A8 2m violet brn ('92) .25 .25
**85** A8 2m red orange ('94) .25 .25
**86** A8 2m yellow grn ('96) .25 .25
**87** A8 4m dk olive grn 11.50 5.75
**88** A8 4m ultra ('92) .25 .25
**89** A8 4m yellow brn ('94) .25 .25
**90** A8 4m blue grn ('96) 1.00 .35
**91** A8 6m dk brown 50.00 15.00
**92** A8 6m pale rose ('92) .25 .25
**93** A8 8m olive bister 35.00 22.00
**94** A8 8m yellow grn ('92) .25 .25
**95** A8 1c yellow brown .30 .25
**96** A8 1c blue grn ('91) .55 .25
**97** A8 1c violet brn ('94) 6.00 .45
**98** A8 1c claret ('96) .65 .25
**99** A8 2c brownish violet 1.00 .85
**100** A8 2c red brown ('92) .95 .25
**101** A8 2c lilac ('94) 2.25 .45
**102** A8 2c orange brn ('96) .65 .25
**103** A8 3c slate blue 7.50 1.00
**104** A8 3c orange ('92) .90 .25
**105** A8 3c ol gray ('94) 6.00 .45
**106** A8 3c blue ('96) 22.00 .35
**107** A8 3c claret brn ('97) .30 .25
**108** A8 4c slate bl ('94) 1.50 .45
**109** A8 4c gray brn ('96) .70 .25
**110** A8 5c brown violet 13.00 .45
**111** A8 5c yellow grn ('94) 5.75 1.10
**112** A8 5c blue green ('92) .90 .25
**113** A8 5c blue ('96) .30 .25
**114** A8 6c orange ('94) .45 .25
**115** A8 6c violet ('96) .35 .25
**116** A8 8c ultra 16.00 1.75
**117** A8 8c gray brown ('92) .25 .25
**118** A8 8c dull vio ('94) 13.00 5.00
**119** A8 8c car rose ('96) 3.00 1.50
**120** A8 10c rose 4.75 1.10
*a.* 10c salmon rose 11.50 2.75
**121** A8 10c lilac rose ('92) 1.50 .35
**122** A8 20c red orange 5.25 4.75
**123** A8 20c lilac ('92) 2.50 .55
**124** A8 20c car rose ('94) 1.50 .45
**125** A8 20c olive gray ('96) 6.75 1.50
**126** A8 40c orange 200.00 57.50
**127** A8 40c slate blue ('92) 5.75 4.00
**128** A8 40c claret ('94) 7.50 13.50
**129** A8 40c salmon ('96) 7.00 1.60
**130** A8 80c yellow green 700.00 240.00
**131** A8 80c orange ('92) 14.50 11.50
**132** A8 80c black ('97) 27.50 23.50

Imperforates of type A8 were not issued and are variously considered to be proofs or printer's waste.

Shades of No. 129 are often mistaken for No. 126. Value for No. 126 is for expertized examples.

For overprints see Nos. 154A-170, MR1-MR13.

Landing of Columbus on Puerto Rico — A9

**1893** **Litho.** ***Perf. 12***

**133** A9 3c dark green 350.00 100.00

400th anniversary, landing of Columbus on Puerto Rico.

This stamp was valid for postage for only one day and for internal use only.

Counterfeits exist.

Alfonso XIII — A10

**1898** **Typo.**

**135** A10 1m orange brown .25 .25
**136** A10 2m orange brown .25 .25
**137** A10 3m orange brown .25 .25
**138** A10 4m orange brown 2.40 .75
**139** A10 5m orange brown .25 .25
**140** A10 1c black violet .25 .25
*a.* Tête bêche pair *1,700.*
**141** A10 2c dk blue green .25 .25
**142** A10 3c dk brown .25 .25
**143** A10 4c orange 2.40 1.60
**144** A10 5c brt rose .30 .25
**145** A10 6c dark blue .85 .25
**146** A10 8c gray brown .30 .25
**147** A10 10c vermilion .30 .25
**148** A10 15c dull olive grn .30 .25
**149** A10 20c maroon 3.00 .75
**150** A10 40c violet 2.25 2.00
**151** A10 60c black 2.25 2.00
**152** A10 80c red brown 8.50 7.25
**153** A10 1p yellow green 18.00 14.50
**154** A10 2p slate blue 50.00 22.00
*Nos. 135-154 (20)* 92.60 53.85

Nos. 135-154 exist imperf. Value, set $1,300.

Stamps of 1890-97 Handstamped in Rose or Violet

**1898**

**154A** A8 ½m dull violet 27.50 11.00
**155** A8 1m deep brown 2.00 1.75
**156** A8 2m yellow green .50 .50
**157** A8 4m blue green .50 .50
**158** A8 1c claret 6.00 5.00
**159** A8 2c orange brown .75 *1.00*
**160** A8 3c blue 55.00 18.00
**161** A8 3c claret brn 4.00 3.25
**162** A8 4c gray brn .80 .80
**163** A8 4c slate blue 29.00 16.50
**164** A8 5c yellow grn 13.00 8.50
**165** A8 5c blue 1.00 .80
**166** A8 6c violet 1.00 .55
**167** A8 8c car rose (V) 2.00 1.00
*a.* Rose overprint 26.00 21.00
**168** A8 20c olive gray 2.50 1.40
**169** A8 40c salmon 4.50 3.25
**170** A8 80c black 60.00 27.50
*Nos. 154A-170 (17)* 210.05 101.30

As usual with handstamps there are many inverted, double and similar varieties. Counterfeits of Nos. 154A-170 abound.

## Issued under U.S. Administration
## LOCAL ISSUES
### Ponce Issue

A11

### Handstamped

**1898** **Unwmk.** ***Imperf.***

**200** A11 5c violet —

No. 200 is a violet handstamp and control mark used on envelopes. Some examples have no control mark. There are two types of circular markings known, and two control marks. Uses on 2¢ U.S. stamps on cover were strictly as a cancellation, not as local postage. Because genuine usage is extremely difficult to authenticate with certainty, certification by competent authorities is essential.

### Coamo Issue

A12

**Typeset, setting of 10**

**1898, Aug.**

**201** A12 5c black 700. *1,250.*

See the Scott U.S. Specialized Catalogue for more detailed listings.

The stamps bear the control mark "F. Santiago" in violet. About 500 were issued.

Dangerous forgeries exist.

### Regular Issue

United States Nos. 279, 279Bf, 281, 272 and 282C Overprinted in Black at 36 degree angle

**1899** **Wmk. 191** ***Perf. 12***

**210** A87 1c yellow green 6.00 1.40
Never hinged 13.00
*a.* Overprint at 25 degree angle 8.00 2.25
Never hinged 17.50
**211** A88 2c redsh car, type IV 5.00 1.25
Never hinged 11.00
*a.* Overprint at 25 degree angle, *Mar. 15* 6.50 2.25
Never hinged 14.00
**212** A91 5c blue 12.50 2.50
Never hinged 27.50
**213** A93 8c violet brown 40.00 17.50
Never hinged 90.00
*a.* Overprint at 25 degree angle 45.00 19.00
Never hinged 100.00
*c.* "PORTO RIC" 150.00 110.00
**214** A94 10c brown, type I 22.50 6.00
Never hinged 50.00
*Nos. 210-214 (5)* 86.00 28.65

Misspellings of the overprint on Nos. 210-214 (PORTO RICU, PORTU RICO, FORTO RICO) are actually broken letters.

United States Nos. 279 and 279B Overprinted Diagonally in Black

**1900**

**215** A87 1c yellow green 7.50 1.40
Never hinged 17.50
**216** A88 2c red, type IV 5.50 2.00
Never hinged 12.50
*b.* Inverted overprint *12,500.*

## POSTAGE DUE STAMPS

United States Nos. J38, J39 and J42 Overprinted in Black at 36 degree angle

**1899** **Wmk. 191** ***Perf. 12***

**J1** D2 1c deep claret 22.50 5.50
Never hinged 50.00
*a.* Overprint at 25 degree angle 22.50 7.50
Never hinged 50.00
**J2** D2 2c deep claret 20.00 6.00
Never hinged 45.00
*a.* Overprint at 25 degree angle 20.00 7.00
Never hinged 45.00
**J3** D2 10c deep claret 180.00 55.00
Never hinged 375.00
*a.* Overprint at 25 degree angle 160.00 75.00
Never hinged 330.00
*Nos. J1-J3 (3)* 222.50 66.50

Stamps of Puerto Rico were replaced by those of the United States.

## WAR TAX STAMPS

Stamps of 1890-94 Overprinted or Surcharged by Handstamp

**1898** **Unwmk.** ***Perf. 14***

**Purple Overprint or Surcharge**

**MR1** A8 1c yellow brn 8.00 5.75
**MR2** A8 2c on 2m orange 3.75 3.00
**MR3** A8 2c on 5c blue grn 5.00 3.50
**MR4** A8 2c dark violet .95 .95
**MR5** A8 2c lilac .90 .90
**MR6** A8 2c red brown .50 .30
**MR7** A8 5c blue green 1.90 1.90
**MR8** A8 5c on 5c bl grn 8.75 6.00

**Rose Surcharge**

**MR9** A8 2c on 2m orange 1.90 1.90
**MR10** A8 5c on 1m dk vio .30 .30
**MR11** A8 5c on 1m dl bl .85 .85

**Magenta Surcharge**

**MR12** A8 5c on 1m dk vio .50 .30
**MR13** A8 5c on 1m dl bl 3.00 3.00
*Nos. MR1-MR13 (13)* 36.30 28.65

Nos. MR2-MR13 were issued as War Tax Stamps (2c on letters or sealed mail; 5c on telegrams) but, during the early days of the American occupation, they were accepted for ordinary postage.

Double, inverted and similar varieties of overprints are numerous in this issue.

Counterfeit overprints exist.

# QATAR

'kät-ər

LOCATION — A peninsula in eastern Arabia
GOVT. — Independent state
AREA — 4,575 sq. mi.
POP. — 580,000 (1998 est.)
CAPITAL — Doha

Qatar was a British protected sheikdom until Sept. 1, 1971, when it declared its independence. Stamps of Muscat were used until 1957.

100 Naye Paise = 1 Rupee
100 Dirhams = 1 Riyal (1967)

**Catalogue values for all unused stamps in this country are for Never Hinged items.**

### Watermarks

Wmk. 368 — JEZ Multiple

**The market for Qatar stamps is extremely volatile, and dealer stocks are quite limited. All values for this country are tentative and *italicized.***

### Great Britain Nos. 317-325, 328, 332-333 and 309-311 Surcharged "QATAR" and New Value in Black

*Perf. 14½x14*

**1957, Apr. 1 Photo. Wmk. 308**

**1** A129 1np on 5p lt brn *.45 .25*
**2** A126 3np on ½p red org *.45 .25*
**3** A126 6np on 1p ultra *.45 .25*
**4** A126 9np on 1½p grn *.45 .25*
**5** A126 12np on 2p red brn *.55 2.50*
**6** A127 15np on 2½p scarlet *.50 .65*
**7** A127 20np on 3p dk pur *.50 .25*
**8** A128 25np on 4p ultra *.70 2.00*
**9** A129 40np on 6p lil rose *.50 .30*
**10** A130 50np on 9p dp ol grn *.80 2.00*
**11** A132 75np on 1sh3p dk grn *1.00 4.00*
**12** A131 1ru on 1sh6p dk bl *14.50 .65*

**Engr. *Perf. 11x12***

**13** A133 2ru on 2sh6p dk brn *5.00 4.00*
**14** A133 5ru on 5sh crimson *6.75 6.50*
**15** A133 10ru on 10sh brt ultra *8.50 15.00*
*Nos. 1-15 (15) 41.10 38.85*

Both typeset and stereotyped overprints were used on Nos. 13-15. The typeset have bars close together and thick, bold letters. The stereotyped have bars wider apart and thinner letters. Value, Nos. 13-15 with stereotyped overprints $95.

### Great Britain Nos. 334-336 Surcharged "QATAR," New Value and Square of Dots in Black

*Perf. 14½x14*

**1957, Aug. 1 Photo. Wmk. 308**

**16** A138 15np on 2½p scarlet *.50 .40*
**17** A138 25np on 4p ultra *.90 .75*
**18** A138 75np on 1sh3p dk grn *1.75 1.50*
*Nos. 16-18 (3) 3.15 2.65*

50th anniv. of the Boy Scout movement and the World Scout Jubilee Jamboree, Aug. 1-12.

### Great Britain Nos. 353-358, 362 Surcharged "QATAR" and New Value

**1960 Wmk. 322 *Perf. 14½x14***

**19** A126 3np on ½p red org *.75 1.75*
**20** A126 6np on 1p ultra *3.00 3.00*
**21** A126 9np on 1½p grn *.80 1.50*
**22** A126 12np on 2p red brn *5.00 6.50*
**23** A127 15np on 2½p scar *2.75 .25*
**24** A127 20np on 3p dk pur *.60 .25*
**25** A129 40np on 6p lil rose *3.00 2.00*
*Nos. 19-25 (7) 15.90 15.25*

Sheik Ahmad bin Ali al Thani — A1

Dhow — A2

Oil Derrick — A3

Designs: 40np, 50np, Peregrine Falcon. 5r, 10r, Mosque.

*Perf. 14½*

**1961, Sept. 2 Unwmk. Photo.**

**26** A1 5np rose carmine *.40 .35*
**27** A1 15np brown black *.50 .35*
**28** A1 20np claret *.50 .35*
**29** A1 30np deep green *.50 .45*
**30** A2 40np red *2.75 .45*
**31** A2 50np sepia *3.50 .60*
**32** A2 75np ultra *1.75 3.00*

**Engr. *Perf. 13***

**33** A3 1ru rose red *3.75 .50*
**34** A3 2ru blue *4.00 2.00*
**35** A3 5ru green *35.00 7.00*
**36** A3 10ru black *70.00 12.00*
*Nos. 26-36 (11) 122.65 27.05*

For surcharges see Nos. 108-108J.

Nos. 31-32, 34-36 Overprinted or Surcharged

**1964, Oct. 25 Photo. *Perf. 14½***

**37** A2 50np sepia *3.00 2.50*
**38** A2 75np ultra *4.50 3.75*

**Engr. *Perf. 13***

**39** A3 1ru on 10r black *6.00 2.00*
**40** A3 2ru blue *14.00 3.75*
**41** A3 5ru green *30.00 10.00*
*Nos. 37-41 (5) 57.50 22.00*

18th Olympic Games, Tokyo, Oct. 10-25.
For surcharges see Nos. 110-110D.

Nos. 31-32, 34-36 with Typographed Overprint or Surcharge

**1964, Nov. 22 Photo. *Perf. 14½***

**42** A2 50np sepia *3.00 1.25*
**43** A2 75np ultra *4.50 1.75*

**Engr. *Perf. 13***

**44** A3 1ru on 10ru blk *6.25 3.00*
**45** A3 2ru blue *13.00 8.00*
**46** A3 5ru green *32.50 13.00*
*Nos. 42-46 (5) 59.25 27.00*

Pres. John F. Kennedy (1917-63).
For surcharges see Nos. 111-111D.

Column — A4

Designs: 2np, 1.50r, Isis Temple and Colonnade, Philae. 3np, 1r, Trajan's kiosk, Philae.

*Perf. 14½x14*

**1965, Jan. 17 Photo. Unwmk.**

**47** A4 1np multicolored *2.25 .60*
**48** A4 2np multicolored *2.75 .60*
**49** A4 3np multicolored *2.75 .60*
**50** A4 1ru multicolored *4.00 1.50*
**51** A4 1.50ru multicolored *8.50 2.50*
**52** A4 2ru multicolored *2.75 2.00*
*Nos. 47-52 (6) 23.00 7.80*

UNESCO world campaign to save historic monuments in Nubia. Nos. 47-52 exist imperf. Value, set $32.50.

Qatar Scout Emblem, Tents and Sheik Ahmad — A5

Scouts Saluting and Sheik Ahmad — A6

Designs: 1np, 4np, Qatar scout emblem.

*Perf. 14 (A5), 14½x14 (A6)*

**1965, May 22 Photo. Unwmk.**

**53** A5 1np ol grn & dk red brn *.90 .45*
**54** A5 2np sal & dk vio bl *.90 .45*
**55** A5 3np dk vio bl & grn *.90 .45*
**56** A5 4np bl & dk red brn *.90 .45*
**57** A5 5np dk vio bl & grnsh bl *.90 .45*
**58** A6 30np multi *8.25 3.50*
**59** A6 40np multi *12.50 5.00*
**60** A6 1ru multi *24.00 10.00*
*Nos. 53-60 (8) 49.25 20.75*

Issued to honor the Qatar Boy Scouts. Nos. 53-60 exist imperf. Value, set $45. Perf. and imperf. souvenir sheets contain one each of Nos. 58-60 with red brown marginal inscription. Size: 108x76mm. Value, perf. $40, imperf. $60.
For surcharges see Nos. 113-113G.

Eiffel Tower, Telstar, ITU Emblem and "Qatar" in Morse Code — A7

Designs: 2np, 1ru, Tokyo Olympic Games emblem and Syncom III. 3np, 40np, Radar tracking station and Relay satellite. 4np, 50np, Post Office Tower, London, and Echo II, Syncom III, Telstar and Relay satellites around globe.

*Perf. 13½x14*

**1965, Oct. 16 Photo. Unwmk.**

**61** A7 1np dk bl & red brn *1.25 .55*
**62** A7 2np bl & dk red brn *1.25 .55*
**63** A7 3np dp yel grn & brt pur *1.25 .55*
**64** A7 4np org brn & brt bl *1.25 .55*
**65** A7 5np dl vio & dk ol bis *1.25 .55*
**66** A7 40np dk car rose & blk *6.50 1.50*
**67** A7 50np sl grn & bis *10.00 1.75*
**68** A7 1ru emer & car *13.00 2.75*
**a.** Souvenir sheet of 2, #67-68 *40.00 40.00*
*Nos. 61-68 (8) 35.75 8.75*

Cent. of the ITU. Nos. 61-68 exist imperf. Value, set $42.50. No. 68a exists imperf. Value $60.
For overprints and surcharges see Nos. 91-98, 114-114G, 117-117G.

Triggerfish — A8

Various Fish, including: 2np, 50np, Clown grunt. 3np, 10ru, Saddleback butterflyfish. 4np, 5ru, Butterflyfish. 15np, 3ru, Paradisefish. 20np, 1ru, Rio Grande perch. 75np, Triggerfish.

**1965, Oct. 18 *Perf. 14x14½***

**69** A8 1np multi & black *.50 .40*
**70** A8 2np multi & black *.50 .40*
**71** A8 3np multi & black *.50 .40*
**72** A8 4np multi & black *.50 .40*
**73** A8 5np multi & black *.50 .40*
**74** A8 15np multi & black *1.50 .40*
**75** A8 20np multi & black *1.75 .40*
**76** A8 30np multi & black *2.50 .60*
**77** A8 40np multi & black *3.00 .75*
**78** A8 50np multi & gold *3.75 1.25*
**79** A8 75np multi & gold *5.00 1.75*
**80** A8 1ru multi & gold *6.00 —*
**81** A8 2ru multi & gold *16.00 4.00*
**82** A8 3ru multi & gold *22.50 6.50*
**83** A8 4ru multi & gold *32.50 8.00*
**84** A8 5ru multi & gold *42.50 10.00*
**85** A8 10ru multi & gold *95.00 14.00*
*Nos. 69-85 (17) 234.50 49.65*

Nos. 69-85 exist imperf. Values about 25-50 percent higher,
For surcharges see Nos. 115-115P.

Basketball — A9

No. 87, Horse jumping. No. 88, Running. No. 89, Soccer. No. 90, Weight lifting.

**1966, Jan. 10 Photo. *Perf. 11½***
**Granite Paper**

**86** A9 1ru gray, blk & dk red *4.25 2.00*
**87** A9 1ru brn & ol grn *4.25 2.00*
**88** A9 1ru dull rose & blue *4.25 2.00*
**89** A9 1ru grn & blk *4.25 2.00*
**90** A9 1ru bl & brn *4.25 2.00*
**a.** Strip of 5, #86-90 *35.00 —*
*Nos. 86-90 (5) 21.25 10.00*

4th Pan Arab Games, Cairo, Sept. 2-11. Nos. 86-90 were printed in sheets of 25 in se-tenant horizontal rows of five. Nos. 86-90 exist imperf. Value, set $25.

### Nos. 61-68 Overprinted in Black

**1966, Feb. 9 Photo. *Perf. 13½x14***

**91** A7 1np dk bl & red brn *1.50 .40*
**92** A7 2np bl & dk red brn *1.50 .40*
**93** A7 3np dp yel grn & brt pur *1.50 .40*
**94** A7 4np org brn & brt bl *1.50 .40*
**95** A7 5np dl vio & dk ol bis *1.50 .40*

**96** A7 40np dk car rose & blk 7.00 .45
**97** A7 50np slate grn & bis 7.50 .55
**98** A7 1ru emer & car 17.50 1.10
*a.* Souvenir sheet of 2, #97-98 55.00 32.50
*Nos. 91-98 (8)* 39.50 4.10

Issued to commemorate the rendezvous in space of Gemini 6 and 7, Dec. 15, 1965. Nos. 91-98 exist overprinted in red. Value, set $200. Nos. 96-98 also exist overprinted in blue. Value, set $150. No. 98a exists imperf. Value, $800 each.

For surcharges see Nos. 117-117G.

Sheik Ahmad — A9a

Designs: 3np, 5np, 40np, 80np, 2ru, 10ru, Reverse of coin with Arabic inscription.

### Litho. & Embossed Gold or Silver Foil

**1966, Feb. 24** *Imperf.*

**99** A9a 1np ol & lil (S) 1.00 .40
**99A** A9a 3np blk & org (S) 1.00 .40
**99B** A9a 4np pur & red 1.00 .40
**99C** A9a 5np brt grn & red brn 1.00 .40

**Diameter: 55mm**

**99D** A9a 10np brn & brt vio (S) 3.00 .40
**99E** A9a 40np org red & bl (S) 4.00 .75
**99F** A9a 70np Prus bl & bl vio 8.00 1.60
**99G** A9a 80np car & grn 8.00 1.60

**Diameter: 65mm**

**99H** A9a 1ru red vio & blk (S) 12.00 2.10
**99J** A9a 2ru bl grn & cl (S) 20.00 4.00
**99K** A9a 5ru red lil & ver 45.00 9.00
**99L** A9a 10ru bl vio & brn car 90.00 21.00
*Nos. 99-99L (12)* 194.00 42.05

John F. Kennedy, UN Headquarters, NY, and ICY Emblem — A10

Designs (ICY emblem and): #100, UN emblem. #100B, Dag Hammarskjold and UN General Assembly. #100C, Jawaharlal Nehru and dove.

**1966, Mar. 8** *Perf. 11½*

**Granite Paper**

**100** A10 40np brt bl, vio bl & red brn 5.00 2.50
**100A** A10 40np brt grn, vio & brn 5.00 2.50
**100B** A10 40np red brn, brt bl & blk 5.00 2.50
**100C** A10 40np dk vio & brt grn 5.00 2.50
*d.* Block of 4, #100-100C 27.50 25.00
*Nos. 100-100C (4)* 20.00 10.00

UN Intl. Cooperation Year, 1965. Printed in sheets of 16 + 9 labels in shape of a cross. Nos. 100-100C exist imperf. Value, set $30. No. 100Cd exists imperf.

An imperf. souvenir sheet of 4 contains one each of Nos. 100-100C. Value $55.

For overprints see Nos. 101E-101H. For surcharges see Nos. 117H-117K.

Telstar, Rocket — A10a

Nos. 100-100C Overprinted in Blue, Black or Red

Designs: No. 101, John F. Kennedy, "In Memoriam / John F. Kennedy / 1917-1963." No. 101A, Olive branches, Churchill quote and "In Memoriam / 1874-1965." No. 101B, like #101 portrait facing left, no overprint. No. 101C, Eternal flame, Arabic inscription. No. 101D, Telstar, Rocket.

**1966, Mar. 8** **Granite Paper**

**101** A10a 5np bl grn, car & blk (BL) 15.00 8.00
*j.* 5np Like #101, bl grn, blk & car (BL) — —
**101A** A10a 5np bl grn, rose & blk 15.00 8.00
*k.* 5np Like #101A (R) — —
**101B** A10a 5np bl grn, car & blk 15.00 8.00
*l.* 5np Like #101B, bl grn, blk & car — —
**101C** A10a 5np bl grn, rose & blk 15.00 8.00
*m.* 5np Like #101C, bl grn, blk & car (R) — —
**101D** A10a 5np bl grn, car & blk 15.00 8.00
*n.* 5np Like #101D, bl grn, blk & car (R) — —
**101E** A10 40np on No. 100 5.00 3.00
*o.* 40np Like #101E (R) — —
**101F** A10 40np on No. 100A 5.00 3.00
*p.* 40np Like #101F (R) — —
**101G** A10 40np on No. 100B 5.00 3.00
*q.* 40np Like #101G (R) — —
**101H** A10 40np on No. 100C 5.00 3.00
*i.* Sheet of 21, #101-101D, 4 ea #101E-101H+4 labels — —
*r.* 40np Like #101H (R) — —
*s.* Sheet of 21, #101j-101Hn, 4 ea #101Eo-101Hr+4 labels — —
*Nos. 101-101H (9)* 95.00 52.00

Nos. 101-101H were made from the sheets of Nos. 100-100C. The 4 outer labels and the center label were surcharged to create Nos. 101-101D. The other 4 labels were overprinted but have no denomination. Kennedy's portrait is in carmine on Nos. 101, 101B and in black on Nos. 101j and 101Bl.

The imperf. souvenir sheet exists with overprint in margin: "IN VICTORY, / MAGNANIMITY. / IN PEACE / GOODWILL / WINSTON CHURCHILL." The margin overprint overlaps onto No. 101A on upper left quarter of stamp.

Nos. 101-101H exist imperf.

For surcharges see Nos. 118-118H.

John F. Kennedy (1917-1963) — A10b

Kennedy and: No. 102c, 10np, No. 102Af, 70np, NYC. No. 102d, 30np, No. 102Ag, 80np, Rocket lifting off at Cape Kennedy. No. 102e, 60np, No. 102Ah, 1ru, Statue of Liberty. No. 102B, Statue of Liberty.

**1966, July 18** *Perf. 13½*

**102** A10b Strip of 3, #c.-e. 4.00 4.00
**102A** A10b Strip of 3, #f.-h. 7.00 7.00

### Souvenir Sheet

*Imperf*

**102B** A10b 50np multicolored 42.50 —

Nos. 102-102A exist imperf. Value, set of 2 strips $17.50.

For surcharges see Nos. 119-119B.

1968 Summer Olympics, Mexico City — A10c

Designs: #103c, 1np, #103Af, 70np, #103B, Equestrian. #103d, 4np, #103Ag, 80np, Running. #103e, 5np, #103Ah, 90np, Javelin.

**1966, July 20** *Perf. 13½*

**103** A10c Strip of 3, #c.-e. 4.00 4.00
**103A** A10c Strip of 3, #f.-h. 10.00 15.00

### Souvenir Sheet

*Imperf*

**103B** A10c 50np multicolored 42.50 —

Nos. 103-103A exist imperf. Value, set $30.

For surcharges see Nos. 120-120B.

A10d



American Astronauts — A10e

Astronaut and space vehicle: No. 104c, 5np, James A. Lovell. d, 10np, Thomas P. Stafford. e, 15np, Alan B. Shepard.

No. 104Af, 20np, John H. Glenn. No. 104Ag, 30np, M. Scott Carpenter. No. 104Ah, 40np, Walter M. Schirra. No. 104Ai, 50np, Virgil I. Grissom. No. 104Aj, 60np, L. Gordon Cooper, Jr.

No. 104B, Stafford, Schirra, Frank Borman, Lovell and diagram of space rendezvous.

**1966, Aug. 20** *Perf. 12*

**104** A10d Strip of 3, #c.-e. 4.00 4.00
**104A** A10e Strip of 5, #f.-j. 12.50 12.50

### Souvenir Sheet

*Imperf*

**Size: 115x75mm**

**104B** A10e 50np multicolored 52.50 —

The name of James A. Lovell is spelled "Lovel" on No. 104c. Nos. 104-104A exist imperf. For surcharges see Nos. 121-121B.

A10h A10i

1966 World Cup Soccer Championships, London

Designs: 1np-4np, Jules Rimet Cup. 60np, #107H, Hands holding Cup, soccer ball. 70np, #107J, Cup, soccer ball. 80np, #107K, Soccer players, ball. 90np, #107L, Wembley Stadium.

**1966, Nov. 27** **Photo.** *Perf. 13½*

**107** A10h 1np blue 5.00 —
**107A** A10h 2np blue 5.00 —
**107B** A10h 3np blue 5.00 —
**107C** A10h 4np blue 5.00 —
*m.* Block of 4, #107-107C 20.00 —
**107D** A10i 60np multi 15.00 —
**107E** A10i 70np multi 15.00 —
**107F** A10i 80np multi 15.00 —
**107G** A10i 90np multi 15.00 —
*n.* Block of 4, #107D-107G 60.00 —

### Souvenir Sheets

*Imperf*

**107H** A10i 25np multi 50.00 50.00
**107J** A10i 25np multi 50.00 50.00
**107K** A10i 25np multi 50.00 50.00
**107L** A10i 25np multi 50.00 50.00
*Nos. 107-107L (12)* 280.00 200.00

Nos. 107-107C are airmail. Issued in sheets of 36 containing 5 #107m and 4 #107n. Nos. 107-107G exist imperf.

### Nos. 26-36 Surcharged with New Currency

**1966, Oct.** *Perf.*

**108** A1 5d on 5np rose car 12.00 7.50
**108A** A1 15d on 15np brn blk 12.00 7.50
**108B** A1 20d on 20np clar 13.00 7.50
**108C** A1 30d on 30np dp grn 45.00 15.00
**108D** A2 40d on 40np red 85.00 27.50
**108E** A2 50d on 50np sepia 95.00 32.50
**108F** A2 75d on 75np ultra 150.00 40.00
**108G** A3 1r on 1ru rose red 175.00 50.00
**108H** A3 2r on 2ru blue 185.00 110.00
**108I** A3 5r on 5ru green 300.00 150.00
**108J** A3 10r on 10ru black 450.00 225.00
*Nos. 108-108J (11)* 1,522. 672.50

### Nos. 37-41 Surcharged with New Currency in Gray or Red

**1966** **Photo.** *Perf. 14½*

**110** A2 50d on 50np #37 (G) 25.00 —
**110A** A2 75d on 75np #38 35.00 —

**Engr.**

*Perf. 13*

**110B** A3 1r on 1ru on 10ru #39 50.00 —
**110C** A3 2r on 2ru #40 75.00 —
**110D** A3 5r on 5ru #41 100.00 —
*Nos. 110-110D (5)* 285.00

### Nos. 42-46 Surcharged with New Currency in Gray or Red

**1966** **Photo.** *Perf. 14½*

**111** A2 50d on 50np #42 (G) 40.00 —
**111A** A2 75d on 75np #43 50.00 —

**Engr.**

*Perf. 13*

**111B** A3 1r on 1ru on 10ru #44 75.00 —
**111C** A3 2r on 2ru #45 100.00 —
**111D** A3 5r on 5ru #46 125.00 —
*Nos. 111-111D (5)* 390.00

### Nos. 53-60 Surcharged with New Currency

*Perf. 14 (A5), 14½x14 (A6)*

**1966** **Photo.**

**113** A5 1d on 1np #53 2.00 —
**113A** A5 2d on 2np #54 3.00 —
**113B** A5 3d on 3np #55 5.00 —
**113C** A5 4d on 4np #56 8.00 —
**113D** A5 5d on 4np #57 10.00 —
**113E** A6 30d on 30np #58 20.00 —
**113F** A6 40d on 40np #59 30.00 —
**113G** A6 1r on 1ru #60 45.00 —
*Nos. 113-113G (8)* 123.00

Exist imperf. Perf and imperf souvenir sheets contain one each of #113E-113G surcharged with new currency.

### Nos. 61-68 Surcharged with New Currency in Black or Red

**1966** *Perf. 13½x14*

**114** A7 1d on 1np #61 2.00 —
**114A** A7 2d on 2np #62 3.00 —
**114B** A7 3d on 3np #63 4.00 —
**114C** A7 4d on 4np #64 6.00 —
**114D** A7 5d on 5np #65 8.00 —
**114E** A7 40d on 40np #66 20.00 —
**114F** A7 50d on 50np #67 30.00 —
**114G** A7 1r on 1ru #68 40.00 —
*Nos. 114-114G (8)* 113.00

Exist imperf.

### Nos. 69-85 Surcharged with New Currency

**1966, Oct.**

**115** A8 1d on 1np multi & black 3.00 1.75
**115A** A8 2d on 2np multi & black 3.00 1.75
**115B** A8 3d on 3np multi & black 3.00 1.75
**115C** A8 4d on 4np multi & black 3.00 1.75
**115D** A8 5d on 5np multi & black 3.00 1.75

115E A8 15d on 15np multi & black 3.50 1.75
115F A8 20d on 20np multi & black 4.00 1.75
115G A8 30d on 30np multi & black 4.00 1.75
115H A8 40d on 40np multi & black 5.00 4.50
115I A8 50d on 50np multi & gold 6.50 6.50
115J A8 75d on 75np multi & gold 7.50 20.00
115K A8 1r on 1 ru multi & gold 75.00 35.00
115L A8 2r on 2ru multi & gold 110.00 45.00
115M A8 3r on 3ru multi & gold 125.00 55.00
115N A8 4r on 4ru multi & gold 200.00 75.00
115O A8 5r on 5 ru multi & gold 225.00 100.00
115P A8 10r on 10ru multi & gold 275.00 150.00
*Nos. 115-115P (17)* 1,056. 505.00

Nos. 69-85 exist imperf. Value, set *$1,600.*

**Nos. 91-98 Surcharged with New Currency**

**1966 Photo. *Perf. 13½x14***

117 A7 1d on 1np #91 — —
117A A7 2d on 2np #92 — —
117B A7 3d on 3np #93 — —
117C A7 4d on 4np #94 — —
117D A7 5d on 5np #95 — —
117E A7 40d on 40np #96 — —
117F A7 50d on 50np #97 — —
117G A7 1r on 1ru #98 — —
*Set, #117-117G (8)* 75.00 —

A sheet similar to No. 98a surcharged in new currency exists. Value, $800.

Nos. 100-100C Surcharged in Black

**1966 *Perf. 11½***

**Granite Paper**

117H A10 40d on 40np #100 — —
117I A10 40d on 40np #100A — —
117J A10 40d on 40np #100B — —
117K A10 40d on 40np #100C — —
*l.* Block of 4, #117H-117K — —

Printed in sheets of 16 + 9 labels in shape of a cross. Nos. 117H-117K exist imperf.

**Nos. 101-101H Surcharged in Black with New Currency Like Nos. 117H-117K**

**1966 Photo. *Perf. 11½***

**Granite Paper**

118 A10a 5d on 5np #101 — —
*j.* 5d on 5np #101j — —
118A A10a 5d on 5np #101A — —
*k.* 5d on 5np #101Ak — —
118B A10a 5d on 5np #101B — —
*l.* 5d on 5np #101Bl — —
118C A10a 5d on 5np #101C — —
*m.* 5d on 5np #101Cm — —
118D A10a 5d on 5np #101D — —
*n.* 5d on 5np #101Dn — —
118E A10 40d on 40np #101E — —
*o.* 40d on 40np #101Eo — —
118F A10 40d on 40np #101F 5.00 3.00
*p.* 40d on 40np #101Fp — —
118G A10 40d on 40np #101G — —
*q.* 40d on 40np #101Gq — —
118H A10 40d on 40np #101H — —
*i.* Sheet of 21, #118-118D, 4 ea #118E-118H+4 labels — —
*r.* 40d on 40np #101Hr — —
*s.* Sheet of 21, #118j-118Dn, 4 ea #118Eo-118Hr+4 labels — —

Exist imperf. Imperf. souvenir sheets mentioned after Nos. 100C, 101H exist surcharged with new currency.

**Nos. 102-102B Surcharged with New Currency**

**1966 *Perf. 13½***

119 Strip of 3 30.00 —
*c.* A10b 10d on 10np #102c 5.00 —
*d.* A10b 30d on 30np #102d 7.50 —
*e.* A10b 60d on 60np #102e 10.00 —
119A Strip of 3 50.00 —
*f.* A10b 70d on 70np #102Af 12.50 —
*g.* A10b 80d on 80np #102Ag 15.00 —
*h.* A10b 1r on 1ru #102Ah 17.50 —

**Souvenir Sheet**

***Imperf***

119B A10b 50d on 50np #102B 80.00 50.00
*Nos. 119-119B (3)* 160.00 50.00

Nos. 119-119A exist imperf.

**Nos. 103-103B Surcharged with New Currency**

**1966 *Perf. 13½***

120 Strip of 3 65.00 —
*c.* A10c 1d on 1np #103c 10.00 —
*d.* A10c 4d on 4np #103d 15.00 —
*e.* A10c 5d on 5np #103e 22.50 —
120A Strip of 3 100.00 —
*f.* A10c 70d on 70np #103Af 25.00 —
*g.* A10c 80d on 80np #103Ag 27.50 —
*h.* A10c 90d on 90np #103Ah 32.50 —

**Souvenir Sheet**

***Imperf***

120B A10c 50d on 50np #103 100.00 —
*Nos. 120-120B (3)* 265.00

Nos. 120-120B exist imperf.

**Nos. 104-104B Surcharged with New Currency**

**1966 *Perf. 12***

121 Strip of 3 30.00 —
*c.* A10d 5d on 5np #104c 5.00 —
*d.* A10d 10d on 10np #104d 7.00 —
*e.* A10d 15d on 15np #104e 8.00 —
121A Strip of 5 75.00 —
*f.* A10e 20d on 20np #104Af 9.00 —
*g.* A10e 30d on 30np #104Ag 10.00 —
*h.* A10e 40d on 40np #104Ah 12.00 —
*i.* A10e 50d on 50np #104Ai 15.00 —
*j.* A10e 60d on 60np #104Aj 17.00 —

**Souvenir Sheet**

***Imperf***

121B A10e 50d on 50np #104B 115.00 —
*Nos. 121-121B (3)* 220.00

Nos. 121-121A printed se-tenant with five labels showing Arabic inscription.

Arab Postal Union Emblem — A11

**1967, Apr. 15 Photo. *Perf. 11x11½***

122 A11 70d magenta & sepia 4.50 2.00
122A A11 80d dull blue & sepia 6.50 2.00

Qatar's joining the Arab Postal Union.

Apollo Project A11a

Designs: 5d, 70d, Two astronauts on Moon. 10d, 80d, Command and lunar modules in lunar orbit. 20d, 1r, Lunar module on Moon. 30d, 1.20r, Lunar module ascending from Moon. 40d, 2r, Saturn 5 rocket.

**1967, May 1 *Perf. 12½***

123 A11a 5d multicolored .75 .35
123A A11a 10d multicolored .75 .35
123B A11a 20d multicolored .75 .35
123C A11a 30d multicolored 1.00 .50
123D A11a 40d multicolored 1.50 .65
123E A11a 70d multicolored 3.00 1.50
123F A11a 80d multicolored 3.25 2.25
123G A11a 1r multicolored 3.50 2.75
123H A11a 1.20r multicolored 4.25 3.00
123J A11a 2r multicolored 6.00 4.00
*Nos. 123-123J (10)* 24.75 15.70

#123J exists in an imperf. souv. sheet of one. Value $30.

Traffic Light and Intersection — A12

**1967, May 24 Litho. *Perf. 13½***

124 A12 20d vio & multi 1.00 .40
124A A12 30d multi 2.00 .65
124B A12 50d multi 3.00 .80
124C A12 1r ultra & multi 5.00 2.50
*Nos. 124-124C (4)* 11.00 4.35

Issued for Traffic Day.

Boy Scouts and Sheik Ahmad A13

Designs: 1d, First Boy Scout camp, Brownsea Island, 1907, and tents, Idaho, US, 1967. 2d, Lord Baden-Powell. 5d, Boy Scout canoeing. 15d, Swimming. 75d, Mountain climbing. 2r, Boy Scout saluting flag and emblem of 12th World Jamboree. 1d and 2d lack head of Sheik Ahmad.

**1967, Sept. 15 Litho. *Perf. 11½x11***

125 A13 1d multicolored 1.00 .45
125A A13 2d buff & multi 1.00 .45

**Litho. and Engr.**

125B A13 3d rose & multi 1.00 .45
125C A13 5d lilac & multi 1.25 .45
125D A13 15d multicolored 2.50 .55
125E A13 75d green & multi 5.00 1.75
125F A13 2r sepia & multi 14.00 6.00
*Nos. 125-125F (7)* 25.75 10.10

Nos. 125-125A for 60th anniv. of the Boy Scouts, Nos. 125B-125F for 12th Boy Scout World Jamboree, Farragut State Park, Idaho, Aug. 1-9.

Viking Ship (from Bayeux Tapestry) A14

Famous Ships: 2d, Santa Maria (Columbus). 3d, San Gabriel (Vasco da Gama). 75d, Victoria (Ferdinand Magellan). 1r, Golden Hind (Sir Francis Drake). 2r, Gipsy Moth IV (Sir Francis Chichester).

**1967, Nov. 27 Litho. *Perf. 13½***

126 A14 1d org & multi .80 .35
126A A14 2d lt bl, tan & blk .90 .35
126B A14 3d lt bl & multi 1.25 .35
126C A14 75d fawn & multi 5.75 1.75
126D A14 1r gray, yel grn & red 7.50 2.75
126E A14 2r multi 14.50 3.75
*Nos. 126-126E (6)* 30.70 9.30

Professional Letter Writer — A15

Designs: 2d, Carrier pigeon and man releasing pigeon, vert. 3d, Postrider. 60d, Mail transport by rowboat, vert. 1.25r, Mailman riding camel, jet plane and modern buildings. 2r, Qatar No. 1, hand holding pen, paper, envelopes and inkwell.

**1968, Feb. 14**

127 A15 1d multicolored .75 .40
127A A15 2d multicolored .75 .40
127B A15 3d multicolored .75 .40
127C A15 60d multicolored 4.00 1.25
127D A15 1.25r multicolored 8.00 2.50
127E A15 2r multicolored 14.00 4.25
*Nos. 127-127E (6)* 28.25 9.20

Ten years of Qatar postal service.

Human Rights Flame and Barbed Wire A16

2d, Arab refugee family leaving concentration camp. 3d, Scales of Justice. 60d, Hands opening gates to the sun. 1.25r, Family and sun, vert. 2r, Stylized family groups.

**1968, Apr. 10**

128 A16 1d gray & multi .60 .30
129 A16 2d multicolored .60 .30
130 A16 3d brt grn, org & blk .75 .30
131 A16 60d org, brn & blk 4.00 2.25
132 A16 1.25r brt grn, blk & yel 5.50 4.75
133 A16 2r multicolored 11.00 6.50
*Nos. 128-133 (6)* 22.45 14.40

International Human Rights Year.

Nurse Attending Premature Baby — A17

Designs (WHO Emblem and): 2d, Operating room. 3d, Dentist. 60d, X-ray examination. 1.25r, Medical laboratory. 2r, State Hospital.

**1968, June 20**

134 A17 1d multi .75 .40
135 A17 2d multi .75 .40
136 A17 3d multi .85 .40
137 A17 60d multi 3.75 .70
138 A17 1.25r multi 8.50 2.25
139 A17 2r multi 14.00 3.25
*Nos. 134-139 (6)* 28.60 7.40

20th anniv. of the World Health Organization.

Olympic Rings and Gymnast A18

Designs (Olympic Rings and): 1d, Discobolus and view of Mexico City. 2d, Runner and flaming torch. 60d, Weight lifting and torch. 1.25r, Olympic flame as a mosaic, vert. 2r, Mythological bird.

**1968, Aug. 24**

140 A18 1d multicolored .55 .50
141 A18 2d multicolored .65 .50
142 A18 3d multicolored 1.00 .50
143 A18 60d multicolored 4.50 1.75
144 A18 1.25r multicolored 8.00 2.75
145 A18 2r multicolored 14.00 4.25
*Nos. 140-145 (6)* 28.70 10.25

19th Olympic Games, Mexico City, 10/12-27.

A19

Sheik Ahmad bin Ali al Thani — A21

Dhow A20

Designs: 40d, Desalination plant. 60d, Loading platform and oil tanker. 70d, Qatar Mosque. 1r, Clock Tower, Market Place, Doha. 1.25r, Doha Fort. 1.50r, Falcon.

**1968 Litho. *Perf. 13½***

| No. | Type | Description | Unused | Used |
|---|---|---|---|---|
| 146 | A19 | 5d blue & green | .50 | .50 |
| 147 | A19 | 10d brt bl & red brn | .65 | .50 |
| 148 | A19 | 20d blk & vermilion | 1.00 | .50 |
| 149 | A19 | 25d brt mag & brt grn | 2.25 | .50 |

**Lithographed and Engraved**

***Perf. 13***

| No. | Type | Description | Unused | Used |
|---|---|---|---|---|
| 150 | A20 | 35d grn & brt pink | 4.00 | .50 |
| 151 | A20 | 40d pur, lt bl & org | 5.00 | .50 |
| 152 | A20 | 60d lt bl, brn & lil | 6.50 | .85 |
| 153 | A20 | 70d blk, lt bl & brt grn | 7.00 | 1.10 |
| 154 | A20 | 1r vio bl, yel & brt grn | 9.00 | 1.40 |
| 155 | A20 | 1.25r ind, brt bl & ocher | 10.00 | 1.75 |
| 156 | A20 | 1.50r lt bl, dk grn & rose lil | 12.50 | 2.10 |

***Perf. 11½***

| No. | Type | Description | Unused | Used |
|---|---|---|---|---|
| 157 | A21 | 2r brn, ocher & bl gray | 17.50 | 3.00 |
| 158 | A21 | 5r grn, lt grn & pur | 30.00 | 7.25 |
| 159 | A21 | 10r ultra, lt bl & sep | 60.00 | 13.50 |
| | | *Nos. 146-159 (14)* | 165.90 | 33.95 |

UN Headquarters, NY, and Flags — A22

1d, Flags. 4d, World map and dove. 60d, Classroom. 1.50r, Farmers, wheat and tractor. 2r, Sec. Gen. U Thant and General Assembly Hall.

**1968, Oct. 24 Litho. *Perf. 13½x13***

| No. | Type | Description | Unused | Used |
|---|---|---|---|---|
| 160 | A22 | 1d multi | .50 | .50 |
| 161 | A22 | 4d multi | .65 | .50 |
| 162 | A22 | 5d multi | .75 | .50 |
| 163 | A22 | 60d multi | 4.75 | 1.50 |
| 164 | A22 | 1.50r multi | 7.50 | 2.40 |
| 165 | A22 | 2r multi | 8.50 | 4.00 |
| | | *Nos. 160-165 (6)* | 22.65 | 9.40 |

United Nations Day, Oct. 24, 1968.

Fishing Vessel Ross Rayyan A23

Progress in Qatar: 4d, Elementary School and children playing. 5d, Doha Intl. Airport. 60d, Cement factory and road building. 1.50r, Power station. 2r, Housing development.

**1969, Jan. 13**

| No. | Type | Description | Unused | Used |
|---|---|---|---|---|
| 166 | A23 | 1d brt bl & multi | .40 | .40 |
| 167 | A23 | 4d green & multi | .40 | .40 |
| 168 | A23 | 5d dl org & multi | .75 | .40 |
| 169 | A23 | 60d lt brn & multi | 4.00 | 1.50 |
| 170 | A23 | 1.50r brt lil & multi | 9.00 | 2.00 |
| 171 | A23 | 2r buff & multi | 13.00 | 3.00 |
| | | *Nos. 166-171 (6)* | 27.55 | 7.70 |

Armored Cars A24

Designs: 2d, Traffic police. 3d, Military helicopter. 60d, Military band. 1.25r, Field gun. 2r, Mounted police.

**1969, May 6 Litho. *Perf. 13½***

| No. | Type | Description | Unused | Used |
|---|---|---|---|---|
| 172 | A24 | 1d multicolored | .75 | .45 |
| 173 | A24 | 2d lt blue & multi | .75 | .45 |
| 174 | A24 | 3d gray & multi | .90 | .50 |
| 175 | A24 | 60d multicolored | 5.00 | 1.50 |
| 176 | A24 | 1.25r multi | 8.50 | 2.25 |
| 177 | A24 | 2r blue & multi | 15.00 | 4.00 |
| | | *Nos. 172-177 (6)* | 30.90 | 9.15 |

Issued to honor the public security forces.

Oil Tanker A25

2d, Research laboratory. 3d, Off-shore oil rig, helicopter. 60d, Oil rig, storage tanks. 1.50r, Oil refinery. 2r, Oil tankers, 1890-1968.

**1969, July 4**

| No. | Type | Description | Unused | Used |
|---|---|---|---|---|
| 178 | A25 | 1d gray & multi | .65 | .40 |
| 179 | A25 | 2d olive & multi | .65 | .40 |
| 180 | A25 | 3d ultra & multi | 1.00 | .40 |
| 181 | A25 | 60d lilac & multi | 4.00 | 1.75 |
| 182 | A25 | 1.50r red brn & multi | 11.00 | 3.25 |
| 183 | A25 | 2r brown & multi | 16.50 | 4.25 |
| | | *Nos. 178-183 (6)* | 33.80 | 10.45 |

Qatar oil industry.

Boy Scouts Building Boats A26

Designs: 2d, Scouts at work and 10 symbolic candles. 3d, Parade. 60d, Gate to camp interior. 1.25r, Main camp gate. 2r, Hoisting Qatar flag, and Sheik Ahmad.

**1969, Sept. 18 Litho. *Perf. 13½x13***

| No. | Type | Description | Unused | Used |
|---|---|---|---|---|
| 184 | A26 | 1d multicolored | .35 | .30 |
| 185 | A26 | 2d multicolored | .35 | .30 |
| 186 | A26 | 3d multicolored | .75 | .30 |
| 187 | A26 | 60d multicolored | 6.00 | 1.10 |
| *a.* | | Souvenir sheet of 4, #184-187 | 40.00 | 20.00 |
| 188 | A26 | 1.25r multicolored | 9.50 | 2.25 |
| 189 | A26 | 2r multicolored | 13.00 | 3.50 |
| | | *Nos. 184-189 (6)* | 29.95 | 7.75 |

10th Qatar Boy Scout Jamboree. No. 187a sold for 1r.

Neil A. Armstrong A27

Designs: 2d, Col. Edwin E. Aldrin, Jr. 3d, Lt. Col. Michael Collins. 60d, Astronaut walking on moon. 1.25r, Blast-off from moon. 2r, Capsule and raft in Pacific, horiz.

**1969, Dec. 6 *Perf. 13x13½, 13½x13***

| No. | Type | Description | Unused | Used |
|---|---|---|---|---|
| 190 | A27 | 1d blue & multi | .50 | .50 |
| 191 | A27 | 2d multicolored | .50 | .50 |
| 192 | A27 | 3d grn & multi | .85 | .50 |
| 193 | A27 | 60d multicolored | 3.50 | 1.25 |
| 194 | A27 | 1.25r pur & multi | 7.00 | 3.00 |
| 195 | A27 | 2r multicolored | 12.50 | 4.75 |
| | | *Nos. 190-195 (6)* | 24.85 | 10.50 |

See note after US No. C76.

UPU Emblem, Boeing Jet Loading in Qatar A28

2d, Transatlantic ocean liner. 3d, Mail truck and mail bags. 60d, Qatar Post Office. 1.25r, UPU Headquarters, Bern. 2r, UPU emblem.

**1970, Jan. 31 Litho. *Perf. 13½x13***

| No. | Type | Description | Unused | Used |
|---|---|---|---|---|
| 196 | A28 | 1d multi | .50 | .50 |
| 197 | A28 | 2d multi | .50 | .50 |
| 198 | A28 | 3d multi | .90 | .50 |
| 199 | A28 | 60d multi | 3.50 | 1.50 |
| 200 | A28 | 1.25r multi | 6.50 | 2.75 |
| 201 | A28 | 2r brt yel grn, blk & lt brn | 11.00 | 3.50 |
| | | *Nos. 196-201 (6)* | 22.90 | 9.25 |

Qatar's admission to the UPU.

Map of Arab League Countries, Flag and Emblem — A28a

**1970, Mar. *Perf. 13x13½***

| No. | Type | Description | Unused | Used |
|---|---|---|---|---|
| 202 | A28a | 35d yellow & multi | 2.25 | .80 |
| 203 | A28a | 60d blue & multi | 3.75 | 1.25 |
| 204 | A28a | 1.25r multi | 7.00 | 2.25 |
| 205 | A28a | 1.50r vio & multi | 9.50 | 4.00 |
| | | *Nos. 202-205 (4)* | 22.50 | 8.30 |

25th anniversary of the Arab League.

VC10 Touching down for Landing A29

Designs: 2d, Hawk, and VC10 in flight. 3d, VC10 and airport. 60d, Map showing route Doha to London. 1.25r, VC10 over Gulftown. 2r, Tail of VC10 with emblem of Gulf Aviation.

**1970, Apr. 5 *Perf. 13½x13***

| No. | Type | Description | Unused | Used |
|---|---|---|---|---|
| 206 | A29 | 1d multi | .45 | .45 |
| 207 | A29 | 2d multi | .75 | .45 |
| 208 | A29 | 3d multi | .85 | .45 |
| 209 | A29 | 60d multi | 5.50 | 1.50 |
| 210 | A29 | 1.25r multi | 10.00 | 3.00 |
| 211 | A29 | 2r multi | 17.50 | 4.50 |
| | | *Nos. 206-211 (6)* | 35.05 | 10.35 |

Issued to publicize the first flight to London from Doha by Gulf Aviation Company.

Education Year Emblem, Spaceship Trajectory, Koran Quotation — A30

**1970, May 24 *Perf. 13x12½***

| No. | Type | Description | Unused | Used |
|---|---|---|---|---|
| 212 | A30 | 35d blue & multi | 4.00 | 1.60 |
| 213 | A30 | 60d blue & multi | 8.00 | 2.50 |

Intl. Education Year. Translation of Koran quotation: "And say, O God, give me more knowledge."

Flowers — A31

**1970, July 2 *Perf. 13x13½***

| No. | Type | Description | Unused | Used |
|---|---|---|---|---|
| 214 | A31 | 1d Freesia | .90 | .45 |
| 215 | A31 | 2d Azalea | .90 | .45 |
| 216 | A31 | 3d Ixia | 1.25 | .45 |
| 217 | A31 | 60d Amaryllis | 5.50 | 1.60 |
| 218 | A31 | 1.25r Cineraria | 9.50 | 3.50 |
| 219 | A31 | 2r Rose | 12.50 | 4.50 |
| | | *Nos. 214-219 (6)* | 30.55 | 10.95 |

For surcharges see Nos. 287-289.

EXPO Emblem and Fisherman on Shikoku Beach — A32

1d, Toyahama fishermen honoring ocean gods. 2d, Map of Japan. 60d, Mt. Fuji. 1.50r, Camphorwood torii. 2r, Tower of Motherhood, EXPO Tower and Mt. Fuji.

***Perf. 13½x13, 13x13½***

**1970, Sept. 29**

| No. | Type | Description | Unused | Used |
|---|---|---|---|---|
| 220 | A32 | 1d multi, horiz. | .45 | .45 |
| 221 | A32 | 2d multi, horiz. | .60 | .45 |
| 222 | A32 | 3d multi | .90 | .45 |
| 223 | A32 | 60d multi | 4.25 | 1.10 |
| *a.* | | Souvenir sheet of 4 | 55.00 | 27.50 |
| 224 | A32 | 1.50r multi, horiz. | 12.00 | 3.50 |
| 225 | A32 | 2r multi | 17.50 | 6.00 |
| | | *Nos. 220-225 (6)* | 35.70 | 11.95 |

EXPO '70 Intl. Exhib., Osaka, Japan, Mar. 15-Sept. 13. No. 223a contains 4 imperf. stamps similar to Nos. 220-223 with simulated perforations. Sold for 1r.

Globe and UN Emblem — A33

UN, 25th anniv.: 2d, Cannon used as flower vase. 3d, Birthday cake and dove. 35d, Emblems of UN agencies forming wall. 1.50r, Trumpet and emblems of UN agencies. 2r, Two men, black and white, embracing, and globe.

**1970, Dec. 7 Litho. *Perf. 14x13½***

| No. | Type | Description | Unused | Used |
|---|---|---|---|---|
| 226 | A33 | 1d blue & multi | .70 | .35 |
| 227 | A33 | 2d multicolored | .70 | .35 |
| 228 | A33 | 3d brt pur & multi | 1.00 | .40 |
| 229 | A33 | 35d green & multi | 3.25 | 1.00 |
| 230 | A33 | 1.50r multi | 9.50 | 2.25 |
| 231 | A33 | 2r brn red & multi | 11.50 | 3.75 |
| | | *Nos. 226-231 (6)* | 26.65 | 8.10 |

Al Jahiz and Old World Map A34

Designs: 2d, Sultan Saladin and palace. 3d, Al Farabi, sailboat and musical instruments. 35d, Iben al Haithum and palace. 1.50r, Al Motanabbi and camels. 2r, Avicenna and old world map.

**1971, Feb. 20** *Perf. 13½x14*

| No. | Type | Description | Unused | Used |
|---|---|---|---|---|
| 232 | A34 | 1d brt pink & multi | .90 | .40 |
| 233 | A34 | 2d pale bl & multi | .90 | .40 |
| 234 | A34 | 3d dl yel & multi | 1.50 | .40 |
| 235 | A34 | 35d lt bl & multi | 5.00 | .95 |
| 236 | A34 | 1.50r yel grn & multi | 20.00 | 3.75 |
| 237 | A34 | 2r pale grn & multi | 25.00 | 5.00 |
| | | *Nos. 232-237 (6)* | 53.30 | 10.90 |

Famous men of Islam.

Cormorant — A35

Designs: 2d, Lizard and prickly pear. 3d, Flamingos and palms. 60d, Oryx and yucca. 1.25r, Gazelle and desert dandelion. 2r, Camel, palm and bronzed chenopod.

**1971, Apr. 14** **Litho.** *Perf. 11x12*

| No. | Type | Description | Unused | Used |
|---|---|---|---|---|
| 238 | A35 | 1d multi | 2.50 | .45 |
| 239 | A35 | 2d multi | 2.50 | .45 |
| 240 | A35 | 3d multi | 2.50 | .50 |
| 241 | A35 | 60d multi | 11.00 | 2.00 |
| 242 | A35 | 1.25r multi | 22.50 | 5.00 |
| 243 | A35 | 2r multi | 30.00 | 7.50 |
| | | *Nos. 238-243 (6)* | 71.00 | 15.90 |

Goonhilly Satellite Tracking Station A36

Designs: 2d, Cable ship, and section of submarine cable. 3d, 35d, London Post Office Tower, and television control room. 4d, Various telephones. 5d, 75d, Video telephone. 3r, Telex machine and tape.

**1971, May 17** *Perf. 13½x13*

| No. | Type | Description | Unused | Used |
|---|---|---|---|---|
| 244 | A36 | 1d vio bl & multi | .40 | .35 |
| 245 | A36 | 2d multicolored | .40 | .35 |
| 246 | A36 | 3d rose red & multi | .40 | .35 |
| 247 | A36 | 4d magenta & multi | .40 | .35 |
| 248 | A36 | 5d rose red & multi | .40 | .35 |
| 249 | A36 | 35d multicolored | 3.25 | 1.00 |
| 250 | A36 | 75d magenta & multi | 4.75 | 1.25 |
| 251 | A36 | 3r ocher & multi | 17.50 | 3.50 |
| | | *Nos. 244-251 (8)* | 27.50 | 7.50 |

3rd World Telecommunications Day.

## State of Qatar

Arab Postal Union Emblem — A37

**1971, Sept. 4** *Perf. 13*

| No. | Type | Description | Unused | Used |
|---|---|---|---|---|
| 252 | A37 | 35d red & multi | 1.25 | .40 |
| 253 | A37 | 55d blue & multi | 2.25 | .80 |
| 254 | A37 | 75d brown & multi | 3.25 | 1.25 |
| 255 | A37 | 1.25r violet & multi | 5.25 | 1.90 |
| | | *Nos. 252-255 (4)* | 12.00 | 4.35 |

25th anniv. of the Conf. of Sofar, Lebanon, establishing the Arab Postal Union.

Boy Reading — A38

**1971, Aug. 10** *Perf. 13x13½*

| No. | Type | Description | Unused | Used |
|---|---|---|---|---|
| 256 | A38 | 35d brown & multi | 2.00 | .40 |
| 257 | A38 | 55d ultra & multi | 4.25 | .75 |
| 258 | A38 | 75d green & multi | 5.75 | 1.10 |
| | | *Nos. 256-258 (3)* | 12.00 | 2.25 |

International Literacy Day, Sept. 8.

Men Splitting Racism A39

2d, 3r, People fighting racism. 3d, Soldier helping war victim. 4d, Men of 4 races rebuilding. 5d, Children on swing. 35d, Wave of racism engulfing people. 75d, like 1d.

*Perf. 13½x13, 13x13½*

**1971, Oct. 12** **Litho.**

| No. | Type | Description | Unused | Used |
|---|---|---|---|---|
| 259 | A39 | 1d multi | .60 | .40 |
| 260 | A39 | 2d multi | .60 | .40 |
| 261 | A39 | 3d multi | .60 | .40 |
| 262 | A39 | 4d multi, vert. | .60 | .40 |
| 263 | A39 | 5d multi, vert. | .60 | .40 |
| 264 | A39 | 35d multi | 3.50 | .90 |
| 265 | A39 | 75d multi | 7.50 | 1.75 |
| 266 | A39 | 3r multi | 17.50 | 3.75 |
| | | *Nos. 259-266 (8)* | 31.50 | 8.40 |

Intl. Year Against Racial Discrimination.

UNICEF Emblem, Mother and Child — A40

UNICEF, 25th anniv.: 2d, Child's head, horiz. 3d, 75d, Child with book. 4d, Nurse and child, horiz. 5d, Mother and child, horiz. 35d, Woman and daffodil. 3r, like 1d.

**1971, Dec. 6** *Perf. 14x13½, 13½x14*

| No. | Type | Description | Unused | Used |
|---|---|---|---|---|
| 267 | A40 | 1d blue & multi | .60 | .50 |
| 268 | A40 | 2d lil rose & multi | .60 | .50 |
| 269 | A40 | 3d blue & multi | .60 | .50 |
| 270 | A40 | 4d yellow & multi | .60 | .50 |
| 271 | A40 | 5d blue & multi | .60 | .50 |
| 272 | A40 | 35d lil rose & multi | 2.50 | .65 |
| 273 | A40 | 75d yellow & multi | 6.75 | 1.50 |
| 274 | A40 | 3r multicolored | 16.00 | 3.50 |
| | | *Nos. 267-274 (8)* | 28.25 | 8.15 |

Sheik Ahmad, Flags of Arab League and Qatar A41

"International Cooperation" A42

75d, Sheik Ahmad, flags of UN and Qatar. 1.25r, Sheik Ahmad bin Ali al Thani.

**1972, Jan. 17** *Perf. 13½x13, 13x13½*

| No. | Type | Description | Unused | Used |
|---|---|---|---|---|
| 275 | A41 | 35d black & multi | 2.00 | .50 |
| 276 | A41 | 75d black & multi | 3.75 | 1.25 |
| 277 | A42 | 1.25r lt brn & blk | 5.50 | 1.50 |
| 278 | A42 | 3r multicolored | 13.00 | 3.50 |
| a. | | Souvenir sheet | 50.00 | 25.00 |
| | | *Nos. 275-278 (4)* | 24.25 | 6.75 |

Independence 1971. No. 278a contains one stamp with simulated perforations.

European Roller — A43

Birds: 2d, European kingfisher. 3d, Rock thrush. 4d, Caspian tern. 5d, Hoopoe. 35d, European bee-eater. 75d, European golden oriole. 3r, Peregrine falcon.

**1972, Mar. 1** **Litho.** *Perf. 12x11*

| No. | Type | Description | Unused | Used |
|---|---|---|---|---|
| 279 | A43 | 1d sepia & multi | 2.00 | .85 |
| 280 | A43 | 2d emerald & multi | 2.25 | .85 |
| 281 | A43 | 3d bister & multi | 2.25 | .85 |
| 282 | A43 | 4d lt blue & multi | 2.50 | .85 |
| 283 | A43 | 5d yellow & multi | 2.50 | .85 |
| 284 | A43 | 35d vio bl & multi | 8.00 | 1.00 |
| 285 | A43 | 75d pink & multi | 18.00 | 2.75 |
| 286 | A43 | 3r blue & multi | 47.50 | 11.00 |
| | | *Nos. 279-286 (8)* | 85.00 | 19.00 |

Nos. 217-219 Surcharged

**1972, Mar. 7** *Perf. 13x13½*

| No. | Type | Description | Unused | Used |
|---|---|---|---|---|
| 287 | A31 | 10d on 60d multi | 5.00 | .80 |
| 288 | A31 | 1r on 1.25r multi | 20.00 | 4.00 |
| 289 | A31 | 5r on 2r multi | 70.00 | 13.00 |
| | | *Nos. 287-289 (3)* | 95.00 | 17.80 |

Sheik Khalifa bin Hamad al Thani
A44 A44a

**1972** **Size: 23x27mm** *Perf. 14*

| No. | Type | Description | Unused | Used |
|---|---|---|---|---|
| 290 | A44 | 5d pur & ultra | .75 | .30 |
| 291 | A44 | 10d brn & rose red | .75 | .60 |
| 291A | A44a | 10d lt brn & lt red | 240.00 | 100.00 |
| 291B | A44a | 25d vio & emer | 240.00 | 100.00 |
| 292 | A44 | 35d org & dl grn | 2.50 | .75 |
| 293 | A44 | 55d brt grn & lil | 4.25 | 1.75 |
| 294 | A44 | 75d vio & lil rose | 5.50 | 2.00 |

**Size: 26½x32mm**

| No. | Type | Description | Unused | Used |
|---|---|---|---|---|
| 295 | A44 | 1r bister & blk | 9.50 | 2.50 |
| 296 | A44 | 1.25r olive & blk | 11.00 | 3.50 |
| 297 | A44 | 5r blue & blk | 40.00 | 10.00 |
| 298 | A44 | 10r red & blk | 70.00 | 24.00 |
| | | *Nos. 290-298 (11)* | 624.25 | |
| | | *Nos. 290-291,292-298 (9)* | 144.25 | 45.40 |

Issued: Type A44, Mar. 7.

Book Year Emblem A45

**1972, Apr. 23** *Perf. 13½x13*

| No. | Type | Description | Unused | Used |
|---|---|---|---|---|
| 299 | A45 | 35d lt ultra & blk | 2.50 | .45 |
| 300 | A45 | 55d lt brown & blk | 3.75 | .75 |
| 301 | A45 | 75d green & blk | 5.00 | 1.10 |
| 302 | A45 | 1.25r violet & blk | 8.25 | 1.75 |
| | | *Nos. 299-302 (4)* | 19.50 | 4.05 |

International Book Year 1972.

Olympic Rings, Soccer A46

2d, 3r, Running. 3d, Bicycling. 4d, Gymnastics. 5d, Basketball. 35d, Discus. 75d, Like 1d.

**1972, June 12** *Perf. 13½x13*

| No. | Type | Description | Unused | Used |
|---|---|---|---|---|
| 303 | A46 | 1d green & multi | .80 | .40 |
| 304 | A46 | 2d yel grn & multi | .80 | .40 |
| 305 | A46 | 3d blue & multi | .80 | .40 |
| 306 | A46 | 4d lilac & multi | .80 | .40 |
| 307 | A46 | 5d blue & multi | .90 | .40 |
| 308 | A46 | 35d gray & multi | 2.25 | .60 |
| a. | | Souvenir sheet of 6 | 40.00 | 25.00 |
| 309 | A46 | 75d green & multi | 4.00 | 1.00 |
| 310 | A46 | 3r multicolored | 15.00 | 4.00 |
| | | *Nos. 303-310 (8)* | 25.35 | 7.60 |

20th Olympic Games, Munich, Aug. 26-Sept. 10. No. 308a contains stamps with simulated perforations similar to Nos. 303-308.

Installation of Underwater Pipe Line — A47

1d, Drilling for oil, vert. 5d, Drilling platform. 35d, Ship searching for oil.

**1972, Aug. 8** **Litho.** *Perf. 13x13½*

| No. | Type | Description | Unused | Used |
|---|---|---|---|---|
| 311 | A47 | 1d multicolored | .65 | .40 |
| 312 | A47 | 4d shown | .65 | .40 |
| 313 | A47 | 5d multicolored | .65 | .40 |
| 314 | A47 | 35d multicolored | 2.75 | .55 |
| 315 | A47 | 75d like 1d, vert. | 5.75 | 1.25 |
| 316 | A47 | 3r like 5d | 27.50 | 6.00 |
| | | *Nos. 311-316 (6)* | 37.95 | 9.00 |

Oil from the sea.

Government Palace — A48

Designs: 35d, Clasped hands, Qatar flag. 75d, Clasped hands, UN flag. 1.25r, Sheik Khalifa bin Hamad al-Thani, vert.

**1972, Sept. 3** *Perf. 13½x13, 13x13½*

| No. | Type | Description | Unused | Used |
|---|---|---|---|---|
| 317 | A48 | 10d yel & multi | 1.50 | .50 |
| 318 | A48 | 35d blk & multi | 4.00 | .65 |
| 319 | A48 | 75d blk & multi | 7.50 | 1.25 |
| 320 | A48 | 1.25r gold & multi | 14.00 | 2.00 |
| a. | | Souvenir sheet of 1 | 42.50 | 22.50 |
| | | *Nos. 317-320 (4)* | 27.00 | 4.40 |

Independence Day, 1st anniv. of independence.

No. 320a contains one stamp with simulated perforations similar to No. 320.

Qatar Flag, Council Emblem and Flag A49

**1972, Dec. 4** **Litho.** *Perf. 14x13½*

| No. | Type | Description | Unused | Used |
|---|---|---|---|---|
| 321 | A49 | 25d blue & multi | 4.00 | 1.00 |
| 322 | A49 | 30d vio bl & multi | 6.00 | 1.50 |

Civil Aviation Council of Arab States, 10th session.

Tracking Station, Satellite, Telephone, ITU and UN Emblems A50

Designs (Agency and UN Emblems): 2d, Surveyor, artist; UNESCO. 3d, Tractor, helicopter, fish, grain and fruit; FAO. 4d, Reading children, teacher; UNICEF. 5d, Weather satellite and map; WMO. 25d, Workers and crane; ILO. 55d, Health clinic; WHO. 1r, Mail plane and post office; UPU.

**1972, Oct. 24** *Perf. 13½x14*

**323** A50 1d multicolored .60 .35
**324** A50 2d multicolored .60 .35
**325** A50 3d multicolored .60 .35
**326** A50 4d multicolored .60 .35
**327** A50 5d multicolored .75 .50
**328** A50 25d multicolored 5.75 1.00
**329** A50 55d multicolored 10.00 3.00
**330** A50 1r multicolored 20.00 6.00
*Nos. 323-330 (8)* 38.90 11.90

United Nations Day, Oct. 24, 1972. Each stamp dedicated to a different UN agency.

Road Building — A51

3d, Housing development. 4d, Operating room. 5d, Telephone operators. 15d, School, classroom. 20d, Television studio. 35d, Sheik Khalifa. 55d, New Gulf Hotel. 1r, Fertilizer plant. 1.35r, Flour mill.

**1973, Feb. 22** **Litho.** *Perf. 13x13½*

**331** A51 2d multicolored .80 .40
**332** A51 3d multicolored .80 .40
**333** A51 4d multicolored .80 .40
**334** A51 5d multicolored .80 .40
**335** A51 15d multicolored 1.75 .40
**336** A51 20d multicolored 2.00 .40
**337** A51 35d multicolored 3.00 .50
**338** A51 55d multicolored 3.75 .80
**339** A51 1r multicolored 5.25 1.60
**340** A51 1.35r multicolored 8.25 2.25
*Nos. 331-340 (10)* 27.20 7.55

1st anniv. of the accession of Sheik Khalifa bin Hamad al Thani as Emir of Qatar.

Aerial Pest Control — A52

WHO, 25th anniv.: 3d, Medicines. 4d, Poliomyelitis prevention. 5d, Malaria control. 55d, Mental health. 1r, Pollution control.

**1973, May 14** **Litho.** *Perf. 14*

**341** A52 2d blue & multi .85 .50
**342** A52 3d blue & multi .85 .50
**343** A52 4d blue & multi .85 .50
**344** A52 5d blue & multi 1.75 .65
**345** A52 55d blue & multi 11.00 2.00
**346** A52 1r blue & multi 25.00 3.75
*Nos. 341-346 (6)* 40.30 7.90

Weather Ship A53

Designs (WMO Emblem and): 3d, Launching of radiosonde balloon. 4d, Plane and meteorological data checking. 5d, Cup anemometers and meteorological station. 10d, Weather plane in flight. 1r, Nimbus I weather satellite. 1.55r, Launching of rocket carrying weather satellite.

**1973, July** **Litho.** *Perf. 14x13*

**347** A53 2d multicolored .60 .40
**348** A53 3d multicolored .60 .40
**349** A53 4d multicolored .60 .40
**350** A53 5d multicolored .60 .40
**351** A53 10d multicolored 2.00 .60
**352** A53 1r multicolored 13.50 1.75
**353** A53 1.55r multicolored 20.00 3.00
*Nos. 347-353 (7)* 37.90 6.95

Cent. of intl. meteorological cooperation.

Sheik Khalifa — A54

Clock Tower, Doha — A55

**1973-74** **Litho.** *Perf. 14*

**Size: 18x27mm**

**354** A54 5d green & multi 1.25 .40
**355** A54 10d lt bl & multi 1.75 .40
**356** A54 20d ver & multi 2.25 .40
**357** A54 25d org & multi 3.00 .40
**358** A54 35d purple & multi 4.00 .75
**359** A54 55d dk gray & multi 6.00 1.00

**Engr.**

***Perf. 13½***

**360** A55 75d lil, bl & yel grn 9.00 2.00

**Photo.**

***Perf. 13***

**Size: 27x32mm**

**360A** A54 1r multicolored 22.50 5.00
**360B** A54 5r multicolored 75.00 24.00
**360C** A54 10r multicolored 160.00 55.00
*Nos. 354-360C (10)* 284.75 89.35

Issue dates: 20d, 75d, July 3, 1973; 1r-10r, July 1974; others, Jan. 27, 1973.

Flag of Qatar, Handclasp, Sheik Khalifa — A56

Flag, Sheik and: 35d, Harvest. 55d, Government Building. 1.35r, Market and Clock Tower, Doha. 1.55r, Illuminated fountain.

**1973, Oct. 4** **Litho.** *Perf. 13*

**361** A56 15d red & multi .45 .30
**362** A56 35d buff & multi .80 .30
**363** A56 55d multi 2.00 .50
**364** A56 1.35r vio & multi 4.50 1.25
**365** A56 1.55r multi 5.00 1.60
*Nos. 361-365 (5)* 12.75 3.95

2nd anniversary of independence.

Planting Tree, Qatar and UN Flags, UNESCO Emblem — A57

Qatar and UN Flags and: 4d, UN Headquarters and flags. 5d, Pipe laying, cement mixer, helicopter and ILO emblem. 35d, Nurse, patient and UNICEF emblem. 1.35r, Telecommunications and ITU emblem. 3r, Cattle, wheat disease analysis and FAO emblem.

**1973, Oct. 24**

**366** A57 2d multi .50 .50
**367** A57 4d multi .50 .50
**368** A57 5d multi .60 .50
**369** A57 35d multi 1.60 .50
**370** A57 1.35r multi 6.50 1.75
**371** A57 3r multi 15.00 5.50
*Nos. 366-371 (6)* 24.70 9.25

United Nations Day.

Prison Gates Opening — A58

4d, Marchers with flags. 5d, Scales of Justice. 35d, Teacher and pupils. 1.35r, UN General Assembly. 3r, Human Rights flame, vert.

**1973, Dec.** **Litho.** *Perf. 13x13½*

**372** A58 2d yellow & multi .45 .40
**373** A58 4d pale lil & multi .45 .40
**374** A58 5d rose & multi .70 .40
**375** A58 35d ocher & multi 2.00 .75
**376** A58 1.35r lt bl & multi 7.00 3.00
**377** A58 3r citron & multi 13.00 4.25
*Nos. 372-377 (6)* 23.60 9.20

25th anniversary of the Universal Declaration of Human Rights.

Highway Overpass — A59

**1974, Feb. 22** *Perf. 14x13½*

**378** A59 2d shown .70 .35
**379** A59 3d Symbol of learning .70 .35
**380** A59 5d Oil field .70 .35
**381** A59 35d Gulf Hotel, Doha 2.25 .50
**382** A59 1.55r Radar station 10.00 3.25
**383** A59 2.25r Sheik Khalifa 13.00 4.00
*Nos. 378-383 (6)* 27.35 8.80

Accession of Sheik Khalifa as Emir, 2nd, anniv.

Mail Truck, Camel Caravan and UPU Emblem — A60

UPU cent.: 3d, Old and new trains, Arab Postal Union emblem. 10d, Old and new ships and Qatar coat of arms. 35d, Old and new planes. 75d, Mail sorting by hand and computer, and Arab Postal Union emblem. 1.25r, Old and new post offices, and Qatar coat of arms.

**1974, May 22** **Litho.** *Perf. 13½*

**384** A60 2d brt yel & multi .85 .45
**385** A60 3d lt bl & multi .85 .45
**386** A60 10d dp org & multi .85 .45
**387** A60 35d slate & multi 3.25 .65
**388** A60 75d yellow & multi 7.75 1.25
**389** A60 1.25r lt bl & multi 11.00 2.25
*Nos. 384-389 (6)* 24.55 5.50

Doha Hospital — A61

**1974, July 13** **Litho.** *Perf. 13½*

**390** A61 5d shown .55 .40
**391** A61 10d WPY emblem and people .55 .40
**392** A61 15d WPY emblem .75 .40
**393** A61 35d World map 1.75 .75
**394** A61 1.75r Clock and infants 6.75 3.00
**395** A61 2.25r Family 9.75 4.00
*Nos. 390-395 (6)* 20.10 8.95

World Population Year 1974.

Television Station — A62

**1974, Sept. 2** *Perf. 13½x13*

**399** A62 5d shown .45 .45
**400** A62 10d Palace of Doha .45 .45
**401** A62 15d Teachers'College .45 .45
**402** A62 75d Clock Tower and Mosque 5.25 1.10
**403** A62 1.55r Traffic circle, Doha 8.50 1.75
**404** A62 2.25r Sheik Khalifa 13.50 2.75
*Nos. 399-404 (6)* 28.60 6.95

3rd anniversary of independence.

Operating Room and WHO Emblem — A63

UN Day: 10d, Satellite earth station and ITU emblem. 20d, Tractor, UN and FAO emblems. 25d, School children, UN and UNESCO emblems. 1.75r, Open air court, UN Headquarters, emblems. 2r, UPU and UN emblems.

**1974, Oct. 24** **Litho.** *Perf. 13x13½*

**405** A63 5d multi .60 .45
**406** A63 10d multi 1.10 .45
**407** A63 20d multi 2.25 .45
**408** A63 25d multi 3.50 .55
**409** A63 1.75r multi 13.50 2.00
**410** A63 2r multi 16.00 2.75
*Nos. 405-410 (6)* 36.95 6.65

VC-10, Gulf Aviation Airliner — A64

Arab League and Qatar Flags, Civil Aviation Emblem — A65

Design: 25d, Doha Airport.

**1974, Dec. 1** **Litho.** *Perf. 13½*

**411** A64 20d multi 3.00 .55
**412** A64 25d yel & dk bl 4.50 .70
**413** A65 30d multi 5.75 .85
**414** A65 50d multi 8.50 1.00
*Nos. 411-414 (4)* 21.75 3.10

Arab Civil Aviation Day.

Caspian Terns, Hoopoes and Shara'o Island — A66

Dhow by Moonlight — A67

5d, Clock Tower, Doha, vert. 15d, Zubara Fort. 35d, Gulf Hotel & sailboats. 75d, Arabian oryx. 1.25r, Khor Al-Udein. 1.75r, Ruins, Wakrah.

**1974, Dec. 21 Litho. *Perf. 13½***

| | | | | |
|---|---|---|---|---|
| **415** | A66 | 5d multi | 1.25 | .40 |
| **416** | A66 | 10d multi | 1.60 | .40 |
| **417** | A66 | 15d multi | 2.00 | .40 |
| **418** | A66 | 35d multi | 3.25 | .40 |
| **419** | A67 | 55d multi | 3.75 | .70 |
| **420** | A66 | 75d multi | 5.75 | 1.00 |
| **421** | A67 | 1.25r multi | 9.50 | 1.60 |
| **422** | A66 | 1.75r multi | 12.50 | 2.00 |
| | | *Nos. 415-422 (8)* | 39.60 | 6.90 |

Traffic Circle, Doha A68

Sheik Khalifa — A69

35d, Pipe line from offshore platform. 55d, Laying underwater pipe line. 1r, Refinery.

**1975, Feb. 22 Litho. *Perf. 13½***

| | | | | |
|---|---|---|---|---|
| **423** | A68 | 10d multi | .40 | .40 |
| **424** | A68 | 35d multi | 2.10 | .85 |
| **425** | A68 | 55d multi | 3.25 | 1.10 |
| **426** | A68 | 1r multi | 6.25 | 1.75 |
| **427** | A69 | 1.35r sil & multi | 7.25 | 2.50 |
| **428** | A69 | 1.55r gold & multi | 9.50 | 3.50 |
| | | *Nos. 423-428 (6)* | 28.75 | 10.10 |

Accession of Sheik Khalifa, 3rd anniv.

Qatar Flag and Arab Labor Charter Emblem — A70

**1975, May 28 Litho. *Perf. 13***

| | | | | |
|---|---|---|---|---|
| **429** | A70 | 10d bl, red brn & blk | .55 | .55 |
| **430** | A70 | 35d multicolored | 4.25 | 1.00 |
| **431** | A70 | 1r green & multi | 11.00 | 2.75 |
| | | *Nos. 429-431 (3)* | 15.80 | 4.30 |

Arab Labor Charter and Constitution, 10th anniversary.

Flintlock Pistol with Ornamental Grip — A71

Designs: 3d, Ornamental mosaic. 35d, View of museum. 75d, Arch and museum, vert. 1.25r, Flint arrowheads and tool. 3r, Gold necklace, vert.

**1975, June 23 *Perf. 13***

| | | | | |
|---|---|---|---|---|
| **432** | A71 | 2d multi | .50 | .40 |
| **433** | A71 | 3d ver blk & gold | 1.00 | .40 |
| **434** | A71 | 35d bis & multi | 2.50 | .50 |
| **435** | A71 | 75d ver & multi | 5.75 | 1.00 |
| **436** | A71 | 1.25r vio & multi | 9.00 | 1.75 |
| **437** | A71 | 3r fawn & multi | 20.00 | 3.25 |
| | | *Nos. 432-437 (6)* | 38.75 | 7.30 |

Opening of Qatar National Museum.

Traffic Signs, Policeman, Doha — A72

Designs: 15d, 55d, Cars, arrows, traffic lights, Doha Clock Tower. 35d, like 5d.

**1975, June 24**

| | | | | |
|---|---|---|---|---|
| **438** | A72 | 5d lt green & multi | .50 | .50 |
| **439** | A72 | 15d lt blue & multi | 3.25 | .50 |
| **440** | A72 | 35d lemon & multi | 7.75 | 1.10 |
| **441** | A72 | 55d lt violet & multi | 13.00 | 1.90 |
| | | *Nos. 438-441 (4)* | 24.50 | 4.00 |

Traffic Week.

Constitution, Arabic Text — A73

5d, Government buildings, horiz. 15d, Museum & Clock Tower, horiz. 55d, 1.25r, Sheik Khalifa & Qatar flag. 75d, Constitution, English text.

**1975, Sept. 2**

| | | | | |
|---|---|---|---|---|
| **442** | A73 | 5d multi | .40 | .40 |
| **443** | A73 | 15d multi | 2.10 | .95 |
| **444** | A73 | 35d multi | 2.50 | .65 |
| **445** | A73 | 55d multi | 4.25 | .95 |
| **446** | A73 | 75d multi | 5.75 | 1.25 |
| **447** | A73 | 1.25r multi | 9.00 | 2.10 |
| | | *Nos. 442-447 (6)* | 24.00 | 6.30 |

4th anniversary of independence.

Satellite over Globe, ITU Emblem — A74

UN, 30th anniv.: 15d, UN Headquarters, NY and UN emblem. 35d, UPU emblem over Eastern Arabia, UN emblem. 1r, Nurses and infant, WHO emblem. 1.25r, Road building equipment, ILO emblem. 2r, Students, UNESCO emblem.

**1975, Oct. 25 Litho. *Perf. 13x13½***

| | | | | |
|---|---|---|---|---|
| **448** | A74 | 5d multi | .55 | .55 |
| **449** | A74 | 15d multi | 1.40 | .55 |
| **450** | A74 | 35d multi | 2.10 | .50 |
| **451** | A74 | 1r multi | 6.25 | 1.40 |
| **452** | A74 | 1.25r multi | 7.00 | 1.60 |
| **453** | A74 | 2r multi | 12.50 | 2.75 |
| | | *Nos. 448-453 (6)* | 29.80 | 7.35 |

Fertilizer Plant — A75

Designs: 10d, Flour mill, vert. 35d, Natural gas plant. 75d, Oil refinery. 1.25r, Cement works. 1.55r, Steel mill.

**1975, Dec. 6**

| | | | | |
|---|---|---|---|---|
| **454** | A75 | 5d salmon & multi | .50 | .50 |
| **455** | A75 | 10d yellow & multi | 1.25 | .50 |
| **456** | A75 | 35d multi | 2.50 | .60 |
| **457** | A75 | 75d multi | 5.00 | 1.50 |
| **458** | A75 | 1.25r mag & multi | 10.00 | 2.50 |
| **459** | A75 | 1.55r multi | 15.00 | 3.50 |
| | | *Nos. 454-459 (6)* | 34.25 | 9.10 |

Modern Building, Doha — A76

10d, 35d, 1.55r, Various modern buildings. 55d, 75d, Sheik Khalifa & Qatar flag, diff.

**1976, Feb. 22 Litho. *Perf. 13***

| | | | | |
|---|---|---|---|---|
| **460** | A76 | 5d multi | .55 | .55 |
| **461** | A76 | 10d multi | .55 | .55 |
| **462** | A76 | 35d multi | 2.25 | .55 |
| **463** | A76 | 55d multi | 4.25 | .85 |
| **464** | A76 | 75d multi | 5.50 | 1.25 |
| **465** | A76 | 1.55r multi | 11.00 | 2.50 |
| | | *Nos. 460-465 (6)* | 24.10 | 6.25 |

Accession of Sheik Khalifa, 4th anniv.

Satellite Earth Station — A77

Designs: 55d, 1r, Satellite. 75d, Like 35d.

**1976, Mar. 1**

| | | | | |
|---|---|---|---|---|
| **466** | A77 | 35d multicolored | 2.50 | .40 |
| **467** | A77 | 55d dp bis & multi | 3.25 | .50 |
| **468** | A77 | 75d vermilion & multi | 4.75 | .70 |
| **469** | A77 | 1r violet & multi | 7.25 | .95 |
| | | *Nos. 466-469 (4)* | 17.75 | 2.55 |

Inauguration of satellite earth station in Qatar.

Telephones, 1876 and 1976 — A78

**1976, Mar. 10**

| | | | | |
|---|---|---|---|---|
| **470** | A78 | 1r rose & multi | 4.75 | 2.00 |
| **471** | A78 | 1.35r lt bl & multi | 6.50 | 2.75 |

Centenary of first telephone call by Alexander Graham Bell, Mar. 10, 1876.

Arabian Soccer League Emblem — A79

Designs: 10d, 1.25r, Stadium, Doha. 35d, Like 5d. 55d, Players. 75d, One player.

**1976, Mar. 25 Litho. *Perf. 13½x13***

| | | | | |
|---|---|---|---|---|
| **472** | A79 | 5d lil & multi | .45 | .45 |
| **473** | A79 | 10d pink & multi | 1.25 | .45 |
| **474** | A79 | 35d bl grn & multi | 2.00 | .60 |
| **475** | A79 | 55d multi | 4.00 | .95 |
| **476** | A79 | 75d multi | 6.75 | 1.40 |
| **477** | A79 | 1.25r multi | 8.75 | 2.40 |
| | | *Nos. 472-477 (6)* | 23.20 | 6.25 |

4th Arabian Gulf Soccer Cup Tournament, Doha, Mar. 22-Apr.

Dhow A80

Designs: Various dhows.

**1976, Apr. 19 *Perf. 13½x14***

| | | | | |
|---|---|---|---|---|
| **478** | A80 | 10d blue & multi | 2.50 | .35 |
| **479** | A80 | 35d blue & multi | 3.00 | .40 |
| **480** | A80 | 80d blue & multi | 9.00 | 1.25 |
| **481** | A80 | 1.25r blue & multi | 13.00 | 2.00 |
| **482** | A80 | 1.50r blue & multi | 15.00 | 2.50 |
| **483** | A80 | 2r blue & multi | 22.50 | 4.00 |
| | | *Nos. 478-483 (6)* | 65.00 | 10.50 |

Soccer — A81

10d, Yachting. 35d, Steeplechase. 80d, Boxing. 1.25r, Weight lifting. 1.50r, Basketball.

**1976, May 15 Litho. *Perf. 14x13½***

| | | | | |
|---|---|---|---|---|
| **484** | A81 | 5d multicolored | .85 | .40 |
| **485** | A81 | 10d blue & multi | .85 | .40 |
| **486** | A81 | 35d orange & multi | .85 | .40 |
| **487** | A81 | 80d bister & multi | 5.50 | .85 |
| **488** | A81 | 1.25r lilac & multi | 9.50 | 1.60 |
| **489** | A81 | 1.50r rose & multi | 12.50 | 2.10 |
| | | *Nos. 484-489 (6)* | 30.05 | 5.75 |

21st Olympic Games, Montreal, Canada, July 17-Aug. 1.

Village and Emblems — A82

35d, Emblems. 80d, Village. 1.25r, Sheik Khalifa.

**1976, May 31 *Perf. 13½x14***

| | | | | |
|---|---|---|---|---|
| **490** | A82 | 10d orange & multi | .65 | .30 |
| **491** | A82 | 35d yellow & multi | 1.75 | .30 |
| **492** | A82 | 80d citron & multi | 4.25 | .70 |
| **493** | A82 | 1.25r dp blue & multi | 7.25 | 2.00 |
| | | *Nos. 490-493 (4)* | 13.90 | 3.30 |

Habitat, UN Conf. on Human Settlements, Vancouver, Canada, May 31-June 11.

Snowy Plover A83

Birds: 10d, Great cormorant. 35d, Osprey. 80d, Flamingo. 1.25r, Rock thrush. 2r, Saker falcon. 35d, 80d, 1.25r, 2r, vertical.

***Perf. 13½x14, 14x13½***

**1976, July 19** **Litho.**

**494** A83 5d multi *1.25 .40*
**495** A83 10d multi *3.00 .55*
**496** A83 35d multi *8.25 .90*
**497** A83 80d multi *17.50 2.00*
**498** A83 1.25r multi *27.50 3.00*
**499** A83 2r multi *30.00 4.00*
*Nos. 494-499 (6) 87.50 10.85*

Sheik Khalifa and Qatar Flag — A84

Government Building — A85

Designs: 10d, like 5d. 80d, Government building. 1.25r, Offshore oil platform. 1.50r, UN emblem and Qatar coat of arms.

**1976, Sept. 2** ***Perf. 14x13½, 13½x14***

**500** A84 5d gold & multi *.50 .50*
**501** A84 10d silver & multi *.50 .50*
**502** A85 40d multicolored *1.90 .60*
**503** A85 80d multicolored *3.50 1.25*
**504** A85 1.25r multicolored *5.50 1.50*
**505** A85 1.50r multicolored *7.50 1.75*
*Nos. 500-505 (6) 19.40 6.10*

5th anniversary of independence.

Qatar Flag and UN Emblem — A86

**1976, Oct. 24** **Litho.** ***Perf. 13½x14***

**506** A86 2r multi *7.00 1.75*
**507** A86 3r multi *9.50 2.50*

United Nations Day 1976.

Sheik Khalifa — A87

**1977, Feb. 22** **Litho.** ***Perf. 14x13½***

**508** A87 20d silver & multi *1.50 .50*
**509** A87 1.80r gold & multi *11.00 2.50*

Accession of Sheik Khalifa, 5th anniv.

Sheik Khalifa — A88

**1977, Mar. 1** **Litho.** ***Perf. 14x14½***

**Size: 22x27mm**

**510** A88 5d multicolored *.50 .30*
**511** A88 10d aqua & multi *.75 .30*
**512** A88 35d orange & multi *1.25 .35*
**513** A88 80d multicolored *2.50 .50*

***Perf. 13½***

**Size: 25x30mm**

**514** A88 1r vio bl & multi *5.00 .75*
**515** A88 5r yellow & multi *16.00 3.25*
**516** A88 10r multicolored *37.50 6.75*
*Nos. 510-516 (7) 63.50 12.20*

Letter, APU Emblem, Flag — A89

**1977, Apr. 12** ***Perf. 14x13½***

**517** A89 35d blue & multi *1.75 .50*
**518** A89 1.35r blue & multi *5.25 2.00*

Arab Postal Union, 25th anniversary.

Waves and Sheik Khalifa A90

**1977, May 17** **Litho.** ***Perf. 13½x14***

**519** A90 35d multi *1.00 .45*
**520** A90 1.80r multi *6.25 2.50*

World Telecommunications Day.

Sheik Khalifa — A90a

***Perf. 13½x13***

**1977, June 29** **Litho.** **Wmk. 368**

**520A** A90a 5d multi *1.00 1.00*
**520B** A90a 10d multi *2.00 2.00*
**520C** A90a 35d multi *3.00 3.00*
**520D** A90a 80d multi *10.00 10.00*
*e.* Bklt. pane, 4 5d, 3 10d, 2 35d, 80d *50.00 25.00*
*Nos. 520A-520D (4) 16.00 16.00*

Issued in booklets only.

Parliament, Clock Tower, Minaret — A91

Designs: No. 522, Main business district, Doha. No. 523, Highway crossings, Doha.

**1977, Sept. 1** **Litho.** ***Perf. 13x13½***

**521** A91 80d multicolored *4.25 1.50*
**522** A91 80d multicolored *4.25 1.50*
**523** A91 80d multicolored *4.25 1.50*
*Nos. 521-523 (3) 12.75 4.50*

6th anniversary of independence.

UN Emblem, Flag — A92

**1977, Oct. 24** **Litho.** ***Perf. 13½x14***

**524** A92 20d green & multi *1.50 .55*
**525** A92 1r blue & multi *6.00 2.25*

United Nations Day.

Surgery — A93

20d, Steel mill. 1r, Classroom. 5r, Sheik Khalifa.

**1978, Feb. 22** **Litho.** ***Perf. 13½x14***

**526** A93 20d multicolored *1.40 .40*
**527** A93 80d multicolored *3.00 .65*
**528** A93 1r multicolored *5.00 1.00*
**529** A93 5r multicolored *16.00 3.00*
*Nos. 526-529 (4) 25.40 5.05*

Accession of Sheik Khalifa, 6th anniv.

Oil Refinery — A94

80d, Office buildings, Doha. 1.35r, Traffic Circle, Doha. 1.80r, Sheik Khalifa and flag.

**1978, Aug. 31** **Litho.** ***Perf. 13½x14***

**530** A94 35d multi *1.00 .40*
**531** A94 80d multi *2.50 .95*
**532** A94 1.35r multi *4.00 1.40*
**533** A94 1.80r multi *5.25 1.90*
*Nos. 530-533 (4) 12.75 4.65*

7th anniversary of independence.

Man Learning to Read — A95

**1978, Sept. 8** **Litho.** ***Perf. 13½x14***

**534** A95 35d multicolored *1.75 .50*
**535** A95 80d multicolored *5.00 1.60*

International Literacy Day.

Flag and UN Emblem — A96

**1978, Oct. 14** ***Perf. 13x13½***

**536** A96 35d multi *1.50 .50*
**537** A96 80d multi *4.50 1.25*

United Nations Day.

Human Rights Emblem — A97

Designs: 80d, like 35d. 1.25r, 1.80r, Scales and Human Rights emblem.

**1978, Dec. 10** **Litho.** ***Perf. 14x13½***

**538** A97 35d multi *1.00 .35*
**539** A97 80d multi *2.50 1.00*
**540** A97 1.25r multi *3.75 1.50*
**541** A97 1.80r multi *5.25 2.25*
*Nos. 538-541 (4) 12.50 5.10*

30th anniversary of Universal Declaration of Human Rights.

IYC Emblem — A98

**Wmk. JEZ Multiple (368)**

**1979, Jan. 1** **Litho.** ***Perf. 13½x13***

**542** A98 35d multi *1.25 1.00*
**543** A98 1.80r multi *4.25 4.00*

International Year of the Child.

A99

**1979, Jan. 15** **Unwmk.** ***Perf. 14***

**544** A99 5d multi *.30 .30*
**545** A99 10d multi *.35 .30*
**546** A99 20d multi *.65 .30*
**547** A99 25d multi *1.00 .30*
**548** A99 35d multi *1.50 .55*
**549** A99 60d multi *1.90 .65*
**550** A99 80d multi *2.50 .70*

**Size: 27x32mm**

**551** A99 1r multi *2.75 1.00*
**552** A99 1.25r multi *3.00 1.10*
**553** A99 1.35r multi *3.25 1.50*
**554** A99 1.80r multi *5.00 1.75*
**555** A99 5r multi *12.00 3.25*
**556** A99 10r multi *22.50 7.00*
*Nos. 544-556 (13) 56.70 18.70*

Sheik Khalifa — A100

**1979, Feb. 22** **Wmk. 368**

**557** A100 35d multi *.80 .50*
**558** A100 80d multi *1.75 1.10*
**559** A100 1r multi *2.75 1.50*
**560** A100 1.25r multi *3.25 1.90*
*Nos. 557-560 (4) 8.55 5.00*

7th anniv. of accession of Sheik Khalifa.

Cables and People — A101

**1979, May 17 Litho. *Perf. 14x13½***

561 A101 2r multi *4.75 2.00*
562 A101 2.80r multi *5.75 3.00*

World Telecommunications Day.

Children Holding Globe, UNESCO Emblem — A102

***Perf. 13x13½***
**1979, July 15 Litho. Unwmk.**

563 A102 35d multicolored *1.00 .45*
564 A102 80d multicolored *4.25 1.10*

International Bureau of Education, Geneva, 50th anniversary.

Rolling Mill — A103

**Wmk. 368**
**1979, Sept. 2 Litho. *Perf. 13½***

565 A103 5d shown *.75 .40*
566 A103 10d Doha, aerial view *1.10 .40*
567 A103 1.25r Qatar flag *4.50 1.25*
568 A103 2r Sheik Khalifa *6.25 1.75*
*Nos. 565-568 (4)* *12.60 3.80*

Independence, 8th anniversary.

UN Day — A104

**1979, Oct. 24 Litho. *Perf. 13½x13***

569 A104 1.25r multi *4.25 1.25*
570 A104 2r multi *7.50 1.75*

Conference Emblem — A105

**1979, Nov. 24 *Perf. 13x13½***

571 A105 35d multi *3.25 1.00*
572 A105 1.80r multi *10.00 2.25*

Hegira (Pilgrimage Year); 3rd World Conference on Prophets.

Sheik Khalifa, 8th Anniversary of Accession — A106

**1980, Feb. 22 Litho. *Perf. 13x13½***

573 A106 20d multi *1.25 .30*
574 A106 60d multi *3.25 .65*
575 A106 1.25r multi *5.00 1.25*
576 A106 2r multi *11.00 2.10*
*Nos. 573-576 (4)* 20.50 4.30

Map of Arab Countries — A107

**1980, Mar. 1 Litho. *Perf. 13½x14***

577 A107 2.35r multi *8.25 1.75*
578 A107 2.80r multi *12.00 2.10*

6th Congress of Arab Town Organization, Doha, Mar. 1-4.

Oil Refinery — A108

**1980, Sept. 2 Litho. *Perf. 14½***

579 A108 10d shown *.75 .40*
580 A108 35d View of Doha *3.00 .50*
581 A108 2r Telecommunications tower *11.00 2.50*
582 A108 2.35r Hospital *13.00 3.75*
*Nos. 579-582 (4)* *27.75 7.15*

9th anniversary of independence.

Men Holding OPEC Emblem — A109

**1980, Sept. 15 *Perf. 14x13½***

583 A109 1.35r multi *4.75 1.40*
584 A109 2r multi *7.00 2.10*

OPEC, 20th anniversary.

United Nations Day 1980 — A110

**1980, Oct. 24**

585 A110 1.35r multi *3.25 1.25*
586 A110 1.80r multi *4.75 1.60*

Hegira (Pilgrimage Year) — A111

**1980, Nov. 8 Litho. *Perf. 14½***

587 A111 10d multi *.50 .50*
588 A111 35d multi *1.00 .65*
589 A111 1.25r multi *2.25 1.50*
590 A111 2.80r multi *5.50 3.75*
*Nos. 587-590 (4)* *9.25 6.40*

International Year of the Disabled — A112

**1981, Jan. 5 Photo. *Perf. 11½***
**Granite Paper**

591 A112 2r multi *4.75 2.75*
592 A112 3r multi *7.25 3.25*

Education Day — A113

***Perf. 14x13½***
**1981, Feb. 22 Litho. Wmk. 368**

593 A113 2r multi *5.50 2.00*
594 A113 3r multi *6.75 2.75*

Sheik Khalifa, 9th Anniversary of Accession — A114

**1981, Feb. 22**

595 A114 10d multi *.50 .40*
596 A114 35d multi *1.50 .40*
597 A114 80d multi *3.00 .70*
598 A114 5r multi *15.00 3.75*
*Nos. 595-598 (4)* *20.00 5.25*

A115

**1981, May 17 Litho. *Perf. 13½x13***

599 A115 2r multi *5.00 1.25*
600 A115 2.80r multi *7.25 2.40*

13th World Telecommunications Day.

A116

Championship emblem.

**1981, June 11 Litho. *Perf. 14x13½***

601 A116 1.25r multi *6.00 1.60*
602 A116 2.80r multi *10.00 3.00*

30th Intl. Military Soccer Championship, Doha.

10th Anniv. of Independence — A117

***Perf. 13½x14***
**1981, Sept. 2 Litho. Wmk. 368**

603 A117 5d multicolored *.75 .40*
604 A117 60d multicolored *2.25 .60*
605 A117 80d multicolored *3.00 .75*
606 A117 5r multicolored *17.50 5.25*
*Nos. 603-606 (4)* *23.50 7.00*

World Food Day A118

**1981, Oct. 16 Litho. *Perf. 13***

607 A118 2r multi *6.50 3.25*
608 A118 2.80r multi *8.50 4.00*

Red Crescent Society — A119

**1982, Jan. 16 Litho. *Perf. 14x13½***

609 A119 20d multi *1.25 .30*
610 A119 2.80r multi *7.75 3.25*

10th Anniv. of Sheik Khalifa's Accession — A120

***Perf. 13½x14***
**1982, Feb. 22 Litho. Wmk. 368**

611 A120 10d multi *1.00 .45*
612 A120 20d multi *2.00 .45*
613 A120 1.25r multi *7.00 1.40*
614 A120 2.80r multi *15.00 3.00*
*Nos. 611-614 (4)* *25.00 5.30*

Sheik Khalifa — A121

Oil Refinery — A122

Designs: 5r, 10r, 15r, Hoda Clock Tower.

**1982, Mar. 1 Photo. *Perf. 11½x12***
**Granite Paper**

| No. | Type | Value | Color | Unused | Used |
|---|---|---|---|---|---|
| **615** | A121 | 5d | multi | .30 | .30 |
| **616** | A121 | 10d | multi | .35 | .30 |
| **617** | A121 | 15d | multi | .40 | .30 |
| **618** | A121 | 20d | multi | .45 | .30 |
| **619** | A121 | 25d | multi | .60 | .30 |
| **620** | A121 | 35d | multi | .85 | .30 |
| **621** | A121 | 60d | multi | 1.25 | .35 |
| **622** | A121 | 80d | multi | 2.00 | .50 |
| **623** | A122 | 1r | multi | 2.25 | .65 |
| **624** | A122 | 1.25r | multi | 3.00 | 1.00 |
| **625** | A122 | 2r | multi | 4.75 | 1.90 |
| **626** | A122 | 5r | multi | 12.50 | 4.50 |
| **627** | A122 | 10r | multi | 22.50 | 9.25 |
| **628** | A122 | 15r | multi | 32.50 | 13.50 |
| | *Nos. 615-628 (14)* | | | *83.70* | *33.45* |

Hamad General Hospital — A123

**1982, Mar. Litho. *Perf. 13x13½***

| No. | Type | Value | Color | Unused | Used |
|---|---|---|---|---|---|
| **629** | A123 | 10d | multi | .75 | .35 |
| **630** | A123 | 2.35r | multi | 6.75 | 3.00 |

6th Anniv. of United Arab Shipping Co. — A124

**1982, Mar. 6 Litho. *Perf. 13x13½***

| No. | Type | Value | Color | Unused | Used |
|---|---|---|---|---|---|
| **631** | A124 | 20d | multi | 1.25 | .35 |
| **632** | A124 | 2.35r | multi | 11.00 | 3.00 |

A125

**1982, Apr. 12 Litho. *Perf. 13½x13***

| No. | Type | Value | Color | Unused | Used |
|---|---|---|---|---|---|
| **633** | A125 | 35d | yellow & multi | 1.50 | .35 |
| **634** | A125 | 2.80r | blue & multi | 10.50 | 2.25 |

30th anniv. of Arab Postal Union.

A126

**1982, Sept. 2 Litho. *Perf. 13½x13***

| No. | Type | Value | Color | Unused | Used |
|---|---|---|---|---|---|
| **635** | A126 | 10d | multi | 1.00 | .30 |
| **636** | A126 | 80d | multi | 2.25 | .60 |
| **637** | A126 | 1.25r | multi | 4.00 | 1.50 |
| **638** | A126 | 2.80r | multi | 7.75 | 2.25 |
| | *Nos. 635-638 (4)* | | | *15.00* | *4.65* |

11th anniv. of Independence.

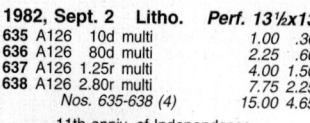

World Communications Year — A127

**1983, Jan. 10 Litho. *Perf. 13½x13***

| No. | Type | Value | Color | Unused | Used |
|---|---|---|---|---|---|
| **639** | A127 | 35d | multi | 1.75 | .50 |
| **640** | A127 | 2.80r | multi | 8.75 | 2.50 |

Gulf Postal Org., 2nd Conference, Doha, Apr. — A128

**1983, Apr. 9 Litho. *Perf. 13½x14***

| No. | Type | Value | Color | Unused | Used |
|---|---|---|---|---|---|
| **641** | A128 | 1r | multi | 4.00 | 1.25 |
| **642** | A128 | 1.35r | multi | 5.75 | 2.00 |

A129

**1983, Sept. 2 Litho. *Perf. 14***

| No. | Type | Value | Color | Unused | Used |
|---|---|---|---|---|---|
| **643** | A129 | 10d | multi | .45 | .45 |
| **644** | A129 | 35d | multi | .90 | .45 |
| **645** | A129 | 80d | multi | 2.00 | .75 |
| **646** | A129 | 2.80r | multi | 6.75 | 2.50 |
| | *Nos. 643-646 (4)* | | | *10.10* | *4.15* |

12th anniv. of Independence.

A130

**1983, Nov. 7 Litho. *Perf. 13½x14***

| No. | Type | Value | Color | Unused | Used |
|---|---|---|---|---|---|
| **647** | A130 | 35d | multi | 3.00 | .50 |
| **648** | A130 | 2.80r | multi | 10.00 | 3.00 |

GCC Supreme Council, 4th regular session.

35th Anniv. of UN Declaration of Human Rights — A131

**1983, Dec. 10 Litho. *Perf. 13½x14***

| No. | Type | Value | Description | Unused | Used |
|---|---|---|---|---|---|
| **649** | A131 | 1.25r | Globe, emblem | 4.00 | 1.50 |
| **650** | A131 | 2.80r | Scale | 7.75 | 2.50 |

A132

A133

**1984, Mar. 1 Litho. *Perf. 13x13½***

| No. | Type | Value | Color | Unused | Used |
|---|---|---|---|---|---|
| **651** | A132 | 15d | multi | .50 | .25 |
| **652** | A132 | 40d | multi | 1.25 | .45 |
| **653** | A132 | 50d | multi | 1.25 | .55 |

***Perf. 14½x13½***

| No. | Type | Value | Color | Unused | Used |
|---|---|---|---|---|---|
| **654** | A133 | 1r | multi | 3.00 | 1.50 |
| **655** | A133 | 1.50r | multi | 3.50 | 1.75 |
| **656** | A133 | 2.50r | multi | 6.00 | 2.75 |
| **657** | A133 | 3r | multi | 8.00 | 3.00 |
| **658** | A133 | 5r | multi | 14.00 | 5.75 |
| **659** | A133 | 10r | multi | 24.00 | 11.00 |
| | *Nos. 651-659 (9)* | | | *61.50* | *27.00* |

See Nos. 707-709, 792-801.

13th Anniv. of Independence — A134

**1984, Sept. 2 Photo. *Perf. 12***

| No. | Type | Value | Color | Unused | Used |
|---|---|---|---|---|---|
| **660** | A134 | 15d | multi | 1.00 | .45 |
| **661** | A134 | 1r | multi | 3.00 | 1.00 |
| **662** | A134 | 2.50r | multi | 6.00 | 2.25 |
| **663** | A134 | 3.50r | multi | 8.75 | 3.25 |
| | *Nos. 660-663 (4)* | | | *18.75* | *6.95* |

Literacy Day, 1984 — A135

**1984, Sept. 8 Litho. *Perf. 14x13½***

| No. | Type | Value | Color | Unused | Used |
|---|---|---|---|---|---|
| **664** | A135 | 1r | lilac & multi | 5.25 | 1.10 |
| **665** | A135 | 1r | orange & multi | 5.25 | 1.10 |

40th Anniv., ICAO — A136

**1984, Dec. 7 Litho. *Perf. 13½x13***

| No. | Type | Value | Color | Unused | Used |
|---|---|---|---|---|---|
| **666** | A136 | 20d | multi | .50 | .40 |
| **667** | A136 | 3.50r | multi | 8.50 | 3.00 |

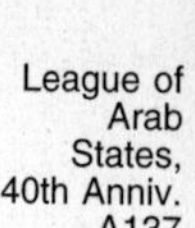

League of Arab States, 40th Anniv. A137

**1985, Mar. 22 Photo. *Perf. 11½***

| No. | Type | Value | Color | Unused | Used |
|---|---|---|---|---|---|
| **668** | A137 | 50d | multi | 1.50 | .40 |
| **669** | A137 | 4r | multi | 7.75 | 3.00 |

Intl. Youth Year — A138

**1985, Mar. 4 *Perf. 11½x12***
**Granite Paper**

| No. | Type | Value | Color | Unused | Used |
|---|---|---|---|---|---|
| **670** | A138 | 50d | multi | 2.25 | .65 |
| **671** | A138 | 1r | multi | 4.75 | 1.25 |

Traffic Crossing — A139

**1985, Mar. 9 *Perf. 14x13½***

| No. | Type | Value | Color | Unused | Used |
|---|---|---|---|---|---|
| **672** | A139 | 1r | lt bl & multi | 4.00 | 1.25 |
| **673** | A139 | 1r | pink & multi | 4.00 | 1.25 |

Gulf Cooperation Council Traffic Safety Week, Mar. 16-22.

Natl. Independence, 14th Anniv. — A140

**1985, Sept. 2 *Perf. 11½x12***
**Granite Paper**

| No. | Type | Value | Description | Unused | Used |
|---|---|---|---|---|---|
| **674** | A140 | 40d | Doha | 1.25 | .35 |
| **675** | A140 | 50d | Earth satellite station | 2.00 | .55 |
| **676** | A140 | 1.50r | Oil refinery | 5.50 | 1.25 |
| **677** | A140 | 4r | Storage facility | 12.50 | 4.00 |
| | *Nos. 674-677 (4)* | | | *21.25* | *6.15* |

Org. of Petroleum Exporting Countries, 25th Anniv. — A141

**1985, Sept. 14 *Perf. 13½x14***

| No. | Type | Value | Color | Unused | Used |
|---|---|---|---|---|---|
| **678** | A141 | 1r | brt yel grn & multi | 5.00 | 1.25 |
| **679** | A141 | 1r | salmon rose & multi | 5.00 | 1.25 |

UN, 40th Anniv. A142

**1985, Oct. 24 Litho. *Perf. 13½x14***

| No. | Type | Value | Color | Unused | Used |
|---|---|---|---|---|---|
| **680** | A142 | 1r | multi | 1.75 | 1.25 |
| **681** | A142 | 3r | multi | 5.00 | 3.50 |

Population and Housing Census — A143

**1986, Mar. 1 Photo. *Perf. 11½x12***
**682** A143 1r multi *3.25 1.25*
**683** A143 3r multi *7.25 4.00*

United Arab Shipping Co., 10th Anniv. — A144

**1986, May 30 Litho. *Perf. 13½x14***
**684** A144 1.50r Qatari ibn al Fuja'a *3.00 2.75*
**685** A144 4r Al Wajba *9.25 6.00*

Natl. Independence, 15th Anniv. — A145

***Perf. 13x13½***
**1986, Sept. 2 Litho. Unwmk.**
**686** A145 40d multi *.75 .55*
**687** A145 50d multi *1.10 .65*
**688** A145 1r multi *2.25 1.25*
**689** A145 4r multi *7.00 4.75*
*Nos. 686-689 (4) 11.10 7.20*

Sheik Khalifa — A146

**1987, Jan. 1 Photo. *Perf. 11½x12***
**Granite Paper**
**690** A146 15r multi *19.00 12.00*
**691** A146 20r multi *24.00 16.00*
**692** A146 30r multi *42.50 25.00*
*Nos. 690-692 (3) 85.50 53.00*

15th Anniv. of Sheik Khalifa's Accession A147

**1987, Feb. 22 *Perf. 12x11½***
**Granite Paper**
**693** A147 50d multi *.95 .50*
**694** A147 1r multi *2.00 1.00*
**695** A147 1.50r multi *2.75 1.40*
**696** A147 4r multi *6.50 4.50*
*Nos. 693-696 (4) 12.20 7.40*

Arab Postal Union, 35th Anniv. — A148

***Perf. 14x13½***
**1987, Apr. 12 Litho. Unwmk.**
**697** A148 1r multi *3.00 1.25*
**698** A148 1.50r multi *3.50 2.00*

Natl. Independence, 16th Anniv. — A149

**1987, Sept. 2 Litho. *Perf. 13x13½***
**699** A149 25d Housing complex *1.00 .35*
**700** A149 75d Water tower, city *3.25 .90*
**701** A149 2r Modern office building *5.00 2.25*
**702** A149 4r Oil refinery *11.00 4.75*
*Nos. 699-702 (4) 20.25 8.25*

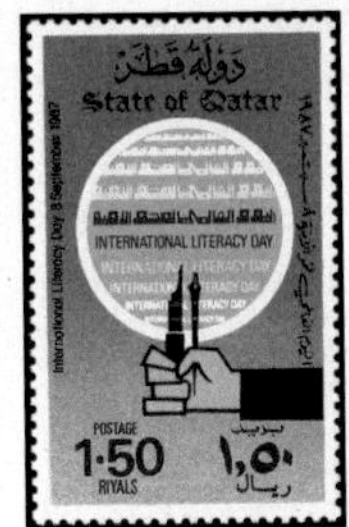


A150

***Perf. 13½x13***
**1987, Sept. 8 Litho. Unwmk.**
**703** A150 1.50r multicolored *2.75 1.25*
**704** A150 4r multicolored *4.75 2.00*

Intl. Literacy Day.

A151

***Perf. 14x13½***
**1987, Apr. 24 Litho. Wmk. 368**
**705** A151 1r multicolored *2.25 1.25*
**706** A151 4r multicolored *5.75 4.00*

Gulf Environment Day.

**Sheik Type of 1984**
**1988, Jan. 1 *Perf. 13x13½***
**Size of 25d, 75d: 22x27mm**
**707** A133 25d multicolored *2.00 .75*
**708** A133 75d multicolored *4.50 2.00*
***Perf. 14½x13***
**709** A133 2r multicolored *15.00 4.75*

WHO, 40th Anniv. — A152

**1988, Apr. 7 *Perf. 14x13½***
**714** A152 1.50r multicolored *3.25 2.25*
**715** A152 2r multicolored *7.00 3.50*

Independence, 17th Anniv. — A153

***Perf. 11½x12***
**1988, Sept. 2 Litho. Unwmk.**
**Granite Paper**
**716** A153 50d multicolored *1.00 .55*
**717** A153 75d multicolored *1.75 .80*
**718** A153 1.50r multicolored *3.00 2.00*
**719** A153 2r multicolored *3.75 2.40*
*Nos. 716-719 (4) 9.50 5.75*

Opening of the Doha General P.O. — A154

**1988, Sept. 3 *Perf. 13x13½***
**720** A154 1.50r multicolored *2.25 2.00*
**721** A154 4r multicolored *5.00 4.75*

Arab Housing Day — A155

**1988, Oct. 3 *Perf. 11½x12***
**Granite Paper**
**722** A155 1.50r multicolored *3.00 1.75*
**723** A155 4r multicolored *7.75 3.75*

A156

***Perf. 14x13½***
**1988, Dec. 10 Wmk. 368**
**724** A156 1.50r multicolored *3.25 2.50*
**725** A156 2r multicolored *4.25 3.75*

Declaration of Human Rights, 40th anniv.

A157

***Perf. 12x11½***
**1989, May 17 Unwmk.**
**Granite Paper**
**726** A157 2r multicolored *3.00 2.25*
**727** A157 4r multicolored *6.00 4.00*

World Telecommunications Day.

Qatar Red Crescent Soc., 10th Anniv. — A158

***Perf. 13½x14***
**1989, Aug. 8 Wmk. 368**
**728** A158 4r multicolored *11.00 4.75*

Natl. Independence, 18th Anniv. — A159

***Perf. 13x13½***
**1989, Sept. 2 Unwmk.**
**729** A159 75d multicolored *1.25 .85*
**730** A159 1r multicolored *2.25 1.50*
**731** A159 1.50r multicolored *2.75 2.00*
**732** A159 2r multicolored *4.00 2.40*
*Nos. 729-732 (4) 10.25 6.75*

Gulf Air, 40th Anniv. A160

**1990, Mar. 24 Litho. *Perf. 13x13½***
**733** A160 50d multicolored *1.25 .50*
**734** A160 75d multicolored *2.00 1.00*
**735** A160 4r multicolored *8.50 4.00*
*Nos. 733-735 (3) 11.75 5.50*

Independence, 19th Anniv. — A161

Designs: 75d, Map, sunburst. 1.50r, 2r, Swordsman, musicians.

**1990, Sept. 2 *Perf. 14x13½***
**736** A161 50d multicolored *1.25 .50*
**737** A161 75d multicolored *1.75 .90*
**738** A161 1.50r multicolored *3.50 1.60*
**739** A161 2r multicolored *5.50 2.75*
*Nos. 736-739 (4) 12.00 5.75*

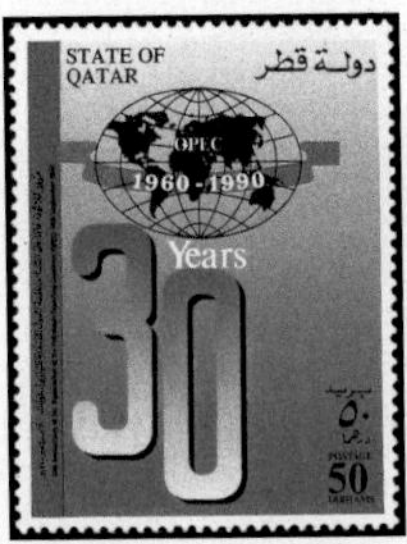


Organization of Petroleum Exporting Countries (OPEC), 30th Anniv. A162

**1990, Sept. 14**
**740** A162 50d shown *2.00 .55*
**741** A162 1.50r Flags *5.00 1.60*

A163

GCC Supreme Council, 11th Regular Session: 1r, Leaders of member nations. 1.50r, Flag, council emblem. 2r, State seal, emblem.

*Perf. 14x13½*

**1990, Dec. 22 Litho. Wmk. 368**

| | | | | |
|---|---|---|---|---|
| **742** | A163 | 50d multicolored | *1.50* | *.50* |
| **743** | A163 | 1r multicolored | *2.50* | *1.10* |
| **744** | A163 | 1.50r multicolored | *4.00* | *1.75* |
| **745** | A163 | 2r multicolored | *4.75* | *2.10* |
| | | *Nos. 742-745 (4)* | *12.75* | *5.45* |

A164

Plants — 10d, Glossonema edule. 25d, Lycium shawii. 50d, Acacia tortilis. 75d, Acacia ehrenbergiana. 1r, Capparis spinosa. 4r, Cymhopogon parkeri.

*Perf. 12½x13½*

**1991, June 20 Litho. Wmk. 368**

| | | | | |
|---|---|---|---|---|
| **747** | A164 | 10d multi | *1.00* | *.35* |
| **748** | A164 | 25d multi | *1.10* | *.40* |
| **749** | A164 | 50d multi | *1.25* | *1.00* |
| **750** | A164 | 75d multi | *2.25* | *1.25* |
| **751** | A164 | 1r multi | *3.25* | *2.50* |
| **752** | A164 | 4r multi | *13.00* | *8.50* |
| | | *Nos. 747-752 (6)* | *21.85* | *14.00* |

Independence, 20th Anniv. — A165

**1991, Aug. 15 Litho. *Perf. 14x14½***
**Granite Paper**

| | | | | |
|---|---|---|---|---|
| **762** | A165 | 25d shown | *.85* | *.30* |
| **763** | A165 | 75d red vio & multi | *1.75* | *.65* |

*Perf. 14½x14*

| | | | | |
|---|---|---|---|---|
| **764** | A165 | 1r Doha skyline, horiz. | *2.50* | *1.00* |
| **765** | A165 | 1.50r Palace, horiz. | *3.75* | *1.75* |
| | | *Nos. 762-765 (4)* | *8.85* | *3.70* |

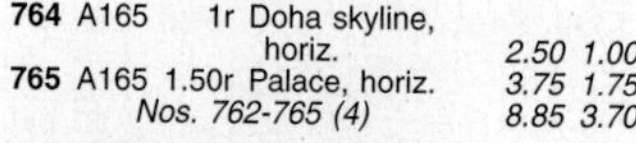

Fish A166

Various species of fish.

**1991, Dec. 1 *Perf. 14x13½***

| | | | | |
|---|---|---|---|---|
| **767** | A166 | 10d multicolored | *1.00* | *.50* |
| **768** | A166 | 15d multicolored | *1.25* | *.55* |
| **769** | A166 | 25d multicolored | *2.00* | *.90* |
| **770** | A166 | 50d multicolored | *4.50* | *1.75* |
| **771** | A166 | 75d multicolored | *6.50* | *2.75* |
| **772** | A166 | 1r multicolored | *8.00* | *4.50* |
| **773** | A166 | 1.50r multicolored | *12.00* | *7.00* |
| **774** | A166 | 2r multicolored | *14.50* | *8.50* |
| | | *Nos. 767-774 (8)* | *49.75* | *26.45* |

A167

Sheik Khalifa, 20th Anniv. of Accession A168

*Perf. 14x13½*

**1992, Feb. 22 Litho. Wmk. 368**

| | | | | |
|---|---|---|---|---|
| **781** | A167 | 25d multicolored | *.75* | *.35* |
| **782** | A167 | 50d multicolored | *1.25* | *.50* |
| **783** | A168 | 75d multicolored | *2.00* | *.75* |
| **784** | A168 | 1.50r multicolored | *3.75* | *1.75* |
| | | *Nos. 781-784 (4)* | *7.75* | *3.35* |

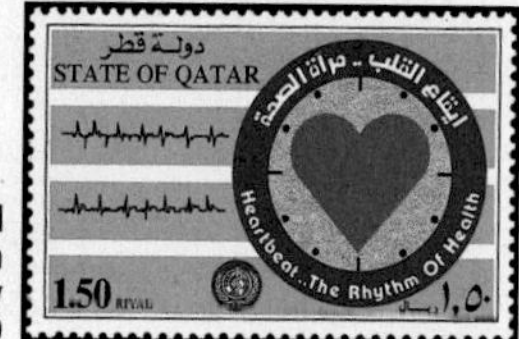

World Health Day A169

**1992, Apr. 7 *Perf. 14x13½, 13½x14***

| | | | | |
|---|---|---|---|---|
| **785** | A169 | 50d Heart with face, vert. | *1.10* | *.60* |
| **786** | A169 | 1.50r shown | *3.00* | *2.00* |

Children's Paintings A170

25d, Girls dancing. 50d, Children playing. 75d, Ships. 1.50r, Fishing from boats.

**1992, June 15 Unwmk. *Perf. 11½***

| | | | | |
|---|---|---|---|---|
| **787** | A170 | 25d multi | *.75* | *.40* |
| **788** | A170 | 50d multi | *1.75* | *.50* |
| **789** | A170 | 75d multi | *3.25* | *.65* |
| **790** | A170 | 1.50r multi | *5.00* | *1.25* |
| *a.* | | Souvenir sheet of 4, #787-790 | *375.00* | *375.00* |
| | | *Nos. 787-790 (4)* | *10.75* | *2.80* |

**Type of 1984 with Smaller Arabic Inscription and**

A171

A172

Designs: 25d, 1.50r, Offshore oil field. 50d, 2r, 5r, Map. 75d, 3r, Storage tanks, horiz. 1r, 4r, 10r, Oil refinery, horiz.

**1992 Litho. *Perf. 13x13½***

| | | | | |
|---|---|---|---|---|
| **791** | A171 | 10d multicolored | *.35* | *.25* |
| **792** | A132 | 25d multicolored | *.35* | *.25* |
| **793** | A132 | 50d multicolored | *.55* | *.50* |

*Perf. 13½x13*

| | | | | |
|---|---|---|---|---|
| **794** | A132 | 75d multicolored | *.95* | *.55* |
| **795** | A132 | 1r multicolored | *1.25* | *.75* |

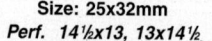

**Size: 25x32mm**
***Perf. 14½x13, 13x14½***

| | | | | |
|---|---|---|---|---|
| **796** | A132 | 1.50r multicolored | *1.60* | *1.10* |
| **797** | A132 | 2r multicolored | *2.10* | *1.25* |
| **798** | A132 | 3r multicolored | *4.25* | *2.50* |
| **799** | A132 | 4r multicolored | *4.75* | *3.00* |
| **800** | A132 | 5r multicolored | *5.50* | *3.75* |
| **801** | A132 | 10r multicolored | *12.00* | *7.00* |
| **802** | A172 | 15r multicolored | *16.00* | *12.00* |
| **803** | A172 | 20r multicolored | *27.50* | *14.00* |
| **804** | A172 | 30r multicolored | *32.50* | *24.00* |
| | | *Nos. 791-804 (14)* | *109.65* | *70.90* |

Issued: 10-50d, 1.50, 2, 5, 15, 30r, 2/15; others, 5/14.

1992 Summer Olympics, Barcelona A174

**1992, July 25 Litho. *Perf. 15***

| | | | | |
|---|---|---|---|---|
| **805** | A174 | 50d Running | *1.50* | *.40* |
| **806** | A174 | 1.50r Soccer | *3.75* | *1.25* |

11th Persian Gulf Soccer Cup A175

**1992, Nov. 27 Litho. *Perf. 14½***

| | | | | |
|---|---|---|---|---|
| **807** | A175 | 50d shown | *1.75* | *.60* |
| **808** | A175 | 1r Ball, net, vert. | *3.50* | *1.25* |

A176

Independence, 21st Anniv. — A177

Sheik Khalifa and: No. 810, "21" in English and Arabic. No. 811, Tree, dhow in harbor. No. 812, Natural gas well, pen, dhow.

**Unwmk.**
**1992, Sept. 2 Litho. *Perf. 12***
**Granite Paper**

| | | | | |
|---|---|---|---|---|
| **809** | A176 | 50d shown | *1.25* | *.55* |
| **810** | A176 | 50d multicolored | *1.25* | *.55* |
| **811** | A177 | 1r multicolored | *2.00* | *1.25* |
| **812** | A177 | 1r multicolored | *2.00* | *1.25* |
| *a.* | | Strip of 8, 2 each #809-812 | *14.00* | *9.00* |
| | | *Nos. 809-812 (4)* | *6.50* | *3.60* |

Intl. Conference on Nutrition, Rome — A178

50d, Globe, emblems, vert. 1r, Cornucopia.

**1992, Dec. 12 *Perf. 14½***

| | | | | |
|---|---|---|---|---|
| **813** | A178 | 50d multicolored | *2.00* | *.40* |
| **814** | A178 | 1r multicolored | *3.25* | *.70* |

Qatar Broadcasting, Silver Jubilee — A179

Designs: 25d, Man at microphone, satellite dish. 50d, Rocket lift-off, satellite. 75d, Communications building. 1r, Technicians working on books.

**1993, June 25 Photo. *Perf. 12x11½***
**Granite Paper**

| | | | | |
|---|---|---|---|---|
| **819** | A179 | 25d multicolored | *1.00* | *.40* |
| **820** | A179 | 50d multicolored | *2.50* | *.75* |
| **821** | A179 | 75d multicolored | *3.25* | *1.00* |
| **822** | A179 | 1r multicolored | *4.75* | *1.25* |
| *a.* | | Souvenir sheet of 4, #819-822 | *225.00* | *225.00* |
| | | *Nos. 819-822 (4)* | *11.50* | *3.40* |

Ruins A180

Mosque with: a, Minaret (at left, shown). b, Minaret with side projections (at right). c, Minaret with catwalk, inside wall. d, Minaret at right, outside wall.

**1993, May 10 Litho. *Perf. 12***
**Granite Paper**

| | | | | |
|---|---|---|---|---|
| **823** | A180 | 1r Strip of 4, #a.-d. | *9.00* | *3.75* |

Independence, 22nd Anniv. — A181

Designs: 25c, Oil pumping station. 50d, Flag, clock tower. 75d, Coat of arms, "22." 1.50r, Flag, fortress tower.

**1993, Sept. 2 Litho. *Perf. 11½***
**Granite Paper**

| | | | | |
|---|---|---|---|---|
| **824** | A181 | 25d multicolored | *.50* | *.30* |
| **825** | A181 | 50d multicolored | *1.00* | *.60* |
| **826** | A181 | 75d multicolored | *1.50* | *1.00* |
| **827** | A181 | 1.50r multicolored | *3.50* | *2.25* |
| | | *Nos. 824-827 (4)* | *6.50* | *4.15* |

Intl. Literacy Day — A182

Designs: 25d, Quill, paper. 50d, Papers with English letters, pen. 75d, Papers with Arabic letters, pen. 1.50r, Scroll, Arabic letters, pen.

*Perf. 14x13½*

**1993, Sept. 2 Litho. Wmk. 368**

| | | | | |
|---|---|---|---|---|
| **828** | A182 | 25d multicolored | *.50* | *.30* |
| **829** | A182 | 50d multicolored | *1.00* | *.60* |
| **830** | A182 | 75d multicolored | *1.50* | *.90* |
| **831** | A182 | 1.50r multicolored | *3.50* | *2.25* |
| | | *Nos. 828-831 (4)* | *6.50* | *4.05* |

Children's Games A183

Designs: 25d, Girls with thread and spinners. 50d, Boys with stick and disk, vert. 75r, Children guiding wheels with sticks, vert. 1.50r, Girls with jump rope.

**1993, Dec. 5 Litho. *Perf. 11½***
**Granite Paper**

| | | | | |
|---|---|---|---|---|
| **832** | A183 | 25d multicolored | .85 | .35 |
| **833** | A183 | 50d multicolored | 1.75 | .50 |
| **834** | A183 | 75d multicolored | 2.75 | .75 |
| *a.* | | Souvenir sheet, 2 each #833, #834 | 90.00 | 90.00 |
| **835** | A183 | 1.50r multicolored | 5.25 | 2.00 |
| *a.* | | Souvenir sheet, 2 each #832, #835 | 90.00 | 90.00 |
| | | *Nos. 832-835 (4)* | 10.60 | 3.60 |

Falcons — A184

**1993, Dec. 22 Granite Paper**

| | | | | |
|---|---|---|---|---|
| **836** | A184 | 25d Lanner | .75 | .40 |
| **837** | A184 | 50d Saker | 1.25 | .50 |
| **838** | A184 | 75d Barbary | 2.25 | .75 |
| **839** | A184 | 1.50r Peregrine | 4.75 | 2.00 |
| *a.* | | Souvenir sheet, #836-839 | 175.00 | |
| | | *Nos. 836-839 (4)* | 9.00 | 3.65 |

A185

Society for Handicapped Welfare and Rehabilition: 75d, Hands above and below handicapped symbol.

**1994, May 6 Litho. *Perf. 14***

| | | | | |
|---|---|---|---|---|
| **840** | A185 | 25d shown | 1.10 | .50 |
| **841** | A185 | 75d multi | 2.75 | 1.10 |

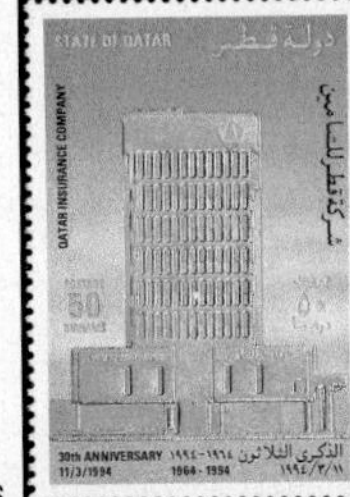
A186

Qatar Insurance Co., 30th Anniv.: 50d, Building. 1.50r, Co. arms, global tourist attractions.

***Perf. 14½***
**1994, Mar. 11 Litho. Unwmk.**

| | | | | |
|---|---|---|---|---|
| **842** | A186 | 50d gold & multi | 1.50 | .40 |
| **843** | A186 | 1.50r gold & multi | 4.50 | 1.60 |

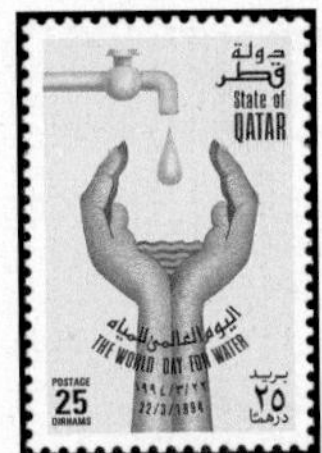
A187

World Day for Water: 1r, UN emblem, hands catching water drop, tower, grain.

**1994, Mar. 22 Litho. *Perf. 11½***

| | | | | |
|---|---|---|---|---|
| **844** | A187 | 25d shown | 1.50 | .40 |
| **845** | A187 | 1r multicolored | 2.75 | 1.50 |

A188

**1994, Mar. 22 Litho. *Perf. 11½***

| | | | | |
|---|---|---|---|---|
| **846** | A188 | 75d shown | 1.25 | .75 |
| **847** | A188 | 2r Scales, gavel | 2.75 | 2.50 |

Intl. Law Conference.

A189

1r, Family, UN emblem.

***Perf. 12x11½***
**1994, July 16 Litho. Unwmk.**

| | | | | |
|---|---|---|---|---|
| **848** | A189 | 25d shown | 1.00 | .65 |
| **849** | A189 | 1r multicolored | 3.00 | 1.25 |

Intl. Year of the Family.

Independence, 23rd Anniv. — A190

25d, 2r, Text. 75d, Island. 1r, Oil drilling plant.

**1994, Sept. 2 Photo. *Perf. 12***
**Granite Paper**

| | | | | |
|---|---|---|---|---|
| **850** | A190 | 25d green & multi | .60 | .35 |
| **851** | A190 | 75d multicolored | 1.25 | .75 |
| **852** | A190 | 1r multicolored | 2.00 | 1.10 |
| **853** | A190 | 2r pink & multi | 4.50 | 2.25 |
| | | *Nos. 850-853 (4)* | 8.35 | 4.45 |

ILO, 75th Anniv. — A191

**1994, May 28 *Perf. 14***

| | | | | |
|---|---|---|---|---|
| **854** | A191 | 25d salmon & multi | .75 | .40 |
| **855** | A191 | 2r green & multi, diff. | 4.75 | 1.60 |

ICAO, 50th Anniv. A192

**1994, Dec. 7 *Perf. 13½x14***

| | | | | |
|---|---|---|---|---|
| **856** | A192 | 25d shown | 1.00 | .40 |
| **857** | A192 | 75d Emblem, airplane | 4.75 | 1.00 |

A193

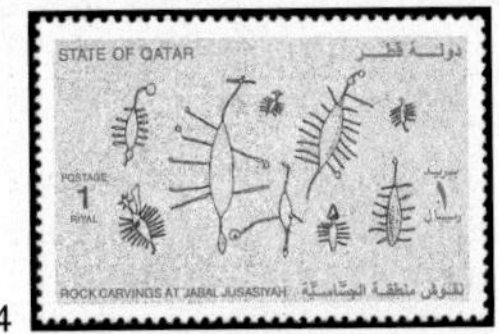
A194

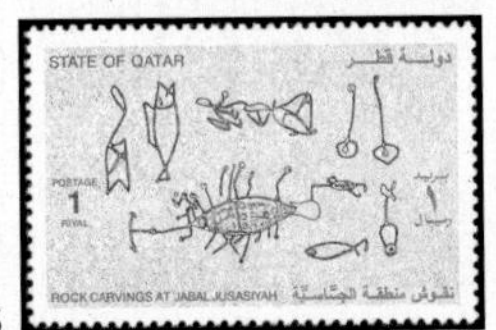
A195

A196

Rock Carvings at Jabal Jusasiyah — A197

**1995, Mar. 18 Litho. *Perf. 14½x15***

| | | | | |
|---|---|---|---|---|
| **858** | A193 | 1r multicolored | 1.40 | .80 |
| **859** | A194 | 1r multicolored | 1.40 | .80 |
| **860** | A195 | 1r multicolored | 1.40 | .80 |
| **861** | A196 | 1r multicolored | 1.40 | .80 |
| **862** | A197 | 1r multicolored | 1.40 | .80 |
| **863** | A197 | 1r multi, diff. | 1.40 | .80 |
| *a.* | | Vert. strip of 6, #858-863 | 11.00 | 8.50 |
| | | *Nos. 858-863 (6)* | 8.40 | 4.80 |

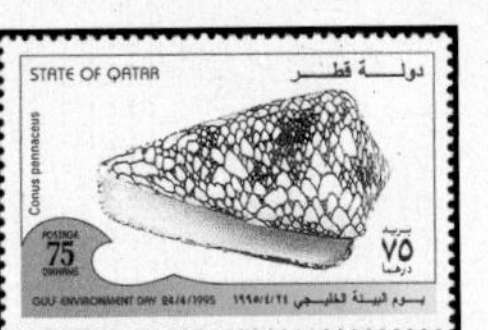
Gulf Environment Day — A198

Shells: No. 864a, Conus pennaceus. b, Cerithidea cingulata. c, Hexaplex kuesterianus. d, Epitonium scalare.

No. 865a, Murex scolopax. b, Thais mutabilis. c, Fusinus arabicus. d, Lambis truncata sebae.

**1995, Apr. 24**

| | | | | |
|---|---|---|---|---|
| **864** | A198 | 75d Strip of 4, #a.-d. | 5.50 | 4.50 |
| **865** | A198 | 1r Strip of 4, #a.-d. | 6.50 | 5.50 |

Intl. Nursing Day — A199

Designs: 1r, Nurse adjusting IV for patient. 1.50r, Injecting shot into arm of infant.

**1995, May 12**

| | | | | |
|---|---|---|---|---|
| **866** | A199 | 1r multicolored | 2.50 | 1.10 |
| **867** | A199 | 1.50r multicolored | 4.25 | 1.60 |

Independence, 24th Anniv. — A200

Designs: a, 1.50r, Shipping dock, city. b, 1r, Children in classroom. c, 1.50r, Aerial view of city. d, 1r, Palm trees.

**1995, Sept. 2 Litho. *Perf. 13½x14***

| | | | | |
|---|---|---|---|---|
| **868** | A200 | Block of 4, #a.-d. | 7.00 | 4.75 |

UN, 50th Anniv. — A201

**1995, Oct. 24 *Perf. 13½***

| | | | | |
|---|---|---|---|---|
| **869** | A201 | 1.50r multicolored | 2.50 | 1.25 |

Gazelles A202

No. 870; a, 75c, Gazella dorcas pelzelni. b, 50d, Dorcatragus megalotis. c, 25d, Gazella dama. d, 1.50r, Gazella spekei. e, 2r, Gazella soemmeringi. f, 1r, Gazella dorcas.

3r, Gazella spekei, gazella dorcas pelzelni, gazella soemmeringi.

**1996, Jan. Litho. *Perf. 11½***

| | | | | |
|---|---|---|---|---|
| **870** | A202 | Strip of 6, #a.-f. | 10.00 | 10.00 |

**Size: 121x81mm**
***Imperf***

| | | | | |
|---|---|---|---|---|
| **871** | A202 | 3r multicolored | 67.50 | 50.00 |

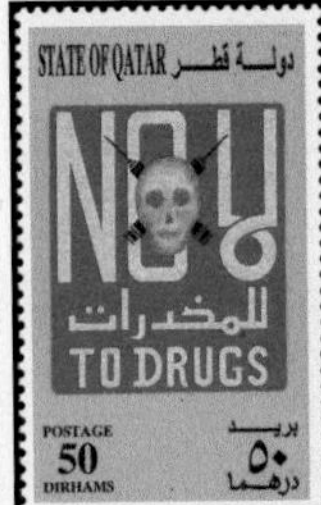

Fight Against Drug Abuse — A203

**1996, June 26 Litho. *Perf. 14x13***

**872** A203 50d shown *1.40 .55*
**873** A203 1r "NO," needles, hand *2.50 1.00*

1996 Summer Olympic Games, Atlanta — A204

a, 10d, Olympic emblem, map of Qatar. b, 15d, Shooting. c, 25d, Bowling. d, 50d, Table tennis. e, 1r, Athletics. f, 1.50r, Yachting.

**1996, July 19 Litho. *Perf. 14x13½***

**874** A204 Strip of 6, #a.-f. *9.00 8.00*

Independence, 25th Anniv. — A204a

**Litho. & Typo.**
**1996, Sept. 2 *Perf. 12***
**Granite Paper**

**875** A204a 1.50r silver & multi *2.50 1.25*
**876** A204a 2r gold & multi *4.75 1.75*

Forts A204b

25d, Al-Wajbah, vert. 75d, Al-Zubarah. 1r, Al-Kout. 3r, Umm Salal Mohammed.

**1997, Jan. 15 Litho. *Perf. 14½***

**877** A204b 25d multicolored *.60 .35*
**878** A204b 75d multicolored *1.50 1.00*
**879** A204b 1r multicolored *2.00 1.25*
**880** A204b 3r multicolored *5.50 4.25*
*Nos. 877-880 (4) 9.60 6.85*

A205 A206

Sheik Hamad — A206a

**1996-2012 (?) Photo. *Perf. 11½x12***
**Granite Paper**

**881** A205 25d pink & multi *.40 .25*
**881A** A205 25d green & multi —
**882** A205 50d green & multi *.65 .40*
**882A** A205 50d org brn & multi —
**883** A205 75d bl grn & multi *1.00 .50*
**884** A205 1r gray & multi *1.25 .60*

***Perf. 11½***

**885** A206 1.50r grn bl & multi *2.25 .90*
**886** A206 2r green & multi *2.50 1.00*
**886A** A206 2r pur brn & multi —
**887** A206 4r ver & multi *4.75 2.50*
**888** A206 5r purple & multi *5.75 5.00*
**888A** A206 5r red vio & multi —
**888B** A206a 5r purple & multi —
**889** A206 10r brown & multi *14.50 7.00*
**889A** A206 10r red & multi —
**889B** A206a 10r brown & multi —
**890** A206 20r blue & multi *25.00 14.00*
**890A** A206a 20r blue & multi —
**890B** A206 20r gray grn & multi —
**891** A206 30r orange & multi *37.50 21.00*
**891A** A206a 30r org & multi —

Issued: Nos. 881-888, 889, 890, 891, 11/16/96; No. 890B, 2012 ? Others, 2009?

A207

UNICEF, 50th Anniv.: No. 893, Children, open book emblem.

**1996, Dec. 11 Litho. *Perf. 14½***

**892** A207 75d blue & multi *1.25 .85*
**893** A207 75d violet & multi *1.25 .85*

A208

17th Session of GCC Supreme Council: 1.50r, Emblem, dove with olive branch, Sheik Khalifa.

**1996, Dec. 7**

**894** A208 1r multicolored *2.00 .75*
**895** A208 1.50r multicolored *3.50 1.50*

Opening of Port of Ras Laffan — A209

**1997, Feb. 24 Litho. *Perf. 13½***

**896** A209 3r multicolored *8.00 3.00*

Arabian Horses A210

25d, Red horse with tan mane. 75d, Black horse. 1r, White horse. 1.50r, Red brown horse. 3r, Mares, foals.

**1997, Mar. 19 Photo. *Perf. 12x11½***

**897** A210 25d multi *1.00 .45*
**898** A210 75d multi *1.75 .90*
**899** A210 1r multi *2.25 1.25*
**900** A210 1.50r multi *3.50 2.00*
*Nos. 897-900 (4) 8.50 4.60*

**Size: 115x75mm**
***Imperf***

**901** A210 3r multi *125.00 65.00*

Independence, 26th Anniv. — A211

**1997, Sept. 2 Photo. *Perf. 11½x12***
**Granite Paper**

**902** A211 1r shown *1.75 .85*
**903** A211 1.50r Oil refinery *2.75 1.25*

Doha '97, Doha-Mena Economic Conference — A212

**1997, Nov. 16 Litho. *Perf. 11***

**904** A212 2r multicolored *2.50 1.25*

Insects — A213

a, Nubian flower bee. b, Domino beetle. c, Seven-spot ladybird. d, Desert giant ant. e, Eastern death's-head hawkmoth. f, Arabian darkling beetle. g, Yellow digger. h, Mole cricket. i, Migratory locust. j, Elegant rhinoceros beetle. k, Oleander hawkmoth. l, American cockroach. m. Girdled skimmer. n, Sabre-toothed beetle. o, Arabian cicada. p, Pinstriped ground weevil. q, Praying mantis. r, Rufous bombardier beetle. s, Diadem. t, Shore earwing.

**1998, July 20 Litho. *Perf. 11½x12***
**Granite Paper**

**905** A213 2r Sheet of 20, #a.-t. *40.00 32.50*
*u.* Souvenir sheet, #905i *22.50 17.50*
*v.* Souvenir sheet, #905s *22.50 17.50*

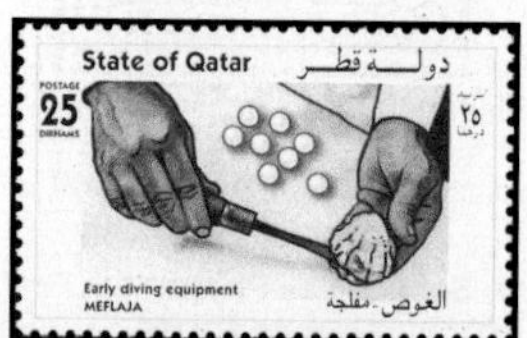


Early Diving Equipment — A214

***Perf. 11½x12, 12x11½***
**1998, Aug. 15 Photo.**
**Granite Paper**

**906** A214 25d Meflaja *.70 .25*
**907** A214 75d Mahar *1.40 .75*
**908** A214 1r Dasta *2.00 1.10*
**909** A214 1.50r Deyen, vert. *3.00 2.00*
*Nos. 906-909 (4) 7.10 4.10*

**Souvenir Sheet**

**910** A214 2r Man seated in boat *16.00 12.00*

Qatar University, 25th Anniv. — A215

**1998, Sept. 2 Litho. *Perf. 13½x13***

**911** A215 1r blue & multi *1.40 .85*
**912** A215 1.50r gray & muti *2.25 1.25*

Independence, 27th Anniv. — A216

**1998, Sept. 2 *Perf. 14***

**913** A216 1r Sheik Khalifa, vert. *1.40 .85*
**914** A216 1.50r Sheik Khalifa *2.25 1.25*

Camels — A217

**1999, Jan. 25 Litho. *Perf. 11½***
**Granite Paper**

**915** A217 25d shown *.25 .25*
**916** A217 75d One standing *1.50 1.25*
**917** A217 1r Three standing *2.10 1.50*
**918** A217 1.50r Four standing, group *3.00 2.50*
*Nos. 915-918 (4) 6.85 5.50*

**Souvenir Sheet**

**919** A217 2r Adult, juvenile *24.50 20.00*

1999 FEI General Assembly Meeting, Doha — A218

**1999 Litho. *Perf. 13¼x13***

**920** A218 1.50r multicolored *3.50 2.00*

Ancient Coins — A219

Obverse, reverse of dirhams — #921: a, Umayyad (shown). b, Umayyad, diff. c, Abbasid (3 lines of text on obv.). d, Abbasid (6 lines of text obv.). e, Umayyad, diff. (small circles near edge at top of obv. & rev.).

Obv., rev. of dinars — #922: a, Abbasid (3 lines of text obv.). b, Umayyad. c, Abbasid (5 lines of text obv.). d, Marabitid. e, Fatimid.

Obverse and reverse of: No. 923, Arab Sasanian dirham. 3r, Umayyad dinar, diff.

**1999 Litho. *Perf. 11½***
**Granite Paper**

**921** A219 1r Strip of 5, #a.-e. *6.00 4.50*
**922** A219 2r Strip of 5, #a.-e. *11.00 7.00*

**Souvenir Sheets**

**923** A219 2r multicolored *16.00 12.00*
**924** A219 3r multicolored *18.00 14.00*

Independence, 28th Anniv. — A220

***Perf. 12¾x13¾***

**1999, Sept. 2 Litho. Wmk. 368**

**925** A220 1r violet & multi *1.40 1.25*
**926** A220 1.50r yellow & multi *2.00 1.75*

A221

UPU, 125th anniv.: 1r, Tree with letters. 1.50r, Building, horiz.

***Perf. 11½***

**1999, Oct. 9 Litho. Unwmk.**

**Granite Paper**

**927** A221 1r multicolored *1.40 1.25*
**928** A221 1.50r multicolored *2.00 1.75*

A222

Fifth Stamp Exhibition for the Arab Gulf Countries: 1r, Emblem, stamps. 1.50r, Emblem, horiz.

**1999, Oct. 30 Granite Paper**

**929** A222 1r multicolored *1.25 .75*
**930** A222 1.50r multicolored *1.75 1.25*

National Committee for Children with Special Needs — A223

***Perf. 12¾x13¼***

**1999, Nov. 2 Litho. Wmk. 368**

**931** A223 1.50r multi *2.40 2.00*

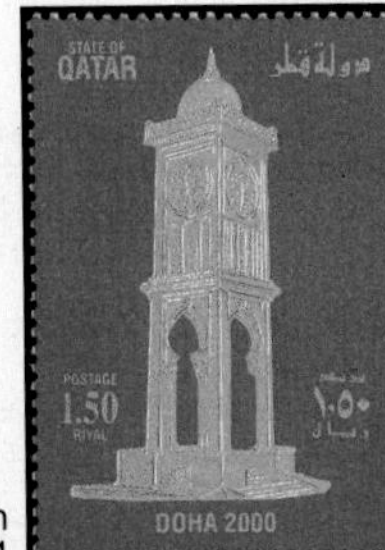


Millennium A224

**Photo. & Embossed**

**2000, Jan. 1 Unwmk. *Perf. 11¾***

**Granite Paper**

**932** A224 1.50r red & gold *2.25 2.00*
**933** A224 2r blue & gold *3.00 2.50*

Qatar Tennis Open — A225

Trophy and: 1r, Stadium. 1.50r, Racquet.

**2000, Jan. 3 Litho. *Perf. 13¼x13½***

**934** A225 1r multi *2.00 1.60*
**935** A225 1.50r multi *2.75 2.40*

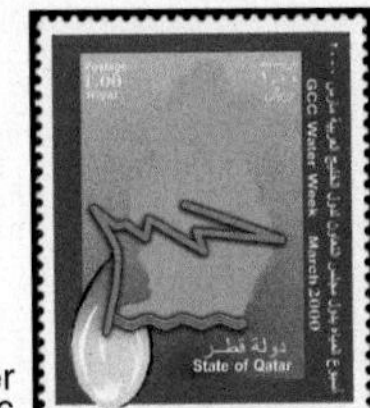


GCC Water Week — A226

**2000, Mar. 1 *Perf. 13¾***

**936** A226 1r Map, water drop *1.60 1.25*
**937** A226 1.50r Hands, water drop *2.40 1.75*

15th Asian Table Tennis Championships, Doha — A227

**2000, May 1 Photo. *Perf. 11¾***

**Granite Paper**

**938** A227 1.50r multi *2.50 2.00*

Independence, 29th Anniv. — A228

Sheik Hamad and: 1r, Fort. 1.50r, Oil derrick, city skyline.

***Perf. 11½x11¾***

**2000, Sept. 2 Photo.**

**Granite Paper**

**939-940** A228 Set of 2 *4.50 4.50*

9th Islamic Summit Conference — A230

Post Office, 50th Anniv. A229

Monument, building and: 1.50r, Bird. 2r, Magnifying glass.

**Photo. & Embossed**

**2000, Oct. 9 *Perf. 11¾***

**Granite Paper**

**941-942** A229 Set of 2 *5.25 5.25*

No. 943: a, 1r, Emblem (size: 21x28mm). b, 1.50r, Emblem, olive branch (size: 45x28mm).

**2000, Nov. 12 Photo.**

**Granite Paper**

**943** A230 Pair, #a-b *4.25 4.25*

Clean Environment Day — A231

Designs: 1r, Qatar Gas emblem, tanker ship, coral reef. 1.50r, RasGas emblem, refinery, antelopes. 2r, Ras Laffan Industrial City emblem, flamingos near industrial complex. 3r, Qatar Petroleum emblem, view of Earth from space.

**2001, Feb. 26 Photo. *Perf. 11½***

**Granite Paper**

**944-947** A231 Set of 4 *9.25 9.25*

Independence, 30th Anniv. — A232

Background colors: 1r, Olive. 1.50r, Blue.

**2001, Sept. 2 Litho. *Perf. 14x14½***

**948-949** A232 Set of 2 *3.75 3.75*

Year of Dialogue Among Civilizations A233

Designs: 1.50r, Shown. 2r, Branch with leaves of many colors.

**2001, Oct. 9 *Perf. 13¼***

**950-951** A233 Set of 2 *6.00 6.00*

4th World Trade Organization Ministerial Conference — A234

Background colors: 1r, Yellow brown. 1.50r, Blue.

**2001, Nov. 9**

**952-953** A234 Set of 2 *5.25 5.25*



Old Doors — A235

Various doors: 25d, 75d, 1.50r, 2r.

**2001, Dec. 30 *Perf. 14½***

**954-957** A235 Set of 4 *6.00 6.00*

**Souvenir Sheet**

**958** A235 3r multi *20.00 20.00*

2002 World Cup Soccer Championships, Japan and Korea — A236

No. 959 — World Cup Posters (except for #959r) from: a, 1930. b, 1934 (Italian). c, 1938. d, 1950. e, 1954. f, 1958. g, 1962. h, 1966. i, 1970. j, 1974. k, 1978. l, 1982. m, 1986. n, 1990. o, 1994. p, 1998. q, 2002. r, World Cup Trophy.

**2002 Litho. *Perf. 14***

**959** Sheet of 18 *52.50 52.50*
*a.-r.* A236 2r Any single *2.00 1.75*
*s.* Souvenir sheet, #959q-959r *8.00 8.00*

Asian Games Emblems — A237

No. 960: a, 1r, 2002 Asian Games emblem, Busan, South Korea. b, 3r, 2006 Asian Games Emblem, Doha, Qatar.

**2002, Sept. 29 Photo. *Perf. 14¼***

**Granite Paper**

**960** A237 Sheet of 2, #a-b *7.00 7.00*

Qatar General Postal Corporation, 1st Anniv. — A238

Background colors: 1r, White. 3r, Light blue.

**2002, Oct. 25 Litho. *Perf. 12½***

**961-962** A238 Set of 2 *5.25 5.25*

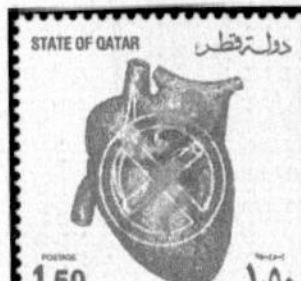


World No Tobacco Day — A239

**2003, May 31 *Perf. 13¼x14***

**963** A239 1.50r red *2.00 2.00*

Qatar Red Crescent, 25th Anniv. — A240

No. 964: a, Red crescent, boy (30mm diameter). b, Headquarters building.

**Litho. With Foil Application**

**2003, July 1 *Perf. 13¼***

**964** A240 75d Horiz. pair, #a-b *4.25 4.25*

Jewelry — A241

Designs: No. 965, 25d, Al-mashmoom. No. 966, 25d, Al-mertash. No. 967, 50d, Khatim. No. 968, 50d, Ishqab. No. 969, 1.50r, Tassa. No. 970, 1.50r, Shmailat.

**Photo. & Embossed**

**2003, Oct. 1** ***Perf. 14½x14¼***
**965-970** A241 Set of 6 *8.25 8.25*

Souvenir Sheet

Powered Flight, Cent. — A242

No. 971: a, Wright Flyer. b, Man with winged glider. c, Qatar Airways jet. d, Plane with propellers.

**2003, Dec. 17 Litho.** ***Perf. 13½***
**971** A242 50d Sheet of 4, #a-d *5.00 5.00*

Intl. Year of the Family, 10th Anniv. A243

**2004, Apr. 15** ***Perf. 14½***
**972** A243 2.50r multi *4.00 4.00*

FIFA (Fédération Internationale de Football Association), Cent. — A244

**2004, May 21** ***Perf. 13***
**973** A244 50d multi *2.00 2.00*

Values are for stamps with selvage adjacent to diagonal sides.

Permanent Constitution — A245

**2004, June 8 Litho.** ***Perf. 13½x13¾***
**974** A245 75d multi *2.25 2.25*

Souvenir Sheet

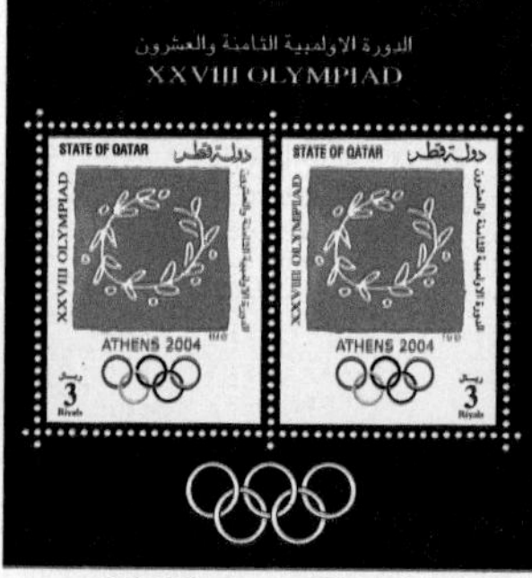

2004 Summer Olympics, Athens — A246

No. 975: a, Denomination at left. b, Denomination at right.

**2004, Aug. 13 Litho.** ***Perf. 13***
**975** A246 3r Sheet of 2, #a-d *5.00 5.00*

Souvenir Sheet

MotoGP 2004 Grand Prix Motorcycle Race — A247

No. 976: a, 3r, Motorcycle, denomination at left. b, 3.50r, Two motorcycles, denomination at right. c, 3.50r, Two motorcycles, denomination at left. d, 3r, Motorcycle, denomination at right.

***Perf. 13x14x14x14, 14x14x13x14***

**2004, Sept. 30**
**976** A247 Sheet of 4, #a-d *8.50 8.50*

Numeral — A248

**2004, Nov. 1 Litho.** ***Perf. 13½x12½***

**Stamp + Label**

| | | | |
|---|---|---|---|
| **977** | A248 50d blue | .50 | .50 |
| **978** | A248 50d red | .50 | .50 |
| **979** | A248 50d orange | .50 | .50 |
| **980** | A248 50d blue green | .50 | .50 |
| **981** | A248 50d olive green | .50 | .50 |
| *a.* | Vert. strip, #977-981, + 5 labels | 3.50 | 3.50 |
| | *Nos. 977-981 (5)* | 2.50 | 2.50 |

National Human Rights Committee — A249

**2004, Nov. 11 Litho.** ***Perf. 13¼x13***
**982** A249 50d multi *.45 .45*

Souvenir Sheet

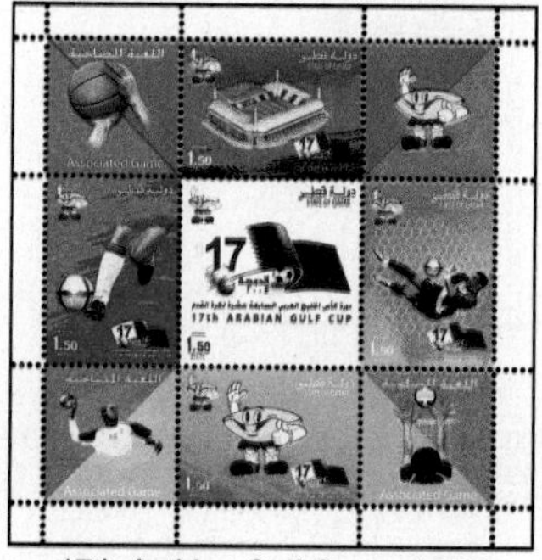
17th Arabian Gulf Cup — A250

No. 983: a, Mascot, emblem, stadium (35x25mm). b, Mascot, emblem, player kicking ball (25x35mm). c, Mascot, emblem (35x35mm). d, Mascot, emblem, goalie catching ball (25x35mm). e, Emblem, two mascots (35x25mm).

**2004, Dec. 10** ***Perf. 12¾x13¼***
**983** A250 1.50r Sheet of 5, #a-e, + 4 labels *7.50 7.50*

2006 Asian Games, Doha — A251

Mascot Orry: Nos. 984, 990a, 50d, Pointing to Doha. Nos. 985, 990b, 1r, On dhow in Doha harbor, horiz. Nos. 986, 990c, 1.50r, Counting down days on calendar, horiz. Nos. 987, 990d, 2r, Carrying torch. Nos. 988, 990e, 3r, Lighting flame. Nos. 989, 990f, Carrying Qatari flag.

***Perf. 13¼x13, 13x13¼***

**2004, Dec. 31 Litho.**
**984-989** A251 Set of 6 8.00 8.00

**Self-Adhesive**

***Serpentine Die Cut 12½***

**990** A251 Booklet pane of 6, #a-f 8.00 8.00

Miniature Sheet

Cars and Trucks — A252

No. 991: a, 1949 DeSoto (green car). b, 1958 Cadillac Sedan de Ville (white car facing left). c, 1938 Buick (white car facing right). d, 1953 Chrysler Windsor (black car). e, 1962 Dodge Powerwagon (red truck facing right). f, 1958 Chevrolet Pickup (orange red truck facing left). g, 1948 Chevrolet Pickup (green truck). h, 1957 Dodge Sweptside (white and red truck).

**2005, Feb. 1** ***Perf. 13½x13¾***
**991** A252 50d Sheet of 8, #a-h 2.75 2.75

Oryx Quest 2005 Catamaran Race — A253

Designs: No. 992, 50d, Qatar 2006. No. 993, 50d, Daedalus. No. 994, 50d, Cheyenne, vert. No. 995, 50d, Geronimo, vert.

**2005, Feb. 1** ***Perf. 14½***
**992-995** A253 Set of 4 1.25 1.25

Expo 2005, Aichi, Japan — A254

Designs: No. 996, 50d, Mascots. No. 997, 50d, Flag of Qatar.

**2005, Mar. 25 Litho.** ***Perf. 13***
**996-997** A254 Set of 2 2.00 2.00

Souvenir Sheet

Doha Development Forum — A255

No. 998: a, Denomination in white. b, Denomination in maroon.

**2005, Apr. 9 Litho.** ***Perf. 12¼x13¼***
**998** A255 6r Sheet of 2, #a-b 7.00 7.00

Souvenir Sheet

Accession of Emir Sheikh Hamad bin Khalifa Al Thani, 10th Anniv. — A256

**Litho. & Embossed with Foil Application**

**2005, June 27** ***Perf. 13¼x13¾***
**999** A256 2.50r multi 2.25 2.25

Friendship Between Doha, Qatar and Sarajevo, Bosnia and Herzegovina — A257

**2005, July 13 Litho.** ***Perf. 13***
**1000** A257 2.50r multi 3.00 3.00

See Bosnia & Herzegovina No. 504.

National Flag — A258

*Serpentine Die Cut 12¾*

**2005, Aug. 1 Self-Adhesive**

**1001** Booklet pane of 6 8.50
*a.* A258 50d maroon .30 .30
*b.* A258 1r maroon .65 .65
*c.* A258 1.50r maroon .95 .95
*d.* A258 2.50r maroon 1.60 1.60
*e.* A258 3r maroon 1.90 1.90
*f.* A258 3.50r maroon 2.25 2.25

Souvenir Sheet

Al Jazeera Children's Channel — A259

No. 1002: a, Children playing. b, Children and balloon. c, Children running. d, Family.

**2005, Sept. 9 Litho. *Perf.***
**1002** A259 50d Sheet of 4, #a-d 1.25 1.25

Souvenir Sheet

Qatar Philatelic and Numismatics Club — A260

No. 1003: a, Denomination in maroon. b, Denomination in blue.

**Litho. & Embossed with Foil Application**

**2005, Dec. 16 *Perf. 12¾***
**1003** A260 1r Sheet of 2, #a-b 1.25 1.25

11th Gulf Cooperation Council Stamp Exhibition — A261

No. 1004: a, Mascots. b, Emblems of exhibition and Qatar General Postal Corporation.

**2005, Dec. 21 Litho. *Perf. 13¾***
**1004** A261 1r Pair, #a-b 1.25 1.25

Intl. Civil Defense Day — A262

Fire trucks and firefighters on: 50d, Metal ladder. 2.50r, Rope ladder.

**2006, Mar. 5 Litho. *Perf. 13x12¾***
**1005-1006** A262 Set of 2 2.10 2.10

A263

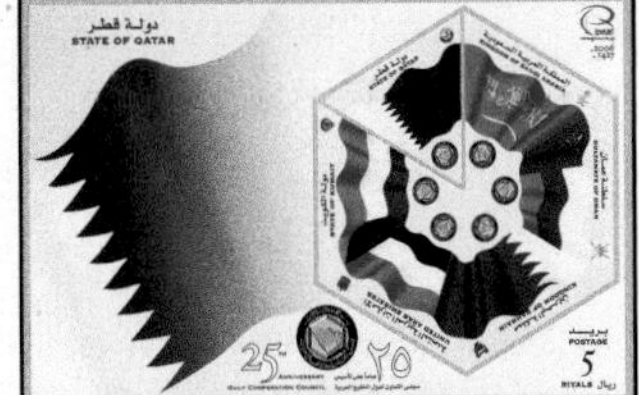

Gulf Cooperation Council, 25th Anniv. — A264

**Litho. with Foil Application**

**2006, May 25 *Perf. 14***
**1007** A263 50d multi .40 .40

***Imperf***

**Size: 165x105mm**

**1008** A264 5r multi 3.25 3.25

See Bahrain Nos. 628-629, Kuwait Nos. 1646-1647, Oman Nos. 477-478, Saudi Arabia No. 1378, and United Arab Emirates Nos. 831-832.

2006 World Cup Soccer Championships, Germany — A265

**2006, June 9 Litho. *Perf. 13¼***
**1009** A265 2r multi + label 1.25 1.25

Printed in sheets of 8 + 8 labels.

2006 Asian Games, Doha — A266

Designs: 50d, Torch bearers. 75d, Volunteers.

**2006, Oct. 8 Litho. *Perf. 13¼x13½***
**1010-1011** A266 Set of 2 .80 .80

2006 Asian Games, Doha A267

Designs: No. 1012, 1.50r, Athlete's village. No. 1013, 1.50r, Khalifa Stadium. No. 1014, 1.50r, Aspire Dome. No. 1015, 1.50r, Al-Dana Club.

5r, Vignettes of Nos. 1012-1015, Khalifa Stadium, vert.

**2006, Nov. 15 Litho. *Perf. 12¾***
**1012-1015** A267 Set of 4 3.50 3.50

***Imperf***

**Size: 126x179mm**

**1016** A267 5r multi 2.75 2.75

Sports of the 2006 Asian Games, Doha — A268

No. 1017: a, Runner breaking tape at finish line. b, Karate. c, Tennis. d, Swimming. e, Cycling.

**2006, Nov. 26 Litho. *Perf. 12¾***
**1017** A268 50d Vert. strip of 5, a-e, + 5 labels 5.50 5.50

Labels on Nos. 1017a-1017e could be personalized.

2006 Asian Games, Doha — A269

Designs: No. 1018, 50d, Mascot Orry playing soccer. No. 1019, 50d, Mascot Orry cycling. No. 1020, 50d, Soccer. No. 1021, 50d, Women's volleyball. No. 1022, 50d, Table tennis.

**2006, Dec. 1 *Perf. 13¼***
**1018-1022** A269 Set of 5 5.50 5.50

Pan-Arab Equestrian Federation General Assembly Meeting, Doha — A270

**2007, Sept. 1 Litho. *Perf. 13¾x14***
**1027** A270 2.50r multi 1.60 1.60

Souvenir Sheet

Doha's Bid For 2016 Summer Olympics and Paralympics — A271

No. 1029: a, Runner in starting position, denomination in red violet. b, Runner in starting position, violet denomination. c, Children with raised arms, orange denomination. d, Children with raised arms, red denomination.

**2007, Oct. 25 Litho. *Perf. 14x14½***
**1029** A271 50d Sheet of 4, #a-d 1.25 1.25

28th Session of Supreme Council of Gulf Cooperation Council — A272

**2007, Dec. 3 Litho. *Perf. 12¾***
**1030** A272 50d multi .30 .30

Miniature Sheet

Qatar Rulers and National Emblem — A273

No. 1031: a, National emblem (light blue panel, 38x28mm). b, Sheikh Hamad bin Khalifa Al Thani (38x55mm). c, National emblem (maroon panel, 38x28mm). d, Sheikh Ali bin Abdullah Al Thani (1895-1974, blue green panel, 38x28mm). e, Sheikh Abdullah bin Jassim Al Thani (1876-1957, pale green panel, 38x28mm). f, Sheikh Khalifa bin Hamad Al Thani (buff panel, 38x28mm). g, Sheikh Ahmad bin Ali Al Thani (1917-77, gray brown panel, 38x28mm).

**Litho. With Foil Application**

**2007, Dec. 18 *Perf. 12¼***
**1031** A273 2.50r Sheet of 7, #a-g, + label 9.75 9.75

Islamic Holy Sites — A274

No. 1032: a, Green Dome of the Holy Prophet, Medina (olive green frame). b, Holy Ka'aba, Mecca (yellow brown frame). c, Dome of the Rock, Jerusalem (blue frame).

**Litho. & Embossed**

**2007, Dec. 19 *Perf. 14x13½***
**1032** A274 Horiz. strip of 3 4.25 4.25
*a.-c.* 2.50r Any single 1.40 1.40

Souvenir Sheet

Holy Ka'aba, Green Dome of the Holy Prophet, and Dome of the Rock — A274a

**Litho. & Embossed**

**2007, Dec. 19 *Perf. 14x13½***
**1033** A274a 5r multi 6.50 6.50

First Arab Stamp Exhibition, Doha
A275

**2008, Jan. 30 Litho. *Perf. 13x12¾***
**1034** A275 50d multi .30 .30

Miniature Sheet

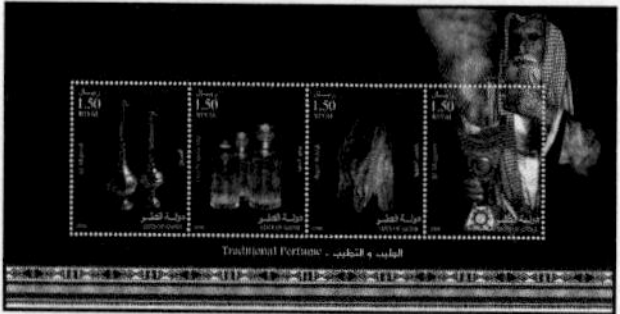

Traditional Perfumes — A276

No. 1035: a, Al Marash. b, Oud perfume oil. c, Agar wood. d, Al Mogbass.

**2008, Mar. 31 *Perf. 13¾***
**1035** A276 1.50r Sheet of 4, #a-d 3.50 3.50

No. 1035 is impregnated with a sandalwood scent.

Miniature Sheet

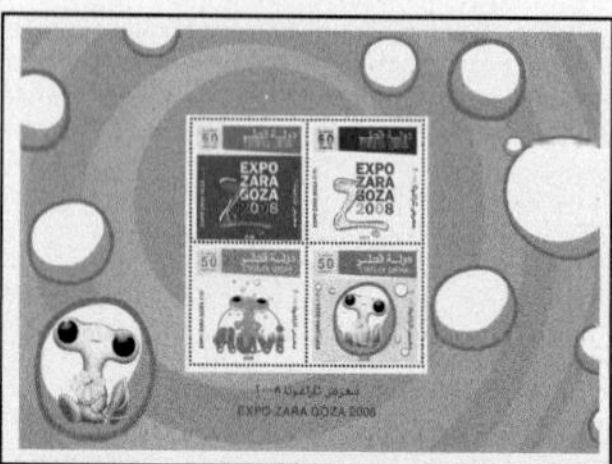


Expo Zaragoza 2008, Zaragoza, Spain — A277

No. 1036: a, Emblem, denomination in Prussian blue. b, Emblem, denomination in dark blue. c, Mascot, denomination in yellow brown. d, Mascot, denomination in gray.

**2008, June 14 *Perf. 14x14¼***
**1036** A277 50d Sheet of 4, #a-d 1.10 1.10

Souvenir Sheet

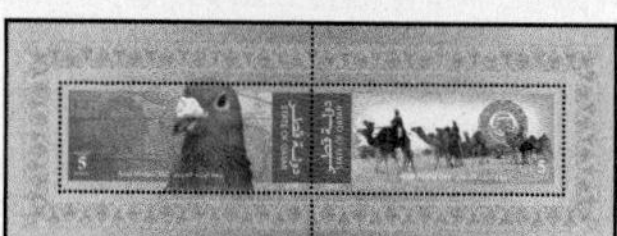

Arab Post Day — A278

No. 1037 — Emblem and: a, World map, pigeon. b, Camel caravan.

**Litho. & Silk-screened With Foil Application**

**2008, Aug. 3 *Perf. 13½x13¼***
**1037** A278 5r Sheet of 2, #a-b 5.50 5.50

Miniature Sheet

2008 Summer Olympics, Beijing — A279

No. 1038 — Beijing Olympics emblem and: a, 50d, Blue background (34x36mm). b, 50d, Green background (34x36mm). c, 3r, Stylized people (69x36mm).

**2008, Aug. 8 Litho. *Perf. 14½***
**1038** A279 Sheet of 3, #a-c 2.25 2.25

14th Gulf Cooperation Council Stamp Exhibition, Doha — A280

**2008, Oct. 14 *Perf. 14x14½***
**1039** A280 50d multi .30 .30

Arab Police Sporting Federation — A281

No. 1040 — Color of denomination. a, White, b, Olive green.

**2008, Oct. 14 *Perf. 13¾x13¼***
**1040** A281 50d Horiz. pair, #a-b .55 .55

Museum of Islamic Art, Doha
A282

**2008, Nov. 22 Litho. *Perf. 13x13¼***
**1041** A282 50d multi .30 .30

**Souvenir Sheet**

**1042** A282 5r multi 2.75 2.75

A283

Souq Waqif
A283a

**2008, Dec. 18 *Perf. 13¾***
**1043** A283 1.50r multi — —
**1044** A283a 1.50r multi — —
**1045** A283b 1.50r multi — —
**1046** A283c 1.50r multi — —

Campaign for Responsible Media — A284

**2009, Jan. 13 Litho. *Perf. 13¼***
**1047** A284 50d multi .30 .30

Tears for Gaza — A285

**2009, Jan. 21 Litho. *Perf. 12¾***
**1048** A285 1r multi .55 .55

First Democratic City Council Elections, 10th Anniv. — A286

**2009, Mar. 15 Litho. *Perf. 13¾***
**1050** A286 50d multi .30 .30

Jerusalem, 2009 Capital of Arab Culture
A287

**2009, Aug. 3 *Perf. 13***
**1051** A287 1r multi .55 .55

Souvenir Sheet

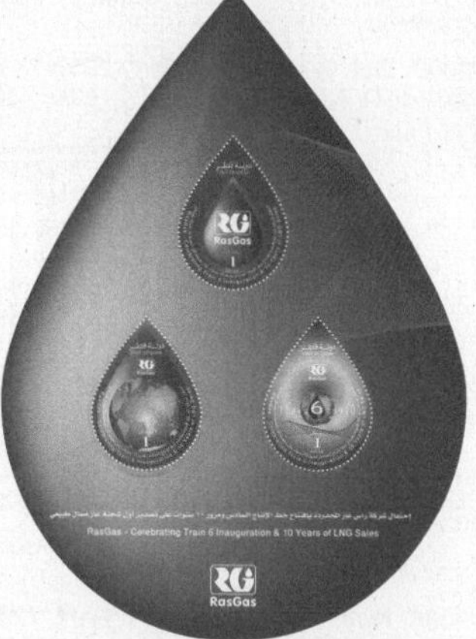


RasGas Liquified Natural Gas Sales, 10th Anniv., and Train 6 Inauguration — A288

No. 1052 — RasGas emblem and: a, Drop. b, Large globe. c, Small glove, numbers 1 to 10.

**2009, Oct. 27 *Perf.***
**1052** A288 1r Sheet of 3, #a-c 1.75 1.75

Birds
A289

Designs: No. 1053, Orphean warbler. No. 1054, Woodchat shrike. No. 1055, Isabelline shrike. No. 1056, Lesser gray shrike. No. 1057, Chiffchaf. No. 1058, Yellow wagtail.

No. 1059: a, Head of Orphean warbler. b, Head of Woodchat shrike. c, Head of Isabelline shrike. d, Head of Lesser gray shrike. e, Head of Chiffchaf. f, Head of Yellow wagtail.

5r, Cream-colored courser.

**2009, Dec. 18 Litho. *Perf. 13***
**1053** A289 50d multi .30 .30
**1054** A289 50d multi .30 .30
**1055** A289 50d multi .30 .30
**1056** A289 50d multi .30 .30
**1057** A289 50d multi .30 .30
**1058** A289 50d multi .30 .30
*Nos. 1053-1058 (6)* 1.80 1.80

**Booklet Stamps**

**1059** Booklet pane of 6 1.80 —
***a.-f.*** A289 50d Any single .30 .30

**Souvenir Sheet**

**1060** A289 5r multi 2.75 2.75

Organization of Petroleum Exporting Countries, 50th Anniv. — A290

**2010, Jan. 28 Litho. *Perf. 13x13¼***
**1061** A290 1r multi .55 .55

Distribution of Mus-haf Qatar (Koran With Calligraphic Writing)
A291

**2010, Mar. 9 *Perf. 12¾x13***
**1062** A291 3r multi 1.75 1.75

2010 Population and Housing Census
A292

**2010, Apr. 20 *Perf. 13¾***
**1063** A292 1r multi .55 .55

25th Universal Postal Union Congress, Doha — A293

**2010, Sept. 24 *Perf. 13¼x13¾***
**1064** A293 50d multi .30 .30

See Nos. 1076, 1084.

A294

Doha, 2010 Capital of Arab Culture — A295

No. 1065: a, Horsemen with flags. b, Masks. c, Open book. d, Stringed instrument and musical notes.
5r, Stylized peacock.

**2010, Oct. 10** *Perf. 14½*
**1065** A294 1.50r Sheet of 4, #a-d 3.50 3.50

**Size:60x100mm**

***Imperf***

**1066** A295 5r multi 2.75 2.75

Souvenir Sheet

2010 Aga Khan Award for Architecture — A296

**2010, Nov. 24** *Perf. 13¼x12¾*
**1067** A296 1.50r multi .85 .85

Souvenir Sheets

A297

A298

A299

Qatar's Annual Production of 77 Million Tonnes of Liquified Natural Gas — A300

**2010, Dec. 13** *Perf. 14x13½*

| | | | | |
|---|---|---|---|---|
| **1068** | A297 | 1r multi | .55 | .55 |
| **1069** | A298 | 1r multi | .55 | .55 |
| **1070** | A299 | 1r multi | .55 | .55 |
| **1071** | A300 | 1r multi | .55 | .55 |
| | | *Nos. 1068-1071 (4)* | 2.20 | 2.20 |

Souvenir Sheet

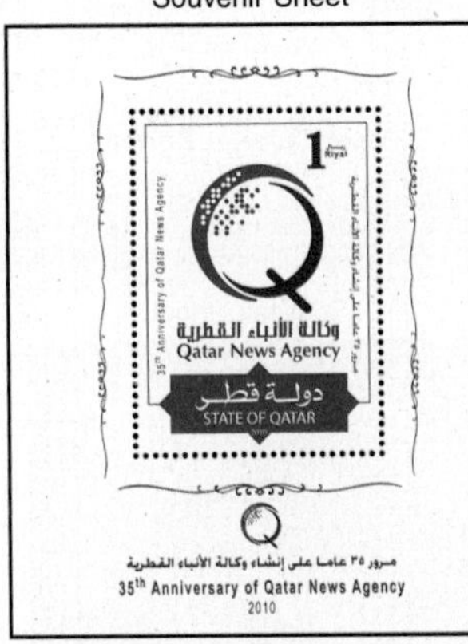

Qatar News Agency, 35th Anniv. — A301

**2010, Dec. 18** *Perf. 13¼*
**1072** A301 1r blue & red .55 .55

Qatar Amateur Radio Society — A302

**2010, Dec. 26** *Perf. 13¾*
**1073** A302 50d multi .30 .30

Arab Deaf Week — A303

**2011, Apr. 20** *Perf. 12¾x13*
**1074** A303 1r multi .55 .55

First Postal Agency, 50th Anniv. — A304

**Litho. With Foil Application**

**2011, May 17** *Perf. 14x13¼*
**1075** A304 50d multi .30 .30

**25th UPU Congress Type of 2010**

**2011, Sept. 24 Litho.** *Perf. 14x14½*
**1076** A293 1r multi .55 .55

Miniature Sheet

11th Qatar Classic Squash Championship — A305

No. 1077 — Color of top panel: a, Light green. b, Tan. c, Light blue. d, Rose lilac.

**2011, Oct. 16** *Perf. 14½x14¾*
**1077** A305 1r Sheet of 4, #a-d 2.25 2.25

2011 Arab Games, Doha — A306

No. 1078 — Text with denomination color in: a, Orange. b, Gray. c, Yellow green.

**2011, Dec. 9** *Perf. 12½*
**1078** A306 50d Vert. strip of 3, #a-c .85 .85

Qatari Endowment Deed, 90th Anniv. — A307

Designs: No. 1079, 50d, Emblem. No. 1080, 50d, Building.
3r, Scroll, vert.

**2012, Mar. 4** *Perf. 13½x13¼*
**1079-1080** A307 Set of 2 .55 .55

**Souvenir Sheet**

***Perf. 13¼x13½***

**1081** A307 3r multi 1.75 1.75

Arab Postal Day A308

**2012, Aug. 3** *Perf. 13¼*
**1082** A308 1r multi .55 .55

**25th UPU Congress Type of 2010**

**2012, Sept. 24 Litho.** *Perf. 14x14½*
**1084** A293 2r multi 1.10 1.10

Falcon, Flags of Qatar and Morocco A310

**2012, Oct. 9** *Perf. 12¾*
**1085** A310 2.50r multi 1.40 1.40

See Morocco No. 1155.

2012 United Nations Climate Change Conference, Doha — A311

**2012, Nov. 1**
**1086** A311 2.50r blue & lt blue 1.40 1.40

First Compressed Natural Gas Bus in Qatar — A312

**2013, Mar. 25 Litho.** *Perf. 12¾*
**1087** A312 50d multi .30 .30

Miniature Sheet

Jeemtv.net — A313

No. 1088: a, Girl, horse made of ribbons, orange panel. b, Boy, automobiles, purple panel. c, Boy in soccer uniform, red panel. d, Girl, stylized butterflies, turquoise green panel.

**2013, June 23 Litho. *Perf. 13¾***
**1088** A313 2.50r Sheet of 4, #a-d 5.50 5.50

World Social Security Forum, Doha — A314

**2013, Nov. 10 Litho. *Perf. 14¼x14***
**1089** A314 3r multi 1.75 1.75

Sheikh Tamim — A315

**2013, Dec. 17 Litho. *Perf. 13¼x13***

**Panel Color at Bottom**

| | | | | | |
|---|---|---|---|---|---|
| **1090** | A315 | 50d pale green | .30 | .30 |
| **1091** | A315 | 1r rose lilac | .55 | .55 |
| **1092** | A315 | 2r brt yel grn | 1.10 | 1.10 |
| **1093** | A315 | 3r pale yel grn | 1.75 | 1.75 |
| **1094** | A315 | 4r pale yellow | 2.25 | 2.25 |
| **1095** | A315 | 5r light blue | 2.75 | 2.75 |

**Size: 25x30mm**

***Perf. 13½x13¼***

| | | | | |
|---|---|---|---|---|
| **1096** | A315 | 10r turq grn | 5.50 | 5.50 |
| **1097** | A315 | 20r pale gray | 11.00 | 11.00 |
| **1098** | A315 | 30r tan | 16.50 | 16.50 |
| | | *Nos. 1090-1098 (9)* | 41.70 | 41.70 |

See Nos. 1113-1115, 1123.

Qatar Insurance Company, 50th Anniv. A316

**Litho. & Embossed With Foil Application**

**2014, Feb. 16 *Perf. 13½***
**1099** A316 1r gold & carmine .55 .55

Souvenir Sheet

Media Training, 10th Anniv. — A317

**Litho. & Embossed With Foil Application**

**2014, Feb. 24 *Perf. 13¾x13½***
**1100** A317 4r multi 2.25 2.25

No. 1100 was printed with three different sheet margins.

Oryx Leucoryx, Vultur Gryphus, Flags of Ecuador and Qatar — A318

**Litho. With Foil Application**

**2014, Oct. 22 *Perf. 12¾x13¼***
**1101** A318 3r silver & gold 1.75 1.75

See Ecuador No. 2133.

Souvenir Sheet

2014 World Arabian Horse Conference, Doha — A319

**2014, Nov. 2 Litho. *Perf. 12¼***
**1102** A319 5r multi 3.25 3.25

Souvenir Sheet

2015 Men's World Handball Championships, Qatar — A321

**2015, Jan. 15 Litho. *Perf. 13x12¾***
**1108** A321 3r copper & blk 1.75 1.75

International Al-Bawasil Diabetic Camp — A322

**2015, Jan. 16 Litho. *Perf. 13½***
**1109** A322 3r multi 1.75 1.75

Souvenir Sheet

Katara Prize for Arabic Novels — A323

**Litho. & Embossed**

**2015, Jan. 18 *Perf. 12¾x13¼***
**1110** A323 5r multi 2.75 2.75

Miniature Sheet

Jeem Cup Children's Soccer Tournament — A324

No. 1111 — Mascot, with panel color of: a, Brown orange. b, Purple. c, Brown red. d, Yellow orange.

**2015, Mar. 16 Litho. *Perf. 13¾***
**1111** A324 2.50r Sheet of 4, #a-d 5.50 5.50

Miniature Sheet

13th United Nations Congress on Crime Prevention and Criminal Justice, Doha — A325

No. 1112 — Emblems and text: a, With red arch at top. b, Without red arch at top.

**2015, Apr. 12 Litho. *Perf. 14½x14¼***
**1112** A325 1r Sheet of 4, 2 each #a-b 2.25 2.25

**Sheikh Tamim Type of 2013**

***Perf. 13½x13¼***

**2015, Aug. 10 Litho.**

**Size: 25x30mm**

**Panel Color at Bottom**

| | | | | |
|---|---|---|---|---|
| **1113** | A315 | 10r light orange | 5.50 | 5.50 |
| **1114** | A315 | 20r red | 11.00 | 11.00 |
| **1115** | A315 | 30r dark blue | 16.50 | 16.50 |
| | | *Nos. 1113-1115 (3)* | 33.00 | 33.00 |

Souvenir Sheet

National Day — A326

***Perf. 13¾x13½***

**2015, Dec. 17 Litho.**
**1116** A326 5r gold & multi 2.75 2.75

20th Gulf Cooperation Council Stamp Exhibition, Doha — A327

Designs: 3r, Gulf Cooperation Council and Exhibition emblems. 5r, Gulf Cooperation Council and Exhibition emblems, triangles.

**2015, Sept. 29 Litho. *Perf. 13¼***
**1117** A327 3r multi 1.75 1.75

**Size: 90x57mm**

***Imperf***

**1118** A327 5r multi 2.75 2.75

National Sports Day — A328

**2016, Feb. 8 Litho. *Perf. 13¼***
**1119** A328 5r multi 2.75 2.75

Miniature Sheet

"With Education, We Build Qatar" — A329

No. 1120: a, Arabic characters. b, Beakers, molecular models and formulas. c, Dhows and buildings. d, Computer keyboard and open book.

***Perf. 13¾ Syncopated***

**2016, Sept. 18 Litho.**
**1120** A329 3.50r Sheet of 4, #a-d 7.75 7.75

Arab Postal Day — A330

No. 1121 — Globe, envelopes and emblem with denomination at: a, LR. b, LL.

**2016, Sept. 25 Litho. *Perf. 12¾***
**1121** A330 4.50r Horiz. pair, #a-b 4.50 4.50

Souvenir Sheet

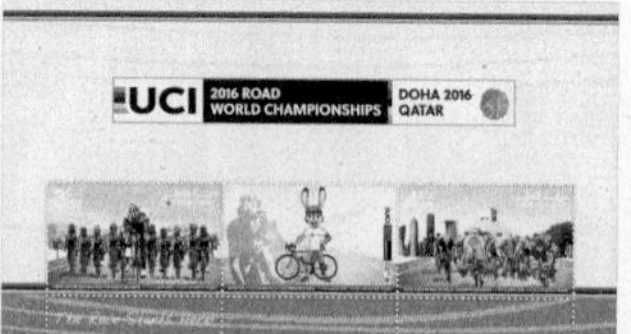

2016 Road Cycling World Championships, Qatar — A331

No. 1122: a, 3.50r, Cyclists wearing same jerseys. b, 4r, Cyclist and mascot. c, 4.50r, Cyclists wearing different jerseys.

***Perf. 13¼x13½***

**2016, Sept. 26 Litho.**
**1122** A331 Sheet of 3, #a-c 6.75 6.75

**Sheikh Tamim Type of 2013**

**2016, Oct. 10 Litho. *Perf. 13¼x13***

**Panel Color at Bottom**

**1123** A315 5r dull mauve 2.75 2.75

Miniature Sheet

QatarDebate Initiative — A332

No. 1124: a, 3.50r, Man and woman debating, magenta frame. b, 4.50r, Man and woman debating, dull blue frame. c, 5r, Woman and two men, magenta background. d, 5r, Woman and two men, greenish blue background.

**2016, Oct. 16 Litho. *Perf. 13¼x13***

**1124** A332 Sheet of 4, 3a-d 10.00 10.00

National Day A333

Denomination in: 50r, Red. 100r, Gold.

**2016, Dec. 17 Litho. *Perf. 14***

**1125-1126** A333 Set of 2 — —

Souvenir Sheet

National Day — A334

No. 1127: a, People pulling on ropes. b, Falcon.

**Litho. With Foil Application**

**2016, Dec. 17 *Perf. 13½x13¼***

**1127** A334 5r Sheet of 2, #a-b 5.50 5.50

Souvenir Sheet

Opening of Port Hamad — A335

No. 1128 — Ship, crane and dock: a, 4.50r. b, 8.50r.

**2017, Jan. 4 Litho. *Perf. 14¼***

**1128** A335 Sheet of 2, #a-b 7.25 7.25

Marine Life — A336

Designs: No. 1129, 50d, Hermit crab. No. 1130, 50d, Cnidaria. No. 1131, 3r, Sea slug. No. 1132, 3r, Crustacean. No. 1133, 4r, Sea anemone. No. 1134, 4r, Coral polyps.

No. 1135, 5r, Sea anemone, diff. No. 1136, 5r, Phylum Annelida.

**2017, Feb. 26 Litho. *Perf. 13¼***

**1129-1134** A336 Set of 6 8.25 8.25

**Size: 100x60mm**

***Imperf***

**1135-1136** A336 Set of 2 5.50 5.50

Education Excellence Day — A337

**2017, Mar. 1 Litho. *Perf. 13¼x14***

**1137** A337 3.50r multi 2.00 2.00

Souvenir Sheet

Qatar Stars Professional Soccer League — A338

No. 1138: a, Soccer ball with red flower designs. b, Stylized soccer player. c, Ring of five colored flower designs.

**2017, Sept, 12 Litho. *Perf. 14***

**1138** A338 4r Sheet of 3, #a-c 6.75 6.75

Miniature Sheet

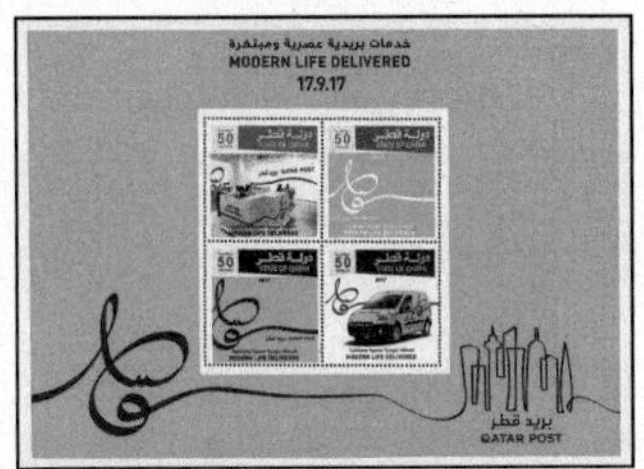


Qatar Post — A339

No. 1139: a, Post office counter. b, Arabic calligraphy and English slogan in white. c, Arabic calligraphy and English slogan in dark blue and blackish purple. d, Mail van.

**2017, Sept. 17 Litho. *Perf. 14x14½***

**1139** A339 50d Sheet of 4, #a-d 1.10 1.10

Souvenir Sheet

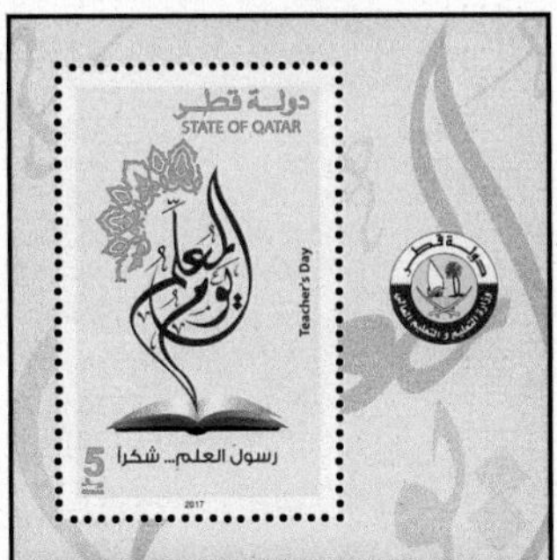


Teacher's Day — A340

**Litho. With Foil Application**

**2017, Oct. 5 *Perf. 13***

**1140** A340 5r silver & multi 2.60 2.60

Miniature Sheet

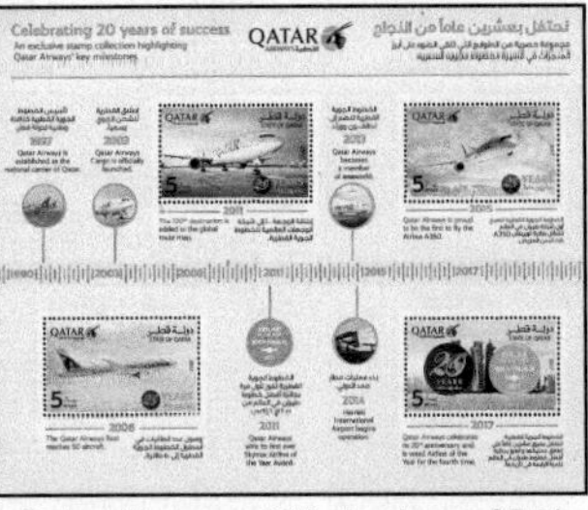


Qatar Airways, 20th Anniv. — A341

No. 1141: a, Jet on runway. b, Front view of jet in flight. c, Side view of jet in flight. d, Doha skyline, 20th anniversary emblem, 2017 Airline of the Year award.

**Litho. & Embossed With Foil Application**

**2017, Nov. 30 *Perf. 13x12¾***

**1141** A341 5r Sheet of 4, #a-d 11.00 11.00

Souvenir Sheet

National Day — A342

No. 1142 — Arabic text and: a, Clouds. b, Doha skyline.

**Litho. With Foil Application**

**2017, Dec. 17 *Perf. 13¾x13¼***

**1142** A342 10r Sheet of 2, #a-b, + central label 11.00 11.00

Souvenir Sheet

Diplomatic Relations Between Qatar and Turkey, 45th Anniv. — A343

No. 1143: a, Rumeli Fortress, Istanbul, and Al Zubara Castle, Qatar. b, Barzan Castle, Qatar, and Ankara Castle, Ankara.

**Litho., Sheet Margin Litho. With Foil Application**

**2018, Feb. 21 *Perf. 13½x13¼***

**1143** A343 8.50r Sheet of 2, #a-b 9.50 9.50

See Turkey No. 3588.

A344

Qatar National Library, Doha — A345

**2018, Apr. 16 Litho. *Perf. 13¼x13¾***

**1144** A344 1r multi — —

**1145** A345 1r multi — —

A346

A347

A348

Al Wadha Arches at 5/6 Interchange, Doha — A349

***Serpentine Die Cut 11 Syncopated***

**Litho. With Foil Application**

**2018, June 5 Self-Adhesive**

**1146** Sheet of 4 —

*a.* A346 3.50r silver & multi — —

*b.* A347 3.50r silver & multi — —

*c.* A348 3.50r silver & multi — —

*d.* A349 3.50r silver & multi — —

Souvenir Sheet

Reign of Sheikh Tamim, 5th Anniv. — A350

No. 1147 — Sheikh Tamim and: a, Flags. b, Building, horiz. c, Emblem of Qatar, horiz.

**Litho. With Foil Application**

**2018, July 2 *Perf. 13***

**1147** A350 25r Sheet of 3, #a-c — —

Miniature Sheet

First Graduates of Qatar Police College — A351

No. 1148: a, Graduates and flag bearer with Qatar Police College flag. b, Graduates standing at attention. c, Graduates marching. d, Graduates and flag bearer with flag of Qatar.

**Litho. (#1148b, 1148c), Litho. With Foil Application (#1148a, 1148d)**

**2019, July 10** ***Perf. 14x13¼***

| | | | | |
|---|---|---|---|---|
| **1148** | A351 4r Sheet of 4, #a-d | | 8.75 | 8.75 |

Flag of Palestinian Authority, Doves and Dome of the Rock, Jerusalem — A352

***Perf. 12¾x12½***

**2019, Nov. 14** **Litho.**

| | | | |
|---|---|---|---|
| **1149** | A352 8.50r multi | 4.75 | 4.75 |

Jerusalem, capital of Palestinian Authority.

Souvenir Sheet

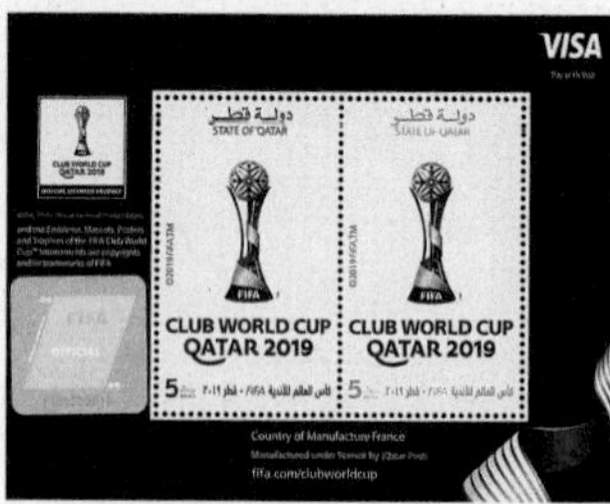

2019 Club World Cup Soccer Championships, Qatar — A353

No. 1150 — Club World cup with denomination and country name in: a, Brown. b, Blue green.

**Litho., Sheet Margin Litho. With Hologram Affixed**

**2019, Dec. 17** ***Perf. 14***

| | | | |
|---|---|---|---|
| **1150** | A353 5r Sheet of 2, #a-b | 5.50 | 5.50 |

Miniature Sheet

Children's Day — A354

No. 1151 — Various children's drawings with top and bottom panels in: a, 4r, Red. b, 4r, Blue. c, 4.50r, Yellow. d, 4.50r, Green.

**2020, Nov. 20** **Litho.** ***Perf. 14¼***

| | | | |
|---|---|---|---|
| **1151** | A354 Sheet of 4, #a-d | 9.50 | 9.50 |

An additional stamp was issued in this set. The editors would like to see any example of it.

A356

A357

A358

A359

A360

United Nations International Mother Language Day — A361

***Perf. 12¾x12½***

**2020, Nov. 30** **Litho.**

| | | | |
|---|---|---|---|
| **1153** | Sheet of 6 | 7.00 | 7.00 |
| *a.* | A356 1r brown & black | .55 | .55 |
| *b.* | A357 1r brown & black | .55 | .55 |
| *c.* | A358 1.50r brown & black | .85 | .85 |
| *d.* | A359 2.50r brown & black | 1.40 | 1.40 |
| *e.* | A360 3r brown & black | 1.75 | 1.75 |
| *f.* | A361 3r brown & black | 1.75 | 1.75 |

Souvenir Sheet

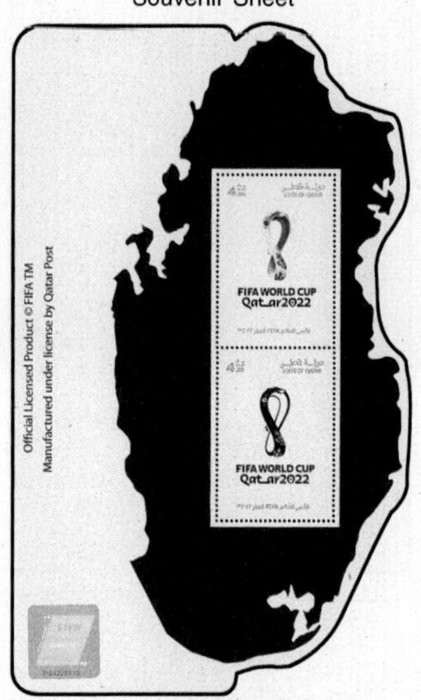

2022 World Cup Soccer Championships, Qatar — A362

No. 1154: a, 4r, Emblem. b, 4.50r, Emblem with colors reversed.

**Litho. With Foil Application, Sheet Margin Litho. With Hologram Affixed**

**2021, Apr. 1** ***Perf. 13¼***

| | | | |
|---|---|---|---|
| **1154** | A362 Sheet of 2, #a-b | 4.75 | 4.75 |

Miniature Sheet

Opening of Doha Metro — A363

No. 1155: a, People at station. b, Front of train. c, Front of train with destination sign. d, Front of train with destination sign, vert.

**Litho. & Embossed With Foil Application**

**2021, July 7** ***Perf. 14x13¼***

| | | | |
|---|---|---|---|
| **1155** | A363 5r Sheet of 4, #a-d | 11.00 | 11.00 |

## QUELIMANE

ˌkel-ə-ˈmän-ə

LOCATION — A district of the Mozambique Province in Portuguese East Africa

GOVT. — Part of the Portuguese East Africa Colony

AREA — 39,800 sq. mi.

POP. — 877,000 (approx.)

CAPITAL — Quelimane

This district was formerly a part of Zambezia. Quelimane stamps were replaced by those of Mozambique.

100 Centavos = 1 Escudo

**Vasco da Gama Issue**

Various Portuguese Colonies Surcharged

**1913** **Unwmk.** ***Perf. 12½ to 16***

**On Stamps of Macao**

| | | | | |
|---|---|---|---|---|
| **1** | CD20 | ¼c on ½a bl grn | 3.50 | 3.50 |
| **2** | CD21 | ½c on 1a red | 3.00 | 2.60 |
| **3** | CD22 | 1c on 2a red vio | 3.00 | 2.60 |
| **4** | CD23 | 2½c on 4a yel grn | 3.00 | 2.60 |
| **5** | CD24 | 5c on 8a dk bl | 3.00 | 2.60 |
| **6** | CD25 | 7½c on 12a vio brn | 5.75 | *4.25* |
| **7** | CD26 | 10c on 16a bis brn | 3.50 | 2.60 |
| **8** | CD27 | 15c on 24a bister | 3.50 | 2.60 |
| | | *Nos. 1-8 (8)* | 28.25 | 23.35 |
| | | Set, never hinged | 67.50 | |

**On Stamps of Portuguese Africa**

| | | | | |
|---|---|---|---|---|
| **9** | CD20 | ¼c on 2½r bl grn | 2.60 | *2.60* |
| **10** | CD21 | ½c on 5r red | 2.60 | *2.60* |
| **11** | CD22 | 1c on 10r red vio | 2.60 | *2.60* |
| *a.* | | Inverted surcharge | 70.00 | 70.00 |
| **12** | CD23 | 2½c on 25r yel grn | 2.60 | *2.60* |
| **13** | CD24 | 5c on 50r dk bl | 2.60 | *2.60* |
| **14** | CD25 | 7½c on 75r vio brn | 5.75 | *4.00* |
| **15** | CD26 | 10c on 100r bister | 3.25 | *2.60* |
| **16** | CD27 | 15c on 150r bister | 3.25 | *2.60* |
| | | *Nos. 9-16 (8)* | 25.25 | 22.20 |
| | | Set, never hinged | 60.00 | |

**On Stamps of Timor**

| | | | | |
|---|---|---|---|---|
| **17** | CD20 | ¼c on ½a bl grn | 3.00 | *3.00* |
| **18** | CD21 | ½c on 1a red | 3.00 | *3.00* |
| **19** | CD22 | 1c on 2a red vio | 3.00 | *3.00* |
| **20** | CD23 | 2½c on 4a yel grn | 3.00 | *3.00* |
| **21** | CD24 | 5c on 8a dk bl | 3.00 | *3.00* |
| **22** | CD25 | 7½c on 12a vio brn | 5.75 | *4.00* |
| **23** | CD26 | 10c on 16a bis brn | 3.50 | *3.00* |
| **24** | CD27 | 15c on 24a bister | 3.50 | *3.00* |
| | | *Nos. 17-24 (8)* | 27.75 | 25.00 |
| | | Set, never hinged | 67.50 | |
| | | *Nos. 1-24 (24)* | 81.25 | 70.55 |
| | | Set, never hinged | 195.00 | |

Ceres — A1

**1914** **Typo.** ***Perf. 15x14***

**Name and Value in Black**

**Chalky Paper**

| | | | | |
|---|---|---|---|---|
| **25** | A1 | ¼c olive brown | 1.60 | *2.25* |
| **26** | A1 | ½c black | 2.25 | *2.25* |
| **27** | A1 | 1c blue green | 2.60 | *2.25* |
| *a.* | | Imperf. | | |
| **28** | A1 | 1½c lilac brown | 3.25 | *2.40* |
| **29** | A1 | 2c carmine | 3.25 | *2.60* |
| **30** | A1 | 2½c light violet | 1.60 | *1.20* |
| **31** | A1 | 5c deep blue | 2.40 | *2.40* |
| **32** | A1 | 7½c yellow brown | 4.00 | *2.40* |
| **33** | A1 | 8c slate | 4.00 | *2.40* |
| **34** | A1 | 10c orange brown | 4.00 | *2.40* |
| **35** | A1 | 15c plum | 4.00 | *3.75* |
| **36** | A1 | 20c yellow green | 6.50 | *2.75* |
| **37** | A1 | 30c brown, *green* | 7.25 | *6.50* |
| **38** | A1 | 40c brown, *pink* | 7.25 | *7.25* |
| **39** | A1 | 50c orange, *salmon* | 8.00 | *8.00* |
| **40** | A1 | 1e green, *blue* | 10.00 | *9.00* |
| | | *Nos. 25-40 (16)* | 71.95 | *59.80* |

**Ordinary Paper**

| | | | | |
|---|---|---|---|---|
| **25B** | A1 | ¼c olive brown | 2.10 | *2.25* |
| **27B** | A1 | 1c blue green | 2.50 | *2.25* |
| **32B** | A1 | 7½c yellow brown | 3.25 | 2.40 |
| **34B** | A1 | 10c orange brown | 2.50 | 2.40 |
| **36B** | A1 | 20c yellow green | 4.00 | *2.10* |
| | | *Nos. 25B-36B (5)* | 14.35 | 11.40 |

# RAS AL KHAIMA

ˌräs al ˈkī-mə

LOCATION — Oman Peninsula, Arabia, on Persian Gulf
GOVT. — Sheikdom under British protection

Ras al Khaima was the 7th Persian Gulf sheikdom to join the United Arab Emirates, doing so in Feb. 1972.
See United Arab Emirates.

100 Naye Paise = 1 Rupee
100 Fils = 1 Rupee (1966)
100 Dirhams = 1 Riyal (1966)

**Catalogue values for all unused stamps in this country are for Never Hinged items.**

**Used values are for canceled to order stamps, except for Nos. 66-141, and where otherwise stated.**

**Imperforate stamps and deluxe sheets are footnoted where they are known to exist. All are believed to have been valid for postage and sold at the post office in Ras Al Khaima, but were produced in limited quanities. Orders were often limited to one set per order or to one set for every 10 regularly perforated sets ordered.**

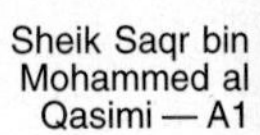

Sheik Saqr bin Mohammed al Qasimi — A1

Seven Palm Trees — A2

Dhow A3

***Perf. 14½x14***

**1964, Dec. 21 Photo. Unwmk.**

| No. | Type | Description | Unused | Used |
|---|---|---|---|---|
| 1 | A1 | 5np brown & black | .25 | .25 |
| 2 | A1 | 15np deep blue & blk | .25 | .25 |
| 3 | A2 | 30np ocher & black | .25 | .35 |
| 4 | A2 | 40np blue & black | .30 | .45 |
| 5 | A2 | 75np brn red & blk | 1.25 | .90 |
| 6 | A3 | 1r lt grn & sepia | 3.75 | 1.25 |
| 7 | A3 | 2r brt vio & sepia | 10.00 | 2.75 |
| 8 | A3 | 5r blue gray & sepia | 25.00 | 8.25 |
| | | *Nos. 1-8 (8)* | 41.05 | 14.45 |

Used values are for postally used examples.
For overprints and surcharges see Nos. 21-29, 66-73, 86-93, 140-141.

Pres. John Kennedy (1917-63), Lyndon Johnson (1908-73), and Astronaut John Glenn (1921-2016) — A4

Pres. John Kennedy (1917-63) A5

Design: Nos. 10 and 13, President John F. Kennedy and Jackie Kennedy shaking hands.

**1965, July 21 Photo. *Perf. 14½***

| No. | Type | Description | Unused | Used |
|---|---|---|---|---|
| 9 | A4 | 2r sepia & bl | .75 | .40 |
| 10 | A4 | 3r sepia, bl & blk | 1.20 | .60 |
| 11 | A5 | 4r sepia & bl | 1.75 | .85 |
| | | *Nos. 9-11 (3)* | 3.70 | 1.85 |

Nos. 9-11 were printed in sheets of six.
For surcharges see Nos. 74-76, 160-162.

| No. | Type | Description | Unused | Used |
|---|---|---|---|---|
| 12 | A4 | 1r sepia & bl | .60 | .25 |
| a. | | Pane of 4 | 2.50 | 1.20 |
| 13 | A4 | 1r sepia, bl & blk | .60 | .25 |
| a. | | Pane of 4 | 2.50 | 1.20 |
| 14 | A5 | 1r sepia & bl | .60 | .25 |
| a. | | Pane of 4 | 2.50 | 1.20 |
| | | *Nos. 12-14 (3)* | 1.80 | .75 |

Nos. 12-14 were printed in sheets of four.
For surcharges see Nos. 77-79, 163-165.

Winston Churchill (1874-1965) — A6

Funeral Procession, Winston Churchill (1874-1965) — A7

Design: Nos. 16 and 19, Winston Churchill with Franklin Roosevelt, horiz.

**1965, Nov. 30 Photo. *Perf. 14½***

| No. | Type | Description | Unused | Used |
|---|---|---|---|---|
| 15 | A6 | 2r sepia, bl & blk | .75 | .40 |
| 16 | A6 | 3r sepia & bl | 1.20 | .60 |
| 17 | A7 | 4r sepia, bl & blk | 1.75 | .85 |
| | | *Nos. 15-17 (3)* | 3.70 | 1.85 |

Nos. 15-17 were printed in sheets of six.
For overprints and surcharges see Nos. 80-82.

**Souvenir Sheets**

| No. | Type | Description | Unused | Used |
|---|---|---|---|---|
| 18 | A6 | 1r sepia, bl & blk | .60 | .25 |
| a. | | Pane of 4 | 2.50 | 1.20 |
| 19 | A6 | 1r sepia & bl | .60 | .25 |
| a. | | Pane of 4 | 2.50 | 1.20 |
| 20 | A7 | 1r sepia, bl & blk | .60 | .25 |
| a. | | Pane of 4 | 2.50 | 1.20 |
| | | *Nos. 18-20 (3)* | 1.80 | .75 |

Nos. 18-20 were printed in sheets of four.
For surcharges see Nos. 83-85.

**Nos. 6-8 Overprinted**

**1965, Oct. 10 *Perf. 14½x14***

| No. | Type | Description | Unused | Used |
|---|---|---|---|---|
| 21 | A3 | 1r lt grn & sepia | .60 | .60 |
| 22 | A3 | 2r brt vio & sepia | 1.20 | 1.20 |
| 23 | A3 | 5r blue gray & sepia | 3.25 | 3.25 |
| | | *Nos. 21-23 (3)* | 5.05 | 5.05 |

Overprinted for the 1964 Tokyo Olympic Games.
Nos. 21-23 exist with inverted or double overprints.

**Nos. 6-8 Overprinted**

**1965, Nov. 1**

| No. | Type | Description | Unused | Used |
|---|---|---|---|---|
| 24 | A3 | 1r lt grn & sepia | .60 | .60 |
| 25 | A3 | 2r brt vio & sepia | 1.20 | 1.20 |
| 26 | A3 | 5r blue gray & sepia | 3.25 | 3.25 |
| | | *Nos. 24-26 (3)* | 5.05 | 5.05 |

Overprinted for the 100th anniversary of the death Abraham Lincoln (1809-65).
Nos. 24-26 exist with inverted or double overprints.

**Nos. 6-8 Overprinted**

**1965, Nov. 30**

| No. | Type | Description | Unused | Used |
|---|---|---|---|---|
| 27 | A3 | 1r lt grn & sepia | .60 | .60 |
| 28 | A3 | 2r brt vio & sepia | 1.20 | 1.20 |
| 29 | A3 | 5r blue gray & sepia | 3.25 | 3.25 |
| | | *Nos. 27-29 (3)* | 5.05 | 5.05 |

Overprinted for the 20th anniversary of the death of Franklin Roosevelt (1882-1945).
Nos. 27-29 exist with inverted or double overprints.

Satellite and Dish — A8

Designs: 15np, 1r, Satellite and satellite dish with radio waves. 50np, 2r, Satellite and tower. 85np, 3r, Satellite and rocket on launch pad.
5r, Two satellites orbiting globe.

**1966, May 10 Litho. *Perf. 13¼x13½***

| No. | Type | Description | Unused | Used |
|---|---|---|---|---|
| 30 | A8 | 15np multi | .25 | .25 |
| 31 | A8 | 50np multi | .45 | .25 |
| 32 | A8 | 85np multi | .95 | .30 |
| 33 | A8 | 1r multi | 1.10 | .40 |
| 34 | A8 | 2r multi | 1.90 | .45 |
| 35 | A8 | 3r multi | 2.25 | .50 |
| | | *Nos. 30-35 (6)* | 6.90 | 2.15 |

**Souvenir Sheet**

***Imperf***

| No. | Type | Description | Unused | Used |
|---|---|---|---|---|
| 36 | A8 | 5r multi | 5.00 | — |

100th anniversary of the ITU.
Nos. 30-35 exist imperf. Value, set $9.
For surcharges see Nos. 94-100.

Running — A9

Designs: 1np, 5np, Running. 2np, 25np, Boxing. 3np, 50np, Soccer. 4np, 75np, 5r, Fencing. 10np, 1r, Swimming.

**1966, June 9 Photo. *Perf. 12***

| No. | Type | Description | Unused | Used |
|---|---|---|---|---|
| 37 | A9 | 1np shown | .25 | .25 |
| 38 | A9 | 2np multi | .25 | .25 |
| 39 | A9 | 3np multi | .25 | .25 |
| 40 | A9 | 4np multi | .25 | .25 |
| 41 | A9 | 5np multi | .25 | .25 |
| 42 | A9 | 10np multi | .25 | .25 |
| 43 | A9 | 25np multi | .40 | .25 |
| 44 | A9 | 50np multi | .75 | .25 |
| 45 | A9 | 75np multi | 1.00 | .25 |
| 46 | A9 | 1r multi | 1.60 | .25 |
| | | *Nos. 37-46 (10)* | 5.25 | 2.50 |

**Souvenir Sheet**

***Imperf***

| No. | Type | Description | Unused | Used |
|---|---|---|---|---|
| 47 | A9 | 5r multi | 5.00 | — |

Pan-Arab Games.
Nos. 37-46 exist imperf. Value, set $6.75.
For surcharges see Nos. 100-111.

Scott Carpenter (1925-2013), Astronaut — A10

Designs: 25np, Scott Carpenter (1925-2013). 50np, John Glenn (1921-2016). 75np, Alan Shepard (1923-98). 1r, Leroy Gordon Cooper (1927-2004). 2r, Virgil Ivan Grissom (1926-67). 3r, Walter Marty Schirra (1923-2007). 4r, Thomas P. Stafford (b. 1930). 5r, James A. Lovell (b. 1928).

**1966, June 30 Photo. *Perf. 12***

| No. | Type | Description | Unused | Used |
|---|---|---|---|---|
| 48 | A10 | 25np gold & multi | .25 | .25 |
| 49 | A10 | 50np silver & multi | .25 | .25 |
| 50 | A10 | 75np silver & multi | .25 | .25 |
| 51 | A10 | 1r silver & multi | .35 | .25 |
| 52 | A10 | 2r silver & multi | .70 | .30 |
| 53 | A10 | 3r gold & multi | 1.00 | .30 |
| 54 | A10 | 4r gold & multi | 1.25 | .40 |
| 55 | A10 | 5r gold & multi | 1.50 | .50 |
| | | *Nos. 48-55 (8)* | 5.55 | 2.50 |

**Souvenir Sheet**
**Size: 155x105mm**

***Simulated Perfs***

| No. | Type | Description | Unused | Used |
|---|---|---|---|---|
| 56 | A10 | 4r multi | 5.00 | *5.00* |
| 57 | A10 | 4r multi | 5.00 | *5.00* |

Nos. 48-55 exist imperf. Value, set $9.
No. 56 is a single 4r stamp containing the designs of Nos. 49-52. No. 57 is a single 4r stamp containing the designs of Nos. 48 and 53-55.
For surcharges and overprints see Nos. 122-131, 173-182.

Sheikh Saqr bin Mohammed al Qasimi (1918-2010) and Sheikh Ahmad — A11

Designs: Sheikh Saqr bin Mohammed al Qasimi (1918-2010) with other world leaders. No. 58, Sheikh Ahmad. No. 59, Sheikh Ahmed Bin Ali Al Thani (1922-77), Qatar. No. 60, Pres. Gamal Abdel Nasser (1918-70), Egypt and the United Arab Republic. No. 61, King Hussein bin Talal (1935-99), Jordan. No. 62, Pres. Lyndon B. Johnson (1908-73), United States. No. 63, Pres. Charles de Gaulle (1890-1970), France. No. 64, Pope Paul VI (1897-1978). No. 65, Prime Minister Harold Wilson (1916-95), Great Britain.

**1966, July 28 Litho. *Perf. 13½x14½***

| No. | Type | Description | Unused | Used |
|---|---|---|---|---|
| 58 | A11 | 1r peach & blk | .65 | .25 |
| 59 | A11 | 1r purple & blk | .65 | .25 |
| 60 | A11 | 1r pink & blk | .65 | .25 |
| 61 | A11 | 1r steel grn & blk | .65 | .25 |
| a. | | Sheet of 4, #58-61, simulated perfs. | 5.00 | — |
| 62 | A11 | 1r yelsh grn & blk | .65 | .25 |
| 63 | A11 | 1r yellow & blk | .65 | .25 |
| 64 | A11 | 1r org & blk | .65 | .25 |

**65** A11 1r steel blue & blk .65 .25
*a.* Sheet of 4, #62-65, simulated perfs. 5.00 —
*Nos. 58-65 (8)* 5.20 2.00

Issued for the 20th anniversary of the United Nations.
Nos. 58-65 exist imperf. Value, set $10.
For surcharges see Nos. 132-139.

Nos. 66-85 were surcharged for the currency change from Rupee to Fils, which occurred on Aug. 1, 1966.
Nos. 30-35 and 58-65 surcharged with Fils are likely bogus. The editors would like more information on these.

**Nos. 1-8 Surcharged New Currency in Fils With Three Bar Obliterators**

**1966, Aug. 1 Photo. *Perf. 14½x14***
**66** A1 5f on 5np — —
**67** A1 15f on 15np — —
**68** A2 30f on 30np — —
**69** A2 40f on 40np — —
**70** A2 75f on 75np — —
**71** A3 100f on 1r — —
**72** A3 200f on 2r — —
**73** A3 500f on 5r — —

See Nos. 86-93. For surcharge see No. 141.

**Nos. 9-11 Surcharged in English and Arabic**

**1966, Aug. 1**
**74** A4 200f on 2r .75 *.75*
**75** A4 300f on 3r 1.00 *1.00*
**76** A5 400f on 4r 1.25 *1.25*
*Nos. 74-76 (3)* 3.00 *3.00*

**Same Surcharge on Nos. 12-14**
Souvenir Sheets
**77** A4 100f on 1r (#12) .50 *.50*
*a.* Pane of 4 2.00 *2.00*
**78** A4 100f on 1r (#13) .50 *.50*
*a.* Pane of 4 2.00 *2.00*
**79** A5 100f on 1r (#14) .50 *.50*
*a.* Pane of 4 2.00 *2.00*
*Nos. 77-79 (3)* 1.50 *1.50*

Nos. 15-17 Surcharged in English and Arabic

**1966, Aug. 1 *Perf. 14½***
**80** A6 200f on 2r .75 *.75*
**81** A6 300f on 3r 1.00 *1.00*
**82** A7 400f on 4r 1.25 *1.25*
*Nos. 80-82 (3)* 3.00 *3.00*

**Same Surcharge on Nos. 18-20**
Souvenir Sheets
**83** A6 100f on 1r (#18) .50 *.50*
*a.* Pane of 4 2.00 *2.00*
**84** A6 100f on 1r (#19) .50 *.50*
*a.* Pane of 4 2.00 *2.00*
**85** A7 100f on 1r (#20) .50 *.50*
*a.* Pane of 4 2.00 *2.00*
*Nos. 83-85 (3)* 1.50 *1.50*

For Nos. 74-79, used values are for postally used examples.

Nos. 86-141 were surcharged for the currency change from Fils to Dirhams, which occurred on Nov. 20, 1966.

Nos. 1-8 Surcharged

**1966 *Perf. 14½x14***
**86** A1 5d on 5np — *5.50*
**87** A1 15d on 15np — *5.50*
**88** A2 30d on 30np — *5.50*
**89** A2 40d on 40np — *5.50*
**90** A2 75d on 75np — *35.00*
**91** A3 1rl on 1r — *10.00*
**92** A3 2rl on 2r — *10.00*
**93** A3 5rl on 5r — *10.00*
*Nos. 86-93 (8)* *87.00*

**Nos. 30-36 Surcharged**

**1966, Nov. 20 *Perf. 13¼x13½***
**94** A8 15d on 15np .35 *.35*
**95** A8 50d on 50np 1.20 *1.20*
**96** A8 85d on 85np 2.25 *2.25*
**97** A8 1rl on 1r 2.40 *2.40*
**98** A8 2rl on 2r 3.75 *3.75*
**99** A8 3rl on 3r 5.00 *5.00*
*Nos. 94-99 (6)* 14.95 *14.95*

**Souvenir Sheet**
***Imperf***
**100** A8 5rl on 5r 20.00 —

Nos. 94-99 exist imperf. Value, set *$25.*

Nos. 37-47 Surcharged

**1966, Nov. 20 *Perf. 12***
**101** A9 1d on 1np .30 *.30*
**102** A9 2d on 2np .30 *.30*
**103** A9 3d on 3np .30 *.30*
**104** A9 4d on 4np .30 *.30*
**105** A9 5d on 5np .30 *.30*
**106** A9 10d on 10np .45 *.45*
**107** A9 25d on 25np .75 *.75*
**108** A9 50d on 50np 1.60 *1.60*
**109** A9 75d on 75np 2.40 *2.40*
**110** A9 1rl on 1r 3.50 *3.50*
*Nos. 101-110 (10)* 10.20 *10.20*

**Souvenir Sheet**
***Simulated Perfs***
**111** A9 5rl on 5r *50.00* —

Nos. 101-110 exist imperf.
For overprints see Nos. 112-121.

**Overprinted "PRO OLYMPIC GAMES MEXICO" Diagonally in English and Arabic on Nos. 101-110**

**1966**
**112** A9 1d on 1np *1.00* —
**113** A9 2d on 2np *1.00* —
**114** A9 3d on 3np *1.00* —
**115** A9 4d on 4np *1.00* —
**116** A9 5d on 5np *1.00* —
**117** A9 10d on 10np *1.00* —
**118** A9 25d on 25np *1.00* —
**119** A9 50d on 50np *1.60* —
**120** A9 75d on 75np *2.40* —
**121** A9 1rl on 1r *3.50* —
*Nos. 112-121 (10)* *14.50*

Nos. 112-121 exist imperf.

Nos. 48-57 Surcharged

**1966, Nov. 20**
**122** A10 25d on 25np *.50* —
**123** A10 50d on 50np *.90* —
**124** A10 75d on 75np *1.25* —
**125** A10 1rl on 1r *1.60* —
**126** A10 2rl on 2r *2.50* —
**127** A10 3rl on 3r *3.25* —
**128** A10 4rl on 4r *3.75* —
**129** A10 5rl on 5r *4.50* —
*Nos. 122-129 (8)* *18.25*

**Souvenir Sheet**
**Size: 155x105mm**
***Simulated Perfs***
**130** A10 4rl on 4r (#56) *30.00* —
**131** A10 4rl on 4r (#57) *30.00* —

Nos. 122-129 exist imperf. Value, set *$27.50.*
For similar surcharges see Nos. 173-182.

**Nos. 58-65 Surcharged**

**1966, Nov. 20**
**132** A11 1rl on 1r (#58) .90 *.90*
**133** A11 1rl on 1r (#59) .90 *.90*
**134** A11 1rl on 1r (#60) .90 *.90*
**135** A11 1rl on 1r (#61) .90 *.90*
*a.* On #61a 5.00 —
**136** A11 1rl on 1r (#62) .90 *.90*
**137** A11 1rl on 1r (#63) .90 *.90*
**138** A11 1rl on 1r (#64) .90 *.90*
**139** A11 1rl on 1r (#65) .90 *.90*
*a.* On #65a 5.00 —
*Nos. 132-139 (8)* 7.20 *7.20*

Nos. 132-139 exist imperf. Value, set $8.

No. 5 Surcharged in Black

**1966**
**140** A2 5d on 75np *150.00*

**No. 70 Surcharged in Black**

**1966**
**141** A2 5d on 75f on 75np — *1,200.*

W.H.O. Headquarters — A12

**1966, Dec. 1 Litho. *Perf. 12***
**142** A12 15d shown .25 .25
**143** A12 35d multi .50 .25
**144** A12 50d multi .60 .25
**145** A12 3rl multi 1.60 .25
*a.* Sheet of 1, imperf. 5.00 *5.00*
*Nos. 142-145 (4)* 2.95 1.00

Nos. 144-145 are airmail.
Nos. 142-145 exist imperf. Value, set $5.

Domestic Cat A13

**1967, Mar. 30 Photo. *Perf. 11¼***
**146** A13 1d shown .25 .25
**147** A13 2d blue & multi .25 .25
**148** A13 3d pink & multi .25 .25
**149** A13 4d green & multi .25 .25
**150** A13 5d brown & multi .25 .25
**151** A13 3rl lilac & multi 3.00 1.25
*Nos. 146-151 (6)* 4.25 2.50

No. 151 is airmail.

Solon and His Students — A14

Designs: 2d, Monarch and Attendants, vert. 3d and 1rl, Al Hairth to Abu Zayd. 4d, Monarch on His Throne, vert. 10d, Herons. 20d, Archangel Israfil, vert. 30d, Two Horsemen.

**1967, May 10 Litho. *Perf. 12***
**152** A14 1d shown .25 .25
**153** A14 2d multi .25 .25
**154** A14 3d multi .25 .25
**155** A14 4d multi .25 .25
**156** A14 10d multi .60 .25
**157** A14 20d multi 1.40 .50
**158** A14 30d multi 1.60 .80
*Nos. 152-158 (7)* 4.60 2.55

**Souvenir Sheet**
***Imperf***
**159** A14 1rl multi 3.50 *3.50*

Nos. 152-158 were issued in sheets of 10.
Nos. 152-158 exist imperf. Value, set $8.
For similar designs see Nos. C10-C16.

**Nos. 9-11 Overprinted in English and Arabic in a Circle and Surcharged**

**1967, June 30**
**160** A4 2rl on 2r 1.60 —
**161** A4 3rl on 3r 2.10 —
**162** A5 4rl on 4r 3.25 —
*Nos. 160-162 (3)* 6.95

**Same Overprinted on Nos. 12-14**
**163** A4 1rl on 1r (#12) 1.00 *1.00*
*a.* Pane of 4 4.00 *4.00*
**164** A4 1rl on 1r (#13) 1.00 *1.00*
*a.* Pane of 4 4.00 *4.00*
**165** A5 1rl on 1r (#14) 1.00 *4.00*
*a.* Pane of 4 4.00 *4.00*
*Nos. 163-165 (3)* 3.00 *6.00*

Nos. 160-162 may exist imperf. The editors would like to examine any examples.

12th Boy Scout Jamboree, Idaho — A15

Designs: 1d, Bugler. 2d and 75d, Sir Baden-Powell (1857-1941). 3d, Campfire and four scouts, horiz. 4d, Three scouts hiking, horiz. 35d, Scout emblem. 1rl, Gemini capsule and boy scout.

**1967, July 20 Litho. *Perf. 12***

| | | | | |
|---|---|---|---|---|
| **166** | A15 | 1d shown | .45 | .25 |
| **167** | A15 | 2d multi | .45 | .25 |
| **168** | A15 | 3d multi | .45 | .25 |
| **169** | A15 | 4d multi | .45 | .25 |
| **170** | A15 | 35d multi | .90 | .75 |
| **171** | A15 | 75d multi | 1.75 | .75 |
| *a.* | | Imperf. sheet of 2, #170-171 | 4.75 | *4.75* |
| **172** | A15 | 1rl multi | 2.10 | .75 |
| *a.* | | Imperf. sheet of 1 | 4.75 | *4.75* |
| | | *Nos. 166-172 (7)* | 6.55 | 3.25 |

Nos. 170-172 are airmail.
Nos. 166-172 exist imperf. Value, set $9.

## Nos. 48-57 Surcharged and Overprinted in English and Arabic

Nos. 173-174, 179

Nos. 175-176, 178, 180

No. 177

**1967, Aug. 20**

| | | | | |
|---|---|---|---|---|
| **173** | A10 | 25d on 25np | .25 | — |
| **174** | A10 | 50d on 50np | .30 | — |
| **175** | A10 | 75d on 75np | .50 | — |
| **176** | A10 | 1rl on 1r | .75 | — |
| **177** | A10 | 2rl on 2r | 1.50 | — |
| **178** | A10 | 3rl on 3r | 2.25 | — |
| **179** | A10 | 4rl on 4r | 3.25 | — |
| **180** | A10 | 5rl on 5r | 4.00 | — |
| | | *Nos. 173-180 (8)* | 12.80 | |

### Souvenir Sheet
### Size: 155x105mm
***Simulated Perfs***

| | | | | |
|---|---|---|---|---|
| **181** | A10 | 4rl on 4r (#56) | 7.00 | — |
| **182** | A10 | 4rl on 4r (#57) | 7.00 | — |

Nos. 173-180 have additional images commemorating the three astronauts killed aboard Apollo 1 were printed in the gutter.

On No. 181 the simulated stamps have Arabic inscription. On No. 182 the simulated stamps have Arabic inscription, whereas #177 has English.

Nos. 173-182 exist imperf. Value, set $35.

Discus thrower and Atlantes of Tula — A16

Designs: Olympic rings, athlete and Mexico tourist attraction. 20d, Weightlifter and Palacio de Bellas Artes. 30d, Soccer player and University of Mexico Library. 40d, Fencer and fishing boats. 1rl, Runner and Guadalajara Cathedral. 2rl, Boxer and Paseo de la Reforma.

**1967, Oct. 20 Photo. *Perf. 12½***

| | | | | |
|---|---|---|---|---|
| **183** | A16 | 10d shown | .25 | .25 |
| **184** | A16 | 20d multi | .25 | .25 |
| **185** | A16 | 30d multi | .25 | .25 |
| **186** | A16 | 40d multi | .25 | .25 |
| **187** | A16 | 1rl multi | .75 | .30 |
| **188** | A16 | 2rl multi | 1.40 | .50 |
| *a.* | | Imperf. sheet of 1 | 4.00 | 2.00 |
| | | *Nos. 183-188 (6)* | 3.15 | 1.80 |

Nos. 187-188 are airmail.
Nos. 183-188 exist imperf. Value, set $8.

Grenoble Olympics, Ice Hockey — A17

Grenoble Olympics A18

Designs: 2d, Ski jumping. 3d, Speed skating. 4d, 2rl, Bobsled. 5d, No. 196, Figure skating pair.

No. 197, Aerial map of Grenoble.

**1967, Dec. 24 Litho. *Perf. 12½***

| | | | | |
|---|---|---|---|---|
| **189** | A17 | 1d shown | .25 | .25 |
| **190** | A17 | 2d multi | .25 | .25 |
| **191** | A17 | 3d multi | .25 | .25 |
| **192** | A17 | 4d multi | .25 | .25 |
| **193** | A17 | 5d multi | .25 | .25 |
| **194** | A18 | 85d shown | .60 | .25 |
| **195** | A17 | 2rl multi | 1.20 | .25 |
| **196** | A17 | 3rl multi | 1.75 | .25 |
| | | *Nos. 189-196 (8)* | 4.80 | 2.00 |

### Souvenir Sheet
***Imperf***

| | | | | |
|---|---|---|---|---|
| **197** | A17 | 3rl multi | 6.50 | *6.50* |

Nos. 194-197 are airmail.
Nos. 189-196 exist imperf. Value, set $8.

Beatrice d'Este, by Leonardo da Vinci — A19

Designs: 30d, The Goldfinch Madonna, by Raphael. 40d, La Donna Velata, by Raphael. 50d, Fabiola, by Jean-Jacques Henner. 1rl, Portrait of Anne Henriette, by Jean-Marc Nattier the Younger, horiz. 2rl, Study, by Jean Honore Fragonard. 3rl, Portrait of Mary Adelaide, by Jean-Marc Nattier the Younger, horiz. 4rl, Virgin with Green Cushion, by Andrea Solari.

5rl, Mona Lisa, by Leonardo da Vinci.

**1968, Mar. 21 Litho. *Perf. 11¼***

| | | | | |
|---|---|---|---|---|
| **198** | A19 | 20d shown | .25 | .25 |
| **199** | A19 | 30d multi | .25 | .25 |
| **200** | A19 | 40d multi | .25 | .25 |
| **201** | A19 | 50d multi | .25 | .25 |
| **202** | A19 | 1rl multi | .25 | .25 |
| **203** | A19 | 2rl multi | .40 | .25 |
| **204** | A19 | 3rl multi | .60 | .25 |
| **205** | A19 | 4rl multi | .90 | .25 |
| | | *Nos. 198-205 (8)* | 3.15 | 2.00 |

### Souvenir Sheet
***Imperf***

| | | | | |
|---|---|---|---|---|
| **206** | A19 | 5rl multi | 8.00 | 1.00 |

Issued in panes of six and 10.
Nos. 202-205 are airmail.
Nos. 198-205 exist imperf. Value, set $8.50. And in imperf. deluxe sheets of one.

No. 206 exists perforated around the design. Without the selvage this becomes simply a label. Value unused, $8, CTO, $1.

Abraham Lincoln (1809-65) — A20

Designs: No. 208, John Kennedy (1917-63). No. 209, Martin Luther King, Jr. (1929-68).

**1968, May 25 Litho. *Perf. 11¼***

| | | | | |
|---|---|---|---|---|
| **207** | A20 | 2rl shown | 1.90 | .50 |
| **208** | A20 | 2rl multi | 1.90 | .50 |
| **209** | A20 | 2rl multi | 1.90 | .50 |
| *a.* | | Imperf. sheet of 3, #207-209 | 7.00 | 1.50 |
| | | *Nos. 207-209 (3)* | 5.70 | 1.50 |

Issued for the International Human Rights Year, in panes of six.

Nos. 207-209 exist imperf. Value, set $7.50. No. 209a exists perforated.

For overprint see No. 312.

Young Child, by Gerard Terborch A21

Designs: Paintings. No. 211, Lady on Horsebock, by Edouard Manet, horiz. 20d, A Little Girl, by Jan Gossaert. 25d, The Hay Wain, by John Constable, horiz. 35d, Helene, by Peter Paul Rubens. 40d, Young Beggars Playing Dice, by Bortolome Esteban Murillo. 45d, A Horse Frightened by Lightning, by Thoedore Gericault, horiz. 60d, Plaster Torso, by Henri Matisse. 70d, Portrait of M. Fourcade, by Henri de Toulouse-Lautrec. 80d, Madonna and Child, by Leonardo da Vinci. 90d, Balerina with Bouquet, by Edgar Degas. 1rl, Concert, by Gerrit van Honthorst. 1.25rl, The Milkmaid, by Jean-Baptiste Greuze. 1.50rl, The Poor Fisherman, by Paul Gauguin. 2.50rl, Sunflowers, by Vincent Van Gogh. 2.75rl, The Land of Cockaigne, by Peter Brueghel.

No. 226a, Pleasure Boat, by Claude Monet. No. 226b, The Bridge at Mantes, by Jean-Baptiste Corot. No. 227a, Girl Reading Letter, by Jan Vermeer. No. 227b, Self-portrait with Saskia, by Rembrandt. No. 228a, The Painter's Daughters, by Thomas Gainsborough. No. 228b, A Child with an Apple, by Jean-Baptiste Greuze. No. 229a, Coeur in the Forest, by Pierre Auguste Renoir. No. 229b, The Negro Scipio, by Paul Cezanne.

**1968, May 25 Litho. *Perf. 11¼***

| | | | | |
|---|---|---|---|---|
| **210** | A21 | 15d shown | .25 | .25 |
| **211** | A21 | 15d multi | .25 | .25 |
| **212** | A21 | 20d multi | .25 | .25 |
| **213** | A21 | 25d multi | .25 | .25 |
| **214** | A21 | 35d multi | .25 | .25 |
| **215** | A21 | 40d multi | .25 | .25 |
| **216** | A21 | 45d multi | .25 | .25 |
| **217** | A21 | 60d multi | .30 | .25 |
| **218** | A21 | 70d multi | .35 | .25 |
| **219** | A21 | 80d multi | .35 | .25 |
| **220** | A21 | 90d multi | .45 | .25 |
| **221** | A21 | 1rl multi | .45 | .25 |
| **222** | A21 | 1.25rl multi | .55 | .25 |
| **223** | A21 | 1.50rl multi | .70 | .25 |
| **224** | A21 | 2.50rl multi | 1.10 | .25 |
| **225** | A21 | 2.75rl multi | 1.25 | .25 |
| | | *Nos. 210-225 (16)* | 7.25 | 4.00 |

### Souvenir Sheets

| | | | | |
|---|---|---|---|---|
| **226** | | Sheet of 2, #a.-b. | 5.00 | *5.00* |
| *a.* | A21 | 2rl multi | 1.50 | *1.50* |
| *b.* | A21 | 3rl multi | 1.50 | *1.50* |
| **227** | | Sheet of 2, #a.-b. | 5.00 | *5.00* |
| *a.* | A21 | 2rl multi | 1.50 | *1.50* |
| *b.* | A21 | 3rl multi | 1.50 | *1.50* |
| **228** | | Sheet of 2, #a.-b. | 5.00 | *5.00* |
| *a.* | A21 | 2rl multi | 1.50 | *1.50* |
| *b.* | A21 | 3rl multi | 1.50 | *1.50* |
| **229** | | Sheet of 2, #a.-b. | 5.00 | *5.00* |
| *a.* | A21 | 2rl multi | 1.50 | *1.50* |
| *b.* | A21 | 3rl multi | 1.50 | *1.50* |
| | | *Nos. 226-229 (4)* | 20.00 | *20.00* |

Nos. 210-225 exist imperf. Value, set $24. Nos. 226-229 exist imperf. Value unused, $5 each, CTO, $1.75 each.

Winter Olympics Champions, Marielle Goitschel — A22

Designs: 1rl, Franco Nones. 1.50rl, Jean-Claude Killy and Guy Perillat. 2rl, Olga Pall. 2.50rl, Nancy Greene. 3rl, Peggy Fleming.

No. 236 Marielle Goitschel, same design as No. 230.

**1968, Aug 31 Litho. *Perf. 11¼***

| | | | | |
|---|---|---|---|---|
| **230** | A22 | 50d shown | .25 | .25 |
| **231** | A22 | 1rl multi | .40 | .25 |
| **232** | A22 | 1.50rl multi | .60 | .25 |
| **233** | A22 | 2rl multi | .75 | .25 |
| **234** | A22 | 2.50rl multi | .90 | .25 |
| **235** | A22 | 3rl multi | 1.00 | .25 |
| | | *Nos. 230-235 (6)* | 3.90 | 1.50 |

### Embossed on Foil Coated Paper
***Perf. 8***

| | | | | |
|---|---|---|---|---|
| **236** | A22 | 50d gold | 15.00 | — |

Printed in panes of 6.

Nos. 230-235 exist imperf. Value, set $7. No. 236 exists imperf. Value, $15. Nos. 230-235 exist in deluxe sheets of one. Value, $13 each. No. 236 exists in an imperf. sheet of one. Value, $23.

See Nos. C22-C23.

Christmas Paintings - The Virgin and Child with John the Baptist, by Sandro Botticelli — A23

Rest during the Flight into Egypt, by Gentile da Fabriano — A24

Adoration of the Child, by Gerrit van Honthorst — A25

Designs: 30d, The Adoration of the Child, by Antonio Correggio. 40d, Nativity, by Carle van Loo. 50d, Adoration, by Susan Tu Luca Ch'en. 60d, Madonna and Child, by Bartolome Estiban Murillo. 1rl, Adoration of the Shepherds, by Gerrit van Horthorst. 3rl, Nativity, by Neri di Bicci. 4rl, Nativity, by unknown Florentine master.

**1968, Dec. Litho. *Perf. 11¼***

| | | | | |
|---|---|---|---|---|
| **237** | A23 | 20d shown | .25 | .25 |
| **238** | A23 | 30d multi | .25 | .25 |
| **239** | A23 | 40d multi | .30 | .25 |
| **240** | A23 | 50d multi | .30 | .25 |
| **241** | A23 | 60d multi | .40 | .25 |
| **242** | A23 | 1rl multi | .60 | .25 |

***Perf. 11***

| | | | | |
|---|---|---|---|---|
| **243** | A24 | 2rl shown | 1.00 | .25 |
| **244** | A24 | 3rl multi | 1.40 | .25 |
| **245** | A24 | 4rl multi | 2.00 | .25 |
| | | *Nos. 237-245 (9)* | 6.50 | 2.25 |

**Souvenir Sheet**

**Size: 120x94mm**

***Simulated Perfs***

| | | | | |
|---|---|---|---|---|
| **246** | A25 | 5rl shown | 3.00 | .75 |
| *a.* | | Size: 132x134mm | *50.00* | — |

Issue dates: Nos. 237-242 and 246, Dec. 10; Nos. 243-245, Dec. 7.

Nos. 237-245 were printed in sheets of five plus one label. The top right and the top left stamps in the pane show parts of the marginal design.

Nos. 243-246 are airmail.

Nos. 237-245 exist imperf. Value, set $15.

Nos. 237-245 exist in deluxe sheets of one. Value, $4.75 each.

Nos. 243-245 exist in sheetlets of five overprinted "APOLLO 8 - XMAS TRIP AROUND THE MOON 25.12.68." This overprint spans the entire miniature sheet. Values for miniature sheets of No. 243 perf. overprinted, $15, imperf., $25; No. 244 perf. overprinted, $20, imperf., $35; No. 245 perf. overprinted, $25, imperf., $40. No. 246 was similarly overprinted. Value, $22.50.

Paintings of Composers, Frederic Chopin, by Eugene Delacroix — A26

Designs: 50d, Hector Berlioz, by Gustave Courbet. 75d, Richard Strauss, by Max Liebermann. 1.50rl, Wolfgang Mozart, by Raoul Dufy. 2.50rl, Giuseppe Verdi, by Giovanni Boldini.

**1969, Jan. 5 Litho. *Perf. 11¼***

| | | | | |
|---|---|---|---|---|
| **247** | A26 | 25d shown | .25 | .25 |
| **248** | A26 | 50d multi | .45 | .25 |
| **249** | A26 | 75d multi | .65 | .25 |
| **250** | A26 | 1.50rl multi | 1.30 | .25 |
| **251** | A26 | 2.50rl multi | 2.40 | .25 |
| | | *Nos. 247-251 (5)* | 5.05 | 1.25 |

Nos. 247-251 were issued in panes of six.

Nos. 247-251 exist imperf. Value, set $6. And as deluxe sheets of one. Value, set $25.

Scenes from Operas, Othello, by Giuseppe Verdi — A27

Designs: 40d, Faust, by Charles Gounod. 60d, Aida, by Giuseppe Verdi. 80d, Madame Butterfly, by Giacomo Puccini. 1rl, Lohengrin, by Richard Wagner. 2rl and 10rl, Abduction of the Seraglio, by Wolfgang Mozart.

**1969, Feb. 5 Litho. *Perf. 11¼***

| | | | | |
|---|---|---|---|---|
| **252** | A27 | 20d shown | .25 | .25 |
| **253** | A27 | 40d multi | .50 | .30 |
| **254** | A27 | 60d multi | .75 | .45 |
| **255** | A27 | 80d multi | 1.00 | .55 |
| **256** | A27 | 1rl multi | 1.25 | .60 |
| **257** | A27 | 2rl multi | 2.25 | .75 |
| | | *Nos. 252-257 (6)* | 6.00 | 2.90 |

**Souvenir Sheet**

| | | | | |
|---|---|---|---|---|
| **258** | A27 | 10rl multi | *12.00* | — |

Nos. 252-257 were issued in panes of six.

Nos. 252-257 exist imperf. Value, set $7.50. Also issued as deluxe sheets of one, Value, set $17.50.

No. 258 exists imperf. Value, $13.

A miniature sheet of 4, depicting "The Four Seasons" by Abel Grimmer (1573-1619) exists both perforated and imperforate. The sheet has a face value of 10rl, printed in the selvage of the sheet. It is uncertain whether this sheet was legitimately issued and valid for postage. The editors are seeking additional information. Value perf., $9, imperf., $17.50.

Famous People and Scenes, Sheikh Ahmed Bin Majid and Ship — A28

Designs: 30d and No. 268, Charles de Gaulle and Europa emblem. 50d, Napoleon Bonaparte and Napoleon on a horse. 1.50rl, Vincent van Gogh with brushes and palette. Nos. 264 and 270, Lord Baden Powell and scout tents. Nos. 265 and 271, Pierre de Coubertin and columns. Nos. 266 and 272, Wernher von Braun with satellite and rocket. Nos. 267, 269 and 273, John Kennedy and United States Capitol building.

**1969, Feb. 5 Litho. *Perf. 12***

| | | | | |
|---|---|---|---|---|
| **260** | A28 | 20d shown | .25 | .25 |
| **261** | A28 | 30d multi | .25 | .25 |
| **262** | A28 | 50d multi | .40 | .25 |
| **263** | A28 | 1.50rl multi | .90 | .25 |
| **264** | A28 | 2rl multi | 1.50 | .25 |
| **265** | A28 | 3rl multi | 1.75 | .25 |
| **266** | A28 | 4rl multi | 2.50 | .25 |
| **267** | A28 | 5rl multi | 3.00 | .25 |
| | | *Nos. 260-267 (8)* | 10.55 | 2.00 |

**Souvenir Sheets**

| | | | | |
|---|---|---|---|---|
| **268** | A28 | 10rl multi | 7.50 | — |
| **269** | A28 | 10rl multi | 7.50 | — |

**Embossed on Foil Coated Paper**

***Perf. 8***

| | | | | |
|---|---|---|---|---|
| **270** | A28 | 2rl gold | 10.00 | — |
| **271** | A28 | 3rl gold | 10.00 | — |
| **272** | A28 | 4rl gold | 10.00 | — |
| **273** | A28 | 5rl gold | 10.00 | — |
| | | *Nos. 270-273 (4)* | 40.00 | |

Nos 263-273 are airmail.

Nos. 260-267 exist imperf. Value, set *$50.* Also exists in deluxe sheets of one. Value, set *$125.*

Nos. 268-269 exist imperf. Value, set *$50.*

Nos. 270-273 exist imperf. Value, $10 each. Also exists in imperf. sheets of one. Value, $20 each.

For overprint see No. C38.

United States No. 1332b — A29

Designs: 25d, Japan No. B28. 35d, Germany No. 988. 40d, Greece No. 670. 50d, United Nations No. 29. 60d, Mali No. C31. 70d, Belgium No. 706. 1rl, France No. 1150. 2rl, Monaco No. 596. 3rl, San Marino No. 653. Nos. 284 and 289, Vatican No. 397. Nos. 285 and 290, Mexico No. 966.

No. 286 as No. 274 in gold.

**1969, Feb. 20 Litho. *Perf. 11***

| | | | | |
|---|---|---|---|---|
| **274** | A29 | Pair, #a.-b. | .25 | .25 |
| *a.-b.* | | 10d either single | .25 | .25 |
| **275** | A29 | 25d multi | .25 | .25 |
| **276** | A29 | 35d multi | .25 | .25 |
| **277** | A29 | 40d multi | .25 | .25 |
| **278** | A29 | 50d multi | .25 | .25 |
| **279** | A29 | 60d multi | .25 | .25 |
| **280** | A29 | 70d multi | .25 | .25 |

***Perf. 11¼***

| | | | | |
|---|---|---|---|---|
| **281** | A29 | 1rl multi | .35 | .25 |
| **282** | A29 | 2rl multi | .65 | .30 |
| **283** | A29 | 3rl multi | .95 | .35 |
| **284** | A29 | 5rl multi | 1.60 | .50 |
| **285** | A29 | 5rl multi | 1.60 | .50 |
| *a.* | | Souvenir sheet of 2, #284-285 | 2.50 | 1.00 |
| | | *Nos. 274-285 (12)* | 6.90 | 3.65 |

**Embossed on Foil Coated Paper**

***Perf. 7½***

| | | | | |
|---|---|---|---|---|
| **286** | A29 | Pair, #a.-b. | 14.00 | — |
| *c.* | | Sheet of 2, imperf. | 20.00 | — |
| *d.* | | With ovpt. "...APOLLO 13" on tab | 50.00 | — |
| *e.* | | As "c," with margin ovpt. "...APOLLO 13" | 50.00 | — |
| **287** | A29 | 2rl gold | 14.00 | — |
| *a.* | | Sheet of 1, imperf. | 20.00 | — |
| *b.* | | As "a," with margin ovpt. "...APOLLO 13..." | 50.00 | — |
| **288** | A29 | 3rl gold | 14.00 | — |
| *a.* | | Sheet of 1, imperf. | 20.00 | — |
| *b.* | | With ovpt. "...U.P.U." | 50.00 | 50.00 |
| *c.* | | As "a," with margin ovpt. "CHRISTMAS 1970" | 60.00 | — |
| *d.* | | As "a," with margin ovpt. "...U.P.U." | 60.00 | — |
| **289** | A29 | 5rl gold | 14.00 | — |
| *a.* | | Sheet of 1, imperf. | 20.00 | — |
| *b.* | | As "a," with margin ovpt. "CHRISTMAS 1970" | 60.00 | — |
| **290** | A29 | 5rl gold | 14.00 | — |
| *a.* | | Sheet of 1, imperf. | 20.00 | — |
| *b.* | | With ovpt. "MUNICH 1972" | 50.00 | — |
| *c.* | | As "a," with margin ovpt. "SUPPORT..." | 60.00 | — |
| *d.* | | As "a," with margin ovpt. "Transmission..." | 60.00 | — |
| | | *Nos. 286-290 (5)* | 70.00 | |

Nos. 281-285 and 287-290 are airmail and are in a larger format than the rest of the set.

Nos. 274-285 exist imperf. Value, set $14.

Nos. 286-290 exist imperf. Value, $14 each.

Nos. 275-285 exist in deluxe sheets of one, No. 274 exists as a deluxe sheet of two. Value, set $120.

No. 285a exists imperf. Value, $2.50.

Nos. 288b and 290b exist imperf. Value, *$50* each.

Soccer — A30

Designs: 2rl, Skiing. 3rl, Ice hockey. 4rl, Running.

10rl, Three gold medalists.

**1969, June 10 Litho. *Perf. 11***

| | | | | |
|---|---|---|---|---|
| **291** | A30 | 1rl shown | .50 | .25 |
| **292** | A30 | 2rl multi | .75 | .25 |
| **293** | A30 | 3rl multi | 1.25 | .25 |
| **294** | A30 | 4rl multi | 1.75 | .25 |
| | | *Nos. 291-294 (4)* | 4.25 | 1.00 |

**Souvenir Sheet**

| | | | | |
|---|---|---|---|---|
| **295** | A30 | 10rl multi | 4.00 | — |

Issued in panes of 10.

Nos. 291-294 exist imperf. Value, set $4.50. Also issued in imperf. deluxe sheets of one. Value, set $10.

No. 295 exists imperf. Value, $12.

Napoleon I Bonaparte, Bicentennial of Birth — A31

Designs: 1.75rl, Bonaparte, Premier Consul, on Horseback, by Antoine-Jean Gros. 2.75rl, Bonaparte, Franchissant les Alpes au Grand Saint-Bernard, by Jacques-Louis David. 3.75rl, Napoleon with the Coronation Dress, by Simon Gerard.

**1969, Aug. 15 Litho. *Perf. 11***

| | | | | |
|---|---|---|---|---|
| **296** | A31 | 75d shown | .35 | .25 |
| **297** | A31 | 1.75rl multi | .80 | .25 |
| **298** | A31 | 2.75rl multi | 1.25 | .25 |
| **299** | A31 | 3.75rl multi | 1.60 | .25 |
| | | *Nos. 296-299 (4)* | 4.00 | 1.00 |

Issued in panes of 16, composed of four strips of four.

No. 296 is airmail.

Nos. 296-299 exist imperf. Value, set $7. An imperf. deluxe sheet of four of Nos. 296-299 exists. Value, $20.

See No. C31.

**Nos. 230-232 Surcharged**

**Method and Perfs as Before**

**1969, Nov.**

| | | | | |
|---|---|---|---|---|
| **299A** | A22 | 5d on 50d | — | *950.* |
| **299B** | A22 | 5d on 1rl | — | *1,250.* |
| **299C** | A22 | 5d on 1.50rl | — | *800.* |

Paintings of Philippe de Champaigne (1602-74) — A32

Designs: Paintings: No. 300, Various paintings of Philippe de Champaigne (1602-74). No. 301, Various paintings of Andrea del Sarto (1486-1531). No. 302, Various paintings of Jean-Battista Tiepolo (1693-1770). No. 303, Various paintings of Barolome Esteban Murillo (1617-82). No. 304, Various paintings of Paul Gauguin (1848-1903). No. 305, Various paintings of Titian (1488-1576).

No. 306, Le Reve D'Elie, by Philippe de Champaigne. No. 307, La Madone des Harpies, by Andrea del Sarto. No. 308, La Crocifissione, by Jean-Battista Tiepelo. No. 309, Rebecca et Elieze, by Barolome Esteban Murillo. No. 310, Nafea Foa Ipoipo, by Paul Gauguin. No. 311, La Vierge Au Lapin, by Titian.

**1970, Jan. 2 Litho. *Perf. 14½***

| | | | | |
|---|---|---|---|---|
| **300** | A32 | Horiz. strip of 3, #a.-c. | 2.00 | .75 |
| *a.* | | 50d multi | .50 | .25 |
| *b.* | | 3rl multi | .50 | .25 |
| *c.* | | 3.50rl multi | .50 | .25 |
| **301** | A32 | Horiz. strip of 3, #a.-c. | 2.00 | .75 |
| *a.* | | 50d multi | .50 | .25 |
| *b.* | | 3rl multi | .50 | .25 |
| *c.* | | 3.50rl multi | .50 | .25 |
| **302** | A32 | Horiz. strip of 3, #a.-c. | 2.00 | .75 |
| *a.* | | 50d multi | .50 | .25 |
| *b.* | | 3rl multi | .50 | .25 |
| *c.* | | 3.50rl multi | .50 | .25 |
| **303** | A32 | Horiz. strip of 3, #a.-c. | 2.00 | .75 |
| *a.* | | 50d multi | .50 | .25 |
| *b.* | | 3rl multi | .50 | .25 |
| *c.* | | 3.50rl multi | .50 | .25 |
| **304** | A32 | Horiz. strip of 3, #a.-c. | 2.00 | .75 |
| *a.* | | 50d multi | .50 | .25 |
| *b.* | | 3rl multi | .50 | .25 |
| *c.* | | 3.50rl multi | .50 | .25 |
| **305** | A32 | Horiz. strip of 3, #a.-c. | 2.00 | .75 |
| *a.* | | 50d multi | .50 | .25 |
| *b.* | | 3rl multi | .50 | .25 |
| *c.* | | 3.50rl multi | .50 | .25 |
| | | *Nos. 300-305 (6)* | 12.00 | 4.50 |

**Souvenir Sheets**

| | | | | |
|---|---|---|---|---|
| **306** | A32 | 10rl multi | 3.50 | 2.25 |
| **307** | A32 | 10rl multi | 3.50 | 2.25 |
| **308** | A32 | 10rl multi | 3.50 | 2.25 |
| **309** | A32 | 10rl multi | 3.50 | 2.25 |
| **310** | A32 | 10rl multi | 3.50 | 2.25 |
| **311** | A32 | 10rl multi | 3.50 | 2.25 |
| | | *Nos. 306-311 (6)* | 21.00 | 13.50 |

Nos. 300-305 we printed in sheets of 12.

The central stamp of Nos. 303 and 311 is inscribed "CHRISTMAS 1969." The central stamp of Nos. 300 and 308 is inscribed "EASTER 1970."

Nos. 300-305 exist imperf. Value, $3 each. Nos. 306-311 exist imperf. Value, $4 each.

Nos. 301-305 exist in imperf. deluxe sheets of 3. Value, $12 each. It is likely that No. 300 also exists in that format. The editors would like to examine any examples.

**No. 208 Overprinted**

**1970, May? *Perf. 11¼***

| | | | | |
|---|---|---|---|---|
| **312** | A20 | 2rl multi | *4.50* | *4.50* |
| *a.* | | Imperf. sheet of 3, #207, 209, 312 | *8.00* | — |

Printed in panes of six.

No. 312 exists imperf. Value, *$8*. No. 312a exists perforated.

No. 312 and 312a exist with the overprint inverted, "29th may" on right. Value, *$15* and *$20*, respectively. This was an intentionally created variety, presumably with a limited print run.

Great Britain Pavilion — A33

Tower of the Sun, Globe and Emblem, Japan No. B34 — A34

Designs: 50d, Japan-Midori-Kan "Astrorama." 55d, Cherry Blossoms, Japan No. B35. 60d, Japan Tower of the Sun and Saudi Arabia pavilion. 65d, Globe and cherry blossoms, Japan Nos. 1024, and 1023. 70d, Federal Republic of Germany pavilion. 75d, The Irises, Japan No. 1025. 80d, France pavilion. 85d, Winter landscape, Japan No. 984, vert. 90d, Japan Gas Association. 95d, Buddah Fugen, Japan No. 953, vert. 1.60rl, United States of America pavilion. 1.65rl, Ichikawa Ebizo, Japan No. 630, vert. 1.85rl, Girl with flute, Japan No. 619, vert. 2rl, Fiji Group, Japan Pavilion.

5rl, Japan Pavilion. 10rl, Japan No. 931.

**1970, June 18 Litho. *Perf. 11¼***

| | | | | |
|---|---|---|---|---|
| **313** | A33 | 40d shown | .25 | .25 |
| **314** | A34 | 45d shown | .25 | .25 |
| **315** | A33 | 50d multi | .25 | .25 |
| **316** | A34 | 55d multi | .40 | .25 |
| **317** | A33 | 60d multi | .40 | .25 |
| **318** | A34 | 65d multi | .40 | .25 |
| **319** | A33 | 70d multi | .50 | .25 |
| **320** | A34 | 75d multi | .50 | .25 |
| **321** | A33 | 80d multi | .50 | .25 |
| **322** | A34 | 85d multi | .55 | .25 |
| **323** | A33 | 90d multi | .60 | .25 |
| **324** | A34 | 95d multi | .60 | .25 |
| **325** | A33 | 1.60rl multi | 1.10 | .25 |
| **326** | A34 | 1.65rl multi | 1.10 | .25 |
| **327** | A34 | 1.85rl multi | 1.20 | .25 |
| **328** | A33 | 2rl multi | 1.25 | .25 |
| | | *Nos. 313-328 (16)* | 9.85 | 4.00 |

**Souvenir Sheets**

| | | | | |
|---|---|---|---|---|
| **329** | A33 | 5rl multi | 7.00 | 1.50 |
| **330** | A34 | 10rl multi | 7.00 | 1.50 |

Issued in panes of six for the World Exhibition EXPO '70 Osaka, Japan.

Nos. 321-330 are airmail.

Nos. 313-328 exist imperf. Value, set $16.

Nos. 329-330 exist imperf. Value, $9 each.

Iris and Birds, by Harunobu Sazuki (1724-70) — A35

Designs: Various Japanese paintings. 55d, Snow, Moon, and Blossoms, by Katsukawa Shunsho (1726-92). 65d, Spring, by Sakai Hoitsu (1761-1828). 75d, Flowering Grasses, by Tatebayashi Kagei. 85d, Ivy-bound Lane, by Fukae Roshu (1699-1755). 95d, Two Beauties, by Katsushika Hokusai (1760-1849). 1.50rl, Spring, by Sakai Hoitsu. 1.75rl, Cock and Hen, by Ito Jakuchu (1713-1800).

5rl, Palm and Children, by Maruyama Ohkyo (1733-95).

**1970, June 18 Litho. *Perf. 14***

| | | | | |
|---|---|---|---|---|
| **331** | A35 | 25d shown | .25 | .25 |
| **332** | A35 | 55d multi | .40 | .25 |
| **333** | A35 | 65d multi | .55 | .25 |
| **334** | A35 | 75d multi | .65 | .25 |
| **335** | A35 | 85d multi | .75 | .25 |
| **336** | A35 | 95d multi | 1.00 | .25 |
| **337** | A35 | 1.50rl multi | 1.40 | .25 |
| **338** | A35 | 1.75rl multi | 2.00 | .25 |
| | | *Nos. 331-338 (8)* | 7.00 | 2.00 |

**Souvenir Sheet**

***Simulated Perfs***

| | | | | |
|---|---|---|---|---|
| **339** | A35 | 5rl multi | 4.00 | 1.25 |

Issued in panes of 10 for the World Exhibition EXPO '70 Osaka, Japan.

Nos. 331, 335-339 are airmail.

Nos. 331-338 exist imperf. Value, set $9. No. 339 exists imperf. Value, *$5.50*.

Nos. 331-338 exist as imperf. deluxe sheets of one, with a white background. Value, *$5* each. Also exists with a yellow background. Value, *$8* each.

Sapporo Olympics 1972, Ice Hockey — A36

**Embossed on Foil Coated Paper**

**1970, June 30 *Perf. 8***

| | | | | |
|---|---|---|---|---|
| **340** | A36 | 3rl gold | *10.00* | — |

No. 340 exists imperf. and in an imperf sheet of one. Values, *$10* and *$12*, respectively.

Stations of the Cross, Jesus Condemned — A37

Designs: a, 10d, Station 1, Jesus condemned b, 20d, Station 2, Jesus carries the cross. c, 30d, Station 3, Jesus falls carrying the cross. d, 40d, Station 4, Jesus carrying the cross, meets Mary. e, 50d, Station 5, Simon of Cyrene helps Jesus carry the cross. f, 60d, Station 6, Veronica wipes the face of Jesus. g, 70d, Station 7, Jesus falls carrying the cross. h, 80d, Station 8, Jesus carrying the cross meets the women of Jerusalem. i, 1rl, Station 9, Jesus falls carrying the cross. j, 1.50rl, Station 10, Jesus' clothes are removed. k, 2rl, Station 11, Jesus is nailed to the cross. l, 2.50rl, Station 12, Jesus dies on the cross. m, 3rl, Station 13, Jesus' body is taken down. n, 3.50rl, Station 14, Jesus is laid in the tomb.

**1970, Aug. 5 Photo. *Perf. 13½***

| | | | | |
|---|---|---|---|---|
| **341** | | Sheet of 14 + label | *40.00* | *5.00* |
| *a.-n.* | A37 | any single | 1.40 | .25 |

Easter.

No. 341 exists imperf. Value, *$75*.

The Life of Jesus Christ — A38

Designs: Paintings of the life of Jesus —5d, Jesus in the Temple, by Duccio di Buoninsegna. 10d, Calling of Peter and Andrew, by Duccio di Buoninsegna. 25d, Sinite Parvulos, by Ludwig Vogel. 50d, Christ at the Sea of Galilee, Jacopo Tintoretto. 1rl, Entry into Jerusalem, by Giotto di Bondone. 2rl, The Kiss of Judas, by Giotto di Bondone. 5rl, The Ascent to Calvary, by Jacopo Tintoretto.

10rl, Adoration of the Magi, by Gentile da Fabriano.

**1970, Nov. 6 Litho. *Perf. 13***

| | | | | |
|---|---|---|---|---|
| **342** | A38 | 5d shown | .25 | .25 |
| **343** | A38 | 10d multi | .25 | .25 |
| **344** | A38 | 25d multi | .25 | .25 |
| **345** | A38 | 50d multi | .30 | .25 |
| **346** | A38 | 1rl multi | .70 | .25 |
| **347** | A38 | 2rl multi | 1.25 | .25 |
| **348** | A38 | 5rl multi | 3.00 | .25 |
| | | *Nos. 342-348 (7)* | 6.00 | 1.75 |

**Souvenir Sheet**

| | | | | |
|---|---|---|---|---|
| **349** | A38 | 10rl multi | 6.00 | 2.50 |

Nos. 342-348 exist imperf. Value, set $9. No. 349 exists imperf. Value, $12.

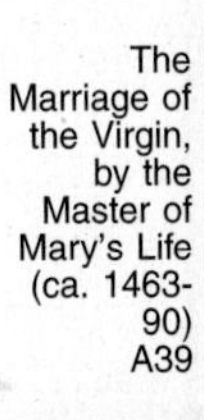

The Marriage of the Virgin, by the Master of Mary's Life (ca. 1463-90) A39

Designs: Paintings of the Life of the Virgin Mary. 15d, The Annunciation, by Fra Angelico. 30d, The Visitation, by the Master of Mary's Life. 60d, The Nativity, by Sandro Botticelli. 75d, Presentation at the Temple, by Hans Memling. 3rl, Madonna and Child Adored by Angels, by the Master of Moulins. 4rl, The Canigiani Madonna, by Raphael.

10rl, Madonna and Child.

**1970, Dec. 5 Litho. *Perf. 13½***

| | | | | |
|---|---|---|---|---|
| **350** | A39 | 10d shown | .25 | .25 |
| **351** | A39 | 15d multi | .25 | .25 |
| **352** | A39 | 30d multi | .25 | .25 |
| **353** | A39 | 60d multi | .60 | .25 |
| **354** | A39 | 75d multi | .75 | .25 |
| **355** | A39 | 3rl multi | 3.00 | .25 |
| **356** | A39 | 4rl multi | 4.00 | .25 |
| | | *Nos. 350-356 (7)* | 9.10 | 1.75 |

**Souvenir Sheet**

| | | | | |
|---|---|---|---|---|
| **357** | A39 | 10rl multi | 5.50 | 1.90 |

No. 357 exists imperf. Value, $8.

---

## AIR POST STAMPS

Wembley Stadium — AP1

Designs: 2r, Goalie diving for ball and another player. 3r, Two players, one dribbling ball. 4r, Presentaion of the Jules Rimet Cup to Bobby Moore by Queen Elizabeth II.

**Perf. 12¼x11¼**

**1966, Dec. 30 Unwmk. Photo.**

| | | | | |
|---|---|---|---|---|
| **C1** | AP1 | 1rl shown | .60 | .25 |
| **C2** | AP1 | 2rl multi | 1.00 | .25 |
| **C3** | AP1 | 3rl multi | 1.50 | .25 |
| **C4** | AP1 | 4rl multi | 2.00 | .25 |
| | | *Nos. C1-C4 (4)* | 5.10 | 1.00 |

Nos. C1-C4 exist imperf. Value, set $7.50.

Nos. C1 and C4 exist as imperf. sheets of one. Value, $3.50 each.

The Magic Garden — AP2

Designs: 70d, Aladdin and the Genie, vert. 1rl, Girl riding a flying black horse. 2rl, Sinbad carried by an eagle, vert. 3rl, Ali Baba surrounded by treasure.

**1967, Feb 1 Litho. *Perf. 12***

| | | | | |
|---|---|---|---|---|
| **C5** | AP2 | 30d shown | .25 | .25 |
| **C6** | AP2 | 70d multi | .25 | .25 |
| **C7** | AP2 | 1rl multi | .45 | .25 |
| **C8** | AP2 | 2rl multi | .90 | .25 |
| **C9** | AP2 | 3rl multi | 1.20 | .25 |
| | | *Nos. C5-C9 (5)* | 3.05 | 1.25 |

Nos. C5-C9 exist imperf. Value, set $5.50.

No. C9 exists as an imperf. sheet of one. Value, $4.

Arab Saddling His Horse, by Eugene Delacroix AP3

Designs: 70d, Pierrot and Harlequin, by Paul Cezanne. 1rl, The Fifer, by Edouard Manet. 2rl, Fishing Boats on the Beach at Saites-Maries, by Vincent van Gogh, horiz. 3rl, A Young Man with a Glove, by Frans Hals. 5rl, Vase of Flowers, by Jean Baptiste Simeon Chardin. Hendrickje Stoffels in the Window, by Rembrandt.

**1967 Litho. *Perf. 12***

| | | | | |
|---|---|---|---|---|
| **C10** | AP3 | 60d shown | .30 | .25 |
| **C11** | AP3 | 70d multi | .30 | .25 |
| *a.* | | Sheet of 2, #C10-C11, imperf. | 9.50 | — |
| **C12** | AP3 | 1rl multi | .50 | .25 |
| **C13** | AP3 | 2rl multi | .75 | .25 |
| **C14** | AP3 | 3rl multi | 1.25 | .25 |
| **C15** | AP3 | 5rl multi | 2.25 | .50 |
| **C16** | AP3 | 10rl multi | 4.25 | 1.00 |
| | | *Nos. C10-C16 (7)* | 9.60 | 2.75 |

Issue Dates: Nos. C10-C13, 5/30; Nos C14-C16, 9/10.

Nos. C10-C16 exist imperf. Value, set *$12.*

Weightlifting — AP4

Designs: Mexican artifacts and athlete. 2rl, Discus throw. 3rl, Shot put. Nos. C20-C21, Running.

**1968, Aug. 31 Litho. *Perf. 11¼***

| | | | | |
|---|---|---|---|---|
| **C17** | AP4 | 1rl shown | .70 | .25 |
| **C18** | AP4 | 2rl multi | 1.40 | .25 |
| **C19** | AP4 | 3rl multi | 2.00 | .25 |
| **C20** | AP4 | 4rl multi | 2.90 | .25 |
| | | *Nos. C17-C20 (4)* | 7.00 | 1.00 |

**Embossed on Foil Coated Paper**

| | | | | |
|---|---|---|---|---|
| **C21** | AP4 | 4rl gold | 12.50 | — |

Nos. C17-C20 exist imperf. Value, set $8.

No. C21 exists imperf. Value, $12.50.

Nos. C17-C20 exist in deluxe sheets of one. Value, $6.50 each.

No. C21 exists in an imperf. sheet of one. Value, $19. Additionally the imperf. sheet of one exists with green overprint "F.I.S./1970/VALGARDENA" in the lower selvage. Value, $35.

Grenoble Olympic Champions, Peggy Flemming with President Lyndon B. Johnson — AP5

Design: 5rl, Jean-Claude Killy (France)

**1968, Aug 31 Litho. *Perf. 11¼***

| | | | | |
|---|---|---|---|---|
| **C22** | AP5 | 2rl shown | .75 | .25 |
| **C23** | AP5 | 5rl multi | 1.15 | .25 |
| *a.* | | Souvenir sheet of 2, #C22-C23 | 3.00 | 1.25 |

Issued in panes of six.

Nos. C22-C23 exist imperf. Value, set *$2.50*. No. C23a exists imperf. Value, *$3*.

Imperf. deluxe sheets of one, and of the pair exist. Values, *$10* and *$6* respectively.

Reverse of United States 1964 50-Cent Coin — AP6

Designs: No. C24-C25, shown. Nos. C26-C27, Obverse of United States 1964 50-cent coin showing John Kennedy.

**Embossed on Foil Coated Paper**

**1968, Nov. 22 *Imperf.***

| | | | | |
|---|---|---|---|---|
| **C24** | AP6 | 2rl black & silver | 6.00 | 6.00 |
| **C25** | AP6 | 2rl gold | 6.00 | 6.00 |
| **C26** | AP6 | 3rl black & silver | 9.00 | 9.00 |
| **C27** | AP6 | 3rl gold | 9.00 | 9.00 |
| | | *Nos. C24-C27 (4)* | 30.00 | 30.00 |

Nos. C24-C27 exist in miniature sheets of one. Value, set $65.

Nos. C25 and C27 were not available on the day of issue, but were made available later. Miniature sheets and singles exist with nine different colored frames in all four designs, totaling 36 singles and 36 miniature sheets. Only 500 sets were issued and came in a vinyl faux leather wallet with 18 stamps. Value for either set of 18 singles, $110. Value for either set of 18 miniature sheets, $200.

Soviet Space Program — AP7

Designs: 2.50rl, Apollo Program. 3.50rl, French Program. 4.50rl, Moonlanding. 10rl, Apollo 11.

**1969, June 19 Litho. *Perf. 11***

| | | | | |
|---|---|---|---|---|
| **C28** | AP7 | 1.50rl shown | .50 | .25 |
| **C29** | AP7 | 2.50rl multi | .75 | .25 |
| **C30** | AP7 | 3.50rl multi | 1.00 | .25 |
| **C31** | AP7 | 4.50rl multi | 1.25 | .25 |
| | | *Nos. C28-C31 (4)* | 3.50 | 1.00 |

**Souvenir Sheet**

| | | | | |
|---|---|---|---|---|
| **C32** | AP7 | 10rl multi | 6.50 | — |

Issued in panes of 10.

Nos. C28-C31 exist imperf. Value, set $7.75. Also exists in imperf. deluxe sheets of one. Value, set $20.

No. C32 exists imperf. Value, $10.

See no. C50.

Coronation of Napoleon — AP8

Napoleon Bonaparte, Bicentennial of Birth — AP9

**1969, Aug. 15 Litho. *Perf. 11***

| | | | | |
|---|---|---|---|---|
| **C33** | AP8 | 10rl multi | 7.00 | 3.00 |

**Embossed on Foil Coated Paper**

***Perf. 7½***

| | | | | |
|---|---|---|---|---|
| **C34** | AP8 | 10rl gold | *10.00* | — |

***Perf. 11***

| | | | | |
|---|---|---|---|---|
| **C35** | AP9 | 10rl gold | *10.00* | — |

No. C33 exists imperf. Value, $9. Nos. C34-C35 exist imperf. and in imperf sheets of one. Value, $7.50 each and $15 each, respectively.

See Nos. 296-299.

Apollo 10 — AP10

Design: C37, Apollo 11.

**1969, Aug. 15 Litho. *Perf. 11***

| | | | | |
|---|---|---|---|---|
| **C36** | | Strip of 4, #a.-d. | 6.00 | 1.00 |
| *a.* | AP10 | 2rl multi | 1.00 | .25 |
| *b.* | AP10 | 3rl multi | 1.00 | .25 |
| *c.* | AP10 | 4rl multi | 1.00 | .25 |
| *d.* | AP10 | 5rl multi | 1.00 | .25 |
| **C37** | | Strip of 4, #a.-d. | 6.00 | 1.00 |
| *a.* | AP10 | 2.50rl multi | 1.00 | .25 |
| *b.* | AP10 | 3.50rl multi | 1.00 | .25 |
| *c.* | AP10 | 4.50rl multi | 1.00 | .25 |
| *d.* | AP10 | 5.50rl multi | 1.00 | .25 |

**Overprint on No. 269**

**Souvenir Sheet**

***Perf. 12***

| | | | | |
|---|---|---|---|---|
| **C38** | A28 | 10rl multi | 7.00 | — |

Issued in sheets of 16 and 20.

Nos. C36-C37 exist imperf. Value, set $15. No. C38 exists imperf. Value, $35.

Nos. C36 and C37 were each produced in imperf. deluxe sheets of four. Value, set $32.

No. C38 exists with intentionally created inverted overprints. Value, $60.

Apollo 10 — AP11

Designs: No. C40, Apollo 11. No. C41 and C43, Apollo 11, lunar research. No. C42 and C44, Apollo 12, inspection of Surveyor, vert.

**Souvenir Sheets**

**1969, Aug. 15 Litho. *Perf. 11***

| | | | | |
|---|---|---|---|---|
| **C39** | AP11 | 10rl shown | 6.00 | 2.00 |
| **C40** | AP11 | 10rl multi | 6.00 | 2.00 |
| **C41** | AP11 | 10rl multi | 6.00 | 2.00 |
| **C42** | AP11 | 10rl multi | 6.00 | 2.00 |

**Embossed on Foil Coated Paper**

***Perf. 11***

| | | | | |
|---|---|---|---|---|
| **C43** | AP11 | 10rl gold | 12.00 | — |

***Perf. 14½***

| | | | | |
|---|---|---|---|---|
| **C44** | AP11 | 10rl gold | 12.00 | — |

Nos. C39-C41 exist imperf. Value, set $7.50.

Nos. C43-C44 exist imperf. Value, set $12. They also exist as miniature sheets of 1. Value, set $20.

Designs: No. C45, As No. C39, with President Kennedy's mouth open. No. C46, As No. C39, with President Kennedy's mouth closed. No. C47, As No. C40.

**Embossed on Foil Coated Paper**

**1969, Aug. 30 *Perf. 8***

| | | | | |
|---|---|---|---|---|
| **C45** | AP11 | 10rl gold | *30.00* | — |
| **C46** | AP11 | 10rl gold | *10.00* | — |
| **C47** | AP11 | 10rl gold | *10.00* | — |

No. C45 was withdrawn from sale due to design flaws.

No. C45 exists imperf. Value, $35. No. C45 exists as a deluxe sheet of one with red inscriptions. Value, $55.

Nos. C46-C47 exist imperf. Value, $12 each. Nos. C46-C47 exist as deluxe sheets of one with red or black inscriptions. Value, $22.50 and $85 each, respectively.

Michael Collins, Apollo 11 — AP12

Designs: 3.25rl, Neil Armstrong. 4.25rl, Edward Aldrin. 5.25rl, Nixon and three Apollo 11 astronauts.

**1969, Aug. 15 Litho. *Perf. 11***

| | | | |
|---|---|---|---|
| **C48** | Strip of 4, #a.-d. | 5.00 | 1.50 |
| *a.* | AP12 2.25rl multi | 1.00 | .25 |
| *b.* | AP12 3.25rl multi | 1.00 | .25 |
| *c.* | AP12 4.25rl multi | 1.00 | .25 |
| *d.* | AP12 5.25rl multi | 1.00 | .25 |

Issued in sheets of 16 and 20.
No. C48 exists imperf. Value, $8. No. C48 exists in imperf. deluxe sheets of four, and as imperf deluxe sheets of one of each value with a white background, and with a pink background.
On No. C48c Edwin Aldrin is misspelled Edward Aldrin.

Apollo 12 — AP13

Designs: 60d, Command center. 2.60rl, Richard F. Gordon Jr. 3.60rl, Charles Conrad, Jr. 4.60rl, Alan L. Bean. 5.60rl, John F. Kennedy, Wernher von Braun, and rocket.

**1969, Aug. Litho. *Perf. 11***

| | | | |
|---|---|---|---|
| **C49** | AP13 Sheet of 5, #a.-e., + 4 labels | 9.50 | 4.25 |
| *a.* | 60d multi | 1.50 | .50 |
| *b.* | 2.60rl multi | 1.50 | .50 |
| *c.* | 3.60rl multi | 1.50 | .50 |
| *d.* | 4.60rl multi | 1.50 | .50 |
| *e.* | 5.60rl multi | 1.50 | .50 |

No. C49 exists imperf. Value, $15.
Nos. C49b-C49e exist in deluxe sheets of one, both perf and imperf. Value, *$65.* No. C49a exists in a deluxe sheet of one plus two labels, both perf. and imperf. Value, *$65.*
See No. C56.

**Type of Soviet Space Progam**
**Embossed on Foil Coated Paper**

**1969, Sept. *Perf. 8***

| | | | |
|---|---|---|---|
| **C50** | AP7 4.50rl gold | 15.00 | — |

No. C50 exists imperf. Value, *$15.* Also exists as an imperf. sheet of one. Value, *$20.*

1968 Mexico Olympics, Mask — AP14

Design: 3rl, Mask with red background.

**1969, Dec. Litho. *Perf. 11¼***

| | | | |
|---|---|---|---|
| **C51** | AP14 2rl shown | .75 | .25 |
| **C52** | AP14 3rl multi | 2.00 | .25 |
| *a.* | Souvenir sheet of 2, #C51-C52 | 3.50 | 1.50 |

Issued in panes of six.
Nos. C51-C52 exist imperf. Value, set $3. No. C52a exists imperf. Value, $3.50.
Imperf. deluxe sheets of one, and of the pair exist. Values, $10 and $6, respectively.

**Type of 1969**

Designs: Apollo 11. No. C53, Apollo 11, eagle and moon. No. C54, Michael Collins, Niel Armstrong and Edwin "Buzz" Aldrin. No. C55, Lunar module and moon.

**Embossed on Foil Coated Paper**

**1970, Jan. 20 *Perf. 7½***

| | | | |
|---|---|---|---|
| **C53** | AP9 10rl gold | 12.00 | — |
| **C54** | AP9 10rl gold | 12.00 | — |
| **C55** | AP9 10rl gold | 12.00 | — |

Nos. C53-C55 exist imperf. Value, $17 each.
Nos. C53-C55 exist as imperf. sheets of one. Value, $25 each.

**Type of Apollo XII**
**Embossed on Foil Coated Paper**

**1970, Feb. 24 *Perf. 14½***

| | | | |
|---|---|---|---|
| **C56** | AP13 5.60rl gold | 12.00 | — |

No. C56 exists imperf, and as an imperf sheet of one. Values, $12 and $15, respectively.

AP15

1970 World Cup, Mexico — AP16

Designs: Various soccer scenes and artifacts. 1rl, red background. 2rl, olive background. 3rl, yellow background. 4rl, green background. 5rl, blue background. 6rl, pink background.

**1970, Mar. 10 Litho. *Perf. 11***

| | | | |
|---|---|---|---|
| **C57** | Block of 6, #a.-f. | 8.00 | 2.25 |
| *a.* | AP15 1rl shown | 1.00 | .25 |
| *b.* | AP15 2rl multi | 1.00 | .25 |
| *c.* | AP15 3rl multi | 1.00 | .25 |
| *d.* | AP15 4rl multi | 1.00 | .25 |
| *e.* | AP15 5rl multi | 1.00 | .25 |
| *f.* | AP15 6rl multi | 1.00 | .25 |

**Souvenir Sheet**

| | | | |
|---|---|---|---|
| **C58** | AP16 10rl multi | 5.75 | 1.50 |

Printed in panes of 12 plus three labels.
No. C57 exists imperf. Value, $11. No. C58 exists imperf. Value, $7.
Nos. C57a-C57f exist in imperf deluxe sheets of one, with an image of a mask and a soccer ball in the margins. Value, $5 each.
For gold foil version see No. C63. For overprints see Nos. C65-C66.

1972 Sapporo Olympics, Downhill Skiing — AP17

Designs: 2rl, Ski jumping. 3rl. Speed skating. 4rl, Slalom skiing. 5rl, Figure skating. 6rl, Ice hockey.
10rl, Downhill skiing.

**1970, Mar. 10 Litho. *Perf. 11***

| | | | |
|---|---|---|---|
| **C59** | Block of 6, #a.-f. | 6.00 | 2.00 |
| *a.* | AP17 1rl shown | .80 | .25 |
| *b.* | AP17 2rl multi | .80 | .25 |
| *c.* | AP17 3rl multi | .80 | .25 |
| *d.* | AP17 4rl multi | .80 | .25 |
| *e.* | AP17 5rl multi | .80 | .25 |
| *f.* | AP17 6rl multi | .80 | .25 |

**Souvenir Sheet**

| | | | |
|---|---|---|---|
| **C60** | AP17 10rl multi | 5.00 | 1.50 |

Printed in panes of 12 plus three labels.
No. C59 exists imperf. Value, $9. No. C60 exists imperf. Value, $5.50.
Nos. C59a-C59f exist in imperf deluxe sheets of one. Value, $5 each.
No. C60 was also overprinted, both perf. and imperf. However the overprint is entirely in the selvage. Value, perf. *$6.* Value, imperf. *$7.*
No. C60 contains one 38x50½.
See No. C64. For overprints see No. C67.

1972 Munich Olympics, Hurdling — AP18

Designs: 2rl, Diving. 3rl, Running. 4rl, High jump. 5rl, Riding. 6rl, Gymnastics.
10rl, Stadium.

**1970, Mar. 10 Litho. *Perf. 11***

| | | | |
|---|---|---|---|
| **C61** | Block of 6, #a.-f. | 7.00 | 3.00 |
| *a.* | AP18 1rl shown | .90 | .35 |
| *b.* | AP18 2rl multi | .90 | .35 |
| *c.* | AP18 3rl multi | .90 | .35 |
| *d.* | AP18 4rl multi | .90 | .35 |
| *e.* | AP18 5rl multi | .90 | .35 |
| *f.* | AP18 6rl multi | .90 | .35 |

**Souvenir Sheet**

| | | | |
|---|---|---|---|
| **C62** | AP18 10rl multi | 5.00 | 1.50 |

Printed in panes of 12 plus three labels.
No. C61 exists imperf. Value, $9. No. C62 exists imperf. Value, $6.
Nos. C61a-C61f exist in imperf deluxe sheets of one. Value, $5 each.
No. C62 contains one 38x50½.
See No. C64. For overprints see Nos. C68-C69.

**Types of 1969-70**

Designs: No. C63, as No. C58. No. C64, as No. C61d.

**Embossed on Foil Coated Paper**

**1970, June 6 *Perf. 13***

| | | | |
|---|---|---|---|
| **C63** | AP16 20rl gold | *7.00* | — |

**1970, July**

| | | | |
|---|---|---|---|
| **C64** | AP18 4rl gold | *8.00* | — |

Nos. C63-C64 exist imperf. Value, $8 each.
Nos. C63-C64 exist in imperf. sheets of one. Value, $10 and $12, respectively.

---

A 25rl and 30rl set of two was issued June 20, 1970, embossed in gold foil and rouletted, bearing the images of the Queen of Saba and a camel, and Winston Churchill and Sheikh Saqr Bin Mohammed Al Qasimi, respectively. The editors question the validity of this issue and would like more information.

---

**No. C57 Overprinted in Gold**

**1970, July Litho. *Perf. 11***

| | | | |
|---|---|---|---|
| **C65** | Block of 6, #a.-f. | 9.50 | — |
| *a* | AP15 1rl shown | 1.25 | — |
| *b.* | AP15 2rl multi | 1.25 | — |
| *c.* | AP15 3rl multi | 1.25 | — |
| *d.* | AP15 4rl multi | 1.25 | — |
| *e.* | AP15 5rl multi | 1.25 | — |
| *f.* | AP15 6rl multi | 1.25 | — |

**No. C58 Overprinted In Blue**

| | | | |
|---|---|---|---|
| **C66** | AP16 10rl multi | 6.50 | — |

Printed in panes of 12 plus three labels.
No. C65 exists imperf. Value, *$13.* No. C66 exists imperf. Value, *$8.50.*
Nos. C65a-C65f exist in imperf. deluxe sheets of one. Value, *$6* each.

**No. C59 Overprinted in Gold**

**1970, July Litho. *Perf. 11***

| | | | |
|---|---|---|---|
| **C67** | Block of 6, #a.-f. | 7.00 | — |
| *a.* | AP17 1rl shown | .90 | — |
| *b.* | AP17 2rl multi | .90 | — |
| *c.* | AP17 3rl multi | .90 | — |
| *d.* | AP17 4rl multi | .90 | — |
| *e.* | AP17 5rl multi | .90 | — |
| *f.* | AP17 6rl multi | .90 | — |

Printed in panes of 12 plus 3 labels.
No. C67 exists imperf. Value, *$12.*
Nos. C67a-C67f exist in imperf. deluxe sheets of one. Value, *$6* each.
See footnote after No. C60.

**Nos. C61-C62 Overprinted in Gold**

**1970, July Litho. *Perf. 11***

| | | | |
|---|---|---|---|
| **C68** | Block of 6, #a.-f. | 8.25 | — |
| *a.* | AP18 1rl shown | 1.10 | — |
| *b.* | AP18 2rl multi | 1.10 | — |
| *c.* | AP18 3rl multi | 1.10 | — |
| *d.* | AP18 4rl multi | 1.10 | — |
| *e.* | AP18 5rl multi | 1.10 | — |
| *f.* | AP18 6rl multi | 1.10 | — |

**Souvenir Sheet**

| | | | |
|---|---|---|---|
| **C69** | AP18 10rl multi | 6.00 | — |

Printed in panes of 12 plus three labels.
No. C68 exists imperf. Value, *$12.* No. C69 exists imperf. Value, *$7.*
Nos. C68a-C68f exist in imperf. deluxe sheets of one. Value, *$6.*

Apollo 12 — AP19

Designs: No. C71, Apollo 13: a, Apollo 13 struck by space debris. b, Nos. C82-C83, command module releasing lunar module. c, command module reentering atmosphere.

No. C72, Symphonie satellites: a, Diamant B, assembly. b, Nos. C84-C85, WIKA satellite. c, Diamant B rocket.

No. C73, Apollo 13: a, Apollo 13 orbiting the moon. b, Apollo 13 astronauts c, Apollo 13 water landing.

No. C74, a, Zond satellite orbitting moon. b, Mars probe and Mars. c, Mariner VII and Mars.

No. C75, a, Vladimir Komarov. b, Soyuz 1. c, Yuri Gagarin.

No. C76, Exploring Surveyor 3. No. C77, Command and lunar modules. No. C78, Intelsat IV. No. C79, Apollo 13 splashdown. No. C80, Mariner VII passes Mars. No. C81, Soyuz 4 and Soyuz 5 join.

**1970, July 22 Litho. *Perf. 14½***

**C70** AP19 Strip of 3, #a.-c. 6.00 .75
*a.* 1rl multi 1.00 .25
*b.* 2rl multi 1.00 .25
*c.* 4rl multi 1.00 .25
**C71** AP19 Strip of 3, #a.-c. 6.00 .75
*a.* 1rl multi 1.00 .25
*b.* 2rl multi 1.00 .25
*c.* 4rl multi 1.00 .25
**C72** AP19 Strip of 3, #a.-c. 6.00 .75
*a.* 1rl multi 1.00 .25
*b.* 2rl multi 1.00 .25
*c.* 4rl multi 1.00 .25
**C73** AP19 Strip of 3, #a.-c. 6.00 .75
*a.* 1rl multi 1.00 .25
*b.* 2rl multi 1.00 .25
*c.* 4rl multi 1.00 .25
**C74** AP19 Strip of 3, #a.-c. 6.00 .75
*a.* 1rl multi 1.00 .25
*b.* 2rl multi 1.00 .25
*c.* 4rl multi 1.00 .25
**C75** AP19 Strip of 3, #a.-c. 6.00 .75
*a.* 1rl multi 1.00 .25
*b.* 2rl multi 1.00 .25
*c.* 4rl multi 1.00 .25
*Nos. C70-C75 (6)* 36.00 4.50

**Souvenir Sheets**

**C76** AP19 10rl multi *16.50* *5.00*
**C77** AP19 10rl multi *16.50* *5.00*
**C78** AP19 10rl multi *16.50* *5.00*
**C79** AP19 10rl multi *16.50* *5.00*
**C80** AP19 10rl multi *16.50* *5.00*
**C81** AP19 10rl multi *16.50* *5.00*
*Nos. C76-C81 (6)* 99.00 30.00

**Embossed on Foil Coated Paper**

***Perf. 13***

**C82** AP19 2rl silver *15.00* —
**C83** AP19 2rl gold *15.00* —
**C84** AP19 2rl silver *15.00* —
**C85** AP19 2rl gold *15.00* —
*Nos. C82-C85 (4)* 60.00

Issued in panes of 12, in 4 strips of 3.

Nos. C70-C75 exist imperf. Value, set *$40*.

Nos. C76-C81 exist imperf. Value, *$25* each.

Nos. C70a-C75c exist as imperf. deluxe sheets of one. Value, *$150* for set of 18.

Nos. C82-C85 exist imperf. Value, *$15* each. Also exists in imperf. deluxe sheets of one. Value, *$25* each.

Napoleon Bonaparte — AP20

Designs: No. C86: a, Napoleon Bonaparte, portrait. b, Napoleon in Tilsit. c, Napoleon in Alexandria.

No. C87: a, Surrender of Madrid. b, Napoleon at the hospice of St. Bernard Pass. c, Napoleon visits the Louvre.

No. C88: a, Napoleon establishes the constitution of the Duchy of Warsaw. b, Napoleon after the Battle of Aspern. c, Napoleon receives the Ambassador of Persia.

No. C89: Louis XIV. a, Portrait as a boy. b, Framed portrait and musical instruments. c, Portrait by Henri Testelin.

No. C90: a, Queen Marie-Louise, portrait. b, Queen Marie-Louise in Compiegne. c, Josephine Bonaparte, portrait.

No. C91: Charles De Gaulle. a, Charles De Gaulle meeting Sir Winston Churchill. b, Charles De Gaulle, Heinrich Lubke and Konrad Adenauer. c, Charles De Gaulle and Dwight D. Eisenhower.

No. C92, Napoleon Meeting the King of Prussia at Tilsit, by Nicolas-Henri Tardieu. No. C93, Napoleon Proclaimed Emperor by Georges Rouget. No. C94, Napoleon Meets the Baron Vincent at Erfurt, by Sylvia Gosse. No. C95, Family of Divinites by Jean Nocret. No. C96, Arrival of Napoleon and Marie-Louise in Tuileries, by Etienne Barthelemy Garnier. No. C97, John F. Kennedy, Charles De Gaulle and Jackie Kennedy.

Nos. C98-C99, design as No. C86a. Nos. C100-C101, design as No. C91b.

**1970, July 22 Litho. *Perf. 14½***

**C86** AP20 Strip of 3, #a.-c. *6.00* *1.75*
*a.* 1rl multi *1.00* *.50*
*b.* 2rl multi *1.00* *.50*
*c.* 4rl multi *1.00* *.50*
**C87** AP20 Strip of 3, #a.-c. *6.00* *1.75*
*a.* 1rl multi *1.00* *.50*
*b.* 2rl multi *1.00* *.50*
*c.* 4rl multi *1.00* *.50*
**C88** AP20 Strip of 3, #a.-c. *6.00* *1.75*
*a.* 1rl multi *1.00* *.50*
*b.* 2rl multi *1.00* *.50*
*c.* 4rl multi *1.00* *.50*
**C89** AP20 Strip of 3, #a.-c. *6.00* *1.75*
*a.* 1rl multi *1.00* *.50*
*b.* 2rl multi *1.00* *.50*
*c.* 4rl multi *1.00* *.50*
**C90** AP20 Strip of 3, #a.-c. *6.00* *1.75*
*a.* 1rl multi *1.00* *.50*
*b.* 2rl multi *1.00* *.50*
*c.* 4rl multi *1.00* *.50*
**C91** AP20 Strip of 3, #a.-c. *6.00* *1.75*
*a.* 1rl multi *1.00* *.50*
*b.* 2rl multi *1.00* *.50*
*c.* 4rl multi *1.00* *.50*
*Nos. C86-C91 (6)* *36.00* *10.50*

**Souvenir Sheets**

**C92** AP20 10rl multi *16.50* *5.00*
**C93** AP20 10rl multi *16.50* *5.00*
**C94** AP20 10rl multi *16.50* *5.00*
**C95** AP20 10rl multi *16.50* *5.00*
**C96** AP20 10rl multi *16.50* *5.00*
**C97** AP20 10rl multi *16.50* *5.00*
*Nos. C92-C97 (6)* 99.00 30.00

**Embossed on Foil Coated Paper**

***Perf. 13***

**C98** AP20 2rl silver *15.00* —
**C99** AP20 2rl gold *15.00* —
**C100** AP20 2rl silver *15.00* —
**C101** AP20 2rl gold *15.00* —
*Nos. C98-C101 (4)* *60.00*

Issued in panes of 12, in four strips of three.

Nos. C86-C91 exist imperf. Nos. C92-C97 exist imperf. Value, *$20* each.

Nos. C86a-C91c exist as imperf. deluxe sheets of one.

Nos. C98-C101 exist imperf. Value, *$15* each. Also exists in imperf. deluxe sheets of one. Value, *$25* each. Nos. C100-C101 deluxe sheets exist with marginal inscription "AUSTERLITZ 1805." Value, *$50* each.

PHILYMPIA '70 London, Belgium No. 726 — AP21

Designs: No. C102: a, Belgium No. 726. b, Nicaragua No. C713. c, Panama No. C363. d, Romania No. 2160. e, United States No. C76. f, El Salvador No. C282. g, Ecuador No. 764E. h, Singapore No. 114. i, Paraguay No. 1240. j, Togo No. 733. k, Monaco No. 772. l, Vatican City No. 481. m, Monaco No. 773. n, Bulgaria No. 1842. o, Rwanda No. 130. p, Chile No. C294. q, Romania No. 2137. r, Romania No. 2177. s, Aden, Kathiri State of Hadhramaut unlisted stamp. t, Monaco No. 757.

No. C103, Musketeer and Cupid, by Pablo Picasso. No. C104, El Salvador No. C276. No. C105, Germany No. 901. No. C106, Togo No. 674.

Nos. C107-C108, design as No. C102e. Nos. C109-C110, design as No. C102o.

**1970, Sept. 30 Litho. *Perf. 11***

**C102** Sheet of 20, #a.-t. *30.00* *15.00*
*a.-d.* AP21 1rl any single *1.25* *.60*
*e.-h.* AP21 1.50rl any single *1.25* *.60*
*i.-l.* AP21 2.50rl any single *1.25* *.60*
*m.-p.* AP21 3rl any single *1.25* *.60*
*q.-t.* AP21 4rl any single *1.25* *.60*

**Souvenir Sheets**

**C103** AP21 10rl multi *27.50* *7.00*
**C104** AP21 10rl multi *9.00* *4.00*
**C105** AP21 10rl multi — *4.00*
**C106** AP21 10rl multi *12.00* *4.00*
*Nos. C103-C106 (4)* *48.50* *19.00*

**Embossed on Foil Coated Paper**

***Perf. 13***

**C107** AP21 1.50rl silver *15.00* —
**C108** AP21 1.50rl gold *15.00* —
**C109** AP21 3rl silver *17.50* —
**C110** AP21 3rl gold *17.50* —
*Nos. C107-C110 (4)* *65.00*

No. C102 exists imperf. Nos. C103-C106 exist imperf. Nos. C107-C110 exist imperf.

Nos. C102a-C102t exist in deluxe sheets of one. Value CTO, perf. $2.50 each. Value CTO, imperf. $2.50 each.

Nos. C107-C110 exist in imperf sheets of one.

# RHODESIA

rō-ˈdē-zh͟ē-͵ə

## (British South Africa)

LOCATION — Southeastern Africa
GOVT. — Administered by the British South Africa Company
AREA — 440,653 sq. mi.
POP. — 1,738,000 (estimated 1921)
CAPITAL — Salisbury

In 1923 the area was divided and the portion south of the Zambezi River became the British Crown Colony of Southern Rhodesia. In the following year the remaining territory was formed into the Protectorate of Northern Rhodesia. The Federation of Rhodesia and Nyasaland (comprising Southern Rhodesia, Northern Rhodesia and Nyasaland) was established Sept. 3, 1953.

12 Pence = 1 Shilling
20 Shillings = 1 Pound

A1

A2

Coat of Arms — A3

**Thin Paper**

**Engr. (A1, A3); Engr., Typo. (A2)**

**1890-94 Unwmk. *Perf. 14, 14½***

**1** A2 ½p blue & ver ('91) 4.75 *5.25*
**2** A1 1p black 19.00 4.50
**3** A2 2p gray grn & ver ('91) 28.00 8.00
**4** A2 3p gray & grn ('91) 25.00 5.00
**5** A2 4p red brn & blk ('91) 47.50 6.50
**6** A1 6p ultra 80.00 28.00
**7** A1 6p deep blue 50.00 4.25
**8** A2 8p rose & bl ('91) 22.50 24.00
**9** A1 1sh gray brown 55.00 16.00
**10** A1 2sh vermilion 77.50 42.50
**11** A1 2sh6p dull lilac 47.50 55.00
Revenue cancellation 1.00
**12** A2 3sh brn & grn ('94) 195.00 100.00
Revenue cancellation 2.50
**13** A2 4sh gray & ver ('93) 48.00 60.00
Revenue cancellation 1.00
**14** A1 5sh yellow 92.50 65.00
Revenue cancellation 1.50
**15** A1 10sh deep green 130.00 *110.00*
Revenue cancellation 1.25
**16** A3 £1 dark blue *325.00* *175.00*
Revenue cancellation 6.75
**17** A3 £2 rose *550.00* *200.00*
Revenue cancellation 22.50
**18** A3 £5 yellow grn *1,775.* *500.00*
Revenue cancellation 50.00
**19** A3 £10 orange brn *3,000.* *800.00*
Revenue cancellation 75.00
*Nos. 1-16 (16)* 1,247. *709.00*

The paper of the 1891 issue has the trademark and initials of the makers in a monogram watermarked in each sheet. Some of the lower values were also printed on a slightly thicker paper without watermark.

Examples of Nos. 16-19 with cancellations removed are frequently offered as unused specimens.

See Nos. 24-25, 58.

For surcharges see Nos. 20-23, 40-42. For overprints see British Central Africa Nos. 1-20.

Nos. 6 and 9 Surcharged in Black

**1891, Mar.**

**20** A1 ½p on 6p ultra 150.00 *525.00*
**21** A1 2p on 6p ultra 195.00 *700.00*
**22** A1 4p on 6p ultra 210.00 *825.00*
**23** A1 8p on 1sh brown 225.00 *925.00*
*Nos. 20-23 (4)* 780.00 *2,975.*

Beware of forged surcharges.

**1895 Thick Soft Paper *Perf. 12½***

**24** A2 2p green & red 32.50 20.00
**25** A2 4p ocher & black 32.50 21.00
*a.* Imperf., pair 2,250.

A4

**1896 Engraved, Typo. *Perf. 14***

**26** A4 ½p slate & vio 5.00 *3.75*
**27** A4 1p scar & emer 14.00 5.50
**28** A4 2p brn & rose lil 30.00 4.00
**29** A4 3p red brn & ultra 11.00 2.50
**30** A4 4p blue & red lil 24.00 .60
*d.* Horiz. pair, imperf. btwn.
**31** A4 6p vio & pale rose 19.00 1.10
**32** A4 8p dp grn & vio, *buff* 20.00 .70
*a.* Imperf. pair *4,500.*
*b.* Horiz. pair, imperf. btwn.
**33** A4 1sh brt grn & ultra 27.50 4.00
**34** A4 2sh dk bl & grn, *buff* 55.00 14.00
**35** A4 2sh6p brn & vio, *yel* 92.50 65.00
**36** A4 3sh grn & red vio, *bl* 90.00 47.50
*a.* Imperf. pair *13,000.*
**37** A4 4sh red & bl, *grn* 75.00 4.00
**38** A4 5sh org red & *grn* 65.00 14.00
**39** A4 10sh sl & car, *rose* 150.00 75.00
*Nos. 26-39 (14)* 678.00 241.65

The plates for this issue were made from two dies. Stamps of die I have a small dot at the right of the tail of the supporter at the right of the shield, and the body of the lion is not fully shaded. Stamps of die II have not the dot and the lion is heavily shaded.

See type A7.

**Nos. 4, 13-14 Surcharged in Black**

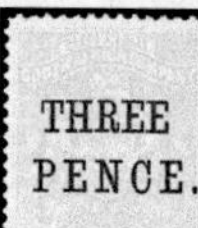


**1896, Apr. *Perf. 14***

**40** A2 1p on 3p 650.00 850.00
*a.* "P" of "Penny" inverted *50,000.*
*b.* "y" of "Penny" inverted —
*c.* Double surcharge —
**41** A2 1p on 4sh 325.00 350.00
*a.* "P" of "Penny" inverted *37,500.*
*b.* Single bar in surch. *1,250.* *1,400.*
*c.* "y" of "Penny" inverted *37,500.*
**42** A1 3p on 5sh yellow 225.00 *275.00*
*a.* "T" of "THREE" inverted *50,000.*
*b.* "R" of "THREE" inverted *37,500.*
*Nos. 40-42 (3)* *1,200.* *1,475.*

Cape of Good Hope Stamps Overprinted in Black



**1896, May 22 Wmk. 16**

**43** A6 ½p slate 20.00 *25.00*
**44** A15 1p carmine 22.50 *29.00*
**45** A6 2p bister brown 27.50 15.00
**46** A6 4p deep blue 34.00 27.50
*a.* "COMPANY" omitted *11,000.*
**47** A3 6p violet 77.50 *90.00*
**48** A6 1sh yellow buff 175.00 *165.00*

**Wmk. 2**

49 A6 3p claret 60.00 *85.00*
*Nos. 43-49 (7)* 416.50 *436.50*

Nos. 42-49 were used at Bulawayo during the Matabele Rebellion.
Forgeries are known.

**Remainders**

Rhodesian authorities made available remainders in large quantities of all stamps in 1897, 1898-1908, 1905, 1909 and 1910 issues, CTO. Some varieties exist only as remainders. See notes following Nos. 100 and 118.

A7

Type A7 differs from type A4 in having the ends of the scroll which is below the shield curved between the hind legs of the supporters instead of passing behind one leg of each. There are other minor differences.

***Perf. 13½ to 16***

**1897 Unwmk. Engr.**

50 A7 ½p slate & violet 7.75 *9.50*
51 A7 1p ver & gray grn 13.00 *11.50*
52 A7 2p brn & lil rose 27.50 4.50
53 A7 3p red brn & gray bl 11.00 .55
*a.* Vert. pair, imperf. btwn. 5,000.
54 A7 4p ultra & red lil 32.50 4.50
*a.* Horiz. pair, imperf. btwn. 18,000. 17,500.
55 A7 6p vio & sal 22.50 4.00
56 A7 8p dk grn & vio, *buff* 32.50 .55
*a.* Vert. pair, imperf. btwn. — 4,000.
57 A7 £1 blk & red, *grn* 450.00 250.00
Revenue cancellation 12.00
*Nos. 50-56 (7)* 146.75 *35.10*

**Thick Paper**

***Perf. 15***

58 A3 £2 bright red *1,900.* 500.00
Revenue cancellation *65.00*

See note on remainders following No. 49.

A8

A9

A10

**1898-1908** ***Perf. 13½ to 16***

59 A8 ½p yel grn ('04) 7.50 4.00
*a.* Imperf. pair 1,000.
*b.* Horiz. pair, imperf. vert. 975.00
*c.* Vert. pair, imperf between 1,675.
60 A8 1p rose (shades) 17.50 1.10
*a.* Horiz. pair, imperf. btwn. 1,150.
*b.* Vert. pair, imperf between 825.00
*c.* Imperf. pair 1,000. 900.00
*d.* 1p red (shades) ('05) 13.00 .80
61 A8 2p brown 14.50 3.00
62 A8 2½p dull blue (shades) 26.00 2.00
*a.* Horiz. pair, imperf vert. 1,100. 1,300.
63 A8 3p clar ('08) 22.50 1.00
*a.* Vert. pair, imperf between 800.00
64 A8 4p ol grn 21.00 .75
*a.* Vert. pair, imperf. between 800.00
65 A8 6p lilac 27.50 3.75
66 A9 1sh bister 42.50 6.00
*a.* Vert. pair, imperf. btwn. 3,500. 3,500.
*b.* Horiz. pair, imperf between 4,000. 4,000.
67 A9 2sh6p bluish gray ('06) 75.00 2.25
*a.* Vert. pair, imperf. between 1,300. 575.00
68 A9 3sh pur ('02) 42.50 4.50
69 A9 5sh org ('01) 70.00 29.00
70 A9 7sh6p blk ('01) 110.00 32.50
71 A9 10sh bluish grn ('08) 65.00 3.00
72 A10 £1 gray vio, perf 15½ ('01) 425.00 170.00
Revenue cancellation 17.50
73 A10 £2 red brn ('08) 130.00 7.50
74 A10 £5 dk blue ('01) *3,750.* *3,000.*
Revenue cancellation 125.00
75 A10 £10 blue lil ('01) *3,750.* *3,000.*
Revenue cancellation 125.00
75A A10 £20 bister ('01?) *22,500.*
Revenue cancellation 175.00
75B A10 £100 cherry red ('01) *185,000.* —
Revenue cancellation *900.00*
*Nos. 59-73 (15)* 1,097. 270.35

For overprints and surcharges see #82-100.
See note on remainders following #49.

Victoria Falls — A11

***Perf. 14, 14½x15 (#78)***

**1905, July 13**

76 A11 1p rose red 9.50 *11.50*
77 A11 2½p ultra 45.00 12.00
78 A11 5p magenta 47.50 *60.00*
79 A11 1sh blue green 42.50 57.50
*a.* Imperf., pair 35,000.
*b.* Horiz. pair, imperf. vert. 37,500.
*c.* Horiz. pair, imperf. btwn. 45,000.
*d.* Vert. pair, imperf. btn. 45,000.
*e.* Perf 14½x15 — 425.00
80 A11 2sh6p black 145.00 *180.00*
81 A11 5sh violet 145.00 50.00
*Nos. 76-81 (6)* 434.50 *371.00*

Opening of the Victoria Falls bridge across the Zambezi River.
See note on remainders following No. 49.

**Stamps of 1898-1908 Overprinted or Surcharged**

**1909** ***Perf. 14, 15***

82 A8 ½p green (shades) 6.50 3.50
83 A8 1p car rose 11.00 1.75
*a.* Horiz. pair, imperf between 525.00
84 A8 2p brown 7.50 *9.00*
85 A8 2½p cobalt blue 5.00 .90
86 A8 3p claret 5.00 3.00
*a.* Double overprint 1,600. *1,600.*
*b.* Inverted overprint — 20.00
87 A8 4p ol grn 17.50 4.25
*a.* Inverted overprint 16.50
88 A8 5p on 6p lilac 16.00 *22.50*
*a.* Violet surcharge 100.00
89 A8 6p lilac 12.00 12.00
*b.* 6p dull purple 27.50 12.00
90 A9 7½p on 2sh6p 7.00 4.25
*a.* Violet surcharge 27.50 11.00
*b.* Double surcharge *10,000.*
91 A9 10p on 3sh pur, vio srch. 9.00 *5.00*
*a.* Black surcharge 18.50 *11.00*
92 A9 1sh dp brnsh bister 18.00 9.00
93 A9 2sh on 5sh org 17.00 8.50
94 A9 2sh6p bluish gray 42.50 14.00
*b.* Inverted overprint 25.00
95 A9 3sh purple 30.00 13.50
96 A9 5sh orange 57.50 *87.50*
97 A9 7sh6p black 110.00 40.00
98 A9 10sh bluish grn 77.50 24.00
99 A10 £1 gray vio 220.00 110.00
*a.* Vert. pair, lower stamp without overprint 47,500.
*b.* Violet overprint 425.00 220.00
100 A10 £2 red brn, *bluish,* perf 14½x15 ('12) *4,500.* 330.00
100B A10 £5 dp blue, *bluish* *9,000.* *5,000.*
*Nos. 82-99 (18)* 669.00 372.65

See note on remainders following No. 49. Nos. 86b, 87a and 94b are from the remainders.

Nos. 82-87, 89, 92, 94, 96 and 98 exist without period after "Rhodesia." See the *Scott Classic Specialized Catalogue of Stamps & Covers* for listings.

Queen Mary and King George V — A12

**1910 Engr.** ***Perf. 14, 15x14, 14x15***

101 A12 ½p green 15.00 2.50
*a.* ½p olive green 45.00 5.50
*b.* Perf. 15 350.00 14.50
*c.* Imperf., pair *16,000.* *8,000.*
*d.* Perf. 13½ 350.00 55.00
102 A12 1p rose car 37.50 4.50
*a.* Vertical pair, imperf. btwn. *22,500.* *14,500.*
*b.* Perf. 15 350.00 10.00
*c.* Perf. 13½ *2,250.* 55.00
103 A12 2p gray & blk 60.00 12.50
*b.* Perf. 15 1,000. 47.50
104 A12 2½p ultra 27.50 12.00
*a.* 2½p light blue 29.00 24.00
*b.* Perf. 15 82.50 45.00
*c.* Perf. 13½ 45.00 *77.50*
105 A12 3p ol yel & vio 50.00 52.00
*a.* Perf. 15 3,650. 82.50
*b.* Perf. 14x15 7,750. 325.00
106 A12 4p org & blk 55.00 27.50
*a.* 4p orange & violet black 95.00 72.50
*b.* Perf. 15x14 550.00
*c.* Perf. 15 65.00 82.50
107 A12 5p ol grn & brn 60.00 60.00
*a.* 5p olive yel & brn (error) 725.00 165.00
*b.* Perf. 15 875.00 115.00
108 A12 6p claret & brn 72.50 25.00
*a.* Perf. 15 1,000. 67.50
109 A12 8p brn vio & gray blk 190.00 110.00
*a.* Perf. 13½ 67.50 *275.00*
110 A12 10p plum & rose red 55.00 55.00
111 A12 1sh turq grn & black 72.50 24.00
*a.* Perf. 14x15 32,500. 3,250.
*b.* Perf. 15 1,325. 62.50
112 A12 2sh gray bl & black 125.00 82.50
*a.* Perf. 15 2,500 400.00
113 A12 2sh6p car rose & blk 400.00 450.00
114 A12 3sh vio & bl grn 250.00 210.00
115 A12 5sh yel grn & brn red 325.00 225.00
116 A12 7sh6p brt bl & car 725.00 500.00
117 A12 10sh red org & bl grn 475.00 550.00
*a.* 10sh red org & myrtle grn 725.00 325.00
118 A12 £1 bluish sl & car 1,650. 775.00
*a.* £1 black & red 1,550. 425.00
*c.* Perf. 15 *19,000.* *4,750.*
*d.* As "a," carmine and reddish mauve (error) 14,500.
*Nos. 101-118 (18)* 4,645. 3,178.

See note on remainders following No. 49. The £1 in plum and red is from the remainders.

King George V — A13

Three dies were used for Nos. 122, 124-138:

I, Outline at top of cap absent or very faint and broken. Left ear not shaded or outlined and appears white.

II, Outline at top of cap faint and broken. Ear shaded all over, with no outline.

III, Outline at top of cap continuous. Ear shaded all over, with continuous outline.

Die types are noted in parentheses.

**1913-23** ***Perf. 14***

119 A13 ½p dp grn 9.25 2.50
*a.* Vert. pair, imperf horiz. 025.00
*b.* Vert. strip of 5, imperf between 4,250.
*d.* ½p blue green, perf 15 9.50 *30.00*
120 A13 1p brn rose 4.50 4.00
*a.* Perf. 15 7.50 *10.00*
*b.* 1p bright rose 7.25 2.50
*c.* As "b," horiz. pair, imperf btwn. 1,100. 950.00
121 A13 1½p bis brn ('17) 6.00 2.50
*a.* Horiz. pair, imperf between 900.00 900.00
*b.* Perf. 15 ('19) 50.00 8.00
*c.* As "b," horiz. pair, imperf between 26,500.
122 A13 2p vio blk & blk (III) '22 13.50 9.00
*a.* 2p gray & black (III) 11.50 4.00
*b.* Perf. 15 (II) 13.50 25.00
*c.* Horiz. pair, imperf. btwn. (III) *6,750.*
*d.* 2p gray & brnish blk (III), perf 15 *6,500.*
123 A13 2½p ultra 8.25 *40.00*
*a.* Perf. 15 17.50 *65.00*
124 A13 3p org yel & blk (III) 20.00 4.75
*a.* 3p yellow & black (III) 17.50 4.25
*b.* Perf. 15 (I) 9.00 *27.50*
125 A13 4p org red & blk (I) 12.00 42.50
*a.* Perf. 15 (I) 175.00 32.50
126 A13 5p yel grn & blk (I) 7.25 *22.50*
127 A13 6p lilac & blk (III) 16.50 8.75
*a.* Perf. 15 (I) 10.50 *12.00*
128 A13 8p gray grn & vio (II) 19.00 *82.50*
*a.* Perf. 15 (III) 77.50
*b.* 8p green & violet (II) 225.00 190.00
129 A13 10p car rose & bl, perf. 15 (II) 16.50 *50.00*
*a.* Perf. 14 (III) '22 18.50 *75.00*
130 A13 1sh turq bl & blk (III) '22 15.00 22.50
*a.* 1sh lt grn & blk (III) ('19) 95.00 60.00
*b.* Perf. 15 (II) 77.50 22.50
132 A13 2sh brn & blk, perf. 14 (III)('19) 22.50 *20.00*
*a.* Perf. 15 (I) 17.50 *55.00*
133 A13 2sh6p ol gray & vio bl (III) '22 65.00 *110.00*
*a.* 2sh6p gray & blue (II) 82.50 60.00
*b.* Perf. 15 (II) 55.00 105.00
134 A13 3sh brt blue & red brn (II) 130.00 *165.00*
*a.* Perf. 15 (III) '23 195.00
135 A13 5sh grn & bl (II) 95.00 *100.00*
*a.* Perf. 15 (II) 210.00 *225.00*
136 A13 7sh6p blk & vio, perf. 15 (II) 175.00 *300.00*
*a.* Perf. 14 (III) '22 250.00 *425.00*
137 A13 10sh yel grn & car (III) '23 275.00 *360.00*
*a.* Perf. 15 (II) 250.00 *425.00*
138 A13 £1 vio & blk (II) 450.00 *675.00*
*a.* £1 magenta & black (III) '23 950.00 *1,250.*
*b.* Perf. 15 (III) '23 1,100.
*c.* Perf. 15, black & purple (II) 1,750. 1,750.
*Nos. 119-138 (19)* 1,360. *2,022.*

**No. 120 Surcharged in Dark Violet**

No. 139

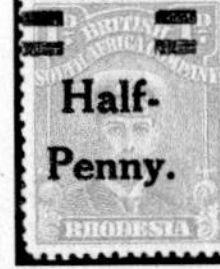

No. 140

**1917**

139 A13 ½p on 1p 2.75 10.50
*a.* Inverted surcharge *1,600.* *1,650.*
140 A13 ½p on 1p 2.00 10.00

Nos. 141-190 are accorded to Rhodesia and Nyasaland.

## RHODESIA & NYASALAND

rō-ˈdē-zh͟ē-ˌə ənˌd͟ nī-ˈa-sə-ˌland

LOCATION — Southern Africa
GOVT. — Federal State in British Commonwealth
AREA — 486,973 sq. mi.
POP. — 8,510,000 (est. 1961)
CAPITAL — Salisbury, Southern Rhodesia

The Federation of Southern Rhodesia, Northern Rhodesia and Nyasaland was created in 1953, dissolved at end of 1963.

12 Pence = 1 Shilling
20 Shillings = 1 Pound

**Catalogue values for all unused stamps in this country are for Never Hinged items.**

A14

A15

Queen Elizabeth II
A16

***Perf. 13½x14 (A14), 13½x13 (A15), 14x13 (A16)***

**1954-56 Engr. Unwmk.**

141 A14 ½p vermilion .25 .25
 a. Booklet pane of 6 1.25
 b. Perf. 12½x14 .75 .50
142 A14 1p ultra .25 .25
 a. Booklet pane of 6 1.25
 b. Perf. 12½x14 1.50 *15.00*
143 A14 2p emerald .25 .25
 a. Booklet pane of 6 1.60
143B A14 2½p ocher ('56) 5.00 .25
144 A14 3p carmine .25 .25
145 A14 4p red brown .60 .25
146 A14 4½p blue green .40 *1.50*
147 A14 6p red lilac 2.00 .25
148 A14 9p purple 2.25 .90
149 A14 1sh gray 2.00 .25
150 A15 1sh3p ultra & ver 6.50 .40
151 A15 2sh brn & dp bl 7.50 5.00
152 A15 2sh6p car & blk 7.50 2.00
153 A15 5sh ol & pur 21.00 6.50
154 A16 10sh red org & aqua 21.00 9.50
155 A16 £1 brn car & ol 37.50 27.50
 *Nos. 141-155 (16)* 114.25 55.30

Issue dates: 2½p, Feb. 15, others, July 1.
Nos. 141b and 142b are coils.

Victoria Falls
A17 A18

**1955, June 15** ***Perf. 13½***

156 A17 3p Plane .80 .35
157 A18 1sh David Livingstone .90 .75

Centenary of discovery of Victoria Falls.

Tea Picking — A19

Rhodes' Grave, Matopos — A20

Designs: 1p, V. H. F. Mast. 2p, Copper mining. 2½p, Kingsley Fairbridge Memorial. 4p, Boat on Lake Bangweulu. 6p, Victoria Falls. 9p, Railroad trains. 1sh, Tobacco. 1sh3p, Ship on Lake Nyasa. 2sh, Chirundu Bridge, Zambezi River. 2sh6p, Salisbury Airport. 5sh, Cecil Rhodes statue, Salisbury. 10sh, Mlanje mountain. £1, Coat of arms.

***Perf. 13½x14, 14x13½***

**1959-63 Engr. Unwmk.**

**Size: 18½x22½mm, 22½x18½mm**

158 A19 ½p emer & blk 1.25 *2.00*
 a. Perf. 12½x13½ 3.50 *5.50*
159 A19 1p blk & rose red .30 .25
 a. Perf. 12½x13½ 3.50 *11.00*
 b. Rose red (center) omitted 325.00
160 A19 2p ocher & vio 2.00 .50
161 A19 2½p slate & lil, perf. 14½ 1.75 *2.00*
162 A20 3p blue & blk 1.00 .25
 a. Booklet pane of 4 ('63) 4.00
 b. Black omitted *30,000.*

***Perf. 14½***

**Size: 24x27mm, 27x24mm**

163 A19 4p ol & mag 1.50 .25
164 A19 6p grn & ultra 2.50 .25
164A A20 9p pur & ocher ('62) 7.50 3.25
165 A20 1sh ultra & yel grn 1.25 .25
166 A20 1sh3p sep & brt grn, perf. 14 4.75 .25
167 A20 2sh lake & grn 4.00 .60
168 A20 2sh6p ocher & bl 9.50 1.00

***Perf. 11½***

**Size: 32x27mm**

169 A20 5sh yel grn & choc 13.00 2.50
170 A20 10sh brt rose & ol 22.50 19.00
171 A20 £1 vio & blk 40.00 *45.00*
 *Nos. 158-171 (15)* 112.80 77.35

Nos. 158a and 159a are coils.
Issue dates: 9p, May 15, others, Aug. 12.

Kariba Gorge, 1955
A21

Designs: 6p, Power lines. 1sh, View of dam. 1sh3p, View of dam and lake. 2sh6p, Power station. 5sh, Dam and Queen Mother Elizabeth.

**1960, May 17 Photo.** ***Perf. 14½x14***

172 A21 3p org & sl grn .80 .25
 a. Orange omitted 6,000.
173 A21 6p yel brn & brn 1.00 .25
174 A21 1sh dull bl & emer 2.25 *4.25*
175 A21 1sh3p grnsh bl & ocher 2.50 *3.50*
176 A21 2sh6p org ver & blk 3.75 *8.50*
177 A21 5sh grnsh bl & lilac 10.00 *12.00*
 *Nos. 172-177 (6)* 20.30 28.75

Miner with Drill — A22

Design: 1sh3p, Mining surface installations.

**1961, May 8 Unwmk.**

178 A22 6p chnt brn & ol grn .75 .25
179 A22 1sh3p lt blue & blk .75 .90

7th Commonwealth Mining and Metallurgical Cong., Apr. 10-May 20.

DH Hercules Biplane
A23

Designs: 1sh3p, Flying boat over Zambezi River. 2sh6p, DH Comet, Salisbury Airport.

**1962, Feb. 6**

180 A23 6p ver & ol grn 2.50 .75
181 A23 1sh3p bl, blk, grn & yel 1.90 .50
182 A23 2sh6p dk pur & car rose 4.25 6.50
 *Nos. 180-182 (3)* 8.65 7.75

30th anniv. of the inauguration of the Rhodesia-London airmail service.

Tobacco Plant — A24

Designs: 6p, Tobacco field. 1sh3p, Auction floor. 2sh6p, Cured tobacco.

**1963, Feb. 18 Photo.** ***Perf. 14x14½***

184 A24 3p gray brown & grn .30 .25
185 A24 6p blue, grn & brn .40 .30
186 A24 1sh3p slate & red brn 1.40 .40
187 A24 2sh6p brown & org yel 1.60 3.00
 *Nos. 184-187 (4)* 3.70 3.95

3rd World Tobacco Scientific Cong., Salisbury, Feb. 18-26 and the 1st Intl. Tobacco Trade Cong., Salisbury, March 6-16.

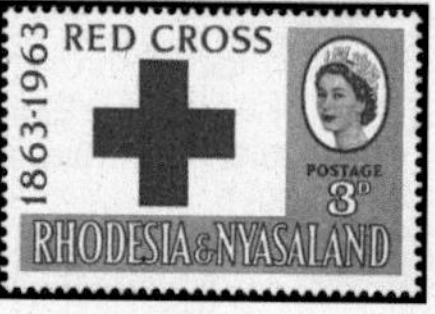
Red Cross
A25

**1963, Aug. 6** ***Perf. 14½x14***

188 A25 3p red 1.10 .25

Centenary of the International Red Cross.

"Round Table" Emblem
A26

**1963, Sept. 11 Unwmk.**

189 A26 6p multicolored .65 *1.25*
190 A26 1sh3p multicolored .90 *.95*

World Council of Young Men's Service Clubs at University College of Rhodesia and Nyasaland, Sept. 8-15.

### POSTAGE DUE STAMPS

D1

***Perf. 12½***

**1961, Apr. 19 Unwmk. Typo.**

J1 D1 1p vermilion 4.25 *5.75*
 a. Horiz. pair, imperf. btwn. *750.00 850.00*
J2 D1 2p dark blue 3.50 *3.50*
J3 D1 4p emerald 3.75 *10.00*
J4 D1 6p dark purple 5.25 *8.00*
 a. Horiz. pair, imperf. btwn. *1,900.*
 *Nos. J1-J4 (4)* 16.75 *27.25*

Nos. 142-143 exist with provisional "Postage Due" handstamp.

## RHODESIA

rō-ˈdē-zh͟ē-ˌə

### Self-Governing State (formerly Southern Rhodesia)

LOCATION — Southeastern Africa, bordered by Zambia, Mozambique, South Africa and Botswana
GOVT. — Self-governing member of British Commonwealth
AREA — 150,333 sq. mi.
POP. — 4,670,000 (est. 1968)
CAPITAL — Salisbury

In Oct. 1964, Southern Rhodesia assumed the name Rhodesia. On Nov. 11, 1965, the white minority government declared Rhodesia independent. Rhodesia became Zimbabwe on Apr. 18, 1980. For earlier issues, see Southern Rhodesia and Rhodesia and Nyasaland.

12 Pence = 1 Shilling
20 Shillings = 1 Pound
100 Cents = 1 Dollar (1967)

**Catalogue values for all unused stamps in this country are for Never Hinged items.**

ITU Emblem, Old and New Communication Equipment — A27

**Unwmk.**

**1965, May 17 Photo.** ***Perf. 14***

200 A27 6p apple grn & brt vio 1.50 .45
201 A27 1sh3p brt vio & dk vio 1.50 .45
202 A27 2sh6p org brn & dk vio 4.50 *4.50*
 *Nos. 200-202 (3)* 7.50 5.40

Cent. of the ITU.

Bangala Dam — A28

Designs: 4p, Irrigation canal through sugar plantation. 2sh6p, Worker cutting sugar cane.

**1965, July 19 Photo.** ***Perf. 14***

203 A28 3p dull bl, grn & ocher .40 .25
204 A28 4p blue, grn & brn 1.25 1.25
205 A28 2sh6p multicolored 2.25 *3.50*
 *Nos. 203-205 (3)* 3.90 5.00

Issued to publicize Conservation Week of the Natural Resources Board.

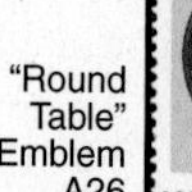

Churchill, Parliament, Quill and Sword — A29

**1965, Aug. 16**

**206** A29 1sh3p ultra & black .70 .45

Sir Winston Spencer Churchill (1874-1965), statesman and WWII leader.

For surcharge see No. 222.

### Issues of Smith Government

Arms of Rhodesia A30

**1965, Dec. 8 Photo. *Perf. 11***

**207** A30 2sh6p violet & multi .35 .25
*a.* Imperf., pair 900.00

Declaration of independence by the government of Prime Minister Ian Smith.

Southern Rhodesia Nos. 95-108 Overprinted

***Perf. 14½***

**1966, Jan. 17 Unwmk. Photo.**

**Size: 23x19mm**

**208** A30 ½p lt bl, yel & grn .25 .25
*a.* Pair, one without overprint *7,500.*
**209** A30 1p ocher & pur .25 .25
**210** A30 2p vio & org yel .25 .25
**211** A30 3p lt blue & choc .25 .25
**212** A30 4p sl grn & org .25 .25

***Perf. 13½x13***

**Size: 27x23mm**

**213** A30 6p dull grn, red & yel .40 .25
*a.* Pair, one without overprint
**214** A30 9p ol grn, yel & brn .45 .25
*a.* Double overprint 800.00
*b.* Pair, one without overprint
**215** A30 1sh ocher & brt grn .50 .25
*a.* Double overprint 800.00
*b.* Pair, one without overprint
**216** A30 1sh3p grn, vio & dk red .60 .40
**217** A30 2sh dull bl & yel .75 *2.75*
**218** A30 2sh6p ultra & red .85 .90
*a.* Red omitted

***Perf. 14½x14***

**Size: 32x27mm**

**Overprint 26mm Wide**

**219** A30 5sh bl, grn, ocher & lt brn 2.25 *5.50*
*a.* Double overprint *850.00*
**220** A30 10sh ocher, blk, red & bl 4.00 2.50
**221** A30 £1 rose, sep, ocher & grn 1.50 *2.50*
*Nos. 208-221 (14)* 12.55 16.55

### No. 206 Surcharged in Red

***Perf. 14***

**222** A29 5sh on 1sh3p *6.25* *14.00*
*a.* "5/-" omitted

Ansellia Orchid — A31

Designs: 1p, Cape Buffalo. 2p, Oranges. 3p, Kudu. 4p, Emeralds. 6p, Flame lily. 9p, Tobacco. 1sh, Corn. 1sh3p, Lake Kyle. 2sh, Aloe. 2sh6p, Tigerfish. 5sh, Cattle. 10sh, Gray-breasted helmet guinea fowl. £1, Arms of Rhodesia.

### Printed by Harrison & Sons, London

**1966, Feb. 9 Photo. *Perf. 14½***

**Size: 23x19mm**

**223** A31 1p ocher & pur .25 .25
**224** A31 2p slate grn & org .25 .25
*b.* Orange omitted *3,250.*
**225** A31 3p lt blue & choc .25 .25
*b.* Queen's head omitted 6,500.
*c.* Booklet pane of 4 1.00
*d.* Lt blue omitted *4,750.*
**226** A31 4p gray & brt grn 1.75 .25

***Perf. 13½x13***

**Size: 27x23mm**

**227** A31 6p dull grn, red & yel .25 .25
**228** A31 9p purple & ocher .75 .25
**229** A31 1sh lt bl, yel & grn .25 .25
**230** A31 1sh3p dull blue & yel .35 .25
*b.* Yellow omitted *4,000.*
**231** A31 1sh6p ol grn, yel & brn 2.25 .35
**232** A31 2sh lt ol grn, vio & dk red .75 *.95*
**233** A31 2sh6p brt grnsh bl, ultra & ver 1.50 .25

***Perf. 14½x14***

**Size: 32x27mm**

**234** A31 5sh bl, grn, ocher & lt brn 1.25 1.00
**235** A31 10sh dl yel, blk, red & bl 4.25 3.75
**236** A31 £1 sal pink, sep, ocher & grn 3.50 *7.50*
*Nos. 223-236 (14)* 17.60 15.80

### Printed by Mardon Printers, Salisbury

**1966-68 Litho. *Perf. 14½***

*223a* A31 1p ocher & pur .25 .25
*224a* A31 2p sl grn & org ('68) 1.00 .50
*225a* A31 3p lt bl & choc ('68) 2.00 .25
*226a* A31 4p sep & brt grn 1.00 .55
*227a* A31 6p gray grn, red & yel 1.00 .50
*228a* A31 9p pur & ocher ('68) .80 .25
*230a* A31 1sh3p dl bl & yel 2.00 .40
*232a* A31 2sh lt ol grn, vio & dk red 2.25 *3.50*

***Perf. 14***

*234a* A31 5sh brt bl, grn, ocher & brn 3.00 *5.00*
*235a* A31 10sh ocher, blk, red & bl *8.50* *15.00*
*236a* A31 £1 sal pink, sep, ocher & grn *12.50* *22.50*
*Nos. 223a-236a (11)* 34.30 48.70

See Nos. 245-248A.

Zeederberg Coach — A32

Designs: 9p, Sir Rowland Hill. 1sh6p, Penny Black. 2sh6p, Rhodesia No. 18, £5.

***Perf. 14½***

**1966, May 2 Litho. Unwmk.**

**237** A32 3p blue, org & blk .30 .25
**238** A32 9p beige & brown .30 .25
**239** A32 1sh6p blue & black .45 .50
**240** A32 2sh6p rose, yel grn & blk .55 *.90*
*a.* Souvenir sheet of 4, #237-240 10.00 *14.00*
*Nos. 237-240 (4)* 1.60 1.90

28th Cong. of the Southern Africa Phil. Fed. and the RHOPEX Exhib., Bulawayo, May 2-7.

No. 240a was printed in sheets of 12 and comes with perforations extending through the margins in four different versions. Many have holes in the top margin made when the sheet was cut into individual panes. Sizes of panes vary. Nos. 237, 240-240a exist imperf.

De Havilland Dragon Rapide A33

Planes: 1sh3p, Douglas DC-3. 2sh6p, Vickers Viscount. 5sh, Jet.

**1966, June 1**

**241** A33 6p multicolored 1.00 .50
**242** A33 1sh3p multicolored 1.25 .60
**243** A33 2sh6p multicolored 2.25 1.50
**244** A33 5sh blue & black 3.25 *4.50*
*Nos. 241-244 (4)* 7.75 7.10

20th anniv. of Central African Airways.

### Dual Currency Issue

Type of 1966 with Denominations in Cents and Pence-Shillings

**1967-68 Litho. *Perf. 14½***

**245** A31 3p/2½c lt blue & choc .75 .25
**246** A31 1sh/10c multi 1.00 .45
**247** A31 1sh6p/15c multi 5.00 1.00
**248** A31 2sh/20c multi 4.75 *6.00*
**248A** A31 2sh6p/25c multi *20.00* *27.50*
*Nos. 245-248A (5)* 31.50 *35.20*

These locally printed stamps were issued to acquaint Rhodesians with the decimal currency to be introduced in 1969-1970.

Issued: 3p, 3/15; 1sh, 11/1/67; 1sh6p, 2sh, 3/11/68; 2sh6p, 12/9/68.

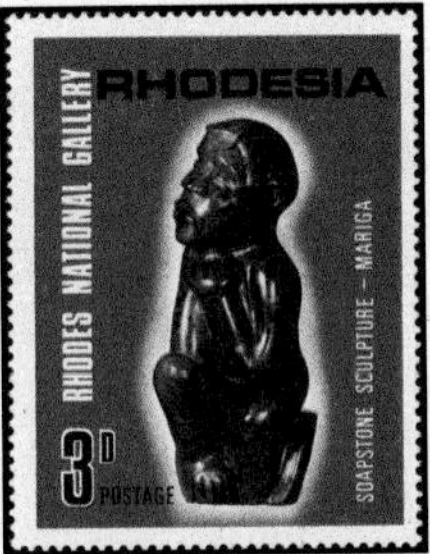

Leander Starr Jameson, by Frank Moss Bennett A34

**1967, May 17**

**249** A34 1sh6p emerald & multi .50 .50

Dr. Leander Starr Jameson (1853-1917), pioneer with Cecil Rhodes and Prime Minister of Cape Colony. See No. 262.

Soapstone Sculpture, by Joram Mariga A35

9p, Head of Burgher of Calais, by Auguste Rodin. 1sh3p, "Totem," by Roberto Crippa. 2sh6p, St. John the Baptist, by Michele Tosini.

**1967, July 12 Litho. *Perf. 14***

**250** A35 3p brn, blk & ol grn .25 .25
**251** A35 9p brt bl, blk & ol grn .30 .25
*a.* Perf. 13½ 8.25 *17.50*
**252** A35 1sh3p multicolored .30 .30
**253** A35 2sh6p multicolored .40 *.50*
*Nos. 250-253 (4)* 1.25 1.30

10th anniv. of the Rhodes Natl. Gallery, Salisbury.

White Rhinoceros — A36

#255, Parrot's beak gladioli, vert. #256, Baobab tree. #257, Elephants.

**1967, Sept. 6 Unwmk. *Perf. 14½***

**254** A36 4p olive & black .25 .25
**255** A36 4p dp orange & blk .35 .25
**256** A36 4p brown & blk .35 .25
**257** A36 4p gray & blk .25 .25
*Nos. 254-257 (4)* 1.20 1.00

Issued to publicize nature conservation.

Wooden Hand Plow, c. 1820 A37

Designs: 9p, Ox-drawn plow, c. 1860. 1sh6p, Steam tractor and plows, c. 1905. 2sh6p, Tractor and moldboard plow, 1968.

**1968, Apr. 26 Litho. *Perf. 14½***

**258** A37 3p multicolored .25 .25
**259** A37 9p multicolored .25 .25
**260** A37 1sh6p multicolored .30 .30
**261** A37 2sh6p multicolored .30 *.75*
*Nos. 258-261 (4)* 1.10 1.55

15th world plowing contest, Kent Estate, Norton.

### Portrait Type of 1967

Design: 1sh6p, Alfred Beit (portrait at left).

**1968, July 15 Unwmk. *Perf. 14½***

**262** A34 1sh6p orange, blk & red .50 .50

Alfred Beit (1853-1906), philanthropist and friend of Cecil Rhodes.

Allan Wilson, Matopos Hills — A38

Matabeleland, 75th Anniversary: 3p, Flag raising, Bulawayo, 1893. 9p, Bulawayo arms, view of Bulawayo.

**1968, Nov. 4 Litho. *Perf. 14½***

**263** A38 3p multicolored .25 .25
**264** A38 9p multicolored .25 .25
**265** A38 1sh6p multicolored .40 .40
*Nos. 263-265 (3)* .90 .90

William Henry Milton (1854-1930), Adminstrator — A39

**1969, Jan. 15**

**266** A39 1sh6p multicolored .50 .50

See Nos. 298-303.

Locomotive, 1890's — A40

Beira-Salisbury Railroad, 70th Anniversary: 9p, Steam locomotive, 1901. 1sh6p, Garratt articulated locomotive, 1950, 2sh6p, Diesel, 1955.

**1969, May 22**

**267** A40 3p multicolored *.75* .25
**268** A40 9p multicolored *1.25* .60
**269** A40 1sh6p multicolored *2.25* .80
**270** A40 2sh6p multicolored *3.00* *4.00*
*Nos. 267-270 (4)* *7.25* 5.65

Low Level Bridge A41

Bridges: 9p, Mpudzi River. 1sh6p, Umniati River. 2sh6p, Birchenough over Sabi River.

**1969, Sept. 18**

| | | | | |
|---|---|---|---|---|
| **271** | A41 | 3p multicolored | .60 | .25 |
| **272** | A41 | 9p multicolored | 1.00 | .50 |
| **273** | A41 | 1sh6p multicolored | 1.75 | 1.25 |
| **274** | A41 | 2sh6p multicolored | 2.50 | *2.75* |
| | | *Nos. 272-274 (3)* | 5.25 | 4.50 |

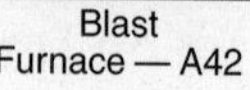

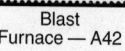

Blast Furnace — A42

Devil's Cataract, Victoria Falls — A43

1c, Wheat harvest. 2½c, Ruins, Zimbabwe. 3c, Trailer truck. 3½c, 4c, Cecil Rhodes statue. 5c, Mining. 6c, Hydrofoil, "Seaflight." 7½c, like 8c. 10c, Yachting, Lake McIlwaine. 12½c, Hippopotamus. 14c, 15c, Kariba Dam. 20c, Irrigation canal. 25c, Bateleur eagles. 50c, Radar antenna and Viscount plane. $1, "Air Rescue." $2, Rhodesian flag.

**1970-73 Litho. *Perf. 14½***

**Size: 22x18mm**

| | | | | |
|---|---|---|---|---|
| **275** | A42 | 1c multicolored | .25 | .25 |
| *a.* | | Booklet pane of 4 | .25 | |
| *b.* | | Min. sheet of 4, Rhophil | 3.75 | |
| **276** | A42 | 2c multicolored | .25 | .25 |
| **277** | A42 | 2½c multicolored | .25 | .25 |
| *a.* | | Booklet pane of 4 | 1.00 | |
| *b.* | | Min. sheet of 4, Rhophil | 3.75 | |
| **278** | A42 | 3c multi ('73) | 1.25 | .25 |
| *a.* | | Booklet pane of 4 | 5.00 | |
| **279** | A42 | 3½c multicolored | .25 | .25 |
| *a.* | | Booklet pane of 4 | 1.00 | |
| *b.* | | Min. sheet of 4, Rhophil | 3.75 | |
| **280** | A42 | 4c multi ('73) | 2.00 | 1.00 |
| *a.* | | Booklet pane of 4 | 8.00 | |
| **281** | A42 | 5c multicolored | .25 | .25 |

**Size: 27x23mm**

| | | | | |
|---|---|---|---|---|
| **282** | A43 | 6c multi ('73) | 4.50 | 4.50 |
| **283** | A43 | 7½c multi ('73) | 7.50 | .80 |
| **284** | A43 | 8c multicolored | .90 | .50 |
| **285** | A43 | 10c multicolored | .75 | .25 |
| **286** | A43 | 12½c multicolored | 1.75 | .25 |
| **287** | A43 | 14c multi ('73) | 12.50 | 1.00 |
| **288** | A43 | 15c multi | 1.50 | .25 |
| **289** | A43 | 20c multicolored | 1.25 | .25 |

**Size: 30x25mm**

| | | | | |
|---|---|---|---|---|
| **290** | A43 | 25c multicolored | 4.25 | .70 |
| **291** | A43 | 50c multicolored | 1.40 | .75 |
| **292** | A43 | $1 multicolored | 5.50 | 3.00 |
| **293** | A43 | $2 multicolored | 9.00 | *16.00* |
| | | *Nos. 275-293 (19)* | 55.30 | 30.75 |

Booklet panes and miniature sheets were made by altering the plates used to print the stamps, eliminating every third horizontal and vertical row of stamps. The perforations extend through the margins in four different versions. In 1972 sheets of 4 overprinted in the margins were issued for Rhophil '72 Philatelic Exhibition.

Issue dates: Feb. 17, 1970, Jan. 1, 1973.

Despatch Rider, c. 1890 A44

Posts and Telecommunications Corporation, Inauguration: 3½c, Loading mail, Salisbury Airport. 15c, Telegraph line construction, c.1890. 25c, Telephone and telecommunications equipment.

**1970, July 1**

| | | | | |
|---|---|---|---|---|
| **294** | A44 | 2½c multicolored | .45 | .25 |
| **295** | A44 | 3½c multicolored | .55 | .55 |
| **296** | A44 | 15c multicolored | .75 | *1.25* |
| **297** | A44 | 25c multicolored | 1.25 | *2.00* |
| | | *Nos. 294-297 (4)* | 3.00 | 4.05 |

**Famous Rhodesians Type of 1969**

13c Dr. Robert Moffat (1795-1883), missionary. #299, Dr. David Livingstone (1813-73), explorer. #300, George Pauling (1854-1919), engineer. #301, Thomas Baines (1820-75), self-portrait. #302, Mother Patrick (1863-1900), Dominican nurse and teacher. #303, Frederick Courteney Selous (1851-1917), explorer, big game hunter.

**1970-75 Litho. *Perf. 14½***

| | | | | |
|---|---|---|---|---|
| **298** | A39 | 13c multi ('72) | .90 | .90 |
| **299** | A39 | 14c multi ('73) | .90 | .90 |
| **300** | A39 | 14c multi ('74) | .90 | .90 |
| **301** | A39 | 14c multi ('75) | .90 | .90 |
| **302** | A39 | 15c multi | .90 | .90 |
| **303** | A39 | 15c multi ('71) | .90 | .90 |
| | | *Nos. 298-303 (6)* | 5.40 | 5.40 |

Issued: 2/14/72; 4/2/73; 5/15/74; 2/12/75; 11/16/70; 3/1/71.

African Hoopoe — A45

Birds: 2½c, Half-collared kingfisher, horiz. 5c, Golden-breasted bunting. 7½c, Carmine bee-eater. 8c, Red-eyed bulbul. 25c, Wattled plover, horiz.

**1971, June 1**

| | | | | |
|---|---|---|---|---|
| **304** | A45 | 2c multicolored | *1.25* | .30 |
| **305** | A45 | 2½c multicolored | *1.50* | .25 |
| **306** | A45 | 5c multicolored | *1.75* | .50 |
| **307** | A45 | 7½c multicolored | *2.00* | .55 |
| **308** | A45 | 8c multicolored | *2.75* | 1.25 |
| **309** | A45 | 25c multicolored | *3.25* | *3.25* |
| | | *Nos. 304-309 (6)* | *12.50* | 6.10 |

Porphyritic Granite — A46

Granite '71, Geological Symposium, 8/30-9/19: 7½c, Muscovite mica, seen through microscope. 15c, Granite, seen through microscope. 25c, Geological map of Rhodesia.

**1971, Aug. 30**

| | | | | |
|---|---|---|---|---|
| **310** | A46 | 2½c multicolored | *.75* | .50 |
| **311** | A46 | 7½c multicolored | *1.25* | .50 |
| **312** | A46 | 15c multicolored | *1.50* | .50 |
| **313** | A46 | 25c multicolored | *2.00* | *3.50* |
| | | *Nos. 310-313 (4)* | *5.50* | 5.00 |

"Be Airwise" A47

Prevent Pollution: 3½c, Antelope (Be Country-wise). 7c, Fish (Be Waterwise). 13c, City (Be Citywise).

**1972, July 17**

| | | | | |
|---|---|---|---|---|
| **314** | A47 | 2½c multicolored | .25 | .25 |
| **315** | A47 | 3½c multicolored | .25 | .25 |
| **316** | A47 | 7c multicolored | .30 | .25 |
| **317** | A47 | 13c multicolored | .35 | .30 |
| | | *Nos. 314-317 (4)* | 1.15 | 1.05 |

The Three Kings — A48

**1972, Oct. 18**

| | | | | |
|---|---|---|---|---|
| **318** | A48 | 2c multicolored | .25 | .25 |
| **319** | A48 | 5c multicolored | .25 | .25 |
| **320** | A48 | 13c multicolored | .40 | .40 |
| | | *Nos. 318-320 (3)* | .90 | .90 |

Christmas.

W.M.O. Emblem — A49

**1973, July 2**

| | | | | |
|---|---|---|---|---|
| **321** | A49 | 3c multicolored | .25 | .25 |
| **322** | A49 | 14c multicolored | .40 | .30 |
| **323** | A49 | 25c multicolored | .75 | *.75* |
| | | *Nos. 321-323 (3)* | 1.40 | 1.30 |

Intl. Meteorological Cooperation, cent.

Arms of Rhodesia A50

**1973, Oct. 10**

| | | | | |
|---|---|---|---|---|
| **324** | A50 | 2½c multicolored | .25 | .25 |
| **325** | A50 | 4c multicolored | .25 | .25 |
| **326** | A50 | 7½c multicolored | .30 | .25 |
| **327** | A50 | 14c multicolored | .45 | *1.00* |
| | | *Nos. 324-327 (4)* | 1.25 | 1.75 |

Responsible Government, 50th Anniversary.

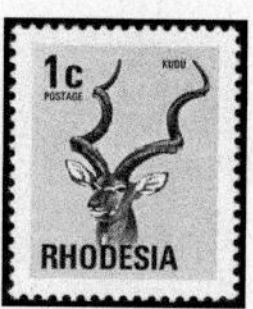

Kudu A51

Thunbergia A52

Pearl Charaxes — A53

**1974-76 Litho. *Perf. 14½***

| | | | | |
|---|---|---|---|---|
| **328** | A51 | 1c shown | .25 | .25 |
| **329** | A51 | 2½c Eland | .75 | .25 |
| **330** | A51 | 3c Roan antelope | .25 | .25 |
| **331** | A51 | 4c Reedbuck | .25 | .25 |
| **332** | A51 | 5c Bushbuck | .30 | *.50* |
| **333** | A52 | 6c shown | .50 | .25 |
| **334** | A52 | 7½c Flame lily | 1.00 | .45 |
| **335** | A52 | 8c like 7½c ('76) | .35 | .25 |
| **336** | A52 | 10c Devil thorn | .30 | .25 |
| **337** | A52 | 12c Hibiscus ('76) | 1.00 | 2.00 |
| **338** | A52 | 12½c Pink sabi star | 1.25 | .45 |
| **339** | A52 | 14c Wild pimpernel | 1.50 | .45 |
| **340** | A52 | 15c like 12½c ('76) | .70 | *1.00* |
| **341** | A52 | 16c like 14c ('76) | .70 | .40 |
| **342** | A53 | 20c shown | 1.25 | .50 |
| **343** | A53 | 24c Yellow pansy ('76) | .85 | .50 |
| **344** | A53 | 25c like 24c | 3.00 | 2.00 |
| **345** | A53 | 50c Queen purple tip | 1.00 | .80 |
| **346** | A53 | $1 Striped sword-tail | 1.50 | 1.00 |
| **347** | A53 | $2 Guinea fowl butterfly | 1.50 | 1.00 |
| | | *Nos. 328-347 (20)* | 18.20 | 12.80 |

Issue dates: Aug. 14, 1974, July 1, 1976.

For surcharges see Nos. 364-366.

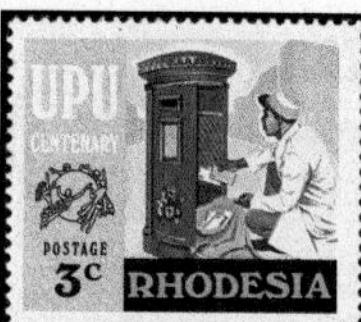

Mail Collection and UPU Emblem A54

**1974, Nov. 20 *Perf. 14½***

| | | | | |
|---|---|---|---|---|
| **348** | A54 | 3c shown | .25 | .25 |
| **349** | A54 | 4c Mail sorting | .25 | .25 |
| **350** | A54 | 7½c Mail delivery | .35 | .30 |
| **351** | A54 | 14c Parcel post | .60 | *.90* |
| | | *Nos. 348-351 (4)* | 1.45 | 1.70 |

Universal Postal Union Centenary.

Euphorbia Confinalis — A55

**1975, July 16**

| | | | | |
|---|---|---|---|---|
| **352** | A55 | 2½c shown | .30 | .30 |
| **353** | A55 | 3c Aloe excelsa | .30 | .30 |
| **354** | A55 | 4c Hoodia lugardii | .35 | .30 |
| **355** | A55 | 7½c Aloe ortholopha | .40 | .30 |
| **356** | A55 | 14c Aloe musapana | .45 | .30 |
| **357** | A55 | 25c Aloe saponaria | .90 | *2.00* |
| | | *Nos. 352-357 (6)* | 2.70 | 3.50 |

Intl. Succulent Cong., Salisbury, July 1975.

Head Injury and Safety Helmet — A56

Occupational Safety: 4c, Bandaged hand and safety glove. 7½c, Injured eye and safety eyeglass. 14c, Blind man and protective shield.

**1975, Oct. 15**

| | | | | |
|---|---|---|---|---|
| **358** | A56 | 2½c multicolored | .25 | .25 |
| **359** | A56 | 4c multicolored | .25 | .25 |
| **360** | A56 | 7½c multicolored | .30 | .25 |
| **361** | A56 | 14c multicolored | .40 | .30 |
| | | *Nos. 358-361 (4)* | 1.20 | 1.05 |

Telephones, 1876 and 1976 — A57

Alexander Graham Bell — A58

**1976, Mar. 10**

| | | | | |
|---|---|---|---|---|
| **362** | A57 | 3c light blue & blk | .25 | .25 |
| **363** | A58 | 14c buff & black | .25 | .25 |

Centenary of first telephone call, by Alexander Graham Bell, Mar. 10, 1876.

**Nos. 334, 339 and 344 Surcharged with New Value and Two Bars**

**1976, July 1**

| | | | | |
|---|---|---|---|---|
| **364** | A52 | 8c on 7½c multi | .30 | .25 |
| **365** | A52 | 16c on 14c multi | .35 | .30 |
| **366** | A53 | 24c on 25c multi | .45 | *.80* |
| | | *Nos. 364-366 (3)* | 1.10 | 1.35 |

Wildlife Protection A59

**1976, July 21**

| | | | | | |
|---|---|---|---|---|---|
| **367** | A59 | 4c | Roan Antelope | .30 | .25 |
| **368** | A59 | 6c | Brown hyena | .40 | *.60* |
| **369** | A59 | 8c | Wild dog | .40 | .30 |
| **370** | A59 | 16c | Cheetah | .50 | .50 |
| | | | *Nos. 367-370 (4)* | 1.60 | 1.65 |

Brachystegia Spiciformis — A60

**1976, Nov. 17**

| | | | | | |
|---|---|---|---|---|---|
| **371** | A60 | 4c | shown | .25 | .25 |
| **372** | A60 | 6c | Red mahogany | .25 | .25 |
| **373** | A60 | 8c | Pterocarpus angolensis | .25 | .25 |
| **374** | A60 | 16c | Rhodesian teak | .30 | *.50* |
| | | | *Nos. 371-374 (4)* | 1.05 | 1.25 |

Flowering trees.

Black-eyed Bulbul — A61

Birds: 4c, Yellow-mantled whydah. 6c, Orange-throated longclaw. 8c, Long-tailed shrike. 16c, Lesser blue-eared starling. 24c, Red-billed wood hoopoe.

**1977, Mar. 16**

| | | | | | |
|---|---|---|---|---|---|
| **375** | A61 | 3c | multicolored | .25 | .25 |
| **376** | A61 | 4c | multicolored | .30 | .25 |
| **377** | A61 | 6c | multicolored | .35 | .30 |
| **378** | A61 | 8c | multicolored | .40 | .35 |
| **379** | A61 | 16c | multicolored | .55 | .35 |
| **380** | A61 | 24c | multicolored | 1.00 | 1.00 |
| | | | *Nos. 375-380 (6)* | 2.85 | 2.50 |

Lake Kyle, by Joan Evans A62

Landscape Paintings: 4c, Chimanimani Mountains, by Evans. 6c, Rocks near Bonsor Reef, by Alice Balfour. 8c, Dwala (rock) near Devil's Pass, by Balfour. 16c, Zimbabwe, by Balfour. 24c, Victoria Falls, by Thomas Baines.

**1977, July 20 Litho. *Perf. 14½***

| | | | | | |
|---|---|---|---|---|---|
| **381** | A62 | 3c | multicolored | .25 | .25 |
| **382** | A62 | 4c | multicolored | .25 | .25 |
| **383** | A62 | 6c | multicolored | .25 | .25 |
| **384** | A62 | 8c | multicolored | .25 | .25 |
| **385** | A62 | 16c | multicolored | .35 | .30 |
| **386** | A62 | 24c | multicolored | .40 | *.65* |
| | | | *Nos. 381-386 (6)* | 1.75 | 1.95 |

Virgin and Child — A63

**1977, Nov. 16**

| | | | | | |
|---|---|---|---|---|---|
| **387** | A63 | 3c | multicolored | .25 | .25 |
| **388** | A63 | 6c | multicolored | .25 | .25 |
| **389** | A63 | 8c | multicolored | .25 | .25 |
| **390** | A63 | 16c | multicolored | .30 | .25 |
| | | | *Nos. 387-390 (4)* | 1.05 | 1.00 |

Christmas.

Fair Spire and Fairgrounds — A64

19th Rhodesian Trade Fair, Bulawayo: 8c, Fair spire.

**1978, Mar. 15**

| | | | | | |
|---|---|---|---|---|---|
| **391** | A64 | 4c | multicolored | .25 | .25 |
| **392** | A64 | 8c | multicolored | .30 | .25 |

Morganite A65

Black Rhinoceros A66

Odzani Falls — A67

**1978, Aug. 16 Litho. *Perf. 14½***

| | | | | | |
|---|---|---|---|---|---|
| **393** | A65 | 1c | shown | .25 | .25 |
| **394** | A65 | 3c | Amethyst | .25 | .25 |
| **395** | A65 | 4c | Garnet | .25 | .25 |
| **396** | A65 | 5c | Citrine | .25 | .25 |
| **397** | A65 | 7c | Blue topaz | .25 | .25 |
| **398** | A66 | 9c | shown | .25 | .25 |
| **399** | A66 | 11c | Lion | .35 | .35 |
| **400** | A66 | 13c | Warthog | .35 | *1.25* |
| **401** | A66 | 15c | Giraffe | .35 | .35 |
| **402** | A66 | 17c | Zebra | .35 | .25 |
| **403** | A67 | 21c | shown | .35 | *.40* |
| **404** | A67 | 25c | Goba Falls | .50 | .25 |
| **405** | A67 | 30c | Inyangombe Falls | .60 | .25 |
| **406** | A67 | $1 | Bridal Veil Falls | 1.25 | .45 |
| **407** | A67 | $2 | Victoria Falls | 1.50 | .65 |
| | | | *Nos. 393-407 (15)* | 7.10 | 5.70 |

Wright's Flyer A A68

**1978, Oct. 18**

| | | | | | |
|---|---|---|---|---|---|
| **408** | A68 | 4c | shown | .25 | .25 |
| **409** | A68 | 5c | Bleriot XI | .25 | .25 |
| **410** | A68 | 7c | Vickers Vimy | .25 | .25 |
| **411** | A68 | 9c | A.W. 15 Atalanta | .25 | .25 |
| **412** | A68 | 17c | Vickers Viking 1B | .35 | .25 |
| **413** | A68 | 25c | Boeing 720 | .45 | *.50* |
| | | | *Nos. 408-413 (6)* | 1.80 | 1.75 |

75th anniversary of powered flight.

### POSTAGE DUE STAMPS

**Type of Rhodesia and Nyasaland, 1961, Inscribed "RHODESIA"**

***Hyphen Hole Perf. 5***

**1965, June 17 Typo. Unwmk.**

| | | | | | |
|---|---|---|---|---|---|
| **J5** | D1 | 1p | vermilion | .60 | *14.00* |
| *a.* | | | Rouletted 9½ | 5.50 | *14.00* |

***Rouletted 9½***

| | | | | | |
|---|---|---|---|---|---|
| **J6** | D1 | 2p | dark blue | .45 | *9.00* |
| **J7** | D1 | 4p | emerald | .60 | *9.00* |
| **J8** | D1 | 6p | purple | .65 | *6.50* |
| | | | *Nos. J5-J8 (4)* | 2.30 | *38.50* |

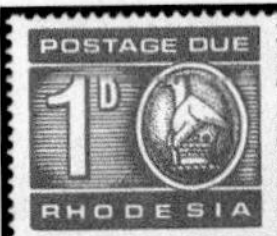


Soapstone Zimbabwe Bird — D2

**1966, Dec. 15 Litho. *Perf. 14½***

| | | | | | |
|---|---|---|---|---|---|
| **J9** | D2 | 1p | crimson | 1.50 | *4.50* |
| **J10** | D2 | 2p | violet blue | 1.75 | *3.00* |
| **J11** | D2 | 4p | emerald | 1.75 | *4.00* |
| **J12** | D2 | 6p | lilac | 1.75 | *2.75* |
| **J13** | D2 | 1sh | dull red brown | 1.75 | *2.75* |
| **J14** | D2 | 2sh | black | 2.00 | *6.00* |
| | | | *Nos. J9-J14 (6)* | 10.50 | *23.00* |

**1970-73 Litho. *Perf. 14½***

**Size: 26x22½mm**

| | | | | | |
|---|---|---|---|---|---|
| **J15** | D2 | 1c | bright green | .90 | *1.50* |
| **J16** | D2 | 2c | ultramarine | .90 | .75 |
| **J17** | D2 | 5c | red violet | 1.75 | *2.75* |
| **J18** | D2 | 6c | lemon | 7.00 | *5.00* |
| **J19** | D2 | 10c | rose red | 1.75 | *5.00* |
| | | | *Nos. J15-J19 (5)* | 12.30 | *15.00* |

Issued: 6c, 5/7/73; others, 2/1/70.

## RIO DE ORO

ˌrē-ō dē ˈōr-ₒ̦ō

LOCATION — On the northwest coast of Africa, bordering on the Atlantic Ocean
GOVT. — Spanish Colony
AREA — 71,600 sq. mi.
POP. — 24,000
CAPITAL — Villa Cisneros

Prior to the issuance of Rio de Oro stamps, Spanish stamps were used 1901-1904, canceled "Rio de Oro."

Rio de Oro became part of Spanish Sahara in 1924.

100 Centimos = 1 Peseta

King Alfonso XIII — A1

**Control Numbers on Back in Blue**

**1905 Unwmk. Typo. *Perf. 14***

| | | | | | |
|---|---|---|---|---|---|
| **1** | A1 | 1c | blue green | 4.00 | 3.00 |
| **2** | A1 | 2c | claret | 5.00 | 3.00 |
| **3** | A1 | 3c | bronze green | 5.00 | 3.00 |
| **4** | A1 | 4c | dark brown | 5.00 | 3.00 |
| **5** | A1 | 5c | orange red | 5.00 | 3.00 |
| **6** | A1 | 10c | dk gray brown | 5.00 | 3.00 |
| **7** | A1 | 15c | red brown | 5.00 | 3.00 |
| **8** | A1 | 25c | dark blue | 95.00 | 32.50 |
| **9** | A1 | 50c | dark green | 45.00 | 13.50 |
| **10** | A1 | 75c | dark violet | 45.00 | 19.00 |
| **11** | A1 | 1p | orange brown | 32.50 | 8.00 |
| **12** | A1 | 2p | buff | 100.00 | 57.50 |
| **13** | A1 | 3p | dull violet | 70.00 | 20.00 |
| **14** | A1 | 4p | blue green | 70.00 | 20.00 |
| **15** | A1 | 5p | dull blue | 100.00 | 45.00 |
| **16** | A1 | 10p | pale red | 250.00 | 150.00 |
| | | | *Nos. 1-16 (16)* | 841.50 | 386.50 |
| | | | Set, never hinged | 1,700. | |

For surcharges see Nos. 17, 34-36, 60-66.

No. 8 Handstamp Surcharged in Rose — a

**1907**

| | | | | | |
|---|---|---|---|---|---|
| **17** | A1 | | 15c on 25c dk blue | 250.00 | 60.00 |
| | | | Never hinged | 400.00 | |

The surcharge exists inverted, double and in violet, normally positioned. Value for each, $450.

King Alfonso XIII — A2

**Control Numbers on Back in Blue**

**1907 Typo.**

| | | | | | |
|---|---|---|---|---|---|
| **18** | A2 | 1c | claret | 3.00 | 2.75 |
| **19** | A2 | 2c | black | 3.50 | 2.75 |
| **20** | A2 | 3c | dark brown | 3.50 | 2.75 |
| **21** | A2 | 4c | red | 3.50 | 2.75 |
| **22** | A2 | 5c | black brown | 3.50 | 2.75 |
| **23** | A2 | 10c | chocolate | 3.50 | 2.75 |
| **24** | A2 | 15c | dark blue | 3.50 | 2.75 |
| **25** | A2 | 25c | deep green | 9.50 | 2.75 |
| **26** | A2 | 50c | black violet | 9.50 | 2.75 |
| **27** | A2 | 75c | orange brown | 9.50 | 2.75 |
| **28** | A2 | 1p | orange | 16.00 | 2.75 |
| **29** | A2 | 2p | dull violet | 5.50 | 2.75 |
| **30** | A2 | 3p | blue green | 5.50 | 2.75 |
| *a.* | | | Cliché of 4p in plate of 3p | 400.00 | 260.00 |
| **31** | A2 | 4p | dark blue | 9.00 | 5.00 |
| **32** | A2 | 5p | red | 9.00 | 5.25 |
| **33** | A2 | 10p | deep green | 9.00 | 12.00 |
| | | | *Nos. 18-33 (16)* | 106.50 | 58.00 |
| | | | Set, never hinged | 250.00 | |

For surcharges see Nos. 38-43, 67-70.

Nos. 9-10 Handstamp Surcharged in Red

**1907**

| | | | | | |
|---|---|---|---|---|---|
| **34** | A1 | | 10c on 50c dk green | 150.00 | 30.00 |
| | | | Never hinged | 235.00 | |
| *a.* | | | "10" omitted | 175.00 | 100.00 |
| | | | Never hinged | 250.00 | |
| **35** | A1 | | 10c on 75c dk violet | 100.00 | 32.00 |
| | | | Never hinged | 175.00 | |

No. 12 Handstamp Surcharged in Violet

**1908**

| | | | | | |
|---|---|---|---|---|---|
| **36** | A1 | | 2c on 2p buff | 75.00 | 24.00 |
| | | | Never hinged | 125.00 | |

No. 36 is found with "1908" measuring 11mm and 12mm.

**Same Surcharge in Red on No. 26**

| | | | | | |
|---|---|---|---|---|---|
| **38** | A2 | | 10c on 50c blk vio | 22.50 | 3.75 |
| | | | Never hinged | 37.50 | |

A 5c on 10c (No. 23) was not officially issued.

**Nos. 25, 27-28 Handstamp Surcharged Type "a" in Red, Violet or Green**

**1908**

| | | | | | |
|---|---|---|---|---|---|
| **39** | A2 | | 15c on 25c dp grn (R) | 25.00 | 3.75 |
| **40** | A2 | | 15c on 75c org brn (V) | 32.50 | 17.50 |
| *a.* | | | Green surcharge | 50.00 | 6.75 |
| | | | Never hinged | 72.50 | |
| **41** | A2 | | 15c on 1p org (V) | 37.50 | 15.00 |
| **42** | A2 | | 15c on 1p org (R) | 35.00 | 15.00 |
| **43** | A2 | | 15c on 1p org (G) | 25.00 | 12.00 |
| | | | *Nos. 39-43 (5)* | 155.00 | 63.25 |
| | | | Set, never hinged | 325.00 | |

As this surcharge is handstamped, it exists in several varieties: double, inverted, in pairs with one surcharge omitted, etc.

A3

**Revenue stamps overprinted and surcharged**

**1908** ***Imperf.***

**44** A3 5c on 50c green (C) 90.00 30.00
Never hinged 160.00
**45** A3 5c on 50c green (V) 130.00 52.50
Never hinged 225.00

The surcharge, which is handstamped, exists in many variations.

Nos. 44-45 are found with and without control numbers on back. Stamps with control numbers sell at about double the above values. Counterfeits exist.

See Spanish Guinea Nos. 98-101C for additional revenue stamps surcharged for postal use.

King Alfonso XIII — A4

**Control Numbers on Back in Blue**

**1909** **Typo.** ***Perf. 14½***

**46** A4 1c red .85 .50
**47** A4 2c orange .85 .50
**48** A4 5c dark green .85 .50
**49** A4 10c orange red .85 .50
**50** A4 15c blue green .85 .50
**51** A4 20c dark violet 2.10 .70
**52** A4 25c deep blue 2.10 .70
**53** A4 30c claret 2.10 .70
**54** A4 40c chocolate 2.10 .70
**55** A4 50c red violet 4.00 .70
**56** A4 1p dark brown 5.25 3.25
**57** A4 4p carmine rose 6.25 4.75
**58** A4 10p claret 14.00 7.75
*Nos. 46-58 (13)* 42.15 21.75
Set, never hinged 100.00

Stamps of 1905 Handstamped in Black

**1910**

**60** A1 10c on 5p dull bl 21.00 8.50
*a.* Red surcharge 90.00 55.00
Never hinged 145.00
**62** A1 10c on 10p pale red 21.00 8.50
*a.* Violet surcharge 145.00 62.50
Never hinged 210.00
*b.* Green surcharge 145.00 62.50
Never hinged 210.00
**65** A1 15c on 3p dull vio 21.00 8.50
*a.* Imperf. 110.00
Never hinged 190.00
**66** A1 15c on 4p blue grn 21.00 8.50
*a.* 10c on 4p bl grn 925.00 275.00
Never hinged 1,300.
*Nos. 60-66 (4)* 84.00 34.00
Set, never hinged 160.00

See note after No. 43.

Nos. 31 and 33 Surcharged in Red or Violet

**1911-13**

**67** A2 2c on 4p dk blue (R) 12.50 9.00
**68** A2 5c on 10p dp grn (V) 37.50 9.00

Nos. 29-30 Surcharged in Black

**69** A2 10c on 2p dull vio 19.00 8.25
**69A** A2 10c on 3p bl grn ('13) 225.00 50.00

**Nos. 30, 32 Handstamped Type "a"**

**69B** A2 15c on 3p bl grn ('13) 200.00 24.00
**70** A2 15c on 5p red 13.50 9.00
*Nos. 67-70 (6)* 507.50 109.25
Set, never hinged 650.00

King Alfonso XIII — A5

**Control Numbers on Back in Blue**

**1912** **Typo.** ***Perf. 13½***

**71** A5 1c carmine rose .40 .35
**72** A5 2c lilac .40 .35
**73** A5 5c deep green .40 .35
**74** A5 10c red .40 .35
**75** A5 15c brown orange .40 .35
**76** A5 20c brown .40 .35
**77** A5 25c dull blue .40 .35
**78** A5 30c dark violet .40 .35
**79** A5 40c blue green .40 .35
**80** A5 50c lake .40 .35
**81** A5 1p red 4.00 .80
**82** A5 4p claret 7.50 4.00
**83** A5 10p dark brown 11.00 6.00
*Nos. 71-83 (13)* 26.50 14.30
Set, never hinged 60.00

For overprints see Nos. 97-109.

King Alfonso XIII — A6

**Control Numbers on Back in Blue**

**1914** ***Perf. 13***

**84** A6 1c olive black .40 .35
**85** A6 2c maroon .40 .35
**86** A6 5c deep green .40 .35
**87** A6 10c orange red .40 .35
**88** A6 15c orange red .40 .35
**89** A6 20c deep claret .40 .35
**90** A6 25c dark blue .40 .35
**91** A6 30c blue green .40 .35
**92** A6 40c brown orange .40 .35
**93** A6 50c dark brown .40 .35
**94** A6 1p dull lilac 3.00 2.40
**95** A6 4p carmine rose 7.25 6.25
**96** A6 10p dull violet 7.50 6.25
*Nos. 84-96 (13)* 21.75 18.40
Set, never hinged 50.00

Nos. 71-83 Overprinted in Black

**1917** ***Perf. 13½***

**97** A5 1c carmine rose 17.50 1.40
**98** A5 2c lilac 17.50 1.40
**99** A5 5c deep green 3.50 1.40
**100** A5 10c red 3.50 1.40
**101** A5 15c orange brn 3.50 1.40
**102** A5 20c brown 3.50 1.40
**103** A5 25c dull blue 3.50 1.40
**104** A5 30c dark violet 3.50 1.40
**105** A5 40c blue green 3.50 1.40
**106** A5 50c lake 3.50 1.40
**107** A5 1p red 19.00 4.75
**108** A5 4p claret 22.50 6.25
**109** A5 10p dark brown 42.50 9.25
*Nos. 97-109 (13)* 147.00 34.25
Set, never hinged 300.00

Nos. 97-109 exist with overprint inverted or double (value 50 percent over normal) and in dark blue (value twice normal). Forgeries exist.

King Alfonso XIII — A7

**Control Numbers on Back in Blue**

**1919** **Typo.** ***Perf. 13***

**114** A7 1c brown 1.25 .55
**115** A7 2c claret 1.25 .55
**116** A7 5c light green 1.25 .55
**117** A7 10c carmine 1.25 .55
**118** A7 15c orange 4.00 2.00
**119** A7 20c orange 1.25 .55
**120** A7 25c blue 1.25 .55
**121** A7 30c green 1.25 .55
**122** A7 40c vermilion 1.25 .55
**123** A7 50c brown 1.25 .55
**124** A7 1p lilac 8.00 4.50
**125** A7 4p rose 14.50 7.50
**126** A7 10p violet 25.00 10.00
*Nos. 114-126 (13)* 62.75 28.95
Set, never hinged 100.00

A8

**Control Numbers on Back in Blue**

**1920** ***Perf. 13***

**127** A8 1c gray lilac 1.10 .55
**128** A8 2c rose 1.10 .55
**129** A8 5c light red 1.10 .55
**130** A8 10c lilac 1.10 .55
**131** A8 15c light brown 1.10 .55
**132** A8 20c greenish blue 1.10 .55
**133** A8 25c yellow 1.10 .55
**134** A8 30c dull blue 6.25 4.50
**135** A8 40c orange 3.75 2.10
**136** A8 50c dull rose 3.75 2.10
**137** A8 1p gray green 5.25 2.10
**138** A8 4p lilac rose 7.00 4.25
**139** A8 10p brown 25.00 10.00
*Nos. 127-139 (13)* 58.70 28.90
Set, never hinged 100.00

A9

**Control Numbers on Back in Blue**

**1922**

**140** A9 1c yellow 1.00 .60
**141** A9 2c red brown 1.00 .60
**142** A9 5c blue green 1.00 .60
**143** A9 10c pale red 1.00 .60
**144** A9 15c myrtle green 1.00 .60
**145** A9 20c turq blue 1.00 .65
**146** A9 25c deep blue 1.00 .65
**147** A9 30c deep rose 1.75 1.25
**148** A9 40c violet 1.75 1.25
**149** A9 50c orange 1.75 1.25
**150** A9 1p lilac 5.50 1.75
**151** A9 4p claret 12.00 4.00
**152** A9 10p dark brown 20.00 8.25
*Nos. 140-152 (13)* 49.75 22.05
Set, never hinged 100.00

For subsequent issues see Spanish Sahara.

---

## RIO MUNI

ˌrē-ō ˈmü-nē

LOCATION — West Africa, bordering on Cameroun and Gabon Republics
GOVT. — Province of Spain
AREA — 9,500 sq. mi.
POP. — 183,377 (1960)
CAPITAL — Bata

Rio Muni and the island of Fernando Po are the two provinces that constitute Spanish Guinea. Separate stamp issues for the two provinces were decreed in 1960.

Spanish Guinea Nos. 1-84 were used only in the territory now called Rio Muni.

Rio Muni united with Fernando Po on Oct. 12, 1968, to form the Republic of Equatorial Guinea.

100 Centimos = 1 Peseta

**Catalogue values for all unused stamps in this country are for Never Hinged items.**

Boy Reading and Missionary — A1

**1960** **Unwmk.** **Photo.** ***Perf. 13x12½***

**1** A1 25c dull vio bl .25 .25
**2** A1 50c gray brown .25 .25
**3** A1 75c dull grysh pur .25 .25
**4** A1 1p scarlet .25 .25
**5** A1 1.50p brt blue grn .25 .25
**6** A1 2p magenta .25 .25
**7** A1 3p slate blue .30 .25
**8** A1 5p red brown 1.00 .25
**9** A1 10p lt olive grn 1.75 .25
*Nos. 1-9 (9)* 4.55 2.25

Quina Plant — A2

Design: 80c, Croton plant.

**1960** ***Perf. 13x12½***

**10** A2 35c olive gray .25 .25
**11** A2 80c dp bluish grn .25 .25

See Nos. B1-B2.

Map of Rio Muni — A3

Designs: 50c, 1p, Gen. Franco. 70c, Government Palace.

**1961, Oct. 1** ***Perf. 12½x13***

**12** A3 25c gray violet .25 .25
**13** A3 50c brown .25 .25
**14** A3 70c yellow green .25 .25
**15** A3 1p org vermilion .25 .25
*Nos. 12-15 (4)* 1.00 1.00

25th anniversary of the nomination of Gen. Francisco Franco as Chief of State.

Rio Muni Headdress — A4

Design: 50c, Rio Muni idol.

**1962, July 10** ***Perf. 13x12½***

**16** A4 25c violet .25 .25
**17** A4 50c green .25 .25
**18** A4 1p orange brown .25 .25
*Nos. 16-18 (3)* .75 .75

Issued for child welfare.

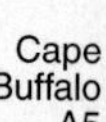
Cape Buffalo A5

Design: 35c, Gorilla, vert.

***Perf. 13x12½, 12½x13***

**1962, Nov. 23** **Photo.** **Unwmk.**

**19** A5 15c olive gray .25 .25
**20** A5 35c deep magenta .25 .25
**21** A5 1p brown red .25 .25
*Nos. 19-21 (3)* .75 .75

Issued for Stamp Day.

Mother and Child — A6

**1963, Jan. 29** ***Perf. 13x12½***

**22** A6 50c green .25 .25
**23** A6 1p brown orange .25 .25

Issued to help the victims of the Seville flood.

Father Joaquin Juanola — A7

50c, Blessing hand, cross and palms.

**1963, July 6** ***Perf. 13x12½***

**24** A7 25c blackish violet .25 .25
**25** A7 50c brown olive .25 .25
**26** A7 1p scarlet .25 .25
*Nos. 24-26 (3)* .75 .75

Issued for child welfare.

Praying Child and Arms — A8

**1963, July 12**

**27** A8 50c gray green .25 .25
**28** A8 1p redsh brown .25 .25

Issued for Barcelona flood relief.

Branch of Copal Tree — A9

50c, Flowering quina, horiz.

***Perf. 13x12½, 12½x13***

**1964, Mar. 6** **Photo.**

**29** A9 25c purple .25 .25
**30** A9 50c brt blue green .25 .25
**31** A9 1p carmine lake .25 .25
*Nos. 29-31 (3)* .75 .75

Issued for Stamp Day 1963.

Tree Pangolin A10

Design: 50c, Chameleon.

**1964, June 1** ***Perf. 13x12½***

**32** A10 25c violet blk .25 .25
**33** A10 50c olive brown .25 .25
**34** A10 1p lake brown .25 .25
*Nos. 32-34 (3)* .75 .75

Issued for child welfare.

Dwarf Crocodile A11

15c, 70c, 3p, Dwarf crocodile. 25c, 1p, 5p, Leopard. 50c, 1.50p, 10p, Black rhinoceros.

**1964, July 1**

**35** A11 15c lt brown .25 .25
**36** A11 25c violet .25 .25
**37** A11 50c olive gray .25 .25
**38** A11 70c green .25 .25
**39** A11 1p brown lake .85 .25
**40** A11 1.50p blue green .90 .25
**41** A11 3p indigo 1.75 .25
**42** A11 5p deep brown 4.50 .50
**43** A11 10p green 8.50 1.10
*Nos. 35-43 (9)* 17.50 3.35

Greshoff's Tree Frog A12

Stamp Day: 1p, Helmet guinea fowl, vert.

***Perf. 13x12½, 12½x13***

**1964, Nov. 23** **Photo.** **Unwmk.**

**44** A12 50c deep dull green .25 .25
**45** A12 1p lake .25 .25
**46** A12 1.50p deep bluish green .25 .25
*Nos. 44-46 (3)* .75 .75

Issued for Stamp Day, 1964.

Woman's Head — A13

Woman Chemist — A14

Design: 1.50p, Logger.

**1964** **Photo.** ***Perf. 13x12½***

**47** A13 50c deep green .25 .25
**48** A14 1p scarlet .25 .25
**49** A14 1.50p deep bluish green .25 .25
*Nos. 47-49 (3)* .75 .75

Issued to commemorate 25 years of peace.

Goliath Beetle A15

Beetle: 1p, Acridoxena hewaniana.

**1965, June 1** **Photo.** ***Perf. 12½x13***

**50** A15 50c slate green .25 .25
**51** A15 1p dark gray brown .25 .25
**52** A15 1.50p black & gray .25 .25
*Nos. 50-52 (3)* .75 .75

Issued for child welfare.

Ring-necked Pheasant — A16

Leopard and Arms of Rio Muni A17

***Perf. 13x12½, 12½x13***

**1965, Nov. 23** **Photo.**

**53** A16 50c brownish black .35 .25
**54** A17 1p sepia .65 .25
**55** A16 2.50p reddish lilac 3.00 .90
*Nos. 53-55 (3)* 4.00 1.40

Issued for Stamp Day, 1965.

Elephant and Parrot A18

Design: 1.50p, Lion and boy.

***Perf. 12½x13***

**1966, June 1** **Photo.** **Unwmk.**

**56** A18 50c sepia .25 .25
**57** A18 1p dk purple .25 .25
**58** A18 1.50p greenish blue .25 .25
*Nos. 56-58 (3)* .75 .75

Issued for child welfare.

Water Chevrotain A19

Designs: 40c, 4p, Tree pangolin, vert.

**1966, Nov. 23** **Photo.** ***Perf. 13***

**59** A19 10c brown & yel brn .25 .25
**60** A19 40c brown & yellow .25 .25
**61** A19 1.50p slate lil & brn lil .25 .25
**62** A19 4p bl & brt yel grn .25 .25
*Nos. 59-62 (4)* 1.00 1.00

Issued for Stamp Day, 1966.

A20

Designs: 40c, 4p, Vine creeper.

**1967, June 1** **Photo.** ***Perf. 13***

**63** A20 10c green & yellow .25 .25
**64** A20 40c blk, rose car & gray grn .25 .25
**65** A20 1.50p brt blue, pink & lake brn .25 .25
**66** A20 4p gray green & black .25 .25
*Nos. 63-66 (4)* 1.00 1.00

Issued for child welfare.

Potto — A21

Designs: 1p, River hog, horiz. 3.50p, African golden cat, horiz.

**1967, Nov. 23** **Photo.** ***Perf. 13***

**67** A21 1p black & red brn .30 .30
**68** A21 1.50p dk brown & grn .30 .30
**69** A21 3.50p org brn & grn .45 .45
*Nos. 67-69 (3)* 1.05 1.05

Issued for Stamp Day 1967.

**Zodiac Issue**

Cancer — A22

1.50p, Taurus. 2.50p, Gemini.

**1968, Apr. 25** **Photo.** ***Perf. 13***

**70** A22 1p brt mag, *lt yel* .30 .30
**71** A22 1.50p red brn, *pink* .30 .30
**72** A22 2.50p dp vio blue, *yel* .75 .75
*Nos. 70-72 (3)* 1.35 1.35

Issued for child welfare.

---

## SEMI-POSTAL STAMPS

### Type of Regular Issue, 1960

Designs: 10c+5c, Croton plant. 15c+5c, Flower and leaves of croton.

**1960** **Unwmk.** **Photo.** ***Perf. 13x12½***

**B1** A2 10c + 5c brn pur .25 .25
**B2** A2 15c + 5c yellow brown .25 .25

The surtax was for child welfare.

Bishop Juan de Ribera — SP1

20c+5c, The clown Pablo de Valladolid by Velazquez. 30c+10c, Juan de Ribera statue.

**1961** ***Perf. 13x12½***

**B3** SP1 10c + 5c dp rose red .25 .25
**B4** SP1 20c + 5c gray green .25 .25
**B5** SP1 30c + 10c brown .25 .25
**B6** SP1 50c + 20c lt brown .25 .25
*Nos. B3-B6 (4)* 1.00 1.00

Issued for Stamp Day, 1960.

Mandrill SP2

Design: 25c+10c, Elephant, vert.

***Perf. 12½x13, 13x12½***

**1961, June 21** **Unwmk.**

**B7** SP2 10c + 5c lake .25 .25
**B8** SP2 25c + 10c gray violet .25 .25
**B9** SP2 80c + 20c dp gray grn .25 .25
*Nos. B7-B9 (3)* .75 .75

The surtax was for child welfare.

Statuette — SP3

Design: 25c+10c, 1p+10c, Male figure.

**1961, Nov. 23** ***Perf. 13x12½***

**B10** SP3 10c + 5c rose brown .25 .25
**B11** SP3 25c + 10c dark purple .25 .25
**B12** SP3 30c + 10c blksh brn .25 .25
**B13** SP3 1p + 10c red orange .25 .25
*Nos. B10-B13 (4)* 1.00 1.00

Issued for Stamp Day 1961.

# ROMANIA

rō-'mā-nēə

## (Rumania, Roumania)

LOCATION — Southeastern Europe, bordering on the Black Sea
GOVT. — Republic
AREA — 91,699 sq. mi.
POP. — 22,600,000 (est. 1984)
CAPITAL — Bucharest

Romania was formed in 1861 from the union of the principalities of Moldavia and Walachia in 1859. It became a kingdom in 1881. Following World War I, the original territory was considerably enlarged by the addition of Bessarabia, Bukovina, Transylvania, Crisana, Maramures and Banat. The republic was established in 1948.

40 Parale = 1 Piaster
100 Bani = 1 Leu (plural "Lei") (1868)

**Catalogue values for unused stamps in this country are for Never Hinged items, beginning with Scott 475 in the regular postage section, Scott B82 in the semi-postal section, Scott C24 in the airpost section, Scott CB1 in the airpost semi-postal section, Scott J82 in the postage due section, Scott O1 in the official section, Scott RA16 in the postal tax section, and Scott RAJ1 in the postal tax postage due section.**

### Watermarks

Wmk. 95 — Wavy Lines

Wmk. 163 — Coat of Arms

Wmk. 164 — PR

Wmk. 165 — PR Interlaced

Wmk. 167 — Coat of Arms Covering 25 Stamps

Wmk. 200 — PR

Wmk. 225 — Crown over PTT, Multiple

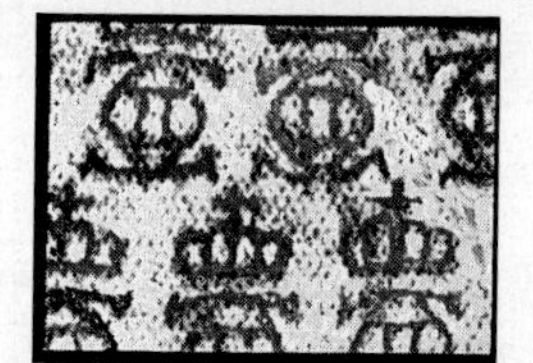
Wmk. 230 — Crowns and Monograms

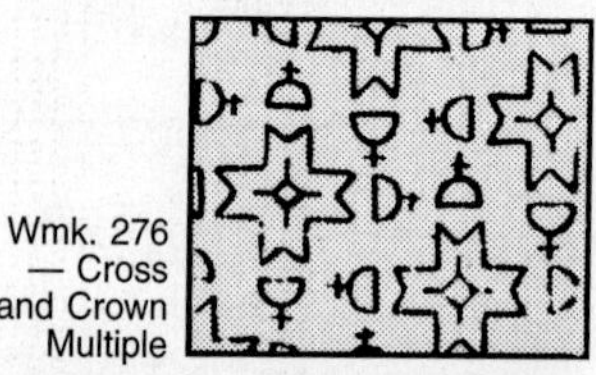
Wmk. 276 — Cross and Crown Multiple

Wmk. 289 — RPR Multiple

Wmk. 358 — RPR Multiple in Endless Rows

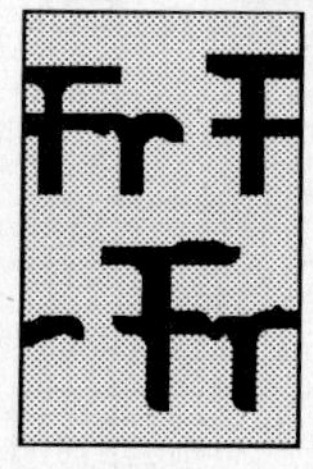
Wmk. 398 — Fr Multiple

Values for unused stamps are for examples with original gum as defined in the catalogue introduction except for Nos. 1-4 which are valued without gum.

### Moldavia

Coat of Arms — A1

**Laid Paper**

**Handstamped**

| 1858, July | | Unwmk. | | *Imperf.* |
|---|---|---|---|---|
| 1 | A1 | 27pa blk, *rose* | *60,000.* | *25,000.* |
| a. | | Tête bêche pair | | |
| 2 | A1 | 54pa blue, *grn* | *15,500.* | *10,000.* |
| 3 | A1 | 108pa blue, *rose* | *35,000.* | *16,000.* |

**Wove Paper**

| | | | | |
|---|---|---|---|---|
| 4 | A1 | 81pa blue, *bl* | *50,000.* | *55,000.* |

Cut to shape or octagonally, Nos. 1-4 sell for one-fourth to one-third of these values.

Coat of Arms — A2

| 1858 | | Bluish Wove Paper | | |
|---|---|---|---|---|
| 5 | A2 | 5pa black | *15,000.* | *15,000.* |
| a. | | Tête bêche pair | | |
| 6 | A2 | 40pa blue | 275. | 225. |
| a. | | Tête bêche pair | *1,300.* | *2,650.* |
| 7 | A2 | 80pa red | *7,750.* | *875.* |
| a. | | Tête bêche pair | | |

| 1859 | | White Wove Paper | | |
|---|---|---|---|---|
| 8 | A2 | 5pa black | *15,000.* | *10,000.* |
| a. | | Tête bêche pair | | |
| b. | | Frame broken at bottom | 175. | |
| c. | | As "b," tête bêche pair | 600. | |
| 9 | A2 | 40pa blue | 175. | 190. |
| b. | | Tête bêche pair | 650. | *1,500.* |
| 10 | A2 | 80pa red | 475. | 300. |
| b. | | Tête bêche pair | *1,750.* | *3,250.* |

Nos. 6-7, 9-10 are inscribed "Posta Scrisorei." No. 8b has a break in the frame at bottom below "A." It was never placed in use.

### Moldavia-Walachia

Coat of Arms — A3

**Printed by Hand from Single Dies**

| 1862 | | White Laid Paper | | |
|---|---|---|---|---|
| 11 | A3 | 3pa orange | 300.00 | *2,250.* |
| a. | | 3pa yellow | 300.00 | *2,250.* |
| 12 | A3 | 6pa carmine | 300.00 | 475.00 |
| 13 | A3 | 6pa red | 300.00 | 475.00 |
| 14 | A3 | 30pa blue | 87.50 | 115.00 |
| | | *Nos. 11-14 (4)* | 987.50 | 3,315. |

**White Wove Paper**

| | | | | |
|---|---|---|---|---|
| 15 | A3 | 3pa orange yel | 85.00 | *275.00* |
| a. | | 3pa lemon | 85.00 | *275.00* |
| 16 | A3 | 6pa carmine | 95.00 | *275.00* |
| 17 | A3 | 6pa vermilion | 77.50 | *225.00* |
| 18 | A3 | 30pa blue | 60.00 | 65.00 |
| | | *Nos. 15-18 (4)* | 317.50 | 840.00 |

**Greenish-Blue Paper**

| | | | | |
|---|---|---|---|---|
| 15C | A3 | 3pa orange yel | — | 2,500. |

**Tête bêche pairs**

| | | | | |
|---|---|---|---|---|
| *11b* | A3 | 3pa orange | 1,550. | |
| *12a* | A3 | 6pa carmine | 1,000. | 1,250. |
| *14a* | A3 | 30pa blue | 190.00 | 1,550. |
| *15b* | A3 | 3pa orange yellow | 210.00 | *1,600.* |
| *16a* | A3 | 6pa carmine | 275.00 | 1,750. |
| *17a* | A3 | 6pa vermilion | 190.00 | 1,600. |
| *18a* | A3 | 30pa blue | 175.00 | 1,600. |

Nos. 11-18 were printed with a hand press, one at a time, from single dies. The impressions were very irregularly placed and occasionally overlapped. Sheets of 32 (4x8). The 3rd and 4th rows were printed inverted, making the second and third rows tête bêche. All values come in distinct shades, frequently even on the same sheet. The paper of this and the following issues through No. 52 often shows a bluish, grayish or yellowish tint.

**White Wove Paper**

| 1864 | | Typographed from Plates | | |
|---|---|---|---|---|
| 19 | A3 | 3pa yellow | 60.00 | *1,500.* |
| a. | | Tête bêche pair | 350.00 | |
| b. | | Pair, one sideways | 150.00 | |
| 20 | A3 | 6pa deep rose | 22.50 | |
| a. | | Tête bêche pair | 52.50 | |
| b. | | Pair, one sideways | 52.50 | |
| 21 | A3 | 30pa deep blue | 17.50 | *100.00* |
| a. | | Tête bêche pair | 57.50 | |
| b. | | Pair, one sideways | 57.50 | 2,650. |
| c. | | Bluish wove paper | *150.00* | |
| | | *Nos. 19-21 (3)* | 100.00 | |

Stamps of 1862 issue range from very clear to blurred impressions but rarely have broken or deformed characteristics. The 1864 issue, though rarely blurred, usually have various imperfections in the letters and numbers. These include breaks, malformations, occasional dots at left of the crown or above the "R" of "PAR," a dot on the middle stroke of the "F," and many other bulges, breaks and spots of color.

The 1864 issue were printed in sheets of 40 (5x8). The first and second rows were inverted. Clichés in the third row were placed sideways, 4 with head to right and 4 with head to left, making one tête bêche pair. The fourth and fifth rows were normally placed.

No. 20 was never placed in use.

All values exist in shades, light to dark.

Counterfeit cancellations exist on #11-21.

Three stamps in this design- 2pa, 5pa, 20pa- were printed on white wove paper in 1864, but never placed in use. Value, set $12.

### Romania

Prince Alexandru Ioan Cuza — A4

TWENTY PARALES:

Type I — The central oval does not touch the inner frame. The "I" of "DECI" extends above and below the other letters.

Type II — The central oval touches the frame at the bottom. The "I" of the "DECI" is the same height as the other letters.

| 1865, Jan. | Unwmk. | Litho. | | *Imperf.* |
|---|---|---|---|---|
| 22 | A4 | 2pa orange | 70.00 | *250.00* |
| a. | | 2pa yellow | 77.50 | *325.00* |
| b. | | 2pa ocher | 325.00 | *325.00* |
| 23 | A4 | 5pa blue | 45.00 | *275.00* |
| 24 | A4 | 20pa red, type I | 35.00 | 47.50 |
| a. | | Bluish paper | 350.00 | |
| 25 | A4 | 20pa red, type II | 35.00 | 40.00 |
| a. | | Bluish paper | 350.00 | |
| | | *Nos. 22-25 (4)* | 185.00 | 612.50 |

The 20pa types are found se-tenant.

**White Laid Paper**

| | | | | |
|---|---|---|---|---|
| 26 | A4 | 2pa orange | 60.00 | *275.00* |
| a. | | 2pa ocher | 125.00 | |
| 27 | A4 | 5pa blue | 95.00 | *450.00* |

Prince Carol — A5

Type I — A6

Type II — A7

TWENTY PARALES:

Type I — A6. The Greek border at the upper right goes from right to left.

Type II — A7. The Greek border at the upper right goes from left to right.

| 1866-67 | | Thin Wove Paper | | |
|---|---|---|---|---|
| 29 | A5 | 2pa blk, *yellow* | 35.00 | *95.00* |
| a. | | Thick paper | 65.00 | *400.00* |
| 30 | A5 | 5pa blk, *dk bl* | 60.00 | *575.00* |
| a. | | 5pa black, *indigo* | 100.00 | — |
| b. | | Thick paper | 70.00 | *525.00* |
| 31 | A6 | 20pa blk, *rose*, (I) | 30.00 | 26.50 |
| a. | | Dot in Greek border, thin paper | 400.00 | 150.00 |
| b. | | Thick paper | 175.00 | 87.50 |
| c. | | Dot in Greek border, thick paper | 125.00 | 72.50 |
| 32 | A7 | 20pa blk, *rose*, (II) | 30.00 | 26.50 |
| a. | | Thick paper | 175.00 | 87.50 |
| | | *Nos. 29-32 (4)* | 155.00 | 723.00 |

The 20pa types are found se-tenant.

Faked cancellations are known on Nos. 22-27, 29-32.

The white dot of Nos. 31a and 31c occurs in extreme upper right border.

Thick paper was used in 1866, thin in 1867.

Prince Carol — A8

**1868-70**

33 A8 2b orange 42.50 40.00
*a.* 2b yellow 45.00 40.00
34 A8 3b violet ('70) 42.50 40.00
35 A8 4b dk blue 55.00 47.50
36 A8 18b scarlet 225.00 30.00
*a.* 18b rose 225.00 30.00
*Nos. 33-36 (4)* 365.00 157.50

Prince Carol — A9

**1869**

37 A9 5b orange yel 72.50 42.50
*a.* 5b deep orange 75.00 *42.50*
38 A9 10b blue 40.00 35.00
*a.* 10b ultramarine 77.50 52.50
*b.* 10b indigo 85.00 40.00
40 A9 15b vermilion 40.00 35.00
41 A9 25b orange & blue 40.00 26.50
42 A9 50b blue & red 150.00 52.50
*a.* 50b indigo & red 175.00 55.00
*Nos. 37-42 (5)* 342.50 191.50

No. 40 on vertically laid paper was not issued. Value $1,250.

Prince Carol — A10

**1871-72** ***Imperf.***

43 A10 5b rose 42.50 35.00
*a.* 5b vermilion 45.00 45.00
44 A10 10b orange yel 55.00 35.00
*a.* Vertically laid paper *450.00 450.00*
45 A10 10b blue 125.00 70.00
46 A10 15b red 210.00 210.00
47 A10 25b olive brown 47.50 47.50
*Nos. 43-47 (5)* 480.00 397.50

**1872**

48 A10 10b ultra 42.50 52.50
*a.* Vertically laid paper 175.00 300.00
*b.* 10b greenish blue 150.00 175.00
49 A10 50b blue & red 225.00 240.00

No. 48 is a provisional issue printed from a new plate in which the head is placed further right.

Faked cancellations are found on No. 49.

**1872 Wove Paper *Perf. 12½***

50 A10 5b rose 65.00 52.50
*a.* 5b vermilion *1,300. 700.00*
51 A10 10b blue 57.50 52.50
*a.* 10b ultramarine 60.00 25.00
52 A10 25b dark brown 47.50 47.50
*Nos. 50-52 (3)* 170.00 152.50

No. 43a with faked perforation is frequently offered as No. 50a.

Prince Carol — A11

**Paris Print, Fine Impression**
**Tinted Paper**

**1872 Typo. *Perf. 14x13½***

53 A11 1½b brnz grn, *bluish* 25.00 5.00
54 A11 3b green, *bluish* 32.50 5.00
55 A11 5b bis, *pale buff* 21.00 4.50
56 A11 10b blue 21.00 5.00
57 A11 15b red brn, *pale buff* 140.00 15.00
58 A11 25b org, *pale buff* 145.00 18.50
59 A11 50b rose, *pale rose* 150.00 42.50
*Nos. 53-59 (7)* 534.50 95.50

Nos. 53-59 exist imperf.

**Bucharest Print, Rough Impression**
***Perf. 11, 11½, 13½, and Compound***

**1876-79**

60 A11 1½b brnz grn, *bluish* 6.50 4.25
61 A11 5b bis, *yelsh* 17.00 3.25
*b.* Printed on both sides *75.00*
62 A11 10b bl, *yelsh* ('77) 27.50 5.00
*a.* 10b pale bl, *yelsh* 25.00 5.00
*b.* 10b dark blue, *yelsh* 42.50 5.00
*d.* Cliché of 5b in plate of 10b ('79) 425.00 425.00
63 A11 10b ultra, *yelsh* ('77) 47.50 5.00
64 A11 15b red brn, *yelsh* 72.50 9.25
*a.* Printed on both sides *100.00*
65 A11 30b org red, *yelsh* ('78) 190.00 50.00
*a.* Printed on both sides *210.00*
*Nos. 60-65 (6)* 361.00 76.75

#60-65 are valued in the grade of fine.

*#62d has been reprinted in dark blue. The originals are in dull blue. Value of reprint, $175.*

***Perf. 11, 11½, 13½ and Compound***

**1879**

66 A11 1½b blk, *yelsh* 6.25 4.25
*b.* Imperf. 12.00
67 A11 3b ol grn, *bluish* 17.50 12.50
*a.* Diagonal half used as 1½b on cover
68 A11 5b green, *bluish* 6.75 4.25
69 A11 10b rose, *yelsh* 13.50 2.50
*b.* Clichê of 5b in plate of 10b 3.75.00 *475.00*
70 A11 15b rose red, *yelsh* 50.00 12.50
71 A11 25b blue, *yelsh* 140.00 25.00
72 A11 50b bister, *yelsh* 120.00 35.00
*Nos. 66-72 (7)* 354.00 96.00

#66-72 are valued in the grade of fine.

There are two varieties of the numerals on the 15b and 50b.

*No. 69b has been reprinted in dark rose. Originals are in pale rose. Value of reprint, $40.*

King Carol I — A12

**1880 White Paper**

73 A12 15b brown 12.50 2.50
74 A12 25b blue 23.50 3.25

#73-74 are valued in the grade of fine.
No. 74 exists imperf.

King Carol I — A13

***Perf. 13½, 11½ & Compound***

**1885-89**

75 A13 1½b black 3.50 1.75
*a.* Printed on both sides
76 A13 3b violet 5.00 1.75
*a.* Half used as 1½b on cover 21.00
77 A13 5b green 75.00 1.75
78 A13 15b red brown 14.50 2.50
79 A13 25b blue 17.00 6.00
*Nos. 75-79 (5)* 115.00 13.75

**Tinted Paper**

80 A13 1½b blk, *bluish* 5.00 1.75
81 A13 3b vio, *bluish* 5.00 1.75
82 A13 3b ol grn, *bluish* 5.00 1.75
83 A13 5b bl grn, *bluish* 5.00 1.75
84 A13 10b rose, *pale buff* 5.00 2.50
85 A13 15b red brn, *pale buff* 18.50 2.75
86 A13 25b bl, *pale buff* 18.50 6.00
87 A13 50b bis, *pale buff* 75.00 21.00
*Nos. 80-87 (8)* 137.00 39.25

**Thin Pale Yellowish Paper**

**1889 Wmk. 163**

88 A13 1½b black 30.00 6.00
89 A13 3b violet 21.00 6.00
90 A13 5b green 21.00 6.00
91 A13 10b rose 21.00 6.00
92 A13 15b red brown 72.50 13.00
93 A13 25b dark blue 47.50 10.00
*Nos. 88-93 (6)* 213.00 47.00

King Carol I — A14

**1890 *Perf. 13½, 11½ & Compound***

94 A14 1½b maroon 5.00 3.50
95 A14 3b violet 25.00 3.50
96 A14 5b emerald 12.00 3.50
97 A14 10b red 13.00 5.00
*a.* 10b rose 17.00 6.75
98 A14 15b dk brown 30.00 3.50
99 A14 25b gray blue 25.00 3.50
100 A14 50b orange 65.00 32.50
*Nos. 94-100 (7)* 175.00 55.00

**1891 Unwmk.**

101 A14 1½b lilac rose 1.75 1.25
*b.* Printed on both sides *65.00*
102 A14 3b lilac 2.00 1.75
*a.* 3b violet 2.25 2.25
*b.* Printed on both sides
*c.* Impressions of 5b on back *100.00 75.00*
103 A14 5b emerald 3.50 1.75
104 A14 10b pale red 21.00 1.75
*a.* Printed on both sides *140.00 110.00*
105 A14 15b gray brown 13.00 1.25
106 A14 25b gray blue 13.00 1.75
107 A14 50b orange 85.00 13.00
*Nos. 101-107 (7)* 139.25 22.50

Nos. 101-107 exist imperf.

King Carol I — A15

**1891**

108 A15 1½b claret 6.00 7.00
109 A15 3b lilac 6.00 7.00
110 A15 5b emerald 7.50 8.50
111 A15 10b red 7.50 8.50
112 A15 15b gray brown 7.50 8.50
*Nos. 108-112 (5)* 34.50 39.50

25th year of the reign of King Carol I.

**1894 Wmk. 164**

113 A14 3b lilac 9.25 5.00
114 A14 5b pale green 9.25 5.00
115 A14 25b gray blue 13.50 6.25
116 A14 50b orange 27.50 12.50
*Nos. 113-116 (4)* 59.50 28.75

King Carol I
A17 A18

A19

A20

A21

A23

**1893-98 Wmk. 164 & 200**

117 A17 1b pale brown 1.25 1.25
118 A17 1½b black .85 1.25
119 A18 3b chocolate 1.25 .85
120 A19 5b blue 1.75 .85
*a.* Clichê of the 25b in the plate of 5b 185.00 *200.00*
121 A19 5b yel grn ('98) 5.00 3.00
*a.* 5b emerald 5.00 3.00
122 A20 10b emerald 2.50 1.75
123 A20 10b rose ('98) 6.00 2.50
124 A21 15b rose 2.50 .85
125 A21 15b black ('98) 6.00 2.00
126 A19 25b violet 3.75 1.25
127 A19 25b indigo ('98) 9.25 3.25
128 A19 40b gray grn 21.00 3.50
129 A19 50b orange 12.50 2.00
130 A23 1 l bis & rose 30.00 2.00
131 A23 2 l orange & brn 35.00 3.25
*Nos. 117-131 (15)* 138.60 29.55

This watermark may be found in four versions (Wmks. 164, 200 and variations). The paper also varies in thickness.

A 3b orange of type A18; 10b brown, type A20; 15b rose, type A21, and 25b bright green with similar but different border, all watermarked "P R," were prepared but never issued. Value, each $15.

See Nos. 132-157, 224-229. For overprints and surcharges see Romanian Post Offices in the Turkish Empire Nos. 1-6, 10-11.

King Carol I — A24

**Thin Paper, Tinted Rose on Back**
***Perf. 11½, 13½ and Compound***

**1900-03 Unwmk.**

132 A17 1b pale brown 1.75 1.75
133 A24 1b brown ('01) 1.75 1.25
134 A24 1b black ('03) 1.75 1.25
135 A18 3b red brown 1.75 .85
136 A19 5b emerald 2.50 .85
137 A20 10b rose 3.00 1.25
138 A21 15b black 2.50 .85
139 A21 15b lil gray ('01) 2.50 .85
140 A21 15b dk vio ('03) 2.50 1.25
141 A19 25b blue 4.25 1.75
142 A19 40b gray grn 8.50 1.75
143 A19 50b orange 17.00 1.75
144 A23 1 l bis & rose ('01) 34.00 3.00
145 A23 1 l grn & blk ('03) 30.00 3.50
146 A23 2 l org & brn ('01) 30.00 3.50
147 A23 2 l red brn & blk ('03) 25.00 4.25
*Nos. 132-147 (16)* 168.75 29.65

#132 inscribed BANI; #133-134 BAN.

**1900, July Wmk. 167**

148 A17 1b pale brown 12.00 5.00
149 A18 3b red brown 12.00 5.50
150 A19 5b emerald 10.00 5.00
151 A20 10b rose 15.00 6.00
152 A21 15b black 17.00 7.25
153 A19 25b blue 19.00 12.50
154 A19 40b gray grn 30.00 12.50
155 A19 50b orange 30.00 12.50
156 A23 1 l bis & rose 34.00 17.00
157 A23 2 l orange & brn 42.50 21.00
*Nos. 148-157 (10)* 221.50 104.25

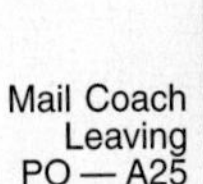
Mail Coach Leaving PO — A25

**Thin Paper, Tinted Rose on Face**

**1903 Unwmk. *Perf. 14x13½***

158 A25 1b gray brown *2.25* 1.60
159 A25 3b brown violet *3.75* 1.60
160 A25 5b pale green *7.50* 2.50
161 A25 10b rose *4.50* 2.50
162 A25 15b black *4.50* 3.25
163 A25 25b blue *22.50* 9.50
164 A25 40b dull green *32.50* 12.50
165 A25 50b orange *37.50* 16.00
*Nos. 158-165 (8)* *115.00* 49.45

Counterfeits are plentiful. See note after No. 172. See No. 428.

King Carol I and Façade of New Post Office — A26

**Thick Toned Paper**

**1903 Engr. *Perf. 13½x14***

166 A26 15b black 5.00 3.75
167 A26 25b blue 11.00 6.50
168 A26 40b gray grn 19.00 9.00
169 A26 50b orange 21.00 11.00
170 A26 1 l dk brown 16.00 9.00

**171** A26 2 l dull red 130.00 65.00
*a.* 2 l orange (error) 180.00 150.00
**172** A26 5 l dull violet 160.00 110.00
*a.* 5 l red violet 80.00 32.50
*Nos. 166-172 (7)* 362.00 214.25

Opening of the new PO in Bucharest (Nos. 158-172).
Counterfeits exist.

Prince Carol Taking Oath of Allegiance, 1866 — A27

Prince in Royal Carriage A28

Prince Carol at Calafat in 1877 — A29

Prince Carol Shaking Hands with His Captive, Osman Pasha — A30

Carol I as Prince in 1866 and King in 1906 — A31

Romanian Army Crossing Danube A32

Romanian Troops Return to Bucharest in 1878 — A33

Prince Carol at Head of His Command in 1877 — A34

King Carol I at the Cathedral in 1896 — A35

King Carol I at Shrine of St. Nicholas, 1904 — A36

**1906** **Engr.** ***Perf. 12***

**176** A27 1b bister & blk .65 .45
**177** A28 3b red brn & blk 1.40 .45
**178** A29 5b dp grn & blk 1.75 .45
**179** A30 10b carmine & blk 1.10 .45
**180** A31 15b dull vio & blk 1.10 .45
**181** A32 25b ultra & blk 7.00 5.25
*a.* 25b olive green & black 9.00 5.25
**182** A33 40b dk brn & blk 1.90 1.60
**183** A34 50b bis brn & blk 2.00 1.60
**184** A35 1 l vermilion & blk 2.25 1.90
**185** A36 2 l orange & blk 2.50 2.40
*Nos. 176-185 (10)* 21.65 15.00

40 years' rule of Carol I as Prince & King.
No. 181a was never placed in use. Cancellations were by favor.

King Carol I — A37

**1906**

**186** A37 1b bister & blk .90 .45
**187** A37 3b red brn & blk 2.25 .85
**188** A37 5b dp grn & blk 1.50 .75
**189** A37 10b carmine & blk 1.50 .75
**190** A37 15b dl vio & blk 1.50 .75
**191** A37 25b ultra & blk 13.50 7.00
**192** A37 40b dk brn & blk 6.00 1.50
**193** A37 50b bis brn & blk 6.00 1.50
**194** A37 1 l red & blk 6.00 1.50
**195** A37 2 l orange & blk 6.00 1.50
*Nos. 186-195 (10)* 45.15 16.55

25th anniversary of the Kingdom.

Plowman and Angel — A38

Exposition Building — A39

Exposition Buildings
A40 A41

King Carol I — A42

Queen Elizabeth (Carmen Sylva) — A43

**1906** **Typo.** ***Perf. 11½, 13½***

**196** A38 5b yel grn & blk 4.50 1.40
**197** A38 10b car & blk 4.50 1.40
**198** A39 15b violet & blk 6.50 2.25
**199** A39 25b blue & blk 6.50 2.25
**200** A40 30b red & blk brn 8.75 2.25
**201** A40 40b grn & blk brn 9.50 2.75
**202** A41 50b orange & blk 8.75 3.25
**203** A41 75b lt brn & dk brn 7.75 3.25
**204** A42 1.50 l red lil & blk brn 97.50 45.00
*a.* Center inverted *450.00*
**205** A42 2.50 l yellow & brn 37.50 26.00
*a.* Center inverted
**206** A43 3 l brn org & brn 28.00 26.00
*Nos. 196-206 (11)* 219.75 115.80

General Exposition. They were sold at post offices July 29-31, 1906, and were valid only for those three days. Those sold at the exposition are overprinted "S E" in black. Remainders were sold privately, both unused and canceled to order, by the Exposition promoters. Value, set: unused or used, $450.

A44

A45

***Perf. 11½, 13½ & Compound***

**1908-18** **Engr.**

**207** A44 5b pale yel grn 2.50 .25
**208** A44 10b carmine .70 .25
**209** A45 15b purple 11.50 2.25
**210** A44 25b deep blue 1.75 .25
**211** A44 40b brt green .85 .25
**212** A44 40b dk brn ('18) 5.25 2.25
**213** A44 50b orange .65 .25
**214** A44 50b lt red ('18) 2.00 .70
**215** A44 1 l brown 2.00 .40
**216** A44 2 l red 10.00 2.50
*Nos. 207-216 (10)* 37.20 9.35

King Carol I — A46

***Perf. 13½x14, 11½, 13½ & Compound***

**1909-18** **Typo.**

**217** A46 1b black .60 .25
**218** A46 3b red brown 1.25 .25
**219** A46 5b yellow grn .60 .25
**220** A46 10b rose 1.25 .25
**221** A46 15b dull violet 21.00 12.50
**222** A46 15b olive green 1.25 .25
**223** A46 15b red brn ('18) 1.10 .65
*Nos. 217-223 (7)* 27.05 14.40

Nos. 217-219, 222 exist imperf.
No. 219 in black is a chemical changeling.
For surcharge and overprints see Nos. 240-242, 245-247, J50-J51, RA1-RA2, RA11-RA12, Romanian Post Offices in the Turkish Empire 7-9.

**Types of 1893-99**

**1911-19** **White Paper** **Unwmk.**

**224** A17 1½b straw 1.75 .45
**225** A19 25b deep blue ('18) 1.00 .85
**226** A19 40b gray brn ('19) 1.25 .85
**227** A19 50b dull red ('19) 1.75 .85
**228** A23 1 l gray grn ('18) 2.25 .50
**229** A23 2 l orange ('18) 2.25 .85
*Nos. 224-229 (6)* 10.25 4.35

For overprints see Romanian Post Offices in the Turkish Empire Nos. 10-11.

Romania Holding Flag — A47

Romanian Crown and Old Fort on Danube — A48

Troops Crossing Danube — A49

View of Turtucaia — A50

Mircea the Great and Carol I — A51

View of Silistra — A52

***Perf. 11½x13½, 13½x11½***

**1913, Dec. 25**

**230** A47 1b black .85 .40
**231** A48 3b ol gray & choc 2.25 .85
**232** A49 5b yel grn & blk brn 1.75 .40
**233** A50 10b org & gray .85 .40
**234** A51 15b bister & vio 2.25 .85
**235** A52 25b blue & choc 3.00 1.25
**236** A49 40b bis & red vio 6.00 4.75
**237** A48 50b yellow & bl 16.00 6.50
**238** A48 1 l bl & ol bis 25.00 14.50
**239** A48 2 l org red & rose 40.00 20.00
*Nos. 230-239 (10)* 97.95 49.90

Romania's annexation of Silistra.

No. 217 Handstamped in Red

***Perf. 13½x14, 11½, 13½ & Compound***

**1918, May 1**

**240** A46 25b on 1b black 2.25 2.25

This handstamp is found inverted.

No. 219 and 220 Overprinted in Black

**1918**

**241** A46 5b yellow green .60 .55
*a.* Inverted overprint 3.25 3.25
*b.* Double overprint 3.25 3.25
**242** A46 10b rose .60 .55
*a.* Inverted overprint 3.25 3.25
*b.* Double overprint 3.25 3.25

Nos. 217, 219 and 220 Overprinted in Red or Black

**1919, Nov. 8**

**245** A46 1b black (R) .40 .25
*a.* Inverted overprint 6.75
*b.* Double overprint 10.00 2.25
**246** A46 5b yel grn (Bk) .40 .25
*a.* Double overprint 10.00 3.25
*b.* Inverted overprint 6.75 2.00
**247** A46 10b rose (Bk) .40 .25
*a.* Inverted overprint 6.75 2.00
*b.* Double overprint 10.00 3.00
*Nos. 245-247 (3)* 1.20 .75

Recovery of Transylvania and the return of the King to Bucharest.

King Ferdinand — A53

**1920-22** **Typo.**

| No. | Design | Description | Unused | Used |
|---|---|---|---|---|
| 248 | A53 | 1b black | .25 | .25 |
| 249 | A53 | 5b yellow grn | .25 | .25 |
| 250 | A53 | 10b rose | .25 | .25 |
| 251 | A53 | 15b red brown | .75 | .25 |
| 252 | A53 | 25b deep blue | 1.50 | .40 |
| 253 | A53 | 25b brown | .75 | .25 |
| 254 | A53 | 40b gray brown | 1.25 | .35 |
| 255 | A53 | 50b salmon | .35 | .25 |
| 256 | A53 | 1 l gray grn | 1.25 | .25 |
| 257 | A53 | 1 l rose | .75 | .25 |
| 258 | A53 | 2 l orange | 1.25 | .25 |
| 259 | A53 | 2 l dp blue | 1.25 | .25 |
| 260 | A53 | 2 l rose ('22) | 3.00 | 1.75 |
| | | *Nos. 248-260 (13)* | 12.85 | 5.00 |

Nos. 248-260 are printed on two papers: coarse, grayish paper with bits of colored fiber, and thinner white paper of better quality.

Nos. 248-251, 253 exist imperf.

King Ferdinand — A54

Type I

Type II

Type III

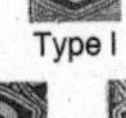

Type I

Type II Type I Type II

TWO LEI:

Type I — The "2" is thin, with tail 2½mm wide. Top of "2" forms a hook.

Type II — The "2" is thick, with tail 3mm wide. Top of "2" forms a ball.

Type III — The "2" is similar to type II. The "E" of "LEI" is larger and about 2mm wide.

THREE LEI:

Type I — Top of "3" begins in a point. Top and middle bars of "E" of "LEI" are without serifs.

Type II — Top of "3" begins in a ball. Top and middle bars of "E" of "LEI" have serifs.

FIVE LEI:

Type I — The "5" is 2½mm wide. The end of the final stroke of the "L" of "LEI" almost touches the vertical stroke.

Type II — The "5" is 3mm wide and the lines are broader than in type I. The end of the final stroke of the "L" of "LEI" is separated from the vertical by a narrow space.

***Perf. 13½x14, 11½, 13½ & Compound***

**1920-26**

| No. | Design | Description | Unused | Used |
|---|---|---|---|---|
| 261 | A54 | 3b black | .25 | .25 |
| 262 | A54 | 5b black | .25 | .25 |
| 263 | A54 | 10b yel grn ('25) | .25 | .25 |
| a. | | 10b olive green ('25) | .40 | |
| 264 | A54 | 25b bister brn | .25 | .25 |
| 265 | A54 | 25b salmon | .25 | .25 |
| 266 | A54 | 30b violet | .25 | .25 |
| 267 | A54 | 50b orange | .25 | .25 |
| 268 | A54 | 60b gray grn | 1.00 | .55 |
| 269 | A54 | 1 l violet | .25 | .25 |
| 270 | A54 | 2 l rose (I) | 1.25 | .25 |
| a. | | 2 l claret (I) | 47.50 | |
| 271 | A54 | 2 l lt green (II) | .70 | .25 |
| a. | | 2 l light green (I) | .95 | .40 |
| b. | | 2 l light green (III) | .80 | .25 |
| 272 | A54 | 3 l blue (I) | 2.60 | .80 |
| 273 | A54 | 3 l buff (II) | 2.60 | .80 |
| a. | | 3 l buff (I) | 12.50 | 2.25 |
| 274 | A54 | 3 l salmon (II) | .25 | .25 |
| a. | | 3 l salmon (I) | 1.60 | 1.25 |
| 275 | A54 | 3 l car rose (II) | .65 | .25 |
| 276 | A54 | 5 l emer (I) | 2.10 | .50 |
| 277 | A54 | 5 l lt brn (II) | .45 | .25 |
| a. | | 5 l light brown (I) | 1.60 | .80 |
| 278 | A54 | 6 l blue | 2.60 | 1.25 |
| 279 | A54 | 6 l carmine | 5.75 | 3.25 |
| 280 | A54 | 6 l ol grn ('26) | 2.50 | .80 |
| 281 | A54 | 7½ l pale bl | 2.10 | .45 |
| 282 | A54 | 10 l deep blue | 2.10 | .45 |
| | | *Nos. 261-282 (22)* | 28.65 | 12.10 |

#273 and 273a, 274 and 274a, exist se-tenant. The 50b exists in three types.

For surcharge see No. Q7.

Alba Iulia Cathedral A55

King Ferdinand A56

Coat of Arms — A57

Queen Marie as Nurse — A58

Michael the Brave and King Ferdinand A59

King Ferdinand A60

Queen Marie — A61

***Perf. 13½x14, 13½, 11½ & Compound***

**1922, Oct. 15** **Photo.** **Wmk. 95**

| No. | Design | Description | Unused | Used |
|---|---|---|---|---|
| 283 | A55 | 5b black | .40 | .30 |
| 284 | A56 | 25b chocolate | 1.25 | .40 |
| 285 | A57 | 50b dp green | 1.25 | .60 |
| 286 | A58 | 1 l olive grn | 1.50 | .85 |
| 287 | A59 | 2 l carmine | 1.50 | .85 |
| 288 | A60 | 3 l blue | 4.00 | 1.25 |
| 289 | A61 | 6 l violet | 11.50 | 8.00 |
| | | *Nos. 283-289 (7)* | 21.40 | 12.25 |

Coronation of King Ferdinand I and Queen Marie on Oct. 15, 1922, at Alba Iulia. All values exist imperforate. Value, set $150, unused or used.

King Ferdinand
A62 A63

**1926, July 1** **Unwmk.** ***Perf. 11***

| No. | Design | Description | Unused | Used |
|---|---|---|---|---|
| 291 | A62 | 10b yellow grn | .35 | .25 |
| 292 | A62 | 25b orange | .35 | .25 |
| 293 | A62 | 50b orange brn | .35 | .25 |
| 294 | A63 | 1 l dk violet | .50 | .25 |
| 295 | A63 | 2 l dk green | .50 | .25 |
| 296 | A63 | 3 l brown car | .50 | .50 |
| 297 | A63 | 5 l black brn | .50 | .50 |
| 298 | A63 | 6 l dk olive | .50 | .50 |
| a. | | 6 l bright blue (error) | 150.00 | 175.00 |
| 300 | A63 | 9 l slate | .75 | .50 |
| 301 | A63 | 10 l brt blue | .75 | .50 |
| b. | | 10 l brown carmine (error) | 150.00 | 175.00 |
| | | *Nos. 291-301 (10)* | 5.05 | 3.75 |

60th birthday of King Ferdinand.

Exist imperf. Value, set unused $150; used $175. Imperf. examples with watermark 95 are proofs.

King Carol I and King Ferdinand A69

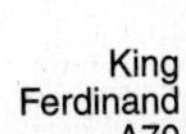

King Ferdinand A70

A71

**1927, Aug. 1** ***Perf. 13½***

| No. | Design | Description | Unused | Used |
|---|---|---|---|---|
| 308 | A69 | 25b brown vio | .50 | .35 |
| 309 | A70 | 30b gray blk | .50 | .35 |
| 310 | A71 | 50b dk green | .50 | .35 |
| 311 | A69 | 1 l bluish slate | .50 | .35 |
| 312 | A70 | 2 l dp green | .50 | .45 |
| 313 | A70 | 3 l violet | .50 | .55 |
| 314 | A71 | 4 l dk brown | .50 | .65 |
| 315 | A71 | 4.50 l henna brn | 3.00 | 2.25 |
| 316 | A70 | 5 l red brown | .50 | .55 |
| 317 | A71 | 6 l carmine | 2.00 | 1.25 |
| 318 | A69 | 7.50 l grnsh bl | .50 | .55 |
| 319 | A69 | 10 l brt blue | 3.00 | 1.10 |
| | | *Nos. 308-319 (12)* | 12.50 | 8.75 |

50th anniversary of Romania's independence from Turkish suzerainty.

Some values exist imperf. All exist imperf. and with value numerals omitted.

King Michael
A72 A73

***Perf. 13½x14 (25b, 50b); 13½***

**1928-29** **Typo.** **Unwmk.**

**Size: 19x25mm**

| No. | Design | Description | Unused | Used |
|---|---|---|---|---|
| 320 | A72 | 25b black | .25 | .25 |
| 321 | A72 | 30b fawn ('29) | .40 | .25 |
| 322 | A72 | 50b olive grn | .25 | .25 |

**Photo.**

**Size: 18½x24½mm**

| No. | Design | Description | Unused | Used |
|---|---|---|---|---|
| 323 | A73 | 1 l violet | .45 | .25 |
| 324 | A73 | 2 l dp green | .45 | .25 |
| 325 | A73 | 3 l brt rose | .90 | .25 |
| 326 | A73 | 5 l red brown | 1.40 | .25 |
| 327 | A73 | 7.50 l ultra | 6.25 | .90 |
| 328 | A73 | 10 l blue | 5.25 | .35 |
| | | *Nos. 320-328 (9)* | 15.60 | 3.00 |

See Nos. 343-345, 353-357. For overprints see Nos. 359-368A.

Parliament House, Bessarabia — A74

Designs: 1 l, 2 l, Parliament House, Bessarabia. 3 l, 5 l, 20 l, Hotin Fortress. 7.50 l, 10 l, Fortress Cetatea Alba.

**1928, Apr. 29** **Wmk. 95** ***Perf. 13½***

| No. | Design | Description | Unused | Used |
|---|---|---|---|---|
| 329 | A74 | 1 l deep green | 1.75 | .65 |
| 330 | A74 | 2 l deep brown | 1.75 | .65 |
| 331 | A74 | 3 l black brown | 1.75 | .65 |
| 332 | A74 | 5 l carmine lake | 2.25 | .80 |
| 333 | A74 | 7.50 l ultra | 2.25 | .80 |
| 334 | A74 | 10 l Prus blue | 5.00 | 2.00 |
| 335 | A74 | 20 l black vio | 8.00 | 2.75 |
| | | *Nos. 329-335 (7)* | 22.75 | 8.30 |

Reunion of Bessarabia with Romania, 10th anniv.

King Carol I and King Michael A77

View of Constanta Harbor A78

Trajan's Monument at Adam Clisi A79

Cernavoda Bridge — A80

**1928, Oct. 25**

| No. | Design | Description | Unused | Used |
|---|---|---|---|---|
| 336 | A77 | 1 l blue green | 1.10 | .45 |
| 337 | A78 | 2 l red brown | 1.10 | .45 |
| 338 | A77 | 3 l gray black | 1.40 | .50 |
| 339 | A79 | 5 l dull lilac | 1.75 | .60 |
| 340 | A79 | 7.50 l ultra | 2.10 | .80 |
| 341 | A80 | 10 l blue | 3.25 | 1.90 |
| 342 | A80 | 20 l carmine rose | 5.50 | 3.25 |
| | | *Nos. 336-342 (7)* | 16.20 | 7.95 |

Union of Dobruja with Romania, 50th anniv.

**Michael Types of 1928-29**

***Perf. 13½x14***

**1928, Sept. 1** **Typo.** **Wmk. 95**

| No. | Design | Description | Unused | Used |
|---|---|---|---|---|
| 343 | A72 | 25b black | .60 | .25 |

**Photo.**

| No. | Design | Description | Unused | Used |
|---|---|---|---|---|
| 344 | A73 | 7.50 l ultra | 2.00 | .75 |
| 345 | A73 | 10 l blue | 4.00 | .60 |
| | | *Nos. 343-345 (3)* | 6.60 | 1.60 |

Ferdinand I; Stephen the Great; Michael the Brave; Corvin and Constantine Brancoveanu — A81

Union with Transylvania A82

Avram Jancu — A83

Prince Michael the Brave — A84

Castle Bran — A85

King Ferdinand I — A86

**1929, May 10 Photo. Wmk. 95**

| No. | Type | Value | Color | Unused | Used |
|---|---|---|---|---|---|
| **347** | A81 | 1 l | dark violet | 2.25 | 1.75 |
| **348** | A82 | 2 l | olive green | 2.25 | 1.75 |
| **349** | A83 | 3 l | violet brown | 2.50 | 1.75 |
| **350** | A84 | 4 l | cerise | 2.75 | 2.25 |
| **351** | A85 | 5 l | orange | 4.50 | 2.25 |
| **352** | A86 | 10 l | brt blue | 7.50 | 4.25 |
| | | | *Nos. 347-352 (6)* | 21.75 | 14.00 |

Union of Transylvania and Romania.

**Michael Type of 1928**

**1930 Unwmk. *Perf. 14½x14***

**Size: 18x23mm**

| No. | Type | Value | Color | Unused | Used |
|---|---|---|---|---|---|
| **353** | A73 | 1 l | deep violet | .80 | .25 |
| **354** | A73 | 2 l | deep green | 1.25 | .25 |
| **355** | A73 | 3 l | carmine rose | 2.40 | .25 |
| **356** | A73 | 7.50 l | ultra | 5.00 | 1.10 |
| **357** | A73 | 10 l | deep blue | 16.00 | 7.00 |
| | | | *Nos. 353-357 (5)* | 25.45 | 8.85 |

Stamps of 1928-30 Overprinted

**On Nos. 320-322, 326, 328**

***Perf. 13½x14, 13½***

**1930, June 8 Typo.**

| No. | Type | Value | Color | Unused | Used |
|---|---|---|---|---|---|
| **359** | A72 | 25b | black | .40 | .25 |
| **360** | A72 | 30b | fawn | .80 | .25 |
| **361** | A72 | 50b | olive green | .80 | .25 |

**Photo.**

**Size: 18½x24½mm**

| No. | Type | Value | Color | Unused | Used |
|---|---|---|---|---|---|
| **362** | A73 | 5 l | red brown | 1.60 | .25 |
| **362A** | A73 | 10 l | brt blue | 8.25 | 1.50 |

**On Nos. 353-357**

***Perf. 14½x14***

**Size: 18x23mm**

| No. | Type | Value | Color | Unused | Used |
|---|---|---|---|---|---|
| **363** | A73 | 1 l | deep violet | .80 | .25 |
| **364** | A73 | 2 l | deep green | .80 | .25 |
| **365** | A73 | 3 l | carmine rose | 1.60 | .25 |
| **366** | A73 | 7.50 l | ultra | 4.00 | .75 |
| **367** | A73 | 10 l | deep blue | 3.25 | .75 |

**On Nos. 343-344**

***Perf. 13½x14, 13½***

**Typo. Wmk. 95**

| No. | Type | Value | Color | Unused | Used |
|---|---|---|---|---|---|
| **368** | A72 | 25b | black | 1.25 | .35 |

**Photo.**

**Size: 18½x24½mm**

| No. | Type | Value | Color | Unused | Used |
|---|---|---|---|---|---|
| **368A** | A73 | 7.50 l | ultra | 5.00 | 1.50 |
| | | | *Nos. 359-368A (12)* | 28.55 | 6.60 |

Accession to the throne by King Carol II.
This overprint exists on Nos. 323, 345.

A87

A88

King Carol II — A89

***Perf. 13½, 14, 14x13½***

**1930 Wmk. 225**

| No. | Type | Value | Color | Unused | Used |
|---|---|---|---|---|---|
| **369** | A87 | 25b | black | 1.10 | .25 |
| **370** | A87 | 50b | chocolate | 3.25 | .45 |
| **371** | A87 | 1 l | dk violet | 2.25 | .25 |
| **372** | A87 | 2 l | gray green | 2.75 | .25 |
| **373** | A88 | 3 l | carmine rose | 2.25 | .25 |
| **374** | A88 | 4 l | orange red | 3.25 | .25 |
| **375** | A88 | 6 l | carmine brn | 4.25 | .25 |
| **376** | A88 | 7.50 l | ultra | 4.25 | .30 |
| **377** | A89 | 10 l | deep blue | 2.25 | .25 |
| **378** | A89 | 16 l | peacock grn | 4.75 | .25 |
| **379** | A89 | 20 l | orange | 1.40 | .60 |
| | | | *Nos. 369-379 (11)* | 31.75 | 3.35 |

Exist imperf. Value, unused or used, $250.
See Nos. 405-414.

A90

A91

**1930, Dec. 24 Unwmk. *Perf. 13½***

| No. | Type | Value | Color | Unused | Used |
|---|---|---|---|---|---|
| **380** | A90 | 1 l | dull violet | 1.25 | .45 |
| **381** | A91 | 2 l | green | 2.25 | .50 |
| **382** | A91 | 4 l | vermilion | 2.50 | .35 |
| **383** | A91 | 6 l | brown carmine | 6.50 | .45 |
| | | | *Nos. 380-383 (4)* | 12.50 | 1.75 |

First census in Romania.

King Carol II — A92

King Carol I — A93

King Ferdinand — A96

King Carol II — A94

King Carol II, King Ferdinand and King Carol I — A95

**1931, May 10 Photo. Wmk. 225**

| No. | Type | Value | Color | Unused | Used |
|---|---|---|---|---|---|
| **384** | A92 | 1 l | gray violet | 2.50 | 1.75 |
| **385** | A93 | 2 l | green | 4.25 | 2.00 |
| **386** | A94 | 6 l | red brown | 11.00 | 3.25 |
| **387** | A95 | 10 l | blue | 16.00 | 6.00 |
| **388** | A96 | 20 l | orange | 22.50 | 8.50 |
| | | | *Nos. 384-388 (5)* | 56.25 | 21.50 |

50th anniversary of Romanian Kingdom.

Using Bayonet — A97

Romanian Infantryman 1870 — A98

Romanian Infantry 1830 — A99

King Carol I A100

Infantry Advance A101

King Ferdinand A102

King Carol II A103

**1931, May 10**

| No. | Type | Value | Color | Unused | Used |
|---|---|---|---|---|---|
| **389** | A97 | 25b | gray black | 1.40 | .75 |
| **390** | A98 | 50b | dk red brn | 2.10 | 1.10 |
| **391** | A99 | 1 l | gray violet | 2.75 | 1.10 |
| **392** | A100 | 2 l | deep green | 4.25 | 1.50 |
| **393** | A101 | 3 l | carmine rose | 10.00 | 3.50 |
| **394** | A102 | 7.50 l | ultra | 13.00 | 9.00 |
| **395** | A103 | 16 l | blue green | 16.00 | 4.00 |
| | | | *Nos. 389-395 (7)* | 49.50 | 20.95 |

Centenary of the Romanian Army.

Naval Cadet Ship "Mircea" A104

10 l, Ironclad. 16 l, Light cruiser. 20 l, Destroyer.

**1931, May 10**

| No. | Type | Value | Color | Unused | Used |
|---|---|---|---|---|---|
| **396** | A104 | 6 l | red brown | 7.00 | 4.00 |
| **397** | A104 | 10 l | blue | 9.50 | 4.50 |
| **398** | A104 | 16 l | blue green | 40.00 | 6.00 |
| **399** | A104 | 20 l | orange | 17.50 | 10.00 |
| | | | *Nos. 396-399 (4)* | 74.00 | 24.50 |

50th anniversary of the Romanian Navy.

King Carol II — A108

**1931 Unwmk. Engr. *Perf. 12***

| No. | Type | Value | Color | Unused | Used |
|---|---|---|---|---|---|
| **400** | A108 | 30 l | ol bis & dk bl | 1.75 | 1.00 |
| **401** | A108 | 50 l | red & dk bl | 4.50 | 1.50 |
| **402** | A108 | 100 l | dk grn & dk bl | 7.25 | 3.50 |
| | | | *Nos. 400-402 (3)* | 13.50 | 6.00 |

Exist imperf. Value, unused or used, $150.

Carol II, Ferdinand, Carol I — A109

**Wmk. 230**

**1931, Nov. 1 Photo. *Perf. 13½***

| No. | Type | Value | Color | Unused | Used |
|---|---|---|---|---|---|
| **403** | A109 | 16 l | Prus green | 12.00 | .90 |

Exists imperf. Value, unused or used, $300.

**Carol II Types of 1930**

***Perf. 13½, 14, 14½ and Compound***

**1932 Wmk. 230**

| No. | Type | Value | Color | Unused | Used |
|---|---|---|---|---|---|
| **405** | A87 | 25b | black | .50 | .25 |
| **406** | A87 | 50b | dark brown | 1.00 | .25 |
| **407** | A87 | 1 l | dark violet | 1.40 | .25 |
| **408** | A87 | 2 l | gray green | 1.75 | .25 |
| **409** | A88 | 3 l | carmine rose | 2.25 | .25 |
| **410** | A88 | 4 l | orange red | 5.25 | .25 |
| **411** | A88 | 6 l | carmine brn | 12.50 | .25 |
| **412** | A88 | 7.50 l | ultra | 21.50 | .75 |
| **413** | A89 | 10 l | deep blue | 125.00 | .90 |
| **414** | A89 | 20 l | orange | 110.00 | 9.00 |
| | | | *Nos. 405-414 (10)* | 281.15 | 12.40 |

Alexander the Good — A110

**1932, May *Perf. 13½***

| No. | Type | Value | Color | Unused | Used |
|---|---|---|---|---|---|
| **415** | A110 | 6 l | carmine brown | 12.00 | 6.00 |

500th death anniv. of Alexander the Good, Prince of Moldavia, 1400-1432.

King Carol II — A111

**1932, June**

| No. | Type | Value | Color | Unused | Used |
|---|---|---|---|---|---|
| **416** | A111 | 10 l | brt blue | 12.00 | .45 |

Exists imperf. Value, unused or used, $200.

Cantacuzino and Gregory Ghika, Founders of Coltea and Pantelimon Hospitals — A112

Session of the Congress A113

Aesculapius and Hygeia — A114

**1932, Sept. *Perf. 13½***

| No. | Type | Value | Color | Unused | Used |
|---|---|---|---|---|---|
| **417** | A112 | 1 l | carmine rose | 7.50 | 7.50 |
| **418** | A113 | 6 l | deep orange | 20.00 | 11.00 |
| **419** | A114 | 10 l | brt blue | 34.00 | 18.50 |
| | | | *Nos. 417-419 (3)* | 61.50 | 37.00 |

9th Intl. History of Medicine Congress, Bucharest.

Bull's Head and Post Horn A116

Lion Rampant and Bridge A117

Dolphins
A118

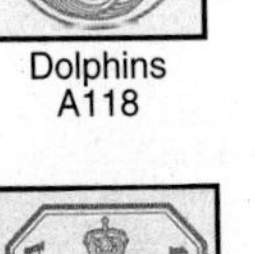

Eagle and Castles
A119

Coat of Arms — A120

Eagle and Post Horn — A121

Bull's Head and Post Horn — A122

**1932, Nov. 20 Typo. *Imperf.***

| No. | Type | Value | Color | Unused | Used |
|---|---|---|---|---|---|
| 421 | A116 | 25b | black | .85 | .40 |
| 422 | A117 | 1 l | violet | 2.00 | .70 |
| 423 | A118 | 2 l | green | 2.50 | .90 |
| 424 | A119 | 3 l | car rose | 2.80 | 1.10 |
| 425 | A120 | 6 l | red brown | 3.50 | 1.25 |
| 426 | A121 | 7.50 l | lt blue | 4.25 | 1.75 |
| 427 | A122 | 10 l | dk blue | 8.00 | 3.00 |
| | | | *Nos. 421-427 (7)* | 23.90 | 9.10 |

75th anniv. of the first Moldavian stamps.

**Mail Coach Type of 1903**

**1932, Nov. 20 *Perf. 13½***

| No. | Type | Value | Color | Unused | Used |
|---|---|---|---|---|---|
| 428 | A25 | 16 l | blue green | 11.00 | 5.50 |

30th anniv. of the opening of the new post office, Bucharest, in 1903.

Arms of City of Turnu-Severin, Ruins of Tower of Emperor Severus — A123

Inauguration of Trajan's Bridge — A124

Prince Carol Landing at Turnu-Severin — A125

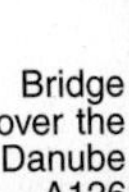

Bridge over the Danube A126

**1933, June 2 Photo. *Perf. 14½x14***

| No. | Type | Value | Color | Unused | Used |
|---|---|---|---|---|---|
| 429 | A123 | 25b | gray green | .75 | .30 |
| 430 | A124 | 50b | dull blue | 1.10 | .45 |
| 431 | A125 | 1 l | black brn | 1.75 | .75 |
| 432 | A126 | 2 l | olive blk | 3.25 | 1.10 |
| | | | *Nos. 429-432 (4)* | 6.85 | 2.60 |

Centenary of the incorporation in Walachia of the old Roman City of Turnu-Severin. Exist imperf. Value, unused or used, $150.

Queen Elizabeth and King Carol I — A127

Profiles of Kings Carol I, Ferdinand and Carol II — A128

Castle Peles, Sinaia A129

**1933, Aug.**

| No. | Type | Value | Color | Unused | Used |
|---|---|---|---|---|---|
| 433 | A127 | 1 l | dark violet | 2.50 | 2.00 |
| 434 | A128 | 3 l | olive brown | 3.00 | 2.75 |
| 435 | A129 | 6 l | vermilion | 4.25 | 3.25 |
| | | | *Nos. 433-435 (3)* | 9.75 | 8.00 |

50th anniversary of the erection of Castle Peles, the royal summer residence at Sinaia. Exist imperf. Value, unused or used, $125.

A130

A131

King Carol II — A132

**1934, Aug. *Perf. 13½***

| No. | Type | Value | Color | Unused | Used |
|---|---|---|---|---|---|
| 436 | A130 | 50b | brown | 1.00 | .40 |
| 437 | A131 | 2 l | gray green | 2.00 | .40 |
| 438 | A131 | 4 l | red | 3.50 | .55 |
| 439 | A132 | 6 l | deep claret | 8.00 | .40 |
| | | | *Nos. 436-439 (4)* | 14.50 | 1.75 |

See Nos. 446-460 for stamps inscribed "Posta." Nos. 436, 439 exist imperf. Value for both, unused or used, $100.

Child and Grapes — A133

Woman and Fruit — A134

**1934, Sept. 14**

| No. | Type | Value | Color | Unused | Used |
|---|---|---|---|---|---|
| 440 | A133 | 1 l | dull green | 5.00 | 2.25 |
| 441 | A134 | 2 l | violet brown | 5.00 | 2.25 |

Natl. Fruit Week, Sept. 14-21. Exist imperf. Value, unused or used, $125.

Crisan, Horia and Closca A135

**1935, Feb. 28**

| No. | Type | Value | Color | Unused | Used |
|---|---|---|---|---|---|
| 442 | A135 | 1 l | shown | .65 | .50 |
| 443 | A135 | 2 l | Crisan | .90 | .60 |
| 444 | A135 | 6 l | Closca | 2.25 | 1.00 |
| 445 | A135 | 10 l | Horia | 5.00 | 2.25 |
| | | | *Nos. 442-445 (4)* | 8.80 | 4.35 |

150th anniversary of the death of three Romanian martyrs. Exist imperf. Value, unused or used, $110.

A139

A140

A141

A142

King Carol II — A143

**Wmk. 230**

**1935-40 Photo. *Perf. 13½***

| No. | Type | Value | Color | Unused | Used |
|---|---|---|---|---|---|
| 446 | A139 | 25b | black brn | .25 | .25 |
| 447 | A142 | 50b | brown | .25 | .25 |
| 448 | A140 | 1 l | purple | .25 | .25 |
| 449 | A141 | 2 l | green | .45 | .25 |
| 449A | A141 | 2 l | dk bl grn ('40) | .65 | .25 |
| 450 | A142 | 3 l | deep rose | .70 | .25 |
| 450A | A142 | 3 l | grnsh bl ('40) | .85 | .30 |
| 451 | A141 | 4 l | vermilion | 1.25 | .25 |
| 452 | A140 | 5 l | rose car ('40) | 1.25 | .80 |
| 453 | A143 | 6 l | maroon | 1.60 | .25 |
| 454 | A140 | 7.50 l | ultra | 1.90 | .30 |
| 454A | A142 | 8 l | magenta ('40) | 1.90 | .70 |
| 455 | A141 | 9 l | brt ultra ('40) | 2.50 | .80 |
| 456 | A142 | 10 l | brt blue | 1.00 | .25 |
| 456A | A143 | 12 l | slate bl ('40) | 1.60 | 1.25 |
| 457 | A139 | 15 l | dk brn ('40) | 1.60 | .95 |
| 458 | A143 | 16 l | Prus blue | 2.10 | .25 |
| 459 | A143 | 20 l | orange | 1.25 | .35 |
| 460 | A143 | 24 l | dk car ('40) | 2.10 | .95 |
| | | | *Nos. 446-460 (19)* | 23.45 | 8.90 |

Exist imperf. Value, unused or used, $240.

Nos. 454, 456 Overprinted in Red

**1936, Dec. 5**

| No. | Type | Value | Color | Unused | Used |
|---|---|---|---|---|---|
| 461 | A140 | 7.50 l | ultra | 9.25 | 6.50 |
| 462 | A142 | 10 l | brt blue | 9.25 | 6.50 |

16th anniversary of the Little Entente. Overprints in silver or gold are fraudulent.

Birthplace of Ion Creanga A144

Ion Creanga A145

**1937, May 15**

| No. | Type | Value | Color | Unused | Used |
|---|---|---|---|---|---|
| 463 | A144 | 2 l | green | 1.25 | .80 |
| 464 | A145 | 3 l | carmine rose | 1.75 | .90 |
| 465 | A144 | 4 l | dp violet | 2.00 | 1.10 |
| 466 | A145 | 6 l | red brown | 5.00 | 2.50 |
| | | | *Nos. 463-466 (4)* | 10.00 | 5.30 |

Creanga (1837-89), writer. Exist imperf. Value, unused or used, $125.

Cathedral at Curtea de Arges — A146

**1937, July 1**

| No. | Type | Value | Color | Unused | Used |
|---|---|---|---|---|---|
| 467 | A146 | 7.50 l | ultra | 2.50 | 1.10 |
| 468 | A146 | 10 l | blue | 3.25 | .80 |

The Little Entente (Romania, Czechoslovakia, Yugoslavia). Exist imperf. Value, unused or used, $125.

**Souvenir Sheet**

A146a

**Surcharged in Black with New Values**

**1937, Oct. 25 Unwmk. *Perf. 13½***

| No. | Type | Value | Color | Unused | Used |
|---|---|---|---|---|---|
| 469 | A146a | | Sheet of 4 | 9.00 | 9.00 |
| a. | | 2 l on 20 l | orange | .35 | .35 |
| b. | | 6 l on 10 l | bright blue | .35 | .35 |
| c. | | 10 l on 6 l | maroon | .45 | .45 |
| d. | | 20 l on 2 l | green | 1.00 | 1.00 |

Promotion of the Crown Prince Michael to the rank of Lieutenant on his 17th birthday.

Arms of Romania, Greece, Turkey and Yugoslavia A147

***Perf. 13x13½***

**1938, Feb. 10 Wmk. 230**

| No. | Type | Value | Color | Unused | Used |
|---|---|---|---|---|---|
| 470 | A147 | 7.50 l | ultra | 1.50 | .90 |
| 471 | A147 | 10 l | blue | 2.00 | .80 |

The Balkan Entente. Exist imperf. Value, unused or used, $100.

A148

King Carol II

A149 A150

**1938, May 10** *Perf. 13½*

| No. | Type | Denomination | Color | Unused | Used |
|---|---|---|---|---|---|
| **472** | A148 | 3 l | dk carmine | .75 | .50 |
| **473** | A149 | 6 l | violet brn | 1.25 | .50 |
| **474** | A150 | 10 l | blue | 2.00 | .90 |
| | | | *Nos. 472-474 (3)* | 4.00 | 1.90 |

New Constitution of Feb. 27, 1938.
Exist imperf. Value, unused or used, $100.

**Catalogue values for unused stamps in this section, from this point to the end of the section, are for Never Hinged items.**

Prince Carol's Calatorie, 1866 A151

Examining Plans for a Monastery A153

Prince Carol and Carmen Sylva (Queen Elizabeth) A155

Sigmaringen and Peles Castles — A154

Prince Carol, Age 6 — A156

Equestrian Statue — A159

Battle of Plevna — A160

On Horseback A161

Cathedral of Curtea de Arges A164

King Carol I and Queen Elizabeth A163

Designs: 50b, At Calafat. 4 l, In 1866. 5 l, In 1877. 12 l, in 1914.

*Perf. 14, 13½*

**1939, Apr. 10** **Wmk. 230**

| No. | Type | Denomination | Color | Unused | Used |
|---|---|---|---|---|---|
| **475** | A151 | 25b | olive blk | .25 | .25 |
| **476** | A151 | 50b | violet brn | .25 | .25 |
| **477** | A153 | 1 l | dk purple | .25 | .25 |
| **478** | A154 | 1.50 l | green | .25 | .25 |
| **479** | A155 | 2 l | myrtle grn | .25 | .25 |
| **480** | A156 | 3 l | red orange | .25 | .25 |
| **481** | A156 | 4 l | rose lake | .25 | .25 |
| **482** | A156 | 5 l | black | .25 | .25 |
| **483** | A159 | 7 l | olive blk | .25 | .25 |
| **484** | A160 | 8 l | dark blue | .25 | .25 |
| **485** | A161 | 10 l | deep mag | .80 | .25 |
| **486** | A161 | 12 l | dull blue | 1.20 | .25 |
| **487** | A163 | 15 l | ultra | 1.20 | .25 |
| **488** | A164 | 16 l | Prus green | 1.20 | .60 |
| | | | *Nos. 475-488 (14)* | 6.90 | 3.85 |

Centenary of the birth of King Carol I.
Nos 475-488 exist imperf. Value, unused or used, $150.

### Souvenir Sheets

**1939** *Perf. 14x13½*

| No. | Description | Unused | Used |
|---|---|---|---|
| **488A** | Sheet of 3, #475-476, 478 | 3.50 | 3.50 |
| *d.* | Imperf. ('40) | 7.00 | 7.00 |

*Perf. 14x15½*

| No. | Description | Unused | Used |
|---|---|---|---|
| **488B** | Sheet of 4, #480-482, 486 | 3.50 | 3.50 |
| *e.* | Imperf. ('40) | 7.00 | 7.00 |
| **488C** | Sheet of 4, #479, 483-485 | 3.50 | 3.50 |
| *f.* | Imperf. ('40) | 7.00 | 7.00 |

No. 488A sold for 20 l, Nos. 488B-488C for 50 l, the surtax for national defense.

Nos. 488A-488C and 488Ad-488Cf were overprintod "PRO-PATRIA 1940" to aid the armament fund. Value, set of 6, $100.

Nos. 488A-488C exist with overprint of "ROMA BERLIN 1940" and bars, but these are not recognized as having been officially issued.

Romanian Pavilion A165

Romanian Pavilion A166

**1939, May 8** *Perf. 14x13½, 13½*

| No. | Type | Denomination | Color | Unused | Used |
|---|---|---|---|---|---|
| **489** | A165 | 6 l | brown carmine | 1.25 | .60 |
| **490** | A166 | 12 l | brt blue | 1.25 | .60 |

New York World's Fair.
Nos 489-490 exist imperf. Value, unused or used, $250.

Mihail Eminescu
A167 A168

**1939, May 22** *Perf. 13½*

| No. | Type | Denomination | Color | Unused | Used |
|---|---|---|---|---|---|
| **491** | A167 | 5 l | olive gray | 3.00 | 1.75 |
| **492** | A168 | 7 l | brown carmine | 3.00 | 1.75 |

Mihail Eminescu, poet, 50th death anniv.
Nos 491-492 exist imperf. Value, unused or used, $300.

Three Types of Locomotives — A169

Modern Train A170

Wood-burning Locomotive A171

Streamlined Locomotive A172

Railroad Terminal A173

**1939, June 10** **Typo.** *Perf. 14*

| No. | Type | Denomination | Color | Unused | Used |
|---|---|---|---|---|---|
| **493** | A169 | 1 l | red violet | 1.75 | .60 |
| **494** | A170 | 4 l | deep rose | 1.75 | .60 |
| **495** | A171 | 5 l | gray lilac | 1.75 | .60 |
| **496** | A171 | 7 l | claret | 1.75 | .60 |
| **497** | A172 | 12 l | blue | 3.50 | 1.75 |
| **498** | A173 | 15 l | green | 3.50 | 2.40 |
| | | | *Nos. 493-498 (6)* | 14.00 | 6.55 |

Romanian Railways, 70th anniversary.
Nos 493-498 exist imperf. Value, unused or used, $200.

Arms of Romania, Greece, Turkey and Yugoslavia — A174

**Wmk. 230**

**1940, May 27** **Photo.** *Perf. 13½*

| No. | Type | Denomination | Color | Unused | Used |
|---|---|---|---|---|---|
| **504** | A174 | 12 l | lt ultra | 1.25 | .75 |
| **505** | A174 | 16 l | dull blue | 1.25 | .75 |

The Balkan Entente.
Nos 504-505 exist imperf. Value, unused or used, $125.

King Michael — A175

**1940-42** **Wmk. 230** *Perf. 14*

| No. | Type | Denomination | Color | Unused | Used |
|---|---|---|---|---|---|
| **506** | A175 | 25b | Prus green | .25 | .25 |
| **506A** | A175 | 50b | dk grn ('42) | .25 | .25 |
| **507** | A175 | 1 l | purple | .25 | .25 |
| **508** | A175 | 2 l | red orange | .25 | .25 |
| **508A** | A175 | 4 l | slate ('42) | .25 | .25 |
| **509** | A175 | 5 l | rose pink | .25 | .25 |
| **509A** | A175 | 7 l | dp blue ('42) | .25 | .25 |
| **510** | A175 | 10 l | dp magenta | .40 | .25 |
| **511** | A175 | 12 l | dull blue | .25 | .25 |
| **511A** | A175 | 13 l | dk vio ('42) | .25 | .25 |
| **512** | A175 | 16 l | Prus blue | .55 | .25 |
| **513** | A175 | 20 l | brown | 1.75 | .25 |
| **514** | A175 | 30 l | yellow grn | .25 | .25 |
| **515** | A175 | 50 l | olive brn | .25 | .25 |
| **516** | A175 | 100 l | rose brown | .75 | .25 |
| | | | *Nos. 506-516 (15)* | 6.20 | 3.75 |

See Nos. 535A-553.

Prince Duca — A176

**1941, Oct. 6** *Perf. 13½*

| No. | Type | Denomination | Color | Unused | Used |
|---|---|---|---|---|---|
| **517** | A176 | 6 l | lt brown | .40 | .40 |
| **518** | A176 | 12 l | dk violet | .80 | .80 |
| **519** | A176 | 24 l | brt blue | 1.10 | 1.10 |
| | | | *Nos. 517-519 (3)* | 2.30 | 2.30 |

Crossing of the Dniester River by Romanian forces invading Russia.

Nos. 517-519 each exist in an imperf., ungummed souvenir sheet of 4. These were prepared by the civil government of Trans-Dniestria to be sold for 300 lei apiece to aid the Red Cross, but were not recognized by the national government at Bucharest. The sheets reached philatelic channels in 1946. Value, set of 3 sheets $40.

See Nos. 554-557.

Hotin Chapel, Bessarabia A177

Sucevita Monastery, Bucovina A179

Designs. 50b, 0.50 l, Hotin Fortress, Bessarabia. 1.50 l, Soroca Fortress, Bessarabia. 2 l, 5.50 l, Tighina Fortress, Bessarabia. 3 l, Dragomirna Monastery, Bucovina. 6.50 l, Cetatea Alba Fortress, Bessarabia. 10 l, 130 l, Putna Monastery, Bucovina. 13 l, Milisauti Monastery, Bucovina. 26 l, St. Nicholas Monastery, Suceava, Bucovina. 39 l, Rughi Monastery, Bessarabia.

**Inscribed "Basarabia" or "Bucovina" at bottom**

**1941, Dec. 1** *Perf. 13½*

| No. | Type | Denomination | Color | Unused | Used |
|---|---|---|---|---|---|
| **520** | A177 | 25b | rose car | .25 | .25 |
| **521** | A179 | 50b | red brn | .25 | .25 |
| **522** | A179 | 1 l | dp vio | .25 | .25 |
| **523** | A179 | 1.50 l | green | .25 | .25 |
| **524** | A179 | 2 l | brn org | .30 | .25 |
| **525** | A177 | 3 l | dk ol grn | .30 | .25 |
| **526** | A177 | 5 l | olive blk | .30 | .25 |
| **527** | A179 | 5.50 l | brown | .30 | .25 |
| **528** | A179 | 6.50 l | magenta | .40 | .25 |
| **529** | A179 | 9.50 l | gray blk | .40 | .25 |
| **530** | A179 | 10 l | dk vio brn | .35 | .25 |
| **531** | A177 | 13 l | slate blue | .70 | .25 |
| **532** | A179 | 17 l | brn car | 1.00 | .25 |
| **533** | A179 | 26 l | gray grn | 1.25 | .40 |
| **534** | A179 | 39 l | bl grn | 1.75 | .60 |
| **535** | A179 | 130 l | yel org | 5.00 | 2.75 |
| | | | *Nos. 520-535,B179-B187 (25)* | 19.50 | 11.75 |

**Type of 1940-42**

**1943-45** **Wmk. 276** *Perf. 14*

| No. | Type | Denomination | Color | Unused | Used |
|---|---|---|---|---|---|
| **535A** | A175 | 25b | Prus grn ('44) | .25 | .25 |
| **536** | A175 | 50b | dk grn ('44) | .25 | .25 |
| **537** | A175 | 1 l | dk vio ('43) | .25 | .25 |
| **538** | A175 | 2 l | red org ('43) | .25 | .25 |
| **539** | A175 | 3 l | red brn ('44) | .25 | .25 |
| **540** | A175 | 3.50 l | brn ('43) | .25 | .25 |
| **541** | A175 | 4 l | slate | .25 | .25 |
| **542** | A175 | 4.50 l | dk brn ('43) | .25 | .25 |
| **543** | A175 | 5 l | rose car | .25 | .25 |
| **544** | A175 | 6.50 l | dl vio | .25 | .25 |
| **545** | A175 | 7 l | dp bl | .25 | .25 |
| **546** | A175 | 10 l | dp mag | .25 | .25 |
| **547** | A175 | 11 l | brt ultra | .25 | .25 |
| **548** | A175 | 12 l | dark blue | .25 | .25 |
| **549** | A175 | 15 l | royal blue | .25 | .25 |
| **550** | A175 | 16 l | dp blue | .25 | .25 |
| **551** | A175 | 20 l | brn ('43) | .25 | .25 |
| **551A** | A175 | 29 l | ultra ('45) | .55 | .35 |
| **552** | A175 | 30 l | yel grn | .25 | .25 |
| **553** | A175 | 50 l | olive blk | .25 | .25 |
| | | | *Nos. 535A-553 (20)* | 5.30 | 5.10 |

### Prince Duca Type of 1941

**1943** *Perf. 13½*

| No. | Type | Value | Color | Unused | Used |
|---|---|---|---|---|---|
| **554** | A176 | 3 l | red org | .40 | *.75* |
| **555** | A176 | 6 l | dl brn | .40 | *.75* |
| **556** | A176 | 12 l | dl vio | .80 | *1.10* |
| **557** | A176 | 24 l | brt bl | 1.10 | *1.50* |
| | *Nos. 554-557 (4)* | | | 2.70 | 4.10 |

Andrei Saguna — A188

Andrei Muresanu A189

Transylvanians: 4.50 l, Samuel Micu. 11 l, Gheorghe Sincai. 15 l, Michael the Brave. 31 l, Gheorghe Lazar. 35 l, Avram Jancu. 41 l, Simeon Barnutiu. 55 l, Three Heroes. 61 l, Petru Maior.

**1945** **Inscribed "1944"** *Perf. 14*

| No. | Type | Value | Color | Unused | Used |
|---|---|---|---|---|---|
| **558** | A188 | 25b | rose red | .60 | *.70* |
| **559** | A189 | 50b | orange | .40 | *.70* |
| **560** | A189 | 4.50 l | brown | .40 | *.70* |
| **561** | A188 | 11 l | lt ultra | .40 | *.70* |
| **562** | A188 | 15 l | Prus grn | .40 | *.70* |
| **563** | A189 | 31 l | dl vio | .40 | *.70* |
| **564** | A188 | 35 l | bl blk | .40 | *.70* |
| **565** | A188 | 41 l | olive gray | 1.10 | *.70* |
| **566** | A189 | 55 l | red brown | .40 | *.70* |
| **567** | A189 | 61 l | deep magenta | .40 | *.70* |
| | *Nos. 558-567,B251 (11)* | | | 5.40 | 7.75 |

Romania's liberation.

A198 A199

King Michael

A200 A201

**1945** **Photo.**

| No. | Type | Value | Color | Unused | Used |
|---|---|---|---|---|---|
| **568** | A198 | 50b | gray blue | .25 | .25 |
| **569** | A199 | 1 l | dl brn | .25 | .25 |
| **570** | A199 | 2 l | violet | .25 | .25 |
| **571** | A198 | 2 l | sepia | .25 | .25 |
| **572** | A199 | 4 l | yel grn | .25 | .25 |
| **573** | A200 | 5 l | dp mag | .25 | .25 |
| **574** | A198 | 10 l | blue | .25 | .25 |
| **575** | A198 | 15 l | magenta | .25 | .25 |
| **576** | A198 | 20 l | dl blue | .25 | .25 |
| **577** | A200 | 25 l | red org | .25 | .25 |
| **578** | A200 | 35 l | brown | .25 | .25 |
| **579** | A200 | 40 l | car rose | .25 | .25 |
| **580** | A199 | 50 l | pale ultra | .25 | .25 |
| **581** | A199 | 55 l | red | .25 | .25 |
| **582** | A200 | 75 l | Prus grn | .25 | .25 |
| **583** | A201 | 80 l | orange | .25 | .25 |
| **584** | A201 | 100 l | dp red brn | .25 | .25 |
| **585** | A201 | 160 l | yel grn | .25 | .25 |
| **586** | A201 | 200 l | dk ol grn | .25 | .25 |
| **587** | A201 | 400 l | dl vio | .25 | .25 |
| | *Nos. 568-587 (20)* | | | 5.00 | 5.00 |

Nos. 571, 573, 580, 581, 585 and 587 are printed on toned paper, Nos. 576, 577, 583, 584 and 586 on both toned and white papers, others on white paper only.

See Nos. 610-624, 651-660.

Mail Carrier A202

Telegraph Operator A203

Lineman A204

Post Office, Bucharest A205

**1945, July 20** **Wmk. 276** *Perf. 13*

| No. | Type | Value | Color | Unused | Used |
|---|---|---|---|---|---|
| **588** | A202 | 100 l | dk brn | 1.00 | 1.00 |
| **589** | A202 | 100 l | gray olive | 1.00 | 1.00 |
| **590** | A203 | 150 l | brown | 1.65 | 1.65 |
| **591** | A203 | 150 l | brt rose | 1.65 | 1.65 |
| **592** | A204 | 250 l | lt gray ol | 2.00 | 2.00 |
| **593** | A204 | 250 l | blue | 2.00 | 2.00 |
| **594** | A205 | 500 l | dp mag | 14.00 | 14.00 |
| | *Nos. 588-594 (7)* | | | 23.30 | 23.30 |

Issued in sheets of 4. Value, set of 7 sheets $150.

I. Ionescu, G. Titeica, A. O. Idachimescu and V. Cristescu — A207

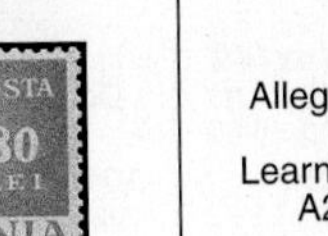

Allegory of Learning A208

**1945, Sept. 5** *Perf. 13½*

| No. | Type | Value | Color | Unused | Used |
|---|---|---|---|---|---|
| **596** | A207 | 2 l | sepia | .25 | .25 |
| **597** | A208 | 80 l | bl blk | .55 | .55 |

50th anniversary of "Gazeta Matematica," mathematics journal.

Cernavoda Bridge, 50th Anniv. — A209

**1945, Sept. 26** *Perf. 14*

| No. | Type | Value | Color | Unused | Used |
|---|---|---|---|---|---|
| **598** | A209 | 80 l | bl blk | .40 | .25 |

Blacksmith and Plowman — A210

**1946, Mar. 6**

| No. | Type | Value | Color | Unused | Used |
|---|---|---|---|---|---|
| **599** | A210 | 80 l | blue | .50 | .25 |
| | *Nos. 599,B326-B329 (5)* | | | 2.10 | 3.25 |

Agrarian reform law of Mar. 23, 1945. See No. CB4.

Atheneum, Bucharest A211

Numeral in Wreath A212

Georges Enescu — A213

**Wmk. 276**

**1946, Apr. 26** **Photo.** *Perf. 13½*

| No. | Type | Value | Color | Unused | Used |
|---|---|---|---|---|---|
| **600** | A211 | 10 l | dk bl | .25 | .25 |
| **601** | A212 | 20 l | red brn | .25 | .25 |
| **602** | A212 | 55 l | peacock bl | .25 | .25 |
| **603** | A213 | 80 l | purple | .40 | .25 |
| *a.* | | | Tête bêche pair | .80 | .80 |
| **604** | A212 | 160 l | red org | .25 | .25 |
| | *Nos. 600-604,B330-B331 (7)* | | | 3.10 | 4.50 |

Philharmonic Society, 25th anniv.

Mechanic — A214

Labor Day: No. 606, Laborer. No. 607, Sower. No. 608, Reaper. 200 l, Students.

**1946, May 1** *Perf. 13½x13*

| No. | Type | Value | Color | Unused | Used |
|---|---|---|---|---|---|
| **605** | A214 | 10 l | Prus grn | .75 | .75 |
| **606** | A214 | 10 l | dk car rose | .25 | .25 |
| **607** | A214 | 20 l | dl bl | .75 | .75 |
| **608** | A214 | 20 l | dk red brn | .25 | .25 |
| **609** | A214 | 200 l | brt red | .40 | .40 |
| | *Nos. 605-609 (5)* | | | 2.40 | 2.40 |

### Michael Types of 1945

**1946** **Wmk. 276** **Photo.** *Perf. 14*

**Toned Paper**

| No. | Type | Value | Color | Unused | Used |
|---|---|---|---|---|---|
| **610** | A198 | 10 l | brt red brn | .25 | .25 |
| **611** | A198 | 20 l | vio brn | .25 | .25 |
| **612** | A201 | 80 l | blue | .25 | .25 |
| **613** | A198 | 137 l | yel grn | .25 | .25 |
| **614** | A201 | 160 l | chalky bl | .25 | .25 |
| **615** | A201 | 200 l | red org | .25 | .25 |
| **616** | A201 | 300 l | sapphire | .25 | .25 |
| **617** | A201 | 360 l | sepia | .25 | .25 |
| **618** | A199 | 400 l | red org | .25 | .25 |
| **619** | A201 | 480 l | brn red | .25 | .25 |
| **620** | A201 | 600 l | dk ol grn | .25 | .25 |
| **621** | A201 | 1000 l | Prus grn | .25 | .25 |
| **622** | A198 | 1500 l | Prus grn | .25 | .25 |
| **623** | A201 | 2400 l | magenta | .25 | .25 |
| **624** | A201 | 3700 l | dull bl | .25 | .25 |
| | *Nos. 610-624 (15)* | | | 3.75 | 3.75 |

Demetrius Cantemir — A219

Designs: 100 l, "Cultural Ties." 300 l, "Economic Ties."

**1946, Oct. 20** *Perf. 13½*

| No. | Type | Value | Color | Unused | Used |
|---|---|---|---|---|---|
| **625** | A219 | 80 l | dk brn | .40 | .40 |
| **626** | A219 | 100 l | dp bl | .40 | .40 |
| **627** | A219 | 300 l | bl blk | .40 | .40 |
| | *Nos. 625-627,B338 (4)* | | | 1.90 | 2.45 |

Romania-Soviet friendship. See No. B339.

Soccer — A222

Designs: 20 l, Diving. 50 l, Running. 80 l, Mountain climbing.

**1946, Sept. 1** *Perf. 11½, Imperf.*

| No. | Type | Value | Color | Unused | Used |
|---|---|---|---|---|---|
| **628** | A222 | 10 l | dp blue | .40 | .40 |
| **629** | A222 | 20 l | brt red | .40 | .40 |
| **630** | A222 | 50 l | dp violet | .40 | .40 |
| **631** | A222 | 80 l | chocolate | .40 | .40 |
| | *Nos. 628-631,B340,C26,CB6 (7)* | | | 4.10 | 4.60 |

Issued in sheets of 16.

Weaving — A226

**Wmk. 276**

**1946, Nov. 20** **Photo.** *Perf. 14*

| No. | Type | Value | Color | Unused | Used |
|---|---|---|---|---|---|
| **636** | A226 | 80 l | dk ol brn | .30 | .30 |
| | *Nos. 636,B342-B345 (5)* | | | 1.70 | 3.30 |

Democratic Women's Org. of Romania. See No. CB7.

Child Receiving Bread — A227

Transporting Relief Supplies — A228

**1947, Jan. 15** *Perf. 13½x14, 14x13½*

| No. | Type | Value | Color | Unused | Used |
|---|---|---|---|---|---|
| **637** | A227 | 300 l | dk ol brn | .40 | .40 |
| **638** | A228 | 600 l | magenta | .40 | .40 |
| | *Nos. 637-638,B346-B347 (4)* | | | 1.40 | 2.00 |

Social relief fund. See #B348.

CGM Congress Emblem — A229

**1947, Feb. 10** *Perf. 13½*

| No. | Type | Value | Color | Unused | Used |
|---|---|---|---|---|---|
| **639** | A229 | 200 l | blue | .55 | .55 |
| **640** | A229 | 300 l | orange | .55 | .55 |
| *a.* | | | Pair, #639-640 | 1.10 | 1.10 |
| *b.* | | | Pair, #640-641 | 1.25 | 1.25 |
| **641** | A229 | 600 l | crimson | .70 | .70 |
| | *Nos. 639-641 (3)* | | | 1.80 | 1.80 |

Congress of the United Labor Unions ("CGM").

Printed in sheets of 18 comprising 3 pairs of each denomination. Sheet yields 3 each of Nos. 640a and 640b.

Peace in Chariot A230

Peace — A231

Flags of US, Russia, GB & Romania — A232

Dove of Peace — A233

**1947, Feb. 25** ***Perf. 14x13½, 13½x14***

| | | | | | |
|---|---|---|---|---|---|
| **642** | A230 | 300 l | dl vio | .50 | .50 |
| **643** | A231 | 600 l | dk org brn | .50 | .50 |
| **644** | A232 | 3000 l | blue | .50 | .50 |
| **645** | A233 | 7200 l | sage grn | .50 | .50 |
| | | *Nos. 642-645 (4)* | | 2.00 | 2.00 |

Signing of the peace treaty of Feb. 10, 1947.

King Michael — A234

**1947** **Size: 25x30mm** ***Perf. 13½***

| | | | | | |
|---|---|---|---|---|---|
| **646** | A234 | 3000 l | blue | .25 | .25 |
| **647** | A234 | 7200 l | dl vio | .25 | .25 |
| **648** | A234 | 15,000 l | brt bl | .40 | .25 |
| **649** | A234 | 21,000 l | magenta | .40 | .25 |
| **650** | A234 | 36,000 l | violet | .75 | .60 |
| | | *Nos. 646-650 (5)* | | 2.05 | 1.60 |

See Nos. 661-664.

**Michael Types of 1945**

**1947** **Wmk. 276** **Photo.** ***Perf. 14***

| | | | | | |
|---|---|---|---|---|---|
| **651** | A199 | 10 l | red brn | .25 | .25 |
| **652** | A200 | 20 l | magenta | .25 | .25 |
| **653** | A198 | 80 l | blue | .25 | .25 |
| **654** | A199 | 200 l | brt red | .25 | .25 |
| **655** | A198 | 500 l | magenta | .25 | .25 |
| **656** | A200 | 860 l | vio brn | .25 | .25 |
| **657** | A199 | 2500 l | ultra | .25 | .25 |
| **658** | A198 | 5000 l | sl gray | .25 | .25 |
| **659** | A198 | 8000 l | Prus grn | .75 | .25 |
| **660** | A201 | 10,000 l | dk brn | 1.00 | .25 |

**Type of 1947**

**Size: 18x21½mm**

| | | | | | |
|---|---|---|---|---|---|
| **661** | A234 | 1000 l | gray bl | .25 | .25 |
| **662** | A234 | 5500 l | yel grn | .25 | .25 |
| **663** | A234 | 20,000 l | ol brn | .55 | .30 |
| **664** | A234 | 50,000 l | red org | 1.00 | .45 |
| | | *Nos. 651-664 (14)* | | 5.80 | 3.75 |

For surcharge see No. B368.

Harvesting Wheat A235

Designs: 1 l, Log raft. 2 l, River steamer. 3 l, Resita. 5 l, Cathedral of Curtea de Arges. 10 l, View of Bucharest. 12 l, 36 l, Cernavoda Bridge. 15 l, 32 l, Port of Constantsa. 20 l, Petroleum field.

**1947, Aug. 15** ***Perf. 14½x14***

| | | | | | |
|---|---|---|---|---|---|
| **666** | A235 | 50b | red org | .25 | .25 |
| **667** | A235 | 1 l | red brn | .25 | .25 |
| **668** | A235 | 2 l | grnsh blue | .25 | .25 |
| **669** | A235 | 3 l | rose crim | .50 | .25 |
| **670** | A235 | 5 l | gray blue | .50 | .25 |
| **671** | A235 | 10 l | Prus blue | .65 | .30 |
| **672** | A235 | 12 l | violet | .85 | .35 |
| **673** | A235 | 15 l | dp vio blue | 1.50 | .35 |
| **674** | A235 | 20 l | dk brown | 2.50 | .50 |
| **675** | A235 | 32 l | violet brn | 5.75 | 2.50 |
| **676** | A235 | 36 l | dk car rose | 6.00 | 2.50 |
| | | *Nos. 666-676 (11)* | | 19.00 | 7.75 |

For overprints & surcharge see #684-694, B369.

Beehive, Savings Emblem — A236

**1947, Oct. 31** ***Perf. 13½***

| | | | | | |
|---|---|---|---|---|---|
| **677** | A236 | 12 l | dk car rose | .55 | .35 |

World Savings Day, Oct. 31, 1947.

**People's Republic**

Map, Workers and Children A237

**1948, Jan. 25** ***Perf. 14½x14***

| | | | | | |
|---|---|---|---|---|---|
| **678** | A237 | 12 l | brt ultra | 1.00 | .30 |

1948 census. For surcharge see #819A.

Government Printing Plant and Press — A238

**1948** ***Perf. 14½x14***

| | | | | | |
|---|---|---|---|---|---|
| **679** | A238 | 6 l | magenta | 2.00 | 1.10 |
| **680** | A238 | 7.50 l | dk Prus grn | 1.10 | .25 |
| *b.* | | Tête bêche pair | | 3.25 | 3.25 |

75th anniversary of Stamp Division of Romanian State Printing Works.

Issued: No. 680, Feb. 12; No. 679, May 20.

Romanian and Bulgarian Peasants Shaking Hands A239

**1948, Mar. 25** **Wmk. 276**

| | | | | | |
|---|---|---|---|---|---|
| **680A** | A239 | 32 l | red brown | 1.50 | .75 |

Romanian-Bulgarian friendship.

For surcharge see No. 696.

Allegory of the People's Republic — A240

**1948, Apr. 8** **Photo.** ***Perf. 14x14½***

| | | | | | |
|---|---|---|---|---|---|
| **681** | A240 | 1 l | car rose | .55 | .40 |
| **682** | A240 | 2 l | dl org | .80 | .55 |
| **683** | A240 | 12 l | deep blue | 2.40 | .90 |
| | | *Nos. 681-683 (3)* | | 3.75 | 1.85 |

New constitution.

For surcharge see No. 820.

**Nos. 666 to 676 Overprinted in Black**

**1948, Mar.** ***Perf. 14½x14***

| | | | | | |
|---|---|---|---|---|---|
| **684** | A235 | 50b | red org | .30 | .25 |
| **685** | A235 | 1 l | red brn | .30 | .25 |
| **686** | A235 | 2 l | bl gray | .60 | .25 |
| **687** | A235 | 3 l | rose crim | .60 | .25 |
| **688** | A235 | 5 l | brt ultra | 1.25 | .30 |
| **689** | A235 | 10 l | brt bl | 1.50 | .30 |
| **690** | A235 | 12 l | violet | 1.75 | .35 |
| **691** | A235 | 15 l | dp ultra | 1.75 | .40 |
| **692** | A235 | 20 l | dk brn | 2.50 | .55 |
| **693** | A235 | 32 l | vio brn | 7.50 | 2.50 |
| **694** | A235 | 36 l | dk car rose | 7.50 | 2.50 |
| | | *Nos. 684-694 (11)* | | 25.55 | 7.90 |

Romanian Newspapers — A241

**1948, Sept. 12**

| | | | | | |
|---|---|---|---|---|---|
| **695** | A241 | 10 l | red brn | .40 | .25 |
| | | *Nos. 695,B396-B398 (4)* | | 3.70 | 3.55 |

Week of the Democratic Press, Sept. 12-19.

**No. 680A Surcharged with New Value in Black**

**1948, Aug. 17**

| | | | | | |
|---|---|---|---|---|---|
| **696** | A239 | 31 l on 32 l | red brn | 1.00 | .35 |

Monument to Soviet Soldier — A242

**1948, Oct. 29** **Photo.** ***Perf. 14x14½***

| | | | | | |
|---|---|---|---|---|---|
| **697** | A242 | 10 l | dk red | .80 | .80 |
| | | *Nos. 697,B399-B400 (3)* | | 6.30 | 8.30 |

Sheets of 50 stamps and 50 labels.

Proclamation of Islaz — A243

**1948, June 1** ***Perf. 14½x14***

| | | | | | |
|---|---|---|---|---|---|
| **698** | A243 | 11 l | car rose | .85 | .25 |
| | | *Nos. 698,B409-B412 (5)* | | 4.30 | 5.05 |

Centenary of Revolution of 1848.

For surcharge see No. 820A.

Arms of Romanian People's Republic — A243a

**1948, July 8** **Wmk. 276**

| | | | | | |
|---|---|---|---|---|---|
| **698A** | A243a | 50b | red ("Lei 0.50") | .30 | .25 |
| **698B** | A243a | 1 l | red brn | .30 | .25 |
| **698C** | A243a | 2 l | dk grn | .30 | .25 |
| **698D** | A243a | 3 l | grnsh blk | .55 | .25 |
| **698E** | A243a | 4 l | chocolate | .55 | .25 |
| **698F** | A243a | 5 l | ultra | .70 | .25 |
| **698G** | A243a | 10 l | dp bl | .85 | .25 |

**"Bani" instead of "Lei"**

| | | | | | |
|---|---|---|---|---|---|
| **698H** | A243a | 50b | red ("Bani 0.50") | .55 | .55 |
| | | *Nos. 698A-698H (8)* | | 4.10 | 2.30 |

See Nos. 712-717.

Nicolae Balcescu (1819-1852), Writer — A244

**1948, Dec. 20** **Wmk. 289**

| | | | | | |
|---|---|---|---|---|---|
| **699** | A244 | 20 l | scarlet | 1.00 | .35 |

Release from Bondage — A245

**1948, Dec. 30** ***Perf. 13½***

| | | | | | |
|---|---|---|---|---|---|
| **700** | A245 | 5 l | brt rose | .55 | .25 |

First anniversary of the Republic.

Lenin, 25th Death Anniv. — A246

**1949, Jan. 21**

| | | | | | |
|---|---|---|---|---|---|
| **701** | A246 | 20 l | black | .70 | .25 |

Exists imperf. Value, unused or used, $1.25.

Folk Dance — A247

**1949, Jan. 24** ***Perf. 13½***

| | | | | | |
|---|---|---|---|---|---|
| **702** | A247 | 10 l | dp bl | .55 | .30 |

90th anniv. of the union of the Danubian Principalities.

Ion C. Frimu and Revolutionary Scene — A248

**1949, Mar. 22** ***Perf. 14½x14***

| | | | | | |
|---|---|---|---|---|---|
| **703** | A248 | 20 l | red | .55 | .25 |

Exists imperf. Value, unused or used, $1.25.

Aleksander S. Pushkin, 150th Birth Anniv. — A249

**1949, May 20** *Perf. 14x14½*
**704** A249 11 l car rose 1.25 .75
**705** A249 30 l Prus grn 1.60 .75

For surcharges see Nos. 821-822.

Globe and Post Horn — A250

Evolution of Mail Transportation — A251

*Perf. 13½, 14½x14*
**1949, June 30 Photo. Wmk. 289**
**706** A250 20 l org brn 2.25 2.25
**707** A251 30 l brt bl 4.75 1.25

UPU, 75th anniv.
For surcharges see Nos. C43-C44.

Russian Army Entering Bucharest, August, 1944 — A252

**1949, Aug. 23** *Perf. 14½x14*
**708** A252 50 l choc, *bl grn* .95 .60

5th anniv. of the liberation of Romania by the Soviet army, Aug. 1944.
Exists imperf. Value, unused or used, $2.

"Long Live Romanian-Soviet Amity" — A253

**1949, Nov. 1** *Perf. 13½x14½*
**709** A253 20 l dp red .65 .35

Natl. week of Romanian-Soviet friendship celebration, 11/1-7/49. Exists imperf. Value, unused or used, $1.50.

Symbols of Transportation A254

**1949, Dec. 10** *Perf. 13½*
**710** A254 11 l blue 1.50 1.50
**711** A254 20 l crimson 1.50 1.50

Intl. Conference of Transportation Unions, Dec. 10, 1949.
Alternate vertical rows of stamps and labels in sheet. Exist imperf. Value for set, unused or used, $3.75.

**Arms Type of 1948**

**1949-50 Wmk. 289** *Perf. 14x13½*
**712** A243a 50b red ("Lei 0.50") .40 .25
**713** A243a 1 l red brn .40 .25
**714** A243a 2 l dk grn .40 .25
**714A** A243a 3 l grnsh blk .65 .25
**715** A243a 5 l ultra .50 .25
**716** A243a 5 l rose vio ('50) .80 .25
**717** A243a 10 l dp blue 1.00 .25
*Nos. 712-717 (7)* 4.15 1.75

Joseph V. Stalin — A256

**1949, Dec. 21** *Perf. 13½*
**718** A256 31 l olive black .65 .25

Stalin's 70th birthday. Exists imperf. Value, unused or used, $1.60.

Mihail Eminescu — A257

Poem: "Life" — A258

No. 721, "Third Letter." No. 722, "Angel and Demon." No. 723, "Emperor and Proletariat."

**1950, Jan. 15 Photo. Wmk. 289**
**719** A257 11 l blue 1.00 .30
**720** A258 11 l purple 1.75 .65
**721** A258 11 l dk grn 1.00 .30
**722** A258 11 l red brn 1.00 .30
**723** A258 11 l rose pink 1.00 .30
*Nos. 719-723 (5)* 5.75 1.85

Birth cent. of Mihail Eminescu, poet.
For surcharges see Nos. 823-827.

Fair at Dragaica A259

Ion Andreescu (Self-portrait) A260

Village Well A261

**1950, Mar. 25** *Perf. 14½x14, 14x14½*
**724** A259 5 l dk gray grn 1.00 .60
**725** A260 11 l ultra 1.60 .60
**726** A261 20 l brown 1.75 1.00
*Nos. 724-726 (3)* 4.35 2.20

Birth cent. of Ion Andreescu, painter. No. 725 also exists imperf. Value, unused or used, $3.50.
For surcharges see Nos. 827A-827B.

Graph and Factories A262

Design: 31 l, Tractor and Oil Derricks.

**Inscribed: "Planul de Stat 1950."**

*Perf. 14½x14*
**1950, Apr. 23 Wmk. 289**
**727** A262 11 l red .60 .25
**728** A262 31 l violet 1.10 .50

1950 plan for increased industrial production. No. 727 exists imperf. Value, unused or used, $2.
For surcharges see Nos. 827C-827D.

Young Man Holding Flag — A263

**1950, May 1** *Perf. 14x14½*
**729** A263 31 l orange red .65 .25

Labor Day, May 1.
Exists imperf. Value, unused or used, $1.25.
For surcharge see No. 827E.

> Canceled to Order
> Canceled sets of new issues have long been sold by the government. Values in the second ("used") column are for these canceled-to-order stamps. Postally used stamps are worth more.

Arms of Republic — A264

**1950 Photo.** *Perf. 12½*
**730** A264 50b black .25 .25
**731** A264 1 l red orange .25 .25
**732** A264 2 l ol gray .25 .25
**733** A264 3 l violet .25 .25
**734** A264 4 l rose lilac .25 .25
**735** A264 5 l red brn .25 .25
**736** A264 6 l dp grn .25 .25
**737** A264 7 l vio brn .25 .25
**738** A264 7.50 l blue .40 .25
**739** A264 10 l dk brn .80 .25
**740** A264 11 l rose car .80 .25
**741** A264 15 l dp bl .40 .25
**742** A264 20 l Prus grn .40 .25
**743** A264 31 l dl grn .80 .25
**744** A264 36 l dk org brn 1.25 .30
*Nos. 730-744 (15)* 6.85 3.80

See Nos. 947-961 which have similar design with white denomination figures.
For overprint & surcharges see Nos. 758, 828-841.

Bugler and Drummer A265

Designs: 11 l, Three school children. 31 l, Drummer, flag-bearer and bugler.

**1950, May 25** *Perf. 14½x14*
**745** A265 8 l blue 1.40 .60
**746** A265 11 l rose vio 1.75 1.00
**747** A265 31 l org ver 3.00 2.00
*Nos. 745-747 (3)* 6.15 3.60

Young Pioneers, 1st anniv.
For surcharges see Nos. 841A-841C.

Factory Worker — A266

**1950, July 20 Photo.** *Perf. 14x14½*
**748** A266 11 l red brn .50 .35
**749** A266 11 l red .85 .35
**750** A266 11 l blue .50 .35
**751** A266 11 l blk brn .85 .35
*Nos. 748-751 (4)* 2.70 1.40

Nationalization of industry, 2nd anniv.

Aurel Vlaicu and his First Plane — A267

**1950, July 22 Wmk. 289** *Perf. 12½*
**752** A267 3 l dk grn .40 .25
**753** A267 6 l dk bl .60 .25
**754** A267 8 l ultra .75 .35
*Nos. 752-754 (3)* 1.75 .85

Aurel Vlaicu (1882-1913), pioneer of Romanian aviation.
For surcharges see Nos. 842-844.

Mother and Child — A268

Lathe and Operator — A269

**1950, Sept. 9** *Perf. 13½*
**755** A268 11 l rose red .40 .25
**756** A269 20 l dk ol brn .45 .25

Congress of the Committees for the Struggle for Peace.
For surcharge see No. 844A.

Statue of Soviet Soldier — A270

**1950, Oct. 6** *Perf. 14x14½*
**757** A270 30 l red brn .85 .35

Celebration of Romanian-Soviet friendship, Oct. 7-Nov. 7, 1950.

No. 741 Overprinted in Carmine

**1950, Oct. 6** *Perf. 12½*
**758** A264 15 l deep blue 1.10 .35

Romanian-Hungarian friendship.

"Agriculture," "Manufacturing" and Sports Badge — A271

5 l, Student workers & badge. 11 l, Track team & badge. 31 l, Calisthenics & badge.

**1950, Oct. 30** *Perf. 14½x14*

**759** A271 3 l rose car 1.40 1.40
**760** A271 5 l red brn 1.00 1.00
**761** A271 5 l brt bl 1.00 1.00
**762** A271 11 l green 1.00 1.00
**763** A271 31 l brn ol 2.50 2.50
*Nos. 759-763 (5)* 6.90 6.90

For surcharge see No. 845.

A272

**1950, Nov. 2** *Perf. 13½*

**764** A272 11 l blue .50 .35
**765** A272 11 l red org .50 .35

3rd Soviet-Romanian Friendship Congress.

"Industry" — A273

"Agriculture" — A274

*Perf. 14x14½, 14½x14*

**1951, Feb. 9** **Photo.** **Wmk. 289**

**766** A273 11 l red brn .40 .25
**767** A274 31 l deep bl .75 .35

Industry and Agriculture Exposition. Exist imperf. Value for set, unused or used, $2.

For surcharge see No. 846.

Ski Jump — A275

Ski Descent A276

5 l, Skating. 20 l, Hockey. 31 l, Bobsledding.

**1951, Jan. 28** *Perf. 13½*

**768** A275 4 l blk brn 1.50 1.50
**769** A275 5 l vermilion 1.25 1.25
**770** A276 11 l dp bl 1.25 1.25
**771** A275 20 l org brn 1.25 1.25
**772** A275 31 l dk gray grn 3.50 3.25
*Nos. 768-772 (5)* 8.75 8.50

9th World University Winter Games.

For surcharges see Nos. 847-848.

Medal for Work — A277

Orders: 4 l, Star of the Republic, Classes III, IV & V. 11 l, Work. 35 l, As 4 l, Classes I & II.

**1951, May 1** *Perf. 13½*

**773** A277 2 l ol gray .25 .25
**774** A277 4 l blue .35 .25
**775** A277 11 l crimson .50 .25
**776** A277 35 l org brn .75 .40
*Nos. 773-776 (4)* 1.85 1.15

Labor Day. Exist imperf. Value for set, unused or used, $2.50.

For surcharges see Nos. 849-852.

Camp of Young Pioneers A278

Pioneers Greeting Stalin — A279

Admitting New Pioneers A280

**1951, May 8** *Perf. 14x14½, 14½x14*

**777** A278 1 l gray grn 1.00 .45
**778** A279 11 l blue 1.00 .45
**779** A280 35 l red 1.50 .70
*Nos. 777-779 (3)* 3.50 1.60

Romanian Young Pioneers Organization.

For surcharge see No. 853.

Woman Orator and Flags — A281

**1951, Mar. 8** *Perf. 14x14½*

**780** A281 11 l org brn .50 .25

Woman's Day, March 8. Exists imperf. Value, unused or used, 80c.

Ion Negulici — A282

**1951, June 20** *Perf. 14x14½*

**781** A282 35 l rose red 3.50 2.10

Death cent. of Ion Negulici, painter.

Bicyclists A283

**1951, July 9** *Perf. 14½x14*

**782** A283 11 l chnt brn 2.10 .80
*a.* Tête bêche pair 7.00 7.00

The 1951 Bicycle Tour of Romania.

Festival Badge — A284

Boy and Girl with Flag — A285

Youths Encircling Globe — A286

**1951, Aug. 1** *Perf. 13½*

**783** A284 1 l scarlet .80 .40
**784** A285 5 l deep blue 1.50 .40
**785** A286 11 l deep plum 2.25 .80
*Nos. 783-785 (3)* 4.55 1.60

3rd World Youth Festival, Berlin.

Filimon Sarbu — A287

**1951, July 23** *Perf. 14x14½*

**786** A287 11 l dk brn .70 .25

10th death anniv. of Filimon Sarbu, patriot.

"Romania Raising the Masses" — A288

"Revolutionary Romania" — A289

**1951, July 23** *Perf. 14x14½, 14½x14*

**787** A288 11 l yel brn 2.00 .75
**788** A288 11 l rose vio 2.00 .75
**789** A289 11 l dk grn 2.00 .75
**790** A289 11 l org red 2.00 .75
*Nos. 787-790 (4)* 8.00 3.00

Death cent. of C. D. Rosenthal, painter.

Scanteia Building A290

**1951, Aug. 16** *Perf. 14½x14*

**791** A290 11 l blue .75 .35

20th anniv. of the newspaper Scanteia.

Miner in Dress Uniform — A291

Design: 11 l, Miner in work clothes.

**1951, Aug. 12** *Perf. 14x14½*

**792** A291 5 l blue .60 .35
**793** A291 11 l plum .70 .25

Miner's Day. For surcharge see No. 854.

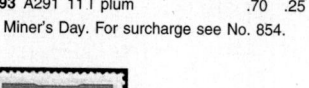

Order for National Defense — A293

**1951, Aug. 12** *Perf. 14x14½*

**794** A293 10 l crimson .55 .25

For surcharge see No. 855.

Choir — A294

Music Week Emblem — A295

Design: No. 796, Orchestra and dancers.

**Wmk. 358**

**1951, Sept. 22** **Photo.** *Perf. 13½*

**795** A294 11 l blue .50 .35
**796** A294 11 l red brown .75 .40
**797** A295 11 l purple .50 .35
*Nos. 795-797 (3)* 1.75 1.10

Music Week, Sept. 22-30, 1951.

Soldier — A296

**1951, Oct. 2**

**798** A296 11 l blue .55 .25

Army Day, Oct. 2, 1951.

Oil Field — A297

Designs: 2 l, Coal mining. 3 l, Romanian soldier. 4 l, Smelting ore. 5 l, Agricultural machinery. 6 l, Canal construction. 7 l, Agriculture. 8 l, Self-education. 11 l, Hydroelectric production. 35 l, Manufacturing.

**1951-52**

**799** A297 1 l black brn .70 .25
**800** A297 2 l chocolate .40 .25
**801** A297 3 l scarlet .75 .45
**802** A297 4 l yel brn ('52) .50 .25
**803** A297 5 l green .50 .25
**804** A297 6 l brt bl ('52) 2.00 1.10
**805** A297 7 l emerald 1.10 .50
**806** A297 8 l brown ('52) .90 .50
**807** A297 11 l blue .90 .25
**808** A297 35 l purple 1.25 .75
*Nos. 799-808,C35-C36 (12)* 15.75 10.05

1951-55 Five Year Plan.
2 l and 11 l exist with wmk. 289. Values same.
For surcharges see Nos. 860-869.

Arms of Soviet Union and Romania A298

**1951, Oct. 7** **Wmk. 358**

**809** A298 4 l chestnut brn, *cr* .40 .25
**810** A298 35 l orange red .85 .45

Month of Romanian-Soviet friendship, Oct. 7-Nov. 7.
For surcharges see Nos. 870-871.

Pavel Tcacenco — A299

**1951, Dec. 15** ***Perf. 14x14½***

**811** A299 10 l ol brn & dk brn .75 .40

Revolutionary, 26th death anniv.
For surcharge see No. 872.

Railroad Conductor — A300

**1952, Mar. 24** ***Perf. 13½***

**812** A300 55b dark brown 3.00 .40

Railroad Workers' Day, Feb. 16.

Ion L. Caragiale — A301

Announcing Caragiale Celebration — A302

Designs: No. 814, Book and painting "1907." No. 815, Bust and wreath.

**Inscribed: ". . . . I. L. Caragiale."**

**1952, Apr. 1** ***Perf. 13½, 14½x14***

**813** A301 55b chalky blue 1.50 .55
**814** A302 55b scarlet 1.50 .55
**815** A302 55b deep green 1.50 .55
**816** A302 1 l brown 4.00 .70
*Nos. 813-816 (4)* 8.50 2.35

Birth cent. of Ion L. Caragiale, dramatist.
For surcharges see Nos. 817-819.

**Types of 1952 Surcharged with New Value in Black or Carmine**

**1952-53**

**817** A302 20b on 11 l scar (as #814) 1.25 .65
**818** A302 55b on 11 l dp grn (as #815) (C) 1.75 .80
**819** A301 75b on 11 l chlky bl (C) 3.00 1.10

**Various Issues Surcharged with New Values in Carmine or Black**

**On No. 678, Census**

***Perf. 14x13½***

**819A** A237 50b on 12 l ultra 3.25 2.00

**On No. 683, New Constitution**

***Perf. 14***

**820** A240 50b on 12 l dp bl 4.00 1.25

**On No. 698, Revolution**

**820A** A243 1.75 l on 11 l car rose (Bk) 18.00 5.00

**On Nos. 704-705, Pushkin**

**1952** **Wmk. 358**

**821** A249 10b on 1 l (Bk) 4.00 1.75
**822** A249 10b on 30 l 4.00 1.75

**On Nos. 719-723, Eminescu**

***Perf. 13½x13, 13x13½***

**823** A257 10b on 11 l blue 3.00 1.90
**824** A258 10b on 11 l pur 3.00 1.90
**825** A258 10b on 11 l dk grn 3.00 1.90
**826** A258 10b on 11 l red brn (Bk) 3.00 1.90
**827** A258 10b on 11 l rose pink (Bk) 3.00 1.90

**On Nos. 724-725, Andreescu**

***Perf. 14***

**827A** A259 55b on 5 l dk gray grn 10.00 3.25
**827B** A260 55b on 11 l ultra 10.00 3.25

**On Nos. 727-728, Production Plan**

***Perf. 14½x14***

**827C** A262 20b on 11 l red (Bk) 4.00 1.25
**827D** A262 20b on 31 l vio 4.00 1.25

**On No. 729, Labor Day**

***Perf. 14***

**827E** A263 55b on 31 l (Bk) 5.00 3.25

**On Nos. 730-739 and 741-744, National Arms**

***Perf. 12½***

**828** A264 3b on 1 l red (Bk) 2.50 1.10
**829** A264 3b on 2 l ol gray (Bk) 2.50 1.10
**830** A264 3b on 4 l rose lil (Bk) 2.50 1.10
**831** A264 3b on 5 l red brn (Bk) 2.50 1.10
**832** A264 3b on 7.50 l bl (Bk) 2.50 1.10
**833** A264 3b on 10 l dk brn (Bk) 2.50 1.10
**834** A264 55b on 50b blk brn 7.00 1.90
**835** A264 55b on 3 l vio 7.00 1.90
**836** A264 55b on 6 l dp grn 7.00 1.90
**837** A264 55b on 7 l vio brn 7.00 1.90
**838** A264 55b on 15 l dp bl 9.00 1.90
**839** A264 55b on 20 l Prus grn 7.00 1.90
**840** A264 55b on 31 l dl grn 7.00 1.90
**841** A264 55b on 36 l dk org brn 9.00 1.90

**On Nos. 745-747, Young Pioneers**

***Perf. 14***

**841A** A265 55b on 8 l 10.00 5.75
**841B** A265 55b on 11 l 10.00 5.75
**841C** A265 55b on 31 l (Bk) 10.00 5.75

**On Nos. 752-754, Vlaicu**

***Perf. 12½***

**842** A267 10b on 3 l dk grn 3.00 1.10
**843** A267 10b on 6 l dk bl 3.00 1.10
**844** A267 10b on 8 l ultra 3.00 1.10

Original denomination canceled with an "X."

**On No. 756, Peace Congress**

***Perf. 13½***

**844A** A269 20b on 20 l 4.00 1.90

**On No. 759, Sports**

***Perf. 14½x14***

**845** A271 55b on 3 l (Bk) 24.00 15.00

**On No. 767, Exposition**

**846** A274 55b on 31 l dp bl 6.00 3.75

**On Nos. 771-772, Winter Games**

***Perf. 13½***

**847** A275 55b on 20 l (Bk) 35.00 15.00
**848** A275 55b on 31 l 35.00 15.00

**On Nos. 773-776, Labor Medals**

**849** A277 20b on 2 l 5.00 2.40
**850** A277 20b on 4 l 5.00 2.40
**851** A277 20b on 11 l (Bk) 5.00 2.40
**852** A277 20b on 35 l (Bk) 5.00 2.40

**On Nov. 779, Young Pioneers**

***Perf. 14x14½***

**853** A280 55b on 35 l (Bk) 10.00 4.75

**On No. 792, Miners' Day**

**854** A291 55b on 5 l bl 10.00 2.75

**On No. 794, Defense Order**

**855** A293 55b on 10 l (Bk) 10.00 2.75

**On Nos. B409-B412, 1848 Revolution**

**1952** **Wmk. 276** ***Perf. 13x13½***

**856** SP280 1.75 l on 2 l + 2 l (Bk) 18.00 4.75
**857** SP281 1.75 l on 5 l + 5 l 18.00 4.75
**858** SP282 1.75 l on 10 l + 10 l 18.00 4.75
**859** SP280 1.75 l on 36 l + 18 l 18.00 4.75

**On Nos. 799-808, 5-Year Plan**

**Wmk. 358** ***Perf. 13½***

**860** A297 35b on 1 l blk brn 2.10 .95
**861** A297 35b on 2 l choc 2.50 .95
**862** A297 35b on 3 l scar (Bk) 4.50 2.00
**863** A297 35b on 4 l yel brn (Bk) 5.25 2.25
*a.* Red surcharge 25.00 15.00
**864** A297 35b on 5 l grn 4.25 4.00
**865** A297 1 l on 6 l brt bl 6.25 5.00
**866** A297 1 l on 7 l emer 6.25 2.25
**867** A297 1 l on 8 l brn 6.25 5.00
**868** A297 1 l on 11 l bl 6.25 2.75
**869** A297 1 l on 35 l pur 8.00 2.25

Nos. 861, 868 exist with wmk. 289.

**On Nos. 809-810, Romanian-Soviet Friendship**

**870** A298 10b on 4 l (Bk) 2.25 1.25
**871** A298 10b on 35 l (Bk) 2.25 1.25

**On No. 811, Tcacenco**

***Perf. 13½x14***

**872** A299 10b on 10 l 2.25 1.00

A302a

***Perf. 13½x13***

**1952, Apr. 14** **Photo.** **Wmk. 358**

**873** A302a 1 l Ivan P. Pavlov 2.75 .40

Meeting of Romanian-Soviet doctors in Bucharest.

Labor Day — A303

**1952, May 1**

**874** A303 55b Hammer & sickle medal 2.75 .25

Medal for Motherhood A304

Medals: 55b, Maternal glory. 1.75 l, Mother-Heroine.

**1952, Apr. 7** ***Perf. 13x13½***

**875** A304 20b plum & sl gray .90 .25
**876** A304 55b henna brn 2.00 .45
**877** A304 1.75 l rose red & brn buff 4.25 .55
*Nos. 875-877 (3)* 7.15 1.25

International Women's Day.

Leonardo da Vinci — A305

**1952, July 3**

**878** A305 55b purple 5.00 .55

500th birth anniv. of Leonardo da Vinci.

Gogol and Scene from Taras Bulba A306

Nikolai V. Gogol — A307

**1952, Apr. 1** ***Perf. 13½x14, 14x13½***

**879** A306 55b deep blue 2.25 .35
**880** A307 1.75 l olive gray 2.75 .55

Gogol, Russian writer, death cent.

Pioneers Saluting — A308

Labor Day Paraders Returning A309

Design: 55b, Pioneers studying nature.

**1952, May 21** *Perf. 14*

**881** A308 20b brown 1.50 .25
**882** A308 55b dp green 4.00 .25
**883** A309 1.75 l blue 7.00 .55
*Nos. 881-883 (3)* 12.50 1.05

Third anniversary of Romanian Pioneers.

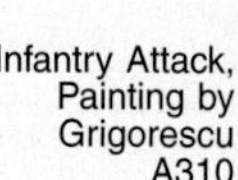

Infantry Attack, Painting by Grigorescu A310

1.10 l, Romanian and Russian soldiers.

**1952, June 7** *Perf. 13x13½*

**884** A310 50b rose brown 1.10 .25
**885** A310 1.10 l blue 1.75 .50

Independence Proclamation of 1877, 75th anniv.

Miner — A311

**1952, Aug. 11** **Wmk. 358**

**902** A311 20b rose red 2.00 .45
**903** A311 55b purple 2.00 .40

Day of the Miner.

Book and Globe — A312

Chemistry Student A313

Students in Native Dress — A314

Design: 55b, Students playing soccer.

*Perf. 13½x13, 13½x14, 13x13½*

**1952, Sept. 5**

**904** A312 10b deep blue .50 .25
**905** A313 20b orange 2.75 .35
**906** A312 55b deep green 2.75 .45
**907** A314 1.75 l rose red 5.50 1.10
*Nos. 904-907 (4)* 11.50 2.15

Intl. Student Union Congr., Bucharest, Sept.

Soldier, Sailor and Aviator — A316

**1952, Oct. 2** *Perf. 14*

**909** A316 55b blue 1.75 .25

Armed Forces Day, Oct. 2, 1952.

"Russia" Leading Peace Crusade — A317

Allegory: Romanian-Soviet Friendship — A318

**1952, Oct. 7** *Perf. 13½x13, 13x13½*

**910** A317 55b vermilion 1.10 .25
**911** A318 1.75 l black brown 3.00 .60

Month of Romanian-Soviet friendship, Oct.

Rowing on Lake Snagov — A319

1.75 l, Athletes marching with flags.

**1952, Oct. 20**

**912** A319 20b deep blue 5.00 .50
**913** A319 1.75 l rose red 8.00 1.10

Values are for stamps with poor perforations.

Nicolae Balcescu — A320

**1952, Nov. 29**

**914** A320 55b gray 4.00 .50
**915** A320 1.75 l lemon bister 8.00 1.25

Death cent. of Nicolae Balcescu, poet.

Arms of Republic — A321

**1952, Dec. 6** **Wmk. 358**

**916** A321 55b dull green 1.75 .35

5th anniversary of socialist constitution.

Arms and Industrial Symbols A322

**1953, Jan. 8** *Perf. 12½x13½*

**917** A322 55b blue, yellow & red 3.50 .50

5th anniv. of the proclamation of the People's Republic.

Matei Millo, Costache Caragiale and Aristita Romanescu A323

**1953, Feb.** **Photo.** *Perf. 13x13½*

**918** A323 55b brt ultra 3.50 .35

National Theater of I. L. Caragiale, cent.

Iron Foundry Worker — A324

Worker — A325

Design: No. 921, Driving Tractor.

**1953, Feb.** *Perf. 13½x13, 13x13½*

**919** A324 55b slate green 1.25 .25
**920** A325 55b black brown 1.25 .25
**921** A325 55b orange 1.50 .55
*Nos. 919-921 (3)* 4.00 1.05

3rd Congress of the Syndicate of the Romanian People's Republic.

"Strike at Grivita," Painted by G. Miclossy A326

**1953, Feb. 16** *Perf. 13x13½*

**922** A326 55b chestnut 2.75 .25

Oil industry strike, Feb. 16, 1933, 20th anniv.

Arms of Romanian People's Republic — A327

**1953** *Perf. 12½*

**923** A327 5b crimson .80 .25
**924** A327 55b purple 1.40 .25

Flags of Romania and Russia, Farm Machinery A328

**1953, Mar. 24** *Perf. 14*

**925** A328 55b dk brn, *bl* 4.00 .50

5th anniv. of the signing of a treaty of friendship and mutual assistance between Russia and Romania.

Map and Medal — A329

**1953, Mar. 24**

**926** A329 55b dk gray green 10.00 1.75
**927** A329 55b chestnut 10.00 1.75

20th World Championship Table Tennis Matches, Budapest, 1953.

Ceramics — A330

Costume of Campulung (Muscel) — A330a

Folk Dance — A330b

Designs: 55b, Apuseni Mts. costume. 1 l, Rug.

**Inscribed: "Arta Populara Romaneasca"**

**1953**

**928** A330 10b deep green 1.00 .25
**929** A330a 20b red brown 1.75 .25
**929A** A330b 35b purple 3.00 .25
**930** A330a 55b violet blue 4.00 .25
**931** A330 1 l brt red violet 6.00 .35
*Nos. 928-931 (5)* 15.75 1.35

Romanian Folk Arts.

Karl Marx — A331

**1953, May 21** *Perf. 13½x13*

**932** A331 1.55 l olive brown 3.50 .45

70th death anniv. of Karl Marx.

Children Planting Tree — A332

Physics Class A333

Design: 55b, Flying model planes.

**1953, May 21** *Perf. 14*

**933** A332 35b deep green 1.75 .25
**934** A332 55b dull blue 2.10 .30
**935** A333 1.75 l brown 4.00 .65
*Nos. 933-935 (3)* 7.85 1.20

Women and Flags — A334

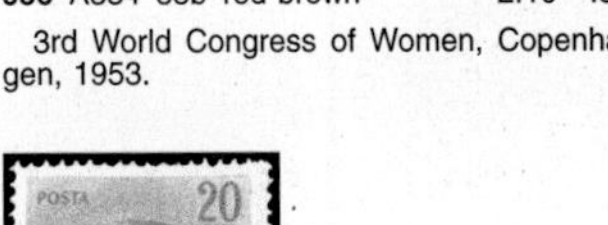

**1953, June 18** *Perf. 13½x13*

| | | | | |
|---|---|---|---|---|
| **936** | A334 | 55b red brown | 2.10 | .30 |

3rd World Congress of Women, Copenhagen, 1953.

Discus Thrower — A335

Students Offering Teacher Flowers A336

Designs: 55b, Students reaching toward dove. 1.75 l, Dance in local costumes.

**1953, Aug. 2** **Wmk. 358** *Perf. 14*

| | | | | |
|---|---|---|---|---|
| **937** | A335 | 20b orange | 1.00 | .35 |
| **938** | A335 | 55b deep blue | 1.75 | .75 |
| **939** | A336 | 65b scarlet | 2.25 | 1.10 |
| **940** | A336 | 1.75 l red violet | 6.50 | 1.75 |
| | | *Nos. 937-940 (4)* | 11.50 | 3.95 |

4th World Youth Festival, Bucharest, 8/2-16.

Waterfall — A337

Wheat Field — A338

Design: 55b, Forester holding seedling.

**1953, July 29** **Photo.**

| | | | | |
|---|---|---|---|---|
| **941** | A337 | 20b violet blue | 1.25 | .25 |
| **942** | A338 | 38b dull green | 3.00 | 1.00 |
| **943** | A337 | 55b lt brown | 3.50 | .35 |
| | | *Nos. 941-943 (3)* | 7.75 | 1.60 |

Month of the Forest.

Vladimir V. Mayakovsky, 60th Birth Anniv. — A339

**1953, Aug. 22**

| | | | | |
|---|---|---|---|---|
| **944** | A339 | 55b brown | 2.50 | .50 |

Miner Using Drill A340

**1953, Sept. 19**

| | | | | |
|---|---|---|---|---|
| **945** | A340 | 1.55 l slate black | 4.00 | .50 |

Miners' Day.

Arms of Republic — A342

**Size: 20x24mm**

**1952-53** *Perf. 12½*

| | | | | |
|---|---|---|---|---|
| **947** | A342 | 3b deep orange | .60 | .25 |
| **948** | A342 | 5b crimson | .80 | .25 |
| **949** | A342 | 7b dk blue grn | .80 | .25 |
| **950** | A342 | 10b chocolate | 1.00 | .25 |
| **951** | A342 | 20b deep blue | 1.25 | .25 |
| **952** | A342 | 35b black brn | 2.75 | .25 |
| **953** | A342 | 50b dk gray grn | 3.25 | .25 |
| **954** | A342 | 55b purple | 7.25 | .25 |

**Size: 24x29mm**

| | | | | |
|---|---|---|---|---|
| **955** | A342 | 1.10 l dk brown | 6.50 | .30 |
| **956** | A342 | 1.75 l violet | 26.00 | .50 |
| **957** | A342 | 2 l olive black | 6.75 | .60 |
| **958** | A342 | 2.35 l orange brn | 8.00 | .40 |
| **959** | A342 | 2.55 l dp orange | 10.00 | .50 |
| **960** | A342 | 3 l dk gray grn | 10.00 | .40 |
| **961** | A342 | 5 l deep crimson | 13.00 | .75 |
| | | *Nos. 947-961 (15)* | 97.95 | 5.45 |

Stamps of similar design with value figures in color are Nos. 730-744.

Postal Administration Building and Telephone Employees — A343

Designs: 55b, Postal Adm. Bldg. and Letter carrier. 1 l, Map and communications symbols. 1.55 l, Postal Adm. Bldg. and Telegraph employees.

**1953, Oct. 20** **Wmk. 358** *Perf. 14*

| | | | | |
|---|---|---|---|---|
| **964** | A343 | 20b dk red brn | .40 | .25 |
| **965** | A343 | 55b olive green | .75 | .25 |
| **966** | A343 | 1 l brt blue | 1.75 | .25 |
| **967** | A343 | 1.55 l rose brown | 3.25 | .50 |
| | | *Nos. 964-967 (4)* | 6.15 | 1.25 |

50th anniv. of the construction of the Postal Administration Building.

Liberation Medal — A344

**1953, Oct. 20** *Perf. 14x13½*

| | | | | |
|---|---|---|---|---|
| **968** | A344 | 55b dark brown | 1.75 | .25 |

9th anniv. of the liberation of Romania.

Soldier and Flag — A345

**1953, Oct. 2** *Perf. 13½*

| | | | | |
|---|---|---|---|---|
| **969** | A345 | 55b olive green | 1.75 | .25 |

Army Day, Oct. 2.

Girl with Model Plane A346

Civil Aviation: 20b, Parachute landing. 55b, Glider and pilot. 1.75 l, Plane in flight.

**1953, Oct. 20** *Perf. 14*

| | | | | |
|---|---|---|---|---|
| **970** | A346 | 10b org & dk gray grn | 3.00 | .40 |
| **971** | A346 | 20b org brn & dk ol grn | 5.75 | .25 |
| **972** | A346 | 55b dk scar & rose lil | 9.50 | .60 |
| **973** | A346 | 1.75 l dk rose vio & brn | 12.50 | .90 |
| | | *Nos. 970-973 (4)* | 30.75 | 2.15 |

Workers and Flags — A347

1.55 l, Spasski Tower, lock on Volga-Don Canal.

**1953, Nov. 25** *Perf. 13x13½*

| | | | | |
|---|---|---|---|---|
| **974** | A347 | 55b brown | 1.10 | .25 |
| **975** | A347 | 1.55 l rose brown | 1.60 | .35 |

Month of Romanian-Soviet friendship, Oct. 7-Nov. 7.

Hemispheres and Clasped Hands — A348

Workers, Flags and Globe — A349

**1953, Nov. 25** *Perf. 14*

| | | | | |
|---|---|---|---|---|
| **976** | A348 | 55b dark olive | .90 | .25 |
| **977** | A349 | 1.25 l crimson | 1.75 | .45 |

World Congress of Trade Unions.

Ciprian Porumbescu A350

**1953, Dec. 16**

| | | | | |
|---|---|---|---|---|
| **978** | A350 | 55b purple | 8.50 | .45 |

Ciprian Porumbescu (1853-1883), composer.

Harvesting Machine A351

Designs: 35b, Tractor in field. 2.55 l, Cattle.

*Perf. 13x13½*

**1953, Dec. 16** **Wmk. 358**

| | | | | |
|---|---|---|---|---|
| **979** | A351 | 10b sepia | .30 | .25 |
| **980** | A351 | 35b dark green | .50 | .25 |
| **981** | A351 | 2.55 l orange brown | 3.75 | .80 |
| | | *Nos. 979-981 (3)* | 4.55 | 1.30 |

Aurel Vlaicu — A352

**1953, Dec. 26** *Perf. 14*

| | | | | |
|---|---|---|---|---|
| **982** | A352 | 50b violet blue | 1.75 | .25 |

Vlaicu, aviation pioneer, 40th death anniv.

Lenin — A353

**1954, Jan. 21** *Perf. 13½*

| | | | | |
|---|---|---|---|---|
| **983** | A353 | 55b dk red brn, *buff* | 2.00 | .25 |

30th death anniv. of Lenin.

Red Deer — A354

Designs: 55b, Children planting trees. 1.75 l, Mountain scene.

**Yellow Surface-colored Paper**

**1954, Apr. 1**

| | | | | |
|---|---|---|---|---|
| **984** | A354 | 20b dark brown | 4.00 | .45 |
| **985** | A354 | 55b violet | 3.25 | .45 |
| **986** | A354 | 1.75 l dark blue | 5.75 | 1.00 |
| | | *Nos. 984-986 (3)* | 13.00 | 1.90 |

Month of the Forest.

Calimanesti Rest Home — A355

Workers' Rest Homes: 1.55 l, Sinaia. 2 l, Predeal. 2.35 l, Tusnad. 2.55 l, Govora.

**1954, Apr. 15** *Perf. 14*

| | | | | |
|---|---|---|---|---|
| **987** | A355 | 5b blk brn, *cream* | .40 | .25 |
| **988** | A355 | 1.55 l dk vio brn, *bl* | 2.00 | .25 |
| **989** | A355 | 2 l dk grn, *pink* | 3.00 | .30 |
| **990** | A355 | 2.35 l ol blk, *grnsh* | 3.00 | .60 |
| **991** | A355 | 2.55 l dk red brn, *cit* | 4.00 | .80 |
| | | *Nos. 987-991 (5)* | 12.40 | 2.20 |

Octav Bancila — A356

**1954, May 26** *Perf. 13½*

| | | | | |
|---|---|---|---|---|
| **992** | A356 | 55b red brn & dk grn | 6.50 | 2.75 |

10th death anniv. of Octav Bancila, painter.

Globe, Child, Dove and Flowers
A357

**1954, June 1** *Perf. 13x13½*
**993** A357 55b brown 1.75 .25

Children's Day, June 1.

Girl Feeding Calf
A358

Designs: 55b, Girl holding sheaf of grain. 1.75 l, Young students.

**1954, July 5** *Perf. 14*
**994** A358 20b grnsh blk .45 .25
**995** A358 55b blue .80 .30
**996** A358 1.75 l car rose 2.50 .50
*Nos. 994-996 (3)* 3.75 1.05

Stephen the Great — A359

**1954, July 10**
**997** A359 55b violet brown 2.75 .45

Stephen of Moldavia (1433?-1504).

Loading Coal on Conveyor Belt — A360

**1954, Aug. 8** *Perf. 13x13½*
**998** A360 1.75 l black 3.00 .50

Miners' Day.

Victor Babes — A361

**1954, Aug. 15** *Perf. 14*
**999** A361 55b rose red 2.25 .40

Birth cent. of Victor Babes, serologist.

Applicant Requesting Loan — A362

Design: 55b, Mutual aid declaration.

**1954, Aug. 20**
**1000** A362 20b deep violet .40 .25
**1001** A362 55b dk redsh brn .80 .25

5th anniv. of the Mutual Aid Organization.

Sailor and Naval Scene — A363

**1954, Aug. 19** *Perf. 13x13½*
**1002** A363 55b deep blue 1.75 .35

Navy Day.

Monument to Soviet Soldier — A364

**1954, Aug. 23** *Perf. 13½x13*
**1003** A364 55b scarlet & purple 1.50 .30

10th anniv. of Romania's liberation.

House of Culture
A365

Academy of Music, Bucharest — A366

55b, Scanteia building. 1.55 l, Radio station.

**1954, Sept. 6** *Perf. 14, 13½x13*
**1004** A365 20b violet blue .50 .25
**1005** A366 38b violet 1.00 .30
**1006** A365 55b violet brown 1.00 .30
**1007** A366 1.55 l red brown 2.00 .30
*Nos. 1004-1007 (4)* 4.50 1.15

Publicizing Romania's cultural progress during the decade following liberation.

Aviator — A367

*Perf. 13½x13*
**1954, Sept. 13** **Wmk. 358**
**1008** A367 55b blue 2.75 .40

Aviation Day.

Chemical Plant and Oil Derricks
A368

**1954, Sept. 21** *Perf. 13x13½*
**1009** A368 55b gray 2.50 .40

Intl. Conference of chemical and petroleum workers, Bucharest, Sept. 1954.

Dragon Pillar, Peking — A369

**1954, Oct. 7** *Perf. 14*
**1010** A369 55b dk ol grn, *cream* 2.50 .40

Week of Chinese Culture.

Dumitri T. Neculuta — A370

**1954, Oct. 17** *Perf. 13½x13*
**1011** A370 55b purple 2.00 .30

Neculuta, poet, 50th death anniv.

ARLUS Emblem — A371

65b, Romanian & Russian women embracing.

**1954, Oct. 22** *Perf. 14*
**1012** A371 55b rose carmine .70 .25
**1013** A371 65b dark purple 1.00 .25

Month of Romanian-Soviet Friendship.

Gheorghe Tattarescu — A372

**1954, Oct. 24** *Perf. 13½x13*
**1014** A372 55b cerise 2.50 .40

Gheorghe Tattarescu (1820-1894), painter.

Barbu Iscovescu — A373

**1954, Nov. 3** *Perf. 14*
**1015** A373 1.75 l red brown 3.25 .60

Death cent. of Barbu Iscovescu, painter.

Wild Boar — A374

Month of the Forest: 65b, Couple planting tree. 1.20 l, Logging.

*Perf. 13½x13*
**1955, Mar. 15** **Wmk. 358**
**1016** A374 35b brown 1.40 .25
**1017** A374 65b turq blue 1.60 .30
**1018** A374 1.20 l dark red 3.50 .65
*Nos. 1016-1018 (3)* 6.50 1.20

Globe and Clasped Hands — A375

**1955, Apr. 5** **Photo.**
**1019** A375 25b carmine rose .70 .25

Intl. Conference of Universal Trade Unions (Federation Syndicale Mondiale), Vienna, Apr. 1955.

Teletype — A376

**1954, Dec. 31** *Perf. 13½x13*
**1020** A376 50b redsh pur 1.75 .30

Romanian telegraph system, cent.

Lenin — A377

Various Portraits of Lenin.

**1955, Apr. 22** *Perf. 13½x14*
**1021** A377 20b ol bis & brn .65 .25
**1022** A377 55b copper brown 1.25 .30
**1023** A377 1 l vermilion 2.00 .35
*Nos. 1021-1023 (3)* 3.90 .90

85th anniversary of the birth of Lenin.

Chemist — A378

Designs: 5b, Steelworker. 10b, Aviator. 20b, Miner. 30b, Tractor driver. 35b, Pioneer. 40b, Girl student. 55b, Mason. 1 l, Sailor. 1.55 l, Spinner. 2.35 l, Soldier. 2.55 l, Electrician.

**1955-56** **Wmk. 358** *Perf. 14*
**1024** A378 3b blue .40 .25
**1025** A378 5b violet .25 .25
**1026** A378 10b chocolate .40 .25
**1027** A378 20b lilac rose .50 .25
**1027A** A378 30b vio bl ('56) 1.00 .25
**1028** A378 35b grnsh blue .75 .25
**1028A** A378 40b slate 1.60 .25
**1029** A378 55b ol gray 1.50 .25
**1030** A378 1 l purple 2.00 .25
**1031** A378 1.55 l brown lake 3.00 .25
**1032** A378 2.35 l bister brn 4.00 .75
**1033** A378 2.55 l slate 6.25 .55
*Nos. 1024-1033 (12)* 21.65 3.80

Volleyball — A379

Design: 1.75 l, Woman volleyball player.

**1955, June 17**

**1034** A379 55b red vio, *pink* 5.00 .80
**1035** A379 1.75 l lil rose, *cr* 11.00 .80

European Volleyball Championships, Bucharest.

Globe, Flag and Dove — A379a

**1955, May 7 Photo. *Perf. 13½***

**1035A** A379a 55b ultra 1.75 .25

Peace Congress, Helsinki.

Girls with Dove and Flag — A380

**1955, June 1 *Perf. 13½x14***

**1036** A380 55b dark red brown 1.60 .25

International Children's Day, June 1.

Russian War Memorial, Berlin — A381

**1955, May 9**

**1037** A381 55b deep blue 1.40 .25

Victory over Germany, 10th anniversary.

Theodor Aman Museum A382

Bucharest Museums: 55b, Lenin and Stalin Museum. 1.20 l, Popular Arts Museum. 1.75 l, Arts Museum. 2.55 l, Simu Museum.

**1955, June 28 *Perf. 13½, 14***

**1038** A382 20b rose lilac .45 .25
**1039** A382 55b brown .70 .25
**1040** A382 1.20 l gray black 1.60 .45
**1041** A382 1.75 l slate green 2.50 .45
**1042** A382 2.55 l rose violet 4.75 .60
*Nos. 1038-1042 (5)* 10.00 2.00

#1038, 1040, 1042 measure 29x24½mm, #1039, 1041 32½x23mm.

Sharpshooter A383

**1955, Sept. 11 *Perf. 13½***

**1043** A383 1 l pale brn & sepia 6.00 .60

European Sharpshooting Championship meeting, Bucharest, Sept. 11-18.

Fire Truck, Farm and Factory — A384

**1955, Sept. 13 Wmk. 358**

**1044** A384 55b carmine 2.50 .35

Firemen's Day, Sept. 13.

Bishop Dosoftei A385

Romanian writers: No. 1046, Stolnicul Constantin Cantacuzino. No. 1047, Dimitrie Cantemir. No. 1048, Enachita Vacarescu. No. 1049, Anton Pann.

**1955, Sept. 9 Photo.**

**1045** A385 55b bluish gray 1.25 .30
**1046** A385 55b dp vio 1.25 .30
**1047** A385 55b ultra 1.25 .30
**1048** A385 55b rose vio 1.25 .30
**1049** A385 55b ol gray 1.25 .30
*Nos. 1045-1049 (5)* 6.25 1.50

Mother and Child — A386

**1955, July 7 *Perf. 13½x14***

**1050** A386 55b ultra 1.75 .30

World Congress of Mothers, Lausanne.

Pioneers and Train Set — A387

Designs: 20b, Pioneers studying nature. 55b, Home of the Pioneers.

**1955 *Perf. 12½***

**1051** A387 10b brt ultra .70 .25
**1052** A387 20b grnsh bl 1.40 .25
**1053** A387 55b dp plum 3.00 .30
*Nos. 1051-1053 (3)* 5.10 .80

Fifth anniversary of the Pioneer headquarters, Bucharest.

Rowing — A388

**1955, Aug. 22 *Perf. 13x13½***

**1054** A388 55b shown 8.00 .60
**1055** A388 1 l Sculling 14.00 1.00

European Women's Rowing Championship on Lake Snagov, Aug. 4-7.

Insect Pest Control A389

20b, Orchard. 55b, Vineyard. 1 l, Truck garden.

**1955, Oct. 15 *Perf. 14x13½***

**1056** A389 10b brt grn 1.00 .25
**1057** A389 20b lil rose 1.00 .25
**1058** A389 55b vio bl 2.50 .30
**1059** A389 1 l dp claret 3.50 .40
*Nos. 1056-1059 (4)* 8.00 1.20

Quality products of Romanian agriculture. See Nos. 1068-1071.

I. V. Michurin — A390

**1955, Oct. 25 *Perf. 13½x14***

**1060** A390 55b Prus bl 1.75 .30

Birth cent. of I. V. Michurin, Russian agricultural scientist.

Congress Emblem A391

**1955, Oct. 20 *Perf. 13x13½***

**1061** A391 20b cream & ultra 1.00 .25

4th Soviet-Romanian Cong., Bucharest, Oct.

Globes and Olive Branches — A392

1 l, Three workers holding FSM banner.

**1955, Oct. 1 *Perf. 13½x13***

**1062** A392 55b dk ol grn .50 .25
**1063** A392 1 l ultra .80 .25

Intl. Trade Union Org. (Federation Syndicale Mondiale), 10th anniv.

Sugar Beets — A393

20b, Cotton. 55b, Flax. 1.55l, Sunflower.

**1955, Nov. 10 *Perf. 13½***

**1064** A393 10b plum .75 .25
**1065** A393 20b sl grn 1.00 .30
**1066** A393 55b brt ultra 2.25 .70
**1067** A393 1.55 l dk red brn 4.75 1.00
*Nos. 1064-1067 (4)* 8.75 2.25

Sheep and Shepherd A394

Stock Farming: 10b, Pigs. 35b, Cattle. 55b, Horses.

**1955, Dec. 10 *Perf. 14x13½***

**1068** A394 5b yel grn & brn 1.00 .25
**1069** A394 10b ol bis & dk vio 1.00 .25
**1070** A394 35b brick red & brn 2.75 .50
**1071** A394 55b dk ol bis & brn 3.25 .70
*Nos. 1068-1071 (4)* 8.00 1.70

Animal husbandry.

Hans Christian Andersen — A395

Portraits: 55b, Adam Mickiewicz. 1 l, Friedrich von Schiller. 1.55 l, Baron de Montesquieu. 1.75 l, Walt Whitman. 2 l, Miguel de Cervantes.

***Perf. 13½x14***

**1955, Dec. 17 Engr. Unwmk.**

**1072** A395 20b sl bl .50 .25
**1073** A395 55b dp ultra 1.25 .25
**1074** A395 1 l grnsh blk 2.25 .30
**1075** A395 1.55 l vio brn 4.00 .55
**1076** A395 1.75 l dl vio 4.25 .90
**1077** A395 2 l rose lake 5.25 1.00
*Nos. 1072-1077 (6)* 17.50 3.25

Anniversaries of famous writers.

Bank Book and Savings Bank A396

***Perf. 14x13½***

**1955, Dec. 29 Photo. Wmk. 358**

**1078** A396 55b dp vio 2.75 .50
**1079** A396 55b blue 8.25 4.50

Advantages of systematic saving in a bank.

Census Date — A397

Family Group — A397a

**Inscribed: "Recensamintul Populatiei"**

**1956, Feb. 3 *Perf. 13½***

**1080** A397 55b dp org .45 .25
**1081** A397a 1.75 l emer & red brn 1.90 .35
*a.* Center inverted *550.00 500.00*

National Census, Feb. 21, 1956.

Ring-necked Pheasant A398

Great Bustard — A399

Animals: No. 1082, Hare. No. 1083, Bustard. 35b, Trout. 50b, Boar. No. 1087, Brown bear. 1 l, Lynx. 1.55 l, Red squirrel. 2 l, Chamois. 3.25 l, Pintail (duck). 4.25 l, Fallow deer.

**1956 Wmk. 358 *Perf. 14***

| No. | Type | Description | Unused | Used |
|---|---|---|---|---|
| **1082** | A398 | 20b grn & blk | 2.50 | .40 |
| **1083** | A399 | 20b cit & gray blk | 2.50 | .40 |
| **1084** | A399 | 35b brt bl & blk | 2.50 | .40 |
| **1085** | A398 | 50b dp ultra & brn blk | 2.50 | .40 |
| **1086** | A398 | 55b ol bis & ind | 2.50 | .40 |
| **1087** | A398 | 55b dk bl grn & dk red brn | 2.50 | .40 |
| **1088** | A398 | 1 l dk grn & red brn | 4.75 | .75 |
| **1089** | A399 | 1.55 l lt ultra & red brn | 4.75 | .75 |
| **1090** | A399 | 1.75 l sl grn & dk brn | 4.75 | .75 |
| **1091** | A398 | 2 l ultra & brn blk | 17.50 | 15.00 |
| **1092** | A398 | 3.25 l lt grn & blk brn | 17.50 | 15.00 |
| **1093** | A399 | 4.25 l brn org & dk brn | 17.50 | 15.00 |
| | | *Nos. 1082-1093 (12)* | 81.75 | 49.65 |

Exist imperf. in changed colors. Value, set $50.

Street Fighting, Paris, 1871 — A400

**1956, May 29 *Perf. 13½***

| No. | Type | Description | Unused | Used |
|---|---|---|---|---|
| **1094** | A400 | 55b vermilion | 1.75 | .35 |

85th anniversary of Commune of Paris.

Globe and Child — A400a

**1956, June 1 Photo. *Perf. 13½x14***

| No. | Type | Description | Unused | Used |
|---|---|---|---|---|
| **1095** | A400a | 55b dp vio | 2.50 | .30 |

Intl. Children's Day. The sheet of 100 contains 10 labels, each with "Peace" printed on it in one of 10 languages. Value for stamp with label, unused or used, $20.

Oak Tree — A401

Design: 55b, Logging train in timberland.

**1956, June 11 Litho. Wmk. 358**

| No. | Type | Description | Unused | Used |
|---|---|---|---|---|
| **1096** | A401 | 20b dk bl grn, *pale grn* | 1.40 | .25 |
| **1097** | A401 | 55b brn blk, *pale grn* | 4.00 | .50 |

Month of the Forest.

Romanian Academy A402

**1956, June 19 Photo. *Perf. 14***

| No. | Type | Description | Unused | Used |
|---|---|---|---|---|
| **1098** | A402 | 55b dk grn & dl yel | 1.75 | .30 |

90th anniversary of Romanian Academy.

Red Cross Worker — A403

**1956, June 7**

| No. | Type | Description | Unused | Used |
|---|---|---|---|---|
| **1099** | A403 | 55b olive & red | 2.75 | .40 |

Romanian Red Cross Congress, June 7-9.

Woman Speaker and Globe — A404

**1956, June 14**

| No. | Type | Description | Unused | Used |
|---|---|---|---|---|
| **1100** | A404 | 55b dk bl grn | 1.75 | .30 |

Intl. Conference of Working Women, Budapest, June 14-17.

Traian Vuia and Planes — A405

**1956, June 21 *Perf. 13x13½***

| No. | Type | Description | Unused | Used |
|---|---|---|---|---|
| **1101** | A405 | 55b grnsh blk & brn | 2.25 | .30 |

1st flight by Vuia, near Paris, 50th anniv.

Ion Georgescu A406

**1956, June 25 *Perf. 14x13½***

| No. | Type | Description | Unused | Used |
|---|---|---|---|---|
| **1102** | A406 | 55b dk red brn & dk grn | 2.75 | .30 |

Ion Georgescu (1856-1898), sculptor.

White Cabbage Butterfly A407

June Bug — A408

Design: 55b, Colorado potato beetle.

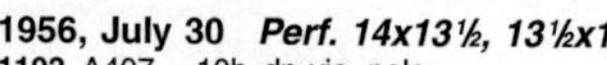

**1956, July 30 *Perf. 14x13½, 13½x14***

| No. | Type | Description | Unused | Used |
|---|---|---|---|---|
| **1103** | A407 | 10b dp vio, pale yel & blk | 3.75 | .45 |
| **1104** | A407 | 55b ol blk & yel | 5.50 | .50 |
| **1105** | A408 | 1.75 l lt ol & dp plum | 15.00 | 10.00 |
| **1106** | A408 | 1.75 l gray ol & dk vio brn | 12.00 | 1.25 |
| | | *Nos. 1103-1106 (4)* | 36.25 | 12.20 |

Campaign against insect pests.

Girl Holding Sheaf of Wheat — A409

**1956 *Perf. 13½x14***

| No. | Type | Description | Unused | Used |
|---|---|---|---|---|
| **1107** | A409 | 55b "1949-1956" | 2.75 | .40 |
| *a.* | | "1951-1956" (error) | 12.00 | 12.00 |

7th anniversary of collective farming.

Dock Workers on Strike — A410

**1956, Aug. 6**

| No. | Type | Description | Unused | Used |
|---|---|---|---|---|
| **1108** | A410 | 55b dk red brn | 1.75 | .30 |

Dock workers' strike at Galati, 50th anniv.

Title Page and Printer — A411

**1956, Aug. 13 *Perf. 13½***

| No. | Type | Description | Unused | Used |
|---|---|---|---|---|
| **1109** | A411 | 55b ultra | 1.50 | .25 |

25th anniv. of the publication of "Scanteia" (The Spark).

Maxim Gorki — A412

**1956, Aug. 29 *Perf. 13½x14***

| No. | Type | Description | Unused | Used |
|---|---|---|---|---|
| **1110** | A412 | 55b brown | 1.75 | .30 |

Maxim Gorki (1868-1936), Russian writer.

Theodor Aman — A413

**1956, Sept. 24 Engr.**

| No. | Type | Description | Unused | Used |
|---|---|---|---|---|
| **1111** | A413 | 55b gray blk | 2.75 | .30 |

Aman, painter, 125th birth anniv.

Primrose and Snowdrops — A414

55b, Daffodil and violets. 1.75 l, Snapdragon and bellflowers. 3 l, Poppies and lilies of the valley.

**Flowers in Natural Colors**

**1956, Sept. 26 Photo. *Perf. 14x14½***

| No. | Type | Description | Unused | Used |
|---|---|---|---|---|
| **1112** | A414 | 5b bl, yel & red | 1.00 | .40 |
| **1113** | A414 | 55b blk, yel & red | 3.00 | .80 |
| **1114** | A414 | 1.75 l ind, pink & yel | 7.00 | 1.00 |
| **1115** | A414 | 3 l bl grn, dk bl grn & yel | 12.00 | 1.75 |
| | | *Nos. 1112-1115 (4)* | 23.00 | 3.95 |

Olympic Rings and Torch — A415

Designs: 55b, Water polo. 1 l, Gymnastics. 1.55 l, Canoeing. 1.75 l, High jump.

**1956, Oct. 25 *Perf. 13½x14***

| No. | Type | Description | Unused | Used |
|---|---|---|---|---|
| **1116** | A415 | 20b vermilion | .55 | .25 |
| **1117** | A415 | 55b ultra | .80 | .25 |
| **1118** | A415 | 1 l lil rose | 1.60 | .30 |
| **1119** | A415 | 1.55 l lt bl grn | 2.10 | .30 |
| **1120** | A415 | 1.75 l dp pur | 3.00 | .40 |
| | | *Nos. 1116-1120 (5)* | 8.05 | 1.50 |

16th Olympic Games, Melbourne, 11/22-12/8.

See Nos. 1448-1451. The vertical inscriptions on Nos. 1116-1120 are different than on Nos. 1448-1451.

Janos Hunyadi — A416

**1956, Oct. Wmk. 358**

| No. | Type | Description | Unused | Used |
|---|---|---|---|---|
| **1121** | A416 | 55b dp vio | 1.40 | .30 |

Janos Hunyadi (1387-1456), national hero of Hungary. No. 1121 is found se-tenant with label showing Hunyadi Castle. Value for stamp with label, unused or used, $20.

Benjamin Franklin — A417

Portraits: 35b, Sesshu (Toyo Oda). 40b, G. B. Shaw. 50b, Ivan Franco. 55b, Pierre Curie. 1 l, Henrik Ibsen. 1.55 l, Fedor Dostoevski. 1.75 l, Heinrich Heine. 2.55 l, Mozart. 3.25 l, Rembrandt.

**1956 Unwmk.**

| No. | Type | Description | Unused | Used |
|---|---|---|---|---|
| **1122** | A417 | 20b vio bl | .50 | .25 |
| **1123** | A417 | 35b rose lake | .60 | .25 |
| **1124** | A417 | 40b chocolate | .70 | .25 |
| **1125** | A417 | 50b brn blk | .90 | .25 |
| **1126** | A417 | 55b dk ol | .90 | .25 |
| **1127** | A417 | 1 l dk bl grn | 1.75 | .25 |
| **1128** | A417 | 1.55 l dp pur | 2.50 | .25 |
| **1129** | A417 | 1.75 l brt bl | 3.25 | .25 |

**1130** A417 2.55 l rose vio 4.50 .40
**1131** A417 3.25 l dk bl 4.75 .90
*Nos. 1122-1131 (10)* 20.35 3.30

Great personalities of the world.

George Enescu as a Boy — A418

Portrait: 1.75 l, George Enescu as an adult.

**1956, Dec. 29** **Engr.**
**1132** A418 55b ultramarine 1.25 .30
**1133** A418 1.75 l deep claret 2.25 .40

75th birth anniv. of George Enescu, musician and composer.

A419

Fighting Peasants, by Octav Bancila.

**1957, Feb. 28** **Photo.** **Wmk. 358**
**1134** A419 55b dk bl gray 1.50 .30

50th anniversary of Peasant Uprising.

A420

**1957, Apr. 24** ***Perf. 13½x14***
**1147** A420 55b brown 1.25 .25
**1148** A420 55b olive black .75 .40

Enthronement of Stephen the Great, Prince of Moldavia, 500th anniv.

Dr. George Marinescu, Marinescu Institute and Congress Emblem — A421

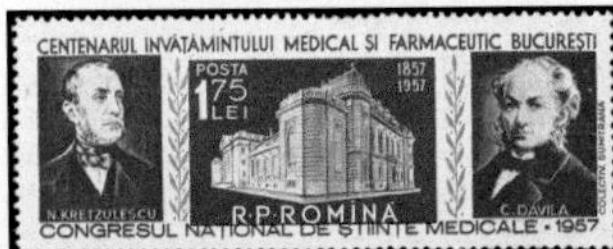


Dr. N. Kretzulescu, Medical School, Dr. C. Davila — A422

35b, Dr. I. Cantacuzino & Cantacuzino Hospital. 55b, Dr. V. Babes & Babes Institute.

**1957, May 5** ***Perf. 14x13½***
**1149** A421 20b dp grn .45 .25
**1150** A421 35b dp red brn .60 .25
**1151** A421 55b red lil 1.00 .30
**1152** A422 1.75 l brt ultra & dk red 3.75 .70
*Nos. 1149-1152 (4)* 5.80 1.50

National Congress of Medical Science, Bucharest, May 5-6.

No. 1152 also for centenary of medical and pharmaceutical teaching in Bucharest. It measures 66x23mm.

Dove and Handle Bars — A423

**1957, May 29** ***Perf. 13½x14***
**1153** A423 20b shown .40 .25
**1154** A423 55b Cyclist 1.25 .30

10th International Bicycle Peace Race.

Woman Watching Gymnast — A424

Woman Gymnast on Bar — A425

**1957, May 21** ***Perf. 13½***
**1155** A424 20b shown .60 .25
**1156** A425 35b shown .90 .25
**1157** A425 55b Vaulting horse 1.75 .30
**1158** A424 1.75 l Acrobat 5.00 .75
*Nos. 1155-1158 (4)* 8.25 1.55

European Women's Gymnastic meet, Bucharest.

Slide Rule, Caliper & Atomic Symbol — A426

**Wmk. 358**
**1957, May 29** **Photo.** ***Perf. 14***
**1159** A426 55b blue 1.40 .25
**1160** A426 55b brn red 1.60 .30

2nd Congress of the Society of Engineers and Technicians, Bucharest, May 29-31.

Rhododendron Hirsutum — A427

Carpathian Mountain Flowers: 10b, Daphne Blagayana. 20b, Lilium Bulbiferum L. 35b, Leontopodium Alpinum. 55b, Gentiana Acaulis L. 1 l, Dianthus Callizonus. 1.55 l, Primula Carpatica Griseb. 1.75 l, Anemone Montana Hoppe.

**Light Gray Background**

**1957, June 22** **Litho.** **Unwmk.**
**1161** A427 5b brt rose .35 .25
**1162** A427 10b dk grn .45 .25
**1163** A427 20b red org .50 .25
**1164** A427 35b olive .90 .25
**1165** A427 55b ultra 1.25 .25
**1166** A427 1 l red 2.50 .25
**1167** A427 1.55 l yellow 2.50 .30
**1168** A427 1.75 l dk pur 4.25 .45
*Nos. 1161-1168 (8)* 12.70 2.25

Nos. 1161-1168 also come se-tenant with a decorative label. Value, set $50.

"Oxcart" by Grigorescu A428

Nicolae Grigorescu — A429

Painting: 1.75 l, Battle scene.

**1957, June 29** **Photo.** **Wmk. 358**
**1169** A428 20b dk bl grn .60 .25
**1170** A429 55b deep brown 1.50 .25
**1171** A428 1.75 l chalky blue 5.50 .70
*Nos. 1169-1171 (3)* 7.60 1.20

Grigorescu, painter, 50th death anniv.

Warship A430

**1957, Aug. 3** ***Perf. 13x13½***
**1172** A430 1.75 l Prus bl 2.00 .30

Navy Day.

Young Couple — A431

Festival Emblem — A432

Folk Dance — A433

Design: 55b, Girl with flags on hoop.

***Perf. 14x14½, 14x14x12½ (A432), 13½x12½ (A433)***

**1957, July 28**
**1173** A431 20b red lilac .25 .25
**1174** A431 55b emerald .45 .25
**1175** A432 1 l red orange 1.10 .30
**1176** A433 1.75 l ultra 1.75 .25
*Nos. 1173-1176 (4)* 3.55 1.05

Moscow 1957 Youth Festival. No. 1173 measures 23x34mm, No. 1174 22x38mm.

No. 1175 was printed in sheets of 50, alternating with 40 labels inscribed "Peace and Friendship" in 20 languages. Value for stamp with label, unused or used, $10.

Bugler — A434

**1957, Aug. 30** **Wmk. 358** ***Perf. 14***
**1177** A434 20b brt pur 2.50 .50

80th anniv. of the Russo-Turkish war.

Girl Holding Dove — A435

**1957, Sept. 3** ***Perf. 13½***
**1178** A435 55b Prus grn & red 2.75 .50

Honoring the Red Cross.

Battle Scene A436

**1957, Aug. 31**
**1179** A436 1.75 l brown 1.75 .30

Battle of Marasesti, 40th anniv.

Jumper and Dove — A437

55b, Javelin thrower, bison. 1.75 l, Runner, stag.

**1957, Sept. 14** **Photo.** ***Perf. 13½***
**1180** A437 20b brt bl & blk .40 .25
**1181** A437 55b yel & blk 1.25 .25
**1182** A437 1.75 l brick red & blk 3.50 .50
*Nos. 1180-1182 (3)* 5.15 1.00

International Athletic Meet, Bucharest.

Statue of Ovid, Constanta A438

**1957, Sept. 20** **Photo.** **Wmk. 358**
**1183** A438 1.75 l vio bl 2.75 .60

2000th anniv. of the birth of the Roman poet Publius Ovidius Naso.

Oil Field — A439

Design: 55b, Horse pulling drill, 1857.

**1957, Oct. 5**

1184 A439 20b dl red brn .45 .25
1185 A439 20b indigo .45 .25
1186 A439 55b vio blk 1.10 .30
*Nos. 1184-1186 (3)* 2.00 .80

Centenary of Romanian oil industry.

Congress Emblem A440

**1957, Sept. 28**

1187 A440 55b ultra 1.00 .25

4th Intl. Trade Union Cong., Leipzig, 10/4-15.

Young Couple, Lenin Banner — A441

35b, Lenin & Flags. 55b, Lenin statue.

**1957, Nov. 6** ***Perf. 14x14½, 14½x14***

1188 A441 10b crimson .30 .25
1189 A441 35b plum, horiz. .60 .25
1190 A441 55b brown .90 .25
*Nos. 1188-1190 (3)* 1.80 .75

Russian Revolution, 40th anniversary.

Endre Ady — A442

**1957, Dec. 5** ***Perf. 14***

1191 A442 55b ol brn 1.25 .25

Ady, Hungarian poet, 80th birth anniv.

Oath of Bobilna A443

Bobilna Monument — A444

**1957, Nov. 30**

1192 A443 50b deep plum .35 .25
1193 A444 55b slate blue .50 .25

520th anniversary of the insurrection of the peasants of Bobilna in 1437.

Black-winged Stilt — A445

Animals: 10b, Great white egret. 20b, White spoonbill. 50b, Sturgeon. 55b, Ermine, horiz. 1.30 l, White pelican, horiz.

***Perf. 13½x14, 14x13½***

**1957, Dec. 27 Photo. Wmk. 358**

1194 A445 5b red brn & gray .25 .25
1195 A445 10b emer & ocher .25 .25
1196 A445 20b brt red & ocher .35 .25
1197 A445 50b bl grn & ocher .65 .25
1198 A445 55b dp cl & gray 1.00 .25
1199 A445 1.30 l pur & org 1.75 .30
*Nos. 1194-1199,C53-C54 (8)* 14.00 3.80

Sputnik 2 and Laika A446

**1957, Dec. 20** ***Perf. 14x13½***

1200 A446 1.20 l bl & dk brn 5.00 .60
1201 A446 1.20 l grnsh bl & choc 5.00 .60

Dog Laika, "first space traveler."

Romanian Arms, Flags — A447

Designs: 55b, Arms, "Industry and Agriculture." 1.20 l, Arms, "Art, Science and Sport (soccer)."

**1957, Dec. 30** ***Perf. 13½***

1202 A447 25b ultra, red & ocher .35 .25
1203 A447 55b dull yellow .60 .25
1204 A447 1.20 l crimson rose 1.25 .30
*Nos. 1202-1204 (3)* 2.20 .80

Proclamation of the Peoples' Republic, 10th anniv.

Flag and Wreath — A448

**1958, Feb. 15 Unwmk.** ***Perf. 13½***

1205 A448 1 l dk bl & red, *buff* .90 .25
1206 A448 1 l brn & red, *buff* .90 .25

Grivita Strike, 25th anniversary.

Television, Radio Antennas A449

Design: 1.75 l, Telegraph pole and wires.

**1958, Mar. 21** ***Perf. 14x13½***

1207 A449 55b brt vio .50 .25
1208 A449 1.75 l dp mag 1.00 .30

Telecommunications Conference, Moscow, Dec. 3-17, 1957.

Nicolae Balcescu — A450

Romanian Writers: 10b, Ion Creanga. 35b, Alexandru Vlahuta. 55b, Mihail Eminescu. 1.75 l, Vasile Alecsandri. 2 l, Barbu S. Delavrancea.

**1958 Wmk. 358** ***Perf. 14x14½***

1209 A450 5b bluish blk .35 .25
1210 A450 10b int blk .35 .25
1211 A450 35b dk bl .35 .25
1212 A450 55b dk red brn .60 .25
1213 A450 1.75 l blk brn 1.25 .30
1214 A450 2 l dk sl grn 2.10 .35
*Nos. 1209-1214 (6)* 5.00 1.65

See Nos. 1309-1314.

Fencer in Global Mask A451

**1958, Apr. 5** ***Perf. 14½x14***

1215 A451 1.75 l brt pink 1.75 .30

Youth Fencing World Championships, Bucharest.

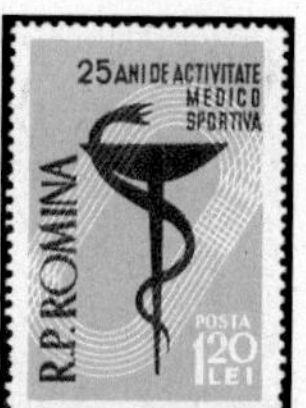


Stadium and Health Symbol — A452

**1958, Apr. 16** ***Perf. 14x14½***

1216 A452 1.20 l lt grn & red 1.75 .30

25 years of sports medicine.

Globe and Dove — A453

**1958, May 15 Photo.**

1217 A453 55b brt bl 1.10 .25

4th Congress of the Intl. Democratic Women's Federation, June 1958.

Carl von Linné — A454

Portraits: 20b, Auguste Comte. 40b, William Blake. 55b, Mikhail I. Glinka. 1 l, Henry W. Longfellow. 1.75 l, Carlo Goldoni. 2 l, Jan A. Komensky.

***Perf. 14x14½***

**1958, May 31 Unwmk.**

1218 A454 10b Prus grn .25 .25
1219 A454 20b brown .35 .25
1220 A454 40b dp lil .60 .25
1221 A454 55b dp bl .90 .25
1222 A454 1 l dp mag 1.25 .25
1223 A454 1.75 l dp vio bl 1.50 .30
1224 A454 2 l olive 2.75 .35
*Nos. 1218-1224 (7)* 7.60 1.90

Great personalities of the world.

Clavaria Aurea — A456

Mushrooms: 5b, Lepiota Procera. 20b, Amanita caesarea. 30b, Lactarius deliciosus. 35b, Armillaria mellea. 55b, Coprinus comatus. 1 l, Morchella conica. 1.55 l, Psalliota campestris. 1.75 l, Boletus edulis. 2 l, Cantharellus cibarius.

**1958, July Litho. Unwmk.**

1225 A456 5b gray bl & brn .25 .25
1226 A456 10b ol, ocher & brn .25 .25
1227 A456 20b gray, red & yel .45 .25
1228 A456 30b grn & dp org .60 .25
1229 A456 35b lt bl & yel brn .65 .25
1230 A456 55b pale grn, fawn & brn .90 .25
1231 A456 1 l bl grn, ocher & brn 1.25 .25
1232 A456 1.55 l gray, lt gray & pink 2.10 .30
1233 A456 1.75 l emer, brn & buff 2.40 .35
1234 A456 2 l dl bl & org yel 3.50 .40
*Nos. 1225-1234 (10)* 12.35 2.80

Antarctic Map and Emil Racovita A457

Design: 1.20 l, Cave and Racovita.

**1958, July 30 Photo.** ***Perf. 14½x14***

1235 A457 55b indigo & lt bl 1.10 .30
1236 A457 1.20 l ol bis & dk vio 2.50 .30

90th birth anniv. of Emil Racovita, explorer and naturalist.

Armed Forces Monument — A458

Designs: 75b, Soldier guarding industry. 1.75 l, Sailor raising flag and ship.

**1958, Oct. 2** ***Perf. 13½x13***

1237 A458 55b orange brown .30 .25
1238 A458 75b deep magenta .45 .25
1239 A458 1.75 l bright blue 1.00 .25
*Nos. 1237-1239,C55 (4)* 3.35 1.25

Armed Forces Day.

Woman & Man from Oltenia — A459

Regional Costumes: 40b, Tara Oasului. 50b, Transylvania. 55b, Muntenia. 1 l, Banat. 1.75 l, Moldavia. Pairs: "a" woman, "b" man.

**1958 Unwmk. Litho.** ***Perf. 13½x14***

1240 A459 35b Pair, #a.-b. + label .75 .25
1241 A459 40b Pair, #a.-b. + label .75 .25
1242 A459 50b Pair, #a.-b. + label .95 .25
1243 A459 55b Pair, #a.-b. + label 1.50 .25
1244 A459 1 l Pair, #a.-b. + label 3.25 .45

| | | | | | |
|---|---|---|---|---|---|
| 1245 | A459 | 1.75 l | Pair, #a.-b. + label | 3.75 | .55 |
| | | | *Nos. 1240-1245 (6)* | 10.95 | 2.00 |

Nos. 1240-1245 exist imperf. Value, set $20, unused or used.

Printer and Hand Press A461

Moldavia Stamp of 1858 A462

55b, Scissors cutting strips of 1858 stamps. 1.20 l, Postilion, mail coach. 1.30 l, Postilion blowing horn, courier on horseback. 1.75 l, 2 l, 3.30 l, Various denominations of 1858 issue.

**1958, Nov. 15 Engr. *Perf. 14½x14***

| | | | | | |
|---|---|---|---|---|---|
| 1252 | A461 | 35b | vio bl | .30 | .25 |
| 1253 | A461 | 55b | dk red brn | .50 | .25 |
| 1254 | A461 | 1.20 l | dull bl | .90 | .25 |
| 1255 | A461 | 1.30 l | brown vio | 1.20 | .25 |
| 1256 | A462 | 1.55 l | gray brn | 1.50 | .25 |
| 1257 | A462 | 1.75 l | claret | 1.50 | .25 |
| 1258 | A462 | 2 l | dull vio | 1.90 | .50 |
| 1259 | A462 | 3.30 l | dull red brn | 2.50 | .60 |
| | | | *Nos. 1252-1259 (8)* | 10.30 | 2.60 |

Cent. of Romanian stamps. See No. C57. Exist imperf. Value, set $25.

Bugler — A463

**1958, Dec. 10 Photo. *Perf. 13½x13***

| | | | | | |
|---|---|---|---|---|---|
| 1260 | A463 | 55b | crimson rose | .75 | .30 |

Decade of teaching reforms.

Runner — A464

***Perf. 13½x14***

**1958, Dec. 9 Wmk. 358**

| | | | | | |
|---|---|---|---|---|---|
| 1261 | A464 | 1 l | deep brown | 1.25 | .30 |

Third Youth Spartacist Sports Meet. For overprint, see No. 1287.

Building and Flag — A465

**1958, Dec. 16**

| | | | | | |
|---|---|---|---|---|---|
| 1262 | A465 | 55b | dk car rose | .80 | .25 |

Workers' Revolution, 40th anniversary.

Prince Alexandru Ioan Cuza A466

***Perf. 14x13½***

**1959, Jan. 27 Unwmk.**

| | | | | | |
|---|---|---|---|---|---|
| 1263 | A466 | 1.75 l | dk blue | 1.50 | .30 |

Centenary of the Romanian Union.

Friedrich Handel — A467

Portraits: No. 1265, Robert Burns. No. 1266, Charles Darwin. No. 1267, Alexander Popov. No. 1268, Shalom Aleichem.

**1959, Apr. 25 Photo. *Perf. 13½x14***

| | | | | | |
|---|---|---|---|---|---|
| 1264 | A467 | 55b | brown | .60 | .25 |
| 1265 | A467 | 55b | indigo | .60 | .25 |
| 1266 | A467 | 55b | slate | .60 | .25 |
| 1267 | A467 | 55b | carmine | .60 | .25 |
| 1268 | A467 | 55b | purple | .60 | .25 |
| | | | *Nos. 1264-1268,C59 (6)* | 7.00 | 1.85 |

Various cultural anniversaries in 1959.

Corn — A468

Sheep A469

No. 1270, Sunflower and bee. No. 1271, Sugar beet and refinery. No. 1273, Cattle. No. 1274, Rooster and hens. No. 1275, Tractor and grain. No. 1276, Loaded farm wagon. No. 1277, Farm couple and "10."

***Perf. 13½x14, 14x13½***

**1959, June 1 Photo. Wmk. 358**

| | | | | | |
|---|---|---|---|---|---|
| 1269 | A468 | 55b | brt green | .40 | .25 |
| 1270 | A468 | 55b | red org | .40 | .25 |
| 1271 | A468 | 55b | red lilac | .40 | .25 |
| 1272 | A469 | 55b | olive grn | .40 | .25 |
| 1273 | A469 | 55b | red brown | .40 | .25 |
| 1274 | A469 | 55b | yellow brn | .40 | .25 |
| 1275 | A469 | 55b | blue | .40 | .25 |
| 1276 | A469 | 55b | brown | .40 | .25 |

**Unwmk.**

| | | | | | |
|---|---|---|---|---|---|
| 1277 | A469 | 5 l | dp red lilac | 3.00 | .60 |
| | | | *Nos. 1269-1277 (9)* | 6.20 | 2.60 |

10th anniv. of collective farming. Sizes: #1272-1276 33x23mm; #1277 38x27mm.

Young Couple — A470

Design: 1.60 l, Dancer in folk costume.

***Perf. 13½x14***

**1959, July 15 Unwmk.**

| | | | | | |
|---|---|---|---|---|---|
| 1278 | A470 | 1 l | brt blue | .75 | .25 |
| 1279 | A470 | 1.60 l | car rose | 1.00 | .25 |

7th World Youth Festival, Vienna, 7/26-8/14.

Steel Worker and Farm Woman — A471

**1959, Aug. 23 Litho. *Perf. 13½x14***

| | | | | | |
|---|---|---|---|---|---|
| 1280 | A471 | 55b | multicolored | .60 | .25 |
| *a.* | | | Souvenir sheet of 1 | 1.75 | .65 |

15th anniv. of Romania's liberation from the Germans.

No. 1280a is ungummed and imperf. The blue, yellow and red vignette shows large "XV" and Romanian flag. Brown 1.20 l denomination and inscription in margin.

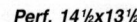

Prince Vlad Tepes and Document — A472

Designs: 40b, Nicolae Balcescu Street. No. 1283, Atheneum. No. 1284, Printing Combine. 1.55 l, Opera House. 1.75 l, Stadium.

**1959, Sept. 20 Photo.**

**Centers in Gray**

| | | | | | |
|---|---|---|---|---|---|
| 1281 | A472 | 20b | blue | .95 | .25 |
| 1282 | A472 | 40b | brown | 1.40 | .25 |
| 1283 | A472 | 55b | bister brn | 1.60 | .25 |
| 1284 | A472 | 55b | rose lilac | 2.00 | .35 |
| 1285 | A472 | 1.55 l | pale violet | 4.25 | .60 |
| 1286 | A472 | 1.75 l | bluish grn | 4.75 | .85 |
| | | | *Nos. 1281-1286 (6)* | 14.95 | 2.55 |

500th anniversary of the founding of Bucharest. See No. C71.

**No. 1261 Overprinted with Shield in Silver, inscribed: "Jocurile Bucaresti Balcanice 1959"**

**1959, Sept. 12 Wmk. 358**

| | | | | | |
|---|---|---|---|---|---|
| 1287 | A464 | 1 l | deep brown | 10.00 | 3.50 |

Balkan Games.

Soccer — A473

Motorcycle Race — A474

***Perf. 13½***

**1959, Oct. 5 Unwmk. Litho.**

| | | | | | |
|---|---|---|---|---|---|
| 1288 | A473 | 20b | shown | .25 | .25 |
| 1289 | A474 | 35b | shown | .30 | .25 |
| 1290 | A474 | 40b | Ice hockey | .40 | .25 |
| 1291 | A473 | 55b | Handball | .45 | .25 |
| 1292 | A473 | 1 l | Horse race | .80 | .25 |
| 1293 | A473 | 1.50 l | Boxing | 1.40 | .25 |
| 1294 | A474 | 1.55 l | Rugby | 1.60 | .25 |
| 1295 | A474 | 1.60 l | Tennis | 2.00 | .30 |
| | | | *Nos. 1288-1295,C72 (9)* | 9.70 | 2.55 |

Russian Icebreaker "Lenin" A475

***Perf. 14½x13½***

**1959, Oct. 25 Photo.**

| | | | | | |
|---|---|---|---|---|---|
| 1296 | A475 | 1.75 l | blue vio | 2.50 | .40 |

First atomic ice-breaker.

Stamp Album and Magnifying Glass — A476

**1959, Nov. 15 Wmk. 358 *Perf. 14***

| | | | | | |
|---|---|---|---|---|---|
| 1297 | A476 | 1.60 l | + 40b label | 1.25 | .40 |

Issued for Stamp Day.

Stamp and label were printed alternately in sheet. The 40b went to the Romanian Association of Philatelists.

Purple Foxglove — A477

**1959, Dec. 15 Typo. Unwmk.**

**Medicinal Flowers in Natural Colors**

| | | | | | |
|---|---|---|---|---|---|
| 1298 | A477 | 20b | shown | .25 | .25 |
| 1299 | A477 | 40b | Peppermint | .30 | .25 |
| 1300 | A477 | 55b | Cornflower | .50 | .25 |
| 1301 | A477 | 55b | Daisies | .65 | .25 |
| 1302 | A477 | 1 l | Autumn crocus | .90 | .25 |
| 1303 | A477 | 1.20 l | Monkshood | 1.00 | .25 |
| 1304 | A477 | 1.55 l | Poppies | 1.50 | .25 |
| 1305 | A477 | 1.60 l | Linden | 1.50 | .30 |
| 1306 | A477 | 1.75 l | Dog rose | 1.50 | .30 |
| 1307 | A477 | 3.20 l | Buttercup | 2.50 | .50 |
| | | | *Nos. 1298-1307 (10)* | 10.60 | 2.85 |

Cuza University, Jassy, Centenary A478

**1959, Nov. 26 Photo. Wmk. 358**

| | | | | | |
|---|---|---|---|---|---|
| 1308 | A478 | 55b | brown | .70 | .25 |

**Romanian Writers Type of 1958**

20b, Gheorghe Cosbuc. 40b, Ion Luca Caragiale. 50b, Grigore Alexandrescu. 55b, Alexandru Donici. 1 l, Costache Negruzzi. 1.55 l, Dimitrie Bolintineanu.

**1960, Jan. 20 *Perf. 14***

| | | | | | |
|---|---|---|---|---|---|
| 1309 | A450 | 20b | bluish blk | .25 | .25 |
| 1310 | A450 | 40b | dp lilac | .55 | .25 |
| 1311 | A450 | 50b | brown | .65 | .25 |
| 1312 | A450 | 55b | violet brn | .65 | .25 |
| 1313 | A450 | 1 l | violet | 1.10 | .25 |
| 1314 | A450 | 1.55 l | dk blue | 1.50 | .35 |
| | | | *Nos. 1309-1314 (6)* | 4.70 | 1.60 |

Huchen (Salmon) — A480

55b, Greek tortoise. 1.20 l, Shelduck.

**1960, Feb. 1 Engr. Unwmk.**

| | | | | | |
|---|---|---|---|---|---|
| 1315 | A480 | 20b | blue | .30 | .25 |
| 1316 | A480 | 55b | brown | .50 | .25 |
| 1317 | A480 | 1.20 l | dk purple | 1.25 | .30 |
| | | | *Nos. 1315-1317,C76-C78 (6)* | 7.30 | 2.10 |

Woman, Dove and Globe — A481

**1960, Mar. 1 Photo. *Perf. 14***

| | | | | | |
|---|---|---|---|---|---|
| 1318 | A481 | 55b | violet blue | .50 | .25 |

50 years of Intl. Women's Day, Mar. 8.

A482

40b, Lenin. 55b, Lenin statue, Bucharest. 1.55 l, Head of Lenin.

**1960, Apr. 22 Wmk. 358 *Perf. 13½***

| | | | | | |
|---|---|---|---|---|---|
| 1319 | A482 | 40b | magenta | .35 | .25 |
| 1320 | A482 | 55b | violet blue | .50 | .25 |

**Souvenir Sheet**

| | | | | | |
|---|---|---|---|---|---|
| 1321 | A482 | 1.55 l | carmine | 3.00 | 2.00 |

90th birth anniv. of Lenin.

A483

40b, Heroes Monument. 55b, Soviet war memorial.

**1960, May 9 Wmk. 358 *Perf. 14***

| | | | | | |
|---|---|---|---|---|---|
| 1322 | A483 | 40b | multicolored | .35 | .25 |
| 1323 | A483 | 55b | multicolored | .45 | .25 |
| *a.* | | | Strip of 2, #1322-1323 + label | 1.50 | .75 |

15th anniversary of the liberation.

Nos. 1322-1323 exist imperf., printed in deep magenta. Value, set $3.25; label strip, $4.50.

Swimming A484

Sports: 55b, Women's gymnastics. 1.20 l, High jump. 1.60 l, Boxing. 2.45 l, Canoeing.

**1960, June Unwmk. Typo. *Perf. 14***

**Gray Background**

| | | | | | |
|---|---|---|---|---|---|
| 1326 | A484 | 40b | blue & yel | 3.00 | 3.00 |
| 1327 | A484 | 55b | blk, yel & emer | 3.00 | 3.00 |
| 1328 | A484 | 1.20 l | emer & brick red | 3.00 | 3.00 |
| *a.* | | | Strip of 3, #1326-1328 | 10.00 | 10.00 |
| 1329 | A484 | 1.60 l | blue, yel & blk | 3.00 | 3.00 |
| 1330 | A484 | 2.45 l | blk, emer & brick red | 3.00 | 3.00 |
| *a.* | | | Pair, #1329-1330 + 2 labels | 10.00 | 10.00 |
| | | | *Nos. 1326-1330 (5)* | 15.00 | 15.00 |

17th Olympic Games, Rome, 8/25-9/11.

Nos. 1326-1330 were printed in one sheet, the top half containing No. 1328a, the bottom half No. 1330a, with gutter between. When the two strips are placed together, the Olympic rings join in a continuous design.

Exist imperf. (3.70 l replaced 2.45 l). Value, set, two strips $35.

Swimming — A485

Olympic Flame, Stadium — A486

40b, Women's gymnastics. 55b, High jump. 1 l, Boxing. 1.60 l, Canoeing. 2 l, Soccer.

**1960 Photo. Wmk. 358**

| | | | | | |
|---|---|---|---|---|---|
| 1331 | A485 | 20b | chalky blue | .25 | .25 |
| 1332 | A485 | 40b | dk brn red | .35 | .25 |
| 1333 | A485 | 55b | blue | .55 | .25 |
| 1334 | A485 | 1 l | rose red | .75 | .25 |
| 1335 | A485 | 1.60 l | rose lilac | 1.00 | .25 |
| 1336 | A485 | 2 l | dull violet | 1.50 | .35 |
| | | | *Nos. 1331-1336 (6)* | 4.40 | 1.60 |

**Souvenir Sheets**

***Perf. 11½***

| | | | | | |
|---|---|---|---|---|---|
| 1337 | A486 | 5 l | ultra | 12.50 | 7.00 |

***Imperf***

| | | | | | |
|---|---|---|---|---|---|
| 1338 | A486 | 6 l | dull red | 20.00 | 10.00 |

17th Olympic Games.

A487

***Perf. 13½***

**1960, June 20 Unwmk. Litho.**

| | | | | | |
|---|---|---|---|---|---|
| 1339 | A487 | 55b | red org & dk car | .50 | .25 |

Romanian Workers' Party, 3rd congress.

A488

Portraits: 10b, Leo Tolstoy. 20b, Mark Twain. 35b, Hokusai. 40b, Alfred de Musset. 55b, Daniel Defoe. 1 l, Janos Bolyai. 1.20 l, Anton Chekov. 1.55 l, Robert Koch. 1.75 l, Frederick Chopin.

**1960 Wmk. 358 Photo. *Perf. 14***

| | | | | | |
|---|---|---|---|---|---|
| 1340 | A488 | 10b | dull pur | .25 | .25 |
| 1341 | A488 | 20b | olive | .30 | .25 |
| 1342 | A488 | 35b | blue | .40 | .25 |
| 1343 | A488 | 40b | slate green | .50 | .25 |
| 1344 | A488 | 55b | dull brn vio | .75 | .25 |
| 1345 | A488 | 1 l | Prus grn | 1.25 | .45 |
| 1346 | A488 | 1.20 l | dk car rose | 1.40 | .25 |
| 1347 | A488 | 1.55 l | gray blue | 1.60 | .25 |
| 1348 | A488 | 1.75 l | brown | 2.25 | .50 |
| | | | *Nos. 1340-1348 (9)* | 8.70 | 2.70 |

Various cultural anniversaries.

Students A489

Piano and Books A490

Designs: 5b, Diesel locomotive. 10b, Dam. 20b, Miner with drill. 30b, Ambulance and doctor. 35b, Textile worker. 50b, Nursery. 55b, Timber industry. 60b, Harvester. 75b, Feeding cattle. 1 l, Atomic reactor. 1.20 l, Oil derricks. 1.50 l, Coal mine. 1.55 l, Loading ship. 1.60 l, Athlete. 1.75 l, Bricklayer. 2 l, Steam roller. 2.40 l, Chemist. 3 l, Radio and television.

**1960 Wmk. 358 Photo. *Perf. 14***

| | | | | | |
|---|---|---|---|---|---|
| 1349 | A489 | 3b | brt lil rose | .25 | .25 |
| 1350 | A489 | 5b | olive bis | .25 | .25 |
| 1351 | A489 | 10b | violet gray | .25 | .25 |
| 1352 | A489 | 20b | blue vio | .25 | .25 |
| 1353 | A489 | 30b | vermilion | .25 | .25 |
| 1354 | A489 | 35b | crimson | .25 | .25 |
| 1355 | A490 | 40b | ocher | .25 | .25 |
| 1356 | A489 | 50b | bluish vio | .25 | .25 |
| 1357 | A489 | 55b | blue | .25 | .25 |
| 1358 | A490 | 60b | green | .25 | .25 |
| 1359 | A490 | 75b | gray ol | .30 | .25 |
| 1360 | A489 | 1 l | car rose | .50 | .25 |
| 1361 | A489 | 1.20 l | black | .40 | .25 |
| 1362 | A489 | 1.50 l | plum | .50 | .25 |
| 1363 | A490 | 1.55 l | Prus grn | .50 | .25 |
| 1364 | A490 | 1.60 l | dp blue | .55 | .25 |
| 1365 | A489 | 1.75 l | red brown | .75 | .25 |
| 1366 | A489 | 2 l | dk ol gray | 1.00 | .25 |
| 1367 | A489 | 2.40 l | brt lilac | 1.25 | .25 |
| 1368 | A489 | 3 l | grysh blue | 1.75 | .25 |
| | | | *Nos. 1349-1368,C86 (21)* | 11.50 | 5.25 |

Ovid Statue at Constanta A491

Black Sea Resorts: 35b, Constanta harbor. 40b, Vasile Rosita beach and vase. 55b, Ionian column and Mangalia beach. 1 l, Eforie at night. 1.60 l, Eforie and sailboat.

**1960, Aug. 2 Litho. Unwmk.**

| | | | | | |
|---|---|---|---|---|---|
| 1369 | A491 | 20b | multicolored | .25 | .25 |
| 1370 | A491 | 35b | multicolored | .25 | .25 |
| 1371 | A491 | 40b | multicolored | .25 | .25 |
| 1372 | A491 | 55b | multicolored | .30 | .25 |
| 1373 | A491 | 1 l | multicolored | .75 | .25 |
| 1374 | A491 | 1.60 l | multicolored | 1.10 | .25 |
| | | | *Nos. 1369-1374,C87 (7)* | 4.40 | 2.00 |

Emblem — A492

Petrushka, Russian Puppet — A493

Designs: Various Puppets.

**1960, Aug. 20 Typo.**

| | | | | | |
|---|---|---|---|---|---|
| 1375 | A492 | 20b | multi | .25 | .25 |
| 1376 | A493 | 40b | multi | .25 | .25 |
| 1377 | A493 | 55b | multi | .25 | .25 |
| 1378 | A493 | 1 l | multi | .50 | .25 |
| 1379 | A493 | 1.20 l | multi | .50 | .25 |
| 1380 | A493 | 1.75 l | multi | .75 | .25 |
| | | | *Nos. 1375-1380 (6)* | 2.50 | 1.50 |

International Puppet Theater Festival.

Children on Sled — A494

Children's Sports: 35b, Boys playing ball, horiz. 55b, Ice skating, horiz. 1 l, Running. 1.75 l, Swimming, horiz.

**Unwmk.**

**1960, Oct. 1 Litho. *Perf. 14***

| | | | | | |
|---|---|---|---|---|---|
| 1381 | A494 | 20b | multi | .25 | .25 |
| 1382 | A494 | 35b | multi | .25 | .25 |
| 1383 | A494 | 55b | multi | .30 | .25 |
| 1384 | A494 | 1 l | multi | .45 | .25 |
| 1385 | A494 | 1.75 l | multi | .90 | .25 |
| | | | *Nos. 1381-1385 (5)* | 2.15 | 1.25 |

Globe and Peace Banner — A495

***Perf. 13½x14***

**1960, Nov. 26 Photo. Wmk. 358**

| | | | | | |
|---|---|---|---|---|---|
| 1386 | A495 | 55b | brt bl & yel | .40 | .25 |

Intl. Youth Federation, 15th anniv.

Worker and Flags A496

***Perf. 14x13***

**1960, Nov. 26 Litho. Unwmk.**

| | | | | | |
|---|---|---|---|---|---|
| 1387 | A496 | 55b | dk car & red org | .40 | .25 |

40th anniversary of the general strike.

Carp A497

Fish: 20b, Pikeperch. 40b, Black Sea turbot. 55b, Allis shad. 1 l, Wels (catfish). 1.20 l, Sterlet. 1.60 l, Huchen (salmon).

**1960, Dec. 5 Typo.**

| | | | | | |
|---|---|---|---|---|---|
| 1388 | A497 | 10b | multi | .25 | .25 |
| 1389 | A497 | 20b | multi | .30 | .25 |
| 1390 | A497 | 40b | multi | .35 | .25 |
| 1391 | A497 | 55b | multi | .40 | .25 |
| 1392 | A497 | 1 l | multi | 1.00 | .25 |
| 1393 | A497 | 1.20 l | multi | 1.10 | .25 |
| 1394 | A497 | 1.60 l | multi | 1.75 | .35 |
| | | | *Nos. 1388-1394 (7)* | 5.15 | 1.85 |

Kneeling Woman and Grapes — A498

Designs: 30b, Farmers drinking, horiz. 40b, Loading grapes into basket, horiz. 55b, Woman cutting grapes. 75b, Vintner with basket. 1 l, Woman filling basket with grapes. 1.20 l, Vintner with jug. 5 l, Antique wine jug.

**1960, Dec. 20 Litho. *Perf. 14***

| | | | | | |
|---|---|---|---|---|---|
| 1395 | A498 | 20b | brn & gray | .25 | .25 |
| 1396 | A498 | 30b | red org & pale grn | .30 | .25 |
| 1397 | A498 | 40b | dp ultra & gray ol | .40 | .25 |
| 1398 | A498 | 55b | emer & buff | .50 | .25 |
| 1399 | A498 | 75b | dk car rose & pale grn | .50 | .25 |
| 1400 | A498 | 1 l | Prus grn & gray ol | .65 | .25 |
| 1401 | A498 | 1.20 l | org brn & pale bl | 1.00 | .30 |
| | | | *Nos. 1395-1401 (7)* | 3.60 | 1.80 |

### Souvenir Sheet
*Imperf*

**1402** A498 5 l dk car rose & bis 4.00 1.90

Each stamp represents a different wine-growing region: Dragasani, Dealul Mare, Odobesti, Cotnari, Tirnave, Minis, Murfatlar and Pietroasa.

Steelworker by I. Irimescu — A499

Modern Sculptures: 10b, G. Doja, I. Vlad. 20b, Meeting, B. Caragea. 40b, George Enescu, A. Anghel. 50b, Mihail Eminescu, C. Baraschi. 55b, Peasant Revolt, 1907, M. Constantinescu, horiz. 1 l, "Peace," I. Jalea. 1.55 l, Building Socialism, C. Medrea. 1.75 l, Birth of an Idea, A. Szobotka.

*Perf. 13½x14, 14x13½*

**1961, Feb. 16 Photo. Unwmk.**

**1403** A499 5b car rose .25 .25
**1404** A499 10b violet .25 .25
**1405** A499 20b ol blk .25 .25
**1406** A499 40b ol bis .35 .25
**1407** A499 50b blk brn .40 .25
**1408** A499 55b org ver .60 .25
**1409** A499 1 l dp plum .80 .25
**1410** A499 1.55 l brt ultra 1.00 .25
**1411** A499 1.75 l green 1.40 .25
*Nos. 1403-1411 (9)* 5.30 2.25

Peter Poni, and Chemical Apparatus — A500

Romanian Scientists: 20b, A. Saligny and Danube bridge, Cernavoda. 55b, C. Budeanu and electrical formula. 1.55 l, Gh. Titeica and geometrical symbol.

**1961, Apr. 11 Litho.** *Perf. 13½x13*

**Portraits in Brown Black**

**1412** A500 10b pink & vio bl .25 .25
**1413** A500 20b citron & mar .25 .25
**1414** A500 55b blue & red .30 .25
**1415** A500 1.55 l ocher & lilac 1.00 .25
*Nos. 1412-1415 (4)* 1.80 1.00

Freighter "Galati" A501

Ships: 40b, Passenger ship "Oltenita." 55b, Motorboat "Tomis." 1 l, Freighter "Arad." 1.55 l, Tugboat. 1.75 l, Freighter "Dobrogea."

**1961, Apr. 25 Typo.** *Perf. 14x13*

**1416** A501 20b multi .25 .25
**1417** A501 40b multi .25 .25
**1418** A501 55b multi .40 .25
**1419** A501 1 l multi .50 .25
**1420** A501 1.55 l multi .75 .25
**1421** A501 1.75 l multi 1.10 .25
*Nos. 1416-1421 (6)* 3.25 1.50

Marx, Lenin and Engels on Red Flag — A502

Designs: 55b, Workers. 1 l, "Industry and Agriculture" and Workers Party Emblem.

**1961, Apr. 29 Litho.**

**1422** A502 35b red, bl & ocher .40 .25
**1423** A502 55b mar, red & gray .60 .25

### Souvenir Sheet
*Imperf*

**1424** A502 1 l multi 1.75 .70

40th anniv. of the Romanian Communist Party. #1424 contains one 55x33mm stamp.

Roe Deer and Bronze Age Hunting Scene — A503

Lynx and Prehistoric Hunter A504

35b, Boar, Roman hunter. 40b, Brown bear, Roman tombstone. 55b, Red deer, 16th cent. hunter. 75b, Red fox, feudal hunter. 1 l, Black goat, modern hunter. 1.55 l, Rabbit, hunter with dog. 1.75 l, Badger, hunter. 2 l, Roebuck, hunter.

**1961, July** *Perf. 13x14, 14x13*

**1425** A503 10b multi .25 .25
**1426** A504 20b multi .25 .25
**1427** A504 35b multi .35 .25
**1428** A504 40b multi .60 .25
**1429** A503 55b multi .75 .25
**1430** A504 75b multi .90 .25
**1431** A503 1 l multi 1.00 .25
**1432** A503 1.55 l multi 1.25 .25
**1433** A503 1.75 l multi 1.50 .30
**1434** A503 2 l multi 1.75 .45
*Nos. 1425-1434 (10)* 8.60 2.75

Georges Enescu A505

**1961, Sept. 7 Litho.** *Perf. 14x13*

**1435** A505 3 l pale vio & vio brn 1.40 .30

2nd Intl. George Enescu Festival, Bucharest.

Peasant Playing Panpipe — A506

Peasants playing musical instruments: 20b, Alpenhorn, horiz. 40b, Flute. 55b, Guitar. 60b, Bagpipe. 1 l, Zither.

*Perf. 13x14, 14x13*

**1961 Unwmk. Typo.**

**Tinted Paper**

**1436** A506 10b multi .25 .25
**1437** A506 20b multi .25 .25
**1438** A506 40b multi .25 .25
**1439** A506 55b multi .45 .25
**1440** A506 60b multi .45 .25
**1441** A506 1 l multi .70 .25
*Nos. 1436-1441 (6)* 2.35 1.50

Heraclitus — A507

Portraits: 20b, Francis Bacon. 40b, Rabindranath Tagore. 55b, Domingo F. Sarmiento. 1.35 l, Heinrich von Kleist. 1.75 l, Mikhail V. Lomonosov.

*Perf. 13½x13*

**1961, Oct. 25 Photo. Wmk. 358**

**1442** A507 10b maroon .25 .25
**1443** A507 20b brown .25 .25
**1444** A507 40b Prus grn .25 .25
**1445** A507 55b cerise .25 .25
**1446** A507 1.35 l brt bl .75 .25
**1447** A507 1.75 l purple 1.00 .25
*Nos. 1442-1447 (6)* 2.75 1.50

Swimming — A508

Gold Medal, Boxing A509

No. 1449, Olympic torch. No. 1450, Water polo, Melbourne. No. 1451, Women's high jump, Rome.

*Perf. 14x14½*

**1961, Oct. 30 Photo. Unwmk.**

**1448** A508 20b bl gray .25 .25
**1449** A508 20b vermilion .25 .25
**1450** A508 55b ultra .60 .25
**1451** A508 55b blue .60 .25
*Nos. 1448-1451 (4)* 1.70 1.00

*Perf. 10½*

**Size: 33x33mm**

Gold Medals: 35b, Pistol shooting, Melbourne. 40b, Sharpshooting, Rome. 55b, Wrestling. 1.35 l, Woman's high jump. 1.75 l, Three medals for canoeing.

**Medals in Ocher**

**1452** A509 10b Prus grn .25 .25
**1453** A509 35b brown .40 .25
**1454** A509 40b plum .45 .25
**1455** A509 55b org red .60 .25
**1456** A509 1.35 l dp ultra .90 .25

**Size: 46x32mm**

**1457** A509 1.75 l dp car rose 1.75 .35
*Nos. 1452-1457 (6)* 4.35 1.60
*Nos. 1448-1457 (10)* 6.05 2.60

Romania's gold medals in 1956, 1960 Olympics.

Nos. 1452-1457 exist imperf. Value, set: unused $5; used $3.50.

A souvenir sheet of one 4 l dark red & ocher was issued. Value, unused $5.50, canceled $4.50.

See Nos. 1116-1120. The vertical inscriptions on Nos. 1448-1451 are different than on Nos. 1116-1120.

Congress Emblem — A510

**1961, Dec. Litho.** *Perf. 13½x14*

**1458** A510 55b dk car rose .50 .25

5th World Congress of Trade Unions, Moscow, Dec. 4-16.

Primrose A511

Designs: 20b, Sweet William. 25b, Peony. 35b, Prickly pear. 40b, Iris. 55b, Buttercup. 1 l, Hepatica. 1.20 l, Poppy. 1.55 l, Gentian. 1.75 l, Carol Davilla and Dimitrie Brindza. 20b, 25b, 40b, 55b, 1.20 l, 1.55 l, are vertical.

*Perf. 14x13½, 13½x14*

**1961, Sept. 15**

**1459** A511 10b multi .25 .25
**1460** A511 20b multi .25 .25
**1461** A511 25b multi .25 .25
**1462** A511 35b multi .30 .25
**1463** A511 40b multi .30 .25
**1464** A511 55b multi .35 .25
**1465** A511 1 l multi .50 .25
**1466** A511 1.20 l multi .65 .25
**1467** A511 1.55 l multi 1.10 .25
*Nos. 1459-1467 (9)* 3.95 2.25

### Souvenir Sheet
*Imperf*

**1468** A511 1.75 l car, blk & grn 4.50 3.00

Bucharest Botanical Garden, cent.
No. 1459-1467 exist imperf. Value, set $12.

United Nations Emblem — A512

Designs: 20b, Map of Balkan peninsula and dove. 40b, Men of three races.

**1961, Nov. 27** *Perf. 13½x14*

**1469** A512 20b bl, yel & pink .25 .25
**1470** A512 40b multi .55 .25
**1471** A512 55b org, lil & yel .80 .25
*Nos. 1469-1471 (3)* 1.60 .75

UN, 15th anniv. Nos. 1469-1470 are each printed with alternating yellow labels.

Exist imperf. Value, set: unused $2.75; used $2.

Cock and Savings Book — A513

Savings Day: 55b, Honeycomb, bee and savings book.

**1962, Feb. 15 Typo.** *Perf. 13½*

**1472** A513 40b multi .30 .25
**1473** A513 55b multi .30 .25

Soccer Player and Map of Europe — A514

**1962, Apr. 20 Litho.** *Perf. 13x14*

**1474** A514 55b emer & red brn 2.00 .75

European Junior Soccer Championships, Bucharest. For surcharge see No. 1510.

Wheat, Map and Tractor — A515

Designs: 55b, Medal honoring agriculture. 1.55Nl, Sheaf of wheat, hammer & sickle.

**1962, Apr. 27** *Perf. 13½x14*

| | | | | |
|---|---|---|---|---|
| **1475** A515 | 40b org & dk car | .25 | .25 |
| **1476** A515 | 55b yel, car & brn | .25 | .25 |
| **1477** A515 | 1.55 l multi | .85 | .25 |
| | *Nos. 1475-1477 (3)* | 1.35 | .75 |

Collectivization of agriculture.

Canoe Race A516

20b, Kayak. 40b, 8-man shell. 55b, 2-man skiff. 1 l, Yachts. 1.20 l, Motorboats. 1.55 l, Sailboat. 3 l, Water slalom.

**1962, May 15 Photo.** *Perf. 14x13*

**Vignette in Bright Blue**

| | | | |
|---|---|---|---|
| **1478** A516 | 10b lil rose | .25 | .25 |
| **1479** A516 | 20b ol gray | .25 | .25 |
| **1480** A516 | 40b red brn | .25 | .25 |
| **1481** A516 | 55b ultra | .25 | .25 |
| **1482** A516 | 1 l red | .30 | .25 |
| **1483** A516 | 1.20 l dp plum | .70 | .25 |
| **1484** A516 | 1.55 l orange | 1.00 | .25 |
| **1485** A516 | 3 l violet | 1.75 | .25 |
| | *Nos. 1478-1485 (8)* | 4.75 | 2.00 |

These stamps were also issued imperf. with color of denomination and inscription changed. Value, set unused $6, canceled $2.75.

Ion Luca Caragiale — A517

40b, Jean Jacques Rousseau. 1.75 l, Aleksander I. Herzen. 3.30 l, Ion Luca Caragiale (as a young man).

**1962, June 9** *Perf. 13½x14*

| | | | |
|---|---|---|---|
| **1486** A517 | 40b dk sl grn | .25 | .25 |
| **1487** A517 | 55b magenta | .25 | .25 |
| **1488** A517 | 1.75 l dp bl | .75 | .25 |
| | *Nos. 1486-1488 (3)* | 1.25 | .75 |

**Souvenir Sheet**

*Perf. 11½*

| | | | |
|---|---|---|---|
| **1489** A517 | 3.30 l brown | 4.25 | 4.25 |

Rousseau, French philosopher, 250th birth anniv.; Caragiale, Romanian author, 50th death anniv.; Herzen, Russian writer, 150th birth anniv. No. 1489 contains one 32x55mm stamp.

Globes Surrounded with Flags — A518

**1962, July 6 Typo.** *Perf. 11*

| | | | |
|---|---|---|---|
| **1490** A518 | 55b multi | .60 | .25 |

8th Youth Festival for Peace and Friendship, Helsinki, July 28-Aug. 6.

Traian Vuia — A519

Portraits: 20b, Al. Davila. 35b, Vasile Pirvan. 40b, Ion Negulici. 55b, Grigore Cobilcescu. 1 l, Dr. Gheorghe Marinescu. 1.20 l, Ion Cantacuzino. 1.35 l, Victor Babes. 1.55 l, C. Levaditi.

*Perf. 13½x14*

**1962, July 20 Photo. Wmk. 358**

| | | | |
|---|---|---|---|
| **1491** A519 | 15b brown | .25 | .25 |
| **1492** A519 | 20b dl red brn | .25 | .25 |
| **1493** A519 | 35b brn mag | .25 | .25 |
| **1494** A519 | 40b bl vio | .25 | .25 |
| **1495** A519 | 55b brt bl | .25 | .25 |
| **1496** A519 | 1 l dp ultra | .30 | .25 |
| **1497** A519 | 1.20 l crimson | .45 | .25 |
| **1498** A519 | 1.35 l Prus grn | .60 | .25 |
| **1499** A519 | 1.55 l purple | 1.10 | .25 |
| | *Nos. 1491-1499 (9)* | 3.70 | 2.25 |

Fieldball Player and Globe — A520

*Perf. 13x14*

**1962, May 12 Litho. Unwmk.**

| | | | |
|---|---|---|---|
| **1500** A520 | 55b yel & vio | 2.50 | .50 |

2nd Intl. Women's Fieldball Championships, Bucharest.

No. 1500 Surcharged in Violet Blue

**1962, July 31**

| | | | |
|---|---|---|---|
| **1501** A520 | 5 l on 55b yel & vio | 7.50 | 5.00 |
| *a.* | Pair, one without surcharge | 500.00 | |

Romanian victory in the 2nd Intl. Women's Fieldball Championships.

Rod Fishing A521

Various Fishing Scenes.

**1962, July 25** *Perf. 14x13*

| | | | |
|---|---|---|---|
| **1502** A521 | 10b multi | .25 | .25 |
| **1503** A521 | 25b multi | .25 | .25 |
| **1504** A521 | 40b bl & brick red | .25 | .25 |
| **1505** A521 | 55b multi | .25 | .25 |
| **1506** A521 | 75b sl, gray & bl | .40 | .25 |
| **1507** A521 | 1 l multi | .55 | .25 |
| **1508** A521 | 1.75 l multi | .90 | .25 |
| **1509** A521 | 3.25 l multi | 1.50 | .25 |
| | *Nos. 1502-1509 (8)* | 4.35 | 2.00 |

**No. 1474 Surcharged "1962 Campioana Europeana 2 lei" in Dark Blue**

**1962, July 31**

| | | | |
|---|---|---|---|
| **1510** A514 | 2 l on 55b | 3.75 | 3.75 |

Romania's victory in the European Junior Soccer Championships, Bucharest.

Child and Butterfly — A522

Designs: 30b, Girl feeding bird. 40b, Boy and model sailboat. 55b, Children writing, horiz. 1.20 l, Girl at piano, and boy playing violin. 1.55 l, Pioneers camping, horiz.

*Perf. 13x14, 14x13*

**1962, Aug. 25 Litho.**

| | | | |
|---|---|---|---|
| **1511** A522 | 20b lt bl, red & brn | .35 | .25 |
| **1512** A522 | 30b org, bl & red brn | .35 | .25 |
| **1513** A522 | 40b chalky bl, dp org & Prus bl | .35 | .25 |
| **1514** A522 | 55b citron, bl & red | .45 | .25 |
| **1515** A522 | 1.20 l car, brn & dk vio | .65 | .25 |
| **1516** A522 | 1.55 l bis, red & vio | 1.25 | .25 |
| | *Nos. 1511-1516 (6)* | 3.40 | 1.50 |

Handicraft — A523

Designs: 10b, Food and drink. 20b, Chemical industry. 40b, Chinaware. 55b, Leather industry. 75b, Textiles. 1 l, Furniture. 1.20 l, Electrical appliances. 1.55 l, Household goods (sewing machine and pots).

**1962, Oct. 12** *Perf. 13x14*

| | | | |
|---|---|---|---|
| **1517** A523 | 5b multi | .25 | .25 |
| **1518** A523 | 10b multi | .25 | .25 |
| **1519** A523 | 20b multi | .25 | .25 |
| **1520** A523 | 40b multi | .25 | .25 |
| **1521** A523 | 55b multi | .25 | .25 |
| **1522** A523 | 75b multi | .25 | .25 |
| **1523** A523 | 1 l multi | .40 | .25 |
| **1524** A523 | 1.20 l multi | .75 | .25 |
| **1525** A523 | 1.55 l multi | 1.10 | .25 |
| | *Nos. 1517-1525,C126 (10)* | 5.25 | 2.50 |

4th Sample Fair, Bucharest.

Lenin — A524

**1962, Nov. 7** *Perf. 10½*

| | | | |
|---|---|---|---|
| **1526** A524 | 55b vio bl, red & bis | .50 | .25 |

Russian October Revolution, 45th anniv.

Bull — A525

Designs: 20b, Sheep, horiz. 40b, Merino ram, horiz. 1 l, York pig. 1.35 l, Cow. 1.55 l, Heifer, horiz. 1.75 l, Pigs, horiz.

**1962, Nov. 20** *Perf. 14x13, 13x14*

| | | | |
|---|---|---|---|
| **1527** A525 | 20b ultra & blk | .25 | .25 |
| **1528** A525 | 40b bl, yel & sep | .30 | .25 |
| **1529** A525 | 55b ocher, buff & sl grn | .50 | .25 |
| **1530** A525 | 1 l gray, yel & brn | .75 | .25 |
| **1531** A525 | 1.35 l dl grn, choc & blk | 1.25 | .25 |
| **1532** A525 | 1.55 l org red, dk brn & blk | 1.25 | .25 |
| **1533** A525 | 1.75 l dk vio bl, yel & org | 2.00 | .30 |
| | *Nos. 1527-1533 (7)* | 6.30 | 1.80 |

Arms, Factory and Harvester A526

*Perf. 14½x13½*

**1962, Dec. 30 Litho.**

| | | | |
|---|---|---|---|
| **1534** A526 | 1.55 l multi | .85 | .25 |

Romanian People's Republic, 15th anniv.

Strikers at Grivita, 1933 A527

**1963, Feb. 16** *Perf. 14x13½*

| | | | |
|---|---|---|---|
| **1535** A527 | 1.75 l red, vio & yel | .80 | .25 |

30th anniv. of the strike of railroad and oil industry workers at Grivita.

Tractor Driver and "FAO" Emblem A528

55b, Farm woman, cornfield & combine. 1.55 l, Child drinking milk & milking machine. 1.75 l, Woman with basket of grapes & vineyard.

**1963, Mar. 21 Photo.** *Perf. 14½x13*

| | | | |
|---|---|---|---|
| **1536** A528 | 40b vio bl | .25 | .25 |
| **1537** A528 | 55b bis brn | .25 | .25 |
| **1538** A528 | 1.55 l rose red | .50 | .25 |
| **1539** A528 | 1.75 l green | .85 | .25 |
| | *Nos. 1536-1539 (4)* | 1.85 | 1.00 |

FAO "Freedom from Hunger" campaign.

Tomatoes — A529

40b, Hot peppers. 55b, Radishes. 75b, Eggplant. 1.20 l, Mild peppers. 3.25 l, Cucumbers, horiz.

*Perf. 13½x14, 14x13½*

**1963, Apr. 25 Litho. Unwmk.**

| | | | |
|---|---|---|---|
| **1540** A529 | 35b multi | .25 | .25 |
| **1541** A529 | 40b multi | .25 | .25 |
| **1542** A529 | 55b multi | .25 | .25 |
| **1543** A529 | 75b multi | .25 | .25 |
| **1544** A529 | 1.20 l multi | .70 | .25 |
| **1545** A529 | 3.25 l multi | 1.50 | .30 |
| | *Nos. 1540-1545 (6)* | 3.20 | 1.55 |

Woman Swimmer at Start — A530

Designs: 30b, Crawl, horiz. 55b, Butterfly stroke, horiz. 1 l, Backstroke, horiz. 1.35 l, Breaststroke, horiz. 1.55 l, Woman diver. 2 l, Water polo.

**1963, June 15** *Perf. 13x14, 14x13*

| No. | Type | Value | Color | Unused | Used |
|---|---|---|---|---|---|
| 1546 | A530 | 25b | yel brn, emer & gray | .25 | .25 |
| 1547 | A530 | 30b | ol grn, gray & yel | .25 | .25 |
| 1548 | A530 | 55b | bl, gray & red | .25 | .25 |
| 1549 | A530 | 1 l | grn, gray & red | .25 | .25 |
| 1550 | A530 | 1.35 l | ultra, car & gray | .40 | .25 |
| 1551 | A530 | 1.55 l | pur, gray & org | .85 | .25 |
| 1552 | A530 | 2 l | car rose, gray & org | .90 | .35 |
| | | | *Nos. 1546-1552 (7)* | 3.15 | 1.85 |

Chicks — A531

Domestic poultry: 30b, Hen. 40b, Goose. 55b, White cock. 70b, Duck. 1 l, Hen. 1.35 l, Tom turkey. 3.20 l, Hen.

**Fowl in Natural Colors; Inscription in Dark Blue**

**1963, May 23** *Perf. 10½*

| No. | Type | Value | Color | Unused | Used |
|---|---|---|---|---|---|
| 1553 | A531 | 20b | ultra | .25 | .25 |
| 1554 | A531 | 30b | tan | .25 | .25 |
| 1555 | A531 | 40b | org brn | .25 | .25 |
| 1556 | A531 | 55b | brt grn | .25 | .25 |
| 1557 | A531 | 70b | lilac | .25 | .25 |
| 1558 | A531 | 1 l | blue | .35 | .25 |
| 1559 | A531 | 1.35 l | ocher | .50 | .25 |
| 1560 | A531 | 3.20 l | yel grn | 1.10 | .35 |
| | | | *Nos. 1553-1560 (8)* | 3.20 | 2.10 |

Women and Globe A532

**1963, June 15 Photo.** *Perf. 14x13*

| No. | Type | Value | Color | Unused | Used |
|---|---|---|---|---|---|
| 1561 | A532 | 55b | dark blue | .40 | .25 |

Intl. Women's Cong., Moscow, June 24-29.

William M. Thackeray, Writer A533

Portraits: 50b, Eugene Delacroix, painter. 55b, Gheorghe Marinescu, physician. 1.55 l, Giuseppe Verdi, composer. 1.75 l, Stanislavski, actor and producer.

**1963, July Unwmk.** *Perf. 14x13*

**Portrait in Black**

| No. | Type | Value | Color | Unused | Used |
|---|---|---|---|---|---|
| 1562 | A533 | 40b | pale vio | .25 | .25 |
| 1563 | A533 | 50b | bister brn | .25 | .25 |
| 1564 | A533 | 55b | olive | .25 | .25 |
| 1565 | A533 | 1.55 l | rose brn | .50 | .25 |
| 1566 | A533 | 1.75 l | pale vio bl | .85 | .25 |
| | | | *Nos. 1562-1566 (5)* | 2.10 | 1.25 |

Walnuts A534

Designs: 20b, Plums. 40b, Peaches. 55b, Strawberries. 1 l, Grapes. 1.55 l, Apples. 1.60 l, Cherries. 1.75 l, Pears.

**1963, Sept. 15 Litho.** *Perf. 14x13½*

**Fruits in Natural Colors**

| No. | Type | Value | Color | Unused | Used |
|---|---|---|---|---|---|
| 1567 | A534 | 10b | pale yel & brn ol | .25 | .25 |
| 1568 | A534 | 20b | pale pink & red org | .25 | .25 |
| 1569 | A534 | 40b | lt bl & bl | .25 | .25 |
| 1570 | A534 | 55b | dl yel & rose car | .25 | .25 |
| 1571 | A534 | 1 l | pale vio & vio | .25 | .25 |
| 1572 | A534 | 1.55 l | yel grn & ultra | .45 | .25 |
| 1573 | A534 | 1.60 l | yel & bis | .75 | .25 |
| 1574 | A534 | 1.75 l | lt bl & grn | .75 | .25 |
| | | | *Nos. 1567-1574 (8)* | 3.20 | 2.00 |

Women Playing Volleyball and Map of Europe — A535

40b, 3 men players. 55b, 3 women players. 1.75 l, 2 men players. 3.20 l, Europa Cup.

**1963, Oct. 22** *Perf. 13½x14*

| No. | Type | Value | Color | Unused | Used |
|---|---|---|---|---|---|
| 1575 | A535 | 5b | gray & lil rose | .25 | .25 |
| 1576 | A535 | 40b | gray & vio bl | .25 | .25 |
| 1577 | A535 | 55b | gray & grnsh bl | .30 | .25 |
| 1578 | A535 | 1.75 l | gray & org brn | .55 | .25 |
| 1579 | A535 | 3.20 l | gray & vio | 1.25 | .35 |
| | | | *Nos. 1575-1579 (5)* | 2.60 | 1.35 |

European Volleyball Championships, Oct. 22-Nov. 4.

Pine Tree, Branch and Cone A536

Design: 1.75 l, Beech forest and branch.

*Perf. 13½*

**1963, Dec. 5 Unwmk. Photo.**

| No. | Type | Value | Color | Unused | Used |
|---|---|---|---|---|---|
| 1580 | A536 | 55b | dk grn | .25 | .25 |
| 1581 | A536 | 1.75 l | dk bl | .60 | .25 |

Reforestation program.

Silkworm Moth — A537

Designs: 20b, Chrysalis, moth and worm. 40b, Silkworm on leaf. 55b, Bee over mountains, horiz. 60b, 1.20 l, 1.35 l, 1.60 l, Bees pollinating various flowers, horiz.

**1963, Dec. 12 Litho.** *Perf. 13x14*

| No. | Type | Value | Color | Unused | Used |
|---|---|---|---|---|---|
| 1582 | A537 | 10b | multi | .30 | .25 |
| 1583 | A537 | 20b | multi | .30 | .25 |
| 1584 | A537 | 40b | multi | .30 | .25 |
| 1585 | A537 | 55b | multi | .40 | .25 |
| 1586 | A537 | 60b | multi | .50 | .25 |
| 1587 | A537 | 1.20 l | multi | .80 | .25 |
| 1588 | A537 | 1.35 l | multi | 1.00 | .25 |
| 1589 | A537 | 1.60 l | multi | 1.40 | .25 |
| | | | *Nos. 1582-1589 (8)* | 5.00 | 2.00 |

18th Century House, Ploesti — A538

Peasant Houses from Village Museum, Bucharest: 40b, Oltenia, 1875, horiz. 55b, Hunedoara, 19th Cent., horiz. 75b, Oltenia, 19th Cent. 1 l, Brasov, 1847. 1.20 l, Bacau, 19th Cent. 1.75 l, Arges, 19th Cent.

**1963, Dec. 25 Engr.** *Perf. 13*

| No. | Type | Value | Color | Unused | Used |
|---|---|---|---|---|---|
| 1590 | A538 | 20b | claret | .35 | .25 |
| 1591 | A538 | 40b | blue | .35 | .25 |
| 1592 | A538 | 55b | dl vio | .35 | .25 |
| 1593 | A538 | 75b | green | .35 | .25 |
| 1594 | A538 | 1 l | brn & mar | .65 | .25 |
| 1595 | A538 | 1.20 l | gray ol | .80 | .25 |
| 1596 | A538 | 1.75 l | dk brn & ultra | 1.60 | .25 |
| | | | *Nos. 1590-1596 (7)* | 4.45 | 1.75 |

Ski Jump A539

20b, Speed skating. 40b, Ice hockey. 55b, Women's figure skating. 60b, Slalom. 75b, Biathlon. 1 l, Bobsledding. 1.20 l, Cross-country skiing.

**1963, Nov. 25 Litho.** *Perf. 14*

| No. | Type | Value | Color | Unused | Used |
|---|---|---|---|---|---|
| 1597 | A539 | 10b | red & dk bl | .30 | .25 |
| 1598 | A539 | 20b | ultra & red brn | .30 | .25 |
| 1599 | A539 | 40b | emer & red brn | .30 | .25 |
| 1600 | A539 | 55b | vio & red brn | .40 | .25 |
| 1601 | A539 | 60b | org & vio bl | .65 | .25 |
| 1602 | A539 | 75b | lil rose & dk bl | .80 | .25 |
| 1603 | A539 | 1 l | bis & vio bl | 1.50 | .30 |
| 1604 | A539 | 1.20 l | grnsh bl & vio | 1.60 | .40 |
| | | | *Nos. 1597-1604 (8)* | 5.85 | 2.20 |

9th Winter Olympic Games, Innsbruck, Jan. 29-Feb. 9, 1964.

Exist imperf. in changed colors. Value, set $6.50.

A souvenir sheet contains one imperf. 1.50 l ultramarine and red stamp showing the Olympic Ice Stadium at Innsbruck and the Winter Games emblem. Value $6.50.

Elena Teodorini as Carmen — A540

Designs: 10b, George Stephanescu, founder of Romanian opera. 35b, Ion Bajenaru as Petru Rares. 40b, D. Popovici as Alberich. 55b, Hariclea Darclée as Tosca. 75b, George Folescu as Boris Godunov. 1 l, Jean Athanasiu as Rigoletto. 1.35 l, Traian Grosavescu as Duke in Rigoletto. 1.55 l, N. Leonard as Hoffmann.

**1964, Jan. 20 Photo.** *Perf. 13*

**Portrait in Dark Brown**

| No. | Type | Value | Color | Unused | Used |
|---|---|---|---|---|---|
| 1605 | A540 | 10b | olive | .25 | .25 |
| 1606 | A540 | 20b | ultra | .25 | .25 |
| 1607 | A540 | 35b | green | .25 | .25 |
| 1608 | A540 | 40b | grnsh bl | .25 | .25 |
| 1609 | A540 | 55b | car rose | .30 | .25 |
| 1610 | A540 | 75b | lilac | .30 | .25 |
| 1611 | A540 | 1 l | blue | .65 | .25 |
| 1612 | A540 | 1.35 l | brt vio | .90 | .25 |
| 1613 | A540 | 1.55 l | red org | 1.00 | .25 |
| | | | *Nos. 1605-1613 (9)* | 4.15 | 2.25 |

Munteanu Murgoci and Congress Emblem — A541

**1964, Feb. 5 Unwmk.** *Perf. 13*

| No. | Type | Value | Color | Unused | Used |
|---|---|---|---|---|---|
| 1614 | A541 | 1.60 l | brt bl, ind & bis | .80 | .25 |

8th Intl. Soil Congress, Bucharest.

Asculaphid A542

Insects: 10b, Thread-waisted wasp. 35b, Wasp. 40b, Rhyparioides metelkana moth. 55b, Tussock moth. 1.20 l, Kanetisa circe butterfly. 1.55 l, Beetle. 1.75 l, Horned beetle.

**1964, Feb. 20 Litho.** *Perf. 14x13*

**Insects in Natural Colors**

| No. | Type | Value | Color | Unused | Used |
|---|---|---|---|---|---|
| 1615 | A542 | 5b | pale lilac | .25 | .25 |
| 1616 | A542 | 10b | lt bl & red | .25 | .25 |
| 1617 | A542 | 35b | pale grn | .25 | .25 |
| 1618 | A542 | 40b | olive green | .25 | .25 |
| 1619 | A542 | 55b | ultra | .30 | .25 |
| 1620 | A542 | 1.20 l | pale grn & red | .50 | .25 |
| 1621 | A542 | 1.55 l | yel & brn | .70 | .25 |
| 1622 | A542 | 1.75 l | orange & red | .75 | .25 |
| | | | *Nos. 1615-1622 (8)* | 3.25 | 2.00 |

Tobacco Plant — A543

Garden flowers: 20b, Geranium. 40b, Fuchsia. 55b, Chrysanthemum. 75b, Dahlia. 1 l, Lily. 1.25 l, Day lily. 1.55 l, Marigold.

**1964, Mar. 25** *Perf. 13x14*

| No. | Type | Value | Color | Unused | Used |
|---|---|---|---|---|---|
| 1623 | A543 | 10b | dk bl, grn & bis | .25 | .25 |
| 1624 | A543 | 20b | gray, grn & red | .25 | .25 |
| 1625 | A543 | 40b | pale grn, grn & red | .25 | .25 |
| 1626 | A543 | 55b | grn, lt grn & lil | .30 | .25 |
| 1627 | A543 | 75b | cit, red & grn | .35 | .25 |
| 1628 | A543 | 1 l | dp cl, rose cl, grn & org | .50 | .25 |
| 1629 | A543 | 1.25 l | sal, vio bl & grn | .60 | .25 |
| 1630 | A543 | 1.55 l | red brn, yel & grn | .70 | .25 |
| | | | *Nos. 1623-1630 (8)* | 3.20 | 2.00 |

Jumping — A544

Horse Show Events: 40b, Dressage, horiz. 1.35 l, Jumping. 1.55 l, Galloping, horiz.

**Unwmk.**

**1964, Apr. 25 Photo.** *Perf. 13*

| No. | Type | Value | Color | Unused | Used |
|---|---|---|---|---|---|
| 1631 | A544 | 40b | lt bl, rose brn & blk | .25 | .25 |
| 1632 | A544 | 55b | lil, red & brn | .25 | .25 |
| 1633 | A544 | 1.35 l | brt grn, red & dk brn | .65 | .25 |
| 1634 | A544 | 1.55 l | pale yel, bl & dp claret | .90 | .25 |
| | | | *Nos. 1631-1634 (4)* | 2.05 | 1.00 |

Hogfish A545

Fish (Constanta Aquarium): 10b, Peacock blenny. 20b, Mediterranean scad. 40b, Sturgeon. 50b, Sea horses. 55b, Yellow gurnard. 1 l, Beluga. 3.20 l, Stingray.

**1964, May 10 Litho.** *Perf. 14*

| No. | Type | Value | Color | Unused | Used |
|---|---|---|---|---|---|
| 1635 | A545 | 5b | multi | .40 | .25 |
| 1636 | A545 | 10b | multi | .40 | .25 |
| 1637 | A545 | 20b | multi | .40 | .25 |
| 1638 | A545 | 40b | multi | .40 | .25 |
| 1639 | A545 | 50b | multi | .40 | .25 |
| 1640 | A545 | 55b | multi | .40 | .25 |
| 1641 | A545 | 1 l | multi | 1.10 | .25 |
| 1642 | A545 | 3.20 l | multi | 2.50 | .25 |
| | | | *Nos. 1635-1642 (8)* | 6.00 | 2.00 |

Mihail Eminescu — A546

Portraits: 20b, Ion Creanga. 35b, Emil Girleanu. 55b, Michelangelo. 1.20 l, Galileo Galilei. 1.75 l, William Shakespeare.

**1964, June 20 Photo. *Perf. 13***

**Portraits in Dark Brown**

**1643** A546 5b green .25 .25
**1644** A546 20b magenta .25 .25
**1645** A546 35b vermilion .25 .25
**1646** A546 55b bister .35 .25
**1647** A546 1.20 l ultra .60 .25
**1648** A546 1.75 l violet 1.00 .25
*Nos. 1643-1648 (6)* 2.70 1.50

50th death anniv. of Emil Girleanu, writer; the 75th death anniversaries of Ion Creanga and Mihail Eminescu, writers; the 400th anniv. of the death of Michelangelo and the births of Galileo and Shakespeare.

Road through Gorge — A547

Tourist Publicity: 55b, Lake Bilea and cottage. 1 l, Ski lift, Polana Brasov. 1.35 l, Ceahlaul peak and Lake Dicaz, horiz. 1.75 l, Hotel Alpin.

**1964, June 29 Engr.**

**1649** A547 40b rose brn .25 .25
**1650** A547 55b dk bl .25 .25
**1651** A547 1 l dl pur .40 .25
**1652** A547 1.35 l pale brn .55 .25
**1653** A547 1.75 l green .65 .25
*Nos. 1649-1653 (5)* 2.10 1.25

High Jump — A548

1964 Balkan Games: 40b, Javelin throw. 55b, Running. 1 l, Discus throw. 1.20 l, Hurdling. 1.55 l, Map and flags of Balkan countries.

**Size: 23x37½mm**

**1964, July 28 Photo.**

**1654** A548 30b ver, yel & yel grn .25 .25
**1655** A548 40b grn, yel, brn & vio .25 .25
**1656** A548 55b gldn brn, yel & bl grn .25 .25
**1657** A548 1 l brt bl, yel, brn & red .50 .25
**1658** A548 1.20 l pur, yel, brn & grn .65 .25

**Litho.**

**Size: 23x45mm**

**1659** A548 1.55 l multi 1.00 .25
*Nos. 1654-1659 (6)* 2.90 1.50

Factory — A549

55b, Flag, Coat of Arms, vert. 75b, Combine. 1.20 l, Apartment buildings. 2 l, Flag, coat of arms, industrial & agricultural scenes. 55b, 2 l, Inscribed "A XX A aniversare a eliberarii patriei!"

**1964, Aug. 23 Photo. *Perf. 13***

**1660** A549 55b multi .25 .25
**1661** A549 60b multi .25 .25
**1662** A549 75b multi .25 .25
**1663** A549 1.20 l multi .60 .25
*Nos. 1660-1663 (4)* 1.35 1.00

**Souvenir Sheet**

***Imperf***

**1664** A549 2 l multi 1.50 .50

20th anniv. of Romania's liberation. No. 1664 contains one stamp 110x70mm.

High Jump — A550

Sport: 30b, Wrestling. 35b, Volleyball. 40b, Canoeing. 55b, Fencing. 1.20 l, Women's gymnastics. 1.35 l, Soccer. 1.55 l, Sharpshooting.

**Olympic Rings in Blue, Yellow, Black, Green and Red**

**1964, Sept. 1 Litho.**

**1665** A550 20b yel & blk .25 .25
**1666** A550 30b lilac & blk .25 .25
**1667** A550 35b grnsh bl & blk .25 .25
**1668** A550 40b pink & blk .25 .25
**1669** A550 55b lt yel grn & blk .45 .25
**1670** A550 1.20 l org & blk .75 .25
**1671** A550 1.35 l ocher & blk 1.00 .25
**1672** A550 1.55 l bl & blk 1.10 .35
*Nos. 1665-1672 (8)* 4.30 2.10

18th Olympic Games, Tokyo, Oct. 10-25.
Nos. 1665-1669 exist imperf., in changed colors. Three other denominations exist, 1.60 l, 2 l and 2.40 l, imperf. Value, set of 8, unused $7, canceled $5.
An imperf. souvenir sheet contains a 3.25 l stamp showing a runner. Value unused $7 canceled $6.

George Enescu, Piano Keys and Neck of Violin — A551

Designs: 55b, Enescu at piano. 1.60 l, Enescu Festival medal. 1.75 l, Enescu bust by G. Anghel.

**1964, Sept. 5 Engr.**

**1673** A551 10b bl grn .30 .25
**1674** A551 55b vio blk 1.00 .25
**1675** A551 1.60 l dk red brn 1.50 .65
**1676** A551 1.75 l dk bl 2.00 .40
*Nos. 1673-1676 (4)* 4.30 1.55

3rd Intl. George Enescu Festival, Bucharest, Sept., 1964.

Black Swans A552

5b, Indian python. 35b, Ostriches. 40b, Crowned cranes. 55b, Tigers. 1 l, Lions. 1.55 l, Grevy's zebras. 2 l, Bactrian camels.

***Perf. 14x13***

**1964, Sept. 28 Litho. Unwmk.**

**1677** A552 5b multi .25 .25
**1678** A552 10b multi .25 .25
**1679** A552 35b multi .25 .25
**1680** A552 40b multi .25 .25
**1681** A552 55b multi .25 .25
**1682** A552 1 l multi .45 .25
**1683** A552 1.55 l multi .90 .25
**1684** A552 2 l multi 1.25 .25
*Nos. 1677-1684 (8)* 3.85 2.00

Issued to publicize the Bucharest Zoo. No. 1683 inscribed "BANI."

C. Brincoveanu, Stolnicul Cantacuzino, Gheorghe Lazar and Academy — A553

Designs: 40b, Alexandru Ioan Cuza, medal and University. 55b, Masks, curtain, harp, keyboard and palette, vert. 75b, Women students in laboratory and auditorium. 1 l, Savings Bank building.

***Perf. 13x13½, 13½x13***

**1964, Oct. 14 Photo.**

**1685** A553 20b multi .25 .25
**1686** A553 40b multi .25 .25
**1687** A553 55b multi .25 .25
**1688** A553 75b multi .25 .25
**1689** A553 1 l dk brn, yel & org .50 .25
*Nos. 1685-1689 (5)* 1.50 1.25

No. 1685 for 250th anniv. of the Royal Academy; Nos. 1686, 1688 cent. of the University of Bucharest; No. 1687 cent. of the Academy of Art and No. 1689 cent. of the Savings Bank.

Soldier's Head and Laurel — A554

**1964, Oct. 25 Litho. *Perf. 12x12½***

**1690** A554 55b ultra & lt bl .40 .25

Army Day.

Canadian Kayak Singles Gold Medal, Melbourne, 1956 A555

Romanian Olympic Gold Medals: 30b, Boxing, Melbourne, 1956. 35b, Rapid Silhouette Pistol, Melbourne, 1956. 40b, Women's High Jump, Rome, 1960. 55b, Wrestling, Rome, 1960. 1.20 l, Clay Pigeon Shooting, Rome, 1960. 1.35 l, Women's High Jump, Tokyo, 1964. 1.55 l, Javelin, Tokyo, 1964.

**1964, Nov. 30 Photo. *Perf. 13½***

**Medals in Gold and Brown**

**1691** A555 20b pink & ultra .25 .25
**1692** A555 30b yel grn & ultra .25 .25
**1693** A555 35b bluish grn & ultra .25 .25
**1694** A555 40b lil & ultra .50 .25
**1695** A555 55b org & ultra .60 .25
**1696** A555 1.20 l ol grn & ultra .90 .25
**1697** A555 1.35 l gldn brn & ultra 1.00 .25
**1698** A555 1.55 l rose lil & ultra 1.50 .35
*Nos. 1691-1698 (8)* 5.25 2.10

Romanian athletes who won gold medals in three Olympic Games.
Nos. 1691-1695 exist imperf., in changed colors. Three other denominations exist, 1.60 l, 2 l and 2.40 l, imperf. Value, set of 8, unused $7, canceled $5.
A 10 l souvenir sheet shows the 1964 Olympic gold medal and world map. Value unused $7, canceled $5.

Strawberries A556

Designs: 35b, Blackberries. 40b, Raspberries. 55b, Rose hips. 1.20 l, Blueberries. 1.35 l, Cornelian cherries. 1.55 l, Hazelnuts. 2.55 l, Cherries.

**1964, Dec. 20 Litho. *Perf. 13½x14***

**1703** A556 5b gray, red & grn .25 .25
**1704** A556 35b ocher, grn & dk vio bl .25 .25
**1705** A556 40b pale vio, car & grn .30 .25
**1706** A556 55b yel grn, grn & red .30 .25
**1707** A556 1.20 l sal pink, grn, brn & ind .50 .25
**1708** A556 1.35 l lt bl, grn & red .60 .25
**1709** A556 1.55 l gldn brn, grn & ocher 1.00 .25
**1710** A556 2.55 l ultra, grn & red 1.25 .25
*Nos. 1703-1710 (8)* 4.45 2.00

Syncom 3 — A557

Space Satellites: 40b, Syncom 3 over TV antennas. 55b, Ranger 7 reaching moon, horiz. 1 l, Ranger 7 and moon close-up, horiz. 1.20 l, Voskhod. 5 l, Konstantin Feoktistov, Vladimir M. Komarov, Boris B. Yegorov and Voskhod.

***Perf. 13x14, 14x13***

**1965, Jan. 5 Litho. Unwmk.**

**Size: 22x38mm, 38x22mm**

**1711** A557 30b multi .30 .25
**1712** A557 40b multi .30 .25
**1713** A557 55b multi .50 .25
**1714** A557 1 l multi .60 .25
**1715** A557 1.20 l multi, horiz. .90 .25

***Perf. 13½x13***

**Size: 52x30mm**

**1716** A557 5 l multi 2.10 .75
*Nos. 1711-1716 (6)* 4.70 2.00

For surcharge see No. 1737.

UN Headquarters, NY — A558

1.60 l, Arms, flag of Romania, UN emblem.

**1965, Jan. 25 *Perf. 12x12½***

**1717** A558 55b ultra, red & gold .45 .25
**1718** A558 1.60 l ultra, red, gold & yel .80 .25

20th anniv. of the UN and 10th anniv. of Romania's membership in the UN.

Greek Tortoise — A559

Reptiles: 10b, Bull lizard. 20b, Three-lined lizard. 40b, Sand lizard. 55b, Slow worm. 60b, Sand viper. 1 l, Desert lizard. 1.20 l, Orsini's viper. 1.35 l, Caspian whipsnake. 3.25 l, Four-lined snake.

**1965, Feb. 25 Photo. *Perf. 13½***

| | | | | |
|---|---|---|---|---|
| **1719** A559 | 5b | multi | .25 | .25 |
| **1720** A559 | 10b | multi | .25 | .25 |
| **1721** A559 | 20b | multi | .25 | .25 |
| **1722** A559 | 40b | multi | .40 | .25 |
| **1723** A559 | 55b | multi | .40 | .25 |
| **1724** A559 | 60b | multi | .45 | .25 |
| **1725** A559 | 1 l | multi | .60 | .25 |
| **1726** A559 | 1.20 l | multi | .70 | .25 |
| **1727** A559 | 1.35 l | multi | .90 | .25 |
| **1728** A559 | 3.25 l | multi | 1.75 | .25 |
| | | *Nos. 1719-1728 (10)* | 5.95 | 2.50 |

White Persian Cats — A560

Designs: 1.35 l, Siamese cat. Others; Various European cats. (5b, 10b, 3.25 l, horiz.)

**1965, Mar. 20 Litho.**

**Size: 41x29mm, 29x41mm**

**Cats in Natural Colors**

| | | | | |
|---|---|---|---|---|
| **1729** A560 | 5b | brn org & blk | .25 | .25 |
| **1730** A560 | 10b | brt bl & blk | .25 | .25 |
| **1731** A560 | 40b | yel grn, yel & blk | .40 | .25 |
| **1732** A560 | 55b | rose red & blk | .55 | .25 |
| **1733** A560 | 60b | yel & blk | .90 | .25 |
| **1734** A560 | 75b | lt vio & blk | 1.10 | .25 |
| **1735** A560 | 1.35 l | red org & blk | 1.40 | .25 |

***Perf. 13x13½***

**Size: 62x29mm**

| | | | | |
|---|---|---|---|---|
| **1736** A560 | 3.25 l | blue | 2.50 | .75 |
| | | *Nos. 1729-1736 (8)* | 7.35 | 2.50 |

**No. 1714 Surcharged in Violet**

**1965, Apr. 25 *Perf. 14x13***

| | | | | |
|---|---|---|---|---|
| **1737** A557 | 5 l on 1 l | multi | 14.00 | 14.00 |

Flight of the US rocket Ranger 9 to the moon, Mar. 24, 1965.

Dante Alighieri — A561

40b, Ion Bianu, philologist and historian. 55b, Anton Bacalbasa, writer. 60b, Vasile Conta, philosopher. 1 l, Jean Sibelius, Finnish composer. 1.35 l, Horace, Roman poet.

**1965, May 10 Photo. *Perf. 13½***

**Portrait in Black**

| | | | | |
|---|---|---|---|---|
| **1738** A561 | 40b | chalky blue | .25 | .25 |
| **1739** A561 | 55b | bister | .25 | .25 |
| **1740** A561 | 60b | light lilac | .25 | .25 |
| **1741** A561 | 1 l | dl red brn | .45 | .25 |
| **1742** A561 | 1.35 l | olive | .60 | .25 |
| **1743** A561 | 1.75 l | orange red | 1.10 | .25 |
| | | *Nos. 1738-1743 (6)* | 2.90 | 1.50 |

ITU Emblem, Old and New Communication Equipment — A562

**1965, May 15 Engr.**

| | | | | |
|---|---|---|---|---|
| **1744** A562 | 1.75 l | ultra | .90 | .40 |

ITU, centenary.

Iron Gate, Danube — A562a

Arms of Yugoslavia and Romania and Djerdap Dam — A562b

55b (50d), Iron Gate hydroelectric plant & dam.

***Perf. 12½x12***

**1965, Apr. 30 Litho. Unwmk.**

| | | | | |
|---|---|---|---|---|
| **1745** A562a | 30b (25d) | lt bl & grn | .25 | .25 |
| **1746** A562a | 55b (50d) | lt bl & dk red | .45 | .25 |

**Miniature Sheet**

***Perf. 13½x13***

| | | | | |
|---|---|---|---|---|
| **1747** A562b | | Sheet of 4 | 3.00 | 2.25 |
| *a.* | | 80b multi | .35 | .35 |
| *b.* | | 1.20 l multi | .70 | .70 |

Issued simultaneously by Romania and Yugoslavia for the start of construction of the Iron Gate hydroelectric plant and dam. Valid for postage in both countries.

No. 1747 contains one each of Nos. 1747a, 1747b and Yugoslavia Nos. 771a and 771b. Only Nos. 1747a and 1747b were valid in Romania. Sold for 4 l. See Yugoslavia Nos. 769-771.

Small-bore Rifle Shooting, Kneeling — A563

Designs: 40b, Rifle shooting, prone. 55b, Rapid-fire pistol and map of Europe. 1 l, Free pistol and map of Europe. 1.60 l, Small-bore rifle, standing, and map of Europe. 2 l, 5 l, Marksmen in various shooting positions (all horizontal).

***Perf. 12x12½, 12½x12***

**1965, May 30 Litho. Unwmk.**

**Size: 23x43mm, 43x23mm**

| | | | | |
|---|---|---|---|---|
| **1748** A563 | 20b | multi | .25 | .25 |
| **1749** A563 | 40b | dl grn, pink & blk | .25 | .25 |
| **1750** A563 | 55b | multi | .25 | .25 |
| **1751** A563 | 1 l | pale grn, blk & ocher | .35 | .25 |
| **1752** A563 | 1.60 l | multi | .60 | .25 |

***Perf. 13½***

**Size: 51x28mm**

| | | | | |
|---|---|---|---|---|
| **1753** A563 | 2 l | multi | .70 | .25 |
| | | *Nos. 1748-1753 (6)* | 2.40 | 1.50 |

European Shooting Championships, Bucharest.

Nos. 1749-1752 were issued imperf. in changed colors. Two other denominations exist, 3.25 l and 5 l, imperf. Value, set of 6, unused $5, canceled $2.

Fat-Frumos and the Giant A564

Fairy Tales: 40b, Fat-Frumos on horseback and Ileana Cosinzeana. 55b, Harap Alb and the Bear. 1 l, "The Moralist Wolf." 1.35 l, "The Ox and the Calf." 2 l, Wolf and bear pulling sled.

**1965, June 25 Photo. *Perf. 13***

| | | | | |
|---|---|---|---|---|
| **1756** A564 | 20b | multi | .25 | .25 |
| **1757** A564 | 40b | multi | .25 | .25 |
| **1758** A564 | 55b | multi | .30 | .25 |
| **1759** A564 | 1 l | multi | .45 | .25 |
| **1760** A564 | 1.35 l | multi | .70 | .25 |
| **1761** A564 | 2 l | multi | 1.00 | .25 |
| | | *Nos. 1756-1761 (6)* | 2.95 | 1.50 |

Bee and Blossoms — A565

Design: 1.60 l, Exhibition Hall, horiz.

***Perf. 12x12½, 12½x12***

**1965, July 28 Litho. Unwmk.**

| | | | | |
|---|---|---|---|---|
| **1762** A565 | 55b | org, bl & pink | .35 | .25 |
| **1763** A565 | 1.60 l | multi | .60 | .25 |

20th Congress of the Intl Federation of Beekeeping Assocs. (Apimondia), Bucharest, Aug. 26-31.

Space Achievements A566

Designs: 1.75 l, Col. Pavel Belyayev, Lt. Col. Alexei Leonov and Voskhod 2. 2.40 l, Early Bird over globe. 3.20 l, Lt. Col. Gordon Cooper and Lt. Com. Charles Conrad, Gemini 3 and globe.

**1965, Aug. 25 Litho. *Perf. 12x12½***

| | | | | |
|---|---|---|---|---|
| **1764** A566 | 1.75 l | dk bl, bl & ver | .80 | .25 |
| **1765** A566 | 2.40 l | multi | 1.10 | .25 |
| **1766** A566 | 3.20 l | dk bl, lt bl & ver | 2.25 | .35 |
| | | *Nos. 1764-1766 (3)* | 4.15 | .85 |

European Quail — A567

Birds: 10b, Eurasian woodcock. 20b, Eurasian snipe. 40b, Turtle dove. 55b, Mallard. 60b, White-fronted goose. 1 l, Eurasian crane. 1.20 l, Glossy ibis. 1.35 l, Mute swan. 3.25 l, White pelican.

**1965, Sept. 10 Photo. *Perf. 13½***

**Size: 34x34mm**

**Birds in Natural Colors**

| | | | | |
|---|---|---|---|---|
| **1767** A567 | 5b | red brn & rose lil | .25 | .25 |
| **1768** A567 | 10b | red brn & yel grn | .25 | .25 |
| **1769** A567 | 20b | brn & bl grn | .25 | .25 |
| **1770** A567 | 40b | lil & org brn | .25 | .25 |
| **1771** A567 | 55b | brt grn & lt brn | .25 | .25 |
| **1772** A567 | 60b | dl org & bl | .30 | .25 |
| **1773** A567 | 1 l | red & lil | .40 | .25 |
| **1774** A567 | 1.20 l | dk brn & grn | .60 | .25 |
| **1775** A567 | 1.35 l | org & ultra | .80 | .25 |

**Size: 32x73mm**

| | | | | |
|---|---|---|---|---|
| **1776** A567 | 3.25 l | ultra & sep | 2.10 | .30 |
| | | *Nos. 1767-1776 (10)* | 5.45 | 2.55 |

Marx and Lenin — A568

**1965, Sept. 6 Photo.**

| | | | | |
|---|---|---|---|---|
| **1777** A568 | 55b | red, blk & yel | .50 | .25 |

6th Conference of Postal Ministers of Communist Countries, Peking, June 21-July 15.

Vasile Alecsandri — A569

**1965, Oct. 9 Unwmk. *Perf. 13½***

| | | | | |
|---|---|---|---|---|
| **1778** A569 | 55b | red brn, dk brn & gold | .50 | .25 |

Alecsandri (1821-1890), statesman and poet.

Bird-of-Paradise Flower — A570

Flowers from Cluj Botanical Gardens: 10b, Stanhope orchid. 20b, Paphiopedilum insigne. 30b, Zanzibar water lily, horiz. 40b, Ferocactus, horiz. 55b, Cotton blossom, horiz. 1 l, Hibiscus, horiz. 1.35 l, Gloxinia. 1.75 l, Victoria water lily, horiz. 2.30 l, Hibiscus, bird-of-paradise flower and greenhouse.

*Perf. 12x12½, 12½x12*

**1965, Oct. 25** **Litho.**

**Size: 23x43mm, 43x23mm**

**Flowers in Natural Colors**

| | | | | |
|---|---|---|---|---|
| **1779** | A570 | 5b brown | .25 | .25 |
| **1780** | A570 | 10b green | .25 | .25 |
| **1781** | A570 | 20b dk bl | .30 | .25 |
| **1782** | A570 | 30b vio bl | .30 | .25 |
| **1783** | A570 | 40b red brn | .30 | .25 |
| **1784** | A570 | 55b dk red | .30 | .25 |
| **1785** | A570 | 1 l ol grn | .45 | .25 |
| **1786** | A570 | 1.35 l violet | .60 | .25 |
| **1787** | A570 | 1.75 l dk grn | 1.00 | .25 |

***Perf. 13½***

**Size: 52x30mm**

| | | | | |
|---|---|---|---|---|
| **1788** | A570 | 2.30 l green | 1.50 | .35 |
| | | *Nos. 1779-1788 (10)* | 5.25 | 2.60 |

The orchid on No. 1780 is attached to the bottom of the limb.

Running — A571

**1965, Nov. 10** **Photo.** ***Perf. 13½***

| | | | | |
|---|---|---|---|---|
| **1789** | A571 | 55b shown | .25 | .25 |
| **1790** | A571 | 1.55 l Soccer | .50 | .25 |
| **1791** | A571 | 1.75 l Woman diver | .65 | .25 |
| **1792** | A571 | 2 l Mountaineering | .70 | .25 |
| **1793** | A571 | 5 l Canoeing, horiz. | 1.60 | .40 |
| | | *Nos. 1789-1793 (5)* | 3.70 | 1.40 |

Spartacist Games. No. 1793 commemorates the Romanian victory in the European Kayak Championships.

Pigeon and Post Horn — A572

Designs: 1 l, Pigeon on television antenna and post horn, horiz. 1.75 l, Flying pigeon and post horn, horiz.

**1965, Nov. 15** **Engr.**

| | | | | |
|---|---|---|---|---|
| **1794** | A572 | 55b + 45b label | .50 | .25 |
| **1795** | A572 | 1 l green & brown | .50 | .25 |
| **1796** | A572 | 1.75 l ol grn & sepia | 1.00 | .25 |
| | | *Nos. 1794-1796 (3)* | 2.00 | .75 |

Issued for Stamp Day. No. 1794 is printed with alternating label showing post rider and emblem of Romanian Philatelists' Association and 45b additional charge. Stamp and label are imperf. between.

Chamois and Hunting Trophy A573

Hunting Trophy and: 1 l, Brown bear. 1.60 l, Red deer. 1.75 l, Wild boar. 3.20 l, Antlers of red deer.

**1965, Dec. 10** **Photo.** ***Perf. 13½***

**Size: 37x22mm**

| | | | | |
|---|---|---|---|---|
| **1797** | A573 | 55b rose lil, yel & brn | .35 | .25 |
| **1798** | A573 | 1 l brt grn, red & brn | .45 | .25 |
| **1799** | A573 | 1.60 l lt vio bl, org & brn | 1.25 | .25 |
| **1800** | A573 | 1.75 l rose, grn & blk | 1.60 | .25 |

**Size: 48x36½mm**

| | | | | |
|---|---|---|---|---|
| **1801** | A573 | 3.20 l gray, gold, blk & org | 2.50 | .40 |
| | | *Nos. 1797-1801 (5)* | 6.15 | 1.40 |

Probe III Photographing Moon — A574

Designs: 5b, Proton I space station, vert. 15b, Molniya I telecommunication satellite, vert. 3.25 l, Mariner IV and Mars picture, vert. 5 l, Gemini 5.

***Perf. 12x12½, 12½x12***

**1965, Dec. 25** **Litho.**

| | | | | |
|---|---|---|---|---|
| **1802** | A574 | 5b multi | .25 | .25 |
| **1803** | A574 | 10b vio bl, red & gray | .25 | .25 |
| **1804** | A574 | 15b pur, gray & org | .25 | .25 |
| **1805** | A574 | 3.25 l vio bl, blk & red | 2.25 | .25 |
| **1806** | A574 | 5 l dk bl, gray & red org | 3.50 | .45 |
| | | *Nos. 1802-1806 (5)* | 6.50 | 1.45 |

Achievements in space research.

Cocker Spaniel — A575

Hunting Dogs: 5b, Dachshund (triangle). 40b, Retriever. 55b, Terrier. 60b, Red setter. 75b, White setter. 1.55 l, Pointers (rectangle). 3.25 l, Duck hunter with retriever (rectangle).

**1965, Dec. 28** **Photo.** ***Perf. 13½***

**Size: 30x42mm**

| | | | | |
|---|---|---|---|---|
| **1807** | A575 | 5b multi | .25 | .25 |

**Size: 33½x33½mm**

| | | | | |
|---|---|---|---|---|
| **1808** | A575 | 10b multi | .25 | .25 |
| **1809** | A575 | 40b multi | .30 | .25 |
| **1810** | A575 | 55b multi | .45 | .25 |
| **1811** | A575 | 60b multi | .65 | .25 |
| **1812** | A575 | 75b multi | .90 | .25 |

**Size: 43x28mm**

| | | | | |
|---|---|---|---|---|
| **1813** | A575 | 1.55 l multi | 1.75 | .25 |
| **1814** | A575 | 3.25 l multi | 3.50 | .75 |
| | | *Nos. 1807-1814 (8)* | 8.05 | 2.50 |

Chessboard, Queen and Jester — A576

Chessboard and: 20b, 1.60 l, Pawn and emblem. 55b, 1 l, Rook and knight on horseback.

**1966, Feb. 25** **Litho.** ***Perf. 13***

| | | | | |
|---|---|---|---|---|
| **1815** | A576 | 20b multi | .25 | .25 |
| **1816** | A576 | 40b multi | .30 | .25 |
| **1817** | A576 | 55b multi | .45 | .25 |
| **1818** | A576 | 1 l multi | .75 | .25 |
| **1819** | A576 | 1.60 l multi | 1.25 | .25 |
| **1820** | A576 | 3.25 l multi | 2.00 | 1.60 |
| | | *Nos. 1815-1820 (6)* | 5.00 | 2.85 |

Chess Olympics in Cuba.

Tractor, Grain and Sun — A577

**1966, Mar. 5**

| | | | | |
|---|---|---|---|---|
| **1821** | A577 | 55b lt grn & ocher | .40 | .25 |

Founding congress of the National Union of Cooperative Farms.

Gheorghe Gheorghiu-Dej A578

**1966, Mar.** **Photo.** ***Perf. 13½***

| | | | | |
|---|---|---|---|---|
| **1822** | A578 | 55b gold & blk | .60 | .40 |
| *a.* | | 5 l souvenir sheet | 4.50 | 3.75 |

1st death anniv. of Pres. Gheorghe Gheorghiu-Dej (1901-65). No. 1822a contains design similar to No. 1822 with signature of Gheorghiu-Dej.

Congress Emblem — A579

**1966, Mar. 21** ***Perf. 13x14½***

| | | | | |
|---|---|---|---|---|
| **1823** | A579 | 55b yel & red | .40 | .25 |

1966 Congress of Communist Youth.

Folk Dancers of Moldavia — A580

Folk Dances: 40b, Oltenia. 55b, Maramaros. 1 l, Muntenia. 1.60 l, Banat. 2 l, Transylvania.

**1966, Apr. 4** **Engr.** ***Perf. 13½***

**Center in Black**

| | | | | |
|---|---|---|---|---|
| **1824** | A580 | 30b lilac | .25 | .25 |
| **1825** | A580 | 40b brick red | .25 | .25 |
| **1826** | A580 | 55b brt bl grn | .30 | .25 |
| **1827** | A580 | 1 l maroon | .50 | .25 |
| **1828** | A580 | 1.60 l dk bl | 1.00 | .25 |
| **1829** | A580 | 2 l yel grn | 1.75 | .30 |
| | | *Nos. 1824-1829 (6)* | 4.05 | 1.55 |

Soccer Game — A581

Designs: 10b, 15b, 55b, 1.75 l, Scenes of soccer play. 4 l, Jules Rimet Cup.

**1966, Apr. 25** **Litho.** **Unwmk.**

| | | | | |
|---|---|---|---|---|
| **1830** | A581 | 5b multi | .25 | .25 |
| **1831** | A581 | 10b multi | .25 | .25 |
| **1832** | A581 | 15b multi | .25 | .25 |
| **1833** | A581 | 55b multi | .45 | .25 |
| **1834** | A581 | 1.75 l multi | 1.10 | .25 |
| **1835** | A581 | 4 l gold & multi | 2.50 | .60 |
| *a.* | | 10 l souv. sheet | 6.00 | 5.50 |
| | | *Nos. 1830-1835 (6)* | 4.80 | 1.85 |

World Cup Soccer Championship, Wembley, England, July 11-30.

No. 1835a contains one imperf. 10 l multicolored stamp in design of 4 l, but larger (32x46mm). No gum. Issued June 20.

Symbols of Industry A582

**1966, May 14** **Photo.**

| | | | | |
|---|---|---|---|---|
| **1836** | A582 | 55b multi | .40 | .25 |

Romanian Trade Union Congress.

Red-breasted Flycatcher A583

Song Birds: 10b, Red crossbill. 15b, Great reed warbler. 20b, European redstart. 55b, European robin. 1.20 l, White-spotted bluethroat. 1.55 l, Yellow wagtail. 3.20 l, Common penduline tit.

**1966, May 25** **Photo.** ***Perf. 13½***

| | | | | |
|---|---|---|---|---|
| **1837** | A583 | 5b gold & multi | .40 | .25 |
| **1838** | A583 | 10b sil & multi | .40 | .25 |
| **1839** | A583 | 15b gold & multi | .40 | .25 |
| **1840** | A583 | 20b sil & multi | .40 | .25 |
| **1841** | A583 | 55b sil & multi | .50 | .25 |
| **1842** | A583 | 1.20 l gold & multi | .75 | .25 |
| **1843** | A583 | 1.55 l sil & multi | 2.25 | .30 |
| **1844** | A583 | 3.20 l gold & multi | 3.50 | .50 |
| | | *Nos. 1837-1844 (8)* | 8.60 | 2.30 |

Venera 3 (USSR) — A584

Designs: 20b, FR-1 (France). 1.60 l, Luna 9 (USSR). 5 l, Gemini 6 and 7 (US).

**1966, June 25**

| | | | | |
|---|---|---|---|---|
| **1845** | A584 | 10b dp vio, gray & red | .30 | .25 |
| **1846** | A584 | 20b ultra, blk & red | .30 | .25 |
| **1847** | A584 | 1.60 l dk bl, blk & red | .85 | .25 |
| **1848** | A584 | 5 l bl, blk, brn & red | 2.25 | .40 |
| | | *Nos. 1845-1848 (4)* | 3.70 | 1.15 |

International achievements in space.

Urechia Nestor — A585

Portraits: 5b, George Cosbuc. 10b, Gheorghe Sincai. 40b, Aron Pumnul. 55b, Stefan Luchian. 1 l, Sun Yat-sen. 1.35 l, Gottfried Wilhelm Leibnitz. 1.60 l, Romain Rolland. 1.75 l, Ion Ghica. 3.25 l, Constantin Cantacuzino.

**1966, June 28**

| No. | Type | Description | Unused | Used |
|---|---|---|---|---|
| **1849** | A585 | 5b grn, blk & dk bl | .25 | .25 |
| **1850** | A585 | 10b rose car, grn & blk | .25 | .25 |
| **1851** | A585 | 20b grn, plum & blk | .25 | .25 |
| **1852** | A585 | 40b vio bl, brn & blk | .25 | .25 |
| **1853** | A585 | 55b brn org, bl grn & blk | .25 | .25 |
| **1854** | A585 | 1 l ocher, vio & blk | .25 | .25 |
| **1855** | A585 | 1.35 l bl & blk | .35 | .25 |
| **1856** | A585 | 1.60 l brt grn, dl vio & blk | .55 | .25 |
| **1857** | A585 | 1.75 l org, dl vio & blk | .55 | .25 |
| **1858** | A585 | 3.25 l bl, dk car & blk | 1.00 | .25 |
| | | *Nos. 1849-1858 (10)* | 3.95 | 2.50 |

Cultural anniversaries.

Country House, by Gheorghe Petrascu — A586

Paintings: 10b, Peasant Woman, by Nicolae Grigorescu, vert. 20b, Reapers at Rest, by Camil Ressu. 55b, Man with the Blue Cap, by Van Eyck, vert. 1.55 l, Train Compartment, by Daumier. 3.25 l, Betrothal of the Virgin, by El Greco, vert.

**1966, July 25** **Unwmk.**

**Gold Frame**

| No. | Type | Description | Unused | Used |
|---|---|---|---|---|
| **1859** | A586 | 5b Prus grn & brn org | .25 | .25 |
| **1860** | A586 | 10b red brn & crim | .25 | .25 |
| **1861** | A586 | 20b brn & brt grn | .30 | .25 |
| **1862** | A586 | 55b vio bl & lil | .40 | .25 |
| **1863** | A586 | 1.55 l dk sl grn & org | 1.90 | .40 |
| **1864** | A586 | 3.25 l vio & ultra | 4.00 | 1.25 |
| | | *Nos. 1859-1864 (6)* | 7.10 | 2.65 |

See Nos. 1907-1912.

Hottonia Palustris A587

Marine Flora: 10b, Ceratophyllum submersum. 20b, Aldrovanda vesiculosa. 40b, Callitriche verna. 55b, Vallisneria spiralis. 1 l, Elodea Canadensis rich. 1.55 l, Hippuris vulgaris. 3.25 l, Myriophyllum spicatum.

**1966, Aug. 25** **Litho.** ***Perf. 13½***

**Size: 28x40mm**

| No. | Type | Description | Unused | Used |
|---|---|---|---|---|
| **1865** | A587 | 5b multi | .25 | .25 |
| **1866** | A587 | 10b multi | .25 | .25 |
| **1867** | A587 | 20b multi | .25 | .25 |
| **1868** | A587 | 40b multi | .25 | .25 |
| **1869** | A587 | 55b multi | .25 | .25 |
| **1870** | A587 | 1 l multi | .45 | .25 |
| **1871** | A587 | 1.55 l multi | .70 | .25 |

**Size: 28x50mm**

| No. | Type | Description | Unused | Used |
|---|---|---|---|---|
| **1872** | A587 | 3.25 l multi | 1.40 | .35 |
| | | *Nos. 1865-1872 (8)* | 3.80 | 2.10 |

Derivation of the Meter — A588

Design: 1 l, Metric system symbols.

**1966, Sept. 10** **Photo.** ***Perf. 13½***

| No. | Type | Description | Unused | Used |
|---|---|---|---|---|
| **1873** | A588 | 55b salmon & ultra | .30 | .25 |
| **1874** | A588 | 1 l lt grn & vio | .40 | .25 |

Introduction of metric system in Romania, centenary.

Statue of Ovid and Medical School Emblem — A589

Line Integral Denoting Work — A590

I. H. Radulescu, M. Kogalniceanu and T. Savulescu — A591

Design: 1 l, Academy centenary medal.

**1966, Sept. 30** **Size: 22x27mm**

| No. | Type | Description | Unused | Used |
|---|---|---|---|---|
| **1875** | A589 | 40b lil gray, ultra, sep & gold | .25 | .25 |
| **1876** | A590 | 55b gray, brn, red & gold | .25 | .25 |

**Size: 22x34mm**

| No. | Type | Description | Unused | Used |
|---|---|---|---|---|
| **1877** | A589 | 1 l ultra, brn & gold | .45 | .25 |

**Size: 66x28mm**

| No. | Type | Description | Unused | Used |
|---|---|---|---|---|
| **1878** | A591 | 3 l org, dk brn & gold | 1.10 | .30 |
| | | *Nos. 1875-1878 (4)* | 2.05 | 1.05 |

Centenary of the Romanian Academy.

Stone Crab A592

Molluscs and Crustaceans:5b, Crawfish. 10b, Nassa reticulata, vert. 40b, Campylaea trizona. 55b, Helix lucorum. 1.35 l, Mytilus galloprovincialis. 1.75 l, Lymnaea stagnalis. 3.25 l, Anodonta cygnaea. (10b, 40b, 55b, 1.75 l, are snails; 1.35 l, 3.25 l, are bivalves).

**1966, Oct. 15**

**Animals in Natural Colors**

| No. | Type | Description | Unused | Used |
|---|---|---|---|---|
| **1879** | A592 | 5b dp org | .25 | .25 |
| **1880** | A592 | 10b lt bl | .25 | .25 |
| **1881** | A592 | 20b pale lil | .25 | .25 |
| **1882** | A592 | 40b yel grn | .25 | .25 |
| **1883** | A592 | 55b car rose | .25 | .25 |
| **1884** | A592 | 1.35 l brt grn | .55 | .25 |
| **1885** | A592 | 1.75 l ultra | .65 | .25 |
| **1886** | A592 | 3.25 l brt org | 1.60 | .35 |
| | | *Nos. 1879-1886 (8)* | 4.05 | 2.10 |

Cave Bear A593

Prehistoric Animals: 10b, Mammoth. 15b, Bison. 55b, Cave elephant. 1.55 l, Stags. 4 l, Dinotherium.

**1966, Nov. 25** **Size: 36x22mm**

| No. | Type | Description | Unused | Used |
|---|---|---|---|---|
| **1887** | A593 | 5b ultra, bl grn & red brn | .25 | .25 |
| **1888** | A593 | 10b vio, emer & brn | .25 | .25 |
| **1889** | A593 | 15b ol, grn & dk brn | .25 | .25 |
| **1890** | A593 | 55b lil, emer & brn | .30 | .25 |
| **1891** | A593 | 1.55 l ultra, grn & brn | .95 | .25 |

**Size: 43x27mm**

| No. | Type | Description | Unused | Used |
|---|---|---|---|---|
| **1892** | A593 | 4 l rose car, grn & brn | 1.50 | .50 |
| | | *Nos. 1887-1892 (6)* | 3.50 | 1.75 |

Putna Monastery, 500th Anniv. A594

**1966** **Photo.** ***Perf. 13½***

| No. | Type | Description | Unused | Used |
|---|---|---|---|---|
| **1893** | A594 | 2 l multi | .70 | .25 |

Yuri A. Gagarin and Vostok 1 — A595

Russian Achievements in Space: 10b, Trajectory of Sputnik 1 around globe, horiz. 25b, Valentina Tereshkova and globe with trajectory of Vostok 6. 40b, Andrian G. Nikolayev, Pavel R. Popovich and globe with trajectory of Vostok 3 and 4. 55b, Alexei Leonov walking in space.

**1967, Feb. 15** **Photo.** ***Perf. 13½***

| No. | Type | Description | Unused | Used |
|---|---|---|---|---|
| **1894** | A595 | 10b silver & multi | .25 | .25 |
| **1895** | A595 | 20b silver & multi | .25 | .25 |
| **1896** | A595 | 25b silver & multi | .25 | .25 |
| **1897** | A595 | 40b silver & multi | .35 | .25 |
| **1898** | A595 | 55b silver & multi | .45 | .25 |
| | | *Nos. 1894-1898,C163-C166 (9)* | 5.40 | 2.85 |

Ten years of space exploration.

Barn Owl A596

Birds of Prey: 20b, Eagle owl. 40b, Saker falcon. 55b, Egyptian vulture. 75b, Osprey. 1 l, Griffon vulture. 1.20 l, Lammergeier. 1.75 l, Cinereous vulture.

**1967, Mar. 20** **Photo.** **Unwmk.**

**Birds in Natural Colors**

| No. | Type | Description | Unused | Used |
|---|---|---|---|---|
| **1899** | A596 | 10b vio & olive | .30 | .25 |
| **1900** | A596 | 20b bl & org | .35 | .25 |
| **1901** | A596 | 40b emer & org | .30 | .25 |
| **1902** | A596 | 55b yel grn & ocher | .35 | .25 |
| **1903** | A596 | 75b rose lil & grn | .35 | .25 |
| **1904** | A596 | 1 l yel org & blk | .70 | .25 |
| **1905** | A596 | 1.20 l claret & yel | 1.25 | .25 |
| **1906** | A596 | 1.75 l sal pink & gray | 1.75 | .50 |
| | | *Nos. 1899-1906 (8)* | 5.35 | 2.25 |

**Painting Type of 1966**

10b, Woman in Fancy Dress, by Ion Andreescu. 20b, Washwomen, by J. Al. Steriadi. 40b, Women weavers, by St. Dimitrescu, vert. 1.55 l, Venus and Amor, by Lucas Cranach, vert. 3.20 l, Hercules & the Lion of Nemea, by Rubens. 5 l, Haman Asking Esther's Forgiveness, by Rembrandt, vert.

**1967, Mar. 30** ***Perf. 13½***

**Gold Frame**

| No. | Type | Description | Unused | Used |
|---|---|---|---|---|
| **1907** | A586 | 10b dp bl & rose red | .25 | .25 |
| **1908** | A586 | 20b dp grn & bis | .25 | .25 |
| **1909** | A586 | 40b carmine & bl | .25 | .25 |
| **1910** | A586 | 1.55 l dp plum & lt ultra | .50 | .25 |
| **1911** | A586 | 3.20 l brown & grn | .90 | .25 |
| **1912** | A586 | 5 l ol grn & org | 2.00 | .45 |
| | | *Nos. 1907-1912 (6)* | 4.15 | 1.70 |

Mlle. Pogany, by Brancusi A597

Sculptures: 5b, Girl's head. 10b, The Sleeping Muse, horiz. 20b, The Infinite Column. 40b, The Kiss, horiz. 55b, Earth Wisdom (seated woman). 3.25 l, Gate of the Kiss.

**1967, Apr. 27** **Photo.** ***Perf. 13½***

| No. | Type | Description | Unused | Used |
|---|---|---|---|---|
| **1913** | A597 | 5b dl yel, blk brn & ver | .25 | .25 |
| **1914** | A597 | 10b bl grn, blk & lil | .25 | .25 |
| **1915** | A597 | 20b lt bl, blk & rose red | .25 | .25 |
| **1916** | A597 | 40b pink, sep & brt grn | .25 | .30 |
| **1917** | A597 | 55b yel grn, blk & ultra | .35 | .25 |
| **1918** | A597 | 1.20 l bluish lil, ol blk & org | .85 | .25 |
| **1919** | A597 | 3.25 l emer, blk & cer | 1.50 | .75 |
| | | *Nos. 1913-1919 (7)* | 3.70 | 2.30 |

Constantin Brancusi (1876-1957), sculptor.

Coins of 1867 A598

Design: 1.20 l, Coins of 1966.

**1967, May 4**

| No. | Type | Description | Unused | Used |
|---|---|---|---|---|
| **1920** | A598 | 55b multicolored | .25 | .25 |
| **1921** | A598 | 1.20 l multicolored | 1.00 | .25 |

Centenary of Romanian monetary system.

Infantry Soldier, by Nicolae Grigorescu A599

**1967, May 9**

| No. | Type | Description | Unused | Used |
|---|---|---|---|---|
| **1922** | A599 | 55b multicolored | .70 | .25 |

90th anniv. of Romanian independence.

Peasants Marching, by Stefan Luchian — A600

Painting: 40b, Fighting Peasants, by Octav Bancila, vert.

**1967, May 20** **Unwmk.** ***Perf. 13½***

| No. | Type | Description | Unused | Used |
|---|---|---|---|---|
| **1923** | A600 | 40b multicolored | .25 | .25 |
| **1924** | A600 | 1.55 l multicolored | 1.10 | .70 |

60th anniversary of Peasant Uprising.

Centaury — A601

Carpathian Flora: 40b, Hedge mustard. 55b, Columbine. 1.20 l, Alpine violet. 1.75 l, Bell flower. 4 l, Dryas, horiz.

**1967, June 10** **Photo.**
**Flowers in Natural Colors**

**1925** A601 20b ocher .30 .25
**1926** A601 40b violet .30 .25
**1927** A601 55b bis & brn red .30 .25
**1928** A601 1.20 l yel & red brn .50 .25
**1929** A601 1.75 l bluish grn & car .70 .25
**1930** A601 4 l lt ultra 2.00 .25
*Nos. 1925-1930 (6)* 4.10 1.50

Fortifications, Sibiu — A602

Map of Romania and ITY Emblem — A603

Designs: 40b, Cris Castle. 55b, Wooden Church, Plopis. 1.60 l, Ruins of Nuamtulua Fortress. 1.75 l, Mogosoaia Palace. 2.25 l, Voronet Church.

**1967, June 29** **Photo.** ***Perf. 13½***
**Size: 33x33mm**

**1931** A602 20b ultra & multi .40 .25
**1932** A602 40b vio & multi .60 .25
**1933** A602 55b multi .85 .25
**1934** A602 1.60 l multi 1.50 .25
**1935** A602 1.75 l multi 1.75 .35

**Size: 48x36mm**

**1936** A602 2.25 l bl & multi 2.75 1.50
*Nos. 1931-1936 (6)* 7.85 2.85

**Souvenir Sheet**
***Imperf***

**1937** A603 5 l lt bl, ultra & blk 4.50 4.50

International Tourist Year.

The Attack at Marasesti, by E. Stoica — A604

**1967, July 24** **Unwmk.** ***Perf. 13½***

**1938** A604 55b gray, Prus bl & brn .45 .25

Battle of Marasesti & Oituz, 50th anniv.

Dinu Lipatti, Pianist — A605

Designs: 20b, Al. Orascu, architect. 40b, Gr. Antipa, zoologist. 55b, M. Kogalniceanu, statesman. 1.20 l, Jonathan Swift, writer. 1.75 l, Marie Curie, scientist.

**1967, July 29** **Photo.** ***Perf. 13½***

**1939** A605 10b ultra, blk & pur .25 .25
**1940** A605 20b org brn, blk & ultra .25 .25
**1941** A605 40b bl grn, blk & org brn .25 .25
**1942** A605 55b dp rose, blk & dk ol grn .25 .25
**1943** A605 1.20 l ol, blk & brn .40 .25
**1944** A605 1.75 l dl bl, blk & bl grn .80 .25
*Nos. 1939-1944 (6)* 2.20 1.50

Cultural anniversaries.

Wrestlers A606

Designs: 20b, 55b, 1.20 l, 2 l, Various fight scenes and world map (20b, 2 l horizontal); on 2 l maps are large and wrestlers small.

**1967, Aug. 28**

**1945** A606 10b olive & multi .25 .25
**1946** A606 20b citron & multi .25 .25
**1947** A606 55b bister & multi .25 .25
**1948** A606 1.20 l multi .25 .25
**1949** A606 2 l ultra, gold & dp car 1.00 .30
*Nos. 1945-1949 (5)* 2.00 1.30

World Greco-Roman Wrestling Championships, Bucharest.

Congress Emblem — A607

**1967, Aug. 28**

**1950** A607 1.60 l lt bl, ultra & dp car .70 .40

Intl. Linguists' Cong., Bucharest, 8/28-9/2.

Ice Skating — A608

Designs: 40b, Biathlon. 55b, 5 l, Bobsledding. 1 l, Skiing. 1.55 l, Ice Hockey. 2 l, Emblem of 10th Winter Olympic Games. 2.30 l, Ski jump.

**1967, Sept. 28** **Photo.** ***Perf. 13½x13***

**1951** A608 20b lt bl & multi .25 .25
**1952** A608 40b multi .25 .25
**1953** A608 55b bl & multi .25 .25
**1954** A608 1 l lil & multi .25 .25
**1955** A608 1.55 l multi .30 .25
**1956** A608 2 l gray & multi .50 .25
**1957** A608 2.30 l multi .85 .35
*Nos. 1951-1957 (7)* 2.65 1.85

**Souvenir Sheet**
***Imperf***

**1958** A608 5 l lt bl & multi 3.25 2.75

10th Winter Olympic Games, Grenoble, France, Feb. 6-18, 1968.

Nos. 1951-1957 issued in sheets of 10 (5x2) and 5 labels.

Curtea de Arges Monastery, 450th Anniv. — A609

**1967, Nov. 1** **Unwmk.** ***Perf. 13½***

**1959** A609 55b multicolored .40 .25

Romanian Academy Library, Bucharest, Cent. — A610

**1967, Sept. 25** **Litho.**

**1960** A610 55b ocher, gray & dk bl .40 .25

Karl Marx and Title Page — A611

**1967, Nov. 4** **Photo.**

**1961** A611 40b rose claret, blk & yel .40 .25

Centenary of the publication of "Das Kapital" by Karl Marx.

Lenin — A612

**1967, Nov. 3**

**1962** A612 1.20 l red, blk & gold .40 .25

Russian October Revolution, 50th anniv.

Monorail Leaving US EXPO Pavilion A613

Designs: 1 l, EXPO emblem and atom symbol. 1.60 l, Cup, world map and EXPO emblem. 2 l, EXPO emblem.

**1967, Nov. 28** **Photo.**

**1963** A613 55b grnsh bl, vio & blk .25 .25
**1964** A613 1 l red, blk & gray .25 .25
**1965** A613 1.60 l multicolored .40 .25
**1966** A613 2 l multicolored .60 .25
*Nos. 1963-1966 (4)* 1.50 1.00

EXPO '67 Intl. Exhib., Montreal, Apr. 28-Oct. 27. No. 1965 also for Romania's victory in the World Fencing Championships in Montreal. Issued in sheets of four.

Truck — A614

Arms of the Republic — A615

Diesel Locomotive — A616

Map Showing Telephone Network A617

Designs: 10b, Communications emblem, vert. 20b, Train. 35b, Plane. 50b, Telephone, vert. 60b, Small loading truck. 1.20 l, Autobus. 1.35 l, Helicopter. 1.50 l, Trolley bus. 1.55 l, Radio station and tower. 1.75 l, Highway. 2 l, Mail truck. 2.40 l, Television tower. 3.20 l, Jet plane. 3.25 l, Steamship. 4 l, Electric train. 5 l, World map and teletype.

**Photo.; Engr. (type A615)**
**1967-68** ***Perf. 13½***

**1967** A614 5b lt ol grn ('68) .25 .25
**1968** A614 10b henna brn ('68) .25 .25
**1969** A614 20b gray ('68) .25 .25
**1970** A614 35b bl blk ('68) .25 .25
**1971** A615 40b violet blue .25 .25
**1972** A614 50b orange ('68) .25 .25
**1973** A615 55b dull orange .25 .25
**1974** A614 60b orange brn ('68) .25 .25

**Size: 22½x28mm, 28x22½mm**

**1975** A616 1 l emerald ('68) .25 .25
**1976** A617 1.20 l red lil ('68) .25 .25
**1977** A617 1.35 l brt blue ('68) .30 .25
**1978** A616 1.50 l rose red ('68) .35 .25
**1979** A616 1.55 l dk brown ('68) .35 .25
**1980** A615 1.60 l rose red .40 .25
**1981** A617 1.75 l dp green ('68) .40 .25
**1982** A617 2 l citron ('68) .60 .25
**1983** A616 2.40 l dk blue ('68) .75 .25
**1984** A617 3 l grnsh blue .75 .25
**1985** A617 3.20 l ocher ('68) 1.00 .25
**1986** A616 3.25 l ultra ('68) 1.00 .25
**1987** A617 4 l lil rose ('68) 1.25 .25
**1988** A617 5 l violet ('68) 1.40 .25
*Nos. 1967-1988 (22)* 11.05 5.50

Issue dates: 1967, Nov. 6, Nos. 1971, 1973, 1980; 1967, Dec. 20, No. 1984; 1968, Jan. 20, Nos. 1975, 1976, 1978, 1979, 1981; 1968, Feb. 6, all others.

40th anniv. of the first automatic telephone exchange; introduction of automatic telephone service (No. 1984).

See Nos. 2078-2079, 2269-2284 and design A792.

Coat of Arms, Symbols of Agriculture and Industry A618

55b, Coat of arms. 1.60 l, Romanian flag. 1.75 l, Coat of arms, symbols of arts and education.

**1967, Dec. 26 Photo. *Perf. 13½***

**Size: 27x48mm**

| | | | | | |
|---|---|---|---|---|---|
| **1989** | A618 | 40b | multicolored | .25 | .25 |
| **1990** | A618 | 55b | multicolored | .25 | .25 |

**Size: 33½x48mm**

| | | | | | |
|---|---|---|---|---|---|
| **1991** | A618 | 1.60 l | multicolored | .50 | .25 |

**Size: 27x48mm**

| | | | | | |
|---|---|---|---|---|---|
| **1992** | A618 | 1.75 l | multicolored | 1.00 | .55 |
| | | | *Nos. 1989-1992 (4)* | 2.00 | 1.30 |

20th anniversary of the republic.

Souvenir Sheet

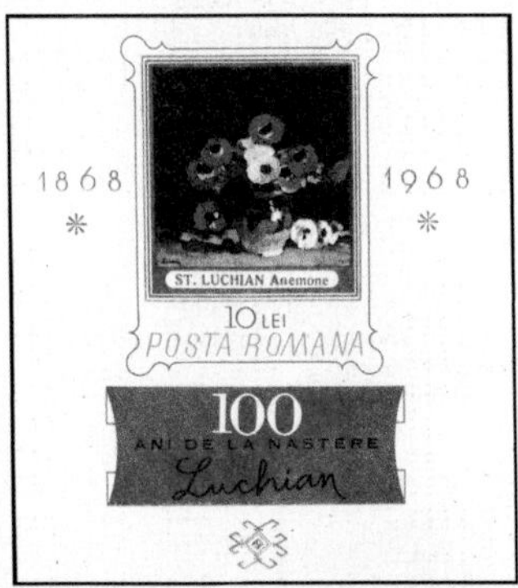


Anemones, by Stefan Luchian — A619

**1968, Mar. 30 Litho. *Imperf.***

| | | | | | |
|---|---|---|---|---|---|
| **1993** | A619 | 10 l | multi | 6.00 | 6.00 |

Stefan Luchian, Romanian painter, birth cent.

Portrait of a Lady, by Misu Popp A620

Paintings: 10b, The Reveille of Romania, by Gheorghe Tattarescu. 20b, Composition, by Teodorescu Sionion, horiz. 35b, The Judgment of Paris, by Hendrick van Balen, horiz. 55b, Little Girl with Red Kerchief, by Nicolae Grigorescu. 60b, The Mystical Betrothal of St. Catherine, by Lamberto Sustris, horiz. 1 l, Old Nicolas, the Zither Player, by Stefan Luchian. 1.60 l, Man with a Skull, by Dierick Bouts (?). 1.75 l, Madonna and Child with Fruit Basket, by Jan van Bylert. 2.40 l, Medor and Angelica, by Sebastiano Ricci, horiz. 3 l, Summer, by Jacob Jordaens, horiz. 3.20 l, 5 l, Ecce Homo, by Titian.

**Gold Frame**

**Size: 28x49mm**

**1968 Photo. *Perf. 13½***

| | | | | | |
|---|---|---|---|---|---|
| **1994** | A620 | 10b | multi | .25 | .25 |

**Size: 48½x36½mm, 36x48½mm**

| | | | | | |
|---|---|---|---|---|---|
| **1995** | A620 | 20b | multi | .25 | .25 |
| **1996** | A620 | 35b | multi | .25 | .25 |
| **1997** | A620 | 40b | multi | .25 | .25 |
| **1998** | A620 | 55b | multi | .25 | .25 |
| **1999** | A620 | 60b | multi | .25 | .25 |
| **2000** | A620 | 1 l | multi | .65 | .25 |
| **2001** | A620 | 1.60 l | multi | .80 | .25 |
| **2002** | A620 | 1.75 l | multi | 1.10 | .25 |
| **2003** | A620 | 2.40 l | multi | 1.25 | .30 |
| **2004** | A620 | 3 l | multi | 2.50 | .50 |
| **2005** | A620 | 3.20 l | multi | 2.25 | .70 |
| | | | *Nos. 1994-2005 (12)* | 10.05 | 3.75 |

**Miniature Sheet**

***Imperf***

| | | | | | |
|---|---|---|---|---|---|
| **2006** | A620 | 5 l | multi | 5.00 | 5.00 |

Issued: 40, 55b, 1, 1.60, 2.40, 3.20, 5 l, 3/28; others, 9/9.

See Nos. 2088-2094, 2124-2130.

Human Rights Flame — A621

**1968, May 9 Unwmk. *Perf. 13½***

| | | | | | |
|---|---|---|---|---|---|
| **2007** | A621 | 1 l | multicolored | .45 | .25 |

Intl. Human Rights Year.

WHO Emblem — A622

**1968, May 14 Photo.**

| | | | | | |
|---|---|---|---|---|---|
| **2008** | A622 | 1.60 l | multi | .50 | .25 |

WHO, 20th anniversary.

"Prince Dragos Hunting Bison," by Nicolae Grigorescu — A623

**1968, May 17**

| | | | | | |
|---|---|---|---|---|---|
| **2009** | A623 | 1.60 l | multi | .70 | .25 |

15th Hunting Cong., Mamaia, May 23-29.

Pioneers and Liberation Monument — A624

Pioneers: 40b, receiving scarfs. 55b, building model planes and boat. 1 l, as radio amateurs. 1.60 l, folk dancing. 2.40 l, Girl Pioneers in camp.

**1968, June 9 Photo. *Perf. 13½***

| | | | | | |
|---|---|---|---|---|---|
| **2010** | A624 | 5b | multi | .25 | .25 |
| **2011** | A624 | 40b | multi | .25 | .25 |
| **2012** | A624 | 55b | multi | .25 | .25 |
| **2013** | A624 | 1 l | multi | .30 | .25 |
| **2014** | A624 | 1.60 l | multi | .50 | .25 |
| **2015** | A624 | 2.40 l | multi | .70 | .25 |
| | | | *Nos. 2010-2015 (6)* | 2.25 | 1.50 |

Ion Ionescu de la Brad — A625

Designs: 55b, Emil Racovita. 1.60 l, Prince Mircea of Walachia.

**1968 Size: 28x43mm**

| | | | | | |
|---|---|---|---|---|---|
| **2016** | A625 | 40b | multicolored | .25 | .25 |
| **2017** | A625 | 55b | green & multi | .25 | .25 |

**Size: 28x48mm**

| | | | | | |
|---|---|---|---|---|---|
| **2018** | A625 | 1.60 l | gold & multi | .55 | .25 |
| | | | *Nos. 2016-2018 (3)* | 1.05 | .75 |

Ion Ionescu de la Brad (1818-91); Emil Racovita (1868-1947), explorer and naturalist; 1.60 l, Prince Mircea (1386-1418). Issue dates: 40b, 55b, June 24; 1.60 l, June 22.

Geranium A626

Designs: Various geraniums.

**1968, July 20 Photo. *Perf. 13½***

| | | | | | |
|---|---|---|---|---|---|
| **2019** | A626 | 10b | multicolored | .25 | .25 |
| **2020** | A626 | 20b | multicolored | .25 | .25 |
| **2021** | A626 | 40b | multicolored | .25 | .25 |
| **2022** | A626 | 55b | multicolored | .25 | .25 |
| **2023** | A626 | 60b | multicolored | .25 | .25 |
| **2024** | A626 | 1.20 l | multicolored | .25 | .25 |
| **2025** | A626 | 1.35 l | multicolored | .35 | .25 |
| **2026** | A626 | 1.60 l | multicolored | .75 | .25 |
| | | | *Nos. 2019-2026 (8)* | 2.60 | 2.00 |

Avram Iancu, by B. Iscovescu and Demonstrating Students — A627

Demonstrating Students and: 55b, Nicolae Balcescu, by Gheorghe Tattarescu. 1.60 l, Vasile Alecsandri, by N. Livaditti.

**1968, July 25**

| | | | | | |
|---|---|---|---|---|---|
| **2027** | A627 | 55b | gold & multi | .25 | .25 |
| **2028** | A627 | 1.20 l | gold & multi | .45 | .25 |
| **2029** | A627 | 1.60 l | gold & multi | .70 | .25 |
| | | | *Nos. 2027-2029 (3)* | 1.40 | .75 |

120th anniversary of 1848 revolution.

Boxing — A628

Aztec Calendar Stone and: 10b, Javelin, Women's. 20b, Woman diver. 40b, Volleyball. 60b, Wrestling. 1.20 l, Fencing. 1.35 l, Canoeing. 1.60 l, Soccer. 5 l, Running.

**1968, Aug. 28**

| | | | | | |
|---|---|---|---|---|---|
| **2030** | A628 | 10b | multi | .25 | .25 |
| **2031** | A628 | 20b | multi | .25 | .25 |
| **2032** | A628 | 40b | multi | .25 | .25 |
| **2033** | A628 | 55b | multi | .25 | .25 |
| **2034** | A628 | 60b | multi | .25 | .25 |
| **2035** | A628 | 1.20 l | multi | .35 | .25 |
| **2036** | A628 | 1.35 l | multi | .40 | .25 |
| **2037** | A628 | 1.60 l | multi | .65 | .25 |
| | | | *Nos. 2030-2037 (8)* | 2.65 | 2.00 |

**Souvenir Sheet**

***Imperf***

| | | | | | |
|---|---|---|---|---|---|
| **2038** | A628 | 5 l | multi | 3.00 | 2.00 |

19th Olympic Games, Mexico City, 10/12-17.

Atheneum and Harp — A629

**1968, Aug. 20 Litho. *Perf. 12x12½***

| | | | | | |
|---|---|---|---|---|---|
| **2039** | A629 | 55b | multicolored | .40 | .25 |

Centenary of the Philharmonic Orchestra.

Globe and Emblem — A630

**1968, Oct. 4 Litho. *Perf. 13½***

| | | | | | |
|---|---|---|---|---|---|
| **2040** | A630 | 1.60 l | ultra & gold | .60 | .25 |

Intl. Fed. of Photograpic Art, 20th anniv.

Moldovita Monastery Church — A631

Historic Monuments: 10b, "The Triumph of Trajan," Roman metope, vert. 55b, Cozia monastery church. 1.20 l, Court of Tirgoviste Palace. 1.55 l, Palace of Culture, Jassy. 1.75 l, Corvinus Castle, Hunedoara.

**1968, Nov. 25 Engr. *Perf. 13½***

| | | | | | |
|---|---|---|---|---|---|
| **2041** | A631 | 10b | dk bl, ol & brn | .25 | .25 |
| **2042** | A631 | 40b | rose car, bl & brn | .25 | .25 |
| **2043** | A631 | 55b | ol, brn & vio | .25 | .25 |
| **2044** | A631 | 1.20 l | yel, mar & gray | .30 | .25 |
| **2045** | A631 | 1.55 l | vio brn, dk bl & lt grn | .50 | .25 |
| **2046** | A631 | 1.75 l | org, blk & ol | 1.00 | .25 |
| | | | *Nos. 2041-2046 (6)* | 2.55 | 1.50 |

Mute Swan — A632

Protected Birds and Animals: 20b, European stilts. 40b, Sheldrakes. 55b, Egret feeding young. 60b, Golden eagle. 1.20 l, Great bustards. 1.35 l, Chamois. 1.60 l, Bison.

**1968, Dec. 20 Photo. *Perf. 13½***

| | | | | | |
|---|---|---|---|---|---|
| **2047** | A632 | 10b | pink & multi | .30 | .25 |
| **2048** | A632 | 20b | multicolored | .30 | .25 |
| **2049** | A632 | 40b | lilac & multi | .30 | .25 |
| **2050** | A632 | 55b | olive & multi | .30 | .25 |
| **2051** | A632 | 60b | multicolored | .30 | .25 |
| **2052** | A632 | 1.20 l | multicolored | .65 | .25 |

**2053** A632 1.35 l blue & multi .75 .25
**2054** A632 1.60 l multicolored .90 .25
*Nos. 2047-2054 (8)* 3.80 2.00

Michael the Brave's Entry into Alba Iulia, by D. Stoica — A633

Designs: 1 l, "The Round Dance of Union," by Theodor Aman. 1.75 l, Assembly of Alba Iulia.

**1968, Dec. 1 Litho. *Perf. 13½***

**2055** A633 55b gold & multi .25 .25
**2056** A633 1 l gold & multi .40 .25
**2057** A633 1.75 l gold & multi .60 .35
*a.* Souv. sheet of 3, #2055-2057, imperf. 1.75 1.50
*Nos. 2055-2057 (3)* 1.25 .85

50th anniv. of the union of Transylvania and Romania. No. 2057a sold for 4 l.

Woman from Neamt — A634

Regional Costumes: 40b, Man from Neamt. 55b, Woman from Hunedoara. 1 l, Man from Hunedoara. 1.60 l, Woman from Brasov. 2.40 l, Man from Brasov.

**1968, Dec. 28 *Perf. 12x12½***

**2058** A634 5b orange & multi .25 .25
**2059** A634 40b blue & multi .25 .25
**2060** A634 55b multi .25 .25
**2061** A634 1 l brown & multi .25 .25
**2062** A634 1.60 l brown & multi .50 .25
**2063** A634 2.40 l multi .95 .35
*Nos. 2058-2063 (6)* 2.45 1.60

**1969, Feb. 15**

Regional Costumes: 5b, Woman from Dolj. 40b, Man from Dolj. 55b, Woman from Arges. 1 l, Man from Arges. 1.60 l, Woman from Timisoara. 2.40 l, Man from Timisoara.

**2064** A634 5b multi .25 .25
**2065** A634 40b multi .25 .25
**2066** A634 55b lil & multi .25 .25
**2067** A634 1 l rose & multi .25 .25
**2068** A634 1.60 l multi .55 .25
**2069** A634 2.40 l brn & multi 1.00 .25
*Nos. 2064-2069 (6)* 2.55 1.50

Fencing — A635

Sports: 20b, Women's javelin. 40b, Canoeing. 55b, Boxing. 1 l, Volleyball. 1.20 l, Swimming. 1.60 l, Wrestling. 2.40 l, Soccer.

**1969, Mar. 10 Photo. *Perf. 13½***

**Denominations Black, Athletes in Gray**

**2070** A635 10b pale brown .25 .25
**2071** A635 20b violet .25 .25
**2072** A635 40b blue .25 .25
**2073** A635 55b red .25 .25
**2074** A635 1 l green .25 .25
**2075** A635 1.20 l brt blue .25 .25
**2076** A635 1.60 l cerise .45 .25
**2077** A635 2.40 l dp green .85 .25
*Nos. 2070-2077 (8)* 2.80 2.00

### Type of Regular Issue

**1969, Jan. 10 Photo. *Perf. 13½***

**2078** A614 40b Power lines, vert. .25 .25
**2079** A614 55b Dam, vert. .25 .25

### Painting Type of 1968

Paintings (Nudes): 10b, Woman Carrying Jug, by Gheorghe Tattarescu. 20b, Reclining Woman, by Theodor Pallady, horiz. 35b, Seated Woman, by Nicolae Tonitza. 60b, Venus and Amor, 17th century Flemish School. 1.75 l, 5 l, Diana and Endimion, by Marco Liberi. 3 l, The Three Graces, by Hans von Aachen.

**1969, Mar. 27 Photo. *Perf. 13½***

**Gold Frame**

**Size: 37x49mm, 49x37mm**

**2088** A620 10b multi .25 .25
**2089** A620 20b multi .25 .25
**2090** A620 35b multi .25 .25
**2091** A620 60b multi .30 .25
**2092** A620 1.75 l multi .80 .25

**Size: 27½x48½mm**

**2093** A620 3 l multi 1.75 .45
*Nos. 2088-2093 (6)* 3.60 1.70

**Miniature Sheet**

***Imperf***

**2094** A620 5 l multi 4.50 4.50

No. 2094 contains one stamp 36½x48½mm. with simulated perforations.

No. 2093 is incorrectly inscribed Hans von Achen.

ILO, 50th Anniv. — A636

**1969, Apr. 9 Photo. *Perf. 13½***

**2095** A636 55b multicolored .50 .25

Symbolic Head — A637

**1969, Apr. 28**

**2096** A637 55b ultra & multi .35 .25
**2097** A637 1.50 l red & multi 1.00 .35

Romania's cultural and economic cooperation with European countries.

Communications Symbol — A638

**1969, May 12 Photo. *Perf. 13½***

**2098** A638 55b vio bl & bluish gray .40 .25

7th Session of the Conference of Postal and Telecommunications Ministers, Bucharest.

Boxers, Referee and Map of Europe A639

Map of Europe and: 40b, Two boxers. 55b, Sparring. 1.75 l, Referee declaring winner.

**1969, May 24**

**2099** A639 35b multicolored .25 .25
**2100** A639 40b multicolored .25 .25
**2101** A639 55b multicolored .25 .25
**2102** A639 1.75 l blue & multi .60 .25
*Nos. 2099-2102 (4)* 1.35 1.00

European Boxing Championships, Bucharest, May 31-June 8.

Apatura Ilia — A640

Designs: Various butterflies and moths.

**1969, June 25 Photo. *Perf. 13½***

**Insects in Natural Colors**

**2103** A640 5b yellow grn .30 .25
**2104** A640 10b rose mag .30 .25
**2105** A640 20b violet .30 .25
**2106** A640 40b blue grn .30 .25
**2107** A640 55b brt blue .30 .25
**2108** A640 1 l blue .45 .25
**2109** A640 1.20 l violet bl .60 .25
**2110** A640 2.40 l yellow bis 1.25 .25
*Nos. 2103-2110 (8)* 3.80 2.00

Communist Party Flag — A641

**1969, Aug. 6 Photo. *Perf. 13½***

**2111** A641 55b multicolored .40 .25

10th Romanian Communist Party Congress.

Torch, Atom Diagram and Book — A642

Designs: 40b, Symbols of agriculture, science and industry. 1.75 l, Pylon, smokestack and cogwheel.

**1969, Aug. 10**

**2112** A642 35b multicolored .25 .25
**2113** A642 40b green & multi .25 .25
**2114** A642 1.75 l multicolored .50 .25
*Nos. 2112-2114 (3)* 1.00 .75

Exhibition showing the achievements of Romanian economy during the last 25 years.

Broken Chain — A643

55b, Construction work. 60b, Flags.

**1969, Aug. 23**

**2115** A643 10b multicolored .25 .25
**2116** A643 55b yellow & multi .25 .25
**2117** A643 60b multicolored .25 .25
*Nos. 2115-2117 (3)* .75 .75

25th anniversary of Romania's liberation from fascist rule.

Juggler on Unicycle — A644

Circus Performers: 20b, Clown. 35b, Trapeze artists. 60b, Dressage and woman trainer. 1.75 l, Woman in high wire act. 3 l, Performing tiger and trainer.

**1969, Sept. 29 Photo. *Perf. 13½***

**2118** A644 10b lt blue & multi .25 .25
**2119** A644 20b lemon & multi .25 .25
**2120** A644 35b lilac & multi .25 .25
**2121** A644 60b multicolored .25 .25
**2122** A644 1.75 l multicolored .55 .25
**2123** A644 3 l ultra & multi .90 .35
*Nos. 2118-2123 (6)* 2.45 1.60

### Painting Type of 1968

10b, Venetian Senator, Tintoretto School. 20b, Sofia Kretzulescu, by Gheorghe Tattarescu. 35b, Phillip IV, by Velazquez. 60b, Man Reading and Child, by Hans Memling. 1.75 l, Doamnei d'Aguesseau, by Madame Vigée-Lebrun. 3 l, Portrait of a Woman, by Rembrandt. 5 l, The Return of the Prodigal Son, by Bernardino Licinio, horiz.

**Gold Frame**

**1969 Size: 36½x49mm**

**2124** A620 10b multi .25 .25
**2125** A620 20b multi .25 .25
**2126** A620 35b multi .25 .25
**2127** A620 60b multi .40 .25
**2128** A620 1.75 l multi .80 .25
**2129** A620 3 l multi 1.40 .40
*Nos. 2124-2129 (6)* 3.35 1.65

**Miniature Sheet**

***Imperf***

**2130** A620 5 l gold & multi 3.00 2.25

No. 2130 contains one stamp with simulated perforations.

Issue dates: 5 l, July 31. Others, Oct. 1.

Masks — A645

**1969, Nov. 24 Photo. *Perf. 13½***

**2131** A645 40b Branesti .25 .25
**2132** A645 55b Tudora .25 .25
**2133** A645 1.55 l Birsesti .50 .25
**2134** A645 1.75 l Rudaria .60 .25
*Nos. 2131-2134 (4)* 1.60 1.00

Armed Forces Memorial A646

**1969, Oct. 25**

**2135** A646 55b red, blk & gold .40 .25

25th anniversary of the People's Army.

Locomotives of 1869 and 1969 — A647

**1969, Oct. 31**

**2136** A647 55b silver & multi .40 .25

Bucharest-Filaret-Giurgevo railroad, cent.

A648

Apollo 12 landing module.

**1969, Nov. 24**

**2137** A648 1.50 l multi .50 .40

2nd landing on the moon, Nov. 19, 1969, astronauts Captains Alan Bean, Charles Conrad, Jr. and Richard Gordon.

Printed in sheets of 4 with 4 labels (one label with names of astronauts, one with Apollo 12 emblem and 2 silver labels with picture of landing module, Intrepid). Value, unused $2.50; used $2.25.

A649

New Year: 40b, Mother Goose in Goat Disguise. 55b, Children singing and decorated tree, Sorcova. 1.50 l, Drummer, and singer, Buhaiul. 2.40 l, Singer and bell ringer, Plugusurol.

**1969, Dec. 25 Photo. *Perf. 13½***

**2138** A649 40b bister & multi .25 .25
**2139** A649 55b lilac & multi .25 .25
**2140** A649 1.50 l blue & multi .60 .25
**2141** A649 2.40 l multicolored 1.10 .25
*Nos. 2138-2141 (4)* 2.20 1.00

The Last Judgment (detail), Voronet Monastery — A650

North Moldavian Monastery Frescoes: 10b, Stephen the Great and family, Voronet. 20b, Three prophets, Sucevita. 60b, St. Nicholas (scene from his life), Sucevita, vert. 1.75 l, Siege of Constantinople, 7th century, Moldovita. 3 l, Plowman, Voronet, vert.

**1969, Dec. 15**

**2142** A650 10b gold & multi .25 .25
**2143** A650 20b gold & multi .25 .25
**2144** A650 35b gold & multi .25 .25
**2145** A650 60b gold & multi .30 .25
**2146** A650 1.75 l gold & multi .50 .25
**2147** A650 3 l gold & multi 1.40 .25
*Nos. 2142-2147 (6)* 2.95 1.50

Ice Hockey A651

Designs: 55b, Goalkeeper. 1.20 l, Two players with puck. 2.40 l, Player and goalkeeper.

**1970, Jan. 20 *Perf. 13½***

**2148** A651 20b yellow & multi .25 .25
**2149** A651 55b multicolored .25 .25
**2150** A651 1.20 l pink & multi .50 .25
**2151** A651 2.40 l lt blue & multi 1.10 .30
*Nos. 2148-2151 (4)* 2.10 1.05

World Ice Hockey Championships, Bucharest and Galati, Feb. 24-Mar. 5.

Pasqueflower A652

Flowers: 10b, Adonis vernalis. 20b, Thistle. 40b, Almond tree blossoms. 55b, Iris. 1 l, Flax. 1.20 l, Sage. 2.40 l, Peony.

**1970, Feb. 25 Photo. *Perf. 13½***

**2152** A652 5b yellow & multi .25 .25
**2153** A652 10b green & multi .25 .25
**2154** A652 20b lt bl & multi .25 .25
**2155** A652 40b violet & multi .25 .25
**2156** A652 55b ultra & multi .25 .25
**2157** A652 1 l multicolored .25 .25
**2158** A652 1.20 l red & multi .45 .25
**2159** A652 2.40 l multicolored .95 .25
*Nos. 2152-2159 (8)* 2.90 2.00

Japanese Print and EXPO '70 Emblem A653

Design: 1 l, Pagoda, EXPO '70 emblem.

**1970, Mar. 23**

**2160** A653 20b gold & multi .25 .25

**Size: 29x92mm**

**2161** A653 1 l gold & multi .50 .25

EXPO '70 Intl. Exhib., Osaka, Japan, Mar. 15-Sept. 13.

A souvenir sheet exists with perforated label in pagoda design of 1 l. Issued Nov. 28, 1970. Value $3.

Camille, by Claude Monet (Maximum Card) — A654

**1970, Apr. 19 Photo. *Perf. 13½***

**2162** A654 1.50 l gold & multi .55 .25

Franco-Romanian Maximafil Phil. Exhib.

Cuza, by C. Popp de Szathmary — A655

**1970, Apr. 20 *Perf. 13½***

**2163** A655 55b gold & multi .35 .25

Alexandru Ioan Cuza (1820-1866), prince of Romania.

Lenin (1870-1924) A656

**1970, Apr. 21 Photo. *Perf. 13½***

**2164** A656 40b dk red & multi .35 .25

Map of Europe with Capital Cities A657

**1970, Apr. 28**

**2165** A657 40b grn, brn org & blk .50 .35
**2166** A657 1.50 l ultra, yel brn & blk 1.00 .70

Inter-European cultural and economic cooperation.

Victory Monument, Romanian and Russian Flags — A658

**1970, May 9**

**2167** A658 55b red & multi .35 .25

25th anniv. of victory over the Germans.

Greek Silver Drachm, 5th Century B.C. — A659

Coins: 20b, Getic-Dacian silver didrachm, 2nd-1st centuries B.C. 35b, Emperor Trajan's copper sestertius, 106 A.D. 60b, Mircea ducat, 1400. 1.75 l, Stephen the Great's silver groschen, 1460. 3 l, Brasov klippe-taler, 1601, vert.

**1970, May 15**

**2168** A659 10b ultra, blk & sil .25 .25
**2169** A659 20b hn brn, blk & sil .25 .25
**2170** A659 35b grn, dk brn & gold .25 .25
**2171** A659 60b brn, blk & sil .25 .25
**2172** A659 1.75 l brt bl, blk & sil .50 .25
**2173** A659 3 l dk car, blk & sil 1.00 .25
*Nos. 2168-2173 (6)* 2.50 1.50

Soccer Players and Ball — A660

Soccer ball & various scenes from soccer game.

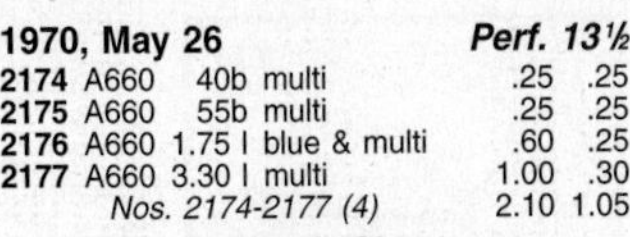

**1970, May 26 *Perf. 13½***

**2174** A660 40b multi .25 .25
**2175** A660 55b multi .25 .25
**2176** A660 1.75 l blue & multi .60 .25
**2177** A660 3.30 l multi 1.00 .30
*Nos. 2174-2177 (4)* 2.10 1.05

**Souvenir Sheet**

**2178** Sheet of 4 3.00 2.00
*a.* A660 1.20 l multi .35 .25
*b.* A660 1.50 l multi .50 .25
*c.* A660 1.55 l multi .60 .25
*d.* A660 1.75 l multi .60 .25

9th World Soccer Championships for the Jules Rimet Cup, Mexico City, May 30-June 21. No. 2178 contains 4 stamps similar to Nos. 2174-2177, but with only one quarter of the soccer ball on each stamp, forming one large ball in the center of the block.

Moldovita Monastery — A661

Frescoes from North Moldavian Monasteries.

**1970, June 29 *Perf. 13½***

**Size: 36½x49mm**

**2179** A661 10b gold & multi .25 .25

**Size: 27½x49mm**

**2180** A661 20b gold & multi .25 .25

**Size: 36½x49mm, 48x37mm**

**2181** A661 40b gold & multi .25 .25
**2182** A661 55b gold & multi .25 .25
**2183** A661 1.75 l gold & multi .35 .25
**2184** A661 3 l gold & multi 1.00 .35
*Nos. 2179-2184 (6)* 2.35 1.60

**Miniature Sheet**

**2185** A661 5 l gold & multi 2.50 2.25

Friedrich Engels (1820-1895), German Socialist — A662

**1970, July 10 Photo. *Perf. 13½***

**2186** A662 1.50 l multi .45 .25

Aerial View of Iron Gate Power Station A663

**1970, July 13**

**2187** A663 35b blue & multi .30 .25

Hydroelectric plant at the Iron Gate of the Danube.

Cargo Ship A664

**1970, July 17**

**2188** A664 55b blue & multi .30 .25

Romanian merchant marine, 75th anniv.

Exhibition Hall and Oil Derrick A665

**1970, July 20**

**2189** A665 1.50 l multi .45 .25

International Bucharest Fair, Oct. 13-24.

Opening of UPU Headquarters, Bern — A666

**1970, Aug. 17 Photo.** ***Perf. 13½***

**2190** A666 1.50 l ultra & slate green .45 .25

Education Year Emblem — A667

**1970, Aug. 17**

**2191** A667 55b black, pur & red .40 .25

International Education Year.

Iceberg Rose — A668

Roses: 35b, Wiener charme. 55b, Pink luster. 1 l, Piccadilly. 1.50 l, Orange Delbard. 2.40 l, Sibelius.

**1970, Aug. 21**

**2192** A668 20b dk red, grn & yel .25 .25
**2193** A668 35b vio, yel & grn .25 .25
**2194** A668 55b blue, rose & grn .25 .25
**2195** A668 1 l grn, car rose & yel .40 .25
**2196** A668 1.50 l dk bl, red & grn .55 .25
**2197** A668 2.40 l brt bl, dp red & grn 1.00 .25
*Nos. 2192-2197 (6)* 2.70 1.50

Spaniel and Pheasant, by Jean B. Oudry A669

Paintings: 10b, The Hunt, by Domenico Brandi. 35b, The Hunt, by Jan Fyt. 60b, After the Chase, by Jacob Jordaens. 1.75 l, 5 l, Game Merchant, by Frans Snyders (horiz.). 3 l, The Hunt, by Adriaen de Gryeff. Sizes: 37x49mm (10b, 35b); 35x33mm (20b, 60b, 3 l); 49x37mm (1.75 l, 3 l).

**1970, Sept. 20 Photo.** ***Perf. 13½***

**2198** A669 10b gold & multi .25 .25
**2199** A669 20b gold & multi .25 .25
**2200** A669 35b gold & multi .25 .25
**2201** A669 60b gold & multi .40 .25
**2202** A669 1.75 l gold & multi .90 .30
**2203** A669 3 l gold & multi 1.75 .60
*Nos. 2198-2203 (6)* 3.80 1.90

**Miniature Sheet**

**2204** A669 5 l gold & multi 3.75 3.25

UN Emblem — A670

**1970, Sept. 29**

**2205** A670 1.50 l lt bl, ultra & blk .60 .25

25th anniversary of the United Nations.

Mother and Child — A671

Designs: 1.50 l, Red Cross relief trucks and tents. 1.75 l, Rebuilding houses.

**1970, Sept. 25**

**2206** A671 55b bl gray, blk & ol .25 .25
**2207** A671 1.50 l ol, blk & car .45 .25
*a.* Strip of 3, #2206-2207, C179 1.40 .55
**2208** A671 1.75 l blue & multi .70 .25
*Nos. 2206-2208, C179 (4)* 1.65 1.00

Plight of the Danube flood victims.

Ludwig van Beethoven (1770-1827), Composer — A673

**1970, Nov. 2**

**2215** A673 55b multicolored 1.25 .25

Arabian Thoroughbred — A672

Horses: 35b, American trotter. 55b, Ghidran (Anglo-American). 1 l, Northern Moravian. 1.50 l, Trotter thoroughbred. 2.40 l, Lippizaner.

**1970, Oct. 10 Photo.** ***Perf. 13½***

**2209** A672 20b blk & multi .25 .25
**2210** A672 35b blk & multi .25 .25
**2211** A672 55b blk & multi .25 .25
**2212** A672 1 l blk & multi .30 .25
**2213** A672 1.50 l blk & multi .50 .25
**2214** A672 2.40 l blk & multi 1.10 .25
*Nos. 2209-2214 (6)* 2.65 1.50

Abstract, by Joan Miró — A674

**1970, Dec. 10 Photo.** ***Perf. 13½***

**2216** A674 3 l ultra & multi 2.75 2.75

**Souvenir Sheet**

***Imperf***

**2217** A674 5 l ultra & multi 5.00 5.00

Plight of the Danube flood victims. No. 2216 issued in sheets of 5 stamps and label with signature of Miró and date of flood. No. 2217 contains one stamp with simulated perforation.

The Sense of Sight, by Gonzales Coques A675

"The Senses," paintings by Gonzales Coques (1614-1684): 20b, Hearing. 35b, Smell. 60b, Taste. 1.75 l, Touch. 3 l, Bruckenthal Museum, Sibiu. 5 l, View of Sibiu, 1808, horiz.

**1970, Dec. 15 Photo.** ***Perf. 13½***

**2218** A675 10b gold & multi .25 .25
**2219** A675 20b gold & multi .25 .25
**2220** A675 35b gold & multi .25 .25
**2221** A675 60b gold & multi .25 .25
**2222** A675 1.75 l gold & multi .60 .25
**2223** A675 3 l gold & multi 1.00 .45
*Nos. 2218-2223 (6)* 2.60 1.70

**Miniature Sheet**

***Imperf***

**2224** A675 5 l gold & multi 2.75 2.50

Men of Three Races A676

**1971, Feb. 23 Photo.** ***Perf. 13½***

**2225** A676 1.50 l multi .60 .25

Intl. year against racial discrimination.

Tudor Vladimirescu, by Theodor Aman — A677

**1971, Feb. 20**

**2226** A677 1.50 l gold & multi .60 .25

Vladimirescu, patriot, 150th death anniv.

German Shepherd A677a

Dogs: 35b, Bulldog. 55b, Fox terrier. 1 l, Setter. 1.50 l, Cocker spaniel. 2.40 l, Poodle.

**1971, Feb. 22**

**2227** A677a 20b blk & multi .25 .25
**2228** A677a 35b blk & multi .25 .25
**2229** A677a 55b blk & multi .25 .25
**2230** A677a 1 l blk & multi .40 .25
**2231** A677a 1.50 l blk & multi .65 .25
**2232** A677a 2.40 l blk & multi 1.25 .40
*Nos. 2227-2232 (6)* 3.05 1.65

Paris Commune — A678

**1971, Mar. 15 Photo.** ***Perf. 13½***

**2233** A678 40b multicolored .40 .25

Centenary of the Paris Commune.

Congress Emblem — A679

**1971, Mar. 23**

**2234** A679 55b multicolored .40 .25

Romanian Trade Unions Congress.

Rock Formation A680

Designs: 10b, Bicazului Gorge, vert. 55b, Winter resort. 1 l, Danube Delta view. 1.50 l, Lakeside resort. 2.40 l, Venus, Jupiter, Neptune Hotels on Black Sea.

**Size: 23x38mm, 38x23mm**

**1971, Apr. 15**

**2235** A680 10b multi .25 .25
**2236** A680 40b multi .25 .25
**2237** A680 55b multi .25 .25
**2238** A680 1 l multi .30 .25
**2239** A680 1.50 l multi .50 .25

**Size: 76½x28mm**

**2240** A680 2.40 l multi 1.00 .35
*Nos. 2235-2240 (6)* 2.55 1.60

Tourist publicity.

Arrow Pattern A681

Design: 1.75 l, Wave pattern.

**1971, Apr. 28 Photo. *Perf. 13½***

| | | | | |
|---|---|---|---|---|
| **2241** | A681 | 55b multi | .75 | .60 |
| **2242** | A681 | 1.75 l multi | 1.50 | 1.00 |

Inter-European Cultural and Economic Collaboration. Sheets of 10.

Historical Museum — A682

**1971, May 7 Photo. *Perf. 13½***

| | | | | |
|---|---|---|---|---|
| **2243** | A682 | 55b blue & multi | .40 | .25 |

For Romania's Historical Museum.

Communist Party Emblem — A683

Demonstration, by A. Anastasiu — A684

35b, Reading Proclamation, by Stefan Szonyi.

**1971, May 8**

| | | | | |
|---|---|---|---|---|
| **2244** | A684 | 35b multicolored | .25 | .25 |
| **2245** | A683 | 40b multicolored | .25 | .25 |
| **2246** | A684 | 55b multicolored | .25 | .25 |
| | | *Nos. 2244-2246 (3)* | .75 | .75 |

Romanian Communist Party, 50th anniv.

Souvenir Sheets

Motra Tone, by Kole Idromeno A685

Dancing the Hora, by Theodor Aman — A686

Designs: b, Girl from Kalotina, by V. Dimitrov-Maystora. c, Rosa Botzaris, by Joseph Stieler. d, Woman in Costume, by Katarina Ivanovic. e, Argeseanca, by Carol Popp de Szathmary. f, Woman in Modern Dress, by Ibrahim Calli.

**1971, May 25 Photo. *Perf. 13½***

| | | | | |
|---|---|---|---|---|
| **2247** | A685 | Sheet of 6 | 4.00 | 3.50 |
| *a.-f.* | | 1.20 l any single | .55 | .40 |
| **2248** | A686 | 5 l multicolored | 3.00 | 3.00 |

Balkanphila III Stamp Exhibition, Bucharest, June 27-July 2.

No. 2247 contains 6 stamps in 3 rows and 6 labels showing exhibition emblem and "60b."

Pomegranate Flower — A687

Flowers: 35b, Slipperwort. 55b, Lily. 1 l, Mimulus. 1.50 l, Morning-glory. 2.40 l, Leaf cactus, horiz.

**1971, June 20**

| | | | | |
|---|---|---|---|---|
| **2249** | A687 | 20b ultra & multi | .25 | .25 |
| **2250** | A687 | 35b red & multi | .25 | .25 |
| **2251** | A687 | 55b ultra & multi | .25 | .25 |
| **2252** | A687 | 1 l car & multi | .45 | .25 |
| **2253** | A687 | 1.50 l car & multi | .75 | .25 |
| **2254** | A687 | 2.40 l ultra & multi | 1.10 | .30 |
| | | *Nos. 2249-2254 (6)* | 3.05 | 1.55 |

Nude, by Iosif Iser A688

Paintings of Nudes: 20b, by Camil Ressu. 35b, by Nicolae Grigorescu. 60b, by Eugene Delacroix (odalisque). 1.75 l, by Auguste Renoir. 3 l, by Palma il Vecchio (Venus and Amor). 5 l, by Il Bronzino (Venus and Amor). 60b, 3 l, 5 l, horiz.

**1971, July 25 Photo. *Perf. 13½***
**Size: 38x50mm, 49x39mm, 29x50mm (20b)**

| | | | | |
|---|---|---|---|---|
| **2255** | A688 | 10b gold & multi | .25 | .25 |
| **2256** | A688 | 20b gold & multi | .25 | .25 |
| **2257** | A688 | 35b gold & multi | .25 | .25 |
| **2258** | A688 | 60b gold & multi | .25 | .25 |
| **2259** | A688 | 1.75 l gold & multi | .35 | .25 |
| **2260** | A688 | 3 l gold & multi | 1.40 | .35 |
| | | *Nos. 2255-2260 (6)* | 2.75 | 1.60 |

**Miniature Sheet**

***Imperf***

| | | | | |
|---|---|---|---|---|
| **2261** | A688 | 5 l gold & multi | 3.25 | 3.25 |

Ships in Storm, by B. Peters — A689

Paintings of Ships by: 20b, Ludolf Backhuysen. 35b, Andries van Eertvelt. 60b, M. W. Arnold. 1.75 l, Ivan Konstantinovich Aivazovski. 3 l, Jean Steriadi. 5 l, N. Darascu, vert.

**1971, Sept. 15 Photo. *Perf. 13½***

| | | | | |
|---|---|---|---|---|
| **2262** | A689 | 10b gold & multi | .25 | .25 |
| **2263** | A689 | 20b gold & multi | .25 | .25 |
| **2264** | A689 | 35b gold & multi | .25 | .25 |
| **2265** | A689 | 60b gold & multi | .25 | .25 |
| **2266** | A689 | 1.75 l gold & multi | .45 | .25 |
| **2267** | A689 | 3 l gold & multi | 1.00 | .35 |
| | | *Nos. 2262-2267 (6)* | 2.45 | 1.60 |

**Miniature Sheet**

| | | | | |
|---|---|---|---|---|
| **2268** | A689 | 5 l gold & multi | 2.50 | 2.50 |

**Type of Regular Issue**

Designs as Before and: 3.60 l, Mail collector. 4.80 l, Mailman. 6 l, Ministry of Posts.

**1971 Photo. *Perf. 13½***
**Size: 16½x23mm, 23x16½mm**

| | | | | |
|---|---|---|---|---|
| **2269** | A616 | 1 l emerald | .25 | .25 |
| **2270** | A617 | 1.20 l red lilac | .25 | .25 |
| **2271** | A617 | 1.35 l brt blue | .30 | .25 |
| **2272** | A616 | 1.50 l orange red | .35 | .25 |
| **2273** | A616 | 1.55 l sepia | .35 | .25 |
| **2274** | A617 | 1.75 l deep green | .40 | .25 |
| **2275** | A617 | 2 l citron | .45 | .25 |
| **2276** | A616 | 2.40 l dark blue | .55 | .25 |
| **2277** | A617 | 3 l greenish bl | .75 | .25 |
| **2278** | A617 | 3.20 l ocher | .75 | .25 |
| **2279** | A616 | 3.25 l ultra | .85 | .25 |
| **2280** | A616 | 3.60 l blue | .90 | .25 |
| **2281** | A617 | 4 l lilac rose | 1.10 | .25 |
| **2282** | A616 | 4.80 l grnsh blue | 1.20 | .25 |
| **2283** | A617 | 5 l violet | 1.25 | .25 |
| **2284** | A616 | 6 l dp magenta | 1.60 | .25 |
| | | *Nos. 2269-2284 (16)* | 11.30 | 4.00 |

Prince Neagoe Basarab A690

**1971, Sept. 20 *Perf. 13½***

| | | | | |
|---|---|---|---|---|
| **2288** | A690 | 60b gold & multi | .40 | .25 |

450th anniversary of the death of Prince Neagoe Basarab of Walachia.

Theodor Pallady (Painter) — A691

Portraits of: 55b, Benvenuto Cellini (1500-1571), sculptor. 1.50 l, Antoine Watteau (1684-1721), painter. 2.40 l, Albrecht Dürer (1471-1528), painter.

**1971, Oct. 12 Photo. *Perf. 13½***

| | | | | |
|---|---|---|---|---|
| **2289** | A691 | 40b gold & multi | .25 | .25 |
| **2290** | A691 | 55b gold & multi | .25 | .25 |
| **2291** | A691 | 1.50 l gold & multi | .50 | .25 |
| **2292** | A691 | 2.40 l gold & multi | 1.00 | .25 |
| | | *Nos. 2289-2292 (4)* | 2.00 | 1.00 |

Anniversaries of famous artists.

Proclamation of Cyrus the Great — A692

**1971, Oct. 12**

| | | | | |
|---|---|---|---|---|
| **2293** | A692 | 55b multicolored | .50 | .25 |

2500th anniversary of the founding of the Persian empire by Cyrus the Great.

Figure Skating — A693

Designs: 20b, Ice hockey. 40b, Biathlon (skier). 55b, Bobsledding. 1.75 l, Skiing. 3 l, Sapporo '72 emblem. 5 l, Olympic flame and emblem.

**1971, Oct. 25**

| | | | | |
|---|---|---|---|---|
| **2294** | A693 | 10b lt bl, blk & red | .25 | .25 |
| **2295** | A693 | 20b multicolored | .25 | .25 |
| **2296** | A693 | 40b multicolored | .25 | .25 |
| **2297** | A693 | 55b lt bl, blk & red | .25 | .25 |
| **2298** | A693 | 1.75 l lt bl, blk & red | .50 | .25 |
| **2299** | A693 | 3 l lt bl, blk & red | .80 | .25 |
| | | *Nos. 2294-2299 (6)* | 2.30 | 1.50 |

**Miniature Sheet**

***Imperf***

| | | | | |
|---|---|---|---|---|
| **2300** | A693 | 5 l multicolored | 2.75 | 2.75 |

11th Winter Olympic Games, Sapporo, Japan, Feb. 3-13, 1972. Nos. 2294-2296 printed se-tenant in sheets of 15 (5x3); Nos. 2297-2298 printed se-tenant in sheets of 10 (5x2). No. 2300 contains one stamp 37x50mm.

St. George and the Dragon A694

Frescoes from North Moldavian Monasteries: 10b, 20b, 40b, Moldovita. 55b, 1.75 l, 5 l, Voronet. 3 l, Arborea, horiz.

**1971, Nov. 30 Photo. *Perf. 13½***

| | | | | |
|---|---|---|---|---|
| **2301** | A694 | 10b gold & multi | .25 | .25 |
| **2302** | A694 | 20b gold & multi | .25 | .25 |
| **2303** | A694 | 40b gold & multi | .25 | .25 |
| **2304** | A694 | 55b gold & multi | .25 | .25 |
| **2305** | A694 | 1.75 l gold & multi | .70 | .25 |
| **2306** | A694 | 3 l gold & multi | 1.00 | .40 |
| | | *Nos. 2301-2306 (6)* | 2.70 | 1.65 |

**Miniature Sheet**

***Imperf***

| | | | | |
|---|---|---|---|---|
| **2307** | A694 | 5 l gold & multi | 2.50 | 2.50 |

No. 2307 contains one stamp 44x56mm.

Ferdinand Magellan A695

Designs: 55b, Johannes Kepler and observation tower. 1 l, Yuri Gagarin and rocket orbiting earth. 1.50 l, Baron Ernest R. Rutherford, atom, nucleus and chemical apparatus.

**1971, Dec. 20**

| | | | | |
|---|---|---|---|---|
| **2308** | A695 | 40b grn, brt rose & dk bl | .25 | .25 |
| **2309** | A695 | 55b lil, bl & gray grn | .25 | .25 |
| **2310** | A695 | 1 l violet & multi | .35 | .25 |
| **2311** | A695 | 1.50 l red brn, grn & bl | .60 | .25 |
| | | *Nos. 2308-2311 (4)* | 1.45 | 1.00 |

Magellan (1480?-1521), navigator; Kepler (1571-1630), astronomer; Gagarin, 1st man in space, 10th anniv.; Ernest R. Rutherford (1871-1937), British physicist.

Matei Millo — A696

Design: 1 l, Nicolae Iorga.

**1971, Dec.**

| | | | | |
|---|---|---|---|---|
| **2312** | A696 | 55b blue & multi | .25 | .25 |
| **2313** | A696 | 1 l purple & multi | .30 | .25 |

Millo (1814-1896), playwright; Iorga (1871-1940), historian and politician.

Young Communists Union Emblem — A697

**1972, Feb.**

| | | | | |
|---|---|---|---|---|
| **2314** | A697 | 55b dk bl, red & gold | .40 | .25 |

Young Communists Union, 50th anniv.

Young Animals — A698

**1972, Mar. 10 Photo. *Perf. 13½***

| | | | | |
|---|---|---|---|---|
| **2315** | A698 | 20b Lynx | .25 | .25 |
| **2316** | A698 | 35b Foxes | .25 | .25 |
| **2317** | A698 | 55b Roe fawns | .25 | .25 |
| **2318** | A698 | 1 l Wild pigs | .25 | .25 |
| **2319** | A698 | 1.50 l Wolves | .50 | .25 |
| **2320** | A698 | 2.40 l Bears | 1.00 | .25 |
| | | *Nos. 2315-2320 (6)* | 2.50 | 1.50 |

Wrestling — A699

Olympic Rings and: 20b, Canoeing. 55b, Soccer. 1.55 l, Women's high jump. 2.90 l, Boxing. 6.70 l, Field ball.

**1972, Apr. 25 Photo. *Perf. 13½***

| | | | | |
|---|---|---|---|---|
| **2321** | A699 | 10b yel & multi | .25 | .25 |
| **2322** | A699 | 20b multicolored | .25 | .25 |
| **2323** | A699 | 55b gray & multi | .25 | .25 |
| **2324** | A699 | 1.55 l grn & multi | .35 | .25 |
| **2325** | A699 | 2.90 l multicolored | .80 | .25 |
| **2326** | A699 | 6.70 l lil & multi | 1.25 | .50 |
| | | *Nos. 2321-2326 (6)* | 3.15 | 1.75 |

20th Olympic Games, Munich, Aug. 26-Sept. 10. See Nos. C186-C187.

Stylized Map of Europe and Links A700

Design: 2.90 l, Entwined arrows and links.

**1972, Apr. 28**

| | | | | |
|---|---|---|---|---|
| **2327** | A700 | 1.75 l dp car, gold & blk | 1.10 | .75 |
| **2328** | A700 | 2.90 l grn, gold & blk | 1.50 | 1.00 |
| *a.* | | Pair, #2327-2328 | 2.60 | 2.00 |

Inter-European Cultural and Economic Collaboration.

UIC Emblem and Trains A701

**1972, May 20 Photo. *Perf. 13½***

| | | | | |
|---|---|---|---|---|
| **2329** | A701 | 55b dp car rose, blk & gold | .35 | .25 |

50th anniv., Intl. Railroad Union (UIC).

Souvenir Sheet

"Summer," by Peter Brueghel, the Younger — A702

**1972, May 20 *Perf. 13x13½***

| | | | | |
|---|---|---|---|---|
| **2330** | A702 | 6 l gold & multi | 3.00 | 3.00 |

Belgica 72, Intl. Phil. Exhib., Brussels, June 24-July 9.

Peony — A703

Protected Flowers: 40b, Pink. 55b, Edelweiss. 60b, Nigritella rubra. 1.35 l, Narcissus. 2.90 l, Lady's slipper.

**1972, June 5 Photo. *Perf. 13***

**Flowers in Natural Colors**

| | | | | |
|---|---|---|---|---|
| **2331** | A703 | 20b dk vio bl | .25 | .25 |
| **2332** | A703 | 40b chocolate | .25 | .25 |
| **2333** | A703 | 55b dp blue | .25 | .25 |
| **2334** | A703 | 60b dk green | .30 | .25 |
| **2335** | A703 | 1.35 l violet | .65 | .25 |
| **2336** | A703 | 2.90 l dk Prus bl | 1.25 | .40 |
| | | *Nos. 2331-2336 (6)* | 2.95 | 1.65 |

Saligny Bridge, Cernavoda — A704

Danube Bridges: 1.75 l, Giurgeni Bridge, Vadul. 2.75 l, Friendship Bridge, Giurgiu-Ruse.

**1972, June 25 Photo. *Perf. 13½***

| | | | | |
|---|---|---|---|---|
| **2337** | A704 | 1.35 l multi | .35 | .25 |
| **2338** | A704 | 1.75 l multi | .50 | .25 |
| **2339** | A704 | 2.75 l multi | .85 | .25 |
| | | *Nos. 2337-2339 (3)* | 1.70 | .75 |

North Railroad Station, Bucharest, Cent. A705

**1972, July 4**

| | | | | |
|---|---|---|---|---|
| **2340** | A705 | 55b ultra & multi | .35 | .25 |

Water Polo and Olympic Rings A706

Olympic Rings and: 20b, Pistol shoot. 55b, Discus. 1.55 l, Gymnastics, women's. 2.75 l, Canoeing. 6.40 l, Fencing.

**1972, July 5 Photo. *Perf. 13½***

| | | | | |
|---|---|---|---|---|
| **2341** | A706 | 10b ol, gold & lil | .25 | .25 |
| **2342** | A706 | 20b red, gold & grn | .25 | .25 |
| **2343** | A706 | 55b grn, gold & brn | .25 | .25 |
| **2344** | A706 | 1.55 l vio, gold & ol | .40 | .25 |
| **2345** | A706 | 2.75 l bl, gold & gray | .70 | .25 |
| **2346** | A706 | 6.40 l pur, gold & gray | 1.50 | .45 |
| | | *Nos. 2341-2346 (6)* | 3.35 | 1.70 |

20th Olympic Games, Munich, Aug. 26-Sept. 11. See No. C187.

Stamp Printing Press — A707

**1972, July 25**

| | | | | |
|---|---|---|---|---|
| **2347** | A707 | 55b multicolored | .35 | .25 |

Centenary of the stamp printing office.

Stefan Popescu, Self-portrait — A708

**1972, Aug. 10**

| | | | | |
|---|---|---|---|---|
| **2348** | A708 | 55b shown | .25 | .25 |
| **2349** | A708 | 1.75 l Octav Bancila | .25 | .25 |
| **2350** | A708 | 2.90 l Gheorghe Petrascu | .50 | .25 |
| **2351** | A708 | 6.50 l Ion Andreescu | 1.25 | .30 |
| | | *Nos. 2348-2351 (4)* | 2.25 | 1.05 |

Self-portraits by Romanian painters.

Runner with Torch, Olympic Rings — A709

**1972, Aug. 13**

| | | | | |
|---|---|---|---|---|
| **2352** | A709 | 55b sil, bl & claret | .75 | .25 |

Olympic torch relay from Olympia, Greece, to Munich, Germany, passing through Romania.

City Hall Tower, Sibiu — A710

Designs: 1.85 l, St. Michael's Cathedral, Cluj. 2.75 l, Sphinx Rock, Mt. Bucegi, horiz. 3.35 l, Heroes' Monument, Bucharest. 3.45 l, Sinaia Castle, horiz. 5.15 l, Hydroelectric Works, Arges, horiz. 5.60 l, Church of the Epiphany, Iasi. 6.20 l, Bran Castle. 6.40 l, Hunedoara Castle, horiz. 6.80 l, Polytechnic Institute, Bucharest, horiz. 7.05 l, Black Church, Brasov. 8.45 l, Atheneum, Bucharest. 9.05 l, Excavated Coliseum, Sarmizegetusa, horiz. 9.10 l, Hydroelectric Station, Iron Gate, horiz. 9.85 l, Monument, Cetatea. 11.90 l, Republic Palace, horiz. 12.75 l, Television Station. 13.30 l, Arch, Alba Iulia, horiz. 16.20 l, Clock Tower, Sighisoara.

**1972 Photo. *Perf. 13***

**Size: 23x18mm, 17x24mm**

| | | | | |
|---|---|---|---|---|
| **2353** | A710 | 1.85 l brt purple | .25 | .25 |
| **2354** | A710 | 2.75 l gray | .40 | .25 |
| **2355** | A710 | 3.35 l magenta | .55 | .25 |
| **2356** | A710 | 3.45 l green | .55 | .25 |
| **2357** | A710 | 5.15 l brt blue | .80 | .25 |
| **2358** | A710 | 5.60 l blue | 1.00 | .25 |
| **2359** | A710 | 6.20 l cerise | 1.00 | .25 |
| **2360** | A710 | 6.40 l sepia | 1.00 | .25 |
| **2361** | A710 | 6.80 l rose red | 1.25 | .25 |
| **2362** | A710 | 7.05 l black | 1.25 | .25 |
| **2363** | A710 | 8.45 l rose red | 1.50 | .25 |
| **2364** | A710 | 9.05 l dull green | 1.40 | .25 |
| **2365** | A710 | 9.10 l ultra | 1.40 | .25 |
| **2366** | A710 | 9.85 l green | 1.60 | .25 |

**Size: 19½x29mm, 29x21mm**

| | | | | |
|---|---|---|---|---|
| **2367** | A710 | 10 l dp brown | 1.60 | .25 |
| **2368** | A710 | 11.90 l bluish blk | 1.75 | .25 |
| **2369** | A710 | 12.75 l dk violet | 1.75 | .25 |
| **2370** | A710 | 13.30 l dull red | 2.10 | .25 |
| **2371** | A710 | 16.20 l olive grn | 2.75 | .25 |
| | | *Nos. 2353-2371,C193 (20)* | 25.40 | 5.15 |

View of Satu-Mare — A711

**1972, Oct. 5**

| | | | | |
|---|---|---|---|---|
| **2372** | A711 | 55b multicolored | .50 | .25 |

Millennium of Satu-Mare.

Tennis Racket and Davis Cup A712

**1972, Oct. 10** ***Perf. 13½***
**2373** A712 2.75 l multi 1.40 .25

Davis Cup finals between Romania and US, Bucharest, Oct. 13-15.

Venice, by Gheorge Petrascu — A713

Paintings of Venice by: 20b, N. Darascu. 55b, Petrascu. 1.55 l, Marius Bunescu. 2.75 l, N. Darascu, vert. 6 l, Petrascu. 6.40 l, Marius Bunescu.

**1972, Oct. 20**
**2374** A713 10b gray & multi .25 .25
**2375** A713 20b gray & multi .25 .25
**2376** A713 55b gray & multi .25 .25
**2377** A713 1.55 l gray & multi .25 .25
**2378** A713 2.75 l gray & multi .55 .25
**2379** A713 6.40 l gray & multi 1.40 .35
*Nos. 2374-2379 (6)* 2.95 1.60

**Souvenir Sheet**

**2380** A713 6 l gray & multi 2.00 2.00

Fencing, Bronze Medal — A714

20b, Team handball, bronze medal. 35b, Boxing, silver medal. 1.45 l, Hurdles, women's, silver medal. 2.75 l, Pistol shoot, silver medal. 6.20 l, Wrestling, gold medal.

**1972, Oct. 28**
**2381** A714 10b red org & multi .25 .25
**2382** A714 20b lt grn & multi .25 .25
**2383** A714 35b multicolored .25 .25
**2384** A714 1.45 l multi .25 .25
**2385** A714 2.75 l ocher & multi .85 .25
**2386** A714 6.20 l bl & multi 2.00 .45
*Nos. 2381-2386 (6)* 3.85 1.70

Romanian medalists at 20th Olympic Games. See No. C191. For surcharge see No. 2493.

Charity Labels

Stamp day issues frequently have an attached, fully perforated label with a face value. These are Romanian Philatelic Association charity labels. They are inscribed "AFR." The stamps are valued with label attached. When the "label" is part of the stamp, the stamp is listed in the semi-postal section. See Nos. B426-B430.

**Stamp Day Semi-Postal Type of 1968**

Design: Traveling Gypsies, by Emil Volkers.

**1972, Nov. 15 Photo.** ***Perf. 13½***
**2386A** SP288 1.10 l + 90b label 1.00 .40

Stamp Day.

Apollo 1, 2 and 3 — A715

**1972, Dec. 27 Photo.** ***Perf. 13½***
**2387** A715 10b shown .25 .25
**2388** A715 35b Grissom, Chaffee and White, 1967 .25 .25
**2389** A715 40b Apollo 4, 5, 6 .25 .25
**2390** A715 55b Apollo 7, 8 .25 .25
**2391** A715 1 l Apollo 9, 10 .25 .25
**2392** A715 1.20 l Apollo 11, 12 .25 .25
**2393** A715 1.85 l Apollo 13, 14 .35 .25
**2394** A715 2.75 l Apollo 15, 16 .60 .25
**2395** A715 3.60 l Apollo 17 1.10 .30
*Nos. 2387-2395 (9)* 3.55 2.30

Highlights of US Apollo space program. See No. C192.

"25" and Flags — A716

Designs: 1.20 l, "25" and national emblem. 1.75 l, "25" and factory.

**1972, Dec. 25**
**2396** A716 55b blue & multi .25 .25
**2397** A716 1.20 l yel & multi .35 .25
**2398** A716 1.75 l ver & multi .60 .25
*Nos. 2396-2398 (3)* 1.20 .75

25th anniversary of the Republic.

European Bee-eater A717

Globeflowers A718

Nature Protection: No. 2400, Red-breasted goose. No. 2401, Penduline tit. No. 2403, Garden Turk's-cap. No. 2404, Gentian.

**1973, Feb. 5 Photo.** ***Perf. 13***
**2399** A717 1.40 l gray & multi .25 .25
**2400** A717 1.85 l multi .35 .25
**2401** A717 2.75 l blue & multi .70 .25
*a.* Strip of 3, #2399-2401 1.40 .60
**2402** A718 1.40 l multi .25 .25
**2403** A718 1.85 l yellow & multi .35 .25
**2404** A718 2.75 l multi .70 .25
*a.* Strip of 3, #2402-2404 1.40 .60

Nicolaus Copernicus — A719

**1973, Feb. 19 Photo.** ***Perf. 13x13½***
**2405** A719 2.75 l multi 1.00 .35

Nicolaus Copernicus (1473-1543), Polish astronomer. Printed with alternating label publicizing Intl. Phil. Exhib., Poznan, 8/19-9/2.

Suceava Woman A720

Regional Costumes: 40b, Suceava man. 55b, Harghita woman. 1.75 l, Harghita man. 2.75 l, Gorj woman. 6.40 l, Gorj man.

**1973, Mar. 15**
**2406** A720 10b lt bl & multi .25 .25
**2407** A720 40b multicolored .25 .25
**2408** A720 55b bis & multi .25 .25
**2409** A720 1.75 l lil & multi .30 .25
**2410** A720 2.75 l multi .45 .25
**2411** A720 6.40 l multi 1.25 .35
*Nos. 2406-2411 (6)* 2.75 1.60

D. Paciurea (Sculptor) — A721

Portraits: 40b, I. Slavici (1848-1925), writer. 55b, G. Lazar (1779-1823), writer. 6.40 l, A. Flechtenmacher (1823-1898), composer.

**1973, Mar. 26**
**2412** A721 10b multi .25 .25
**2413** A721 40b multi .25 .25
**2414** A721 55b multi .25 .25
**2415** A721 6.40 l multi 1.25 .40
*Nos. 2412-2415 (4)* 2.00 1.15

Anniversaries of famous artists.

Map of Europe A722

Design: 3.60 l, Symbol of collaboration.

**1973, Apr. 28 Photo.** ***Perf. 13½***
**2416** A722 3.35 l dp bl & gold 1.10 .70
**2417** A722 3.60 l brt mag & gold 1.25 1.00
*a.* Pair, #2416-2417 2.40 2.00

Inter-European cultural and economic cooperation. Printed in sheets of 10 with blue marginal inscription.

Souvenir Sheet

The Rape of Proserpina, by Hans von Aachen — A723

**1973, May 5**
**2418** A723 12 l gold & multi 3.50 3.25

IBRA Munchen 1973, Intl. Stamp Exhib., Munich, May 11-20.

Prince Alexander I. Cuza — A724

**1973, May 5 Photo.** ***Perf. 13½***
**2419** A724 1.75 l multi .50 .25

Alexander Ioan Cuza (1820-1873), prince of Romania, Moldavia and Walachia.

Hand with Hammer and Sickle — A725

**1973, May 5**
**2420** A725 40b gold & multi .40 .25

Workers and Peasants Party, 25th anniv.

Romanian Flag, Bayonets Stabbing Swastika — A726

**1973, May 5**
**2421** A726 55b multicolored .40 .25

Anti-fascist Front, 40th anniversary.

WMO Emblem, Weather Satellite — A727

**1973, June 15**
**2422** A727 2 l ultra & multi .60 .25

Intl. meteorological cooperation, cent.

Dimitrie Ralet Holding Letter — A728

Portraits with letters. 60b, Enachita Vacarescu, by A. Chladek. 1.55 l, Serdarul Dimitrie Aman, by C. Lecca.

**1973, June 20**
**2423** A728 40b multi .25 .25
**2424** A728 60b multi .25 .25
**2425** A728 1.55 l multi .50 .25
*Nos. 2423-2425,B432 (4)* 2.50 1.35

"The Letter on Romanian Portraits." Socfilex III Philatelic Exhibition, Bucharest, July 20-29. See No. B433.

Dimitrie Cantemir — A729

6 l, Portrait of Cantemir in oval frame.

**1973, June 25**

| | | | | |
|---|---|---|---|---|
| **2426** | A729 | 1.75 l multi | .50 | .25 |

**Souvenir Sheet**

| | | | | |
|---|---|---|---|---|
| **2427** | A729 | 6 l multi | 2.50 | 1.75 |

Dimitrie Cantemir (1673-1723), Prince of Moldavia, writer. No. 2427 contains one 38x50mm stamp.

Plate — A730

Designs: 10b, Fibulae, vert. 55b, Jug, vert. 1.55 l, Necklaces and fibula. 2.75 l, Plate, vert. 6.80 l, Octagonal bowl with animal handles. 12 l, Breastplate, vert.

**1973, July 25 Photo. *Perf. 13½***

| | | | | |
|---|---|---|---|---|
| **2428** | A730 | 10b vio bl & multi | .25 | .25 |
| **2429** | A730 | 20b green & multi | .25 | .25 |
| **2430** | A730 | 55b red & multi | .25 | .25 |
| **2431** | A730 | 1.55 l multi | .35 | .25 |
| **2432** | A730 | 2.75 l plum & multi | .55 | .25 |
| **2433** | A730 | 6.80 l multi | 1.50 | .35 |
| | | *Nos. 2428-2433 (6)* | 3.15 | 1.60 |

**Souvenir Sheet**

| | | | | |
|---|---|---|---|---|
| **2434** | A730 | 12 l multi | 3.00 | 2.75 |

Roman gold treasure of Pietroasa, 4th century.

Symbolic Flower, Map of Europe A731

Design: 5 l, Map of Europe, symbolic tree.

**1973, Oct. 2 Photo. *Perf. 13½***

| | | | | |
|---|---|---|---|---|
| **2435** | A731 | 2.75 l multi | 1.10 | .70 |
| **2436** | A731 | 5 l multi | 1.75 | 1.00 |
| *a.* | | Sheet, 2 each + 2 labels | 5.25 | 5.25 |

Conference for European Security and Cooperation, Helsinki, Finland, July 1973.

Jug and Cloth, Oboga — A732

Designs: 20b, Plate and Pitcher, Vama. 55b, Bowl, Marginea. 1.55 l, Pitcher and plate, Sibiu-Saschiz. 2.75 l, Bowl and jug, Pisc. 6.80 l, Figurine (fowl), Oboga.

**1973, Oct. 15 *Perf. 13***

| | | | | |
|---|---|---|---|---|
| **2437** | A732 | 10b multi | .25 | .25 |
| **2438** | A732 | 20b multi | .25 | .25 |
| **2439** | A732 | 55b multi | .25 | .25 |
| **2440** | A732 | 1.55 l multi | .35 | .25 |
| **2441** | A732 | 2.75 l multi | .55 | .25 |
| **2442** | A732 | 6.80 l multi | 1.25 | .35 |
| | | *Nos. 2437-2442 (6)* | 2.90 | 1.60 |

Pottery and cloths from various regions of Romania.

Postilion, by A. Verona A732a

**1973, Nov. 15 Photo. *Perf. 13½***

| | | | | |
|---|---|---|---|---|
| **2442A** | A732a | 1.10 l + 90b label | .50 | .25 |

Stamp Day.

Women Workers, by G. Saru A733

Paintings of Workers: 20b, Construction Site, by M. Bunescu, horiz. 55b, Shipyard Workers, by H. Catargi, horiz. 1.55 l, Worker, by Catargi. 2.75 l, Miners, by A. Phoebus. 6.80 l, Spinner, by Nicolae Grigorescu. 12 l, Farmers at Rest, by Stefan Popescu, horiz.

**1973, Nov. 26 Photo. *Perf. 13½***

| | | | | |
|---|---|---|---|---|
| **2443** | A733 | 10b gold & multi | .25 | .25 |
| **2444** | A733 | 20b gold & multi | .25 | .25 |
| **2445** | A733 | 55b gold & multi | .25 | .25 |
| **2446** | A733 | 1.55 l gold & multi | .25 | .25 |
| **2447** | A733 | 2.75 l gold & multi | .50 | .25 |
| **2448** | A733 | 6.80 l gold & multi | 1.25 | .35 |
| | | *Nos. 2443-2448 (6)* | 2.75 | 1.60 |

**Miniature Sheet**

| | | | | |
|---|---|---|---|---|
| **2449** | A733 | 12 l gold & multi | 3.00 | 2.75 |

City Hall, Craiova — A734

Tugboat under Bridge — A735

Designs: 10b, Infinite Column, by Constantin Brancusi, vert. 20b, Heroes' Mausoleum, Marasesti. 35b, Risnov Citadel. 40b, Densus Church, vert. 50b, Dej Church, vert. 55b, Maldaresti Fortress. 60b, National Theater, Iasi. 1 l, Curtea-de-Arges Monastery, vert. 1.20 l, Tirgu-Mures Citadel. 1.45 l, Cargoship Dimbovita. 1.50 l, Muntenia passenger ship. 1.55 l, Three-master Mircea. 1.75 l, Motorship Transilvania. 2.20 l, Ore carrier Oltol. 3.65 l, Trawler Mures. 4.70 l, Tanker Arges.

**1973-74 Photo. *Perf. 13***

| | | | | |
|---|---|---|---|---|
| **2450** | A734 | 5b lake | .25 | .25 |
| **2451** | A734 | 10b brt blue | .25 | .25 |
| **2452** | A734 | 20b orange | .25 | .25 |
| **2453** | A734 | 35b green | .25 | .25 |
| **2454** | A734 | 40b dk violet | .25 | .25 |
| **2455** | A734 | 50b ultra | .25 | .25 |
| **2456** | A734 | 55b orange brn | .25 | .25 |
| **2457** | A734 | 60b carmine | .25 | .25 |
| **2458** | A734 | 1 l dp ultra | .25 | .25 |
| **2459** | A734 | 1.20 l olive grn | .30 | .25 |
| **2460** | A735 | 1.35 l gray | .35 | .25 |
| **2461** | A735 | 1.45 l dull blue | .35 | .25 |
| **2462** | A735 | 1.50 l car rose | .35 | .25 |
| **2463** | A735 | 1.55 l violet bl | .35 | .25 |
| **2464** | A735 | 1.75 l slate grn | .45 | .25 |
| **2465** | A735 | 2.20 l brt blue | .60 | .25 |
| **2466** | A735 | 3.65 l dull lilac | 1.00 | .25 |
| **2467** | A735 | 4.70 l violet brn | 1.40 | .25 |
| | | *Nos. 2450-2467 (18)* | 7.40 | 4.50 |

Issued: #2450-2459, 12/15/73; #2460-2467, 1/28/74.

Boats at Montfleur, by Claude Monet — A736

Impressionistic paintings: 40b, Church of Moret, by Alfred Sisley, vert. 55b, Orchard in Bloom, by Camille Pissarro. 1.75 l, Portrait of Jeanne, by Pissarro, vert. 2.75 l, Landscape, by Auguste Renoir. 3.60 l, Portrait of a Girl, by Paul Cezanne, vert. 10 l, Women Taking Bath, by Renoir, vert.

**1974, Mar. 15 Photo. *Perf. 13½***

| | | | | |
|---|---|---|---|---|
| **2468** | A736 | 20b blue & multi | .25 | .25 |
| **2469** | A736 | 40b blue & multi | .25 | .25 |
| **2470** | A736 | 55b blue & multi | .25 | .25 |
| **2471** | A736 | 1.75 l blue & multi | .40 | .25 |
| **2472** | A736 | 2.75 l blue & multi | .60 | .25 |
| **2473** | A736 | 3.60 l blue & multi | .80 | .25 |
| | | *Nos. 2468-2473 (6)* | 2.55 | 1.50 |

**Souvenir Sheet**

| | | | | |
|---|---|---|---|---|
| **2474** | A736 | 10 l blue & multi | 2.25 | 2.00 |

Harness Racing A737

Designs: Various horse races.

**1974, Apr. 5 Photo. *Perf. 13½***

| | | | | |
|---|---|---|---|---|
| **2475** | A737 | 40b ver & multi | .25 | .25 |
| **2476** | A737 | 55b bis & multi | .25 | .25 |
| **2477** | A737 | 60b multi | .25 | .25 |
| **2478** | A737 | 1.55 l multi | .35 | .25 |
| **2479** | A737 | 2.75 l multi | .60 | .25 |
| **2480** | A737 | 3.45 l multi | .80 | .30 |
| | | *Nos. 2475-2480 (6)* | 2.50 | 1.55 |

Centenary of horse racing in Romania.

Nicolae Titulescu (1883-1941) A738

**1974, Apr. 16**

| | | | | |
|---|---|---|---|---|
| **2481** | A738 | 1.75 l multi | .50 | .25 |

Interparliamentary Session, Bucharest, Apr. 1974. Titulescu was the first Romanian delegate to the League of Nations.

Souvenir Sheet

1850 ANI
DE LA RIDICAREA ASEZARII
NAPOCA - CLVJ
LA RANG DE MVNICIPIV

Roman Memorial with First Reference to Napoca (Cluj) — A739

**1974, Apr. 18 Photo. *Perf. 13***

| | | | | |
|---|---|---|---|---|
| **2482** | A739 | 10 l multi | 2.50 | 2.50 |

1850th anniv. of the elevation of the Roman settlement of Napoca (Cluj) to a municipality.

Stylized Map of Europe A740

Design: 3.45 l, Satellite over earth.

**1974, Apr. 25 Photo. *Perf. 13½x13***

| | | | | |
|---|---|---|---|---|
| **2483** | A740 | 2.20 l multi | 1.00 | .70 |
| **2484** | A740 | 3.45 l multi | 1.50 | 1.00 |
| *a.* | | Pair, #2483-2484 | 2.50 | 2.00 |

Inter-European Cultural Economic Cooperation.

Young Pioneers with Banners, by Pepene Cornelia — A741

**1974, Apr. 25 Photo. *Perf. 13½***

| | | | | |
|---|---|---|---|---|
| **2485** | A741 | 55b multicolored | .50 | .25 |

25th anniv. of the Romanian Pioneers Org.

Mail Motorboat, UPU Emblem A742

UPU Emblem and: 40b, Mail train. 55b, Mailplane and truck. 1.75 l, Mail delivery by motorcycle. 2.75 l, Mailman delivering letter to little girl. 3.60 l, Young stamp collectors. 4 l, Mail collection. 6 l, Modern post office.

**1974, May 15**

| | | | | |
|---|---|---|---|---|
| **2486** | A742 | 20b gray & multi | .25 | .25 |
| **2487** | A742 | 40b multicolored | .25 | .25 |
| **2488** | A742 | 55b ultra & multi | .25 | .25 |
| **2489** | A742 | 1.75 l multi | .50 | .25 |
| **2490** | A742 | 2.75 l brn & multi | .70 | .25 |
| **2491** | A742 | 3.60 l org & multi | 1.00 | .30 |
| | | *Nos. 2486-2491 (6)* | 2.95 | 1.55 |

**Souvenir Sheet**

| | | | | |
|---|---|---|---|---|
| **2492** | | Sheet of 2 | 3.00 | 2.75 |
| *a.* | | A742 4 l multi | .90 | |
| *b.* | | A742 6 l multi | 1.60 | |

Centenary of Universal Postal Union. Size of stamps of No. 2492, 28x24mm.

An imperf airmail UPU souvenir sheet of one (10 l) exists. The multicolored stamp is 49x38mm. This sheet is not known to have been sold to the public at post offices. Value, unused $30, used $27.50.

### No. 2382 Surcharged with New Value and Overprinted: "ROMÂNIA / CAMPIOANA / MONDIALĂ / 1974"

**1974, May 13**

| | | | | | |
|---|---|---|---|---|---|
| **2493** | A714 | 1.75 l on 20b multi | | 2.50 | 1.75 |

Romania's victory in World Handball Championship, 1974.

Soccer and Games Emblem A743

Designs: Games emblem and various scenes from soccer game.

**1974, June 25** *Perf. 13½*

| | | | | | |
|---|---|---|---|---|---|
| **2494** | A743 | 20b | purple & multi | .25 | .25 |
| **2495** | A743 | 40b | multi | .25 | .25 |
| **2496** | A743 | 55b | ultra & multi | .25 | .25 |
| **2497** | A743 | 1.75 l | brn & multi | .25 | .25 |
| **2498** | A743 | 2.75 l | multi | .50 | .25 |
| **2499** | A743 | 3.60 l | vio & multi | .75 | .30 |
| | | | *Nos. 2494-2499 (6)* | 2.25 | 1.55 |

**Souvenir Sheet**

| | | | | | |
|---|---|---|---|---|---|
| **2500** | A743 | 10 l | multi | 2.50 | 2.00 |

World Cup Soccer Championship, Munich, June 13-July 7. No. 2500 contains one horizontal stamp 50x38mm.

An imperf. 10 l airmail souvenir sheet exists showing a globe as soccer ball and satellite. Gray blue margin showing Soccer Cup, radio tower and stadium; black control number. Value, unused or used, $65.

"25" — A744

**1974, June 10**

| | | | | | |
|---|---|---|---|---|---|
| **2501** | A744 | 55b | blue & multi | .40 | .25 |

25th anniv. of the Council for Mutual Economic Assistance (COMECON).

UN Emblem and People — A745

**1974, June 25** **Photo.** *Perf. 13½*

| | | | | | |
|---|---|---|---|---|---|
| **2502** | A745 | 2 l | multicolored | .60 | .25 |

World Population Year.

Hand Drawing Peace Dove — A746

**1974, June 28**

| | | | | | |
|---|---|---|---|---|---|
| **2503** | A746 | 2 l | ultra & multi | .60 | .25 |

25 years of the National and Intl. Movement to Uphold the Cause of Peace.

Ioan, Prince of Wallachia — A747

Soldier, Industry and Agriculture A748

Hunedoara Iron and Steel Works — A749

Designs: 1.10 l, Avram Iancu (1824-1872). 1.30 l, Dr. C. I. Parhon (1874-1969). 1.40 l, Bishop Dosoftei (1624-1693).

**1974** **Photo.** *Perf. 13*

| | | | | | |
|---|---|---|---|---|---|
| **2504** | A747 | 20b | blue | .25 | .25 |
| **2505** | A748 | 55b | carmine rose | .25 | .25 |
| **2506** | A749 | 1 l | slate green | .25 | .25 |
| **2507** | A747 | 1.10 l | dk gray olive | .25 | .25 |
| **2508** | A747 | 1.30 l | deep magenta | .30 | .25 |
| **2509** | A747 | 1.40 l | dark violet | .35 | .25 |
| | | | *Nos. 2504-2509 (6)* | 1.65 | 1.50 |

No. 2505 for Army Day, No. 2506 for 220th anniv. of Hunedoara Iron and Steel works; others for anniversaries of famous Romanians.

Issue dates: 1l, June 17; others June 25.

Romanians and Flags — A750

Design: 40b, Romanian and Communist flags forming "XXX," vert.

**1974, Aug. 20**

| | | | | | |
|---|---|---|---|---|---|
| **2510** | A750 | 40b | gold, ultra & car | .25 | .25 |
| **2511** | A750 | 55b | yellow & multi | .25 | .25 |

Romania's liberation from Fascist rule, 30th anniv.

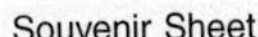

**Souvenir Sheet**

View, Stockholm — A751

**1974, Sept. 10** **Photo.** *Perf. 13*

| | | | | | |
|---|---|---|---|---|---|
| **2512** | A751 | 10 l | multicolored | 2.50 | 2.50 |

Stockholmia 74 International Philatelic Exhibition, Stockholm, Sept. 21-29.

Thistle — A752

Nature Protection: 40b, Checkered lily. 55b, Yew. 1.75 l, Azalea. 2.75 l, Forget-me-not. 3.60 l, Pinks.

**1974, Sept. 15**

| | | | | | |
|---|---|---|---|---|---|
| **2513** | A752 | 20b | plum & multi | .25 | .25 |
| **2514** | A752 | 40b | multi | .25 | .25 |
| **2515** | A752 | 55b | multi | .25 | .25 |
| **2516** | A752 | 1.75 l | multi | .50 | .25 |
| **2517** | A752 | 2.75 l | brn & multi | .70 | .25 |
| **2518** | A752 | 3.60 l | multi | 1.00 | .30 |
| | | | *Nos. 2513-2518 (6)* | 2.95 | 1.55 |

Isis, First Century A.D. A753

Archaeological art works excavated in Romania: 40b, Serpent, by Glycon. 55b, Emperor Trajan, bronze bust. 1.75 l, Roman woman, statue, 3rd century. 2.75 l, Mithraic bas-relief. 3.60 l, Roman man, statue, 3rd century.

**1974, Oct. 20** **Photo.** *Perf. 13*

| | | | | | |
|---|---|---|---|---|---|
| **2519** | A753 | 20b | gold & multi | .25 | .25 |
| **2520** | A753 | 40b | ultra & multi | .25 | .25 |
| **2521** | A753 | 55b | multi | .25 | .25 |
| **2522** | A753 | 1.75 l | multi | .40 | .25 |
| **2523** | A753 | 2.75 l | brn & multi | .60 | .25 |
| **2524** | A753 | 3.60 l | multi | .85 | .30 |
| | | | *Nos. 2519-2524 (6)* | 2.60 | 1.55 |

Romanian Communist Party Emblem — A754

Design: 1 l, similar to 55b.

**1974, Nov. 20**

| | | | | | |
|---|---|---|---|---|---|
| **2525** | A754 | 55b | blk, red & gold | .25 | .25 |
| **2526** | A754 | 1 l | blk, red & gold | .30 | .25 |

9th Romanian Communist Party Congress.

Discobolus and Olympic Rings — A755

**1974, Nov. 11**

| | | | | | |
|---|---|---|---|---|---|
| **2527** | A755 | 2 l | ultra & multi | .75 | .25 |

Romanian Olympic Committee, 60th anniv.

Skylab A756

**1974, Dec. 14** **Photo.** *Perf. 13*

| | | | | | |
|---|---|---|---|---|---|
| **2528** | A756 | 2.50 l | multi | .70 | .35 |

Skylab, manned US space laboratory. No. 2528 printed in sheets of 4 stamps and 4 labels. A 10 l imperf. souvenir sheet exists showing Skylab. Value, unused or used, $65.

Field Ball and Games' Emblem A757

Designs: 1.75 l, 2.20 l, Various scenes from field ball; 1.75 l, vert.

**1975, Jan. 3**

| | | | | | |
|---|---|---|---|---|---|
| **2529** | A757 | 55b | ultra & multi | .25 | .25 |
| **2530** | A757 | 1.75 l | yellow & multi | .30 | .25 |
| **2531** | A757 | 2.20 l | multi | .45 | .25 |
| | | | *Nos. 2529-2531 (3)* | 1.00 | .75 |

World University Field Ball Championship.

Rocks and Birches, by Andreescu A758

Paintings by Ion Andreescu (1850-1882): 40b, Farm Woman with Green Kerchief. 55b, Winter in the Woods. 1.75 l, Winter in Barbizon, horiz. 2.75 l, Self-portrait. 3.60 l, Main Road, horiz.

**1975, Jan. 24**

| | | | | | |
|---|---|---|---|---|---|
| **2532** | A758 | 20b | multi | .25 | .25 |
| **2533** | A758 | 40b | multi | .25 | .25 |
| **2534** | A758 | 55b | multi | .25 | .25 |
| **2535** | A758 | 1.75 l | multi | .40 | .25 |
| **2536** | A758 | 2.75 l | multi | .60 | .25 |
| **2537** | A758 | 3.60 l | multi | .85 | .30 |
| | | | *Nos. 2532-2537 (6)* | 2.60 | 1.55 |

Torch with Flame in Flag Colors and Coat of Arms — A759

**1975, Feb. 1**
**2538** A759 40b multicolored .40 .25

Romanian Socialist Republic, 10th anniv.

Vaslui Battle, by O. Obedeanu A760

**1975, Feb. 25 Photo. *Perf. 13½***
**2539** A760 55b gold & multi .40 .25

Battle at the High Bridge, Stephan the Great's victory over the Turks, 500th anniv.

Woman Spinning, by Nicolae Grigorescu — A761

**1975, Mar. 1**
**2540** A761 55b gold & multi .40 .25

International Women's Year.

Michelangelo, Self-portrait A762

**1975, Mar. 10**
**2541** A762 5 l multicolored 1.40 .30

Michelangelo Buonarroti (1475-1564), Italian sculptor, painter and architect.
For overprint see No. 2581.

Souvenir Sheet

Escorial Palace and España 75 Emblem — A763

**1975, Mar. 15 Photo. *Perf. 13***
**2542** A763 10 l multi 2.50 2.25

Espana 75 Intl. Phil. Exhib., Madrid, 4/4-13.

Letter with Postal Code, Pigeon A764

**1975, Mar. 26 Photo. *Perf. 13½***
**2543** A764 55b blue & multi .40 .25

Introduction of postal code system.

Children's Science Pavilion — A765

**1975, Apr. 10 Photo. *Perf. 13***
**2544** A765 4 l multicolored 1.20 .25

Oceanexpo 75, International Exhibition, Okinawa, July 20, 1975-Jan. 1976.

Peonies, by N. Tonitza A766

3.45 l, Chrysanthemums, by St. Luchian.

**1975, Apr. 28**
**2545** A766 2.20 l gold & multi .85 .50
**2546** A766 3.45 l gold & multi 1.25 .95
*a.* Pair, #2545-2546 2.25 1.75

Inter-European Cultural and Economic Cooperation. Printed checkerwise in sheets of 10 (2x5).

1875 Meter Convention Emblem — A767

**1975, May 10 Photo. *Perf. 13***
**2547** A767 1.85 l bl, blk & gold .65 .25

Cent. of Intl. Meter Convention, Paris, 1875.

Mihail Eminescu and his Home — A768

**1975, June 5**
**2548** A768 55b multicolored .40 .25

Mihail Eminescu (1850-1889), poet.

Marble Plaque and Dacian Coins 1st-2nd Centuries — A769

**1975, May 26**
**2549** A769 55b multicolored .40 .25

2000th anniv. of the founding of Alba Iulia (Apulum).

Souvenir Sheet

"On the Bank of the Seine," by Th. Pallady — A770

**1975, May 26**
**2550** A770 10 l multicolored 2.25 1.75

ARPHILA 75, Paris, June 6-16.

Dr. Albert Schweitzer (1875-1965), Medical Missionary — A771

**1974, Dec. 20 Photo. *Perf. 13½***
**2551** A771 40b black brown .40 .25

Ana Ipatescu — A772

**1975, June 2 Photo. *Perf. 13½***
**2552** A772 55b lilac rose .40 .25

Ana Ipatescu, fighter in 1848 revolution.

Policeman with Walkie-talkie — A773

**1975, Sept. 1**
**2553** A773 55b brt blue .40 .25

Publicity for traffic rules.

Monument and Projected Reconstruction, Adam Clissi — A777

Roman Monuments: 55b, Emperor Trajan, bas-relief, vert. 1.20 l, Trajan's column, Rome, vert. 1.55 l, Governor Decibalus, bas-relief, vert. 2 l, Excavated Roman city, Turnu-Severin. 2.25 l, Trajan's Bridge, ruin and projected reconstruction. No. 2569, Roman fortifications, vert.

**1975, June 26 Photo. *Perf. 13½***
**2563** A777 55b red brn & blk .25 .25
**2564** A777 1.20 l vio bl & blk .25 .25
**2565** A777 1.55 l green & blk .35 .25
**2566** A777 1.75 l dl rose & multi .50 .25
**2567** A777 2 l dl yel & blk .60 .25
**2568** A777 2.25 l brt bl & blk 1.10 .25
*Nos. 2563-2568 (6)* 3.05 1.50

**Souvenir Sheet**

**2569** A777 10 l multicolored 4.50 3.75

European Architectural Heritage Year.
An imperf. 10 l gold and dark brown souvenir sheet exists showing the Roman wolf suckling Romulus and Remus. Value $70, unused or used.
A similar souvenir sheet was issued in 1978 to honor the Essen International Stamp Fair. It contains a 10 l stamp, depicting the design of the stamp described above, within a blue frame. Value $10, unused or used.

Michael the Brave, by Sadeler A778

Michael the Brave Statue — A779

Designs: 1.20 l, Ottoman Messengers Offering Gifts to Michael the Brave, by Theodor Aman, horiz. 2.75 l, Michael the Brave in Battle of Calugareni, by Aman.

**1975, July 7**
**2571** A778 55b gold & blk .25 .25
**2572** A778 1.20 l gold & multi .25 .25
**2573** A778 2.75 l gold & multi .65 .25
*Nos. 2571-2573 (3)* 1.15 .75

### Souvenir Sheet
*Imperf*

**2574** A779 10 l gold & multi 20.00 20.00

First political union of Romanian states under Michael the Brave, 375th anniv.
No. 2574 issued Sept. 20.

Larkspur — A780

**1975, Aug. 15 Photo. *Perf. 13½***

**2575** A780 20b shown .25 .25
**2576** A780 40b Field poppies .25 .25
**2577** A780 55b Xeranthemum annuum .25 .25
**2578** A780 1.75 l Rockrose .30 .25
**2579** A780 2.75 l Meadow sage .60 .25
**2580** A780 3.60 l Wild chicory .75 .25
*Nos. 2575-2580 (6)* 2.40 1.50

No. 2541 Overprinted in Red

**1975, Aug. 23**

**2581** A762 5 l multicolored 4.50 4.50

Intl. Phil. Exhib., Riccione, Italy, Aug. 23-25.

Map Showing Location of Craiova, 1750 — A781

**1975, Sept. 15 Photo. *Perf. 13½***

**2582** A781 Strip of 3 .65 .30
*a.* 20b ocher, yellow, red & black .25 .25
*b.* 55b ocher, yellow, red & black .25 .25
*c.* 1 l ocher, yellow, red & black .25 .25

1750th anniv. of first documentation of Daco-Getian settlement of Pelendava and 500th anniversary of documentation of Craiova.
Size of Nos. 2582a, 2582c: 25x32mm; of No. 2582b: 80x32mm.

Muntenian Rug — A782

Romanian Peasant Rugs: 40b, Banat. 55b, Oltenia. 1.75 l, Moldavia. 2.75 l, Oltenia. 3.60 l, Maramures.

**1975, Oct. 5 Photo. *Perf. 13½***

**2583** A782 20b dk bl & multi .25 .25
**2584** A782 40b black & multi .25 .25
**2585** A782 55b multicolored .25 .25
**2586** A782 1.75 l black & multi .30 .25
**2587** A782 2.75 l multicolored .55 .25
**2588** A782 3.60 l black & multi .70 .25
*Nos. 2583-2588 (6)* 2.30 1.50

Minibus A783

**1975, Nov. 5 Photo. *Perf. 13½***

**2589** A783 20b shown .25 .25
**2590** A783 40b Gasoline truck .25 .25
**2591** A783 55b Jeep .25 .25
**2592** A783 1.75 l Flat-bed truck .40 .25
**2593** A783 2.75 l Dacia automobile .55 .25
**2594** A783 3.60 l Dump truck .70 .25
*Nos. 2589-2594 (6)* 2.40 1.50

Souvenir Sheet

Winter, by Peter Brueghel, the Younger — A784

**1975, Nov. 25 Photo. *Perf. 13½***

**2595** A784 10 l multicolored 3.25 3.00

THEMABELGA Intl. Topical Phil. Exhib., Brussels, Dec. 13-21.

Luge and Olympic Games' Emblem — A785

Innsbruck Olympic Games' Emblem and: 40b, Biathlon, vert. 55b, Woman skier. 1.75 l, Ski jump. 2.75 l, Woman figure skater. 3.60 l, Ice hockey. 10 l, Two-man bobsled.

**1976, Jan. 12 Photo. *Perf. 13½***

**2596** A785 20b blue & multi .25 .25
**2597** A785 40b multicolored .25 .25
**2598** A785 55b multicolored .25 .25
**2599** A785 1.75 l ol & multi .40 .25
**2600** A785 2.75 l multi .60 .25
**2601** A785 3.60 l multi .80 .35
*Nos. 2596-2601 (6)* 2.55 1.60

### Souvenir Sheet

**2602** A785 10 l multi 4.50 4.25

12th Winter Olympic Games, Innsbruck, Austria, Feb. 4-15. An imperf. 10 l souvenir sheet exists showing slalom; Romanian flag, Games' emblem. Values: unused $50; used, $30.

Washington at Valley Forge, by W. T. Trego — A786

Paintings: 40b, Washington at Trenton, by John Trumbull, vert. 55b, Washington Crossing the Delaware, by Emanuel Leutze. 1.75 l, The Capture of the Hessians, by Trumbull. 2.75 l, Jefferson, by Thomas Sully, vert. 3.60 l, Surrender of Cornwallis at Yorktown, by Trumbull. 10 l, Signing of the Declaration of Independence, by Trumbull.

**1976, Jan. 25 Photo. *Perf. 13½***

**2603** A786 20b gold & multi .25 .25
**2604** A786 40b gold & multi .25 .25
**2605** A786 55b gold & multi .30 .25
**2606** A786 1.75 l gold & multi .40 .25
**2607** A786 2.75 l gold & multi .80 .30
**2608** A786 3.60 l gold & multi 1.00 .35
*Nos. 2603-2608 (6)* 3.00 1.65

### Souvenir Sheet

**2609** A786 10 l gold & multi 3.00 2.50

American Bicentennial. No. 2609 also for Interphil 76 Intl. Phil. Exhib., Philadelphia, Pa., May 20-June 6. Printed in horizontal rows of 4 stamps with centered label showing Bicentennial emblem.

Prayer, by Brancusi A787

Designs: 1.75 l, Architectural Assembly, by Brancusi. 3.60 l, Constantin Brancusi.

**1976, Feb. 15 Photo. *Perf. 13½***

**2610** A787 55b purple & multi .25 .25
**2611** A787 1.75 l blue & multi .30 .25
**2612** A787 3.60 l multicolored .85 .35
*Nos. 2610-2612 (3)* 1.40 .85

Constantin Brancusi (1876-1957), sculptor.
For surcharge see No. B440.

Anton Davidoglu A788

Archives Museum A789

55b, Vlad Tepes. 1.20 l, Costache Negri.

**1976, Feb. 25**

**2613** A788 40b green & multi .25 .25
**2614** A788 55b green & multi .25 .25
**2615** A788 1.20 l green & multi .25 .25
**2616** A789 1.75 l green & multi .25 .25
*Nos. 2613-2616 (4)* 1.00 1.00

Anniversaries: Anton Davidoglu (1876-1958), mathematician; Prince Vlad Tepes, commander in war against the Turks (d. 1476); Costache Negri (1812-1876), Moldavian freedom fighter; Romanian National Archives Museum, founded 1926.

Dr. Carol Davila — A790

1.75 l, Nurse with patient. 2.20 l, First aid.

**1976, Apr. 20**

**2617** A790 55b multi .25 .25
**2618** A790 1.75 l multi .40 .25
**2619** A790 2.20 l yellow & multi .50 .25
*Nos. 2617-2619,C199 (4)* 1.85 1.00

Romanian Red Cross cent.

Vase with King Decebalus Portrait — A791

Design: 3.45 l, Vase with portrait of King Michael the Bold.

**1976, May 13**

**2620** A791 2.20 l bl & multi .35 .35
**2621** A791 3.45 l multi .35 .35

Inter-European Cultural Economic Cooperation. Nos. 2620-2621 each printed in sheets of 4 with marginal inscriptions.

Coat of Arms — A792

**1976, June 12**

**2622** A792 1.75 l multi .75 .25

See design A615.

Spiru Haret — A793

**1976, June 25**

**2628** A793 20b multicolored .40 .25

Spiru Haret (1851-1912), mathematician.

Woman Athlete — A794

Romanian Olympic Emblem and: 40b, Boxing. 55b, Team handball. 1.75 l, 2-man scull, horiz. 2.75 l, Gymnast on rings, horiz. 3.60 l, 2-man canoe, horiz. 10 l, Woman gymnast, horiz.

**1976, June 25 Photo. *Perf. 13½***

**2629** A794 20b org & multi .25 .25
**2630** A794 40b multi .25 .25
**2631** A794 55b multi .25 .25
**2632** A794 1.75 l multi .35 .25
**2633** A794 2.75 l vio & multi .50 .25
**2634** A794 3.60 l bl & multi .75 .45
*Nos. 2629-2634 (6)* 2.35 1.70

### Souvenir Sheet

**2635** A794 10 l rose & multi 3.25 2.25

21st Olympic Games, Montreal, Canada, July 17-Aug. 1. No. 2635 contains one stamp 49x37mm.
An imperf. airmail 10 l souvenir sheet exists showing Olympic Stadium, Montreal. Values: unused $40; used $25.

Inscribed Stone Tablets, Banat — A795

Designs: 40b, Hekate, Bacchus, bas-relief. 55b, Ceramic fragment, bowl, coins. 1.75 l, Bowl, urn and cup. 2.75 l, Sword, lance and tombstone. 3.60 l, Lances, urn. 10 l, Clay vessel and silver coins.

**1976, July 25**

| No. | Type | Value | Description | Unused | Used |
|---|---|---|---|---|---|
| **2636** | A795 | 20b | multi | .25 | .25 |
| **2637** | A795 | 40b | multi | .25 | .25 |
| **2638** | A795 | 55b | org & multi | .25 | .25 |
| **2639** | A795 | 1.75 l | multi | .40 | .25 |
| **2640** | A795 | 2.75 l | fawn & multi | .60 | .25 |
| **2641** | A795 | 3.60 l | multi | .85 | .35 |
| | | | *Nos. 2636-2641 (6)* | 2.60 | 1.60 |

**Souvenir Sheet**

| No. | Type | Value | Description | Unused | Used |
|---|---|---|---|---|---|
| **2642** | A795 | 10 l | yel & multi | 3.25 | 2.25 |

Daco-Roman archaeological treasures. No. 2642 issued Mar. 25. An imperf. 10 l souvenir sheet exists showing a silver and gold vase and silver coins. Values: unused $10; used $6.

Wolf Statue, 4th Century Map A796

**1976, Aug. 25**

| No. | Type | Value | Description | Unused | Used |
|---|---|---|---|---|---|
| **2643** | A796 | 55b | multi | .40 | .25 |

Founding of Buzau, 1600th anniv.

Game A797

**1976, Sept. 20**

| No. | Type | Value | Description | Unused | Used |
|---|---|---|---|---|---|
| **2644** | A797 | 20b | Red deer | .25 | .25 |
| **2645** | A797 | 40b | Brown bear | .25 | .25 |
| **2646** | A797 | 55b | Chamois | .25 | .25 |
| **2647** | A797 | 1.75 l | Boar | .40 | .25 |
| **2648** | A797 | 2.75 l | Red fox | .60 | .25 |
| **2649** | A797 | 3.60 l | Lynx | .85 | .25 |
| | | | *Nos. 2644-2649 (6)* | 2.60 | 1.50 |

Dan Grecu, Bronze Medal — A798

Nadia Comaneci — A799

40b, Fencing, bronze medal. 55b Gheorge Megelea (Javelin), bronze medal. 1.75 l, Handball, silver medal. 2.75 l, Boxing, 1 bronze, 2 silver medals. 3.60 l, Wrestling, silver and bronze medals. 10 l, Vasile Daba (kayak), gold and silver medals, vert.

**1976, Oct. 20 Photo. *Perf. 13½***

| No. | Type | Value | Description | Unused | Used |
|---|---|---|---|---|---|
| **2650** | A798 | 20b | multi | .25 | .25 |
| **2651** | A798 | 40b | car & multi | .25 | .25 |
| **2652** | A798 | 55b | grn & multi | .25 | .25 |
| **2653** | A798 | 1.75 l | red & multi | .25 | .25 |
| **2654** | A798 | 2.75 l | bl & multi | .40 | .25 |
| **2655** | A798 | 3.60 l | multi | .60 | .30 |
| **2656** | A799 | 5.70 l | multi | 1.50 | .45 |
| | | | *Nos. 2650-2656 (7)* | 3.50 | 2.00 |

**Souvenir Sheet**

| No. | Type | Value | Description | Unused | Used |
|---|---|---|---|---|---|
| **2657** | A798 | 10 l | multi | 3.25 | 2.25 |

Romanian Olympic medalists. No. 2657 contains one 37x50mm stamp.

An imperf airmail 10 l souvenir sheet exists picturing gymnast, Nadia Comaneci. Values: unused $45; used $25.

Milan Cathedral — A800

**1976, Oct. 20 Photo. *Perf. 13½***

| No. | Type | Value | Description | Unused | Used |
|---|---|---|---|---|---|
| **2658** | A800 | 4.75 l | multi | 1.00 | .40 |

ITALIA 76 Intl. Phil. Exhib., Milan, 10/14-24.

Oranges and Carnations, by Luchian — A801

Paintings by Stefan Luchian (1868-1916): 40b, Flower arrangement. 55b, Vase with flowers. 1.75 l, Roses. 2.75 l, Cornflowers. 3.60 l, Carnations in vase.

**1976, Nov. 5**

| No. | Type | Value | Description | Unused | Used |
|---|---|---|---|---|---|
| **2659** | A801 | 20b | multi | .25 | .25 |
| **2660** | A801 | 40b | multi | .25 | .25 |
| **2661** | A801 | 55b | multi | .25 | .25 |
| **2662** | A801 | 1.75 l | multi | .25 | .25 |
| **2663** | A801 | 2.75 l | multi | .35 | .25 |
| **2664** | A801 | 3.60 l | multi | .65 | .35 |
| | | | *Nos. 2659-2664 (6)* | 2.00 | 1.60 |

Arms of Alba — A802

Designs: Arms of Romanian counties.

**1976-77 Photo. *Perf. 13½***

| No. | Type | Value | Description | Unused | Used |
|---|---|---|---|---|---|
| **2665** | A802 | 55b | shown | .25 | .25 |
| **2666** | A802 | 55b | Arad | .25 | .25 |
| **2667** | A802 | 55b | Arges | .25 | .25 |
| **2668** | A802 | 55b | Bacau | .25 | .25 |
| **2669** | A802 | 55b | Bihor | .25 | .25 |
| **2670** | A802 | 55b | Bistrita-Nasaud | .25 | .25 |
| **2671** | A802 | 55b | Botosani | .25 | .25 |
| **2672** | A802 | 55b | Brasov | .25 | .25 |
| **2673** | A802 | 55b | Braila | .25 | .25 |
| **2674** | A802 | 55b | Buzau | .25 | .25 |
| **2675** | A802 | 55b | Caras-Severin | .25 | .25 |
| **2676** | A802 | 55b | Cluj | .25 | .25 |
| **2677** | A802 | 55b | Constanta | .25 | .25 |
| **2678** | A802 | 55b | Covasna | .25 | .25 |
| **2679** | A802 | 55b | Dimbovita | .25 | .25 |
| **2680** | A802 | 55b | Dolj | .25 | .25 |
| **2681** | A802 | 55b | Galati | .25 | .25 |
| **2682** | A802 | 55b | Gorj | .25 | .25 |
| **2683** | A802 | 55b | Harghita | .25 | .25 |
| **2684** | A802 | 55b | Hunedoara | .25 | .25 |
| **2685** | A802 | 55b | Ialomita | .25 | .25 |
| **2686** | A802 | 55b | Iasi | .25 | .25 |
| **2687** | A802 | 55b | Ilfov | .25 | .25 |
| **2688** | A802 | 55b | Maramures | .25 | .25 |
| **2689** | A802 | 55b | Mehedinti | .25 | .25 |
| **2690** | A802 | 55b | Mures | .25 | .25 |
| **2691** | A802 | 55b | Neamt | .25 | .25 |
| **2692** | A802 | 55b | Olt | .25 | .25 |
| **2693** | A802 | 55b | Prahova | .25 | .25 |
| **2694** | A802 | 55b | Salaj | .25 | .25 |
| **2695** | A802 | 55b | Satu-Mare | .25 | .25 |
| **2696** | A802 | 55b | Sibiu | .25 | .25 |
| **2697** | A802 | 55b | Suceava | .25 | .25 |
| **2698** | A802 | 55b | Teleorman | .25 | .25 |
| **2699** | A802 | 55b | Timis | .25 | .25 |
| **2700** | A802 | 55b | Tulcea | .25 | .25 |
| **2701** | A802 | 55b | Vaslui | .25 | .25 |
| **2702** | A802 | 55b | Vilcea | .25 | .25 |
| **2703** | A802 | 55b | Vrancea | .25 | .25 |
| **2704** | A802 | 55b | Postal emblem | .25 | .25 |
| | | | *Nos. 2665-2704 (40)* | 10.00 | 10.00 |

Sheets of 50 (10x5) contain 5 designs: Nos. 2665-2669; 2670-2674; 2675-2679; 2680-2684; 2685-2689; 2690-2694; 2695-2699; 2700-2704. Each row of 10 contains 5 pairs of each design.

Issued: #2665-2679, 12/20; #2680-2704, 9/5/77.

Oxcart, by Grigorescu — A803

Paintings by Nicolae Grigorescu (1838-1907): 1 l, Self-portrait, vert. 1.50 l, Shepherdess. 2.15 l, Woman Spinning with Distaff. 3.40 l, Shepherd, vert. 4.80 l, Rest at Well.

**1977, Jan. 20 Photo. *Perf. 13½***

| No. | Type | Value | Description | Unused | Used |
|---|---|---|---|---|---|
| **2705** | A803 | 55b | gray & multi | .25 | .25 |
| **2706** | A803 | 1 l | gray & multi | .25 | .25 |
| **2707** | A803 | 1.50 l | gray & multi | .25 | .25 |
| **2708** | A803 | 2.15 l | gray & multi | .40 | .25 |
| **2709** | A803 | 3.40 l | gray & multi | .55 | .30 |
| **2710** | A803 | 4.80 l | gray & multi | .85 | .35 |
| | | | *Nos. 2705-2710 (6)* | 2.55 | 1.65 |

Cheia Telecommunications Station — A804

**1977, Feb. 1**

| No. | Type | Value | Description | Unused | Used |
|---|---|---|---|---|---|
| **2711** | A804 | 55b | multi | .25 | .25 |

Red Deer A805

Protected Birds and Animals: 1 l, Mute swan. 1.50 l, Egyptian vulture. 2.15 l, Bison. 3.40 l, White-headed ruddy duck. 4.80 l, Kingfisher.

**1977, Mar. 20 Photo. *Perf. 13½***

| No. | Type | Value | Description | Unused | Used |
|---|---|---|---|---|---|
| **2712** | A805 | 55b | multi | .25 | .25 |
| **2713** | A805 | 1 l | multi | .25 | .25 |
| **2714** | A805 | 1.50 l | multi | .25 | .25 |
| **2715** | A805 | 2.15 l | multi | .40 | .25 |
| **2716** | A805 | 3.40 l | multi | .60 | .25 |
| **2717** | A805 | 4.80 l | multi | .85 | .25 |
| | | | *Nos. 2712-2717 (6)* | 2.60 | 1.50 |

Calafat Artillery Unit, by Sava Hentia — A806

Paintings: 55b, Attacking Infantryman, by Oscar Obedeanu, vert. 1.50 l, Infantry Attack in Winter, by Stefan Luchian, vert. 2.15 l, Battle of Plevna (after etching). 3.40 l, Artillery, by Nicolae Ion Grigorescu. 10 l, Battle of Grivita, 1877.

**1977**

| No. | Type | Value | Description | Unused | Used |
|---|---|---|---|---|---|
| **2718** | A806 | 55b | gold & multi | .25 | .25 |
| **2719** | A806 | 1 l | gold & multi | .25 | .25 |
| **2720** | A806 | 1.50 l | gold & multi | .25 | .25 |
| **2721** | A806 | 2.15 l | gold & multi | .60 | .25 |
| **2722** | A806 | 3.40 l | gold & multi | .75 | .25 |
| | | | *Nos. 2718-2722,B442 (6)* | 3.60 | 1.65 |

**Souvenir Sheet**

| No. | Type | Value | Description | Unused | Used |
|---|---|---|---|---|---|
| **2723** | A806 | 10 l | gold & multi | 3.00 | 2.25 |

Centenary of Romania's independence. A 10 l imperf. souvenir sheet exists showing victorious return of army, Dobruja, 1878. Values: unused $10; used, $6.

Issued: #2718-2722, May 9; #2723, Apr. 25.

Sinaia, Carpathian Mountains — A807

Design: 2.40 l, Hotels, Aurora, Black Sea.

**1977, May 17**

| No. | Type | Value | Description | Unused | Used |
|---|---|---|---|---|---|
| **2724** | A807 | 2 l | gold & multi | 1.00 | .85 |
| **2725** | A807 | 2.40 l | gold & multi | 1.40 | 1.25 |

Inter-European Cultural and Economic Cooperation. Nos. 2724-2725 printed in sheets of 4 with marginal inscriptions.

Petru Rares — A808

**1977, June 10 Photo.** ***Perf. 13½***

**2726** A808 40b multi .35 .25

450th anniversary of the elevation of Petru Rares to Duke of Moldavia.

Ion Luca Caragiale — A809

**1977, June 10**

**2727** A809 55b multi .35 .25

Ion Luca Caragiale (1852-1912), writer.

Red Cross Nurse, Children, Emblems A810

**1977, June 10**

**2728** A810 1.50 l multi .40 .25

23rd Intl. Red Cross Conf., Bucharest.

Arch of Triumph, Bucharest A811

**1977, June 10**

**2729** A811 2.15 l multi .75 .25

Battles of Marasesti and Oituz, 60th anniv.

Peaks of San Marino, Exhibition Emblem — A812

**1977, Aug. 28 Photo.** ***Perf. 13½***

**2730** A812 4 l brt bl & multi 1.20 .25

Centenary of San Marino stamps, and San Marino '77 Phil. Exhib., San Marino, 8/28-9/4.

Man on Pommel Horse — A813

Gymnasts: 40b, Woman dancer. 55b, Man on parallel bars. 1 l, Woman on balance beam. 2.15 l, Man on rings. 4.80 l, Woman on double bars.

**1977, Sept. 25 Photo.** ***Perf. 13½***

| | | | | |
|---|---|---|---|---|
| **2731** | A813 | 20b multi | .25 | .25 |
| **2732** | A813 | 40b multi | .25 | .25 |
| **2733** | A813 | 55b multi | .25 | .25 |
| **2734** | A813 | 1 l multi | .25 | .25 |
| **2735** | A813 | 2.15 l multi | .35 | .25 |
| **2736** | A813 | 4.80 l multi | 1.25 | .25 |
| | | *Nos. 2731-2736 (6)* | 2.60 | 1.50 |

"Carpati" near Cazane, Iron Gate — A814

Designs: 1 l, "Mircesti" at Orsova. 1.50 l, "Oltenita" at Calafat. 2.15 l, Water bus at Giurgiu. 3 l, "Herculane" at Tulcea. 3.40 l, "Muntenia" in Nature preserve, Sulina. 4.80 l, Map of Danube Delta with Sulina Canal. 10 l, Danubius, god of Danube, from Trajan's Column, Rome, vert.

**1977, Dec. 28**

| | | | | |
|---|---|---|---|---|
| **2737** | A814 | 55b multi | .25 | .25 |
| **2738** | A814 | 1 l multi | .25 | .25 |
| **2739** | A814 | 1.50 l multi | .25 | .25 |
| **2740** | A814 | 2.15 l multi | .40 | .25 |
| **2741** | A814 | 3 l multi | .60 | .25 |
| **2742** | A814 | 3.40 l multi | .65 | .25 |
| **2743** | A814 | 4.80 l multi | 1.25 | .30 |
| | | *Nos. 2737-2743 (7)* | 3.65 | 1.80 |

**Souvenir Sheet**

**2744** A814 10 l multi 2.75 2.00

European Danube Commission.

A 10 l imperf. souvenir sheet exists showing map of Danube from Regensburg to the Black Sea. Value, unused or used, $50.

Flag and Arms of Romania A815

Designs: 1.20 l, Computer production in Romania. 1.75 l, National Theater, Craiova.

**1977, Dec. 30**

| | | | | |
|---|---|---|---|---|
| **2745** | A815 | 55b multi | .25 | .25 |
| **2746** | A815 | 1.20 l multi | .25 | .25 |
| **2747** | A815 | 1.75 l multi | .40 | .25 |
| | | *Nos. 2745-2747 (3)* | .90 | .75 |

Proclamation of Republic, 30th anniversary.

Dancers A816

Designs: Romanian male folk dancers.

**1977, Nov. 28 Photo.** ***Perf. 13½***

| | | | | |
|---|---|---|---|---|
| **2748** | A816 | 20b multi | .25 | .25 |
| **2749** | A816 | 40b multi | .25 | .25 |
| **2750** | A816 | 55b multi | .25 | .25 |
| **2751** | A816 | 1 l multi | .25 | .25 |
| **2752** | A816 | 2.15 l multi | .35 | .25 |
| **2753** | A816 | 4.80 l multi | 1.25 | .25 |
| | | *Nos. 2748-2753 (6)* | 2.60 | 1.50 |

**Souvenir Sheet**

**2754** A816 10 l multi 2.50 2.25

Firiza Dam A817

Hydroelectric Stations and Dams: 40b, Negovanu. 55b, Piatra Neamt. 1 l, Izvorul Muntelui-Bicaz. 2.15 l, Vidraru. 4.80 l, Iron Gate.

**1978, Mar. 10 Photo.** ***Perf. 13½***

| | | | | |
|---|---|---|---|---|
| **2755** | A817 | 20b multi | .25 | .25 |
| **2756** | A817 | 40b multi | .25 | .25 |
| **2757** | A817 | 55b multi | .25 | .25 |
| **2758** | A817 | 1 l multi | .25 | .25 |
| **2759** | A817 | 2.15 l multi | .35 | .25 |
| **2760** | A817 | 4.80 l multi | 1.00 | .25 |
| | | *Nos. 2755-2760 (6)* | 2.35 | 1.50 |

Soccer and Argentina '78 Emblem A818

Various soccer scenes & Argentina '78 emblem.

**1978, Apr. 15**

| | | | | |
|---|---|---|---|---|
| **2761** | A818 | 55b bl & multi | .25 | .25 |
| **2762** | A818 | 1 l org & multi | .25 | .25 |
| **2763** | A818 | 1.50 l yel grn & multi | .25 | .25 |
| **2764** | A818 | 2.15 l ver & multi | .30 | .25 |
| **2765** | A818 | 3.40 l bl grn & multi | .50 | .25 |
| **2766** | A818 | 4.80 l lil rose & multi | 1.00 | .25 |
| | | *Nos. 2761-2766 (6)* | 2.55 | 1.50 |

11th World Cup Soccer Championship, Argentina '78, June 1-25. See No. C222.

King Decebalus of Dacia Statue, Deva A819

Design: 3.40 l, King Mircea the Elder of Wallachia statue, Tulcea, and ship.

**1978, May 22 Photo.** ***Perf. 13½***

| | | | | |
|---|---|---|---|---|
| **2767** | A819 | 1.30 l gold & multi | .90 | .70 |
| **2768** | A819 | 3.40 l gold & multi | 1.60 | 1.25 |

Inter-European Cultural and Economic Cooperation. Each printed in sheet of 4.

Worker, Factory, Flag — A821

**1978, June 11 Photo.** ***Perf. 13½***

**2770** A821 55b multi .35 .25

Nationalization of industry, 30th anniv.

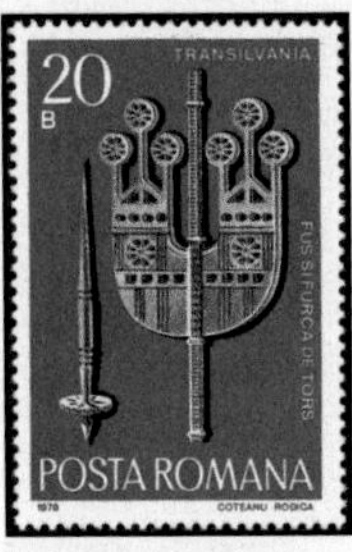


Spindle and Handle, Transylvania A822

Wood Carvings: 40b, Cheese molds, Muntenia. 55b, Spoons, Oltenia. 1 l, Barrel, Moldavia. 2.15 l, Ladle and mug, Transylvania. 4.80 l, Water bucket, Oltenia.

**1978, June 20**

| | | | | |
|---|---|---|---|---|
| **2771** | A822 | 20b multi | .25 | .25 |
| **2772** | A822 | 40b multi | .25 | .25 |
| **2773** | A822 | 55b multi | .25 | .25 |
| **2774** | A822 | 1 l multi | .25 | .25 |
| **2775** | A822 | 2.15 l multi | .30 | .25 |
| **2776** | A822 | 4.80 l multi | 1.00 | .25 |
| | | *Nos. 2771-2776 (6)* | 2.30 | 1.50 |

Danube Delta — A823

Tourist Publicity: 1 l, Bran Castle, vert. 1.50 l, Monastery, Suceava, Moldavia. 2.15 l, Caves, Oltenia. 3.40 l, Ski lift, Brasov. 4.80 l, Mangalia, Black Sea. 10 l, Strehaia Fortress, vert.

**1978, July 20 Photo.** ***Perf. 13½***

| | | | | |
|---|---|---|---|---|
| **2777** | A823 | 55b multi | .25 | .25 |
| **2778** | A823 | 1 l multi | .25 | .25 |
| **2779** | A823 | 1.50 l multi | .25 | .25 |
| **2780** | A823 | 2.15 l multi | .30 | .25 |
| **2781** | A823 | 3.40 l multi | .50 | .25 |
| **2782** | A823 | 4.80 l multi | 1.00 | .35 |
| | | *Nos. 2777-2782 (6)* | 2.55 | 1.60 |

**Miniature Sheet**

**2783** A823 10 l multi 3.00 2.50

No. 2783 contains one 37x51mm stamp. Issued July 30.

Electronic Microscope A824

Designs: 40b, Hydraulic excavator. 55b, Computer center. 1.50 l, Oil derricks. 3 l, Harvester combine. 3.40 l, Petrochemical plant.

**1978, Aug. 15 Photo.** ***Perf. 13½***

| | | | | |
|---|---|---|---|---|
| **2784** | A824 | 20b multi | .25 | .25 |
| **2785** | A824 | 40b multi | .25 | .25 |
| **2786** | A824 | 55b multi | .25 | .25 |
| **2787** | A824 | 1.50 l multi | .25 | .25 |

**2788** A824 3 l multi, horiz. .55 .25
**2789** A824 3.40 l multi .70 .25
*Nos. 2784-2789 (6)* 2.25 1.50

Industrial development.

Polovraci Cave, Carpathians A825

Caves: 1 l, Topolnita. 1.50 l, Ponoare. 2.15 l, Ratei, Mt. Bucegi. 3.40 l, Closani, Mt. Motrului. 4.80 l, Epuran. 1 l, 1.50 l, 4.80 l, Mt. Mehedinti.

**1978, Aug. 25 Photo. *Perf. 13½***
**2790** A825 55b multi .25 .25
**2791** A825 1 l multi .25 .25
**2792** A825 1.50 l multi .25 .25
**2793** A825 2.15 l multi .30 .25
**2794** A825 3.40 l multi .50 .25
**2795** A825 4.80 l multi 1.00 .25
*Nos. 2790-2795 (6)* 2.55 1.50

"Racial Equality" — A826

**1978, Sept. 28**
**2796** A826 3.40 l multi .70 .25

Anti-Apartheid Year.

Gold Bas-relief — A827

Designs: 40b, Gold armband. 55b, Gold cameo ring. 1 l, Silver bowl. 2.15 l, Eagle from Roman standard, vert. 4.80 l, Silver armband.

**1978, Sept. 25**
**2797** A827 20b multi .25 .25
**2798** A827 40b multi .25 .25
**2799** A827 55b multi .25 .25
**2800** A827 1 l multi .25 .25
**2801** A827 2.15 l multi .30 .25
**2802** A827 4.80 l multi 1.00 .35
*Nos. 2797-2802 (6)* 2.30 1.60

Daco-Roman archaeological treasures. An imperf. 10 l souvenir sheet exists showing gold helmet, vert. Values: unused $10; used $6.

Woman Gymnast, Games' Emblem A828

1 l, Running. 1.50 l, Skiing. 2.15 l, Equestrian. 3.40 l, Soccer. 4.80 l, Handball.

**1978, Sept. 15**
**2803** A828 55b multi .25 .25
**2804** A828 1 l multi .25 .25
**2805** A828 1.50 l multi .25 .25
**2806** A828 2.15 l multi .30 .25
**2807** A828 3.40 l multi .50 .25
**2808** A828 4.80 l multi 1.00 .25
*Nos. 2803-2808 (6)* 2.55 1.50

Ptolemaic Map of Dacia A829

Designs: 55b, Meeting House of Romanian National Council, Arad. 1.75 l, Pottery vases, 8th-9th centuries, found near Arad.

**1978, Oct. 21 Photo. *Perf. 13½***
**2809** A829 40b multi .25 .25
**2810** A829 55b multi .25 .25
**2811** A829 1.75 l multi .35 .25
*b.* Strip of 3, #2809-2811 .50 .30

2,000th anniversary of founding of Arad.

Dacian Warrior, from Trajan's Column, Rome — A829a

**1978, Nov. 5 Photo. *Perf. 13x13½***
**2811A** A829a 6 l + 3 l label 1.60 .85

NATIONALA '78 Phil. Exhib., Bucharest. Stamp Day.

Assembly at Alba Iulia, 1919 — A830

Design: 1 l, Open book and Romanian flag.

**1978, Dec. 1**
**2812** A830 55b gold & multi .25 .25
**2813** A830 1 l gold & multi .25 .25

60th anniversary of national unity.

Warrior, Bas-relief — A831

1.50 l, Warrior on horseback, bas-relief.

**1979 Photo. *Perf. 13½***
**2814** A831 55b multi .25 .25
**2815** A831 1.50 l multi .25 .25

2,050 years since establishment of first centralized and independent Dacian state.

"Heroes of Vaslui" — A832

Children's Drawings: 1 l, Building houses. 1.50 l, Folk music of Tica. 2.15 l, Industrial landscape, horiz. 3.40 l, winter customs, horiz. 4.80 l, Pioneer festival, horiz.

**1979, Mar. 1**
**2816** A832 55b multi .25 .25
**2817** A832 1 l multi .25 .25
**2818** A832 1.50 l multi .25 .25
**2819** A832 2.15 l multi .30 .25
**2820** A832 3.40 l multi .50 .25
**2821** A832 4.80 l multi .75 .25
*Nos. 2816-2821 (6)* 2.30 1.50

International Year of the Child.

A833

1.30 l, Ice Hockey, Globe, Emblem. 3.40 l, Ice hockey players, globe & emblem.

**1979, Mar. 16 Photo. *Perf. 13½***
**2822** 1.30 l multi .30 .25
**2823** 3.40 l multi .55 .25
*a.* A833 Pair, #2822-2823 .85 .50

European Youth Ice Hockey Championship, Miercurea-Ciuc (1.30 l) and World Ice Hockey Championship, Galati (3.40 l).

Dog's-tooth Violet — A834

Protected Flowers: 1 l, Alpine violet. 1.50 l, Linum borzaeanum. 2.15 l, Persian bindweed. 3.40 l, Primula auricula. 4.80 l, Transylvanian columbine.

**1979, Apr. 25 Photo. *Perf. 13½***
**2824** A834 55b multi .25 .25
**2825** A834 1 l multi .25 .25
**2826** A834 1.50 l multi .25 .25
**2827** A834 2.15 l multi .35 .25
**2828** A834 3.40 l multi .50 .25
**2829** A834 4.80 l multi .75 .25
*Nos. 2824-2829 (6)* 2.35 1.50


Mail Coach and Post Rider, 19th Century A835

**1979, May 3 Photo. *Perf. 13***
**2830** A835 1.30 l multi .40 .25

Inter-European Cultural and Economic Cooperation. Printed in sheets of 4.
See No. C231.

Oil Rig and Refinery — A836

**1979, May 24 Photo. *Perf. 13***
**2832** A836 3.40 l multi .60 .25

10th World Petroleum Congress, Bucharest.

Girl Pioneer — A837

**1979, June 20**
**2833** A837 55b multi .35 .25

30th anniversary of Romanian Pioneers.

Children with Flowers, IYC Emblem A838

IYC Emblem and: 1 l, Kindergarten. 2 l, Pioneers with rabbit. 4.60 l, Drummer, trumpeters, flags.

**1979, July 18 Photo. *Perf. 13½***
**2834** A838 40b multi .25 .25
**2835** A838 1 l multi .25 .25
**2836** A838 2 l multi .30 .25
**2837** A838 4.60 l multi .70 .25
*Nos. 2834-2837 (4)* 1.50 1.00

International Year of the Child.

Lady in a Garden, by Tattarescu A839

Paintings by Gheorghe Tattarescu: 40b, Mountain woman. 55b, Mountain man. 1 l, Portrait of Gh. Magheru. 2.15 l, The artist's daughter. 4.80 l, Self-portrait.

**1979, June 16**
**2838** A839 20b multi .25 .25
**2839** A839 40b multi .25 .25
**2840** A839 55b multi .25 .25
**2841** A839 1 l multi .25 .25
**2842** A839 2.15 l multi .30 .25
**2843** A839 4.80 l multi .90 .25
*Nos. 2838-2843 (6)* 2.20 1.50

Stefan Gheorghiu — A840

Designs: 55b, Gheorghe Lazar monument. 2.15 l, Lupeni monument. 4.60 l, Women in front of Memorial Arch.

**1979, Aug.**

| | | | | |
|---|---|---|---|---|
| **2844** | A840 | 40b multi | .25 | .25 |
| **2845** | A840 | 55b multi | .25 | .25 |
| **2846** | A840 | 2.15 l multi | .40 | .25 |
| **2847** | A840 | 4.60 l multi | 1.10 | .25 |
| | | *Nos. 2844-2847 (4)* | 2.00 | 1.00 |

State Theater, Tirgu-Mures — A841

Modern Architecture: 40b, University, Brasov. 55b, Political Administration Buildings, Baia Mare. 1 l, Stefan Gheorghiu Academy, Bucharest. 2.15 l, Political Administration Building, Botosani. 4.80 l, House of Culture, Tirgoviste.

**1979, June 25**

| | | | | |
|---|---|---|---|---|
| **2848** | A841 | 20b multi | .25 | .25 |
| **2849** | A841 | 40b multi | .25 | .25 |
| **2850** | A841 | 55b multi | .25 | .25 |
| **2851** | A841 | 1 l multi | .25 | .25 |
| **2852** | A841 | 2.15 l multi | .25 | .25 |
| **2853** | A841 | 4.80 l multi | .70 | .25 |
| | | *Nos. 2848-2853 (6)* | 1.95 | 1.50 |

Flags of Russia and Romania — A842

1 l, Workers' Militia, by L. Suhar, horiz.

**1979, Aug. 20 Photo. *Perf. 13½***

| | | | | |
|---|---|---|---|---|
| **2854** | A842 | 55b multi | .25 | .25 |
| **2855** | A842 | 1 l multi | .25 | .25 |

Liberation from Fascism, 35th anniversary.

Cargo Ship Galati A843

Romanian Ships: 1 l, Cargo ship Bucuresti. 1.50 l, Ore carrier Resita. 2.15 l, Ore carrier Tomis. 3.40 l, Tanker Dacia. 4.80 l, Tanker Independenta.

**1979, Aug. 27 Photo. *Perf. 13½***

| | | | | |
|---|---|---|---|---|
| **2856** | A843 | 55b multi | .25 | .25 |
| **2857** | A843 | 1 l multi | .25 | .25 |
| **2858** | A843 | 1.50 l multi | .25 | .25 |
| **2859** | A843 | 2.15 l multi | .25 | .25 |
| **2860** | A843 | 3.40 l multi | .45 | .25 |
| **2861** | A843 | 4.80 l multi | .90 | .25 |
| | | *Nos. 2856-2861 (6)* | 2.35 | 1.50 |

Olympic Stadium, Melbourne, 1956, Moscow '80 Emblem — A844

Moscow '80 Emblem and Olympic Stadiums: 1 l, Rome, 1960. 1.50 l, Tokyo, 1964. 2.15 l, Mexico City, 1968. 3.40 l, Munich, 1972. 4.80 l, Montreal, 1976. 10 l, Moscow, 1980.

**1979, Oct. 23 Photo. *Perf. 13½***

| | | | | |
|---|---|---|---|---|
| **2862** | A844 | 55b multi | .25 | .25 |
| **2863** | A844 | 1 l multi | .25 | .25 |
| **2864** | A844 | 1.50 l multi | .25 | .25 |
| **2865** | A844 | 2.15 l multi | .30 | .25 |
| **2866** | A844 | 3.40 l multi | .45 | .25 |
| **2867** | A844 | 4.80 l multi | .65 | .25 |
| | | *Nos. 2862-2867 (6)* | 2.15 | 1.50 |

**Souvenir Sheet**

| | | | | |
|---|---|---|---|---|
| **2868** | A844 | 10 l multi | 3.00 | 2.50 |

22nd Summer Olympic Games, Moscow, July 19-Aug. 3, 1980. No. 2868 contains one 50x38mm stamp.

No. 2868 airmail.

Imperf 10 l souvenir sheets exist for the European Sports Conference and 1980 Olympics. Value for former, unused or used, $15. Value for latter, unused or used, $20.

Arms of Alba Iulia — A845

Designs: Arms of Romanian cities.

**1979, Oct. 25**

| | | | | |
|---|---|---|---|---|
| **2869** | A845 | 1.20 l shown | .30 | .25 |
| **2870** | A845 | 1.20 l Arad | .30 | .25 |
| **2871** | A845 | 1.20 l Bacau | .30 | .25 |
| **2872** | A845 | 1.20 l Baia-Mare | .30 | .25 |
| **2873** | A845 | 1.20 l Birlad | .30 | .25 |
| **2874** | A845 | 1.20 l Botosani | .30 | .25 |
| **2875** | A845 | 1.20 l Braila | .30 | .25 |
| **2876** | A845 | 1.20 l Brasov | .30 | .25 |
| **2877** | A845 | 1.20 l Buzau | .30 | .25 |
| **2878** | A845 | 1.20 l Calarasi | .30 | .25 |
| **2879** | A845 | 1.20 l Cluj | .30 | .25 |
| **2880** | A845 | 1.20 l Constanta | .30 | .25 |
| **2881** | A845 | 1.20 l Craiova | .30 | .25 |
| **2882** | A845 | 1.20 l Dej | .30 | .25 |
| **2883** | A845 | 1.20 l Deva | .30 | .25 |
| **2884** | A845 | 1.20 l Turnu-Severin | .30 | .25 |
| **2885** | A845 | 1.20 l Focsani | .30 | .25 |
| **2886** | A845 | 1.20 l Galati | .30 | .25 |
| **2887** | A845 | 1.20 l Gheorghe Gheorghiu-Dej | .30 | .25 |
| **2888** | A845 | 1.20 l Giurgiu | .30 | .25 |
| **2889** | A845 | 1.20 l Hunedoara | .30 | .25 |
| **2890** | A845 | 1.20 l Iasi | .30 | .25 |
| **2891** | A845 | 1.20 l Lugoj | .30 | .25 |
| **2892** | A845 | 1.20 l Medias | .30 | .25 |
| **2893** | A845 | 1.20 l Odorheiu Seguiesc | .30 | .25 |

**1980, Jan. 5**

| | | | | |
|---|---|---|---|---|
| **2894** | A845 | 1.20 l Oradea | .30 | .25 |
| **2895** | A845 | 1.20 l Petrosani | .30 | .25 |
| **2896** | A845 | 1.20 l Piatra-Neamt | .30 | .25 |
| **2897** | A845 | 1.20 l Pitesti | .30 | .25 |
| **2898** | A845 | 1.20 l Ploiesti | .30 | .25 |
| **2899** | A845 | 1.20 l Resita | .30 | .25 |
| **2900** | A845 | 1.20 l Rimnicu-Vilcea | .30 | .25 |
| **2901** | A845 | 1.20 l Roman | .30 | .25 |
| **2902** | A845 | 1.20 l Satu-Mare | .30 | .25 |
| **2903** | A845 | 1.20 l Sibiu | .30 | .25 |
| **2904** | A845 | 1.20 l Siget-Marmatiei | .30 | .25 |
| **2905** | A845 | 1.20 l Sighisoara | .30 | .25 |
| **2906** | A845 | 1.20 l Suceava | .30 | .25 |
| **2907** | A845 | 1.20 l Tecuci | .30 | .25 |
| **2908** | A845 | 1.20 l Timisoara | .30 | .25 |
| **2909** | A845 | 1.20 l Tirgoviste | .30 | .25 |
| **2910** | A845 | 1.20 l Tirgu-Jiu | .30 | .25 |
| **2911** | A845 | 1.20 l Tirgu-Mures | .30 | .25 |
| **2912** | A845 | 1.20 l Tulcea | .30 | .25 |
| **2913** | A845 | 1.20 l Turda | .30 | .25 |
| **2914** | A845 | 1.20 l Turnu Magurele | .30 | .25 |
| **2915** | A845 | 1.20 l Bucharest | .30 | .25 |
| | | *Nos. 2869-2915 (47)* | 14.10 | 11.75 |

A846

Regional Costumes: 20b, Maramures Woman. 40b, Maramures man. 55b, Vrancea woman. 1.50 l, Vrancea man. 3 l, Padureni woman. 3.40 l, Padureni man.

**1979, Oct. 27**

| | | | | |
|---|---|---|---|---|
| **2916** | A846 | 20b multi | .25 | .25 |
| **2917** | A846 | 40b multi | .25 | .25 |
| **2918** | A846 | 55b multi | .25 | .25 |
| **2919** | A846 | 1.50 l multi | .25 | .25 |
| **2920** | A846 | 3 l multi | .40 | .25 |
| **2921** | A846 | 3.40 l multi | .45 | .25 |
| | | *Nos. 2916-2921 (6)* | 1.85 | 1.50 |

A847

Flower Paintings by Stefan Luchian: 40b, Snapdragons. 60b, Triple chrysanthemums. 1.55 l, Potted flowers on stairs.

**1979, July 27**

| | | | | |
|---|---|---|---|---|
| **2922** | A847 | 40b multi | .25 | .25 |
| **2923** | A847 | 60b multi | .25 | .25 |
| **2924** | A847 | 1.55 l multi | .25 | .25 |
| | | *Nos. 2922-2924,B445 (4)* | 1.85 | 1.85 |

Socfilex, International Philatelic Exhibition, Bucharest. See No. B446.

Souvenir Sheet

Romanian Communist Party, 12th Congress — A848

**1979, Oct.**

| | | | | |
|---|---|---|---|---|
| **2925** | A848 | 5 l multi | 1.75 | .70 |

Figure Skating, Lake Placid '80 Emblem, Olympic Rings — A849

**1979, Dec. 27 Photo. *Perf. 13½***

| | | | | |
|---|---|---|---|---|
| **2926** | A849 | 55b shown | .25 | .25 |
| **2927** | A849 | 1 l Downhill skiing | .25 | .25 |
| **2928** | A849 | 1.50 l Biathlon | .25 | .25 |
| **2929** | A849 | 2.15 l Two-man bobsledding | .25 | .25 |
| **2930** | A849 | 3.40 l Speed skating | .50 | .25 |
| **2931** | A849 | 4.80 l Ice hockey | 1.00 | .25 |
| | | *Nos. 2926-2931 (6)* | 2.50 | 1.50 |

**Souvenir Sheet**

| | | | | |
|---|---|---|---|---|
| **2932** | A849 | 10 l Ice hockey, diff. | 3.25 | 2.50 |

13th Winter Olympic Games, Lake Placid, NY, Feb. 12-24, 1980. No. 2932 contains one 38x50mm stamp. An imperf. 10 l air post souvenir sheet exists showing four-man bobsledding. Value, unused or used, $30.

"Calugareni", Expo Emblem — A850

No. 2934, "Orleans". No. 2935, #1059, type fawn. No. 2936, #15021, type 1E. No. 2937, "Pacific". No. 2938, Electric engine 060-EA. 10 l, Diesel electric.

**1979, Dec. 29**

| | | | | |
|---|---|---|---|---|
| **2933** | A850 | 55b multicolored | .25 | .25 |
| **2934** | A850 | 1 l multicolored | .25 | .25 |
| **2935** | A850 | 1.50 l multicolored | .25 | .25 |
| **2936** | A850 | 2.15 l multicolored | .35 | .25 |
| **2937** | A850 | 3.40 l multicolored | .60 | .25 |
| **2938** | A850 | 4.80 l multicolored | .80 | .25 |
| | | *Nos. 2933-2938 (6)* | 2.50 | 1.50 |

**Souvenir Sheet**

| | | | | |
|---|---|---|---|---|
| **2939** | A850 | 10 l multicolored | 3.00 | 2.50 |

Intl. Transport Expo., Hamburg, June 8-July 1. #2939 contains one 50x40mm stamp.

Dacian Warrior, Trajan's Column, Rome — A851

Design: 1.50 l, Two warriors.

**1980, Feb. 9 Photo. *Perf. 13½***

| | | | | |
|---|---|---|---|---|
| **2940** | A851 | 55b multi | .25 | .25 |
| **2941** | A851 | 1.50 l multi | .30 | .25 |

2,050 years since establishment of first centralized and independent Dacian state.

Kingfisher — A852

1 l, Great white heron, vert. 1.50 l, Red-breasted goose. 2.15 l, Red deer, vert. 3.40 l, Roe deer. 4.80 l, European bison, vert.

**1980, Mar. 25 Photo. *Perf. 13½***

| | | | | |
|---|---|---|---|---|
| **2942** | A852 | 55b multicolored | .25 | .25 |
| **2943** | A852 | 1 l multicolored | .25 | .25 |
| **2944** | A852 | 1.50 l multicolored | .25 | .25 |
| **2945** | A852 | 2.15 l multicolored | .25 | .25 |
| **2946** | A852 | 3.40 l multicolored | .45 | .25 |
| **2947** | A852 | 4.80 l multicolored | .90 | .25 |
| | | *Nos. 2942-2947 (6)* | 2.35 | 1.50 |

European Nature Protection Year. A 10 l imperf. souvenir sheet exists showing bears; red control number. Value, unused or used, $30.

See No. C232.

Souvenir Sheets

George Enescu — A853

**1980, May 6**

| | | | | |
|---|---|---|---|---|
| **2948** | A853 | Sheet of 4 | 3.50 | 3.00 |
| *a.* | | 1.30 l Playing violin | .70 | .25 |
| *b.* | | 1.30 l Conducting | .70 | .25 |
| *c.* | | 1.30 l Playing piano | .70 | .25 |
| *d.* | | 1.30 l Composing | .70 | .25 |

**2949** A853 Sheet of 4 3.50 3.00
*a.* 3.40 l Beethoven in library .70 .25
*b.* 3.40 l Portrait .70 .25
*c.* 3.40 l At piano .70 .25
*d.* 3.40 l Composing .70 .25

Inter-European Cultural and Economic Cooperation.

Vallota Purpurea — A854

1 l, Eichhornia crasipes. 1.50 l, Sprekelia formosissima. 2.15 l, Hypericum calycinum. 3.40 l, Camellia japonica. 4.80 l, Nelumbo nucifera.

**1980, Apr. 10 Photo. *Perf. 13½***

**2950** A854 55b multicolored .25 .25
**2951** A854 1 l multicolored .25 .25
**2952** A854 1.50 l multicolored .25 .25
**2953** A854 2.15 l multicolored .40 .25
**2954** A854 3.40 l multicolored .60 .25
**2955** A854 4.80 l multicolored 1.00 .25
*Nos. 2950-2955 (6)* 2.75 1.50

Tudor Vladimirescu A855

55b, Mihail Sadoveanu. 1.50 l, Battle against Hungarians. 2.15 l, Tudor Arghezi. 3 l, Horea.

**1980, Apr. 24**

**2956** A855 40b multicolored .25 .25
**2957** A855 55b multicolored .25 .25
**2958** A855 1.50 l multicolored .25 .25
**2959** A855 2.15 l multicolored .40 .25
**2960** A855 3 l multicolored .50 .25
*Nos. 2956-2960 (5)* 1.65 1.25

Anniversaries: 40b, Tudor Vladimirescu (1780-1821), leader of 1821 revolution; 55b, Mihail Sadoveanu (1880-1961), author; 1.50 l, Victory of Posada; 2.15 l, Tudor Arghezi (1880-1967), poet; 3 l, Horea (1730-1785), leader of 1784 uprising.

A856

Dacian fruit bowl and cup.

**1980, May 8**

**2961** A856 1 l multicolored .35 .25

Petrodava City, 2000th anniversary.

A857

**1980, June 20 Photo. *Perf. 13½***

**2962** A857 55b Javelin .25 .25
**2963** A857 1 l Fencing .25 .25
**2964** A857 1.50 l Shooting .30 .25
**2965** A857 2.15 l Kayak .35 .25
**2966** A857 3.40 l Wrestling .55 .25
**2967** A857 4.80 l Rowing .80 .25
*Nos. 2962-2967 (6)* 2.50 1.50

**Souvenir Sheet**

**2968** A857 10 l Handball 2.75 2.25

22nd Summer Olympic Games, Moscow, July 19-Aug. 3. No. 2968 contains one 38x50mm stamp. An imperf. 10 l air post souvenir sheet exists showing gymnast. Value, unused or used, $27.50.

Congress Emblem — A858

**1980, Aug. 10 Photo. *Perf. 13½***

**2969** A858 55b multicolored .50 .50

15th Intl. Historical Sciences Congress, Bucharest.

Fireman Rescuing Child — A859

**1980, Aug. 25**

**2970** A859 55b multicolored .35 .25

Firemen's Day, Sept. 13.

Chinese and Romanian Young Pioneers at Stamp Show — A860

**1980, Sept. 18**

**2971** A860 1 l multicolored .35 .25

Romanian-Chinese Phil. Exhib., Bucharest.

Souvenir Sheet

Parliament Building, Bucharest — A861

**1980, Sept. 30**

**2972** A861 10 l multicolored 2.00 1.65

European Security Conference, Madrid. An imperf. 10 l air post souvenir sheet exists showing Plaza Mayor, Madrid. Value, unused or used, $20.

Knights and Chessboard — A862

**1980, Oct. 1 Photo. *Perf. 13½***

**2973** A862 55b shown .25 .25
**2974** A862 1 l Rooks .25 .25
**2975** A862 2.15 l Man .30 .25
**2976** A862 4.80 l Woman 1.00 .25
*Nos. 2973-2976 (4)* 1.80 1.00

Chess Olympiad, Valletta, Malta, Nov. 20-Dec. 8.

Dacian Warrior — A863

40b, Moldavian soldier, 15th cent. 55b, Walachian horseman, 17th cent. 1 l, Flag bearer, 19th cent. 1.50 l, Infantryman, 19th cent. 2.15 l, Lancer, 19th cent. 4.80 l, Mounted Elite Corps Guard, 19th cent.

**1980, Oct. 15**

**2977** A863 20b multi .25 .25
**2978** A863 40b multi .25 .25
**2979** A863 55b multi .25 .25
**2980** A863 1 l multi .25 .25
**2981** A863 1.50 l multi .25 .25
**2982** A863 2.15 l multi .35 .25
**2983** A863 4.80 l multi .75 .35
*Nos. 2977-2983 (7)* 2.35 1.85

Burebista Sculpture — A864

**1980, Nov. 5 Photo. *Perf. 13½***

**2984** A864 2 l multicolored .35 .25

2050 years since establishment of first centralized and independent Dacian state.

George Oprescu (1881-1969), Art Critic — A865

Famous Men: 2.15 l, Marius Bunescu (1881-1971), painter. 3.40 l, Ion Georgescu (1856-1898), sculptor.

**1981, Feb. 20 Photo. *Perf. 13½***

**2985** A865 1.50 l multicolored .25 .25
**2986** A865 2.15 l multicolored .40 .25
**2987** A865 3.40 l multicolored .70 .25
*Nos. 2985-2987 (3)* 1.35 .75

National Dog Show — A866

Designs: Dogs — 40b, Mountain sheepdog, horiz. 55b, Saint Bernard. 1 l, Fox terrier, horiz. 1.50 l, German shepherd, horiz. 2.15 l, Boxer. 3.40 l, Dalmatian, horiz. 4.80 l, Poodle.

**1981, Mar. 15**

**2988** A866 40b multicolored .25 .25
**2989** A866 55b multicolored .25 .25
**2990** A866 1 l multicolored .25 .25
**2991** A866 1.50 l multicolored .25 .25
**2992** A866 2.15 l multicolored .45 .25
**2993** A866 3.40 l multicolored .70 .25
**2994** A866 4.80 l multicolored 1.00 .25
*Nos. 2988-2994 (7)* 3.15 1.75

River Steamer Stefan cel Mare — A867

1 l, Vas de Supraveghere. 1.50 l, Tudor Vladimirescu. 2.15 l, Dredger Sulina. 3.40 l, Republica Populara Romana. 4.80 l, Sulina Canal.
10 l, Galati.

**1981, Mar. 25**

**2995** A867 55b multi .25 .25
**2996** A867 1 l multi .25 .25
**2997** A867 1.50 l multi .25 .25
**2998** A867 2.15 l multi .25 .25
**2999** A867 3.40 l multi .40 .25
**3000** A867 4.80 l multi .80 .35
*Nos. 2995-3000 (6)* 2.20 1.60

**Souvenir Sheet**

**3001** A867 10 l multi 2.00 2.00

European Danube Commission, 125th anniv. An imperf. 10 l souvenir sheet exists showing map of Danube. Value, unused or used, $22.50.

Carrier Pigeon A868

Various carrier pigeons and doves.

**1981, Apr. 15 Photo. *Perf. 13½***

**3002** A868 40b multi .25 .25
**3003** A868 55b multi .25 .25
**3004** A868 1 l multi .25 .25
**3005** A868 1.50 l multi .25 .25
**3006** A868 2.15 l multi .30 .25
**3007** A868 3.40 l multi .60 .25
*Nos. 3002-3007 (6)* 1.90 1.50

Romanian Communist Party, 60th Anniv. — A869

**1981, Apr. 22 Photo. *Perf. 13½***

| | | | | |
|---|---|---|---|---|
| **3008** | A869 | 1 l multicolored | .35 | .25 |

Folkdance, Moldavia — A870

Designs: Regional folkdances.

**1981, May 4 Photo. *Perf. 13½***

| | | | | |
|---|---|---|---|---|
| **3009** | | Sheet of 4 | 2.50 | 2.50 |
| *a.* | A870 2.50 l shown | | .45 | .45 |
| *b.* | A870 2.50 l Transylvania | | .45 | .45 |
| *c.* | A870 2.50 l Banat | | .45 | .45 |
| *d.* | A870 2.50 l Muntenia | | .45 | .45 |
| **3010** | | Sheet of 4 | 2.50 | 2.50 |
| *a.* | A870 2.50 l Maramures | | .45 | .45 |
| *b.* | A870 2.50 l Dobruja | | .45 | .45 |
| *c.* | A870 2.50 l Oltenia | | .45 | .45 |
| *d.* | A870 2.50 l Crisana | | .45 | .45 |

Inter-European Cultural and Economic Cooperation.

Singing Romania Festival — A871

**1981, July 15**

| | | | | | |
|---|---|---|---|---|---|
| **3011** | A871 | 55b | Industry | .25 | .25 |
| **3012** | A871 | 1.50 l | Electronics | .25 | .25 |
| **3013** | A871 | 2.15 l | Agriculture | .35 | .25 |
| **3014** | A871 | 3.40 l | Culture | .50 | .30 |
| | | | *Nos. 3011-3014 (4)* | 1.35 | 1.05 |

University '81 Games, Bucharest — A872

**1981, July 17**

| | | | | | |
|---|---|---|---|---|---|
| **3015** | A872 | 1 l | Book, flag | .25 | .25 |
| **3016** | A872 | 2.15 l | Emblem | .35 | .25 |
| **3017** | A872 | 4.80 l | Stadium, horiz. | .75 | .35 |
| | | | *Nos. 3015-3017 (3)* | 1.35 | .85 |

Theodor Aman, Artist, Birth Sesquicentennial — A873

Aman Paintings: 40b, Self-portrait. 55b, Battle of Giurgiu. 1 l, The Family Picnic. 1.50 l, The Painter's Studio. 2.15 l, Woman in Interior. 3.40 l, Aman Museum, Bucharest. 55b, 1 l, 1.50 l, 3.40 l horiz.

**1981, July 28**

| | | | | | |
|---|---|---|---|---|---|
| **3018** | A873 | 40b | multi | .25 | .25 |
| **3019** | A873 | 55b | multi | .25 | .25 |
| **3020** | A873 | 1 l | multi | .25 | .25 |
| **3021** | A873 | 1.50 l | multi | .25 | .25 |
| **3022** | A873 | 2.15 l | multi | .30 | .25 |
| **3023** | A873 | 3.40 l | multi | .50 | .25 |
| | | | *Nos. 3018-3023 (6)* | 1.80 | 1.50 |

Thinker of Cernavoda, 3rd Cent. BC — A874

**1981, July 30**

| | | | | |
|---|---|---|---|---|
| **3024** | A874 | 3.40 l multi | .65 | .30 |

16th Science History Congress.

Blood Donation Campaign — A875

**1981, Aug. 15 Photo. *Perf. 13½***

| | | | | |
|---|---|---|---|---|
| **3025** | A875 | 55b multicolored | .35 | .25 |

Bucharest Central Military Hospital Sesquicentennial — A876

**1981, Sept. 1**

| | | | | |
|---|---|---|---|---|
| **3026** | A876 | 55b multicolored | .35 | .25 |

Romanian Musicians — A877

Designs: 40b, George Enescu (1881-1955). 55b, Paul Constantinescu (1909-1963). 1 l, Dinu Lipatti (1917-1950). 1.50 l, Ionel Periea (1900-1970). 2.15 l, Ciprian Porumbescu (1853-1883). 3.40 l, Mihail Jora (1891-1971).

**1981, Sept. 20**

| | | | | | |
|---|---|---|---|---|---|
| **3027** | A877 | 40b | multi | .25 | .25 |
| **3028** | A877 | 55b | multi | .25 | .25 |
| **3029** | A877 | 1 l | multi | .25 | .25 |
| **3030** | A877 | 1.50 l | multi | .25 | .25 |
| **3031** | A877 | 2.15 l | multi | .35 | .25 |
| **3032** | A877 | 3.40 l | multi | .50 | .25 |
| | | | *Nos. 3027-3032 (6)* | 1.85 | 1.50 |

Stamp Day A879

**1981, Nov. 5 Photo. *Perf. 13½***

| | | | | |
|---|---|---|---|---|
| **3034** | A879 | 2 l multicolored | .35 | .25 |

Children's Games — A880

Illustrations by Eugen Palade (40b, 55b, 1 l) and Norman Rockwell (1.50 l, 2.15 l, 3 l, 4 l).

40b, Hopscotch. 55b, Soccer. 1 l, Riding stick horse. 1.50 l, Snagging the Big One. 2.15 l, A Patient Friend. 3 l, Doggone It. 4 l, Puppy Love.

**1981, Nov. 25**

| | | | | | |
|---|---|---|---|---|---|
| **3035** | A880 | 40b | multicolored | .25 | .25 |
| **3036** | A880 | 55b | multicolored | .25 | .25 |
| **3037** | A880 | 1 l | multicolored | .25 | .25 |
| **3038** | A880 | 1.50 l | multicolored | .25 | .25 |
| **3039** | A880 | 2.15 l | multicolored | .30 | .25 |
| **3040** | A880 | 3 l | multicolored | .40 | .25 |
| **3041** | A880 | 4 l | multicolored | .45 | .35 |
| | | | *Nos. 3035-3041,C243 (8)* | 2.85 | 2.55 |

A881

**1981, Dec. 28**

| | | | | | |
|---|---|---|---|---|---|
| **3042** | A881 | 55b | multi | .25 | .25 |
| **3043** | A881 | 1 l | multi | .25 | .25 |
| **3044** | A881 | 1.50 l | multi | .25 | .25 |
| **3045** | A881 | 2.15 l | multi | .35 | .25 |
| **3046** | A881 | 3.40 l | multi | .40 | .25 |
| **3047** | A881 | 4.80 l | multi | .65 | .35 |
| | | | *Nos. 3042-3047 (6)* | 2.15 | 1.60 |

### Souvenir Sheet

| | | | | |
|---|---|---|---|---|
| **3048** | A881 | 10 l multi | 2.00 | 2.00 |

Espana '82 World Cup Soccer.

No. 3048 contains one 38x50mm stamp. An imperf. 10 l air post souvenir sheet exists showing game. Value, unused or used, $27.50.

A882

Designs: 1 l, Prince Alexander the Good of Moldavia (ruled 1400-1432). 1.50 l, Bogdan Petriceicu Hasdeu (1838-1907), scholar. 2.15 l, Nicolae Titulescu (1882-1941), diplomat.

**1982, Jan. 30 Photo. *Perf. 13½***

| | | | | | |
|---|---|---|---|---|---|
| **3049** | A882 | 1 l | multi | .25 | .25 |
| **3050** | A882 | 1.50 l | multi | .25 | .25 |
| **3051** | A882 | 2.15 l | multi | .40 | .25 |
| | | | *Nos. 3049-3051 (3)* | .90 | .75 |

Bucharest Subway System A883

60b, Union Square station entrance. 2.40 l, Heroes' Station platform.

**1982, Feb. 25**

| | | | | | |
|---|---|---|---|---|---|
| **3052** | A883 | 60b | multi | .25 | .25 |
| **3053** | A883 | 2.40 l | multi | .45 | .25 |

60th Anniv. of Communist Youth Union — A884

1.20 l, Construction worker. 1.50 l, Farm workers. 2 l, Research. 2.50 l, Workers. 3 l, Musicians, dancers.

**1982**

| | | | | | |
|---|---|---|---|---|---|
| **3054** | A884 | 1 l | shown | .25 | .25 |
| **3055** | A884 | 1.20 l | multicolored | .25 | .25 |
| **3056** | A884 | 1.50 l | multicolored | .25 | .25 |
| **3057** | A884 | 2 l | multicolored | .30 | .25 |
| **3058** | A884 | 2.50 l | multicolored | .35 | .25 |
| **3059** | A884 | 3 l | multicolored | .40 | .25 |
| | | | *Nos. 3054-3059 (6)* | 1.80 | 1.50 |

Dog Sled A885

55b, Dog rescuing child. 1 l, Shepherd, dog, vert. 3 l, Hunting dog, vert. 4 l, Spitz, woman, vert. 4.80 l, Guide dog, woman, vert. 5 l, Dalmatian, girl, vert. 6 l, Saint Bernard.

**1982, Mar. 28 Photo. *Perf. 13½***

| | | | | | |
|---|---|---|---|---|---|
| **3060** | A885 | 55b | multicolored | .25 | .25 |
| **3061** | A885 | 1 l | multicolored | .25 | .25 |
| **3062** | A885 | 3 l | multicolored | .45 | .25 |
| **3063** | A885 | 3.40 l | shown | .55 | .25 |
| **3064** | A885 | 4 l | multicolored | .60 | .25 |
| **3065** | A885 | 4.80 l | multicolored | .70 | .25 |
| **3066** | A885 | 5 l | multicolored | .75 | .25 |
| **3067** | A885 | 6 l | multicolored | .90 | .25 |
| | | | *Nos. 3060-3067 (8)* | 4.45 | 2.00 |

Bran Castle, Brasov, 1377 A886

**1982, May 6**

| | | | | |
|---|---|---|---|---|
| **3068** | | Sheet of 4 | 1.75 | 1.75 |
| *a.* | A886 2.50 l shown | | .35 | .35 |
| *b.* | A886 2.50 l Hunedoara, Corvinilor, 1409 | | .35 | .35 |
| *c.* | A886 2.50 l Sinaia, 1873 | | .35 | .35 |
| *d.* | A886 2.50 l Iasi, 1905 | | .35 | .35 |
| **3069** | | Sheet of 4 | 1.75 | 1.75 |
| *a.* | A886 2.50 l Neuschwanstein | | .35 | .35 |
| *b.* | A886 2.50 l Stolzenfels | | .35 | .35 |
| *c.* | A886 2.50 l Katz-Loreley | | .35 | .35 |
| *d.* | A886 2.50 l Linderhof | | .35 | .35 |

Inter-European Cultural and Economic Cooperation.

Souvenir Sheet

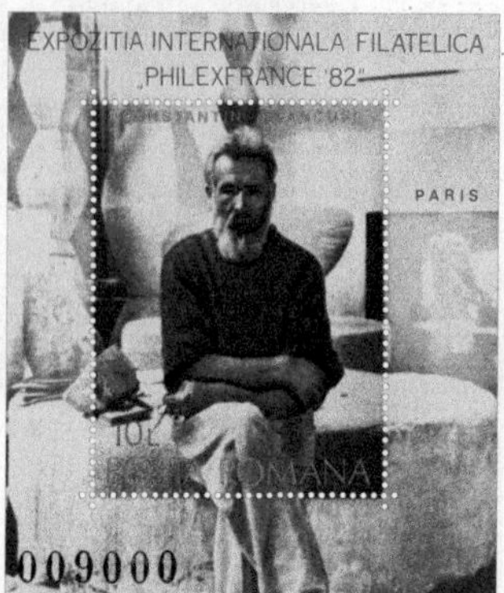

Constantin Brancusi in Paris Studio — A887

**1982, June 5**

| | | | | |
|---|---|---|---|---|
| **3070** | A887 | 10 l multicolored | 2.50 | 2.00 |

PHILEXFRANCE '82 Intl. Stamp Exhibition, Paris, June 11-21.

For surcharge see No. 6067.

Gloria C-16 Combine Harvester — A888

**1982, June 29**

| | | | | |
|---|---|---|---|---|
| **3071** | A888 | 50b shown | .25 | .25 |
| **3072** | A888 | 1 l Dairy farm | .25 | .25 |
| **3073** | A888 | 1.50 l Apple orchard | .25 | .25 |
| **3074** | A888 | 2.50 l Vineyard | .30 | .25 |
| **3075** | A888 | 3 l Irrigation | .50 | .25 |
| | | *Nos. 3071-3075,C250 (6)* | 2.15 | 1.50 |

**Souvenir Sheet**

| | | | | |
|---|---|---|---|---|
| **3076** | A888 | 10 l Village | 2.50 | 2.00 |

Agricultural modernization. No. 3076 contains one 50x38mm stamp.

A890

Resort Hotels and Beaches. 1 l, 2.50 l, 3 l, 5 l horiz.

**1982, Aug. 30 Photo. *Perf. 13½***

| | | | | |
|---|---|---|---|---|
| **3078** | A890 | 50b Baile Felix | .25 | .25 |
| **3079** | A890 | 1 l Predeal | .25 | .25 |
| **3080** | A890 | 1.50 l Baile Herculane | .25 | .25 |
| **3081** | A890 | 2.50 l Eforie Nord | .40 | .25 |
| **3082** | A890 | 3 l Olimp | .50 | .25 |
| **3083** | A890 | 5 l Neptun | .85 | .30 |
| | | *Nos. 3078-3083 (6)* | 2.50 | 1.55 |

A891

Designs: 1 l, Legend, horiz. 1.50 l, Contrasts, horiz. 3.50 l, Relay Runner, horiz. 4 l, Genesis of Romanian People, by Sabin Balasa.

**1982, Sept. 6**

| | | | | |
|---|---|---|---|---|
| **3084** | A891 | 1 l multicolored | .25 | .25 |
| **3085** | A891 | 1.50 l multicolored | .25 | .25 |
| **3086** | A891 | 3.50 l multicolored | .65 | .25 |
| **3087** | A891 | 4 l multicolored | .80 | .35 |
| | | *Nos. 3084-3087 (4)* | 1.95 | 1.10 |

An imperf. 10 l souvenir sheet showing a rainbow over a map of Europe was issued 1982, Sept. 25, with limited distribtuion. Value, $12.

Souvenir Sheet

Merry Peasant Girl, by Nicolae Grigorescu (d. 1907) — A892

**1982, Sept. 30 Photo. *Perf. 13½***

| | | | | |
|---|---|---|---|---|
| **3088** | A892 | 10 l multicolored | 2.50 | 2.50 |

Bucharest Intl. Fair A893

**1982, Oct. 2**

| | | | | |
|---|---|---|---|---|
| **3089** | A893 | 2 l Exhibition Hall, flag | .40 | .25 |

Savings Week, Oct. 25-31 — A894

**1982, Oct. 25**

| | | | | |
|---|---|---|---|---|
| **3090** | A894 | 1 l Girl holding bank book | .25 | .25 |
| **3091** | A894 | 2 l Poster | .35 | .25 |

Stamp Day — A895

**1982, Nov. 10**

| | | | | |
|---|---|---|---|---|
| **3092** | A895 | 1 l Woman letter carrier | .25 | .25 |
| **3093** | A895 | 2 l Mailman | .35 | .25 |

Scene from Ileana Sinziana, by Petre Ispirescu A896

Fairytales: 50b, The Youngest Child and the Golden Apples, by Petre Ispirescu. 1 l, The Bear Hoaxed by the Fox, by Ion Creanga. 1.50 l, The Prince of Tear, by Mihai Eminescu. 2.50 l, The Little Bag with Two Coins Inside, by Ion Creanga. 3 l, Ileana Simziana, by Petre Ispirescu. 5 l, Danila Prepeleac, by Ion Creanga.

**1982, Nov. 30**

| | | | | |
|---|---|---|---|---|
| **3094** | A896 | 50b multicolored | .25 | .25 |
| **3095** | A896 | 1 l multicolored | .25 | .25 |
| **3096** | A896 | 1.50 l multicolored | .25 | .25 |
| **3097** | A896 | 2.50 l multicolored | .40 | .25 |
| **3098** | A896 | 3 l multicolored | .40 | .25 |
| **3099** | A896 | 5 l multicolored | .80 | .30 |
| | | *Nos. 3094-3099 (6)* | 2.35 | 1.55 |

Arms, Colors, Book — A897

**1982, Dec. 16**

| | | | | |
|---|---|---|---|---|
| **3100** | A897 | 1 l Closed book | .25 | .25 |
| **3101** | A897 | 2 l Open book | .35 | .25 |

Natl. Communist Party Conference, Bucharest, Dec. 16-18.

A898

50b, Wooden flask, Suceava. 1 l, Ceramic plate, Radauti. 1.50 l, Wooden scoop, Valea Mare, horiz. 2 l, Plate, jug, Vama. 3 l, Butter churn, wooden bucket, Moldavia. 3.50 l, Ceramic plates, Leheceni, horiz. 4 l, Wooden spoon, platter, Cluj. 5 l, Bowl, pitcher, Marginea. 6 l, Jug, flask, Bihor. 7 l, Spindle, shuttle, Transylvania. 7.50 l, Water buckets, Suceava. 8 l, Jug, Oboga; plate, Horezu. 10 l, Water buckets, Hunedoara, Suceava, horiz. 20 l, Wooden flask, beakers, Horezu. 30 l, Wooden spoons, Alba, horiz. 50 l, Ceramic dishes, Horezu.

**1982, Dec. 22 Photo. *Perf. 13½***

| | | | | |
|---|---|---|---|---|
| **3102** | A898 | 50b red orange | .25 | .25 |
| **3103** | A898 | 1 l dark blue | .25 | .25 |
| **3104** | A898 | 1.50 l orange brn | .25 | .25 |
| **3105** | A898 | 2 l brt blue | .30 | .25 |
| **3106** | A898 | 3 l olive green | .40 | .25 |
| **3107** | A898 | 3.50 l dk green | .55 | .25 |
| **3108** | A898 | 4 l lt brown | .60 | .25 |
| **3109** | A898 | 5 l gray blue | .75 | .25 |

**Size: 23x29mm, 29x23mm**

| | | | | |
|---|---|---|---|---|
| **3110** | A898 | 6 l blue | .90 | .25 |
| **3111** | A898 | 7 l lake | 1.10 | .25 |
| **3112** | A898 | 7.50 l red violet | 1.25 | .25 |
| **3113** | A898 | 8 l brt green | 1.25 | .25 |
| **3114** | A898 | 10 l red | 1.50 | .25 |
| **3115** | A898 | 20 l purple | 3.25 | .25 |
| **3116** | A898 | 30 l Prus blue | 4.50 | .35 |
| **3117** | A898 | 50 l dark brown | 8.00 | .65 |
| | | *Nos. 3102-3117 (16)* | 25.10 | 4.50 |

35th Anniv. of Republic — A899

**1982, Dec. 27**

| | | | | |
|---|---|---|---|---|
| **3118** | A899 | 1 l Symbols of development | .25 | .25 |
| **3119** | A899 | 2 l Flag | .35 | .25 |

Grigore Manolescu (1857-92), as Hamlet — A900

Actors or Actresses in Famous Roles: 50b, Matei Millo (1814-1896) in The Discontented. 1 l, Mihail Pascaly (1829-1882) in Director Milo. 1.50 l, Aristizza Romanescu (1854-1918), in The Dogs. 2 l, C. I. Nottara (1859-1935) in Snowstorm. 3 l, Agatha Birsescu (1857-1939) in Medea. 4 l, Ion Brezeanu (1869-1940) in The Lost Letter. 5 l, Aristide Demetriad (1872-1930) in The Despotic Prince.

**1983, Feb. 28**

| | | | | |
|---|---|---|---|---|
| **3120** | A900 | 50b multi | .25 | .25 |
| **3121** | A900 | 1 l multi | .25 | .25 |
| **3122** | A900 | 1.50 l multi | .30 | .25 |
| **3123** | A900 | 2 l multi | .35 | .25 |
| **3124** | A900 | 2.50 l multi | .45 | .25 |
| **3125** | A900 | 3 l multi | .60 | .25 |
| **3126** | A900 | 4 l multi | .70 | .25 |
| **3127** | A900 | 5 l multi | .90 | .25 |
| | | *Nos. 3120-3127 (8)* | 3.80 | 2.00 |

Hugo Grotius (1583-1645), Dutch Jurist — A901

**1983, Apr. 30**

| | | | | |
|---|---|---|---|---|
| **3128** | A901 | 2 l brown | .45 | .25 |

Romanian-Made Vehicles — A902

50b, ARO-10. 1 l, Dacia, 1300 station wagon. 1.50 l, ARO-242 jeep. 2.50 l, ARO-244. 4 l, Dacia 1310. 5 l, OLTCIT club passenger car.

**1983, May 3**

| | | | | |
|---|---|---|---|---|
| **3129** | A902 | 50b multi | .25 | .25 |
| **3130** | A902 | 1 l multi | .25 | .25 |
| **3131** | A902 | 1.50 l multi | .35 | .25 |
| **3132** | A902 | 2.50 l multi | .60 | .25 |
| **3133** | A902 | 4 l multi | .95 | .35 |
| **3134** | A902 | 5 l multi | 1.20 | .40 |
| | | *Nos. 3129-3134 (6)* | 3.60 | 1.75 |

Johannes Kepler (1571-1630) — A903

Famous Men: No. 3135: b, Alexander von Humboldt (1769-1859), explorer. c, Goethe (1749-1832). d, Richard Wagner (1813-1883), composer.

No. 3136: a, Ioan Andreescu (1850-1882), painter. b, George Constantinescu (1881-1965), engineer. c, Tudor Arghezi (1880-1967), poet. d, C.I. Parhon (1874-1969), endocrinologist.

**1983, May 16**

| | | | |
|---|---|---|---|
| **3135** | Sheet of 4 | 2.50 | 2.50 |
| *a.-d.* | A903 3 l Any single | .55 | .55 |
| **3136** | Sheet of 4 | 2.50 | 2.50 |
| *a.-d.* | A903 3 l Any single | .55 | .55 |

Inter-European Cultural and Economic Cooperation.

Workers' Struggle, 50th Anniv. — A904

**1983, July 22 Photo. *Perf. 13½***

| | | | |
|---|---|---|---|
| **3137** | A904 2 l silver & multi | .35 | .25 |

Birds — A905

50b, Luscinia svecica. 1 l, Sturnus roseus. 1.50 l, Coracias garrulus. 2.50 l, Merops apiaster. 4 l, Emberiza schoeniclus. 5 l, Lanius minor.

**1983, Oct. 28 Photo. *Perf. 13½***

| | | | | |
|---|---|---|---|---|
| **3138** | A905 | 50b multi | .25 | .25 |
| **3139** | A905 | 1 l multi | .25 | .25 |
| **3140** | A905 | 1.50 l multi | .35 | .25 |
| **3141** | A905 | 2.50 l multi | .50 | .25 |
| **3142** | A905 | 4 l multi | .80 | .35 |
| **3143** | A905 | 5 l multi | 1.00 | .40 |
| | | *Nos. 3138-3143 (6)* | 3.15 | 1.75 |

Water Sports A906

**1983, Sept. 16 Photo. *Perf. 13½***

| | | | | |
|---|---|---|---|---|
| **3144** | A906 | 50b Kayak | .25 | .25 |
| **3145** | A906 | 1 l Water polo | .25 | .25 |
| **3146** | A906 | 1.50 l Canadian one-man canoes | .35 | .25 |
| **3147** | A906 | 2.50 l Diving | .60 | .25 |
| **3148** | A906 | 4 l Singles rowing | .95 | .25 |
| **3149** | A906 | 5 l Swimming | 1.20 | .25 |
| | | *Nos. 3144-3149 (6)* | 3.60 | 1.50 |

Stamp Day A907

1 l, Mailman on bicycle. 3.50 l, with 3 l label, flag.

10 l, Unloading mail plane.

**1983, Oct. 24**

| | | | | |
|---|---|---|---|---|
| **3150** | A907 | 1 l multicolored | .25 | .25 |
| **3151** | A907 | 3.50 l multicolored | 1.00 | .55 |

**Souvenir Sheet**

| | | | | |
|---|---|---|---|---|
| **3152** | A907 | 10 l multicolored | 3.00 | 3.00 |

#3152 is airmail, contains one 38x51mm stamp.

Geum Reptans A908

Flora (No. 3154): b, Papaver dubium. c, Carlina acaulis. d, Paeonia peregrina. e, Gentiana excisa. Fauna (No. 3155): a, Sciurus vulgaria. b, Grammia quenselii. c, Dendrocopos medius. d, Lynx. e, Tichodroma muraria.

**1983, Oct. 28 Photo. *Perf. 13½***

| | | | |
|---|---|---|---|
| **3154** | Strip of 5 | 2.25 | 2.25 |
| *a.-e.* | A908 1 l Any single | .45 | .45 |
| **3155** | Strip of 5 | 2.25 | 2.25 |
| *a.-e.* | A908 1 l Any single | .45 | .45 |

Issued in sheets of 15.

Lady with Feather, by Cornelius Baba — A909

**1983, Nov. 3**

| | | | | |
|---|---|---|---|---|
| **3156** | A909 | 1 l shown | .25 | .25 |
| **3157** | A909 | 2 l Citizens | .40 | .25 |
| **3158** | A909 | 3 l Farmers, horiz. | .60 | .25 |
| **3159** | A909 | 4 l Resting in the Field, horiz. | .80 | .25 |
| | | *Nos. 3156-3159 (4)* | 2.05 | 1.00 |

A910

**1983, Nov. 30**

| | | | | |
|---|---|---|---|---|
| **3160** | A910 | 1 l Banner, emblem | .25 | .25 |
| **3161** | A910 | 2 l Congress building, flags | .40 | .25 |

Pact with Romania, 65th anniv.

A911

Designs: 1 l, Flags of participating countries, post office, mailman. 2 l, Congress building, woman letter carrier. 10 l, Flags, Congress building.

**1983, Dec. 17**

| | | | | |
|---|---|---|---|---|
| **3162** | A911 | 1 l multicolored | *.25* | *.25* |
| **3163** | A911 | 2 l multicolored | *.45* | *.25* |

**Souvenir Sheet**

| | | | | |
|---|---|---|---|---|
| **3164** | A911 | 10 l multicolored | *2.25* | *2.25* |

BALKANFILA '83 Stamp Exhibition, Bucharest. #3164 contains one 38x50mm stamp.

**Souvenir Sheet**

Orient Express Centenary (Paris-Istanbul) — A912

Leaving Gara de Nord, Bucharest, 1883

**1983, Dec. 30**

| | | | |
|---|---|---|---|
| **3165** | A912 10 l multi | 3.25 | 3.25 |

1984 Winter Olympics A913

**1984, Jan. 14**

| | | | | |
|---|---|---|---|---|
| **3166** | A913 | 50b Cross-country skiing | .25 | .25 |
| **3167** | A913 | 1 l Biathlon | .25 | .25 |
| **3168** | A913 | 1.50 l Figure skating | .25 | .25 |
| **3169** | A913 | 2 l Speed skating | .30 | .25 |
| **3170** | A913 | 3 l Hockey | .40 | .25 |
| **3171** | A913 | 3.50 l Bobsledding | .50 | .25 |
| **3172** | A913 | 4 l Luge | .60 | .25 |
| **3173** | A913 | 5 l Skiing | .75 | .30 |
| | | *Nos. 3166-3173 (8)* | 3.30 | 2.05 |

A 10 l imperf souvenir sheet exists showing ski jumping. Value, unused or used, $27.50.

**Souvenir Sheet**

Prince Alexandru Ioan Cuza, Arms — A914

**1984, Jan. 24 Photo. *Perf. 13½***

| | | | |
|---|---|---|---|
| **3174** | A914 10 l multi | 2.25 | 2.25 |

Union of Moldavia and Walachia Provinces, 125th anniv.

Palace of Udriste Nasturel (1596-1658), Chancery Official — A915

Miron Costin (1633-91), Poet — A916

Famous Men: 1.50 l, Crisan (Marcu Giurgiu), (1733-85), peasant revolt leader. 2 l, Simion Barnutiu (1808-64), scientist. 3.50 l, Duiliu Zamfirescu (1858-1922), poet. 4 l, Nicolas Milescu (1636-1708), Court official.

**1984, Feb. 8**

| | | | | |
|---|---|---|---|---|
| **3175** | A915 | 50b multi | .25 | .25 |
| **3176** | A916 | 1 l multi | .25 | .25 |
| **3177** | A916 | 1.50 l multi | .35 | .25 |
| **3178** | A916 | 2 l multi | .35 | .25 |
| **3179** | A916 | 3.50 l multi | .50 | .25 |
| **3180** | A916 | 4 l multi | .75 | .25 |
| | | *Nos. 3175-3180 (6)* | 2.45 | 1.50 |

See Nos. 3210-3213.

**Souvenir Sheet**

15th Balkan Chess Match, Herculane A917

4 successive moves culminating in checkmate.

**1984, Feb. 20 Photo. *Perf. 13½***

| | | | |
|---|---|---|---|
| **3181** | Sheet of 4 | 4.50 | 4.50 |
| *a.-d.* | A917 3 l, any single | 1.00 | 1.00 |

Bridges A918

No. 3182 — Romanian bridges: a, Orsova Bridge. b, Arges Bridge. c, Basarabi Bridge. d, Ohaba Bridge.

No. 3183 — Foreign bridges: a, Kohlbrand Bridge, Germany. b, Bosfor (Bosporus) Bridge, Turkey. c, Europa Bridge, Austria. d, Turnului (Tower Bridge), England.

**1984, Apr. 24**

| | | | |
|---|---|---|---|
| **3182** | Sheet of 4 | 2.50 | 2.50 |
| *a.-d.* | A918 3 l Any single | .55 | .55 |
| **3183** | Sheet of 4 | 2.50 | 2.50 |
| *a.-d.* | A918 3 l Any single | .55 | .55 |

Inter-European Cultural and Economic Cooperation.

Summer Olympics — A919

**1984, May 25 Photo. *Perf. 13½***

| | | | | |
|---|---|---|---|---|
| **3184** | A919 | 50b High jump | .25 | .25 |
| **3185** | A919 | 1 l Swimming | .25 | .25 |
| **3186** | A919 | 1.50 l Running | .25 | .25 |
| **3187** | A919 | 3 l Handball | .50 | .30 |
| **3188** | A919 | 4 l Rowing | .70 | .40 |
| **3189** | A919 | 5 l 2-man canoe | .85 | .50 |
| | | *Nos. 3184-3189 (6)* | 2.80 | 1.95 |

A 10 l imperf. airmail souvenir sheet containing a vert. stamp picturing a gymnast exists. Value, unused or used, $27.50.

Environmental Protection — A920

**1984, Apr. 26 Photo. *Perf. 13½***

| | | | | |
|---|---|---|---|---|
| **3190** | A920 | 1 l Sunflower | .25 | .25 |
| **3191** | A920 | 2 l Stag | .45 | .25 |
| **3192** | A920 | 3 l Fish | .70 | .25 |
| **3193** | A920 | 4 l Bird | .90 | .30 |
| | | *Nos. 3190-3193 (4)* | 2.30 | 1.05 |

Danube Flowers — A921

50b, Sagittaria sagittifolia. 1 l, Iris pseudacorus. 1.50 l, Butomus umbellatus. 3 l, Nymphaea alba, horiz. 4 l, Nymphoides peltata, horiz. 5 l, Nuphar luteum, horiz.

**1984, Apr. 30 Photo. *Perf. 13½***

**3194** A921 50b multi .25 .25
**3195** A921 1 l multi .25 .25
**3196** A921 1.50 l multi .40 .25
**3197** A921 3 l multi .70 .25
**3198** A921 4 l multi 1.00 .30
**3199** A921 5 l multi 1.10 .45
*Nos. 3194-3199 (6)* 3.70 1.75

45th Anniv., Youth Anti-Fascist Committee A922

**1984, Apr. 30 Photo. *Perf. 13½***

**3200** A922 2 l multicolored .65 .25

25th Congress, Ear, Nose and Throat Medicine — A923

**1984, May 30 Photo. *Perf. 13½***

**3201** A923 2 l Congress seal .40 .25

Souvenir Sheets

European Soccer Cup Championships A923a

Soccer players and flags of: c, Romania. d, West Germany. e, Portugal. f, Spain. g, France. h, Belgium. i, Yugoslavia. j, Denmark.

**1984, June 7 Photo. *Perf. 13½***

**3201A** Sheet of 4 2.50 2.50
***c.-f.*** A923a 3 l, any single .60 .60
**3201B** Sheet of 4 2.50 2.50
***g.-j.*** A923a 3 l, any single .60 .60

Summer Olympics — A924

**1984, July 2 Photo. *Perf. 13½***

**3202** A924 50b Boxing .25 .25
**3203** A924 1 l Rowing .25 .25
**3204** A924 1.50 l Team handball .25 .25
**3205** A924 2 l Judo .25 .25
**3206** A924 3 l Wrestling .40 .25
**3207** A924 3.50 l Fencing .50 .25
**3208** A924 4 l Kayak .65 .25
**3209** A924 5 l Swimming .75 .30
*Nos. 3202-3209 (8)* 3.30 2.05

Two imperf. 10 l airmail souvenir sheets, showing long jumping and gymnastics exist. Value for each sheet, unused or used, $15.

**Famous Romanians Type**

**1984, July 28 Photo. *Perf. 13½***

**3210** A916 1 l Mihai Ciuca .25 .25
**3211** A916 2 l Petre Aurelian .35 .25
**3212** A916 3 l Alexandru Vlahuta .50 .25
**3213** A916 4 l Dimitrie Leonida .70 .30
*Nos. 3210-3213 (4)* 1.80 1.05

40th Anniv., Romanian Revolution A925

**1984, Aug. 17 Photo. *Perf. 13½***

**3214** A925 2 l multicolored .40 .25

Romanian Horses — A926

**1984, Aug. 30 Photo. *Perf. 13½***

**3215** A926 50b Lippizaner .25 .25
**3216** A926 1 l Hutul .25 .25
**3217** A926 1.50 l Bucovina .30 .25
**3218** A926 2.50 l Nonius .50 .25
**3219** A926 4 l Arabian 1.00 .30
**3220** A926 5 l Romanian Mixed-breed .80 .40
*Nos. 3215-3220 (6)* 3.10 1.70

1784 Uprisings, 200th Anniv. — A927

**1984, Nov. 1 Photo. *Perf. 13½***

**3221** A927 2 l Monument .40 .25

Children A928

Paintings: 50b, Portrait of Child, by T. Aman. 1 l, Shepherd, by N. Grigorescu. 2 l, Girl with Orange, by S. Luchian. 3 l, Portrait of Child, by N. Tonitza. 4 l, Portrait of Boy, by S. Popp. 5 l, Portrait of Girl, by I. Tuculescu.

**1984, Nov. 10 Photo. *Perf. 13½***

**3222** A928 50b multicolored .25 .25
**3223** A928 1 l multicolored .25 .25
**3224** A928 2 l multicolored .35 .25
**3225** A928 3 l multicolored .50 .25
**3226** A928 4 l multicolored .70 .30
**3227** A928 5 l multicolored .85 .35
*Nos. 3222-3227 (6)* 2.90 1.65

Stamp Day A929

**1984, Nov. 15 Photo. *Perf. 13½***

**3228** A929 2 l + 1 l label .50 .30

Souvenir Sheet

13th Party Congress — A930

**1984, Nov. 17 Photo. *Perf. 13½***

**3229** A930 10 l Party symbols 4.00 4.00

Souvenir Sheets

Romanian Medalists, 1984 Summer Olympic Games — A931

No. 3230: a, Ecaterina Szabo, gymnastic floor exercise. b, 500-meter four-women kayak. c, Anisoara Stanciu, long jump. d, Greco-Roman wrestling. e, Mircea Fratica, half middleweight judo. f, Corneliu Ion, rapid fire pistol.

No. 3231: a, 1000-meter two-man scull. b, Weight lifting. c, Women's relays. d, Canoeing, pair oars without coxswain. e, Fencing, team foil. f, Ecaterina Szabo, all-around gymnastics.

**1984, Oct. 29 Photo. *Perf. 13½***

**3230** Sheet of 6 3.25 3.25
***a.-f.*** A931 3 l, any single .50 .50
**3231** Sheet of 6 3.25 3.25
***a.-f.*** A931 3 l, any single .50 .50

A932

Pelicans of the Danube Delta.

**1984, Dec. 15**

**3232** A932 50b Flying .25 .25
**3233** A932 1 l On ground .55 .25
**3234** A932 1 l In water .65 .25
**3235** A932 2 l Nesting .95 .45
*Nos. 3232-3235 (4)* 2.40 1.20

A933

Famous Men: 50b, Dr. Petru Groza (1884-1958). 1 l, Alexandru Odobescu (1834-1895). 2 l, Dr. Carol Davila (1828-1884). 3 l, Dr. Nicolae G. Lupu (1884-1966). 4 l, Dr. Daniel Danielopolu (1884-1955). 5 l, Panait Istrati (1884-1935).

**1984, Dec. 26**

**3236** A933 50b multi .25 .25
**3237** A933 1 l multi .25 .25
**3238** A933 2 l multi .35 .25
**3239** A933 3 l multi .50 .25
**3240** A933 4 l multi .70 .30
**3241** A933 5 l multi .85 .35
*Nos. 3236-3241 (6)* 2.90 1.65

Timisoara Power Station, Electric Street Lights, Cent. A934

**1984, Dec. 29**

**3242** A934 1 l Generator, 1884 .25 .25
**3243** A934 2 l Street arc lamp, Timisoara, 1884, vert. .35 .25

Souvenir Sheets

European Music Year — A935

Composers and opera houses, No. 3244a, Moscow Theater, Tchaichovsky (1840-1893). b, Bucharest Theater, George Enescu (1881-1955). c, Dresden Opera, Wagner (1813-1883). d, Warsaw Opera, Stanislaw Moniuszko (1819-1872).

No. 3245a, Paris Opera, Gounod (1818-1893). b, Munich Opera, Strauss (1864-1949). c, Vienna Opera, Mozart (1756-1791). d, La Scala, Milan, Verdi (1813-1901).

**1985, Mar. 28**

**3244** A935 Sheet of 4 2.50 2.50
***a.-d.*** 3 l, any single .60 .60
**3245** A935 Sheet of 4 2.50 2.50
***a.-d.*** 3 l, any single .60 .60

August T. Laurian (1810-1881), Linguist and Historian — A936

Famous men: 1 l, Grigore Alexandrescu (1810-1885), author. 1.50 l, Gheorghe Pop de Basesti (1835-1919), politician. 2 l, Mateiu Caragiale (1885-1936), author. 3 l, Gheorghe Ionescu-Sisesti (1885-1967), scientist. 4 l, Liviu Rebreanu (1885-1944), author.

**1985, Mar. 29**

| | | | | |
|---|---|---|---|---|
| **3246** | A936 | 50b multi | .25 | .25 |
| **3247** | A936 | 1 l multi | .25 | .25 |
| **3248** | A936 | 1.50 l multi | .25 | .25 |
| **3249** | A936 | 2 l multi | .35 | .25 |
| **3250** | A936 | 3 l multi | .50 | .30 |
| **3251** | A936 | 4 l multi | .70 | .40 |
| | | *Nos. 3246-3251 (6)* | 2.30 | 1.70 |

Intl. Youth Year — A937

**1985, Apr. 15**

| | | | | |
|---|---|---|---|---|
| **3252** | A937 | 1 l Scientific research | .25 | .25 |
| **3253** | A937 | 2 l Construction | .35 | .25 |

**Souvenir Sheet**

| | | | | |
|---|---|---|---|---|
| **3254** | A937 | 10 l Intl. solidarity | 2.50 | 2.25 |

No. 3254 contains one 54x42mm stamp.

Wildlife Conservation A938

**1985, May 6**

| | | | | |
|---|---|---|---|---|
| **3255** | A938 | 50b Nyctereutes procyonoides | .25 | .25 |
| **3256** | A938 | 1 l Perdix perdix | .25 | .25 |
| **3257** | A938 | 1.50 l Nyctea scandiaca | .30 | .25 |
| **3258** | A938 | 2 l Martes martes | .40 | .25 |
| **3259** | A938 | 3 l Meles meles | .65 | .25 |
| **3260** | A938 | 3.50 l Lutra lutra | .80 | .25 |
| **3261** | A938 | 4 l Tetrao urogallus | .90 | .30 |
| **3262** | A938 | 5 l Otis tarda | 1.10 | .35 |
| | | *Nos. 3255-3262 (8)* | 4.65 | 2.15 |

End of World War II, 40th Anniv. — A939

War monument, natl. and party flags.

**1985, May 9**

| | | | | |
|---|---|---|---|---|
| **3263** | A939 | 2 l multicolored | .50 | .25 |

Union of Communist Youth, 12th Congress A940

**1985, May 14**

| | | | | |
|---|---|---|---|---|
| **3264** | A940 | 2 l Emblem | .35 | .25 |

An imperf. 10 l EUROPA souvenir sheet showing a man, a woman and a baby with arms raised was issued 1985, June 3, with limited distribution. Value, $16.

Danube-Black Sea Canal Opening, May 26, 1984 — A942

1 l, Canal, map. 2 l, Bridge over lock, Cernavoda. 3 l, Bridge over canal, Medgidea. 4 l, Agigea lock, bridge.
10 l, Opening ceremony, Cernavoda, Ceaucescu.

**1985, June 7** *Perf. 13½*

| | | | | |
|---|---|---|---|---|
| **3266** | A942 | 1 l multi | .25 | .25 |
| **3267** | A942 | 2 l multi | .50 | .25 |
| **3268** | A942 | 3 l multi | .70 | .25 |
| **3269** | A942 | 4 l multi | 1.00 | .35 |
| | | *Nos. 3266-3269 (4)* | 2.45 | 1.10 |

**Souvenir Sheet**

| | | | | |
|---|---|---|---|---|
| **3270** | A942 | 10 l multi | 4.50 | 4.00 |

No. 3270 contains one 54x42mm stamp.

Audubon Birth Bicentenary — A943

American bird species — 50b, Turdus migratorius. 1 l, Pelecanus occidentalis. 1.50 l, Nyctanassa violarea. 2 l, Icterus galbula. 3 l, Podiceps grisegena. 4 l, Anas platyrhynchos.
Nos. 3272-3275 vert.

**1985, June 26**

| | | | | |
|---|---|---|---|---|
| **3271** | A943 | 50b multi | .25 | .25 |
| **3272** | A943 | 1 l multi | .25 | .25 |
| **3273** | A943 | 1.50 l multi | .30 | .25 |
| **3274** | A943 | 2 l multi | .35 | .25 |
| **3275** | A943 | 3 l multi | .70 | .25 |
| **3276** | A943 | 4 l multi | .95 | .35 |
| | | *Nos. 3271-3276 (6)* | 2.80 | 1.60 |

20th Century Paintings by Ion Tuculescu — A944

**1985, July 13**

| | | | | |
|---|---|---|---|---|
| **3277** | A944 | 1 l Fire, vert. | .25 | .25 |
| **3278** | A944 | 2 l Circuit, vert. | .35 | .25 |
| **3279** | A944 | 3 l Interior | .50 | .25 |
| **3280** | A944 | 4 l Sunset | .65 | .35 |
| | | *Nos. 3277-3280 (4)* | 1.75 | 1.10 |

Butterflies A945

**1985, July 15**

| | | | | |
|---|---|---|---|---|
| **3281** | A945 | 50b Inachis io | .25 | .25 |
| **3282** | A945 | 1 l Papilio machaon | .25 | .25 |
| **3283** | A945 | 2 l Vanessa atalanta | .40 | .25 |
| **3284** | A945 | 3 l Saturnia pavonia | .60 | .30 |
| **3285** | A945 | 4 l Ammobiota festiva | .80 | .40 |
| **3286** | A945 | 5 l Smerinthus ocellatus | 1.00 | .50 |
| | | *Nos. 3281-3286 (6)* | 3.30 | 1.95 |

Natl. Communist Party Achievements — A946

Natl. and party flags, and: 1 l, Transfagarasan Mountain Road. 2 l, Danube-Black Sea Canal. 3 l, Bucharest Underground Railway. 4 l, Irrigation.

**1985, July 29**

| | | | | |
|---|---|---|---|---|
| **3287** | A946 | 1 l multicolored | .25 | .25 |
| **3288** | A946 | 2 l multicolored | .50 | .25 |
| **3289** | A946 | 3 l multicolored | .75 | .25 |
| **3290** | A946 | 4 l multicolored | 1.00 | .35 |
| | | *Nos. 3287-3290 (4)* | 2.50 | 1.10 |

20th annivs.: Election of Gen.-Sec. Nicolae Ceausescu; Natl. Communist Congress.

Romanian Socialist Constitution, 20th Anniv. — A947

**1985, Aug. 5**

| | | | | |
|---|---|---|---|---|
| **3291** | A947 | 1 l Arms, wheat, dove | .25 | .25 |
| **3292** | A947 | 2 l Arms, torch | .60 | .25 |

1986 World Cup Soccer Preliminaries — A948

Flags of participants; Great Britain, Northern Ireland, Romania, Finland, Turkey and: 50b, Sliding tackle. 1 l, Trapping the ball. 1.50 l, Heading the ball. 2 l, Dribble. 3 l, Tackle. 4 l, Scissor kick. 10 l, Dribble, diff.

**1985, Oct. 15**

| | | | | |
|---|---|---|---|---|
| **3293** | A948 | 50b multi | .25 | .25 |
| **3294** | A948 | 1 l multi | .25 | .25 |
| **3295** | A948 | 1.50 l multi | .30 | .25 |
| **3296** | A948 | 2 l multi | .35 | .25 |
| **3297** | A948 | 3 l multi | .55 | .30 |
| **3298** | A948 | 4 l multi | .70 | .35 |
| | | *Nos. 3293-3298 (6)* | 2.40 | 1.65 |

An imperf airmail 10 l souvenir sheet exists, showing flags, stadium and soccer players. Value, unused or used, $13.

Souvenir Sheet

Motorcycle Centenary — A949

**1985, Aug. 22** **Photo.** *Perf. 13½*

| | | | | |
|---|---|---|---|---|
| **3300** | A949 | 10 l 1885 Daimler Einspur | 2.25 | 2.25 |

Retezat Natl. Park, 50th Anniv. — A950

50b, Senecio glaberrimus. 1 l, Rupicapra rupicapra. 2 l, Centaurea retezatensis. 3 l, Viola dacica. 4 l, Marmota marmota. 5 l, Aquila chrysaetos.
10 l, Lynx lynx.

**1985, Aug. 29**

| | | | | |
|---|---|---|---|---|
| **3301** | A950 | 50b multi | .25 | .25 |
| **3302** | A950 | 1 l multi | .25 | .25 |
| **3303** | A950 | 2 l multi | .35 | .25 |
| **3304** | A950 | 3 l multi | .55 | .25 |
| **3305** | A950 | 4 l multi | .80 | .35 |
| **3306** | A950 | 5 l multi | 1.00 | .45 |
| | | *Nos. 3301-3306 (6)* | 3.20 | 1.80 |

**Souvenir Sheet**

| | | | | |
|---|---|---|---|---|
| **3307** | A950 | 10 l multi | 3.00 | 2.75 |

No. 3307 contains one 42x54mm stamp.

Tractors Manufactured by Universal — A951

**1985, Sept. 10**

| | | | | |
|---|---|---|---|---|
| **3308** | A951 | 50b 530 DTC | .25 | .25 |
| **3309** | A951 | 1 l 550 M HC | .25 | .25 |
| **3310** | A951 | 1.50 l 650 Super | .25 | .25 |
| **3311** | A951 | 2 l 850 | .30 | .25 |
| **3312** | A951 | 3 l S 1801 IF | .60 | .25 |
| **3313** | A951 | 4 l A 3602 IF | .75 | .30 |
| | | *Nos. 3308-3313 (6)* | 2.40 | 1.55 |

Folk Costumes — A952

Women's and men's costumes from same region printed in continuous design.

**1985, Sept. 28**

| | | | |
|---|---|---|---|
| **3314** | 50b Muscel woman | .25 | .25 |
| **3315** | 50b Muscel man | .25 | .25 |
| *a.* | A952 Pair, #3314-3315 | .25 | .25 |
| **3316** | 1.50 l Bistrita-Nasaud woman | .25 | .25 |
| **3317** | 1.50 l Bistrita-Nasaud man | .25 | .25 |
| *a.* | A952 Pair, #3316-3317 | .50 | .30 |
| **3318** | 2 l Vrancea woman | .35 | .25 |
| **3319** | 2 l Vrancea man | .35 | .25 |
| *a.* | A952 Pair, #3318-3319 | .70 | .30 |
| **3320** | 3 l Vilcea woman | .50 | .25 |
| **3321** | 3 l Vilcea man | .50 | .25 |
| *a.* | A952 Pair, #3320-3321 | 1.00 | .50 |
| | *Nos. 3314-3321 (8)* | 2.70 | 2.00 |

Admission to UN, 30th Anniv. — A953

**1985, Oct. 21**

| | | | | |
|---|---|---|---|---|
| **3322** | A953 | 2 l multicolored | .40 | .25 |

UN, 40th Anniv. — A954

**1985, Oct. 21**

| | | | | |
|---|---|---|---|---|
| **3323** | A954 | 2 l multicolored | .35 | .25 |

Mineral Flowers — A955

50b, Quartz and calcite, Herja. 1 l, Copper, Altin Tepe. 2 l, Gypsum, Cavnic. 3 l, Quartz, Ocna de Fier. 4 l, Stibium, Baiut. 5 l, Tetrahedrite, Cavnic.

**1985, Oct. 28**

| | | | | |
|---|---|---|---|---|
| **3324** | A955 | 50b multi | .25 | .25 |
| **3325** | A955 | 1 l multi | .25 | .25 |
| **3326** | A955 | 2 l multi | .30 | .25 |
| **3327** | A955 | 3 l multi | .60 | .30 |
| **3328** | A955 | 4 l multi | .75 | .40 |
| **3329** | A955 | 5 l multi | .90 | .50 |
| | | *Nos. 3324-3329 (6)* | 3.05 | 1.95 |

Stamp Day — A956

**1985, Oct. 29**

| | | | | |
|---|---|---|---|---|
| **3330** | A956 | 2 l + 1 l label | .40 | .25 |

A Connecticut Yankee in King Arthur's Court, by Mark Twain — A957

The Three Brothers, by Jacob and Wilhelm Grimm — A958

Disney characters in classic fairy tales — No. 3331, Hank Morgan awakes in Camelot. No. 3332, Predicts eclipse of sun. No. 3333, Mounting horse. No. 3334, Sir Sagramor. No. 3335, Fencing with shadow. No. 3336, Fencing, father. No. 3337, Shoeing a horse. No. 3338, Barber, rabbit. No. 3339, Father, three sons.

No. 3340, Tournament of knights. No. 3341, Cottage.

**1985, Nov. 28**

| | | | | |
|---|---|---|---|---|
| **3331** | A957 | 50b multi | 2.00 | 2.00 |
| **3332** | A957 | 50b multi | 2.00 | 2.00 |
| **3333** | A957 | 50b multi | 2.00 | 2.00 |
| **3334** | A957 | 50b multi | 2.00 | 2.00 |
| **3335** | A958 | 1 l multi | 4.50 | 4.50 |
| **3336** | A958 | 1 l multi | 4.50 | 4.50 |
| **3337** | A958 | 1 l multi | 4.50 | 4.50 |
| **3338** | A958 | 1 l multi | 4.50 | 4.50 |
| **3339** | A958 | 1 l multi | 4.50 | 4.50 |
| | | *Nos. 3331-3339 (9)* | 30.50 | 30.50 |

**Souvenir Sheets**

| | | | | |
|---|---|---|---|---|
| **3340** | A957 | 5 l multi | 15.00 | 15.00 |
| **3341** | A958 | 5 l multi | 15.00 | 15.00 |

Miniature Sheets

Intereuropa 1986 — A959

Fauna & flora: #3343: a, Felis silvestris. b, Mustela erminea. c, Tetrao urogallus. d, Urso arctos.

#3344: a, Dianthus callizonus. b, Pinus cembra. c, Salix sp. d, Rose pendulina.

**1986, Mar. 25 Photo. *Perf. 13½***

| | | | | |
|---|---|---|---|---|
| **3343** | A959 | Sheet of 4 | 2.50 | 2.50 |
| *a.-d.* | | 3 l, any single | .60 | .60 |
| **3344** | A959 | Sheet of 4 | 2.50 | 2.50 |
| *a.-d.* | | 3 l, any single | .60 | .60 |

Inventors and Adventurers — A960

Designs: 1 l, Orville and Wilbur Wright, Wright Flyer. 1.50 l, Jacques Cousteau, research vessel Calypso. 2 l, Amelia Earhart, Lockheed Electra. 3 l, Charles Lindbergh, Spirit of St. Louis. 3.50 l, Sir Edmund Hillary (1919- ), first man to reach Mt. Everest summit. 4 l, Robert Edwin Peary, Arctic explorer. 5 l, Adm. Richard Byrd, explorer. 6 l, Neil Armstrong, first man on moon.

**1985, Dec. 25 Photo. *Perf. 13½***

| | | | | |
|---|---|---|---|---|
| **3345** | A960 | 1 l multi | .25 | .25 |
| **3346** | A960 | 1.50 l multi | .30 | .25 |
| **3347** | A960 | 2 l multi | .40 | .30 |
| **3348** | A960 | 3 l multi | .60 | .40 |
| **3349** | A960 | 3.50 l multi | .65 | .50 |
| **3350** | A960 | 4 l multi | .75 | .60 |
| **3351** | A960 | 5 l multi | 1.00 | .70 |
| **3352** | A960 | 6 l multi | 1.25 | .85 |
| | | *Nos. 3345-3352 (8)* | 5.20 | 3.85 |

Paintings by Nicolae Tonitza — A961

**1986, Mar. 12 Photo. *Perf. 13½***

| | | | | |
|---|---|---|---|---|
| **3353** | A961 | 1 l Nina in Green | .25 | .25 |
| **3354** | A961 | 2 l Irina | .40 | .25 |
| **3355** | A961 | 3 l Woodman's Daughter | .55 | .25 |
| **3356** | A961 | 4 l Woman on the Verandah | .75 | .30 |
| | | *Nos. 3353-3356 (4)* | 1.95 | 1.05 |

Color Animated Films, 50th Anniv. — A962

Walt Disney characters in the Band Concert, 1935 — No. 3357, Clarabelle. No. 3358, Mickey Mouse. No. 3359, Paddy and Peter. No. 3360, Goofy. No. 3361, Donald Duck. No. 3362, Mickey Mouse, diff. No. 3363, Mickey and Donald. No. 3364, Horace. No. 3365, Donald and trombonist.

No. 3366, Finale.

**1986, Apr. 10 Photo. *Perf. 13½***

| | | | | |
|---|---|---|---|---|
| **3357** | A962 | 50b multi | 2.00 | 2.00 |
| **3358** | A962 | 50b multi | 2.00 | 2.00 |
| **3359** | A962 | 50b multi | 2.00 | 2.00 |
| **3360** | A962 | 50b multi | 2.00 | 2.00 |
| **3361** | A962 | 1 l multi | 4.50 | 4.50 |
| **3362** | A962 | 1 l multi | 4.50 | 4.50 |
| **3363** | A962 | 1 l multi | 4.50 | 4.50 |
| **3364** | A962 | 1 l multi | 4.50 | 4.50 |
| **3365** | A962 | 1 l multi | 4.50 | 4.50 |
| | | *Nos. 3357-3365 (9)* | 30.50 | 30.50 |

**Souvenir Sheet**

| | | | | |
|---|---|---|---|---|
| **3366** | A962 | 5 l multi | 15.00 | 15.00 |

1986 World Cup Soccer Championships, Mexico — A963

Various soccer plays and flags: 50b, Italy vs. Bulgaria. 1 l, Mexico vs. Belgium. 2 l, Canada vs. France. 3 l, Brazil vs. Spain. 4 l, Uruguay vs. Germany. 5 l, Morocco vs. Poland.

**1986, May 9**

| | | | | |
|---|---|---|---|---|
| **3367** | A963 | 50b multi | .25 | .25 |
| **3368** | A963 | 1 l multi | .25 | .25 |
| **3369** | A963 | 2 l multi | .30 | .25 |
| **3370** | A963 | 3 l multi | .45 | .25 |
| **3371** | A963 | 4 l multi | .90 | .25 |
| **3372** | A963 | 5 l multi | 1.00 | .35 |
| | | *Nos. 3367-3372 (6)* | 3.15 | 1.60 |

An imperf. 10 l airmail souvenir sheet exists picturing stadium, flags of previous winners, satellite and map. Value, unused or used, $22.50.

Hotels — A964

50b, Diana, Herculane. 1 l, Termal, Felix. 2 l, Delfin, Meduza and Steaua de Mare, Eforie Nord. 3 l, Caciulata, Calimanesti Caciulata. 4 l, Palas, Slanic Moldova. 5 l, Bradet, Sovata.

**1986, Apr. 23 Photo. *Perf. 13½***

| | | | | |
|---|---|---|---|---|
| **3373** | A964 | 50b multi | .25 | .25 |
| **3374** | A964 | 1 l multi | .25 | .25 |
| **3375** | A964 | 2 l multi | .35 | .25 |
| **3376** | A964 | 3 l multi | .50 | .25 |
| **3377** | A964 | 4 l multi | .70 | .25 |
| **3378** | A964 | 5 l multi | 1.00 | .35 |
| | | *Nos. 3373-3378 (6)* | 3.05 | 1.60 |

Nicolae Ceausescu, Party Flag — A965

**1986, May 8 Photo. *Perf. 13½***

| | | | | |
|---|---|---|---|---|
| **3379** | A965 | 2 l multicolored | 1.00 | .75 |

Natl. Communist Party, 65th anniv.

Flowers — A966

**1986, June 25 Photo. *Perf. 13½***

| | | | | |
|---|---|---|---|---|
| **3380** | A966 | 50b Tulipa gesneriana | .25 | .25 |
| **3381** | A966 | 1 l Iris hispanica | .25 | .25 |
| **3382** | A966 | 2 l Rosa hybrida | .35 | .25 |
| **3383** | A966 | 3 l Anemone coronaria | .55 | .25 |
| **3384** | A966 | 4 l Freesia refracta | .80 | .25 |
| **3385** | A966 | 5 l Chrysanthemum indicum | 1.00 | .35 |
| | | *Nos. 3380-3385 (6)* | 3.20 | 1.60 |

Mircea the Great, Ruler of Wallachia, 1386-1418 — A967

**1986, July 17 Photo. *Perf. 13½***

| | | | | |
|---|---|---|---|---|
| **3386** | A967 | 2 l multicolored | .60 | .30 |

Ascent to the throne, 600th anniv.

Open Air Museum of Historic Dwellings, Bucharest, 50th Anniv. — A968

**1986, July 21**

**3387** A968 50b Alba .25 .25
**3388** A968 1 l Arges .25 .25
**3389** A968 2 l Constantia .35 .25
**3390** A968 3 l Timis .55 .25
**3391** A968 4 l Neamt .80 .25
**3392** A968 5 l Gorj 1.00 .35
*Nos. 3387-3392 (6)* 3.20 1.60

Polar Research — A969

Exploration: 50b, Julius Popper, exploration of Tierra del Fuego (1886-93). 1 l, Bazil G. Assan, exploration of Spitzbergen (1896). 2 l, Emil Racovita, Antarctic expedition (1897-99). 3 l, Constantin Dumbrava, exploration of Greenland (1927-8). 4 l, Romanians with the 17th Soviet Antarctic expedition (1971-72). 5 l, Research on krill fishing (1977-80).

**1986, July 23 Photo. *Perf. 13½***

**3393** A969 50b multi .25 .25
**3394** A969 1 l multi .25 .25
**3395** A969 2 l multi .35 .25
**3396** A969 3 l multi .55 .25
**3397** A969 4 l multi .80 .25
**3398** A969 5 l multi 1.00 .35
*Nos. 3393-3398 (6)* 3.20 1.60

Natl. Cycling Championships A970

Various athletes.

**1986, Aug. 29**

**3399** A970 1 l multicolored .25 .25
**3400** A970 2 l multicolored .35 .25
**3401** A970 3 l multicolored .55 .25
**3402** A970 4 l multicolored .75 .30
*Nos. 3399-3402 (4)* 1.90 1.05

**Souvenir Sheet**

**3403** A970 10 l multicolored 2.50 1.25

No. 3403 contains one 42x54mm stamp.

Souvenir Sheet

Intl. Peace Year — A971

**1986, July 25**

**3404** A971 5 l multicolored 1.25 .60

Fungi — A972

50b, Amanita rubescens. 1 l, Boletus luridus. 2 l, Lactarius piperatus. 3 l, Lepiota clypeolaria. 4 l, Russula cyanoxantha. 5 l, Tremiscus helvelloides.

**1986, Aug. 15**

**3405** A972 50b multi .25 .25
**3406** A972 1 l multi .25 .25
**3407** A972 2 l multi .35 .25
**3408** A972 3 l multi .55 .25
**3409** A972 4 l multi .80 .25
**3410** A972 5 l multi 1.00 .35
*Nos. 3405-3410 (6)* 3.20 1.60

An imperf. 10 l EUROPA souvenir sheet with an oval stamp inscribed "CSCE" was issued, 1986, Oct. 28, with limited distribtion. Value, $20.

A973

Famous Men: 50b, Petru Maior (c. 1761-1821), historian. 1 l, George Topirceanu (1886-1937), doctor. 2 l, Henri Coanda (1886-1972), engineer. 3 l, Constantin Budeanu (1886-1959), engineer.

**1986, Nov. 10 Photo. *Perf. 13½***

**3411** A973 50b dl cl, gold & dk bl grn .25 .25
**3412** A973 1 l sl grn, gold & dk lil rose .25 .25
**3413** A973 2 l rose cl, gold & brt bl .45 .25
**3414** A973 3 l chlky bl, gold & choc .70 .25
*Nos. 3411-3414 (4)* 1.65 1.00

UNESCO, 40th Anniv. A974

**1986, Nov. 10**

**3415** A974 4 l multicolored .75 .35

Stamp Day — A975

**1986, Nov. 15**

**3416** A975 2 l + 1 l label 1.20 .25

Industry A976

50b, F-300 oil rigs, vert. 1 l, Promex excavator. 2 l, Pitesti refinery, vert. 3 l, 110-ton dump truck. 4 l, Coral computer, vert. 5 l, 350-megawatt turbine.

**1986, Nov. 28**

**3417** A976 50b multi .25 .25
**3418** A976 1 l multi .25 .25
**3419** A976 2 l multi .40 .25
**3420** A976 3 l multi .55 .25
**3421** A976 4 l multi .80 .25
**3422** A976 5 l multi 1.00 .35
*Nos. 3417-3422 (6)* 3.25 1.60

Folk Costumes — A977

**1986, Dec. 26**

**3423** A977 50b Capra .25 .25
**3424** A977 1 l Sorcova .25 .25
**3425** A977 2 l Plugusorul .35 .25
**3426** A977 3 l Buhaiul .55 .25
**3427** A977 4 l Caiutii .80 .25
**3428** A977 5 l Uratorii 1.00 .35
*Nos. 3423-3428 (6)* 3.20 1.60

Recycling Campaign — A978

**1986, Dec. 30**

**3429** A978 1 l Metal .25 .25
**3430** A978 2 l Trees .50 .25

Young Communists' League, 65th Anniv. — A979

**1987, Mar. 18 Photo. *Perf. 13½***

**3431** A979 1 l Flags, youth .25 .25
**3432** A979 2 l Emblem .45 .25
**3433** A979 3 l Flags, youth, diff. .65 .40
*Nos. 3431-3433 (3)* 1.35 .90

Miniature Sheets

Intereuropa — A980

Modern architecture: No. 3434a, Exposition Pavilion, Bucharest. b, Intercontinental Hotel, Bucharest. c, Europa Hotel, Black Sea coast. d, Polytechnic Institute, Bucharest.

No. 3435a, Administration Building, Satu Mare. b, House of Young Pioneers, Bucharest. c, Valahia Hotel, Tirgoviste. d, Caciulata Hotel, Caciulata.

**1987, May 18 Photo. *Perf. 13½***

**3434** A980 Sheet of 4 2.50 2.50
***a.-d.*** 3 l, any single .60 .60
**3435** A980 Sheet of 4 2.50 2.50
***a.-d.*** 3 l, any single .60 .60

Collective Farming, 25th Anniv. — A981

**1987, Apr. 25 Photo. *Perf. 13½***

**3436** A981 2 l multicolored .50 .25

Birch Trees by the Lakeside, by I. Andreescu — A982

Paintings in Romanian museums: 1 l, Young Peasant Girls Spinning, by N. Grigorescu. 2 l, Washerwoman, by S. Luchian. 3 l, Inside the Peasant's Cottage, by S. Dimitrescu. 4 l, Winter Landscape, by A. Ciucurencu. 5 l, Winter in Bucharest, by N. Tonitza, vert.

**1987, Apr. 28**

**3437** A982 50b multicolored .25 .25
**3438** A982 1 l multicolored .25 .25
**3439** A982 2 l multicolored .35 .25
**3440** A982 3 l multicolored .50 .25
**3441** A982 4 l multicolored .75 .35
**3442** A982 5 l multicolored 1.00 .50
*Nos. 3437-3442 (6)* 3.10 1.85

Peasant Uprising of 1907, 80th Anniv. — A983

**1987, May 30**

**3443** A983 2 l multicolored .50 .25

Men's World Handball Championships — A984

Various plays.

**1987, July 15**

**3444** A984 50b multi, vert. .25 .25
**3445** A984 1 l multi .25 .25
**3446** A984 2 l multi, vert. .35 .25
**3447** A984 3 l multi .50 .25
**3448** A984 4 l multi, vert. .75 .35
**3449** A984 5 l multi 1.00 .50
*Nos. 3444-3449 (6)* 3.10 1.85

A985

Natl. Currency — A986

**1987, July 15**

| | | | | |
|---|---|---|---|---|
| **3450** | A985 | 1 l multicolored | .25 | .25 |

**Souvenir Sheet**

| | | | | |
|---|---|---|---|---|
| **3451** | A986 | 10 l multicolored | 2.50 | 2.50 |

Landscapes — A987

50b, Pelicans over the Danube Delta. 1 l, Transfagarasan Highway. 2 l, Hairpin curve, Bicazului. 3 l, Limestone peaks, Mt. Ceahlau. 4 l, Lake Capra, Mt. Fagaras. 5 l, Orchard, Borsa.

**1987, July 31 Photo. *Perf. 13½***

| | | | | |
|---|---|---|---|---|
| **3452** | A987 | 50b multi | .25 | .25 |
| **3453** | A987 | 1 l multi | .25 | .25 |
| **3454** | A987 | 2 l multi | .35 | .25 |
| **3455** | A987 | 3 l multi | .50 | .25 |
| **3456** | A987 | 4 l multi | .70 | .35 |
| **3457** | A987 | 5 l multi | .90 | .50 |
| | | *Nos. 3452-3457 (6)* | 2.95 | 1.85 |

A988

Scenes from Fairy Tale by Peter Ispirescu (b. 1887) — A988a

**1987, Sept. 25 Photo. *Perf. 13½***

| | | | | |
|---|---|---|---|---|
| **3458** | A988 | 50b shown | .25 | .25 |
| **3459** | A988 | 1 l multi, diff. | .25 | .25 |
| **3460** | A988 | 2 l multi, diff. | .35 | .25 |
| **3461** | A988 | 3 l multi, diff. | .50 | .25 |
| **3462** | A988 | 4 l multi, diff. | .70 | .35 |
| **3463** | A988 | 5 l multi, diff. | .85 | .40 |
| | | *Nos. 3458-3463 (6)* | 2.90 | 1.75 |

**Souvenir Sheet**

| | | | | |
|---|---|---|---|---|
| **3464** | A988a | 10 l shown | 2.50 | 2.50 |

Miniature Sheets

Flora and Fauna A989

Flora: No. 3465a, Aquilegia alpina. b, Pulsatilla vernalis. c, Aster alpinus. d, Soldanella pusilla baumg. e, Lilium bulbiferum. f, Arctostaphylos uva-ursi. g, Crocus vernus. h, Crepis aurea. i, Cypripedium calceolus. j, Centaurea nervosa. k, Dryas octopetala. l, Gentiana excisa.

Fauna: No. 3466a, Martes martes. b, Felis lynx. c, Ursus maritimus. d, Lutra lutra. e, Bison bonasus. f, Branta ruficollis. g, Phoenicopterus ruber. h, Otis tarda. i, Lyrurus tetrix. j, Gypaetus barbatus. k, Vormela peregusna. l, Oxyura leucocephala.

**1987, Oct. 16 Sheets of 12**

| | | | | |
|---|---|---|---|---|
| **3465** | A989 | 1 l #a.-l. | 4.50 | 4.50 |
| **3466** | A989 | 1 l #a.-l. | 4.50 | 4.50 |

Souvenir Sheet

PHILATELIA '87, Cologne — A990

**1987, Oct. 19**

| | | | | |
|---|---|---|---|---|
| **3467** | A990 | Sheet of 2 + 2 labels | 2.50 | 2.50 |
| *a.* | | 3 l Bucharest city seal | 1.00 | 1.00 |
| *b.* | | 3 l Cologne city arms | 1.00 | 1.00 |

Locomotives — A991

**1987, Oct. 15**

| | | | | |
|---|---|---|---|---|
| **3468** | A991 | 50b L 45 H | .25 | .25 |
| **3469** | A991 | 1 l LDE 125 | .25 | .25 |
| **3470** | A991 | 2 l LDH 70 | .40 | .25 |
| **3471** | A991 | 3 l LDE 2100 | .65 | .30 |
| **3472** | A991 | 4 l LDE 3000 | .90 | .40 |
| **3473** | A991 | 5 l LE 5100 | 1.00 | .50 |
| | | *Nos. 3468-3473 (6)* | 3.45 | 1.95 |

Folk Costumes — A992

**1987, Nov. 7**

| | | | | |
|---|---|---|---|---|
| **3474** | | 1 l Tirnave (woman) | .25 | .25 |
| **3475** | | 1 l Tirnave (man) | .25 | .25 |
| *a.* | A992 | Pair, #3474-3475 | .40 | .25 |
| **3476** | | 2 l Buzau (woman) | .40 | .25 |
| **3477** | | 2 l Buzau (man) | .40 | .25 |
| *a.* | A992 | Pair, #3476-3477 | .80 | .30 |
| **3478** | | 3 l Dobrogea (woman) | .60 | .30 |
| **3479** | | 3 l Dobrogea (man) | .60 | .30 |
| *a.* | A992 | Pair, #3478-3479 | 1.25 | .60 |
| **3480** | | 4 l Ilfov (woman) | .80 | .40 |
| **3481** | | 4 l Ilfov (man) | .80 | .40 |
| *a.* | A992 | Pair, #3480-3481 | 1.60 | .80 |
| | | *Nos. 3474-3481 (8)* | 4.10 | 2.40 |

Postwoman Delivering Mail — A993

**1987, Nov. 15 Photo. *Perf. 13½***

| | | | | |
|---|---|---|---|---|
| **3482** | A993 | 2 l + 1 l label | .75 | .35 |

Stamp Day.

Apiculture — A994

1 l, Apis mellifica carpatica. 2 l, Bee pollinating sunflower. 3 l, Hives, Danube Delta. 4 l, Apiculture complex, Bucharest.

**1987, Nov. 16 Photo. *Perf. 13½***

| | | | | |
|---|---|---|---|---|
| **3483** | A994 | 1 l multi | .25 | .25 |
| **3484** | A994 | 2 l multi | .50 | .25 |
| **3485** | A994 | 3 l multi | .75 | .35 |
| **3486** | A994 | 4 l multi | 1.00 | .50 |
| | | *Nos. 3483-3486 (4)* | 2.50 | 1.35 |

1988 Winter Olympics, Calgary A995

**1987, Dec. 28 Photo. *Perf. 13½***

| | | | | |
|---|---|---|---|---|
| **3487** | A995 | 50b Biathlon | .25 | .25 |
| **3488** | A995 | 1 l Slalom | .25 | .25 |
| **3489** | A995 | 1.50 l Ice hockey | .25 | .25 |
| **3490** | A995 | 2 l Luge | .25 | .25 |
| **3491** | A995 | 3 l Speed skating | .45 | .25 |
| **3492** | A995 | 3.50 l Women's figure skating | .45 | .25 |
| **3493** | A995 | 4 l Downhill skiing | .60 | .25 |
| **3494** | A995 | 5 l Two-man bob-sled | .75 | .35 |
| | | *Nos. 3487-3494 (8)* | 3.25 | 2.10 |

An imperf. 10 l souvenir sheet picturing ski jumping also exists. Value, unused or used, $20.

Traffic Safety A996

Designs: 50b, Be aware of children riding bicycles in the road. 1 l, Young Pioneer girl as crossing guard. 2 l, Do not open car doors in path of moving traffic. 3 l, Be aware of pedestrian crossings. 4 l, Observe the speed limit; do not attempt curves at high speed. 5 l, Protect small children.

**1987, Dec. 10 Photo. *Perf. 13½***

| | | | | |
|---|---|---|---|---|
| **3495** | A996 | 50b multicolored | .25 | .25 |
| **3496** | A996 | 1 l multicolored | .25 | .25 |
| **3497** | A996 | 2 l multicolored | .40 | .25 |
| **3498** | A996 | 3 l multicolored | .65 | .30 |
| **3499** | A996 | 4 l multicolored | .85 | .40 |
| **3500** | A996 | 5 l multicolored | 1.00 | .45 |
| | | *Nos. 3495-3500 (6)* | 3.40 | 1.90 |

October Revolution, Russia, 70th Anniv. — A997

**1987, Dec. 26**

| | | | | |
|---|---|---|---|---|
| **3501** | A997 | 2 l multicolored | .60 | .25 |

40th Anniv. of the Romanian Republic — A998

**1987, Dec. 30**

| | | | | |
|---|---|---|---|---|
| **3502** | A998 | 2 l multicolored | .50 | .25 |

70th Birthday of President Nicolae Ceausescu — A999

**1988, Jan. 26**

| | | | | |
|---|---|---|---|---|
| **3503** | A999 | 2 l multicolored | .90 | .45 |

Pottery A1000

**1988, Feb. 26 Photo. *Perf. 13½***

| | | | | |
|---|---|---|---|---|
| **3504** | A1000 | 50b Marginea | .25 | .25 |
| **3505** | A1000 | 1 l Oboga | .25 | .25 |
| **3506** | A1000 | 2 l Horezu | .35 | .25 |
| **3507** | A1000 | 3 l Curtea De Arges | .55 | .25 |
| **3508** | A1000 | 4 l Birsa | .75 | .25 |
| **3509** | A1000 | 5 l Vama | 1.00 | .35 |
| | | *Nos. 3504-3509 (6)* | 3.15 | 1.60 |

### Miniature Sheets

Intereuropa — A1001

Transportation and communication: No. 3510a, Mail coach. b, ECS telecommunications satellite. c, Oltcit automobile. d, ICE high-speed electric train.

No. 3511a, Santa Maria, 15th cent. b, Cheia Ground Station satellite dish receivers. c, Bucharest subway. d, Airbus-A320.

**1988, Apr. 27 Photo. *Perf. 13½***

**3510** A1001 Sheet of 4 2.50 2.50
*a.-d.* 3 l any single .60 .60
**3511** A1001 Sheet of 4 2.50 2.50
*a.-d.* 3 l any single .60 .60

1988 Summer Olympics, Seoul — A1002

**1988, Jun. 28**

**3512** A1002 50b Gymnastics .25 .25
**3513** A1002 1.50 l Boxing .30 .25
**3514** A1002 2 l Tennis .35 .25
**3515** A1002 3 l Judo .50 .25
**3516** A1002 4 l Running .80 .25
**3517** A1002 5 l Rowing 1.00 .40
*Nos. 3512-3517 (6)* 3.20 1.65

An imperf. 10 l souvenir sheet exists. Value, unused or used, $12.

19th-20th Cent. Clocks in the Ceasului Museum, Ploesti A1003

50b, Arad Region porcelain. 1.50 l, French bronze. 2 l, French bronze, diff. 3 l, Gothic bronze. 4 l, Saxony porcelain. 5 l, Bohemian porcelain.

**1988, May 20 Photo. *Perf. 13½***

**3518** A1003 50b multicolored .25 .25
**3519** A1003 1.50 l multicolored .25 .25
**3520** A1003 2 l multicolored .40 .25
**3521** A1003 3 l multicolored .55 .25
**3522** A1003 4 l multicolored .85 .25
**3523** A1003 5 l multicolored 1.00 .35
*Nos. 3518-3523 (6)* 3.30 1.60

20th cent. timepiece (50b); others 19th cent.

### Miniature Sheets

European Soccer Championships, Germany — A1003a

Soccer players and flags of: c, Federal Republic of Germany. d, Spain. e, Italy. f, Denmark. g, England. h, Netherlands. i, Ireland. j, Soviet Union.

**1988, June 9 Litho. *Perf. 13½***

**3523A** A1003a Sheet of 4 3.25 3.25
*c.-f.* 3 l any single .80 .80
**3523B** A1003a Sheet of 4 3.25 3.25
*g.-j.* 3 l any single .80 .80

Accession of Constanin Brincoveanu as Prince Regent of Wallachia, 1688-1714, 300th Anniv. — A1004

**1988, June 20**

**3524** A1004 2 l multicolored .50 .25

1988 Summer Olympics, Seoul — A1005

50b, Women's running. 1 l, Canoeing. 1.50 l, Women's gymnastics. 2 l, Kayaking. 3 l, Weight lifting. 3.50 l, Women's swimming. 4 l, Fencing. 5 l, Women's rowing (double).

**1988, Sept. 1 Photo. *Perf. 13½***

**3525** A1005 50b multicolored .25 .25
**3526** A1005 1 l multicolored .25 .25
**3527** A1005 1.50 l multicolored .25 .25
**3528** A1005 2 l multicolored .25 .25
**3529** A1005 3 l multicolored .40 .25
**3530** A1005 3.50 l multicolored .50 .25
**3531** A1005 4 l multicolored .60 .25
**3532** A1005 5 l multicolored .75 .30
*Nos. 3525-3532 (8)* 3.25 2.05

An imperf. 10 l souvenir sheet exists picturing women's gymnastics. Value, unused or used, $20.

Romania-China Philatelic Exhibition — A1006

**1988, Aug. 5 Photo. *Perf. 13½***

**3533** A1006 2 l multicolored .50 .25

### Souvenir Sheet

PRAGA '88 — A1007

**1988, Aug. 26**

**3534** A1007 5 l Carnations, by Stefan Luchian 2.00 2.00

### Miniature Sheets

Orchids — A1008

#3535: a, Oncidium lanceanum. b, Cattleya trianae. c, Sophronitis cernua. d, Bulbophyllum lobbii. e, Lycaste cruenta. f, Mormolyce ringens. g, Phragmipedium schlimii. h, Angraecum sesquipedale. i, Laelia crispa. j, Encyclia atropurpurea. k, Dendrobium nobile. l, Oncidium splendidum.

#3536: a, Brassavola perrinii. b, Paphiopedilum maudiae. c, Sophronitis coccinea. d, Vandopsis lissochiloides. e, Phalaenopsis lueddemanniana. f, Chysis bractescens. g, Cochleanthes discolor. h, Phalaenopsis amabilis. i, Pleione pricei. j, Sobralia macrantha. k, Aspasia lunata. l, Cattleya citrina.

**1988, Oct. 24**

**3535** A1008 Sheet of 12 4.00 4.00
*a.-l.* 1 l any single .30 .30
**3536** A1008 Sheet of 12 4.00 4.00
*a.-l.* 1 l any single .30 .30

### Miniature Sheets

Events Won by Romanian Athletes at the 1988 Seoul Olympic Games A1009

Sporting event and medal: No. 3537a, Women's gymnastics. b, Free pistol shooting. c, Weight lifting (220 pounds). d, Featherweight boxing.

No. 3538a, Women's 1500 and 3000-meter relays. b, Women's 200 and 400-meter individual swimming medley. c, Wrestling (220 pounds). d, Rowing, coxless pairs and coxed fours.

**1988, Dec. 7 Photo. *Perf. 13½***

**3537** Sheet of 4 3.00 3.00
*a.-d.* A1009 3 l any single .75 .75
**3538** Sheet of 4 3.00 3.00
*a.-d.* A1009 3 l any single .75 .75

Stamp Day — A1010

**1988, Nov. 13 Photo. *Perf. 13½***

**3539** A1010 2 l + 1 l label .75 .35

Unitary Natl. Romanian State, 70th Anniv. A1011

**1988, Dec. 29**

**3540** A1011 2 l multicolored .50 .40

Anniversaries — A1012

Designs: 50b, Athenaeum, Bucharest. 1.50 l, Trajan's Bridge, Drobeta, on a Roman bronze sestertius used in Romania from 103 to 105 A.D. 2 l, Ruins, Suceava. 3 l, Pitesti municipal coat of arms, scroll, architecture. 4 l, Trajan's Column (detail), 113 A.D. 5 l, Gold helmet discovered in Prahova County.

**1988, Dec. 30**

**3541** A1012 50b shown .25 .25
**3542** A1012 1.50 l multi .25 .25
**3543** A1012 2 l multi .35 .25
**3544** A1012 3 l multi .50 .25
**3545** A1012 4 l multi .80 .25
**3546** A1012 5 l multi 1.00 .35
*Nos. 3541-3546 (6)* 3.15 1.60

Athenaeum, Bucharest, cent. (50b), Suceava, capital of Moldavia from 1401-1565, 600th anniv. (2 l), & Pitesti municipal charter, 600th anniv. (3 l).

### Miniature Sheets

Grand Slam Tennis Championships — A1013

No. 3547: a, Men's singles, stadium in Melbourne. b, Men's singles, scoreboard. c, Mixed doubles, spectators. d, Mixed doubles, Roland Garros stadium.

No. 3548: a, Women's singles, stadium in Wimbledon. b, Women's singles, spectators. c, Men's doubles, spectators. d, Men's doubles, stadium in Flushing Meadows.

**1988, Aug. 22 Photo. *Perf. 13½***

**3547** A1013 Sheet of 4 3.00 3.00
*a.-d.* 3 l any single .75 .75
**3548** A1013 Sheet of 4 3.00 3.00
*a.-d.* 3 l any single .75 .75

Australian Open (Nos. 3547a-3547b), French Open (Nos. 3547c-3547d), Wimbledon (Nos. 3548a-3548b) and US Open (Nos. 3548c-3548d).

Architecture — A1014

Designs: 50b, Zapodeni, Vaslui, 17th cent. 1.50 l, Berbesti, Maramures, 18th cent. 2 l, Voitinel, Suceava, 18th cent. 3 l, Chiojdu mic, Buzau, 18th cent. 4 l, Cimpanii de sus, Bihor, 19th cent. 5 l, Naruja, Vrancea, 19th cent.

**1989, Feb. 8 Photo. *Perf. 13½***

**3549** A1014 50b multi .25 .25
**3550** A1014 1.50 l multi .25 .25
**3551** A1014 2 l multi .35 .25
**3552** A1014 3 l multi .50 .25
**3553** A1014 4 l multi .80 .25
**3554** A1014 5 l multi 1.00 .35
*Nos. 3549-3554 (6)* 3.15 1.60

Rescue and Relief Services — A1015

50b, Relief worker. 1.50 l, Fireman, child. 2 l, Fireman's carry. 3 l, Rescue team on skis. 3.50 l, Mountain rescue. 4 l, Water rescue. 5 l, Water safety.

**1989, Feb. 25**

| | | | | | |
|---|---|---|---|---|---|
| **3555** | A1015 | 50b multicolored | .25 | .25 |
| **3556** | A1015 | 1 l multicolored | .25 | .25 |
| **3557** | A1015 | 1.50 l multicolored | .25 | .25 |
| **3558** | A1015 | 2 l multicolored | .30 | .25 |
| **3559** | A1015 | 3 l multicolored | .50 | .25 |
| **3560** | A1015 | 3.50 l multicolored | .60 | .25 |
| **3561** | A1015 | 4 l multicolored | .70 | .30 |
| **3562** | A1015 | 5 l multicolored | .85 | .35 |
| | | *Nos. 3555-3562 (8)* | 3.70 | 2.15 |

Nos. 3555, 3557-3558, 3560-3561 vert.

Industries — A1016

Designs: 50b, Fasca Bicaz cement factory. 1.50 l, Bridge on the Danube near Cernavoda. 2 l, MS-2-2400/450-20 synchronous motor. 3 l, Bucharest subway. 4 l, Mangalia-Constanta ferry. 5 l, *Gloria* marine platform.

**1989, Apr. 10 Photo. *Perf. 13½***

| | | | | |
|---|---|---|---|---|
| **3563** | A1016 | 50b multi | .25 | .25 |
| **3564** | A1016 | 1.50 l multi | .25 | .25 |
| **3565** | A1016 | 2 l multi | .40 | .25 |
| **3566** | A1016 | 3 l multi | .55 | .25 |
| **3567** | A1016 | 4 l multi | .75 | .25 |
| **3568** | A1016 | 5 l multi | .85 | .35 |
| | | *Nos. 3563-3568 (6)* | 3.05 | 1.60 |

Anti-fascist March, 50th Anniv. — A1017

**1989, May 1 Photo. *Perf. 13½***

**3569** A1017 2 l shown .50 .25

**Souvenir Sheet**

**3570** A1017 10 l Patriots, flag 4.00 4.00

Souvenir Sheet

BULGARIA '89, Sofia, May 22-31 — A1018

**1989, May 20**

**3571** A1018 10 l Roses 2.50 2.50

Miniature Sheets

Intereuropa 1989 — A1019

Children's activities and games: No. 3572a, Swimming. No. 3572b, Water slide. No. 3572c, Seesaw. No. 3572d, Flying kites. No. 3573a, Playing with dolls. No. 3573b, Playing ball. No. 3573c, Playing in the sand. No. 3573d, Playing with toy cars.

**1989, June 15**

| | | | | |
|---|---|---|---|---|
| **3572** | A1019 | Sheet of 4 | 2.25 | 2.25 |
| *a.-d.* | | 3 l any single | .55 | .55 |
| **3573** | A1019 | Sheet of 4 | 2.25 | 2.25 |
| *a.-d.* | | 3 l any single | .55 | .55 |

Socialist Revolution in Romania, 45th Anniv. A1020

**1989, Aug. 21 Photo. *Perf. 13½***

**3574** A1020 2 l multicolored .50 .25

Cartoons — A1021

50b, Pin-pin. 1 l, Maria. 1.50 l, Gore and Grigore. 2 l, Pisoiul, Balanel, Manole and Monk. 3 l, Gruia Lui Novac. 3.50 l, Mihaela. 4 l, Harap alb. 5 l, Homo sapiens.

**1989, Sept. 25**

| | | | | |
|---|---|---|---|---|
| **3575** | A1021 | 50b multi | .25 | .25 |
| **3576** | A1021 | 1 l multi | .25 | .25 |
| **3577** | A1021 | 1.50 l multi | .30 | .25 |
| **3578** | A1021 | 2 l multi | .35 | .25 |
| **3579** | A1021 | 3 l multi | .55 | .25 |
| **3580** | A1021 | 3.50 l multi | .60 | .25 |
| **3581** | A1021 | 4 l multi | .65 | .25 |
| **3582** | A1021 | 5 l multi | .75 | .30 |
| | | *Nos. 3575-3582 (8)* | 3.70 | 2.05 |

Famous Romanians A1022

Portraits: 1 l, Ion Creanga (1837-1889). 2 l, Mihail Eminescu (1850-1889), poet. 3 l, Nicolae Teclu (1839-1916), chemist and inventor.

**1989, Aug. 18 Photo. *Perf. 13½***

| | | | | |
|---|---|---|---|---|
| **3583** | A1022 | 1 l multicolored | .25 | .25 |
| **3584** | A1022 | 2 l multicolored | .45 | .25 |
| **3585** | A1022 | 3 l multicolored | .65 | .35 |
| | | *Nos. 3583-3585 (3)* | 1.35 | .85 |

Stamp Day — A1023

**1989, Oct. 7**

**3586** A1023 2 l + 1 l label .75 .30

No. 3586 has a second label picturing posthorn.

Storming of the Bastille, 1789 A1024

Emblems of PHILEXFRANCE '89 and the Revolution — A1025

Designs: 1.50 l, Gavroche. 2 l, Robespierre. 3 l, *La Marseillaise,* by Rouget de Lisle. 4 l, Diderot. 5 l, 1848 Uprising, Romania.

**1989, Oct. 14**

| | | | | |
|---|---|---|---|---|
| **3587** | A1024 | 50b shown | .25 | .25 |
| **3588** | A1024 | 1.50 l multicolored | .30 | .25 |
| **3589** | A1024 | 2 l multicolored | .40 | .25 |
| **3590** | A1024 | 3 l multicolored | .60 | .25 |
| **3591** | A1024 | 4 l multicolored | .80 | .30 |
| **3592** | A1024 | 5 l multicolored | 1.00 | .40 |
| | | *Nos. 3587-3592 (6)* | 3.35 | 1.70 |

**Souvenir Sheet**

**3593** A1025 10 l shown 2.50 2.50

French revolution, bicent.

14th Romanian Communist Party Congress — A1025a

**1989, Nov. 20 Photo. *Perf. 13½***

**3593A** A1025a 2 l multicolored .60 .25

**Souvenir Sheet**

**3593B** A1025a 10 l multicolored 3.50 3.50

Revolution of Dec. 22, 1989 — A1026

**1990, Jan. 8 Photo. *Perf. 13½***

**3594** A1026 2 l multicolored .45 .25

For surcharge, see No. 3633.

World Cup Soccer Preliminaries, Italy — A1027

Various soccer players in action.

**1990, Mar. 19 Photo. *Perf. 13½***

| | | | | |
|---|---|---|---|---|
| **3595** | A1027 | 50b multicolored | .25 | .25 |
| **3596** | A1027 | 1.50 l multicolored | .30 | .25 |
| **3597** | A1027 | 2 l multicolored | .40 | .25 |
| **3598** | A1027 | 3 l multicolored | .60 | .25 |
| **3599** | A1027 | 4 l multicolored | .80 | .30 |
| **3600** | A1027 | 5 l multicolored | 1.00 | .35 |
| | | *Nos. 3595-3600 (6)* | 3.35 | 1.65 |

An imperf. 10 l airmail souvenir sheet exists. Value, $10

Souvenir Sheet

First Postage Stamp, 150th Anniv. — A1028

**1990, May 2 Litho. *Perf. 13½***

**3601** A1028 10 l multicolored 3.00 3.00

Stamp World London '90. For surcharge, see No. 5681.

World Cup Soccer Championships, Italy — A1029

Various soccer players in action.

**1990, May 7 Photo. *Perf. 13½***

| | | | | |
|---|---|---|---|---|
| **3602** | A1029 | 50b multicolored | .25 | .25 |
| **3603** | A1029 | 1 l multicolored | .25 | .25 |
| **3604** | A1029 | 1.50 l multicolored | .25 | .25 |
| **3605** | A1029 | 2 l multicolored | .30 | .25 |
| **3606** | A1029 | 3 l multicolored | .45 | .25 |
| **3607** | A1029 | 3.50 l multicolored | .50 | .25 |

| | | | | | |
|---|---|---|---|---|---|
| 3608 | A1029 | 4 l | multicolored | .55 | .25 |
| 3609 | A1029 | 5 l | multicolored | .65 | .25 |
| | | | *Nos. 3602-3609 (8)* | 3.20 | 2.00 |

An imperf. 10 l airmail souvenir sheet showing Olympic Stadium, Rome exists. Value, $10.

Intl. Dog Show, Brno, Czechoslovakia — A1030

50b, German shepherd. 1 l, English setter. 1.50 l, Boxer. 2 l, Beagle. 3 l, Doberman pinscher. 3.50 l, Great Dane. 4 l, Afghan hound. 5 l, Yorkshire terrier.

**1990, June 6**

| | | | | | |
|---|---|---|---|---|---|
| 3610 | A1030 | 50b | multicolored | .25 | .25 |
| 3611 | A1030 | 1 l | multicolored | .25 | .25 |
| 3612 | A1030 | 1.50 l | multicolored | .30 | .25 |
| 3613 | A1030 | 2 l | multicolored | .35 | .25 |
| 3614 | A1030 | 3 l | multicolored | .60 | .25 |
| 3615 | A1030 | 3.50 l | multicolored | .75 | .25 |
| 3616 | A1030 | 4 l | multicolored | .80 | .25 |
| 3617 | A1030 | 5 l | multicolored | 1.00 | .25 |
| | | | *Nos. 3610-3617 (8)* | 4.30 | 2.00 |

Riccione '90, Intl. Philatelic Exhibition A1031

**1990, Aug. 24**

| | | | | | |
|---|---|---|---|---|---|
| 3618 | A1031 | 2 l | multicolored | .50 | .25 |

See No. 3856.

Romanian-Chinese Philatelic Exhibition, Bucharest — A1032

**1990, Sept. 8 Photo. *Perf. 13½***

| | | | | | |
|---|---|---|---|---|---|
| 3619 | A1032 | 2 l | multicolored | .40 | .25 |

For surcharge see No. 4186.

Paintings Damaged in 1989 Revolution — A1033

Designs: 50b, Old Nicolas, the Zither Player, by Stefan Luchian. 1.50 l, Woman in Blue by Ion Andreescu. 2 l, The Gardener by Luchian. 3 l, Vase of Flowers by Jan Brueghel, the Elder. 4 l, Springtime by Peter Brueghel, the Elder, horiz. 5 l, Madonna and Child by G. B. Paggi.

**1990. Oct. 25 Photo. *Perf. 13½***

| | | | | | |
|---|---|---|---|---|---|
| 3620 | A1033 | 50b | multicolored | .25 | .25 |
| 3621 | A1033 | 1.50 l | multicolored | .25 | .25 |
| 3622 | A1033 | 2 l | multicolored | .25 | .25 |
| 3623 | A1033 | 3 l | multicolored | .40 | .25 |
| 3624 | A1033 | 4 l | multicolored | .55 | .25 |
| 3625 | A1033 | 5 l | multicolored | .70 | .30 |
| | | | *Nos. 3620-3625 (6)* | 2.40 | 1.55 |

For surcharges see #4365-4369.

Stamp Day — A1033a

**1990, Nov. 10 Photo. *Perf. 13½***

| | | | | | |
|---|---|---|---|---|---|
| 3625A | A1033a | 2 l + 1 l | label | 1.00 | .70 |

Famous Romanians A1034

Designs: 50b, Prince Constantin Cantacuzino (1640-1716). 1.50 l, Ienachita Vacarescu (c. 1740-1797), historian. 2 l, Titu Maiorescu (1840-1917), writer. 3 l, Nicolae Iorga (1871-1940), historian. 4 l, Martha Bibescu (1890-1973). 5 l, Stefan Procopiu (1890-1972), scientist.

**1990, Nov. 27 Photo. *Perf. 13½***

| | | | | | |
|---|---|---|---|---|---|
| 3626 | A1034 | 50b | sepia & dk bl | .25 | .25 |
| 3627 | A1034 | 1.50 l | grn & brt pur | .25 | .25 |
| 3628 | A1034 | 2 l | claret & dk bl | .30 | .25 |
| 3629 | A1034 | 3 l | dk bl & brn | .40 | .25 |
| 3630 | A1034 | 4 l | brn & dk bl | .50 | .25 |
| 3631 | A1034 | 5 l | brt pur & grn | .65 | .25 |
| | | | *Nos. 3626-3631 (6)* | 2.35 | 1.50 |

For surcharges see #4356-4360.

National Day — A1035

**1990, Dec. 1 Photo. *Perf. 13½***

| | | | | | |
|---|---|---|---|---|---|
| 3632 | A1035 | 2 l | multicolored | .40 | .25 |

No. 3594 Surcharged in Brown

**1990, Dec. 22 Photo. *Perf. 13½***

| | | | | | |
|---|---|---|---|---|---|
| 3633 | A1026 | 4 l on 2 l | | .65 | .25 |

Vincent Van Gogh, Death Cent. — A1036

Paintings: 50b, Field of Irises. 2 l, Artist's Room. 3 l, Night on the Coffee Terrace, vert. 3.50 l, Blossoming Fruit Trees. 5 l, Vase with Fourteen Sunflowers, vert.

**1991, Mar. 29 Photo. *Perf. 13½***

| | | | | | |
|---|---|---|---|---|---|
| 3634 | A1036 | 50b | multicolored | .25 | .25 |
| 3635 | A1036 | 2 l | multicolored | .25 | .25 |
| 3636 | A1036 | 3 l | multicolored | .35 | .25 |
| 3637 | A1036 | 3.50 l | multicolored | .40 | .25 |
| 3638 | A1036 | 5 l | multicolored | .60 | .25 |
| | | | *Nos. 3634-3638 (5)* | 1.85 | 1.25 |

For surcharges see #4371-4372.

A1037

Birds: 50b, Larus marinus. 1 l, Sterna hirundo. 1.50 l, Recurvirostra avosetta. 2 l, Stercorarius pomarinus. 3 l, Vanellus vanellus. 3.50 l, Mergus serrator. 4 l, Egretta garzetta. 5 l, Calidris alpina. 6 l, Limosa limosa. 7 l, Childonias hybrida.

**1991, Apr. 3 Photo. *Perf. 13½***

| | | | | | |
|---|---|---|---|---|---|
| 3639 | A1037 | 50b | ultra | .25 | .25 |
| 3640 | A1037 | 1 l | blue green | .25 | .25 |
| 3641 | A1037 | 1.50 l | bister | .25 | .25 |
| 3642 | A1037 | 2 l | dark blue | .25 | .25 |
| 3643 | A1037 | 3 l | light green | .25 | .25 |
| 3644 | A1037 | 3.50 l | dark green | .30 | .25 |
| 3645 | A1037 | 4 l | purple | .30 | .25 |
| 3646 | A1037 | 5 l | brown | .35 | .25 |
| 3647 | A1037 | 6 l | yel brown | .70 | .25 |
| 3648 | A1037 | 7 l | light blue | .65 | .25 |
| | | | *Nos. 3639-3648 (10)* | 3.55 | 2.50 |

A1038

**1991, Apr. 5 Photo. *Perf. 13½***

| | | | | | |
|---|---|---|---|---|---|
| 3649 | A1038 | 4 l | multicolored | .35 | .25 |

Easter.

Europa — A1039

**1991, May 10 Photo. *Perf. 13½***

| | | | | | |
|---|---|---|---|---|---|
| 3650 | A1039 | 4.50 l | Eutelsat I | 2.00 | .80 |

For surcharge see No. 4185.

Posthorn — A1040

**1991, May 24 Photo. *Perf. 13½***

| | | | | | |
|---|---|---|---|---|---|
| 3651 | A1040 | 4.50 l | blue | .40 | .25 |

Gymnastics A1041

**1991, June 14**

| | | | | | |
|---|---|---|---|---|---|
| 3652 | A1041 | 1 l | Rings | .25 | .25 |
| 3653 | A1041 | 1 l | Parallel bars | .25 | .25 |
| 3654 | A1041 | 4.50 l | Vault | .25 | .25 |
| 3655 | A1041 | 4.50 l | Uneven parallel bars | .25 | .25 |
| 3656 | A1041 | 8 l | Floor exercise | .45 | .25 |
| 3657 | A1041 | 9 l | Balance beam | .60 | .25 |
| | | | *Nos. 3652-3657 (6)* | 2.05 | 1.50 |

For surcharge on 5 l see No. 3735. For other surcharges see Nos. 3944, 3946, 4237-4238.

Monasteries — A1042

**1991, July 4 Photo. *Perf. 13½***

| | | | | | |
|---|---|---|---|---|---|
| 3658 | A1042 | 1 l | Curtea de Arges, vert. | .25 | .25 |
| 3659 | A1042 | 1 l | Putna, vert. | .25 | .25 |
| 3660 | A1042 | 4.50 l | Varatec, vert. | .25 | .25 |
| 3661 | A1042 | 4.50 l | Agapia | .25 | .25 |
| 3662 | A1042 | 8 l | Golia | .45 | .25 |
| 3663 | A1042 | 9 l | Sucevita | .60 | .25 |
| | | | *Nos. 3658-3663 (6)* | 2.05 | 1.50 |

For surcharges see #4354-4355.

Hotels, Lodges, and Resorts
A1043 A1044

Designs: 1 l, Hotel Continental, Timisoara, vert. 2 l, Valea Caprei Lodge, Fagaras. 4 l, Hotel Intercontinental, Bucharest, vert. 5 l, Lebada Hotel, Crisan. 6 l, Muntele Rosu Lodge, Ciucas. 8 l, Transylvania Hotel, Cluj-Napoca. 9 l, Hotel Orizont, Predeal. 10 l, Hotel Roman, Herculane, vert. 18 l, Rarau Lodge, Rarau, vert. 20 l, Alpine Hotel, Poiana Brasov. 25 l, Constanta Casino. 30 l, Miorija Lodge, Bucegi. 45 l, Sura Dacilor Lodge, Poiana Brasov. 60 l, Valea Draganului, Tourist Complex,. 80 l, Hotel Florica, Venus Health Resort. 120 l, International Hotel, Baile Felix, vert. 160 l, Hotel Egreta, Tulcea, vert. 250 l, Motel Valea de Pesti, Valea Jiului. 400 l, Tourist Complex, Baisoara. 500 l, Hotel Bradul, Covasna. 800 l, Hotel Gorj, Tirgu Jiu.

**1991 Photo. *Perf. 13½***

| | | | | | |
|---|---|---|---|---|---|
| 3664 | A1043 | 1 l | blue | .25 | .25 |
| 3665 | A1043 | 2 l | dark green | .25 | .25 |
| 3666 | A1043 | 4 l | carmine | .25 | .25 |
| 3667 | A1043 | 5 l | violet | .25 | .25 |
| 3668 | A1043 | 6 l | olive brown | .25 | .25 |
| 3669 | A1043 | 8 l | brown | .25 | .25 |
| 3670 | A1043 | 9 l | red brown | .60 | .25 |
| 3671 | A1043 | 10 l | olive green | .65 | .25 |
| 3672 | A1043 | 18 l | bright red | .40 | .25 |
| 3673 | A1043 | 20 l | brown org | .30 | .25 |
| 3674 | A1043 | 25 l | bright blue | .65 | .25 |
| 3675 | A1043 | 30 l | magenta | .85 | .25 |
| 3676 | A1043 | 45 l | dark blue | .75 | .30 |
| 3677 | A1044 | 60 l | brown olive | 1.00 | .40 |
| 3678 | A1044 | 80 l | purple | 1.25 | .55 |

**Size: 27x41mm, 41x27mm**

**3679** A1044 120 l gray bl & dk bl vio 1.50 .25
**3680** A1044 160 l lt ver & dk ver 2.00 .25
**3681** A1044 250 l lt bl & dk bl 2.50 .25
**3682** A1044 400 l tan & dk brn 3.25 .30
**3683** A1044 500 l lt bl grn & dk bl grn 3.75 .35
**3684** A1044 800 l pink & dk lil rose 4.50 .40
*Nos. 3664-3684 (21)* 25.45 6.05

Issued: 1 l, 5 l, 9 l, 10 l, 8/27; 2 l, 4 l, 18 l, 25 l, 30 l, 10/8; 6 l, 8 l, 20 l, 45 l, 60 l, 80 l, 11/14; 120 l, 160 l, 250 l, 400 l, 500 l, 800 l, 12/5.

For surcharges see Nos. 4167-4174, 4204-4219, 4384.

Riccone '91, Intl. Philatelic Exhibition — A1045

**1991, Aug. 27**
**3685** A1045 4 l multicolored .40 .25

A1046

Vases: a, Decorated with birds. b, Decorated with flowers.

**1991, Sept. 12**
**3686** A1046 5 l Pair, #a.-b. .80 .35

Romanian-Chinese Philatelic Exhibition.

A1047

**1991, Sept. 17**
**3687** A1047 1 l blue .35 .25

Romanian Academy, 125th anniv.
For surcharges, see Nos. 4266-4267.

A1048

Balkanfila '91 Philatelic Exhibition: 4 l, Flowers, by Nicu Enea. 5 l, Peasant Girl of Vlasca, by Georghe Tattarescu. 20 l, Sports Center, Bacau.

**1991, Sept. 20**
**3688** A1048 4 l multicolored .35 .25
**3689** A1048 5 l multicolored .35 .25

**Souvenir Sheet**

**3690** A1048 20 l multicolored 1.50 1.50

No. 3689 printed se-tenant with 2 l Romanian Philatelic Assoc. label. No. 3690 contains one 54x42mm stamp.

For surcharge see No. 4463.

Miniature Sheets

A1049

Birds: No. 3691a, Cissa erythrorhyncha. b, Malaconotus blanchoti. c, Sialia sialis. d, Sturnella neglecta. e, Harpactes fasciatus. f, Upupa epops. g, Malurus cyaneus. h, Brachypteracias squamigera. i, Leptopterus madagascariensis. j, Phoeniculus bollei. k, Melanerpes erythrocephalus. l, Pericrocotus flammeus.

No. 3692a, Melithreptus laetior. b, Rhynochetos jubatus. c, Turdus migratorius. d, Copsychus saularis. e, Monticola saxatilis. f, Xanthocephalus xanthocephalus. g, Scotopelia peli. h, Ptilogonys caudatus. i, Todus mexicanus. j, Copsychus malabaricus. k, Myzomela erythrocephala. l, Gymnostinops montezuma.

**1991, Oct. 7** **Sheets of 12**
**3691** A1049 2 l #a.-l. 2.50 2.50
**3692** A1049 2 l #a.-l. 2.50 2.50

Natl. Census — A1050

**1991, Oct. 15**
**3693** A1050 5 l multicolored .35 .25

Phila Nippon '91 — A1051

**1991, Nov. 13** **Photo.** ***Perf. 13½***
**3694** A1051 10 l Sailing ship .65 .25
**3695** A1051 10 l Bridge building .65 .25

Miniature Sheets

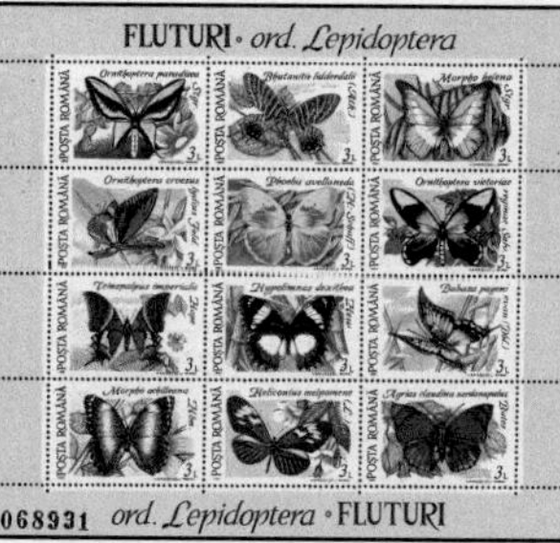


Butterflies and Moths — A1052

Designs: No. 3696a, Ornithoptera paradisea. b, Bhutanitis lidderdalii. c, Morpho helena. d, Ornithoptera croesus. e, Phoebis avellaneda. f, Ornithoptera victoriae. g, Teinopalpus imperialis. h, Hypolimnas dexithea. i, Dabasa payeni. j, Morpho achilleana. k, Heliconius melpomene. l, Agrias claudina sardanapalus.

No. 3697a, Graellsia isabellae. b, Antocharis cardamines. c, Ammobiota festiva. d, Polygonia c-album. e, Catocala promisa. f, Rhyparia purpurata. g, Arctia villica. h, Polyommatus daphnis. i, Zerynthia polyxena. j, Daphnis nerii. k, Licaena dispar rutila. l, Pararge roxelana.

**1991, Nov. 30** **Photo.** ***Perf. 13½***
**Sheets of 12**
**3696** A1052 3 l #a.-l. 3.00 3.00
**3697** A1052 3 l #a.-l. 3.00 3.00

A1053

**1991, Nov. 21** **Photo.** ***Perf. 13½***
**3698** A1053 1 l Running .25 .25
**3699** A1053 4 l Long jump .25 .25
**3700** A1053 5 l High jump .25 .25
**3701** A1053 5 l Runner in blocks .25 .25
**3702** A1053 9 l Hurdles .45 .25
**3703** A1053 10 l Javelin .50 .25
*Nos. 3698-3703 (6)* 1.95 1.50

World Track and Field Championships, Tokyo.

A1054

Famous People: 1 l, Mihail Kogalniceanu (1817-1891), politician. 4 l, Nicolae Titulescu (1882-1941), politician. No. 3706, Andrei Mureseanu (1816-1863), author. No. 3707, Aron Pumnul (1818-1866), author. 9 l, George Bacovia (1881-1957), author. 10 l, Perpessicius (1891-1971), writer.

**1991, Dec. 10** **Photo.** ***Perf. 13½***
**3704** A1054 1 l multi .25 .25
**3705** A1054 4 l multi .25 .25
**3706** A1054 5 l multi .25 .25
**3707** A1054 5 l multi .25 .25
**3708** A1054 9 l multi .60 .25
**3709** A1054 10 l multi .70 .25
*Nos. 3704-3709 (6)* 2.30 1.50

See Nos. 3759-3761, 3776-3781.
For surcharges see Nos. 4238A-4248.

Stamp Day — A1055

**1991, Dec. 20**
**3710** A1055 8 l + 2 l label .50 .25

Central University Library, Bucharest, Cent. A1056

**1991, Dec. 23**
**3711** A1056 8 l red brown .50 .25

Christmas A1057

**1991, Dec. 25** **Photo.** ***Perf. 13½***
**3712** A1057 8 l multicolored .50 .25

See No. 3874.

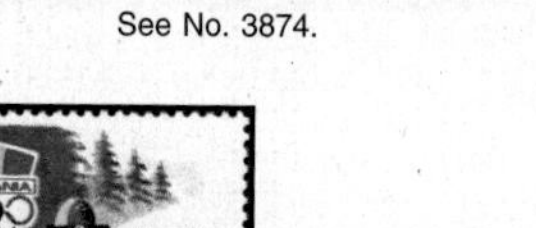

1992 Winter Olympics, Albertville A1058

**1992, Feb. 1** **Photo.** ***Perf. 13½***
**3713** A1058 4 l Biathlon .25 .25
**3714** A1058 5 l Alpine skiing .25 .25
**3715** A1058 8 l Cross-country skiing .25 .25
**3716** A1058 10 l Two-man luge .25 .25
**3717** A1058 20 l Speed skating .35 .25
**3718** A1058 25 l Ski jumping .40 .25
**3719** A1058 30 l Ice hockey .50 .25
**3720** A1058 45 l Men's figure skating .65 .25
*Nos. 3713-3720 (8)* 2.90 2.00

**Souvenir Sheets**

**3721** A1058 75 l Women's figure skating 2.50 2.50

***Imperf***

**3722** A1058 125 l 4-Man bobsled 7.00 7.00

No. 3721 is airmail and contains one 42x54mm stamp.
For surcharge see No. 4464.

Porcelain — A1059

Designs: 4 l, Sugar and cream service. 5 l, Tea service. 8 l, Goblet and pitcher, vert. 30 l, Tea service, diff. 45 l, Vase, vert.

**1992, Feb. 20** **Photo.** ***Perf. 13½***
**3723** A1059 4 l multicolored .25 .25
**3724** A1059 5 l multicolored .25 .25
**3725** A1059 8 l multicolored .25 .25
**3726** A1059 30 l multicolored .45 .25
**3727** A1059 45 l multicolored .65 .35
*Nos. 3723-3727 (5)* 1.85 1.35

Fish A1060

Designs: 4 l, Scomber scombrus. 5 l, Tinca tinca. 8 l, Salvelinus fontinalis. 10 l, Romanichthys valsanicola. 30 l, Chondrostoma nasus. 45 l, Mullus barbatus ponticus.

**1992, Feb. 28** **Photo.** ***Perf. 13½***
**3728** A1060 4 l multicolored .25 .25
**3729** A1060 5 l multicolored .25 .25
**3730** A1060 8 l multicolored .25 .25
**3731** A1060 10 l multicolored .25 .25
**3732** A1060 30 l multicolored .35 .25
**3733** A1060 45 l multicolored .60 .25
*Nos. 3728-3733 (6)* 1.95 1.50

A1060a

**1992, Mar. 11 Photo. *Perf. 13½***
**3734** A1060a 90 l on 5 l multi 1.50 .35

No. 3734 not issued without surcharge.

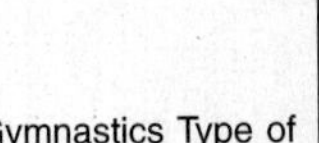
Gymnastics Type of 1991 Surcharged

**1992, Mar. 11 Photo. *Perf. 13½***
**3735** A1041 90 l on 5 l like #3657 1.50 .35

No. 3735 not issued without surcharge.

Horses A1061

Various stylized drawings of horses walking, running, or jumping.

**1992, Mar. 17 Photo. *Perf. 13½***
**3736** A1061 6 l multi, vert. .25 .25
**3737** A1061 7 l multi .25 .25
**3738** A1061 10 l multi, vert. .25 .25
**3739** A1061 25 l multi, vert. .35 .25
**3740** A1061 30 l multi .45 .25
**3741** A1061 50 l multi, vert. .65 .25
*Nos. 3736-3741 (6)* 2.20 1.50

Miniature Sheet

Discovery of America, 500th Anniv. — A1062

Columbus and ships: a, Green background. b, Violet background. c, Blue background. d, Ship approaching island.

**1992, Apr. 22 Photo. *Perf. 13½***
**3742** A1062 35 l Sheet of 4, #a.-d. *17.50 17.50*

Europa.

Granada '92, Philatelic Exhibition — A1063

a, 25 l, Spain No. 1 and Romania No. 1. b, 10 l, Expo emblem. c, 30 l, Building and courtyard, Granada

**1992, Apr. 24 Photo. *Perf. 13½***
**3743** A1063 Sheet of 3, #a.-c. 1.60 1.60

Icon of Christ's Descent into Hell, 1680 — A1064

**1992, Apr. 24 Photo. *Perf. 13½***
**3744** A1064 10 l multicolored .35 .25

Easter.

Fire Station, Bucharest, Cent. — A1065

**1992, May 2**
**3745** A1065 10 l multicolored .50 .25

Chess Olympiad, Manila — A1066

No. 3747, Building, chess board. 75 l, Shore, chess board.

**1992, June 7 *Perf. 13½***
**3746** A1066 10 l shown .30 .25
**3747** A1066 10 l multicolored .30 .25

**Souvenir Sheet**

**3748** A1066 75 l multicolored 1.75 1.75

No. 3748 contains one 42x54mm stamp.

1992 Summer Olympics, Barcelona — A1067

**1992, July 17 Photo. *Perf. 13½***
**3749** A1067 6 l Shooting, vert. .25 .25
**3750** A1067 7 l Weight lifting, vert. .25 .25
**3751** A1067 9 l Two-man canoing .25 .25
**3752** A1067 10 l Handball, vert. .25 .25
**3753** A1067 25 l Wrestling .25 .25
**3754** A1067 30 l Fencing .35 .25
**3755** A1067 50 l Running, vert. .40 .25
**3756** A1067 55 l Boxing .50 .25
*Nos. 3749-3756 (8)* 2.50 2.00

**Souvenir Sheets**

**3757** A1067 100 l Rowing 1.00 1.00

***Imperf***

**3758** A1067 200 l Gymnastics 5.00 5.00

Nos. 3757-3758 are airmail. No. 3757 contains one 54x42mm stamp, No. 3758 one 40x53mm stamp.

**Famous People Type of 1991**

Designs: 10 l, Ion I. C. Bratianu (1864-1927), prime minister. 25 l, Ion Gh. Duca (1879-1933). 30 l, Grigore Gafencu (1892-1957), journalist and politician.

**1992, July 27 Photo. *Perf. 13½***
**3759** A1054 10 l green & violet .25 .25
**3760** A1054 25 l blue & lake .25 .25
**3761** A1054 30 l lake & blue .25 .25
*Nos. 3759-3761 (3)* .75 .75

Expo '92, Seville A1068

Designs: 6 l, The Thinker, Cernavoda. 7 l, Trajan's bridge, Drobeta. 10 l, Mill. 25 l, Railroad bridge, Cernavoda. 30 l, Trajan Vuia's flying machine. 55 l, Herman Oberth's rocket. 100 l, Prayer sculpture, by C. Brancusi.

**1992, Sept. 1**
**3762** A1068 6 l multicolored .25 .25
**3763** A1068 7 l multicolored .25 .25
**3764** A1068 10 l multicolored .25 .25
**3765** A1068 25 l multicolored .25 .25
**3766** A1068 30 l multicolored .25 .25
**3767** A1068 55 l multicolored .50 .25
*Nos. 3762-3767 (6)* 1.75 1.50

**Souvenir Sheet**

**3768** A1068 100 l multicolored .75 .75

No. 3768 contains one 42x54mm stamp.

World Post Day — A1069

**1992, Oct. 9**
**3769** A1069 10 l multicolored .35 .25

For surcharge see No. 3945.

Discovery of America, 500th Anniv. — A1070

Columbus and: 6 l, Santa Maria. 10 l, Nina. 25 l, Pinta. 55 l, Arrival in New World. 100 l, Sailing ship, vert.

**1992, Oct. 30 Photo. *Perf. 13½***
**3770** A1070 6 l multicolored .25 .25
**3771** A1070 10 l multicolored .25 .25
**3772** A1070 25 l multicolored .30 .25
**3773** A1070 55 l multicolored .50 .25
*Nos. 3770-3773 (4)* 1.30 1.00

**Souvenir Sheet**

**3774** A1070 100 l multicolored 1.00 1.00

No. 3774 contains one 42x54mm stamp.

Romanian Postal Reorganization, 1st Anniv. — A1071

**1992, Nov. 5 Photo. *Perf. 13½***
**3775** A1071 10 l multicolored .35 .25

For surcharge see No. 4113.

**Famous People Type of 1991**

Designs: 6 l, Iacob Negruzzi (1842-1932), author. 7 l, Grigore Antipa (1867-1944), naturalist. 9 l, Alexe Mateevici (1888-1917), poet. 10 l, Cezar Petrescu (1892-1961), author. 25 l, Octav Onicescu (1892-1983), mathematician. 30 l, Ecaterina Teodoroiu (1894-1917), World War I soldier.

**1992, Nov. 9 Photo. *Perf. 13½***
**3776** A1054 6 l green & violet .25 .25
**3777** A1054 7 l lilac & green .25 .25
**3778** A1054 9 l gray blue & pur .25 .25
**3779** A1054 10 l brown & blue .25 .25
**3780** A1054 25 l blue & brown .25 .25
**3781** A1054 30 l slate & blue .30 .25
*Nos. 3776-3781 (6)* 1.55 1.50

Wild Animals — A1072

Designs: 6 l, Haliaeetus leucocephalus, vert. 7 l, Strix occidentalis, vert. 9 l, Ursus arctos, vert. 10 l, Haematopus bachmani. 25 l, Canis lupus. 30 l, Odocoileus virginianus. 55 l, Alces alces.

**1992, Nov. 16 Litho. *Perf. 13½***
**3782** A1072 6 l multicolored .25 .25
**3783** A1072 7 l multicolored .25 .25
**3784** A1072 9 l multicolored .25 .25
**3785** A1072 10 l multicolored .25 .25
**3786** A1072 25 l multicolored .25 .25
**3787** A1072 30 l multicolored .30 .25
**3788** A1072 55 l multicolored .60 .25
*Nos. 3782-3788 (7)* 2.15 1.75

**Souvenir Sheet**

**3789** A1072 100 l Orcinus orca .90 .90

Romanian Anniversaries and Events — A1073

7 l, Building, Galea Victoria St., 300th anniv. 9 l, Statue, School of Commerce, 600th anniv. 10 l, Curtea de Arges Monastery, 475th anniv. 25 l, School of Architecture, Bucharest, 80th anniv.

**1992, Dec. 3 Photo. *Perf. 13½***
**3790** A1073 7 l multicolored .25 .25
**3791** A1073 9 l multicolored .25 .25
**3792** A1073 10 l multicolored .25 .25
**3793** A1073 25 l multicolored .25 .25
*Nos. 3790-3793 (4)* 1.00 1.00

For surcharges see No. 4465-4466.

Natl. Arms — A1074

**1992, Dec. 7**
**3794** A1074 15 l multicolored .25 .25

Christmas A1075

**1992, Dec. 15**
**3795** A1075 15 l multicolored .35 .25

For surcharge see No. 4249.

New Telephone Numbering System A1076

**1992, Dec. 28** **Photo.** ***Perf. 13½***
**3796** A1076 15 l blue, blk & red .35 .25

For surcharges see #4268-4272.

Souvenir Sheets

1992 Summer Olympics, Barcelona A1077

No. 3797: a, Shooting. b, Wrestling. c, Weight lifting. d, Boxing.
No. 3798: a, Women's gymnastics. b, Fourman sculls. c, Fencing. d, High jump.

**1992, Dec. 30** **Photo.** ***Perf. 13½***
**3797** A1077 35 l Sheet of 4, #a.-d. *1.00 1.00*
**3798** A1077 35 l Sheet of 4, #a.-d. *1.00 1.00*

Historic Sites, Bucharest — A1078

Designs: 10 l, Mihai Voda Monastery. 15 l, Vacaresti Monastery. 25 l, Multi-purpose hall. 30 l, Mina Minovici Medical Institute.

**1993, Feb. 11** **Photo.** ***Perf. 13½***
**3799** A1078 10 l multicolored .25 .25
**3800** A1078 15 l multicolored .25 .25
**3801** A1078 25 l multicolored .25 .25
**3802** A1078 30 l multicolored .25 .25
*Nos. 3799-3802 (4)* 1.00 1.00

Easter — A1079

**1993, Mar. 25**
**3803** A1079 15 l multicolored .25 .25

Medicinal Plants — A1080

10 l, Crataegus monogyna. 15 l, Gentiana phlogifolia. 25 l, Hippophae rhamnoides. 30 l, Vaccinium myrtillus. 50 l, Arnica montana. 90 l, Rosa canina.

**1993, Mar. 30**
**3804** A1080 10 l multi .25 .25
**3805** A1080 15 l multi .25 .25
**3806** A1080 25 l multi .25 .25
**3807** A1080 30 l multi .25 .25
**3808** A1080 50 l multi .35 .25
**3809** A1080 90 l multi .65 .25
*Nos. 3804-3809 (6)* 2.00 1.50

Nichita Stanescu (1933-1983), Poet — A1081

**1993, Mar. 31**
**3810** A1081 15 l brown and blue .25 .25

Souvenir Sheet

Polska '93 — A1082

**1993, Apr. 28** **Photo.** ***Perf. 13½***
**3811** A1082 200 l multicolored 1.10 1.10

Birds A1083

5 l, Pica pica. 10 l, Aquila chrysaetos. 15 l, Pyrrhula pyrrhula. 20 l, Upupa epops. 25 l, Dendrocopos major. 50 l, Oriolus oriolus. 65 l, Loxia leucoptera. 90 l, Hirundo rustica. 160 l, Parus cyanus. 250 l, Sturnus roseus.

**1993, Apr. 30**
**3812** A1083 5 l multi .25 .25
**3813** A1083 10 l multi .25 .25
**3814** A1083 15 l multi .25 .25
**3815** A1083 20 l multi .25 .25
**3816** A1083 25 l multi .25 .25
**3817** A1083 50 l multi .25 .25
**3818** A1083 65 l multi .25 .25
**3819** A1083 90 l multi .30 .25
**3820** A1083 160 l multi .50 .25
**3821** A1083 250 l multi .65 .25
*Nos. 3812-3821 (10)* 3.20 2.50

Nos. 3812-3813 are horiz.

Cats — A1084

Various cats.

**1993, May 24** **Photo.** ***Perf. 13½***
**3822** A1084 10 l multicolored .25 .25
**3823** A1084 15 l multicolored .25 .25
**3824** A1084 30 l multicolored .25 .25
**3825** A1084 90 l multicolored .35 .25
**3826** A1084 135 l multicolored .45 .25
**3827** A1084 160 l multicolored .60 .25
*Nos. 3822-3827 (6)* 2.15 1.50

Souvenir Sheet

Europa — A1085

Paintings and sculpture by: a, Pablo Picasso. b, Constantin Brancusi. c, Ion Irimescu. d, Alexandru Ciucurencu.

**1993, May 31** **Photo.** ***Perf. 13½***
**3828** A1085 280 l Sheet of 4, #a.-d. *4.00 4.00*

A1086

**1993, June 30** **Photo.** ***Perf. 13½***
**3829** A1086 10 l Vipera berus .25 .25
**3830** A1086 15 l Lynx lynx .25 .25
**3831** A1086 25 l Tadorna tadorna .25 .25
**3832** A1086 75 l Hucho hucho .40 .25
**3833** A1086 105 l Limenitis populi .50 .25
**3834** A1086 280 l Rosalia alpina .75 .25
*Nos. 3829-3834 (6)* 2.40 1.50

Nos. 3829, 3831-3834 are horiz.

A1087

10 l, Martes martes. 15 l, Oryctolagus cuniculus. 20 l, Sciurus vulgaris. 25 l, Rupicapra rupicapra. 30 l, Vulpes vulpes. 40 l, Ovis ammon. 75 l, Genetta genetta. 105 l, Eliomys quercinus. 150 l, Mustela erminea. 280 l, Herpestes ichneumon.

**1993, June 30**
**3835** A1087 10 l multi .25 .25
**3836** A1087 15 l multi .25 .25
**3837** A1087 20 l multi .25 .25
**3838** A1087 25 l multi .25 .25
**3839** A1087 30 l multi .25 .25
**3840** A1087 40 l multi .25 .25
**3841** A1087 75 l multi .25 .25
**3842** A1087 105 l multi .40 .25
**3843** A1087 150 l multi .45 .25
**3844** A1087 280 l multi 1.00 .25
*Nos. 3835-3844 (10)* 3.60 2.50

Nos. 3836, 3839, 3843-3844 are horiz.
For surcharges see Nos. 4427-4428.

Dinosaurs — A1088

**1993, July 30** **Photo.** ***Perf. 13½***
**3845** A1088 29 l Brontosaurus .25 .25
**3846** A1088 46 l Plesiosaurus .25 .25
**3847** A1088 85 l Triceratops .30 .25
**3848** A1088 171 l Stegosaurus .65 .25
**3849** A1088 216 l Tyrannosaurus .75 .25
**3850** A1088 319 l Archaeopteryx 1.00 .25
*Nos. 3845-3850 (6)* 3.20 1.50

Souvenir Sheet

Telafila '93, Israel-Romanian Philatelic Exhibition — A1089

Woman with Eggs, by Marcel Iancu.

**1993, Aug. 21**
**3851** A1089 535 l multicolored 1.75 1.75

Icons — A1090

Designs: 75 l, St. Stephen. 171 l, Martyrs from Brancoveanu and Vacarescu families. 216 l, St. Anthony.

**1993, Aug. 31**
**3852** A1090 75 l multicolored .25 .25
**3853** A1090 171 l multicolored .30 .25
**3854** A1090 216 l multicolored .70 .35
*Nos. 3852-3854 (3)* 1.25 .85

Rural Mounted Police, Cent. — A1091

**1993, Sept. 1**

| | | | | |
|---|---|---|---|---|
| **3855** | A1091 | 29 l multicolored | .25 | .25 |

**No. 3618 Surcharged in Red**

**1993, Sept. 3**

| | | | | |
|---|---|---|---|---|
| **3856** | A1031 | 171 l on 2 l multi | .60 | .25 |

Souvenir Sheet

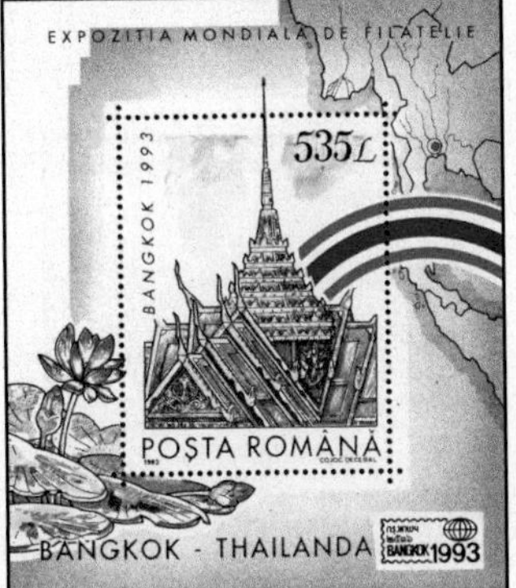


Bangkok '93 — A1092

**1993, Sept. 20**

| | | | | |
|---|---|---|---|---|
| **3857** | A1092 | 535 l multicolored | 1.75 | 1.75 |

Famous Men — A1093

Designs: 29 l, George Baritiu (1812-93), politician. 46 l, Horia Creanga (1892-1943), architect. 85 l, Armand Calinescu (1893-1939), politician. 171 l, Dumitru Bagdasar (1893-1946), physician. 216 l, Constantin Brailoiu (1893-1958), musician. 319 l, Iuliu Maniu (1873-1953), politician.

**1993, Oct. 8**

| | | | | |
|---|---|---|---|---|
| **3858** | A1093 | 29 l multicolored | .25 | .25 |
| **3859** | A1093 | 46 l multicolored | .25 | .25 |
| **3860** | A1093 | 85 l multicolored | .25 | .25 |
| **3861** | A1093 | 171 l multicolored | .30 | .25 |
| **3862** | A1093 | 216 l multicolored | .35 | .25 |
| **3863** | A1093 | 319 l multicolored | .60 | .25 |
| | | *Nos. 3858-3863 (6)* | 2.00 | 1.50 |

For surcharge see No. 4407.

Souvenir Sheet

Romanian Entry into Council of Europe — A1094

**1993, Nov. 26** **Photo.** ***Perf. 13½***

| | | | | |
|---|---|---|---|---|
| **3864** | A1094 | 1590 l multi | 3.50 | 3.50 |

Expansion of Natl. Borders, 75th Anniv. — A1095

Government leaders: 115 l, Iancu Flondor (1865-1924). 245 l, Ion I. C. Bratianu (1864-1927). 255 l, Iuliu Maniu (1873-1953). 325 l, Pantelimon Halippa (1883-1979). 1060 l, King Ferdinand I (1865-1927).

**1993-94**

| | | | | |
|---|---|---|---|---|
| **3865** | A1095 | 115 l multi | .25 | .25 |
| **3866** | A1095 | 245 l multi | .50 | .25 |
| **3867** | A1095 | 255 l multi | .50 | .25 |
| **3868** | A1095 | 325 l multi | .75 | .35 |
| | | *Nos. 3865-3868 (4)* | 2.00 | 1.10 |

**Souvenir Sheet**

| | | | | |
|---|---|---|---|---|
| **3869** | A1095 | 1060 l Romania in one color | 2.50 | 2.50 |
| *a.* | | Romania in four colors | *8.00* | *8.00* |

No. 3869a was redrawn because of an error in the map.

Issued: No. 3869, Feb. 1994; Nos. 3865-3868, 3869a, Dec. 1, 1993.

For surcharge see No. 4472.

Anniversaries and Events A1096

Designs: 115 l, Emblem of the Diplomatic Alliance. 245 l, Statue of Johannes Honterus, founder of first Humanitarian School. 255 l, Arms, seal of Slatina, Olt River Bridge. 325 l, Map, arms of Braila.

**1993, Dec. 15**

| | | | | |
|---|---|---|---|---|
| **3870** | A1096 | 115 l multicolored | .25 | .25 |
| **3871** | A1096 | 245 l multicolored | .55 | .25 |
| **3872** | A1096 | 255 l multicolored | .55 | .25 |
| **3873** | A1096 | 325 l multicolored | .55 | .30 |
| | | *Nos. 3870-3873 (4)* | 1.90 | 1.05 |

Diplomatic Alliance, 75th anniv. (#3870). Birth of Johannes Honterus, 450th anniv. (#3871). City of Slatina, 625th anniv. (#3872). County of Braila, 625th anniv. (#3873).

For surcharge see No. 4473.

**Christmas Type of 1991**

**1993, Dec. 20**

| | | | | |
|---|---|---|---|---|
| **3874** | A1057 | 45 l like #3712 | .25 | .25 |

Insects, Wildlife from Movile Cavern — A1097

Designs: 29 l, Clivina subterranea. 46 l, Nepa anophthalma. 85 l, Haemopis caeca. 171 l, Lascona cristiani. 216 l, Semisalsa dobrogica. 319 l, Armadillidium tabacarui. 535 l, Exploring cavern, vert.

**1993, Dec. 27**

| | | | | |
|---|---|---|---|---|
| **3875** | A1097 | 29 l multicolored | .25 | .25 |
| **3876** | A1097 | 46 l multicolored | .25 | .25 |
| **3877** | A1097 | 85 l multicolored | .25 | .25 |
| **3878** | A1097 | 171 l multicolored | .40 | .25 |
| **3879** | A1097 | 216 l multicolored | .55 | .25 |
| **3880** | A1097 | 319 l multicolored | .80 | .25 |
| | | *Nos. 3875-3880 (6)* | 2.50 | 1.50 |

**Souvenir Sheet**

| | | | | |
|---|---|---|---|---|
| **3881** | A1097 | 535 l multicolored | 1.50 | 1.50 |

Alexandru Ioan Cuza — A1098

**1994, Jan. 24** **Photo.** ***Perf. 13***

| | | | | |
|---|---|---|---|---|
| **3882** | A1098 | 45 l multicolored | .25 | .25 |

Historic Buildings, Bucharest — A1099

115 l, Opera House. 245 l, Vacaresti Monastery. 255 l, Church of St. Vineri. 325 l, Dominican House, Vacaresti Monastery.

**1994, Feb. 7**

| | | | | |
|---|---|---|---|---|
| **3883** | A1099 | 115 l multicolored | .25 | .25 |
| **3884** | A1099 | 245 l multicolored | .45 | .25 |
| **3885** | A1099 | 255 l multicolored | .60 | .25 |
| **3886** | A1099 | 325 l multicolored | .60 | .25 |
| | | *Nos. 3883-3886 (4)* | 1.90 | 1.00 |

For surcharge see No. 4482.

1994 Winter Olympics, Lillehammer A1100

**1994, Feb. 12** ***Perf. 13½***

| | | | | |
|---|---|---|---|---|
| **3887** | A1100 | 70 l Speed skating | .25 | .25 |
| **3888** | A1100 | 115 l Slalom skiing | .25 | .25 |
| **3889** | A1100 | 125 l Bobsled | .30 | .25 |
| **3890** | A1100 | 245 l Biathlon | .40 | .25 |
| **3891** | A1100 | 255 l Ski jumping | .40 | .25 |
| **3892** | A1100 | 325 l Figure skating | .60 | .25 |
| | | *Nos. 3887-3892 (6)* | 2.20 | 1.50 |

**Souvenir Sheet**

| | | | | |
|---|---|---|---|---|
| **3893** | A1100 | 1590 l Luge | 3.00 | 3.00 |

No. 3893 contains one 43x54mm stamp.

Mills — A1101

**1994, Mar. 31** ***Perf. 13***

| | | | | |
|---|---|---|---|---|
| **3894** | A1101 | 70 l Sarichioi | .25 | .25 |
| **3895** | A1101 | 115 l Valea Nucarilor | .25 | .25 |
| **3896** | A1101 | 125 l Caraorman | .30 | .25 |
| **3897** | A1101 | 245 l Romanii de Jos | .40 | .25 |
| **3898** | A1101 | 255 l Enisala, horiz. | .45 | .25 |
| **3899** | A1101 | 325 l Nistoresti | .60 | .30 |
| | | *Nos. 3894-3899 (6)* | 2.25 | 1.55 |

For surcharges see Nos. 4431-4434.

Dinosaurs — A1102

90 l, Struthiosaurs. 130 l, Megalosaurs. 150 l, Parasaurolophus. 280 l, Stenonychosaurus. 500 l, Camarasaurus. 635 l, Gallimimus.

**1994, Apr. 30** **Photo.** ***Perf. 13½***

| | | | | |
|---|---|---|---|---|
| **3900** | A1102 | 90 l multi | .25 | .25 |
| **3901** | A1102 | 130 l multi | .25 | .25 |
| **3902** | A1102 | 150 l multi | .30 | .25 |
| **3903** | A1102 | 280 l multi | .40 | .25 |
| **3904** | A1102 | 500 l multi | .50 | .25 |
| **3905** | A1102 | 635 l multi | .60 | .30 |
| | | *Nos. 3900-3905 (6)* | 2.30 | 1.55 |

For surcharge see No. 4467.

Romanian Legends A1103

Designs: 70 l, Calin the Madman. 115 l, Ileana Cosanzeana. 125 l, Ileana Cosanzeana, diff. 245 l, Ileana Cosanzeana, diff. 255 l, Agheran the Brave. 325 l, Wolf as Prince Charming, Ileana Cosanzeana.

**1994, Apr. 8** **Photo.** ***Perf. 13½***

| | | | | |
|---|---|---|---|---|
| **3906** | A1103 | 70 l multicolored | .25 | .25 |
| **3907** | A1103 | 115 l multicolored | .25 | .25 |
| **3908** | A1103 | 125 l multicolored | .30 | .25 |
| **3909** | A1103 | 245 l multicolored | .45 | .25 |
| **3910** | A1103 | 255 l multicolored | .45 | .25 |
| **3911** | A1103 | 325 l multicolored | .65 | .30 |
| | | *Nos. 3906-3911 (6)* | 2.35 | 1.55 |

For surcharge see No. 4474.

Easter A1104

**1994, Apr. 21**

| | | | | |
|---|---|---|---|---|
| **3912** | A1104 | 60 l multicolored | .25 | .25 |

Trees — A1105

No. 3913, Abies alba. No. 3914, Pinus sylvestris. No. 3915, Populus alba. No. 3916, Quercus robur. No. 3917, Larix decidua. No. 3918, Fagus sylvatica. No. 3919, Acer pseudoplatanus. No. 3920, Fraxinus excelsior. No. 3921, Picea abies. No. 3922, Tilia platyphyllos.

**Wmk. 398**

**1994, May 27 Photo. *Perf. 13¼***

| | | | | | |
|---|---|---|---|---|---|
| **3913** | A1105 | 15 l | multi | .25 | .25 |
| **3914** | A1105 | 35 l | multi | .25 | .25 |
| **3915** | A1105 | 45 l | multi | .25 | .25 |
| **3916** | A1105 | 60 l | multi | .25 | .25 |
| **3917** | A1105 | 70 l | multi | .25 | .25 |
| **3918** | A1105 | 125 l | multi | .25 | .25 |
| **3919** | A1105 | 350 l | multi | .40 | .25 |
| **3920** | A1105 | 940 l | multi | 1.25 | .25 |
| **3921** | A1105 | 1440 l | multi | 1.75 | .25 |
| **3922** | A1105 | 3095 l | multi | 3.50 | .25 |
| | | | *Nos. 3913-3922 (10)* | 8.40 | 2.50 |

For surcharges see Nos. 4221-4224, 4422-4424.

1994 World Cup Soccer Championships, US — A1106

**1994, June 17 Unwmk.**

| | | | | | |
|---|---|---|---|---|---|
| **3923** | A1106 | 90 l | Group A | .25 | .25 |
| **3924** | A1106 | 130 l | Group B | .25 | .25 |
| **3925** | A1106 | 150 l | Group C | .30 | .25 |
| **3926** | A1106 | 280 l | Group D | .50 | .25 |
| **3927** | A1106 | 500 l | Group E | .55 | .25 |
| **3928** | A1106 | 635 l | Group F | .70 | .25 |
| | | | *Nos. 3923-3928 (6)* | 2.55 | 1.50 |

**Souvenir Sheet**

| | | | | | |
|---|---|---|---|---|---|
| **3929** | A1106 | 2075 l | Action scene | 3.00 | 3.00 |

No. 3929 is airmail and contains one 54x42mm stamp.

Intl. Olympic Committee, Cent. — A1107

Ancient Olympians: 150 l, Torchbearer. 280 l, Discus thrower. 500 l, Wrestlers. 635 l, Arbitrator.

2075 l, Runners, emblem of Romanian Olympic Committee.

**1994, June 23**

| | | | | | |
|---|---|---|---|---|---|
| **3930** | A1107 | 150 l | multicolored | .25 | .25 |
| **3931** | A1107 | 280 l | multicolored | .45 | .25 |
| **3932** | A1107 | 500 l | multicolored | .60 | .25 |
| **3933** | A1107 | 635 l | multicolored | 1.20 | .25 |
| | | | *Nos. 3930-3933 (4)* | 2.50 | 1.00 |

**Souvenir Sheet**

| | | | | | |
|---|---|---|---|---|---|
| **3934** | A1107 | 2075 l | multicolored | 3.00 | 3.00 |

No. 3934 contains one 54x42mm stamp. Romanian Olympic Committee, 80th anniv. (#3934).

Miniature Sheets

Mushrooms — A1108

Edible: No. 3935a, 30 l, Craterellus cornucopiodes. b, 60 l, Lepista nuda. c, 150 l, Boletus edulis. d, 940 l, Lycoperdon perlatum.

Poisonous: No. 3936a, 90 l, Boletus satanas. b, 280 l, Amanita phalloides. c, 350 l, Inocybe patonillardi. d, 500 l, Amanita muscaria.

**1994, Aug. 8 Photo. *Perf. 13½***

| | | | | | |
|---|---|---|---|---|---|
| **3935** | A1108 | Sheet of 4, #a.-d. | | 2.00 | 2.00 |
| **3936** | A1108 | Sheet of 4, #a.-d. | | 2.00 | 2.00 |
| | | Complete booklet, #3935-3936 | | 4.50 | |

PHILAKOREA '94 — A1109

**1994, Aug. 16 *Perf. 13½***

| | | | | | |
|---|---|---|---|---|---|
| **3937** | A1109 | 60 l | Tuning fork | .30 | .25 |

**Souvenir Sheet**

| | | | | | |
|---|---|---|---|---|---|
| **3938** | A1109 | 2075 l | Korean drummer | 2.75 | 2.75 |

No. 3938 contains one 42x54mm stamp.

Environmental Protection in Danube River Delta — A1110

Designs: 150 l, Huso huso. 280 l, Vipera ursini. 500 l, Haliaeetus albicilla. 635 l, Mustela lutreola.

2075 l, Periploca graeca.

**1994, Aug. 31**

| | | | | | |
|---|---|---|---|---|---|
| **3939** | A1110 | 150 l | multicolored | .25 | .25 |
| **3940** | A1110 | 280 l | multicolored | .50 | .25 |
| **3941** | A1110 | 500 l | multicolored | .95 | .30 |
| **3942** | A1110 | 635 l | multicolored | 1.10 | .35 |
| | | | *Nos. 3939-3942 (4)* | 2.80 | 1.15 |

**Souvenir Sheet**

| | | | | | |
|---|---|---|---|---|---|
| **3943** | A1110 | 2075 l | multi | 3.00 | 3.00 |

No. 3943 contains one 54x42mm stamp.

Nos. 3654-3655 Surcharged

No. 3769 Surcharged

**1994 *Perfs., Etc. as Before***

| | | | | | |
|---|---|---|---|---|---|
| **3944** | A1041 | 150 l on 4.50 l #3654 | | .25 | .25 |
| **3945** | A1069 | 150 l on 10 l #3769 | | .30 | .25 |
| **3946** | A1041 | 525 l on 4.50 l #3655 | | .90 | .30 |
| | | *Nos. 3944-3946 (3)* | | 1.45 | .80 |

Issued: #3944, 3946 9/9/94; #3945, 10/7/94.

Circus Animal Acts — A1111

Designs: 90 l, Elephant. 130 l, Bear, vert. 150 l, Monkeys. 280 l, Tiger. 500 l, Tightrope walker, dogs. 635 l, Horse.

**1994, Sept. 15 Photo. *Perf. 13***

| | | | | | |
|---|---|---|---|---|---|
| **3947** | A1111 | 90 l | multicolored | .25 | .25 |
| **3948** | A1111 | 130 l | multicolored | .25 | .25 |
| **3949** | A1111 | 150 l | multicolored | .30 | .25 |
| **3950** | A1111 | 280 l | multicolored | .50 | .25 |
| **3951** | A1111 | 500 l | multicolored | .65 | .25 |
| **3952** | A1111 | 635 l | multicolored | .90 | .25 |
| | | | *Nos. 3947-3952 (6)* | 2.85 | 1.50 |

20th Intl. Fair, Bucharest — A1112

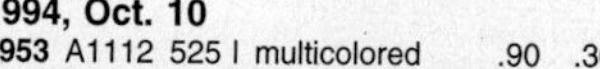

**1994, Oct. 10**

| | | | | | |
|---|---|---|---|---|---|
| **3953** | A1112 | 525 l | multicolored | .90 | .30 |

Fish A1113

World Wildlife Fund: 150 l, Acipenser ruthenus. 280 l, Acipenser guldenstaedti. 500 l, Acipenser stellatus. 635 l, Acipenser sturio.

**1994, Oct. 29 Photo. *Perf. 13½***

| | | | | | |
|---|---|---|---|---|---|
| **3954** | A1113 | 150 l | multicolored | .30 | .25 |
| **3955** | A1113 | 280 l | multicolored | .50 | .25 |
| **3956** | A1113 | 500 l | multicolored | .75 | .25 |
| **3957** | A1113 | 635 l | multicolored | 1.00 | .25 |
| | | | *Nos. 3954-3957 (4)* | 2.55 | 1.00 |

Issued in sheets of 10.

Chinese-Romanian Philatelic Exhibition — A1114

**1994, Oct. 29 Photo. *Perf. 13½***

| | | | | | |
|---|---|---|---|---|---|
| **3958** | A1114 | 150 l | Serpent | .30 | .25 |
| **3959** | A1114 | 1135 l | Dragon | 1.60 | .30 |
| *a.* | | Pair, #3958-3959 + label | | 2.00 | .60 |

Romanian State Railway, 125th Anniv. A1115

**1994, Oct. 31**

| | | | | | |
|---|---|---|---|---|---|
| **3960** | A1115 | 90 l | multicolored | .25 | .25 |

Famous People A1116

Designs: 30 l, Alexandru Orascu (1817-94). 60 l, Gh. Polizu (1819-86). 90 l, Gheorghe Tattarescu (1820-94), politician, prime minister. 150 l, Iulia Hasdeu (1869-88). 280 l, S. Mehedinti (1869-1962). 350 l, Camil Petrescu (1894-1957). 500 l, N. Paulescu (1869-1931). 940 l, L. Grigorescu (1894-1965).

**1994 Photo. *Perf. 13½***

| | | | | | |
|---|---|---|---|---|---|
| **3961** | A1116 | 30 l | multicolored | .25 | .25 |
| **3962** | A1116 | 60 l | multicolored | .25 | .25 |
| **3962A** | A1116 | 90 l | multicolored | .25 | .25 |
| **3963** | A1116 | 150 l | multicolored | .30 | .25 |
| **3964** | A1116 | 280 l | multicolored | .30 | .25 |
| **3965** | A1116 | 350 l | multicolored | .45 | .25 |
| **3966** | A1116 | 500 l | multicolored | .50 | .25 |
| **3967** | A1116 | 940 l | multicolored | 1.25 | .25 |
| | | | *Nos. 3961-3967 (8)* | 3.55 | 2.00 |

Issued; 90 l, 12/28/94; others, 11/30/94.

Christmas — A1117

**1994, Dec. 14 *Perf. 13½***

| | | | | | |
|---|---|---|---|---|---|
| **3968** | A1117 | 60 l | multicolored | .30 | .25 |

For surcharge see No. 4250.

St. Mary's Romanian Orthodox Church, Cleveland, Ohio, 90th Anniv. — A1118

**1994, Dec. 21 Photo. *Perf. 13½***

| | | | | | |
|---|---|---|---|---|---|
| **3969** | A1118 | 610 l | multicolored | .85 | .30 |

World Tourism Organization, 20th Anniv. — A1119

**1994, Dec. 22**

| | | | | | |
|---|---|---|---|---|---|
| **3970** | A1119 | 525 l | multicolored | 1.00 | .30 |

Miniature Sheet

Romanian Military Decorations — A1120

Year of medal — No. 3971: a, 30 l, Distinguished Flying Cross, 1938. b, 60 l, Military Cross, 3rd class, 1916. c, 150 l, Distinguished Serivce Medal, 1st Class, 1880. d, 940 l, Order of the Romanian Star, 1877.

**1994, Dec. 23**

| | | | | |
|---|---|---|---|---|
| **3971** | A1120 | Sheet of 4, #a.-d. | 2.00 | 2.00 |

Baby Animals A1121

**1994, Dec. 27 Photo. *Perf. 13x½***

| | | | | | |
|---|---|---|---|---|---|
| **3972** | A1121 | 90 l | Kittens | .25 | .25 |
| **3973** | A1121 | 130 l | Puppies | .25 | .25 |
| **3974** | A1121 | 150 l | Kid goat | .25 | .25 |
| **3975** | A1121 | 280 l | Foal | .30 | .25 |
| **3976** | A1121 | 500 l | Bunnies | .60 | .25 |
| **3977** | A1121 | 635 l | Lambs | .75 | .25 |
| | | | *Nos. 3972-3977 (6)* | 2.40 | 1.50 |

For surcharge see No. 4468.

A1122

**1995, Jan. 31 Photo. *Perf. 13½***

| | | | | | |
|---|---|---|---|---|---|
| **3978** | A1122 | 60 l | dark blue | .35 | .25 |

Save the Children organization.

A1123

The Young Men of Brasov: 40 l, Tanar. 60 l, Batran. 150 l, Curcan. 280 l, Dorobant. 350 l, Brasovechean. 500 l, Rosior. 635 l, Albior.

**1995, Feb. 25 Photo. *Perf. 13½***

| | | | | | |
|---|---|---|---|---|---|
| **3979** | A1123 | 40 l | multicolored | .25 | .25 |
| **3980** | A1123 | 60 l | multicolored | .25 | .25 |
| **3981** | A1123 | 150 l | multicolored | .25 | .25 |
| **3982** | A1123 | 280 l | multicolored | .30 | .25 |
| **3983** | A1123 | 350 l | multicolored | .50 | .25 |
| **3984** | A1123 | 500 l | multicolored | .60 | .25 |
| **3985** | A1123 | 635 l | multicolored | .75 | .25 |
| | | | *Nos. 3979-3985 (7)* | 2.90 | 1.75 |

Liberation of Concentration Camps, 50th Anniv. — A1124

**1995, Mar. 24 *Perf. 13½***

| | | | | | |
|---|---|---|---|---|---|
| **3986** | A1124 | 960 l | black & red | .85 | .30 |

FAO & UN, 50th Anniv. A1125

Designs: 675 l, FAO emblem, grain. 960 l, "50," UN emblem. 1615 l, Hand holding pen with flags of UN Charter countries.

**1995, Apr. 12 *Perf. 13½***

| | | | | | |
|---|---|---|---|---|---|
| **3987** | A1125 | 675 l | multicolored | .50 | .25 |
| **3988** | A1125 | 960 l | multicolored | .75 | .25 |
| **3989** | A1125 | 1615 l | multicolored | 1.50 | .25 |
| | | | *Nos. 3987-3989 (3)* | 2.75 | .75 |

Easter A1126

**1995, Apr. 14**

| | | | | | |
|---|---|---|---|---|---|
| **3990** | A1126 | 60 l | multicolored | .25 | .25 |

Romanian Fairy Tales — A1127

Designs: 90 l, King riding horse across town. 130 l, Woman feeding animals, vert. 150 l, Man riding on winged horse. 280 l, Old man, young man. 500 l, Archer aiming at apple tree, vert. 635 l, Two people riding log pulled by galloping horses.

**1995, Apr. 20 *Perf. 13½***

| | | | | | |
|---|---|---|---|---|---|
| **3991** | A1127 | 90 l | multicolored | .25 | .25 |
| **3992** | A1127 | 130 l | multicolored | .25 | .25 |
| **3993** | A1127 | 150 l | multicolored | .25 | .25 |
| **3994** | A1127 | 280 l | multicolored | .35 | .25 |
| **3995** | A1127 | 500 l | multicolored | .60 | .25 |
| **3996** | A1127 | 635 l | multicolored | .75 | .25 |
| | | | *Nos. 3991-3996 (6)* | 2.45 | 1.50 |

For surcharge see No. 4405.

Georges Enescu (1881-1955), Composer — A1128

**1995, May 5 *Perf. 13½***

| | | | | | |
|---|---|---|---|---|---|
| **3997** | A1128 | 960 l | blk & dp yel | .75 | .30 |

Peace & Freedom A1129

Europa: 150 l, Dove carryng piece of rainbow. 4370 l, Dove under rainbow with wings forming "Europa."

**1995, May 8**

| | | | | | |
|---|---|---|---|---|---|
| **3998** | A1129 | 150 l | multicolored | .25 | .25 |
| **3999** | A1129 | 4370 l | multicolored | 6.00 | 6.00 |

Lucian Blaga (1895-1961), Poet — A1130

**1995, May 9**

| | | | | | |
|---|---|---|---|---|---|
| **4000** | A1130 | 150 l | multicolored | .35 | .25 |

See Nos. 4017-4021.

Methods of Transportation — A1131

Designs: 470 l, Bucharest Metro subway train, 1979. 675 l, Brasov aerial cable car, vert. 965 l, Sud Aviation SA 330 Puma helicopter. 2300 l, 1904 Trolleybus. 2550 l, Steam locomotive, 1869. 3410 l, Boeing 737-300.

**1995, May 30 Photo. *Perf. 13½***

| | | | | | |
|---|---|---|---|---|---|
| **4001** | A1131 | 470 l | blk, gray & yel | .40 | .25 |
| **4002** | A1131 | 675 l | blk, gray & red | .55 | .25 |
| **4003** | A1131 | 965 l | bl, blk & gray | .80 | .25 |
| **4004** | A1131 | 2300 l | blk, gray & grn | 2.00 | .25 |
| **4005** | A1131 | 2550 l | blk, gray & red | 2.00 | .25 |
| **4006** | A1131 | 3410 l | bl, blk & gray | 2.90 | .25 |
| | | | *Nos. 4001-4006 (6)* | 8.65 | 1.50 |

Nos. 4003, 4006 are airmail. No. 4006, 75th anniversary of Romanian air transportation.

See Nos. 4055-4060.

Romanian Maritime Service, Cent. — A1132

Ships: 90 l, Dacia, liner, vert. 130 l, Imparatul Traian, steamer. 150 l, Romania, steamer. 280 l, Costinesti, tanker. 960 l, Caransebes, container ship. 3410 l, Tutova, car ferry.

**1995, May 31 Photo. *Perf. 13½***

| | | | | | |
|---|---|---|---|---|---|
| **4007** | A1132 | 90 l | multicolored | .25 | .25 |
| **4008** | A1132 | 130 l | multicolored | .25 | .25 |
| **4009** | A1132 | 150 l | multicolored | .25 | .25 |
| **4010** | A1132 | 280 l | multicolored | .25 | .25 |
| **4011** | A1132 | 960 l | multicolored | .60 | .25 |
| **4012** | A1132 | 3410 l | multicolored | 2.25 | .50 |
| | | | *Nos. 4007-4012 (6)* | 3.85 | 1.75 |

For surcharge see No. 4469.

A1133

European Nature Conservation Year: 150 l, Dama dama. 280 l, Otis tarda. 960 l, Cypripedium caiceolus. 1615 l, Ghetarul scarisoara (stalagmites).

**1995, June 5**

| | | | | | |
|---|---|---|---|---|---|
| **4013** | A1133 | 150 l | multicolored | .25 | .25 |
| **4014** | A1133 | 280 l | multicolored | .25 | .25 |
| **4015** | A1133 | 960 l | multicolored | .35 | .50 |
| **4016** | A1133 | 1615 l | multicolored | 1.25 | .50 |
| | | | *Nos. 4013-4016 (4)* | 2.10 | 1.50 |

**Famous Romanians Type of 1995**

Designs: 90 l, D.D. Rosca (1895-1980). 130 l, Vasile Conta (1845-1882). 280 l, Ion Barbu (1895-1961). 960 l, Iuliu Hatieganu (1885-1959). 1650 l, Dimitrie Brandza (1846-95).

**1995, June 26 Photo. *Perf. 13½***

| | | | | | |
|---|---|---|---|---|---|
| **4017** | A1130 | 90 l | multicolored | .25 | .25 |
| **4018** | A1130 | 130 l | multicolored | .25 | .25 |
| **4019** | A1130 | 280 l | multicolored | .25 | .25 |
| **4020** | A1130 | 960 l | multicolored | .70 | .25 |
| **4021** | A1130 | 1650 l | multicolored | 1.00 | .25 |
| | | | *Nos. 4017-4021 (5)* | 2.45 | 1.25 |

For surcharge see No. 4470.

A1134

**1995, July 10 Photo. *Perf. 13½***

| | | | | | |
|---|---|---|---|---|---|
| **4022** | A1134 | 1650 l | multicolored | 1.25 | .40 |

European Youth Olympic days.

Stamp Day — A1135

**1995, July 15**

| | | | | | |
|---|---|---|---|---|---|
| **4023** | A1135 | 960 l +715 l label | | 2.00 | .50 |

Cernavoda Bridge, Cent. — A1136

**1995, July 27** **Photo.** ***Perf. 13½***

| | | | | | |
|---|---|---|---|---|---|
| **4024** | A1136 | 675 l | multicolored | .75 | .40 |

A1137

Fowl: 90 l, Anas platyrhynchos. 130 l, Gallus gallus (hen). 150 l, Numida meleagris. 280 l, Meleagris gallopavo. 960 l, Anser anser. 1650 l, Gallus gallus (rooster).

**1995, July 31** **Photo.** ***Perf. 13½***

| | | | | | |
|---|---|---|---|---|---|
| **4025** | A1137 | 90 l | multicolored | .25 | .25 |
| **4026** | A1137 | 130 l | multicolored | .25 | .25 |
| **4027** | A1137 | 150 l | multicolored | .25 | .25 |
| **4028** | A1137 | 280 l | multicolored | .30 | .25 |
| **4029** | A1137 | 960 l | multicolored | .85 | .25 |
| **4030** | A1137 | 1650 l | multicolored | 1.25 | .25 |
| | | | *Nos. 4025-4030 (6)* | 3.15 | 1.50 |

For surcharge see No. 4471.

A1138

Institute of Air Medicine, 75th Anniv.: Gen. Dr. Victor Anastasiu (1886-1972).

**1995, Aug. 5** **Photo.** ***Perf. 13½***

| | | | | | |
|---|---|---|---|---|---|
| **4031** | A1138 | 960 l | multicolored | .80 | .35 |

Battle of Calugareni, 400th Anniv. — A1139

**1995, Aug. 13**

| | | | | | |
|---|---|---|---|---|---|
| **4032** | A1139 | 100 l | multicolored | .35 | .25 |

Romanian Buildings — A1140

Structure, year completed: 250 l, Giurgiu Castle, 1395. 500 l, Neamtului Castle, 1395, vert. 960 l, Sebes-Alba Mill, 1245. 1615 l, Dorohoi Church, 1495, vert. 1650 l, Military Observatory, Bucharest, 1895, vert.

**1995, Aug. 28**

| | | | | | |
|---|---|---|---|---|---|
| **4033** | A1140 | 250 l | multicolored | .25 | .25 |
| **4034** | A1140 | 500 l | multicolored | .30 | .25 |
| **4035** | A1140 | 960 l | multicolored | .50 | .25 |
| **4036** | A1140 | 1615 l | multicolored | .75 | .25 |
| **4037** | A1140 | 1650 l | multicolored | .90 | .25 |
| | | | *Nos. 4033-4037 (5)* | 2.70 | 1.25 |

A1141

Buildings in Manastirea: 675 l, Moldovita Monastery. 960 l, Hurez Monastery. 1615 l, Biertan Castle, horiz.

**1995, Aug. 31**

| | | | | | |
|---|---|---|---|---|---|
| **4038** | A1141 | 675 l | multicolored | .30 | .25 |
| **4039** | A1141 | 960 l | multicolored | .60 | .25 |
| **4040** | A1141 | 1615 l | multicolored | .90 | .30 |
| | | | *Nos. 4038-4040 (3)* | 1.80 | .80 |

A1142

**1995, Sept. 8**

| | | | | | |
|---|---|---|---|---|---|
| **4041** | A1142 | 1020 l | multicolored | .85 | .50 |

Romania Open Tennis Tournament, Bucharest.

Magazine "Mathematics," Cent. — A1143

Design: Ion N. Ionescu, founder.

**1995, Sept. 15**

| | | | | | |
|---|---|---|---|---|---|
| **4042** | A1143 | 100 l | multicolored | .35 | .25 |

Plants from Bucharest Botantical Garden — A1144

Designs: 50 l, Albizia julibrissin. 100 l, Taxus baccata. 150 l, Paulownia tomentosa. 500 l, Strelitzia reginae. 960 l, Victoria amazonica. 2300 l, Rhododendron indicum.

**1995, Sept. 29** **Photo.** ***Perf. 13½***

| | | | | | |
|---|---|---|---|---|---|
| **4043** | A1144 | 50 l | multicolored | .25 | .25 |
| **4044** | A1144 | 100 l | multicolored | .25 | .25 |
| **4045** | A1144 | 150 l | multicolored | .25 | .25 |
| **4046** | A1144 | 500 l | multicolored | .30 | .25 |
| **4047** | A1144 | 960 l | multicolored | .60 | .25 |
| **4048** | A1144 | 2300 l | multicolored | 1.20 | .30 |
| | | | *Nos. 4043-4048 (6)* | 2.85 | 1.55 |

Church of St. John — A1145

**1995, Oct. 1** **Photo.** ***Perf. 13½***

| | | | | | |
|---|---|---|---|---|---|
| **4049** | A1145 | 250 l | multi | .75 | .50 |

City of Piatra Neamt, 600th anniv.

A1146

Emigres: 150 l, George Apostu (1934-86), sculptor. 250 l, Emil Cioran (1911-95), philosopher. 500 l, Eugen Ionescu (1909-94), writer. 960 l, Elena Vacarescu (1866-1947), writer. 1650 l, Mircea Eliade (1907-86), philosopher.

**1995, Nov. 9**

| | | | | | |
|---|---|---|---|---|---|
| **4050** | A1146 | 150 l | grn, gray & blk | .25 | .25 |
| **4051** | A1146 | 250 l | bl, gray & blk | .25 | .25 |
| **4052** | A1146 | 500 l | tan, brn & blk | .40 | .25 |
| **4053** | A1146 | 960 l | lake, mag & blk | .80 | .25 |
| **4054** | A1146 | 1650 l | tan, brn & blk | 1.20 | .25 |
| | | | *Nos. 4050-4054 (5)* | 2.90 | 1.25 |

### Transportation Type of 1995

285 l, IAR 80 fighter planes. 630 l, Training ship, Mesagerul. 715 l, IAR-316 Red Cross helicopter. 755 l, Cargo ship, Razboieni. 1575 l, IAR-818H seaplane. 1615 l, First electric tram, Bucharest, 1896, vert.

**1995, Nov. 16**

| | | | | | |
|---|---|---|---|---|---|
| **4055** | A1131 | 285 l | blk, gray & grn | .25 | .25 |
| **4056** | A1131 | 630 l | bl & red | .35 | .25 |
| **4057** | A1131 | 715 l | gray bl & red | .35 | .25 |
| **4058** | A1131 | 755 l | blk, bl & gray | .40 | .25 |
| **4059** | A1131 | 1575 l | blk, grn & gray | .90 | .25 |
| **4060** | A1131 | 1615 l | blk, grn & gray | .75 | .25 |
| | | | *Nos. 4055-4060 (6)* | 3.00 | 1.50 |

Nos. 4055, 4057, 4059 are air mail.
For surcharges see Nos. 4475-4477.

1996 Summer Olympics, Atlanta — A1147

**1995, Dec. 8**

| | | | | | |
|---|---|---|---|---|---|
| **4061** | A1147 | 50 l | Track | .25 | .25 |
| **4062** | A1147 | 100 l | Gymnastics | .25 | .25 |
| **4063** | A1147 | 150 l | Two-man canoe | .25 | .25 |
| **4064** | A1147 | 500 l | Fencing | .50 | .25 |
| **4065** | A1147 | 960 l | Rowing-eights | .85 | .25 |
| **4066** | A1147 | 2300 l | Boxing | 2.00 | .35 |
| | | | *Nos. 4061-4066 (6)* | 4.10 | 1.60 |

**Souvenir Sheet**

| | | | | | |
|---|---|---|---|---|---|
| **4067** | A1147 | 2610 l | Gymnastics | 2.50 | 2.50 |

No. 4067 contains one 42x54mm stamp.

Christmas A1148

100 l, The Holy Family.

**1995, Dec. 15** **Photo.** ***Perf. 13½***

| | | | | | |
|---|---|---|---|---|---|
| **4068** | A1148 | 100 l | multicolored | .35 | .25 |

Folk Masks & Costumes — A1149

**1996, Jan. 31**

| | | | | | |
|---|---|---|---|---|---|
| **4069** | A1149 | 250 l | Maramures | .30 | .25 |
| **4070** | A1149 | 500 l | Moldova | .50 | .25 |
| **4071** | A1149 | 960 l | Moldova, vert. | .80 | .25 |
| **4072** | A1149 | 1650 l | Moldova, diff., vert. | 1.20 | .25 |
| | | | *Nos. 4069-4072 (4)* | 2.80 | 1.00 |

Tristan Tzara (1896-1963), Writer — A1151

1500 l, Anton Pann (1796-1854), writer.

**1996, Mar. 27** **Photo.** ***Perf. 13½***

| | | | | | |
|---|---|---|---|---|---|
| **4078** | A1151 | 150 l | multicolored | .25 | .25 |
| **4079** | A1151 | 1500 l | multicolored | 1.25 | .25 |

Easter A1152

**1996, Mar. 29**

| | | | | | |
|---|---|---|---|---|---|
| **4080** | A1152 | 150 l | multicolored | .35 | .25 |

Romfilex '96, Romanian-Israeli Philatelic Exhibition — A1153

Paintings: a, 370 l, On the Terrace at Sinaia, by Theodor Aman. b, 150 l, The Post Office, by

M. Stoican. c, 1500 l, Old Jerusalem, by Reuven Rubin.

**1996, Apr. 5**

**4081** A1153 Sheet of 3, #a.-c. 5.50 5.00

For surcharges see No. 4202.

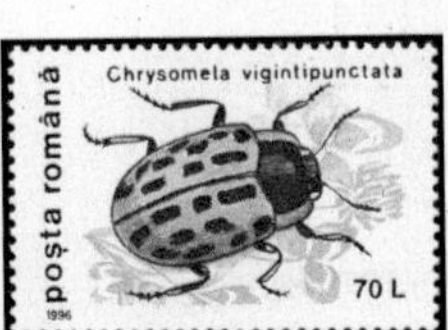


Insects A1154

Designs: 70 l, Chrysomela vigintipunctata. 220 l, Cerambyx cerdo. 370 l, Entomoscelis adonidis. 650 l, Coccinella bipunctata. 700 l, Calosoma sycophanta. 740 l, Hedobia imperialis. 960 l, Oryctes nasicornis. 1000 l, Trichius fasciatus. 1500 l, Purpuricenus kaehleri. 2500 l, Anthaxia salicis.

**1996**

**4082** A1154 70 l multicolored .25 .25
**4083** A1154 220 l multicolored .25 .25
**4084** A1154 370 l multicolored .25 .25
**4085** A1154 650 l multicolored .30 .25
**4086** A1154 700 l multicolored .30 .25
**4087** A1154 740 l multicolored .45 .25
**4088** A1154 960 l multicolored .60 .25
**4089** A1154 1000 l multicolored .60 .25
**4090** A1154 1500 l multicolored .90 .25
**4091** A1154 2500 l multicolored 1.20 .30
*Nos. 4082-4091 (10)* 5.10 2.55

Issued: 220, 740, 960, 1000, 1500 l, 4/16/96; 70, 370, 650, 700, 2500 l, 6/10/96.
For surcharges see Nos. 4283-4289, 4375-4377.

Souvenir Sheet

Dumitru Prunariu, First Romanian Cosmonaut — A1155

**1996, Apr. 22**

**4092** A1155 2720 l multicolored 1.50 1.50

ESPAMER '96, Aviation and Space Philatelic Exhibition, Seville, Spain.
For surcharges see Nos. 4829-4830.

1996 Summer Olympic Games, Atlanta — A1158

**1996, July 12 Photo. *Perf. 13½***

**4093** A1158 220 l Boxing .25 .25
**4094** A1158 370 l Athletics .25 .25
**4095** A1158 740 l Rowing .40 .25
**4096** A1158 1500 l Judo .80 .25
**4097** A1158 2550 l Gymnastics 1.75 .30
*Nos. 4093-4097 (5)* 3.45 1.30

**Souvenir Sheet**

**4098** A1158 4050 l Gymnastics, diff. 2.75 2.00

No. 4098 is airmail and contains one 54x42mm stamp. Olymphilex '96 (#4098).
For surcharge see No. 4877.

UNESCO World Heritage Sites — A1159

Designs: 150 l, Arbore Church. 1500 l, Voronet Monastery. 2550 l, Humor Monastery.

**1996, Apr. 24 Photo. *Perf. 13½***

**4099** A1159 150 l multicolored .25 .25
**4100** A1159 1500 l multicolored .80 .25
**4101** A1159 2550 l multicolored 1.50 .35
*Nos. 4099-4101 (3)* 2.55 .85

Famous Women — A1160

Europa: 370 l, Ana Aslan (1897-1988), physician. 4140 l, Lucia Bulandra (1873-1961), actress.

**1996, May 6**

**4102** A1160 370 l multicolored .25 .25
**4103** A1160 4140 l multicolored 3.75 2.25
*a.* Pair, #4102-4103 + 2 labels 4.00 2.50

UNICEF, 50th Anniv. — A1161

Children's paintings: 370 l, Mother and children. 740 l, Winter Scene. 1500 l, Children and Sun over House. 2550 l, House on Stilts.

**1996, May 25**

**4104** A1161 370 l multi .25 .25
**4105** A1161 740 l multi .45 .25
**4106** A1161 1500 l multi .80 .25
**4107** A1161 2550 l multi, vert. 1.20 .25
*Nos. 4104-4107 (4)* 2.70 1.00

Habitat II (#4107).

Euro '96, European Soccer Championships, Great Britain — A1162

Designs: a, 220 l, Goal keeper, ball. b, 370 l, Player with ball. c, Two players, ball. d, 1500 l, Three players, ball. e, 2550 l, Player dribbling ball.
4050 l, Two players, four balls.

**1996, May 27**

**4108** A1162 Strip of 5, #a.-e. 3.75 1.25

**Souvenir Sheet**

**4109** A1162 4050 l multicolored 2.75 2.10

No. 4109 contains one 42x54mm stamp.

CAPEX '96 — A1163

Designs: 150 l, Toronto Convention Center. 4050 l, CN Tower, Skydome, Toronto skyline.

**1996, May 29**

**4110** A1163 150 l multicolored .25 .25

**Souvenir Sheet**

**4111** A1163 4050 l multicolored 2.75 2.10

No. 4111 contains 42x54mm stamp.

Resita Factory, 225th Anniv. A1164

**1996, June 20 Photo. *Perf. 13½***

**4112** A1164 150 l dark red brown .35 .25

**No. 3775 Surcharged**

**1996, June 22**

**4113** A1071 150 l on 10 l multi .35 .25

Stamp Day — A1165

**1996, July 15**

**4114** A1165 1500 l + 650 l label 1.25 .25

Conifers — A1166

70 l, Picea glauca. 150 l, Picea omorica. 220 l, Picea pungeus. 740 l, Picea sitchensis. 1500 l, Pinus sylvestris. 3500 l, Pinus pinaster.

**1996, Aug. 1**

**4115** A1166 70 l multi .25 .25
**4116** A1166 150 l multi .25 .25
**4117** A1166 220 l multi .25 .25
**4118** A1166 740 l multi .45 .25
**4119** A1166 1500 l multi .85 .25
**4120** A1166 3500 l multi 2.00 .30
*Nos. 4115-4120 (6)* 4.05 1.55

For surcharge see No. 4403.

Wildlife — A1167

Designs: 70 l, Natrix natrix, vert. 150 l, Testudo hermanni, vert. 220 l, Alauda arvensis. 740 l, Vulpes vulpes. 1500 l, Phocaena phocaena, vert. 3500 l, Aquila chrysaetos, vert.

**1996, Sept. 12 Photo. *Perf. 13½***

**4121** A1167 70 l multicolored .25 .25
**4122** A1167 150 l multicolored .25 .25
**4123** A1167 220 l multicolored .25 .25
**4124** A1167 740 l multicolored .45 .25
**4125** A1167 1500 l multicolored .85 .25
**4126** A1167 3500 l multicolored 2.00 .30
*Nos. 4121-4126 (6)* 4.05 1.55

For surcharge see No. 4348.

Famous Men — A1168

100 l, Stan Golestan (1875-1956). 150 l, Corneliu Coposu (1914-95). 370 l, Vintila Horia (1915-92). 1500 l, Alexandru Papana (1906-46).

**1996, Nov. 29**

**4127** A1168 100 l black & rose red .25 .25
**4128** A1168 150 l black & lake .25 .25
**4129** A1168 370 l blk & yel brn .35 .25
**4130** A1168 1500 l black & ver 1.00 .40
*Nos. 4127-4130 (4)* 1.85 1.15

Madonna and Child — A1169

**1996, Nov. 27**

**4131** A1169 150 l multicolored .35 .25

Antique Automobiles — A1170

No. 4132: a, 280 l, 1933 Mercedes Benz. b, 70 l, 1930 Ford Spider. c, 150 l, 1932 Citroen. d, 220 l, 1936 Rolls Royce.
No. 4133: a, 2550 l, 1936 Mercedes Benz 500k Roadster. b, 2550 l, 1934 Bugatti "Type 59." c. 2550 l, 1931 Alfa Romeo 8C. d, 120 l, 1937 Jaguar SS 100.

**1996, Dec. 19 Photo. *Perf. 13½***

**4132** A1170 Sheet of 4, #a.-d. .80 .40
**4133** A1170 Sheet of 4, #a.-d. 7.00 3.50

Souvenir Sheet

Deng Xiaoping, China, and Margaret Thatcher, Great Britain — A1171

**1997, Jan. 20 Photo. *Perf. 13½***
**4134** A1171 1500 l multicolored .75 .75

Hong Kong '97.

Fur-Bearing Animals — A1172

Designs: 70 l, Mustela erminea. 150 l, Alopex lagopus. 220 l, Nyctereutes procyonoides. 740 l, Lutra lutra. 1500 l, Ondatra zibethica. 3500 l, Martes martes.

**1997, Feb. 14**
**4135** A1172 70 l multicolored .25 .25
**4136** A1172 150 l multicolored .25 .25
**4137** A1172 220 l multicolored .25 .25
**4138** A1172 740 l multicolored .25 .25
**4139** A1172 1500 l multicolored .40 .25
**4140** A1172 3500 l multicolored 1.00 .25
*Nos. 4135-4140 (6)* 2.40 1.50

For surcharge see No. 4349.

Greenpeace, 25th Anniv. — A1173

Various views of MV Greenpeace.

**1997, Mar. 6**
**4141** A1173 150 l multicolored .25 .25
**4142** A1173 370 l multicolored .25 .25
**4143** A1173 1940 l multicolored .50 .25
**4144** A1173 2500 l multicolored .75 .25
*Nos. 4141-4144 (4)* 1.75 1.00

**Souvenir Sheet**

**4145** A1173 4050 l multicolored 1.50 .85

No. 4145 contains one 49x38mm stamp.

Famous People — A1174

Designs: 200 l, Thomas A. Edison. 400 l, Franz Schubert. 3600 l, Miguel de Cervantes Saavedra (1547-1616), Spanish writer.

**1997, Mar. 27 Photo. *Perf. 13½***
**4146** A1174 200 l multicolored .25 .25
**4147** A1174 400 l multicolored .25 .25
**4148** A1174 3600 l multicolored 1.75 .25
*Nos. 4146-4148 (3)* 2.25 .75

Inauguration of Mobile Telephone Network in Romania — A1175

**1997, Apr. 7 Photo. *Perf. 13½***
**4149** A1175 400 l multicolored .35 .25

Churches — A1176

**1997, Apr. 21 Photo. *Perf. 13½***
**4150** A1176 200 l Surdesti .25 .25
**4151** A1176 400 l Plopis .25 .25
**4152** A1176 450 l Bogdan Voda .25 .25
**4153** A1176 850 l Rogoz .25 .25
**4154** A1176 3600 l Calinesti .80 .25
**4155** A1176 6000 l Birsana 1.50 .30
*Nos. 4150-4155 (6)* 3.30 1.55

A1177

Shakespeare Festival, Craiova: a, 400 l, Constantin Serghe (1819-87) as Othello, 1855. b, 200 l, Al. Demetrescu Dan (1870-1948) as Hamlet, 1916. c, 3600 l, Ion Manolescu (1881-1959) as Hamlet, 1924. d, 2400 l, Gheorghe Cozorici (1933-93) as Hamlet, 1957.

**1997, Apr. 23 Photo. *Perf. 13½***
**4156** A1177 Sheet of 4, #a.-d. + 4 labels 2.25 1.50

A1178

Europa (Stories and Legends): 400 l, Vlad Tepes (Vlad the Impaler), prince upon whom legend of Dracula said to be based. 4250 l, Dracula.

**1997, May 5**
**4157** A1178 400 l multicolored .25 .25
**4158** A1178 4250 l multicolored 1.90 1.90
*a.* Pair, #4157-4158 + label 2.00 2.00

A1179

Natl. Theater, Cathedral, Statue of Mihai Viteazul.

**1997, June 27 Photo. *Perf. 13½***
**4159** A1179 450 l multicolored .35 .25

Balcanmax '97, Maximum Cards Exhibition, Cluj-Napoca.

Cacti A1180

Designs: 100 l, Dolichothele uberiformis. 250 l, Rebutia. 450 l, Echinofossulocactus lamellosus. 500 l, Ferocactus glaucescens. 650 l, Thelocactus. 6150 l, Echinofossulocactus albatus.

**1997, June 27**
**4160** A1180 100 l multicolored .25 .25
**4161** A1180 250 l multicolored .25 .25
**4162** A1180 450 l multicolored .25 .25
**4163** A1180 500 l multicolored .25 .25
**4164** A1180 650 l multicolored .25 .25
**4165** A1180 6150 l multicolored 2.40 .25
*Nos. 4160-4165 (6)* 3.65 1.50

Stamp Day — A1181

**1997, July 15 Photo. *Perf. 13½***
**4166** A1181 3600 l + 1500 l label 1.75 .40

Ten different labels exist.

Nos. 3664-3670, 3672 Srchd. in Brnish Purple (#4167-4171, 4174) or Black (#4172-4173)

**1997, July 17**
**4167** A1043 250 l on 1 l #3664 .25 .25
**4168** A1043 250 l on 2 l #3665 .25 .25
**4169** A1043 250 l on 4 l #3666 .25 .25
**4170** A1043 450 l on 5 l #3667 .25 .25
**4171** A1043 450 l on 6 l #3668 .25 .25
**4172** A1043 450 l on 18 l #3672 .25 .25
**4173** A1043 950 l on 9 l #3670 .25 .25
**4174** A1043 3600 l on 8 l #3669 .75 .25
*Nos. 4167-4174 (8)* 2.50 2.00

Castle Dracula, Sighisoara — A1181a

Designs: 650 l, Clocktower on Town Hall. 3700 l, Steps leading to castle and clocktower.

**1997, July 31**
**4175** A1181a 250 l shown .25 .25
**4175A** A1181a 650 l multi .25 .25
**4175B** A1181a 3700 l multi 1.20 .25
*Nos. 4175-4175B (3)* 1.70 .75

A1181b

Tourism Monument, Banat.

**1997, Aug. 3**
**4175C** A1181b 950 l multi .35 .25

A1181c

**1997, Aug. 13**
**4175D** A1181c 450 l multi .35 .25

Stamp Printing Works, 125th anniv.

Belgian Antarctic Expedition, Cent. — A1181d

"Belgica" sailing ship and: 450 l, Emil Racovita, biologist. 650 l, Frederick A. Cook, anthropologist, photographer. 1600 l, Roald Amundsen. 3700 l, Adrien de Gerlache, expedition commander.

**1997, Aug. 18**
**4175E** A1181d 450 l multi .25 .25
**4175F** A1181d 650 l multi .25 .25
**4175G** A1181d 1600 l multi .40 .25
**4175H** A1181d 3700 l multi 1.50 .25
*Nos. 4175E-4175H (4)* 2.40 1.00

Sports A1182

500 l, Rugby. 700 l, American football, vert. 1750 l, Baseball. 3700 l, Mountain climbing, vert.

**1997, Nov. 21 Photo. *Perf. 13½***
**4176** A1182 500 l multi .25 .25
**4177** A1182 700 l multi .25 .25
**4178** A1182 1750 l multi .45 .25
**4179** A1182 3700 l multi 1.40 .30
*Nos. 4176-4179 (4)* 2.35 1.05

Romanian Scouts A1183

300 l, Tents at campsite. 700 l, Scouting emblem. 1050 l, Hands reaching toward each other. 1750 l, Carvings. 3700 l, Scouts seated around campfire.

**1997, Oct. 25 Photo. *Perf. 13½***

| | | | | |
|---|---|---|---|---|
| **4180** | A1183 | 300 l multicolored | .25 | .25 |
| **4181** | A1183 | 700 l multicolored | .25 | .25 |
| **4182** | A1183 | 1050 l multicolored | .30 | .25 |
| **4183** | A1183 | 1750 l multicolored | .45 | .25 |
| **4184** | A1183 | 3700 l multicolored | 1.10 | .25 |
| *a.* | | Strip of 5, #4180-4184 | 2.50 | 1.00 |

**No. 3650 Surcharged in Red**

**1997, Sept. 27**

| | | | | |
|---|---|---|---|---|
| **4185** | A1039 | 1050 l on 4.50 l | .60 | .25 |

**No. 3619 Surcharged in Red**

**1997, Oct. 28 Photo. *Perf. 13½***

| | | | | |
|---|---|---|---|---|
| **4186** | A1032 | 500 l on 2 l multi | .25 | .25 |

Ion Mihalache (1882-1963), Politician — A1184

Design: 1050 l, King Carol I (1866-1914).

**1997, Nov. 8**

| | | | | |
|---|---|---|---|---|
| **4187** | A1184 | 500 l multi | .25 | .25 |
| **4188** | A1184 | 1050 l pink & multi | .35 | .30 |

**King Carol I Type of 1997**

Designs: Nos. 4188A-4188C, King Carol I.

**1997, Nov. 8 Litho. *Perf. 13½***

| | | | | |
|---|---|---|---|---|
| **4188A** | A1184 | 1050 l blue & multi | .35 | .35 |
| **4188B** | A1184 | 1050 l clar & multi | .35 | .35 |
| **4188C** | A1184 | 1050 l blk & multi | .35 | .35 |

Chamber of Commerce and Industry, Bucharest, 130th Anniv. — A1185

**1998, Jan. 29 Photo. *Perf. 13½***

| | | | | |
|---|---|---|---|---|
| **4189** | A1185 | 700 l multicolored | .35 | .25 |

No. 4189 is printed se-tenant with label.

1998 Winter Olympic Games, Nagano A1186

**1998, Feb. 5**

| | | | | |
|---|---|---|---|---|
| **4190** | A1186 | 900 l Skiing | .30 | .25 |
| **4191** | A1186 | 3900 l Figure skating | 1.25 | .65 |

**Souvenir Sheet**

Flag Day — A1187

**1998, Feb. 24 Photo. *Perf. 13½***

| | | | | |
|---|---|---|---|---|
| **4192** | A1187 | 900 l multicolored | .60 | .25 |

National Festivals and Holidays — A1188

**1998, Feb. 26 Photo. *Perf. 13x13½***

| | | | | |
|---|---|---|---|---|
| **4193** | A1188 | 900 l 4-Leaf clover | .80 | 1.00 |
| **4194** | A1188 | 3900 l Heart | 17.50 | 22.50 |

Europa.

Famous People and Events of the 20th Century A1189

Designs: 700 l, Alfred Nobel, creation of Nobel Foundation, 1901. 900 l, Guglielmo Marconi, first radio transmission across Atlantic, 1901. 1500 l, Albert Einstein, theory of relativity, 1905. 3900 l, Trajan Vuia, flying machine, 1906.

**1998, Mar. 31 Photo. *Perf. 13½***

| | | | | |
|---|---|---|---|---|
| **4195** | A1189 | 700 l multicolored | .40 | .25 |
| **4196** | A1189 | 900 l multicolored | .40 | .25 |
| **4197** | A1189 | 1500 l multicolored | .50 | .25 |
| **4198** | A1189 | 3900 l multicolored | 1.40 | .40 |
| | | *Nos. 4195-4198 (4)* | 2.70 | 1.15 |

See Nos. 4261-4265, 4312-4319, 4380-4383.

Roadside Shrines — A1190

**1998, Apr. 17**

| | | | | |
|---|---|---|---|---|
| **4199** | A1190 | 700 l Cluj | .25 | .25 |
| **4200** | A1190 | 900 l Prahova | .25 | .25 |
| **4201** | A1190 | 1500 l Arges | .50 | .25 |
| | | *Nos. 4199-4201 (3)* | 1.00 | .75 |

No. 4081 Surcharged in Red

Designs: a, 900 l on 370 l. b, 700 l on 150 l, c, 3900 l on 1500 l.

**1998, May 12**

| | | | | |
|---|---|---|---|---|
| **4202** | A1153 | Sheet of 3, #a.-c. | 2.50 | 1.25 |

Surcharge on #4202a, 4202c does not include '98 show emblem. This appears in the selvage to the right and left of the stamps.

Romanian Surgical Society, Cent. — A1191

Thoma Ionescu (1860-1926), founder.

**1998, May 18**

| | | | | |
|---|---|---|---|---|
| **4203** | A1191 | 1050 l multicolored | .50 | .25 |

**Nos. 3665-3669, 3672, 3676 Surcharged in Black, Red, Bright Green, Violet, Red Violet, Orange Brown, Dark Green, Violet Brown or Deep Blue**

**1998 Photo. *Perf. 13½***

| | | | | |
|---|---|---|---|---|
| **4204** | A1043 | 50 l on 2 l #3665 (R) | .25 | .25 |
| **4205** | A1043 | 100 l on 8 l #3669 (BG) | .25 | .25 |
| **4206** | A1043 | 200 l on 4 l #3666 | .25 | .25 |
| **4207** | A1043 | 250 l on 45 l #3676 (Bl) | .25 | .25 |
| **4208** | A1043 | 350 l on 45 l #3676 | .25 | .25 |
| **4209** | A1043 | 400 l on 6 l #3668 (V) | .25 | .25 |
| **4210** | A1043 | 400 l on 45 l #3676 (BG) | .25 | .25 |
| **4211** | A1043 | 450 l on 45l #3676 (RV) | .25 | .25 |
| **4212** | A1043 | 500 l on 18 l #3672 (Bl) | .25 | .25 |
| **4213** | A1043 | 850 l on 45 l #3676 (OB) | .75 | .35 |
| **4214** | A1043 | 900 l on 45 l #3676 (V) | .75 | .35 |
| **4215** | A1043 | 1000 l on 45 l #3676 (DkG) | .75 | .35 |
| **4216** | A1043 | 1000 l on 9 l #3670 | .40 | .40 |
| **4217** | A1043 | 1500 l on 5 l #3667 (R) | .40 | .40 |
| **4218** | A1043 | 1600 l on 45 l #3676 (VB) | 1.75 | .40 |
| **4219** | A1043 | 2500 l on 45 l #3676 (R) | 3.00 | .75 |
| | | *Nos. 4204-4219 (16)* | 10.05 | 5.25 |

Obliterator varies on Nos. 4204-4219.
Issued: Nos. 4204-4206, 4209, 4212, 5/21; Nos. 4216-4217, 7/6; others, 1998.

1998 World Cup Soccer Championships, France — A1192

Various soccer plays, stadium: a, 800 l. b, 1050 l. c, 1850 l. d, 4150 l.

**1998, June 10 Photo. *Perf. 13½***

| | | | | |
|---|---|---|---|---|
| **4220** | A1192 | Sheet of 4, #a.-d. | 2.25 | 1.10 |

Nos. 3913-3915, 3918 Surcharged in Red Violet, Blue, Black, or Red

**Wmk. 398**

**1998, June 30 Photo. *Perf. 13***

**Design A1105**

| | | | | |
|---|---|---|---|---|
| **4221** | 700 l on 125 l #3918 (RV) | .25 | .25 |
| **4222** | 800 l on 35 l #3914 (Bl) | .25 | .25 |
| **4223** | 1050 l on 45 l #3915 (Blk) | .35 | .25 |
| **4224** | 4150 l on 15 l #3913 (R) | 1.25 | .65 |
| | *Nos. 4221-4224 (4)* | 2.10 | 1.40 |

Night Birds A1193

Designs: 700 l, Apteryx australis, vert. 1500 l, Tyto alba, vert. 1850 l, Rallus aquaticus. 2450 l, Caprimulgus europaeus.

**1998, Aug. 12 Unwmk.**

| | | | | |
|---|---|---|---|---|
| **4225** | A1193 | 700 l multicolored | .30 | .30 |
| **4226** | A1193 | 1500 l multicolored | .30 | .30 |
| *a.* | | Complete booklet, 4 each, #4225-4226 | 3.00 | |
| **4227** | A1193 | 1850 l multicolored | .30 | .30 |
| **4228** | A1193 | 2450 l multicolored | 1.10 | 1.10 |
| *a.* | | Complete booklet, 4 each, #4227-4228 | 5.75 | |
| | | *Nos. 4225-4228 (4)* | 2.00 | 2.00 |

Stamp Day A1194

**1998, July Litho. *Perf. 13½***

| | | | | |
|---|---|---|---|---|
| **4229** | A1194 | 700 l Romania #4 | .25 | .25 |
| **4230** | A1194 | 1050 l Romania #1 | .35 | .25 |
| *a.* | | Complete booklet, #4225, 4 #4226 | 3.50 | |

**Souvenir Sheet**

| | | | | |
|---|---|---|---|---|
| **4231** | A1194 | 4150 l +850 l Romania #2-3 | 1.60 | .80 |

No. 4231 contains one 54x42mm stamp.

Natl. Uprising, 150th Anniv. — A1195

**1998, Sept. 28 Photo. *Perf. 13½***

| | | | | |
|---|---|---|---|---|
| **4232** | A1195 | 1050 l multicolored | .35 | .25 |

A1196

German Personalities in Banat: 800 l, Nikolaus Lenau (1802-50). 1850 l, Stefan Jäger (1877-1962). 4150 l, Adam Müller-Guttenbrunn (1852-1923).

**1998, Oct. 16**

**4233** A1196 800 l multicolored .25 .25
**4234** A1196 1850 l multicolored .50 .25
**4235** A1196 4150 l multicolored 1.00 .50
*Nos. 4233-4235 (3)* 1.75 1.00

A1197

**1998, Nov. 4 Photo. *Perf. 13½***

**4236** A1197 1100 l multicolored .40 .25

Intl. Year of the Ocean.

Nos. 3652-3653, 3704-3709, 3776-3779, 3781, 3795, 3968 Srchd. in Green, Black, Red, Red Violet or Deep Blue

**1998 Photo. *Perf. 13½***

**4237** A1041 50 l on #3652 (G) .25 .25
**4238** A1041 50 l on #3653 (Blk) .25 .25
**4238A** A1054 50 l on 1 l #3704 (Blk) .25 .25
**4239** A1054 50 l on #3705 (R) .90 .25
**4240** A1054 50 l on #3706 (R) .25 .25
**4241** A1054 50 l on #3707 (Blk) .25 .25
**4242** A1054 50 l on #3708 (Blk) .25 .25
**4243** A1054 50 l on #3709 (R) .25 .25
**4244** A1054 50 l on #3776 (RV) .25 .25
**4245** A1054 50 l on #3777 (DB) .25 .25
**4246** A1054 50 l on #3778 (Blk) .25 .25
**4247** A1054 50 l on #3779 (G) .25 .25
**4248** A1054 50 l on #3781 (R) .25 .25
**4249** A1075 2000 l on #3795 (G) .80 .50
**4250** A1117 2600 l on #3968 (R) .80 .50
*Nos. 4237-4250 (15)* 5.50 4.25

Obliterator varies on Nos. 4237-4250.
Issued: 4237-4238, 11/10; 4238A, 11/27; 4249-4250, 12/22.

A1198

Lighthouses.

**1998, Dec. 28**

**4251** A1198 900 l Genovez .25 .25
**4252** A1198 1000 l Constanta .30 .25
**4253** A1198 1100 l Sfantu Gheorghe .35 .25
**4254** A1198 2600 l Sulina 1.00 .40
*Nos. 4251-4254 (4)* 1.90 1.15

A1199

Flowers: 350 l, Tulipa gesneriana. 850 l, Dahlia variabilis. 1100 l, Lillium martagon. 4450 l, Rosa centifolia.

**1998, Nov. 25**

**4255** A1199 350 l multicolored .25 .25
**4256** A1199 850 l multicolored .30 .25
**4257** A1199 1100 l multicolored .30 .25
**4258** A1199 4450 l multicolored 1.00 .65
*Nos. 4255-4258 (4)* 1.85 1.40

Universal Declaration of Human Rights, 50th Anniv. — A1200

**1998, Dec. 10**

**4259** A1200 700 l multicolored .35 .25

Dimitrie Paciurea (1873-1932), Sculptor — A1200a

**1998, Dec. 11 Photo. *Perf. 13¼***

**4259A** A1200a 850 l ocher & blk .40 .25

Total Eclipse of the Sun, Aug. 11, 1999 — A1201

**1998, Dec. 17**

**4260** A1201 1100 l multi + label .35 .25

### Events of the 20th Cent. Type

Designs: 350 l, Sinking of the Titanic, 1912. 1100 l, "Coanda 1910" aircraft with air-reactive (jet) engine, 1919, by Henri Coanda (1886-1972). 1600 l, Louis Blériot's (1872-1936) Calais-Dover flight, 1909. 2000 l, Opening of the Panama Canal, 1914. 2600 l, Russian Revolution, 1917.

**1998, Dec. 22 Photo. *Perf. 13½***

**4261** A1189 350 l multicolored .25 .25
**4262** A1189 1100 l multicolored .30 .25
**4263** A1189 1600 l multicolored .30 .25
**4264** A1189 2000 l multicolored .30 .30
**4265** A1189 2600 l multicolored .75 .40
*Nos. 4261-4265 (5)* 1.90 1.45

No. 3687 Surcharged in Red or Black

**1999, Feb. 10 Photo. *Perf. 13½***

**4266** A1047 100 l on 1 l (R) .30 .25
**4267** A1047 250 l on 1 l (Blk) .30 .25

Obliterator is a guitar on #4266 and a saxophone on #4267.

No. 3796 Surcharged in Black, Red, Green, or Brown

**1999, Jan. 22**

**4268** A1076 50 l on 15 l (Blk) .25 .25
**4269** A1076 50 l on 15 l (R) .25 .25
**4270** A1076 400 l on 15 l (Grn) .25 .25
**4271** A1076 2300 l on 15 l (Brn) .50 .35
**4272** A1076 3200 l on 15 l (Blk) 1.00 .50
*Nos. 4268-4272 (5)* 2.25 1.60

Obliterator varies on Nos. 4268-4272.

Monasteries — A1203

**1999, Jan. 17**

**4273** A1203 500 l Arnota .25 .25
**4274** A1203 700 l Bistrita .25 .25
**4275** A1203 1100 l Dintr'un Lemn .25 .25
**4276** A1203 2100 l Govora .50 .30
**4277** A1203 4850 l Tismana 1.40 .70
*Nos. 4273-4277 (5)* 2.65 1.75

Shrub Flowers A1204

350 l, Magnolia x soulangiana. 1000 l, Stewartia malacodendron. 1100 l, Hibiscus rosa-sinensis. 5350 l, Clematis patens.

**1999, Feb. 15**

**4278** A1204 350 l multicolored .25 .25
**4279** A1204 1000 l multicolored .25 .25
**4280** A1204 1100 l multicolored .25 .25
**4281** A1204 5350 l multicolored 1.50 .75
*Nos. 4278-4281 (4)* 2.25 1.50

Easter A1205

**1999, Mar. 15 Photo. *Perf. 13¼***

**4282** A1205 1100 l multi .35 .25

### No. 4082 Surcharged in Bright Pink, Red, Violet, Black, Green or Blue

**1999, Mar. 22 Litho. *Perf. 13½***

**4283** A1154 100 l on 70 l (BP) .25 .25
**4284** A1154 100 l on 70 l (R) .25 .25
**4285** A1154 200 l on 70 l (V) .25 .25
**4286** A1154 1500 l on 70 l .50 .25
**4287** A1154 1600 l on 70 l (G) .50 .25
**4288** A1154 3200 l on 70 l (Bl) 1.10 .45
**4289** A1154 6000 l on 70 l (G) 1.90 .90
*Nos. 4283-4289 (7)* 4.75 2.60

Obliterators on Nos. 4283-4289 are various dinosaurs.

Jewelry — A1206

Designs: 1200 l, Keys on chain. 2100 l, Key holder. 2600 l, Necklace. 3200 l, Necklace, horiz.

**1999, Mar. 29 Photo. *Perf. 13¼***

**4290-4293** A1206 Set of 4 1.75 .90

Birds — A1207

***Perf. 13½x13¼***

**1999, Apr. 26 Photo.**

**4294** A1207 1100 l Ara macao .30 .25
**4295** A1207 2700 l Pavo albus .60 .35
**4296** A1207 3700 l Pavo cristatus .80 .45
**4297** A1207 5700 l Cacatua galerita 1.25 .65
*Nos. 4294-4297 (4)* 2.95 1.70

Council of Europe, 50th Anniv. — A1208

**1999, May 5 Photo. *Perf. 13¼***

**4298** A1208 2300 l multi + label .60 .35

A1209

Visit of Pope John Paul II to Romania: a, 6300 l, Pope John Paul II. b, 1300 l, St. Peter's Basilica. c, 1600 l, Patriarchal Cathedral, Bucharest. d, 2300 l, Patriarch Teoctist.

**1999, May 7**

**4299** A1209 Sheet of 6, #a.-d. 2.50 1.90

Issued in sheets containing one strip of #4299a-4299d, 1 ea #4299a, 4299d + 2 labels.

A1210

Europa: 1100 l, Anas clypeata. 5700 l, Ciconia nigra.

**1999, May 17**

**4300** A1210 1100 l multicolored .25 .25
**4301** A1210 5700 l multicolored 1.50 1.25

Nos. 4300-4301 printed with se-tenant label.

Famous Personalities — A1211

Designs: 600 l, Gheorghe Cartan (1849-1911). 1100 l, George Calinescu (1899-1965), writer. 2600 l, Johann Wolfgang von Goethe (1749-1832), poet. 7300 l, Honoré de Balzac (1799-1850), novelist.

**1999, May 31**

**4302** A1211 600 l multicolored .25 .25
**4303** A1211 1100 l multicolored .25 .25
**4304** A1211 2600 l multicolored .40 .25
**4305** A1211 7300 l multicolored 1.50 .75
*Nos. 4302-4305 (4)* 2.40 1.50

Total Solar Eclipse, Aug. 11 — A1212

**1999, June 21 Photo. *Perf. 13¼***

**4306** A1212 1100 l multicolored .50 .25

No. 4306 printed se-tenant with label.

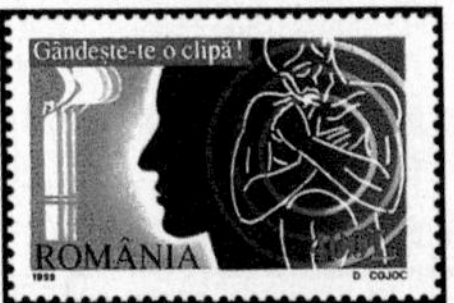


Health Dangers A1213

**1999, July 29 Photo. *Perf. 13¼***

**4307** A1213 400 l Smoking .25 .25
**4308** A1213 800 l Alcohol .25 .25
**4309** A1213 1300 l Drugs .25 .25
**4310** A1213 2500 l AIDS .50 .25
*Nos. 4307-4310 (4)* 1.25 1.00

Luciano Pavarotti Concert in Bucharest on Day of Solar Eclipse — A1214

**1999, Aug. 9**

**4311** A1214 8100 l multi 1.60 .80

**Events of the 20th Century Type**

Designs: 800 l, Alexander Fleming discovers penicillin, 1928. 3000 l, League of Nations, 1920. 7300 l, Harold C. Urey discovers heavy water, 1931. 17,000 l, First marine oil drilling platform, off Beaumont, Texas, 1934.

**1999, Aug. 30**

**4312** A1189 800 l multi .25 .25
**4313** A1189 3000 l multi .50 .40
**4314** A1189 7300 l multi 1.25 .85
**4315** A1189 17,000 l multi 3.50 1.90
*Nos. 4312-4315 (4)* 5.50 3.40

**1999, Sept. 24 Photo. *Perf. 13¼***

1500 l, Karl Landsteiner (1868-1943), discoverer of blood groups. 3000 l, Nicolae C. Paulescu (1869-1931), diabetes researcher. 7300 l, Otto Hahn (1879-1968), discoverer of nuclear fission. 17,000 l, Ernst Ruska (1906-88), inventor of electron microscope.

**4316** A1189 1500 l multi .30 .25
**4317** A1189 3000 l multi .55 .30
**4318** A1189 7300 l multi 1.40 .70
**4319** A1189 17,000 l multi 3.25 1.60
*Nos. 4316-4319 (4)* 5.50 2.85

UPU, 125th Anniv. — A1215

**1999, Oct. 9**

**4320** A1215 3100 l multi .70 .35

Comic Actors — A1216

Designs: 900 l, Grigore Vasiliu Birlic. 1500 l, Toma Caragiu. 3100 l, Constantin Tanase. 7950 l, Charlie Chaplin. 8850 l, Oliver Hardy and Stan Laurel, horiz.

**1999, Oct. 21**

**4321** A1216 900 l blk & brn red .25 .25
**4322** A1216 1500 l blk & brn red .25 .25
**4323** A1216 3100 l blk & brn red .40 .35
**4324** A1216 7950 l blk & brn red 1.20 .95
**4325** A1216 8850 l blk & brn red 1.60 1.00
*Nos. 4321-4325 (5)* 3.70 2.80

Stavropoleos Church, 275th Anniv. — A1217

**1999, Oct. 29**

**4326** A1217 2100 l multi .50 .25

New Olympic Sports A1218

**1999, Nov. 10**

**4327** A1218 1600 l Snowboarding .25 .25
**4328** A1218 1700 l Softball .35 .25
**4329** A1218 7950 l Taekwondo 1.40 .70
*Nos. 4327-4329 (3)* 2.00 1.20

Christmas — A1219

Designs: 1500 l, Christmas tree, bell. 3100 l, Santa Claus.

**1999, Nov. 29 Photo. *Perf. 13¼***

**4330-4331** A1219 Set of 2 .80 .40

UN Rights of the Child Convention, 10th Anniv. — A1220

Children's art by: 900 l, A. Vieriu. 3400 l, A. M. Bulete, vert. 8850 l, M. L. Rogojeanu.

**1999, Nov. 30 Photo. *Perf. 13¼***

**4332** A1220 900 l multi .25 .25
**4333** A1220 3400 l multi .60 .30
**4334** A1220 8850 l multi 1.50 .75
*Nos. 4332-4334 (3)* 2.35 1.30

Princess Diana — A1221

**1999, Dec. 2**

**4335** A1221 6000 l multi 1.00 .60

Issued in sheets of 4. For surcharge, see No. 5992.

Ferrari Automobiles — A1222

Designs: 1500 l, 1968 365 GTB/4. 1600 l, 1970 Dino 246 GT. 1700 l, 1973 365 GT/4 BB. 7950 l, Mondial 3.2. 8850 l, 1994 F 355. 14,500 l, 1998 456M GT.

**1999, Dec. 17**

**4336** A1222 1500 l multi .25 .25
**4337** A1222 1600 l multi .30 .25
**4338** A1222 1700 l multi .30 .25
**4339** A1222 7950 l multi 1.40 .70
**4340** A1222 8850 l multi 1.50 .75
**4341** A1222 14,500 l multi 2.50 1.25
*Nos. 4336-4341 (6)* 6.25 3.45

Romanian Revolution, 10th Anniv. — A1223

**1999, Dec. 21 *Perf. 13¼***

**4342** A1223 2100 l multi .50 .25

Start of Accession Negotiations With European Union — A1224

**2000, Jan. 13 Photo. *Perf. 13¼***

**4343** A1224 6100 l multi 1.00 .50

Souvenir Sheet

Mihail Eminescu (1850-89), Poet — A1225

Scenes from poems and Eminescu: a, At R, clean-shaven. b, At R, with mustache. c, At L, with trimmed mustache. d, At L, with handlebar mustache.

**2000, Jan. 15**

**4344** A1225 Sheet of 4 4.75 1.10
*a.-d.* 3400 l Any single .55 .25

Valentine's Day — A1226

**2000, Feb. 1 Photo. *Perf. 13¼***

**4345** A1226 1500 l Cupid .25 .25
**4346** A1226 7950 l Couple kissing 1.25 .65

Easter — A1227

**2000, Feb. 29**

**4347** A1227 1700 l multi .35 .25

Nos. 4121, 4135 Surcharged in Red

**Methods and Perfs. as Before**

**2000**

**4348** A1167 1700 l on 70 l multi .35 .25
**4349** A1172 1700 l on 70 l multi .35 .25

Issued: No. 4348, 3/14; No. 4349, 3/13. Obliterator on No. 4349 is a crown.

Birds A1228

Designs: 1700 l, Paradisaea apoda. 2400 l, Diphyllodes magnificus. 9050 l, Lophorina superba. 10,050 l, Cicinnurus regius.

**2000, Mar. 20 Photo. *Perf. 13¼***

**4350** A1228 1700 l multi .25 .25
**4351** A1228 2400 l multi .35 .25
**4352** A1228 9050 l multi 1.40 .70
**4353** A1228 10,050 l multi 1.50 .75
*Nos. 4350-4353 (4)* 3.50 1.95

Nos. 3658-3659 Surcharged in Red

**Methods & Perfs. as Before**

**2000, Mar. 31**

| | | | | |
|---|---|---|---|---|
| **4354** | A1042 | 1900 l on 1 l (#3658) | .30 | .25 |
| **4355** | A1042 | 2000 l on 1 l (#3659) | .30 | .25 |

Nos. 3626-3630 Surcharged

**Methods & Perfs. as Before**

**2000, Apr. 12**

| | | | | |
|---|---|---|---|---|
| **4356** | A1034 | 1700 l on 50b | .30 | .30 |
| **4357** | A1034 | 1700 l on 1.50 l | .30 | .30 |
| **4358** | A1034 | 1700 l on 2 l | .30 | .30 |
| **4359** | A1034 | 1700 l on 3 l | .30 | .30 |
| **4360** | A1034 | 1700 l on 4 l | .30 | .30 |
| | | *Nos. 4356-4360 (5)* | 1.50 | 1.50 |

Appearance of obliterator varies.

Flowers — A1229

Designs: 1700 l, Senecio cruentus. 3100 l, Clivia miniata. 5800 l, Plumeria rubra. 10,050 l, Fuchsia hybrida.

**2000, Apr. 20** **Photo.** ***Perf. 13¼***

| | | | | |
|---|---|---|---|---|
| **4361** | A1229 | 1700 l multi | .25 | .25 |
| **4362** | A1229 | 3100 l multi | .40 | .25 |
| **4363** | A1229 | 5800 l multi | .80 | .40 |
| **4364** | A1229 | 10,050 l multi | 1.40 | .70 |
| | | *Nos. 4361-4364 (4)* | 2.85 | 1.60 |

**Nos. 3620-3624 Surcharged**

**Methods & Perfs. as Before**

**2000, Apr. 24**

| | | | | |
|---|---|---|---|---|
| **4365** | A1033 | 1700 l on 50b | .30 | .30 |
| **4366** | A1033 | 1700 l on 1.50 l | .30 | .30 |
| **4367** | A1033 | 1700 l on 2 l | .30 | .30 |
| **4368** | A1033 | 1700 l on 3 l | .30 | .30 |
| **4369** | A1033 | 1700 l on 4 l | .30 | .30 |
| | | *Nos. 4365-4369 (5)* | 1.50 | 1.50 |

**Europa Issue**

Common Design Type

**2000, May 9** **Photo.** ***Perf. 13¼***

| | | | | |
|---|---|---|---|---|
| **4370** | CD17 | 10,150 l multi | 2.50 | 1.25 |

**Nos. 3634, 3637 Surcharged in Red**

**Methods and Perfs as Before**

**2000, May 17**

| | | | | |
|---|---|---|---|---|
| **4371** | A1036 | 1700 l on 50b | .40 | .25 |
| **4372** | A1036 | 1700 l on 3.50 l | .40 | .25 |

Unification of Walachia, Transylvania and Moldavia by Michael the Brave, 400th Anniv. — A1230

**2000, May 19** **Photo.** ***Perf. 13¼***

| | | | | |
|---|---|---|---|---|
| **4373** | A1230 | 3800 l multi | .50 | .25 |

Printing of Bible in Latin by Johann Gutenberg, 550th Anniv. — A1231

**2000, May 19**

| | | | | |
|---|---|---|---|---|
| **4374** | A1231 | 9050 l multi | 1.25 | .60 |

**No. 4084 Surcharged in Red**

**2000, May 31** **Photo.** ***Perf. 13¼***

| | | | | |
|---|---|---|---|---|
| **4375** | A1154 | 10,000 l on 370 l | 1.40 | .70 |
| **4376** | A1154 | 19,000 l on 370 l | 2.50 | 1.25 |
| **4377** | A1154 | 34,000 l on 370 l | 4.75 | 2.40 |
| | | *Nos. 4375-4377 (3)* | 8.65 | 4.35 |

Souvenir Sheet

2000 European Soccer Championships — A1232

No. 4378: a, 3800 l, Romania vs. Portugal (red and green flag). b, 3800 l, England (red and white flag) vs. Romania. c, 10,150 l, Romania vs. Germany. d, 10,150 l, Goalie.

**2000, June 20**

| | | | | |
|---|---|---|---|---|
| **4378** | A1232 | Sheet of 4, #a-d | 3.75 | 1.90 |

First Zeppelin Flight, Cent. A1233

**2000, July 12**

| | | | | |
|---|---|---|---|---|
| **4379** | A1233 | 2100 l multi | .35 | .25 |

Stamp Day.

**20th Century Type of 1998**

2100 l, Enrico Fermi, formula, 1st nuclear reactor, 1942. 2200 l, Signing of UN Charter, 1945. 2400 l, Edith Piaf sings "La Vie en Rose," 1947. 6000 l, 1st ascent of Mt. Everest, by Sir Edmund Hillary and Tenzing Norgay, 1953.

**2000, July 12**

| | | | | |
|---|---|---|---|---|
| **4380-4383** | A1189 | Set of 4 | 1.60 | .80 |

No. 3680 Surcharged in Green

**Methods and Perfs as Before**

**2000, July 31**

| | | | | |
|---|---|---|---|---|
| **4384** | A1044 | 1700 l on 160 l | .30 | .25 |

**20th Century Type of 1998**

Designs: 1700 l, First artificial satellite, 1957. 3900 l, Yuri Gagarin, first man in space, 1961. 6400 l, First heart transplant perfromed by Christiaan Barnard, 1967. 11,300 l, Neil Armstrong, first man on the moon, 1969.

**2000, Aug. 28** **Photo.** ***Perf. 13¼***

| | | | | |
|---|---|---|---|---|
| **4385-4388** | A1189 | Set of 4 | 3.50 | 1.75 |

2000 Summer Olympics, Sydney A1234

Designs: 1700 l, Boxing. 2200 l, High jump. 3900 l, Weight lifting. 6200 l, Gymnastics.

**2000, Sept. 7**

| | | | | |
|---|---|---|---|---|
| **4389-4392** | A1234 | Set of 4 | 2.25 | 1.00 |

**Souvenir Sheet**

| | | | | |
|---|---|---|---|---|
| **4393** | A1234 | 11,300 l Runner | 1.40 | .70 |

No. 4393 contains one 42x54mm stamp.

Souvenir Sheet

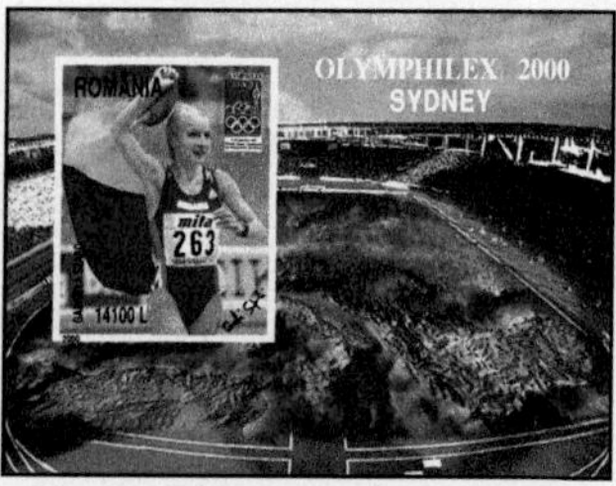


Olymphilex 2000, Sydney — A1235

**2000, Sept. 7** ***Imperf.***

| | | | | |
|---|---|---|---|---|
| **4394** | A1235 | 14,100 l Gabriela Szabo | 2.40 | .85 |

Bucharest Palaces A1236

Designs: 1700 l, Agricultural Ministry Palace, vert. 2200 l, Cantacuzino Palace. 2400 l, Grigore Ghica Palace. 3900 l, Stirbei Palace.

**2000, Sept. 29** ***Perf. 13¼***

| | | | | |
|---|---|---|---|---|
| **4395-4398** | A1236 | Set of 4 | 1.60 | .80 |

**No. 4115 Surcharged in Brown**

**2000, Oct. 11** **Photo.** ***Perf. 13½***

| | | | | |
|---|---|---|---|---|
| **4403** | A1166 | 300 l on 70 l multi | .25 | .25 |

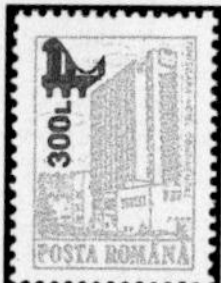


No. 3664 Surcharged in Blue

**2000, Oct. 26** ***Perf. 13½***

| | | | | |
|---|---|---|---|---|
| **4404** | A1043 | 300 l on 1 l blue | .35 | .25 |

**No. 3991 Surcharged in Red Violet**

**2000, Nov. 3** ***Perf. 13½***

| | | | | |
|---|---|---|---|---|
| **4405** | A1127 | 2000 l on 90 l multi | .35 | .25 |

European Human Rights Convention, 50th Anniv. — A1237

**2000, Nov. 3** *Perf. 13¼*
**4406** A1237 11,300 l multi 2.25 2.25

No. 3858 Surcharged

**2000, Nov. 28** *Perf. 13½*
**4407** A1093 2000 l on 29 l multi .60 .25

Endangered Wild Cats — A1238

Designs: 1200 l, Panthera pardus. 2000 l, Panthera uncia. 2200 l, Panthera leo. 2300 l, Lynx rufus. 4200 l, Puma concolor. 6500 l, Panthera tigris.
14,100 l, Panthera leo.

**2000, Nov. 29** **Photo.** *Perf. 13½*
**4408** A1238 1200 l multi .25 .25
**4409** A1238 2000 l multi .25 .25
**4410** A1238 2200 l multi .25 .25
**4411** A1238 2300 l multi .25 .25
**4412** A1238 4200 l multi .40 .25
**4413** A1238 6500 l multi 1.20 .25
*Nos. 4408-4413 (6)* 2.60 1.50

**Souvenir Sheet**

**4414** A1238 14,100 l multi 2.00 .60

No. 4414 contains one 54x42mm stamp.

Self-portraits A1239

Designs: 2000 l, Camil Ressu (1880-1962), 2400 l, Jean A. Steriadi (1880-1956). 4400 l, Nicolae Tonitza ( 1886-1940). 15,000 l, Nicolae Grigorescu (1838-1907).

**2000** **Photo.** *Perf. 13½*
**4415** A1239 2000 l multi .25 .25
**4416** A1239 2400 l multi .25 .25
**4417** A1239 4400 l multi .40 .25
**4418** A1239 15,000 l multi 2.00 .75
*Nos. 4415-4418 (4)* 2.90 1.50

Issued: 2000 l, 12/8; others, 12/13.

Christmas — A1240

**2000, Dec. 15** **Photo.** *Perf. 13½*
**4419** A1240 4400 l multi .35 .25

Christianity, 2000th Anniv. — A1241

Stained glass windows: 2000 l, Resurrection of Jesus. 7000 l, Holy Trinity (22x38mm).

**2000, Dec. 22** **Photo.** *Perf. 13¼*
**4420-4421** A1241 Set of 2 1.10 .40

No. 3922 Surcharged in Red Brown

**Wmk. 398**

**2000, Dec. 28** **Photo.** *Perf. 13¼*
**4422** A1105 7000 l on 3095 l multi 1.10 .30
**4423** A1105 10,000 l on 3095 l multi .75 .45
**4424** A1105 11,500 l on 3095 l multi 1.10 .55
*Nos. 4422-4424 (3)* 2.95 1.30

Obliterator on No. 4423 is a bear and on No. 4424 a bison.

Advent of the Third Millennium — A1242

*Perf. 13½*

**2001, Jan. 19** **Photo.** **Unwmk.**
**4425** A1242 11,500 l multi 1.90 .60

Sculptures by Constantin Brancusi (1876-1957) — A1243

No. 4426: a, 4600 l, b, 7200 l.

**2001, Feb. 2**
**4426** A1243 Horiz. pair, #a-b 1.50 .55

**No. 3844 Surcharged in Black or Red**

**Methods and Perfs as Before**

**2001, Feb. 9**
**4427** A1087 7400 l on 280 l multi .75 .35
**4428** A1087 13,000 l on 280 l multi (R) 1.25 .60

Obliterator on No. 4428 is snake on branch.

Valentine's Day — A1244

Designs: 2200 l, Heart of rope. 11,500 l, Rope running through heart.

**2001, Feb. 15** **Photo.** *Perf. 13½*
**4429-4430** A1244 Set of 2 1.50 .75

Nos. 3894, 3895, 3897 Surcharged in Brown or Green

**Methods and Perfs as Before**

**2001, Feb. 21**
**4431** A1101 1300 l on 245 l .25 .25
**4432** A1101 2200 l on 115 l .25 .25
**4433** A1101 5000 l on 115 l (G) .50 .25
**4434** A1101 16,500 l on 70 l 2.00 .75
*Nos. 4431-4434 (4)* 3.00 1.50

Appearance of obliterators differ. Obliterators on Nos 4432-4433 are ears of corn.

Famous People A1245

Designs: 1300 l, Hortensia Papadat-Bengescu (1876-1955), writer. 2200 l, Eugen Lovinescu (1881-1943), writer. 2400 l, Ion Minulescu (1881-1944), writer. 4600 l, André Malraux (1901-76), writer. 7200 l, George H. Gallup (1901-84), pollster. 35,000 l, Walt Disney (1901-66), film producer.

**2001** **Photo.** *Perf. 13¼*
**4435-4440** A1245 Set of 6 8.00 3.00

Issued: 2200 l, 4600 l, 7200 l, 3/9; others 3/15.

Easter — A1246

**2001, Mar. 23**
**4441** A1246 2200 l multi .35 .25

Fruit — A1247

Designs: 2200 l, Prunus spinosa. 4600 l, Ribes rubrum. 7400 l, Ribes uva-crispa. 11,500 l, Vaccinium vitis-idaea.

**2001, Apr. 12**
**4442-4445** A1247 Set of 4 3.00 1.25

Gheorge Hagi, Soccer Player — A1248

Designs: 2200 l, Wearing uniform. 35,000 l, Wearing team jacket.

**2001, Apr. 23** *Perf. 13¼*
**4446** A1248 2200 l multi .50 .25

**Souvenir Sheet**

***Imperf***

**Without Gum**

**4447** A1248 35,000 l multi 4.75 1.40

No. 4447 is airmail and contains one 43x28mm stamp.

Europa — A1249

**2001, May 4** *Perf. 13¼*
**4448** A1249 13,000 l multi 1.75 .85

Dogs A1250

Designs: 1300 l, Collie. 5000 l, Basset hound. 8000 l, Siberian husky. 13,500 l, Sheepdog.

**2001, June 16**
**4449-4452** A1250 Set of 4 2.75 1.40

Romanian Presidency of Organization for Security and Cooperation in Europe — A1251

**2001, July 6**
**4453** A1251 11,500 l multi 1.25 .45

Millennium — A1252

Events of the 20th Century: 1300 l, Mariner 9, 1971. 1500 l, Telephone pioneer Augustin Maior and circuit diagram, 1906. 2400 l, Discovery of cave drawings in Ardeche, France, 1994. 5000 l, First Olympic perfect score of gymnast Nadia Comaneci, 1976. 5300 l, Pioneer 10, 1972. 8000 l, Fall of the Iron Curtain, 1989. 13,500 l, First microprocessor, 1971. 15,500 l, Hubble Space Telescope, 1990.

**2001**
**4454-4461** A1252 Set of 8 5.50 2.75

Issued: 1300 l, 2400 l, 5000 l, 8000 l, 7/13; others, 9/25.

UN High Commissioner for Refugees, 50th Anniv. — A1253

**2001, July 26**
**4462** A1253 13,500 l multi 1.50 .60

Nos. 3688, 3713, 3790, 3791, 3865, 3870, 3900, 3907, 3972, 4007, 4017, 4025, 4057, 4058, and 4060 Surcharged in Black, Red, Green or Blue

**2001 Photo. *Perf. 13½***
**4463** A1048 300 l on 4 l #3688 .40 .25
**4464** A1058 300 l on 4 l #3713 (R) .40 .25
**4465** A1073 300 l on 7 l #3790 (R) .40 .25
**4466** A1073 300 l on 9 l #3791 (R) .40 .25
**4467** A1102 300 l on 90 l #3900 .40 .25
**4468** A1121 300 l on 90 l #3972 (G) .40 .25
**4469** A1132 300 l on 90 l #4007 .40 .25
**4470** A1130 300 l on 90 l #4017 .40 .25
**4471** A1137 300 l on 90 l #4025 (G) .40 .25
**4472** A1095 300 l on 115 l #3865 (R) .40 .25
**4473** A1096 300 l on 115 l #3870 (R) .40 .25
**4474** A1103 300 l on 115 l #3907 (R) .40 .25
**4475** A1131 2500 l on 715 l #4057 (R) .40 .25
**4476** A1131 2500 l on 755 l #4058 (Bl) .40 .25
**4477** A1131 2500 l on 1615 l #4060 .40 .25
*Nos. 4463-4477 (15)* 6.00 3.75

Numbers have been reserved for additional surcharges. Design and location of obliterators and new value varies.

Issued: No. 4472, 8/20; No. 4473, 8/24; Nos. 4467, 4469, 8/28; No. 4470, 8/29; Nos. 4463, 4464, 4465, 4466, Nos. 4468, 4471, 4474-4477, 8/31.

Equestrian Sports A1254

Designs: 1500 l, Harness racing. 2500 l, Dressage. 5300 l, Steeplechase. 8300 l, Racing.

**2001, Aug. 21 Photo. *Perf. 13¼***
**4478-4481** A1254 Set of 4 2.00 1.00

**No. 3883 Surcharged**

**2001, Aug. 29 Photo. *Perf. 13½***
**4482** A1099 300 l on 115 l multi .25 .25

Souvenir Sheets

Corals and Anemones — A1255

No. 4483: a, 2500 l, Porites porites. b, 8300 l, Condylactis gigantea. c, 13,500 l, Anemonia telia. 37,500 l, Gorgonia ventalina.

No. 4484: a, 9000 l, Corallium rubrum. b, 9000 l, Acropora palmata. c, 16,500 l, Actinia equina. d, 16,500 l, Metridium senile.

**2001-02 Sheets of 4, #a-d**
**4483-4484** A1255 Set of 2 10.50 5.25

Issued: No. 4483, 9/27/01; No. 4484, 1/30/02.

Year of Dialogue Among Civilizations A1256

**2001, Oct. 9**
**4485** A1256 8300 l multi .80 .40

Comic Strip A1257

No. 4486: a, Cat, bear, king. b, Fox with drum, cat. c, Fox plays drum for king. d, Cat gives drum to fox. e, Fox, exploding drum.

**2001, Oct. 31**
**4486** Horiz. strip of 5 7.00 3.50
*a.-e.* A1257 13,500 l Any single 1.40 .70

Christmas A1258

No. 4487: a, Ribbon extending from wreath. b, No ribbon extending from wreath.

**2001, Nov. 5**
**4487** A1258 2500 l Pair, #a-b .35 .25
Booklet, 5 #4487 2.00

Zodiac Signs A1259

Designs: No. 4488, 1500 l, Scorpio. No. 4489, 1500 l, Aries. No. 4490, 2500 l, Libra. No. 4491, 2500 l, Taurus. No. 4492, 5500 l, Capricorn. No. 4493, 5500 l, Gemini. 8700 l, Cancer. No. 4495, 9000 l, Pisces. No. 4496, 9000 l, Leo. 13,500 l, Aquarius. 16,500 l, Sagittarius. 23,500 l, Virgo.

**2001-02**
**4488-4499** A1259 Set of 12 10.00 5.00

Issued: Nos. 4488, 4490, 4492, 4495, 4497, 4498, 11/23/01; others 1/4/02.

Bucharest Post Office, Cent. — A1260

No. 4500: a, Building. b, Medal.

**2001, Dec. 18 Photo. *Perf. 13¼***
**4500** A1260 5500 l Horiz. pair, #a-b 1.20 .55

Emanuil Gojdu (1802-70), Promoter of Romanian Orthodox Church in Hungary A1261

**2002, Feb. 6**
**4501** A1261 2500 l multi .35 .25

Valentine's Day A1262

Designs: 5500 l, Mice. 43,500 l, Elephants.

**2002, Feb. 8**
**4502-4503** A1262 Set of 2 4.25 2.00

Famous Men A1263

Designs: 1500 l, Ion Mincu (1852-1912), architect. 2500 l, Costin D. Nenitescu (1902-70), chemist. 5500 l, Alexandre Dumas père (1802-70), writer. 9000 l, Serban Cioculescu (1902-88), writer. 16,500 l, Leonardo da Vinci (1452-1519), artist. 34,000 l, Victor Hugo (1802-85), writer.

**2002, Mar. 1**
**4504-4509** A1263 Set of 6 6.50 3.25

United We Stand — A1264

No. 4510: a, Statue of Liberty, US flag. b, Romanian flag.

**2002, Mar. 22**
**4510** A1264 25,500 l Horiz. pair, #a-b 5.00 3.25

German Fortresses in Romania — A1265

Designs: 1500 l, Saschiz, vert. 2500 l, Darjiu, vert. 6500 l, Viscri. 10,500 l, Vorumloc. 13,500 l, Calnic, vert. 17,500 l, Prejmer, vert.

**2002, Apr. 2**
**4511-4516** A1265 Set of 6 4.50 2.75

Easter — A1266

Designs: 2500 l, Crucifixion. 10,500 l, Resurrection.

**2002, Apr. 12 Photo. *Perf. 13¼***
**4517-4518** A1266 Set of 2 1.25 .55

Souvenir Sheet

Proclamation of Independence, 125th Anniv. — A1267

**2002, May 9**
**4519** A1267 25,500 l multi 2.50 1.75

Europa — A1268

Clown with: 17,500 l, Yellow hair. 25,500 l, Brown hair.

**2002, May 9**
**4520-4521** A1268 Set of 2 4.50 2.00

Souvenir Sheet

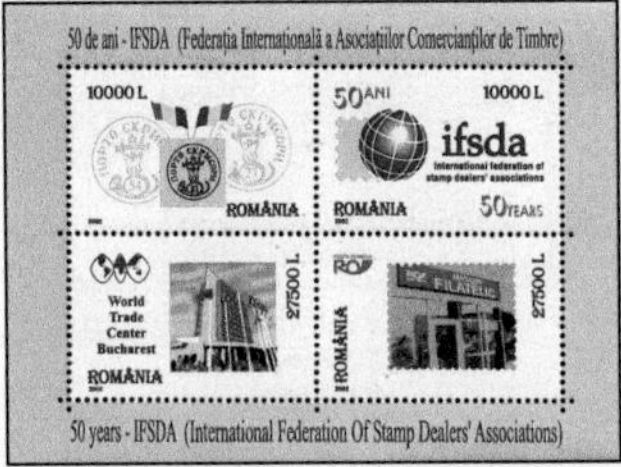

Intl. Federation of Stamp Dealers' Associations, 50th Anniv. — A1269

No. 4522: a, 10,000 l, Romanian flags, #1, 2 and 4. b, 10,000 l, IFSDA emblem. c, 27,500 l, World Trade Center, Bucharest. d, 27,500 l, Romanian philatelic store.

**2002, June 10**

**4522** A1269 Sheet of 4, #a-d 6.00 3.50

Intl. Year of Mountains A1270

**2002, June 14**

**4523** A1270 2000 l multi .30 .25

Intl. Year of Ecotourism A1271

**2002, June 14**

**4524** A1271 3000 l multi .40 .25

Sports A1272

Designs: 7000 l, Cricket. 11,000 l, Polo. 15,500 l, Golf. 19,500 l, Baseball.

**2002, July 11**

**4525-4528** A1272 Set of 4 4.50 2.25

Stamp Day — A1273

No. 4529: a, Ion Luca Caragiale (1852-1912), writer. b, National Theater, Bucharest, 150th anniv.

**2002, July 15**

**4529** A1273 10,000 l Horiz. pair, #a-b 1.75 .85

A1274

A1275

A1276

A1277

Postal Services A1278

**2002, Aug. 9**

| | | | | |
|---|---|---|---|---|
| **4530** | A1274 | 2000 l multi | .25 | .25 |
| **4531** | A1275 | 3000 l multi | .35 | .25 |
| **4532** | A1276 | 10,000 l multi | .85 | .40 |
| **4533** | A1277 | 15,500 l multi | 1.50 | .75 |
| **4534** | A1278 | 27,500 l multi | 2.25 | 1.10 |
| | | *Nos. 4530-4534 (5)* | 5.20 | 2.75 |

See Nos. 4543-4545.

Souvenir Sheet

Butterflies — A1279

No. 4535: a, Boloria pales carpathomeridionalis. b, Erebia pharte romaniae. c, Peridea korbi herculana. d, Tomares nogelli dobrogensis.

**2002, Sept. 2 Photo. *Perf. 13¼***

**4535** A1279 44,500 l Sheet of 4, #a-d 13.00 13.00

Locomotives — A1280

Designs: 4500 l, Series 50115, 1930. 6500 l, Series 50025, 1921. 7000 l, Series 230128, 1933. 11,000 l, Series 764493, 1956. 19,500 l, Series 142072, 1939. 44,500 l, Series 704209, 1909.

72,500 l, Locomotive #1, 1872, vert.

**2002, Sept. 22 Photo. *Perf. 13¼***

**4536-4541** A1280 Set of 6 6.75 3.75

**Souvenir Sheet**

**4542** A1280 72,500 l multi 5.25 3.25

No. 4542 contains one 54x41mm stamp.

A1281

A1282

Postal Services A1283

**2002, Oct. 1**

| | | | | |
|---|---|---|---|---|
| **4543** | A1281 | 8000 l multi | .60 | .35 |
| **4544** | A1282 | 13,000 l multi | .90 | .55 |
| **4545** | A1283 | 20,500 l multi | 1.50 | 1.00 |
| | | *Nos. 4543-4545 (3)* | 3.00 | 1.90 |

Souvenir Sheet

35th Chess Olympiad, Bled, Slovenia — A1284

No. 4546: a, Knight and bishop. b, Queen and knight. c, King and rook.

**2002, Oct. 23**

**4546** A1284 20,500 l Sheet of 3, #a-c 4.50 2.50

Fruit — A1285

Designs: 15,500 l, Cydonia oblonga. 20,500 l, Armeniaca vulgaris. 44,500 l, Cerasus vulgaris. 73,500 l, Morus nigra.

**2002, Nov. 11**

**4547-4550** A1285 Set of 4 12.00 6.00

Christmas A1286

Santa Claus and helper: 3000 l, With gifts. 15,500 l, At computers.

**2002, Nov. 19**

**4551-4552** A1286 Set of 2 1.40 .80

Invitation to Join NATO A1287

**Litho. With Hologram Applied**

**2002, Nov. 22 *Perf. 12¾***

**4553** A1287 131,000 l multi 10.00 10.00

Printed in sheets of 2 + central label. Value, $20.

Paintings — A1288

Designs: 4500 l, Portul Braila, by J.A. Steriadi. 6500 l, Balcic, by N. Darascu. 30,500 l, Conversatie, by N. Vermont. 34,000 l, Dalmatia, by N. Darascu. 46,500 l, Barci Pescaresti, by Steriadi. 53,000 l, Nude, by B. Pietris.

83,500 l, Femeie pe Malul Marii, by N. Grigorescu, vert.

**2003, Jan. 22 Photo. *Perf. 13¼***

**4554-4559** A1288 Set of 6 12.00 7.00

**Souvenir Sheet**

**4560** A1288 83,500 l multi 6.00 3.25

No. 4560 contains one 41x54mm stamp.

Natl. Military Palace, 80th Anniv. A1289

**2003, Jan. 28**

**4561** A1289 5000 l multi .60 .30

St. Valentine's Day A1290

Designs: 3000 l, Ladybug with heart-shaped spots. 5000 l, Man with ladder, vert.

**2003, Feb. 14**

**4562-4563** A1290 Set of 2 .80 .40

Admission to European Union, 10th Anniv. A1291

**2003, Feb. 20**

**4564** A1291 142,000 l multi 10.00 5.00

Famous Men — A1292

Designs: 6000 l, Ion Irimescu, sculptor, cent. of birth. 18,000 l, Hector Berlioz (1803-69), composer. 20,000 l, Vincent Van Gogh (1853-90), painter. 36,000 l, Dr. Georges de Bellio (1828-94), art collector.

**2003, Feb. 27**

**4565-4568** A1292 Set of 4 5.00 3.00

See also Nos. 4587-4590.

Buildings in Bucharest A1293

Designs: 4500 l, Postal Palace. 5500 l, Economics House. 10,000 l, National Bank of Romania, horiz. 15,500 l, Stock Exchange. 20,500 l, Carol I University. 46,500 l, Atheneum.
73,500 l, Palace of Justice.

**2003, Mar. 27 Photo. *Perf. 13¼***
**4569-4574** A1293 Set of 6 7.00 4.00

**Souvenir Sheet**

**4575** A1293 73,500 l multi 5.50 2.75

No. 4575 contains one 42x53mm stamp.

Natl. Map and Book Museum, Bucharest — A1294

No. 4576 — Map of Dacia by Petrus Kaerius: a, Northwestern Dacia. b, Northeastern Dacia. c, Southwestern Dacia. d, Southeastern Dacia.
46,500 l, Museum, vert.

**2003, Apr. 4 Photo. *Perf. 13¼***
**4576** A1294 30,500 l Sheet of 4, #a-d 9.00 4.50

**Souvenir Sheet**

**4577** A1294 46,500 l multi 4.00 2.00

No. 4577 contains one 42x54mm stamp.

Easter — A1295

**2003, Apr. 10**
**4578** A1295 3000 l multi .35 .25

Owls — A1296

Designs: 5000 l, Otus scops. 8000 l, Strix uralensis. 10,000 l, Glaucidium passerinum. 13,000 l, Asio flammeus. 15,500 l, Asio otus. 20,500 l, Aegolius funereus.

**2003, Apr. 25**
**4579-4584** A1296 Set of 6 4.75 2.75

Europa A1297

Poster art: 20,500 l, Butterfly emerging from chrysalis. 73,500 l, Man holding framed picture.

**2003, May 9**
**4585-4586** A1297 Set of 2 5.75 5.75

**Famous Men Type of 2003**

Designs: 4500 l, Dumitru Staniloae (1903-93), theologian. 8000 l, Alexandru Ciucurecu (1903-77), painter. 30,500 l, Ilarie Voronca (1903-46), writer. 46,500 l, Victor Brauner (1903-66), painter.

**2003, June 6 Photo. *Perf. 13¼***
**4587-4590** A1292 Set of 4 5.75 3.25

Paintings by Victor Brauner — A1298

No. 4591 — Unidentified paintings: a, Two dragons in foreground. b, White and black arcs (20x30mm). c, Spheres at left. d, Landscape with house with red roof in center. e, Abstract with fish head (20x30mm). f, Landscape with white clouds at left and right. g, Mountain with rings. h, Line drawing of man (20x30mm). i, Fire-breathing dragon. j, Man standing (20x30mm).

**2003, June 24**
**4591** A1298 10,000 l Sheet, #a-i, 3 #j 10.00 5.00

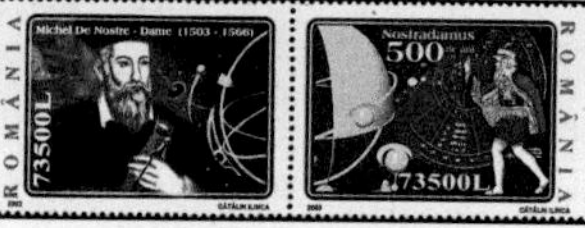


Nostradamus (1503-66), Astrologer — A1299

No. 4592: a, Nostradamus, denomination at left. b, Astrological chart, denomination at bottom.

**2003, July 2**
**4592** A1299 73,500 l Horiz. pair, #a-b 9.00 5.00

Stamp Day A1300

**2003, July 15**
**4593** A1300 5000 l multi .40 .25

**Souvenir Sheets**

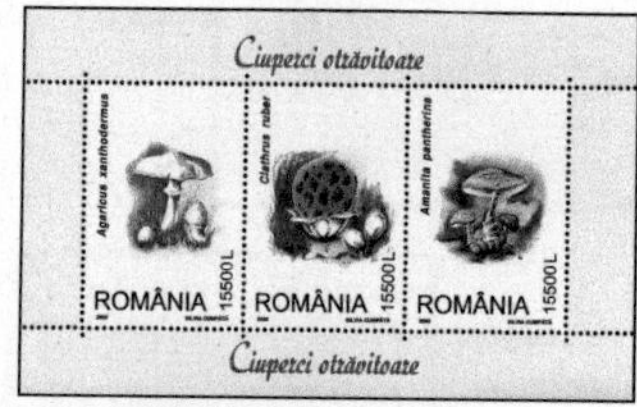


Mushrooms — A1301

No. 4594, 15,500 l: a, Agaricus xanthodermus. b, Clathrus ruber. c, Amanita pantherina.
No. 4595, 20,500 l: a, Leccinum aurantiacum. b, Laetiporus sulphureus. c, Russula xerampelina.

**2003, Sept. 19 Sheets of 3, #a-c**
**4594-4595** A1301 Set of 2 7.50 3.75

Extreme Sports A1302

Designs: 5000 l, Skydiving, vert. 8000 l, Windsurfing. 10,000 l, Motorcycle racing. 30,500 l, Skiing, vert.

**2003, Sept. 30**
**4596-4599** A1302 Set of 4 3.50 1.75

Reptiles and Amphibians — A1303

No. 4600: a, Lacerta viridis. b, Hyla arborea. c, Ablepharus kitaibelii stepanekii. d, Rana temporaria.

**2003, Oct. 28**
**4600** A1303 18,000 l Sheet of 4, #a-d 6.50 3.25

Musical Instruments — A1304

Designs: 1000 l, Lute (cobza). 4000 l, Horn (bucium). 6000 l, Fiddle with horn (vioara cu goarna).

**2003, Oct. 31**
**4601-4603** A1304 Set of 3 .80 .40

Granting of Dobruja Region to Romania, 125th Anniv. — A1305

**2003, Nov. 11**
**4604** A1305 16,000 l multi 1.10 .55

Pope John Paul II and Patriarch Teoctist — A1306

No. 4605: a, Holding crosses. b, Embracing.

**2003, Nov. 29**
**4605** Horiz. pair with 2 central labels 2.00 1.25
***a.-b.*** A1306 16,000 l Either single 1.00 .60

Pontificate of Pope John Paul II, 25th anniv.

Christmas — A1307

No. 4606: a, Santa Claus. b, Snowman.

**2003, Dec. 5**
**4606** A1307 4000 l Horiz. pair, #a-b .50 .25

Women's Fashions in the 20th Century — A1308

No. 4607, 4000 l: a, 1921-30. b, 1931-40.
No. 4608, 21,000 l: a, 1901-10. b, 1911-20.

**2003, Dec. 13**
**Horiz. Pairs, #a-b, + Label**
**4607-4608** A1308 Set of 2 5.50 2.75

FIFA (Fédération Internationale de Football Association), Cent. (in 2004) — A1309

Designs: 3000 l, Women soccer players. 4000 l, Soccer players, television camera. 6000 l, Men, FIFA charter. 10,000 l, Players, equipment. 34,000 l, Rule book, field diagram.

**2003, Dec. 22 Photo. *Perf. 13¼***
**4609-4613** A1309 Set of 5 3.50 1.75

Miniature Sheet

Birds — A1310

No. 4614 — UPU emblem and: a, Ardea cinerea. b, Anas platyrhynchos. c, Podiceps cristatus. d, Pelecanus onocrotalus.

**2004, Jan. 23 Photo. *Perf. 13¼***
**4614** A1310 16,000 l Sheet of 4, #a-d 4.75 2.10

Miniature Sheet

Information Technology — A1311

No. 4615 — UPU emblem and: a, Earth, satellite, compact disc. b, Computer screen showing computer user. c, Earth, satellite dish. d, Computer keyboard, diskette.

**2004, Jan. 26**
**4615** A1311 20,000 l Sheet of 4, #a-d 5.00 2.50

Amerigo Vespucci (1454-1512), Explorer — A1312

Designs: 16,000 l, Vespucci. 31,000 l, Ship.

**2004, Jan. 31**
**4616-4617** A1312 Set of 2 3.00 1.50

St. Valentine's Day — A1313

**2004, Feb. 10**
**4618** A1313 21,000 l multi 1.40 .70

23rd UPU Congress, Bucharest — A1314

No. 4619: a, UPU emblem. b, Congress emblem.

**2004, Feb. 20**
**4619** A1314 31,000 l Horiz. pair, #a-b 4.00 2.00

Easter — A1315

**2004, Mar.5**
**4620** A1315 4000 l multi .35 .25

High Speed Trains A1316

UPU Congress emblem and: 4000 l, Bullet Train, Japan. 6000 l, TGV, France. 10,000 l, KTX, South Korea. 16,000 l, AVE, Spain. 47,000 l, ICE, Germany. 56,000 l, Eurostar, Europe.
77,000 l, Sageata Albastra, Romania.

**2004, Mar. 11**
**4621-4626** A1316 Set of 6 9.00 4.50

**Souvenir Sheet**

**4627** A1316 77,000 l multi 5.00 2.50

No. 4627 contains one 54x42mm stamp.

Admission to NATO — A1317

**2004, Mar. 24**
**4628** A1317 4000 l multi *2.00 1.00*

**Women's Fashions Type of 2003**

No. 4629, 5000 l: a, 1941-50. b, 1951-60.
No. 4630, 21,000 l: a, 1981-90. b, 1991-2000.
No. 4631, 31,000 l: a, 1961-70. b, 1971-80.

**2004, Mar. 31**
**Horiz. Pairs, #a-b + Label**
**4629-4631** A1308 Set of 3 8.00 4.00

Intl. Council for Game and Wildlife Conservation, 51st General Assembly A1318

No. 4632 — Emblem and: a, Hunter. b, Dog and pheasant. c, Buck. d, Mountain goat. e, Bear.
No. 4633, Buck, horiz.

**2004, Apr. 24**
**4632** Horiz. strip of 5 5.75 2.75
*a.-e.* A1318 16,000 l Any single 1.10 .55

**Souvenir Sheet**

**4633** A1318 16,000 l multi 1.10 .55

No. 4633 contains one 54x42mm stamp.

Europa A1319

Stylized sun and: 21,000 l, Beach. 77,000 l, Mountains.

**2004, May 7 Photo. *Perf. 13¼***
**4634-4635** A1319 Set of 2 6.50 3.25

Michael the Brave (1558-1601), Prince of Walachia — A1320

**2004, May 14**
**4636** A1320 3000 l multi .25 .25

National Philatelic and Romanian History Museum — A1321

**2004, May 21**
**4637** A1321 4000 l multi .30 .25

Souvenir Sheet

Dracula — A1322

No. 4638: a, Bram Stoker, author of Dracula. b, Dracula and cross. c, Dracula and woman. d, Dracula in coffin.

**2004, May 21**
**4638** A1322 31,000 l Sheet of 4, #a-d 8.50 4.25

23rd UPU Congress, Bucharest. Exists imperf.

Famous People A1323

Designs: 4000 l, Anghel Saligny (1854-1925), civil engineer. 16,000 l, Gheorghe D. Anghel (1904-66), sculptor. 21,000 l, George Sand (1804-76), author. 31,000 l, Oscar Wilde (1854-1900), writer.

**2004, May 27**
**4639-4642** A1323 Set of 4 5.00 2.25

Romanian Athenaeum — A1324

**2004, May 28**
**4643** A1324 10,000 l multi .60 .30

Johnny Weissmuller (1904-84), Olympic Swimming Gold Medalist, Actor — A1325

**2004, June 2 Photo. *Perf. 13¼***
**4644** A1325 21,000 l multi 1.40 .70

TAROM Airlines, 50th Anniv. A1326

**2004, June 7**
**4645** A1326 16,000 l multi 1.10 .55

FIFA (Fédération Internationale de Football Association), Cent. — A1327

**2004, June 15**
**4646** A1327 31,000 l multi 2.10 1.00

Miniature Sheets

Stephen the Great (1437-1504), Prince of Moldavia — A1328

No. 4647, 10,000 l: a, Portrait of Stephen the Great, Dobrovat-Iasi Monastery Church. b, Sucevei Fortress. c, Portrait of Stephen the Great, Putna Monastery.
No. 4648, 16,000 l: a, Putna Monastery. b, Stephen the Great. c, Neamtului Fortress.

**2004, June 16**
**Sheets of 3, #a-c**
**4647-4648** A1328 Set of 2 5.00 2.50

Famous Men A1329

Designs: 2000 l, Alexandru Macedonski (1854-1920), writer. 3000 l, Victor Babes (1854-1926), bacteriologist. 6000 l, Arthur Rimbaud (1854-91), writer. 56,000 l, Salvador Dali (1904-89), painter.

**2004, June 30**
**4649-4652** A1329 Set of 4 5.00 2.25

Flight of Zeppelin LZ-127 Over Brasov, 75th Anniv. A1330

**2004, July 29**

**4653** A1330 31,000 l multi 2.10 1.00

Savings Banks, 140th Anniv. A1331

**2004, July 30**

**4654** A1331 5000 l multi .35 .25

Fire Fighters — A1332

No. 4655: a, Fire fighters leaving truck. b, Fire fighters in protective suits.

**Horiz. pair, #a-b, + flanking label**

**2004, Aug. 12**

**4655** A1332 12,000 l multi 1.50 .75

2004 Summer Olympics, Athens — A1333

Designs: 7000 l, Rowing. 12,000 l, Fencing. 21,000 l, Swimming. 31,000 l+9000 l, Gymnastics.

**2004, Aug. 20 Litho. *Perf. 13¼***

**4656-4659** A1333 Set of 4 5.50 2.75

Olymphilex Philatelic Exhibition (#4659).

23rd UPU Congress, Bucharest A1334

Stamps commemorating UPU Congresses: 8000 l, Romania #4619b. 10,000 l, Switzerland #590. 19,000 l, South Korea #1794, horiz. 31,000 l, People's Republic of China #2868. 47,000 l, United States #2434, horiz. 77,000 l, Brazil #1629.

**2004, Sept. 10**

**4660-4665** A1334 Set of 6 12.50 6.25

Sculptures by Idel Ianchelevici (1909-94) A1335

Designs: 21,000 l, L'appel. 31,000 l, Perennis Perdurat Poeta.

**2004, Sept. 20**

**4666-4667** A1335 Set of 2 3.00 1.50

Each stamp printed in sheets of 8 + 2 labels. See Belgium Nos. 2036-2037.

Chinese and Romanian Handicrafts — A1336

No. 4668: a, Drum with tigers and birds, China. b, Cucuteni pottery jar, Romania.

**2004, Sept. 24**

**4668** A1336 5000 l Pair, #a-b .70 .35

See People's Republic of China Nos. 3390-3391.

Souvenir Sheet

23rd UPU Congress, Bucharest — A1337

No. 4669: a, Gerardus Mercator and Jodocus Hondius, cartographers. b, UPU emblem. c, Amerigo Vespucci (1454-1512), explorer.

**2004, Oct. 5 *Perf. 13½***

**4669** A1337 118,000 l Sheet of 3, #a-c 24.00 12.00

For surcharge see No. 4755.

Details From Trajan's Column, Rome A1338

Various details: 7000 l, 12,000 l, 19,000 l, 21,000 l, 31,000 l, 56,000 l, 145,000 l.

**2004 *Perf. 13¼***

**4670-4676** A1338 Set of 7 20.00 10.00

Issued: 7000 l, 12,000 l, 19,000 l, 56,000 l, 10/15; others, 12/4.

Roses — A1339

Designs: 8000 l, Simfonia. 15,000 l, Foc de Tabara. 25,000 l, Golden Elegance. 36,000 l, Doamna in Mov.

**2004, Oct. 25**

**4677-4680** A1339 Set of 4 6.00 3.00

*4680a* Souvenir sheet, #4677-4680 6.00 3.00

Ilie Nastase, Tennis Player — A1340

**2004, Nov. 16 *Perf. 13¼***

**4681** A1340 10,000 l multi .75 .35

**Souvenir Sheets**

***Perf. 13¼x13¾***

**4682** A1340 72,000 l Nastase, diff. 5.25 2.60

***Imperf***

**4683** A1340 72,000 l Like No. 4682 5.25 2.60

No. 4682 contains one 42x51mm stamp. No. 4683 contains one 37x48mm stamp.

Christmas — A1341

**2004, Nov. 27 *Perf. 13¼***

**4684** A1341 5000 l multi .40 .25

Organizations A1342

Prince Dimitrie Cantemir (1673-1723), Writer — A1343

Designs: 12,000 l, Romanian Boy Scouts. 16,000 l, Lions International. 19,000 l, Red Cross and Red Crescent.

**2004, Dec. 8 *Perf. 13¼***

**4685-4687** A1342 Set of 3 3.25 1.60

**Souvenir Sheet**

***Perf. 13¼x13¾***

**4688** A1343 87,000 l multi 6.00 3.00

Olympic Gold Medalists A1344

Designs: 5000 l, Iolanda Balas, high jump. 33,000 l, Elisabeta Lipa, rowing. 77,000 l, Ivan Pazaichin, canoeing.

**2004, Dec. 15 *Perf. 13¼***

**4689-4691** A1344 Set of 3 7.00 4.50

Values are for stamps with surrounding selvage.

Souvenir Sheets

Modern Paintings — A1345

No. 4692, 7000 l: a, Tristan Tzara, by M. H. Maxy. b, Baroness, by Merica Ramniceanu. c, Portrait of a Woman, by Jean David.

No. 4693, 12,000 l: a, Composition, by Marcel Iancu. b, Femele Care Viseaza, by Victor Brauner. c, Composition, by Hans Mattis-Teutsch.

**2004, Dec. 16 Litho.**

**Sheets of 3, #a-c**

**4692-4693** A1345 Set of 2 4.25 2.10

Famous People — A1346

Designs: 15,000 l, Gen. Gheorghe Magheru (1804-80), politician. 25,000 l, Christian Dior (1905-57), fashion designer. 35,000 l, Henry Fonda (1905-82), actor. 72,000 l, Greta Garbo (1905-90), actress. 77,000 l, George Valentin Bibescu (1880-1941), first president of Romanian Auto Club.

**2005, Jan. 20 Litho. *Perf. 13¼***

**4694-4698** A1346 Set of 5 15.50 7.75

See Nos. 4722-4726.

Rotary International, Cent. A1347

**2005, Feb. 23**

**4699** A1347 21,000 l multi 1.60 .80

Printed in sheets of 4.

Pottery — A1348

Pottery from: 3000 l, Oboga, Olt. 5000 l, Sacel, Maramures. 7000 l, Romana, Olt. 8000 l, Vadul Crisului, Bihor. 10,000 l, Tara Barsei, Brasov. 12,000 l, Horezu, Valcea. 16,000 l, Corund, Harghita.

**2005 Litho. *Perf. 13¼***

**Pottery Actual Color; Background Color:**

| | | | | | |
|---|---|---|---|---|---|
| **4700** | A1348 | 3000 l | lilac | .25 | .25 |
| **4701** | A1348 | 5000 l | lt blue | .45 | .25 |
| **4702** | A1348 | 7000 l | lt green | .55 | .25 |
| **4703** | A1348 | 8000 l | rose brn | .70 | .35 |
| **4704** | A1348 | 10,000 l | orange | .80 | .40 |

**4705** A1348 12,000 l green 1.00 .50
**4706** A1348 16,000 l lt brown 1.40 .70
*Nos. 4700-4706 (7)* 5.15 2.70

Issued: 3000 l, 5000 l, 12,000 l, 16,000 l, 2/24. 7000 l, 8000 l, 10,000 l, 3/24.

See Nos. 4767-4775, 4804-4811, 4844-4847.

Dinosaurs — A1349

Designs: 21,000 l, Elopteryx nopcsai. 31,000 l, Telmatosaurus transsylvanicus. 35,000 l, Struthiosaurus transilvanicus. 47,000 l, Hatzegopteryx thambema.

**2005, Feb. 25 Litho. *Perf. 13¼***
**4707-4710** A1349 Set of 4 10.00 5.00
*4710a* Souvenir sheet, #4707-4710, + 2 labels 10.00 5.00

Fish — A1350

Designs: 21,000 l, Carassius auratus. 31,000 l, Symphysodon discus. 36,000 l, Labidochromis. 47,000 l, Betta splendens.

**2005, Mar. 1 Stamp + Label**
**4711-4714** A1350 Set of 4 10.00 5.00
*4714a* Souvenir sheet, #4711-4714, + 4 labels 10.00 5.00

Jules Verne (1828-1905), Writer — A1351

Scenes from stories: 19,000 l, The Castle in the Carpathians. 21,000 l, The Danube Pilot. 47,000 l, Claudius Bombarnac. 56,000 l, Keraban, the Inflexible.

**2005, Mar. 29 Litho. *Perf. 13¼***
**4715-4718** A1351 Set of 4 10.50 5.25
*4718a* Souvenir sheet, #4715-4718, + 2 labels 10.50 5.25

Easter — A1352

No. 4719: a, Last Supper. b, Crucifixion (30mm diameter). c, Resurrection.

**2005, Apr. 1**
**4719** A1352 Horiz. strip of 3 1.50 .55
***a.-c.*** 5000 l Any single .40 .25

Pope John Paul II (1920-2005) — A1353

Pope John Paul II and: 5000 l, Dove, map of Romania. 21,000 l, St. Peter's Basilica.

**2005, Apr. 8 Litho. *Perf. 13¼***
**4720-4721** A1353 Set of 2 2.10 1.00
*4721a* Souvenir sheet, 2 each #4720-4721 4.50 2.25

**Famous People Type of 2005**

Designs: 3000 l, Hans Christian Andersen (1805-75), author. 5000 l, Jules Verne (1828-1905), writer. 12,000 l, Albert Einstein (1879-1955), physicist. 21,000 l, Dimitrie Gusti (1880-1955), sociologist. 22,000 l, George Enescu (1881-1955), composer.

**2005, Apr. 18**
**4722-4726** A1346 Set of 5 4.75 2.40

Romanian Accession to European Union — A1354

No. 4727: a, Map in gold. b, Map in silver.

**2005, Apr. 25**
**4727** A1354 Pair .80 .40
***a.-b.*** 5000 l Either single .40 .25
***c.*** Souvenir sheet, 2 each #4727a-4727b 1.75 .85

**Pair of No. 3921 Surcharged in Red and Silver**

No. 4728 — "Sprijin Pentru Semeni": a, In box. b, Reading up at left.

**Wmk. 398**
**2005, May 9 Photo. *Perf. 13¼***
**4728** A1105 Horiz. pair .80 .40
***a.-b.*** 5000 l on 1440 l Either single .40 .25

Nos. 4728a-4728b also have face values expressed in revalued leu currency that was used as of July 1.

Europa — A1355

Designs: 21,000 l, Map of Dacia, archer on horseback, duck and stew pot. 77,000 l, Map, hunting dog, roasted game bird, vegetables, glass of wine.

***Perf. 13¼***
**2005, May 9 Litho. Unwmk.**
**4729-4730** A1355 Set of 2 6.75 3.25
*4730a* Souvenir sheet, 2 each #4729-4730, #4729 at UL 13.50 6.75
*4730b* As "a," #4730 at UL 13.50 6.75

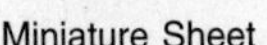

Miniature Sheet

Viticulture — A1356

No. 4731: a, Feteasca alba. b, Grasa de Cotnari. c, Fetesaca neagra. d, Victoria.

**2005, May 27**
**4731** A1356 21,000 l Sheet of 4, #a-d, + 2 labels 6.50 3.25

Nos. 4731a-4731d also have face values expressed in revalued leu currency that was used as of July 1.

Scouting A1357

Designs: No. 4732, 22,000 l, Scout climbing rocks. No. 4733, 22,000 l, Scout following marked trail. No. 4734, 22,000 l, Scouts building campfire. No. 4735, 22,000 l, Scouts reading map.

**2005, June 15**
**4732-4735** A1357 Set of 4 6.00 3.00
*4735a* Horiz. strip of 4, #4732-4735 6.00 3.00
*4735b* Souvenir sheet of 4, #4732-4735 6.00 3.00

Nos. 4732-4735 also have face values expressed in revalued leu currency that was used as of July 1.

July 1 Currency Devaluation — A1358

National Bank of Romania, new and old coins or banknotes depicting revaluation of: 30b, 100 old lei to 1 new ban. 50b, 10,000 old lei to 1 new leu. 70b, 500 old lei to 5 new bani. 80b, 50,000 old lei to 5 new lei. 1 l, 100,000 old lei to 10 new lei. 1.20 l, 500,000 old lei to 50 new lei. 1.60 l, 1,000,000 old lei to 100 new lei. 2.10 l, 1000 old lei to 10 new bani. 2.20 l, 5,000,000 old lei to 500 new lei. 3.10 l, 5000 old lei to 50 new bani.

In the pairs, the "a" stamp has the colored denomination panel on the left and shows the obverse of coins at left and reverse of coins at right, or the obverse side of banknotes. The "b" stamp has the panel on the right, shows the reverse of coins at left and obverse of coins at right, or the reverse side of banknotes.

**2005, July 1 Litho.**
**Horiz. or Vert. Pairs, #a-b**
**Panel Color**

**4736** A1358 30b gray .40 .25
**4737** A1358 50b emerald .70 .35
**4738** A1358 70b blue .95 .45
**4739** A1358 80b red brown 1.10 .55
**4740** A1358 1 l red violet 1.40 .70
**4741** A1358 1.20 l dull brown 1.60 .80
**4742** A1358 1.60 l olive green 2.25 1.10
**4743** A1358 2.10 l blue green 2.75 1.40
**4744** A1358 2.20 l bister 3.00 1.50
**4745** A1358 3.10 l purple 4.25 2.10
***c.*** Miniature sheet of 10 horiz. pairs, #4736-4745 18.50 9.25

Military Ships — A1359

No. 4746: a, Training ship Constanta. b, Corvette Contraadmiral Horia Macellariu. c, Monitor ship Mihail Kogalniceanu. d, Frigate Marasesti.

**2005, July 15 *Perf. 13¼***
**4746** Vert. strip of 4 6.00 3.00
***a.-d.*** A1359 2.20 l Any single 1.50 .75
***e.*** Souvenir sheet of 4, #4746a-4746d 6.00 3.00

Stamp Day.

Rainbow and Genesis 1:9 — A1360

**2005, Aug. 2**
**4747** A1360 50b multi + label .45 .25

July 2005 floods in Romania.

Election of Joseph Cardinal Ratzinger as Pope Benedict XVI — A1361

Ratzinger in vestments of: 1.20 l, Cardinal. 2.10 l, Pope.

**2005, Aug. 18**
**4748-4749** A1361 Set of 2 2.75 1.40
*4749a* Souvenir sheet, #4748-4749 2.75 1.40

European Philatelic Cooperation, 50th Anniv. (in 2006) — A1362

No. 4750 — Christopher Columbus and: a, Denomination to right of face. b, Ship, denomination at lower right. c, Ship, denomination at lower left. d, Denomination to left of face.

**2005, Aug. 22 *Perf. 13¼***
**4750** A1362 Horiz. strip of 4 13.50 6.75
***a.-d.*** 4.70 l Any single 3.25 1.60
***e.*** Souvenir sheet, #4750a-4750d +2 labels 13.50 6.75

Europa stamps, 50th anniv. (in 2006). The vignettes of Nos. 4750a and 4750d are inside a 31x27mm perf. 13 hexagon. Values for singles of these stamps are for examples with surrounding selvage.

No. 4750 exists imperf.

Children's Art — A1363

Designs: 30b, Forest Mailman, by Bianca Paul. 40b, The Road to You, by Daniel Ciornei. 60b, A Messenger of Peace, by Stefan Ghiliman, horiz. 1 l, Good News for Everybody, by Adina Elena Mocanu, horiz.

**2005, Aug. 31 Litho. *Perf. 13¼***
**4751-4754** A1363 Set of 4 1.75 .85

### No. 4669 Surcharged in Black and Blue

No. 4755: a, Gerardus Mercator and Jodocus Hondius, cartographers. b, UPU emblem. c, Amerigo Vespucci, explorer.

**2005, Sept. 26** ***Perf. 13½***

**4755** A1337 11.80 l on 118,000 25.00 25.00

Visit of members of European Philatelic Academy to Bucharest.

Dogs — A1364

No. 4756: a, Jagd terrier. b, Rhodesian ridgeback. c, Munsterlander. d, Bloodhound. e, Transylvanian hound (Copoi ardelenesc). f, Pointer.

**2005, Sept. 28** ***Perf. 13¼***

**4756** A1364 Block of 6 10.50 5.25
*a.-f.* 2.20 l Any single 1.75 .85
*g.* Sheet, #4756a-4756f 10.50 5.25

Natl. Philatelic Museum, 1st Anniv. — A1365

**2005, Sept. 30**

**4757** A1365 40b multi .40 .25

World Summit on the Information Society, Tunis — A1366

**2005, Oct. 10**

**4758** A1366 5.60 l multi 4.75 2.25

United Nations — A1367

Dove, UN emblem, Romanian flag and: 40b, Flags. 1.50 l, Security Council. 2.20 l, General Assembly building.

**2005, Oct. 24**

**4759-4761** A1367 Set of 3 3.50 1.75
*4761a* Souvenir sheet, #4759-4761 3.50 1.75

Romania's admission to UN, 50th anniv. (#4759); Romania's presidency of Security Council, 2004-05 (#4760); UN, 60th anniv. (#4761).

Birthplace of Dimitrie Butculescu, Romanian Philatelic Federation Emblem — A1368

Dimitrie Butculescu, Founder of Romanian Philatelic Society — A1369

Design: No. 4762b, Butculescu, September 1892 edition of Romanian Philatelic Society Monitor.

**2005, Nov. 4** ***Perf. 13¼***

**4762** Horiz. pair with flanking labels .85 .40
*a.-b.* A1368 50b Either single + label .40 .25

### Souvenir Sheet

***Imperf***

**4763** A1369 9 l multi 7.50 3.75

Central University Library, 110th Anniv. — A1370

No. 4764: a, Library building (47x32mm). b, Statue (23x32mm).

**2005, Nov. 10** ***Perf. 13¼***

**4764** A1370 60b Horiz. pair, #a-b 1.00 .50
*c.* Souvenir sheet, #4764a-4764b 1.00 .50

### Souvenir Sheet

Pigeon Breeds — A1371

No. 4765: a, English Pouter (green frame). b, Parlor rollers (lilac frame). c, Standard carrier (green frame). d, Andalusian (yellow orange frame).

**2005, Nov. 18** **Litho.**

**4765** A1371 2.50 l Sheet of 4, #a-d 8.25 4.00

UNESCO, 60th Anniv. — A1372

**2005, Nov. 21**

**4766** A1372 60b multi + label 1.25 .60

### Pottery Type of 2005

Pottery from: 30b, Leheceni, Bihor. 50b, Vladesti, Valcea. 1 l, Curtea de Arges, Arges. 1.20 l, Vamu, Satu Mare. 2.20 l, Barsa, Arad. 2.50 l, Corund, Harghita. 4.70 l, Targu Neamt, Neamt. 5.60 l, Polana Deleni, Iasi. 14.50 l, Valea Izei, Maramures.

**2005** ***Perf. 13¼***

### Pottery Actual Color; Background Color:

| | | | | |
|---|---|---|---|---|
| **4767** | A1348 | 30b greenish yel | .25 | .25 |
| **4768** | A1348 | 50b blue green | .40 | .25 |
| **4769** | A1348 | 1 l red orange | .85 | .40 |
| **4770** | A1348 | 1.20 l pale salmon | 1.00 | .50 |
| **4771** | A1348 | 2.20 l gray | 1.75 | .85 |
| **4772** | A1348 | 2.50 l pink | 2.10 | 1.00 |
| **4773** | A1348 | 4.70 l blue violet | 4.00 | 2.00 |
| **4774** | A1348 | 5.60 l red | 4.75 | 2.25 |
| **4775** | A1348 | 14.50 l lt bl grn | 12.00 | 6.00 |
| | | *Nos. 4767-4775 (9)* | 27.10 | 13.50 |

Issued: 4.70 l, 5.60 l, 12/19; others, 11/24.

Christmas — A1373

No. 4776: a, The Annunciation (23x32mm). b, Nativity (47x32mm). c, Madonna and Child with Angels (23x32mm).

**2005, Dec. 2**

**4776** A1373 50b Horiz. strip of 3, #a-c 1.00 .50

Modern Art — A1374

No. 4777: a, Inscriptions, by Virgil Preda. b, The Suspended Garden, by Alin Gheorghiu. c, Still Life with Bottle, by Constantin Ceraceanu. d, Monster 1, by Cristian Paleologu.

**2005, Dec. 12**

**4777** A1374 1.50 l Block of 4, #a-d 5.00 2.50

Cats A1375

Designs: 30b, Norwegian Forest. 50b, Turkish Van. 70b, Siamese. 80b, Ragdoll. 1.20 l, Persian. 1.60 l, Birman.

**2006, Jan. 20** ***Perf. 13¼***

**4778-4783** A1375 Set of 6 4.25 2.10
*4783a* Souvenir sheet, #4778-4783, imperf. 4.25 2.10

Famous People — A1376

Designs: 50b, Wolfgang Amadeus Mozart (1756-91), composer. 1.20 l, Ion C. Bratianu (1821-91), Prime Minister. 2.10 l, Grigore Moisil (1906-73), mathematician.

**2006, Jan. 27** ***Perf. 13¼***

**4784-4786** A1376 Set of 3 3.25 1.60

See Nos. 4825-4827.

### Souvenir Sheet

2006 Winter Olympics, Turin — A1377

No. 4787: a, Figure skating. b, Downhill skiing. c, Bobsled. d, Biathlon.

**2006, Feb. 1**

**4787** A1377 1.60 l Sheet of 4, #a-d 5.50 2.75

Gold Coins — A1378

Coin obverse and reverse: 30b, 1868 20 lei. 50b, 1906 50 lei. 70b, 1906 100 lei. 1 l, 1922 50 lei. 1.20 l, 1939 100 lei. 2.20 l, 1940 100 lei.

**2006, Feb. 22**

**4788-4793** A1378 Set of 6 5.00 2.50
*4788a* Sheet of 7 + 2 labels 1.75 .85
*4789a* Sheet of 7 + 2 labels 3.00 1.50
*4790a* Sheet of 7 + 2 labels 4.00 2.00
*4791a* Sheet of 7 + 2 labels 6.00 3.00
*4792a* Sheet of 7 + 2 labels 7.00 3.50
*4793a* Sheet of 7 + 2 labels 13.00 6.50

A1379

A1380

A1381

A1382

Easter A1383

**2006, Mar. 15 Litho. *Perf. 13¼***

| | | | |
|---|---|---|---|
| **4794** A1379 50b multi | | .40 | .25 |
| **4795** A1380 50b multi | | .40 | .25 |
| **4796** A1381 50b multi | | .40 | .25 |
| **4797** A1382 50b multi | | .40 | .25 |
| **4798** A1383 50b multi | | .40 | .25 |
| *a.* | Souvenir sheet, #4794-4798, + 4 labels, with red labels at UL and LR | 2.00 | 1.00 |
| *b.* | As "a," with red labels at UR and LL | 2.00 | 1.00 |
| | Complete booklet, 4 each #4794-4798 | 8.00 | |
| | *Nos. 4794-4798 (5)* | 2.00 | 1.25 |

First Flight of Traian Vuia, Cent. — A1384

Outline drawings of aircraft and: 70b, Traian Vuia. 80b, Vuia I aircraft. 1.60 l, Vuia II aircraft. 4.70 l, Vuia in airplane, vert.

**2006, Mar. 18 *Perf. 13¼***

| | | | |
|---|---|---|---|
| **4799-4801** A1384 Set of 3 | | 2.50 | 1.25 |
| *4799a* | Sheet of 8 + label | 4.75 | 2.40 |
| *4800a* | Sheet of 8 + label | 5.50 | 2.75 |
| *4801a* | Souvenir sheet, #4799-4801 + label | 2.50 | 1.25 |
| *4801b* | Sheet of 8 + label | 11.00 | 5.50 |

**Souvenir Sheet**

***Perf. 13¼x14***

**4802** A1384 4.70 l multi 4.00 2.00

No. 4802 contains one 42x52mm stamp.

Léopold Sédar Senghor (1906-2001), First President of Senegal — A1385

**2006, Mar. 20 *Perf. 13¼***

| | | | |
|---|---|---|---|
| **4803** A1385 2.10 l multi | | 1.75 | .85 |
| *a.* | Souvenir sheet of 4 | 7.00 | 3.50 |

**Pottery Type of 2005**

Pottery from: 30b, Oboga, Olt. 40b, Radauti, Suceava. 60b, Poienita, Arges. 70b, Oboga, Olt, diff. 80b, Oboga, Olt, diff. 1.60 l, Romana, Olt. 2.50 l, Vladesti, Valcea. 3.10 l, Jupanesti, Timis.

**2006 *Perf. 13¼***

**Pottery Actual Color; Background Color:**

| | | | |
|---|---|---|---|
| **4804** A1348 30b lilac | | .25 | .25 |
| *a.* | Sheet of 9 | 2.25 | 1.10 |
| **4805** A1348 40b yellow | | .35 | .25 |
| *a.* | Sheet of 9 | 3.25 | 1.60 |
| **4806** A1348 60b pale salmon | | .50 | .25 |
| *a.* | Sheet of 9 | 4.50 | 2.25 |
| **4807** A1348 70b bister | | .60 | .30 |
| *a.* | Sheet of 9 | 5.50 | 2.75 |
| **4808** A1348 80b gray blue | | .70 | .35 |
| *a.* | Sheet of 9 | 6.25 | 3.00 |
| **4809** A1348 1.60 l gray | | 1.25 | .60 |
| *a.* | Sheet of 9 | 11.50 | 5.75 |
| **4810** A1348 2.50 l light green | | 2.10 | 1.00 |
| *a.* | Sheet of 9 | 19.00 | 9.50 |
| **4811** A1348 3.10 l light blue | | 2.50 | 1.25 |
| *a.* | Sheet of 9 | 22.50 | 11.00 |
| | *Nos. 4804-4811 (8)* | 8.25 | 4.25 |

Issued: 60b, 70b, 80b, 1.60 l, 3/30; others 4/20.

Tulip Varieties — A1386

Designs: 30b, Turkestanica. 50b, Ice Follies. 1 l, Cardinal. 1.50 l, Yellow Empress, horiz. (47x32mm). 2.10 l, Donna Bella. 3.60 l, Don Quixote, horiz. (47x32mm).

**2006, Apr. 14 Litho. *Perf. 13¼***

| | | | |
|---|---|---|---|
| **4812-4817** A1386 Set of 6 | | 7.50 | 3.75 |
| *a.* | Block of 6, #4812-4817 | 7.50 | 3.75 |
| *b.* | Souvenir sheet of 6, #4812-4817 | 7.50 | 3.75 |
| *c.* | Miniature sheet, 2 each #4812-4817 | 15.00 | 7.50 |

Europa — A1387

Children's drawings: 2.10 l, Children, house, sun. 3.10 l, People, house, fence.

**2006, May 4**

| | | | |
|---|---|---|---|
| **4818-4819** A1387 Set of 2 | | 4.50 | 2.25 |
| *4819a* | Souvenir sheet, 2 each #4818-4819, #4818 at UL | 9.00 | 4.50 |
| *4819b* | Souvenir sheet, 2 each #4818-4819, #4819 at UL | 9.00 | 4.50 |

Romanian Stamps Depicting Royalty A1388

Crown and: 30b, Prince Carol I (#29). 1 l, King Ferdinand I (#248). 2.10 l, King Carol II (#376). 2.50 l, King Michael (#513).
4.70 l, Carol I as Prince and King (#180), horiz.

**2006, May 8**

| | | | |
|---|---|---|---|
| **4820-4823** A1388 Set of 4 | | 5.00 | 2.50 |
| *4823a* | Miniature sheet, #4820-4823 | 5.00 | 2.50 |

**Souvenir Sheet**

***Perf. 14x13¼***

**4824** A1388 4.70 l multi 4.00 2.00

Foundation of Romanian royal dynasty, 140th anniv., Proclamation of Romanian kingdom, 125th anniv. No. 4824 contains one 51x41mm stamp.

**Famous People Type of 2006**

Designs: 50b, Christopher Columbus (1451-1506), explorer. 1 l, Paul Cézanne (1839-1906), painter. 1.20 l, Henrik Ibsen (1828-1906), writer.

**2006, May 17 *Perf. 13¼***

**4825-4827** A1376 Set of 3 2.25 1.10

Dimitrie Gusti National Village Museum, 70th Anniv. A1389

**2006, May 17**

| | | | |
|---|---|---|---|
| **4828** A1389 2.20 l multi | | 1.90 | .95 |
| *a.* | Sheet of 8 + central label | 13.00 | 6.50 |

**No. 4092 Surcharged in Gold or Silver**

**2006, May 19 *Perf. 13½***

| | | |
|---|---|---|
| **4829** A1155 2.10 l on 2720 l #4092 (G) | 1.75 | .85 |
| **4830** A1155 2.10 l on 2720 l #4092 (S) | 1.75 | .85 |

First Romanian in space, 25th anniv.

1906 General Exhibition and Carol I Park, Bucharest, Cent. — A1390

Designs: 30b, Main entrance to Carol I Park. 50b, Tepes Castle. 1 l, Post Office Pavilion. 1.20 l, European Danube Commission Pavilion. 1.60 l, Industry Palace. No. 4836, 2.20 l, Roman arenas.
No. 4837, Arts Palace.

**2006, June 6 *Perf. 13¼***

| | | | |
|---|---|---|---|
| **4831-4836** A1390 Set of 6 | | 5.75 | 2.75 |
| *4836a* | Miniature sheet, #4831-4836 | 5.75 | 2.75 |

**Souvenir Sheet**

***Perf. 14x13¼***

**4837** A1390 2.20 l multi 1.90 .95

No. 4837 contains one 51x41mm stamp.

Composers — A1391

No. 4838: a, Béla Bartók (1881-1945) and Hungarian flag. b, George Enescu (1881-1955) and Romanian flag.

**2006, June 8 *Perf. 13¼***

| | | | |
|---|---|---|---|
| **4838** A1391 1.20 l Horiz. pair, #a-b | | 2.00 | 1.00 |
| *c.* | Souvenir sheet, #4838 | 2.00 | 1.00 |
| *d.* | Sheet of 6 pairs | 10.50 | 5.25 |

The stamps on No. 4838d are arranged so that the stamps in the middle of the sheet are tete-beche pairs of the same stamp. No. 4838d exists with two arrangements of the stamps, one with No. 4838a as the stamps in the middle of the sheet, the other with No. 4838b as the stamps in the middle of the sheet.

2006 World Cup Soccer Championships, Germany — A1392

Designs: 30b, World Cup. 50b, Ball in goal. 1 l, Player dribbling ball. 1.20 l, Player lifting World Cup.

**2006, June 9**

| | | | |
|---|---|---|---|
| **4839-4842** A1392 Set of 4 | | 2.50 | 1.25 |
| *4842a* | Souvenir sheet, #4839-4842 | 2.50 | 1.25 |

Intl. Day Against Drug Abuse and Illegal Trafficking — A1393

**2006, June 26**

**4843** A1393 2.20 l multi 1.90 .95

**Pottery Type of 2005**

Pottery from: 30b, Golesti, Arges. 70b, Romana, Olt. 1 l, Oboga, Olt. 2.20 l, Vama, Satu Mare.

**2006, July 10 *Perf. 13¼***

**Pottery Actual Color; Background Color:**

| | | | |
|---|---|---|---|
| **4844** A1348 30b tan | | .25 | .25 |
| *a.* | Sheet of 9 | 2.25 | 1.10 |
| **4845** A1348 70b yel orange | | .60 | .30 |
| *a.* | Sheet of 9 | 5.50 | 2.75 |
| **4846** A1348 1 l green | | .85 | .40 |
| *a.* | Sheet of 9 | 7.75 | 3.75 |
| **4847** A1348 2.20 l blue green | | 1.90 | .95 |
| *a.* | Sheet of 9 | 17.00 | 8.50 |
| | *Nos. 4844-4847 (4)* | 3.60 | 1.90 |

Decebalus (d. 106), Dacian King — A1394

Map and: 30b, Coins and Decebalus. 50b, Head of Decebalus. 1.20 l, Dacian helmet. 3.10 l, Decebalus, diff.

**2006, July 15**

| | | | |
|---|---|---|---|
| **4848-4851** A1394 Set of 4 | | 4.25 | 2.10 |
| *4851a* | Souvenir sheet, #4848-4851 | 4.25 | 2.10 |

Stamp Day.

Minerals — A1395

Designs: 30b, Fluorite. 50b, Quartz. 1 l, Agate. 1.20 l, Blende. 1.50 l, Amethyst. 2.20 l, Stibnite.

**2006, Aug. 7**

| | | | |
|---|---|---|---|
| **4852-4857** A1395 Set of 6 | | 5.50 | 2.75 |
| *4857a* | Souvenir sheet, #4852-4857 | 5.50 | 2.75 |

Nos. 4852-4857 were each printed in sheets of 18 + 3 labels.

Bats — A1396

Designs: 30b, Myotis myotis. 50b, Rhinolophus hipposideros. 1 l, Plecotus auritus. 1.20 l, Pipistrellus pipistrellus. 1.60 l, Nyctalus lasiopterus. 2.20 l, Barbastella barbastellus.

**2006, Aug. 15**

**4858-4863** A1396 Set of 6 5.50 2.75
*4863a* Souvenir sheet, #4858-4863 5.50 2.75

Railroads in Romania, 150th Anniv. — A1397

Locomotives: 30b, StEG111 Wartberg, 1854. 50b, D. B. S. R. 1 Ovidiu, 1860. 1 l, L. C. J. E. 56 Curierulu, 1869. 1.20 l, C. F. R. 1 Berlad, 1869. 1.50 l, B. M. 1 Unirea, 1877. 1.60 l, Fulger and King Carol I Pullman Express, 1933.
2.20 l, StEG 500 Steyerdorf.

**2006, Aug. 23**

**4864-4869** A1397 Set of 6 5.00 2.50

**Souvenir Sheet**

**4870** A1397 2.20 l multi 1.90 .95

No. 4870 contains one 71x32mm stamp.

EFIRO 2008 World Philatelic Exhibition, Bucharest A1398

Exhibition emblem and: 30b, Romania #1. 50b, Romania #2. 1.20 l, Romania #4. 1.60 l, Romania #3.
2.20 l, Bull and vignette of Romania #1.

**2006, Aug. 30**

**4871-4874** A1398 Set of 4 4.00 2.00

**Souvenir Sheet**

***Perf. 13¼x14***

**4875** A1398 2.20 l multi 1.90 .95

No. 4875 contains one 41x51mm stamp. Nos. 4871-4874 were each printed in sheets of 16 + 8 labels.

National Lottery, Cent. A1399

**2006, Sept. 14** ***Perf. 13¼***

**4876** A1399 1 l multi .85 .40

Printed in sheets of 27 + 1 label.

**No. 4098 Surcharged in Gold**

**2006, Sept. 16** **Litho.** ***Perf. 13½***

**4877** A1159 5.60 l on 4050 l #4098 4.75 2.25

Sculptures by Constantin Brancusi (1876-1957) — A1400

Designs: 2.10 l, Sleeping Muse. 3.10 l, Sleep.

**2006, Sept. 25** ***Perf. 13¼***

**4878-4879** A1400 Set of 2 4.50 2.25
*4878a* Sheet of 12 18.00 9.00
*4879a* Souvenir sheet, #4878-4879 4.50 2.25
*4879b* Sheet of 12 27.00 13.50

The third stamp down in the middle column of Nos. 4870a and 4879b is inverted in relation to the other stamps in the sheet.
See France Nos. 3245-3246.

11th Francophone Summit, Bucharest A1401

**2006, Sept. 28** ***Perf. 13¼***

**4880** A1401 1.20 l multi 1.00 .50

**Souvenir Sheet**

***Perf. 13¼x14***

**4881** A1401 5.60 l multi 4.75 2.25

No. 4881 contains one 41x51mm stamp.

Romanian Peasant Museum, Cent. — A1402

Designs: 40b, Headdress, 20th cent. 70b, Turkish belt, 19th cent. 1.60 l, Coin necklace, 19th cent. 3.10 l, Musuem founder Alexandru Tzgara-Samurcas.

**2006, Oct. 5** ***Perf. 13¼***

**4882-4885** A1402 Set of 4 5.00 2.50

Souvenir Sheet

Romanian Division of Intl. Police Association, 10th Anniv. — A1403

**2006, Oct. 7**

**4886** A1403 8.70 l multi 7.25 3.50

Worldwide Fund for Nature (WWF) — A1404

Platalea leucorodia: No. 4887, 80b, Adult and chicks at nest. No. 4888, 80b, Birds in flight. No. 4889, 80b, Birds at water. No. 4890, 80b, Two birds.

**2006, Oct. 20**

**4887-4890** A1404 Set of 4 3.25 2.25
*4890a* Souvenir sheet, #4887-4890 3.25 3.25

Nos. 4887-4890 each were printed in sheets of 10 + 2 labels.

Romanian Orders — A1405

Designs: 30b, Order of Loyal Service. 80b, Order of Romanian Star. 2.20 l, Order of Merit. 2.50 l, First Class Order of Merit in Sports.

**2006, Oct. 30** ***Perf. 13¼x14***

**4891-4894** A1405 Set of 4 5.00 2.50

A small star-shaped hole was punched into Nos. 4891-4894.

Actors and Actresses A1406

Designs: 40b, Radu Beligan. 1 l, Carmen Stanescu. 1.50 l, Dina Cocea. 2.20 l, Colea Rautu.

**2006, Nov. 15** ***Perf. 13¼***

**4895-4898** A1406 Set of 4 4.25 2.10

Christmas A1407

Designs: No. 4899, 50b, Madonna and Child (shown). No. 4900, 50b, Adoration of the Magi. No. 4901, 50b, Madonna and Child enthroned with angels.

**2006, Nov. 17**

**4899-4901** A1407 Set of 3 1.25 .60
*4901a* Sheet of 9, 3 each #4899-4901 3.75 1.90

Art by Ciprian Paleologu — A1408

Designs: 30b, Ad Perpetuam Rei Memoriam. 1.50 l, Cui Bono? 3.60 l, Usqve Ad Finem.

**2006, Nov. 30**

**4902-4904** A1408 Set of 3 4.50 2.25

2007 Admission of Romania and Bulgaria into European Union — A1409

Designs: 50b, "EU" in colors of Bulgarian and Romanian flags. 2.10 l, Flags of Bulgaria and Romania, map of Europe, European Union ballot box.

**2006, Nov. 26** **Litho.** ***Perf. 13¼***

**4905-4906** A1409 Set of 2 2.00 1.00
*4906a* Sheet of 8, 4 each #4905-4906, + label 8.00 4.00

See Bulgaria Nos. 4412-4413.

**Currency Devaluation Type of 2005**

1,000,000 old lei bank notes and 200 lei note: 50b, Obverses of notes. 1.20 l, Reverses of notes.

**2006, Dec. 1** **Litho.** ***Perf. 13¼***

**4907-4908** A1358 Set of 2 1.40 .70
*4908a* Sheet of 16, 8 each #4907-4908 11.50 5.75

UNICEF, 60th Anniv. — A1410

**2006, Dec. 11**

**4909** A1410 3.10 l multi 2.50 1.25

Admission into European Union — A1411

**2007, Jan. 3** **Litho.** ***Perf. 13¼***

**4910** A1411 2.20 l multi + label 1.75 .85
*a.* Sheet of 8 + 8 labels 14.00 7.00

Biospeleology, Cent. — A1412

Designs: 40b, Altar Rock Cave. 1.60 l, Emil Racovita (1868-1947), founder of Biospeleology Institute. 7.20 l, Ursus spelaeus. 8.70 l, Typhlocirolana moraguesi.

**2007, Jan. 19**

**4911-4914** A1412 Set of 4 14.00 7.00
*4914a* Souvenir sheet, #4911-4914 14.00 7.00

Intl. Holocaust Remembrance Day — A1413

**2007, Jan. 27**

**4915** A1413 3.30 l multi 2.60 1.40

Printed in sheets of 32 + 4 labels.

Black Sea Fauna A1414

Designs: 70b, Hypocampus hypocampus. 1.50 l, Delphinus delphis. 3.10 l, Caretta caretta. 7.70 l, Trigla lucerna.

**2007, Feb. 9**

**4916-4919** A1414 Set of 4 10.50 5.25
*4919a* Souvenir sheet, #4916-4919 10.50 5.25

Famous People — A1415

Designs: 60b, Gustave Eiffel (1832-1923), engineer. 80b, Maria Cutarida (1857-1919), physician. 2.10 l, Virginia Woolf (1882-1941), writer. 3.50 l, Nicolae Titulescu (1882-1941), politician.

**2007, Feb. 23**

**4920-4923** A1415 Set of 4 5.50 2.75

Easter — A1416

No. 4924: a, Decorated Easter egg, Olt (30mm diameter). b, Detail from painted glass icon. c, Decorated Easter egg, Bucovina (30mm diameter).

**2007, Mar. 9**

**4924** A1416 50b Horiz. strip of 3, #a-c 1.25 .60
*d.* Miniature sheet, 3 each #4924a-4924c 3.75 1.90

Orchids A1417

Designs: 30b, Cephalanthera rubra. 1.20 l, Epipactis palustris. 1.60 l, Dactylorhiza maculata. 2.50 l, Anacamptis pyramidalis. 2.70 l, Limodorum abortivum. 6 l, Ophrys scolopax.

**2007, Mar. 23**

**4925-4930** A1417 Set of 6 11.50 5.75
*a.* Souvenir sheet, #4925-4930 11.50 5.75

Nos. 4925-4930 each were printed in sheets of 21. The right column of stamps in each sheet have 3 perforation holes separating the stamp from the right selvage, which promotes the 2008 Efiro Intl. Philatelic Exhibition, Bucharest.

Peasant Plates — A1418

Plates from: 70b, Oboga, Olt. 1 l, Varna, Satu Mare. 2.10 l, Valea Izei, Maramures. 2.20 l, Fagaras, Brasov.

**2007, Apr. 13**

**4931** A1418 70b blue & multi .60 .30
*a.* Miniature sheet of 6 3.75 1.90
**4932** A1418 1 l fawn & multi .85 .40
*a.* Miniature sheet of 6 5.25 2.60
**4933** A1418 2.10 l lt grn & multi 1.75 .85
*a.* Miniature sheet of 6 10.50 5.25
**4934** A1418 2.20 l yel & multi 1.90 .95
*a.* Miniature sheet of 6 11.50 5.75
*Nos. 4931-4934 (4)* 5.10 2.50

See Nos. 4950-4957.

Birds of Prey — A1419

Designs: 50b, Accipiter nisus. 80b, Circus aeruginosus. 1.60 l, Aquila pomarina. 2.50 l, Buteo buteo. 3.10 l, Athene noctua. 4.70 l, Falco subbuteo.

**2007, Apr. 19 Litho. *Perf. 13¼***

**4935-4939** A1419 Set of 5 7.00 3.50

**Souvenir Sheet**

***Perf. 13¼x14***

**4940** A1419 4.70 l multi 4.00 2.00

No. 4940 contains one 42x52mm stamp.

Europa A1420

Designs: 2.10 l, Scouts. 7.70 l, Lord Robert Baden-Powell.

**2007, May 3 Litho. *Perf. 13¼***

**4941-4942** A1420 Set of 2 8.00 4.00
*4942a* Souvenir sheet, 2 each #4941-4942, #4941 at UL 16.00 8.00
*4942b* As "a," #4942 at UL 16.00 8.00

Scouting, cent. Nos. 4941-4942 each printed in sheets of 6.

Old Bucharest — A1421

Designs: 30b, Vlad Tepes, Old Court, document mentioning Bucharest for first time. 50b, Sturdza Palace and arms. 70b, National Military Circle building and arms. 1.60 l, National Theater, Prince Alexandru Ioan Cuza. 3.10 l, I. C. Bratianu Square, King Carol I. 4.70 l, Senate Square and arms.
5.60 l, Romanian Athenaeum.

**2007, May 15 *Perf. 13¼***

**4943-4948** A1421 Set of 6 9.00 4.50
*4948a* Miniature sheet, #4943-4948, + 3 labels 9.00 4.50

**Souvenir Sheet**

***Perf. 14x13¼***

**4949** A1421 5.60 l multi 4.75 2.40

No. 4949 contains one 42x42mm stamp

**Peasant Plates Type of 2007**

Plates from: 60b, Tirgu Lapus, Maramures. 70b, Vladesti, Valcea. No. 4952, 80b, Vistea, Brasov. No. 4953, 80b, Luncavita, Tulcea. 1.10 l, Horezu, Valcea. No. 4955, 1.60 l, Tansa, Iasi. No. 4956, 1.60 l, Radauti, Suceava. 3.10 l, Romana, Olt.

**2007 *Perf. 13¼***

**4950** A1418 60b gray & multi .50 .25
*a.* Miniature sheet of 6 3.00 1.50
**4951** A1418 70b bl grn & multi .60 .30
*a.* Miniature sheet of 6 3.75 1.90
**4952** A1418 80b org & multi .65 .35
*a.* Miniature sheet of 6 4.00 2.00
**4953** A1418 80b pink & multi .70 .35
*a.* Miniature sheet of 6 4.25 2.10
**4954** A1418 1.10 l gray & multi .95 .45
*a.* Miniature sheet of 6 5.75 2.75
**4955** A1418 1.60 l grn & multi 1.40 .70
*a.* Miniature sheet of 6 8.50 4.25
**4956** A1418 1.60 l yel org & multi 1.40 .70
*a.* Miniature sheet of 6 8.50 4.25
**4957** A1418 3.10 l pink & multi 2.60 1.25
*a.* Miniature sheet of 6 16.00 8.00
*Nos. 4950-4957 (8)* 8.80 4.35

Issued: Nos. 4950, 4953, 4954, 4956, 8/3; Nos. 4951, 4952, 4955, 4957, 6/5.

Steaua Sports Club, 60th Anniv. — A1422

**2007, June 7**

**4958** A1422 7.70 l multi 6.50 3.25

Printed in sheets of 8 + label.

Romanian Savings Bank Building, 110th Anniv. — A1423

Various views of building with frame color of: 4.70 l, Brown. 5.60 l, Olive green.

**2007, June 8**

**4959** A1423 4.70 l multi 4.00 2.00

**Souvenir Sheet**

**4960** A1423 5.60 l multi + label 4.75 2.40

No. 4959 printed in sheets of 12 with one stamp tete-beche in relation to others.

Sibiu, 2007 European Cultural Capital — A1424

Designs: 30b, Altemberger House, knights from church altar, Dupus. 50b, Liars' Bridge and Council Tower, 18th cent. Transylvanian Saxons. 60b, Parochial Evangelical Church, painting of the Crucifixion. 70b, Grand Square, 1780, 18th cent. peasants. 2.10 l, Brukenthal Palace, statue of St. Nepomuk, portrait of Samuel von Brukenthal. 5.60 l, Sibiu, 1790, Cisnadie Gate Tower.
4.70 l, Sibiu Fortress.

**2007, June 11 *Perf. 13¼***

**4961-4966** A1424 Set of 6 8.50 4.25
*4966a* Miniature sheet, #4961-4966, + 3 labels 8.50 4.25

**Souvenir Sheet**

***Perf. 14x13¼***

**4967** A1424 4.70 l multi 4.25 2.10

No. 4967 contains one 52x42mm stamp.

Ducks and Geese — A1425

Designs: 40b, Anser erythropus. 60b, Branta ruficollis. 1.60 l, Anas acuta. 2.10 l, Anser albifrons. 3.60 l, Netta rufina. 4.70 l, Anas querquedula.
5.60 l, Anas clypeata.

**2007, July 12 *Perf. 13¼***

**4968-4973** A1425 Set of 6 11.50 5.75
*4973a* Miniature sheet, #4968-4973 11.50 5.75

**Souvenir Sheet**

***Imperf***

**4974** A1425 5.60 l multi 5.00 2.50

Nos. 4968-4973 each printed in sheets of 10 + 5 labels. No. 4974 contains one 52x42mm stamp.

Bistra Resort Local Postage Stamps, Cent. — A1426

Designs: 50b, Carriage, Upper Colony cabins, 6 heller stamp. 2.10 l, Lower Colony cabins, postman, 2 heller stamp.

**2007, July 18 *Perf. 13¼***

**4975-4976** A1426 Set of 2 2.25 1.10

Teoctist (1915-2007), Patriarch of Romanian Orthodox Church A1427

**2007, Aug. 3 Litho.**

**4977** A1427 80b multi .70 .35

Printed in sheets of 4 + 2 labels.

Pottery Baskets, Cups and Pitchers — A1428

Designs: 1.40 l, Basket, Horezu, Valcea. 1.80 l, Cup, Baia Mare, Maramures. 2.10 l, Pitcher, Transylvania. 2.90 l, Cup, Oboga, Olt. 3.10 l, Pitcher, Horezu, Valcea. 7.20 l, Cup, Obarsa, Hunedoara. 7.10 l, Cup, Baia Mare, Maramures, diff. 8.70 l, Cup, Baia Mare, Maramures, diff.

**2007** ***Perf. 13¼***

| | | | |
|---|---|---|---|
| **4978** | A1428 1.40 l gray & multi | 1.25 | .60 |
| *a.* | Miniature sheet of 4 | 5.00 | 2.50 |
| **4979** | A1428 1.80 l pink & multi | 1.60 | .80 |
| *a.* | Miniature sheet of 4 | 6.50 | 3.25 |
| **4980** | A1428 2.10 l blue & multi | 1.75 | .90 |
| *a.* | Miniature sheet of 4 | 7.00 | 3.75 |
| **4981** | A1428 2.90 l bis & multi | 2.50 | 1.25 |
| *a.* | Miniature sheet of 4 | 10.00 | 5.00 |
| **4982** | A1428 3.10 l lilac & multi | 2.60 | 1.25 |
| *a.* | Miniature sheet of 4 | 10.50 | 5.00 |
| **4983** | A1428 7.20 l yel & multi | 6.00 | 3.00 |
| *a.* | Miniature sheet of 4 | 24.00 | 12.00 |
| **4984** | A1428 7.70 l gray grn & multi | 6.75 | 3.50 |
| *a.* | Miniature sheet of 4 | 27.00 | 14.00 |
| **4985** | A1428 8.70 l lt grn & multi | 7.50 | 3.75 |
| *a.* | Miniature sheet of 4 | 30.00 | 15.00 |
| | *Nos. 4978-4985 (8)* | 29.95 | 15.05 |

Issued: Nos. 4978, 4979, 4981, 4984, 8/10. Nos. 4980, 4982, 4983, 4985, 11/7.

See Nos. 5027-5030.

EFIRO 2008 World Philatelic Exhibition, Bucharest — A1429

EFIRO emblem and: 1.10 l, Romania #8. 2.10 l, Romania #9. 3.30 l, Romania #10. 5.60 l, Star, bull's head and post horn.

**2007, Aug. 17** **Litho.** ***Perf. 13¼***

**Stamp + Label**

**4986-4988** A1429 Set of 3 5.50 2.75

**Souvenir Sheet**

***Perf. 13¼x13¾***

**4989** A1429 5.60 l multi 4.75 2.40

No. 4989 contains one 42x52mm stamp.

Famous Germans Born in Romania A1430

Designs: 1.90 l, Johannes Honterus (1498-1549), author, cartographer. 2.10 l, Hermann Oberth (1894-1989), rocket scientist. 3.90 l, Stephan Ludwig Roth (1796-1849), educator.

**2007, Aug. 24** **Litho.** ***Perf. 13¼***

**4990-4992** A1430 Set of 3 6.75 3.25

Nos. 4990-4992 each printed in sheets of 8 + label.

Casa Luxemburg, Sibiu — A1431

Various views of building.

**2007, Sept. 3** ***Perf. 13¼***

**4993** A1431 3.60 l multi 3.00 1.50

**Souvenir Sheet**

***Perf. 14x13¼***

**4994** A1431 4.30 l multi 3.75 1.90

No. 4994 contains one 52x42mm stamp.

See Luxembourg No. 1222.

Modern Romanian Monetary System, 140th Anniv. — A1432

Coins: 3.90 l, Reverse of 1867 1-ban coin. 5.60 l, Reverse of 1870 1-leu coin.

**2007, Sept. 12** **Litho.** ***Perf. 13¼***

**4995** A1432 3.90 l multi 3.25 1.60

**Souvenir Sheet**

***Perf.***

**4996** A1432 5.60 l multi 4.75 2.40

Values for No. 4995 are for stamps with surrounding selvage.

2007 Rugby World Cup, France — A1433

Various players: 1.80 l, 3.10 l.

**2007, Sept. 25** ***Perf. 13¼***

**4997-4998** A1433 Set of 2 4.25 2.10

Nos. 4997-4998 each printed in sheets of 8 + label.

Launch of Sputnik 1, 50th Anniv. — A1434

Sputnik 1 and: 3.10 l, Earth and Moon. 5.60 l, Earth.

**2007, Oct. 4** ***Perf. 13¼***

**4999** A1434 3.10 l multi 2.60 1.25

**Souvenir Sheet**

***Perf. 14x13¼***

**5000** A1434 5.60 l multi 4.75 2.40

No. 4999 printed in sheets of 8 + label.

Christmas — A1435

**2007, Nov. 3** ***Perf. 13¼***

**5001** A1435 80b multi .70 .35

Printed in sheets of 8 + label.

Support for the Blind — A1436

**2007, Nov. 13** **Litho.** ***Perf. 13¼***

**5002** A1436 5.60 l multi 4.75 2.40

Printed in sheets of 10 + 2 labels.

Danube River Harbors and Ships — A1437

Ships and: 1 l, Orsova, Romania 1.10 l, Novi Sad, Serbia.

No. 5005 — Ships: a, Orsova. b, Sirona.

**2007, Nov. 14**

**5003-5004** A1437 Set of 2 1.75 .90

**Souvenir Sheet**

**5005** A1437 2.10 l Sheet of 2, #a-b, + 2 labels 3.50 1.75

Nos. 5003 and 5004 each were printed in sheets of 10 + 5 labels. See Serbia Nos. 412-414.

Arctic Animals — A1438

Designs: 30b, Ursus maritimus. 50b, Pagophilus groenlandicus, vert. 1.90 l, Alopex lagopus, vert. 3.30 l, Aptenodytes forsteri. 3.60 l, Balaenoptera musculus. 4.30 l, Odobenus rosmarus, vert.

**2007, Dec. 12** **Litho.** ***Perf. 13¼***

**5006-5011** A1438 Set of 6 11.50 5.75

Edible and Poisonous Mushrooms A1439

Designs: 1.20 l, Lepiota rhacodes. 1.40 l, Lactarius deliciosus. 2 l, Morchella esculenta. 2.40 l, Paxillus involutus. 3 l, Gyromitra exculenta. 4.50 l, Russula emetica.

**2008, Jan. 18** **Litho.** ***Perf. 13¼***

**5012-5017** A1439 Set of 6 11.50 5.75

*5017a* Miniature sheet of 6, #5012-5017 11.50 5.75

Henri Farman (1874-1958) and Voisin-Farman I Bis Airplane — A1440

**2008, Jan. 25**

**5018** A1440 5 l multi 4.00 2.00

Printed in sheets of 8 + label. First flight of one kilometer over a circular course, cent.

Firearms in Natl. Military Museum A1441

Designs: 50b, Four-barreled flint pistol, 18th cent. 1 l, Flint pistol, 18th cent. 2.40 l, Mannlicher carbine pistol, 1903. 5 l, 8mm revolver, 1915.

**2008, Feb. 8** **Litho.** ***Perf. 13¼***

**5019-5022** A1441 Set of 4 7.25 3.75

*5022a* Souvenir sheet of 4, #5019-5022, + 2 labels 7.25 3.75

No. 5022a exists with top gun in top label pointing either left or right.

1958 Space Exploration Missions, 50th Anniv. — A1442

Designs: 1 l, Explorer 1. 2.40 l, Sputnik 3. 3.10 l, Jupiter AM-13.

**2008, Feb. 22**

**5023-5025** A1442 Set of 3 5.00 5.00

Nos. 5023-5025 each were printed in sheets of 8 + central label.

Easter — A1443

**2008, Mar. 12**

**5026** A1443 1 l multi .85 .40

Printed in sheets of 8 + central label.

**Pottery Cups and Pitchers Type of 2007**

Designs: 2 l, Cup, Cosesti, Arges. 2.40 l, Pitcher, Radauti, Suceava. 6 l, Pitcher, Baia Mare, Maramures. 7.60 l, Lidded pot, Vladesti, Valcea.

**2008, Mar. 21** ***Perf. 13¼***

| | | | |
|---|---|---|---|
| **5027** | A1428 2 l multi | 1.75 | .85 |
| *a.* | Miniature sheet of 4 | 7.00 | 3.50 |
| **5028** | A1428 2.40 l multi | 2.10 | 1.10 |
| *a.* | Miniature sheet of 4 | 8.50 | 4.50 |
| **5029** | A1428 6 l multi | 5.25 | 2.60 |
| *a.* | Miniature sheet of 4 | 21.00 | 10.50 |
| **5030** | A1428 7.60 l multi | 6.50 | 3.25 |
| *a.* | Miniature sheet of 4 | 26.00 | 13.00 |
| | *Nos. 5027-5030 (4)* | 15.60 | 7.80 |

NATO Summit, Bucharest A1444

**2008, Apr. 2** **Litho.**

**Color of NATO Emblem**

**5031** A1444 6 l blue 5.25 2.60

**Litho. With Foil Application**

**5032** A1444 6 l gold 5.25 2.60
**5033** A1444 6 l silver 5.25 2.60
*Nos. 5031-5033 (3)* 15.75 7.80

Nos. 5032-5033 each were printed in sheets of 8 + central label.

Bears — A1445

Designs: 60b, Helarctos malayanus. 1.20 l, Ursus americanus, horiz. 1.60 l, Ailuropoda melanoleuca, horiz. 3 l, Melursus ursinus, horiz. 5 l, Tremarctos ornatus. 9.10 l, Ursus arctos.

**2008, Apr. 21** **Litho.** ***Perf. 13¼***

**5034-5038** A1445 Set of 5 9.75 4.50

**Souvenir Sheet**

***Perf. 13¼x13¾***

**5039** A1445 9.10 l multi 7.75 3.75

Nos. 5034-5038 each were printed in sheets of 8 + label. No. 5039 contains one 42x52mm stamp.

Miniature Sheet

2008 Summer Olympics, Beijing — A1446

No. 5040: a, Track. b, Gymnastics. c, Swimming. d, Canoeing.

**2008, May 1** ***Perf. 13¼***

**5040** A1446 1 l Sheet of 4, #a-d 3.50 1.75

Europa — A1447

Designs: 1.60 l, Envelope, map of Europe. 8.10 l, Stamped cover, European Union flag.

**2008, May 8**

**5041-5042** A1447 Set of 2 8.25 4.00
*5042a* Souvenir sheet of 4, 2 each #5041-5042, with #5041 at UL 16.50 8.25
*5042b* As "a," with #5042 at UL 16.50 8.25

Grigore Antipa Natl. Natural History Museum, Cent. — A1448

Designs: 2.40 l, Flora and fauna. 3 l, Grigore Antipa (1867-1944), biologist.

**2008, May 20**

**5043-5044** A1448 Set of 2 4.75 2.40

Nos. 5043-5044 each were printed in sheets of 8 + label.

European Central Bank, 10th Anniv. — A1449

**2008, May 26**

**5045** A1449 3.10 l multi 2.00 2.00
*a.* Sheet of 6 + 6 labels 14.00 14.00

No. 5045 was printed in sheets of 40 stamps + 20 labels.

A1450

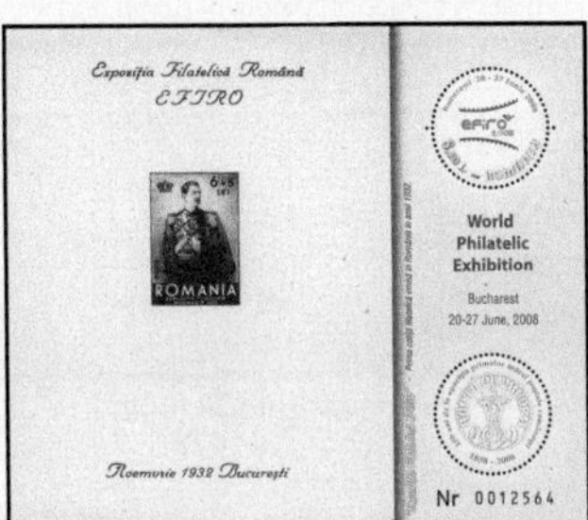
EFIRO 2008 World Philatelic Exhibition, Bucharest — A1451

Romanian stamps: 50b, #5. 1 l, #12. 2.40 l, #22. 3.10 l, #108. 4.50 l, #158. 6 l, #415.

**2008, June 20** ***Perf. 13¼***

**5046** A1450 50b multi + label .45 .25
*a.* Tete-beche pair .90 .40
**5047** A1450 1 l multi + label .90 .45
*a.* Tete-beche pair 1.80 .90
**5048** A1450 2.40 l multi + label 2.10 1.10
*a.* Tete-beche pair 4.20 2.20
**5049** A1450 3.10 l multi + label 2.75 1.40
*a.* Tete-beche pair 5.50 2.80
**5050** A1450 4.50 l multi + label 4.00 2.00
*a.* Tete-beche pair 8.00 4.00
**5051** A1450 6 l multi + label 5.25 2.60
*a.* Tete-beche pair 10.50 5.20
*b.* Miniature sheet, #5046-5051, + 6 labels 15.50 7.75
*Nos. 5046-5051 (6)* 15.45 7.80

**Souvenir Sheet**

***Perf.***

**5052** A1451 8.10 l multi 7.00 3.00

Labels of Nos. 5046-5051 are separated from stamps by two sets of three perforation holes.

Diplomatic Relations Between Romania and Kuwait, 45th Anniv. — A1452

No. 5053: a, Romanian woman weaving. b, Kuwaiti man building ship model. 3.30 l, Romanian oil well fire vehicle.

**2008, June 21**

**5053** Horiz. pair + 2 labels 3.50 1.75
*a.-b.* A1452 2 l Either single 1.75 .85
*c.* Miniature sheet, 2 #5053 7.00 3.50

**Souvenir Sheet**

**5054** A1452 3.30 l multi 3.00 1.50

Labels of Nos. 5053a and 5053b are separated from stamps by a partial row of perforations. The labels show the flags on top and also at the bottom. On No. 5053c, both labels are shown adjacent to the two similar stamps. See Kuwait Nos. 1678-1679.

Selection of "7 Arts" as Best Animated Film at Tours Film Festival, 50th Anniv. — A1453

Designs: 1.40 l, Characters from film. 4.70 l, Character, award, and Ion Popescu-Gopo, director.

**2008, June 22** ***Perf. 13¼***

**5055-5056** A1453 Set of 2 5.25 2.60
*5056a* Souvenir sheet, #5055-5056 5.25 2.60

Cathedrals A1454

UNESCO World Heritage Sites: 3 l, St. George's Cathedral, Voronets Monastery, Romania, and chrismon. 4.30 l, St. Demetrius's Cathedral, Vladimir, Russia, and winged beast.

**2008, June 23**

**5057-5058** A1454 Set of 2 6.50 3.25
*5058a* Souvenir sheet, #5057-5058, + 4 labels 6.50 3.25

Nos. 5057-5058 each were printed in sheets of 10 stamps + 2 labels. See Russia No. 7074.

Castles — A1455

Designs: 1 l, Fagaras Castle, Fagaras. 2.10 l, Peles Castle, Sinaia. 3 l, Huniad Castle, Hunedoara. 5 l, Bethlen Castle, Cris.

**2008, June 24**

**5059-5062** A1455 Set of 4 9.75 4.75
*5062a* Miniature sheet of 4, #5059-5062 9.75 4.75

Nos. 5059-5062 each were printed in sheets of 9 stamps + 3 labels.

Printing of First Book in Romania, 500th Anniv. A1456

Designs: 4.30 l, Page from Macarie's Missal. 9.10 l, Two pages from Macarie's Missal.

**2008, June 25** ***Perf. 13¼***

**5063** A1456 4.30 l multi 3.75 1.90

**Souvenir Sheet**

***Perf. 13¾x13¼***

**5064** A1456 9.10 l multi 8.00 4.00

No. 5063 was printed in sheets of 9 stamps + 3 labels. No. 5064 contains one 52x42mm stamp.

Iasi, 600th Anniv. of Mention in Documents — A1457

Buildings in Iasi: 1 l, Church of the Three Holy Hierarchs. 1.60 l, Metropolitan Cathedral. 2.10 l, Vasile Alecsandri National Theater. 3.10 l, Museum of Unification. 7.60 l, Palace of Culture, vert.

**2008, June 26** ***Perf. 13¼***

**Stamps + Label**

**5065-5068** A1457 Set of 4 6.75 3.25
*5068a* Miniature sheet of 4, #5065-5068, + 4 labels 6.75 3.25

**Souvenir Sheet**

***Perf. 13¼x13¾***

**5069** A1457 7.60 l multi 6.75 3.25

Nos. 5065-5068 have labels to both the right and left of the stamp. No. 5069 contains one 42x52mm stamp.

Queen Marie (1875-1938) A1458

**2008, July 15** ***Perf. 13¼***

**Color of Queen**

**5070** A1458 1 l maroon .90 .45
*a.* Sheet of 8 + central label 7.25 3.75
**5071** A1458 3 l gray green 2.75 1.40
*a.* Sheet of 8 + central label 22.00 11.50
*b.* Souvenir sheet of 2, #5070-5071 3.75 1.90

Nos. 5070-5071 each were printed in sheets of 16 stamps + 4 labels.

Regional Coats of Arms
A1459

Arms of: 60b, Moldavia (Moldova). 1 l, Wallachia (Tara Romaneasca). 3 l, Transylvania. 3.10 l, Bucharest.
6 l, Seal of Bucharest, vert.

**2008, Sept. 4** *Perf. 13¼*
**5072** A1459 60b multi .50 .25
*a.* Sheet of 8 + central label 4.00 2.00
**5073** A1459 1 l multi .80 .40
*a.* Sheet of 8 + central label 6.50 3.25
**5074** A1459 3 l multi 2.40 1.25
*a.* Sheet of 8 + central label 19.50 10.00
**5075** A1459 3.10 l multi 2.50 1.25
*a.* Sheet of 8 + central label 20.00 10.00
*b.* Miniature sheet of 4, #5072-5075 6.25 3.25
*Nos. 5072-5075 (4)* 6.20 3.15

**Souvenir Sheet**
***Perf. 13¼x13¾***

**5076** A1459 6 l multi 4.75 2.40

Nos. 5072-5075 each were printed in sheets of 16 stamps + 4 labels. No. 5076 contains one 42x52mm stamp.

Nuclearelectrica Power Company, 10th Anniv. — A1460

**2008, Oct. 21** *Perf. 13¼*
**5077** A1460 2.10 l multi + label 1.50 .75

Radio Romania, 80th Anniv.
A1461

**2008, Oct. 28** **Litho.** *Perf. 13½*
**5078** A1461 2.40 l multi 1.75 .85
*a.* Souvenir sheet of 2 3.50 1.75

No. 5078 was printed in sheets of 16 having adjacent stamps rotated 90 degrees from each other.

Christmas
A1462

**2008, Nov. 5** **Litho.** *Perf. 13¼*
**5079** A1462 1 l multi .70 .35

Flora and Fauna of Paraul Petea Nature Reserve
A1463

Designs: 1.40 l, Nymphaea lotus thermalis. 1.60 l, Scardinius racovitzai. 3.10 l, Melanopsis parreyssi.

**2008, Dec. 8** **Litho.** *Perf. 13½*
**5081-5083** A1463 Set of 3 4.25 2.10
*5083a* Souvenir sheet, #5081-5083 4.25 2.10

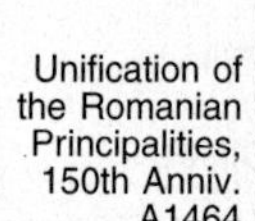

Unification of the Romanian Principalities, 150th Anniv.
A1464

Various arms of the United Romanian Principalities.

**2009, Jan. 24** *Perf. 13½*
**5084** A1464 2.40 l multi 1.50 .75

**Souvenir Sheet**
***Perf.***

**5085** A1464 9.10 l multi 5.50 2.75

Value for No. 5084 is for stamp with surrounding selvage.

Introduction of the Euro, 10th Anniv. — A1465

**2009, Jan. 30** **Litho.** *Perf. 13¼*
**5086** A1465 3 l multi 1.90 .95

**Litho. With Foil Application**

**5087** A1465 3 l multi 1.90 .95

Easter — A1466

No. 5088: a, Crucifixion. b, Resurrection. c, Ascension.

**2009, Feb. 26** **Litho.** *Perf. 13½*
**5088** A1466 1 l Horiz. strip of 3, #a-c 1.90 .95

Birds of the Danube Delta — A1467

Designs: 50b, Alcedo atthis atthis. 1.60 l, Himantopus himantopus, horiz. (48x33mm). 2.10 l, Egretta alba, horiz. (48x33mm). 3.10 l, Falco cherrug.
8.10 l, Haliaeetus albicilla.

**2009, Feb. 28** *Perf. 13¼*
**5089-5092** A1467 Set of 4 4.50 2.25
*5092a* Sheet of 4, #5089-5092 4.50 2.25

**Souvenir Sheet**
***Perf. 13½***

**5093** A1467 8.10 l multi 4.75 2.40

No. 5093 contains one 50x50mm diamond-shaped stamp.

Preservation of Polar Regions and Glaciers
A1468

Designs: 1.60 l, Penguin, eye and teardrop. 8.10 l, Map of Antarctica, iceberg.

**2009, Mar. 21** *Perf. 13¼*
**5094** A1468 1.60 l multi 1.10 .55
*a.* Tete-beche pair 2.20 1.10
**5095** A1468 8.10 l multi 5.25 2.60
*a.* Tete-beche pair 10.50 5.25
*b.* Souvenir sheet, #5094-5095 6.50 3.75

Flowers of the Rodna Mountains
A1469

Designs: 30b, Leontopodium alpinum. 60b, Aster alpinus. 1 l, Dianthus superbus. 1.20 l, Silene nivalis. 2.40 l, Campanula persicifolia. 3.10 l, Lilium martagon.

**2009, Mar. 28** *Perf. 13½*
**5096** A1469 30b multi .25 .25
*a.* Sheet of 8 + central label 1.60 .80
**5097** A1469 60b multi .40 .25
*a.* Sheet of 8 + central label 3.25 1.60
**5098** A1469 1 l multi .65 .30
*a.* Sheet of 8 + central label 5.25 2.60
**5099** A1469 1.20 l multi .80 .40
*a.* Sheet of 8 + central label 6.50 3.25
**5100** A1469 2.40 l multi 1.60 .80
*a.* Sheet of 8 + central label 13.00 6.50
**5101** A1469 3.10 l multi 2.00 1.00
*a.* Sheet of 8 + central label 16.00 8.00
*Nos. 5096-5101 (6)* 5.70 3.00

Romgaz, Cent. — A1470

**2009, Apr. 24** *Perf. 13¼*
**5102** A1470 2.40 l multi 1.50 .75
*a.* Sheet of 6 + 3 central labels 9.00 4.50

Europa — A1471

Designs: 2.40 l, Galileo and his telescope, Leaning Tower of Pisa. 9.10 l, Map of constellations.

**2009, May 6** **Litho.**
**5103** A1471 2.40 l multi 1.60 .80
**5104** A1471 9.10 l multi 6.00 3.00
*a.* Sheet of 4, 2 each #5103-5104, #5103 at UL 15.50 7.75
*b.* As "a," with #5104 at UL 15.50 7.75

Intl. Year of Astronomy. Nos. 5103-5104 were each printed in sheets of 6 with and without an illustrated margin.

Council of Europe, 60th Anniv. — A1472

**2009, May 11** *Perf. 13¼*
**5105** A1472 6 l multi 4.00 2.00

31st Conference of Police Agencies of European Capitals, Bucharest — A1473

Conference emblem, map of Bucharest and: 1 l, Bucharest coat of arms. 1.60 l, Emblem of Romanian Police.

**2009, May 25**
**5106** A1473 1 l multi .70 .35
*a.* Tete-beche pair 1.40 .70
**5107** A1473 1.60 l multi 1.10 .55
*a.* Tete-beche pair 2.20 1.10
*b.* Horiz. pair, #5106-5107 1.80 .90

Romania as Source of European Energy — A1474

Designs: 80b, Electric street light, electric tram and Timisoara Cathedral. 2.10 l, Gas street lamp and Orthodox Cathedral, Turda. 3 l, Iron Gates I Hydroelectric Station, power lines.

**2009, June 2**
**5108-5110** A1474 Set of 3 4.00 2.00
*5110a* Sheet of 3, #5108-5110 4.00 2.00

First Man on the Moon, 40th Anniv.
A1475

Designs: 3 l, Astronaut stepping onto Moon. 14.50 l, Bootprint on Moon.

**2009, July 20** *Perf. 13¼*
**5111** A1475 3 l multi 2.00 1.00

**Souvenir Sheet**
***Perf.***

**5112** A1475 14.50 l multi 9.75 5.00

No. 5111 was printed in sheets of 8 + label. Values of No. 5111 are for stamps with surrounding selvage.

Historic Center of Sigisoara, UNESCO World Heritage Site — A1476

Arms of Sigisoara and: 1 l, Church on the Hill. 1.60 l, Historic city center. 6 l, Clock Tower, vert.
7.60 l, Aerial view of Sigisoara.

**2009, July 24** *Perf. 13¼*
**5113-5115** A1476 Set of 3 6.00 3.00
*5115a* Sheet of 3 #5113-5115 6.00 3.00

**Souvenir Sheet**
***Perf. 14x13¼***

**5116** A1476 7.60 l multi 5.25 2.60

Nos. 5113-5115 were each printed in sheets of 8 + central label. No. 5116 contains one 51x41mm stamp.

Stamp Day — A1477

Anghel I. Saligny (1854-1925), engineer and: 2.10 l, Cernavoda Railroad Bridge. 2.40 l, Cernavoda Railroad Bridge and statue.

**2009, July 30** *Perf. 13¼*

**5117-5118** A1477 Set of 2 3.00 1.50

Electric Trams of European Cities A1478

Arms and trams from: 80b, Frankfurt-am-Main, Germany. 1.20 l, Bucharest. 1.60 l, Vienna. 2.10 l, Brailia, Romania. 2.40 l, London.
8.10 l, Berlin.

**2009, Aug. 14**

**5119-5123** A1478 Set of 5 5.50 2.75

**Souvenir Sheet**

**5124** A1478 8.10 l multi 5.50 2.75

No. 5124 contains one 48x33mm stamp.

Protected Animals — A1479

Designs: 30b, Aquila chrysaetos. 50b, Lynx lynx, vert. 60b, Cervus elaphus. 1.40 l, Huso huso, vert. 3 l, Testudo graeca ibera. 6 l, Otis tarda, vert.

**2009, Aug. 28** *Perf. 13¼*

**5125-5130** A1479 Set of 6 8.00 4.00

Nos. 5125-5130 were each printed in sheets of 8 + label.

Miniature Sheet

Treasures of Romania — A1480

No. 5131: a, Dimitrie Cantemir (1673-1723), prince of Moldavia and writer. b, George Enescu (1881-1955), composer. c, Church of the Three Hierarchs, Iasi. d, Black Church, Brasov. e, Pelican and water lily, Danube Delta. f, Retezat National Park. g, Viticulture. h, Maramures pottery and wood carving.

**2009, Sept. 16**

**5131** A1480 3 l Sheet of 8, #a-h, stamps adjacent 17.00 8.50

*i.* As No. 5131, stamps separated 17.00 8.50

Bucharest, 550th Anniv. — A1481

Designs: 30b, Buna Vestire Church. 80b, Coltea Hospital. 3 l, Sutu Palace. 4.70 l, School of Architecture.
8.10 l, Bucharest Patriarchal Cathedral.

**2009, Sept. 18** *Perf. 13¼*

**5132-5135** A1481 Set of 4 6.25 3.25

*5135a* Sheet of 4, #5132-5135 6.25 3.25

**Souvenir Sheet**

***Perf. 14x13¼***

**5136** A1481 8.10 l multi 5.75 3.00

No. 5136 contains one 51x41mm stamp.

Intl. Day of Non-violence — A1482

**2009, Oct. 6** *Perf. 13¼*

**5137** A1482 3 l multi 2.10 1.10

*a.* Tete-beche pair 4.20 2.20

*b.* Sheet of 6 13.00 6.75

Transgaz, 35th Anniv. — A1483

**2009, Oct. 14** **Litho.**

**5138** A1483 5 l multi 3.50 1.75

*a.* Souvenir sheet of 3 10.50 5.25

General Staff of the Romanian Armed Forces, 150th Anniv. A1484

**2009, Nov. 12**

**5139** A1484 7.60 l multi 5.25 2.60

*a.* Sheet of 6 32.00 16.00

No. 5139 was printed in sheets of 8 + central label.

Christmas A1485

**2009, Nov. 20** **Litho.** *Perf. 13¼*

**5140** A1485 1 l multi .70 .35

*a.* Sheet of 4, perf. 13¼ on 3 sides 2.80 1.40

No. 5140 was printed in sheets of 8 + central label.

University of Bucharest Law Faculty, 150th Anniv. — A1486

**2009, Nov. 25**

**5141** A1486 9.10 l multi 6.50 3.25

*a.* Souvenir sheet of 2 13.00 6.50

No. 5141 was printed in sheets of 8 + central label.

First Yiddish Theater, Iasi — A1487

**2009, Nov. 26**

**5142** A1487 3.10 l multi 2.25 1.10

*a.* Souvenir sheet of 2 4.50 2.25

No. 5142a contains two stamps, one with its label to the left of the stamp. The labels on No. 5142a have a complete column of perforations separating them from the adjacent stamps.
See Israel No. 1797.

Constanta Harbor, Cent. — A1488

Designs: 1 l, Ship "Mircea." 5 l, King Carol I Lighthouse.

**2009, Dec. 23**

**5143-5144** A1488 Set of 2 4.25 2.10

*5144a* Sheet of 2, #5143-5144 4.25 2.10

Honeybees A1489

Designs: 50b, Apis mellifera mellifera. 2.10 l, Apis mellifera ligustica. 3.10 l, Apis mellifera carnica. 4.30 l, Apis mellifera caucasica.

**2010, Jan. 22** *Perf. 13¼*

**5145** A1489 50b multi .35 .25

*a.* Sheet of 4, perf. 13¼ on 2 or 3 sides 1.40 .70

**5146** A1489 2.10 l multi 1.50 .75

*a.* Sheet of 4, perf. 13¼ on 2 or 3 sides 6.00 3.00

**5147** A1489 3.10 l multi 2.10 1.10

*a.* Sheet of 4, perf. 13¼ on 2 or 3 sides 8.50 4.50

**5148** A1489 4.30 l multi 3.00 1.50

*a.* Sheet of 4, perf. 13¼ on 2 or 3 sides 12.00 6.00

*Nos. 5145-5148 (4)* 6.95 3.60

2010 Winter Olympics, Vancouver A1490

Designs: 60b, Cross-country skiing. 80b, Speed skating. 1 l, Skeleton, horiz. 7.60 l, Bobsled, horiz.

**2010, Feb. 12** *Perf. 13¼*

**5149-5152** A1490 Set of 4 6.75 3.50

Nos. 5149-5152 each were printed in sheets of 4.

Tarantulas A1491

Designs: 50b, Brachypelma albopilosum. 80b, Haplopelma lividum. 1.20 l, Brachypelma smithi. 9.10 l, Grammostola rosea.

**2010, Feb. 19**

**5153-5156** A1491 Set of 4 7.75 4.00

Nos. 5153-5156 each were printed in sheets of 8 + central label.

Lighthouses A1492

Designs: 60b, Genoese Lighthouse, Constanta. 80b, Old Lighthouse, Sulina. 1.20 l, Mangalia Lighthouse. 1.60 l, Landing Lighthouse, Tuzla. 8.10 l, White Lighthouse, Constanta North Harbor.

**2010, Mar. 5** *Perf. 13¼*

**5157-5161** A1492 Set of 5 8.25 4.25

Nos. 5157-5161 each were printed in sheets of 8 + label.

Easter A1493

**2010, Mar. 12**

**5162** A1493 1 l multi .65 .35

Printed in sheets of 8 + central label.

Intl. Civil Aviation Organization, 65th Anniv. — A1494

**2010, Mar. 29** *Perf. 13¼x14*

**5163** A1494 8.10 l multi 5.50 2.75
*a.* Souvenir sheet of 2 11.00 5.50

No. 5163 was printed in sheets of 8 + 2 labels

Romanian Gendarmerie, 160th Anniv. — A1495

**2010, Apr. 7** *Perf. 13¼*

**5164** A1495 9.10 l multi 6.00 3.00
*a.* Souvenir sheet of 2 12.00 6.00

No. 5164 was printed in sheets of 8 + central label.

Souvenir Sheet

Eugeniu Carada (1836-1910), Founder of National Bank of Romania — A1496

**2010, Apr. 29**

**5165** A1496 9.10 l multi 6.00 3.00

Europa A1497

Designs: 4.30 l, Little Red Riding Hood and Wolf. 7.60 l, Boy and Dragon.

**2010, May 6**

**5166-5167** A1497 Set of 2 7.25 3.75
*5167a* Sheet of 4, 2 each #5166-5167, #5166 at UL 14.50 7.25
*5167b* As "a," #5167 at UL 14.50 7.25

Coats of Arms and Landmarks of Countries Along the Danube River — A1498

Mother Baar with Her Daughter, the Young Danube, Sculpture by Adolf Heer, Donaueschingen, Germany — A1499

Design on stamps and attached labels: 1.40 l, Melk Abbey, arms of Austria. 2.40 l, Bratislava Castle, arms of Slovakia. 3.10 l, Ilok Fortress, arms of Croatia. 4.30 l, Parliament Building, arms of Hungary.

**2010, May 8**

**5168-5171** A1498 Set of 4 6.50 3.25
*5171a* Souvenir sheet of 4, #5168-5171 6.50 3.25

**Souvenir Sheet**

**5172** A1499 14.50 l multi 8.25 4.25

Minerals A1500

Designs: 50b, Quartz and calcite. 1.40 l, Quartz and gold. 1.60 l, Quartz and rhodochrosite. 2.40 l, Calcite. 7.60 l, Red barite.

**2010, May 21** **Litho.**

**5173-5177** A1500 Set of 5 7.75 4.00

Nos. 5173-5177 each were printed in sheets of 4.

Horse Breeds — A1501

Designs: 60b, Huçul. 1 l, Arabian thoroughbred. 2 l, Lippizaner, vert. 2.10 l, Furioso North Star. 5 l, Shagya Arab.

**2010, May 29** *Perf. 13¼*

**5178-5182** A1501 Set of 5 6.25 3.25

Nos. 5178-5182 each were printed in sheets of 8 + label.

Protected Fauna of the Danube Region — A1502

Designs: 1.40 l, Vipera ursinii. 1.60 l, Phalacrocorax pygmaeus. 2 l, Huso huso. 7.60 l, Pelecanus crispus.

**2010, June 9**

**5183-5186** A1502 Set of 4 7.25 3.75
*5186a* Souvenir sheet of 4, #5183-5186 7.25 3.25

Nos. 5183-5186 each were printed in sheets of 8 + central label.

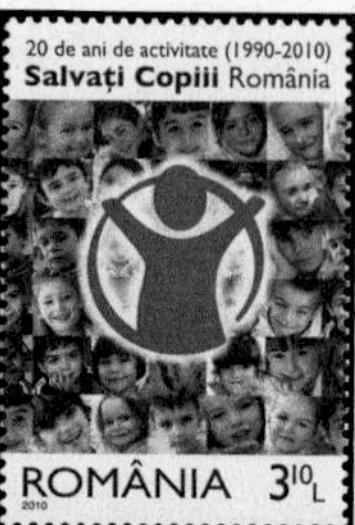

Save the Children Romania, 20th Anniv. A1503

**2010, June 9**

**5187** A1503 3.10 l multi 1.75 .90

Printed in sheets of 8 + central label.

Ceramic Tiles — A1504

Tile from: 2.10 l, Portugal, 18th cent. 3.10 l, Romania, 19th cent.

**2010, June 30**

**5188-5189** A1504 Set of 2 3.25 1.60

Nos. 5188-5189 each were printed in sheets of 8 + central label, with or without an illustrated margin. Stamps from sheets with illustrated margins are perforated on 2 or 3 sides. See Portugal No. 3236.

Recognition of Romanian Orthodox Church Autocephaly, 125th Anniv. A1505

**2010, July 15**

**5190** A1505 6 l multi 3.75 1.90

Stamp Day. Printed in sheets of 8 + central label.

Botanical Garden of Bucharest, 150th Anniv. — A1506

Dr. Dimitrie Brandza (1846-95), Founder of Botanical Garden — A1507

Designs: 1.60 l, Clivia miniata. 2.10 l, Magnolia kobus. 2.40 l, Strelitzia juncea. 3 l, Hepatica transsilvanica. 3.10 l, Dicentra spectabilis.

**2010, July 23**

**5191-5195** A1506 Set of 5 7.50 3.75

**Souvenir Sheet**

**5196** A1507 7.60 l multi 4.75 2.40

A1508

Carpathian Garden — A1509

Designs: 1 l, Tourist looking at Carpathian Sphinx. 1.60 l, Tourist looking at valley. 9.10 l, Valley.

***Perf. 13¼x14 on 3 Sides***

**2010, July 29**

**Stamp + Label**

**5197-5198** A1508 Set of 2 1.60 .80
*5198a* Sheet, #5197-5198, perf. 13¼x14, + 2 labels 1.60 .80

**Souvenir Sheet**

***Perf. 13¼x14***

**5199** A1509 9.10 l multi + label 5.75 2.75

Souvenir Sheet

2010 Youth Olympics, Singapore — A1510

**2010, Aug. 12** *Perf. 13¼*

**5200** A1510 8.10 l multi 5.00 2.50

Mountain Lakes A1511

Designs: 2.10 l, Lake Nahuel Huapi, Argentina. 3.10 l, Lake Balea, Romania.

**2010, Aug. 14** *Perf. 13¼x14*

**5201-5202** A1511 Set of 2 3.25 1.60

Nos. 5201-5202 were each printed in sheets of 4. See Argentina Nos. 2588-2589.

National Bank of Romania, 130th Anniv. — A1512

100-lei banknote of 1896: 2.40 l, Obverse. 4.30 l, Reverse.

**2010, Sept. 5** *Perf. 14x13¼*

**5203** A1512 2.40 l multi 1.50 .75
*a.* Tete-beche pair 3.00 1.50

**5204** A1512 4.30 l multi 2.60 1.25
*a.* Tete-beche pair 5.20 2.50
*b.* Souvenir sheet of 2, #5203-5204 4.25 2.10

Nos. 5203-5204 each have a star punched into the paper next to denomination.

Orient Express — A1513

Locomotive and view of: 2.40 l, Salzburg, Austria. 4.70 l, Sinaia, Romania.

**2010, Sept. 6** ***Perf. 13¼***
**5205-5206** A1513 Set of 2 4.25 2.10
*5206a* Souvenir sheet of 2, #5205-5206 4.25 2.10

See Austria No. 2275.

Ratification of UN Convention on the Rights of the Child, 20th Anniv. — A1514

**2010, Sept. 27**
**5207** A1514 6 l multi 4.00 2.00

Printed in sheets of 8 + central label.

**Danube River Countries Types of 2010**

Designs of stamps and attached labels: 1.40 l, Ram Fortress, Serbia, arms of Serbia. 2.40 l, Sava Ognyanov Drama Theater, Ruse, Bulgaria, arms of Bulgaria. 3.10 l, Bogdan Petriceicu Hasdeu State University, Cahul, Moldova, arms of Moldova. 4.30 l, Assumption of the Virgin Church, Izmail, Ukraine, arms of Ukraine.
14.50 l, Navigation Palace, Galati, Romania.

**2010, Oct. 1 Litho.** ***Perf. 13¼***
**5208-5211** A1498 Set of 4 7.25 3.75
*5211a* Souvenir sheet of 4, #5208-5211 7.25 3.25

**Souvenir Sheet**

**5212** A1499 14.50 l multi 9.50 4.75

Nos. 5208-5211 each were printed in sheets of 8 + central label. No. 5212 contains one 48x33mm stamp.

Souvenir Sheet

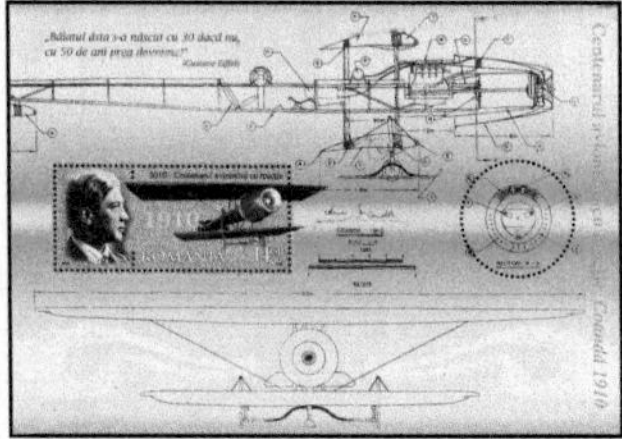
Henri Coanda (1886-1972), Aviation Pioneer and His 1910 Jet Airplane — A1515

**2010, Oct. 15**
**5213** A1515 14.50 l multi + 2 labels 9.50 4.75

National Grand Masonic Lodge, 130th Anniv. — A1516

Designs: 3 l, Arms. 5 l, Compass and square.

**2010, Nov. 4**
**5214-5215** A1516 Set of 2 5.25 2.60

Nos. 5214-5215 each were printed in sheets of 8 + central label.

Viticulture A1517

Designs: 2.10 l, Wine barrels, wine glass. 3.10 l, Grapes, pitcher.

**2010, Nov. 10**
**5216-5217** A1517 Set of 2 3.50 1.75
*5217a* Souvenir sheet of 2, #5216-5217, perf. 13¼ on 3 sides 3.50 1.75

Nos. 5216-5217 each were printed in sheets of 8 + label. See Cyprus No. 1139.

Christmas A1518

Paintings: 1 l, The Birth of Jesus, by Gheorghe Tattarescu. 3.10 l, The Nativity and Adoration of the Shepherds, by the School of Murillo.

**2010, Nov. 15** ***Perf. 13¼***
**5218-5219** A1518 Set of 2 2.60 1.25

Nos. 5218-5219 each were printed in sheets of 8 + central label. See Vatican City Nos. 1458-1461.

Romanian Innovations — A1519

Designs: 3 l, Brad-Barza gold mine ore car on track with switch, 16th cent. 4.30 l, Horizontal water wheel, 13th-14th cent. 5 l, Petrarche Poenaru and his fountain pen, 1827. 8.10 l, 1923 aerodynamic automobile designed by Aurel Persu.

**2010, Dec. 17**
**5220-5223** A1519 Set of 4 13.00 6.50

Nos. 5220-5223 each were printed in sheets of 8 + central label.

Reptiles A1520

Designs: 60b, Zamenis longissimus. 2.40 l, Podarcis taurica. 3 l, Vipera ammodytes ammodytes. 9.10 l, Vipera ursinii moldavica.

**2011, Jan. 19**
**5224** A1520 60b multi .40 .25
*a.* Souvenir sheet of 4 1.60 .80
**5225** A1520 2.40 l multi 1.60 .80
*a.* Souvenir sheet of 4 6.50 3.25
**5226** A1520 3 l multi 1.90 .95
*a.* Souvenir sheet of 4 7.75 4.00
**5227** A1520 9.10 l multi 6.00 3.00
*a.* Souvenir sheet of 4 24.00 12.00
*Nos. 5224-5227 (4)* 9.90 5.00

Nos. 5224-5227 each were printed in sheets of 8 + central label.

Paintings in the National Bank of Romania Collection A1521

Designs: 1.40 l, Mercury, by George Demetrescu Mirea. 2.10 l, Marine, by Eugeniu Voinescu. 3 l, Rodica, by Nicolae Grigorescu. 7.60 l, Prometheus, by Mirea.

**2011, Jan. 28** ***Perf. 13¼x13¾***
**5228** A1521 1.40 l multi .90 .45
*a.* Souvenir sheet of 4 3.75 1.90
*b.* Tete-beche pair 1.80 .90
**5229** A1521 2.10 l multi 1.40 .70
*a.* Souvenir sheet of 4 5.75 3.00
*b.* Tete-beche pair 2.80 1.40
**5230** A1521 3 l multi 1.90 .95
*a.* Souvenir sheet of 4 7.75 4.00
*b.* Tete-beche pair 3.80 1.90
**5231** A1521 7.60 l multi 5.00 2.50
*a.* Souvenir sheet of 4 20.00 10.00
*b.* Tete-beche pair 10.00 5.00
*Nos. 5228-5231 (4)* 9.20 4.60

Nos. 5228-5231 each were printed in sheets of 8.

Caves A1522

Designs: 30b, Ursilor Cave. 50b, Closani Cave. 60b, Muierii Cave. 3 l, Meziad Cave, horiz. 3.10 l, Vantului Cave, horiz. 8.70 l, Sura Mare Cave, horiz.

**2011, Feb. 17** ***Perf. 13¼***
**5232** A1522 30b multi .25 .25
*a.* Sheet of 8 + central label 1.60 .80
**5233** A1522 50b multi .35 .25
*a.* Sheet of 8 + central label 3.00 1.50
**5234** A1522 60b multi .40 .25
*a.* Sheet of 8 + central label 3.25 1.60
**5235** A1522 3 l multi 2.00 1.00
*a.* Sheet of 8 + central label 16.00 8.00
**5236** A1522 3.10 l multi 2.10 1.10
*a.* Sheet of 8 + central label 17.00 8.50
**5237** A1522 8.70 l multi 5.75 3.00
*a.* Sheet of 8 + central label 47.50 24.00
*Nos. 5232-5237 (6)* 10.85 5.85

Parrots A1523

Designs: 1.60 l, Ara illiger. 2.10 l, Ara macao. 2.40 l, Primolius auricollis. 4.70 l, Platycercus eximius. 5 l, Melopsittacus undulatus.
9.10 l, Nymphicus hollandicus.

**2011, Feb. 24**
**5238** A1523 1.60 l multi 1.10 .55
*a.* Sheet of 8 + label 9.00 4.50
**5239** A1523 2.10 l multi 1.40 .70
*a.* Sheet of 8 + label 11.50 5.75
**5240** A1523 2.40 l multi 1.60 .80
*a.* Sheet of 8 + label 13.00 6.50
**5241** A1523 4.70 l multi 3.25 1.60
*a.* Sheet of 8 + label 26.00 13.00
**5242** A1523 5 l multi 3.50 1.75
*a.* Sheet of 8 + label 28.00 14.00
*Nos. 5238-5242 (5)* 10.85 5.40

**Souvenir Sheet**

**5243** A1523 9.10 l multi 6.00 3.00

World Down Syndrome Day — A1524

**2011, Mar. 14**
**5244** A1524 3 l multi 2.10 1.10

Easter — A1525

**2011, Mar. 24** **Litho.**
**5245** A1525 1 l multi .70 .35

Printed in sheets of 8 + central label.

Peonies A1526

Designs: 1 l, Paeonia peregrina. 2.10 l, Paeonia tenuifolia.

**2011, Mar. 30** ***Perf. 13¼***
**5246** A1526 1 l multi .70 .35

**Souvenir Sheet**

**5247** A1526 2.10 l multi 1.50 .75

No. 5246 was printed in sheets of 4.

Butterflies and Moths — A1527

Designs: 50b, Parnassius apollo. 60b, Greta oto, vert. 2.40 l, Morpho nestira. 3 l, Papilio macahon. 4.50 l, Attacus atlas. 5 l, Inachis io. 8.10 l, Iphiclides podalirius.

**2011, Apr. 12**
**5248** A1527 50b multi .35 .25
*a.* Sheet of 8 + central label 3.00 1.50
**5249** A1527 60b multi .45 .25
*a.* Sheet of 8 + central label 3.75 1.90
**5250** A1527 2.40 l multi 1.75 .85
*a.* Sheet of 8 + central label 14.00 7.00
**5251** A1527 3 l multi 2.10 1.10
*a.* Sheet of 8 + central label 17.00 8.50
**5252** A1527 4.50 l multi 3.25 1.60
*a.* Sheet of 8 + central label 26.00 13.00
**5253** A1527 5 l multi 3.50 1.75
*a.* Sheet of 8 + central label 28.00 14.00
*Nos. 5248-5253 (6)* 11.40 5.80

**Souvenir Sheet**

**5254** A1527 8.10 l multi 5.75 3.00

Palace of the Parliament, Bucharest — A1528

Designs: 30b, Exterior. 50b, Senate entrance. 60b, Senate chamber. 3 l, Human

Rights Room. 4.30 l, Chamber of Deputies. 7.60 l, Exterior, diff.

**2011, Apr. 26**

5255 A1528 30b multi .25 .25
a. Sheet of 8 + central label 1.60 .80
5256 A1528 50b multi .35 .25
a. Sheet of 8 + central label 3.00 1.50
5257 A1528 60b multi .45 .25
a. Sheet of 8 + central label 3.75 1.90
5258 A1528 3 l multi 2.10 1.10
a. Sheet of 8 + central label 17.00 8.50
5259 A1528 4.30 l multi 3.00 1.50
a. Sheet of 8 + central label 24.00 12.00
5260 A1528 7.60 l multi 5.50 2.75
a. Sheet of 8 + central label 45.00 22.50
b. Souvenir sheet of 6, #5255-5260, + label 12.00 6.00
*Nos. 5255-5260 (6)* 11.65 6.10

Europa A1529

Forest and: 2.40 l, Buck. 9.10 l, Squirrel.

**2011, Apr. 27**

5261 A1529 2.40 l multi 1.75 .85
a. Sheet of 6 10.50 5.25
5262 A1529 9.10 l multi 6.50 3.25
a. Sheet of 6 39.00 19.50
b. Souvenir sheet of 4, 2 each #5261-5262, #5261 at upper left 16.50 8.25
c. As "b," with #5262 at upper left 16.50 8.25

Intl Year of Forests.

Signs of the Zodiac A1530

**2011, May 5**

5263 A1530 30b Aries .25 .25
a. Sheet of 8 + central label 1.60 .80
5264 A1530 50b Taurus .35 .25
a. Sheet of 8 + central label 3.00 1.50
5265 A1530 60b Gemini .45 .25
a. Sheet of 8 + central label 3.75 1.90
5266 A1530 80b Cancer .55 .25
a. Sheet of 8 + central label 4.50 2.25
5267 A1530 1.40 l Leo 1.00 .50
a. Sheet of 8 + central label 8.00 4.00
5268 A1530 14.50 l Virgo 10.00 5.00
a. Sheet of 8 + central label 80.00 40.00
b. Souvenir sheet of 6, #5263-5268 13.00 6.50
*Nos. 5263-5268 (6)* 12.60 6.50

See Nos. 5303-5308.

First Man in Space, 50th Anniv. — A1531

Designs: 3 l, Dumitru Dorin Prunariu, first Romanian in space, Soyuz 40 rocket on launch pad. 4.70 l, Yuri Gagarin, first man in space, Vostok 1 on launch pad.
8.70, Earth as seen from space.

**2011, May 9** *Perf. 13¼*

5269 A1531 3 l multi 2.10 1.10
a. Sheet of 8 + central label 17.00 8.50
5270 A1531 4.70 l multi 3.25 1.60
a. Sheet of 8 + central label 26.00 13.00

**Souvenir Sheet**

***Perf.***

5271 A1531 8.70 l multi 6.00 3.00

Circus A1532

Designs: 50b, Circus tent, clown's face. 8.10 l, Clown with top hat.

**2011, June 1** *Perf. 13¼*

5272 A1532 50b multi .35 .25
a. Sheet of 8 + central label 3.00 1.50
5273 A1532 8.10 l multi 5.75 3.00
a. Sheet of 8 + central label 46.00 23.00
b. Souvenir sheet of 2, #5272-5273 6.25 3.25

Campaign Against AIDS and HIV, 30th Anniv. — A1533

**2011, June 8** **Litho.**

5274 A1533 3 l multi 2.10 1.10

Opening of Basarab Overpass, Bucharest — A1534

**2011, June 21**

5275 A1534 5 l multi 3.50 1.75
a. Souvenir sheet of 2 7.00 3.50
b. Sheet of 8 28.00 14.00

Peach Blossoms A1535

Blossoms of Prunus persica with denomination at: No. 5276, 50b, UL. No. 5277, 50b, UR.

**2011, June 30**

5276-5277 A1535 Set of 2 .70 .35

Nos. 5276-5277 were printed in sheets of 6, containing 3 of each stamp.

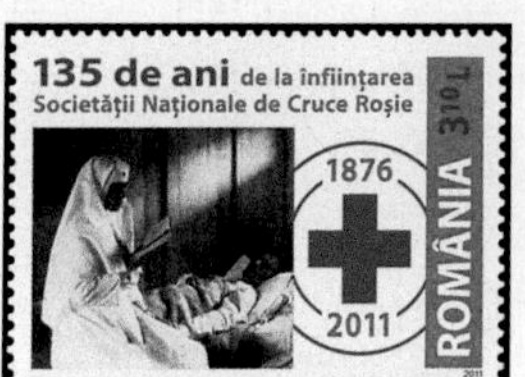


Romanian Red Cross, 135th Anniv. — A1536

**2011, July 3**

5278 A1536 3.10 l multi 2.10 1.10
a. Sheet of 8 + central label 17.00 8.50

Transylvanian Association for Romanian Literature and Culture of the Romanian People, 150th Anniv. — A1537

Anniversary emblem and: 3 l, Metropolitan Andrei Saguna (1808-73), first president of association. 9.10 l, Association library, Sibiu.

**2011, July 15** *Perf. 13¼*

5279 A1537 3 l multi 2.10 1.10
a. Sheet of 8 + central label 17.00 9.00
5280 A1537 9.10 l multi 6.25 3.25
a. Sheet of 8 + central label 50.00 26.00

Stamp Day.

Animals and Birds in Nature Preserves — A1538

Designs: 30b, Canis lupus. 4.50 l, Ardea purpurea. 5 l, Tetrao urogallus. 8.10 l, Nyctereutes procyonoides.

**2011, July 25**

5281 A1538 30b multi .25 .25
a. Sheet of 8 + label 2.00 2.00
5282 A1538 4.50 l multi 3.00 1.50
a. Sheet of 8 + label 24.00 12.00
5283 A1538 5 l multi 3.50 1.75
a. Sheet of 8 + label 28.00 14.00
5284 A1538 8.10 l multi 5.50 2.75
a. Sheet of 8 + label 44.00 22.00
b. Souvenir sheet of 4, #5281-5284 12.50 6.25
*Nos. 5281-5284 (4)* 12.25 6.25

Stained Glass Windows A1539

Windows in Dumitru Furnica-Minovici Western Old Art Museum of the Romanian Academy, Bucharest: 3.60 l, The Artist, 18th cent. Austrian window. 4.30 l, St. Catherine, 19th cent. Austrian window. 4.50 l, Hunter, 19th cent. Austrian window. 4.70 l, Lady in Green, 17th cent. German window.
St. Hieronymus and Resurrection of Lazarus, 15th cent. Tyrolean windows.

**2011, Aug. 18**

5285 A1539 3.60 l multi 2.40 1.25
a. Sheet of 8 + central label 19.50 9.75
5286 A1539 4.30 l multi 2.75 1.40
a. Sheet of 8 + central label 22.00 11.00
5287 A1539 4.50 l multi 3.00 1.50
a. Sheet of 8 + central label 24.00 12.00
5288 A1539 4.70 l multi 3.00 1.50
a. Sheet of 8 + central label 24.00 12.00
*Nos. 5285-5288 (4)* 11.15 5.65

**Souvenir Sheet**

5289 A1539 8.10 l multi 5.25 2.60

Locomotives — A1540

Designs: 2 l, CFR 103 Romania, 1869. 3 l, CFR 28 Codaesti, 1887. 3.30 l, CFR 185 Domnita Maria, 1875. 9.10 l, CFR 001 Lespezi, 1884.
8.10 l, CFR 8008, 1901.

**2011, Aug. 26**

5290 A1540 2 l multi 1.25 .60
a. Sheet of 8 + label 10.00 5.00
5291 A1540 3 l multi 1.90 .95
a. Sheet of 8 + label 15.50 7.75
5292 A1540 3.30 l multi 2.10 1.10
a. Sheet of 8 + label 17.00 9.00
5293 A1540 9.10 l multi 5.75 3.00
a. Sheet of 8 + label 46.00 24.00
*Nos. 5290-5293 (4)* 11.00 5.65

**Souvenir Sheet**

***Perf. 14x13¼***

5294 A1540 8.10 l multi 5.25 2.60

No. 5294 contains one 52x42mm stamp.

20th George Enescu Intl. Music Festival and Competition — A1541

Designs: 1.40 l, Conductor, concert hall. 3 l, Musical score, Enescu's signature, opera libretto. 7.60 l, Romanian Athenaeum.

**2011, Sept. 1** *Perf. 13¼*

5295 A1541 1.40 l multi .90 .45
a. Sheet of 8 7.25 3.75
5296 A1541 3 l multi 1.90 .95
a. Sheet of 8 15.50 7.75
5297 A1541 7.60 l multi 5.00 2.50
a. Sheet of 8 40.00 20.00
b. Souvenir sheet of 3, #5295-5297 8.00 4.00
*Nos. 5295-5297 (3)* 7.80 3.90

New National Arena, Bucharest — A1542

**2011, Sept. 6** *Perf. 14x13¼*

5298 A1542 5 l multi 3.25 1.60
a. Souvenir sheet of 2 6.50 3.25
b. Sheet of 10 32.50 16.00

Biertan Church Castle UNESCO World Heritage Site — A1543

**2011, Sept. 15** *Perf. 13¼*

**Granite Paper**

5299 A1543 2.10 l multi 1.40 .70
a. Sheet of 2 + label 2.80 1.40

See Germany No. 2638.

Franz-Joseph Müller von Reichenstein (c. 1740-1825), Discoverer of Tellurium, Diagram of Tellurium Atom — A1544

**2011, Sept. 26** **Litho.**

| No. | Description | Unused | Used |
|---|---|---|---|
| 5300 | A1544 5 l multi | 3.25 | 1.60 |
| a. | Sheet of 8 + central label | 26.00 | 13.00 |

Intl. Year of Chemistry.

Diplomatic Relations Between Romania and Moldova, 20th Anniv. A1545

Designs: 1 l, Holy Gates, Chisinau, Moldova. 3.10 l, Arch of Triumph, Bucharest.

**2011, Oct. 11** ***Perf. 13¼***

| No. | Description | Unused | Used |
|---|---|---|---|
| 5301 | A1545 1 l multi | .65 | .30 |
| a. | Sheet of 8 + central label | 5.25 | 2.60 |
| 5302 | A1545 3.10 l multi | 2.00 | 1.00 |
| a. | Sheet of 8 + central label | 16.00 | 8.00 |
| b. | Souvenir sheet of 2, #5301-5302 | 2.75 | 1.40 |

See Moldova Nos. 728-729.

### Signs of the Zodiac Type of 2011

**2011, Oct. 14**

| No. | Description | Unused | Used |
|---|---|---|---|
| 5303 | A1530 50b Libra | .35 | .25 |
| a. | Sheet of 8 + central label | 3.00 | 2.00 |
| 5304 | A1530 60b Scorpio | .40 | .25 |
| a. | Sheet of 8 + central label | 3.25 | 2.00 |
| 5305 | A1530 80b Sagittarius | .50 | .25 |
| a. | Sheet of 8 + central label | 4.00 | 2.00 |
| 5306 | A1530 3 l Capricorn | 1.90 | .95 |
| a. | Sheet of 8 + central label | 15.50 | 7.75 |
| 5307 | A1530 6 l Aquarius | 3.75 | 1.90 |
| a. | Sheet of 8 + central label | 30.00 | 15.50 |
| 5308 | A1530 8.10 l Pisces | 5.25 | 2.60 |
| a. | Sheet of 8 + central label | 42.00 | 21.00 |
| b. | Souvenir sheet of 6, #5303-5308 | 12.50 | 6.25 |
| | *Nos. 5303-5308 (6)* | 12.15 | 6.20 |

European Day of Civil Justice — A1546

**2011, Oct. 25**

| No. | Description | Unused | Used |
|---|---|---|---|
| 5309 | A1546 5 l multi | 3.25 | 1.60 |
| a. | Sheet of 8 + central label | 26.00 | 13.00 |

Christmas A1547

**2011, Nov. 18**

| No. | Description | Unused | Used |
|---|---|---|---|
| 5310 | A1547 1 l multi | .65 | .30 |
| a. | Sheet of 8 + central label | 5.25 | 2.60 |

Handicrafts A1548

Designs: No. 5311, Painted Easter eggs, Romania. No. 5312, Dough figurines, Hong Kong.

**2011, Nov. 24**

| No. | Description | Unused | Used |
|---|---|---|---|
| 5311 | A1548 2 l multi | 1.25 | .60 |
| a. | Sheet of 8 | 10.00 | 5.00 |
| 5312 | A1548 2 l multi | 1.25 | .60 |
| a. | Sheet of 8 | 10.00 | 5.00 |
| b. | Souvenir sheet of 2, #5311-5312 | 2.50 | 1.25 |

Romanians and Their Innovations — A1549

Designs: 1.40 l, Stefan Odobleja (1902-78), neurologist, and computer chip. 1.60 l, Ioan Cantacuzino (1863-1934), discoverer of anti-cholera vaccine, bacillae and microscope. 2.10 l, Anastase Dragomir (1896-1966), inventor of airplane ejector seat. 7.60 l, Grigore Antipa (1867-1944), creator of biological dioramas for museums, and animals.

**2011, Dec. 15**

| No. | Description | Unused | Used |
|---|---|---|---|
| 5313 | A1549 1.40 l multi | .85 | .40 |
| a. | Sheet of 8 + central label | 7.00 | 3.50 |
| 5314 | A1549 1.60 l multi | 1.00 | .50 |
| a. | Sheet of 8 + central label | 8.00 | 4.00 |
| 5315 | A1549 2.10 l multi | 1.25 | .60 |
| a. | Sheet of 8 + central label | 10.00 | 5.00 |
| 5316 | A1549 7.60 l multi | 4.75 | 2.40 |
| a. | Sheet of 8 + central label | 38.00 | 19.50 |
| | *Nos. 5313-5316 (4)* | 7.85 | 3.90 |

Cotroceni Palace A1550

Stained-glass windows in Union Hall: 50b, Tara Romaneasca window. 60b, Prince Basarab I window, pillar. 80b, Moldova window. 1 l, Prince Bogdan I window, pillar. 2.40 l, Transilvania window. 3.10 l, Prince Michael the Brave (Mihai Viteazul) window, pillar.
14.50 l, Cotroceni Palace.

**2011, Dec. 21** ***Perf. 13¼***

| No. | Description | Unused | Used |
|---|---|---|---|
| 5317 | A1550 50b multi | .30 | .25 |
| a. | Sheet of 8 + central label | 2.40 | 2.00 |
| 5318 | A1550 60b multi | .40 | .25 |
| a. | Sheet of 8 + central label | 3.25 | 2.00 |
| 5319 | A1550 80b multi | .50 | .25 |
| a. | Sheet of 8 + central label | 4.00 | 2.00 |
| 5320 | A1550 1 l multi | .60 | .30 |
| a. | Sheet of 8 + central label | 5.00 | 2.40 |
| 5321 | A1550 2.40 l multi | 1.50 | .75 |
| a. | Sheet of 8 + central label | 12.00 | 6.00 |
| 5322 | A1550 3.10 l multi | 1.90 | .95 |
| a. | Sheet of 8 + central label | 15.50 | 7.75 |
| | *Nos. 5317-5322 (6)* | 5.20 | 2.75 |

### Souvenir Sheet

***Imperf***

| No. | Description | Unused | Used |
|---|---|---|---|
| 5323 | A1550 14.50 l multi | 8.75 | 4.50 |

Flowers A1551

Designs: 50b, Eritrichium nanum and snake. 60b, Amaranthus caudatus and turkey. 1 l, Pulmonaria officinalis and bear. 1.20 l, Ranunculus repens and chicken. 1.60 l, Borago officinalis and lamb. 2 l, Potentilla anserina and lobster. 3.30 l, Antirrhinum majus and lion. 3.60 l, Oxalis acetosella and rabbit. 4.70 l, Callistephus chinensis and cow. 7.60 l, Convolvulus arvensis and bird.

**2012** **Litho.** ***Perf. 13¼***

| No. | Description | Unused | Used |
|---|---|---|---|
| 5324 | A1551 50b multi | .30 | .25 |
| a. | Sheet of 8 + central label | 2.40 | 1.25 |
| 5325 | A1551 60b multi | .40 | .25 |
| a. | Sheet of 8 + central label | 3.25 | 1.60 |
| 5326 | A1551 1 l multi | .60 | .30 |
| a. | Sheet of 8 + central label | 5.00 | 2.50 |
| 5327 | A1551 1.20 l multi | .75 | .35 |
| a. | Sheet of 8 + central label | 6.00 | 3.00 |
| 5328 | A1551 1.60 l multi | 1.00 | .50 |
| a. | Sheet of 8 + central label | 8.00 | 4.00 |
| 5329 | A1551 2 l multi | 1.25 | .60 |
| a. | Sheet of 8 + central label | 10.00 | 5.00 |
| 5330 | A1551 3.30 l multi | 2.00 | 1.00 |
| a. | Sheet of 8 + central label | 16.00 | 8.00 |
| 5331 | A1551 3.60 l multi | 2.25 | 1.10 |
| a. | Sheet of 8 + central label | 18.00 | 9.00 |
| 5332 | A1551 4.70 l multi | 3.00 | 1.50 |
| a. | Sheet of 8 + central label | 24.00 | 12.00 |
| 5333 | A1551 7.60 l multi | 4.75 | 2.40 |
| a. | Sheet of 8 + central label | 38.00 | 19.50 |
| | *Nos. 5324-5333 (10)* | 16.30 | 8.25 |

Issued: 50b, 60b, 1.60 l, 2 l, 1/19; 1 l, 1.20 l, 3.30 l, 3.60 l, 4.70 l, 7.60 l, 1/17.

Ion Luca Caragiale (1852-1912), Writer — A1552

Designs: 5 l, Caragiale. 9.10 l, Sculpture of Caragiale by Ioan Bolborea, horiz.

**2012, Jan. 30** ***Perf. 13¼***

| No. | Description | Unused | Used |
|---|---|---|---|
| 5334 | A1552 5 l multi | 3.00 | 1.50 |
| a. | Sheet of 8 + central label | 24.00 | 12.00 |

### Souvenir Sheet

***Perf. 14x13¼***

| No. | Description | Unused | Used |
|---|---|---|---|
| 5335 | A1552 9.10 l multi | 5.50 | 2.75 |

No. 5335 contains one 53x42mm stamp.

Selection of Bucharest as Capital of Romania, 150th Anniv. — A1553

Designs: 14.50 l, Sutu Palace, Bucharest coat of arms.
8.10 l, Prince Alexandru Ioan Cuza.

**2012, Feb. 3** ***Perf. 13¼***

| No. | Description | Unused | Used |
|---|---|---|---|
| 5336 | A1553 14.50 l multi | 9.00 | 4.50 |
| a. | Sheet of 8 + central label | 72.00 | 36.00 |

### Souvenir Sheet

***Perf. 14x13¼***

| No. | Description | Unused | Used |
|---|---|---|---|
| 5337 | A1553 8.10 l multi | 5.00 | 2.50 |

No. 5337 contains one 53x42mm stamp.

Portraits on Romanian Banknotes — A1554

Portrait of: 80b, Nicolae Iorga (1871-1940), writer. 1.40 l, George Enescu (1881-1955), composer. 2.10 l, Nicolae Grigorescu (1838-1907), painter. 2.40 l, Aurel Vlaicu (1882-1913), aviation pioneer. 3 l, Ion Luca Caragiale (1852-1912), writer. 3.10 l, Lucian Blaga (1895-1961), writer. 6 l, Mihai Eminescu (1850-89), poet.

**2012, Feb. 10** ***Perf. 13¼***

| No. | Description | Unused | Used |
|---|---|---|---|
| 5338 | A1554 80b multi | .50 | .25 |
| a. | Souvenir sheet of 4 | 2.00 | 1.00 |
| 5339 | A1554 1.40 l multi | .85 | .40 |
| a. | Souvenir sheet of 4 | 3.50 | 1.60 |
| 5340 | A1554 2.10 l multi | 1.25 | .65 |
| a. | Souvenir sheet of 4 | 5.00 | 2.60 |
| 5341 | A1554 2.40 l multi | 1.50 | .75 |
| a. | Souvenir sheet of 4 | 6.00 | 3.00 |
| 5342 | A1554 3 l multi | 1.90 | .95 |
| a. | Souvenir sheet of 4 | 7.75 | 4.00 |
| 5343 | A1554 3.10 l multi | 1.90 | .95 |
| a. | Souvenir sheet of 4 | 7.75 | 4.00 |
| 5344 | A1554 6 l multi | 3.75 | 1.90 |
| a. | Souvenir sheet of 4 | 15.00 | 7.75 |
| | *Nos. 5338-5344 (7)* | 11.65 | 5.85 |

Irons A1555

Iron from: 50b, France, 18th cent. 80b, Germany, 18th cent. 1.40 l, United States, 19th cent. 4.70 l, Scotland, 19th cent. 5 l, Romania, 19th cent.
14.50 l, Romania, 20th cent.

**2012, Feb. 17** ***Perf. 13¼***

| No. | Description | Unused | Used |
|---|---|---|---|
| 5345 | A1555 50b multi | .30 | .25 |
| a. | Sheet of 8 + central label | 2.40 | 1.25 |
| 5346 | A1555 80b multi | .50 | .25 |
| a. | Sheet of 8 + central label | 4.00 | 2.00 |
| 5347 | A1555 1.40 l multi | .85 | .40 |
| a. | Sheet of 8 + central label | 7.00 | 3.50 |
| 5348 | A1555 4.70 l multi | 3.00 | 1.50 |
| a. | Sheet of 8 + central label | 24.00 | 12.00 |
| 5349 | A1555 5 l multi | 3.00 | 1.50 |
| a. | Sheet of 8 + central label | 24.00 | 12.00 |
| | *Nos. 5345-5349 (5)* | 7.65 | 3.90 |

### Souvenir Sheet

***Perf. 13¼x14***

| No. | Description | Unused | Used |
|---|---|---|---|
| 5350 | A1555 14.50 l multi | 9.00 | 4.50 |

No. 5350 contains one 42x52mm stamp.
See Nos. 5384-5389.

Easter — A1556

**2012, Mar. 16** ***Perf. 13¼***

| No. | Description | Unused | Used |
|---|---|---|---|
| 5351 | A1556 1 l multi | .60 | .30 |
| a. | Sheet of 8 + central label | 5.00 | 2.50 |

First Mention of Timisoara in Documents, 800th Anniv. A1557

Designs: 2.10 l, Roman Catholic Cathedral. 5 l, Timisoara Fortress, horiz. 7.60 l, Hunyadi Castle, horiz. 14.50 l, Orthodox Metropolitan Cathedral.

**2012, Mar. 26** **Litho.**

| No. | Description | Unused | Used |
|---|---|---|---|
| 5352 | A1557 2.10 l multi | 1.25 | .60 |
| a. | Sheet of 8 + central label | 10.00 | 5.00 |
| 5353 | A1557 5 l multi | 3.00 | 1.50 |
| a. | Sheet of 8 + central label | 24.00 | 12.00 |
| 5354 | A1557 7.60 l multi | 4.75 | 2.40 |
| a. | Sheet of 8 + central label | 38.00 | 19.50 |
| 5355 | A1557 14.50 l multi | 8.75 | 4.25 |
| a. | Sheet of 8 + central label | 70.00 | 35.00 |
| b. | Souvenir sheet of 1 | 8.75 | 4.25 |
| | *Nos. 5352-5355 (4)* | 17.75 | 8.75 |

Europa
A1558

Map of Romania and: 1.40 l, Crane in Danube Delta. 8.10 l, Castle and mountains.

**2012, Apr. 6**

**5356** A1558 1.40 l multi .85 .40
*a.* Sheet of 6 5.25 2.40
**5357** A1558 8.10 l multi 5.00 2.50
*a.* Sheet of 6 30.00 15.00
*b.* Souvenir sheet of 4, 2 each #5356-5357, #5356 at UL 12.00 6.00
*c.* As "b," with #5357 at UL 12.00 6.00

Romanian Athletic Federation, Cent. — A1559

**2012, Apr. 20** ***Perf. 13¼***

**5358** A1559 1.40 l multi .85 .40
*a.* Sheet of 8 + central label 7.00 3.50

Ministry of Foreign Affairs, 150th Anniv. A1560

**2012, Apr. 25**

**5359** A1560 2.10 l multi 1.25 .60
*a.* Sheet of 8 + central label 10.00 5.00
*b.* Souvenir sheet of 1 + label 1.25 .60

Fruits and Vegetables A1561

Designs: 50b, Grapes, peach, tomatoes, garlic. 1.60 l, Apples. 2.10 l, Peppers.

**2012, May 3**

**5360** A1561 50b multi .30 .25
*a.* Sheet of 8 + central label 2.40 1.25
**5361** A1561 1.60 l multi .95 .50
*a.* Sheet of 8 + central label 7.75 4.00
**5362** A1561 2.10 l multi 1.25 .60
*a.* Sheet of 8 + central label 10.00 5.00
*Nos. 5360-5362 (3)* 2.50 1.35

The upper right stamp in Nos. 5360a-5362a is tete-beche in relation to the other stamps in the sheet.

Intl. Children's Day — A1562

**2012, June 1**

**5363** A1562 2.40 l multi 1.40 .70
*a.* Sheet of 8 + central label 11.50 5.75

Fish A1563

Designs: 1.40 l, Poecilia sphenops. 3 l, Eupomotis gibbosus. 3.10 l, Macropodus opercularis. 14.50 l, Thorichthys meeki.

**2012, June 15**

**5364** A1563 1.40 l multi .80 .40
*a.* Sheet of 8 + central label 6.50 3.25
**5365** A1563 3 l multi 1.60 .80
*a.* Sheet of 8 + central label 13.00 6.50
**5366** A1563 3.10 l multi 1.75 .85
*a.* Sheet of 8 + central label 14.00 7.00
**5367** A1563 14.50 l multi 8.00 4.00
*a.* Sheet of 8 + central label 65.00 32.50
*Nos. 5364-5367 (4)* 12.15 6.05

Birds — A1564

Designs: 1 l, Merops apiaster. 1.20 l, Egretta garzetta. 2.10 l, Ardeola ralloides. 8.10 l, Branta ruficollis. 9.10 l, Pelecanus onocrotalus.

**2012, July 6** ***Perf. 14x13¼***

**5368** A1564 1 l multi .55 .25
*a.* Sheet of 9 + label 5.00 2.50
**5369** A1564 1.20 l multi .65 .30
*a.* Sheet of 9 + label 6.00 3.00
**5370** A1564 2.10 l multi 1.25 .60
*a.* Sheet of 9 + label 11.50 5.50
**5371** A1564 8.10 l multi 4.50 2.25
*a.* Sheet of 9 + label 41.00 21.00
**5372** A1564 9.10 l multi 5.00 2.50
*a.* Sheet of 9 + label 45.00 22.50
*b.* Souvenir sheet of 1 5.00 2.50
*Nos. 5368-5372 (5)* 11.95 5.90

Eleventh meeting of the Conference of the Parties to the Convention on Wetlands of International Importance, Bucharest.

Victor Babes National Institute, 125th Anniv. — A1565

Designs: 3.10 l, Building, Bucharest. 7.60, Babes (1854-1926), physician, and flasks.

**2012, July 16** ***Perf. 13¼***

**5373** A1565 3.10 l multi 1.75 .85
*a.* Sheet of 8 + central label 14.00 7.00
**5374** A1565 7.60 l multi 4.25 2.10
*a.* Sheet of 8 + central label 34.00 17.00
*b.* Souvenir sheet of 2, #5373-5374 6.00 3.00

2012 Summer Olympics, London — A1566

Designs: 1.20 l, Gymnastics. 1.40 l, Canoeing. 2.10 l, Fencing. 6 l, Javelin.

**2012, July 27** **Litho.**

**5375-5378** A1566 Set of 4 5.75 3.00

Nos. 5374-5378 each were printed in sheets of 4.

Dogs — A1567

Designs: 4.50 l, Short-haired dachshund. 5 l, Golden retriever. 8.10 l, Romanian Mioritic shepherd. 9.10 l, Romanian Carpathian shepherd.

**2012, Aug. 10**

**5379** A1567 4.50 l multi 2.60 1.40
*a.* Sheet of 8 + central label 21.00 11.50
**5380** A1567 5 l multi 3.00 1.50
*a.* Sheet of 8 + central label 24.00 12.00
**5381** A1567 8.10 l multi 4.75 2.40
*a.* Sheet of 8 + central label 38.00 19.50
**5382** A1567 9.10 l multi 5.25 2.60
*a.* Sheet of 8 + central label 42.00 21.00
*b.* Souvenir sheet of 4, #5379-5382 16.00 8.00
*Nos. 5379-5382 (4)* 15.60 7.90

Hagigadar Monastery, Moara, 500th Anniv. — A1568

**2012, Aug. 11**

**5383** A1568 4.70 l multi 2.75 1.40
*a.* Sheet of 8 + central label 22.00 11.50
*b.* Souvenir sheet of 2 + 2 labels 5.50 2.75

Examples of No. 5383b with gold foil applied were printed in limited quantities and sold for 135 l. See Armenia No. 911.

**Irons Type of 2012**

Irons from: 80b, Burma, 19th cent. 1 l, Sweden, 18th cent. 1.20 l, Belgium, 18th cent. 1.60 l, Italy, 18th cent. 5 l, Switzerland, 19th cent. 14.50 l, United States, 19th cent.

**2012, Sept. 1**

**5384** A1555 80b multi .45 .25
*a.* Sheet of 8 + central label 3.75 2.00
**5385** A1555 1 l multi .60 .30
*a.* Sheet of 8 + central label 5.00 2.40
**5386** A1555 1.20 l multi .70 .35
*a.* Sheet of 8 + central label 5.75 3.00
**5387** A1555 1.60 l multi .95 .45
*a.* Sheet of 8 + central label 7.75 3.75
**5388** A1555 5 l multi 3.00 1.50
*a.* Sheet of 8 + central label 24.00 12.00
**5389** A1555 14.50 l multi 8.50 4.25
*a.* Sheet of 8 + central label 68.00 34.00
*b.* Souvenir sheet of 1, imperf. 8.50 4.25
*Nos. 5384-5389 (6)* 14.20 7.10

Romanian Post, 150th Anniv. — A1569

Designs: 1 l, Romania #11, 12, 14. 8.10 l, Posthorn, Postal headquarters, Bucharest.

**2012, Sept. 24**

**5390** A1569 1 l multi .60 .30
*a.* Sheet of 8 + central label 5.00 2.40
**5391** A1569 8.10 l multi 4.75 2.40
*a.* Sheet of 8 + central label 38.00 19.50
*b.* Souvenir sheet of 1, imperf. 4.75 2.40

A sheet containing Nos. 5390-5391 was printed in limited quantities.

Treaty Between Romania and Germany, 20th Anniv. — A1570

**2012, Oct. 4**

**5392** A1570 2.10 l multi 1.25 .60
*a.* Sheet of 8 + central label 10.00 5.00

Curtea de Arges Monastery Church, 500th Anniv. — A1571

Designs: 4.50 l, Church and icons. 14.50 l, Church.

**2012, Oct. 12**

**5393** A1571 4.50 l multi 2.60 1.40
*a.* Sheet of 8 + central label 21.00 11.50
**5394** A1571 14.50 l multi 8.25 4.25
*a.* Sheet of 8 + central label 66.00 34.00
*b.* Souvenir sheet of 4, 2 each #5393-5394, + 2 labels 22.00 11.50

Mammals A1572

Designs: No. 5395, Capra pyrenaica. No. 5396, Cervus elaphus.

**2012, Oct. 19**

**5395** A1572 3.10 l multi 1.75 .90
*a.* Sheet of 8 + central label 14.00 7.25
**5396** A1572 3.10 l multi 1.75 .90
*a.* Sheet of 8 + central label 14.00 7.25

A sheet containing Nos. 5395-5396 was printed in limited quantities. See Spain No. 3878.

Christmas A1573

**2012, Nov. 15**

| | | | | |
|---|---|---|---|---|
| 5397 | A1573 1 l multi | | .60 | .30 |
| a. | Sheet of 8 + central label | | 5.00 | 2.40 |

A souvenir sheet of 2 No. 5397 was printed in limited quantities.

Stone Churches A1574

Designs: 3 l, St. Nicholas Church, Densus. 5 l, Strei Church, Hunedoara. 7.60 l, Mintia Church, Vetel. 14.50 l, Colt Church, Suseni.

**2012, Nov. 16**

| | | | | |
|---|---|---|---|---|
| 5398 | A1574 | 3 l multi | 1.75 | .85 |
| a. | Sheet of 8 + central label | | 14.00 | 7.00 |
| 5399 | A1574 | 5 l multi | 3.00 | 1.50 |
| a. | Sheet of 8 + central label | | 24.00 | 12.00 |
| 5400 | A1574 | 7.60 l multi | 4.50 | 2.25 |
| a. | Sheet of 8 + central label | | 36.00 | 18.00 |
| 5401 | A1574 | 14.50 l multi | 8.25 | 4.25 |
| a. | Sheet of 8 + central label | | 66.00 | 34.00 |
| | *Nos. 5398-5401 (4)* | | 17.50 | 8.85 |

Young Animals A1575

Designs: 4.30 l, Bear cub. 5 l, Fawn. 9.10 l, Fox pup. 14.50 l, Wolf pup.

**2012, Dec. 7**

| | | | | |
|---|---|---|---|---|
| 5402 | A1575 | 4.30 l multi | 2.50 | 1.25 |
| a. | Sheet of 8 + central label | | 20.00 | 10.00 |
| 5403 | A1575 | 5 l multi | 3.00 | 1.50 |
| a. | Sheet of 8 + central label | | 24.00 | 12.00 |
| 5404 | A1575 | 9.10 l multi | 5.25 | 2.60 |
| a. | Sheet of 8 + central label | | 42.00 | 21.00 |
| 5405 | A1575 | 14.50 l multi | 8.25 | 4.25 |
| a. | Sheet of 8 + central label | | 66.00 | 34.00 |
| b. | Sheet of 4, #5402-5405 | | 19.00 | 9.75 |
| | *Nos. 5402-5405 (4)* | | 19.00 | 9.60 |

Seal of Mircea cel Batran and Arms of Sovereign Military Order of Malta — A1576

**2012, Dec. 14**

| | | | | |
|---|---|---|---|---|
| 5406 | A1576 8.10 l multi | | 5.00 | 2.50 |
| a. | Sheet of 8 + central label | | 40.00 | 20.00 |

Romanian relations with Sovereign Military Order of Malta, 80th anniv. A souvenir sheet of two No. 5406 exists from a limited printing.

Anti-terrorist Fighter's Day — A1577

Crest of Romanian Anti-terrorist Brigade and: 1 l, Soldier. 8.10 l, Five soldiers.

**2012, Dec. 21**

| | | | | |
|---|---|---|---|---|
| 5407 | A1577 | 1 l multi | .60 | .30 |
| a. | Sheet of 8 + 4 labels | | 5.00 | 2.40 |
| 5408 | A1577 | 8.10 l multi | 5.00 | 2.50 |
| a. | Sheet of 8 + 4 labels | | 40.00 | 20.00 |
| b. | Souvenir sheet of 1 | | 5.00 | 2.50 |

Self-portraits A1578

Self-portrait of: 4.50 l, Stefan Luchian (1868-1916). 9.10 l, Nicolae Grigorescu (1838-1907).

**2013, Jan. 18**

| | | | | |
|---|---|---|---|---|
| 5409 | A1578 | 4.50 l multi | 2.75 | 1.40 |
| a. | Sheet of 8 + central label | | 22.00 | 11.50 |
| 5410 | A1578 | 9.10 l multi | 5.75 | 2.75 |
| a. | Sheet of 8 + central label | | 46.00 | 22.00 |
| b. | Souvenir sheet of 1 | | 5.75 | 2.75 |

Flowers and Clocks — A1579

Designs: 60b, Papaver rhoeas, French mantel clock, 19th cent. 80b, Cichorium intybus, Austrian carriage clock, 19th cent. 1 l, Scorzonera rosea, French table clock, 19th cent. 1.60 l, Caltha palustris, German table clock, 20th cent. 2.40 l, Helianthus annuus, French portico clock, 19th cent. 5 l, Veronica chamaedrys, French table clock, 19th cent.

**2013, Jan. 25**

| | | | | |
|---|---|---|---|---|
| 5411 | A1579 | 60b multi | .40 | .25 |
| a. | Sheet of 8 + central label | | 3.25 | 2.00 |
| 5412 | A1579 | 80b multi | .50 | .25 |
| a. | Sheet of 8 + central label | | 4.00 | 2.00 |
| 5413 | A1579 | 1 l multi | .65 | .30 |
| a. | Sheet of 8 + central label | | 5.25 | 2.40 |
| 5414 | A1579 | 1.60 l multi | 1.00 | .50 |
| a. | Sheet of 8 + central label | | 8.00 | 4.00 |
| 5415 | A1579 | 2.40 l multi | 1.50 | .75 |
| a. | Sheet of 8 + central label | | 12.00 | 6.00 |
| 5416 | A1579 | 5 l multi | 3.25 | 1.60 |
| a. | Sheet of 8 + central label | | 26.00 | 13.00 |
| | *Nos. 5411-5416 (6)* | | 7.30 | 3.65 |

A sheet of six containing Nos. 5412-5417 exists in a limited printing. See Nos. 5454-5459.

Radauti Synagogue, 130th Anniv. — A1580

Synagogue and: 8.10 l, Star of David. 14.50 l, Menorah.

**2013, Feb. 8 Litho. *Perf. 13¼***

| | | | | |
|---|---|---|---|---|
| 5417 | A1580 | 8.10 l multi | 5.00 | 2.50 |
| a. | Sheet of 8 + central label | | 40.00 | 20.00 |
| 5418 | A1580 | 14.50 l multi | 8.75 | 4.50 |
| a. | Sheet of 8 + central label | | 70.00 | 36.00 |

A sheet of two containing Nos. 5417-5418 exists in a limited printing.

Romanian Athenaeum. 125th Anniv. — A1581

Designs: 5 l, Stage. 9.10 l, Exterior.

***Perf. 13¾x13¼***

**2013, Feb. 22 Litho.**

| | | | | |
|---|---|---|---|---|
| 5419 | A1581 | 5 l multi | 3.00 | 1.50 |
| a. | Sheet of 10 | | 30.00 | 15.00 |
| 5420 | A1581 | 9.10 l multi | 5.50 | 2.75 |
| a. | Sheet of 10 | | 55.00 | 27.50 |
| b. | Souvenir sheet of 1 | | 5.50 | 2.75 |

Crowns A1582

Crown of: 3.30 l, King Carol I. 4.30 l, Queen Elizabeth. 14.50 l, Queen Marie.

**2013, Feb. 28 Litho. *Perf. 13¼***

| | | | | |
|---|---|---|---|---|
| 5421 | A1582 | 3.30 l multi | 2.00 | 1.00 |
| a. | Sheet of 6 | | 12.00 | 6.00 |
| 5422 | A1582 | 4.30 l multi | 2.60 | 1.40 |
| a. | Sheet of 6 | | 16.00 | 8.50 |
| 5423 | A1582 | 14.50 l multi | 8.75 | 4.50 |
| a. | Sheet of 6 | | 52.50 | 27.00 |
| | *Nos. 5421-5423 (3)* | | 13.35 | 6.90 |

Values are for stamps with surrounding selvage. A souvenir sheet of three containing Nos. 5421-5423 exists in a limited printing.

Tourist Attractions in Transylvania — A1583

Arms of Transylvania and: 3.30 l, Fortified Church, Viscri. 3.60 l, House, Valea Zalanului, vert. 4.30 l, Hosman, vert. 5 l, St. Michael's Church, Cluj.

**2013, Mar. 15 Litho. *Perf. 13¼***

| | | | | |
|---|---|---|---|---|
| 5424 | A1583 | 3.30 l multi | 1.90 | .95 |
| a. | Sheet of 8 + central label | | 15.50 | 7.75 |
| 5425 | A1583 | 3.60 l multi | 2.10 | 1.10 |
| a. | Sheet of 8 + central label | | 17.00 | 9.00 |
| 5426 | A1583 | 4.30 l multi | 2.50 | 1.25 |
| a. | Sheet of 8 + central label | | 20.00 | 10.00 |
| 5427 | A1583 | 5 l multi | 3.00 | 1.50 |
| a. | Sheet of 8 + central label | | 24.00 | 12.00 |
| | *Nos. 5424-5427 (4)* | | 9.50 | 4.80 |

A sheet of four containing Nos. 5424-5427 exists in a limited printing.

Cameras A1584

Designs: 50b, Goldmann camera, Austria. 80b, Suter camera, Switzerland. 1.40 l, Plaubel Makina camera, Germany. 2 l, Ernemann Tropen-Klapp camera, Germany. 2.10 l, Balda Pontina camera, Germany. 14.50 l, Welta camera, Germany.

**2013, Mar. 29 Litho. *Perf. 13¼***

| | | | | |
|---|---|---|---|---|
| 5428 | A1584 | 50b multi | .30 | .25 |
| a. | Sheet of 8 + central label | | 2.40 | 1.25 |
| 5429 | A1584 | 80b multi | .50 | .25 |
| a. | Sheet of 8 + central label | | 4.00 | 2.00 |
| 5430 | A1584 | 1.40 l multi | .80 | .40 |
| a. | Sheet of 8 + central label | | 6.50 | 3.25 |
| 5431 | A1584 | 2 l multi | 1.25 | .60 |
| a. | Sheet of 8 + central label | | 10.00 | 5.00 |
| 5432 | A1584 | 2.10 l multi | 1.25 | .60 |
| a. | Sheet of 8 + central label | | 10.00 | 5.00 |
| 5433 | A1584 | 14.50 l multi | 8.50 | 4.25 |
| a. | Sheet of 8 + central label | | 68.00 | 34.00 |
| | *Nos. 5428-5433 (6)* | | 12.60 | 6.35 |

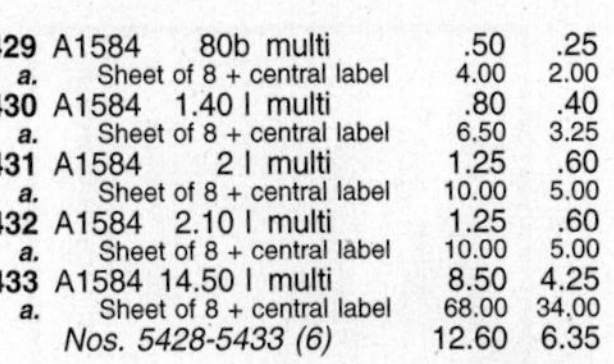


Easter — A1585

**2013, Apr. 5 Litho. *Perf. 13¼***

| | | | | |
|---|---|---|---|---|
| 5434 | A1585 1 l multi | | .60 | .30 |
| a. | Sheet of 8 + central label | | 4.80 | 2.40 |

King Carol I and Bucharest University of Economic Studies — A1586

**2013, Apr. 6 Litho. *Perf. 13¼***

| | | | | |
|---|---|---|---|---|
| 5435 | A1586 8.10 l multi | | 5.00 | 2.50 |
| a. | Sheet of 8 + central label | | 40.00 | 20.00 |

Bucharest University of Economic Studies, cent.

National Bank of Romania, Bucharest — A1587

Designs: 3.10 l, Exterior. 3.60 l, Marble Hall. 4.50 l, Main hallway. 4.70 l, Staircase.

**2013, Apr. 17 Litho. *Perf. 13¼***

| | | | | |
|---|---|---|---|---|
| 5436 | A1587 | 3.10 l multi | 1.90 | .95 |
| a. | Sheet of 6 | | 11.50 | 5.75 |
| 5437 | A1587 | 3.60 l multi | 2.25 | 1.10 |
| a. | Sheet of 6 | | 13.50 | 6.75 |
| 5438 | A1587 | 4.50 l multi | 2.75 | 1.40 |
| a. | Sheet of 6 | | 16.50 | 8.50 |
| 5439 | A1587 | 4.70 l multi | 3.00 | 1.50 |
| a. | Sheet of 6 | | 18.00 | 9.00 |
| b. | Souvenir sheet of 4, #5436-5439 | | 10.00 | 5.00 |
| | *Nos. 5436-5439 (4)* | | 9.90 | 4.95 |

Earth Day — A1588

**2013, Apr. 22 Litho. *Perf. 13¼***

| | | | | |
|---|---|---|---|---|
| 5440 | A1588 5 l multi | | 3.00 | 1.50 |
| a. | Sheet of 8 + central label | | 24.00 | 12.00 |

Famous Women — A1589

Designs: 1 l, Stefania Maracineanu (1882-1944), physicist. 3.30 l, Josephine Cochrane (1839-1913), inventor of dishwasher. 9.10 l, Rear Admiral Grace Murray Hopper (1906-92), computer scientist.

**2013, Apr. 26 Litho. *Perf. 13¼***

| | | | | |
|---|---|---|---|---|
| 5441 | A1589 | 1 l multi | .60 | .30 |
| *a.* | | Sheet of 6 | 3.60 | 1.80 |
| 5442 | A1589 | 3.30 l multi | 2.00 | 1.00 |
| *a.* | | Sheet of 6 | 12.00 | 6.00 |
| 5443 | A1589 | 9.10 l multi | 5.50 | 2.75 |
| *a.* | | Sheet of 6 | 33.00 | 16.50 |
| | | *Nos. 5441-5443 (3)* | 8.10 | 4.05 |

Europa — A1590

Designs: 2.10 l, Biplane with airmail envelopes as wings. 14.50 l, Postman on bicycle delivering letter to driver of automobile.

**2013, Apr. 30 Litho. *Perf. 13¼***

| | | | | |
|---|---|---|---|---|
| 5444 | A1590 | 2.10 l multi | 1.25 | .60 |
| *a.* | | Sheet of 6 | 7.50 | 3.75 |
| 5445 | A1590 | 14.50 l multi | 9.00 | 4.50 |
| *a.* | | Sheet of 6 | 54.00 | 27.00 |
| *b.* | | Souvenir sheet of 4, 2 each #5444-5445, #5444 at UL | 20.50 | 10.50 |
| *c.* | | As "b," #5445 at UL | 20.50 | 10.50 |

Edict of Milan, 1700th Anniv. — A1591

Emperor Constantine the Great and Empress Helen on: 4.70 l, Byzantine era icon. 9.10 l, Icon by Otilia Michail Otetelesanu from 1960s.

**2013, May 21 Litho. *Perf. 13¼***

| | | | | |
|---|---|---|---|---|
| 5446 | A1591 | 4.70 l multi | 3.00 | 1.50 |
| *a.* | | Sheet of 6 | 18.00 | 9.00 |
| 5447 | A1591 | 9.10 l multi | 5.50 | 2.75 |
| *a.* | | Sheet of 6 | 33.00 | 16.50 |

First Mention of Suceava in Documents, 625th Anniv. — A1592

Anniversary emblem and: 4.30 l, St. George's Church (Mirauti Church). 14.50 l, Suceava Fortress.

**2013, May 30 Litho. *Perf. 13¼***

| | | | | |
|---|---|---|---|---|
| 5448 | A1592 | 4.30 l multi | 2.60 | 1.40 |
| *a.* | | Sheet of 8 + label | 21.00 | 11.50 |
| 5449 | A1592 | 14.50 l multi | 8.75 | 4.50 |
| *a.* | | Sheet of 8 + label | 70.00 | 36.00 |

A souvenir sheet of two containing Nos. 5448-5449 was printed in limited quantities.

Healthy Foods A1593

Jar of honey and: 1 l, Walnuts, cinnamon sticks. 1.40 l, Hazelnuts. 6 l, Raspberries and blackberries. 8.10 l, Walnuts, cinnamon sticks, hazelnuts, raspberries and blackberries.

**2013, June 7 Litho. *Perf. 13¼***

| | | | | |
|---|---|---|---|---|
| 5450 | A1593 | 1 l multi | .60 | .30 |
| *a.* | | Sheet of 8 + label | 5.00 | 2.40 |
| 5451 | A1593 | 1.40 l multi | .85 | .40 |
| *a.* | | Sheet of 8 + label | 7.00 | 3.25 |
| 5452 | A1593 | 6 l multi | 3.75 | 1.90 |
| *a.* | | Sheet of 8 + label | 30.00 | 15.50 |
| 5453 | A1593 | 8.10 l multi | 5.00 | 2.50 |
| *a.* | | Sheet of 8 + label | 40.00 | 20.00 |
| | | *Nos. 5450-5453 (4)* | 10.20 | 5.10 |

A souvenir sheet of four containing Nos. 5450-5453 was printed in limited quantities.

**Flowers and Clocks Type of 2013**

Designs: 50b, Anthericum ramosum, French table clock, 19th cent. 1.20 l, Mirabilis jalapa, German table clock, 19th cent. 1.40 l, Datura stramonium, Swiss pocket watch, 18th cent. 3 l, Silene latifolia, Austrian traveler's clock, 19th cent. 3.10 l, Nicotiana alata, French chimney clock, 19th cent. 4.70 l, Oenothera biennis, French miniature table clock, 19th cent.

**2013, June 21 Litho. *Perf. 13¼***

| | | | | |
|---|---|---|---|---|
| 5454 | A1579 | 50b multi | .30 | .25 |
| *a.* | | Sheet of 8 + central label | 2.40 | 1.25 |
| 5455 | A1579 | 1.20 l multi | .70 | .35 |
| *a.* | | Sheet of 8 + central label | 5.75 | 3.00 |
| 5456 | A1579 | 1.40 l mulkti | .85 | .40 |
| *a.* | | Sheet of 8 + central label | 7.00 | 3.25 |
| 5457 | A1579 | 3 l multi | 1.75 | .85 |
| *a.* | | Sheet of 8 + central label | 14.00 | 7.00 |
| 5458 | A1579 | 3.10 l multi | 1.90 | .95 |
| *a.* | | Sheet of 8 + central label | 15.50 | 7.75 |
| 5459 | A1579 | 4.70 l multi | 2.75 | 1.40 |
| *a.* | | Sheet of 8 + central label | 22.00 | 11.50 |
| | | *Nos. 5454-5459 (6)* | 8.25 | 4.20 |

A sheet of six containing Nos. 5454-5459 exists in a limited printing.

Owls — A1594

Designs: 2 l, Athene noctua. 3.30 l, Asio otus. 4.50 l, Strix uralensis. 9.10 l, Strix nebulosa, horiz.

**2013, June 28 Litho. *Perf. 13¼***

| | | | | |
|---|---|---|---|---|
| 5460 | A1594 | 2 l multi | 1.25 | .60 |
| *a.* | | Sheet of 6 | 7.50 | 3.75 |
| 5461 | A1594 | 3.30 l multi | 2.00 | 1.00 |
| *a.* | | Sheet of 6 | 12.00 | 6.00 |
| 5462 | A1594 | 4.50 l multi | 2.75 | 1.40 |
| *a.* | | Sheet of 6 | 16.50 | 8.50 |
| 5463 | A1594 | 9.10 l multi | 5.50 | 2.75 |
| *a.* | | Sheet of 6 | 33.00 | 16.50 |
| | | *Nos. 5460-5463 (4)* | 11.50 | 5.75 |

Treaty of Friendly Relations and Cooperation Between Romania and Russia, 10th Anniv. — A1595

**2013, July 9 Litho. *Perf. 13¾x13¼***

| | | | | |
|---|---|---|---|---|
| 5464 | A1595 | 8.10 l multi | 4.75 | 2.40 |
| *a.* | | Sheet of 6 + 2 labels | 28.50 | 14.50 |
| *b.* | | Souvenir sheet of 1 | 4.75 | 2.40 |

Sport Hunting and Fishing A1596

Designs: 2 l, Mouflon. 2.10 l, European hare. 6 l, Chamois. 7.60 l, Trout.

**2013, July 9 Litho. *Perf. 13¼***

| | | | | |
|---|---|---|---|---|
| 5465 | A1596 | 2 l multi | 1.25 | .60 |
| *a.* | | Sheet of 8 + label | 10.00 | 5.00 |
| 5466 | A1596 | 2.10 l multi | 1.25 | .60 |
| *a.* | | Sheet of 8 + label | 10.00 | 5.00 |
| 5467 | A1596 | 6 l multi | 3.50 | 1.75 |
| *a.* | | Sheet of 8 + label | 28.00 | 14.00 |
| 5468 | A1596 | 7.60 l multi | 4.50 | 2.25 |
| *a.* | | Sheet of 8 + label | 36.00 | 18.00 |
| | | *Nos. 5465-5468 (4)* | 10.50 | 5.20 |

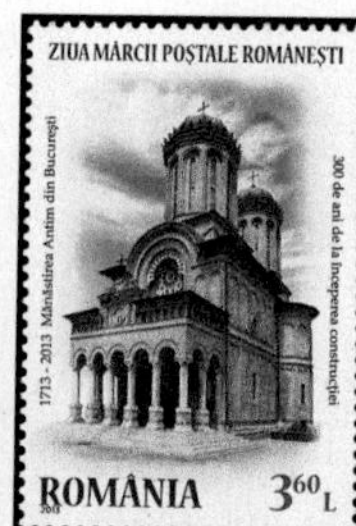

Antim Monastery, 300th Anniv. — A1597

Designs: 3.60 l, Monastery. 14.50 l, Bishop Antim Ivireanu (1650-1716).

**2013, July 15 Litho. *Perf. 13¼***

| | | | | |
|---|---|---|---|---|
| 5469 | A1597 | 3.60 l multi | 2.10 | 1.10 |
| *a.* | | Sheet of 4 | 8.50 | 4.50 |
| 5470 | A1597 | 14.50 l multi | 8.75 | 4.50 |
| *a.* | | Sheet of 4 | 35.00 | 18.00 |

A sheet of two containing Nos. 5469-5470 exists in a limited printing.

Romanian Gold Coins A1598

20-lei coins from: 3.30 l, 1870. 4.30 l, 1906. 4.50 l, 1922. 8.10 l, 1939.

**2013, July 26 Litho. *Perf. 13¼***

| | | | | |
|---|---|---|---|---|
| 5471 | A1598 | 3.30 l multi | 2.00 | 1.00 |
| *a.* | | Sheet of 6 | 12.00 | 6.00 |
| 5472 | A1598 | 4.30 l multi | 2.60 | 1.40 |
| *a.* | | Sheet of 6 | 16.00 | 8.50 |
| 5473 | A1598 | 4.50 l multi | 2.75 | 1.40 |
| *a.* | | Sheet of 6 | 16.50 | 8.50 |
| 5474 | A1598 | 8.10 l multi | 5.00 | 2.50 |
| *a.* | | Sheet of 6 | 30.00 | 15.00 |
| | | *Nos. 5471-5474 (4)* | 12.35 | 6.30 |

Religion and Law — A1599

Designs: 1.20 l, Statue of Moses, by Michelangelo. 1.40 l, Ten Commandments. 3 l, Torahs, Great Synagogue of Bucharest. 14.50 l, St. Catherine's Monastery, Mount Sinai, Egypt.

**2013, Aug. 14 Litho. *Perf. 13¼***

| | | | | |
|---|---|---|---|---|
| 5475 | A1599 | 1.20 l multi | .75 | .35 |
| *a.* | | Sheet of 8 + central label | 6.00 | 3.00 |
| 5476 | A1599 | 1.40 l multi | .85 | .40 |
| *a.* | | Sheet of 8 + central label | 7.00 | 3.25 |
| 5477 | A1599 | 3 l multi | 1.75 | .90 |
| *a.* | | Sheet of 8 + central label | 14.00 | 7.25 |
| 5478 | A1599 | 14.50 l multi | 8.75 | 4.50 |
| *a.* | | Sheet of 8 + central label | 70.00 | 36.00 |
| | | *Nos. 5475-5478 (4)* | 12.10 | 6.15 |

A sheet of 4 containing Nos. 5475-5478 exists in a limited printing.

Mention of Oradea in Documents, 900th Anniv. — A1600

Designs: 2.10 l, Assumption of the Virgin Orthodox Cathedral. 4.30 l, Roman Catholic Cathedral. 4.70 l, Queen Marie Theater, horiz. 9.10 l, Oradea City Hall, horiz.

**2013, Aug. 30 Litho. *Perf. 13¼***

| | | | | |
|---|---|---|---|---|
| 5479 | A1600 | 2.10 l multi | 1.25 | .60 |
| *a.* | | Sheet of 8 + central label | 10.00 | 5.00 |
| 5480 | A1600 | 4.30 l multi | 2.60 | 1.40 |
| *a.* | | Sheet of 8 + central label | 21.00 | 11.50 |
| 5481 | A1600 | 4.70 l multi | 3.00 | 1.50 |
| *a.* | | Sheet of 8 + central label | 24.00 | 12.00 |
| 5482 | A1600 | 9.10 l multi | 5.50 | 2.75 |
| *a.* | | Sheet of 8 + central label | 44.00 | 22.00 |
| *b.* | | Souvenir sheet of 1 | 5.50 | 2.75 |
| | | *Nos. 5479-5482 (4)* | 12.35 | 6.25 |

A sheet of four containing Nos. 5479-5482 exists in a limited printing.

Traditional Costumes of Romania and Poland — A1601

***Perf. 13¾x13¼***

**2013, Sept. 11 Litho.**

| | | | | |
|---|---|---|---|---|
| 5483 | A1601 | 8.10 l multi | 5.00 | 2.50 |
| *a.* | | Sheet of 10 | 50.00 | 25.00 |
| *b.* | | Souvenir sheet of 1 | 5.00 | 2.50 |

See Poland No. 4092.

Statues of the National Bank of Romania A1602

Designs: 2 l, Justice. 3.30 l, Commerce. 3.60 l, Industry. 4.50 l, Agriculture. 8.10 l, Bust of bank founder Eugeniu Carada (1836-1910), by Ioan Bolborea.

**2013, Sept. 20 Litho. *Perf. 13¼***

| | | | | |
|---|---|---|---|---|
| 5484 | A1602 | 2 l multi | 1.25 | .60 |
| *a.* | | Sheet of 6 | 7.50 | 3.75 |
| 5485 | A1602 | 3.30 l multi | 2.00 | 1.00 |
| *a.* | | Sheet of 6 | 12.00 | 6.00 |
| 5486 | A1602 | 3.60 l multi | 2.25 | 1.10 |
| *a.* | | Sheet of 6 | 2.25 | 1.10 |
| 5487 | A1602 | 4.50 l multi | 2.75 | 1.40 |
| *a.* | | Sheet of 6 | 16.50 | 8.50 |
| | | *Nos. 5484-5487 (4)* | 8.25 | 4.10 |

**Souvenir Sheet**

***Perf. 13¼x13¾***

| | | | | |
|---|---|---|---|---|
| 5488 | A1602 | 8.10 l multi | 5.00 | 2.50 |

No. 5488 contains one 42x52mm stamp. A sheet of four containing Nos. 5484-5487 exists in a limited printing, as does and example of No. 5488 with gold foil.

Maria Tanase (1913-63), Singer — A1603

**2013, Sept. 25 Litho. *Perf. 13¼***

5489 A1603 9.10 l multi 5.50 2.75
a. Sheet of 8 44.00 22.00
b. Souvenir sheet of 1 5.50 2.75

No. 5489a exists with two different marginal illustrations. Values are for either illustration.

Rogoz Wooden Church From Wooden Churches of Maramures UNESCO World Heritage Site — A1604

**2013, Sept. 27 Litho. *Perf. 13¼***

5490 A1604 8.10 l multi 5.00 2.50
a. Sheet of 6 30.00 15.00

Rogoz Wooden Church, 350th anniv.

Transylvanian Association for Romanian Literature and Culture Museum of Traditional Folk Civilization, 50th Anniv. — A1605

**2013, Oct. 4 Litho. *Perf. 13¼***

5491 A1605 14.50 l multi 9.00 4.50
a. Sheet of 4 + 2 labels 36.00 18.00

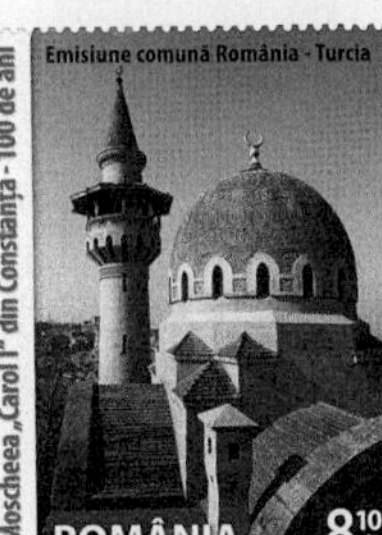

King Carol I Mosque, Constanta, Cent. A1606

**2013, Oct. 10 Litho. *Perf. 13¼x13¾***

5492 A1606 8.10 l multi 5.00 2.50
a. Sheet of 6 30.00 15.00
b. Souvenir sheet of 1 5.00 2.50

No. 5492b exists with a different sheet margin on a first day cover in a limited printing.

See Turkey No. 3365.

Fauna A1607

Designs: 3.30 l, Marmota marmota. 4.30 l, Picoides tridactylus. 4.50 l, Lynx lynx. 9.10 l, Bison bonasus.

**2013, Oct. 25 Litho. *Perf. 13¼***

5493 A1607 3.30 l multi 2.00 1.00
a. Sheet of 5 + label 10.00 5.00
5494 A1607 4.30 l multi 2.60 1.40
a. Sheet of 5 + label 13.00 7.00
5495 A1607 4.50 l multi 2.75 1.40
a. Sheet of 5 + label 14.00 7.00
5496 A1607 9.10 l multi 5.50 2.75
a. Sheet of 5 + label 27.50 14.00
*Nos. 5493-5496 (4)* 12.85 6.55

Radio Romania, 85th Anniv. A1608

Designs: 1 l, Nicolae Iorga (1871-1940), writer and prime minister. 14.50 l, Elena Vacarescu (1866-1947), writer.

**2013, Nov. 4 Litho. *Perf. 13¼***

5497 A1608 1 l multi .60 .30
a. Sheet of 4 2.40 1.25
5498 A1608 14.50 l multi 8.75 4.50
a. Sheet of 4 35.00 18.00
b. Sheet of 2, #5497-5498, + 14 labels 9.50 4.75

Christmas — A1609

**2013, Nov. 22 Litho. *Perf. 13¼***

5499 A1609 1 l multi .60 .30
a. Sheet of 8 + central label 5.00 2.40
Complete booklet, 8 #5499 5.00

A sheet containing four No. 5499 exists in a limited printing.

Chess Pieces and Emblem of Integrated Intelligence Office — A1610

**2013, Nov. 29 Litho. *Perf. 13¼***

5500 A1610 8.10 l multi 5.00 2.50
a. Sheet of 6 + 3 labels 30.00 15.00

Paintings of Roses — A1611

Designs: 1 l, Roses, by Nicolae Grigorescu. 3.60 l, Roses, by Theodor Aman. 4.50 l, Roses, by Stefan Luchian, horiz. 14.50 l, Roses, by Ion Andreescu, horiz.

**2013, Dec. 12 Litho. *Perf. 13¼***

5501 A1611 1 l multi .60 .30
a. Sheet of 6 + 2 labels 3.75 1.90
5502 A1611 3.60 l multi 2.25 1.10
a. Sheet of 6 + 2 labels 13.50 6.75
5503 A1611 4.50 l multi 2.75 1.40
a. Sheet of 6 + 2 labels 16.50 8.50
5504 A1611 14.50 l multi 9.00 4.50
a. Sheet of 6 + 2 labels 54.00 27.00
*Nos. 5501-5504 (4)* 14.60 7.30

A sheet of four containing Nos. 5501-5504 exists in a limited printing.

Corund Ceramics A1612

Designs: 3.30 l, Plate. 3.60 l, Cup. 5 l, Bowl. 8.10 l, Vase.

**2013, Dec. 20 Litho. *Perf. 13¼***

5505 A1612 3.30 l multi 2.00 1.00
a. Sheet of 6 12.00 6.00
5506 A1612 3.60 l multi 2.25 1.10
a. Sheet of 6 13.50 6.75
5507 A1612 5 l multi 3.00 1.50
a. Sheet of 6 18.00 9.00
5508 A1612 8.10 l multi 5.00 2.50
a. Sheet of 6 30.00 15.00
*Nos. 5505-5508 (4)* 12.25 6.10

Churches A1613

Designs: 1 l, Church of the Savior, Berestovo, Ukraine. 9.10 l, Church of the Sucevita Monastery, Romania.

**2013, Dec. 21 Litho. *Perf. 13¼***

5509 A1613 1 l multi .60 .30
a. Sheet of 8 + central label 4.80 2.40
5510 A1613 9.10 l multi 5.50 2.75
a. Sheet of 8 + central label 44.00 22.00

See Ukraine No. 952.

Mihai Eminescu (1850-89), Poet — A1614

**2014, Jan. 15 Litho. *Perf. 13¼***

5511 A1614 9.10 l multi 5.50 2.75
a. Souvenir sheet of 1 5.50 2.75
b. Miniature sheet of 6 33.00 16.50

National Culture Day.

Buildings in Arad — A1615

Arms of Arad and: 2 l, City Hall. 2.10 l, Old Orthodox Cathedral, vert. 3.60 l, Evangelical Lutheran Church, vert. 14.50 l, Ioan Slavici Classical Theater.

**2014, Jan. 23 Litho. *Perf. 13¼***

5512 A1615 2 l multi 1.25 .60
a. Sheet of 5 + label 6.25 3.00
5513 A1615 2.10 l multi 1.25 .65
a. Sheet of 5 + label 6.25 3.25
5514 A1615 3.60 l multi 2.25 1.10
a. Sheet of 5 + label 11.50 5.50
5515 A1615 14.50 l multi 8.75 4.50
a. Sheet of 5 + label 44.00 22.50
*Nos. 5512-5515 (4)* 13.50 6.85

Desert Flowers A1616

Designs: 1 l, Echinocereus triglochidiatus. 1.40 l, Baileya multiradiata. 8.10 l, Solanum elaeagnifolium. 14.50 l, Hibiscus denudatus.

**2014, Jan. 29 Litho. *Perf. 13¼***

5516 A1616 1 l multi .60 .30
a. Sheet of 4 2.40 1.20
5517 A1616 1.40 l multi .85 .40
a. Sheet of 4 3.50 1.60
5518 A1616 8.10 l multi 5.00 2.50
a. Sheet of 4 20.00 10.00
5519 A1616 14.50 l multi 8.75 4.50
a. Sheet of 4 35.00 18.00
*Nos. 5516-5519 (4)* 15.20 7.70

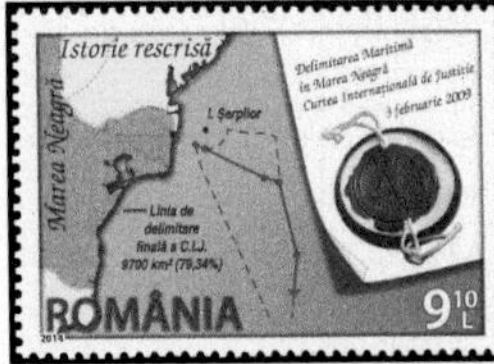

Favorable Judgement in Black Sea Boundary Dispute With Ukraine, 5th Anniv. — A1617

**2014, Feb. 3 Litho. *Perf. 13¼***

5520 A1617 9.10 l multi 5.50 2.75
a. Souvenir sheet of 1 5.50 2.75
b. Sheet of 10 + 2 labels 55.00 27.50

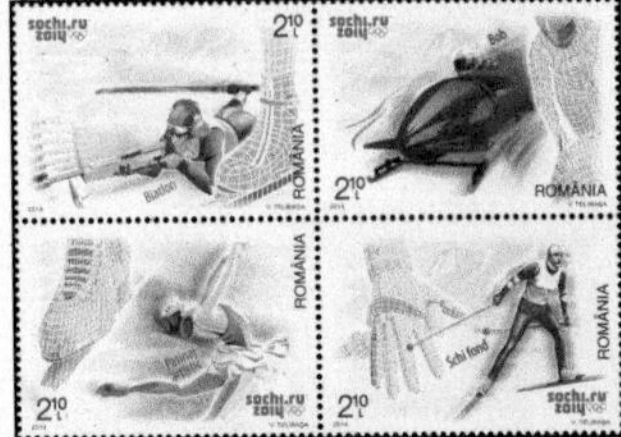

2014 Winter Olympics, Sochi, Russia — A1618

No. 5521: a, Biathlon. b, Bobsledding. c, Figure skating. d, Skiing.

**2014, Feb. 7 Litho. *Perf. 13¼***

5521 A1618 2.10 l Block of 4, #a-d 5.25 2.60

No. 5521 was printed in sheets containing two tete-beche blocks.

Miniature Sheet

Paintings of Roma People — A1619

No. 5522 — Painting of various Roma people by: a, 3.50 l, Iosif Iser (1881-1958). b, 4.30 l, Nicolae Grigorescu (1838-1907). c, 4.50 l, Pierre Bellet (1865-1924). d, 8.10 l, Nicolae Vermont (1836-1932).

**2014, Feb. 20 Litho. *Perf. 13¼x14***

5522 A1619 Sheet of 4, #a-d 12.50 6.25

Actors and Actresses A1620

Designs: No. 5523, Draga Olteanu Matei. No. 5524, Florin Piersic. No. 5525, Olga Tudorache. No. 5526, Marin Moraru. No. 5527, Mircea Albulescu. No. 5528, Ileana Stana Ionescu. No. 5529, Tamara Buciuceanu-Botez. No. 5530, Mitica Popescu. No. 5531, Sebastian Papaiani. No. 5532, Valeria Gagealov. No. 5533, George Motoi. No. 5534, Sanda Toma.

**2014, Mar. 1 Litho. *Perf. 13¼***

**5523** A1620 1.60 l multi 1.00 .50
*a.* Sheet of 4 4.00 2.00
**5524** A1620 1.60 l multi 1.00 .50
*a.* Sheet of 4 4.00 2.00
**5525** A1620 1.60 l multi 1.00 .50
*a.* Sheet of 4 4.00 2.00
**5526** A1620 1.60 l multi 1.00 .50
*a.* Sheet of 4 4.00 2.00
**5527** A1620 1.60 l multi 1.00 .50
*a.* Sheet of 4 4.00 2.00
**5528** A1620 1.60 l multi 1.00 .50
*a.* Sheet of 4 4.00 2.00
**5529** A1620 1.60 l multi 1.00 .50
*a.* Sheet of 4 4.00 2.00
**5530** A1620 1.60 l multi 1.00 .50
*a.* Sheet of 4 4.00 2.00
**5531** A1620 1.60 l multi 1.00 .50
*a.* Sheet of 4 4.00 2.00
**5532** A1620 1.60 l multi 1.00 .50
*a.* Sheet of 4 4.00 2.00
**5533** A1620 1.60 l multi 1.00 .50
*a.* Sheet of 4 4.00 2.00
**5534** A1620 1.60 l multi 1.00 .50
*a.* Sheet of 4 4.00 2.00
*b.* Sheet of 12, #5523-5534, + 4 central labels 12.00 6.00
*Nos. 5523-5534 (12)* 12.00 6.00

See Nos. 5882-5887.

Easter — A1621

**2014, Mar. 20 Litho. *Perf. 13¼***

**5535** A1621 1 l multi .65 .30
*a.* Sheet of 8 + central label 5.25 2.60

Ducks A1622

Designs: 1.20 l, Anas platyrhynchos. 1.40 l, Aythya fuligula. 8.10 l, Anas clypeata. 14.50 l, Anas crecca.

**2014, Mar. 24 Litho. *Perf. 13¼***

**5536** A1622 1.20 l multi .75 .35
*a.* Sheet of 5 + label 3.75 1.75
**5537** A1622 1.40 l multi .85 .45
*a.* Sheet of 5 + label 4.25 2.25
**5538** A1622 8.10 l multi 5.00 2.50
*a.* Sheet of 5 + label 25.00 12.50
**5539** A1622 14.50 l multi 9.00 4.50
*a.* Sheet of 5 + label 45.00 22.50
*Nos. 5536-5539 (4)* 15.60 7.80

Admission to North Atlantic Treaty Organization, 10th Anniv. — A1623

**2014, Apr. 2 Litho. *Perf. 13¼***

**5540** A1623 9.10 l multi 5.75 3.00
*a.* Sheet of 6 35.00 18.00
*b.* Souvenir sheet of 1 5.75 3.00

No. 5540 has 13 perforation holes within stamp; No. 5540b, has 5.

Traditional Foods A1624

Designs: 1 l, Red eggs and cozonac. 3.60 l, Fish on fir tree branches. 4.50 l, Roast lamb and vegetables. 8.10 l, Cheeses and vegetables.

**2014, Apr. 18 Litho. *Perf. 13¼***

**5541** A1624 1 l multi .65 .30
*a.* Sheet of 5 + 3 labels 3.25 1.50
**5542** A1624 3.60 l multi 2.25 1.10
*a.* Sheet of 5 + 3 labels 11.50 5.50
**5543** A1624 4.50 l multi 3.00 1.50
*a.* Sheet of 5 + 3 labels 15.00 7.50
**5544** A1624 8.10 l multi 5.00 2.50
*a.* Sheet of 5 + 3 labels 25.00 12.50
*Nos. 5541-5544 (4)* 10.90 5.40

Europa — A1625

Musicians playing: 2.10 l, Tulnics. 14.50 l, Lutes.

**2014, May 5 Litho. *Perf. 13¼***

**5545** A1625 2.10 l multi 1.40 .70
*a.* Sheet of 6 8.50 4.25
**5546** A1625 14.50 l multi 9.00 4.50
*a.* Sheet of 6 54.00 27.00
*b.* Souvenir sheet of 4, 2 each #5545-5546, #5545 at UL 21.00 10.50
*c.* As "b," #5546 at UL 21.00 10.50

World Conference of Masonic Regular Grand Lodges, Romania A1626

Emblem and: 3.30 l, Olive branch. 9.10 l, Sever Frentiu (1931-97), painter.

**2014, May 14 Litho. *Perf. 13¼***

**5547** A1626 3.30 l multi 2.10 1.10
*a.* Sheet of 4 8.50 4.50
**5548** A1626 9.10 l multi 5.75 3.00
*a.* Sheet of 4 23.00 12.00

Training Ship Mircea, 75th Anniv. — A1627

Designs: 1 l, Mircea with sails up. No. 5550, Mircea and military order, vert.
No. 5551, Mircea with sails down.

**2014, May 24 Litho. *Perf. 13¼***

**5549** A1627 1 l multi .65 .30
*a.* Sheet of 6 4.00 2.00
**5550** A1627 14.50 l multi 9.00 4.50
*a.* Sheet of 6 54.00 27.00

**Souvenir Sheet**

**5551** A1627 14.50 l multi + label 9.00 4.50

Theodor Aman (1831-91), Founder of National University of Arts, Bucharest A1628

**2014, May 28 Litho. *Perf. 13¼***

**5552** A1628 8.10 l multi 5.00 2.50
*a.* Sheet of 6 30.00 15.00
*b.* Souvenir sheet of 1 5.00 2.50

National University of Arts, 150th anniv.

UNICEF Campaign To End Violence Against Children A1629

**2014, June 2 Litho. *Perf. 13¼***

**5553** A1629 4.30 l aqua blue 2.75 1.40
*a.* Sheet of 8 + central label 22.00 11.50

Emblem of Court of Accounts A1630

Emblem of Court of Accounts, Prince Alexandru Ioan Cuza (1820-73) — A1631

**2014, June 6 Litho. *Perf. 13¾***

**5554** A1630 2.40 l multi 1.50 .75
*a.* Sheet of 8 + central label 12.00 6.00
**5555** A1631 4.50 l gray grn & multi 3.00 1.50
*a.* Sheet of 8 + central label 24.00 12.00

**Souvenir Sheet**

**5556** A1631 14.50 l beige & multi 9.00 4.50

Court of Accounts, 150th anniv.

2014 World Cup Soccer Championships, Brazil — A1632

No. 5557: a, Two players, denomination at UR. b, Goaltender, denomination at UL. c, Two players, diff., denomination at LL. d, Two players, diff. denomination at LR.

**2014, June 12 Litho. *Perf. 13¼***

**5557** A1632 2.40 l Block of 4, #a-d 6.00 3.00
*e.* Souvenir sheet of 4, #5557a-5557d 6.00 3.00

Romanian Senate, 150th Anniv. — A1633

Designs: 1 l, Senate Building and emblem. 14.50 l, Emblem.

**2014, June 17 Litho. *Perf. 13¼***

**5558** A1633 1 l multi .65 .30
*a.* Sheet of 8 + 2 labels 5.25 2.40

**Souvenir Sheet**

**5559** A1633 14.50 l multi 9.00 4.50

No. 5559 contains one 36x36mm stamp.

Gymnastics Personalities A1634

Designs: 2.10 l, Octavian Bellu, head coach of national team. 9.10 l, Mariana Bitang, coach and trainer.

**2014, June 20 Litho. *Perf. 13¼***

**5560** A1634 2.10 l multi 1.40 .70
*a.* Sheet of 6 8.50 4.25
**5561** A1634 9.10 l multi 5.75 3.00
*a.* Sheet of 6 35.00 18.00
*b.* Souvenir sheet of 2, #5560-5561 7.25 3.75

Maramures Tourist Attractions A1635

Designs: 2 l, Stephen's Tower. 3.30 l, Berbesti roadside cross. 8.10 l, Wooden church, Sugatag. 14.50 l, Cemetery with decorations, Sapanta.

**2014, July 4 Litho. *Perf. 13¼***

**5562** A1635 2 l multi 1.25 .60
*a.* Sheet of 5 + label 6.25 3.00
**5563** A1635 3.30 l multi 2.00 1.00
*a.* Sheet of 5 + label 10.00 5.00
**5564** A1635 8.10 l multi 5.00 2.50
*a.* Sheet of 5 + label 25.00 12.50
**5565** A1635 14.50 l multi 8.75 4.50
*a.* Sheet of 5 + label 44.00 22.50
*Nos. 5562-5565 (4)* 17.00 8.60

A1636

Church of the Three Holy Hierarchs Monastery, Iasi — A1637

**2014, July 15 Litho. *Perf. 13¼***

5566 A1636 14.50 l multi 8.75 4.50
*a.* Sheet of 8 + central label 70.00 36.00

**Souvenir Sheet**

5567 A1637 8.10 l multi 5.00 2.50

Stamp Day.

University of Bucharest, 150th Anniv. — A1638

Designs: 8.10 l. University building and statue.14.50 l, Watercolor depicting University Buildings by Alexandru Orascu.

**2014, July 16 Litho. *Perf. 13¼***

5568 A1638 8.10 l multi 5.00 2.50
*a.* Sheet of 8 40.00 20.00

**Souvenir Sheet**

5569 A1638 14.50 l multi + label 8.75 4.50

Remembrance of National Heroes — A1639

Designs: 1 l, Order of Michael the Brave first class, King Ferdinand I, Gen. Alexandru Averescu. 3.60 l, Heroes' Cross Monument, vert. 14.50 l, Mausoleum of Marasesti.

**2014, July 25 Litho. *Perf. 13¼***

5570 A1639 1 l multi .60 .30
*a.* Sheet of 6 3.75 1.90
5571 A1639 3.60 l multi 2.25 1.10
*a.* Sheet of 6 13.50 6.75
5572 A1639 14.50 l multi 8.75 4.50
*a.* Sheet of 6 52.50 27.00
*Nos. 5570-5572 (3)* 11.60 5.90

UNESCO Intangible Cultural Heritage in Romania — A1640

Designs: 3.10 l, Doina musician, sheep in pasture. 6 l, Calus dancers. No. 5575, Colindat Christmas ritual.
No. 5576, Horezu plate and potter.

**2014, Aug. 7 Litho. *Perf. 13¼***

5573 A1640 3.10 l multi 1.75 .90
*a.* Sheet of 6 10.50 5.50
5574 A1640 6 l multi 3.75 1.90
*a.* Sheet of 6 22.50 11.50
5575 A1640 9.10 l multi 5.50 2.75
*a.* Sheet of 6 33.00 16.50
*Nos. 5573-5575 (3)* 11.00 5.55

**Souvenir Sheet**

5576 A1640 9.10 l multi 5.50 2.75

Martyrdom of the Brancoveanu Saints, 300th Anniv. — A1641

Designs: 2.40 l, Constantin Brancoveanu (1654-1714), Prince of Wallachia. 5 l, Icon depicting martyrs and Ianache Vacarescu, vert. 14.50 l, St. George's New Church, Bucharest.

**2014, Aug. 16 Litho. *Perf. 13¼***

5577 A1641 2.40 l multi 1.50 .75
*a.* Sheet of 6 9.00 4.50
5578 A1641 5 l multi 3.00 1.50
*a.* Sheet of 6 18.00 9.00
5579 A1641 14.50 l multi 8.75 4.50
*a.* Sheet of 6 52.50 27.00
*Nos. 5577-5579 (3)* 13.25 6.75

An imperforate sheet of Nos. 5577-5579 was printed in a limited edition.

Paintings — A1642

Designs: 4.70 l, Spring, by Pieter Breughel the Younger. 5 l, Summer, by Breughel the Younger. 7.60 l, The Marriage of the Virgin, by El Greco, vert. 8.10 l, The Martyrdom of St. Maurice and the 10,000 Thebans, by El Greco, vert.

**2014, Aug. 22 Litho. *Perf. 13¼***

5580 A1642 4.70 l multi 2.75 1.40
*a.* Sheet of 4 11.00 5.75
5581 A1642 5 l multi 3.00 1.50
*a.* Sheet of 4 12.00 6.00
5582 A1642 7.60 l multi 4.50 2.25
*a.* Sheet of 4 18.00 9.00
5583 A1642 8.10 l multi 5.00 2.50
*a.* Sheet of 4 20.00 10.00
*Nos. 5580-5583 (4)* 15.25 7.65

Oltenia Tourism — A1643

Arms of Oltenia and: 2.40 l, Cula Greceanu, Maldaresti Museum complex, Valcea. 3 l, Art Museum of Craiova. 3.30 l, Tismana Monastery. 4.30 l, Biserica Monastery, Hurezi. 4.50 l, Horezu ceramics. 14.50 l, Grapes and vineyard.

**2014, Aug. 29 Litho. *Perf. 13¼***

5584 A1643 2.40 l multi 1.50 .75
*a.* Sheet of 5 + label 7.50 3.75
5585 A1643 3 l multi 1.75 .90
*a.* Sheet of 5 + label 8.75 4.50
5586 A1643 3.30 l multi 2.00 1.00
*a.* Sheet of 5 + label 10.00 5.00
5587 A1643 4.30 l multi 2.60 1.25
*a.* Sheet of 5 + label 13.00 6.25
5588 A1643 4.50 l multi 2.75 1.40
*a.* Sheet of 5 + label 14.00 7.00
5589 A1643 14.50 l multi 8.75 4.50
*a.* Sheet of 5 + label 44.00 22.50
*Nos. 5584-5589 (6)* 19.35 9.80

Animals and Their Food — A1644

Designs: 1.40 l, Squirrel and hazel nuts. 2 l, Boar and acorns, vert. 8.10 l, Bear and berries, vert. 14.50 l, Starling and grapes.

**2014, Sept. 5 Litho. *Perf. 13¼***

5590 A1644 1.40 l multi .80 .40
*a.* Sheet of 5 + label 4.00 2.00
5591 A1644 2 l multi 1.25 .60
*a.* Sheet of 5 + label 6.25 3.00
5592 A1644 8.10 l multi 4.75 2.40
*a.* Sheet of 5 + label 24.00 12.00
5593 A1644 14.50 l multi 8.50 4.25
*a.* Sheet of 5 + label 42.50 21.50
*Nos. 5590-5593 (4)* 15.30 7.65

Romanian Olympic Committee, Cent. — A1645

"100" and: 1 l, Romanian Olympic Committee emblem. 14.50 l, Torch.

**2014, Sept. 12 Litho. *Perf. 13¼***

5594 A1645 1 l multi .60 .30
*a.* Sheet of 8 + central label 4.80 2.40

**Souvenir Sheet**

5595 A1645 14.50 l multi 8.50 4.25

Bucharest, 555th Anniv. — A1646

Designs: 3.30 l, National Bank of Romania. 4.30 l, Palace of the Patriarchate. 4.50 l, Toma Stelian House. 5 l, Kretulescu Palace. 6 l, Carol Davila University of Medicine and Pharmacy. No. 5601, National Geology Museum.
No. 5602, Zodiac Fountain.

**2014, Sept. 20 Litho. *Perf. 13¼***

5596 A1646 3.30 l multi 1.90 .95
*a.* Sheet of 5 + 5 labels 9.50 4.75
5597 A1646 4.30 l multi 2.50 1.25
*a.* Sheet of 5 + 5 labels 12.50 6.25
5598 A1646 4.50 l multi 2.60 1.25
*a.* Sheet of 5 + 5 labels 13.00 6.25
5599 A1646 5 l multi 3.00 1.50
*a.* Sheet of 5 + 5 labels 15.00 7.50
5600 A1646 6 l multi 3.50 1.75
*a.* Sheet of 5 + 5 labels 17.50 8.75
5601 A1646 9.10 l multi 5.25 2.60
*a.* Sheet of 5 + 5 labels 26.50 13.00
*Nos. 5596-5601 (6)* 18.75 9.30

**Souvenir Sheet**

5602 A1646 9.10 l multi 5.25 2.60

Clock Towers A1647

Designs: 3 l, Oradea City Hall. 3.10 l, Trumpeters' Tower, Medias. 3.30 l, Palace of Culture Tower, Iasi. 3.60 l, Communal Palace Tower, Buzau. 4.70 l, City Council Tower, Brasov. 14.50 l, Peles Castle Central Tower, Sinaia.

**2014, Oct. 3 Litho. *Perf. 13¼***

5603 A1647 3 l multi 1.75 .85
*a.* Sheet of 4 7.00 3.50
5604 A1647 3.10 l multi 1.75 .85
*a.* Sheet of 4 7.00 3.50
5605 A1647 3.30 l multi 1.90 .95
*a.* Sheet of 4 7.75 4.00
5606 A1647 3.60 l multi 2.00 1.00
*a.* Sheet of 4 8.00 4.00
5607 A1647 4.70 l multi 2.75 1.40
*a.* Sheet of 4 11.00 5.75
5608 A1647 14.50 l multi 8.25 4.25
*a.* Sheet of 4 33.00 17.00
*Nos. 5603-5608 (6)* 18.40 9.30

Wild Cats — A1648

Designs; 3.30 l, Felis silvestris ocreata. 3.60 l, Felis silvestris ornata. 7.60 l, Felis silvestris. 8.10 l, Felis silvestris cafra.

**2014, Oct. 10 Litho. *Perf. 13¼***

5609 A1648 3.30 l multi 1.90 .95
*a.* Sheet of 5 + label 9.50 4.75
5610 A1648 3.60 l multi 2.00 1.00
*a.* Sheet of 5 + label 10.00 5.00
5611 A1648 7.60 l multi 4.25 2.10
*a.* Sheet of 5 + label 21.50 10.50
5612 A1648 8.10 l multi 4.75 2.40
*a.* Sheet of 5 + label 24.00 12.00
*Nos. 5609-5612 (4)* 12.90 6.45

Coins From National Bank of Romania Numismatic Collection — A1649

Obverse and reverse of: 2 l, Dacian gold koson. 2.40 l, Istrian drachm. 8.10 l, Thaler. 14.50 l, Venetian gold ducat.

**2014, Oct. 24 Litho. *Perf. 13¼***

5613 A1649 2 l multi 1.10 .55
*a.* Sheet of 6 6.75 3.50
5614 A1649 2.40 l multi 1.40 .70
*a.* Sheet of 6 8.50 4.25
5615 A1649 8.10 l multi 4.75 2.40
*a.* Sheet of 6 28.50 14.50
5616 A1649 14.50 l multi 8.25 4.25
*a.* Sheet of 6 49.50 25.50
*Nos. 5613-5616 (4)* 15.50 7.90

A souvenir sheet of 4 containing Nos. 5613-5616 was printed in limited quantities.

King Michael, 93rd Birthday A1650

Designs: 4.70 l, King Michael and monogram. 14.50 l, King Michael and Queen Anne.

**2014, Oct. 25 Litho. *Perf. 13¼***

5617 A1650 4.70 l multi 2.75 1.40
*a.* Sheet of 8 + central label 22.00 11.50

**Souvenir Sheet**

***Perf. 13¼x14***

5618 A1650 14.50 l multi 8.25 4.25

No. 5618 contains one 42x52mm stamp and exists imperforate.

Tourist Attractions in Tulcea — A1651

Designs: 3 l, Independence Monument. 3.30 l, Spiru Haret College in Dobrogea, horiz. 4.30 l, Aziziye Mosque, horiz. 14.50 l, St. Nicholas Episcopal Cathedral.

**2014, Oct. 31 Litho. *Perf. 13¼***

5619 A1651 3 l multi 1.75 .85
a. Sheet of 5 + label 8.75 4.25
5620 A1651 3.30 l multi 1.90 .95
a. Sheet of 5 + label 9.50 4.75
5621 A1651 4.30 l multi 2.40 1.25
a. Sheet of 5 + label 12.00 6.25
5622 A1651 14.50 l multi 8.25 4.25
a. Sheet of 5 + label 41.50 21.50
*Nos. 5619-5622 (4)* 14.30 7.30

Carol I University Foundation, Cent. — A1652

Designs: 9.10 l, University Library, statue of King Carol I.
14.50 l, University Foundation Palace, horiz.

**2014, Nov. 7 Litho. *Perf. 13¼***

5623 A1652 9.10 l multi 5.25 2.60
a. Sheet of 4 21.00 10.50

**Souvenir Sheet**

***Perf. 14x13¼***

5624 A1652 14.50 l multi 8.25 4.25

No. 5624 contains one 52x42mm stamp. No. 5623a was printed with two different sheet margins.

Fortified Churches A1653

Designs: 1 l, St. Nicholas Church, Komiza, Croatia. 9.10 l, Evangelical Church, Cristian.

**2014, Nov. 14 Litho. *Perf. 13¼***

5625 A1653 1 l multi .55 .30
a. Sheet of 8 + central label 4.50 2.40
5626 A1653 9.10 l multi 5.25 2.60
a. Sheet of 8 + central label 42.00 21.00

See Croatia No. 930.

Hammer and Sickle, "XXV" — A1654

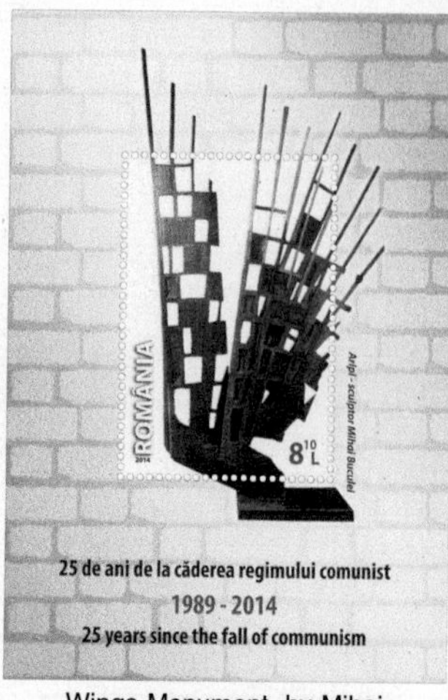


Wings Monument, by Mihai Buculei — A1655

**2014, Nov. 20 Litho. *Perf. 13¼***

5627 A1654 14.50 l multi 8.25 4.25
a. Sheet of 5 + label 41.50 21.50

**Souvenir Sheet**

5628 A1655 8.10 l multi 4.50 2.25

Fall of Communism, 25th anniv.

Christmas A1656

**2014, Nov. 21 Litho. *Perf. 13¼***

5629 A1656 1 l multi .55 .30
a. Sheet of 8 + central label 4.50 2.40

No. 5629 exists imperforate in a limited printing. A souvenir sheet of 2 was printed in limited quantities.

Romanian Savings Bank, 150th Anniv. — A1657

Designs: 8.10 l, Building. 14.50 l, Decorative frieze on Savings Bank.

**2014, Nov. 28 Litho. *Perf. 13¼***

5630 A1657 8.10 l multi 4.50 2.25
a. Sheet of 8 36.00 18.00

**Souvenir Sheet**

5631 A1657 14.50 l gold & multi 8.25 4.25

No. 5631 contains one 36x36mm stamp.

Writers — A1658

Writers: 3.30 l, Ion Creanga (1837-89). 4.50 l, Vasile Alecsandri (1821-90). 7.60 l, George Cosbuc (1866-1918). 8.10 l, George Bacovia (1881-1957).

**2014, Dec. 5 Litho. *Perf. 14x13¼***

5632 A1658 3.30 l multi 1.75 .90
a. Sheet of 5 + label 8.75 4.50
5633 A1658 4.50 l multi 2.40 1.25
a. Sheet of 5 + label 12.00 6.25
5634 A1658 7.60 l multi 4.25 2.10
a. Sheet of 5 + label 21.50 10.50
5635 A1658 8.10 l multi 4.50 2.25
a. Sheet of 5 + label 22.50 11.50
*Nos. 5632-5635 (4)* 12.90 6.50

Inventors and Scientists — A1659

Designs: 3.30 l, Nikola Tesla (1856-1943), electrical engineer, induction motor. 3.60 l, Thomas Alva Edison (1847-1931), inventor, incandescent light bulb. 4.30 l, Albert Einstein (1879-1955), physicist, mass-energy equivalence equation. 14.50 l, Leonardo da Vinci (1452-1519), inventor and painter, irrigation machine.

**2014, Dec. 17 Litho. *Perf. 13¼***

5636 A1659 3.30 l multi 1.75 .90
a. Sheet of 5 + label 8.75 4.50
5637 A1659 3.60 l multi 2.00 1.00
a. Sheet of 5 + label 10.00 5.00
5638 A1659 4.30 l multi 2.40 1.25
a. Sheet of 5 + label 12.00 6.25
5639 A1659 14.50 l multi 7.75 4.00
a. Sheet of 5 + label 39.00 20.00
*Nos. 5636-5639 (4)* 13.90 7.15

Handicrafts A1660

Rugs and: 1 l, Copper vessel from Lahich, Azerbaijan. 9.10 l, Pottery jug from Horezu, Romania.

**2014, Dec. 19 Litho. *Perf. 13¼***

5640 A1660 1 l multi .55 .25
a. Sheet of 6 3.50 1.50
5641 A1660 9.10 l multi 5.00 2.50
a. Sheet of 6 30.00 15.00

See Azerbaijan No. 1075.

Wildlife A1661

Designs: 3.60 l, Antidorcas marsupialis. 4.30 l, Puma concolor. 8.10 l, Orcinus orca. 9.10 l, Acinonyx jubatus.

**2015, Jan. 16 Litho. *Perf. 13¼***

5642-5645 A1661 Set of 4 13.00 6.50
*5645a* Souvenir sheet of 4, #5642-5645 13.00 6.50

Paintings and Sculptures — A1662

Designs: 3.10 l, Hagar in the Desert, by Gheorghe Tattarescu (1820-94). 3.30 l, Girl with Tambourine, by Tattarescu, vert. 4.50 l, The Kiss, sculpture, by Auguste Rodin (1840-1917), vert. 14.50 l, The Spring, sculpture by Rodin.

***Perf. 14x13¼, 13¼x14***

**2015, Jan. 23 Litho.**

5646 A1662 3.10 l gold & multi 1.60 .80
a. Sheet of 4 + 2 labels 6.50 3.25
5647 A1662 3.30 l gold & multi 1.75 .85
a. Sheet of 4 + 2 labels 7.00 3.50
5648 A1662 4.50 l sil & multi 2.40 1.25
a. Sheet of 4 + 2 labels 9.75 5.00
5649 A1662 14.50 l sil & multi 7.50 3.75
a. Sheet of 4 + 2 labels 30.00 15.00
*Nos. 5646-5649 (4)* 13.25 6.65

Romanian Royalty A1663

Royalty and their monograms: 3.10 l, King Carol I (1839-1914), Queen Elisabeth (1843-1916). 3.30 l, King Ferdinand (1865-1927), Queen Marie (1875-1938). 6 l, King Carol II (1893-1953), Queen Helen (1896-1982). 14.50 l, King Michael, Queen Anne.

**2015, Jan. 30 Litho. *Perf. 13¼x14***

5650 A1663 3.10 l multi 1.60 .80
a. Sheet of 4 + 2 labels 6.50 3.25
5651 A1663 3.30 l multi 1.75 .85
a. Sheet of 4 + 2 labels 7.00 3.50
5652 A1663 6 l multi 3.25 1.60
a. Sheet of 4 + 2 labels 13.00 6.50
5653 A1663 14.50 l multi 7.50 3.75
a. Sheet of 4 + 2 labels 30.00 15.00
*Nos. 5650-5653 (4)* 14.10 7.00

The royal monograms on Nos. 5650-5653 are surrounded by perforations within the stamp. A souvenir sheet of 4 containing Nos. 5650-5653 was printed in limited quantities.

Songbirds A1664

Designs: 4.50 l, Coccothraustes cocothraustes. 5 l, Emberiza citrinella. 8.10 l, Bombycilla garrulus. 9.10 l, Pyrrhula pyrrhula.

**2015, Feb. 6 Litho. *Perf. 13¼***

5654 A1664 4.50 l multi 2.25 1.10
a. Sheet of 5 + label 11.50 5.50
5655 A1664 5 l multi 2.50 1.25
a. Sheet of 5 + label 12.50 6.25
5656 A1664 8.10 l multi 4.00 2.00
a. Sheet of 5 + label 20.00 10.00
5657 A1664 9.10 l multi 4.50 2.25
a. Sheet of 5 + label 22.50 11.50
*Nos. 5654-5657 (4)* 13.25 6.60

A souvenir sheet of 4 containing Nos. 5654-5657 was printed in a limited quantity.

Letters and Flowers A1665

Designs: 3 l, "T," roses. 3.10 l, "I," irises. 3.30 l, "M," poppies. 4.30 l, "B," begonias. 4.70 l, "R," flowering tobacco. 14.50 l, "E," purple coneflowers.

**2015, Feb. 20 Litho. *Perf. 13¼***

5658 A1665 3 l multi 1.50 .75
a. Sheet of 5 + label 7.50 3.75
5659 A1665 3.10 l multi 1.60 .80
a. Sheet of 5 + label 8.00 4.00
5660 A1665 3.30 l multi 1.75 .85
a. Sheet of 5 + label 8.75 4.25

**5661** A1665 4.30 l multi 2.25 1.10
*a.* Sheet of 5 + label 11.50 5.50
**5662** A1665 4.70 l multi 2.40 1.25
*a.* Sheet of 5 + label 12.00 6.25
**5663** A1665 14.50 l multi 7.25 3.75
*a.* Sheet of 5 + label 36.50 19.00
*b.* Souvenir sheet of 6, #5658-5663 17.00 8.50
*Nos. 5658-5663 (6)* 16.75 8.50

Easter A1666

Designs: 1 l, Icon depicting crucifixion from Nicula Monastery.
9.10 l, Icon depicting resurrection from Transylvanian Museum of Ethnography.

**2015, Mar. 12 Litho. *Perf. 13¼***
**5664** A1666 1 l multi .50 .25
*a.* Sheet of 4 2.00 1.00
*b.* Sheet of 8 + central label 4.00 2.00

**Souvenir Sheet**

**5665** A1666 9.10 l multi 4.50 2.25

No. 5664a was printed with two different sheet margins. Two souvenir sheets of 2, one containing Nos. 5664-5665, and the other containing 2 No. 5664, were printed in limited quantities.

Archaeological Artifacts of Dinogetia — A1667

Designs: 3 l, Rings, bracelet, loop of gold wire. 4.50 l, Gold coins, chain. 9.10 l, Ring, bracelet, loop of gold wire. 14.50 l, Reliquary cross.

**2015, Mar. 20 Litho. *Perf. 14x13¼***
**5666** A1667 3 l multi 1.50 .75
*a.* Sheet of 4 6.00 3.00
**5667** A1667 4.50 l multi 2.25 1.10
*a.* Sheet of 4 9.00 4.50
**5668** A1667 9.10 l multi 4.50 2.25
*a.* Sheet of 4 18.00 9.00
**5669** A1667 14.50 l multi 7.25 3.75
*a.* Sheet of 4 29.00 15.00
*b.* Souvenir sheet of 4, #5666-5669, + 2 labels 15.50 8.00
*Nos. 5666-5669 (4)* 15.50 7.85

Romanian Intelligence Service, 25th Anniv. — A1668

Designs: 8.10 l, Emblem, map of Romania. 14.50 l, Emblem.

**2015, Mar. 23 Litho. *Perf. 13¼***
**5670** A1668 8.10 l multi 4.00 2.00
*a.* Sheet of 6 24.00 12.00

**Souvenir Sheet**
***Perf.***

**5671** A1668 14.50 l multi 7.25 3.75

No. 5671 contains one 30mm diameter stamp.

Pelicans — A1669

Designs: 3.60 l, Six Pelecanus onocrotalus. 5 l, Two Pelecanus crispus. 8.10 l, Two Pelecanus onocrotalus. No. 5675, 9.10 l, Two Pelecanus cripsus, close up of face.
No. 5676, 9.10 l, Head of Pelecanus crispus.

**2015, Apr. 10 Litho. *Perf. 13¼***
**5672** A1669 3.60 l multi 1.90 .95
*a.* Sheet of 5 + label 9.50 4.75
**5673** A1669 5 l multi 2.60 1.40
*a.* Sheet of 5 + label 13.00 7.00
**5674** A1669 8.10 l multi 4.25 2.10
*a.* Sheet of 5 + label 21.50 10.50
**5675** A1669 9.10 l multi 4.75 2.40
*a.* Sheet of 5 + label 24.00 12.00
*Nos. 5672-5675 (4)* 13.50 6.85

**Souvenir Sheet**
***Perf. 14x13¼***

**5676** A1669 9.10 l multi 4.75 2.40

No. 5676 contains one 52x42mm stamp. A souvenir sheet of 4 containing Nos. 5672-5675 was printed in limited quantities.

Europa A1670

Designs: 2.10 l, Wooden toys. 14.50 l, Rocking horse, tricycle.

**2015, Apr. 17 Litho. *Perf. 13¼***
**5677** A1670 2.10 l multi 1.10 .55
*a.* Sheet of 6 6.75 3.50
**5678** A1670 14.50 l multi 7.50 3.75
*a.* Sheet of 6 45.00 22.50
*b.* Sheet of 4, 2 each #5677-5678, #5677 at UL 17.50 8.75
*c.* As "b," #5678 at UL 17.50 8.75

Quill Pen, Book, Hand Touching Tablet Screen — A1671

**2015, Apr. 30 Litho. *Perf. 13¼***
**5679** A1671 4.70 l multi 2.40 1.25
*a.* Sheet of 5 + label 12.00 6.25

The Group, 10th anniv.

Victory in World War II, 70th Anniv. — A1672

**2015, May 9 Litho. *Perf. 13¼***
**5680** A1672 4.30 l multi 2.25 1.10
*a.* Sheet of 8 + central label 18.00 9.00

No. 5680a was printed with two different central labels.

**No. 3601 Surcharged in Gold**

**Methods and Perfs. As Before**
**2015, May 13**

**5681** A1028 9.10 l on 10 l #3601 4.50 2.25

Europhilex 2015 Intl. Stamp Exhibition, London.

University of Medicine and Pharmacy, Tirgu Mures, 70th Anniv. — A1673

Designs: 3.30 l, University building, emblem with 1945 date. 8.10 l, University building, emblem, without oval.
9.10 l, University building, emblem without oval, vert.

**2015, May 15 Litho. *Perf. 13¼***
**5682** A1673 3.30 l gold & multi 1.75 .85
*a.* Sheet of 5 + label 8.75 4.25
**5683** A1673 8.10 l gold & multi 4.00 2.00
*a.* Sheet of 5 + label 20.00 10.00

**Souvenir Sheet**
***Perf. 13¼x14***

**5684** A1673 9.10 l gold & multi 4.50 2.25

No. 5684 contains one 42x52mm stamp.

Romanian Mint, 145th Anniv. — A1674

Designs: 8.10 l, Mint building, horse and carriage, 1870 1-leu coin.
14.50 l, 1870 gold 20-lei coin.

**2015, May 19 Litho. *Perf. 13¼***
**5685** A1674 8.10 l multi 4.00 2.00
*a.* Imperf. 4.00 2.00
*b.* Sheet of 4 #5685 + 8 labels 16.00 8.00
*c.* Sheet of 5, #5685a, 4 #5685 20.00 10.00

**Souvenir Sheet**

**5686** A1674 14.50 l multi 7.25 3.75

No. 5686 contains one 36x36mm stamp. A ring of perforations surrounds the image of the coin on No. 5685. The ring of perforations is not on No. 5685a. A souvenir sheet of 2 containing Nos. 5685-5686 was produced in limited quantities.

National Institute for Research and Development in Informatics, 45th Anniv. — A1675

**2015, June 5 Litho. *Perf. 14x13¼***
**5687** A1675 7.60 l multi 3.75 1.90
*a.* Sheet of 5 + label 19.00 9.50

National Grand Masonic Lodge of Romania, 135th Anniv. — A1676

Designs: 2.10 l, Masonic and astrological symbols. 14.50 l, Lodge, horiz.

**2015, June 16 Litho. *Perf. 13¼***
**5688** A1676 2.10 l multi 1.10 .55
*a.* Sheet of 4 4.50 2.25
**5689** A1676 14.50 l multi 7.25 3.75
*a.* Sheet of 4 29.00 15.00
*b.* Sheet of 2, #5688-5689, imperf. 8.50 4.25

A souvenir sheet of 2 containing perforated examples of No. 5688-5689 was produced in limited quantities.

Flowers in Botanical Gardens A1677

Designs: 1 l, Astragalus peterfii. 3.30 l, Iris brandzae. 8.10 l, Paeonia peregrina. 9.10 l, Hepatica transsilvanica.

**2015, July 3 Litho. *Perf. 13¼***
**5690** A1677 1 l multi .50 .25
*a.* Sheet of 5 + label 2.50 1.25
**5691** A1677 3.30 l multi 1.60 .80
*a.* Sheet of 5 + label 8.00 4.00
**5692** A1677 8.10 l multi 4.00 2.00
*a.* Sheet of 5 + label 20.00 10.00
**5693** A1677 9.10 l multi 4.50 2.25
*a.* Sheet of 5 + label 22.50 11.50
*Nos. 5690-5693 (4)* 10.60 5.30

Autocephaly of Romanian Orthodox Church, 130th Anniv. — A1678

Designs: 5 l, Drawing for under-construction Romanian People's Salvation Cathedral. 8.10 l, Cathedral, arms of Patriarchate.

**2015, July 15 Litho. *Perf. 13¼***
**5694** A1678 5 l multi 2.50 1.25
*a.* Sheet of 8 + central label 20.00 10.00

**Souvenir Sheet**
***Perf. 14x13¼***

**5695** A1678 8.10 l multi 4.00 2.00

No. 5695 contains one 52x42mm stamp. An souvenir sheet containing two imperforate examples of No. 5694 was printed in limited quantities.

Paintings Depicting Horses — A1679

Details of paintings: 3.60 l, The Plowing, by Ioan Andeescu (1850-82). 8.10 l, Mounted

Ranger Officer, by Nicolae Grigorescu (1838-1907), vert. 9.10 l, Peasant with a Carriage, by Rudolf Schweitzer-Cumpana (1886-1975).

*Perf. 14x13¼, 13¼x14*

**2015, July 24** **Litho.**

**5696** A1679 3.60 l gold & multi 1.90 .95
*a.* Sheet of 4 7.75 4.00
**5697** A1679 8.10 l gold & multi 4.00 2.00
*a.* Sheet of 4 16.00 8.00
**5698** A1679 9.10 l gold & multi 4.50 2.25
*a.* Sheet of 4 18.00 9.00
*Nos. 5696-5698 (3)* 10.40 5.20

Medicinal Plants — A1680

Designs: 1.20 l , Hypericum perforatum. 2 l, Lavandula angustifolia. 2.40 l, Calendula officinalis. 14.50 l, Matricaria chamomilla.

**2015, Aug. 7** **Litho.** ***Perf. 13¼***

**5699** A1680 1.20 l multi .60 .30
*a.* Sheet of 5 + 4 labels 3.00 1.50
**5700** A1680 2 l multi 1.00 .50
*a.* Sheet of 5 + 4 labels 5.00 2.50
**5701** A1680 2.40 l multi 1.25 .60
*a.* Sheet of 5 + 4 labels 6.25 3.00
**5702** A1680 14.50 l multi 7.50 3.75
*a.* Sheet of 5 + 4 labels 37.50 19.00
*b.* Souvenir sheet of 4, #5699-5702 10.50 5.25
*Nos. 5699-5702 (4)* 10.35 5.15

Nicula Monastery A1681

Designs: 1 l, Icon of Virgin Mary and Child. 4.50 l, Wooden church.

**2015, Aug. 15** **Litho.** ***Perf. 13¼***

**5703** A1681 1 l multi .50 .25
*a.* Sheet of 8 + central label 4.00 2.00
**5704** A1681 4.50 l multi 2.40 1.25
*a.* Sheet of 8 + central label 19.50 10.00

A souvenir sheet of 2 containing Nos. 5703-5704 was printed in limited quantities.

Birds A1682

Designs: 3.30 l, Sterna hirundo. 4.30 l, Larus michahellis. 4.70 l, Recurvirostra avosetta. 8.10 l, Tadorna ferruginea. 9.10 l, Cygnus olor.

**2015, Aug. 21** **Litho.** ***Perf. 13¼***

**5705** A1682 3.30 l multi 1.75 .85
*a.* Sheet of 5 + label 8.75 4.25
**5706** A1682 4.30 l multi 2.25 1.10
*a.* Sheet of 5 + label 11.50 5.50
**5707** A1682 4.70 l multi 2.40 1.25
*a.* Sheet of 5 + label 12.00 6.25
**5708** A1682 8.10 l multi 4.25 2.10
*a.* Sheet of 5 + label 21.50 10.50
*Nos. 5705-5708 (4)* 10.65 5.30

**Souvenir Sheet**

**5709** A1682 9.10 l multi 4.75 2.40

A souvenir sheet of 5 containing Nos. 5705-5709 was printed in limited quantities.

Moldavian Tourist Attractions — A1683

Arms and: 3.30 l, Cucuteni Eneolithic Art Museum, Piatra Neamt, Cucuteni ceramic piece. 3.60 l, Neamt Fortress, sculpture of Stephen the Great. 6 l, St. Nicholas Church, Iasi, sculpture of Metropolitan Dosoftei. 9.10 l, Alexandru Ioan Cuza Palace, Ruginoasa, Prince Alexandru Ioan I

**2015, Sept. 8** **Litho.** ***Perf. 13¼***

**5710** A1683 3.30 l multi 1.75 .85
*a.* Sheet of 5 + label 8.75 4.25
**5711** A1683 3.60 l multi 1.90 .95
*a.* Sheet of 5 + label 9.50 4.75
**5712** A1683 6 l multi 3.00 1.50
*a.* Sheet of 5 + label 15.00 7.50
**5713** A1683 9.10 l multi 4.75 2.40
*a.* Sheet of 5 + label 24.00 12.00
*Nos. 5710-5713 (4)* 11.40 5.70

A souvenir sheet of 4 containing Nos. 5710-5713 was printed in limited quantities.

Dobrudja Tourist Attractions — A1684

Map and: 2 l, Tropaeum Traiani, Adamclisi. 4.70 l, Enisala Fortress ruins and coins. 7.60 l, Church of St. Andrew, St. Andrew's Cave pilgrimage site. 8.10 l, Boats and pelican in Danube Delta.

**2015, Sept. 18** **Litho.** ***Perf. 13¼***

**5714** A1684 2 l multi 1.00 .50
*a.* Sheet of 5 + label 5.00 2.50
**5715** A1684 4.70 l multi 2.40 1.25
*a.* Sheet of 5 + label 12.00 6.25
**5716** A1684 7.60 l multi 4.00 2.00
*a.* Sheet of 5 + label 20.00 10.00
**5717** A1684 8.10 l multi 4.25 2.10
*a.* Sheet of 5 + label 21.50 10.50
*Nos. 5714-5717 (4)* 11.65 5.85

A souvenir sheet of 4 containing Nos. 5714-5717 was printed in limited quantities.

National Bank of Romania, 135th Anniv. — A1685

Designs: 3.30 l, Obverse of 1881 20-lei banknote, Ion I. Campineanu, first governor of bank. 9.10 l, Reverse of 1881 20-lei banknote, Emil Costinescu, first director of Banknote Manufacturing and Accounting Service.

**2015, Sept. 29** **Litho.** ***Perf. 13¼***

**5718** A1685 3.30 l multi 1.75 .85
*a.* Sheet of 4 7.00 3.50
**5719** A1685 9.10 l multi 4.75 2.40
*a.* Sheet of 4 19.00 9.75
*b.* Souvenir sheet of 2, #5718-5719 6.50 3.25

A numbered souvenir sheet of 2 containing Nos. 5718-5719 with gold foil was printed in limited quantities.

Peles Castle Stained-Glass Windows — A1686

Windows depicting hunters hunting: 2 l, Boar. 3.30 l, Stags. 4.30 l, Hares. 14.50 l, Bear.

**2015, Oct. 9** **Litho.** ***Perf. 14x13¼***

**5720** A1686 2 l multi 1.00 .50
*a.* Sheet of 4 + 2 labels 4.00 2.00
**5721** A1686 3.30 l multi 1.75 .85
*a.* Sheet of 4 + 2 labels 7.00 3.50
**5722** A1686 4.30 l multi 2.25 1.10
*a.* Sheet of 4 + 2 labels 9.00 4.50
**5723** A1686 14.50 l multi 7.25 3.75
*a.* Sheet of 4 + 2 labels 29.00 15.00
*Nos. 5720-5723 (4)* 12.25 6.20

A souvenir sheet of 4 containing Nos. 5720-5723 was printed in limited quantities.

Ion Tiriac, Tennis Player — A1687

Designs: 2.10 l, Tiriac, tennis ball. 9.10 l, Tiriac.

**2015, Oct. 16** **Litho.** ***Perf. 13¼***

**5724** A1687 2.10 l multi 1.10 .55
*a.* Sheet of 8 + central label 9.00 4.50

**Souvenir Sheet**

**5725** A1687 9.10 l multi 4.50 2.25

No. 5724a was printed with two different central labels.

Christmas A1688

**2015, Nov. 6** **Litho.** ***Perf. 13¼***

**5726** A1688 1 l multi .50 .25
*a.* Sheet of 8 4.00 2.00
*b.* Sheet of 8 + central label 4.00 2.00

Values are for stamps with surrounding selvage.

Flags of Romania and United States, King Carol I and Pres. Rutherford B. Hayes — A1689

**2015, Nov. 18** **Litho.** ***Perf. 13¼***

**5727** A1689 3.60 l multi 1.75 .85
*a.* Sheet of 7 + 2 labels 12.50 6.00

Diplomatic relations between Romania and the United States, 135th anniv.

Oct. 30, 2015 Bucharest Night Club Fire — A1690

**2015, Nov. 20** **Litho.** ***Perf. 13¼***

**5728** A1690 1 l multi .50 .25
*a.* Sheet of 9 4.50 2.25

Dogs A1691

Designs: 2.40 l, German shepherd. 5 l, Malinois. 8.10 l, Labrador retriever. 9.10 l, Rottweiler.

**2015, Nov. 20** **Litho.** ***Perf. 13¼***

**5729** A1691 2.40 l multi 1.25 .60
*a.* Sheet of 5 + label 6.25 3.00
**5730** A1691 5 l multi 2.40 1.25
*a.* Sheet of 5 + label 12.00 6.25
**5731** A1691 8.10 l multi 4.00 2.00
*a.* Sheet of 5 + label 20.00 10.00
**5732** A1691 9.10 l multi 4.50 2.25
*a.* Sheet of 5 + label 22.50 11.50
*Nos. 5729-5732 (4)* 12.15 6.10

Alba Iulia A1692

Designs: 3 l, Roman 13th Twin Legion Fortress. 3.30 l, Third Gate. 8.10 l, St. Michael's Cathedral. 9.10 l, Coronation Cathedral, King Ferdinand.

**2015, Nov. 27** **Litho.** ***Perf. 13¼***

**5733** A1692 3 l multi 1.50 .75
*a.* Sheet of 5 + label 7.50 3.75
**5734** A1692 3.30 l multi 1.60 .80
*a.* Sheet of 5 + label 8.00 4.00
**5735** A1692 8.10 l multi 4.00 2.00
*a.* Sheet of 5 + label 20.00 10.00
**5736** A1692 9.10 l multi 4.50 2.25
*a.* Sheet of 5 + label 22.50 11.50
*Nos. 5733-5736 (4)* 11.60 5.80

A souvenir sheet of 4 containing Nos. 5733-5736 was printed in limited quantities.

Coins in Numismatic Collection of National Bank of Romania — A1693

Designs: 2 l, Dacian silver coins. 2.40 l, Imperial Roman gold coins. 8.10 l, Dutch ducats. 14.50 l, Polish silver coins.

**2015, Dec. 4** **Litho.** ***Perf. 13¼***

**5737** A1693 2 l multi 1.00 .50
*a.* Sheet of 6 6.00 3.00
**5738** A1693 2.40 l multi 1.25 .60
*a.* Sheet of 6 7.50 3.75
**5739** A1693 8.10 l multi 4.00 2.00
*a.* Sheet of 6 24.00 12.00
**5740** A1693 14.50 l multi 7.00 3.50
*a.* Sheet of 6 42.00 21.00
*Nos. 5737-5740 (4)* 13.25 6.60

A souvenir sheet of 4 containing Nos. 5737-5740 was printed in limited quantities.

Romania in United Nations, 60th Anniv. — A1694

**2015, Dec. 15 Litho. *Perf. 13¼***

5741 A1694 4.50 l shown 2.25 1.10
a. Sheet of 7 + 2 labels 16.00 7.75

**Souvenir Sheet**

***Perf.***

5742 A1694 8.10 l Globe 4.00 2.00

No. 5742 contains one 30mm diameter stamp.

Sculptures Depicting Eve — A1695

Sculpture by: 1 l, Gheorghe Leonida. 9.10 l, Victor Brecheret, horiz.

**2015, Dec. 21 Litho. *Perf. 13¼***

5743 A1695 1 l multi .50 .25
a. Sheet of 6 3.00 1.50
5744 A1695 9.10 l multi 4.50 2.25
a. Sheet of 6 27.00 13.50

See Brazil No. 3321.

Flemish Paintings in Brukenthal National Museum — A1696

Designs: 4.70 l, St. Jerome in Scriptorium, by Marinus Claeszoon van Reymerswaele. 5 l, Ceres, Bacchus and Venus, by Abraham Janssens van Nuyssen. 7.60 l, Lion in Front of the Cave, by Roelant Savery. 9.10 l, Still Life with Fruits and Parrot, by Jan Fyt.

**2016, Jan. 6 Litho. *Perf. 13¼***

5745 A1696 4.70 l multi 2.25 1.10
a. Sheet of 5 + label 11.50 5.50
5746 A1696 5 l multi 2.50 1.25
a. Sheet of 5 + label 12.50 6.25
5747 A1696 7.60 l multi 3.75 1.90
a. Sheet of 5 + label 19.00 9.50
5748 A1696 9.10 l multi 4.50 2.25
a. Sheet of 5 + label 22.50 11.50
*Nos. 5745-5748 (4)* 13.00 6.50

Flowers A1697

Designs: 4.70 l, Dipsacus fullonum. 5 l, Centaurea solstitialis. 6 l, Echinops ruthenicus. 8.10 l, Ononis spinosa.

**2016, Jan. 14 Litho. *Perf. 13¼***

5749 A1697 4.70 l multi 2.25 1.10
a. Sheet of 4 9.00 4.50
5750 A1697 5 l multi 2.50 1.25
a. Sheet of 4 10.00 5.00
5751 A1697 6 l multi 3.00 1.50
a. Sheet of 4 12.00 6.00
5752 A1697 8.10 l multi 4.00 2.00
a. Sheet of 4 16.00 8.00
*Nos. 5749-5752 (4)* 11.75 5.85

Prehistoric Animals — A1698

Designs: 2 l, Balaur bondoc. 3 l, Theriosuchus sympiestodon. 3.30 l, Magyarosaurus dacus. 14.50 l, Kogaionon ungureanui.

**2016, Jan. 22 Litho. *Perf. 13¼***

5753 A1698 2 l multi 1.00 .50
a. Sheet of 5 + label 5.00 2.50
5754 A1698 3 l multi 1.50 .75
a. Sheet of 5 + label 7.50 3.75
5755 A1698 3.30 l multi 1.60 .80
a. Sheet of 5 + label 8.00 4.00
5756 A1698 14.50 l multi 7.00 3.50
a. Sheet of 5 + label 35.00 17.50
*Nos. 5753-5756 (4)* 11.10 5.55

Woodpeckers A1699

Designs: 2 l, Picoides tridactylus. 4.50 l, Picus viridis. 5 l, Dryocopus martius. 14.50 l, Jynx torquilla.

**2016, Feb. 9 Litho. *Perf. 13¼***

5757 A1699 2 l multi 1.00 .50
a. Sheet of 5 + label 5.00 2.50
5758 A1699 4.50 l multi 2.25 1.10
a. Sheet of 5 + label 11.50 5.50
5759 A1699 5 l multi 2.50 1.25
a. Sheet of 5 + label 12.50 6.25
5760 A1699 14.50 l multi 7.00 3.50
a. Sheet of 5 + label 35.00 17.50
*Nos. 5757-5760 (4)* 12.75 6.35

Brasov Tourist Attractions — A1700

Arms of Brasov and: 3 l, Black Church. 3.30 l, Catherine's Gate. 5 l, First Romanian school. 14.50 l, Council Hall.

**2016, Feb. 17 Litho. *Perf. 13¼***

5761 A1700 3 l multi 1.50 .75
a. Sheet of 5 + label 7.50 3.75
5762 A1700 3.30 l multi 1.60 .80
a. Sheet of 5 + label 8.00 4.00
5763 A1700 5 l multi 2.50 1.25
a. Sheet of 5 + label 12.50 6.25
5764 A1700 14.50 l multi 7.00 3.50
a. Sheet of 5 + label 35.00 17.50
*Nos. 5761-5764 (4)* 12.60 6.30

A souvenir sheet containing Nos. 5761-5764 was printed in limited quantities.

Romanian Superlatives and Curiosities — A1701

Designs: 3 l, World's smallest and lowest-valued banknotes. 3.30 l, Gold from Gold Museum, Brad. 5 l, Buchholz Organ, Black Church, Brasov, largest mechanical organ in Romania, vert. 14.50 l, Sculpture of King Decebalus, largest stone sculpture in Europe, vert.

**2016, Feb. 24 Litho. *Perf. 13¼***

5765 A1701 3 l multi 1.50 .75
a. Sheet of 5 + label 7.50 3.75
5766 A1701 3.30 l multi 1.60 .80
a. Sheet of 5 + label 8.00 4.00
5767 A1701 5 l multi 2.50 1.25
a. Sheet of 5 + label 12.50 6.25
5768 A1701 14.50 l multi 7.00 3.50
a. Sheet of 5 + label 35.00 17.50
*Nos. 5765-5768 (4)* 12.60 6.30

Letters and Flowers A1702

Designs: 1.20 l, "C," chrysanthemums. 1.40 l, "U," houseleeks. 1.60 l, "D," dahlias. 4.50 l, "R," yellow pheasant's eye. 8 l, "A," azaleas. 16 l, "G," gladiolas.

**2016, Mar. 8 Litho. *Perf. 13¼***

5769 A1702 1.20 l multi .65 .30
a. Sheet of 5 + label 3.25 1.50
5770 A1702 1.40 l multi .75 .35
a. Sheet of 5 + label 3.75 1.75
5771 A1702 1.60 l multi .85 .40
a. Sheet of 5 + label 4.25 2.00
5772 A1702 4.50 l multi 2.40 1.25
a. Sheet of 5 + label 12.00 6.25
5773 A1702 8 l multi 4.00 2.00
a. Sheet of 5 + label 20.00 10.00
5774 A1702 16 l multi 8.25 4.25
a. Sheet of 5 + label 41.50 21.50
b. Sheet of 6, #5769-5774 17.00 8.75
*Nos. 5769-5774 (6)* 16.90 8.55

Famous Romanians A1703

Designs: 1 l, Constantin Brâncusi (1876-1957), sculptor. 2 l, George Enescu (1881-1955), composer. 3.50 l, George Emil Palade (1912-2008), 1974 Nobel laureate for Physiology or Medicine. 4 l, George Constantinescu (1881-1965), inventor. 12 l, Ana Aslan (1897-1988), gerontologist. 31 l, Dumitru Staniloae (1903-93), theologian.

**2016, Mar. 18 Litho. *Perf. 13¼***

5775 A1703 1 l multi .50 .25
a. Sheet of 3 + label 1.50 .75
5776 A1703 2 l multi 1.00 .50
a. Sheet of 3 + label 3.00 1.50
5777 A1703 3.50 l multi 1.75 .90
a. Sheet of 3 + label 5.25 2.75
5778 A1703 4 l multi 2.10 1.10
a. Sheet of 3 + label 6.50 3.50
5779 A1703 12 l multi 6.25 3.25
a. Sheet of 3 + label 19.00 9.75
5780 A1703 31 l multi 16.00 8.00
a. Sheet of 3 + label 48.00 24.00
*Nos. 5775-5780 (6)* 27.60 14.00

Easter A1704

Designs: No. 5781, Icon depicting crucifixion. No. 5782, Easter flowers. 8 l, Crucifixion, diff.

**2016, Mar. 23 Litho. *Perf. 13¼***

5781 A1704 1 l multi .50 .25
b. Sheet of 8 + central label 4.00 2.00
5782 A1704 1 l multi .50 .25
a. Sheet of 8, 4 each #5781-5782 4.00 2.00
b. Sheet of 8 + central label 4.00 2.00

**Souvenir Sheet**

***Perf.***

5783 A1704 8 l multi 4.00 2.00

Values are for stamps with surrounding selvage. A souvenir sheet of 2 containing Nos. 5781-5782 and a souvenir sheet of 3 containing No. 5781 and two No. 5782 were printed in limited quantities.

Romanian Academy, 150th Anniv. — A1705

Designs: 5 l, Romanian Academy building. 8 l, Building façade and goddess Minerva, vert.

**2016, Apr. 4 Litho. *Perf. 13¼***

5784 A1705 5 l multi 2.60 1.25
a. Sheet of 6 + 3 labels 16.00 7.50

**Souvenir Sheet**

***Perf. 13¼x14***

5785 A1705 8 l multi 4.25 2.10

No. 5785 contains one 42x53mm stamp.

Butterflies — A1706

Designs: 3 l, Lycaena dispar. 3.50 l, Scolitantides orion. 5 l, Argynnis paphia. 15 l, Plebejus argus.

**2016, Apr. 15 Litho. *Perf. 14x13¼***

5786 A1706 3 l multi 1.60 .80
a. Sheet of 5 + label 8.00 4.00
5787 A1706 3.50 l multi 1.75 .90
a. Sheet of 5 + label 8.75 4.50
5788 A1706 5 l multi 2.60 1.40
a. Sheet of 5 + label 13.00 7.00
5789 A1706 15 l multi 7.75 4.00
a. Sheet of 5 + label 39.00 20.00
*Nos. 5786-5789 (4)* 13.70 7.10

A souvenir sheet containing Nos. 5786-5789 was printed in limited quantities.

Romania in Interparliamentary Union, 125th Anniv. — A1707

Designs: 3 l, Vasile A. Urechia, member of Romanian delegation to 1891 conference. 12 l, Interparliamentary Union emblem.

**2016, Apr. 18 Litho. *Perf. 13¼***

5790 A1707 3 l multi 1.60 .80
a. Sheet of 8 + central label 13.00 6.50

**Souvenir Sheet**

***Perf.***

5791 A1707 12 l multi 6.25 3.25

No. 5791 contains one 30mm diameter stamp.

A1708

Europa — A1709

**2016, May 4 Litho. *Perf. 13¼***

| No. | Type | Description | Unused | Used |
|---|---|---|---|---|
| **5792** | A1708 | 5 l multi | 2.50 | 1.25 |
| *a.* | | Sheet of 6 | 15.00 | 7.50 |
| **5793** | A1709 | 12 l multi | 2.50 | 1.25 |
| *a.* | | Sheet of 6 | 36.00 | 18.00 |
| *b.* | | Sheet of 4, 2 each #5792-5793, #5792 at UL | 17.00 | 8.50 |
| *c.* | | As "b," #5793 at UL | 17.00 | 8.50 |

Think Green Issue.

Romanian Dynasty, 150th Anniv. A1710

Designs: 4.50 l, Collar of the Order of Carol I. 16 l, Scepter of King Ferdinand I. 8 l, King Carol I and royal family, horiz.

**2016, May 10 Litho. *Perf. 13¼x14***

| No. | Type | Description | Unused | Used |
|---|---|---|---|---|
| **5794** | A1710 | 4.50 l multi | 2.25 | 1.10 |
| *a.* | | Sheet of 5 + label | 11.50 | 5.50 |
| **5795** | A1710 | 16 l multi | 8.00 | 4.00 |
| *a.* | | Sheet of 5 + label | 40.00 | 20.00 |

**Souvenir Sheet**

***Perf. 14x13¼***

| No. | Type | Description | Unused | Used |
|---|---|---|---|---|
| **5796** | A1710 | 8 l multi | 4.00 | 2.00 |

A souvenir sheet of 2 containing Nos. 5794-5795 was printed in limited quantities.

The Four Seasons at the Village Museum, Bucharest — A1711

Designs: 2 l, Sfintii Voievozi Church, flower. 2.40 l, Chiojdu-Mic Homestead, sunflower. 8 l, Jurilovca Homestead, autumn leaves. 15 l, Surdesti Homestead in winter.

**2016, May 20 Litho. *Perf. 13¼***

| No. | Type | Description | Unused | Used |
|---|---|---|---|---|
| **5797** | A1711 | 2 l multi | 1.00 | .50 |
| *a.* | | Sheet of 6 | 6.00 | 3.00 |
| **5798** | A1711 | 2.40 l multi | 1.25 | .60 |
| *a.* | | Sheet of 6 | 7.50 | 3.75 |
| **5799** | A1711 | 8 l multi | 4.00 | 2.00 |
| *a.* | | Sheet of 6 | 24.00 | 12.00 |
| **5800** | A1711 | 15 l multi | 7.50 | 3.75 |
| *a.* | | Sheet of 6 | 45.00 | 22.50 |
| *b.* | | Souvenir sheet of 4, #5797-5800 + 2 labels | 14.00 | 7.00 |
| | | *Nos. 5797-5800 (4)* | 13.75 | 6.85 |

Village Museum, 80th anniv.

Souvenir Sheet

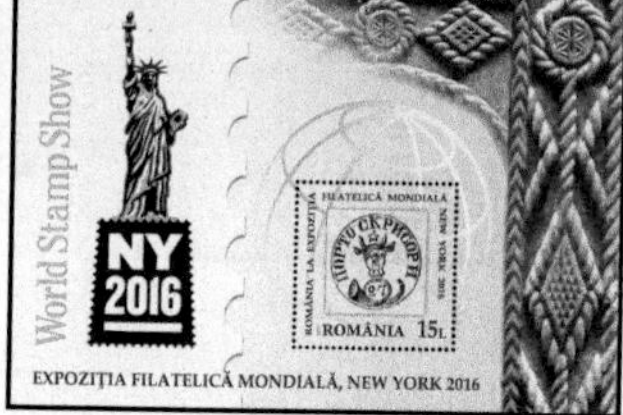


2016 World Stamp Show, New York — A1712

**2016, May 28 Litho. *Perf. 13¼***

| No. | Type | Description | Unused | Used |
|---|---|---|---|---|
| **5801** | A1712 | 15 l Romania #1 | 7.50 | 3.75 |

Children's Stories — A1713

Characters from: 2 l, Two Penny Bag, by Ion Creanga. 2.40 l, Neghinita, by Barbu Stefanescu Delavrancea. 8 l, Prince Charming and Ileana Cosanzeanna, by Petre Ispirecu, vert. 15 l. Mr. Goe, by I. L. Caragiale, vert.

**2016, June 1 Litho. *Perf. 13¼***

| No. | Type | Description | Unused | Used |
|---|---|---|---|---|
| **5802** | A1713 | 2 l multi | 1.00 | .50 |
| *a.* | | Sheet of 5 + label | 5.00 | 2.50 |
| **5803** | A1713 | 2.40 l multi | 1.25 | .60 |
| *a.* | | Sheet of 5 + label | 6.25 | 3.00 |
| **5804** | A1713 | 8 l multi | 4.00 | 2.00 |
| *a.* | | Sheet of 5 + label | 20.00 | 10.00 |
| **5805** | A1713 | 15 l multi | 7.50 | 3.75 |
| *a.* | | Sheet of 5 + label | 37.50 | 19.00 |
| | | *Nos. 5802-5805 (4)* | 13.75 | 6.85 |

Sibiu International Theater Festival — A1714

Masked character from festival poster and Sibiu towers: 5 l, Council Tower. 8 l, Potter's Tower.

**2016, June 10 Litho. *Perf. 13¼***

| No. | Type | Description | Unused | Used |
|---|---|---|---|---|
| **5806** | A1714 | 5 l multi | 2.50 | 1.25 |
| *a.* | | Sheet of 5 + label | 12.50 | 6.25 |
| **5807** | A1714 | 8 l multi | 4.00 | 2.00 |
| *a.* | | Sheet of 5 + label | 20.00 | 10.00 |

2016 European Soccer Championships, France — A1715

Various soccer players, flags of Romania and group opponents: 3 l, France. 3.50 l, Switzerland. 4.50 l, Albania. 16 l, France, Switzerland and Albania.

**2016, June 10 Litho. *Perf. 13¼***

| No. | Type | Description | Unused | Used |
|---|---|---|---|---|
| **5808** | A1715 | 3 l multi | 1.50 | .75 |
| *a.* | | Sheet of 5 + label | 7.50 | 3.75 |
| **5809** | A1715 | 3.50 l multi | 1.75 | .85 |
| *a.* | | Sheet of 5 + label | 8.75 | 4.25 |
| **5810** | A1715 | 4.50 l multi | 2.25 | 1.10 |
| *a.* | | Sheet of 5 + label | 11.50 | 5.50 |
| **5811** | A1715 | 16 l multi | 8.00 | 4.00 |
| *a.* | | Sheet of 5 + label | 40.00 | 20.00 |
| | | *Nos. 5808-5811 (4)* | 13.50 | 6.70 |

Famous Romanian Women Wearing Traditional Blouses — A1716

Designs: 3.50 l, Queen Elisabeth (1843-1916), blouse from Olt County. 4 l, Queen Marie (1875-1938), blouse from Dolj County. 4.50 l, Smaranda Braescu (1897-1948), parachutist, blouse from Muscel. 16 l, Maria Tanase (1913-63), singer, blouse from Padureni.

**2016, June 22 Litho. *Perf. 14x13¼***

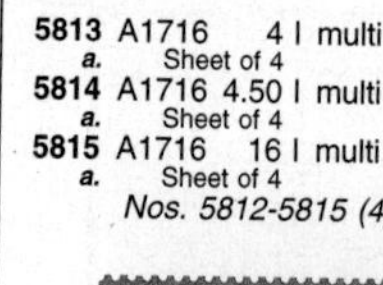

| No. | Type | Description | Unused | Used |
|---|---|---|---|---|
| **5812** | A1716 | 3.50 l multi | 1.75 | .85 |
| *a.* | | Sheet of 4 | 7.00 | 3.50 |
| **5813** | A1716 | 4 l multi | 2.00 | 1.00 |
| *a.* | | Sheet of 4 | 8.00 | 4.00 |
| **5814** | A1716 | 4.50 l multi | 2.25 | 1.10 |
| *a.* | | Sheet of 4 | 9.00 | 4.50 |
| **5815** | A1716 | 16 l multi | 8.00 | 4.00 |
| *a.* | | Sheet of 4 | 32.00 | 16.00 |
| | | *Nos. 5812-5815 (4)* | 14.00 | 6.95 |

Putna Monastery, 550th Anniv. — A1717

Designs: 3 l, Prince Stephen the Great, Putna Monastery. 15 l, Putna Monastery. 12 l, Tomb of Stephen the Great.

**2016, July 5 Litho. *Perf. 13¼***

| No. | Type | Description | Unused | Used |
|---|---|---|---|---|
| **5816** | A1717 | 3 l multi | 1.50 | .75 |
| *a.* | | Sheet of 5 + label | 7.50 | 3.75 |
| **5817** | A1717 | 15 l multi | 7.50 | 3.75 |
| *a.* | | Sheet of 5 + label | 37.50 | 19.00 |

**Souvenir Sheet**

| No. | Type | Description | Unused | Used |
|---|---|---|---|---|
| **5818** | A1717 | 12 l multi | 6.00 | 3.00 |

No. 5818 contains one 36x36mm stamp.

First Documented Reference to Town of Sibiu, 825th Anniv. — A1718

Details from *General View of Sibiuy in 1808,* by Franz Neuhauser the Younger, with arms of Sibiu at: 3 l, Left. 15 l, Right.

**2016, July 15 Litho. *Perf. 13¼***

| No. | Type | Description | Unused | Used |
|---|---|---|---|---|
| **5819** | A1718 | 3 l multi | 1.50 | .75 |
| *a.* | | Sheet of 5 + label | 7.50 | 3.75 |
| **5820** | A1718 | 15 l multi | 7.50 | 3.75 |
| *a.* | | Sheet of 5 + label | 37.50 | 19.00 |

Stamp Day. A souvenir sheet of 2 containing Nos. 5819-5820 was printed in limited quantities.

Awarding of First Perfect Score in Olympic Women's Gymnastics to Nadia Comaneci, 40th Anniv. — A1719

Designs: 4.50 l, Comaneci and "10." No. 5822, Comaneci with leg extended, denomination in black. No. 5823, Comaneci with leg raised, denomination in white.

**2016, July 18 Litho. *Perf. 13¼***

| No. | Type | Description | Unused | Used |
|---|---|---|---|---|
| **5821** | A1719 | 4.50 l multi | 2.25 | 1.10 |
| *a.* | | Sheet of 5 + label | 11.50 | 5.50 |

**Souvenir Sheets**

| No. | Type | Description | Unused | Used |
|---|---|---|---|---|
| **5822** | A1719 | 31 l multi | 15.50 | 7.75 |

***Imperf***

| No. | Type | Description | Unused | Used |
|---|---|---|---|---|
| **5823** | A1719 | 31 l multi | 15.50 | 7.75 |

Nos. 5822 and 5823 each contain one 36x36mm stamp.

2016 Summer Olympics, Rio de Janeiro A1720

Designs: 3 l, Judo. 4 l. Fencing. 8 l, Long jump. 16 l, Shooting.

**2016, Aug. 5 Litho. *Perf. 13¼***

| No. | Type | Description | Unused | Used |
|---|---|---|---|---|
| **5824** | A1720 | 3 l multi | 1.50 | .75 |
| *a.* | | Sheet of 5 + label | 7.50 | 3.75 |
| **5825** | A1720 | 4 l multi | 2.00 | 1.00 |
| *a.* | | Sheet of 5 + label | 10.00 | 5.00 |
| **5826** | A1720 | 8 l multi | 4.00 | 2.00 |
| *a.* | | Sheet of 5 + label | 20.00 | 10.00 |
| **5827** | A1720 | 16 l multi | 8.00 | 4.00 |
| *a.* | | Sheet of 5 + label | 40.00 | 20.00 |
| *b.* | | Souvenir sheet of 4, #5824-5827 + 2 labels | 15.50 | 7.75 |
| | | *Nos. 5824-5827 (4)* | 15.50 | 7.75 |

Transalpina, Highest Road in Romania A1721

Designs: 8 l, Hairpin turn. 15 l, Road and village, horiz.

**2016, Aug. 12 Litho. *Perf. 13¼***

| No. | Type | Description | Unused | Used |
|---|---|---|---|---|
| **5828** | A1721 | 8 l multi | 4.00 | 2.00 |
| *a.* | | Sheet of 8 + central label | 32.00 | 16.00 |

**Souvenir Sheet**

| No. | Type | Description | Unused | Used |
|---|---|---|---|---|
| **5829** | A1721 | 15 l multi | 7.50 | 3.75 |

No. 5829 contains one 48x35mm stamp.

Cluj-Napoca Tourist Attractions A1722

Arms of Cluj- Napoca and: 3.50 l, Dormition of the Virgin Mary Orthodox Metropolitan Cathedral. 4 l, Tailor's Bastion. 4.50 l, Lucian Blaga National Theater, horiz. 15 l, Babes-Bolyai University, horiz.

**2016, Aug. 19 Litho. *Perf. 13¼***

| No. | Type | Description | Unused | Used |
|---|---|---|---|---|
| **5830** | A1722 | 3.50 l multi | 1.75 | .90 |
| *a.* | | Sheet of 5 + label | 8.75 | 4.50 |
| **5831** | A1722 | 4 l multi | 2.00 | 1.00 |
| *a.* | | Sheet of 5 + label | 10.00 | 5.00 |
| **5832** | A1722 | 4.50 l multi | 2.25 | 1.10 |
| *a.* | | Sheet of 5 + label | 11.50 | 5.50 |
| **5833** | A1722 | 15 l multi | 7.50 | 3.75 |
| *a.* | | Sheet of 5 + label | 37.50 | 19.00 |
| | | *Nos. 5830-5833 (4)* | 13.50 | 6.75 |

A souvenir sheet of 4 containing Nos. 5830-5833 was printed in limited quantities.

Romanian Chapter of International Police Association, 20th Anniv. — A1723

Designs: 8 l, Emblem, map and flag of Romania. 15 l, Emblem and flag of Romania.

**2016, Aug. 24 Litho. *Perf. 13¼***

| No. | Type | Description | Unused | Used |
|---|---|---|---|---|
| **5834** | A1723 | 8 l multi | 4.00 | 2.00 |
| *a.* | | Sheet of 8 + central label | 32.00 | 16.00 |

**Souvenir Sheet**

***Perf.***

| No. | Type | Description | Unused | Used |
|---|---|---|---|---|
| **5835** | A1723 | 15 l multi | 7.50 | 3.75 |

No. 5835 contains one 30mm diameter stamp.

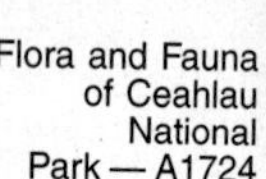

Flora and Fauna of Ceahlau National Park — A1724

Park emblem and: 80b, Edelweiss. 90b, Red crossbill, vert. 1.10 l, Liverwort. 1.20 l, Chamois, vert. 1.30 l, Arnica. 1.40 l, Brown bear, vert. 1.50 l, European robin. 1.60 l, Great yellow gentian, vert. 1.70 l, Water pipit. 1.80 l, Lady's slipper orchid, vert. 2.70 l, Common kingfisher. 16 l, Martagon lily, vert.

**2016, Sept. 1 Litho. *Perf. 13¼***

**5836** A1724 80b multi .40 .25
*a.* Sheet of 4 1.60 .80
**5837** A1724 90b multi .45 .25
*a.* Sheet of 4 1.90 1.00
**5838** A1724 1.10 l multi .55 .25
*a.* Sheet of 4 2.25 1.00
**5839** A1724 1.20 l multi .60 .30
*a.* Sheet of 4 2.40 1.25
**5840** A1724 1.30 l multi .65 .30
*a.* Sheet of 4 2.60 1.25
**5841** A1724 1.40 l multi .70 .35
*a.* Sheet of 4 3.00 1.40
**5842** A1724 1.50 l multi .75 .40
*a.* Sheet of 4 3.00 1.60
**5843** A1724 1.60 l multi .80 .40
*a.* Sheet of 4 3.25 1.60
**5844** A1724 1.70 l multi .85 .40
*a.* Sheet of 4 3.50 1.60
**5845** A1724 1.80 l multi .90 .45
*a.* Sheet of 4 3.75 1.90
**5846** A1724 2.70 l multi 1.40 .70
*a.* Sheet of 4 5.75 3.00
**5847** A1724 16 l multi 8.00 4.00
*a.* Sheet of 4 32.00 16.00
*Nos. 5836-5847 (12)* 16.05 8.05

Bats A1725

Designs: 2.50 l, Plecotus auritus. 4.50 l, Pipistrellus pipistrellus. 8 l, Miniopterus schreibersii. 15 l, Nyctalus noctula, vert.

**2016, Sept. 9 Litho. *Perf. 13¼***

**5848** A1725 2.50 l multi 1.25 .60
*a.* Sheet of 5 + label 6.25 3.00
**5849** A1725 4.50 l multi 2.25 1.10
*a.* Sheet of 5 + label 11.50 5.50
**5850** A1725 8 l multi 4.00 2.00
*a.* Sheet of 5 + label 20.00 10.00
**5851** A1725 15 l multi 7.50 3.75
*a.* Sheet of 5 + label 37.50 19.00
*Nos. 5848-5851 (4)* 15.00 7.45

A souvenir sheet of 4 containing Nos. 5848-5851 was printed in limited quantities.

Anti-Aircraft Artillery, Cent. — A1726

**2016, Sept. 19 Litho. *Perf. 13¼***

**5852** A1726 8 l multi 4.00 2.00
*a.* Sheet of 6 24.00 12.00

Military Aircraft, Cent. — A1727

Designs: 4.50 l, IAR-93. 15 l, IAR-99. 16 l, F-16.

**2016, Oct. 7 Litho. *Perf. 13¼***

**5853** A1727 4.50 l multi 2.25 1.10
*a.* Sheet of 4 9.00 4.50
**5854** A1727 15 l multi 7.50 3.75
*a.* Sheet of 4 30.00 15.00

**Souvenir Sheet**

***Perf. 14x13¼***

**5855** A1727 16 l multi 8.00 4.00

No. 5855 contains one 52x42mm stamp.

Laser Valley Land of Lights Research Laboratory, Magurele — A1728

Designs: 4.50 l, Horia Hulubei (1896-1972), physicist. 8 l, Ion L. Agârbiceanu (1907-71), physicist.
15 l, Laser Valley Laboratory.

**2016, Oct. 11 Litho. *Perf. 13¼***

**5856** A1728 4.50 l multi 2.25 1.10
*a.* Sheet of 5 + label 11.50 5.50
**5857** A1728 8 l multi 4.00 2.00
*a.* Sheet of 5 + label 20.00 10.00

**Souvenir Sheet**

***Perf. 14x13¼***

**5858** A1728 15 l multi 7.50 3.75

No. 5858 contains one 52x42mm stamp.

Muntenia Tourist Attractions A1729

Arms of Muntenia and: 2.50 l, Curtea de Arges Monastery, founder Neagoe Basarab. 3.50 l, Constantin Brancoveanu (1654-1714), Prince of Wallachia, and building details. 8 l, Woman wearing traditional costume, carpets & decorative motifs, stone decorations. 15 l, Buildings, sculpture of Prime Minister Ion C. Bratianu.

**2016, Oct. 14 Litho. *Perf. 13¼***

**5859** A1729 2.50 l multi 1.25 .60
*a.* Sheet of 5 + label 6.25 3.00
**5860** A1729 3.50 l multi 1.75 .85
*a.* Sheet of 5 + label 8.75 4.25
**5861** A1729 8 l multi 4.00 2.00
*a.* Sheet of 5 + label 20.00 10.00
**5862** A1729 15 l multi 7.50 3.75
*a.* Sheet of 5 + label 37.50 19.00
*Nos. 5859-5862 (4)* 14.50 7.20

A souvenir sheet of 4 containing Nos. 5859-5862 was printed in limited quantities.

Corkscrews A1730

Corkscrew from: 1.80 l, Italy, 19th cent. 2.20 l, France, 18th cent. 2.70 l, Great Britain, 19th cent. 3.50 l, Germany, 19th cent. 4.50 l, United States, 20th cent. 8 l, Netherlands, 19th cent.
16 l, Romanian corkscrew, 20th cent., horiz,

**2016, Oct. 27 Litho. *Perf. 13¼***

**5863** A1730 1.80 l multi .90 .45
*a.* Sheet of 8 + central label 7.25 3.75
*b.* Sheet of 13 + 2 labels 12.00 6.00
**5864** A1730 2.20 l multi 1.10 .55
*a.* Sheet of 8 + central label 9.00 4.50
*b.* Sheet of 13 + 2 labels 14.50 7.25
**5865** A1730 2.70 l multi 1.40 .70
*a.* Sheet of 8 + central label 11.50 5.75
*b.* Sheet of 13 + 2 labels 18.50 9.25
**5866** A1730 3.50 l multi 1.75 .85
*a.* Sheet of 8 + central label 14.00 7.00
*b.* Sheet of 13 + 2 labels 23.00 11.50
**5867** A1730 4.50 l multi 2.25 1.10
*a.* Sheet of 8 + central label 18.00 9.00
*b.* Sheet of 13 + 2 labels 29.50 14.50
**5868** A1730 8 l multi 4.00 2.00
*a.* Sheet of 8 + central label 32.00 16.00
*b.* Sheet of 13 + 2 labels 52.00 26.00

**Souvenir Sheet**

***Imperf***

**5869** A1730 16 l multi 8.00 4.00

No. 5869 contains one 52x42mm stamp. See Nos. 5921-5927.

Transportation of King Michael — A1731

King Michael and: 4 l, Aero 30 Roadster. 4.50 l, Motorcycle, vert. 8 l, Automobile, with Queen Anne, vert. 15 l, Airplane.

**2016, Oct. 27 Litho. *Perf. 14x13¼***

**5870** A1731 4 l multi 2.00 1.00
*a.* Sheet of 5 + label 10.00 5.00
**5871** A1731 4.50 l multi 2.25 1.10
*a.* Sheet of 5 + label 11.50 5.50
**5872** A1731 8 l multi 4.00 2.00
*a.* Sheet of 5 + label 20.00 10.00
**5873** A1731 15 l multi 7.50 3.75
*a.* Sheet of 5 + label 37.50 19.00
*Nos. 5870-5873 (4)* 15.75 7.85

A souvenir sheet of 4 containing Nos. 5870-5873 was printed in limited quantities.

World Bank in Romania, 25th Anniv. A1732

**2016, Nov. 1 Litho. *Perf. 13¼x14***

**5874** A1732 12 l multi 6.00 3.00
*a.* Sheet of 5 + label 30.00 15.00

Christmas A1733

Designs: No. 5875, Nativity icon from Putna Monastery. No. 5876, Poinsettia.
12 l, Madonna and Child icon from Putna Monastery.

**2016, Nov. 11 Litho. *Perf. 13¼***

**5875** A1733 1.30 l multi .65 .30
*a.* Sheet of 8 + central label 5.25 2.40
**5876** A1733 1.30 l multi .65 .30
*a.* Sheet of 8 + central label 5.25 2.40

**Souvenir Sheet**

**5877** A1733 12 l multi 5.75 3.00

Souvenir sheets of 2 containing one each of Nos. 5875-5876 and souvenir sheets of 3 containing No. 5875 and 2 examples of No. 5876 were printed in limited quantities.

Foods of the Bible A1734

Designs: 1.60 l, Wheat and bread. 4.50 l, Figs and pomegranates. 8 l, Grapes. 15 l, Olives and olive oil.

**2016, Nov. 24 Litho. *Perf. 13¼***

**5878** A1734 1.60 l multi .75 .40
*a.* Sheet of 5 + label 3.75 2.00
**5879** A1734 4.50 l multi 2.25 1.10
*a.* Sheet of 5 + label 11.50 5.50
**5880** A1734 8 l multi 3.75 1.90
*a.* Sheet of 5 + label 19.00 9.50
**5881** A1734 15 l multi 7.25 3.75
*a.* Sheet of 5 + label 36.50 19.00
*Nos. 5878-5881 (4)* 14.00 7.15

**Actors and Actresses Type of 2014**

Designs: No. 5882, Adela Marculescu. No. 5883, Florina Cercel. No. 5884, Ilinca Tomoroveanu. No. 5885, Ion Caramitru. No. 5886, Costel Constantin. No. 5887, Alexandru Arsinel.

**2016, Dec. 19 Litho. *Perf. 13¼***

**5882** A1620 4.50 l multi 2.10 1.10
*a.* Sheet of 4 8.50 4.50
**5883** A1620 4.50 l multi 2.10 1.10
*a.* Sheet of 4 8.50 4.50
**5884** A1620 4.50 l multi 2.10 1.10
*a.* Sheet of 4 8.50 4.50
**5885** A1620 4.50 l multi 2.10 1.10
*a.* Sheet of 4 8.50 4.50
**5886** A1620 4.50 l multi 2.10 1.10
*a.* Sheet of 4 8.50 4.50
**5887** A1620 4.50 l multi 2.10 1.10
*a.* Sheet of 4 8.50 4.50
*b.* Souvenir sheet of 6, #5882-5887 + 3 labels 13.00 6.75
*Nos. 5882-5887 (6)* 12.60 6.60

New Year's Customs — A1735

Designs: 2.20 l, Plugusorul (man pushing plow decorated with Christmas tree). 2.50 l, Buhaiul (carolers and drummer). 8 l, Ursul (dancers with bear costumes). 15 l, Capra (goat dance).

**2016, Dec. 21 Litho. *Perf. 13¼***

**5888** A1735 2.20 l multi 1.00 .50
*a.* Sheet of 5 + label 5.00 2.50
**5889** A1735 2.50 l multi 1.25 .60
*a.* Sheet of 5 + label 6.25 3.00
**5890** A1735 8 l multi 3.75 1.90
*a.* Sheet of 5 + label 19.00 9.50
**5891** A1735 15 l multi 7.00 3.50
*a.* Sheet of 5 + label 35.00 17.50
*Nos. 5888-5891 (4)* 13.00 6.50

Palace of Culture, Iasi — A1736

Designs: 2.20 l, Palace at night. 2.50 l, Voivode Hall. 8 l, Henri Coanda Room. 15 l, Palace in daytime.

**2017, Jan. 10 Litho. *Perf. 13¼***

**5892** A1736 2.20 l multi 1.10 .55
*a.* Sheet of 5 + label 5.50 2.75
**5893** A1736 2.50 l multi 1.25 .60
*a.* Sheet of 5 + label 6.25 3.00
**5894** A1736 8 l multi 3.75 1.90
*a.* Sheet of 5 + label 19.00 9.50
**5895** A1736 15 l multi 7.25 3.50
*a.* Sheet of 5 + label 36.50 17.50
*Nos. 5892-5895 (4)* 13.35 6.55

Orchids A1737

Designs: 2.20 l, Epipactis atrorubens. 4.50 l, Cephalanthera damasonium. 8 l, Orchis purpurea. 15 l, Epipactis helleborine.

**2017, Jan. 25 Litho. *Perf. 13¼***

**5896** A1737 2.20 l multi 1.10 .55
*a.* Sheet of 4 4.50 2.25
**5897** A1737 4.50 l multi 2.10 1.10
*a.* Sheet of 4 8.50 4.50
**5898** A1737 8 l multi 3.75 1.90
*a.* Sheet of 4 15.00 7.75
**5899** A1737 15 l multi 7.25 3.75
*a.* Sheet of 4 29.00 15.00
*Nos. 5896-5899 (4)* 14.20 7.30

A souvenir sheet of 4 containing Nos. 5896-5899 was printed in limited quantities.

Romania in European Union, 10th Anniv. — A1738

**2017, Jan. 27 Litho. *Perf. 13¼***

5900 A1738 8 l multi 3.75 1.90
*a.* Sheet of 6 22.50 11.50

Birds A1739

Designs: 2.50 l, Corvus monedula. 4.50 l, Garrulus glandarius. 8 l, Corvus frugilegus. 15 l, Pica pica.

**2017, Feb. 10 Litho. *Perf. 13¼***

5901 A1739 2.50 l multi 1.25 .60
*a.* Sheet of 5 + label 6.25 3.00
5902 A1739 4.50 l multi 2.10 1.10
*a.* Sheet of 5 + label 10.50 5.50
5903 A1739 8 l multi 3.75 1.90
*a.* Sheet of 5 + label 19.00 9.50
5904 A1739 15 l multi 7.00 3.50
*a.* Sheet of 5 + label 35.00 17.50
*Nos. 5901-5904 (4)* 14.10 7.10

A souvenir sheet of 4 containing Nos. 5901-5904 was produced in limited quantities.

National Brukenthal Museum, 200th Anniv. — A1740

Baron Samuel von Brukenthal (1721-1803), governor of Transylvania, and: 2.20 l, Pocket watch. 2.50 l, Brukenthal Palace. 8 l, Brukenthal family crest. 15 l, Pocket watch, diff.

**2017, Feb. 17 Litho. *Perf. 13¼***

5905 A1740 2.20 l multi 1.10 .55
*a.* Sheet of 5 + label 5.50 2.75
5906 A1740 2.50 l multi 1.25 .60
*a.* Sheet of 5 + label 6.25 3.00
5907 A1740 8 l multi 3.75 1.90
*a.* Sheet of 5 + label 19.00 9.50
5908 A1740 15 l multi 7.00 3.50
*a.* Sheet of 5 + label 35.00 17.50
*Nos. 5905-5908 (4)* 13.10 6.55

Postcrossing — A1741

**2017, Feb. 24 Litho. *Perf. 13¼***

5909 A1741 4 l multi 1.90 .95
*a.* Sheet of 8 + central label 15.50 7.75

A1742

Easter A1743

Design: 12 l, The Resurrection - The Harrowing of Hell.

**2017, Mar. 10 Litho. *Perf. 13¼***

5910 A1742 1.30 l multi .60 .30
*a.* Sheet of 8 + central label 5.00 2.40
5911 A1743 1.30 l multi .60 .30
*a.* Sheet of 8 + central label 5.00 2.40
*b.* Sheet of 8, 4 each #5910-5911 5.00 2.40

### Souvenir Sheet

5912 A1743 12 l multi 5.75 3.00

Two souvenir sheets of 3 containing No. 5912 and imperforate examples of Nos. 5190-5911, and the other containing Nos. 5910-5911 and one imperforate example of No. 5912 were printed in limited quantities.

National Flowers, Flags and Maps — A1744

Designs: 1.50 l, Paeonia peregrina, flag and map of Romania. 4.50 l, Ocimum basilicum, flag and map of Moldova. 8 l, Iris croatica, flag and map of Croatia. 15 l, Rosa damascena, flag and map of Bulgaria.

**2017, Mar. 17 Litho. *Perf. 13¼***

5913 A1744 1.50 l multi .70 .35
*a.* Sheet of 5 + label 3.50 1.75
5914 A1744 4.50 l multi 2.10 1.10
*a.* Sheet of 5 + label 10.50 5.50
5915 A1744 8 l multi 3.75 1.90
*a.* Sheet of 5 + label 19.00 9.50
5916 A1744 15 l multi 7.00 3.50
*a.* Sheet of 5 + label 35.00 17.50
*Nos. 5913-5916 (4)* 13.55 6.85

Decorated Weapons of the 18th Century — A1745

Designs: 2.50 l, Persian gun. 4.50 l, Italian flintlock pistol. 8 l, Turkish flintlock pistol. 15 l, Turkish pistol, diff.

**2017, Mar. 24 Litho. *Perf. 14x13¼***

5917 A1745 2.50 l multi 1.25 .60
*a.* Sheet of 5 + label 6.25 3.00
5918 A1745 4.50 l multi 2.10 1.10
*a.* Sheet of 5 + label 10.50 5.50
5919 A1745 8 l multi 3.75 1.90
*a.* Sheet of 5 + label 19.00 9.50
5920 A1745 15 l multi 7.00 3.50
*a.* Sheet of 5 + label 35.00 17.50
*Nos. 5917-5920 (4)* 14.10 7.10

### Corkscrews Type of 2016

Designs: 1.60 l, Pocket corkscrew,France, 18th cent. 2.70 l, Agate & gold corkscrew, France, 18th cent. 3.50 l, Bell type corkscrew, England, 19th cent. 4 l, Single lever corkscrew, France, 20th cent. 4.50 l, Zig-zag corkscrew, England, 19th cent. 8 l, Pistol corkscrew, France, 19th cent.

16 l, Corkscrew from Denmark, 20th cent., horiz.

**2017, Mar. 29 Litho. *Perf. 13¼***

5921 A1730 1.60 l multi .75 .35
*a.* Sheet of 8 + central label 6.00 3.00
*b.* Sheet of 13 + 2 labels 9.75 4.75
5922 A1730 2.70 l multi 1.25 .65
*a.* Sheet of 8 + central label 10.00 5.25
*b.* Sheet of 13 + 2 labels 16.50 8.50
5923 A1730 3.50 l multi 1.75 .85
*a.* Sheet of 8 + central label 14.00 7.00
*b.* Sheet of 13 + 2 labels 23.00 11.50
5924 A1730 4 l multi 1.90 .95
*a.* Sheet of 8 + central label 15.50 7.75
*b.* Sheet of 13 + 2 labels 25.00 12.50
5925 A1730 4.50 l multi 2.10 1.10
*a.* Sheet of 8 + central label 17.00 9.00
*b.* Sheet of 13 + 2 labels 27.50 14.50
5926 A1730 8 l multi 3.75 1.90
*a.* Sheet of 8 + central label 30.00 15.50
*b.* Sheet of 13 + 2 labels 49.00 25.00
*Nos. 5921-5926 (6)* 11.50 5.80

### Souvenir Sheet

***Imperf***

5927 A1730 16 l multi 7.50 3.75

No. 5927 contains one 52x42mm stamp.

Symphony of Tulips Floral Exhibition, Pitesti — A1746

Tulips and: 2.50 l, Pitesti City Hall. 4 l, County Museum. 4.50 l, Rudolf Schwietzer-Cumpana Art Gallery. 16 l, Court of Appeals.

**2017, Apr. 7 Litho. *Perf. 13¼***

5928 A1746 2.50 l multi 1.25 .60
*a.* Sheet of 5 + label 6.25 3.00
5929 A1746 4 l multi 2.00 1.00
*a.* Sheet of 5 + label 10.00 5.00
5930 A1746 4.50 l multi 2.25 1.10
*a.* Sheet of 5 + label 11.50 5.50
5931 A1746 16 l multi 7.75 4.00
*a.* Sheet of 5 + label 39.00 20.00
*Nos. 5928-5931 (4)* 13.25 6.70

Europa — A1747

Designs: 4.50 l, Hunyadi Castle, Hunedoara. 15 l, Károlyi Castle, Carei.

**2017, Apr. 12 Litho. *Perf. 13¼***

5932 A1747 4.50 l multi 2.25 1.10
*a.* Sheet of 5 + label 11.50 5.50
5933 A1747 15 l multi 7.25 3.75
*a.* Sheet of 5 + label 37.00 18.00
*b.* Souvenir sheet of 4, 2 each #5932-5933, #5932 at UL 19.00 9.75
*c.* As "b," #5933 at UL 19.00 9.75

Recently Extinct Animals — A1748

Designs: 2.70 l, Ectopistes migratorius, 1914. 3.50 l, Thylacinus cynocephalus, 1936. 8 l, Panthera tigris sondaica, 1976. 15 l, Lipotes vexillifer, 2002.

**2017, Apr. 21 Litho. *Perf. 13¼***

5934 A1748 2.70 l multi 1.40 .70
*a.* Sheet of 5 + label 7.00 3.50
5935 A1748 3.50 l multi 1.75 .85
*a.* Sheet of 5 + label 8.75 4.25
5936 A1748 8 l multi 4.00 2.00
*a.* Sheet of 5 + label 20.00 10.00
5937 A1748 15 l multi 7.25 3.75
*a.* Sheet of 5 + label 37.00 19.00
*Nos. 5934-5937 (4)* 14.40 7.30

Iasi A1749

Iasi coat of arms and: 2.50 l, Ghica-Comanesti House. 4.50 l, National Theater. 8 l, University of Iasi. 15 l, Rosetti-Roznovanu Palace.

16 l, Iasi coat of arms, vert.

**2017, Apr. 26 Litho. *Perf. 13¼***

5938 A1749 2.50 l multi 1.25 .60
*a.* Sheet of 6 7.50 3.75
5939 A1749 4.50 l multi 2.25 1.10
*a.* Sheet of 6 13.50 6.75
5940 A1749 8 l multi 4.00 2.00
*a.* Sheet of 6 24.00 12.00
5941 A1749 15 l multi 7.25 3.75
*a.* Sheet of 6 43.50 22.50
*Nos. 5938-5941 (4)* 14.75 7.45

### Souvenir Sheet

5942 A1749 16 l multi 7.75 4.00

No. 5942 contains one 27x42mm stamp. A souvenir sheet of 4 containing Nos. 5938-5941 was printed in limited quantities.

Endangered Species — A1750

Designs: 2.20 l, Aquila heliaca. 2.50 l, Falco columbarius. 2.70 l, Lutra lutra. 16 l, Huso huso.

**2017, May 11 Litho. *Perf. 13¼***

5943 A1750 2.20 l multi 1.10 .55
*a.* Sheet of 5 + label 5.50 2.75
5944 A1750 2.50 l multi 1.25 .60
*a.* Sheet of 5 + label 6.25 3.00
5945 A1750 2.70 l multi 1.40 .70
*a.* Sheet of 5 + label 7.00 3.50
5946 A1750 16 l multi 8.00 4.00
*a.* Sheet of 5 + label 40.00 20.00
*b.* Souvenir sheet of 4, #5943-5946 12.00 6.00
*Nos. 5943-5946 (4)* 11.75 5.85

National Museum of Romanian Literature, 60th Anniv. — A1751

Designs: 8 l, Dumitru Panaitescu (Perpessicius) (1891-1971), poet, and museum emblem. 16 l, Museum emblem, vert.

**2017, May 17 Litho. *Perf. 13¼***

5947 A1751 8 l multi 4.00 2.00
*a.* Sheet of 8 + central label 32.00 16.00

### Souvenir Sheet

5948 A1751 16 l multi 8.00 4.00

Ancient Jewelry — A1752

Designs: 4 l, Earrings, 7th cent. 4.50 l, Bell pendants, 5th cent., vert. 8 l, Earrings, 5th cent., vert. 12 l, Spiral bracelet, 1st cent. B.C. 15 l, Tubular bracelet, 4th cent. B.C.

**2017, May 26 Litho. *Perf. 13¼***

5949 A1752 4 l multi 2.00 1.00
*a.* Sheet of 5 + label 10.00 5.00
5950 A1752 4.50 l multi 2.25 1.10
*a.* Sheet of 5 + label 11.50 5.50
5951 A1752 8 l multi 4.00 2.00
*a.* Sheet of 5 + label 20.00 10.00
5952 A1752 12 l multi 6.00 3.00
*a.* Sheet of 5 + label 30.00 15.00
*Nos. 5949-5952 (4)* 14.25 7.10

### Souvenir Sheet

5953 A1752 15 l multi 7.50 3.75

Children at Play — A1753

Children: 3.50 l, Cycling. 4 l, Playing with balls. 4.50 l, Playing hopscotch. 15 l, Sledding and building snowman.

**2017, May 31 Litho. *Perf. 13¼***

| | | | | |
|---|---|---|---|---|
| **5954** | A1753 3.50 l multi | | 1.75 | .85 |
| *a.* | Sheet of 5 + label | | 8.75 | .85 |
| **5955** | A1753 4 l multi | | 2.00 | 1.00 |
| *a.* | Sheet of 5 + label | | 10.00 | 5.00 |
| **5956** | A1753 4.50 l multi | | 2.25 | 1.10 |
| *a.* | Sheet of 5 + label | | 11.50 | 5.50 |
| **5957** | A1753 15 l multi | | 7.50 | 3.75 |
| *a.* | Sheet of 5 + label | | 37.50 | 19.00 |

Steaua Soccer Team, 70th Anniv. — A1754

**2017, June 6 Litho. *Perf. 13¼***

| | | | |
|---|---|---|---|
| **5958** | A1754 8 l multi | 4.00 | 2.00 |
| *a.* | Sheet of 8 + central label | 32.00 | 16.00 |

Titu Maiorescu (1840-1937), Literary Critic — A1755

Designs: 4.50 l, Maiorescu and cover of *Convorbiri Literare.* 8 l, Maiorescu, vert.

**2017, June 21 Litho. *Perf. 13¼***

| | | | |
|---|---|---|---|
| **5959** | A1755 4.50 l multi | 2.25 | 1.10 |
| *a.* | Sheet of 5 + label | 11.50 | 5.50 |
| **5960** | A1755 8 l multi | 4.00 | 2.00 |
| *a.* | Sheet of 5 + label | 20.00 | 10.00 |

Bucharest Municipality Museums — A1756

Designs: 2.50 l, 14th cent. Wallachian coin, Greek vase, 500 B.C., George Severeanu Museum. 2.70 l, Cherries, by Theodore Aman (1831-91), and his bust, Theodor Aman Museum. 3.50 l, Decorated plate, Nicolae Minovici Museum. 4 l, Stained-glass window, Vasile Urseanu Astronomical Observatory. 4.50 l, Microscope, paper on bacteriology, Victor Babes (1854-1926), bacteriologist, Victor Babes Museum. 15 l, Sign and Filipescu-Cesianu House.
16 l, Sutu Palace.

**2017, June 29 Litho. *Perf. 13¼***

| | | | |
|---|---|---|---|
| **5961** | A1756 2.50 l multi | 1.25 | .60 |
| *a.* | Sheet of 4 | 5.00 | 2.40 |
| **5962** | A1756 2.70 l multi | 1.40 | .70 |
| *a.* | Sheet of 4 | 5.75 | 3.00 |
| **5963** | A1756 3.50 l multi | 1.75 | .85 |
| *a.* | Sheet of 4 | 7.00 | 3.50 |
| **5964** | A1756 4 l multi | 2.00 | 1.00 |
| *a.* | Sheet of 4 | 8.00 | 4.00 |
| **5965** | A1756 4.50 l multi | 2.25 | 1.10 |
| *a.* | Sheet of 4 | 9.00 | 4.50 |

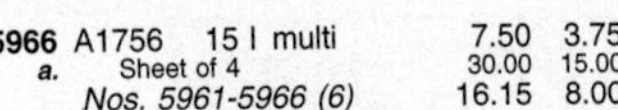

| | | | |
|---|---|---|---|
| **5966** | A1756 15 l multi | 7.50 | 3.75 |
| *a.* | Sheet of 4 | 30.00 | 15.00 |
| | *Nos. 5961-5966 (6)* | 16.15 | 8.00 |

**Souvenir Sheet**

| | | | |
|---|---|---|---|
| **5967** | A1756 16 l multi | 8.00 | 4.00 |

No. 5967 contains one 96x33mm stamp.

Seascape Paintings — A1757

Designs: 2.20 l, City by Sea (Naples), by Nicolae Grigorescu (1838-1907). 2.70 l, Balchik, by Cecelia Citescu-Storck (1879-1969). 8 l, Balchik, by Dumitru Ghiata (1888-1972). 15 l, Shipwreck, by Ivan Aivazovsky (1817-1900), vert.

**2017, July 7 Litho. *Perf. 13¾x13¼***

| | | | |
|---|---|---|---|
| **5968** | A1757 2.20 l multi | 1.25 | .60 |
| *a.* | Sheet of 5 + label | 6.25 | 3.00 |
| **5969** | A1757 2.70 l multi | 1.40 | .70 |
| *a.* | Sheet of 5 + label | 7.00 | 3.50 |
| **5970** | A1757 8 l multi | 4.25 | 2.10 |
| *a.* | Sheet of 5 + label | 21.50 | 10.50 |

***Perf. 13¼x13¾***

| | | | |
|---|---|---|---|
| **5971** | A1757 15 l multi | 7.75 | 4.00 |
| *a.* | Sheet of 5 + label | 39.00 | 20.00 |
| | *Nos. 5968-5971 (4)* | 14.65 | 7.40 |

Heroes of World War I — A1758

Flag, soldiers and: 4.50 l, Ecaterina Teodoroiu (1894-1917), and cannon. 8 l, General Eremia Grigorescu (1863-1919), and fortress.

**2017, July 14 Litho. *Perf. 13¼***

| | | | |
|---|---|---|---|
| **5972** | A1758 4.50 l multi | 2.40 | 1.25 |
| *a.* | Sheet of 5 + label | 12.00 | 6.25 |
| **5973** | A1758 8 l multi | 4.25 | 2.10 |
| *a.* | Sheet of 5 + label | 21.50 | 10.50 |

Stamp Day. A souvenir sheet of 2 containing Nos. 5972-5973 was printed in limited quantities.

Tourism — A1759

Designs: 2.50 l, Egret at Danube River Delta. 2.70 l, Pitcher, Clock Tower, Sighisoara, vert. 3.50 l, Deer, Bigar Waterfall. 4 l, Blouse, Voronet Monastery. 4.50 l, Woodpecker, train on Mocanita Narrow-Gauge Railway, vert. 15 l, Rugs from Oltenia, Horezu ceramics.

**2017, July 26 Litho. *Perf. 13¼***

| | | | |
|---|---|---|---|
| **5974** | A1759 2.50 l multi | 1.40 | .70 |
| *a.* | Sheet of 5 + label | 7.00 | 3.50 |
| **5975** | A1759 2.70 l multi | 1.40 | .70 |
| *a.* | Sheet of 5 + label | 7.00 | 3.50 |
| **5976** | A1759 3.50 l multi | 1.90 | .95 |
| *a.* | Sheet of 5 + label | 9.50 | 4.75 |
| **5977** | A1759 4 l multi | 2.10 | 1.10 |
| *a.* | Sheet of 5 + label | 10.50 | 5.50 |
| **5978** | A1759 4.50 l multi | 2.40 | 1.25 |
| *a.* | Sheet of 5 + label | 12.00 | 6.25 |
| **5979** | A1759 15 l multi | 7.75 | 4.00 |
| *a.* | Sheet of 5 + label | 39.00 | 20.00 |
| *b.* | Souvenir sheet of 6, #5974-5979, imperf. | 17.00 | 8.75 |
| | *Nos. 5974-5979 (6)* | 16.95 | 8.70 |

Sixth National Jamboree of Romanian Scouts — A1760

Jamboree emblem and: 2.20 l, Church tower, Cristian. 3.50 l, Tents at Jamboree site. 8 l, Scouts around campfire. 15 l, Scout salute.

**2017, Aug. 4 Litho. *Perf. 13¼***

| | | | |
|---|---|---|---|
| **5980** | A1760 2.20 l multi | 1.25 | .60 |
| *a.* | Sheet of 5 + label | 6.25 | 3.00 |
| **5981** | A1760 3.50 l multi | 1.90 | .95 |
| *a.* | Sheet of 5 + label | 9.50 | 4.75 |
| **5982** | A1760 8 l multi | 4.25 | 2.10 |
| *a.* | Sheet of 5 + label | 21.50 | 10.50 |
| **5983** | A1760 15 l multi | 7.75 | 4.00 |
| *a.* | Sheet of 5 + label | 39.00 | 20.00 |
| | *Nos. 5980-5983 (4)* | 15.15 | 7.65 |

Medias, 750th Anniv. of Mention in Document A1761

Arms and: 2.50 l, Stephan Ludwig Roth High School and its Gemini symbol. 4 l, Orthodox Cathedral, Tailor's Bastion Tower, statue of spinner. 4.50 l, Franciscan Architectural Complex, bas-relief. 16 l, Church of St. Margaret, sculpture of lion at Schuller House.

**2017, Aug. 11 Litho. *Perf. 13¼***

| | | | |
|---|---|---|---|
| **5984** | A1761 2.50 l multi | 1.40 | .70 |
| *a.* | Sheet of 5 + label | 7.00 | 3.50 |
| **5985** | A1761 4 l multi | 2.10 | 1.10 |
| *a.* | Sheet of 5 + label | 10.50 | 5.50 |
| **5986** | A1761 4.50 l multi | 2.40 | 1.25 |
| *a.* | Sheet of 5 + label | 12.00 | 6.25 |
| **5987** | A1761 16 l multi | 8.25 | 4.25 |
| *a.* | Sheet of 5 + label | 41.50 | 21.50 |
| | *Nos. 5984-5987 (4)* | 14.15 | 7.30 |

A souvenir sheet of 4 containing Nos. 5984-5987 was printed in limited quantities.

Antique Automobiles in Ion Tiriac Collection — A1762

Designs: 2.20 l, 1899 Hurtu 3½ Quadricycle. 3.50 l, 1920 Delage Type CO. 8 l, 1930 Duesenberg Model J Torpedo Berline Convertible. 15 l, 1937 Cord 812 Custom Berverly.

***Perf. 13¾x13¼***

**2017, Aug. 30 Litho.**

| | | | |
|---|---|---|---|
| **5988** | A1762 2.20 l multi | 1.25 | .60 |
| *a.* | Sheet of 5 + label | 6.25 | 3.00 |
| **5989** | A1762 3.50 l multi | 1.90 | .95 |
| *a.* | Sheet of 5 + label | 9.50 | 4.75 |
| **5990** | A1762 8 l multi | 4.25 | 2.10 |
| *a.* | Sheet of 5 + label | 21.50 | 10.50 |
| **5991** | A1762 15 l multi | 7.75 | 4.00 |
| *a.* | Sheet of 5 + label | 39.00 | 20.00 |
| | *Nos. 5988-5991 (4)* | 15.15 | 7.65 |

A souvenir sheet of 4 containing Nos. 5988-5991 was printed in limited quantities.

No. 4335 Surcharged in Metallic Magenta

**Method and Perf. As Before**

**2017, Aug. 31**

| | | | |
|---|---|---|---|
| **5992** | A1221 8 l on 6000 l #4335 (MR) | 4.25 | 2.10 |

Mihail Kogalniceanu (1817-91), Prime Minister — A1763

Designs: 4.50 l, Kogalniceanu and *Danube Star* newspaper. 8 l, Portrait of Kogalniceanu, vert.

**2017, Sept. 6 Litho. *Perf. 13¼***

| | | | |
|---|---|---|---|
| **5993** | A1763 4.50 l multi | 2.40 | 1.25 |
| *a.* | Sheet of 5 + label | 12.00 | 6.25 |
| **5994** | A1763 8 l multi | 4.25 | 2.10 |
| *a.* | Sheet of 5 + label | 21.50 | 10.50 |

Cacti A1764

Flowers of: 3.50 l, Lophocereus schottii forma Monstruosus. 4 l, Opuntia aciculata. 4.50 l, Coryphantha sulcata. 15 l, Echinocactus horizonthaonius.

**2017, Sept. 15 Litho. *Perf. 13¼***

| | | | |
|---|---|---|---|
| **5995** | A1764 3.50 l multi | 1.90 | .95 |
| *a.* | Sheet of 4 | 7.75 | 4.00 |
| **5996** | A1764 4 l multi | 2.10 | 1.10 |
| *a.* | Sheet of 4 | 8.50 | 4.50 |
| **5997** | A1764 4.50 l multi | 2.40 | 1.25 |
| *a.* | Sheet of 4 | 9.75 | 5.00 |
| **5998** | A1764 15 l multi | 7.75 | 4.00 |
| *a.* | Sheet of 4 | 31.00 | 16.00 |
| | *Nos. 5995-5998 (4)* | 14.15 | 7.30 |

A souvenir sheet of 4 containing Nos. 5995-5998 was printed in limited quantities.

Statue of Ion Heliade Radulescu and Bucharest University Building — A1765

Alexandru Ioan Cuza (1820-73), Domnitor of Romania — A1766

**2017, Sept. 20 Litho. *Perf. 13¼***

| | | | |
|---|---|---|---|
| **5999** | A1765 8 l multi | 4.25 | 2.10 |
| *a.* | Sheet of 8 + central label | 34.00 | 17.00 |

**Souvenir Sheet**

***Perf. 13¼x13¾***

| | | | |
|---|---|---|---|
| **6000** | A1766 16 l multi + 2 labels | 8.25 | 4.25 |

Bucharest as capital of Romania, 155th anniv.

Berries A1767

Designs: 2.20 l, Hippophae rhamnoides. 3.50 l, Crategus monogyna. 8 l, Rosa canina. 15 l, Fragaria vesca.

**2017, Sept. 29 Litho. *Perf. 13¼***

| | | | |
|---|---|---|---|
| **6001** | A1767 2.20 l multi | 1.10 | .55 |
| *a.* | Sheet of 5 + label | 5.50 | 2.75 |
| **6002** | A1767 3.50 l multi | 1.90 | .95 |
| *a.* | Sheet of 5 + label | 9.50 | 4.75 |
| **6003** | A1767 8 l multi | 4.25 | 2.10 |
| *a.* | Sheet of 5 + label | 21.50 | 10.50 |
| **6004** | A1767 15 l multi | 7.75 | 4.00 |
| *a.* | Sheet of 5 + label | 39.00 | 20.00 |
| | *Nos. 6001-6004 (4)* | 15.00 | 7.60 |

Mushrooms A1768

Designs: 2.50 l, Amanita caesarea. 4.50 l, Amanita rubescens. 8 l, Leccinum aurantiacum. 15 l, Macrolepiota procera.

**2017, Oct. 6 Litho. *Perf. 13¼***

| | | | |
|---|---|---|---|
| **6005** | A1768 2.50 l multi | 1.25 | .65 |
| *a.* | Sheet of 5 + label | 6.25 | 3.25 |
| **6006** | A1768 4.50 l multi | 2.25 | 1.10 |
| *a.* | Sheet of 5 + label | 11.50 | 5.50 |
| **6007** | A1768 8 l multi | 4.00 | 2.00 |
| *a.* | Sheet of 5 + label | 20.00 | 10.00 |
| **6008** | A1768 15 l multi | 7.75 | 4.00 |
| *a.* | Sheet of 5 + label | 39.00 | 20.00 |
| | *Nos. 6005-6008 (4)* | 15.25 | 7.75 |

A souvenir sheet of 4 containing Nos. 6005-6008 was printed in limited quantities.

Sheep Breeds A1769

Designs: 3.50 l, Merinos de Palas. 4 l, Tigaie Ruginie. 4.50 l, Teleorman Black Head. 16 l, Turcana.

**2017, Oct. 13 Litho. *Perf. 13¼***

| | | | |
|---|---|---|---|
| **6009** | A1769 3.50 l multi | 1.75 | .90 |
| *a.* | Sheet of 5 + label | 8.75 | 4.50 |
| **6010** | A1769 4 l multi | 2.00 | 1.00 |
| *a.* | Sheet of 5 + label | 10.00 | 5.00 |
| **6011** | A1769 4.50 l multi | 2.25 | 1.10 |
| *a.* | Sheet of 5 + label | 11.50 | 5.50 |
| **6012** | A1769 16 l multi | 8.25 | 4.25 |
| *a.* | Sheet of 5 + label | 42.00 | 21.50 |
| | *Nos. 6009-6012 (4)* | 14.25 | 7.25 |

Royal Tableware — A1770

Designs: 3.50 l, Goody & Co. porcelain fruit dish. 4 l, Martin Hall & Co. egg service, vert. 4.50 l, Baccarat crystal punch bowl, vert. 15 l, Meissen candy dish.

***Perf. 14x13¼, 13¼x14***

**2017, Oct. 20 Litho.**

| | | | |
|---|---|---|---|
| **6013** | A1770 3.50 l multi | 1.75 | .90 |
| *a.* | Sheet of 5 + label | 8.75 | 4.50 |
| **6014** | A1770 4 l multi | 2.00 | 1.00 |
| *a.* | Sheet of 5 + label | 10.00 | 5.00 |
| **6015** | A1770 4.50 l multi | 2.25 | 1.10 |
| *a.* | Sheet of 5 + label | 11.50 | 5.50 |
| **6016** | A1770 15 l multi | 7.75 | 4.00 |
| *a.* | Sheet of 5 + label | 39.00 | 20.00 |
| | *Nos. 6013-6016 (4)* | 13.75 | 7.00 |

A souvenir sheet of 4 containing Nos. 6013-6016 was printed in limited quantities.

Mosaics Depicting Saints From Patriarchal Cathedral A1771

Designs: 1.80 l, St. Luke. 4 l, St. John Chrysostom. 16 l, St. Demetrius the New.

**2017, Oct. 27 Litho. *Perf. 13¼***

| | | | |
|---|---|---|---|
| **6017** | A1771 1.80 l multi | .90 | .45 |
| *a.* | Sheet of 5 + label | 4.50 | 2.25 |
| **6018** | A1771 4 l multi | 2.00 | 1.00 |
| *a.* | Sheet of 5 + label | 10.00 | 5.00 |

**Size: 42x52mm**

***Perf. 13¼x14***

| | | | |
|---|---|---|---|
| **6019** | A1771 16 l multi | 8.25 | 4.25 |
| *a.* | Sheet of 5 + label | 42.00 | 21.50 |
| | *Nos. 6017-6019 (3)* | 11.15 | 5.70 |

Conference of Francophone Women, Bucharest — A1772

**2017, Nov. 1 Litho. *Perf. 13¼***

| | | | |
|---|---|---|---|
| **6020** | A1772 8 l multi | 4.00 | 2.00 |
| *a.* | Sheet of 8 + label | 32.00 | 16.00 |

Bucharest Circus A1773

Designs: 3.50 l, Clown with "Star Circus" drum. 4 l, Horse show. 4.50 l, Contortionist acrobat. 15 l, Clown face and trapeze act.

**2017, Nov. 6 Litho. *Perf. 13¼x13¾***

| | | | |
|---|---|---|---|
| **6021** | A1773 3.50 l multi | 1.75 | .90 |
| *a.* | Sheet of 5 + label | 8.75 | 4.50 |
| **6022** | A1773 4 l multi | 2.00 | 1.00 |
| *a.* | Sheet of 5 + label | 10.00 | 5.00 |
| **6023** | A1773 4.50 l multi | 2.25 | 1.10 |
| *a.* | Sheet of 5 + label | 11.50 | 5.50 |
| **6024** | A1773 15 l multi | 7.50 | 3.75 |
| *a.* | Sheet of 5 + label | 37.50 | 19.00 |
| | *Nos. 6021-6024 (4)* | 13.50 | 6.75 |

Geraniums A1774

Designs: 2.20 l, Pelargonium peltatum. 2.50 l, Red Pelargonium zonale. 8 l, Pelargonium grandiflorum. 15 l, Pink Pelargonium zonale.

**2017, Nov. 17 Litho. *Perf. 13¼***

| | | | |
|---|---|---|---|
| **6025** | A1774 2.20 l multi | 1.10 | .55 |
| *a.* | Sheet of 5 + label | 5.50 | 2.75 |
| **6026** | A1774 2.50 l multi | 1.25 | .65 |
| *a.* | Sheet of 5 + label | 6.50 | 3.25 |
| **6027** | A1774 8 l multi | 4.00 | 2.00 |
| *a.* | Sheet of 5 + label | 20.00 | 10.00 |
| **6028** | A1774 15 l multi | 7.50 | 3.75 |
| *a.* | Sheet of 5 + label | 37.50 | 19.00 |
| | *Nos. 6025-6028 (4)* | 13.85 | 6.95 |

A souvenir sheet of 4 containing Nos. 6025-6028 was printed in limited quantities.

The Holy Family Recieving the Shepherds A1775

Madona and Child A1776

**2017, Nov. 21 Litho. *Perf. 13¼***

| | | | |
|---|---|---|---|
| **6029** | A1775 1.30 l multi | .65 | .35 |
| *a.* | Sheet of 9, #6030, 8 #6029 | 6.00 | 3.25 |
| **6030** | A1776 1.30 l multi | .65 | .35 |
| *a.* | Sheet of 9, #6029, 8 #6030 | 6.00 | 3.25 |

A souvenir sheet of 2 containing Nos. 6029-6030 was printed in limited quantities.

Trees — A1777

Designs: No. 6031, Sorbus aucuparia. No. 6032, Picea abies.

**2017, Nov. 24 Litho. *Perf. 13¼***

| | | | |
|---|---|---|---|
| **6031** | A1777 8 l multi | 4.00 | 2.00 |
| *a.* | Sheet of 5 + label | 20.00 | 10.00 |
| **6032** | A1777 8 l multi | 4.00 | 2.00 |
| *a.* | Sheet of 5 + label | 20.00 | 10.00 |

Joint Issue between Romania and Estonia. See Estonia Nos. 855-856.

Venomous Animals A1778

Designs: 3.50 l, Hapalochlaena maculosa. 4 l, Phyllobates terribilis. 4.50 l, Chironex fleckeri. 16 l, Oxyuranus microlepidotus.

**2017, Dec. 7 Litho. *Perf. 13¼***

| | | | |
|---|---|---|---|
| **6033** | A1778 3.50 l multi | 1.75 | .90 |
| *a.* | Sheet of 5 + label | 8.75 | 4.50 |
| **6034** | A1778 4 l multi | 2.00 | 1.00 |
| *a.* | Sheet of 5 + label | 10.00 | 5.00 |
| **6035** | A1778 4.50 l multi | 2.25 | 1.10 |
| *a.* | Sheet of 5 + label | 11.50 | 5.50 |
| **6036** | A1778 16 l multi | 8.25 | 4.25 |
| *a.* | Sheet of 5 + label | 42.00 | 21.50 |
| | *Nos. 6033-6036 (4)* | 14.25 | 7.25 |

A souvenir sheet of 4 containing Nos. 6033-6036 was printed in limited quantities.

King Michael I (1921-2017) — A1779

**2017, Dec. 13 Litho. *Perf. 13¼***

| | | | |
|---|---|---|---|
| **6037** | A1779 8 l multi | 4.00 | 2.00 |
| *a.* | Sheet of 7 + 2 labels | 28.00 | 14.00 |

Heroes of World War I — A1780

Designs: 3.50 l, Ioan Dragalina (1860-1916), general. 4 l, David Praporgescu (1865-1916), general. 4.50 l, Radu R. Rosetti (1877-1949), general. 16 l, Constantin Nazarie (1865-1926), army archpriest.

**2017, Dec. 14 Litho. *Perf. 13¼***

| | | | |
|---|---|---|---|
| **6038** | A1780 3.50 l multi | 1.75 | .90 |
| *a.* | Sheet of 5 + label | 8.75 | 4.50 |
| **6039** | A1780 4 l multi | 2.00 | 1.00 |
| *a.* | Sheet of 5 + label | 10.00 | 5.00 |
| **6040** | A1780 4.50 l multi | 2.25 | 1.10 |
| *a.* | Sheet of 5 + label | 11.50 | 5.50 |
| **6041** | A1780 16 l multi | 8.25 | 4.25 |
| *a.* | Sheet of 5 + label | 42.00 | 21.50 |
| | *Nos. 6038-6041 (4)* | 14.25 | 7.25 |

Stars of the Stage and Screen A1781

Designs: No. 6042, Maia Morgenstern. No. 6043, Oana Pellea. No. 6044, Luminita Gheorghiu. No. 6045, George Mihaita. No. 6046, Horatiu Malaele. No. 6047, Marcel Iures.

**2017, Dec. 20 Litho. *Perf. 13¼***

| | | | |
|---|---|---|---|
| **6042** A1781 8 l multi | 4.00 | 2.00 |
| *a.* Sheet of 4 | 16.00 | 8.00 |
| **6043** A1781 8 l multi | 4.00 | 2.00 |
| *a.* Sheet of 4 | 16.00 | 8.00 |
| **6044** A1781 8 l multi | 4.00 | 2.00 |
| *a.* Sheet of 4 | 16.00 | 8.00 |
| **6045** A1781 8 l multi | 4.00 | 2.00 |
| *a.* Sheet of 4 | 16.00 | 8.00 |
| **6046** A1781 8 l multi | 4.00 | 2.00 |
| *a.* Sheet of 4 | 16.00 | 8.00 |
| **6047** A1781 8 l multi | 4.00 | 2.00 |
| *a.* Sheet of 4 | 16.00 | 8.00 |
| *b.* Souvenir sheet of 6, #6042-6047 | 24.00 | 12.00 |
| *Nos. 6042-6047 (6)* | 24.00 | 12.00 |

Monument, Central Military Cemetery of the Royal Romanian Army, Zvolen, Slovakia — A1782

**2018, Jan. 5 Litho. *Perf. 13¼***

| | | |
|---|---|---|
| **6048** A1782 8 l multi | 4.25 | 2.10 |
| *a.* Sheet of 5 + label | 21.50 | 10.50 |

Diplomatic relations between Romania and Slovakia, 25th anniv. See Slovakia No. 783.

Cranes — A1783

Designs: 3.50 l, Antigone rubicunda. 4 l, Grus japonensis, horiz. 4.50 l, Anthropoides virgo, horiz. 15 l, Leucogeranus leucogeranus. 16 l, Balearica pavonina, horiz.

**2018, Jan. 12 Litho. *Perf. 13¼***

| | | |
|---|---|---|
| **6049** A1783 3.50 l multi | 1.75 | .90 |
| *a.* Sheet of 5 + label | 8.75 | 4.50 |
| **6050** A1783 4 l multi | 2.00 | 1.00 |
| *a.* Sheet of 5 + label | 10.00 | 5.00 |
| **6051** A1783 4.50 l multi | 2.25 | 1.10 |
| *a.* Sheet of 5 + label | 11.50 | 5.50 |
| **6052** A1783 15 l multi | 7.75 | 4.00 |
| *a.* Sheet of 5 + label | 39.00 | 20.00 |
| *Nos. 6049-6052 (4)* | 13.75 | 7.00 |

**Souvenir Sheet**

| | | |
|---|---|---|
| **6053** A1783 16 l multi | 8.25 | 4.25 |

A souvenir sheet of 4 containing Nos. 6049-6052, was issued in limited quantities.

No. 6053 contains a 48x33mm stamp.

Braila, 650th Anniv. of Documented Existence A1784

Designs: 2.20 l, Baroque clock. 3.50 l The Nativity of Our Lord Cathedral. 4 l, Kinetic Fountain, horiz. 4.50 l, Maria Filotti Theater, horiz. 15 l, Panait Istrati Memorial House, horiz.

**2018, Jan. 19 Litho. *Perf. 13¼***

| | | |
|---|---|---|
| **6054** A1784 2.20 l multi | 1.10 | .60 |
| *a.* Sheet of 5 + label | 5.50 | 2.75 |
| **6055** A1784 3.50 l multi | 1.75 | .90 |
| *a.* Sheet of 5 + label | 9.00 | 4.50 |
| **6056** A1784 4 l multi | 2.00 | 1.00 |
| *a.* Sheet of 5 + label | 10.00 | 5.00 |
| **6057** A1784 4.50 l multi | 2.25 | 1.10 |
| *a.* Sheet of 5 + label | 11.50 | 5.50 |
| **6058** A1784 15 l multi | 7.75 | 4.00 |
| *a.* Sheet of 5 + label | 39.00 | 20.00 |
| *Nos. 6054-6058 (5)* | 14.85 | 7.60 |

A souvenir sheet of 5 containing Nos. 6054-6058 was issued in limited quantities.

Mircea the Elder — A1785

Designs: 8 l, Statue. 16 l, Fresco from Bradetu Church.

**2018, Jan. 31 Litho. *Perf. 13¼***

| | | |
|---|---|---|
| **6059** A1785 8 l multi | 4.25 | 2.10 |
| *a.* Sheet of 8 + central label | 34.00 | 17.00 |

**Souvenir Sheet**

***Perf. 13¼x14***

| | | |
|---|---|---|
| **6060** A1785 16 l multi | 8.50 | 4.25 |

No. 6060 contains one 42x52mm stamp.

2018 Winter Olympics, PyeongChang, South Korea — A1786

Designs: 2.50 l, Bobsled. 4.50 l, Alpine skiing. 8 l, Cross country skiing. 15 l, Ski jumping.

**2018, Feb. 9 Litho. *Perf. 13¼***

| | | |
|---|---|---|
| **6061** A1786 2.50 l multi | 1.25 | .60 |
| *a.* Sheet of 5 + label | 6.25 | 3.00 |
| **6062** A1786 4.50 l multi | 2.40 | 1.25 |
| *a.* Sheet of 5 + label | 12.00 | 6.25 |
| **6063** A1786 8 l multi | 4.25 | 2.10 |
| *a.* Sheet of 5 + label | 21.50 | 10.50 |
| **6064** A1786 15 l multi | 8.00 | 4.00 |
| *a.* Sheet of 5 + label | 40.00 | 20.00 |
| *b.* Souvenir sheet of 4, #6061-6064 | 16.00 | 8.00 |
| *Nos. 6061-6064 (4)* | 15.90 | 7.95 |

The Romanian Renaissance, by Gheorghe Tattarescu (1818-94) A1787

Self-portrait, by Tattarescu — A1788

**2018, Feb. 16 Litho. *Perf. 13¼***

| | | |
|---|---|---|
| **6065** A1787 8 l multi | 4.25 | 2.10 |
| *a.* Sheet of 8 + central label | 34.00 | 17.00 |

**Souvenir Sheet**

***Imperf***

| | | |
|---|---|---|
| **6066** A1788 15 l multi | 8.00 | 4.00 |

**No. 3070 Surcharged in Gold**

***Method and Perf. As Before***

**2018, Feb. 19**

| | | |
|---|---|---|
| **6067** A887 31 l on 10 l multi | 16.50 | 8.25 |

Marin Constantin (1925-2011), Founder of Madrigal Choir — A1789

**2018, Feb. 27 Litho. *Perf. 13¼***

| | | |
|---|---|---|
| **6068** A1789 8 l multi | 4.25 | 2.10 |
| *a.* Sheet of 8 + central label | 34.00 | 17.00 |

Madrigal Choir, 55th anniv.

Easter A1790

Alba Iulia Cathedral icons: No. 6069, The Entrance to Jerusalem. No. 6070, The Resurrection of Jesus Christ.

12 l, The Crucifixion of Lord Jesus Christ.

**2018, Mar. 9 Litho. *Perf. 13¼***

| | | |
|---|---|---|
| **6069** A1790 1.30 l multi | .70 | .35 |
| *a.* Sheet of 8 + central label | 5.75 | 3.00 |
| **6070** A1790 1.30 l multi | .70 | .35 |
| *a.* Sheet of 8 + central label | 5.75 | 3.00 |
| *b.* Sheet of 10, 5 each #6069-6070 + 2 labels | 7.00 | 3.50 |

**Souvenir Sheet**

| | | |
|---|---|---|
| **6071** A1790 12 l multi | 6.25 | 3.25 |

A souvenir sheet of 3 containing Nos. 6069-6071, and a souvenir sheet containing No. 6071 and imperforate examples of Nos. 6069-6070, were printed in limited quantities.

Famous Romanians — A1791

Romanian Coat of Arms — A1792

Designs: 2.60 l, Miron Cristea (1868-1939), patriarch of Romanian Orthodox church. 4.50 l, Bishop Iuliu Hossu (1885-1970). 8 l, Iuliu Maniu (1873-1953), Prime Minister. 15 l, Ion I. C. Bratianu (1864-1927), Prime Minister.

**2018, Mar. 20 Litho. *Perf. 13¼***

| | | |
|---|---|---|
| **6072** A1791 2.60 l multi | 1.40 | .70 |
| *a.* Sheet of 6 + 6 labels | 8.50 | 4.25 |
| **6073** A1791 4.50 l multi | 2.40 | 1.25 |
| *a.* Sheet of 6 + 6 labels | 14.50 | 7.50 |
| **6074** A1791 8 l multi | 4.25 | 2.10 |
| *a.* Sheet of 6 + 6 labels | 25.50 | 13.00 |
| **6075** A1791 15 l multi | 8.00 | 4.00 |
| *a.* Sheet of 6 + 6 labels | 48.00 | 24.00 |
| *Nos. 6072-6075 (4)* | 16.05 | 8.05 |

**Souvenir Sheet**

***Imperf***

| | | |
|---|---|---|
| **6076** A1792 16 l multi | 8.50 | 4.25 |

No. 6076 contains one 30mm diameter stamp. See Nos. 6178-6182.

Unification of Bessarabia and Romania, Cent. — A1793

Designs: 4 l, Alexandru Marghiloman (1854-1925), politician. 8 l, Ion Inculet (1884-1940), politician.

16 l, Pantelimon Halippa (1883-1979), journalist and politician.

**2018, Mar. 27 Litho. *Perf. 13¼***

| | | |
|---|---|---|
| **6077** A1793 4 l multi | 2.10 | 1.10 |
| *a.* Sheet of 5 + label | 10.50 | 5.50 |
| **6078** A1793 8 l multi | 4.25 | 2.10 |
| *a.* Sheet of 5 + label | 21.50 | 10.50 |

**Souvenir Sheet**

| | | |
|---|---|---|
| **6079** A1793 16 l multi | 8.50 | 4.25 |

No. 6079 contains one 24x33mm stamp.

Household Items to Hold Hot Objects A1794

Designs: 2.20 l, Iron rest. 2.50 l, Iron protection. 2.70 l, Ornamental plate. 3.50 l, Support with grate. 4 l, Plate with floral motif. 15 l, Plate with central foot plate.
16 l, Detail of plate with central foot plate.

**2018, Mar. 29 Litho. *Perf. 13¼***

| | | | |
|---|---|---|---|
| **6080** | A1794 2.20 l multi | 1.25 | .60 |
| *a.* | Sheet of 8 + central label | 10.00 | 5.00 |
| *b.* | Sheet of 13 + 2 labels | 16.50 | 8.00 |
| **6081** | A1794 2.50 l multi | 1.40 | .70 |
| *a.* | Sheet of 8 + central label | 11.50 | 5.75 |
| *b.* | Sheet of 13 + 2 labels | 18.50 | 9.25 |
| **6082** | A1794 2.70 l multi | 1.50 | .75 |
| *a.* | Sheet of 8 + central label | 12.00 | 6.00 |
| *b.* | Sheet of 13 + 2 labels | 19.50 | 9.75 |
| **6083** | A1794 3.50 l multi | 1.90 | .95 |
| *a.* | Sheet of 8 + central label | 15.50 | 7.75 |
| *b.* | Sheet of 13 + 2 labels | 25.00 | 12.50 |
| **6084** | A1794 4 l multi | 2.10 | 1.10 |
| *a.* | Sheet of 8 + central label | 17.00 | 9.00 |
| *b.* | Sheet of 13 + 2 labels | 27.50 | 14.50 |
| **6085** | A1794 15 l multi | 8.00 | 4.00 |
| *a.* | Sheet of 8 + central label | 64.00 | 32.00 |
| *b.* | Sheet of 13 + 2 labels | 105.00 | 52.50 |
| | *Nos. 6080-6085 (6)* | 16.15 | 8.10 |

**Souvenir Sheet**

***Imperf***

| | | | |
|---|---|---|---|
| **6086** | A1794 16 l multi | 8.50 | 4.25 |

No. 6086 contains one 55x45mm stamp, with detail of object illustrated in No. 6085.
No. 6086 with gold foil embellishment was printed in limited quantities.
See Nos. 6235-6241.

Europa — A1795

Designs: 3.50 l, Bridge of Lies, Sibiu. 16 l, Anghel Saligny Bridge.

**2018, Apr. 12 Litho. *Perf. 13¼***

| | | | |
|---|---|---|---|
| **6087** | A1795 3.50 l multi | 1.90 | .95 |
| *a.* | Sheet of 6 | 11.50 | 5.75 |
| **6088** | A1795 16 l multi | 8.50 | 4.25 |
| *a.* | Sheet of 6 | 51.00 | 25.50 |
| *b.* | Sheet of 4, 2 each #6087-6088, #6087 in UL | 21.00 | 10.50 |
| *c.* | As "b," #6088 in UL | 21.00 | 10.50 |

A sheet of 2 containing imperforate examples of Nos. 6087-6088 was produced in limited quantities.

Famous Men — A1796

Romanian Athenaeum, Bucharest, and: 4 l, George Enescu (1881-1955), composer. 4.50 l, Eduard Wachmann (1836-1908), conductor. 8 l, Albert Galleron (1846-1930), architect of Romanian Athenaeum.

**2018, Apr. 20 Litho. *Perf. 13¼***

| | | | |
|---|---|---|---|
| **6089** | A1796 4 l multi | 2.10 | 1.10 |
| *a.* | Sheet of 5 + label | 10.50 | 5.50 |
| **6090** | A1796 4.50 l multi | 2.40 | 1.25 |
| *a.* | Sheet of 5 + label | 12.00 | 6.25 |
| **6091** | A1796 8 l multi | 4.25 | 2.10 |
| *a.* | Sheet of 5 + label | 21.50 | 11.00 |
| | *Nos. 6089-6091 (3)* | 8.75 | 4.45 |

George Enescu Festival, 60th anniv. (No. 6089); George Enescu Philharmonic, 150th anniv. (No. 6090); Romanian Athenaeum building, 150th anniv. (No. 6091).

A1797


Comic Opera for Children, 20th Anniv. — A1798

**2018, Apr. 25 Litho. *Perf. 13¼***

| | | | |
|---|---|---|---|
| **6092** | A1797 8 l multi | 4.25 | 2.10 |
| *a.* | Sheet of 5 + 5 labels | 21.50 | 10.50 |

**Souvenir Sheet**

***Perf. 14x13¼***

| | | | |
|---|---|---|---|
| **6093** | A1798 16 l multi | 8.50 | 4.25 |

Bucharest Municipality Pinacotheque, 85th Anniv. — A1799

Paintings: 4 l, Zinnias, by Gheorghe Petrascu. 4.50 l, Cornflowers, by Stefan Luchian. 8 l, Peasant Women, by Theodor Pallady, vert. 12 l, Woman with Red Scar, by Nicolae Grigorescu, vert.

**2018, Apr. 27 Litho. *Perf. 14x13¼***

| | | | |
|---|---|---|---|
| **6094** | A1799 4 l multi | 2.10 | 1.10 |
| *a.* | Sheet of 5 + label | 10.50 | 5.50 |
| **6095** | A1799 4.50 l multi | 2.40 | 1.25 |
| *a.* | Sheet of 5 + label | 12.00 | 6.25 |

***Perf. 13¼x14***

| | | | |
|---|---|---|---|
| **6096** | A1799 8 l multi | 4.25 | 2.10 |
| *a.* | Sheet of 5 + label | 21.50 | 10.50 |
| **6097** | A1799 12 l multi | 6.50 | 3.25 |
| *a.* | Sheet of 5 + label | 32.50 | 16.50 |
| | *Nos. 6094-6097 (4)* | 15.25 | 7.70 |

World War I Medals and Decorations — A1800

Designs: 2.90 l, Star of Romania National Order. 3 l, Crown of Romania National Order. 4.50 l, Military Virtue Medal. 16 l, Commemorative Cross of the 1916-1918 War Medal.

**2018, May 7 Litho. *Perf. 13¼x14***

| | | | |
|---|---|---|---|
| **6098** | A1800 2.90 l multi | 1.50 | .75 |
| *a.* | Sheet of 6 | 9.00 | 4.50 |
| **6099** | A1800 3 l multi | 1.60 | .80 |
| *a.* | Sheet of 6 | 9.75 | 5.00 |
| **6100** | A1800 4.50 l multi | 2.40 | 1.25 |
| *a.* | Sheet of 6 | 14.50 | 7.50 |
| **6101** | A1800 16 l multi | 8.25 | 4.25 |
| *a.* | Sheet of 6 | 50.00 | 25.50 |
| | *Nos. 6098-6101 (4)* | 13.75 | 7.05 |

Contemorary Art — A1801

Designs: 2.90 l, Dantesca I, sculpture by Daniela Fainis. 3 l, The Kiss, painting by Vladimir Zamfirescu. 15 l, Germination, sculpture by Ioan Nemtoi.

**2018, May 11 Litho. *Perf. 13¼x14***

| | | | |
|---|---|---|---|
| **6102** | A1801 2.90 l multi | 1.50 | .75 |
| *a.* | Sheet of 5 + label | 7.50 | 3.75 |
| **6103** | A1801 3 l multi | 1.60 | .80 |
| *a.* | Sheet of 5 + label | 8.00 | 4.00 |
| **6104** | A1801 15 l multi | 7.75 | 4.00 |
| *a.* | Sheet of 5 + label | 39.00 | 20.00 |
| | *Nos. 6102-6104 (3)* | 10.85 | 5.55 |

Romanian Judo Federation, 50th Anniv. A1802

Designs: 2.90 l, Judoka in white on top. 12 l, Judoka in blue on top.

**2018, May 18 Litho. *Perf. 13¼***

| | | | |
|---|---|---|---|
| **6105** | A1802 2.90 l multi | 1.50 | .75 |
| *a.* | Sheet of 5 + label | 7.50 | 3.75 |
| **6106** | A1802 12 l multi | 6.25 | 3.00 |
| *a.* | Sheet of 5 + label | 31.50 | 15.00 |

Church Art Miniatures A1803

Designs: 2.90 l, The Last Supper, by unknown artist. 3 l, Holy Trinity, by Picu Patrut (1818-1872). 15 l, Christ Pantocrator, by Patrut.

**2018, May 25 Litho. *Perf. 13¼***

| | | | |
|---|---|---|---|
| **6107** | A1803 2.90 l multi | 1.50 | .75 |
| *a.* | Sheet of 6 | 9.00 | 4.50 |
| **6108** | A1803 3 l multi | 1.60 | .80 |
| *a.* | Sheet of 6 | 9.75 | 5.00 |
| **6109** | A1803 15 l multi | 7.75 | 4.00 |
| *a.* | Sheet of 6 | 46.50 | 24.00 |
| | *Nos. 6107-6109 (3)* | 10.85 | 5.55 |

Vertical pairs are tête-bêche on Nos. 6107a-6109a.

Romanian Man, Woman and Flag — A1804

Thailand Man, Woman and Flag — A1805

**2018, May 31 Litho. *Perf. 13¼***

| | | | |
|---|---|---|---|
| **6110** | Pair | 1.50 | .70 |
| *a.* | A1804 1.50 l multi | .75 | .35 |
| *b.* | A1805 1.50 l multi | .75 | .35 |
| *c.* | Sheet of 8, 4 each #6110a-6110b | 6.00 | 3.00 |

Diplomatic relations between Romania and Thailand, 45th anniv. See Thailand No. 3010.

2018 World Cup Soccer Championships, Russia — A1806

Designs: 2018 World Cup emblem and various players.

**2018, June 7 Litho. *Perf. 13¼***

| | | | |
|---|---|---|---|
| **6111** | A1806 1.70 l multi | .85 | .40 |
| *a.* | Sheet of 6 | 5.25 | 2.40 |
| **6112** | A1806 2 l multi | 1.00 | .50 |
| *a.* | Sheet of 6 | 6.00 | 3.00 |
| **6113** | A1806 3 l multi | 1.50 | .75 |
| *a.* | Sheet of 6 | 9.00 | 4.50 |
| **6114** | A1806 8.50 l multi | 4.25 | 2.10 |
| *a.* | Sheet of 6 | 25.50 | 13.00 |
| *b.* | Souvenir sheet of 4, #6111-6114 | 7.75 | 3.75 |
| | *Nos. 6111-6114 (4)* | 7.60 | 3.75 |

Famous Romanians — A1807

Designs: 1 l, Sofia Ionescu-Ogrezeanu (1920-2008), neurosurgeon. 1.20 l, Dimitrie Gusti (1880-1955), sociologist. 1.50 l, Ion Cantacuzino (1863-1934), microbiologist. 1.70 l, Nichita Stanescu (1933-83), writer. 2 l, Aurel Vlaicu (1882-1913), aviator. 3 l, Lucian Blaga (1895-1961), writer. 7 l, Traian Vuia (1872-1950), airplane designer. 8.50 l, Spiru Haret (1851-1912), mathematician and educator. 28.50 l, Henri Coanda (1886-1972), inventor.

**2018, June 15 Litho. *Perf. 13¼***

| | | | |
|---|---|---|---|
| **6115** | A1807 1 l multi | .50 | .25 |
| *a.* | Sheet of 3 + label | 1.50 | .75 |
| **6116** | A1807 1.20 l multi | .60 | .30 |
| *a.* | Sheet of 3 + label | 1.90 | .90 |
| **6117** | A1807 1.50 l multi | .75 | .35 |
| *a.* | Sheet of 3 + label | 2.25 | 1.10 |
| **6118** | A1807 1.70 l multi | .85 | .40 |
| *a.* | Sheet of 3 + label | 2.60 | 1.25 |
| **6119** | A1807 2 l multi | 1.00 | .50 |
| *a.* | Sheet of 3 + label | 3.00 | 1.50 |
| **6120** | A1807 3 l multi | 1.50 | .75 |
| *a.* | Sheet of 3 + label | 4.50 | 2.25 |
| **6121** | A1807 7 l multi | 3.50 | 1.75 |
| *a.* | Sheet of 3 + label | 10.50 | 5.25 |
| **6122** | A1807 8.50 l multi | 4.25 | 2.10 |
| *a.* | Sheet of 3 + label | 13.00 | 6.50 |
| **6123** | A1807 28.50 l multi | 14.50 | 7.25 |
| *a.* | Sheet of 3 + label | 44.00 | 22.00 |
| | *Nos. 6115-6123 (9)* | 27.45 | 13.65 |

A booklet containing a pane of Nos. 6115-6123 was produced in limited quantities. See Nos. 6137-6145.

Traditional Embroidered Blouses — A1808

Blouses from: 3 l, Bihor and Oas. 5 l, Suceava and Vrancea. 7 l, Lugoj and Padureni. 11.50 l, Mehedinti and Râmnicu Sarat.

*Perf. 13¾x13¼*

**2018, June 22 Litho.**

**6124** A1808 3 l multi 1.50 .75
*a.* Sheet of 4 6.00 3.00
**6125** A1808 5 l multi 2.50 1.25
*a.* Sheet of 4 10.00 5.00
**6126** A1808 7 l multi 3.50 1.75
*a.* Sheet of 4 14.00 7.00
**6127** A1808 11.50 l multi 5.75 3.00
*a.* Sheet of 4 23.00 12.00
*b.* Souvenir sheet of 4, #6124-6127 13.50 6.75
*Nos. 6124-6127 (4)* 13.25 6.75

Minerals A1809

Designs: 2 l, Pyrite and quartz. 5 l, Galena and semseyite. 8.50 l, Gypsum and calcite. 12 l, Quartz and calcite.

**2018, June 29 Litho. *Perf. 13¼***

**6128** A1809 2 l multi 1.00 .50
*a.* Sheet of 5 + label 5.00 2.50
**6129** A1809 5 l multi 2.50 1.25
*a.* Sheet of 5 + label 12.50 6.25
**6130** A1809 8.50 l multi 4.25 2.10
*a.* Sheet of 5 + label 21.50 10.50
**6131** A1809 12 l multi 6.00 3.00
*a.* Sheet of 5 + label 30.00 15.00
*Nos. 6128-6131 (4)* 13.75 6.85

A sheet containing Nos. 6128-6131 was printed in limited quantities.

Stamp Day — A1810

Horse-drawn mail coach and: 1.50 l, Romania #1. 2 l, Romania #5. 3 l, Romania #7. 5 l, Romania #34. 19 l, Romania #51.

**2018, July 13 Litho. *Perf. 13¼***

**6132** A1810 1.50 l multi .75 .40
*a.* Sheet of 5 + label 3.75 2.00
*b.* Sheet of 3, imperf. 2.25 1.25
**6133** A1810 2 l multi 1.00 .50
*a.* Sheet of 5 + label 5.00 2.50
*b.* Sheet of 3, imperf. 3.00 1.50
**6134** A1810 3 l multi 1.50 .75
*a.* Sheet of 5 + label 7.50 3.75
*b.* Sheet of 3, imperf. 4.50 2.25
**6135** A1810 5 l multi 2.50 1.25
*a.* Sheet of 5 + label 12.50 6.25
*b.* Sheet of 3, imperf. 7.50 3.75
**6136** A1810 19 l multi 9.75 4.75
*a.* Sheet of 5 + label 49.00 24.00
*b.* Sheet of 3, imperf. 30.00 14.50
*Nos. 6132-6136 (5)* 15.50 7.65

A sheet containing Nos. 6132-6136 was printed in limited quantities.

**Famous Romanians Type of 2018**

Designs: 1.10 l, Cella Delavrancea (1887-1991), pianist. 1.40 l, Dimitrie Paciurea (1873-1932), sculptor. 1.60 l, Victor Brauner (1903-66), painter. 2.60 l, George Apostu (1934-86), sculptor. 2.90 l, Elvira Popesco (1894-1993), actress. 5 l, Marcel Iancu (1895-1984), architect. 11.50 l, Dimitrie Cantemir (1673-1723), historian. 12 l, Nicolae Iorga (1871-1940), Prime Minister. 19 l, Nicolae Titulescu (1882-1941), minister of foreign affairs.

**2018, July 17 Litho. *Perf. 13¼***

**6137** A1807 1.10 l multi .55 .30
*a.* Sheet of 3 + label 1.65 .90
**6138** A1807 1.40 l multi .70 .35
*a.* Sheet of 3 + label 2.10 1.10
**6139** A1807 1.60 l multi .80 .40
*a.* Sheet of 3 + label 2.40 1.25
**6140** A1807 2.60 l multi 1.40 .70
*a.* Sheet of 3 + label 4.25 2.10
**6141** A1807 2.90 l multi 1.50 .75
*a.* Sheet of 3 + label 4.50 2.25
**6142** A1807 5 l multi 2.50 1.25
*a.* Sheet of 3 + label 7.50 3.75
**6143** A1807 11.50 l multi 6.00 3.00
*a.* Sheet of 3 + label 18.00 9.00
**6144** A1807 12 l multi 6.25 3.25
*a.* Sheet of 3 + label 19.00 9.75
**6145** A1807 19 l multi 9.75 4.75
*a.* Sheet of 3 + label 30.00 14.50
*Nos. 6137-6145 (9)* 29.45 14.75

A booklet containing a pane of Nos. 6137-6145 was produced in limited quantities.

Queen Marie (1875-1938) A1811

Lilies and Queen Marie wearing: 3 l, Crown. 11.50 l, Tiara.
19 l, Queen Marie with arm on pedestal.

**2018, July 20 Litho. *Perf. 13¼***

**6146** A1811 3 l multi 1.50 .75
*a.* Sheet of 6 9.00 4.50
**6147** A1811 11.50 l multi 6.00 3.00
*a.* Sheet of 6 36.00 18.00

**Souvenir Sheet**

***Imperf***

**6148** A1811 19 l multi 9.75 4.75

No. 6148 contains one 42x56mm stamp. A sheet of 2 containing imperforate examples of Nos. 6146-6147 was printed in limited quantities.

Writers — A1812

Designs: 2 l, Urmuz (1883-1923). 3 l, Geo Bogza (1908-93). 19 l, Gellu Naum (1915-2001).

**2018, July 27 Litho. *Perf. 13¼***

**6149** A1812 2 l multi 1.00 .50
*a.* Sheet of 5 + label 5.00 2.50
**6150** A1812 3 l multi 1.50 .75
*a.* Sheet of 5 + label 7.50 3.75
**6151** A1812 19 l multi 9.75 4.75
*a.* Sheet of 5 + label 49.00 24.00
*Nos. 6149-6151 (3)* 12.25 6.00

Emblem of Romanian Records Museum A1813

Emblem of Romanian Philatelic Collection A1814

Emblem of International Federation of Philately A1815

**2018, Aug. 3 Litho. *Perf. 13¼***

**6152** A1813 1.60 l multi .80 .40
*a.* Sheet of 8 + central label 6.50 3.25
**6153** A1814 2 l multi 1.00 .50
*a.* Sheet of 8 + central label 8.00 4.00
**6154** A1815 11.50 l multi 5.75 3.00
*a.* Sheet of 8 + central label 46.00 24.00
*Nos. 6152-6154 (3)* 7.55 3.90

**Souvenir Sheet**

***Imperf***

**6155** A1813 19 l multi 9.50 4.75

Romania Breaking Off Her Chains on the Field of Liberty, by Constantin Daniel Rosenthal (1820-51) A1816

Revolutionary Romania, by Rosenthal — A1817

**2018, Aug. 10 Litho. *Perf. 13¼***

**6156** A1816 5 l multi 2.50 1.25
*a.* Sheet of 5 + label 12.50 6.25

**Souvenir Sheet**

***Imperf***

**6157** A1817 28.50 l multi 14.50 7.25

Flora and Fauna of Domogled-Cerna Valley National Park — A1818

Designs: 1.60 l, Edraianthus graminifolius ssp. kitaibelii. 2 l, Primula auricula ssp. serratifolia. 5 l, Testudo hermanni, horiz. 19 l, Lucanus cervus, horiz.
28.50 l, Zamenis longissimus, horiz.

**2018, Aug. 17 Litho. *Perf. 13¼***

**6158** A1818 1.60 l multi .80 .40
*a.* Sheet of 5 + label 4.00 2.00
**6159** A1818 2 l multi 1.00 .50
*a.* Sheet of 5 + label 5.00 2.50
**6160** A1818 5 l multi 2.50 1.25
*a.* Sheet of 5 + label 12.50 6.25
**6161** A1818 19 l multi 9.50 4.75
*a.* Sheet of 5 + label 47.50 24.00
*Nos. 6158-6161 (4)* 13.80 6.90

**Souvenir Sheet**

**6162** A1818 28.50 l multi 14.50 7.25

A sheet containing Nos. 6158-6161 was printed in limited quantities.

Narrow-Gauge Steam Locomotives — A1819

Locomotive on: 1.60 l, Brad-Criscior line. 7 l, Moldovita line. 8.50 l, Sovata line. 12 l, Vaser Valley line.
19 l, Sovata-Comandau line.

**2018, Aug. 24 Litho. *Perf. 13¼***

**6163** A1819 1.60 l multi .80 .40
*a.* Sheet of 5 + label 4.00 2.00
**6164** A1819 7 l multi 3.50 1.75
*a.* Sheet of 5 + label 17.50 8.75
**6165** A1819 8.50 l multi 4.25 2.10
*a.* Sheet of 5 + label 21.50 10.50
**6166** A1819 12 l multi 6.00 3.00
*a.* Sheet of 5 + label 30.00 15.00
*Nos. 6163-6166 (4)* 14.55 7.25

**Souvenir Sheet**

**6167** A1819 19 l multi 9.50 4.75

A sheet containing Nos. 6163-6166 was printed in limited quantities.

Simona Halep, 2018 French Open Women's Singles Champion — A1820

Designs: 5 l, Halep playing tennis. 28.50 l, Halep lifting trophy, vert.

**2018, Aug. 29 Litho. *Perf. 13¼***

**6168** A1820 5 l multi 2.50 1.25
*a.* Sheet of 4 10.00 5.00

**Souvenir Sheet**

**6169** A1820 28.50 l multi 14.50 7.25

Winning Art in Children's Olympic Games Stamp Design Contest — A1821

Designs: 2 l, Chromatic Dynamics, by Gabriel roman. 3 l, Tennis, by Sofia Fluerasu, vert. 5 l, Young Hopes, by Anna Rocsana Adumitroaie. 19 l, Grace and Elegance, by Diana Aveloiu, vert.

*Perf. 13¾x13¼, 13¼x13¾*

**2018, Sept. 4 Litho.**

**6170** A1821 2 l multi 1.00 .50
*a.* Sheet of 4 4.00 2.00
**6171** A1821 3 l multi 1.50 .75
*a.* Sheet of 4 6.00 3.00
**6172** A1821 5 l multi 2.50 1.25
*a.* Sheet of 4 10.00 5.00
**6173** A1821 19 l multi 9.50 4.75
*a.* Sheet of 4 38.00 19.00
*Nos. 6170-6173 (4)* 14.50 7.25

Camouflage of Birds — A1822

Designs: 2 l, Burhinus oedicnemus facing right. 3 l, Dendrocopos syriacus facing right. 5 l, Caprimulgus europaeus facing right. 19 l, Picus viridis facing left.

***Perf. 13¼x13¾***

**2018, Sept. 14** **Litho.**

**6174** A1822 2 l multi 1.00 .50
 *a.* Bird facing left 1.00 .50
 *b.* Sheet of 5, #6174a, 4 #6174 + label 5.00 2.50
**6175** A1822 3 l multi 1.50 .75
 *a.* Bird facing left 1.50 .75
 *b.* Sheet of 5, #6175a, 4 #6175 + label 7.50 3.75
**6176** A1822 5 l multi 2.50 1.25
 *a.* Bird facing left 2.50 1.25
 *b.* Sheet of 5, #6176a, 4 #6176 + label 12.50 6.25
**6177** A1822 19 l multi 9.50 4.75
 *a.* Bird facing right 9.50 4.75
 *b.* Sheet of 5, #6177a, 4 #6177 + label 47.50 24.00
 *Nos. 6174-6177 (4)* 14.50 7.25

A sheet containing Nos. 6174-6177 was printed in limited quantities.

**Famous Romanians and Romanian Coat of Arms Types of 2018**

Designs: 2 l, Gheorghe Pop de Basesti (1835-1919), politician. 5 l, Alexandru Vaida-Voevod (1872-1950), prime minister. 8.50 l, Iancu Flondor (1865-1924), politician. 11.50 l, Take Ionescu (1858-1922), prime minister.

19 l, Coat of arms of the Union of Transylvania and Romania.

**2018, Sept. 17** **Litho.** ***Perf. 13¼***

**6178** A1791 2 l multi 1.00 .50
 *a.* Sheet of 6 + 6 labels 6.00 3.00
**6179** A1791 5 l multi 2.50 1.25
 *a.* Sheet of 6 + 6 labels 15.00 7.50
**6180** A1791 8.50 l multi 4.25 2.10
 *a.* Sheet of 6 + 6 labels 25.50 13.00
**6181** A1791 11.50 l multi 5.75 3.00
 *a.* Sheet of 6 + 6 labels 34.50 18.00
 *Nos. 6178-6181 (4)* 13.50 6.85

**Souvenir Sheet**

***Imperf***

**6182** A1792 19 l multi 9.50 4.75

No. 6182 contains one 30mm diameter stamp.

Rights of the Child A1823

**2018, Sept. 28** **Litho.** ***Perf. 13¼***

**6183** A1823 5 l multi 2.50 1.25
 *a.* Sheet of 8 + central label 20.00 10.00

Birds A1824

Designs: 2 l, Haliaeetus albicilla. 5 l, Dryocopus martius, vert. 8.50 l, Bubo bubo. 12 l, Pelecanus crispus, vert.

**2018, Oct. 5** **Litho.** ***Perf. 13¼***

**6184** A1824 2 l multi 1.00 .50
 *a.* Sheet of 5 + label 5.00 2.50
**6185** A1824 5 l multi 2.50 1.25
 *a.* Sheet of 5 + label 12.50 6.25
**6186** A1824 8.50 l multi 4.25 2.10
 *a.* Sheet of 5 + label 21.50 10.50
**6187** A1824 12 l multi 6.00 3.00
 *a.* Sheet of 5 + label 30.00 15.00
 *Nos. 6184-6187 (4)* 13.75 6.85

A sheet containing Nos. 6184-6187 was printed in limited quantities.

Monuments in Bucharest A1825

Designs: 1.40 l, Monument to Railway Heroes. 1.60 l, Monument to the Sanitary Heroes. 2 l, Tomb of the Unknown Soldier. 8.50 l, Monument to Air Heroes. 19 l, Monument to Military Engineers.

**2018, Oct. 12** **Litho.** ***Perf. 13¼***

**6188** A1825 1.40 l multi .70 .35
 *a.* Sheet of 5 + label 3.50 1.75
**6189** A1825 1.60 l multi .80 .40
 *a.* Sheet of 5 + label 4.00 2.00
**6190** A1825 2 l multi 1.00 .50
 *a.* Sheet of 5 + label 5.00 2.50
**6191** A1825 8.50 l multi 4.25 2.10
 *a.* Sheet of 5 + label 21.50 10.50
**6192** A1825 19 l multi 9.25 4.75
 *a.* Sheet of 5 + label 46.50 24.00
 *Nos. 6188-6192 (5)* 16.00 8.10

Beatification of Vladimir Ghika (1873-1954), 5th Anniv. — A1826

Designs: 5 l, Ghika. 28.50 l, Postage stamp design drawn by Ghika in 1918.

**2018. Oct. 15** **Litho.** ***Perf. 13¼***

**6193** A1826 5 l multi 2.50 1.25
 *a.* Sheet of 8 + central label 20.00 10.00

**Souvenir Sheet**

**6194** A1826 28.50 l multi 14.00 7.00

Nicoae Minovici (1868-1941), Medical Examiner A1827

Designs: 2 l, Minovici. 12 l, Minovici and Dr. Nicolae Minovici Folk Art Museum, Bucharest, horiz.

**2018, Oct. 23** **Litho.** ***Perf. 13¼***

**6195** A1827 2 l multi 1.00 .50
 *a.* Sheet of 5 + label 5.00 2.50
**6196** A1827 12 l multi 6.00 3.00
 *a.* Sheet of 5 + label 30.00 15.00

Souvenir Sheet

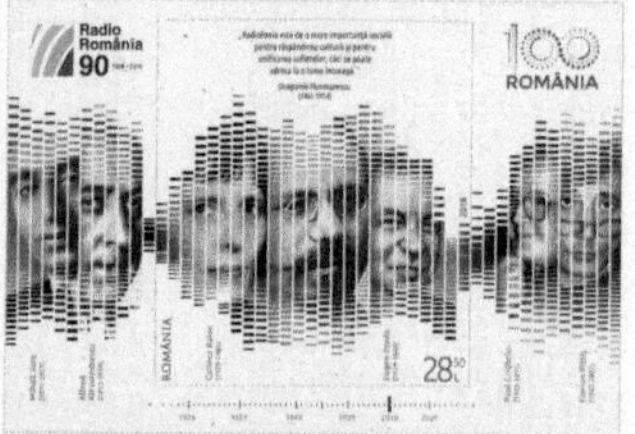


Romanian Radio Broadcasting Company, 90th Anniv. — A1828

**2018, Nov. 1** **Litho.** ***Imperf.***

**6197** A1828 28.50 l multi 14.00 7.00

Annunciation Icon From Bucharest Patriarchal Residence Chapel A1829

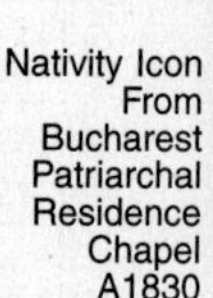

Nativity Icon From Bucharest Patriarchal Residence Chapel A1830

**2018, Nov. 9** **Litho.** ***Perf. 13¼***

**6198** A1829 1.50 l multi .75 .35
**6199** A1830 1.50 l multi .75 .35
 *a.* Sheet of 8, 4 each #6198-6199, + central label, #6198 at UR 6.00 3.00
 *b.* As "a," with #6199 at UR 6.00 3.00

Christmas. Perforate and imperforare sheets of 2 of Nos. 6198-6199 were printed in limited quantites.

Souvenlr Sheet

Vase of Flowers and Hands of Queen Marie and King Ferdinand — A1831

***Perf. 13¼x13¾***

**2018, Nov. 16** **Litho.**

**6200** A1831 28.50 l multi 14.00 7.00

Union of Transylvania With Romania, cent. Imperforate examples of No. 6200 were printed in limited quantities.

General Henri M. Berthelot (1861-1931) — A1832

Berthelot: 5 l, Decorating Romanian officers, 1917. 8.50 l, And his house in Hunedoara.

**2018, Nov. 27** **Litho.** ***Perf. 13¼***

**6201** A1832 5 l multi 2.50 1.25
 *a.* Sheet of 8 + central label 20.00 10.00
**6202** A1832 8.50 l multi 4.25 2.10
 *a.* Sheet of 8 + central label 34.00 17.00

See France Nos. 5568-5569.

Consecration of the Altar of Salvation National Cathedral — A1833

Designs: 5 l. Cathedral and icon of the Apostle Andrew. 28.50 l, Icon of the Ascension.

***Perf. 13¼x13¾***

**2018, Nov. 29** **Litho.**

**6203** A1833 5 l gold & multi 2.50 1.25
 *a.* Sheet of 5 + label 12.50 6.25

**Souvenir Sheet**

***Perf. 13¾x13¼***

**6204** A1833 28.50 l gold & multi 14.00 7.00

No. 6204 contains one 52x84mm stamp.

Holiday Season Traditions A1834

Designs: 2 l, Child mailing letter to Santa Claus. 3 l, Boy glving gift to girl. 11.50 l, People singing carols. 12 l, Snowman wlth Sorcova stick, skiers.

**2018, Dec. 7** **Litho.** ***Perf. 13¼***

**6205** A1834 2 l multi 1.00 .50
 *a.* Sheet of 5 + label 5.00 2.50
**6206** A1834 3 l multi 1.50 .75
 *a.* Sheet of 5 + label 7.50 3.75
**6207** A1834 11.50 l multi 5.75 3.00
 *a.* Sheet of 5 + label 29.00 15.00
**6208** A1834 12 l multi 6.00 3.00
 *a.* Sheet of 5 + label 30.00 15.00
 *Nos. 6205-6208 (4)* 14.25 7.25

Souvenir Sheet

Gen. Nicolae Condeescu (1876-1936), Head of Intelligence Office — A1835

**2018, Dec. 14** **Litho.** ***Perf. 13¼***

**6209** A1835 28.50 l multi + 2 labels 14.00 7.00

Romanian Presidency of the Council of the European Union — A1836

**2019, Jan. 4 Litho. *Perf. 13¼***

| No. | Description | Unused | Used |
|---|---|---|---|
| 6210 | A1836 5 l multi | 2.40 | 1.25 |
| a. | Sheet of 10 | 24.00 | 12.50 |

Romanian Treasures — A1837

Designs: 2 l, Constantin Brancusi (1876-1957), sculptor, and his sculptures. 2.60 l, Romanian Athenaeum Concert Hall, coat of arms of Bucharest. 2.90 l, Henri Coanda (1886-1972), and Coanda 1910 airplane. 3 l, Birds and Danube Delta. 8.50 l. Palace of Culture, coat of arms of Iasi. 12 l, Eagle and Retezat National Park.

**2019, Jan. 16 Litho. *Perf. 13¾x13¼***

| No. | Description | Unused | Used |
|---|---|---|---|
| 6211 | A1837 2 l multi | 1.00 | .50 |
| a. | Sheet of 5 + label | 5.00 | 2.50 |
| 6212 | A1837 2.60 l multi | 1.25 | .60 |
| a. | Sheet of 5 + label | 6.25 | 3.00 |
| 6213 | A1837 2.90 l multi | 1.40 | .70 |
| a. | Sheet of 5 + label | 7.00 | 3.50 |
| 6214 | A1837 3 l multi | 1.50 | .75 |
| a. | Sheet of 5 + label | 7.50 | 3.75 |
| 6215 | A1837 8.50 l multi | 4.25 | 2.10 |
| a. | Sheet of 5 + label | 21.50 | 10.50 |
| 6216 | A1837 12 l multi | 5.75 | 3.00 |
| a. | Sheet of 5 + label | 29.00 | 15.00 |
| b. | Souvenir sheet of 6, #6211-6216 | 15.50 | 7.75 |
| | *Nos. 6211-6216 (6)* | 15.15 | 7.65 |

**Souvenir Sheet**

Alexandru Ioan Cuza (1820-73), Ruling Prince of United Principalities of Moldavia and Wallachia — A1838

**2019, Jan. 23 Litho. *Perf. 13¼x13¾***

| No. | Description | Unused | Used |
|---|---|---|---|
| 6217 | A1838 28.50 l multi | 14.00 | 7.00 |

United Provinces of Moldavia and Wallachia, 160th Anniv.

Adult and Juvenile Animals A1839

Adult and juvenile: 3 l, Loxondonta africana, map of Africa. 5 l, Phascolarctos cinereus, map of Australia and New Zealand, horiz. 7 l, Panthera uncia, map of Asia. 12 l, Ursus arctos, map of Europe, horiz.

**2019, Feb. 8 Litho. *Perf. 13¼***

| No. | Description | Unused | Used |
|---|---|---|---|
| 6218 | A1839 3 l multi | 1.50 | .75 |
| a. | Sheet of 5 + label | 7.50 | 3.75 |
| 6219 | A1839 5 l multi | 2.40 | 1.25 |
| a. | Sheet of 5 + label | 12.00 | 6.25 |
| 6220 | A1839 7 l multi | 3.50 | 1.75 |
| a. | Sheet of 5 + label | 17.50 | 8.75 |
| 6221 | A1839 12 l multi | 5.75 | 3.00 |
| a. | Sheet of 5 + label | 29.00 | 15.00 |
| | *Nos. 6218-6221 (4)* | 13.15 | 6.75 |

Paintings of Nudes by Nicolae Grigorescu (1838-1907) — A1840

Designs: 2 l, Bacanta. 3 l, After the Bath. 5 l, Entering the Bath. 19 l, Before the Bath.

***Perf. 13¼x13¾***

**2019, Feb. 15 Litho.**

| No. | Description | Unused | Used |
|---|---|---|---|
| 6222 | A1840 2 l gold & multi | .95 | .50 |
| a. | Sheet of 4 | 4.00 | 2.00 |
| 6223 | A1840 3 l gold & multi | 1.50 | .75 |
| a. | Sheet of 4 | 6.00 | 3.00 |
| 6224 | A1840 5 l gold & multi | 2.40 | 1.25 |
| a. | Sheet of 4 | 9.75 | 5.00 |
| 6225 | A1840 19 l gold & multi | 9.00 | 4.50 |
| a. | Sheet of 4 | 36.00 | 18.00 |
| | *Nos. 6222-6225 (4)* | 13.85 | 7.00 |

Dog Breeds A1841

Designs: 3 l, Romanian Mioritic shepherd. 5 l, Romanian Carpathian shepherd. 8.50 l, Romanian Bucovina shepherd. 12 l, Romanian Raven shepherd.

**2019, Feb. 22 Litho. *Perf. 13¼***

| No. | Description | Unused | Used |
|---|---|---|---|
| 6226 | A1841 3 l multi | 1.50 | .75 |
| a. | Sheet of 5 + label | 7.50 | 3.75 |
| 6227 | A1841 5 l multi | 2.40 | 1.25 |
| a. | Sheet of 5 + label | 12.00 | 6.25 |
| 6228 | A1841 8.50 l multi | 4.00 | 2.00 |
| a. | Sheet of 5 + label | 20.00 | 10.00 |
| 6229 | A1841 12 l multi | 5.75 | 3.00 |
| a. | Sheet of 5 + label | 29.00 | 15.00 |
| | *Nos. 6226-6229 (4)* | 13.65 | 7.00 |

A sheet containing Nos. 6226-6229 was printed in limited quantities.

Cecilia Cutescu-Storck (1879-1969), Painter — A1842

Designs: 5 l, Self-portrait. 28.50 l, Sculpture of Cutescu-Storck, by her husband, Frederic Storck (1872-1942).

**2019, Mar. 14 Litho. *Perf. 13¼***

| No. | Description | Unused | Used |
|---|---|---|---|
| 6230 | A1842 5 l multi | 2.40 | 1.25 |
| a. | Sheet of 8 + central label | 19.50 | 10.00 |

**Souvenir Sheet**

| No. | Description | Unused | Used |
|---|---|---|---|
| 6231 | A1842 28.50 l multi | 13.50 | 6.75 |

Crucifixion A1843

Resurrection of Jesus Christ A1844

Crucifixion — A1845

**2019, Mar. 22 Litho. *Perf. 13¼***

| No. | Description | Unused | Used |
|---|---|---|---|
| 6232 | A1843 1.50 l multi | .70 | .35 |
| a. | Sheet of 8 + central label | 5.75 | 3.00 |
| 6233 | A1844 1.50 l multi | .70 | .35 |
| a. | Sheet of 8 + central label | 5.75 | 3.00 |

**Souvenir Sheet**

***Perf. 13¼x13¾***

| No. | Description | Unused | Used |
|---|---|---|---|
| 6234 | A1845 28.50 l multi | 13.50 | 6.75 |

Perforated and imperforate sheets of 2 containing Nos. 6232-6233 were printed in limited quantities, as was a perforated sheet of 3 containing Nos. 6232-6234 and a label.

**Household Items to Hold Hot Objects Type of 2018**

Designs: 1.40 l, Saint Valentine trivet (hearts), 19th cent. 1.60 l, Musical symbols support, 19th cent. 1.70 l, Trivet with grape bunch design, 20th cent. 7 l, Trivet with legs, 19th cent. 8.50 l, Artistic leaf-shaped support, 20th cent. 12 l, 19 l, Trivet with horseshoe and Masonic emblems, 19th cent.

**2019, Mar. 29 Litho. *Perf. 13¼***

| No. | Description | Unused | Used |
|---|---|---|---|
| 6235 | A1794 1.40 l multi | .65 | .30 |
| a. | Sheet of 8 + central label | 5.25 | 2.40 |
| b. | Sheet of 13 + 2 labels | 8.50 | 4.00 |
| 6236 | A1794 1.60 l multi | .75 | .40 |
| a. | Sheet of 8 + central label | 6.00 | 3.25 |
| b. | Sheet of 13 + 2 labels | 9.75 | 5.25 |
| 6237 | A1794 1.70 l multi | .80 | .40 |
| a. | Sheet of 8 + central label | 6.50 | 3.25 |
| b. | Sheet of 13 + 2 labels | 10.50 | 5.25 |
| 6238 | A1794 7 l multi | 3.25 | 1.60 |
| a. | Sheet of 8 + central label | 26.00 | 13.00 |
| b. | Sheet of 13 + 2 labels | 42.50 | 21.00 |
| 6239 | A1794 8.50 l multi | 4.00 | 2.00 |
| a. | Sheet of 8 + central label | 32.00 | 16.00 |
| b. | Sheet of 13 + 2 labels | 52.00 | 26.00 |
| 6240 | A1794 12 l multi | 5.75 | 3.00 |
| a. | Sheet of 8 + central label | 46.00 | 24.00 |
| b. | Sheet of 13 + 2 labels | 75.00 | 39.00 |
| | *Nos. 6235-6240 (6)* | 15.20 | 7.70 |

**Souvenir Sheet**

***Imperf***

| No. | Description | Unused | Used |
|---|---|---|---|
| 6241 | A1794 19 l multi | 9.00 | 4.50 |

No. 6241 contains one 55x45mm stamp. An embellished example of No. 6241 was printed in limited quantities.

Articles of the Romanian Constitution — A1846

Designs: 1.70 l, Article 12 regarding flag and national symbols. 1.80 l, Article 32 regarding right to education. 1.90 l, Article 34 regarding right to health and welfare. 2.40 l, Article 35 regarding right to healthy environment. 2.50 l, Article 21 regarding right to seek justice. 2.80 l, Article 30 regarding freedom of expression. 3.10 l, Article 25 regarding right to free movement. 7 l, Article 24 regarding right to defend oneself at trial. 19 l, Article 38 regarding right to be elected to Eueopean Parliament.

**2019, Apr. 8 Litho. *Perf. 13¼***

| No. | Description | Unused | Used |
|---|---|---|---|
| 6242 | A1846 1.70 l multi | .75 | .40 |
| a. | Sheet of 5 + label | 3.75 | 2.00 |
| 6243 | A1846 1.80 l multi | .85 | .40 |
| a. | Sheet of 5 + label | 4.25 | 2.00 |
| 6244 | A1846 1.90 l multi | .90 | .45 |
| a. | Sheet of 5 + label | 4.50 | 2.25 |
| 6245 | A1846 2.40 l multi | 1.10 | .55 |
| a. | Sheet of 5 + label | 5.50 | 2.75 |
| 6246 | A1846 2.50 l multi | 1.25 | .60 |
| a. | Sheet of 5 + label | 6.25 | 3.00 |
| 6247 | A1846 2.80 l multi | 1.40 | .70 |
| a. | Sheet of 5 + label | 7.00 | 3.50 |
| 6248 | A1846 3.10 l multi | 1.50 | .75 |
| a. | Sheet of 5 + label | 7.50 | 3.75 |
| 6249 | A1846 7 l multi | 3.25 | 1.60 |
| a. | Sheet of 5 + label | 16.50 | 8.00 |
| 6250 | A1846 19 l multi | 9.00 | 4.50 |
| a. | Sheet of 5 + label | 45.00 | 22.50 |
| b. | Sheet of 9, #6242-6250 + 9 labels | 20.00 | 10.00 |
| | *Nos. 6242-6250 (9)* | 20.00 | 9.95 |

A booklet containing Nos. 6242-6250 was printed in limited quantities.

Europa A1847

Designs: 1.80 l, Alauda arvensis. 19 l, Aquila chrysaetos.

**2019, Apr. 12 Litho. *Perf. 13¼***

| No. | Description | Unused | Used |
|---|---|---|---|
| 6251 | A1847 1.80 l multi | .85 | .40 |
| a. | Sheet of 6 | 5.25 | 2.40 |
| 6252 | A1847 19 l multi | 9.00 | 4.50 |
| a. | Sheet of 6 | 54.00 | 27.00 |
| b. | Souvenir sheet of 4, 2 each #6251-6252, #6251 at UL | 20.00 | 10.00 |
| c. | Souvenir sheet of 4, 2 each #6251-6252, #6252 at UL | 20.00 | 10.00 |

A sheet of 2 containing imperforate examples of Nos. 6251-6252 was printed in limited quantities.

Grampet Group Rail Company, 20th Anniv. — A1848

Locomotive and: 3.10 l, Tanker cars. 5 l, Shipping containers on flat cars. 7 l, Freight cars. 12 l, Automobile carrier cars.

28.50 l, Train and overhead wires.

**2019, Apr. 19 Litho. *Perf. 13¼***

| No. | Description | Unused | Used |
|---|---|---|---|
| 6253 | A1848 3.10 l multi | 1.50 | .75 |
| a. | Sheet of 5 + label | 7.50 | 3.75 |
| 6254 | A1848 5 l multi | 2.40 | 1.25 |
| a. | Sheet of 5 + label | 12.00 | 6.25 |
| 6255 | A1848 7 l multi | 3.25 | 1.60 |
| a. | Sheet of 5 + label | 16.50 | 8.00 |
| 6256 | A1848 12 l multi | 5.75 | 3.00 |
| a. | Sheet of 5 + label | 29.00 | 15.00 |
| | *Nos. 6253-6256 (4)* | 12.90 | 6.60 |

**Souvenir Sheet**

| No. | Description | Unused | Used |
|---|---|---|---|
| 6257 | A1848 28.50 l multi | 13.50 | 6.75 |

Protected Animals
A1849

Designs: 1.60 l, Lyruris tetrix. 1.90 l, Lynx lynx. 2.90 l, Ursus arctos. 5 l, Cervus elaphus. 7 l, Tetrao urogsallus. 12 l, Rupicapra rupicapra.
28.50 l, Bison bonasus, horiz.

**2019, Apr. 25 Litho. *Perf. 13¼***

**6258** A1849 1.60 l multi .75 .40
*a.* Sheet of 5 + label 3.75 2.00
**6259** A1849 1.90 l multi .90 .45
*a.* Sheet of 5 + label 4.50 2.25
**6260** A1849 2.90 l multi 1.40 .70
*a.* Sheet of 5 + label 7.00 3.50
**6261** A1849 5 l multi 2.40 1.25
*a.* Sheet of 5 + label 12.00 6.25
**6262** A1849 7 l multi 3.25 1.60
*a.* Sheet of 5 + label 16.50 8.00
**6263** A1849 12 l multi 5.75 3.00
*a.* Sheet of 5 + label 29.00 15.00
*Nos. 6258-6263 (6)* 14.45 7.40

**Souvenir Sheet**

**6264** A1849 28.50 l multi 13.50 6.75

A souvenir sheet containing Nos. 6258-6263 was printed in limited quantities.

Souvenir Sheet

Alexandru Romalo (1819-75), Judge — A1850

**2019, May 7 Litho. *Perf. 13¼***

**6265** A1850 28.50 l multi + 2 labels 13.50 6.75

Tourist Attractions — A1851

Designs: 1.60 l, Sturdza Castle, Miclauseni. 1.80 l, Hunyad Castle, Hunedoara. 1.90 l, Peles Castle, Sinaia. 5 l, Barsana Monastery, Barsana. 8.50 l, Rupea Fortress, Rupea. 12 l, Neamt Monastery, Targu Neamt.
28.50 l, City Hall, Sibiu, vert.

**2019, May 9 Litho. *Perf. 13¾x13¼***

**6266** A1851 1.60 l multi .75 .40
*a.* Sheet of 5 + label 3.75 2.00
**6267** A1851 1.80 l multi .85 .45
*a.* Sheet of 5 + label 4.25 2.25
**6268** A1851 1.90 l multi .90 .45
*a.* Sheet of 5 + label 4.50 2.25
**6269** A1851 5 l multi 2.40 1.25
*a.* Sheet of 5 + label 12.00 6.25
**6270** A1851 8.50 l multi 4.00 2.00
*a.* Sheet of 5 + label 20.00 10.00
**6271** A1851 12 l multi 5.75 3.00
*a.* Sheet of 5 + label 29.00 15.00
*b.* Souvenir sheet of 6, #6266-6271, imperf. 15.00 7.75
*Nos. 6266-6271 (6)* 14.65 7.55

**Souvenir Sheet**
***Perf. 13¼x13¾***

**6272** A1851 28.50 l multi 13.50 6.75

Peafowl — A1852

Designs: No. 6273, Afropavo congensis facing left. No. 6273A, Afropavo congensis facing right. No. 6274, Pavo muticus, with beak at right. No. 6274A, Pavo muticus, with beak at left. No. 6275, Pavo cristatus (white bird), with beak at right. No. 6275A, Pavo cristatus (white bird), with beak at left. No. 6276, Pavo cristatus (multicolored bird), with beak at left. No. 6276A, Pavo cristatus (multicolored bird), with beak at right.

**2019, May 17 Litho. *Perf. 13¼***

**6273** A1852 1.80 l multi .85 .45
**6273A** A1852 1.80 l multi .85 .45
*b.* Sheet of 5, #6273A, 4 #6273 + label 4.25 2.25
**6274** A1852 5 l multi 2.40 1.25
**6274A** A1852 5 l multi 2.40 1.25
*b.* Sheet of 5, #6274A, 4 #6274 + label 12.00 6.25
**6275** A1852 8.50 l multi 4.00 2.00
**6275A** A1852 8.50 l multi 4.00 2.00
*b.* Sheet of 5, #6275A, 4 #6275 + label 20.00 10.00
**6276** A1852 12 l multi 5.75 3.00
**6276A** A1852 12 l multi 5.75 3.00
*b.* Sheet of 5, #6276A, 4 #6276 + label 29.00 15.00
*Nos. 6273-6276A (8)* 26.00 13.40

A souvenir sheet containing Nos. 6273, 6274, 6275 and 6276 was printed in limited quantities.

Souvenir Sheet

Visit to Romania of Pope Francis — A1853

**2019, May 31 Litho. *Perf. 13¼***

**6277** A1853 11.50 multi l 5.50 2.75

See Vatican City No. 1720.

Souvenir Sheet

Cross and Seven Stars — A1854

**2019, June 2 Litho. *Perf. 13¼***

**6278** A1854 28.50 l multi + 8 labels 13.50 6.75

Beatification of seven Romanian Greek martyrs.

Melliferous Flowers — A1855

Designs: 1.90 l, Tilia tomentosa. 2.80 l, Robinia pseudoacacia. 5 l, Helianthus annuus. 8.50 l, Brassica rapa subsp. oleifera. 12 l, Malus domestica.

**2019, June 11 Litho. *Perf. 13¼***

**6279** A1855 1.90 l multi .90 .45
*a.* Sheet of 5 + label 4.50 2.25
**6280** A1855 2.80 l multi 1.40 .70
*a.* Sheet of 5 + label 7.00 3.50
**6281** A1855 5 l multi 2.40 1.25
*a.* Sheet of 5 + label 12.00 6.25
**6282** A1855 8.50 l multi 4.25 2.10
*a.* Sheet of 5 + label 21.50 10.50
**6283** A1855 12 l multi 5.75 3.00
*a.* Sheet of 5 + label 29.00 15.00
*Nos. 6279-6283 (5)* 14.70 7.50

A souvenir sheet containing Nos. 6279-6283 was printed in limited quantities.

Souvenir Sheet

Bust of Gheorghe Lazar (1779-1823), Founder of First Romanian Technical School — A1856

***Perf. 13¾x13¼***

**2019, June 18 Litho.**

**6284** A1856 28.50 l multi 14.00 7.00

Politehnica University of Bucharest, 200th anniv. (in 2018).

Paintings of the Danube River — A1857

Designs: 2.80 l, Danube Reaching the Cauldrons Area, by Marius Bunescu (1881-1971). 5 l, Landscape on the Danube, by Petre Iorgulescu Yor (1890-1939). 8.50 l, Danube at Turtucaia, by Gheorghe Petrascu (1872-1949). 12 l, Danube Landscape at Turtucaia, by Iosif Iser (1881-1958).

***Perf. 13¾x13¼***

**2019, June 28 Litho.**

**6285** A1857 2.80 l multi 1.40 .70
*a.* Sheet of 4 5.75 3.00
**6286** A1857 5 l multi 2.40 1.25
*a.* Sheet of 4 9.75 5.00
**6287** A1857 8.50 l multi 4.25 2.10
*a.* Sheet of 4 17.00 8.50
**6288** A1857 12 l multi 5.75 3.00
*a.* Sheet of 4 23.00 12.00
*Nos. 6285-6288 (4)* 13.80 7.05

Souvenir Sheet

Visit of King Ferdinand and Queen Mary to Oradea, Cent. — A1858

**2019, July 9 Litho. *Perf. 13¾x13¼***

**6289** A1858 28.50 l multi 13.50 6.75

End of World War I, cent. (in 2018).

First Man on the Moon, 50th Anniv. — A1859

Designs: 5 l, Launch of Apollo 11, Command and Lunar Modules above Moon. 8.50 l, Astronaut on ladder of Lunar Module, Apollo 11 patch, Hermann Oberth (1894-1989) and Wernher von Braun (1912-77), aerospace engineers.
28.50 l, Astronaut on Moon.

**2019, July 11 Litho. *Perf. 13¾x13¼***

**6290** A1859 5 l multi 2.40 1.25
*a.* Sheet of 5 + label 12.00 6.25
**6291** A1859 8.50 l multi 4.00 2.00
*a.* Sheet of 5 + label 20.00 10.00

***Imperf***

**Souvenir Sheet**

**6292** A1859 28.50 multi l 13.50 6.75

No. 6292 contains one 107x50mm stamp with simulated perforations.

Romanian Rulers and Their Seals — A1860

Portrait and seal of: 3.10 l, Alexander the Good (c. 1375-1432). 7 l, Stephen the Great (c. 1433-1504). 8.50 l, Petru Rares (c. 1483-1546). 11.50 l, Vasile Lupu (1595-1661).

**2019, July 15 Litho. *Perf. 13¼***

**6293** A1860 3.10 l multi 1.50 .75
*a.* Sheet of 5 + label 7.50 3.75
**6294** A1860 7 l multi 3.25 1.60
*a.* Sheet of 5 + label 16.50 8.00
**6295** A1860 8.50 l multi 4.00 2.00
*a.* Sheet of 5 + label 20.00 10.00
**6296** A1860 11.50 l multi 5.50 2.75
*a.* Sheet of 5 + label 27.50 14.00
*Nos. 6293-6296 (4)* 14.25 7.10

A sheet containing imperforate examples of Nos. 6293-6296 was printed in limited quantities.

Souvenir Sheets

A1861

Simona Halep, 2019 Wimbledon Women's Singles Champion — A1862

**2019, July 26 Litho. *Perf. 13¼***

| | | | | |
|---|---|---|---|---|
| **6297** | A1861 | 28.50 l multi | 13.50 | 6.75 |

**Litho., Sheet Margin Litho. With Foil Application**

***Imperf***

| | | | | |
|---|---|---|---|---|
| **6298** | A1862 | 53.50 l multi | 25.00 | 12.50 |

Flowers A1863

Designs: 1.40 l, Daphne blagayana. 1.60 l, Fritillaria meleagris. 1.70 l, Aster alpinus. 3.10 l, Trollius europaeus. 5 l, Silene nivalis. 19 l, Linaria alpina.

**2019, Aug. 8 Litho. *Perf. 13¼***

| | | | | |
|---|---|---|---|---|
| **6299** | A1863 | 1.40 l multi | .65 | .30 |
| *a.* | | Sheet of 5 + label | 3.25 | 1.50 |
| **6300** | A1863 | 1.60 l multi | .75 | .35 |
| *a.* | | Sheet of 5 + label | 3.75 | 1.75 |
| **6301** | A1863 | 1.70 l multi | .80 | .40 |
| *a.* | | Sheet of 5 + label | 4.00 | 2.00 |
| **6302** | A1863 | 3.10 l multi | 1.50 | .75 |
| *a.* | | Sheet of 5 + label | 7.50 | 3.75 |
| **6303** | A1863 | 5 l multi | 2.40 | 1.25 |
| *a.* | | Sheet of 5 + label | 12.00 | 6.25 |
| **6304** | A1863 | 19 l multi | 8.75 | 4.50 |
| *a.* | | Sheet of 5 + label | 44.00 | 22.50 |
| | | *Nos. 6299-6304 (6)* | 14.85 | 7.55 |

Exotic Birds A1864

Designs: 1.40 l, Paradisaea apoda. 1.60 l, Pharomachrus mocinno, vert. 1.70 l, Ramphastos dicolorus, vert. 3.10 l, Onychorhynchus mexicanus, vert. 5 l, Phoenicopterus ruber, vert. 19 l, Ptiloris magnificus.

**2019, Aug. 14 Litho. *Perf. 13¼***

| | | | | |
|---|---|---|---|---|
| **6305** | A1864 | 1.40 l multi | .65 | .30 |
| *a.* | | Sheet of 5 + label | 3.25 | 1.50 |
| **6306** | A1864 | 1.60 l multi | .75 | .35 |
| *a.* | | Sheet of 5 + label | 3.75 | 1.75 |
| **6307** | A1864 | 1.70 l multi | .80 | .40 |
| *a.* | | Sheet of 5 + label | 4.00 | 2.00 |
| **6308** | A1864 | 3.10 l multi | 1.50 | .75 |
| *a.* | | Sheet of 5 + label | 7.50 | 3.75 |
| **6309** | A1864 | 5 l multi | 2.40 | 1.25 |
| *a.* | | Sheet of 5 + label | 12.00 | 6.25 |
| **6310** | A1864 | 19 l multi | 8.75 | 4.50 |
| *a.* | | Sheet of 5 + label | 44.00 | 22.50 |
| | | *Nos. 6305-6310 (6)* | 14.85 | 7.55 |

A sheet containing imperforate examples of Nos. 6305-6310 was printed in limited quantities.

Flowers on Mount Cozia A1865

Designs: 1.40 l, Leontopodium alpinium. 1.60 l, Hypericum richeri. 1.70 l, Erythronium dens-canis. 7 l, Primula elatior. 8.50 l, Gentiana acaulis. 11.50 l, Dictammus albus.

**2019, Aug. 23 Litho. *Perf. 13¼***

| | | | | |
|---|---|---|---|---|
| **6311** | A1865 | 1.40 l multi | .65 | .30 |
| *a.* | | Sheet of 4 | 2.60 | 1.25 |
| **6312** | A1865 | 1.60 l multi | .75 | .35 |
| *a.* | | Sheet of 4 | 3.00 | 1.40 |
| **6313** | A1865 | 1.70 l multi | .80 | .40 |
| *a.* | | Sheet of 4 | 3.25 | 1.60 |
| **6314** | A1865 | 7 l multi | 3.25 | 1.60 |
| *a.* | | Sheet of 4 | 13.00 | 6.50 |
| **6315** | A1865 | 8.50 l multi | 4.00 | 2.00 |
| *a.* | | Sheet of 4 | 16.00 | 8.00 |
| **6316** | A1865 | 11.50 l multi | 5.50 | 2.75 |
| *a.* | | Sheet of 4 | 22.00 | 11.00 |
| | | *Nos. 6311-6316 (6)* | 14.95 | 7.40 |

A sheet containing imperforate examples of Nos. 6311-6316 was printed in limited quantities.

Romanian Lottery, 113th Anniv. A1866

**2019, Sept. 13 Litho. *Perf. 13¼***

| | | | | |
|---|---|---|---|---|
| **6317** | A1866 | 8.50 l multi | 4.00 | 2.00 |
| *a.* | | Sheet of 5 + label | 20.00 | 10.00 |

EFIRO 2019 Philatelic Exhibition, Bucharest A1867

EFIRO emblem and: 1.70 l, Romania #C71. 3.10 l, 1858 cover, two examples of Romania #1. 12 l, Globe, letters, modes of mail transport.

28.50 l, Romania #B40.

**2019, Sept. 19 Litho. *Perf. 13¼***

| | | | | |
|---|---|---|---|---|
| **6318** | A1867 | 1.70 l multi | .80 | .40 |
| *a.* | | Sheet of 8 + central label | 6.50 | 3.25 |
| *b.* | | Sheet of 13 + 2 labels | 10.50 | 5.25 |
| **6319** | A1867 | 3.10 l multi | 1.50 | .75 |
| *a.* | | Sheet of 8 + central label | 12.00 | 6.00 |
| *b.* | | Sheet of 13 + 2 labels | 19.50 | 9.75 |
| **6320** | A1867 | 12 l multi | 5.50 | 2.75 |
| *a.* | | Sheet of 8 + central label | 44.00 | 12.00 |
| *b.* | | Sheet of 13 + 2 labels | 71.50 | 36.00 |
| | | *Nos. 6318-6320 (3)* | 7.80 | 3.90 |

**Souvenir Sheet**

***Imperf***

| | | | | |
|---|---|---|---|---|
| **6321** | A1867 | 28.50 l multi | 13.00 | 6.50 |

No. 6321 contains one 55x45mm stamp.

Ferdinand Magellan (c. 1480-1521), Explorer, His Ship, Victoria, and World Map — A1868

Design: 28.50 l, Magellan and ship's wheel.

**2019, Sept. 24 Litho. *Perf. 13¼***

| | | | | |
|---|---|---|---|---|
| **6322** | A1868 | 7 l multi | 3.25 | .60 |
| *a.* | | Sheet of 8 + central label | 26.00 | 13.00 |

**Souvenir Sheet**

***Imperf***

| | | | | |
|---|---|---|---|---|
| **6323** | A1868 | 28.50 l multi | 13.00 | 6.50 |

Start of Magellan's circumnavigatory expedition, 500th anniv. No. 6323 contains one 34x24mm stamp.

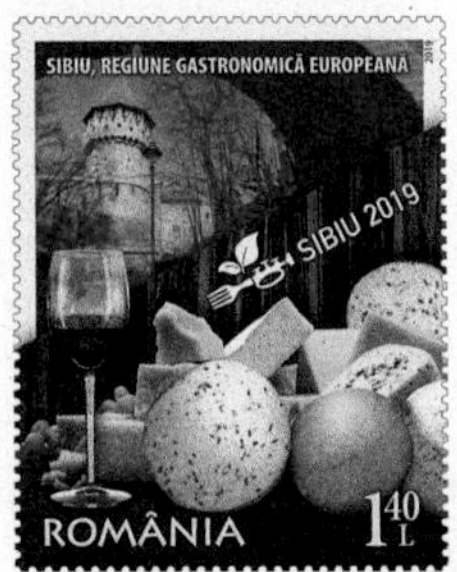


Sibiu, 2019 Region of European Gastronomy — A1869

Designs: 1.40 l, Carpenter's Tower, glass of wine, and cheeses. 3.10 l, Turmul Sfatului, sausages and pork bellies. 5 l, Evangelical Church, red onions, bean and sausage stew. 19 l, Council Square, tray of meats, cheeses, vegetables and spreads.

**2019, Oct. 1 Litho. *Perf. 13¼x13¾***

| | | | | |
|---|---|---|---|---|
| **6324** | A1869 | 1.40 l multi | .65 | .30 |
| *a.* | | Sheet of 5 + label | 3.25 | 1.50 |
| **6325** | A1869 | 3.10 l multi | 1.50 | .75 |
| *a.* | | Sheet of 5 + label | 7.50 | 3.75 |
| **6326** | A1869 | 5 l multi | 2.40 | 1.25 |
| *a.* | | Sheet of 5 + label | 12.00 | 6.25 |
| **6327** | A1869 | 19 l multi | 8.75 | 4.50 |
| *a.* | | Sheet of 5 + label | 44.00 | 22.50 |
| | | *Nos. 6324-6327 (4)* | 13.30 | 6.80 |

Paintings of Romanian Rulers A1870

Portrait of: 1.50 l, Constantin Brancoveanu (1654-1714), by unknown artist. 1.60 l, Grigore II Ghica (1695-1752), by Theodor Aman. 7 l, Michael the Brave (1558-1601), by Misu Popp. 19 l, Stephen the Great (c. 1433-1504), by Constantin Lecca.

**2019, Oct. 11 Litho. *Perf. 13¼x13¾***

| | | | | |
|---|---|---|---|---|
| **6328** | A1870 | 1.50 l multi | .70 | .35 |
| *a.* | | Sheet of 4 | 3.00 | 1.40 |
| **6329** | A1870 | 1.60 l multi | .75 | .35 |
| *a.* | | Sheet of 4 | 3.00 | 1.40 |
| **6330** | A1870 | 7 l multi | 3.25 | 1.60 |
| *a.* | | Sheet of 4 | 13.00 | 6.50 |
| **6331** | A1870 | 19 l multi | 9.00 | 4.50 |
| *a.* | | Sheet of 4 | 36.00 | 18.00 |
| | | *Nos. 6328-6331 (4)* | 13.70 | 6.80 |

Palaces — A1871

Flags of Romania and Malta and: 1.70 l, Mogosoaia Palace, Romania. 8.50 l, Verdala Palace, Malta.

**2019, Oct. 14 Litho. *Perf. 13¼***

| | | | | |
|---|---|---|---|---|
| **6332** | A1871 | 1.70 l multi | .80 | .40 |
| *a.* | | Sheet of 5 + label | 4.00 | 2.00 |
| **6333** | A1871 | 8.50 l multi | 4.00 | 2.00 |
| *a.* | | Sheet of 5 + label | 20.00 | 10.00 |

Joint Issue between Romania and Malta.

A sheet containing imperforate examples of Nos. 6332-6333 was printed in limited quantities. See Malta No. 1672.

Romanian Higher Education in Cluj-Napoca, Cent. — A1872

Designs: 3.10 l, Babes-Bolyai University building and emblem. 12 l, Cluj-Napoca University of Medicine and Pharmacy building and emblem, Iuliu Hatieganu (1885-1959), first dean (72x33mm).

28.50 l, Emblem of Babes-Bolyai University, spray from fountain in its botanical garden.

**2019, Nov. 1 Litho. *Perf. 13¼***

| | | | | |
|---|---|---|---|---|
| **6334** | A1872 | 3.10 l multi | 1.50 | .75 |
| *a.* | | Sheet of 8 | 12.00 | 6.00 |
| **6335** | A1872 | 12 l multi | 5.75 | 3.00 |
| *a.* | | Sheet of 8 | 46.00 | 24.00 |

**Souvenir Sheet**

***Imperf***

| | | | | |
|---|---|---|---|---|
| **6336** | A1872 | 28.50 l multi | 13.50 | 6.75 |

No. 6336 contains one 36x36mm stamp.

Parks of Romania and Gibraltar — A1873

Designs: 7 l, Retezat National Park, Romania. 8 l, Upper Rock Nature Reserve, Gibraltar.

**2019, Nov. 12 Litho. *Perf. 13¼***

| | | | | |
|---|---|---|---|---|
| **6337** | A1873 | 7 l multi | 3.25 | 1.60 |
| *a.* | | Sheet of 5 + label | 16.50 | 8.00 |
| **6338** | A1873 | 8 l multi | 4.00 | 2.00 |
| *a.* | | Sheet of 5 + label | 20.00 | 10.00 |

Joint Issue between Romania and Gibraltar.

A sheet containing imperforate examples of Nos. 6337-6338 was printed in limited quantities. See Gibraltar No. 1740.

Christmas — A1874

No. 6339 — Images from *Akathist Hymn of the Mother of God*: a, Nativity scene (denomination in green). b, Magi (denomination in red).

28.50 l, Madonna and Child, vert.

**2019, Nov. 15 Litho. *Perf. 13¼***

**6339** A1874 1.70 l Pair, #a-b 1.60 .80
*c.* Sheet of 8, 4 each #6339a-6339b, + central label, #6339a at UL 13.00 6.50
*d.* As "c," #6339b at UL 13.00 6.50

**Souvenir Sheet**

***Perf. 13¾x13¼***

**6340** A1874 28.50 l multi 13.50 6.75

No. 6340 contains one 52x84mm stamp.

Animals and Thought Balloons A1875

Designs: 1.60 l, Polar bears and "Ocrotire" (protection) in balloon. 3.10 l, Berber macaque and "Nostalgie" (nostalgia) in balloon. 5 l, St. Bernard, kittens and "Prietenie" (friendliness) in balloon. 19 l, Elephants and "Bucurie" (joy) in balloon.

**2019, Nov. 19 Litho. *Perf. 13¼***

**6341** A1875 1.60 l multi .75 .35
*a.* Sheet of 5 + label 3.75 1.75
**6342** A1875 3.10 l multi 1.50 .75
*a.* Sheet of 5 + label 7.50 3.75
**6343** A1875 5 l multi 2.40 1.25
*a.* Sheet of 5 + label 12.00 6.25
**6344** A1875 19 l multi 8.75 4.50
*a.* Sheet of 5 + label 44.00 22.50
*Nos. 6341-6344 (4)* 13.40 6.85

A sheet containing imperforate examples of Nos. 6341-6344 was printed in limited quantities.

Romanian Legal Education, 160th Anniv. — A1876

Designs: 8.50 l, University of Bucharest Faculty of Law emblem. 28.50 l, Emblem and building of University of Bucharest Faculty of Law, horiz.

**2019, Nov. 21 Litho. *Perf. 13¼***

**6345** A1876 8.50 l multi 4.00 2.00
*a.* Sheet of 5 + label 20.00 10.00

**Souvenir Sheet**

**6346** A1876 28.50 l multi 13.50 6.75

No. 6346 contains one 108x36mm stamp.

Romanian Royalty in Uniforms A1877

Designs: 3.10 l, King Carol I (1839-1914). 7 l, King Ferdinand (1865-1927). 8.50 l, King Carol II (1893-1953). 11.50 l, King Michael (1921-2017).
28.50 l, King Carol I riding horse, horiz.

**2019, Dec. 5 Litho. *Perf. 13¼***

**6347** A1877 3.10 l multi 1.50 .75
*a.* Sheet of 4 6.00 3.00
**6348** A1877 7 l multi 3.25 1.60
*a.* Sheet of 4 13.00 6.50
**6349** A1877 8.50 l multi 4.00 2.00
*a.* Sheet of 4 16.00 8.00
**6350** A1877 11.50 l multi 5.50 2.75
*a.* Sheet of 4 22.00 11.00
*Nos. 6347-6350 (4)* 14.25 7.10

**Souvenir Sheet**

***Perf. 13¼x13¾***

**6351** A1877 28.50 l multi 13.50 6.75

No. 6351 contains one 84x52mm stamp. A sheet containing imperforate examples of Nos. 6347-6350 was printed in limited quantities.

Souvenir Sheet

Industrial and Aesthetic Design Education in Romania, 50th Anniv. — A1878

**2019, Dec. 11 Litho. *Perf. 13¼***

**6352** A1878 28.50 l multi 13.50 6.75

Gramophones A1879

Gramophone from: 1.40 l, Germany, 1908. 1.60 l, United States, 1900. 1.80 l, Germany, 1910. 7 l, Switzerland, 1907. 8.50 l, Germany, 1903. 12 l, Germany, 1908, diff.
28.50 l, Germany, 1910, horiz.

**2019, Dec. 12 Litho. *Perf. 13¼***

**6353** A1879 1.40 l multi .65 .35
*a.* Sheet of 8 + central label 5.25 3.00
*b.* Sheet of 13 + 2 labels 8.50 4.75
**6354** A1879 1.60 l multi .75 .35
*a.* Sheet of 8 + central label 6.00 3.00
*b.* Sheet of 13 + 2 labels 9.75 4.75
**6355** A1879 1.80 l multi .85 .40
*a.* Sheet of 8 + central label 7.00 3.25
*b.* Sheet of 13 + 2 labels 11.50 5.25
**6356** A1879 7 l multi 3.25 1.60
*a.* Sheet of 8 + central label 26.00 13.00
*b.* Sheet of 13 + 2 labels 42.50 21.00
**6357** A1879 8.50 l multi 4.00 2.00
*a.* Sheet of 8 + central label 32.00 16.00
*b.* Sheet of 13 + 2 labels 52.00 26.00
**6358** A1879 12 l multi 5.75 3.00
*a.* Sheet of 8 + central label 46.00 24.00
*b.* Sheet of 13 + 2 labels 75.00 39.00
*Nos. 6353-6358 (6)* 15.25 7.70

**Souvenir Sheet**

***Imperf***

**6359** A1879 28.50 l multi 13.50 6.75

No. 6359 contains one 54x44mm stamp. See Nos. 6388-6394.

Flowers — A1880

Inscriptions: 1.80 l, Lalea (tulip). 1.90 l, Narcisa (daffodil). 2.20 l, Floare de piersic (peach blossom). 2.70 l, Dalie (dahlia). 3.30 l, Mac (poppy). 53.50 l, Anemona (anemone).

**2020, Jan. 7 Litho. *Perf. 13¼***

**6360** A1880 1.80 l multi .85 .40
*a.* Sheet of 5 + label 4.25 2.00
**6361** A1880 1.90 l multi .90 .45
*a.* Sheet of 5 + label 4.50 2.25
**6362** A1880 2.20 l multi 1.00 .50
*a.* Sheet of 5 + label 5.00 2.50
**6363** A1880 2.70 l multi 1.25 .60
*a.* Sheet of 5 + label 6.25 3.00
**6364** A1880 3.30 l multi 1.60 .80
*a.* Sheet of 5 + label 8.00 4.00
**6365** A1880 53.50 l multi 25.00 12.50
*a.* Sheet of 5 + label 125.00 62.50
*Nos. 6360-6365 (6)* 30.60 15.25

Mihai Eminescu (1850-89), and His Lover, Veronica Micle (1850-89), Writers — A1881

Couple with denomination at: 5 l, LL. 11.50 l, LR.
28.50, Couple, diff.

**2020, Jan. 15 Litho. *Perf. 13¼***

**6366** A1881 5 l muti 2.40 1.25
*a.* Sheet of 5 + label 12.00 6.25
**6367** A1881 11.50 l muti 5.50 2.75
*a.* Sheet of 5 + label 27.50 14.00

**Souvenir Sheet**

***Imperf***

**6368** A1881 28.50 l muti 13.50 6.75

Buildings and Coat of Arms of Botosani — A1882

Designs: 1.40 l, Popauti Monastery. 1.90 l, City Hall. 5 l, County Museum of History. 19 l, Nicolae Iorga House.

**2020, Jan. 21 Litho. *Perf. 13¼***

**6369** A1882 1.40 l multi .65 .30
*a.* Sheet of 5 + label 3.25 1.50
**6370** A1882 1.90 l multi .90 .45
*a.* Sheet of 5 + label 4.50 2.25
**6371** A1882 5 l multi 2.40 1.25
*a.* Sheet of 5 + label 12.00 6.25
**6372** A1882 19 l multi 8.75 4.50
*a.* Sheet of 5 + label 44.00 22.50
*Nos. 6369-6372 (4)* 12.70 6.50

A sheet containing Nos. 6369-6372 was printed in limited quantities.

New Year 2020 (Year of the Rat) — A1883

Rat looking: 8.50 l, Left. 28.50 l, Right.

**2020, Jan. 23 Litho. *Perf. 13¼***

**6373** A1883 8.50 l multi 4.00 2.00
*a.* Sheet of 8 32.00 16.00

**Souvenir Sheet**

***Imperf***

**6374** A1883 28.50 l multi + 12 labels 13.50 6.75

No. 6373a contains two tete-beche pairs and a block of 4 with each stamp rotated ninety degrees. No. 6374 contains one 58x58mm stamp.

Animals of Arctic Areas — A1884

Designs: 1.80 l, Canis lupus arctos. 2 l, Bubo scandiacus, horiz. 7 l, Vulpes lagopus, horiz. 19 l, Lepus arcticus.

**2020, Jan. 28 Litho. *Perf. 13¼***

**6375** A1884 1.80 l multi .85 .40
*a.* Sheet of 5 + label 4.25 2.00
**6376** A1884 2 l multi .95 .45
*a.* Sheet of 5 + label 4.75 2.25
**6377** A1884 7 l multi 3.25 1.60
*a.* Sheet of 5 + label 16.50 8.00
**6378** A1884 19 l multi 8.75 4.50
*a.* Sheet of 5 + label 44.00 22.50
*Nos. 6375-6378 (4)* 13.80 6.95

A souvenir sheet containing imperforate examples of Nos. 6375-6378 was printed in limited quantities.

Cats — A1885

Designs: 1.80 l, Persian. 2 l, Siamese, horiz. 3.30 l, British shorthair. 5 l, Bengal. 8.50 l, British shorthair, diff. 11.50 l, Sphinx.

**2020, Feb. 7 Litho. *Perf. 13¼***

**6379** A1885 1.80 l multi .85 .40
*a.* Sheet of 5 + label 4.25 2.00
**6380** A1885 2 l multi .95 .45
*a.* Sheet of 5 + label 4.75 2.25
**6381** A1885 3.30 l multi 1.60 .80
*a.* Sheet of 5 + label 8.00 4.00
**6382** A1885 5 l multi 2.40 1.25
*a.* Sheet of 5 + label 12.00 6.25
**6383** A1885 8.50 l multi 4.00 2.00
*a.* Sheet of 5 + label 20.00 10.00
**6384** A1885 11.50 l multi 5.50 2.75
*a.* Sheet of 5 + label 27.50 14.00
*Nos. 6379-6384 (6)* 15.30 7.65

A souvenir sheet containing Nos. 6379-6384 was printed in limited quantities.

St. Nectarios of Aegina (1846-1920) — A1886

**2020, Feb. 14 Litho. *Perf. 13¼x14***

**6385** A1886 8.50 l gold & multi 4.00 2.00
*a.* Sheet of 4 16.00 8.00

Polytechnic University of Timisoara, Cent. — A1887

Designs: 8.50 l, Rectorate Building. 28.50 l, Centenary emblem and King Ferdinand (1865-1927).

**2020, Feb. 18 Litho. *Perf. 13¼***

**6386** A1887 8.50 l multi 4.00 2.00
*a.* Sheet of 5 + label 20.00 10.00

**Souvenir Sheet**

**6387** A1887 28.50 l multi 13.50 6.75

No. 6387 contains one 63x27mm stamp.

**Gramophones Type of 2019**

Gramophone or phonograph from: 1.80 l, France, 1880. 1.90 l, United States, 1896. 2 l, United Kingdom, 1904. 3.30 l, United States, 1918. 5 l, France, 1896. 19 l, Germany, 1898.

28.50 l, United States, 1911, vert.

**2020, Feb. 25 Litho. *Perf. 13¼***

| | | | |
|---|---|---|---|
| 6388 | A1879 1.80 l multi | .85 | .40 |
| a. | Sheet of 8 + central label | 7.00 | 3.25 |
| b. | Sheet of 13 + 2 labels | 11.50 | 5.25 |
| 6389 | A1879 1.90 l multi | .90 | .45 |
| a. | Sheet of 8 + central label | 7.25 | 3.75 |
| b. | Sheet of 13 + 2 labels | 12.00 | 6.00 |
| 6390 | A1879 2 l multi | .95 | .45 |
| a. | Sheet of 8 + central label | 7.75 | 3.75 |
| b. | Sheet of 13 + 2 labels | 12.50 | 6.00 |
| 6391 | A1879 3.30 l multi | 1.60 | .80 |
| a. | Sheet of 8 + central label | 13.00 | 6.50 |
| b. | Sheet of 13 + 2 labels | 21.00 | 10.50 |
| 6392 | A1879 5 l multi | 2.40 | 1.25 |
| a. | Sheet of 8 + central label | 19.50 | 10.00 |
| b. | Sheet of 13 + 2 labels | 31.50 | 16.50 |
| 6393 | A1879 19 l multi | 8.75 | 4.50 |
| a. | Sheet of 8 + central label | 70.00 | 36.00 |
| b. | Sheet of 13 + 2 labels | 115.00 | 60.00 |
| | *Nos. 6388-6393 (6)* | 15.45 | 7.85 |

**Souvenir Sheet**

***Perf. 13¼x13¾***

| | | | |
|---|---|---|---|
| 6394 | A1879 28.50 l multi | 13.50 | 6.75 |

A souvenir sheet containing Nos. 6388-6393 was printed in limited quantities. No. 6394 contains one 43x53mm stamp.

Flowers A1888

Designs: 2.20 l, Magnolia liliflora. 2.70 l, Mammillaria magnimamma, horiz. 3.30 l, Tulipa sylvestris subsp. australis. 20.50 l, Rosa "Hocus Pocus," horiz.

**2020, Mar. 3 Litho. *Perf. 13¼***

| | | | |
|---|---|---|---|
| 6395 | A1888 2.20 l multi | 1.10 | .55 |
| a. | Sheet of 5 + label | 5.50 | 2.75 |
| 6396 | A1888 2.70 l multi | 1.25 | .65 |
| a. | Sheet of 5 + label | 6.25 | 3.25 |
| 6397 | A1888 3.30 l multi | 1.60 | .80 |
| a. | Sheet of 5 + label | 8.00 | 4.00 |
| 6398 | A1888 20.50 l multi | 9.50 | 4.75 |
| a. | Sheet of 5 + label | 47.50 | 24.00 |
| | *Nos. 6395-6398 (4)* | 13.45 | 6.75 |

Dimitrie Brandza Botanical Garden, Bucharest, 160th anniv.

Easter A1889

Paintings of: No. 6399, The Last Supper. No. 6400, The Holy Myrrhbearing Women at the Holy Grave.

29 l, Jesus Entering Jerusalem, vert.

**2020, Mar. 12 Litho. *Perf. 13¼***

| | | | |
|---|---|---|---|
| 6399 | A1889 1.90 l multi | .85 | .40 |
| a. | Sheet of 8 + central label | 7.00 | 3.25 |
| 6400 | A1889 1.90 l multi | .85 | .40 |
| a. | Sheet of 8 + central label | 7.00 | 3.25 |

**Souvenir Sheet**

| | | | |
|---|---|---|---|
| 6401 | A1889 29 l multi | 13.00 | 6.50 |

No. 6401 contains one 36x72mm stamp.

May 21, 1860 Medal for Military Valor A1890

Domnitor Alexandru Ioan Cuza (1820-73) A1891

**2020, Mar. 20 Litho. *Perf. 13¼x14***

**Stamps With or Without Star-shaped Hole in Vignette**

| | | | |
|---|---|---|---|
| 6402 | A1890 5 l multi | 2.25 | 1.10 |
| a. | Sheet of 4 | 9.00 | 4.50 |
| 6403 | A1891 12 l multi | 5.50 | 1.10 |
| a. | Sheet of 4 | 22.00 | 11.00 |
| b. | Sheet of 4, 2 each #6402-6403, #6402 at UL | 15.50 | 7.75 |
| c. | As"b,", #6403 at UL | 15.50 | 7.75 |

Bible and Masonic Items — A1892

Constantin Moroiu (1837-1918), First Romanian Grand Master — A1893

Emblem of National Grand Lodge — A1893a

**2020, Apr. 3 Litho. *Perf. 13¼***

| | | | |
|---|---|---|---|
| 6404 | A1892 1.80 l multi | .80 | .40 |
| a. | Sheet of 5 + label | 4.00 | 2.00 |
| 6405 | A1893 20.50 l multi | 9.25 | 4.75 |
| a. | Sheet of 5 + label | 46.50 | 24.00 |

**Souvenir Sheet**

| | | | |
|---|---|---|---|
| 6406 | A1893a 29 l multi | 13.00 | 6.50 |

National Grand Masonic Lodge of Romania, 140th anniv.

Europa A1894

Map showing old postal routes and: 1.90 l, Seal of Romanian Telegraph Office and post riders. 20.50 l, Seal of Post Office Directorate of Wallachia and postal coach.

**2020, Apr. 9 Litho. *Perf. 13¼***

| | | | |
|---|---|---|---|
| 6407 | A1894 1.90 l multi | .90 | .45 |
| a. | Sheet of 5 + label | 4.50 | 2.25 |
| 6408 | A1894 20.50 l multi | 9.25 | 4.75 |
| a. | Sheet of 5 + label | 46.50 | 24.00 |
| b. | Sheet of 4, 2 each #6407-6408, #6407 at UL | 20.50 | 10.50 |
| c. | As "b," #6408 at UL | 20.50 | 10.50 |

AEROMFILA 2020 Philatelic Exhibition, Bucharest A1895

Designs: 2.20 l, Biplanes and 1920 route map of CFRNA, world's first international transcontinental airline. 2.70 l, Emblem of Aerophilately Commission of the Association of Romanian Philatelists. 20.50 l, Coudron C-63 biplane and map of Romania.

29 l, Biplanes and 1920 route of CFRNA, horiz.

**2020, Apr. 23 Litho. *Perf. 13¼***

| | | | |
|---|---|---|---|
| 6409 | A1895 2.20 l multi | 1.00 | .50 |
| a. | Sheet of 8 + central label | 8.00 | 4.00 |
| b. | Sheet of 13 + 2 labels | 13.00 | 6.50 |
| 6410 | A1895 2.70 l multi | 1.25 | .60 |
| a. | Sheet of 8 + central label | 10.00 | 5.00 |
| b. | Sheet of 13 + 2 labels | 16.50 | 8.00 |
| 6411 | A1895 20.50 l multi | 9.25 | 4.75 |
| a. | Sheet of 8 + central label | 74.00 | 38.00 |
| b. | Sheet of 13 + 2 labels | 125.00 | 62.00 |
| | *Nos. 6409-6411 (3)* | 11.50 | 5.85 |

**Souvenir Sheet**

***Perf. 14x13¼***

| | | | |
|---|---|---|---|
| 6412 | A1895 29 l multi | 13.50 | 6.75 |

No. 6412 contains one 52x42mm stamp.

Souvenir Sheet

Diplomatic Relations Between Romania and Holy See, Cent. — A1896

**2020, May 5 Litho. *Perf. 13¼***

| | | | |
|---|---|---|---|
| 6413 | A1896 29 l multi | 13.50 | 6.75 |

Romanian Medals and Orders A1897

Designs: 3.30 l, Military Virtue Medal. 5 l, Project Order of the Union. 8.50 l, Order of the Union. 12 l, Star of Romania National Order.

**2020, May 14 Litho. *Perf. 13¼x13¾***

| | | | |
|---|---|---|---|
| 6414 | A1897 3.30 l multi | 1.50 | .75 |
| a. | Sheet of 5 + label | 7.50 | 3.25 |
| 6415 | A1897 5 l multi | 2.40 | 1.25 |
| a. | Sheet of 5 + label | 7.50 | 6.25 |
| 6416 | A1897 8.50 l multi | 4.00 | 2.00 |
| a. | Sheet of 5 + label | 20.00 | 10.00 |
| 6417 | A1897 12 l multi | 5.50 | 2.75 |
| a. | Sheet of 5 + label | 27.50 | 14.00 |
| | *Nos. 6414-6417 (4)* | 13.40 | 6.75 |

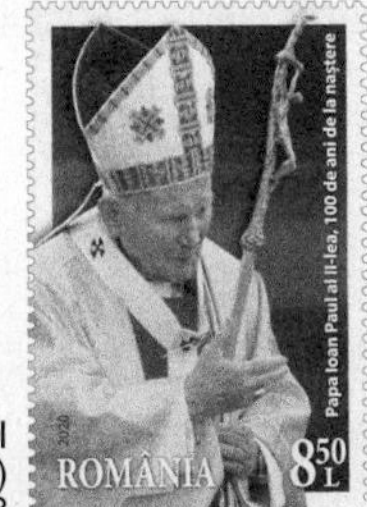


St. John Paul II (1920-2005) A1898

St. John Paul II wearing: 8.50 l, Miter. 29 l, Zucchetto, horiz.

**2020, May 18 Litho. *Perf. 13¼***

| | | | |
|---|---|---|---|
| 6418 | A1898 8.50 l multi | 4.00 | 2.00 |
| a. | Sheet of 5 + label | 20.00 | 10.00 |

**Souvenir Sheet**

| | | | |
|---|---|---|---|
| 6419 | A1898 29 l multi | 13.50 | 6.75 |

A souvenir sheet of 2 containing imperforate examples of Nos. 6418-6419 was printed in limited quantities.

Pheasants A1899

Designs: 1.90 l, Chrysolophus pictus. 5 l, Chrysolophus amherstiae, horiz. 8.50 l, Syrmaticus reevesii. 12 l, Phasianus versicolor, horiz.

**2020, May 22 Litho. *Perf. 13¼***

| | | | |
|---|---|---|---|
| 6420 | A1899 1.90 l multi | .90 | .45 |
| a. | Sheet of 5 + label | 4.50 | 2.25 |
| 6421 | A1899 5 l multi | 2.40 | 1.25 |
| a. | Sheet of 5 + label | 12.00 | 6.25 |
| 6422 | A1899 8.50 l multi | 4.00 | 2.00 |
| a. | Sheet of 5 + label | 20.00 | 10.00 |
| 6423 | A1899 12 l multi | 5.50 | 2.75 |
| a. | Sheet of 5 + label | 27.50 | 14.00 |
| | *Nos. 6420-6423 (4)* | 12.80 | 6.45 |

Squirrels A1900

Designs: 3.30 l, Ratufa indica. 5 l, Funambulus palmarum. 8.50 l, Sciurus carolinensis. 12 l, Sciurus vulgaris.

**2020, June 10 Litho. *Perf. 13¼***

| | | | |
|---|---|---|---|
| 6424 | A1900 3.30 l multi | 1.60 | .80 |
| a. | Sheet of 5 + label | 8.00 | 4.00 |
| 6425 | A1900 5 l multi | 2.40 | 1.25 |
| a. | Sheet of 5 + label | 12.00 | 6.25 |
| 6426 | A1900 8.50 l multi | 4.00 | 2.00 |
| a. | Sheet of 5 + label | 20.00 | 10.00 |
| 6427 | A1900 12 l multi | 5.75 | 2.75 |
| a. | Sheet of 5 + label | 29.00 | 14.00 |
| | *Nos. 6424-6427 (4)* | 13.75 | 6.80 |

Mihai Eminescu (1850-89), Writer — A1901

Statue of Eminescu and: No. 6428, Poem *Rugaciune* (Prayer). No. 6429, Putna Monastery.

**2020, June 15 Litho. *Perf. 13¼***

| No. | Description | Unused | Used |
|---|---|---|---|
| 6428 | A1901 8.50 l multi | 4.00 | 2.00 |
| *a.* | Sheet of 5 + label | 20.00 | 10.00 |
| 6429 | A1901 8.50 l multi | 4.00 | 2.00 |
| *a.* | Sheet of 5 + label | 20.00 | 10.00 |

Speleology — A1902

Designs: 3.30 l, Ancient painting of woolly rhinoceros from Coliboaia Cave, wooly rhinoceros. 5 l, Calcite columns from Piatra Altarului Cave, bat, vert. 8.50 l, Cave bear skull from Rece Cave, cave bear. 12 l, Spelunker on Sura Mare Cave rimstone, spelunker on rope, vert.

**2020, June 18 Litho. *Perf. 13¼***

| No. | Description | Unused | Used |
|---|---|---|---|
| 6430 | A1902 3.30 l multi | 1.60 | .80 |
| *a.* | Sheet of 4 | 6.50 | 3.25 |
| 6431 | A1902 5 l multi | 2.40 | 1.25 |
| *a.* | Sheet of 4 | 9.75 | 5.00 |
| 6432 | A1902 8.50 l multi | 4.00 | 2.00 |
| *a.* | Sheet of 4 | 16.00 | 8.00 |
| 6433 | A1902 12 l multi | 5.75 | 2.75 |
| *a.* | Sheet of 4 | 23.00 | 11.00 |
| | *Nos. 6430-6433 (4)* | 13.75 | 6.80 |

Emil Racovita Institute of Speleology, cent.

Wedding Clothes A1903

Bride and groom from: 1.90 l, Bucovina Region. 2.20 l, Oas Region. 3.30 l, Vlasca Region. 20.50 l, Banat Region.

***Perf. 13¼x13¾***

**2020, June 24 Litho.**

| No. | Description | Unused | Used |
|---|---|---|---|
| 6434 | A1903 1.90 l multi | .90 | .45 |
| *a.* | Sheet of 4 | 3.75 | 1.90 |
| 6435 | A1903 2.20 l multi | 1.10 | .55 |
| *a.* | Sheet of 4 | 4.50 | 2.25 |
| 6436 | A1903 3.30 l multi | 1.60 | .80 |
| *a.* | Sheet of 4 | 6.50 | 3.25 |
| 6437 | A1903 20.50 l multi | 9.50 | 4.75 |
| *a.* | Sheet of 4 | 38.00 | 19.00 |
| | *Nos. 6434-6437 (4)* | 13.10 | 6.55 |

Spotted Animals — A1904

Designs: 1.90 l, Stigmochelys pardalis. 5 l, Hydrurga leptonyx. 8.50 l, Triakis semifasciata. 12 l, Zamenis situla.

**2020, July 2 Litho. *Perf. 13¼***

| No. | Description | Unused | Used |
|---|---|---|---|
| 6438 | A1904 1.90 l multi | .95 | .45 |
| *a.* | Sheet of 5 + label | 4.75 | 2.25 |
| 6439 | A1904 5 l multi | 2.50 | 1.25 |
| *a.* | Sheet of 5 + label | 12.50 | 6.25 |
| 6440 | A1904 8.50 l multi | 4.25 | 2.10 |
| *a.* | Sheet of 5 + label | 21.50 | 10.50 |
| 6441 | A1904 12 l multi | 6.00 | 3.00 |
| *a.* | Sheet of 5 + label | 30.00 | 15.00 |
| | *Nos. 6438-6441 (4)* | 13.70 | 6.80 |

Royalty in Uniform A1905

Designs: 3.30 l, King Carol I (1839-1914). 5 l, King Ferdinand I (1865-1927). 8.50 l, King Carol II (1893-1953). 12 l, King Michael (1921-2017).

29 l, King Carol II, diff.

**2020, July 15 Litho. *Perf. 13¼***

| No. | Description | Unused | Used |
|---|---|---|---|
| 6442 | A1905 3.30 l multi | 1.60 | .80 |
| *a.* | Sheet of 4 | 6.50 | 3.25 |
| 6443 | A1905 5 l multi | 2.50 | 1.25 |
| *a.* | Sheet of 4 | 10.00 | 5.00 |
| 6444 | A1905 8.50 l multi | 4.25 | 2.10 |
| *a.* | Sheet of 4 | 17.00 | 8.50 |
| 6445 | A1905 12 l multi | 6.00 | 3.00 |
| *a.* | Sheet of 4 | 24.00 | 12.00 |
| | *Nos. 6442-6445 (4)* | 14.35 | 7.15 |

**Souvenir Sheet**

***Perf. 13¾x13¼***

| No. | Description | Unused | Used |
|---|---|---|---|
| 6446 | A1905 29 l multi | 14.00 | 7.00 |

A sheet of 8 containing a perforated and imperforate example of Nos. 6442-6445 was printed in limited quantities. No. 6446 contains one 52x85mm stamp, and a reproduction of Romania No. B40 in black that is not valid for postage.

National Theater of Iasi, 180th Anniv. — A1906

Designs: 5 l, Theater exterior and Vasile Alecsandri (1821-90), poet. 12 l, Theater interior, Mihail Kogalniceanu (1817-91), Prime Minister, and Costache Negruzzi (1808-68), writer.

**2020, July 21 Litho. *Perf. 13¼***

| No. | Description | Unused | Used |
|---|---|---|---|
| 6447 | A1906 5 l multi | 2.50 | 1.25 |
| *a.* | Sheet of 6 + 3 labels | 15.00 | 7.50 |
| 6448 | A1906 12 l multi | 6.00 | 3.00 |
| *a.* | Sheet of 6 + 3 labels | 36.00 | 18.00 |

A1907

Ludwig van Beethoven (1770-1827), Composer A1908

**2020, July 28 Litho. *Perf. 13¼***

| No. | Description | Unused | Used |
|---|---|---|---|
| 6449 | A1907 8.50 l multi | 4.25 | 2.10 |
| *a.* | Sheet of 5 + label | 21.50 | 11.50 |
| *b.* | Tete-beche pair | 8.50 | 8.50 |
| 6450 | A1908 8.50 l multi | 4.25 | 2.10 |
| *a.* | Sheet of 5 + label | 21.50 | 11.50 |
| *b.* | Souvenir sheet of 4, 2 each #6449-6450 | 17.00 | 8.50 |
| *c.* | Tete-beche pair | 8.50 | 8.50 |

Orchids A1909

Designs: 3.30 l, Neotinea ustulata var. aestivalis. 5 l, Cephalanthera rubra. 8.50 l, Anacamptis pyramidalis. 10.50 l, Nigritella miniata.

**2020, Aug. 6 Litho. *Perf. 13¼x14***

| No. | Description | Unused | Used |
|---|---|---|---|
| 6451 | A1909 3.30 l multi | 1.75 | .85 |
| *a.* | Sheet of 5 + label | 8.75 | 4.25 |
| 6452 | A1909 5 l multi | 2.50 | .85 |
| *a.* | Sheet of 5 + label | 12.50 | 6.25 |
| 6453 | A1909 8.50 l multi | 4.25 | 2.10 |
| *a.* | Sheet of 5 + label | 21.50 | 10.50 |
| 6454 | A1909 10.50 l multi | 5.25 | 2.60 |
| *a.* | Sheet of 5 + label | 26.50 | 13.00 |
| | *Nos. 6451-6454 (4)* | 13.75 | 6.40 |

Owls — A1910

Designs: 1.90 l, Glaucidium passerinum. 3.30 l, Athene noctua. 5 l, Athene cunicularia. 19 l, Ninox theomacha.

**2020, Aug. 12 Litho. *Perf. 13¼***

| No. | Description | Unused | Used |
|---|---|---|---|
| 6455 | A1910 1.90 l multi | .95 | .45 |
| *a.* | Sheet of 5 + label | 4.75 | 2.25 |
| 6456 | A1910 3.30 l multi | 1.75 | .85 |
| *a.* | Sheet of 5 + label | 8.75 | 4.25 |
| 6457 | A1910 5 l multi | 2.50 | 1.25 |
| *a.* | Sheet of 5 + label | 12.50 | 6.25 |
| 6458 | A1910 19 l multi | 9.50 | 4.75 |
| *a.* | Sheet of 5 + label | 47.50 | 24.00 |
| | *Nos. 6455-6458 (4)* | 14.70 | 7.30 |

A souvenir sheet containing partially perforated examples of Nos. 6455-6458 was printed in limited quantities.

Protected Flowers — A1911

Designs: 1.90 l, Soldanella oreodoxa. 3.30 l, Cypripedium calceolus. 5 l, Paeonia peregrina. 19 l, Gentiana lutea.

**2020, Aug. 19 Litho. *Perf. 13¼***

| No. | Description | Unused | Used |
|---|---|---|---|
| 6459 | A1911 1.90 l multi | .95 | .45 |
| *a.* | Sheet of 5 + label | 4.75 | 2.25 |
| 6460 | A1911 3.30 l multi | 1.75 | .85 |
| *a.* | Sheet of 5 + label | 8.75 | 4.25 |
| 6461 | A1911 5 l multi | 2.50 | 1.25 |
| *a.* | Sheet of 5 + label | 12.50 | 6.25 |
| 6462 | A1911 19 l multi | 9.50 | 4.75 |
| *a.* | Sheet of 5 + label | 47.50 | 24.00 |
| | *Nos. 6459-6462 (4)* | 14.70 | 7.30 |

Alexandru Ioan Cuza University Building, Cuza (1820-73), Prince of Wallachia and Moldavia, and Gheorghe Asachi (1788-1869), Educator — A1912

Alexandru Ioan Cuza University Building and Crest — A1913

**2020, Aug. 26 Litho. *Perf. 13¼***

| No. | Description | Unused | Used |
|---|---|---|---|
| 6463 | A1912 8.50 l multi + label | 4.25 | 2.10 |
| *a.* | Sheet of 6 + 3 labels | 25.50 | 13.00 |
| 6464 | A1913 8.50 l multi + label | 4.25 | 2.10 |
| *a.* | Sheet of 6 + 3 labels | 25.50 | 13.00 |
| *b.* | Sheet of 6, 3 each #6463-6464, + 3 labels | 25.50 | 13.00 |

Alexandru Ioan Cuza University of Iasi, 160th anniv.

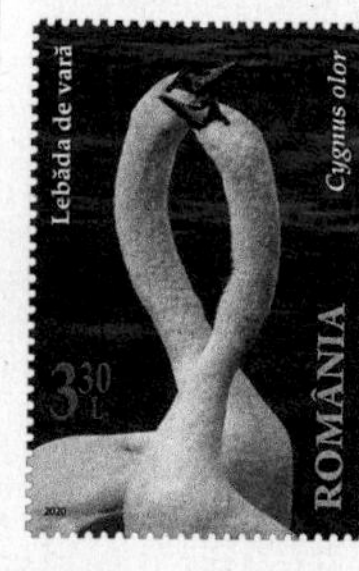


Cygnus Olor — A1914

Cygnus olor: 3.30 l, Heads of two swans. 5 l, Swan in flight, horiz. 8.50 l, Swan above water, horiz. 10.50 l, Head of swan.

**2020, Sept. 1 Litho. *Perf. 13¼***

| No. | Description | Unused | Used |
|---|---|---|---|
| 6465 | A1914 3.30 l multi | 1.75 | .85 |
| *a.* | Sheet of 4 | 7.00 | 3.50 |
| 6466 | A1914 5 l multi | 2.50 | 1.25 |
| *a.* | Sheet of 4 | 10.00 | 5.00 |
| 6467 | A1914 8.50 l multi | 4.25 | 2.10 |
| *a.* | Sheet of 4 | 17.00 | 8.50 |
| 6468 | A1914 10.50 l multi | 5.25 | 2.60 |
| *a.* | Sheet of 4 | 21.00 | 10.50 |
| | *Nos. 6465-6468 (4)* | 13.75 | 6.80 |

A souvenir sheet with imperforate examples of Nos. 6465-6468 was printed in limited quantities.

A1915

Rapahael (1483-1520), Painter A1916

**2020, Sept. 9 Litho. *Perf. 13¼***

| No. | Description | Unused | Used |
|---|---|---|---|
| 6469 | A1915 8.50 l multi | 4.25 | 2.10 |
| *a.* | Sheet of 5 + label | 21.50 | 11.50 |
| *b.* | Tete-beche pair | 8.50 | 8.50 |
| 6470 | A1916 8.50 l multi | 4.25 | 2.10 |
| *a.* | Sheet of 5 + label | 21.50 | 11.50 |
| *b.* | Souvenir sheet of 4, 2 each #6469-6470 | 17.00 | 8.50 |
| *c.* | Tete-beche pair | 8.50 | 8.50 |

Romanian Queens A1917

Designs: 1.90 l, Queen Elizabeth (1843-1916). 3.30 l, Queen Marie (1875-1938). 5 l, Queen Elena (1896-1982). 19 l, Queen Anne (1923-2016).

**2020, Sept. 15 Litho. *Perf. 13¼***

| No. | Description | Unused | Used |
|---|---|---|---|
| 6471 | A1917 1.90 l multi | .95 | .45 |
| *a.* | Sheet of 4 | 4.00 | 1.90 |

**6472** A1917 3.30 l multi 1.60 .80
*a.* Sheet of 4 6.50 3.25
**6473** A1917 5 l multi 2.40 1.25
*a.* Sheet of 4 9.75 5.00
**6474** A1917 19 l multi 9.25 4.75
*a.* Sheet of 4 37.00 19.00
*Nos. 6471-6474 (4)* 14.20 7.25

A souvenir sheet containing perforate and imperforate examples of Nos. 6471-6474 was printed in limited quantities.

Traditional Wedding Costumes A1918

Bride and groom from: 1.40 l, Maramures Region. 3.30 l, Muscel Region. 5 l, Arad Region. 19 l, Vâlcea Region.

**2020, Sept. 24 Litho. *Perf. 13¼x14***

**6475** A1918 1.40 l multi .70 .35
*a.* Sheet of 4 2.80 1.40
**6476** A1918 3.30 l multi 1.60 .80
*a.* Sheet of 4 6.50 3.25
**6477** A1918 5 l multi 2.40 1.25
*a.* Sheet of 4 9.75 5.00
**6478** A1918 19 l multi 9.25 4.75
*a.* Sheet of 4 37.00 19.00
*Nos. 6475-6478 (4)* 13.95 7.15

Chameleons A1919

Designs: 2.20 l, Chamaeleo csalyptratus. 3.30 l, Furcifer pardalis, horiz. 5 l, Trioceros jacksonii, horiz. 19 l, Furcifer pardalis, diff.

**2020, Oct. 1 Litho. *Perf. 13¼***

**6479** A1919 2.20 l multi 1.10 .55
*a.* Sheet of 5 + label 5.50 2.75
**6480** A1919 3.30 l multi 1.60 .80
*a.* Sheet of 5 + label 8.00 4.00
**6481** A1919 5 l multi 2.40 1.25
*a.* Sheet of 5 + label 12.00 6.25
**6482** A1919 19 l multi 9.25 4.75
*a.* Sheet of 5 + label 47.00 24.00
*Nos. 6479-6482 (4)* 14.35 7.35

Music Boxes A1920

Music box from: 1.70 l, Switzerland, 1890. 1.90 l, Germany, 1910. 2.20 l, United States, 1900. 3.30 l, Germany, 1900. 5 l, Germany, 1905. 19 l, Spain, 1950.
29 l, France, 1890, vert.

**2020, Oct. 9 Litho. *Perf. 13¼***

**6483** A1920 1.70 l multi .85 .40
*a.* Sheet of 8 + central label 7.00 3.25
*b.* Sheet of 13 + 2 labels 11.50 5.25
**6484** A1920 1.90 l multi .90 .45
*a.* Sheet of 8 + central label 7.25 3.75
*b.* Sheet of 13 + 2 labels 12.00 6.00
**6485** A1920 2.20 l multi 1.10 .55
*a.* Sheet of 8 + central label 9.00 4.50
*b.* Sheet of 13 + 2 labels 14.50 7.25
**6486** A1920 3.30 l multi 1.60 .80
*a.* Sheet of 8 + central label 13.00 6.50
*b.* Sheet of 13 + 2 labels 21.00 10.50
**6487** A1920 5 l multi 2.40 1.25
*a.* Sheet of 8 + central label 19.50 10.00
*b.* Sheet of 13 + 2 labels 21.00 16.50
**6488** A1920 19 l multi 9.00 4.50
*a.* Sheet of 8 + central label 72.00 36.00
*b.* Sheet of 13 + 2 labels 120.00 60.00
*Nos. 6483-6488 (6)* 15.85 7.95

**Souvenir Sheet**

***Perf. 13¼x14***

**6489** A1920 29 l multi 14.00 7.00

No. 6489 contains one 42x52mm stamp.

National Bank of Romania, 140th Anniv. — A1921

Bank branch offices in: 1.40 l, Constanta. 1.90 l, Cluj. 3.30 l, Craiova, horiz. 5 l, Iasi, horiz. 8.50 l, Timisoara, horiz. 10.50 l, Bucharest, horiz.
29 l, New central headquarters, Bucharest, horiz.

**2020, Oct. 21 Litho. *Perf. 13¼***

**6490** A1921 1.40 l multi .70 .35
*a.* Sheet of 5 + label 3.50 1.75
**6491** A1921 1.90 l multi .90 .45
*a.* Sheet of 5 + label 4.50 2.25
**6492** A1921 3.30 l multi 1.60 .80
*a.* Sheet of 5 + label 8.00 4.00
**6493** A1921 5 l multi 2.40 1.25
*a.* Sheet of 5 + label 12.00 6.25
**6494** A1921 8.50 l multi 4.25 2.10
*a.* Sheet of 5 + label 21.50 10.50
**6495** A1921 10.50 l multi 5.00 2.50
*a.* Sheet of 5 + label 25.00 12.50
*b.* Souvenir sheet of 6, #6490-6495 15.00 7.50
*Nos. 6490-6495 (6)* 14.85 7.45

**Souvenir Sheet**

***Imperf***

**6496** A1921 29 l multi 14.00 7.00

Ion Pelivan (1876-1954), Head of Bessarabian Delegation at Paris Peace Conference A1922

Nicolae Titulescu (1882-1941), Diplomat, and Grand Trianon Palace, Versailles, France — A1923

Arms of Romania, King Ferdinand (1865-1927) and Queen Marie (1875-1938) — A1924

Take Ionescu (1858-1922), Minister of Foreign Affairs, Prime Minister — A1925

**2020, Oct. 28 Litho. *Perf. 13¼***

**6497** A1922 8.50 l multi 4.25 2.10
*a.* Sheet of 5 + label 21.50 10.50
**6498** A1923 8.50 l multi 4.25 2.10
*a.* Sheet of 5 + label 21.50 10.50

**Souvenir Sheets**

**6499** A1924 29 l multi 14.00 7.00

***Imperf***

**6500** A1925 29 l multi 14.00 7.00

Paris Peace Conference and signing of the Treaty of Trianon, cent.

Annunciation A1926

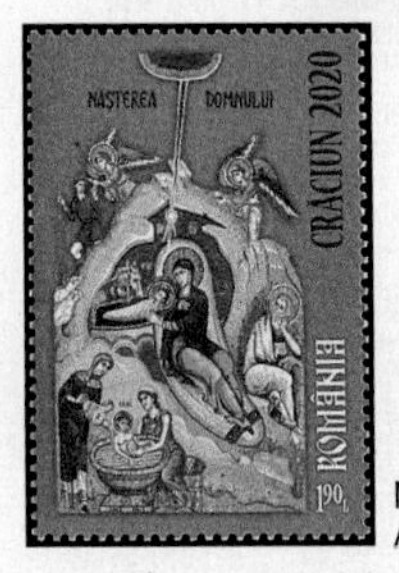


Nativity A1927

Design: 29 l, Madonna and Child.

**2020, Nov. 12 Litho. *Perf. 13¼***

**6501** A1926 1.90 l multi .95 .45
*a.* Sheet of 8 + central label 7.75 3.75
**6502** A1927 1.90 l multi .95 .45
*a.* Sheet of 8 + central label 7.75 3.75

**Souvenir Sheet**

***Imperf***

**6503** A1927 29 l multi 14.50 7.25

Christmas. No. 6503 contains one 57x57mm stamp. A sheet containing imperforate examples of Nos. 6501-6503 was produced in limited quantities.

Crocodilians — A1928

Designs: 2.20 l, Alligator mississipiensis. 2.70 l, Caiman yacare. 5 l, Gavialis gangeticus. 19 l, Crocoylus rhombifer.

**2020, Nov. 19 Litho. *Perf. 13¼***

**6504** A1928 2.20 l multi 1.10 .55
*a.* Tete-beche pair 2.20 1.10
*b.* Sheet of 5 + label 5.50 2.75
**6505** A1928 2.70 l multi 1.40 .70
*a.* Tete-beche pair 2.80 1.40
*b.* Sheet of 5 + label 7.00 3.50
**6506** A1928 5 l multi 2.50 1.25
*a.* Tete-beche pair 5.00 2.50
*b.* Sheet of 5 + label 12.50 6.25
**6507** A1928 19 l multi 9.50 4.75
*a.* Tete-beche pair 19.00 9.50
*b.* Sheet of 5 + label 47.50 24.00
*Nos. 6504-6507 (4)* 14.50 7.25

Paintings of Nudes by Theodor Pallady (1871-1956) — A1929

Paintings: 2.20 l, Toujours du Baudelaire. 3.30 l, Nude Woman. 5 l, Lady on the Couch. 19 l, Nude by the Sea.

**2020, Nov. 25 Litho. *Perf. 13¼***

**6508** A1929 2.20 l multi 1.10 .55
*a.* Sheet of 4 4.50 2.25
**6509** A1929 3.30 l multi 1.60 .80
*a.* Sheet of 4 6.50 3.25
**6510** A1929 5 l multi 2.50 1.25
*a.* Sheet of 4 10.00 5.00
**6511** A1929 19 l multi 9.50 4.75
*a.* Sheet of 4 38.00 19.00
*Nos. 6508-6511 (4)* 14.70 7.35

Bears A1930

Ursus arctos and: 2 l, Pine cone on branch. 3.30 l, Wild strawberries, vert. 5 l, Blueberries. 19 l, Rowanberries, vert.

**2020, Dec. 3 Litho. *Perf. 13¼***

**6512** A1930 2 l multi 1.00 .50
*a.* Tete-beche pair 2.00 1.00
*b.* Sheet of 4 4.00 2.00
**6513** A1930 3.30 l multi 1.75 .85
*a.* Tete-beche pair 3.50 1.75
*b.* Sheet of 4 7.00 3.50
**6514** A1930 5 l multi 2.60 1.30
*a.* Tete-beche pair 5.25 2.60
*b.* Sheet of 4 10.50 5.25
**6515** A1930 19 l multi 9.75 4.75
*a.* Tete-beche pair 19.50 9.50
*b.* Sheet of 4 39.00 19.00
*Nos. 6512-6515 (4)* 15.10 7.40

Winter Flowers A1931

Designs: 2 l, Euphorbia pulcherrima. 2.20 l, Eranthis hyemalis. 5 l, Hippeastrum sp. 19 l, Helleborus niger.

**2020, Dec. 10 Litho. *Perf. 13¼***

**6516** A1931 2 l multi 1.00 .50
*a.* Sheet of 5 + label 5.00 2.50
**6517** A1931 2.20 l multi 1.10 .55
*a.* Sheet of 5 + label 5.50 2.75
**6518** A1931 5 l multi 2.60 1.30
*a.* Sheet of 5 + label 13.00 6.50
**6519** A1931 19 l multi 9.75 4.75
*a.* Sheet of 5 + label 49.00 24.00
*Nos. 6516-6519 (4)* 14.45 7.10

Simu Museum, Bucharest — A1932

Museum building and: 3.30 l, Bust of Anastase Simu (1854-1935), by Frederic Storck (1872-1942). 5 l, Pears, painting by Marius Bunescu (1881-1971). 8.50 l, Marine, painting by Eugen Voinescu (1842-1909). 10.50 l, Venice, painting by Stefan Popescu (1872-1948).

**2021, Jan. 8 Litho. *Perf. 13¼***

**6520** A1932 3.30 l multi + label 1.75 .85
*a.* Sheet of 4 + 4 labels 7.00 3.50
**6521** A1932 5 l multi + label 2.50 1.25
*a.* Sheet of 4 + 4 labels 10.00 5.00
**6522** A1932 8.50 l multi + label 4.25 2.10
*a.* Sheet of 4 + 4 labels 17.00 8.50
**6523** A1932 10.50 l multi + label 5.25 2.60
*a.* Sheet of 4 + 4 labels 21.00 10.50
*Nos. 6520-6523 (4)* 13.75 6.80

National Culture Day — A1933

Putna Monastery and: 2.70 l, Mihai Eminescu (1850-89), poet. 8.50 l, Ioan Slavici (1848-1925), writer. 10.50 l, Ciprian Porumbescu (1853-83), composer.

**2021, Jan. 15 Litho. *Perf. 13¼***

**6524** A1933 2.70 l multi 1.40 .70
*a.* Sheet of 5 + label 7.00 3.50
**6525** A1933 8.50 l multi 4.25 2.10
*a.* Sheet of 5 + label 21.50 10.50
**6526** A1933 10.50 l multi 5.25 2.60
*a.* Sheet of 5 + label 26.50 13.00
*b.* Souvenir sheet of 3, #6524-6526 11.00 5.50
*Nos. 6524-6526 (3)* 10.90 5.40

Kings of Romania A1934

Designs: 1.40 l, King Carol I (1839-1914) on horse. 1.70 l, King Ferdinand (1865-1927), with flowers. 10.50 l, King Carol II (1893-1953) with stamps and stock book. 19 l, King Michael (1921-2017) in airplane cockpit.

**2021, Jan. 22 Litho. *Perf. 13¼x14***

**6527** A1934 1.40 l multi .70 .35
*a.* Sheet of 5 + label 3.50 1.75
**6528** A1934 1.70 l multi .85 .40
*a.* Sheet of 5 + label 4.25 2.00
**6529** A1934 10.50 l multi 5.25 2.60
*a.* Sheet of 5 + label 26.50 13.00
**6530** A1934 19 l multi 9.50 4.75
*a.* Sheet of 5 + label 47.50 24.00
*Nos. 6527-6530 (4)* 16.30 8.10

A souvenir sheet containing Nos. 6527-6530 was produced in limited quantities.

Birds — A1935

Designs: 2 l, Ardeola ralloides. 2.10 l, Nycticorax nycticorax, vert. 3.40 l, Calidris pugnax, vert. 5.50 l, Vanellus vanellus. 9 l, Circus aeruginosus, vert. 10.50 l, Sterna hirundo. 19.50 l, Egretta garzetta, vert.

**2021, Feb. 3 Litho. *Perf. 13¼***

**6531** A1935 2 l multi 1.00 .50
*a.* Tete-beche pair 2.00 1.00
*b.* Sheet of 5 + label 5.00 2.50
**6532** A1935 2.10 l multi 1.10 .55
*a.* Tete-beche pair 2.25 1.10
*b.* Sheet of 5 + label 5.50 2.75
**6533** A1935 3.40 l multi 1.75 .85
*a.* Tete-beche pair 3.50 1.75
*b.* Sheet of 5 + label 8.75 4.25
**6534** A1935 5.50 l multi 2.75 1.40
*a.* Tete-beche pair 5.50 2.80
*b.* Sheet of 5 + label 14.00 7.00
**6535** A1935 9 l multi 4.50 2.25
*a.* Tete-beche pair 9.00 4.50
*b.* Sheet of 5 + label 22.50 11.50
**6536** A1935 10.50 l multi 5.25 2.60
*a.* Tete-beche pair 10.50 5.25
*b.* Sheet of 5 + label 26.50 13.00
**6537** A1935 19.50 l multi 9.75 4.75
*a.* Tete-beche pair 19.50 9.50
*b.* Sheet of 5 + label 49.00 24.00
*Nos. 6531-6537 (7)* 26.10 12.90

A souvenir sheet containing Nos. 6531-6537 was produced in limited quantities.

Falcons A1936

Designs: 2.20 l, Micrastur ruficollis. 2.60 l, Polihierax semitorquatus. 5.50 l, Falco columbarius. 19.50 l, Falco peregrinus.

**2021, Feb. 12 Litho. *Perf. 13¼***

**6538** A1936 2.20 l multi 1.10 .55
*a.* Tete-beche pair 2.25 1.10
*b.* Sheet of 5 + label 5.50 2.75
**6539** A1936 2.60 l multi 1.30 .65
*a.* Tete-beche pair 2.60 1.30
*b.* Sheet of 5 + label 6.50 3.25
**6540** A1936 5.50 l multi 2.75 1.40
*a.* Tete-beche pair 5.50 2.80
*b.* Sheet of 5 + label 14.00 7.00
**6541** A1936 19.50 l multi 9.75 4.75
*a.* Tete-beche pair 19.50 9.50
*b.* Sheet of 5 + label 49.00 24.00
*Nos. 6538-6541 (4)* 14.90 7.35

Mention of Buzau in Historic Documents, 590th Anniv. — A1937

Buzau coat of arms and: 2.10 l, Communal Palace. 7 l, Marghiloman Mansion. 9 l, Archdiocesan Cathedral. 10.50 l, Bogdan P. Hasdeu National College.

**2021, Feb. 23 Litho. *Perf. 13¼***

**6542** A1937 2.10 l multi 1.10 .55
*a.* Sheet of 5 + label 5.50 2.75
**6543** A1937 7 l multi 3.50 1.75
*a.* Sheet of 5 + label 17.50 8.75
**6544** A1937 9 l multi 4.50 2.25
*a.* Sheet of 5 + label 22.50 11.50
**6545** A1937 10.50 l multi 5.25 2.60
*a.* Sheet of 5 + label 26.50 13.00
*Nos. 6542-6545 (4)* 14.35 7.15

Famous Women A1938

Designs: 1.40 l, Alice Voinescu (1885-1961), writer. 1.50 l, Smaranda Braescu (1897-1948), skydiver. 19.50 l, Sarmiza Bilescu (1867-1935), first female lawyer in Romania.

**2021, Mar. 5 Litho. *Perf. 13¼***

**6546** A1938 1.40 l multi .70 .35
*a.* Sheet of 3 + label 2.10 1.10
**6547** A1938 1.50 l multi .75 .35
*a.* Sheet of 3 + label 2.25 1.10
**6548** A1938 19.50 l multi 9.50 4.75
*a.* Sheet of 3 + label 2.25 14.50
*Nos. 6546-6548 (3)* 10.95 5.45

Flowers A1939

Designs: 1.70 l, Gentianella bulgarica. 2.20 l, Crambe maritima. 5.50 l, Centaurea jankae. 19.50 l, Nitraria schoberi.

**2021, Mar. 12 Litho. *Perf. 13¼***

**6549** A1939 1.70 l multi .85 .40
*a.* Tete-beche pair 1.75 .80
*b.* Sheet of 5 + label 4.25 2.00
**6550** A1939 2.20 l multi 1.10 .55
*a.* Tete-beche pair 2.25 1.10
*b.* Sheet of 5 + label 5.50 2.75
**6551** A1939 5.50 l multi 2.75 1.40
*a.* Tete-beche pair 5.50 2.80
*b.* Sheet of 5 + label 14.00 7.00
**6552** A1939 19.50 l multi 9.50 4.75
*a.* Tete-beche pair 19.00 9.50
*b.* Sheet of 5 + label 47.50 24.00
*Nos. 6549-6552 (4)* 14.20 7.10

A souvenir sheet containing Nos. 6549-6552 was produced in limited quantities.

Paintings by Theodor Aman (1831-91) — A1940

Designs: 2 l, Grapes and Apples. 2.20 l, Woman in Vernil, vert. 5.50 l, Odalisque. 19.50 l, Vase with Roses, vert.

***Perf. 14x13¼, 13¼x14***

**2021, Mar. 24 Litho.**

**6553** A1940 2 l multi .95 .50
*a.* Sheet of 4 3.80 2.00
**6554** A1940 2.20 l multi 1.10 .55
*a.* Sheet of 4 4.50 2.25
**6555** A1940 5.50 l multi 2.75 1.40
*a.* Sheet of 4 11.00 5.75
**6556** A1940 19.50 l multi 9.50 4.75
*a.* Sheet of 4 38.00 19.00
*Nos. 6553-6556 (4)* 14.30 7.20

A souvenir sheet containing Nos. 6553-6556 was produced in limited quantities.

Entry of Jesus into Jerusalem A1941

Resurrection of Jesus A1942

The Last Supper — A1943

**2021, Apr. 2 Litho. *Perf. 13¼***

**6557** A1941 2 l gold & multi 1.00 .50
*a.* Sheet of 8 + central label 8.00 4.00
**6558** A1942 2 l gold & multi 1.00 .50
*a.* Sheet of 8 + central label 8.00 4.00

**Souvenir Sheet**

***Perf. 13¼x13¾***

**6559** A1943 31.50 l gold & multi 15.50 7.75

Easter. A sheet containing imperforate examples of Nos. 6557-6559 was printed in limited quantities.

Paintings by Theodor Pallady (1871-1956) — A1944

Designs: 2.20 l, Still Life with a Mask. 5.50 l, Street Landscape (Paris). 9 l, Static Nature. 10.50 l, Still Life.
31.50 l, Still Life with Tulips, horiz.

**2021, Apr. 14 Litho. *Perf. 13¼x13¾***

**6560** A1944 2.20 l multi 1.10 .55
*a.* Sheet of 4 4.50 2.25
**6561** A1944 5.50 l multi 2.75 1.40
*a.* Sheet of 4 11.00 5.75
**6562** A1944 9 l multi 4.50 2.25
*a.* Sheet of 4 18.00 9.00
**6563** A1944 10.50 l multi 5.25 2.60
*a.* Sheet of 4 21.00 10.50
*Nos. 6560-6563 (4)* 13.60 6.80

**Souvenir Sheet**

***Perf. 13¾x13¼***

**6564** A1944 31.50 l multi 15.50 7.75

Europa A1945

Endangered animals: 3.40 l, Mustela lutreola. 19.50 l, Otis tarda.

**2021, Apr. 22 Litho. *Perf. 13¼***

**6565** A1945 3.40 l multi 1.75 .85
*a.* Tete-beche pair 3.50 1.75
*b.* Sheet of 5 + label 8.75 4.25
**6566** A1945 19.50 l multi 9.50 4.75
*a.* Tete-beche pair 19.00 9.50
*b.* Sheet of 5 + label 47.50 24.00
*c.* Souvenir sheet of 4, 2 each #6565-6566, #6565 at UL 26.00 13.00
*d.* Souvenir sheet of 4, 2 each #6565-6566, #6566 at UL 26.00 13.00

A sheet containing 2 imperforate examples each of Nos. 6565-6566 was printed in limited quantities.

Mushrooms A1946

Designs: 1.70 l, Geastrum fimbriatum. 2 l, Clathrus archeri. 2.20 l, Lycoperdon echinatum. 5.50 l, Entoloma hochstetteri. 9 l, Clathrus ruber. 10.50 l, Phallus indusiatus.

**2021, May 6 Litho. *Perf. 13¼***

**6567** A1946 1.70 l multi .85 .40
*a.* Sheet of 5 + label 4.25 2.00
**6568** A1946 2 l multi 1.00 .50
*a.* Sheet of 5 + label 5.00 2.50
**6569** A1946 2.20 l multi 1.10 .55
*a.* Sheet of 5 + label 5.50 2.75
**6570** A1946 5.50 l multi 2.75 1.40
*a.* Sheet of 5 + label 14.00 7.00
**6571** A1946 9 l multi 4.50 2.25
*a.* Sheet of 5 + label 22.50 11.50
**6572** A1946 10.50 l multi 5.25 2.60
*a.* Sheet of 5 + label 26.50 13.00
*Nos. 6567-6572 (6)* 15.45 7.70

Space Exploration — A1947

Designs: 2.20 l, Spaceflight of Yuri Gagarin (1934-68), first man in space, 60th anniv. 19.50 l, Spaceflight of Dumitru-Dorin Prunariu, first Romanian cosmonaut, 40th anniv., vert.
31.50 l, Prunariu, horiz.

**2021, May 14 Litho. *Perf. 13¼***

| | | | | |
|---|---|---|---|---|
| **6573** | A1947 | 2.20 l multi | 1.10 | .55 |
| *a.* | | Sheet of 5 + label | 5.50 | 2.75 |
| **6574** | A1947 | 19.50 l multi | 9.75 | 5.00 |
| *a.* | | Sheet of 5 + label | 49.00 | 25.00 |

**Souvenir Sheet**

***Perf. 13¾x13¼***

| | | | | |
|---|---|---|---|---|
| **6575** | A1947 | 31.50 l multi | 16.00 | 8.00 |

No. 6575 contains one 52x42mm stamp.

Wives of the Romanian Princes A1948

Designs: 2 l, Lady Mara, wife of Mircea the Elder. 2.20 l, Lady Chiajna (1525-88), wife of Mircea the Shepherd. 5.50 l, Lady Elina (1598-1653), wife of Matei Basarab. 19.50 l, Lady Maria Voichita (1457-1511), wife of Stephen the Great.

**2021, May 21 Litho. *Perf. 13¼***

| | | | | |
|---|---|---|---|---|
| **6576** | A1948 | 2 l multi | 1.00 | .50 |
| *a.* | | Sheet of 4 | 4.00 | 2.00 |
| **6577** | A1948 | 2.20 l multi | 1.10 | .55 |
| *a.* | | Sheet of 4 | 4.50 | 2.25 |
| **6578** | A1948 | 5.50 l multi | 2.75 | 1.40 |
| *a.* | | Sheet of 4 | 11.00 | 5.75 |
| **6579** | A1948 | 19.50 l multi | 9.75 | 5.00 |
| *a.* | | Sheet of 4 | 39.00 | 20.00 |
| | | *Nos. 6576-6579 (4)* | 14.60 | 7.45 |

Nos. 6576-6579 were each printed in sheets of 28 + 7 central labels.

Iasi County Palaces — A1949

Designs: 1.70 l, Rosetti-Roznovanu Palace, Iasi. 2 l, Alexandru I. Cuza Palace, Ruginoasa. 5.50 l, Sturdza Palace, Miclauseni. 19.50 l, Palace of Culture, Iasi.

**2021, June 4 Litho. *Perf. 13¾x13¼***

| | | | | |
|---|---|---|---|---|
| **6580** | A1949 | 1.70 l multi | .85 | .40 |
| *a.* | | Sheet of 5 + label | 4.25 | 2.00 |
| **6581** | A1949 | 2 l multi | 1.00 | .50 |
| *a.* | | Sheet of 5 + label | 5.00 | 2.50 |
| **6582** | A1949 | 5.50 l multi | 2.75 | 1.40 |
| *a.* | | Sheet of 5 + label | 14.00 | 7.00 |
| **6583** | A1949 | 19.50 l multi | 9.50 | 4.75 |
| *a.* | | Sheet of 5 + label | 47.50 | 24.00 |
| | | *Nos. 6580-6583 (4)* | 14.10 | 7.05 |

People and Dogs A1950

Designs: 2 l, Dog and baby. 2.20 l, Guide dog and blind man. 5.50 l, Dog with girl in wheelchair. 19.50 l, Dog and child.

**2021, June 11 Litho. *Perf. 13¼***

| | | | | |
|---|---|---|---|---|
| **6584** | A1950 | 2 l multi | 1.00 | .50 |
| *a.* | | Tete-beche pair | 2.00 | 1.00 |
| *b.* | | Sheet of 4 + 4 labels | 4.00 | 2.00 |
| **6585** | A1950 | 2.20 l multi | 1.10 | .55 |
| *a.* | | Tete-beche pair | 2.25 | 1.10 |
| *b.* | | Sheet of 4 + 4 labels | 4.50 | 2.25 |
| **6586** | A1950 | 5.50 l multi | 2.75 | 1.40 |
| *a.* | | Tete-beche pair | 5.50 | 2.80 |
| *b.* | | Sheet of 4 + 4 labels | 11.00 | 5.75 |
| **6587** | A1950 | 19.50 l multi | 9.50 | 4.75 |
| *a.* | | Tete-beche pair | 19.00 | 9.50 |
| *b.* | | Sheet of 4 + 4 labels | 38.00 | 19.00 |
| | | *Nos. 6584-6587 (4)* | 14.35 | 7.20 |

Tudor Vladimirescu (c. 1780-1821), Leader of 1821 Wallachian Uprising A1951

Design: 31.50 l, Vladimirescu wearing light colored shirt.

**2021, June 22 Litho. *Perf. 13¼***

| | | | | |
|---|---|---|---|---|
| **6588** | A1951 | 9 l multi | 4.50 | 2.25 |
| *a.* | | Sheet of 5 + label | 22.50 | 11.50 |

**Souvenir Sheet**

| | | | | |
|---|---|---|---|---|
| **6589** | A1951 | 31.50 l multi | 15.50 | 7.75 |

No. 6589 contains one 24x33mm stamp. A sheet containing Nos. 6588-6589 was produced in limited quantities.

Ion D. Berindei (1871-1928), Architect — A1952

Berindei and Bucharest buildings he designed: 2 l, Assan House. 7 l, Titulescu House. 9 l, Cantacuzino Palace. 10.50 l, Admiral Vasile Urseanu Astronomical Observatory.

**2021, July 2 Litho. *Perf. 13¼***

| | | | | |
|---|---|---|---|---|
| **6590** | A1952 | 2 l multi | 1.00 | .50 |
| *a.* | | Sheet of 5 + label | 5.00 | 2.50 |
| **6591** | A1952 | 7 l multi | 3.50 | 1.75 |
| *a.* | | Sheet of 5 + label | 17.50 | 8.75 |
| **6592** | A1952 | 9 l multi | 4.50 | 2.25 |
| *a.* | | Sheet of 5 + label | 22.50 | 11.50 |
| **6593** | A1952 | 10.50 l multi | 5.25 | 2.60 |
| *a.* | | Sheet of 5 + label | 26.50 | 13.00 |
| | | *Nos. 6590-6593 (4)* | 14.25 | 7.10 |

Romanian Rulers and Their Seals — A1953

Portrait and seal of: 1.40 l, Petru Cercel (c. 1545-90). 1.50 l, Radu Mihnea (1586-1626). 7 l, Grigore I Ghica (1628-75). 19.50 l, Constantin Brâncoveanu (1654-1714).
31.50 l, Obverse and reverse of chrysobull of Grigore I Ghica, vert.

**2021, July 15 Litho. *Perf. 13¼***

| | | | | |
|---|---|---|---|---|
| **6594** | A1953 | 1.40 l multi | .70 | .35 |
| *a.* | | Sheet of 5 + label | 3.50 | 1.75 |
| **6595** | A1953 | 1.50 l multi | .75 | .35 |
| *a.* | | Sheet of 5 + label | 3.75 | 1.75 |
| **6596** | A1953 | 7 l multi | 3.50 | 1.75 |
| *a.* | | Sheet of 5 + label | 17.50 | 8.75 |
| **6597** | A1953 | 19.50 l multi | 9.50 | 4.75 |
| *a.* | | Sheet of 5 + label | 47.50 | 24.00 |
| | | *Nos. 6594-6597 (4)* | 14.45 | 7.20 |

**Souvenir Sheet**

***Imperf***

| | | | | |
|---|---|---|---|---|
| **6598** | A1953 | 31.50 l multi + label | 15.50 | 7.75 |

A sheet containing imperforate examples of Nos. 6594-6597 was printed in limited quantities.

2020 Summer Olympics, Tokyo — A1954

Designs: 1.70 l, Soccer. 2 l, Women's rowing. 2.20 l, Swimming. 7 l, Discus. 9 l, Women's tennis. 10.50 l, Table tennis.
31.50 l, Fencing, horiz.

**2021, July 23 Litho. *Perf. 13¼***

| | | | | |
|---|---|---|---|---|
| **6599** | A1954 | 1.70 l multi | .85 | .40 |
| *a.* | | Sheet of 5 + label | 4.25 | 2.00 |
| **6600** | A1954 | 2 l multi | 1.00 | .50 |
| *a.* | | Sheet of 5 + label | 5.00 | 2.50 |
| **6601** | A1954 | 2.20 l multi | 1.10 | .55 |
| *a.* | | Sheet of 5 + label | 5.50 | 2.75 |
| **6602** | A1954 | 7 l multi | 3.50 | 1.75 |
| *a.* | | Sheet of 5 + label | 17.50 | 8.75 |
| **6603** | A1954 | 9 l multi | 4.50 | 2.25 |
| *a.* | | Sheet of 5 + label | 22.50 | 11.50 |
| **6604** | A1954 | 10.50 l multi | 5.25 | 2.60 |
| *a.* | | Sheet of 5 + label | 26.50 | 13.00 |
| | | *Nos. 6599-6604 (6)* | 16.20 | 8.05 |

**Souvenir Sheet**

| | | | | |
|---|---|---|---|---|
| **6605** | A1954 | 31.50 l multi | 15.50 | 7.75 |

No. 6605 contains one 48x33mm stamp. The 2020 Summer Olympics were postponed until 2021 because of the COVID-19 pandemic.

Romanian Membership in UNESCO, 65th Anniv. — A1955

Wildlife of the Danube Delta UNESCO World Heritage Site: 1.40 l, Ciconia nigra. 1.50 l, Troglodytes troglodytes. 7 l, Castor fiber. 19.50 l, Pelecanus crispus.

**2021, July 27 Litho. *Perf. 13¼***

| | | | | |
|---|---|---|---|---|
| **6606** | A1955 | 1.40 l multi | .70 | .35 |
| *a.* | | Sheet of 5 + label | 3.50 | 1.75 |
| **6607** | A1955 | 1.50 l multi | .75 | .35 |
| *a.* | | Sheet of 5 + label | 3.75 | 1.75 |
| **6608** | A1955 | 7 l multi | 3.50 | 1.75 |
| *a.* | | Sheet of 5 + label | 17.50 | 8.75 |
| **6609** | A1955 | 19.50 l multi | 9.50 | 4.75 |
| *a.* | | Sheet of 5 + label | 47.50 | 24.00 |
| | | *Nos. 6606-6609 (4)* | 14.45 | 7.20 |

Neagoe Basarab (1482-1521), Prince of Wallachia A1957

**2021, Aug. 5 Litho. *Perf. 13¼***

| | | | | |
|---|---|---|---|---|
| **6611** | A1957 | 9 l multi | 4.50 | 2.25 |
| *a.* | | Sheet of 5 + label | 22.50 | 11.50 |

**Souvenir Sheet**

| | | | | |
|---|---|---|---|---|
| **6612** | A1957 | 31.50 l Basarab, diff. | 15.00 | 7.50 |

No. 6612 contains one 27x42mm stamp.

Desert Animals — A1958

Designs: 2 l, Camelus dromedarius. 7 l, Pseudotrapelus sinaitus. 9 l, Vulpes zerda, vert. 10.50 l, Addax nasomaculatus, vert.

**2021, Aug. 12 Litho. *Perf. 13¼***

| | | | | |
|---|---|---|---|---|
| **6613** | A1958 | 2 l multi | .95 | .50 |
| *a.* | | Sheet of 5 + label | 4.75 | 2.50 |
| **6614** | A1958 | 7 l multi | 3.50 | 1.75 |
| *a.* | | Sheet of 5 + label | 17.50 | 8.75 |
| **6615** | A1958 | 9 l multi | 4.50 | 2.25 |
| *a.* | | Sheet of 5 + label | 22.50 | 11.50 |
| **6616** | A1958 | 10.50 l multi | 5.00 | 2.50 |
| *a.* | | Sheet of 5 + label | 25.00 | 12.50 |
| | | *Nos. 6613-6616 (4)* | 13.95 | 7.00 |

Romanian Medalists at the 2020 Summer Olympics — A1959

Designs: 2 l, Ancuta Bodnar and Simona Radis, women's rowing gold medalists. 7 l, Ana-Maria Popescu, women's fencing silver medalist. 9 l, Marius Cozmiuc and Ciprian Tudosa, men's rowing silver medalists. 10.50 l, Cosmin Pascari, Stefan Berariu, Mugurel Semciuc, and Mihaita Tiganescu, men's rowing silver medalists.
31.50 l, Bodnar and Radis with gold medals.

**2021, Aug. 18 Litho. *Perf. 13¼***

| | | | | |
|---|---|---|---|---|
| **6617** | A1959 | 2 l multi | .95 | .50 |
| *a.* | | Sheet of 5 + label | 4.75 | 2.50 |
| **6618** | A1959 | 7 l multi | 3.50 | 1.75 |
| *a.* | | Sheet of 5 + label | 17.50 | 8.75 |
| **6619** | A1959 | 9 l multi | 4.50 | 2.25 |
| *a.* | | Sheet of 5 + label | 22.50 | 11.50 |
| **6620** | A1959 | 10.50 l multi | 5.00 | 2.50 |
| *a.* | | Sheet of 5 + label | 25.00 | 12.50 |
| | | *Nos. 6617-6620 (4)* | 13.95 | 7.00 |

**Souvenir Sheet**

***Perf. 13¾x13¼***

| | | | | |
|---|---|---|---|---|
| **6621** | A1959 | 31.50 l multi | 15.00 | 7.50 |

No. 6621 contains one 52x42mm stamp. The 2020 Summer Olympics were postponed until 2021 because of the COVID-19 pandemic.

Flamingos A1960

Designs: 1.40 l, Phoenicoparrus andinus. 1.70 l, Phoenicopterus chilensis. 7 l, Phoeniconaias minor. 19.50 l, Phoenicopterus roseus.

**2021, Aug. 25 Litho. *Perf. 13¼***

| | | | | |
|---|---|---|---|---|
| **6622** | A1960 | 1.40 l multi | .70 | .35 |
| *a.* | | Tete-beche pair | 1.40 | .70 |
| *b.* | | Sheet of 5 + label | 3.50 | 1.75 |
| **6623** | A1960 | 1.70 l multi | .85 | .40 |
| *a.* | | Tete-beche pair | 1.75 | .80 |
| *b.* | | Sheet of 5 + label | 4.25 | 2.00 |
| **6624** | A1960 | 7 l multi | 3.50 | 1.75 |
| *a.* | | Tete-beche pair | 7.00 | 3.50 |
| *b.* | | Sheet of 5 + label | 17.50 | 8.75 |
| **6625** | A1960 | 19.50 l multi | 9.50 | 4.75 |
| *a.* | | Tete-beche pair | 19.00 | 9.50 |
| *b.* | | Sheet of 5 + label | 47.50 | 24.00 |
| | | *Nos. 6622-6625 (4)* | 14.55 | 7.25 |

A sheet containing imperforate examples of Nos. 6622-6625 was printed in limited quantities.

Targu Mures A1961

Arms of Targu Mures and: 1.50 l, Administrative Palace. 2 l, Medieval Citadel. 5.50 l, Palace of Culture. 19.50 l, Bolyai Farkas High School.

**2021, Sept. 3 Litho. *Perf. 13¼***

| No. | Type | Description | Unused | Used |
|---|---|---|---|---|
| **6626** | A1961 | 1.50 l multi | .70 | .35 |
| *a.* | | Sheet of 5 + label | 3.50 | 1.75 |
| **6627** | A1961 | 2 l multi | .95 | .45 |
| *a.* | | Sheet of 5 + label | 4.75 | 2.25 |
| **6628** | A1961 | 5.50 l multi | 2.60 | 1.30 |
| *a.* | | Sheet of 5 + label | 13.00 | 6.50 |
| **6629** | A1961 | 19.50 l multi | 9.25 | 4.75 |
| *a.* | | Sheet of 5 + label | 46.50 | 24.00 |
| | | *Nos. 6626-6629 (4)* | 13.50 | 6.85 |

European Year of Rail — A1962

Designs: 1.40 l, Resicza No. 2 steam locomotive. 2 l, Train at Henri Coanda Airport Railroad Station. 5.50 l, 060 DA Diesel locomotive. 19.50 l, 060 EA electric locomotive.

**2021, Sept. 10 Litho. *Perf. 13¼***

| No. | Type | Description | Unused | Used |
|---|---|---|---|---|
| **6630** | A1962 | 1.40 l multi | .65 | .30 |
| *a.* | | Sheet of 5 + label | 3.25 | 1.50 |
| **6631** | A1962 | 2 l multi | .95 | .45 |
| *a.* | | Sheet of 5 + label | 4.75 | 2.25 |
| **6632** | A1962 | 5.50 l multi | 2.60 | 1.30 |
| *a.* | | Sheet of 5 + label | 13.00 | 6.50 |
| **6633** | A1962 | 19.50 l multi | 9.25 | 4.75 |
| *a.* | | Sheet of 5 + label | 46.50 | 24.00 |
| | | *Nos. 6630-6633 (4)* | 13.45 | 6.80 |

Nos. 6630-6633 were each printed in sheets of 28 + 7 central labels. A sheet containing imperforate examples of Nos. 6630-6633 was printed in limited quantities.

Eduard Novak, Cycling Silver Medalist at 2020 Summer Paralympics A1963

Alexandru Bologa, Judo Bronze Medalist at 2020 Summer Paralympics A1964

**2021, Sept. 16 Litho. *Perf. 13¼***

| No. | Type | Description | Unused | Used |
|---|---|---|---|---|
| **6634** | A1963 | 9 l multi | 4.25 | 2.10 |
| *a.* | | Sheet of 5 + label | 21.50 | 10.50 |
| **6635** | A1964 | 9 l multi | 4.25 | 2.10 |
| *a.* | | Sheet of 5 + label | 21.50 | 10.50 |

The 2020 Summer Paralympics were postponed until 2021 because of the COVID-19 pandemic.

Turtles — A1965

Designs: 1.70 l, Geochelone elegans. 2 l, Mauremys sinensis. 5.50 l, Testudo graeca ibera. 19.50 l, Testudo horsfieldii.

**2021, Sept. 22 Litho. *Perf. 13¼***

| No. | Type | Description | Unused | Used |
|---|---|---|---|---|
| **6636** | A1965 | 1.70 l multi | .80 | .40 |
| *a.* | | Tete-beche pair | 1.60 | .80 |
| *b.* | | Sheet of 5 + label | 4.00 | 2.00 |
| **6637** | A1965 | 2 l multi | .95 | .45 |
| *a.* | | Tete-beche pair | 1.90 | .90 |
| *b.* | | Sheet of 5 + label | 4.75 | 2.25 |
| **6638** | A1965 | 5.50 l multi | 2.60 | 1.30 |
| *a.* | | Tete-beche pair | 5.25 | 2.60 |
| *b.* | | Sheet of 5 + label | 13.00 | 6.50 |
| **6639** | A1965 | 19.50 l multi | 9.25 | 4.75 |
| *a.* | | Tete-beche pair | 18.50 | 9.50 |
| *b.* | | Sheet of 5 + label | 46.50 | 24.00 |
| | | *Nos. 6636-6639 (4)* | 13.60 | 6.90 |

Items in Peles Castle Collection A1966

Designs: 1.40 l, Vase made by Emile Gallé. 1.50 l, Tea set made by Goldschmidt Workshop. 3.40 l, Cup made by Jacob Tostrup Workshop. 7 l, Silver box made by Christofle Workshop. 9 l, Carafe made by Edmund Wollenweber Workshop. 10.50 l, Silver figurine depicting a queen.

31.50 l, Fruit bowl made by Salviati Workshop.

**2021, Oct. 5 Litho. *Perf. 13¼x13¾***

| No. | Type | Description | Unused | Used |
|---|---|---|---|---|
| **6640** | A1966 | 1.40 l multi | .65 | .35 |
| *a.* | | Sheet of 5 + label | 3.25 | 1.75 |
| **6641** | A1966 | 1.50 l multi | .70 | .35 |
| *a.* | | Sheet of 5 + label | 3.50 | 1.75 |
| **6642** | A1966 | 3.40 l multi | 1.60 | .80 |
| *a.* | | Sheet of 5 + label | 8.00 | 4.00 |
| **6643** | A1966 | 7 l multi | 3.25 | 1.60 |
| *a.* | | Sheet of 5 + label | 16.50 | 8.00 |
| **6644** | A1966 | 9 l multi | 4.25 | 2.10 |
| *a.* | | Sheet of 5 + label | 21.50 | 10.50 |
| **6645** | A1966 | 10.50 l multi | 5.00 | 2.50 |
| *a.* | | Sheet of 5 + label | 25.00 | 12.50 |
| | | *Nos. 6640-6645 (6)* | 15.45 | 7.70 |

**Souvenir Sheet**

***Perf. 13¾x13¼***

| No. | Type | Description | Unused | Used |
|---|---|---|---|---|
| **6646** | A1966 | 31.50 l multi | 15.00 | 7.50 |

No. 6646 contains one 52x84mm stamp. A sheet containing imperforate examples of Nos. 6640-6645 was printed in limited quantities.

Pigeons A1967

Designs: 1.70 l, Ptilinopus jambu. 2 l, Goura victoria. 5.50 l, Chalcophaps indica. 19.50 l, Caloenas nicobarica.

**2021, Oct. 14 Litho. *Perf. 13¼***

| No. | Type | Description | Unused | Used |
|---|---|---|---|---|
| **6647** | A1967 | 1.70 l multi | .80 | .40 |
| *a.* | | Sheet of 5 + label | 4.00 | 2.00 |
| **6648** | A1967 | 2 l multi | .95 | .45 |
| *a.* | | Sheet of 5 + label | 4.75 | 2.25 |
| **6649** | A1967 | 5.50 l multi | 2.60 | 1.30 |
| *a.* | | Sheet of 5 + label | 13.00 | 6.50 |
| **6650** | A1967 | 19.50 l multi | 9.25 | 4.50 |
| *a.* | | Sheet of 5 + label | 46.50 | 22.50 |
| | | *Nos. 6647-6650 (4)* | 13.60 | 6.65 |

A1968

King Michael (1921-2017) and Peles Castle — A1969

**2021, Oct. 25 Litho. *Perf. 13¼***

| No. | Type | Description | Unused | Used |
|---|---|---|---|---|
| **6651** | A1968 | 9 l multi | 4.25 | 2.10 |
| *a.* | | Sheet of 5 + label | 21.50 | 10.50 |
| **6652** | A1969 | 9 l multi | 4.25 | 2.10 |
| *a.* | | Sheet of 5 + label | 21.50 | 10.50 |
| *b.* | | Pair, #6651-6652 | 8.50 | 4.25 |
| *c.* | | Souvenir sheet of 2, #6651-6652, + 2 labels | 8.50 | 4.25 |

Ion Cantacuzino (1863-1934), Bacteriologist — A1971

**2021, Nov. 5 Litho. *Perf. 13¼***

| No. | Type | Description | Unused | Used |
|---|---|---|---|---|
| **6654** | A1971 | 9 l multi | 4.25 | 2.10 |
| *a.* | | Sheet of 5 + label | 21.50 | 10.50 |

Cantacuzino National Medical-Military Research and Development Institute, cent.

60th Birthday of Nadia Comaneci, Gymnastics Gold Medalist at 1976 and 1980 Summer Olympics — A1972

**2021, Nov. 12 Litho. *Perf. 13¼***

| No. | Type | Description | Unused | Used |
|---|---|---|---|---|
| **6655** | A1972 | 9 l multi | 4.25 | 2.10 |
| *a.* | | Sheet of 5 + label | 21.50 | 10.50 |

**Souvenir Sheet**

***Imperf***

| No. | Type | Description | Unused | Used |
|---|---|---|---|---|
| **6656** | A1972 | 31.50 l Comaneci, diff. | 14.50 | 7.25 |

No. 6656 contains one 28x43mm stamp.

Christmas A1973

Designs: 2.60 l, Adoration of the Magi. 31.50 l, Madonna and Child with Angels.

**2021, Nov. 19 Litho. *Perf. 13¼***

| No. | Type | Description | Unused | Used |
|---|---|---|---|---|
| **6657** | A1973 | 2.60 l multi | 1.25 | .60 |
| *a.* | | Sheet of 8 + central label | 10.00 | 5.00 |

**Souvenir Sheet**

| No. | Type | Description | Unused | Used |
|---|---|---|---|---|
| **6658** | A1973 | 31.50 l multi | 14.50 | 7.25 |

A souvenir sheet containing imperforate examples of Nos. 6657-6658 was printed in limited quantities.

Viticulture A1974

Designs: 2 l, Zghihara grapes and wine pitcher. 9 l, Rara Neagra grapes and flask.

**2021, Nov. 24 Litho. *Perf. 13¼***

| No. | Type | Description | Unused | Used |
|---|---|---|---|---|
| **6659** | A1974 | 2 l multi | .95 | .45 |
| *a.* | | Sheet of 5 + label | 4.75 | 2.25 |
| **6660** | A1974 | 9 l multi | 4.25 | 2.10 |
| *a.* | | Sheet of 5 + label | 21.50 | 10.50 |

See Moldova Nos.

Arch of Triumph, Bucharest, 80th Anniv. — A1975

**2021, Dec. 1 Litho. *Perf. 13¼***

| No. | Type | Description | Unused | Used |
|---|---|---|---|---|
| **6661** | A1975 | 10 l multi | 4.75 | 2.40 |
| *a.* | | Sheet of 5 + 10 labels | 24.00 | 24.00 |

No. 6661 was printed in sheets of 32 + 8 central labels.

Politehnica Timisoara Sports Society, Cent. — A1976

**2021, Dec. 2 Litho. *Perf. 13¼***

| No. | Type | Description | Unused | Used |
|---|---|---|---|---|
| **6662** | A1976 | 10 l multi | 4.75 | 2.40 |
| *a.* | | Tete-beche pair | 9.50 | 4.80 |
| *b.* | | Sheet of 6 + 6 labels | 28.50 | 14.50 |

Horses A1977

Various depictions of adult and juvenile horses. Nos. 6664-6666 are horiz.

**2021, Dec. 3 Litho. *Perf. 13¼***

| No. | Type | Description | Unused | Used |
|---|---|---|---|---|
| **6663** | A1977 | 2.60 l multi | 1.25 | .60 |
| *a.* | | Sheet of 5 + label | 6.25 | 3.00 |
| **6664** | A1977 | 4.50 l multi | 2.10 | 1.10 |
| *a.* | | Sheet of 5 + label | 10.50 | 5.50 |
| **6665** | A1977 | 6.50 l multi | 3.00 | 1.50 |
| *a.* | | Sheet of 5 + label | 15.00 | 7.50 |
| **6666** | A1977 | 16 l multi | 7.50 | 3.75 |
| *a.* | | Sheet of 5 + label | 37.50 | 19.00 |
| | | *Nos. 6663-6666 (4)* | 13.85 | 6.95 |

Romanian Kings as Hunters — A1978

Peles and Foisor Castles stained-glass windows and: 3 l, King Carol I (1839-1914). 6.50 l, King Ferdinand (1867-1927). 10 l, King Carol II (1893-1953). 10.50 l, King Michael (1921-2017).

**2021, Dec. 15 Litho. *Perf. 13¼***

| No. | Type | Description | Unused | Used |
|---|---|---|---|---|
| **6667** | A1978 | 3 l multi | 1.40 | .70 |
| *a.* | | Sheet of 5 + label | 7.00 | 3.50 |
| **6668** | A1978 | 6.50 l multi | 3.00 | 1.50 |
| *a.* | | Sheet of 5 + label | 15.00 | 7.50 |
| **6669** | A1978 | 10 l multi | 4.75 | 2.40 |
| *a.* | | Sheet of 5 + label | 24.00 | 12.00 |
| **6670** | A1978 | 10.50 l multi | 5.00 | 2.50 |
| *a.* | | Sheet of 5 + label | 25.00 | 12.50 |
| | | *Nos. 6667-6670 (4)* | 14.15 | 7.10 |

Nos. 6667-6670 were each printed in sheets of 28 + 7 central labels. A souvenir sheet of 4 containing imperforate examples of Nos. 6667-6670 was printed in limited quantities.

## SEMI-POSTAL STAMPS

Queen Elizabeth Spinning — SP1

*Perf. 11½, 11½x13½*

**1906, Jan. 14 Typo. Unwmk.**

| | | | | |
|---|---|---|---|---|
| **B1** | SP1 | 3b (+ 7b) brown | 6.00 | 3.75 |
| **B2** | SP1 | 5b (+ 10b) lt grn | 6.00 | 3.75 |
| **B3** | SP1 | 10b (+ 10b) rose red | 29.00 | 11.00 |
| **B4** | SP1 | 15b (+ 10b) violet | 20.00 | 7.50 |
| | | *Nos. B1-B4 (4)* | 61.00 | 26.00 |

The Queen Weaving — SP2

**1906, Mar. 18**

| | | | | |
|---|---|---|---|---|
| **B5** | SP2 | 3b (+ 7b) org brn | 6.00 | 3.75 |
| **B6** | SP2 | 5b (+ 10b) bl grn | 6.00 | 3.75 |
| **B7** | SP2 | 10b (+ 10b) car | 29.00 | 11.00 |
| **B8** | SP2 | 15b (+ 10b) red vio | 20.00 | 7.50 |
| | | *Nos. B5-B8 (4)* | 61.00 | 26.00 |

Queen as War Nurse SP3

**1906, Mar. 23** ***Perf. 11½, 13½x11½***

| | | | | |
|---|---|---|---|---|
| **B9** | SP3 | 3b (+ 7b) org brn | 6.00 | 3.75 |
| **B10** | SP3 | 5b (+ 10b) bl grn | 6.00 | 3.75 |
| **B11** | SP3 | 10b (+ 10b) car | 29.00 | 11.00 |
| **B12** | SP3 | 15b (+ 10b) red vio | 20.00 | 7.50 |
| | | *Nos. B9-B12 (4)* | 61.00 | 26.00 |
| | | *Nos. B1-B12 (12)* | 183.00 | 78.00 |

Booklet panes of 4 exist of Nos. B1-B3, B5-B7, B9-B12.

Counterfeits of Nos. B1-B12 are plentiful. Examples of Nos. B1-B12 with smooth, even gum are counterfeits.

SP4

**1906, Aug. 4** ***Perf. 12***

| | | | | |
|---|---|---|---|---|
| **B13** | SP4 | 3b (+ 7b) ol brn, buff & bl | 3.25 | 1.50 |
| **B14** | SP4 | 5b (+ 10b) grn, rose & buff | 3.25 | 1.50 |
| **B15** | SP4 | 10b (+ 10b) rose red, buff & bl | 5.00 | 3.00 |
| **B16** | SP4 | 15b (+ 10b) vio, buff & bl | 13.00 | 3.75 |
| | | *Nos. B13-B16 (4)* | 24.50 | 9.75 |

Guardian Angel Bringing Poor to Crown Princess Marie SP5

**1907, Feb. Engr.** ***Perf. 11***

**Center in Brown**

| | | | | |
|---|---|---|---|---|
| **B17** | SP5 | 3b (+ 7b) org brn | 4.00 | 1.50 |
| **B18** | SP5 | 5b (+ 10b) dk grn | 4.00 | 1.50 |
| **B19** | SP5 | 10b (+ 10b) dk car | 4.00 | 1.50 |
| **B20** | SP5 | 15b (+ 10b) dl vio | 4.00 | 1.50 |
| | | *Nos. B17-B20 (4)* | 16.00 | 6.00 |

Nos. B1-B20 were sold for more than face value. The surtax, shown in parenthesis, was for charitable purposes.

Map of Romania SP9

Stephen the Great SP10

Michael the Brave SP11

Kings Carol I and Ferdinand SP12

Adam Clisi Monument — SP13

**1927, Mar. 15 Typo.** ***Perf. 13½***

| | | | | |
|---|---|---|---|---|
| **B21** | SP9 | 1 l + 9 l lt vio | 4.25 | 1.60 |
| **B22** | SP10 | 2 l + 8 l Prus grn | 4.25 | 1.60 |
| **B23** | SP11 | 3 l + 7 l dp rose | 4.25 | 1.60 |
| **B24** | SP12 | 5 l + 5 l dp bl | 4.25 | 1.60 |
| **B25** | SP13 | 6 l + 4 l ol grn | 6.25 | 2.50 |
| | | *Nos. B21-B25 (5)* | 23.25 | 8.90 |

50th anniv. of the Royal Geographical Society. The surtax was for the benefit of that society. The stamps were valid for postage only from 3/15-4/14.

Boy Scouts in Camp — SP15

The Rescue — SP16

Prince Nicholas Chief Scout — SP16a

Designs: 3 l+3 l, Swearing in a Tenderfoot. 6 l+6 l, King Carol II in Scout's Uniform.

**1931, July 15 Photo. Wmk. 225**

| | | | | |
|---|---|---|---|---|
| **B26** | SP15 | 1 l + 1 l car rose | 3.75 | 2.50 |
| **B27** | SP16 | 2 l + 2 l dp grn | 5.00 | 3.00 |
| **B28** | SP15 | 3 l + 3 l ultra | 6.00 | 3.00 |
| **B29** | SP16a | 4 l + 4 l ol gray | 7.50 | 8.00 |
| **B30** | SP16a | 6 l + 6 l red brn | 10.00 | 8.00 |
| | | *Nos. B26-B30 (5)* | 32.25 | 24.50 |

The surtax was for the benefit of the Boy Scout organization.

### Boy Scout Jamboree Issue

Scouts in Camp SP20

Semaphore Signaling SP21

Trailing — SP22

Camp Fire — SP23

King Carol II — SP24

King Carol II and Prince Michael — SP25

**1932, June 8 Wmk. 230**

| | | | | |
|---|---|---|---|---|
| **B31** | SP20 | 25b + 25b pck grn | 3.00 | 1.10 |
| **B32** | SP21 | 50b + 50b brt bl | 4.00 | 2.25 |
| **B33** | SP22 | 1 l + 1 l ol grn | 4.50 | 3.25 |
| **B34** | SP23 | 2 l + 2 l org red | 7.50 | 4.50 |
| **B35** | SP24 | 3 l + 3 l Prus bl | 14.00 | 9.00 |
| **B36** | SP25 | 6 l + 6 l blk brn | 16.00 | 11.50 |
| | | *Nos. B31-B36 (6)* | 49.00 | 31.60 |

For overprints see Nos. B44-B49.

Tuberculosis Sanatorium — SP26

Memorial Tablet to Postal Employees Who Died in World War I — SP27

Carmen Sylva Convalescent Home — SP28

**1932, Nov. 1**

| | | | | |
|---|---|---|---|---|
| **B37** | SP26 | 4 l + 1 l dk grn | 5.00 | 4.00 |
| **B38** | SP27 | 6 l + 1 l chocolate | 5.50 | 4.75 |
| **B39** | SP28 | 10 l + 1 l dp bl | 10.00 | 8.00 |
| | | *Nos. B37-B39 (3)* | 20.50 | 16.75 |

The surtax was given to a fund for the employees of the postal and telegraph services.

### Philatelic Exhibition Issue

Souvenir Sheet

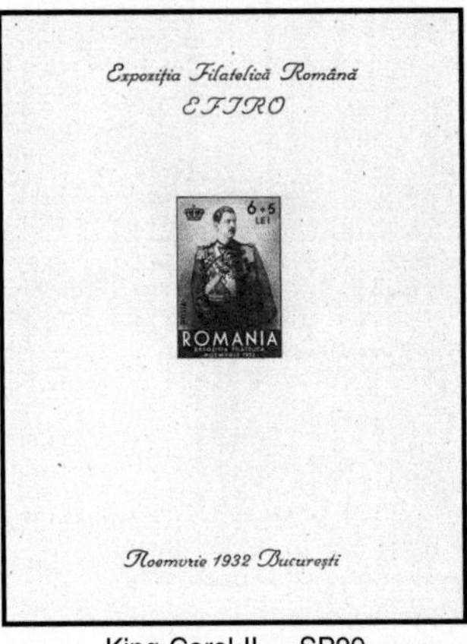

King Carol II — SP29

**1932, Nov. 20 Unwmk.** ***Imperf.***

| | | | | |
|---|---|---|---|---|
| **B40** | SP29 | 6 l + 5 l dk ol grn | 50.00 | 50.00 |

Intl. Phil. Exhib. at Bucharest, Nov. 20-24, 1932. Each holder of a ticket of admission to the exhibition could buy an example of No. B40. The ticket cost 20 lei.

Roadside Shrine SP31

Woman Spinning SP33

Woman Weaving SP32

**1934, Apr. 16 Wmk. 230** ***Perf. 13½***

| | | | | |
|---|---|---|---|---|
| **B41** | SP31 | 1 l + 1 l dk brn | 1.00 | .90 |
| **B42** | SP32 | 2 l + 1 l blue | 1.25 | 1.10 |
| **B43** | SP33 | 3 l + 1 l slate grn | 1.75 | 1.50 |
| | | *Nos. B41-B43 (3)* | 4.00 | 3.50 |

Weaving Exposition.

### Boy Scout Mamaia Jamboree Issue

Semi-Postal Stamps of 1932 Overprinted in Black or Gold

**1934, July 8**

| | | | | |
|---|---|---|---|---|
| **B44** | SP20 | 25b + 25b pck grn | 3.75 | 2.50 |
| **B45** | SP21 | 50b + 50b brt bl (G) | 5.00 | 3.00 |
| **B46** | SP22 | 1 l + 1 l ol grn | 6.00 | 4.75 |
| **B47** | SP23 | 2 l + 2 l org red | 7.50 | 5.50 |
| **B48** | SP24 | 3 l + 3 l Prus bl (G) | 16.00 | 7.00 |
| **B49** | SP25 | 6 l + 6 l blk brn (G) | 18.00 | 9.50 |
| | | *Nos. B44-B49 (6)* | 56.25 | 32.25 |

Sea Scout Saluting SP34

Scout Bugler SP35

Sea and Land Scouts SP36

King Carol II — SP37

Sea, Land and Girl Scouts — SP38

**1935, June 8**

| No. | Type | Description | Unused | Used |
|---|---|---|---|---|
| **B50** | SP34 | 25b ol blk | 1.25 | 1.00 |
| **B51** | SP35 | 1 l violet | 2.75 | 2.25 |
| **B52** | SP36 | 2 l green | 3.50 | 3.00 |
| **B53** | SP37 | 6 l + 1 l red brn | 5.00 | 4.50 |
| **B54** | SP38 | 10 l + 2 l dk ultra | 14.00 | 13.00 |
| | | *Nos. B50-B54 (5)* | 26.50 | 23.75 |

Fifth anniversary of accession of King Carol II, and a national sports meeting held June 8. Surtax aided the Boy Scouts.

Nos. B50-B54 exist imperf. Value $250.

King Carol II — SP39

**1936, May**

| No. | Type | Description | Unused | Used |
|---|---|---|---|---|
| **B55** | SP39 | 6 l + 1 l rose car | .75 | .55 |

Bucharest Exhibition and 70th anniversary of the dynasty. Exists imperf. Value $125

Girl of Oltenia — SP40

Girl of Saliste — SP42

Youth from Gorj — SP44

Designs: 1 l+1 l, Girl of Banat. 3 l+1 l, Girl of Hateg. 6 l+3 l, Girl of Neamt. 10 l+5 l, Youth and girl of Bucovina.

**1936, June 8**

| No. | Type | Description | Unused | Used |
|---|---|---|---|---|
| **B56** | SP40 | 50b + 50b brown | .60 | .60 |
| **B57** | SP40 | 1 l + 1 l violet | .60 | .60 |
| **B58** | SP42 | 2 l + 1 l Prus grn | .60 | *.70* |
| **B59** | SP42 | 3 l + 1 l car rose | .60 | *.90* |
| **B60** | SP44 | 4 l + 2 l red org | 1.00 | .90 |
| **B61** | SP40 | 6 l + 3 l ol gray | 1.00 | *1.20* |
| **B62** | SP42 | 10 l + 5 l brt bl | 2.25 | *2.40* |
| | | *Nos. B56-B62 (7)* | 6.65 | *7.30* |

6th anniv. of accession of King Carol II. The surtax was for child welfare. Exist imperf. Value $300, unused or used.

Insignia of Boy Scouts SP47 SP48

Jamboree Emblem — SP49

**1936, Aug. 20**

| No. | Type | Description | Unused | Used |
|---|---|---|---|---|
| **B63** | SP47 | 1 l + 1 l brt bl | 3.00 | *5.25* |
| **B64** | SP48 | 3 l + 3 l ol gray | 4.50 | *5.25* |
| **B65** | SP49 | 6 l + 6 l car rose | 6.00 | *5.25* |
| | | *Nos. B63-B65 (3)* | 13.50 | *15.75* |

Boy Scout Jamboree at Brasov (Kronstadt). Exist imperf. Value $350, unused or used.

Submarine "Delfinul" SP50

Designs: 3 l+2 l, Training ship "Mircea." 6 l+3 l, Steamship "S.M.R."

**1936, Oct.**

| No. | Type | Description | Unused | Used |
|---|---|---|---|---|
| **B66** | SP50 | 1 l + 1 l pur | 2.75 | 2.50 |
| **B67** | SP50 | 3 l + 2 l ultra | 2.50 | *3.00* |
| **B68** | SP50 | 6 l + 3 l car rose | 3.50 | *4.25* |
| | | *Nos. B66-B68 (3)* | 8.75 | *9.75* |

Marine Exhibition at Bucharest. Exist imperf. Value $325, unused or used.

Soccer SP53

Swimming SP54

Throwing the Javelin — SP55

Skiing — SP56

King Carol II Hunting — SP57

Rowing SP58

Horsemanship SP59

Founding of the U.F.S.R. SP60

**1937, June 8 Wmk. 230 *Perf. 13½***

| No. | Type | Description | Unused | Used |
|---|---|---|---|---|
| **B69** | SP53 | 25b + 25b ol blk | 1.00 | .35 |
| **B70** | SP54 | 50b + 50b brown | 1.00 | .45 |
| **B71** | SP55 | 1 l + 50b violet | 1.20 | .50 |
| **B72** | SP56 | 2 l + 1 l slate grn | 1.50 | .55 |
| **B73** | SP57 | 3 l + 1 l rose lake | 2.20 | .70 |
| **B74** | SP58 | 4 l + 1 l red org | 3.60 | 1.10 |
| **B75** | SP59 | 6 l + 2 l dp claret | 4.25 | 1.90 |
| **B76** | SP60 | 10 l + 4 l brt blue | 5.25 | 2.25 |
| | | *Nos. B69-B76 (8)* | 20.00 | 7.80 |

25th anniversary of the Federation of Romanian Sports Clubs (U.F.S.R.); 7th anniversary of the accession of King Carol II.

Exist imperf. Value $200, unused or used.

Start of Race — SP61

Javelin Thrower — SP62

Designs: 4 l+1 l, Hurdling. 6 l+1 l, Finish of race. 10 l+1 l, High jump.

**1937, Sept. 1 Wmk. 230 *Perf. 13½***

| No. | Type | Description | Unused | Used |
|---|---|---|---|---|
| **B77** | SP61 | 1 l + 1 l purple | .75 | *.90* |
| **B78** | SP62 | 2 l + 1 l green | .95 | *1.25* |
| **B79** | SP61 | 4 l + 1 l vermilion | 1.25 | *1.75* |
| **B80** | SP62 | 6 l + 1 l maroon | 1.40 | *1.90* |
| **B81** | SP61 | 10 l + 1 l brt bl | 4.25 | 3.50 |
| | | *Nos. B77-B81 (5)* | 8.60 | *9.30* |

8th Balkan Games, Bucharest. Exist imperf. Value $200, unused or used.

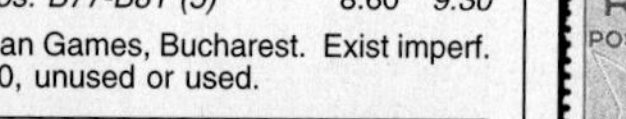
**Catalogue values for unused stamps in this section, from this point to the end of the section, are for Never Hinged items.**

King Carol II — SP66

**1938, May 24**

| No. | Type | Description | Unused | Used |
|---|---|---|---|---|
| **B82** | SP66 | 6 l + 1 l deep magenta | 1.50 | .45 |

Bucharest Exhibition (for local products), May 19-June 19, celebrating 20th anniversary of the union of Rumanian provinces.

Exists imperf. Value $200, unused or used.

Dimitrie Cantemir — SP67

Maria Doamna — SP68

Mircea the Great SP69

Constantine Brancoveanu SP70

Stephen the Great — SP71

Prince Cuza — SP72

Michael the Brave — SP73

Queen Elizabeth — SP74

King Carol II — SP75

King Ferdinand I — SP76

King Carol I — SP77

**1938, June 8 *Perf. 13½***

| No. | Type | Description | Unused | Used |
|---|---|---|---|---|
| **B83** | SP67 | 25b + 25b ol blk | .80 | .35 |
| **B84** | SP68 | 50b + 50b brn | 1.25 | .35 |
| **B85** | SP69 | 1 l + 1 l blk vio | 1.25 | .35 |
| **B86** | SP70 | 2 l + 2 l dk yel grn | 1.40 | .35 |
| **B87** | SP71 | 3 l + 2 l dp mag | 1.40 | .35 |
| **B88** | SP72 | 4 l + 2 l scarlet | 1.40 | .35 |
| **B89** | SP73 | 6 l + 2 l vio brn | 1.50 | .45 |
| **B90** | SP74 | 7.50 l gray bl | 1.75 | .60 |
| **B91** | SP75 | 10 l brt bl | 2.25 | .60 |
| **B92** | SP76 | 16 l dk slate grn | 3.50 | 2.00 |
| **B93** | SP77 | 20 l vermilion | 4.75 | 2.00 |
| | | *Nos. B83-B93 (11)* | 21.25 | 7.75 |

8th anniv. of accession of King Carol II. Surtax was for Straja Tarii, a natl. org. for boys. Exist imperf. Value $175, unused or used.

"The Spring" — SP78

"Escorting Prisoners" SP79

"Rodica, the Water Carrier" SP81

Nicolae Grigorescu SP82

Design: 4 l+1 l, "Returning from Market."

**1938, June 23** ***Perf. 13½***

**B94** SP78 1 l + 1 l brt bl 2.25 .70
**B95** SP79 2 l + 1 l yel grn 2.25 1.25
**B96** SP79 4 l + 1 l vermilion 2.25 1.25
**B97** SP81 6 l + 1 l lake 3.00 2.25
**B98** SP82 10 l + 1 l brt bl 6.75 2.50
*Nos. B94-B98 (5)* 16.50 7.95

Birth centenary of Nicolae Grigorescu, Romanian painter.
Exist imperf. Value $200, unused or used.

St. George and the Dragon — SP83

**1939, June 8** **Photo.**

**B99** SP83 25b + 25b ol gray .60 .45
**B100** SP83 50b + 50b brn .60 .45
**B101** SP83 1 l + 1 l pale vio .60 .45
**B102** SP83 2 l + 2 l lt grn .60 .45
**B103** SP83 3 l + 2 l red vio 1.00 .45
**B104** SP83 4 l + 2 l red org 1.40 .55
**B105** SP83 6 l + 2 l car rose 1.50 .55
**B106** SP83 8 l gray vio 1.75 .55
**B107** SP83 10 l brt bl 1.90 .70
**B108** SP83 12 l brt ultra 2.10 1.40
**B109** SP83 16 l bl grn 2.25 1.75
*Nos. B99-B109 (11)* 14.30 7.75

9th anniv. of accession of King Carol II. Exist imperf. Value $175, unused or used.

King Carol II
SP87 SP88

SP89 SP90

SP91

**Wmk. 230**

**1940, June 8** **Photo.** ***Perf. 13½***

**B113** SP87 1 l + 50b dl pur .75 .30
**B114** SP88 4 l + 1 l fawn .75 .45
**B115** SP89 6 l + 1 l blue .75 .45
**B116** SP90 8 l rose brn 1.10 .65
**B117** SP89 16 l ultra 1.25 .90
**B118** SP91 32 l dk vio brn 2.00 1.25
*Nos. B113-B118 (6)* 6.60 4.00

10th anniv. of accession of King Carol II. Exist imperf. Value $200, unused or used.

King Carol II
SP92 SP93

**1940, June 1**

**B119** SP92 1 l + 50b dk grn .25 .25
**B120** SP92 2.50 l + 50b Prus grn .25 .25
**B121** SP93 3 l + 1 l rose car .35 .25
**B122** SP92 3.50 l + 50b choc .35 .35
**B123** SP93 4 l + 1 l org brn .50 .35
**B124** SP93 6 l + 1 l sapphire .75 .25
**B125** SP93 9 l + 1 l brt bl .85 .70
**B126** SP93 14 l + 1 l dk bl grn 1.10 .90
*Nos. B119-B126 (8)* 4.40 3.30

Surtax was for Romania's air force. Exist imperf. Value $200, unused or used.

View of Danube SP94

Greco-Roman Ruins — SP95

Designs: 3 l+1 l, Hotin Castle. 4 l+1 l, Hurez Monastery. 5 l+1 l, Church in Bucovina. 8 l+1 l, Tower. 12 l+2 l, Village church, Transylvania. 16 l+2 l, Arch in Bucharest.

**Inscribed: "Straja Tarii 8 Junie 1940"**

**1940, June 8** ***Perf. 14½x14, 14x14½***

**B127** SP94 1 l + 1 l dp vio .40 .25
**B128** SP95 2 l + 1 l red brn .45 .30
**B129** SP94 3 l + 1 l yel grn .50 .35
**B130** SP94 4 l + 1 l grnsh blk .55 .40
**B131** SP95 5 l + 1 l org ver .60 .45
**B132** SP95 8 l + 1 l brn car .85 .60
**B133** SP95 12 l + 2 l ultra 1.75 1.10
**B134** SP95 16 l + 2 l dk bl gray 3.00 2.00
*Nos. B127-B134 (8)* 8.10 5.45

Issued to honor Straja Tarii, a national organization for boys. Exist imperf. Value $140, unused or used.

King Michael — SP102

**1940-42** **Photo.** **Wmk. 230**

**B138** SP102 1 l + 50b yel grn .25 .25
**B138A** SP102 2 l + 50b yel grn .25 .25
**B139** SP102 2.50 l + 50b dk bl grn .25 .25
**B140** SP102 3 l + 1 l pur .25 .25
**B141** SP102 3.50 l + 50b rose pink .25 .25
**B141A** SP102 4 l + 50b org ver .25 .25
**B142** SP102 4 l + 1 l brn .25 .25
**B142A** SP102 5 l + 1 l dp plum 1.25 .25
**B143** SP102 6 l + 1 l lt ultra .25 .25
**B143A** SP102 7 l + 1 l sl grn .50 .25
**B143B** SP102 8 l + 1 l dp vio .25 .25
**B143C** SP102 12 l + 1 l brn vio .50 .25
**B144** SP102 14 l + 1 l brt bl .50 .25
**B144A** SP102 19 l + 1 l lil rose 1.00 .25
*Nos. B138-B144A (14)* 6.00 3.50

Issue years: Nos. B138A, B141A, B142A, B143A, B143B, B143C, B144A, 1942; others, 1940.

Corneliu Codreanu — SP103

**1940, Nov. 8** **Unwmk.** ***Perf. 13½***

**B145** SP103 7 l + 30 l dk grn 6.00 *9.00*

13th anniv. of the founding of the Iron Guard by Corneliu Codreanu.

Vasile Marin — SP104

Design: 15 l+15 l, Ion Mota.

**1941, Jan. 13**

**B146** SP104 7 l + 7 l rose brn 3.50 *6.00*
**B147** SP104 15 l + 15 l slate bl 5.00 *9.00*

**Souvenir Sheet**

***Imperf***

**B148** Sheet of 2 75.00 *125.00*
*a.* SP104 7 l + 7 l Prus grn 15.00 *35.00*
*b.* SP104 15 l + 15 l Prus green 15.00 *35.00*

Vasile Marin and Ion Mota, Iron Guardists who died in the Spanish Civil War.
No. B148 sold for 300 lei.

Crown, Leaves and Bible — SP107

Designs: 2 l+43 l, Library shelves. 7 l+38 l, Carol I Foundation, Bucharest. 10 l+35 l, King Carol I. 16 l+29 l, Kings Michael and Carol I.

**Inscribed: "1891 1941"**

**Wmk. 230**

**1941, May 9** **Photo.** ***Perf. 13½***

**B149** SP107 1.50 l + 43.50 l pur 1.60 *2.50*
**B150** SP107 2 l + 43 l rose brn 1.60 *2.50*
**B151** SP107 7 l + 38 l rose 1.60 *2.50*
**B152** SP107 10 l + 35 l ol blk 1.60 *2.50*
**B153** SP107 16 l + 29 l brown 1.60 *2.50*
*Nos. B149-B153 (5)* 8.00 *12.50*

50th anniv. of the Carol I Foundation, established to endow research and stimulate the arts.

Same Overprinted in Red or Black

**1941, Aug.**

**B154** SP107 1.50 l + 43.50 l (R) 2.00 *4.00*
**B155** SP107 2 l + 43 l 2.00 *4.00*
**B156** SP107 7 l + 38 l 2.00 *4.00*
**B157** SP107 10 l + 35 l (R) 2.00 *4.00*
**B158** SP107 16 l + 29 l 2.00 *4.00*

Occupation of Cernauti, Bucovina.

Same Overprinted in Red or Black

**1941, Aug.**

**B159** SP107 1.50 l + 43.50 l (R) 2.00 *4.00*
**B160** SP107 2 l + 43 l 2.00 *4.00*
**B161** SP107 7 l + 38 l 2.00 *4.00*
**B162** SP107 10 l + 35 l (R) 2.00 *4.00*
**B163** SP107 16 l + 29 l 2.00 *4.00*
*Nos. B154-B163 (10)* 20.00 *40.00*

Occupation of Chisinau, Bessarabia.

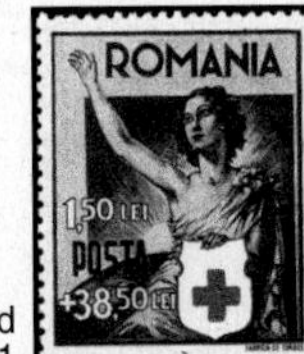

Romanian Red Cross — SP111

**1941, Aug.** ***Perf. 13½***

**B164** SP111 1.50 l + 38.50 l 1.20 *2.00*
**B165** SP111 2 l + 38 l 1.20 *2.00*
**B166** SP111 5 l + 35 l 1.20 *2.00*
**B167** SP111 7 l + 33 l 1.20 *2.00*
**B168** SP111 10 l + 30 l 1.50 *2.00*
*Nos. B164-B168 (5)* 6.30 *10.00*

**Souvenir Sheet**

***Imperf***

**Without Gum**

**B169** Sheet of 2 20.00 20.00
*a.* SP111 7 l + 33 l brown & red 2.75 *3.50*
*b.* SP111 10 l + 30 l brt blue & red 2.75 *3.50*

The surtax on Nos. B164-B169 was for the Romanian Red Cross.
No. B169 sold for 200 l.

King Michael and Stephen the Great SP113

Hotin and Akkerman Castles SP114

Romanian and German Soldiers SP115

Soldiers SP116

SP118

**1941, Oct. 11** ***Perf. 14½x13½***

| | | | | |
|---|---|---|---|---|
| **B170** | SP113 | 10 l + 30 l ultra | 2.25 | *3.00* |
| **B171** | SP114 | 12 l + 28 l dl org red | 2.25 | *3.00* |
| **B172** | SP115 | 16 l + 24 l lt brn | 2.50 | *3.00* |
| **B173** | SP116 | 20 l + 20 l dk vio | 2.50 | *3.00* |
| | | *Nos. B170-B173 (4)* | 9.50 | *12.00* |

**Souvenir Sheet**

***Imperf***

**Without Gum**

| | | | | |
|---|---|---|---|---|
| **B174** | SP118 | Sheet of 2 | 12.00 | *17.50* |
| *a.* | | 16 l blue gray | 1.50 | *4.50* |
| *b.* | | 20 l brown carmine | 1.50 | *4.50* |

No. B174 sold for 200 l. The surtax aided the Anti-Bolshevism crusade.

**Nos. B170-B174 Overprinted**

**1941, Oct.** ***Perf. 14½x13½***

| | | | | |
|---|---|---|---|---|
| **B175** | SP113 | 10 l + 30 l ultra | 2.00 | *3.00* |
| **B176** | SP114 | 12 l + 28 l dl org red | 2.00 | *3.00* |
| **B177** | SP115 | 16 l + 24 l lt brn | 2.50 | *3.00* |
| **B178** | SP116 | 20 l + 20 l dk vio | 2.50 | *3.00* |
| | | *Nos. B175-B178 (4)* | 9.00 | *12.00* |

**Souvenir Sheet**

***Imperf***

**Without Gum**

| | | | | |
|---|---|---|---|---|
| **B178A** | SP118 | Sheet of 2 | 17.50 | *25.00* |

Occupation of Odessa, Russia.

**Types of Regular Issue, 1941**

Designs: 3 l+50b, Sucevita Monastery, Bucovina. 5.50 l+50b, Rughi Monastery, Soroca, Bessarabia. 5.50 l+1 l, Tighina Fortress, Bessarabia. 6.50 l+1 l, Soroca Fortress, Bessarabia. 8 l+1 l, St. Nicholas Monastery, Suceava, Bucovina. 9.50 l+1 l, Milisauti Monastery, Bucovina. 10.50 l+1 l, Putna Monastery, Bucovina. 16 l+1 l, Cetatea Alba Fortress, Bessarabia. 25 l+1 l, Hotin Fortress, Bessarabia.

**1941, Dec. 1** **Wmk. 230** ***Perf. 13½***

| | | | | |
|---|---|---|---|---|
| **B179** | A179 | 3 l + 50b rose brn | .45 | .25 |
| **B180** | A179 | 5.50 l + 50b red org | .60 | .50 |
| **B181** | A179 | 5.50 l + 1 l blk | .60 | .50 |
| **B182** | A179 | 6.50 l + 1 l dk brn | .75 | .75 |
| **B183** | A179 | 8 l + 1 l lt bl | .60 | .40 |
| **B184** | A177 | 9.50 l + 1 l gray bl | .75 | .60 |
| **B185** | A179 | 10.50 l + 1 l dk bl | .80 | .40 |
| **B186** | A179 | 16 l + 1 l vio | .90 | .65 |
| **B187** | A179 | 25 l + 1 l gray blk | 1.00 | .70 |
| | | *Nos. B179-B187 (9)* | 6.45 | 4.75 |

Titu Maiorescu SP128

**1942, Oct. 5**

| | | | | |
|---|---|---|---|---|
| **B188** | SP128 | 9 l + 11 l dl vio | .70 | *1.00* |
| **B189** | SP128 | 20 l + 20 l yel brn | 1.75 | *2.50* |
| **B190** | SP128 | 20 l + 30 l blue | 2.00 | *3.00* |
| | | *Nos. B188-B190 (3)* | 4.45 | *6.50* |

**Souvenir Sheet**

***Imperf***

**Without Gum**

| | | | | |
|---|---|---|---|---|
| **B191** | SP128 | Sheet of 3 | 9.00 | *15.00* |

The surtax aided war prisoners.

No. B191 contains one each of Nos. B188-B190, imperf. Sold for 200 l.

Statue of Miron Costin at Jassy — SP130

**1942, Dec.** ***Perf. 13½***

| | | | | |
|---|---|---|---|---|
| **B192** | SP130 | 6 l + 44 l sepia | 1.75 | *2.75* |
| **B193** | SP130 | 12 l + 38 l violet | 1.75 | *2.75* |
| **B194** | SP130 | 24 l + 26 l blue | 1.75 | *2.75* |
| | | *Nos. B192-B194 (3)* | 5.25 | *8.25* |

Anniv. of the conquest of Transdniestria, and for use only in this territory which includes Odessa and land beyond the Duiester.

Michael, Antonescu, Hitler, Mussolini and Bessarabia Map SP131

Michael, Antonescu and (inset) Stephen of Moldavia SP132

Romanian Troops Crossing Pruth River to Retake Bessarabia — SP133

**1942** **Wmk. 230** **Photo.** ***Perf. 13½***

| | | | | |
|---|---|---|---|---|
| **B195** | SP131 | 9 l + 41 l red brn | 2.75 | *3.50* |
| **B196** | SP132 | 18 l + 32 l ol gray | 2.75 | *3.50* |
| **B197** | SP133 | 20 l + 30 l brt ultra | 2.75 | *3.50* |
| | | *Nos. B195-B197 (3)* | 8.25 | *10.50* |

First anniversary of liberation of Bessarabia.

Bucovina Coats of Arms
SP134 SP135

Design: 20 l+30 l, Bucovina arms with triple-barred cross.

**1942, Nov. 1**

| | | | | |
|---|---|---|---|---|
| **B198** | SP134 | 9 l + 41 l brt ver | 2.75 | *3.50* |
| **B199** | SP135 | 18 l + 32 l blue | 2.75 | *3.50* |
| **B200** | SP135 | 20 l + 30 l car rose | 2.75 | *3.50* |
| | | *Nos. B198-B200 (3)* | 8.25 | *10.50* |

First anniversary of liberation of Bucovina.

Andrei Muresanu SP137

**1942, Dec. 30**

| | | | | |
|---|---|---|---|---|
| **B201** | SP137 | 5 l + 5 l violet | 1.00 | *1.75* |

80th death anniv. of Andrei Muresanu, writer.

Avram Jancu, National Hero — SP138

**1943, Feb. 15**

| | | | | |
|---|---|---|---|---|
| **B202** | SP138 | 16 l + 4 l brown | 1.00 | *1.75* |

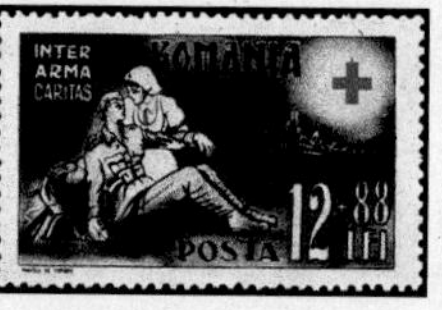

Nurse Aiding Wounded Soldier SP139

**1943, Mar. 1** ***Perf. 14½x14***

| | | | | |
|---|---|---|---|---|
| **B203** | SP139 | 12 l + 88 l red brn & ultra | 1.00 | *1.25* |
| **B204** | SP139 | 16 l + 84 l brt ultra & red | 1.00 | *1.25* |
| **B205** | SP139 | 20 l + 80 l ol gray & red | 1.00 | *1.25* |
| | | *Nos. B203-B205 (3)* | 3.00 | *3.75* |

**Souvenir Sheet**

***Imperf***

| | | | | |
|---|---|---|---|---|
| **B206** | | Sheet of 2 | 8.00 | *9.00* |
| *a.* | SP139 | 16 l + 84 l bright ultra & red | 2.00 | *2.50* |
| *b.* | SP139 | 20 l + 80 l olive gray & rod | 2.00 | *2.50* |

Surtax on Nos. B203-B206 aided the Romanian Red Cross.
No. B206 sold for 500 l.

Sword Hilt — SP141

Sword Severing Chain — SP142

Soldier and Family, Guardian Angel — SP143

***Perf. 14x14½***

**1943, June 22** **Wmk. 276**

| | | | | |
|---|---|---|---|---|
| **B207** | SP141 | 36 l + 164 l brn | 3.75 | *4.50* |
| **B208** | SP142 | 62 l + 138 l brt bl | 3.75 | *4.50* |
| **B209** | SP143 | 76 l + 124 l ver | 3.75 | *4.50* |
| | | *Nos. B207-B209 (3)* | 11.25 | *13.50* |

**Souvenir Sheet**

***Imperf***

| | | | | |
|---|---|---|---|---|
| **B210** | | Sheet of 2 | 20.00 | 20.00 |
| *a.* | SP142 | 62 l + 138 l deep blue | 5.75 | 5.75 |
| *b.* | SP143 | 76 l + 124 l red org | 5.75 | 5.75 |

2nd anniv. of Romania's entrance into WWII. No. B210 sold for 600 l.

Petru Maior — SP145

Horea, Closca and Crisan SP148

32 l+118 l, Gheorghe Sincai. 36 l+114 l, Timotei Cipariu. 91 l+109 l, Gheorghe Cosbuc.

***Perf. 13½; 14½x14 (No. B214)***

**1943, Aug. 15** **Photo.** **Wmk. 276**

| | | | | |
|---|---|---|---|---|
| **B211** | SP145 | 16 l + 134 l red org | .70 | *1.40* |
| **B212** | SP145 | 32 l + 118 l lt bl | .70 | *1.40* |
| **B213** | SP145 | 36 l + 114 l vio | .70 | *1.40* |
| **B214** | SP148 | 62 l + 138 l car rose | .70 | *1.40* |
| **B215** | SP145 | 91 l + 109 l dk brn | .70 | *1.40* |
| | | *Nos. B211-B215 (5)* | 3.50 | *7.00* |

See Nos. B219-B223.

King Michael and Ion Antonescu SP150

**1943, Sept. 6**

| | | | | |
|---|---|---|---|---|
| **B216** | SP150 | 16 l + 24 l blue | 2.50 | *3.50* |

3rd anniv. of the government of King Michael and Marshal Ion Antonescu.

Symbols of Sports — SP151

**1943, Sept. 26** ***Perf. 13½***

| | | | | |
|---|---|---|---|---|
| **B217** | SP151 | 16 l + 24 l ultra | .75 | *1.00* |
| **B218** | SP151 | 16 l + 24 l red brn | .75 | *1.00* |

Surtax for the benefit of Romanian sports.

**Portrait Type of 1943**

Designs: 16 l+134 l, Samuel Micu. 51 l+99 l, George Lazar. 56 l+144 l, Octavian Goga. 76 l+ 124 l, Simeon Barnutiu. 77 l+123 l, Andrei Saguna.

**1943, Oct. 1**

| | | | | |
|---|---|---|---|---|
| **B219** | SP145 | 16 l + 134 l red vio | .60 | *1.20* |
| **B220** | SP145 | 51 l + 99 l orange | .60 | *1.20* |
| **B221** | SP145 | 56 l + 144 l rose car | .60 | *1.20* |
| **B222** | SP145 | 76 l + 124 l slate bl | .60 | *1.20* |
| **B223** | SP145 | 77 l + 123 l brown | .60 | *1.20* |
| | | *Nos. B219-B223 (5)* | 3.00 | *6.00* |

The surtax aided refugees.

Calafat, 1877 — SP157

Designs: 2 l +2 l, World War I scene. 3.50 l+3.50 l, Stalingrad, 1943. 4 l+4 l, Tisza, 1919. 5 l+5 l, Odessa, 1941. 6.50 l+6.50 l, Caucasus, 1942. 7 l+7 l, Sevastopol, 1942. 20 l+20 l, Prince Ribescu and King Michael.

**1943, Nov. 10** **Photo.** ***Perf. 13½***

| | | | | |
|---|---|---|---|---|
| **B224** | SP157 | 1 l + 1 l red brn | .30 | *.50* |
| **B225** | SP157 | 2 l + 2 l dl vio | .30 | *.50* |
| **B226** | SP157 | 3.50 l + 3.50 l lt ultra | .30 | *.50* |
| **B227** | SP157 | 4 l + 4 l mag | .30 | *.50* |
| **B228** | SP157 | 5 l + 5 l red org | .70 | *1.25* |
| **B229** | SP157 | 6.50 l + 6.50 l bl | .70 | *1.25* |

**B230** SP157 7 l + 7 l dp vio .80 *2.25*
**B231** SP157 20 l + 20 l crim 1.25 *3.75*
*Nos. B224-B231 (8)* 4.65 *10.50*

Centenary of Romanian Artillery.

Emblem of Romanian Engineers' Association — SP165

**1943, Dec. 19** ***Perf. 14***
**B232** SP165 21 l + 29 l sepia 1.10 *1.75*

Society of Romanian Engineers, 25th anniv.

Motorcycle, Truck and Post Horn — SP166

Post Wagon SP167

Roman Post Chariot SP168

Post Rider — SP169

**1944, Feb. 1** **Wmk. 276** ***Perf. 14***
**B233** SP166 1 l + 49 l org red 2.00 *3.00*
**B234** SP167 2 l + 48 l lil rose 2.00 *3.00*
**B235** SP168 4 l + 46 l ultra 2.00 *3.00*
**B236** SP169 10 l + 40 l dl vio 2.00 *3.00*
*Nos. B233-B236 (4)* 8.00 *12.00*

**Souvenir Sheets**

***Perf. 14***

**B237** Sheet of 3 8.00 *12.50*
***a.*** SP166 1 l + 49 l orange red .80 *1.20*
***b.*** SP167 2 l + 48 l orange red .80 *1.20*
***c.*** SP168 4 l + 46 l orange red .80 *1.20*

***Imperf***

**B238** Sheet of 3 8.00 *12.50*
***a.*** SP166 1 l + 49 l dull violet .80 *1.20*
***b.*** SP167 2 l + 48 l dull violet .80 *1.20*
***c.*** SP168 4 l + 46 l dull violet .80 *1.20*

The surtax aided communications employees.
No. B238 is imperf. between the stamps.
Nos. B237-B238 each sold for 200 l.

**Nos. B233-B238 Overprinted**

**1944, Feb. 28**
**B239** SP166 1 l + 49 l org red 4.50 *6.50*
**B240** SP167 2 l + 48 l lil rose 4.50 *6.50*
**B241** SP168 4 l + 46 l ultra 4.50 *6.50*
**B242** SP169 10 l + 40 l dl vio 4.50 *6.50*
*Nos. B239-B242 (4)* 18.00 *26.00*

**Souvenir Sheets**

***Perf. 14***

**B243** Sheet of 3 17.50 *25.00*

***Imperf***

**B244** Sheet of 3 17.50 *25.00*

Rugby Player — SP171

**1944, Mar. 16** ***Perf. 15***
**B245** SP171 16 l + 184 l crimson 4.75 *7.50*

30th anniv. of the Romanian Rugby Assoc. The surtax was used to encourage the sport.

Dr. N. Cretzulescu SP172

**1944, Mar. 1** **Photo.** ***Perf. 13½***
**B246** SP172 35 l + 65 l brt ultra 1.10 *1.75*

Centenary of medical teaching in Romania.

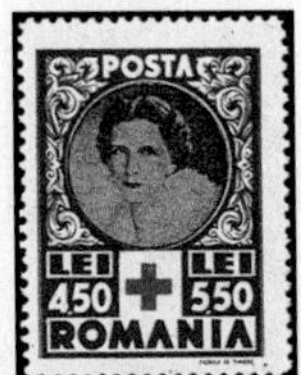

Queen Mother Helen — SP173

**1945, Feb. 10**
**B247** SP173 4.50 l + 5.50 l multi .35 *.70*
**B248** SP173 10 l + 40 l multi .45 *.90*
**B249** SP173 15 l + 75 l multi .70 *1.40*
**B250** SP173 20 l + 80 l multi 1.00 *2.00*
*Nos. B247-B250 (4)* 2.50 *5.00*

The surtax aided the Romanian Red Cross.

Kings Ferdinand and Michael and Map SP174

**1945, Feb.** ***Perf. 14***
**B251** SP174 75 l + 75 l dk ol brn .50 *.75*

Romania's liberation.

Stefan Tomsa Church, Radaseni SP175

Municipal Home SP176

Gathering Fruit — SP177

School SP178

**1944** **Wmk. 276** **Photo.** ***Perf. 14***
**B252** SP175 5 l + 145 l brt bl 1.00 1.00
**B253** SP176 12 l + 138 l car rose 1.00 1.00
**B254** SP177 15 l + 135 l red org 1.00 1.00
**B255** SP178 32 l + 118 l dk brn 1.00 1.00
*Nos. B252-B255 (4)* 4.00 4.00

King Michael and Carol I Foundation, Bucharest — SP179

Design: 200 l, King Carol I and Foundation.

**1945, Feb. 10** ***Perf. 13***
**B256** SP179 20 l + 180 l dp org .50 *.75*
**B257** SP179 25 l + 175 l slate .50 *.75*
**B258** SP179 35 l + 165 l cl brn .50 *.75*
**B259** SP179 75 l + 125 l pale vio .50 *.75*
*Nos. B256-B259 (4)* 2.00 *3.00*

**Souvenir Sheet**

***Imperf***

**Without Gum**

**B260** SP179 200 l blue 7.50 *15.00*

Surtax was to aid in rebuilding the Public Library, Bucharest.
#B256-B259 were printed in sheets of 4.
No. B260 sold for 1200 l.

Ion G. Duca SP181

16 l+184 l, Virgil Madgearu. 20 l+180 l, Nikolai Jorga. 32 l+168 l, Ilie Pintilie. 35 l+165 l, Bernath Andrei. 36 l+164 l, Filimon Sarbu.

**1945, Apr. 30** ***Perf. 13***
**B261** SP181 12 l + 188 l dk bl .70 *1.00*
**B262** SP181 16 l + 184 l cl brn .70 *1.00*
**B263** SP181 20 l + 180 l blk brn .70 *1.00*
**B264** SP181 32 l + 168 l brt red .70 *1.00*
**B265** SP181 35 l + 165 l Prus bl .70 *1.00*
**B266** SP181 36 l + 164 l lt vio .70 *1.00*
*Nos. B261-B266 (6)* 4.20 *6.00*

**Souvenir Sheet**

***Imperf***

**B267** Sheet of 2 24.00 *40.00*
***a.*** SP181 32 l + 168 l mag 4.75 *7.50*
***b.*** SP181 35 l + 165 l mag 4.75 *7.50*

Honoring six victims of Nazi terrorism.
No. B267 sold for 1,000 l.

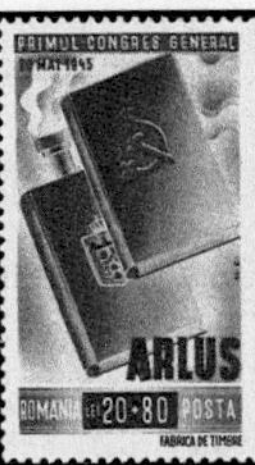

Books and Torch — SP188

Designs: #B269, Flags of Russia and Romania. #B270, Kremlin, Moscow. #B271, Tudor Vladimirescu and Alexander Nevsky.

**1945, May 20** ***Perf. 14***
**B268** SP188 20 l + 80 l ol grn .40 *.60*
**B269** SP188 35 l + 165 l brt rose .40 *.60*
**B270** SP188 75 l + 225 l blue .40 *.60*
**B271** SP188 80 l + 420 l cl brn .40 *.60*
*Nos. B268-B271 (4)* 1.60 *2.40*

**Souvenir Sheet**

***Imperf***

**Without Gum**

**B272** Sheet of 2 8.50 *17.50*
***a.*** SP189 35 l + 165 l bright red 2.00 *3.50*
***b.*** SP190 75 l + 225 l bright red 2.00 *3.50*

1st Soviet-Romanian Cong., May 20, 1945.
No. B272 sold for 900 l.

Karl Marx — SP193

120 l+380 l, Friedrich Engels. 155 l+445 l, Lenin.

**1945, June 30** ***Perf. 13½***
**B273** SP193 75 l + 425 l car rose 3.00 *6.00*
**B274** SP193 120 l + 380 l bl 3.00 *6.00*
**B275** SP193 155 l + 445 l dk vio brn 3.00 *6.00*

***Imperf***

**B276** SP193 75 l + 425 l bl 8.50 *15.00*
**B277** SP193 120 l + 380 l dk vio brn 8.50 *15.00*
**B278** SP193 155 l + 445 l car rose 8.50 *15.00*
*Nos. B273-B278 (6)* 34.50 *63.00*

Nos. B276-B278 were printed in sheets of 4.

Woman Throwing Discus — SP196

Designs: 16 l+184 l, Diving. 20 l+180 l, Skiing. 32 l+168 l, Volleyball. 35 l+165 l, Worker athlete.

**Wmk. 276**

**1945, Aug. 5** **Photo.** ***Perf. 13***
**B279** SP196 12 l +188 l ol gray 2.00 *4.00*
**B280** SP196 16 l +184 l lt ultra 2.00 *4.00*
**B281** SP196 20 l +180 l dp grn 2.00 *4.00*
**B282** SP196 32 l +168 l mag 2.00 *4.00*
**B283** SP196 35 l +165 l brt bl 2.00 *4.00*

***Imperf***

**B284** SP196 12 l +188 l org red 2.00 *4.00*
**B285** SP196 16 l +184 l vio brn 2.00 *4.00*
**B286** SP196 20 l +180 l dp vio 2.00 *4.00*
**B287** SP196 32 l +168 l yel grn 2.00 *4.00*
**B288** SP196 35 l +165 l dk ol grn 2.00 *4.00*
*Nos. B279-B288 (10)* 20.00 *40.00*

Printed in sheets of 9.

Mail Plane and Bird Carrying Letter SP201

**1945, Aug. 5** — *Perf. 13½*

| | | | | |
|---|---|---|---|---|
| **B289** | SP201 | 200 l + 1000 l bl & dk bl | 25.00 | *45.00* |
| *a.* | | With label | 67.50 | *160.00* |

The surtax on Nos. B279-B289 was for the Office of Popular Sports.

Issued in sheets of 30 stamps and 10 labels, arranged 10x4 with second and fourth horizontal rows each having five alternating labels.

Agriculture and Industry United — SP202

King Michael SP203

**1945, Aug. 23** — *Perf. 14*

| | | | | |
|---|---|---|---|---|
| **B290** | SP202 | 100 l + 400 l red | .80 | *2.00* |
| **B291** | SP203 | 200 l + 800 l blue | .85 | *2.00* |

The surtax was for the Farmers' Front. For surcharges see Nos. B318-B325.

Political Amnesty SP204

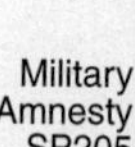

Military Amnesty SP205

Agrarian Amnesty SP206

Tudor Vladimirescu SP207

Nicolae Horia SP208

Reconstruction — SP209

**1945, Aug.** — *Perf. 13*

| | | | | |
|---|---|---|---|---|
| **B292** | SP204 | 20 l + 580 l choc | 10.00 | 10.00 |
| **B293** | SP204 | 20 l + 580 l mag | 10.00 | 10.00 |
| **B294** | SP205 | 40 l + 560 l blue | 10.00 | 10.00 |
| **B295** | SP205 | 40 l + 560 l sl grn | 10.00 | 10.00 |
| **B296** | SP206 | 55 l + 545 l red | 10.00 | 10.00 |
| **B297** | SP206 | 55 l + 545 l dk vio brn | 10.00 | 10.00 |
| **B298** | SP207 | 60 l + 540 l ultra | 10.00 | 10.00 |
| **B299** | SP207 | 60 l + 540 l choc | 10.00 | 10.00 |
| **B300** | SP208 | 80 l + 520 l red | 10.00 | 10.00 |
| **B301** | SP208 | 80 l + 520 l mag | 10.00 | 10.00 |
| **B302** | SP209 | 100 l + 500 l sl grn | 10.00 | 10.00 |
| **B303** | SP209 | 100 l + 500 l red brn | 10.00 | 10.00 |
| | | *Nos. B292-B303 (12)* | 120.00 | 120.00 |

1st anniv. of Romania's armistice with Russia. Issued in panes of four.

Nos. B292-B303 also exist on coarse grayish paper, ungummed (same value).

Electric Train SP210

Coats of Arms SP211

Truck on Mountain Road SP212

Oil Field SP213



"Agriculture" — SP214

**1945, Oct. 1** — *Perf. 14*

| | | | | |
|---|---|---|---|---|
| **B304** | SP210 | 10 l + 490 l ol grn | .70 | .70 |
| **B305** | SP211 | 20 l + 480 l red brn | .70 | .70 |
| **B306** | SP212 | 25 l + 475 l brn vio | .70 | .70 |
| **B307** | SP213 | 55 l + 445 l ultra | .70 | .70 |
| **B308** | SP214 | 100 l + 400 l brn | .70 | .70 |

***Imperf***

| | | | | |
|---|---|---|---|---|
| **B309** | SP210 | 10 l + 490 l blue | .70 | .70 |
| **B310** | SP211 | 20 l + 480 l vio | .70 | .70 |
| **B311** | SP212 | 25 l + 475 l bl grn | .70 | .70 |
| **B312** | SP213 | 55 l + 445 l gray | .70 | .70 |
| **B313** | SP214 | 100 l + 400 l dp mag | .70 | .70 |
| | | *Nos. B304-B313 (10)* | 7.00 | 7.00 |

16th Congress of the General Assoc. of Romanian Engineers.

"Brotherhood" — SP215

160 l+1840 l, "Peace." 320 l+1680 l, Hammer crushing Nazism. 440 l+2560 l, "World Unity."

**1945, Dec. 5** — *Perf. 14*

| | | | | |
|---|---|---|---|---|
| **B314** | SP215 | 80 l + 920 l mag | 17.50 | *25.00* |
| **B315** | SP215 | 160 l + 1840 l org brn | 17.50 | *25.00* |
| **B316** | SP215 | 320 l + 1680 l vio | 17.50 | *25.00* |
| **B317** | SP215 | 440 l + 2560 l yel grn | 17.50 | *25.00* |
| | | *Nos. B314-B317 (4)* | 70.00 | *100.00* |

World Trade Union Congress at Paris, Sept. 25-Oct. 10, 1945.

### Nos. B290 and B291 Surcharged in Various Colors

**1946, Jan. 20**

| | | | | |
|---|---|---|---|---|
| **B318** | SP202 | 10 l + 90 l (Bk) | .85 | *1.75* |
| **B319** | SP203 | 10 l + 90 l (R) | .85 | *1.75* |
| **B320** | SP202 | 20 l + 80 l (G) | .85 | *1.75* |
| **B321** | SP203 | 20 l + 80 l (Bk) | .85 | *1.75* |
| **B322** | SP202 | 80 l + 120 l (Bl) | .85 | *1.75* |
| **B323** | SP203 | 80 l + 120 l (Bk) | .85 | *1.75* |
| **B324** | SP202 | 100 l + 150 l (Bk) | .85 | *1.75* |
| **B325** | SP203 | 100 l + 150 l (R) | .85 | *1.75* |
| | | *Nos. B318-B325 (8)* | 6.80 | *14.00* |

Re-distribution of Land — SP219

Sower SP220

Ox Team Drawing Hay SP221

Old and New Plowing Methods SP222

**1946, Mar. 6**

| | | | | |
|---|---|---|---|---|
| **B326** | SP219 | 50 l + 450 l red | .40 | *.75* |
| **B327** | SP220 | 100 l + 900 l purple | .40 | *.75* |
| **B328** | SP221 | 200 l + 800 l orange | .40 | *.75* |
| **B329** | SP222 | 400 l + 1600 l dk grn | .40 | *.75* |
| | | *Nos. B326-B329 (4)* | 1.60 | *3.00* |

Agrarian reform law of Mar. 23, 1945.

### Philharmonic Types of Regular Issue

*Perf. 13, 13½x13*

**1946, Apr. 26** — **Photo.** — **Wmk. 276**

| | | | | |
|---|---|---|---|---|
| **B330** | A211 | 200 l + 800 l brt red | .80 | *1.50* |
| *a.* | | Sheet of 12 | 22.50 | *25.00* |
| **B331** | A213 | 350 l + 1650 l dk bl | .90 | *1.75* |
| *a.* | | Sheet of 12 | 22.50 | *25.00* |

Issued in sheets containing 12 stamps and 4 labels, with bars of music in the margins.

Agriculture SP223

Designs: 10 l+200 l, Hurdling. 80 l+200 l, Research. 80 l+300 l, Industry. 200 l+400 l, Workers and flag.

**Wmk. 276**

**1946, July 28** — **Photo.** — *Perf. 11½*

| | | | | |
|---|---|---|---|---|
| **B332** | SP223 | 10 l + 100 l dk org brn & red | .40 | *.75* |
| **B333** | SP223 | 10 l + 200 l bl & red brn | .40 | *.75* |
| **B334** | SP223 | 80 l + 200 l brn vio & brn | .40 | *.75* |
| **B335** | SP223 | 80 l + 300 l dk org brn & rose lil | .40 | *.75* |
| **B336** | SP223 | 200 l + 400 l Prus bl & red | .40 | *.75* |
| | | *Nos. B332-B336 (5)* | 2.00 | *3.75* |

Issued in panes of 4 stamps with marginal inscription.

Dove — SP228

**1946, Oct. 20** — *Perf. 13½x13, Imperf.*

| | | | | |
|---|---|---|---|---|
| **B338** | SP228 | 300 l + 1200 l scar | .70 | *1.25* |

**Souvenir Sheet**

*Perf. 14x14½*

| | | | | |
|---|---|---|---|---|
| **B339** | SP228 | 1000 l scarlet | 5.00 | *10.00* |

Romanian-Soviet friendship. No. B339 sold for 6000 lei.

Skiing — SP230

**1946, Sept. 1** — *Perf. 11½, Imperf.*

| | | | | |
|---|---|---|---|---|
| **B340** | SP230 | 160 l + 1340 l dk grn | .50 | *.75* |

Surtax for Office of Popular Sports.

Spinning SP231

Reaping SP232

Riding — SP233

Water Carrier — SP234

**1946, Nov. 20** ***Perf. 14***

**B342** SP231 80 l + 320 l brt red .35 *.75*
**B343** SP232 140 l + 360 l dp org .35 *.75*
**B344** SP233 300 l + 450 l brn ol .35 *.75*
**B345** SP234 600 l + 900 l ultra .35 *.75*
*Nos. B342-B345 (4)* 1.40 *3.00*

Democratic Women's Org. of Romania.

Angel with Food and Clothing SP235

Bread for Hungry Family SP236

Care for Needy — SP237

**1947, Jan. 15** ***Perf. 13½x14***

**B346** SP235 1500 l + 3500 l red org .30 *.60*
**B347** SP236 3700 l + 5300 l dp vio .30 *.60*

**Miniature Sheet**

***Imperf***

**Without Gum**

**B348** SP237 5000 l + 5000 l ultra 7.50 *15.00*

Surtax helped the social relief fund. No. B348 is miniature sheet of one.

Student Reciting SP238

Allegory of Education — SP242

SP243

#B350, Weaving class. #B351, Young machinist. #B352, Romanian school.

***Perf. 14x13½***

**1947, Mar. 5** **Photo.** **Wmk. 276**

**B349** SP238 200 l + 200 l vio bl .25 *.35*
**B350** SP238 300 l + 300 l red brn .25 *.35*
**B351** SP238 600 l + 600 l Prus grn .25 *.35*
**B352** SP238 1200 l + 1200 l ultra .25 *.35*
**B353** SP242 1500 l + 1500 l dp rose .25 *.35*
*Nos. B349-B353 (5)* 1.25 *1.75*

**Souvenir Sheet**

***Imperf***

**B354** SP243 3700 l + 3700 l dl brn & dl bl 2.25 *5.00*

Romania's vocational schools, 50th anniv.

Victor Babes — SP244

#B356, Michael Eminescu. #B357, Nicolae Grigorescu. #B358, Peter Movila. #B359, Aleksander S. Pushkin. #B360, Mikhail V. Lomonosov. #B361, Peter I. Tchaikovsky. #B362, Ilya E. Repin.

**1947, Apr. 18** ***Perf. 14***

**B355** SP244 1500 l + 1500 l red org .25 .25
**B356** SP244 1500 l + 1500 l dk ol grn .25 .25
**B357** SP244 1500 l + 1500 l dk bl .25 .25
**B358** SP244 1500 l + 1500 l dp plum .25 .25
**B359** SP244 1500 l + 1500 l scar .25 .25
**B360** SP244 1500 l + 1500 l rose brn .25 .25
**B361** SP244 1500 l + 1500 l ultra .25 .25
**B362** SP244 1500 l + 1500 l choc .25 .25
*Nos. B355-B362 (8)* 2.00 2.00

Transportation — SP252

Labor Day: No. B364, Farmer. No. B365, Farm woman. No. B366, Scientist and Romanian Academy of Sciences. No. B367, Laborer and factory.

**1947, May 1**

**B363** SP252 1000 l + 1000 l dk ol brn .30 *.50*
**B364** SP252 1500 l + 1500 l red brn .30 *.50*
**B365** SP252 2000 l + 2000 l blue .30 *.50*
**B366** SP252 2500 l + 2500 l red vio .30 *.50*
**B367** SP252 3000 l + 3000 l crim rose .30 *.50*
*Nos. B363-B367 (5)* 1.50 *2.50*

No. 650 Surcharged in Carmine

**1947, Sept. 6** ***Perf. 13½***

**B368** A234 2 l + 3 l on 36,000 l vio 1.00 *2.00*

Balkan Games of 1947, Bucharest.

**Type of 1947 Surcharged in Carmine**

Design: Cathedral of Curtea de Arges.

**1947, Oct. 30** ***Imperf.***

**B369** A235 5 l + 5 l brt ultra .70 *1.00*

Soviet-Romanian Congress, Nov. 1-7.

Plowing — SP257

***Perf. 14x14½***

**1947, Oct. 5** **Photo.** **Wmk. 276**

**B370** SP257 1 l + 1 l shown .25 .25
**B371** SP257 2 l + 2 l Sawmill .25 .25
**B372** SP257 3 l + 3 l Refinery .25 .25
**B373** SP257 4 l + 4 l Steel mill .25 .25
*Nos. B370-B373,CB12 (5)* 1.70 1.70

17th Congress of the General Assoc. of Romanian Engineers.

Allegory of Industry, Science and Agriculture — SP258

Winged Man Holding Hammer and Sickle SP259

**1947, Nov. 10** ***Perf. 14½x14***

**B374** SP258 2 l + 10 l rose lake .30 .30
**B375** SP259 7 l + 10 l bluish blk .30 .30

2nd Trade Union Conf., Nov. 10.

SP260

SP264

Designs: 1 l+1 l, Convoy of Food for Moldavia. 2 l+2 l, "Everything for the Front-Everything for Victory." 3 l+3 l, Woman, child and hospital. 4 l+4 l, "Help the Famine-stricken Regions." 5 l+5 l, "Three Years of Action."

**1947, Nov. 7** ***Perf. 14***

**B376** SP260 1 l + 1 l dk gray bl .30 *.35*
**B377** SP260 2 l + 2 l dk brn .30 *.35*
**B378** SP260 3 l + 3 l rose lake .30 *.35*
**B379** SP260 4 l + 4 l brt ultra .30 *.35*
**B380** SP264 5 l + 5 l red .30 *.35*
*Nos. B376-B380 (5)* 1.50 *1.75*

Issued in sheets of eight.

Discus Thrower — SP265

Balkan Games of 1947: 2 l+2 l, Runner. 5 l+5 l, Boy and girl athletes.

**Wmk. 276**

**1948, Feb.** **Photo.** ***Perf. 13½***

**B381** SP265 1 l + 1 l dk brn .45 *.50*
**B382** SP265 2 l + 2 l car lake .60 *.65*
**B383** SP265 5 l + 5 l blue 1.00 *1.25*
*Nos. B381-B383,CB13-CB14 (5)* 5.05 *4.10*

Labor — SP266

Youths Following Filimon Sarbu Banner — SP269

3 l+3 l, Agriculture. 5 l+5 l, Education.

**1948, Mar. 15**

**B384** SP266 2 l + 2 l dk sl bl .35 *.70*
**B385** SP266 3 l + 3 l gray grn .40 *.70*
**B386** SP266 5 l + 5 l red brn .50 *.70*

***Imperf***

**B387** SP269 8 l + 8 l dk car rose .70 *.70*
*Nos. B384-B387,CB15 (5)* 3.05 *3.40*

No. B387 issued in triangular sheets of 4.

Gliders — SP270

Sailboat Race SP271

Designs: No. B389, Early plane. No. B390, Plane over farm. No. B391, Transport plane. B393, Training ship, Mircea. B394, Danube ferry. B395, S.S. Transylvania.

**1948, July 26** ***Perf. 14x14½***

**B388** SP270 2 l + 2 l blue 1.50 1.50
**B389** SP270 5 l + 5 l pur 1.50 1.50
**B390** SP270 8 l + 8 l dk car rose 2.50 2.50
**B391** SP270 10 l + 10 l choc 3.25 3.25
**B392** SP271 2 l + 2 l dk grn 1.50 1.50
**B393** SP271 5 l + 5 l slate 1.50 1.50
**B394** SP271 8 l + 8 l brt bl 2.50 2.50
**B395** SP271 10 l + 10 l ver 3.25 3.25
*Nos. B388-B395 (8)* 17.50 17.50

Air and Sea Communications Day.

**Type of Regular Issue and**

Torch, Pen, Ink and Flag
SP272

Alexandru Sahia — SP273

***Perf. 14x13½, 13½x14***

**1948, Sept. 12**

| | | | | |
|---|---|---|---|---|
| **B396** | A241 | 5 l + 5 l crimson | .70 | .70 |
| **B397** | SP272 | 10 l + 10 l violet | 1.10 | 1.10 |
| **B398** | SP273 | 15 l + 15 l blue | 1.50 | 1.50 |
| | | *Nos. B396-B398 (3)* | 3.30 | 3.30 |

Week of the Democratic Press, Sept. 12-19.

Nos. B396-B398 were also issued imperf. Value, unused $4.50, used $7.

1,500 sets of Nos. 695, B396-B398 perf and B396-B398 imperf were overprinted at "The Week of the Democratic Press" exposition. These stamps were not recognized by the Romanian PTT, although some examples were used on items mailed from the exposition post office.

Romanian-Soviet Association Emblem — SP274

Design: 15 l+15 l, Spasski Tower, Kremlin.

**1948, Oct. 29** ***Perf. 14***

| | | | | |
|---|---|---|---|---|
| **B399** | SP274 | 10 l + 10 l gray grn | 2.50 | *3.00* |
| **B400** | SP274 | 15 l + 15 l dp ultra | 3.00 | *4.50* |

No. B399 was issued in sheets of 50 stamps and 50 labels.

Symbols of United Labor
SP275

Agriculture
SP276

Industry — SP277

**1948, May 1** ***Perf. 14x13½, 13½x14***

| | | | | |
|---|---|---|---|---|
| **B401** | SP275 | 8 l + 8 l red | 1.50 | *2.00* |
| **B402** | SP276 | 10 l + 10 l ol grn | 1.75 | *2.50* |
| **B403** | SP277 | 12 l + 12 l red brn | 3.00 | *3.75* |
| | | *Nos. B401-B403 (3)* | 6.25 | *8.25* |

Labor Day, May 1. See No. CB17.

Automatic Riflemen — SP278

Soldiers Cutting Barbed Wire
SP279

No. B406, Field Artillery. No. B407, Tank. No. B408, Warship.

**Flags and Dates: 23 Aug 1944-9 Mai 1945**

**1948, May 9**

| | | | | |
|---|---|---|---|---|
| **B404** | SP278 | 1.50 l + 1.50 l shown | .35 | .35 |
| **B405** | SP279 | 2 l + 2 l shown | .35 | .35 |
| **B406** | SP279 | 4 l + 4 l multi | .65 | .65 |
| **B407** | SP279 | 7.50 l + 7.50 l multi | 1.25 | 1.25 |
| **B408** | SP279 | 8 l + 8 l multi | 1.40 | 1.40 |
| | | *Nos. B404-B408,CB18-CB19 (7)* | 18.00 | 18.00 |

Honoring the Romanian Army.

Nicolae Balcescu — SP280

Balcescu and Revolutionists
SP281

Balcescu, Sandor Petöfi and Revolutionists — SP282

Revolution of 1848: #B412, Balcescu and revolutionists.

**1948, June 1** ***Perf. 13x13½***

| | | | | |
|---|---|---|---|---|
| **B409** | SP280 | 2 l + 2 l car lake | .40 | *.60* |
| **B410** | SP281 | 5 l + 5 l dk vio | .55 | *.70* |
| **B411** | SP282 | 10 l + 10 l dk ol brn | .75 | *1.25* |
| **B412** | SP280 | 36 l + 18 l dp bl | 1.75 | *2.25* |
| | | *Nos. B409-B412 (4)* | 3.45 | *4.80* |

For surcharges see Nos. 856-859.

Loading Freighter
SP283

Designs: 3 l+3 l, Lineman. 11 l+11 l, Transport plane. 15 l+15 l, Railroad train.

**Wmk. 289**

**1948, Dec. 10** **Photo.** ***Perf. 14***

**Center in Black**

| | | | | |
|---|---|---|---|---|
| **B413** | SP283 | 1 l + 1 l dk grn | .65 | *1.10* |
| **B414** | SP283 | 3 l + 3 l redsh brn | .75 | *1.10* |
| **B415** | SP283 | 11 l + 11 l dp bl | 3.50 | 3.00 |
| **B416** | SP283 | 15 l + 15 l red | 4.00 | *4.50* |
| *a.* | | Sheet of 4 | 20.00 | *25.00* |
| | | *Nos. B413-B416 (4)* | 8.90 | *9.70* |

No. B416a contains four imperf. stamps similar to Nos. B413-B416 in changed colors, center in brown. No gum.

Runners — SP284

Parade of Athletes
SP285

**1948, Dec. 31** ***Perf. 13x13½, 13½x13***

| | | | | |
|---|---|---|---|---|
| **B421** | SP284 | 5 l + 5 l grn | 3.50 | 3.50 |
| **B422** | SP285 | 10 l + 10 l brn vio | 5.75 | 5.75 |

***Imperf***

| | | | | |
|---|---|---|---|---|
| **B423** | SP284 | 5 l + 5 l brown | 3.50 | 3.50 |
| **B424** | SP285 | 10 l + 10 l red | 5.75 | 5.75 |
| | | *Nos. B421-B424,CB20-CB21 (6)* | 48.50 | 48.50 |

Nos. B421-B424 were issued in sheets of 4.

**Souvenir Sheet**

SP286

**1950, Jan. 27**

| | | | | |
|---|---|---|---|---|
| **B425** | SP286 | 10 l carmine | 5.00 | 3.25 |

Philatelic exhib., Bucharest. Sold for 50 lei.

Crossing the Buzau, by Denis Auguste Marie Raffet — SP287

**1967, Nov. 15** **Engr.** ***Perf. 13½***

| | | | | |
|---|---|---|---|---|
| **B426** | SP287 | 55b + 45b ocher & indigo | .90 | .45 |

Stamp Day.

Old Bucharest, 18th Century Painting — SP288

**1968, Nov. 15** **Photo.** ***Perf. 13½***

| | | | | |
|---|---|---|---|---|
| **B427** | SP288 | 55b + 45b label | 1.10 | .60 |

Stamp Day. Simulated label has printed perforations. See Nos. 2386A, B428-B429.

**1969, Nov. 15**

Design: Courtyard, by M. Bouquet.

| | | | | |
|---|---|---|---|---|
| **B428** | SP288 | 55b + 45b label | 1.00 | .60 |

Stamp Day. Simulated label at right of stamp has printed perforations.

**1970, Nov. 15**

Mail Coach in the Winter, by Emil Volkers.

| | | | | |
|---|---|---|---|---|
| **B429** | SP288 | 55b + 45b multi | 1.10 | .70 |

Stamp Day. No simulated label.

Lady with Letter, by Sava Hentia
SP289

**1971, Nov. 15** **Photo.** ***Perf. 13½***

| | | | | |
|---|---|---|---|---|
| **B430** | SP289 | 1.10 l + 90b multi | 1.25 | .75 |

Stamp Day. Label portion below stamp has printed perforations and shows Romania No. 12.

**Portrait Type of Regular Issue**

Designs: 4 l+2 l, Aman at his Desk, by B. Iscovescu. 6 l+2 l, The Poet Alecsandri with his Family, by N. Livaditti.

**1973, June 20** **Photo.** ***Perf. 13½***

| | | | | |
|---|---|---|---|---|
| **B432** | A728 | 4 l + 2 l multi | 1.50 | .60 |

**Souvenir Sheet**

| | | | | |
|---|---|---|---|---|
| **B433** | A728 | 6 l + 2 l multi | 3.00 | 3.00 |

No. B433 contains one 38x50mm stamp.

Map of Europe with Emblem Marking Bucharest
SP291

**1974, June 25** **Photo.** ***Perf. 13½***

| | | | | |
|---|---|---|---|---|
| **B435** | SP291 | 4 l + 3 l multi | 1.50 | .50 |

EUROMAX, European Exhibition of Maximaphily, Bucharest, Oct. 6-13.

Marketplace, Sibiu — SP292

**1974, Nov. 15** **Photo.** ***Perf. 13½***

| | | | | |
|---|---|---|---|---|
| **B436** | SP292 | 2.10 l + 1.90 l multi | 1.10 | .40 |

Stamp Day.

**No. B436 Overprinted in Red: "EXPOZITIA FILATELICA 'NATIONALA '74' / 15-24 noiembrie / Bucuresti"**

**1974, Nov. 15**

| | | | | |
|---|---|---|---|---|
| **B437** | SP292 | 2.10 l + 1.90 l multi | 2.25 | 2.25 |

NATIONALA '74 Philatelic Exhibition, Bucharest, Nov. 15-24.

Post Office, Bucharest
SP293

Stamp Day: 2.10 l+1.90 l, like No. B438, side view.

**1975, Nov. 15 Photo. *Perf. 13½***
**B438** SP293 1.50 l + 1.50 l multi .85 .45
**B439** SP293 2.10 l + 1.90 l multi 1.40 .65

### No. 2612 Surcharged and Overprinted "EXPOZITIA FILATELICA / BUCURESTI / 12-19.IX.1976"

**1976, Sept. 12 Photo. *Perf. 13½***
**B440** A787 3.60 l + 1.80 l 4.00 3.25

Philatelic Exhibition, Bucharest, Sept. 12-19.

Elena Cuza, by Theodor Aman — SP294

**1976, Nov. 15 Photo. *Perf. 13½***
**B441** SP294 2.10 l + 1.90 l multi 1.10 .70

Stamp Day.

### Independence Type of 1977

Stamp Day: Battle of Rahova, after etching.

**1977, May 9 Photo. *Perf. 13½***
**B442** A806 4.80 l + 2 l multi 1.50 .40

Dispatch Rider Handing Letter to Officer — SP295

**1977, Nov. Photo. *Perf. 13½***
**B443** SP295 2.10 l + 1.90 l multi 1.25 .85

### Socfilex Type of 1979

Flower Paintings by Luchian: 4 l+2 l, Field flowers. 10 l+5 l, Roses.

**1979, July 27 Photo. *Perf. 13½***
**B445** A847 4 l + 2 l multi 1.10 1.10

### Souvenir Sheet

**B446** A847 10 l + 5 l multi 3.00 3.00

Socfilex Intl. Phil. Exhib., Bucharest, Oct. 26-Nov. 1. #B446 contains one 50x38mm stamp.

Stamp Day SP297

**1979, Dec. 12 Photo. *Perf. 13½***
**B447** SP297 2.10 l + 1.90 l multi .80 .25

### Souvenir Sheet

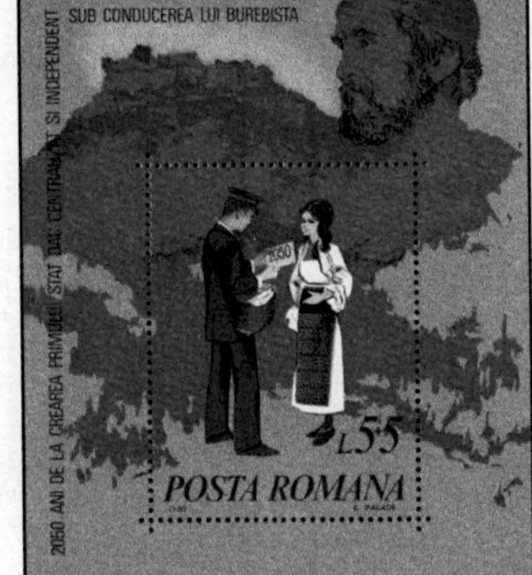

Stamp Day — SP298

**1980, July 1 Photo. *Perf. 13½***
**B448** SP298 5 l + 5 l multi 2.00 2.00

December 1989 Revolution — SP299

Designs: 50b+50b, Palace on fire, Bucharest. 1 l+ 1 l, Crowd, Timisoara. 1.50 l+1 l, Soldiers & crowd, Tirgu Mures. 2 l+1 l, Soldiers in Bucharest, vert. 3 l+1 l, Funeral, Timisoara. 3.50 l+1 l, Crowd celebrating, Brasov, vert. 4 l+1 l, Crowd with flags, Sibiu. No. B456, Cemetery, Bucharest. No. B457, Foreign aid.

**1990, Oct. 1 Photo. *Perf. 13½***
**B449** SP299 50b +50b multi .25 .25
**B450** SP299 1 l +1 l multi .25 .25
**B451** SP299 1.50 l +1 l multi .25 .25
**B452** SP299 2 l +1 l multi .30 .25
**B453** SP299 3 l +1 l multi .35 .25
**B454** SP299 3.50 l +1 l multi .40 .25
**B455** SP299 4 l +1 l multi .45 .25
**B456** SP299 5 l +2 l multi .60 .25
*Nos. B449-B456 (8)* 2.85 2.00

### Souvenir Sheet

**B457** SP299 5 l +2 l multi 1.25 1.25

No. B457 contains one 54x42mm stamp.

Stamp Day — SP300

**1992, July 15 Photo. *Perf. 13½***
**B458** SP300 10 l +4 l multi .25 .25

For surcharge see No. B460.

Stamp Day — SP301

**1993, Apr. 26 Photo. *Perf. 13½***
**B459** SP301 15 l +10 l multi .25 .25

### No. B458 Surcharged in Red

**1993, Nov. 9 Photo. *Perf. 13½***
**B460** SP300 70 l +45 l on 10 l+4 l .50 .50

National History Museum, Bucharest SP302

**1994, July 15 Photo. *Perf. 13½***
**B461** SP302 90 l +60 l multi .30 .25

Stamp Day.

### Souvenir Sheet

Romanian Olympic Committee, 90th Anniv. — SP303

No. B462: a, Pierre de Coubertin. b, Greece #125 (54x42mm). c, George V. Bibescu.

**2004, Mar. 25 Photo. *Perf. 13¼***
**B462** SP303 16,000 l +5000 l Sheet of 3, #a-c 4.25 4.25

First Romanian Philatelic Exhibition, 80th Anniv. — SP304

**2004, July 15 Photo. *Perf. 13¼***
**B463** SP304 21,000 l +10,000 l multi 2.40 2.40

### Litho. *Imperf*

**B464** SP304 21,000 l +10,000 l multi 2.40 2.40

---

## AIR POST STAMPS

Capt. C. G. Craiu's Airplane AP1

### Wmk. 95 Vertical

**1928 Photo. *Perf. 13½***
**C1** AP1 1 l red brown 3.00 2.50
**C2** AP1 2 l brt blue 3.00 2.50
**C3** AP1 5 l carmine rose 3.00 2.50

### Wmk. 95 Horizontal

**C4** AP1 1 l red brown 4.00 3.25
**C5** AP1 2 l brt blue 4.00 3.25
**C6** AP1 5 l carmine rose 4.00 3.25
*Nos. C1-C6 (6)* 21.00 17.25

Nos. C4-C6 also come with white gum.

### Nos. C4-C6 Overprinted

**1930**
**C7** AP1 1 l red brown 8.00 6.75
**C8** AP1 2 l brt blue 8.00 6.75
*a.* Vert. pair, imperf. btwn. *175.00*
**C9** AP1 5 l carmine rose 8.00 6.75
*Nos. C7-C9 (3)* 24.00 20.25

### Same Overprint on Nos. C1-C3
### Wmk. 95 Vertical

**C10** AP1 1 l red brown 50.00 50.00
**C11** AP1 2 l brt blue 50.00 50.00
**C12** AP1 5 l carmine rose 50.00 50.00
*Nos. C10-C12 (3)* 150.00 150.00
*Nos. C7-C12 (6)* 174.00 170.25

Nos. C7-C12 for the accession of King Carol II.

Excellent connterfeits are known of Nos. C10-C12.

King Carol II — AP2

### Bluish Paper

**1930, Oct. 4 Unwmk.**
**C13** AP2 1 l dk violet 2.00 3.50
**C14** AP2 2 l gray green 2.50 3.50
**C15** AP2 5 l red brown 5.00 3.50
**C16** AP2 10 l brt blue 9.00 3.50
*Nos. C13-C16 (4)* 18.50 14.00
Set, never hinged 36.50

Junkers Monoplane AP3

Monoplanes AP7

Designs: 3 l, Monoplane with biplane behind. 5 l, Biplane. 10 l, Monoplane flying leftward.

**1931, Nov. 4 Wmk. 230**
**C17** AP3 2 l dull green 1.50 1.25
**C18** AP3 3 l carmine 2.00 1.75
**C19** AP3 5 l red brown 2.50 2.00
**C20** AP3 10 l blue 6.00 4.50
**C21** AP7 20 l dk violet 15.00 6.00
*Nos. C17-C21 (5)* 27.00 15.50
Set, never hinged 40.00

Exist imperforate. Value $350, unused or used.

Souvenir Sheets

Plane over Resita — AP8

Plane over Sinaia — AP9

**Wmk. 276**

**1945, Oct. 1 Photo.** ***Perf. 13***

**Without Gum**

**C22** AP8 80 l slate green 17.50 25.00

***Imperf***

**C23** AP9 80 l magenta 10.00 17.50

16th Congress of the General Assoc. of Romanian Engineers.

**Catalogue values for unused stamps in this section, from this point to the end of the section, are for Never Hinged items.**

Plane AP10

Design: 500 l, Aviator and planes.

**1946, Sept. 5** ***Perf. 13½x13***

**C24** AP10 200 l yel grn & bl 3.00 6.00
**C25** AP10 500 l org red & dl bl 3.00 6.00

Sheets of four with marginal inscription.

Lockheed 12 Electra — AP12

**1946, Oct.** ***Perf. 11½***

**C26** AP12 300 l crimson 1.00 1.00
*a.* Pair, #C26, CB6 2.25 2.25

Sheet contains 8 each of Nos. C26 and CB6, arranged so se-tenant or normal pairs are available.

CGM Congress Emblem — AP13

**1947, Mar. Wmk. 276** ***Perf. 13x14***

**C27** AP13 1100 l blue .50 1.00

Congress of the United Labor Unions ("CGM"). Printed in sheets of 15.

"May 1" Supported by Parachutes AP14

Designs: No. C29, Air Force monument. No. C30, Plane over rural road.

**1947, May 4** ***Perf. 11½***

**C28** AP14 3000 l vermilion .30 .60
**C29** AP14 3000 l grnsh gray .30 .60
**C30** AP14 3000 l blk brown .30 .60
*Nos. C28-C30 (3)* .90 1.80

Printed in sheets of four with marginal inscriptions.

Plane and Conference Banner — AP17

**1947, Nov. 10** ***Perf. 14***

**C31** AP17 11 l bl & dp car 1.25 1.25

2nd Trade Union Conference, Nov. 10.

Emblem of the Republic and Factories AP18

Industry and Agriculture — AP19

Transportation — AP20

***Perf. 14x13½***

**1948, Nov. 22 Wmk. 289 Photo.**

**C32** AP18 30 l cerise .75 .25
*a.* 30 l carmine ('50) .85 .45
**C33** AP19 50 l dk slate grn 1.25 .50
**C34** AP20 100 l ultra 3.75 1.50
*Nos. C32-C34 (3)* 5.75 2.25

No. C32a issued May 10. For surcharges see Nos. C37-C39.

Agriculture — AP21

Design: 50 l, Transportation.

**1951-52 Wmk. 358** ***Perf. 13½***

**C35** AP21 30 l dk green ('52) 3.75 3.00
**C36** AP21 50 l red brown 3.00 2.50

1951-55 Five Year Plan.
For surcharges see Nos. C40-C41.

**Nos. C32-C36 Surcharged in Blue or Carmine**

**1952 Wmk. 289** ***Perf. 14x13½***

**C37** AP18 3b on 30 l car (Bl) 3.00 2.25
*a.* 3b on 30 l cerise (Bl) *12.00 8.50*
**C38** AP19 3b on 50 l dk sl grn 1.00 .70
**C39** AP20 3b on 100 l ultra 1.00 .70

***Perf. 13½***

**Wmk. 358**

**C40** AP21 1 l on 30 l dk grn *8.00 1.50*
**C41** AP21 1 l on 50 l red brn *8.00 1.50*
*Nos. C37-C41 (5) 21.00 6.65*

Nos. 706 and 707 Surcharged in Blue or Carmine

**1953 Wmk. 289** ***Perf. 13½, 14***

**C43** A250 3 l on 20 l org brn *35.00 25.00*
**C44** A251 5 l on 30 l brt bl (C) *45.00 32.50*

Plane facing right and surcharge arranged to fit design on No. C44.

Plane over City — AP22

Designs: 55b, Plane over Mountains. 1.75 l, over Harvest fields. 2.25 l, over Seashore.

***Perf. 14½x14***

**1956, Dec. 15 Photo. Wmk. 358**

**C45** AP22 20b brt bl, org & grn .55 .80
**C46** AP22 55b brt bl, grn & ocher 1.25 .80
**C47** AP22 1.75 l brt bl & red org 3.75 1.25
**C48** AP22 2.55 l brt bl & red org 5.25 2.00
*Nos. C45-C48 (4)* 10.80 4.85

Sputnik 1 and Earth — AP23

3.75 l, Sputniks 1 and 2 circling globe.

**1957, Nov. 6** ***Perf. 14***

**C49** AP23 25b brt ultra .65 .25
**C50** AP23 25b dk bl grn .65 .25
**C51** AP23 3.75 l brt ultra 3.50 .60
*a.* Pair, #C49, C51 + label 6.00 3.75
**C52** AP23 3.75 l dk bl grn 3.50 .60
*a.* Pair, #C50, C52 + label 6.00 3.75
*Nos. C49-C52 (4)* 8.30 1.70

Each sheet contains 27 triptychs with the center rows arranged tete-beche.

In 1958 Nos. C49-C52 were overprinted: 1.) "Expozitia Universal a Bruxelles 1958" and star. 2.) Large star. 3.) Small star. Value, both pairs: unused $30, used $20. Exist imperf. Value, both pairs: unused $60, used $50.

**Animal Type of Regular Issue, 1957**

Birds: 3.30 l, Black-headed gull, horiz. 5 l, Sea eagle, horiz.

***Perf. 14x13½***

**1957, Dec. 27 Wmk. 358**

**C53** A445 3.30 l ultra & gray 4.00 1.00
**C54** A445 5 l carmine & org 5.75 1.25

**Armed Forces Type of Regular Issue**

Design: Flier and planes.

***Perf. 13½x13***

**1958, Oct. 2 Unwmk. Photo.**

**C55** A458 3.30 l brt violet 1.60 .50

Day of the Armed Forces, Oct. 2.

Earth and Sputnik 3 Orbit AP24

**1958, Sept. 20** ***Perf. 14x13½***

**C56** AP24 3.25 l indigo & ocher 3.75 .75

Launching of Sputnik 3, May 15, 1958.

**Type of Regular Issue, 1958**

Souvenir Sheet

Design: Tête bêche pair of 27pa of 1858.

***Perf. 11½***

**1958, Nov. 15 Unwmk. Engr.**

**C57** A462 10 l blue, bluish 35.00 35.00

A similar sheet, printed in dull red and imperf., exists. Values, unused $45; used $22.50.

No. C57 on bluish and white papers was overprinted in 1959 in vermilion to commemorate the 10th anniv. of the State Philatelic Trade. Values: unused $100; used $125.

Lunik I Leaving Earth AP25

**1959, Feb. 4 Photo.** ***Perf. 14***

**C58** AP25 3.25 l vio bl, *pnksh* 15.00 2.00

Launching of the "first artificial planet of the solar system."
For surcharge see No. C70.

Frederic Joliot-Curie — AP26

**1959, Apr. 25** ***Perf. 13½x14***

**C59** AP26 3.25 l ultra 4.00 .60

Frederic Joliot-Curie; 10th anniv. of the World Peace Movement.

Rock Thrush AP27

Birds: 20b, European golden oriole. 35b, Lapwing. 40b, Barn swallow. No. C64, Goldfinch. No. C65, Great spotted woodpecker. No. C66, Great tit. 1 l, Bullfinch. 1.55 l, Long-tailed tit. 5 l, Wall creeper. Nos. C62-C67 vertical.

**1959, June 25 Litho.** ***Perf. 14***

**Birds in Natural Colors**

**C60** AP27 10b gray, *cr* .25 .25
**C61** AP27 20b gray, *grysh* .25 .25
**C62** AP27 35b gray, *grysh* .30 .25
**C63** AP27 40b gray & red, *pnksh* .40 .25
**C64** AP27 55b gray, *buff* .55 .25
**C65** AP27 55b gray, *grnsh* .55 .25
**C66** AP27 55b gray & ol, *grysh* .55 .25
**C67** AP27 1 l gray and red, *cr* 2.00 .25

**C68** AP27 1.55 l gray & red, *pnksh* 2.50 .25
**C69** AP27 5 l gray, *grnsh* 6.00 2.25
*Nos. C60-C69 (10)* 13.35 4.50

No. C58 Surcharged in Red

**1959, Sept. 14 Photo. Unwmk.**
**C70** AP25 5 l on 3.25 l 13.50 3.75

1st Russian rocket to reach the moon, 9/14/59.

Miniature Sheet

Prince Vlad Tepes and Document — AP28

**1959, Sept. 15 Engr. *Perf. 11½x11***
**C71** AP28 20 l violet brn *150.00 150.00*

500th anniv. of the founding of Bucharest.

**Sport Type of Regular Issue, 1959**

**1959, Oct. 5 Litho. *Perf. 13½***
**C72** A474 2.80 l Boating 2.50 .50

Soviet Rocket, Globe, Dog and Rabbit — AP29

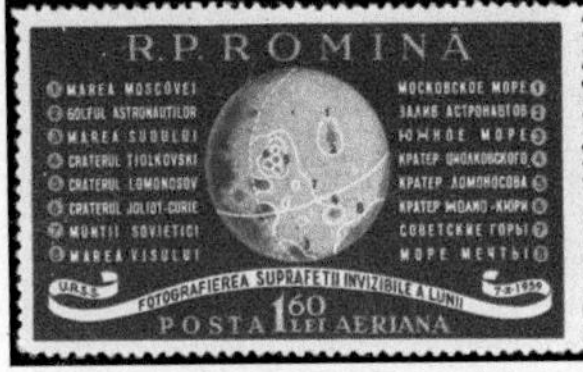
Photograph of Far Side of the Moon — AP30

Design: 1.75 l, Trajectory of Lunik 3, which hit the moon.

***Perf. 14, 13½ (AP30)***
**1959, Dec. Photo. Wmk. 358**
**C73** AP29 1.55 l dk blue 3.00 .35
**C74** AP30 1.60 l dk vio bl, *buff* 3.50 .55
**C75** AP29 1.75 l dk blue 3.50 .55
*Nos. C73-C75 (3)* 10.00 1.45

Soviet conquest of space.

**Animal Type of Regular Issue, 1960.**

Designs: 1.30 l, Golden eagle. 1.75 l, Black grouse. 2 l, Lammergeier.

**Unwmk.**
**1960, Mar. 3 Engr. *Perf. 14***
**C76** A480 1.30 l dk blue 1.75 .40
**C77** A480 1.75 l olive grn 1.75 .40
**C78** A480 2 l dk carmine 1.75 .50
*Nos. C76-C78 (3)* 5.25 1.30

Aurel Vlaicu and Plane of 1910 AP31

Bucharest Airport and Turbo-Jet — AP32

Designs: 20b, Plane and Aurel Vlaicu. 35b, Amphibian ambulance plane. 40b, Plane spraying crops. 55b, Pilot and planes, vert. 1.75 l, Parachutes at aviation sports meet.

**1960, June 15 Litho. Unwmk.**
**C79** AP31 10b yellow & brn .25 .25
**C80** AP31 20b red org & brn .25 .25

**Photo. Wmk. 358**
**C81** AP31 35b crimson .40 .25
**C82** AP31 40b violet .55 .25
**C83** AP31 55b blue .80 .25

**Litho. Unwmk.**
**C84** AP32 1.60 l vio bl, yel & emer 2.00 .40
**C85** AP32 1.75 l bl, red, brn & pale grn 2.50 .55
*Nos. C79-C85 (7)* 6.75 2.20

50th anniv. of the first Romanian airplane flight by Aurel Vlaicu.
For surcharge see No. C145.

Bucharest Airport — AP33

**1960 Wmk. 358 Photo. *Perf. 14***
**C86** AP33 3.20 l brt ultra 1.50 .25

**Type of Regular Issue, 1960**

Black Sea Resort: 2 l, Beach at Mamaia.

**1960, Aug. 2 Litho. Unwmk.**
**C87** A491 2 l grn, org & lt bl 1.50 .50

Sputnik 4 Flying into Space AP34

**1960, June 8 Photo. Wmk. 358**
**C88** AP34 55b deep blue 2.50 .25

Launching of Sputnik 4, May 15, 1960.

Saturnia Pyri AP35

Papilio Machaon AP36

Limenitis Populi — AP37

Designs: 40b, Chrisophanus virgaureae. 1.60 l, Acherontia atropos. 1.75 l, Apatura iris.

***Perf. 13, 14x12½, 14***
**1960, Oct. 10 Typo. Unwmk.**
**C89** AP35 10b multi .25 .25
**C90** AP37 20b multi .25 .25
**C91** AP37 40b multi .35 .25
**C92** AP36 55b multi .65 .25
**C93** AP36 1.60 l multi 2.00 .35
**C94** AP36 1.75 l multi, horiz. 2.75 .35
*Nos. C89-C94 (6)* 6.25 1.70

Compass Rose and Jet — AP38

***Perf. 13½x14***
**1960, Nov. 1 Photo. Wmk. 358**
**C95** AP38 55b brt bl + 45b label .50 .25

Stamp Day.

Skier AP39

Slalom — AP40

Designs: 25b, Skiers going up. 40b, Bobsled. 55b, Ski jump. 1 l, Mountain climber. 1.55 l, Long-distance skier.

***Perf. 14x13½, 13½x14***
**1961, Mar. 18 Litho. Unwmk.**
**C96** AP39 10b olive & gray .25 .25
**C97** AP40 20b gray & dk red .25 .25
**C98** AP40 25b gray & bl grn .35 .25
**C99** AP40 40b gray & pur .35 .25
**C100** AP39 55b gray & ultra .45 .25
**C101** AP40 1 l gray & brn lake .75 .25
**C102** AP39 1.55 l gray & brn 1.10 .25
*Nos. C96-C102 (7)* 3.50 1.75

Exist imperf. with changed colors. Value, set $5.

Maj. Yuri A. Gagarin — AP41

Design: 3.20 l, Gagarin in space capsule and globe with orbit, horiz.

***Perf. 14x14½, 14½x14***
**1961, Apr. 19 Photo. Unwmk.**
**C103** AP41 1.35 l brt blue 1.00 .30
**C104** AP41 3.20 l ultra 2.25 .60

No. C104 exists imperf. in dark carmine rose. Value unused $7.50, canceled $3.25.

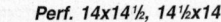

Eclipse over Republic Palace Place, Bucharest AP42

1.75 l, Total Eclipse, Scinteia House, telescope.

***Perf. 14x13½***
**1961, June 13 Wmk. 358**
**C106** AP42 1.60 l ultra 1.25 .30
**C107** AP42 1.75 l dk blue 1.50 .30

Total solar eclipse of Feb. 15, 1961.

Maj. Gherman S. Titov — AP43

55b, "Peace" and Vostok 2 rocket. 1.75 l, Yuri A. Gagarin and Gherman S. Titov, horiz.

***Perf. 13½x14***
**1961, Sept. 11 Unwmk.**
**C108** AP43 55b dp blue .55 .25
**C109** AP43 1.35 l dp purple .80 .25
**C110** AP43 1.75 l dk carmine 1.25 .25
*Nos. C108-C110 (3)* 2.60 .75

Issued to honor the Russian space navigators Y. A. Gagarin and G. S. Titov.

Globe and Stamps — AP44

**1961, Nov. 15 Litho. *Perf. 13½x14***
**C111** AP44 55b multi + 45b label 1.00 .25

Stamp Day.

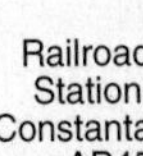

Railroad Station, Constanta AP45

Buildings: 20b, Tower, RPR Palace place, vert. 55b, Congress hall, Bucharest. 75b, Mill, Hunedoara. 1 l, Apartment houses, Bucharest. 1.20 l, Circus, Bucharest. 1.75 l, Worker's Club, Mangalia.

***Perf. 13½x14, 14x13½***
**1961, Nov. 20 Typo.**
**C112** AP45 20b multi .25 .25
**C113** AP45 40b multi .25 .25
**C114** AP45 55b multi .25 .25
**C115** AP45 75b multi .30 .25
**C116** AP45 1 l multi .40 .25
**C117** AP45 1.20 l multi .75 .25
**C118** AP45 1.75 l multi 1.10 .25
*Nos. C112-C118 (7)* 3.30 1.75

Space Exploration Stamps and Dove AP46

Design: Each stamp shows a different group of Romanian space exploration stamps.

**1962, July 27** ***Perf. 14x13½***

| | | | | |
|---|---|---|---|---|
| **C119** | AP46 | 35b yellow brn | .25 | .25 |
| **C120** | AP46 | 55b green | .30 | .25 |
| **C121** | AP46 | 1.35 l blue | .60 | .25 |
| **C122** | AP46 | 1.75 l rose red | 1.10 | .25 |
| *a.* | | Sheet of 4 | 3.00 | 1.50 |
| | | *Nos. C119-C122 (4)* | 2.25 | 1.00 |

Peaceful space exploration.

No. C122a contains four imperf. stamps similar to Nos. C119-C122 in changed colors and with one dove covering all four stamps. Stamps are printed together without space between.

Andrian G. Nikolayev — AP47

Designs: 1.60 l, Globe and trajectories of Vostoks 3 and 4. 1.75 l, Pavel R. Popovich.

***Perf. 13½x14***

**1962, Aug. 20** **Photo.** **Unwmk.**

| | | | | |
|---|---|---|---|---|
| **C123** | AP47 | 55b purple | .30 | .25 |
| **C124** | AP47 | 1.60 l dark blue | .90 | .30 |
| **C125** | AP47 | 1.75 l rose claret | 1.25 | .30 |
| | | *Nos. C123-C125 (3)* | 2.45 | .85 |

1st Russian group space flight of Vostoks 3 and 4, Aug. 11-15, 1962.

Exhibition Hall — AP48

**1962, Oct. 12** **Litho.** ***Perf. 14x13***

| | | | | |
|---|---|---|---|---|
| **C126** | AP48 | 1.60 l bl, vio bl & org | 1.50 | .25 |

4th Sample Fair, Bucharest.

The Coachmen by Szatmary — AP49

**1962, Nov. 15** ***Perf. 13½x14***

| | | | | |
|---|---|---|---|---|
| **C127** | AP49 | 55b + 45b label | 1.25 | .35 |

Stamp Day. Alternating label shows No. 14 on cover.

**No. C127 Overprinted in Violet**

**1963, Mar. 30**

| | | | | |
|---|---|---|---|---|
| **C128** | AP49 | 55b + 45b label | 3.50 | 2.00 |

Romanian Philatelists' Assoc. meeting at Bucharest, Mar. 30.

Sighisoara Glass and Crockery Factory AP50

Industrial Plants: 40b, Govora soda works. 55b, Tirgul-Jiu wood processing factory. 1 l, Savinesti chemical plant (synthetic fibers). 1.55 l, Hunedoara metal factory. 1.75 l, Brazi thermal power station.

***Perf. 14x13***

**1963, Apr. 10** **Unwmk.** **Photo.**

| | | | | |
|---|---|---|---|---|
| **C129** | AP50 | 30b dk bl & red | .30 | .25 |
| **C130** | AP50 | 40b sl grn & pur | .30 | .25 |
| **C131** | AP50 | 55b brn red & dp bl | .30 | .25 |
| **C132** | AP50 | 1 l vio & brn | .30 | .25 |
| **C133** | AP50 | 1.55 l ver & dk bl | .70 | .25 |
| **C134** | AP50 | 1.75 l dk bl & magenta | 1.00 | .25 |
| | | *Nos. C129-C134 (6)* | 2.90 | 1.50 |

Industrial achievements.

Lunik 4 Approaching Moon — AP51

**1963, Apr. 29** ***Perf. 13½x14***

| | | | | |
|---|---|---|---|---|
| **C135** | AP51 | 55b dk ultra & red | .45 | .25 |

***Imperf***

| | | | | |
|---|---|---|---|---|
| **C136** | AP51 | 1.75 l vio & red | 1.00 | .25 |

Moon flight of Lunik 4, Apr. 2, 1963.

Steam Locomotive AP52

Designs: 55b, Diesel locomotive. 75b, Trolley bus. 1.35 l, Passenger ship. 1.75 l, Plane.

**1963, July 10** **Litho.** ***Perf. 14½x13***

| | | | | |
|---|---|---|---|---|
| **C137** | AP52 | 40b multi | .35 | .25 |
| **C138** | AP52 | 55b multi | .40 | .25 |
| **C139** | AP52 | 75b multi | .60 | .25 |
| **C140** | AP52 | 1.35 l multi | 1.00 | .30 |
| **C141** | AP52 | 1.75 l multi | 1.40 | .25 |
| | | *Nos. C137-C141 (5)* | 3.75 | 1.30 |

Valeri Bykovski AP53

Designs: 1.20 l, Bykovski, vert. 1.60 l, Tereshkova, vert. 1.75 l, Valentina Tereshkova.

**1963** **Photo.**

| | | | | |
|---|---|---|---|---|
| **C142** | AP53 | 55b blue | .30 | .25 |
| **C143** | AP53 | 1.75 l rose red | 1.40 | .30 |

**Souvenir Sheet**

***Perf. 13***

| | | | | |
|---|---|---|---|---|
| **C144** | | Sheet of 2 | 2.75 | .80 |
| *a.* | AP53 | 1.20 l ultra | .60 | .30 |
| *b.* | AP53 | 1.60 l ultra | .75 | .40 |

Space flights of Valeri Bykovski, June 14-19, and Valentina Tereshkova, first woman cosmonaut, June 16-19, 1963.

**No. C79 Surcharged and Overprinted "1913-1963 50 ani de la moarte"**

**Unwmk.**

**1963, Sept. 15** **Litho.** ***Perf. 14***

| | | | | |
|---|---|---|---|---|
| **C145** | AP31 | 1.75 l on 10b | 2.50 | .95 |

50th death anniv. of Aurel Vlaicu, aviation pioneer.

Exists with "i" of "lei," missing.

Centenary Stamp of 1958 AP54

Stamps on Stamps: 40b, Sputnik 2 and Laika, No. 1200. 55b, Yuri A. Gagarin, No. C104a. 1.20 l, Nikolayev and Popovich, Nos. C123, C125. 1.55 l, Postal Administration Bldg. and letter carrier, No. 965.

**1963, Nov. 15** **Photo.** ***Perf. 14x13½***

**Size: 38x26mm**

| | | | | |
|---|---|---|---|---|
| **C146** | AP54 | 20b lt bl & dk brn | .25 | .25 |
| **C147** | AP54 | 40b brt pink & dk bl | .25 | .25 |
| **C148** | AP54 | 55b lt ultra & dk car rose | .25 | .25 |
| **C149** | AP54 | 1.20 l ocher & pur | .45 | .25 |
| **C150** | AP54 | 1.55 l sal pink & ol gray | .65 | .25 |
| | | *Nos. C146-C150,CB22 (6)* | 4.60 | 1.75 |

15th UPU Congress, Vienna.

Pavel R. Popovich AP55

Astronauts and flag: 5b, Yuri A. Gagarin. 10b, Gherman S. Titov. 20b, John H. Glenn, Jr. 35b, M. Scott Carpenter. 40b, Andrian G. Nikolayev. 60b, Walter M. Schirra. 75b, L. Gordon Cooper. 1 l, Valeri Bykovski. 1.40 l, Valentina Tereshkova. (5b, 10b, 20b, 35b, 60b and 75b are diamond shaped).

***Perf. 13½***

**1964, Jan. 15** **Litho.** **Unwmk.**

**Light Blue Background**

| | | | | |
|---|---|---|---|---|
| **C151** | AP55 | 5b red, yel & vio bl | .30 | .25 |
| **C152** | AP55 | 10b red, yel & pur | .30 | .25 |
| **C153** | AP55 | 20b red, ultra & ol gray | .30 | .25 |
| **C154** | AP55 | 35b red, ultra & sl bl | .30 | .25 |
| **C155** | AP55 | 40b red, yel & ultra | .30 | .25 |
| **C156** | AP55 | 55b red, yel & ultra | .60 | .25 |
| **C157** | AP55 | 60b ultra, red & sep | .60 | .25 |
| **C158** | AP55 | 75b red, ultra & dk bl | .65 | .25 |
| **C159** | AP55 | 1 l red, yel & mar | .95 | .25 |
| **C160** | AP55 | 1.40 l red, yel & mar | 1.10 | .25 |
| | | *Nos. C151-C160 (10)* | 5.40 | 2.50 |

Nos. C151-C160 exist imperf. in changed colors. Value, set $8 unused, $3 used.

A miniature sheet contains one imperf. horizontal 2 l ultramarine and yellow stamp. Size of stamp: 59½x43mm. Value unused $8.50, canceled $4.25.

Modern and 19th Century Post Office Buildings AP56

**Engr. & Typo.**

**1964, Nov. 15** ***Perf. 13½***

| | | | | |
|---|---|---|---|---|
| **C161** | AP56 | 1.60 l ultra + 40b label | 1.25 | .50 |

Stamp Day. Stamp and label are imperf. between.

Plane Approaching Airport and Coach Leaving Gate — AP57

**Engr. & Typo.**

**1966, Oct. 20** ***Perf. 13½***

| | | | | |
|---|---|---|---|---|
| **C162** | AP57 | 55b + 45b label | .90 | .50 |

Stamp Day.

**Space Exploration Type of Regular Issue**

US Achievements in Space: 1.20 l, Early Bird satellite and globe. 1.55 l, Mariner 4 transmitting pictures of the moon. 3.25 l, Gemini 6 & 7, rendezvous in space. 5 l, Gemini 8 meeting Agena rocket, and globe.

**1967, Feb. 15** **Photo.** ***Perf. 13½***

| | | | | |
|---|---|---|---|---|
| **C163** | A595 | 1.20 l silver & multi | .60 | .25 |
| **C164** | A595 | 1.55 l silver & multi | .75 | .25 |
| **C165** | A595 | 3.25 l silver & multi | 1.00 | .35 |
| **C166** | A595 | 5 l silver & multi | 1.50 | .75 |
| | | *Nos. C163-C166 (4)* | 3.85 | 1.50 |

10 years of space exploration.

Plane Spraying Crops — AP58

Designs: 55b, Aerial ambulance over river, horiz. 1 l, Red Cross and plane. 2.40 l, Biplane and Mircea Zorileanu, aviation pioneer.

***Perf. 12x12½, 12½x12***

**1968, Feb. 28** **Litho.** **Unwmk.**

| | | | | |
|---|---|---|---|---|
| **C167** | AP58 | 40b bl grn, blk & yel brn | .25 | .25 |
| **C168** | AP58 | 55b multicolored | .30 | .25 |
| **C169** | AP58 | 1 l ultra, pale grn & red org | .30 | .25 |
| **C170** | AP58 | 2.40 l brt rose lil & multi | .75 | .30 |
| | | *Nos. C167-C170 (4)* | 1.60 | 1.05 |

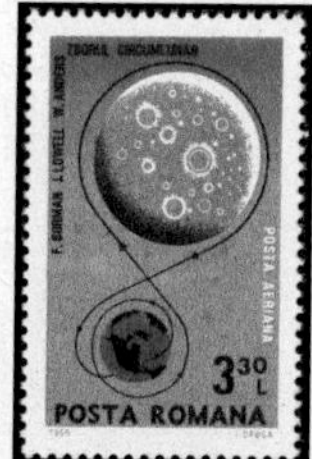


Moon, Earth and Path of Apollo 8 — AP59

Design: No. C172, Soyuz 4 and 5 over globe with map of Russia.

**1969** **Photo.** ***Perf. 13½***

| | | | | |
|---|---|---|---|---|
| **C171** | AP59 | 3.30 l multi | 1.60 | 1.60 |
| **C172** | AP59 | 3.30 l multi | 1.60 | 1.60 |

1st manned flight around the Moon, Dec. 21-27, 1968, and the first team flights of the Russian spacecrafts Soyuz 4 and 5, Jan. 16, 1969. See note after Hungary No. C284.

Issued in sheets of 4.

Issued: #C171, Jan. 17, #C172, Mar. 28.

Apollo 9 and Lunar Landing Module over Earth AP60

Design: 2.40 l, Apollo 10 and lunar landing module over moon, vert.

**1969, June 15 Photo. *Perf. 13½***
**C173** AP60 60b multi .25 .25
**C174** AP60 2.40 l multi 1.75 .35

US space explorations, Apollo 9 and 10.

First Man on Moon — AP61

**1969, July 24 Photo. *Perf. 13½***
**C175** AP61 3.30 l multi 1.90 1.90

Man's first landing on the moon July 20, 1969, US astronauts Neil A. Armstrong and Col. Edwin E. Aldrin, Jr., with Lieut. Col. Michael Collins piloting Apollo 11. Printed in sheets of 4.

**1970, June 29**

1.50 l, Apollo 13 capsule splashing down in Pacific.

**C176** AP61 1.50 l multi .75 .60

Flight and safe landing of Apollo 13, Apr. 11-17, 1970. Printed in sheets of 4.

BAC 1-11 Jet AP62

Design: 2 l, Fuselage BAC 1-11 and control tower, Bucharest airport.

**1970, Apr. 6**
**C177** AP62 60b multi .35 .25
**C178** AP62 2 l multi .80 .25

50th anniv. of Romanian civil aviation.

**Flood Relief Type of Regular Issue**

Design: 60b, Rescue by helicopter.

**1970, Sept. 25 Photo. *Perf. 13½***
**C179** A671 60b bl gray, blk & olive .25 .25

Publicizing the plight of victims of the Danube flood. See No. 2207a.

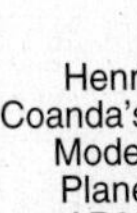

Henri Coanda's Model Plane AP63

**1970, Dec. 1**
**C180** AP63 60b multicolored 1.10 .30

Henri Coanda's first flight, 60th anniversary.

Luna 16 on Moon AP64

No. C182, Lunokhod 1, unmanned vehicle on moon. No. C183, US astronaut & vehicle on moon.

**1971, Mar. 5 Photo. *Perf. 13½***
**C181** AP64 3.30 l silver & multi 1.00 1.00
**C182** AP64 3.30 l silver & multi 1.00 1.00
*a.* Pair, #C181-C182 + 2 labels 2.75 2.75
**C183** AP64 3.30 l silver & multi 1.50 1.50
*Nos. C181-C183 (3)* 3.50 3.50

No. C181 commemorates Luna 16 Russian unmanned, automatic moon mission, Sept. 12-24, 1970 (labels are incorrectly inscribed Oct. 12-24). No. C182 commemorates Lunokhod 1 (Luna 17), Nov. 10-17, 1970. Nos. C181-C182 printed in sheets of 4 stamps, arranged checkerwise, and 4 labels. No. C183 commemorates Apollo 14 moon landing, Jan. 31-Feb. 9. Printed in sheets of 4 with 4 labels showing portraits of US astronauts Alan B. Shepard, Edgar D. Mitchell, Stuart A. Roosa, and Apollo 14 emblem.

Souvenir Sheet

Cosmonauts Patsayev, Dobrovolsky and Volkov — AP65

**1971, July 26 Litho. *Perf. 13½***
**C184** AP65 6 l black & ultra 6.50 5.00

In memory of Russian cosmonauts Viktor I. Patsayev, Georgi T. Dobrovolsky and Vladislav N. Volkov, who died during Soyuz 11 space mission, June 6-30, 1971.

No. C184 exists imperf. in black & blue green; Size: 130x90mm. Value, unused or used, $150.

Lunar Rover on Moon AP66

**1971, Aug. 26 Photo.**
**C185** AP66 1.50 l blue & multi 1.50 1.50

US Apollo 15 moon mission, July 26-Aug. 7, 1971. No. C185 printed in sheets of 4 stamps and 4 labels showing astronauts David Scott, James Irwin, Alfred Worden and Apollo 15 emblem with dates.

No. C185 exists imperf. in green & multicolored. The sheet has a control number. Values: unused $150; used $110.

**Olympics Type of Regular Issue**
Souvenir Sheets

Designs: No. C186, Torchbearer and map of Romania. No. C187, Soccer.

**1972 Photo. *Perf. 13½***
**C186** A699 6 l pale grn & multi 7.50 7.50
**C187** A699 6 l blue & multi 7.50 7.50

20th Olympic Games, Munich, Aug. 26-Sept. 11. No. C186 contains one stamp 50x38mm. No. C187 contains one stamp 48½x37mm.

Issued: #C186, Apr. 25; #C187, Sept. 29.

Two imperf. 6 l souvenir sheets exist, one showing equestrian, the other a satellite over globe. Value for either sheet, unused or used, $80.

Lunar Rover on Moon — AP67

**1972, May 10 Photo. *Perf. 13½***
**C188** AP67 3 l vio bl, rose & gray grn 1.10 .85

Apollo 16 US moon mission, Apr. 15-27, 1972. No. C188 printed in sheets of 4 stamps and 4 gray green and black labels showing Capt. John W. Young, Lt. Comdr. Thomas K. Mattingly 2nd, Col. Charles M. Duke, Jr., and Apollo 16 badge.

Aurel Vlaicu and Monoplane — AP68

Romanian Aviation Pioneers: 3 l, Traian Vuia and his flying machine.

**1972, Aug. 15**
**C189** AP68 60b multicolored .25 .25
**C190** AP68 3 l multicolored 1.00 .40

**Olympic Medals Type of Regular Issue**
Souvenir Sheet

Olympic silver and gold medals, horiz.

**1972, Sept. 29 Litho. *Perf. 13½***
**C191** A714 6 l multicolored 7.50 7.50

Romanian medalists at 20th Olympic Games. An imperf. 6 l souvenir sheet exists showing gold medal. Value, unused or used, $70.

**Apollo Type of Regular Issue**
Souvenir Sheet

Design: 6 l, Lunar rover, landing module, rocket and astronauts on moon, horiz.

**1972, Dec. 27 Photo. *Perf. 13½***
**C192** A715 6 l vio bl, bis & dl grn 10.00 10.00

No. C192 contains one stamp 48½x36mm.

An imperf. 6 l souvenir sheet exists showing surface of moon with landing sites of last 6 Apollo missions and landing capsule. Value, unused or used, $80.

**Type of Regular Issue, 1972**

Design: Otopeni Airport, horiz.

**1972, Dec. 20 Photo. *Perf. 13***
**Size: 29x21mm**
**C193** A710 14.60 l brt blue 1.50 .40

Apollo and Soyuz Spacecraft — AP69

3.25 l, Apollo and Soyuz after link-up.

**1975, July 14 Photo. *Perf. 13½***
**C196** AP69 1.75 l vio bl, red & ol 1.25 1.25
**C197** AP69 3.25 l vio bl, red & ol 1.25 1.25

Apollo Soyuz space test project (Russo-American cooperation), launching July 15; link-up, July 17. Nos. C196-C197 printed in sheets of 4 stamps, arranged checkerwise, and 4 rose lilac labels showing Apollo-Soyuz emblem.

European Security and Cooperation Conference — AP70

**1975, July 30 Photo. *Perf. 13½***
**C198** AP70 Sheet of 4 2.50 2.50
*a.* 2.75 l Map of Europe .35 .35
*b.* 2.75 l Peace doves .35 .35
*c.* 5 l Open book .75 .75
*d.* 5 l Children playing .75 .75

European Security and Cooperation Conference, Helsinki, July 30-Aug. 1. No. C198b inscribed "posta aeriana."

An imperf. 10 l souvenir sheet exists showing Helsinki on map of Europe. Value, unused or used, $95.

**Red Cross Type of 1976**

Design: Blood donors, Red Cross plane.

**1976, Apr. 20 Photo. *Perf. 13½***
**C199** A790 3.35 l multi .70 .25

De Havilland DH-9 — AP71

Airplanes: 40b, I.C.A.R. Comercial. 60b, Douglas DC-3. 1.75 l, AN-24. 2.75 l, IL-62. 3.60 l, Boeing 707.

**1976, June 24 Photo. *Perf. 13½***
**C200** AP71 20b blue & multi .25 .25
**C201** AP71 40b blue & multi .25 .25
**C202** AP71 60b multi .25 .25
**C203** AP71 1.75 l multi .40 .25
**C204** AP71 2.75 l blue & multi .55 .25
**C205** AP71 3.60 l multi .85 .30
*Nos. C200-C205 (6)* 2.55 1.55

Romanian Airline, 50th anniversary.

Glider I.C.A.R.-1 — AP72

Gliders: 40b, I.S.-3d. 55b, R.G.-5. 1.50 l, I.S.-11. 3 l, I.S.-29D. 3.40 l, I.S.-28B.

**1977, Feb. 20 Photo. *Perf. 13***
**C206** AP72 20b multi .25 .25
**C207** AP72 40b multi .25 .25
**C208** AP72 55b multi .25 .25
**C209** AP72 1.50 l bl & multi .25 .25
**C210** AP72 3 l multi .60 .25
**C211** AP72 3.40 l multi .95 .25
*Nos. C206-C211 (6)* 2.55 1.50

Souvenir Sheet

Boeing 707 over Bucharest Airport and Pioneers — AP73

**1977, June 28 Photo. *Perf. 13½***
**C212** AP73 10 l multi 2.50 2.50

European Security and Cooperation Conference, Belgrade.

An imperf. 10 l souvenir sheet exists showing Boeing 707, map of Europe and buildings. Value, unused or used, $35.

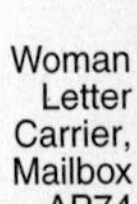

Woman Letter Carrier, Mailbox AP74

30 l, Plane, newspapers, letters, packages.

**1977 Photo. *Perf. 13½***
**C213** AP74 20 l multicolored 3.50 1.00
**C214** AP74 30 l multicolored 5.50 1.75

Issue dates: 20 l, July 25, 30 l, Sept. 10.

LZ-1 over Friedrichshafen, 1900 — AP75

Airships: 1 l, Santos Dumont's dirigible over Paris, 1901. 1.50 l, British R-34 over New York and Statue of Liberty, 1919. 2.15 l, Italia over North Pole, 1928. 3.40 l, Zeppelin LZ-127 over Brasov, 1929. 4.80 l, Zeppelin over Sibiu, 1929. 10 l, Zeppelin over Bucharest, 1929.

**1978, Mar. 20 Photo. *Perf. 13½***

| | | | | |
|---|---|---|---|---|
| **C215** | AP75 | 60b multi | .25 | .25 |
| **C216** | AP75 | 1 l multi | .25 | .25 |
| **C217** | AP75 | 1.50 l multi | .35 | .25 |
| **C218** | AP75 | 2.15 l multi | .40 | .25 |
| **C219** | AP75 | 3.40 l multi | .75 | .25 |
| **C220** | AP75 | 4.80 l multi | 1.10 | .25 |
| | | *Nos. C215-C220 (6)* | 3.10 | 1.50 |

**Souvenir Sheet**

| | | | | |
|---|---|---|---|---|
| **C221** | AP75 | 10 l multi | 2.50 | 2.50 |

History of airships. No. C221 contains one 50x37½mm stamp.

**Soccer Type of 1978**
Souvenir Sheet

10 l, 2 soccer players, Argentina '78 emblem.

**1978, Apr. 15 Photo. *Perf. 13½***

| | | | | |
|---|---|---|---|---|
| **C222** | A818 | 10 l blue & multi | 3.00 | 3.00 |

11th World Cup Soccer Championship, Argentina, June 1-25. No. C222 contains one stamp 37x50mm. A 10 l imperf souvenir sheet exists showing goalkeeper. Values: unused $30; used $20.

Wilbur and Orville Wright, Flyer A — AP76

Aviation History: 1 l, Louis Blériot and his plane over English Channel, 1909. 1.50 l, Anthony Fokker and Fokker F-VII trimotor, 1926. 2.15 l, Andrei N. Tupolev and ANT-25 monoplane, 1937. 3 l, Otto Lilienthal and glider, 1891-96. 3.40 l, Traian Vuia and his plane, Montesson, France, 1906. 4.80 l, Aurel Vlaicu and 1st Romanian plane, 1910. 10 l, Henri Coanda and his "jet," 1910.

**1978, Dec. 18 Photo. *Perf. 13½***

| | | | | |
|---|---|---|---|---|
| **C223** | AP76 | 55b multi | .25 | .25 |
| **C224** | AP76 | 1 l multi | .25 | .25 |
| **C225** | AP76 | 1.50 l multi | .25 | .25 |
| **C226** | AP76 | 2.15 l multi | .35 | .25 |
| **C227** | AP76 | 3 l multi | .35 | .25 |
| **C228** | AP76 | 3.40 l multi | .40 | .25 |
| **C229** | AP76 | 4.80 l multi | .45 | .25 |
| | | *Nos. C223-C229 (7)* | 2.30 | 1.75 |

**Souvenir Sheet**

| | | | | |
|---|---|---|---|---|
| **C230** | AP76 | 10 l multi | 2.25 | 2.25 |

No. C230 contains one stamp 50x38mm.

**Inter-Europa Type of 1979**

3.40 l, Jet, mail truck and motorcycle.

**1979, May 3 Photo. *Perf. 13***

| | | | | |
|---|---|---|---|---|
| **C231** | A835 | 3.40 l multi | .40 | .40 |

Issued in sheets of 4.

**Animal Type of 1980**
Souvenir Sheet

**1980, Mar. 25 Photo. *Perf. 13½***

| | | | | |
|---|---|---|---|---|
| **C232** | A852 | 10 l Pelicans | 2.25 | 2.25 |

No. C232 contains one stamp 38x50mm.

Mercury AP77

**1981, June 30 Photo. *Perf. 13½***

| | | | | |
|---|---|---|---|---|
| **C233** | AP77 | 55b shown | .25 | .25 |
| **C234** | AP77 | 1 l Venus, Earth, Mars | .25 | .25 |
| **C235** | AP77 | 1.50 l Jupiter | .25 | .25 |
| **C236** | AP77 | 2.15 l Saturn | .30 | .25 |
| **C237** | AP77 | 3.40 l Uranus | .60 | .25 |
| **C238** | AP77 | 4.80 l Neptune, Pluto | .75 | .30 |
| | | *Nos. C233-C238 (6)* | 2.40 | 1.55 |

**Souvenir Sheet**

| | | | | |
|---|---|---|---|---|
| **C239** | AP77 | 10 l Earth | 2.25 | 2.25 |

No. C239 contains one stamp 37x50mm. An imperf. 10 l souvenir sheet exists showing planets in orbit. Value, unused or used, $30.

Romanian-Russian Space Cooperation — AP78

55b, Soyuz 40. 3.40 l, Salyut 6, Soyuz 40. 10 l, Cosmonauts, spacecraft.

**1981 Photo. *Perf. 13½***

| | | | | |
|---|---|---|---|---|
| **C240** | AP78 | 55b multicolored | .25 | .25 |
| **C241** | AP78 | 3.40 l multicolored | .50 | .25 |

**Souvenir Sheet**

| | | | | |
|---|---|---|---|---|
| **C242** | AP78 | 10 l multicolored | 2.25 | 2.25 |

No. C242 contains one stamp 50x39mm. Issued: 55b, 3.40 l, May 14; 10 l, June 30.

---

An imperforate souvenir sheet titled "C.S.C.E. in EUROPA" was issued with limited distribution 1981, Oct. 28. The souvenir sheet contains three stamps showing a map of Europe, an airplane over a globe, and Madrid, respectively. Each stamp has a face value of 5 l. Value for sheet, $16.

---

**Children's Games Type of 1981**

**1981, Nov. 25**

| | | | | |
|---|---|---|---|---|
| **C243** | A880 | 4.80 l Flying model planes | .70 | .70 |

Standard Glider — AP79

**1982, June 20 Photo. *Perf. 13½***

| | | | | |
|---|---|---|---|---|
| **C244** | AP79 | 50b shown | .25 | .25 |
| **C245** | AP79 | 1 l Excelsior D | .25 | .25 |
| **C246** | AP79 | 1.50 l Dedal I | .25 | .25 |
| **C247** | AP79 | 2.50 l Enthusiast | .45 | .25 |
| **C248** | AP79 | 4 l AK-22 | .60 | .25 |
| **C249** | AP79 | 5 l Grifrom | .75 | .30 |
| | | *Nos. C244-C249 (6)* | 2.55 | 1.55 |

**Agriculture Type of 1982**

**1982, June 29**

| | | | | |
|---|---|---|---|---|
| **C250** | A888 | 4 l Helicopter spraying insecticide | .60 | .25 |

Vlaicu's Glider, 1909 — AP80

Aurel Vlaicu (1882-19), Aviator: 1 l, Memorial, Banesti-Prahova, vert. 2.50 l, Hero Aviators Memorial, by Kotzebue and Fekete, vert. 3 l, Vlaicu-1 glider, 1910.

**1982, Sept. 27 Photo. *Perf. 13½***

| | | | | |
|---|---|---|---|---|
| **C251** | AP80 | 50b multi | .25 | .25 |
| **C252** | AP80 | 1 l multi | .25 | .25 |
| **C253** | AP80 | 2.50 l multi | .40 | .25 |
| **C254** | AP80 | 3 l multi | .45 | .25 |
| | | *Nos. C251-C254 (4)* | 1.35 | 1.00 |

25th Anniv. of Space Flight AP81

Designs: 50b, H. Coanda, reaction motor, 1910. 1 l, H. Oberth, rocket, 1923. 1.50 l, Sputnik I, 1957. 2.50 l, Vostok I, 1961. 4 l, Apollo 11, 1969. 5 l, Columbia space shuttle, 1982. 10 l, Globe.

**1983, Jan. 24**

| | | | | |
|---|---|---|---|---|
| **C255** | AP81 | 50b multi | .25 | .25 |
| **C256** | AP81 | 1 l multi | .25 | .25 |
| **C257** | AP81 | 1.50 l multi | .30 | .25 |
| **C258** | AP81 | 2.50 l multi | .45 | .25 |
| **C259** | AP81 | 4 l multi | .70 | .25 |
| **C260** | AP81 | 5 l multi | .90 | .25 |
| | | *Nos. C255-C260 (6)* | 2.85 | 1.50 |

**Souvenir Sheet**

| | | | | |
|---|---|---|---|---|
| **C261** | AP81 | 10 l multi | 2.50 | 2.50 |

No. C261 contains one stamp 41x53mm.

First Romanian-built Jet Airliner — AP82

**1983, Jan. 25 Photo. *Perf. 13½***

| | | | | |
|---|---|---|---|---|
| **C262** | AP82 | 11 l Rombac 1-11 | 2.75 | .40 |

World Communications Year — AP83

**1983, July 25 Photo. *Perf. 13½***

| | | | | |
|---|---|---|---|---|
| **C263** | AP83 | 2 l Boeing 707, Postal van | .40 | .25 |

---

An imperf. 10 l souvenir sheet showing a dove above the Palacic de Congresos de Madrid building was issued 1983, nov. 28 with limited distribution for EUROPA. Value, $20.

---

40th Anniv., Intl. Civil Aviation Organization — AP84

**1984, Aug. 15 Photo. *Perf. 13½***

| | | | | |
|---|---|---|---|---|
| **C265** | AP84 | 50b Lockheed L-14 | .25 | .25 |
| **C266** | AP84 | 1.50 l BN-2 Islander | .35 | .25 |
| **C267** | AP84 | 3 l Rombac | .70 | .25 |
| **C268** | AP84 | 6 l Boeing 707 | 1.25 | .35 |
| | | *Nos. C265-C268 (4)* | 2.55 | 1.10 |

Halley's Comet — AP85

**1986, Jan. 27 Photo. *Perf. 13½***

| | | | | |
|---|---|---|---|---|
| **C269** | AP85 | 2 l shown | .60 | .40 |
| **C270** | AP85 | 4 l Space probes | 1.50 | .65 |

An imperf. 10 l air post souvenir sheet exists showing comet and space probes, red control number. Value, unused or used, $10. For surcharge, see No. C302.

Souvenir Sheet

Plane of Alexandru Papana, 1936 — AP86

**1986, May 15 Photo. *Perf. 13½***

| | | | | |
|---|---|---|---|---|
| **C271** | AP86 | 10 l multi | 2.25 | 2.25 |

AMERIPEX '86.

Aircraft AP87

50b, Henri Auguste glider, 1909. 1 l, Sky diver, IS-28 B2 glider. 2 l, IS-29 D-2 glider. 3 l, IS-32 glider. 4 l, IAR-35 glider. 5 l, IS-28 M2, route.

**1987, Aug. 10**

| | | | | |
|---|---|---|---|---|
| **C272** | AP87 | 50b multi | .25 | .25 |
| **C273** | AP87 | 1 l multi | .25 | .25 |
| **C274** | AP87 | 2 l multi | .35 | .25 |
| **C275** | AP87 | 3 l multi | .55 | .25 |
| **C276** | AP87 | 4 l multi | .80 | .25 |
| **C277** | AP87 | 5 l multi | 1.00 | .30 |
| | | *Nos. C272-C277 (6)* | 3.20 | 1.55 |

1st Moon Landing, 20th Anniv. — AP88

Designs: 50b, C. Haas. 1.50 l, Konstantin Tsiolkovski (1857-1935), Soviet rocket science pioneer. 2 l, H. Oberth and equations. 3 l, Robert Goddard and diagram on blackboard. 4 l, Sergei Korolev (1906-66), Soviet aeronautical engineer. 5 l, Wernher von Braun (1912-77), lunar module.

**1989, Oct. 25 Photo. *Perf. 13½***

| | | | | |
|---|---|---|---|---|
| **C278** | AP88 | 50b multicolored | .25 | .25 |
| **C279** | AP88 | 1.50 l multicolored | .35 | .25 |
| **C280** | AP88 | 2 l multicolored | .45 | .25 |
| **C281** | AP88 | 3 l multicolored | .65 | .25 |

| | | | | |
|---|---|---|---|---|
| **C282** | AP88 | 4 l multicolored | .85 | .25 |
| **C283** | AP88 | 5 l multicolored | 1.10 | .25 |
| | | *Nos. C278-C283 (6)* | 3.65 | 1.50 |

A 10 l souvenir sheet picturing Armstrong and *Eagle* lunar module was also issued. Value, unused or used, $22.50.

Souvenir Sheet

World Stamp Expo '89, Washington, DC, Nov. 17-Dec. 3 — AP89

**1989, Nov. 17 Photo. *Perf. 13½***
**C284** AP89 5 l Postal coach 1.75 1.75

Captured Balloons — AP90

Balloons captured by Romanian army: 30 l, German balloon, Draken, 1903. 90 l, French balloon, Caquot, 1917.

**1993, Feb. 26 Photo. *Perf. 13½***

| | | | | |
|---|---|---|---|---|
| **C285** | AP90 | 30 l multicolored | .25 | .25 |
| **C286** | AP90 | 90 l multicolored | .70 | .25 |

Souvenir Sheet

European Inventions, Discoveries — AP91

Europa: a, 240 l, Hermann Oberth (1894-1989), rocket scientist. b, 2100 l, Henri Coanda (1886-1972), aeronautical engineer.

**1994, May 25 Photo. *Perf. 13***
**C287** AP91 Sheet of 2, #a.-b. + 2 labels 4.50 4.50

ICAO, 50th Anniv. AP92

Aircraft: 110 l, Traian Vuia, 1906. 350 l, Rombac 1-11. 500 l, Boeing 737-300. 635 l, Airbus A310.

**1994. Aug. 12 Photo. *Perf. 13***

| | | | | |
|---|---|---|---|---|
| **C288** | AP92 | 110 l multicolored | .25 | .25 |
| **C289** | AP92 | 350 l multicolored | .60 | .25 |
| **C290** | AP92 | 500 l multicolored | 1.00 | .25 |
| **C291** | AP92 | 635 l multicolored | 1.25 | .25 |
| | | *Nos. C288-C291 (4)* | 3.10 | 1.00 |

For surcharges see #C294-C297.

French-Romanian Aeronautical Agreement, 75th Anniv. — AP93

**1995, Mar. 31 Photo. *Perf. 13x13¼***

| | | | | |
|---|---|---|---|---|
| **C292** | AP93 | 60 l shown | .25 | .25 |
| **C293** | AP93 | 960 l Biplane Potez IX | 1.25 | .25 |

**No. C291 Surcharged in Red**

**Methods and Perfs as Before**

**2000, May 19**

| | | | | |
|---|---|---|---|---|
| **C294** | AP92 | 1700 l on 635 l multi | .25 | .25 |
| **C295** | AP92 | 2000 l on 635 l multi | .40 | .25 |
| **C296** | AP92 | 3900 l on 635 l multi | .65 | .25 |
| **C297** | AP92 | 9050 l on 635 l multi | 1.40 | .60 |
| | | *Nos. C294-C297 (4)* | 2.70 | 1.35 |

**No. C293 Surcharged in Red**

**2000, Oct. 27 Photo. *Perf. 13¼***

| | | | | |
|---|---|---|---|---|
| **C298** | AP93 | 2000 l on 960 l multi | .25 | .25 |
| **C299** | AP93 | 4200 l on 960 l multi | .45 | .25 |
| **C300** | AP93 | 4600 l on 960 l multi | .45 | .25 |
| **C301** | AP93 | 6500 l on 960 l multi | .65 | .25 |
| | | *Nos. C298-C301 (4)* | 1.80 | 1.00 |

**Souvenir Sheet Footnoted Under No. C270 Surcharged in Gold**

**Litho. With Foil Application**

**2016, Apr. 22 *Imperf.***
**C302** AP85 31 l on 10 l multi 16.00 8.00

---

**AIR POST SEMI-POSTAL STAMPS**

**Catalogue values for unused stamps in this section are for Never Hinged items.**

Corneliu Codreanu SPAP1

**Unwmk.**

**1940, Dec. 1 Photo. *Perf. 14***
**CB1** SPAP1 20 l + 5 l Prus grn 4.50 3.25

Propaganda for the Rome-Berlin Axis.

No. CB1 exists with overprint "1 Mai 1941 Jamboreea Nationala." This was a private overprint, not authorized by the Romanian Postal Service.

Plane over Sinaia — SPAP2

200 l+800 l, Plane over Mountains.

**1945, Oct. 1 Wmk. 276 *Imperf.***

| | | | | |
|---|---|---|---|---|
| **CB2** | SPAP2 | 80 l + 420 l gray | 2.50 | *2.50* |
| **CB3** | SPAP2 | 200 l + 800 l ultra | 2.50 | *2.50* |

16th Congress of the General Assoc. of Romanian Engineers.

Souvenir Sheet

Re-distribution of Land — SPAP4

**1946, May 4 Photo. *Perf. 14***
**CB4** SPAP4 80 l blue 14.00 *25.00*

Agrarian reform law of Mar. 23, 1945. The sheet sold for 100 lei.

Souvenir Sheet

Plane Skywriting — SPAP5

**1946, May 1 *Perf. 13***
**CB5** SPAP5 200 l bl & brt red 12.00 *22.50*

Labor Day. The sheet sold for 10,000 lei.

Lockheed 12 Electra — SPAP6

**1946, Sept. 1 *Perf. 11½***
**CB6** SPAP6 300 l + 1200 l dp bl 1.00 *1.25*

For se-tenant see No. C26a and note after No. C26.

The surtax was for the Office of Popular Sports.

Miniature Sheet

Women of Wallachia, Transylvania and Moldavia — SPAP7

**1946, Dec. 20 Wmk. 276 *Imperf.***
**CB7** SPAP7 500 l + 9500 l choc & red 6.00 6.00

Democratic Women's Org. of Romania.

SPAP8

**1946, Oct. *Imperf.***
**CB8** SPAP8 300 l deep plum 17.50 *17.50*

The surtax was for the Office of Popular Sports. Sheets of four. Stamp sold for 1300 l.

Laborer with Torch — SPAP9

**1947, Mar. 1**
**CB9** SPAP9 3000 l + 7000 l choc .80 1.50

Sheets of four with marginal inscription.

Plane — SPAP10

**1947, June 27 *Imperf.***
**CB10** SPAP10 15,000 l + 15,000 l .80 .80

Sheets of four with marginal inscription.

Plane above Shore Line — SPAP11

**1947, May 1 *Perf. 14x13***
**CB11** SPAP11 3000 l + 12,000 l bl .60 .60

Planes over Mountains
SPAP12

**1947, Oct. 5** *Perf. 14x14½*

**CB12** SPAP12 5 l + 5 l blue .70 .70

17th Congress of the General Assoc. of Romanian Engineers.

Plane over Athletic Field — SPAP13

**Wmk. 276**

**1948, Feb. 20 Photo.** *Perf. 13½*

**CB13** SPAP13 7 l + 7 l vio 1.00 .70

*Imperf*

**CB14** SPAP13 10 l + 10 l Prus grn 2.00 1.00

Balkan Games. Sheets of four with marginal inscription.

Swallow and Plane
SPAP14

**1948, Mar. 15** *Perf. 14x13½*

**CB15** SPAP14 12 l + 12 l blue 1.10 .60

Bucharest-Moscow Passenger Plane, Douglas DC-3 Dakota — SPAP15

**1948, Oct. 29** *Perf. 14*

**CB16** SPAP15 20 l + 20 l dp bl 10.00 10.00

Printed in sheets of 8 stamps and 16 small, red brown labels. Sheet yields 8 triptychs, each comprising 1 stamp flanked by label with Bucharest view and label with Moscow view.

Douglas DC-4 — SPAP16

**1948, May 1** *Perf. 13½x14*

**CB17** SPAP16 20 l + 20 l blue 10.00 8.00

Issued to publicize Labor Day, May 1, 1948.

Pursuit Plane and Victim — SPAP17

**1948, May 9** *Perf. 13*

**CB18** SPAP17 3 l + 3 l shown 6.00 6.00
**CB19** SPAP17 5 l + 5 l Bomber 8.00 8.00

Issued to honor the Romanian army.

Launching Model Plane — SPAP18

**1948, Dec. 31** *Perf. 13x13½*

**CB20** SPAP18 20 l + 20 l dp ultra 15.00 15.00

*Imperf*

**CB21** SPAP18 20 l + 20 l Prus bl 15.00 15.00

Nos. CB20 and CB21 were issued in sheets of four stamps, with ornamental border and "1948" in contrasting color.

### UPU Type of Air Post Issue, 1963

Design: 1.60 l+50b, Globe, map of Romania, planes and UPU monument.

*Perf. 14x13½*

**1963, Nov. 15 Litho. Unwmk.**

**Size: 75x27mm**

**CB22** AP54 1.60 l + 50b multi 2.75 .50

Surtax for the Romanian Philatelic Federation.

---

## POSTAGE DUE STAMPS

D1

***Perf. 11, 11½, 13½ and Compound***

**1881 Typo. Unwmk.**

**J1** D1 2b brown 4.00 1.50
**J2** D1 5b brown 22.50 2.50
*a.* Tête bêche pair 190.00 75.00
**J3** D1 10b brown 30.00 1.50
**J4** D1 30b brown 32.50 1.50
**J5** D1 50b brown 26.00 2.75
**J6** D1 60b brown 21.00 4.00
*Nos. J1-J6 (6)* 136.00 13.75

**1885**

**J7** D1 10b pale red brown 8.00 .50
**J8** D1 30b pale red brown 8.00 .50

**1887-90**

**J9** D1 2b gray green 4.00 1.00
**J10** D1 5b gray green 8.00 3.50
**J11** D1 10b gray green 8.00 3.50
**J12** D1 30b gray green 8.00 1.00
*Nos. J9-J12 (4)* 28.00 9.00

**1888**

**J14** D1 2b green, *yellowish* .90 .75
**J15** D1 5b green, *yellowish* 2.25 2.25
**J16** D1 10b green, *yellowish* 32.50 2.75
**J17** D1 30b green, *yellowish* 17.50 1.25
*Nos. J14-J17 (4)* 53.15 7.00

**1890-96 Wmk. 163**

**J18** D1 2b emerald 1.60 .45
**J19** D1 5b emerald .80 .45
**J20** D1 10b emerald 1.25 .45
**J21** D1 30b emerald 2.00 .45
**J22** D1 50b emerald 6.50 .95
**J23** D1 60b emerald 8.75 3.25
*Nos. J18-J23 (6)* 20.90 6.00

**1898 Wmk. 200**

**J24** D1 2b blue green .70 .45
**J25** D1 5b blue green .90 .30
**J26** D1 10b blue green 1.40 .30
**J27** D1 30b blue green 1.90 .30
**J28** D1 50b blue green 4.75 .90
**J29** D1 60b blue green 5.50 1.75
*Nos. J24-J29 (6)* 15.15 4.00

**1902-10 Unwmk.**

**Thin Paper, Tinted Rose on Back**

**J30** D1 2b green .85 .25
**J31** D1 5b green .50 .25
**J32** D1 10b green .40 .25
**J33** D1 30b green .50 .25
**J34** D1 50b green 2.50 .90
**J35** D1 60b green 5.25 2.25
*Nos. J30-J35 (6)* 10.00 4.15

**1908-11 White Paper**

**J36** D1 2b green .80 .50
**J37** D1 5b green .60 .50
*a.* Tête bêche pair 12.00 12.00
**J38** D1 10b green .40 .30
*a.* Tête bêche pair 12.00 12.00
**J39** D1 30b green .50 .30
*a.* Tête bêche pair 12.00 12.00
**J40** D1 50b green 2.00 1.25
*Nos. J36-J40 (5)* 4.30 2.85

D2

**1911 Wmk. 165**

**J41** D2 2b dark blue, *green* .25 .25
**J42** D2 5b dark blue, *green* .25 .25
**J43** D2 10b dark blue, *green* .25 .25
**J44** D2 15b dark blue, *green* .25 .25
**J45** D2 20b dark blue, *green* .25 .25
**J46** D2 30b dark blue, *green* .25 .25
**J47** D2 50b dark blue, *green* .50 .30
**J48** D2 60b dark blue, *green* .60 .40
**J49** D2 2 l dark blue, *green* 1.00 .80
*Nos. J41-J49 (9)* 3.60 3.00

The letters "P.R." appear to be embossed instead of watermarked. They are often faint or entirely invisible.

The 20b, type D2, has two types, differing in the width of the head of the "2." This affects Nos. J45, J54, J58, and J63.

See Nos. J52-J77, J82, J87-J88. For overprints see Nos. J78-J81, RAJ1-RAJ2, RAJ20-RAJ21, 3NJ1-3NJ7.

Regular Issue of 1908 Overprinted

**1918 Unwmk.**

**J50** A46 5b yellow green 1.40 .40
*a.* Inverted overprint 5.00 5.00
**J51** A46 10b rose 1.40 .40
*a.* Inverted overprint 3.75 3.75

### Postage Due Type of 1911

**1920 Wmk. 165**

**J52** D2 5b black, *green* .25 .25
**J53** D2 10b black, *green* .25 .25
**J54** D2 20b black, *green* 4.00 .60
**J55** D2 30b black, *green* 1.10 .40
**J55A** D2 50b black, *green* 3.00 .90
*Nos. J52-J55A (5)* 8.60 2.40

***Perf. 11½, 13½ and Compound***

**1919 Unwmk.**

**J56** D2 5b black, *green* .30 .25
**J57** D2 10b black, *green* .30 .25
**J58** D2 20b black, *green* 1.00 .25
**J59** D2 30b black, *green* .90 .25
**J60** D2 50b black, *green* 2.25 .40
*Nos. J56-J60 (5)* 4.75 1.40

**1920-26 White Paper**

**J61** D2 5b black .25 .25
**J62** D2 10b black .25 .25
**J63** D2 20b black .25 .25
**J64** D2 30b black .25 .25
**J65** D2 50b black .40 .40
**J66** D2 60b black .25 .25
**J67** D2 1 l black .30 .30
**J68** D2 2 l black .25 .25
**J69** D2 3 l black ('26) .25 .25
**J70** D2 6 l black ('26) .30 .30
*Nos. J61-J70 (10)* 2.75 2.75

**1923-24**

**J74** D2 1 l black, *pale green* .25 .25
**J75** D2 2 l black, *pale green* .45 .25
**J76** D2 3 l black, *pale green* ('24) 1.25 .60
**J77** D2 6 l blk, *pale green* ('24) 1.75 .60
*Nos. J74-J77 (4)* 3.70 1.70

Postage Due Stamps of 1920-26 Overprinted

**1930** *Perf. 13½*

**J78** D2 1 l black .25 .25
**J79** D2 2 l black .25 .25
**J80** D2 3 l black .35 .25
**J81** D2 6 l black .60 .30
*Nos. J78-J81 (4)* 1.45 1.05

Accession of King Carol II.

**Catalogue values for unused stamps in this section, from this point to the end of the section, are for Never Hinged items.**

### Type of 1911 Issue

**1931 Wmk. 225**

**J82** D2 2 l black .90 .35

D3

**1932-37 Wmk. 230**

**J83** D3 1 l black .25 .25
**J84** D3 2 l black .25 .25
**J85** D3 3 l black ('37) .25 .25
**J86** D3 6 l black ('37) .25 .25
*Nos. J83-J86 (4)* 1.00 1.00

See Nos. J89-J98.

### Type of 1911 Issue

**1942 Typo.** *Perf. 13½*

**J87** D2 50 l black .35 .25
**J88** D2 100 l black .50 .25

### Type of 1932

**1946-47 Unwmk.** *Perf. 14*

**J89** D3 20 l black .60 .55
**J90** D3 100 l black ('47) .45 .25
**J91** D3 200 l black 1.10 .55
*Nos. J89-J91 (3)* 2.15 1.35

**1946-47 Wmk. 276**

**J92** D3 20 l black .25 .25
**J93** D3 50 l black .25 .25
**J94** D3 80 l black .25 .25
**J95** D3 100 l black .25 .25
**J96** D3 200 l black .60 .35
**J97** D3 500 l black .90 .50
**J98** D3 5000 l black ('47) 2.50 1.25
*Nos. J92-J98 (7)* 5.00 3.10

Crown and King Michael — D3a

*Perf. 14½x13½*

**1947 Typo. Wmk. 276**

**J98A** D3a 2 l carmine .40 .25
**J98B** D3a 4 l gray blue .75 .30
**J98C** D3a 5 l black 1.10 .45
**J98D** D3a 10 l violet brown 2.00 .75
*Nos. J98A-J98D (4)* 4.25 1.75

### Nos. J98A-J98D Overprinted

**1948**

J98E D3a 2 l carmine .30 .25
J98F D3a 4 l gray blue .75 .25
J98G D3a 5 l black 1.00 .30
J98H D3a 10 l violet brown 1.75 .55
*Nos. J98E-J98H (4)* 3.80 1.35

In use, Nos. J98A-J106 and following issues were torn apart, one half being affixed to the postage due item and the other half being pasted into the postman's record book. Values are for unused and canceled-to-order pairs.

Communications Badge and Postwoman — D4

**1950 Unwmk. Photo. *Perf. 14½x14***

J99 D4 2 l orange vermilion .75 .75
J100 D4 4 l deep blue .75 .75
J101 D4 5 l dark gray green 1.25 1.25
J102 D4 10 l orange brown 1.50 1.50

**Wmk. 358**

J103 D4 2 l orange vermilion 7.50 7.50
J104 D4 4 l deep blue 7.50 7.50
J105 D4 5 l dark gray green 3.50 3.50
J106 D4 10 l orange brown 2.00 2.00
*Nos. J99-J106 (8)* 24.75 24.75

**Postage Due Stamps of 1950 Surcharged with New Values in Black or Carmine**

**1952 Unwmk.**

J107 D4 4b on 2 l .40 .40
J108 D4 10b on 4 l (C) .40 .40
J109 D4 20b on 5 l (C) 1.00 1.00
J110 D4 50b on 10 l 1.50 1.50
*Nos. J107-J110 (4)* 3.30 3.30

**Wmk. 358**

J111 D4 4b on 2 l
J112 D4 10b on 4 l (C)
J113 D4 20b on 5 l (C) *7.50 7.50*
J114 D4 50b on 10 l *7.50 7.50*

The existence of Nos. J111-J112 has been questioned.

See note after No. J98H.

General Post Office and Post Horn — D5

**1957 Wmk. 358 *Perf. 14***

J115 D5 3b black .25 .25
J116 D5 5b red orange .25 .25
J117 D5 10b red lilac .25 .25
J118 D5 20b brt red .25 .25
J119 D5 40b lt bl grn .50 .25
J120 D5 1 l brt ultra 2.00 .40
*Nos. J115-J120 (6)* 3.50 1.65

See note after No. J98H.

General Post Office and Post Horn — D6

**1967, Feb. 25 Photo. *Perf. 13***

J121 D6 3b brt grn .25 .25
J122 D6 5b brt bl .25 .25
J123 D6 10b lilac rose .25 .25
J124 D6 20b vermilion .25 .25
J125 D6 40b brown .25 .25
J126 D6 1 l violet .55 .25
*Nos. J121-J126 (6)* 1.80 1.50

See note after No. J98H.

**1970, Mar. 10 Unwmk.**

J127 D6 3b brt grn .25 .25
J128 D6 5b brt bl .25 .25
J129 D6 10b lilac rose .25 .25
J130 D6 20b vermilion .25 .25
J131 D6 40b brown .25 .25
J132 D6 1 l violet .35 .25
*Nos. J127-J132 (6)* 1.60 1.50

See note after No. J98H.

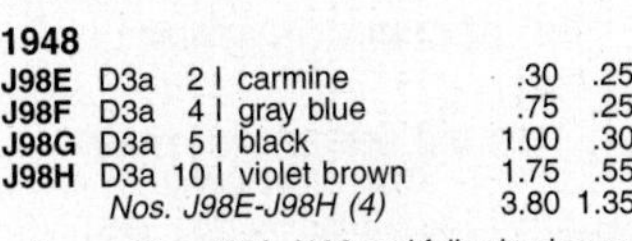

Symbols of Communications — D7

Designs: 10b, Like 5b. 20b, 40b, Pigeons, head of Mercury and post horn. 50b, 1 l, General Post Office, post horn and truck.

**1974, Jan. 1 Photo. *Perf. 13***

J133 D7 5b brt bl .25 .25
J134 D7 10b olive .25 .25
J135 D7 20b lilac rose .25 .25
J136 D7 40b purple .25 .25
J137 D7 50b brown .25 .25
J138 D7 1 l orange .35 .25
*Nos. J133-J138 (6)* 1.60 1.50

See note after No. J98H.

See #J139-J144. For surcharges see #J147-J151.

**1982, Dec. 23 Photo. *Perf. 13½***

J139 D7 25b like #J135 .25 .25
J140 D7 50b like #J133 .25 .25
J141 D7 1 l like #J135 .25 .25
J142 D7 2 l like #J137 .45 .25
J143 D7 3 l like #J133 .70 .25
J144 D7 4 l like #J137 1.00 .25
*Nos. J139-J144 (6)* 2.90 1.50

See note after No. J98H.

Post Horn — D8

**1992, Feb. 3 Photo. *Perf. 13½***

J145 D8 4 l red .50 .25
J146 D8 8 l blue .50 .25

See note after No. J98H.

D9

**1994, Dec. 10 Photo. *Perf. 13¼***

J146A D9 10 l brown .25 .25
J146B D9 45 l orange .40 .25

See note after No. J98H.

**Nos. J140-J142, J144 Surcharged in Green, Deep Blue, or Black**

**1999, Mar. 12 Photo. *Perf. 13½***

J147 D7 50 l on 50b #J140 (G) .25 .25
J148 D7 50 l on 1 l #J141 (DBl) .25 .25
J149 D7 100 l on 2 l #J142 .25 .25
J150 D7 700 l on 1 l #J141 .30 .25
J151 D7 1100 l on 4 l #J144 .45 .25
*Nos. J147-J151 (5)* 1.50 1.25

**Nos. J145, J146B Surcharged**

**2001, Jan. 17 Photo. *Perf. 13¼***

J152 D8 500 l on 4 l red .25 .25
J153 D8 1000 l on 4 l red .25 .25
J154 D9 2000 l on 45 l org .25 .25
*Nos. J152-J154 (3)* .75 .75

See note after No. J98H.

## OFFICIAL STAMPS

**Catalogue values for unused stamps in this section are for Never Hinged items.**

Eagle Carrying National Emblem — O1

**1929 Photo. Wmk. 95 *Perf. 13½***

O1 O1 25b red orange .25 .25
O2 O1 50b dk brown .25 .25
O3 O1 1 l dk violet .30 .25
O4 O1 2 l olive grn .30 .25
O5 O1 3 l rose car .45 .25
O6 O1 4 l dk olive .45 .25
O7 O1 6 l Prus blue 2.50 .25
O8 O1 10 l deep blue .80 .25
O9 O1 25 l carmine brn 1.60 1.25
O10 O1 50 l purple 4.75 3.50
*Nos. O1-O10 (10)* 11.65 6.75

Type of Official Stamps of 1929 Overprinted

**1930 Unwmk.**

O11 O1 25b red orange .25 .25
O12 O1 50b dk brown .25 .25
O13 O1 1 l dk violet .35 .25
O14 O1 3 l rose carmine .50 .25
*Nos. O11-O14 (4)* 1.35 1.00

Nos. O11-O14 were not placed in use without overprint.

**Same Overprint on Nos. O1-O10**

**Wmk. 95**

O15 O1 25b red orange .25 .25
O16 O1 50b dk brown .25 .25
O17 O1 1 l dk violet .25 .25
O18 O1 2 l dp green .25 .25
O19 O1 3 l rose carmine .60 .25
O20 O1 4 l olive black .75 .25
O21 O1 6 l Prus blue 2.00 .25
O22 O1 10 l deep blue .80 .25
O23 O1 25 l carmine brown 3.00 2.50
O24 O1 50 l purple 4.00 3.50
*Nos. O15-O24 (10)* 12.15 8.00

Accession of King Carol II to the throne of Romania (Nos O11-O24).

Coat of Arms — O2

***Perf. 13½, 13½x14½***

**1931-32 Typo. Wmk. 225**

O25 O2 25b black .30 .25
O26 O2 1 l lilac .30 .25
O27 O2 2 l emerald .60 .40
O28 O2 3 l rose 1.00 .70
*Nos. O25-O28 (4)* 2.20 1.60

**1932 Wmk. 230 *Perf. 13½***

O29 O2 25b black .30 .25
O30 O2 1 l violet .40 .35
O31 O2 2 l emerald .65 .55
O32 O2 3 l rose .80 .65
O33 O2 6 l red brown 1.25 1.00
*Nos. O29-O33 (5)* 3.40 2.80

## PARCEL POST STAMPS

PP1

***Perf. 11½, 13½ and Compound***

**1895 Wmk. 163 Typo.**

Q1 PP1 25b brown red 12.50 2.25

**1896**

Q2 PP1 25b vermilion 10.00 1.25

***Perf. 13½ and 11½x13½***

**1898 Wmk. 200**

Q3 PP1 25b brown red 7.00 1.25
 a. Tête bêche pair
Q4 PP1 25b vermilion 7.00 .90

**Thin Paper**

Tinted Rose on Back

**1905 Unwmk. *Perf. 11½***

Q5 PP1 25b vermilion 7.50 1.25

**1911 White Paper**

Q6 PP1 25b pale red 7.50 1.25

No. 263 Surcharged in Carmine

**1928 *Perf. 13½***

Q7 A54 5 l on 10b yellow green 1.50 .30

## POSTAL TAX STAMPS

Regular Issue of 1908 Overprinted

***Perf. 11½, 13½, 11½x13½***

**1915 Unwmk.**

RA1 A46 5b green .25 .25
RA2 A46 10b rose .40 .25

The "Timbru de Ajutor" stamps represent a tax on postal matter. The money obtained from their sale was turned into a fund for the assistance of soldiers' families.

Until 1923 the only "Timbru de Ajutor" stamps used for postal purposes were the 5b and 10b. Stamps of higher values with this inscription were used to pay the taxes on railway and theater tickets and other fiscal taxes. In 1923 the postal rate was advanced to 25b.

The Queen Weaving — PT1

**1916-18 Typo.**

RA3 PT1 5b gray blk .25 .25
RA4 PT1 5b green ('18) .70 .40
RA5 PT1 10b brown .40 .25
RA6 PT1 10b gray blk ('18) 1.00 .45
*Nos. RA3-RA6 (4)* 2.35 1.35

For overprints see Nos. RA7-RA8, RAJ7-RAJ9, 3NRA1-3NRA8.

Stamps of 1916 Overprinted in Red or Black

**1918 *Perf. 13½***

RA7 PT1 5b gray blk (R) .70 .25
 a. Double overprint 5.00
 c. Black overprint 5.00
RA8 PT1 10b brn (Bk) .70 .25
 a. Double overprint 5.00
 b. Double overprint, one inverted 5.00
 c. Inverted overprint 5.00

**Same Overprint on RA1 and RA2**

**1919**

| | | | |
|---|---|---|---|
| **RA11** | A46 5b yel grn (R) | 19.00 | 12.50 |
| **RA12** | A46 10b rose (Bk) | 19.00 | 12.50 |

Charity — PT3

***Perf. 13½, 11½, 13½x11½***

**1921-24 Typo. Unwmk.**

| | | | |
|---|---|---|---|
| **RA13** | PT3 10b green | .25 | .25 |
| **RA14** | PT3 25b blk ('24) | .25 | .25 |

**Type of 1921-24 Issue**

**1928 Wmk. 95**

| | | | |
|---|---|---|---|
| **RA15** | PT3 25b black | 1.00 | .45 |

Nos. RA13, RA14 and RA15 are the only stamps of type PT3 issued for postal purposes. Other denominations were used fiscally.

**Catalogue values for unused stamps in this section, from this point to the end of the section, are for Never Hinged items.**

Airplane — PT4

**1931 Photo. Unwmk.**

| | | | |
|---|---|---|---|
| **RA16** | PT4 50b Prus bl | .45 | .25 |
| *a.* | Double impression | 15.00 | |
| **RA17** | PT4 1 l dk red brn | .75 | .25 |
| **RA18** | PT4 2 l ultra | 1.00 | .25 |
| | *Nos. RA16-RA18 (3)* | 2.20 | .75 |

The use of these stamps, in addition to the regular postage, was obligatory on all postal matter for the interior of the country. The money thus obtained was to augment the National Fund for Aviation. When the stamps were not used to prepay the special tax, it was collected by means of Postal Tax Due stamps Nos. RAJ20 and RAJ21.

Nos. RA17 and RA18 were also used for other than postal tax.

Head of Aviator — PT5

**1932 Wmk. 230 *Perf. 14 x 13½***

| | | | |
|---|---|---|---|
| **RA19** | PT5 50b Prus bl | .30 | .25 |
| **RA20** | PT5 1 l red brn | .45 | .25 |
| **RA21** | PT5 2 l ultra | .70 | .25 |
| | *Nos. RA19-RA21 (3)* | 1.45 | .75 |

See notes after No. RA18.

After 1937 use of Nos. RA20-RA21 was limited to other than postal matter.

Nos. RA19-RA21 exist imperf.

Four stamps similar to type PT5 were issued in 1936: 10b sepia, 20b violet, 3 l green and 5 l red. These were used for purposes other than postal tax.

Aviator — PT5A

**1936-37 *Perf. 13¾x14½***

| | | | |
|---|---|---|---|
| **RA19A** | PT5A 10b orange | 1.00 | .25 |
| **RA20A** | PT5A 20b reddish pur ('37) | 1.00 | .25 |
| **RA21A** | PT5A 50b rose | 1.50 | .45 |
| | *Nos. RA19A-RA21A (3)* | 3.50 | .95 |

Aviator — PT6

**1937 *Perf. 13½***

| | | | |
|---|---|---|---|
| **RA22** | PT6 50b Prus grn | .25 | .25 |
| **RA23** | PT6 1 l red brn | .35 | .25 |
| **RA24** | PT6 2 l ultra | .45 | .25 |
| | *Nos. RA22-RA24 (3)* | 1.05 | .75 |

Stamps overprinted or inscribed "Fondul Aviatiei" other than Nos. RA22, RA23 or RA24 were used to pay taxes on other than postal matters.

King Michael — PT7

**1943 Wmk. 276 Photo. *Perf. 14***

| | | | |
|---|---|---|---|
| **RA25** | PT7 50b org ver | .25 | .25 |
| **RA26** | PT7 1 l lil rose | .25 | .25 |
| **RA27** | PT7 2 l brown | .25 | .25 |
| **RA28** | PT7 4 l lt ultra | .25 | .25 |
| **RA29** | PT7 5 l dull lilac | .25 | .25 |
| **RA30** | PT7 8 l yel grn | .25 | .25 |
| **RA31** | PT7 10 l blk brn | .25 | .25 |
| | *Nos. RA25-RA31 (7)* | 1.75 | 1.75 |

The tax was obligatory on domestic mail.

Examples of these stamps with an overprint consisting of a red cross and text are unissued franchise stamps.

Protection of Homeless Children — PT8

**1945**

| | | | |
|---|---|---|---|
| **RA32** | PT8 40 l Prus bl | .35 | .25 |

PT9

**Black Surcharge**

**1947 Unwmk. Typo. *Perf. 14x14½***

| | | | |
|---|---|---|---|
| **RA33** | PT9 1 l on 2 l + 2 l pink | .30 | .25 |
| *a.* | Inverted surcharge | 25.00 | 25.00 |
| **RA34** | PT9 5 l on 1 l + 1 l gray grn | 2.50 | 2.50 |

"Hope" — PT10

**1948 *Perf. 14***

| | | | |
|---|---|---|---|
| **RA35** | PT10 1 l rose | .90 | .35 |
| **RA36** | PT10 1 l rose violet | 1.00 | .35 |

A 2 lei blue and 5 lei ocher in type PT10 were issued primarily for revenue purposes.

---

## POSTAL TAX DUE STAMPS

**Catalogue values for unused stamps in this section are for Never Hinged items.**

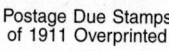

Postage Due Stamps of 1911 Overprinted

***Perf. 11½, 13½, 11½x13½***

**1915 Unwmk.**

| | | | |
|---|---|---|---|
| **RAJ1** | D2 5b dk bl, *grn* | .75 | .25 |
| **RAJ2** | D2 10b dk bl, *grn* | .75 | .25 |
| *a.* | Wmk. 165 | 10.00 | 1.00 |

PTD1

**1916 Typo. Unwmk.**

| | | | |
|---|---|---|---|
| **RAJ3** | PTD1 5b brn, *grn* | .40 | .25 |
| **RAJ4** | PTD1 10b red, *grn* | .40 | .25 |

See Nos. RAJ5-RAJ6, RAJ10-RAJ11. For overprint see No. 3NRAJ1.

**1918**

| | | | |
|---|---|---|---|
| **RAJ5** | PTD1 5b red, *grn* | .25 | .25 |
| *a.* | Wmk. 165 | 1.00 | .25 |
| **RAJ6** | PTD1 10b brn, *grn* | .25 | .25 |
| *a.* | Wmk. 165 | 1.75 | .25 |

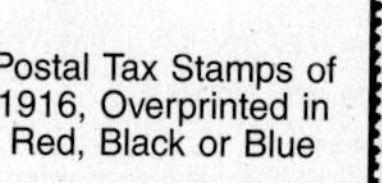

Postal Tax Stamps of 1916, Overprinted in Red, Black or Blue

| | | | |
|---|---|---|---|
| **RAJ7** | PT1 5b gray blk (R) | .40 | .25 |
| *a.* | Inverted overprint | 7.50 | |
| **RAJ8** | PT1 10b brn (Bk) | .80 | .25 |
| *a.* | Inverted overprint | 7.50 | |
| **RAJ9** | PT1 10b brn (Bl) | *5.00* | *5.00* |
| *a.* | Vertical overprint | *20.00* | *15.00* |
| | *Nos. RAJ7-RAJ9 (3)* | 6.20 | 5.50 |

**Type of 1916**

**1921**

| | | | |
|---|---|---|---|
| **RAJ10** | PTD1 5b red | .50 | .25 |
| **RAJ11** | PTD1 10b brown | .50 | .25 |

PTD2

**1922-25 Greenish Paper Typo.**

| | | | |
|---|---|---|---|
| **RAJ12** | PTD2 10b brown | .25 | .25 |
| **RAJ13** | PTD2 20b brown | .25 | .25 |
| **RAJ14** | PTD2 25b brown | .25 | .25 |
| **RAJ15** | PTD2 50b brown | .25 | .25 |
| | *Nos. RAJ12-RAJ15 (4)* | 1.00 | 1.00 |

**1923-26**

| | | | |
|---|---|---|---|
| **RAJ16** | PTD2 10b lt brn | .25 | .25 |
| **RAJ17** | PTD2 20b lt brn | .25 | .25 |
| **RAJ18** | PTD2 25b brown ('26) | .25 | .25 |
| **RAJ19** | PTD2 50b brown ('26) | .25 | .25 |
| | *Nos. RAJ16-RAJ19 (4)* | 1.00 | 1.00 |

J82 and Type of 1911 Postage Due Stamps Overprinted in Red

**1931 Wmk. 225 *Perf. 13½***

| | | | |
|---|---|---|---|
| **RAJ20** | D2 1 l black | .25 | .25 |
| **RAJ21** | D2 2 l black | .25 | .25 |

When the Postal Tax stamps for the Aviation Fund issue (Nos. RA16 to RA18) were not used to prepay the obligatory tax on letters, etc., it was collected by affixing Nos. RAJ20 and RAJ21.

---

## OCCUPATION STAMPS

### ISSUED UNDER AUSTRIAN OCCUPATION

Austria Military Stamps Nos. M51-M67 Surcharged

No. M51

No. M65

**1917 Unwmk. Engr. *Perf. 12½***

| | | | |
|---|---|---|---|
| **1N1** | M3 3b on 3h ol gray | 2.00 | 3.00 |
| **1N2** | M3 5b on 5h ol grn | 2.00 | 3.00 |
| **1N3** | M3 6b on 6h violet | 2.00 | 3.00 |
| **1N4** | M3 10b on 10h org brn | .40 | .70 |
| **1N5** | M3 12b on 12h dp blue | 1.50 | 2.50 |
| **1N6** | M3 15b on 15h brt rose | 1.50 | 2.50 |
| **1N7** | M3 20b on 20h red brn | .40 | .70 |
| **1N8** | M3 25b on 25h ultra | .40 | .70 |
| **1N9** | M3 30b on 30h grnsh slate | .70 | 1.00 |
| **1N10** | M3 40b on 40h ol bis | .70 | 1.00 |
| *a.* | Perf. 11½ | 100.00 | 175.00 |
| *b.* | Perf. 11½x12½ | 100.00 | 175.00 |
| **1N11** | M3 50b on 50h dp grn | .40 | .70 |
| **1N12** | M3 60b on 60h car rose | .40 | .70 |
| **1N13** | M3 80b on 80h dl bl | .35 | .65 |
| **1N14** | M3 90b on 90h dk vio | .70 | 1.00 |
| **1N15** | M4 2 l on 2k rose, *straw* | 1.10 | 1.60 |
| **1N16** | M4 3 l on 3k grn, *bl* | 1.10 | 2.00 |
| **1N17** | M4 4 l on 4k rose, *grn* | 1.50 | 2.50 |
| | *Nos. 1N1-1N17 (17)* | 17.15 | 27.25 |

Nos. 1N1-1N14 have "BANI" surcharged in red.

Nos. 1N1-1N17 also exist imperforate. Value, set $125.

OS3

OS4

**1918**

| | | | |
|---|---|---|---|
| **1N18** | OS3 3b ol gray | .35 | .85 |
| **1N19** | OS3 5b ol grn | .35 | .85 |
| **1N20** | OS3 6b violet | .35 | .85 |
| **1N21** | OS3 10b org brn | .35 | .85 |
| **1N22** | OS3 12b dp bl | .35 | .85 |
| **1N23** | OS3 15b brt rose | .35 | .85 |
| **1N24** | OS3 20b red brn | .35 | .85 |
| **1N25** | OS3 25b ultra | .35 | .85 |
| **1N26** | OS3 30b slate | .35 | .85 |
| **1N27** | OS3 40b ol bis | .35 | .85 |
| **1N28** | OS3 50b dp grn | .35 | .85 |
| **1N29** | OS3 60b rose | .35 | .85 |
| **1N30** | OS3 80b dl bl | .35 | .85 |
| **1N31** | OS3 90b dk vio | .35 | .85 |
| **1N32** | OS4 2 l rose, *straw* | .35 | .85 |
| **1N33** | OS4 3 l grn, *bl* | .75 | 2.25 |
| **1N34** | OS4 4 l rose, *grn* | 1.00 | 2.25 |
| | *Nos. 1N18-1N34 (17)* | 7.00 | 17.25 |

Exist. imperf. Value, set $80.

The complete series exists with "BANI" or "LEI" inverted, also with those words and the numerals of value inverted. Neither of these sets was regularly issued.

Austrian Nos. M69-M82 Overprinted In Black

**1918 Typo. *Perf. 12½***

| | | | |
|---|---|---|---|
| **1N35** | M5 | 1h grnsh blue | 40.00 |
| **1N36** | M5 | 2h orange | 25.00 |
| **1N37** | M5 | 3h olive gray | 47.50 |
| **1N38** | M5 | 5h yellow green | 25.00 |
| **1N39** | M5 | 10h dark brown | 70.00 |
| **1N40** | M5 | 20h red | 70.00 |
| **1N41** | M5 | 25h blue | 27.50 |
| **1N42** | M5 | 30h bister | 47.50 |
| **1N43** | M5 | 45h dark slate | 52.50 |
| **1N44** | M5 | 50h deep green | 60.00 |
| **1N45** | M5 | 60h violet | 1,000. |
| **1N46** | M5 | 80h rose | 80.00 |
| **1N47** | M5 | 90h brown violet | 80.00 |
| | | *Nos. 1N35-1N47 (13)* | 1,625. |

Nos. 1N35-1N47 were on sale at the Vienna post office for a few days before the Armistice signing. They were never issued at the Army Post Offices.

## ISSUED UNDER BULGARIAN OCCUPATION

Dobruja District

Bulgarian Stamps of 1915-16 Overprinted in Red or Blue

**1916 Unwmk. *Perf. 11½, 14***

| | | | | |
|---|---|---|---|---|
| **2N1** | A20 | 1s dk blue grn (R) | .25 | .25 |
| **2N2** | A23 | 5s grn & vio brn (R) | 3.00 | 1.75 |
| **2N3** | A24 | 10s brn & brnsh blk (Bl) | .30 | .25 |
| **2N4** | A26 | 25s indigo & blk (Bl) | .30 | .25 |
| | | *Nos. 2N1-2N4 (4)* | 3.85 | 2.50 |

Many varieties of overprint exist.

## ISSUED UNDER GERMAN OCCUPATION

German Stamps of 1905-17 Surcharged

**1917 Wmk. 125 *Perf. 14***

| | | | | |
|---|---|---|---|---|
| **3N1** | A22 | 15b on 15pf dk vio (R) | 1.00 | 1.00 |
| **3N2** | A16 | 25b on 20pf ultra (Bk) | 1.00 | 1.00 |
| **3N3** | A16 | 40b on 30pf org & blk, *buff* (R) | 17.50 | 17.50 |
| | | *Nos. 3N1-3N3 (3)* | 19.50 | 19.50 |

"M.V.iR." are the initials of "Militär Verwaltung in Rumänien" (Military Administration of Romania).

German Stamps of 1905-17 Surcharged

**1917-18**

| | | | | |
|---|---|---|---|---|
| **3N4** | A16 | 10b on 10pf car | 1.10 | 1.40 |
| **3N5** | A22 | 15b on 15pf dk vio | 5.50 | 4.50 |
| **3N6** | A16 | 25b on 20pf ultra | 3.00 | 4.00 |
| **3N7** | A16 | 40b on 30pf org & blk, *buff* | 1.00 | 1.40 |
| *a.* | | "40" omitted | 90.00 | *350.00* |
| | | *Nos. 3N4-3N7 (4)* | 10.60 | 11.30 |

German Stamps of 1905-17 Surcharged

**1918**

| | | | | |
|---|---|---|---|---|
| **3N8** | A16 | 5b on 5pf grn | .60 | 1.75 |
| **3N9** | A16 | 10b on 10pf car | .60 | 1.50 |
| **3N10** | A22 | 15b on 15pf dk vio | .25 | .40 |
| **3N11** | A16 | 25b on 20pf bl vio | .60 | 1.50 |
| *a.* | | 25b on 20pf blue | 2.50 | 8.00 |
| **3N12** | A16 | 40b on 30pf org & blk, *buff* | .30 | .35 |
| | | *Nos. 3N8-3N12 (5)* | 2.35 | 5.50 |

German Stamps of 1905-17 Overprinted

**1918**

| | | | | |
|---|---|---|---|---|
| **3N13** | A16 | 10pf carmine | 8.75 | *40.00* |
| **3N14** | A22 | 15pf dk vio | 13.00 | *35.00* |
| **3N15** | A16 | 20pf blue | 1.25 | *1.75* |
| **3N16** | A16 | 30pf org & blk, *buff* | 13.00 | *22.50* |
| | | *Nos. 3N13-3N16 (4)* | 36.00 | *99.25* |

## POSTAGE DUE STAMPS ISSUED UNDER GERMAN OCCUPATION

Postage Due Stamps and Type of Romania Overprinted in Red

***Perf. 11½, 13½ and Compound***

**1918 Wmk. 165**

| | | | | |
|---|---|---|---|---|
| **3NJ1** | D2 | 5b dk bl, *grn* | 20.00 | 60.00 |
| **3NJ2** | D2 | 10b dk bl, *grn* | 20.00 | 60.00 |

The 20b, 30b and 50b with this overprint are fraudulent.

**Unwmk.**

| | | | | |
|---|---|---|---|---|
| **3NJ3** | D2 | 5b dk bl, *grn* | 8.00 | 10.50 |
| **3NJ4** | D2 | 10b dk bl, *grn* | 8.00 | 10.50 |
| **3NJ5** | D2 | 20b dk bl, *grn* | 3.00 | 2.75 |
| **3NJ6** | D2 | 30b dk bl, *grn* | 3.00 | 2.75 |
| **3NJ7** | D2 | 50b dk bl, *grn* | 3.00 | 2.75 |
| | | *Nos. 3NJ1-3NJ7 (7)* | 65.00 | 149.25 |

## POSTAL TAX STAMPS ISSUED UNDER GERMAN OCCUPATION

**Romanian Postal Tax Stamps and Type of 1916**

Overprinted in Red or Black

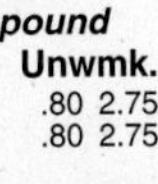

***Perf. 11½, 13½ and Compound***

**1917 Unwmk.**

| | | | | |
|---|---|---|---|---|
| **3NRA1** | PT1 | 5b gray blk (R) | .80 | 2.75 |
| **3NRA2** | PT1 | 10b brown (Bk) | .80 | 2.75 |

Same, Overprinted

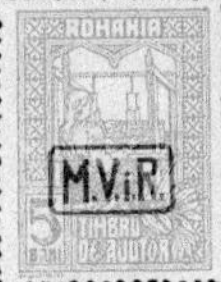


**1917-18**

| | | | | |
|---|---|---|---|---|
| **3NRA3** | PT1 | 5b gray blk (R) | 1.50 | 3.50 |
| *a.* | | Black overprint | 57.00 | *750.00* |
| **3NRA4** | PT1 | 10b brown (Bk) | 9.00 | 19.00 |
| **3NRA5** | PT1 | 10b violet (Bk) | 1.50 | 5.00 |
| | | *Nos. 3NRA3-3NRA5 (3)* | 12.00 | 27.50 |

Same, Overprinted in Red or Black

**1918**

| | | | | |
|---|---|---|---|---|
| **3NRA6** | PT1 | 5b gray blk (R) | *45.00* | 30.00 |
| **3NRA7** | PT1 | 10b brown (Bk) | *45.00* | 30.00 |

Same, Overprinted

**1918**

| | | | | |
|---|---|---|---|---|
| **3NRA8** | PT1 | 10b violet (Bk) | .80 | 2.75 |

## POSTAL TAX DUE STAMP ISSUED UNDER GERMAN OCCUPATION

Type of Romanian Postal Tax Due Stamp of 1916 Overprinted

***Perf. 11½, 13½, and Compound***

**1918 Wmk. 165**

| | | | | |
|---|---|---|---|---|
| **3NRAJ1** | PTD1 | 10b red, *green* | 2.50 | 3.00 |

## ROMANIAN POST OFFICES IN THE TURKISH EMPIRE

40 Paras = 1 Piaster

**Romania Nos. 120, 122 & 126 Surcharged**

***Perf. 11½, 13½ and Compound***

**1896 Wmk. 200 Black Surcharge**

| | | | | |
|---|---|---|---|---|
| **1** | A19 | 10pa on 5b blue | 32.50 | 30.00 |
| **2** | A20 | 20pa on 10b emer | 24.00 | 22.50 |
| **3** | A19 | 1pa on 25b violet | 24.00 | 22.50 |
| | | *Nos. 1-3 (3)* | 80.50 | 75.00 |

**Violet Surcharge**

| | | | | |
|---|---|---|---|---|
| **4** | A19 | 10pa on 5b blue | 17.00 | 15.00 |
| **5** | A20 | 20pa on 10b emer | 17.00 | 15.00 |
| **6** | A19 | 1pa on 25b violet | 17.00 | 15.00 |
| | | *Nos. 4-6 (3)* | 51.00 | 45.00 |

Romanian Stamps of 1908-18 Overprinted in Black or Red

**1919 Typo. Unwmk.**

| | | | | |
|---|---|---|---|---|
| **7** | A46 | 5b yellow grn | .50 | .50 |
| **8** | A46 | 10b rose | .65 | .65 |
| **9** | A46 | 15b red brown | .75 | .75 |
| **10** | A19 | 25b dp blue (R) | 1.00 | 1.00 |
| **11** | A19 | 40b gray brn (R) | 2.75 | 2.75 |
| | | *Nos. 7-11 (5)* | 5.65 | 5.65 |

All values exist with inverted overprint.

## ROMANIAN POST OFFICES IN THE TURKISH EMPIRE POSTAL TAX STAMP

Romanian Postal Tax Stamp of 1918 Overprinted

**1919 Unwmk. *Perf. 11½, 11½x13½***

| | | | | |
|---|---|---|---|---|
| **RA1** | PT1 | 5b green | 2.50 | 2.50 |

# ROUAD, ILE

ēl-ru-ad

(Arwad)

LOCATION — An island in the Mediterranean, off the coast of Latakia, Syria

GOVT. — French Mandate

In 1916, while a French post office was maintained on Ile Rouad, stamps were issued by France.

25 Centimes = 1 Piaster

French Offices in the Levant 1902-06 Stamps Ovptd.

***Perf. 14x13½***

**1916, Jan. 12 Unwmk.**

| | | | | |
|---|---|---|---|---|
| **1** | A2 | 5c green | 550.00 | 275.00 |
| **2** | A3 | 10c rose red | 550.00 | 275.00 |
| **3** | A5 | 1pi on 25c blue | 550.00 | 275.00 |

Dangerous counterfeits exist.

A 40c and 2pi-on-50c exist but were not regularly issued. Most examples have favor cancels. Value so canceled, $700 each.

Stamps of French Offices in the Levant, 1902-06, Overprinted Horizontally

**1916, Dec.**

| | | | | |
|---|---|---|---|---|
| **4** | A2 | 1c gray | 1.40 | 1.40 |
| **5** | A2 | 2c lilac brown | 1.50 | 1.50 |
| **6** | A2 | 3c red orange | 1.60 | 1.60 |
| *a.* | | Double overprint | 210.00 | |
| **7** | A2 | 5c green | 1.75 | 1.75 |
| **8** | A3 | 10c rose | 2.00 | 2.00 |
| **9** | A3 | 15c pale red | 2.00 | 2.00 |
| **10** | A3 | 20c brown violet | 3.75 | 3.75 |
| **11** | A5 | 1pi on 25c blue | 2.75 | 2.75 |
| **12** | A3 | 30c violet | 2.50 | 2.50 |
| **13** | A4 | 40c red & pale bl | 6.00 | 6.00 |
| **14** | A6 | 2pi on 50c bis brn & lavender | 9.00 | 9.00 |
| **15** | A6 | 4pi on 1fr cl & ol grn | 16.00 | 16.00 |
| **16** | A6 | 20pi on 5fr dk bl & buff | 40.00 | 40.00 |
| | | *Nos. 4-16 (13)* | 90.25 | 90.25 |

There is a wide space between the two words of the overprint on Nos. 13 to 16 inclusive. Nos. 4, 5 and 6 are on white and coarse, grayish (G. C.) papers.

(Note on G. C. paper follows France No. 184.)

# RUANDA-URUNDI

rü-,än-də ü'rün-dē

## (Belgian East Africa)

LOCATION — In central Africa, bounded by Congo, Uganda and Tanganyika
GOVT. — Former United Nations trusteeship administered by Belgium
AREA — 20,540 sq. mi.
POP. — 4,700,000 (est. 1958)
CAPITAL — Usumbura

See German East Africa in Vol. 3 for stamps issued under Belgian occupation.

In 1962 the two parts of the trusteeship became independent states, the Republic of Rwanda and the Kingdom of Burundi.

100 Centimes = 1 Franc

**Catalogue values for unused stamps in this country are for Never Hinged items, beginning with Scott 151 in the regular postage section, Scott B26 in the semi-postal section, and Scott J8 in the postage due section.**

Stamps of Belgian Congo, 1923-26, Overprinted

**1924-26** *Perf. 12*

| No. | Type | Description | Unused | Used |
|---|---|---|---|---|
| 6 | A32 | 5c orange yel | .25 | .25 |
| 7 | A32 | 10c green | .25 | .25 |
| a. | | Double overprint | 70.00 | 70.00 |
| 8 | A32 | 15c olive brn | .25 | .25 |
| 9 | A32 | 20c olive grn | .25 | .25 |
| 10 | A44 | 20c green ('26) | .25 | .25 |
| 11 | A44 | 25c red brown | .40 | .25 |
| 12 | A44 | 30c rose red | .35 | .35 |
| 13 | A44 | 30c olive grn ('25) | .25 | .25 |
| 14 | A32 | 40c violet ('25) | .35 | .35 |
| a. | | Inverted overprint | 95.00 | 95.00 |
| 15 | A44 | 50c gray blue | .35 | .35 |
| 16 | A44 | 50c buff ('25) | .40 | .35 |
| 17 | A44 | 75c red org | .65 | .60 |
| 18 | A44 | 75c gray blue ('25) | .60 | .45 |
| 19 | A44 | 1fr bister brown | .70 | .60 |
| 20 | A44 | 1fr dull blue ('26) | .75 | .50 |
| 21 | A44 | 3fr gray brown | 6.00 | 2.50 |
| 22 | A44 | 5fr gray | 12.00 | 8.50 |
| 23 | A44 | 10fr gray black | 25.00 | 19.00 |
| | | *Nos. 6-23 (18)* | 49.05 | 35.30 |
| | | Set, never hinged | 160.00 | |

Belgian Congo Nos. 112-113 Overprinted in Red or Black

**1925-27** *Perf. 12½*

| No. | Type | Description | Unused | Used |
|---|---|---|---|---|
| 24 | A44 | 45c dk vio (R) ('27) | .30 | .30 |
| 25 | A44 | 60c car rose (Bk) | .50 | .50 |
| | | Set, never hinged | 1.75 | |

Stamps of Belgian Congo, 1923-1927, Overprinted

**1927-29**

| No. | Type | Description | Unused | Used |
|---|---|---|---|---|
| 26 | A32 | 10c green ('29) | .60 | .60 |
| 27 | A32 | 15c ol brn ('29) | 1.60 | 1.60 |
| 28 | A44 | 35c green | .35 | .35 |
| 29 | A44 | 75c salmon red | .50 | .45 |
| 30 | A44 | 1fr rose red | .60 | .50 |
| 31 | A32 | 1.25fr dull blue | .85 | .75 |
| 32 | A32 | 1.50fr dull blue | .85 | .75 |
| 33 | A32 | 1.75fr dull blue | 3.00 | 1.90 |

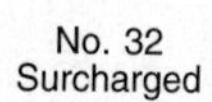

No. 32 Surcharged

| No. | Type | Description | Unused | Used |
|---|---|---|---|---|
| 34 | A32 | 1.75fr on 1.50fr dl bl | .85 | .75 |
| | | *Nos. 26-34 (9)* | 9.20 | 7.65 |
| | | Set, never hinged | 23.50 | |

No. 30 Surcharged

No. 33 Surcharged

**1931**

| No. | Type | Description | Unused | Used |
|---|---|---|---|---|
| 35 | A44 | 1.25fr on 1fr rose red | 3.00 | 1.50 |
| 36 | A32 | 2fr on 1.75fr dl bl | 4.50 | 2.50 |
| | | Set, never hinged | 17.50 | |

Porter — A1

Mountain Scene — A2

Designs: 5c, 60c, Porter. 15c, Warrior. 25c, Kraal. 40c, Cattle herders. 50c, Cape buffalo. 75c, Bahutu greeting. 1fr, Urundi women. 1.25fr, Bahutu mother. 1.50fr, 2fr, Making wooden vessel. 2.50fr, 3.25fr, Preparing hides. 4fr, Watuba potter. 5fr, Mututsi dancer. 10fr, Watusi warriors. 20fr, Urundi prince.

**1931-38** **Engr.** *Perf. 11½*

| No. | Type | Description | Unused | Used |
|---|---|---|---|---|
| 37 | A1 | 5c dp lil rose ('38) | .25 | .25 |
| 38 | A2 | 10c gray | .25 | .25 |
| 39 | A2 | 15c pale red | .25 | .25 |
| 40 | A2 | 25c brown vio | .25 | .25 |
| 41 | A1 | 40c green | .50 | .50 |
| 42 | A2 | 50c gray lilac | .25 | .25 |
| 43 | A1 | 60c lilac rose | .25 | .25 |
| 44 | A1 | 75c gray black | .25 | .25 |
| 45 | A2 | 1fr rose red | .40 | .25 |
| 46 | A1 | 1.25fr red brown | .40 | .25 |
| 47 | A2 | 1.50fr brown vio ('37) | .25 | .25 |
| 48 | A2 | 2fr deep blue | .50 | .25 |
| 49 | A2 | 2.50fr dp blue ('37) | .60 | .60 |
| 50 | A2 | 3.25fr brown vio | .65 | .30 |
| 51 | A2 | 4fr rose | .65 | .45 |
| 52 | A1 | 5fr gray | .65 | .50 |
| 53 | A1 | 10fr brown violet | 1.50 | 1.50 |
| 54 | A1 | 20fr brown | 5.00 | 5.00 |
| | | *Nos. 37-54 (18)* | 12.85 | 11.60 |
| | | Set, never hinged | 25.00 | |

### King Albert Memorial Issue

King Albert — A16

**1934** **Photo.**

| No. | Type | Description | Unused | Used |
|---|---|---|---|---|
| 55 | A16 | 1.50fr black | .65 | .65 |
| | | Never hinged | 2.50 | |

Stamps of 1931-38 Surcharged in Black

**1941**

| No. | Type | Description | Unused | Used |
|---|---|---|---|---|
| 56 | A1 | 5c on 40c green | 9.00 | 9.00 |
| 57 | A2 | 60c on 50c gray lil | 5.00 | 5.00 |
| 58 | A2 | 2.50fr on 1.50fr brn vio | 5.00 | 5.00 |
| 59 | A2 | 3.25fr on 2fr dp bl | 26.00 | 26.00 |
| | | *Nos. 56-59 (4)* | 45.00 | 45.00 |
| | | Set, never hinged | 130.00 | |

Belgian Congo No. 173 Overprinted in Black

**1941** *Perf. 11*

| No. | Type | Description | Unused | Used |
|---|---|---|---|---|
| 60 | A70 | 10c light gray | 10.00 | 10.00 |
| | | Never hinged | 27.50 | |

Inverts exist. Values: $45 hinged; $70 never hinged.

Belgian Congo Nos. 179, 181 Overprinted in Black

**1941**

| No. | Type | Description | Unused | Used |
|---|---|---|---|---|
| 61 | A70 | 1.75fr orange | 6.00 | 6.00 |
| 62 | A70 | 2.75fr vio bl | 6.00 | 6.00 |
| | | Set, never hinged | 52.50 | |

For surcharges see Nos. 64-65.

Belgian Congo No. 168 Surcharged in Black

**1941** *Perf. 11½*

| No. | Type | Description | Unused | Used |
|---|---|---|---|---|
| 63 | A66 | 5c on 1.50fr dp red brn & blk | .25 | .25 |
| | | Never hinged | .35 | |

Inverts exist. Value $19.

### Nos. 61-62 Surcharged with New Values and Bars in Black

**1942**

| No. | Type | Description | Unused | Used |
|---|---|---|---|---|
| 64 | A70 | 75c on 1.75fr org | 1.75 | 1.75 |
| 65 | A70 | 2.50fr on 2.75fr vio bl | 5.75 | 5.75 |
| | | Set, never hinged | 30.00 | |

Inverts exist. Value $55.

### Belgian Congo Nos. 167, 183 Surcharged in Black

**1942** *Perf. 11, 11½*

| No. | Type | Description | Unused | Used |
|---|---|---|---|---|
| 66 | A65 | 75c on 90c car & brn | 1.25 | 1.25 |
| a. | | Inverted surcharge | 25.00 | 25.00 |
| 67 | A70 | 2.50fr on 10fr rose red | 2.50 | 1.90 |
| a. | | Inverted surcharge | 22.00 | 22.00 |
| | | Set, never hinged | 7.50 | |
| | | Nos. 66a-67a, never hinged | 90.00 | |

Oil Palms — A17

Oil Palms — A18

Watusi Chief — A19

Leopard A20

Askari — A21

Zebra — A22

Askari — A23

Design: 100fr, Watusi chief.

**1942-43** **Engr.** *Perf. 12½*

| No. | Type | Description | Unused | Used |
|---|---|---|---|---|
| 68 | A17 | 5c red | .25 | .25 |
| 69 | A18 | 10c ol grn | .25 | .25 |
| 70 | A18 | 15c brn car | .25 | .25 |
| 71 | A18 | 20c dp ultra | .25 | .25 |
| 72 | A18 | 25c brn vio | .25 | .25 |
| 73 | A18 | 30c dull blue | .25 | .25 |
| 74 | A18 | 50c dp grn | .25 | .25 |
| 75 | A18 | 60c chestnut | .25 | .25 |
| 76 | A19 | 75c dl lil & blk | .25 | .25 |
| 77 | A19 | 1fr dk brn & blk | .35 | .25 |
| 78 | A19 | 1.25fr rose red & blk | .40 | .40 |
| 79 | A20 | 1.75fr dk gray brn | 1.00 | .75 |
| 80 | A20 | 2fr ocher | 1.00 | .50 |
| 81 | A20 | 2.50fr carmine | 1.00 | .25 |
| 82 | A21 | 3.50fr dk ol grn | .65 | .35 |
| 83 | A21 | 5fr orange | .80 | .50 |
| 84 | A21 | 6fr brt ultra | .80 | .50 |
| 85 | A21 | 7fr black | .80 | .50 |
| 86 | A21 | 10fr dp brn | 1.00 | .65 |
| 87 | A22 | 20fr org brn & blk | 2.50 | 2.50 |

| | | | | |
|---|---|---|---|---|
| **88** | A23 | 50fr red & blk ('43) | 2.50 | 2.50 |
| **89** | A23 | 100fr grn & blk ('43) | 7.50 | 7.50 |
| | | *Nos. 68-89 (22)* | 22.55 | 19.40 |
| | | Set, never hinged | 45.00 | |

Nos. 68-89 exist imperforate, but have no franking value. Value, set never hinged $225, value set hinged $110.

Miniature sheets of Nos. 72, 76, 77 and 83 were printed in 1944 by the Belgian Government in London and given to the Belgian political review, "Message," which distributed them to its subscribers, one a month. Values, each: $65 hinged; $150 never hinged.

See note after Belgian Congo No. 225.

For surcharges see Nos. B17-B20.

Baluba Mask — A25

Carved Figures and Masks of Baluba Tribe: 10c, 50c, 2fr, 10fr, "Ndoha," figure of tribal king. 15c, 70c, 2.50fr, "Tshimanyi," an idol. 20c, 75c, 3.50fr, "Buangakokoma," statue of a kneeling beggar. 25c, 1fr, 5fr, "Mbuta," sacred double cup carved with two faces, Man and Woman. 40c, 1.25fr, 6fr, "Ngadimuashi," female mask. 1.50fr, 50fr, "Buadi-Muadi," mask with squared features (full face). 20fr, 100fr, "Mbowa," executioner's mask with buffalo horns.

**1948-50 Unwmk. *Perf. 12x12½***

| | | | | |
|---|---|---|---|---|
| **90** | A25 | 10c dp org | .25 | .25 |
| **91** | A25 | 15c ultra | .25 | .25 |
| **92** | A25 | 20c brt bl | .25 | .25 |
| **93** | A25 | 25c rose car | .30 | .25 |
| **94** | A25 | 40c violet | .25 | .25 |
| **95** | A25 | 50c ol brn | .25 | .25 |
| **96** | A25 | 70c yel grn | .25 | .25 |
| **97** | A25 | 75c magenta | .25 | .25 |
| **98** | A25 | 1fr yel org & dk vio | .30 | .25 |
| **99** | A25 | 1.25fr lt bl grn & mag | .30 | .25 |
| **100** | A25 | 1.50fr ol & mag ('50) | 1.00 | .75 |
| **101** | A25 | 2fr org & mag | .30 | .25 |
| **102** | A25 | 2.50fr brn red & bl grn | .40 | .25 |
| **103** | A25 | 3.50fr lt bl & blk | .50 | .30 |
| **104** | A25 | 5fr bis & mag | 1.00 | .30 |
| **105** | A25 | 6fr brn org & ind | 1.00 | .25 |
| **106** | A25 | 10fr pale vio & red brn | 1.25 | .50 |
| **107** | A25 | 20fr red org & vio brn | 1.90 | .80 |
| **108** | A25 | 50fr dp org & blk | 4.75 | 3.50 |
| **109** | A25 | 100fr crim & blk brn | 8.50 | 7.50 |
| | | *Nos. 90-109 (20)* | 23.25 | 16.90 |
| | | Set, never hinged | 110.00 | |

**Nos. 102 and 105 Surcharged with New Value and Bars in Black**

**1949**

| | | | | |
|---|---|---|---|---|
| **110** | A25 | 3fr on 2.50fr | .40 | .30 |
| **111** | A25 | 4fr on 6fr | .45 | .35 |
| **112** | A25 | 6.50fr on 6fr | .60 | .50 |
| | | *Nos. 110-112 (3)* | 1.45 | 1.15 |
| | | Set, never hinged | 2.75 | |

St. Francis Xavier — A26

**1953, Apr. 9 *Perf. 12½x13***

| | | | | |
|---|---|---|---|---|
| **113** | A26 | 1.50fr ultra & gray blk | .50 | .50 |
| | | Never hinged | .75 | |

Death of St. Francis Xavier, 400th anniv.

Dissotis — A27

Flowers: 15c, Protea. 20c, Vellozia. 25c, Littonia. 40c, Ipomoea. 50c, Angraecum. 60c, Euphorbia. 75c, Ochna. 1fr, Hibiscus. 1.25fr, Protea. 1.50fr, Schizoglossum. 2fr, Ansellia. 3fr, Costus. 4fr, Nymphaea. 5fr, Thunbergia. 7fr, Gerbera. 8fr, Gloriosa. 10fr, Silene. 20fr, Aristolochia.

**Flowers in Natural Colors**

**1953 Unwmk. Photo. *Perf. 11½***

| | | | | |
|---|---|---|---|---|
| **114** | A27 | 10c plum & ocher | .25 | .25 |
| **115** | A27 | 15c red & yel grn | .25 | .25 |
| **116** | A27 | 20c green & gray | .25 | .25 |
| **117** | A27 | 25c dk grn & dl org | .25 | .25 |
| **118** | A27 | 40c grn & sal | .25 | .25 |
| **119** | A27 | 50c dk car & aqua | .25 | .25 |
| **120** | A27 | 60c bl grn & pink | .25 | .25 |
| **121** | A27 | 75c dp plum & gray | .25 | .25 |
| **122** | A27 | 1fr car & yel | .45 | .25 |
| **123** | A27 | 1.25fr dk grn & bl | .70 | .65 |
| **124** | A27 | 1.50fr vio & ap grn | .25 | .25 |
| **125** | A27 | 2fr ol grn & buff | 2.25 | .25 |
| **126** | A27 | 3fr ol grn & pink | .70 | .25 |
| **127** | A27 | 4fr choc & lil | .70 | .25 |
| **128** | A27 | 5fr dp plum & lt bl grn | 1.00 | .25 |
| **129** | A27 | 7fr dk grn & fawn | 1.10 | .65 |
| **130** | A27 | 8fr grn & lt yel | 1.75 | .90 |
| **131** | A27 | 10fr dp plum & pale ol | 3.00 | 1.10 |
| **132** | A27 | 20fr vio bl & dl sal | 4.75 | 2.50 |
| | | *Nos. 114-132 (19)* | 18.65 | 9.30 |
| | | Set, never hinged | 47.50 | |

For overprints see Burundi Nos. 1-8.

King Baudouin and Tropical Scene A28

Designs: Various African Views.

**1955 Engr. & Photo.**

**Portrait Photo. in Black**

| | | | | |
|---|---|---|---|---|
| **133** | A28 | 1.50fr rose carmine | 2.75 | 1.25 |
| **134** | A28 | 3fr green | 2.75 | 1.25 |
| **135** | A28 | 4.50fr ultra | 2.75 | 1.25 |
| **136** | A28 | 6.50fr deep claret | 3.75 | 1.25 |
| | | *Nos. 133-136 (4)* | 12.00 | 5.00 |
| | | Set, never hinged | 27.50 | |

Nos. 133-136 exist imperf. Value, set $110.

Mountain Gorilla — A29

Cape Buffaloes A30

Animals: 40c, 2fr, Black-and-white colobus (monkey). 50c, 6.50fr, Impalas. 1fr, Mountain gorilla. 3fr, 8fr, Elephants. 5fr, 10fr, Eland and Zebras. 20fr, Leopard. 50fr, Lions.

**1959-61 Unwmk. Photo. *Perf. 11½***

**Granite Paper**

**Size: 23x33mm, 33x23mm**

| | | | | |
|---|---|---|---|---|
| **137** | A29 | 10c brn, crim, & blk brn | .25 | .25 |
| **138** | A30 | 20c blk, gray & ap grn | .25 | .25 |
| **139** | A29 | 40c mag, blk & gray grn | .25 | .25 |
| **140** | A30 | 50c grn, org yel & brn | .25 | .25 |
| **141** | A29 | 1fr brn, ultra & blk | .25 | .25 |
| **142** | A30 | 1.50fr blk, gray & org | .25 | .25 |
| **143** | A29 | 2fr grnsh bl, ind & brn | .25 | .25 |
| **144** | A30 | 3fr brn, dp car & blk | .25 | .25 |
| **145** | A30 | 5fr brn, dl yel, grn & blk | .25 | .25 |
| **146** | A30 | 6.50fr red, org yel & brn | .40 | .45 |
| **147** | A30 | 8fr bl, mag & blk | .50 | .60 |
| **148** | A30 | 10fr multi | .50 | .60 |

**Size: 45x26½mm**

| | | | | |
|---|---|---|---|---|
| **149** | A30 | 20fr multi ('61) | .90 | .90 |
| **150** | A30 | 50fr multi ('61) | 1.25 | 1.60 |
| | | *Nos. 137-150 (14)* | 5.80 | 6.40 |
| | | Set, never hinged | 8.00 | |

Nos. 137-150 exist imperf. Value, set $150.

For surcharge see No. 153.

For overprints see Burundi Nos. 9-24.

**Catalogue values for unused stamps in this section, from this point to the end of the section, are for Never Hinged items.**

Map of Africa and Symbolic Honeycomb A31

**1960, Feb.19 Unwmk. *Perf. 11½***

**Inscription in French**

| | | | | |
|---|---|---|---|---|
| **151** | A31 | 3fr ultra & red | .50 | .25 |

**Inscription in Flemish**

| | | | | |
|---|---|---|---|---|
| **152** | A31 | 3fr ultra & red | .50 | .25 |

10th anniversary of the Commission for Technical Co-operation in Africa South of the Sahara (C. C. T. A.).

Nos. 151-152 exist imperf. Value, set $27.50.

For surcharges and overprints see Burundi Nos. 34-39.

**No. 144 Surcharged with New Value and Bars**

**1960**

| | | | | |
|---|---|---|---|---|
| **153** | A30 | 3.50fr on 3fr red, blk, brn | .30 | .25 |

---

## SEMI-POSTAL STAMPS

Belgian Congo Nos. B10-B11 Overprinted

**1925 Unwmk. *Perf. 12½***

| | | | | |
|---|---|---|---|---|
| **B1** | SP1 | 25c + 25c car & blk | .75 | .50 |
| **B2** | SP1 | 25c + 25c car & blk | .75 | .50 |
| | | Set, never hinged | 2.75 | |

No. B2 inscribed "BELGISCH CONGO."

Commemorative of the Colonial Campaigns in 1914-1918. Nos. B1 and B2 alternate in the sheet.

Belgian Congo Nos. B12-B20 Overprinted in Blue or Red

**1930 *Perf. 11½***

| | | | | |
|---|---|---|---|---|
| **B3** | SP3 | 10c + 5c ver | 1.00 | 1.00 |
| **B4** | SP3 | 20c + 10c dk brn | 2.00 | 2.00 |
| **B5** | SP5 | 35c + 15c dp grn | 3.50 | 3.50 |
| **B6** | SP5 | 60c + 30c dl vio | 4.00 | 4.00 |
| **B7** | SP3 | 1fr + 50c dk car | 6.00 | 6.00 |
| **B8** | SP5 | 1.75fr + 75c dp bl (R) | 7.50 | 7.50 |
| **B9** | SP5 | 3.50fr + 1.50fr rose lake | 17.50 | 17.50 |
| **B10** | SP5 | 5fr + 2.50fr red brn | 15.00 | 15.00 |
| **B11** | SP5 | 10fr + 5fr gray blk | 16.00 | 16.00 |
| | | *Nos. B3-B11 (9)* | 72.50 | 72.50 |
| | | Set, never hinged | 175.00 | |

On Nos. B3, B4 and B7 there is a space of 26mm between the two words of the overprint.

The surtax was for native welfare.

Queen Astrid with Native Children — SP1

**1936 Photo.**

| | | | | |
|---|---|---|---|---|
| **B12** | SP1 | 1.25fr + 5c dk brn | .50 | .50 |
| **B13** | SP1 | 1.50fr + 10c dl rose | .50 | .50 |
| **B14** | SP1 | 2.50fr + 25c dk bl | 1.00 | 1.00 |
| | | *Nos. B12-B14 (3)* | 2.00 | 2.00 |
| | | Set, never hinged | 6.50 | |

Issued in memory of Queen Astrid. The surtax was for the National League for Protection of Native Children.

Lion of Belgium and Inscription "Belgium Shall Rise Again" — SP2

**1942 Engr. *Perf. 12½***

| | | | | |
|---|---|---|---|---|
| **B15** | SP2 | 10fr + 40fr blue | 2.00 | 2.00 |
| **B16** | SP2 | 10fr + 40fr dark red | 2.00 | 2.00 |
| | | Set, never hinged | 9.00 | |

**Nos. 74, 78, 79 and 82 Surcharged in Red**

a

b

c

**1945 Unwmk. *Perf. 12½***

| | | | | |
|---|---|---|---|---|
| **B17** | A18 (a) | 50c + 50fr | 1.00 | 1.00 |
| **B18** | A19 (b) | 1.25fr + 100fr | 1.50 | 1.50 |
| **B19** | A20 (c) | 1.75fr + 100fr | 1.00 | 1.00 |
| **B20** | A21 (b) | 3.50fr + 100fr | 1.50 | 1.50 |
| | | *Nos. B17-B20 (4)* | 5.00 | 5.00 |
| | | Set, never hinged | 19.00 | |

Mozart at Age 7 — SP3

Queen Elizabeth and Mozart Sonata — SP4

**1956** **Engr.** ***Perf. 11½***

| | | | | |
|---|---|---|---|---|
| **B21** | SP3 | 4.50fr + 1.50fr bluish vio | 1.50 | *1.50* |
| **B22** | SP4 | 6.50fr + 2.50fr claret | 3.50 | *3.50* |
| | | Set, never hinged | 10.00 | |

200th anniv. of the birth of Wolfgang Amadeus Mozart.

Surtax for the Pro-Mozart Committee.

Nurse and Children — SP5

Designs: 4.50fr+50c, Patient receiving injection. 6.50fr+50c, Patient being bandaged.

**1957** **Photo.** ***Perf. 13x10½***

**Cross in Carmine**

| | | | | |
|---|---|---|---|---|
| **B23** | SP5 | 3fr + 50c dk blue | .30 | .30 |
| **B24** | SP5 | 4.50fr + 50c dk grn | .45 | .45 |
| **B25** | SP5 | 6.50fr + 50c red brn | .65 | .65 |
| | | *Nos. B23-B25 (3)* | 1.40 | 1.40 |
| | | Set, never hinged | 3.00 | |

The surtax was for the Red Cross.

**Catalogue values for unused stamps in this section, from this point to the end of the section, are for Never Hinged items.**

Soccer SP6

Sports: #B26, High Jumper. #B27, Hurdlers. #B29, Javelin thrower. #B30, Discus thrower.

**1960** **Unwmk.** ***Perf. 13½***

| | | | | |
|---|---|---|---|---|
| **B26** | SP6 | 50c + 25c int bl & maroon | .30 | .25 |
| **B27** | SP6 | 1.50fr + 50c dk car & blk | .45 | .25 |
| **B28** | SP6 | 2fr + 1fr blk & dk car | .50 | .25 |
| **B29** | SP6 | 3fr + 1.25fr org ver & grn | 1.75 | 1.00 |
| **B30** | SP6 | 6.50fr + 3.50fr ol grn & red | 1.75 | 1.00 |
| | | *Nos. B26-B30 (5)* | 4.75 | 2.75 |

17th Olympic Games, Rome, Aug. 25-Sept. 11. The surtax was for the youth of Ruanda-Urundi.

Usumbura Cathedral — SP7

Designs: 1fr+50c, 5fr+2fr, Cathedral, sideview. 1.50fr+75c, 6.50fr+3fr, Stained glass window.

**1961, Dec. 18** ***Perf. 11½***

| | | | | |
|---|---|---|---|---|
| **B31** | SP7 | 50c + 25c brn & buff | .25 | .25 |
| **B32** | SP7 | 1fr + 50c grn & pale grn | .25 | .25 |
| **B33** | SP7 | 1.50fr + 75c multi | .25 | .25 |
| **B34** | SP7 | 3.50fr + 1.50fr lt bl & brt bl | .25 | .25 |
| **B35** | SP7 | 5fr + 2fr car & sal | .25 | .25 |
| **B36** | SP7 | 6.50fr + 3fr multi | .45 | .35 |
| | | *Nos. B31-B36 (6)* | 1.70 | 1.60 |

The surtax went for the construction and completion of the Cathedral at Usumbura.

## POSTAGE DUE STAMPS

Belgian Congo Nos. J1-J7 Overprinted

**1924-27** **Unwmk.** ***Perf. 14***

| | | | | |
|---|---|---|---|---|
| **J1** | D1 | 5c black brn | .25 | .25 |
| | *a.* | Double overprint | 75.00 | 75.00 |
| **J2** | D1 | 10c deep rose | .25 | .25 |
| **J3** | D1 | 15c violet | .30 | .25 |
| | *a.* | Double overprint | 75.00 | 75.00 |
| **J4** | D1 | 30c green | .50 | .30 |
| **J5** | D1 | 50c ultra | .50 | .40 |
| **J6** | D1 | 50c brt blue ('27) | .80 | .45 |
| **J7** | D1 | 1fr gray | .70 | .55 |
| | | *Nos. J1-J7 (7)* | 3.30 | 2.45 |
| | | Set, never hinged | 5.50 | |

**Catalogue values for unused stamps in this section, from this point to the end of the section, are for Never Hinged items.**

Belgian Congo Nos. J8-J12 Overprinted in Carmine

**1943** ***Perf. 14x14½, 12½***

| | | | | |
|---|---|---|---|---|
| **J8** | D2 | 10c olive green | .25 | .25 |
| **J9** | D2 | 20c dk ultra | .25 | .25 |
| **J10** | D2 | 50c green | .25 | .25 |
| **J11** | D2 | 1fr dark brown | .45 | .40 |
| **J12** | D2 | 2fr yellow orange | .55 | .50 |
| | | *Nos. J8-J12 (5)* | 1.75 | 1.65 |

Nos. J8-J12 values are for stamps perf. 14x14½. Value, set perf. 12½ $10.

Belgian Congo Nos. J13-J19 Overprinted

**1959** **Engr.** ***Perf. 11½***

| | | | | |
|---|---|---|---|---|
| **J13** | D3 | 10c olive brown | .25 | .25 |
| **J14** | D3 | 20c claret | .25 | .25 |
| **J15** | D3 | 50c green | .25 | .25 |
| **J16** | D3 | 1fr lt blue | .25 | .25 |
| **J17** | D3 | 2fr vermilion | .40 | .35 |
| **J18** | D3 | 4fr purple | .80 | .70 |
| **J19** | D3 | 6fr violet blue | .85 | .75 |
| | | *Nos. J13-J19 (7)* | 3.05 | 2.80 |

Both capital and lower-case U's are found in this overprint.

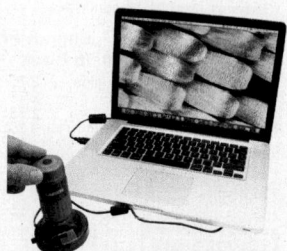

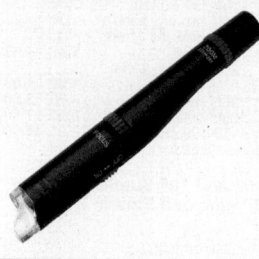

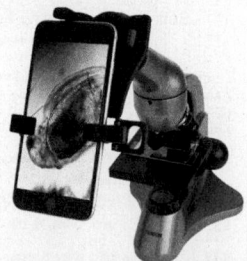

# RUSSIA

'rəsh-ə

(Union of Soviet Socialist Republics)

LOCATION — Eastern Europe and Northern Asia
GOVT. — Republic
AREA — 6,592,691 sq. mi.
POP. — 147,100,000 (1999 est.)
CAPITAL — Moscow

An empire until 1917, the government was overthrown in that year and a socialist union of republics was formed under the name of the Union of Soviet Socialist Republics. The USSR includes the following autonomous republics which have issued their own stamps: Armenia, Azerbaijan, Georgia and Ukraine.

With the breakup of the Soviet Union on Dec. 26, 1991, eleven former Soviet republics established the Commonwealth of Independent States. Stamps inscribed "Rossija" are issued by the Russian Republic.

100 Kopecks = 1 Ruble

**Catalogue values for unused stamps in this country are for Never Hinged items, beginning with Scott 1021 in the regular postage section, Scott B58 in the semi-postal section, and Scott C82 in the airpost section.**

## Watermarks

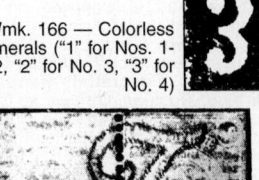

Wmk. 166 — Colorless Numerals ("1" for Nos. 1-2, "2" for No. 3, "3" for No. 4)

Wmk. 168 — Cyrillic EZGB & Wavy Lines

Wmk. 169 — Lozenges

Wmk. 171 — Diamonds

Wmk. 170 — Greek Border and Rosettes

Wmk. 226 — Diamonds Enclosing Four Dots

Wmk. 293 — Hammer and Sickle, Multiple

Wmk. 383 — Cyrillic Letters in Shield

## Empire

Coat of Arms — A1

**Wmk. 166**

**1857, Dec. 10** **Typo.** ***Imperf.***

| No. | Description | Unused | Used |
|---|---|---|---|
| **1** | A1 10k brown & blue | *62,500.* | 950. |
| | No gum | *21,000.* | |
| | Pen cancellation | | 475. |
| | Penmark & postmark | | 475. |
| | Straight line town cancellation, *from* | | 650. |
| | Circular datestamp cancellation, *from* | | 900. |

Genuine unused examples of No. 1 are exceedingly rare. Most of those offered are used with pen cancellation removed. The unused value is for an example without gum. The very few known stamps with original gum sell for much more.

See Poland for similar stamp inscribed "ZALOT KOP. 10."

**1858, Jan. 10** ***Perf. 14½, 15***

| No. | Description | Unused | Used |
|---|---|---|---|
| **2** | A1 10k brown & blue | 14,000. | 175. |
| | No gum | *4,400.* | |
| **3** | A1 20k blue & orange | 13,000. | 1,700. |
| | No gum | *4,250.* | |
| **4** | A1 30k carmine & green | 18,500. | 2,500. |
| | No gum | *5,750.* | |

Coat of Arms — A2

**Wove Paper**

**1858-64** **Unwmk.** ***Perf. 12½***

| No. | Description | Unused | Used |
|---|---|---|---|
| **5** | A2 1k blk & yel ('64) | 170.00 | 67.50 |
| *a.* | 1k black & orange | 340.00 | 55.00 |
| **6** | A2 3k blk & grn ('64) | 1,100. | 100.00 |
| **7** | A2 5k blk & lil ('64) | 1,000. | 90.00 |
| **8** | A1 10k brown & blue | 275.00 | 13.50 |
| **9** | A1 20k blue & orange | 1,000. | 80.00 |
| *a.* | Half used as 10k on cover | | — |
| **10** | A1 30k car & grn | 1,175. | 125.00 |
| | *Nos. 5-10 (6)* | 4,720. | 476.00 |

Coat of Arms — A3

**1863**

| No. | Description | Unused | Used |
|---|---|---|---|
| **11** | A3 5k black & blue | 30.00 | *160.00* |

No. 11 was issued to pay local postage in St. Petersburg and Moscow. It is known to have been used in other cities. In Aug. 1864 it was authorized for use on mail addressed to other destinations.

**1865, June 2** ***Perf. 14½, 15***

| No. | Description | Unused | Used |
|---|---|---|---|
| **12** | A2 1k black & yellow | 375.00 | 37.50 |
| *a.* | 1k black & orange | 400.00 | 42.50 |
| **13** | A2 3k black & green | 350.00 | 17.50 |
| **14** | A2 5k black & lilac | 375.00 | 40.00 |
| **15** | A1 10k brown & blue | 925.00 | 3.00 |
| *a.* | Thick paper | 975.00 | 7.50 |
| **17** | A1 20k blue & orange | 2,750. | 40.00 |
| *a.* | Thick paper | 3,000. | 45.00 |
| **18** | A1 30k car & grn | 1,950. | 40.00 |
| *a.* | Thick paper | 2,100. | 45.00 |
| | *Nos. 12-18 (6)* | 6,725. | 178.00 |

**Horizontally Laid Paper**

**1866-70** **Wmk. 168**

| No. | Description | Unused | Used |
|---|---|---|---|
| **19** | A2 1k blk & yel | 10.00 | 1.10 |
| *a.* | 1k black & orange | 12.00 | 1.25 |
| *b.* | Imperf. | | *3,000.* |
| *c.* | Vertically laid | 315.00 | 45.00 |
| *d.* | Groundwork inverted | *5,500.* | *5,500.* |
| *e.* | Thick paper | 75.00 | 55.00 |
| *f.* | As "c," imperf. | 7,500. | 7,250. |
| *g.* | As "b," "c" & "d" | *11,000.* | *17,000.* |
| *h.* | 1k blk & org, vert. laid paper | 350.00 | 42.50 |
| **20** | A2 3k blk & dp grn | 12.50 | 1.50 |
| *a.* | 3k black & yellow green | 12.50 | 1.50 |
| *b.* | Imperf. | | *3,400.* |
| *c.* | Vertically laid | 400.00 | 50.00 |
| *d.* | V's in groundwork (error) ('70) | 2,000. | 40.00 |
| *e.* | 3k black & blue green | 12.50 | 1.50 |
| **22** | A2 5k black & lilac | 15.00 | 2.00 |
| *a.* | 5k black & gray | 240.00 | 32.50 |
| *b.* | Imperf. | | 4,250. |
| *c.* | Vertically laid | 10,000. | 160.00 |
| *d.* | As "c," imperf. | — | — |
| **23** | A1 10k brn & blue | 45.00 | 1.75 |
| *a.* | Vertically laid | 525.00 | 16.50 |
| *b.* | Center inverted | | *50,000.* |
| *c.* | Imperf. | | *22,500.* |
| **24** | A1 20k blue & org | 100.00 | 15.00 |
| *a.* | Vertically laid | 5,250. | 160.00 |
| **25** | A1 30k car & grn | 100.00 | 30.00 |
| *a.* | Vertically laid | 1,000. | 120.00 |
| | *Nos. 19-25 (6)* | 282.50 | 51.35 |

Arms — A4

**1875-82** **Horizontally Laid Paper**

| No. | Description | Unused | Used |
|---|---|---|---|
| **26** | A2 2k black & red | 25.00 | 1.60 |
| *a.* | Vertically laid | 6,750. | 160.00 |
| | No gum | 1,275. | |
| *b.* | Groundwork inverted | | *57,500.* |
| **27** | A4 7k gray & rose ('79) | 20.00 | 1.00 |
| *a.* | Imperf. | | *8,500.* |
| *b.* | Vertically laid | 2,000. | 65.00 |
| | No gum | 600.00 | |
| *c.* | Wmkd. hexagons ('79) | | *170,000.* |
| *d.* | Center inverted | | — |
| *e.* | Center omitted | — | — |
| *f.* | 7k black & carmine ('80) | 21.00 | .85 |
| *g.* | 7k pale gray & carmine ('82) | 21.00 | .85 |
| **28** | A4 8k gray & rose | 25.00 | 1.60 |
| *a.* | Vertically laid | 2,500. | 82.50 |
| | No gum | 600.00 | |
| *b.* | Imperf. | | *22,500.* |
| *c.* | "C" instead of "B" in "Bocem" | 650.00 | *250.* |
| **29** | A4 10k brn & blue | 50.00 | 5.75 |
| *a.* | Center inverted | | *60,000.* |

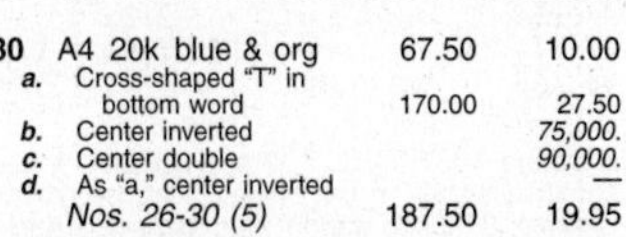

| No. | Description | Unused | Used |
|---|---|---|---|
| **30** | A4 20k blue & org | 67.50 | 10.00 |
| *a.* | Cross-shaped "T" in bottom word | 170.00 | 27.50 |
| *b.* | Center inverted | | *75,000.* |
| *c.* | Center double | | *90,000.* |
| *d.* | As "a," center inverted | | — |
| | *Nos. 26-30 (5)* | 187.50 | 19.95 |

The hexagon watermark of No. 27c is that of revenue stamps. No. 27c exists with Perm and Riga postmarks.

**See Finland for stamps similar to designs A4-A15, which have "dot in circle" devices or are inscribed "Markka," "Markkaa," "Pen.," or "Pennia."**

Imperial Eagle and Post Horns

A5 A6

***Perf. 14 to 15 and Compound***

**1883-88** **Wmk. 168**

**Horizontally Laid Paper**

| No. | Description | Unused | Used |
|---|---|---|---|
| **31** | A5 1k orange | 10.00 | 1.20 |
| *a.* | Imperf. | | 62,500. |
| *b.* | Groundwork inverted | | *9,000.* |
| *c.* | 1k yellow | 6.75 | 1.20 |
| **32** | A5 2k dark green | 4.00 | 1.20 |
| *a.* | 2k yellow green ('88) | 32.50 | 4.00 |
| *b.* | Imperf. | 1,100. | 700.00 |
| *c.* | Wove paper | — | — |
| *d.* | Groundwork inverted | | *31,500.* |
| **33** | A5 3k carmine | 12.50 | 1.20 |
| *a.* | Imperf. | — | — |
| *b.* | Groundwork inverted | | *30,000.* |
| *c.* | Wove paper | — | — |
| **34** | A5 5k red violet | 8.00 | .90 |
| *a.* | Groundwork inverted | | *8,500.* |
| **35** | A5 7k blue | 10.00 | .90 |
| *a.* | Imperf. | 800.00 | 475.00 |
| *b.* | Groundwork inverted | 2,000. | 1,900. |
| *c.* | Double impression of frame and center | — | — |
| **36** | A6 14k blue & rose | 85.00 | 2.50 |
| *a.* | Imperf. | 4,000. | 3,000. |
| *b.* | Center inverted | — | *6,250.* |
| *c.* | Diagonal half surcharge "7" in red, on cover ('84) | | — |

37 A6 35k vio & grn 60.00 6.50
38 A6 70k brn & org 67.50 9.50
*Nos. 31-38 (8)* 257.00 23.90

Before 1882 the 1, 2, 3 and 5 kopecks had small numerals in the background; beginning with No. 31 these denominations have a background of network, like the higher values.

No. 36c is handstamped. It is known with cancellations of Tiflis and Kutais, both in Georgia. It is believed to be of philatelic origin.

A7

**1884** ***Perf. 13½, 13½x11½***

**Vertically Laid Paper**

39 A7 3.50r blk & gray 1,200. 625.
 a. Horiz. laid *175,000.* 15,000.
 b. Inverted center — —
40 A7 7r blk & org 800. 675.

Forgeries exist, both unused and used.

A8

Imperial Eagle and Post Horns with Thunderbolts — A9

**With Thunderbolts Across Post Horns**

***Perf. 14 to 15 and Compound***

**1889, May 14**

**Horizontally Laid Paper**

41 A8 4k rose 12.00 .45
 a. Groundwork inverted — *16,000.*
 b. Double impression of center — —
 c. Double impression of frame — —
42 A8 10k dark blue 20.00 .45
43 A8 20k blue & carmine 21.00 1.20
 a. Groundwork inverted — —
44 A8 50k violet & green 16.00 1.50

***Perf. 13½***

45 A9 1r lt brn, brn & org 47.50 2.50
 a. Horiz. pair, imperf. btwn. 900.00 450.00
 b. Vert. pair, imperf. btwn. 850.00 425.00
 c. Center omitted — —
*Nos. 41-45 (5)* 116.50 6.10

See #57C, 60, 63, 66, 68, 82, 85, 87, 126, 129, 131. For surcharges see #216, 219, 223, 226.

A10

A11

A12

**With Thunderbolts Across Post Horns**

**1889-92** ***Perf. 14½x15***

**Horizontally Laid Paper**

46 A10 1k orange 3.25 .50
 a. Imperf. 850.00 —
47 A10 2k green 4.00 .50
 a. Imperf. 800.00
 b. Groundwork inverted 800.00 *17,000.*
48 A10 3k carmine 8.00 .50
 a. Imperf. 425.00 350.00
49 A10 5k red vio 8.00 .60
 b. Groundwork omitted or inverted 850.00 650.00
50 A10 7k dk blue 5.25 .50
 a. Imperf. 425.00 *9,000.*
 b. Groundwork inverted *16,000.* *11,250.*
 c. Groundwork omitted 250.00 200.00
51 A11 14k blue & rose 16.00 .50
 a. Center inverted *6,750.* *4,500.*
 b. Center omitted 850.00
52 A11 35k vio & grn 67.50 6.00

***Perf. 13½***

53 A12 3.50r blk & gray 50.00 8.00
 a. Center inverted — *12,750.*
54 A12 7r blk & yel 190.00 11.00
 a. Dbl. impression of black *45,000.*
*Nos. 46-54 (9)* 352.00 28.10

***Perf. 14 to 15 and Compound***

**1902-05** **Vertically Laid Paper**

55 A10 1k orange 4.50 .35
 a. Imperf. 1,100. *1,100.*
 b. Groundwork inverted — —
 c. Groundwork omitted — —
56 A10 2k yel grn 4.50 .35
 a. 2k deep green 8.00 .70
 b. Groundwork omitted — —
 c. Groundwork inverted — —
 d. Groundwork double *375.00* *375.00*
57 A10 3k rose red 10.50 .35
 a. Groundwork omitted — —
 b. Double impression 275.00 250.00
 d. Imperf. *1,350.* —
 e. Groundwork inverted — —
 f. Groundwork double 275.00
57C A8 4k rose red ('04) 9.00 .85
 f. Double impression 340.00 275.00
 g. Groundwork inverted — *16,500.*
58 A10 5k red vio 19.00 .60
 a. 5k dull violet 12.50 2.25
 b. Groundwork inverted — *30,000.*
 c. Imperf. — —
 d. Groundwork omitted 675.00 150.00
 e. Groundwork double *1,350.* 100.00
59 A10 7k dk blue 10.50 .35
 a. Groundwork omitted 315.00 *275.00*
 b. Imperf. 675.00 600.00
 c. Groundwork inverted — —
60 A8 10k dk blue ('04) 4.00 .50
 a. Groundwork inverted 42.50 17.50
 b. Groundwork omitted 600.00 85.00
 c. Groundwork double 175.00 85.00

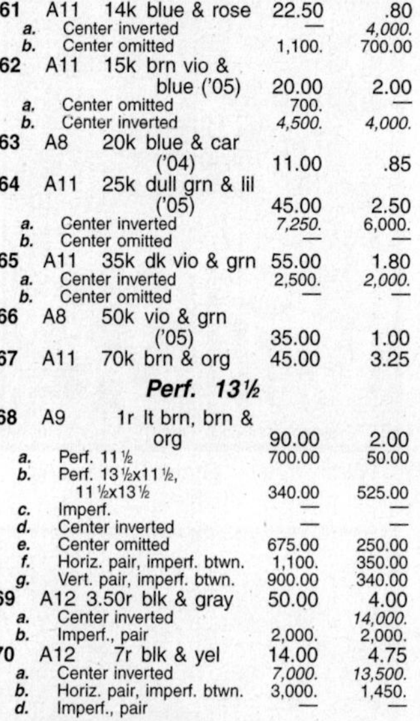

61 A11 14k blue & rose 22.50 .80
 a. Center inverted — *4,000.*
 b. Center omitted 1,100. 700.00
62 A11 15k brn vio & blue ('05) 20.00 2.00
 a. Center omitted 700. —
 b. Center inverted *4,500.* *4,000.*
63 A8 20k blue & car ('04) 11.00 .85
64 A11 25k dull grn & lil ('05) 45.00 2.50
 a. Center inverted *7,250.* 6,000.
 b. Center omitted — —
65 A11 35k dk vio & grn 55.00 1.80
 a. Center inverted 2,500. *2,000.*
 b. Center omitted — —
66 A8 50k vio & grn ('05) 35.00 1.00
67 A11 70k brn & org 45.00 3.25

***Perf. 13½***

68 A9 1r lt brn, brn & org 90.00 2.00
 a. Perf. 11½ 700.00 50.00
 b. Perf. 13½x11½, 11½x13½ 340.00 525.00
 c. Imperf. — —
 d. Center inverted — —
 e. Center omitted 675.00 250.00
 f. Horiz. pair, imperf. btwn. 1,100. 350.00
 g. Vert. pair, imperf. btwn. 900.00 340.00
69 A12 3.50r blk & gray 50.00 4.00
 a. Center inverted *14,000.*
 b. Imperf., pair 2,000. 2,000.
70 A12 7r blk & yel 14.00 4.75
 a. Center inverted *7,000.* *13,500.*
 b. Horiz. pair, imperf. btwn. 3,000. 1,450.
 d. Imperf., pair — —

A13

**1906** ***Perf. 13½***

71 A13 5r dk blue, grn & pale blue 50.00 4.50
 a. Perf. 11½ 500.00 275.00
72 A13 10r car rose, yel & gray 350.00 10.50
*Nos. 55-72 (19)* 849.50 41.30

The design of No. 72 differs in many details from the illustration. Nos. 71-72 were printed in sheets of 25.

See Nos. 80-81, 83-84, 86, 108-109, 125, 127-128, 130, 132-135, 137-138. For surcharges see Nos. 217-218, 220-222, 224-225, 227-229.

A14 A15

**Vertical Lozenges of Varnish on Face**

**1909-12** **Unwmk.** ***Perf. 14x14½***

**Wove Paper**

73 A14 1k dull org yel .45 .45
 a. 1k orange yellow ('09) 2.50 .45
 c. Double impression 90.00 —
74 A14 2k dull green .25 .25
 a. 2k green ('09) 1.60 .25
 b. Double impression 100.00 —
75 A14 3k carmine .25 .25
 a. 3k rose red ('09) 1.40 .25
76 A15 4k carmine .25 .25
 a. 4k carmine rose ('09) 1.40 .25
77 A14 5k claret 2.50 .25
 a. 5k lilac ('12) .25 .25
 b. Double impression 95.00
78 A14 7k blue .25 .25
 a. 7k light blue ('09) 2.50 .45
 b. Imperf. 1,250.
79 A15 10k dark blue .25 .25
 a. 10k light blue ('09) *80.00* *8.00*
 b. 10k pale blue 8.00 2.00
80 A11 14k dk blue & car .85 .25
 a. 14k blue & rose ('09) 1.40 .25
81 A11 15k red brn & dp blue .25 .25
 a. 15k dull violet & blue ('09) 1.40 .25
 c. Center omitted 170.00 —
 d. Center double 50.00 —
82 A8 20k dull bl & dk car .25 .25
 a. 20k blue & carmine ('10) 1.40 .45
 b. Groundwork omitted 42.50
 c. Center double 175.00
 d. Center and value omitted — —
83 A11 25k dl grn & dk vio .25 .25
 a. 25k green & violet ('09) 1.40 .45
 b. Center omitted 170.00
 c. Center double 175.00 —

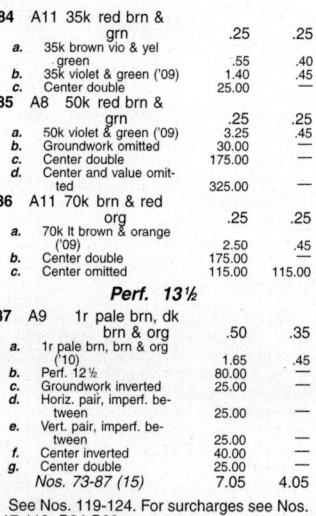

84 A11 35k red brn & grn .25 .25
 a. 35k brown vio & yel green .55 .40
 b. 35k violet & green ('09) 1.40 .45
 c. Center double 25.00 —
85 A8 50k red brn & grn .25 .25
 a. 50k violet & green ('09) 3.25 .45
 b. Groundwork omitted 30.00 —
 c. Center double 175.00 —
 d. Center and value omitted 325.00 —
86 A11 70k brn & red org .25 .25
 a. 70k lt brown & orange ('09) 2.50 .45
 b. Center double 175.00 —
 c. Center omitted 115.00 115.00

***Perf. 13½***

87 A9 1r pale brn, dk brn & org .50 .35
 a. 1r pale brn, brn & org ('10) 1.65 .45
 b. Perf. 12½ 80.00 —
 c. Groundwork inverted 25.00 —
 d. Horiz. pair, imperf. between 25.00 —
 e. Vert. pair, imperf. between 25.00 —
 f. Center inverted 40.00 —
 g. Center double 25.00 —
*Nos. 73-87 (15)* 7.05 4.05

See Nos. 119-124. For surcharges see Nos. 117-118, B24-B29.

No. 87a was issued in sheets of 40 stamps, while Nos. 87 and 87b came in sheets of 50. Nos. 87g-87k are listed below No. 138a.

Nearly all values of this issue are known without the lines of varnish.

The 7k has two types:

I — The scroll bearing the top inscription ends at left with three short lines of shading beside the first letter. Four pearls extend at lower left between the leaves and denomination panel.

II — Inner lines of scroll at top left end in two curls; three pearls at lower left.

Three clichés of type II (an essay) were included by mistake in the plate used for the first printing. Value of pair, type I with type II, unused $4,500.

**SURCHARGES**

**Russian stamps of types A6-A15 with various surcharges may be found listed under Armenia, Batum, Far Eastern Republic, Georgia, Latvia, Siberia, South Russia, Transcaucasian Federated Republics, Ukraine, Russian Offices in China, Russian Offices in the Turkish Empire and Army of the Northwest.**

Peter I — A16

Alexander II — A17

Alexander III — A18

Peter I — A19

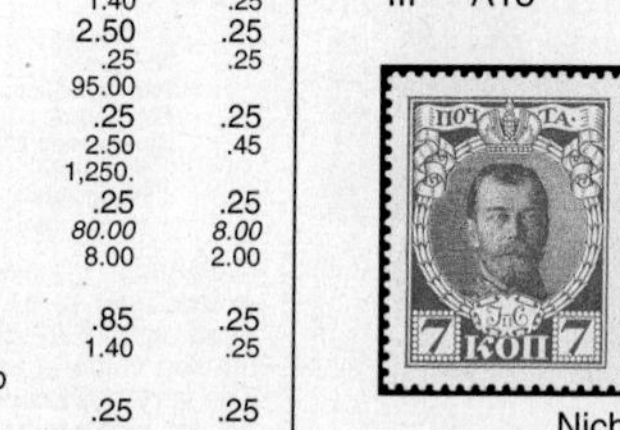

Nicholas II

A20 A21

Catherine II — A22

Nicholas I — A23

Alexander I — A24

Alexis Mikhailovich A25

Paul I A26

Elizabeth Petrovna A27

Michael Feodorovich A28

The Kremlin — A29

Winter Palace — A30

Romanov Castle — A31

Nicholas II — A32

**Without Lozenges of Varnish**

**1913, Jan. 2 Typo. *Perf. 13½***

**88** A16 1k brn org 1.60 .25
**89** A17 2k yellow green 4.25 .25
**90** A18 3k rose red 4.25 .25
*b.* Double impression 600.00
**91** A19 4k dull red 1.60 .25
**92** A20 7k brown 1.60 .25
*b.* Double impression 675.00 —
**93** A21 10k deep blue 4.25 .25
**94** A22 14k blue green 4.25 .40
**95** A23 15k yellow brown 8.00 .60
**96** A24 20k olive green 26.50 .70
**97** A25 25k red violet 8.00 1.10
**98** A26 35k gray vio & dk grn 2.50 .70
**99** A27 50k brn & slate 10.75 1.90
**100** A28 70k yel grn & brn 8.00 1.90

**Engr.**

**101** A29 1r deep green 40.00 6.25
**102** A30 2r red brown 65.00 11.00
**103** A31 3r dark violet 50.00 11.00
**104** A32 5r black brown 40.00 19.00
*Nos. 88-104 (17)* 280.55 56.05
Set, never hinged 650.00

**Imperf**

*88a* A16 1k brown orange 800.00 —
*89a* A17 2k yellow green 800.00 —
*90a* A18 3k rose red 800.00
*91a* A19 4k dull red 1,900.
*92a* A20 7k brown 425.00
*93a* A21 10k deep blue 800.00
*94a* A22 14k blue green 1,900.
*101a* A29 1r deep green 1,600.
*102a* A30 2r red brown 800.00
*103b* A31 3r dark violet 800.00
*104a* A32 5r dark violet 1,900.

Tercentenary of the founding of the Romanov dynasty.

See Nos. 105-107, 112-116, 139-141. For surcharges see Nos. 110-111, Russian Offices in the Turkish Empire 213-227.

**Arms and 5-line Inscription on Back**

No. 107 Back

**Thin Cardboard**
**Without Gum**

**1915, Oct. Typo. *Perf. 13½***

**105** A21 10k blue 2.50 *32.50*
**106** A23 15k brown 2.50 *32.50*
**107** A24 20k olive green 2.50 *32.50*
*Nos. 105-107 (3)* 7.50 *97.50*

***Imperf***

*105a* A21 10k 550.00
*106a* A23 15k 200.00 —
*107a* A24 20k 175.00

Nos. 105-107, 112-116 and 139-141 were issued for use as paper money, but contrary to regulations were often used for postal purposes. Back inscription means: "Having circulation on par with silver subsidiary coins."

**Types of 1906 Issue**
**Vertical Lozenges of Varnish on Face**

**1915 *Perf. 13½, 13½x13***

**108** A13 5r ind, grn & lt blue 1.40 .50
*a.* 5r dk bl, grn & pale bl ('15) 13.50 1.60
*b.* Perf. 12½ 20.00 6.75
*c.* Center double 60.00
*d.* Pair, imperf. between *100.00* —
**109** A13 10r car lake, yel & gray 2.00 .50
*a.* 10r carmine, yel & light gray 2.00 .50
*b.* 10r rose red, yel & gray ('15) 6.75 .85
*c.* 10r car, yel & gray blue (error) *2,700.*
*d.* Groundwork inverted *450.00*
*e.* Center double 60.00 —

Nos. 108a and 109b were issued in sheets of 25. Nos. 108, 108b, 109 and 109a came in sheets of 50. Chemical forgeries of No. 109c exist. Genuine examples usually are centered to upper right.

Nos. 92, 94 Surcharged

**1916**

**110** A20 10k on 7k brown .85 .50
*a.* Inverted surcharge 210.00
**111** A22 20k on 14k bl grn .85 .45

***Imperf***

*110b* A20 10k on 7k brown *425.00* —
*111a* A22 20k on 14k bl grn *425.00* —

**Types of 1913 Issue**
**Arms, Value & 4-line inscription on Back**
**Surcharged Large Numerals on Nos. 112-113**
**Thin Cardboard**

**1916-17 Without Gum**

**112** A16 1 on 1k brn org ('17) 2.50 *40.00*
**113** A17 2 on 2k yel green ('17) 2.50 *40.00*

**Without Surcharge**

**114** A16 1k brown orange 50.00 —
**115** A17 2k yellow green 52.50 —
**116** A18 3k rose red 2.50 *32.50*

See note after No. 107.

**Nos. 78a, 80a Surcharged**

a

b

**1917 *Perf. 14x14½***

**117** A14 10k on 7k lt blue .85 .45
*a.* Inverted surcharge 150.00 —
*b.* Double surcharge 60.00 —
*c.* Imperforate *375.00* —
**118** A11 20k on 14k bl & rose 1.20 .45
*a.* Inverted surcharge 250.00 —

**Provisional Government**
**Civil War**
**Type of 1889-1912 Issues**
**Vertical Lozenges of Varnish on Face**

Two types of 7r:
Type I — Single outer frame line.
Type II — Double outer frame line.

**Wove Paper**

**1917 Typo. *Imperf.***

**119** A14 1k orange 1.10 .25
**120** A14 2k gray green .25 .25
**121** A14 3k red .25 .25
**122** A15 4k carmine .85 2.50
**123** A14 5k claret .25 .25
**124** A15 10k dark blue 20.00 20.00
**125** A11 15k red brn & dp blue .40 .25
*a.* Center omitted 175.00
**126** A8 20k blue & car .35 .35
*a.* Groundwork omitted 42.50 —
**127** A11 25k grn & gray vio .50 1.00
**128** A11 35k red brn & grn .50 .35
**129** A8 50k brn vio & grn .45 .25
*a.* Groundwork omitted 42.50 —
**130** A11 70k brn & org .45 .35
*a.* Center omitted 100.00
**131** A9 1r pale brn, brn & red org .35 .25
*a.* Center inverted 25.00 —
*b.* Center omitted 25.00 —
*c.* Center double 25.00 —
*d.* Groundwork double 150.00 —
*e.* Groundwork inverted 60.00 —
*f.* Groundwork omitted 60.00 —
*g.* Frame double 25.00 —
**132** A12 3.50r mar & lt grn 1.10 .25
**133** A13 5r dk blue, grn & pale blue 1.25 .35
*a.* 5r dk bl, grn & yel (error) 900.00
*b.* Groundwork inverted *3,600.*
**134** A12 7r dk grn & pink (I) 1.20 1.15
*a.* Center inverted *30,000.*
**135** A13 10r scar, yel & gray 45.00 35.00
*a.* 10r scarlet, green & gray (error) 1,125.
*Nos. 119-135 (17)* 74.25 63.05

Beware of trimmed examples of No. 109 offered as No. 135.

**Vertical Lozenges of Varnish on Face**

**1917 *Perf. 13½, 13½x13***

**137** A12 3.50r mar & lt grn .50 .25
**138** A12 7r dk grn & pink (II) 2.50 .50
*d.* Type I 40.00 6.75

***Perf. 12½***

*137a* A12 3.50r maroon & lt grn 14.00 2.75
*138a* A12 7r dk grn & pink (II) 17.00 4.75

**Horizontal Lozenges of Varnish on Face**

***Perf. 13½x13***

*87h* A9 1r pale brown, brn & red orange 1.35 .30
*i.* Imperf. 17.50 —
*j.* As "i," center omitted 45.00 —
*k.* As "i," center inverted 22.50 —
*m.* As "i," center double 22.50 —
*137b* A12 3.50r mar & lt green 2.50 .50
*d.* Imperf. 2,250.
*138b* A12 7r dk grn & pink (II) 1.35 .25
*c.* Imperf. 1,550.

Nos. 87g, 137b and 138b often show the eagle with little or no embossing.

**Types of 1913 Issue**

No. 88 Surcharged Large Numeral

No. 139 Back

No. 140 Back

The backside of Nos. 139-140 have surcharge & 4-line inscription.

**1917**

**Thin Cardboard, Without Gum**

**139** A16 1 on 1k brown org 3.00 *40.00*
**140** A17 2 on 2k yel green 3.00 *40.00*
*a.* Imperf. 525.00 —
Pair *1,700.*

**Without Surcharge**

**141** A18 3k rose red 3.00 *40.00*
*Nos. 139-141 (3)* 9.00 *120.00*

See note after No. 107.

Stamps overprinted with a Liberty Cap on Crossed Swords or with reduced facsimiles of pages of newspapers were a private speculation and without official sanction.

**RUSSIAN TURKESTAN**

Russian stamps of 1917-18 surcharged as above are frauds.

## Russian Soviet Federated Socialist Republic

Severing Chain of Bondage — A33

**1918 Typo. *Perf. 13½***
**149** A33 35k blue .45 *6.25*
*a.* Imperf., pair 1,600.
**150** A33 70k brown .50 *7.25*
*a.* Imperf., pair *16,500.*

For surcharges see Nos. B18-B23, J1-J9 and note following No. B17.

A 15k stamp exists but was not regularly issued. Value, $30,000.

During 1918-22, the chaotic conditions of revolution and civil war brought the printing of stamps by the central government to a halt. Stocks of old tsarist Arms type stamps and postal stationery remained in use, and postal savings and various revenue stamps were authorized for postage use. During this period, stamps were sold and used at different rates at different times: 1918-20, sold at face value; from March, 1920, sold at 100 times face value; from Aug. 15, 1921, sold at 250r each, regardless of face value; from April, 1922, sold at 10,000r per 1k or 1r. In Oct. 1922, these issues were superseded by gold currency stamps.

See Nos. AR1-AR25 for fiscal stamps used as postage stamps during this period.

Symbols of Agriculture — A40

Symbols of Industry — A41

Soviet Symbols of Agriculture and Industry — A42

Science and Arts — A43

**1921 Unwmk. Litho. *Imperf.***
**177** A40 1r orange 1.00 *140.00*
*b.* 1r pale orange 90.00
**178** A40 2r lt brown 1.00 *140.00*
*a.* Double impression *800.00*
**179** A41 5r gray blue 2.25 *140.00*
*a.* Double impression —
**180** A42 20r blue, ordinary wove paper 2.00 *140.00*
*a.* Double impression 250.00
*b.* Pelure paper 8.00 *150.00*
**180C** A42 20r ultra, pelure paper 5.00 140.00
*d.* Double impression 275.00 —
**181** A40 100r orange .25 *.25*
*a.* Double impression 200.00
*b.* Pelure paper .25 .45
*c.* As "b," double impression 200.00
**182** A40 200r lt brown .50 *.25*
*a.* Double impression 180.00
*b.* Triple impression 150.00
*c.* 200r gray brown 25.00
**183** A43 250r dull violet .25 *.25*
*a.* Tête bêche pair 25.00
*b.* Double impression 90.00
*c.* Pelure paper .25 *.45*
*d.* As "c," tête bêche pair 32.50 —
*e.* As "c," double impression 100.00
*f.* Chalk surfaced paper 12.50 *5.00*
**184** A40 300r green .60 *1.10*
*a.* Double impression 425.00
*b.* Pelure paper 12.00 22.50
**185** A41 500r blue 1.00 .30
*a.* Double impression —
**186** A41 1000r carmine .25 *.30*
*a.* Double impression 110.00
*b.* Triple impression 135.00
*c.* Pelure paper .85 *.30*
*d.* As "c," double impression 90.00
*e.* Thick paper 2.50 *2.75*
*f.* Chalk surfaced paper .25 *.50*
*Nos. 177-186 (10)* 9.10 562.45

Nos. 177-180 were on sale only in Petrograd, Moscow and Kharkov. Used values are for cancelled-to-order stamps. Postally used examples are worth substantially more.

Nos. 183a and 183d are from printings in which one of the two panes of 25 in the sheet were inverted. Thus, they are horizontal pairs, with a vertical gutter.

See Nos. 203, 205. For surcharges see Nos. 191-194, 196-199, 201, 210, B40, B43-B47, J10.

New Russia Triumphant A44

Type I — 37½mm by 23½mm.
Type II — 38½mm by 23¼mm.

**1921, Aug. 10 Wmk. 169 Engr.**
**187** A44 40r slate, type II 1.90 *160.00*
*a.* Type I 1.90 *160.00*

The types are caused by paper shrinkage. One type has the watermark sideways in relation to the other.

For surcharges see Nos. 195, 200.

Initials Stand for Russian Soviet Federated Socialist Republic — A45

**1921 Litho. Unwmk.**
**188** A45 100r orange .85 .85
**189** A45 250r violet .85 .85
**190** A45 1000r carmine rose 1.75 1.40
*Nos. 188-190 (3)* 3.45 3.10

4th anniversary of Soviet Government.

A 200r was not regularly issued. Values: unused $60, never hinged $100.

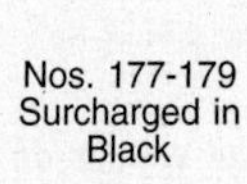
Nos. 177-179 Surcharged in Black

**1922**
**191** A40 5000r on 1r org 3.00 .80
*a.* Inverted surcharge 140.00 32.50
*b.* Double surch., red & blk 800.00 —
*c.* Pair, one without surcharge 250.00 —
**192** A40 5000r on 2r lt brn 3.00 1.10
*a.* Inverted surcharge 110.00 90.00
*b.* Double surcharge 145.00
**193** A41 5000r on 5r ultra 3.00
*a.* Inverted surcharge — *450.00*
*b.* Double surcharge 145.00

Beware of digitally created forgeries of the errors of Nos. 191-193 and 196-199.

No. 180 Surcharged

**194** A42 5000r on 20r blue 2.10 2.25
*a.* Pelure paper 16.50 3.25
*b.* Pair, one without surcharge *125.00*

### Nos. 177-180, 187-187a Surcharged in Black or Red

**Wmk. Lozenges (169)**
**195** A44 10,000r on 40r, type I 70.00 50.00
*a.* Inverted surcharge 225.00
*b.* Type II 67.50 50.00
*c.* "1.0000" instead of "10.000" 2,750.
*d.* Double surcharge *8,500.*

**Red Surcharge**

**Unwmk.**
**196** A40 5000r on 1r org 5.75 5.75
*a.* Inverted surcharge 50.00 25.00
**197** A40 5000r on 2r lt brn 5.75 5.75
*a.* Inverted surcharge 125.00 30.00
**198** A41 5000r on 5r ultra 5.75 5.75
**199** A42 5000r on 20r blue 3.00 2.25
*a.* Inverted surcharge 200.00 50.00
*b.* Pelure paper 4.00 5.00

**Wmk. Lozenges (169)**
**200** A44 10,000r on 40r, type I (R) 2.25 1.25
*a.* Inverted surcharge 160.00 40.00
*b.* Double surcharge 125.00 —
*c.* With periods after Russian letters 1,100. 450.00
*d.* Type II 2.25 2.75
*e.* As "a," type II 125.00 40.00
*f.* As "c," type II 200.00 —

No. 183 Surcharged in Black or Blue Black

**1922, Mar. Unwmk.**
**201** A43 7500r on 250r (Bk) .25 .25
*a.* Pelure paper .25 .25
*b.* Chalk surfaced paper .45 .45
*c.* Blue black surcharge .50 .25
*d.* Surch. typographed 250.00 —
*e.* As "c," surch. lithographed 850.00 —
*f.* As "d," surch. inverted *3,250.* —
*Nos. 191-201 (11)* 103.85 75.15

Nos. 201, 201a and 201b exist with surcharge inverted (value about $20 each), and double (about $25 each).

The horizontal surcharge was prepared but not issued. Values: $11 unused, $20 never hinged. The horizontal surcharge also exists on pelure paper. Values: $70 unused, $175 never hinged.

### Type of 1921 and

"Workers of the World Unite" A46

**1922 Litho. Wmk. 171**
**202** A46 5000r dark violet 1.90 .60
**203** A42 7500r blue .50 .50
**204** A46 10,000r blue 17.50 3.00

**Unwmk.**
**205** A42 7500r blue, *buff* .50 .50
*a.* Double impression 250.00
**206** A46 22,500r dk vio, *buff* .50 .60
*Nos. 202-206 (5)* 20.90 5.20

For surcharges see Nos. B41-B42.

No. 183 Surcharged Diagonally

**1922 Unwmk. *Imperf.***
**210** A43 100,000r on 250r .50 .50
*a.* Inverted surcharge 200.00 .50
*b.* Pelure paper .50 .50
*c.* Chalk surfaced paper 2.25 1.65
*d.* As "b," inverted surcharge 225.00 —

Marking 5th Anniversary of October Revolution — A48

**1922 Typo.**
**211** A48 5r ocher & black .60 *.25*
**212** A48 10r brown & black .60 *.25*
**213** A48 25r violet & black 1.60 *.60*
**214** A48 27r rose & black 5.50 *2.00*
**215** A48 45r blue & black 3.60 *2.00*
*Nos. 211-215 (5)* 11.90 *5.10*

**Pelure Paper**
*211a* A48 5r ocher & black 82.50
*212a* A48 10r brown & black 120.00
*213a* A48 25r violet & black 82.50
*214a* A48 27r rose & black 82.50
*215a* A48 45r blue & black 60.00

5th anniv. of the October Revolution. Sold in the currency of 1922 which was valued at 10,000 times that of the preceding years.

For surcharges see Nos. B38-B39.

Nos. 81, 82a, 85-86, 125-126, 129-130 Surcharged

**1922-23 *Perf. 14½x15***
**216** A8 5r on 20k .45 6.00
*a.* Inverted surcharge 50.00 *90.00*
*b.* Double surcharge 100.00 —
*c.* Pair, one without surch. 165.00
**217** A11 20r on 15k 1.90 2.00
*a.* Inverted surcharge 120.00 *90.00*
*b.* Pair, one without surch. 165.00
**218** A11 20r on 70k .25 .35
*a.* Inverted surcharge 60.00 *45.00*
*b.* Double surcharge 50.00 50.00
*c.* Pair, one without surch. 165.00
**219** A8 30r on 50k 1.75 .50
*a.* Inverted surcharge *67.50* *67.50*
*c.* Groundwork omitted *50.00* *50.00*
*d.* Double surcharge *100.00* *100.00*
**220** A11 40r on 15k 1.00 .35
*a.* Inverted surcharge 67.50 *67.50*
*b.* Double surcharge *90.00* *90.00*
*c.* Pair, one without surch. 165.00
**221** A11 100r on 15k 1.00 .35
*a.* Inverted surcharge *90.00* *67.50*
*b.* Double surcharge *90.00* *67.50*
*c.* Pair, one without surch. 225.00
**222** A11 200r on 15k 2.75 .35
*a.* Inverted surcharge 57.50 *45.00*
*b.* Double surcharge 67.50 *45.00*
*c.* Pair, one without surch. 225.00

Nos. 221-222 exist with triple surcharge; No. 221 with double surcharge, one inverted. Value, each $100.

***Imperf***
**223** A8 5r on 20k 32.50 25.00
**224** A11 20r on 15k *9,500.*
**225** A11 20r on 70k .90 1.75
*a.* Inverted surcharge 82.50
**226** A8 30r on 50k brn vio & grn .50 1.00
**227** A11 40r on 15k .30 .30
*a.* Inverted surcharge 140.00 —
*b.* Double surcharge 100.00 —
**228** A11 100r on 15k 1.00 .50
*a.* Inverted surcharge 190.00 —
**229** A11 200r on 15k .75 .50
*a.* Inverted surcharge — —
*b.* Double surcharge 140.00 —
*Nos. 216-223,225-229 (13)* 45.05 38.95

Forgeries of No. 223-229 exist, including a dangerous digital forgery of No. 224.

Worker A49

Soldier A50

| **1922-23** | | **Typo.** | ***Imperf.*** | |
|---|---|---|---|---|
| **230** | A49 | 10r blue | .25 | .25 |
| **231** | A50 | 50r brown | .25 | .25 |
| **232** | A50 | 70r brown violet | .25 | .25 |
| **233** | A50 | 100r red | .25 | .25 |
| | | *Nos. 230-233 (4)* | 1.00 | 1.00 |

| **1923** | | ***Perf. 14x14½*** | | |
|---|---|---|---|---|
| **234** | A49 | 10r dp bl, perf. 13½ | .25 | 2.75 |
| *a.* | | Perf. 14 | 32.50 | 4.00 |
| *b.* | | Perf. 12½ | 1.40 | 2.75 |
| **235** | A50 | 50r brown | .25 | 2.75 |
| *a.* | | Perf. 12½ | 7.50 | 3.25 |
| *b.* | | Perf. 13½ | 2.25 | 2.75 |
| **236** | A50 | 70r brown violet | .25 | 2.75 |
| *a.* | | Perf. 12½ | 4.00 | 2.75 |
| **237** | A50 | 100r red | .25 | .25 |
| *a.* | | Cliché of 70r in plate of 100r | 50.00 | 30.00 |
| *b.* | | Corrected cliché | — | — |
| | | *Nos. 234-237 (4)* | 1.00 | 8.50 |

No. 237b has extra broken line at right.

Nos. 230-233 were surcharged for use in Far Eastern Republic. See Far Eastern Republic Nos. 66-70.

Soldier — Worker — Peasant
A51 A52 A53

| **1923** | | ***Perf. 14½x15*** | | |
|---|---|---|---|---|
| **238** | A51 | 3r rose | .25 | .25 |
| **239** | A52 | 4r brown | .25 | .25 |
| **240** | A53 | 5r light blue | .25 | .25 |
| *a.* | | Double impression | *82.50* | — |
| **241** | A51 | 10r gray | .25 | .25 |
| *e.* | | Double impression | 95.00 | — |
| **241A** | A51 | 20r brown violet | .50 | .35 |
| *b.* | | Double impression | *140.00* | — |
| | | *Nos. 238-241A (5)* | 1.50 | 1.35 |

***Imperf***

| | | | | |
|---|---|---|---|---|
| *238a* | A51 | 3r rose | 12.50 | — |
| *239a* | A52 | 4r brown | 30.00 | — |
| *b.* | | As "a," double impression | *150.00* | |
| *240b* | A53 | 5r light blue | 8.00 | — |
| *241d* | A51 | 10r gray | 8.00 | — |
| *f.* | | As "d," double impression | 115.00 | — |
| *241c* | A51 | 20r brown violet | 275.00 | — |

Stamps of 1r buff, type A52, and 2r green, type A53, perf. 12 and imperf. were prepared but not put in use.

The imperfs of Nos. 238-241A were sold only by the philatelic bureau in Moscow.

Stamps of 20r, type A51, printed in gray black or dull violet are essays. Value, $200 each.

The stamps of this and the following issues were sold for the currency of 1923, one ruble of which was equal to 100 rubles of 1922 and 1,000,000 rubles of 1921.

## Union of Soviet Socialist Republics

Reaping — A54

Sowing — A55

Fordson Tractor A56

Symbolical of the Exhibition — A57

| **1923, Aug. 19** | | **Litho.** | ***Imperf.*** | |
|---|---|---|---|---|
| **242** | A54 | 1r brown & orange | 4.50 | 2.50 |
| **243** | A55 | 2r dp grn & pale grn | 5.00 | 2.00 |
| **244** | A56 | 5r dp bl & pale blue | 5.00 | 3.75 |
| **245** | A57 | 7r rose & pink | 5.00 | 4.50 |

***Perf. 12½, 13½***

| | | | | |
|---|---|---|---|---|
| **246** | A54 | 1r brown & orange | 5.00 | *3.75* |
| *a.* | | Perf. 12½ | 42.50 | *37.50* |
| **247** | A55 | 2r dp grn & pale grn, perf. 12½ | 6.00 | *3.75* |
| **248** | A56 | 5r dp bl & pale bl | 14.00 | *3.75* |
| *a.* | | Perf. 13½ | 13.50 | *8.00* |
| **249** | A57 | 7r rose & pink | 5.00 | *6.00* |
| *a.* | | Perf. 12½ | 24.00 | *12.50* |
| | | *Nos. 242-249 (8)* | 49.50 | *30.00* |

1st Agriculture and Craftsmanship Exhibition, Moscow.

Worker — Soldier — Peasant
A58 A59 A60

| **1923** | | **Unwmk. Litho.** | ***Imperf.*** | |
|---|---|---|---|---|
| **250** | A58 | 1k orange | 2.50 | .45 |
| **251** | A60 | 2k green | 2.50 | .45 |
| **252** | A59 | 3k red brown | 2.50 | 1.40 |
| **253** | A58 | 4k deep rose | 24.00 | 1.25 |
| **254** | A58 | 5k lilac | 2.50 | .65 |
| **255** | A60 | 6k light blue | 2.75 | .45 |
| **256** | A59 | 10k dark blue | 35.00 | 3.75 |
| **257** | A58 | 20k yellow green | 12.00 | .75 |
| **258** | A60 | 50k dark brown | 19.00 | 2.50 |
| **259** | A59 | 1r red & brown | 50.00 | 5.00 |
| | | *Nos. 250-259 (10)* | 152.75 | 16.65 |

| **1924** | | ***Perf. 14½x15*** | | |
|---|---|---|---|---|
| **261** | A58 | 4k deep rose | 110.00 | — |
| **262** | A59 | 10k dark blue | 165.00 | — |
| **263** | A60 | 30k violet | 25.00 | *4.00* |
| **264** | A59 | 40k slate gray | 25.00 | *4.00* |
| | | *Nos. 261-264 (4)* | 325.00 | *8.00* |

See Nos. 273-290, 304-321. For surcharges see Nos. 349-350.

Vladimir Ilyich Ulyanov (Lenin) — A61

| **1924** | | ***Imperf.*** | | |
|---|---|---|---|---|
| **265** | A61 | 3k red & black | 8.25 | 2.40 |
| **266** | A61 | 6k red & black | 7.00 | 2.00 |
| **267** | A61 | 12k red & black | 5.50 | 2.00 |
| **268** | A61 | 20k red & black | 11.50 | 2.00 |
| | | *Nos. 265-268 (4)* | 32.25 | 8.40 |

Three printings of Nos. 265-268 differ in size of red frame.

***Perf. 13½***

| | | | | |
|---|---|---|---|---|
| **269** | A61 | 3k red & black | 6.75 | 4.00 |
| **270** | A61 | 6k red & black | 6.75 | 2.00 |
| **271** | A61 | 12k red & black | 12.00 | 2.00 |
| **272** | A61 | 20k red & black | 8.00 | 2.50 |
| | | *Nos. 269-272 (4)* | 33.50 | 10.50 |
| | | *Nos. 265-272 (8)* | 65.75 | 18.90 |

Death of Lenin (1870-1924).
Forgeries of Nos. 265-272 exist.

**Types of 1923**

Worker — A62

There are small differences between the lithographed stamps of 1923 and the typographed of 1924-25. On a few values this may be seen in the numerals.

Type A58: Lithographed. The two white lines forming the outline of the ear are continued across the cheek. Typographed. The outer lines of the ear are broken where they touch the cheek.

Type A59: Lithographed. At the top of the right shoulder a white line touches the frame at the left. Counting from the edge of the visor of the cap, lines 5, 6 and sometimes 7 touch at their upper ends. Typographed. The top line of the shoulder does not reach the frame. On the cap lines 5, 6 and 7 run together and form a white spot.

Type A60: In the angle above the first letter "C" there is a fan-shaped ornament enclosing four white dashes. On the lithographed stamps these dashes reach nearly to the point of the angle. On the typographed stamps the dashes are shorter and often only three are visible.

On unused examples of the typographed stamps the raised outlines of the designs can be seen on the backs of the stamps.

| **1924-25** | | **Typo.** | ***Imperf.*** | |
|---|---|---|---|---|
| **273** | A59 | 3k red brown | 6.75 | 1.40 |
| **274** | A58 | 4k deep rose | 3.00 | 1.50 |
| **275** | A59 | 10k dark blue | 4.00 | 1.25 |
| **275A** | A60 | 50k brown | *6,750.* | 25.00 |

Other typographed and imperf. values include: 2k green, 5k lilac, 6k light blue, 20k green and 1r red and brown. Value, unused: $150, $100, $150, $200 and $1,000, respectively.

Nos. 273-275A were regularly issued. The 7k, 8k, 9k, 30k, 40k, 2r, 3r, and 5r also exist imperf. Value, set of 8, $75.

***Perf. 14½x15***

**Typo.**

| | | | | |
|---|---|---|---|---|
| **276** | A58 | 1k orange | 175.00 | 8.00 |
| **277** | A60 | 2k green | 2.00 | .45 |
| **278** | A59 | 3k red brown | 2.00 | .45 |
| **279** | A58 | 4k deep rose | 2.00 | .45 |
| **280** | A58 | 5k lilac | 160.00 | 5.00 |
| **281** | A60 | 6k lt blue | 2.00 | .45 |
| **282** | A59 | 7k chocolate | 2.00 | .45 |
| **283** | A58 | 8k brn ol | 1.80 | .45 |
| **284** | A60 | 9k orange red | 4.50 | .45 |
| **285** | A59 | 10k dark blue | 4.00 | .45 |
| **286** | A58 | 14k slate blue | 225.00 | 2.50 |
| **287** | A60 | 15k yellow | *25,000.* | *210.00* |
| **288** | A58 | 20k gray green | 5.25 | .45 |
| **288A** | A60 | 30k violet | 400.00 | *4.00* |
| **288B** | A59 | 40k slate gray | 800.00 | *4.00* |
| **289** | A60 | 50k brown | 225.00 | *10.00* |
| **290** | A59 | 1r red & brn | 19.00 | *1.00* |
| **291** | A62 | 2r grn & rose | 12.00 | *2.00* |
| | | *Nos. 276-286,288-291 (17)* | 2,042. | 40.55 |

See No. 323. Forgeries of No. 287 exist.

| **1925** | | ***Perf. 12*** | | |
|---|---|---|---|---|
| *276a* | A58 | 1k orange | 2.50 | 1.00 |
| *277a* | A60 | 2k green | 21.50 | 1.00 |
| *278a* | A59 | 3k red brown | 3.50 | 9.00 |
| *279a* | A58 | 4k deep rose | 275.00 | *25.00* |
| *280a* | A58 | 5k lilac | 5.50 | 1.00 |
| *282a* | A59 | 7k chocolate | 10.00 | 1.00 |
| *283a* | A58 | 8k brown olive | 1,375. | 5.00 |
| *284a* | A60 | 9k orange red | *20.00* | *2.50* |
| *285a* | A59 | 10k dark blue | *5.00* | 2.00 |
| *286a* | A58 | 14k slate blue | 2.50 | 1.00 |
| *287a* | A60 | 15k yellow | 6.75 | 1.00 |
| *288c* | A58 | 20k gray green | 27.50 | 1.00 |
| *288d* | A60 | 30k violet | 22.50 | *1.50* |
| *288e* | A59 | 40k slate gray | 110.00 | *2.50* |
| *289a* | A60 | 50k brown | 16.50 | *1.00* |
| *290a* | A59 | 1r red & brown | *2,000.* | *3,000.* |
| | | *Nos. 276a-290a (16)* | 3,904. | 3,056. |

Soldier — A63

Worker — A64

| **1924-25** | | ***Perf. 13½*** | | |
|---|---|---|---|---|
| **292** | A63 | 3r blk brn & grn | 19.00 | 2.50 |
| *a.* | | Perf. 10 | 5,500. | 145.00 |
| *b.* | | Perf. 13½x10 | *2,750.* | — |
| **293** | A64 | 5r dk bl & gray brn | 200.00 | 12.50 |
| *a.* | | Perf. 10½ | 70.00 | — |

See Nos. 324-325.

Lenin Mausoleum, Moscow — A65

**Wmk. 170**

| **1925, Jan.** | | **Photo.** | ***Imperf.*** | |
|---|---|---|---|---|
| **294** | A65 | 7k deep blue | 9.00 | 2.50 |
| **295** | A65 | 14k dark green | 25.00 | 4.00 |
| **296** | A65 | 20k carmine rose | 14.00 | 5.00 |
| **297** | A65 | 40k red brown | 25.00 | 7.00 |
| | | *Nos. 294-297 (4)* | 73.00 | 18.50 |

***Perf. 13½x14***

| | | | | |
|---|---|---|---|---|
| **298** | A65 | 7k deep blue | 5.50 | 4.50 |
| **299** | A65 | 14k dark green | 25.00 | 6.75 |
| **300** | A65 | 20k carmine rose | 20.00 | 5.25 |
| **301** | A65 | 40k red brown | 26.00 | 6.25 |
| | | *Nos. 298-301 (4)* | 76.50 | 22.75 |
| | | *Nos. 294-301 (8)* | 149.50 | 41.25 |

First anniversary of Lenin's death.

Nos. 294-301 are found on both ordinary and thick paper. Those on thick paper sell for twice as much, except for No. 301, which is scarcer on ordinary paper.

Lenin — A66

**Wmk. 170**

| **1925, July** | | **Engr.** | ***Perf. 13½*** | |
|---|---|---|---|---|
| **302** | A66 | 5r red brown | 40.00 | 6.75 |
| *a.* | | Perf. 12½ | 165.00 | 25.00 |
| *b.* | | Perf. 10½ ('26) | 82.50 | 11.00 |
| **303** | A66 | 10r indigo | 40.00 | 10.00 |
| *a.* | | Perf. 12½ | 1,250. | 175.00 |
| *b.* | | Perf. 10½ ('26) | 200.00 | 11.00 |

Imperfs. exist. Value, set $75.

See Nos. 407-408, 621-622

### Types of 1923 Issue

**1925-27 Wmk. 170 Typo. *Perf. 12***

**304** A58 1k orange 1.60 .35
**305** A60 2k green 1.60 .35
**306** A59 3k red brown 1.60 .35
**307** A58 4k deep rose 1.60 .35
**308** A58 5k lilac 1.60 .35
**309** A60 6k lt blue 1.60 .75
**310** A59 7k chocolate 3.25 .75
**311** A58 8k brown olive 17.00 1.40
*a.* Perf. 14½x15 325.00 27.50
**312** A60 9k red 6.50 .75
**313** A59 10k dark blue 3.50 .75
*a.* 10k pale blue ('27) 9.00 4.50
**314** A58 14k slate blue 4.00 1.25
**315** A60 15k yellow 9.50 1.25
**316** A59 18k violet 17.00 1.75
**317** A58 20k gray green 9.50 1.25
**318** A60 30k violet 17.00 1.25
**319** A59 40k slate gray 17.00 1.75
**320** A60 50k brown 17.00 1.75
**321** A59 1r red & brown 19.00 4.00
*a.* Perf. 14½x15 325.00 *50.00*
**323** A62 2r grn & rose red 75.00 11.00
*a.* Perf. 14½x15 18.00 5.00

***Perf. 13½***

**324** A63 3r blk brn & grn 27.50 9.50
*a.* Perf. 12½ *475.00* 82.50
**325** A64 5r dk blue & gray brn 35.00 12.50
*Nos. 304-325 (21)* 287.35 53.40

Nos. 304-315, 317-325 exist imperf. Value, set $125.

Mikhail V. Lomonosov and Academy of Sciences — A67

**1925, Sept. Photo. *Perf. 12½, 13½***

**326** A67 3k orange brown 7.50 2.00
*a.* Perf. 12½x12 40.00 6.75
*c.* Perf. 13½ 50.00 9.00
**327** A67 15k dk olive green 14.00 2.25
*a.* Perf. 12½ 20.00 5.00

Russian Academy of Sciences, 200th anniv. Exist unwatermarked, on thick paper with yellow gum, perf. 13½. These are essays, later perforated and gummed. Value, each $50.

Prof. Aleksandr S. Popov (1859-1905), Radio Pioneer — A68

**1925, Oct. *Perf. 13½***

**328** A68 7k deep blue 6.25 1.00
**329** A68 14k green 10.00 1.50

For surcharge see No. 353.

Decembrist Exiles — A69

Street Rioting in St. Petersburg — A70

Revolutionist Leaders — A71

**1925, Dec. 28 *Imperf.***

**330** A69 3k olive green 5.00 *1.00*
**331** A70 7k brown 32.50 *3.50*
**332** A71 14k carmine lake 19.00 *5.00*

***Perf. 13½***

**333** A69 3k olive green 4.50 1.25
*a.* Perf. 12½ *100.00* *50.00*
**334** A70 7k brown 16.50 *3.50*
**335** A71 14k carmine lake 19.50 5.50
*Nos. 330-335 (6)* 97.00 19.75

Centenary of Decembrist revolution.
For surcharges see Nos. 354, 357.

Revolters Parading — A72

Speaker Haranguing Mob — A73

Street Barricade, Moscow — A74

**1925, Dec. 20 *Imperf.***

**336** A72 3k olive green 5.00 *7.50*
**337** A73 7k brown 17.50 *8.75*
**338** A74 14k carmine lake 12.50 *2.75*

***Perf. 12½, 12x12½***

**339** A72 3k olive green 5.50 *3.00*
*a.* Perf. 13½ 37.50 *8.00*
**340** A73 7k brown 35.00 *5.00*
*a.* Perf. 13½ 17.50 *5.25*
*b.* Horiz. pair, imperf. btwn. — —
**341** A74 14k carmine lake 6.75 3.75
*a.* Perf. 13½ 40.00 7.50
*Nos. 336-341 (6)* 82.25 30.75

20th anniversary of Revolution of 1905.
For surcharges see Nos. 355, 358.

Lenin — A75

**1926 Wmk. 170 Engr. *Perf. 10½***

**342** A75 1r dark brown 37.50 4.00
*a.* Perf. 12½ 2,250. —
**343** A75 2r black violet 35.00 5.75
*a.* Perf. 12½ 2,250. —
**344** A75 3r dark green 37.50 5.75
*a.* Perf. 12½ 4,250. —
*b.* Horiz. pair, imperf. btwn. — *5,000.*
*Nos. 342-344 (3)* 110.00 15.50

Nos. 342-343 exist imperf.
See Nos. 406, 620.

Liberty Monument, Moscow — A76

**1926, July Litho. *Perf. 12x12½***

**347** A76 7k blue green & red 10.00 2.75
**348** A76 14k blue green & vio 12.50 2.75

6th International Esperanto Congress at Leningrad. Exist perf. 11½. Value, set $8,500.
For surcharge see No. 356.

Nos. 282, 282a and 310 Surcharged in Black

Two types of overprint: Type I, 2mm space between lines of surcharge; Type II, .7mm space between lines of surcharge.

**1927, June Unwmk. *Perf. 14½x15***

**349** A59 8k on 7k choc (I) 22.50 4.00
*a.* Perf. 12x12¼ 27.50 3.75
*b.* Inverted surcharge *300.00* —
*c.* Type II *2,750.* 140.00
*d.* As "b," surcharge inverted *275.00*

***Perf. 12***

**Wmk. 170**

**350** A59 8k on 7k chocolate 8.00 2.50
*a.* Inverted surcharge *150.00*
*b.* Type II *10,500.* 70.00
*c.* As "b," surcharge inverted *350.00*

The surcharge on Nos. 349-350 comes in two types: With space of 2mm between lines, and with space of ¾mm. The latter is much scarcer.

### Same Surcharge on Stamps of 1925-26 in Black or Red

***Perf. 13½, 12½, 12x12½***

**353** A68 8k on 7k dp bl (R) 6.75 2.25
*a.* Inverted "8" 110.00 *50.00*
**354** A70 8k on 7k brown 12.50 *4.75*
**355** A73 8k on 7k brown 20.00 *6.25*
**356** A76 8k on 7k bl grn & red 21.50 8.50

***Imperf***

**357** A70 8k on 7k brown 11.00 4.00
**358** A73 8k on 7k brown 19.00 7.00
*Nos. 349-350,353-358 (8)* 121.25 39.25

Postage Due Stamps of 1925 Surcharged

Two settings: A's aligned (shown), bottom A to left.

### Lithographed or Typographed

**1927, June Unwmk. *Perf. 12***

**359** D1 8k on 1k red, typo. 4.50 *2.00*
*a.* Litho. *2,750.* *150.00*
**360** D1 8k on 2k violet 4.50 *2.00*
*a.* Inverted surcharge 275.00 —

***Perf. 12, 14½x14***

**361** D1 8k on 3k lt blue 4.50 *2.00*
*a.* Inverted surcharge 275.00 —
**362** D1 8k on 7k orange 4.25 *1.25*
**363** D1 8k on 8k green 4.50 *2.00*
*a.* Inverted surcharge — *1,750.*
**364** D1 8k on 10k dk blue 4.00 *1.25*
*a.* Inverted surcharge 275.00 —
**365** D1 8k on 14k brown 3.75 4.00
*a.* Inverted surcharge 350.00 —
*Nos. 359-365 (7)* 30.00 14.50

**Wmk. 170**

**1927, June Typo. *Perf. 12***

**366** D1 8k on 1k red 4.50 *1.00*
**367** D1 8k on 2k violet 4.50 *1.00*
**368** D1 8k on 3k lt blue 4.50 *1.00*
**369** D1 8k on 7k orange 4.50 *1.00*
**370** D1 8k on 8k green 4.50 *1.00*
**371** D1 8k on 10k dk blue 4.50 *1.00*
*a.* Inverted surcharge *3,500.* —
**372** D1 8k on 14k brown 4.50 *1.00*
*a.* Inverted surcharge — *1,750.*
*Nos. 366-372 (7)* 31.50 *7.00*

Nos. 366, 368-370 exist with inverted surcharge.

Dr. L. L. Zamenhof A77

**1927 Photo. *Perf. 10½***

**373** A77 14k yel grn & brn 11.00 2.25

**Unwmk.**

**374** A77 14k yel grn & brn 11.00 2.25
*a.* Perf. 10 325.00 52.50
*b.* Perf. 10x10½ 175.00 75.00
*c.* Imperf. 950.00 —
*d.* Vert. pair, imperf. btwn., never hinged *8,250.* —

40th anniversary of creation of Esperanto.

Worker, Soldier, Peasant — A78

Worker and Sailor — A81

Lenin in Car Guarded by Soldiers A79

Smolny Institute, Leningrad A80

Map of the USSR A82

Men of Various Soviet Republics — A83

Workers of Different Races; Kremlin in Background — A84

**Typo. (3k, 8k, 18k), Engr. (7k), Litho. (14k), Photo. (5k, 28k)**
***Perf. 13½, 12½x12, 11***

**1927, Oct. Unwmk.**

**375** A78 3k bright rose 5.50 1.10
*a.* Imperf., pair *5,000.*
**376** A79 5k deep brown 14.00 2.25
*a.* Imperf. 1,650. *500.00*
*b.* Perf. 12½ 125.00 12.50
*c.* Perf. 12½x10½ 55.00 5.00
**377** A80 7k myrtle green 14.00 4.00
*a.* Perf. 11½ 32.50 7.50
*b.* Imperf., pair *1,500.*
**378** A81 8k brown & black 8.00 1.50
*a.* Perf. 10½x12½ *42.50* *2.75*
**379** A82 14k dull blue & red 6.75 2.75
**380** A83 18k blue 4.75 1.25
*a.* Imperf. 275.00
**381** A84 28k olive brown 18.00 5.00
*a.* Perf. 10 45.00 8.00
*Nos. 375-381 (7)* 71.00 17.85

10th anniversary of October Revolution.
The paper of No. 375 has an overprint of pale yellow wavy lines.
No. 377b exists with watermark 170. Value, $1,000.

Worker — A85

Peasant — A86

Lenin — A87

**1927-28 Typo. *Perf. 13½***

**Chalk Surfaced Paper**

| No. | Type | Description | Unused | Used |
|---|---|---|---|---|
| 382 | A85 | 1k orange | 1.10 | .35 |
| *a.* | | Imperf. | 1,750. | — |
| 383 | A86 | 2k apple green | 4.25 | .35 |
| *a.* | | Imperf. | 1,750. | — |
| 385 | A85 | 4k bright blue | 1.10 | .35 |
| 386 | A86 | 5k brown | 1.10 | .35 |
| *a.* | | Imperf. | 1,750. | — |
| 388 | A86 | 7k dark red ('28) | 1.10 | .35 |
| *a.* | | Double impression | 475.00 | — |
| 389 | A85 | 8k green | 7.00 | .60 |
| 391 | A85 | 10k light brown | 5.00 | .35 |
| *a.* | | Imperf. | 1,325. | — |
| 392 | A87 | 14k dark green ('28) | 10.75 | 4.00 |
| 393 | A87 | 18k olive green | 12.00 | 1.25 |
| *a.* | | Imperf. | *3,750.* | — |
| 394 | A87 | 18k dark blue ('28) | 11.00 | 1.70 |
| 395 | A86 | 20k dark gray green | 16.50 | .35 |
| 396 | A85 | 40k rose red | 20.00 | 2.00 |
| 397 | A86 | 50k bright blue | 24.00 | 1.10 |
| 399 | A85 | 70k gray green | 11.00 | 2.00 |
| 400 | A86 | 80k orange | 15.00 | 2.75 |
| | | *Nos. 382-400 (15)* | 140.90 | 17.85 |

Soldier and Kremlin — A88

Sailor and Flag — A89

Cavalryman A90

Aviator A91

**1928, Feb. 6**

**Chalk Surfaced Paper**

| No. | Type | Description | Unused | Used |
|---|---|---|---|---|
| 402 | A88 | 8k light brown | 4.75 | .85 |
| *a.* | | Imperf. | 1,200. | — |
| 403 | A89 | 14k deep blue | 12.00 | 1.50 |
| 404 | A90 | 18k carmine rose | 6.50 | 1.60 |
| *a.* | | Imperf. | *7,000.* | |
| 405 | A91 | 28k yellow green | 15.00 | 2.25 |
| | | *Nos. 402-405 (4)* | 38.25 | 6.20 |

10th anniversary of the Soviet Army.

**Lenin Types of 1925-26**

**Wmk. 169**

**1928-29 Engr. *Perf. 10½***

| No. | Type | Description | Unused | Used |
|---|---|---|---|---|
| 406 | A75 | 3r dark green ('29) | 52.50 | 3.50 |
| *a.* | | Perf. 10 | 52.50 | 6.75 |
| *b.* | | Imperf. | 3,250. | — |
| 407 | A66 | 5r red brown | 19.00 | 3.75 |
| *a.* | | Perf. 10 | 105.00 | 14.00 |
| *b.* | | Imperf. | *20,000.* | — |
| 408 | A66 | 10r indigo | 19.00 | *4.50* |
| *a.* | | Perf. 10 | 27.50 | 6.75 |
| *b.* | | Imperf. | *20,000.* | — |
| | | *Nos. 406-408 (3)* | 90.50 | 11.75 |

Bugler Sounding Assembly
A92 A93

***Perf. 12½x12***

**1929, Aug. 18 Photo. Wmk. 170**

| No. | Type | Description | Unused | Used |
|---|---|---|---|---|
| 411 | A92 | 10k olive brown | 32.50 | 6.25 |
| *a.* | | Perf. 10½ | 140.00 | 27.50 |
| *b.* | | Perf. 12½x12x10½x12 | 140.00 | 75.00 |
| 412 | A93 | 14k slate | 5.50 | 2.75 |
| *a.* | | Perf. 12½x12x10½x12 | 425.00 | 95.00 |

First All-Soviet Assembly of Pioneers.

Factory Worker A95

Peasant A96

Farm Worker A97

Soldier A98

Worker, Soldier, Peasant A100

Worker A103

Lenin A104

Peasant A107

Factory Worker A109

Farm Worker A111

***Perf. 12x12½***

**1929-31 Typo. Wmk. 170**

| No. | Type | Description | Unused | Used |
|---|---|---|---|---|
| 413 | A103 | 1k orange | 1.25 | .25 |
| *a.* | | Perf. 10½ | 19.00 | 4.00 |
| *b.* | | Perf. 12x12¼ | 8.00 | 1.60 |
| 414 | A95 | 2k yellow green | 1.25 | .25 |
| 415 | A96 | 3k blue | 2.75 | .25 |
| *a.* | | Perf. 12x12¼ | 82.50 | *25.00* |
| 416 | A97 | 4k claret | 2.75 | .45 |
| 417 | A98 | 5k orange brown | 2.75 | .45 |
| *a.* | | Perf. 10½ | 190.00 | *25.00* |
| 418 | A100 | 7k scarlet | 2.75 | .90 |
| 419 | A103 | 10k olive green | 2.75 | .50 |
| *a.* | | Perf. 10½ | 400.00 | 40.00 |

**Unwmk.**

| No. | Type | Description | Unused | Used |
|---|---|---|---|---|
| 420 | A104 | 14k indigo | 5.50 | 1.00 |
| *a.* | | Perf. 10½ | 17.50 | 3.25 |

**Wmk. 170**

| No. | Type | Description | Unused | Used |
|---|---|---|---|---|
| 421 | A100 | 15k dk ol grn ('30) | 2.75 | .85 |
| 422 | A107 | 20k green | 2.75 | .85 |
| *a.* | | Perf. 10½ | — | — |
| 423 | A109 | 30k dk violet | 14.00 | 1.75 |
| 424 | A111 | 50k dp brown | 14.00 | 2.50 |
| 425 | A98 | 70k dk red ('30) | 8.00 | 2.50 |
| 426 | A107 | 80k red brn ('31) | 8.00 | 2.50 |
| | | *Nos. 413-426 (14)* | 71.25 | 15.00 |

Nos. 422, 423, 424 and 426 have a background of fine wavy lines in pale shades of the colors of the stamps.

See Nos. 456-466, 613A-619A. For surcharge see No. 743.

Symbolical of Industry A112

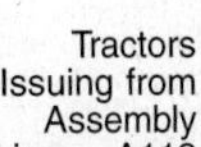

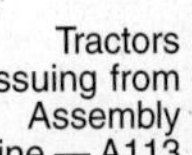

Tractors Issuing from Assembly Line — A113

Iron Furnace (Inscription reads, "More Metal More Machines") A114

Blast Furnace and Chart of Anticipated Iron Production A115

**1929-30 *Perf. 12x12½***

| No. | Type | Description | Unused | Used |
|---|---|---|---|---|
| 427 | A112 | 5k orange brown | 3.25 | *.90* |
| 428 | A113 | 10k olive green | 9.50 | *1.80* |

***Perf. 12½x12***

| No. | Type | Description | Unused | Used |
|---|---|---|---|---|
| 429 | A114 | 20k dull green | 9.50 | *3.00* |
| *a.* | | Perf. 10¾ | *8,000.* | 400.00 |
| 430 | A115 | 28k violet black | 4.25 | 2.00 |
| | | *Nos. 427-430 (4)* | 26.50 | 7.70 |

Publicity for greater industrial production. No. 429 exists perf. 10½. Value *$4,000.*

Red Cavalry in Polish Town after Battle A116

Cavalry Charge A117

Staff Officers of 1st Cavalry Army A118

Plan of Action for 1st Cavalry Army — A119

**1930, Feb. *Perf. 12x12½***

| No. | Type | Description | Unused | Used |
|---|---|---|---|---|
| 431 | A116 | 2k yellow green | 3.25 | *1.80* |
| 432 | A117 | 5k light brown | 7.00 | *1.80* |
| 433 | A118 | 10k olive gray | 14.00 | *2.75* |
| 434 | A119 | 14k indigo & red | 5.50 | *2.50* |
| | | *Nos. 431-434 (4)* | 29.75 | *8.85* |

1st Red Cavalry Army, 10th anniversary.

Students Preparing a Poster Newspaper A120

**1930, Aug. 15**

| No. | Type | Description | Unused | Used |
|---|---|---|---|---|
| 435 | A120 | 10k olive green | 8.00 | *1.80* |

Educational Exhibition, Leningrad, 7/1-8/15/30.

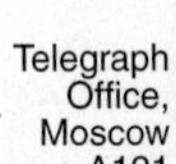

Telegraph Office, Moscow A121

Lenin Hydroelectric Power Station on Volkhov River A122

**1930 Photo. Wmk. 169 *Perf. 12¼***

| No. | Type | Description | Unused | Used |
|---|---|---|---|---|
| 436 | A121 | 1r deep blue | 19.00 | *5.00* |

**Wmk. 170**

| No. | Type | Description | Unused | Used |
|---|---|---|---|---|
| 437 | A122 | 3r yel grn & blk brn | 10.50 | *5.00* |

See Nos. 467, 469.

Battleship Potemkin A123

Inside Presnya Barricade A124

Moscow Barricades in 1905 — A125

**1930 Typo. *Perf. 12x12½, 12½x12***

| No. | Type | Description | Unused | Used |
|---|---|---|---|---|
| 438 | A123 | 3k red | 1.75 | .50 |
| 439 | A124 | 5k blue | 3.25 | .70 |
| 440 | A125 | 10k dk green & red | 9.50 | 1.75 |
| | | *Nos. 438-440 (3)* | 14.50 | 2.95 |

**1931 *Imperf.***

| No. | Type | Description | Unused | Used |
|---|---|---|---|---|
| 452 | A123 | 3k red | 11.00 | *5.00* |
| 453 | A124 | 5k deep blue | 11.00 | *9.00* |
| 454 | A125 | 10k dk green & red | 22.00 | *17.50* |
| | | *Nos. 452-454 (3)* | 44.00 | *31.50* |
| | | *Nos. 438-454 (6)* | 58.50 | 34.45 |

Revolution of 1905, 25th anniversary.

**Types of 1929-31 Regular Issue**

**1931-32 *Imperf.***

| No. | Type | Description | Unused | Used |
|---|---|---|---|---|
| 456 | A103 | 1k orange | 4.00 | 1.00 |
| 457 | A95 | 2k yellow green | 4.00 | 1.00 |
| 458 | A96 | 3k blue | 5.50 | 1.00 |
| 459 | A97 | 4k claret | 47.50 | 14.00 |
| 460 | A98 | 5k orange brown | 5.50 | 2.50 |
| 462 | A103 | 10k olive green | 55.00 | 22.50 |
| 464 | A100 | 15k dk olive green | 35.00 | *25.00* |
| 466 | A109 | 30k dull violet | 40.00 | *35.00* |
| 467 | A121 | 1r dark blue | 200.00 | *35.00* |
| | | *Nos. 456-467 (9)* | 396.50 | 137.00 |

Nos. 459, 462-467 were sold only by the philatelic bureau.

**Type of 1930 Issue**

**1931 Wmk. 170 *Perf. 12x12½***

| No. | Type | Description | Unused | Used |
|---|---|---|---|---|
| 469 | A121 | 1r dark blue | 8.00 | 1.50 |
| | | Never hinged | 12.00 | |

Maxim Gorki — A133

**1932-33** **Photo.**

| | | | |
|---|---|---|---|
| 470 | A133 15k dark brown | 8.00 | *1.75* |
| *a.* | Imperf. | 140.00 | *67.50* |
| 471 | A133 35k dp ultra ('33) | 35.00 | *14.50* |
| | Set, never hinged | 90.00 | |

40th anniversary of Gorki's literary activity.

Lenin Addressing the People A134

Revolution in Petrograd (Leningrad) A135

Dnieper Hydroelectric Power Station A136

Asiatics Saluting the Soviet Flag — A139

Designs (dated 1917 1932): 15k, Collective farm. 20k, Magnitogorsk metallurgical plant in Urals. 30k, Radio tower and heads of 4 men.

**1932-33** ***Perf. 12½x12; 12½ (30k)***

| | | | |
|---|---|---|---|
| 472 | A134 3k dark violet | 4.25 | 1.25 |
| 473 | A135 5k dark brown | 4.25 | 1.25 |
| 474 | A136 10k ultra | 7.00 | 4.25 |
| 475 | A136 15k dark green | 4.25 | 1.50 |
| 476 | A136 20k lake ('33) | 4.25 | 1.50 |
| 477 | A136 30k dk gray ('33) | 55.00 | *15.00* |
| 478 | A139 35k gray black | 95.00 | *55.00* |
| | *Nos. 472-478 (7)* | 174.00 | 79.75 |
| | Set, never hinged | 325.00 | |

October Revolution, 15th anniversary.

Breaking Prison Bars — A140

**1932, Nov.** **Litho.** ***Perf. 12½x12***

| | | | |
|---|---|---|---|
| 479 | A140 50k dark red | 32.50 | 9.50 |
| | Never hinged | 67.50 | |

Intl. Revolutionaries' Aid Assoc., 10th anniv.

Trier, Birthplace of Marx — A141

Grave, Highgate Cemetery, London — A142

35k, Portrait & signature of Karl Marx (1818-83).

***Perf. 12x12½, 12½x12***

**1933, Mar.** **Photo.**

| | | | |
|---|---|---|---|
| 480 | A141 3k dull green | 4.00 | 1.80 |
| 481 | A142 10k black brown | 10.00 | 2.25 |
| 482 | A142 35k brown violet | 67.50 | 14.50 |
| | *Nos. 480-482 (3)* | 81.50 | 18.55 |
| | Set, never hinged | 145.00 | |

Fine Arts Museum, Moscow — A145

**1932, Dec.** ***Perf. 12½***

| | | | |
|---|---|---|---|
| 485 | A145 15k black brown | 5.00 | 6.00 |
| 486 | A145 35k ultra | 90.00 | 52.50 |
| *a.* | Perf. 10½ | 67.50 | 32.50 |
| | Set, never hinged | 240.00 | |

Moscow Philatelic Exhibition, 1932.

Nos. 485 and 486 were also issued in imperf. sheets of 4 containing 2 of each value, on thick paper for presentation purposes. They were not valid for postage. Value, from $19,500. Replicas of the sheet were made for Moscow 97 by the Canadian Society of Russian Philately.

**Nos. 485 and 486a Surcharged**

**1933, Mar.** ***Perf. 12½***

| | | | |
|---|---|---|---|
| 487 | A145 30k on 15k blk brn | 50.00 | 15.00 |
| | ***Perf. 10½*** | | |
| 488 | A145 70k on 35k ultra | 275.00 | 200.00 |
| | Set, never hinged | 500.00 | |

Leningrad Philatelic Exhibition, 1933.

**Peoples of the Soviet Union**

Kazaks A146

Lezghians A147

Tungus A150

Crimean Tartars A148

Jews, Birobidzhan A149

Buryats — A151

Yakuts — A156

Chechens A152

Abkhas A153

Georgians A154

Nientzians A155

Great Russians — A157

Tadzhiks — A158

Transcaucasians — A159

Turkmen — A160

Ukrainians — A161

Uzbeks — A162

Byelorussians — A163

Koryaks A164

Bashkirs A165

Chuvashes A166

***Perf. 12, 12x12½, 12½x12, 11x12, 12x11***

**1933, Apr.** **Photo.**

| | | | |
|---|---|---|---|
| 489 | A146 1k black brown | 9.00 | 2.00 |
| 490 | A147 2k ultra | 5.00 | 2.00 |
| 491 | A148 3k gray green | 18.00 | 2.00 |
| 492 | A149 4k gray black | 5.00 | 2.00 |
| 493 | A150 5k brown violet | 5.00 | 2.00 |
| 494 | A151 6k indigo | 5.00 | 2.00 |
| 495 | A152 7k black brown | 5.00 | 2.00 |
| 496 | A153 8k rose red | 11.00 | 2.00 |
| 497 | A154 9k ultra | 35.00 | 2.00 |
| 498 | A155 10k black brown | 5.00 | 2.00 |
| 499 | A156 14k olive green | 5.00 | 2.00 |
| 500 | A157 15k orange | 16.00 | 2.00 |
| 501 | A158 15k ultra | 13.00 | 2.00 |
| 502 | A159 15k dark brown | 13.00 | 2.00 |
| 503 | A160 15k rose red | 13.00 | 2.00 |
| 504 | A161 15k violet brown | 16.00 | 2.00 |
| 505 | A162 15k gray black | 13.00 | 2.00 |
| 506 | A163 15k dull green | 16.00 | 2.00 |
| 507 | A164 20k dull blue | 18.00 | *2.00* |
| 508 | A165 30k brown violet | 15.00 | *3.00* |
| 509 | A166 35k black | 15.00 | *3.00* |
| | *Nos. 489-509 (21)* | 256.00 | 44.00 |
| | Set, never hinged | 495.00 | |

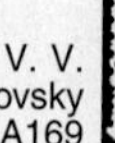

V. V. Vorovsky A169

3k, V. M. Volodarsky. 5k, M. S. Uritzky.

**1933, Oct.** ***Perf. 12x12½***

| | | | |
|---|---|---|---|
| 514 | A169 1k dull green | 4.00 | 1.00 |
| 515 | A169 3k blue black | 8.00 | 1.25 |
| 516 | A169 5k olive brown | 9.00 | 2.00 |
| | *Nos. 514-516 (3)* | 21.00 | 4.25 |
| | Set, never hinged | 42.50 | |

10th anniv, of the murder of Soviet Representative Vorovsky; 15th anniv. of the murder of the Revolutionists Volodarsky and Uritzky.

See Nos. 531-532, 580-582.

Order of the Red Banner, 15th Anniv. — A173

**1933, Nov. 17 Unwmk. *Perf. 14***

| | | | |
|---|---|---|---|
| **518** A173 20k black, red & yel | 15.00 | 3.50 |
| Never hinged | 40.00 | |

No. 518, perf. 9½, is a proof. Values: unused, $4,000; never hinged, $8,000.

Commissar Schaumyan A174

Commissar Prokofii A. Dzhaparidze A175

Commissars Awaiting Execution — A176

Designs: 35k, Monument to the 26 Commissars. 40k, Worker, peasant and soldier dipping flags in salute.

**1933, Dec. 1**

| | | |
|---|---|---|
| **519** A174 4k brown | 30.00 | 2.00 |
| **520** A175 5k dark gray | 25.00 | 2.00 |
| **521** A176 20k purple | 8.00 | 2.00 |
| **522** A176 35k ultra | 80.00 | *17.50* |
| **523** A176 40k carmine | 25.00 | *7.00* |
| *Nos. 519-523 (5)* | 168.00 | 30.50 |
| Set, never hinged | 440.00 | |

15th anniv. of the execution of 26 commissars at Baku. No. 521 exists imperf. Many part-perf varieties exist on all values of this issue, including imperf between pairs of several values.

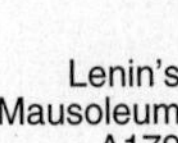

Lenin's Mausoleum A179

**1934, Feb. 7 Engr. *Perf. 14***

| | | |
|---|---|---|
| **524** A179 5k brown | 20.00 | 2.50 |
| *a.* Imperf. | 675.00 | — |
| **525** A179 10k slate blue | 90.00 | 10.00 |
| *a.* Imperf. | 675.00 | — |
| **526** A179 15k dk carmine | 32.50 | 7.00 |
| **527** A179 20k green | 6.00 | 5.25 |
| **528** A179 35k dark brown | 32.50 | 8.00 |
| *Nos. 524-528 (5)* | 181.00 | 32.75 |
| Set, never hinged | 360.00 | |

10th anniversary of Lenin's death.

Ivan Fedorov A180

**1934, Mar. 5**

| | | |
|---|---|---|
| **529** A180 20k carmine rose | 55.00 | 10.00 |
| *a.* Imperf. | 675.00 | — |
| **530** A180 40k indigo | 17.50 | 10.00 |
| *a.* Imperf. | 675.00 | — |
| Set, never hinged | 150.00 | |

350th anniv. of the death of Ivan Fedorov, founder of printing in Russia.

### Portrait Type of 1933

Designs: 10k, Yakov M. Sverdlov. 15k, Victor Pavlovich Nogin.

**1934, Mar. Photo. Wmk. 170**

| | | |
|---|---|---|
| **531** A169 10k ultra | 27.50 | 6.00 |
| **532** A169 15k red | 200.00 | 37.50 |
| Set, never hinged | 475.00 | |

Deaths of Yakov M. Sverdlov, chairman of the All-Russian Central Executive Committee of the Soviets, 15th anniv., Victor Pavlovich Nogin, chairman Russian State Textile Syndicate, 10th anniv.

A184

Dmitri Ivanovich Mendeleev A185

**1934, Sept. 15 Wmk. 170 *Perf. 14***

| | | |
|---|---|---|
| **536** A184 5k emerald | 22.00 | 3.00 |
| **537** A185 10k black brown | 100.00 | 13.00 |
| **538** A185 15k vermilion | 140.00 | 18.00 |
| **539** A184 20k ultra | 22.00 | 5.50 |
| *Nos. 536-539 (4)* | 284.00 | 39.50 |
| Set, never hinged | 525.00 | |

Prof. D. I. Mendeleev (1834-1907), chemist who discovered the Periodic Law of Classification of the Elements.

Imperfs. exist of 5k (value $400) and 15k (value $400).

Lenin as Child and Youth A186 A187

Demonstration before Lenin Mausoleum — A190

Designs: 5k, Lenin in middle age. 10k, Lenin the orator. 30k, Lenin and Stalin.

**1934, Nov. 23 Unwmk. *Perf. 14***

| | | |
|---|---|---|
| **540** A186 1k indigo & black | 22.00 | 4.00 |
| **541** A187 3k indigo & black | 11.00 | 4.00 |
| *a.* Horiz. pair, imperf. btwn. | — | *5,000.* |
| **542** A187 5k indigo & black | 50.00 | 3.00 |
| **543** A187 10k indigo & black | 16.50 | 2.50 |
| **544** A190 20k brn org & ultra | 11.00 | 8.50 |
| **545** A190 30k brn org & car | 240.00 | 35.00 |
| *Nos. 540-545 (6)* | 350.50 | 57.00 |
| Set, never hinged | 760.00 | |

First decade without Lenin.

See Nos. 931-935, 937.

Bombs Falling on City A192

"Before War and Afterwards" A194

Designs: 10k, Refugees from burning town. 20k, "Plowing with the sword." 35k, "Comradeship."

**1935, Jan. 1 Wmk. 170 *Perf. 14***

| | | |
|---|---|---|
| **546** A192 5k violet black | 28.00 | 3.00 |
| **547** A192 10k ultra | 130.00 | 15.00 |
| **548** A194 15k green | 150.00 | 20.00 |
| **549** A194 20k dark brown | 19.00 | 3.75 |
| **550** A194 35k carmine | 220.00 | 30.00 |
| *Nos. 546-550 (5)* | 547.00 | 71.75 |
| Set, never hinged | 1,050. | |

Anti-war propaganda, the designs symbolize the horrors of modern warfare.

Subway Tunnel A197

Subway Station Cross Section A198

Subway Station A199

Train in Station — A200

**1935, Feb. 25 Wmk. 170 *Perf. 14***

| | | |
|---|---|---|
| **551** A197 5k orange | 42.50 | 7.50 |
| **552** A198 10k dark ultra | 32.50 | 8.50 |
| **553** A199 15k rose carmine | 300.00 | 32.50 |
| **554** A200 20k emerald | 32.50 | 10.00 |
| *Nos. 551-554 (4)* | 407.50 | 58.50 |
| Set, never hinged | 815.00 | |

Completion of Moscow subway.

Friedrich Engels (1820-1895), German Socialist and Collaborator of Marx — A201

**1935, May Wmk. 170 *Perf. 14***

| | | |
|---|---|---|
| **555** A201 5k carmine | 14.00 | 4.00 |
| **556** A201 10k dark green | 25.00 | 6.00 |
| **557** A201 15k dark blue | 70.00 | 14.00 |
| **558** A201 20k brown black | 13.50 | 6.00 |
| *Nos. 555-558 (4)* | 122.50 | 30.00 |
| Set, never hinged | 230.00 | |

Running — A202

Designs: 2k, Diving. 3k, Rowing. 4k, Soccer. 5k, Skiing. 10k, Bicycling. 15k, Tennis. 20k, Skating. 35k, Hurdling. 40k, Parade of athletes.

**1935, Apr. 22 Unwmk. *Perf. 14***

| | | |
|---|---|---|
| **559** A202 1k org & ultra | 20.00 | 4.25 |
| **560** A202 2k black & ultra | 16.00 | 2.50 |
| **561** A202 3k grn & blk brn | 22.00 | 3.00 |
| **562** A202 4k rose red & ultra | 17.00 | 5.25 |
| **563** A202 5k pur & blk brn | 20.00 | 2.50 |
| **564** A202 10k rose red & vio | 20.00 | 5.25 |
| **565** A202 15k blk & blk brn | 190.00 | 42.50 |
| **566** A202 20k blk brn & ultra | 22.00 | 5.00 |
| **567** A202 35k ultra & blk brn | 125.00 | 35.00 |
| **568** A202 40k blk brn & car | 20.00 | 8.50 |
| *Nos. 559-568 (10)* | 472.00 | 113.75 |
| Set, never hinged | 925.00 | |

International Spartacist Games, Moscow. The games never took place.

Silver Plate of Sassanian Dynasty A212

**1935, Sept. 10 Wmk. 170**

| | | |
|---|---|---|
| **569** A212 5k orange red | 57.50 | 3.50 |
| **570** A212 10k dk yel grn | 22.50 | 5.25 |
| **571** A212 15k dark violet | 22.50 | 8.50 |
| **572** A212 35k black brown | 57.50 | 10.00 |
| *Nos. 569-572 (4)* | 160.00 | 27.25 |
| Set, never hinged | 300.00 | |

3rd International Congress of Persian Art, Leningrad, Sept. 12-18, 1935.

Kalinin, the Worker — A213

Mikhail Kalinin — A216

Kalinin as: 5k, farmer. 10k, orator.

**1935, Nov. 20 Unwmk. *Perf. 14***

| | | |
|---|---|---|
| **573** A213 3k rose lilac | 3.75 | 1.25 |
| *a.* Horiz. pair, imperf. btwn. | — | *4,500.* |
| **574** A213 5k green | 3.75 | 1.25 |
| **575** A213 10k blue slate | 7.50 | 1.75 |
| **576** A216 20k brown black | 16.00 | 3.50 |
| *a.* Imperf. | *1,500.* | |
| *Nos. 573-576 (4)* | 31.00 | 7.75 |
| Set, never hinged | 52.50 | |

60th birthday of Mikhail Kalinin, chairman of the Central Executive Committee of the USSR.

A217

Leo Tolstoy — A218

Design: 20k, Statue of Tolstoy.

**1935, Dec. 4** *Perf. 14*

**577** A217 3k ol black & vio 7.00 2.50
*b.* Horiz. pair, imperf. btwn. — *2,000.*
**578** A218 10k vio blk & blk brn 11.00 1.50
*b.* Vert. pair, imperf. btwn. — *2,250.*
**579** A217 20k dk grn & blk brn 12.50 3.00
*Nos. 577-579 (3)* 30.50 7.00
Set, never hinged 57.50

***Perf. 11***

*577a* A217 3k 7.00 4.00
*c.* Horiz. pair, imperf. btwn. *2,000.* *850.00*
*578a* A218 10k 26.00 3.00
*579a* A217 20k 9.00 4.50
*b.* Vert. pair, imperf. btwn. *1,600.* *1,100.*
*Nos. 577a-579a (3)* 42.00 11.50
Set, never hinged 80.00

25th anniv. of the death of Count Leo N. Tolstoy (1828-1910).

### Portrait Type of 1933

Designs: 2k, Mikhail V. Frunze. 4k, N. E. Bauman. 40k, Sergei M. Kirov.

**1935, Nov. Wmk. 170** *Perf. 11*

**580** A169 2k purple 11.00 5.50
**581** A169 4k brown violet 7.00 5.00
**582** A169 40k black brown 19.00 5.00
*Nos. 580-582 (3)* 37.00 15.50
Set, never hinged 65.00

***Perf. 14***

*580a* A169 2k 10.00 1.50
*b.* Vert. pair, imperf. btwn. *2,250.* —
*581a* A169 4k 22.50 3.00
*582a* A169 40k 60.00 4.00
*b.* Vert. pair, imperf. btwn. — *2,750.*
*Nos. 580a-582a (3)* 92.50 8.50
Set, never hinged 200.00

Death of three revolutionary heroes.

Nos. 580-582 exist imperf. but were not regularly issued. Values, set: unused, $1,800; never hinged, $3,250.

Pioneers Preventing Theft from Mailbox A223

Designs: 3k, 5k, Pioneers preventing destruction of property. 10k, Helping recover kite. 15k, Girl Pioneer saluting.

**1936, Apr. Unwmk.** *Perf. 14*

**583** A223 1k yellow green 2.00 1.00
*b.* Vert. pair, imperf. btwn. — *1,650.*
**584** A223 2k copper red 2.50 .85
*b.* Vert. pair, imperf. btwn. *1,750.* *1,650.*
**585** A223 3k slate blue 2.75 .85
**586** A223 5k rose lake 4.50 1.40
**587** A223 10k gray blue 6.75 2.50
*b.* Horiz. pair, imperf. btwn. *2,650.* —
**588** A223 15k brown olive 40.00 10.00
*Nos. 583-588 (6)* 58.50 16.60
Set, never hinged 135.00

***Perf. 11***

*583a* A223 1k 2.00 1.00
*c.* Vert. pair, imperf. btwn. — *1,200.*
*584a* A223 2k 2.50 1.00
*c.* Vert. pair, imperf. btwn. *1,750.* *1,900.*
*585a* A223 3k 2.25 1.00
*b.* Vert. pair, imperf. btwn. *1,750.* *1,650.*
*586a* A223 5k 22.50 2.25
*587a* A223 10k 11.50 3.00
*c.* Vert. pair, imperf. btwn. — *2,750.*
*d.* Horiz. pair, imperf. btwn. *1,750.* *1,650.*
*588a* A223 15k 17.50 5.50
*Nos. 583a-588a (6)* 58.25 13.75
Set, never hinged 105.00

Nikolai A. Dobrolyubov, Writer and Critic, Birth Cent. — A227

**1936, Aug. 13 Typo.** *Perf. 11½*

**589** A227 10k rose lake 10.50 5.50
Never hinged 20.00
*a.* Perf. 14 8.50 3.50
Never hinged 17.00

Aleksander Sergeyevich Pushkin — A228

Statue of Pushkin, Moscow — A229

### Chalky Paper

**1937, Feb. 1**

***Line Perf 12¼***

**590** A228 10k yellow brown 3.50 .75
**591** A228 20k Prus green 3.50 .75
**592** A228 40k rose lake 3.50 .75
**593** A229 50k blue 8.25 2.00
**594** A229 80k carmine rose 42.50 6.00
**595** A229 1r green 82.50 8.50
*Nos. 590-595 (6)* 143.75 18.75
Set, never hinged 254.75

### Chalky or Ordinary Paper

***Comb Perf 12¼x11¾***

**590A** A228 10k yellow brown 7.00 2.00
**591A** A228 20k Prus green 7.00 3.00
**592A** A228 40k rose lake 12.00 3.00
**593A** A229 50k blue 21.00 7.00
**594A** A229 80k carmine rose 7.00 2.00
*Nos. 590A-594A (5)* 54.00 17.00
Set, never hinged 120.00

***Line Perf 13¾x12¼***

**590B** A228 10k yellow brown 9.50 .75
**591B** A228 20k Prus green 6.00 .75
**592B** A228 40k rose lake 2.00 1.75
**593B** A229 50k blue 27.00 4.75
**594B** A229 80k carmine rose 22.50 6.00
**595B** A229 1r green 52.50 8.50
*Nos. 590B-595B (6)* 119.50 22.50
Set, never hinged 120.00

***Line Perf 11x12¼***

**590C** A228 10k yellow brown 37.50 2.25
**591C** A228 20k Prus green 165.00 14.50
**592C** A228 40k rose lake 145.00 14.50
**593C** A229 50k blue 37.50 11.00
**594C** A229 80k carmine rose 35.00 2.25
**595C** A229 1r green 42.50 5.50
*Nos. 590C-595C (6)* 462.50 50.00
Set, never hinged 120.00

***Line Perf 13¾***

**590D** A228 10k yellow brown 82.50 —
**591D** A228 20k Prus green 60.00 —
**592D** A228 40k rose lake 82.50 —
*Nos. 590D-592D (3)* 225.00
Set, never hinged 120.00

***Line Perf 11***

**590E** A228 10k yellow brown 187.50 *22.50*
**592E** A228 40k rose lake 140.00 *22.50*
*Nos. 590E-592E (2)* 327.50 45.00
Set, never hinged 120.00

### Souvenir Sheet

***Imperf***

**596** Sheet of 2 25.00 *75.00*
Never hinged 50.00
*a.* A228 10k brown 4.00 *20.00*
*b.* A229 50k brown 4.00 *27.50*

Pushkin (1799-1837), writer and poet.

Tchaikovsky Concert Hall — A230

Hotel Moscow — A231

Designs: 5k, 15k, Telegraph Agency House. 10k, Tchaikovsky Concert Hall. 20k, 50k, Red Army Theater. 40k, Palace of the Soviets.

### Nos. 697-601, 604 Sizes: 41.25mm x 25mm
### Nos. 602-603 Sizes: 44.5mm x 27mm

### Unwmk.

**1937, June Photo.** *Perf. 12*

**597** A230 3k brown violet 5.75 .75
*b.* Imperf. 285.00 145.00
**598** A230 5k henna brown 2.90 1.75
*b.* Imperf. 285.00 105.00
**599** A230 10k dark brown 6.00 .75
*b.* Imperf. 700.00 285.00
**600** A230 15k black 65.00 .75
*b.* Imperf. 1,050. 475.00
**601** A230 20k olive green 11.50 1.75
*b.* Imperf. 82.50 325.00
**602** A231 30k gray black 8.25 2.25
*a.* Perf. 11 82.50 *12.50*
*b.* Imperf. — —
**603** A231 40k violet 11.50 1.75
*a.* Souv. sheet of 4, imperf. 29.00 *25.00*
*b.* Imperf. 1,425. —
**604** A230 50k dark brown 11.50 6.00
*b.* Imperf. 1,650. 425.00
*Nos. 597-604 (8)* 122.40 15.75
Set, never hinged 450.00

First Congress of Soviet Architects. The 30k is watermarked Greek Border and Rosettes (170).

Nos. 602-603 are sized 44½x27mm, rest in set are sized 41¼x25mm.

Values for No. 603b are for stamps with large margins to ensure that they are from No. 603a.

Feliks E. Dzerzhinski — A235

**1937, July 27 Typo.** *Perf. 12*

**606** A235 10k yellow brown 3.00 1.20
*a.* Imperf. 1,500.
**607** A235 20k Prus green 6.75 1.20
*a.* Imperf. 1,500.
**608** A235 40k rose lake 14.00 2.25
*a.* Imperf. 1,500.
**609** A235 80k carmine 12.00 3.75
*a.* Imperf. 1,500.
*Nos. 606-609 (4)* 35.75 8.40
Set, never hinged 80.00

Dzerzhinski, organizer of Soviet secret police, 10th death anniv.

Shota Rustaveli — A236

***Line Perf 12¼***

**1938, Feb. Unwmk. Photo.**

**610** A236 20k deep green 7.25 1.00
Never hinged 13.00
*a.* Comb perf. 12½x12 *1,450.* 375.00
*b.* Imperf. *2,100.* —

750th anniversary of the publication of the poem "Knight in the Tiger Skin," by Shota Rustaveli, Georgian poet.

Statue Surmounting Pavilion A237

Soviet Pavilion at Paris Exposition A238

**1938** **Typo.**

**611** A237 5k red 1.25 .60
*a.* Imperf. *1,650.*
**612** A238 20k rose 1.75 .50
**613** A237 50k dark blue 19.50 3.75
*Nos. 611-613 (3)* 22.50 4.85
Set, never hinged 42.50

USSR participation in the 1937 International Exposition at Paris.

### Types of 1929-32 and Lenin Types of 1925-26

**1937-52 Unwmk.** *Perf. 11½x12, 12*

**613A** A103 1k dull org ('40) 7.50 *2.50*
**614** A95 2k yel grn ('39) 6.75 *1.00*
**615** A97 4k claret ('40) 65.00 *3.50*
*b.* Imperf. 950.00
**615A** A98 5k org brn ('46) 65.00 *10.00*
**616** A109 10k blue ('38) 1.25 *.50*
*b.* Imperf. 725.00
**616A** A103 10k olive ('40) 145.00 *12.50*
*b.* Imperf. 1,875.
**616B** A109 10k black ('52) .25 .25
**617** A97 20k dull green 1.25 .40
*b.* Imperf. 2,950.
**617A** A107 20k green ('39) 100.00 *6.25*
*b.* Imperf. 600.00
**618** A109 30k claret ('39) 45.00 1.75
*b.* Imperf. 600.00
**619** A104 40k indigo ('38) 6.50 *.75*
*b.* Imperf. 375.00
**619A** A111 50k dp brn ('40) 6.50 *1.00*

### Engr.

**620** A75 3r dk grn ('39) 2.50 .50
*a.* Horiz. pair, imperf. btwn. *2,850.* —
**621** A66 5r red brn ('39) 8.50 2.50
**622** A66 10r indigo ('39) 3.75 1.50
*Nos. 613A-622 (15)* 464.75 44.90
Set, never hinged 800.00

No. 616B was re-issued in 1954-56 in slightly smaller format, 14½x21mm, and in gray black. See note after No. 738.

Airplane Route from Moscow to North Pole — A239

Soviet Flag and Airplanes at North Pole — A240

**1938, Feb. 25 Litho.** *Perf. 12*

**625** A239 10k brn & black 3.75 .75
**626** A239 20k blue gray & blk 7.25 2.25

### Typo.

**627** A240 40k dl grn & car 18.00 3.75
*a.* Imperf. 1,450.
**628** A240 80k rose car & car 4.00 .80
*a.* Imperf. 150.00
*b.* Double impression of flag *2,000.*
*Nos. 625-628 (4)* 33.00 7.55
Set, never hinged 57.50

Soviet flight to the North Pole.

Infantryman
A241

Soldier
A242

Stalin Reviewing Cavalry A246

Chapayev and Boy — A247

Designs: 30k, Sailor, 40k, Aviator. 50k, Antiaircraft soldier.

**Unwmk.**

**1938, Mar. Photo. *Perf. 12***

**629** A241 10k gray blk & dk red 5.50 .75
**630** A242 20k gray blk & dk red 8.25 .80
**631** A242 30k gray blk & dk red 10.50 1.20
**632** A242 40k gray blk & dk red 14.50 1.90
**633** A242 50k gray blk & dk red 14.50 1.90
**634** A246 80k gray blk & dk red 19.00 3.75

**Typo.**

***Perf. 12x12½***

**635** A247 1r blk & car 6.00 2.00
*a.* Imperf. 1,150. —
*Nos. 629-635 (7)* 78.25 12.30
Set, never hinged 140.00

Workers' & Peasants' Red Army, 20th anniv.

Aviators Chkalov, Baidukov, Beliakov and Flight Route — A248

**1938, Apr. 10 Photo.**

**636** A248 10k black & red 8.25 .75
*a.* Imperf. 5,250. 3,600.
**637** A248 20k brn blk & red 12.00 .75
*a.* Imperf. 1,050. 375.00
**638** A248 40k brown & red 12.00 2.00
*a.* Imperf. 1,050. 375.00
**639** A248 50k brn vio & red 15.00 3.75
*a.* Imperf. 1,050. 375.00
*Nos. 636-639 (4)* 47.25 7.25
Set, never hinged 95.00

First Trans-Polar flight, June 18-20, 1937, from Moscow to Vancouver, Wash.

Aviators Gromov, Danilin, Yumashev and Flight Route — A249

**1938, Apr. 13**

**640** A249 10k claret 10.00 .75
*a.* Imperf. 825.00
**641** A249 20k brown black 12.00 1.75
*a.* Imperf. 725.00 —
**642** A249 50k dull violet 13.00 5.00
*a.* Imperf. *23,000.*
*Nos. 640-642 (3)* 35.00 7.50
Set, never hinged 60.00

First Trans-Polar flight, July 12-14, 1937, from Moscow to San Jacinto, Calif.

Arrival of the Rescuing Ice-breakers Taimyr and Murmansk A250

Ivan Papanin and His Men Aboard Ice-breaker Yermak — A251

**1938, June 21 Typo. *Perf. 12, 12½***

**643** A250 10k violet brown 6.00 1.25
*a.* Imperf. 2,250.
**644** A250 20k dark blue 8.25 1.50
*a.* Imperf. 2,250.

**Photo.**

**645** A251 30k olive brown 21.00 3.75
*a.* Imperf. 3,250.
**646** A251 50k ultra 16.50 6.00
*a.* Imperf. 2,350.
*Nos. 643-646 (4)* 51.75 12.50
Set, never hinged 110.00

Rescue of Papanin's North Pole Expedition.

Arms of Armenia — A252

Arms of USSR A253

No. 650

No. 651

No. 652

No. 653

No. 654

No. 655

No. 656

Designs: Different arms on each stamp.

***Perf. 12, 12½***

**1937-38 Unwmk. Typo.**

**647** A252 20k dp bl (Armenia) 10.50 2.00
**648** A252 20k dl vio (Azerbaijan) 10.50 2.00
**649** A252 20k brn org (Byelorussia) 10.50 2.00
**650** A252 20k car rose (Georgia) 10.50 2.00
**651** A252 20k bl grn (Kazakh) 10.50 2.00
**652** A252 20k emer (Kirghiz) 10.50 2.00
**653** A252 20k yel org (Uzbek) 10.50 2.00
**654** A252 20k bl (R.S.F.S.R.) 10.50 2.00
**655** A252 20k claret (Tadzhik) 10.50 2.00
**656** A252 20k car (Turkmen) 10.50 2.00
**657** A252 20k red (Ukraine) 10.50 2.00

**Engr.**

**658** A253 40k brown red 9.25 2.00
*Nos. 647-658 (12)* 124.75 24.00
Set, never hinged 240.00

Constitution of USSR. No. 649 has inscriptions in Yiddish, Polish, Byelorussian and Russian.

Issue dates: 40k, 1937. Others, 1938. See Nos. 841-842.

Nurse Weighing Child — A264

Children at Lenin's Statue — A265

Biology Lesson A266

Health Camp A267

Young Model Builders A268

**1938, Sept. 15 Unwmk. *Perf. 12***

**659** A264 10k dk blue green 12.00 2.00
**660** A265 15k dk blue green 3.50 3.50
**661** A266 20k violet brown 13.00 2.50
**662** A267 30k claret 13.00 2.50
**663** A266 40k light brown 13.00 2.50
**664** A268 50k deep blue 12.00 *5.00*
**665** A268 80k light green 13.00 *4.50*
*Nos. 659-665 (7)* 79.50 22.50
Set, never hinged 145.00

Child welfare.

View of Yalta A269

Crimean Shoreline — A272

Designs: No. 667, View along Crimean shore. No. 668, Georgian military highway. No, 670, View near Yalta. No. 671, "Swallows' Nest" Castle. 20k, Dzerzhinski Rest House for workers. 30k, Sunset in Crimea. 40k, Alupka. 50k, Gursuf. 80k, Crimean Gardens. 1r, "Swallows' Nest" Castle, horiz.

**Unwmk.**

**1938, Sept. 21 Photo. *Perf. 12***

**666** A269 5k brown 4.75 *1.00*
**667** A269 5k black brown 4.75 *1.00*
**668** A269 10k slate green 4.75 *1.00*
**669** A272 10k brown 4.75 *1.00*
**670** A269 15k black brown 6.00 *1.75*
**671** A272 15k black brown 6.00 *1.75*
**672** A269 20k dark brown 10.00 *1.75*
**673** A272 30k black brown 12.00 *1.75*
**674** A269 40k brown 12.00 *1.75*
**675** A272 50k slate green 12.00 *1.75*
*a.* Horiz. pair, imperf. btwn. 2,175.
*b.* Vert. pair, imperf. btwn. 2,175.
**676** A269 80k brown 12.00 *1.75*
**677** A269 1r slate green 120.00 *20.00*
*Nos. 666-677 (12)* 209.00 36.25
Set, never hinged 400.00

Children Flying Model Plane A281

Glider A282

Captive Balloon — A283

Dirigible over Kremlin — A284

Parachute Jumpers — A285

Hydroplane A286

Balloon in Flight — A287

Balloon Ascent — A288

Four-motor Plane A289

**Unwmk.**

| **1938, Oct. 7** | **Typo.** | | *Perf. 12* |
|---|---|---|---|
| **678** A281 | 5k violet brown | 3.75 | 1.50 |
| **679** A282 | 10k olive gray | 3.75 | 1.50 |
| **680** A283 | 15k pink | 6.00 | 1.50 |
| **681** A284 | 20k deep blue | 6.00 | 1.50 |
| **682** A285 | 30k claret | 12.00 | 1.50 |
| **683** A286 | 40k deep blue | 14.50 | 1.50 |
| **684** A287 | 50k blue green | 12.00 | 2.50 |
| **685** A288 | 80k brown | 14.50 | 2.50 |
| **686** A289 | 1r blue green | 82.50 | 10.00 |
| | *Nos. 678-686 (9)* | 155.00 | 24.00 |
| | Set, never hinged | 270.00 | |

For overprints see Nos. C76-C76D.

Mayakovsky Station, Moscow Subway — A290

Sokol Terminal — A291

Kiev Station — A292

Dynamo Station A293

Train in Tunnel A294

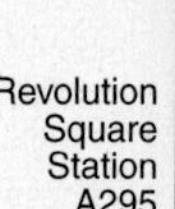

Revolution Square Station A295

**Unwmk.**

| **1938, Nov. 7** | **Photo.** | | *Perf. 12* |
|---|---|---|---|
| **687** A290 | 10k dp red vio | 3.00 | 2.00 |
| *a.* | Vert. pair, imperf. btwn. | 2,175. | — |
| **688** A291 | 15k dark brown | 6.00 | 2.00 |
| **689** A292 | 20k black brown | 14.50 | 2.50 |
| **690** A293 | 30k dark red violet | 21.00 | 4.75 |
| *a.* | Vert. pair, imperf. btwn. | — | *3,600.* |
| **691** A294 | 40k black brown | 21.00 | 4.75 |
| **692** A295 | 50k dark brown | 24.00 | 7.25 |
| | *Nos. 687-692 (6)* | 89.50 | 23.25 |
| | Set, never hinged | 155.00 | |

Second line of the Moscow subway opening.

Girl with Parachute A296

Young Miner A297

Harvesting A298

Designs: 50k, Students returning from school. 80k, Aviator and sailor.

| **1938, Dec. 7** | **Typo.** | | *Perf. 12* |
|---|---|---|---|
| **693** A296 | 20k deep blue | 13.00 | 2.50 |
| **694** A297 | 30k deep claret | 13.00 | 2.50 |
| **695** A298 | 40k violet brown | 10.50 | 2.50 |
| **696** A298 | 50k deep rose | 35.00 | 8.25 |
| **697** A298 | 80k deep blue | 8.25 | 6.00 |
| | *Nos. 693-697 (5)* | 79.75 | 21.75 |
| | Set, never hinged | 140.00 | |

20th anniv. of the Young Communist League (Komsomol).

Diving — A301

Discus Thrower — A302

Designs: 15k, Tennis. 20k, Acrobatic motorcyclists. 30k, Skier. 40k, Runners. 50k, Soccer. 80k, Physical culture.

**Unwmk.**

| **1938, Dec. 28** | **Photo.** | | *Perf. 12* |
|---|---|---|---|
| **698** A301 | 5k scarlet | 3.50 | 1.25 |
| **699** A302 | 10k black | 3.50 | 1.25 |
| **700** A302 | 15k brown | 6.00 | 1.75 |
| **701** A302 | 20k green | 6.00 | 1.75 |
| **702** A302 | 30k dull violet | 30.00 | 2.00 |
| **703** A302 | 40k deep green | 15.00 | 2.00 |
| **704** A302 | 50k blue | 82.50 | 10.00 |
| **705** A302 | 80k deep blue | 10.50 | 5.00 |
| | *Nos. 698-705 (8)* | 157.00 | 25.00 |
| | Set, never hinged | 290.00 | |

Gorki Street, Moscow — A309

Dynamo Subway Station A315

Moscow scenes: 20k, Council House & Hotel Moscow. 30k, Lenin Library. 40k, Crimea Bridge. 50k, Bridge over Moscow River. 80k, Khimki River Terminal.

**Paper with network as in parenthesis**

| **1939, Mar.** | **Typo.** | | *Perf. 12* |
|---|---|---|---|
| **706** A309 | 10k brn *(red brown)* | 1.25 | 1.25 |
| **707** A309 | 20k dk sl grn *(lt blue)* | 1.50 | 1.50 |
| **708** A309 | 30k brn vio *(red brn)* | 2.25 | 1.50 |
| **709** A309 | 40k blue *(lt blue)* | 5.00 | 2.50 |
| **710** A309 | 50k rose lake *(red brn)* | 5.00 | 3.00 |
| **711** A309 | 80k gray ol *(lt blue)* | 47.50 | 5.75 |
| **712** A315 | 1r dk blue *(lt blue)* | 47.50 | 7.50 |
| | *Nos. 706-712 (7)* | 110.00 | 23.00 |
| | Set, never hinged | 250.00 | |

"New Moscow." On 30k, denomination is at upper right.

Foundry-man — A316

| **1939, Mar.** | | | |
|---|---|---|---|
| **713** A316 | 15k dark blue | 7.50 | .75 |
| | Never hinged | 14.50 | |
| *a.* | Imperf. | 2,000. | |
| | Never hinged | 3,000. | |

Statue on USSR Pavilion — A317

USSR Pavilion A318

| **1939, May** | | | **Photo.** |
|---|---|---|---|
| **714** A317 | 30k indigo & red | 2.75 | 1.00 |
| *a.* | Imperf. ('40) | 3.00 | 1.00 |
| **715** A318 | 50k blue & bister brn | 5.50 | 1.00 |
| *a.* | Imperf. ('40) | 6.00 | 1.25 |
| | Set, never hinged | 15.00 | |

Russia's participation in the NY World's Fair.

Paulina Osipenko A318a

Marina Raskova A318b

Design: 60k, Valentina Grizodubova.

| **1939, Mar.** | | | |
|---|---|---|---|
| **718** A318a | 15k green | 8.25 | 2.00 |
| **719** A318b | 30k brown violet | 14.50 | 3.75 |
| **720** A318b | 60k red | 14.50 | 7.50 |
| | *Nos. 718-720 (3)* | 37.25 | 13.25 |
| | Set, never hinged | 65.00 | |

Non-stop record flight from Moscow to the Far East.

Exist imperf. Value, each unused $2,100.

Shevchenko, Early Portrait — A319

Monument at Kharkov — A321

30k, Shevchenko portrait in later years.

| **1939, Mar. 9** | | | |
|---|---|---|---|
| **721** A319 | 15k black brn & blk | 7.50 | 1.50 |
| **722** A319 | 30k dark red & blk | 13.00 | 2.25 |
| **723** A321 | 60k green & dk brn | 14.50 | 3.00 |
| | *Nos. 721-723 (3)* | 35.00 | 6.75 |
| | Set, never hinged | 80.00 | |

Taras G. Shevchenko (1814-1861), Ukrainian poet and painter.

Milkmaid with Prize Cow — A322

Tractor-plow at Work on Abundant Harvest A323

Designs: 20k, Shepherd tending sheep. No. 727, Fair pavilion. No. 728, Fair emblem. 45k, Turkmen picking cotton. 50k, Drove of horses. 60k, Symbolizing agricultural wealth. 80k, Kolkhoz girl with sugar beets. 1r, Hunter with Polar foxes.

| **1939, Aug.** | | | |
|---|---|---|---|
| **724** A322 | 10k rose pink | 3.50 | .45 |
| **725** A323 | 15k red brown | 3.50 | .45 |
| **726** A323 | 20k slate black | 9.50 | 2.00 |
| **727** A323 | 30k purple | 5.75 | 1.00 |
| **728** A322 | 30k red orange | 3.50 | .45 |
| **729** A322 | 45k dark green | 9.50 | 1.25 |
| *a.* | Horiz. pair, imperf. btwn. | *1,750.* | |
| **730** A322 | 50k copper red | 2.00 | .45 |
| *a.* | Horiz. pair, imperf. btwn. | *1,500.* | |
| **731** A322 | 60k bright purple | 7.00 | 1.00 |
| **732** A322 | 80k dark violet | 7.00 | 1.00 |
| **733** A322 | 1r dark blue | 19.00 | 2.00 |
| *a.* | Horiz. pair, imperf. btwn. | *2,350.* | |
| *b.* | Vert. pair, imperf. btwn. | *1,500.* | |
| | Nos. 724-733 (10) | 70.25 | 10.05 |
| | Set, never hinged | 128.00 | |

Soviet Agricultural Fair.

Worker A331

Soldier A332

Aviator — A333

Arms of USSR A334 A335

*Perf. 11¾x12¼*

**1939-43 Unwmk. Typo.**

| | | | |
|---|---|---|---|
| **734** | A331 5k red | .40 | .25 |
| **735** | A332 15k dark green | .45 | .25 |
| **736** | A333 30k deep blue | .80 | .25 |
| **737** | A334 60k fawn ('43) | 5.25 | 9.00 |

**Photo.**

| | | | |
|---|---|---|---|
| **738** | A335 60k rose carmine | .80 | .50 |
| | *Nos. 734-738 (5)* | 7.70 | 10.25 |
| | Set, never hinged | 15.00 | |

No. 734 was re-issued in 1954-56 in slightly smaller format: 14x21½mm, instead of 14¾x22¼mm. Other values reissued in smaller format: 10k, 15k, 20k, 25k, 30k, 40k and 1r. (See notes following Nos. 622, 1260, 1347 and 1689.)

**No. 416 Surcharged with New Value in Black**

**1939 Wmk. 170 *Perf. 12x12½***

| | | | |
|---|---|---|---|
| **743** | A97 30k on 4k claret | 25.00 | 12.50 |
| *a.* | Unwmkd. | 250.00 | 37.50 |

M.E. Saltykov (N. Shchedrin)
A336 A337

**Unwmk.**

**1939, Sept. Typo. *Perf. 12***

| | | | |
|---|---|---|---|
| **745** | A336 15k claret | 3.00 | .75 |
| **746** | A337 30k dark green | 3.75 | .75 |
| **747** | A336 45k olive gray | 8.75 | 1.50 |
| **748** | A337 60k dark blue | 8.75 | 2.25 |
| | *Nos. 745-748 (4)* | 24.25 | 5.25 |
| | Set, never hinged | 80.00 | |

Mikhail E. Saltykov (1826-89), writer & satirist who used pen name of N. Shchedrin.

Sanatorium of the State Bank — A338

Designs: 10k, 15k, Soviet Army sanatorium. 20k, Rest home, New Afyon. 30k, Clinical Institute. 50k, 80k, Sanatorium for workers in heavy industry. 60k, Rest home, Sukhumi.

**1939, Nov. Photo. *Perf. 12***

| | | | |
|---|---|---|---|
| **749** | A338 5k dull brown | 2.00 | .25 |
| **750** | A338 10k carmine | 2.00 | .25 |
| **751** | A338 15k yellow green | 3.50 | .45 |
| **752** | A338 20k dk slate green | 7.00 | .45 |
| **753** | A338 30k bluish black | 3.50 | .45 |
| *a.* | Horiz. pair, imperf. between | *2,500.* | |
| **754** | A338 50k gray black | 3.50 | 1.75 |
| **755** | A338 60k brown violet | 9.50 | 1.75 |
| **756** | A338 80k orange red | 7.00 | 1.75 |
| | *Nos. 749-756 (8)* | 38.00 | 7.10 |
| | Set, never hinged | 125.00 | |

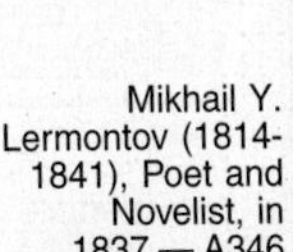

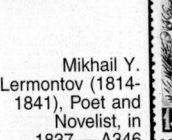

Mikhail Y. Lermontov (1814-1841), Poet and Novelist, in 1837 — A346

Portrait in 1838 — A347

Portrait in 1841 — A348

**1939, Dec.**

| | | | |
|---|---|---|---|
| **757** | A346 15k indigo & sepia | 8.25 | 1.25 |
| *a.* | Vert. pair, imperf. between | — | 1,650. |
| **758** | A347 30k dk grn & dull blk | 12.00 | 3.00 |
| *a.* | Vert. pair, imperf. between | — | 1,650. |
| **759** | A348 45k brk red & indigo | 8.25 | 1.25 |
| | *Nos. 757-759 (3)* | 28.50 | 5.50 |
| | Set, never hinged | 60.00 | |

Nikolai Chernyshevski A349

**1939, Dec. Photo.**

| | | | |
|---|---|---|---|
| **760** | A349 15k dark green | 9.50 | 1.25 |
| **761** | A349 30k dull violet | 14.50 | 1.25 |
| **762** | A349 60k Prus green | 14.50 | 3.00 |
| | *Nos. 760-762 (3)* | 38.50 | 5.50 |
| | Set, never hinged | 50.00 | |

50th anniversary of the death of Nikolai Chernyshevski, scientist and critic.

Anton Chekhov — A350

Design: 20k, 30k, Portrait with hat.

**1940, Feb. Unwmk. *Perf. 12***

| | | | |
|---|---|---|---|
| **763** | A350 10k dark yellow green | 2.00 | 1.50 |
| **764** | A350 15k ultra | 3.75 | 1.50 |
| **765** | A350 20k violet | 3.75 | 1.50 |
| **766** | A350 30k copper brown | 14.50 | 1.50 |
| | *Nos. 763-766 (4)* | 24.00 | 6.00 |
| | Set, never hinged | 40.00 | |

Chekhov (1860-1904), playwright.

Welcome to Red Army by Western Ukraine and Western Byelorussia A352

Designs: 30k, Villagers welcoming tank crew. 50k, 60k, Soldier giving newspapers to crowd. 1r, Crowd waving to tank column.

**1940, Apr.**

| | | | |
|---|---|---|---|
| **767** | A352 10k deep rose | 1.90 | .75 |
| **768** | A352 30k myrtle green | 3.25 | 1.00 |
| **769** | A352 50k gray black | 3.75 | 1.25 |
| **770** | A352 60k indigo | 13.00 | 2.50 |
| **771** | A352 1r red | 9.75 | 2.00 |
| | *Nos. 767-771 (5)* | 31.65 | 7.50 |
| | Set, never hinged | 60.00 | |

Liberation of the people of Western Ukraine and Western Byelorussia.

Ice-breaker "Josef Stalin," Captain Beloussov and Chief Ivan Papanin A356

Badigin and Papanin A358

Map of the Drift of the Sedov and Crew Members — A359

Design: 30k, Icebreaker Georgi Sedov, Captain Vadygin and First Mate Trofimov.

**1940, Apr.**

| | | | |
|---|---|---|---|
| **772** | A356 15k dull yel green | 3.50 | .75 |
| **773** | A356 30k dull purple | 10.50 | 1.25 |
| *b.* | Vert. pair, imperf. between | — | *7,250.* |
| **774** | A358 50k copper brown | 6.50 | 1.50 |
| **775** | A359 1r dark ultra | 12.50 | 2.50 |
| | *Nos. 772-775 (4)* | 33.00 | 6.00 |
| | Set, never hinged | 57.50 | |

Heroism of the Sedov crew which drifted in the Polar Basin for 812 days.

A360

Vladimir V. Mayakovsky — A361

**1940, June *Line Perf. 12¼***

| | | | |
|---|---|---|---|
| **776** | A360 15k deep red | 4.75 | 1.25 |
| **777** | A360 30k copper brown | 4.75 | 1.25 |
| **778** | A361 60k dark gray blue | 12.00 | 2.00 |
| **779** | A361 80k bright ultra | 9.50 | 1.25 |
| | *Nos. 776-779 (4)* | 31.00 | 5.75 |
| | Set, never hinged | 57.50 | |

Mayakovsky, poet (1893-1930).

K.A. Timiryazev and Academy of Agricultural Sciences A362

In the Laboratory of Moscow University A363

Last Portrait A364

Monument in Moscow — A365

**1940, June**

| | | | |
|---|---|---|---|
| **780** | A362 10k indigo | 3.00 | 1.25 |
| **781** | A363 15k purple | 12.00 | 1.25 |
| **782** | A364 30k dk violet brown | 4.75 | 1.75 |
| **783** | A365 60k dark green | 4.75 | 2.50 |
| | *Nos. 780-783 (4)* | 24.50 | 6.75 |
| | Set, never hinged | 40.00 | |

20th anniversary of the death of K. A. Timiryasev, scientist and professor of agricultural and biological sciences.

Relay Race A366

Sportswomen Marching — A367

Children's Sport Badge — A368

Skier — A369

Throwing the Grenade A370

**1940, July 21 *Line Perf. 12½***

| | | | |
|---|---|---|---|
| **784** | A366 15k carmine rose | 4.25 | .75 |
| **785** | A367 30k sepia | 8.25 | 3.00 |
| **786** | A368 50k dk violet blue | 4.75 | .75 |
| **787** | A369 60k dk violet blue | 12.00 | 3.00 |
| **788** | A370 1r grayish green | 14.50 | .75 |
| | *Nos. 784-788 (5)* | 43.75 | 8.25 |
| | Set, never hinged | 85.00 | |

Tchaikovsky Museum at Klin A371

Tchaikovsky & Passage from his Fourth Symphony A372

Peter Ilich Tchaikovsky and Excerpt from Eugene Onegin — A373

*Comb Perf. 12¼x11¾*

**1940, Aug. Unwmk. Typo.**

| | | | |
|---|---|---|---|
| **789** | A371 15k Prus green | 5.50 | 1.50 |
| **790** | A372 20k brown | 6.00 | 1.50 |
| **791** | A372 30k dark blue | 5.50 | 2.00 |
| **792** | A371 50k rose lake | 14.50 | 3.50 |
| **793** | A373 60k red | 12.00 | 7.00 |
| | *Nos. 789-793 (5)* | 43.50 | 15.50 |
| | Set, never hinged | 85.00 | |

Tchaikovsky (1840-1893), composer.

Volga Provinces Pavilion A374

Northeast Provinces Pavilion — A376

ПАВИЛЬОН МОСКОВСКОЙ, РЯЗАНСКОЙ И ТУЛЬСКОЙ ОБЛ.

No. 797

ПАВИЛЬОН УКРАИНСКОЙ ССР

No. 798

ПАВИЛЬОН БЕЛОРУССКОЙ ССР

No. 799

ПАВИЛЬОН АЗЕРБАЙДЖАНСКОЙ ССР

No. 800

ПАВИЛЬОН ГРУЗИНСКОЙ ССР

No. 801

ПАВИЛЬОН АРМЯНСКОЙ ССР

No. 802

У ВХОДА В ПАВИЛЬОН УЗБЕКСКОЙ ССР

No. 803

ПАВИЛЬОН ТУРКМЕНСКОЙ ССР

No. 804

ПАВИЛЬОН ТАДЖИКСКОЙ ССР

No. 805

ПАВИЛЬОН КИРГИЗСКОЙ ССР

No. 806

ПАВИЛЬОН КАЗАХСКОЙ ССР

No. 807

ПАВИЛЬОН КАРЕЛО-ФИНСКОЙ ССР

No. 808

No. 795, Far East Provinces. No. 797, Central Regions. No. 798, Ukrainian. No. 799, Byelorussian. No. 800, Azerbaijan. No. 801, Georgian. No. 802, Armenian. No. 803, Uzbek. No. 804, Turkmen. No. 805, Tadzhik. No. 806, Kirghiz. No. 807, Kazakh. No. 808, Karelian Finnish. No. 809, Main building. No. 810, Mechanizaton Pavilion, Stalin statue.

**1940, Oct. Typo. *Line Perf. 12¼***

| | | | | |
|---|---|---|---|---|
| **794** | A374 | 10k shown | 9.50 | .55 |
| **795** | A374 | 15k multicolored | 9.50 | .55 |
| **796** | A376 | 30k shown | 12.00 | .55 |
| **797** | A376 | 30k multicolored | 14.50 | .55 |
| **798** | A376 | 30k multicolored | 3.50 | .55 |
| **799** | A376 | 30k multicolored | 3.50 | .55 |
| **800** | A376 | 30k multicolored | 3.50 | .55 |
| **801** | A374 | 30k multicolored | 7.00 | .55 |
| **802** | A376 | 30k multicolored | 7.00 | .55 |
| **803** | A376 | 30k multicolored | 3.50 | .55 |
| **804** | A374 | 30k multicolored | 9.50 | .55 |
| **805** | A376 | 30k multicolored | 3.50 | .55 |
| **806** | A376 | 30k multicolored | 3.50 | .55 |
| **807** | A376 | 30k multicolored | 3.50 | .55 |
| **808** | A376 | 30k multicolored | 9.50 | .55 |
| **809** | A376 | 50k multicolored | 16.50 | 1.50 |
| **810** | A376 | 60k multicolored | 19.00 | 2.50 |
| | | *Nos. 794-810 (17)* | 138.50 | 12.25 |
| | | Set, never hinged | 215.00 | |

All-Union Agricultural Fair.

Nos. 796-808 printed in three sheet formats with various vertical and horizontal se-tenant combinations.

Monument to Red Army Heroes — A391

Map of War Operations and M. V. Frunze — A393

Heroic Crossing of the Sivash A394

Designs: 15k, Grenade thrower. 60k, Frunze's headquarters, Stroganovka. 1r, Victorious soldier.

**1940** ***Imperf.***

| | | | | |
|---|---|---|---|---|
| **811** | A391 | 10k dark green | 2.25 | .55 |
| **812** | A391 | 15k orange ver | 2.25 | .55 |
| **813** | A393 | 30k dull brown & car | 6.25 | 1.50 |
| **814** | A394 | 50k violet brn | 3.50 | 1.00 |
| **815** | A394 | 60k indigo | 3.50 | 1.00 |
| **816** | A391 | 1r gray black | 4.25 | 1.50 |
| | | *Nos. 811-816 (6)* | 22.00 | 6.10 |
| | | Set, never hinged | 35.00 | |

***Perf. 12***

| | | | | |
|---|---|---|---|---|
| **811A** | A391 | 10k dark green | 2.75 | .55 |
| **812A** | A391 | 15k orange ver | 2.75 | .55 |
| **813A** | A393 | 30k dull brown & car | 3.75 | 1.00 |
| **814A** | A394 | 50k violet brn | 2.75 | .65 |
| **815A** | A394 | 60k indigo | 3.75 | 1.00 |
| **816A** | A391 | 1r gray black | 3.75 | 1.00 |
| | | *Nos. 811A-816A (6)* | 19.50 | 4.75 |
| | | Set, never hinged | 32.50 | |

20th anniversary of battle of Perekop.

Coal Miners — A397

Blast Furnace — A398

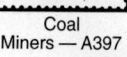

Bridge over Moscow-Volga Canal — A399

Three New Type Locomotives A400

Workers on a Collective Farm — A401

Automobiles and Planes A402

Oil Derricks — A403

**1941, Jan.** ***Perf. 12***

| | | | | |
|---|---|---|---|---|
| **817** | A397 | 10k deep blue | 2.00 | 1.00 |
| **818** | A398 | 15k dark violet | 2.25 | 1.25 |
| **819** | A399 | 20k deep blue | 2.75 | 1.50 |
| **820** | A400 | 30k dark brown | 3.00 | 1.50 |
| **821** | A401 | 50k olive brown | 3.75 | 1.75 |
| **822** | A402 | 60k olive brown | 4.50 | 2.50 |
| **823** | A403 | 1r dark blue green | 6.75 | 6.00 |
| | | *Nos. 817-823 (7)* | 25.00 | 15.50 |
| | | Set, never hinged | 60.00 | |

Soviet industries.

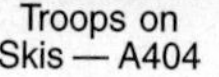

Troops on Skis — A404

Sailor — A405

Soldiers with Cannon A406

20k, Cavalry. 30k, Machine gunners. 45k, Army horsemen. 50k, Aviator. 1r, 3r, Marshal's Star.

**1941-43**

| | | | | |
|---|---|---|---|---|
| **824** | A404 | 5k dark violet | 2.00 | .25 |
| **825** | A405 | 10k deep blue | 2.00 | .25 |
| **826** | A406 | 15k brt yellow green | 1.00 | .25 |
| **827** | A404 | 20k vermilion | 1.00 | .25 |
| **828** | A404 | 30k dull brown | 1.00 | .25 |
| **829** | A406 | 45k gray green | 4.00 | .50 |
| **830** | A404 | 50k dull blue | 1.50 | .75 |
| **831** | A404 | 1r dull blue green | 2.50 | 1.00 |
| **831A** | A404 | 3r myrtle grn ('43) | 10.00 | 1.75 |
| | | *Nos. 824-831A (9)* | 25.00 | 5.25 |
| | | Set, never hinged | 70.00 | |

Army & Navy of the USSR, 23rd anniv.

Battle of Ismail — A412

Field Marshal Aleksandr Suvorov — A413

**1941 Unwmk. *Perf. 12***

| | | | | |
|---|---|---|---|---|
| **832** | A412 | 10k dark green | 3.00 | .25 |
| **833** | A412 | 15k carmine rose | 3.00 | .30 |
| **834** | A413 | 30k blue black | 1.00 | .70 |
| **835** | A413 | 1r olive brown | 3.00 | 3.00 |
| | | *Nos. 832-835 (4)* | 10.00 | 4.25 |
| | | Set, never hinged | 25.00 | |

150th anniversary of the capture of the Turkish fortress, Ismail.

Kirghiz Horse Breeder A414

Kirghiz Miner A415

**1941, Mar. *Perf. 12, 12x12½***

| | | | | |
|---|---|---|---|---|
| **836** | A414 | 15k dull brown | 2.50 | .45 |
| **837** | A415 | 30k dull purple | 3.50 | .60 |
| | | Set, never hinged | 15.00 | |

15th anniversary of the Kirghizian Soviet Socialist Republic.

Prof. N. E. Zhukovski A416

Zhukovski Lecturing A418

Military Air Academy A417

**1941, Mar.**

| | | | | |
|---|---|---|---|---|
| **838** | A416 | 15k deep blue | 3.50 | .35 |
| **839** | A417 | 30k carmine rose | 3.00 | .65 |
| **840** | A418 | 50k brown violet | 3.50 | 1.00 |
| | | *Nos. 838-840 (3)* | 10.00 | 2.00 |
| | | Set, never hinged | 20.00 | |

Prof. Zhukovski, scientist (1847-1921).

**Arms Type of 1938**

Karelian-Finnish Soviet Socialist Republic.

**1941, Mar.**

| | | | | |
|---|---|---|---|---|
| **841** | A252 | 30k rose | 2.75 | .75 |
| **842** | A252 | 45k dark blue green | 3.25 | 1.25 |
| | | Set, never hinged | 15.00 | |

1st anniversary of the Karelian-Finnish Soviet Socialist Republic.

Spasski Tower, Kremlin — A420

Kremlin and Moscow River A421

**1941, May Typo. Unwmk.**

| | | | | |
|---|---|---|---|---|
| **843** | A420 | 1r dull red | .75 | .50 |
| **844** | A421 | 2r brown orange | 1.25 | 1.00 |
| | | Set, never hinged | 5.00 | |

"Suvorov's March through the Alps, 1799" A422

Vasili Ivanovich Surikov, Self-portrait A424

"Stepan Rasin on the Volga" A423

**1941, June Photo. *Perf. 12***

| | | | | |
|---|---|---|---|---|
| **845** | A422 | 20k black | 12.00 | 1.25 |
| **846** | A423 | 30k scarlet | 6.00 | 2.75 |
| **847** | A422 | 50k dk vio brn | 45.00 | 8.00 |
| **848** | A423 | 1r gray green | 45.00 | 11.00 |
| **849** | A424 | 2r brown | 45.00 | 13.00 |
| | | *Nos. 845-849 (5)* | 153.00 | 36.00 |
| | | Set, never hinged | 250.00 | |

Surikov (1848-1916), painter.

Mikhail Y. Lermontov, Poet, Death Centenary — A425

**1941, July**

| No. | Type | Description | Unused | Used |
|---|---|---|---|---|
| **850** | A425 | 15k Prus green | *20.00* | *4.00* |
| **851** | A425 | 30k dark violet | *25.00* | *6.00* |
| | | Set, never hinged | 125.00 | |

Visitors in Lenin Museum A426

Lenin Museum A427

**1941-42**

| No. | Type | Description | Unused | Used |
|---|---|---|---|---|
| **852** | A426 | 15k rose red | 14.00 | 6.00 |
| **853** | A427 | 30k dark violet ('42) | 40.00 | 18.00 |
| **854** | A426 | 45k Prus green | 21.00 | 9.00 |
| **855** | A427 | 1r org brn ('42) | 45.00 | 17.00 |
| | | *Nos. 852-855 (4)* | 120.00 | 50.00 |
| | | Set, never hinged | 250.00 | |

Fifth anniversary of Lenin Museum.

Mother's Farewell to a Soldier Son ("Be a Hero!") — A428

**1941, Aug.**

| No. | Type | Description | Unused | Used |
|---|---|---|---|---|
| **856** | A428 | 30k carmine | 15.00 | 15.00 |
| | | Never hinged | 35.00 | |

Alisher Navoi — A429

**1942, Jan.**

| No. | Type | Description | Unused | Used |
|---|---|---|---|---|
| **857** | A429 | 30k brown | 90.00 | 25.00 |
| **858** | A429 | 1r dark violet | 60.00 | 25.00 |
| | | Set, never hinged | *300.00* | |

Alisher Navoi, Uzbekian poet, 500th birth anniv.

People's Militia — A430

**1941, Dec.** **Typo.**

| No. | Type | Description | Unused | Used |
|---|---|---|---|---|
| **859** | A430 | 30k dull blue | 125.00 | 75.00 |
| | | Never hinged | 300.00 | |

Junior Lieutenant Talalikhin Ramming German Plane in Midair A431

Captain Gastello and Burning Plane Diving into Enemy Gasoline Tanks A432

Major General Dovator and Cossack Cavalry in Action A433

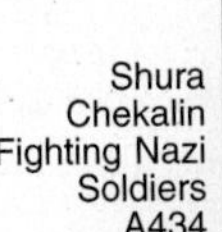

Shura Chekalin Fighting Nazi Soldiers A434

Nazi Soldiers Leading Zoya Kosmodemjanskaja to her Death — A435

**1942-44 Unwmk. Photo. *Perf. 12***

| No. | Type | Description | Unused | Used |
|---|---|---|---|---|
| **860** | A431 | 20k bluish black | 2.50 | 1.75 |
| **860A** | A431 | 30k Prus grn ('44) | 2.50 | 1.75 |
| **861** | A432 | 30k bluish black | 2.50 | 1.75 |
| **861A** | A432 | 30k dp ultra ('44) | 2.50 | 1.75 |
| **862** | A433 | 30k black | 2.50 | 1.75 |
| **863** | A434 | 30k black | 2.50 | 1.75 |
| **863A** | A434 | 30k brt yel grn ('44) | 2.50 | 1.75 |
| **864** | A435 | 30k black | 2.50 | 1.75 |
| **864A** | A435 | 30k rose vio ('44) | 2.50 | 1.75 |
| **865** | A434 | 1r slate green | 32.50 | 11.00 |
| **866** | A435 | 2r slate green | 45.00 | 30.00 |
| | | *Nos. 860-866 (11)* | 100.00 | 56.75 |
| | | Set, never hinged | 200.00 | |

Issued to honor Soviet heroes.
For surcharges see Nos. C80-C81.

Anti-tank Artillery A436

Signal Corps in Action A437

Defense of Leningrad A440

Guerrilla Fighters A438

War Worker A439

Red Army Scouts A441

**1942-43**

| No. | Type | Description | Unused | Used |
|---|---|---|---|---|
| **867** | A436 | 20k black | 2.50 | *1.50* |
| **868** | A437 | 30k sappire | 2.50 | *1.50* |
| **869** | A438 | 30k Prus grn ('43) | 2.50 | *1.50* |
| **870** | A439 | 30k dull red brn ('43) | 2.50 | *1.50* |
| **871** | A440 | 60k blue black | 30.00 | 10.00 |
| **872** | A441 | 1r black brown | 30.00 | 6.00 |
| | | *Nos. 867-872 (6)* | 70.00 | 22.00 |
| | | Set, never hinged | 120.00 | |

Women Workers and Soldiers A442

Flaming Tank A443

Women Preparing Food Shipments A444

Sewing Equipment for Red Army — A445

Anti-Aircraft Battery in Action — A446

**1942-43 Typo. Unwmk.**

| No. | Type | Description | Unused | Used |
|---|---|---|---|---|
| **873** | A442 | 20k dark blue | 1.25 | 1.00 |
| **874** | A443 | 20k dull rose violet | 1.25 | 1.00 |
| **875** | A444 | 30k brn vio ('43) | 1.75 | 1.75 |
| **876** | A445 | 45k dull rose red | 7.00 | 5.00 |
| **877** | A446 | 45k dp dl blue ('43) | 7.00 | 5.00 |
| | | *Nos. 873-877 (5)* | 18.25 | 13.75 |
| | | Set, never hinged | 30.00 | |

Manufacturing Explosives — A447

Designs: 10k, Agriculture. 15k, Group of Fighters. 20k, Storming the Palace. 30k, Lenin and Stalin. 60k, Tanks. 1r, Lenin. 2r, Revolution scene.

**Inscribed: "1917 XXV 1942"**

**1943, Jan. Photo. *Perf. 12***

| No. | Type | Description | Unused | Used |
|---|---|---|---|---|
| **878** | A447 | 5k black brown | 1.00 | .50 |
| **879** | A447 | 10k black brown | 1.00 | .50 |
| **880** | A447 | 15k blue black | 1.00 | .50 |
| **881** | A447 | 20k blue black | 1.50 | .50 |
| **882** | A447 | 30k black brown | 2.25 | .60 |
| **883** | A447 | 60k black brown | 3.50 | 1.50 |
| **884** | A447 | 1r dull red brown | 4.00 | 2.00 |
| **885** | A447 | 2r black | 11.00 | 3.50 |
| | | *Nos. 878-885 (8)* | 25.25 | 9.60 |
| | | Set, never hinged | 65.00 | |

25th anniversary of October Revolution.

Mount St. Elias, Alaska A455

Bering Sea and Bering's Ship — A456

**1943, Apr.**

| No. | Type | Description | Unused | Used |
|---|---|---|---|---|
| **886** | A455 | 30k chalky blue | .90 | .50 |
| **887** | A456 | 60k Prus green | 1.75 | .65 |
| **888** | A455 | 1r yellow green | 4.00 | .80 |
| **889** | A456 | 2r bister brown | 8.00 | 1.25 |
| | | *Nos. 886-889 (4)* | 14.65 | 3.20 |
| | | Set, never hinged | 25.00 | |

200th anniv. of the death of Vitus Bering, explorer (1681-1741).

Medical Corpsmen and Wounded Soldier A457

Trench Mortar A458

Army Scouts A459

Repulsing Enemy Tanks A460

Snipers A461

**1943**

| No. | Type | Description | Unused | Used |
|---|---|---|---|---|
| **890** | A457 | 30k blue gray | 1.25 | 1.00 |
| **891** | A458 | 30k brown bister | 1.25 | 1.00 |
| **892** | A459 | 30k blue gray | 1.25 | 1.00 |
| **893** | A460 | 60k myrtle green | 2.00 | 1.90 |
| **894** | A461 | 60k chalky blue | 2.00 | 1.90 |
| | | *Nos. 890-894 (5)* | 7.75 | 6.80 |
| | | Set, never hinged | 20.00 | |

Maxim Gorki (1868-1936), Writer A462

**1943, June**

| No. | Type | Description | Unused | Used |
|---|---|---|---|---|
| **895** | A462 | 30k green | .80 | .40 |
| **896** | A462 | 60k slate black | 1.25 | .50 |
| | | Set, never hinged | 5.00 | |

Patriotic War Medal A463

Order of Field Marshal Suvorov A464

**1943, July** **Engr.**

**897** A463 1r black 1.00 1.00
**898** A464 10r dk olive green 4.00 4.00
Set, never hinged 8.00

Sailors A465

Designs: 30k, Navy gunner and warship. 60k, Soldiers and tank.

**1943, Oct.** **Photo.**

**899** A465 20k golden brown .35 .30
**900** A465 30k dark myrtle green .35 .30
**901** A465 60k brt yellow green .75 .60
**902** A465 3r chalky blue 2.50 1.75
*Nos. 899-902 (4)* 3.95 2.95
Set, never hinged 7.00

25th anniv. of the Red Army and Navy.

Karl Marx — A468

**1943, Sept.**

**903** A468 30k blue black 1.50 .25
**904** A468 60k dk slate green 2.50 .25
Set, never hinged 8.00

125th anniv. of the birth of Karl Marx.

Vladimir V. Mayakovsky — A469

**1943, Oct.**

**905** A469 30k red orange 1.50 .40
**906** A469 60k deep blue 1.50 .60
Set, never hinged 6.00

Mayakovsky, poet, 50th birth anniv.

Flags of US, Britain, and USSR A470

**1943, Nov.**

**907** A470 30k blk, dp red & dk bl .40 .30
**908** A470 3r sl blue, red & lt blue 2.60 .85
Set, never hinged 5.00

The Tehran conference.

Ivan Turgenev (1818-83), Poet — A471

**1943, Oct.**

**909** A471 30k myrtle green 20.00 20.00
**910** A471 60k dull purple 25.00 25.00
Set, never hinged 125.00

Map of Stalingrad A472

Harbor of Sevastopol and Statue of Lenin A473

Leningrad A474

Odessa A475

**1944, Mar.** ***Perf. 12***

**911** A472 30k dull brown & car 1.75 .50
**912** A473 30k dark blue 1.75 .50
**913** A474 30k dk slate green 1.75 .50
**914** A475 30k yel green 1.75 .50
*Nos. 911-914 (4)* 7.00 2.00
Set, never hinged 22.50

Honoring the defenders of Stalingrad, Leningrad, Sevastopol and Odessa.
See No. 959.
No. 911 measures 33x22mm and also exists in smaller size: 32x21 ½mm.

USSR War Heroes A476

**1944, Apr.**

**915** A476 30k deep ultra .50 .25
Never hinged 2.00

Sailor Loading Gun — A477

Tanks — A478

Soldier Bayoneting a Nazi A479

Infantryman A480

Soldier Throwing Hand Grenade — A481

**1943-44** **Photo.**

**916** A477 15k deep ultra .30 .25
**917** A478 20k red orange ('44) .30 .25
**918** A479 30k dull brn & dk red ('44) .30 .25
**919** A480 1r brt yel green 2.00 .40
**920** A481 2r blue gray ('44) 2.00 1.00
*Nos. 916-920 (5)* 4.90 2.15
Set, never hinged 15.00

25th anniversary of the Young Communist League (Komsomol).

Flags of US, USSR, Great Britain — A482

**1944, May 30** **Unwmk.** ***Perf. 12***

**921** A482 60k black, red & blue .50 .30
**922** A482 3r dk bl, red & lt bl 2.75 1.10
Set, never hinged 5.00

Day of the Nations United Against Germany, June 14, 1944.

Patriotic War Order — A483

Order of Prince Alexander Nevsky — A484

Order of Field Marshal Suvorov — A485

Order of Field Marshal Kutuzov — A486

**Paper with network as in parenthesis**

**1944** **Typo.** ***Perf. 12***

**923** A483 15k dull red *(rose)* .35 .25
**924** A484 20k blue *(lt blue)* .35 .25
**925** A485 30k green *(green)* .50 .25
**926** A486 60k dull red *(rose)* .75 .40
*Nos. 923-926 (4)* 1.95 1.15
Set, never hinged 10.00

***Imperf***

**923A** A483 15k dull red *(rose)* .35 .25
**924A** A484 20k blue *(lt blue)* .35 .25
**925A** A485 30k green *(green)* .50 .25
**926A** A486 60k dull red *(rose)* .75 .40
*Nos. 923A-926A (4)* 1.95 1.15
Set, never hinged 10.00

Beware of bogus perforation "errors" created from imperfs.

Order of Patriotic War — A487

Order of Prince, Alexander Nevski — A488

Order of Field Marshal Kutuzov A489

Order of Field Marshal Suvorov A490

**1944, June** **Unwmk.** **Engr.** ***Perf. 12***

**927** A487 1r black .50 .40
**928** A488 3r blue black 1.10 1.00
**929** A489 5r dark olive green 1.75 1.25
**930** A490 10r dark red 3.50 2.00
*Nos. 927-930 (4)* 6.85 4.65
Set, never hinged 20.00

**Types of 1934, Inscribed 1924-1944 and**

Lenin's Mausoleum — A491

30k (#931), 3r, Lenin & Stalin. 50k, Lenin in middle age. 60k, Lenin, the orator.

**1944, June** **Photo.**

**931** A190 30k orange & car .30 .25
**932** A186 30k slate & black .30 .25
**933** A187 45k slate & black .50 .30
**934** A187 50k slate & black .50 .30
**935** A187 60k slate & black .50 .40
**936** A491 1r indigo & brn blk 2.50 .75
**937** A190 3r bl blk & dull org 3.00 1.25
*Nos. 931-937 (7)* 7.60 3.50
Set, never hinged 30.00

20 years without Lenin.

Nikolai Rimski-Korsakov
A492 A493

**1944, June** ***Perf. 12***

**938** A492 30k gray black .25 .25
**939** A493 60k slate green .25 .25
**940** A492 1r brt blue green .55 .35
**941** A493 3r purple 1.25 .40
*Nos. 938-941 (4)* 2.30 1.25
Set, never hinged 4.00

*Imperf*

**938A** A492 30k gray black .25 .25
**939A** A493 60k slate green .25 .25
**940A** A492 1r brt blue green .55 .35
**941A** A493 3r purple 1.25 .40
*Nos. 938A-941A (4)* 2.30 1.25
Set, never hinged 5.00

Rimski-Korsakov (1844-1909), composer.

N.A. Shchors — A494

Heroes of the 1918 Civil War: No. 943, V.I. Chapayev. No. 944, S.G. Lazo.

**1944, Sept.** *Perf. 12*

**942** A494 30k gray black .35 .30
**943** A494 30k dark slate green .35 .30
**944** A494 30k brt yellow green .35 .30
*Nos. 942-944 (3)* 1.05 .90
Set, never hinged 3.00

See Nos. 1209-1211, 1403.

Sergei A. Chaplygin — A497

**1944, Sept.**

**945** A497 30k gray .50 .30
**946** A497 1r lt brown 1.50 .75
Set, never hinged 3.00

75th anniversary of the birth of Sergei A. Chaplygin, scientist and mathematician.

Khanpasha Nuradilov A498

A. Matrosov A499

F. Louzan A500

M. S. Polivanova and N. V. Kovshova A501

Pilot B. Safonov — A502

**1944, July**

**947** A498 30k slate green 1.00 .60
**948** A499 60k dull purple 1.75 .60
**949** A500 60k dull blue 1.75 .60
**950** A501 60k bright green 3.00 .60
**951** A502 60k slate black 3.00 .60
*Nos. 947-951 (5)* 10.50 3.00
Set, never hinged 20.00

Soviet war heroes.

Ilya E. Repin — A503

Ivan A. Krylov — A505

"Cossacks' Reply to Sultan Mohammed IV" — A504

**1944, Nov.** *Perf. 12½*

**952** A503 30k slate green .65 .30
**953** A504 50k dk blue green .75 .30
**954** A504 60k chalky blue .75 .30
**955** A503 1r dk org brn 1.00 .30
**956** A504 2r dark purple 2.00 .60
*Nos. 952-956 (5)* 5.15 1.80
Set, never hinged 14.00

*Imperf*

**952A** A503 30k slate green .65 .30
**953A** A504 50k dk blue green .75 .30
**954A** A504 60k chalky blue .75 .30
**955A** A503 1r dk org brn 1.00 .30
**956A** A504 2r dark purple 2.00 .60
*Nos. 952A-956A (5)* 5.15 1.80
Set, never hinged 14.00

I. E. Repin (1844-1930), painter.

**1944, Nov.** *Perf. 12*

**957** A505 30k yellow brown .50 .25
**958** A505 1r dk violet blue .50 .25
Set, never hinged 3.00

Krylov, fable writer, death centenary.

**Leningrad Type of 1944**
Souvenir Sheet

**1944, Dec. 6** *Imperf.*

**959** Sheet of 4 10.00 4.75
Never hinged 25.00
*a.* Marginal inscriptions inverted 6,500.
*b.* Marginal inscriptions double, one inverted 30,000.
*c.* A474 30k dark slate green 1.00 .60

Relief of the siege of Leningrad, Jan. 27, 1944.

Partisan Medal — A507

Order for Bravery — A508

Order of Bogdan Chmielnicki A509

Order of Victory A510

Order of Ushakov A511

Order of Nakhimov A512

**Paper with network as in parenthesis**
*Perf. 12½*

**1945, Jan.** **Typo.** **Unwmk.**

**960** A507 15k black *(green)* .25 .30
**961** A508 30k dp blue *(lt blue)* .35 .30
**962** A509 45k dk blue .35 .30
**963** A510 60k dl rose *(pale rose)* .45 .30
**964** A511 1r dull blue *(green)* .80 .40
**965** A512 1r yel green *(blue)* .80 .40
*Nos. 960-965 (6)* 3.00 2.00
Set, never hinged 7.00

*Imperf*

**960A** A507 15k black *(green)* .25 .30
**961A** A508 30k dp blue *(lt blue)* .35 .30
**962A** A509 45k dk blue .35 .30
**963A** A510 60k dl rose *(pale rose)* .45 .30
**964A** A511 1r dull blue *(green)* .80 .40
**965A** A512 1r yel green *(blue)* .80 .40
*Nos. 960A-965A (6)* 3.00 2.00
Set, never hinged 5.00

Beware of bogus perforation "errors" created from imperfs.

Aleksandr S. Griboedov — A513

**1945, Jan.** **Photo.** *Perf. 12½*

**966** A513 30k dk slate green .35 .25
**967** A513 60k gray brown .65 .30
Set, never hinged 4.00

Griboedov (1795-1829), poet & statesman.

Red Army Soldier — A514

**1945, Mar.**

**968** A514 60k gray blk & henna .50 .55
**969** A514 3r gray blk & henna 1.50 1.10
Set, never hinged 3.00

**Souvenir Sheet**
*Imperf*

**970** Sheet of 4 60.00 40.00
Never hinged 100.00
*a.* A514 3r gray brown & henna 9.00 7.50
Never hinged 15.00

Second anniv. of victory at Stalingrad.

Order for Bravery A516

Order of Bogdan Chmielnicki A517

Order of Victory — A518

**1945** **Engr.** *Perf. 12*

**971** A516 1r indigo .50 .35
**972** A517 2r black 1.75 .90
**973** A518 3r henna 1.60 .75
*Nos. 971-973 (3)* 3.85 2.00
Set, never hinged 7.50

See Nos. 1341-1342. For overprints see Nos. 992, 1709.

A519

A520

A521

A522

A523

Battle Scenes A524

**1945, Apr.** **Photo.** *Perf. 12½*

**974** A519 20k sl grn, org red & black .75 .60
**975** A520 30k bl blk & dull org .75 .60
**976** A521 30k blue black .75 .60
**977** A522 60k orange red 1.50 1.50
**978** A523 1r sl grn & org red 6.00 2.75
**979** A524 1r slate green 6.00 2.75
*Nos. 974-979 (6)* 15.75 8.80
Set, never hinged 25.00

Red Army successes against Germany.

Parade in Red Square, Nov. 7, 1941 — A525

Designs: 60k, Soldiers and Moscow barricade, Dec. 1941. 1r, Air battle, 1941.

**1945, June**

**980** A525 30k dk blue violet .30 .25
**981** A525 60k olive black .70 .35
**982** A525 1r black brown 2.00 1.40
*Nos. 980-982 (3)* 3.00 2.00
Set, never hinged 5.00

3rd anniversary of the victory over the Germans before Moscow.

Elite Guard Badge and Cannons — A528

**1945, Apr.** **Typo.**

**983** A528 60k red 1.00 .50
Never hinged 4.00

Motherhood Medal — A529

Motherhood Glory Order — A530

Mother-Heroine Order — A531

**Paper with network as in parenthesis**

**1945** **Size: 22x33¼mm** ***Perf. 12½***

**984** A529 20k brown *(lt blue)* .40 .40
**985** A530 30k yel brown *(green)* .50 .40
**986** A531 60k dull rose *(pale rose)* .80 .40

***Imperf***

**984A** A529 20k brown *(lt blue)* .40 .40
**985A** A530 30k yel brown *(green)* .50 .40
**986D** A531 60k dull rose *(pale rose)* .80 .40

***Perf. 12½***

**Engr.**

**Size: 20x38mm**

**986A** A529 1r blk brn *(green)* .80 .40
**986B** A530 2r dp bl *(lt blue)* 1.75 .70
**986C** A531 3r brn red *(lt blue)* 2.00 1.20
*Nos. 984-986D (9)* 7.95 4.70
Set, never hinged 20.00

Academy Building, Moscow — A532

Academy at Leningrad and M. V. Lomonosov A533

**1945, June** **Photo.** ***Perf. 12½***

**987** A532 30k blue violet .50 .30
*a.* Horiz. pair, imperf. between 90.00
**988** A533 2r grnsh black 1.50 .65
Set, never hinged 4.00

Academy of Sciences, 220th anniv.

Popov and his Invention A534

Aleksandr S. Popov A535

**1945, July** **Unwmk.**

**989** A534 30k dp blue violet .50 .25
**990** A534 60k dark red 1.00 .35
**991** A535 1r yellow brown 1.75 .50
*Nos. 989-991 (3)* 3.25 1.10
Set, never hinged 5.00

"Invention of radio" by A. S. Popov, 50th anniv.

No. 973 Overprinted in Blue

**1945, Aug.** ***Perf. 12***

**992** A518 3r henna 2.00 1.00

Victory of the Allied Nations in Europe.

Yakovlev-3 Fighter — A536

Petliakov-2 Dive Bombers — A537

Ilyushin-2 Bombers A538

#992A, 995, Yakovlev-3 Fighter. #992B, 1000, Petliakov-2 dive bombers. #992C, 996, Ilyushin-2 bombers. #992D, 993, Petliakov-8 heavy bomber. #992E, 1001, Tupolev-2 bombers. #992F, 997, Ilyushin-4 bombers. #992G, 999, Polikarpov-2 biplane. #992H, 998, Lavochkin-7 fighters. #992I, 994, Yakovlev-3 fighter in action.

**1945-46** **Unwmk.** **Photo.** ***Perf. 12***

**992A** A536 5k dk violet ('46) .40 .25
**992B** A537 10k hen brn ('46) .40 .25
**992C** A538 15k hen brn ('46) .80 .25
**992D** A538 15k Prus grn ('46) .80 .25
**992E** A538 20k gray brn ('46) .80 .50
**992F** A538 30k violet ('46) 1.60 .50
**992G** A538 30k brown ('46) 1.60 .50
**992H** A538 50k blue vio ('46) 2.25 1.25
**992I** A536 60k dl bl vio ('46) 3.00 1.50
**993** A536 1r gray black 3.50 .60
**994** A536 1r henna brown 3.50 .60
**995** A536 1r brown 3.50 .60
**996** A538 1r deep brown 3.50 .60
**997** A538 1r intense black 3.50 .60
**998** A538 1r orange ver 3.50 .60
**999** A538 1r bright green 3.50 .60
**1000** A537 1r deep brown 3.50 .60
**1001** A538 1r violet blue 3.50 .60
*Nos. 992A-1001 (18)* 43.15 10.65
Set, never hinged 75.00

Issued: #992A-992I, 3/26; #993-1001, 8/19.

A545

Lenin, 75th Birth Anniv. — A546

Various Lenin portraits.

**Dated "1870-1945"**

**1945, Sept.** ***Perf. 12½***

**1002** A545 30k bluish black .60 .35
**1003** A546 50k gray brown .75 .35
**1004** A546 60k orange brown .85 .35
**1005** A546 1r greenish black 2.00 .35
**1006** A546 3r sepia 6.00 1.25
*Nos. 1002-1006 (5)* 10.20 2.65
Set, never hinged 25.00

Prince M. I. Kutuzov — A550

**1945, Sept. 16**

**1007** A550 30k blue violet .60 .40
**1008** A550 60k brown 1.40 .60
Set, never hinged 4.00

Field Marshal Prince Mikhail Illarionovich Kutuzov (1745-1813).

Aleksandr Ivanovich Herzen A551

**1945, Oct. 26**

**1009** A551 30k dark brown .50 .40
**1010** A551 2r black 1.50 .60
Set, never hinged 5.00

Herzen, author, revolutionist, 75th death anniv.

Ilya Mechnikov — A552

**1945, Nov. 27**

**1011** A552 30k brown .65 .40
**1012** A552 1r greenish black 1.25 .60
Set, never hinged 5.00

Ilya I. Mechnikov, zoologist and bacteriologist (1845-1916).

Friedrich Engels — A553

**1945, Nov.** **Unwmk.** ***Perf. 12½***

**1013** A553 30k dark brown 1.00 .40
**1014** A553 60k Prussian green 2.00 .60
Set, never hinged 5.00

125th anniversary of the birth of Friedrich Engels, collaborator of Karl Marx.

Tank Leaving Assembly Line — A554

Designs: 30k, Harvesting wheat. 60k, Airplane designing. 1r, Moscow fireworks.

**1945, Dec. 25** **Photo.**

**1015** A554 20k indigo & brown 1.00 .25
**1016** A554 30k blk & org brn 1.00 .40
**1017** A554 60k brown & green 1.75 .60
**1018** A554 1r dk blue & org 2.25 .90
*Nos. 1015-1018 (4)* 6.00 2.15
Set, never hinged 15.00

Artillery Observer and Guns A558

Heavy Field Pieces A559

**1945, Dec.**

**1019** A558 30k brown 1.00 .50
**1020** A559 60k sepia 2.00 .75
Set, never hinged 7.00

Artillery Day, Nov. 19, 1945.

**Catalogue values for unused stamps in this section, from this point to the end of the section, are for Never Hinged items.**

Victory Medal — A560

Soldier with Victory Flag — A561

**1946, Jan. 23**

**1021** A560 30k dk violet .75 .25
**1022** A560 30k brown .75 .25
**1023** A560 60k greenish black 1.10 .25
**1024** A560 60k henna 1.10 .25
**1025** A561 60k black & dull red 3.75 1.10
*Nos. 1021-1025 (5)* 7.45 2.10

Arms of USSR — A562

Red Square — A563

**1946, Feb. 10**

**1026** A562 30k henna 1.00 .25
**1027** A563 45k henna 1.50 .25
**1028** A562 60k greenish black 2.50 .50
*Nos. 1026-1028 (3)* 5.00 1.00

Elections to the Supreme Soviet of the USSR, Feb. 10, 1946.

Artillery in Victory Parade — A564

Victory Parade A565

**1946, Feb. 23**

**1029** A564 60k dark brown 5.00 .50
**1030** A564 2r dull violet 15.00 1.00
**1031** A565 3r black & red 15.00 1.50
*Nos. 1029-1031 (3)* 35.00 3.00

Victory Parade, Moscow, June 24, 1945.

Order of Lenin — A566

Order of Red Star — A567

Medal of Hammer and Sickle A568

Order of Token of Veneration A569

Gold Star Medal — A570

Order of Red Banner — A571

Order of the Red Workers' Banner — A572

**Paper with network as in parenthesis**

**1946 Unwmk. Typo.** ***Perf. 12½x12***

**1032** A566 60k myr grn *(green)* 1.40 1.10
**1033** A567 60k dk vio brn *(brown)* 1.40 1.10
**1034** A568 60k plum *(pink)* 1.40 1.10
**1035** A569 60k dp blue *(green)* 1.40 1.10
**1036** A570 60k dk car *(salmon)* 1.40 1.10
**1037** A571 60k red *(salmon)* 1.40 1.10
**1038** A572 60k dk brn vio *(buff)* 1.40 1.10
*Nos. 1032-1038 (7)* 9.80 7.70

See Nos. 1650-1654.

Workers' Achievement of Distinction A573

Workers' Gallantry A574

Marshal's Star — A575

Defense of Soviet Trans-Arctic Regions — A576

Meritorious Service in Battle A577

Defense of Caucasus A578

Defense of Moscow — A579

Bravery — A580

**Paper with network as in parenthesis**

**1946**

**1039** A573 60k choc *(salmon)* 3.00 1.25
**1040** A574 60k brown *(salmon)* 3.00 1.25
**1041** A575 60k blue *(pale blue)* 3.00 1.25
**1042** A576 60k dk grn *(green)* 3.00 1.25
**1043** A577 60k dk blue *(green)* 3.00 1.25
**1044** A578 60k dk yel grn *(grn)* 3.00 1.25
**1045** A579 60k carmine *(pink)* 3.00 1.25
**1046** A580 60k dk violet *(blue)* 3.00 1.25
*Nos. 1039-1046 (8)* 24.00 10.00

A581

Maxim Gorki A582

**1946, June 18** **Photo.**

**1047** A581 30k brown 1.50 .25
**1048** A582 60k dark green 2.50 .25

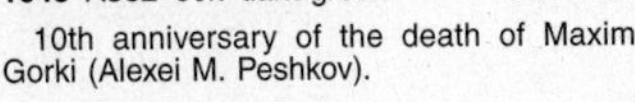
10th anniversary of the death of Maxim Gorki (Alexei M. Peshkov).

Kalinin — A583

**1946, June**

**1049** A583 20k sepia 2.00 .60

Mikhail Ivanovich Kalinin (1875-1946).

Chebyshev — A584

**1946, May 25**

**1050** A584 30k brown 1.25 .35
**1051** A584 60k gray brown 1.75 .65

Pafnuti Lvovich Chebyshev (1821-94), mathematician.

View of Sukhumi A585

Sanatorium at Sochi — A587

Designs: #1053, Promenade at Gagri. 45k, New Afyon Sanatorium.

**1946, June 18**

**1052** A585 15k dark brown 1.25 .25
**1053** A585 30k dk slate green 2.50 .25
**1054** A587 30k dark green 2.50 .25
**1055** A585 45k chestnut brown 3.75 .50
*Nos. 1052-1055 (4)* 10.00 1.25

All-Union Parade of Physical Culturists — A589

**1946, July 21**

**1056** A589 30k dark green 6.00 2.00

Tank Divisions in Red Square A590

**1946, Sept. 8**

**1057** A590 30k dark green 1.50 .40
**1058** A590 60k brown 2.50 .60

Honoring Soviet tankmen.

Belfry of Ivan the Great, Kremlin — A591

Bolshoi Theater, Moscow — A592

Hotel Moscow A593

Red Square — A597

Spasski Tower and Statues of Minin and Pozharski — A598

Moscow scenes: 20k, Bolshoi Theater, Sverdlov Square. 45k, View of Kremlin. 50k, Lenin Museum.

**1946, Sept. 5**

**1059** A591 5k brown 1.00 .25
**1060** A592 10k sepia 1.00 .25
**1061** A593 15k chestnut 1.00 .25
**1062** A593 20k light brown 2.00 .25
**1063** A593 45k dark green 4.50 .45
**1064** A593 50k brown 4.50 .50
**1065** A597 60k blue violet 10.00 .60
**1066** A598 1r chestnut brown 15.00 1.00
*Nos. 1059-1066 (8)* 39.00 3.55

Workers' Achievement of Distinction A599

Workers' Gallantry A600

Partisan of the Patriotic War — A601

Defense of Soviet Trans-Arctic Regions — A602

Meritorious Service in Battle A603

Defense of Caucasus A604

Defense of Moscow — A605

Bravery — A606

**1946, Sept. 5** **Engr.**

| | | | | |
|---|---|---|---|---|
| **1067** | A599 | 1r dark violet brown | 3.75 | 1.50 |
| **1068** | A600 | 1r dark carmine | 3.75 | 1.50 |
| **1069** | A601 | 1r carmine | 3.75 | 1.50 |
| **1070** | A602 | 1r blue black | 3.75 | 1.50 |
| **1071** | A603 | 1r black | 3.75 | 1.50 |
| **1072** | A604 | 1r black brown | 3.75 | 1.50 |
| **1073** | A605 | 1r olive black | 3.75 | 1.50 |
| **1074** | A606 | 1r deep claret | 3.75 | 1.50 |
| | | *Nos. 1067-1074 (8)* | 30.00 | 12.00 |

See Nos. 1650-1654.

Give the Country Each Year: 127 Million Tons of Grain A607

60 Million Tons of Oil — A608

60 Million Tons of Steel — A610

500 Million Tons of Coal — A609

50 Million Tons of Cast Iron — A611

***Perf. 12½x12***

**1946, Oct. 6** **Photo.** **Unwmk.**

| | | | | |
|---|---|---|---|---|
| **1075** | A607 | 5k olive brown | .25 | .25 |
| **1076** | A608 | 10k dk slate green | .50 | .25 |
| **1077** | A609 | 15k brown | .75 | .25 |
| **1078** | A610 | 20k dk blue violet | 1.50 | .25 |
| **1079** | A611 | 30k brown | 3.00 | .25 |
| | | *Nos. 1075-1079 (5)* | 6.00 | 1.25 |

Symbols of Transportation, Map and Stamps — A612

Early Soviet Stamp A613

Stamps of Soviet Russia — A614

**1946, Nov. 6** ***Perf. 12½***

| | | | | |
|---|---|---|---|---|
| **1080** | A612 | 15k blk & dk red | 2.00 | .55 |
| | *a.* | Sheet of 4, imperf. | 100.00 | 50.00 |
| **1081** | A613 | 30k dk grn & brn | 3.00 | .60 |
| | *a.* | Sheet of 4, imperf. | 100.00 | 50.00 |
| **1082** | A614 | 60k dk grn & blk | 5.00 | .85 |
| | *a.* | Sheet of 4, imperf. | 100.00 | 50.00 |
| | | *Nos. 1080-1082 (3)* | 10.00 | 2.00 |

1st Soviet postage stamp, 25th anniv.

Lenin and Stalin — A615

**1946** **Photo.** ***Perf. 12½***

| | | | | |
|---|---|---|---|---|
| **1083** | A615 | 30k dp brown org | 2.00 | 1.00 |
| | *a.* | Sheet of 4, imperf. | 75.00 | 35.00 |
| | *b.* | Single, imperf | 5.00 | 1.50 |
| **1084** | A615 | 30k dk green | 2.00 | 1.00 |
| | *a.* | Single, imperf | 5.00 | 1.50 |

October Revolution, 29th anniv.
Issued: #1083b-1084a, 11/6; #1083-1084, 12/18; #1083a, 6/47.

Dnieprostroy Dam and Power Station — A616

**1946, Dec. 23** ***Perf. 12½***

| | | | | |
|---|---|---|---|---|
| **1085** | A616 | 30k sepia | 2.00 | .60 |
| **1086** | A616 | 60k chalky blue | 4.00 | .90 |

Aleksandr P. Karpinsky — A617

**1947, Jan. 17** **Unwmk.**

| | | | | |
|---|---|---|---|---|
| **1087** | A617 | 30k dark green | 1.25 | .75 |
| **1088** | A617 | 50k sepia | 2.75 | 1.00 |

Karpinsky (1847-1936), geologist.

Canceled to Order

Canceled sets of new issues have long been sold by the government. Values in the second ("used") column are for these canceled-to-order stamps. Postally used stamps are worth more.

Nikolai A. Nekrasov — A618

**1946, Dec. 4**

| | | | | |
|---|---|---|---|---|
| **1089** | A618 | 30k sepia | 1.50 | .25 |
| **1090** | A618 | 60k brown | 2.50 | .75 |

Nikolai A. Nekrasov (1821-1878), poet.

Lenin's Mausoleum A619

Lenin — A620

**1947, Jan. 21**

| | | | | |
|---|---|---|---|---|
| **1091** | A619 | 30k slate blue | 2.50 | .65 |
| **1092** | A619 | 30k dark green | 2.50 | .65 |
| **1093** | A620 | 50k dark brown | 5.00 | 1.25 |
| | | *Nos. 1091-1093 (3)* | 10.00 | 2.55 |

23rd anniversary of the death of Lenin.
See Nos. 1197-1199.

F. P. Litke and Sailing Vessel A621

N. M. Przewalski, Mare and Foal — A622

**1947, Jan. 27**

| | | | | |
|---|---|---|---|---|
| **1094** | A621 | 20k blue violet | 4.75 | 1.10 |
| **1095** | A621 | 20k sepia | 4.75 | 1.10 |
| **1096** | A622 | 60k olive brown | 10.50 | 1.40 |
| **1097** | A622 | 60k sepia | 10.50 | 1.40 |
| | | *Nos. 1094-1097 (4)* | 30.50 | 5.00 |

Soviet Union Geographical Society, cent.

Nikolai E. Zhukovski (1847-1921), Scientist A623

**1947, Jan. 17**

| | | | | |
|---|---|---|---|---|
| **1098** | A623 | 30k sepia | 1.50 | .30 |
| **1099** | A623 | 60k blue violet | 2.25 | .45 |

Stalin Prize Medal — A624

**1946, Dec. 21** **Photo.**

| | | | | |
|---|---|---|---|---|
| **1100** | A624 | 30k black brown | 7.50 | .50 |

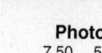

Russian Soldier A625

Military Instruction A626

Aviator, Sailor and Soldier A627

***Perf. 12x12½, 12½x12***

**1947, Feb. 23** **Unwmk.**

| | | | | |
|---|---|---|---|---|
| **1101** | A625 | 20k sepia | 2.50 | .50 |
| **1102** | A626 | 30k slate blue | 3.75 | .75 |
| **1103** | A627 | 30k brown | 3.75 | .75 |
| | | *Nos. 1101-1103 (3)* | 10.00 | 2.00 |

***Imperf***

| | | | | |
|---|---|---|---|---|
| **1101A** | A625 | 20k sepia | 2.50 | .50 |
| **1102A** | A626 | 30k slate blue | 3.75 | .75 |
| **1103A** | A627 | 30k brown | 3.75 | .75 |
| | | *Nos. 1101A-1103A (3)* | 10.00 | 2.00 |

29th anniversary of the Soviet Army.

Reprints

From here through 1953 many sets exist in two distinct printings from different plates.

**Arms of**

Russian Socialist Federated Soviet Republic — A628

Armenian SSR — A629

Azerbaijan SSR — A630

Byelorussian SSR — A631

Estonian SSR — A632

Georgian SSR — A633

Karelo Finnish SSR — A634

Kazakh SSR — A635

Kirghiz SSR — A636

Latvian SSR — A637

Lithuanian SSR — A638

Moldavian SSR — A639

Tadzhkistan SSR — A640

Turkmen SSR — A641

Ukrainian SSR — A642

Uzbek SSR — A643

Soviet Union — A644

**1947 Unwmk. Photo.** *Perf. 12½*

| | | | | |
|---|---|---|---|---|
| **1104** | A628 | 30k henna brown | 3.25 | .50 |
| **1105** | A629 | 30k chestnut | 3.25 | .50 |
| **1106** | A630 | 30k olive brown | 3.25 | .50 |
| **1107** | A631 | 30k olive green | 3.25 | .50 |
| **1108** | A632 | 30k violet black | 3.25 | .50 |
| **1109** | A633 | 30k dark vio brown | 3.25 | .50 |
| **1110** | A634 | 30k dark violet | 3.25 | .50 |
| **1111** | A635 | 30k deep orange | 3.25 | .50 |
| **1112** | A636 | 30k dark violet | 3.25 | .50 |
| **1113** | A637 | 30k yellow brown | 3.25 | .50 |
| **1114** | A638 | 30k dk ol grn | 3.25 | .50 |
| **1115** | A639 | 30k dk vio brn | 3.25 | .50 |
| **1116** | A640 | 30k dark green | 3.25 | .50 |
| **1117** | A641 | 30k gray black | 3.25 | .50 |
| **1118** | A642 | 30k blue violet | 3.25 | .50 |
| **1119** | A643 | 30k brown | 3.25 | .50 |

**Litho.**

| | | | | |
|---|---|---|---|---|
| **1120** | A644 | 1r dk brn, bl, gold & red | 8.00 | 2.00 |
| | | *Nos. 1104-1120 (17)* | 60.00 | 10.00 |

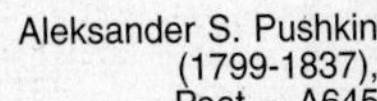
Aleksander S. Pushkin (1799-1837), Poet — A645

**1947, Feb. Photo.** *Perf. 12*

| | | | | |
|---|---|---|---|---|
| **1121** | A645 | 30k sepia | 2.00 | .35 |
| **1122** | A645 | 50k dk yellow green | 3.00 | .75 |

Classroom A646

Parade of Women — A647

**1947, Mar. 11**

| | | | | |
|---|---|---|---|---|
| **1123** | A646 | 15k bright blue | 2.00 | .60 |
| **1124** | A647 | 30k red | 3.00 | .90 |

Intl. Day of Women, Mar. 8, 1947.

Moscow Council Building A648

**1947** *Perf. 12½*

| | | | | |
|---|---|---|---|---|
| **1125** | A648 | 30k sep, gray blue & brick red | 3.00 | 1.00 |

30th anniversary of the Moscow Soviet. Exists imperf. The imperf. exists also with gray blue omitted.

Both perf. and imperf. stamps exist in two sizes: 40x27mm and 41x27mm.

May Day Parade in Red Square — A649

**1947, June 10** *Perf. 12½*

| | | | | |
|---|---|---|---|---|
| **1126** | A649 | 30k scarlet | 1.50 | .60 |
| **1127** | A649 | 1r dk olive green | 4.50 | 2.00 |

Labor Day, May 1, 1947.

**Nos. 1062, 1064-1066 Ovptd. in Red**

**1947, Sept.** *Perf. 12½x12*

| | | | | |
|---|---|---|---|---|
| **1128** | A593 | 20k lt brown | 2.00 | .40 |
| **1129** | A593 | 50k brown | 4.00 | 1.00 |
| **1130** | A597 | 60k blue violet | 6.00 | 1.20 |
| **1131** | A598 | 1r chestnut brown | 8.00 | 1.40 |
| | | *Nos. 1128-1131 (4)* | 20.00 | 4.00 |

Overprint arranged in 4 lines on No. 1131.

Crimea Bridge, Moscow — A650

Gorki Street, Moscow A651

View of Kremlin, Moscow — A652

Designs: No. 1134, Central Telegraph Building. No. 1135, Kiev Railroad Station. No. 1136, Kazan Railroad Station. No. 1137, Kaluga St. No. 1138, Pushkin Square. 50k, View of Kremlin. No. 1141, Grand Kremlin Palace. No. 1142, "Old Moscow," by Vasnetsov. No. 1143, St. Basil Cathedral. 2r, View of Kremlin. 3r, View of Kremlin. 5r, Hotel Moscow and government building.

**1947 Photo.** *Perf. 12½*

**Various Frames, Dated 1147-1947**

| | | | | |
|---|---|---|---|---|
| **1132** | A650 | 5k dk bl & dk brn | *.50* | .50 |
| **1133** | A651 | 10k red brn & brn blk | *.50* | .50 |
| **1134** | A650 | 30k brown | *1.20* | .80 |
| **1135** | A650 | 30k dk Prus blue | *1.20* | .80 |
| **1136** | A650 | 30k ultra | *1.20* | .80 |
| **1137** | A650 | 30k dp yel green | *1.20* | .80 |
| **1138** | A651 | 30k yel green | *1.20* | .80 |
| **1139** | A650 | 50k dp yel green | *1.80* | 1.00 |
| **1140** | A652 | 60k red brn & brn blk | *1.90* | 1.20 |
| **1141** | A651 | 60k gray blue | *2.75* | 1.50 |
| **1142** | A651 | 1r dark violet | *4.25* | 2.50 |

**Typo.**

**Colors: Blue, Yellow and Red**

| | | | | |
|---|---|---|---|---|
| **1143** | A651 | 1r multicolored | *4.25* | 2.50 |
| **1144** | A651 | 2r multicolored | *8.50* | 6.00 |
| **1145** | A650 | 3r multicolored | *15.00* | 8.00 |
| *a.* | | Souv. sheet of 4, imperf. | *35.00* | 20.00 |
| **1146** | A650 | 5r multicolored | *25.00* | 16.00 |
| | | *Nos. 1132-1146 (15)* | *70.45* | 43.70 |

Nos. 1128-1146 for founding of Moscow, 800th anniv.

Nos. 1143-1146 were printed in a single sheet containing a row of each denomination plus a row of labels.

Karamyshevsky Dam — A653

Map Showing Moscow-Volga Canal — A654

Designs: No. 1148, Direction towers, Yakromsky Lock. 45k, Yakromsky Pumping Station. 50k, Khimki Terminal. 1r, Lock #8.

**1947, Sept. 7 Photo.**

| | | | | |
|---|---|---|---|---|
| **1147** | A653 | 30k sepia | 2.50 | .50 |
| **1148** | A653 | 30k red brown | 2.50 | .50 |
| **1149** | A653 | 45k henna brown | 3.25 | .50 |
| **1150** | A653 | 50k bright ultra | 3.75 | .50 |
| **1151** | A654 | 60k bright rose | 4.25 | .50 |
| **1152** | A653 | 1r violet | 7.75 | 1.00 |
| | | *Nos. 1147-1152 (6)* | 24.00 | 3.50 |

Moscow-Volga Canal, 10th anniversary.

Elektrozavodskaya Station — A655

Mayakovsky Station — A656

Moscow Subway scenes: No. 1154, Ismailovsky Station. No. 1155, Sokol Station. No. 1156, Stalinsky Station. No. 1158, Kiev Station.

**1947, Sept.**

| | | | | |
|---|---|---|---|---|
| **1153** | A655 | 30k sepia | 2.40 | .55 |
| **1154** | A655 | 30k blue black | 2.40 | .55 |
| **1155** | A655 | 45k yellow brown | 3.00 | .60 |
| **1156** | A655 | 45k deep violet | 3.00 | .60 |
| **1157** | A656 | 60k henna brown | 4.50 | .80 |
| **1158** | A655 | 60k deep yel grn | 4.50 | .80 |
| | | *Nos. 1153-1158 (6)* | 19.80 | 3.90 |

Planes and Flag — A657

**1947, Sept. 1**

| | | | | |
|---|---|---|---|---|
| **1159** | A657 | 30k deep violet | 3.00 | .40 |
| **1160** | A657 | 1r bright ultra | 7.00 | .60 |

Day of the Air Fleet. For overprints see Nos. 1246-1247.

Spasski Tower, Kremlin — A658

*Perf. 12½*

**1947, Nov. Unwmk. Typo.**

| | | | | |
|---|---|---|---|---|
| **1161** | A658 | 60k dark red | 18.00 | 4.50 |

See No. 1260.

Agave Plant at Sukhumi — A659

Gullripsh Sanatorium, Sukhumi A660

Peasants', Livadia A661

New Riviera A662

Russian sanatoria: No. 1166, Abkhasia, New Afyon. No. 1167, Kemeri, near Riga. No. 1168, Kirov Memorial, Kislovodsk. No. 1169, Voroshilov Memorial, Sochi. No. 1170, Riza, Gagri. No. 1171, Zapadugol, Sochi.

**1947, Nov.** **Photo.**

| | | | | |
|---|---|---|---|---|
| **1162** | A659 | 30k dark green | 3.50 | .50 |
| **1163** | A660 | 30k violet | 3.50 | .50 |
| **1164** | A661 | 30k olive | 3.50 | .50 |
| **1165** | A662 | 30k brown | 3.50 | .50 |
| **1166** | A660 | 30k red brown | 3.50 | .50 |
| **1167** | A660 | 30k black violet | 3.50 | .50 |
| **1168** | A660 | 30k bright ultra | 3.50 | .50 |
| **1169** | A660 | 30k dk brown violet | 3.50 | .50 |
| **1170** | A659 | 30k dk yel green | 3.50 | .50 |
| **1171** | A660 | 30k sepia | 3.50 | .50 |
| | | *Nos. 1162-1171 (10)* | 35.00 | 5.00 |

Blast Furnaces, Constantine A663

Tractor Plant, Kharkov A664

Tractor Plant, Stalingrad A665

Maxim Gorki Theater, Stalingrad A666

20k, No. 1180, Kirov foundry, Makeevka. Nos. 1175, 1179, Agricultural machine plant, Rostov.

**1947, Nov.** ***Perf. 12½***

| | | | | |
|---|---|---|---|---|
| **1172** | A663 | 15k yellow brown | .35 | .25 |
| **1173** | A663 | 20k sepia | .60 | .25 |
| **1174** | A663 | 30k violet brown | .85 | .25 |
| **1175** | A663 | 30k dark green | .85 | .25 |
| **1176** | A664 | 30k brown | .85 | .25 |
| **1177** | A665 | 30k black brown | .85 | .25 |
| **1178** | A666 | 60k violet brown | 1.60 | .70 |
| **1179** | A663 | 60k yellow brown | 1.60 | .70 |
| **1180** | A663 | 1r orange red | 3.50 | 1.40 |
| **1181** | A664 | 1r red | 3.50 | 1.40 |
| **1182** | A665 | 1r violet | 3.50 | 1.40 |
| | | *Nos. 1172-1182 (11)* | 18.05 | 7.10 |

***Imperf***

| | | | | |
|---|---|---|---|---|
| **1172A** | A663 | 15k yellow brown | .35 | .25 |
| **1173A** | A663 | 20k sepia | .60 | .25 |
| **1174A** | A663 | 30k violet brown | .85 | .25 |
| **1175A** | A663 | 30k dark green | .85 | .25 |
| **1176A** | A664 | 30k brown | .85 | .25 |
| **1177A** | A665 | 30k black brown | .85 | .25 |
| **1178A** | A666 | 60k violet brown | 1.60 | .70 |
| **1179A** | A663 | 60k yellow brown | 1.60 | .70 |
| **1180A** | A663 | 1r orange red | 3.50 | 1.40 |
| **1181A** | A664 | 1r red | 3.50 | 1.40 |
| **1182A** | A665 | 1r violet | 3.50 | 1.40 |
| | | *Nos. 1172A-1182A (11)* | 18.05 | 7.10 |

Reconstruction of war-damaged cities and factories, and as Five-Year-Plan publicity.

Revolutionists — A667

Designs: 30k, No. 1185, Revolutionists. 50k, 1r, Industry. No. 1186, 2r, Agriculture.

**1947, Nov.** ***Perf. 12½***

**Frame in Dark Red**

| | | | | |
|---|---|---|---|---|
| **1183** | A667 | 30k greenish black | 2.00 | .30 |
| **1184** | A667 | 50k blue black | 3.00 | .40 |
| **1185** | A667 | 60k brown black | 5.00 | .55 |
| **1186** | A667 | 60k brown | 5.00 | .55 |
| **1187** | A667 | 1r black | 8.00 | .95 |
| **1188** | A667 | 2r greenish black | 15.00 | 1.50 |
| | | *Nos. 1183-1188 (6)* | 38.00 | 4.25 |

***Imperf***

| | | | | |
|---|---|---|---|---|
| **1183A** | A667 | 30k greenish black | 1.00 | .30 |
| **1184A** | A667 | 50k blue black | 1.50 | .40 |
| **1185A** | A667 | 60k brown black | 2.50 | .55 |
| **1186A** | A667 | 60k brown | 2.50 | .55 |
| **1187A** | A667 | 1r black | 4.00 | .95 |
| **1188A** | A667 | 2r greenish black | 7.50 | 1.50 |
| | | *Nos. 1183A-1188A (6)* | 19.00 | 4.25 |

30th anniversary of October Revolution.

Palace of the Arts (Winter Palace) A668

Peter I Monument — A669

Designs (Leningrad in 1947): 60k, Sts. Peter and Paul Fortress. 1r, Smolny Institute.

**1948, Jan. 10** ***Perf. 12½***

| | | | | |
|---|---|---|---|---|
| **1189** | A668 | 30k violet | 3.00 | 1.10 |
| **1190** | A669 | 50k dk slate green | 5.00 | 1.25 |
| **1191** | A668 | 60k sepia | 6.00 | 2.40 |
| **1192** | A669 | 1r dk brown violet | 11.00 | 3.25 |
| | | *Nos. 1189-1192 (4)* | 25.00 | 8.00 |

5th anniversary of the relief of the siege of Leningrad from the German blockade.

Government Building, Kiev — A670

50k, Dnieprostroy Dam. 60k, Wheat field, granary. 1r, Steel mill, coal mine.

**1948, Jan. 25** ***Perf. 12½***

| | | | | |
|---|---|---|---|---|
| **1193** | A670 | 30k indigo | 2.00 | .40 |
| **1194** | A670 | 50k violet | 2.75 | .50 |
| **1195** | A670 | 60k golden brown | 4.00 | .85 |
| **1196** | A670 | 1r sepia | 6.25 | 2.25 |
| | | *Nos. 1193-1196 (4)* | 15.00 | 4.00 |

Ukrainian SSR, 30th anniv.

**Lenin Types of 1947 Inscribed "1924-1948"**

**1948, Jan. 21** **Unwmk.**

| | | | | |
|---|---|---|---|---|
| **1197** | A619 | 30k brown violet | 8.00 | 3.00 |
| **1198** | A619 | 60k dark gray blue | 8.00 | 3.00 |
| **1199** | A620 | 60k dp yel grn | 8.00 | 3.00 |
| | | *Nos. 1197-1199 (3)* | 24.00 | 9.00 |

24th anniversary of the death of Lenin.

Vasili I. Surikov — A672

**1948, Feb. 15** **Photo.** ***Perf. 12***

| | | | | |
|---|---|---|---|---|
| **1201** | A672 | 30k red brown | 3.50 | .75 |
| **1202** | A672 | 60k dark green | 6.50 | 1.25 |

Vasili Ivanovich Surikov, artist, birth cent.

Soviet Soldier and Artillery — A675

Fliers and Planes A676

No. 1206, Soviet sailor. 60k, Military class.

**1948, Feb. 23**

| | | | | |
|---|---|---|---|---|
| **1205** | A675 | 30k brown | 2.50 | .65 |
| **1206** | A675 | 30k gray | 2.50 | .65 |
| **1207** | A676 | 30k violet blue | 2.50 | .65 |
| **1208** | A676 | 60k red brown | 7.50 | 2.00 |
| | | *Nos. 1205-1208 (4)* | 15.00 | 3.95 |

**Hero Types of 1944**

Designs: No. 1209, N.A. Shchors. No. 1210, V.I. Chapayev. No. 1211, S.G. Lazo.

**1948, Feb. 23**

| | | | | |
|---|---|---|---|---|
| **1209** | A494 | 60k deep green | 6.50 | 1.75 |
| **1210** | A494 | 60k yellow brown | 6.50 | 1.75 |
| **1211** | A494 | 60k violet blue | 6.50 | 1.75 |
| | | *Nos. 1209-1211 (3)* | 19.50 | 5.25 |

Nos. 1205-1211 for Soviet army, 30th anniv.

Karl Marx, Friedrich Engels and Communist Manifesto A677

**1948, Apr.**

| | | | | |
|---|---|---|---|---|
| **1212** | A677 | 30k black | 1.50 | .25 |
| **1213** | A677 | 50k henna brown | 3.50 | .30 |

Centenary of the Communist Manifesto.

Miner A678

Marine A679

Aviator A680

Woman Farmer A681

Arms of USSR A682

Scientist A683

Spasski Tower, Kremlin A684

Soldier A685

**1948** **Photo.**

| | | | | |
|---|---|---|---|---|
| **1214** | A678 | 5k sepia | .50 | .30 |
| **1215** | A679 | 10k violet | .85 | .30 |
| **1216** | A680 | 15k bright blue | 1.25 | .85 |
| **1217** | A681 | 20k brown | 1.50 | .75 |
| **1218** | A682 | 30k henna brown | 2.50 | 1.25 |
| **1219** | A683 | 45k brown violet | 5.00 | 1.90 |
| **1220** | A684 | 50k bright blue | 7.00 | 3.00 |
| **1221** | A685 | 60k bright green | 8.50 | 4.25 |
| | | *Nos. 1214-1221 (8)* | 27.10 | 12.60 |

See Nos. 1306, 1343-1347, 1689.

May Day Parade in Red Square — A686

**1948, June 5** ***Perf. 12***

| | | | | |
|---|---|---|---|---|
| **1222** | A686 | 30k deep car rose | 5.00 | .80 |
| **1223** | A686 | 60k bright blue | 15.00 | 1.25 |

Labor Day, May 1, 1948.

Vissarion G. Belinski (1811-48), Literary Critic — A687

**1948, June 7** **Unwmk.** ***Perf. 12***

| | | | | |
|---|---|---|---|---|
| **1224** | A687 | 30k brown | 5.00 | 1.00 |
| **1225** | A687 | 50k dark green | 7.50 | 2.00 |
| **1226** | A687 | 60k purple | 15.00 | 2.00 |
| | | *Nos. 1224-1226 (3)* | 27.50 | 5.00 |

Aleksandr N. Ostrovski
A690 A691

**1948, June 10 Photo. *Perf. 12***

**1227** A690 30k bright green 4.50 2.50
**1228** A691 60k brown 9.00 4.50
**1229** A691 1r brown violet 15.00 8.00
*Nos. 1227-1229 (3)* 28.50 15.00

Ostrovski (1823-1886), playwright. Exist imperf. Value, set $250.

Ivan I. Shishkin (1832-1898), Painter — A692

"Field of Rye," by Shishkin A693

60k, "Bears in a Forest," by Shishkin.

**Photo. (30k, 1r), Typo. (50k, 60k)**
**1948, June 12**

**1230** A692 30k dk grn & vio brn 13.00 3.50
**1231** A693 50k multicolored 20.00 7.50
**1232** A693 60k multicolored 30.00 8.00
**1233** A692 1r brn & bl blk 37.50 21.00
*Nos. 1230-1233 (4)* 100.50 40.00

Industrial Expansion A694

Public Gathering at Leningrad — A695

**Photo., Frames Litho. in Carmine**
**1948, June 25**

**1234** A694 15k red brown 3.50 1.00
**1235** A695 30k slate 4.50 1.50
**1236** A694 60k brown black 7.00 2.75
*Nos. 1234-1236 (3)* 15.00 5.25

Industrial five-year plan.

Planting Crops A696

Nos. 1238, 1243, Gathering vegetables. Nos. 1239, 1241, Baling cotton. No. 1240, Planting Crops. No. 1242, Harvesting grain.

**1948, July 12 Photo.**

**1237** A696 30k carmine rose .75 .30
**1238** A696 30k blue green .75 .30
**1239** A696 45k red brown 1.50 .70
**1240** A696 50k brown black 2.25 .70
**1241** A696 60k dark green 2.10 .80
**1242** A696 60k dk blue green 2.10 .80
**1243** A696 1r purple 5.50 1.40
*Nos. 1237-1243 (7)* 14.95 5.00

Agricultural five-year plan.

Arms and Citizens of USSR — A697

**Photo., Frames Litho. in Scarlet**
**1948, July 25**

**1244** A697 30k blue black 10.00 2.50
**1245** A697 60k greenish black 15.00 5.00

25th anniv. of the USSR.

Nos. 1159 and 1160 Overprinted in Red

**1948, Aug. 24 *Perf. 12½***

**1246** A657 30k deep violet 3.00 2.50
**1247** A657 1r bright ultra 10.00 2.50

Air Fleet Day, 1948. On sale one day.

Soviet Miners — A698

Miner's Day, Aug. 29: 60k, Scene in mine. 1r, Miner's badge.

**1948, Aug. Photo. *Perf. 12½x12***

**1248** A698 30k blue 3.00 .35
**1249** A698 60k purple 6.00 .45
**1250** A698 1r green 11.00 1.20
*Nos. 1248-1250 (3)* 20.00 2.00

A. A. Zhdanov — A699

**1948, Sept. 3**

**1251** A699 40k slate 4.00 2.00

Andrei A. Zhdanov, statesman, 1896-1948.

Soviet Sailor — A700

**1948, Sept. 12 *Perf. 12***

**1252** A700 30k blue green 6.00 3.00
**1253** A700 60k bright blue 14.00 5.00

Navy Day, Sept. 12.

Slalom A701

Motorcyclist — A702

Designs: No. 1254, Foot race. 30k, Soccer game. 45k, Motorboat race. 50k, Diving.

**1948, Sept. 15 *Perf. 12½x12***

**1253A** A701 15k dark blue 2.50 .25
**1254** A702 15k violet 1.00 .25
**1254A** A702 20k dk slate blue 3.50 .55
**1255** A701 30k brown 2.00 .25
**1256** A701 45k sepia 3.00 .35
**1257** A702 50k blue 3.00 .35
*Nos. 1253A-1257 (6)* 15.00 2.00

Tankmen Group A703

Design: 1r, Tank parade.

**1948, Sept. 25**

**1258** A703 30k sepia 4.50 1.50
**1259** A703 1r rose 10.50 3.50

Day of the Tankmen, Sept. 25.

**Spasski Tower Type of 1947**

**1948 Litho. *Perf. 12x12½***

**1260** A658 1r brown red 2.00 .25

No. 1260 was re-issued in 1954-56 in slightly smaller format: 14½x21½mm, instead of 14¾x22mm and in a paler shade. See note after No. 738.

Train — A704

Transportation 5-year plan: 60k, Auto and bus at intersection. 1r, Steamships at anchor.

**1948, Sept. 30 Photo. *Perf. 12½x12***

**1261** A704 30k brown 30.00 7.50
**1262** A704 50k dark green 60.00 10.00
**1263** A704 60k blue 100.00 12.50
**1264** A704 1r blue violet 100.00 20.00
*Nos. 1261-1264 (4)* 290.00 50.00

Horses A705

Livestock 5-year plan: 60k, Dairy farm.

**1948, Sept. 30 *Perf. 12***

**1265** A705 30k slate gray 11.00 4.00
**1266** A705 60k bright green 19.00 6.50
**1267** A705 1r brown 35.00 9.50
*Nos. 1265-1267 (3)* 65.00 20.00

Pouring Molten Metal A706

Designs: 60k, 1r, Iron pipe manufacture.

**1948, Oct. 14 *Perf. 12½***

**1268** A706 30k purple 3.00 .75
**1269** A706 50k brown 3.00 1.00
**1270** A706 60k carmine 3.00 1.25
**1271** A706 1r dull blue 3.00 2.00
*Nos. 1268-1271 (4)* 12.00 5.00

Heavy Machinery Plant A707

Design: 60k, Pump station interior.

**1948, Oct. 14**

**1272** A707 30k purple 10.00 .75
**1273** A707 50k sepia 5.00 1.25
**1274** A707 60k brown 10.00 1.40
*Nos. 1272-1274 (3)* 25.00 3.40

Nos. 1268-1274 publicize the 5-year plan for steel, iron and machinery industries.

Khachatur Abovian (1809-1848), Armenian Writer and Poet — A708

**1948, Oct. 16 *Perf. 12x12½***

**1275** A708 40k purple 7.00 2.50
**1276** A708 50k deep green 8.00 2.50

Farkhatz Hydroelectric Station A709

Design: 60k, Zouiev Hydroelectric Station.

**1948, Oct. 24 *Perf. 12½***

**1277** A709 30k green 15.00 5.00
**1278** A709 60k red 15.00 5.00
**1279** A709 1r carmine rose 15.00 5.00
*Nos. 1277-1279 (3)* 45.00 15.00

Electrification five-year plan.

Coal Mine — A710

Designs: Nos. 1282, 1283, Oil field and tank cars.

**1948, Oct. 24**

**1280** A710 30k sepia 25.00 1.25
**1281** A710 60k brown 35.00 2.50
**1282** A710 60k red brown 35.00 2.50
**1283** A710 1r blue green 115.00 3.75
*Nos. 1280-1283 (4)* 210.00 10.00

Coal mining and oil production 5-year plan.

Flying Model Planes — A712

Marching Pioneers A713

Pioneers Saluting — A714

60k, Pioneer bugler. 1r, Pioneers at campfire.

**1948, Oct. 26** ***Perf. 12½***

| | | | | |
|---|---|---|---|---|
| 1284 | A712 | 30k dark bl grn | 30.00 | 4.25 |
| 1285 | A713 | 45k dark violet | 40.00 | 5.50 |
| 1286 | A714 | 45k deep carmine | 32.50 | 4.75 |
| 1287 | A714 | 60k deep ultra | 45.00 | 7.25 |
| 1288 | A713 | 1r deep blue | 100.00 | 13.00 |
| | | *Nos. 1284-1288 (5)* | 247.50 | 34.75 |

Young Pioneers, a Soviet youth organization, and governmental supervision of children's summer vacations.

Marching Youths A715

Farm Girl — A716

League Members and Flag — A717

Designs: 50k, Communist students. 1r, Flag and badges. 2r, Young worker.

**Inscribed: "1918 1948 XXX"**

**1948, Oct. 29** ***Perf. 12½***

| | | | | |
|---|---|---|---|---|
| 1289 | A715 | 20k violet brown | 12.50 | 1.25 |
| 1290 | A716 | 25k rose red | 13.50 | 1.60 |
| 1291 | A717 | 40k brown & red | 22.50 | 2.00 |
| 1292 | A715 | 50k blue green | 29.00 | 3.25 |
| 1293 | A717 | 1r multicolored | 95.00 | 14.50 |
| 1294 | A716 | 2r purple | 50.00 | 11.00 |
| | | *Nos. 1289-1294 (6)* | 222.50 | 33.60 |

30th anniversary of the Young Communist League (Komsomol).

Stage of Moscow Art Theater A719

K. S. Stanislavski, V. I. Nemirovich Danchenko A720

**1948, Nov. 1** ***Perf. 12½***

| | | | | |
|---|---|---|---|---|
| 1295 | A719 | 40k gray blue | 6.50 | 3.50 |
| 1296 | A720 | 1r violet brown | 9.50 | 4.50 |

Moscow Art Theater, 50th anniv.

Flag and Moscow Buildings — A721

**1948, Nov. 7** ***Perf. 12½***

| | | | | |
|---|---|---|---|---|
| 1297 | A721 | 40k red | 5.00 | 2.25 |
| 1298 | A721 | 1r green | 10.00 | 2.75 |

31st anniversary of October Revolution.

House of Unions, Moscow A722

Player's Badge (Rook and Chessboard) A723

**1948, Nov. 20** ***Perf. 12½***

| | | | | |
|---|---|---|---|---|
| 1299 | A722 | 30k greenish blue | 2.50 | .35 |
| 1300 | A723 | 40k violet | 6.25 | .50 |
| 1301 | A722 | 50k orange brown | 6.25 | .90 |
| | | *Nos. 1299-1301 (3)* | 15.00 | 1.75 |

16th Chess Championship.

Artillery Salute A724

**1948, Nov. 19** ***Perf. 12½***

| | | | | |
|---|---|---|---|---|
| 1302 | A724 | 30k blue | 30.00 | 10.00 |
| 1303 | A724 | 1r rose carmine | 70.00 | 25.00 |

Artillery Day, Nov. 19, 1948.

Vasili Petrovich Stasov — A725

Stasov and Barracks of Paul's Regiment, Petrograd A726

**1948, Nov. 27** **Unwmk.**

| | | | | |
|---|---|---|---|---|
| 1304 | A725 | 40k brown | 6.50 | 1.75 |
| 1305 | A726 | 1r sepia | 13.50 | 3.25 |

Stasov (1769-1848), architect.

**Arms Type of 1948**

**1948** **Litho.** ***Perf. 12x12½***

| | | | | |
|---|---|---|---|---|
| 1306 | A682 | 40k brown red | 50.00 | 3.00 |

See No. 1689.

Y. M. Sverdlov Monument A727

Design: 40k, Lenin Street, Sverdlovsk.

**1948** **Photo.** ***Perf. 12½***

| | | | | |
|---|---|---|---|---|
| 1307 | A727 | 30k blue | 1.00 | .25 |
| 1308 | A727 | 40k purple | 1.25 | .35 |
| 1309 | A727 | 1r bright green | 2.50 | .60 |
| | | *Nos. 1307-1309 (3)* | 4.75 | 1.20 |

225th anniv. of the city of Sverdlovsk (before 1924, Ekaterinburg). Exist imperf. Value, set $20.00.

"Swallow's Nest," Crimea A729

Hot Spring, Piatigorsk A730

Shoreline, Sukhumi A731

Tree-lined Walk, Sochi A732

Formal Gardens, Sochi A733

Stalin Highway, Sochi — A734

Colonnade, Kislovodsk A735

Seascape, Gagri — A736

**1948, Dec. 30** ***Perf. 12½***

| | | | | |
|---|---|---|---|---|
| 1310 | A729 | 40k brown | 6.25 | .60 |
| 1311 | A730 | 40k bright red violet | 6.25 | .60 |
| 1312 | A731 | 40k dark green | 6.25 | .60 |
| 1313 | A732 | 40k violet | 6.25 | .60 |
| 1314 | A733 | 40k dark purple | 6.25 | .60 |
| 1315 | A734 | 40k dark blue green | 6.25 | .60 |
| 1316 | A735 | 40k bright blue | 6.25 | .60 |
| 1317 | A736 | 40k dark blue green | 6.25 | .60 |
| | | *Nos. 1310-1317 (8)* | 50.00 | 4.80 |

Byelorussian S.S.R. Arms — A737

**1949, Jan. 4**

| | | | | |
|---|---|---|---|---|
| 1318 | A737 | 40k henna brown | 6.00 | 2.00 |
| 1319 | A737 | 1r blue green | 9.00 | 3.00 |

Byelorussian SSR, 30th anniv.

Mikhail V. Lomonosov — A738

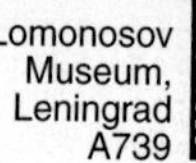

Lomonosov Museum, Leningrad A739

**1949, Jan. 10**

| | | | | |
|---|---|---|---|---|
| 1320 | A738 | 40k red brown | 7.00 | *3.50* |
| 1321 | A738 | 50k green | 9.00 | 3.50 |
| 1322 | A739 | 1r deep blue | 20.00 | 8.00 |
| | | *Nos. 1320-1322 (3)* | 36.00 | 15.00 |

Cape Dezhnev (East Cape) A740

Design: 1r, Map and Dezhnev's ship.

**1949, Jan. 30**

| | | | | |
|---|---|---|---|---|
| 1323 | A740 | 40k olive green | 12.50 | 5.00 |
| 1324 | A740 | 1r gray | 27.50 | 10.00 |

300th anniv. of the discovery of the strait between Asia and America by S. I. Dezhnev.

**Souvenir Sheet**

A741

**1949, Dec.** ***Imperf.***

| | | | | |
|---|---|---|---|---|
| 1325 | A741 | Sheet of 4 | 500.00 | 300.00 |
| | | Hinged | 200.00 | |
| *a.* | | 40k Stalin's birthplace, Gorki | 25.00 | *35.00* |
| *b.* | | 40k Lenin & Stalin, Leningrad, 1917 | 25.00 | *35.00* |
| *c.* | | 40k Lenin & Stalin, Gorki | 25.00 | *35.00* |
| *d.* | | 40k Marshal Stalin | 25.00 | *35.00* |

70th birthday of Joseph V. Stalin.

Lenin Mausoleum — A742

**1949, Jan. 21** ***Perf. 12½***

| | | | | |
|---|---|---|---|---|
| 1326 | A742 | 40k ol grn & org brn | 15.00 | 7.50 |
| 1327 | A742 | 1r gray blk & org brn | 25.00 | 12.50 |
| *a.* | | Sheet of 4 | 600.00 | 500.00 |

25th anniversary of the death of Lenin.

No. 1327a exists imperf. Value $975 mint, $3,000 used.

Admiral S. O. Makarov — A743

**1949, Mar. 15**

**1328** A743 40k blue 8.00 4.00
**1329** A743 1r red brown 17.00 6.00

Centenary of the birth of Admiral Stepan Osipovich Makarov, shipbuilder.

Kirov Military Medical Academy A744

Professors Botkin, Pirogov and Sechenov A745

**1949, Mar. 24**

**1330** A744 40k red brown 6.00 3.00
**1331** A745 50k blue 12.00 5.00
**1332** A744 1r blue green 12.00 6.50
*Nos. 1330-1332 (3)* 30.00 14.50

150th anniversary of the foundation of Kirov Military Medical Academy, Leningrad.

Soviet Soldier A746

**1949, Mar. 16** **Photo.**

**1333** A746 40k rose red 20.00 10.00

31st anniversary of the Soviet army.

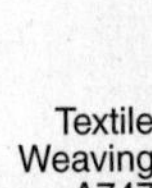

Textile Weaving A747

Political Leadership — A748

Designs: 25k, Preschool teaching. No. 1337, School teaching. No. 1338, Farm women. 1r, Women athletes.

**Inscribed: "8 MAPTA 1949r"**

**1949, Mar. 8** ***Perf. 12½***

**1334** A747 20k dark violet .45 .25
**1335** A747 25k blue .60 .25
**1336** A748 40k henna brown .80 .25
**1337** A747 50k slate gray 1.50 .35
**1338** A747 50k brown 1.50 .35
**1339** A747 1r green 4.00 .50
**1340** A748 2r copper red 6.00 1.50
*Nos. 1334-1340 (7)* 14.85 3.45

International Women's Day, Mar. 8.

**Medal Types of 1945**

**1948-49** **Engr.**

**1341** A517 2r green ('49) 12.00 5.00
**1341A** A517 2r violet brown 11.00 5.25
**1342** A518 3r brown car ('49) 8.00 .75
*Nos. 1341-1342 (3)* 31.00 11.00

For overprint see No. 1709.

**Types of 1948**

**1949** **Litho.** ***Perf. 12x12½***

**1343** A678 15k black 2.00 1.00
**1344** A681 20k green 3.00 1.25
**1345** A680 25k dark blue 2.50 1.00
**1346** A683 30k brown 3.50 1.50
**1347** A684 50k deep blue 90.00 20.00
*Nos. 1343-1347 (5)* 101.00 24.75

The 20k, 25k and 30k were re-issued in 1954-56 in slightly smaller format. The 20k measures 14x21mm, instead of 15x22mm; 25k, 14½x21mm, instead of 14½x21¾mm, and 30k, 14½x21mm, instead of 15x22mm.

The smaller-format 20k is olive green, the 25k, slate blue. The 15k was reissued in 1959 (?) in smaller format: 14x21mm, instead of 14½x22mm. See note after No. 738.

Vasili R. Williams (1863-1939), Agricultural Scientist A749

**1949, Apr. 18** **Photo.** ***Perf. 12½***

**1348** A749 25k blue green 5.00 2.75
**1349** A749 50k brown 10.00 4.25

Russian Citizens and Flag — A750

**1949, Apr. 30** ***Perf. 12½***

**1350** A750 40k scarlet 3.00 1.00
**1351** A750 1r blue green 16.00 6.00

Labor Day, May 1, 1949.

A. S. Popov and Radio — A751

Popov Demonstrating Radio to Admiral Makarov — A752

**1949, May** **Unwmk.**

**1352** A751 40k purple 8.00 3.25
**1353** A752 50k brown 16.00 6.25
**1354** A751 1r blue green 16.00 10.00
*Nos. 1352-1354 (3)* 40.00 19.50

54th anniversary of Popov's discovery of the principles of radio.

Soviet Publications A753

Reading Pravda A754

**1949, May 4**

**1355** A753 40k crimson 11.00 3.75
**1356** A754 1r dark violet 29.00 8.00

Soviet Press Day.

Ivan V. Michurin — A755

**1949, July 28**

**1357** A755 40k blue gray 7.00 1.50
**1358** A755 1r bright green 13.00 3.50

Michurin (1855-1925), agricultural scientist.

A. S. Pushkin, 1822 — A756

Pushkin Reading Poem A757

No. 1360, Pushkin portrait by Kiprensky, 1827. 1r, Pushkin Museum, Boldino.

**1949, June** **Unwmk.**

**1359** A756 25k indigo & sepia 3.75 .75
**1360** A756 40k org brn & sep 8.75 1.75
*a.* Souv. sheet of 4, 2 each #1359, 1360, imperf. 200.00 40.00
**1361** A757 40k brn red & dk violet 8.75 2.00
**1362** A757 1r choc & slate 21.00 4.00
**1363** A757 2r brn & vio bl 32.50 6.50
*Nos. 1359-1363 (5)* 74.75 15.00

150th anniversary of the birth of Aleksander S. Pushkin.

Horizontal rows of Nos. 1361 and 1363 contain alternate stamps and labels.

No. 1360a issued July 20.

River Tugboat A758

1r, Freighter, motorship "Bolshaya Volga."

**1949, July 13**

**1364** A758 40k slate blue 25.00 5.00
**1365** A758 1r red brown 50.00 15.00

Centenary of the establishment of the Sormovo Machine and Boat Works.

VCSPS No. 3, Kislovodsk A759

State Sanatoria for Workers: No. 1367, Communications, Khosta. No. 1368, Sanatorium No. 3, Khosta. No. 1369, Electric power, Khosta. No. 1370, Sanatorium No. 1, Kislovodsk. No. 1371, State Theater, Sochi. No. 1372, Frunze Sanatorium, Sochi. No. 1373, Sanatorium at Machindzhaury. No. 1374, Clinical, Chaltubo. No. 1375, Sanatorium No. 41, Zheleznovodsk.

**1949, Sept. 10** **Photo.** ***Perf. 12½***

**1366** A759 40k violet 1.00 .25
**1367** A759 40k black 1.00 .25
**1368** A759 40k carmine 1.00 .25
**1369** A759 40k blue 1.00 .25
**1370** A759 40k violet brown 1.00 .25
**1371** A759 40k red orange 1.00 .25
**1372** A759 40k dark brown 1.00 .25
**1373** A759 40k green 1.00 .25
**1374** A759 40k red brown 1.00 .25
**1375** A759 40k blue green 1.00 .25
*Nos. 1366-1375 (10)* 10.00 2.50

Regatta A760

Sports, "1949": 25k, Kayak race. 30k, Swimming. 40k, Bicycling. No. 1380, Soccer. 50k, Mountain climbing. 1r, Parachuting. 2r, High jump.

**1949, Aug. 7**

**1376** A760 20k bright blue .70 .25
**1377** A760 25k blue green .70 .25
**1378** A760 30k violet 1.20 .25
**1379** A760 40k red brown 1.20 .25
**1380** A760 40k green 1.20 .25
**1381** A760 50k dk blue gray 1.50 .25
**1382** A760 1r carmine rose 4.50 .70
**1383** A760 2r gray black 8.75 1.10
*Nos. 1376-1383 (8)* 19.75 3.30

V. V. Dokuchayev and Fields A761

**1949, Aug. 8**

**1384** A761 40k brown 1.00 .30
**1385** A761 1r green 2.00 .45

Vasili V. Dokuchayev (1846-1903), pioneer soil scientist.

Vasili Bazhenov and Lenin Library, Moscow A762

**1949, Aug. 14** **Photo.** ***Perf. 12½***

**1386** A762 40k violet 4.00 .35
**1387** A762 1r red brown 6.00 .45

Bazhenov, architect, 150th death anniv.

A. N. Radishchev — A763

**1949, Aug. 31**

**1388** A763 40k blue green 15.00 6.00
**1389** A763 1r gray 35.00 9.00

200th anniversary of the birth of Aleksandr N. Radishchev, writer.

Ivan P. Pavlov A764

**1949, Sept. 30** **Unwmk.**

**1390** A764 40k deep brown 5.00 .75
**1391** A764 1r gray black 10.00 1.25

Pavlov (1849-1936), Russian physiologist.

Globe Encircled by Letters A765

**1949, Oct.** *Perf. 12½*

**1392** A765 40k org brn & indigo 2.50 .30
*a.* Imperf. 25.00 5.00
**1393** A765 50k indigo & gray vio 2.50 .30
*a.* Imperf. 25.00 5.00

75th anniv. of the UPU.

Cultivators A766

Map of European Russia — A767

Designs: No. 1395, Peasants in grain field. 50k, Rural scene. 2r, Old man and children.

**1949, Oct. 18** *Perf. 12½*

**1394** A766 25k green 31.00 12.50
**1395** A766 40k violet 7.75 2.75
**1396** A767 40k gray grn & blk 9.00 5.50
**1397** A766 50k deep blue 8.00 4.50
**1398** A766 1r gray black 20.00 9.00
**1399** A766 2r dark brown 25.00 12.50
*Nos. 1394-1399 (6)* 100.75 46.75

Encouraging agricultural development.
Nos. 1394, 1398, 1399 measure 33x19mm.
Nos. 1395, 1397 measure 33x22mm.

Maly (Little) Theater, Moscow A768

M. N. Ermolova, I. S. Mochalov, A. N. Ostrovski, M. S. Shchepkin and P. M. Sadovsky A769

**1949, Oct. 27**

**1400** A768 40k green 2.50 .25
**1401** A768 50k red orange 3.75 .40
**1402** A769 1r deep brown 8.75 .85
*Nos. 1400-1402 (3)* 15.00 1.50

125th anniversary of the Maly Theater (State Academic Little Theater).

**Chapayev Type of 1944**

**1949, Oct. 22** **Photo.**

**1403** A494 40k brown orange 75.00 30.00

30th anniversary of the death of V. I. Chapayev, a hero of the 1918 civil war.
Portrait and outer frame same as type A494. Dates "1919 1949" are in upper corners. Other details differ.

125th Anniv. of the Birth of Ivan Savvich Nikitin, Russian Poet (1824-1861) — A770

**1949, Oct. 24** **Unwmk.**

**1404** A770 40k brown 1.50 .25
**1405** A770 1r slate blue 2.50 .35

Spasski Tower and Russian Citizens A771

**1949, Oct. 29** *Perf. 12½*

**1406** A771 40k brown orange 6.00 4.00
**1407** A771 1r deep green 10.00 6.00

October Revolution, 32nd anniversary.

Sheep, Cattle and Farm Woman — A772

**1949, Nov. 2**

**1408** A772 40k chocolate 8.00 .40
**1409** A772 1r violet 12.00 .60

Encouraging better cattle breeding in Russia.

Arms and Flag of USSR — A773

**1949, Nov. 30** **Engr.** *Perf. 12*

**1410** A773 40k carmine 20.00 6.00

Constitution Day.

Electric Trolley Car — A774

40k, 1r, Diesel train. 50k, Steam train.

**1949, Nov. 19** **Photo.** *Perf. 12½*

**1411** A774 25k red 4.00 .50
**1412** A774 40k violet 7.00 .50
**1413** A774 50k brown 9.00 .75
**1414** A774 1r Prus green 30.00 1.25
*Nos. 1411-1414 (4)* 50.00 3.00

Ski Jump — A775

Designs: 40k, Girl on rings. 50k, Ice hockey. 1r, Weight lifter. 2r, Wolf hunt.

**1949, Nov. 12** **Unwmk.**

**1415** A775 20k dark green 1.20 .55
**1416** A775 40k orange red 2.40 .65
**1417** A775 50k deep blue 3.00 .80
**1418** A775 1r red 6.00 .90
**1419** A775 2r violet 12.00 1.10
*Nos. 1415-1419 (5)* 24.60 4.00

Textile Mills — A776

Designs: 25k, Irrigation system. 40k, 1r, Government buildings, Stalinabad. 50k, University of Medicine.

**1949, Dec. 7** **Photo.** *Perf. 12*

**1420** A776 20k blue 3.00 .25
**1421** A776 25k green 3.00 .25
**1422** A776 40k red orange 4.50 .25
**1423** A776 50k violet 7.50 .40
**1424** A776 1r gray black 12.00 1.00
*Nos. 1420-1424 (5)* 30.00 2.15

Tadzhik Republic, 20th anniv.

"Russia" versus "War" — A777

**1949, Dec. 25**

**1425** A777 40k rose carmine 3.00 .25
**1426** A777 50k blue 4.00 .75

Issued to portray Russia as the defender of world peace.

Byelorussians and Flag — A778

Design: No. 1428, Ukrainians and flag.

**Inscribed: "1939 1949"**

**1949, Dec. 23** **Unwmk.**

**1427** A778 40k orange red 37.50 5.00
**1428** A778 40k deep orange 37.50 5.00

Return of western territories to the Byelorussian and Ukrainian Republics, 10th anniv.

Teachers College A779

25k, State Theater. #1431, Government House. #1432, Navol Street, Tashkent. 1r, Fergana Canal. 2r, Kuigonyarsk Dam.

**1950, Jan. 3**

**1429** A779 20k blue 1.00 .25
**1430** A779 25k gray black 1.00 .25
**1431** A779 40k red orange 2.00 .25
**1432** A779 40k violet 1.50 .25
**1433** A779 1r green 4.00 1.00
**1434** A779 2r brown 6.00 1.00
*Nos. 1429-1434 (6)* 15.50 3.00

Uzbek Republic, 25th anniversary.

Lenin at Razliv — A780

Lenin's Office, Kremlin A781

Design: 1r, Lenin Museum.

**1950, Jan.** **Unwmk.** **Litho.** *Perf. 12*

**1435** A780 40k dk grn & dk brn 3.00 .50
**1436** A781 50k dk brn, red brn & grn 4.00 .50
**1437** A781 1r dk brn, dk grn & cream 9.00 2.00
*Nos. 1435-1437 (3)* 16.00 3.00

26th anniversary of the death of Lenin.

Textile Factory, Ashkhabad A782

Designs: 40k, 1r, Power dam and Turkmenian arms. 50k, Rug making.

**1950, Jan. 7** **Photo.**

**1438** A782 25k gray black 3.50 1.00
**1439** A782 40k brown 5.00 .75
**1440** A782 50k green 6.50 1.25
**1441** A782 1r purple 15.00 2.50
*Nos. 1438-1441 (4)* 30.00 5.50

Turkmen Republic, 25th anniversary.

Motion Picture Projection A783

**1950, Feb.**

**1442** A783 25k brown 40.00 25.00

Soviet motion picture industry, 30th anniv.

Voter — A784

Kremlin — A785

**1950, Mar. 8**

**1443** A784 40k green, *yellow* 20.00 4.00
**1444** A785 1r rose carmine 40.00 6.00

Supreme Soviet elections, Mar. 12, 1950.

Morozov Monument, Moscow — A786

**1950, Mar. 16** *Perf. 12½*

**1445** A786 40k black brn & red 20.00 3.25
**1446** A786 1r dk green & red 30.00 7.50

Unveiling of a monument to Pavlik Morozov, Pioneer.

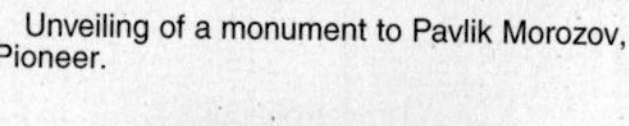

Globes and Communication Symbols — A787

**1950, Apr. 1**

**1447** A787 40k deep green, *blue* 10.00 4.50
**1448** A787 50k deep blue, *blue* 12.00 5.50

Meeting of the Post, Telegraph, Telephone and Radio Trade Unions.

State Polytechnic Museum A788

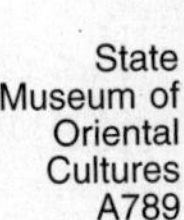

State Museum of Oriental Cultures A789

State University Museum — A790

Pushkin Museum A791

Museums: No. 1451, Tretiakov Gallery. No. 1452, Timiryazev Biology Museum. No. 1453, Lenin Museum. No. 1454, Museum of the Revolution. No. 1456, State History Museum.

**Inscribed: "MOCKBA 1949" in Top Frame**

**Multicolored Centers**

**1950, Mar. 28 Litho. *Perf. 12½***

**1449** A788 40k dark blue 6.00 .50
**1450** A789 40k dark blue 6.00 .50
**1451** A789 40k green 6.00 .50
**1452** A789 40k dark brown 6.00 .50
**1453** A789 40k olive brown 6.00 .50
**1454** A789 40k claret 6.00 .50
**1455** A790 40k red 6.00 .50
**1456** A790 40k chocolate 6.00 .50
**1457** A791 40k brown violet 6.00 .50
*Nos. 1449-1457 (9)* 54.00 4.50

Soviets of Three Races — A792

1r, 4 Russians and communist banner, horiz.

**1950, May 1 Photo. *Perf. 12½***

**1458** A792 40k org red & gray 15.00 2.25
**1459** A792 1r red & gray black 20.00 5.00

Labor Day, May 1, 1950.

A. S. Shcherbakov A793

**1950, May Unwmk.**

**1460** A793 40k black, *pale blue* 8.00 1.00
**1461** A793 1r dk green, *buff* 12.50 2.00

Shcherbakov, political leader (1901-1945).

Monument A794

Victory Medal A795

***Perf. 12x12½***

**1950 Photo. Wmk. 293**

**1462** A794 40k dk brown & red 37.50 4.00

**Unwmk.**

**1463** A795 1r carmine rose 37.50 8.00

5th Intl. Victory Day, May 9, 1950.

A. V. Suvorov — A796

50k, Suvorov crossing Alps, 32½x47mm. 60k, Badge, flag and marchers, 24x39½mm. 2r, Suvorov facing left, 19x33½mm.

**Various Designs and Sizes Dated "1800 1950"**

**1950 *Perf. 12, 12½x12***

**1464** A796 40k blue, *pink* 15.00 4.00
**1465** A796 50k brown, *pink* 19.00 8.00
**1466** A796 60k gray black, *pale gray* 19.00 8.00
**1467** A796 1r dk brn, *lemon* 23.00 12.00
**1468** A796 2r greenish blue 50.00 18.00
*Nos. 1464-1468 (5)* 126.00 50.00

Field Marshal Count Aleksandr V. Suvorov (1730-1800).

Farmers Studying Agronomic Techniques A797

No. 1470, 1r, Sowing on collective farm.

**1950, June *Perf. 12½***

**1469** A797 40k dk grn, *pale grn* 7.50 2.00
**1470** A797 40k gray black, *buff* 7.50 2.00
**1471** A797 1r blue, *lemon* 15.00 4.00
*Nos. 1469-1471 (3)* 30.00 8.00

George M. Dimitrov — A798

**1950, July 2**

**1472** A798 40k gray blk, *citron* 6.00 3.00
**1473** A798 1r gray blk, *salmon* 14.00 6.00

Dimitrov (1882-1949), Bulgarian-born revolutionary leader and Comintern official.

Opera and Ballet Theater, Baku — A799

Designs: 40k, Azerbaijan Academy of Science. 1r, Stalin Avenue, Baku.

**1950, July Photo. *Perf. 12½***

**1474** A799 25k dp grn, *citron* 15.00 1.50
**1475** A799 40k brn, *pink* 10.00 5.00
**1476** A799 1r gray blk, *buff* 15.00 8.50
*Nos. 1474-1476 (3)* 40.00 15.00

Azerbaijan SSR, 30th anniversary.

Victory Theater — A800

Lenin Street A801

Designs: 50k, Gorky Theater. 1r, Monument marking Stalingrad defense line.

**1950, June**

**1477** A800 20k dark blue 5.00 1.50
**1478** A801 40k green 5.00 2.25
**1479** A801 50k red orange 10.00 3.50
**1480** A801 1r gray 10.00 6.00
*Nos. 1477-1480 (4)* 30.00 13.25

Restoration of Stalingrad.

Moscow Subway Stations: "Park of Culture" A802

#1482, Kaluzskaya station. #1483, Taganskaya. #1484, Kurskaya. #1485, Paveletskaya. #1486, Park of Culture. #1487, Taganskaya.

**1950, July 30 Size: 33½x23mm**

**1481** A802 40k deep carmine 5.50 .90
**1482** A802 40k dk grn, *buff* 5.50 .90
**1483** A802 40k deep blue, *buff* 5.50 .90
**1484** A802 1r dark brn, *citron* 8.25 3.00
**1485** A802 1r purple 8.25 3.00
**1486** A802 1r dark grn, *citron* 8.25 3.00

**Size: 33x18½mm**

**1487** A802 1r black, *pink* 8.25 3.25
*Nos. 1481-1487 (7)* 49.50 14.95

Socialist Peoples and Flags A803

**1950, Aug. 4 Unwmk. *Perf. 12½***

**1488** A803 40k multicolored 1.75 .25
**1489** A803 50k multicolored 3.50 .30
**1490** A803 1r multicolored 4.75 .50
*Nos. 1488-1490 (3)* 10.00 1.05

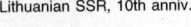

Trade Union Building, Riga — A804

Opera and Ballet Theater, Riga — A805

Designs: 40k, Latvian Cabinet building. 50k, Monument to Jan Rainis. 1r, Riga State Univ. 2r, Latvian Academy of Sciences.

**1950 Photo. *Perf. 12½***

**1491** A804 25k dark brown 3.00 1.50
**1492** A804 40k scarlet 5.00 2.50
**1493** A804 50k dark green 10.00 3.50
**1494** A805 60k deep blue 12.00 4.00
**1495** A805 1r lilac 15.00 6.00
**1496** A804 2r sepia 30.00 10.00
*Nos. 1491-1496 (6)* 75.00 27.50

Latvian SSR, 10th anniv.

Lithuanian Academy of Sciences A806

Marite Melnik — A807

Design: 1r, Cabinet building.

**1950**

**1497** A806 25k dp bl, *bluish* 6.00 2.50
**1498** A807 40k brown 12.00 7.50
**1499** A806 1r scarlet 42.00 15.00
*Nos. 1497-1499 (3)* 60.00 25.00

Lithuanian SSR, 10th anniv.

Stalingrad Square, Tallinn A808

Victor Kingisepp — A809

Designs: 40k, Government building, Tallinn. 50k, Estonia Theater, Tallinn.

**1950**

**1500** A808 25k dark green 5.00 2.00
**1501** A808 40k scarlet 5.00 3.00
**1502** A808 50k blue, *yellow* 10.00 5.00
**1503** A809 1r brown, *blue* 30.00 12.00
*Nos. 1500-1503 (4)* 50.00 22.00

Estonian SSR, 10th anniv.

Citizens Signing Appeal for Peace A810

Children and Governess — A811

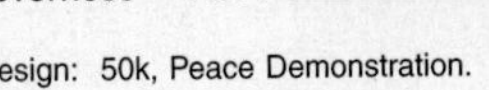

Design: 50k, Peace Demonstration.

**1950, Oct. 16** **Photo.**

| No. | Type | Description | Unused | Used |
|---|---|---|---|---|
| 1504 | A810 | 40k red, *salmon* | 4.00 | 3.00 |
| 1505 | A811 | 40k black | 4.00 | 3.00 |
| 1506 | A811 | 50k dark red | 8.50 | 5.00 |
| 1507 | A810 | 1r brown, *salmon* | 24.00 | 9.00 |
| | | *Nos. 1504-1507 (4)* | 40.50 | 20.00 |

F. G. Bellingshausen, M. P. Lazarev and Globe — A812

Route of Antarctic Expedition — A813

**Blue Paper**

**1950, Oct. 25** **Unwmk.** ***Perf. 12½***

| No. | Type | Description | Unused | Used |
|---|---|---|---|---|
| 1508 | A812 | 40k dark carmine | 35.00 | 15.00 |
| 1509 | A813 | 1r purple | 65.00 | 35.00 |

130th anniversary of the Bellingshausen-Lazarev expedition to the Antarctic.

M. V. Frunze — A814

**1950, Oct. 31**

| No. | Type | Description | Unused | Used |
|---|---|---|---|---|
| 1510 | A814 | 40k blue, *buff* | 10.00 | 3.00 |
| 1511 | A814 | 1r brown, *blue* | 30.00 | 12.00 |

Frunze, military strategist, 25th death anniv.

M. I. Kalinin — A815

**1950, Nov. 20** **Engr.**

| No. | Type | Description | Unused | Used |
|---|---|---|---|---|
| 1512 | A815 | 40k deep green | 10.00 | 1.50 |
| 1513 | A815 | 1r reddish brown | 10.00 | 2.50 |
| 1514 | A815 | 5r violet | 35.00 | 6.00 |
| | | *Nos. 1512-1514 (3)* | 55.00 | 10.00 |

75th anniversary of the birth of M. I. Kalinin, Soviet Russia's first president.

Gathering Grapes A816

Armenian Government Building A817

G. M. Sundukian — A818

**1950, Nov. 29** **Photo.** ***Perf. 12½***

| No. | Type | Description | Unused | Used |
|---|---|---|---|---|
| 1515 | A816 | 20k dp blue, *buff* | 5.00 | 1.00 |
| 1516 | A817 | 40k red org, *blue* | 32.50 | 8.50 |
| 1517 | A818 | 1r ol gray, *yellow* | 7.50 | 3.50 |
| | | *Nos. 1515-1517 (3)* | 45.00 | 13.00 |

Armenian Republic, 30th anniv. 1r also for birth of Sundukian, playwright.

Apartment Building, Koteljnicheskaya Quay — A819

Hotel, Kalanchevkaya Square — A820

**Various Buildings**
**Inscribed: "Mockba, 1950"**

**1950, Dec. 2** **Unwmk.**

| No. | Type | Description | Unused | Used |
|---|---|---|---|---|
| 1518 | A819 | 1r red brn, *buff* | 57.50 | 22.00 |
| 1519 | A819 | 1r gray black | 57.50 | 22.00 |
| 1520 | A819 | 1r brown, *blue* | 57.50 | 22.00 |
| 1521 | A819 | 1r dk green, *blue* | 57.50 | 22.00 |
| 1522 | A820 | 1r dp blue, *buff* | 57.50 | 22.00 |
| 1523 | A820 | 1r black, *buff* | 57.50 | 22.00 |
| 1524 | A820 | 1r red orange | 57.50 | 22.00 |
| 1525 | A819 | 1r dk grn, *yellow* | 57.50 | 22.00 |
| | | *Nos. 1518-1525 (8)* | 460.00 | 176.00 |
| | | Set, hinged | 250.00 | |

Skyscrapers planned for Moscow.

Spasski Tower, Kremlin — A821

**1950, Dec. 4**

| No. | Type | Description | Unused | Used |
|---|---|---|---|---|
| 1526 | A821 | 1r dk grn, red brn & yel brown | 75.00 | 5.00 |

October Revolution, 33rd anniversary.

Golden Autumn by Levitan A822

I. I. Levitan (1861-90), Painter A823

**1950, Dec. 6** **Litho.** ***Perf. 12½***

| No. | Type | Description | Unused | Used |
|---|---|---|---|---|
| 1527 | A822 | 40k multicolored | 10.00 | .55 |

***Perf. 12***
**Photo.**

| No. | Type | Description | Unused | Used |
|---|---|---|---|---|
| 1528 | A823 | 50k red brown | 15.00 | .55 |

Black Sea by Aivazovsky — A824

Ivan K. Aivazovsky (1817-1900) Painter A825

Design: 50k, "Ninth Surge."

**1950, Dec. 6** **Litho.**
**Multicolored Centers**

| No. | Type | Description | Unused | Used |
|---|---|---|---|---|
| 1529 | A824 | 40k chocolate | 3.50 | .30 |
| 1530 | A824 | 50k chocolate | 4.50 | .50 |
| 1531 | A825 | 1r indigo | 8.50 | 1.25 |
| | | *Nos. 1529-1531 (3)* | 16.50 | 2.05 |

Flags and Newspapers Iskra and Pravda — A826

1r, Flag and profiles of Lenin and Stalin.

**1950, Dec. 23** **Photo.**

| No. | Type | Description | Unused | Used |
|---|---|---|---|---|
| 1532 | A826 | 40k gray blk & red | 50.00 | 15.00 |
| 1533 | A826 | 1r dk brn & red | 100.00 | 35.00 |

1st issue of the newspaper Iskra, 50th anniv.

Presidium of Supreme Soviet, Alma-Ata A827

Design: 1r, Opera and Ballet Theater.

**Inscribed: "ALMA-ATA" in Cyrillic**

**1950, Dec. 27**

| No. | Type | Description | Unused | Used |
|---|---|---|---|---|
| 1534 | A827 | 40k gray black, *blue* | 10.00 | 7.50 |
| 1535 | A827 | 1r red brn, *yellow* | 25.00 | 7.50 |

Kazakh Republic, 30th anniversary. Cyrillic charcters for "ALMA-ATA" are above building in vignette on 40k, immediately below building on right on 1r.

Decembrists and Senatskaya Square, Leningrad — A828

**1950, Dec. 30** **Unwmk.**

| No. | Type | Description | Unused | Used |
|---|---|---|---|---|
| 1536 | A828 | 1r blk brn, *yellow* | 30.00 | 10.00 |

Decembrist revolution of 1825.

Lenin at Razliv A829

Design: 1r, Lenin and young communists.

**Multicolored Centers**

**1951, Jan. 21** **Litho.** ***Perf. 12½***

| No. | Type | Description | Unused | Used |
|---|---|---|---|---|
| 1537 | A829 | 40k olive green | 7.00 | .30 |
| 1538 | A829 | 1r indigo | 13.00 | .70 |

27th anniversary of the death of Lenin.

Mountain Pasture A830

Government Building, Frunze A831

**1951, Feb. 2** **Photo.** ***Perf. 12½***

| No. | Type | Description | Unused | Used |
|---|---|---|---|---|
| 1539 | A830 | 25k dk brown, *blue* | 10.00 | 3.50 |
| 1540 | A831 | 40k dp green, *blue* | 20.00 | 6.50 |

Kirghiz Republic, 25th anniv.

Government Building, Tirana A832

**1951, Jan. 6** **Unwmk.** ***Perf. 12***

| No. | Type | Description | Unused | Used |
|---|---|---|---|---|
| 1541 | A832 | 40k green, *bluish* | 50.00 | 40.00 |

Honoring the Albanian People's Republic.

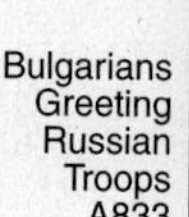

Bulgarians Greeting Russian Troops A833

Lenin Square, Sofia — A834

Design: 60k, Monument to Soviet soldiers.

**1951, Jan. 13**

| No. | Type | Description | Unused | Used |
|---|---|---|---|---|
| 1542 | A833 | 25k gray blk, *bluish* | 12.00 | 5.00 |
| 1543 | A834 | 40k org red, *sal* | 17.50 | 10.00 |
| 1544 | A834 | 60k blk brn, *sal* | 30.00 | 15.00 |
| | | *Nos. 1542-1544 (3)* | 59.50 | 30.00 |

Honoring the Bulgarian People's Republic.

Choibalsan State University — A835

State Theater, Ulan Bator A836

Mongolian Republic Emblem and Flag — A837

**1951, Mar. 12**

| | | | | |
|---|---|---|---|---|
| 1545 | A835 | 25k purple, *salmon* | .55 | .65 |
| 1546 | A836 | 40k dp orange, *yellow* | 1.25 | 1.00 |
| 1547 | A837 | 1r multicolored | 3.25 | 1.50 |
| | | *Nos. 1545-1547 (3)* | 5.05 | 3.15 |

Honoring the Mongolian People's Republic.

D. A. Furmanov (1891-1926) Writer — A838

Furmanov at Work A839

**1951, Mar. 17** ***Perf. 12½***

| | | | | |
|---|---|---|---|---|
| 1548 | A838 | 40k brown | 22.50 | 2.00 |
| 1549 | A839 | 1r gray black, *buff* | 27.50 | 3.00 |

Russian War Memorial, Berlin — A840

**1951, Mar. 21** ***Perf. 12***

| | | | | |
|---|---|---|---|---|
| 1550 | A840 | 40k dk gray grn & dk red | 40.00 | 6.00 |
| 1551 | A840 | 1r brn blk & red | 50.00 | 14.00 |

Stockholm Peace Conference.

Kirov Machine Works A841

**1951, May 19** **Photo.** ***Perf. 12½***

| | | | | |
|---|---|---|---|---|
| 1552 | A841 | 40k brown, *cream* | 17.50 | 3.00 |

Kirov Machine Works, 150th anniv.

Bolshoi Theater, Moscow — A842

Russian Composers A843

**1951, May** **Unwmk.**

| | | | | |
|---|---|---|---|---|
| 1553 | A842 | 40k multicolored | 10.00 | 1.00 |
| 1554 | A843 | 1r multicolored | 10.00 | 1.25 |

Bolshoi Theater, Moscow, 175th anniv.

Liberty Bridge, Budapest A844

Monument to Liberators — A845

Budapest Buildings: 40k, Parliament. 60k, National Museum.

**1951, June 9** ***Perf. 12***

| | | | | |
|---|---|---|---|---|
| 1555 | A844 | 25k emerald | 5.00 | 4.00 |
| 1556 | A844 | 40k bright blue | 5.00 | 4.00 |
| 1557 | A844 | 60k sepia | 10.00 | 6.00 |
| 1558 | A845 | 1r sepia, *salmon* | 20.00 | 10.00 |
| | | *Nos. 1555-1558 (4)* | 40.00 | 24.00 |

Honoring the Hungarian People's Republic.

Harvesting Wheat A846

Designs: 40k, Apiary. 1r, Gathering citrus fruits. 2r, Cotton picking.

**1951, June 25**

| | | | | |
|---|---|---|---|---|
| 1559 | A846 | 25k dark green | 6.50 | 3.50 |
| 1560 | A846 | 40k green, *bluish* | 6.50 | 3.50 |
| 1561 | A846 | 1r brown, *yellow* | 6.50 | 5.00 |
| 1562 | A846 | 2r dk grn, *sal* | 30.00 | 14.00 |
| | | *Nos. 1559-1562 (4)* | 49.50 | 26.00 |

Kalinin Museum, Moscow — A847

Mikhail I. Kalinin — A848

Design: 1r, Kalinin statue.

**1951, Aug. 4** ***Perf. 12x12½, 12½x12***

| | | | | |
|---|---|---|---|---|
| 1563 | A847 | 20k org brn & black | 1.50 | .25 |
| 1564 | A848 | 40k dp green & choc | 3.00 | .50 |
| 1565 | A848 | 1r vio blue & gray | 5.50 | .75 |
| | | *Nos. 1563-1565 (3)* | 10.00 | 1.50 |

5th anniv. of the death of Kalinin.

F. E. Dzerzhinski, 25th Death Anniv. — A849

Design: 1r, Profile of Dzerzhinski.

**1951, Aug. 4** **Engr.** ***Perf. 12x12½***

| | | | | |
|---|---|---|---|---|
| 1566 | A849 | 40k brown red | 12.00 | 3.00 |
| 1567 | A849 | 1r gray black | 18.00 | 5.00 |

Aleksandr M. Butlerov — A850

A. Kovalevski A850a

P. K. Kozlov A850b

N. S. Kurnakov — A850c

P. N. Lebedev A850d

N. I. Lobachevski A850e

A. N. Lodygin A850f

A. N. Severtsov A850g

K. E. Tsiolkovsky A850h

Russian Scientists: No. 1570 Sonya Kovalevskaya. No. 1572, S. P. Krasheninnikov. No. 1577, D. I. Mendeleev. No. 1578, N. N. Miklukho-Maklai. No. 1580, A. G. Stoletov. No. 1581, K. A. Timiryasev. No. 1583, P. N. Yablochkov.

**1951, Aug. 15** **Photo.** ***Perf. 12½***

| | | | | |
|---|---|---|---|---|
| 1568 | A850 | 40k org red, *bluish* | 12.50 | 1.25 |
| 1569 | A850a | 40k dk blue, *sal* | 4.75 | .50 |
| 1570 | A850 | 40k pur, *salmon* | 4.75 | .50 |
| 1571 | A850b | 40k orange red | 4.75 | .50 |
| 1572 | A850 | 40k purple | 4.75 | .50 |
| 1573 | A850c | 40k brn, *sal* | 4.75 | .50 |
| 1574 | A850d | 40k blue | 4.75 | .50 |
| 1575 | A850e | 40k brown | 4.75 | .50 |
| 1576 | A850f | 40k green | 4.75 | .50 |
| 1577 | A850 | 40k deep blue | 4.75 | .50 |
| 1578 | A850 | 40k org red, *sal* | 4.75 | .50 |
| 1579 | A850g | 40k sepia, *sal* | 4.75 | .50 |
| 1580 | A850 | 40k grn, *sal* | 4.75 | .50 |
| 1581 | A850 | 40k brn, *sal* | 4.75 | .50 |
| 1582 | A850h | 40k gray blk, *blue* | 20.00 | 1.40 |
| 1583 | A850 | 40k sepia | 4.75 | .50 |
| | | *Nos. 1568-1583 (16)* | 99.00 | 9.65 |

Two printings exist in differing stamp sizes of most of this issue.

A. A. Aliabiev — A851

Design: No. 1585, V. S. Kalinnikov.

**1951, Aug. 28**

| | | | | |
|---|---|---|---|---|
| 1584 | A851 | 40k brown, *salmon* | 50.00 | 15.00 |
| 1585 | A851 | 40k gray, *salmon* | 50.00 | 15.00 |

Russian composers.

Opera and Ballet Theater, Tbilisi — A852

Gathering Citrus Fruit — A853

40k, Principal street, Tbilisi. 1r, Picking tea.

**1951** **Unwmk.** ***Perf. 12½***

| | | | | |
|---|---|---|---|---|
| 1586 | A852 | 20k dp grn, *yellow* | 5.00 | 1.60 |
| 1587 | A853 | 25k pur, org & brn | 5.00 | 1.60 |
| 1588 | A853 | 40k dk brn, *blue* | 22.50 | 3.50 |
| 1589 | A853 | 1r red brn & dk grn | 17.50 | 8.00 |
| | | *Nos. 1586-1589 (4)* | 50.00 | 14.70 |

Georgian Republic, 30th anniversary.

Emblem of Aviation Society — A854

Planes and Emblem — A855

60k, Flying model planes. 1r, Parachutists.

**1951, Sept. 19 Litho. *Perf. 12½***
**Dated: "1951"**

| | | | | |
|---|---|---|---|---|
| **1590** | A854 | 40k multicolored | 3.00 | .25 |
| **1591** | A854 | 60k emer, lt bl & brn | 10.00 | .45 |
| **1592** | A854 | 1r blue, sal & lilac | 12.50 | .45 |
| **1593** | A855 | 2r multicolored | 22.50 | 1.00 |
| | | *Nos. 1590-1593 (4)* | 48.00 | 2.15 |

Promoting interest in aviation.

Victor M. Vasnetsov (1848-1926), Painter — A856

Three Heroes, by Vasnetsov — A857

**1951, Oct. 15**

| | | | | |
|---|---|---|---|---|
| **1594** | A856 | 40k dk bl, brn & buff | 12.00 | .75 |
| **1595** | A857 | 1r multicolored | 18.00 | 1.25 |

Hydroelectric Station, Lenin and Stalin — A858

Design: 1r, Spasski Tower, Kremlin.

**1951, Nov. 6 Photo. *Perf. 12½***
**Dated: "1917-1951"**

| | | | | |
|---|---|---|---|---|
| **1596** | A858 | 40k blue vio & red | 35.00 | 10.00 |
| **1597** | A858 | 1r dk brown & red | 65.00 | 35.00 |

34th anniversary of October Revolution.

Map, Dredge and Khakhovsky Hydroelectric Station A859

Map, Volga Dam and Tugboat — A860

Designs (each showing map): 40k, Stalingrad Dam. 60k, Excavating Turkmenian canal. 1r, Kuibyshev dam.

**1951, Nov. 28 *Perf. 12½***

| | | | | |
|---|---|---|---|---|
| **1598** | A859 | 20k multicolored | *18.00* | *3.00* |
| **1599** | A860 | 30k multicolored | *27.00* | *4.50* |
| **1600** | A860 | 40k multicolored | *32.50* | *6.50* |
| **1601** | A860 | 60k multicolored | *55.00* | *9.50* |
| **1602** | A860 | 1r multicolored | *115.00* | *15.00* |
| | | *Nos. 1598-1602 (5)* | *247.50* | *38.50* |

Flag and Citizens Signing Peace Appeal — A861

**1951, Nov. 30 *Perf. 12½***

| | | | | |
|---|---|---|---|---|
| **1603** | A861 | 40k gray & red | 20.00 | 7.00 |

Third All-Union Peace Conference.

Mikhail V. Ostrogradski, Mathematician, 150th Birth Anniv. — A862

**1951, Dec. 10 Unwmk.**

| | | | | |
|---|---|---|---|---|
| **1604** | A862 | 40k black brn, *pink* | 17.50 | 10.00 |

Monument to Jan Zizka, Prague — A863

Monument to Soviet Liberators A864

25k, Monument to Soviet Soldiers, Ostrava. 40k, Julius Fucik. 60k, Smetana Museum, Prague.

**1951, Dec. 10 *Perf. 12½***

| | | | | |
|---|---|---|---|---|
| **1605** | A863 | 20k vio blue, *sal* | 16.00 | 3.00 |
| **1606** | A863 | 25k copper red, *yel* | 35.00 | 12.50 |
| **1607** | A863 | 40k red org, *sal* | 60.00 | 7.50 |
| **1608** | A863 | 60k brnsh gray, *buff* | 35.00 | 6.00 |
| **1609** | A864 | 1r brnsh gray, *buff* | 30.00 | 9.00 |
| | | *Nos. 1605-1609 (5)* | 176.00 | 38.00 |

Soviet-Czechoslovakian friendship.

Volkhovski Hydroelectric Station and Lenin Statue — A865

**1951, Dec. 19**

| | | | | |
|---|---|---|---|---|
| **1610** | A865 | 40k dk bl, gray & yel | 6.00 | .25 |
| **1611** | A865 | 1r pur, gray & yel | 14.00 | .55 |

25th anniv. of the opening of the Lenin Volkhovski hydroelectric station.

Lenin as a Schoolboy A866

Horizontal Designs: 60k, Lenin among children. 1r, Lenin and peasants.

**1952, Jan. 24 Photo. *Perf. 12½***
**Multicolored Centers**

| | | | | |
|---|---|---|---|---|
| **1612** | A866 | 40k dk blue green | 2.25 | .55 |
| **1613** | A866 | 60k violet blue | 3.25 | .55 |
| **1614** | A866 | 1r orange brown | 4.50 | .65 |
| | | *Nos. 1612-1614 (3)* | 10.00 | 1.75 |

28th anniversary of the death of Lenin.

Semenov — A867

**1952, Feb. 1**

| | | | | |
|---|---|---|---|---|
| **1615** | A867 | 1r sepia, *blue* | 15.00 | 8.00 |

Petr Petrovich Semenov-Tianshanski (1827-1914), traveler and geographer who explored the Tian Shan mountains.

Kovalevski — A868

**1952, Mar. 3 Unwmk.**

| | | | | |
|---|---|---|---|---|
| **1616** | A868 | 40k sepia, *yellow* | 25.00 | 10.00 |

V. O. Kovalevski (1843-1883), biologist and palaeontologist.

Skaters A869

**1952, Mar. 3**

| | | | | |
|---|---|---|---|---|
| **1617** | A869 | 40k shown | 4.00 | .40 |
| **1618** | A869 | 60k Skiers | 6.00 | .60 |

N. V. Gogol and Characters from "Taras Bulba" — A870

Designs: 60k, Gogol and V. G. Belinski. 1r, Gogol and Ukrainian peasants.

**1952, Mar. 4 Dated: "1852-1952"**

| | | | | |
|---|---|---|---|---|
| **1619** | A870 | 40k sepia, *blue* | 5.00 | .50 |
| **1620** | A870 | 60k multicolored | 5.00 | .50 |
| **1621** | A870 | 1r multicolored | 15.00 | 1.00 |
| | | *Nos. 1619-1621 (3)* | 25.00 | 2.00 |

Death centenary of N. V. Gogol, writer.

G. K. Ordzhonikidze A871

**1952, Apr. 23 Photo. *Perf. 12½***

| | | | | |
|---|---|---|---|---|
| **1622** | A871 | 40k dp green, *pink* | 19.00 | 8.50 |
| **1623** | A871 | 1r sepia, *blue* | 11.00 | 3.50 |

15th anniv. of the death of Grigori K. Ordzhonikidze, Georgian party worker.

Workers and Soviet Flag — A872

Workers' Rest Home A873

No. 1626, Aged citizens. No. 1627, Schoolgirl.

**1952, May 15 Unwmk.**

| | | | | |
|---|---|---|---|---|
| **1624** | A872 | 40k red & blk, *cream* | 40.00 | 10.00 |
| **1625** | A873 | 40k red & dk grn, *pale gray* | 80.00 | 18.00 |
| **1626** | A873 | 40k red & brown, *pale gray* | 40.00 | 10.00 |
| **1627** | A872 | 40k red & black, *pale gray* | 40.00 | 10.00 |
| | | *Nos. 1624-1627 (4)* | 200.00 | 48.00 |

Adoption of Stalin constitution., 15th anniv

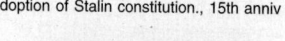

A. S. Novikov-Priboy and Ship — A874

**1952, June 5**

| | | | | |
|---|---|---|---|---|
| **1628** | A874 | 40k blk, pale cit & bl grn | 1.00 | .30 |

Novikov-Priboy, writer, 75th birthanniv.

150th anniv. of Birth of Victor Hugo (1802-1855), French Writer — A875

**1952, June 5 Unwmk. *Perf. 12½***
**1629** A875 40k brn org, gray & black 2.00 .25

Julaev — A876

**1952, June 28**
**1630** A876 40k rose red, *pink* 1.00 .25

200th anniversary of the birth of Salavat Julaev, Bashkir hero who took part in the insurrection of 1773-1775.

Sedov — A877

**1952, July 4**
**1631** A877 40k dk bl, dk brn & blue green 37.50 8.00

Georgi J. Sedov, Arctic explorer (1877-1914).

Arms and Flag of Romania — A878

University Square, Bucharest A879

Design: 60k, Monument to Soviet soldiers.

**1952, July 26**
**1632** A878 40k multicolored 4.50 1.00
**1633** A878 60k dk green, *pink* 7.50 2.50
**1634** A879 1r bright ultra 13.00 5.00
*Nos. 1632-1634 (3)* 25.00 8.50

Zhukovski — A880

Design: No. 1636, K. P. Bryullov.

**1952, July 26 Pale Blue Paper**
**1635** A880 40k gray black 10.00 .50
**1636** A880 40k brt blue green 10.00 .50

V. A. Zhukovski, poet, and Bryullov, painter (1799-1852).

Ogarev — A881

**1952, Aug. 29**
**1637** A881 40k deep green .75 .25

75th anniversary of the death of N. P. Ogarev, poet and revolutionary.

Uspenski — A882

**1952, Sept. 4**
**1638** A882 40k indigo & blk brn 2.00 .50

Gleb Ivanovich Uspenski (1843-1902), writer.

Nakhimov — A883

**1952, Sept. 9**
**1639** A883 40k multicolored 5.00 2.00

Adm. Paul S. Nakhimov (1802-1855).

University Building, Tartu — A884

**1952, Oct. 2**
**1640** A884 40k black brn, *sal* 20.00 *3.00*

150th anniversary of the enlargement of the University of Tartu, Estonia.

Kajum Nasyri — A885

**1952, Nov. 5**
**1641** A885 40k brown, *yellow* 15.00 5.00

Nasyri (1825-1902), Tartar educator.

A. N. Radishchev — A886

**1952, Oct. 23**
**1642** A886 40k blk, brn & dk red 6.00 1.00

Radishchev, writer, 150th death anniv.

M.S. Joseph Stalin at Entrance to Volga-Don Canal — A887

Design: 1r, Lenin, Stalin and red banners.

**1952, Nov. 6 *Perf. 12½***
**1643** A887 40k multicolored 15.00 6.00
**1644** A887 1r brown, red & yel 25.00 9.00

35th anniversary of October Revolution.

Pavel Andreievitch Fedotov (1815-52), Artist — A888

**1952, Nov. 26**
**1645** A888 40k red brn & black 2.00 .50

V. D. Polenov, Artist, 25th Death Anniv. — A889

"Moscow Courtyard" — A890

**1952, Dec. 6**
**1646** A889 40k red brown & buff 3.50 .35
**1647** A890 1r multicolored 4.50 .65

A. I. Odoyevski (1802-39) Poet — A891

**1952, Dec. 8**
**1648** A891 40k gray blk & red org 5.00 .50

D. N. Mamin-Sibiryak — A892

**1952, Dec. 15**
**1649** A892 40k dp green, *cream* 2.00 .50

Centenary of the birth of Dimitrii N. Mamin-Sibiryak (1852-1912), writer.

**Composite Medal Types of 1946**
**Frames as A599-A606**
**Centers as Indicated**

Medals: 1r, Token of Veneration. 2r, Red Star. 3r, Red Workers' Banner. 5r, Red Banner. 10r, Lenin.

**1952-59 Engr. *Perf. 12½***
**1650** A569 1r dark brown 9.00 7.00
**1651** A567 2r red brown 1.40 .55
**1652** A572 3r dp blue violet 2.00 .95
**1653** A571 5r dk car ('53) 2.50 .95
**1654** A566 10r bright rose 4.50 1.90
*a.* 10r dull red ('59) 5.00 2.00
*Nos. 1650-1654 (5)* 19.40 11.35

Vladimir M. Bekhterev (1857-1927), Neuropathologist A893

**1952, Dec. 24 Photo.**
**1655** A893 40k vio bl, slate & blk 3.00 .50

Byelorusskaya Station — A894

Designs (Moscow Subway stations): 40k, Botanical Garden Station. 40k, Novoslobodskaya Station. 40k, Komsomolskaya Station.

**1952, Dec. 30**
**Multicolored Centers**
**1656** A894 40k dull violet 3.50 .50
**1657** A894 40k light ultra 3.50 .50
**1658** A894 40k blue gray 3.50 .50
**1659** A894 40k dull green 3.50 .50
*a.* Horiz. strip of 4, #1656-1659 15.00 4.00

USSR Emblem and Flags of 16 Union Republics — A895

**1952, Dec. 30**
**1660** A895 1r grn, dk red & brn 25.00 4.50

30th anniversary of the USSR.

Lenin — A896

**1953, Jan. 26**
**1661** A896 40k multicolored 10.00 4.00

29 years without Lenin.

Stalin Peace Medal — A897

**1953, Apr. 30** ***Perf. 12½***
**1662** A897 40k red brn, bl & dull yel 12.00 6.00

Valerian V. Kuibyshev A898

**1953, June 6**
**1663** A898 40k red brn & black 3.00 .55

Kuibyshev (1888-1935), Bolshevik leader.

A899

**1953, July 21**
**1664** A899 40k buff & dk brown 20.00 1.25

Nikolai G. Chernyshevski (1828-1889), writer and radical leader; exiled to Siberia for 24 years.

A900

**1953, July 19**
**1665** A900 40k ver & gray brown 8.00 2.00

60th anniv. of the birth of Vladimir V. Mayakovsky, poet.

Tsymijanskaja Dam — A901

Volga-Don Canal: No. 1666, Lock No. 9, Volga-Don Canal. No. 1667, Lock 13. No. 1668, Lock 15. No. 1669, Volga River lighthouse. No. 1671, M. S. "Joseph Stalin" in canal.

**1953, Aug. 29** **Litho.**
**1666** A901 40k multicolored 4.00 1.00
**1667** A901 40k multicolored 4.00 2.00
**1668** A901 40k multicolored 4.00 1.00
**1669** A901 40k multicolored 4.00 2.00
**1670** A901 40k multicolored 4.00 1.00
**1671** A901 1r multicolored 5.00 1.00
*Nos. 1666-1671 (6)* 25.00 8.00

V. G. Korolenko (1853-1921), Writer — A902

**1953, Aug. 29** **Photo.** ***Perf. 12x12½***
**1672** A902 40k brown 2.00 .25

Count Leo N. Tolstoy (1828-1910), Writer — A903

**1953, Sept.** ***Perf. 12***
**1673** A903 1r dark brown 15.00 5.00

Moscow University and Two Youths — A904

1r, Komsomol badge and four orders.

**1953, Oct. 29** ***Perf. 12½x12***
**1674** A904 40k multicolored 12.50 2.00
**1675** A904 1r multicolored 22.50 3.00

35th anniversary of the Young Communist League (Komsomol).

Nationalities of the Soviet Union — A905

60k, Lenin and Stalin at Smolny.

**1953, Nov. 6**
**1676** A905 40k multicolored 30.00 10.00
**1677** A905 60k multicolored 50.00 15.00

36th anniversary of October Revolution.
No. 1676 measures 25½x38mm; No. 1677, 25½x42mm.

Lenin and His Writings — A906

1r, Lenin facing left and pages of "What to Do."

**1953**
**1678** A906 40k multicolored 8.00 4.00
**1679** A906 1r dk brn, org brn & red 14.00 8.50

Communist Party formation, 50th anniv. (40k). 2nd cong. of the Russian Socialist Party, 50th anniv. (1r).
Issued: 40k, 11/12; 1r, 12/14.

Lenin Statue — A907

Peter I Statue, Decembrists' Square — A908

Leningrad Views: Nos. 1681 & 1683, Admiralty building. Nos. 1685 & 1687, Smolny Institute.

**1953, Nov. 23**
**1680** A907 40k brn blk, *yellow* 8.00 4.00
**1681** A907 40k vio brn, *yellow* 8.00 4.00
**1682** A907 40k dk brn, *pink* 6.00 3.00
**1683** A907 40k brn blk, *cream* 6.00 3.00
**1684** A908 1r dk brn, *blue* 17.50 10.00
**1685** A908 1r dk green, *pink* 17.50 10.00
**1686** A908 1r violet, *yellow* 14.00 9.00
**1687** A908 1r blk brn, *blue* 14.00 9.00
*Nos. 1680-1687 (8)* 91.00 52.00

See Nos. 1944-1945, 1943a.

"Pioneers" and Model of Lomonosov Moscow University — A909

**1953, Dec. 22** **Litho.** ***Perf. 12***
**1688** A909 40k dk sl grn, dk brn & red 5.00 1.75

**Arms Type of 1948**

**1954-57**
**1689** A682 40k scarlet 1.00 .50
*a.* 8 ribbon turns on wreath at left ('54) 4.25 1.65

No. 1689 was re-issued in 1954-56 typographed in slightly smaller format: 14½x21¾mm, instead of 14¾x21¾mm, and in a lighter shade. See note after No. 738.
No. 1689 has 7 ribbon turns on left side of wreath.

Aleksandr S. Griboedov, Writer (1795-1829) A910

**1954, Mar. 4** **Photo.**
**1690** A910 40k dp claret, *cream* 2.25 .75
**1691** A910 1r black, *green* 5.75 2.00

Kremlin View — A911

**1954, Mar. 7** **Litho.** ***Perf. 12½x12***
**1692** A911 40k red & gray 12.00 3.00

1954 elections to the Supreme Soviet.

V. P. Chkalov — A912

**1954, Mar. 16** ***Perf. 12***
**1693** A912 1r gray, vio bl & dk brown 20.00 10.00

50th anniversary of the birth of Valeri P. Chkalov (1904-1938), airplane pilot.

Lenin — A913

Lenin at Smolny A914

Designs: No. 1696, Lenin's home (later museum), Ulyanovsk. No. 1697, Lenin addressing workers. No. 1698, Lenin among students, University of Kazan.

**1954, Apr. 16** **Photo.**
**1694** A913 40k multicolored 6.00 2.00

**Size: 38x27½mm**

**1695** A914 40k multicolored 6.00 2.00
**1696** A914 40k multicolored 6.00 2.00

**Size: 48x35mm**

**1697** A914 40k multicolored 6.00 2.00
**1698** A914 40k multicolored 6.00 2.00
*Nos. 1694-1698 (5)* 30.00 10.00

30th anniversary of the death of Lenin.
For overprint see No. 2060.

Joseph V. Stalin — A915

**1954, Apr. 30 Unwmk. *Perf. 12***

**1699** A915 40k dark brown 15.00 2.00

First anniversary of the death of Stalin.

Supreme Soviet Buildings in Kiev and Moscow A916

T. G. Shevchenko Statue, Kharkov — A917

Designs: No. 1701, University building, Kiev. No. 1702, Opera, Kiev. No. 1703, Ukranian Academy of Science. No. 1705, Bogdan Chmielnicki statue, Kiev. No. 1706 Flags of Soviet Russia and Ukraine. No. 1707, T. G. Shevchenko statue, Kanev. No. 1708, Chmielnicki proclaming reunion of Ukraine and Russia, 1654.

**1954, May 10 Litho.**

**Size: 37½x26mm, 26x37½mm**

**1700** A916 40k red brn, sal, cream & black 2.50 .25
**1701** A916 40k ultra, vio bl & brn 2.50 .25
**1702** A916 40k red brn, buff, blue brown 2.50 .25
**1703** A916 40k org brn, cream & grn 2.50 .25
**1704** A917 40k red, blk, yel & brown 2.25 .25
**1705** A917 60k multicolored 3.00 .30
**1706** A917 1r multicolored 5.00 .50

**Size: 42x28mm**

**1707** A916 1r multicolored 3.50 .75

**Size: 45x29½mm**

**1708** A916 1r multicolored, *pink* 5.00 .75

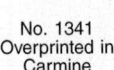

No. 1341 Overprinted in Carmine

**1709** A517 2r green 9.00 1.75
*Nos. 1700-1709 (10)* 37.75 5.30

300th anniversary of the union between the Ukraine and Russia.

Sailboat Race A918

Basketball A919

No. 1711, Hurdle race. No. 1712, Swimmers. No. 1713, Cyclists. No. 1714, Track. No. 1715, Skier. No. 1716, Mountain climbing.

**1954, May 29**

**Frames in Orange Brown**

**1710** A918 40k blue & black 2.25 .35
**1711** A918 40k vio gray & blk 2.25 .35
**1712** A918 40k dk blue & black 2.25 .35
**1713** A918 40k dk brn & buff 2.25 .35
**1714** A918 40k black brn & buff 2.25 .35
**1715** A918 1r blue & black 5.50 .95
**1716** A918 1r blue & black 5.50 .90
**1717** A919 1r dk brn & brn 7.50 1.50
*Nos. 1710-1717 (8)* 29.75 5.10

For overprint see No. 2170.

Cattle A920

No. 1719, Potato planting and cultivation. No. 1720, Kolkhoz hydroelectric station.

**1954, June 8**

**1718** A920 40k brn, cream, ind & blue gray 3.75 1.00
**1719** A920 40k gray grn, buff & brown 3.75 1.00
**1720** A920 40k blk, bl grn & vio bl 3.75 1.00
*Nos. 1718-1720 (3)* 11.25 3.00

Anton P. Chekhov, Writer, 50th Death Anniv. — A921

**1954, July 15**

**1721** A921 40k green & black brn 5.00 .50

F. A. Bredichin, V. J. Struve, A. A. Belopolski and Observatory — A922

**1954, July 26**

**1722** A922 40k vio bl, blk & blue 10.00 1.00

Restoration of Pulkov Observatory.

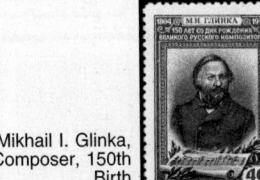

Mikhail I. Glinka, Composer, 150th Birth Anniv. — A923

Pushkin and Zhukovsky Visiting Glinka A924

**1954, July 26**

**1723** A923 40k dp cl, pink & blk brown 6.00 1.00
**1724** A924 60k multicolored 9.00 2.00

Nikolai A. Ostrovsky (1904-36), Blind Writer — A925

**1954, Sept. 29 Photo. *Perf. 12½x12***

**1725** A925 40k brn, dark red & yel 7.00 1.00

Monument to Sunken Ships — A926

Defenders of Sevastopol — A927

Design: 1r, Admiral P. S. Nakhimov.

**1954, Oct. 17 *Perf. 12½***

**1726** A926 40k blue grn, blk & ol brown 4.00 1.10
**1727** A927 60k org brn, blk & brn 5.50 1.60
**1728** A926 1r brn, blk & ol green 10.50 2.25
*Nos. 1726-1728 (3)* 20.00 4.95

Centenary of the defense of Sevastopol during the Crimean War.

Sculpture at Exhibition Entrance — A928

Agriculture Pavilion — A929

Cattle Pavilion A929a

Designs: No. 1732, Machinery pavilion. No. 1733, Main entrance. No. 1734, Main pavilion.

***Perf. 12½, 12½x12, 12x12½***

**1954, Nov. 5 Litho.**

**Size: 26x37mm**

**1729** A928 40k multicolored 2.00 .50

**Size: 40x29mm**

**1730** A929 40k multicolored 2.00 .50
**1731** A929a 40k multicolored 2.00 .50
**1732** A929 40k multicolored 2.00 .50

**Size: 40½x33mm**

**1733** A929 1r multicolored 6.00 2.00

**Size: 28½x40½mm**

**1734** A928 1r multicolored 6.00 2.00
*Nos. 1729-1734 (6)* 20.00 6.00

1954 Agricultural Exhibition.

Marx, Engels, Lenin and Stalin — A930

**1954, Nov. 6 Photo. *Perf. 12½x12***

**1735** A930 1r dk brn, pale org & red 6.00 2.50

37th anniversary of October Revolution.

Kazan University Building A931

**1954, Nov. 11 *Perf. 12x12½***

**1736** A931 40k deep blue 1.75 .50
**1737** A931 60k claret 3.25 1.00

Founding of Kazan University, 150th anniv.

Salome Neris A932

**1954, Nov. 17 *Perf. 12½x12***

**1738** A932 40k red, org & ol gray 4.00 1.50

50th anniversary of the birth of Salome Neris (1904-1945), Lithuanian poet.

Vegetables and Garden A933

Cultivating Flax — A934

Designs: No. 1741, Tractor plowing field. No. 1742, Loading ensilage.

**1954, Dec. 12 Litho. *Perf. 12x12½***

| | | | | |
|---|---|---|---|---|
| **1739** | A933 | 40k multicolored | 1.60 | .50 |
| **1740** | A934 | 40k multicolored | 1.60 | .50 |
| **1741** | A933 | 40k multicolored | 1.60 | .50 |
| **1742** | A934 | 60k multicolored | 7.25 | .50 |
| | | *Nos. 1739-1742 (4)* | 12.05 | 2.00 |

Joseph Stalin, 75th Birth Anniv. — A935

**1954, Dec. 21 Engr. *Perf. 12½x12***

| | | | | |
|---|---|---|---|---|
| **1743** | A935 | 40k rose brown | 1.50 | .50 |
| **1744** | A935 | 1r dark blue | 3.50 | .60 |

Anton G. Rubinstein (1829-94), Composer A936

**1954, Dec. 30 Photo.**

| | | | | |
|---|---|---|---|---|
| **1745** | A936 | 40k claret, gray & blk | 4.00 | 1.00 |

Vsevolod M. Garshin (1855-1888), Writer — A937

**Lithographed and Photogravure**

**1955, Mar. 2 Unwmk. *Perf. 12***

| | | | | |
|---|---|---|---|---|
| **1746** | A937 | 40k buff, blk brn & green | 2.00 | .50 |

K. A. Savitsky and Painting A938

**1955, Mar. 21 Photo.**

| | | | | |
|---|---|---|---|---|
| **1747** | A938 | 40k multicolored | 3.00 | .30 |
| *a.* | | Sheet of 4, black inscription | 35.00 | 35.00 |
| *b.* | | As "a," red brown inscription | 35.00 | 35.00 |

K. A. Savitsky (1844-1905), painter. Size: Nos. 1747a, 1747b, 152x108mm.

Globe and Clasped Hands — A939

**1955, Apr. 9 Litho.**

| | | | | |
|---|---|---|---|---|
| **1748** | A939 | 40k multicolored | 2.00 | .50 |

International Conference of Public Service Unions, Vienna, April 1955.

Poets Pushkin and Mickiewicz — A940

Brothers in Arms Monument, Warsaw — A941

Palace of Culture and Science, Warsaw A942

Copernicus, Painting by Jan Matejko (in Medallion) — A943

**Unwmk.**

**1955, Apr. 22 Photo. *Perf. 12***

| | | | | |
|---|---|---|---|---|
| **1749** | A940 | 40k chalky blue, vio & black | 2.50 | .35 |
| **1750** | A941 | 40k violet black | 2.50 | .35 |
| **1751** | A942 | 1r brt red & gray black | 5.50 | 1.25 |
| **1752** | A943 | 1r multicolored | 5.50 | 1.25 |
| | | *Nos. 1749-1752 (4)* | 16.00 | 3.20 |

Polish-USSR treaty of friendship, 10th anniv.

Lenin at Shushinskoe — A944

Lenin at Secret Printing House — A945

Design: 1r, Lenin and Krupskaya with peasants at Gorki, 1921.

**1955, Apr. 22**

**Frame and Inscription in Dark Red**

| | | | | |
|---|---|---|---|---|
| **1753** | A944 | 60k multicolored | 1.50 | .50 |
| **1754** | A944 | 1r multicolored | 3.00 | .75 |
| **1755** | A945 | 1r multicolored | 3.00 | .75 |
| | | *Nos. 1753-1755 (3)* | 7.50 | 2.00 |

85th anniversary of the birth of Lenin.

Friedrich von Schiller — A946

**1955, May 10**

| | | | | |
|---|---|---|---|---|
| **1756** | A946 | 40k chocolate | 2.00 | .50 |

150th anniversary of the death of Friedrich von Schiller, German poet.

A. G. Venezianov and "Spring on the Land" — A947

**1955, June 21 Photo.**

| | | | | |
|---|---|---|---|---|
| **1757** | A947 | 1r multicolored | 5.00 | .50 |
| *a.* | | Souvenir sheet of 4 | 45.00 | 25.00 |

Venezianov, painter, 175th birth anniv.

Anatoli K. Liadov (1855-1914), Composer — A948

**1955, July 5 Litho.**

| | | | | |
|---|---|---|---|---|
| **1758** | A948 | 40k red brn, blk & lt brn | 2.50 | .50 |

Aleksandr Popov — A949

**1955, Nov. 5**

**Portraits Multicolored**

| | | | | |
|---|---|---|---|---|
| **1759** | A949 | 40k light ultra | 1.75 | .50 |
| **1760** | A949 | 1r gray brown | 3.25 | .50 |

60th anniv. of the construction of a coherer for detecting Hertzian electromagnetic waves by A. S. Popov, radio pioneer.

Lenin — A950

Storming the Winter Palace — A951

Design: 1r, Lenin addressing the people.

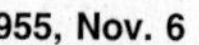

**1955, Nov. 6**

| | | | | |
|---|---|---|---|---|
| **1761** | A950 | 40k multicolored | 3.00 | 1.00 |
| **1762** | A951 | 40k multicolored | 3.00 | 1.00 |
| **1763** | A951 | 1r multicolored | 7.50 | 2.00 |
| | | *Nos. 1761-1763 (3)* | 13.50 | 4.00 |

38th anniversary of October Revolution.

Apartment Houses, Magnitogorsk — A952

**1955, Nov. 29**

| | | | | |
|---|---|---|---|---|
| **1764** | A952 | 40k multicolored | 3.00 | 1.00 |

25th anniversary of the founding of the industrial center, Magnitogorsk.

Arctic Observation Post — A953

Design: 1r, Scientist at observation post.

**1955, Nov. 29 *Perf. 12½x12***

| | | | | |
|---|---|---|---|---|
| **1765** | A953 | 40k multicolored | 6.00 | 2.00 |
| **1766** | A953 | 60k multicolored | 6.00 | 2.00 |
| **1767** | A953 | 1r multicolored | 6.00 | 2.00 |
| *a.* | | Souvenir sheet of 4 ('58) | 35.00 | 50.00 |
| | | *Nos. 1765-1767 (3)* | 18.00 | 6.00 |

Publicizing the Soviet scientific drifting stations at the North Pole.

In 1962, No. 1767a was overprinted in red "1962" on each stamp and, in the lower sheet margin, a three-line Russian inscription meaning "25 years from the beginning of the work of "NP-1" station."

Sheet value, $75 unused, $100 canceled.

Fedor Ivanovich Shubin (1740-1805), Sculptor — A954

**1955, Dec. 22 *Perf. 12***

| | | | | |
|---|---|---|---|---|
| **1768** | A954 | 40k green & multi | 1.00 | .35 |
| **1769** | A954 | 1r brown & multi | 1.00 | .35 |

Federal Socialist Republic Pavilion (R.S.F.S.R.) — A955

ПАВИЛЬОН ТАДЖИКСКОЙ ССР

No. 1771

ПАВИЛЬОН БЕЛОРУССКОЙ ССР

No. 1772

ПАВИЛЬОН АЗЕРБАЙДЖАНСКОЙ ССР

No. 1773

ПАВИЛЬОН ГРУЗИНСКОЙ ССР

No. 1774

ПАВИЛЬОН АРМЯНСКОЙ ССР

No. 1775

ПАВИЛЬОН ТУРКМЕНСКОЙ ССР

No. 1776

No. 1777

No. 1778

No. 1779

No. 1780

No. 1781

No. 1782

No. 1783

No. 1784

No. 1785

Designs: Pavilions.

**1955 Litho. Unwmk.**

**Centers in Natural Colors; Frames in Blue Green and Olive**

| | | | | |
|---|---|---|---|---|
| **1770** | A955 40k shown | | 1.00 | .50 |
| *a.* | Sheet of 4 | | 15.00 | 15.00 |
| **1771** | A955 40k Tadzhik | | 1.00 | .50 |
| **1772** | A955 40k Byelorussian | | 1.00 | .50 |
| *a.* | Sheet of 4 | | 15.00 | 15.00 |
| **1773** | A955 40k Azerbaijan | | 1.00 | .50 |
| **1774** | A955 40k Georgian | | 1.00 | .50 |
| **1775** | A955 40k Armenian | | 1.00 | .50 |
| **1776** | A955 40k Turkmen | | 1.00 | .50 |
| **1777** | A955 40k Uzbek | | 1.00 | .50 |
| **1778** | A955 40k Ukrainian | | 1.00 | .50 |
| *a.* | Sheet of 4 | | 15.00 | 15.00 |
| **1779** | A955 40k Kazakh | | 1.00 | .50 |
| **1780** | A955 40k Kirghiz | | 1.00 | .50 |
| **1781** | A955 40k Karelo-Finnish | | 1.00 | .50 |
| **1782** | A955 40k Moldavian | | 1.00 | .50 |
| **1783** | A955 40k Estonian | | 1.00 | .50 |
| **1784** | A955 40k Latvian | | 1.00 | .50 |
| **1785** | A955 40k Lithuanian | | 1.00 | .50 |
| | *Nos. 1770-1785 (16)* | | 16.00 | 8.00 |

All-Union Agricultural Fair.

Nos. 1773-1785 were printed in sheets containing various stamps, providing a variety of horizontal se-tenant pairs and strips. Value, $50 per sheet.

Lomonosov Moscow State University, 200th Anniv. — A956

Design: 1r, New University buildings.

**1955, June 9** ***Perf. 12***

| | | | |
|---|---|---|---|
| **1786** | A956 40k multicolored | 2.00 | .25 |
| *a.* | Sheet of 4 ('56) | 10.00 | *10.00* |
| **1787** | A956 1r multicolored | 4.00 | .50 |
| *a.* | Sheet of 4 ('56) | 20.00 | *20.00* |

Vladimir V. Mayakovsky — A957

**1955, May 31**

| | | | |
|---|---|---|---|
| **1788** | A957 40k multicolored | 2.00 | .50 |

Mayakovsky, poet, 25th death anniv.

Race Horse — A958

Trotter A959

**1956, Jan. 9**

| | | | |
|---|---|---|---|
| **1789** | A958 40k dark brown | 3.00 | .40 |
| **1790** | A958 60k Prus grn & blue green | 4.50 | .60 |
| **1791** | A959 1r dull pur & blue vio | 7.50 | 1.00 |
| | *Nos. 1789-1791 (3)* | 15.00 | 2.00 |

International Horse Races, Moscow, Aug. 14-Sept. 4, 1955.

Alexei N. Krylov (1863-1945), Mathematician, Naval Architect — A960

**1956, Jan. 9**

| | | | |
|---|---|---|---|
| **1792** | A960 40k gray, brown & black | 2.00 | .50 |

Symbol of Spartacist Games, Stadium and Factories — A961

**1956, Jan. 18**

| | | | |
|---|---|---|---|
| **1793** | A961 1r red vio & lt grn | 2.00 | .50 |

5th All-Union Spartacist Games of Soviet Trade Union sport clubs, Moscow, Aug. 12-18, 1955.

Atomic Power Station A962

Design: 60k, Atomic Reactor.

**1956, Jan. 31**

| | | | |
|---|---|---|---|
| **1794** | A962 25k multicolored | 1.25 | .40 |
| **1795** | A962 60k multicolored | 3.25 | 1.00 |
| **1796** | A962 1r multicolored | 5.50 | 1.75 |
| | *Nos. 1794-1796 (3)* | 10.00 | 3.15 |

Establishment of the first Atomic Power Station of the USSR Academy of Science. Inscribed in Russian: "Atomic Energy in the service of the people."

Statue of Lenin, Kremlin and Flags A963

**1956, Feb.**

| | | | |
|---|---|---|---|
| **1797** | A963 40k multicolored | 5.00 | .50 |
| **1798** | A963 1r ol, buff & red org | 7.00 | 1.50 |

20th Congress of the Communist Party of the Soviet Union.

Khachatur Abovian, Armenian Writer, 150th Birth Anniv. — A964

**1956, Feb. 25 Unwmk. *Perf. 12***

| | | | |
|---|---|---|---|
| **1799** | A964 40k black brn, *bluish* | 5.00 | .50 |

Workers with Red Flag — A965

**1956, Mar. 14**

| | | | |
|---|---|---|---|
| **1800** | A965 40k multicolored | 6.00 | .75 |

Revolution of 1905, 50th anniversary.

Nikolai A. Kasatkin — A966

**1956, Apr. 30**

| | | | |
|---|---|---|---|
| **1801** | A966 40k carmine lake | 2.00 | .50 |

Kasatkin (1859-1930), painter.

"On the Oka River" A967

**1956, Apr. 30**

**Center Multicolored**

| | | | |
|---|---|---|---|
| **1802** | A967 40k bister & black | 5.00 | .40 |
| **1803** | A967 1r ultra & black | 7.00 | .60 |

A. E. Arkhipov, painter.

I. P. Kulibin, Inventor, 220th Birth Anniv. — A968

**1956, May 12**

| | | | |
|---|---|---|---|
| **1804** | A968 40k multicolored | 2.00 | .25 |

Vassili Grigorievitch Perov (1833-82), Painter — A969

"Birdcatchers" — A970

Painting: No. 1807, "Hunters at Rest."

**1956, May 12**

**Multicolored Centers**

| | | | |
|---|---|---|---|
| **1805** | A969 40k green | 3.00 | .40 |
| **1806** | A970 1r brown | 6.00 | .80 |
| **1807** | A970 1r orange brown | 6.00 | .80 |
| | *Nos. 1805-1807 (3)* | 15.00 | 2.00 |

Ural Pavilion A971

No. 1809

No. 1810

No. 1811

No. 1812

No. 1813

No. 1814

No. 1815

No. 1816

No. 1817

No. 1818

No. 1819

ПАВИЛЬОН МОСКОВСКОЙ, ТУЛЬСКОЙ, КАЛУЖСКОЙ, РЯЗАНСКОЙ И БРЯНСКОЙ ОБЛАСТЕЙ

No. 1820

Pavilions: No. 1809, Tatar Republic. No. 1810, Volga District. No. 1811, Central Black Earth Area. No. 1812, Northeastern District. No. 1813, Northern Caucasus. No. 1814, Bashkir Republic. No. 1815, Far East. No. 1816, Central Asia. No. 1817, Young Naturalists. No. 1818, Siberia. No. 1819, Leningrad and Northwestern District. No. 1820, Moscow, Tula, Kaluga, Ryazan and Bryansk Districts.

**1956, Apr. 25**

**Multicolored Centers**

**1808** A971 1r yel green & pale yel 3.00 .50
**1809** A971 1r blue grn & pale yel 3.00 .50
**1810** A971 1r dk blue grn & pale yel 3.00 .50
**1811** A971 1r dk bl grn & yel grn 3.00 .50
**1812** A971 1r dk blue grn & buff 3.00 .50
**1813** A971 1r ol gray & pale yel 3.00 .50
**1814** A971 1r olive & yellow 3.00 .50
**1815** A971 1r olive grn & lemon 3.00 .50
**1816** A971 1r olive brn & lemon 3.00 .50
**1817** A971 1r olive brn & lemon 3.00 .50
**1818** A971 1r brown & yellow 3.00 .50
**1819** A971 1r redsh brown & yel 3.00 .50
**1820** A971 1r dk red brn & yel 3.00 .50
*Nos. 1808-1820 (13)* 39.00 6.50

All-Union Agricultural Fair, Moscow.

Six of the Pavilion set were printed se-tenant in one sheet of 30 (6x5), the strip containing Nos. 1809, 1816, 1817, 1813, 1818 and 1810 in that order. Two others, Nos. 1819-1820, were printed se-tenant in one sheet of 35. Value, $50 per sheet.

Lenin — A972

**1956, May 25**

**1821** A972 40k lilac & multi 6.00 1.00

86th anniversary of the birth of Lenin.

Lobachevski A973

**1956, June 4**

**1822** A973 40k black brown 2.00 .25

Nikolai Ivanovich Lobachevski (1793-1856), mathematician.

Nurse and Textile Factory A974

No. 1824, First aid instruction.

**1956, June 4** **Unwmk.**

**1823** A974 40k lt ol grn, grnsh bl & red 3.00 .25
**1824** A974 40k red brn, lt bl & red 3.00 .25

Red Cross and Red Crescent. No. 1823 measures 37x25mm; No. 1824, 40x28mm.

V. K. Arseniev (1872-1930), Explorer and Writer — A975

**1956, June 15** **Litho.** ***Perf. 12***

**1825** A975 40k violet, black & rose 3.00 .50

I. M. Sechenov (1829-1905), Physiologist A976

**1956, June 15**

**1826** A976 40k multicolored 2.00 .50

A. K. Savrasov, Painter — A977

**1956, June 22**

**1827** A977 1r dull yel & brown 3.00 .50

I. V. Michurin, Scientist, Birth Centenary A978

Design: 60k, I. V. Michurin with Pioneers.

**1956, June 22**

**Center Multicolored**

**1828** A978 25k dark brown .55 .25
**1829** A978 60k green & lt blue 1.10 .40
**1830** A978 1r light blue 2.25 .55
*Nos. 1828-1830 (3)* 3.90 1.20

Nos. 1828 and 1830 measure 32x25mm. No. 1829 measures 47x26mm.

Nadezhda K. Krupskaya A979

**1956, June 28**

**1831** A979 40k brn, lt blue & pale brown 8.00 2.00

Krupskaya (1869-1939), teacher and wife of Lenin.

See Nos. 1862, 1886, 1983, 2028.

S. M. Kirov (1886-1934), Revolutionary A980

**1956, June 28**

**1832** A980 40k red, buff & brown 2.00 .50

Nikolai S. Leskov (1831-1895), Novelist — A981

**1956, July 10**

**1833** A981 40k olive bister & brn 1.50 .25
**1834** A981 1r green & dk brown 3.50 .75

Aleksandr A. Blok (1880-1921), Poet — A982

**1956, July 10**

**1835** A982 40k olive & brn, *cream* 2.00 .50

Farm Machinery Factory A983

**1956, July 23** ***Perf. 12½x12***

**1836** A983 40k multicolored 2.00 .50

Rostov Farm Machinery Works, 25th anniv.

A984

**1956, July 23** **Unwmk.**

**1837** A984 40k brown & rose vio 5.00 .50

G. N. Fedotova (1846-1925), actress. See No. 2026.

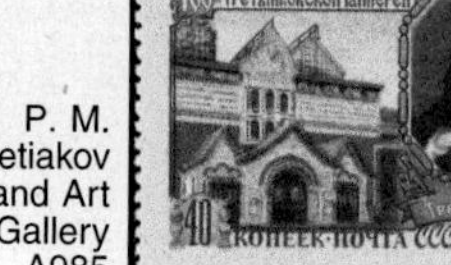

P. M. Tretiakov and Art Gallery A985

"The Rooks Have Arrived" by A. K. Savrasov A986

**1956, July 31** ***Perf. 12***

**1838** A985 40k multicolored 5.00 1.00
**1839** A986 40k multicolored 5.00 1.00

Tretiakov Art Gallery, Moscow, cent.

Relay Race A987

Volleyball — A988

#1842, Rowing. #1843, Swimming. #1844, Medal with heads of man and woman. #1845, Tennis. #1846, Soccer. #1847, Fencing. #1848, Bicycle race. #1849, Stadium and flag. #1850, Diving. #1851, Boxing. #1852, Gymnast. 1r, Basketball.

**1956, Aug. 5**

**1840** A987 10k carmine rose .40 .25
**1841** A988 25k dk orange brn .60 .25
**1842** A988 25k brt grnsh blue .60 .25
**1843** A988 25k grn, blue & lt brn .60 .25
**1844** A988 40k org, pink, bis & yellow 1.25 .25
**1845** A988 40k orange brown 1.25 .25
**1846** A987 40k brt yel grn & dk brown 1.25 .25
**1847** A987 40k grn, brt grn & dk brn, *grnsh* 1.25 .25
**1848** A987 40k blue green 1.25 .25
**1849** A988 40k brt yel grn & red 1.25 .25
**1850** A988 40k greenish blue 1.25 .25
**1851** A988 60k violet 1.75 .25
**1852** A987 60k brt violet 1.75 .25
**1853** A987 1r red brown 2.50 .40
*Nos. 1840-1853 (14)* 16.95 3.65

All-Union Spartacist Games, Moscow, Aug. 5-16.

Parachute Landing — A989

**1956, Aug. 5** ***Perf. 12x12½***

**1854** A989 40k multicolored 2.00 1.00

Third World Parachute Championships, Moscow, July 1956.

Building under Construction A990

Builders' Day: 60k, Building a factory. 1r, Building a dam.

**1956 Photo. *Perf. 12***

**1855** A990 40k deep orange 1.50 .50
**1856** A990 60k brown carmine 1.00 .50
**1857** A990 1r intense blue 2.50 .50
*Nos. 1855-1857 (3)* 5.00 1.50

Ivan Franko — A991

**1956, Aug. 27**

**1858** A991 40k deep claret 1.25 .25
**1859** A991 1r bright blue 1.75 .30

Franko, writer (1856-1916).

Makhmud Aivazov — A992

Type I Type II

Two types:
I — Three lines in panel with "148."
II — Two lines in panel with "148."

**1956, Aug. 27**

**1860** A992 40k emerald (II) 5.00 3.00
*a.* Type I 21.00 18.00

148th birthday of Russia's oldest man, an Azerbaijan collective farmer.

Robert Burns, Scottish Poet, 160th Death Anniv. — A993

**1956-57 Photo.**

**1861** A993 40k yellow brown 6.00 2.00

**Engr.**

**1861A** A993 40k lt ultra & brn ('57) 4.00 1.00

For overprint see No. 2174.

**Portrait Type of 1956**

Lesya Ukrainka (1871-1913), Ukrainian writer.

**1956, Aug. 27 Litho.**

**1862** A979 40k olive, blk & brown 4.00 1.00

Statue of Nestor — A995

**1956, Sept. 22 *Perf. 12x12½***

**1863** A995 40k multicolored 1.50 .25
**1864** A995 1r multicolored 3.50 .50

900th anniversary of the birth of Nestor, first Russian historian.

Aleksandr Andreevich Ivanov (1806-58), Painter — A996

**1956, Sept. 22 Unwmk.**

**1865** A996 40k gray & brown 2.00 .25

I. E. Repin and "Volga River Boatmen" — A997

"Cossacks Writing a Letter to the Turkish Sultan" — A998

**1956, Aug. 21**

**Multicolored Centers**

**1866** A997 40k org brn & black 7.00 1.00
**1867** A998 1r chalky blue & blk 13.00 3.00

Ilya E. Repin (1844-1930), painter.

Chicken Farm A999

Designs: No. 1869, Harvest. 25k, Harvesting corn. No. 1871, Women in corn field. No. 1872, Farm buildings. No. 1873, Cattle. No. 1874, Farm workers, inscriptions and blast furnances.

**1956, Oct. 7**

**1868** A999 10k multicolored .50 .25
**1869** A999 10k multicolored .50 .25
**1870** A999 25k multicolored 1.00 .25
**1871** A999 40k multicolored 2.25 .50
**1872** A999 40k multicolored 2.25 .50
**1873** A999 40k multicolored 2.25 .50
**1874** A999 40k multicolored 2.25 .50
*Nos. 1868-1874 (7)* 11.00 2.75

#1868, 1872, 1873 measure 37x25½mm; #1869-1871 37x27½mm; #1874 37x21mm.

Benjamin Franklin — A1000

G. B Shaw A1000a

Dostoevski A1000b

Portraits: #1876 Sesshu (Toyo Oda). #1877, Rembrandt. #1879, Mozart. #1880, Heinrich Heine. #1882, Ibsen. #1883, Pierre Curie.

**1956, Oct. 17 Photo.**

**Size: 25x37mm**

**1875** A1000 40k copper brn 3.75 1.60
**1876** A1000 40k brt orange 3.75 1.60
**1877** A1000 40k black 3.75 1.60
**1878** A1000a 40k black 3.75 1.60

**Size: 21x32mm**

**1879** A1000 40k grnsh blue 3.75 1.60
**1880** A1000 40k violet 3.75 1.60
**1881** A1000b 40k green 3.75 1.60
**1882** A1000 40k brown 3.75 1.60
**1883** A1000 40k brt green 3.75 1.60
*Nos. 1875-1883 (9)* 33.75 14.40

Great personalities of the world.

Antarctic Bases — A1001

**1956, Oct. 22 Litho. *Perf. 12x12½***

**1884** A1001 40k slate, grnsh bl & red 2.00 .50

Soviet Scientific Antarctic Expedition.

G. I. Kotovsky (1881-1925), Military Commander A1002

**1956, Oct. 30**

**1885** A1002 40k magenta 2.50 1.00

**Portrait Type of 1956**

Portrait: Julia A. Zemaite (1845-1921), Lithuanian novelist.

**1956, Oct. 30 *Perf. 12***

**1886** A979 40k lt ol green & brn 3.00 1.00

Fedor A. Bredichin (1831-1904), Astronomer — A1004

**1956, Oct. 30**

**1887** A1004 40k sepia & ultra 3.00 .75

Field Marshal Count Aleksandr V. Suvorov (1730-1800) A1005

**1956, Nov. 17 Engr.**

**1888** A1005 40k org & maroon .75 .25
**1889** A1005 1r ol & dk red brn 1.75 .30
**1890** A1005 3r lt red brn & black 2.50 .75
*Nos. 1888-1890 (3)* 5.00 1.30

Shatura Power Station A1006

**1956 Litho. *Perf. 12½x12***

**1891** A1006 40k multicolored 6.00 .50

30th anniv. of the Shatura power station.

Kryakutni's Balloon, 1731 — A1007

**1956, Nov. 17**

**1892** A1007 40k lt brn, sepia & yel 5.00 .50

225th anniv. of the 1st balloon ascension of the Russian inventor, Kryakutni.

A1008

**1956, Dec. 3 Unwmk. *Perf. 12***

**1893** A1008 40k ultra & brown 1.00 .50

Yuli M. Shokalski (1856-1940), oceanographer and geodesist.

Apollinari M. Vasnetsov and "Winter Scene" A1009

**1956, Dec. 30**

**1894** A1009 40k multicolored 2.00 .50

Vasnetsov (1856-1933), painter.

Indian Building and Books — A1010

**1956, Dec. 26**

**1895** A1010 40k deep carmine 2.00 .50

Kalidasa, 5th century Indian poet.

Ivan Franko, Ukrainian Writer — A1011

**1956, Dec. 26** **Engr.**
**1896** A1011 40k dk slate green 2.00 .50

See Nos. 1858-1859.

Leo N. Tolstoy A1012

Portraits of Writers: No. 1898, Mikhail V. Lomonosov. No. 1899, Aleksander S. Pushkin. No. 1900, Maxim Gorki. No. 1901, Shota Rustaveli. No. 1902, Vissarion G. Belinski. No. 1903, Mikhail Y. Lermontov, poet, and Darjal Ravine in Caucasus.

**1956-57** **Litho.** ***Perf. 12½x12***

**Size: 37½x27½mm**

**1897** A1012 40k brt grnsh blue & brown 2.10 .25
**1898** A1012 40k dk red, ol & brn olive 2.10 .25

**Size: 35½x25½mm**

**1899** A1012 40k dk gray blue & brown 2.10 .25
**1900** A1012 40k black & brn car 2.10 .25
**1901** A1012 40k ol, brn & ol gray 2.10 .25
**1902** A1012 40k bis, dl vio & brn ('57) 2.10 .25
**1903** A1012 40k indigo & ol ('57) 2.10 .25
*Nos. 1897-1903 (7)* 14.70 1.75

Famous Russian writers.
See Nos. 1960-1962, 2031, 2112.

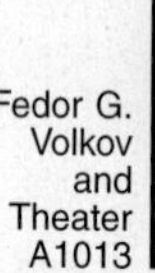

Fedor G. Volkov and Theater A1013

**1956, Dec. 31** **Unwmk.**
**1904** A1013 40k mag, gray & yel 1.00 .30

200th anniversary of the founding of the St. Petersburg State Theater.

Vitus Bering and Map of Bering Strait A1016

**1957, Feb. 6**
**1905** A1016 40k brown & blue 2.00 .50

275th anniversary of the birth of Vitus Bering, Danish navigator and explorer.

Dmitri I. Mendeleev A1017

**1957, Feb. 6** ***Perf. 12x12½***
**1906** A1017 40k gray & gray brn 3.00 1.00

D. I. Mendeleev (1834-1907), chemist.

Mikhail I. Glinka — A1018

Design: 1r, Scene from opera Ivan Susanin.

**1957, Feb. 23** ***Perf. 12***
**1907** A1018 40k dk red, buff & sep 1.50 .30
**1908** A1018 1r multicolored 2.50 .50

Mikhail I. Glinka (1804-1857), composer.

All-Union Festival of Soviet Youth, Moscow — A1019

**1957, Feb. 23**
**1909** A1019 40k dk blue, red & ocher .75 .35

23rd Ice Hockey World Championship, Moscow — A1020

Designs: 25k, Emblem. 40k, Player. 60k, Goalkeeper.

**1957, Feb. 24** **Photo.**
**1910** A1020 25k deep violet 1.00 .25
**1911** A1020 40k bright blue 1.00 .25
**1912** A1020 60k emerald 1.00 .35
*Nos. 1910-1912 (3)* 3.00 .85

Dove and Festival Emblem — A1021

**1957** **Litho.** ***Perf. 12***
**1913** A1021 40k multicolored .40 .25
**1914** A1021 60k multicolored .60 .25

6th World Youth Festival, Moscow. Exist imperf. Value, each $30.

Assembly Line — A1022

**1957, Mar. 15**
**1915** A1022 40k Prus grn & dp org 3.00 .75

Moscow Machine Works centenary.

Black Grouse A1023

Axis Deer — A1024

No. 1916, Gray partridge. No. 1918, Polar bear. No. 1920, Bison. No. 1921, Mallard. No. 1922, European elk. No. 1923, Sable.

**1957, Mar. 28**

**Center in Natural Colors**

**1916** A1024 10k yel brown .85 .35
**1917** A1023 15k brown .85 .35
**1918** A1023 15k slate blue .90 .35
**1919** A1024 20k red orange .90 .35
**1920** A1023 30k ultra .90 .35
**1921** A1023 30k dk olive grn .90 .35
**1922** A1023 40k dk olive grn 2.25 .40
**1923** A1024 40k violet blue 2.25 .40
*Nos. 1916-1923 (8)* 9.80 2.90

See Nos. 2213-2219, 2429-2431.

Wooden Products, Hohloma A1025

National Handicrafts: No. 1925, Lace maker, Vologda. No. 1926, Bone carver, North Russia. No. 1927, Woodcarver, Moscow area. No. 1928, Rug weaver, Turkmenistan. No. 1929, Painting.

**1957-58** **Unwmk.**
**1924** A1025 40k red org, yel & black 3.00 .80
**1925** A1025 40k brt car, yel & brown 3.00 .80
**1926** A1025 40k ultra, buff & gray 3.00 .80
**1927** A1025 40k brn, pale yel & hn brown 3.00 .80
**1928** A1025 40k buff, brn, bl & org ('58) 1.50 .90
**1929** A1025 40k multicolored ('58) 1.50 .90
*Nos. 1924-1929 (6)* 15.00 5.00

Aleksei Nikolaievitch Bach (1857-1946), Biochemist A1026

**1957, Apr. 6** **Litho.** ***Perf. 12***
**1930** A1026 40k ultra, brn & buff 5.00 .30

Georgi Valentinovich Plekhanov (1856-1918), Political Philosopher A1027

**1957, Apr. 6** **Engr.**
**1931** A1027 40k dull purple .60 .30

Leonhard Euler A1028

**1957, Apr. 17** **Litho.**
**1932** A1028 40k lilac & gray 2.00 .50

Leonhard Euler (1707-1783), Swiss mathematician and physicist.

Lenin, 87th Birth Anniv. — A1029

Designs: No. 1934, Lenin talking to soldier and sailor. No. 1935, Lenin participating in a subbotnik, a voluntary neighborhood clean-up.

**1957, Apr. 22**

**Multicolored Centers**

**1933** A1029 40k magenta & bis 3.00 1.00
**1934** A1029 40k magenta & bis 3.00 1.00
**1935** A1029 40k magenta & bis 3.00 1.00
*Nos. 1933-1935 (3)* 9.00 3.00

Youths of All Races Carrying Festival Banner — A1030

Design: 20k, Sculptor with motherhood statue. 40k, Young couples dancing. 1r, Festival banner and fireworks over Moscow University.

**1957, May 27** ***Perf. 12x12½***
**1936** A1030 10k emer, pur & yel .25 .25
**1937** A1030 20k multicolored .60 .25
**1938** A1030 25k emer, pur & yel .90 .25
**1939** A1030 40k rose, bl grn & bis brn .90 .25
**1940** A1030 1r multicolored 1.40 .25
*Nos. 1936-1940 (5)* 4.05 1.25

6th World Youth Festival in Moscow. The 10k, 20k, and 1r exist imperf. Value: 10k, 20k, each $20; 1r $200.

Marine Museum Place and Neva — A1031

Designs: No. 1942, Lenin monument. No. 1943, Nevski Prospect and Admiralty.

**1957, May 27 Photo. *Perf. 12***

**1941** A1031 40k blue green 1.50 .40
**1942** A1031 40k reddish brown 1.50 .40
**1943** A1031 40k bluish violet 1.50 .40
*a.* Souv. sheet of 3, red border 35.00 20.00
*Nos. 1941-1943 (3)* 4.50 1.20

250th anniversary of Leningrad.

No. 1943a contains imperf. stamps similar to #1941, 1680 (in reddish brown), 1943, and is for 40th anniv. of the October Revolution. Issued Nov. 7, 1957. A similar sheet is listed as No. 2002a.

**Type of 1953 Overprinted in Red**

No. 1944

No. 1945

Designs: No. 1944, Peter I Statue, Decembrists' Square. No. 1945, Smolny Institute.

**1957, May 27 *Perf. 12½x12***

**1944** A908 1r black brn, *greenish* 1.50 .25
**1945** A908 1r green, *pink* 1.50 .25

250th anniversary of Leningrad.
The overprint is in one line on No. 1945.

Henry Fielding — A1032

**1957, June 20 Litho.**

**1946** A1032 40k multicolored 1.00 .50

Fielding (1707-54), English playwright, novelist.

William Harvey — A1033

**1957, May 20 Photo.**

**1947** A1033 40k brown 1.00 .50

300th anniversary of the death of the English physician William Harvey, discoverer of blood circulation.

M. A. Balakirev (1836-1910), Composer A1034

**1957, May 20 Engr.**

**1948** A1034 40k bluish black 2.00 .50

A. I. Herzen and N. P. Ogarev A1035

**1957, May 20 Litho.**

**1949** A1035 40k blk vio & dk ol gray 1.00 .50

Centenary of newspaper Kolokol (Bell).

Kazakhstan Workers' Medal — A1036

**1957, May 20**

**1950** A1036 40k lt blue, blk & yel 1.00 .35

A1037 A1037a A1037b

Portraits: No. 1951, A. M. Liapunov. No. 1952, V. Mickevicius Kapsukas, writer. No. 1953, G. Bashindchagian, Armenian painter. No. 1954, Yakub Kolas, Byelorussian poet. No. 1955, Carl von Linné, Swedish botanist.

**1957 Various Frames Photo.**

**1951** A1037 40k dull red brown 6.50 1.00
**1952** A1037a 40k sepia 5.00 1.00
**1953** A1037 40k sepia 5.00 1.00
**1954** A1037b 40k gray 5.00 1.00
**1955** A1037 40k brown black 5.00 1.00
*Nos. 1951-1955 (5)* 26.50 5.00

See Nos. 2036-2038, 2059.

Bicyclist A1038

**1957, June 20 Litho.**

**1956** A1038 40k claret & vio blue 1.00 .50

10th Peace Bicycle Race.

Telescope A1039

Designs: No. 1958, Comet and observatory. No. 1959, Rocket leaving earth.

**1957, July 4 Size: 25½x37mm**

**1957** A1039 40k brn, ocher & blue 2.00 .35
**1958** A1039 40k indigo, lt bl & yel 2.00 .35

**Size: 14½x21mm**

**1959** A1039 40k blue violet 2.00 .35
*Nos. 1957-1959 (3)* 6.00 1.05

International Geophysical Year, 1957-58. See Nos. 2089-2091.

Folksinger A1040

**1957, May 20**

**1960** A1040 40k multicolored 5.00 1.00

"The Song of Igor's Army," Russia's oldest literary work.

Taras G. Shevchenko, Ukrainian Poet — A1041

Design: No. 1962, Nikolai G. Chernyshevski, writer and politician.

**1957, July 20**

**1961** A1041 40k grn & dk red brn 1.00 .35
**1962** A1041 40k orange brn & grn 1.00 .35

Woman Gymnast — A1043

25k, Wrestling. No. 1965, Stadium. No. 1966, Youths of three races. 60k, Javelin thrower.

**1957, July 15 Litho. *Perf. 12***

**1963** A1043 20k bluish vio & org brn .60 .25
**1964** A1043 25k brt grn & claret .75 .25
**1965** A1043 40k Prus bl, ol & red 1.20 .25
**1966** A1043 40k crimson & violet 1.20 .25
**1967** A1043 60k ultra & brown 1.60 .40
*Nos. 1963-1967 (5)* 5.35 1.40

Third International Youth Games, Moscow.

Javelin Thrower — A1044

Designs: No. 1969, Sprinter. 25k, Somersault. No. 1971, Boxers. No. 1972, Soccer players, horiz. 60k, Weight lifter.

**1957, July 20 Unwmk.**

**1968** A1044 20k lt ultra & ol blk .45 .25
**1969** A1044 20k brt grn, red vio & black .45 .25
**1970** A1044 25k orange, ultra & blk .60 .25
**1971** A1044 40k rose vio & blk .90 .30
**1972** A1044 40k dp pink, bl, buff & black .90 .30
**1973** A1044 60k lt violet & brn 1.50 .40
*Nos. 1968-1973 (6)* 4.80 1.75

Success of Soviet athletes at the 16th Olympic Games, Melbourne.

Kupala — A1045

**1957, July 27 Photo.**

**1974** A1045 40k dark gray 10.00 5.00

Yanka Kupala (1882-1942), poet.

Kremlin A1046

Moscow Views: No. 1976, Stadium. No. 1977, University. No. 1978, Bolshoi Theater.

**Center in Black**

**1957, July 27 Litho.**

**1975** A1046 40k dull red brown .35 .25
**1976** A1046 40k brown violet .35 .25
**1977** A1046 1r red 1.10 .25
**1978** A1046 1r brt violet blue 1.10 .25
*Nos. 1975-1978 (4)* 2.90 1.00

Sixth World Youth Festival, Moscow.

Lenin Library A1047

**1957, July 27 Photo.**

**1979** A1047 40k brt grnsh blue .75 .35
*a.* Souvenir sheet of 2, light blue, imperf. 20.00 *20.00*

Intl. Phil. Exhib., Moscow, July 29-Aug. 11.
No. 1979 exists imperf. Value $7.50.

Pierre Jean de Beranger(1780-1857), French Song Writer — A1048

**1957, Aug. 9**

**1980** A1048 40k brt blue green .75 .35

Globe, Dove and Olive Branch — A1049

**1957, Aug. 8 Litho.**

**1981** A1049 40k bl, grn & bis brn 2.50 1.00
**1982** A1049 1r violet, grn & brn 5.50 2.00

Publicity for world peace.

### Portrait Type of 1956

Portrait: 40k, Clara Zetkin (1857-1933), German communist.

**1957, Aug. 9**

**1983** A979 40k gray blue, brn & blk 5.00 1.00

Krenholm Factory, Narva A1050

**1957, Sept. 8** **Photo.**

**1984** A1050 40k black brown 2.00 .50

Centenary of Krenholm textile factory, Narva, Estonia.

Carrier Pigeon and Globes A1051

**1957, Sept. 26** **Unwmk.** ***Perf. 12***

**1985** A1051 40k blue .40 .25
**1986** A1051 60k lilac .60 .25

Intl. Letter Writing Week, Oct. 6-12.

Vyborzhets Factory, Lenin Statue A1052

**1957, Sept. 23** **Litho.**

**1987** A1052 40k dark blue 2.00 1.00

Krasny Vyborzhots factory, Leningrad, cent.

Vladimir Vasilievich Stasov (1824-1906), Art and Music Critic — A1053

**1957, Sept. 23** **Engr.**

**1988** A1053 40k brown .50 .25
**1989** A1053 1r bluish black 1.00 .30

Congress Emblem A1054

**1957, Oct. 7** **Litho.** ***Perf. 12***

**1990** A1054 40k gray blue & blk, *bluish* 1.00 .35

4th International Trade Union Congress, Leipzig, Oct. 4-15.

Konstantin E. Tsiolkovsky and Rockets A1055

**1957, Oct. 7**

**1991** A1055 40k dk blue & pale brown 3.50 .50

Tsiolkovsky (1857-1935), rocket and astronautics pioneer.

For overprint see No. 2021.

Sputnik 1 Circling Globe — A1056

**1957** **Photo.**

**1992** A1056 40k indigo, *bluish* 1.40 .50
**1993** A1056 40k bright blue 1.40 .50

Launching of first artificial earth satellite, Oct. 4. Issue dates: No. 1992, Nov. 5; No. 1993, Dec. 28.

Turbine Wheel, Kuibyshev Hydroelectric Station — A1057

**1957, Nov. 20** **Litho.**

**1994** A1057 40k red brown 1.00 .35

All-Union Industrial Exhib. See #2030.

Meteor — A1058

**1957, Nov. 20**

**1995** A1058 40k multicolored 10.00 1.00

Falling of Sikhote Alinj meteor, 10th anniv.

Lenin — A1059

Design: 60k, Lenin reading Pravda, horiz.

**1957, Oct. 30** **Engr.**

**1996** A1059 40k blue 1.00 .25
**1997** A1059 60k rose red 1.00 .25

40th anniversary of October Revolution.

Students and Moscow University — A1060

Miner and Railroad A1061

No. 1999, Red flag, Lenin. No. 2000, Lenin addressing workers and peasants. No. 2002, Harvester.

***Perf. 12½x12, 12x12½, 12½***

**1957, Oct. 15** **Litho.**

**1998** A1060 10k buff, sepia & red .40 .25
**1999** A1060 40k buff, red, sep & yel .80 .25
**2000** A1060 40k red, black & yel .80 .25
**2001** A1061 40k red, yel & green .80 .25
**2002** A1061 60k red, ocher & vio brn 1.25 .25
*a.* Souvenir sheet of 3, #2000-2002, imperf. 50.00 25.00
*Nos. 1998-2002 (5)* 4.05 1.25

40th anniv. of the October Revolution. A similar sheet is listed as No. 1943a.

Nos. 1998-2002 exist imperf. Value, set $12.50.

Federal Socialist Republic A1062

Uzbek Republic — A1063

Republic: No. 2005, Tadzhik (building, peasant girl). No. 2006, Byelorussia (truck). No. 2007, Azerbaijan (buildings). No. 2008, Georgia (valley, palm, couple). No. 2009, Armenia, (fruit, power line, mountains). No. 2010, Turkmen (couple, lambs). No. 2011, Ukraine (farmers). No. 2012, Kazakh (harvester, combine). No. 2013, Kirghiz (horseback rider, building). No. 2014, Moldavia (automatic sorting machine). No. 2015, Estonia (girl in national costume). No. 2016, Latvia (couple, sea, field). No. 2017, Lithuania (farm, farmer couple).

**1957, Oct. 25**

**2003** A1062 40k multicolored 1.00 .35
**2004** A1063 40k multicolored 1.00 .35
**2005** A1062 40k multicolored 1.00 .35
**2006** A1062 40k multicolored 1.00 .35
**2007** A1062 40k multicolored 1.00 .35
**2008** A1062 40k multicolored 1.00 .35
**2009** A1062 40k multicolored 1.00 .35
**2010** A1062 40k multicolored 1.00 .35
**2011** A1063 40k multicolored 1.00 .35
**2012** A1062 40k multicolored 1.00 .35
**2013** A1062 40k multicolored 1.00 .35
**2014** A1062 40k multicolored 1.00 .35
**2015** A1063 40k multicolored 1.00 .35
**2016** A1062 40k multicolored 1.00 .35
**2017** A1062 40k multicolored 1.00 .35
*Nos. 2003-2017 (15)* 15.00 5.25

40th anniversary of the October Revolution.

Artists and Academy of Art — A1064

Red Army Monument, Berlin — A1065

1r, Worker and Peasant monument, Moscow.

**1957, Dec. 16**

**2018** A1064 40k black, *pale salmon* .60 .25
**2019** A1065 60k black .90 .30
**2020** A1065 1r black, *pink* 1.50 .45
*Nos. 2018-2020 (3)* 3.00 1.00

200th anniversary of the Academy of Arts, Leningrad. Artists on 40k are K. P. Bryulov, Ilya Repin and V. I. Surikov.

No. 1991 Overprinted in Black

**1957, Nov. 28**

**2021** A1055 40k 40.00 5.00

Launching of Sputnik 1.

Ukrainian Arms, Symbolic Figures A1066

**1957, Dec. 24**

**2022** A1066 40k yel, red & blue .75 .35

Ukrainian Soviet Republic, 40th anniv.

Edvard Grieg — A1067

**1957, Dec. 24** **Photo.**

**2023** A1067 40k black, *buff* 3.00 1.00

Grieg, Norwegian composer, 50th death anniv.

Giuseppe Garibaldi — A1068

**1957, Dec. 24** **Litho.**

**2024** A1068 40k plum, lt grn & blk 1.00 .35

Garibaldi, (1807-1882) Italian patriot.

Vladimir Lukich Borovikovsky (1757-1825), Painter — A1069

**1957, Dec. 24** **Photo.**

**2025** A1069 40k brown 1.00 .50

### Portrait Type of 1956

Portrait: 40k, Mariya Nikolayevna Ermolova (1853-1928), actress.

**1957, Dec. 28** **Litho.**

**2026** A984 40k red brn & brt vio 1.00 .30

Kuibyshev Hydroelectric Station and Dam A1070

**1957, Dec. 28**

**2027** A1070 40k dark blue, *buff* 3.00 .50

### Type of 1956

Portrait: 40k, Rosa Luxemburg (1870-1919), German socialist.

**1958, Jan. 8**

**2028** A979 40k blue & brown 1.50 .60

Chi Pai-shih — A1070a

**1958, Jan. 8** **Photo.**

**2029** A1070a 40k deep violet 10.00 1.00

Chi Pai-shih (1864-1957), Chinese painter.

Flag and Symbols of Industry A1070b

**1958, Jan. 8** **Litho.**

**2030** A1070b 60k gray vio, red & black 2.00 .50

All-Union Industrial Exhib. Exists imperf. Value, $250.

Aleksei N. Tolstoi, Novelist & Dramatist (1883-1945) A1071

**1958, Jan. 28** **Photo.** ***Perf. 12***

**2031** A1071 40k brown olive 1.00 .30

See Nos. 2112, 2175-2178C.

Symbolic Figure Greeting Sputnik 2 — A1072

**1957-58** **Figure in Buff** **Litho.**

**2032** A1072 20k black & rose .75 .25
**2033** A1072 40k black & grn ('58) 1.00 .25
**2034** A1072 60k blk & lt brn ('58) 1.25 .25
**2035** A1072 1r black & blue 2.00 .50
*Nos. 2032-2035 (4)* 5.00 1.25

Launching of Sputnik 2, Nov. 3, 1957.

### Small Portrait Type of 1957

No. 2036, Henry W. Longfellow, American poet. No. 2037, William Blake, English artist, poet, mystic. No. 2038, E. Charents, Armenian poet.

**1958, Mar.** **Unwmk.** ***Perf. 12***
**Various Frames**

**2036** A1037 40k gray black 5.00 2.25
**2037** A1037 40k gray black 5.00 2.25
**2038** A1037 40k sepia 5.00 2.25
*Nos. 2036-2038 (3)* 15.00 6.75

Victory at Pskov A1073

Soldier and Civilian — A1074

Designs: No. 2040, Airman, sailor and soldier. No. 2042, Sailor and soldier. 60k, Storming of Berlin Reichstag building.

**1958, Feb. 21**

**2039** A1073 25k multicolored .50 .40
**2040** A1073 40k multicolored 1.00 .40
**2041** A1074 40k multicolored 1.00 .40
**2042** A1074 40k multicolored 1.00 .40
**2043** A1073 60k multicolored 1.50 .40
*Nos. 2039-2043 (5)* 5.00 2.00

40th anniversary of Red Armed Forces.

Peter Ilich Tchaikovsky A1075

Swan Lake Ballet A1076

Design: 1r, Tchaikovsky, pianist and violinist.

**1958, Mar. 18**

**2044** A1075 40k grn, bl, brn & red .60 .25
**2045** A1076 40k grn, ultra, red & yel .60 .25
**2046** A1075 1r lake & emerald 2.00 .50
*Nos. 2044-2046 (3)* 3.20 1.00

Honoring Tchaikovsky and for the Tchaikovsky competitions for pianists and violinists. Exist imperf. Value, set $10.

Nos. 2044-2045 were printed in sheets of 30, including 15 stamps of each value and 5 se-tenant pairs. Value, pairs $10.

V. F. Rudnev — A1077

**1958, Mar. 25** **Unwmk.**

**2047** A1077 40k green, blk & ocher 1.00 .50

Rudnev, naval commander.

Maxim Gorki — A1078

**1958, Apr. 3** **Litho.** ***Perf. 12***

**2048** A1078 40k multicolored .75 .50

Gorki, writer, 90th birth anniv.

Spasski Tower — A1079

**1958, Apr. 9**

**2049** A1079 40k dp violet, *pinkish* .75 .25
**2050** A1079 60k rose red 1.25 .25

13th Congress of the Young Communist League (Komsomol).

Russian Pavilion, Brussels A1080

**1958, Apr.**

**2051** A1080 10k multicolored .45 .25
**2052** A1080 40k multicolored .55 .25

Universal and International Exhibition at Brussels. Exist imperf. Value $5.

Lenin — A1081

**1958, Apr. 22** **Engr.**

**2053** A1081 40k dk blue gray 1.00 .65
**2054** A1081 60k rose brown 1.50 .65
**2055** A1081 1r brown 2.50 .65
*Nos. 2053-2055 (3)* 5.00 1.95

88th anniversary of the birth of Lenin.

**1958, May 5**

Portrait: Nos. 2056-2058, Karl Marx.

**2056** A1081 40k brown 1.00 .25
**2057** A1081 60k dark blue 1.50 .25
**2058** A1081 1r dark red 2.50 .40
*Nos. 2056-2058 (3)* 5.00 .90

140th anniversary of the birth of Marx.

Jan A. Komensky (Comenius) — A1082

**1958, Apr. 17** **Photo.**

**2059** A1082 40k green 3.00 1.00

### No. 1695 Overprinted in Blue

**1958, Apr. 22**

**2060** A914 40k multicolored 4.50 1.00

Academy of Arts, Moscow, 200th anniv.

Lenin Order — A1083

**1958, Apr. 30** **Litho.**

**2061** A1083 40k brn, yel & red 1.00 .50

Carlo Goldoni — A1084

**1958, Apr. 28** **Photo.**

**2062** A1084 40k blue & dk gray .75 .35

Carlo Goldoni, Italian dramatist.

Radio Tower, Ship and Planes A1085

**1958, May 7**

**2063** A1085 40k blue grn & red 5.00 .50

Issued for Radio Day, May 7.

Globe and Dove — A1086

**1958, May 6** **Litho.**

**2064** A1086 40k blue & black .40 .25
**2065** A1086 60k ultra & black .60 .25

4th Congress of the Intl. Democratic Women's Federation, June, 1958, at Vienna.

Ilya Chavchavadze A1087

**1958, May 12** **Photo.**

**2066** A1087 40k black & blue .80 .35

50th anniversary of the death of Ilya Chavchavadze, Georgian writer.

Flags and Communication Symbols — A1088

**1958-59** **Litho.**

**2067** A1088 40k blue, red, yel & blk 8.00 3.00
*a.* Red half of Czech flag at bottom 8.00 3.00

Communist ministers' meeting on social problems in Moscow, Dec. 1957.

On No. 2067, the Czech flag (center flag in vertical row of five) is incorrectly pictured with red stripe on top. This error is corrected on No. 2067a.

Bugler — A1089

Pioneers: 25k, Boy with model plane.

**1958, May 29 Unwmk. *Perf. 12***

**2068** A1089 10k ultra, red & red brn .50 .25
**2069** A1089 25k ultra, yel & red brn .50 .25

Children of Three Races — A1090

Design: No. 2071, Child and bomb.

**1958, May 29**

**2070** A1090 40k car, ultra & brn .50 .25
**2071** A1090 40k car & brn .50 .25

Intl. Day for the Protection of Children.

Soccer Players and Globe — A1091

**1958, June 5**

**2072** A1091 40k blue, red & buff .75 .25
**2073** A1091 60k blue, red & buff 2.25 .30

6th World Soccer Championships, Stockholm, June 8-29. Exist imperf. Value $5.

Rimski-Korsakov A1092

**1958, June 5 Photo.**

**2074** A1092 40k blue & brown 3.00 .50

Nikolai Andreevich Rimski-Korsakov (1844-1908), composer.

Girl Gymnast — A1093

No. 2076, Gymnast on rings and view.

**1958, June 24 Litho.**

**2075** A1093 40k ultra, red & buff 1.00 .25
**2076** A1093 40k blue, red buff & grn 1.00 .25

14th World Gymnastic Championships, Moscow, July 6-10.

Bomb, Globe, Atom, Sputniks, Ship A1094

**1958, July 1**

**2077** A1094 60k dk blue, blk & org 9.00 1.00

Conference for peaceful uses of atomic energy, held at Stockholm.

Street Fighters — A1095

**1958, July 5**

**2078** A1095 40k red & violet blk 2.00 .30

Communist Party in the Ukraine, 40th anniv.

Moscow State University A1096

Congress Emblem — A1097

**1958, July 8 *Perf. 12***

**2079** A1096 40k red & blue .75 .25
**2080** A1097 60k lt grn, blue & red 1.25 .30
*a.* Souvenir sheet of 2 10.00 7.00

5th Congress of the International Architects' Organization, Moscow.

No. 2080a contains Nos. 2079-2080, imperf., with background design in yellow, brown, blue and red. Issued Sept. 8, 1958.

Young Couple A1098

**1958, June 25**

**2081** A1098 40k blue & ocher .75 .30
**2082** A1098 60k yel green & ocher 1.25 .45

Day of Soviet Youth.

Sputnik 3 Leaving Earth A1099

**1958, June 16**

**2083** A1099 40k vio blue, grn & rose 2.50 .35

Launching of Sputnik 3, May 15. Printed in sheets with alternating labels, giving details of launching.

Sadriddin Aini — A1100

**1958, July 15**

**2084** A1100 40k rose, black & buff 3.00 .50

80th birthday of Aini, Tadzhik writer.

Emblem A1101

**1958, July 21 Typo. *Perf. 12***

**2085** A1101 40k lilac & blue .75 .35

1st World Trade Union Conference of Working Youths, Prague, July 14-20.

### Type of 1958-59 and

TU-104 and Globe A1102

Design: 1r, Turbo-propeller liner AN-10.

**1958, Aug. Litho.**

**2086** A1102 60k blue, red & bis .75 .25
**2087** A1123 1r yel, red & black 1.25 .25

Soviet civil aviation. Exist imperf. Value, set $5.50. See Nos. 2147-2151.

L. A. Kulik A1103

**1958, Aug. 12**

**2088** A1103 40k sep, bl, yel & claret 2.00 .50

50th anniv. of the falling of the Tungus meteor and the 75th anniv. of the birth of L. A. Kulik, meteorist.

### IGY Type of 1957

Designs: No. 2089, Aurora borealis and camera. No. 2090, Schooner "Zarja" exploring's earth magnetism. No. 2091, Weather balloon and radar.

**1958, July 29 Size: 25½x37mm**

**2089** A1039 40k blue & brt yel 1.40 .35
**2090** A1039 40k blue green 1.40 .35
**2091** A1039 40k bright ultra 1.40 .35
*Nos. 2089-2091 (3)* 4.20 1.05

International Geophysical Year, 1957-58.

Crimea Observatory A1104

Moscow University A1105

Design: 1r, Telescope.

**1958, Aug. Photo.**

**2092** A1104 40k brn & brt grnsh bl 2.00 .35
**2093** A1105 60k lt blue, vio & yel 2.50 .35
**2094** A1104 1r dp blue & org brn 3.50 .35
*Nos. 2092-2094 (3)* 8.00 1.05

10th Congress of the International Astronomical Union, Moscow.

Postilion, 16th Century A1106

Designs: No. 2095, 15th cent. letter writer. No. 2097, A. L. Ordyn-Natshokin and sleigh mail coach, 17th cent. No. 2098, Mail coach and post office, 18th cent. No. 2099, Troika, 19th cent. No. 2100, Lenin stamp, ship and Kremlin. No. 2101, Jet plane and troika. No. 2102, Leningrad Communications Museum, vert. No. 2103, V. N. Podbielski and letter carriers. No. 2104, Mail train. No. 2105, Loading mail on plane. No. 2106, Ship, plane, train and globe.

**1958, Aug. Unwmk. Litho. *Perf. 12***

**2095** A1106 10k red, blk, yel & lil .25 .25
**2096** A1106 10k multicolored .25 .25
**2097** A1106 25k ultra & slate .60 .30
**2098** A1106 25k black & ultra .60 .30
**2099** A1106 40k car lake & brn blk 1.20 .45
**2100** A1106 40k blk, mag & brn 1.20 .45
**2101** A1106 40k red, org & gray 1.20 .45
**2102** A1106 40k sal & brn 1.20 .45
**2103** A1106 60k grnsh blue & red lil 1.50 .35
**2104** A1106 60k grnsh bl & lilac 1.50 .35
**2105** A1106 1r multicolored 3.25 .70
**2106** A1106 1r multicolored 3.25 .70
*Nos. 2095-2106 (12)* 16.00 5.00

Centenary of Russian postage stamps.

Two imperf. souvenir sheets exist, measuring 155x106mm. One contains one each of Nos. 2095-2099, with background design in red, ultramarine, yellow and brown. The other contains one each of Nos. 2100, 2103-2106, with background design in blue, gray, ocher, pink and brown. Value for both, $50 unused, $10 canceled.

Nos. 2096, 2100-2101 exist imperf. Value for both, $20 unused, $10 canceled.

M. I. Chigorin, Chess Player, 50th Death Anniv. — A1107

**1958, Aug. 30 Photo.**

**2107** A1107 40k black & emerald 2.00 .50

Golden Gate, Vladimir A1108

60k, Gorki Street with trolley bus and truck.

**1958, Aug. 23 Litho.**

**2108** A1108 40k multicolored .80 .40
**2109** A1108 60k lt violet, yel & blk 1.20 .60

850th anniv. of the city of Vladimir.

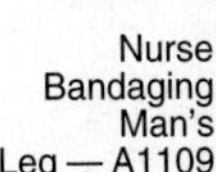
Nurse Bandaging Man's Leg — A1109

No. 2111, Hospital, & people of various races.

**1958, Sept. 15**

**2110** A1109 40k multicolored .75 .30
**2111** A1109 40k ol, lem & red .75 .30

40 years of Red Cross-Red Crescent work.

**Portrait Type of 1958**

Mikhail E. Saltykov (Shchedrin), writer.

**1958, Sept. 15**

**2112** A1071 40k brn black & mar 5.00 1.00

Rudagi — A1110

**1958, Oct. 10 Litho. *Perf. 12***

**2113** A1110 40k multicolored 2.00 .50

1100th anniversary of the birth of Rudagi, Persian poet.

V. V. Kapnist — A1111

**1958, Sept. 30**

**2114** A1111 40k blue & gray 1.00 .50

200th anniversary of the birth of V. V. Kapnist, poet and dramatist.

Book, Torch, Lyre, Flower A1112

**1958, Oct. 4**

**2115** A1112 40k red org, ol & blk 2.00 .50

Conf. of Asian & African Writers, Tashkent.

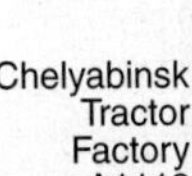
Chelyabinsk Tractor Factory A1113

Designs: No. 2117, Zaporozstal foundry. No. 2118, Ural machine building plant.

**1958, Oct. 20 Photo.**

**2116** A1113 40k green & yellow 1.50 .30
**2117** A1113 40k brown red & yel 1.50 .30
**2118** A1113 40k blue 1.50 .30
*Nos. 2116-2118 (3)* 4.50 .90

Pioneers of Russian Industry.

Ancient Georgian on Horseback A1114

**1958, Oct. 18 Litho.**

**2119** A1114 40k ocher, ultra & red 2.00 .50

1500th anniv. of Tbilisi, capital of Georgia.

Red Square, Moscow — A1115

АЛМА-АТА · ПЛОЩАДЬ им. В. И. ЛЕНИНА
No. 2121

ТБИЛИСИ · ПРОСПЕКТ РУСТАВЕЛИ
No. 2125

ФРУНЗЕ · УНИВЕРСИТЕТСКАЯ ПЛОЩАДЬ
No. 2127

ОБЩИЙ ВИД ГОРОДА ЕРЕВАН
No. 2128

МИНСК · КРУГЛАЯ ПЛОЩАДЬ
No. 2131

Capitals of Soviet Republics: No. 2121, Lenin Square, Alma Ata. No. 2122, Lenin statue, Ashkhabad. No. 2123, Lenin statue, Tashkent. No. 2124, Lenin Square, Stalinabad. No. 2125, Rustaveli Ave., Tbilisi. No. 2126, View from Dvina River, Riga. No. 2127, University Square, Frunze. No. 2128, View, Yerevan. No. 2129, Communist Street, Baku. No. 2130, Lenin Prospect, Kishinev. No. 2131, Round Square, Minsk. No. 2132, Viru Gate, Tallinn. No. 2133, Main Street, Kiev. No. 2134, View, Vilnius.

**1958 Engr.**

**2120** A1115 40k violet 1.00 .45
**2121** A1115 40k brt blue green 1.00 .45
**2122** A1115 40k greenish gray 1.00 .45
**2123** A1115 40k dark gray 1.00 .45
**2124** A1115 40k blue 1.00 .45
**2125** A1115 40k violet blue 1.00 .45
**2126** A1115 40k brown red 1.00 .45
**2127** A1115 40k dk blue gray 1.00 .45
**2128** A1115 40k brown 1.00 .45
**2129** A1115 40k purple 1.00 .45
**2130** A1115 40k olive 1.00 .45
**2131** A1115 40k gray brown 1.00 .45
**2132** A1115 40k emerald 1.00 .45
**2133** A1115 40k lilac rose 1.00 .45
**2134** A1115 40k orange ver 1.00 .45
*Nos. 2120-2134 (15)* 15.00 6.75

See No. 2836.

Young Civil War Soldier, 1919 — A1116

20k, Industrial brigade. 25k, Youth in World War II. 40k, Girl farm worker. 60k, Youth building new towns. 1r, Students, fighters for culture.

**1958, Oct. 25 Litho.**

**2135** A1116 10k multicolored .40 .25
**2136** A1116 20k multicolored .75 .25
**2137** A1116 25k multicolored .90 .25
**2138** A1116 40k multicolored 1.50 .25
**2139** A1116 60k multicolored 2.25 .25
**2140** A1116 1r multicolored 4.50 1.00
*Nos. 2135-2140 (6)* 10.30 2.25

40th anniversary of the Young Communist League (Komsomol).

Marx and Lenin — A1117

Lenin, Intellectual, Peasant and Miner A1118

**1958, Oct. 31**

**2141** A1117 40k multicolored .50 .25
**2142** A1118 1r multicolored 1.50 .30

41st anniversary of Russian Revolution.

Torch, Wreath and Family A1119

**1958, Nov. 5**

**2143** A1119 60k blk, beige & dull bl 1.00 .50

10th anniversary of the Universal Declaration of Human Rights.

Sergei Esenin (1895-1925), Poet — A1120

**1958, Nov. 29**

**2144** A1120 40k multicolored 1.00 .50

G. K. Ordzhonikidze A1121

**1958, Dec. 12 *Perf. 12***

**2145** A1121 40k multicolored 1.00 .50

G. K. Ordzhonikidze (1886-1937), Georgian party worker.

Kuan Han-ching — A1122

**1958, Dec. 5**

**2146** A1122 40k dk blue & gray 3.00 1.00

700th anniversary of the theater of Kuan Han-ching, Chinese dramatist.

Airliner IL-14 and Globe A1123

Soviet civil aviation: No. 2148, Jet liner TU-104. No. 2149, Turbo-propeller liner TU-114. 60k, Jet liner TU-110. 2r, Turbo-propeller liner IL-18.

**1958-59**

**2147** A1123 20k ultra, blk & red .40 .25
**2148** A1123 40k bl grn, blk & red .60 .25
**2149** A1123 40k brt bl, blk & red .60 .25
**2150** A1123 60k rose car & black .60 .25
**2151** A1123 2r plum, red & black ('59) 1.75 .25
*Nos. 2147-2151 (5)* 3.95 1.25

Exist imperf.; value $10.
See Nos. 2086-2087.

Eleonora Duse — A1124

**1958, Dec. 26**

**2152** A1124 40k blue grn & gray 1.00 .50

Duse, Italian actress, birth cent.

John Milton — A1125

**1958, Dec. 17**

**2153** A1125 40k brown 1.00 .50

John Milton (1608-1674), English poet.

K. F. Rulye — A1126

**1958, Dec. 26**

**2154** A1126 40k ultra & black 1.00 .50

Rulye, educator, death cent.

Fuzuli — A1127

**1958, Dec. 23 Photo.**

**2155** A1127 40k grnsh bl & brn 1.00 .50

400th anniv. of the death of Fuzuli (Mehmet Suleiman Oglou), Azerbaijani poet.

Census Emblem and Family — A1128

Design: No. 2157, Census emblem.

**1958, Dec.** **Litho.**

**2156** A1128 40k multicolored .75 .25
**2157** A1128 40k yel, gray, bl & red .75 .25

1959 Soviet census.

Lunik and Sputniks over Kremlin — A1129

Designs: 40k, Lenin and view of Kremlin. 60k, Workers and Lenin power plant on Volga.

**1959, Jan.** **Unwmk.** ***Perf. 12***

**2158** A1129 40k multicolored 1.50 .25
**2159** A1129 60k multicolored 2.50 .75
**2160** A1129 1r red, yel & vio bl 7.00 1.50
*Nos. 2158-2160 (3)* 11.00 2.50

21st Cong. of the Communist Party and "the conquest of the cosmos by the Soviet people."

Lenin Statue, Minsk Buildings — A1130

**1958, Dec. 20**

**2161** A1130 40k red, buff & brn .75 .35

Byelorussian Republic, 40th anniv.

Atomic Icebreaker "Lenin" A1131

Design: 60k, Diesel Locomotive "TE-3."

**1958, Dec. 31**

**2162** A1131 40k multicolored 1.75 1.00
**2163** A1131 60k multicolored 2.75 1.25

Shalom Aleichem — A1132

**1959, Feb. 10**

**2164** A1132 40k chocolate .75 .35

Aleichem, Yiddish writer, birth cent.

Evangelista Torricelli — A1133

Scientists: No. 2166, Charles Darwin, English biologist. No. 2167, N. F. Gamaleya, microbiologist.

**1959, Feb.** **Various Frames**

**2165** A1133 40k blue green & blk .75 .25
**2166** A1133 40k chalky blue & brn .75 .25
**2167** A1133 40k dk red & black .75 .25
*Nos. 2165-2167 (3)* 2.25 .75

Woman Skater — A1134

**1959, Feb. 5**

**2168** A1134 25k ultra, black & ver .75 .25
**2169** A1134 40k ultra & black 1.25 .30

Women's International Ice Skating Championships, Sverdlovsk.

No. 1717 Overprinted in Orange Brown

**1959, Feb. 12**

**2170** A919 1r dk brn & brn 7.50 5.00

"Victory of the USSR Basketball Team — Chile 1959." However, the 3rd World Basketball Championship honors went to Brazil when the Soviet team was disqualified for refusing to play Nationalist China.

Frederic Joliot-Curie A1135

**1959, Mar. 3** **Litho.** ***Perf. 12***

**2171** A1135 40k turq bl & gray brn, *beige* 1.00 .25

Joliot-Curie (1900-58), French scientist.

Selma Lagerlöf — A1136

**1959, Feb. 26**

**2172** A1136 40k red brn & blk .75 .35

Lagerlöf (1858-1940), Swedish writer.

Peter Zwirka — A1137

**1959, Mar. 3**

**2173** A1137 40k hn brn & blk, *yel* .75 .35

Zwirka (1909-1947), Lithuanian writer.

**No. 1861A Overprinted in Red: "1759 1959"**

**1959, Feb. 26** **Engr.**

**2174** A993 40k lt ultra & brown 10.00 10.00

200th anniversary of the birth of Robert Burns, Scottish poet.

**Type of 1958**

Russian Writers: No. 2175, A. S. Griboedov. No. 2176, A. N. Ostrovski. No. 2177, Anton Chekhov. No. 2178, I. A. Krylov. No. 2178A, Nikolai V. Gogol. No. 2178B, S. T. Aksakov. No. 2178C, A. V. Koltzov. poet, and reaper.

**1959** **Litho.**

**2175** A1071 40k buff, cl, blk & vio .75 .40
**2176** A1071 40k vio & brown .75 .40
**2177** A1071 40k slate & hn brn .75 .40
**2178** A1071 40k ol bister & brn .75 .40
**2178A** A1071 40k ol, gray & bis .75 .40
**2178B** A1071 40k brn, vio & bis .75 .40
**2178C** A1071 40k violet & black .75 .40
*Nos. 2175-2178C (7)* 5.25 2.80

No. 2178A for the 150th birth anniv. of Nikolai V. Gogol, writer, No. 2178B the centenary of the death of S. T. Aksakov, writer.

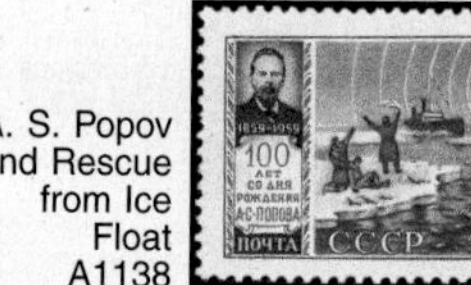

A. S. Popov and Rescue from Ice Float A1138

60k, Radio broadcasting "Peace" in 5 languages.

**1959, Mar. 13**

**2179** A1138 40k brn, blk & dk blue .75 .25
**2180** A1138 60k multicolored 1.25 .25

Centenary of the birth of A. S. Popov, pioneer in radio research.

M.S. Rossija at Odessa A1139

Ships: 10k, Steamer, Vladivostok-Petropavlovsk-Kamchatka line. 20k, M.S. Feliks Dzerzhinski, Odessa-Latakia line. No. 2184, Ship, Murmansk-Tyksi line. 60k, M.S. Mikhail Kalinin at Leningrad. 1r, M.S. Baltika, Leningrad-London line.

**1959** **Litho.** **Unwmk.**

**2181** A1139 10k multicolored .30 .25
**2182** A1139 20k red, lt grn & dk bl .40 .25
**2183** A1139 40k multicolored .75 .25
**2184** A1139 40k blue, buff & red 1.25 .25
**2185** A1139 60k bl grn, red & buff 1.50 .30
**2186** A1139 1r ultra, red & yel 1.75 1.00
*Nos. 2181-2186 (6)* 5.95 2.30

Honoring the Russian fleet.

Globe and Luna 1 A1140

Luna 1, launched Jan. 2, 1959: No. 2188, Globe and route of Luna 1.

**1959, Apr. 13**

**2187** A1140 40k red brown & rose 2.50 .50
**2188** A1140 40k ultra & blue 2.50 .50

Compare with type A1175.

Saadi and "Gulistan" A1141

**1959, Mar. 20** **Photo.**

**2189** A1141 40k dk blue & black .75 .35

Persian poet Saadi (Muslih-ud-Din) and 700th anniv. of his book, "Gulistan" (1258).

Sulhan S. Orbeliani — A1142

**1959, Apr. 2**

**2190** A1142 40k dull rose & black .75 .35

Orbeliani (1658-1725), Georgian writer.

Drawing by Korin — A1143

**1959, Apr. 10** **Litho.**

**2191** A1143 40k multicolored 5.00 1.50

Ogata Korin (1653?-1716), Japanese artist.

Lenin — A1144

**1959, Apr. 17** **Engr.**

**2192** A1144 40k sepia 1.00 .50

89th anniversary of the birth of Lenin.

Cachin — A1146

**1959, Apr. 27** **Photo.**

**2194** A1146 60k dark brown 1.00 .30

Marcel Cachin (1869-1958), French Communist Party leader.

Joseph Haydn — A1147

**1959, May 8**

**2195** A1147 40k dk bl, gray & brn black 5.00 .50

Sesquicentennial of the death of Joseph Haydn, Austrian composer.

Alexander von Humboldt — A1148

**1959, May 6**

**2196** A1148 40k violet & brown .75 .35

Alexander von Humboldt, German naturalist and geographer, death centenary.

Three Races Carrying Flag of Peace — A1149

**1959, Apr. 30** **Litho.**

**2199** A1149 40k multicolored 1.00 .25

10th anniv. of World Peace Movement.

Mountain Climber — A1150

Sports and Travel: No. 2201, Tourists reading map. No. 2202, Canoeing, horiz. No. 2203, Skiers.

**1959, May 15**

**2200** A1150 40k multicolored .50 .25
**2201** A1150 40k multicolored .50 .25
**2202** A1150 40k multicolored .50 .25
**2203** A1150 40k multicolored .50 .25
*Nos. 2200-2203 (4)* 2.00 1.00

I. E. Repin Statue, Moscow — A1151

Statues: No. 2205, Lenin, Ulyanovsk. 20k, V. V. Mayakovsky, Moscow. 25k, Alexander Pushkin, Leningrad. 60k, Maxim Gorki, Moscow. 1r, Tchaikovsky, Moscow.

**1959** **Photo.** **Unwmk.**

**2204** A1151 10k ocher & sepia .25 .25
**2205** A1151 10k red & black .25 .25
**2206** A1151 20k violet & sepia .35 .25
**2207** A1151 25k grnsh blue & blk .45 .25
**2208** A1151 60k lt green & slate .75 .25
**2209** A1151 1r lt ultra & gray 1.75 .45
*Nos. 2204-2209 (6)* 3.80 1.70

N. Y. Coliseum and Spasski Tower — A1152

**1959, June 25** **Litho.** ***Perf. 12***

**2210** A1152 20k multicolored .30 .25
**2211** A1152 40k multicolored .70 .25
*a.* Souv. sheet of 1, imperf. 5.00 .50

Soviet Exhibition of Science, Technology and Culture, New York, June 20-Aug. 10. No. 2211a issued July 20.

### Animal Types of 1957

No. 2213, Hare. No. 2214, Siberian horse. No. 2215, Tiger. No. 2216, Red squirrel. No. 2217, Pine marten. No. 2218, Hazel hen. No. 2219, Mute swan.

**1959-60** **Litho.** ***Perf. 12***

**Center in Natural Colors**

**2213** A1023 20k vio blue ('60) .60 .25
**2214** A1023 25k blue black .60 .25
**2215** A1023 25k brown .60 .25
**2216** A1023 40k deep green .80 .25
**2217** A1023 40k dark green .80 .25
**2218** A1024 60k dark green 1.25 .40
**2219** A1023 1r bright blue 1.75 .85
*Nos. 2213-2219 (7)* 6.40 2.50

Louis Braille — A1153

**1959, July 16**

**2220** A1153 60k blue grn, bis & brn .75 .35

150th anniversary of the birth of Louis Braille, French educator of the blind.

Musa Djalil — A1154

**1959, July 16** **Photo.**

**2221** A1154 40k violet & black 1.75 .35

Musa Djalil, Tatar poet.

Sturgeon A1155

**1959, July 16**

**2222** A1155 40k shown .75 .25
**2223** A1155 60k Chum salmon 1.25 .25

See Nos. 2375-2377.

Gymnast A1156

Athletes Holding Spartacist Games emblem — A1157

Designs: 25k, Runner. 60k, Water polo.

**1959, Aug. 7**

**2224** A1156 15k lilac rose & gray .30 .25
**2225** A1156 25k yel green & red brn .60 .25
**2226** A1157 30k brt red & gray .75 .25
**2227** A1156 60k blue & org yel 1.25 .25
*Nos. 2224-2227 (4)* 2.90 1.00

2nd National Spartacist Games.

Globe and Hands — A1158

**1959, Aug. 12** **Litho.**

**2228** A1158 40k yel, blue & red .75 .35

2nd Intl. Conf. of Public Employees Unions.

Cathedral and Modern Building A1159



**1959, Aug. 21** **Unwmk.** ***Perf. 12***

**2229** A1159 40k blue, ol, yel & red 1.00 .25

1100th anniv. of the city of Novgorod.

Schoolboys in Workshop — A1160



Design: 1r, Workers in night school.

**1959, Aug. 27** **Photo.**

**2230** A1160 40k dark purple .25 .25
**2231** A1160 1r dark blue .50 .25

Strengthening the connection between school and life.

Glacier Survey — A1161

Rocket and Observatory A1162

Designs: 25k, Oceanographic ship "Vityaz" and map. 40k, Plane over Antarctica, camp and emperor penguin.

**1959**

**2232** A1161 10k blue green .25 .25
**2233** A1161 25k brt blue & red .30 .25
**2234** A1161 40k ultra & red .50 .25
**2235** A1162 1r ultra & buff 1.50 .30
*Nos. 2232-2235 (4)* 2.55 1.05

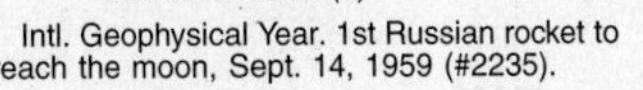

Intl. Geophysical Year. 1st Russian rocket to reach the moon, Sept. 14, 1959 (#2235).

Workers and Farmers Holding Atom Symbol — A1163

**1959, Sept. 23** **Litho.**

**2236** A1163 40k red org & bister .75 .35

All-Union Economic Exhibition, Moscow.

Russian and Chinese Students A1164

40k, Russian miner and Chinese steel worker.

**1959, Sept. 25** **Litho.** ***Perf. 12***

**2237** A1164 20k multicolored .80 .30
**2238** A1164 40k multicolored 1.20 .45

People's Republic of China, 10th anniv.

Letter Carrier A1165

**1959, Sept.**

**2239** A1165 40k dk car rose & black .40 .25
**2240** A1165 60k blue & black .60 .25

Intl. Letter Writing Week, Oct. 4-10.

Makhtumkuli A1166

**1959, Sept. 30** **Photo.**

**2241** A1166 40k brown 1.00 .25

225th anniversary of the birth of Makhtumkuli, Turkmen writer.

East German Emblem and Workers A1167

City Hall, East Berlin — A1168

**1959, Oct. 6** **Litho.**

**2242** A1167 40k multicolored .35 .25

**Photo.**

**2243** A1168 60k dp claret & buff .45 .25

German Democratic Republic, 10th anniv.

Steel Production — A1169

7-Year Production Plan (Industries): No. 2244, Chemicals. No. 2245, Spasski Tower, hammer and sickle. No. 2246, Home building. No. 2247, Meat production, woman with farm animals. No. 2248, Man working machinery. No. 2249, Grain production, woman tractor driver. No. 2250, Oil. No. 2251, Textiles. No. 2252, Steel. No. 2253, Coal. No. 2254, Iron. No. 2255, Electric power.

**1959-60** **Litho.**

**2244** A1169 10k vio, grnsh blue & maroon .50 .25
**2245** A1169 10k orange & dk car .50 .25
**2246** A1169 15k brn, yel & red .50 .25
**2247** A1169 15k brn, grn & mar .50 .25
**2248** A1169 20k bl grn, yel & red .50 .25
**2249** A1169 20k green, yel & red .50 .25
**2250** A1169 30k lilac, sal & red .50 .25
**2251** A1169 30k gldn brn, lil, red & green ('60) .50 .25
**2252** A1169 40k vio bl, yel & org .50 .25
**2253** A1169 40k dk blue, pink & dp rose .50 .25
**2254** A1169 60k org red, yel, bl & maroon .50 .25
**2255** A1169 60k ultra, buff & red .50 .25
*Nos. 2244-2255 (12)* 6.00 3.00

Arms of Tadzhikistan A1170

**1959, Oct. 13**

**2258** A1170 40k red, emer, ocher & black .75 .35

Tadzhikistan statehood, 30th anniversary.

Path of Luna 3 and Electronics Laboratory A1171

**1959, Oct. 12**

**2259** A1171 40k violet 1.50 .50

Flight of Luna 3 around the moon, Oct. 4, 1959.

Red Square, Moscow A1172

**1959, Oct. 26** **Engr.**

**2260** A1172 40k dark red 1.00 .50

42nd anniversary of October Revolution.

US Capitol, Globe and Kremlin — A1173

**1959, Oct. 27** **Photo.**

**2261** A1173 60k blue & yellow 1.00 .50

Visit of Premier Nikita Khrushchev to the US, Sept., 1959.

Helicopter — A1174

25k, Diver. 40k, Motorcyclist. 60k, Parachutist.

**1959, Oct. 28**

**2262** A1174 10k vio blue & mar .25 .25
**2263** A1174 25k blue & brown .60 .25
**2264** A1174 40k red brn & indigo 1.00 .25
**2265** A1174 60k blue & ol bister 1.25 .25
*Nos. 2262-2265 (4)* 3.10 1.00

Honoring voluntary aides of the army.

Moon, Earth and Path of Rocket A1175

No. 2267, Kremlin and diagram showing rocket and positions of moon and earth.

**1959, Nov. 1** **Litho.**

**2266** A1175 40k bl, dk bl, red & bis 1.50 .25
**2267** A1175 40k gray, pink & red 1.50 .25

Landing of the Soviet rocket on the moon, Sept. 14, 1959. Compare with type A1140.

Sandor Petőfi A1176

Victory Statue and View of Budapest — A1177

**1959, Nov. 9** ***Perf. 12x12½, 12½x12***

**2268** A1176 20k gray & ol bister .50 .25
**2269** A1177 40k multicolored 1.50 .50

Soviet-Hungarian friendship.
For overprint see No. 2308.

Manolis Glezos and Acropolis A1178

**1959, Nov. 12** **Photo.** ***Perf. 12x12½***

**2270** A1178 40k ultra & brown 9.00 3.00

Manolis Glezos, Greek communist.

A. A. Voskresensky, Chemist, 150th Birth Anniv. — A1179

**1959, Dec. 7** ***Perf. 12½x12***

**2271** A1179 40k ultra & brown .75 .35

Chusovaya River, Ural — A1180

No. 2273, Lake Ritza, Caucasus. No. 2274, Lena River, Siberia. No. 2275, Seashore, Far East. No. 2276, Lake Iskander, Central Asia. No. 2277, Lake Baikal, Siberia. No. 2278, Belukha Mountain, Altai range. No. 2279, Khibiny Mountains. No. 2280, Gursuf region, Crimea.

**1959, Dec.** **Engr.** ***Perf. 12½***

**2272** A1180 10k purple .25 .25
**2273** A1180 10k rose carmine .25 .25
**2274** A1180 25k dark blue .65 .25
**2275** A1180 25k olive .65 .25
**2276** A1180 25k dark red .65 .25
**2277** A1180 40k claret 1.50 .25
**2278** A1180 60k Prus blue 2.25 .35
**2279** A1180 1r olive green 4.50 .75
**2280** A1180 1r deep orange 4.50 .75
*Nos. 2272-2280 (9)* 15.20 3.35

"Trumpeters of 1st Cavalry" by M. Grekov — A1181

**1959, Dec. 30** **Litho.** ***Perf. 12½x12***

**2283** A1181 40k multicolored 2.00 1.00

40th anniversary of the 1st Cavalry.

Farm Woman — A1182

Designs: 25k, Architect. 60k, Steel worker.

**1958-60** **Engr.** ***Perf. 12½***

**2286** A1182 20k slate grn ('59) 7.00 3.75
**2287** A1182 25k sepia ('59) 3.25 1.60
**2288** A1182 60k carmine 9.25 4.25

***Perf. 12x12½***

**Litho.**

**2290** A1182 20k green ('60) .25 .25
**2291** A1182 25k sepia ('60) .75 .25
**2292** A1182 60k vermilion ('59) .25 .25
**2293** A1182 60k blue ('60) 1.50 .25
*Nos. 2286-2293 (7)* 22.25 10.60

Mikhail V. Frunze (1885-1925), Revolutionary A1183

**1960, Jan. 25** **Photo.** ***Perf. 12½***

**2295** A1183 40k dark red brown 1.00 .35

G.N. Gabrichevski, Microbiologist, Birth Cent. — A1184

***Perf. 12½x12***

**1960, Jan. 30** **Unwmk.**

**2296** A1184 40k brt vio & brn 1.00 .35

Anton Chekhov and Moscow Home A1185

40k, Chekhov in later years, Yalta home.

**1960, Jan. 20** **Litho.** ***Perf. 12x12½***

**2297** A1185 20k red, gray & vio bl .40 .25
**2298** A1185 40k dk blue, buff & brn .70 .25

Anton P. Chekhov (1860-1904), playwright.

Vera Komissarzhevskaya (1864-1910), Actress — A1186

**1960, Feb. 5** **Photo.** ***Perf. 12½x12***

**2299** A1186 40k chocolate 1.00 .50

8th Olympic Winter Games, Squaw Valley, Calif., Feb. 18-29 A1187

Sports: 10k, Ice hockey. 25k, Speed skating. 40k, Skier. 60k, Woman figure skater. 1r, Ski jumper.

**1960, Feb. 18** **Litho.** ***Perf. 11½***

**2300** A1187 10k ocher & vio blue .25 .25
**2301** A1187 25k multicolored .50 .25
**2302** A1187 40k org, rose lil & vio blue .75 .25
**2303** A1187 60k vio, grn & buff 1.25 .25
**2304** A1187 1r bl, grn & brn 2.25 .35
*Nos. 2300-2304 (5)* 5.00 1.35

Sword into Plowshare Statue, UN, NY — A1188

**1960** ***Perf. 12x12½***
**2305** A1188 40k grnsh bl, yel & brown 1.00 .50
*a.* Souvenir sheet, imperf. 2.00 .50

No. 2305a for Premier Nikita Khrushchev's visit to the 15th General Assembly of the UN in NYC.

Women of Various Races A1189

**1960, Mar. 8**
**2306** A1189 40k multicolored 1.00 .35

50 years of Intl. Woman's Day, Mar. 8.

Planes in Combat and Timur Frunze A1190

**1960, Feb. 23** ***Perf. 12½x12***
**2307** A1190 40k multicolored 2.00 1.50

Lieut. Timur Frunze, World War II hero.

No. 2269 Overprinted in Red

**1960, Apr. 4**
**2308** A1177 40k multicolored 4.50 2.50

15th anniversary of Hungary's liberation from the Nazis.

Lunik 3 Photographing Far Side of Moon — A1191

Design: 60k, Far side of the moon.

**1960** **Photo.** ***Perf. 12x12½***
**2309** A1191 40k pale bl, dk bl & yel 1.75 .30

**Litho.**
**2310** A1191 60k lt bl, dk bl & citron 2.25 .30

Photographing of the far side of the moon, Oct. 7, 1959.

Lenin as Child A1192

Various Lenin Portraits and: 20k, Lenin with children and Christmas tree. 30k, Flag, workers and ship. 40k, Kremlin, banners and marchers. 60k, Map of Russia, buildings and ship. 1r, Peace proclamation and globe.

**1960, Apr. 10** **Litho.** ***Perf. 12½x12***
**2311** A1192 10k multicolored .25 .25
**2312** A1192 20k red, green & blk .30 .25
**2313** A1192 30k multicolored .50 .25
**2314** A1192 40k multicolored .75 .25
**2315** A1192 60k multicolored 1.00 .30
**2316** A1192 1r red, vio bl & brn 2.00 .45
*Nos. 2311-2316 (6)* 4.80 1.75

90th anniversary of the birth of Lenin.

Steelworker A1193

**1960, Apr. 30** **Photo.**
**2317** A1193 40k brown & red 1.00 .50

Industrial overproduction by 50,000,000r during the 1st year of the 7-year plan.

Government House, Baku A1194

**1960, Apr.** **Litho.** ***Perf. 12x12½***
**2318** A1194 40k bister & brown 1.00 .30

Azerbaijan, 40th anniv.
For surcharge see #2898.

Brotherhood Monument, Prague — A1195

Design: 60k, Charles Bridge, Prague.

**1960, Apr. 29** **Photo.** ***Perf. 12½x12***
**2319** A1195 40k brt blue & blk .25 .25
**2320** A1195 60k blk brn & yel .75 .30

Czechoslovak Republic, 15th anniv.

Radio Tower and Popov Central Museum of Communications, Leningrad — A1196

**1960, May 6** **Litho.**
**2321** A1196 40k blue, ocher & brn 1.00 .50

Radio Day.

Gen. I. D. Tcherniakovski and Soldiers — A1197

**1960, May 4**
**2322** A1197 1r multicolored 1.00 .50

Gen. I. D. Tcherniakovski, World War II hero and his military school.

Robert Schumann (1810-56), German Composer A1198

**1960, May 20** **Photo.** ***Perf. 12x12½***
**2323** A1198 40k ultra & black 1.00 .50

Yakov M. Sverdlov (1885-1919), 1st USSR Pres. — A1199

**1960, May 24** ***Perf. 12½x12***
**2324** A1199 40k dk brn & org brn 1.00 .50

Stamp of 1957 Under Magnifying Glass A1200

**1960, May 28** **Litho.** ***Perf. 11½***
**2325** A1200 60k multicolored 1.00 .50

Stamp Day.

Karl Marx Avenue, Petrozavodsk, Karelian Autonomous Republic — A1201

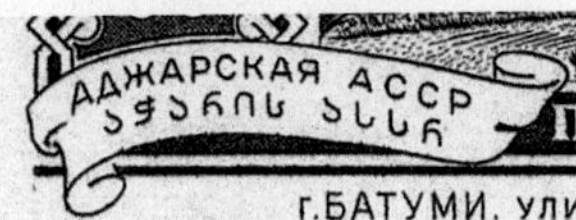


No. 2327

No. 2329

No. 2330

No. 2332

No. 2333

No. 2339

No. 2341

No. 2342

Capitals, Soviet Autonomous Republics: No. 2327, Lenin street, Batum, Adzhar. No. 2328, Cultural Palace, Izhevsk, Udmurt. No. 2329, August street, Grozny, Chechen-Ingush. No. 2330, Soviet House, Cheboksary, Chuvash. No. 2331, Buinak Street, Makhachkala, Dagestan. No. 2332, Soviet street, Ioshkar Ola, Mari. No. 2333, Chkalov street, Dzaudzhikau, North Ossetia. No. 2334, October street, Yakutsk, Yakut. No. 2335, House of Ministers, Nukus, Kara-Kalpak.

**1960** **Engr.** ***Perf. 12½***
**2326** A1201 40k Prus green 1.10 .50
**2327** A1201 40k violet blue 1.10 .50
**2328** A1201 40k green 1.10 .50
**2329** A1201 40k maroon 1.10 .50
**2330** A1201 40k dull red 1.10 .50
**2331** A1201 40k carmine .90 .30
**2332** A1201 40k dark brown .90 .30
**2333** A1201 40k orange brown .90 .30
**2334** A1201 40k dark blue .90 .30
**2335** A1201 40k brown .90 .30
*Nos. 2326-2335 (10)* 10.00 4.00

See Nos. 2338-2344C. For overprints see Nos. 2336-2337.

**No. 2326 Overprinted in Red**

**1960, June 4**
**2336** A1201 40k Prus green 5.00 3.00

Karelian Autonomous Rep., 40th anniv.

**No. 2328 Overprinted in Red**

**1960, Nov. 4**
**2337** A1201 40k green 5.00 3.00

Udmurt Autonomous Rep., 40th anniv.

**1961-62** ***Perf. 12½, 12½x12***

Capitals, Soviet Autonomous Republics: No. 2338, Rustaveli Street, Sukhumi, Abkhazia. No. 2339, House of Soviets, Nalchik, Kabardino-Balkar. No. 2340, Lenin Street, Ulan-Ude, Buriat. No. 2341, Soviet Street, Syktyvkar, Komi. No. 2342, Lenin Street, Nakhichevan, Nakhichevan. No. 2343, Elista, Kalmyk. No. 2344, Ufa, Bashkir. No. 2344A, Lobachevsky Square, Kazan, Tartar. No. 2344B, Kizil, Tuvinia. No. 2344C, Saransk, Mordovia.

**2338** A1201 4k orange ver .30 .25
**2339** A1201 4k dark violet .30 .25
**2340** A1201 4k dark blue .30 .25
**2341** A1201 4k gray .30 .25
**2342** A1201 4k dk car rose .30 .25
**2343** A1201 4k olive green .30 .25
**2344** A1201 4k dull purple .30 .25
**2344A** A1201 4k grnsh blk ('62) .40 .25
**2344B** A1201 4k claret ('62) .40 .25
**2344C** A1201 4k deep grn ('62) .40 .25
*Nos. 2338-2344C (10)* 3.30 2.50

Denominations of Nos. 2338-2344C are in the revalued currency.

Children's Friendship A1202

Drawings by Children: 20k, Collective farm, vert. 25k, Winter joys. 40k, "In the Zoo."

***Perf. 12x12½, 12½x12***

**1960, June 1** **Litho.**

| | | | | |
|---|---|---|---|---|
| **2345** | A1202 10k multicolored | .50 | .25 |
| **2346** | A1202 20k multicolored | .50 | .25 |
| **2347** | A1202 25k multicolored | .50 | .25 |
| **2348** | A1202 40k multicolored | .50 | .25 |
| | *Nos. 2345-2348 (4)* | 2.00 | 1.00 |

Lomonosov University and Congress Emblem — A1203

**1960, June 17 Photo.** ***Perf. 12½x12***

**2349** A1203 60k yel & dk brn 1.25 .40

1st congress of the International Federation for Automation Control, Moscow.

Sputnik 4 and Globe — A1204

**1960, June 17** ***Perf. 12x12½***

**2350** A1204 40k vio blue & dp org 3.00 .55

Launching on May 15, 1960, of Sputnik 4, which orbited the earth with a dummy cosmonaut.

Kosta Hetagurov (1859-1906), Ossetian Poet — A1205

**1960, June 20 Litho.** ***Perf. 12½***

**2351** A1205 40k gray blue & brn 1.00 .50

Flag and Tallinn, Estonia A1206

Soviet Republics, 20th Annivs.: No. 2353, Flag and Riga, Latvia. No. 2354, Flag and Vilnius, Lithuania.

***Perf. 12x12½, 12½ (#2353)***

**1960** **Photo.**

**2352** A1206 40k red & ultra .65 .25

**Typo.**

**2353** A1206 40k blue, gray & red .65 .25

**Litho.**

**2354** A1206 40k blue, red & grn .65 .25
*Nos. 2352-2354 (3)* 1.95 .75

Cement Factory, Belgorod A1207

Design: 40k, Factory, Novy Krivoi.

**1960, June 28** ***Perf. 12½x12***

| | | | |
|---|---|---|---|
| **2355** | A1207 25k ultra & black | .40 | .25 |
| **2356** | A1207 40k rose brn & blk | .60 | .25 |

"New buildings of the 1st year of the 7-year plan."

Automatic Production Line and Roller Bearing A1208

No. 2358, Automatic production line and gear.

**1960, June 13** ***Perf. 11½***

| | | | |
|---|---|---|---|
| **2357** | A1208 40k rose violet | .50 | .25 |
| **2358** | A1208 40k Prus green | .50 | .25 |

Publicizing mechanization and automation of factories.

Running A1209

Sports: 10k, Wrestling. 15k, Basketball. 20k, Weight lifting. 25k, Boxing. No. 2364, Fencing. No. 2365, Diving. No. 2366, Women's gymnastics. 60k, Canoeing. 1r, Steeplechase.

**1960, Aug. 1** **Litho.** ***Perf. 11½***

| | | | |
|---|---|---|---|
| **2359** | A1209 5k multicolored | .25 | .25 |
| **2360** | A1209 10k brn, blue & yel | .25 | .25 |
| **2361** | A1209 15k multicolored | .25 | .25 |
| **2362** | A1209 20k blk, crim & sal | .30 | .25 |
| **2363** | A1209 25k lake, sl & rose | .30 | .25 |
| **2364** | A1209 40k vio bl, bl & bis | .40 | .25 |
| **2365** | A1209 40k vio, gray & pink | .40 | .25 |
| **2366** | A1209 40k multicolored | .50 | .25 |
| **2367** | A1209 60k multicolored | .60 | .25 |
| **2368** | A1209 1r brn, lil & pale grn | .90 | .45 |
| | *Nos. 2359-2368 (10)* | 4.15 | 2.70 |

17th Olympic Games, Rome, 8/25-9/11.

No. 2365 Overprinted in Red

**1960, Aug. 23**

**2369** A1209 40k vio, gray & pink 10.00 7.50

12th San Marino-Riccione Stamp Fair.

Kishinev, Moldavian Republic A1210

**1960, Aug. 2** ***Perf. 12x12½***

**2370** A1210 40k multicolored 1.00 .50

20th anniversary of Moldavian Republic.

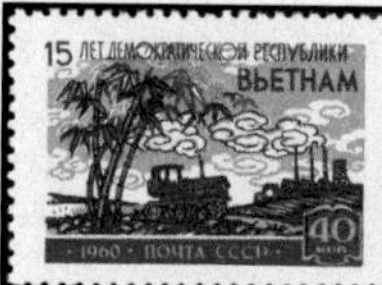
Tractor and Factory A1211

Book Museum, Hanoi — A1212

***Perf. 12x12½, 12½x12***

**1960, Aug. 25**

| | | | |
|---|---|---|---|
| **2371** | A1211 40k green, ocher & blk | .60 | .25 |
| **2372** | A1212 60k blue, lilac & brn | .90 | .25 |

15th anniversary of North Viet Nam.

Gregory N. Minkh, Microbiologist, 125th Birth Anniv. — A1213

**1960, Aug. 25 Photo.** ***Perf. 12½x12***

**2373** A1213 60k bister brn & dk brn 1.00 .50

"March," by I. I. Levitan A1214

**1960, Aug. 29**

**2374** A1214 40k ol bister & black .75 .30

I. I. Levitan, painter, birth cent.

**Fish Type of 1959**

Designs: 20k, Pikeperch. 25k, Fur seals. 40k, Ludogan whitefish.

**1960, Sept. 3** ***Perf. 12½***

| | | | |
|---|---|---|---|
| **2375** | A1155 20k blue & black | .40 | .25 |
| **2376** | A1155 25k vio gray & red brn | .40 | .25 |
| **2377** | A1155 40k rose lil & pur | .75 | .25 |
| | *Nos. 2375-2377 (3)* | 1.55 | .75 |

Forest by I. I. Shishkin — A1215

**1960, Aug. 29** **Engr.**

**2378** A1215 1r red brown 2.00 .50

5th World Forestry Congress, Seattle, Wash., Aug. 29-Sept. 10.

Globe with USSR and Letter A1216

**1960, Sept. 10 Litho.** ***Perf. 12x12½***

| | | | |
|---|---|---|---|
| **2379** | A1216 40k multicolored | .40 | .25 |
| **2380** | A1216 60k multicolored | .50 | .30 |

Intl. Letter Writing Week, Oct. 3-9.

Farmer, Worker, Scientist A1217

**1960, Oct. 4** **Typo.** ***Perf. 12½***

**2381** A1217 40k multicolored .60 .25

Kazakh SSR, 40th anniv.

Globes and Olive Branch — A1218

**1960, Sept. 29 Litho.** ***Perf. 12½x12***

**2382** A1218 60k pale vio, bl & gray .70 .25

World Federation of Trade Unions, 15th anniv.

Kremlin, Sputnik 5 and Dogs Belka and Strelka A1219

**1960, Sept. 29** **Photo.**

| | | | |
|---|---|---|---|
| **2383** | A1219 40k brt pur & yellow | .75 | .30 |
| **2384** | A1219 1r blue & salmon | 2.25 | .40 |

Flight of Sputnik 5, Aug. 19-20, 1960.

Passenger Ship "Karl Marx" A1220

Ships: 40k, Turbo-electric ship "Lenin." 60k, Speedboat "Raketa" (Rocket).

**1960, Oct. 24 Litho.** ***Perf. 12x12½***

| | | | |
|---|---|---|---|
| **2385** | A1220 25k bl, blk, red & yel | .40 | .25 |
| **2386** | A1220 40k blue, black & red | .60 | .25 |
| **2387** | A1220 60k blue, blk & rose | 1.00 | .35 |
| | *Nos. 2385-2387 (3)* | 2.00 | .85 |

A. N. Voronikhin and Kasansky Cathedral, Leningrad A1221

**1960, Oct. 24** **Photo.**

**2388** A1221 40k gray & brn black 1.00 .50

Voronikhin, architect, 200th birth anniv.

J. S. Gogebashvili A1222

**1960, Oct. 29**

**2389** A1222 40k dk gray & mag 1.00 .50

120th anniversary of the birth of J. S. Gogebashvili, Georgian teacher and publicist.

Red Flag, Electric Power Station and Factory — A1223

**1960, Oct. 29** **Litho.**
**2390** A1223 40k red, yel & brown .70 .25

43rd anniversary of October Revolution.

Leo Tolstoy A1224

Designs: 40k, Tolstoy in Yasnaya Polyana. 60k, Portrait, vert.

***Perf. 12x12½, 12½x12***

**1960, Nov. 14**
**2391** A1224 20k violet & brown .30 .25
**2392** A1224 40k blue & lt brown .70 .25
**2393** A1224 60k dp clar & sep 1.00 .35
*Nos. 2391-2393 (3)* 2.00 .85

50th anniversary of the death of Count Leo Tolstoy, writer.

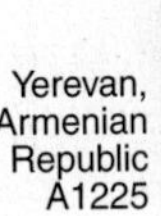

Yerevan, Armenian Republic A1225

**1960, Nov. 14** ***Perf. 12x12½***
**2394** A1225 40k bl, red, buff & brn 1.00 .50

Armenian Soviet Rep., 40th anniv.

Friedrich Engels, 140th Birth Anniv. — A1226

**1960, Nov. 25** **Engr.** ***Perf. 12½***
**2395** A1226 60k slate 1.00 .50

Badge of Youth Federation A1227

**1960, Nov. 2** **Litho.**
**2396** A1227 60k brt pink, blk & yel .50 .25

Intl. Youth Federation, 15th anniv.

40-ton Truck MAL-530 A1228

Automotive Industry: 40k, "Volga" car. 60k, "Moskvitch 407" car. 1r, "Tourist LAS-697" Bus.

**1960, Oct. 29** **Photo.** ***Perf. 12x12½***
**2397** A1228 25k ultra & gray .40 .25
**2398** A1228 40k ol bister & ultra .60 .25
**2399** A1228 60k Prus green & dp car .90 .25

**Litho.**

**2400** A1228 1r multicolored 1.40 .35
*Nos. 2397-2400 (4)* 3.30 1.10

N. I. Pirogov — A1229

**1960, Dec. 13** **Photo.** ***Perf. 12½x12***
**2401** A1229 40k grn & brn blk 1.00 .50

Pirogov, surgeon, 125th birth anniv.

Friendship University and Students A1230

**1960, Nov.** ***Perf. 12x12½***
**2402** A1230 40k brown carmine 1.00 .50

Completion of Friendship of Nations University in Moscow.

For surcharge see No. 2462.

Mark Twain A1231

**1960, Nov. 30** ***Perf. 12½x12***
**2403** A1231 40k dp org & brown 2.00 .90

Mark Twain, 125th birth anniv.

Dove and Globe — A1232

**1960, Oct. 29** **Photo.**
**2404** A1232 60k maroon & gray 1.00 .50

Intl. Democratic Women's Fed, 15th anniv.

Akaki Tsereteli — A1233

**1960, Dec. 27**
**2405** A1233 40k vio & blk brn 1.00 .30

Tsereteli, Georgian poet, 120th birth anniv.

Frederic Chopin, after Delacroix A1234

**1960, Dec. 24** ***Perf. 12x11½***
**2406** A1234 40k bister & brown 1.10 .25

Chopin, Polish composer, 150th birth anniv.

North Korean Flag and Flying Horse — A1235

**1960, Dec. 24** **Litho.** ***Perf. 12½x12***
**2407** A1235 40k multicolored 1.00 .50

15th anniversary of "the liberation of the Korean people by the Soviet army."

Crocus — A1236

Asiatic Flowers: No. 2409, Tulip. No. 2410, Trollius. No. 2411, Tulip. No. 2412, Ginseng. No. 2413, Iris. No. 2414, Hypericum. 1r, Dog rose.

**1960** ***Perf. 12x12½***

**Flowers in Natural Colors**

**2408** A1236 20k green & violet .30 .25
**2409** A1236 20k vio blue & black .30 .25
**2410** A1236 25k gray .35 .25
**2411** A1236 40k ol bister & black .40 .25
**2412** A1236 40k grn & blk, wmkd. .40 .25
**2413** A1236 60k yel, green & red .75 .25
**2414** A1236 60k bluish grn & blk .75 .25
**2415** A1236 1r slate grn & blk 1.25 .25
*Nos. 2408-2415 (8)* 4.50 2.00

The watermark on No. 2412 consists of vertical rows of chevrons.

Lithuanian Costumes A1237

Regional Costumes: 60k, Uzbek.

***Perf. 12½ (10k), 11½ (60k)***

**1960, Dec. 24** **Typo.** **Unwmk.**
**2416** A1237 10k multicolored .25 .25
**2417** A1237 60k multicolored 1.00 .40

**Currency Revalued**

**1961-62** **Litho.** ***Perf. 11½***

Regional Costumes: No. 2418, Moldavia. No. 2419, Georgia. No. 2420, Ukrainia. No. 2421, White Russia. No. 2422, Kazakhstan. No. 2422A, Latvia. 4k, Koryak. 6k, Russia. 10k, Armenia. 12k, Estonia.

**2418** A1237 2k buff, brn & ver .25 .25
**2419** A1237 2k red, brn, ocher & black .25 .25
**2420** A1237 3k ultra, buff, red & brown .30 .25
**2421** A1237 3k red org, ocher & black .30 .25
**2422** A1237 3k buff, brn, grn & red .30 .25
**2422A** A1237 3k org red, gray ol & blk ('62) .30 .25
**2423** A1237 4k multicolored .50 .25
**2424** A1237 6k multicolored .60 .30
**2425** A1237 10k brn, ol bis & vermilion .90 .35
**2426** A1237 12k red, ultra & black 1.25 .45
*Nos. 2418-2426 (10)* 4.95 2.85

See Nos. 2723-2726.

Lenin and Map Showing Electrification — A1238

**1961** ***Perf. 12½x12***
**2427** A1238 4k blue, buff & brown .50 .25
**2428** A1238 10k red org & blue blk 1.00 .35

State Electrification Plan, 40th anniv. (in 1960).

**Animal Types of 1957**

**1961, Jan. 7** ***Perf. 12½***
**2429** A1024 1k Brown bear .75 .25
**2430** A1023 6k Beaver 2.25 .70
**2431** A1023 10k Roe deer 3.00 .95
*Nos. 2429-2431 (3)* 6.00 1.90

Georgian Flag and Views A1239

**1961, Feb. 15** ***Perf. 12½x12***
**2432** A1239 4k multicolored .40 .25

40th anniv. of Georgian SSR.

Nikolai D. Zelinski, Chemist, Birth Cent. A1240

**1961, Feb. 6** **Photo.** ***Perf. 12x12½***
**2433** A1240 4k rose violet .50 .25

Nikolai A. Dobrolyubov (1836-61), Journalist and Critic — A1241

**1961, Feb. 5** ***Perf. 11½x12***
**2434** A1241 4k brt blue & brown .55 .25

A1242

Designs: 3k, Cattle. 4k, Tractor in cornfield. 6k, Mechanization of Grain Harvest. 10k, Women picking apples.

**1961** ***Perf. 12x12½, 12x11½***
**2435** A1242 3k blue & magenta .30 .25
**2436** A1242 4k green & dk gray .30 .25
**2437** A1242 6k vio blue & brn .70 .25
**2438** A1242 10k maroon & ol grn 1.00 .40
*Nos. 2435-2438 (4)* 2.30 1.15

Agricultural development.

A1243

Designs: 1k, "Labor" Holding Peace Flag. 2k, Harvester and silo. 3k, Space rockets. 4k, Arms and flag of USSR. 6k, Kremlin tower. 10k, Workers' monument. 12k, Minin and Pozharsky Monument and Spasski tower. 16k, Plane over power station and dam.

***Perf. 12x12½; 12x11½ (Nos. 2439A, 2442 & 12k)***

**1961-65 Engr. Unwmk.**

| | | | | | |
|---|---|---|---|---|---|
| **2439** | A1243 | 1k olive bister | 1.00 | .25 |
| | | **Litho.** | | |
| **2439A** | A1243 | 1k olive bister | 1.00 | .25 |
| **2440** | A1243 | 2k green | .35 | .30 |
| **2441** | A1243 | 3k dk violet | 2.50 | .25 |
| | | **Engr.** | | |
| **2442** | A1243 | 3k dk violet | 5.25 | 2.50 |
| | | **Litho.** | | |
| **2443** | A1243 | 4k red | .75 | .25 |
| **2443A** | A1243 | 4k org brn ('65) | 13.00 | 9.00 |
| **2444** | A1243 | 6k vermilion | 6.00 | .90 |
| **2445** | A1243 | 6k dk car rose | 2.00 | .25 |
| **2446** | A1243 | 10k orange | 3.75 | .25 |
| | | **Photo.** | | |
| **2447** | A1243 | 12k brt magenta | 3.50 | .30 |
| | | **Litho.** | | |
| **2448** | A1243 | 16k ultra | 4.50 | .80 |
| | | *Nos. 2439-2448 (12)* | 43.60 | 15.30 |

V. P. Miroshnitchenko — A1244

**1961, Feb. 23 Photo. *Perf. 12½x12***
**2449** A1244 4k violet brn & slate .75 .40

Soldier hero of World War II.
See Nos. 2570-2571.

Taras G. Shevchenko and Birthplace — A1245

Shevchenko Statue, Kharkov — A1246

6k, Book, torch and Shevchenko with beard.

***Perf. 12½, 11½x12***

**1961, Mar. Litho.; Photo. (4k)**

| | | | | |
|---|---|---|---|---|
| **2450** | A1245 3k brown & violet | .50 | .25 |
| **2451** | A1246 4k red org & gray | .40 | .25 |
| **2452** | A1245 6k blk, grn & red brn | .85 | .30 |
| | *Nos. 2450-2452 (3)* | 1.75 | .80 |

Shevchenko, Ukrainian poet, death cent.
No. 2452 was printed with alternating green and black label, containing a quotation.
See No. 2852.

Andrei Rubljov — A1247

**1961, Mar. 13 Litho. *Perf. 12½x12***
**2453** A1247 4k ultra, bister & brn 1.00 .50

Rubljov, painter, 600th birth anniv.

N. V. Sklifosovsky A1248

**1961, Mar. 26 Photo. *Perf. 11½x12***
**2454** A1248 4k ultra & black 1.00 .35

Sklifosovsky, surgeon, 125th birth anniv.

Robert Koch — A1249

**1961, Mar. 26**
**2455** A1249 6k dark brown 2.00 .50

Koch, German microbiologist, 59th death anniv.

Globe and Sputnik 8 — A1250

10k, Venera 1 space probe and its path to Venus.

**1961, Apr. Litho. *Perf. 11½***

| | | | |
|---|---|---|---|
| **2456** | A1250 6k dk & lt blue & org | .65 | .25 |
| | **Photo.** | | |
| **2457** | A1250 10k vio blue & yel | .90 | .35 |

Launching of the Venera 1 space probe, 2/12/61.

Open Book and Globe A1251

**1961, Apr. 7 Litho. *Perf. 12½x12***
**2458** A1251 6k ultra & sepia .75 .25

Centenary of the magazine "Around the World."

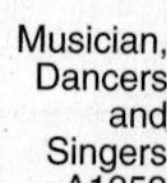

Musician, Dancers and Singers A1252

**1961, Apr. 7 Unwmk.**
**2459** A1252 4k yel, red & black .50 .25

Russian National Choir, 50th anniv.

African Breaking Chains and Map — A1253

6k, Globe, torch & black & white handshake.

**1961, Apr. 15 *Perf. 12½***

| | | | |
|---|---|---|---|
| **2460** | A1253 4k multicolored | .60 | .25 |
| **2461** | A1253 6k blue, pur & org | .60 | .25 |

Africa Day and 3rd Conference of Independent African States, Cairo, Mar. 25-31.

No. 2402 Surcharged in Red

**1961, Apr. 15 Photo. *Perf. 12x12½***
**2462** A1230 4k on 40k brn car 1.00 .40

Naming of Friendship University, Moscow, in memory of Patrice Lumumba, Premier of Congo.

Maj. Yuri A. Gagarin A1254

6k, Kremlin, rockets and radar equipment. 10k, Rocket, Gagarin with helmet and Kremlin.

**1961, Apr. *Perf. 11½ (3k), 12½x12***

| | | | |
|---|---|---|---|
| **2463** | A1254 3k Prus blue | .35 | .25 |
| | **Litho.** | | |
| **2464** | A1254 6k blue, vio & red | .70 | .25 |
| **2465** | A1254 10k red, blue grn & brn | 1.20 | .25 |
| | *Nos. 2463-2465 (3)* | 2.25 | .75 |

1st man in space, Yuri A. Gagarin, Apr. 12, 1961. No. 2464 printed with alternating light blue and red label.
Nos. 2463-2465 exist imperf. Value $5.

Lenin — A1255

**1961, Apr. 22 Litho. *Perf. 12x12½***
**2466** A1255 4k dp car, sal & blk .75 .25

91st anniversary of Lenin's birth.

Rabindranath Tagore — A1256

**1961, May 8 Engr. *Perf. 11½x12***
**2467** A1256 6k bis, maroon & blk 1.00 .25

Tagore, Indian poet, birth cent.

The Hunchbacked Horse — A1257

Fairy Tales: 1k, The Geese and the Swans. 3k, Fox, Hare and Cock. 6k, The Peasant and the Bear. 10k, Ruslan and Ludmilla.

**1961 Litho. *Perf. 12½***

| | | | |
|---|---|---|---|
| **2468** | A1257 1k multicolored | .25 | .25 |
| **2469** | A1257 3k multicolored | .75 | .35 |
| **2470** | A1257 4k multicolored | .50 | .25 |
| **2471** | A1257 6k multicolored | .90 | .40 |
| **2472** | A1257 10k multicolored | 1.10 | .45 |
| | *Nos. 2468-2472 (5)* | 3.50 | 1.70 |

"Man Conquering Space" A1258

Design: 6k, Giuseppe Garibaldi.

**1961, May 24 Photo.**

| | | | |
|---|---|---|---|
| **2481** | A1258 4k orange brown | .40 | .30 |
| **2482** | A1258 6k lilac & salmon | .60 | .30 |

International Labor Exposition, Turin.

Lenin — A1259

Various portraits of Lenin.

**1961 Photo. *Perf. 12½x12***
**Olive Bister Frame**

| | | | |
|---|---|---|---|
| **2483** | A1259 20k dark green | 1.75 | 1.00 |
| **2484** | A1259 30k dark blue | 2.75 | 2.00 |
| **2485** | A1259 50k rose red | 8.00 | 6.00 |
| | *Nos. 2483-2485 (3)* | 12.50 | 9.00 |

Patrice Lumumba — A1260

**1961, May 29** **Litho.**

**2486** A1260 2k yellow & brown .50 .25

Lumumba (1925-61), premier of Congo.

Kindergarten — A1261

Children's Day: 3k, Young Pioneers in camp. 4k, Young Pioneers, vert.

***Perf. 12½x12, 12x12½***

**1961, May 31** **Photo.**

**2487** A1261 2k orange & ultra .25 .25
**2488** A1261 3k ol bister & purple .60 .30
**2489** A1261 4k red & gray 1.00 .25
*Nos. 2487-2489 (3)* 1.85 .80

Dog Zvezdochka and Sputnik 10 — A1263

Sputniks 9 and 10: 4k, Dog Chernushka and Sputnik 9, vert.

**1961, June 8** **Litho.** ***Perf. 12½, 11½***

**2491** A1263 2k vio, Prus blue & blk 5.00 2.50

**Photo.**

**2492** A1263 4k Prus blue & brt grn 5.00 2.50

Vissarion G. Belinski, Author, 150th Birth. Anniv. — A1265

**Engraved and Photogravure**

**1961, June 13** ***Perf. 11½x12***

**2493** A1265 4k carmine & black .75 .35

Lt. Gen. D.M. Karbishev A1266

**1961, June 22** **Litho.** ***Perf. 12½***

**2494** A1266 4k black, red & yel .35 .25

Karbishev was tortured to death in the Nazi prison camp at Mauthausen, Austria.

Hydro-meteorological Map and Instruments — A1267

**1961, June 21** ***Perf. 12x12½***

**2495** A1267 6k ultra & green .50 .35

40th anniversary of hydro-meteorological service in Russia.

Gliders A1268

6k, Motorboat race. 10k, Motorcycle race.

**1961, July 5** **Photo.** ***Perf. 12½***

**2497** A1268 4k dk slate grn & crim .30 .25

**Litho.**

**2498** A1268 6k slate & vermilion .45 .25
**2499** A1268 10k slate & vermilion 1.40 .35
*Nos. 2497-2499 (3)* 2.15 .85

USSR Technical Sports Spartakiad.

Javelin Thrower A1269

**1961, Aug. 8** **Photo.** ***Perf. 12½x12***

**2500** A1269 6k dp car & pink .50 .25

7th Trade Union Spartacist Games.

S. I. Vavilov — A1270

**1961, July 25**

**2501** A1270 4k lt green & sepia .60 .25

Vavilov, president of Academy of Science.

Vazha Pshavela — A1271

**1961** **Photo.** ***Perf. 11½x12***

**2502** A1271 4k dk brn & cream .75 .35

Pshavela, Georgian poet, birth cent.

Scientists at Control Panel for Rocket — A1272

Globe and Youth Activities A1273

Design: 2k, Men pushing tank into river.

**1961** **Unwmk.** ***Perf. 11½***

**2503** A1273 2k orange & sepia .25 .25
**2504** A1272 4k lilac & dk green .60 .40
**2505** A1273 6k ultra & citron 1.00 .60
*Nos. 2503-2505 (3)* 1.85 1.25

International Youth Forum, Moscow.

Arms of Mongolian Republic and Sukhe Bator Statue A1274

**1961, July 25** **Litho.** ***Perf. 12½x12***

**2506** A1274 4k multicolored 1.00 .50

Mongol national revolution, 40th anniv.

Knight Kalevipoeg A1275

**1961, July 31**

**2507** A1275 4k black, blue & yel .75 .35

1st publication of "Kalevipoeg," Estonian national saga, recorded by R. K. Kreutzwald, Estonian writer, cent.

Symbols of Biochemistry A1276

**1961, July 31**

**2508** A1276 6k multicolored .75 .35

5th Intl. Biochemistry Congress, Moscow.

Major Titov and Vostok 2 — A1277

4k, Globe with orbit and cosmonaut.

**1961, Aug.** **Photo.** ***Perf. 11½***

**2509** A1277 4k vio blue & dp plum .35 .25
**2510** A1277 6k brown, grn & org .65 .25

1st manned space flight around the world, Maj. Gherman S. Titov, Aug. 6-7, 1961. Nos. 2509-2510 exist imperf. Value, set $10.

A. D. Zacharov and Admiralty Building, Leningrad A1278

**1961, Aug. 8** ***Perf. 12x11½***

**2511** A1278 4k blue, dk brn & buff .50 .25

Zacharov (1761-1811), architect.

Defense of Brest, 1941 A1279

Designs: No. 2512, Defense of Moscow. No. 2514, Defense of Odessa. No. 2514A, Defense of Sevastopol. No. 2514B, Defense of Leningrad. No. 2514C, Defense of Kiev. No. 2514D, Battle of the Volga (Stalingrad).

**1961-63** **Photo.** ***Perf. 12½x12***

**2512** A1279 4k blk & red brn (Moscow) .50 .25

**Litho.**

**2513** A1279 4k (Brest) .50 .25
**2514** A1279 4k (Odessa) .50 .25
**2514A** A1279 4k (Sevastopol; '62) .50 .25
**2514B** A1279 4k brn, dl bl & bis (Leningrad; '63) .50 .25
**2514C** A1279 4k blk & multi (Kiev; '63) .50 .25
**2514D** A1279 4k dl org & multi (Volga; '63) .50 .25
*Nos. 2512-2514D (7)* 3.50 1.75

"War of Liberation," 1941-1945.

See Nos. 2757-2758.

Students' Union Emblem A1280

**1961, Aug. 8** **Litho.** ***Perf. 12½***

**2515** A1280 6k ultra & red .75 .35

15th anniversary of the founding of the International Students' Union.

Soviet Stamps A1281

Stamps and background different on each denomination.

**1961, Aug.** ***Perf. 12½x12***

**2516** A1281 2k multicolored .40 .25
**2517** A1281 4k multicolored .75 .30
**2518** A1281 6k multicolored 1.25 .35
**2519** A1281 10k multicolored 2.00 .50
*Nos. 2516-2519 (4)* 4.40 1.40

40 years of Soviet postage stamps.

Nikolai A. Schors Statue, Kiev — A1282

Statue: 4k, Gregori I. Kotovski, Kishinev.

**1961 Photo. *Perf. 11½x12***

**2520** A1282 2k lt ultra & sepia .50 .25
**2521** A1282 4k rose vio & sepia .50 .25

Letters and Means of Transportation — A1283

**1961, Sept. 15 *Perf. 11½***

**2522** A1283 4k dk car & black .50 .25

International Letter Writing Week.

Angara River Bridge, Irkutsk A1284

**1961, Sept. 15 Litho. *Perf. 12½x12***

**2523** A1284 4k ol bis, lil & blk 2.00 .50

300th anniversary of Irkutsk.

Lenin, Marx, Engels and Marchers — A1285

3k, Obelisk commemorating conquest of space and Moscow University. #2526, Harvester combine. #2527, Industrial control center. #2528, Worker pointing to globe.

**1961 Litho.**

**2524** A1285 2k ver, yel & brown .40 .25
**2525** A1285 3k org & deep blue 2.25 .40
**2526** A1285 4k mar, bis & red brown .75 .40
**2527** A1285 4k car rose, brn, org & blue .75 .40
**2528** A1285 4k red & dk brown .75 .40
*Nos. 2524-2528 (5)* 4.90 1.85

22nd Congress of the Communist Party of the USSR, Oct. 17-31.

Soviet Soldier Monument, Berlin — A1286

**1961, Sept. 28 Photo. *Perf. 12x12½***

**2529** A1286 4k red & gray violet .75 .30

10th anniversary of the International Federation of Resistance, FIR.

Workers Studying Mathematics — A1287

Designs: 2k, Communist labor team. 4k, Workers around piano.

**1961, Sept. 28 Litho. *Perf. 12½x12***

**2530** A1287 2k plum & red, *cream* .50 .35
**2531** A1287 3k brn & red, *yellow* 1.00 .50
**2532** A1287 4k vio blue & red, *cr* 1.50 .65
*Nos. 2530-2532 (3)* 3.00 1.50

Publicizing Communist labor teams in their efforts for labor, education and relaxation.

Rocket and Stars — A1288

**Engraved on Aluminum Foil**

**1961, Oct. 17 *Perf. 12½***

**2533** A1288 1r black & red 25.00 25.00

Soviet scientific and technical achievements in exploring outer space.

**Overprinted in Red**

**1961, Oct. 23**

**2534** A1288 1r black & red 27.50 27.50

Communist Party of the USSR, 22nd cong.

Amangaldi Imanov — A1289

**1961, Oct. 25 Photo. *Perf. 11½x12***

**2535** A1289 4k green, buff & brn .75 .25

Amangaldi Imanov (1873-1919), champion of Soviet power in Kazakhstan.

Franz Liszt (1811-86), Composer A1290

**1961, Oct. 31 *Perf. 12x11½***

**2536** A1290 4k mar, dk brn & ocher 5.00 2.00

Flags and Slogans A1291

**1961, Nov. 4 *Perf. 11½***

**2537** A1291 4k red, yel & dark red .75 .35

44th anniversary of October Revolution.

Hand Holding Hammer — A1292

Congress Emblem A1293

Designs: Nos. 2538, 2542, Congress emblem. Nos. 2539, 2543, African breaking chains. No. 2541, Three hands holding globe.

**1961, Nov. *Perf. 12, 12½, 11½***

**2538** A1293 2k scarlet & bister .25 .25
**2539** A1293 2k dk purple & gray .25 .25
**2540** A1292 4k plum, org & blue .60 .25
**2541** A1292 4k blk, lt blue & pink .75 .25
**2542** A1293 6k grn, bister & red .75 .25
**2543** A1293 6k ind, dull yel & red .75 .25
*Nos. 2538-2543 (6)* 3.35 1.50

Fifth World Congress of Trade Unions, Moscow, Dec. 4-16.

Lomonosov Statue — A1294

Designs: 6k, Lomonosov at desk. 10k, Lomonosov, his birthplace and Leningrad Academy of Science, horiz.

***Perf. 11½x12, 12x11½***

**1961, Nov. 19 Photo. & Engr.**

**2544** A1294 4k Prus blue, yel grn & brown .60 .25
**2545** A1294 6k grn, yel & blk 1.00 .35
**2546** A1294 10k mar, slate & brn 1.25 .60
*Nos. 2544-2546 (3)* 2.85 1.20

250th anniversary of the birth of M. V. Lomonosov, scientist and poet.

Hands Holding Hammer and Sickle — A1295

**1961, Nov. 27 Litho. *Perf. 12x12½***

**2547** A1295 4k red & yellow .60 .30

USSR constitution, 25th anniv.

Romeo and Juliet Ballet — A1296

Ballets: 2k, Red Flower. 3k, Paris Flame. 10k, Swan Lake.

**1961-62 *Perf. 12x12½***

**2548** A1296 2k brn, car & lt green ('62) .25 .25
**2549** A1296 3k multi ('62) .45 .25
**2550** A1296 6k dk brn, bis & vio .65 .25
**2551** A1296 10k blue, pink & dk brn 1.00 .30
*Nos. 2548-2551 (4)* 2.35 1.05

Honoring the Russian Ballet.

Linemen A1297

**1961 *Perf. 12½***

**2552** A1297 3k shown .75 .25
**2553** A1297 4k Welders .75 .25
**2554** A1297 6k Surveyor 1.50 .35
*Nos. 2552-2554 (3)* 3.00 .85

Honoring self-sacrificing work of youth in the 7-year plan.

Andrejs Pumpurs (1841-1902), Latvian Poet and Satirist A1298

**1961, Dec. 20 *Perf. 12x11½***

**2555** A1298 4k gray & claret 2.00 .50

Bulgarian Couple, Flag, Emblem and Building A1299

**1961, Dec. 28 *Perf. 12½x12***

**2556** A1299 4k multicolored 1.00 .50

Bulgarian People's Republic, 15th anniv.

Fridtjof Nansen A1300

**1961, Dec. 30 Photo. *Perf. 11½***

**2557** A1300 6k dk blue & brown 2.00 .60

Centenary of the birth of Fridtjof Nansen, Norwegian Polar explorer.

Mihael Ocipovich Dolivo-Dobrovolsky — A1301

**1962, Jan. 25 *Perf. 12x11½***

**2558** A1301 4k bister & dark blue .50 .25

Dolivo-Dobrovolsky, scientist and electrical engineer, birth cent.

Woman and Various Activities A1302

**1962, Jan. 26 *Perf. 11½***

**2559** A1302 4k bister, blk & dp org .50 .25

Honoring Soviet Women.

Aleksander S. Pushkin, 125th Death Anniv. — A1303

**1962, Jan. 26 Litho. *Perf. 12½x12***
**2560** A1303 4k buff, dk brn & ver .50 .25

Dancers A1304

**1962, Feb. 6 *Perf. 12x12½***
**2561** A1304 4k bister & ver .50 .25

State ensemble of folk dancers, 25th anniv.

Speed Skating, Luzhniki Stadium A1305

***Perf. 11½***
**1962, Feb. 17 Unwmk. Photo.**
**2562** A1305 4k orange & ultra .60 .25

Intl. Winter Sports Championships, Moscow.

No. 2562 Overprinted

**1962, Mar. 3**
**2563** A1305 4k orange & ultra 2.40 1.50

Victories of I. Voronina and V. Kosichkin, world speed skating champions, 1962.

Ski Jump A1305a

10k, Woman long distance skier, vert.

**1962, May 31 *Perf. 11½***
**2564** A1305a 2k ultra, brn & red .30 .25
**2565** A1305a 10k org, ultra & black .70 .25

Intl. Winter Sports Championships, Zakopane.

**Hero Type of 1961**

4k, V. S. Shalandin. 6k, Magomet Gadgiev.

**1962, Feb. 22 *Perf. 12½x12***
**2570** A1244 4k dk blue & brown 3.00 .80
**2571** A1244 6k brn & slate grn 1.00 .80

Soldier heroes of World War II.

Skier A1306

**1962, Mar. 3 *Perf. 11½***
**2572** A1306 4k shown .40 .25
**2573** A1306 6k Ice hockey .50 .25
**2574** A1306 10k Ice skating 1.00 .40
*Nos. 2572-2574 (3)* 1.90 .90

First People's Winter Games, Sverdlovsk.
For overprints see Nos. 2717, 3612.

Aleksandr Ivanovich Herzen (1812-70), Political Writer A1307

**1962, Mar. 28 Litho. *Perf. 12x12½***
**2575** A1307 4k ultra, black & buff .50 .25

Lenin — A1308

Design: 6k, Lenin, horiz.

**1962, Mar. 28 *Perf. 12x12½, 12½x12***
**2576** A1308 4k brown, red & yel .30 .25
**2577** A1308 6k blue, org & brn .50 .25

14th congress of the Young Communist League (Komsomol).

Vostok 1 — A1309

**1962, Apr. Unwmk. *Perf. 11x11½***
**2578** A1309 10k multicolored .50 .35

1st anniv. of Yuri A. Gagarin's flight into space.

No. 2578 was printed in sheets of 20 stamps alternating with 20 labels.

No. 2578 was also issued imperf. Value $2.25.

Bust of Tchaikovsky A1310

**1962, Apr. 19 Photo. *Perf. 11½x12***
**2579** A1310 4k blue, blk & bis 1.00 .30

Second International Tchaikovsky Competition in Moscow.

Youths of 3 Races, Broken Chain, Globe A1311

**1962, Apr. 19 *Perf. 11½***
**2580** A1311 6k black, brn & yel .50 .25

International Day of Solidarity of Youth against Colonialism.

Ulyanov (Lenin) Family Portrait A1312

Lenin A1313

**1962, Apr. 21 *Perf. 12x11½***
**2581** A1312 4k gray, red & dk brn .40 .25

**Typographed and Embossed**
***Perf. 12½***
**2582** A1313 10k dk red, gray & blk .90 .35
*a.* Souv. sheet of 2, perf. 12 5.00 3.00

92nd anniversary of the birth of Lenin.
No. 2582a for 94th anniv. of the birth of Lenin. Issued Nov. 6, 1964.

Cosmos 3 Satellite — A1314

**1962, Apr. 26 Litho. *Perf. 12½x12***
**2586** A1314 6k blk, lt blue & vio .50 .25

Cosmos 3 earth satellite launching, Apr. 24.

Charles Dickens — A1315

No. 2589, Jean Jacques Rousseau.

**1962, Apr. 29**
**2588** A1315 6k blue, brn & pur .50 .25

***Perf. 11½x12***
**Photo.**
**2589** A1315 6k gray, lilac & brn .50 .25

Charles Dickens, English writer, 150th birth anniv., and Jean Jacques Rousseau, French writer, 250th birth anniv.

Karl Marx Monument, Moscow — A1316

**1962, Apr. 29 *Perf. 12x12½***
**2590** A1316 4k deep ultra & gray .50 .25

Pravda, Lenin, Revolutionists A1317

Lenin Reading Pravda — A1318

No. 2592, Pravda, Lenin and rocket.

**1962, May 4 Litho.**
**2591** A1317 4k blk, bis & red .65 .25
**2592** A1317 4k red, blk & ocher .65 .25

***Perf. 11½***
**Photo.**
**2593** A1318 4k ocher, dp clar & red .65 .25
*Nos. 2591-2593 (3)* 1.95 .75

50th anniversary of Pravda, Russian newspaper founded by Lenin.

Malaria Eradication Emblem and Mosquito A1319

**1962**
**2594** A1319 4k Prus blue, red & blk .50 .25
**2595** A1319 6k ol grn, red & blk .50 .35

WHO drive to eradicate malaria.
Issue dates: 4k, May 6; 6k, June 23.
No. 2595 exists imperf. Value $1.75.

Pioneers Taking Oath before Lenin and Emblem A1320

Designs (Emblem and): 3k, Lenja Golikov and Valja Kotik. No. 2598, Pioneers building rocket model. No. 2599, Red Cross, Red Crescent and nurse giving health instruction. 6k, Pioneers of many races and globe.

**1962, May 19 Litho. *Perf. 12½x12***
**2596** A1320 2k green, red & brn .30 .25
**2597** A1320 3k multicolored .30 .25
**2598** A1320 4k multicolored .50 .25
**2599** A1320 4k multicolored .50 .25
**2600** A1320 6k multicolored .80 .25
*Nos. 2596-2600 (5)* 2.40 1.25

All-Union Lenin Pioneers, 40th anniv.

Mesrob — A1321

**1962, May 27 Photo.** ***Perf. 12½x12***
**2601** A1321 4k yel & dk brn 1.00 .25

"1600th" anniversary of the birth of Bishop Mesrob (350?-439), credited as author of the Armenian and Georgian alphabets.

Ivan A. Goncharov A1322

**1962, June 18**
**2602** A1322 4k gray & brown .75 .35

Ivan Aleksandrovich Goncharov (1812-91), novelist, 150th birth anniv.

Volleyball — A1323

2k, Bicyclists, horiz. 10k, Eight-man shell. 12k, Goalkeeper, soccer, horiz. 16k, Steeplechase.

**1962, June 27** ***Perf. 11½***
**2603** A1323 2k lt brn, blk & ver .25 .25
**2604** A1323 4k brn org, black & buff .30 .25
**2605** A1323 10k ultra, black & yel .85 .25
**2606** A1323 12k lt blue, brn & yel .95 .35
**2607** A1323 16k lt green, blk & red 1.10 .45
*Nos. 2603-2607 (5)* 3.45 1.55

Intl. Summer Sports Championships, 1962.

Louis Pasteur — A1324

**1962, June 30** ***Perf. 12½x12***
**2608** A1324 6k blk & brn org .60 .25

Invention of the sterilization process by Louis Pasteur, French chemist, cent.

Library, 1862 A1325

Design: No. 2610, New Lenin Library.

**1962, June 30 Photo.**
**2609** A1325 4k slate & black .40 .25
**2610** A1325 4k slate & black .40 .25
*a.* Pair, #2609-2610 2.00 .75

Centenary of the Lenin Library, Moscow.

Auction Building and Ermine — A1326

**1962, June 30 Litho.**
**2611** A1326 6k multicolored 1.00 .25

International Fur Auction, Leningrad.

Young Couple, Lenin, Kremlin — A1327

Workers of Three Races and Dove — A1328

**1962, June 30** ***Perf. 12x12½***
**2612** A1327 2k multicolored .40 .30
**2613** A1328 4k multicolored .60 .30

Program of the Communist Party of the Soviet Union for Peace and Friendship among all people.

Hands Breaking Bomb A1329

**1962, July 7** ***Perf. 11½***
**2614** A1329 6k blue, blk & olive .50 .35

World Congress for Peace and Disarmament, Moscow, July 9-14.

Yakub Kolas and Yanka Kupala A1330

**1962, July 7 Photo.** ***Perf. 12½x12***
**2615** A1330 4k henna brn & buff .50 .35

Byelorussian poets. Kolas (1882-1956), and Kupala (1882-1942).

Alekper Sabir (1862-1911), Azerbaijani Poet, Satirist — A1331

**1962, July 16** ***Perf. 11½***
**2616** A1331 4k buff, dk brn & blue .70 .35

Examples inscribed "Azerbajanyn" were withdrawn before release. Value, $250.

Cancer Congress Emblem A1332

**1962, July 16 Litho.** ***Perf. 12½***
**2617** A1332 6k grnsh blue, blk & red .50 .35

8th Anti-Cancer Cong., Moscow, July 1962.

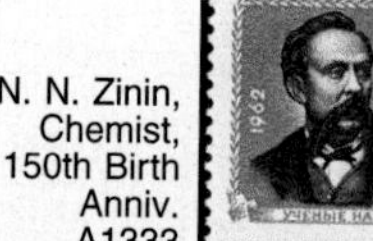

N. N. Zinin, Chemist, 150th Birth Anniv. A1333

**1962, July 16 Photo.** ***Perf. 12x11½***
**2618** A1333 4k violet & dk brown .35 .25

I. M. Kramskoy, Painter — A1334

I. D. Shadr, Sculptor A1335

M. V. Nesterov, Painter A1336

**1962, July 28** ***Perf. 11½x12, 12x12½***
**2619** A1334 4k gray, mar & dk brn .50 .30
**2620** A1335 4k blk & red brn .50 .30
**2621** A1336 4k multicolored .50 .30
*Nos. 2619-2621 (3)* 1.50 .90

Vostok 2 Going into Space — A1337

***Perf. 11½***
**1962, Aug. 7 Unwmk. Photo.**
**2622** A1337 10k blk, lilac & blue .50 .25
**2623** A1337 10k blk, org & blue .50 .25

1st anniv. of Gherman Titov's space flight. Issued imperf. on Aug. 6. Value, set $4.

Friendship House, Moscow A1338

**1962, Aug. 15** ***Perf. 12x12½***
**2624** A1338 6k ultra & gray .50 .25

Moscow State University and Atom Symbol — A1339

Design: 6k, Map of Russia, atom symbol and "Peace" in 10 languages.

**1962, Aug. 15 Litho.** ***Perf. 12½x12***
**2625** A1339 4k multicolored .50 .25
**2626** A1339 6k multicolored .50 .25

Use of atomic energy for peace.

Andrian G. Nikolayev A1340

Cosmonauts in Space Helments — A1341

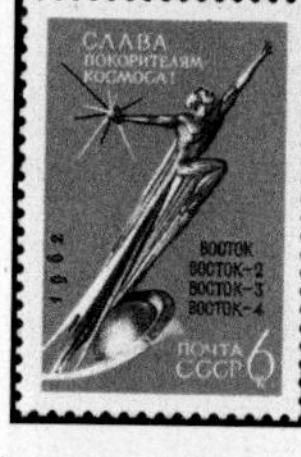

"To Space" Monument by G. Postnikov — A1342

Design: No. 2628, Pavel R. Popovich, with inscription at left and dated "12-15-VIII, 1962."
1r, Monument and portraits of Gagarin, Titov, Nikolayev and Popovich.

**1962 Photo.** ***Perf. 11½***
**2627** A1340 4k blue, brn & red .40 .25
**2628** A1340 4k blue, brn & red .40 .25

***Perf. 12½x12***
**Litho.**
**2629** A1341 6k dk bl, lt bl, org & yellow 1.00 .30

***Perf. 11½***
**Photo.**
**2630** A1342 6k brt blue & multi .70 .25
**2631** A1342 10k violet & multi .90 .35
*Nos. 2627-2631 (5)* 3.40 1.40

**Souvenir Sheet**

**1962, Nov. 27 Litho.** ***Perf. 12½***
**2631A** A1342 1r brt bl, blk & sil 35.00 5.00

Nos. 2627-2631A honor the four Russian "conquerors of space," with Nos. 2627-2629 for the 1st group space flight, by Vostoks 3 and 4, Aug. 11-15, 1962. Also issued imperf. Value, set $6, souvenir sheet $50.
For overprint see No. 2662.

Carp and Bream — A1343

Design: 6k, Freshwater salmon.

**1962, Aug. 28 Photo.** ***Perf. 11½x12***

**2632** A1343 4k blue & orange .45 .25
**2633** A1343 6k blue & orange .60 .30

Fish preservation in USSR.

Feliks E. Dzerzhinski — A1344

**1962, Sept. 6 Litho.** ***Perf. 12½x12***

**2634** A1344 4k ol grn & dk blue .50 .25

Dzerzhinski (1877-1926), organizer of Soviet secret police, 85th birth anniv.

O. Henry and New York Skyline A1345

**1962, Sept. 10 Photo.** ***Perf. 12x11½***

**2635** A1345 6k yel, red brn & black .55 .35

O. Henry (William Sidney Porter, 1862-1910), American writer.

Barclay de Tolly, Mikhail I. Kutuzov, Petr I. Bagration A1346

4k, Denis Davidov leading partisans. 6k, Battle of Borodino. 10k, Wasilisa Kozhina and partisans.

**1962, Sept. 25** ***Perf. 12½x12***

**2636** A1346 3k orange brown .30 .25
**2637** A1346 4k ultra .30 .25
**2638** A1346 6k blue gray .65 .25
**2639** A1346 10k violet .75 .25
*Nos. 2636-2639 (4)* 2.00 1.00

War of 1812 against the French, 150th anniv.

Street in Vinnitsa A1347

**1962, Sept. 25 Photo.**

**2640** A1347 4k yel bister & black .50 .25

Town of Vinnitsa, Ukraine, 600th anniv.

"Mail and Transportation" — A1348

**1962, Sept. 25** ***Perf. 11½***

**2641** A1348 4k blue grn, blk & lil .50 .25

Intl. Letter Writing Week, Oct. 7-13.

Cedar — A1349

4k, Canna. 6k, Arbutus. 10k, Chrysanthemum.

**1962, Sept. 27 Engr. & Photo.**

**2642** A1349 3k ver, black & grn .75 .25
**2643** A1349 4k multicolored .75 .25
**2644** A1349 6k multicolored 1.25 .25
**2645** A1349 10k multicolored 2.25 .25
*Nos. 2642-2645 (4)* 5.00 1.00

Nikitsky Botanical Gardens, 150th anniv.

Construction Worker — A1350

Designs: No. 2647, Hiker. No. 2648, Surgeon. No. 2649, Worker and lathe. No. 2650, Agricultural worker. No. 2651, Textile worker. No. 2652, Modern home.

**1962, Sept. 29 Litho.** ***Perf. 12x12½***

**2646** A1350 4k org, gray & vio blue .25 .25
**2647** A1350 4k yel, gray, grn & blue .25 .25
**2648** A1350 4k grn, gray & lilac rose .25 .25
**2649** A1350 4k ver, gray & lilac .25 .25
**2650** A1350 4k bl, gray & emer .25 .25
**2651** A1350 4k brt pink, gray & vio .25 .25
**2652** A1350 4k yel, gray, dp vio, red & brown .25 .25
*Nos. 2646-2652 (7)* 1.75 1.75

Sputnik and Stars A1351

**1962, Oct. 4** ***Perf. 12½x12***

**2653** A1351 10k multicolored .80 .30

5th anniversary, launching of Sputnik 1.

M. F. Ahundov, Azerbaijan Poet and Philosopher, 150th Birth Anniv. — A1352

**1962, Oct. 2 Photo.**

**2654** A1352 4k lt grn & dk brn .50 .25

Farm and Young Couple with Banner A1353

Designs: No. 2656, Tractors, map and surveyor. No. 2657, Farmer, harvester and map.

**1962, Oct. 18 Litho.** ***Perf. 12½x12***

**2655** A1353 4k multicolored .75 .25
**2656** A1353 4k multicolored .75 .25
**2657** A1353 4k brown, yel & red .75 .25
*Nos. 2655-2657 (3)* 2.25 .75

Honoring pioneer developers of virgin soil.

N. N. Burdenko A1354

V. P. Filatov A1355

**1962, Oct. 20** ***Perf. 12½x12***

**2658** A1354 4k red brn, lt brn & blk .50 .25
**2659** A1355 4k multicolored .50 .25

Scientists and academicians.

Lenin Mausoleum, Red Square — A1356

**1962, Oct. 26 Litho.**

**2660** A1356 4k multicolored .60 .25

92nd anniversary of Lenin's birth.

Worker, Flag and Factories A1357

**1962, Oct. 29** ***Perf. 12x12½***

**2661** A1357 4k multicolored .50 .25

45th anniv. of the October Revolution.

No. 2631 Overprinted in Dark Violet

**1962, Nov. 3 Photo.** ***Perf. 11½***

**2662** A1342 10k violet & multi 3.00 2.50

Launching of a rocket to Mars.

Togolok Moldo (1860-1942), Kirghiz Poet A1358

Sajat Nova (1712-1795), Armenian Poet A1359

**1962, Nov. 17** ***Perf. 12x12½***

**2663** A1358 4k brn red & black 1.00 .25
**2664** A1359 4k ultra & black 1.00 .25

Arms, Hammer & Sickle and Map of USSR A1360

**1962, Nov. 17** ***Perf. 11½***

**2665** A1360 4k red, org & dk red .50 .25

USSR founding, 40th anniv.

Space Rocket, Earth and Mars — A1361

**1962, Nov. 17** ***Perf. 12½x12***

**Size: 73x27mm**

**2666** A1361 10k purple & org red 1.00 .40

Launching of a space rocket to Mars, Nov. 1, 1962.

Electric Power Industry — A1362

Designs: No. 2668, Machines. No. 2669, Chemicals and oil. No. 2670, Factory construction. No. 2671, Transportation. No. 2672, Telecommunications and space. No. 2673, Metals. No. 2674, Grain farming. No. 2675, Dairy, poultry and meat.

**1962 Litho.** ***Perf. 12½x12***

**2667** A1362 4k ultra, red, blk & gray .60 .25
**2668** A1362 4k ultra, gray, yel & cl .60 .25
**2669** A1362 4k yel, pink, blk, gray & brown .60 .25
**2670** A1362 4k yel, blue, red brn & gray .45 .25
**2671** A1362 4k mar, yel, red & blue .45 .25
**2672** A1362 4k brt yel, blue & brn .45 .25
**2673** A1362 4k lil, org, yel & dk brn .45 .25
**2674** A1362 4k vio, bis, org red & dk brown .45 .25
**2675** A1362 4k emer, dk brn, brn & gray .45 .25
*Nos. 2667-2675 (9)* 4.50 2.25

"Great decisions of the 22nd Communist Party Congress" and Russian people at work. Issued: #2667-2669, 11/19; others, 12/28.

Queen, Rook and Knight — A1363

*Perf. 12½*

**1962, Nov. 24 Unwmk. Photo.**

**2676** A1363 4k org yel & blk .60 .40

30th Russian Chess Championships.

Gen. Vasili Blucher A1364

**1962, Nov. 27** ***Perf. 11½***

**2677** A1364 4k multicolored 3.00 .25

General Vasili Konstantinovich Blucher (1889-1938).

V. N. Podbelski (1887-1920), Minister of Posts — A1365

**1962, Nov. 27** ***Perf. 12½x12***

**2678** A1365 4k red brn, gray & blk .60 .25

Makarenko A1366

Dove and Globe — A1368

Gaidar A1367

**1962, Nov. 30** ***Perf. 11½x12***

**2679** A1366 4k multicolored .65 .45
**2680** A1367 4k multicolored .65 .45

A. S. Makharenko (1888-1939) and Arkadi Gaidar (1904-1941), writers.

**1962, Dec. 22 Litho.** ***Perf. 12½x12***

**2681** A1368 4k multicolored 1.00 .50

New Year 1963. Has alternating label inscribed "Happy New Year!" Issued imperf. on Dec. 20. Value $2.

D. N. Prjanishnikov A1369

**1962, Dec. 22** ***Perf. 12x12½***

**2682** A1369 4k multicolored 1.00 .25

Prjanishnikov, founder of Russian agricultural chemistry.

Rose-colored Starlings — A1370

4k, Red-breasted geese. 6k, Snow geese. 10k, White storks. 16k, Greater flamingos.

**1962, Dec. 26 Photo.** ***Perf. 11½***

**2683** A1370 3k grn, blk & pink .35 .25
**2684** A1370 4k brn, blk & dp org .50 .25
**2685** A1370 6k gray, blk & red .60 .25
**2686** A1370 10k blue, blk & red .90 .30
**2687** A1370 16k lt bl, rose & blk 1.50 .50
*Nos. 2683-2687 (5)* 3.85 1.55

FIR Emblem A1371

**1962, Dec. 26** ***Perf. 12x12½***

**2688** A1371 4k violet & red .45 .25
**2689** A1371 6k grnsh blue & red .45 .25

4th Cong. of the Intl. Federation of Resistance.

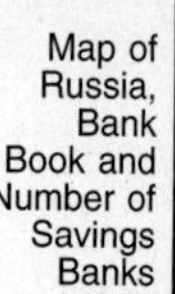

Map of Russia, Bank Book and Number of Savings Banks A1372

Design: 6k, as 4k, but with depositors.

**1962, Dec. 30 Litho.** ***Perf. 12½x12***

**2690** A1372 4k multicolored .75 .25
**2691** A1372 6k multicolored 1.25 .30

40th anniv. of Russian savings banks.

Rustavsky Fertilizer Plant — A1373

Hydroelectric Power Stations: No. 2693, Bratskaya. No. 2964, Volzhskaya.

**1962, Dec. 30 Photo.** ***Perf. 12½***

**2692** A1373 4k ultra, lt blue & black .70 .25
**2693** A1373 4k yel grn, bl grn & blk .70 .25
**2694** A1373 4k gray bl, brt bl & blk .70 .25
*Nos. 2692-2694 (3)* 2.10 .75

Stanislavski A1374

*Perf. 12½*

**1963, Jan. 15 Unwmk. Engr.**

**2695** A1374 4k slate green .50 .25

Stanislavski (professional name of Konstantin Sergeevich Alekseev, 1863-1938), actor, producer and founder of the Moscow Art Theater.

A. S. Serafimovich (1863-1949), Writer — A1375

**1963, Jan. 19 Photo.** ***Perf. 11½***

**2696** A1375 4k mag, dk brn & gray .50 .25

Children in Nursery A1376

Designs: No. 2698, Kindergarten. No. 2699, Pioneers marching and camping. No. 2700, Young people studying and working.

**1963, Jan. 31**

**2697** A1376 4k brn org, org red & black .70 .25
**2698** A1376 4k blue, mag & org .70 .25
**2699** A1376 4k brt grn, red & brn .70 .25
**2700** A1376 4k multicolored .70 .25
*Nos. 2697-2700 (4)* 2.80 1.00

Wooden Dolls and Toys, Russia — A1377

National Handicrafts: 6k, Pottery, Ukraine. 10k, Bookbinding, Estonia. 12k, Metalware, Dagestan.

**1963, Jan. 31 Litho.** ***Perf. 12x12½***

**2701** A1377 4k multicolored .45 .25
**2702** A1377 6k multicolored .60 .25
**2703** A1377 10k multicolored .90 .35
**2704** A1377 12k ultra, org & black 1.00 .40
*Nos. 2701-2704 (4)* 2.95 1.25

Gen. Mikhail N. Tukhachevski — A1378

Designs: No. 2706, U. M. Avetisian. No. 2707, A. M. Matrosov. No. 2708, J. V. Panfilov. No. 2709, Y. F. Fabrisciuss.

*Perf. 12½x12*

**1963, Feb. Photo. Unwmk.**

**2705** A1378 4k blue grn & slate grn .60 .25
**2706** A1378 4k org brown & blk .60 .25
**2707** A1378 4k ultra & dk brown .60 .25
**2708** A1378 4k dp rose & black .60 .25
**2709** A1378 4k rose lil & vio bl .60 .25
*Nos. 2705-2709 (5)* 3.00 1.25

45th anniv. of the Soviet Army and honoring its heroes. No. 2705 for Gen. Mikhail Nikolaevich Tukhachevski (1893-1937).

M. A. Pavlov — A1379

E. O. Paton and Dnieper Bridge, Kiev — A1379a

Portraits: No. 2711, I. V. Kurchatov. No. 2712, V. I. Vernadski. No. 2713, Aleksei N. Krylov. No. 2714, V. A. Obrutchev, geologist.

**1963** ***Perf. 11½x12***

**Size: 21x32mm**

**2710** A1379 4k gray, buff & dk bl .50 .25
**2711** A1379 4k slate & brown .50 .25

*Perf. 12*

**2712** A1379 4k lil gray & lt brn .50 .25

*Perf. 11½*

**Size: 23x34½mm**

**2713** A1379 4k dk blue, sep & red .50 .25
**2714** A1379 4k brn ol, gray & red .50 .25
**2715** A1379a 4k grnsh bl, blk & red .50 .25
*Nos. 2710-2715 (6)* 3.00 1.50

Members of the Russian Academy of Science. No. 2715 for Eugene Oskarovich Paton (1870-1953), bridge building engineer.

Winter Sports A1380

**1963, Feb. 28** ***Perf. 11½***

**2716** A1380 4k brt blue, org & blk .50 .25

5th Trade Union Spartacist Games. Printed in sheets of 50 (5x10) with every other row inverted.

No. 2573 Overprinted

**1963, Mar. 20**

**2717** A1306 6k Prus blue & plum 3.00 1.00

Victory of the Soviet ice hockey team in the World Championships, Stockholm. For overprint see No. 3612.

Victor Kingisepp A1381

**1963, Mar. 24** ***Perf. 12x12½***

**2718** A1381 4k blue gray & choc .50 .25

75th anniversary of the birth of Victor Kingisepp, communist party leader. Exists imperf.

Rudolfs Blaumanis (1863-1908), Latvian Writer — A1382

**1963, Mar. 24** *Perf. 12½x12*
**2719** A1382 4k ultra & dk red brn .50 .25

Flower and Globe — A1383

Designs: 6k, Atom diagram and power line. 10k, Rocket in space.

**1963, Mar. 26** *Perf. 11½*
**2720** A1383 4k red, ultra & grn .50 .25
**2721** A1383 6k red, grn & lilac 1.00 .35
**2722** A1383 10k red, vio & lt blue 1.50 .45
*Nos. 2720-2722 (3)* 3.00 1.05

"World without Arms and Wars."
The 10k exists imperf. Value: $2 mint; $1 used.
For overprint see No. 2754.

**Costume Type of 1960-62**

Regional Costumes: 3k, Tadzhik. No. 2724, Kirghiz. No. 2725, Azerbaijan. No. 2726, Turkmen.

**1963, Mar. 31** **Litho.** *Perf. 11½*
**2723** A1237 3k blk, red, ocher & org 1.25 .30
**2724** A1237 4k brown, ver, ocher & ultra 1.25 .30
**2725** A1237 4k blk, ocher, red & grn 1.25 .30
**2726** A1237 4k red, lil, ocher & blk 1.25 .30
*Nos. 2723-2726 (4)* 5.00 1.20

Lenin A1384

**1963, Mar. 30** **Engr.** *Perf. 12*
**2727** A1384 4k red & brown 3.50 1.00

93rd anniversary of the birth of Lenin.

Luna 4 Approaching Moon — A1385

**1963, Apr. 2** **Photo.**
**2728** A1385 6k black, lt blue & red 1.00 .25

Soviet rocket to the moon, Apr. 2, 1963. Exists imperforate. Values: unused, $2; used, $1.
For overprint see No. 3160.

Woman and Beach Scene A1386

Designs: 4k, Young man's head and factory. 10k, Child's head and kindergarden.

**1963, Apr. 7** **Litho.** *Perf. 12½x12*
**2729** A1386 2k multicolored .35 .25
**2730** A1386 4k multicolored .40 .30
**2731** A1386 10k multicolored .70 .40
*Nos. 2729-2731 (3)* 1.45 .95

15th anniversary of World Health Day.

A1387

No. 2732: a, d, Sputnik & Earth. b, e, Vostok 1, earth & moon. c, f, Rocket & Sun.

**1963, Apr. 12**
**2732** Block of 6 5.00 1.50
*a.* A1387 10k "10k" blk, blue & lil rose .70 .25
*b.* A1387 10k "10k" lil rose, blue & blk .70 .25
*c.* A1387 10k "10k" black, red & yel .70 .25
*d.* A1387 10k "10k" blue .70 .25
*e.* A1387 10k "10k" lilac rose .70 .25
*f.* A1387 10k "10k" yellow .70 .25

Cosmonauts' Day.

Demian Bednii (1883-1945), Poet — A1388

**1963, Apr. 13** **Photo.**
**2735** A1388 4k brown & black .50 .25

Soldiers on Horseback and Cuban Flag — A1389

Soviet-Cuban friendship: 6k, Cuban flag, hands with gun and book. 10k, Cuban and USSR flags and crane lifting tractor.

**1963, Apr. 25** *Perf. 11½*
**2736** A1389 4k blk, red & ultra .30 .25
**2737** A1389 6k blk, red & ultra .40 .25
**2738** A1389 10k red, ultra & blk .80 .25
*Nos. 2736-2738 (3)* 1.50 .75

Karl Marx — A1390

**1963, May 9** *Perf. 12x12½*
**2739** A1390 4k dk red brn & blk .50 .25

145th anniversary of the birth of Marx.

Hasek — A1391

**1963, Apr. 29** *Perf. 11½x12*
**2740** A1391 4k black .75 .25

Jaroslav Hasek (1883-1923), Czech writer.

Moscow P.O. for Foreign Mail A1392

**1963, May 9** *Perf. 11½*
**2741** A1392 6k brt vio & red brn .50 .25

5th Conference of Communications Ministers of Socialist countries, Budapest.

King and Pawn A1393

6k, Queen, bishop. 16k, Rook, knight.

**1963, May 22** **Photo.**
**2742** A1393 4k multicolored .60 .25
**2743** A1393 6k ultra, brt pink & grnsh blue 1.00 .30
**2744** A1393 16k brt plum, brt pink & black 2.40 .55
*Nos. 2742-2744 (3)* 4.00 1.10

25th Championship Chess Match, Moscow. Exists imperf., issued May 18. Value $6.

Richard Wagner — A1394

Design: No. 2745A, Giuseppe Verdi.

**1963** **Unwmk.** *Perf. 11½x12*
**2745** A1394 4k black & red 1.50 .50
**2745A** A1394 4k red & violet brn 1.50 .50

150th annivs. of the births of Wagner and Verdi, German and Italian composers.

15th European Boxing Championships, Moscow A1395

4k, Boxers. 6k, Referee proclaiming victor.

**1963, May 29** **Litho.** *Perf. 12½*
**2746** A1395 4k multicolored .60 .25
**2747** A1395 6k multicolored .90 .35

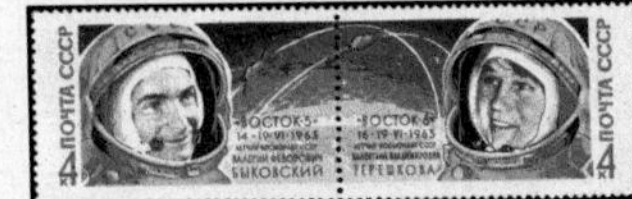
A1396

Valentina Tereshkova — A1397

Designs: No. 2748, Valeri Bykovski. No. 2749, Valentina Tereshkova. No. 2751, Bykovski. No. 2752, Symbolic man and woman fliers. No. 2753, Valentina Tereshkova, vert.

**Litho. (A1396); Photo. (A1397)**

**1963** *Perf. 12½x12, 12x12½*
**2748** 4k multicolored .90 .25
**2749** 4k multicolored .90 .25
*a.* A1396 Pair #2748-2749 1.80 .80
**2750** A1397 6k grn & dk car rose .75 .25
**2751** A1397 6k purple & brown .75 .25
**2752** A1397 10k blue & red 1.50 .40
**2753** A1396 10k multicolored 2.10 .50
*Nos. 2748-2753 (6)* 6.90 1.90

Space flights of Valeri Bykovski, June 14-19, and Valentina Tereshkova, 1st woman cosmonaut, June 16-19, 1963, in Vostoks 5 and 6.
No. 2749a has continuous design.
Nos. 2750-2753 exist imperf. Value $9.

No. 2720 Overprinted in Red

**1963, June 24** **Photo.** *Perf. 11½*
**2754** A1383 4k red, ultra & green .90 .50

Intl. Women's Cong., Moscow, June 24-29.

Globe, Camera and Film A1398

**1963, July 7** **Photo.** *Perf. 11½*
**2755** A1398 4k gray & ultra .90 .35

3rd International Film Festival, Moscow.

Vladimir V. Mayakovsky, Poet, 70th Birth Anniv. — A1399

**1963, July 19** **Engr.** *Perf. 12½*
**2756** A1399 4k red brown .90 .25

Tanks and Map A1400

Design: 6k, Soldier, tanks and flag.

**1963, July** **Litho.** *Perf. 12½x12*
**2757** A1400 4k sepia & orange .75 .25
**2758** A1400 6k org, slate green & blk 1.00 .35

20th anniversary of the Battle of Kursk in the "War of Liberation," 1941-1945.

Bicyclist — A1401

Sports: 4k, Long jump. 6k, Women divers, horiz. 12k, Basketball. 16k, Soccer.

**1963, July 27** ***Perf. 12½x12, 12x12½***

**2759** A1401 3k multicolored .25 .25
**2760** A1401 4k multicolored .25 .25
**2761** A1401 6k multicolored .40 .25
**2762** A1401 12k multicolored .85 .25
**2763** A1401 16k multicolored 1.25 .30
*a.* Souvenir sheet of 4, imperf. 15.00 3.00
*Nos. 2759-2763 (5)* 3.00 1.30

3rd Spartacist Games.
Exist imperf. Value $5.
No. 2763a contains stamps similar to the 3k, 4k, 12k and 16k, with colors changed. Issued Dec. 22.

Ice Hockey — A1402

**1963, July 27** ***Photo.***

**2764** A1402 6k red & gray blue .50 .25

World Ice Hockey Championship, Stockholm.
For overprint see No. 3012.

Lenin — A1403

**1963, July 29**

**2765** A1403 4k red & black .50 .25

60th anniversary of the 2nd Congress of the Social Democratic Labor Party.

Freighter and Relief Shipment — A1404

Design: 12k, Centenary emblem.

**1963, Aug. 8** ***Perf. 12½***

**2766** A1404 6k Prus green & red .35 .25
**2767** A1404 12k dark blue & red .90 .25

Centenary of International Red Cross.

Lapp Reindeer Race A1405

Designs: 4k, Pamir polo, vert. 6k, Burjat archery. 10k, Armenian wrestling, vert.

**1963, Aug. 8** ***Perf. 11½***

**2768** A1405 3k lt vio bl, brn & red .45 .25
**2769** A1405 4k bis brn, red & blk .60 .25
**2770** A1405 6k yel, black & red .75 .25
**2771** A1405 10k sepia, blk & dk red 1.25 .35
*Nos. 2768-2771 (4)* 3.05 1.10

A. F. Mozhaisky (1825-1890), Pioneer Airplane Builder — A1406

Aviation Pioneers: 10k, P. N. Nesterov (1887-1914), pioneer stunt flyer. 16k, N. E. Zhukovski (1847-1921), aerodynamics pioneer, and pressurized air tunnel.

**1963, Aug. 18** ***Engr. & Photo.***

**2772** A1406 6k black & brt blue .30 .25
**2773** A1406 10k black & brt blue .60 .25
**2774** A1406 16k black & brt blue 1.00 .25
*Nos. 2772-2774 (3)* 1.90 .75

Alexander S. Dargomyzhski and Scene from "Rusalka" — A1408

S. S. Gulak-Artemovsky and Scene from "Cossacks on the Danube" — A1409

No. 2777, Georgi O. Eristavi and theater.

***Perf. 11½x12, 12x12½***

**1963, Sept. 10** ***Photo.***

**2776** A1408 4k violet & black .50 .25
**2777** A1408 4k gray violet & brn .60 .25
**2778** A1409 4k red & black .50 .25
*Nos. 2776-2778 (3)* 1.60 .75

Dargomyzhski, Ukrainian composer; Eristavi, Georgian writer, and Gulak-Artemovsky, Ukrainian composer, 150th birth annivs.

Map of Antarctica, Penguins, Research Ship and Southern Lights — A1410

Designs: 4k, Map, southern lights and snocats (trucks). 6k, Globe, camp and various planes. 12k, Whaler and whales.

**1963, Sept. 16** ***Litho.*** ***Perf. 12½x12***

**2779** A1410 3k multicolored .40 .25
**2780** A1410 4k multicolored .60 .30
**2781** A1410 6k vio, blue & red 1.00 .40
**2782** A1410 12k multicolored 2.00 .75
*Nos. 2779-2782 (4)* 4.00 1.70

"The Antarctic - Continent of Peace."

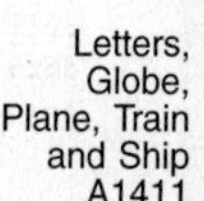

Letters, Globe, Plane, Train and Ship A1411

**1963, Sept. 20** ***Photo.*** ***Perf. 11½***

**2783** A1411 4k violet, black & org .75 .25

International Letter Writing Week.

Denis Diderot — A1412

**1963, Oct. 10** ***Unwmk.*** ***Perf. 11½***

**2784** A1412 4k dk blue, brn & yel bister .75 .25

Denis Diderot (1713-84), French philosopher and encyclopedist.

Gleb Uspenski — A1414

Portraits: No. 2787, N. P. Ogarev. No. 2788, V. Brusov. No. 2789, F. Gladkov

**1963, Oct. 10**

**2786** A1414 4k buff, red brn & dk brown .75 .25
**2787** A1414 4k blk & pale grn .75 .25
**2788** A1414 4k car, brown & gray .75 .25
**2789** A1414 4k car, ol brn & gray .75 .25
*Nos. 2786-2789 (4)* 3.00 1.00

Gleb Ivanovich Uspenski (1843-1902), historian and writer; Ogarev, politician, 150th birth anniv.; Brusov, poet, 90th birth anniv., Fyodor Gladkov (1883-1958), writer.

"Peace" Worker, Student, Astronaut and Lenin — A1415

Designs: No. 2794, "Labor," automatic controls. No. 2795, "Liberty," painter, lecturer, woman reading newspaper. No. 2796, "Equality," elections, regional costumes. No. 2797, "Brotherhood," Recognition of achievement. No. 2798, "Happiness," Family.

**1963, Oct. 15** ***Litho.*** ***Perf. 12½x12***

**2793** A1415 4k dk red, red & blk .55 .35
**2794** A1415 4k red, dk red & blk .55 .35
**2795** A1415 4k dk red, red & blk .55 .35
**2796** A1415 4k dk red, red & blk .55 .35
**2797** A1415 4k dk red, red & blk .55 .35
**2798** A1415 4k dk red, red & blk .55 .35
*a.* Strip of 6, #2793-2798 4.00 3.00

Proclaiming Peace, Labor, Liberty, Equality, Brotherhood and Happiness.

Kirghiz Academy and Moscow State University A1416

**1963, Oct. 22** ***Perf. 12x12½***

**2799** A1416 4k red, yel & vio blue .50 .25

Russia's annexation of Kirghizia, cent.

Lenin and Young Workers A1417

Design: No. 2801, Lenin and Palace of Congresses, the Kremlin.

**1963, Oct. 24** ***Photo.*** ***Perf. 11½***

**2800** A1417 4k crimson & black .50 .25
**2801** A1417 4k carmine & black .50 .25

13th Congr. of Soviet Trade Unions, Moscow.

Olga Kobylyanskaya, Ukrainian Novelist, Birth Cent. — A1418

**1963, Oct. 24** ***Perf. 11½x12***

**2802** A1418 4k tan & dk car rose .60 .30

Ilya Mechnikov A1419

6k, Louis Pasteur. 12k, Albert Calmette.

**1963, Oct. 28** ***Perf. 12***

**2803** A1419 4k green & bister .50 .35
**2804** A1419 6k purple & bister .70 .35
**2805** A1419 12k blue & bister 1.40 .35
*Nos. 2803-2805 (3)* 2.60 1.05

Pasteur Institute, Paris, 75th anniv; 12k for Albert Calmette (1863-1933), bacteriologist.

Cruiser Aurora and Rockets A1420

**1963, Nov. 1**

**2806** A1420 4k mar, blk, gray & red orange .45 .25
**2807** A1420 4k mar, blk, gray & brt rose red .55 .25

Development of the Armed Forces, and 46th anniv. of the October Revolution. The bright rose red ink of No. 2807 is fluorescent.

Mausoleum Gur Emir, Samarkand
A1421

Architecture in Samarkand, Uzbekistan: #2809, Shakhi-Zinda Necropolis. 6k, Registan Square.

**1963, Nov. 14 Litho. *Perf. 12***

**Size: 27½x27½mm**

**2808** A1421 4k bl, yel & red brn .50 .25
**2809** A1421 4k bl, yel & red brn .50 .25

**Size: 55x27½mm**

**2810** A1421 6k bl, yel & red brn 1.00 .25
*Nos. 2808-2810 (3)* 2.00 .75

Proclamation, Spasski Tower and Globe
A1422

**1963, Nov. 15 Photo. *Perf. 12x11½***

**2811** A1422 6k purple & lt blue .50 .25

Signing of the Nuclear Test Ban Treaty between the US and the USSR.

Pushkin Monument, Kiev — A1423

M. S. Shchepkin
A1424

Portrait: No. 2814, V. L. Durov (1863-1934), circus clown.

**1963 Engr. *Perf. 12x12½***

**2812** A1423 4k dark brown 1.50 .25
**2813** A1424 4k brown 1.50 .25
**2814** A1424 4k brown black 2.00 .25
*Nos. 2812-2814 (3)* 5.00 .75

No. 2813 for M. S. Shchepkin, actor, 75th birth anniv.

Yuri M. Steklov, 1st Editor of Izvestia, 90th Birth Anniv.
A1425

**1963, Nov. 17 Photo. *Perf. 11½***

**2815** A1425 4k black & lilac rose .60 .25

Vladimir G. Shuhov and Moscow Radio Tower — A1426

**1963, Nov. 17 *Perf. 12½x12***

**2816** A1426 4k green & black .50 .30

Shuhov, scientist, 110th birth anniv.

USSR and Czech Flags, Kremlin and Hradcany
A1427

**1963, Nov. 25 *Perf. 11½***

**2817** A1427 6k red, ultra & brown .50 .25

Russo-Czechoslovakian Treaty, 20th anniv.

Fyodor A. Poletaev — A1428

**1963, Nov. 25 Litho. *Perf. 12½x12***

**2818** A1428 4k multicolored .50 .30

F. A. Poletaev, Hero of the Soviet Union, National Hero of Italy, and holder of the Order of Garibaldi.

Julian Grimau and Worker Holding Flag — A1429

**1963, Nov. 29 Photo. *Perf. 11½***

**Flag and Name Panel Embossed**

**2819** A1429 6k vio black, red & buff 1.00 .25

Spanish anti-fascist fighter Julian Grimau.

Rockets, Sky and Tree — A1430

**1963, Dec. 12 Litho. *Perf. 12x12½***

**2820** A1430 6k multicolored 1.00 .25

"Happy New Year!" — A1431

**Photogravure and Embossed**

**1963, Dec. 20 *Perf. 11½***

**2821** A1431 4k grn, dk blue & red .50 .25
**2822** A1431 6k grn, dk bl & fluor. rose red .60 .30

Nos. 2820-2822 issued for New Year 1964.

Mikas J. Petrauskas, Lithuanian Composer, 90th Birth Anniv.
A1432

**1963, Dec. 20 Photo. *Perf. 11½x12***

**2823** A1432 4k brt grn & brn .75 .35

Topaz — A1433

Precious stones of the Urals: 4k, Jasper. 6k, Amethyst. 10k, Emerald. 12k, Rhodonite. 16k, Malachite.

**1963, Dec. 26 Litho. *Perf. 12***

**2824** A1433 2k brn, yel & blue .30 .25
**2825** A1433 4k multicolored .40 .30
**2826** A1433 6k red & purple .50 .30
**2827** A1433 10k multicolored .80 .40
**2828** A1433 12k multicolored 1.10 .50
**2829** A1433 16k multicolored 1.40 .60
*Nos. 2824-2829 (6)* 4.50 2.35

Coat of Arms and Sputnik
A1434

Rockets: No. 2831, Luna I. No. 2832, Rocket around the moon. No. 2833, Vostok I, first man in space. No. 2834, Vostok III & IV. No. 2835, Vostok VI, first woman astronaut.

**1963, Dec. 27 Litho. & Embossed**

**2830** A1434 10k red, gold & gray .80 .30
**2831** A1434 10k red, gold & gray .80 .30
**2832** A1434 10k red, gold & gray .80 .30
**2833** A1434 10k red, gold & gray .80 .30
**2834** A1434 10k red, gold & gray .80 .30
**2835** A1434 10k red, gold & gray .80 .30
*a.* Vert. strip of 6, #2830-2835 5.50 2.50

Soviet achievements in space.

Dyushambe, Tadzhikistan — A1435

**1963, Dec. 30 Engr.**

**2836** A1435 4k dull blue .60 .30

No. 2836 was issued after Stalinabad was renamed Dyushambe.

For overprint see No. 2943.

Flame, Broken Chain and Rainbow
A1436

**1963, Dec. 30 Litho.**

**2837** A1436 6k multicolored .75 .25

15th anniversary of the Universal Declaration of Human Rights.

F. A. Sergeev
A1437

**1963, Dec. 30 Photo. *Perf. 12x12½***

**2838** A1437 4k gray & red .50 .25

80th anniversary of the birth of the revolutionist Artjem (F. A. Sergeev).

Sun and Radar
A1438

6k, Sun, Earth, vert. 10k, Earth, Sun.

**1964, Jan. 1 Photo. *Perf. 11½***

**2839** A1438 4k brt mag, org & blk .45 .35
**2840** A1438 6k org yel, red & bl .60 .35
**2841** A1438 10k blue, vio & org .90 .35
*Nos. 2839-2841 (3)* 1.95 1.05

International Quiet Sun Year, 1964-65.

Christian Donalitius
A1439

**1964, Jan. 1 Unwmk. *Perf. 12***

**2842** A1439 4k green & black .50 .25

Lithuanian poet Christian Donalitius (Donelaitis), 250th birth anniv.

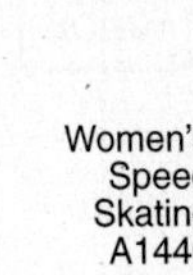

Women's Speed Skating
A1440

Designs: 4k, Women's cross country skiing. 6k, 1964 Olympic emblem and torch. 10k, Biathlon. 12k, Figure skating pair.

**1964, Feb. 4 *Perf. 11½, Imperf.***

**2843** A1440 2k ultra, blk & lil rose .25 .25
**2844** A1440 4k lil rose, blk & ultra .40 .25
**2845** A1440 6k dk bl, red & blk .50 .25
**2846** A1440 10k grn, lil & blk .90 .30
**2847** A1440 12k lil, blk & grn .90 .35
*Nos. 2843-2847 (5)* 2.95 1.40

9th Winter Olympic Games, Innsbruck Jan. 29-Feb. 9, 1964. Exists imperf. Values: unused, $4; used, $3. See Nos. 2865, 2867-2870.

Anna S. Golubkina (1864-1927), Sculptor — A1441

**1964, Feb. 4** **Photo.**

**2848** A1441 4k gray, brn & buff .50 .25

**No. 2450 Overprinted**

and

Taras G. Shevchenko A1443

Designs: 4k, Shevchenko statue, Kiev. 10k, Shevchenko by Ilya Repin. (Portrait on 6k by I. Kramskoi.)

**1964** **Litho.** ***Perf. 12***

**2852** A1245 3k brown & violet 3.00 2.00

**Engr.**

**2853** A1443 4k magenta .30 .25
**2854** A1443 4k deep green .30 .25
**2855** A1443 6k red brown .40 .25
**2856** A1443 6k indigo .40 .25

**Photo.**

**2857** A1443 10k bister & brown .50 .25
**2858** A1443 10k buff & dull violet .50 .25
*Nos. 2852-2858 (7)* 5.40 3.50

Shevchenko, Ukrainian poet, 150th birth anniv.

Issued: #2852, 2857-2858, 2/22; Others, 3/1.

K. S. Zaslonov A1444

Soviet Heroes: No. 2860, N. A. Vilkov. No. 2861, J. V. Smirnov. No. 2862, V. S. Khorujaia (heroine). No. 2862A, I. M. Sivko. No. 2862B, I. S. Polbin.

**1964-65** **Photo.**

**2859** A1444 4k hn brn & brn blk .50 .35
**2860** A1444 4k Prus bl & vio blk .50 .35
**2861** A1444 4k brn red & ind .50 .35
**2862** A1444 4k bluish gray & dk brown .50 .35
**2862A** A1444 4k lil & blk ('65) .50 .35
**2862B** A1444 4k blue & dk brn ('65) .50 .35
*Nos. 2859-2862B (6)* 3.00 2.10

Printer Inking Form, 16th Century A1445

6k, Statue of Ivan Fedorov, 1st Russian printer.

**1964, Mar. 1** **Litho.** **Unwmk.**

**2863** A1445 4k multicolored .60 .25
**2864** A1445 6k multicolored .80 .25

400th anniv. of book printing in Russia.

Nos. 2843-2847 Overprinted

and

Ice Hockey A1446

Olympic Gold Medal, "11 Gold, 8 Silver, 6 Bronze" A1447

Design: 3k, Ice hockey.

**1964, Mar. 9** **Photo.** ***Perf. 11½***

**2865** A1440 2k ultra, blk & lilac rose .25 .25
**2866** A1446 3k blk, bl grn & red .30 .25
**2867** A1440 4k lil rose, blk & ultra .35 .25
**2868** A1440 6k dk bl, red & blk .75 .25
**2869** A1440 10k grn, lil & blk .85 .30
**2870** A1440 12k lilac, blk & grn .95 .35

***Perf. 12***

**2871** A1447 16k org red & gldn brown 1.40 .40
*Nos. 2865-2871 (7)* 4.85 2.05

Soviet victories at the 9th Winter Olympic Games.

On Nos. 2865, 2867-2870 the black overprints commemorate victories in various events and are variously arranged in 3 to 6 lines, with "Innsbruck" in Russian added below "1964" on 2k, 4k, 10k and 12k.

Rubber Industry — A1448

Designs: No. 2873, Textile industry. No. 2874, Cotton, wheat, corn and helicopter spraying land.

**1964** **Litho.** ***Perf. 12x12½***

**2872** A1448 4k org, lilac, ultra & blk .65 .25
**2873** A1448 4k org, blk, grn & ultra .65 .25
**2874** A1448 4k dull yel, ol, red & bl .65 .25
*Nos. 2872-2874 (3)* 1.95 .75

Importance of the chemical industry to the Soviet economy.

Issued: #2872, 2/10; #2873-2874, 3/27.

Regular and Volunteer Militiamen A1449

**1964, Mar. 27** **Photo.** ***Perf. 12***

**2875** A1449 4k red & deep ultra .75 .35

Day of the Militia.

Sailor and Odessa Lighthouse — A1450

Liberation Monument, Minsk — A1451

No. 2877, Lenin statue and Leningrad.

**1964** **Litho.** ***Perf. 12½x12***

**2876** A1450 4k red, lt grn, ultra & black .80 .35
**2877** A1450 4k red, yel, grn, brn & black .80 .35
**2878** A1451 4k bl, gray, red & emer .80 .35
*Nos. 2876-2878 (3)* 2.40 1.05

Liberation of Odessa (#2876), Leningrad (#2877), Byelorussia (#2878), 20th anniv.

Issued: #2876, 4/10; #2877, 5/9; #2878, 6/30.

First Soviet Sputniks A1452

F. A. Tsander — A1453

Designs: 6k, Mars 1 spacecraft. No. 2886, Konstantin E. Tsiolkovsky. No. 2887, N. I. Kibaltchitch. No. 2888, Statue honoring 3 balloonists killed in 1934 accident. 12k, Gagarin and satellite.

***Perf. 11½, Imperf.***

**1964, Apr.** **Photo.**

**2883** A1452 4k red org, blk & blue green .40 .25
**2884** A1452 6k dk bl & org red .65 .25
**2885** A1453 10k grn, blk & fluor. pink .80 .30
**2886** A1453 10k dk bl grn, blk & fluor. pink .80 .30
**2887** A1453 10k lilac, blk & lt grn .80 .30
**2888** A1453 10k blue & black .80 .30
**2889** A1452 12k blue grn, org brn & black 1.25 .40
*Nos. 2883-2889 (7)* 5.50 2.10

Leaders in rocket theory and technique.

Lenin, 94th Birth Anniv. A1454

**Engraved and Photogravure**

**1964-65** ***Perf. 12x11½***

**2890** A1454 4k blk, buff & lilac rose 4.50 3.50
*a.* Re-engraved ('65) 3.50 3.50

On No. 2890a, the portrait shading is much heavier. Lines on collar are straight and unbroken, rather than dotted.

For souvenir sheet see No. 2582a.

William Shakespeare, 400th Birth Anniv. — A1455

**1964, Apr. 23** ***Perf. 11½***

**2891** A1455 10k gray & red brn 1.00 .40

See Nos. 2985-2986.

"Irrigation" — A1456

**1964, May 12** **Litho.** ***Perf. 12x12½***

**2892** A1456 4k multicolored .65 .25

A1457

***Perf. 12½x11½***

**1964, May 12** **Photo.**

**2893** A1457 4k blue & gray brn .50 .25

Y. B. Gamarnik, army commander, 70th birth anniv.

D. I. Gulia A1458

Portraits: No. 2895, Hamza Hakim-Zade Nijazi. No. 2896, Saken Seifullin. No. 2896A, M. M. Kotsyubinsky. No. 2896B, Stepanos Nazaryan. No. 2896C, Toktogil Satyiganov.

**Engraved and Photogravure**

**1964** **Unwmk.** ***Perf. 12x11½***

**2894** A1458 4k grn, buff & blk .80 .35
**2895** A1458 4k red, buff & blk .80 .35
**2896** A1458 4k brn, ocher, buff & black .80 .35
**2896A** A1458 4k brn lake, blk & buff .80 .35
**2896B** A1458 4k blue, pale bl, blk & buff .80 .35
**2896C** A1458 4k red brn & blk .80 .35
*Nos. 2894-2896C (6)* 4.80 2.10

Abkhazian poet Gulia, 90th birth anniv.; Uzbekian writer and composer Nijazi, 75th birth anniv.; Kazakian poet Seifullin, 70th birth anniv.; Ukrainian writer Kotsyubinsky (1864-1913); Armenian writer Nazaryan (1814-1879); Kirghiz poet Satylganov (1864-1933).

Arkadi Gaidar (1904-41) A1459

Writers: No. 2897A, Nikolai Ostrovsky (1904-36) and battle scene (portrait at left).

**1964 Photo. Perf. 12**

2897 A1459 4k red orange & gray .50 .25

**Engr.**

2897A A1459 4k brn lake & blk .50 .25

No. 2318 Surcharged

**1964, May 27 Litho. Perf. 12**

2898 A1194 4k on 40k bis & brn 4.00 2.00

Azerbaijan's joining Russia, 150th anniv.

"Romania" A1460

No. 2900, "Poland," (map, Polish eagle, industrial and agricultural symbols). No. 2901, "Bulgaria" (flag, rose, industrial and agricultural symbols). No. 2902, Soviet and Yugoslav soldiers and embattled Belgrade. No. 2903, "Czechoslovakia" (view of Prague, arms, Russian soldier and woman). No. 2903A, Map and flag of Hungary, Liberty statue. No. 2903B, Statue of Russian Soldier and Belvedere Palace, Vienna. No. 2904, Buildings under construction, Warsaw; Polish flag and medal.

**1964-65 Litho. Perf. 12**

2899 A1460 6k gray & multi .60 .25
2900 A1460 6k ocher, red & brn .60 .25
2901 A1460 6k tan, grn & red .60 .25
2902 A1460 6k gray, blk, dl bl, ol & red .60 .25
2903 A1460 6k ultra, black & red ('65) .60 .25
2903A A1460 6k brn, red & green ('65) .60 .25
2903B A1460 6k dp org, gray bl & black ('65) .60 .25
2904 A1460 6k blue, red, yel & bister ('65) .60 .25
*Nos. 2899-2904 (8)* 4.80 2.00

20th anniversaries of liberation from German occupation of Romania, Poland, Bulgaria, Belgrade, Czechoslovakia, Hungary, Vienna and Warsaw.

Elephant A1461

Designs: 2k, Giant panda, horiz. 4k, Polar bear. 6k, European elk. 10k, Pelican. 12k, Tiger. 16k, Lammergeier.

***Perf. 12x12½, 12½x12, Imperf.***

**1964 Photo.**

**Size: 25x36mm, 36x25mm**

2905 A1461 1k red & black .25 .25
2906 A1461 2k tan & black .25 .25

***Perf. 12***

**Size: 26x28mm**

2907 A1461 4k grnsh gray, black & tan .25 .25

***Perf. 12x12½***

**Size: 25x36mm**

2908 A1461 6k ol, dk brn & tan .60 .25

***Perf. 12***

**Size: 26x28mm**

2909 A1461 10k ver, gray & blk .90 .40

***Perf. 12½x12, 12x12½***

**Size: 36x25mm, 25x36mm**

2910 A1461 12k brn, ocher & blk 1.25 .40
2911 A1461 16k ultra, blk, bis & yellow 1.60 .60
*Nos. 2905-2911 (7)* 5.10 2.40

100th anniv. of the Moscow zoo.
Issue dates: Perf., June 18. Imperf., May.

Leningrad Post Office A1462

**1964, June 30 Litho. Perf. 12**

2912 A1462 4k citron, blk & red .75 .25

Leningrad postal service, 250th anniv.

Corn — A1463

**1964 Photo. Perf. 11½, Imperf.**

2913 A1463 2k shown .25 .25
2914 A1463 3k Wheat .35 .25
2915 A1463 4k Potatoes .35 .25
2916 A1463 6k Beans .55 .25
2917 A1463 10k Beets .90 .25
2918 A1463 12k Cotton 1.10 .30
2919 A1463 16k Flax 1.50 .35
*Nos. 2913-2919 (7)* 5.00 1.90

Issue dates: Perf., July 10. Imperf., June 25.

Thorez — A1464

**1964, July 31**

2920 A1464 4k black & red .60 .40

Maurice Thorez, chairman of the French Communist party.

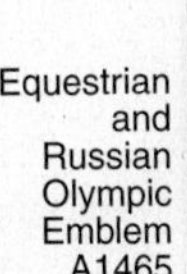

Equestrian and Russian Olympic Emblem A1465

Designs: 4k, Weight lifter. 6k, High jump. 10k, Canoeing. 12k, Girl gymnast. 16k, Fencing.

**1964, July Perf. 11½, Imperf.**

2921 A1465 3k lt yel grn, red, brn & black .25 .25
2922 A1465 4k yel, black & red .25 .25
2923 A1465 6k lt blue, blk & red .35 .25
2924 A1465 10k bl grn, red & blk .50 .25
2925 A1465 12k gray, blk & red .70 .25
2926 A1465 16k lt ultra, blk & red .90 .25
*Nos. 2921-2926 (6)* 2.95 1.50

18th Olympic Games, Tokyo, 10/10-25/64.
Two 1r imperf. souvenir sheets exist, showing emblem, woman gymnast and stadium. Size: 91x71mm.
Value, red sheet, $7 unused, $3 canceled; green sheet, $200 unused, $300 canceled.

Three Races — A1466

**1964, Aug. 8 Photo. Perf. 12**

2929 A1466 6k orange & black .50 .40

International Congress of Anthropologists and Ethnographers, Moscow.

Indian Prime Minister Jawaharlal Nehru (1889-1964) A1467

**1964, Aug. 20 Perf. 11½**

2930 A1467 4k brown & black .75 .25

Souvenir Sheet

Conquest of Space

**1964, Aug. 20 Perf. 11½x12**

2930A Sheet of 6 5.00 3.00
*b.* On glossy paper 15.00 5.00

Marx and Engels — A1468

Designs: No. 2932 Lenin and title page of "CPSS Program." No. 2933, Worker breaking chains around the globe. No. 2934, Title pages of "Communist Manifesto" in German and Russian. No. 2935, Globe and banner inscribed "Workers of the World Unite."

**1964, Aug. 27 Photo. Perf. 11½x12**

2931 A1468 4k red, dk red & brown .60 .25
2932 A1468 4k red, brn & slate .60 .25
2933 A1468 4k blue, fluor. brt rose & black .60 .25

***Perf. 12½x12***

**Litho.**

2934 A1468 4k ol blk, blk & red .60 .25
2935 A1468 4k bl, red & ol bis .60 .25
*Nos. 2931-2935 (5)* 3.00 1.25

Centenary of First Socialist International.

A. V. Vishnevsky A1469

Portraits: No. 2937, N. A. Semashko. No. 2938, D. Ivanovsky.

**Size: 23½x35mm**

**1964 Photo. Perf. 11½**

2936 A1469 4k gray & brown .65 .30
2937 A1469 4k buff, sepia & red .65 .30

**Litho.**

**Size: 22x32½mm**

2938 A1469 4k tan, gray & brown .65 .30
*Nos. 2936-2938 (3)* 1.95 .90

90th birth annivs. Vishnevsky, surgeon, and Semashko, founder of the Russian Public Health Service; Ivanovsky (1864-1920), biologist.

Palmiro Togliatti (1893-1964), General Secretary of the Italian Communist Party — A1470

**1964, Sept. 15 Perf. 12½x12**

2939 A1470 4k black & red .50 .25

Letter, Aerogram and Globe A1471

**1964, Sept. 20 Litho.**

2940 A1471 4k tan, lil rose & ultra .50 .25

Intl. Letter Writing Week, Oct. 5-11.

Arms of German Democratic Republic, Factories, Ship and Train — A1472

**1964, Oct. 7 Perf. 12**

2942 A1472 6k blk, yel, red & bis .50 .25

German Democratic Republic, 15th anniv.

**No. 2836 Overprinted in Red**

**1964, Oct. 7 Engr.**

2943 A1435 4k dull blue 5.00 5.00

40th anniversary of Tadzhik Republic.

Woman Holding Bowl of Grain and Fruit A1473

Uzbek Farm Couple and Arms — A1474

Turkmen Woman Holding Arms — A1475

**1964, Oct.** **Litho.**

**2944** A1473 4k red, green & brn .75 .25
**2945** A1474 4k red yel & claret .75 .25
**2946** A1475 4k red, black & red brn .75 .25
*Nos. 2944-2946 (3)* 2.25 .75

40th anniv. of the Moldavian, Uzbek and Turkmen Socialist Republics.

Issue dates: #2944, Oct. 7; others, Oct. 26.

Soldier and Flags A1476

**1964, Oct. 14**

**2947** A1476 4k red, bis, dk brn & bl .75 .25

Liberation of the Ukraine, 20th anniv.

Mikhail Y. Lermontov (1814-41), Poet — A1477

Designs: 4k, Birthplace of Tarchany. 10k, Lermontov and Vissarion G. Belinski.

**1964, Oct. 14** **Engr.; Litho. (10k)**

**2948** A1477 4k violet black .40 .25
**2949** A1477 6k black .50 .25
**2950** A1477 10k dk red brn & buff 1.10 .30
*Nos. 2948-2950 (3)* 2.00 .80

Hammer and Sickle A1478

**1964, Oct. 14** **Litho.**

**2951** A1478 4k dk blue, red, ocher & yellow .50 .25

47th anniversary of October Revolution.

Col. Vladimir M. Komarov A1479

Komarov, Feoktistov and Yegorov — A1480

Designs: No. 2953, Boris B. Yegorov, M.D. No. 2954, Konstantin Feoktistov, scientist. 10k, Spacecraft Voskhod I and cosmonauts. 50k, Red flag with portraits of Komarov, Feoktistov and Yegorov, and trajectory around earth.

***Perf. 11½ (A1479), 12½x12***

**1964** **Photo.**

**2952** A1479 4k bl grn, blk & org .45 .25
**2953** A1479 4k bl grn, blk & org .45 .25
**2954** A1479 4k bl grn, blk & org .45 .25

**Size: 73x23mm**

**2955** A1480 6k vio & dk brn .80 .25
**2956** A1480 10k dp ultra & pur 1.25 .25

***Imperf***

**Litho.**

**Size: 90x45½mm**

**2957** A1480 50k vio, red & gray 5.00 2.50
*Nos. 2952-2957 (6)* 8.40 3.75

3-men space flight of Komarov, Yegorov and Feoktistov, Oct. 12-13. Issued: #2952-2954, 10/19; #2955, 10/17; #2956, 10/13; #2957, 11/20.

A. I. Yelizarova-Ulyanova — A1482

Portrait: No. 2961, Nadezhda K. Krupskaya.

**1964, Nov. 6** **Photo.** ***Perf. 11½***

**2960** A1482 4k brn, org & indigo .50 .25
**2961** A1482 4k indigo, red & brn .50 .25

Yelizarova-Ulyanova, Lenin's sister, birth cent. & Krupskaya, Lenin's wife, 95th birth anniv.

Farm Woman, Sheep, Flag of Mongolia A1483

**1964, Nov. 20** **Litho.** ***Perf. 12***

**2962** A1483 6k multicolored .50 .25

Mongolian People's Republic, 40th anniv.

Mushrooms A1484

Designs: Various mushrooms.

**1964, Nov. 25** **Litho.** ***Perf. 12***

**2963** A1484 2k ol grn, red brn & yellow .25 .25
**2964** A1484 4k green & yellow .50 .25
**2965** A1484 6k bluish grn, brn & yellow .75 .25
**2966** A1484 10k grn, org red & brn 1.20 .40
**2967** A1484 12k ultra, yel & grn 2.25 .50
*Nos. 2963-2967 (5)* 4.95 1.65

Nos. 2963-2967 exist varnished, printed in sheets of 25 with 10 labels in outside vertical rows. Issued Nov. 30. Value, set: mint $7.50; used $3.

A. P. Dovzhenko — A1485

Design: 6k, Scene from "Chapayev" (man and boy with guns).

**1964, Nov. 30** **Photo.** ***Perf. 12***

**2968** A1485 4k gray & dp ultra 1.00 .35
**2968A** A1485 6k pale olive & blk 1.00 .35

Dovzhenko (1894-1956), film producer, and 30th anniv. of the production of the film "Chapayev."

"Happy New Year" — A1486

**Photogravure and Engraved**

**1964, Nov. 30** ***Perf. 11½***

**2969** A1486 4k multicolored 1.00 .50

New Year 1965. The bright rose ink is fluorescent.

V. J. Struve — A1487

Portraits: No. 2971, N. P. Kravkov. No. 2971A, P. K. Sternberg. No. 2971B, Ch. Valikhanov. No. 2971C, V. A. Kistjakovski.

**1964-65** **Photo.** ***Perf. 12½x11½***

**2970** A1487 4k sl bl & dk brn .55 .25

**Litho.**

**2971** A1487 4k brn, red & blk .55 .25

**Photo.**

***Perf. 11½***

**2971A** A1487 4k dk bl & dk brn .55 .25

***Perf. 12***

**2971B** A1487 4k rose vio & blk .55 .25

**Litho.**

**2971C** A1487 4k brn vio, blk & cit .55 .25
*Nos. 2970-2971C (5)* 2.75 1.25

Astronomer Struve (1793-1864), founder of Pulkov Observatory; Kravkov (1865-1924), pharmacologist; Sternberg (1865-1920), astronomer; Valikhanov (1835-1865), Kazakh scientist; Kistjakovski (1865-1952), chemist.

Issued: #2970, 11/30; #2971, 1/31/65; #2971A-2971B, 9/21/65; #2971C, 12/24.

S. V. Ivanov and Skiers A1488

**1964, Dec. 22** **Engr.** ***Perf. 12½***

**2972** A1488 4k black & brown .75 .35

S. V. Ivanov (1864-1910), painter.

Chemical Industry: Fertilizers and Pest Control — A1489

Importance of the chemical industry for the national economy: 6k, Synthetics factory.

**1964, Dec. 25** **Photo.** ***Perf. 12***

**2973** A1489 4k olive & lilac rose .50 .25
**2974** A1489 6k dp ultra & black .50 .25

European Cranberries A1490

Wild Berries: 3k, Huckleberries. 4k, Mountain ash. 10k, Blackberries. 16k, Cranberries.

**1964, Dec. 25** ***Perf. 11½x12***

**2975** A1490 1k pale grn & car .25 .25
**2976** A1490 3k gray, vio bl & grn .30 .25
**2977** A1490 4k gray, org red & brown .30 .25
**2978** A1490 10k lt grn, dk vio blue & claret .90 .25
**2979** A1490 16k gray, brt green & car rose 1.25 .25
*Nos. 2975-2979 (5)* 3.00 1.25

Academy of Science Library A1491

**1964, Dec. 25** **Typo.** ***Perf. 12x12½***

**2980** A1491 4k blk, pale grn & red .75 .35

250th anniv. of the founding of the Academy of Science Library, Leningrad.

Congress Palace, Kremlin — A1492

**1964, Dec. 25**

**2981** A1492 1r dark blue 4.50 1.25

Khan Tengri — A1493

Mountains: 6k, Kazbek, horiz. 12k, Twin peaks of Ushba.

**1964, Dec. 29** **Photo.** ***Perf. 11½***

**2982** A1493 4k grnsh bl, vio bl & buff .70 .35
**2983** A1493 6k yel, dk brn & ol .75 .35
**2984** A1493 12k lt yel, grn & pur 1.50 .35
*Nos. 2982-2984 (3)* 2.95 1.05

Development of mountaineering in Russia.

**Portrait Type of 1964**

Design: 6k, Michelangelo. 12k, Galileo.

**Engraved and Photogravure**

**1964, Dec. 30** ***Perf. 11½***

**2985** A1455 6k sep, red brn & org .75 .25
**2986** A1455 12k dk brn & green 2.25 .30

Michelangelo Buonarotti, artist, 400th death anniv. and Galileo Galilei, astronomer and physicist, 400th birth anniv.

Helmet
A1494

Treasures from Kremlin Treasury: 6k, Quiver. 10k, Jeweled fur crown. 12k, Gold ladle. 16k, Bowl.

**1964, Dec. 30** **Litho.**

**2987** A1494 4k multicolored .25 .25
**2988** A1494 6k multicolored .35 .25
**2989** A1494 10k multicolored .50 .25
**2990** A1494 12k multicolored 1.25 .25
**2991** A1494 16k multicolored 1.40 .25
*Nos. 2987-2991 (5)* 3.75 1.25

Dante Alighieri (1265-1321), Italian Poet — A1495

**1965, Jan. 29** **Photo.** ***Perf. 11½***

**2995** A1495 4k dk red brn & ol bis .50 .25

Blood Donor — A1496

Honoring blood donors: No. 2997, Hand holding carnation, and donors' emblem.

**1965, Jan. 31** **Litho.** ***Perf. 12***

**2996** A1496 4k dk car, red, vio bl & bl .60 .25
**2997** A1496 4k brt grn, red & dk grn .60 .25

Bandy — A1497

6k, Figure skaters and Moscow Sports Palace.

**1965, Feb.** **Photo.** ***Perf. 11½x12***

**2998** A1497 4k blue, red & yellow .50 .25
**2999** A1497 6k green, blk & red .50 .25

4k issued Feb. 21, for the victory of the Soviet team in the World Bandy Championship, Moscow, Feb. 21-27; 6k issued Feb. 12, for the European Figure Skating Championship. For overprint see No. 3017.

Police Dog — A1498

Dogs: 1k, Russian hound. 2k, Irish setter. No. 3003, Pointer. No. 3004, Fox terrier. No. 3005, Sheepdog. No. 3006, Borzoi. 10k, Collie. 12k, Husky. 16k, Caucasian sheepdog. (1k, 2k, 4k, 12k and No. 3006 horiz.)

***Perf. 12x11½, 11½x12 (Photo. stamps); 12x12½, 12½x12 (Litho.)***
**Photo., Litho. (1k, 10k, 12k, 16k)**

**1965, Feb. 26**

**3000** A1498 1k blk, yel & mar .25 .25
**3001** A1498 2k ultra, blk & red brown .45 .25
**3002** A1498 3k blk, ocher & org red .45 .25
**3003** A1498 4k org, yel grn & blk .70 .25
**3004** A1498 4k brn, blk & lt grn .70 .25
**3005** A1498 6k chalky blue, sep & red 1.20 .25
**3006** A1498 6k chalky bl, org brn & black 1.20 .25
**3007** A1498 10k yel green, ocher & red 1.90 .35
**3008** A1498 12k gray, blk & ocher 2.10 .45
**3009** A1498 16k multicolored 2.75 .60
*Nos. 3000-3009 (10)* 11.70 3.15

Richard Sorge (1895-1944), Soviet spy and Hero of the Soviet Union — A1499

**1965, Mar. 6** **Photo.** ***Perf. 12x12½***

**3010** A1499 4k hn brn & blk 3.00 1.00

Communications Symbols — A1500

**1965, Mar. 6** ***Perf. 12½x12***

**3011** A1500 6k grnsh blue, vio & brt purple .60 .30

Intl. Telecommunication Union, cent.

No. 2764 Overprinted

**1965, Mar. 20** **Photo.** ***Perf. 12***

**3012** A1402 6k red & gray blue 2.50 1.00

Soviet victory in the European and World Ice Hockey Championships.

Lt. Col. Alexei Leonov Taking Movies in Space — A1501

1r, Leonov walking in space and Voskhod 2.

**1965, Mar. 23** **Photo.** ***Perf. 12***
**Size: 73x23mm**

**3015** A1501 10k brt ultra, org & gray .75 .35

First man walking in space, Lt. Col. Alexei Leonov, Mar. 17, 1965 ("18 March" on stamp). Exists imperf. Value $2.

**Souvenir Sheet**

**1965, Apr. 12** **Litho.**

**3016** A1501 1r multicolored 6.00 2.00

Space flight of Voskhod 2. No. 3016 contains one 81x27mm stamp.

No. 2999 Overprinted

**1965, Mar. 26** ***Perf. 11½x12***

**3017** A1497 6k grn, blk & red 3.00 1.00

Soviet victory in the World Figure Skating Championships.

Flags of USSR and Poland A1502

**1965, Apr. 12** **Photo.** ***Perf. 12***

**3018** A1502 6k bister & red .50 .25

20th anniversary of the signing of the Polish-Soviet treaty of friendship, mutual assistance and postwar cooperation.

Tsiolkovsky Monument, Kaluga; Globe and Rockets — A1503

Rockets, Radio Telescope, TV Antenna A1504

Designs: 12k, Space monument, Moscow. 16k, Cosmonauts' monument, Moscow. No. 3023, Globe with trajectories, satellite and astronauts.

**1965, Apr. 12** ***Perf. 11½***

**3019** A1503 4k pale grn, black & brt rose .25 .25
**3020** A1503 12k vio, pur & brt rose .55 .25
**3021** A1503 16k multicolored .85 .25

**Lithographed on Aluminum Foil**
***Perf. 12½x12***

**3022** A1504 20k black & red 5.00 4.00
**3023** A1504 20k blk, blue & red 5.00 4.00
*Nos. 3019-3023 (5)* 11.65 8.75

National Cosmonauts' Day. On Nos. 3019-3021 the bright rose is fluorescent.

Lenin — A1505

**1965, Apr. 16** **Engr.** ***Perf. 12***

**3024** A1505 10k tan & indigo .75 .25

95th anniversary of the birth of Lenin.

Poppies — A1506

Flowers: 3k, Daisies. 4k, Peony. 6k, Carnation. 10k, Tulips.

**1965, Apr. 23** **Photo.** ***Perf. 11***

**3025** A1506 1k mar, red & grn .25 .25
**3026** A1506 3k dk brn, yel & grn .40 .25
**3027** A1506 4k blk, grn & lilac .75 .25
**3028** A1506 6k dk sl grn, grn & red 1.00 .25
**3029** A1506 10k dk plum, yel & grn 1.50 .25
*Nos. 3025-3029 (5)* 3.90 1.25

Soviet Flag, Broken Swastikas, Fighting in Berlin A1507

Designs: 2k, "Fatherland Calling!" (woman with proclamation) by I. Toidze. 3k, "Attack on Moscow" by V. Bogatkin. No. 3033, "Rest after the Battle" by Y. Neprintsev. No. 3034, "Mother of Partisan" by S. Gerasimov. 6k, "Our Flag — Symbol of Victory" (soldiers with banner) by V. Ivanov. 10k, "Tribute to the Hero" (mourners at bier) by F. Bogorodsky. 12k, "Invincible Nation and Army" (worker and soldier holding shell) by V. Koretsky. 16k, "Victory celebration on Red Square" by K. Yuan. 20k, Soldier and symbols of war.

**1965** ***Perf. 11½***

**3030** A1507 1k red, blk & gold .25 .25
**3031** A1507 2k crim, blk & gold .25 .25
**3032** A1507 3k ultra & gold .40 .25
**3033** A1507 4k green & gold .45 .25
**3034** A1507 4k violet & gold .45 .25
**3035** A1507 6k dp claret & gold .75 .25
**3036** A1507 10k plum & gold 1.10 .25
**3037** A1507 12k blk, red & gold 1.40 .35
**3038** A1507 16k lilac rose & gold 1.90 .40
**3039** A1507 20k red, blk & gold 2.25 .50
*Nos. 3030-3039 (10)* 9.20 3.00

20th anniv. of the end of World War II. Issued Apr. 25-May 1.

**Souvenir Sheet**

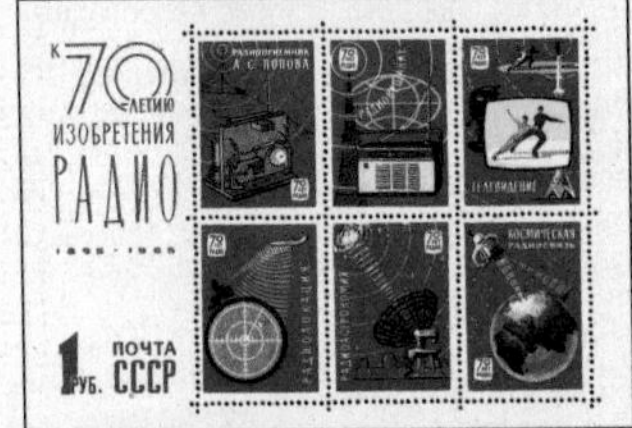

From Popov's Radio to Space Telecommunications — A1508

**1965, May 7** **Litho.** ***Perf. 11½***

**3040** A1508 1r blue & multi 5.00 1.00

70th anniv. of Aleksandr S. Popov's radio pioneer work. No. 3040 contains 6 labels without denominations or country name.

Marx, Lenin and Crowd with Flags — A1509

**1965, May 9 Photo. *Perf. 12x12½***
**3041** A1509 6k red & black .50 .25

6th conference of Postal Ministers of Communist Countries, Peking, June 21-July 15.

Bolshoi Theater, Moscow — A1510

**1965, May 20 *Perf. 11x11½***
**3042** A1510 6k grnsh blue, bis & blk 1.00 .25

International Theater Day.

Col. Pavel Belyayev A1511

Design: No. 3044, Lt. Col. Alexei Leonov.

**1965, May 23 *Perf. 12x11½***
**3043** A1511 6k magenta & silver .60 .25
**3044** A1511 6k purple & silver .60 .25

Space flight of Voskhod 2, Mar. 18-19, 1965, and the 1st man walking in space, Lt. Col. Alexei Leonov.

Sverdlov — A1512

Portrait: No. 3046, Juldash Akhunbabaev.

**Photogravure and Engraved**
**1965, May 30 *Perf. 11½x12***
**3045** A1512 4k orange brn & blk 1.50 .35
**3046** A1512 4k lt violet & blk 1.50 .35

Yakov M. Sverdlov, 1885-1919, 1st pres. of USSR, and J. Akhunbabaev, 1885-1943, pres. of Uzbek Republic.

Grotewohl — A1513

**1965, June 12 Photo. *Perf. 12***
**3051** A1513 4k black & magenta .50 .25

Otto Grotewohl, prime minister of the German Democratic Republic (1894-1964).

Maurice Thorez — A1514

**1965, June 12**
**3052** A1514 6k brown & red .50 .25

Maurice Thorez (1900-1964), chairman of the French Communist party.

Communication by Satellite — A1515

Designs: No. 3054, Pouring ladle, steel mill and map of India. No. 3055, Stars, satellites and names of international organizations.

**1965, June 15 Litho.**
**3053** A1515 3k olive, blk & gold .50 .30
**3054** A1515 6k emer, dk grn & gold .50 .30
**3055** A1515 6k vio blue, gold & blk .50 .30
*Nos. 3053-3055 (3)* 1.50 .90

Emphasizing international cooperation through communication, economic cooperation and international organizations.

Symbols of Chemistry A1516

**1965, June 15 Photo. *Perf. 11½***
**3056** A1516 4k blk, brt rose & brt bl .45 .25

20th Cong. of the Intl. Union of Pure and Applied Chemistry (IUPAC), Moscow. The bright rose ink is fluorescent.

V. A. Serov A1517

Design: 6k, Full-length portrait of Feodor Chaliapin, the singer, by Serov.

**1965, June 25 Typo. *Perf. 12½***
**3057** A1517 4k red brn, buff & blk .50 .25
**3058** A1517 6k ol bis & blk .50 .25

Serov (1865-1911), historical painter.

Abay Kunanbaev, Kazakh Poet — A1518

Designs (writers and poets): No. 3060, Vsevolod Ivanov (1895-1963). No. 3060A, Eduard Vilde, Estonian writer. No. 3061, Mark Kropivnitsky, Ukrainian playwright. No. 3062, Manuk Apeghyan, Armenian writer and critic. No. 3063, Musa Djalil, Tartar poet. No. 3064, Hagop Hagopian, Armenian poet. No. 3064A, Djalil Mamedkulizade, Azerbaijan writer.

**1965-66 Photo. *Perf. 12½x12***
**3059** A1518 4k lt violet & blk .55 .30
**3060** A1518 4k rose lilac & blk .55 .30
**3060A** A1518 4k gray & black .55 .30
**3061** A1518 4k black & org brn .55 .30

***Perf. 12½***
**Typo.**
**3062** A1518 4k crim, blue grn & blk .55 .30

***Perf. 11½***
**Photogravure and Engraved**
**3063** A1518 4k black & org brn ('66) .55 .30
**3064** A1518 4k grn & blk ('66) .55 .30

**Photo.**
**3064A** A1518 4k Prus green & blk ('66) .55 .30
*Nos. 3059-3064A (8)* 4.40 2.40

Sizes: Nos. 3059-3062, 38x25mm. Nos. 3063-3064A, 35x23mm.

Jan Rainis A1518a

**1965, Sept. 8 Photo. *Perf. 12½x12***
**3064B** A1518a 4k dl blue & blk .50 .25

Rainis (1865-1929), Latvian playwright. "Rainis" was pseudonym of Jan Plieksans.

Film, Screen, Globe and Star A1519

**1965, July 5 Litho. *Perf. 12***
**3065** A1519 6k brt blue, gold & blk .50 .25

4th Intl. Film Festival, Moscow: "For Humanism in Cinema Art, for Peace and Friendship among Nations."

Concert Bowl, Tallinn A1520

"Lithuania" A1521

"Latvia" A1522

**1965, July *Perf. 12x11½, 11½x12***
**3066** A1520 4k ultra, blk, red & ocher 1.00 .25
**3067** A1521 4k red & brown 1.00 .25
**3068** A1522 4k yel, red & blue 1.00 .25
*Nos. 3066-3068 (3)* 3.00 .75

25th anniversaries of Estonia, Lithuania and Latvia as Soviet Republics. Issued: #3066, 7/7; #3067, 7/14; #3068, 7/16.

"Keep Peace" — A1523

**1965, July 10 Photo. *Perf. 11x11½***
**3069** A1523 6k yel, blk & blue .55 .25

Protesting Women and Czarist Eagle A1524

Designs: No. 3071, Soldier attacking distributor of handbills. No. 3072, Fighters on barricades with red flag. No. 3073, Monument for sailors of Battleship "Potemkin," Odessa.

**1965, July 20 Litho. *Perf. 11½***
**3070** A1524 4k blk, red & ol grn .50 .25
**3071** A1524 4k red, ol grn & blk .50 .25
**3072** A1524 4k red, black & brn .50 .25
**3073** A1524 4k red & violet blue .50 .25
*Nos. 3070-3073 (4)* 2.00 1.00

60th anniversary of the 1905 revolution.

Gheorghe Gheorghiu-Dej (1901-1965), President of Romanian State Council (1961-1965) A1525

**1965, July 26 Photo. *Perf. 12***
**3074** A1525 4k black & red .40 .25

Relay Race A1526

Sport: No. 3076, Bicycle race. No. 3077, Gymnast on vaulting horse.

**1965, Aug. 5 Litho. *Perf. 12½x12***
**3075** A1526 4k vio blue, bis brn & red brown 1.00 .25
**3076** A1526 4k buff, red brn, gray & maroon 1.00 .25
**3077** A1526 4k bl, mar, buff & lt brn 1.00 .25
*Nos. 3075-3077 (3)* 3.00 .75

8th Trade Union Spartacist Games.

Electric Power A1527

Designs: 2k, Metals in modern industry. 3k, Modern chemistry serving the people. 4k, Mechanization, automation and electronics.

6k, New materials for building industry. 10k, Mechanization and electrification of agriculture. 12k, Technological progress in transportation. 16k, Application of scientific discoveries to industry.

**1965, Aug. 5 Photo. *Perf. 12x11½***

**3078** A1527 1k olive, bl & blk .25 .25
**3079** A1527 2k org, blk & yel .25 .25
**3080** A1527 3k yel, vio & bister .25 .25
**3081** A1527 4k ultra, ind & red .25 .25
**3082** A1527 6k ultra & bister .40 .25
**3083** A1527 10k yel, org & red brn .75 .25
**3084** A1527 12k Prus blue & red .60 .25
**3085** A1527 16k rose lilac, blk & violet blue 1.00 .25
*Nos. 3078-3085 (8)* 3.75 2.00

Creation of the material and technical basis of communism.

Gymnast — A1528

Design: 6k, Bicycling.

**1965, Aug. 12 *Perf. 11½***

**3086** A1528 4k multi & red 1.00 .25
**3087** A1528 6k grnsh bl, red & brn 1.00 .25

9th Spartacist Games for school children.

Javelin and Running — A1529

Designs: 6k, High jump and shot put. 10k, Hammer throwing and hurdling.

**1965, Aug. 27**

**3088** A1529 4k brn, lilac & red .50 .25
**3089** A1529 6k brn, yel green & red .50 .25
**3090** A1529 10k brn, chlky bl & red 1.00 .25
*Nos. 3088-3090 (3)* 2.00 .75

US-Russian Track and Field Meet, Kiev.

Worker and Globe — A1530

Designs: No 3092, Heads of three races and torch. No. 3093, Woman with dove.

**1965, Sept. 1**

**3091** A1530 6k dk purple & tan .35 .25
**3092** A1530 6k brt bl, brn & red org .35 .25
**3093** A1530 6k Prus green & tan .35 .25
*Nos. 3091-3093 (3)* 1.05 .75

Intl. Fed. of Trade Unions (#3091), Fed. of Democratic Youth (#3092), Democratic Women's Fed. (#3093), 20th annivs.

Flag of North Viet Nam, Factory and Palm — A1531

**1965, Sept. 1 Litho. *Perf. 12***

**3094** A1531 6k red, yel, brn & gray .35 .25

Republic of North Viet Nam, 20th anniv.

Scene from Film "Potemkin" A1532

Film Scenes: 6k, "Young Guard." 12k, "Ballad of a Soldier."

**1965, Sept. 29 Litho. *Perf. 12½x12***

**3095** A1532 4k blue, blk & red 1.25 .25
**3096** A1532 6k multicolored 1.50 .25
**3097** A1532 12k multicolored 2.25 .25
*Nos. 3095-3097 (3)* 5.00 .75

Post Rider, 16th Century — A1533

History of the Post: No. 3099, Mail coach, 17th-18th centuries. 2k, Train, 19th century. 4k, Mail truck, 1920. 6k, Train, ship and plane. 12k, New Moscow post office, helicopter, automatic sorting and canceling machines. 16k, Lenin, airport and map of USSR.

**1965 Photo. Unwmk. *Perf. 11½x12***

**3098** A1533 1k org brn, dk gray & dk green .50 .25
**3099** A1533 1k gray, ocher & dk brown .50 .25
**3100** A1533 2k dl lil, brt bl & brn .35 .25
**3101** A1533 4k bis, rose lake & blk .55 .25
**3102** A1533 6k pale brn, Prus grn & black .65 .25
**3103** A1533 12k lt ultra, lt brn & blk 1.50 .25
**3104** A1533 16k gray, rose red & vio black 1.50 .25
*Nos. 3098-3104 (7)* 5.55 1.75

For overprint see No. 3175.

Scientific Conquests of the Arctic and Antarctic — A1534

No. 3106, Icebreakers "Taimir" and "Vaigitch". No. 3107, Atomic Icebreaker "Lenin." 6k, Dickson Settlement. 10k, Sailing ships "Vostok" and "Mirni," Bellinghausen-Lazarev expedition & icebergs. 16k, Vostok South Pole station.

**1965, Oct. 23 Litho. *Perf. 12***

**Size: 37x25mm**

**3106** 4k bl, blk & org .45 .25
**3107** 4k bl, blk & org .45 .25
*a.* A1534 Pair #3106-3107 1.00 .50
**3108** A1534 6k sepia & dk vio 1.10 .25

**Size: 33x33mm**

**3109** A1534 10k red, black & buff 1.40 .25

**Size: 37x25mm**

**3110** A1534 16k vio blk & red brn 1.60 .50
*Nos. 3106-3110 (5)* 5.00 1.50

Souvenir Sheet

Basketball, Map of Europe and Flags — A1535

**1965, Oct. 29 Litho. *Imperf.***

**3111** A1535 1r multicolored 5.00 1.50

14th European Basketball Championship, Moscow.

Timiryazev Agriculture Academy, Moscow — A1536

**1965, Oct. 30 Photo. *Perf. 11***

**3112** A1536 4k brt car, gray & vio bl .50 .25

Agriculture Academy, Moscow, cent.

Souvenir Sheet

Lenin — A1537

**Lithographed and Engraved**

**1965, Oct. 30 *Imperf.***

**3113** A1537 10k sil, blk & dp org 10.00 1.25

48th anniv. of the October Revolution.

Nicolas Poussin (1594-1665), French Painter — A1538

**1965, Nov. 16 Photo. *Perf. 11½***

**3114** A1538 4k gray blue, dk bl & dk brown .50 .25

Kremlin A1539

**1965, Nov. 16 *Perf. 12x11½***

**3115** A1539 4k black, ver & silver 1.00 .25

New Year 1966.

Mikhail Ivanovich Kalinin (1875-1946), USSR President (1923-1946) A1540

**1965, Nov. 19 *Perf. 12½***

**3116** A1540 4k dp claret & red .35 .25

Klyuchevskaya Sopka — A1541

Kamchatka Volcanoes: 12k, Karumski erupting, vert. 16k, Koryakski snowcovered.

**1965, Nov. 30 Litho. *Perf. 12***

**3117** A1541 4k multicolored .60 .25
**3118** A1541 12k multicolored 1.60 .30
**3119** A1541 16k multicolored 2.75 .45
*Nos. 3117-3119 (3)* 4.95 1.00

October Subway Station, Moscow — A1542

Subway Stations: No. 3121, Lenin Avenue, Moscow. No. 3122, Moscow Gate, Leningrad. No. 3123, Bolshevik Factory, Kiev.

**1965, Nov. 30 Engr.**

**3120** A1542 6k indigo .75 .30
**3121** A1542 6k brown .75 .30
**3122** A1542 6k gray brown .75 .30
**3123** A1542 6k slate green .75 .30
*Nos. 3120-3123 (4)* 3.00 1.20

Buzzard — A1543

Birds: 2k, Kestrel. 3k, Tawny eagle. 4k, Red kite. 10k, Peregrine falcon. 12k, Golden eagle, horiz. 14k, Lammergeier, horiz. 16k, Gyrfalcon.

**1965 Photo. *Perf. 11½x12***

| | | | | |
|---|---|---|---|---|
| **3124** A1543 | 1k gray grn & black | .25 | .25 |
| **3125** A1543 | 2k pale brn & blk | .25 | .25 |
| **3126** A1543 | 3k lt ol grn & black | .25 | .25 |
| **3127** A1543 | 4k lt gray brn & blk | .35 | .25 |
| **3128** A1543 | 10k lt vio brn & blk | 1.00 | .25 |
| **3129** A1543 | 12k blue & black | 1.25 | .25 |
| **3130** A1543 | 14k bluish gray & blk | 1.40 | .25 |
| **3131** A1543 | 16k dl red brn & blk | 1.75 | .30 |
| | *Nos. 3124-3131 (8)* | 6.50 | 2.05 |

Issued: 4k, 10k, Nov.; 1k, 2k, 12k, 14k, 12/24; 3k, 16k, 12/29.

Red Star Medal, War Scene and View of Kiev A1544

Red Star Medal, War Scene and view of: No. 3133, Leningrad. No. 3134, Odessa. No. 3135, Moscow. No. 3136, Brest Litovsk. No. 3137, Volgograd (Stalingrad). No. 3138, Sevastopol.

**1965, Dec. *Perf. 11½***

**Red, Gold and**

| | | | |
|---|---|---|---|
| **3132** A1544 10k brown | .50 | .25 |
| **3133** A1544 10k dark blue | .50 | .25 |
| **3134** A1544 10k Prussian blue | .50 | .25 |
| **3135** A1544 10k dark violet | .50 | .25 |
| **3136** A1544 10k dark brown | .50 | .25 |
| **3137** A1544 10k black | .50 | .25 |
| **3138** A1544 10k gray | .50 | .25 |
| *Nos. 3132-3138 (7)* | 3.50 | 1.75 |

Honoring the heroism of various cities during World War II.

Issued: #3136-3138, 12/30; others, 12/20.

Map and Flag of Yugoslavia, and National Assembly Building A1545

**1965, Dec. 30 Litho. *Perf. 12***

**3139** A1545 6k vio blue, red & bis .70 .25

Republic of Yugoslavia, 20th anniv.

Collective Farm Watchman by S.V. Gerasimov A1547

Painting: 16k, "Major's Courtship" by Pavel Andreievitch Fedotov, horiz.

**1965, Dec. 31 Engr.**

| | | | |
|---|---|---|---|
| **3145** A1547 12k red & sepia | 1.50 | .35 |
| **3146** A1547 16k red & dark blue | 2.50 | .65 |

Painters: Gerasimov, 80th birth anniv; Pavel A. Fedotov (1815-52).

Turkeys, Geese, Chicken and Globe A1548

Congress Emblems: No. 3147, Microscope and Moscow University. No. 3149, Crystals. No. 3150, Oceanographic instruments and ship. No. 3151, Mathematical symbols.

**1966 Photo. *Perf. 11½***

| | | | |
|---|---|---|---|
| **3147** A1548 6k dull bl, blk & red | .60 | .25 |
| **3148** A1548 6k gray, pur & black | .60 | .25 |
| **3149** A1548 6k ol bis, blk & bl | .60 | .25 |
| **3150** A1548 6k grnsh blue & blk | .60 | .25 |
| **3151** A1548 6k dull yel, red brn & blk | .60 | .25 |
| *Nos. 3147-3151 (5)* | 3.00 | 1.25 |

Intl. congresses to be held in Moscow: 9th Cong. of Microbiology (#3147); 13th Cong. on Poultry Raising (#3148); 7th Cong. on Crystallography (#3149); 2nd Intl. Cong. of Oceanography (#3150); Intl. Cong. of Mathematicians (#3151).

See Nos. 3309-3310.

Mailman and Milkmaid, 19th Century Figurines — A1549

**1966, Jan. 28 Litho.**

| | | | |
|---|---|---|---|
| **3152** A1549 6k shown | .40 | .25 |
| **3153** A1549 10k Tea set | .60 | .25 |

Bicentenary of Dimitrov Porcelain Works.

Romain Rolland (1866-1944), French Writer — A1550

Portrait: No. 3155, Eugène Pottier (1816-1887), French poet and author of the "International."

**1966 Photo. & Engr. *Perf. 11½***

| | | | |
|---|---|---|---|
| **3154** A1550 4k dk blue & brn org | .75 | .25 |
| **3155** A1550 4k sl, red & dk red brn | .75 | .25 |

Horseback Rider, and Flags of Mongolia and USSR — A1551

**1966, Jan. 31 Litho. *Perf. 12½x12***

**3159** A1551 4k red, ultra & vio brn .50 .25

20th anniversary of the signing of the Mongolian-Soviet treaty of friendship and mutual assistance.

No. 2728 Overprinted in Silver

**1966, Feb. 5 Photo. *Perf. 12***

**3160** A1385 6k blk, lt blue & red 5.00 4.00

1st soft landing on the moon by Luna 9, Feb. 3, 1966.

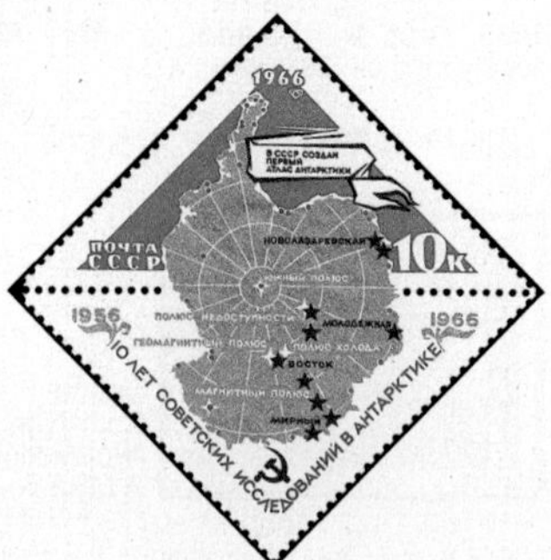


Map of Antarctica With Soviet Stations — A1552

Diesel Ship "Ob" and Emperor Penguins — A1553

No. 3164, Snocat tractors and aurora australis.

**1966, Feb. 14 Photo. *Perf. 11***

| | | | |
|---|---|---|---|
| **3162** A1552 10k sky bl, sil & dk car | 1.50 | 1.00 |
| **3163** A1553 10k silver & dk car | 1.50 | 1.00 |
| **3164** A1553 10k dk car, sil & sky bl | 1.50 | 1.00 |
| *a.* Strip of 3, #3162-3164 | 5.00 | 5.00 |

10 years of Soviet explorations in Antarctica. No. 3162 has horizontal rows of perforation extending from either mid-side up to the map.

Lenin A1554

**1966, Feb. 22 Photo. *Perf. 12x11½***

| | | | |
|---|---|---|---|
| **3165** A1554 10k grnsh black & gold | 1.00 | .50 |
| **3166** A1554 10k dk red & silver | 1.00 | .25 |

96th anniversary of the birth of Lenin.

N.Y. Iljin, Guardsman A1555

Soviet Heroes: #3168, Lt. Gen. G. P. Kravchenko. #3169, Pvt. Anatoli Uglovsky.

**1966 *Perf. 11½x12***

| | | | |
|---|---|---|---|
| **3167** A1555 4k dp org & vio black | .65 | .25 |
| **3168** A1555 4k grnsh bl & dk pur | .65 | .25 |
| **3169** A1555 4k green & brown | .65 | .25 |
| *Nos. 3167-3169 (3)* | 1.95 | .75 |

Kremlin Congress Hall — A1556

**1966, Feb. 28 Typo. *Perf. 12***

**3172** A1556 4k gold, red & lt ultra .50 .25

23rd Communist Party Congress.

Hamlet and Queen from Film "Hamlet" A1557

Film Scene: 4k, Two soldiers from "The Quick and the Dead."

**1966, Feb. 28 Litho.**

| | | | |
|---|---|---|---|
| **3173** A1557 4k red, blk & ol | 1.00 | .25 |
| **3174** A1557 10k ultra & black | 1.00 | .25 |

**No. 3104 Overprinted**

**1966, Mar. 10 Photo. *Perf. 11½x12***

**3175** A1533 16k multicolored 5.00 2.50

Constituent assembly of the All-Union Society of Philatelists, 1966.

Emblem and Skater — A1558

Designs: 6k, Emblem and ice hockey. 10k, Emblem and slalom skier.

**1966, Mar. 11 *Perf. 11***

| | | | |
|---|---|---|---|
| **3176** A1558 4k ol, brt ultra & red | .35 | .25 |
| **3177** A1558 6k bluish lilac, red & dk brown | .60 | .25 |
| **3178** A1558 10k lt bl, red & dk brn | .95 | .25 |
| *Nos. 3176-3178 (3)* | 1.90 | .75 |

Second Winter Spartacist Games, Sverdlovsk. The label-like upper halves of Nos. 3176-3178 are separated from the lower halves by a row of perforations.

Electric Locomotive — A1559

Designs: 6k, Map of the Lenin Volga-Baltic Waterway, Admiralty, Leningrad, and Kremlin. 10k, Ship passing through lock in waterway, vert. 12k, M.S. Aleksander Pushkin. 16k, Passenger liner and globe.

**1966 Litho. *Perf. 12½x12, 12x12½***

**3179** A1559 4k multicolored .65 .25
**3180** A1559 6k gray, ultra, red & black .65 .25
**3181** A1559 10k Prus bl, gray brn & black .90 .25
**3182** A1559 12k blue, ver & blk 1.40 .25
**3183** A1559 16k blue & multi 1.40 .25
*Nos. 3179-3183 (5)* 5.00 1.25

Modern transportation.
Issued: #3179-3181, 8/6; #3182-3183, 3/25.

Supreme Soviet Building, Frunze — A1560

**1966, Mar. 25 Photo. *Perf. 12***

**3184** A1560 4k deep red .50 .25

40th anniv. of the Kirghiz Republic.

Sergei M. Kirov — A1561

Portraits: No. 3186, Grigori Ordzhonikidze. No. 3187, Ion Yakir.

**1966 Engr. *Perf. 12***

**3185** A1561 4k dk red brown 1.00 .30
**3186** A1561 4k slate green 1.00 .30
**3187** A1561 4k dark gray violet 1.00 .30
*Nos. 3185-3187 (3)* 3.00 .90

Kirov (1886-1934), revolutionist and Secretary of the Communist Party Central Committee; Ordzhonikidze (1886-1937), a political leader of the Red Army and government official; Yakir, military leader in October Revolution, 70th birth anniv.

Issued: #3185, 3/27; #3186, 6/22; #3187, 7/30.

Souvenir Sheet

Lenin — A1563

**Embossed and Typographed**

**1966, Mar. 29 *Imperf.***

**3188** A1563 50k red & silver 5.00 1.00

23rd Communist Party Congress.

Aleksandr E. Fersman (1883-1945), Mineralogist A1564

Soviet Scientists: No. 3190, D. K. Zabolotny (1866-1929), microbiologist. No. 3191, M. A. Shatelen (1866-1957), physicist. No. 3191A, Otto Yulievich Schmidt (1891-1956), scientist and arctic explorer.

**1966, Mar. 30 Litho. *Perf. 12½x12***

**3189** A1564 4k vio blue & multi .75 .30
**3190** A1564 4k red brn & multi .75 .30
**3191** A1564 4k lilac & multi .75 .30
**3191A** A1564 4k Prus bl & brn .75 .30
*Nos. 3189-3191A (4)* 3.00 1.20

**Overprinted in Red**

**1966, Apr. 3 Typo. *Imperf.***

**3192** A1565 10k gold, blk, brt bl & brt rose 2.00 1.50

Launching of the 1st artificial moon satellite, Luna 10. The bright rose ink is fluorescent on Nos. 3192-3194.

Luna 10 Automatic Moon Station — A1565

Design: 12k, Station on moon.

**1966, Apr. 12 *Perf. 12***

**3193** A1565 10k multicolored .80 .30
**3194** A1565 12k multicolored 1.20 .30

Day of Space Research, Apr. 12, 1966.

Molniya 1 and Television Screens A1566

**1966, Apr. 12 Litho. *Perf. 12½***

**3195** A1566 10k gold, blk, brt bl & red 1.00 .30

Launching of the communications satellite "Lightning 1," Apr. 23, 1965.

Ernst Thälmann — A1567

Portraits: No. 3197, Wilhelm Pieck. No. 3198, Sun Yat-sen. No. 3199, Sen Katayama.

**1966-67 Engr. *Perf. 12½x12***

**3196** A1567 6k rose claret 1.25 .25
**3197** A1567 6k blue violet 1.25 .25
**3198** A1567 6k reddish brown 1.25 .25

**Photo.**

**3199** A1567 6k gray green ('67) 1.25 .25
*Nos. 3196-3199 (4)* 5.00 1.00

Thälmann (1886-1944), German Communist leader; Pieck (1876-1960), German Dem. Rep. Pres.; Sun Yat-sen (1866-1925), leader of the Chinese revolution; Katayama (1859-1933), founder of Social Democratic Party in Japan in 1901.

Issued: No. 3196, 4/16; No. 3197-3198, 6/22; No. 3199, 11/2/67.

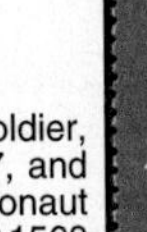

Soldier, 1917, and Astronaut A1568

**1966, Apr. 30 Litho. *Perf. 11½***

**3200** A1568 4k brt rose & black .50 .25

15th Congress of the Young Communist League (Komsomol).

Ice Hockey Player — A1569

**1966, Apr. 30**

**3201** A1569 10k red, ultra, gold & black .50 .25

Soviet victory in the World Ice Hockey Championships. For souvenir sheet see No. 3232. For overprint see No. 3315.

Nicolai Kuznetsov A1570

Heroes of Guerrilla Warfare during WWII (Gold Star of Hero of the Soviet Union and): No. 3203, Imant Sudmalis. No. 3204, Anya Morozova. No. 3205, Filipp Strelets. No. 3206, Tikhon Bumazhkov.

**1966, May 9 Photo. *Perf. 12x12½***

**3202** A1570 4k green & black .60 .25
**3203** A1570 4k ocher & black .60 .25
**3204** A1570 4k blue & black .60 .25
**3205** A1570 4k brt rose & black .60 .25
**3206** A1570 4k violet & black .60 .25
*Nos. 3202-3206 (5)* 3.00 1.25

Peter I. Tchaikovsky A1571

4k, Moscow State Conservatory, Tchaikovsky monument. 16k, Tchaikovsky House, Klin.

**1966, May 26 Typo. *Perf. 12½***

**3207** A1571 4k red, yel & black 1.00 .25
**3208** A1571 6k yel, red & black 1.25 .30
**3209** A1571 16k red, bluish gray & black 3.00 .35
*Nos. 3207-3209 (3)* 5.25 .90

Third International Tchaikovsky Contest, Moscow, May 30-June 29.

Runners — A1572

Designs: 6k, Weight lifters. 12k, Wrestlers.

**1966, May 26 Photo. *Perf. 11x11½***

**3210** A1572 4k emer, olive & brn .50 .25
**3211** A1572 6k org, blk & lt brn .75 .25
**3212** A1572 12k grnsh bl, brn ol & black 1.00 .25
*Nos. 3210-3212 (3)* 2.25 .75

No. 3210, Znamensky Brothers Intl. Track Competitions; No. 3211, Intl. Weightlifting Competitions; No. 3212, Intl. Wrestling Competitions for Ivan Poddubny Prize.

Jules Rimet World Soccer Cup, Ball and Laurel — A1573

Chessboard, Gold Medal, Pawn and King A1574

Designs: No. 3214, Soccer. 12k, Fencers. 16k, Fencer, mask, foil and laurel branch.

**1966, May 31 Litho. *Perf. 11½***

**3213** A1573 4k rose red, gold & blk .30 .25
**3214** A1573 6k emer, tan, blk & red .45 .25
**3215** A1574 6k brn, gold, blk & white 1.75 .75
**3216** A1573 12k brt bl, ol & blk 1.10 .25
**3217** A1573 16k multicolored 1.40 .30
*Nos. 3213-3217 (5)* 5.00 1.80

Nos. 3213-3214 for World Cup Soccer Championship, Wembley, England, July 11-30; No. 3215 the World Chess Title Match between Tigran Petrosian and Boris Spassky; Nos. 3216-3217 the World Fencing Championships. For souvenir sheet see No. 3232.

Sable and Lake Baikal, Map of Barguzin Game Reserve — A1575

Design: 6k, Map of Lake Baikal region and Game Reserve, brown bear on lake shore.

**1966, June 25 Photo. *Perf. 12***

**3218** A1575 4k steel blue & black 1.50 .25
**3219** A1575 6k rose lake & black 1.50 .25

Barguzin Game Reserve, 50th anniv.

Pink Lotus — A1576

6k, Palms and cypresses. 12k, Victoria cruziana.

**1966, June 30** ***Perf. 11½***

**3220** A1576 3k grn, pink & yel .25 .25
**3221** A1576 6k grnsh bl, ol brn & dk brn 1.00 .25
**3222** A1576 12k multicolored 1.75 .25
*Nos. 3220-3222 (3)* 3.00 .75

Sukhum Botanical Garden, 125th anniv.

Dogs Ugolek and Veterok after Space Flight A1577

Designs: No. 3224, Diagram of Solar System, globe and medal of Venera 3 flight. No. 3225, Luna 10, earth and moon.

**1966, July 15** ***Perf. 12x11½***

**3223** A1577 6k ocher, ind & org brn 1.00 .25
**3224** A1577 6k crim, blk & silver 1.00 .25

***Perf. 12x12½***

**3225** A1577 6k dk blue & bis brn 1.00 .25
*Nos. 3223-3225 (3)* 3.00 .75

Soviet achievements in space.

Itkol Hotel, Mount Cheget and Map of USSR A1578

Arch of General Headquarters, Winter Palace and Alexander Column A1579

Resort Areas: 4k, Ship on Volga River and Zhigul Mountain. 10k, Castle, Kislovodsk. 12k, Ismail Samani Mausoleum, Bukhara, Uzbek. 16k, Hotel Caucasus, Sochi.

**1966 Litho.** ***Perf. 12½x12, 12½ (6k)***

**3226** A1578 1k multicolored .25 .25
**3227** A1578 4k multicolored .35 .25
**3228** A1579 6k multicolored .40 .25
**3229** A1578 10k multicolored .65 .25
**3230** A1578 12k multicolored .90 .25
**3231** A1578 16k multicolored 1.40 .30
*Nos. 3226-3231 (6)* 3.95 1.55

Issue dates: 10k, Sept. 14; others, July 20.

Souvenir Sheet

A1580

**1966, July 26 Litho.** ***Perf. 11½***

**3232** A1580 Sheet of 4 10.00 2.00
*a.* 10k Fencers 2.00 .40
*b.* 10k Chess 2.00 .40
*c.* 10k Soccer cup 2.00 .40
*d.* 10k Ice hockey 2.00 .40

World fencing, chess, soccer and ice hockey championships.
See Nos. 3201, 3213-3217.

Congress Emblem, Congress Palace and Kremlin Tower — A1581

**1966, Aug. 6 Photo.** ***Perf. 11½x12***

**3233** A1581 4k brown & yellow .35 .25

Consumers' Cooperative Societies, 7th Cong.

Dove, Crane, Russian and Japanese Flags A1582

**1966, Aug. 9** ***Perf. 12½x11½***

**3234** A1582 6k gray & red 1.00 .25

Soviet-Japanese friendship, and 2nd meeting of Russian and Japanese delegates at Khabarovsk.

"Knight Fighting with Tiger" by Rustaveli A1583

Designs: 4k, Shota Rustaveli, bas-relief. 6k, "Avtandil at a Mountain Spring." 50k, Shota Rustaveli Monument and design of 3k stamp.

**1966, Aug. 31 Engr.** ***Perf. 11½x12½***

**3235** A1583 3k blk, *olive green* .75 .25
**3236** A1583 4k brown, *yellow* .90 .25
**3237** A1583 6k bluish black, *lt ultra* 1.40 .25
*Nos. 3235-3237 (3)* 3.05 .75

**Souvenir Sheet**

***Imperf***

**Engraved and Photogravure**

**3238** A1583 50k slate grn & bis 4.00 1.25

800th anniv. of the birth of Shota Rustaveli, Georgian poet, author of "The Knight in the Tiger's Skin." No. 3238 contains one 32x49mm stamp; dark green margin with design of 6k stamp.

Coat of Arms and Fireworks over Moscow A1584

**Lithographed (Lacquered)**

**1966, Sept. 14** ***Perf. 11½***

**3239** A1584 4k multicolored .50 .25

49th anniversary of October Revolution.

Grayling A1585

Designs (Fish and part of design of 6k stamp): 4k, Sturgeon. 6k, Trawler, net and map of Lake Baikal, vert. 10k, Two Baikal cisco. 12k, Two Baikal whitefish.

**1966, Sept. 25** ***Photo. & Engr.***

**3240** A1585 2k multicolored .25 .25
**3241** A1585 4k multicolored .25 .25
**3242** A1585 6k multicolored .35 .25
**3243** A1585 10k multicolored .50 .25
**3244** A1585 12k gray, dk grn & red brown .75 .25
*Nos. 3240-3244 (5)* 2.10 1.25

Fish resources of Lake Baikal.

Map of USSR and Symbols of Transportation and Communication — A1586

Designs (map of USSR and): No. 3246, Technological education. No. 3247, Agriculture and mining. No. 3248, Increased productivity through five-year plan. No. 3249, Technology and inventions.

**1966, Sept. 29 Photo.** ***Perf. 11½x12***

**3245** A1586 4k ultra & silver .60 .25
**3246** A1586 4k car & silver .60 .25
**3247** A1586 4k red brn & silver .60 .25
**3248** A1586 4k red & silver .60 .25
**3249** A1586 4k dp green & silver .60 .25
*Nos. 3245-3249 (5)* 3.00 1.25

23rd Communist Party Congress decisions.

Government House, Kishinev, and Moldavian Flag — A1587

**1966, Oct. 8 Litho.** ***Perf. 12½x12***

**3250** A1587 4k multicolored .50 .50

500th anniversary of Kishinev.

Symbolic Water Cycle A1588

**1966, Oct. 12** ***Perf. 11½***

**3251** A1588 6k multicolored 1.00 .25

Hydrological Decade (UNESCO), 1965-1974.

Nikitin Monument in Kalinin, Ship's Prow and Map — A1589

**1966, Oct. 12** ***Photo.***

**3252** A1589 4k multicolored .50 .25

Afanasii Nikitin's trip to India, 500th anniv.

Scene from Opera "Nargiz" by M. Magomayev — A1590

No. 3254, Scene from opera "Kerogli" by Y. Gadjubekov (knight on horseback and armed men).

**1966, Oct. 12**

**3253** A1590 4k black & ocher .75 .25
**3254** A1590 4k blk & blue green .75 .25
*a.* Pair, #3253-3254 2.00 .50

Azerbaijan opera. Printed in checkerboard arrangement.

Fighters A1591

**1966, Oct. 26**

**3255** A1591 6k red, blk & ol bister .50 .25

30th anniversary of Spanish Civil War.

National Militia — A1592

**1966, Oct. 26 Litho.** ***Perf. 12x12½***

**3256** A1592 4k red & dark brown .50 .25

25th anniv. of the National Militia.

Protest Rally — A1592a

**1966, Oct. 26** ***Perf. 12***
**3256A** A1592a 6k yel, black & red .50 .30

"Hands off Viet Nam!"

Soft Landing on Moon, Luna 9 — A1593

Symbols of Agriculture and Chemistry A1594

Designs: 1k, Congress Palace, Moscow, and map of Russia. 3k, Boy, girl and Lenin banner. 4k, Flag. 6k, Plane and Ostankino Television Tower. 10k, Soldier and Soviet star. 12k, Steel worker. 16k, "Peace," woman with dove. 20k, Demonstrators in Red Square, flags, carnation and globe. 50k, Newspaper, plane, train and Communications Ministry. 1r, Lenin and industrial symbols.

**Inscribed "1966"**

**1966** **Litho.** ***Perf. 12***
**3257** A1593 1k dk red brown .25 .25
**3258** A1593 2k violet .25 .25
**3259** A1593 3k red lilac .25 .25
**3260** A1593 4k bright red .25 .25
**3261** A1593 6k ultra .25 .25
**3262** A1593 10k olive .40 .25
**3263** A1593 12k red brown 1.10 .25
**3264** A1593 16k violet blue 1.40 .25

***Perf. 11½***

**Photo.**

**3265** A1594 20k bis, red & dk bl 2.00 .25
**3266** A1594 30k dp grn & green 2.50 .30
**3267** A1594 50k blue & violet bl 4.50 .35
**3268** A1594 1r black & red 7.00 .55
*Nos. 3257-3268 (12)* 20.15 3.45

No. 3260 was issued on fluorescent paper in 1969.
See Nos. 3470-3481.

Ostankino Television Tower, Molniya 1 Satellite and Kremlin A1595

**1966, Nov. 19** **Litho.** ***Perf. 12***
**3273** A1595 4k multicolored 1.00 .25

New Year, 1967, the 50th anniversary of the October Revolution.

Diagram of Luna 9 Flight — A1596

Arms of Russia and Pennant Sent to Moon — A1597

No. 3276, Luna 9 & photograph of moonscape.

**1966, Nov. 25** **Typo.** ***Perf. 12***
**3274** A1596 10k black & silver .65 .25
**3275** A1597 10k red & silver .65 .25
**3276** A1596 10k black & silver .65 .25
***a.*** Strip of 3, #3274-3276 2.00 1.00

Soft landing on the moon by Luna 9, Jan. 31, 1966, and the television program of moon pictures on Feb. 2.

Battle of Moscow, 1941 — A1598

Details from "Defense of Moscow" Medal and Golden Star Medal A1599

25th anniv. of Battle of Moscow: 10k, Sun rising over Kremlin. Ostankino Tower, chemical plant and rockets.

***Perf. 12, 11½ (A1599)***

**1966, Dec. 1** **Photo.**
**3277** A1598 4k red brown .25 .25
**3278** A1599 6k bister & brown 1.00 .25
**3279** A1598 10k dp bister & yel 1.75 .25
*Nos. 3277-3279 (3)* 3.00 .75

Cervantes and Don Quixote A1600

**1966, Dec. 15** **Photo.** ***Perf. 11½***
**3280** A1600 6k gray & brown .50 .25

Miguel Cervantes Saavedra (1547-1616), Spanish writer.

Bering's Ship and Map of Voyage to Commander Islands — A1601

Far Eastern Territories: 2k, Medny Island and map. 4k, Petropavlosk-Kamchatski Harbor. 6k, Geyser, Kamchatka, vert. 10k, Avachinskaya Bay, Kamchatka. 12k, Fur seals, Bering Island. 16k, Guillemots in bird sanctuary, Kuril Islands.

**1966, Dec. 25** **Litho.** ***Perf. 12***
**3281** A1601 1k bister & multi .45 .25
**3282** A1601 2k bister & multi .50 .25
**3283** A1601 4k dp blue & multi .60 .25
**3284** A1601 6k multicolored .75 .25
**3285** A1601 10k dp blue & multi 1.00 .25
**3286** A1601 12k olive & multi 1.00 .40
**3287** A1601 16k lt blue & multi 1.25 .75
*Nos. 3281-3287 (7)* 5.55 2.40

Communications Satellite, Molniya 1 — A1602

Design: No. 3289, Luna 11 moon probe, moon, earth and Soviet emblem.

**1966, Dec. 29** **Photo.** ***Perf. 12x11½***
**3288** A1602 6k blk, vio bl & brt rose 1.00 .30
**3289** A1602 6k black & brt rose 1.00 .30

Space explorations. The bright rose is fluorescent.

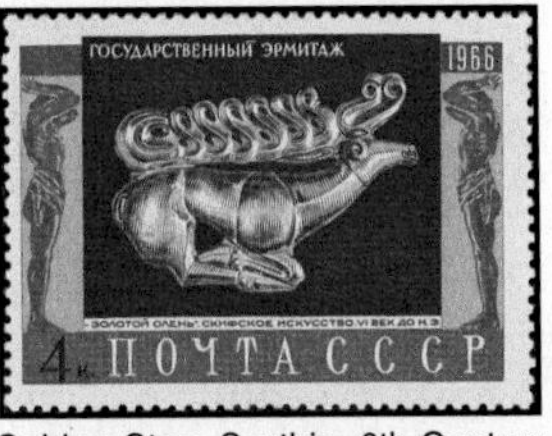

Golden Stag, Scythia, 6th Century B.C. — A1603

Treasures from the Hermitage, Leningrad: 6k, Silver jug, Persia, 5th Century A.D. 10k, Statue of Voltaire by Jean Antoine Houdon. 12k, Malachite vase, Ural, 1840. 16k, "The Lute Player," by Michelangelo de Caravaggio. (6k, 10k, 12k are vertical).

**1966, Dec. 29** **Engr.** ***Perf. 12***
**3290** A1603 4k yellow & black .45 .25
**3291** A1603 6k gray & black .60 .25
**3292** A1603 10k dull vio & black .90 .25
**3293** A1603 12k emer & black 1.25 .30
**3294** A1603 16k ocher & black 1.75 .35
*Nos. 3290-3294 (5)* 4.95 1.40

Sea Water Converter and Pavilion at EXPO '67 A1604

Pavilion and: 6k, Splitting atom, vert. 10k, "Proton" space station. 30k, Soviet pavilion.

**1967, Jan. 25** **Litho.** ***Perf. 12***
**3295** A1604 4k multicolored .75 .25
**3296** A1604 6k multicolored .75 .25
**3297** A1604 10k multicolored 1.50 .25
*Nos. 3295-3297 (3)* 3.00 .75

**Souvenir Sheet**

**3298** A1604 30k multicolored 3.00 1.25

EXPO '67, Intl. Exhib., Montreal, 4/28-10/27.

1st Lieut. B. I. Sizov A1605

Design: No. 3300, Sailor V. V. Khodyrev.

**1967, Feb. 16** **Photo.** ***Perf. 12x11½***
**3299** A1605 4k dull yel & ocher .40 .25
**3300** A1605 4k gray & dk gray .40 .25

Heroes of World War II.

Woman's Head and Pavlov Shawl — A1606

**1967, Feb. 16** ***Perf. 11***
**3301** A1606 4k vio, red & grn 1.00 .25

International Woman's Day, Mar. 8.

Movie Camera and Film — A1607

**1967, Feb. 16** **Photo.** ***Perf. 11½***
**3302** A1607 6k multicolored .50 .25

5th Intl. Film Festival, Moscow, July 5-20.

Trawler Fish Factory and Fish — A1608

Designs: No. 3304, Refrigerationship. No. 3305, Crab canning ship. No. 3306, Fishing trawler. No. 3307, Black Sea seiner.

**1967, Feb. 28** **Litho.** ***Perf. 12x11½***

**Ships in Black and Red**

**3303** A1608 6k blue & gray .60 .25
**3304** A1608 6k blue & gray .60 .25
**3305** A1608 6k blue & gray .60 .25
**3306** A1608 6k blue & gray .60 .25
**3307** A1608 6k blue & gray .60 .25
***a.*** Vert. strip of 5, #3303-3307 3.25 1.50

Soviet fishing industry.

Newspaper Forming Hammer and Sickle, Red Flag — A1609

**1967, Mar. 13** **Litho.** ***Perf. 12x12½***
**3308** A1609 4k cl brn, red, yel & brn .40 .25

50th anniversary of newspaper Izvestia.

**Congress Type of 1966**

Congress Emblems and: No. 3309, Moscow State University, construction site and star. No. 3310, Pile driver, mining excavator, crossed hammers, globe and "V."

**1967, Mar. 10** **Photo.** ***Perf. 11½***
**3309** A1548 6k ultra, brt blue & blk .50 .25
**3310** A1548 6k blk, org red & blue .50 .25

Intl. congresses to be held in Moscow: 7th General Assembly Session of the Intl. Standards Association (#3309); 5th Intl. Mining Cong. (#3310).

International Tourist Year Emblem and Travel Symbols — A1610

**1967, Mar. 10** ***Perf. 11***

**3314** A1610 4k blk, sky bl & sil .50 .25

International Tourist Year, 1967.

**No. 3201 Overprinted**

**1967, Mar. 29** **Litho.** ***Perf. 11½***

**3315** A1569 10k multicolored 2.00 1.00

Victory of the Soviet team in the Ice Hockey Championships, Vienna, Mar. 18-29. Overprint reads: "Vienna-1967."

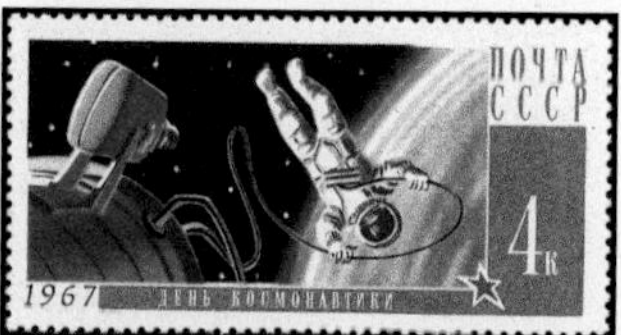


Space Walk — A1611

Designs: 10k, Rocket launching from satellite. 16k, Spaceship over moon, and earth.

**1967, Mar. 30** **Litho.** ***Perf. 12***

**3316** A1611 4k bister & multi .50 .25
**3317** A1611 10k black & multi 1.00 .25
**3318** A1611 16k lilac & multi 1.50 .30
*Nos. 3316-3318 (3)* 3.00 .80

National Cosmonauts' Day.

Lenin as Student, by V. Tsigal A1612

Sculptures of Lenin: 3k, Monument at Ulyanovsk by M. Manizer. 4k, Lenin in Razliv, by V. Pinchuk, horiz. 6k, Head, by G. Neroda. 10k, Lenin as Leader, statue, by N. Andreyev.

**1967** **Photo.** ***Perf. 12x11½, 11½x12***

**3319** A1612 2k ol grn, sepia & buff .30 .25
**3320** A1612 3k maroon & brn .30 .25
**3321** A1612 4k ol black & gold .45 .25
**3322** A1612 6k dk bl, sil & blk .60 .25
**3323** A1612 10k sil, gray bl & blk 1.10 .25
**3323A** A1612 10k gold, gray & black 1.10 .25
*Nos. 3319-3323A (6)* 3.85 1.50

97th anniversary of the birth of Lenin. Issued: #3323A, Oct. 25; others, Apr. 22.

Lt. M. S. Kharchenko and Battle Scenes — A1613

Designs: No. 3325, Maj. Gen. S. V. Rudnev. No. 3326, M. Shmyrev.

**1967, Apr. 24** ***Perf. 12x11½***

**3324** A1613 4k brt pur & ol bis .40 .25
**3325** A1613 4k ultra & ol bister .40 .25
**3326** A1613 4k org brn & ol bister .40 .25
*Nos. 3324-3326 (3)* 1.20 .75

Partisan heroes of WWII.

Marshal S. S. Biryuzov, Hero of the Soviet Union — A1614

**1967, May 9** **Photo.** ***Perf. 12***

**3327** A1614 4k ocher & sl grn .35 .25

Driver Crossing Lake Ladoga A1615

**1967, May 9** ***Perf. 11½***

**3328** A1615 4k plum & blue gray .35 .25

25th anniversary of siege of Leningrad.

Views of Old and New Minsk A1616

**1967, May 9**

**3329** A1616 4k sl grn & blk .35 .25

900th anniversary of Minsk.

Red Cross and Tulip — A1617

**1967, May 15** ***Perf. 12***

**3330** A1617 4k yel brn & red .50 .25

Centenary of the Russian Red Cross.

Stamps of 1918 and 1967 — A1618

**1967** **Photo.** ***Perf. 11½***

**3331** A1618 20k blue & black 1.00 .30
*a.* Souv. sheet of 2, imperf. 3.00 1.25

All-Union Philatelic Exhibition "50 Years of the Great October," Moscow, Oct. 1-10. Se-tenant with label showing exhibition emblem.

Issue dates: 20k, May 25. Sheet, Oct. 1.

No. 3331 was re-issued Oct. 3 with "Oct. 1-10" printed in blue on the label. Value $2.

Komsomolsk-on-Amur and Map of Amur River — A1619

**1967, June 12** ***Perf. 12x12½***

**3332** A1619 4k red & brown .60 .25

35th anniv. of the Soviet youth town, Komsomolsk-on-Amur. Printed with label showing boy and girl of Young Communist League and tents.

Souvenir Sheet

Sputnik Orbiting Earth — A1620

**1967, June 24** **Litho.** ***Perf. 13x12***

**3333** A1620 30k black & multi 7.50 6.00

10th anniv. of the launching of Sputnik 1, the 1st artificial satellite, Oct. 4, 1957.

Motorcyclist A1621

**Photogravure and Engraved**

**1967, June 24** ***Perf. 12x11½***

**3334** A1621 10k multicolored .35 .25

Intl. Motor Rally, Moscow, July 19.

G. D. Gai (1887-1937), Corps Commander of the First Cavalry, 1920 — A1622

**1967, June 30** **Photo.** ***Perf. 12***

**3335** A1622 4k red & black .35 .25

Children's Games Emblem and Trophy A1623

**1967, July 8** ***Perf. 11½***

**3336** A1623 4k silver, red & black .35 .25

10th National Athletic Games of School Children, Leningrad, July, 1967.

Games Emblem and Trophy A1624

No. 3338, Cup and gymnast. No. 3339, Cup and bicyclists. No. 3340, Cup and diver.

**1967, July 20**

**3337** A1624 4k silver, red & black .25 .25
**3338** A1624 4k silver, red & black .25 .25
*a.* Pair, #3337-3338 1.00 .35
**3339** A1624 4k silver, red & black .25 .25
**3340** A1624 4k silver, red & black .25 .25
*a.* Pair, #3339-3340 1.00 .35

4th Natl. Spartacist Games, & USSR 50th anniv.

Se-tenant in checkerboard arrangement.

V. G. Klochkov (1911-41), Hero of the Soviet Union — A1625

**1967, July 20** ***Perf. 12½x12***

**3341** A1625 4k red & black .75 .30

Alternating label shows citation.

Soviet Flag, Arms and Moscow Views A1626

Arms of USSR and Laurel — A1627

АРМЯНСКАЯ ССР
ՀԱՅԿԱԿԱՆ ՍՍՀ

No. 3343

АЗЕРБАЙДЖАНСКАЯ ССР
АЗӘРБАЈҸАН ССР

No. 3344

БЕЛОРУССКАЯ ССР
БЕЛАРУСКАЯ ССР

No. 3345

ГРУЗИНСКАЯ ССР
საქართველოს სსრ

No. 3347

КИРГИЗСКАЯ ССР
КЫРГЫЗ ССР

No. 3349

МОЛДАВСКАЯ ССР
РСС МОЛДОВЕНЯСКЭ

No. 3352

ТАДЖИКСКАЯ ССР
РСС ТОҶИКИСТОН

No. 3353

ТУРКМЕНСКАЯ ССР
ТУРКМЕНИСТАН ССР

No. 3354

УКРАИНСКАЯ ССР
УКРАЇНСЬКА РСР

No. 3355

УЗБЕКСКАЯ ССР
ЎЗБЕКИСТОН ССР

No. 3356

Flag, Crest and Capital of Republic.

**1967, Aug. 4 Litho. *Perf. 12½x12***

**3342** A1626 4k shown .60 .25
**3343** A1626 4k Armenia .60 .25
**3344** A1626 4k Azerbaijan .60 .25
**3345** A1626 4k Byelorussia .60 .25
**3346** A1626 4k Estonia .60 .25
**3347** A1626 4k Georgia .60 .25
**3348** A1626 4k Kazakhstan .60 .25
**3349** A1626 4k Kirghizia .60 .25
**3350** A1626 4k Latvia .60 .25
**3351** A1626 4k Lithuania .60 .25
**3352** A1626 4k Moldavia .60 .25
**3353** A1626 4k Tadzhikistan .60 .25
**3354** A1626 4k Turkmenistan .60 .25
**3355** A1626 4k Ukraine .60 .25
**3356** A1626 4k Uzbekistan .60 .25
**3357** A1627 4k red, gold & black .60 .25
*Nos. 3342-3357 (16)* 9.60 4.00

50th anniversary of October Revolution.

Communication Symbols — A1628

**1967, Aug. 16 Photo. *Perf. 12***

**3358** A1628 4k crimson & silver 1.00 .50

Development of communications in USSR.

Flying Crane, Dove and Anniversary Emblem — A1629

**1967, Aug. 20 *Perf. 12½x12***

**3359** A1629 16k silver, red & blk 1.00 .30

Russo-Japanese Friendship Meeting, held at Khabarovsk. Emblem is for 50th anniv. of October Revolution.

Karl Marx and Title Page of "Das Kapital" — A1630

**1967, Aug. 22 Engr. *Perf. 12½x12***

**3360** A1630 4k sepia & dk red 3.00 .30

Centenary of the publication of "Das Kapital" by Karl Marx.

Russian Checkers Players A1631

Design: 6k, Woman gymnast.

**Photogravure and Engraved**

**1967, Sept. 9 *Perf. 12x11½***

**3361** A1631 1k lt brn, dp brn & sl .50 .25
**3362** A1631 6k ol bister & maroon .50 .25

World Championship of Russian Checkers (Shashki) at Moscow, and World Championship of Rhythmic Gymnastics.

Javelin A1632

**1967, Sept. 9 Engr. *Perf. 12x12½***

**3363** A1632 2k shown .65 .25
**3364** A1632 3k Running .65 .25
**3365** A1632 4k Jumping .65 .25
*Nos. 3363-3365 (3)* 1.95 .75

Europa Cup Championships, Kiev, Sept. 15-17.

Ice Skating and Olympic Emblem A1633

Designs: 3k, Ski jump. 4k, Emblem of Winter Olympics, vert. 10k, Ice hockey. 12k, Long-distance skiing.

**Photogravure and Engraved**

**1967, Sept. 20 *Perf. 11½***

**3366** A1633 2k gray, blk & bl .25 .25
**3367** A1633 3k bis, ocher, blk & green .25 .25
**3368** A1633 4k gray, bl, red & blk .25 .25
**3369** A1633 10k bis, brn, bl & blk .75 .25
**3370** A1633 12k gray, blk, lil & grn 1.50 .25
*Nos. 3366-3370 (5)* 3.00 1.25

10th Winter Olympic Games, Grenoble, France, Feb. 6-18, 1968.

Arctic Blue Fox A1634

Fur-bearing Animals: 4k, Silver Fox. 6k, Red fox, horiz. 10k, Muskrat, horiz. 12k, Ermine. 16k, Sable. 20k, Mink, horiz.

**1967, Sept. 20 Photo.**

**3371** A1634 2k brn, blk & gray blue .25 .25
**3372** A1634 4k tan, dk brn & gray blue .30 .25
**3373** A1634 6k gray grn, ocher & black .45 .25
**3374** A1634 10k yel grn, dk brn & ocher .65 .25
**3375** A1634 12k lilac, blk & bis .75 .25
**3376** A1634 16k org, brn & black .80 .25
**3377** A1634 20k gray blue, blk & dk brown 1.00 .30
*Nos. 3371-3377 (7)* 4.20 1.80

International Fur Auctions in Leningrad.

Young Guards Memorial — A1635

**1967, Sept. 23**

**3378** A1635 4k magenta, org & blk .50 .25

25th anniv. of the fight of the Young Guards at Krasnodon against the Germans.

Map of Cedar Valley Reservation and Snow Leopard — A1636

**1967, Oct. 14 *Perf. 12***

**3379** A1636 10k ol bister & black 1.00 .25

Far Eastern Cedar Valley Reservation.

Planes and Emblem A1637

**1967, Oct. 14 *Perf. 11½***

**3380** A1637 6k dp blue, red & gold .50 .25

French Normandy-Neman aviators, who fought on the Russian Front, 25th anniv.

Militiaman and Soviet Emblem A1638

**1967, Oct. 14 *Perf. 12½x12***

**3381** A1638 4k ver & ultra .35 .25

50th anniversary of the Soviet Militia.

Space Station Orbiting Moon — A1639

Science Fiction: 6k, Explorers on the moon, horiz. 10k, Rocket flying to the stars. 12k, Landscape on Red Planet, horiz. 16k, Satellites from outer space.

**1967 Litho. *Perf. 12x12½, 12½x12***

**3382** A1639 4k multicolored .25 .25
**3383** A1639 6k multicolored .35 .25
**3384** A1639 10k multicolored .45 .25
**3385** A1639 12k multicolored .60 .25
**3386** A1639 16k multicolored .65 .25
*Nos. 3382-3386 (5)* 2.30 1.25

Emblem of USSR and Red Star — A1640

Lenin Addressing 2nd Congress of Soviets, by V. A. Serov — A1641

Builders of Communism, by L. M. Merpert and Y. N. Skripkov — A1641a

Paintings: No. 3389, Lenin pointing to Map, by L. A. Schmatjko, 1957. No. 3390, The First Cavalry Army, by M. B. Grekov, 1924. No. 3391, Working Students on the March, by B. V. Yoganson, 1928. No. 3392, Russian Friendship for the World, by S. M. Karpov, 1924. No. 3393, Five-Year Plan Morning, by Y. D. Romas, 1934. No. 3394, Farmers' Holiday, by S. V. Gerasimov, 1937. No. 3395, Victory in the Great Patriotic War, by Y. K. Korolev, 1965.

**Lithographed and Embossed**

**1967, Oct. 25 *Perf. 11½***

**3387** A1640 4k gold, yel, red & dk brown .50 .25
**3388** A1641 4k gold & multi .50 .25
**3389** A1641 4k gold & multi .50 .25
**3390** A1641 4k gold & multi .50 .25
**3391** A1641 4k gold & multi .50 .25
**3392** A1641 4k gold & multi .50 .25
**3393** A1641 4k gold & multi .50 .25
**3394** A1641 4k gold & multi .50 .25
**3395** A1641 4k gold & multi .50 .25
**3396** A1641a 4k gold & multi .50 .25
*a.* Souvenir sheet of 2 4.25 1.00
*Nos. 3387-3396 (10)* 5.00 2.50

50th anniversary of October Revolution. No. 3396a contains two 40k imperf. stamps similar to Nos. 3388 and 3396. Issued Nov. 5.

Souvenir Sheet

Hammer, Sickle and Sputnik — A1642

**1967, Nov. 5 Engr. *Perf. 12½x12***

**3397** A1642 1r lake 5.00 2.00

50th anniv. of the October Revolution. Margin contains "50" as a watermark.

Ostankino Television Tower — A1643

**1967, Nov. 5 Litho. *Perf. 11½***

**3398** A1643 16k gray, org & black .35 .25

Jurmala Resort and Hepatica A1644

Health Resorts of the Baltic Region: 6k, Narva-Joesuu and Labrador tea. 10k, Druskininkai and cranberry blossoms. 12k, Zelenogradsk and Scotch heather, vert. 16k, Svetlogorsk and club moss, vert.

***Perf. 12½x12, 12x12½***

**1967, Nov. 30 Litho.**

**Flowers in Natural Colors**

**3399** A1644 4k blue & black .25 .25
**3400** A1644 6k ocher & black .35 .25
**3401** A1644 10k green & black .60 .25
**3402** A1644 12k gray olive & blk .75 .25
**3403** A1644 16k brown & black 1.10 .25
*Nos. 3399-3403 (5)* 3.05 1.25

Emergency Commission Emblem — A1645

**1967, Dec. 11 Photo. *Perf. 11½***

**3404** A1645 4k ultra & red .75 .25

All-Russia Emergency Commission (later the State Security Commission), 50th anniv.

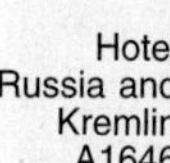

Hotel Russia and Kremlin A1646

**1967, Dec. 14**

**3405** A1646 4k silver, dk brn & brt pink 2.00 .25

New Year 1968. The pink is fluorescent.

Soldiers, Sailors, Congress Building, Kharkov, and Monument to the Men of Arsenal — A1647

Designs: 6k, Hammer and sickle and scenes from industry and agriculture. 10k, Ukrainians offering bread and salt, monument of the Unknown Soldier, Kiev, and Lenin monument in Zaporozhye.

**1967, Dec. 20 Litho. *Perf. 12½***

**3406** A1647 4k multicolored .30 .25
**3407** A1647 6k multicolored .65 .25
**3408** A1647 10k multicolored .80 .25
*Nos. 3406-3408 (3)* 1.75 .75

50th anniv. of the Ukrainian SSR.

Three Kremlin Towers A1648

Kremlin: 6k, Cathedral of the Annunciation, horiz. 10k, Konstantin and Elena, Nabatnaya and Spasski towers. 12k, Ivan the Great bell tower. 16k, Kutafya and Troitskaya towers.

**Engraved and Photogravure**

**1967, Dec. 25 *Perf. 12x11½, 11½x12***

**3409** A1648 4k dk brn & claret .25 .25
**3410** A1648 6k dk brn, yel & grn .35 .25
**3411** A1648 10k maroon & slate .65 .25
**3412** A1648 12k sl grn, yel & vio .90 .25
**3413** A1648 16k brn, pink & red 1.00 .25
*Nos. 3409-3413 (5)* 3.15 1.25

Coat of Arms, Lenin's Tomb and Rockets A1649

Designs: No. 3415, Agricultural Progress: Wheat, reapers and silo. No. 3416, Industrial Progress: Computer tape, atom symbol, cogwheel and factories. No. 3417, Scientific Progress: Radar, microscope, university buildings. No. 3418, Communications progress: Ostankino TV tower, railroad bridge, steamer and Aeroflot emblem, vert.

**1967, Dec. 25 Engr. *Perf. 12½***

**3414** A1649 4k maroon .30 .25
**3415** A1649 4k green .30 .25
**3416** A1649 4k red brown .30 .25
**3417** A1649 4k violet blue .30 .25
**3418** A1649 4k dark blue .30 .25
*Nos. 3414-3418 (5)* 1.50 1.25

Material and technical basis of Russian Communism.

Monument to the Unknown Soldier, Moscow — A1650

**1967, Dec. 25**

**3419** A1650 4k carmine .50 .25

Dedication of the Monument of the Unknown Soldier of WWII in the Kremlin Wall.

Seascape by Ivan Aivazovsky — A1651

Paintings: 3k, Interrogation of Communists by B. V. Yoganson, 1933. No. 3422, The Lacemaker, by V. A. Tropinin, 1823, vert. No. 3423, Bread-makers, by T. M. Yablonskaya, 1949. No. 3424, Alexander Nevsky, by P. D. Korin, 1942-43, vert. No. 3425, The Boyar Morozov Going into Exile by V. I. Surikov, 1887. No. 3426, The Swan Maiden, by M. A. Vrubel, 1900, vert. No. 3427, The Arrest of a Propagandist by Ilya E. Repin, 1878. 16k, Moscow Suburb in February by G. G. Nissky, 1957.

***Perf. 12½x12, 12x12½, 12, 11½***

**1967, Dec. 29 Litho.**

**Size: 47x33mm, 33x47mm**

**3420** A1651 3k multicolored .25 .25
**3421** A1651 4k multicolored .30 .25
**3422** A1651 4k multicolored .30 .25

**Size: 60x35mm, 35x60mm**

**3423** A1651 6k multicolored .40 .25
**3424** A1651 6k multicolored .40 .25
**3425** A1651 6k multicolored .40 .25

**Size: 47x33mm, 33x47mm**

**3426** A1651 10k multicolored .70 .25
**3427** A1651 10k multicolored .70 .25
**3428** A1651 16k multicolored 1.10 .40
*Nos. 3420-3428 (9)* 4.55 2.40

Tretiakov Art Gallery, Moscow.

Globe, Wheel and Workers of the World — A1652

**1968, Jan. 18 Photo. *Perf. 12***

**3429** A1652 6k ver & green .50 .25

14th Trade Union Congress.

Lt. S. Baikov and Velikaya River Bridge A1653

Heroes of WWII (War Memorial and): No. 3431. Lt. A. Pokalchuk. No. 3432, P. Gutchenko.

**1968, Jan. 20 *Perf. 12½x12***

**3430** A1653 4k blue gray & black .35 .25
**3431** A1653 4k rose & black .35 .25
**3432** A1653 4k gray green & black .35 .25
*Nos. 3430-3432 (3)* 1.05 .75

Thoroughbred and Horse Race — A1654

Horses: 6k, Arab mare and dressage, vert. 10k, Orlovski trotters. 12k, Altekin horse performing, vert. 16k, Donskay race horse.

**1968, Jan. 23 *Perf. 11½***

**3433** A1654 4k ultra, blk & red lil .40 .25
**3434** A1654 6k crim, blk & ultra .65 .25
**3435** A1654 10k grnsh blue, blk & orange .95 .40
**3436** A1654 12k org brn, black & apple green 1.25 .50
**3437** A1654 16k ol grn, blk & red 1.75 .70
*Nos. 3433-3437 (5)* 5.00 2.10

Horse breeding.

Maria I. Ulyanova (1878-1937), Lenin's Sister — A1655

**1968, Jan. 30 *Perf. 12x12½***

**3438** A1655 4k indigo & pale green .50 .25

Soviet Star and Flags of Army, Air Force and Navy A1656

Lenin Addressing Troops in 1919 — A1657

No. 3441, Dneprostroi Dam & sculpture "On Guard." No. 3442, 1918 poster & marching volunteers. No. 3443, Red Army entering Vladivostok, 1922, & soldiers' monument in Primorie. No. 3444, Poster "Red Army as Liberator," Western Ukraine. No. 3445, Poster "Westward," defeat of German army. No. 3446, "Battle of Stalingrad" monument & German prisoners of war. No. 3447, Victory parade on Red Square, May 24, 1945, & Russian War Memorial, Berlin. Nos. 3448-3449, Modern weapons and Russian flag.

**1968, Feb. 20 Typo. *Perf. 12x12½***

**3439** A1656 4k gold & multi .30 .25

**Photo.**

***Perf. 11½x12***

**3440** A1657 4k blk, red, pink & silver .30 .25
**3441** A1657 4k gold, black & red .30 .25

**Litho.**

***Perf. 12½x12***

**3442** A1657 4k yel grn, blk, red & buff .30 .25
**3443** A1657 4k grn, dk brn, red & bis .30 .25
**3444** A1657 4k green & multi .30 .25
**3445** A1657 4k yel green & multi .30 .25

***Perf. 11½x12, 12x11½***

**Photo.**

**3446** A1657 4k blk, silver & red .30 .25
**3447** A1657 4k gold, blk, pink & red .30 .25
**3448** A1656 4k blk, red & silver .30 .25
*Nos. 3439-3448 (10)* 3.00 2.50

**Souvenir Sheet**

**1968, Feb. 23 Litho. *Imperf.***

**3449** A1656 1r blk, silver & red 4.50 1.50

50th anniv. of the Armed Forces of the USSR. No. 3449 contains one 25x37½mm stamp with simulated perforations.

Maxim Gorki (1868-1936), Writer — A1658

**1968, Feb. 29** **Photo.** ***Perf. 12***
**3450** A1658 4k gray ol & dk brown .50 .25

Fireman, Fire Truck and Boat — A1659

**1968, Mar. 30** **Photo.** ***Perf. 12x12½***
**3451** A1659 4k red & black .60 .25

50th anniversary of Soviet Fire Guards.

Link-up of Cosmos 186 and 188 Satellites — A1660

**1968, Mar. 30** ***Perf. 11½***
**3452** A1660 6k blk, dp lilac rose & gold .50 .25

First link-up in space of two satellites, Cosmos 186 and Cosmos 188, Oct. 30, 1967.

N. N. Popudrenko — A1661

Design: No. 3454, P. P. Vershigora.

**1968, Mar. 30** ***Perf. 12½x12***
**3453** A1661 4k gray green & black .30 .25
**3454** A1661 4k lt purple & black .30 .25

Partisan heroes of World War II.

Globe and Hand Shielding from War A1662

**1968, Apr. 11** ***Perf. 11½***
**3455** A1662 6k sil, mar, ver & black .60 .35

Emergency session of the World Federation of Trade Unions and expressing solidarity with the people of Vietnam.

Space Walk A1663

6k, Docking operation of Kosmos 186 & Kosmos 188. 10k, Exploration of Venus.

**1968, Apr. 12** **Litho.**
**3456** A1663 4k multicolored .50 .25
**3457** A1663 6k multicolored .50 .25
**3458** A1663 10k multicolored 1.00 .25
*a.* Block of 3, #3456-3458 + 3 labels 3.50 .50

National Astronauts' Day.

Lenin, 1919 A1664

Lenin Portraits: No. 3460, Addressing crowd on Red Square, Nov. 7, 1918. No. 3461, Full-face portrait, taken in Petrograd, Jan. 1918.

**Engraved and Photogravure**

**1968, Apr. 16** ***Perf. 12x11½***
**3459** A1664 4k gold, brown & red 1.00 .25
**3460** A1664 4k gold, red & black 1.00 .25
**3461** A1664 4k gold, brn, buff & red 1.00 .25
*Nos. 3459-3461 (3)* 3.00 .75

98th anniversary of the birth of Lenin.

Alisher Navoi, Uzbek Poet, 525th Birth Anniv. — A1665

**1968, Apr. 29** **Photo.** ***Perf. 12x12½***
**3462** A1665 4k deep brown .50 .25

Karl Marx (1818-83) A1666

**1968, May 5** **Engr.** ***Perf. 11½x12***
**3463** A1666 4k black & red .50 .25

Frontier Guard — A1667

Jubilee Badge — A1668

**1968, May 22** **Photo.** ***Perf. 11½***
**3464** A1667 4k sl grn, ocher & red 1.00 .25
**3465** A1668 6k sl grn, blk & red brn 1.00 .25

Russian Frontier Guards, 50th anniv.

Crystal and Congress Emblem A1669

Congress Emblems and: No. 3467, Power lines and factories. No. 3468, Ground beetle. No. 3469, Roses and carbon rings.

**1968, May 30**
**3466** A1669 6k blue, dk blue & grn .50 .25
**3467** A1669 6k org, gold & dk brn .50 .25
**3468** A1669 6k red brn, gold & blk .50 .25
**3469** A1669 6k lil rose, org & blk .50 .25
*Nos. 3466-3469 (4)* 2.00 1.00

Intl. congresses, Leningrad: 8th Cong. for Mineral Research; 7th World Power Conf.; 13th Entomological Cong.; 4th Cong. for the Study of Volatile Oils.

**Types of 1966**

Designs as before.

**1968, June 20** **Engr.** ***Perf. 12***
**3470** A1593 1k dk red brown .45 .25
**3471** A1593 2k deep violet .45 .25
**3472** A1593 3k plum .55 .25
**3473** A1593 4k bright red .60 .25
**3474** A1593 6k blue .80 .30
**3475** A1593 10k olive 1.00 .40
**3476** A1593 12k red brown 1.10 .45
**3477** A1593 16k violet blue 1.40 .60

***Perf. 12½***
**3478** A1594 20k red 1.60 .75
**3479** A1594 30k bright green 2.75 .90
**3480** A1594 50k violet blue 5.75 1.10

***Perf. 12x12½***
**3481** A1594 1r gray, red brn & black 8.50 2.75
*Nos. 3470-3481 (12)* 24.95 8.25

Sadriddin Aini A1670

**1968, June 30** **Photo.** ***Perf. 12½x12***
**3482** A1670 4k olive bister & mar .50 .25

Aini (1878-1954), Tadzhik poet.

Post Rider and C.C.E.P. Emblem A1671

#3484, Modern means of communications (train, ship, planes and C.C.E.P. emblem).

**1968, June 30**
**3483** A1671 6k gray & red brown .50 .25
**3484** A1671 6k org brn & bis .50 .25

Annual session of the Council of the Consultative Commission on Postal Investigation of the UPU (C.C.E.P.), Moscow, 9/20-10/5.

Bolshevik Uprising, Kiev — A1672

**1968, July 5** ***Perf. 11½***
**3485** A1672 4k gold, red & plum .50 .25

Ukrainian Communist Party, 50th anniv.

Athletes A1673

**1968, July 9**
**3486** A1673 4k yel, dp car & bis .50 .25

1st Youth Summer Sports Games for 50th anniv. of the Leninist Young Communists League.

Field Ball — A1674

Table Tennis A1675

Designs: 6k, 20th Baltic Regatta. 10k, Soccer player and cup. 12k, Scuba divers.

***Perf. 12x12½, 12½x12***

**1968, July 18** **Litho.**
**3487** A1674 2k red & multi .25 .25
**3488** A1675 4k purple & multi .30 .25
**3489** A1674 6k blue & multi .60 .25
**3490** A1674 10k multicolored .90 .25
**3491** A1675 12k green & multi 1.00 .25
*Nos. 3487-3491 (5)* 3.05 1.25

European youth sports competitions.

Rhythmic Gymnast A1676

6k, Weight lifting. 10k, Rowing. 12k, Women's hurdling. 16k, Fencing. 40k, Running.

**1968, July 31** **Photo.** ***Perf. 11½***
**Gold Background**
**3492** A1676 4k blue & green .30 .25
**3493** A1676 6k dp rose & pur .45 .25
**3494** A1676 10k yel grn & grn .60 .25
**3495** A1676 12k org & red brn .75 .25
**3496** A1676 16k ultra & pink 1.00 .25
*Nos. 3492-3496 (5)* 3.10 1.25

**Souvenir Sheet**

*Perf. 12½x12*

**Lithographed and Photogravure**

**3497** A1676 40k gold, grn, org & gray 3.00 1.00

19th Olympic Games, Mexico City, 10/12-27.

Gediminas Tower, Vilnius — A1677

**1968, Aug. 14 Photo. *Perf. 11½***

**3498** A1677 4k mag, tan & red .50 .25

Soviet power in Lithuania, 50th anniv.

Tbilisi State University A1678

**1968, Aug. 14 *Perf. 12***

**3499** A1678 4k slate grn & lt brn .50 .25

Tbilisi State University, Georgia, 50th anniv.

Laocoon — A1679

**1968, Aug. 16 *Perf. 11½***

**3500** A1679 6k sepia, blk & mar 3.50 .50

"Promote solidarity with Greek democrats."

Red Army Man, Cavalry Charge and Order of the Red Banner of Battle — A1680

Designs: 3k, Young man and woman, Dneprostroi Dam and Order of the Red Banner of Labor. 4k, Soldier, storming of the Reichstag, Berlin, and Order of Lenin. 6k, "Restoration of National Economy" (workers), and Order of Lenin. 10k, Young man and woman cultivating virgin land and Order of Lenin. 50k, like 2k.

**1968, Aug. 25 Litho. *Perf. 12½x12***

**3501** A1680 2k gray, red & ocher .25 .25
**3502** A1680 3k multicolored .50 .25
**3503** A1680 4k org, ocher & rose car .50 .25
**3504** A1680 6k multicolored .75 .25
**3505** A1680 10k olive & multi 1.25 .25
*Nos. 3501-3505 (5)* 3.25 1.25

**Souvenir Sheet**

***Imperf***

**3506** A1680 50k ultra, red & bister 2.00 .50

50th anniv. of the Lenin Young Communist League, Komsomol.

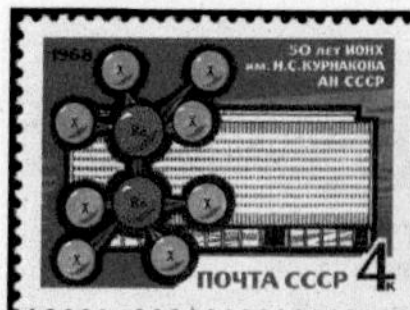

Chemistry Institute and Dimeric Molecule A1681

**1968, Sept. 3 Photo. *Perf. 11½***

**3507** A1681 4k vio bl, dp lil rose & black .50 .25

50th anniversary of Kurnakov Institute for General and Inorganic Chemistry.

Letter, Compass Rose, Ship and Plane A1682

Compass Rose and Stamps of 1921 and 1965 A1683

**1968, Sept. 16 Photo. *Perf. 11½***

**3508** A1682 4k dk car rose, brn & brt red .50 .25
**3509** A1683 4k dk blue, blk & bister .50 .25

No. 3508 for Letter Writing Week, Oct. 7-13, and No. 3509 for Stamp Day and the Day of the Collector.

The 26 Baku Commissars, Sculpture by Merkurov — A1684

**1968, Sept. 20**

**3510** A1684 4k multicolored .50 .25

50th anniversary of the shooting of the 26 Commissars, Baku, Sept. 20, 1918.

Toyvo Antikaynen (1898-1941), Finnish Workers' Organizer — A1685

**1968, Sept. 30 *Perf. 12***

**3511** A1685 6k gray & sepia .60 .25

Russian Merchant Marine Emblem A1686

**1968, Sept. 30 *Perf. 12x11½***

**3512** A1686 6k blue, red & indigo .50 .25

Russian Merchant Marine.

Order of the October Revolution — A1687

**Typographed and Embossed**

**1968, Sept. 30 *Perf. 12x12½***

**3513** A1687 4k gold & multi .50 .25

51st anniv. of the October Revolution. Printed with alternating label.

Pavel P. Postyshev — A1688

Designs: No. 3515, Stepan G. Shaumyan (1878-1918). No. 3516, Akmal Ikramov (1898-1938). No. 3516A, N. G. Markin (1893-1918). No. 3516B, P. E. Dybenko (1889-1938). No. 3516C, S. V. Kosior (1889-1939). No. 3516D, Vasili Kikvidze (1895-1919).

**Size: 21½x32½mm**

**1968-70 Engr. *Perf. 12½x12***

**3514** A1688 4k bluish black .65 .25
**3515** A1688 4k bluish black .65 .25
**3516** A1688 4k gray black .65 .25
**3516A** A1688 4k black .65 .25
**3516B** A1688 4k dark car ('69) .65 .25
**3516C** A1688 4k indigo ('69) .65 .25
**3516D** A1688 4k dk brown ('70) .65 .25
*Nos. 3514-3516D (7)* 4.55 1.75

Honoring outstanding workers for the Communist Party and the Soviet State.

Issued: #3514-3516, 9/30/68; #3516A, 12/31/68; #3516D, 9/24/70; others, 5/15/69.

See #3782.

American Bison and Zebra A1689

Designs: No. 3518, Purple gallinule and lotus. No. 3519, Great white egrets, vert. No. 3520, Ostrich and golden pheasant, vert. No. 3521, Eland and guanaco. No. 3522, European spoonbill and glossy ibis.

***Perf. 12½x12, 12x12½***

**1968, Oct. 16 Litho.**

**3517** A1689 4k ocher, brn & blk .65 .30
**3518** A1689 4k ocher & multi .65 .30
**3519** A1689 6k olive & black .75 .30
**3520** A1689 6k gray & multi .75 .30
**3521** A1689 10k dp grn & multi 1.10 .40
**3522** A1689 10k emerald & multi 1.10 .40
*Nos. 3517-3522 (6)* 5.00 2.00

Askania Nova and Astrakhan state reservations.

Ivan S. Turgenev (1818-83), Writer — A1690

**1968, Oct. 10 Engr. *Perf. 12x12½***

**3523** A1690 4k green 4.50 .50

Warrior, 1880 B.C. and Mt. Ararat — A1691

Design: 12k, David Sasountsi monument, Yerevan, and Mt. Ararat.

**Engraved and Photogravure**

**1968, Oct. 18 *Perf. 11½***

**3524** A1691 4k blk & dk blue, *gray* .35 .25
**3525** A1691 12k dk brn & choc, *bis* .45 .25

Yerevan, capital of Armenia, 2,750th anniv.

First Radio Tube Generator and Laboratory A1692

**1968, Oct. 26 Photo. *Perf. 11½***

**3526** A1692 4k dk bl, dp bis & blk .50 .25

50th anniversary of Russia's first radio laboratory at Gorki (Nizhni Novgorod).

Prospecting Geologist and Crystals A1693

6k, Prospecting for metals: seismographic test apparatus with shock wave diagram, plane, truck. 10k, Oil derrick in the desert.

**1968, Oct. 31 Litho. *Perf. 11½***

**3527** A1693 4k blue & multi .50 .25
**3528** A1693 6k multicolored .30 .25
**3529** A1693 10k multicolored .70 .25
*Nos. 3527-3529 (3)* 1.50 .75

Geology Day. Printed with alternating label.

Borovoe, Kazakhstan — A1694

Landscapes: No. 3531, Djety-Oguz, Kirghizia, vert. No. 3532, Issyk-kul Lake, Kirghizia. No. 3533, Borovoe, Kazakhstan, vert.

***Perf. 12½x12, 12x12½***

**1968, Nov. 20 Typo.**

**3530** A1694 4k dk red brn & multi .35 .25
**3531** A1694 4k gray & multi .35 .25
**3532** A1694 6k dk red brn & multi .35 .25
**3533** A1694 6k black & multi .35 .25
*Nos. 3530-3533 (4)* 1.40 1.00

Recreational areas in the Kazakh and Kirghiz Republics.

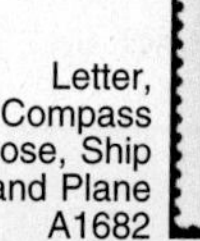

Medals and Cup, Riccione, 1952, 1961 and 1965 — A1695

4k, Medals, Eiffel Tower and Arc de Triomphe, Paris, 1964. 6k, Porcelain plaque, gold medal and Brandenburg Gate, Debria, Berlin, 1950, 1959. 12k, Medal and prize-winning stamp #2888, Buenos Aires. 16k, Cups and medals, Rome, 1952, 1954. 20k, Medals, awards and views, Vienna, 1961, 1965. 30k, Trophies, Prague, 1950, 1955, 1962.

**1968, Nov. 27 Photo. *Perf. 11½x12***

| | | | | |
|---|---|---|---|---|
| **3534** | A1695 4k dp cl, sil & blk | .25 | .25 |
| **3535** | A1695 6k dl bl, gold & blk | .25 | .25 |
| **3536** | A1695 10k lt ultra, gold & blk | .30 | .35 |
| **3537** | A1695 12k blue, sil & blk | .35 | .25 |
| **3538** | A1695 16k red, gold & blk | .55 | .25 |
| **3539** | A1695 20k brt blue, gold & blk | .60 | .25 |
| **3540** | A1695 30k org brn, gold & blk | .90 | .30 |
| | *Nos. 3534-3540 (7)* | 3.20 | 1.90 |

Awards to Soviet post office at foreign stamp exhibitions.

Worker with Banner — A1696

**1968, Nov. 29 *Perf. 12x12½***
**3541** A1696 4k red & black .50 .35

Estonian Workers' Commune, 50th anniv.

V. K. Lebedinsky and Radio Tower — A1697

**1968, Nov. 29 *Perf. 11½x12***
**3542** A1697 4k gray grn, blk & gray .50 .25

V. K. Lebedinsky (1868-1937), scientist.

Souvenir Sheet

Communication via Satellite — A1698

**1968, Nov. 29 Litho. *Perf. 12***

| | | | |
|---|---|---|---|
| **3543** | A1698 Sheet of 3 | 3.00 | .75 |
| ***a.*** | 16k Molniya I | .70 | .25 |
| ***b.*** | 16k Map of Russia | .70 | .25 |
| ***c.*** | 16k Ground Station "Orbite" | .70 | .25 |

Television transmission throughout USSR with the aid of the earth satellite Molniya I.

Sprig, Spasski Tower, Ministry of Foreign Affairs and Library A1699

**1968, Dec. 1 *Perf. 11½***
**3544** A1699 4k ultra, sil, grn & red .25 .30

New Year 1969.

Maj. Gen. Georgy Beregovoi A1700

**1968, Dec. 14 Photo. *Perf. 11½***
**3545** A1700 10k Prus blue, blk & red .50 .25

Flight of Soyuz 3, Oct. 26-30.

Rail-laying and Casting Machines A1701

Soviet railroad transportation: 4k, Railroad map of the Soviet Union and Train.

**1968, Dec. 14 *Perf. 12½x12***
**3546** A1701 4k rose mag & org .60 .25
**3547** A1701 10k brown & emerald .60 .25

Newspaper Banner and Monument A1702

**1968, Dec. 23 *Perf. 11½***
**3548** A1702 4k tan, red & dk brn 1.00 .25

Byelorussian communist party, 50th anniv.

The Reapers, by A. Venetzianov A1703

Knight at the Crossroads, by Viktor M. Vasnetsov — A1704

Paintings: 2k, The Last Day of Pompeii, by Karl P. Bryullov. 4k, Capture of a Town in Winter, by Vasili I. Surikov. 6k, On the Lake, by I.I. Levitan. 10k, Alarm, 1919 (family), by K. Petrov-Vodkin. 16k, Defense of Sevastopol, 1942, by A. Deineka. 20k, Sculptor with a Bust of Homer, by G. Korzhev. 30k, Celebration on Uritsky Square, 1920, by G. Koustodiev. 50k, Duel between Peresvet and Chelubey, by Avilov.

***Perf. 12x12½, 12½***
**1968, Dec. 25 Litho.**

| | | | | |
|---|---|---|---|---|
| **3549** | A1703 1k multicolored | .25 | .25 |
| **3550** | A1704 2k multicolored | .25 | .25 |
| **3551** | A1704 3k multicolored | .25 | .25 |
| **3552** | A1704 4k multicolored | .25 | .25 |
| **3553** | A1704 6k multicolored | .40 | .25 |
| **3554** | A1703 10k multicolored | .70 | .25 |
| **3555** | A1704 16k multicolored | 1.10 | .25 |
| **3556** | A1703 20k multicolored | 1.25 | .25 |
| **3557** | A1704 30k multicolored | 2.00 | .40 |
| **3558** | A1704 50k multicolored | 3.50 | .80 |
| | *Nos. 3549-3558 (10)* | 9.95 | 3.20 |

Russian State Museum, Leningrad.

House, Zaoneje, 1876 — A1705

Russian Architecture: 4k, Carved doors, Gorki Oblast, 1848. 6k, Church, Kizhi Pogost, 1714. 10k, Fortress wall, Rostov-Yaroslav, 16th-17th centuries. 12k, Gate, Tsaritsino, 1785. 16k, Architect Rossi Street, Leningrad.

**1968, Dec. 27 Engr. *Perf. 12x12½***

| | | | |
|---|---|---|---|
| **3559** | A1705 3k dp brown, *ocher* | .35 | .25 |
| **3560** | A1705 4k green, *yellow* | .35 | .25 |
| **3561** | A1705 6k vio, *gray violet* | .60 | .25 |
| **3562** | A1705 10k dl bl, *grnsh gray* | .95 | .30 |
| **3563** | A1705 12k car, *gray* | 1.20 | .40 |
| **3564** | A1705 16k black, *yellowish* | 1.50 | .50 |
| | *Nos. 3559-3564 (6)* | 4.95 | 1.95 |

Banners of Young Communist League, October Revolution Medal — A1707

**1968, Dec. 31 Litho. *Perf. 12***
**3566** A1707 12k red, yel & black .60 .30

Award of Order of October Revolution to the Young Communist League on its 50th anniversary.

Soldiers on Guard — A1708

**1969, Jan. 1 *Perf. 12x12½***
**3567** A1708 4k orange & claret .40 .25

Latvian Soviet Republic, 50th anniv.

Revolutionaries and Monument — A1709

Designs: 4k, Partisans and sword. 6k, Workers and Lenin Medals.

**1969, Jan. Photo. *Perf. 11½***

| | | | |
|---|---|---|---|
| **3568** | A1709 2k ocher & rose clar | .30 | .25 |
| **3569** | A1709 4k ocher & red | .30 | .25 |
| **3570** | A1709 6k dk ol, mag & red | .30 | .25 |
| | *Nos. 3568-3570 (3)* | .90 | .75 |

Byelorussian Soviet Republic, 50th anniv.

Souvenir Sheet

Vladimir Shatalov, Boris Volynov, Alexei S. Elisseyev, Evgeny Khrunov — A1710

**1969, Jan. 22 *Imperf.***
**3571** A1710 50k dp bis & dk brn 2.00 .75

1st team flights of Soyuz 4 and 5, 1/16/69.

Leningrad University A1711

**1969, Jan. 23 Photo. *Perf. 12½x12***
**3572** A1711 10k black & maroon .40 .25

University of Leningrad, 150th anniv.

Ivan A. Krylov (1769?-1844), Fable Writer — A1712

**1969, Feb. 13 Litho. *Perf. 12x12½***
**3573** A1712 4k black & multi .50 .30

Nikolai Filchenkov A1713

Designs: No. 3575, Alexander Kosmodemiansky. No. 3575A, Otakar Yarosh, member of Czechoslovak Svoboda Battalion.

**1969 Photo.**

| | | | |
|---|---|---|---|
| **3574** | A1713 4k dl rose & blk | .25 | .25 |
| **3575** | A1713 4k emer & dk brn | .25 | .25 |
| **3575A** | A1713 4k blue & black | .25 | .25 |
| | *Nos. 3574-3575A (3)* | .75 | .75 |

Heroes of World War II. Issued: #3575A, May 9; others, Feb. 23.

"Shoulder to the Wheel," Parliament, Budapest A1714

Design: "Shoulder to the Wheel" is a sculpture by Zigmond Kisfaludi-Strobl.

**1969, Mar. 21 Typo. *Perf. 11½***
**3576** A1714 6k black, ver & lt grn .50 .25

Hungarian Soviet Republic, 50th anniv.

Oil Refinery and Salavat Tualeyev Monument — A1715

**1969, Mar. 22 Litho. *Perf. 12***
**3577** A1715 4k multicolored .40 .25

50th anniv. of the Bashkir Autonomous Socialist Republic.

Sergei P. Korolev, Sputnik 1, Space Monument, Moscow — A1716

Vostok on Launching Pad — A1717

Natl. Cosmonauts' Day: No. 3579, Zond 2 orbiting moon, and photograph of earth made by Zond 5. 80k, Spaceship Soyuz 3.

***Perf. 12½x12, 12x12½***
**1969, Apr. 12 Litho.**

| | | | | |
|---|---|---|---|---|
| **3578** | A1716 | 10k black, vio & grn | .65 | .25 |
| **3579** | A1716 | 10k dk brn, yel & brn red | .65 | .25 |
| **3580** | A1717 | 10k multicolored | .65 | .25 |
| | | *Nos. 3578-3580 (3)* | 1.95 | .75 |

**Souvenir Sheet**
***Perf. 12***

**3581** A1716 80k vio, green & red 2.00 .75

No. 3581 contains one 37x24mm stamp.

Lenin University, Kazan, and Kremlin A1718

Lenin House, Kuibyshev A1718a

Lenin House, Pskov A1718b

Lenin House, Shushensko — A1718c

Smolny Institute, Leningrad A1718d

Places Connected with Lenin: #3586, Straw Hut, Razliv. #3587, Lenin Museum, Gorki. #3589, Lenin's room, Kremlin. #3590, Lenin Museum, Ulyanovsk. #3591, Lenin House, Ulyanovsk.

**1969 Photo. *Perf. 11½***

| | | | | |
|---|---|---|---|---|
| **3582** | A1718 | 4k pale rose & multi | .35 | .25 |
| **3583** | A1718a | 4k beige & multi | .35 | .25 |
| **3584** | A1718b | 4k bis brn & multi | .35 | .25 |
| **3585** | A1718c | 4k gray vio & multi | .35 | .25 |
| **3586** | A1718 | 4k violet & multi | .35 | .25 |
| **3587** | A1718 | 4k blue & multi | .35 | .25 |
| **3588** | A1718d | 4k brick red & multi | .35 | .25 |
| **3589** | A1718 | 4k rose red & multi | .35 | .25 |
| **3590** | A1718 | 4k lt red brn & multi | .35 | .25 |
| **3591** | A1718 | 4k dull grn & multi | .35 | .25 |
| | | *Nos. 3582-3591 (10)* | 3.50 | 2.50 |

99th anniv. of the birth of Lenin.

Telephone, Transistor Radio and Trademark — A1719

**1969, Apr. 25 *Perf. 12½x12***
**3592** A1719 10k sepia & dp org .50 .25

50th anniversary of VEF Electrical Co.

ILO Emblem and Globe — A1720

**1969, May 9 *Perf. 11***
**3593** A1720 6k car rose & gold .40 .25

50th anniversary of the ILO.

Suleiman Stalsky A1721

**1969, May 15 Photo. *Perf. 12½x12***
**3595** A1721 4k tan & ol green .40 .25

Stalsky (1869-1937), Dagestan poet.

Yasnaya Polyana Rose A1722

4k, "Stroynaya" lily. 10k, Cattleya orchid. 12k, "Listopad" dahlia. 14k, "Ural Girl" gladioli.

**1969, May 15 Litho. *Perf. 11½***

| | | | | |
|---|---|---|---|---|
| **3596** | A1722 | 2k multicolored | .25 | .25 |
| **3597** | A1722 | 4k multicolored | .45 | .25 |
| **3598** | A1722 | 10k multicolored | 1.10 | .25 |
| **3599** | A1722 | 12k multicolored | 1.40 | .25 |
| **3600** | A1722 | 14k multicolored | 1.50 | .25 |
| | | *Nos. 3596-3600 (5)* | 4.70 | 1.25 |

Work of the Botanical Gardens of the Academy of Sciences.

Ukrainian Academy of Sciences A1723

**1969, May 22 Photo. *Perf. 12½x12***
**3601** A1723 4k brown & yellow .50 .25

Ukrainian Academy of Sciences, 50th anniv.

Film, Camera and Medal A1724

Ballet Dancers A1725

**1969, June 3 Litho. *Perf. 12x12½***

| | | | | |
|---|---|---|---|---|
| **3602** | A1724 | 6k rose car, blk & gold | .30 | .25 |
| **3603** | A1725 | 6k dk brown & multi | .30 | .25 |

Intl. Film Festival in Moscow, and 1st Intl. Young Ballet Artists' Competitions.

Congress Emblem and Cell Division — A1726

**1969, June 10 Photo. *Perf. 11½***
**3605** A1726 6k dp clar, lt bl & yel .50 .30

Protozoologists, 3rd Intl. Cong., Leningrad.

Estonian Singer and Festival Emblem — A1727

**1969, June 14 *Perf. 12x12½***
**3606** A1727 4k ver & bister .90 .25

Centenary of the Estonian Song Festival.

Mendeleev and Formula with Author's Corrections — A1728

30k, Dmitri Ivanovich Mendeleev, vert.

**Engraved and Lithographed**
**1969, June 20 *Perf. 12***
**3607** A1728 6k brown & rose .90 .30

**Souvenir Sheet**

**3608** A1728 30k carmine rose 5.00 1.25

Cent. of the Periodic Law (classification of elements), formulated by Dimitri I. Mendeleev (1834-1907). No. 3608 contains one engraved 29x37mm stamp.

Hand Holding Peace Banner and World Landmarks A1729

**1969, June 20 Photo. *Perf. 11½***
**3609** A1729 10k bl, dk brn & gold .40 .25

20th anniversary of the Peace Movement.

Laser Beam Guiding Moon Rocket — A1730

**1969, June 20**
**3610** A1730 4k silver, black & red .50 .25

Soviet scientific inventions, 50th anniv.

Ivan Kotlyarevski (1769-1838), Ukrainian Writer — A1731

**Typographed and Photogravure**
**1969, June 25 *Perf. 12½x12***
**3611** A1731 4k blk, olive & lt brn .50 .25

No. 2717 Overprinted in Vermilion

**1969, June 25 Photo. *Perf. 11½***
**3612** A1306 6k Prus blue & plum 4.00 1.50

Soviet victory in the Ice Hockey World Championships, Stockholm, 1969.

"Hill of Glory" Monument and Minsk Battle Map A1732

**1969, July 3 Litho. *Perf. 12x12½***
**3613** A1732 4k red & olive .40 .25

25th anniv. of the liberation of Byelorussia from the Germans.

Eagle, Flag and Map of Poland A1733

No. 3615, Hands holding torch, flags of Bulgaria, USSR, Bulgarian coat of arms.

**1969, July 10 Photo. *Perf. 12***
**3614** A1733 6k red & bister .60 .25

**Litho.**

**3615** A1733 6k bis, red, grn & blk .60 .25

25th anniv. of the Polish Republic; liberation of Bulgaria from the Germans.

Monument to 68 Heroes — A1734

**1969, July 15 Photo. *Perf. 12***
**3616** A1734 4k red & maroon .50 .30

25th anniversary of the liberation of Nikolayev from the Germans.

Old Samarkand A1735

Design: 6k, Intourist Hotel, Samarkand.

**1969, July 15 Typo.**
**3617** A1735 4k multicolored .35 .25
**3618** A1735 6k multicolored .35 .25

2500th anniversary of Samarkand.

Volleyball — A1736

Design: 6k, Kayak race.

**Photogravure and Engraved**

**1969, July 20 *Perf. 11½***
**3619** A1736 4k dp org & red brn .35 .25
**3620** A1736 6k multicolored .35 .25

Championships: European Junior Volleyball; European Rowing.

Munkascy & "Woman Churning Butter" — A1737

**1969, July 20 Photo.**
**3621** A1737 6k dk brn, blk & org .40 .25

Mihaly von Munkascy (1844-1900), Hungarian painter.

Miners' Monument A1738

**1969, July 30**
**3622** A1738 4k silver & magenta .40 .25

Centenary of the founding of the city of Donetsk, in the Donets coal basin.

Machine Gun Cart, by Mitrofan Grekov — A1739

**1969, July 30 Engr. *Perf. 12½x12***
**3623** A1739 4k red brn & brn red 1.00 .25

First Mounted Army, 50th anniv.

Barge Pullers Along the Volga, by Repin — A1740

Ilya E. Repin (1844-1930), Self-portrait A1741

Repin Paintings: 6k, "Not Expected." 12k, Confession. 16k, Dnieper Cossacks.

***Perf. 12½x12, 12x12½***

**1969, Aug. 5 Litho.**
**3624** A1740 4k multicolored .75 .25
**3625** A1740 6k multicolored .75 .25
**3626** A1741 10k bis, red brn & blk 1.00 .25
**3627** A1740 12k multicolored 1.50 .25
**3628** A1740 16k multicolored 2.00 .25
*Nos. 3624-3628 (5)* 6.00 1.25

Runner — A1742

Design: 10k, Athlete on rings.

**1969, Aug. 9 *Perf. 12x12½***
**3629** A1742 4k red, green & blk .30 .25
**3630** A1742 10k grn, lt bl & blk .30 .25

**Souvenir Sheet**

***Imperf***

**3631** A1742 20k red, bister & blk 2.50 .60

9th Trade Union Spartakiad, Moscow.

Komarov — A1743

**1969, Aug. 22 Photo. *Perf. 12x11½***
**3632** A1743 4k olive & brown .40 .25

V. L. Komarov (1869-1945), botanist.

Hovannes Tumanian, Armenian Landscape — A1744

**1969, Sept. 1 Typo. *Perf. 12½x12***
**3633** A1744 10k blk & peacock blue 1.50 .25

Tumanian (1869-1923), Armenian poet.

Turkmenian Wine Horn, 2nd Century — A1745

Designs: 6k, Persian Simurg vessel (giant anthropomorphic bird), 13th century. 12k, Head of goddess Kannon, Korea, 8th century. 16k, Bodhisattva, Tibet, 7th century. 20k, Statue of Ebisu and fish (tai), Japan, 17th century.

**1969, Sept. 3 Litho. *Perf. 12x12½***
**3634** A1745 4k blue & multi .25 .25
**3635** A1745 6k lilac & multi .25 .25
**3636** A1745 12k red & multi .40 .25
**3637** A1745 16k blue vio & multi .55 .25
**3638** A1745 20k pale grn & multi .70 .30
*Nos. 3634-3638 (5)* 2.15 1.30

Treasures from the State Museum of Oriental Art.

Mahatma Gandhi (1869-1948) A1746

**1969, Sept. 10 Engr.**
**3639** A1746 6k deep brown .90 .35

Black Stork Feeding Young A1747

Belovezhskaya Forest reservation: 6k, Doe and fawn (red deer). 10k, Fighting bison. 12k, Lynx and cubs. 16k, Wild pig and piglets.

**1969, Sept. 10 Photo. *Perf. 12***
**Size: 75x23mm, 10k; 35x23mm, others**

**3640** A1747 4k blk, yel grn & red .50 .25
**3641** A1747 6k blue grn, dk brn & ocher .75 .25
**3642** A1747 10k dk brn, dull org & dp org 1.50 .25
**3643** A1747 12k dk & yel green, brn & gray 1.50 .25
**3644** A1747 16k gray, yel grn & dk brown 2.00 .25
*Nos. 3640-3644 (5)* 6.25 1.25

Komitas A1748

**1969, Sept. 18 Typo. *Perf. 12½x12***
**3645** A1748 6k blk, gray & sal .50 .30

Komitas (S. N. Sogomonian, 1869-1935), Armenian composer.

Lisa Chaikina A1749

A. Cheponis, J. Aleksonis and G. Borisa A1750

#3647, Major S. I. Gritsevets & fighter planes.

**1969, Sept. 20 Photo. *Perf. 12½x12***
**3646** A1749 4k olive & brt green .35 .25
**3647** A1749 4k gray & black .35 .25

*Perf. 11½*

**3648** A1750 4k hn brn, brn & buff .35 .25
*Nos. 3646-3648 (3)* 1.05 .75

Heroes of the Soviet Union.

Ivan Petrovich Pavlov (1849-1936), Physiologist A1751

**1969, Sept. 26**

**3649** A1751 4k multicolored .50 .25

East German Arms, TV Tower and Brandenburg Gate — A1752

**1969, Oct. 7 Litho. *Perf. 12***

**3650** A1752 6k red, black & yel .60 .25

German Democratic Republic, 20th anniv.

Aleksei Vasilievich Koltsov (1809-42), Poet — A1753

**1969, Oct. 14 Photo. *Perf. 12x12½***

**3652** A1753 4k lt blue & brown .50 .25

National Emblem A1754

**1969, Oct. 14 *Perf. 12x11½***

**3653** A1754 4k gold & red .50 .30

25th anniversary of the liberation of the Ukraine from the Nazis.

Stars, Hammer and Sickle A1755

**1969, Oct. 21 Typo. *Perf. 11½***

**3654** A1755 4k vio blue, gold, yel & red .50 .25

52nd anniversary of October Revolution.

Georgy Shonin and Valery Kubasov A1756

Designs: No. 3656, Anatoly Filipchenko, Vladislav Volkov and Viktor Gorbatko. No. 3657, Vladimir Shatalov and Alexey Elisyev.

**1969, Oct. 22 Photo. *Perf. 12½x12***

**3655** A1756 10k black & gold .65 .25
**3656** A1756 10k black & gold .65 .25
**3657** A1756 10k black & gold .65 .25
*a.* Strip of 3, #3655-3657 2.00 .60

Group flight of the space ships Soyuz 6, Soyuz 7 and Soyuz 8, Oct. 11-13.

Lenin as a Youth A1757

**1969, Oct. 25 Engr. *Perf. 11½***

**3658** A1757 4k dark red, *pink* .50 .25

1st Soviet Youth Philatelic Exhibition, Kiev, dedicated to Lenin's 100th birthday.

Emblem of Communications Unit of Army — A1758

**1969, Oct. 30 Photo.**

**3659** A1758 4k dk red, red & bister .50 .25

50th anniversary of the Communications Troops of Soviet Army.

Souvenir Sheet

Lenin and Quotation — A1759

**Lithographed and Embossed**

**1969, Nov. 6 *Imperf.***

**3660** A1759 50k red, gold & pink 3.00 .75

52nd anniv. of the October Revolution.

Cover of "Rules of the Kolkhoz" and Farm Woman's Monument — A1760

**1969, Nov. 18 Photo. *Perf. 12½x12***

**3661** A1760 4k brown & gold .50 .25

3rd All Union Collective Farmers' Congress, Moscow, Nov.-Dec.

Vasilissa, the Beauty, by Ivan Y. Bilibin A1761

Designs (Book Illustrations by Ivan Y. Bilibin): 10k, Marya Morevna. 16k, Finist, the Fine Fellow, horiz. 20k, Tale of the Golden Cockerel. 50k, The Tale of Tsar Sultan. The inscriptions on the 16k and 20k are transposed. 4k, 10k, 16k are fairy tales; 20k and 50k are tales by Pushkin.

**1969, Nov. 20 Litho. *Perf. 12***

**3662** A1761 4k gray & multi .25 .25
**3663** A1761 10k gray & multi .60 .50
**3664** A1761 16k gray & multi .75 .75
**3665** A1761 20k gray & multi .85 .85
**3666** A1761 50k gray & multi 3.00 1.40
*a.* Strip of 5, #3662-3666 6.50 5.50

Illustrator and artist Ivan Y. Bilibin.

USSR Emblems Dropped on Venus, Radar Installation and Orbits A1762

6k, Interplanetary station, space capsule, orbits.

**1969, Nov. 25 Photo. *Perf. 12x11½***

**3667** A1762 4k bis, blk & red .35 .25
**3668** A1762 6k gray, lil rose & blk .35 .25

Completion of the fights of the space stations Venera 5 and Venera 6.

Flags of USSR and Afghanistan — A1763

**1969, Nov. 30 Photo. *Perf. 11½***

**3669** A1763 6k red, blk & grn .50 .25

50th anniversary of diplomatic relations between Russia and Afghanistan.

Russian State Emblem and Star — A1764

**Coil Stamp**

**1969, Nov. 13 *Perf. 11x11½***

**3670** A1764 4k red 2.00 .30

MiG Jet and First MiG Fighter Plane — A1765

**1969, Dec. 12 *Perf. 11½x12***

**3671** A1765 6k red, black & gray .60 .25

Soviet aircraft builders.

Lenin and Flag A1766

**Typographed and Lithographed**

**1969, Dec. 25 *Perf. 11½***

**3672** A1766 4k gold, blue, red & blk .40 .25

Happy New Year 1970, birth cent. of Lenin.

Antonov 2 — A1767

Aircraft: 3k, PO-2. 4k, ANT-9. 6k, TsAGI 1-EA. 10k, ANT-20 "Maxim Gorki." 12k, Tupolev-104. 16k, Mi-10 helicopter. 20k, Ilyushin-62. 50k, Tupolev-144.

**Photogravure and Engraved**

**1969 *Perf. 11½x12***

**3673** A1767 2k bister & multi .25 .25
**3674** A1767 3k multicolored .25 .25
**3675** A1767 4k multicolored .25 .25
**3676** A1767 6k multicolored .30 .25
**3677** A1767 10k lt vio & multi .50 .25
**3678** A1767 12k multicolored .70 .25
**3679** A1767 16k multicolored .85 .25
**3680** A1767 20k multicolored .90 .25
*Nos. 3673-3680 (8)* 4.00 2.00

**Souvenir Sheet**

***Imperf***

**3681** A1767 50k blue & multi 3.00 1.00

History of national aeronautics and aviation. No. 3681 margin contains signs of the zodiac, partly overlapping the stamp.

Issued: #3679, 3681, 12/31; others 12/25.

Photograph of Earth by Zond 7 — A1768

Designs: No. 3683a, same as 10k. No. 3683b, Photograph of moon.

**1969, Dec. 26 Photo. *Perf. 12x11½***

**3682** A1768 10k black & multi .40 .30

**Souvenir Sheet**

**Litho.** ***Imperf.***

| | | | |
|---|---|---|---|
| **3683** | Sheet of 2 | 4.00 | 1.50 |
| *a.* | A1768 50k indigo & multi | 1.65 | .90 |
| *b.* | A1768 50k dark brown & multi | 1.65 | .90 |

Space explorations of the automatic stations Zond 6, Nov. 10-17, 1968, and Zond 7, Aug. 8-14, 1969. No. 3683 contains 27x40mm stamps with simulated perforations.

Model Aircraft — A1769

Technical Sports: 4k, Motorboats. 6k, Parachute jumping.

**1969, Dec. 26 Engr.** ***Perf. 12½x12***

| | | | |
|---|---|---|---|
| **3684** | A1769 3k bright magenta | .45 | .25 |
| **3685** | A1769 4k dull blue green | .45 | .25 |
| **3686** | A1769 6k red orange | .45 | .25 |
| | *Nos. 3684-3686 (3)* | 1.35 | .75 |

Romanian Arms and Soviet War Memorial, Bucharest A1770

**1969, Dec. 31 Photo.** ***Perf. 11½***

**3687** A1770 6k rose red & brown .60 .35

25th anniversary of Romania's liberation from fascist rule.

Ostankino Television Tower, Moscow A1771

**1969, Dec. 31 Typo.** ***Perf. 12***

**3688** A1771 10k multicolored 1.00 .35

Conversation with Lenin, by A. Shirokov (in front of red table) — A1772

Paintings: No. 3689, Lenin, by N. Andreyev. No. 3690, Lenin at Marxist Meeting, St. Petersburg, by A. Moravov (behind table). No. 3691, Lenin at Second Party Congress, by Y. Vinogradov (next to table). No. 3692, First Day of Soviet Power, by N. Babasyuk (leading crowd). No. 3694, Farmers' Delegation Meeting Lenin, by F. Modorov (seated at desk). No. 3695, With Lenin, by V. A. Serov (with cap, in background). No. 3696, Lenin on May 1, 1920, by I. Brodsky (with cap, in foreground). No. 3697, Builder of Communism, by a group of painters (in red). No. 3698, Mastery of Space, by A. Deyneka (rockets).

**1970, Jan. 1 Litho.** ***Perf. 12***

| | | | |
|---|---|---|---|
| **3689** | A1772 4k multicolored | .35 | .25 |
| **3690** | A1772 4k multicolored | .35 | .25 |
| **3691** | A1772 4k multicolored | .35 | .25 |
| **3692** | A1772 4k multicolored | .35 | .25 |
| **3693** | A1772 4k multicolored | .35 | .25 |
| **3694** | A1772 4k multicolored | .35 | .25 |
| **3695** | A1772 4k multicolored | .35 | .25 |
| **3696** | A1772 4k multicolored | .35 | .25 |
| **3697** | A1772 4k multicolored | .35 | .25 |
| **3698** | A1772 4k multicolored | .35 | .25 |
| | *Nos. 3689-3698 (10)* | 3.50 | 2.50 |

Centenary of birth of Lenin (1870-1924).

Map of Antarctic, "Mirny" and "Vostok" A1773

Design: 16k, Camp and map of the Antarctic with Soviet Antarctic bases.

**1970, Jan. 27 Photo.** ***Perf. 11½***

| | | | |
|---|---|---|---|
| **3699** | A1773 4k multicolored | .30 | .25 |
| **3700** | A1773 16k multicolored | 1.50 | .25 |

150th anniversary of the Bellingshausen-Lazarev Antarctic expedition.

F. W. Sychkov and "Tobogganing" — A1774

**1970, Jan. 27** ***Perf. 12½x12***

**3701** A1774 4k sepia & vio blue .50 .25

F. W. Sychkov (1870-1958), painter.

Col. V. B. Borsoyev A1775

Design: No. 3703, Sgt. V. Peshekhonov.

**1970, Feb. 10** ***Perf. 12x12½***

| | | | |
|---|---|---|---|
| **3702** | A1775 4k brown olive & brn | .30 | .25 |
| **3703** | A1775 4k dark gray & plum | .30 | .25 |

Heroes of the Soviet Union.

Geographical Society Emblem and Globes — A1776

**1970, Feb. 26 Photo.** ***Perf. 11½***

**3704** A1776 6k bis, Prus bl & dk brn .50 .30

Russian Geographical Society, 125th anniv.

Torch of Peace — A1777

**1970, Mar. 3 Litho.** ***Perf. 12***

**3705** A1777 6k blue green & tan .50 .25

Intl. Women's Solidarity Day, Mar. 8.

Symbols of Russian Arts and Crafts — A1778

Lenin — A1779

Designs: 6k, Russian EXPO '70 pavilion. 10k, Boy holding model ship.

**1970, Mar. 10 Photo.** ***Perf. 11½***

| | | | |
|---|---|---|---|
| **3706** | A1778 4k dk blue grn, red & black | .25 | .25 |
| **3707** | A1778 6k blk, silver & red | .25 | .25 |
| **3708** | A1778 10k vio bl, sil & red | .25 | .25 |
| | *Nos. 3706-3708 (3)* | .75 | .75 |

**Souvenir Sheet**

**Engr. & Litho.**

***Perf. 12x12½***

**3709** A1779 50k dark red 2.00 1.00

EXPO '70 Intl. Exhibition, Osaka, Japan, 3/15-4/13.

Lenin — A1780

**1970, Mar. 14 Photo.** ***Perf. 11½***

**3710** A1780 4k red, blk & gold .50 .30

**Souvenir Sheet**

**Photogravure and Embossed**

***Imperf***

**3711** A1780 20k red, blk & gold 5.00 2.00

USSR Philatelic Exhibition dedicated to the centenary of the birth of Lenin.

Friendship Tree, Sochi — A1781

**1970, Mar. 18 Litho.** ***Perf. 11½***

**3712** A1781 10k multicolored .50 .30

Friendship among people. Printed with alternating label.

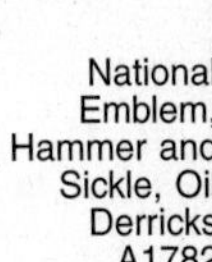

National Emblem, Hammer and Sickle, Oil Derricks A1782

**1970, Mar. 18 Photo.** ***Perf. 11½***

**3713** A1782 4k dk car rose & gold .75 .25

Azerbaijan Republic, 50th anniversary.

Ice Hockey Players A1783

**1970, Mar. 18**

**3714** A1783 6k blue & slate green .35 .25

World Ice Hockey Championships, Sweden.

Overprinted in Red

**1970, Apr. 1 Photo.** ***Perf. 11½***

**3715** A1783 6k blue & slate green 1.00 .25

Soviet hockey players as the tenfold world champions.

D. N. Medvedev A1784

Portrait: No. 3717, K. P. Orlovsky.

**1970, Mar. 26 Engr.** ***Perf. 12x12½***

| | | | |
|---|---|---|---|
| **3716** | A1784 4k chocolate | .30 | .25 |
| **3717** | A1784 4k dk redsh brown | .30 | .25 |

Heroes of the Soviet Union.

Worker, Books, Globes and UNESCO Symbol A1785

**1970, Mar. 26 Photo.** ***Perf. 12½x12***

**3718** A1785 6k car lake & ocher .50 .25

UNESCO-sponsored Lenin Symposium, Tampere, Finland, Apr. 6-10.

Hungarian Arms, Budapest Landmarks A1786

**1970, Apr. 4 Typo. *Perf. 11½***
**3719** A1786 6k multicolored .50 .25

Liberation of Hungary, 25th anniv.
See No. 3738.

Cosmonauts' Emblem A1787

**1970, Apr. 12 Litho. *Perf. 11½***
**3720** A1787 6k buff & multi .50 .25

Cosmonauts' Day.

Lenin, 1891 — A1788

Designs: Various portraits of Lenin.

**Lithographed and Typographed**

**1970, Apr. 15 *Perf. 12x12½***

| | | | | |
|---|---|---|---|---|
| **3721** | A1788 | 2k green & gold | .25 | .25 |
| **3722** | A1788 | 2k ol gray & gold | .25 | .25 |
| **3723** | A1788 | 4k vio blue & gold | .25 | .25 |
| **3724** | A1788 | 4k lake & gold | .25 | .25 |
| **3725** | A1788 | 6k red brn & gold | .25 | .25 |
| **3726** | A1788 | 6k lake & gold | .25 | .25 |
| **3727** | A1788 | 10k dk brn & gold | .25 | .25 |
| **3728** | A1788 | 10k dk rose brn & gold | .35 | .25 |
| **3729** | A1788 | 12k blk, sil & gold | .45 | .25 |

**Photo.**

| | | | | |
|---|---|---|---|---|
| **3730** | A1788 | 12k red & gold | .45 | .25 |
| | | *Nos. 3721-3730 (10)* | 3.00 | 2.50 |

**Souvenir Sheet**

**1970, Apr. 22 Litho. & Typo.**
**3731** A1788 20k blk, silver & gold 3.00 1.50

Cent. of the birth of Lenin. Issued in sheets of 8 stamps surrounded by 16 labels showing Lenin-connected buildings, books, coats of arms and medals. Value, $50. No. 3731 contains one stamp in same design as No. 3729.

Order of Victory — A1789

Designs: 2k, Monument to the Unknown Soldier, Moscow. 3k, Victory Monument, Berlin-Treptow. 4k, Order of the Great Patriotic War. 10k, Gold Star of the Order of Hero of the Soviet Union and Medal of Socialist Labor. 30k, Like 1k.

**1970, May 8 Photo. *Perf. 11½***

| | | | | |
|---|---|---|---|---|
| **3732** | A1789 | 1k red lil, gold & gray | .25 | .25 |
| **3733** | A1789 | 2k dark brn, gold & red | .25 | .25 |
| **3734** | A1789 | 3k dark brn, gold & red | .40 | .25 |
| **3735** | A1789 | 4k dark brn, gold & red | .70 | .25 |
| **3736** | A1789 | 10k red lil, gold & red | 1.40 | .25 |
| | | *Nos. 3732-3736 (5)* | 3.00 | 1.25 |

**Souvenir Sheet**

***Imperf***

**3737** A1789 30k dk red, gold & gray 2.00 .60

25th anniv. of victory in WWII. No. 3737 has simulated perforations.

**Arms-Landmark Type of 1970**

Czechoslovakia arms and view of Prague.

**1970, May 8 Typo. *Perf. 12½***
**3738** A1786 6k dk brown & multi .50 .25

25th anniversary of the liberation of Czechoslovakia from the Germans.

Young Fighters, and Youth Federation Emblem A1791

**1970, May 20 Litho. *Perf. 12***
**3739** A1791 6k blue & black .50 .25

25th anniversary of the World Federation of Democratic Youth.

Lenin A1792

**1970, May 20 Photo. *Perf. 11½***
**3740** A1792 6k red .50 .25

Intl. Youth Meeting dedicated to the cent. of the birth of Lenin, UN, NY, June 1970.

Komsomol Emblem with Lenin — A1793

**1970, May 20 Litho. *Perf. 12***
**3741** A1793 4k red, yel & purple .50 .25

16th Congress of the Young Communist League, May 26-30.

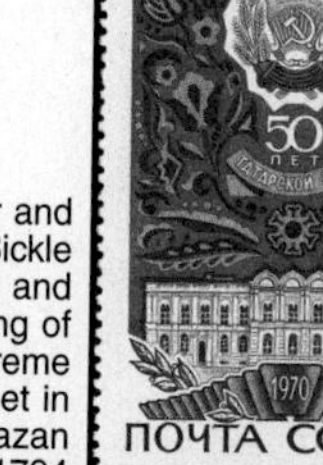


Hammer and Sickle Emblem and Building of Supreme Soviet in Kazan A1794

No. 3744

No. 3744B

No. 3744C

Designs (Hammer-Sickle Emblem and Supreme Soviet Building in): No. 3743, Petrozavodsk. No. 3744, Cheboksary. No. 3744A, Elista. No. 3744B, Izhevsk. No. 3744C, Yoshkar-Ola.

**1970 Engr. *Perf. 12x12½***

| | | | | |
|---|---|---|---|---|
| **3742** | A1794 | 4k violet blue | .50 | .25 |
| **3743** | A1794 | 4k green | .50 | .25 |
| **3744** | A1794 | 4k dark carmine | .50 | .25 |
| **3744A** | A1794 | 4k red | .50 | .25 |
| **3744B** | A1794 | 4k dark green | .50 | .25 |
| **3744C** | A1794 | 4k dark carmine | .50 | .25 |
| | | *Nos. 3742-3744C (6)* | 3.00 | 1.50 |

50th annivs. of the Tatar (#3742), Karelian (#3743), Chuvash (#3744), Kalmyk (#3744A), Udmurt (#3744B) and Mari (#3744C) autonomous SSRs.

Issued: #3742, 5/27; #3743, 6/5; #3744, 6/24; #3744A-3744B, 10/22; #3744C, 11/4.

See Nos. 3814-3823, 4286, 4806.

9th World Soccer Championships for the Jules Rimet Cup, Mexico City, May 29-June 21 — A1795

10k, Woman athlete on balancing bar.

**1970, May 31 Photo. *Perf. 11½***

| | | | | |
|---|---|---|---|---|
| **3745** | A1795 | 10k lt gray & brt rose | .40 | .25 |
| **3746** | A1795 | 16k dk grn & org brn | .65 | .25 |

17th World Gymnastics Championships, Ljubljana, Oct. 22-27 (#3745).

Sword into Plowshare Statue, UN, NY — A1796

**1970, June 1 Litho. *Perf. 12x12½***
**3747** A1796 12k gray & lake .50 .25

25th anniversary of the United Nations.

Soyuz 9, Andrian Nikolayev, Vitaly Sevastyanov A1797

**1970, June 7 Photo. *Perf. 12x11½***
**3748** A1797 10k multicolored .50 .25

424 hour space flight of Soyuz 9, June 1-19.

Friedrich Engels A1798

**1970, June 16 Engr. *Perf. 12x12½***
**3749** A1798 4k chocolate & ver .50 .25

Friedrich Engels (1820-1895), German socialist, collaborator with Karl Marx.

Armenian Woman and Symbols of Agriculture and Industry A1799

Design: No. 3751, Kazakh woman and symbols of agriculture and industry.

**1970, June 16 Photo. *Perf. 11½***

| | | | | |
|---|---|---|---|---|
| **3750** | A1799 | 4k red brn & silver | .30 | .30 |
| **3751** | A1799 | 4k brt rose lilac & gold | .30 | .30 |

50th anniv. of the Armenian & Kazakh Soviet Socialist Republics.

Missile Cruiser "Grozny" — A1800

Soviet Warships: 3k, Cruiser "Aurora." 10k, Cruiser "October Revolution." 12k, Missile cruiser "Varyag." 20k, Atomic submarine "Leninsky Komsomol."

**1970, July 26 Photo. *Perf. 11½x12***

| | | | | |
|---|---|---|---|---|
| **3752** | A1800 | 3k lilac, pink & blk | .25 | .25 |
| **3753** | A1800 | 4k yellow & black | .25 | .25 |
| **3754** | A1800 | 10k rose & black | .45 | .25 |
| **3755** | A1800 | 12k buff & dk brown | .45 | .25 |
| **3756** | A1800 | 20k blue grn, dk brn & vio blue | .90 | .25 |
| | | *Nos. 3752-3756 (5)* | 2.30 | 1.25 |

Navy Day.

Soviet and Polish Workers and Flags — A1801

**1970, July 26 *Perf. 12***
**3757** A1801 6k red & slate .50 .25

25th anniversary of the Treaty of Friendship, Collaboration and Mutual Assistance between USSR and Poland.

"History," Petroglyphs, Sputnik and Emblem — A1802

**1970, Aug. 16 *Perf. 11½***
**3758** A1802 4k red brn, buff & blue .50 .25

13th International Congress of Historical Sciences in Moscow.

Mandarin Ducks A1803

Animals from the Sikhote-Alin Reserve: 6k, Pine marten. 10k, Asiatic black bear, vert. 16k, Red deer. 20k, Ussurian tiger.

*Perf. 12½x12, 12x12½*

**1970, Aug. 19** **Litho.**

**3759** A1803 4k multicolored .55 .25
**3760** A1803 6k multicolored .65 .25
**3761** A1803 10k multicolored .80 .30
**3762** A1803 16k ultra & multi 1.25 .45
**3763** A1803 20k gray & multi 1.75 .60
*Nos. 3759-3763 (5)* 5.00 1.85

Magnifying Glass over Stamp, and Covers — A1804

**1970, Aug. 31** **Photo.** ***Perf. 12x12½***

**3764** A1804 4k red & silver .50 .25

2nd All-Union Philatelists' Cong., Moscow.

Pioneers' Badge — A1805

Soviet general education: 2k, Lenin and Children, monument. 4k, Star and scenes from play "Zarnitsa."

**1970, Sept. 24** **Photo.** ***Perf. 11½***

**3765** A1805 1k gray, red & gold .35 .25
**3766** A1805 2k brn red & slate grn .35 .25
**3767** A1805 4k lt ol, car & gold .35 .25
*Nos. 3765-3767 (3)* 1.05 .75

Yerevan University A1806

**1970, Sept. 24** **Photo.** ***Perf. 12½x12***

**3768** A1806 4k ultra & salmon pink .50 .25

Yerevan State University, 50th anniv.

Library Bookplate, Vilnius University A1807

**1970, Oct.** **Typo.** ***Perf. 12x12½***

**3772** A1807 4k silver, gray & blk .50 .25

Vilnius University Library, 400th anniv.

Woman Holding Flowers — A1808

**1970, Oct. 30** **Photo.**

**3773** A1808 6k blue & lt brown .50 .25

25th anniversary of the International Democratic Federation of Women.

Farm Woman, Cattle Farm — A1809

Designs: No. 3775, Farmer and mechanical farm equipment. No. 3776, Farmer, fertilization equipment and plane.

**1970, Oct. 30** ***Perf. 11½x12***

**3774** A1809 4k olive, yellow & red .35 .25
**3775** A1809 4k ocher, yellow & red .35 .25
**3776** A1809 4k lt vio, yellow & red .35 .25
*Nos. 3774-3776 (3)* 1.05 .75

Aims of the new agricultural 5-year plan.

Lenin — A1810

**Lithographed and Embossed**

**1970, Nov. 3** ***Perf. 12½x12***

**3777** A1810 4k red & gold .50 .25

**Souvenir Sheet**

**3778** A1810 30k red & gold 2.00 .75

53rd anniv. of the October Revolution.

**No. 3389 Overprinted in Gold**

**1970, Nov. 3** ***Perf. 11½***

**3779** A1641 4k gold & multi 1.00 .50

50th anniversary of the GOELRO Plan for the electrification of Russia.

Spasski Tower and Fir Branch — A1811

**1970, Nov. 23** **Litho.** ***Perf. 12x12½***

**3780** A1811 6k multicolored .50 .25

New Year, 1971.

A. A. Baykov — A1812

**1970, Nov. 25** **Photo.** ***Perf. 12½x12***

**3781** A1812 4k sepia & golden brn .50 .25

Baykov (1870-1946), metallurgist and academician.

**Portrait Type of 1968**

Portrait: No. 3782, A. D. Tsyurupa.

**1970, Nov. 25** **Photo.** ***Perf. 12x12½***

**3782** A1688 4k brown & salmon .50 .25

Tsyurupa (1870-1928), First Vice Chairman of the Soviet of People's Commissars.

Vasily Blazhenny Church, Red Square A1813

Tourist publicity: 6k, Performance of Swan Lake. 10k, Two deer. 12k, Folk art. 14k, Sword into Plowshare statue, by E. Vouchetich, and museums. 16k, Automobiles and woman photographer.

**Photogravure and Engraved**

**1970, Nov. 29** ***Perf. 12x11½***

**Frame in Brown Orange**

**3783** A1813 4k multicolored .25 .25
**3784** A1813 6k multicolored .25 .25
**3785** A1813 10k brn org & sl green .35 .25
**3786** A1813 12k multicolored .45 .25
**3787** A1813 14k multicolored .50 .25
**3788** A1813 16k multicolored .65 .25
*Nos. 3783-3788 (6)* 2.45 1.50

Daisy — A1814

**1970, Nov. 29** **Litho.** ***Perf. 11½***

**3789** A1814 4k shown .25 .25
**3790** A1814 6k Dahlia .25 .25
**3791** A1814 10k Phlox .40 .25
**3792** A1814 12k Aster .50 .25
**3793** A1814 16k Clementis .85 .25
*Nos. 3789-3793 (5)* 2.25 1.25

UN Emblem, African Mother and Child, Broken Chain — A1815

**1970, Dec. 10** **Photo.** ***Perf. 12x12½***

**3794** A1815 10k blue & dk brown .50 .25

United Nations Declaration on Colonial Independence, 10th anniversary.

Ludwig van Beethoven (1770-1827), Composer — A1816

**1970, Dec. 16** **Engr.** ***Perf. 12½x12***

**3795** A1816 10k deep claret, *pink* .50 .30

Skating — A1817

Design: 10k, Skiing.

**1970, Dec. 18** **Photo.** ***Perf. 11½***

**3796** A1817 4k lt gray, ultra & dk red .35 .25
**3797** A1817 10k lt gray, brt grn & brn .65 .25

1971 Trade Union Winter Games.

Luna 16 — A1818

Designs: No. 3799, 3801b, Luna 16 leaving moon. No. 3800, 3801c, Capsule landing on earth. No. 3801a, like No. 3798.

**1970, Dec.** **Photo.** ***Perf. 11½***

**3798** A1818 10k gray blue .40 .25
**3799** A1818 10k dk purple .40 .25
**3800** A1818 10k gray blue .40 .25
*Nos. 3798-3800 (3)* 1.20 .75

**Souvenir Sheet**

**3801** Sheet of 3 4.00 1.00
*a.* A1818 20k blue 1.00 .25
*b.* A1818 20k dark purple 1.00 .25
*c.* A1818 20k blue 1.00 .25

Luna 16 unmanned, automatic moon mission, Sept. 12-24, 1970.

Nos. 3801a-3801c have attached labels (no perf. between vignette and label). Issue dates: No. 3801. Dec. 18; Nos. 3798-3800, Dec. 28.

The Conestabile Madonna, by Raphael A1819

Paintings: 4k, Apostles Peter and Paul, by El Greco. 10k, Perseus and Andromeda, by Rubens, horiz. 12k, The Prodigal Son, by Rembrandt. 16k, Family Portrait, by van Dyck. 20k, The Actress Jeanne Samary, by Renoir. 30k, Woman with Fruit, by Gauguin. 50k, The Little Madonna, by da Vinci. All paintings from the Hermitage in Leningrad, except 20k from Pushkin Museum, Moscow.

*Perf. 12x12½, 12½x12*

**1970, Dec. 23** **Litho.**

**3802** A1819 3k gray & multi .25 .25
**3803** A1819 4k gray & multi .25 .25
**3804** A1819 10k gray & multi .60 .25
**3805** A1819 12k gray & multi .60 .25
**3806** A1819 16k gray & multi .70 .25
**3807** A1819 20k gray & multi .85 .25
**3808** A1819 30k gray & multi 1.75 .25
*Nos. 3802-3808 (7)* 5.00 1.75

**Souvenir Sheet**

***Imperf***

**3809** A1819 50k gold & multi 3.00 .90

Harry Pollitt and Shipyard A1820

**1970, Dec. 31 Photo. *Perf. 12***

**3810** A1820 10k maroon & brown .40 .30

Pollitt (1890-1960), British labor leader.

International Cooperative Alliance A1821

**1970, Dec. 31 *Perf. 11½x12***

**3811** A1821 12k yel green & red .50 .30

Intl. Cooperative Alliance, 75th anniv.

Lenin — A1822

**1971, Jan. 1 *Perf. 12***

**3812** A1822 4k red & gold .50 .25

Year of the 24th Congress of the Communist Party of the Soviet Union.

Georgian Republic Flag A1823

**1971, Jan. 12 Litho. *Perf. 11½***

**3813** A1823 4k ol bister & multi .50 .25

Georgian SSR, 50th anniversary.

**Republic Anniversaries Type of 1970**

No. 3816

No. 3818

Designs (Hammer-Sickle Emblem and): No. 3814, Supreme Soviet Building, Makhachkala. No. 3815, Fruit, ship, mountain, conveyor. No. 3816, Grapes, refinery, ship. No. 3817, Supreme Soviet Building, Nalchik. No. 3818, Supreme Soviet Building, Syktyvkar, and lumber industry. No. 3819, Natural resources, dam, mining. No. 3820, Industrial installations and natural products. No. 3821, Ship, "industry." No. 3822, Grapes, pylons and mountains. No. 3823, Kazbek Mountain, industrial installations, produce.

**Engraved; Litho. (#3815, 3823)**

**1971-74 *Perf. 12x12½***

**3814** A1794 4k dk blue green 1.00 .25
**3815** A1794 4k rose red 1.00 .25
**3816** A1794 4k red 1.00 .25
**3817** A1794 4k blue 1.00 .25
**3818** A1794 4k green 1.00 .25
**3819** A1794 4k brt bl ('72) 1.00 .25
**3820** A1794 4k car rose ('72) 1.00 .25
**3821** A1794 4k brt ultra ('73) 1.00 .25
**3822** A1794 4k golden brn ('74) 1.00 .25
**3823** A1794 4k dark red ('74) 1.00 .25
*Nos. 3814-3823 (10)* 10.00 2.50

50th annivers. of Dagestan (No. 3814), Abkazian (No. 3815), Adzhar (No. 3816), Kabardino-Balkarian (No. 3817), Komi (No. 3818), Yakut (No. 3819), Checheno-Ingush (No. 3820), Buryat (No. 3821), Nakhichevan (No. 3822), and North Ossetian (No. 3823) autonomous SSRs.

No. 3823 also for bicentenary of Ossetia's union with Russia.

Issued: No. 3814, 1/20; No. 3815, 3/3; No. 3816, 6/16; Nos. 3817-3818, 8/17; No. 3819, 4/20; No. 3820, 11/22; No. 3821, 5/24; No. 3822, 2/6; No. 3823, 7/7.

Tower of Genoa, Cranes, Hammer and Sickle A1824

**1971, Jan. 28 Typo. *Perf. 12***

**3824** A1824 10k dk red, gray & yel .50 .25

Founding of Feodosiya, Crimea, 2500th anniv.

Palace of Culture, Kiev — A1825

**1971, Feb. 16 Photo. *Perf. 11½***

**3825** A1825 4k red, bister & blue .50 .25

Ukrainian Communist Party, 24th cong.

N. Gubin, I. Chernykh, S. Kosinov A1826

**1971, Feb. 16 *Perf. 12½x12***

**3826** A1826 4k slate grn & vio brn .50 .25

Heroes of the Soviet Union.

"Industry and Agriculture" A1827

**1971, Feb. 16 *Perf. 12x12½***

**3827** A1827 6k olive bister & red .50 .25

State Planning Organization, 50th anniv.

Lesya Ukrayinka (1871-1913), Ukrainian Poet — A1828

**1971, Feb. 25**

**3828** A1828 4k orange red & bister .50 .25

"Summer" Dance — A1829

Dancers of Russian Folk Dance Ensemble: No. 3830, "On the Skating Rink." No. 3831, Ukrainian dance "Hopak." No. 3832, Adzharian dance. No. 3833, Gypsy dance.

**1971, Feb. 25 Litho. *Perf. 12½x12***

**3829** A1829 10k bister & multi .40 .25
**3830** A1829 10k olive & multi .40 .25
**3831** A1829 10k olive bis & multi .40 .25
**3832** A1829 10k gray & multi .40 .25
**3833** A1829 10k grnsh gray & multi .40 .25
*Nos. 3829-3833 (5)* 2.00 1.25

Luna 17 on Moon A1830

Designs: No. 3835, Ground control. No. 3836, Separation of Lunokhod 1 and carrier. 16k, Lunokhod 1 in operation.

**1971, Mar. 16 Photo. *Perf. 11½***

**3834** A1830 10k dp vio & sepia .35 .25
**3835** A1830 12k dk blue & sepia .50 .25
**3836** A1830 12k dk blue & sepia .50 .25
**3837** A1830 16k dp vio & sepia .65 .25
*a.* Souv. sheet of 4 2.50 1.00
*Nos. 3834-3837 (4)* 2.00 1.00

Luna 17 unmanned, automated moon mission, Nov. 10-17, 1970.

No. 3837a contains Nos. 3834-3837, size 32x21mm each.

Paris Commune, Cent. — A1831

**1971, Mar. 18 Litho. *Perf. 12***

**3838** A1831 6k red & black .50 .25

Industry, Science, Culture A1832

**1971, Mar. 29 *Perf. 11½***

**3839** A1832 6k bister, brn & red .50 .25

24th Communist Party Cong., 3/30-4/3.

Yuri Gagarin Medal A1833

**1971, Mar. 30 Photo. *Perf. 11½***

**3840** A1833 10k brown & lemon .50 .25

10th anniv. of man's first flight into space.

Space Research A1834

**1971, Mar. 30**

**3841** A1834 12k slate bl & vio brn .50 .25

Cosmonauts' Day, Apr. 12.

Ernests Birznieks-Upitis (1871-1960), Latvian Writer — A1835

**1971, Apr. 1 *Perf. 12x12½***

**3842** A1835 4k red brown & gray .35 .25

Bee and Blossom — A1836

**1971, Apr. 1 *Perf. 11½***

**3843** A1836 6k olive & multi .90 .25

23rd International Beekeeping Congress, Moscow, Aug. 22-Sept. 2.

Souvenir Sheet

Cosmonauts and Spacecraft — A1837

Designs: 10k, Vostok. No. 3844b, Yuri Gagarin. No. 3844c, First man walking in space. 16k, First orbital station.

**1971, Apr. 12 Litho. *Perf. 12***

**3844** A1837 Sheet of 4 2.50 1.00
*a.* 10k violet brown .45 .25
*b.-c.* 12k Prussian green .45 .25
*d.* 16k violet brown .50 .25

10th anniv. of man's 1st flight into space. Size of stamps: 26x19mm.

Lenin Memorial, Ulyanovsk — A1838

**1971, Apr. 16 Photo. *Perf. 12***

**3845** A1838 4k cop red & ol bister .40 .25

Lenin's birthday. Memorial was built for centenary celebration of his birth.

Lt. Col. Nikolai I. Vlasov — A1839

**1971, May 9 Photo. *Perf. 12x12½***

**3846** A1839 4k gray olive & brn .40 .25

Hero of the Soviet Union.

Khafiz Shirazi, Tadzhik-Persian Poet, 650th Birth Anniv. — A1840

**1971, May 9 Litho.**

**3847** A1840 4k olive, brn & black .50 .25

GAZ-66 — A1841

Soviet Cars: 3k, BelAZ-540 truck. No. 3850, Moskvich-412. No. 3851, ZAZ-968. 10k, Volga.

**1971, May 12 Photo. *Perf. 11x11½***

| | | | | | |
|---|---|---|---|---|---|
| **3848** | A1841 | 2k | yellow & multi | .25 | .25 |
| **3849** | A1841 | 3k | lt blue & multi | .25 | .25 |
| **3850** | A1841 | 4k | lt lilac & multi | .25 | .25 |
| **3851** | A1841 | 4k | lt gray & multi | .25 | .25 |
| **3852** | A1841 | 10k | lt lilac & multi | .25 | .25 |
| | | | *Nos. 3848-3852 (5)* | 1.25 | 1.25 |

Bogomolets A1842

**1971, May 24 Photo. *Perf. 12***

**3853** A1842 4k orange & black .50 .25

A. A. Bogomolets, physician, 90th birth anniv.

Satellite — A1843

**1971, June 9 *Perf. 11½***

**3854** A1843 6k blue & multi .60 .25

15th General Assembly of the International Union of Geodesics and Geophysics.

Symbols of Science and History A1844

**1971, June 9 *Perf. 12***

**3855** A1844 6k green & gray .50 .25

13th Congress of Science History.

Oil Derrick & Symbols A1845

**1971, June 9 *Perf. 11½***

**3856** A1845 6k multicolored .60 .25

8th World Oil Congress.

Sukhe Bator Monument — A1846

**1971, June 16 Typo. *Perf. 12***

**3857** A1846 6k red, gold & black .60 .25

50th anniversary of Mongolian revolution.

Monument of Defenders of Liepaja A1847

**1971, June 21 Photo.**

**3858** A1847 4k gray, black & brn .50 .25

30th anniversary of the defense of Liepaja (Libau) against invading Germans.

Map of Antarctica and Station — A1848

**Engraved and Photogravure**

**1971, June 21 *Perf. 11½***

**3859** A1848 6k black, grn & ultra 1.25 .30

Antarctic Treaty pledging peaceful uses of & scientific co-operation in Antarctica, 10th anniv.

Weather Map, Plane, Ship and Satellite — A1849

**1971, June 21**

**3860** A1849 10k black, red & ultra .50 .30

50th anniversary of Soviet Hydrometeorological service.

FIR Emblem, "Homeland" by E. Vouchetich A1850

**1971, June 21 Photo. *Perf. 12x12½***

**3861** A1850 6k dk red & slate .50 .25

International Federation of Resistance Fighters (FIR), 20th anniversary.

Discus and Running A1851

Designs: 4k, Archery (women). 6k, Dressage. 10k, Basketball. 12k, Wrestling.

**Lithographed and Engraved**

**1971, June 24 *Perf. 11½***

| | | | | | |
|---|---|---|---|---|---|
| **3862** | A1851 | 3k | vio blue, *rose* | .25 | .25 |
| **3863** | A1851 | 4k | slate grn, *pale pink* | .25 | .25 |
| **3864** | A1851 | 6k | red brn, *apple grn* | .25 | .25 |
| **3865** | A1851 | 10k | dk pur, *gray blue* | .35 | .25 |
| **3866** | A1851 | 12k | red brn, *yellow* | .40 | .25 |
| | | | *Nos. 3862-3866 (5)* | 1.50 | 1.25 |

5th Summer Spartakiad.

Benois Madonna, by da Vinci A1852

Paintings: 4k, Mary Magdalene, by Titian. 10k, The Washerwoman, by Jean Simeon Chardin, horiz. 12k, Portrait of a Young Man, by Frans Hals. 14k, Tancred and Arminia, by Nicolas Poussin, horiz. 16k, Girl with Fruit, by Murillo. 20k, Girl with Ball, by Picasso.

***Perf. 12x12½, 12½x12***

**1971, July 7 Litho.**

| | | | | | |
|---|---|---|---|---|---|
| **3867** | A1852 | 2k | bister & multi | .25 | .25 |
| **3868** | A1852 | 4k | bister & multi | .25 | .25 |
| **3869** | A1852 | 10k | bister & multi | .40 | .25 |
| **3870** | A1852 | 12k | bister & multi | .45 | .25 |
| **3871** | A1852 | 14k | bister & multi | .55 | .25 |
| **3872** | A1852 | 16k | bister & multi | .65 | .25 |
| **3873** | A1852 | 20k | bister & multi | .75 | .25 |
| | | | *Nos. 3867-3873 (7)* | 3.30 | 1.75 |

Foreign master works in Russian museums.

Kazakhstan Flag, Lenin Badge — A1853

**1971, July 7 Photo. *Perf. 11½***

**3874** A1853 4k blue, red & brown .50 .25

50th anniversary of the Kazakh Communist Youth League.

Star Emblem and Letters A1854

**1971, July 14**

**3875** A1854 4k oliver, blue & black .50 .25

International Letter Writing Week.

Nikolai A. Nekrasov, by Ivan N. Kramskoi A1855

Portraits: No. 3877, Aleksandr Spendiarov, by M. S. Saryan. 10k, Fedor M. Dostoevski, by Vassili G. Perov.

**1971, July 14 Litho. *Perf. 12x12½***

| | | | | | |
|---|---|---|---|---|---|
| **3876** | A1855 | 4k | citron & multi | .25 | .25 |
| **3877** | A1855 | 4k | gray blue & multi | .25 | .25 |
| **3878** | A1855 | 10k | multicolored | .40 | .25 |
| | | | *Nos. 3876-3878 (3)* | .90 | .75 |

Nikolai Alekseevitch Nekrasov (1821-1877), poet, Fedor Mikhailovich Dostoevski (1821-1881), novelist, Spendiarov (1871-1928), Armenian composer.

See Nos. 4056-4057.

Zachary Paliashvili (1871-1933), Georgian Composer and Score — A1856

**1971, Aug. 3 Photo. *Perf. 12x12½***

**3879** A1856 4k brown .50 .25

Gorki Kremlin, Stag and Hydrofoil A1857

**1971, Aug. 3 Litho. *Perf. 12***

**3880** A1857 16k multicolored .50 .25

Gorki (formerly Nizhni Novgorod), 750th anniv. See Nos. 3889, 3910-3914.

Federation Emblem and Students A1858

**1971, Aug. 3 Photo. *Perf. 11½***
**3881** A1858 6k ultra & multi .50 .25

Intl. Students Federation, 25th anniv.

Common Dolphins A1859

Sea Mammals: 6k, Sea otter. 10k, Narwhals. 12k, Walrus. 14k, Ribbon seals.

**Photogravure and Engraved**

**1971, Aug. 12 *Perf. 11½***
**3882** A1859 4k silver & multi .40 .25
**3883** A1859 6k silver & multi .40 .25
**3884** A1859 10k silver & multi .60 .25
**3885** A1859 12k silver & multi .70 .25
**3886** A1859 14k silver & multi .90 .25
*Nos. 3882-3886 (5)* 3.00 1.25

Miner's Star of Valor — A1860

**1971, Aug. 17 Photo. *Perf. 11½***
**3887** A1860 4k bister, black & red .50 .25

250th anniversary of the discovery of coal in the Donets Basin.

Ernest Rutherford and Diagram of Movement of Atomic Particles A1861

**1971, Aug. 24 Photo. *Perf. 12***
**3888** A1861 6k magenta & dk ol .75 .25

Rutherford (1871-1937), British physicist.

Gorki and Gorki Statue — A1862

**1971, Sept. 14 *Perf. 11½***
**3889** A1862 4k steel blue & multi .50 .25

Gorki (see No. 3880).

Troika and Spasski Tower A1863

**1971, Sept. 14**
**3890** A1863 10k black, red & gold .50 .25

New Year 1972.

Automatic Production Center — A1864

#3892, Agricultural development. #3893, Family in shopping center. #3894, Hydro-generators, thermoelectric station. #3895, Marchers, flags, books inscribed Marx and Lenin.

**1971, Sept. 29 Photo. *Perf. 12x11½***
**3891** A1864 4k purple, red & blk .40 .25
**3892** A1864 4k ocher, red & brn .40 .25
**3893** A1864 4k yel, olive & red .40 .25
**3894** A1864 4k bister, red & brn .40 .25
**3895** A1864 4k ultra, red & slate .40 .25
*Nos. 3891-3895 (5)* 2.00 1.25

Resolutions of 24th Soviet Union Communist Party Congress.

The Meeting, by Vladimir Y. Makovsky A1865

Ivan N. Kramskoi, Self-portrait — A1866

Paintings: 4k, Woman Student, by Nikolai A. Yaroshenko. 6k, Woman Miner, by Nikolai A. Kasatkin. 10k, Harvest, by G. G. Myasoyedov, horiz. 16k, Country Road, by A. K. Savrasov. 20k, Pine Forest, by I. I. Shishkin, horiz.

***Perf. 12x12½, 12½x12***

**1971, Oct. 14 Litho.**

**Frame in Light Gray**
**3896** A1865 2k multicolored .25 .25
**3897** A1865 4k multicolored .25 .25
**3898** A1865 6k multicolored .25 .25
**3899** A1865 10k multicolored .50 .25
**3900** A1865 16k multicolored .55 .25
**3901** A1865 20k multicolored 1.10 .25
*Nos. 3896-3901 (6)* 2.90 1.50

**Souvenir Sheet**

**Lithographed and Gold Embossed**
**3902** A1866 50k dk green & multi 2.00 .60

History of Russian painting.

V. V. Vorovsky, Bolshevik Party Leader and Diplomat, Birth Cent. — A1867

**1971, Oct. 14 Engr. *Perf. 12***
**3903** A1867 4k red brown .50 .25

Cosmonauts Dobrovolsky, Volkov and Patsayev — A1868

**1971, Oct. 20 Photo. *Perf. 11½x12***
**3904** A1868 4k black, lilac & org .50 .25

In memory of cosmonauts Lt. Col. Georgi T. Dobrovolsky, Vladislav N. Volkov and Viktor I. Patsayev, who died during the Soyuz 11 space mission, June 6-30, 1971.

Order of October Revolution — A1869

**1971, Oct. 20 Litho. *Perf. 12***
**3905** A1869 4k red, yel & black .50 .25

54th anniversary of October Revolution.

E. Vakhtangov and "Princess Turandot" A1870

Designs: No. 3907, Boris Shchukin and scene from "Man with Rifle (Lenin)," horiz. No. 3908, Ruben Simonov and scene from "Cyrano de Bergerac," horiz.

***Perf. 12x12½, 12½x12***

**1971, Oct. 26 Photo.**
**3906** A1870 10k mar & red brn .35 .25
**3907** A1870 10k brown & dull yel .35 .25
**3908** A1870 10k red brn & ocher .35 .25
*Nos. 3906-3908 (3)* 1.05 .75

Vakhtangov Theater, Moscow, 50th anniv.

Dzhambul Dzhabayev(1846-1945), Kazakh Poet — A1871

**1971, Nov. 16 *Perf. 12x12½***
**3909** A1871 4k orange & brown .50 .25

**Gorki Kremlin Type, 1971**

Designs: 3k, Pskov Kremlin and Velikaya River. 4k, Novgorod Kremlin and eternal flame memorial. 6k, Smolensk Fortress and liberation monument. 10k, Kolomna Kremlin and buses. 50k, Moscow Kremlin.

**1971, Nov. 16 Litho. *Perf. 12***
**3910** A1857 3k multicolored .75 .25
**3911** A1857 4k multicolored .75 .25
**3912** A1857 6k gray & multi .75 .25
**3913** A1857 10k olive & multi .75 .25
*Nos. 3910-3913 (4)* 3.00 1.00

**Souvenir Sheet**

**Engraved and Lithographed**

***Perf. 11½***
**3914** A1857 50k yellow & multi 1.50 .75

Historic buildings. No. 3914 contains one 21½x32mm stamp.

William Foster, View of New York A1872

**1971 Litho. *Perf. 12***
**3915** A1872 10k brn & blk ("-1961") 1.00 .25
*a.* "-1964" 20.00 7.25

William Foster (1881-1961), chairman of Communist Party of US.

No. 3915a was issued Nov. 16 with incorrect death date (1964). No. 3915, with corrected date (1961), was issued Dec. 8.

Aleksandr Fadeyev and Cavalrymen — A1873

**1971, Nov. 25 Photo. *Perf. 12½x12***
**3916** A1873 4k slate & orange .50 .25

Aleksandr Fadeyev (1901-1956), writer.

Amethyst and Diamond Brooch A1874

Precious Jewels: No. 3918, Engraved Shakh diamond, India, 16th cent. No. 3919, Diamond daffodils, 18th cent. No. 3920, Amethyst & diamond pendant. No. 3921, Diamond rose made for centenary of Lenin's birth. No. 3922, Diamond & pearl pendant.

**1971, Dec. 8 Litho. *Perf. 11½***
**3917** A1874 10k brt blue & multi .35 .25
**3918** A1874 10k dk red & multi .35 .25
**3919** A1874 10k grnsh black & multi .35 .25
**3920** A1874 20k grnsh black & multi .70 .30
**3921** A1874 20k rose red & multi .70 .30
**3922** A1874 30k black & multi 1.00 .45
*Nos. 3917-3922 (6)* 3.45 1.80

Souvenir Sheet

Workers with Banners, Congress Hall and Spasski Tower — A1875

**1971, Dec. 15 Photo. *Perf. 11x11½***
**3923** A1875 20k red, pale grn & brn 2.00 1.00

See note after No. 3895. No. 3923 contains one partially perforated stamp.

Vanda Orchid — A1876

Flowers: No. 3924, No. 3929b, shown. No. 3925, Anthurium. No. 3926, No. 3929c, Flowering crab cactus. No. 3927, No. 3929a, Amaryllis. No. 3928, No. 3929d, Medinilla magnifica.

**1971, Dec. 15 Litho. *Perf. 12x12½***

| No. | Type | Description | Unused | Used |
|---|---|---|---|---|
| **3924** | A1876 | 1k olive & multi | .25 | .25 |
| **3925** | A1876 | 2k green & multi | .25 | .25 |
| **3926** | A1876 | 4k blue & multi | .40 | .25 |
| **3927** | A1876 | 12k multicolored | .50 | .25 |
| **3928** | A1876 | 14k multicolored | .65 | .25 |
| | | *Nos. 3924-3928 (5)* | 2.05 | 1.25 |

**Miniature Sheet**

***Perf. 12***

| No. | Type | Description | Unused | Used |
|---|---|---|---|---|
| **3929** | | Sheet of 4 | 1.50 | .75 |
| ***a.-d.*** | A1876 | 10k any single | .40 | .25 |

Nos. 3929a-3929d have white background, black frame line and inscription. Size of stamps 19x57mm.

Issued: Nos. 3924-3928, 12/15; No. 3929, 12/30.

Peter I Reviewing Fleet, 1723 — A1877

History of Russian Fleet: 4k, Oriol, first ship built in Eddinovo, 1668, vert. 10k, Battleship Poltava, 1712, vert. 12k, Armed ship Ingermanland, 1715, vert. 16k, Frigate Vladimir, 1848.

***Perf. 11½x12, 12x11½***

**1971, Dec. 15 Engr. & Photo.**

| No. | Type | Description | Unused | Used |
|---|---|---|---|---|
| **3930** | A1877 | 1k multicolored | .30 | .25 |
| **3931** | A1877 | 4k brown & multi | .45 | .30 |
| **3932** | A1877 | 10k multicolored | 1.20 | .75 |
| **3933** | A1877 | 12k multicolored | 1.40 | .75 |
| **3934** | A1877 | 16k lt green & multi | 1.90 | 1.00 |
| | | *Nos. 3930-3934 (5)* | 5.25 | 3.05 |

Ice Hockey A1878

**1971, Dec. 15 Litho. *Perf. 12½***

| No. | Type | Description | Unused | Used |
|---|---|---|---|---|
| **3935** | A1878 | 6k multicolored | .50 | .25 |

25th anniversary of Soviet ice hockey.

A1879

Oil rigs and causeway in Caspian Sea.

**1971, Dec. 30 *Perf. 11½***

| No. | Type | Description | Unused | Used |
|---|---|---|---|---|
| **3936** | A1879 | 4k dp blue, org & blk | .50 | .25 |

Baku oil industry.

A1880

**1972, Jan. 5 Engr. *Perf. 12***

| No. | Type | Description | Unused | Used |
|---|---|---|---|---|
| **3937** | A1880 | 4k yellow brown | .50 | .25 |

G. M. Krzhizhanovsky (1872-1959), scientist and co-worker with Lenin.

Alexander Scriabin (1872-1915), Composer A1881

**1972, Jan. 6 Photo. *Perf. 12x12½***

| No. | Type | Description | Unused | Used |
|---|---|---|---|---|
| **3938** | A1881 | 4k indigo & olive | .50 | .25 |

Bering's Cormorant A1882

Birds: 6k, Ross' gull, horiz. 10k, Barnacle geese. 12k, Spectacled eiders, horiz. 16k, Mediterranean gull.

**1972, Jan. 12 *Perf. 11½***

| No. | Type | Description | Unused | Used |
|---|---|---|---|---|
| **3939** | A1882 | 4k dk grn, blk & yel | .30 | .25 |
| **3940** | A1882 | 6k ind, pink & blk | .50 | .25 |
| **3941** | A1882 | 10k grnsh blue, blk & brown | .80 | .35 |
| **3942** | A1882 | 12k multicolored | .95 | .45 |
| **3943** | A1882 | 16k ultra, gray & red | 1.25 | .60 |
| | | *Nos. 3939-3943 (5)* | 3.80 | 1.90 |

Waterfowl of the USSR.

11th Winter Olympic Games, Sapporo, Japan, Feb. 3-13 — A1883

Designs (Olympic Rings and): 4k, Speed skating. 6k, Women's figure skating. 10k, Ice hockey. 12k, Ski jump. 16k, Long-distance skiing. 50k, Sapporo '72 emblem.

**1972, Jan. 20 Litho. *Perf. 12x12½***

| No. | Type | Description | Unused | Used |
|---|---|---|---|---|
| **3944** | A1883 | 4k bl grn, red & brn | .25 | .25 |
| **3945** | A1883 | 6k yel grn, blue & dp orange | .25 | .25 |
| **3946** | A1883 | 10k vio, bl & dp org | .40 | .25 |
| **3947** | A1883 | 12k light blue, blue & brick red | .50 | .25 |
| **3948** | A1883 | 16k gray, bl & brt rose | .60 | .25 |
| | | *Nos. 3944-3948 (5)* | 2.00 | 1.25 |

**Souvenir Sheet**

| No. | Type | Description | Unused | Used |
|---|---|---|---|---|
| **3949** | A1883 | 50k multicolored | 1.50 | .75 |

For overprint see No. 3961.

Heart, Globe and Exercising Family — A1884

**1972, Feb. 9 Photo.**

| No. | Type | Description | Unused | Used |
|---|---|---|---|---|
| **3950** | A1884 | 4k brt grn & rose red | .50 | .25 |

Heart Month sponsored by the WHO.

Leipzig Fair Emblem and Soviet Pavilion — A1885

**1972, Feb. 22 *Perf. 11½***

| No. | Type | Description | Unused | Used |
|---|---|---|---|---|
| **3951** | A1885 | 16k red & gold | .75 | .25 |

50th anniversary of the participation of the USSR in the Leipzig Trade Fair.

Hammer, Sickle and Cogwheel Emblem — A1886

**1972, Feb. 29 *Perf. 12x12½***

| No. | Type | Description | Unused | Used |
|---|---|---|---|---|
| **3952** | A1886 | 4k rose red & lt brn | .50 | .25 |

15th USSR Trade Union Congress, Moscow, March 1972.

Aloe — A1887

Medicinal Plants: 2k, Horn poppy. 4k, Groundsel. 6k, Orthosiphon stamineus. 10k, Nightshade.

**1972, Mar. 14 Litho. *Perf. 12x12½***

**Flowers in Natural Colors**

| No. | Type | Description | Unused | Used |
|---|---|---|---|---|
| **3953** | A1887 | 1k olive bister | .80 | .25 |
| **3954** | A1887 | 2k slate green | .80 | .25 |
| **3955** | A1887 | 4k brt purple | .80 | .25 |
| **3956** | A1887 | 6k violet blue | .80 | .25 |
| **3957** | A1887 | 10k dk brown | .80 | .25 |
| | | *Nos. 3953-3957 (5)* | 4.00 | 1.25 |

Aleksandra Kollontai — A1888

No. 3959, Georgy Chicherin. No. 3960, Kamo (pseudonym of S.A. Ter-Petrosyan).

**1972, Mar. 20 Engr. *Perf. 12½x12***

| No. | Type | Description | Unused | Used |
|---|---|---|---|---|
| **3958** | A1888 | 4k red brown | .35 | .25 |
| **3959** | A1888 | 4k claret | .35 | .25 |
| **3960** | A1888 | 4k olive bister | .35 | .25 |
| | | *Nos. 3958-3960 (3)* | 1.05 | .75 |

Outstanding workers of the Communist Party of the Soviet Union and for the State.

**No. 3949 Overprinted**

Souvenir Sheet

**1972, Mar. 20 Litho. *Perf. 12x12½***

| No. | Type | Description | Unused | Used |
|---|---|---|---|---|
| **3961** | A1883 | 50k multicolored | 4.00 | 2.00 |

Victories of Soviet athletes in the 11th Winter Olympic Games (8 gold, 5 silver, 3 bronze medals).

For similar overprints see Nos. 4028, 4416.

Orbital Station Salyut and Spaceship Soyuz Docking Above Earth — A1889

Designs: No. 3963, Mars 2 approaching Mars, and emblem dropped on Mars. 16k, Mars 3, which landed on Mars, Dec. 2, 1971.

**1972, Apr. 5 Photo. *Perf. 11½x12***

| No. | Type | Description | Unused | Used |
|---|---|---|---|---|
| **3962** | A1889 | 6k vio, blue & silver | .40 | .25 |
| **3963** | A1889 | 6k pur, ocher & sil | .40 | .25 |
| **3964** | A1889 | 16k pur, blue & sil | 1.20 | .25 |
| | | *Nos. 3962-3964 (3)* | 2.00 | .75 |

Cosmonauts' Day.

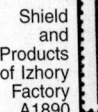

Shield and Products of Izhory Factory A1890

**1972, Apr. 20 *Perf. 12½x12***

| No. | Type | Description | Unused | Used |
|---|---|---|---|---|
| **3965** | A1890 | 4k purple & silver | .50 | .25 |

250th anniversary of Izhory Factory, founded by Peter the Great.

Leonid Sobinov in "Eugene Onegin," by Tchaikovsky — A1891

**1972, Apr. 20**

| No. | Type | Description | Unused | Used |
|---|---|---|---|---|
| **3966** | A1891 | 10k dp brown & buff | .50 | .25 |

Sobinov (1872-1934), opera singer.

Book, Torch, Children and Globe A1892

**1972, May 5** ***Perf. 11½***

**3967** A1892 6k brn, grnsh bl & buff .35 .25

International Book Year 1972.

Girl in Laboratory and Pioneers A1893

Designs: 1k, Pavlik Morosov (Pioneer hero), Pioneers saluting and banner. 3k, Pioneers with wheelbarrow, Chukchi boy, and Chukotka Pioneer House. 4k, Pioneer Honor Guard and Parade. 30k, Pioneer Honor Guard, vert.

**1972, May 10**

**3968** A1893 1k red & multi .50 .25
**3969** A1893 2k multicolored .50 .25
**3970** A1893 3k multicolored .50 .25
**3971** A1893 4k gray & multi .50 .25
*Nos. 3968-3971 (4)* 2.00 1.00

**Souvenir Sheet**

***Perf. 12x12½***

**3972** A1893 30k multicolored 1.50 .75

50th anniversary of the Lenin Pioneer Organization of the USSR.

Pioneer Bugler A1894

**1972, May 27** **Photo.** ***Perf. 11½***

**3973** A1894 4k red, ocher & plum .50 .25

2nd Youth Philatelic Exhibition, Minsk, and 50th anniv. of Lenin Pioneer Org.

M. S. Ordubady (1872-1950), Azerbaijan Writer and Social Worker — A1895

**1972, May 25** ***Perf. 12x12½***

**3974** A1895 4k orange & rose brn .50 .25

Globe A1896

**1972, May 25** ***Perf. 11½***

**3975** A1896 6k multicolored .50 .30

European Safety and Cooperation Conference, Brussels.

Cossack Leader, by Ivan Nikitin A1897

Paintings: 4k, Fedor G. Volkov (actor), by Anton Losenko. 6k, V. Majkov (poet), by Fedor Rokotov. 10k, Nikolai I. Novikov (writer), by Dimitri Levitsky. 12k, Gavriil R. Derzhavin (poet, civil servant), by Vladimir Borovikovsky. 16k, Peasants' Supper, by Mikhail Shibanov, horiz. 20k, View of Moscow, by Fedor Alexeyev, horiz.

***Perf. 12x12½, 12½x12***

**1972, June 7** **Litho.**

**3976** A1897 2k gray & multi .25 .25
**3977** A1897 4k gray & multi .25 .25
**3978** A1897 6k gray & multi .25 .25
**3979** A1897 10k gray & multi .30 .25
**3980** A1897 12k gray & multi .30 .25
**3981** A1897 16k gray & multi .45 .25
**3982** A1897 20k gray & multi .60 .25
*Nos. 3976-3982 (7)* 2.40 1.75

History of Russian painting. See Nos. 4036-4042, 4074-4080, 4103-4109.

George Dimitrov (1882-1949), Bulgarian Communist Party Leader — A1898

**1972, June 15** **Photo.** ***Perf. 12½x12***

**3983** A1898 6k brown & ol bister .50 .25

20th Olympic Games, Munich, 8/26-9/11 A1899

Olympic Rings and: 4k, Fencing. 6k, Women's gymnastics. 10k, Canoeing. 14k, Boxing. 16k, Running. 50k, Weight lifting.

**1972, July 1** ***Perf. 12x11½***

**3984** A1899 4k brt mag & gold .25 .25
**3985** A1899 6k dp green & gold .25 .25
**3986** A1899 10k brt blue & gold .55 .25
**3987** A1899 14k Prus bl & gold .60 .25
**3988** A1899 16k red & gold .85 .25
*Nos. 3984-3988 (5)* 2.50 1.25

**Souvenir Sheet**

***Perf. 11½***

**3989** A1899 50k gold & multi 1.50 .60

No. 3989 contains one 25x35mm stamp. For overprint see No. 4028.

Congress Palace, Kiev A1900

**1972, July 1** **Photo. & Engr.**

**3990** A1900 6k Prus blue & bister .50 .25

9th World Gerontology Cong., Kiev, 7/2-7.

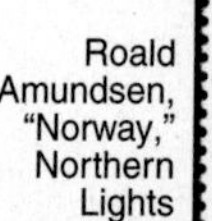

Roald Amundsen, "Norway," Northern Lights A1901

**1972, July 13** **Photo.** ***Perf. 11½***

**3991** A1901 6k vio blue & dp bister 1.00 .25

Roald Amundsen (1872-1928), Norwegian polar explorer.

17th Century House, Chernigov A1902

Designs: 4k, Market Square, Lvov, vert. 10k, Kovnirov Building, Kiev. 16k, Fortress, Kamenets-Podolski, vert.

***Perf. 12x12½, 12½x12***

**1972, July 18** **Litho.**

**3992** A1902 4k citron & multi .25 .25
**3993** A1902 6k gray & multi .25 .25
**3994** A1902 10k ocher & multi .60 .25
**3995** A1902 16k salmon & multi .80 .25
*Nos. 3992-3995 (4)* 1.90 1.00

Historic and architectural treasures of the Ukraine.

Asoka Pillar, Indian Flag, Red Fort, New Delhi A1903

**1972, July 27** **Photo.** ***Perf. 11½***

**3996** A1903 6k dk blue, emer & red .50 .25

25th anniversary of India's independence.

Miners' Emblem A1904

**1972, Aug. 10**

**3997** A1904 4k violet gray & red .50 .25

25th Miners' Day.

Far East Fighters' Monument A1905

Designs: 4k, Monument for Far East Civil War heroes, industrial view. 6k, Vladivostok rostral column, Pacific fleet ships.

**1972, Aug. 10**

**3998** A1905 3k red org, car & black .50 .25
**3999** A1905 4k yel, sepia & blk .50 .25
**4000** A1905 6k pink, dk car & black .50 .25
*Nos. 3998-4000 (3)* 1.50 .75

50th anniversary of the liberation of the Far Eastern provinces.

Boy with Dog, by Murillo A1906

Paintings from the Hermitage, Leningrad: 4k, Breakfast, Velazquez. 6k, Milkmaid's Family, Louis Le Nain. 16k, Sad Woman, Watteau. 20k, Moroccan Saddling Steed, Delacroix. 50k, Self-portrait, Van Dyck. 4k, 6k horiz.

***Perf. 12½x12, 12x12½***

**1972, Aug. 15** **Litho.**

**4001** A1906 4k multicolored .25 .25
**4002** A1906 6k multicolored .25 .25
**4003** A1906 10k multicolored .40 .25
**4004** A1906 16k multicolored .60 .25
**4005** A1906 20k multicolored .90 .25
*Nos. 4001-4005 (5)* 2.40 1.25

**Souvenir Sheet**

***Perf. 12***

**4006** A1906 50k multicolored 2.50 1.00

Sputnik 1 — A1907

No. 4008, Launching of Vostok 2. No. 4009, Lenov floating in space. No. 4010, Lunokhod on moon. No. 4011, Venera 7 descending to Venus. No. 4012, Mars & descending to Mars.

**1972, Sept. 14** **Litho.** ***Perf. 12x11½***

**4007** A1907 6k shown .35 .25
**4008** A1907 6k multicolored .35 .25
**4009** A1907 6k multicolored .35 .25
**4010** A1907 6k multicolored .35 .25
**4011** A1907 6k multicolored .35 .25
**4012** A1907 6k multicolored .35 .25
*Nos. 4007-4012 (6)* 2.10 1.50

15 years of space era. Sheets of 6.

Konstantin Aleksandrovich Mardzhanishvili (1872-1933), Theatrical Producer A1908

**1972, Sept. 20** **Engr.** ***Perf. 12x12½***

**4013** A1908 4k slate green .50 .25

Museum Emblem, Communications Symbols — A1909

**1972, Sept. 20** **Photo.** ***Perf. 11½***

**4014** A1909 4k slate green & multi .50 .25

Centenary of the A. S. Popov Central Museum of Communications.

"Stamp" and Topical Collecting Symbols
A1910

**Engraved and Lithographed**

**1972, Oct. 4** *Perf. 12*

**4015** A1910 4k yel, black & red .50 .25

Philatelic Exhibition in honor of 50th anniversary of the USSR.

Lenin
A1911

**1972, Oct. 12** **Photo.** *Perf. 11½*

**4016** A1911 4k gold & red .50 .25

55th anniversary of October Revolution.

Militia Badge — A1912

**1972, Oct. 12**

**4017** A1912 4k gold, red & dk brn .30 .25

55th anniv. of the Militia of the USSR.

Arms of USSR
A1913

USSR, 50th anniv.: No. 4019, Arms and industrial scene. No. 4020, Arms, Supreme Soviet, Kremlin. No. 4021, Lenin. No. 4022, Arms, worker, book (Constitution).
30k, Coat of arms and Spasski Tower, horiz.

**1972, Oct. 28** *Perf. 12x11½*

| | | | | |
|---|---|---|---|---|
| **4018** | A1913 | 4k multicolored | .30 | .25 |
| **4019** | A1913 | 4k multicolored | .30 | .25 |
| **4020** | A1913 | 4k multicolored | .30 | .25 |
| **4021** | A1913 | 4k multicolored | .30 | .25 |
| **4022** | A1913 | 4k multicolored | .30 | .25 |
| | | *Nos. 4018-4022 (5)* | 1.50 | 1.25 |

**Souvenir Sheet**

**Lithographed; Embossed**

*Perf. 12*

**4023** A1913 30k red & gold 1.50 .40

Kremlin and Snowflake
A1914

**Engraved and Photogravure**

**1972, Nov. 15** *Perf. 11½*

**4024** A1914 6k multicolored 1.00 .25

New Year 1973.

Savings Bank Book — A1915

**1972, Nov. 15** **Photo.** *Perf. 12x12½*

**4025** A1915 4k lilac & slate .50 .25

50th anniv. of savings banks in the USSR.

Soviet Olympic Emblem and Laurel
A1916

Design: 30k, Soviet Olympic emblem and obverse of gold, silver and bronze medals.

**1972, Nov. 15** *Perf. 11½*

**4026** A1916 20k brn ol, red & gold .50 .40

**4027** A1916 30k dp car, gold & brn 1.00 .60

**No. 3989 Overprinted in Red**

Souvenir Sheet

**1972, Nov. 15**

**4028** A1899 50k gold & multi 2.50 1.25

Soviet medalists at 20th Olympic Games.

Battleship Peter the Great, 1872 — A1917

History of Russian Fleet: 3k, Cruiser Varyag, 1899. 4k, Battleship Potemkin, 1900. 6k, Cruiser Ochakov, 1902. 10k, Mine layer Amur, 1907.

**Engraved and Photogravure**

**1972, Nov. 22** *Perf. 11½x12*

| | | | | |
|---|---|---|---|---|
| **4029** | A1917 | 2k multicolored | .35 | .25 |
| **4030** | A1917 | 3k multicolored | .35 | .25 |
| **4031** | A1917 | 4k multicolored | .45 | .25 |
| **4032** | A1917 | 6k multicolored | .70 | .25 |
| **4033** | A1917 10k | multicolored | 1.10 | .25 |
| | | *Nos. 4029-4033 (5)* | 2.95 | 1.25 |

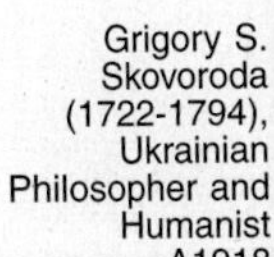

Grigory S. Skovoroda (1722-1794), Ukrainian Philosopher and Humanist
A1918

**1972, Dec. 7** **Engr.** *Perf. 12*

**4034** A1918 4k dk violet blue .50 .25

Child Reading Traffic Rules — A1919

**1972, Dec. 7** **Photo.** *Perf. 11½*

**4035** A1919 4k Prus blue, blk & red .50 .25

Traffic safety campaign.

**Russian Painting Type of 1972**

2k, Meeting of Village Party Members, by E. M. Cheptsov, horiz. 4k, Pioneer Girl, by Nicolai A. Kasatkin. 6k, Woman Delegate, by G. G. Ryazhsky. 10k, Winter's End, by K. F. Yuon, horiz. 16k, The Partisan A. G. Lunev, by N. I. Strunnikov. 20k, Igor E. Grabar, self-portrait. 50k, Blue Space (seascape with flying geese), by Arcadi A. Rylov, horiz.

*Perf. 12x12½, 12½x12*

**1972, Dec. 7** **Litho.**

| | | | | |
|---|---|---|---|---|
| **4036** | A1897 | 2k olive & multi | .25 | .25 |
| **4037** | A1897 | 4k olive & multi | .25 | .25 |
| **4038** | A1897 | 6k olive & multi | .25 | .25 |
| **4039** | A1897 | 10k olive & multi | .25 | .25 |
| **4040** | A1897 | 16k olive & multi | .40 | .25 |
| **4041** | A1897 | 20k olive & multi | .60 | .25 |
| | | *Nos. 4036-4041 (6)* | 2.00 | 1.50 |

**Souvenir Sheet**

*Perf. 12*

**4042** A1897 50k multicolored 1.75 1.25

History of Russian painting.

Symbolic of Theory and Practice — A1920

**Engraved and Photogravure**

**1972, Dec. 7** *Perf. 11½*

**4043** A1920 4k sl grn, yel & red brn .50 .25

Centenary of Polytechnic Museum, Moscow.

Venera 8 and Parachute
A1921

**1972, Dec. 28** **Photo.** *Perf. 11½*

**4044** A1921 6k dl claret, bl & blk .50 .25

**Souvenir Sheet**

*Imperf*

| | | | | |
|---|---|---|---|---|
| **4045** | | Sheet of 2 | 7.00 | 2.00 |
| *a.* | A1921 | 50k Venera 8 | 3.00 | .90 |
| *b.* | A1921 | 50k Mars 3 | 3.00 | .90 |

Soviet space research. No. 4045 contains 2 40x20mm stamps with simulated perforations.

Globe, Torch and Palm — A1922

**1973, Jan. 5** *Perf. 11x11½*

**4046** A1922 10k tan, vio blue & red .50 .30

15th anniversary of Afro-Asian Peoples' Solidarity Organization (AAPSO).

I. V. Babushkin — A1923

**1973, Jan. 10** **Engr.** *Perf. 12*

**4047** A1923 4k greenish black .50 .25

Babushkin (1873-1906), revolutionary.

"30," Map and Admiralty Tower, Leningrad
A1924

**1973, Jan. 10** **Photo.** *Perf. 11½*

**4048** A1924 4k pale brn, ocher & blk .50 .25

30th anniversary of the breaking of the Nazi blockade of Leningrad.

TU-154 Turbojet Passenger Plane — A1925

**1973, Jan. 10** **Litho.** *Perf. 12*

**4049** A1925 6k multicolored .75 .25

50th anniversary of Soviet Civil Aviation.

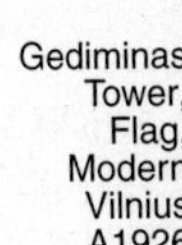

Gediminas Tower, Flag, Modern Vilnius
A1926

**1973, Jan. 10** **Photo.** *Perf. 11½*

**4050** A1926 10k gray, red & green .50 .30

650th anniversary of Vilnius.

Heroes' Memorial, Stalingrad — A1927

Designs (Details from Monument): 3k, Man with rifle and "Mother Russia," vert. 10k, Mourning mother and child. 12k, Arm with torch, vert. No. 4055a, Red star, hammer and sickle emblem and statuary like 3k. No. 4055b, "Mother Russia," vert.

**1973, Feb. 1 Litho. *Perf. 11½***

| | | | | |
|---|---|---|---|---|
| **4051** | A1927 | 3k dp org & blk | 1.25 | .25 |
| **4052** | A1927 | 4k dp yel & blk | 1.25 | .25 |
| **4053** | A1927 | 10k olive & multi | 1.25 | .25 |
| **4054** | A1927 | 12k dp car & black | 1.25 | .25 |
| | | *Nos. 4051-4054 (4)* | 5.00 | 1.00 |

**Souvenir Sheet**

***Perf. 12x12½, 12½x12***

| | | | | |
|---|---|---|---|---|
| **4055** | | Sheet of 2 | 3.00 | 1.00 |
| ***a.-b.*** | A1927 | 20k any single | .75 | .25 |

30th anniv. of the victory over the Germans at Stalingrad. #4055 contains 2 40x18mm stamps.

**Large Portrait Type of 1971**

Designs: 4k, Mikhail Prishvin (1873-1954), author. 10k, Fedor Chaliapin (1873-1938), opera singer, by K. Korovin.

**1973 Litho. *Perf. 11½x12***

| | | | | |
|---|---|---|---|---|
| **4056** | A1855 | 4k pink & multi | .50 | .25 |
| **4057** | A1855 | 10k lt blue & multi | .50 | .25 |

Issue dates: 4k, Feb. 1; 10k, Feb. 8.

"Mayakovsky Theater" — A1928

"Mossovet Theater" — A1929

**1973, Feb. 1 Photo. *Perf. 11½***

| | | | | |
|---|---|---|---|---|
| **4058** | A1928 | 10k red, gray & indigo | .50 | .25 |
| **4059** | A1929 | 10k red, mag & gray | .50 | .25 |

50th anniversary of the Mayakovsky and Mossovet Theaters in Moscow.

Copernicus and Solar System A1930

**1973, Feb. 8 Engr. & Photo.**

| | | | | |
|---|---|---|---|---|
| **4060** | A1930 | 10k ultra & sepia | .75 | .25 |

500th anniversary of the birth of Nicolaus Copernicus (1473-1543), Polish astronomer.

Ice Hockey A1931

Design: 50k, Two players, vert.

**1973, Mar. 14 Photo. *Perf. 11½***

| | | | | |
|---|---|---|---|---|
| **4061** | A1931 | 10k gold, blue & sep | .50 | .25 |

**Souvenir Sheet**

| | | | | |
|---|---|---|---|---|
| **4062** | A1931 | 50k bl grn, gold & sep | 2.00 | 1.00 |

European and World Ice Hockey Championships, Moscow.
See No. 4082.

Athletes and Banners of Air, Land and Naval Forces — A1932

**1973, Mar. 14**

| | | | | |
|---|---|---|---|---|
| **4063** | A1932 | 4k bright blue & multi | .50 | .25 |

Sports Society of Soviet Army, 50th anniv.

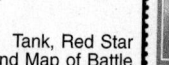

Tank, Red Star and Map of Battle of Kursk — A1933

**1973, Mar. 14**

| | | | | |
|---|---|---|---|---|
| **4064** | A1933 | 4k gray, black & red | .50 | .25 |

30th anniversary of Soviet victory in the Battle of Kursk during World War II.

Nikolai E. Bauman (1873-1905), Bolshevist Revolutionary A1934

**1973, Mar. 20 Engr. *Perf. 12½x12***

| | | | | |
|---|---|---|---|---|
| **4065** | A1934 | 4k brown | .50 | .25 |

Red Cross and Red Crescent — A1935

6k, Theater curtain & mask. 16k, Youth Festival emblem & young people.

**1973, Mar. 20 Photo. *Perf. 11***

| | | | | |
|---|---|---|---|---|
| **4066** | A1935 | 4k gray grn & red | .45 | .25 |
| **4067** | A1935 | 6k violet blue & red | .45 | .25 |
| **4068** | A1935 | 16k multicolored | 1.10 | .25 |
| | | *Nos. 4066-4068 (3)* | 2.00 | .75 |

Union of Red Cross and Red Crescent Societies of the USSR, 50th annivs.; 15th Cong. of the Intl. Theater Institute; 10th World Festival of Youth and Students, Berlin.

Aleksandr N. Ostrovsky, by V. Perov A1936

**1973, Apr. 5 Litho. *Perf. 12x12½***

| | | | | |
|---|---|---|---|---|
| **4069** | A1936 | 4k tan & multi | .50 | .25 |

Ostrovsky (1823-1886), dramatist.

Earth Satellite "Interkosmos" A1937

Lunokhod 2 on Moon and Lenin Moon Plaque A1938

**1973, Apr. 12 Photo. *Perf. 11½***

| | | | | |
|---|---|---|---|---|
| **4070** | A1937 | 6k brn ol & dull cl | .25 | .25 |
| **4071** | A1938 | 6k vio blue & multi | .25 | .25 |

**Souvenir Sheets**

***Perf. 12x11½***

| | | | | |
|---|---|---|---|---|
| **4072** | | Sheet of 3, purple & multi | 1.50 | .75 |
| ***a.*** | A1938 | 20k Lenin plaque | .40 | .25 |
| ***b.*** | A1938 | 20k Lunokhod 2 | .40 | .25 |
| ***c.*** | A1938 | 20k Telecommunications | .40 | .25 |
| **4073** | | Sheet of 3, slate grn & multi | 1.50 | .75 |
| ***a.*** | A1938 | 20k Lenin plaque | .40 | .25 |
| ***b.*** | A1938 | 20k Lunokhod 2 | .40 | .25 |
| ***c.*** | A1938 | 20k Telecommunications | .40 | .25 |

Cosmonauts' Day. No. 4070 for cooperation in space research by European communist countries.

Souvenir sheets contain 3 50x21mm stamps.

**Russian Painting Type of 1972**

Paintings: 2k, Guitarist, V. A. Tropinin. 4k, Young Widow, by P. A. Fedotov. 6k, Self-portrait, by O. A. Kiprensky. 10k, Woman with Grapes ("An Afternoon in Italy") by K. P. Bryullov. 12k, Boy with Dog ("That was my Father's Dinner"), by A. Venetsianov. 16k, "Lower Gallery of Albano," by A. A. Ivanov. 20k, Soldiers ("Conquest of Siberia"), by V. I. Surikov, horiz.

***Perf. 12x12½, 12½x12***

**1973, Apr. 18 Litho.**

| | | | | |
|---|---|---|---|---|
| **4074** | A1897 | 2k gray & multi | .25 | .25 |
| **4075** | A1897 | 4k gray & multi | .25 | .25 |
| **4076** | A1897 | 6k gray & multi | .25 | .25 |
| **4077** | A1897 | 10k gray & multi | .25 | .25 |
| **4078** | A1897 | 12k gray & multi | .45 | .25 |
| **4079** | A1897 | 16k gray & multi | .60 | .25 |
| **4080** | A1897 | 20k gray & multi | .70 | .25 |
| | | *Nos. 4074-4080 (7)* | 2.75 | 1.75 |

Athlete, Ribbon of Lenin Order — A1939

**1973, Apr. 18 Photo. *Perf. 11½***

| | | | | |
|---|---|---|---|---|
| **4081** | A1939 | 4k blue, red & ocher | .50 | .25 |

50th anniversary of Dynamo Sports Society.

**No. 4062 with Blue Green Inscription and Ornaments Added in Margin**

Souvenir Sheet

**1973, Apr. 26 Photo. *Perf. 11½***

| | | | | |
|---|---|---|---|---|
| **4082** | A1931 | 50k multicolored | 5.00 | 2.00 |

Soviet victory in European and World Ice Hockey Championships, Moscow.

"Mikhail Lermontov," Route Leningrad to New York — A1940

**1973, May 20 Photo. *Perf. 11½***

| | | | | |
|---|---|---|---|---|
| **4083** | A1940 | 16k multicolored | .60 | .25 |

Inauguration of transatlantic service Leningrad to New York.

Ernest E. T. Krenkel, Polar Stations and Ship Chelyuskin A1941

**1973, May 20 Litho. & Engr.**

| | | | | |
|---|---|---|---|---|
| **4084** | A1941 | 4k dull blue & olive | 1.00 | .30 |

Krenkel (1903-1971), polar explorer.

Emblem and Sports — A1942

**1973, May 20 Litho. *Perf. 12x12½***

| | | | | |
|---|---|---|---|---|
| **4085** | A1942 | 4k multicolored | .65 | .25 |

Sports Association for Labor and Defense.

Latvian Song Festival, Cent. — A1943

**1973, May 24**

| | | | | |
|---|---|---|---|---|
| **4086** | A1943 | 10k Singers | .65 | .25 |

Throwing the Hammer — A1944

Designs: 3k, Athlete on rings. 4k, Woman diver. 16k, Fencing. 50k, Javelin.

**1973, June 14 Litho. *Perf. 11½***

| | | | | |
|---|---|---|---|---|
| **4087** | A1944 | 2k lemon & multi | .25 | .25 |
| **4088** | A1944 | 3k blue & multi | .25 | .25 |
| **4089** | A1944 | 4k citron & multi | .25 | .25 |
| **4090** | A1944 | 16k lilac & multi | .35 | .25 |
| | | *Nos. 4087-4090 (4)* | 1.10 | 1.00 |

**Souvenir Sheet**

| | | | | |
|---|---|---|---|---|
| **4091** | A1944 | 50k gold & multi | 1.75 | 1.25 |

Universiad, Moscow, 1973.

Souvenir Sheet

Valentina Nikolayeva-Tereshkova — A1945

**1973, June 14 Photo. *Perf. 12x11½***

| | | | | |
|---|---|---|---|---|
| **4092** | A1945 | Sheet of 3 + label | 3.00 | 1.25 |
| ***a.*** | | 20k as cosmonaut | .55 | .25 |
| ***b.*** | | 20k with Indian and African women | .55 | .25 |
| ***c.*** | | 20k with daughter | .55 | .25 |

Flight of the 1st woman cosmonaut, 10th anniv.

European Bison — A1946

**1973, July 26 Photo. *Perf. 11x11½***

| | | | | |
|---|---|---|---|---|
| **4093** | A1946 | 1k shown | .25 | .25 |
| **4094** | A1946 | 3k Ibex | .25 | .25 |
| **4095** | A1946 | 4k Caucasian snowcock | .25 | .25 |
| **4096** | A1946 | 6k Beaver | .25 | .25 |
| **4097** | A1946 | 10k Deer and fawns | .25 | .25 |
| | | *Nos. 4093-4097 (5)* | 1.25 | 1.25 |

Caucasus and Voronezh wildlife reserves.

Party Membership Card with Lenin Portrait — A1947

**1973, July 26 Litho. *Perf. 11½***

**4098** A1947 4k multicolored .50 .25

70th anniversary of 2nd Congress of the Russian Social Democratic Workers' Party.

Abu-al-Rayhan al-Biruni (973-1048), Arabian (Persian) Scholar and Writer — A1948

**1973, Aug. 9 Engr. *Perf. 12x12½***

**4099** A1948 6k red brown .50 .25

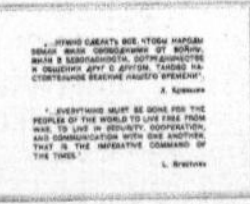
White House, Spasski Tower, Hemispheres — A1949

#4101, Eiffel Tower, Spasski Tower, globe. #4102, Schaumburg Palace, Bonn, Spasski Tower, globe. Stamps show representative buildings of Moscow, Washington, New York, Paris & Bonn.

**1973, Aug. 10 Photo. *Perf. 11½x12***

| | | | | |
|---|---|---|---|---|
| **4100** | A1949 | 10k magenta & multi | 1.00 | .50 |
| **4101** | A1949 | 10k brown & multi | 1.00 | .50 |
| **4102** | A1949 | 10k dp car & multi | 1.00 | .50 |
| *a.* | | Souv. sheet of 3 + 3 labels | 4.50 | 2.50 |
| | | *Nos. 4100-4102 (3)* | 3.00 | 1.50 |

Visit of General Secretary Leonid I. Brezhnev to Washington, Paris and Bonn. Nos. 4100-4102 each printed with se-tenant label with different statements by Brezhnev in Russian and English, French and German, respectively.

No. 4102a contains 4k stamps similar to Nos. 4100-4102 in changed colors. Issued Nov. 26.

See Nos. 4161-4162.

**Russian Painting Type of 1972**

2k, S. T. Konenkov, sculptor, by P. D. Korin. 4k, Tractor Operators at Supper, by A. A. Plastov. 6k, Letter from the Front, by A. I. Laktionov. 10k, Mountains, by M. S. Saryan. 16k, Wedding on a Future Street, by Y. I. Pimenov. 20k, Ice Hockey, mosaic by A. A. Deineka. 50k, Lenin at 3rd Congress of Young Communist League, by B. V. Yoganson.

**1973, Aug. 22 Litho. *Perf. 12x12½***
**Frame in Light Gray**

| | | | | |
|---|---|---|---|---|
| **4103** | A1897 | 2k multicolored | .25 | .25 |
| **4104** | A1897 | 4k multicolored | .25 | .25 |
| **4105** | A1897 | 6k multicolored | .25 | .25 |
| **4106** | A1897 | 10k multicolored | .25 | .25 |
| **4107** | A1897 | 16k multicolored | .45 | .25 |
| **4108** | A1897 | 20k multicolored | .55 | .25 |
| | | *Nos. 4103-4108 (6)* | 2.00 | 1.50 |

**Souvenir Sheet**
***Perf. 12***

**4109** A1897 50k multicolored 3.00 1.50

History of Russian Painting.

Museum, Tashkent A1950

**1973, Aug. 23 Photo. *Perf. 12x12½***

**4110** A1950 4k multicolored .50 .25

Lenin Central Museum, Tashkent branch.

Y. M. Steklov — A1951

**1973, Aug. 27 Photo. *Perf. 11½x12***

**4111** A1951 4k multicolored .50 .25

Steklov (1873-1941), party worker, historian, writer.

Book, Pen and Torch — A1952

**1973, Aug. 31 *Perf. 11½***

**4112** A1952 6k multicolored .50 .25

Conf. of Writers of Asia & Africa, Alma-Ata.

Echinopanax Elatum — A1953

Medicinal Plants: 2k, Ginseng. 4k, Orchis maculatus. 10k, Arnica montana. 12k, Lily of the valley.

**1973, Sept. 5 Litho. *Perf. 12x12½***

| | | | | |
|---|---|---|---|---|
| **4113** | A1953 | 1k yellow & multi | .25 | .25 |
| **4114** | A1953 | 2k lt blue & multi | .25 | .25 |
| **4115** | A1953 | 4k gray & multi | .25 | .25 |
| **4116** | A1953 | 10k sepia & multi | .25 | .25 |
| **4117** | A1953 | 12k green & multi | .25 | .25 |
| | | *Nos. 4113-4117 (5)* | 1.25 | 1.25 |

Imadeddin Nasimi, Azerbaijani Poet, 600th Birth Anniv. — A1954

**1973, Sept. 5 Engr.**

**4118** A1954 4k sepia .50 .25

Cruiser Kirov — A1955

Soviet Warships: 4k, Battleship October Revolution. 6k, Submarine Krasnogvardeyets. 10k, Torpedo boat Soobrazitelny. 16k, Cruiser Red Caucasus.

**Engraved and Photogravure**
**1973, Sept. 12 *Perf. 11½x12***

| | | | | |
|---|---|---|---|---|
| **4119** | A1955 | 3k violet & multi | .25 | .25 |
| **4120** | A1955 | 4k green & multi | .25 | .25 |
| **4121** | A1955 | 6k multicolored | .25 | .25 |
| **4122** | A1955 | 10k blue grn & multi | .40 | .25 |
| **4123** | A1955 | 16k multicolored | .60 | .25 |
| | | *Nos. 4119-4123 (5)* | 1.75 | 1.25 |

Globe and Red Flag Emblem — A1956

**1973, Sept. 25 Photo. *Perf. 11½***

**4124** A1956 6k gold, buff & red .50 .25

15th anniversary of the international communist review "Problems of Peace and Socialism," published in Prague.

Emelyan I. Pugachev and Peasant Army — A1957

**Engraved and Photogravure**
**1973, Sept. 25 *Perf. 11½x12***

**4125** A1957 4k brn, bister & red .75 .25

Bicentenary of peasant revolt of 1773-75 led by Emelyn Ivanovich Pugachev.

Crystal, Institute Emblem and Building A1958

**1973, Oct. 5 *Perf. 11½***

**4126** A1958 4k black & multi .50 .25

Leningrad Mining Institute, 150th anniv.

Palm, Globe, Flower — A1959

**1973, Oct. 5 Photo.**

**4127** A1959 6k red, gray & dk blue .50 .25

World Cong. of Peace-loving Forces, Moscow.

Elena Stasova — A1960

**1973, Oct. 5 *Perf. 11½x12***

**4128** A1960 4k deep claret .50 .25

Elena Dmitriyevna Stasova (1873-1966), communist party worker.

See Nos. 4228-4229.

Order of Friendship — A1961

**1973, Oct. 5 Litho. *Perf. 12***

**4129** A1961 4k red & multi .75 .25

56th anniv. of the October Revolution. Printed se-tenant with coupon showing Arms of USSR and proclamation establishing Order of Friendship of People, in 1972, on the 50th anniv. of the USSR.

Marshal Malinovsky A1962

**1973, Oct. 5 Engr.**

**4130** A1962 4k slate .50 .25

Rodion Y. Malinovsky (1898-1967).

See Nos. 4203-4205.

Ural Man, Red Guard, Worker — A1963

**1973, Oct. 17 Photo. *Perf. 11½***

**4131** A1963 4k red, gold & black .50 .25

250th anniversary of the city of Sverdlovsk.

Dimitri Cantemir (1673-1723), Prince of Moldavia, Writer — A1964

**1973, Oct. 17 Engr. *Perf. 12x12½***

**4132** A1964 4k rose claret .50 .25

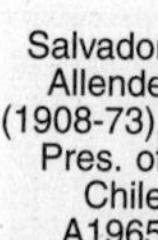

Salvador Allende (1908-73), Pres. of Chile A1965

**1973, Nov. 26 Photo. *Perf. 11½***

**4133** A1965 6k rose brn & black .50 .25

Spasski Tower, Kremlin — A1966

**1973, Nov. 30 Litho. *Perf. 12x12½***

**4134** A1966 6k brt blue & multi 1.00 .25

New Year 1974.

Nariman Narimanov A1967

**1973, Nov. 30 Engr. *Perf. 12***

**4135** A1967 4k slate green .50 .25

Nariman Narimanov (1870-1925), Chairman of Executive Committee of USSR.

Russo-Balt, 1909 — A1968

Designs: 3k, AMO-F15 truck, 1924. 4k, Spartak, NAMI-1 car, 1927. 12k, Ya-6 autobus, 1929. 16k, GAZ-A car, 1932.

**1973, Nov. 30 Photo. *Perf. 12x11½***

**4136** A1968 2k purple & multi .25 .25
**4137** A1968 3k olive & multi .25 .25
**4138** A1968 4k ocher & multi .25 .25
**4139** A1968 12k vio blue & multi .40 .25
**4140** A1968 16k red & multi .50 .25
*Nos. 4136-4140 (5)* 1.65 1.25

Development of Russian automotive industry. See Nos. 4216-4220, 4325-4329, 4440-4444.

Still Life, by Frans Snyders — A1969

Paintings: 6k, Woman Trying on Earrings, by Rembrandt, vert. 10k, Sick Woman and Physician, by Jan Steen, vert. 12k, Still Life with Sculpture, by Jean-Baptiste Chardin. 14k, Lady in Garden, by Claude Monet. 16k, Young Love, by Jules Bastien-Lepage, vert. 20k Girl with Fan, by Auguste Renoir, vert. 50k, Flora, by Rembrandt, vert.

***Perf. 12x11½, 11½x12***

**1973, Dec. 12 Litho.**

**4141** A1969 4k bister & multi .25 .25
**4142** A1969 6k bister & multi .25 .25
**4143** A1969 10k bister & multi .40 .25
**4144** A1969 12k bister & multi .45 .25
**4145** A1969 14k bister & multi .50 .25
**4146** A1969 16k bister & multi .55 .25
**4147** A1969 20k bister & multi .70 .25
*Nos. 4141-4147 (7)* 3.10 1.75

**Souvenir Sheet**

***Perf. 12***

**4148** A1969 50k multicolored 2.00 1.00

Foreign paintings in Russian museums.

Pablo Picasso (1881-1973), Painter A1970

**1973, Dec. 20 Photo. *Perf. 12x11½***

**4149** A1970 6k gold, slate grn & red .75 .25

Organ Pipes and Dome, Riga — A1971

No. 4151, Small Trakai Castle, Lithuania. No. 4152, Great Sea Gate, Tallinn, Estonia. 10k, Town Hall and "Old Thomas" weather vane, Tallinn.

**1973, Dec. 20 Engr. *Perf. 12x12½***

**4150** A1971 4k blk, red & slate grn .25 .25
**4151** A1971 4k gray, red & buff .25 .25
**4152** A1971 4k black, red & grn .25 .25
**4153** A1971 10k sep, grn, red & blk .25 .25
*Nos. 4150-4153 (4)* 1.00 1.00

Architecture of the Baltic area.

I. G. Petrovsky A1972

L. A. Artsimovich A1973

No. 4154, I. G. Petrovsky (1901-73), mathematician, rector of Moscow State University. No. 4155, L. A. Artsimovich (1909-73), physicist, academician. No. 4156, K. D. Ushinsky (1824-71), teacher. No. 4157, M. D. Millionschikov (1913-73), vice president of Academy of Sciences.

**1973-74 Photo. *Perf. 11½***

**4154** A1972 4k orange & multi .50 .25
**4155** A1973 4k blk brn & olive .50 .25

**Engr.**

***Perf. 12½x12***

**4156** A1973 4k multicolored .50 .25

**Litho.**

***Perf. 12***

**4157** A1973 4k multicolored .50 .25
*Nos. 4154-4157 (4)* 2.00 1.00

Issued: #4154, 12/28/73; others, 2/6/74.

Flags of India and USSR, Red Fort, Taj Mahal and Kremlin — A1974

Design: No. 4162, Flags of Cuba and USSR, José Marti Monument, Moncada Barracks and Kremlin.

**1973-74 Litho. *Perf. 12***

**4161** A1974 4k lt ultra & multi 1.00 .25
**4162** A1974 4k lt grn & multi ('74) 1.00 .25

Visit of General Secretary Leonid I. Brezhnev to India and Cuba. Nos. 4161-4162 each printed with se-tenant label with different statements by Brezhnev in Russian and Hindi, and Russian and Spanish respectively.

Red Star, Soldier, Newspaper A1975

**1974, Jan. 1 Photo. *Perf. 11x11½***

**4166** A1975 4k gold, red & black .50 .25

50th anniversary of the Red Star newspaper.

Victory Monument, Peter-Paul Fortress, Statue of Peter I — A1976

**1974, Jan. 16 Litho. *Perf. 11½***

**4167** A1976 4k multicolored 1.00 .25

30th anniversary of the victory over the Germans near Leningrad.

Oil Workers, Refinery — A1977

**1974, Jan. 16 Photo. *Perf. 11½***

**4168** A1977 4k dull blue, red & blk .50 .25

10th anniversary of the Tyumen oilfields.

Comecon Building — A1978

**1974, Jan. 16 Photo. *Perf. 11½***

**4169** A1978 16k red brn, ol & red .50 .25

25th anniversary of the Council for Mutual Economic Assistance.

Skaters and Rink, Medeo A1979

**1974, Jan. 28**

**4170** A1979 6k slate, brn red & bl .50 .25

European Women's Skating Championships, Medeo, Alma-Ata.

Art Palace, Leningrad, Academy, Moscow A1980

**1974, Jan. 30 Photo. & Engr.**

**4171** A1980 10k multicolored .50 .25

25th anniversary of the Academy of Sciences of the USSR.

3rd Winter Spartiakad Emblem — A1981

**1974, Mar. 20 Photo. *Perf. 11½***

**4172** A1981 10k gold & multi .50 .25

Third Winter Spartiakad.

Young People and Emblem — A1982

**1974, Mar. 20 Photo. & Engr.**

**4173** A1982 4k multicolored .50 .25

Youth scientific-technical work.

Azerbaijan Theater — A1983

**1974, Mar. 20 Photo. *Perf. 11½***

**4174** A1983 6k org, red brn & brn .50 .25

Centenary of Azerbaijan Theater.

Meteorological Satellite "Meteor" — A1984

Cosmonauts V. G. Lazarev and O. G. Makarov and Soyuz 12 — A1985

Design: No. 4177, Cosmonauts P. I. Klimuk and V. V. Lebedev, and Soyuz 13.

**1974, Mar. 27 *Perf. 11½***

**4175** A1984 6k violet & multi .60 .25

***Perf. 12x11½***

**4176** A1985 10k grnsh bl & multi .70 .25
**4177** A1985 10k dull yel & multi .70 .25
*Nos. 4175-4177 (3)* 2.00 .75

Cosmonauts' Day.

Odessa by Moonlight, by Aivazovski — A1986

Seascapes by Aivazovski: 4k, Battle of Chesma, 1848, vert. 6k, St. George's Monastery. 10k, Stormy Sea. 12k, Rainbow (shipwreck). 16k, Shipwreck. 50k, Portrait of Aivazovski, by Kramskoy, vert.

***Perf. 12x11½, 11½x12***

**1974, Mar. 30 Litho.**

**4178** A1986 2k gray & multi .25 .25
**4179** A1986 4k gray & multi .25 .25
**4180** A1986 6k gray & multi .25 .25
**4181** A1986 10k gray & multi .30 .25
**4182** A1986 12k gray & multi .45 .25
**4183** A1986 16k gray & multi .70 .25
*Nos. 4178-4183 (6)* 2.20 1.50

**Souvenir Sheet**

**4184** A1986 50k gray & multi 2.00 .90

Ivan Konstantinovich Aivazovski (1817-1900), marine painter. Sheets of Nos. 4178-4183 each contain 2 labels with commemorative inscriptions.

See Nos. 4230-4234.

Young Man and Woman, Banner A1987

**1974, Mar. 30 Litho. *Perf. 12½x12***

**4185** A1987 4k red, yel & brown .50 .25

17th Cong. of the Young Communist League.

Lenin, by V. E. Tsigal A1988

**1974, Mar. 30**

**4186** A1988 4k yel, red & brown .50 .25

50th anniversary of naming the Komsomol (Young Communist League) after Lenin.

Souvenir Sheet

Lenin at the Telegraph, by Igor E. Grabar — A1989

**1974, Apr. 16 Litho. *Perf. 12***

**4187** A1989 50k multicolored 2.00 .90

104th anniv. of the birth of Lenin.

Rainbow, Swallow over Clouds — A1990

6k, Fish in water. 10k, Crystal. 16k, Rose. 20k, Fawn. 50k, Infant.

**1974, Apr. 24 Photo. *Perf. 11½***

**4188** A1990 4k lilac & multi .25 .25
**4189** A1990 6k multicolored .25 .25
**4190** A1990 10k multicolored .35 .25
**4191** A1990 16k blue & multi .55 .25
**4192** A1990 20k citron & multi .60 .25
*Nos. 4188-4192 (5)* 2.00 1.25

**Souvenir Sheet**

**Litho.**

***Perf. 12x12½***

**4193** A1990 50k blue & multi 2.00 .80

EXPO '74 World's Fair, theme "Preserve the Environment," Spokane, WA, May 4-Nov. 4.

Congress Emblem and Clover — A1991

**1974, May 7 Photo. *Perf. 11½***

**4194** A1991 4k green & multi .50 .25

12th International Congress on Meadow Cultivation, Moscow, 1974.

"Cobblestones, Weapons of the Proletariat," by I. D. Shadr — A1992

**1974, May 7**

**4195** A1992 4k gold, red & olive .50 .25

50th anniversary of the Lenin Central Revolutionary Museum of the USSR.

Saiga — A1993

Fauna of USSR: 3k, Koulan (wild ass). 4k, Desman. 6k, Sea lion. 10k, Greenland whale.

**1974, May 22 Litho. *Perf. 11½***

**4196** A1993 1k olive & multi .40 .25
**4197** A1993 3k green & multi .80 .35
**4198** A1993 4k multicolored .80 .35
**4199** A1993 6k multicolored 1.10 .50
**4200** A1993 10k multicolored 1.90 .60
*Nos. 4196-4200 (5)* 5.00 2.05

Peter Ilich Tchaikovsky — A1994

**1974, May 22 Photo. *Perf. 11½***

**4201** A1994 6k multicolored .50 .25

5th International Tchaikovsky Competition, Moscow.

Souvenir Sheet

Aleksander S. Pushkin, by O. A. Kiprensky — A1995

**1974, June 4 Litho. *Imperf.***

**4202** A1995 50k multicolored 2.00 .80

Aleksander S. Pushkin (1799-1837).

**Marshal Type of 1973**

Designs: No. 4203, Marshal F. I. Tolbukhin (1894-1949); No. 4204, Admiral I. S. Isakov (1894-1967); No. 4205, Marshal S. M. Budenny (1883-1973).

**1974 Engr. *Perf. 12***

**4203** A1962 4k olive green .50 .25
**4204** A1962 4k indigo .50 .25
**4205** A1962 4k slate green .50 .25
*Nos. 4203-4205 (3)* 1.50 .75

Issued: #4203, 6/5; #4204, 7/18; #4205, 8/20.

Stanislavski and Nemirovich-Danchenko — A1996

**1974, June 12 Litho. *Perf. 12***

**4211** A1996 10k yel, black & dk red .50 .25

75th anniv. of the Moscow Arts Theater.

Runner, Track, Open Book A1997

**1974, June 12 Photo. *Perf. 11½***

**4212** A1997 4k multicolored .50 .25

13th Natl. School Spartakiad, Alma-Ata.

Railroad Car A1998

**1974, June 12**

**4213** A1998 4k multicolored 1.00 .25

Egorov Railroad Car Factory, cent.

Victory Monument, Minsk — A1999

No. 4215, Monument & Government House, Kiev.

**1974, June 20**

**4214** A1999 4k violet, black & yel .50 .25
**4215** A1999 4k blue, black & yel .50 .25

30th anniversary of liberation of Byelorussia (No. 4214), and of Ukraine (No. 4215).

Issued: #4214, June 20; #4215, July 18.

**Automotive Type of 1973**

Designs: 2k, GAZ AA truck, 1932. 3k, GAZ 03-30 bus, 1933. 4k, Zis 5 truck, 1933. 14k, Zis 8 bus, 1934. 16k, Zis 101 car, 1936.

**1974, June 20 *Perf. 12x11½***

**4216** A1968 2k brown & multi .25 .25
**4217** A1968 3k multicolored .25 .25
**4218** A1968 4k orange & multi .25 .25
**4219** A1968 14k multicolored .50 .25
**4220** A1968 16k multicolored .60 .25
*Nos. 4216-4220 (5)* 1.85 1.25

Soviet automotive industry.

Liberation Monument, Poltava — A2000

**1974, July 7 *Perf. 11½***

**4221** A2000 4k dull red & sepia .50 .25

800th anniversary of city of Poltava.

Nike Monument, Warsaw and Polish Flag — A2001

**1974, July 7 Litho.** ***Perf. 12½x12***

**4222** A2001 6k olive & red .50 .25

Polish People's Republic, 30th anniversary.

Mine Layer — A2002

Soviet Warships: 4k, Landing craft. 6k, Anti-submarine destroyer and helicopter. 16k, Anti-submarine cruiser.

**Engraved and Photogravure**

**1974, July 25** ***Perf. 11½x12***

| | | | | |
|---|---|---|---|---|
| **4223** | A2002 | 3k multicolored | .25 | .25 |
| **4224** | A2002 | 4k multicolored | .70 | .25 |
| **4225** | A2002 | 6k multicolored | 1.00 | .25 |
| **4226** | A2002 | 16k multicolored | 2.00 | .25 |
| | | *Nos. 4223-4226 (4)* | 3.95 | 1.00 |

Pentathlon A2003

**1974, Aug. 7 Photo.** ***Perf. 11½***

**4227** A2003 16k gold, blue & brown .50 .25

World Pentathlon Championships, Moscow.

**Portrait Type of 1973**

No. 4228, Dimitri Ulyanov (1874-1943), Soviet official and Lenin's brother. No. 4229, V. Menzhinsky (1874-1934), Soviet official.

**1974, Aug. 7 Engr.** ***Perf. 12½x12***

**4228** A1960 4k slate green .50 .25

**Litho.**

***Perf. 12x11½***

**4229** A1960 4k rose lake .50 .25

**Painting Type of 1974**

Russian paintings: 4k, Lilac, by W. Kontchalovski. 6k, "Towards the Wind" (sailboats), by E. Kalnins. 10k, "Spring" (girl and landscape), by O. Zardarjan. 16k, Northern Harbor, G. Nissky. 20k, Kirghiz Girl, by S. Chuikov, vert.

***Perf. 12x11½, 11½x12***

**1974, Aug. 20** **Litho.**

| | | | | |
|---|---|---|---|---|
| **4230** | A1986 | 4k gray & multi | .25 | .25 |
| **4231** | A1986 | 6k gray & multi | .25 | .25 |
| **4232** | A1986 | 10k gray & multi | .55 | .25 |
| **4233** | A1986 | 16k gray & multi | .80 | .25 |
| **4234** | A1986 | 20k gray & multi | 1.10 | .25 |
| | | *Nos. 4230-4234 (5)* | 2.95 | 1.25 |

Printed in sheets of 18 stamps and 2 labels.

Page of First Russian Primer — A2004

**1974, Aug. 20 Photo.** ***Perf. 11½***

**4235** A2004 4k black, red & gold .50 .25

1st printed Russian primer, 400th anniv.

Monument, Russian and Romanian Flags — A2005

**1974, Aug. 23**

**4236** A2005 6k dk blue, red & yel .50 .25

Romania's liberation from Fascist rule, 30th anniversary.

Vitebsk A2006

**1974, Sept. 4 Litho.** ***Perf. 12***

**4237** A2006 4k dk car & olive .50 .25

Millennium of city of Vitebsk.

Kirghiz Republic A2007

50th Anniv. of Founding of Republics (Flags, industrial and agricultural themes): No. 4239, Moldavia. No. 4240, Turkmen. No. 4241, Uzbek. No. 4242, Tadzhik.

**1974, Sept. 4** ***Perf. 11½x11***

| | | | | |
|---|---|---|---|---|
| **4238** | A2007 | 4k vio blue & multi | 1.00 | .25 |
| **4239** | A2007 | 4k maroon & multi | 1.00 | .25 |
| **4240** | A2007 | 4k yellow & multi | 1.00 | .25 |
| **4241** | A2007 | 4k green & multi | 1.00 | .25 |
| **4242** | A2007 | 4k lt blue & multi | 1.00 | .25 |
| | | *Nos. 4238-4242 (5)* | 5.00 | 1.25 |

Arms and Flag of Bulgaria — A2008

**Photogravure and Engraved**

**1974, Sept. 4** ***Perf. 11½***

**4243** A2008 6k gold & multi .50 .25

30th anniv. of the Bulgarian revolution.

Arms of DDR and Soviet War Memorial, Treptow A2009

**1974, Sept. 4 Photo.**

**4244** A2009 6k multicolored .50 .25

German Democratic Republic, 25th anniv.

Souvenir Sheet

Soviet Stamps and Exhibition Poster — A2010

**1974, Sept. 4 Litho.** ***Perf. 12x12½***

**4245** A2010 50k multicolored *7.50 3.00*

3rd Cong. of the Phil. Soc. of the USSR.

Maly State Theater — A2011

**1974, Oct. 3 Photo.** ***Perf. 11x11½***

**4246** A2011 4k red, black & gold .50 .25

150th anniversary of the Lenin Academic Maly State Theater, Moscow.

"Guests from Overseas," by N. K. Roerich — A2012

**1974, Oct. 3 Litho.** ***Perf. 12***

**4247** A2012 6k multicolored .50 .25

Nicholas Konstantin Roerich (1874-1947), painter and sponsor of Roerich Pact and Banner of Peace.

UPU Monument, Bern, and Arms of USSR A2013

Development of Postal Service — A2014

UPU Cent.: No. 4248, Ukrainian coat of arms, letters, UPU emblem and headquarters, Bern. No. 4249, Arms of Byelorussia, UPU emblem, letters, stagecoach and rocket.

**Photogravure and Engraved**

**1974, Oct. 9** ***Perf. 12x11½***

| | | | | |
|---|---|---|---|---|
| **4248** | A2013 | 10k red & multi | .35 | .25 |
| **4249** | A2013 | 10k red & multi | .35 | .25 |
| **4250** | A2013 | 10k red & multi | .35 | .25 |
| | | *Nos. 4248-4250 (3)* | 1.05 | .75 |

**Souvenir Sheet**

**Typo.**

***Perf. 11½x12***

| | | | | |
|---|---|---|---|---|
| **4251** | A2014 | Sheet of 3 | 5.00 | 2.50 |
| *a.* | | 30k Jet and UPU emblem | 1.25 | .75 |
| *b.* | | 30k Mail coach, UPU emblem | 1.25 | .75 |
| *c.* | | 40k UPU emblem | 1.25 | .75 |

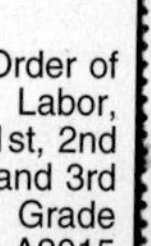

Order of Labor, 1st, 2nd and 3rd Grade A2015

KAMAZ Truck Leaving Kama Plant — A2016

Design: No. 4254, Nurek Hydroelectric Plant.

**1974, Oct. 16 Litho.** ***Perf. 12½x12***

| | | | | |
|---|---|---|---|---|
| **4252** | A2015 | 4k multicolored | .65 | .25 |
| **4253** | A2016 | 4k multicolored | .65 | .25 |
| **4254** | A2016 | 4k multicolored | .65 | .25 |
| | | *Nos. 4252-4254 (3)* | 1.95 | .75 |

Space Stations Mars 4-7 over Mars A2017

P. R. Popovich, Y. P. Artyukhin and Soyuz 14 — A2018

Design: No. 4257, Cosmonauts G. V. Sarafanov and L. S. Demin, Soyuz 15, horiz.

***Perf. 12x11½, 11½***

**1974, Oct. 28** **Photo.**

| | | | | |
|---|---|---|---|---|
| **4255** | A2017 | 6k multicolored | .25 | .25 |
| **4256** | A2018 | 10k multicolored | .40 | .25 |
| **4257** | A2018 | 10k multicolored | .40 | .25 |
| | | *Nos. 4255-4257 (3)* | 1.05 | .75 |

Russian explorations of Mars (6k); flight of Soyuz 14 (No. 4256) and of Soyuz 15, Aug. 26-28 (No. 4257).

Mongolian Flag and Arms A2019

**1974, Nov. 14 Photo.** ***Perf. 11½***

**4258** A2019 6k gold & multi .50 .25

Mongolian People's Republic, 50th anniv.

Guards' Ribbon, Estonian Government Building, Tower — A2020

**1974, Nov. 14**

| | | | | |
|---|---|---|---|---|
| **4259** | A2020 | 4k multicolored | .50 | .25 |

Liberation of Estonia, 30th anniversary.

Tanker, Passenger and Cargo Ships — A2021

**1974, Nov. 14 Typo.** ***Perf. 12½x12***

| | | | | |
|---|---|---|---|---|
| **4260** | A2021 | 4k multicolored | .50 | .25 |

USSR Merchant Marine, 50th anniversary.

Spasski Tower Clock — A2022

**1974, Nov. 14 Litho.** ***Perf. 12***

| | | | | |
|---|---|---|---|---|
| **4261** | A2022 | 4k multicolored | .50 | .25 |

New Year 1975.

The Fishmonger, by Pieters A2023

Paintings: 4k, The Marketplace, by Beuckelaer, 1564, horiz. 10k, A Drink of Lemonade, by Gerard Terborch. 14k, Girl at Work, by Gabriel Metsu. 16k, Saying Grace, by Jean Chardin. 20k, The Spoiled Child, by Jean Greuze. 50k, Self-portrait, by Jacques Louis David.

***Perf. 12x12½, 12½x12***

**1974, Nov. 20 Litho.**

| | | | | |
|---|---|---|---|---|
| **4262** | A2023 | 4k bister & multi | .25 | .25 |
| **4263** | A2023 | 6k bister & multi | .25 | .25 |
| **4264** | A2023 | 10k bister & multi | .25 | .25 |
| **4265** | A2023 | 14k bister & multi | .50 | .25 |
| **4266** | A2023 | 16k bister & multi | .55 | .25 |
| **4267** | A2023 | 20k bister & multi | .70 | .25 |
| | | *Nos. 4262-4267 (6)* | 2.50 | 1.50 |

**Souvenir Sheet**

***Perf. 12***

| | | | | |
|---|---|---|---|---|
| **4268** | A2023 | 50k multicolored | 2.00 | .75 |

Foreign paintings in Russian museums. Printed in sheets of 16 stamps and 4 labels.

Morning Glory — A2024

Designs: Flora of the USSR.

**1974, Nov. 20** ***Perf. 12x12½***

| | | | | |
|---|---|---|---|---|
| **4269** | A2024 | 1k red brn & multi | .25 | .25 |
| **4270** | A2024 | 2k green & multi | .25 | .25 |
| **4271** | A2024 | 4k multicolored | .25 | .25 |
| **4272** | A2024 | 10k brown & multi | .25 | .25 |
| **4273** | A2024 | 12k dk blue & multi | .25 | .25 |
| | | *Nos. 4269-4273 (5)* | 1.25 | 1.25 |

Ivan S. Nikitin (1824-1861), Poet — A2025

**1974, Dec. 11 Photo.** ***Perf. 11½***

| | | | | |
|---|---|---|---|---|
| **4274** | A2025 | 4k gray grn, grn & blk | .50 | .25 |

Leningrad Mint — A2026

**Photogravure and Engraved**

**1974, Dec. 11** ***Perf. 11***

| | | | | |
|---|---|---|---|---|
| **4275** | A2026 | 6k silver & multi | .50 | .25 |

250th anniversary of the Leningrad Mint.

Mozhajsky Plane, 1882 — A2027

Early Russian Aircraft: No. 4277, Grizidubov-N biplane, 1910. No. 4278, Russia-A, 1910. No. 4279, Russian Vityaz (Sikorsky), 1913. No. 4280, Grigorovich flying boat, 1914.

**1974, Dec. 25 Photo.** ***Perf. 11½x12***

| | | | | |
|---|---|---|---|---|
| **4276** | A2027 | 6k olive & multi | .60 | .25 |
| **4277** | A2027 | 6k ultra & multi | .60 | .25 |
| **4278** | A2027 | 6k magenta & multi | .60 | .25 |
| **4279** | A2027 | 6k red & multi | .60 | .25 |
| **4280** | A2027 | 6k brown & multi | .60 | .25 |
| | | *Nos. 4276-4280 (5)* | 3.00 | 1.25 |

Russian aircraft history, 1882-1914.

Souvenir Sheet

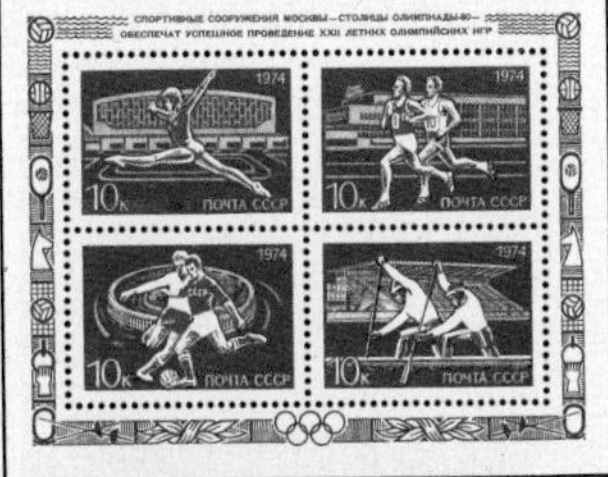

Sports and Sport Buildings, Moscow — A2028

**1974, Dec. 25** ***Perf. 11½***

| | | | | |
|---|---|---|---|---|
| **4281** | A2028 | Sheet of 4 | 1.00 | .50 |
| *a.* | | 10k Woman gymnast | .25 | .25 |
| *b.* | | 10k Running | .25 | .25 |
| *c.* | | 10k Soccer | .25 | .25 |
| *d.* | | 10k Canoeing | .25 | .25 |

Moscow preparing for Summer Olympic Games, 1980.

Rotary Press, Masthead A2029

**1975, Jan. 20**

| | | | | |
|---|---|---|---|---|
| **4282** | A2029 | 4k multicolored | .50 | .25 |

Komsomolskaya Pravda newspaper, 50th anniv.

Masthead and Pioneer Emblems — A2030

**1975, Jan. 20**

| | | | | |
|---|---|---|---|---|
| **4283** | A2030 | 4k red, blk & silver | .50 | .25 |

Pioneers' Pravda newspaper, 50th anniv.

Spartakiad Emblem and Skiers — A2031

**1975, Jan. 20**

| | | | | |
|---|---|---|---|---|
| **4284** | A2031 | 4k blue & multi | .50 | .25 |

8th Winter Spartakiad of USSR Trade Unions.

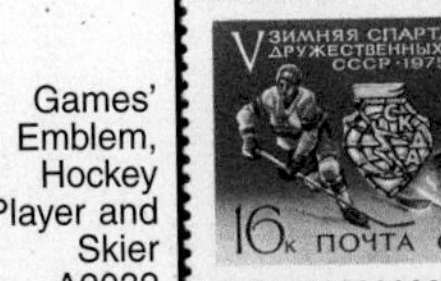


Games' Emblem, Hockey Player and Skier A2032

**1975, Jan. 20**

| | | | | |
|---|---|---|---|---|
| **4285** | A2032 | 16k multicolored | .50 | .25 |

5th Winter Spartakiad of Friendly Armies, Feb. 23-Mar. 1.

**Republic Anniversaries Type of 1970**

Design (Hammer-Sickle Emblem and): No. 4286, Landscape and produce.

**1975, Jan. 24 Engr.** ***Perf. 12x12½***

| | | | | |
|---|---|---|---|---|
| **4286** | A1794 | 4k green | .50 | .25 |

50th anniversary of Karakalpak Autonomous Soviet Socialist Republic.

David, by Michelangelo — A2033

Michelangelo, Self-portrait — A2034

Works by Michelangelo: 6k, Squatting Boy. 10k, Rebellious Slave. 14k, The Creation of Adam. 20k, Staircase, Laurentian Library, Florence. 30k, The Last Judgment.

**Lithographed and Engraved**

**1975, Feb. 27** ***Perf. 12½x12***

| | | | | |
|---|---|---|---|---|
| **4296** | A2033 | 4k slate grn & grn | .25 | .25 |
| **4297** | A2033 | 6k red brn & bister | .25 | .25 |
| **4298** | A2033 | 10k slate grn & grn | .30 | .25 |
| *a.* | | Min. sheet, 2 ea #4296-4298 | 5.00 | 5.00 |
| **4299** | A2033 | 14k red brn & bister | .50 | .25 |
| **4300** | A2033 | 20k slate grn & grn | .70 | .25 |
| **4301** | A2033 | 30k red brn & bister | 1.00 | .25 |
| *a.* | | Min. sheet, 2 ea #4299-4301 | 5.00 | 2.00 |
| | | *Nos. 4296-4301 (6)* | 3.00 | 1.50 |

**Souvenir Sheet**

***Perf. 12x11½***

| | | | | |
|---|---|---|---|---|
| **4302** | A2034 | 50k gold & multi | 4.00 | .80 |

Michelangelo Buonarroti (1475-1564), Italian sculptor, painter and architect. Issued only in the min. sheets of 6.

Mozhajski, Early Plane and Supersonic Jet TU-144 — A2035

**1975, Feb. 27 Photo.** ***Perf. 12x11½***

| | | | | |
|---|---|---|---|---|
| **4303** | A2035 | 6k violet blue & ocher | .50 | .25 |

A. F. Mozhajski (1825-1890), pioneer aircraft designer, birth sesquicentennial.

"Metric System" A2036

**1975, Mar. 14** ***Perf. 11½***

| | | | | |
|---|---|---|---|---|
| **4304** | A2036 | 6k blk, vio blue & org | .50 | .25 |

Intl. Meter Convention, Paris, 1875, cent.

Spartakiad Emblem and Sports A2037

**1975, Mar. 14**

| | | | | |
|---|---|---|---|---|
| **4305** | A2037 | 6k red, silver & black | .50 | .25 |

6th Summer Spartakiad.

Liberation Monument, Parliament, Arms — A2038

Charles Bridge Towers, Arms and Flags — A2039

**1975, Mar. 14**

**4306** A2038 6k gold & multi .25 .25
**4307** A2039 6k gold & multi .25 .25

30th anniv. of liberation from fascism, Hungary (#4306) & Czechoslovakia (#4307).

Flags of France and USSR — A2040

**1975, Mar. 25 Litho.** ***Perf. 12***

**4308** A2040 6k lilac & multi .50 .25

50th anniv. of the establishment of diplomatic relations between France and USSR, 1st foreign recognition of Soviet State.

Yuri A. Gagarin, by L. Kerbel — A2041

A. V. Filipchenko, N.N. Rukavishnikov, Russo-American Space Emblem, Soyuz 16 — A2042

Cosmonauts' Day: 10k, A. A. Gubarev, G. M. Grechko aboard Soyuz 17 & orbital station Salyut 4.

***Perf. 11½x12, 12x11½***

**1975, Mar. 28 Photo.**

**4309** A2041 6k blue, sil & red .25 .25
**4310** A2042 10k blk, blue & red .50 .25
**4311** A2042 16k multicolored .75 .25
*Nos. 4309-4311 (3)* 1.50 .75

Warsaw Treaty Members' Flags — A2043

**1975, Apr. 16 Litho.** ***Perf. 12***

**4312** A2043 6k multicolored .50 .25

Signing of the Warsaw Treaty (Bulgaria, Czechoslovakia, German Democratic Rep., Hungary, Poland, Romania, USSR), 20th anniv.

Lenin on Steps of Winter Palace, by V. G. Zyplakow A2044

**1975, Apr. 22** ***Perf. 12x12½***

**4313** A2044 4k multicolored .60 .25

105th anniversary of the birth of Lenin.

Communications Emblem and Exhibition Pavilion — A2045

**1975, Apr. 22** ***Perf. 11½***

**4314** A2045 6k ultra, red & silver .50 .25

International Communications Exhibition, Sokolniki Park, Moscow, May 1975.

Lenin and Red Flag — A2046

Order of Victory — A2047

No. 4316, Eternal Flame and guard. No. 4317, Woman munitions worker. No. 4318, Partisans. No. 4319, Soldier destroying swastika. No. 4320, Soldier with gun and banner.

**1975, Apr. 22 Typo.** ***Perf. 12***

**4315** A2046 4k shown .25 .25
**4316** A2046 4k multicolored .25 .25
**4317** A2046 4k multicolored .25 .25
**4318** A2046 4k multicolored .25 .25
**4319** A2046 4k multicolored .25 .25
**4320** A2046 4k multicolored .25 .25
*Nos. 4315-4320 (6)* 1.50 1.50

**Souvenir Sheet**

**Litho., Typo. & Photo.**

***Imperf***

**4321** A2047 50k multicolored 2.00 1.00

World War II victory, 30th anniversary.

War Memorial, Berlin-Treptow A2048

**1975, Apr. 25 Litho.** ***Perf. 12x12½***

**4322** A2048 6k buff & multi .50 .25

**Souvenir Sheet**

**4323** A2048 50k dull blue & multi 2.00 .60

Socfilex 75 Intl. Phil. Exhib. honoring 30th anniv. of WWII victory, Moscow, May 8-18.

Soyuz-Apollo Docking Emblem and Painting by Cosmonaut A. A. Leonov — A2049

**1975, May 23 Photo.** ***Perf. 12x11½***

**4324** A2049 20k multicolored .50 .30

Russo-American space cooperation.

**Automobile Type of 1973**

2k, GAZ-M-I car, 1936. 3k, 5-ton truck, YAG-6, 1936. 4k, ZIZ-16, autobus, 1938. 12k, KIM-10 car, 1940. 16k, GAZ-67B jeep, 1943.

**1975, May 23 Photo.** ***Perf. 12x11½***

**4325** A1968 2k dp org & multi .25 .25
**4326** A1068 3k green & multi .25 .25
**4327** A1968 4k dk green & multi .25 .25
**4328** A1968 12k maroon & multi .30 .25
**4329** A1968 16k olive & multi .45 .25
*Nos. 4325-4329 (5)* 1.50 1.25

Canal, Emblem, Produce — A2050

**1975, May 23** ***Perf. 11½***

**4330** A2050 6k multicolored .50 .25

9th Intl. Congress on Irrigation and Drainage, Moscow, and International Commission on Irrigation and Drainage, 25th anniv.

Flags and Arms of Poland and USSR, Factories A2051

**1975, May 23**

**4331** A2051 6k multicolored .50 .25

Treaty of Friendship, Cooperation and Mutual Assistance between Poland & USSR, 30th anniv.

Man in Space and Earth A2052

**1975, May 23**

**4332** A2052 6k multicolored .50 .25

First man walking in space, Lt. Col. Alexei Leonov, 10th anniversary.

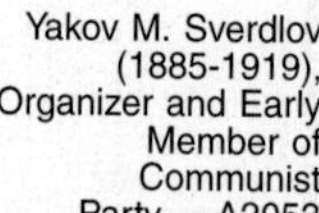

Yakov M. Sverdlov (1885-1919), Organizer and Early Member of Communist Party — A2053

**1975, June 4**

**4333** A2053 4k multicolored .50 .25

Congress, Emblem, Forest and Field A2054

**1975, June 4**

**4334** A2054 6k multicolored .50 .25

8th International Congress for Conservation of Plants, Moscow.

Symbolic Flower with Plants and Emblem A2055

**1975, June 20 Litho.** ***Perf. 11½***

**4335** A2055 6k multicolored .50 .25

12th International Botanical Congress.

**Souvenir Sheet**

UN Emblem — A2056

**1975, June 20 Photo.** ***Perf. 11½x12***

**4336** A2056 50k gold & blue 2.00 1.00

30th anniversary of United Nations.

Globe and Film A2057

**1975, June 20 Photo.** ***Perf. 11½***

**4337** A2057 6k multicolored .50 .25

9th Intl. Film Festival, Moscow, 1975.

Soviet and American Astronauts and Flags — A2058

Apollo and Soyuz After Link-up and Earth — A2059

Soyuz Launch A2060

Designs: No. 4340, Spacecraft before link-up, earth and project emblem. 50k, Soviet Mission Control Center.

**1975, July 15 Litho. *Perf. 11½***

| | | | | |
|---|---|---|---|---|
| **4338** | A2058 10k multicolored | | .35 | .25 |
| **4339** | A2059 12k multicolored | | .45 | .25 |
| **4340** | A2059 12k multicolored | | .45 | .25 |
| *a.* | Vert. pair, #4339-4340 | | 1.50 | .50 |
| **4341** | A2060 16k multicolored | | .75 | .40 |
| | *Nos. 4338-4341 (4)* | | 2.00 | 1.15 |

**Souvenir Sheet**

**Photo.**

***Perf. 12x11½***

| | | | |
|---|---|---|---|
| **4342** | A2058 50k multicolored | 3.00 | 1.25 |

Apollo-Soyuz space test project (Russo-American space cooperation), launching, July 15; link-up July 17.

No. 4342 contains one 50x21mm stamp.

See US Nos. 1569-1570.

Sturgeon, Caspian Sea, Oceanexpo 75 Emblem — A2061

Designs (Oceanexpo 75 Emblem and): 4k, Salt-water shell, Black Sea. 6k, Eel, Baltic Sea. 10k, Sea duck, Arctic Sea. 16k, Crab, Far Eastern waters. 20k, Chrisipther (fish), Pacific Ocean.

**1975, July 22 Photo. *Perf. 11***

| | | | |
|---|---|---|---|
| **4343** | A2061 3k multicolored | .25 | .25 |
| **4344** | A2061 4k multicolored | .25 | .25 |
| **4345** | A2061 6k green & multi | .25 | .25 |
| **4346** | A2061 10k dk blue & multi | .35 | .25 |
| **4347** | A2061 16k purple & multi | .65 | .25 |
| **4348** | A2061 20k multicolored | 1.50 | .25 |
| | *Nos. 4343-4348 (6)* | 3.25 | 1.50 |

**Souvenir Sheet**

***Perf. 12x11½***

| | | | |
|---|---|---|---|
| **4349** | Sheet of 2 | 2.00 | .90 |
| *a.* | A2061 30k Dolphin rising | .75 | .30 |
| *b.* | A2061 30k Dolphin diving | .75 | .30 |

Oceanexpo 75, 1st Intl. Oceanographic Exhib., Okinawa, July 20, 1975-Jan. 1976. No. 4349 contains 55x25mm stamps.

Parade, Red Square, 1941, by K. F. Yuon — A2062

Paintings: 2k, Morning of Industrial Moscow, by Yuon. 6k, Soldiers Inspecting Captured Artillery, by Lansere. 10k, Excavating Metro Tunnel, by Lansere. 16k, Pushkin and His Wife at Court Ball, by Ulyanov, vert. 20k, De Lauriston at Kutuzov's Headquarters, by Ulyanov.

**1975, July 22 Litho. *Perf. 12½x11½***

| | | | |
|---|---|---|---|
| **4350** | A2062 1k gray & multi | .25 | .25 |
| **4351** | A2062 2k gray & multi | .25 | .25 |
| **4352** | A2062 6k gray & multi | .25 | .25 |
| **4353** | A2062 10k gray & multi | .25 | .25 |
| **4354** | A2062 16k gray & multi | .50 | .25 |
| **4355** | A2062 20k gray & multi | .70 | .25 |
| | *Nos. 4350-4355 (6)* | 2.20 | 1.50 |

Konstantin F. Yuon (1875-1958), Yevgeni Y. Lansere (1875-1946), Nikolai P. Ulyanov (1875-1949).

Nos. 4350-4355 issued in sheets of 16 plus 4 labels.

Finlandia Hall, Map of Europe, Laurel — A2063

**1975, Aug. 18 Photo. *Perf. 11½***

| | | | |
|---|---|---|---|
| **4356** | A2063 6k brt blue, gold & blk | .50 | .25 |

European Security and Cooperation Conference, Helsinki, July 30-Aug. 1. Printed se-tenant with label with quotation by Leonid I. Brezhnev, first secretary of Communist party.

Ciurlionis, Waves and Lighthouse A2064

**1975, Aug. 20 Photo. & Engr.**

| | | | |
|---|---|---|---|
| **4357** | A2064 4k grn, indigo & gold | .50 | .25 |

M. K. Ciurlionis, Lithuanian composer, birth centenary.

Avetik Isaakyan, by Martiros Saryan A2065

**1975, Aug. 20 Litho. *Perf. 12x12½***

| | | | |
|---|---|---|---|
| **4358** | A2065 4k multicolored | .50 | .25 |

Isaakyan (1875-1957), Armenian poet.

Jacques Duclos — A2066

**1975, Aug. 20 Photo. *Perf. 11½x12***

| | | | |
|---|---|---|---|
| **4359** | A2066 6k maroon & silver | .50 | .25 |

Duclos (1896-1975), French labor leader.

al-Farabi — A2067

**1975, Aug. 20 *Perf. 11½***

| | | | |
|---|---|---|---|
| **4360** | A2067 6k grnsh blue, brn & bis | .50 | .25 |

Nasr al-Farabi (870?-950), Arab philosopher.

Male Ruffs A2068

**1975, Aug. 25 Litho. *Perf. 12½x12***

| | | | |
|---|---|---|---|
| **4361** | A2068 1k shown | .25 | .25 |
| **4362** | A2068 4k Altai roebuck | .25 | .25 |
| **4363** | A2068 6k Siberian marten | .25 | .25 |
| **4364** | A2068 10k Old squaw (duck) | .40 | .25 |
| **4365** | A2068 16k Badger | .55 | .25 |
| | *Nos. 4361-4365 (5)* | 1.70 | 1.25 |

Berezina River and Stolby wildlife reservations, 50th anniversary.

A2069 A2070

Designs: No. 4366, Flags of USSR, North Korea, arms of N. K., Liberation monument, Pyongyang. No. 4367, Flags of USSR, North Viet Nam, arms of N.V., industrial development.

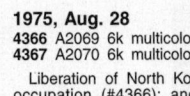

**1975, Aug. 28 *Perf. 12***

| | | | |
|---|---|---|---|
| **4366** | A2069 6k multicolored | .30 | .25 |
| **4367** | A2070 6k multicolored | .30 | .25 |

Liberation of North Korea from Japanese occupation (#4366); and establishment of Democratic Republic of Viet Nam (#4367), 30th annivs.

P. Klimuk and V. Sevastyanov, Soyuz 18 and Salyut 4 Docking — A2071

**1975, Sept. 12 Photo. *Perf. 12x11½***

| | | | |
|---|---|---|---|
| **4368** | A2071 10k ultra, blk & dp org | .50 | .25 |

Docking of space ship Soyuz 18 and space station Salyut 4.

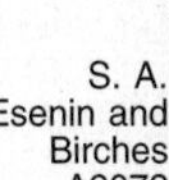

S. A. Esenin and Birches A2072

**Photogravure and Engraved**

**1975, Sept. 12 *Perf. 11½***

| | | | |
|---|---|---|---|
| **4369** | A2072 6k brown & ocher | .50 | .25 |

Sergei A. Esenin (1895-1925), poet.

Standardization Symbols — A2073

**1975, Sept. 12 Photo. *Perf. 11½***

| | | | |
|---|---|---|---|
| **4370** | A2073 4k red & multi | .50 | .25 |

USSR Committee for Standardization of Communications Ministry, 50th anniversary.

Karakul Lamb A2074

**1975, Sept. 22 Photo. *Perf. 11½***

| | | | |
|---|---|---|---|
| **4371** | A2074 6k black, yel & grn | .50 | .25 |

3rd International Symposium on astrakhan production, Samarkand, Sept. 22-27.

Dr. M. P. Konchalovsky A2075

**1975, Sept. 30 *Perf. 11½x12***

| | | | |
|---|---|---|---|
| **4372** | A2075 4k brown & red | .50 | .25 |

Konchalovsky (1875-1942), physician.

Exhibition Emblem — A2076

**1975, Sept. 30** *Perf. 11½*

**4373** A2076 4k deep blue & red .50 .25

3rd All-Union Youth Phil. Exhib., Yerevan.

IWY Emblem and Rose — A2077

**1975, Sept. 30 Litho.** *Perf. 12x11½*

**4374** A2077 6k multicolored .50 .25

International Women's Year 1975.

Yugoslavian Flag and Parliament A2078

**1975, Sept. 30 Photo.** *Perf. 11½*

**4375** A2078 6k gold, red & blue .50 .25

Republic of Yugoslavia, 30th anniv.

Illustration from 1938 Edition, by V. A. Favorsky — A2079

**1975, Oct. 20 Typo.** *Perf. 12*

**4376** A2079 4k buff, red & black .50 .25

175th anniversary of the 1st edition of the old Russian saga "Slovo o polku Igoreve."

Mikhail Ivanovich Kalinin — A2080

No. 4378, Anatoli Vasilievich Lunacharski.

**1975, Oct. 20 Engr.** *Perf. 12*

**4377** A2080 4k sepia .25 .25
**4378** A2080 4k sepia .25 .25

Kalinin (1875-1946), chairman of Central Executive Committee and Presidium of Supreme Soviet; Lunacharski (1875-1933), writer, commissar for education.

Hand Holding Torch and Lenin Quotation — A2081

**1975, Oct. 20** **Engr.**

**4379** A2081 4k red & olive .50 .25

First Russian Revolution (1905), 70th anniv.

Building Baikal-Amur Railroad — A2082

Novolipetsk Metallurgical Plant — A2083

Nevynomyssk Chemical Plant, Fertilizer Formula — A2084

**1975, Oct. 30 Photo.** *Perf. 11½*

**4380** A2082 4k gold & multi .40 .25
**4381** A2083 4k red, gray & sl grn .40 .25
**4382** A2084 4k red, blue & silver .40 .25
*Nos. 4380-4382 (3)* 1.20 .75

58th anniversary of October Revolution.

Bas-relief of Decembrists and "Decembrists at the Senate Square," by D. N. Kardovsky — A2085

**1975, Nov. 12 Litho. & Engr.**

**4383** A2085 4k gray & multi .50 .25

Sesquicentennial of Decembrist rising.

Star and "1976" — A2086

**1975, Nov. 12 Litho.** *Perf. 12x12½*

**4384** A2086 4k green & multi .50 .25

New Year 1976.

Village Street, by F. A. Vasilev A2087

Paintings by Vasilev: 4k, Road in Birch Forest. 6k, After the Thunderstorm. 10k, Swamp, horiz. 12k, In the Crimean Mountains. 16k, Meadow, horiz. 50k, Portrait, by Kramskoi.

*Perf. 12x12½, 12½x12*

**1975, Nov. 25**

**4385** A2087 2k gray & multi .25 .25
**4386** A2087 4k gray & multi .25 .25
**4387** A2087 6k gray & multi .25 .25
**4388** A2087 10k gray & multi .30 .25
**4389** A2087 12k gray & multi .55 .25
**4390** A2087 16k gray & multi .60 .25
*Nos. 4385-4390 (6)* 2.20 1.50

**Souvenir Sheet**

*Perf. 12*

**4391** A2087 50k gray & multi 2.00 .90

Fedor Aleksandrovich Vasilev (1850-1873), landscape painter. Nos. 4385-4390 printed in sheets of 7 stamps and one label.

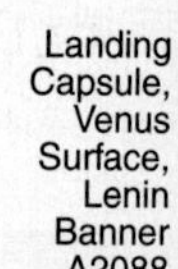

Landing Capsule, Venus Surface, Lenin Banner A2088

**1975, Dec. 8 Photo.** *Perf. 11½*

**4392** A2088 10k multicolored .50 .25

Flights of Soviet interplanetary stations Venera 9 and Venera 10.

Gabriel Sundoukian — A2089

**1975, Dec. 8 Litho.** *Perf. 12*

**4393** A2089 4k multicolored .50 .30

Sundoukian (1825-1912), Armenian playright.

Polar Poppies, Taiga A2090

Regional Flowers: 6k, Globeflowers, tundra. 10k, Buttercups, oak forest. 12k, Wood anemones, steppe. 16k, Eminium Lehmannii, desert.

**Photogravure and Engraved**

**1975, Dec. 25** *Perf. 12x11½*

**4394** A2090 4k black & multi .25 .25
**4395** A2090 6k black & multi .50 .25
**4396** A2090 10k black & multi .60 .25
**4397** A2090 12k black & multi 1.20 .25
**4398** A2090 16k black & multi 1.75 .25
*Nos. 4394-4398 (5)* 4.30 1.25

A. L. Mints (1895-1974), Academician A2091

**1975, Dec. 31 Photo.** *Perf. 11½x12*

**4399** A2091 4k dp brown & gold .50 .25

Demon, by A. Kochupalov A2092

Paintings: 6k, Vasilisa the Beautiful, by I. Vakurov. 10k, Snow Maiden, by T. Zubkova. 16k, Summer, by K. Kukulieva. 20k, The Fisherman and the Goldfish, by I. Vakurov, horiz.

**1975, Dec. 31 Litho.** *Perf. 12*

**4400** A2092 4k bister & multi .25 .25
**4401** A2092 6k bister & multi .35 .25
**4402** A2092 10k bister & multi .60 .25
**4403** A2092 16k bister & multi .75 .25
**4404** A2092 20k bister & multi 1.00 .25
*a.* Strip of 5, #4400-4404 5.00 1.25

Palekh Art State Museum, Ivanov Region.

Wilhelm Pieck (1876-1960), Pres. of German Democratic Republic — A2093

**1976, Jan. 3 Engr.** *Perf. 12½x12*

**4405** A2093 6k greenish black .50 .25

M. E. Saltykov-Shchedrin, by I.N. Kramskoi — A2094

**1976, Jan. 14 Litho.** *Perf. 12x12½*

**4406** A2094 4k multicolored .50 .25

Mikhail Evgrafovich Saltykov-Shchedrin (1826-1889), writer and revolutionist.

Congress Emblem — A2095

**1976, Feb. 2 Photo.** *Perf. 11½*

**4407** A2095 4k red, gold & mar .50 .25

**Souvenir Sheet**

***Perf. 11½x12***

**4408** A2095 50k red, gold & mar 1.75 .65

25th Congress of the Communist Party of the Soviet Union.

Lenin Statue, Kiev — A2096

**1976, Feb. 2** ***Perf. 11½***

**4409** A2096 4k red, black & blue .50 .25

Ukrainian Communist Party, 25th Congress.

Ice Hockey, Games' Emblem A2097

Designs (Winter Olympic Games' Emblem and): 4k, Cross-country skiing. 6k, Figure skating, pairs. 10k, Speed skating. 20k, Luge. 50k, Winter Olympic Games' emblem, vert.

**1976, Feb. 4 Litho.** ***Perf. 12½x12***

**4410** A2097 2k multicolored .25 .25
**4411** A2097 4k multicolored .25 .25
**4412** A2097 6k multicolored .25 .25
**4413** A2097 10k multicolored .35 .25
**4414** A2097 20k multicolored .90 .30
*Nos. 4410-4414 (5)* 2.00 1.30

**Souvenir Sheet**

***Perf. 12x12½***

**4415** A2097 50k vio bl, org & red 2.00 1.00

12th Winter Olympic Games, Innsbruck, Austria, Feb. 4-15. No. 4415 contains one stamp; silver and violet blue margin showing designs of Nos. 4410-4414. Size: 90x80mm.

**No. 4415 Overprinted in Red**

Souvenir Sheet

**1976, Mar. 24**

**4416** A2097 50k multicolored 3.00 2.00

Success of Soviet athletes in 12th Winter Olympic Games. Translation of overprint: "Glory to Soviet Sport! The athletes of the USSR have won 13 gold, 6 silver and 8 bronze medals."

K.E. Voroshilov A2098

**1976, Feb. 4 Engr.** ***Perf. 12***

**4417** A2098 4k slate green .50 .25

Kliment Efremovich Voroshilov (1881-1969), pres. of revolutionary military council, commander of Leningrad front, USSR pres. 1953-60. See Nos. 4487-4488, 4545-4548.

Flag over Kremlin Palace of Congresses, Troitskaya Tower A2099

**Photogravure on Gold Foil**

**1976, Feb. 24** ***Perf. 12x11½***

**4418** A2099 20k gold, grn & red 3.50 1.00

25th Congress of the Communist Party of the Soviet Union (CPSU).

Lenin on Red Square, by P. Vasiliev — A2100

**1976, Mar. 10 Litho.** ***Perf. 12½x12***

**4419** A2100 4k yellow & multi .50 .25

106th anniversary of the birth of Lenin.

Atom Symbol and Dubna Institute — A2101

**1976, Mar. 10 Photo.** ***Perf. 11½***

**4420** A2101 6k vio bl, red & silver .50 .25

Joint Institute of Nuclear Research, Dubna, 20th anniversary.

Bolshoi Theater — A2102

**1976, Mar. 24 Litho.** ***Perf. 11x11½***

**4421** A2102 10k yel, blue & dk brn .50 .25

Bicentenary of Bolshoi Theater.

Back from the Fair, by Konchalovsky — A2103

Paintings by P. P. Konchalovsky: 2k, The Green Glass. 6k, Peaches. 16k, Meat, Game and Vegetables. 20k, Self-portrait, 1943, vert.

**1976, Apr. 6** ***Perf. 12½x12, 12x12½***

**4422** A2103 1k yellow & multi .25 .25
**4423** A2103 2k yellow & multi .25 .25
**4424** A2103 6k yellow & multi .30 .25
**4425** A2103 16k yellow & multi .60 .25
**4426** A2103 20k yellow & multi .75 .30
*Nos. 4422-4426 (5)* 2.15 1.30

Birth centenary of P. P. Konchalovsky.

Vostok, Salyut-Soyuz Link-up — A2104

Yuri A. Gagarin — A2105

Designs: 6k, Meteor and Molniya Satellites, Orbita Ground Communications Center. 10k, Cosmonauts on board Salyut space station and Mars planetary station. 12k, Interkosmos station and Apollo-Soyuz linking.

**Lithographed and Engraved**

**1976, Apr. 12** ***Perf. 11½***

**4427** A2104 4k multicolored .25 .25
**4428** A2104 6k multicolored .35 .25
**4429** A2104 10k multicolored .50 .25
**4430** A2104 12k multicolored .90 .25
*Nos. 4427-4430 (4)* 2.00 1.00

**Souvenir Sheet**

**Engr.** ***Perf. 12***

**4431** A2105 50k black 10.00 2.00

1st manned flight in space, 15th anniv.

I. A. Dzhavakhishvili A2106

**1976, Apr. 20 Photo.** ***Perf. 11½x12***

**4432** A2106 4k multicolored .50 .25

Dzhavakhishvili (1876-1940), scientist.

Samed Vurgun and Derrick — A2107

**1976, Apr. 20** ***Perf. 11½***

**4433** A2107 4k multicolored .50 .25

Vurgun (1906-56), natl. poet of Azerbaijan.

1st All-Union Festival of Amateur Artists — A2108

USSR Flag, Worker and Farmer Monument.

**1976, May 12 Litho.** ***Perf. 11½x12***

**4434** A2108 4k multicolored .50 .25

Intl. Federation of Philately, 50th Anniv. — A2109

**1976, May 12 Photo.** ***Perf. 11½***

**4435** A2109 6k FIP Emblem .50 .25

Souvenir Sheet

V. A. Tropinin, Self-portrait — A2110

**1976, May 12 Litho.** ***Perf. 12***

**4436** A2110 50k multicolored 1.50 1.00

Vasily Andreevich Tropinin (1776-1857), painter.

Emblem, Dnieper Bridge — A2111

**1976, May 20 Photo.** ***Perf. 11½***

**4437** A2111 4k Prus blue, gold & blk .50 .25

Bicentenary of Dnepropetrovsk.

Dr. N. N. Burdenko — A2112

**1976, May 20** ***Perf. 11½x12***

**4438** A2112 4k deep brown & red .50 .25

Burdenko (1876-1946), neurosurgeon.

K. A. Trenev (1876-1945), Playwright A2113

**1976, May 20** ***Perf. 11½***

**4439** A2113 4k black & multi .50 .25

**Automobile Type of 1973**

2k, ZIS-110 passenger car. 3k, GAZ-51 Gorky truck. 4k, GAZ-M-20 Pobeda passenger car. 12k, ZIS-150 Moscow Motor Works truck. 16k, ZIS-154 Moscow Motor Works bus.

**1976, June 15** **Photo.** ***Perf. 12x11½***

**4440** A1968 2k grnsh bl & multi .25 .25
**4441** A1968 3k bister & multi .25 .25
**4442** A1968 4k dk blue & multi .25 .25
**4443** A1968 12k brown & multi .55 .25
**4444** A1968 16k deep car & multi .70 .25
*Nos. 4440-4444 (5)* 2.00 1.25

Canoeing A2114

USSR National Olympic Committee Emblem and: 6k, Basketball, vert. 10k, Greco-Roman wrestling. 14k, Women's discus, vert. 16k, Target shooting. 50k, Olympic medal, obverse and reverse.

***Perf. 12½x12, 12x12½***

**1976, June 23** **Litho.**

**4445** A2114 4k red & multi .25 .25
**4446** A2114 6k red & multi .25 .25
**4447** A2114 10k red & multi .35 .25
**4448** A2114 14k red & multi .25 .25
**4449** A2114 16k red & multi .25 .25
*Nos. 4445-4449 (5)* 1.35 1.25

**Souvenir Sheet**

**4450** A2114 50k red & multi 3.00 .75

21st Olympic Games, Montreal, Canada, July 17-Aug. 1.

For overprint see No. 4472.

Electric Trains, Overpass A2115

**1976, June 23** **Photo.** ***Perf. 11½***

**4451** A2115 4k multicolored 1.00 .25

Electrification of USSR railroads, 50th anniversary.

L. Emilio Recabarren — A2116

**1976, July 6**

**4452** A2116 6k gold, red & blk .50 .25

Luis Emilio Recabarren (1876-1924), founder of Chilean Communist Party.

Ljudmilla Mikhajlovna Pavlichenko (1916-1974), WWII Heroine — A2117

**1976, July 6**

**4453** A2117 4k dp brn, silver & yel .50 .25

Pavel Andreevich Fedotov (1815-1852), Painter A2118

Paintings: 2k, New Partner, by P. A. Fedotov. 4k, The Fastidious Fiancée, horiz. 6k, Aristocrat's Breakfast. 10k, Gamblers, horiz. 16k, The Outing. 50k, Self-portrait.

***Perf. 12x12½, 12½x12***

**1976, July 15** **Litho.**

**4454** A2118 2k black & multi .25 .25
**4455** A2118 4k black & multi .25 .25
**4456** A2118 6k black & multi .25 .25
**4457** A2118 10k black & multi .50 .25
**4458** A2118 16k black & multi .75 .25
*Nos. 4454-4458 (5)* 2.00 1.25

**Souvenir Sheet**

***Perf. 12***

**4459** A2118 50k multicolored 1.50 .75

Nos. 4454-4458 each printed in sheets of 20 stamps and center label with black commemorative inscription.

S. S. Nametkin — A2119

**1976, July 20** **Photo.** ***Perf. 11½x12***

**4460** A2119 4k blue, black & buff .50 .25

Sergei Semenovich Nametkin (1876-1950), organic chemist.

Squacco Heron — A2120

Waterfowl: 3k, Arctic loon. 4k, European coot. 6k, Atlantic puffin. 10k, Slender-billed gull.

**1976, Aug. 18** **Litho.** ***Perf. 12x12½***

**4465** A2120 1k dk green & multi .25 .25
**4466** A2120 3k ol green & multi .50 .50
**4467** A2120 4k orange & multi .80 .80
**4468** A2120 6k purple & multi 1.10 1.10
**4469** A2120 10k brt blue & multi 2.40 2.40
*Nos. 4465-4469 (5)* 5.05 5.05

Nature protection.

Peace Dove A2121

**1976, Aug. 25** **Photo.** ***Perf. 11½***

**4470** A2121 4k salmon, gold & blue .50 .25

2nd Stockholm appeal and movement to stop arms race.

Resistance Movement Emblem A2122

**1976, Aug. 25**

**4471** A2122 6k dk bl, blk & gold .50 .25

Intl. Resistance Movement Fed., 25th anniv.

**No. 4450 Overprinted in Gold**

**Souvenir Sheet**

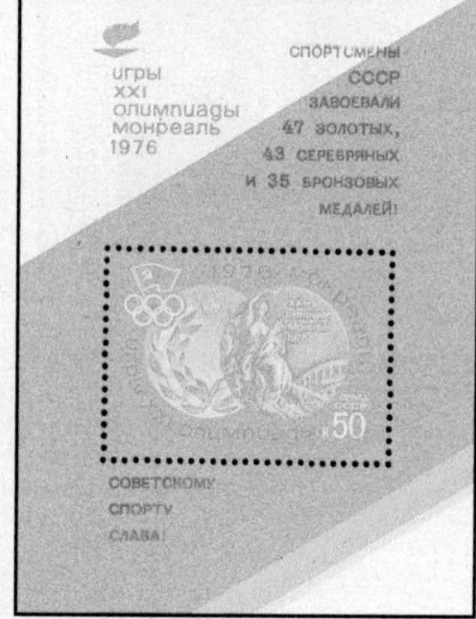

**1976, Aug. 25** **Litho.** ***Perf. 12½x12***

**4472** A2114 50k red & multi 3.00 .75

Victories of Soviet athletes in 21st Olympic Games (47 gold, 43 silver and 35 bronze medals).

Flags of India and USSR — A2123

**1976, Sept. 8** ***Perf. 12***

**4473** A2123 4k multicolored .50 .25

Friendship and cooperation between USSR and India.

UN, UNESCO Emblems, Open Book — A2124

**1976, Sept. 8** **Engr.** ***Perf. 12x12½***

**4474** A2124 16k multicolored .50 .30

UNESCO, 30th anniv.

B. V. Volynov, V. M. Zholobov, Star Circling Globe — A2125

**1976, Sept. 8** **Photo.** ***Perf. 12x11½***

**4475** A2125 10k brn, blue & black .50 .35

Exploits of Soyuz 21 and Salyut space station.

"Industry" — A2126

**1976, Sept. 17**

**4476** A2126 4k shown .40 .25
**4477** A2126 4k Farm industry .40 .25
**4478** A2126 4k Science .40 .25
**4479** A2126 4k Transport & communications .40 .25
**4480** A2126 4k Intl. cooperation .40 .25
*Nos. 4476-4480 (5)* 2.00 1.25

25th Congress of the Communist Party of the Soviet Union.

Victory, by I. I. Vakurov A2127

Paintings: 2k, Plower, by I. I. Golikov, horiz. 4k, Au (woman), by I. V. Markichev. 12k, Firebird, by A. V. Kotuhin, horiz. 14k, Festival, by A. I. Vatagin.

***Perf. 12½x12, 12x12½***

**1976, Sept. 22** **Litho.**

**4481** A2127 2k black & multi .25 .25
**4482** A2127 4k black & multi .25 .25
**4483** A2127 12k black & multi 1.25 .25
**4484** A2127 14k black & multi 1.40 .25
**4485** A2127 20k black & multi 1.75 .35
*Nos. 4481-4485 (5)* 4.90 1.35

Palekh Art State Museum, Ivanov Region.

Shostakovich, Score from 7th Symphony, Leningrad — A2128

**1976, Sept. 25 Engr. *Perf. 12½x12***

**4486** A2128 6k dk vio blue .50 .25

Dimitri Dimitrievich Shostakovich (1906-1975), composer.

### Voroshilov Type of 1976

No. 4487, Zhukov. No. 4488, Rokossovsky.

**1976, Oct. 7 Engr. *Perf. 12***

**4487** A2098 4k slate green .25 .25
**4488** A2098 4k brown .25 .25

Marshal Georgi Konstantinovich Zhukov (1896-1974), commander at Stalingrad and Leningrad and Deputy of Supreme Soviet; Marshal Konstantin K. Rokossovsky (1896-1968), commander at Stalingrad.

Intercosmos-14 A2129

10k, India's satellite Arryabata. 12k, Soyuz-19 and Apollo before docking. 16k, French satellite Aureole and Northern Lights. 20k, Docking of Soyuz-Apollo, Intercosmos-14 and Aureole.

**1976, Oct. 15 Photo. *Perf. 11½***

**4489** A2129 6k black & multi .25 .25
**4490** A2129 10k black & multi .30 .25
**4491** A2129 12k black & multi .40 .25
**4492** A2129 16k black & multi .45 .25
**4493** A2129 20k black & multi .60 .25
*Nos. 4489-4493 (5)* 2.00 1.25

Interkosmos Program for Scientific and Experimental Research.

Vladimir I. Dahl A2130

### Photogravure and Engraved

**1976, Oct. 15 *Perf. 11½***

**4494** A2130 4k green & dk grn .50 .25

Vladimir I. Dahl (1801-1872), physician, writer, compiled Russian Dictionary.

Electric Power Industry A2131

No. 4496, Balashovo textile mill. No. 4497, Laying of drainage pipes and grain elevator.

**1976, Oct. 20 Photo. *Perf. 11½***

**4495** A2131 4k dk blue & multi .50 .25
**4496** A2131 4k rose brn & multi .50 .25
**4497** A2131 4k slate grn & multi .50 .25
*Nos. 4495-4497 (3)* 1.50 .75

59th anniversary of the October Revolution.

Petrov Tumor Research Institute A2132

M. A. Novinski — A2133

**1976, Oct. 28**

**4498** A2132 4k vio blue & gold .50 .25

***Perf. 11½x12***

**4499** A2133 4k dk brn, buff & blue .50 .25

Petrov Tumor Research Institute, 50th anniversary, and 135th birth anniversary of M. A. Novinski, cancer research pioneer.

Aviation Emblem, Gakkel VII, 1911 A2134

Russian Aircraft (Russian Aviation Emblem and): 6k, Gakkel IX, 1912. 12k, I. Steglau No. 2, 1912. 14k, Dybovski's Dolphin, 1913. 16k, Iliya Muromets, 1914.

### Lithographed and Engraved

**1976, Nov. 4 *Perf. 12x12½***

**4500** A2134 3k multicolored .25 .25
**4501** A2134 6k multicolored .25 .25
**4502** A2134 12k multicolored .50 .35
**4503** A2134 14k multicolored .55 .35
**4504** A2134 16k multicolored .60 .50
*Nos. 4500-4504 (5)* 2.15 1.70

See Nos. C109-C120.

Saffron A2135

Flowers of the Caucasus: 2k, Pasqueflowers. 3k, Gentian. 4k, Columbine. 6k, Checkered lily.

**1976, Nov. 17 *Perf. 12x11½***

**4505** A2135 1k multicolored .40 .40
**4506** A2135 2k multicolored .40 .40
**4507** A2135 3k multicolored .40 .40
**4508** A2135 4k multicolored .40 .40
**4509** A2135 6k multicolored .40 .40
*Nos. 4505-4509 (5)* 2.00 2.00

Spasski Tower Clock, Greeting Card A2136

**1976, Nov. 25 Litho. *Perf. 12½x12***

**4510** A2136 4k multicolored .60 .25

New Year 1977.

Parable of the Workers in the Vineyard, by Rembrandt — A2137

Rembrandt Paintings in Russian Museums: 6k, Danae. 10k, David and Jonathan, vert. 14k, Holy Family, vert. 20k, Rembrandt's brother Adrian, 1654, vert. 50k, Artaxerxes, Esther and Haman.

***Perf. 12½x12, 12x12½***

**1976, Nov. 25 Photo.**

**4511** A2137 4k multicolored .25 .25
**4512** A2137 6k multicolored .35 .25
**4513** A2137 10k multicolored .60 .25
**4514** A2137 14k multicolored .90 .25
**4515** A2137 20k multicolored 1.40 .25
*Nos. 4511-4515 (5)* 3.50 1.25

### Souvenir Sheet

**4516** A2137 50k multicolored 6.50 2.00

Rembrandt van Rijn (1606-69). Nos. 4511 and 4515 printed in sheets of 7 stamps and decorative label.

Armed Forces Order A2138

Worker and Farmer, by V. I. Muhina A2139

Marx and Lenin, by Fridman and Belostotsky A2140

Council for Mutual Economic Aid Building A2141

Lenin, 1920 Photograph A2142

Globe and Sputnik Orbits A2143

Designs: 2k, Golden Star and Hammer and Sickle medals. 4k, Coat of arms and "CCCP." 6k, TU-154 plane, globe and airmail envelope. 10k, Order of Labor. 12k, Space exploration medal with Gagarin portrait. 16k, Lenin Prize medal.

**1976 Engr. *Perf. 12x12½***

**4517** A2138 1k greenish black .25 .25
**4518** A2138 2k brt magenta .25 .25
**4519** A2139 3k red .25 .25
**4520** A2138 4k brick red .25 .25
**4521** A2139 6k Prus blue .25 .25
**4522** A2138 10k olive green .45 .25
**4523** A2139 12k violet blue .50 .25
**4524** A2139 16k deep green .60 .25

***Perf. 12½x12***

**4525** A2140 20k brown red .80 .25
**4526** A2141 30k brick red 1.10 .25
**4527** A2142 50k brown 1.90 .25
**4528** A2143 1r dark blue 4.00 .25
*Nos. 4517-4528 (12)* 10.60 3.00

Issued: Nos. 4517-4524, 12/17; Nos. 4525-4528, 8/10.

See Nos. 4596-4607. For overprint see No. 5720.

Luna 24 Emblem and Moon Landing A2144

**1976, Dec. 17 Photo. *Perf. 11½***

**4531** A2144 10k multicolored .50 .25

Moon exploration of automatic station Luna 24.

Icebreaker "Pilot" — A2145

Icebreakers: 6k, Ermak, vert. 10k, Fedor Litke. 16k, Vladimir Ilich, vert. 20k, Krassin.

***Perf. 12x11½, 11½x12***

**1976, Dec. 22 Litho. & Engr.**

**4532** A2145 4k multicolored .25 .25
**4533** A2145 6k multicolored .35 .25
**4534** A2145 10k multicolored .55 .25
**4535** A2145 16k multicolored .75 .25
**4536** A2145 20k multicolored 1.10 .30
*Nos. 4532-4536 (5)* 3.00 1.30

See Nos. 4579-4585.

Soyuz 22 Emblem, Cosmonauts V. F. Bykovsky and V. V. Aksenov — A2146

**1976, Dec. 28 Photo. *Perf. 12x11½***

**4537** A2146 10k multicolored .50 .25

Soyuz 22 space flight, Sept. 15-23.

Society Emblem — A2147

**1977, Jan. 1 *Perf. 11½***

**4538** A2147 4k multicolored .50 .25

Red Banner Voluntary Soc., supporting Red Army, Navy & Air Force, 50th anniv.

S. P. Korolev, Vostok Rocket and Satellite A2148

**1977, Jan. 12**

**4539** A2148 4k multicolored .50 .25

Sergei Pavlovich Korolev (1907-1966), creator of first Soviet rocket space system.

Globe and Palm A2149

**1977, Jan. 12**

**4540** A2149 4k multicolored .50 .25

World Congress of Peace Loving Forces, Moscow, Jan. 1977.

Sedov and "St. Foka" A2150

**1977, Jan. 25 Photo. *Perf. 11½***

**4541** A2150 4k multicolored .50 .25

G.Y. Sedov (1877-1914), polar explorer and hydrographer.

Worker and Farmer Monument and Izvestia Front Page — A2151

**1977, Jan. 25**

**4542** A2151 4k silver, black & red .50 .25

60th anniversary of newspaper Izvestia.

Ship Sailing Across the Oceans — A2152

**1977, Jan. 25**

**4543** A2152 6k deep blue & gold .50 .25

24th Intl. Navigation Cong., Leningrad.

Congress Hall and Troitskaya Tower, Kremlin — A2153

**1977, Feb. 9 Photo. *Perf. 11½***

**4544** A2153 4k red, gold & black .50 .25

16th Congress of USSR Trade Unions.

**Voroshilov Type of 1976**

Marshals of the Soviet Union: No. 4545, Leonid A. Govorov (1897-1955). No. 4546, Ivan S. Koniev. No. 4547, K. A. Merezhkov. No. 4548, W. D. Sokolovsky.

| **1977** | **Engr.** | ***Perf. 12*** | | |
|---|---|---|---|---|
| **4545** | A2098 4k brown | | .40 | .25 |
| **4546** | A2098 4k slate green | | .40 | .25 |
| **4547** | A2098 4k brown | | .40 | .25 |
| **4548** | A2098 4k black | | .40 | .25 |
| | *Nos. 4545-4548 (4)* | | 1.60 | 1.00 |

Issue dates: #4545, Feb. 9; others, June 7.

Academy, Crest, Anchor and Ribbons A2155

**Photogravure and Engraved**

**1977, Feb. 9 *Perf. 11½***

**4549** A2155 6k multicolored .50 .25

A. A. Grechko Naval Academy, Leningrad, sesquicentennial.

Jeanne Labourbe — A2156

**1977, Feb. 25 Photo. *Perf. 11½***

**4550** A2166 4k multicolored .50 .25

Jeanne Labourbe (1877-1919), leader of French communists in Moscow.

Queen and Knights — A2157

**1977, Feb. 25**

**4551** A2157 6k multicolored .50 .25

4th European Chess Championships.

Cosmonauts V. D. Zudov and V. I. Rozhdestvensky — A2158

**1977, Feb. 25 *Perf. 12x11½***

**4552** A2158 10k multicolored .50 .25

Soyuz 23 space flight, Oct. 14-16, 1976.

A. S. Novikov-Priboy (1877-1944), Writer — A2159

**1977, Mar. 16 Photo. *Perf. 11½***

**4553** A2159 4k multicolored .50 .25

Welcome, by M. N. Soloninkin A2160

Folk Tale Paintings from Fedoskino Artists' Colony: 6k, Along the Street, by V. D. Antonov, horiz. 10k, Northern Song, by J. V. Karapaev. 12k, Tale of Tsar Saltan, by A. I. Kozlov. 14k, Summer Troika, by V. A. Nalimov, horiz. 16k, Red Flower, by V. D. Lipitsky.

***Perf. 12x12½, 12½x12***

| **1977, Mar. 16** | | **Litho.** | |
|---|---|---|---|
| **4554** | A2160 4k black & multi | .45 | .25 |
| **4555** | A2160 6k black & multi | .45 | .25 |
| **4556** | A2160 10k black & multi | .65 | .25 |
| **4557** | A2160 12k black & multi | .95 | .25 |
| **4558** | A2160 14k black & multi | 1.10 | .25 |
| **4559** | A2160 16k black & multi | 1.40 | .30 |
| | *Nos. 4554-4559 (6)* | 5.00 | 1.55 |

Lenin on Red Square, by K.V. Filatov — A2161

**1977, Apr. 12 *Perf. 12½x11½***

**4560** A2161 4k multicolored .50 .25

107th anniversary of the birth of Lenin.

Electricity Congress Emblem A2162

**1977, Apr. 12 Photo. *Perf. 11½***

**4561** A2162 6k blue, red & gray .50 .25

World Electricity Congress, Moscow 1977.

Yuri Gagarin, Sputnik, Soyuz and Salyut — A2163

**1977, Apr. 12 *Perf. 12x11½***

**4562** A2163 6k multicolored .50 .25

Cosmonauts' Day.

N. I. Vavilov — A2164

**1977, Apr. 26 Photo. *Perf. 11½***

**4563** A2164 4k multicolored .50 .25

Vavilov (1887-1943), agricultural geneticist.

Feliks E. Dzerzhinski A2165

**1977, May 12 Engr. *Perf. 12½x12***

**4564** A2165 4k black .50 .25

Feliks E. Dzerzhinski (1877-1926), organizer and head of secret police (OGPU).

Saxifraga Sibirica — A2166

Siberian Flowers: 3k, Dianthus repena. 4k, Novosieversia glactalis. 6k, Cerasticum maxinicem. 16k, Golden rhododendron.

| **1977, May 12** | **Litho.** | ***Perf. 12x12½*** | |
|---|---|---|---|
| **4565** | A2166 2k multicolored | .25 | .25 |
| **4566** | A2166 3k multicolored | .25 | .25 |
| **4567** | A2166 4k multicolored | .25 | .25 |
| **4568** | A2166 6k multicolored | .35 | .25 |
| **4569** | A2166 16k multicolored | .90 | .25 |
| | *Nos. 4565-4569 (5)* | 2.00 | 1.25 |

V. V. Gorbatko, Y. N. Glazkov, Soyuz 24 Rocket A2167

**1977, May 16 Photo. *Perf. 12x11½***

**4570** A2167 10k multicolored .50 .25

Space explorations of cosmonauts on Salyut 5 orbital station, launched with Soyuz 24 rocket.

Film and Globe — A2168

**1977, June 21 Photo. *Perf. 11½***

**4571** A2168 6k multicolored .50 .25

10th Intl. Film Festival, Moscow 1977.

Lion Hunt, by Rubens — A2169

Rubens Paintings, Hermitage, Leningrad: 4k, Lady in Waiting, vert. 10k, Workers in Quarry. 12k, Alliance of Water and Earth, vert. 20k, Landscape with Rainbow. 50k, Self-portrait.

*Perf. 12x12½, 12½x12*

**1977, June 24** **Litho.**

| | | | | |
|---|---|---|---|---|
| **4572** | A2169 | 4k yellow & multi | .30 | .25 |
| **4573** | A2169 | 6k yellow & multi | .30 | .25 |
| **4574** | A2169 | 10k yellow & multi | .60 | .25 |
| **4575** | A2169 | 12k yellow & multi | .75 | .25 |
| **4576** | A2169 | 20k yellow & multi | 1.00 | .30 |
| | | *Nos. 4572-4576 (5)* | 2.95 | 1.30 |

**Souvenir Sheet**

| | | | | |
|---|---|---|---|---|
| **4577** | A2169 | 50k yellow & multi | 2.00 | .60 |

Peter Paul Rubens (1577-1640), painter. Sheets of No. 4575 contain 2 labels with commemorative inscriptions and Atlas statue from Hermitage entrance.

Souvenir Sheet

Judith, by Giorgione — A2170

**1977, July 15** **Litho.** ***Perf. 12x12½***

| | | | | |
|---|---|---|---|---|
| **4578** | A2170 | 50k multicolored | 2.00 | 1.00 |

Il Giorgione (1478-1511), Venetian painter.

**Icebreaker Type of 1976**

Icebreakers: 4k, Aleksandr Sibiryakov. 6k, Georgi Sedov. 10k, Sadko. 12k, Dezhnev. 14k, Siberia. 16k, Lena. 20k, Amguyema.

**Lithographed and Engraved**

**1977, July 27** ***Perf. 12x11½***

| | | | | |
|---|---|---|---|---|
| **4579** | A2145 | 4k multicolored | .25 | .25 |
| **4580** | A2145 | 6k multicolored | .40 | .25 |
| **4581** | A2145 | 10k multicolored | .75 | .25 |
| **4582** | A2145 | 12k multicolored | 1.00 | .25 |
| **4583** | A2145 | 14k multicolored | 1.25 | .25 |
| **4584** | A2145 | 16k multicolored | 1.50 | .35 |
| **4585** | A2145 | 20k multicolored | 1.75 | .45 |
| | | *Nos. 4579-4585 (7)* | 6.90 | 2.05 |

Souvenir Sheet

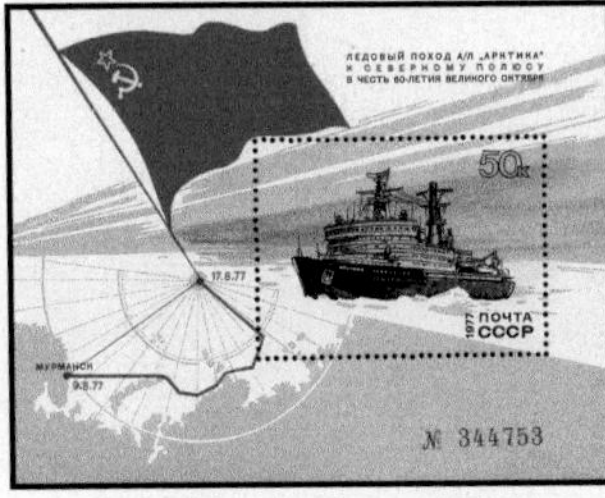


Icebreaker Arctica — A2171

**Lithographed and Engraved**

**1977, Sept. 15** ***Perf. 12½x12***

| | | | | |
|---|---|---|---|---|
| **4586** | A2171 | 50k multicolored | 5.00 | 3.00 |

Arctica, first ship to travel from Murmansk to North Pole, Aug. 9-17.

View and Arms of Stavropol — A2172

**1977, Aug. 16** **Photo.** ***Perf. 11½***

| | | | | |
|---|---|---|---|---|
| **4587** | A2172 | 6k multicolored | .50 | .25 |

200th anniversary of Stavropol.

Stamps and Exhibition Emblem — A2173

**1977, Aug. 16**

| | | | | |
|---|---|---|---|---|
| **4588** | A2173 | 4k multicolored | .50 | .25 |

October Revolution Anniversary Philatelic Exhibition, Moscow.

Yuri A. Gagarin and Spacecraft — A2174

No. 4590, Alexei Leonov floating in space. No. 4591, Orbiting space station, cosmonauts at control panel.

Nos. 4592-4594, Various spacecraft: No. 4592, International cooperation for space research. No. 4593, Interplanetary flights. No. 4594, Exploring earth's atmosphere.

50k, "XX," laurel, symbolic Sputnik with Red Star.

**1977, Oct. 4** **Photo.** ***Perf. 11½x12***

| | | | | |
|---|---|---|---|---|
| **4589** | A2174 | 10k sepia & multi | .25 | .25 |
| **4590** | A2174 | 10k gray & multi | .25 | .25 |
| **4591** | A2174 | 10k gray green & multi | .25 | .25 |
| **4592** | A2174 | 20k green & multi | .45 | .35 |
| **4593** | A2174 | 20k vio bl & multi | .45 | .35 |
| **4594** | A2174 | 20k bister & multi | .45 | .35 |
| | | *Nos. 4589-4594 (6)* | 2.10 | 1.80 |

**Souvenir Sheet**

| | | | | |
|---|---|---|---|---|
| **4595** | A2174 | 50k claret & gold | *5.00* | *5.00* |

20th anniv. of space research. No. 4595 contains one stamp, size: 22x32mm.

**Types of 1976**

Designs: 15k, Communications emblem and globes; others as before.

**1977-78** **Litho.** ***Perf. 12x12½***

| | | | | |
|---|---|---|---|---|
| **4596** | A2138 | 1k olive green | .25 | .25 |
| **4597** | A2138 | 2k lilac rose | .25 | .25 |
| **4598** | A2139 | 3k brick red | .25 | .25 |
| **4599** | A2138 | 4k vermilion | .25 | .25 |
| **4600** | A2139 | 6k Prus blue | .30 | .25 |
| **4601** | A2138 | 10k gray green | .50 | .25 |
| **4602** | A2139 | 12k vio blue | .65 | .25 |
| **4602A** | A2139 | 15k blue ('78) | 5.00 | .25 |
| **4603** | A2139 | 16k slate green | .80 | .25 |

***Perf. 12½x12***

| | | | | |
|---|---|---|---|---|
| **4604** | A2140 | 20k brown red | .80 | .25 |
| **4605** | A2141 | 30k dull brick red | 1.10 | .25 |
| **4606** | A2142 | 50k brown | 1.25 | .25 |
| **4607** | A2143 | 1r dark blue | 3.75 | .25 |
| | | *Nos. 4596-4607 (13)* | 15.15 | 3.25 |

Nos. 4596-4602A, 4604-4607 were printed on dull and shiny paper.

For overprint see No. 5720. For surcharges see Uzbekistan Nos. 16-17, 23, 27-29, 61A.

Souvenir Sheet

Bas-relief, 12th Century, Cathedral of St. Dimitri, Vladimir — A2175

6k, Necklace, Ryazan excavations, 12th cent. 10k, Mask, Cathedral of the Nativity, Suzdal, 13th cent. 12k, Archangel Michael, 15th cent. icon. 16k, Chalice by Ivan Fomin, 1449. 20k, St. Basil's Cathedral, Moscow, 16th cent.

**1977, Oct. 12** **Litho.** ***Perf. 12***

| | | | | |
|---|---|---|---|---|
| **4608** | | Sheet of 6 | 3.00 | 1.25 |
| *a.* | A2175 | 4k gold & black | .25 | .25 |
| *b.* | A2175 | 6k gold & multi | .25 | .25 |
| *c.* | A2175 | 10k gold & multi | .25 | .25 |
| *d.* | A2175 | 12k gold & multi | .25 | .25 |
| *e.* | A2175 | 16k gold & multi | .35 | .25 |
| *f.* | A2175 | 20k gold & multi | .35 | .25 |

Masterpieces of old Russian culture.

Fir, Snowflake, Molniya Satellite — A2176

**1977, Oct. 12** ***Perf. 12x12½***

| | | | | |
|---|---|---|---|---|
| **4609** | A2176 | 4k multicolored | 1.00 | .25 |

New Year 1978.

Cruiser Aurora and Torch A2177

60th Anniversary of Revolution Medal — A2178

60th Anniv. of October Revolution: No. 4611, Lenin speaking at Finland Station (monument), 1917. No. 4612, 1917 Peace Decree, Brezhnev's book about Lenin. No. 4613, Kremlin tower with star and fireworks.

**1977, Oct. 26** **Photo.** ***Perf. 12x11½***

| | | | | |
|---|---|---|---|---|
| **4610** | A2177 | 4k gold, red & blk | .25 | .25 |
| **4611** | A2177 | 4k gold, red & blk | .25 | .25 |
| **4612** | A2177 | 4k gold, red & blk | .25 | .25 |
| **4613** | A2177 | 4k gold, red & blk | .25 | .25 |
| | | *Nos. 4610-4613 (4)* | 1.00 | 1.00 |

**Souvenir Sheet**

***Perf. 11½***

| | | | | |
|---|---|---|---|---|
| **4614** | A2178 | 30k gold, red & blk | 1.50 | .60 |

Flag of USSR, Constitution (Book) with Coat of Arms — A2179

Designs: No. 4616, Red banner, people and cover of constitution. 50k, Constitution, Kremlin and olive branch.

**1977, Oct. 31** **Litho.** ***Perf. 12½x12***

| | | | | |
|---|---|---|---|---|
| **4615** | A2179 | 4k red, black & yel | .25 | .25 |
| **4616** | A2179 | 4k red, black & yel | .25 | .25 |

**Souvenir Sheet**

***Perf. 11½x12½***

**Lithographed and Embossed**

| | | | | |
|---|---|---|---|---|
| **4617** | A2179 | 50k red, gold & yel | 2.00 | 1.00 |

Adoption of new constitution. No. 4617 contains one 70x50mm stamp.

Souvenir Sheet

Leonid Brezhnev — A2180

**Lithographed and Embossed**

**1977, Nov. 2** ***Perf. 11½x12***

| | | | | |
|---|---|---|---|---|
| **4618** | A2180 | 50k gold & multi | 4.00 | 1.00 |

Adoption of new constitution, General Secretary Brezhnev, chairman of Constitution Commission.

Postal Official and Postal Code — A2181

Mail Processing (Woman Postal Official and): No. 4620, Mail collection and Moskvich 430 car. No. 4621, Automatic letter sorting machine. No. 4622, Mail transport by truck, train, ship and planes. No. 4623, Mail delivery in city and country.

**Lithographed and Engraved**

**1977, Nov. 16** ***Perf. 12½x12***

| | | | | |
|---|---|---|---|---|
| **4619** | A2181 | 4k multicolored | .35 | .25 |
| **4620** | A2181 | 4k multicolored | .35 | .25 |
| **4621** | A2181 | 4k multicolored | .35 | .25 |
| **4622** | A2181 | 4k multicolored | .35 | .25 |
| **4623** | A2181 | 4k multicolored | .35 | .25 |
| | | *Nos. 4619-4623 (5)* | 1.75 | 1.25 |

Capital, Asoka Pillar, Red Fort — A2182

**1977, Dec. 14** **Photo.** ***Perf. 11½***

| | | | | |
|---|---|---|---|---|
| **4624** | A2182 | 6k maroon, gold & red | .60 | .25 |

30th anniversary of India's independence.

Proclamation Monument, Charkov A2183

**1977, Dec. 14** **Litho.** ***Perf. 12x12½***

| | | | | |
|---|---|---|---|---|
| **4625** | A2183 | 6k multicolored | .50 | .25 |

60th anniv. of Soviet power in the Ukraine.

Lebetina Viper — A2184

Protected Fauna: 1k to 12k, Venomous snakes, useful for medicinal purposes. 16k, Polar bear and cub. 20k, Walrus and calf. 30k, Tiger and cub.

**Photogravure and Engraved**

**1977, Dec. 16** ***Perf. 11½x12***

| | | | | |
|---|---|---|---|---|
| **4626** | A2184 | 1k black & multi | .25 | .25 |
| **4627** | A2184 | 4k black & multi | .25 | .25 |
| **4628** | A2184 | 6k black & multi | .25 | .25 |
| **4629** | A2184 | 10k black & multi | .35 | .25 |
| **4630** | A2184 | 12k black & multi | .45 | .25 |
| **4631** | A2184 | 16k black & multi | .55 | .25 |
| **4632** | A2184 | 20k black & multi | .75 | .25 |
| **4633** | A2184 | 30k black & multi | 1.00 | .35 |
| | | *Nos. 4626-4633 (8)* | 3.85 | 2.10 |

Wheat, Combine, Silos — A2185

**1978, Jan. 27** **Photo.** ***Perf. 11½***

| | | | | |
|---|---|---|---|---|
| **4634** | A2185 | 4k multicolored | .50 | .25 |

Gigant collective grain farm, Rostov Region, 50th anniversary.

Congress Palace, Spasski Tower — A2186

**1978, Jan. 27** **Litho.** ***Perf. 12x12½***

| | | | | |
|---|---|---|---|---|
| **4635** | A2186 | 4k multicolored | .50 | .25 |

Young Communist League, Lenin's Komsomol, 60th anniv. and its 25th Cong.

Liberation Obelisk, Emblem, Dove — A2187

**1978, Jan. 27** **Photo.** ***Perf. 11½***

| | | | | |
|---|---|---|---|---|
| **4636** | A2187 | 6k multicolored | .50 | .25 |

8th Congress of International Federation of Resistance Fighters, Minsk, Belorussia.

Soldiers Leaving for the Front — A2188

Designs: No. 4638, Defenders of Moscow Monument, Lenin banner. No. 4639, Soldier as defender of the people.

**1978, Feb. 21** **Litho.** ***Perf. 12½x12***

| | | | | |
|---|---|---|---|---|
| **4637** | A2188 | 4k red & multi | .50 | .25 |
| **4638** | A2188 | 4k red & multi | .50 | .25 |
| **4639** | A2188 | 4k red & multi | .50 | .25 |
| | | *Nos. 4637-4639 (3)* | 1.50 | .75 |

60th anniversary of USSR Military forces.

Celebration in Village — A2189

Kustodiev Paintings: 6k, Shrovetide (winter landscape). 10k, Morning, by Kustodiev. 12k, Merchant's Wife Drinking Tea. 20k, Bolshevik. 50k, Self-portrait, vert.

**1978, Mar. 3** ***Perf. 11½***

**Size: 70x33mm**

| | | | | |
|---|---|---|---|---|
| **4640** | A2189 | 4k lilac & multi | .25 | .25 |
| **4641** | A2189 | 6k lilac & multi | .30 | .25 |

**Size: 47x32mm**

***Perf. 12½x12***

| | | | | |
|---|---|---|---|---|
| **4642** | A2189 | 10k lilac & multi | .50 | .25 |
| **4643** | A2189 | 12k lilac & multi | .65 | .25 |
| **4644** | A2189 | 20k lilac & multi | .85 | .25 |
| | | *Nos. 4640-4644 (5)* | 2.55 | 1.25 |

**Souvenir Sheet**

***Perf. 11½x12½***

| | | | | |
|---|---|---|---|---|
| **4644A** | A2189 | 50k lilac & multi | 2.00 | .75 |

Boris Mikhailovich Kustodiev (1878-1927), painter. Nos. 4642-4644 have se-tenant label showing museum where painting is kept. No. 4644A has label giving short biography.

Docking in Space, Intercosmos Emblem A2190

Designs: 6k, Rocket, Soviet Cosmonaut Aleksei Gubarev and Czechoslovak Capt. Vladimir Remek on launching pad. 32k, Parachute, helicopter, Intercosmos emblem, USSR and Czechoslovakian flags.

**1978, Mar. 10** **Litho.** ***Perf. 12x12½***

| | | | | |
|---|---|---|---|---|
| **4645** | A2190 | 6k multicolored | .25 | .25 |
| **4646** | A2190 | 15k multicolored | .60 | .25 |
| **4647** | A2190 | 32k multicolored | 1.20 | .40 |
| | | *Nos. 4645-4647 (3)* | 2.05 | .90 |

Intercosmos, Soviet-Czechoslovak cooperative space program.

Festival Emblem — A2191

**1978, Mar. 17** **Litho.** ***Perf. 12x12½***

| | | | | |
|---|---|---|---|---|
| **4648** | A2191 | 4k blue & multi | .50 | .25 |

11th Youth & Students' Cong., Havana.

Tulip, Bolshoi Theater A2192

Moscow Flowers: 2k, Rose "Moscow morning" and Lomonosov University. 4k, Dahlia "Red Star" and Spasski Tower. 10k, Gladiolus "Moscovite" and VDNH Building. 12k, Ilich anniversary iris and Lenin Central Museum.

**1978, Mar. 17** ***Perf. 12½x12***

| | | | | |
|---|---|---|---|---|
| **4649** | A2192 | 1k multicolored | .40 | .25 |
| **4650** | A2192 | 2k multicolored | .40 | .25 |
| **4651** | A2192 | 4k multicolored | .40 | .25 |
| **4652** | A2192 | 10k multicolored | .40 | .25 |
| **4653** | A2192 | 12k multicolored | .40 | .25 |
| | | *Nos. 4649-4653 (5)* | 2.00 | 1.25 |

IMCO Emblem and Waves — A2193

**1978, Mar. 17** **Litho.** ***Perf. 12x12½***

| | | | | |
|---|---|---|---|---|
| **4654** | A2193 | 6k multicolored | .50 | .25 |

Intergovernmental Maritime Consultative Org., 20th anniv., and World Maritime Day.

Spaceship, Orbits of Salyut 5, Soyuz 26 and 27 — A2194

**1978, Apr. 12** **Photo.** ***Perf. 12***

| | | | | |
|---|---|---|---|---|
| **4655** | A2194 | 6k blue, dk blue & gold | .50 | .25 |

Cosmonauts' Day, Apr. 12.

World Federation of Trade Unions Emblem — A2195

**1978, Apr. 16** ***Perf. 12***

| | | | | |
|---|---|---|---|---|
| **4656** | A2195 | 6k multicolored | .50 | .25 |

9th World Trade Union Congress, Prague.

2-2-0 Locomotive, 1845, Petersburg and Moscow Stations — A2196

Locomotives: 1k, 1st Russian model by E. A. and M. W. Cherepanov, vert. 2k, 1-3-0 freight, 1845. 16k, Aleksandrov 0-3-0, 1863. 20k, 2-2-0 passenger and Sergievsk Pustyn platform, 1863.

**1978, Apr. 20** **Litho.** ***Perf. 11½***

| | | | | |
|---|---|---|---|---|
| **4657** | A2196 | 1k orange & multi | .25 | .25 |
| **4658** | A2196 | 2k ultra & multi | .25 | .25 |
| **4659** | A2196 | 3k yellow & multi | .30 | .25 |
| **4660** | A2196 | 16k green & multi | 1.20 | .25 |
| **4661** | A2196 | 20k rose & multi | 1.00 | .25 |
| | | *Nos. 4657-4661 (5)* | 3.00 | 1.25 |

**Souvenir Sheet**

Lenin, by V. A. Serov — A2197

**1978, Apr. 22** ***Perf. 12x12½***

| | | | | |
|---|---|---|---|---|
| **4662** | A2197 | 50k multicolored | 2.00 | .75 |

108th anniversary of the birth of Lenin.

A2198

No. 4663, Soyuz and Salyut 6 docking in space. No. 4664, Y. V. Romanenko and G. M. Grechko.

**1978, June 15** ***Perf. 12***

| | | | | |
|---|---|---|---|---|
| **4663** | | 15k multicolored | .40 | .25 |
| **4664** | | 15k multicolored | .40 | .25 |
| ***a.*** | | A2198 Pair, #4663-4664 | 1.00 | .40 |

Photographic survey and telescopic observations of stars by crews of Soyuz 26, Soyuz 27 and Soyuz 28, Dec. 10, 1977-Mar. 16, 1978. Nos. 4663-4664 printed se-tenant with label showing schematic pictures of various experiments.

Space Meteorology, Rockets, Spaceship, Earth — A2200

No. 4665, Natural resources of earth and Soyuz. No. 4667, Space communications, "Orbita" Station and Molnyia satellite. No. 4668, Man, earth and Vostok. 50k, Study of magnetosphere, Prognoz over earth.

**1978, June 23** ***Perf. 12x12½***

| | | | | |
|---|---|---|---|---|
| **4665** | A2200 | 10k green & multi | .50 | .25 |
| **4666** | A2200 | 10k blue & multi | .50 | .25 |
| **4667** | A2200 | 10k violet & multi | .50 | .25 |
| **4668** | A2200 | 10k rose lil & multi | .50 | .25 |
| | | *Nos. 4665-4668 (4)* | 2.00 | 1.00 |

**Souvenir Sheet**

***Perf. 11½x12½***

| | | | | |
|---|---|---|---|---|
| **4669** | A2200 | 50k multicolored | 2.00 | .75 |

Space explorations of the Intercosmos program. #4669 contains one 36x51mm stamp.

Soyuz Rocket on Carrier — A2201

Designs (Flags of USSR and Poland, Intercosmos Emblem): 15k, Crystal, spaceship (Sirena, experimental crystallogenesis in space). 32k, Research ship "Cosmonaut Vladimir Komarov," spaceship, world map and paths of Salyut 6, Soyuz 29-30.

**1978, Litho. *Perf. 12½x12***
**4670** A2201 6k multicolored .25 .25
**4671** A2201 15k multicolored .40 .25
**4672** A2201 32k multicolored .80 .40
*Nos. 4670-4672 (3)* 1.45 .90

Intercosmos, Soviet-Polish cooperative space program. Issued: 6k, 6/28; 15k, 6/30; 32k, 7/5.

Lenin, Awards Received by Komsomol A2202

Kamaz Car, Train, Bridge, Hammer and Sickle — A2203

**1978, July 5 *Perf. 12x12½***
**4673** A2202 4k multicolored .25 .25
**4674** A2203 4k multicolored .25 .25

Leninist Young Communist League (Komsomol), 60th anniv. (#4673); Komsomol's participation in 5-year plan (#4674).
For overprint see No. 4703.

M. V. Zaharov (1898-1972), Marshal of the Soviet Union — A2204

**1978, July 5 Engr. *Perf. 12***
**4675** A2204 4k sepia .50 .25

Torch, Flags of Participants A2205

**1978, July 25 Litho. *Perf. 12x12½***
**4676** A2205 4k multicolored .50 .25

Construction of Soyuz gas-pipeline (Friendship Line), Orenburg. Flags of participating countries shown: Bulgaria, Hungary, German Democratic Republic, Poland, Romania, USSR, Czechoslovakia.

Dr. William Harvey (1578-1657), Discoverer of Blood Circulation — A2206

**1978, July 25 *Perf. 12***
**4677** A2206 6k blue, blk & dp grn .50 .25

Nikolai Gavilovich Chernyshevsky (1828-1889), Revolutionary — A2207

**1978, July 30 Engr. *Perf. 12x12½***
**4678** A2207 4k brown, *yellow* .50 .25

Whitewinged Petrel A2208

Antarctic Fauna: 1k, Crested penguin, horiz. 4k, Emperor penguin and chick. 6k, White-blooded pikes. 10k, Sea elephant, horiz.

***Perf. 12x11½, 11½x12***
**1978, July 30 Litho.**
**4679** A2208 1k multicolored 1.00 .25
**4680** A2208 3k multicolored 1.00 .25
**4681** A2208 4k multicolored 1.00 .25
**4682** A2208 6k multicolored 1.00 .25
**4683** A2208 10k multicolored 1.00 .25
*Nos. 4679-4683 (5)* 5.00 1.25

The Red Horse, by Petrov-Votkin — A2209

Paintings by Petrov-Votkin: 6k, Mother and Child, Petrograd, 1918. 10k, Death of the Commissar. 12k, Still-life with Fruit. 16k, Still-life with Teapot and Flowers. 50k, Self-portrait, 1918, vert.

**1978, Aug. 16 Litho. *Perf. 12½x12***
**4684** A2209 4k silver & multi .25 .25
**4685** A2209 6k silver & multi .35 .25
**4686** A2209 10k silver & multi .55 .25
**4687** A2209 12k silver & multi .85 .25
**4688** A2209 16k silver & multi 1.00 .25
*Nos. 4684-4688 (5)* 3.00 1.25

**Souvenir Sheet**

***Perf. 11½x12***
**4689** A2209 50k silver & multi 1.50 .75

Kozma Sergeevich Petrov-Votkin (1878-1939), painter. Nos. 4684-4688 have se-tenant labels. No. 4689 has label the size of stamp.

Soyuz 31 in Shop, Intercosmos Emblem, USSR and DDR Flags A2210

Designs (Intercosmos Emblem, USSR and German Democratic Republic Flags and): 15k, Pamir Mountains photographed from space; Salyut 6, Soyuz 29 and 31 complex and spectrum. 32k, Soyuz 31 docking, photographed from Salyut 6.

**1978 Litho. *Perf. 12x12½***
**4690** A2210 6k multicolored .25 .25
**4691** A2210 15k multicolored .40 .25
**4692** A2210 32k multicolored 1.00 .45
*Nos. 4690-4692 (3)* 1.65 .95

Intercosmos, Soviet-East German cooperative space program.
Issued: 6k, 8/27; 15k, 8/31; 32k, 9/3.

PRAGA '78 Emblem, Plane, Radar, Spaceship A2211

**Photogravure and Engraved**
**1978, Aug. 29 *Perf. 11½***
**4693** A2211 6k multicolored .50 .25

PRAGA '78 International Philatelic Exhibition, Prague, Sept. 8-17.

Leo Tolstoi (1828-1910), Novelist and Philosopher A2212

**1978, Sept. 7 Engr. *Perf. 12x12½***
**4694** A2212 4k slate green 1.40 .90

Stag, Conference Emblem — A2213

**1978 Photo. *Perf. 11½***
**4695** A2213 4k multicolored .50 .25

14th General Assembly of the Society for Wildlife Preservation, Ashkhabad.

Bronze Figure, Erebuni, 8th Century A2214

Armenian Architecture: 6k, Etchmiadzin Cathedral, 4th century. 10k, Stone crosses, Dzaghkatzor, 13th century. 12k, Library, Erevan, horiz. 16k, Lenin statue, Lenin Square, Erevan, horiz.

**1978 Litho. *Perf. 12x12½, 12½x12***
**4696** A2214 4k multicolored .25 .25
**4697** A2214 6k multicolored .25 .25
**4698** A2214 10k multicolored .30 .25
**4699** A2214 12k multicolored .40 .25
**4700** A2214 16k multicolored .50 .25
*Nos. 4696-4700 (5)* 1.70 1.25

Issued: 4k, 10k, 16k, 9/12; others, 10/14.

Memorial, Messina, Russian Warships A2215

**1978, Sept. 12 Photo. *Perf. 11½***
**4701** A2215 6k multicolored .50 .25

70th anniversary of aid given by Russian sailors during Messina earthquake.

Communications Emblem, Ostankino TV Tower — A2216

**1978, Sept. 20 Photo. *Perf. 11½***
**4702** A2216 4k multicolored .50 .25

Organization for Communication Cooperation of Socialist Countries, 20th anniv.

No. 4673 Overprinted

**1978, Sept. 20 Litho. *Perf. 12x12½***
**4703** A2202 4k multicolored 2.00 .70

Philatelic Exhibition for the Leninist Young Communist League.

**Souvenir Sheet**

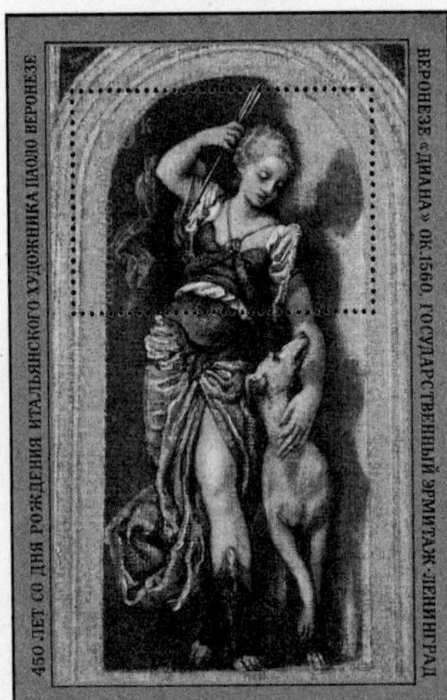
Diana, by Paolo Veronese — A2217

**1978, Sept. 28 Litho. *Perf. 12x11½***
**4704** A2217 50k multicolored 2.00 1.00

Veronese (1528-88), Italian painter.

Souvenir Sheet

Kremlin, Moscow — A2218

**Lithographed and Embossed**

**1978, Oct. 7** ***Perf. 11½x12***
**4705** A2218 30k gold & multi 2.00 .65

Russian Constitution, 1st anniversary.

Stepan Georgevich Shaumyan (1878-1918), Communist Party Functionary A2219

**1978, Oct. 11** **Engr.** ***Perf. 12½x12***
**4706** A2219 4k slate green .50 .25

Ferry, Russian and Bulgarian Colors — A2220

**1978, Oct. 14** **Photo.** ***Perf. 11½***
**4707** A2220 6k multicolored .50 .25

Opening of Ilychovsk-Varna Ferry.

Hammer and Sickle, Flags — A2221

**1978, Oct. 26** **Photo.** ***Perf. 11½***
**4708** A2221 4k gold & multi .50 .25

61st anniversary of October Revolution.

Silver Gilt Cup, Novgorod, 12th Century — A2222

Old Russian Art: 10k, Pokrowna Nerli Church, 12th century, vert. 12k, St. George Slaying the Dragon, icon, Novgorod, 15th century, vert. 16k, The Czar, cannon, 1586.

***Perf. 12½x12, 12x12½***

**1978, Nov. 28** **Litho.**
**4709** A2222 6k multicolored .25 .25
**4710** A2222 10k multicolored .45 .25
**4711** A2222 12k multicolored .50 .25
**4712** A2222 16k multicolored .75 .25
*Nos. 4709-4712 (4)* 1.95 1.00

Oncology Institute, Emblem — A2223

**1978, Dec. 1** **Photo.** ***Perf. 11½***
**4713** A2223 4k multicolored .50 .25

P.A. Herzen Tumor Institute, 75th anniv.

Savior Tower, Kremlin — A2224

**1978, Dec. 20** **Litho.** ***Perf. 12x12½***
**4714** A2224 4k silver, blue & red .50 .25

New Year 1979.

Nestor Pechersky, Chronicler, c. 885 — A2225

History of Postal Service: 6k, Birch bark letter and stylus. 10k, Messenger with trumpet and staff, from 14th century Psalm book. 12k, Winter traffic, from 16th century book by Sigizmund Gerberstein. 16k, Prikaz post office, from 17th century icon.

**Lithographed and Engraved**

**1978, Dec. 20** ***Perf. 12½x12***
**4715** A2225 4k multicolored .25 .25
**4716** A2225 6k multicolored .25 .25
**4717** A2225 10k multicolored .50 .25
**4718** A2225 12k multicolored .55 .25
**4719** A2225 16k multicolored .65 .25
*Nos. 4715-4719 (5)* 2.20 1.25

Kovalenok and Ivanchenkov, Salyut 6-Soyuz — A2226

**1978, Dec. 20** **Photo.** ***Perf. 11½x12***
**4720** A2226 10k multicolored .50 .25

Cosmonauts V. V. Kovalenok and A. S. Ivanchenkov spent 140 days in space, June 15-Nov. 2, 1978.

Vasilii Pronchishchev — A2227

Icebreakers: 6k, Captain Belousov, 1954, vert. 10k, Moscow. 12k, Admiral Makarov, 1974. 16k, Lenin, 1959, vert. 20k, Nuclear-powered Arctica.

***Perf. 11½x12, 12x11½***

**1978, Dec. 20** **Photo. & Engr.**
**4721** A2227 4k multicolored .25 .25
**4722** A2227 6k multicolored .35 .25
**4723** A2227 10k multicolored .45 .25
**4724** A2227 12k multicolored .60 .25
**4725** A2227 16k multicolored .70 .25
**4726** A2227 20k multicolored .80 .25
*Nos. 4721-4726 (6)* 3.15 1.50

Souvenir Sheet

Mastheads and Globe with Russia — A2228

**1978, Dec. 28** **Litho.** ***Perf. 12***
**4727** A2228 30k multicolored 1.50 .35

Distribution of periodicals through the Post and Telegraph Department, 60th anniversary.

Cuban Flags Forming Star — A2229

**1979, Jan. 1** **Photo.** ***Perf. 11½***
**4728** A2229 6k multicolored .50 .25

Cuban Revolution, 20th anniversary.

Russian and Byelorussian Flags, Government Building, Minsk — A2230

**1979, Jan. 1**
**4729** A2230 4k multicolored .50 .25

Byelorussian SSR and Byelorussian Communist Party, 60th annivs.

Ukrainian and Russian Flags, Reunion Monument A2231

**1979, Jan. 16**
**4730** A2231 4k multicolored .50 .25

Reunion of Ukraine & Russia, 325th anniv.

Old and New Vilnius University Buildings A2232

**1979, Jan. 16** **Photo. & Engr.**
**4731** A2232 4k black & salmon .50 .25

400th anniversary of University of Vilnius.

Bulgaria No. 1 and Exhibition Hall A2233

**1979, Jan. 25** **Litho.** ***Perf. 12½x12***
**4732** A2233 15k multicolored .50 .25

Filaserdica '79 Philatelic Exhibition, Sofia, for centenary of Bulgarian postal service.

Sputniks, Soviet Radio Hams Emblem — A2234

**1979, Feb. 23** **Photo.** ***Perf. 11½***
**4733** A2234 4k multicolored .50 .25

Sputnik satellites Radio 1 and Radio 2, launched, Oct. 1978.

1-3-0 Locomotive, 1878 — A2235

Locomotives: 3k, 1-4-0, 1912. 4k, 2-3-1, 1915. 6k, 1-3-1, 1925. 15k, 1-5-0, 1947.

**1979, Feb. 23** **Litho.** ***Perf. 11½***
**4734** A2235 2k multicolored .25 .25
**4735** A2235 3k multicolored .25 .25
**4736** A2235 4k multicolored .25 .25
**4737** A2235 6k multicolored .40 .25
**4738** A2235 15k multicolored 1.00 .25
*Nos. 4734-4738 (5)* 2.15 1.25

Souvenir Sheet

Medal for Land Development — A2236

**1979, Mar. 14** ***Perf. 11½x12½***
**4739** A2236 50k multicolored 2.00 .75

25th anniv. of drive to develop virgin lands.

Venera 11 and 12 over Venus — A2237

**1979, Mar. 16 Photo. *Perf. 11½***
**4740** A2237 10k multicolored .50 .25

Interplanetary flights of Venera 11 and Venera 12, December 1978.

Albert Einstein, Equation and Signature A2238

**1979, Mar. 16**
**4741** A2238 6k multicolored .50 .25

Einstein (1879-1955), theoretical physicist.

Congress Emblem A2239

**1979, Mar. 16**
**4742** A2239 6k multicolored .50 .25

21st World Veterinary Congress, Moscow.

"To Arms," by Robert Berény (1887-1953) — A2240

**1979, Mar. 21**
**4743** A2240 4k multicolored .50 .25

Soviet Republic of Hungary, 60th anniv.

Salyut 6, Soyuz, Research Ship, Letters — A2241

**1979, Apr. 12 Litho. *Perf. 11½x12***
**4744** A2241 15k multicolored .50 .25

Cosmonauts' Day.

Souvenir Sheet

Ice Hockey — A2242

**1979, Apr. 14 Photo. *Perf. 12x11½***
**4745** A2242 50k multicolored 2.00 .75

World and European Ice Hockey Championships, Moscow, Apr. 14-27.
For overprint see No. 4751.

Souvenir Sheet

Lenin — A2243

**1979, Apr. 18**
**4746** A2243 50k red, gold & brn 1.50 .75

109th anniversary of the birth of Lenin.

Astronauts' Training Center A2244

Design: 32k, Astronauts, landing capsule, radar, helicopter and emblem.

**1979, Apr. 12 Litho. *Perf. 11½***
**4747** A2244 6k multicolored .30 .25
**4748** A2244 32k multicolored .70 .40

Joint Soviet-Bulgarian space flight.

Exhibition Emblem — A2245

**1979, Apr. 18 Photo. *Perf. 11½***
**4749** A2245 15k sil, red & vio blue 1.00 .25

National USSR Exhibition in the United Kingdom. Se-tenant label with commemorative inscription.

Blast Furnace, Pushkin Theater, "Tent" Sculpture — A2246

**1979, May 24 Photo. *Perf. 11½***
**4750** A2246 4k multicolored .50 .25

50th anniversary of Magnitogorsk City.

**No. 4745 Overprinted in Red**

**1979, May 24 *Perf. 12x11½***
**4751** A2242 50k multicolored 2.00 .80

Victory of Soviet team in World and European Ice Hockey Championships.

Infant, Flowers, IYC Emblem — A2247

**1979, June 1 Litho. *Perf. 12x12½***
**4752** A2247 4k multicolored .50 .25

International Year of the Child.

Horn Player and Bears Playing Balalaika, Bogorodsk Wood Carvings — A2248

Folk Art: 3k, Decorated wooden bowls, Khokhloma. 4k, Tray decorated with flowers, Zhestovo. 6k, Carved bone boxes, Kholmogory. 15k, Lace, Vologda.

**1979, June 14 Litho. *Perf. 12½x12***
**4753** A2248 2k multicolored .25 .25
**4754** A2248 3k multicolored .25 .25
**4755** A2248 4k multicolored .25 .25
**4756** A2248 6k multicolored .25 .25
**4757** A2248 15k multicolored .25 .25
*Nos. 4753-4757 (5)* 1.25 1.25

Nos. 4753-4757 printed in sheets of 7 stamps and decorative label. Value, set with attached labels, $3.

V. A. Djanibekov, O. G. Makarov, Spacecraft A2249

**1979, June *Perf. 12x11½***
**4758** A2249 4k multicolored .50 .25

Flights of Soyuz 26-27 and work on board of orbital complex Salyut 6.

COMECON Building, Members' Flags — A2250

**1979, June 26 *Perf. 12***
**4759** A2250 16k multicolored .50 .25

Council for Mutual Economic Aid of Socialist Countries, 30th anniversary.

Scene from "Potemkin" and Festival Emblem — A2251

**Photogravure and Engraved**

**1979, July *Perf. 11½***
**4760** A2251 15k multicolored .50 .25

11th International Film Festival, Moscow, and 60th anniversary of Soviet film industry.

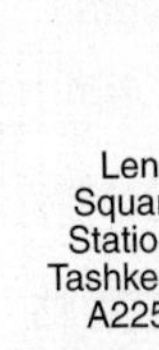

Lenin Square Station, Tashkent A2252

**1979, July Litho. *Perf. 12***
**4761** A2252 4k multicolored .50 .25

Tashkent subway.

### Souvenir Sheets

Atom Symbol, Factories, Dam — A2253

**1979, July 23 Photo.** ***Perf. 11½x12***

**4762** A2253 30k multicolored 2.00 .45

50th anniversary of 1st Five-Year Plan.

USSR Philatelic Society Emblem — A2254

**1979, July 25 Litho.** ***Perf. 12x12½***

**4763** A2254 50k gray grn & red 2.00 .70

4th Cong. of USSR Phil. Soc., Moscow.

Exhibition Hall, Scene from "Chapayev" A2255

**1979, Aug. 8 Photo.** ***Perf. 11½***

**4764** A2255 4k multicolored .50 .25

60th anniversary of Soviet Film and Exhibition of History of Soviet Film.

Roses, by P. P. Konchalovsky, 1955 — A2256

Russian Flower Paintings: 1k, Flowers and Fruit, by I. F. Khrutsky, 1830. 2k, Phlox, by I. N. Kramskoi, 1884. 3k, Lilac, by K. A. Korovin, 1915. 15k, Bluebells, by S. V. Gerasimov, 1944. 2k, 3k, 15k, vert.

***Perf. 12½x12, 12x12½***

**1979, Aug. 16 Litho.**

**4765** A2256 1k multicolored .25 .25
**4766** A2256 2k multicolored .25 .25
**4767** A2256 3k multicolored .25 .25
**4768** A2256 15k multicolored .30 .25
**4769** A2256 32k multicolored .45 .30
*Nos. 4765-4769 (5)* 1.50 1.30

John Maclean — A2257

**1979, Aug. 29 Litho.** ***Perf. 11½***

**4770** A2257 4k red & black .50 .25

John Maclean (1879-1923), Scottish Communist labor leader.

Soviet Circus Emblem — A2258

**1979, Sept.**

**4771** A2258 4k multicolored .50 .25

Soviet Circus, 60th anniversary.

Friendship — A2259

Children's Drawings: 3k, Children and Horses. 4k, Dances. 15k, The Excursion.

**1979, Sept. 10** ***Perf. 12½x12***

**4772** A2259 2k multicolored .50 .25
**4773** A2259 3k multicolored .50 .25
**4774** A2259 4k multicolored .50 .25
**4775** A2259 15k multicolored .50 .25
*Nos. 4772-4775 (4)* 2.00 1.00

International Year of the Child.
Exist imperf. Value, $50 each.

Oriolus oriolus — A2260

Birds: 3k, Dendrocopus minor. 4k, Parus cristatus. 10k, Tyto alba. 15k, Caprimulgus europaeus.

**1979, Sept. 18**

**4776** A2260 2k multicolored .25 .25
**4777** A2260 3k multicolored .25 .25
**4778** A2260 4k multicolored .45 .25
**4779** A2260 10k multicolored .90 .25
**4780** A2260 15k multicolored 1.40 .25
*Nos. 4776-4780 (5)* 3.25 1.25

German Arms, Marx, Engels, Lenin, Berlin A2261

**1979, Oct. 7 Photo.** ***Perf. 11½***

**4781** A2261 6k multicolored .50 .25

German Democratic Republic, 30th anniv.

Valery Ryumin, Vladimir Lyakhov, Salyut 6 — A2262

Design: No. 4783, Spacecraft.

**1979, Oct. 10** ***Perf. 12x11½***

**4782** A2262 15k multicolored .50 .25
**4783** A2262 15k multicolored .50 .25
*a.* Pair, #4782-4783 1.25 .75

175 days in space, Feb. 25-Aug. 19. No. 4783a has continuous design.

Star — A2264

**1979, Oct. 18** ***Perf. 11½***

**4784** A2264 4k multicolored .50 .25

USSR Signal Troops, 60th anniversary.

Hammer and Sickle — A2265

**1979, Oct. 18**

**4785** A2265 4k multicolored .50 .25

October Revolution, 62nd anniversary.

Katherina, by T. G. Shevchenko A2266

Ukrainian Paintings: 3k, Working Girl, by K.K. Kostandi. 4k, Lenin's Return to Petrograd, by A.M. Lopuhov. 10k, Soldier's Return, by N.V. Kostetsky. 15k, Going to Work, by M.G. Belsky.

**1979, Nov. 18 Litho.** ***Perf. 12x12½***

**4786** A2266 2k multicolored .25 .25
**4787** A2266 3k multicolored .25 .25
**4788** A2266 4k multicolored .25 .25
**4789** A2266 10k multicolored .50 .25
**4790** A2266 15k multicolored .75 .25
*Nos. 4786-4790 (5)* 2.00 1.25

Shabolovka Radio Tower, Moscow — A2267

**1979, Nov. 28 Photo.** ***Perf. 12***

**4791** A2267 32k multicolored .50 .35

Radio Moscow, 50th anniversary.

Mischa Holding Stamp — A2268

**1979, Nov. 28** ***Perf. 12x12½***

**4792** A2268 4k multicolored .90 .25

New Year 1980.

Hand Holding Peace Message A2269

Peace Program in Action: No. 4794, Hands holding cultural symbols. No. 4795, Hammer and sickle, flag.

**1979, Dec. 5 Litho.** ***Perf. 12***

**4793** A2269 4k multicolored .65 .25
**4794** A2269 4k multicolored .65 .25
**4795** A2269 4k multicolored .65 .25
*Nos. 4793-4795 (3)* 1.95 .75

Policeman, Patrol Car, Helicopter A2270

Traffic Safety: 4k, Car, girl and ball. 6k, Speeding cars.

**1979, Dec. 20** ***Perf. 12x12½***

**4796** A2270 3k multicolored .50 .25
**4797** A2270 4k multicolored .50 .25
**4798** A2270 6k multicolored .50 .25
*Nos. 4796-4798 (3)* 1.50 .75

Vulkanolog — A2271

Research Ships and Portraits: 2k, Professor Bogorov. 4k, Ernst Krenkel. 6k, Vladislav Volkov. 10k, Cosmonaut Yuri Gagarin. 15k, Academician E.B. Kurchatov.

### Lithographed and Engraved

**1979, Dec. 25** ***Perf. 12x11½***

**4799** A2271 1k multicolored .25 .25
**4800** A2271 2k multicolored .25 .25
**4801** A2271 4k multicolored .25 .25
**4802** A2271 6k multicolored .30 .25
**4803** A2271 10k multicolored .35 .25
**4804** A2271 15k multicolored .60 .25
*Nos. 4799-4804 (6)* 2.00 1.50

See Nos. 4881-4886.

Souvenir Sheet

Explorers Raising Red Flag at North Pole — A2272

**1979, Dec. 25 Photo. *Perf. 11½x12***
**4805** A2272 50k multicolored 2.00 .75

Komsomolskaya Pravda North Pole expedition.

**Type of 1970**

4k, Coat of arms, power line, factories.

**1980, Jan. 10 Litho. *Perf. 12x12½***
**4806** A1794 4k carmine .50 .25

Mordovian Autonomous SSR, 50th anniv.

Freestyle Skating A2273

**1980, Jan. 22 *Perf. 12x12½, 12½x12***

| | | | | | |
|---|---|---|---|---|---|
| **4807** | A2273 | 4k | Speed skating, vert. | .25 | .25 |
| **4808** | A2273 | 6k | shown | .25 | .25 |
| **4809** | A2273 | 10k | Ice hockey | .25 | .25 |
| **4810** | A2273 | 15k | Downhill skiing | .35 | .25 |
| **4811** | A2273 | 20k | Luge, vert. | .50 | .35 |
| | | | *Nos. 4807-4811 (5)* | 1.60 | 1.35 |

**Souvenir Sheet**

**4812** A2273 50k Cross-country skiing, vert. 2.00 1.00

13th Winter Olympic Games, Lake Placid, NY, Feb. 12-24.
Nos. 4808, 4809 exist imperf. Value, $50 for both.

Nikolai Ilyitch Podvoiski (1880-1948), Revolutionary A2274

**1980, Feb. 16 Engr. *Perf. 12½x12***
**4813** A2274 4k claret brown 1.00 .25

Rainbow, by A.K. Savrasov — A2275

No. 4815, Summer Harvest, by A.G. Venetsianov, vert. No. 4816, Old Erevan, by M.S. Saryan.

**1980, Mar. 4 Litho. *Perf. 11½***

| | | | | | |
|---|---|---|---|---|---|
| **4814** | A2275 | 6k | multicolored | .35 | .25 |
| **4815** | A2275 | 6k | multicolored | .35 | .25 |
| **4816** | A2275 | 6k | multicolored | .35 | .25 |
| | | | *Nos. 4814-4816 (3)* | 1.05 | .75 |

Souvenir Sheet

Cosmonaut Alexei Leonov — A2276

**1980, Mar. 18 Litho. *Perf. 12½x12***
**4817** A2276 50k multicolored 1.50 .75

Man's first walk in space (Voskhod 2, Mar. 18-19, 1965).

Georg Ots, Estonian Artist — A2277

**1980, Mar. 21 Engr.**
**4818** A2277 4k slate blue .50 .25

Lenin Order, 50th Anniversary A2278

**1980, Apr. 6 Photo. *Perf. 11½***
**4819** A2278 4k multicolored .50 .25

Souvenir Sheet

Cosmonauts, Salyut 6 and Soyuz — A2279

**1980, Apr. 12 Litho. *Perf. 12***
**4820** A2279 50k multicolored 1.50 1.00

Intercosmos cooperative space program.

Flags and Arms of Azerbaijan, Government House — A2280

**1980, Apr. 22 Photo.**
**4821** A2280 4k multicolored .50 .25

Azerbaijan Soviet Socialist Republic, Communist Party of Azerbaijan, 60th anniv.

Souvenir Sheet

Lenin, 110th Birth Anniversary — A2281

**1980, Apr. 22 *Perf. 12x11½***
**4822** A2281 30k multicolored 1.50 .75

"Mother Russia," Fireworks over Moscow — A2282

No. 4824, Soviet War Memorial, Berlin, raising of Red flag. No. 4825, Parade, Red Square, Moscow.

**1980, Apr. 25 Litho.**

| | | | | | |
|---|---|---|---|---|---|
| **4823** | A2282 | 4k | multicolored | .35 | .25 |
| **4824** | A2282 | 4k | multicolored | .35 | .25 |
| **4825** | A2282 | 4k | multicolored | .35 | .25 |
| | | | *Nos. 4823-4825 (3)* | 1.05 | .75 |

35th anniv. of victory in World War II.
Nos. 4823, 4824 exist imperf. Value, $25 for both.

Workers' Monument A2283

**1980, May 12 Litho. *Perf. 12***
**4826** A2283 4k multicolored .50 .25

Workers' Delegates in Ivanovo-Voznesensk, 75th anniversary.

"XXV" — A2284

**1980, May 14 Photo. *Perf. 11½***
**4827** A2284 32k multicolored .50 .35

Signing of Warsaw Pact (Bulgaria, Czechoslovakia, German Democratic Rep., Hungary, Poland, Romania, USSR), 25th anniv.

YaK-24 Helicopter, 1953 — A2285

**1980, May 15 Litho. *Perf. 12½x12***

| | | | | | |
|---|---|---|---|---|---|
| **4828** | A2285 | 1k | shown | .25 | .25 |
| **4829** | A2285 | 2k | MI-8, 1962 | .25 | .25 |
| **4830** | A2285 | 3k | KA-26, 1965 | .25 | .25 |
| **4831** | A2285 | 6k | MI-6, 1957 | .25 | .25 |
| **4832** | A2285 | 15k | MI-10 | .35 | .25 |
| **4833** | A2285 | 32k | V-12 | .65 | .40 |
| | | | *Nos. 4828-4833 (6)* | 2.00 | 1.65 |

Nos 4832-4833 exist imperf. Value, $50 for both.

David Anhaght, Illuminated Manuscript A2286

**1980, May 16 *Perf. 12***
**4834** A2286 4k multicolored .50 .25

David Anacht, Armenian philosopher, 1500th birth anniversary.

Emblem, Training Lab — A2287

15k, Cosmonauts meeting. 32k, Press conference.

**1980, June 4**

| | | | | | |
|---|---|---|---|---|---|
| **4835** | A2287 | 6k | shown | .25 | .25 |
| **4836** | A2287 | 15k | multicolored | .40 | .25 |
| **4837** | A2287 | 32k | multicolored | .85 | .55 |
| | | | *Nos. 4835-4837 (3)* | 1.50 | 1.05 |

Intercosmos cooperative space program (USSR-Hungary).

Polar Fox A2288

2k, Dark silver fox, vert. 6k, Mink. 10k, Azerbaijan nutria, vert. 15k, Black sable.

**1980, June 25 Litho. *Perf. 12x12½***

| | | | | | |
|---|---|---|---|---|---|
| **4838** | A2288 | 2k | multicolored | .25 | .25 |
| **4839** | A2288 | 4k | shown | .25 | .25 |
| **4840** | A2288 | 6k | multicolored | .25 | .25 |
| **4841** | A2288 | 10k | multicolored | .25 | .25 |
| **4842** | A2288 | 15k | multicolored | .25 | .25 |
| | | | *Nos. 4838-4842 (5)* | 1.25 | 1.25 |

Factory, Buildings, Arms of Tatar A.S.S.R. A2289

**1980, June 25 *Perf. 12***
**4843** A2289 4k multicolored .50 .25

Tatar Autonomous SSR, 60th anniv.

College — A2290

**1980, July 1** **Photo.** ***Perf. 11½***
**4844** A2290 4k multicolored .50 .25

Bauman Technological College, Moscow, 150th anniversary.

Ho Chi Minh — A2291

**1980, July 7**
**4845** A2291 6k multicolored .50 .25

Red Flag, Lithuanian Arms, Flag, Red Guards Monument A2292

**1980, July 12** **Litho.** ***Perf. 12***
**4846** A2292 4k multicolored .50 .25

Lithuanian SSR, 40th anniv.

Russian Flag and Arms, Latvian Flag, Monument, Buildings A2293

Design: No. 4848, Russian flag and arms, Estonian flag, monument, buildings.

**1980, July 21** **Litho.** ***Perf. 12***
**4847** A2293 4k multicolored .35 .25
**4848** A2293 4k multicolored .35 .25

Restoration of Soviet power.

Cosmonauts Boarding Soyuz A2294

**1980, July 24** ***Perf. 12x12½***
**4849** A2294 6k shown .25 .25
**4850** A2294 15k Working aboard spacecraft .45 .25
**4851** A2294 32k Return flight .80 .55
*Nos. 4849-4851 (3)* 1.50 1.05

Center for Cosmonaut Training, 20th anniv.

Avicenna (980-1037), Philosopher and Physician — A2295

**Photogravure and Engraved**

**1980, Aug. 16** ***Perf. 11½***
**4852** A2295 4k multicolored .50 .25

Soviet Racing Car KHADI-7 — A2296

**1980, Aug. 25** **Litho.** ***Perf. 12***
**4853** A2296 2k shown .25 .25
**4854** A2296 6k KHADI-10 .25 .25
**4855** A2296 15k KHADI-113 .25 .25
**4856** A2296 32k KHADI-133 .25 .25
*Nos. 4853-4856 (4)* 1.00 1.00

No. 4856 exists imperf. Value, $50.

Kazakhstan Republic, 60th Anniversary A2297

**1980, Aug. 26**
**4857** A2297 4k multicolored .50 .25

Ingres, Self-portrait, and Nymph A2298

**1980, Aug. 29** ***Perf. 12x12½***
**4858** A2298 32k multicolored .50 .35

Jean Auguste Dominique Ingres (1780-1867), French painter.
Exists imperf. Value, $25.

Morning on the Field of Kulikovo, by A. Bubnov — A2299

**1980, Sept. 6** **Litho.** ***Perf. 12***
**4859** A2299 4k multicolored .50 .25

Battle of Kulikovo, 600th anniversary.

Town Hall, Tartu — A2300

**1980, Sept. 15** **Photo.** ***Perf. 11½***
**4860** A2300 4k multicolored .50 .25

Tartu, 950th anniversary.

Y.V. Malyshev, V.V. Aksenov A2301

**1980, Sept. 15** **Litho.** ***Perf. 12x12½***
**4861** A2301 10k multicolored .50 .25

Soyuz T-2 space flight.

Flight Training, Yuri Gagarin — A2302

**1980, Sept. 15** **Photo.** ***Perf. 11½x12***
**4862** A2302 6k shown .25 .25
**4863** A2302 15k Space walk .40 .25
**4864** A2302 32k Endurance test .85 .45
*Nos. 4862-4864 (3)* 1.50 .95

Gagarin Cosmonaut Training Center, 20th anniversary.

Intercosmos A2303

6k, Intercosmos Emblem, Flags of USSR and Cuba, and Cosmonauts training. 15k, Inside weightless cabin. 32k, Landing.

**1980, Sept. 15** **Litho.** ***Perf. 12x12½***
**4865** A2303 6k multicolored .25 .25
**4866** A2303 15k multicolored .40 .25
**4867** A2303 32k multicolored .85 .45
*Nos. 4865-4867 (3)* 1.50 .95

Intercosmos cooperative space program (USSR-Cuba).

October Revolution, 63rd Anniversary A2304

**1980, Sept. 20** **Photo.** ***Perf. 11½***
**4868** A2304 6k multicolored .50 .25

David Guramishvili (1705-1792), Poet — A2305

**1980, Sept. 20**
**4869** A2305 6k multicolored .50 .25

Family with Serfs, by N.V. Nevrev (1830-1904) — A2305a

Design: No. 4869B, Countess Tarakanova, by K.D. Flavitsky (1830-1866), vert.

**1980, Sept. 25** **Litho.** ***Perf. 11½***
**4869A** A2305a 6k multicolored .50 .25
**4869B** A2305a 6k multicolored .50 .25

A.F. Ioffe (1880-1960), Physicist — A2306

**1980, Sept. 29**
**4870** A2306 4k multicolored .50 .25

Siberian Pine A2307

**1980, Sept. 29** **Litho.** ***Perf. 12½x12***
**4871** A2307 2k shown .25 .25
**4872** A2307 4k Oak .25 .25
**4873** A2307 6k Lime tree, vert. .25 .25
**4874** A2307 10k Sea bucthorn .50 .25
**4875** A2307 15k European ash .75 .25
*Nos. 4871-4875 (5)* 2.00 1.25

A.M. Vasilevsky (1895-1977), Soviet Marshal — A2308

**1980, Sept. 30** **Engr.** ***Perf. 12***
**4876** A2308 4k dark green .50 .25

Souvenir Sheet

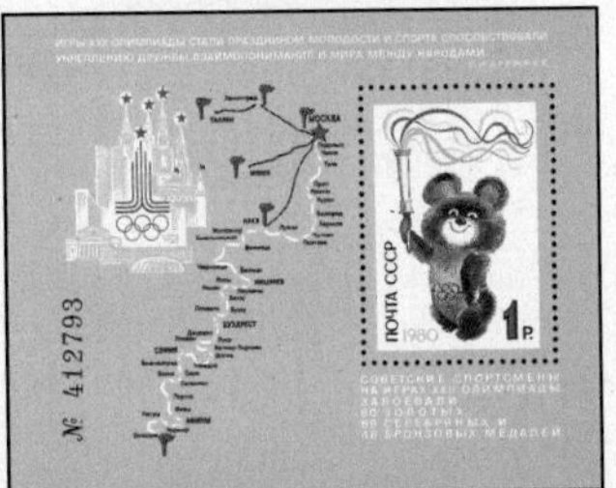

Mischa Holding Olympic Torch — A2309

**1980, Nov. 24** ***Perf. 12x12½***
**4877** A2309 1r multicolored 5.00 1.75

Completion of 22nd Summer Olympic Games, Moscow, July 19-Aug. 3.

A.V. Suvorov (1730-1800), General and Military Theorist A2310

**1980, Nov. 24** **Engr.**
**4878** A2310 4k slate .50 .25

A2311

**1980, Nov. 24** **Litho.** ***Perf. 12***
**4879** A2311 4k multicolored .50 .25

Armenian SSR & Armenian Communist Party, 60th annivs.

Aleksandr Blok (1880-1921), Poet — A2312

**1980, Nov. 24**
**4880** A2312 4k multicolored .50 .25

**Research Ship Type of 1979**

**Lithographed and Engraved**

**1980, Nov. 24** ***Perf. 12x11½***
**4881** A2271 2k Aju Dag, Fleet arms .25 .25
**4882** A2271 3k Valerian Urywaev .25 .25
**4883** A2271 4k Mikhail Somov .25 .25
**4884** A2271 6k Sergei Korolev .25 .25
**4885** A2271 10k Otto Schmidt .25 .25
**4886** A2271 15k Mstislav Keldysh .25 .25
*Nos. 4881-4886 (6)* 1.50 1.50

For overprint see No. 5499.

Russian Flag — A2313

**1980, Dec. 1** **Engr.** ***Perf. 12x12½***
**4887** A2313 3k orange red 2.00 .25

Soviet Medical College, 50th Anniversary A2314

**1980, Dec. 1** **Photo.** ***Perf. 11½***
**4888** A2314 4k multicolored .50 .25

New Year 1981 A2315

**1980, Dec. 1** **Litho.** ***Perf. 12***
**4889** A2315 4k multicolored .50 .25

Lenin, Electrical Plant A2316

**1980, Dec. 18**
**4890** A2316 4k multicolored .50 .25

60th anniversary of GOELRO (Lenin's electro-economic plan).

A.N. Nesmeyanov (1899-1980), Chemist — A2317

**1980, Dec. 19** ***Perf. 12½x12***
**4891** A2317 4k multicolored .50 .25

Nagatinski Bridge, Moscow — A2318

**Photogravure and Engraved**

**1980, Dec. 23** ***Perf. 11½x12***
**4892** A2318 4k shown .25 .25
**4893** A2318 6k Luzhniki Bridge .25 .25
**4894** A2318 15k Kalininski Bridge .25 .25
*Nos. 4892-4894 (3)* .75 .75

S.K. Timoshenko (1895-1970), Soviet Marshal — A2319

**1980, Dec. 25** **Engr.** ***Perf. 12***
**4895** A2319 4k rose lake .50 .25

Flags of India and USSR, Government House, New Delhi A2320

**1980, Dec. 30** **Litho.** ***Perf. 12x12½***
**4896** A2320 4k multicolored .50 .35

Visit of Pres. Brezhnev to India. Printed se-tenant with inscribed label.

Mirny Base — A2321

6k, Earth station, rocket. 15k, Map, supply ship.

**1981, Jan. 5** ***Perf. 12***
**4897** A2321 4k shown .25 .25
**4898** A2321 6k multicolored .35 .25
**4899** A2321 15k multicolored .90 .25
*Nos. 4897-4899 (3)* 1.50 .75

Soviet Antarctic research, 25th anniv.

Dagestan Soviet Socialist Republic, 60th Anniversary A2322

**1981, Jan. 20**
**4900** A2322 4k multicolored .50 .25

Bandy World Championship, Khabarovsk — A2323

**1981, Jan. 20**
**4901** A2323 6k multicolored .50 .25

26th Congress of Ukrainian Communist Party A2324

**1981, Jan. 23** **Photo.** ***Perf. 11½***
**4902** A2324 4k multicolored .50 .25

Lenin, "XXVI" A2325

**1981** **Photo.** ***Perf. 11½***
**4903** A2325 4k multicolored .50 .25

Lenin and Congress Building — A2326

Banner and Kremlin — A2327

**Photogravure and Embossed**

**1982** ***Perf. 11½x12***
**4904** A2326 20k multicolored 1.50 .75

**Souvenir Sheet**

**Litho.**

***Perf. 12x12½***

**4905** A2327 50k multicolored 1.50 .75

26th Communist Party Congress. Issue dates: 4k, 20k, Jan. 22; 50k, Feb. 16.

Mstislav V. Keldysh — A2328

**Photogravure and Engraved**

**1981, Feb. 10** ***Perf. 11½x12***
**4906** A2328 4k multicolored .50 .25

Mstislav Vsevolodovich Keldysh (1911-1978), mathematician.

Freighter, Flags of USSR and India — A2329

**1981, Feb. 10** **Litho.** ***Perf. 12***
**4907** A2329 15k multicolored .50 .30

Soviet-Indian Shipping Line, 25th anniv.

Baikal-Amur Railroad and Map — A2330

10th Five-Year Plan Projects (1976-1980): No. 4909, Gas plant, Urengoi (spherical tanks). No. 4910, Enisei River power station (dam). No. 4911, Atomic power plant. No. 4912, Paper mill. No. 4913, Coal mining, Ekibstyi.

**1981, Feb. 18** ***Perf. 12½x12***
**4908** A2330 4k multicolored .25 .25
**4909** A2330 4k multicolored .25 .25
**4910** A2330 4k multicolored .25 .25
**4911** A2330 4k multicolored .25 .25

**4912** A2330 4k multicolored .25 .25
**4913** A2330 4k multicolored .25 .25
*Nos. 4908-4913 (6)* 1.50 1.50

Georgian Soviet Socialist Republic, 60th Anniv. A2331

**1981, Feb. 25** ***Perf. 12***
**4914** A2331 4k multicolored .50 .25

Abkhazian Autonomous Soviet Socialist Republic, 60th Anniv. — A2332

**1981, Mar. 4**
**4915** A2332 4k multicolored .50 .25

Exists imperf.

Communications Institute — A2333

**1981, Mar. 12** **Photo.** ***Perf. 11½***
**4916** A2333 4k multicolored .50 .25

Moscow Electrotechnical Institute of Communications, 60th anniv.

Satellite, Radio Operator — A2334

**1981, Mar. 12**
**4917** A2334 4k multicolored .50 .25

30th All-Union Amateur Radio Designers Exhibition.

Cosmonauts L.I. Popov and V.V. Ryumin A2335

**1981, Mar. 20** **Litho.** ***Perf. 12***
**4918** A2335 15k shown .25 .25
**4919** A2335 15k Spacecraft complex .25 .25
*a.* Pair, #4918-4919 + label 1.00 .50

185-day flight of Cosmos 35-Salyut 6-Cosmos 37 complex, Apr. 9-Oct. 11, 1980. No. 4919a has a continuous design.

Cosmonauts O. Makarov, L. Kizim and G. Strekalov — A2336

**1981, Mar. 20** ***Perf. 12½x12***
**4920** A2336 10k multicolored .50 .25

Soyuz T-3 flight, Nov. 27-Dec. 10, 1980.

Lift-Off, Baikonur Base — A2337

15k, Mongolians watching flight on TV. 32k, Re-entry.

**1981, Mar. 23**
**4921** A2337 6k shown .25 .25
**4922** A2337 15k multicolored .40 .25
**4923** A2337 32k multicolored .85 .50
*Nos. 4921-4923 (3)* 1.50 1.00

Intercosmos cooperative space program (USSR-Mongolia).

Vitus Bering A2338

**1981, Mar. 25** **Engr.** ***Perf. 12x12½***
**4924** A2338 4k dark blue .50 .25

Bering (1680-1741), Danish navigator.

Yuri Gagarin and Earth — A2339

Yuri Gagarin — A2340

**1981, Apr. 12** **Photo.** ***Perf. 11½x12***
**4925** A2339 6k shown .25 .25
**4926** A2339 15k S.P. Korolev (craft designer) .40 .25
**4927** A2339 32k Monument .65 .25
*Nos. 4925-4927 (3)* 1.30 .75

**Souvenir Sheet**

**4928** A2340 50k shown 5.00 1.00

Soviet space flights, 20th anniv. Nos. 4925-4927 each se-tenant with label.

Salyut Orbital Station, 10th Anniv. of Flight A2341

**1981, Apr. 19** **Litho.** ***Perf. 12x12½***
**4929** A2341 32k multicolored .50 .35

**Souvenir Sheet**

111th Birth Anniv. of Lenin — A2342

**1981, Apr. 22** ***Perf. 11½x12½***
**4930** A2342 50k multicolored 1.50 .60

Sergei Prokofiev (1891-1953), Composer A2343

**1981, Apr. 23** **Engr.** ***Perf. 12***
**4931** A2343 4k dark violet .50 .25

New Hofburg Palace, Vienna — A2344

**1981, May 5** **Litho.**
**4932** A2344 15k multicolored .50 .25

WIPA 1981 Phil. Exhib., Vienna, May 22-31.

Adzhar Autonomous Soviet Socialist Republic, 60th Anniv. — A2345

**1981, May 7**
**4933** A2345 4k multicolored .50 .25

Centenary of Welding (Invented by N.N. Benardos) A2346

**Lithographed and Engraved**

**1981, May 12** ***Perf. 11½***
**4934** A2346 6k multicolored .50 .25

Intl. Architects Union, 14th Congress, Warsaw — A2347

**1981, May 12** **Photo.**
**4935** A2347 15k multicolored .50 .25

Albanian Girl, by A.A. Ivanov A2348

No. 4937, Horseman, by F.A. Roubeau. No. 4938, The Demon, by M.A. Vrubel, horiz. No. 4939, Sunset over the Sea, by N.N. Ge, horiz.

**1981, May 15** **Litho.** ***Perf. 12x12½***
**4936** A2348 10k multicolored .50 .25
**4937** A2348 10k multicolored .50 .25
**4938** A2348 10k multicolored .50 .25
**4939** A2348 10k multicolored .50 .25
*Nos. 4936-4939 (4)* 2.00 1.00

Cosmonauts in Training A2349

**1981, May 15**
**4940** A2349 6k shown .25 .25
**4941** A2349 15k In space .40 .25
**4942** A2349 32k Return .85 .50
*Nos. 4940-4942 (3)* 1.50 1.00

Intercosmos cooperative space program (USSR-Romania).

Dwarf Primrose — A2350

Flowers of the Carpathian Mountains: 6k, Great carline thistle. 10k, Mountain parageum. 15k, Alpine bluebell. 32k, Rhododendron kotschyi.

**1981, May 20** *Perf. 12*

| | | | | |
|---|---|---|---|---|
| **4943** | A2350 | 4k multicolored | .25 | .25 |
| **4944** | A2350 | 6k multicolored | .25 | .25 |
| **4945** | A2350 | 10k multicolored | .25 | .25 |
| **4946** | A2350 | 15k multicolored | .40 | .25 |
| **4947** | A2350 | 32k multicolored | .85 | .50 |
| | | *Nos. 4943-4947 (5)* | 2.00 | 1.50 |

Luigi Longo, Italian Labor Leader, 1st Death Anniv. — A2351

**1981, May 24** **Photo.** *Perf. 11½*

**4948** A2351 6k multicolored .50 .25

Nizami Gjanshevi (1141-1209), Azerbaijan Poet — A2352

**1981, May 25** **Photo. & Engr.**

**4949** A2352 4k multicolored .50 .25

A2353

**1981, June 18** **Litho.** *Perf. 12*

| | | | | |
|---|---|---|---|---|
| **4950** | A2353 | 4k Running | .25 | .25 |
| **4951** | A2353 | 6k Soccer | .25 | .25 |
| **4952** | A2353 | 10k Discus throwing | .25 | .25 |
| **4953** | A2353 | 15k Boxing | .30 | .25 |
| **4954** | A2353 | 32k Diving | .45 | .35 |
| | | *Nos. 4950-4954 (5)* | 1.50 | 1.35 |

Mongolian Revolution, 60th anniv. — A2354

**1981, July 6**

**4955** A2354 6k multicolored .75 .25

12th Intl. Film Festival, Moscow — A2355

**1981, July 6** **Photo.** *Perf. 11½*

**4956** A2355 15k multicolored .50 .30

River Tour Boat Lenin A2356

6k, Cosmonaut Gagarin. 15k, Valerian Kuibyshev. 32k, Freighter Baltijski.

**1981, July 9** **Litho.** *Perf. 12½*

| | | | | |
|---|---|---|---|---|
| **4957** | A2356 | 4k shown | .25 | .25 |
| **4958** | A2356 | 6k multicolored | .25 | .25 |
| **4959** | A2356 | 15k multicolored | .35 | .25 |
| **4960** | A2356 | 32k multicolored | .65 | .45 |
| | | *Nos. 4957-4960 (4)* | 1.50 | 1.20 |

Icebreaker Maligin — A2357

**Photogravure and Engraved**

**1981, July 9** *Perf. 11½x12*

**4961** A2357 15k multicolored .50 .30

26th Party Congress Resolutions (Intl. Cooperation) — A2358

**1981, July 15** **Photo.** *Perf. 12x11½*

| | | | | |
|---|---|---|---|---|
| **4962** | A2358 | 4k shown | .25 | .25 |
| **4963** | A2358 | 4k Industry | .25 | .25 |
| **4964** | A2358 | 4k Energy | .25 | .25 |
| **4965** | A2358 | 4k Agriculture | .25 | .25 |
| **4966** | A2358 | 4k Communications | .25 | .25 |
| **4967** | A2358 | 4k Arts | .25 | .25 |
| | | *Nos. 4962-4967 (6)* | 1.50 | 1.50 |

I.N. Ulyanov (Lenin's Father), 150th Anniv. of Birth — A2359

**1981, July 25** **Engr.** *Perf. 11½*

**4968** A2359 4k multicolored .50 .25

Leningrad Theater, 225th Anniv. — A2360

**1981, Aug. 12** **Photo.** *Perf. 11½*

**4969** A2360 6k multicolored .50 .25

A.M. Gerasimov, Artist, Birth Centenary A2361

**1981, Aug. 12** **Litho.** *Perf. 12*

**4970** A2361 4k multicolored .50 .25

Physical Chemistry Institute, Moscow Academy of Science, 50th Anniv. A2362

**1981, Aug. 12** **Photo.** *Perf. 11½*

**4971** A2362 4k multicolored .50 .25

Siberian Tit A2363

Song birds — 10k, Tersiphone paradisi, vert. 15k, Emberiza jankovski. 20k, Sutora webbiana, vert. 32k, Saxicola torquata, vert.

*Perf. 12½x12, 12x12½*

**1981, Aug. 20** **Litho.**

| | | | | |
|---|---|---|---|---|
| **4972** | A2363 | 6k shown | .25 | .25 |
| **4973** | A2363 | 10k multicolored | .30 | .25 |
| **4974** | A2363 | 15k multicolored | .40 | .25 |
| **4975** | A2363 | 20k multicolored | .45 | .30 |
| **4976** | A2363 | 32k multicolored | .60 | .35 |
| | | *Nos. 4972-4976 (5)* | 2.00 | 1.40 |

60th Anniv. of Komi Autonomous Soviet Socialist Republic — A2364

**1981, Aug. 22** *Perf. 12*

**4977** A2364 4k multicolored .50 .25

Svyaz-'81 Intl. Communications Exhibition — A2365

**Photogravure and Engraved**

**1981, Aug. 22** *Perf. 11½*

**4978** A2365 4k multicolored .50 .25

60th Anniv. of Kabardino-Balkar Autonomous Soviet Socialist Republic — A2366

**1981, Sept. 1** **Litho.** *Perf. 12*

**4979** A2366 4k multicolored .50 .25

War Veterans' Committee, 25th Anniv. — A2367

**1981, Sept. 1** **Photo.** *Perf. 11½*

**4980** A2367 4k multicolored .50 .25

Schooner Kodor — A2368

Training ships — 4k, 4-masted bark Tovarich I. 6k, Barkentine Vega I. 15k, 3-masted bark Tovarich. 20k, 4-masted bark Kruzenstern. 32k, 4-masted bark Sedov.

4k, 6k, 15k, 20k, horiz.

*Perf. 12½x12, 12x12½*

**1981, Sept. 18** **Litho.**

| | | | | |
|---|---|---|---|---|
| **4981** | A2368 | 4k multicolored | .25 | .25 |
| **4982** | A2368 | 6k multicolored | .25 | .25 |
| **4983** | A2368 | 10k shown | .25 | .25 |
| **4984** | A2368 | 15k multicolored | .30 | .25 |
| **4985** | A2368 | 20k multicolored | .45 | .25 |
| **4986** | A2368 | 32k multicolored | .60 | .30 |
| | | *Nos. 4981-4986 (6)* | 2.10 | 1.55 |

A2369

**1981, Oct. 10** *Perf. 12*

**4987** A2369 4k multicolored .50 .25

Kazakhstan's Union with Russia, 250th Anniv.

A2370

**1981, Oct. 10** **Photo.** *Perf. 11½*

**4988** A2370 4k multicolored .50 .25

Mikhail Alekseevich Lavrentiev (1900-80), mathematician. Exists imperf.

64th Anniv. of October Revolution — A2371

**1981, Oct. 15** **Litho.**
**4989** A2371 4k multicolored .50 .25

Ekran Satellite TV Broadcasting System — A2372

**1981, Oct. 15** ***Perf. 12***
**4990** A2372 4k multicolored .50 .25

Salyut 6-Soyuz flight of V.V. Kovalionok and V.P. Savinykh A2373

**1981, Oct. 15**
**4991** 10k Text .40 .25
**4992** 10k Cosmonauts .40 .25
*a.* A2373 Pair, #4991-4992 1.00 .30

Souvenir Sheet

Birth Centenary of Pablo Picasso — A2375

**1981, Oct. 25** ***Perf. 12x12½***
**4993** A2375 50k multicolored 2.00 .75

A2376

**Photogravure and Engraved**

**1981, Nov. 5** ***Perf. 11½***
**4994** A2376 4k multicolored .50 .25

Sergei Dmitrievich Merkurov (1881-1952), artist.

Autumn, by Niko Piromanashvili, 1913 — A2377

Paintings: 6k, Gurian Woman, by S.G. Kikodze, 1921. 10k, Fellow Travelers, by U.M. Dzhaparidze, 1936, horiz. 15k, Shota Rustaveli, by S.S. Kobuladze, 1938. 32k, Collecting Tea, by V.D. Gudiashvili, 1964, horiz.

***Perf. 12x12½, 12½x12***

**1981, Nov. 5** **Litho.**
**4995** A2377 4k multicolored .25 .25
**4996** A2377 6k multicolored .25 .25
**4997** A2377 10k multicolored .30 .25
**4998** A2377 15k multicolored .40 .25
**4999** A2377 32k multicolored 1.00 .40
*Nos. 4995-4999 (5)* 2.20 1.40

New Year 1982 — A2378

**1981, Dec. 2** **Litho.** ***Perf. 12***
**5000** A2378 4k multicolored 1.00 .25

Public Transportation 19th-20th Cent. — A2379

**Photogravure and Engraved**

**1981, Dec. 10** ***Perf. 11½x12***
**5001** A2379 4k Sled .25 .25
**5002** A2379 6k Horse-drawn trolley .25 .25
**5003** A2379 10k Coach .25 .25
**5004** A2379 15k Taxi, 1926 .25 .25
**5005** A2379 20k Bus, 1926 .35 .30
**5006** A2379 32k Trolley, 1912 .50 .40
*Nos. 5001-5006 (6)* 1.85 1.70

Souvenir Sheet

Kremlin and New Delhi Parliament — A2380

**1981, Dec. 17** **Photo.**
**5007** A2380 50k multicolored 1.50 .75

1st direct telephone link with India.

A2381

A2382

**1982, Jan. 11** **Litho.** ***Perf. 12***
**5008** A2381 4k multicolored .50 .25
**5009** A2382 4k multicolored .50 .25

60th anniv. of Checheno-Ingush Autonomous SSR and of Yakutsk Autonomous SSR.

1500th Anniv. of Kiev — A2383

**1982, Jan. 12** **Photo.** ***Perf. 11½x12***
**5010** A2383 10k multicolored .50 .25

S.P. Korolev (1907-66), Rocket Designer — A2384

**1982, Jan. 12** ***Perf. 11½***
**5011** A2384 4k multicolored .50 .25

Nazym Khikmet (1902-1963), Turkish Poet — A2385

**1982, Jan. 20** **Litho.** ***Perf. 12***
**5012** A2385 6k multicolored .50 .25

10th World Trade Union Congress, Havana — A2386

**1982, Feb. 1** **Photo.** ***Perf. 11½***
**5013** A2386 15k multicolored .50 .25

17th Soviet Trade Union Congress A2387

**1982, Feb. 10** **Litho.**
**5014** A2387 4k multicolored .50 .25

Edouard Manet (1832-1883) A2388

**1982, Feb. 10** ***Perf. 12x12½***
**5015** A2388 32k multicolored 1.00 .45

Equestrian Sports A2389

**1982, Feb. 16** **Photo.** ***Perf. 11½***
**5016** A2389 4k Hurdles .25 .25
**5017** A2389 6k Riding .30 .25
**5018** A2389 15k Racing .45 .25
*Nos. 5016-5018 (3)* 1.00 .75

No. 5016 exists imperf. Value, $25.

2nd Death Anniv. of Marshal Tito of Yugoslavia A2390

**1982, Feb. 25** **Litho.** ***Perf. 12***
**5019** A2390 6k olive black .50 .25

350th Anniv. of State University of Tartu A2392

**1982, Mar. 4** **Photo.** ***Perf. 11½***
**5020** A2392 4k multicolored .50 .25

9th Intl. Cardiologists Congress, Moscow — A2393

**1982, Mar. 4**
**5021** A2393 15k multicolored .50 .25

Souvenir Sheet

Biathlon, Speed Skating — A2394

**1982, Mar. 6 Litho. *Perf. 12½x12***
**5022** A2394 50k multicolored 1.50 .70

5th Natl. Athletic Meet.

Blueberry Bush — A2395

4k, Cloudberries. 10k, Brambles. 15k, Cornelian cherries. 32k, Wild strawberries.

**1982, Mar. 10 Litho. *Perf. 12x12½***

| | | | | | |
|---|---|---|---|---|---|
| **5023** | A2395 | 4k | multicolored | .25 | .25 |
| **5024** | A2395 | 6k | shown | .25 | .25 |
| **5025** | A2395 | 10k | multicolored | .25 | .25 |
| **5026** | A2395 | 15k | multicolored | .25 | .25 |
| **5027** | A2395 | 32k | multicolored | .50 | .25 |
| | | | *Nos. 5023-5027 (5)* | 1.50 | 1.25 |

Venera 13 and Venera 14 Flights — A2396

**1982, Mar. 10 Photo. *Perf. 11½***
**5028** A2396 10k multicolored .50 .25

Marriage Ceremony, by V.V. Pukirev (1832-1890) A2397

Paintings: No. 5030, M.I. Lopukhina, by V. L. Borovikovsky (1757-1825). No. 5031, E.V. Davidov, by O.A. Kiprensky (1782-1836). No. 5032, Oak Trees, by I.I. Shishkin (1832-1898).

**1982, Mar. 18 *Perf. 12***

| | | | | | |
|---|---|---|---|---|---|
| **5029** | A2397 | 6k | multicolored | .25 | .25 |
| **5030** | A2397 | 6k | multicolored | .25 | .25 |
| **5031** | A2397 | 6k | multicolored | .25 | .25 |
| **5032** | A2397 | 6k | multicolored | .25 | .25 |
| | | | *Nos. 5029-5032 (4)* | 1.00 | 1.00 |

K.I. Chukovsky (1882-1969), Writer — A2398

**1982, Mar. 31 Engr.**
**5033** A2398 4k gray & black .50 .25

Cosmonauts' Day — A2399

**1982, Apr. 12 Photo. *Perf. 12x11½***
**5034** A2399 6k multicolored .50 .25

Souvenir Sheet

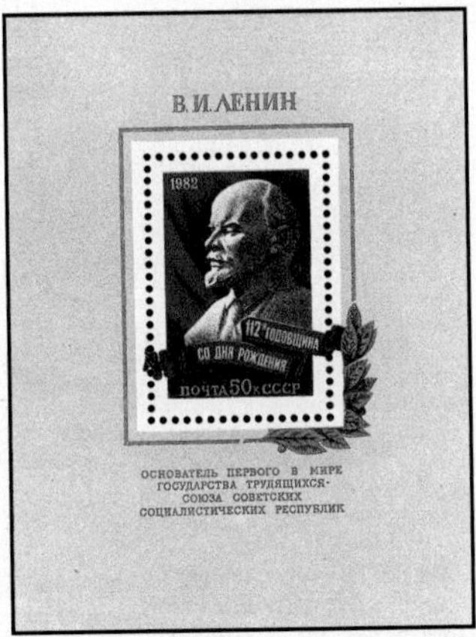


112th Birth Anniv. of Lenin — A2400

**1982, Apr. 22 Photo. *Perf. 11½x12***
**5035** A2400 50k multicolored 1.50 .70

V.P. Soloviev-Sedoi (1907-79), Composer A2401

**1982, Apr. 25 Engr. *Perf. 12***
**5036** A2401 4k brown .50 .25

G. Dimitrov (1882-1949), 1st Bulgarian Prime Minister — A2402

**1982, Apr. 25**
**5037** A2402 6k green .50 .25

Kremlin Tower, Moscow — A2403

**1982 Litho. *Perf. 12½x12***
**5038** A2403 45k brown 1.00 .65
*a.* Engraved 1.00 .65

Issued: #5038, Apr. 25. #5038a, Oct. 12.

70th Anniv. of Pravda Newspaper A2404

**1982, May 5 Photo. *Perf. 12x11½***
**5039** A2404 4k multicolored .50 .25

UN Conf. on Human Environment, 10th anniv. — A2405

**1982, May 10 *Perf. 11½***
**5040** A2405 6k multicolored .50 .25

Pioneers' Org., 60th anniv. — A2406

**1982, May 19**
**5041** A2406 4k multicolored .50 .25

Communist Youth Org., 19th Cong. — A2407

**1982, May 19**
**5042** A2407 4k multicolored .50 .25

ITU Delegates Conf., Nairobi — A2408

**1982, May 19**
**5043** A2408 15k multicolored .50 .25

TUL-80 Electric Locomotive — A2409

**1982, May 20 *Perf. 12x11½***

| | | | | | |
|---|---|---|---|---|---|
| **5044** | A2409 | 4k | shown | .25 | .25 |
| **5045** | A2409 | 6k | TEP-75 diesel | .25 | .25 |
| **5046** | A2409 | 10k | TEP-7 diesel | .30 | .25 |
| **5047** | A2409 | 15k | WL-82m electric | .45 | .30 |
| **5048** | A2409 | 32k | EP-200 electric | .95 | .45 |
| | | | *Nos. 5044-5048 (5)* | 2.20 | 1.50 |

1982 World Cup — A2410

**1982, June 4 *Perf. 11½x12***
**5049** A2410 20k olive & purple .50 .30

Rare Birds — A2411

18th Ornithological Cong., Moscow — 2k, Grus Monacha. 4k, Haliaeetus pelagicus. 6k, Eurynorhynchus. 10k, Eulabeia indica. 15k, Chettusia gregaria. 32k, Ciconia boyciana.

**1982, June 10 Litho. *Perf. 12x12½***

| | | | | | |
|---|---|---|---|---|---|
| **5050** | A2411 | 2k | multicolored | .25 | .25 |
| **5051** | A2411 | 4k | multicolored | .25 | .25 |
| **5052** | A2411 | 6k | multicolored | .25 | .25 |
| **5053** | A2411 | 10k | multicolored | .25 | .25 |
| **5054** | A2411 | 15k | multicolored | .30 | .25 |
| **5055** | A2411 | 32k | multicolored | .70 | .35 |
| | | | *Nos. 5050-5055 (6)* | 2.00 | 1.60 |

Komomolsk-on-Amur City, 50th Anniv. — A2412

**Photogravure and Engraved**

**1982, June 10 *Perf. 11½***
**5056** A2412 4k multicolored .50 .25

Tatchanka, by M.B. Grekov (1882-1934) — A2413

**1982, June 15 Litho. *Perf. 12½x12***
**5057** A2413 6k multicolored .50 .25

2nd UN Conference on Peaceful Uses of Outer Space, Vienna, Aug. 9-21 — A2414

**1982, June 15 Photo. *Perf. 11½***
**5058** A2414 15k multicolored .50 .25

Exists in a miniature sheet of 8. Value, $75.

Intercosmos Cooperative Space Program (USSR-France) — A2415

**1982 Litho. *Perf. 12½x12***

**5059** A2415 6k Cosmonauts .25 .25
*a.* Miniature sheet of 8 75.00
**5060** A2415 20k Rocket, globe .35 .25
*a.* Miniature sheet of 8 75.00
**5061** A2415 45k Satellites .80 .40
*a.* Miniature sheet of 8 75.00
*Nos. 5059-5061 (3)* 1.40 .90

**Souvenir Sheet**

**5062** A2415 50k Emblem, satellite 1.50 .75

No. 5062 contains one 41x29mm stamp. Issue dates: 6k, 50k, June 24. 20k, 45k, July 2.

The Tale of the Golden Cockerel, by P. Sosin, 1968 — A2416

Lacquerware Paintings, Ustera: 10k, Minin's Appeal to Count Posharski, by J. Fomichev, 1953. 15k, Two Peasants, by A. Kotyagin, 1933. 20k, The Fisherman, by N. Klykov, 1933, 32k, The Arrest of the Propagandists, by N. Shishakov, 1968.

**1982, July 6 Litho. *Perf. 12½x12***

**5063** A2416 6k multicolored .25 .25
**5064** A2416 10k multicolored .25 .25
**5065** A2416 15k multicolored .30 .25
**5066** A2416 20k multicolored .50 .25
**5067** A2416 32k multicolored .75 .30
*Nos. 5063-5067 (5)* 2.05 1.30

Telephone Centenary A2417

**1982, July 13 *Perf. 12***

**5068** A2417 4k Phone, 1882 .50 .25

P. Schilling's Electro-magnetic Telegraph Sesquicentennial — A2418

**Photogravure and Engraved**

**1982, July 16 *Perf. 11½***

**5069** A2418 6k Voltaic cells .50 .25

Intervision Gymnastics Contest A2419

**1982, Aug. 10 Photo.**

**5070** A2419 15k multicolored .50 .30

Gliders A2420

4k, Mastjahart Glider, 1923. 6k, Red Star, 1930. 10k, ZAGI-2, 1934.
20k, Stakhanovets, 1939. 32k, Troop carrier GR-29, 1941.

**1982, Aug. 20 Litho. *Perf. 12½x12***

**5071** A2420 4k multicolored .25 .25
**5072** A2420 6k multicolored .25 .25
**5073** A2420 10k multicolored .30 .25

**Size: 60x28mm**

***Perf. 11½x12***

**5074** A2420 20k multicolored .60 .25
**5075** A2420 32k multicolored .75 .35
*Nos. 5071-5075 (5)* 2.15 1.35

See Nos. 5118-5122.

Garibaldi (1807-1882) A2421

**1982, Aug. 25 Photo. *Perf. 11½***

**5076** A2421 6k multicolored .50 .25

Exists imperf. Value, $25.

Intl. Atomic Energy Authority, 25th Anniv. — A2422

**1982, Aug. 30**

**5077** A2422 20k multicolored .50 .25

Marshal B.M. Shaposhnikov (1882-1945) A2423

**1982, Sept. 10 Engr. *Perf. 12***

**5078** A2423 4k red brown .50 .25

World Chess Championship A2424

**1982, Sept. 10 Photo. *Perf. 11½***

**5079** A2424 6k King .50 .25
**5080** A2424 6k Queen .50 .25

See #5084.

African Natl. Congress, 70th Anniv. — A2425

**1982, Sept. 10**

**5081** A2425 6k multicolored .50 .25

S.P. Botkin (1832-89), Physician — A2426

**1982, Sept. 17 Engr. *Perf. 12½x12***

**5082** A2426 4k green .50 .25

**Souvenir Sheet**

25th Anniv. of Sputnik — A2427

**1982, Sept. 17 Litho. *Perf. 12x12½***

**5083** A2427 50k multicolored 2.00 .65

**No. 5079 Overprinted in Gold for Karpov's Victory**

**1982, Sept. 22 Photo. *Perf. 11½***

**5084** A2424 6k multicolored 1.00 .30

World War II Warships — A2428

4k, Submarine S-56. 6k, Minelayer Gremjashtsky. 15k, Mine sweeper T-205. 20k, Cruiser Red Crimea. 45k, Sebastopol.

**Photogravure and Engraved**

**1982, Sept. 22 *Perf. 11½x12***

**5085** A2428 4k multicolored .25 .25
**5086** A2428 6k multicolored .25 .25
**5087** A2428 15k multicolored .30 .25
**5088** A2428 20k multicolored .40 .25
**5089** A2428 45k multicolored .80 .45
*Nos. 5085-5089 (5)* 2.00 1.45

65th Anniv. of October Revolution A2429

**1982, Oct. 12 Litho. *Perf. 12***

**5090** A2429 4k multicolored .50 .25

House of the Soviets, Moscow — A2430

60th Anniv. of USSR: No. 5092, Dnieper Dam, Komosomol Monument, Statue of worker. No. 5093, Soviet War Memorial, resistance poster. No. 5094, Worker at podium, decree text. No. 5095, Workers' Monument, Moscow, Rocket, jet. No. 5096, Arms, Kremlin.

**1982, Oct. 25 Photo. *Perf. 11½x12***

**5091** A2430 10k multicolored .50 .25
**5092** A2430 10k multicolored .50 .25
**5093** A2430 10k multicolored .50 .25
**5094** A2430 10k multicolored .50 .25
**5095** A2430 10k multicolored .50 .25
**5096** A2430 10k multicolored .50 .25
*Nos. 5091-5096 (6)* 3.00 1.50

**No. 5095 Overprinted in Red for All-Union Philatelic Exhibition, 1984**

**1982, Nov. 10**

**5097** A2430 10k multicolored 1.00 .25

Portrait of an Actor, by Domenico Fetti A2431

Paintings from the Hermitage: 10k, St. Sebastian, by Perugino. 20k, Danae, by Titian, horiz. 45k, Portrait of a Woman, by Correggio. No. 5102, Self-portrait, by Capriolo. No. 5103a, Portrait of a Young Woman, by Melzi.

***Perf. 12x12½***

**1982, Nov. 25 Litho. Wmk. 383**

**5098** A2431 4k multicolored .25 .25
**5099** A2431 10k multicolored .25 .25
**5100** A2431 20k multicolored .30 .25
**5101** A2431 45k multicolored .50 .40
**5102** A2431 50k multicolored .75 .55
*Nos. 5098-5102 (5)* 2.05 1.70

**Souvenir Sheet**

**5103** Sheet of 2 2.50 1.65
*a.* A2431 50k multicolored 1.00 .65

Printed in sheets of 24 stamps + label and 15 stamps + label. Value, sheet of 15 stamps + label, $75.

See Nos. 5129-5134, 5199-5204, 5233-5238, 5310-5315, 5335-5340.

New Year 1983 — A2432

**1982, Dec. 1** **Unwmk.**
**5104** A2432 4k multicolored .50 .25
*a.* Miniature sheet of 8 100.00

Exists imperf. Value, $50.

Souvenir Sheet

60th Anniv. of USSR — A2433

**1982, Dec. 3** ***Perf. 12½x12***
**5105** A2433 50k multicolored 2.00 .90

Souvenir Sheet

Mountain Climbers Scaling Mt. Everest — A2434

**1982, Dec. 20** **Photo.** ***Perf. 11½x12***
**5106** A2434 50k multicolored 2.00 .90

Lighthouses A2435

**1982, Dec. 29** **Litho.** ***Perf. 12***

| | | | | | |
|---|---|---|---|---|---|
| **5107** | A2435 | 6k | green & multi | .50 | .25 |
| **5108** | A2435 | 6k | lilac & multi | .50 | .25 |
| **5109** | A2435 | 6k | salmon & multi | .50 | .25 |
| **5110** | A2435 | 6k | lt gldn brn & multi | .50 | .25 |
| **5111** | A2435 | 6k | lt brown & multi | .50 | .25 |
| | | | *Nos. 5107-5111 (5)* | 2.50 | 1.25 |

No. 5111 exists imperf. Value, $25.
See Nos. 5179-5183, 5265-5269.

Mail Transport — A2436

**1982, Dec. 22** ***Perf. 12***
**5112** A2436 5k greenish blue 5.00 1.00

**1983, May 20** **Litho.** ***Perf. 12***
**5113** A2436 5k blue 1.75 .25

For surcharge see Uzbekistan #61E.

Iskra Newspaper Masthead A2438

**1983, Jan. 5** **Litho.** ***Perf. 12x12½***
**5114** A2438 4k multicolored .50 .25

80th anniv. of 2nd Congress of Social-Democratic Workers' Party.

Fedor P. Tolstoi (1783-1873), Painter — A2439

**1983, Jan. 5** **Photo.** ***Perf. 11½***
**5115** A2439 4k multicolored .50 .25

65th Anniv. of Armed Forces — A2440

**1983, Jan. 25** **Litho.** ***Perf. 12***
**5116** A2440 4k multicolored .50 .25

Exists imperf. Value, $25.

Souvenir Sheet

60th Anniv. of Aeroflot Airlines — A2441

**1983, Feb. 9** ***Perf. 12x12½***
**5117** A2441 50k multicolored 1.50 1.00

**Glider Type of 1982**

**1983, Feb. 10** ***Perf. 12½x12***

| | | | | | |
|---|---|---|---|---|---|
| **5118** | A2420 | 2k | A-9, 1948 | .25 | .25 |
| **5119** | A2420 | 4k | KAJ-12, 1957 | .25 | .25 |
| **5120** | A2420 | 6k | A-15, 1960 | .25 | .25 |
| **5121** | A2420 | 20k | SA-7, 1970 | .40 | .25 |
| **5122** | A2420 | 45k | LAJ-12, 1979 | .75 | .60 |
| | | | *Nos. 5118-5122 (5)* | 1.90 | 1.60 |

Tashkent Bimillennium — A2442

**1983, Feb. 17** ***Perf. 12½x12***
**5123** A2442 4k View .50 .25

B.N. Petrov (1913-1980), Scientist — A2443

**1983, Feb. 17**
**5124** A2443 4k multicolored .50 .25

Holy Family, by Raphael A2444

**1983, Feb. 17** ***Perf. 12x12½***
**5125** A2444 50k multicolored .50 .25
*a.* Miniature sheet of 15 + label 20.00

Soyuz T-7-Salyut 7-Soyuz T-5 Flight A2445

10k, L. Popov, A. Serebrov, S. Savitskaya.

**1983, Mar. 10** ***Perf. 12x12½***
**5126** A2445 10k multicolored .50 .25

Souvenir Sheet

World Communications Year — A2446

**1983, Mar. 10** **Photo.** ***Perf. 11½***
**5127** A2446 50k multicolored 2.00 1.25

A.W. Aleksandrov, Natl. Anthem Composer — A2447

**1983, Mar. 22** **Litho.** ***Perf. 12***
**5128** A2447 4k multicolored .50 .25

Exists imperf. Value, $50.

**Hermitage Type of 1982**

Rembrandt Paintings, Hermitage, Leningrad: 4k, Portrait of an Old Woman. 10k, Portrait of a Learned Man. 20k, Old Warrior. 45k, Portrait of Mrs. B. Martens Doomer. No. 5133, Sacrifice of Abraham. No. 5134a, Portrait of an Old Man in a Red Garment.

***Perf. 12x12½***

**1983, Mar. 25** **Wmk. 383**

| | | | | | |
|---|---|---|---|---|---|
| **5129** | A2431 | 4k | multicolored | .25 | .25 |
| **5130** | A2431 | 10k | multicolored | .25 | .25 |
| **5131** | A2431 | 20k | multicolored | .70 | .35 |
| **5132** | A2431 | 45k | multicolored | 1.40 | .70 |
| **5133** | A2431 | 50k | multicolored | 1.50 | .75 |
| | | | *Nos. 5129-5133 (5)* | 4.10 | 2.30 |

**Souvenir Sheet**

**Lithographed and Embossed**

**5134** Sheet of 2 + label 2.00 1.50
*a.* A2431 50k multicolored .75 .75

Nos. 5129-5133 printed in sheets of 24 + label and in miniature sheets of 15 + label. Value, set of miniature sheets, $75.

Souvenir Sheet

Cosmonauts' Day — A2449

*Perf. 12½x12*

**1983, Apr. 12 Litho. Unwmk.**

**5135** A2449 50k Soyuz T *2.00* 2.00

Souvenir Sheet

113th Birth Anniv. of Lenin — A2450

**Photogravure and Engraved**

**1983, Apr. 22** ***Perf. 11½x12***

**5136** A2450 50k multicolored 1.50 .80

A. Berezovoy, V. Lebedev — A2451

Salyut 7-Soyuz T Spacecraft — A2452

**1983, Apr. 25 Litho.** ***Perf. 12½x12***

**5137** A2451 10k multicolored .50 .25
**5138** A2452 10k multicolored .50 .25
*a.* Pair, #5137-5138 1.00 .50

Salyut 7-Soyuz T 211-Day Flight. Exists se-tenant with label.

Karl Marx (1818-1883) A2453

**1983, May 5** ***Perf. 12x12½***

**5139** A2453 4k multicolored .50 .25

View of Rostov-on-Don — A2454

**1983, May 5 Photo.** ***Perf. 11½***

**5140** A2454 4k multicolored .50 .25

Exists imperf. Value, $50.

Buriat Autonomous Soviet Socialist Republic, 60th Anniv. — A2455

**1983, May 12 Litho.** ***Perf. 12***

**5141** A2455 4k multicolored .50 .25

Kirov Opera and Ballet Theater, Leningrad, 200th Anniv. — A2456

**Photogravure and Engraved**

**1983, May 12** ***Perf. 11½x12***

**5142** A2456 4k multicolored .50 .25

Emblem of Motorcycling, Auto Racing, Shooting, Motorboating, Parachuting Organization — A2457

**1983, May 20 Litho.** ***Perf. 11½***

**5143** A2457 6k multicolored .50 .25

A.I. Khachaturian (1903-1978), Composer — A2458

**1983, May 25 Engr.** ***Perf. 12½x12***

**5144** A2458 4k violet brown 1.00 .30

Chelyabinsk Tractor Plant, 50th Anniv. — A2459

**1983, June 1 Photo.** ***Perf. 11½***

**5145** A2459 4k multicolored .50 .25

Simon Bolivar Bicentenary A2460

**Photogravure and Engraved**

**1983, June 10** ***Perf. 12***

**5146** A2460 6k brown & dk brown .50 .25

City of Sevastopol, 200th Anniv. — A2461

**1983, June 14 Photo.** ***Perf. 11½x12***

**5147** A2461 5k multicolored .50 .25

Spring Flowers — A2462

**1983, June 14 Litho.** ***Perf. 12x12½***

**5148** A2462 4k multicolored .25 .25
**5149** A2462 6k multicolored .25 .25
**5150** A2462 10k multicolored .30 .25
**5151** A2462 15k multicolored .50 .30
**5152** A2462 20k multicolored .70 .35
*Nos. 5148-5152 (5)* 2.00 1.40

Valentina Tereshkova's Spaceflight, 20th Anniv. — A2463

**1983, June 16 Litho.** ***Perf. 12***

**5153** A2463 10k multicolored .50 .25
*a.* Miniature sheet of 8 200.00

P.N. Pospelov (1898-1979), Academician A2464

**Photogravure and Engraved**

**1983, June 20** ***Perf. 11½***

**5154** A2464 4k multicolored .50 .25

10th European Cong. of Rheumatologists A2465

**1983, June 21 Photo.** ***Perf. 11½***

**5155** A2465 4k multicolored .50 .25

13th International Film Festival, Moscow — A2466

**1983, July 7 Litho.** ***Perf. 12***

**5156** A2466 20k multicolored .50 .25

Ships of the Soviet Fishing Fleet — A2467

4k, Two trawlers. 6k, Refrigerated trawler. 10k, Large trawler. 15k, Large refrigerated ship. 20k, Base ship.

**Photogravure and Engraved**

**1983, July 20** ***Perf. 12x11½***

**5157** A2467 4k multicolored .25 .25
**5158** A2467 6k multicolored .25 .25
**5159** A2467 10k multicolored .35 .25
**5160** A2467 15k multicolored .50 .25
**5161** A2467 20k multicolored .65 .25
*Nos. 5157-5161 (5)* 2.00 1.25

E.B. Vakhtangov (1883-1922), Actor and Producer — A2468

**1983, July 20 Photo.** ***Perf. 11½***

**5162** A2468 5k multicolored .50 .25

"USSR-1" Stratospheric Flight, 50th Anniv. — A2469

**1983, July 25 Photo.** ***Perf. 12***

**5163** A2469 20k multicolored .50 .40
*a.* Miniature sheet of 8 100.00

Food Fish A2470

4k, Oncorhynchus nerka. 6k, Perciformes. 15k, Anarhichas minor. 20k, Neogobius fluviatilis, 45k, Platichthys stellatus.

**1983, Aug. 5 Litho.** ***Perf. 12½x12***

**5164** A2470 4k multicolored .25 .25
**5165** A2470 6k multicolored .25 .25
**5166** A2470 15k multicolored .25 .25
**5167** A2470 20k multicolored .30 .30
**5168** A2470 45k multicolored .50 .60
*Nos. 5164-5168 (5)* 1.55 1.65

A2471

SOZPHILEX '83 Philatelic Exhibition — A2472

**1983, Aug. 18 Photo. *Perf. 11½***
**5169** A2471 6k multicolored .50 .25

**Souvenir Sheet**

**5170** A2472 50k Moscow Skyline 2.00 .80

Miniature Sheet

First Russian Postage Stamp, 125th Anniv. — A2473

**Photogravure and Engraved**

**1983, Aug. 25 *Perf. 11½x12***
**5171** A2473 50k pale yel & black 2.00 .70

**No. 5171 Ovptd. in Red for the 5th Philatelic Society Congress**

**1984, Oct. 1**
**5171A** A2473 50k pale yel & blk 4.00 3.50

Namibia Day — A2474

**1983, Aug. 26 Photo. *Perf. 11½***
**5172** A2474 5k multicolored .50 .25

Palestinian Solidarity — A2475

**1983, Aug. 29 Photo. *Perf. 11½***
**5173** A2475 5k multicolored .50 .25

1st European Championship of Radio-Telegraphy, Moscow — A2476

**1983, Sept. 1 Photo. *Perf. 11½***
**5174** A2476 6k multicolored .50 .25

Exists imperf. Value, $50.

4th UNESCO Council on Communications Development — A2477

**1983, Sept. 2 Photo. *Perf. 12x11½***
**5175** A2477 10k multicolored .50 .25

Muhammad Al-Khorezmi, Uzbek Mathematician, 1200th Birth Anniv. — A2478

**Photogravure and Engraved**

**1983, Sept. 6 *Perf. 11½***
**5176** A2478 4k multicolored .50 .25

Marshal A.I. Egorov (1883-1939) A2479

**1983, Sept. 8 Engr. *Perf. 12***
**5177** A2479 4k brown violet .50 .25

Union of Georgia and Russia, 200th Anniv. — A2480

**1983, Sept. 8 Photo. *Perf. 11½***
**5178** A2480 6k multicolored .50 .25

**Lighthouse Type of 1982**

Baltic Sea lighthouses.

**1983, Sept. 19 Litho. *Perf. 12***

| | | | | | |
|---|---|---|---|---|---|
| **5179** | A2435 | 1k | Kipu | .25 | .25 |
| **5180** | A2435 | 5k | Keri | .25 | .25 |
| **5181** | A2435 | 10k | Stirsudden | .30 | .25 |
| **5182** | A2435 | 12k | Tahkun | .50 | .25 |
| **5183** | A2435 | 20k | Tallinn | .70 | .30 |
| | | | *Nos. 5179-5183 (5)* | 2.00 | 1.30 |

Early Spring, by V.K. Bialynicki-Birula, 1912 — A2481

Belorussian Paintings: 4k, Portrait of the Artist's Wife with Fruit and Flowers, by J.F. Khrutzky, 1838. 15k, Young Partisan, by E.A. Zaitsev, 1943. 20k, Partisan Madonna, by M.A. Savitsky, 1967. 45k, Harvest, by V.K. Tsvirko, 1972. 15k, 20k, vert.

***Perf. 12½x12, 12x12½***

**1983, Sept. 28**

| | | | | | |
|---|---|---|---|---|---|
| **5184** | A2481 | 4k | multicolored | .25 | .25 |
| **5185** | A2481 | 6k | multicolored | .25 | .25 |
| **5186** | A2481 | 15k | multicolored | .25 | .25 |
| **5187** | A2481 | 20k | multicolored | .30 | .25 |
| **5188** | A2481 | 45k | multicolored | .40 | .25 |
| | | | *Nos. 5184-5188 (5)* | 1.45 | 1.25 |

Hammer and Sickle Steel Mill, Moscow, Centenary A2482

**1983, Oct. 1 Photo. *Perf. 11½***
**5189** A2482 4k multicolored .50 .25

Natl. Food Program A2483

**1983, Oct. 10**

| | | | | | |
|---|---|---|---|---|---|
| **5190** | A2483 | 5k | Wheat production | .50 | .25 |
| **5191** | A2483 | 5k | Cattle, dairy products | .50 | .25 |
| **5192** | A2483 | 5k | Produce | .50 | .25 |
| | | | *Nos. 5190-5192 (3)* | 1.50 | .75 |

October Revolution, 66th anniv. — A2484

**1983, Oct. 12 Litho. *Perf. 12***
**5193** A2484 4k multicolored .50 .25

Ivan Fedorov — A2485

**1983, Oct. 12 Engr. *Perf. 12x12½***
**5194** A2485 4k dark brown .50 .25

Ivan Fedorov, first Russian printer (Book of the Apostles), 400th death anniv.

Urengoy-Uzgorod Transcontinental Gas Pipeline Completion — A2486

**1983, Oct. 12 Photo. *Perf. 12x11½***
**5195** A2486 5k multicolored .50 .25

A.W. Sidorenko (1917-82), Geologist — A2487

**1983, Oct. 19 Litho. *Perf. 12***
**5196** A2487 4k multicolored .50 .25

Campaign Against Nuclear Weapons — A2488

**1983, Oct. 19 Photo. *Perf. 11½***
**5197** A2488 5k Demonstration .50 .25

Exists imperf. Value $50.

Maktumkuli, Turkmenistan Poet, 250th Birth Anniv. — A2489

**1983, Oct. 27**
**5198** A2489 5k multicolored .50 .25

**Hermitage Painting Type of 1982**

Paintings by Germans: 4k, Madonna and Child with Apple Tree, by Lucas Cranach the Elder. 10k, Self-portrait, by Anton R. Mengs. 20k, Self-portrait, by Jüurgen Ovens. 45k, Sailboat, by Caspar David Friedrich. No. 5203, Rape of the Sabines, by Johann Schoenfeld, horiz. No. 5204a, Portrait of a Young Man, by Ambrosius Holbein.

***Perf. 12x12½, 12½x12***

**1983, Nov. 10 Litho. Wmk. 383**

| | | | | | |
|---|---|---|---|---|---|
| **5199** | A2431 | 4k | multicolored | .25 | .25 |
| **5200** | A2431 | 10k | multicolored | .25 | .25 |
| **5201** | A2431 | 20k | multicolored | .30 | .25 |
| **5202** | A2431 | 45k | multicolored | .60 | .40 |
| **5203** | A2431 | 50k | multicolored | .70 | .50 |
| | | | *Nos. 5199-5203 (5)* | 2.10 | 1.65 |

**Souvenir Sheet**

**5204** Sheet of 2 + label 3.00 1.50
*a.* A2431 50k multicolored 1.50 .50

Nos. 5199-5203 with labels, value $5.
Printed in sheets of 24+label and 15+label. Value, each $75.

Physicians Against Nuclear War Movement A2490

***Perf. 11½***

**1983, Nov. 17 Photo. Unwmk.**
**5205** A2490 5k Baby, dove, sun .50 .25

Sukhe Bator (1893-1923), Mongolian People's Rep. Founder — A2491

**1983, Nov. 17**
**5206** A2491 5k Portrait .50 .25

New Year 1984 A2492

**1983, Dec. 1**
**5207** A2492 5k Star, snowflakes .50 .25

Exists imperf; Value, $50.
Printed in sheets of 50. Also exist in miniature sheets of 16. Value, $150.

Newly Completed Buildings, Moscow — A2493

3k, Children's Musical Theater. 4k, Tourist Hotel, vert. 6k, Council of Ministers. 20k, Ismaelovo Hotel. 45k, Novosti Press Agency.

***Perf. 12½x12, 12x12½***

**1983, Dec. 15 Engr.**
**5208** A2493 3k multicolored .25 .25
**5209** A2493 4k multicolored .25 .25
**5210** A2493 6k multicolored .25 .25
**5211** A2493 20k multicolored .40 .30
**5212** A2493 45k multicolored .75 .50
*Nos. 5208-5212 (5)* 1.90 1.55

Souvenir Sheet

Environmental Protection Campaign — A2494

**1983, Dec. 20 Photo. *Perf. 11½***
**5213** A2494 50k multicolored 1.50 1.50

Moscow Local Broadcasting Network, 50th anniv. — A2495

**1984, Jan. 1**
**5214** A2495 4k multicolored .50 .25

European Women's Skating Championships — A2496

**1984, Jan. 1 *Perf. 12x11½***
**5215** A2496 5k multicolored .50 .25

Exists imperf. Value, $50.

Cuban Revolution, 25th Anniv. A2497

**1984, Jan. 1 *Perf. 11½***
**5216** A2497 5k Flag, "25" .50 .25

Exists imperf. Value, $50.

World War II Tanks — A2498

**1984, Jan. 25 Litho. *Perf. 12½x12***
**5217** A2498 10k KW .60 .25
**5218** A2498 10k IS-2 .60 .25
**5219** A2498 10k T-34 .60 .25
**5220** A2498 10k ISU-152 .60 .25
**5221** A2498 10k SU-100 .60 .25
*Nos. 5217-5221 (5)* 3.00 1.25

No. 5220 exists imperf. Value, $50.

1984 Winter Olympics — A2499

**1984, Feb. 8 Photo. *Perf. 11½x12***
**5222** A2499 5k Biathlon .25 .25
*a.* Miniature sheet of 8 45.00
**5223** A2499 10k Speed skating .25 .25
*a.* Miniature sheet of 8 45.00
**5224** A2499 20k Hockey .25 .25
*a.* Miniature sheet of 8 45.00
**5225** A2499 45k Figure skating .25 .25
*a.* Miniature sheet of 8 45.00
*Nos. 5222-5225 (4)* 1.00 1.00

Exist imperf. Value, each $50.

Moscow Zoo, 120th Anniv. — A2500

**1984, Feb. 16 Litho. *Perf. 12½x12***
**5226** A2500 2k Mandrill .25 .25
**5227** A2500 3k Gazelle .25 .25
**5228** A2500 4k Snow leopard .25 .25
**5229** A2500 5k Crowned crane .25 .25
**5230** A2500 20k Macaw .25 .25
*Nos. 5226-5230 (5)* 1.25 1.25

Yuri Gagarin (1934-68) — A2501

**1984, Mar. 9 Engr. *Perf. 12½x12***
**5231** A2501 15k Portrait, Vostok .50 .25
*a.* Miniature sheet of 8 150.00

Souvenir Sheet

Mass Development of Virgin and Unused Land, 30th Anniv. — A2502

**1984, Mar. 14 Photo. *Perf. 11½x12***
**5232** A2502 50k multicolored 1.50 .75

**Hermitage Painting Type of 1982**

Paintings by English Artists: 4k, E.K. Vorontsova, by George Hayter. 10k, Portrait of Mrs. Greer, by George Romney. 20k, Before a Thunderstorm, by George Morland, horiz. 45k, Portrait of an Unknown Man, by Marcus Gheeraerts Jr. No. 5237, Cupid and Venus, by Joshua Reynolds. No. 5238a, Portrait of a Lady in Blue, by Thomas Gainsborough.

***Perf. 12x12½, 12½x12***

**1984, Mar. 20 Litho. Wmk. 383**
**5233** A2431 4k multicolored .25 .25
**5234** A2431 10k multicolored .25 .25
**5235** A2431 20k multicolored .30 .25
**5236** A2431 45k multicolored .70 .40
**5237** A2431 50k multicolored .80 .45
*Nos. 5233-5237 (5)* 2.30 1.60

**Souvenir Sheet**

**5238** Sheet of 2 2.00 1.00
*a.* A2431 50k multicolored .50 .40

Nos. 5233-5237 each se-tenant with label showing text and embossed emblem. Value, set of pairs with label, $5. Exists also in miniature sheets of 15 + label. Value, set, $75.

S.V. Ilyushin — A2503

***Perf. 11½***

**1984, Mar. 23 Photo. Unwmk.**
**5239** A2503 5k Aircraft designer, (1894-1977) .50 .25

Andrei S. Bubnov — A2504

**1984, Apr. 3 *Perf. 11½x12***
**5240** A2504 5k Statesman, (1884-1940) .50 .25

Intercosmos Cooperative Space Program (USSR-India) A2505

Designs: 5k, Weather Station M-100 launch. 20k, Geodesy (satellites, observatory). 45k, Rocket, satellites, dish antenna. 50k, Flags, cosmonauts.

**1984 *Perf. 12x11½***
**5241** A2505 5k multicolored .25 .25
**5242** A2505 20k multicolored .35 .25
**5243** A2505 45k multicolored .40 .25
*Nos. 5241-5243 (3)* 1.00 .75

**Souvenir Sheet**

**5244** A2505 50k multicolored 1.50 .75

No. 5244 contains one 25x36mm stamp. Issue dates: 50k, Apr. 5; others, Apr. 3.

Cosmonauts' Day — A2506

**1984, Apr. 12 *Perf. 11½x12***
**5245** A2506 10k Futuristic spaceman .50 .25

Tchelyuskin Arctic Expedition, 50th Anniv. — A2507

**Photogravure and Engraved**

**1984, Apr. 13 *Perf. 11½x12***
**5246** A2507 6k Ship .25 .25
*a.* Miniature sheet of 8 *40.00*

5247 A2507 15k Shipwreck .50 .25
a. Miniature sheet of 8 40.00
5248 A2507 45k Rescue 1.50 .70
a. Miniature sheet of 8 40.00
*Nos. 5246-5248 (3)* 2.25 1.20

**Souvenir Sheet**

**Photo.**

5249 A2507 50k Hero of Soviet Union medal 1.50 .70

First HSU medal awarded to rescue crew. No. 5249 contains one 27x39mm stamp.

Souvenir Sheet

114th Birth Anniv. of Lenin — A2508

**1984, Apr. 22 Litho. *Perf. 11½x12½***
5250 A2508 50k Portrait 1.50 .70

Aquatic Plants — A2509

1k, Lotus. 2k, Euriola. 3k, Water lilies, horiz. 10k, White nymphaea, horiz. 20k, Marsh-flowers, horiz.

**1984, May 5 *Perf. 12x12½, 12½x12***
5251 A2509 1k multicolored .25 .25
5252 A2509 2k multicolored .25 .25
5253 A2509 3k multicolored .25 .25
5254 A2509 10k multicolored .25 .25
a. Miniature sheet of 8 30.00
5255 A2509 20k multicolored .45 .25
*Nos. 5251-5255 (5)* 1.45 1.25

Soviet Peace Policy — A2510

No. 5256, Marchers, banners (at left). No. 5257, Text. No. 5258, Marchers, banners (at right).

**1984, May 8 Photo. *Perf. 11½***
5256 A2510 5k multicolored .35 .25
5257 A2510 5k multicolored .35 .25
5258 A2510 5k multicolored .35 .25
a. Strip of 3, #5256-5258 2.00 .50

A2511

**1984, May 15 Photo. *Perf. 11½***
5259 A2511 10k multicolored .50 .25

E.O. Paton Institute of Electric Welding, 50th anniv.

A2512

**1984, May 21**
5260 A2512 10k multicolored .50 .30

25th Conf. for Electric and Postal Communications Cooperation.

A2513

**1984, May 29**
5261 A2513 5k violet brown .50 .25

Maurice Bishop, Grenada Prime Minister (1944-83).

A2514

**1984, May 31**
5262 A2514 5k multicolored 1.00 .25

V.I. Lenin Central Museum, 60th anniv.

City of Archangelsk, 400th Anniv. — A2515

**1984, June 1 Photo. & Engr.**
5263 A2515 5k multicolored .50 .25

European Youth Soccer Championship — A2516

**1984, June 1 Photo. *Perf. 12x11½***
5264 A2516 15k multicolored .50 .30

**Lighthouse Type of 1982**

Far Eastern seas lighthouses.

**1984, June 14 Litho. *Perf. 12***
5265 A2435 1k Petropavlovsk .40 .25
5266 A2435 2k Tokarev .40 .25
5267 A2435 4k Basargin .40 .25
5268 A2435 5k Kronitsky .40 .25
5269 A2435 10k Marekan .40 .25
*Nos. 5265-5269 (5)* 2.00 1.25

Salyut 7-Soyuz T-9 150-Day Flight — A2517

**1984, June 27 Litho. *Perf. 12***
5270 A2517 15k multicolored .50 .25

A2518

**Photogravure and Engraved**

**1984, July 1 *Perf. 11½***
5271 A2518 10k multicolored .50 .25

Morflot, Merchant & Transport Fleet, 60th anniv.

60th Anniv. of Awarding V.I. Lenin Name to Youth Communist League — A2519

**1984, July 1 Photo. *Perf. 11½x12***
5272 A2519 5k multicolored .50 .25

Liberation of Byelorussia, 40th Anniv. A2520

**1984, July 3 Photo. *Perf. 12x11½***
5273 A2520 5k multicolored .50 .25

CMEA Conference, Moscow — A2521

**1984, June 12 Photo. *Perf. 11½***
5274 A2521 5k CMEA Building & Kremlin .50 .25

A2522

**1984, July 20 Photo. *Perf. 11½***
5275 A2522 5k Convention seal .50 .25

27th Intl. Geological Cong., Moscow.

A2523

**1984, July 22 Photo. *Perf. 11½***
5276 A2523 5k Arms, draped flag .50 .25

People's Republic of Poland, 40th anniv.

B. V. Asafiev (1884-1949), Composer — A2524

**1984, July 25 Engr. *Perf. 12½x12***
5277 A2524 5k greenish black .50 .25

Relations with Mexico, 60th Anniv. A2525

**1984, Aug. 4 Litho. *Perf. 12***
5278 A2525 5k USSR, Mexican flags .50 .25

Miniature Sheet

Russian Folk Tales A2526

Designs: a, 3 archers. b, Prince and frog. c, Old man and prince. d, Crowd and swans. e, Wolf and men. f, Bird and youth. g, Youth on white horse. h, Couple with Tsar. i, Village scene. j, Man on black horse. k, Old man. l, Young woman.

**1984, Aug. 10 Litho. *Perf. 12x12½***
5279 Sheet of 12 5.00 2.00
a.-l. A2526 5k, any single .30 .25

Friendship '84 Games A2527

**1984, Aug. 15 Photo. *Perf. 11½***

| | | | | |
|---|---|---|---|---|
| **5280** | A2527 | 1k Basketball | .25 | .25 |
| **5281** | A2527 | 5k Gymnastics, vert. | .25 | .25 |
| **5282** | A2527 | 10k Weightlifting | .25 | .25 |
| **5283** | A2527 | 15k Wrestling | .25 | .25 |
| **5284** | A2527 | 20k High jump | .25 | .25 |
| | | *Nos. 5280-5284 (5)* | 1.25 | 1.25 |

A2528

**1984, Aug. 23 Litho. *Perf. 12***

**5285** A2528 5k Flag, monument .50 .25

Liberation of Romania, 40th anniv.

A2529

Designs: 35k, Sable. 2r, Ship, arctic map. 3r, Child and globe. 5r, Palm frond and globe.

Subjects: 35k, 3r, Environmental protection. 2r, Arctic development. 5r, World peace.

**1984, Sept. 5 Litho. *Perf. 12½x12***

| | | | | |
|---|---|---|---|---|
| **5286** | A2529 | 35k grayish olive | .65 | .35 |
| **5287** | A2529 | 2r dark gray | .80 | .45 |

**Engr.**

| | | | | |
|---|---|---|---|---|
| **5288** | A2529 | 3r gray | 4.00 | 1.10 |
| **5289** | A2529 | 5r blue | 5.00 | 1.90 |
| | | *Nos. 5286-5289 (4)* | 10.45 | 3.80 |

Nos. 5286 and 5287 were issued in 1984 on chalky paper, which fluoresces under UV light. Reprints on ordinary paper were made in 1988 and 1991, respectively. Values above are for the later printings. The 1984 printings are valued, mint or used, at 90c for No. 5286, and $3 for No. 5287.

See Nos. 6016B-6017A.

World Chess Championships A2530

No. 5290, Motherland statue, Volgograd. No. 5291, Spasski Tower, Moscow.

**1984, Sept. 7 Photo. *Perf. 11½***

| | | | | |
|---|---|---|---|---|
| **5290** | A2530 | 15k multicolored | .50 | .30 |
| **5291** | A2530 | 15k multicolored | .50 | .30 |

Bulgarian Revolution, 40th Anniv. — A2531

**1984, Sept. 9 Photo. *Perf. 11½***

**5292** A2531 5k Bulgarian arms .50 .25

Ethiopian Revolution, 10th Anniv. A2532

**1984, Sept. 12 Litho. *Perf. 12***

**5293** A2532 5k Ethiopian flag, seal .50 .25

Novokramatorsk Machinery Plant, 50th Anniv. — A2533

**Photogravure and Engraved**

**1984, Sept. 20 *Perf. 11½***

**5294** A2533 5k Excavator .50 .25

Nakhichevan ASSR, 60th Anniv. — A2534

**1984, Sept. 20 Litho. *Perf. 12***

**5295** A2534 5k Arms .50 .25

Television from Space, 25th Anniv. A2535

**1984, Oct. 4 Photo. *Perf. 11½***

| | | | | |
|---|---|---|---|---|
| **5296** | A2535 | 5k Luna 3 | .25 | .25 |
| **5297** | A2535 | 20k Venera 9 | .35 | .25 |
| **5298** | A2535 | 45k Meteor satellite | .40 | .25 |
| | | *Nos. 5296-5298 (3)* | 1.00 | .75 |

**Souvenir Sheet**

***Perf. 11½x12***

**5299** A2535 50k Camera, space walker, vert. 1.50 .75

No. 5299 contains one 26x37mm stamp.

German Democratic Republic, 35th Anniv. A2536

**1984, Oct. 7 Photo. *Perf. 11½***

**5300** A2536 5k Flag, arms .50 .25

Ukrainian Liberation, 40th Anniv. A2537

**1984, Oct. 8 Photo. *Perf. 12x11½***

**5301** A2537 5k Motherland statue, Kiev .50 .25

Soviet Republics and Parties, 60th Anniv. A2538

SSR Flags & Arms: No. 5302, Moldavian. No. 5303, Kirgiz. No. 5304, Tadzhik. No. 5305, Uzbek. No. 5306, Turkmen.

**1984 Litho. *Perf. 12***

| | | | | |
|---|---|---|---|---|
| **5302** | A2538 | 5k multicolored | .25 | .25 |
| **5303** | A2538 | 5k multicolored | .25 | .25 |
| **5304** | A2538 | 5k multicolored | .25 | .25 |
| **5305** | A2538 | 5k multicolored | .25 | .25 |
| **5306** | A2538 | 5k multicolored | .25 | .25 |
| | | *Nos. 5302-5306 (5)* | 1.25 | 1.25 |

Issued: No. 5302, 10/12; Nos. 5303-5304, 10/14; Nos. 5305-5306, 10/27.

Kremlin, 1917 Flag — A2539

**1984, Oct. 23 Photo. *Perf. 11½***

**5307** A2539 5k multicolored .50 .25

October Revolution, 67th anniv.

Aircraft, Spacecraft A2540

**1984, Nov. 6 Photo. *Perf. 11½***

**5308** A2540 5k multicolored .50 .25

M. Frunze Inst. of Aviation & Cosmonautics.

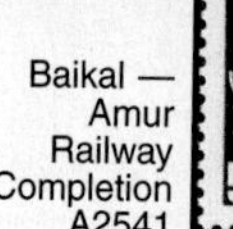

Baikal — Amur Railway Completion A2541

5k, Workers, map, engine.

**1984, Nov. 7 Photo. *Perf. 11½***

**5309** A2541 5k multicolored .50 .25

**Hermitage Type of 1982**

Paintings by French Artists: 4k, Girl in a Hat, by Jean Louis Voille. 10k, A Stolen Kiss, by Jean-Honore Fragonard. 20k, Woman Combing her Hair, by Edgar Degas. 45k, Pigmalion and Galatea, by Francois Boucher. 50k, Landscape with Polyphenus, by Nicholas Poussin. No. 5315a, Child with a Whip, by Pierre-Auguste Renoir.

***Perf. 12x12½, 12½x12***

**1984, Nov. 20 Litho. Wmk. 383**

| | | | | |
|---|---|---|---|---|
| **5310** | A2431 | 4k multicolored | .25 | .25 |
| **5311** | A2431 | 10k multi, horiz. | .35 | .25 |
| **5312** | A2431 | 20k multicolored | .55 | .45 |
| **5313** | A2431 | 45k multi, horiz. | .85 | .55 |
| **5314** | A2431 | 50k multi, horiz. | 1.00 | .65 |
| | | *Nos. 5310-5314 (5)* | 3.00 | 2.15 |

**Souvenir Sheet**

| | | | |
|---|---|---|---|
| **5315** | Sheet of 2 | 3.00 | 1.50 |
| *a.* | A2431 50k multicolored | 1.00 | .50 |

Nos. 5310-5314 exist se-tenant with label. Value, set, $5. Also exists in miniature sheets of 15 + label. Value, set of sheets, $75.

Mongolian Peoples' Republic, 60th Anniv. — A2542

5k, Mongolian flag, arms.

***Perf. 11½***

**1984, Nov. 26 Photo. Unwmk.**

**5316** A2542 5k multicolored .50 .25

New Year 1985 — A2543

5k, Kremlin, snowflakes.

**1984, Dec. 4 Litho. *Perf. 11½***

| | | | |
|---|---|---|---|
| **5317** | A2543 5k multicolored | .50 | .25 |
| *a.* | Miniature sheet of 8 | 110.00 | |

**Souvenir Sheet**

Environmental Protection — A2544

50k, Leaf, pollution sources.

**1984, Dec. 4 Litho. *Perf. 12½x12***

**5318** A2544 50k multicolored 2.00 .75

Russian Fire Vehicles — A2545

3k, Crew wagon, 19th cent. 5k, Pumper, 19th cent. 10k, Ladder truck, 1904. 15k, Pumper, 1904. 20k, Ladder truck, 1913.

**Photogravure and Engraved**

**1984, Dec. 12 *Perf. 12x11½***

| | | | | |
|---|---|---|---|---|
| **5319** | A2545 | 3k multicolored | .25 | .25 |
| **5320** | A2545 | 5k multicolored | .25 | .25 |
| **5321** | A2545 | 10k multicolored | .55 | .25 |
| **5322** | A2545 | 15k multicolored | .75 | .25 |
| **5323** | A2545 | 20k multicolored | 1.20 | .25 |
| | | *Nos. 5319-5323 (5)* | 3.00 | 1.25 |

See Nos. 5410-5414.

Intl. Venus-Halley's Comet Project — A2546

15k, Satellite, flight path.

**1984, Dec. 15 Photo. *Perf. 12x11½***

| | | | |
|---|---|---|---|
| **5324** | A2546 15k multicolored | 1.00 | .25 |
| *a.* | Miniature sheet of 8 | *75.00* | |

Indira Gandhi (1917-1984), Indian Prime Minister — A2547

**1984, Dec. 28 Litho. *Perf. 12***
**5325** A2547 5k Portrait .50 .25

1905 Revolution A2548

5k, Flag, Moscow memorial.

**1985, Jan. 22 Photo. *Perf. 11½***
**5326** A2548 5k multicolored .50 .25

A2549

**1985, Jan. 24**
**5327** A2549 5k multicolored .50 .25

Patrice Lumumba Peoples' Friendship University, 25th Anniv.

Mikhail Vasilievich Frunze (1885-1925), Party Leader — A2550

**1985, Feb. 2**
**5328** A2550 5k bluish, blk & ocher .50 .25

Karakalpak ASSR, 60th Anniv. A2551

**1985, Feb. 16 *Perf. 12***
**5329** A2551 5k Republic arms .50 .25

10th Winter Spartakiad of Friendly Armies — A2552

**1985, Feb. 23 *Perf. 11½***
**5330** A2552 5k Hockey player, emblem .50 .25

Kalevala, 150th Anniv. A2553

**1985, Feb. 25 Litho. *Perf. 12***
**5331** A2553 5k Rune singer, frontispiece .50 .25

Finnish Kalevala, collection of Karelian epic poetry compiled by Elias Lonrot.

Yakov M. Sverdlov (1885-1919), Party Leader — A2554

**1985, Mar. 3 Engr. *Perf. 12½x12***
**5332** A2554 5k rose lake .50 .25

Yakov M. Sverdlov (1885-1919), party leader.

Pioneer Badge, Awards — A2555

**1985, Mar. 6 Photo. *Perf. 11½***
**5333** A2555 5k multicolored .50 .25

Pionerskaya Pravda, All-Union children's newspaper, 60th Anniv.

Maria Alexandrovna Ulyanova (1835-1916), Lenin's Mother — A2556

**1985, Mar. 6 Engr. *Perf. 12½x12***
**5334** A2556 5k black .50 .25

**Hermitage Type of 1982**

Paintings by Spanish artists: 4k, The Young Virgin Praying, vert., by Francisco de Zurbaran (1598-1664). 10k, Still-life, by Antonio Pereda (c. 1608-1678). 20k, The Immaculate Conception, vert., by Murillo (1617-1682). 45k, The Grinder, by Antonio Puga. No. 5339, Count Olivares, vert., by Diego Velazques (1599-1660). No. 5340a, Portrait of the actress Antonia Zarate, vert., by Goya (1746-1828).

***Perf. 12x12½, 12½x12***

**1985, Mar. 14 Litho. Wmk. 383**
**5335** A2431 4k multicolored .25 .25
**5336** A2431 10k multicolored .30 .25
**5337** A2431 20k multicolored .50 .40
**5338** A2431 45k multicolored 1.25 .90
**5339** A2431 50k multicolored 1.40 .95
*Nos. 5335-5339 (5)* 3.70 2.75

**Souvenir Sheet**

**Lithographed and Embossed**

**5340** Sheet of 2 + label 3.00 2.00
*a.* A2431 50k multicolored 1.10 .75

Nos. 5335-5339 exist in miniature sheets of 15 + label. Value, set of sheets, $75.

EXPO '85, Tsukuba, Japan A2557

Soviet exhibition, Expo '85 emblems and: 5k, Cosmonauts in space. 10k, Communications satellite. 20k, Alternative energy sources development. 45k, Future housing systems. 50k, Soviet exhibition emblem, globe.

***Perf. 12x11½***

**1985, Mar. 17 Photo. Unwmk.**
**5341** A2557 5k multicolored .25 .25
**5342** A2557 10k multicolored .25 .25
**5343** A2557 20k multicolored .50 .35
**5344** A2557 45k multicolored 1.00 .70
*Nos. 5341-5344 (4)* 2.00 1.55

**Souvenir Sheet**

**5345** A2557 50k multicolored 1.50 .90

Nos. 5341-5344 issued in sheets of 25. Miniature sheets of 8 exist. Value, set, $100.

Souvenir Sheet

Johann Sebastian Bach (1685-1750), Composer — A2558

**Photogravure and Engraved**

**1985, Mar. 21 *Perf. 12x11½***
**5346** A2558 50k black 1.50 1.00

Natl. Crest, Budapest Memorial — A2559

**1985, Apr. 4 Litho. *Perf. 12***
**5347** A2559 5k multi .50 .25

Hungary liberated from German occupation, 40th Anniv.

Emblem — A2560

**1985, Apr. 5 Photo. *Perf. 11½***
**5348** A2560 15k multi .50 .30

Society for Cultural Relations with Foreign Countries, 60th anniv.

Victory over Fascism, 40th Anniv. A2561

#5349, Battle of Moscow, soldier, Kremlin, portrait of Lenin. #5350, Soldier, armed forces. #5351, Armaments production, worker. #5352, Partisan movement, cavalry. #5353, Berlin-Treptow war memorial, German Democratic Republic. #5354, Order of the Patriotic War, second class.

**1985, Apr. 20 *Perf. 12x11½***
**5349** A2561 5k multicolored .25 .25
**5350** A2561 5k multicolored .25 .25
**5351** A2561 5k multicolored .25 .25
**5352** A2561 5k multicolored .25 .25
**5353** A2561 5k multicolored .25 .25
*Nos. 5349-5353 (5)* 1.25 1.25

**Souvenir Sheet**

***Perf. 11½***

**5354** A2561 50k multicolored 1.50 .50

No. 5354 contains one 28x40mm stamp. Issued in sheets of 25. Exists in miniature sheets of 8. Value, set, $25.

No. 5353 Ovptd. in Red for 40th Year Since World War II Victory All-Union Philatelic Exhibition

**1985, Apr. 29 Photo. *Perf. 12x11½***
**5354A** A2561 5k brn lake, gold & vermilion 2.00 .50

Yuri Gagarin Center for Training Cosmonauts, 25th Anniv. — A2562

Cosmonauts day: Portrait, cosmonauts, Soyuz-T spaceship.

**1985, Apr. 12 Photo. *Perf. 11½x12***
**5355** A2562 15k multicolored .50 .25
*a.* Miniature sheet of 8 *125.00*

12th World Youth Festival, Moscow A2563

**1985, Apr. 15 Litho. *Perf. 12x12½***

5356 A2563 1k Three youths .25 .25
5357 A2563 3k African girl .25 .25
5358 A2563 5k Girl, rainbow .25 .25
*a.* Miniature sheet of 8 10.00
5359 A2563 20k Asian youth, camera .35 .35
5360 A2563 45k Emblem .75 .35
*Nos. 5356-5360 (5)* 1.85 1.45

**Souvenir Sheet**

**1985, July 4**

5361 A2563 30k Emblem 1.50 1.00

115th Birth Anniv. of Lenin — A2564

Portrait and: No. 5362, Lenin Museum, Tampere, Finland. No. 5363, Memorial apartment, Paris, France.

**1985, Apr. 22 Photo. *Perf. 11½x12***

5362 A2564 5k multicolored .25 .25
5363 A2564 5k multicolored .25 .25

**Souvenir Sheet**

**Litho.**

***Perf. 12x12½***

5364 A2564 30k Portrait 1.50 1.00

No. 5364 contains one 30x42mm stamp.

Order of Victory — A2565

**Photogravure and Engraved**

**1985, May 9 *Perf. 11½***

5365 A2565 20k sil, royal bl, dk red & gold .60 .35

Allied World War II victory over Germany and Japan, 40th anniv.

Arms — A2566

**1985, May 9 Litho. *Perf. 12½x12***

5366 A2566 5k multicolored .50 .25

Liberation of Czechoslovakia from German occupation, 40th Anniv.

Flags of Member Nations — A2567

**1985, May 14 Photo. *Perf. 11½***

5367 A2567 5k multicolored .50 .25

Warsaw Treaty Org., 30th anniv.

Mikhail Alexandrovich Sholokhov (1905-1984), Novelist & Nobel Laureate — A2568

Portraits and book covers: No. 5368, Tales from the Don, Quiet Flows the Don, A Human Tragedy. No. 5369, The Quiet Don, Virgin Lands Under the Plow, Thus They Have Fought for Their Homeland. No. 5370, Portrait.

**1985, May 24 Litho. *Perf. 12½x12***

5368 A2568 5k Portrait at left .35 .25
5369 A2568 5k Portrait at right .35 .25

**Photo.**

***Perf. 12x11½***

**Size: 37x52mm**

5370 A2568 5k brn, gold & black .35 .25
*Nos. 5368-5370 (3)* 1.05 .75

INTERCOSMOS Project Halley-Venus — A2570

15k, Spacecraft, satellites, Venus.

**1985, June 11 Litho. *Perf. 12***

5372 A2570 15k multicolored .50 .25
*a.* Miniature sheet of 8 125.00

Artek Pioneer Camp, 60th Anniv. A2571

4k, Camp, badges, Lenin Pioneers emblem.

**1985, June 14 Photo. *Perf. 11½***

5373 A2571 4k multicolored .50 .25

Mutiny on the Battleship Potemkin, 80th Anniv. — A2572

**Photogravure and Engraved**

**1985, June 16 *Perf. 11½x12***

5374 A2572 5k dk red, gold & black .50 .25

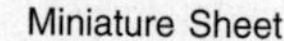

Miniature Sheet

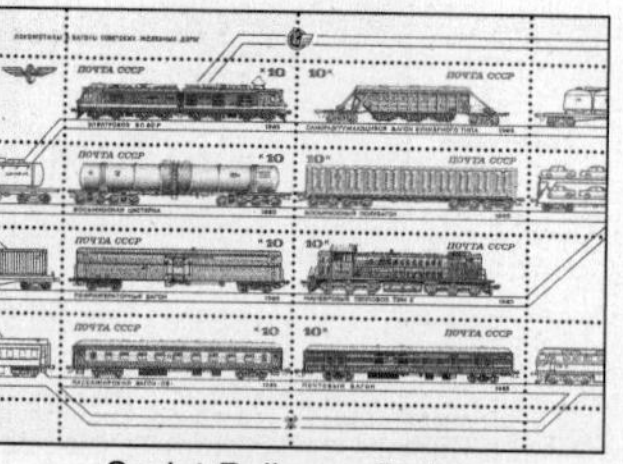

Soviet Railways Rolling Stock — A2573

Designs: a, Electric locomotive WL 80-R (grn). b, Tanker car (bl). c, Refrigerator car (bl). d, Sleeper car (brn). e, Tipper car (brn). f, Box car (brn). g, Shunting diesel locomotive (bl). h, Mail car (grn).

**1985, June 15 Engr. *Perf. 12½x12***

5375 A2573 Sheet of 8 3.00 1.65
*a.-h.* 10k any single .35 .25

Cosmonauts L. Kizim, V. Soloviov, O. Atkov and Salyut-7 Spacecraft — A2574

**1985, June 25 Litho.**

5376 A2574 15k multicolored .50 .25
*a.* Miniature sheet of 8 50.00

Soyuz T-10, Salyut-7 and Soyuz T-11 flights, Feb. 8-Oct. 2, 1984.

Beating Sword into Plowshares, Sculpture Donated to UN Hdqtrs. by USSR — A2575

**Photogravure and Engraved**

**1985, June 26 *Perf. 11½***

5377 A2575 45k multicolored .50 .35

UN 40th anniv.

Intl. Youth Year A2576

**1985, June 26 Photo. *Perf. 12***

5378 A2576 10k multicolored .50 .25

Medicinal Plants from Siberia — A2577

2k, O. dictiocarpum. 3k, Thermopsis lanceolata. 5k, Rosa acicularis lindi. 20k, Rhaponticum carthamoides. 45k, Bergenia crassifolia fritsch.

**1985, July 10 Litho. *Perf. 12½x12***

5379 A2577 2k multicolored .25 .25
5380 A2577 3k multicolored .25 .25
5381 A2577 5k multicolored .25 .25
5382 A2577 20k multicolored .50 .35
*a.* Miniature sheet of 8 35.00
5383 A2577 45k multicolored .75 .50
*Nos. 5379-5383 (5)* 2.00 1.60

Cosmonauts V. A. Dzhanibekov, S. E. Savistskaya, and I. P. Volk, Soyuz T-12 Mission, July 17-29, 1984 — A2578

**1985, July 17**

5384 A2578 10k multicolored .50 .25
*a.* Miniature sheet of 8 100.00

1st woman's free flight in space.

A2579

Caecilienhof Palace, Potsdam, Flags of UK, USSR, & US.

**1985, July 17**

5385 A2579 15k multicolored .50 .25

Potsdam Conference, 40th anniv.

Finlandia Hall, Helsinki — A2580

**1985, July 25 Photo. *Perf. 11½***

5386 A2580 20k multicolored .50 .30
*a.* Miniature sheet of 8 100.00

Helsinki Conference on European security and cooperation, 10th anniv.

Flags of USSR, North Korea, Liberation Monument in Pyongyang A2581

**1985, Aug. 1**

5387 A2581 5k multicolored .50 .25

Socialist Rep. of North Korea, 40th anniv.

Endangered Wildlife — A2582

Designs: 2k, Sorex bucharensis, vert. 3k, Cardiocranius paradoxus. 5k, Selevinia betpakdalensis, vert. 20k, Felis caracal. 45k, Gazella subgutturosa. 50k, Panthera pardus.

***Perf. 12x12½, 12½x12***

**1985, Aug. 15 Litho.**

5388 A2582 2k multicolored .25 .25
5389 A2582 3k multicolored .25 .25
5390 A2582 5k multicolored .25 .25

**Size: 47x32mm**

**5391** A2582 20k multicolored .60 .30
*a.* Miniature sheet of 8 100.00
**5392** A2582 45k multicolored 1.20 .60
*Nos. 5388-5392 (5)* 2.55 1.65

**Souvenir Sheet**

**5393** A2582 50k multicolored 2.50 .75

Youth World Soccer Cup Championships, Moscow — A2583

**1985, Aug. 24** ***Perf. 12***
**5394** A2583 5k multicolored .50 .25

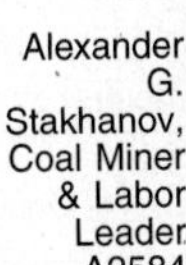

Alexander G. Stakhanov, Coal Miner & Labor Leader A2584

**1985, Aug. 30 Photo.** ***Perf. 11½***
**5395** A2584 5k multicolored .50 .25

Stakhanovite Movement for high labor productivity, 50th anniv.

Bryansk Victory Memorial, Buildings, Arms A2585

**1985, Sept. 1**
**5396** A2585 5k multicolored .50 .25

Millennium of Bryansk.

Socialist Republic of Vietnam, 40th Anniv. — A2586

**1985, Sept. 2 Litho.** ***Perf. 12½x12***
**5397** A2586 5k Arms .50 .25

A2587

**1985, Sept. 2 Photo.** ***Perf. 11½***
**5398** A2587 10k multicolored .50 .25

1985 World Chess Championship match, A. Karpov Vs. G. Kasparov, Moscow.

Lutsk City, Ukrainian SSR, 900th Anniv. — A2588

**1985, Sept. 14**
**5399** A2588 5k Lutsk Castle .50 .25

Open Book, the Weeping Jaroslavna and Prince Igor's Army — A2589

**Photogravure and Engraved**

**1985, Sept. 14** ***Perf. 11½x12***
**5400** A2589 10k multicolored .50 .25

The Song of Igor's Campaign, epic poem, 800th anniv.

Sergei Vasilievich Gerasimov (1885-1964), Painter A2590

**1985, Sept. 26** ***Perf. 12x11½***
**5401** A2590 5k Portrait .50 .25

October Revolution, 68th Anniv. — A2591

**1985, Oct. 10 Photo.** ***Perf. 11½***
**5402** A2591 5k multicolored .50 .25

UN 40th Anniv. — A2592

**1985, Oct. 24**
**5403** A2592 15k multicolored .50 .25

Krisjanis Barons (1835-1923), Latvian Folklorist — A2593

**Lithographed and Engraved**

**1985, Oct. 31**
**5404** A2593 5k beige & black .50 .25

Lenin, Laborer Breaking Chains A2594

**1985, Nov. 20** **Photo.**
**5405** A2594 5k multicolored .50 .25

Petersburg Union struggle for liberation of the working classes, founded by Lenin, 90th anniv.

Largest Soviet Telescope, 10th Anniv. — A2595

**1985, Nov. 20 Engr.** ***Perf. 12½x12***
**5406** A2595 10k dark blue .50 .25

Soviet Observatory inauguration.

A2596

**1985, Nov. 25** **Photo.**
**5407** A2596 5k multicolored .50 .25

Angolan Independence, 10th anniv.

A2597

**1985, Nov. 29** ***Perf. 11½***
**5408** A2597 5k multicolored .50 .25

Socialist Federal Republic of Yugoslavia, 40th anniv.

New Year — A2598

**1985, Dec. 3 Litho.** ***Perf. 12***
**5409** A2598 5k multicolored 1.00 .25
*a.* Miniature sheet of 8 22.50

**Vehicle Type of 1984**

**1985, Dec. 18 Photo.** ***Perf. 12x11½***
**5410** A2545 3k AMO-F15, 1926 .25 .25
**5411** A2545 5k PMZ-1, 1933 .25 .25
**5412** A2545 10k AC-40, 1977 .35 .25
**5413** A2545 20k AL-30, 1970 .55 .35
**5414** A2545 45k AA-60, 1978 1.10 .70
*Nos. 5410-5414 (5)* 2.50 1.80

Samantha Smith — A2599

**1985, Dec. 25** ***Perf. 12***
**5415** A2599 5k vio blue, choc & ver .50 .25

American student invited to meet with Soviet leaders in 1984.

A2600

**1985, Dec. 30** **Litho.**
**5416** A2600 5k multicolored .50 .25

N.M. Emanuel (1915-1984), chemist.

A2601

**1985, Dec. 30**
**5417** A2601 5k Sightseeing .50 .25
**5418** A2601 5k Sports .50 .25

Family leisure activities.

Intl. Peace Year — A2602

**1986, Jan. 2 Photo.** ***Perf. 11½***
**5419** A2602 20k brt blue, bluish grn & silver .50 .30

Flags, Congress Palace, Carnation A2603

Lenin, Spasskaya Tower, Congress Palace A2604

Lenin — A2605

**1986, Jan. 3**

**5420** A2603 5k multicolored .25 .25

**Photogravure and Engraved**

***Perf. 12x11½***

**5421** A2604 20k multicolored 1.00 .30

**Souvenir Sheet**

**Photo.**

***Perf. 11½***

**5422** A2605 50k multicolored 2.50 .70

27th Communist Party Congress.

A2606

**1986, Jan. 10** ***Perf. 11½x12***

**5423** A2606 15k multicolored .50 .25

*a.* Miniature sheet of 8 20.00

Modern Olympic Games, 90th anniv.

A2607

Flora of Russian Steppes, different.

***Perf. 12½x12, 12x12½***

**1986, Jan. 15** **Litho.**

**5424** A2607 4k multicolored .25 .25

**5425** A2607 5k multi, horiz. .25 .25

**5426** A2607 10k multicolored .35 .25

**5427** A2607 15k multicolored .50 .30

**5428** A2607 20k multicolored .60 .35

*a.* Miniature sheet of 8 *32.50*

*Nos. 5424-5428 (5)* 1.95 1.40

A2608

Vodovzvodnaya Tower, Grand Kremlin Palace.

**1986, Jan. 20** ***Perf. 12½x12***

**5429** A2608 50k grayish green 1.50 .70

A2609

**1986, Feb. 20** ***Perf. 11½***

**5430** A2609 5k multicolored .50 .25

Voronezh City, 400th anniv.

A2610

**1986, Feb. 20** **Engr.** ***Perf. 12***

**5431** A2610 10k bluish black .50 .25

Bela Kun (1886-1939), Hungarian party leader.

A2611

**1986, Feb. 28** ***Perf. 12½x12***

**5432** A2611 5k grayish black .50 .25

Karolis Pozhela (1896-1926), Lithuanian party founder.

Intercosmos Project Halley, Final Stage — A2612

15k, Vega probe, comet. 50k, Vega I, comet.

**1986, Mar. 6** **Litho.** ***Perf. 12***

**5433** A2612 15k multi .50 .25

*a.* Miniature sheet of 8 *125.00*

**Souvenir Sheet**

***Perf. 12½x12***

**5434** A2612 50k multi 5.00 .75

No. 5434 contains one 42x30mm stamp.

Butterflies A2613

4k, Utetheisa pulchella. 5k, Allancastria caucasica. 10k, Zegris eupheme. 15k, Catocala sponsa. 20k, Satyrus bischoffi.

**1986, Mar. 18** ***Perf. 12x12½***

**5435** A2613 4k multicolored .25 .25

**5436** A2613 5k multicolored .25 .25

**5437** A2613 10k multicolored .40 .25

**5438** A2613 15k multicolored .50 .50

**5439** A2613 20k multicolored .65 .55

*a.* Miniature sheet of 8 *60.00*

*Nos. 5435-5439 (5)* 2.05 1.80

EXPO '86, Vancouver A2614

**1986, Mar. 25** **Photo.** ***Perf. 12x11½***

**5440** A2614 20k Globe, space station .50 .30

*a.* Miniature sheet of 8 20.00

S.M. Kirov (1886-1934), Party Leader — A2615

**1986, Mar. 27** **Engr.** ***Perf. 12½x12***

**5441** A2615 5k black .50 .25

Cosmonauts' Day — A2616

Designs: 5k, Konstantin E. Tsiolkovsky (1857-1935), aerodynamics innovator, and futuristic space station. 10k, Sergei P. Korolev (1906-1966), rocket scientist, and Vostok spaceship, vert. 15k, Yuri Gagarin, 1st cosmonaut, Sputnik I and Vega probe.

***Perf. 12½x12, 12x12½***

**1986, Apr. 12** **Litho.**

**5442** A2616 5k multicolored .50 .25

*a.* Miniature sheet of 8 50.00

**5443** A2616 10k multicolored .50 .25

*a.* Miniature sheet of 8 50.00

**5444** A2616 15k multicolored .75 .25

*a.* Miniature sheet of 7 + label 50.00

*Nos. 5441-5444 (4)* 2.25 1.00

No. 5444 printed se-tenant with label picturing Vostok and inscribed for the 25th anniv. of first space flight.

1986 World Ice Hockey Championships, Moscow — A2617

**1986, Apr. 12** **Photo.** ***Perf. 11½***

**5445** A2617 15k multicolored .50 .25

Ernst Thalmann (1886-1944), German Communist Leader — A2618

**1986, Apr. 16** **Engr.** ***Perf. 12½x12***

**5446** A2618 10k dark brown .35 .25

**5447** A2618 10k reddish brown .35 .25

Lenin, 116th Birth Anniv. — A2619

Portraits and architecture: No. 5448, Socialist-Democratic People's House, Prague. No. 5449, Lenin Museum, Leipzig. No. 5450, Lenin Museum, Poronino, Poland.

**1986, Apr. 22** **Photo.** ***Perf. 11½x12***

**5448** A2619 5k multicolored .35 .25

**5449** A2619 5k multicolored .35 .25

**5450** A2619 5k multicolored .35 .25

*Nos. 5448-5450 (3)* 1.05 .75

Tambov City, 350th Anniv. A2620

**1986, Apr. 27** ***Perf. 11½***

**5451** A2620 5k Buildings, city arms .50 .25

Soviet Peace Fund, 25th Anniv. A2621

**1986, Apr. 27**

**5452** A2621 10k lt chalky bl, gold & brt ultra .50 .25

29th World Cycle Race, May 6-22 — A2622

**1986, May 6**

**5453** A2622 10k multicolored .50 .25

Toadstools A2623

No. 5454, Amanita phalloides. No. 5455, Amanita muscaria. No. 5456, Amanita pantherina. No. 5457, Tylopilus felleus. No. 5458, Hypholoma fasciculare.

**1986, May 15** **Litho.** ***Perf. 12***

**5454** A2623 4k multi .25 .25

*a.* Miniature sheet of 8 10.00

**5455** A2623 5k multi .25 .25

*a.* Miniature sheet of 8 10.00

**5456** A2623 10k multi .45 .25

*a.* Miniature sheet of 8 10.00

**5457** A2623 15k multi .50 .30

*a.* Miniature sheet of 8 10.00

**5458** A2623 20k multi .65 .35

*a.* Miniature sheet of 8 10.00

*Nos. 5454-5458 (5)* 2.10 1.40

A2624

**1986, May 19** **Photo.** ***Perf. 11½***
**5459** A2624 10k multicolored .50 .25

UNESCO Campaign, Man and Biosphere.

A2625

**1986, May 20**
**5460** A2625 10k multicolored .50 .25

9th Soviet Spartakiad.

A2626

Design: Lenin's House, Eternal Glory and V. I. Chapaiev monuments, Gorky State Academic Drama Theater.

**1986, May 24**
**5461** A2626 5k multicolored .50 .25

City of Kuibyshev, 400th anniv.

A2627

**1986, May 25**
**5462** A2627 5k multicolored .50 .25

"COMMUNICATION '86, Moscow."

1986 World Cup Soccer Championships, Mexico — A2628

5k, 10k, Various soccer plays. 15k, World Cup on FIFA commemorative gold medal.

**1986, May 31**
**5463** A2628 5k multicolored .25 .25
*a.* Miniature sheet of 8 15.00
**5464** A2628 10k multicolored .30 .25
*a.* Miniature sheet of 8 15.00
**5465** A2628 15k multicolored .45 .25
*a.* Miniature sheet of 8 15.00
*Nos. 5463-5465 (3)* 1.00 .75

Paintings in the Tretyakov Gallery, Moscow — A2629

Designs: 4k, Lane in Albano. 1837, by M.I. Lebedev, vert. 5k, View of the Kremlin in Foul Weather, 1851, by A.K. Savrasov. 10k, Sunlit Pine Trees, 1896, by I.I. Shishkin, vert. 15k, Return, 1896, by A.E. Arkhipov. 45k, Wedding Procession in Moscow, the 17th Century, 1901, by A.P. Ryabushkin.

***Perf. 12x12½, 12½x12***

**1986, June 11** **Litho.**
**5466** A2629 4k multicolored .25 .25
*a.* Miniature sheet of 8 10.00
**5467** A2629 5k multicolored .25 .25
*a.* Miniature sheet of 8 10.00
**5468** A2629 10k multicolored .35 .25
*a.* Miniature sheet of 8 10.00

**Size: 74x37mm**

***Perf. 11½***

**5469** A2629 15k multicolored .40 .30
*a.* Miniature sheet of 8 10.00
**5470** A2629 45k multicolored 1.10 .75
*a.* Miniature sheet of 8 10.00
*Nos. 5466-5470 (5)* 2.35 1.80

Irkutsk City, 300th Anniv. — A2630

**1986, June 28** **Photo.** ***Perf. 11½***
**5471** A2630 5k multicolored .50 .25

Goodwill Games, Moscow, July 5-20 A2631

**1986, July 4** **Photo.** ***Perf. 11½***
**5472** A2631 10k Prus bl, gold & blk .50 .25
**5473** A2631 10k brt blue, gold & blk .50 .25

UNESCO Projects in Russia — A2632

Designs: 5k, Information sciences. 10k, Geological correlation. 15k, Inter-governmental oceanographic commission. 35k, Intl. hydrologic program.

**1986, July 15**
**5474** A2632 5k multicolored .25 .25
**5475** A2632 10k multicolored .40 .25
**5476** A2632 15k multicolored .50 .30
**5477** A2632 35k multicolored .95 .55
*Nos. 5474-5477 (4)* 2.10 1.35

Tyumen, 400th Anniv. A2633

**1986, July 27**
**5478** A2633 5k multicolored .50 .25

A2634

**1986, Aug. 1** **Photo.** ***Perf. 11½***
**5479** A2634 10k multicolored .50 .25

Olof Palme (1927-86), Prime Minister of Sweden.

A2635

**1986, Aug. 8**
**5480** A2635 15k multicolored .50 .25

10th World Women's Basketball Championships, Moscow, Aug. 15-17.

Natl. Sports Committee Intl. Alpinist Camps — A2636

4k, Mt. Lenin. 5k, Mt. E. Korzhenevskaya. 10k, Mt. Belukha. 15k, Mt. Communism. 30k, Mt. Elbrus.

**1986, Sept. 5** **Litho.** ***Perf. 12***
**5481** A2636 4k multi .25 .25
**5482** A2636 5k multi .25 .25
*a.* Miniature sheet of 8 *35.00*
**5483** A2636 10k multi .35 .25
**5484** A2636 15k multi .40 .25
**5485** A2636 30k multi .70 .30
*Nos. 5481-5485 (5)* 1.95 1.30

See Nos. 5532-5535.

Souvenir Sheet

Red Book, Rainbow, Earth — A2637

**1986, Sept. 10** ***Perf. 11½***
**5486** A2637 50k multicolored 2.00 .75

Nature preservation.

A2638

**1986, Sept. 13** **Photo.**
**5487** A2638 5k multicolored .50 .25

Chelyabinsk, 250th anniv.

A2639

**1986, Sept. 23**
**5488** A2639 15k multicolored .50 .25

Mukran, DDR to Klaipeda, Lithuania, Train Ferry, inauguration.

A2640

**1986, Sept. 26**
**5489** A2640 5k multicolored .50 .25

Siauliai, Lithuanian SSR, 750th anniv.

Trucks — A2641

No. 5490, Ural-375D, 1964. No. 5491, GAZ-53A, 1965. No. 5492, KrAZ-256B, 1966. No.

5493, MAZ-515B, 1974. No. 5494, ZIL-133GY, 1979.

**1986, Oct. 15** *Perf. 11½x12*

| | | | | |
|---|---|---|---|---|
| **5490** | A2641 | 4k multicolored | .25 | .25 |
| **5491** | A2641 | 5k multicolored | .25 | .25 |
| **5492** | A2641 | 10k multicolored | .60 | .25 |
| *a.* | | Miniature sheet of 8 | 25.00 | |
| **5493** | A2641 | 15k multicolored | .75 | .30 |
| **5494** | A2641 | 20k multicolored | 1.25 | .35 |
| | | *Nos. 5490-5494 (5)* | 3.10 | 1.40 |

October Revolution, 69th anniv. — A2642

Design: Lenin Monument in October Square, Kremlin, Moscow.

**1986, Oct. 1** **Litho.** *Perf. 12*

**5495** A2642 5k multicolored .50 .25

A2643

5k, Icebreaker, helicopters. 10k, Mikhail Somov port side.

**1986, Oct. 10** **Photo.** *Perf. 11½*

| | | | | |
|---|---|---|---|---|
| **5496** | | 5k multicolored | .40 | .25 |
| **5497** | | 10k multicolored | .40 | .25 |
| *a.* | A2643 | Pair, #5496-5497 | 1.00 | .25 |
| *b.* | | Miniature sheet of 8, 4 each | 75.00 | |

**Souvenir Sheet**

*Perf. 12½x11½*

**5498** A2643 50k Trapped in ice 3.00 .65

Mikhail Somov trapped in the Antarctic.

No. 5497a has a continuous design. No. 5498 contains one 51½x36½mm stamp.

**No. 4883 Ovptd. in Black for Rescue of the Mikhail Somov**

**Lithographed & Engraved**

**1986, Oct. 10** *Perf. 12x11½*

**5499** A2271 4k multicolored 1.00 .25

Locomotives — A2644

4k, EU 684-37, 1929. 5k, FD 21-3000, 1941. 10k, OV-5109, 1907. 20k, C017-1613, 1944. 30k, FDP 20-578, 1941.

**1986, Oct. 15** **Litho.** *Perf. 12*

| | | | | |
|---|---|---|---|---|
| **5500** | A2644 | 4k multi | .25 | .25 |
| **5501** | A2644 | 5k multi | .25 | .25 |
| **5502** | A2644 | 10k multi | .55 | .25 |
| *a.* | | Miniature sheet of 8 | 25.00 | |
| **5503** | A2644 | 20k multi | .85 | .40 |
| **5504** | A2644 | 30k multi | 1.10 | .65 |
| | | *Nos. 5500-5504 (5)* | 3.00 | 1.80 |

Grigori Konstantinovich Ordzhonikidze (1886-1937), Communist Party Leader — A2645

**1986, Oct. 18** **Engr.** *Perf. 12½x12*

**5505** A2645 5k dark blue green .50 .25

A.G. Novikov (1896-1984), Composer — A2646

**1986, Oct. 30**

**5506** A2646 5k dark brown 1.00 .25

A2647

**1986, Nov. 4** **Photo.** *Perf. 11½*

**5507** A2647 10k blue & silver .50 .25

UNSECO, 40th anniv.

A2648

**1986, Nov. 12**

**5508** A2648 5k lt grnsh gray & blk .50 .25

Sun Yat-sen (1866-1925), Chinese statesman.

Mikhail Vasilyevich Lomonosov, Scientist A2649

**1986, Nov. 19** **Engr.** *Perf. 12x12½*

**5509** A2649 5k dk violet brown .50 .25

Aircraft by A.S. Yakovlev — A2650

**1986, Nov. 25** **Photo.** *Perf. 11½x12*

| | | | | |
|---|---|---|---|---|
| **5510** | A2650 | 4k 1927 | .25 | .25 |
| **5511** | A2650 | 5k 1935 | .25 | .25 |
| *a.* | | Miniature sheet of 8 | 50.00 | |
| **5512** | A2650 | 10k 1946 | .40 | .25 |
| **5513** | A2650 | 20k 1972 | .65 | .35 |
| **5514** | A2650 | 30k 1981 | .95 | .50 |
| | | *Nos. 5510-5514 (5)* | 2.50 | 1.60 |

New Year 1987 A2651

**1986, Dec. 4** **Litho.** *Perf. 11½*

**5515** A2651 5k Kremlin towers .50 .25

*a.* Miniature sheet of 8 35.00

27th Communist Party Cong., 2/25-3/6 — A2652

Red banner and: No. 5516, Computers. No. 5517, Engineer, computer, dish receivers. No. 5518, Aerial view of city. No. 5519, Council for Mutual Economic Assistance building, workers. No. 5520, Spasski Tower, Kremlin Palace.

**1986, Dec. 12** **Photo.** *Perf. 11½x12*

| | | | | |
|---|---|---|---|---|
| **5516** | A2652 | 5k multicolored | .25 | .25 |
| **5517** | A2652 | 5k multicolored | .25 | .25 |
| **5518** | A2652 | 5k multicolored | .25 | .25 |
| **5519** | A2652 | 5k multicolored | .25 | .25 |
| **5520** | A2652 | 5k multicolored | .25 | .25 |
| | | *Nos. 5516-5520 (5)* | 1.25 | 1.25 |

A2653

**1986, Dec. 24** **Engr.** *Perf. 12½x12*

**5521** A2653 5k black .50 .25

Alexander Yakovlevich Parkhomenko (1886-1921), revolution hero.

A2654

**1986, Dec. 25** **Photo.** *Perf. 11½*

**5522** A2654 5k brown & buff .50 .25

Samora Moises Machel (1933-1986) Pres. of Mozambique.

**Miniature Sheet**

Palace Museums in Leningrad — A2655

**1986, Dec. 25** **Engr.** *Perf. 12*

| | | | | |
|---|---|---|---|---|
| **5523** | A2655 | Sheet of 5 + label | 3.00 | 1.40 |
| *a.* | | 5k State Museum, 1898 | .25 | .25 |
| *b.* | | 10k The Hermitage, 1764 | .35 | .25 |
| *c.* | | 15k Petrodvorets, 1728 | .45 | .30 |
| *d.* | | 20k Yekaterininsky, 1757 | .55 | .35 |
| *e.* | | 50k Pavlovsk, restored c. 1945 | 1.25 | .75 |

18th Soviet Trade Unions Congress, Feb. 24-28 — A2656

**1987, Jan. 7** **Photo.** *Perf. 11½*

**5524** A2656 5k multicolored .50 .25

Butterflies A2657

4k, Atrophaneura alcinous. 5k, Papilio machaon. 10k, Papilio alexanor. 15k, Papilio maackii. 30k, Iphiclides podalirius.

**1987, Jan. 15** **Litho.** *Perf. 12x12½*

| | | | | |
|---|---|---|---|---|
| **5525** | A2657 | 4k multicolored | .25 | .25 |
| **5526** | A2657 | 5k multicolored | .25 | .25 |
| **5527** | A2657 | 10k multicolored | .30 | .25 |
| **5528** | A2657 | 15k multicolored | .40 | .30 |
| **5529** | A2657 | 30k multicolored | .80 | .50 |
| | | *Nos. 5525-5529 (5)* | 2.00 | 1.55 |

A2658

**1987, Jan. 31** *Perf. 12½x12*

**5530** A2658 5k multicolored .50 .25

Karlis Miyesniyek (1887-1977), Artist.

A2659

**1987, Feb. 4** *Perf. 12*
5531 A2659 5k buff & lake .50 .25

Stasis Shimkus (1887-1943), composer.

**Alpinist Camps Type of 1986**

4k, Chimbulak Gorge. 10k, Shavla Gorge. 20k, Mts. Donguz-orun, Nakra-tau. 35k, Mt. Kazbek.

**1987, Feb. 4**
5532 A2636 4k multicolored .25 .25
5533 A2636 10k multicolored .30 .25
a. Miniature sheet of 8 15.00
5534 A2636 20k multicolored .40 .25
5535 A2636 35k multicolored .65 .40
*Nos. 5532-5535 (4)* 1.60 1.15

Vasily Ivanovich Chapayev (1887-1919), Revolution Hero — A2660

**1987, Feb. 9** **Engr.**
5536 A2660 5k dark red brown .50 .25

Heino Eller (1887-1970), Estonian Composer — A2661

**1987, Mar. 7** **Litho.** *Perf. 12*
5537 A2661 5k buff & brown .50 .25

A2662

**1987, Mar. 8** **Photo.** *Perf. 11½*
5538 A2662 5k multicolored .40 .25

**Souvenir Sheet**

*Perf. 11½x12*

5539 A2662 50k "XX," and colored bands 2.00 .75

All-Union Leninist Young Communist League 20th Congress, Moscow. No. 5539 contains one 26x37mm stamp.

A2663

**Photogravure and Engraved**

**1987, Mar. 20** *Perf. 11½*
5540 A2663 5k buff & sepia .50 .25

Iosif Abgarovich Orbeli (1887-1961), first president of the Armenian Academy of Sciences.

World Wildlife Fund — A2664

Polar bears.

**1987, Mar. 25** **Photo.** *Perf. 11½x12*
5541 A2664 5k multicolored .30 .25
a. Miniature sheet of 8 150.00
5542 A2664 10k multicolored .40 .25
a. Miniature sheet of 8 150.00
5543 A2664 20k multicolored .90 .40
a. Miniature sheet of 8 150.00
5544 A2664 35k multicolored 1.40 .75
a. Miniature sheet of 8 150.00
*Nos. 5541-5544 (4)* 3.00 1.65

Cosmonauts' Day — A2665

**1987, Apr. 12** *Perf. 11½*
5545 A2665 10k Sputnik, 1957 .35 .25
5546 A2665 10k Vostok 3 and 4, 1962 .35 .25
5547 A2665 10k Mars 1, 1962 .35 .25
a. Miniature sheet of 8 50.00
*Nos. 5545-5547 (3)* 1.05 .75

UN Emblem, ESCAP Headquarters, Bangkok — A2666

**1987, Apr. 21**
5548 A2666 10k multicolored .50 .25

UN Economic and Social Commission for Asia and the Pacific, 40th anniv.

Lenin, 117th Birth Anniv. — A2667

Paintings: No. 5549, Lenin's Birthday, by N.A. Sysoyev. No. 5550, Lenin with Delegates at the 3rd Congress of the Soviet Young Communist League, by P.O. Belousov. No. 5551a, Lenin's Underground Activity (Lenin, lamp), by D.A. Nalbandyan. No. 5551b, Before the Assault (Lenin standing at table), by S.P. Viktorov. No. 5551c, We'll Show the Earth the New Way (Lenin, soldiers, flags), by A.G. Lysenko. No. 5551d, Lenin in Smolny, October 1917 (Lenin seated), by M.G. Sokolov. No. 5551e, Lenin, by N.A. Andreyev.

**1987, Apr. 22** **Litho.** *Perf. 12½x12*
5549 A2667 5k multicolored .50 .25
5550 A2667 5k multicolored .50 .25

**Souvenir Sheet**

*Perf. 12*

5551 Sheet of 5 2.00 .75
a.-e. A2667 10k any single .30 .25

Sizes: Nos. 5551a-5551d, 40x28mm; No. 5551e, 40x56mm.

A2668

**1987, May 5** **Photo.** *Perf. 11½*
5552 A2668 10k multicolored .50 .25

European Gymnastics Championships, Moscow, May 18-26.

Bicycle Race — A2669

**1987, May 6**
5553 A2669 10k multicolored .50 .25

40th Peace Bicycle Race, Poland-Czechoslovakia-German Democratic Republic, May.

Fauna — A2670

5k, Menzbira marmot. 10k, Bald badger, horiz. 15k, Snow leopard.

*Perf. 12½x12 (#5554), 12x12½*

**1987, May 15** **Litho.**
5554 A2670 5k multicolored .50 .25
a. Miniature sheet of 8 35.00
5555 A2670 10k multicolored .60 .25

**Size: 32x47mm**

5556 A2670 15k multicolored .90 .25
*Nos. 5554-5556 (3)* 2.00 .75

Passenger Ships — A2671

5k, Maxim Gorki. 10k, Alexander Pushkin. 30k, The Soviet Union.

**1987, May 20** **Photo.** *Perf. 12x11½*
5557 A2671 5k multicolored .25 .25
5558 A2671 10k multicolored .50 .25
a. Miniature sheet of 8 125.00
5559 A2671 30k multicolored 1.25 .45
*Nos. 5557-5559 (3)* 2.00 .95

Paintings by Foreign Artists in the Hermitage Museum A2672

4k, Portrait of a Woman, by Lucas Cranach Sr. (1472-1553). 5k, St. Sebastian, by Titian. 10k, Justice, by Durer. 30k, Adoration of the Magi, by Pieter Brueghel the Younger (c. 1564-1638). 50k, Ceres, by Rubens.

*Perf. 12x12½, 12½x12*

**1987, June 5** **Litho.**
5560 A2672 4k multicolored .25 .25
5561 A2672 5k multicolored .25 .25
a. Miniature sheet of 8 175.00
5562 A2672 10k multicolored .25 .25
a. Miniature sheet of 8 175.00
5563 A2672 30k multicolored .60 .40
5564 A2672 50k multicolored .75 .50
*Nos. 5560-5564 (5)* 2.10 1.65

Tolyatti City, 250th Anniv. — A2673

Design: Zhiguli car, Volga Motors factory, Lenin Hydroelectric plant.

**1987, June 6** **Photo.** *Perf. 11½*
5565 A2673 5k multicolored .50 .25

Aleksander Pushkin (1799-1837), Poet — A2674

**1987, June 6** **Litho.**
5566 A2674 5k buff, yel brn & deep brown .50 .25

Printed se-tenant with label. Value pair, stamp + label, $1.

A2675

**1987, June 7** **Engr.** *Perf. 12½x12*
5567 A2675 5k black .50 .25

Maj.-Gen. Sidor A. Kovpak (1887-1967), Vice-Chairman of the Ukranian SSR.

A2676

**1987, June 23** **Photo.** *Perf. 11½*
5568 A2676 10k multicolored .50 .25

Women's World Congress on Nuclear Disarmament, Moscow, June 23-27.

Tobolsk City, 400th Anniv. — A2677

Design: Tobolsk kremlin, port, theater and Ermak Monument.

**1987, June 25**

**5569** A2677 5k multicolored .50 .25

Mozambique-USSR Treaty of Friendship and Cooperation, 10th anniv. — A2678

No. 5570, Flag of Frelimo, man. No. 5571, Flags of Mozambique, USSR.

**1987, June 25**

**5570** 5k multicolored .40 .25
**5571** 5k multicolored .40 .25
*a.* A2678 Pair, #5570-5571 1.00 .30

Ferns — A2679

4k, Scolopendrium vulgare. 5k, Ceterach officinarum. 10k, Salvinia natans, horiz. 15k, Matteuccia struthiopteris. 50k, Adiantum pedatum.

**1987, July 2 Litho. *Perf. 12***

**5572** A2679 4k multicolored .25 .25
**5573** A2679 5k multicolored .25 .25
**5574** A2679 10k multicolored .30 .25
**5575** A2679 15k multicolored .30 .30
**5576** A2679 50k multicolored 1.00 .75
*Nos. 5572-5576 (5)* 2.10 1.80

A2680

No. 5577, Kremlin and 2000 Year-old Coin of India. No. 5578, Red Fort, Delhi, Soviet hammer & sickle.

**1987, July 3**

**5577** A2680 5k shown .40 .25
**5578** A2680 5k muticolored .40 .25
*a.* Pair, #5577-5578 1.00 .30

Festivals 1987-88: India in the USSR (No. 5577) and the USSR in India (No. 5578).

15th Intl. Film Festival, July 16-17, Moscow — A2681

**1987, July 6 Photo. *Perf. 11½***

**5579** 2681 10k multicolored .50 .25

Joint Soviet-Syrian Space Flight A2682

Mir Space Station — A2683

Flags, Intercosmos emblem and: 5k, Cosmonaut training and launch. 10k, Mir space station, Syrian parliament and cosmonauts. 15k, Gagarin Memorial, satellite dishes and cosmonauts wearing space suits.

**1987 Litho. *Perf. 12x12½***

**5580** A2682 5k multicolored .25 .25
**5581** A2682 10k multicolored .50 .25
**5582** A2682 15k multicolored .75 .25
*Nos. 5580-5582 (3)* 1.50 .75

**Souvenir Sheet**

**5583** A2683 50k multicolored 1.50 .75

Issued: 5k, 7/22; 10k, 7/24; 15k, 50k 7/30.

Intl. Atomic Energy Agency, 30th Anniv. A2684

**1987, July 29 Photo. *Perf. 11½***

**5584** A2684 20k multicolored .50 .25

14th-16th Century Postrider — A2685

Designs: 5k, 17th cent. postman and 17th cent. kibitka (sled). 10k, 16th-17th cent. ship and 18th cent. packet. 30k, Railway station and 19th cent. mailcars. 35k, AMO-F-15 bus and car, 1905. 50k, Postal headquarters, Moscow, and modern postal delivery trucks.

**Photo. & Engr.**

**1987, Aug. 25 *Perf. 11½x12***

**5585** A2685 4k buff & black .25 .25
**5586** A2685 5k buff & black .25 .25
**5587** A2685 10k buff & black .35 .25
**5588** A2685 30k buff & black .75 .25
**5589** A2685 35k buff & black 1.00 .40
*Nos. 5585-5589 (5)* 2.60 1.40

**Souvenir Sheet**

**5590** A2685 50k pale yel, dull gray grn & blk 2.00 .90

A2686

October Revolution, 70th Anniv. — A2687

Paintings by Russian artists: No. 5591, Long Live the Socialist Revolution! by V.V. Kuznetsov. No. 5592, V.I. Lenin Proclaims the Soviet Power (Lenin pointing), by V.A. Serov. No. 5593, V.I. Lenin (with pencil), by P.V. Vasiliev. No. 5594, On the Eve of the Storm (Lenin, Trotsky, Dzerzhinski), by V.V. Pimenov. No. 5595, Taking the Winter Palace by Storm, by V.A. Serov.

**1987, Aug. 25 Litho. *Perf. 12½x12***

**5591** A2686 5k shown .30 .25
*a.* Miniature sheet of 8 5.00
**5592** A2686 5k multicolored .30 .25
*a.* Miniature sheet of 8 5.00
**5593** A2686 5k multicolored .30 .25
*a.* Miniature sheet of 8 5.00

**Size: 70x33mm**

***Perf. 11½***

**5594** A2686 5k multicolored .30 .25
*a.* Miniature sheet of 8 5.00
**5595** A2686 5k multicolored .30 .25
*a.* Miniature sheet of 8 5.00
*Nos. 5591-5595 (5)* 1.50 1.25

**Souvenir Sheet**

**Photo. & Engr.**

***Perf. 12x11½***

**5596** A2687 30k gold & black 1.50 .45

For overprint see No. 5604.

Souvenir Sheet

Battle of Borodino, 175th Anniv. — A2688

**1987, Sept. 7 Litho. *Perf. 12½x12***

**5597** A2688 1r blk, yel brn & blue gray 3.00 1.50

A2689

**1987, Sept. 18 Engr.**

**5598** A2689 5k intense blue .50 .25

Pavel Petrovich Postyshev (1887-1939), party leader.

Moscow, 840th Anniv. — A2690

Design: 5k, Monument to founder Yuri Dolgoruki, by sculptor S. Orlov, A. Antropov, N. Stamm and architect V. Andreyev, in Sovetskaya Square, and buildings in Moscow.

**1987, Sept. 19 Photo. *Perf. 11½***

**5599** A2690 5k dk red brn, cr & dk org .50 .25

Scientists — A2691

Designs: No. 5600, Muhammed Taragai Ulugh Begh (1394-1449), Uzbek astronomer and mathematician. No. 5601, Sir Isaac Newton (1642-1727), English physicist and mathematician. No. 5602, Marie Curie (1867-1934), physicist, chemist, Nobel laureate.

**1987, Oct. 3 Photo. & Engr.**

**5600** A2691 5k dk bl, org brn & blk .50 .25
**5601** A2691 5k dull grn, blk & dk ultra .50 .25
**5602** A2691 5k brn & dp blue .50 .25
*Nos. 5600-5602 (3)* 1.50 .75

Nos. 5600-5602 each printed se-tenant with inscribed label.

Souvenir Sheet

COSPAS-SARSAT Intl. Satellite System for Tracking Disabled Planes and Ships — A2692

**1987, Oct. 15 Photo.**

**5603** A2692 50k multicolored 3.00 .75

**No. 5595 Overprinted in Gold**

**1987, Oct. 17** **Litho.**
**5604** A2686 5k multicolored 1.50 .40

All-Union Philatelic Exhibition and the 70th Anniv. of the October Revolution.
Sheet of 8 No. 5595 has the overprint in the margin.

My Quiet Homeland, by V.M. Sidorov — A2693

The Sun Above Red Square, by P.P. Ossovsky — A2694

Paintings by Soviet artists exhibited at the 7th Republican Art Exhibition, Moscow, 1985: 4k, There Will be Cities in the Taiga, by A.A. Yakovlev. 5k, Mother, by V.V. Shcherbakov. 30k, On Jakutian Soil, by A.N. Osipov. 35k, Ivan's Return, by V.I. Yerofeyev.

**1987, Oct. 20** ***Perf. 12x12½, 12½x12***
**5605** A2693 4k multi, vert. .25 .25
**5606** A2693 5k multi, vert. .25 .25
**5607** A2693 10k multicolored .35 .25
**5608** A2693 30k multicolored .75 .45
**5609** A2693 35k multicolored .85 .50
*Nos. 5605-5609 (5)* 2.45 1.70

**Souvenir Sheet**
***Perf. 11½x12½***
**5610** A2694 50k multicolored 3.00 1.00

John Reed (1887-1920), American Journalist — A2695

**1987, Oct. 22** ***Perf. 11½***
**5611** A2695 10k buff & dk brn .50 .25

Samuil Yakovlevich Marshak (1887-1964), Author — A2696

**1987, Nov. 3** **Engr.** ***Perf. 12½x12***
**5612** A2696 5k deep claret .50 .25

A2697

**1987, Nov. 8**
**5613** A2697 5k slate blue .50 .25

Ilja Grigorjevich Chavchavadze (1837-1907), Georgian author.

Indira Gandhi (1917-1984) A2698

**1987, Nov. 19** **Photo.** ***Perf. 11½***
**5614** A2698 5k black & brown .50 .25

A2699

**1987, Nov. 25** ***Perf. 12½x12***
**5615** A2699 5k black .50 .25

Vadim Nikolaevich Podbelsky (1887-1920), revolution leader.

A2700

**1987, Nov. 25**
**5616** A2700 5k dark blue gray .50 .25

Nikolai Ivanovich Vavilov (1887-1943), botanist.

A2701

Modern Science: 5k, TOKAMAK, a controlled thermonuclear reactor. 10k, Kola Project (Earth strata study). 20k, RATAN-600 radiotelescope.

**Photo. & Engr.**
**1987, Nov. 25** ***Perf. 11½***
**5617** A2701 5k grnsh gray & brn .25 .25
**5618** A2701 10k dull grn, lt blue gray & dark blue .35 .25
**5619** A2701 20k gray olive, blk & buff .50 .30
*Nos. 5617-5619 (3)* 1.10 .80

U.S. and Soviet Flags, Spasski Tower and US Capitol — A2702

**1987, Dec. 17** **Photo.**
**5620** A2702 10k multicolored .50 .25

INF Treaty (eliminating intermediate-range nuclear missiles) signed by Gen.-Sec. Gorbachev and Pres. Reagan, Dec. 8.

New Year 1988 A2703

**1987, Dec. 2** **Litho.** ***Perf. 12x12½***
**5621** A2703 5k Kremlin .50 .25
*a.* Miniature sheet of 8 17.50

Marshal Ivan Khristoforovich Bagramyan (1897-1982) A2704

**1987, Dec. 2** **Engr.** ***Perf. 12½x12***
**5622** A2704 5k black .50 .25

**Miniature Sheet**

18th-19th Cent. Naval Commanders and War Ships — A2705

Designs: 4k, Adm. Grigori Andreyevich Spiridov (1713-1790), Battle of Chesmen. 5k, Fedor Fedorovich Ushakov (1745-1817), Storming of Corfu. 10k, Adm. Dimitiri Nikolayevich Senyavin (1763-1831) and flagship at the Battle of Afon off Mt. Athos. 25k, Mikhail Petrovich Lazarev (1788-1851), Battle of Navarin. 30k, Adm. Pavel Stepanovich Nakhimov (1802-1855), Battle of Sinop.

**1987, Dec. 22**
**5623** A2705 Sheet of 5 + label 5.00 1.25
*a.* 4k dark blue & indigo .35 .25
*b.* 5k maroon & indigo .35 .25
*c.* 10k maroon & indigo .50 .25
*d.* 25k dark blue & indigo 1.00 .40
*e.* 30k dark blue & indigo 1.25 .50

No. 5623 contains corner label (LR) picturing ensign of period Russian Navy vessels and anchor.
See No. 5850.

Asia-Africa Peoples Solidarity Organization, 30th Anniv. — A2706

**1987, Dec. 26** **Photo.** ***Perf. 11½***
**5624** A2706 10k multicolored .50 .25

1st Soviet Postage Stamp, 70th Anniv. — A2707

**1988, Jan. 4** **Photo.** ***Perf. 11½***
**5625** A2707 10k #149, #150 UR .50 .25
**5626** A2707 10k #150, #149 UR .50 .25
*a.* Pair, #5625-5626 1.00 .30

Lettering in brown on No. 5625, in blue on No. 5626.

A2708

5k, Biathlon. 10k, Cross-country skiing. 15k, Slalom. 20k, Pairs figure skating. 30k, Ski jumping.
50k, Ice hockey, horiz.

**1988, Jan. 4**
**5627** A2708 5k multi .25 .25
*a.* Miniature sheet of 8 80.00
**5628** A2708 10k multi .30 .25
*a.* Miniature sheet of 8 80.00
**5629** A2708 15k multi .40 .30
*a.* Miniature sheet of 8 80.00
**5630** A2708 20k multi .50 .35
*a.* Miniature sheet of 8 80.00
**5631** A2708 30k multi .70 .50
*a.* Miniature sheet of 8 80.00
*Nos. 5627-5631 (5)* 2.15 1.65

**Souvenir Sheet**
**5632** A2708 50k multi 2.00 1.00

1988 Winter Olympics, Calgary.
For overprint see No. 5665.

A2709

**1988, Jan. 7**
**5633** A2709 35k blue & gold 1.00 .65

World Health Org., 40th anniv.

Lord Byron (1788-1824), English Poet A2710

**Photo. & Engr.**

**1988, Jan. 22** ***Perf. 12x11½***

**5634** A2710 15k Prus blue, blk & grn black .50 .30

A2711

**1988, Jan. 27** **Photo.** ***Perf. 11½***

**5635** A2711 20k multicolored .50 .40

Cultural, Technical and Educational Agreement with the US, 30th anniv.

A2712

**1988, Feb. 5**

**5636** A2712 5k black & tan .50 .25

G.I. Lomov-Oppokov (1888-1938), party leader. See Nos. 5649, 5660, 5666, 5673, 5700, 5704, 5721, 5812.

Animated Soviet Cartoons — A2713

1k, Little Humpback Horse, 1947. 3k, Winnie-the-Pooh, 1969. 4k, Gena, the Crocodile, 1969. 5k, Just you Wait! 1969. 10k, Hedgehog in the Mist, 1975.
30k, Post, 1929.

**1988, Feb. 18** **Litho.** ***Perf. 12½x12***

| | | | | |
|---|---|---|---|---|
| **5637** | A2713 | 1k multicolored | .25 | .25 |
| **5638** | A2713 | 3k multicolored | .25 | .25 |
| **5639** | A2713 | 4k multicolored | .25 | .25 |
| **5640** | A2713 | 5k multicolored | .25 | .25 |
| **5641** | A2713 | 10k multicolored | .30 | .25 |
| | | *Nos. 5637-5641 (5)* | 1.30 | 1.25 |

**Souvenir Sheet**

**5642** A2713 30k multicolored 2.00 .60

A2714

**1988, Feb. 21** **Photo.** ***Perf. 11½***

**5643** A2714 10k buff & black .50 .25

Mikhail Alexandrovich Bonch-Bruevich (1888-1940), broadcast engineer.

A2715

**1988, Feb. 25**

**5644** A2715 15k blk, brt bl & dk red .50 .30

*a.* Miniature sheet of 8 40.00

Intl. Red Cross and Red Crescent Organizations, 125th annivs.

World Speed Skating Championships, Mar. 5-6, Alma-Ata — A2716

**1988, Mar. 13** **Photo.** ***Perf. 11½***

**5645** A2716 15k blk, vio & brt blue .50 .30

No. 5645 printed se-tenant with label picturing Alma-Ata skating rink, Medeo.

A2717

**1988, Mar. 13** **Litho.** ***Perf. 12½x12***

**5646** A2717 10k dark olive green .50 .25

Anton Semenovich Makarenko (1888-1939), teacher, youth development expert.

Franzisk Skorina (b. 1488), 1st Printer in Byelorussia A2718

**1988, Mar. 17** **Engr.** ***Perf. 12x12½***

**5647** A2718 5k gray black .50 .25

Labor Day — A2719

**1988, Mar. 22** **Photo.** ***Perf. 11½***

**5648** A2719 5k multicolored .50 .25

**Party Leader Type of 1988**

**1988, Mar. 24** **Engr.** ***Perf. 12***

**5649** A2712 5k dark green .50 .25

Victor Eduardovich Kingisepp (1888-1922).

Organized Track and Field Events in Russia, Cent. A2721

**1988, Mar. 24** **Photo.** ***Perf. 11½***

**5650** A2721 15k multicolored .50 .30

Marietta Sergeyevna Shaginyan (1888-1982), Author — A2722

**1988, Apr. 2** **Litho.** ***Perf. 12½x12***

**5651** A2722 10k brown .50 .25

Soviet-Finnish Peace Treaty, 40th Anniv. — A2723

**1988, Apr. 6** **Photo.** ***Perf. 11½***

**5652** A2723 15k multicolored .50 .30

Cosmonaut's Day — A2724

MIR space station, Soyuz TM transport ship, automated cargo ship *Progress* & *Quant* module.

**1988, Apr. 12** ***Perf. 11½x12***

**5653** A2724 15k multicolored .50 .30

*a.* Miniature sheet of 8 40.00

*Victory*, 1948, Painted by P.A. Krivonogov A2725

**1988, Apr. 20** **Litho.** ***Perf. 12x12½***

**5654** A2725 5k multicolored .50 .25

Victory Day (May 9).

Sochi City, 150th Anniv. A2726

**1988, Apr. 20** **Photo.** ***Perf. 11½***

**5655** A2726 5k multicolored .50 .25

Branches of the Lenin Museum — A2727

Portrait of Lenin and: No. 5656, Central museum, Moscow, opened May 15, 1926. No. 5657, Branch, Leningrad, opened in 1937. No. 5658, Branch, Kiev, opened in 1938. No. 5659, Branch, Krasnoyarsk, opened in 1987.

**1988, Apr. 22** **Litho.** ***Perf. 12***

| | | | | |
|---|---|---|---|---|
| **5656** | A2727 | 5k vio brown & gold | .25 | .25 |
| **5657** | A2727 | 5k brn vio, vio brown & gold | .25 | .25 |
| **5658** | A2727 | 5k dp brn ol & gold | .25 | .25 |
| **5659** | A2727 | 5k dark green & gold | .25 | .25 |
| *a.* | | Block of 4, Nos. 5656-5659 | 1.00 | .40 |

See Nos. 5765-5767, 5885-5887.

**Party Leader Type of 1988**

**1988, Apr. 24** **Photo.** ***Perf. 11½***

**5660** A2712 5k blue black .50 .25

Ivan Alexeyevich Akulov (1888-1939).

EXPO '88, Brisbane, Australia — A2729

**1988, Apr. 30**

**5661** A2729 20k multicolored .50 .35

Karl Marx — A2730

**1988, May 5** **Engr.** ***Perf. 12***

**5662** A2730 5k chocolate .50 .25

Social and Economic Reforms — A2731

Designs: No. 5663, Cruiser *Aurora*, revolutionary soldiers, workers and slogans Speeding Up, Democratization, and Glasnost against Kremlin Palace. No. 5664, Worker, agriculture and industries.

**1988, May 5 Photo. *Perf. 12x11½***
**5663** A2731 5k multicolored .25 .25
**5664** A2731 5k multicolored .25 .25

### No. 5632 Ovptd. in Dark Red
Souvenir Sheet

**1988, May 12 Photo. *Perf. 11½***
**5665** A2708 50k multicolored 2.00 1.25

Victory of Soviet athletes at the 1988 Winter Olympics, Calgary. No. 5665 overprinted below stamp on souvenir sheet margin. Soviet sportsmen won 11 gold, 9 silver and 9 bronze medals.

### Party Leader Type of 1988

**1988, May 19 Engr. *Perf. 12***
**5666** A2712 5k black .50 .25

Nikolai Mikhailovich Shvernik (1888-1970).

Hunting Dogs — A2733

Designs: 5k, Russian borzoi, fox hunt. 10k, Kirghiz greyhound, falconry. 15k, Russian retrievers. 20k, Russian spaniel, duck hunt. 35k, East Siberian husky, bear hunt.

**1988, May 20 Litho.**
**5667** A2733 5k multicolored .25 .25
**5668** A2733 10k multicolored .40 .25
**5669** A2733 15k multicolored .55 .25
**5670** A2733 20k multicolored .75 .40
**5671** A2733 35k multicolored 1.00 .50
*Nos. 5667-5671 (5)* 2.95 1.65

A2734

**1988, May 29 Photo. *Perf. 11½***
**5672** A2734 5k multicolored .50 .25

Soviet-US Summit Conf., May 29-June 2, Moscow.

### Party Leader Type of 1988

**1988, June 6 Engr. *Perf. 12***
**5673** A2712 5k brown black .50 .25

Valerian Vladimirovich Kuibyshev (1888-1935).

A2736

Design: Flags, Mir space station and Soyuz TM spacecraft.

**1988, June 7 Photo. *Perf. 11½***
**5674** A2736 15k multicolored .50 .35

Shipka '88, USSR-Bulgarian joint space flight, June 7.

A2737

Design: Natl. & Canadian flags, skis & globe.

**1988, June 16**
**5675** A2737 35k multicolored .50 .35

Soviet-Canada transarctic ski expedition, May-Aug.

A2738

**1988, June 16**
**5676** A2738 5k multicolored .50 .25

For a world without nuclear weapons.

A2739

A2740

19th All-union Communist Party Conference, Moscow — A2741

**1988, June 16 Litho. *Perf. 12***
**5677** A2739 5k multicolored .25 .25

**Photo.**
***Perf. 11½***
**5678** A2740 5k multicolored .25 .25

### Souvenir Sheet
***Perf. 11½x12***
**5679** A2741 50k multicolored 2.00 .75

1988 Summer Olympics, Seoul A2742

**1988, June 29 Litho. *Perf. 12***
**5680** A2742 5k Hurdling .25 .25
*a.* Miniature sheet of 8 25.00
**5681** A2742 10k Long jump .25 .25
*a.* Miniature sheet of 8 25.00
**5682** A2742 15k Basketball .40 .30
*a.* Miniature sheet of 8 25.00
**5683** A2742 20k Rhythmic gymnastics .50 .35
*a.* Miniature sheet of 8 25.00
**5684** A2742 30k Swimming .60 .50
*a.* Miniature sheet of 8 25.00
*Nos. 5680-5684 (5)* 2.00 1.65

### Souvenir Sheet
**5685** A2742 50k Soccer 1.50 1.00

For overprint see No. 5722.

Phobos Intl. Space Project — A2743

10k, Satellite, space probe.

**1988, July 7 Photo. *Perf. 11½x12***
**5686** A2743 10k multicolored .50 .25

For the study of Phobos, a satellite of Mars.

Flowers Populating Deciduous Forests — A2744

5k, Campanula latifolia. 10k, Orobus vernus, horiz. 15k, Pulmonaria obscura. 20k, Lilium martagon. 35k, Ficaria verna.

**1988, July 7 Litho. *Perf. 12***
**5687** A2744 5k multicolored .25 .25
**5688** A2744 10k multicolored .35 .25
**5689** A2744 15k multicolored .50 .35
**5690** A2744 20k multicolored .65 .45
**5691** A2744 35k multicolored 1.10 .75
*Nos. 5687-5691 (5)* 2.85 2.05

A2745

**1988, July 14 Photo. *Perf. 11½***
**5692** A2745 5k multicolored .50 .25

Leninist Young Communist League (Komsomol), 70th anniv. For overprint see No. 5699.

A2746

**1988, July 18**
**5693** A2746 10k multicolored .50 .25

Nelson Mandela (1918-2013), South African anti-apartheid leader.

Paintings in the Timiriazev Equestrian Museum of the Moscow Agricultural Academy — A2747

Paintings: 5k, *Light Gray Arabian Stallion,* by N.E. Sverchkov, 1860. 10k, *Konvoets, a Kabardian,* by M.A. Vrubel, 1882, vert. 15k, *Horsewoman Riding an Orlov-Rastopchinsky,* by N.E. Sverchkov. 20k, *Letuchya, a Gray Orlov Trotter,* by V.A. Serov, 1886, vert. 30k, *Sardar, an Akhaltekinsky Stallion,* by A.B. Villevalde, 1882.

**1988, July 20 Litho. *Perf. 12½x12***
**5694** A2747 5k multicolored .25 .25
**5695** A2747 10k multicolored .25 .25
**5696** A2747 15k multicolored .40 .25
**5697** A2747 20k multicolored .55 .35
**5698** A2747 30k multicolored .90 .65
*Nos. 5694-5698 (5)* 2.35 1.75

No. 5692 Ovptd. for the All-Union Philatelic Exhibition, Moscow, Aug. 10-17

**1988, Aug. 10 Photo. *Perf. 11½***
**5699** A2745 5k multicolored .50 .30

### Party Leader Type of 1988

**1988, Aug. 13 Engr. *Perf. 12½x12***
**5700** A2712 5k black .50 .25

Petr Lazarevich Voykov (1888-1927), economic and trade union plenipotentiary.

МЕЖДУНАРОДНАЯ НЕДЕЛЯ ПИСЬМА 1988 ПОЧТА СССР 5к

Intl. Letter-Writing Week — A2749

**1988, Aug. 25 Photo. *Perf. 11½***

**5701** A2749 5k blue grn & dark blue green .50 .25

Earth, Mir space station and Soyuz-TM A2750

**1988, Aug. 29**

**5702** A2750 15k multicolored .50 .30

Soviet-Afghan joint space flight.

A2751

**1988, Sept. 1 Photo. *Perf. 11½***

**5703** A2751 10k multicolored .50 .25

*Problems of Peace and Socialism* magazine, 30th anniv.

**Party Leader Type of 1988**

**1988, Sept. 13 Engr. *Perf. 12***

**5704** A2712 5k black .50 .25

Emmanuil Ionovich Kviring (1888-1937).

A2753

A2753a

A2753b

A2753c

A2753d

Designs: No. 5705, *Ilya Muromets,* Russian lore. No. 5706, *Ballad of the Cossack Golota,* Ukrainian lore. No. 5707, *Musician-Magician,* a Byelorussian fairy tale. No. 5708, *Koblandy-batyr,* a poem from Kazakh. No. 5709, *Alpamysh,* a fairy tale from Uzbek.

***Perf. 12x12½, 12½x12***

**1988, Sept. 22 Litho.**

**5705** A2753 10k multicolored .25 .25
**5706** A2753a 10k multicolored .25 .25
**5707** A2753b 10k multicolored .25 .25
**5708** A2753c 10k multicolored .25 .25
**5709** A2753d 10k multicolored .25 .25
*Nos. 5705-5709 (5)* 1.25 1.25

Nos. 5705-5709 each printed se-tenant with inscribed labels. See design A2795.

Appeal of the Leader, 1947, by I.M. Toidze A2754

**1988, Oct. 5 *Perf. 12x12½***

**5710** A2754 5k multicolored .40 .25

October Revolution, 71st anniv.

A2755

**1988, Oct. 18 Engr. *Perf. 12***

**5711** A2755 10k black .50 .25

Andrei Timofeyevich Bolotov (1738-1833), agricultural scientist, publisher.

A2756

**1988, Oct. 18**

**5712** A2756 10k steel blue .50 .25

Andrei Nikolayevich Tupolev (1888-1972), aeronautical engineer.

A2757

20k, Map of expedition route, atomic icebreaker *Sibirj* & expedition members.

**1988, Oct. 25 Litho.**

**5713** A2757 20k multicolored .50 .35

North Pole expedition (in 1987). Exists imperf. Value, $35.

A2758

**1988, Oct. 30 Engr.**

**5714** A2758 5k brown black .40 .25

Dmitry F. Ustinov (1908-84), minister of defense.

Soviet-Vietnamese Treaty, 10th Anniv. — A2759

**1988, Nov. 3 Photo. *Perf. 11½***

**5715** A2759 10k multicolored .50 .25

State Broadcasting and Sound Recording Institute, 50th Anniv. — A2760

**1988, Nov. 3**

**5716** A2760 10k multicolored .50 .25

UN Declaration of Human Rights, 40th Anniv. A2761

**1988, Nov. 21**

**5717** A2761 10k multicolored .50 .25

New Year 1989 — A2762

Design: Preobrazhensky Regiment bodyguard riding to announce Peter the Great's decree to celebrate new year's eve as of January 1, 1700.

**1988, Nov. 24 Litho. *Perf. 12x11½***

**5718** A2762 5k multicolored .50 .25

Soviet-French Joint Space Flight — A2763

**1988, Nov. 26 Photo. *Perf. 11½***

**5719** A2763 15k Space walkers .50 .30

No. 4607 Overprinted in Red

**1988, Dec. 16 Litho. *Perf. 12½x12***

**5720** A2143 1r dark blue 5.00 2.25

Space mail.

**Party Leader Type of 1988**

**1988, Dec. 16 Engr.**

**5721** A2712 5k slate green .50 .25

Martyn Ivanovich Latsis (1888-1938).

**No. 5685 Overprinted in Bright Blue**

Souvenir Sheet

**1988, Dec. 20 Litho. *Perf. 12***

**5722** A2742 50k multicolored 2.00 1.00

Victory of Soviet athletes at the 1988 Summer Olympics, Seoul. Overprint on margin of No. 5722 specifies that Soviet athletes won 55 gold, 31 silver and 46 bronze medals.

Post Rider — A2765

Designs: 3k, Cruiser *Aurora.* 4k, Spasski Tower, Lenin Mausoleum. 5k, Natl. flag, crest. 10k, *The Worker and the Collective Farmer,* 1935, sculpture by V.I. Mukhina. 15k, Satellite dish. 20k, Lyre, art tools, quill pen, parchment (arts and literature). 25k, *Discobolus,* 5th cent. sculpture by Myron (c. 480-440 B.C.). 30k, Map of the Antarctic, penguins. 35k, *Mercury,* sculpture by Giambologna (1529-1608). 50k, White cranes (nature conservation). 1r, UPU emblem.

**1988, Dec. 22 Engr. *Perf. 12x11½***

**5723** A2765 1k dark brown .25 .25
**5724** A2765 3k dark blue green .25 .25
**5725** A2765 4k indigo .25 .25
**5726** A2765 5k red .25 .25
**5727** A2765 10k claret .25 .25
**5728** A2765 15k deep blue .30 .25
**5729** A2765 20k olive gray .35 .30
**5730** A2765 25k dark green .40 .35
**5731** A2765 30k dark blue .50 .40
**5732** A2765 35k dark red brown .60 .50
**5733** A2765 50k sapphire .80 .50

***Perf. 12x12½***

**5734** A2765 1r blue gray 1.60 1.25
*Nos. 5723-5734 (12)* 5.80 4.80

See Nos. 5838-5849, 5984-5987. For surcharges see Uzbekistan #15, 22, 25-26, 61B, 61D, 61F.

Fountains of Petrodvorets A2766

Designs: 5k, Samson Fountain, 1723, and Great Cascade. 10k, Adam Fountain, 1722, and sculptures, 1718, by D. Bonazza. 15k, Golden Mountain Cascade, by N. Miketti (1721-1723) and M.G. Zemtsov. 30k, Roman Fountains, 1763. 50k, Oak Tree Fountain, 1735.

**1988, Dec. 25 Engr. *Perf. 11½x12***

**5735** A2766 5k myrtle green .25 .25
**5736** A2766 10k myrtle green .25 .25
**5737** A2766 15k myrtle green .30 .25
**5738** A2766 30k myrtle green .60 .40
**5739** A2766 50k myrtle green 1.00 .70
*a.* Pane of 5, #5735-5739 5.00 1.50

Panes have photogravure margin. Panes are printed bilaterally and separated in the center by perforations so that stamps in the 2nd pane are arranged in reverse order from the 1st pane.

19th Communist Party Congress — A2767

**1988, Dec. 30 Photo. *Perf. 12x11½***
**Multicolored and**

**5740** A2767 5k deep car (power) .50 .25
**5741** A2767 5k dp bl vio (industry) .50 .25
**5742** A2767 5k green (land) .50 .25
*Nos. 5740-5742 (3)* 1.50 .75

Souvenir Sheet

Inaugural Flight of the *Buran* Space Shuttle, Nov. 15 — A2768

**1988, Dec. 30 *Perf. 11½x12***
**5743** A2768 50k multicolored 2.00 .75

*Luna 1,* 30th Anniv. — A2769

**1989, Jan. 2 Photo. *Perf. 11½***
**5744** A2769 15k multicolored .50 .30

Jalmari Virtanen (1889-1939), Karelian Poet — A2770

**1989, Jan. 8**
**5745** A2770 5k olive brown .50 .25

Council for Mutual Economic Assistance, 40th Anniv. A2771

**1989, Jan. 8**
**5746** A2771 10k multicolored .50 .25

Environmental Protection — A2772

**1989, Jan. 18 Litho. *Perf. 12½x12***
**5747** A2772 5k Forest .30 .25
**5748** A2772 10k Arctic deer .50 .25
**5749** A2772 15k Stop desert encroachment .70 .30
*Nos. 5747-5749 (3)* 1.50 .80

Nos. 5747-5749 printed se-tenant with inscribed labels picturing maps.

Samovars A2773

Samovars in the State Museum, Leningrad: 5k, Pear-shaped urn, late 18th cent. 10k, Barrel-shaped urn by Ivan Listisin, early 19th cent. 20k, "Kabachok" urn by the Sokolov Bros., Tula, c. 1830. 30k, Vase-shaped urn by the Nikolari Malikov Studio, Tula, c. 1840.

**1989, Feb. 8 Photo. *Perf. 11½***
**5750** A2773 5k multicolored .25 .25
**5751** A2773 10k multicolored .30 .25
**5752** A2773 20k multicolored .60 .30
**5753** A2773 30k multicolored .85 .45
*Nos. 5750-5753 (4)* 2.00 1.25

Modest Petrovich Mussorgsky (1839-1881), Composer — A2774

**1989, Feb. 15 Litho. *Perf. 12½x12***
**5754** A2774 10k dull vio & vio brn 1.00 .25

P.E. Dybenko (1889-1938), Military Commander A2775

**1989, Feb. 28 Engr. *Perf. 12***
**5755** A2775 5k black .50 .25

T.G. Shevchenko (1814-1861), Poet A2776

**1989, Mar. 6 Litho. *Perf. 11½***
**5756** A2776 5k pale grn, blk & brn .50 .25

Exists imperf. Value, $25.

Cultivated Lilies — A2777

**1989, Mar. 15 *Perf. 12½x12***
**5757** A2777 5k Lilium speciosum .25 .25
**5758** A2777 10k African queen .25 .25
**5759** A2777 15k Eclat du soir .30 .25
**5760** A2777 30k White tiger .80 .55
*Nos. 5757-5760 (4)* 1.60 1.30

Souvenir Sheet

Labor Day, Cent. — A2778

**1989, Mar. 25 *Perf. 11½x12***
**5761** A2778 30k multicolored 2.00 .60

*Victory Banner,* by P. Loginov and V. Pamfilov A2779

**1989, Apr. 5 Litho. *Perf. 12x12½***
**5762** A2779 5k multicolored .50 .25

World War II Victory Day.

Cosmonauts' Day — A2780

**1989, Apr. 12 Photo. *Perf. 11x11½***
**5763** A2780 15k Mir space station .50 .30

A2781

**1989, Apr. 14 *Perf. 11½***
**5764** A2781 10k multicolored .75 .25

Bering Bridge Soviet-American Expedition, Anadyr and Kotzebue.

**Type of 1988**

Portraits and branches of the Lenin Central Museum: No. 5765, Kazan. No. 5766, Kuibyshev. No. 5767, Frunze.

**1989, Apr. 14 Litho. *Perf. 12***
**5765** A2727 5k rose brown & multi .25 .25
**5766** A2727 5k olive gray & multi .25 .25
**5767** A2727 5k deep brown & multi .25 .25
*Nos. 5765-5767 (3)* .75 .75

Lenin's 119th Birth Anniv.

Souvenir Sheet

Launch of Interplanetary Probe *Phobos* — A2783

**1989, Apr. 24 *Perf. 11½x12***
**5768** A2783 50k multicolored 1.75 .85

A2784

**1989, May 5 Photo. *Perf. 11½***
**5769** A2784 5k multicolored .50 .25

Hungarian Soviet Republic, 70th anniv.

A2785

**1989, May 5 Photo. & Engr.**
**5770** A2785 5k multicolored .40 .25

Volgograd, 400th anniv.

Honeybees A2786

No. 5771, Drone. No. 5772, Workers, flowers, man-made hive. No. 5773, Worker collecting pollen. No. 5774, Queen, drones, honeycomb.

**1989, May 18 Litho. *Perf. 12***

| | | | | | |
|---|---|---|---|---|---|
| **5771** | A2786 | 5k multi | | .25 | .25 |
| **5772** | A2786 | 10k multi | | .25 | .25 |
| **5773** | A2786 | 20k multi | | .50 | .25 |
| **5774** | A2786 | 35k multi | | .90 | .50 |
| | | *Nos. 5771-5774 (4)* | | 1.90 | 1.25 |

No. 5771 exists imperf. Value, $30.

Photography, 150th Anniv. — A2787

**1989, May 24 Photo. *Perf. 11½***

**5775** A2787 5k multicolored .50 .25

I.A. Kuratov (1839-1875), Author — A2788

**1989, June 26 Litho. *Perf. 12½x12***

**5776** A2788 5k dk golden brn .40 .25

Jean Racine (1639-1699), French Dramatist A2789

**Photo. & Engr.**

**1989, June 16 *Perf. 12x11½***

**5777** A2789 15k multicolored .50 .25

Europe, Our Common Home — A2790

Designs: 5k, Map of Europe, stylized bird. 10k, Crane, two men completing a bridge, globe. 15k, Stork's nest, globe.

**1989, June 20 Photo. *Perf. 11½***

| | | | | | |
|---|---|---|---|---|---|
| **5778** | A2790 | 5k | multicolored | .25 | .25 |
| **5779** | A2790 | 10k | multicolored | .30 | .25 |
| **5780** | A2790 | 15k | multicolored | .50 | .35 |
| | | | *Nos. 5778-5780 (3)* | 1.05 | .85 |

Mukhina, by Nesterov A2791

**1989, June 25 Litho. *Perf. 12x12½***

**5781** A2791 5k chalky blue .50 .25

Vera I. Mukhina (1889-1953), sculptor.

13th World Youth and Student Festival, Pyongyang A2792

**1989, July 1 Litho. *Perf. 12***

**5782** A2792 10k multicolored .40 .25

Ducks A2793

No. 5783, Tadorna tadorna. No. 5784, Anas crecca. No. 5785, Tadorna ferruginea.

**1989, July 1**

| | | | | | |
|---|---|---|---|---|---|
| **5783** | A2793 | 5k | multicolored | .25 | .25 |
| **5784** | A2793 | 15k | multicolored | .35 | .25 |
| **5785** | A2793 | 20k | multicolored | .40 | .30 |
| *a.* | | Min. sheet, 2 5k, 4 15k, 3 20k | | 5.00 | 3.00 |
| | | | *Nos. 5783-5785 (3)* | 1.00 | .80 |

French Revolution, Bicent. A2794

Designs: 5k, PHILEXFRANCE '89 emblem and Storming of the Bastille. 15k, Marat, Danton, Robespierre. 20k, "La Marseillaise," from the Arc de Triomphe carved by Francois Rude (1784-1855).

**Photo. & Engr., Photo. (15k)**

**1989, July 7 *Perf. 11½***

| | | | | | |
|---|---|---|---|---|---|
| **5786** | A2794 | 5k | multicolored | .25 | .25 |
| **5787** | A2794 | 15k | multicolored | .35 | .25 |
| **5788** | A2794 | 20k | multicolored | .40 | .30 |
| *a.* | | Miniature sheet of 8 | | 9.00 | |
| | | | *Nos. 5786-5788 (3)* | 1.00 | .80 |

A2795

A2795a

A2795b

A2795c

Folklore and Legends A2795d

Designs: No. 5789, *Amiraniani*, Georgian lore. No. 5790, *Koroglu*, Azerbaijan lore. No. 5791, *Fir, Queen of the Grass-snakes*, Lithuanian lore. No. 5792, *Mioritsa*, Moldavian lore. No. 5793, *Lachplesis*, Latvian lore.

**1989, July 12 Litho. *Perf. 12x12½***

| | | | | | |
|---|---|---|---|---|---|
| **5789** | A2795 | 10k | multicolored | .40 | .25 |
| **5790** | A2795a | 10k | multicolored | .40 | .25 |
| **5791** | A2795b | 10k | multicolored | .40 | .25 |
| **5792** | A2795c | 10k | multicolored | .40 | .25 |
| **5793** | A2795d | 10k | multicolored | .40 | .25 |
| | | | *Nos. 5789-5793 (5)* | 2.00 | 1.25 |

Each printed with a se-tenant label. See types A2753-A2753d & #5890-5894.

Tallinn Zoo, 50th Anniv. — A2796

**1989, July 20 Photo. *Perf. 11½***

**5794** A2796 10k Lynx .50 .25

Intl. Letter Writing Week — A2797

**1989, July 20 Litho. *Perf. 12***

**5795** A2797 5k multicolored .40 .25

Exists imperf. Value, $35.

Pulkovskaya Observatory, 150th Anniv. — A2798

**Photo. & Engr.**

**1989, July 20 *Perf. 11½***

**5796** A2798 10k multicolored .50 .25

**Souvenir Sheet**

Peter the Great and Battle Scene — A2799

**1989, July 27 Photo. *Perf. 11½x12***

**5797** A2799 50k dk bl & dk brn 1.50 1.00

Battle of Hango, 275th anniv.

City of Nikolaev, Bicent. A2800

**1989, Aug. 3 Photo. *Perf. 11½***

**5798** A2800 5k multicolored .50 .25

80th Birth Anniv. of Kwame Nkrumah, 1st Pres. of Ghana — A2801

**1989, Aug. 9**

**5799** A2801 10k multicolored .40 .25

6th Congress of the All-Union Philatelic Soc., Moscow A2802

**1989, Aug. 9 *Perf. 12***

**5800** A2802 10k bl, blk & pink .50 .25

Printed se-tenant with label picturing simulated stamps and congress emblem.

James Fenimore Cooper (1789-1851), American Novelist A2803

**Photo. & Engr.**

**1989, Aug. 19 *Perf. 12x11½***

**5801** A2803 15k multicolored .50 .35

A2804

Soviet Circus Performers — A2805

Performers and scenes from their acts: 1k, V.L. Durov, clown and trainer. 3k, M.N. Rumyantsev, clown. 4k, V.I. Filatov, bear trainer. 5k, E.T. Kio, magician. 10k, V.E. Lazarenko, acrobat and clown. 30k, Moscow Circus, Tsvetnoi Boulevard.

**1989, Aug. 22 Litho. *Perf. 12***

| | | | | |
|---|---|---|---|---|
| **5802** | A2804 | 1k multicolored | .40 | .25 |
| **5803** | A2804 | 3k multicolored | .40 | .25 |
| **5804** | A2804 | 4k multicolored | .40 | .25 |
| **5805** | A2804 | 5k multicolored | .40 | .25 |
| **5806** | A2804 | 10k multicolored | .40 | .25 |
| | | *Nos. 5802-5806 (5)* | 2.00 | 1.25 |

**Souvenir Sheet**

***Perf. 12x12½***

| | | | | |
|---|---|---|---|---|
| **5807** | A2805 | 30k multicolored | 2.00 | .70 |

Nos. 5802-5806 exist imperf. Value, $30 each.

5th World Boxing Championships, Moscow — A2806

**1989, Aug. 25 Photo. *Perf. 11½***

| | | | | |
|---|---|---|---|---|
| **5808** | A2806 | 15k multicolored | .50 | .35 |

Aleksandr Popov (1859-1905), Inventor of Radio in Russia — A2807

Design: *Demonstration of the First Radio Receiver,* 1895, by N. Sysoev.

**1989, Oct. 5 Litho. *Perf. 12x12½***

| | | | | |
|---|---|---|---|---|
| **5809** | A2807 | 10k multicolored | .50 | .25 |

A2808

**1989, Oct. 7 Photo. *Perf. 11½***

| | | | | |
|---|---|---|---|---|
| **5810** | A2808 | 5k multicolored | .40 | .25 |

German Democratic Republic, 40th anniv.

Polish People's Republic, 45th Anniv. A2809

**1989, Oct. 7**

| | | | | |
|---|---|---|---|---|
| **5811** | A2809 | 5k multicolored | .50 | .25 |

**Party Leader Type of 1988**

**1989, Oct. 10 Engr. *Perf. 12***

| | | | | |
|---|---|---|---|---|
| **5812** | A2712 | 5k black | .40 | .25 |

S.V. Kosior (1889-1939).

A2811

**1989, Oct. 10**

| | | | | |
|---|---|---|---|---|
| **5813** | A2811 | 15k dark red brown | .60 | .25 |

Jawaharlal Nehru, 1st prime minister of independent India.

*Guardsmen of October,* by M.M. Chepik — A2812

**1989, Oct. 14 Litho. *Perf. 12½x12***

| | | | | |
|---|---|---|---|---|
| **5814** | A2812 | 5k multicolored | .40 | .25 |

October Revolution, 72nd anniv. Exists imperf. Value, $30.

Kosta Khetagurov (1859-1906), Ossetic Poet — A2813

**1989, Oct. 14**

| | | | | |
|---|---|---|---|---|
| **5815** | A2813 | 5k dark red brown | .40 | .25 |

Exists imperf.

A2814

**1989, Oct. 14 Photo. *Perf. 11½***

| | | | | |
|---|---|---|---|---|
| **5816** | A2814 | 5k buff, sepia & black | .50 | .25 |

Li Dazhao (1889-1927), communist party leader of China.

A2815

**1989, Oct. 20 Engr. *Perf. 12***

| | | | | |
|---|---|---|---|---|
| **5817** | A2815 | 5k black | .40 | .25 |

Jan Karlovich Berzin (1889-1938), army intelligence leader.

Russian — A2816

Musical Instruments: No. 5819, Byelorussian. No. 5820, Ukrainian. No. 5821, Uzbek.

**Photo. & Engr.**

**1989, Oct. 20 *Perf. 12x11½***

**Denomination Color**

| | | | | |
|---|---|---|---|---|
| **5818** | A2816 | 10k blue | .25 | .25 |
| **5819** | A2816 | 10k brown | .25 | .25 |
| **5820** | A2816 | 10k lemon | .25 | .25 |
| **5821** | A2816 | 10k blue green | .25 | .25 |
| | | *Nos. 5818-5821 (4)* | 1.00 | 1.00 |

See Nos. 5929-5932, 6047-6049.

Scenes from Novels by James Fenimore Cooper A2817

Designs: No. 5822, *The Hunter,* (settlers, canoe). No. 5823, *Last of the Mohicans* (Indians, settlers). No. 5824, *The Pathfinder,* (couple near cliff). No. 5825, *The Pioneers* (women, wild animals). No. 5826, *The Prairie* (injured Indians, horse).

**1989, Nov. 17 Litho. *Perf. 12x12½***

| | | | | |
|---|---|---|---|---|
| **5822** | A2817 | 20k multicolored | .60 | .40 |
| **5823** | A2817 | 20k multicolored | .60 | .40 |
| **5824** | A2817 | 20k multicolored | .60 | .40 |
| **5825** | A2817 | 20k multicolored | .60 | .40 |
| **5826** | A2817 | 20k multicolored | .60 | .40 |
| *a.* | | Strip of 5, #5822-5826 | 3.00 | 2.00 |

Printed in a continuous design.

Monuments A2818

No. 5827, Pokrovsky Cathedral, St. Basil's, statue of K. Minin and D. Pozharsky, Moscow. No. 5828, Petropavlovsky Cathedral, statue of Peter the Great, Leningrad. No. 5829, Sofiisky Cathedral, Bogdan Chmielnicki monument, Kiev. No. 5830, Khodzha Akhmed Yasavi Mausoleum, Turkestan. No. 5831, Khazret-Khyzr Mosque, Samarkand.

**1989, Nov. 20 *Perf. 11½***

**Color of "Sky"**

| | | | | |
|---|---|---|---|---|
| **5827** | A2818 | 15k tan | .40 | .30 |
| **5828** | A2818 | 15k gray green | .40 | .30 |
| **5829** | A2818 | 15k blue green | .40 | .30 |
| **5830** | A2818 | 15k violet blue | .40 | .30 |
| **5831** | A2818 | 15k bright blue | .40 | .30 |
| | | *Nos. 5827-5831 (5)* | 2.00 | 1.50 |

New Year 1990 A2819

**1989, Nov. 22 *Perf. 12***

| | | | | |
|---|---|---|---|---|
| **5832** | A2819 | 5k multicolored | .50 | .25 |

Space Achievements A2820

Designs: Nos. 5833, 5837a, Unmanned Soviet probe on the Moon. Nos. 5834, 5837b, American astronaut on Moon, 1969. Nos. 5835, 5837c, Soviet cosmonaut and American astronaut on Mars. Nos. 5836, 5837d, Mars, planetary body, diff.

**1989, Nov. 24**

| | | | | |
|---|---|---|---|---|
| **5833** | A2820 | 25k multicolored | .75 | .55 |
| **5834** | A2820 | 25k multicolored | .75 | .55 |
| **5835** | A2820 | 25k multicolored | .75 | .55 |
| **5836** | A2820 | 25k multicolored | .75 | .55 |
| *a.* | | Block of 4, #5833-5836 | 3.00 | 2.20 |

**Souvenir Sheet**

***Imperf***

| | | | | |
|---|---|---|---|---|
| **5837** | | Sheet of 4 | 2.25 | 1.50 |
| *a.-d.* | | A2820 25k any single | .50 | .35 |

World Stamp Expo '89, Washington DC, Nov. 17-Dec. 3; 20th UPU Cong.

See US No. C126.

**Type of 1988**

**Dated 1988**

**1989, Dec. 25 Litho. *Perf. 12x12½***

| | | | | |
|---|---|---|---|---|
| **5838** | A2765 | 1k dark brown | .25 | .25 |
| **5839** | A2765 | 3k dark blue green | .25 | .25 |
| **5840** | A2765 | 4k indigo | .25 | .25 |
| **5841** | A2765 | 5k red | .25 | .25 |
| **5842** | A2765 | 10k claret | .30 | .25 |
| **5843** | A2765 | 15k deep blue | .45 | .30 |
| **5844** | A2765 | 20k olive gray | .60 | .40 |
| **5845** | A2765 | 25k dark green | .75 | .50 |
| **5846** | A2765 | 30k dark blue | .90 | .60 |
| **5847** | A2765 | 35k dark red brown | 1.00 | .70 |
| **5848** | A2765 | 50k sapphire | 1.50 | 1.00 |
| **5849** | A2765 | 1r blue gray | 3.50 | 2.00 |
| | | *Nos. 5838-5849 (12)* | 10.00 | 6.75 |

For surcharges see Uzbekistan #15, 22, 25-26, 61B, 61D, 61F.

**Admirals Type of 1987**

**Miniature Sheet**

Admirals & battle scenes: 5k, V.A. Kornilov (1806-54). 10k, V.I. Istomin (1809-55). 15k, G.I. Nevelskoi (1813-76). 20k, G.I. Butakov (1820-82). 30k, A.A. Popov (1821-98). 35k, Stepan O. Makarov (1849-1904).

**1989, Dec. 28 Engr. *Perf. 12½x12***

| | | | | |
|---|---|---|---|---|
| **5850** | | Sheet of 6 | 6.00 | 2.00 |
| *a.* | A2705 | 5k brown & Prus blue | .25 | .25 |
| *b.* | A2705 | 10k brown & Prus blue | .25 | .25 |
| *c.* | A2705 | 15k dark blue & Prus blue | .40 | .25 |
| *d.* | A2705 | 20k dark blue & Prus blue | .50 | .05 |
| *e.* | A2705 | 30k brown & Prus blue | .85 | .50 |
| *f.* | A2705 | 35k brown & Prus blue | 1.00 | .60 |

Global Ecology — A2821

10k, Flower dying, industrial waste entering the environment. 15k, Bird caught in industrial waste, Earth. 20k, Sea of chopped trees.

**1990, Jan. 5 Photo. *Perf. 11½***

| | | | | |
|---|---|---|---|---|
| **5851** | A2821 | 10k multicolored | .35 | .25 |
| **5852** | A2821 | 15k multicolored | .50 | .35 |
| **5853** | A2821 | 20k multicolored | .65 | .45 |
| | | *Nos. 5851-5853 (3)* | 1.50 | 1.05 |

**Capitals of the Republics**

A2822

A2822a

A2822b

A2822c

A2822d

A2822e

A2822f

A2822g

A2822h

A2822i

A2822j

A2822k

A2822l

A2822m

A2822n

**1990, Jan. 18 Litho. *Perf. 12x12½***

| | | | | | |
|---|---|---|---|---|---|
| **5854** | A2822 | 5k | Moscow | .30 | .25 |
| **5855** | A2822a | 5k | Tallinn | .30 | .25 |
| **5856** | A2822b | 5k | Riga | .30 | .25 |
| **5857** | A2822c | 5k | Vilnius | .30 | .25 |
| **5858** | A2822d | 5k | Minsk | .30 | .25 |
| **5859** | A2822e | 5k | Kiev | .30 | .25 |
| **5860** | A2822f | 5k | Kishinev | .30 | .25 |
| **5861** | A2822g | 5k | Tbilisi | .30 | .25 |
| **5862** | A2822h | 5k | Yerevan | .30 | .25 |
| **5863** | A2822i | 5k | Baku | .30 | .25 |
| **5864** | A2822j | 5k | Alma-Ata | .30 | .25 |
| **5865** | A2822k | 5k | Tashkent | .30 | .25 |
| **5866** | A2822l | 5k | Frunze | .30 | .25 |
| **5867** | A2822m | 5k | Ashkhabad | .30 | .25 |
| **5868** | A2822n | 5k | Dushanbe | .30 | .25 |
| | | | *Nos. 5854-5868 (15)* | 4.50 | 3.75 |

A2823

**1990, Feb. 3 *Perf. 11½***

| | | | | | |
|---|---|---|---|---|---|
| **5869** | A2823 | 10k | black & brown | .50 | .25 |

Ho Chi Minh (1890-1969).

A2824

**1990, Feb. 3 Photo.**

| | | | | | |
|---|---|---|---|---|---|
| **5870** | A2824 | 5k | multicolored | .50 | .25 |

Vietnamese Communist Party, 60th anniv.

Owls
A2825

***Perf. 12x12½, 12½x12***

**1990, Feb. 8 Litho.**

| | | | | | |
|---|---|---|---|---|---|
| **5871** | A2825 | 10k | Nyctea scandiaca | .30 | .25 |
| *a.* | | | Miniature sheet of 8 | 6.00 | |
| **5872** | A2825 | 20k | Bubo bubo, vert. | .60 | .40 |
| **5873** | A2825 | 35k | Asio otus | 1.60 | 1.00 |
| | | | *Nos. 5871-5873 (3)* | 2.50 | 1.65 |

Penny Black, 150th Anniv.
A2826

Emblems and various Penny Blacks: No. 5875, Position TP. No. 5876, Position TF. No. 5877, Position AH. No. 5878, Position VK. No. 5879, Position AE.

**1990, Feb. 15 Photo. *Perf. 11½***

| | | | | | |
|---|---|---|---|---|---|
| **5874** | A2826 | 10k | shown | .35 | .25 |
| **5875** | A2826 | 20k | gold & black | .50 | .35 |
| *a.* | | | Miniature sheet of 8 | 6.50 | |
| **5876** | A2826 | 20k | gold & black | .50 | .35 |
| *a.* | | | Miniature sheet of 8 | 6.50 | |
| **5877** | A2826 | 35k | multicolored | .85 | .55 |
| **5878** | A2826 | 35k | multicolored | .85 | .55 |
| | | | *Nos. 5874-5878 (5)* | 3.05 | 2.05 |

**Souvenir Sheet**

***Perf. 12x11½***

| | | | | | |
|---|---|---|---|---|---|
| **5879** | A2826 | 1r | dk green & blk | 4.00 | 2.00 |

Stamp World London '90 (35k).
No. 5879 contains one 37x26mm stamp.

ITU, 125th Anniv.
A2827

**1990, Feb. 20 Photo. *Perf. 11½***

| | | | | | |
|---|---|---|---|---|---|
| **5880** | A2827 | 20k | multicolored | .50 | .35 |

Labor Day
A2828

**1990, Mar. 28 Photo. *Perf. 11½***

| | | | | | |
|---|---|---|---|---|---|
| **5881** | A2828 | 5k | multicolored | .40 | .25 |

*Victory, 1945*, by A. Lysenko
A2829

**1990, Mar. 28 Litho. *Perf. 12x12½***

| | | | | | |
|---|---|---|---|---|---|
| **5882** | A2829 | 5k | multicolored | .50 | .25 |

End of World War II, 45th anniv.

Mir Space Station, Cosmonaut
A2830

**1990, Apr. 12**

| | | | | | |
|---|---|---|---|---|---|
| **5883** | A2830 | 20k | multicolored | .50 | .35 |
| *a.* | | | Miniature sheet of 8 | 5.00 | |

Cosmonauts' Day.

Lenin, 120th Birth Anniv. — A2831

**1990, Apr. 14 Engr. *Perf. 11½***

| | | | | | |
|---|---|---|---|---|---|
| **5884** | A2831 | 5k | red brown | .40 | .25 |

LENINIANA '90 all-union philatelic exhibition.

**Lenin Birthday Type of 1988**

Portrait of Lenin and: No. 5885, Lenin Memorial (birthplace), Ulyanovsk. No. 5886, Branch of the Central Lenin Museum, Baku. No. 5887, Branch of the Central Lenin Museum, Tashkent.

**1990, Apr. 14 Litho. *Perf. 12***

| | | | | | |
|---|---|---|---|---|---|
| **5885** | A2727 | 5k | dark car & multi | .30 | .25 |
| **5886** | A2727 | 5k | rose vio & multi | .30 | .25 |
| **5887** | A2727 | 5k | dark grn & multi | .30 | .25 |
| | | | *Nos. 5885-5887 (3)* | .90 | .75 |

Lenin, 120th Birth Anniv.

Tchaikovsky, Scene from *Iolanta* — A2832

**1990, Apr. 25 Engr. *Perf. 12½x12***

| | | | | | |
|---|---|---|---|---|---|
| **5888** | A2832 | 15k | black | 1.00 | .35 |

Tchaikovsky (1840-1893), composer.

Kalmyk Legend *Dzhangar*, 550th Anniv. — A2833

**1990, May 22 Litho. *Perf. 12x12½***

| | | | | | |
|---|---|---|---|---|---|
| **5889** | A2833 | 10k | blk & blk brn | .50 | .25 |

**Folklore Type of 1989**

Designs: No. 5890, *Manas*, Kirghiz legend (Warrior with saber leading battle). No. 5891, *Guraguli*, Tadzhik legend (Armored warriors and elephant). No. 5892, *David Sasunsky*, Armenian legend (Men, arches), vert. No. 5893, *Gerogly*, Turkmen legend (Sleeping woman, man with lute), vert. No. 5894, *Kalevipoeg*, Estonian legend (Man with boards), vert. Nos. 5890-5894 printed se-tenant with descriptive label.

**1990, May 22 *Perf. 12½x12, 12x12½***

| | | | | | |
|---|---|---|---|---|---|
| **5890** | A2795 | 10k | multicolored | .40 | .25 |
| **5891** | A2795 | 10k | multicolored | .40 | .25 |
| **5892** | A2795 | 10k | multicolored | .40 | .25 |
| **5893** | A2795 | 10k | multicolored | .40 | .25 |
| **5894** | A2795 | 10k | multicolored | .40 | .25 |
| | | | *Nos. 5890-5894 (5)* | 2.00 | 1.25 |

World Cup Soccer Championships, Italy 1990 — A2834

Various soccer players.

**1990, May 25 *Perf. 12x12½***

| | | | | | |
|---|---|---|---|---|---|
| **5895** | A2834 | 5k | multicolored | .25 | .25 |
| *a.* | | | Miniature sheet of 8 | 4.00 | |
| **5896** | A2834 | 10k | multicolored | .30 | .25 |
| *a.* | | | Miniature sheet of 8 | 6.00 | |
| **5897** | A2834 | 15k | multicolored | .40 | .30 |
| **5898** | A2834 | 25k | multicolored | .70 | .55 |
| **5899** | A2834 | 35k | multicolored | .90 | .75 |
| *a.* | | | Strip of 5, #5895-5899 | 3.00 | 2.00 |

A2835

**1990, June 5 Litho. *Perf. 11½***

| | | | | | |
|---|---|---|---|---|---|
| **5900** | A2835 | 15k | multicolored | .50 | .30 |

Final agreement, European Conference on Security and Cooperation, 15th anniv.

45th World Shooting Championships, Moscow — A2836

**1990, June 5 Photo.**

| | | | | | |
|---|---|---|---|---|---|
| **5901** | A2836 | 15k | multicolored | .50 | .30 |

Cooperation in Antarctic Research
A2837

**1990, June 13 Litho. *Perf. 12x12½***

| | | | | | |
|---|---|---|---|---|---|
| **5902** | A2837 | 5k | Scientists on ice | .35 | .25 |
| **5903** | A2837 | 50k | Krill | 1.60 | 1.00 |
| *a.* | | | Souv. sheet of 2, #5902-5903 | 2.00 | |

See Australia Nos. 1182-1183.

Goodwill Games
A2838

**1990, June 14 Litho. *Perf. 11½***

| | | | | | |
|---|---|---|---|---|---|
| **5904** | A2838 | 10k | multicolored | .50 | .25 |

Souvenir Sheet

Battle of the Neva River, 750th Anniv. — A2839

**1990, June 20 Litho. *Perf. 12½x12***
**5905** A2839 50k multicolored 2.00 1.25

Duck Conservation — A2840

5k, Anas platyrhychos. 15k, Bucephala clangula. 20k, Netta rufina.

**1990, July 1 Litho. *Perf. 12***
**5906** A2840 5k multicolored .25 .25
**5907** A2840 15k multicolored .30 .25
**5908** A2840 20k multicolored .45 .25
*a.* Miniature sheet of 9 4.00
*Nos. 5906-5908 (3)* 1.00 .75

Nos. 5906-5908 exists imperf.

Poultry A2841

5k, Obroshinsky geese. 10k, Adler rooster & hen. 15k, North Caucasian turkeys.

**1990, July 1 *Perf. 12x12½***
**5909** A2841 5k multicolored .30 .25
**5910** A2841 10k multicolored .30 .25
**5911** A2841 15k multicolored .30 .35
*Nos. 5909-5911 (3)* .90 .85

Spaso-Efrosinievsky Monastery, Polotsk — A2842

Statue of Nicholas Baratashvili and Pantheon, Mtasminda A2843

Palace of Shirvanshahs, Baku A2844

Statue of Stefan III the Great, Kishinev — A2845

St. Nshan's Church, Akhpat — A2846

Historic Architecture: No. 5915, Cathedral, Vilnius. No. 5917, St. Peter's Church, Riga. No. 5919, Niguliste Church, Tallinn.

**1990, Aug. 1 Litho. *Perf. 11½***
**5912** A2842 15k multicolored .40 .25
**5913** A2843 15k multicolored .40 .25
**5914** A2844 15k multicolored .40 .25
**5915** A2842 15k multicolored .40 .25
**5916** A2845 15k multicolored .40 .25
**5917** A2842 15k multicolored .40 .25
**5918** A2846 15k multicolored .40 .25
**5919** A2842 15k multicolored .40 .25
*Nos. 5912-5919 (8)* 3.20 2.00

See Nos. 5968-5970.

Prehistoric Animals — A2847

**1990, Aug. 15**
**5920** A2847 1k Sordes .25 .25
**5921** A2847 3k Chalicotherium .25 .25
**5922** A2847 5k Indricotherium .25 .25
**5923** A2847 10k Saurolophus .25 .25
**5924** A2847 20k Thyestes .50 .35
*Nos. 5920-5924 (5)* 1.50 1.35

Nos. 5921-5923 vert.

Indian Child's Drawing of the Kremlin A2848

No. 5926, Russian child's drawing of India.

**1990, Aug. 15 *Perf. 12***
**5925** A2848 10k multicolored .40 .25
**5926** A2848 10k multicolored .40 .25
*a.* Pair, #5925-5926 1.00 .50

See India Nos. 1318-1319.

Letter Writing Week — A2849

**1990, Sept. 12 Engr. *Perf. 12x11½***
**5927** A2849 5k blue .50 .25

Traffic Safety — A2850

**1990, Sept. 12 Litho. *Perf. 11½***
**5928** A2850 5k multicolored .50 .25

**Musical Instruments Type of 1989**

#5929, Kazakh. #5930, Georgian. #5931, Azerbaijanian. #5932, Lithuanian.

**Photo. & Engr.**
**1990, Sept. 20 *Perf. 12x11½***
**Denomination Color**
**5929** A2816 10k brown .35 .25
**5930** A2816 10k green .35 .25
**5931** A2816 10k orange .35 .25
**5932** A2816 10k blue .35 .25
*Nos. 5929-5932 (4)* 1.40 1.00

Killer Whales A2855

Northern Sea Lions A2856

Sea Otter A2857

Common Dolphin A2858

**1990, Oct. 3 Litho. *Perf. 12x11½***
**5933** A2855 25k multicolored .45 .30
**5934** A2856 25k multicolored .45 .30
**5935** A2857 25k multicolored .45 .30
**5936** A2858 25k multicolored .45 .30
*a.* Block of 4, #5933-5936 2.00 1.50

See US Nos. 2508-2511.

October Revolution, 73rd Anniv. — A2859

Design: Lenin Among the Delegates to the 2nd Congress of Soviets, by S.V. Gerasimov.

**1990, Oct. 10 Litho. *Perf. 12x12½***
**5937** A2859 5k multicolored .50 .25

Nobel Laureates in Literature — A2860

#5938, Ivan A. Bunin (1870-1953). #5939, Boris Pasternak (1890-1960). #5940, Mikhail A. Sholokov (1905-1984).

**1990, Oct. 22 *Perf. 12***
**5938** A2860 15k brown olive .50 .25
**5939** A2860 15k bluish black .50 .25
**5940** A2860 15k black .50 .25
*Nos. 5938-5940 (3)* 1.50 .75

Submarines — A2861

**1990, Nov. 14 Litho. *Perf. 12***
**5941** A2861 5k Sever-2 .25 .25
**5942** A2861 10k Tinro-2 .25 .25
**5943** A2861 15k Argus .25 .25
**5944** A2861 25k Paisis .60 .45
**5945** A2861 35k Mir .75 .50
*Nos. 5941-5945 (5)* 2.10 1.70

A2862

Armenia-Mother Monument by E. Kochar.

**1990, Nov. 27 Litho. *Perf. 11½***
**5946** A2862 10k multicolored .50 .25

Armenia '90 Philatelic Exhibition.

A2863

Soviet Agents: #5947, Rudolf I. Abel (1903-71). #5948, Kim Philby (1912-88). #5949, Konon T. Molody (1922-70). #5950, S.A. Vaupshasov (1899-1976). #5951, I.D. Kudrya (1912-42).

**1990, Nov. 29 Photo. *Perf. 11½***
**5947** A2863 5k black & brown .40 .25
**5948** A2863 5k black & bluish blk .40 .25
**5949** A2863 5k black & yel brown .40 .25
**5950** A2863 5k black & yel green .40 .25
**5951** A2863 5k black & brown .40 .25
*Nos. 5947-5951 (5)* 2.00 1.25

Joint Soviet-Japanese Space Flight — A2864

**1990, Dec. 2 Litho. *Perf. 12***
**5952** A2864 20k multicolored .75 .50

Happy New Year — A2865

**1990, Dec. 3 *Perf. 11½***
**5953** A2865 5k multicolored .50 .25
*b.* Miniature sheet of 8 4.00

Charter for a New Europe — A2865a

**1990, Dec. 31 Litho. *Perf. 11½***

**5953A** A2865a 30k Globe, Eiffel Tower .75 .50

Marine Life A2866

4k, Rhizostoma pulmo. 5k, Anemonia sulcata. 10k, Squalus acanthias. 15k, Engraulis encrasicolus. 20k, Tursiops truncatus.

**1991, Jan. 4 Litho. *Perf. 12***

**5954** A2866 4k multicolored .25 .25
**5955** A2866 5k multicolored .25 .25
**5956** A2866 10k multicolored .35 .25
**5957** A2866 15k multicolored .50 .35
**5958** A2866 20k multicolored .65 .45
*Nos. 5954-5958 (5)* 2.00 1.55

Chernobyl Nuclear Disaster, 5th Anniv. A2867

**1991, Jan. 22 *Perf. 11½***

**5959** A2867 15k multicolored .50 .25

Sorrento Coast with View of Capri, 1826, by S.F. Shchedrin (1791-1830) — A2868

Evening in the Ukraine, 1878, by A.I. Kuindzhi (1841-1910) — A2869

Paintings: No. 5961, New Rome, St. Angel's Castle, 1823, by Shchedrin. No. 5963, Birch Grove, 1879, by Kuindzhi.

**1991, Jan. 25 *Perf. 12½x12***

**5960** A2868 10k multicolored .35 .25
**5961** A2868 10k multicolored .35 .25
*a.* Pair, #5960-5961+label .75 .50
**5962** A2869 10k multicolored .35 .25
**5963** A2869 10k multicolored .35 .25
*a.* Pair, #5962-5963+label .75 .50
*Nos. 5960-5963 (4)* 1.40 1.00

Paul Keres (1916-1975), Chess Grandmaster — A2870

**1991, Jan. 7 Litho. *Perf. 11½***

**5964** A2870 15k dark brown .50 .35

Environmental Protection — A2871

Designs: 10k, Bell tower near Kaliazin, Volga River region. 15k, Lake Baikal. 20k, Desert zone of former Aral Sea.

**1991, Feb. 5 Litho. *Perf. 11½***

**5965** A2871 10k multicolored .35 .25
**5966** A2871 15k multicolored .50 .35
**5967** A2871 20k multicolored .65 .45
*Nos. 5965-5967 (3)* 1.50 1.05

Moslem Tower, Uzgen, Kirghizia A2872

Mukhammed Bashar Mausoleum, Tadzhikstan A2873

Talkhatan-baba Mosque, Turkmenistan A2874

**1991, Mar. 5**

**5968** A2872 15k multicolored .30 .25
**5969** A2873 15k multicolored .30 .25
**5970** A2874 15k multicolored .30 .25
*Nos. 5968-5970 (3)* .90 .75

See Nos. 5912-5919.

Russian Settlements in America — A2875

Designs: 20k, G. I. Shelekhov (1747-1795), Alaska colonizer. 30k, A. A. Baranov, (1746-1819), first governor of Russian America. 50k, I. A. Kuskov, founder of Fort Ross, California.

**1991, Mar. 14 *Perf. 12x11½***

**5971** A2875 20k brt blue & black .35 .25
**5972** A2875 30k olive brn & blk .65 .45
**5973** A2875 50k red brn & black 1.10 .60
*Nos. 5971-5973 (3)* 2.10 1.30

Yuri A. Gagarin A2876

Inscription, Nos. 5977c, 5977e

**1991, Apr. 6 *Perf. 11½x12***

**5974** A2876 25k Pilot .75 .50
**5975** A2876 25k Cosmonaut .75 .50
**5976** A2876 25k Pilot, wearing hat .75 .50
**5977** A2876 25k As civilian .75 .50
*a.* Block of 4, #5974-5977 3.00 2.50
*b.* Sheet of 4, #5974-5977, imperf. 4.00 2.80
*c.* As "b," inscribed 10.00 5.00
*d.* Sheet, 2 each, #5974-5977, Perf. 12x11½ 10.00 6.00
*e.* As "d," inscribed 10.00 6.00

Nos. 5977b-5977c have simulated perforations.

May 1945 by A. and S. Tkachev A2877

**1991, Apr. 10 *Perf. 12***

**5978** A2877 5k multicolored .50 .25

World War II Victory Day.

Asia and Pacific Transport Network, 10th Anniv. — A2878

**1991, Apr. 15 *Perf. 11½***

**5979** A2878 10k multicolored .50 .25

**Type of 1988 Dated 1991**

Designs: 2k, Early ship, train, and carriage. 7k, Airplane, helicopter, ocean liner, cable car, van. 12k, Space shuttle. 13k, Space station.

**1991, Apr. 15 Litho. *Perf. 12x12½***

**5984** A2765 2k orange brown .50 .25
*a.* Imperf .50 .25
**5985** A2765 7k bright blue .50 .25
*a.* Perf. 12x11½, photo. .50 .25
**5986** A2765 12k dk lilac rose .90 .30
**5987** A2765 13k deep violet 1.00 .35
*Nos. 5984-5987 (4)* 2.90 1.15

Nos. 5984-5987 were also issued on chalky paper. Vaue, $4.

For surcharges see Tadjikistan #10-11, Uzbekistan #18, 61C.

Lenin, 121st Birth Anniv. A2879

Painting: Lenin working on "Materialism and Empirical Criticism" by P.P. Belousov.

**1991, Apr. 22 Litho. *Perf. 12***

**5992** A2879 5k multicolored .50 .25

Sergei Prokofiev (1891-1953), Composer — A2880

**1991, Apr. 23 *Perf. 12½x12***

**5993** A2880 15k brown .60 .40

Orchids — A2881

3k, Cypripedium calceolus. 5k, Orchis purpurea. 10k, Ophrys apifera. 20k, Calypso bulbosa. 25k, Epipactis palustris.

**1991, May 7 *Perf. 12***

**5994** A2881 3k multicolored .25 .25
**5995** A2881 5k multicolored .25 .25
**5996** A2881 10k multicolored .25 .25
**5997** A2881 20k multicolored .30 .25
**5998** A2881 25k multicolored .45 .25
*Nos. 5994-5998 (5)* 1.50 1.25

A2882

Nobel Prize Winners: No. 5999, Ivan P. Pavlov (1849-1936), 1904, Physiology. No. 6000, Elie Metchnikoff (1845-1916), 1908, Physiology. No. 6001, Andrei D. Sakharov, (1921-89), 1975, Peace.

**1991, May 14**

**5999** A2882 15k black .50 .30
**6000** A2882 15k black .50 .30
**6001** A2882 15k blue black .50 .30
*Nos. 5999-6001 (3)* 1.50 .90

William Saroyan (1908-1981), American Writer — A2883

**1991, May 22 *Perf. 11½***

**6002** A2883 1r multicolored 3.00 2.25

See United States No. 2538.

Russia-Great Britain Joint Space Mission — A2884

**1991, May 18 Litho. *Perf. 12***

**6003** A2884 20k multicolored .75 .50

Cultural Heritage A2885

Designs: 10k, Miniature from "Ostomirov Gospel," by Sts. Cyril & Methodius, 1056-1057. 15k, "Russian Truth," manuscript, 11th-13th century by Jaroslav Mudrin. 20k, Sergei Radonezhski by Troitse Sergeiev Lavra, 1424. 25k, Trinity, icon by Andrei Rublev, c. 1411. 30k, Illustration from "Book of the Apostles," by Ivan Feodorov and Petr Mstislavetz, 1564.

**1991, June 20 Litho. *Perf. 12x12½***

**6004** A2885 10k multicolored .35 .25
**6005** A2885 15k multicolored .55 .35
**6006** A2885 20k multicolored .70 .50
*a.* Miniature sheet of 8 4.00
**6007** A2885 25k multicolored .90 .60
*a.* Miniature sheet of 8 4.00
**6008** A2885 30k multicolored 1.00 .80
*a.* Strip of #6004-6008 5.00 3.00

Ducks A2886

Designs: 5k, Anas acuta. 15k, Aythya marila. 20k, Oxyura leucocephala.

**1991, July 1 *Perf. 12***

**6009** A2886 5k multicolored .25 .25
**6010** A2886 15k multicolored .35 .35
**6011** A2886 20k multicolored .45 .45
*a.* Min. sheet of 9, 2 #6009, 4 #6010, 3 #6011 4.25 3.25
*Nos. 6009-6011 (3)* 1.05 1.05

Airships A2887

Designs: 1k, Albatross, 1910, vert. 3k, GA-42, 1987, vert. 4k, Norge, 1923. 5k, Victory, 1944. 20k, Graf Zeppelin, 1928.

**1991, July 18**

**6012** A2887 1k multicolored .40 .25
**6013** A2887 3k multicolored .40 .25
**6014** A2887 4k multicolored .40 .25
**6015** A2887 5k multicolored .40 .25
**6016** A2887 20k multicolored .40 .25
*a.* Miniature sheet of 8 4.00
*Nos. 6012-6016 (5)* 2.00 1.25

**Types of 1984**

2r, Ship, Arctic map. 3r, Child & globe. 5r, Palm frond and globe.

**1991-92 Litho. *Perf. 12½x12***

**6016B** A2529 2r dark gray .50 .25
*c.* Imperf. 1.00 .50
**6017** A2529 3r gray 5.00 2.50
**6017A** A2529 5r blue 4.00 1.50
*Nos. 6016B-6017A (3)* 9.50 4.25

Issued: 3r, 6/25; 5r, 11/10; No. 6016B, 8/22/91; No. 6016Bc, 4/20/92.

Conf. on Security and Cooperation in Europe — A2888

**1991, July 1 Photo. *Perf. 11½***

**6018** A2888 10k multicolored .50 .25

Bering & Chirikov's Voyage to Alaska, 250th Anniv. — A2889

Design: No. 6020, Sailing ship, map.

**1991, July 27 *Perf. 12x11½***

**6019** A2889 30k multicolored .50 .25
**6020** A2889 30k multicolored .50 .25

A2890

**1991, Aug. 1 *Perf. 12***

**6021** A2890 30k multicolored .50 .25

Ukrainian declaration of sovereignty.

A2891

**1991, Aug. 1 *Perf. 12x11½***

**6022** A2891 7k brown 1.00 .25

Letter Writing Week.

1992 Summer Olympic Games, Barcelona A2892

**1991, Sept. 4 Litho. *Perf. 12x12½***

**6023** A2892 10k Canoeing .25 .25
*a.* Miniature sheet of 8 5.00
**6024** A2892 20k Running .30 .25
*a.* Miniature sheet of 8 5.00
**6025** A2892 30k Soccer .45 .25
*a.* Miniature sheet of 8 5.00
*Nos. 6023-6025 (3)* 1.00 .75

Victims of Aug. 1991 Failed Coup — A2893

Citizens Protecting Russian "White House" — A2893a

No. 6026, Vladimir Usov, b. 1954. No. 6027, Illya Krichevsky, b. 1963. No. 6028, Dmitry Komar, b. 1968.

**1991, Oct. 11 Litho. *Perf. 11½***

**6026** A2893 7k multicolored .30 .25
**6027** A2893 7k multicolored .30 .25
**6028** A2893 7k multicolored .30 .25
*Nos. 6026-6028 (3)* .90 .75

**Souvenir Sheet**

**6029** A2893a 50k multicolored 2.00 .50

USSR-Austria Joint Space Mission — A2894

**1991, Oct. 2 Litho. *Perf. 11½***

**6030** A2894 20k multicolored .50 .25

**Folk Holidays**

Ascension, Armenia A2895

New Year, Azerbaijan A2895a

Ivan Kupala Day, Byelorussia A2895b

New Year, Estonia A2895c

Berikaoba, Georgia A2895d

Kazakhstan — A2895e

Kys Kumai, Kirgizia — A2895f

Ivan Kupala Day, Latvia — A2895g

Palm Sunday, Lithuania A2895h

Plugushorul, Moldavia A2895i

Shrovetide, Russia — A2895j

New Year, Tadzhikistan A2895k

Harvest, Turkmenistan — A2895l

Christmas, Ukraine — A2895m

Spring Tulips, Uzbekistan A2895n

***Perf. 12x12½, 12½x12***

**1991, Oct. 4** **Litho.**

| | | | | |
|---|---|---|---|---|
| **6031** | A2895 | 15k multicolored | .25 | .25 |
| **6032** | A2895a | 15k multicolored | .25 | .25 |
| **6033** | A2895b | 15k multicolored | .25 | .25 |
| **6034** | A2895c | 15k multicolored | .25 | .25 |
| **6035** | A2895d | 15k multicolored | .25 | .25 |
| **6036** | A2895e | 15k multicolored | .25 | .25 |
| **6037** | A2895f | 15k multicolored | .25 | .25 |
| **6038** | A2895g | 15k multicolored | .25 | .25 |
| **6039** | A2895h | 15k multicolored | .25 | .25 |
| **6040** | A2895i | 15k multicolored | .25 | .25 |
| **6041** | A2895j | 15k multicolored | .25 | .25 |
| **6042** | A2895k | 15k multicolored | .25 | .25 |
| **6043** | A2895l | 15k multicolored | .25 | .25 |
| **6044** | A2895m | 15k multicolored | .25 | .25 |
| **6045** | A2895n | 15k multicolored | .25 | .25 |
| *a.* | | Min. sheet, 2 each #6031-6045 | *10.00* | |
| | | *Nos. 6031-6045 (15)* | 3.75 | 3.75 |

A2896

**1991, Oct. 29** **Litho.** ***Perf. 11½***

| | | | | |
|---|---|---|---|---|
| **6046** | A2896 | 7k multicolored | .50 | .25 |

Election of Boris Yeltsin, 1st president of Russian Republic, June 12, 1991.

**Musical Instruments Type of 1989**

Musical Instruments: No. 6047, Moldavia. No. 6048, Latvia. No. 6049, Kirgiz.

**Photo. & Engr.**

**1991, Nov. 19** ***Perf. 12x11½***

**Denomination Color**

| | | | | |
|---|---|---|---|---|
| **6047** | A2816 | 10k red | .50 | .25 |
| **6048** | A2816 | 10k brt greenish bl | .50 | .25 |
| **6049** | A2816 | 10k red lilac | .50 | .25 |
| | | *Nos. 6047-6049 (3)* | 1.50 | .75 |

New Year 1992 A2897

**1991, Dec. 8** **Litho.** ***Perf. 12x12½***

| | | | | |
|---|---|---|---|---|
| **6050** | A2897 | 7k multicolored | .50 | .25 |
| *a.* | | Miniature sheet of 8 | 4.00 | |

A2899

Russian Historians: No. 6052, V. N. Tatischev (1686-1750). No. 6053, N. M. Karamzin (1766-1826). No. 6054, S. M. Soloviev (1820-79). No. 6055, Vasili O. Klyuchevsky (1841-1911).

**1991, Dec. 12** **Photo. & Engr.**

| | | | | |
|---|---|---|---|---|
| **6052** | A2899 | 10k multicolored | .50 | .25 |
| **6053** | A2899 | 10k multicolored | .50 | .25 |
| **6054** | A2899 | 10k multicolored | .50 | .25 |
| **6055** | A2899 | 10k multicolored | .50 | .25 |
| | | *Nos. 6052-6055 (4)* | 2.00 | 1.00 |

**With the breakup of the Soviet Union on Dec. 26, 1991, eleven former Soviet republics established the Commonwealth of Independent States. Stamps inscribed "Rossija" are issued by the Russian Republic.**

1992 Winter Olympics, Albertville — A2900

14k, Cross-country skiing, ski jumping. 1r, Freestyle skiing. 2r, Bobsleds.

**1992, Jan. 10** **Litho.** ***Perf. 11½x12***

| | | | | |
|---|---|---|---|---|
| **6056** | A2900 | 14k multicolored | .45 | .25 |
| *a.* | | Miniature sheet of 8 | 2.75 | |
| **6057** | A2900 | 1r multicolored | .50 | .25 |
| *a.* | | Miniature sheet of 8 | 3.25 | |
| **6058** | A2900 | 2r multicolored | 1.00 | .25 |
| *a.* | | Miniature sheet of 8 | 5.00 | |
| | | *Nos. 6056-6058 (3)* | 1.95 | .75 |

Souvenir Sheet

Battle on the Ice, 750th Anniv. — A2901

**1992, Feb. 20** **Litho.** ***Perf. 12½x12***

| | | | | |
|---|---|---|---|---|
| **6059** | A2901 | 50k multicolored | 1.00 | .65 |

A2902

Designs: 10k, Golden Portal, Vladimir. 15k, Kremlin, Pskov. 20k, 50k, St. George Slaying the Dragon. 25k, 55k, Triumph Gate, Moscow. 30k, 80k, "Millennium of Russia," by M.O. Mikeshin, Novgorod. 60k, Minin-Posharsky Monument, Moscow. 1r, Church, Kizhi. 1.50r, Monument to Peter the Great, St. Petersburg. 2r, St. Basil's Cathedral, Moscow. 3r, Tretyakov Gallery, Moscow. 5r, Morosov House, Moscow. 10r, St. Isaac's Cathedral, St. Petersburg. 25r, Monument to Yuri Dolgoruky, Moscow. 100r, Kremlin, Moscow.

***Perf. 12½x12, 11½x12 (15k, 25k, 3r)***

**1992** **Litho.**

| | | | | |
|---|---|---|---|---|
| **6060** | A2902 | 10k salmon | .45 | .25 |
| **6060A** | A2902 | 15k dark brn | .45 | .25 |
| **6061** | A2902 | 20k red | .45 | .25 |
| **6062** | A2902 | 25k red brown | .45 | .25 |
| **6063** | A2902 | 30k black | .45 | .25 |
| **6064** | A2902 | 50k dark blue | .45 | .25 |
| **6065** | A2902 | 55k dark bl grn | .45 | .25 |
| **6066** | A2902 | 60k blue green | .45 | .25 |
| **6066A** | A2902 | 80k lake | .45 | .25 |
| **6067** | A2902 | 1r yel brown | .45 | .25 |
| **6067A** | A2902 | 1.50r olive | .50 | .25 |
| **6068** | A2902 | 2r blue | .45 | .25 |
| **6068A** | A2902 | 3r red | .45 | .25 |
| **6069** | A2902 | 5r dark brn | .75 | .25 |
| **6070** | A2902 | 10r bright blue | .80 | .25 |
| **6071** | A2902 | 25r dark red | 3.00 | .50 |
| **6071A** | A2902 | 100r brt olive | 4.50 | 1.00 |
| | | *Nos. 6060-6071A (17)* | 14.95 | 5.25 |

Issued: 20k, 30k, 2/26; 10k, 60k, 2r, 4/20; 25r, 5/25; 10r, 100r, May; 1r, 1.50r, 5r, 6/25; 55k, 8/11; 50k, 80k, 8/18; 15k, 25k, 3r, 9/10.

Nos. 6060-6071A were also issued on chalky paper. Value, same.

See Nos. 6109-6124.

Victory by N. N. Baskakov A2903

**1992, Mar. 5** ***Perf. 12x12½***

| | | | | |
|---|---|---|---|---|
| **6072** | A2903 | 5k multicolored | .50 | .25 |

End of World War II, 47th anniv.

Prioksko-Terrasny Nature Reserve — A2904

**1992, Mar. 12** ***Perf. 12***

| | | | | |
|---|---|---|---|---|
| **6073** | A2904 | 50k multicolored | .25 | .25 |

Russia-Germany Joint Space Mission — A2905

**1992, Mar. 17**

| | | | | |
|---|---|---|---|---|
| **6074** | A2905 | 5r multicolored | 1.00 | .30 |

Souvenir Sheet

Discovery of America, 500th Anniv. — A2906

**1992, Mar. 18** ***Perf. 12x11½***

| | | | | |
|---|---|---|---|---|
| **6075** | A2906 | 3r Ship, Columbus | 1.00 | .80 |

Characters from Children's Books A2907

**1992, Apr. 22** **Litho.** ***Perf. 12***

| | | | | |
|---|---|---|---|---|
| **6076** | A2907 | 25k Pinocchio | .50 | .25 |
| **6077** | A2907 | 30k Cipollino | .50 | .25 |
| **6078** | A2907 | 35k Dunno | .50 | .25 |
| **6079** | A2907 | 50k Karlson | .50 | .25 |
| | | *Nos. 6076-6079 (4)* | 2.00 | 1.00 |

Space Accomplishments A2908

Designs: No. 6081, Astronaut, Russian space station and space shuttle. No. 6082, Sputnik, Vostok, Apollo Command and Lunar modules. No. 6083, Soyuz, Mercury and Gemini spacecraft.

**1992, May 29** **Litho.** ***Perf. 11½x12***

| | | | | |
|---|---|---|---|---|
| **6080** | A2908 | 25r multicolored | .60 | .25 |
| **6081** | A2908 | 25r multicolored | .60 | .25 |
| **6082** | A2908 | 25r multicolored | .60 | .25 |
| **6083** | A2908 | 25r multicolored | .60 | .25 |
| *a.* | | Block of 4, #6080-6083 | 3.00 | 1.25 |

See US Nos. 2631-2634.

1992 Summer Olympics, Barcelona A2909

***Perf. 11½x12, 12x11½***

**1992, June 5** **Photo.**

| | | | | |
|---|---|---|---|---|
| **6084** | A2909 | 1r Team handball, vert. | .25 | .25 |
| *a.* | | Miniature sheet of 8 | 1.50 | 1.50 |
| **6085** | A2909 | 2r Fencing | .30 | .25 |
| *a.* | | Miniature sheet of 8 | 3.50 | 2.00 |
| **6086** | A2909 | 3r Judo | .50 | .25 |
| *a.* | | Miniature sheet of 8 | 5.00 | 2.00 |
| | | *Nos. 6084-6086 (3)* | 1.05 | .75 |

Explorers — A2910

Designs: 55r, L. A. Zagoskin, Alaska-Yukon. 70r, N. N. Miklucho-Maklai, New Guinea. 1r, G. I. Langsdorf, Brazil.

**1992, June 23** **Litho.** ***Perf. 12x11½***

| | | | | |
|---|---|---|---|---|
| **6087** | A2910 | 55k multicolored | .30 | .25 |
| **6088** | A2910 | 70k multicolored | .30 | .25 |
| **6089** | A2910 | 1r multicolored | .30 | .25 |
| | | *Nos. 6087-6089 (3)* | .90 | .75 |

Ducks A2911

**1992, July 1** ***Perf. 12***

| | | | | |
|---|---|---|---|---|
| **6090** | A2911 | 1r Anas querquedula | .30 | .25 |
| **6091** | A2911 | 2r Aythya ferina | .30 | .25 |
| **6092** | A2911 | 3r Anas falcata | .30 | .25 |
| *a.* | | Min. sheet of 9, 3 #6090, 4 #6091, 2 #6092 | 3.00 | 2.10 |
| | | *Nos. 6090-6092 (3)* | .90 | .75 |

The Saviour, by Andrei Rublev A2912

**1992, July 3** ***Perf. 12x12½***
**6093** A2912 1r multicolored .50 .25
*a.* Miniature sheet of 8 3.00 1.60

The Taj Mahal Mausoleum in Agra, by Vasili Vereshchagin (1842-1904) — A2913

Design: No. 6095, Let Me Approach (detail), by Vereshchagin.

**1992, July 3** ***Perf. 12½x12***
**6094** A2913 1.50r multicolored .30 .25
**6095** A2913 1.50r multicolored .30 .25
*a.* Pair, #6094-6095 + label .90 .30

Cathedral of the Assumption, Moscow A2914

Cathedral of the Annunciation, Moscow A2915

No. 6098, Archangel Cathedral, Moscow.

**1992, Sept. 3** **Litho.** ***Perf. 11½***
**6096** A2914 1r multicolored .30 .25
*a.* Miniature sheet of 9 3.00
**6097** A2915 1r multicolored .30 .25
*a.* Miniature sheet of 9 3.00
**6098** A2915 1r multicolored .30 .25
*a.* Miniature sheet of 9 3.00
*Nos. 6096-6098 (3)* .90 .75

The Nutcracker, by Tchaikovsky, Cent. — A2916

Designs: No. 6099, Nutcrackers, one holding rifle. No. 6100, Nutcrackers, diff. No. 6101, Pas de deux before Christmas tree. No. 6102, Ballet scene.

**1992, Nov. 4** **Litho.** ***Perf. 12½x12***
**6099** A2916 10r multicolored .50 .25
**6100** A2916 10r multicolored .50 .25
**6101** A2916 25r multicolored 1.00 .50
**6102** A2916 25r multicolored 1.00 .50
*a.* Block of 4, #6099-6102 4.00 2.00

A2917

A2918

A2919

Icons — A2920

Christmas: No. 6103, Joachim and Anna, 16th cent. No. 6104, Madonna and Child, 14th cent. No. 6105, Archangel Gabriel, 12th cent. No. 6106, St. Nicholas, 16th cent.

**1992, Nov. 27** ***Perf. 11½***
**6103** A2917 10r multicolored .40 .25
**6104** A2918 10r multicolored .40 .25
**6105** A2919 10r multicolored .40 .25
**6106** A2920 10r multicolored .40 .25
*a.* Block of 4, #6103-6106 2.25 1.25

See Sweden Nos. 1979-1982.

New Year 1993 A2921

**1992, Dec. 2** **Litho.** ***Perf. 12x12½***
**6107** A2921 50k multicolored .30 .25
*a.* Miniature sheet of 9 3.00

Discovery of America, 500th Anniv. — A2922

**1992, Dec. 29** ***Perf. 11½x12***
**6108** A2922 15r Flags, sculpture .50 .35

## Monuments Type of 1992

Designs: 4r, Church, Kizhi. 6r, Monument to Peter the Great, St. Petersburg. 15r, 45r, The Horsebreaker, St. Petersburg. 50r, Kremlin, Rostov. 75r, Monument to Yuri Dolgoruky, Moscow. 150r, Golden Gate of Vladimir. 250r, Church, Bogolyubovo. 300r, Monument of Minin and Pozharsky. 500r, Lomonosov University, Moscow. 750r, State Library, Moscow. 1000r, Fortress of St. Peter and St. Paul, St. Petersburg. 1500r, Pushkin Museum, Moscow. 2500r, Admiralty, St. Petersburg. 5000r, Bolshoi Theater, Moscow.

**Litho., Photo. (50r, 250r, 500r)**
***Perf. 12½x12, 12x11½ (1000r)***
**1992-95**
**6109** A2902 4r red brown .25 .25
**6110** A2902 6r gray blue .25 .25
**6111** A2902 15r brown .30 .25
*a.* Photo. .30 .25
**6112** A2902 45r slate 1.40 .45
**6113** A2902 50r purple .40 .25
**6114** A2902 75r red brown 2.75 .70
**6115** A2902 150r blue .35 .25
**6116** A2902 250r green 4.00 .30
**6117** A2902 300r red brown .70 .45
**6118** A2902 500r violet 8.00 .60
**6119** A2902 750r olive grn .60 .35
**6120** A2902 1000r slate .70 .50
**6121** A2902 1500r green 1.10 .60
**6122** A2902 2500r olive brn 1.75 1.00
**6123** A2902 5000r blue grn 3.50 2.00
*Nos. 6109-6123 (15)* 26.05 8.20

Issued: #6111a, 6113, 6116, 6118, 12/25/92; #6109-6110, 6/4/93; #6112, 6114, 1/25/93; 150r, 300r, 12/30/93; 1000r, 1/27/95; 750r, 1500r, 2500r, 5000r, 2/21/95.
For surcharge see #6529.

Communications Satellites — A2928

Ballets: No. 6126, Paquita (1847). No. 6127, Sleeping Beauty (1890). No. 6128, Swan Lake (1895). No. 6129, Raymonda (1898).

**1993, Jan. 14** **Litho.** ***Perf. 12½x12***
**6126** A2923 25r multicolored .75 .25
**6127** A2923 25r multicolored .75 .25
**6128** A2923 25r multicolored .75 .25
**6129** A2923 25r multicolored .75 .25
*a.* Block of 4, #6126-6129 4.00 2.00

A2924

Characters from Children's Books: a, 2r, Scrub and Rub. b, 3r, Big Cockroach. c, 10r, The Buzzer Fly. d, 15r, Doctor Doolittle. e, 25r, Barmalei.

**1993, Feb. 25** **Litho.** ***Perf. 12½x12***
**6130** A2924 Strip of 5, #a.-e. 1.00 .75

No. 6130 printed in continuous design.

A2925

**1993, Mar. 18** **Photo.** ***Perf. 11½x12***
**6131** A2925 10r Vyborg Castle .50 .25

City of Vyborg, 700th anniv.

Battle of Kursk, 50th Anniv. A2926

**1993, Mar. 25** ***Perf. 12x12½***
**6132** A2926 10r multicolored .50 .25

Victory Day.

Flowers — A2927

10r, Saintpaulia ionantha. 15r, Hibiscus rosa-sinensis. 25r, Cyclamen persicum. 50r, Fuchsia hybrida. 100r, Begonia semperflorens.

**1993, Mar. 25** ***Perf. 12½x12***
**6133** A2927 10r multicolored .25 .25
**6134** A2927 15r multicolored .25 .25
**6135** A2927 25r multicolored .25 .25
**6136** A2927 50r multicolored .40 .30
*a.* Miniature sheet of 8 5.00
**6137** A2927 100r multicolored .85 .60
*a.* Miniature sheet of 8 10.00
*Nos. 6133-6137 (5)* 2.00 1.65

See Nos. 6196-6200.

**1993, Apr. 12** **Photo.** ***Perf. 11½***
**6138** A2928 25r Molniya-3 .25 .25
**6139** A2928 45r Ekran-M .30 .25
**6140** A2928 50r Gorizont .30 .25
**6141** A2928 75r Luch .50 .35
**6142** A2928 100r Express .65 .50
*Nos. 6138-6142 (5)* 2.00 1.60

### Souvenir Sheet
***Perf. 12x11½***
**6143** A2928 250r Ground station, horiz. 2.00 1.40

No. 6143 contains one 37x26mm stamp.

Antique Silver A2929

15r, Snuff box, 1820, mug, 1849. 25r, Tea pot, 1896-1908. 45r, Vase, 1896-1908. 75r, Tray, candlestick holder, 1896-1908. 100r, Coffee pot, cream and sugar set, 1852. 250r, Sweet dish, 1896-1908, biscuit dish, 1844.

**1993, May 5** **Litho.** ***Perf. 11½***
**6144** A2929 15r multicolored .25 .25
**6145** A2929 25r multicolored .25 .25
*a.* Miniature sheet of 9 3.50
**6146** A2929 45r multicolored .30 .25
**6147** A2929 75r multicolored .50 .35
**6148** A2929 100r multicolored .70 .45
*a.* Miniature sheet of 9 6.50
*Nos. 6144-6148 (5)* 2.00 1.55

### Souvenir Sheet
***Perf. 12½x12***
**6149** A2929 250r multicolored 2.50 1.25

No. 6149 contains one 52x37mm stamp.

A2930

Novgorod Kremlin A2931

Designs: No. 6150, Kremlin towers, 14th-17th cent. No. 6151, St. Sofia's Temple, 11th cent. No. 6152, Belfry of St. Sophia's, 15th-18th cent. 250r, Icon, "Sign of the Virgin," 12th cent.

**1993, June 4** **Litho.** ***Perf. 12***
**6150** A2930 25r multicolored .50 .25
**6151** A2931 25r multicolored .50 .25
**6152** A2931 25r multicolored .50 .25
*a.* Sheet, 3 each #6150-6152 5.00 3.00
*Nos. 6150-6152 (3)* 1.50 .75

### Souvenir Sheet
***Perf. 12½x12***
**6153** A2930 250r multicolored 3.00 1.75

No. 6153 contains one 42x30mm stamp.

Russian-Danish Relations, 500th Anniv. — A2932

**1993, June 17** ***Perf. 11½***

| | | | |
|---|---|---|---|
| **6154** | A2932 90r grn & light grn | .75 | .25 |

See Denmark No. 985.

Ducks A2933

90r, Somateria stelleri. 100r, Somateria mollissima. 250r, Somateria spectabilis.

**1993, July 1** **Litho.** ***Perf. 12***

| | | | |
|---|---|---|---|
| **6155** | A2933 90r multicolored | .50 | .25 |
| **6156** | A2933 100r multicolored | .50 | .25 |
| **6157** | A2933 250r multicolored | 1.00 | .30 |
| *a.* | Min. sheet, 4 each #6155-6156, 1 #6157 | 4.50 | |
| | *Nos. 6155-6157 (3)* | 2.00 | .80 |

Sea Life A2934

50r, Pusa hispida. 60r, Paralithodes brevipes. 90r, Todarodes pacificus. 100fr, Oncorhynchus masu. 250r, Fulmarus glacialis.

**1993, July 6**

| | | | |
|---|---|---|---|
| **6158** | A2934 50r multicolored | .25 | .25 |
| **6159** | A2934 60r multicolored | .25 | .25 |
| **6160** | A2934 90r multicolored | .40 | .25 |
| **6161** | A2934 100r multicolored | .40 | .25 |
| **6162** | A2934 250r multicolored | 1.10 | .75 |
| *a.* | Sheet, #6162, 2 each #6158-6161 | 5.00 | |
| | *Nos. 6158-6162 (5)* | 2.40 | 1.75 |

Natl. Museum of Applied Arts and Folk Crafts, Moscow — A2935

Designs: No. 6163, Skopino earthenware candlestick. No. 6164, Painted tray, horiz. No. 6165, Painted box, distaff. No. 6166, Enamel icon of St. Dmitry of Solun. 250r, Fedoskino lacquer miniature Easter egg depicting the Resurrection.

***Perf. 12x12½, 12½x12***

**1993, Aug. 11** **Litho.**

| | | | |
|---|---|---|---|
| **6163** | A2935 50r multicolored | .25 | .25 |
| **6164** | A2935 50r multicolored | .25 | .25 |
| **6165** | A2935 100r multicolored | .35 | .25 |
| **6166** | A2935 100r multicolored | .35 | .25 |
| **6167** | A2935 250r multicolored | .75 | .45 |
| | *Nos. 6163-6167 (5)* | 1.95 | 1.45 |

Goznak (Bank Note Printer and Mint), 175th Anniv. A2936

**1993, Sept. 2** **Litho.** ***Perf. 12***

| | | | |
|---|---|---|---|
| **6168** | A2936 100r multicolored | 1.00 | .25 |

Shipbuilders — A2937

No. 6169, Peter the Great (1672-1725), Goto Predestinatsia. No. 6170, K.A. Shilder (1786-1854), first all-metal submarine. No. 6171, I.A. Amosov (1800-78), screw steamship Archimedes. No. 6172, I.G. Bubnov (1872-1919), submarine Bars. No. 6173, B.M. Malinin (1889-1949), submarine Dekabrist. No. 6174, A.I. Maslov (1894-1968), cruiser Kirov.

**1993, Sept. 7**

| | | | |
|---|---|---|---|
| **6169** | A2937 100r multicolored | .50 | .25 |
| **6170** | A2937 100r multicolored | .50 | .25 |
| **6171** | A2937 100r multicolored | .50 | .25 |
| **6172** | A2937 100r multicolored | .50 | .25 |
| **6173** | A2937 100r multicolored | .50 | .25 |
| **6174** | A2937 100r multicolored | .50 | .25 |
| *a.* | Block of 6, #6169-6174 | 5.00 | 1.50 |

A2938

Moscow Kremlin A2939

No. 6175, Granovitaya Chamber (1487-91). No. 6176, Church of Rizpolozheniye (1484-88). No. 6177, Teremnoi Palace (1635-36).

**1993, Oct. 28** **Litho.** ***Perf. 12***

| | | | |
|---|---|---|---|
| **6175** | A2938 100r multicolored | .45 | .25 |
| *a.* | Miniature sheet of 9 | 4.50 | |
| **6176** | A2939 100r multicolored | .45 | .25 |
| *a.* | Miniature sheet of 9 | 4.50 | |
| **6177** | A2939 100r multicolored | .45 | .25 |
| *a.* | Miniature sheet of 9 | 4.50 | |
| | *Nos. 6175-6177 (3)* | 1.35 | .75 |

Panthera Tigris A2940

Designs: 100r, Adult in woods. 250r, Two cubs. 500r, Adult in snow.

**1993, Nov. 25** **Litho.** ***Perf. 12½x12***

| | | | |
|---|---|---|---|
| **6178** | A2940 50r multicolored | .35 | .25 |
| **6179** | A2940 100r multicolored | .35 | .25 |
| **6180** | A2940 250r multicolored | .50 | .25 |
| **6181** | A2940 500r multicolored | 1.25 | .60 |
| *a.* | Block of 4, #6178-6181 | 3.00 | 1.75 |
| *b.* | Miniature sheet, 2 #6181a | 6.00 | |

World Wildlife Fund.

New Year 1994 — A2941

**1993, Dec. 2** **Photo.** ***Perf. 11½***

| | | | |
|---|---|---|---|
| **6182** | A2941 25r multicolored | 1.00 | .25 |
| *a.* | Sheet of 8 | 50.00 | |

A2942

**1993, Nov. 25** **Photo.** ***Perf. 11½x12***

| | | | |
|---|---|---|---|
| **6183** | A2942 90r gray, blk & red | .75 | .25 |

Prevention of AIDS.

Wildlife — A2943

No. 6184, Phascolarctos cinereus. No. 6185, Monachus schauinslandi. No. 6186, Haliaeetus leucocephalus. No. 6187, Elephas maximus. No. 6188, Grus vipio. No. 6189, Ailuropoda melanoleuca. No. 6190, Phocoenoides dalli. No. 6191, Eschrichtius robustus.

**1993, Dec. 30** **Litho.** ***Perf. 12½x12***

| | | | |
|---|---|---|---|
| **6184** | A2943 250r multicolored | .50 | .25 |
| **6185** | A2943 250r multicolored | .50 | .25 |
| **6186** | A2943 250r multicolored | .50 | .25 |
| **6187** | A2943 250r multicolored | .50 | .25 |
| **6188** | A2943 250r multicolored | .50 | .25 |
| **6189** | A2943 250r multicolored | .50 | .25 |
| **6190** | A2943 250r multicolored | .50 | .25 |
| **6191** | A2943 250r multicolored | .50 | .25 |
| *a.* | Min. sheet of 8, #6184-6191 | 7.50 | |
| | *Nos. 6184-6191 (8)* | 4.00 | 2.00 |

Nikolai Rimsky-Korsakov (1844-1908), Scene from "Sadko" — A2944

Scenes from operas: No. 6193, "Golden Cockerel," 1907. No. 6194, "The Czar's Bride," 1898. No. 6195, "The Snow Maiden," 1881.

**1994, Jan. 20** **Litho.** ***Perf. 12½x12***

| | | | |
|---|---|---|---|
| **6192** | A2944 250r multicolored | 1.25 | .50 |
| **6193** | A2944 250r multicolored | 1.25 | .50 |
| **6194** | A2944 250r multicolored | 1.25 | .50 |
| **6195** | A2944 250r multicolored | 1.25 | .50 |
| *a.* | Block of 4, #6192-6195 | 5.00 | 2.00 |

### Flower Type of 1993

Designs: 50r, Epiphyllum peacockii. No. 6197, Mammillaria swinglei. No. 6198, Lophophora williamsii. No. 6199, Opuntia basilaris. No. 6200, Selenicereus grandiflorus.

**1994, Feb. 25** **Litho.** ***Perf. 12½x12***

| | | | |
|---|---|---|---|
| **6196** | A2927 50r multicolored | .25 | .25 |
| **6197** | A2927 100r multicolored | .35 | .25 |
| *a.* | Min. sheet of 8 | 7.50 | 4.00 |
| **6198** | A2927 100r multicolored | .35 | .25 |
| *a.* | Min. sheet of 8 | 7.50 | 4.00 |
| **6199** | A2927 250r multicolored | .50 | .25 |
| **6200** | A2927 250r multicolored | .50 | .25 |
| | *Nos. 6196-6200 (5)* | 1.95 | 1.25 |

Cathedral of St. Peter, York, Great Britain — A2945

Metropolis Church, Athens — A2946

Gothic Church, Roskilde, Denmark A2947

Notre Dame Cathedral, Paris — A2948

St. Peter's Basilica, Vatican City — A2949

Cologne Cathedral, Germany A2950

St. Basil's Cathedral, Moscow — A2951

Seville Cathedral, Spain — A2952

No. 6207, St. Patrick's Cathedral, NYC, US.

**1994, Mar. 24 Litho. *Perf. 12x12½***

| | | | | |
|---|---|---|---|---|
| **6201** | A2945 150r multicolored | .25 | .25 |
| **6202** | A2946 150r multicolored | .25 | .25 |
| **6203** | A2947 150r multicolored | .25 | .25 |
| **6204** | A2948 150r multicolored | .25 | .25 |
| **6205** | A2949 150r multicolored | .25 | .25 |
| **6206** | A2950 150r multicolored | .25 | .25 |
| **6207** | A2950 150r multicolored | .25 | .25 |
| **6208** | A2951 150r multicolored | .25 | .25 |
| *a.* | Min. sheet of 9 | *5.00* | *5.00* |
| **6209** | A2952 150r multicolored | .25 | .25 |
| *a.* | Min. sheet of 9, #6201-6209 | *5.00* | *5.00* |
| | *Nos. 6201-6209 (9)* | 2.25 | 2.25 |

Space Research A2953

Designs: 100r, TS-18 Centrifuge, Soyuz landing module during re-entry. 250r, Soyuz spacecraft docked at Mir space station. 500r, Training in hydrolaboratory, cosmonaut during space walk.

**1994, Apr. 12 Litho. *Perf. 12x11½***

| | | | |
|---|---|---|---|
| **6210** | A2953 100r multicolored | .25 | .25 |
| **6211** | A2953 250r multicolored | .30 | .25 |
| **6212** | A2953 500r multicolored | .45 | .25 |
| | *Nos. 6210-6212 (3)* | 1.00 | .75 |

Liberation of Soviet Areas, 50th Anniv. A2954

Battle maps and: a, Katyusha rockets, liberation of Russia. b, Fighter planes, liberation of Ukraine. c, Combined offensive, liberation of Belarus.

**1994, Apr. 26 *Perf. 12***

| | | | |
|---|---|---|---|
| **6213** | A2954 100r Block of 3, #a.-c., + label | 2.00 | .45 |

See Belarus No. 78, Ukraine No. 195.

Russian Architecture A2955

Structure, architect: 50r, Krasniye Vorota, Moscow, Prince D.V. Ukhtomsky (1719-74). 100r, Academy of Science, St. Petersburg, Giacomo Quarenghi (1744-1817). 150r, Trinity Cathedral, St. Petersburg, V.P. Stasov (1769-1848). 300r, Church of Christ the Saviour, Moscow, K.A. Ton (1794-1881).

**1994, May 25 Litho. *Perf. 12½x12***

| | | | |
|---|---|---|---|
| **6214** | A2955 50r lt brown & blk | .50 | .25 |
| **6215** | A2955 100r red brn & blk | .50 | .25 |
| **6216** | A2955 150r olive grn & blk | .50 | .25 |
| **6217** | A2955 300r gray vio & blk | .50 | .25 |
| | *Nos. 6214-6217 (4)* | 2.00 | 1.00 |

**Painting Type of 1992**

Paintings by V. D. Polenov (1844-1927): No. 6218, Christ and the Adultress, 1886-87. No. 6219, Golden Autumn, 1893.

**1994, June 1 Litho. *Perf. 12½x12***

| | | | |
|---|---|---|---|
| **6218** | A2913 150r multicolored | .25 | .25 |
| **6219** | A2913 150r multicolored | .25 | .25 |
| *a.* | Pair, #6218-6219 + label | .50 | .35 |

Ducks A2956

**1994, July 1 *Perf. 12***

| | | | |
|---|---|---|---|
| **6220** | A2956 150r Anas penelope | .30 | .25 |
| **6221** | A2956 250r Aythya fuligula | .40 | .25 |
| **6222** | A2956 300r Anas formosa | .60 | .25 |
| *a.* | Min. sheet, 3 #6220, 4 #6221, 2 #6222 | *5.00* | 2.00 |
| *b.* | As "a," overprinted | *10.00* | 2.00 |
| | *Nos. 6220-6222 (3)* | 1.30 | .75 |

No. 6222b is overprinted in sheet margin: "World Philatelic Exhibition Moscow-97" in Cyrillic and Latin with four exhibition emblems.

A2957

**1994, July 5 Photo. *Perf. 11½x12***

| | | | |
|---|---|---|---|
| **6223** | A2957 100r multicolored | 1.00 | .25 |

1994 Goodwill Games, St. Petersburg.

A2958

Nobel Prize Winners in Physics: No. 6224, P.L. Kapitsa (1894-1984). No. 6225, P.A. Cherenkov (1904-90).

**1994, July 5 Litho. *Perf. 12***

| | | | |
|---|---|---|---|
| **6224** | A2958 150r sepia | .50 | .25 |
| **6225** | A2958 150r sepia | .50 | .25 |

Intl. Olympic Committee, Cent. A2959

**1994, July 5**

| | | | |
|---|---|---|---|
| **6226** | A2959 250r multicolored | 1.00 | .25 |

Russian Postal Day — A2960

**1994, July 8 *Perf. 11½x12***

| | | | |
|---|---|---|---|
| **6227** | A2960 125r multicolored | 1.00 | .25 |

Porcelain A2961

Designs: 50r, Snuff box, 1752. 100r, Candlestick, 1750-1760. 150r, Statue of watercarrier, 1818. 250r, Vase, 19th cent. 300r, Statue of lady with mask, 1910. 500r, Monogramed dinner service, 1848.

**1994, Aug. 10 Litho. *Perf. 11½***

| | | | |
|---|---|---|---|
| **6228** | A2961 50r multicolored | .40 | .25 |
| *a.* | Min. sheet of 9 | 5.00 | 2.50 |
| *b.* | As "a," overprinted | 5.00 | 3.00 |
| **6229** | A2961 100r multicolored | .40 | .25 |
| **6230** | A2961 150r multicolored | .40 | .25 |
| **6231** | A2961 250r multicolored | .40 | .25 |
| **6232** | A2961 300r multicolored | .40 | .25 |
| | *Nos. 6228-6232 (5)* | 2.00 | 1.25 |

**Souvenir Sheet**

| | | | |
|---|---|---|---|
| **6233** | A2961 500r multicolored | 3.00 | 1.00 |

No. 6228b is overprinted in sheet margin: "World Philatelic Exhibition Moscow 97" in Cyrillic and Latin with four exhibition logos.

Integration of Tuva into Russia, 50th Anniv. — A2962

**1994, Oct. 13 Photo. *Perf. 11½12***

| | | | |
|---|---|---|---|
| **6234** | A2962 125r multicolored | 1.00 | .25 |

Russian Voyages of Exploration — A2963

Sailing ships and: No. 6235, V.M. Golovnin, Kurile Islands expedition, 1811. No. 6236, I.F. Kruzenstern, trans-global expedition, 1803-06. No. 6237, F.P. Wrangel, North American expedition, 1829-35. No. 6238, F.P. Litke, Novaya Zemlya expedition, 1821-24.

**Photo. & Engr.**

**1994, Nov. 22 *Perf. 12x11½***

| | | | |
|---|---|---|---|
| **6235** | A2963 250r multicolored | .50 | .25 |
| **6236** | A2963 250r multicolored | .50 | .25 |
| *a.* | Miniature sheet of 8 | 5.00 | 1.10 |
| **6237** | A2963 250r multicolored | .50 | .25 |
| **6238** | A2963 250r multicolored | .50 | .25 |
| | *Nos. 6235-6238 (4)* | 2.00 | 1.00 |

Russian Fleet, 300th anniv. (#6236a).

New Year 1995 — A2964

**1994, Dec. 6 Photo. *Perf. 12x11½***

| | | | |
|---|---|---|---|
| **6239** | A2964 125r multicolored | 1.00 | .25 |
| *a.* | Min. sheet of 8 | 8.00 | 2.00 |

Alexander Griboedov (1795-1829), Poet, Diplomat A2965

**1995, Jan. 5 Litho. *Perf. 11½***

| | | | |
|---|---|---|---|
| **6240** | A2965 250r sepia & black | .75 | .25 |

No. 6240 printed se-tenant with label.

A2966

Mikhail Fokine (1880-1942), Choreographer — A2967

Scenes from ballets: No. 6241, Scheherazade. No. 6242, The Fire Bird. No. 6243, Petrouchka.

**1995, Jan. 18 Litho. *Perf. 12½x12***

| | | | |
|---|---|---|---|
| **6241** | A2966 500r multicolored | .50 | .25 |
| **6242** | A2967 500r multicolored | .50 | .25 |
| **6243** | A2967 500r multicolored | .50 | .25 |
| *a.* | Block of 3 + label | 5.00 | 1.00 |

Mikhail Kutuzov (1745-1813), Field Marshal — A2968

**1995, Jan. 20**

| | | | |
|---|---|---|---|
| **6244** | A2968 300r multicolored | .50 | .25 |
| *a.* | Miniature sheet of 8 | 4.00 | 3.00 |

16th-17th Cent. Architecture, Moscow A2969

Designs: 125r, English Yard, Varvarka St. 250r, Averki Kirillov's house, Bersenevskaya Embankment. 300r, Volkov's house, Kharitonievsky Lane.

**1995, Feb. 15 Litho. *Perf. 12x12½***

| | | | |
|---|---|---|---|
| **6245** | A2969 125r multicolored | 1.00 | .25 |
| **6246** | A2969 250r multicolored | 1.00 | .25 |
| **6247** | A2969 300r multicolored | 1.00 | .25 |
| *a.* | Min. sheet, 2 #6245, 4 #6246, 3 #6247 | *15.00* | *15.00* |
| *b.* | Min. sheet, as "a," diff. margin | *55.00* | *55.00* |
| | *Nos. 6245-6247 (3)* | 3.00 | .75 |

Sheet margin on No. 6247b has emblems and inscriptions in Cyrillic and Latin for "World Philatelic Exhibition Moscow '97."

UN Fight Against Drug Abuse — A2970

**1995, Mar. 1** *Perf. 12½x12*
6248 A2970 150r multicolored .60 .25

Endangered Species — A2971

a, Shoreline. b, Pusa hispida. c, Lynx. d, River, trees.

**1995, Mar. 1** *Perf. 12x12½*
6249 A2971 250r Block of 4, #a.-d. 1.50 .75

Nos. 6249a-6249b, 6249c-6249d are continuous designs. See Finland No. 960.

End of World War II, 50th Anniv. A2972

#6250, Churchill, Roosevelt, Stalin at Yalta. #6251, Ruins of Reichstag, Berlin. #6252, Monument to concentration camp victims. #6253, Tomb of the Unknown Soldier, Moscow, vert. #6254, Potsdam Conference, map of divided Germany, vert. #6255, Russian planes over Manchuria. #6256, Victory parade, Moscow, vert.

**1995, Apr. 7** *Perf. 12x12½, 12½x12*
6250 A2972 250r multicolored .35 .25
6251 A2972 250r multicolored .35 .25
6252 A2972 250r multicolored .35 .25
6253 A2972 250r multicolored .35 .25
6254 A2972 250r multicolored .35 .25
6255 A2972 250r multicolored .35 .25

**Size: 37x52mm**

6256 A2972 500r multicolored .35 .25
a. Souv. sheet of 1, perf 11½x12 2.25 1.50
*Nos. 6250-6256 (7)* 2.45 1.75

MIR-Space Shuttle Docking, Apollo-Soyuz Link-Up — A2973

a, Space shuttle Atlantis. b, MIR space station. c, Apollo command module. d, Soyuz spacecraft.

**1995, June 29 Litho.** *Perf. 12x12½*
6257 A2973 1500r Block of 4, #a.-d. 5.00 3.00

No. 6257 is a continuous design.

Radio, Cent. A2974

Design: 250r, Alexander Popov (1859-1905), radio-telegraph.

**1995, May 3 Litho.** *Perf. 11½*
6258 A2974 250r multicolored .50 .25

Flowers — A2975

No. 6259, Campanula patula. No. 6260, Leucanthemum vulgare. No. 6261, Trifolium pratense. No. 6262, Centaurea jacea. 500r, Geranium pratense.

**1995, May 18 Litho.** *Perf. 12½x12*
6259 A2975 250r multicolored .60 .25
6260 A2975 250r multicolored .60 .25
6261 A2975 300r multicolored .60 .25
a. Min. sheet of 8 5.00
b. As "a," different margin 5.00
6262 A2975 300r multicolored .60 .25
6263 A2975 500r multicolored .60 .25
*Nos. 6259-6263 (5)* 3.00 1.25

No. 6261b has emblems and inscriptions in Cyrillic and Latin for "World Philatelic Exhibition Moscow '97."

Songbirds — A2976

No. 6264, Alauda arvensis. No. 6265, Turdus philomelos. No. 6266, Carduelis carduelis. No. 6267, Cyanosylvia svecica. No. 6268, Luscinia luscinia.

**1995, June 15 Litho.** *Perf. 12½x12*
6264 A2976 250r multicolored .40 .25
6265 A2976 250r multicolored .40 .25
6266 A2976 500r multicolored .40 .25
6267 A2976 500r multicolored .40 .25
6268 A2976 750r multicolored .40 .25
a. Min. sheet, 2 each #6264-6265, 1 #6268 + label 5.00 1.10
b. Min. sheet, 2 each #6266-6267, 1 #6268 + label 5.00 1.50
*Nos. 6264-6268 (5)* 2.00 1.25

St. Trinity, Jerusalem A2977

Sts. Peter & Paul, Karlovy Vary — A2978

St. Nicholas, Vienna — A2979

St. Nicholas, New York — A2980

Russian Orthodox Churches abroad: 750r, St. Alexei, Leipzig.

**1995, July 5 Litho.** *Perf. 12x12½*
6269 A2977 300r multicolored .35 .25
6270 A2978 300r multicolored .35 .25
6271 A2979 500r multicolored .35 .25
6272 A2980 500r multicolored .35 .25
6273 A2980 750r multicolored .35 .25
a. Min. sheet, 2 ea #6269-6273 4.00 4.00
*Nos. 6269-6273 (5)* 1.75 1.25

Principality of Ryazan, 900th Anniv. — A2981

**1995, July 20 Photo.** *Perf. 11½*
6274 A2981 250r Kremlin Cathedral .50 .25

Fabergé Jewelry in Kremlin Museums A2982

Designs: 150r, Easter egg, 1909, St. Petersburg. 250r, Goblet, 1899-1908, Moscow. 300r, Cross, 1899-1908, St. Petersburg. 600r, Ladle, 1890, Moscow. 750r, Easter egg, 1910, St. Petersburg.
1500r, Easter egg, 1904-06, St. Petersburg.

**1995, Aug. 15 Litho.** *Perf. 11½*
6275 A2982 150r multicolored .40 .25
6276 A2982 250r multicolored .40 .25
6277 A2982 300r multicolored .40 .25
6278 A2982 500r multicolored .40 .25
6279 A2982 750r multicolored .40 .30
*Nos. 6275-6279 (5)* 2.00 1.30

**Souvenir Sheet**

6280 A2982 1500r multicolored 1.00 1.00

No. 6280 contains one 37x51mm stamp.

**Souvenir Sheet**

Singapore '95 — A2983

**1995, Sept. 1** *Perf. 12½x12*
6281 A2983 2500r multicolored 2.00 1.75

Ducks A2984

Designs: 500r, Histrionicus histrionicus. 750r, Aythya baeri. 1000r, Mergus merganser.

**1995, Sept. 1** *Perf. 12*
6284 A2984 500r multicolored .40 .25
6285 A2984 750r multicolored .60 .25
6286 A2984 1000r multicolored 1.00 .40
a. Miniature sheet, 2 #6284, 4 #6285, 3 #6286 4.00 4.00
*Nos. 6284-6286 (3)* 2.00 .90

Russian Fleet, 300th Anniv. — A2985

Paintings: 250r, Battle of Grengam, 1720. 300r, Bay of Cesme, 1770. 500r, Battle of Revel Roadstead, 1790. 750r, Kronstadt Roadstead, 1840.

**1995, Sept. 14 Litho.** *Perf. 12*
6287 A2985 250r multicolored .25 .25
6288 A2985 300r multicolored .25 .25
6289 A2985 500r multicolored .30 .25
6290 A2985 750r multicolored .40 .25
*Nos. 6287-6290 (4)* 1.20 1.00

Arms & Flag of the Russian Federation — A2986

**1995, Oct. 4 Litho.** *Perf. 12x12½*
6291 A2986 500r multicolored .50 .25

No. 6291 is printed with se-tenant label.

UN, 50th Anniv. — A2987

**1995, Oct. 4**
6292 A2987 500r multicolored .50 .30

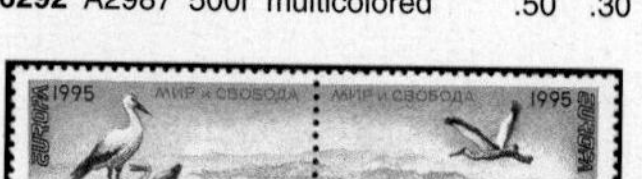

Peace and Freedom — A2988

Europa: No. 6293, Storks in nest, countryside. No. 6294, Stork in flight.

**1995, Nov. 15 Litho.** *Perf. 12x12½*
6293 1500r multicolored 1.00 .75
6294 1500r multicolored 1.00 .75
a. A2988 Pair, Nos. 6293-6294 2.25 1.75

No. 6294a is a continuous design.

Christmas A2989

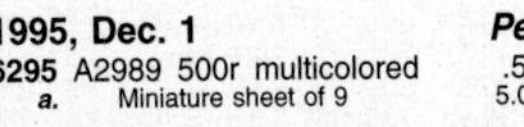

**1995, Dec. 1** *Perf. 12*
**6295** A2989 500r multicolored .50 .25
*a.* Miniature sheet of 9 5.00

A2990

A2990a

A2990b

Early Russian Dukes — A2990c

Designs: No. 6296, Yuri Dolgorouki (1090-1157), Duke of Souzdal, Grand Duke of Kiev, founder of Moscow. No. 6297, Alexander Nevski (1220-63), Duke of Novgorod, Grand Duke of Vladimir. No. 6298, Michael Alexandrovitsch (1333-39), Prince of Tver. No. 6299, Dimitri Donskoi (1350-89), Duke of Moscow, Vladimir. No. 6300, Ivan III (1440-1505), Grand Duke of Moscow.

**Litho. & Engr.**

**1995, Dec. 21** *Perf. 12*
**6296** A2990 1000r multicolored .60 .40
**6297** A2990a 1000r multicolored .60 .40
**6298** A2990b 1000r multicolored .60 .40
**6299** A2990c 1000r multicolored .60 .40
**6300** A2990c 1000r multicolored .60 .40
*Nos. 6296-6300 (5)* 3.00 2.00

See #6359-6362.

A2991

**1996, Jan. 31** **Litho.** *Perf. 12*
**6301** A2991 750r dull olive black .50 .25

Nikolai N. Semenov (1896-1986), chemist.

A2992

Flowers: 500r, Viola wittrockiana. No. 6303, Dianthus barbatus. No. 6304, Lathyrus odoratus. No. 6305, Fritillaria imperialis. No. 6306, Antirrhinum majus.

**1996, Feb. 22** **Litho.** *Perf. 12*
**6302** A2992 500r multicolored .35 .25
**6303** A2992 750r multicolored .45 .25
**6304** A2992 750r multicolored .45 .25
**6305** A2992 1000r multicolored .55 .30
**6306** A2992 1000r multicolored .55 .30
*a.* Min. sheet of 20, 4 each #6302-6306 + 4 labels 12.00 12.00
*Nos. 6302-6306 (5)* 2.35 1.35

Domestic Cats A2993

Designs: No. 6307, European tiger. No. 6308, Russian blue. No. 6309, Persian white. No. 6310, Siamese. No. 6311, Siberian.

**1996, Mar. 21**
**Color of Background**
**6307** A2993 1000r orange .60 .30
**6308** A2993 1000r brown .60 .30
**6309** A2993 1000r red .60 .30
**6310** A2993 1000r blue violet .60 .30
**6311** A2993 1000r green .60 .30
*a.* Sheet, 2 each #6307-6311 7.00 7.00
*Nos. 6307-6311 (5)* 3.00 1.50

Souvenir Sheet

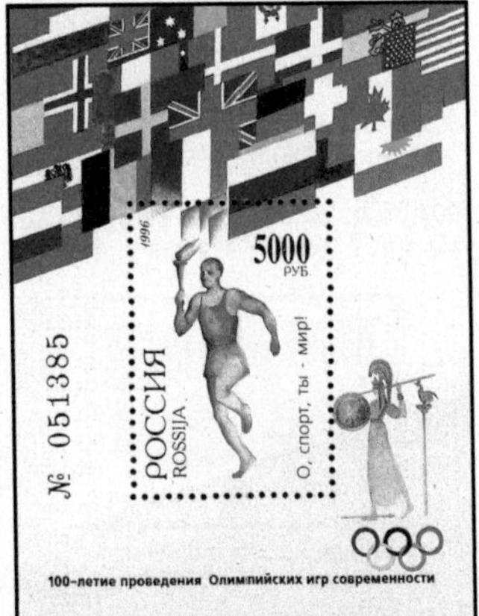

Modern Olympic Games, Cent. — A2994

**1996, Mar. 27**
**6312** A2994 5000r multicolored 3.00 2.00

Victory Day — A2995

Design: Painting, "Plunged Down Banners," by A. S. Mikhailov.

**1996, Apr. 19** **Litho.** *Perf. 12*
**6313** A2995 1000r multicolored .60 .25
*a.* Sheet of 8 + label 8.00

Value of No. 6313 single + label, $2.

Tula, 850th Anniv. A2996

**1996, May 14** *Perf. 12½x12*
**6314** A2996 1500r Tula Kremlin .75 .40

Russian Trams A2997

Designs: 500r, Putilovsky plant. No. 6316, Sormovo, 1912. No. 6317, "X" series, 1928. No. 6318, "KM" series, 1931. No. 6319, LM-57, 1957. 2500r, Model 71-608 K, 1993.

**1996, May 16** **Photo.** *Perf. 11½*
**6315** A2997 500r multicolored .25 .25
**6316** A2997 750r multicolored .30 .25
**6317** A2997 750r multicolored .30 .25
**6318** A2997 1000r multicolored .45 .30
**6319** A2997 1000r multicolored .45 .30
**6320** A2997 2500r multicolored 1.25 .90
*a.* Souvenir sheet 2.00 2.00
*b.* Sheet of 6 7.50 7.50
*Nos. 6315-6320 (6)* 3.00 2.25

A2998

Europa (Famous Women): No. 6321, E.R. Daschkova (1744-1810), scientist. No. 6322, S.V. Kovalevskaya (1850-91), mathematician.

**1996, May 20** **Litho.** *Perf. 12x12½*
**6321** A2998 1500r green & black 1.50 .75
**6322** A2998 1500r lilac & black 1.50 .75

A2999

**1996, June 1** **Litho.** *Perf. 12½x12*
**6323** A2999 1000r multicolored .60 .35

UNICEF, 50th anniv.

Summer, by P.P. Sokolov A3000

Post Troika, by P.N. Gruzinsky A3001

Design: No. 6326, Winter, by Sokolov.

**1996, June 14**
**6324** A3000 1500r multicolored .65 .50
**6325** A3001 1500r multicolored .65 .50
**6326** A3000 1500r multicolored .65 .50
*Nos. 6324-6326 (3)* 1.95 1.50

Moscow, 850th Anniv. — A3002

Paintings of urban views: No. 6327, Yauza River, 1790's. No. 6328, Kremlin Palace, 1797. No. 6329, Kamenny Bridge, 1811. No. 6330, Volkhonka Steet, 1830's. No. 6331, Vorvarka St. 1830-40's. No. 6332, Petrovsky Park, troikas.

**1996, June 20** **Litho.** *Perf. 12*
**6327** A3002 500r multicolored .25 .25
**6328** A3002 500r multicolored .25 .25
**6329** A3002 750r multicolored .35 .25
**6330** A3002 750r multicolored .35 .25
**6331** A3002 1000r multicolored .40 .25
*a.* Sheet, 2 ea #6327, 6330-6331 5.00
**6332** A3002 1000r multicolored .40 .25
*a.* Sheet, 2 ea #6328-6329, 6332 5.00
*b.* Sheet of 6, #6327-6332 5.00
*Nos. 6327-6332 (6)* 2.00 1.50

No. 6332b has emblems and inscriptions in Cyrillic and Latin for "World Philatelic Exhibition Moscow '97."

Traffic Police, 60th Anniv. A3003

a, Pedestrian crossing guard. b, Children receiving traffic safety education. c, Officer writing citation.

**1996, July 3** **Litho.** *Perf. 12x12½*
**6333** A3003 1500r Sheet of 3, #a.-c. 3.00 1.50

1996 Summer Olympic Games, Atlanta — A3004

**1996, July 10** *Perf. 12*
**6334** A3004 500r Basketball .25 .25
**6335** A3004 1000r Boxing .35 .25
**6336** A3004 1000r Swimming .35 .25
**6337** A3004 1500r Women's gymnastics .60 .30
**6338** A3004 1500r Hurdles .60 .30
*a.* Sheet of 8 5.00
*Nos. 6334-6338 (5)* 2.15 1.35

A3005

Russian Navy, 300th Anniv. A3006

Ships: 750r, Yevstafy, 1762. No. 6340, Petropavlovsk, 1894. No. 6341, Novik, 1913. Nos. 6342, 6346a, Galera, 1696. Nos. 6343, 6346d, Aircraft carrier Admiral Kuznetzov, 1985. No. 6344, Tashkent, 1937. No. 6345, Submarine C-13, 1939.

No. 6346: b, Atomic submarine, 1981. c, Sailing ship Azov, 1826.

**Litho. & Engr.**

**1996, July 26** *Perf. 12*
**6339** A3005 750r multicolored .50 .25
**6340** A3005 1000r multicolored .80 .25
**6341** A3005 1000r multicolored .80 .25
**6342** A3006 1000r multicolored .80 .25
**6343** A3006 1000r multicolored .80 .25
*a.* Sheet, 3 each #6342-6343 10.00 10.00
**6344** A3005 1500r multicolored .65 .40
**6345** A3005 1500r multicolored .65 .40
*Nos. 6339-6345 (7)* 5.00 2.05

**Souvenir Sheet**

**6346** A3006 1000r Sheet of 4, #a.-d. + label 2.00 1.25

No. 6346 has blue background.

Aleksandr Gorsky (1871-1924), Choreographer — A3006a

a, 750r, Portrait, scenes from "The Daughter of Gudule," "Salambo." b, 1500r, Don Quixote. c, 1500r, Giselle. d, 750r, La Bayadere.

**1996, Aug. 7 Litho. *Perf. 12½x12***

**6347** A3006a Block of 4, #a.-d. 2.00 1.00
*e.* Sheet of 6, #6347b 10.00 5.00

Treaty Between Russia and Belarus A3006b

**1996, Aug. 27 *Perf. 12x12½***

**6348** A3006b 1500r Natl. flags .50 .30

17th-20th Cent. Enamelwork — A3007

Designs: No. 6349, Chalice, 1679. No. 6350, Aromatic bottle, 17th cent. No. 6351, Ink pot, ink set, 17th-18th cent. No. 6352, Coffee pot, 1750-1760. No. 6353, Perfume bottle, 19th-20th cent.

5000r, Icon, Our Lady of Kazan, 1894.

**1996, Sept. 10 *Perf. 11½***

**6349** A3007 1000r multicolored .50 .25
**6350** A3007 1000r multicolored .50 .25
*a.* Sheet of 9 5.00 2.50
**6351** A3007 1000r multicolored .50 .25
**6352** A3007 1500r multicolored .50 .30
**6353** A3007 1500r multicolored .50 .30
*a.* Sheet of 9 5.00 2.50
*Nos. 6349-6353 (5)* 2.50 1.35

**Souvenir Sheet**

**6354** A3007 5000r multicolored 2.00 1.00

No. 6353a inscribed in sheet margin for Moscow '97.

No. 6354 contains one 35x50mm stamp.

UNESCO, 50th Anniv. A3008

**1996, Oct. 15 *Perf. 12x12½***

**6355** A3008 1000r multicolored .50 .25

No. 6355 issued in sheets of 8.

Icons, Religious Landmarks A3009

Designs: a, Icon of Our Lady of Iverone, Moscow. b, Holy Monastery of Stavrovouni, Cyprus. c, Icon of St. Nicholas, Cyprus. d, Resurrection (Iverone), Gate, Moscow.

**1996, Nov. 13 *Perf. 11½***

**6356** A3009 1500r Block of 4, #a.-d. 3.25 1.60

See Cyprus Nos. 893-896.

New Year 1997 — A3010

Design: Chiming Clock of Moscow, Kremlin.

**1996, Dec. 5**

**6357** A3010 1000r multicolored .50 .25
*a.* Sheet of 8 5.00 2.50

Natl. Ice Hockey Team, 50th Anniv. A3011

Action scenes: a, Two players. b, Three players. c, Three players, referee.

**1996, Dec. 5 *Perf. 12***

**6358** A3011 1500r Strip of 3, #a.-c. 3.00 1.10

Basil III — A3012

Ivan IV (the Terrible) — A3013

Feodor Ivanovich — A3014

Boris Godunov — A3015

**Litho. & Engr.**

**1996, Dec. 20 *Perf. 12***

**6359** A3012 1500r multicolored .75 .35
**6360** A3013 1500r multicolored .75 .35
**6361** A3014 1500r multicolored .75 .35
**6362** A3015 1500r multicolored .75 .35
*Nos. 6359-6362 (4)* 3.00 1.40

See #6296-6300.

Flowers — A3016

Designs: No. 6363, Chaenomeles japonica. No. 6364, Amygdalus triloba. No. 6365, Cytisus scoparius. No. 6366, Rosa pimpinellifolia. No. 6367, Philadelphus coronarius.

**1997, Jan. 21 Litho. *Perf. 12½x12***

**6363** A3016 500r multicolored *.75* .25
**6364** A3016 500r multicolored *.75* .25
**6365** A3016 1000r multicolored *1.25* .55
**6366** A3016 1000r multicolored *1.25* .55
**6367** A3016 1000r multicolored *1.25* .55
*Nos. 6363-6367 (5)* *5.25* 2.15

**Souvenir Sheet**

Moscow, 850th Anniv. — A3017

**1997, Feb. 20 *Perf. 12x12½***

**6368** A3017 3000r Coat of arms 2.00 1.00

Shostakovich Intl. Music Festival — A3018

Dmitri D. Shostakovich (1906-75), composer.

**1997, Feb. 26 *Perf. 12***

**6369** A3018 1000r multicolored .50 .25

**Souvenir Sheet**

Coat of Arms of Russia, 500th Anniv. — A3019

**1997, Mar. 20**

**6370** A3019 3000r multicolored 2.00 .70

Post Emblem — A3020

Designs: 100r, Agriculture. 150r, Oil rig. 250r, Cranes (birds). 300r, Radio/TV tower. 500r, Russian Post emblem. 750r, St. George slaying dragon. 1000r, Natl. flag, arms. 1500r, Electric power. 2000r, Train. 2500r, Moscow Kremlin. 3000r, Satellite. 5000r, Fine arts.

**1997 Chalky Paper *Perf. 12x12½***

**6371** A3020 100r blk & yel brn .25 .25
**6372** A3020 150r blk & red lilac .25 .25
**6373** A3020 250r blk & olive .35 .25
**6374** A3020 300r blk & dk grn .65 .25
**6375** A3020 500r blk & dk bl .55 .25
**6376** A3020 750r blk & brown 1.10 .25
**6377** A3020 1000r blue & red 1.10 .25
**6378** A3020 1500r blk & grn bl 1.60 .30
**6379** A3020 2000r blk & green 1.25 .40
**6380** A3020 2500r blk & red 2.25 .45
**6381** A3020 3000r blk & purple 2.25 .60
**6382** A3020 5000r blk & brown 3.25 1.00
*Nos. 6371-6382 (12)* 14.85 4.50

Nos. 6371-6382 exist on normal (glossy) paper. Values, same.

Issued: 500r, 750r, 1000r, 1500r, 2500r, 3/31; 100r, 150r, 250r, 300r, 2000r, 3000r, 5000r, 4/30.

See Nos. 6423-6433, 6550-6560, 6617-6620.

A3021

**1997, Mar. 31 Litho. *Perf. 12***

**6383** A3021 1000r multicolored *10.00* .25

City of Vologda, 850th anniv.

A3022

Europa (Stories and Legends): Legend of Volga.

**1997, May 5 Litho. *Perf. 12x12½***

**6384** A3022 1500r multicolored 3.50 .80

Moscow, 850th Anniv. — A3023

Historic buildings: a, Cathedral of Christ the Savior. b, Turrets and roofs of the Kremlin. c, Grand Palace of the Kremlin, cathedral plaza. d, St. Basil's Cathedral. e, Icon, St. George slaying the Dragon. f, Text of first chronicled record of Moscow, 1147. g, Prince Aleksandr Nevski, Danilov Monastery. h, 16th cent. miniature of Moscow Kremlin. i, Miniature of coronation of Czar Ivan IV. j, 16th cent. map of Moscow.

**1997, May 22**

**6385** A3023 1000r Sheet of 10, #a.-j. 12.00 12.00

Nos. 6385c, 6385h are 42x42mm.

Helicopters — A3024

**1997, May 28 Litho. *Perf. 12½x12***

**6386** A3024 500r Mi-14 *6.00* 2.50
**6387** A3024 1000r Mi-24 *6.00* 2.50
**6388** A3024 1500r Mi-26 *6.00* 2.50
**6389** A3024 2000r Mi-28 *6.00* 2.50
*a.* Sheet of 6 *45.00*
**6390** A3024 2500r Mi-34 *6.00* 2.50
*Nos. 6386-6390 (5)* *30.00* 12.50

Fairy Tales by Aleksander S. Pushkin — A3025

Designs: 500r, Man holding rope beside lake, devil running, from "The Tale of the Priest and his Workman Balda." 1000r, Two women, two men, from "The Tale of Tsar Saltan." 1500r, Man fishing, fish, man, castle, from "The Tale of the Fisherman and the Fish." 2000r, Princess on steps, old woman holding apple, from "The Tale of the Dead Princess." 3000r, Woman, King bowing while holding scepter, rooster up in air, from "The Tale of the Golden Cockerel."

**Photo. & Engr.**

**1997, June 6** *Perf. 12x12½*

**6391** A3025 500r multicolored *.60* .25
**6392** A3025 1000r multicolored *1.25* .25
**6393** A3025 1500r multicolored *1.75* .30
**6394** A3025 2000r multicolored *2.50* .40
**6395** A3025 3000r multicolored *3.50* .60
*a.* Strip of 5, #6391-6395 *15.00* 12.00
*b.* Sheet of 2 #6395a 40.00 40.00

Diplomatic Relations Between Russia and Thailand A3026

Design: St. Petersburg, Russian flag, Bangkok, Thailand flag.

**1997, June 20 Litho.** *Perf. 12½x12*

**6396** A3026 1500r multicolored 1.00 .30

Wildlife A3027

Designs: a, 500r, Pteromys volans. b, 750r, Felix lynx. c, 1000r, Tetrao urogallus. d, 2000r, Lutra lutra. e, 3000r, Numenius arguata.

**1997, July 10** *Perf. 12*

**6397** A3027 Block of 5, #a.-e., + label 3.00 1.50

Russian Regions A3028

No. 6398, Winter scene, Archangel Oblast. No. 6399, Ocean, beach, Kaliningrad Oblast, vert. No. 6400, Ship, Krasnodarsky Krai. No. 6401, Mountains, Yakutia, vert. No. 6402, Mountain, sailing ship monument, Kamchatka Oblast.

**1997, July 15** *Perf. 12½x12, 12x12½*

**6398** A3028 1500r multicolored .55 .30
**6399** A3028 1500r multicolored .55 .30
**6400** A3028 1500r multicolored .55 .30
**6401** A3028 1500r multicolored .55 .30
**6402** A3028 1500r multicolored .55 .30
*Nos. 6398-6402 (5)* 2.75 1.50

Cartoon Character Kljopa A3029

Kljpoa and: 500r, Rainbow, balloons. 1000r, Hang glider. 1500r, Troika.

**1997, July 25** *Perf. 11½*

**6403** A3029 500r multicolored .50 .25
**6404** A3029 1000r multicolored 1.00 .25

**Size: 45x33mm**

*Perf. 12*

**6405** A3029 1500r multicolored 1.50 .40
*Nos. 6403-6405 (3)* 3.00 .90

World Philatelic Exhibition, Moscow 97 — A3030

Designs: a, No. 1, No. 35. b, No. 6061.

**1997, Aug. 5** *Perf. 11½*

**6406** A3030 1500r Pair, #a.-b. 1.00 .50
*c.* Sheet of 6 stamps 9.00 9.00

A3031

History of Russia, Peter I: No. 6407, Planning new capital. No. 6408, Reforming the military. No. 6409, In Baltic Sea naval battle. No. 6410, Ordering administrative reform. No. 6411, Advocating cultural education.
5000r, Peter I (1672-1725).

**1997, Aug. 15** *Perf. 12x12½*

**6407** A3031 2000r multicolored 1.10 .50
**6408** A3031 2000r multicolored 1.10 .50
**6409** A3031 2000r multicolored 1.10 .50
**6410** A3031 2000r multicolored 1.10 .50
**6411** A3031 2000r multicolored 1.10 .50
*Nos. 6407-6411 (5)* 5.50 2.50

**Souvenir Sheet**

**Litho. & Engr.**

**6411A** A3031 5000r multicolored 4.00 1.50

Indian Independence, 50th Anniv. — A3032

**1997, Aug. 15** *Perf. 12*

**6412** A3032 500r multicolored .50 .25

Russian Pentathlon, 50th Anniv. — A3033

**1997, Sept. 1** *Perf. 12½x12*

**6413** A3033 1000r multicolored .50 .25

Russian Soccer, Cent. A3034

**1997, Sept. 4**

**6414** A3034 2000r multicolored .75 .35

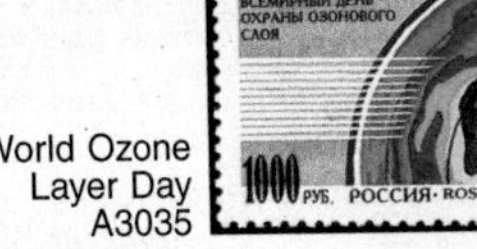

World Ozone Layer Day A3035

**1997, Sept. 16** *Perf. 12x12½*

**6415** A3035 1000r multioclored .50 .25

A3036

**1997, Oct. 1**

**6416** A3036 1000r multicolored 1.00 .50

Russia's admission to European Council. No. 6416 printed with se-tenant label.

**Souvenir Sheet**

Pushkin's "Eugene Onegin," Translated by Abraham Shlonsky — A3038

**1997, Nov. 19 Litho.** *Perf. 12*

**6418** A3038 3000r multicolored 2.00 1.60

See Israel No. 1319.

Russian State Museum, St. Petersburg, Cent. — A3039

500r, Boris and Gleb, 14th cent. icon. 1000r, "The Volga Boatmen," by I. Repin. 1500r, "A Promenade," by Marc Chagall. 2000r, "A Merchant's Wife Having Tea," by Kustodiyev.

**1997, Nov. 12 Litho.** *Perf. 12*

**6419** A3039 500r multi, vert. .25 .25
**6420** A3039 1000r multi, vert. .40 .25
**6421** A3039 1500r multi .60 .30
**6422** A3039 2000r multi, vert. .80 .40
*Nos. 6419-6422 (4)* 2.05 1.20

Nos. 6419-6422 were each issued in sheets of 8 + label.
See Nos. 6446-6450.

**Post Emblem Type of 1997**

**1998, Jan. 1 Litho.** *Perf. 12x12½*

**6423** A3020 10k like #6371 .25 .25
**6424** A3020 15k like #6372 .25 .25
**6425** A3020 25k like #6373 .25 .25
**6426** A3020 30k like #6374 .25 .25
**6427** A3020 50k like #6375 .30 .25
**6428** A3020 1r like #6377 .60 .30
**6429** A3020 1.50r like #6378 .90 .45
**6430** A3020 2r like #6379 1.25 .60
**6431** A3020 2.50r like #6380 1.40 .70
**6432** A3020 3r like #6381 1.75 .90
**6433** A3020 5r like #6382 3.00 1.40
*Nos. 6423-6433 (11)* 10.20 5.60

Nos. 6423-6433 were printed on chalky paper and normal (glossy) paper. Values, same.

Vasily Surikov (1848-1916), V. Vasnetsov (1848-1926), Painters — A3040

Entire paintings or details by Surikov: No. 6434, Menshikov in Berezovo, 1887. No. 6435, Boyarynya Morozova, 1887.
By Vasnetsov, vert.: No. 6436, The Struggle of Slavs with the Nomads, 1881. No. 6437, Ivan Tsarevitch on a Wolf, 1889.

**1998, Jan. 24** *Perf. 12*

**6434** A3040 1.50r multicolored .90 .45
**6435** A3040 1.50r multicolored .90 .45
*a.* Pair, #6434-6435 + label 3.00 .90
**6436** A3040 1.50r multicolored .90 .45
**6437** A3040 1.50r multicolored .90 .45
*a.* Pair, #6436-6437 + label 3.00 .90

1998 Winter Olympic Games, Nagano — A3041

50k, Cross country skiing. 1r, Pairs figure skating. 1.50r, Biathlon.

**1998, Jan. 27 Litho.** *Perf. 12*

**6438** A3041 50k multicolored .40 .25
**6439** A3041 1r multicolored 1.00 .30
**6440** A3041 1.50r multicolored 1.60 .45
*a.* Sheet, 2 each #6438-6440 10.00 3.00
*Nos. 6438-6440 (3)* 3.00 1.00

Aquarium Fish A3042

Designs: No. 6441, Hyphessobrycon callistus. No. 6442, Epalzeorhynchus bicolor. 1r, Synodontis galinae. No. 6444, Botia kristinae. No. 6445, Cichlasoma labiatum.

**1998, Feb. 25 Litho.** *Perf. 12½x12*

**6441** A3042 50k multicolored .35 .25
**6442** A3042 50k multicolored .35 .25
**6443** A3042 1r multicolored .60 .25
*a.* Sheet of 6 *25.00 12.50*
**6444** A3042 1.50r multicolored .90 .30
**6445** A3042 1.50r multicolored .90 .30
*Nos. 6441-6445 (5)* 3.10 1.35

**Russian State Museum, St. Petersburg, Cent., Type of 1997**

Designs: No. 6446, The Last Day of Pompeii, by K.P. Bryullov, 1833. No. 6447, Our Lady of Malevolent Hearts Tenderness, by K.S. Petrov-Vodkin, 1914-15. No. 6448, Mast Pine Grove, by I.I. Shishkin, 1898. No. 6449, The Ninth Wave, by I.K. Aivazovsky, 1850.
3r, The Mihailovksy Palace (detail), by K.P. Beggrov, 1832.

**1998, Mar. 17** *Perf. 12x12½*

| | | | | |
|---|---|---|---|---|
| **6446** | A3039 | 1.50r multicolored | 1.20 | .30 |
| **6447** | A3039 | 1.50r multicolored | 1.20 | .30 |
| **6448** | A3039 | 1.50r multicolored | 1.20 | .30 |
| **6449** | A3039 | 1.50r multicolored | 1.20 | .30 |
| *a.* | | Sheet, 2 each #6446-6449 + label | 10.00 | 5.00 |
| | | *Nos. 6446-6449 (4)* | 4.80 | 1.20 |

**Souvenir Sheet**

| | | | | |
|---|---|---|---|---|
| **6450** | A3039 | 3r multicolored | 2.00 | 1.00 |

Souvenir Sheet

Expo '98, Lisbon — A3043

**1998, Apr. 15** *Perf. 12½x12*

| | | | | |
|---|---|---|---|---|
| **6451** | A3043 | 3r Emblem, dolphins | 2.00 | .75 |

Theater of Arts, Moscow, Cent. — A3044

**1998, Apr. 24** *Perf. 12*

| | | | | |
|---|---|---|---|---|
| **6452** | A3044 | 1.50r multicolored | 1.00 | .40 |

No. 6452 was printed se-tenant with label.

Shrove-tide Natl. Festival — A3045

**1998, May 5 Litho.** *Perf. 12½x12*

| | | | | |
|---|---|---|---|---|
| **6453** | A3045 | 1.50r multicolored | 1.00 | .50 |

Europa.

A3046

A3046a

A3046b

Aleksander S. Pushkin (1799-1837), Poet — A3046c

Pushkin's drawings: No. 6454, Lyceum where Puskin studied 1811-17. No. 6455, A. N. Wolf, contemporary of Pushkin's. No. 6456, Tatyana, heroine of novel, "Eugene Onegin." No. 6457, Cover of 1830 manuscript. No. 6458, Self-portrait.

**Litho. & Engr.**

**1998, May 28** *Perf. 12x12½*

| | | | | |
|---|---|---|---|---|
| **6454** | A3046 | 1.50r multicolored | .60 | .30 |
| **6455** | A3046a | 1.50r multicolored | .60 | .30 |
| **6456** | A3046b | 1.50r multicolored | .60 | .30 |
| **6457** | A3046c | 1.50r multicolored | .60 | .30 |
| **6458** | A3046c | 1.50r multicolored | .60 | .30 |
| *a.* | | Sheet, 2 each #6454-6458 | 20.00 | 5.00 |
| | | *Nos. 6454-6458 (5)* | 3.00 | 1.50 |

City of Ulyanovsk (Simbirsk), 350th Anniv. — A3047

**1998, May 28 Litho.** *Perf. 12½x12*

| | | | | |
|---|---|---|---|---|
| **6459** | A3047 | 1r multicolored | 3.00 | .30 |

Czar Nicholas II (1868-1918) — A3048

**1998, June 30 Litho.** *Perf. 11½*

| | | | | |
|---|---|---|---|---|
| **6460** | A3048 | 3r multicolored | 1.00 | .60 |

Printed se-tenant with label.

City of Taganrog, 300th Anniv. — A3049

**1998, June 10 Litho.** *Perf. 12½x12*

| | | | | |
|---|---|---|---|---|
| **6461** | A3049 | 1r multicolored | .75 | .25 |

Souvenir Sheet

1998 World Youth Games, Moscow — A3049a

**1998, June 25 Litho.** *Perf. 12½x12*

| | | | | |
|---|---|---|---|---|
| **6461A** | A3049a | 3r multicolored | 1.25 | .75 |

A3050

Wild Berries: 50k, Vitis amurensis. 75k, Rubus idaeus. 1r, Schisandra chinensis. 1.50r, Vaccinium vitis-idaea. 2r, Rubus arcticus.

**1998, July 10**

| | | | | |
|---|---|---|---|---|
| **6462** | A3050 | 50k multicolored | .25 | .25 |
| **6463** | A3050 | 75k multicolored | .40 | .25 |
| **6464** | A3050 | 1r multicolored | .50 | .25 |
| **6465** | A3050 | 1.50r multicolored | .75 | .30 |
| **6466** | A3050 | 2r multicolored | 1.00 | .40 |
| | | *Nos. 6462-6466 (5)* | 2.90 | 1.45 |

A3051

**1998, July 15**

| | | | | |
|---|---|---|---|---|
| **6467** | A3051 | 1r multicolored | 1.00 | .25 |

Ekaterinburg, 275th anniv.

Soviet Intelligence Agents — A3052

No. 6468, L. R. Kvasnikov (1905-93). No. 6469, Morris Cohen (1910-95). No. 6470, Leontina Cohen (1913-92). No. 6471, A.A. Yatskov (1913-93).

**1998, Aug. 10 Litho.** *Perf. 12*

| | | | | |
|---|---|---|---|---|
| **6468** | A3052 | 1r green & black | .75 | .25 |
| **6469** | A3052 | 1r brn, bister & blk | .75 | .25 |
| **6470** | A3052 | 1r slate & black | .75 | .25 |
| **6471** | A3052 | 1r claret & black | .75 | .25 |
| | | *Nos. 6468-6471 (4)* | 3.00 | 1.00 |

Orders of Russia — A3053

1r, St. Andrey Pervozvanny. 1.50r St. Catherine. 2r, St. Alexander Nevsky. 2.50r, St. George.

**1998, Aug. 20 Litho.** *Perf. 12x12½*

| | | | | |
|---|---|---|---|---|
| **6472** | A3053 | 1r multi | .35 | .25 |
| **6472A** | A3053 | 1.50r multi | .55 | .25 |
| **6472B** | A3053 | 2r multi | .70 | .35 |
| **6472C** | A3053 | 2.50r multi | .90 | .45 |
| *d.* | | Block of 4, #6472-6472C | 3.50 | 1.75 |
| *e.* | | Souvenir sheet of 4, #6472-6472C + label | 25.00 | 10.00 |

See #6496-6500.

Murmansk Oblast A3054

Khabarovsk Krai — A3055

Karelia Republic — A3056 Buryat Republic — A3057

**1998, Sept. 15 Litho.** *Perf. 12*

| | | | | |
|---|---|---|---|---|
| **6473** | A3054 | 1.50r multicolored | .60 | .30 |
| **6474** | A3055 | 1.50r multicolored | .60 | .30 |
| **6475** | A3056 | 1.50r multicolored | .60 | .30 |
| **6476** | A3057 | 1.50r multicolored | .60 | .30 |
| **6477** | A3054 | 1.50r Primorski Krai | .60 | .30 |
| | | *Nos. 6473-6477 (5)* | 3.00 | 1.50 |

World Stamp Day A3058

**1998, Oct. 9 Litho.** *Perf. 12*

| | | | | |
|---|---|---|---|---|
| **6478** | A3058 | 1r multicolored | .75 | .25 |

Universal Declaration of Human Rights, 50th Anniv. — A3059

**1998, Oct. 15**

| | | | | |
|---|---|---|---|---|
| **6479** | A3059 | 1.50r multicolored | .50 | .30 |

No. 6479 released with se-tenant label.

Menatep Bank, 10th Anniv. — A3060

**1998, Oct. 29**
**6480** A3060 2r multicolored 1.00 .40

A sheet of eight was withdrawn from sale because the Menatep Bank went bankrupt. Value, $50.

20th Cent. Achievements — A3061

**1998, Nov. 12**
**6481** A3061 1r Aviation .50 .25
**6482** A3061 1r Space .50 .25
**6483** A3061 1r Television .50 .25
**6484** A3061 1r Genetics .50 .25
**6485** A3061 1r Nuclear power .50 .25
**6486** A3061 1r Computers .50 .25
*Nos. 6481-6486 (6)* 3.00 1.50

M.I. Koshkin (1898-1940), Tank Designer — A3062

**1998, Nov. 20**
**6487** A3062 1r multicolored 1.00 .25

New Year — A3063

**1998, Dec. 1 Litho. *Perf. 11½***
**6488** A3063 1r multicolored .50 .25
*a.* Sheet of 9 12.00 5.00

Moscow-St. Petersburg Telephone Line, Cent. — A3064

**1999, Jan. 13**
**6489** A3064 1r multicolored .50 .25

Hunting A3065

**1999, Jan. 29 Litho. *Perf. 11¼***
**6490** A3065 1r Wild turkey .25 .25
**6491** A3065 1.50r Ducks .45 .25
**6492** A3065 2r Releasing raptor .55 .25
**6493** A3065 2.50r Wolves .75 .30
**6494** A3065 3r Bear .90 .35
*Nos. 6490-6494 (5)* 2.90 1.40

Souvenir Sheet

Mediterranean Cruise of Feodor F. Ushakov, Bicent. — A3066

**1999, Feb. 19 *Perf. 12½x12***
**6495** A3066 5r multicolored 2.00 .55

**Order of Russia Type of 1998**

1r, St. Vladimir, 1782. 1.50r, St. Anne, 1797. 2r, St. John of Jerusalem, 1798. 2.50r, White Eagles, 1815. 3r, St. Stanislas, 1815.

**1999, Feb. 25 Litho. *Perf. 12x12¼***
**6496** A3053 1r multicolored .35 .25
**6497** A3053 1.50r multicolored .45 .25
**6498** A3053 2r multicolored .60 .25
**6499** A3053 2.50r multicolored .75 .30
**6500** A3053 3r multicolored .90 .40
*a.* Sheet of 5, #6496-6500 40.00 25.00

Children's Paintings — A3067

Designs: No. 6501, Family picnic. No. 6502, City, bridge, boats on water, helicopter. No. 6503, Stylized city, vert.

**1999, Mar. 24 Litho. *Perf. 12¼x12***
**6501** A3067 1.20r multicolored .65 .25
**6502** A3067 1.20r multicolored .65 .25
**6503** A3067 1.20r multicolored .65 .25
*Nos. 6501-6503 (3)* 1.95 .75

Souvenir Sheet

Russian Navy's Use of Flag with St. Andrew's Cross, 300th Anniv. — A3068

**1999, Mar. 24 Litho. *Perf. 12½x12***
**6504** A3068 7r multicolored 2.50 1.00

Souvenir Sheet

Intl. Space Station — A3069

**1999, Apr. 12 *Perf. 11½x12½***
**6505** A3069 7r multicolored 5.00 .60

IBRA '99 World Philatelic Exhibition, Nuremberg — A3070

**1999, Apr. 27 *Perf. 12½x12***
**6506** A3070 3r multicolored .50 .25

Fishermen and Fishing Gear — A3071

**1999, Apr. 30 *Perf. 11¾***
**6507** A3071 1r Raft .25 .25
**6508** A3071 2r Three fishermen .40 .25
**6509** A3071 2r Fisherman, boat .40 .25
**6510** A3071 3r Spear fishing .50 .25
**6511** A3071 3r Ice fishermen .50 .25
*Nos. 6507-6511 (5)* 2.05 1.25

Council of Europe, 50th Anniv. A3072

**1999, May 5 *Perf. 12x12¼***
**6512** A3072 3r multicolored .50 .25

Europa A3073

**1999, May 5 *Perf. 12½x12***
**6513** A3073 5r Bison, Oka Natl. Nature Reserve 2.25 .60

Red Deer — A3074

Designs: a, Bucks. b, Does.

**1999, May 18 *Perf. 12½x12***
**6514** A3074 2.50r Pair, #a.-b. 3.00 .35
Complete booklet #6514 3.00

See People's Republic of China #2958-2959.

Aleksander Pushkin (1799-1837), Poet A3075

Paintings of Pushkin by: 1r, S. G. Chirikov, 1815. 3r, J. E. Vivien, 1826. 5r, Karl P. Bryulov, 1836.
7r, Vasily A. Tropinin, 1827

**Litho. & Engr.**

**1999, May 27 *Perf. 12***
**6515** A3075 1r multicolored .35 .25
**6516** A3075 3r multicolored .55 .25
**6517** A3075 5r multicolored 1.10 .35
*a.* Min. sheet, 2 ea #6515-6517 9.00 3.75
*Nos. 6515-6517 (3)* 2.00 .85

**Souvenir Sheet**

***Perf. 12x12½***
**6518** A3075 7r multicolored 2.00 .60

No. 6518 contains one 30x41mm stamp.

North Ossetia Republic A3076

Stavropol Kray A3077

Evenki Autonomous Okrug — A3078

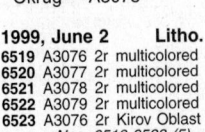

Bashkir Republic — A3079

**1999, June 2 Litho. *Perf. 12***
**6519** A3076 2r multicolored .30 .25
**6520** A3077 2r multicolored .30 .25
**6521** A3078 2r multicolored .30 .25
**6522** A3079 2r multicolored .30 .25
**6523** A3076 2r Kirov Oblast .30 .25
*Nos. 6519-6523 (5)* 1.50 1.25

Roses — A3080

**1999, June 10 *Perf. 12¼x11¾***
**Color of Rose**
**6524** A3080 1.20r pink .25 .25
**6525** A3080 1.20r yellow .25 .25
**6526** A3080 2r red & yellow .30 .25
**6527** A3080 3r white .45 .25
**6528** A3080 4r red .60 .30
*a.* Min. sheet of 5, #6524-6528 10.00 4.50
*b.* Strip of 5, #6524-6528 5.00 2.50
*Nos. 6524-6528 (5)* 1.85 1.30

**No. 6123 Surcharged**

**1999, June 22 Litho. *Perf. 12½x12***
**6529** A2902 1.20r on 5000r 1.00 .30

Rostov-on-Don, 250th Anniv. — A3081

**1999, July 8 Litho. *Perf. 11¾x12¼***
**6530** A3081 1.20r multi *2.50* .25

UPU, 125th Anniv. — A3082

**1999, Aug. 23** ***Perf. 11¾***
**6531** A3082 3r multi .55 .30

Paintings of Karl P. Bryullov (1799-1852) — A3083

Paintings: a, Horsewoman, 1832. b, Portrait of Y. P. Samoilova and Amacillia Paccini.

**1999, Aug. 25 Litho.** ***Perf. 11¾x12***
**6532** A3083 2.50r Pair, #a-b, + central label 2.00 .35

Motorcycles — A3084

Designs: a, 1r, IZ-1, 1929. b, 1.50r, L-300, 1930. c, 2r, M-72, 1941. d, 2.50r, M-1A, 1945. e, 5r, IZ Planet 5, 1987.

**1999, Sept. 9 Litho.** ***Perf. 11¾***
**6533** A3084 Block of 5, #a.-e., + label 3.00 .85
Booklet #6533 5.50

The booklet also contains an unfranked cacheted envelope with First Day Cancel.

Field Marshal Aleksandr Suvorov's Alpine Campaign, Bicent. A3085

Designs: No. 6534, Suvorov and soldiers, monument at Schöllenen Gorge. No. 6535, Suvorov's vanguard at Lake Klöntal.

**1999, Sept. 24 Litho.** ***Perf. 12x11½***
**6534** A3085 2.50r multi *.40 1.50*
*a.* Miniature sheet of 8 40.00
**6535** A3085 2.50r multi *.40 1.50*
*a.* Miniature sheet of 8 40.00

See Switzerland Nos. 1056-1057.

Native Sports — A3086

#6536, Kalmyk wrestling. #6537, Horse racing. #6538, Stick tossing. #6539, Reindeer racing. #6540, Weight lifting.

***Perf. 11¾x11½, 11½x11¾***
**1999, Sept. 30 Litho.**
**6536** A3086 2r multi .40 .25
**6537** A3086 2r multi .40 .25
**6538** A3086 2r multi .40 .25
**6539** A3086 2r multi .40 .25
**6540** A3086 2r multi, vert. .40 .25
*Nos. 6536-6540 (5)* 2.00 1.25

Popular Singers A3087

Designs: No. 6542, Leonid Utesov (1895-1982). No. 6543, Mark Bernes (1911-69). No. 6544, Claudia Shulzhenko (1906-84). No. 6545, Lidia Ruslanova (1900-73). No. 6546, Bulat Okudzhava (1924-97). No. 6547, Vladimir Vysotsky (1938-80). No. 6548, Viktor Tsoi (1962-90). No. 6549, Igor Talkov (1956-91).

**1999, Oct. 6 Litho.** ***Perf. 12x12¼***
**6542** A3087 2r multi .40 .25
**6543** A3087 2r multi .40 .25
**6544** A3087 2r multi .40 .25
**6545** A3087 2r multi .40 .25
**6546** A3087 2r multi .40 .25
**6547** A3087 2r multi .40 .25
**6548** A3087 2r multi .40 .25
**6549** A3087 2r multi .40 .25
*a.* Miniature sheet, #6542-6549 10.00
*Nos. 6542-6549 (8)* 3.20 2.00

**Types of 1997 Redrawn with Microprinting Replacing Vertical Lines**

**1999, Oct. 26 Litho.** ***Perf. 12x12¼***
**Granite Paper**
**6550** A3020 10k Like #6371 .50 .25
**6551** A3020 15k Like #6372 .50 .25
**6552** A3020 25k Like #6373 .50 .25
**6553** A3020 30k Like #6374 .50 .25
**6554** A3020 50k Like #6375 .50 .25
**6555** A3020 1r Like #6377 .50 .25
**6556** A3020 1.50r Like #6378 .50 .25
**6557** A3020 2r Like #6379 .50 .25
**6558** A3020 2.50r Like #6380 .50 .25
**6559** A3020 3r Like #6381 .50 .30
**6560** A3020 5r Like #6382 .50 .40
*Nos. 6550-6560 (11)* 5.50 2.95

Dated 1998.

Spartak, Russian Soccer Champions A3088

**1999, Nov. 27** ***Perf. 12x12¼***
**6561** A3088 2r multi .60 .25

New Year 2000 — A3089

Designs: a, Grandfather Frost, planets. b, Tree, earth in shell.

**1999, Dec. 1** ***Perf. 11½x11¾***
**6562** A3089 1.20r Pair, #a-b 2.25 .25
*c.* Sheet of 6 #6562a *15.00*
*d.* Sheet of 6 #6562b *20.00*

No. 6562 printed in sheets of 30 stamps.

Christianity, 2000th Anniv. — A3090

Paintings: No. 6563, The Raising of the Daughter of Jairus, by Vassili D. Polenov, 1871. No. 6564, Christ in the Wilderness, by Ivan N. Kramskoy, 1872. No. 6565, Christ in the House of Mary and Martha, by G. I. Semiradsky, 1886. No. 6566, What is Truth?, by Nikolai N. Gay, 1890, vert.

7r, Appearance of the Risen Christ, by Alexander A. Ivanov, 1837-57.

**2000, Jan. 1 Litho.** ***Perf. 12***
**6563** A3090 3r multi .50 .25
**6564** A3090 3r multi .50 .25
**6565** A3090 3r multi .50 .25
**6566** A3090 3r multi .50 .25
*Nos. 6563-6566 (4)* 2.00 1.00

**Souvenir Sheet**
***Perf. 12¼x12***
**6567** A3090 7r multi 2.00 1.00

No. 6567 contains one 52x37mm stamp.

Souvenir Sheet

Christianity, 2000th Anniv. — A3091

No. 6568: a, Mother of God mosaic, St. Sofia Cathedral, Kiev, 11th cent. b, Christ Pantocrator fresco, Polotsk, Belarus, 12th cent. c, Volodymyr Madonna, Tretiakov Gallery, Moscow, 12th cent.

**2000, Jan. 5** ***Perf. 12x12¼***
**6568** A3091 3r Sheet of 3, #a-c 3.00 1.25

See Belarus No. 330, Ukraine No. 370.

Nikolai D. Psurtsev (1900-80), Communications Minister — A3092

**Litho. & Engr.**
**2000, Feb. 1** ***Perf. 12x12¼***
**6569** A3092 2.50r multi .50 .25

Souvenir Sheet

Christianity, 2000th Anniv. — A3093

**2000, Feb. 10 Litho.** ***Perf. 12¼***
**6570** A3093 10r Kremlin Cathedrals 5.00 .70

No. 6570 contains two 37x52mm labels.

Polar Explorers — A3094

Designs: No. 6571, R. L. Samoilovich (1881-1940). No. 6572, V. Y. Vize (1886-1954). No. 6573, Mikhail M. Somov (1908-73). No. 6574, P. A. Gordienko (1913-82). No. 6575, A. F. Treshnikov (1914-91).

**2000, Feb. 24** ***Perf. 11¾***
**6571** A3094 2r multi .80 .25
**6572** A3094 2r multi .80 .25
**6573** A3094 2r multi .80 .25
**6574** A3094 2r multi .80 .25
**6575** A3094 2r multi .80 .25
*a.* Miniature sheet of 5, #6571-6575, + label *60.00 60.00*
*Nos. 6571-6575 (5)* 4.00 1.25

National Sporting Milestones of the 20th Century — A3095

No. 6576: a, 25k, N. A. Panin-Kolomenkin, 1st Olympic champion, 1908. b, 30k, Stockholm Olympics, 1912. c, 50k, All-Russian Olympiad, 1913-14. d, 1r, All-Union Spartacist Games, 1928. e, 1.35r, Sports Association for Labor & Defense, 1931. f, 1.50r, Honored Master of Sport award, 1934. g, 2r, Helsinki Olympics, 1952. h, 2.50r, Vladimir P. Kuts, gold medalist at Melbourne Olympics, 1956. i, 3r, Gold medalist soccer team at Melbourne, 1956. j, 4r Mikhail M. Botvinnik, chess champion. k, 5r, Hockey series between Canada and Soviet Union, 1972. l, 6r, Moscow Olympics, 1980.

**2000, Mar. 15** ***Perf. 12¼x12***
**6576** A3095 Sheet of 12, #a-l 7.50 2.50

Souvenir Sheet

World Meteorological Organization, 50th Anniv. — A3096

**2000, Mar. 20**
**6577** A3096 7r multi 2.00 .45

A3097 A3098

End of World War II, 55th Anniv. — A3099

War effort posters: No. 6581, Soldier holding child.

5r, Soldier and medal.

**2000, Apr. 10**
**6578** A3097 1.50r multi .50 .25
**6579** A3098 1.50r multi .50 .25
**6580** A3099 1.50r multi .50 .25
**6581** A3099 1.50r multi .50 .25
*Nos. 6578-6581 (4)* 2.00 1.00

**Souvenir Sheet**
**6582** A3099 5r multi 3.00 .75
*a.* Miniature sheet, #6578-6581, 2 #6582 20.00 10.00

International Space Cooperation A3100

2r, Apollo-Soyuz mission. 3r, Intl. Space Station. 5r, Sea-based launching station.

**2000, Apr. 12** *Perf. 12*

| | | | |
|---|---|---|---|
| **6583** | A3100 2r multi, vert. | .65 | .25 |
| *a.* | Miniature sheet of 6 | 20.00 | 10.00 |
| **6584** | A3100 3r multi | .75 | .25 |
| **6585** | A3100 5r multi, vert. | 1.60 | .25 |
| | *Nos. 6583-6585 (3)* | 3.00 | .75 |

Traffic Safety Week — A3101

**2000, Apr. 20** **Litho.** *Perf. 12x12½*

| | | | |
|---|---|---|---|
| **6586** | A3101 1.75r multi | .50 | .25 |

Holocaust A3102

**2000, May 5** *Perf. 12*

| | | | |
|---|---|---|---|
| **6587** | A3102 2r multi | 7.50 | 2.50 |

Election of Vladimir V. Putin as President — A3103

**2000, May 7** **Litho.** *Perf. 12*

| | | | |
|---|---|---|---|
| **6588** | A3103 1.75r multi | 2.00 | .35 |

**Europa, 2000**

Common Design Type

**2000, May 9** **Litho.** *Perf. 12½x12*

| | | | |
|---|---|---|---|
| **6589** | CD17 7r multi | 4.00 | .85 |
| | Booklet, #6589 | *10.00* | |

Souvenir Sheet

Expo 2000, Hanover — A3104

**2000, May 17** **Litho.** *Perf. 12½x12*

| | | | |
|---|---|---|---|
| **6590** | A3104 10r multi | 3.00 | .60 |

Yamalo-Nenets Autonomous Okrug — A3105

Kalmykia Republic — A3106

Mari El Republic — A3107

Tatarstan Republic — A3108

**2000, May 25** *Perf. 12*

| | | | |
|---|---|---|---|
| **6591** | A3105 3r shown | 1.00 | .50 |
| **6592** | A3105 3r Chuvash Republic | 1.00 | .50 |
| **6593** | A3106 3r shown | 1.00 | .50 |
| **6594** | A3107 3r shown | 1.00 | .50 |
| **6595** | A3108 3r shown | 1.00 | .50 |
| **6596** | A3108 3r Udmurtia Republic | 1.00 | .50 |
| | *Nos. 6591-6596 (6)* | 6.00 | 3.00 |

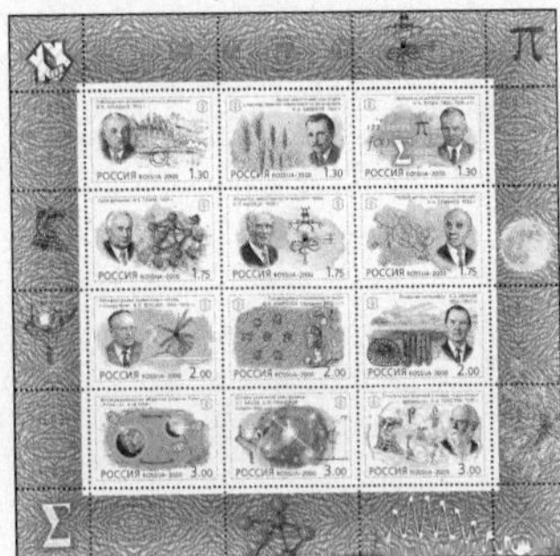

National Scientific Milestones in the 20th Century — A3109

No. 6597: a, 1.30r, Observation of ferromagnetic resonance by V. K. Arkadjev, 1913. b, 1.30r, Botanical diversity studies by N. I. Vavilov, 1920. c, 1.30r, Moscow Mathematical School, N. N. Luzin, 1920-30. d, 1.75r, Theories on light wave emissions by I. Y. Tamm, 1929. e, 1.75r, Discovery of superfluidity of liquid helium, by P. L. Kapitsa, 1938. f, 1.75r, Research in chemical chain reactions by N. N. Semenov, 1934. g, 2r, Phase stability in particle accelerators, by V. I. Veksler, 1944-45. h, 2r, Translation of Mayan texts by Y. V. Knorozov, 1950s. i, 2r, Research into pogonophorans by A. V. Ivanov. j, 3r, Photographing of the dark side of the moon by Luna 3, 1959. k, 3r, Research in quantum electronics by N. G. Basov and A. M. Prokhorov, 1960s. l, 3r, Slavic ethnolinguistic dictionary by N. I. Tolstoi, 1995.

**2000, June 20** *Perf. 12½x12*

| | | | |
|---|---|---|---|
| **6597** | A3109 Sheet of 12, #a-l | 15.00 | 3.50 |

Dogs — A3110

**2000, July 20** *Perf. 12x11¾*

| | | | |
|---|---|---|---|
| **6598** | Horiz. strip of 5 | 3.00 | 1.00 |
| *a.* | A3110 1r Chihuahua | .45 | .25 |
| *b.* | A3110 1.50r Toy terrier | .45 | .25 |
| *c.* | A3110 2r Miniature poodle | .45 | .25 |
| *d.* | A3110 2.50r French bulldog | .50 | .25 |
| *e.* | A3110 3r Japanese chin | .60 | .25 |
| *f.* | Souvenir sheet, #6598e, 2 each #6598a-6598d, perf. 11¾ | 14.00 | 14.00 |

2000 Summer Olympics, Sydney — A3111

Designs: 2r, Fencing. 3r, Synchronized swimming. 5r, Volleyball.

**2000, Aug. 15** **Litho.** *Perf. 12*

| | | | |
|---|---|---|---|
| **6599-6601** | A3111 Set of 3 | 2.00 | .65 |

Geological Service, 300th Anniv. — A3112

Minerals: 1r, Charoite. 2r, Hematite. 3r, Rock crystals. 4r, Gold.

**2000, Aug. 22** *Perf. 11¾*

| | | | |
|---|---|---|---|
| **6602-6605** | A3112 Set of 4 | 1.50 | .60 |

National Cultural Milestones in the 20th Century — A3113

No. 6606: a, 30k, Tours of Russian ballet and opera companies, 1908-14. b, 50k, Black Square on White, by Kazimir S. Malevich, 1913. c, 1r, Battleship Potemkin, movie by Sergein Eisenstein, 1925. d, 1.30r, Maxim Gorki, writer. e, 1.50r, Symbols of socialism. f, 1.75r, Vladimir V. Mayakovsky, poet, and propaganda posters. g, 2r, Vsevolod V. Meyerhold, Konstantin S. Stanislavsky, actors. h, 2.50r, Dmitry D. Shostakovich, composer. i, 3r, Galina S. Ulanova, ballet dancer. j, 4r, A. T. Tvardovsky, poet. k, 5r, Restoration of historical monuments and buildings. l, 6r, D. S. Likhachev, literary critic.

**2000, Sept. 20** **Litho.** *Perf. 12½x12*

| | | | |
|---|---|---|---|
| **6606** | A3113 Sheet of 12, #a-l | 6.00 | 2.00 |

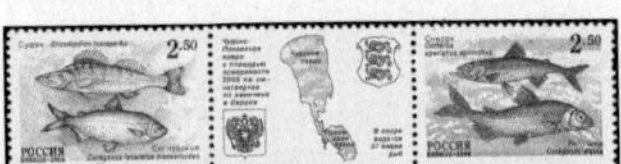

Fish in Lake Peipus — A3114

No. 6607: a, Stizostedion lucioperka, Coregonus lauaretus maenoides. b, Osmerus eperlanus spirinchus, Coregonus albula.

**2000, Oct. 25** *Perf. 12x12¼*

| | | | |
|---|---|---|---|
| **6607** | A3114 Horiz. pair + central label | 2.00 | .50 |
| *a.-b.* | 2.50r Any single | .50 | .25 |
| | Booklet, #6607 | 2.50 | |

See Estonia No. 403.

National Technological Milestones in the 20th Century — A3115

No. 6608: a, 1.50r, Medicine. b, 1.50r, Construction. c, 1.50r, Motor transport. d, 2r, Power generation. e, 2r, Communications. f, 2r, Space technology. g, 3r, Aviation. h, 3r, Rail transport. i, 3r, Sea transport. j, 4r, Metallurgy. k, 4r, Oil refining. l, 4r, Mineral extraction.

**2000, Nov. 28** *Perf. 12½x12*

| | | | |
|---|---|---|---|
| **6608** | A3115 Sheet of 12, #a-l | 5.00 | 2.50 |

Happy New Millennium — A3116

**2000, Dec. 1** *Perf. 12*

| | | | |
|---|---|---|---|
| **6609** | A3116 2r multi | 1.00 | .35 |
| *a.* | Sheet of 6 | 6.00 | 2.50 |

Foreign Intelligence Service, 80th Anniv. — A3117

**2000, Dec. 14** **Litho.** *Perf. 12x12½*

| | | | |
|---|---|---|---|
| **6610** | A3117 2.50r multi | .50 | .25 |

Kabardino-Balkaria Republic — A3118

Dagestan Republic A3119

Samara Oblast A3120

**2001, Jan. 10** *Perf. 12*

| | | | |
|---|---|---|---|
| **6611** | A3118 3r shown | 1.00 | .50 |
| **6612** | A3119 3r shown | 1.00 | .50 |
| **6613** | A3120 3r shown | 1.00 | .50 |
| **6614** | A3118 3r Chita Oblast | 1.00 | .50 |
| **6615** | A3118 3r Komi Republic, vert. | 1.00 | .50 |
| | *Nos. 6611-6615 (5)* | 5.00 | 2.50 |

Souvenir Sheet

Naval Education in Russia, 300th Anniv. — A3121

No. 6616: a, 1.50r, Mathematics and Navigation School, Moscow. b, 2r, Geographical expeditions. c, 8r, St. Petersburg Naval Institute.

**2001, Jan. 10** ***Perf. 12x12¼***

**6616** A3121 Sheet of 3, #a-c 5.00 1.00

### Type of 1997 With Lines of Microprinting for Vertical Lines

Designs: 10r, Ballerina. 25r, Rhythmic gymnast. 50r, Earth and computer. 100r, UPU emblem.

**2001, Jan. 24 Litho.** ***Perf. 11¾x12¼***

| | | | | |
|---|---|---|---|---|
| **6617** | A3020 | 10r multi | .75 | .45 |
| **6618** | A3020 | 25r blk & yel brn | 3.00 | 1.10 |
| **6619** | A3020 | 50r blk & blue | 5.00 | 2.00 |
| **6620** | A3020 | 100r blk & claret | 9.00 | 3.50 |
| | | *Nos. 6617-6620 (4)* | 17.75 | 7.05 |

A3122

A3123

A3124 A3124a

Tulips — A3125

**2001, Feb. 2 Litho.** ***Perf. 12¼x12***

| | | | |
|---|---|---|---|
| **6625** | Horiz. strip of 5 | 3.00 | .75 |
| *a.* | A3122 2r Happy Birthday | .40 | .25 |
| *b.* | A3123 2r Be Happy | .40 | .25 |
| *c.* | A3124 2r Congratulations | .40 | .25 |
| *d.* | A3124a 2r Good luck | .40 | .25 |
| *e.* | A3125 2r With Love | .40 | .25 |
| *f.* | Sheet, #6625a-6625e + label | 10.00 | 2.00 |

Paintings — A3126

No. 6626, 3r (brown background): a, Portrait of P. A. Bulakhov, by Vasily Andreevich Tropinin, 1823. b, Portrait of E. I. Karzinkina, by Tropinin, 1838.

No. 6627, 3r (tan and white background): a, Portrait of I. A. Galitsin, by A. M. Matveev, 1728 . b, Portrait of A. P. Galitsina, by Matveev, 1728.

**2001, Feb. 15 Litho.** ***Perf. 12***

**Pairs, #a-b, + Central Label**

**6626-6627** A3126 Set of 2 3.00 .60

St. Petersburg, 300th Anniv. — A3127

Paintings: 1r, Senate Square and Peter the Great Monumnet, by B. Patersen, 1799. 2r, English Embankment Near senate, by Patersen, 1801. 3r, View of Mikhailovsky Castle From Fontanka Embankment, by Patersen, 1801. 4r, View of the River Moika Near the Stable Department Building, by A. E. Martynov, 1809. 5r, View of the Neva River From the Peter and Paul Fortress, by K. P. Beggrov, 19th cent.

**2001, Mar. 15** ***Perf. 12x11¾***

| | | | | |
|---|---|---|---|---|
| **6628-6632** | A3127 | Set of 5 | 2.00 | .80 |
| *6632a* | | Sheet, #6628-6632, + label | 7.50 | 3.00 |

Dragonflies — A3128

No. 6633: a, 1r, Pyrrhosoma nymphula. b, 1.50r, Epitheca bimaculata. c, 2r, Aeschna grandis. d, 3r, Libellula depressa. e, 5r, Coenagrion hastulatum.

**2001, Apr. 5** ***Perf. 12x12¼***

**6633** A3128 Block of 5, #a-e, + label 3.00 .75

First Manned Space Flight, 40th Anniv. — A3129

No. 6634: a, Cosmonaut Yuri Gagarin and rocket designer Sergei Korolev. b, Gagarin saluting.

**2001, Apr. 12 Litho.** ***Perf. 12½x12***

| | | | |
|---|---|---|---|
| **6634** | A3129 3r Horiz. pair, #a-b | 2.00 | .60 |
| *c.* | Sheet, 3 #6634 | 6.00 | 2.75 |

Europa — A3130

**2001, May 9 Litho.** ***Perf. 11¾***

| | | | |
|---|---|---|---|
| **6635** | A3130 8r multi | 1.00 | .50 |
| *a.* | Sheet of 6 | 10.00 | 5.00 |

Intl. Federation of Philately, 75th Anniv. — A3131

**2001, May 17** ***Perf. 11½***

**6636** A3131 2.50r multi .50 .25

Declaration of State Sovereignty Day — A3132

**Litho. & Embossed**

**2001, June 5** ***Perf. 13¼***

**6637** A3132 5r multi 2.00 1.00

Russian Emblems A3133

Designs: No. 6638a, Flag. No. 6638b, National anthem. Nos. 6638c, 6639a, Arms.

**Litho. & Embossed**

**2001, June 5** ***Perf. 13¼***

| | | | |
|---|---|---|---|
| **6638** | Horiz. strip of 3 | 2.00 | .75 |
| *a.-b.* | A3133 2.50r Any single | .30 | .25 |
| *c.* | A3133 5r multi | .60 | .30 |
| *d.* | Booklet pane of 1, #6638a | — | — |
| *e.* | Booklet pane of 1, #6638b | — | — |

**Souvenir Sheet**

| | | | |
|---|---|---|---|
| **6639** | Sheet of 3, #6638a-6638b, 6639a | 35.00 | 15.00 |
| *a.* | A3133 100r multi | 30.00 | 8.00 |
| *b.* | Booklet pane of 1, #6639a | *100.00* | — |
| | Booklet, #6638d, 6638e, 6639b | *100.00* | |

A souvenir booklet, produced in a quantity of 3,000, exists. It comprises a pane of No. 6639 and panes of 4 each of Nos. 6638a, 6638b and 6639a. Booklets were issued with red, blue or white borders. Value, each $500.

A3134

Houses of Worship — A3135

Designs: No. 6640, Cathedral, Vladimir, 1189. No. 6641, Cathedral, Zvenigorod, 1405. No. 6642, Cathedral, Moscow, 1792. No. 6643, Cathedral, Rostov-on-Don, 1792. No. 6644, Mosque, Ufa, 1830. No. 6645, Church, St. Petersburg, 1838. No. 6646, Mosque, Kazan, 1849. No. 6647, Synagogue, Moscow, 1891. No. 6648, Synagogue, St. Petersburg, 1893. No. 6649, Cathedral, Moscow, 1911. No. 6650, Temple, Ulan-Ude, 1976. No. 6651, Church, Bryansk, 1996. No. 6652, Church, Ryazan, 1996. No. 6653, Church, Lesosibirsk, 1999.

**2001, July 12 Litho.** ***Perf. 11½***

| | | | | |
|---|---|---|---|---|
| **6640** | A3134 | 2.50r multi | .35 | .25 |
| **6641** | A3134 | 2.50r multi | .35 | .25 |
| **6642** | A3134 | 2.50r shown | .35 | .25 |
| **6643** | A3134 | 2.50r multi | .35 | .25 |
| **6644** | A3134 | 2.50r multi | .35 | .25 |
| **6645** | A3134 | 2.50r multi | .35 | .25 |
| **6646** | A3134 | 2.50r multi | .35 | .25 |
| **6647** | A3134 | 2.50r multi | .35 | .25 |
| **6648** | A3134 | 2.50r multi | .35 | .25 |
| **6649** | A3134 | 2.50r multi | .35 | .25 |
| **6650** | A3134 | 2.50r multi | .35 | .25 |
| **6651** | A3135 | 2.50r shown | .35 | .25 |
| **6652** | A3135 | 2.50r multi | .35 | .25 |
| **6653** | A3134 | 2.50r multi | .35 | .25 |
| | | *Nos. 6640-6653 (14)* | 4.90 | 3.50 |

Souvenir Sheet

First Russian Railroad, 150th Anniv. — A3136

**2001, July 25** ***Perf. 12***

**6654** A3136 12r multi 2.00 .50

Flight of Gherman Titov on Vostok 2, 40th Anniv. A3137

**2001, Aug. 6 Litho.** ***Perf. 12¼x12***

| | | | |
|---|---|---|---|
| **6655** | A3137 3r multi | 1.00 | .25 |
| *a.* | Sheet of 6 | 6.00 | 3.00 |

Film Stars A3138

Designs: No. 6656, 2.50r, Mikhail Zharov (1899-1981). No. 6657, 2.50r, Faina Ranevskaya (1896-1984). No. 6658, 2.50r, Nikolai Kryuchkov (1910-94). No. 6659, 2.50r, Nikolai Rybnikov (1930-90). No. 6660, 2.50r, Lubov Orlova (1902-75). No. 6661, 2.50r, Yuri Nikulin (1921-97). No. 6662, 2.50r, Evgeny Leonov (1926-94). No. 6663, 2.50r, Anatoly Papanov (1922-87). No. 6664, 2.50r, Andrei Mironov (1941-87).

**2001, Sept. 20** ***Perf. 12***

| | | | | |
|---|---|---|---|---|
| **6656-6664** | A3138 | Set of 9 | 2.00 | 1.25 |
| *6664a* | | Sheet, #6656-6664 | 10.00 | 5.00 |

Ivan Lazarev (1735-1801) and Institute of Eastern Languages — A3139

**2001, Sept. 26** ***Perf. 11¾***

**6665** A3139 2.50r multi .50 .35

See Armenia No. 635.

Arkady Raikin (1911-87), Comedian — A3140

**2001, Oct. 9** *Perf. 12*
**6666** A3140 2r gray & black .50 .25

Year of Dialogue Among Civilizations A3141

**2001, Oct. 9**
**6667** A3141 5r multi .50 .35

Souvenir Sheet

Vladimir Dal (1801-72), Author — A3142

**2001, Oct. 16** *Perf. 12x12½*
**6668** A3142 10r multi 2.00 .75

Constitutional Court, 10th Anniv. A3143

**2001, Nov. 1** *Perf. 11¾x12*
**6669** A3143 3r multi .50 .25

Savings Bank of Russia, 160th Anniv. — A3144

**2001, Nov. 2** *Perf. 12x11¾*
**6670** A3144 2.20r multi .50 .25

Souvenir Sheet

Defense of Moscow, 60th Anniv. — A3145

**2001, Nov. 15** *Perf. 12x12½*
**6671** A3145 10r multi 3.00 .60

Commonwealth of Independent States, 10th Anniv. — A3146

**2001, Nov. 28** *Perf. 12*
**6672** A3146 2r multi 2.00 .75
*a.* Miniature sheet of 10 20.00

Happy New Year — A3147

**2001, Dec. 4** *Perf. 12x12¼*
**6673** A3147 2.50r multi .50 .25
*a.* Sheet of 6 10.00 5.00

Amur Oblast A3148

Khakassia Republic A3149

Karachay-Cherkessia Republic — A3150

Sakhalin Oblast A3151

Altai Republic — A3152

**2002, Jan. 2** *Perf. 12x12¼, 12¼x12*

| | | | | |
|---|---|---|---|---|
| **6674** | A3148 3r multi | | 1.00 | .50 |
| **6675** | A3149 3r multi | | 1.00 | .50 |
| **6676** | A3150 3r multi | | 1.00 | .50 |
| **6677** | A3151 3r multi | | 1.00 | .50 |
| **6678** | A3152 3r multi | | 1.00 | .50 |
| | *Nos. 6674-6678 (5)* | | 5.00 | 2.50 |

2002 Winter Olympics, Salt Lake City A3153

Designs: 3r, Skier. 4r, Figure skater. 5r, Ski jumper.

**2002, Jan. 24** *Perf. 12x12¼*
**6679-6681** A3153 Set of 3 1.50 .75

World Unity Against Terrorism A3154

**2002, Jan. 30**
**6682** A3154 5r multi .50 .35

Souvenir Sheet

Trans-Siberian Railway, Cent. — A3155

**2002, Jan. 30** *Perf. 12¼x12*
**6683** A3155 12r multi 3.00 .60

New Hermitage, 150th Anniv. A3156

Designs: No. 6684, Ecce Homo, by Peter Paul Rubens, before 1612. No. 6685, Courtesan, by Hendrik Goltzius, 1606. No. 6686, Helmet, by Philippo Negroli, 1530s. No. 6687, Gonzaga Cameo, 3rd Cent. B.C.

15r, New Hermitage, 1861, by Luigi Premazzi.

**Litho. & Embossed**

**2002, Feb. 15** *Perf. 13¼*

| | | | |
|---|---|---|---|
| **6684** | A3156 2.50r multi | .75 | .30 |
| *a.* | Booklet pane of 1 | *20.00* | — |
| **6685** | A3156 2.50r multi | .75 | .30 |
| *a.* | Booklet pane of 1 | *20.00* | — |
| **6686** | A3156 5r multi | 1.50 | .60 |
| *a.* | Booklet pane of 1 | *40.00* | — |
| **6687** | A3156 5r multi | 1.50 | .60 |
| *a.* | Booklet pane of 1 | *40.00* | — |
| | *Nos. 6684-6687 (4)* | 4.50 | 1.80 |

**Souvenir Sheet**

| | | | |
|---|---|---|---|
| **6688** | A3156 15r multi | 3.00 | 1.00 |
| *a.* | Booklet pane of 1 | *125.00* | — |
| | Booklet, #6684a-6688a | *350.00* | |

Lilies
A3157 A3158

Flower color: No. 6690, White. No. 6692, White with red spots. No. 6693, Red and white with red spots.

*Perf. 12¼x11¾*

**2002, Feb. 20** **Litho.**

| | | | |
|---|---|---|---|
| **6689** | A3157 2.50r multi | .50 | .25 |
| **6690** | A3157 2.50r multi | .50 | .25 |
| **6691** | A3158 2.50r multi | .50 | .25 |
| **6692** | A3157 2.50r multi | .50 | .25 |
| **6693** | A3157 2.50r multi | .50 | .25 |
| *b.* | Miniature sheet, #6689-6693 + label | 5.00 | 2.00 |
| | *Nos. 6689-6693 (5)* | 2.50 | 1.25 |

Dogs — A3159

**2002, Mar. 15** *Perf. 11¾*

| | | | |
|---|---|---|---|
| **6694** | Horiz. strip of 5 | 4.00 | 2.00 |
| *a.* | A3159 1r Cane Corso | .60 | .25 |
| *b.* | A3159 2r Shar-pei | .60 | .25 |
| *c.* | A3159 3r Bull mastiff | .60 | .25 |
| *d.* | A3159 4r Fila Brasileiro | .60 | .25 |
| *e.* | A3159 5r Neapolitan mastiff | .60 | .25 |
| *f.* | Miniature sheet of 9, #6694c, 6694d, 6694e, 2 # 6694a, 4 #6694b | 5.00 | 2.00 |

St. Petersburg, 300th Anniv. (in 2003) — A3160

Designs: No. 6695, Kazan Cathedral (semi-circular colonnade), monument to Marshal Barclay de Tolly. No. 6696, St. Isaac's Cathedral and sculpture. No. 6697, Cathedral of the Resurrection, bridge, griffin. No. 6698, St. Peter and Paul Cathedral, angel and cross steeple, vert. No. 6699, Admiralty and ship steeple, vert.

**Litho. & Embossed**

**2002, Apr. 25** *Perf. 13¼*

| | | | |
|---|---|---|---|
| **6695** | A3160 5r multi | 5.00 | 1.50 |
| *a.* | Booklet pane of 1 | *20.00* | — |
| **6696** | A3160 5r multi | 5.00 | 1.50 |
| *a.* | Booklet pane of 1 | *20.00* | — |
| **6697** | A3160 25r multi | 20.00 | 6.50 |
| *a.* | Booklet pane of 1 | *52.50* | — |
| **6698** | A3160 25r multi | 20.00 | 6.50 |
| *a.* | Booklet pane of 1 | *52.50* | — |
| **6699** | A3160 25r multi | 20.00 | 6.50 |
| *a.* | Booklet pane of 1 | *52.50* | — |
| | Booklet, #6695a-6699a | *200.00* | |
| | *Nos. 6695-6699 (5)* | 70.00 | 22.50 |

The embossed portions of the designs of the 25r values bear 22k gold applications.

Security Services, 80th Anniv. — A3161

No. 6700: a, A. K. Artuzov (1891-1937). b, N. I. Demidenko (1896-1934). c, J. K. Olsky (1898-1937). d, S. V. Puzitsky (1895-1937). e,

V. A. Styrne (1897-1937). f, G. S. Syroezhkin (1900-37).

**2002, Apr. 30 Litho. *Perf. 12x12¼***
**6700** A3161 2r Sheet of 6, #a-f 5.00 1.75

Europa A3162

**2002, May 9 *Perf. 12½x12***
**6701** A3162 8r multi 1.00 .50
*a.* Miniature sheet of 6 6.00 3.00

Admiral P. S. Nakhimov (1802-55) — A3163

**2002, May 24 *Perf. 12x11¾***
**6702** A3163 2r multi .50 .25
*a.* Miniature sheet of 8 5.00 2.00

European Organization of Supreme Audit Institutions, 5th Congress — A3164

**2002, May 24 *Perf. 12x12¼***
**6703** A3164 2r multi .50 .25

Kamchatka Peninsula Volcanos — A3165

No. 6704: a, 1r, Steaming geysers. b, 2r, Mud hole. c, 3r, Karymski Volcano. d, 5r, Crater lake.

**2002, June 20 Litho. *Perf. 12***
**6704** A3165 Block of 4, #a-d 1.50 .60

Carriages A3166

Designs: No. 6705a, Russian carriage, 1640s. No. 6705b, Closed sleigh, 1732. Nos. 6705c, 6706a, Coupe carriage, 1746. Nos. 6705d, 6706b, 25r, English calash, 1770s. Nos. 6705e, 6706c, Berline carriage, 1769.

**Litho. & Embossed**

**2002, July 25 *Perf. 13x13¼***
**6705** Block of 5 + label 3.00 .95
*a.-b.* A3166 2.50r Any single .25 .25
*c.-e.* A3166 5r Any single .40 .40
*f.* Booklet pane, #6705a 27.50
*g.* Booklet pane, #6705b 27.50
*h.* Booklet pane, #6705c 57.50
*i.* Booklet pane, #6705d 57.50
*j.* Booklet pane, #6705e 57.50
Booklet, #6705f-6705j 250.00

**Souvenir Sheet**

**6706** A3166 25r Sheet of 3, #a-c 6.00 6.00

Kamov Helicopters — A3167

**2002, Aug. 8 Litho. *Perf. 12½x12***
**6707** Block of 5 + label 3.00 1.00
*a.* A3167 1r KA-10 .45 .25
*b.* A3167 1.50r KA-22 .45 .25
*c.* A3167 2r KA-26 .45 .25
*d.* A3167 2.50r KA-27 .45 .25
*e.* A3167 5r KA-50 .45 .25

Anatoly A. Sobchak, Mayor of St. Petersburg (1937-2000) A3168

**2002, Aug. 10 *Perf. 12x12½***
**6708** A3168 3.25r multi 5.00 .35

Birds — A3169

No. 6709: a, Anthropoides virgo. b, Larus ichthyaetus.

**2002, Aug. 29 *Perf. 12¼x12***
**6709** A3169 2.50r Horiz. pair, #a-b .50 .50

See Kazakhstan No. 385.

Kostroma, 850th Anniv. A3170

**2002, Sept. 2 Litho. *Perf. 12x12¼***
**6710** A3170 2r multi 1.00 .25

Government Ministries, 200th Anniv. — A3171

Arms and/or Russian flag and ministry buildings or symbols: No. 6711, 3r, Defense (light green background, dark green frame). No. 6712, 3r, Foreign Affairs (light blue background, dark green frame). No. 6713, 3r, Internal Affairs (light blue background, dark blue frame). No. 6714, 3r, Education (pink background, red frame). No. 6715, 3r, Finance (lilac background, dark blue frame). No. 6716, 3r, Justice (light yellow background, gray blue frame).

**2002, Sept. 2 *Perf. 12***
**6711-6716** A3171 Set of 6 2.00 .85

Russian State, 1140th Anniv. — A3172

**2002, Sept. 17 *Perf. 11½x11¾***
**6717** A3172 3r multi .50 .25

2002 Census — A3173

**Litho. & Embossed**

**2002, Sept. 17 *Perf. 13¼x13***

**Stamp + label**

**6718** A3173 4r shown 5.00 .75
*a.* Booklet pane of 4, no labels 650.00
Complete booklet, #6718a 750.00

**Litho.**

**Self-Adhesive**

***Serpentine Die Cut 10¾x11***

**6719** A3173 3r Emblem, people 4.50 .50
*a.* Booklet pane of 8, no labels 45.00
Complete booklet, #6719a 50.00

Customs Service — A3174

No. 6720: a, 2r, Customs house, Arkhangelsk, 18th cent. b, 3r, Customs officers, St. Petersburg, 1830s. c, 5r, Kalanchovsky customs warehouse, Moscow, 19th cent.

**2002, Sept. 25 Litho. *Perf. 12x12¼***
**6720** A3174 Sheet of 3, #a-c 5.00 1.00

**Souvenir Sheet**

Battle of Stalingrad, 60th Anniv. — A3175

**2002, Oct. 4**
**6721** A3175 10r multi 3.00 1.00

Eyes Displaying Interest A3176

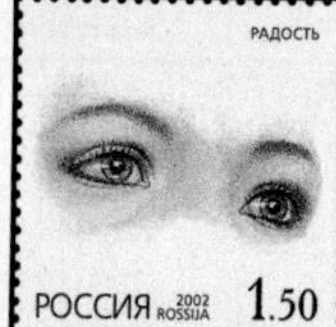

Eyes Displaying Gladness A3177

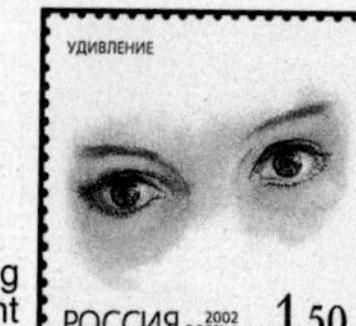

Eyes Displaying Astonishment A3178

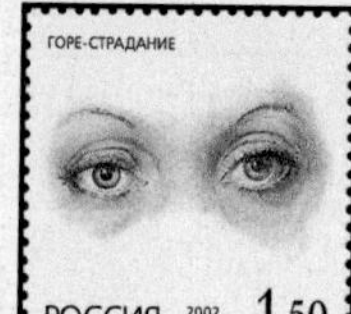

Eyes Displaying Grief — A3179

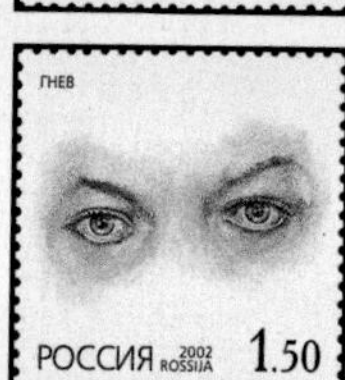

Eyes Displaying Anger — A3180

Eyes Displaying Disgust A3181

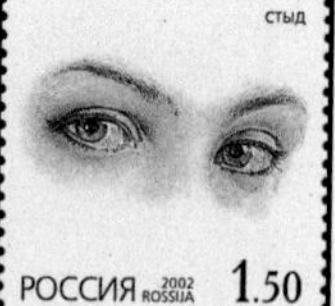

Eyes Displaying Shame — A3182

Eyes Displaying Contempt A3183

Eyes Displaying Guilt — A3184

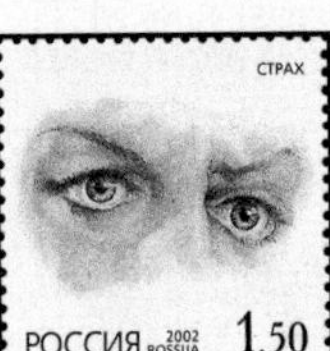
Eyes Displaying Fear — A3185

**2002, Oct. 17** *Perf. 12x11¾*

| | | | |
|---|---|---|---|
| **6722** | Sheet of 10 | 5.00 | 2.50 |
| *a.* | A3176 1.50r multi | .40 | .25 |
| *b.* | A3177 1.50r multi | .40 | .25 |
| *c.* | A3178 1.50r multi | .40 | .25 |
| *d.* | A3179 1.50r multi | .40 | .25 |
| *e.* | A3180 1.50r multi | .40 | .25 |
| *f.* | A3181 1.50r multi | .40 | .25 |
| *g.* | A3182 1.50r multi | .40 | .25 |
| *h.* | A3183 1.50r multi | .40 | .25 |
| *i.* | A3184 1.50r multi | .40 | .25 |
| *j.* | A3185 1.50r multi | .40 | .25 |

Emperor Alexander I (1777-1825) A3186

Alexander I: No. 6723, 4r, And Manifesto of March 12, 1801 (blue frame). No. 6724, 4r, Taking over codification of laws from his secretary Mikhail M. Speransky, Oct. 1809 (green frame). No. 6725, 7r, Receiving historian N. M. Karamzin ( red frame). No. 6726, 7r, Entering Paris with troops, Mar. 1814 (brown frame).

10r, Portrait of Alexander I, by Francois Gérard.

**Litho. & Engr.**

**2002, Nov. 12** *Perf. 12x12½*

**6723-6726** A3186 Set of 4 8.00 1.50

**Souvenir Sheet**

**6727** A3186 10r multi 6.00 1.60

Russian Orthodox Monasteries — A3187

Designs: No. 6728, 5r, Monastery of St. Daniel, 1282. No. 6729, 5r, Sergii Lavra, 1337. No. 6730, 5r, Valaam Monastery, 14th cent. No. 6731, 5r, Monastery of Reverend Savva, 1398. No. 6732, 5r, Pskov Cave Monastery, 1470.

**Litho. & Embossed**

**2002, Nov. 26** *Perf. 12½*

| | | | |
|---|---|---|---|
| **6728-6732** A3187 | Set of 5 | 10.00 | 3.50 |
| *6732a* | Souvenir sheet, #6728-6732 + label | 8.00 | 4.00 |

Nos. 6728-6732 each were issued in sheets of 9 stamps + label. The labels on these sheets differ from the label on No. 6732a. Value, set of 5 sheets $100.

See Nos. 6756-6761, 6818-6822.

A limited edition booklet exists containing booklet panes of one of each of Nos. 6728-6732 and 6756-6761. Value, *$350.*

Happy New Year — A3188

**2002, Dec. 2 Litho.** *Perf. 12¼x11¾*

| | | | |
|---|---|---|---|
| **6733** A3188 3.50r multi | | .50 | .25 |
| *a.* | Sheet of 6 | 7.00 | 3.50 |

Sculpture and Buildings A3189

Designs: 2r, Sculpture "Artemis with Deer," Palace, Arkhangelskoye. 2.50r, Sculpture "Omphala," Chinese Palace, Oranienbaum. 3r, Sculpture of griffin, mansion, Marfino. 4r, Sculpture "Erminia," Grand Palace, Pavlovsk. 5r, Allegorical sculpture of Scamander River, Palace, Kuskovo.

**Town name Panels with Colored Backgrounds**

**Denomination Color**

***Serpentine Die Cut 11***

**2002, Dec. 16** **Self-Adhesive**

| | | | | |
|---|---|---|---|---|
| **6734** A3189 | 2r brown | .50 | .25 |
| **6735** A3189 | 2.50r blue | .75 | .25 |
| **6736** A3189 | 3r indigo | 1.00 | .25 |
| **6737** A3189 | 4r violet | 1.25 | .60 |
| **6738** A3189 | 5r purple | 1.50 | .60 |
| | *Nos. 6734-6738 (5)* | 5.00 | 1.95 |

See also Nos. 6802-6805, 6823-6827.

Nuclear Physicists A3190

Reactor diagrams and: No. 6739, 2.50r, Anatoly P. Alexandrov (1903-94). No. 6740, 2.50r, Igor V. Kurchatov (1903-60).

**2003, Jan. 8** *Perf. 12½x12*

**6739-6740** A3190 Set of 2 2.00 .25

Souvenir Sheet

Antarctic Research — A3191

No. 6741: a, Ice borings, map. b, Vostok research station.

**2003, Jan. 8** *Perf. 11½x12¼*

**6741** A3191 5r Sheet of 2, #a-b 3.00 1.10

Kemerovo Oblast A3192

Kurgan Oblast A3193

Magadan Oblast A3194

Perm Oblast A3195

Ulyanovsk Oblast A3196

Astrakhan Oblast — A3197

**2003, Jan. 10** *Perf. 12x12¼, 12¼x12*

| | | | |
|---|---|---|---|
| **6742** A3192 3r multi | | 1.00 | .50 |
| **6743** A3193 3r multi | | 1.00 | .50 |
| **6744** A3194 3r multi | | 1.00 | .50 |
| **6745** A3195 3r multi | | 1.00 | .50 |
| **6746** A3196 3r multi | | 1.00 | .50 |
| **6747** A3197 3r multi | | 1.00 | .50 |
| | *Nos. 6742-6747 (6)* | 6.00 | 3.00 |

Commonwealth of Independent States Intergovernmental Communications by Courier, 10th Anniv. — A3198

**2003, Jan. 16** *Perf. 12x12½*

**6748** A3198 3r multi .50 .25

Victory at 2002 Davis Cup Tennis Championships — A3199

Designs: 4r, Fans with signs and Russian flags. 8r, Ball and net, fans with Russian flags. 50r, Davis Cup.

**2003, Feb. 19 Litho.** *Perf. 13¼*

**6749-6750** A3199 Set of 2 1.50 .45

**Souvenir Sheet**

**Litho. with Foil Application & Embossed**

***Perf. 13¼x13***

| | | | |
|---|---|---|---|
| **6751** A3199 50r silver & multi | | 8.00 | 2.10 |
| *a.* | Miniature sheet, Nos 6749-6751 | 50.00 | |

No. 6751 contains one 51x39mm stamp.

Yaroslav Mudry (the Wise) (978-1054), Grand Prince of Kiev — A3200

Vladimir II Monomakh (1053-1125), Grand Prince of Kiev — A3201

Daniel Aleksandrovich Moscowsky (1261-1303), Grand Prince of Moscow — A3202

Ivan II Ivanovich Krasny (the Red) (1320-1359), Grand Prince of Moscow — A3203

**Litho. & Engr.**

**2003, Mar. 4** *Perf. 11¾*

| | | | |
|---|---|---|---|
| **6752** A3200 8r multi | | 1.00 | .40 |
| **6753** A3201 8r multi | | 1.00 | .40 |
| **6754** A3202 8r multi | | 1.00 | .40 |
| **6755** A3203 8r multi | | 1.00 | .40 |
| | *Nos. 6752-6755 (4)* | 4.00 | 1.60 |

**Monasteries Type of 2002**

Designs: No. 6756, 5r, Yuriev Monastery, Novgorod, 1030. No. 6757, 5r, Tolgsky Nunnery, 1314. No. 6758, 5r, Kozelsk Optina Pustyn Monastery, 14th-15th cent. No. 6759, 5r, Solovetsky Zosima and Savvatii Monastery, 15th cent. No. 6760, 5r, Novodevichy Nunnery, 1524. No. 6761, 5r, Seraphim Nunnery, Diveyevo, 1780.

**Litho. & Embossed**

**2003, Mar. 26** *Perf. 12½*

| | | | |
|---|---|---|---|
| **6756-6761** A3187 | Set of 6 | 5.00 | 1.10 |
| *6761a* | Souvenir sheet, #6756-6761 | 10.00 | 2.00 |

Nos. 6756-6761 each were issued in sheets of 9 stamps + label. A limited edtion booklet exists containing booklet panes of one of each of Nos. 6728-6732 and 6756-6761. Value, *$450.*

Petrozavodsk, 300th Anniv. — A3204

*Perf. 12¼x11¾*

**2003, Mar. 26** **Litho.**

**6762** A3204 3r multi .50 .25

Novosibirsk, Cent. — A3205

**2003, Apr. 15** ***Perf. 11¾x12¼***
**6763** A3205 3r multi .50 .25

Souvenir Sheet

Baltic Fleet, 300th Anniv. — A3206

**2003, Apr. 15** ***Perf. 12¼x11¾***
**6764** A3206 12r multi 4.00 2.00

Aram Khatchaturian (1903-78), Composer — A3207

**2003, Apr. 23** ***Perf. 12***
**6765** A3207 2.50r multi 1.00 .35

Europa — A3208

**2003, May 5** ***Perf. 12¼x11¾***
**6766** A3208 8r multi .75 .50
*a.* Sheet of 6 9.50 4.75

Carillons — A3209

No. 6767: a, St. Rombout's Cathedral, Mechelen, Belgium, and bells (denomination at left). b, Sts. Peter and Paul Cathedral, St. Petersburg, and bells (denomination at right).

**Litho. & Engr.**

**2003, May 15** ***Perf. 12***
**6767** A3209 5r Horiz. pair, #a-b 1.00 .50
*c.* Sheet, 3 #6767 5.00 2.00

See Belgium No. 1956.

Anichkov Bridge — A3210

Neva River Drawbridge — A3211

Vasilievsky Island — A3212

Palace Square — A3213

Winter Palace — A3214

Summer Garden — A3215

Peter I Monument — A3216

Designs: 75r, 100r, Peter I Monument.

**Litho. & Embossed**

**2003, May 15** ***Perf. 13x13¼***
**6768** A3210 5r multi 2.50 .80
**6769** A3211 5r multi 2.50 .80
**6770** A3212 5r multi 2.50 .80
**6771** A3213 5r multi 2.50 .80
**6772** A3214 5r multi 2.50 .80
**6773** A3215 5r multi 2.50 .80
*Nos. 6768-6773 (6)* 15.00 4.80

**Souvenir Sheet**

***Perf. 13¼***
**6774** A3216 50r multi 15.00 3.50
**6775** A3216 75p multi 15.00 3.25
**6776** A3216 100p multi 20.00 4.25

St. Petersburg, 300th anniv.

Nos. 6775 and 6776 contain one 37x51mm stamp.

A booklet exists containing one pane of Nos. 6768-6773 and one pane of No. 6774 with an extended margin. Value, *$500.*

Space Flight of Valentina Tereshkova, 40th Anniv. — A3217

**2003, May 20 Litho.** ***Perf. 12¼x11¾***
**6777** A3217 3r multi .50 .25
*a.* Sheet of 6 7.00 1.50

Second World Anti-Narcotics Congress — A3218

**2003, May 25 Litho.** ***Perf. 12x12½***
**6778** A3218 3r multi .50 .25

Pskov, 1100th Anniv. — A3219

**2003, June 3** ***Perf. 11¾x12¼***
**6779** A3219 3r multi 1.00 .25

Krasnoyarsk, 375th Anniv. — A3220

**2003, June 10**
**6780** A3220 4r multi 1.00 .25

Symbols of Industry, 5 Ruble Coin — A3221

**2003, June 10** ***Perf. 12½x12***
**6781** A3221 5r multi .50 .25

Promotion of "Transparent Economy."

Souvenir Sheet

Battle of Kursk, 60th Anniv. — A3222

**2003, June 10** ***Perf. 12x12½***
**6782** A3222 10r multi 3.00 1.25

Komi Republic Forests — A3223

No. 6783: a, 2r, Stone pillars, Man-Pupuner Mountain. b, 3r, Kozhim River. c, 5r, Upper Pechora River.

**2003, June 25** ***Perf. 12x12¼***
**6783** A3223 Block of 3, #a-c, + label 5.00 .50

Souvenir Sheet

St. Petersburg Postal Service, 300th Anniv. — A3224

**2003, June 29** ***Perf. 12¼x12***
**6784** A3224 12r multi 3.00 .60

Beetles — A3225

No. 6785: a, Lucanus cervus. b, Calosoma sycophanta. c, Carabus lopatini. d, Carabus constricticollis. e, Carabus caucasicus.

**2003, July 22** ***Perf. 12***
**6785** Horiz. strip of 5 3.00 .85
*a.* A3225 1r multi .40 .25
*b.* A3225 2r multi .40 .25
*c.* A3225 3r multi .50 .25
*d.* A3225 4r multi .65 .25
*e.* A3225 5r multi .85 .25
*f.* Sheet, #6785a-6785e, + label 7.00 3.50

Intl. Association of Academies of Science, 10th Anniv. — A3226

**2003, July 30** ***Perf. 11¼***
**6786** A3226 2.50r multi .50 .25

Chita, 350th Anniv. — A3227

**2003, Aug. 14** ***Perf. 12x12¼***
**6787** A3227 3r multi 1.00 .25

World Conference on Climate Fluctuations, Moscow — A3228

**2003, Aug. 14** ***Perf. 11¾***
**6788** A3228 4r multi 1.00 .45

Mushrooms — A3229

Various mushrooms.

**2003, July 22** ***Perf. 11¾***
**6789** Horiz. strip of 5 3.00 .85
*a.* A3229 2r multi .40 .25
*b.* A3229 2.50r multi .40 .25

*c.* A3229 3r multi .50 .25
*d.* A3229 4r multi .70 .25
*e.* A3229 5r multi .90 .25
*f.* Sheet, #6789a-6789e, + label 7.00 3.00

Fruit
A3230

Designs: No. 6790, 5r, Melon. No. 6791, 5r, Apples. No. 6792, 5r, Pear. No. 6793, 5r, Pineapple. No. 6794, 5r, Strawberries.

**2003, Aug. 27** ***Perf. 13½***
**6790-6794** A3230 Set of 5 3.50 2.50

Nos. 6790-6794 are impregnated with fruit scents. Values are for stamps with surrounding selvage.

Caspian Sea Fauna — A3231

No. 6795: a, Phoca caspica. b, Huso huso.

**2003, Sept. 9** ***Perf. 12½x12***
**6795** A3231 2.50r Horiz. pair, #a-b 2.00 .45
*c.* Sheet, 3 each #6795a-6795b 35.00 10.00

See Iran No. 2873.

Souvenir Sheet

Russian Journalism, 300th Anniv. — A3232

**2003, Sept. 12** ***Perf. 12x12¼***
**6796** A3232 10r multi 3.00 .35

Automobiles — A3233

Designs: a, 3r, 1911 Russo-Balt K 12/20. b, 4r, 1929 NAMI-1. c, 4r, 1939 GAZ-M1. d, 5r, 1946 GAZ-67b. e, 5r, 1954 GAZ-M20 Pobeda.

**2003, Sept. 17** ***Perf. 11¾x11½***
**6797** A3233 Block of 5, #a-e, + label 5.00 1.25

Constitution, 10th Anniv. — A3234

**2003, Oct. 15** ***Perf. 12½x12***
**6798** A3234 3r multi .50 .25

E. T. Krenkel (1903-71), Polar Explorer — A3235

**2003, Oct. 15** ***Perf. 12x12½***
**6799** A3235 4r multi .60 .30

Souvenir Sheet

Battle of Sinop, 150th Anniv. — A3236

**2003, Nov. 5** ***Perf. 12¼x12***
**6800** A3236 12r multi 3.00 .55

Happy New Year — A3237

**2003, Dec. 1** ***Perf. 12½***

**Flocked Paper**

**6801** A3237 7r multi .50 .25

**Sculpture and Buildings Type of 2002**

Designs: 1r, Ostankino Palace. 1.50r, Gatchinsky Palace. 6r, Grand Palace, Petrodvorets. 10r, Empress Catherine's Palace, Tsarskoye Selo.

**2003, Dec. 5** ***Serpentine Die Cut 11***

**Self-Adhesive**

**6802** A3189 1r multi .75 .25
**6803** A3189 1.50r multi .75 .25
**6804** A3189 6r multi 1.25 .25
**6805** A3189 10r multi 2.25 .35
*Nos. 6802-6805 (4)* 5.00 1.10

Legislative Bodies, 10th Anniv. A3238

No. 6806: a, Federation Council (denomination at right). b, State Duma (denomination at left).

**2003, Dec. 10** ***Perf. 12¼x12***
**6806** Horiz. pair + central label 1.00 .25
*a.-b.* A3238 2.50r Either single .40 .25

Belgorod Oblast A3239

Ivanovo Oblast A3240

Lipetsk Oblast A3241

Moscow Oblast A3242

Nenetsky Okrug A3243

Nizhny Novgorod Oblast A3244

**2004, Jan. 6** ***Perf. 12x12¼***
**6807** A3239 5r multi 1.00 .50
**6808** A3240 5r multi 1.00 .50
**6809** A3241 5r multi 1.00 .50
**6810** A3242 5r multi 1.00 .50
**6811** A3243 5r multi 1.00 .50
**6812** A3244 5r multi 1.00 .50
*Nos. 6807-6812 (6)* 6.00 3.00

Souvenir Sheet

World War II Offensives of 1944, 60th Anniv. — A3245

**2004, Jan. 16 Litho.** ***Perf. 12x12¼***
**6813** A3245 10r multi 3.00 .75

V. P. Chkalov (1904-38), Test Pilot — A3246

**2004, Jan. 23** ***Perf. 11¾x12***
**6814** A3246 3r multi .50 .25
*a.* Miniature sheet of 8 8.00

Tales by P. P. Bazhov (1879-1950) — A3247

No. 6815: a, 2r, The Stone Flower. b, 4r, The Malachite Box. c, 6r, The Golden Hair.

**2004, Jan. 27** ***Perf. 12x11¾***
**6815** A3247 Horiz. strip of 3, #a-c 1.50 .60
*d.* Miniature sheet, 2 #6815 7.50 2.75

Yuly B. Khariton (1904-66), Physicist — A3248

**2004, Feb. 12 Litho.** ***Perf. 12¼x12***
**6816** A3248 3r multi .50 .25

Yuri Gagarin (1934-68), First Man in Space — A3249

**2004, Feb. 20** ***Perf. 12***
**6817** A3249 3r multi .50 .25
*a.* Miniature sheet of 8 10.00

**Monasteries Type of 2002**

Designs: No. 6818, 8r, St. Panteleimon Monastery, Mt. Athos, Greece, 11th cent. No. 6819, 8r, Holy Assumption Kiev-Pecherskaya Lavra, Ukraine, 1051. No. 6820, 8r, Convent of the Savior and Efrosinia, Polotsk, Belarus, 1128. No. 6821, 8r, Gorney Convent, Israel, 1886. No. 6822, 8r, Pyukhtitsky Convent of the Assumption, Estonia.

**Litho. & Embossed**

**2004, Mar. 16** ***Perf. 12½***
**6818-6822** A3187 Set of 5 5.00 2.25
*6822a* Miniature sheet, #6818-6822 + label 10.00 3.00

A limited edition booklet exists containing booklet panes of one of Nos. 6818-6822. Value, *$250.*

**Sculptures and Buildings Type of 2002 Redrawn**

Designs as before.

**Town Name Panels At Bottom With White Background**

**Denomination Color**

**2004 Litho.** ***Serpentine Die Cut 11***

**Self-Adhesive**

**6823** A3189 2r brown .50 .25
**6824** A3189 2.50r blue .50 .25
**6825** A3189 3r indigo .50 .25
**6826** A3189 4r violet .70 .25
**6827** A3189 5r purple .80 .25
*Nos. 6823-6827 (5)* 3.00 1.25

Issued: 2r, 4r, 4/5; 2.50r, 5r, 4/12; 3r, 4/15. Nos. 6823-6827 have a crest with stronger lines and vignettes in slightly different shades than Nos. 6734-6738. The background of the town name panels on Nos. 6734-6738 have dots of color, which on some stamps are faint, but are easily seen under magnification.

Kronshtadt, 300th Anniv. — A3250

**2004, Apr. 15** *Perf. 12½x12*

**6828** A3250 4r multi .50 .25

Zodiac Signs A3251

No. 6829: a, Aries. b. Leo. c, Sagittarius.
No. 6830: a, Gemini. b, Aquarius. c, Libra.
No. 6831: a, Capricorn. b, Taurus. c, Virgo.
No. 6832: a, Pisces. b, Cancer. c, Scorpio.

**Litho. & Embossed**

**2004, Apr. 21** *Perf. 13¼x13*

**6829** Horiz. strip of 3 2.50 .65
*a.-c.* A3251 5r Any single .50 .25
**6830** Horiz. strip of 3 2.50 .65
*a.-c.* A3251 5r Any single .50 .25
**6831** Horiz. strip of 3 2.50 .65
*a.-c.* A3251 5r Any single .50 .25
**6832** Horiz. strip of 3 2.50 .65
*a.-c.* A3251 5r Any single .50 .25
*d.* Miniature sheet, #6829a-6829c, 6830a-6830c, 6831a-6831c, 6832a-6832c 15.00 5.00

Empress Catherine II (1729-96) A3252

Catherine the Great: 6r, Watching scientific presentation of Mikhail Lomonosov. 7r, Giving money to support education, vert. 8r, At legislative commission meeting, vert. 9r, Viewing ships at Inkerman Palace, Crimea.
15r, Portrait.

*Perf. 12½x12, 12x12½*

**2004, Apr. 27** **Litho. & Engr.**

**6833-6836** A3252 Set of 4 3.50 1.60

**Souvenir Sheet**

*Perf. 11¾x12¼*

**6837** A3252 15r multi 3.50 1.00

No. 6837 contains one 33x47mm stamp.

Europa A3253

**2004, May 5** **Litho.** *Perf. 11¾x12¼*

**6838** A3253 8r multi *1.25 .50*
*a.* Miniature sheet of 8 *10.00 5.00*

Souvenir Sheet

Defense of Port Arthur (Lüshun, China) in Russo-Japanese War, Cent. — A3254

**2004, May 12** *Perf. 11¼*

**6839** A3254 10r multi 3.00 1.00

Mikhail I. Glinka (1804-57), Composer — A3255

No. 6840: a, Portrait. b, Scene from opera "Life for the Tsar," 1836. c, Scene from opera "Ruslan and Ludmila," 1842.

**2004, May 20** *Perf. 12*

**6840** A3255 4r Block of 3, #a-c, + label 3.00 .60

Russian Crown — A3256

Carved Head — A3257

Treasures from the Amber Room, State Museum, St. Petersburg: No. 6842, Cameo depicting Moses and Pharaoh, vert.
25r, Touch and Smell, Florentine mosaic.

**Litho. & Embossed**

**2004, May 25** *Perf. 13¼*

**6841** A3256 5r multi 1.00 .50
*a.* Miniature sheet of 10 17.50
**6842** A3256 5r multi 1.00 .50
*a.* Miniature sheet of 10 17.50
**6843** A3257 5r multi 1.00 .50
*a.* Miniature sheet of 10 17.50
*Nos. 6841-6843 (3)* 3.00 1.50

**Souvenir Sheet**

*Perf. 13*

**6844** A3257 25r multi 3.00 1.50

A limited edition booklet exists containing booklet panes of one of Nos. 6841-6844. Value, *$150.*

German - Russian Youth Meeting A3258

**2004, June 3** **Litho.** *Perf. 11¼*

**6845** A3258 8r multi 1.00 .50

See Germany No. 2287.

Vladimir K. Kokkinaki (1904-85), Test Pilot — A3259

**2004, June 8** *Perf. 12*

**6846** A3259 3r multi .50 .25
*a.* Miniature sheet of 8 10.00

Victory — A3260

Who Comes With the Sword Will Die by the Sword — A3261

Patriotic paintings by S. Prisekin: No. 6848, Marshal Zhukov. No. 6850, And the Oath of Allegiance We Have Honored, Smolensk, 1812.

**2004, June 8** *Perf. 11¾x11½*

**6847** A3260 5r shown .50 .25
**6848** A3260 5r multi .50 .25

*Perf. 11¾*

**6849** A3261 5r shown .50 .25
**6850** A3261 5r multi .50 .25
*Nos. 6847-6850 (4)* 2.00 1.00

Women's Riding Habits — A3262

Designs: No. 6851, 4r, Three women, horse. No. 6852, 4r, Three women, horse, dog. No. 6853, 4r, Two women, horse, two dogs.

**2004, July 15** *Perf. 12x11¾*

**6851-6853** A3262 Set of 3 2.00 .75
*6853a* Miniature sheet, 2 each #6851-6853 8.00 4.00

2004 Summer Olympics, Athens — A3267

**2004, July 20** *Perf. 12*

**6854** A3267 Horiz. pair with central label 1.00 .50
*a.* 3r Running .25 .25
*b.* 8r Wrestling .75 .35

Souvenir Sheet

Admiralty Shipyard, 300th Anniv. — A3268

**2004, July 22** *Perf. 12x12¼*

**6855** A3268 12r multi 3.00 .60

Miniature Sheet

Children and Road Safety — A3269

No. 6856: a, Ducks crossing street at pedestrian crossing. b, Boy and turtle crossing street with green light. c, Driver near fenced garden. d, Girl playing in street. e, Accident showing eggs flying out of car.

**2004, Aug. 5** *Perf. 12*

**6856** A3269 4r Sheet of 5, #a-e, + label 5.00 1.00

Worldwide Fund for Nature (WWF) — A3270

Gulo gulo: a, With pine branches. b, With dead bird. c, On tree branch. d, With young.

**2004, Aug. 12** *Perf. 11¼*

**6857** A3270 Block of 4 3.00 1.10
*a.-d.* 8r Any single .75 .25
*e.* Miniature sheet, #6857a, 2 each #6857b-6857c, 3 #6857d + label 10.00 5.00

Tomsk, 400th Anniv. — A3271

**2004, Aug. 20** ***Perf. 12¼x12***

**6858** A3271 4r multi .50 .25

ITAR-TASS News Agency, Cent. — A3272

**2004, Aug. 20** ***Perf. 12***

**6859** A3272 4r multi .50 .25

*a.* Miniature sheet of 8 10.00

Famous Men — A3273

Designs: No. 6860, 5r, B. G. Muzrukov (1904-79), organizer of defense industry. No. 6861, 5r, N. L. Dukhov (1904-64), rocket designer.

**2004, Sept. 8**

**6860-6861** A3273 Set of 2 1.00 .50

Tsar Paul I (1754-1801) A3274

Designs: No. 6862, 10r, Seated. No. 6863, 10r, Standing.
20p, Wearing hat.

**Litho. & Engr.**

**2004, Sept. 10** ***Perf. 12***

**6862-6863** A3274 Set of 2 1.00 .50

**Souvenir Sheet**

**6864** A3274 20r multi 3.00 1.00

S. N. Rerikh (1904-93), Painter — A3275

***Perf. 11¾x11½***

**2004, Sept. 16** **Litho.**

**6865** A3275 4r multi .50 .25

Vsevolod III (1154-1212), Grand Prince of Novgorod — A3276

**Litho. & Engr.**

**2004, Oct. 7** ***Perf. 11¾***

**6866** A3276 12r multi 2.00 .55

Kazan State University, 200th Anniv. — A3277

**2004, Oct. 20** **Litho.** ***Perf. 12x11¾***

**6867** A3277 5r multi 1.00 .25

Silver Containers — A3278

Designs: No. 6868, 4.70r, Bowl, c. 1880-1890. No. 6869, 4.70r, Milk container, 1900. No. 6870, 4.70r, Ladle, 1910. No. 6871, 4.70r, Vase, c. 1900-08, vert.

**Litho. & Embossed**

**2004, Oct. 26** ***Perf. 13¼***

**6868-6871** A3278 Set of 4 4.00 1.00

Happy New Year — A3279

***Serpentine Die Cut***

**2004, Nov. 12** **Litho.**

**Self-Adhesive**

**6872** A3279 5r multi 8.00 4.00

*a.* Miniature sheet of 8 75.00

Altai Republic Landscapes — A3280

No. 6873: a, 2r, Belukha Mountain. b, 3r, Katun River. c, 5r, Teletskoye Lake.

**2004, Nov. 18** ***Perf. 12***

**6873** A3280 Block of 3, #a-c, + label 2.00 .50

Baikonur Cosmodrome, 50th Anniv. — A3281

**2004, Dec. 1**

**6874** Horiz. strip of 4 3.00 1.00

*a.* A3281 2.50r R-7 missile .35 .25

*b.* A3281 3.50r Proton rocket .40 .25

*c.* A3281 4r Soyuz rocket .50 .25

*d.* A3281 6r Zenit rocket .75 .30

*e.* Miniature sheet, 2 #6874 10.00 5.00

Mordovian Republic A3282

Smolensk Oblast A3283

Tver Oblast A3284

Chukotsky Autonomous Okrug — A3285

Koryak Autonomous Okrug — A3286

Taimyr Autonomous Okrug — A3287

**2005, Jan. 10**

**6875** A3282 5r multi 1.00 .40

**6876** A3283 5r multi 1.00 .40

**6877** A3284 5r multi 1.00 .40

**6878** A3285 5r multi 1.00 .40

**6879** A3286 5r multi 1.00 .40

**6880** A3287 5r multi 1.00 .40

*Nos. 6875-6880 (6)* 6.00 2.40

Moscow M. V. Lomonosov State University, 250th Anniv. — A3288

**2005, Jan. 12**

**6881** A3288 5r multi 1.00 .25

*a.* Miniature sheet of 9 10.00

**Souvenir Sheet**

Expo 2005, Aichi, Japan — A3289

**2005, Feb. 21** **Litho.** ***Perf. 12½x12***

**6882** A3289 15r multi 5.50 2.75

Archaeological Treasures of Sarmatia — A3290

Designs: No. 6883, 5r, Silver bowl with bull design (shown). No. 6884, 5r, Gold and wood bowl with bear design. No. 6885, 7r, Gold ornament with camel design. No. 6886, 7r, Gold ornament with deer design, vert.

**Litho. & Embossed**

**2005, Feb. 25** ***Perf. 13¼***

**6883-6886** A3290 Set of 4 8.00 4.00

Submarine Force, Cent. A3291

Submarines: 2r, Type M, VI-bis series. 3r, Type S, IX-bis series. 5r, Type Sch, X-bis series. 8r, Type K.

**2005, Mar. 3** **Litho.** ***Perf. 12x12¼***

**6887-6890** A3291 Set of 4 *25.00 12.50*

Kazan, 1000th Anniv. A3292

Designs: No. 6891, 5r, Suyumbike Tower (shown). No. 6892, 5r, Kul Sharif Mosque. 7r, Cathedral of the Annunciation.

**2005, Mar. 10** ***Perf. 11¾x12***

**6891-6893** A3292 Set of 3 2.50 .60

*6893a* Souvenir sheet, #6891-6893 20.00 7.00

Emperor Alexander II (1818-81) A3293

Alexander II and: No. 6894, 10r, Educator Vasily Zhukovsky, pillar (blue frame). No. 6895, 10r, Coronation (red frame). No. 6896, 10r, At desk (green frame). No. 6897, 10r, On horse (brown frame).
25r, Portrait.

**Litho. & Engr.**

**2005, Mar. 28** ***Perf. 12x12½***

| | | | | |
|---|---|---|---|---|
| **6894-6897** | A3293 | Set of 4 | 5.00 | 2.00 |

**Souvenir Sheet**

| | | | | |
|---|---|---|---|---|
| **6898** | A3293 | 25r multi | 3.50 | 1.25 |

Victory in World War II, 60th Anniv. — A3294

Designs: No. 6899, 2r, Soldier at column with grafitti. No. 6900, 2r, Soldiers and tank. No. 6901, 3r, Soldier watching pigeons eat. No. 6902, 3r, Jubilant soldiers return to Moscow. 5r, Soldiers and captured Nazi banners.
10r, Soldiers saluting Soviet flag over Reichstag building.

**2005, Apr. 5** **Litho.** ***Perf. 12***

| | | | | |
|---|---|---|---|---|
| **6899-6903** | A3294 | Set of 5 | 2.00 | .55 |
| *6899a* | | Sheet of 9 + label | 15.00 | 6.00 |
| *6903a* | | Souvenir sheet, #6899-6903, + label | 5.00 | 2.50 |

**Souvenir Sheet**

***Perf. 12x12¼***

| | | | | |
|---|---|---|---|---|
| **6904** | A3294 | 10r multi | 3.00 | 1.50 |

Liberation of Vienna by Soviet Troops, 60th Anniv. A3295

**2005, Apr. 13** **Litho.** ***Perf. 12***

| | | | | |
|---|---|---|---|---|
| **6905** | A3295 | 6r multi | 1.00 | .30 |

**Souvenir Sheet**

Fauna — A3296

No. 6906: a, Aquila danga (eagle). b, Catocala sponsa (butterflies). c, Castor fiber (beaver). d, Meles meles (badger).

**2005, Apr. 15**

| | | | | |
|---|---|---|---|---|
| **6906** | A3296 | 5r Sheet of 4, #a-d, + label | 3.00 | 1.00 |

See Belarus No. 554.

**Souvenir Sheet**

Opening of First Line of Moscow Metro, 70th Anniv. — A3297

No. 6907: a, 5r, Old train, stations, map of first line. b, 10r, Modern train, modern Metro map.

**2005, Apr. 25** ***Perf. 11½x12¼***

| | | | | |
|---|---|---|---|---|
| **6907** | A3297 | Sheet of 2, #a-b | 2.50 | .75 |

Bid of Moscow to Host 2012 Summer Olympics A3298

**2005, May 5** ***Perf. 12***

| | | | | |
|---|---|---|---|---|
| **6908** | A3298 | 4r multi | 1.00 | .25 |

Europa — A3299

**2005, May 5** ***Perf. 12¼x12***

| | | | | |
|---|---|---|---|---|
| **6909** | A3299 | 8r multi | *1.50* | *.75* |
| *a.* | | Sheet of 6 | *9.50* | *4.75* |

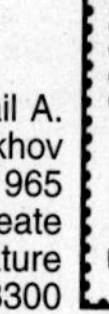

Mikhail A. Sholokhov (1905-84), 1965 Nobel Laureate in Literature A3300

**2005, May 20** ***Perf. 11¾***

| | | | | |
|---|---|---|---|---|
| **6910** | A3300 | 5r multi | 1.00 | .25 |

Fauna A3301

No. 6911: a, Martes zibellina. b, Panthera tigris altaica.

**2005, June 1** ***Perf. 12***

| | | | | |
|---|---|---|---|---|
| **6911** | | Horiz. pair, #a-b, + central label | 2.50 | .75 |
| *a.-b.* | A3301 | 8r Either single | 1.00 | .35 |

See North Korea Nos. 4436-4437.

Bees A3302

**2005, June 15** ***Perf. 11¼***

| | | | | |
|---|---|---|---|---|
| **6912** | | Horiz. strip of 5 | 3.50 | 1.25 |
| *a.* | A3302 | 3r Bombus armeniacus | .40 | .25 |
| *b.* | A3302 | 4r Bombus fragrans | .60 | .25 |
| *c.* | A3302 | 5r Bombus anachoreta | .75 | .30 |
| *d.* | A3302 | 6r Bombus unicus | .60 | .30 |
| *e.* | A3302 | 7r Bombus czerskii | .80 | .35 |
| *f.* | | Souvenir sheet, #6912a-6912e, + label | 10.00 | 5.00 |

Kaliningrad, 750th Anniv. — A3303

**2005, June 23** ***Perf. 12¼x12***

| | | | | |
|---|---|---|---|---|
| **6913** | A3303 | 5r multi | 1.00 | .45 |

N. E. Bauman Moscow State Technical University, 175th Anniv. — A3304

**2005, July 1** ***Perf. 12***

| | | | | |
|---|---|---|---|---|
| **6914** | A3304 | 5r multi | 1.00 | .35 |

Lighthouses — A3305

Map and: 5r, Mudyugsky Lighthouse. 6r, Solovetsky Lighthouse. 8r, Svyatonossky Lighthouse.

**2005, July 4** **Litho.**

| | | | | |
|---|---|---|---|---|
| **6915-6917** | A3305 | Set of 3 | 2.00 | 1.00 |

MiG Fighters A3306

Designs: No. 6918, 5r, MiG-3. No. 6919, 5r, MiG-15. No. 6920, 5r, MiG-21. No. 6921, 5r, MiG-25. No. 6922, 5r, MiG-29.

**2005, July 6**

| | | | | |
|---|---|---|---|---|
| **6918-6922** | A3306 | Set of 5 | 3.00 | 1.25 |
| *6922a* | | Souvenir sheet, #6918-6922, + label | 10.00 | 5.00 |

**Souvenir Sheet**

Battle of Kulikovo, 625th Anniv. — A3307

**2005, Aug. 2** ***Perf. 12½x12***

| | | | | |
|---|---|---|---|---|
| **6923** | A3307 | 15r multi | 2.50 | .75 |

**Souvenir Sheet**

Water — A3308

No. 6924: a, 3r, Hands in water. b, 3.50r, Ocean wave. c, 4r, Iceberg. d, 4.50r, Waterfall. e, 5r, Water droplets on leaf.

**2005, Aug. 16** ***Perf. 12***

| | | | | |
|---|---|---|---|---|
| **6924** | A3308 | Sheet of 5, #a-e, + label | 3.50 | 1.00 |

Field Marshal Aleksandr V. Suvorov (1729-1800) — A3309

**2005, Sept. 15** **Litho.** ***Perf. 12x11¾***

| | | | | |
|---|---|---|---|---|
| **6925** | A3309 | 4r multi | .90 | .25 |
| *a.* | | Miniature sheet of 8 | 9.50 | 3.25 |

Sea Infantry, 300th Anniv. — A3310

No. 6926 — Sea infantrymen from: a, 2r, 18th cent. b, 3r, 19th cent. c, 4r, 20th cent. d, 5r, 21st cent.

**2005, Oct. 19** **Litho.** ***Perf. 11¾***

| | | | | |
|---|---|---|---|---|
| **6926** | A3310 | Block of 4, #a-d | 2.50 | .75 |

Santa Claus (Ded Moroz) A3311

**2005, Oct. 26** ***Perf. 12***

| | | | | |
|---|---|---|---|---|
| **6927** | A3311 | 5r multi | .75 | .25 |

Printed in sheets of 8.

UNESCO, 60th Anniv. A3312

**2005, Nov. 1** ***Perf. 11¼***

| | | | | |
|---|---|---|---|---|
| **6928** | A3312 | 5.60r multi | .75 | .25 |

Christmas and New Year's Day A3313

**2005, Dec. 1**

| | | | | |
|---|---|---|---|---|
| **6929** | A3313 5.60r multi | | .80 | .30 |
| *a.* | Sheet of 9 | | 7.50 | 3.00 |

Antonov Airplanes A3314

Designs: No. 6930, 5.60r, An-3T. No. 6931, 5.60r, An-12. No. 6932, 5.60r, An-24. No. 6933, 5.60r, An-74. No. 6934, 5.60r, An-124.

**2006, Jan. 12** **Litho.** ***Perf. 12***

| | | | | |
|---|---|---|---|---|
| **6930-6934** | A3314 | Set of 5 | 3.50 | 1.50 |
| *6934a* | Sheet, #6930-6934, + label | | 10.00 | 5.00 |

2006 Winter Olympics, Turin A3315

Designs: No. 6935, 4r, Luge. No. 6936, 4r, Speed skating. No. 6937, 4r, Snowboarding.

**2006, Jan. 18**

| | | | | |
|---|---|---|---|---|
| **6935-6937** | A3315 | Set of 3 | 1.50 | .70 |

Armenia Day in Russia — A3316

**2006, Jan. 22** ***Perf. 11¼***

| | | | |
|---|---|---|---|
| **6938** | A3316 10r multi | 1.25 | .60 |

See Armenia No. 723.

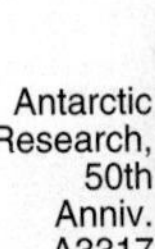

Antarctic Research, 50th Anniv. A3317

Designs: No. 6939, 7r, Underwater researcher, transport vehicle. No. 6940, 7r, Scientific ship, airplane. No. 6941, 7r, Ice-breaker, penguins.

**2006, Jan. 26** ***Perf. 12***

| | | | | |
|---|---|---|---|---|
| **6939-6941** | A3317 | Set of 3 | 2.50 | 1.25 |
| *6941a* | Sheet of 6 #6941 | | 6.50 | 3.25 |

Peter I Interrogating Tsarevich Aleksei, by N. N. Ge (1831-94) — A3318

Design: No. 6943, 5.60r, Portrait of N. N. Ge, by I. E. Repin, vert.

**2006, Feb. 16**

| | | | | |
|---|---|---|---|---|
| **6942-6943** | A3318 | Set of 2 | 2.50 | 1.00 |

Paintings by M. A. Vrubel (1856-1910) A3319

Designs: No. 6944, 5.60r, Tsarevna-Swan (shown). No. 6945, 5.60r, Self-portrait.

**2006, Feb. 27** **Litho.** ***Perf. 12***

| | | | | |
|---|---|---|---|---|
| **6944-6945** | A3319 | Set of 2 | 2.50 | 1.00 |

Russian Submarine Fleet, Cent. A3320

Submarine: 3r, 667A. 4r, 671. 6r, 941. 7r, 949A.

**2006, Feb. 28** ***Perf. 12***

| | | | | |
|---|---|---|---|---|
| **6946-6949** | A3320 | Set of 4 | 12.00 | 5.00 |

Moscow Kremlin Museums, Bicent. A3321

Designs: No. 6950, 5r, No. 6954b, 20r, Throne of Ivan IV. No. 6951, 5r, No. 6954c, 20r, Orb of Tsar Michael. No. 6952, 5r, No. 6954d, 20r, Helmet of Tsar Michael. No. 6953, 5r, No. 6954e, 20r, State sword and shield. No. 6954a, 20r, No. 6955, 15r, Monomakh's cap.

**Litho., Litho. & Embossed (#6954)**

**2006, Mar. 6** ***Perf. 11¾x12***

| | | | | |
|---|---|---|---|---|
| **6950-6953** | A3321 | Set of 4 | 2.50 | 1.00 |
| **6954** | Horiz. strip of 5 | | *45.00* | *45.00* |
| *a.-e.* | A3321 20r Any single | | *8.25* | *8.25* |

**Souvenir Sheet**

***Perf. 11¾x12¼***

| | | | |
|---|---|---|---|
| **6955** | A3321 15r multi | 1.50 | .75 |

Airplanes Designed by Aleksandr S. Yakovlev (1906-89) A3322

Designs: No. 6956, 5r, AIR-1. No. 6957, 5r, Yak-42. No. 6958, 5r, Yak-54. No. 6959, 5r, Yak-130. No. 6960, 5r, Yak-141.

**2006, Mar. 20** **Litho.** ***Perf. 12¼x12***

| | | | | |
|---|---|---|---|---|
| **6956-6960** | A3322 | Set of 5 | 3.25 | 1.25 |
| *6960a* | Souvenir sheet, #6956-6960 | | 10.00 | 5.00 |

Souvenir Sheet

Duma, Cent. — A3323

**2006, Apr. 8** ***Perf. 12½x12***

| | | | |
|---|---|---|---|
| **6961** | A3323 15p multi | 2.00 | 1.00 |

Arms A3324

Flag A3325

**2006, Apr. 20** ***Perf. 14***

| | | | |
|---|---|---|---|
| **6962** | A3324 5.60r multi | 2.50 | .75 |
| | Booklet, 10 #6962 | 25.00 | |
| | Booklet, 15 #6962 | 37.50 | |
| | Booklet, 20 #6962 | 50.00 | |
| **6963** | A3325 5.60r multi | 2.50 | .75 |
| | Booklet, 10 #6963 | 25.00 | |
| | Booklet, 15 #6963 | 37.50 | |
| | Booklet, 20 #6963 | 50.00 | |

Paintings In Tretyakov Gallery, Moscow A3326

Tretyakov Gallery and Statue of Pavel M. Tretyakov — A3327

Designs: No. 6964, 5.60r, Trinity, by Anrrej Roubljov, c. 1420. No. 6965, 5.60r, Girl with Peaches, by V. A. Serov, 1887. No. 6966, 5.60r, Beyond the Eternal Calm, by I. I. Levitan, 1894, horiz. No. 6967, 5.60r, Three Heroes, by V. M. Vasnetsov, 1898, horiz.

***Perf. 11¾x12, 12x11¾***

**2006, Apr. 26** **Litho.**

| | | | | |
|---|---|---|---|---|
| **6964-6967** | A3326 | Set of 4 | 2.75 | 1.25 |

**Souvenir Sheet**

***Perf. 12½x12***

| | | | |
|---|---|---|---|
| **6968** | A3327 15r multi | 1.90 | .85 |

Emperor Alexander III (1845-94) A3328

Designs: No. 6970, 10r, Alexander III and map. No. 6971, 10r, Alexander III, flag and ship.

25r, Alexander III.

**Litho. & Engr.**

**2006, May 4** ***Perf. 12x12½***

| | | | | |
|---|---|---|---|---|
| **6970-6971** | A3328 | Set of 2 | 5.00 | 2.00 |

**Souvenir Sheet**

***Perf. 12x12¼***

| | | | |
|---|---|---|---|
| **6972** | A3328 25r multi | 3.00 | 1.50 |

Blagoveschensk, 150th Anniv. — A3329

**2006, May 11** **Litho.** ***Perf. 12x12¼***

| | | | |
|---|---|---|---|
| **6973** | A3329 5r multi | .80 | .25 |

Souvenir Sheet

Baltic Shipyards, 150th Anniv. — A3330

**2006, May 22** ***Perf. 12x12½***

| | | | |
|---|---|---|---|
| **6974** | A3330 12p multi | 2.00 | .75 |

Luzhniki Olympic Stadium, 50th Anniv. A3331

**2006, May 29** ***Perf. 12***

| | | | |
|---|---|---|---|
| **6975** | A3331 6r multi | .75 | .35 |

Flowers — A3332

No. 6976: a, Spring flowers (denomination at UL). b, Summer flowers (denomination at UR). c, Fall flowers (denomination at LL). d, Winter flowers (denomination at LR).

**2006, June 6** ***Perf. 11½***

| | | | |
|---|---|---|---|
| **6976** | A3332 7r Block of 4, #a-d | 4.00 | 2.00 |

Altai Territories as Part of Russia, 250th Anniv. — A3333

**Litho. & Embossed**

**2006, June 15** ***Perf. 11¼***

**6977** A3333 5r multi .80 .25
*a.* Miniature sheet of 9 10.00

Adygeya Republic — A3334

Vladimir Oblast — A3335

Ryazan Oblast A3336

Kostroma Oblast A3337

Pskov Oblast A3338

ТУЛЬСКАЯ ОБЛАСТЬ

Tula Oblast A3339

**2006, June 20** **Litho.** ***Perf. 12***

**6978** A3334 6r multi .75 .35
**6979** A3335 6r multi .75 .35
**6980** A3336 6r multi .75 .35
**6981** A3337 6r multi .75 .35
**6982** A3338 6r multi .75 .35
**6983** A3339 6r multi .75 .35
*Nos. 6978-6983 (6)* 4.50 2.10

Circumnavigation by the Kruzenshtern, 2005-06 — A3340

**2006, June 29**

**6984** A3340 4r multi 1.00 .50

Arcticcoal, 75th Anniv. A3341

**2006, July 12** ***Perf. 11¼***

**6985** A3341 4r multi .70 .35

**Souvenir Sheet**

Bolshoi Tsarskoselski Palace, 250th Anniv. — A3342

No. 6986: a, 5r, Left portion. b, 6r, Central portion. c, 7r, Right portion.

**2006, July 17** ***Perf. 12x11¾***

**6986** A3342 Sheet of 3, #a-c 3.00 1.00

РОССИЯ
6.00
А.А. ИВАНОВ
1806-1858

Branch, by A. A. Ivanov (1806-58) — A3343

Design: No. 6988, 6r, Portrait of A. A. Ivanov, by S. P. Postnikov, vert.

**2006, July 17** ***Perf. 12***

**6987-6988** A3343 Set of 2 1.25 .60

Novodevichy Monastery, by A. M. Vasnetsov (1856-1933) — A3344

Design: No. 6990, 6r, Portrait of A. M. Vasnetsov, by N.D. Kuznetsov, vert.

**2006, July 24**

**6989-6990** A3344 Set of 2 1.25 .60

Barents Sea Lighthouses — A3345

Designs: 5r, Kaninsky Lighthouse. 6r, Kildinsky North Lighthouse. 8r, Vaidagubsky Lighthouse, vert.

**2006, Aug. 10**

**6991-6993** A3345 Set of 3 2.50 1.25

**Souvenir Sheet**

Russian State Theater, 250th Anniv. — A3346

**2006, Aug. 16** ***Perf. 12¼x12***

**6994** A3346 15r multi 1.75 .75

Fauna of Sakha Republic A3347

Designs: 3r, Rhodostethia rosea. 4r, Grus leucogeranus. 5r, Ursus maritimus. 6r, Equus caballus. 7r, Rangifer tarandus.

**2006, Aug. 29** ***Perf. 11½x11¼***

**6995-6999** A3347 Set of 5 2.75 1.40
*6999a* Souvenir sheet, #6995-6999, + label 3.75 1.90

Russian Language Development International Youth Project — A3348

**2006, Sept. 5** **Litho.** ***Perf. 11¼***

**7000** A3348 7r multi 1.50 .75

D. S. Likhachev (1906-99), Literary Critic — A3349

**2006, Sept. 19** ***Perf. 12***

**7001** A3349 5r multi .60 .35
*a.* Sheet of 6 + 2 labels 3.75 2.00

Nature of the Caucausus Region — A3350

No. 7002: a, 6r, Mountain. b, 7r, Stream. c, 8r, Bison.

**2006, Sept. 22** ***Perf. 12***

**7002** A3350 Block of 3, #a-c, + label 2.50 1.00

Television Broadcasting In Russia, 75th Anniv. A3351

**2006, Oct. 5** ***Perf. 11¼***

**7003** A3351 7r multi .95 .35

Mobile Telephone Communications in Russia, 15th Anniv. — A3352

**2006, Oct. 12** ***Perf. 12***

**7004** A3352 7r multi .80 .35

К ЕДИНОЙ ЕВРОПЕ БЕЗ РАЗДЕЛИТЕЛЬНЫХ ЛИНИЙ
РОССИЯ
RUSSIA
8.00

Admission to European Council, 10th Anniv. — A3353

**2006, Oct. 18** ***Perf. 12x12¼***

**7005** A3353 8r multi .95 .45

Savings Banks, 165th Anniv. — A3354

Designs: 7r, N. A. Kristofari (1802-81), bank founder, and bank building. 15r, Kristofari, vert.

**2006, Oct. 18** ***Perf. 12***

**7006** A3354 7r multi 1.00 .50

**Souvenir Sheet**

***Perf. 12x12½***

**7007** A3354 15r multi 1.75 .85

No. 7007 contains one 30x42mm stamp.

Regional Communications Commonwealth, 15th Anniv. — A3355

**2006, Nov. 9** *Perf. 12¼x12*
**7008** A3355 5r multi 1.25 .30

Ded Moroz (Russian Santa Claus) — A3356

**2006, Nov. 29** *Perf. 11¾*
**7009** A3356 7r multi .95 .35

Printed in sheets of 6.

Russian National Atlas — A3357

**2006, Dec. 7** *Perf. 12x11¾*
**7010** A3357 6r multi .95 .30

New Year 2007 A3358

**2006, Dec. 12** *Perf. 12*
**7011** A3358 7r multi .95 .35
*a.* Souvenir sheet of 6 6.00 3.00

Vladimir M. Bekhterev (1857-1927), Psychoneurologist — A3359

**2007, Jan. 15 Litho.** *Perf. 12*
**7012** A3359 5r multi .70 .30

Ivan I. Shishkin (1832-98), Painter A3360

Designs: No. 7013, 7r, Portrait of Shishkin, by I. N. Kramskoy (shown). No. 7014, 7r, In the North Wild, by Shishkin

**2007, Jan. 25**
**7013-7014** A3360 Set of 2 1.75 .85

Order of St. George, 200th Anniv. A3361

**2007, Feb. 7** **Litho.**
**7015** A3361 10r multi 1.25 .60

**Souvenir Sheet**

**Litho. & Embossed**

**7016** A3361 50r multi 7.00 3.00

No. 7015 was printed in sheets of 8 + label. No. 7016 contains one diamond-shaped 57x57mm stamp.

Russian G. V. Plekhanov Economic Academy, Cent. — A3362

**2007, Feb. 9 Litho.** *Perf. 13¾x13½*
**7017** A3362 5r multi .70 .30

Orest A. Kiprensky (1782-1836), Painter A3363

Paintings by Kiprensky: No. 7018, 7r, Self-portrait (shown). No. 7019, 7r, Poor Eliza.

*Perf. 12, 13½x13¾ (#7019)*

**2007, Mar. 2**
**7018-7019** A3363 Set of 2 1.75 .85

Russian Post Emblem — A3364

**2007, Mar. 12** *Perf. 12¼x12*
**7020** A3364 6.50r blue 1.00 .50
Complete booklet, 10 #7020 15.00
Complete booklet, 20 #7020 30.00

Compare with type A3827.

Souvenir Sheet

Intl. Polar Year — A3365

No. 7021: a, 6r, Icebreaker, scientific station. b, 7r, Glacier. c, 8r, Wildlife and cultural heritage.

**2007, Mar. 21** *Perf. 12*
**7021** A3365 Sheet of 3, #a-c 5.00 1.25

Souvenir Sheet

Famous Men — A3366

No. 7022: a, Arkady Tarkovsky (1907-89), poet. b, Andrei Tarkovsky (1932-86), film director.

**2007, Apr. 4** *Perf. 12¼x12*
**7022** A3366 8r Sheet of 2, #a-b 2.00 1.00

Souvenir Sheet

Space Exploration, 50th Anniv. — A3367

No. 7023: a, 10r, Sputnik 1. b, 20r, Sergei P. Korolev (1907-66), aeronautical engineer. c, 20r, Konstantin E. Tsiolkovsky (1857-1935), scientist.

**2007, Apr. 12** *Perf. 11¾*
**7023** A3367 Sheet of 3, #a-c 6.00 3.00

Bashkiria as Part of Russia, 450th Anniv. — A3368

**2007, Apr. 24** *Perf. 11¼*
**7024** A3368 6.50r multi .80 .35

Pavel P. Chistyakov (1832-1919), Painter A3369

Paintings of Chistyakov by: No. 7025, 7r, I. E. Repin (shown). No. 7026, 7r, V. A. Serov.

**2007, May 11** *Perf. 12*
**7025-7026** A3369 Set of 2 1.50 .85

Vladimir L. Borovikovsky (1757-1825), Painter A3370

Designs: No. 7027, 7r, Portrait of Borovikovsky, by I. V. Bugaevsky-Blagodatny (shown). No. 7028, 7r, Portrait of Sisters Anna and Barbara Gavrilovna.

**2007, May 15**
**7027-7028** A3370 Set of 2 1.50 .85

Souvenir Sheet

First Russian Postage Stamps, 150th Anniv. — A3371

**2007, May 24** *Perf. 12¼x12*
**7029** A3371 10r multi 1.50 .60

Telephones in Russia, 125th Anniv. — A3372

**2007, June 14** *Perf. 14*
**7030** A3372 5r multi .70 .30

Souvenir Sheet

Russian Academy of Arts, 250th Anniv. — A3373

**Litho. & Engr.**

**2007, June 15** ***Perf. 12¼x12***
**7031** A3373 25r multi 3.00 1.50

Emblem of 2007 St. Petersburg World Stamp Exhibition A3374

**2007, June 19 Litho.** ***Perf. 12x12½***
**7032** A3374 5r multi .70 .30
*a.* Perf. 12 1.00 .50

No. 7032a was printed in sheets of 8 + central label.

Souvenir Sheet

Plesetsk Cosmodrome, 50th Anniv. — A3375

**2007, July 2** ***Perf. 12¼x12***
**7033** A3375 12r multi 1.50 .75

Khakassia as Part of Russia, 300th Anniv. — A3376

**2007, July 12 Litho.** ***Perf. 11¼***
**7034** A3376 6.50r multi .70 .45

N. A. Lunin (1907-70), Submariner — A3377

M. I. Gadzhiev (1907-42), Submariner — A3378

**2007, July 25** ***Perf. 12x12¼***
**7035** Horiz. pair + central label 3.00 .85
*a.* A3377 7r multi .75 .40
*b.* A3378 7r multi .75 .40

S. P. Botkin (1832-89), Physician A3379

**2007, Aug. 14** ***Perf. 12x12½***
**7036** A3379 5r blue & black .65 .30

Irkutsk Oblast A3380

Orel Oblast A3381

Altai Kray A3382

Vologda Oblast A3383

Rostov Oblast A3384

Novosibirsk Oblast — A3385

**2007, Aug. 21** ***Perf. 12x12¼***
**7037** A3380 7r multi 1.00 .50
**7038** A3381 7r multi 1.00 .50
**7039** A3382 7r multi 1.00 .50
**7040** A3383 7r multi 1.00 .50
**7041** A3384 7r multi 1.00 .50
**7042** A3385 7r multi 1.00 .50
*Nos. 7037-7042 (6)* 6.00 3.00

Souvenir Sheet

Biblio-Globus Bookstore, 50th Anniv. — A3386

**2007, Aug. 24**
**7043** A3386 12r multi 1.75 .70

Souvenir Sheet

Russian Language Year — A3387

**2007, Sept. 14** ***Perf. 12¼x12***
**7044** A3387 12r multi 1.60 .70

Souvenir Sheet

Flowers — A3388

No. 7045: a, Gladiolus gandavensis. b, Iris ensata. c, Rosa hybrida. d, Nelumbo nucifera.

**2007, Sept. 26 Litho.**
**7045** A3388 6r Sheet of 4, #a-d 3.00 1.50

See North Korea No. 4689.

Worldwide Fund for Nature (WWF) — A3389

Designs: 5r, Ciconia boyciana. 6r, Uncia uncia. 7r, Bison bonasus.

**2007, Oct. 1** ***Perf. 11¼***
**7046-7048** A3389 Set of 3 2.25 1.10
*7048a* Miniature sheet of 8, 2 #7048, 3 each #7046-7047, + label 5.75 2.75

Trucks — A3390

No. 7049: a, 1924 AMO-F-15. b, 1932 GAZ-AA (MM). c, 1942 ZIS-5V.

**2007, Oct. 25** ***Perf. 11¾x11½***
**7049** A3390 Horiz. strip of 3 3.00 1.50
*a.-c.* 8r Any single 1.00 .50
*d.* Miniature sheet of 8, 2 #7049a, 3 each #7049b-7049c, + label 7.75 3.75

Russian House of Science and Culture, Berlin A3391

**2007, Oct. 29** ***Perf. 12***
**7050** A3391 8r multi .90 .45

Russian Language Year.

Horses — A3392

Horse's head and: 6r, Vladimir horse pulling wagon. No. 7052, 7r, Orlov Trotter pulling sulky. No. 7053, 7r, Don horse with rider. 8r, Vyatsky horse jumping.

**2007, Nov. 7** ***Perf. 11¾***
**7051-7054** A3392 Set of 4 2.75 1.25
*7054a* Souvenir sheet, #7051-7054 2.75 1.25

Arctic Deep Sea Exploration A3393

No. 7055: a, Mir-1 bathyscaphe. b, Russian flag on North Pole on map.

**2007, Dec. 7 Litho.** ***Perf. 12***
**7055** A3393 8r Vert. pair, #a-b, + label 1.75 1.00

New Year's Day — A3394

**2007, Dec. 7** ***Perf. 11¾x11½***
**7056** A3394 8r multi .85 .45
*a.* Miniature sheet of 6 6.00 3.00

First Russian Postage Stamps, 150th Anniv. — A3395

**2008, Jan. 10** ***Perf. 12x11¼***
**7057** A3395 8r No. 1 .90 .45

Count Alexei N. Tolstoy (1883-1945), Writer — A3396

**2008, Jan. 10** ***Perf. 12***
**7058** A3396 6r multi .70 .30

Nobel Laureates in Physics A3397

Designs: No. 7059, 6r, Ilya M. Frank (1908-90), 1958 laureate. No. 7060, 6r, Lev D. Landau (1908-68), 1962 laureate.

**2008, Jan. 22** ***Perf. 11¾***
**7059-7060** A3397 Set of 2 1.25 .70

Agustín de Betancourt (1758-1824), Engineer — A3398

**2008, Feb. 1** **Litho.** ***Perf. 12½x12***
**7061** A3398 9r multi 1.00 .50

See note under No. 7097.

Astrakhan, 450th Anniv. — A3399

**2008, Feb. 22** ***Perf. 11¾***
**7062** A3399 9r multi 1.00 .50

Valentin P. Glushko (1908-89), Spacecraft Designer — A3400

**2008, Mar. 17** ***Perf. 12¼x12***
**7063** A3400 8r multi .90 .45

Miniature Sheet

Archaeology — A3401

No. 3401 — Metal plates featuring: a, Mythological beast, 2nd cent. B.C.- 1st cent. A. D. b, Two oxen, 2nd cent. B.C.- 1st cent. A.D. c, Deer, 4th-3rd cents. B.C.

**Litho. & Embossed**

**2008, Mar. 25** ***Perf. 12½x12***
**7064** A3401 12r Sheet of 3, #a-c 4.00 2.00

2008 Summer Olympics, Beijing — A3402

No. 7065 — Various athletes with stripe at upper right corner in: a, Gray. b, Blue. c, Black.

**2008, Apr. 15** **Litho.** ***Perf. 11¾***
**7065** A3402 8r Horiz. strip of 3, #a-c 2.75 1.50
*d.* Souvenir sheet, #7065 2.75 1.50

Souvenir Sheet

Black Sea Naval Fleet, 225th Anniv. — A3403

**2008, Apr. 29** ***Perf. 12x12¼***
**7066** A3403 15r multi 2.00 1.00

Europa A3404

**2008, May 5** ***Perf. 12¼x12***
**7067** A3404 8r multi .70 .35
*a.* Miniature sheet of 6 4.50 2.10

Election of Pres. Dmitry Medvedev A3405

**2008, May 7** ***Perf. 12x12¼***
**7068** A3405 7r multi 1.00 .35

Krasnoyarsk Kray — A3406

Sverdlovsk Oblast — A3407

Penza Oblast A3408

Volgograd Oblast A3409

Yaroslavl Oblast A3410

**2008, May 20** ***Perf. 12¼x12, 12x12¼***
**7069** A3406 8r multi .75 .35
**7070** A3407 8r multi .75 .35
**7071** A3408 8r multi .75 .35
**7072** A3409 8r multi .75 .35
**7073** A3410 8r multi .75 .35
*Nos. 7069-7073 (5)* 3.75 1.75

Cathedrals — A3411

No. 7074: a, St. Demetrius's Cathedral, Vladimir, Russia, 12th cent., and winged beast. b, St. George's Cathedral, Voronets Monastery, Romania, 15th cent., and chrismon.

**2008, June 23** ***Perf. 11½***
**7074** A3411 Horiz. pair, #a-b, + central label 2.75 1.50
*a.-b.* 12r Either single 1.50 .75
*c.* Miniature sheet, 3 #7074 9.00 4.50

See Romania Nos. 5057-5058.

Helicopter Sports in Russia, 50th Anniv. — A3412

**2008, July 12** **Litho.** ***Perf. 11¾***
**7075** A3412 5r multi .50 .25

Pokrovsk Cathedral — A3413

**2008, July 25** ***Perf. 11¾x12¼***
**7076** A3413 7.50r multi .80 .35
Complete booklet, 10 #7076 10.00
Complete booklet, 20 #7076 22.50

Souvenir Sheet

Northern Navy, 75th Anniv. — A3414

**2008, July 26** ***Perf. 12x12½***
**7077** A3414 15r multi 4.00 1.00

Udmurtia as Part of Russia, 450th Anniv. — A3415

**2008, July 28** ***Perf. 11½***
**7078** A3415 7.50r multi .80 .35

Souvenir Sheet

Kizhi UNESCO World Heritage Site — A3416

No. 7079: a, Church, 1714. b, Bell tower, 1862. c, Church, 1694-1764.

**2008, July 31** ***Perf. 11¾x12¼***
**7079** A3416 10r Sheet of 3, #a-c 3.50 1.75

Souvenir Sheet

Emperor Nicholas I (1796-1855) — A3417

**Litho. & Engr.**

**2008, Aug. 8** ***Perf. 12x12½***

**7080** A3417 35r multi 4.00 2.00

Souvenir Sheet

International Polar Year — A3418

No. 7081 — Map of Northern Russia and various ships: a, 6r. b, 7r. c, 8r.

**2008, Aug. 28 Litho.** ***Perf. 12x11½***

**7081** A3418 Sheet of 3, #a-c 5.00 1.25

Wildlife — A3419

***Perf. 12¼x12 Syncopated***

**2008, Aug. 29** **Litho.**

| | | | | | |
|---|---|---|---|---|---|
| **7082** | A3419 | 10k | Hare | .25 | .25 |
| **7083** | A3419 | 15k | Hare | .25 | .25 |
| **7084** | A3419 | 25k | Hare | .25 | .25 |
| **7085** | A3419 | 30k | Fox | .25 | .25 |
| **7086** | A3419 | 50k | Fox | .25 | .25 |
| **7087** | A3419 | 1r | Fox | .25 | .25 |
| **7088** | A3419 | 1.50r | Lynx | .25 | .25 |
| **7089** | A3419 | 2r | Lynx | .25 | .25 |
| **7090** | A3419 | 2.50r | Lynx | .25 | .25 |
| **7091** | A3419 | 3r | Elk | .30 | .25 |
| **7092** | A3419 | 4r | Elk | .40 | .25 |
| **7093** | A3419 | 5r | Elk | .45 | .25 |
| **7094** | A3419 | 6r | Bear | .50 | .25 |
| **7095** | A3419 | 10r | Bear | .85 | .40 |
| **7096** | A3419 | 25r | Bear | 2.10 | 1.00 |
| | *Nos. 7082-7096 (15)* | | | 6.85 | 4.65 |

Souvenir Sheet

Goznak (State Currency Printers), 190th Anniv. — A3420

**Litho. & Embossed With Foil Application**

**2008, Sept. 1** ***Perf.***

**7097** A3420 20r black & gold 3.00 1.10

No. 7097 contains one 33mm diameter stamp.

A booklet containing booklet panes of 1 of Nos. 7061 and 7097 exists. Value, $55.

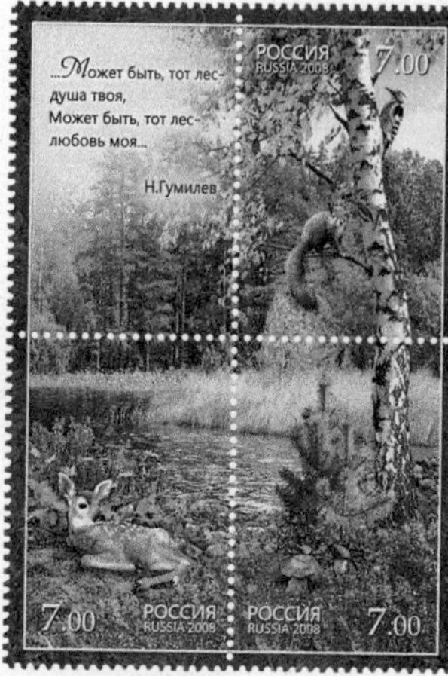


Flora and Fauna — A3421

No. 7098: a, Woodpecker and squirrel in birch tree. b, Fawn. c, Mushrooms, evergreens and birch tree.

**2008, Sept. 12 Litho.** ***Perf. 12x12¼***

**7098** A3421 7r Block of 3, #a-c, + label 3.00 1.25

Leningrad Oblast A3422

**2008, Sept. 17**

**7099** A3422 8r multi .80 .40

Souvenir Sheet

History of the Cossacks — A3423

No. 7100: a, Silver medal. b, Crossed swords and wreath. c, Sword hilt.

**2008, Sept. 17** ***Perf. 11¾x12¼***

**7100** A3423 10r Sheet of 3, #a-c 4.00 1.60

Helicopters — A3424

**2008, Oct. 2** ***Perf. 12¼x12***

**7101** A3424 7r Ka-226 1.00 .40

**7102** A3424 7r Ka-32 1.00 .40

***a.*** Miniature sheet, 3 each #7101-7102 5.50 2.75

Central Sikhote-Alin UNESCO World Heritage Site — A3425

No. 7103 — Various forest views: a, 7r. b, 8r. c, 9r.

**2008, Oct. 15 Litho.** ***Perf. 12***

**7103** A3425 Block of 3, #a-c, + label 3.00 1.25

Federation Council, 15th Anniv. — A3426

State Duma, 15th Anniv. A3427

**2008, Nov. 13** ***Perf. 12½x12***

**7104** A3426 10r multi 1.10 .50

**7105** A3427 10r multi 1.10 .50

Nos. 7104-7105 each were printed in sheets of 14 + label.

Bridges — A3428

Bridges over: 6r, Moscow River, Moscow. 7r, Volga River, Kimry. 8r, Ob River, Surgut. 9r, Neva River, St. Petersburg.

**2008, Nov. 28** ***Perf. 12x12¼***

**7106-7109** A3428 Set of 4 3.00 1.50

*7109a* Miniature sheet of 8, 2 each #7106-7109 6.50 3.00

Shuvalov Swimming School, Cent. A3429

**2008, Dec. 5**

**7110** A3429 8r multi .85 .40

Russia, 2008 World Ice Hockey Champions A3430

**2008, Dec. 5**

**7111** A3430 8r multi .85 .40

For surcharge, see No. 7375.

Bicycles — A3431

Designs: No. 7112, 7r, 1946 bicycle, derailleur. No. 7113, 7r, 1954 bicycle, front chain ring, chain guard and pedals. No. 7114, 7r, 1917 bicycle, saddle. No. 7115, 7r, 1938 bicycle, handlebars.

**2008, Dec. 11 Litho.** ***Perf. 12x11½***

**7112-7115** A3431 Set of 4 3.00 1.50

*7115a* Miniature sheet, 2 each # 7112-7115 5.75 2.75

Nos. 7112-7115 each were printed in sheets of 8 + central label.

A3432

A3433

A3434

Traditional Dagestan Costumes and Decorations A3435

**2008, Dec. 18** ***Perf. 11½x12***

**7116** A3432 7.50r multi .75 .30

**7117** A3433 7.50r multi .75 .30

**7118** A3434 7.50r multi .75 .30

**7119** A3435 7.50r multi .75 .30

***a.*** Miniature sheet, 2 each #7116-7119 6.50 3.00

*Nos. 7116-7119 (4)* 3.00 1.20

Nos. 7116-7119 each were printed in sheets of 11 + label.

New Year 2009 — A3436

**2008, Dec. 18** *Perf. 11¾*
**7120** A3436 7.50r multi .80 .35

Voronezh Oblast A3437

Chelyabinsk Oblast — A3438

Saratov Oblast A3439

**2009, Jan. 17** *Perf. 12*
**7121** A3437 9r multi .90 .35
**7122** A3438 9r multi .90 .35
**7123** A3439 9r multi .90 .35
*Nos. 7121-7123 (3)* 2.70 1.05

Ernesto "Che" Guevara and Cuban Flag — A3440

**2009, Jan. 19** *Perf. 12x12¼*
**7124** A3440 10r multi 2.25 .75

Cuban Revolution, 50th anniv. See Cuba No. 4924A.

Naval Museum, 300th Anniv. — A3441

**2009, Jan. 22** **Litho.** *Perf. 12x11½*
**7125** A3441 7r multi .75 .30

Vasily G. Perov (1834-82), Painter A3442

Designs: No. 7126, 9r, Self-portrait, 1851. No. 7127, 9r, Drinking of Tea in Mytischi, Near Moscow, 1862, horiz.

**2009, Jan. 28** *Perf. 11½x12, 12x11½*
**7126-7127** A3442 Set of 2 1.75 .75

Souvenir Sheet

Dmitri Mendeleev (1834-1907), Chemist — A3443

**2009, Feb. 6** *Perf. 12x12¼*
**7128** A3443 15r multi 1.50 .60

No. 7128 with an 80r surcharge and an overprint in the sheet margin marking 2019 as International Year of the Periodic Table was produced in limited quantities and issued on Mar. 19, 2019.

G. Bakhchivandji (1909-43), Test Pilot — A3444

**2009, Feb. 16** *Perf. 12¼x12*
**7129** A3444 10r multi .80 .45

Yuri Gagarin (1934-68), First Cosmonaut A3445

**2009, Mar. 6** *Perf. 12x12¼*
**7130** A3445 10r multi .80 .45

Printed in sheets of 10 + 2 central labels.

Souvenir Sheet

Aleksandr S. Popov (1859-1905), Electrical Engineer — A3446

**2009, Mar. 16** **Litho.** *Perf.*
**7131** A3446 20r multi 2.00 .85

Scenes From Novels By Nikolai V. Gogol (1809-52) — A3447

Gogol — A3448

No. 7132 — Scenes from: a, 6r, The Inspector General. b, 7r, Dead Souls. c, 8r, The Overcoat. d, 9r, Taras Bulba.

**2009, Apr. 1** *Perf. 12*
**7132** A3447 Sheet of 4, #a-d 3.00 1.40

**Souvenir Sheet**
*Perf. 12x12¼*
**7133** A3448 15r multi 1.75 .60

Weapons of World War II — A3449

Designs: 7r, SRT-40 and ARS-36 rifles. 8r, 1895 Nagan revolver and 1933 Tokarev pistol. 9r, PPS-43 and PPSh-41 machine guns. 10r, DP and SG-43 machine guns.

**2009, Apr. 27** *Perf. 11¾*
**7134-7137** A3449 Set of 4 3.50 1.50
*7137a* Sheet of 8, 2 each #7134-7137 6.00 3.00

A booklet containing four panes of one of Nos. 7134-7137 sold for 225r. Value, $30.

Europa A3450

**2009, May 5** *Perf. 12*
**7138** A3450 9r multi .90 .40
***a.*** Miniature sheet of 9 8.50 3.50

Intl. Year of Astronomy.

Hydrometeorological Service, 175th Anniv. — A3451

Weather map and: 8r, Weather measuring equipment, A. Y. Kupfer (1799-1865), weather scientist. 9r, Weather satellite.

**2009, May 15** *Perf. 12x12¼*
**7139-7140** A3451 Set of 2 1.75 .85
*7140a* Sheet of 8, 4 each #7139-7140 8.00 3.25

Souvenir Sheet

Empress Catherine I (1684-1727) — A3452

**Litho. & Engr.**
**2009, May 21** *Perf. 12x12¼*
**7141** A3452 35r multi 3.25 1.60

Kalmykia as Part of Russia, 400th Anniv. — A3453

**2009, June 2** **Litho.** *Perf. 11½x11¼*
**7142** A3453 7r multi .75 .30

Atomic-powered Icebreakers — A3454

Ships: 7r, Lenin. 8r, Taimyr. 9r, Yamal. 10r, 50 Let Pobedy.

**2009, June 18** **Litho.** *Perf. 12x11½*
**7143-7146** A3454 Set of 4 3.25 1.60

Nos. 7143-7146 each were printed in sheets of 8 + 2 labels.

Souvenir Sheet

Battle of Poltava, 300th Anniv. — A3455

**2009, June 26** *Perf. 11¾x12¼*
**7147** A3455 30r multi 3.00 1.40

Youth Year — A3456

**2009, June 27** *Perf. 12¼x12*
**7148** A3456 8r multi .90 .40

Ingushetia Republic A3457

Chechen Republic A3458

Tomsk Oblast A3459

**2009, July 7** *Perf. 12*
**7149** A3457 9r multi .85 .40
**7150** A3458 9r multi .85 .40
**7151** A3459 9r multi .85 .40
*Nos. 7149-7151 (3)* 2.55 1.20

Miniature Sheet

Helicopters Designed by M. L. Mil (1909-70) — A3460

No. 7152: a, 5r, Mi-1. b, 6r, Mi-4. c, 7r, Mi-8. d, 8r, Mi-34. e, 9r, Mi-28.

**2009, July 10** *Perf. 12¼x12*
**7152** A3460 Sheet of 5, #a-e, + label 3.50 1.75

Zinaida E. Serebryakova (1884-1967), Painter — A3461

Paintings by Serebryakova: No. 7153, 9r, Self-portrait in Dressing Room (shown). No. 7154, 9r, Autumn Field.

**2009, July 15** *Perf. 11½x12*
**7153-7154** A3461 Set of 2 1.75 .85

Andrei A. Gromyko (1909-89), Foreign Affairs Minister of Soviet Union A3462

**2009, July 17 Litho.** *Perf. 11½*
**7155** A3462 7r multi .65 .30

Miniature Sheet

Solovetski Islands — A3463

No. 7156 — Map and: a, St. Troitsky Church, 17th cent., and horse. b, St. Sergiev Church, 19th cent., and cow. c, Solovetski Monastery, 15th cent. d, Andrei Pervozvannyi Church, 18th cent.

**2009, July 27** *Perf. 12*
**7156** A3463 12r Sheet of 4, #a-d 5.00 2.25

Emblem of St. Petersburg A3464

Emblem of Moscow A3465

**2009, Aug. 6 Litho.** *Perf. 11¾x12¼*
**7157** A3464 6.60r multi .65 .30
Complete booklet, 10 #7157 6.50
Complete booklet, 20 #7157 13.00
**7158** A3465 9r multi .85 .45
Complete booklet, 10 #7158 8.50
Complete booklet, 20 #7158 17.00

Bridges — A3466

Designs: 6r, Oka River Bridge, Nizhni Novgorod. 7r, Irtysh River Bridge, Khanty-Mansiysk. 8r, Matsesta River Bridge, Sochi. 9r, Don River Bridge, Rostov-na-Donu.

**2009, Aug. 12 Litho.** *Perf. 12x12¼*
**7159-7162** A3466 Set of 4 2.75 1.40
*7162a* Miniature sheet of 8, 2 each #7159-7162 5.75 2.75

Miniature Sheet

Towns of Military Glory — A3467

No. 7163 — City names at top: a, Belgorod (8 letters in city name, tanks). b, Kursk. c, Orel (4 letters in city name, tanks and guns). d, Polyarny (8 letters in city name, ships). e, Rzhev (4 letters in city name, tanks and trucks).

**Litho. With Foil Application**

**2009, Aug. 24** *Perf. 11¼*
**7163** A3467 10r Sheet of 5, #a-e, + label 4.75 2.40

Souvenir Sheet

Great Novgorod, 1150th Anniv. — A3468

**Litho. & Embossed**

**2009, Sept. 4** *Perf. 12½x12*
**7164** A3468 50r multi 4.75 2.70

Souvenir Sheet

Famous Cossacks — A3469

No. 7165: a, Ermak Timofeevich (c. 1540-1585), explorer of Siberia (with helmet). b, Semen Ivanovich Dezhnev (c. 1605-72), explorer of Siberia (with beard). c, Count Matvei Ivanovich Platov (1757-1818), general (with mustache).

*Perf. 11¾x12¼*

**2009, Sept. 15 Litho.**
**7165** A3469 10r Sheet of 3, #a-c 2.75 1.40

19th Century Headdresses A3470

Designs: No. 7166, 9r, Tver region man wearing hat. No. 7167, 9r, Moscow region woman wearing headdress with blue ribbon (blue background). No. 7168, 9r, Nizhny Novgorod region woman wearing veiled headdress (red background). No. 7169, 9r, Yaroslavl region woman wearing veiled headdress (blue green background).

**2009, Sept. 23** *Perf. 11¼x12*
**7166-7169** A3470 Set of 4 3.50 1.75
*7169a* Miniature sheet of 8, 2 each #7166-7169 7.00 3.50

Nos, 7166-7169 each were printed in sheets of 11 + label.

Kremlins A3471

Kremlins in: 1r, Astrakhan. 1.50r, Zaraisk. 2r, Kazan. 2.50r, Kolomna. 3r, Rostov. 4r, Nizhny Novgorod. 5r, Novgorod. 6r, Pskov. 10r, Moscow. 25r, Ryazan. 50r, Tobolsk. 100r, Tula.

**2009, Oct. 1** *Serpentine Die Cut 11*
**Self-Adhesive**

**7170** A3471 1r multi .30 .25
**7171** A3471 1.50r multi .30 .25
**7172** A3471 2r multi .30 .25
**7173** A3471 2.50r multi .30 .25
**7174** A3471 3r multi .30 .25
**7175** A3471 4r multi .35 .25
**7176** A3471 5r multi .50 .25
**7177** A3471 6r multi .55 .25
**7178** A3471 10r multi .90 .45
**7179** A3471 25r multi 2.50 1.25
*a.* Sheet of 10, #7170-7179 3.50
**7180** A3471 50r multi 5.00 2.50
**7181** A3471 100r multi 9.50 4.75
*a.* Miniature sheet of 12, #7170-7181 21.00
*Nos. 7170-7181 (12)* 20.80 10.95

Issued: No. 7179a, 1/24/14. See Nos. 7847-7848, 7932.

World Food Program — A3472

**2009, Oct. 7** ***Perf. 11¾***
**7182** A3472 10r multi 1.00 .50

Admiral Vladimir Ivanovich Istomin (1809-55) — A3473

**2009, Oct. 14** ***Perf. 12x11½***
**7183** A3473 10r multi 1.00 .50

Traffic Safety A3474

**2009, Oct. 22** ***Perf. 12½x12***
**7184** A3474 9r multi .90 .45

Order of the Hero of the Soviet Union, 75th Anniv. — A3475

**Litho. & Embossed With Foil Application**

**2009, Oct. 29** ***Perf. 12x12¼***
**7185** A3475 9r multi .90 .45

Souvenir Sheet

Empress Elizabeth Petrovna (1709-62) — A3476

**Litho. & Engr.**

**2009, Nov. 6** ***Perf. 12x12¼***
**7186** A3476 40r multi 4.00 2.00

Department of Transportation, 200th Anniv. — A3477

**2009, Nov. 9** **Litho.** ***Perf. 12¼x12***
**7187** A3477 9r multi .90 .45

Shchepkin Drama School, 200th Anniv. A3478

**2009, Nov. 25**
**7188** A3478 10r multi 1.00 .50

Antarctic Treaty, 50th Anniv. A3479

**2009, Nov. 30** **Litho.**
**7189** A3479 15r multi 1.50 .75

New Year's Day — A3480

**2009, Dec. 1** ***Die Cut***

**Self-Adhesive**

**7190** A3480 10r multi 1.00 .50

Strategic Rocket Forces, 50th Anniv. A3481

**2009, Dec. 10** ***Perf. 11¼x12***
**7191** A3481 9r multi 1.00 .45

Fountains A3482

Fountain in: 9r, Verkhnyaya Pyshma. 10r, Nizhny Novgorod. 12r, Novy Urengoi, vert. 15r, Yaroslavl.

***Serpentine Die Cut 11¼***

**2009, Dec. 15** **Self-Adhesive**
**7192-7195** A3482 Set of 4 4.50 2.25

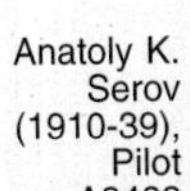

Anatoly K. Serov (1910-39), Pilot A3483

Valentina S. Grizodubova (1910-93), Pilot — A3484

**2010, Jan. 14** **Litho.** ***Perf. 12½x12***
**7196** A3483 10r multi 1.00 .50
**7197** A3484 10r multi 1.00 .50

A3485

Anton P. Chekhov (1860-1904), Writer — A3486

No. 7198 — Characters from: a, 8r, Lady with the Dog. b, 10r, The Seagull. c, 12r, The Artist's Story (The House with the Mezzanine). 20r, Chekhov.

**2010, Jan. 29** **Litho.** ***Perf. 11¾x12¼***
**7198** A3485 Sheet of 3, #a-c 4.00 2.00

**Souvenir Sheet**

***Perf.***

**7199** A3486 20r multi 3.00 1.50

Peoples' Friendship University, Moscow, 50th Anniv. — A3487

**2010, Feb. 5** **Litho.** ***Perf. 12x11½***
**7200** A3487 10r multi 1.00 .50

2010 Winter Olympics, Vancouver — A3488

**Litho. & Embossed**

**2010, Feb. 11** ***Perf. 11½***
**7201** A3488 15r multi 1.25 .60

Paintings by Fedor S. Rokotov (c. 1735-1808) A3489

Portraits of: No. 7202, 10.50r, Prince D. M. Golitsyn. No. 7203, 10.50r, Countess E. A. Musina-Pushkina.

**2010, Mar. 19** **Litho.** ***Perf. 11¼x12***
**7202-7203** A3489 Set of 2 2.00 1.00

Orenburg Oblast A3490

Tuva Republic A3491

**2010, Mar. 24** ***Perf. 12x12¼***
**7204** A3490 10.50r multi 1.00 .50
**7205** A3491 10.50r multi 1.00 .50

Evgeny K. Fedorov (1910-81), Polar Explorer — A3492

**2010, Apr. 9** ***Perf. 12x12¼***
**7206** A3492 12r multi 1.25 .40

Miniature Sheet

Towns of Military Glory — A3493

No. 7207 — City names at top: a, Malgobek (8 letters in city name, airplanes, cannons and cavalry). b, Elnja (5 letters in city name, bazookas, cannons and tanks). c, Elets (4 letters in city name, trucks, cannons and tanks). d, Voronezh (7 letters in city name, airplanes and cannons). e, Luga (4 letters in city name, cannons and tanks).

**Litho. With Foil Application**

**2010, Apr. 15** ***Perf. 11¼***
**7207** A3493 10r Sheet of 5, #a-e, + label 4.25 1.75

World War II Tanks — A3494

Designs: 9r, BT-7M. 10r, T-70. 11r, T-34-85. 12r, IS-2.

**2010, Apr. 20** **Litho.** ***Perf. 13½***
**7208-7211** A3494 Set of 4 4.00 1.50
*7211a* Sheet of 8, 2 each #7208-7211 8.00 3.00

Souvenir Sheet

Soviet Union Order of Victory — A3495

**Litho. & Embossed**

**2010, Apr. 26** ***Perf. 12***
**7212** A3495 50r multi 4.25 1.75

Victory in World War II, 65th anniv.

Europa — A3496

**2010, May 5** **Litho.** ***Perf. 12x12½***
**7213** A3496 10.50r multi .70 .35
*a.* Miniature sheet of 6 5.00 2.10

Modernization of Cyrillic Alphabet, 300th Anniv. — A3497

**2010, May 18** ***Perf. 12x12¼***
**7214** A3497 7.70r multi .75 .25

Souvenir Sheet

Ivan Fedorov (c. 1510-83), Printer — A3498

**Litho. & Engr.**

**2010, May 18** ***Perf. 12½x12***
**7215** A3498 50r multi 4.50 1.60

Miniature Sheet

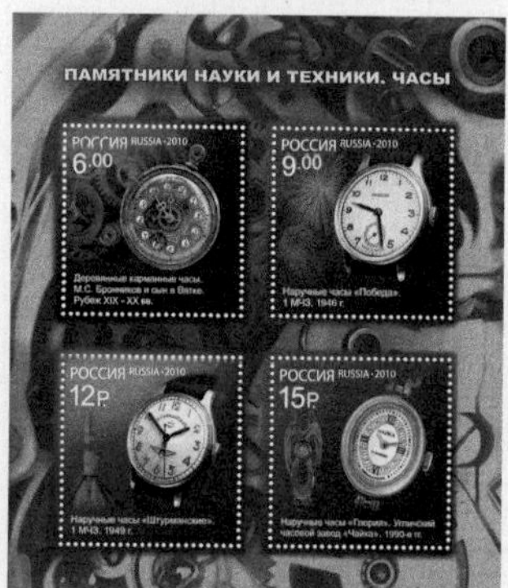

Watches — A3499

No. 7216 — Watch from: a, 6r, Wooden pocket watch by M. S. Bronnikov and Son. 9r, Pobeda wrist watch, 1946. 12r, Shturmanskie wrist watch, 1949. 15r, Chaika wrist watch, 1990.

**2010, May 28** **Litho.** ***Perf. 12¼***
**7216** A3499 Sheet of 4, #a-d 3.75 1.40

Dmitry Levitzky (c.1735-1822), Painter — A3500

Designs: No. 7217, 10.50r, Self-portrait (detail), 1783. No. 7218, 10.50r, Portrait of G. I. Alymova, 1776.

**2010, June 7** ***Perf. 11½x12***
**7217-7218** A3500 Set of 2 2.00 .70

Souvenir Sheet

Valaam Archipelago — A3501

**2010, June 8** ***Perf. 12***
**7219** A3501 25r multi 1.60 .80

Souvenir Sheet

Tsarskoye Selo (Tsar's Village) UNESCO World Heritage Site, 300th Anniv. — A3502

No. 7220: a, Egyptian Gates. b, Pushkin Monument, vert. c, Alexander Palace.

***Perf. 12x12¼, 12¼x12***

**2010, June 18**
**7220** A3502 15r Sheet of 3, #a-c 4.25 1.50

Icons of Russia and Serbia — A3503

No. 7221: a, Archangel Michael, by Andrei Rublev, 15th cent., Russia. b, Odigitria Virgin, Belgrade, Serbia, 14th cent.

**2010, June 28** ***Perf. 11½***
**7221** A3503 15r Pair, #a-b 2.75 1.00

See Serbia No. 515.

Vladivostok, 150th Anniv. — A3504

**2010, July 2** ***Perf. 13½***
**7222** A3504 15r multi 1.40 .50

Bryansk Oblast A3505

Jewish Autonomous Oblast — A3506

**2010, July 14** ***Perf. 12x12¼***
**7223** A3505 10.50r multi .90 .35
**7224** A3506 10.50r multi .90 .35

Curonian Spit UNESCO World Heritage Site — A3507

No. 7225 — Spit with denomination at: a, Left. b, Right.

**2010, June 26** **Litho.** ***Perf. 13½***
**7225** Horiz. pair + central label 4.00 1.00
*a.-b.* A3507 15r Either single 1.75 .50

A gritty substance is affixed to the areas of the stamps and labels showing sand.

A3508

A3509

A3510

Headdresses of Tatarstan A3511

**2010, July 30** **Litho.** ***Perf. 11½x12***
**7226** A3508 11r multi 1.00 .35
**7227** A3509 11r multi 1.00 .35
**7228** A3510 11r multi 1.00 .35
**7229** A3511 11r multi 1.00 .35
*a.* Miniature sheet of 8, 2 each #7226-7229 7.50 3.00
*Nos. 7226-7229 (4)* 3.00 1.40

Nos. 7226-7229 each were printed in sheets of 11 + label.

Souvenir Sheet

Ferapontov Monastery UNESCO World Heritage Site — A3512

**2010, Aug. 2** *Perf. 12½x12*
**7230** A3512 30r multi 3.00 1.00

Nikolai N. Zubov (1885-1960), Arctic Explorer, and Icebreaker Sadko — A3513

**2010, Aug. 12** *Perf. 12x12¼*
**7231** A3513 12r multi 1.25 .40

Souvenir Sheet

Cossacks — A3514

No. 7232: a, Don Cossacks, brown horse. b, Kuban Cossacks, white horse. c, Terek Cossacks, black horse.

**2010, Aug. 20**
**7232** A3514 12r Sheet of 3, #a-c 3.50 1.25

Arms of Vladivostok A3515

Arms of Yaroslavl A3516

**2010, Aug. 27** *Perf. 11¾x12¼*

| | | | |
|---|---|---|---|
| **7233** A3515 7.70r multi | .75 | .25 |
| Complete booklet, 10 #7233 | 7.50 | |
| Complete booklet, 20 #7233 | 15.00 | |
| **7234** A3516 10.50r multi | 1.25 | .35 |
| Complete booklet, 10 #7234 | 12.50 | |
| Complete booklet, 20 #7234 | 25.00 | |

Souvenir Sheet

Fresh Wind, Volga, by Isaac I. Levitan (1860-1900) — A3517

**2010, Aug. 30** *Perf. 12½x12*
**7235** A3517 25r multi 2.50 .85

Memorial to End of World War II, Moscow A3518

**2010, Sept. 2** *Perf. 11½*
**7236** A3518 15r multi 1.50 .50

End of World War II, 65th anniv.

Gherman Titov (1935-2000), Cosmonaut A3519

**2010, Sept. 10** *Perf. 13½*
**7237** A3519 10.50r multi 1.10 .35

No. 7237 was printed in sheets of 6 + 2 labels. For surcharge, see No. 7754.

Souvenir Sheet

Yaroslavl, 1000th Anniv. — A3520

*Serpentine Die Cut 10*

**2010, Sept. 10** **Self-Adhesive**
**7238** A3520 50r multi 5.00 1.60

Bridges — A3521

Designs: 9r, Jubilee Bridge, Yaroslavl. 10r, Matsesta Valley Bridge, Sochi. 11r, Moscow Canal Bridge, Khlebnikovo, Moscow Oblast. 12r, Kola Bay Bridge, Murmansk.

**2010, Sept. 15** *Perf. 12x12¼*
**7239-7242** A3521 Set of 4 4.00 1.40
*7242a* Miniature sheet of 8, 2 each #7239-7242 8.00 2.75

Miniature Sheet

Bank of Russia, 150th Anniv. — A3522

No. 7243: a, 10r, 1855 copper half-kopeck coin. b, 15r, 1895 one-ruble coin. c, 20r, 1924 fifty-kopeck coin. d, 25r, 2006 gold fifty-ruble coin.

**Litho. & Embossed**

**2010, Sept. 22** *Perf. 12¼*
**7243** A3522 Sheet of 4, #a-d 7.00 2.40

Teacher's Year A3523

*Serpentine Die Cut 10*

**2010, Oct. 5** **Self-Adhesive** **Litho.**
**7244** A3523 10.50r multi 1.25 .35

2010 Census — A3524

**2010, Oct. 14** *Serpentine Die Cut 10*
**Self-Adhesive**
**7245** A3524 12r red & blue 1.25 .40

Shokan Valikhanov (1835-65), Diplomat, Ethnologist A3525

**2010, Oct. 21** *Perf. 12x12½*
**7246** A3525 15r multi 1.50 .50

See Kazakhstan No. 628.

Sputnik 5 Spaceflight Carrying Dogs Belka and Strelka, 50th Anniv. — A3526

**2010, Oct. 29** *Perf. 12x12¼*
**7247** A3526 10r multi .90 .35

Khanty-Mansi Autonomous Okrug — A3527

Kursk Oblast A3528

**2010, Nov. 1**
**7248** A3527 10.50r multi .70 .35
**7249** A3528 10.50r multi .70 .35

Soviet Union Victory in UEFA European Soccer Championships, 50th Anniv. — A3529

**2010, Nov. 10** *Perf. 11½*
**7250** A3529 12r multi .80 .40

Printed in sheets of 8 + central label.

Souvenir Sheet

Nikolai I. Pirogov (1810-81), Surgeon — A3530

**2010, Nov. 25** *Perf. 12x12½*
**7251** A3530 20r multi 1.75 .70

Kachino Aviation School, Cent. — A3531

**2010, Nov. 29** ***Perf. 11½***
**7252** A3531 15r multi 1.50 .50

Printed in sheets of 8 + central label.

New Year's Day A3532

**2010, Dec. 1 Self-Adhesive** ***Die Cut***
**7253** A3532 10.50r multi 1.25 .35

Mstislav Keldysh (1911-78), Mathematician and Space Propulsion Pioneer — A3533

**2011, Jan. 25** ***Perf. 12½x12***
**7254** A3533 12r multi .85 .40

Souvenir Sheet

Princess Maria Alexandrovna (1824-80) — A3534

**2011, Feb. 21** ***Perf.***
**7255** A3534 40r multi 4.00 1.50

City of Mariehamn, Aland Islands, 150th anniv. See Finland (Aland Islands) No. 313.

Souvenir Sheet

Sochi, Host City of 2014 Winter Olympics — A3535

**2011, Mar. 15** ***Perf. 12½x12***
**7256** A3535 25r multi 1.90 .95

Novgorod Oblast — A3536

Tyumen Oblast — A3537

Tambov Oblast — A3538

**2011, Mar. 30** ***Perf. 12¼x12***
**7257** A3536 11.80r multi 1.25 .40
**7258** A3537 11.80r multi 1.25 .40
**7259** A3538 11.80r multi 1.25 .40
*Nos. 7257-7259 (3)* 3.75 1.20

Souvenir Sheet

Yuri Gagarin, First Man in Space, 50th Anniv. — A3539

**2011, Apr. 12 Litho.** ***Perf. 12x12¼***
**7260** A3539 50r multi 5.00 1.90

Miniature Sheet

Towns of Military Glory — A3540

No. 7261 — City names at top: a, Vyborg (6 letters in city name, airplanes and tanks). b, Rostov-on-Don (city name with hyphens, cannons). c, Tuapse (6 letters in city name, airplanes, cannons and ships). d, Vladikavkaz (11 letters in name, airplanes and cannons). e, Veliki Novgorod (15 letters in city name, vehicle on skis, cannons and tanks). f, Velikiye Luki (10 letters in city name, biplanes, cannons and tanks).

**Litho. With Foil Application**

**2011, Apr. 20** ***Perf. 11¼***
**7261** A3540 12r Sheet of 6, #a-f 6.50 2.60

Russian Peace Fund, 50th Anniv. A3541

**2011, Apr. 27 Litho.** ***Perf. 13½***
**7262** A3541 8.50r multi .90 .30

World War II Military Aircraft — A3542

Designs: 9r, Yakovlev Yak-3 fighter. 10r, Lavochkin La-5 fighter. 11r, Ilyushin Il-2 attack plane. 12r, Petlyakov Pe-2 bomber.

**2011, Apr. 29**
**7263-7266** A3542 Set of 4 4.00 1.50
*7266a* Sheet of 8, 2 each #7263-7266 8.00 3.00

A booklet containing panes of one of each of the stamps was produced in limited quantities. Value, $30.

Europa A3543

**2011, May 5** ***Perf. 11¼***
**7267** A3543 15r multi 1.50 .55

Intl. Year of Forests.

Miniature Sheet

Clocks — A3544

No. 7268 — Clock at: a, 9r, Central Telegraph Office, Moscow. b, 12r, Admiralty Building, St. Petersburg. c, 15r, Moscow State University. d, 25r, Railway Station, Sochi.

**2011, May 16** ***Perf. 12¼***
**7268** A3544 Sheet of 4, #a-d 6.00 2.25

Kiril I. Shchelkin (1911-68), Physicist A3545

**2011, May 17** ***Perf. 12x12½***
**7269** A3545 12r multi 1.25 .45

Irkutsk Arms A3546

Komi Republic Arms A3547

**2011, May 26** ***Perf. 11¾x12¼***
**7270** A3546 8.50r multi .75 .30
Complete booklet, 10 #7270 7.50
Complete booklet, 20 #7270 15.00
**7271** A3547 11.80r multi 1.00 .40
Complete booklet, 10 #7271 10.00
Complete booklet, 20 #7271 20.00

Kazansky Cathedral, St. Petersburg — A3548

Russian Diplomatic Mission, Cetinje, Montenegro — A3549

**2011, May 26** ***Perf. 12½x12***
**7272** Horiz. pair + central label 3.00 1.10
*a.* A3548 15r multi 1.40 .55
*b.* A3549 15r multi 1.40 .55

See Montenegro Nos. 285-286.

Famous Men — A3550

Designs: No. 7273, 12r, Valery Bryusov (1873-1924), painter. No. 7274, 12r, Hovannes Tumanian (1869-1923), poet.

**2011, June 1** ***Perf. 12x12½***
**7273-7274** A3550 Set of 2 2.25 .85

Nos. 7273-7274 each were printed in sheets of 14 + label. See Armenia Nos. 877-878.

Independence of Venezuela, Bicent. — A3551

**2011, June 20** ***Perf. 12½x12***
**7275** A3551 12r multi 1.25 .45

Irkutsk, 350th Anniv. — A3552

**2011, June 24** *Perf. 12x11½*
**7276** A3552 15r multi 1.40 .55

Buryatia as Part of Russia, 350th Anniv. — A3553

**2011, June 27** *Perf. 11½*
**7277** A3553 11.80r multi 1.25 .40

State Road Inspection, 75th Anniv. A3554

**2011, June 27** **Litho.**
**7278** A3554 15r multi 1.50 .55

Souvenir Sheet

Order of St. Andrew the Apostle — A3555

**2011, July 1** *Perf. 12x12½*
**7279** A3555 50r multi 4.50 1.90

Souvenir Sheet

Pechora-Ilych Nature Reserve — A3556

**2011, July 29** *Perf. 12x12¼*
**7280** A3556 25r multi 2.25 .85

Souvenir Sheet

Malye Korely Museum of Wooden Architecture — A3557

No. 7281: a, 10r, Chapel of St. Makary, 18th cent. b, 15r, Resurrection Church, 17th cent. c, 20r, Windmill, 20th cent.

**2011, Aug. 1**
**7281** A3557 Sheet of 3, #a-c 4.25 1.60

Bridges — A3558

Designs: 9r, Pochtamtsky Bridge, St. Petersburg. 10r, Patriarshy Bridge, Moscow. 12r, Kena River Bridge, Arkhangelsk Oblast. 15r, Vezelka River Bridge, Belgorod.

**2011, Aug. 15** **Litho.**
**7282-7285** A3558 Set of 4 4.25 1.60
*7285a* Souvenir sheet of 8, 2 each #7282-7285 8.50 3.25

Souvenir Sheet

Cossacks — A3559

No. 7286: a, Amur Cossacks (woman holding pail). b, Astrakhan Cossacks (man on horse). c, Volga Cossacks (woman holding jar).

**2011, Aug. 29** *Perf. 12x12¼*
**7286** A3559 15r Sheet of 3, #a-c 4.00 1.50

Recipients of the Order of St. Andrew the Apostle — A3560

Designs: No. 7287, 15r, Dmitry S. Likhachev (1906-99), Russian language and literature scholar. No. 7288, 15r, Lyudmila G. Zykina (1929-2009), singer. No. 7289, 15r, Boris V. Petrovsky (1908-2004), Health minister.

**2011, Sept. 1** *Perf. 12x11¼*
**7287-7289** A3560 Set of 3 4.25 1.50

See Nos. 7369-7371, 7442, 7457, 7478, 7578, 7846, 7995.

Field Marshal Michael Barclay de Tolly (1761-1818) — A3561

**2011, Sept. 9**
**7290** A3561 15r multi 1.50 .50

Printed in sheets of 8 + central label.

Modern Art — A3562

Designs: No. 7291, 14r, Monument to Yuri Nikulin, sculpture by A. I. Rukavishnikov, 2000. No. 7292, 14r, View of Borisoglebsky Monastery, painting by N. I. Borovskoy, 2001. No. 7293, 14r, Seascape, by A. V. Adamov, 2007. No. 7294, 14r, Gymnasts of the U.S.S.R., painting by D.D. Zhilinsky, 1964-65, vert. No. 7295, 14r, Aidan, painting by T.T. Salakhov, 1967, vert. No. 7296, 14r, Akinshino Village, painting by V. Y. Yukin, 1995 (50x50mm).

*Perf. 12x11¼, 11¼x12, 12 (#7296)*
**2011, Sept. 12**
**7291-7296** A3562 Set of 6 8.00 2.75

Souvenir Sheet

Derbent Citadel UNESCO World Heritage Site — A3563

**2011, Sept. 13** *Perf. 12½x12*
**7297** A3563 50r multi 4.50 1.75

A3564

A3565

A3566

Traditional 19th and 20th Century Headdresses of Northern Russia A3567

**2011, Sept. 15** *Perf. 12*
**7298** A3564 12r multi 1.25 .40
**7299** A3565 12r multi 1.25 .40
**7300** A3566 12r multi 1.25 .40
**7301** A3567 12r multi 1.25 .40
*a.* Souvenir sheet of 8, 2 each #7298-7301, perf. 11½x12 10.00 3.25
*Nos. 7298-7301 (4)* 5.00 1.60

Worldwide Fund for Nature (WWF), 50th Anniv. A3568

**2011, Sept. 26** *Perf. 11¼*
**7302** A3568 15r multi 1.50 .50

Tourist Sites in Sochi — A3569

Designs: 15r, Krasnaya Polyana Ski Resort. 20r, Marine Terminal Building. 25r, Watchtower on Bolshoy Akhun Mountain. 30r, Volkonskiy dolmen.

**2011, Sept. 27** *Perf. 12½x12*

**Dated "2011"**

**7303** A3569 15r multi + label 1.25 .50
**7304** A3569 20r multi + label 2.00 .65
**7305** A3569 25r multi + label 2.25 .80
**7306** A3569 30r multi + label 3.00 .95
*a.* Souvenir sheet of 4, #7303-7306, + 4 labels 7.50 3.00
*Nos. 7303-7306 (4)* 8.50 2.90

Sochi, host city of 2014 Winter Olympics. Nos. 7303-7306 each were printed in sheets of 6 + 6 labels, with each label being in one of six languages (Russian, English, Chinese, French, Spanish, German). No. 7306a was printed in six versions, with the inscriptions on the labels in the sheet all being in one of the six languages.

See Nos. 7348-7351.

Eurasian Economin Community Innovative Biotechnologies Program — A3570

**2011, Sept. 30** *Perf. 13½*

**7307** A3570 9r multi 1.00 .30

Sports of the 2014 Winter Olympics, Sochi A3571

Designs: No. 7308, 25r, Cross-country skiing. No. 7309, 25r, Ski jumping. No. 7310, 25r, Short-track speed skating.

**Litho. & Embossed**

**2011, Oct. 3** *Perf. 11¼*

**7308-7310** A3571 Set of 3 7.00 2.40
*7308a* Dated "2014" at right 2.00 .70
*7309a* Dated "2014" at right 2.00 .70
*7310a* Dated "2014" at right 2.00 .70

Nos. 7308-7310 each were printed in sheets of 8 + label.

Issued: Nos. 7308a, 7309a, 7310a, 1/24/14.

Regional Communications Commonwealth, 20th Anniv. — A3572

**2011, Oct. 10 Litho.** *Perf. 12x12½*

**7311** A3572 12r multi 1.25 .40

Arsenal Factory, 300th Anniv. A3573

**2011, Oct. 14** *Perf. 11¼*

**7312** A3573 15r multi 1.50 .50

A3574

Moscow Post Office, 300th Anniv. — A3575

No. 7313: a, Afanasy L. Ordin-Naschokin (c. 1605-80), founder of Russian postal system, horse-drawn mail sleigh, sealed and rolled document . b, Russia #1, 19th cent. stagecoach. c, Russia #856, 5795, postal card, mail box, Moskvich 400-422 mail vehicle. d, Russia #7178, postal cards, Moscow Post Office, mail van.

50r, Wax seal with 300th anniversary emblem.

**2011, Oct. 21 Litho.** *Perf. 12½x12*

**7313** Horiz. strip of 4 4.50 1.60
*a.-d.* A3574 11.80r Any single .90 .40

**Souvenir Sheet**

**Litho. & Embossed**

***Perf.***

**7314** A3575 50r multi 5.00 1.60

State Kremlin Palace (Kremlin Palace of Congresses), 50th Anniv. — A3576

**2011, Oct. 24 Litho.** *Perf. 12x12¼*

**7315** A3576 12r multi 1.25 .40

Constitutional Court, 20th Anniv. — A3577

**2011, Oct. 27**

**7316** A3577 12r multi 1.25 .40

Petr G. Sobolevsky (1782-1841) and People Near Gas Streetlight — A3578

**2011, Oct. 28** *Perf. 12½x12*

**7317** A3578 12r multi 1.25 .40

Gas use in Russia, 200th anniv.

Commonweath of Independent States, 20th Anniv. — A3579

**2011, Nov. 3** *Perf. 12x11½*

**7318** A3579 11.80r multi 1.25 .40

**Souvenir Sheet**

Mikhail V. Lomonosov (1711-65), Scientist — A3580

**Litho. & Engr.**

**2011, Nov. 17** *Perf. 12¼x12*

**7319** A3580 100r multi 10.00 3.25
*a.* Booklet pane of 1 15.00 —
Complete booklet, #7319a 15.00

No. 7319a is rectangular. Complete booklet sold for 200r.

**Souvenir Sheet**

Moskvoretsky Bridge, Painting by Konstantin A. Korovin (1861-1939) — A3581

**2011, Nov. 21 Litho.** *Perf. 12x12½*

**7320** A3581 45r multi 4.50 1.50

Empress Catherine II (1729-96) — A3582

**2011, Nov. 25** *Perf. 12x11½*

**7321** A3582 8.50r multi 1.00 .30

Insurance in Russia, 225th anniv.

Russian Olympic Committee, Cent. — A3583

**2011, Nov. 25** *Perf. 12½x12*

**7322** A3583 15r multi 1.25 .50

Kaluga Oblast A3584

Omsk Oblast A3585

**2011 Litho.** *Perf. 12x12¼*

**7323** A3584 11.80r multi 1.25 .40
**7324** A3585 11.80r multi 1.25 .40

Issued: No. 7323, 11/30; No. 7324, 12/12.

New Year's Day A3586

**Litho. With Foil Application**

**2011, Dec. 1** *Perf. 11¼*

**7325** A3586 20r multi 2.00 .70

Russian-Italian Year of Culture — A3587

**2011, Dec. 10 Litho.** *Perf. 12¼x12*

**7326** A3587 15r multi 1.50 .50

See Italy No. 3110.

Lace — A3588

Lace from: No. 7327, 15r, Belev (brown background). No. 7328, 15r, Elets (red brown background). No. 7329, 15r, Vyatka (purple background). No. 7330, 15r, Vologda (blue background).

*Perf. 11¼x11½*

**2011, Dec. 12 Litho. & Engr.**

**7327-7330** A3588 Set of 4 5.50 1.90

Souvenir Sheet

Tula Small Arms Factory, 300th Anniv. — A3589

**2012, Feb. 1 Litho. *Perf. 12***
**7331** A3589 50r multi 5.00 1.75

Whales — A3590

No. 7332: a, 15r, Orcinus orca. b, 20r, Megaptera novaeangliae.

**2012, Feb. 8 *Perf. 13½***
**7332** A3590 Vert. pair, #a-b 3.25 1.25

Pyotr N. Nesterov (1887-1914), Aeronautical Pioneer — A3591

**2012, Feb. 13 *Perf. 12½x12***
**7333** A3591 15r multi 1.50 .55

No. 7333 was printed in sheets of 10 + 2 central labels.

Souvenir Sheet

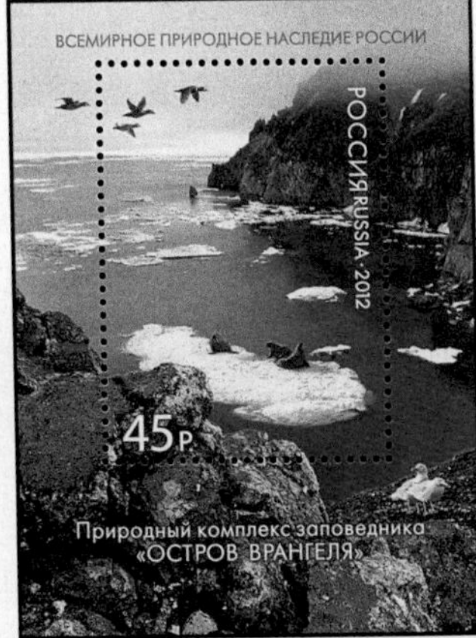

Wrangel Island — A3592

**2012, Feb. 27 *Perf. 12***
**7334** A3592 45r multi 4.50 1.60

Mascots for 2014 Winter Olympics, Sochi — A3593

No. 7335: a, Snow Leopard (48x53mm). b, Zaya the Hare (28x44mm). c, Polar Bear (44x59mm).

**2012, Feb. 27 *Die Cut***
**Self-Adhesive**
**7335** A3593 15r Sheet of 3, #a-c 4.25 1.60

Snowflake and Fire Boy, Mascots for 2014 Winter Paralympics, Sochi — A3594

**2012, Feb. 27 *Die Cut***
**Self-Adhesive**
**7336** A3594 30r multi 3.25 1.10

Gold Star Medal A3596

Order of St. George A3597

Order of Merit for the Fatherland A3598

**Litho. & Embossed**
**2012, Mar. 2 *Perf. 11¾***
**7337** A3596 25r multi 2.50 .85
**7338** A3597 25r multi 2.50 .85
**7339** A3598 25r multi 2.50 .85
*Nos. 7337-7339 (3)* 7.50 2.55

Nos. 7337-7339 each were printed in sheets of 7 + label.

Marina M. Raskova (1912-43), Combat Pilot — A3599

**2012, Mar. 21 Litho. *Perf. 12½x12***
**7340** A3599 15r multi 1.50 .50

No. 7540 was pritned in sheets of 10 + central label.

Pyotr A. Stolypin (1862-1911), Prime Minister A3600

**2012, Apr. 6 *Perf. 11½***
**7341** A3600 15r multi 1.50 .50

World War II Military Vehicles — A3601

Designs: 10r, GAZ-AA truck. 12r, ZIS-5B truck. 14r, GAZ-67B general personnel carrier. 15r, GAZ-M1 automobile.

**2012, Apr. 16 *Perf. 13½***
**7342-7345** A3601 Set of 4 5.00 1.75
*7345a* Souvenir sheet of 8, 2 each #7342-7345 7.00 3.50

A booklet containing panes of one of each of Nos. 7342-7345 was produced in limited quantities. Value, $30.

Miniature Sheet

Towns of Military Glory — A3602

No. 7346 — City names at top: a, Pskov (5 letters in city name with last letter "B", airplanes, cannons and tanks). b, Vyazma (6 letters in city name, airplanes, cannons, artillery launchers). c, Naro-Fominsk (10 letters and hyphen in city name, airplanes, cannons and tanks). d, Tver (5 letters in city name with last letter "b", airplanes, cannons and tanks). e, Kronshtadt (9 letters in city name, cannons, airplanes and ships). f, Dmitrov (7 letters in city name, airplanes, cannons, machine guns).

**Litho. With Foil Application**
**2012, Apr. 20 *Perf. 11¼***
**7346** A3602 15r Sheet of 6, #a-f 9.00 3.25

Emblem of Russian War Veteran's Association — A3603

**2012, Apr. 26 Litho. *Perf. 11½***
**7347** A3603 10r multi 1.10 .35

**Tourist Sites in Sochi Type of 2011**

Designs: 15r, Sail Rock, near Gelendzhik. 20r, Sochi Railway Station. 25r, Gazebo in Botanical Gardens, Sochi. 30r, Orehovsky Waterfall, Sochi.

**2012, Apr. 27 *Perf. 12½x12***
**Dated "2012"**
**7348** A3569 15r multi + label 1.40 .50
**7349** A3569 20r multi + label 1.75 .70
**7350** A3569 25r multi + label 2.25 .85
**7351** A3569 30r multi + label 2.75 1.10
*a.* Souvenir sheet of 4, #7348-7351 + 4 labels 8.50 3.25
*Nos. 7348-7351 (4)* 8.15 3.15

Nos. 7348-7351 each were printed in sheets of 6 + 6 labels, with each label being in one of six languages (Russian, English, Chines, French, Spanish, German). No. 7351a was printed in six versions, with the inscriptions on the labels in the sheet all being in one of the six languages.

Europa A3604

**2012, May 4 *Perf. 11½***
**7352** A3604 15r multi 1.50 .45

Third Inauguration of Pres. Vladimir Putin — A3605

**2012, May 7 Litho. & Embossed**
**7353** A3605 15r multi 1.50 .45

Heroes A3606

Gold Star Medal and: No. 7354, 15r, V. V. Zamaryev (1959-2004). No. 7355, 15r, D. A. Razumovsky (1968-2004). No. 7356, 15r, Irina Janina (1966-99). No. 7357, 15r, A. V. Putsykin (1980-2008). No. 7358, 15r, A. B. Tsydenzhapov (1991-2010).

**2012, May 7 Litho.** ***Perf. 12½x12***
**7354-7358** A3606 Set of 5 7.00 2.40

Nos. 7354-7358 each were printed in sheets of 5 + label.

Souvenir Sheet

Mikhail V. Nesterov (1862-1942), Painter — A3607

**2012, May 17** ***Perf. 12x12½***
**7359** A3607 30r multi 3.00 .95

Ivan N. Kramskoi (1837-87), Painter A3608

Designs: No. 7360, 15r, Self-portrait (detail), 1867. No. 7361, 15r, Portrait of an Unknown Woman, 1883, horiz.

**2012, May 29** ***Perf. 11½x12, 12x11½***
**7360-7361** A3608 Set of 2 3.00 .95

Souvenir Sheet

Ivan A. Goncharov (1812-91), Writer — A3609

**2012, June 4** ***Perf.***
**7362** A3609 30r multi 3.00 .95

First Non-stop Transpolar Flight, 75th Anniv. A3610

**2012, June 6** ***Perf. 11½***
**7363** A3610 13r multi 1.25 .40

No. 7363 was printed in sheets of 8 + central label.

Souvenir Sheet

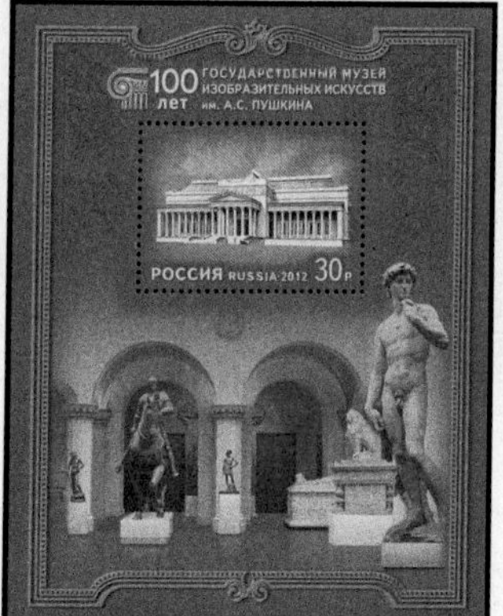

Pushkin Museum of Fine Arts, Moscow, Cent. — A3611

**2012, June 6** ***Perf. 12½x12***
**7364** A3611 30r multi 3.00 .95

Monument to Minin and Pozharsky, Moscow A3612

Triumphal Arch, Moscow A3613

**2012, June 14** ***Perf. 11¾x12¼***
**7365** A3612 9.20r multi .90 .30
Complete booklet, 10 #7365 9.00
Complete booklet, 20 #7365 18.00
**7366** A3613 13r multi 1.40 .40
Complete booklet, 10 #7366 14.00
Complete booklet, 20 #7366 28.00

Newts — A3614

No. 7367: a, Lissotriton vulgaris. b, Triturus cristatus.

**2012, June 25** ***Perf. 11¼x12***
**7367** A3614 13r Pair, #a-b 2.50 .80

See Belarus Nos. 829-830.

Oleg E. Kutafin (1937-2008), Lawyer, and Order of Merit for the Fatherland — A3615

**2012, June 26** ***Perf. 12½x12***
**7368** A3615 15r multi 1.50 .45

Printed in sheets of 14 + label.

**Recipients of the Order of St. Andrew Type of 2011**

Order of St. Andrew and: No. 7369, 15r, Patriarch Aleksei II (1929-2008). No. 7370, 15r, Irina K. Arkhipova (1925-2010), opera singer. No. 7371, 15r, Valeri I. Shumakov (1931-2008), transplant surgery pioneer.

**2012, June 29** ***Perf. 12x11½***
**7369-7371** A3560 Set of 3 4.50 1.40

Nos. 7369-7371 each were printed in sheets of 11 + label.

Souvenir Sheet

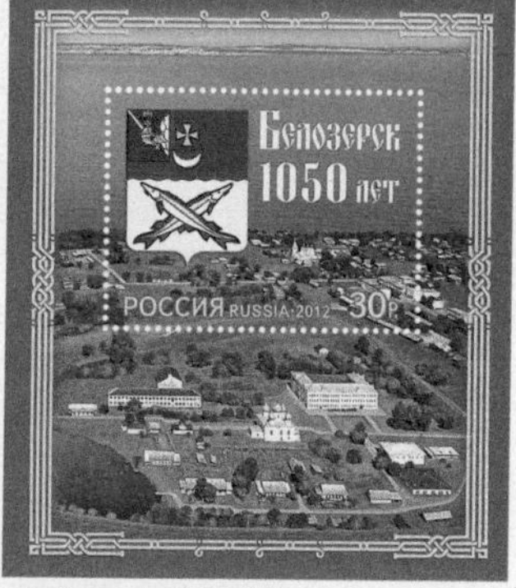

Belozersk, 1050th Anniv. — A3617

**2012, July 4** ***Perf. 12***
**7372** A3617 30r multi 3.00 .95

Souvenir Sheet

Izborsk, 1150th Anniv. — A3618

**2012, July 4** ***Perf. 12¼x12***
**7373** A3618 30r multi 3.00 .95

Record Non-stop Transpolar Flight, 75th Anniv. A3619

**2012, July 6** ***Perf. 11¼***
**7374** A3619 13r multi 1.25 .40

Printed in sheets of 8 + central label.

No. 7111 Srchd.

**Method and Perf. As Before**
**2012, July 6**
**7375** A3430 12r on 8r #7111 *6.00 3.00*

Victory of Russian men's ice hockey team in 2012 World Championships.

Churches — A3620

No. 7376: a, Church of the Savior on Spilled Blood, St. Petersburg, Russia. b, Episcopal Palace, Astorga, Spain.

**2012, July 17 Litho.** ***Perf. 11¼***
**7376** A3620 13r Pair, #a-b 2.50 .85

No. 7376 was printed in sheets containing 4 pairs + central label. See Spain No. 3863.

Mordovia, 1000th Anniv. — A3621

**2012, July 20**
**7377** A3621 13r multi 1.25 .40

Souvenir Sheet

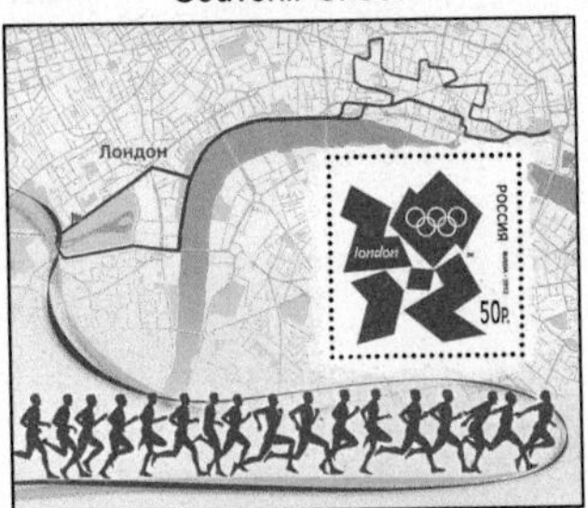

2012 Summer Olympics, London — A3622

**2012, July 26** ***Perf. 11½***
**7378** A3622 50r multi 4.25 1.60

A3623

A3624

Modern Art — A3625

Designs: No. 7379, Warm Day, by Georgy A. Leman, 1996. No. 7380, Cossacks' Send Off, by Sergei A. Gavrilyachenko, 1999. No. 7381, Autumn Interior, by Aleksei N. Sukhovetsky, 1992. No. 7382, Monument to F. I. Shalyapin in Kazan, by Andrei V. Balashov, 1999. No. 7383, Russian Madonna, by Vasily I. Nestorenko, 1992. No. 7384, Mammoths in Khanty-Mansiysk, by Andrei N. Kovalchuk, 2007.

**2012, July 30** ***Perf. 12x11½***
**7379** A3623 15r multi 1.50 .70
**7380** A3623 15r multi 1.50 .70

***Perf. 11½x12***
**7381** A3624 15r multi 1.50 .70
**7382** A3624 15r multi 1.50 .70

***Perf. 11¼***
**7383** A3625 15r multi 1.50 .70
**7384** A3625 15r multi 1.50 .70
*Nos. 7379-7384 (6)* 9.00 4.20

Gleb E. Kotelnikov (1872-1944), Inventor of Packable Parachute — A3626

**2012, Aug. 2** ***Perf. 12½x12***
**7385** A3626 13r multi 1.00 .40

Friedrich A. Tsander (1887-1933), Rocketry Pioneer — A3627

**2012, Aug. 9** **Litho.**
**7386** A3627 9.20r multi 1.00 .30

Russian Air Force, Cent. — A3628

**2012, Aug. 10** ***Perf. 13½***
**7387** A3628 15r multi 1.50 .45

Souvenir Sheet

Rostov, 1150th Anniv. — A3629

**2012, Aug. 20** ***Perf. 11¾***
**7388** A3629 30r multi 3.00 .95

Souvenir Sheet

Cossacks — A3630

No. 7389: a, Enisei Cossacks (woman touching horse). b, Orenburg Cossacks (woman seated). c, Ussuriisk Cossacks (man on horse).

**2012, Aug. 22** ***Perf. 12x12¼***
**7389** A3630 15r Sheet of 3, #a-c 4.50 1.50

Souvenir Sheet

War of 1812, Bicent. — A3631

**2012, Aug. 27** ***Perf. 12***
**7390** A3631 50r multi 5.00 1.60

Souvenir Sheet

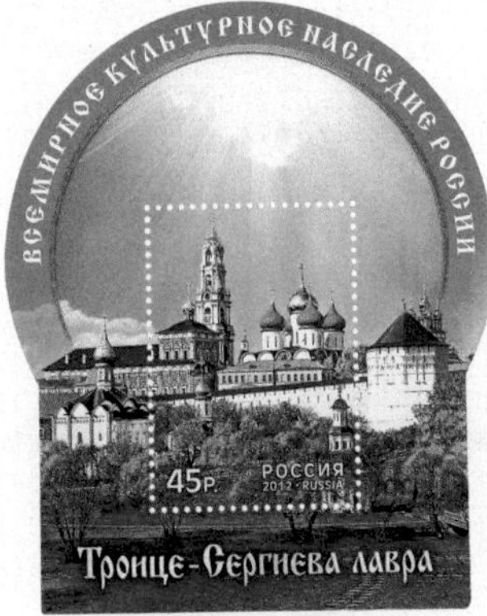

Trinity Monastery of St. Sergius — A3632

**2012, Aug. 30** ***Perf. 12x12¼***
**7391** A3632 45r multi 4.50 1.50

Asia-Pacific Economic Cooperation Summit, Vladivostok — A3633

**2012, Aug. 31** ***Perf. 13½***
**7392** A3633 13r multi 1.25 .40

A booklet containing one pane of two No. 7392 was printed in a limited edition. Value, $20.

Souvenir Sheet

On a Visit, Painting by Abram E. Arkhipov (1862-1930) — A3634

**2012, Sept. 7** ***Perf. 12x12½***
**7393** A3634 50r multi 5.00 1.60

Lawyers A3635

Designs: No. 7394, 15r, Gavrila R. Derzhavin (1741-1816). No. 7395, 15r, Mikhail M. Speransky (1772-1839). No. 7396, 15r, Anatoly F. Koni (1844-1927).

**2012, Sept. 7** ***Perf. 11½***
**7394-7396** A3635 Set of 3 4.50 1.50

Nos. 7394-7396 each were printed in sheets of 8 + label. See Nos. 7499-7500, 7588-7590, 7629, 7702-7704, 7791-7793, 7882-7884, 7975-7977.

Fort Ross, Russian Outpost on California Coast, 200th Anniv. — A3636

**2012, Sept. 11** ***Perf. 12x12¼***
**7397** A3636 13r multi 1.25 .40

Quick Response Code and Emblem of 2014 Winter Olympics, Sochi A3637

***Serpentine Die Cut 10***
**2012, Sept. 18** **Self-Adhesive**
**7398** A3637 25r multi 2.50 .80

Vologda Region Costumes A3639

Russian Statehood (Founding of Rurik Dynasty), 1150th Anniv. — A3638

**2012, Sept. 19** ***Perf. 12x11¼***
**7399** A3638 10r multi 1.25 .30

**2012, Sept. 21** ***Perf. 11½x12***
**7400** A3639 15r multi 1.50 .50

Souvenir Sheet

Russian Railways, 175th Anniv. — A3640

**2012, Sept. 30** *Perf. 11¾*
**7401** A3640 50r multi 5.00 1.60

North Shipyard, Saint Petersburg, Cent. A3641

**2012, Oct. 1** *Perf. 11¼*
**7402** A3641 15r multi 1.50 .50

Souvenir Sheet

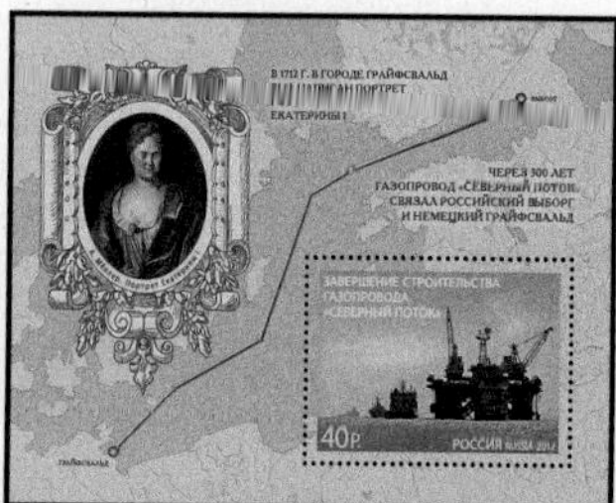


Completion of Gas Pipeline Between Vyborg and Greifswald, Germany — A3642

**2012, Oct. 5** *Perf. 12*
**7403** A3642 40r multi 4.00 1.40

Border Guards, 500th Anniv. A3643

**2012, Oct. 10** *Perf. 12¼x12*
**7404** A3643 13r multi 1.50 .40

No. 7404 was printed in sheets of 11 + 4 labels.

Sports of the 2014 Winter Olympics, Sochi A3644

Designs: No. 7405, 25r, Freestyle skiing. No. 7406, 25r, Alpine (downhill) skiing. No. 7407, 25r, Snowboarding. No. 7408, 25r, Skeleton. No. 7409, 25r, Luge. No. 7410, 25r, Speed skating.

**Litho. & Embossed**

**2012, Oct. 19** *Perf. 11¼*
**7405-7410** A3644 Set of 6 15.00 4.75
*7405a* Dated "2014" at right 2.25 .70
*7406a* Dated "2014" at right 2.25 .70
*7407a* Dated "2014" at right 2.25 .70
*7408a* Dated "2014" at right 2.25 .70
*7409a* Dated "2014" at right 2.25 .70
*7409b* Booklet pane of 3, #7309a, 7408a, 7409a 7.00 —
*7410a* Dated "2014" at right 2.25 .70

Nos. 7405-7410 each were printed in sheets of 8 + central label.

Issued: Nos. 7405a, 7406a, 7407a, 7408a, 7409a, 7409b, 7410a, 1/24/14.

Souvenir Sheet

Restoration of National Unity After "Time of Troubles," 400th Anniv. — A3645

**2012, Nov. 2** **Litho.** *Perf. 12x12½*
**7411** A3645 40r multi 4.00 1.40

A3646

A3647

A3648

Cast Iron Moldings From Kasli — A3649

**Litho. & Thermography**

**2012, Nov. 15**
**7412** A3646 20r blk & green 2.00 1.00
**7413** A3647 20r blk & blue 2.00 1.00
**7414** A3648 20r blk & rose brn 2.00 1.00
**7415** A3649 20r blk & lilac 2.00 1.00
*Nos. 7412-7415 (4)* 8.00 4.00

Nos. 7412-7415 each were printed in sheets of 4.

Souvenir Sheets

Moscow Coat of Arms — A3650

Saint Petersburg Coat of Arms — A3651

**Litho. & Embossed**

**2012, Nov. 30** *Perf. 12*
**7416** A3650 50r multi 5.00 1.60
**7417** A3651 50r multi 5.00 1.60

A booklet containing a pane of No. 7416 and a pane of No. 7417 sold for 226.50r.

Russian Animated Films — A3652

No. 7418: a, Winnie the Pooh (Winnie, Piglet with umbrella, bees). b, Mowgli (Mowgli, with wolf, bear and panther). c, A Kid and Karlson (Man, boy sitting in chair, cat and dog). d, Vovka in the Far-Away Kingdom (boy sitting, two men in polka-dot clothing).

**2012, Dec. 3** **Litho.** *Perf. 12x12¼*
**7418** A3652 10r Block of 4, #a-d 4.00 1.40

New Year 2013 — A3653

**2012, Dec. 3** *Perf. 11¼*
**7419** A3653 13r blue 1.25 .40

Souvenir Sheet

Konstantin Stanislavsky (1863-1938), Theater Director — A3654

**2013, Jan. 17** *Perf.*
**7420** A3654 50r multi 5.00 1.75

Georgy Flyorov (1913-90), Nuclear Physicist A3655

**2013, Jan. 21** *Perf. 12¼x12*
**7421** A3655 15r multi 1.50 .50

Adoption of name of Flevorium (in honor of Flyorov) for element 114.

Rams — A3656

No. 7422: a, Ovis ammon. b, Capra caucasica. c, Capra aegagrus. d, Ovis nivicola.

**2013, Jan. 30** *Perf. 11½*
**7422** A3656 15r Block or strip of 4, #a-d 6.00 2.00

Miniature Sheet

Towns of Military Glory — A3657

No. 7423 — City names at top: a, Arkhangelsk (11 letters in city name, airplanes, artillery and ships). b, Bryansk (6 letters in city name, airplanes, mortars on tripods, and trucks). c, Volokolamsk (11 letters in city name, biplanes, cannons, and tanks). d, Kalach-na-Donu (hyphenated city name, airplanes and tanks). e, Kozelsk (8 letters in city name, biplanes, cannons, and armored locomotives). f, Nalchik (7 letters in city name, mortars and artillery).

**Litho. With Foil Application**

**2013, Jan. 30**
**7423** A3657 15r Sheet of 6, #a-f 9.00 3.00

Penza, 350th Anniv. — A3658

**2013, Feb. 8 Litho.** ***Perf. 12x12¼***
**7424** A3658 15r multi 1.50 .50

Russian Orders — A3659

Designs: No. 7425, 25r, Order of Suvorov (name at top on one line). No. 7426, 25r, Order of Alexander Nevsky (name at top on two lines). No. 7427, 25r, Order of St. Catherine the Great (name at top on three lines).

**Litho. & Embossed**

**2013, Feb. 18** ***Perf. 11¾***
**7425-7427** A3659 Set of 3 7.50 2.50

Nos. 7425-7427 each were printed in sheets of 7 + label.

Alexander I. Pokryshkin (1913-85), Soviet Air Force Marshal — A3660

**2013, Feb. 22 Litho.** ***Perf. 12½x12***
**7428** A3660 15r multi 1.50 .50

No. 7428 was printed in sheets of 10 + central label.

Military Heroes A3661

Designs: No. 7429, 15r, Nikolai S. Maidanov (1956-2000). No. 7430, 15r, Valery I. Shkurny (1959-2000). No. 7431, 15r, Evgeny N. Chernyshev (1963-2010). No. 7432, 15r, Oleg G. Ilyin (1967-2004). No. 7433, 15r, Yuri A. Dmitriev (1978-2002).

**2013, Feb. 22**
**7429-7433** A3661 Set of 5 7.00 2.50

Nos. 7429-7433 each were printed in sheets of 5 + label.

Souvenir Sheet

Uvs Nuur Basin UNESCO World Heritage Site — A3662

**2013, Feb. 27**
**7434** A3662 45r multi 4.50 1.50

A gritty substance was applied to portions of the design.

Conifers — A3663

No. 7435: a, Juniperus davurica. b, Microbiota decussata. c, Larix cajanderi. d, Picea obovata.

**2013, Mar. 4** ***Serpentine Die Cut 11***
**Self-Adhesive**
**7435** A3663 15r Block of 4, #a-d 6.00 2.00

Souvenir Sheet

General Mikhail D. Skobolev on Horse, by Nikolai D. Dmitriev-Orenburgsky — A3664

**2013, Mar. 5** ***Perf. 12x12½***
**7436** A3664 35r multi 3.50 1.10

Russo-Turkish War, 135th anniv. See Bulgaria No. 4626.

Viktor S. Chernomyrdin (1938-2010), Prime Minister — A3665

**2013, Mar. 14** ***Perf. 12½x12***
**7437** A3665 15r multi 1.50 .50

Printed in sheets of 14 + label.

Obukhov State Plant, St. Petersburg, 150th Anniv. A3666

**2013, Mar. 26** ***Perf. 11¼***
**7438** A3666 15r multi 1.50 .50

A booklet containing a pane containing one No. 7438 was printed in limited quantities. Value, $30.

Diplomatic Relations Between Russia and Algeria, 50th Anniv. — A3667

**2013, Apr. 1** ***Perf. 12½x12***
**7439** A3667 10r multi 1.25 .30

Europa — A3668

**2013, Apr. 26** ***Perf. 13½***
**7440** A3668 15r multi 1.50 .50

Winter Palace — A3669

Admiralty and St. Isaac's Cathedral — A3670

Old Stock Exchange, Vasilyevsky Island — A3671

**2013, Apr. 26** ***Perf. 12x12¼***
**7441** Horiz. strip of 3 4.50 1.50
*a.* A3669 10r multi .90 .30
*b.* A3670 15r multi 1.25 .50
*c.* A3671 20r multi 1.75 .70

Historic Center of St. Petersburg UNESCO World Heritage Site.

**Recipients of Order of St. Andrew Type of 2011**

Design: Order of St. Andrew and Heidar Aliyev (1923-2003), Pres. of Azerbaijan.

**2013, May 6** ***Perf. 12x11¼***
**7442** A3560 15r multi .95 .50

No. 7442 was printed in sheets of 11 + label. Compare with No. 7457. See Azerbaijan No. 1022.

World War II Ships — A3672

Designs: 10r, Mine sweeper "Mina." 12r, Escort ship "Metel." 15r, Armored boat "BKA-75." 20r, Gunboat "Usyskin."

**2013, May 8** ***Perf. 13½***
**7443-7446** A3672 Set of 4 5.50 1.90
*7446a* Sheet of 8, 2 each #7443-7446 11.00 4.00

A booklet containing panes of one of each of the stamps was produced in limited quantities. Value, $35.

Souvenir Sheet

Alexandrovskaya Sloboda, 500th Anniv. — A3673

**2013, May 18** ***Perf. 12x12½***
**7447** A3673 50r multi 5.00 1.60

Souvenir Sheet

Mission of Saints Cyril and Methodius to Slavic Lands, 1150th Anniv. — A3674

**2013, May 24** ***Perf. 12¼x12***
**7448** A3674 40r multi 4.00 1.25

Scientific Research Ship "Vyacheslav Tikhonov" — A3675

Oil Tanker "Timofey Guzhenko" — A3676

**2013, June 5** *Perf. 12x11¾*

**7449** A3675 14.25r multi 1.50 .45
**7450** A3676 14.25r multi 1.50 .45

Nos. 7449-7450 each were printed in sheets of 8 + label.

A3677

Modern Art — A3678

Designs: No. 7451, On the Trubezh River, by V. P. Polotnov, 2008. No. 7452, Indian Summer, by D. A. Belyukin, 2003. No. 7453, The Girl and the City, by A. A. Lubavin, 2005.

**2013, June 17** *Perf. 11¼x12*

**7451** A3677 15r multi 1.50 .45

*Perf. 11¼*

**7452** A3678 15r multi 1.50 .45
**7453** A3678 15r multi 1.50 .45
*Nos. 7451-7453 (3)* 4.50 1.35

Arms of Aleksandrov A3679

Arms of Kazan A3680

**2013, June 18** *Perf. 11¾x12¼*

**7454** A3679 10r multi 1.00 .30
Complete booklet, 10 #7454 10.00
Complete booklet, 20 #7454 20.00
**7455** A3680 14.25r multi 1.50 .45
Complete booklet, 10 #7455 15.00
Complete booklet, 20 #7455 30.00

Souvenir Sheet

27th Summer Universiade, Kazan — A3681

**2013, June 25** *Perf. 12x12¼*

**7456** A3681 25r multi 2.50 .80

A booklet containing one example of No. 7456 sold for 255r. Value, $25.

Order of St. Andrew and Rasul G. Gamzatov (1923-2003), Poet — A3682

**2013, June 28** *Perf. 12x11½*

**7457** A3682 15r multi 1.50 .45

No. 7457 was printed in sheets of 11 + label. Compare with No. 7442.

Sports of the 2014 Winter Olympics, Sochi A3683

Designs: No. 7458, 25r, Nordic combined skiing. No. 7459, 25r, Bobsled. No. 7460, 25r, Pairs figure skating.

**Litho. & Embossed**

**2013, June 29** *Perf. 11¼*

**7458-7460** A3683 Set of 3 7.50 2.40
*7458a* Dated "2014" at right 2.50 .70
*7459a* Dated "2014" at right 2.50 .70
*7460a* Dated "2014" at right 2.50 .70
*7460b* Booklet pane of 3, #7407a, 7410a, 7460a 7.50 —

Nos. 7458-7460 each were printed in sheets of 8 + central label.

Issued: Nos. 7458a, 7459a, 7460a, 7460b, 1/24/14.

Gull and Russia No. 2753 — A3684

**2013, July 5** **Litho.** *Perf. 11¾*

**7461** A3684 14.25r multi 1.50 .45

Space flight of Valentina Tereshkova, first woman in space, 50th anniv.

Kerchief From Karabanovo — A3685

Kerchief From Trekhgorny Factory, Moscow — A3686

Kerchief From Orenburg — A3687

Shawl From Pavlovsky Posad — A3688

**2013, July 5** *Perf. 11½*

**7462** A3685 15r multi 1.50 .45
**7463** A3686 15r multi 1.50 .45
**7464** A3687 15r multi 1.50 .45
**7465** A3688 15r multi 1.50 .45
*Nos. 7462-7465 (4)* 6.00 1.80

Nos. 7462-7465 each were printed in sheets of 4.

Souvenir Sheet

The Baptism of Rus, by Viktor M. Vasnetsov (1848-1926) — A3689

**2013, July 28** **Litho.** *Perf. 12*

**7466** A3689 30r multi 3.00 .95

Christianization of Kievan Rus, 1025th anniv. See Belarus No. 870, Ukraine No. 930.

Souvenir Sheet

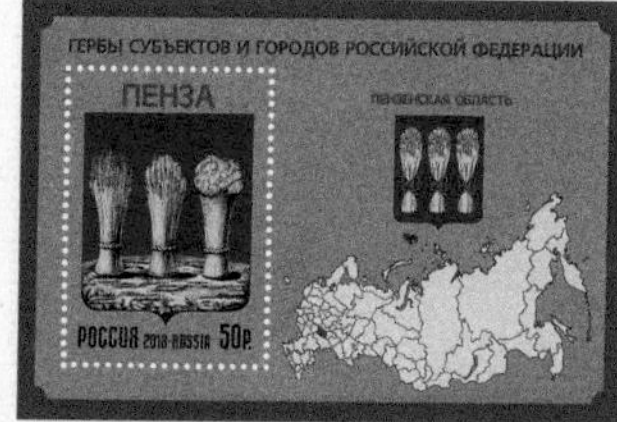


Penza Coat of Arms — A3690

**2013, Aug. 2** **Litho.** *Perf. 12x12½*

**7467** A3690 50r multi 5.00 1.50

MS Princess Anastasia — A3691

**2013, Aug. 5** **Litho.** *Perf. 12*

**7468** A3691 14.25r multi 1.50 .45

See Finland (Aland Islands) No. 347.

18th Intl. Track and Field Championships, Moscow — A3692

**2013, Aug. 10** **Litho.** *Perf. 12¼x12*

**7469** A3692 14.25r multi 1.50 .45

Miniature Sheet

Aircraft Designed by Andrei N. Tupolev (1888-1972) — A3693

No. 7470: a, 10r, Tu-2. b, 13r, Tb-7. c, 15r, Tu-16. d, 17r, Tu-22M3. e, 20r, Tu-95.

**2013, Aug. 13** **Litho.** *Perf. 12¼x12*

**7470** A3693 Sheet of 5, #a-e, + label 7.50 2.10

Kolomna Locomotive Works, 150th Anniv. A3694

**2013, Aug. 15** **Litho.** *Perf. 11¼*

**7471** A3694 15r multi 1.50 .45

Communications Satellite, Arrows and Map of Russia — A3695

**2013, Aug. 21** **Litho.** *Perf. 12¼x12*

**7472** A3695 14.25r multi 1.50 .45

Paintings by Ivan Myasoyedov (Eugen Zotow) (1881-1953) — A3696

No. 7473: a, Voyage of the Argonauts, 1909. b, Silum, 1945.

**2013, Sept. 2** **Litho.** *Perf. 12x11¼*

**7473** A3696 15r Pair, #a-b 3.50 .95

Printed in sheets of 10 containing 5 each #7473a-7473b, + 2 labels. See Liechtenstein No. 1592.

### Souvenir Sheet

Discovery of Severnaya Zemlya Archipelago, Cent. — A3697

No. 7474: a, Icebreaker Vaigach (ship facing left). b, Boris A. Vilkitsky (1885-1961), hydrographer and expedition leader, vert. c, Icebreaker Taimyr (ship facing right).

***Perf. 12x12¼, 12¼x12 (#7474b)***

**2013, Sept. 4** **Litho.**
**7474** A3697 15r Sheet of 3, #a-c 4.00 1.40

A booklet containing three panes, each containing one each of Nos. 7474a-7474c sold for 284r. Value, $35.

18th Conference of Intl. Association of Prosecutors, Moscow — A3698

**2013, Sept. 6** **Litho.** ***Perf. 12x12¼***
**7475** A3698 15r multi 1.50 .45

### Souvenir Sheet

Smolensk, 1150th Anniv. — A3699

**2013, Sept. 21** **Litho.** ***Perf. 12¼x12***
**7476** A3699 50r multi 5.00 1.60

### Souvenir Sheet

Olympic Flame — A3700

**2013, Oct. 7** **Litho.** ***Perf. 12***
**7477** A3700 50r multi 5.00 1.60

2014 Winter Olympics, Sochi.

### Recipients of the Order of St. Andrew Type of 2012

Design: Order of St. Andrew and Sergey V. Mikhalkov (1913-2009), writer.

**2013, Oct. 9** **Litho.** ***Perf. 12x11¼***
**7478** A3560 15r multi 1.50 .45

No. 7478 was printed in sheets of 11 + label.

### Souvenir Sheet

Coat of Arms of Yaroslavl — A3701

**2013, Oct. 11** **Litho.** ***Perf. 12x12½***
**7479** A3701 50r multi 5.00 1.60

### Souvenir Sheet

Battle of Leipzig, by Carl Rechlin — A3702

**2013, Oct. 19** **Litho.** ***Perf. 12x12½***
**7480** A3702 50r multi 5.00 1.60

Battle of Leipzig, 200th anniv.

Modern Art — A3703

Designs: No. 7481, 15r, Monument to A. I. Pokryshkin, by M. V. Pereyaslavets, 2005. No. 7482, 15r, Bouquet, by V. M. Malyi, 2005. No. 7483, 15r, Kerosene, by A. L. Bobykin, 2012, horiz.

***Perf. 11½x12, 12x11½***

**2013, Oct. 25** **Litho.**
**7481-7483** A3703 Set of 3 4.50 1.40

Sports of the 2014 Winter Olympics, Sochi A3704

Designs: No. 7484, Biathlon. No. 7485, Curling. No. 7486, Ice hockey.

**Litho. & Embossed**

**2013-14** ***Perf. 11¼***

**Dated "2013" at Right**

**7484** A3704 25r multi 2.50 .75
*a.* Dated "2014" at right 2.50 .70
*b.* Booklet pane of 3, #7406a, 7459a, 7484a 7.50 —
**7485** A3704 25r multi 2.50 .75
*a.* Dated "2014" at right 2.50 .70
*b.* Booklet pane of 3, #7308a, 7458a, 7485a 7.50 —
**7486** A3704 25r multi 2.50 .75
*a.* Dated "2014" at right 2.50 .70
*b.* Sheet of 15, #7308a, 7309a, 7310a, 7405a, 7406a, 7407a, 7408a, 7409a, 7410a, 7458a, 7459a, 7460a, 7484a, 7485a, 7486a, + label 37.50 10.50
*c.* Booklet pane of 3, #7310a, 7405a, 7486a 7.50 —
Complete booklet, #7409b, 7460b, 7484b, 7485b, 7486c 37.50
*Nos. 7484-7486 (3)* 7.50 2.25

Issued: Nos. 7484-7486, 11/1; Nos. 7484a, 7484b, 7485a, 7485b, 7486a, 7486b, 7486c, 1/24/14.

Nos. 7484-7486 were each printed in sheets of 8 + central label. Complete booklet sold for 595r.

Sambo, 75th Anniv. — A3705

**2013, Nov. 1** **Litho.** ***Perf. 12x12½***
**7487** A3705 10r multi 1.25 .30

Police Uniforms A3706

Designs: No. 7488, 15r, Dragoon and police officer, 1718. No. 7489, 15r, Police officer and captain, 19th cent. No. 7490, 15r, Traffic policeman and militia foreman, 1934. No. 7491, 15r, Police lieutenant and major general, 2012.

**2013, Nov. 8** **Litho.** ***Perf. 11¾***
**7488-7491** A3706 Set of 4 6.00 1.90
*7491a* Souvenir sheet of 8, 2 each #7488-7491 12.00 3.75

### Miniature Sheets

A3707

Sports Legends — A3708

No. 7492: a, Yevgeny Grishin (1931-2005), speed skater. b, Lyudmila Pakhomova (1946-86), ice dancer. c, Vladimir Melanin (1933-94), biathlete. d, Alexander Ragulin (1941-2004), ice hockey player. e, Anatoly Firsov (1941-2000), ice hockey player.

No. 7493: a, Klavdiya Boyarskikh (1939-2009), cross-country skier. b, Vsevolod Bobrov (1922-79), soccer and ice hockey player. c, Tatyana Averina (1950-2001), speed skater. d, Pierre de Coubertin (1863-1937), founder of the Modern Olympic Games. e, Ludwig Guttman (1899-1980), founder of the Paralympic Games.

**2013** **Litho.** ***Perf. 11¾***
**7492** A3707 15r Sheet of 5, #a-e 7.50 2.40
**7493** A3708 15r Sheet of 5, #a-e 7.50 2.40

2014 Winter Olympics, Sochi. Issued: No. 7492, 11/15; No. 7493, 12/14.

New Year 2014 A3709

Mascots of the 2014 Winter Olympics, Sochi: No. 7494, 20r, Leopard. No. 7495, 20r, Hare. No. 7496, 20r, Polar Bear. No. 7497, 20r, Snowflake and Ray of Light.

***Serpentine Die Cut 11***

**2013, Nov. 29** **Litho.**

**Self-Adhesive**

**7494-7497** A3709 Set of 4 8.00 2.50
*7497a* Sheet of 8, 2 each #7494-7497 16.00

### Miniature Sheet

Venues of the 2014 Winter Olympics and Paralympics, Sochi — A3710

No. 7498: a, Crowd outside of Fisht Olympic Stadium. b, Biathletes at Laura Biathlon and Ski Complex. c, Ski jumps at Russki Gorki Jumping Center. d, Crowds and flagpoles outside of Bolshoi Ice Dome. e, Iceberg Skating Palace at night. f, Photographer and crowd outside of Shayba Arena.

**2013, Nov. 30** **Litho.** ***Perf. 11¾***
**7498** A3710 20r Sheet of 6, #a-f 12.50 3.75

### Lawyers Type of 2012

Designs: No. 7499, 15r, Alexander N. Radishchev (1749-1802). No. 7500, 15r, Fedor N. Plevako (1842-1909).

**2013, Dec. 3** **Litho.** ***Perf. 11½***
**7499-7500** A3635 Set of 2 3.00 .95

Nos. 7499-7500 each were printed in sheets of 8 + label.

Automobiles A3711

No. 7501: a, ZiL-111B. b, Sunbeam Alpine.

**2013, Dec. 5** **Litho.** ***Perf. 11½***
**7501** A3711 15r Pair, #a-b 3.00 .95

Printed in sheets containing four each #7501a-7501b + central label. See Monaco No. 2740.

State Duma, 20th Anniv. — A3712

Federation Council, 20th Anniv. — A3713

Constitution, 20th Anniv. — A3714

**2013, Dec. 12 Litho. *Perf. 11½***

| | | | | |
|---|---|---|---|---|
| **7502** | A3712 | 20r multi | 2.00 | .60 |
| **7503** | A3713 | 20r multi | 2.00 | .60 |

**Souvenir Sheet**

***Perf. 12***

| | | | | |
|---|---|---|---|---|
| **7504** | A3714 | 50r multi | 5.00 | 1.60 |

Order of Zhukov A3716

Order of Kutuzov A3717

Order of Ushakov A3718

**Litho. & Embossed**

**2014, Jan. 31 *Perf. 11¾***

| | | | | |
|---|---|---|---|---|
| **7506** | A3716 | 25r multi | 2.50 | .70 |
| **7507** | A3717 | 25r multi | 2.50 | .70 |
| **7508** | A3718 | 25r multi | 2.50 | .70 |
| | | *Nos. 7506-7508 (3)* | 7.50 | 2.10 |

Nos. 7506-7508 each were printed in sheets of 7 + label.

**Souvenir Sheet**

Medals of the 2014 Winter Olympics, Sochi — A3719

No. 7509: a, 25r, Bronze medal. b, 50r, Silver medal. c, 75r, Gold medal, vert.

***Perf. 12x12¼, 12¼x12 (75r)***

**2014, Feb. 7 Litho. & Embossed**

| | | | | |
|---|---|---|---|---|
| **7509** | A3719 | Sheet of 3, #a-c | 15.00 | 4.25 |
| *d.* | | As #7509, overprinted with Cyrillic text in red in sheet margin | 15.00 | 4.25 |

Issued: No. 7509d, 4/25. Overprint on No. 7509d gives medal count of Russian team (13 gold, 11 silver, 9 bronze) at 2014 Winter Olympics.

**Souvenir Sheet**

Moscow Zoo, 150th Anniv. — A3720

**2014, Feb. 13 Litho. *Perf. 12***

| | | | | |
|---|---|---|---|---|
| **7510** | A3720 | 40r multi | 4.00 | 1.10 |

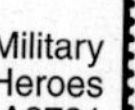

Military Heroes A3721

Designs: No. 7511, 15r, Aleksandr V. Perov (1975-2004) (shown). No. 7512, 15r, Andrei A. Turkin (1975-2004). No. 7513, 15r, Andrei N. Rozhkov (1961-98). No. 7514, 15r, Viktor S. Chechviy (1960-99). No. 7515, 15r, Mikhail Y. Malofeev (1956-2000).

**2014, Feb. 21 Litho. *Perf. 12½x12***

| | | | | |
|---|---|---|---|---|
| **7511-7515** | A3721 | Set of 5 | 7.50 | 2.10 |

Nos. 7511-7515 were each printed in sheets of 5 + label.

**Souvenir Sheet**

Medals of the 2014 Winter Paralympics, Sochi — A3722

No. 7516: a, 25r, Bronze medal. b, 50r, Silver medal. c, 75r, Gold medal, vert.

***Perf. 12x12¼, 12¼x12 (75r)***

**2014 Litho. & Embossed**

| | | | | |
|---|---|---|---|---|
| **7516** | A3722 | Sheet of 3, #a-c | 12.00 | 4.25 |
| *d.* | | As #7516, overprinted with Cyrillic text in red in sheet margin | 12.00 | 4.25 |

Issued: No. 7516, 3/7; No. 7516d, 4/25. Overprint on No. 7516d gives medal count of Russian team (30 gold, 28 silver, 22 bronze) at 2014 Winter Paralympics.

**Souvenir Sheet**

Summer Garden, by Aleksei Mikhailovich Gritsai (1914-98) — A3723

**2014, Mar. 7 Litho. *Perf. 12x12¼***

| | | | | |
|---|---|---|---|---|
| **7517** | A3723 | 50r multi | 5.00 | 1.50 |

Flowers — A3724

No. 7518: a, Chamaenerion angustifolium. b, Lupinus polyphyllus. c, Cichorium intybus. d, Matricaria recutita.

**2014, Mar. 14 Litho. *Perf. 11¼***

| | | | | |
|---|---|---|---|---|
| **7518** | A3724 | 15r Block of 4, #a-d | 6.50 | 1.75 |

Mark L. Gallai (1914-98), Test Pilot, and M-3 Bomber A3725

**2014, Mar. 28 Litho. *Perf. 12½x12***

| | | | | |
|---|---|---|---|---|
| **7519** | A3725 | 15r multi | 1.50 | .40 |

No. 7519 was printed in sheets of 10 + central label.

**Souvenir Sheet**

Liberation of Russia, Belarus and Ukraine From Nazi Occupation, 70th Anniv. — A3726

**2014, Apr. 18 Litho. *Perf. 12x12¼***

| | | | | |
|---|---|---|---|---|
| **7520** | A3726 | 50r multi | 5.00 | 1.50 |

See Belarus No. 898.

Ekaterina I. Zelenko (1916-41), World War II Pilot — A3727

Boris I. Kovzan (1922-85), World War II Pilot — A3728

Alexei S. Khlobystov (1918-43), World War II Pilot — A3729

Petr V. Eremeyev (1911-41), World War II Pilot — A3730

**2014, Apr. 18 Litho. *Perf. 13½***

| | | | | |
|---|---|---|---|---|
| **7521** | A3727 | 15r multi | 1.50 | .40 |
| **7522** | A3728 | 15r multi | 1.50 | .40 |
| **7523** | A3729 | 15r multi | 1.50 | .40 |
| **7524** | A3730 | 15r multi | 1.50 | .40 |
| *a.* | | Sheet of 8, 2 each #7521-7524 | 12.00 | 3.50 |
| | | *Nos. 7521-7524 (4)* | 6.00 | 1.60 |

Nos. 7521-7524 were each printed in sheets of 7 + label.

World War II Artillery — A3731

Designs: 12r, 53-K 45-mm anti-tank gun. 15r, ZIS-3 76-mm divisional gun. 18r, 52-K 85-mm anti-aircraft gun. 20r, M-30 122-mm howitzer.

**2014, Apr. 25 Litho. *Perf. 13½***

| | | | | |
|---|---|---|---|---|
| **7525-7528** | A3731 | Set of 4 | 7.00 | 1.90 |
| *7528a* | | Sheet of 8, 2 each #7525-7528 | 14.00 | 4.00 |

A booklet containing four panes of one of each of Nos. 7525-7528 sold for 350r. Value, $40.

Musicians Playing Balalaika and Accordion A3732

**2014, Apr. 30 Litho. *Perf. 12***

**7529** A3732 18r multi 1.90 .50

Europa.

Yakov B. Zeldovich (1914-87), Physicist A3733

**2014, May 5 Litho. *Perf. 12¼x12***

**7530** A3733 15r multi 1.50 .45

Clock Towers and Clocks — A3734

No. 7531: a, 15r, Zytglogge, Bern, Switzerland. b, 20r, Kazansky Tower, Moscow.

**2014, May 21 Litho. *Perf. 11¼***

**7531** A3734 Pair, #a-b 3.50 1.00

No. 7531 was printed in sheets of 8 (4 of each stamp) + central label. See Switzerland Nos. 1528-1529.

Concord Tower, Magas — A3735

**2014, June 4 Litho. *Perf. 11¼***

**7532** A3735 15r multi 1.50 .45

Souvenir Sheet

St. Petersburg Post Office, 300th Anniv. — A3736

**2014, June 10 Litho. *Perf.***

**7533** A3736 50r multi 5.00 1.50

Crimean Republic A3737

Sevastopol A3738

**2014 Litho. *Perf. 12x12¼***

**7534** A3737 15r multi 1.50 .45

***Perf. 12¼x12***

**7535** A3738 15r multi 1.50 .45

Issued: No. 7534, 6/19; No. 7535, 6/20.

Souvenir Sheet

Hermitage Museum, 250th Anniv. — A3739

**2014, June 20 Litho. *Perf. 11¾***

**7536** A3739 50r multi 5.00 1.50

Arms of Sergiev Posad — A3740

***Perf. 11¾x12¼***

**2014, June 24 Litho.**

| | | | | |
|---|---|---|---|---|
| **7537** | A3740 | 10.50r multi | 1.10 | .30 |
| | | Complete booklet, 10 #7537 | 10.00 | |
| | | Complete booklet, 20 #7537 | 20.00 | |

Topol-M Missile Launcher and Barricades Manufacturing Plant — A3741

**2014, June 26 Litho. *Perf. 11¼***

**7538** A3741 15r multi 1.60 .45

Barricades Manufacturing Plant, Volgograd, cent.

Vladimir N. Chelomey (1914-84). Missile Engineer A3742

**2014, June 27 Litho. *Perf. 12¼x12***

**7539** A3742 15r multi 1.50 .45

Tuva as Part of Russia, Cent. — A3743

**2014, June 27 Litho. *Perf. 11¼***

**7540** A3743 15r multi 1.50 .45

Souvenir Sheet

Approval of Construction of Baikal-Amur Mainline Railway, 40th Anniv. — A3744

**2014, July 2 Litho. *Perf. 12***

**7541** A3744 40r multi 4.00 1.25

A3745

**2014, July 7 Litho. *Perf. 12¼x12***

**7542** A3745 15r multi 1.50 .40

Diplomatic relations between Russia and Bulgaria, 135th anniv. See Bulgaria No. 4684.

Hero of Labor of the Russian Federation Medal — A3746

Medal for the Defense of Leningrad A3747

Medal for the Defense of Sevastopol A3748

Medal for the Defense of Stalingrad A3749

Medal for the Defense of Moscow A3750

**Litho. & Embossed**

**2014, July 7 *Perf. 11¾***

| | | | | |
|---|---|---|---|---|
| **7543** | A3746 | 25r multi | 2.50 | .70 |
| **7544** | A3747 | 25r multi | 2.50 | .70 |
| **7545** | A3748 | 25r multi | 2.50 | .70 |
| **7546** | A3749 | 25r multi | 2.50 | .70 |
| **7547** | A3750 | 25r multi | 2.50 | .70 |
| | | *Nos. 7543-7547 (5)* | 12.50 | 3.50 |

Nos. 7543-7547 were each printed in sheets of 7 + label.

Hugo Chávez (1954-2013), President of Venezuela
A3751

**2014, July 28 Litho.** ***Perf. 12x12¼***
**7548** A3751 15r multi .85 .40

World War I, Cent. — A3752

Designs: No. 7549, 20r, Soldiers charging with rifles with bayonets, map of battle for Osovets Fortress. No. 7550, 20r, Soldiers and cannon, map of battle for Erzum Fortress. No. 7551, 20r, General Aleksei A. Brusilov (seated) and his officers, map of Brusilov Offensive. No. 7552, 20r, Russian Expeditionary Corps in France (with flag), map of Europe and Asia.

**2014, July 31 Litho.** ***Perf. 12***
**7549-7552** A3752 Set of 4 8.00 2.25

Nos. 7549-7552 were each printed in sheets of 11 + label. A booklet containing panes of one of each of the stamps was produced in limited quantities. Value, $40.

Souvenir Sheet

Battle of Gangut, 300th Anniv. — A3753

**2014, Aug. 1 Litho.** ***Perf. 11¾***
**7553** A3753 50r multi 5.00 1.40

Wild Cats — A3754

No. 7554: a, 15r, Otocolobus manul. b, 16r, Felis silvestris. c, 17r, Prionailurus bengalensis euptilurus. d, 18r, Felis chaus.

**2014, Aug. 1 Litho.** ***Perf. 13½***
**7554** A3754 Block or vert. strip of 4, #a-d 7.00 1.90

See No. 7581.

Medal for the Defense of the Caucasus
A3755

Medal for the Defense of Kiev — A3756

Medal for the Defense of Odessa
A3757

Medal for the Defense of the Arctic — A3758

**Litho. & Embossed**

**2014, Aug. 8** ***Perf. 11¾***
**7555** A3755 25r multi 2.50 .70
**7556** A3756 25r multi 2.50 .70
**7557** A3757 25r multi 2.50 .70
**7558** A3758 25r multi 2.50 .70
*Nos. 7555-7558 (4)* 10.00 2.80

Nos. 7555-7558 were each printed in sheets of 7 + label.

Kyzyl, Cent.
A3759

**2014, Aug. 23 Litho.** ***Perf. 12½x12***
**7559** A3759 15r multi 1.50 .40

Icebreaker Vitus Bering — A3760

Tugboat Sadko — A3761

**2014, Aug. 26 Litho.** ***Perf. 12***
**7560** A3760 15r multi 1.50 .40
**7561** A3761 15r multi 1.50 .40

Battles of Khakhin Gol, 75th Anniv. — A3762

**2014, Aug. 28 Litho.** ***Perf. 11½***
**7562** A3762 15r multi 1.50 .40

See Mongolia No. 2816.

Miniature Sheet

Towns of Military Glory — A3763

No. 7563 — City names at top: a, Anapa (5 letters in city name, airplanes, guns and ships). b, Vladivostok (11 letters in city name, airplanes, trucks and ships). c, Kovrov (6 letters in city name, guns and tanks). d, Kolpino (7 letters in city name, airplanes and tanks). e, Stary Oscol (2 words in city name, airplanes, guns and tanks). f, Tikhvin (6 letters in city name, airplanes and tanks).

**Litho. With Foil Application**

**2014, Aug. 28** ***Perf. 11½***
**7563** A3763 20r Sheet of 6, #a-f 12.50 3.25

Uniforms of Postal and Communications Workers
A3764

Designs: No. 7564, 15r, Clerk and postman of Yamskoi Post Office, 1671. No. 7565, 15r, Postman and official from Yamskoi Post Office, 1767. No. 7566, 15r, Official and telegraph operator, 1870. No. 7567, 15r, Postman and operator, 1950.

**2014, Sept. 1 Litho.** ***Perf. 13½***
**7564-7567** A3764 Set of 4 6.00 1.60
*7567a* Souvenir sheet of 8, 2 each #7564-7567 12.00 3.25

Printing in Russia, 450th Anniv. — A3765

**2014, Sept. 3 Litho.** ***Perf. 12x11¼***
**7568** A3765 15r multi 1.50 .40

Souvenir Sheet

Kolomenskoye Church of the Ascenscion UNESCO World Heritage Site — A3766

**2014, Sept. 5 Litho.** ***Perf. 12x12½***
**7569** A3766 45r multi 4.50 1.10

Souvenir Sheet

St. Sergius of Radonezh (1314-92), Monk — A3767

**Litho. & Silk-Screened**

**2014, Sept. 16** ***Perf. 12***
**7570** A3767 70r multi 7.00 1.75

Special Communications Center and Vehicles — A3768

**2014, Sept. 18 Litho.** ***Perf. 12½x12***
**7571** A3768 18r multi 1.90 .45

Souvenir Sheet

Coat of Arms of City of Krasnodar — A3769

**2014, Sept. 25 Litho.** ***Perf. 12x12½***
**7572** A3769 50r multi 5.00 1.25

Ice Hockey — A3770

**2014, Oct. 7 Litho.** ***Perf. 13½***
**7573** A3770 20r multi 2.10 .45

Formula 1 Race Cars — A3771

**2014, Oct. 12 Litho.** ***Perf. 13½***
**7574** A3771 15r multi 1.50 .30

2014 Sochi Grand Prix.

Birds — A3772

**2014, Oct. 12 Litho.** ***Perf. 12½x12***
**7575** A3772 Horiz. pair 3.50 .70
*a.* 15r Accipiter nisus 1.50 .30
*b.* 18r Pandion haliaetus 2.00 .40

See North Korea No.

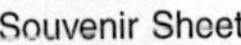

Souvenir Sheet

Mikhail Lermontov (1814-41), Writer — A3773

**2014, Oct. 15 Litho.** ***Perf. 12½x12***
**7576** A3773 50r multi 2.25 1.10

Arms of Sochi — A3774

**2014, Oct. 21 Litho.** ***Perf. 11¾x12¼***
**7577** A3774 15r multi 1.50 .30
Complete booklet, 10 #7577 15.00
Complete booklet, 20 #7577 30.00

**Recipients of the Order of St. Andrew Type of 2011**

Design: Order of St. Andrew and General Mikhail Kalashnikov (1919-2013), arms designer.

**2014, Oct. 24 Litho.** ***Perf. 12x11¼***
**7578** A3560 15r multi 1.50 .30

No. 7578 was printed in sheets of 11 + label.

Galina Vishnevskaya (1926-2012), Opera Singer — A3775

**2014, Oct. 24 Litho.** ***Perf. 12½x12***
**7579** A3775 15r multi 1.50 .30

No. 7579 was printed in sheets of 14 + label.

Souvenir Sheet

Imperial Orthodox Palestine Society — A3776

No. 7580: a, Grand Duchess Elizabeth (1864-1918), holy martyr of Russian Orthodox Church. b, Society emblem. c, Sergei Imperial Hospice, Russian Compound, Jerusalem.

**2014, Oct. 29 Litho.** ***Perf. 12x12¼***
**7580** A3776 20r Sheet of 3, #a-c 6.00 1.40

**Wild Cats Type of 2014**

No. 7581: a, 15r, Uncia uncia. b, 18r, Panthera pardus orientalis. c, 20r, Panthera tigris altaica.

**2014, Nov. 7 Litho.** ***Perf. 11¾***
**7581** A3754 Horiz. strip of 3, #a-c 6.50 1.25

Georgi N. Babakin (1914-71), Designer of Spacecraft A3777

**2014, Nov. 13 Litho.** ***Perf. 12½x12***
**7582** A3777 15r multi 1.50 .30

Souvenir Sheet

2014 World Cup Soccer Championships, Brazil — A3778

**2014, Nov. 25 Litho.** ***Perf.***
**7583** A3778 50r multi 5.00 .95

Kerzhensky Nature Reserve — A3779

**2014, Nov. 25 Litho.** ***Perf. 12x12¼***
**7584** A3779 15r multi 1.50 .30

Carved Wooden Door Trim From Nizhny Novgorod — A3780

Carved Wooden Door Trim From Pskov — A3781

Nos. 7585 and 7586: a, Denomination at left. b, Denomination at right.

**2014, Nov. 28 Litho.** ***Perf. 11½***
**7585** A3780 20r Horiz. pair, #a-b 4.25 .75
**7586** A3781 20r Horiz. pair, #a-b 4.25 .75

A varnish applied to parts of the vignette has a rough feel.

Souvenir Sheet

Coat of Arms of City of Tver — A3782

**2014, Dec. 2 Litho.** ***Perf. 12x12½***
**7587** A3782 50r multi 5.00 .95

**Lawyers Type of 2012**

Designs: No. 7588, 15r, Count Pavel I. Yaguzhinsky (1683-1736). No. 7589, 15r, Fedor F. Martens (1845-1909). No. 7590, 15r, Sergei A. Muromtsev (1850-1910).

**2014, Dec. 3 Litho.** ***Perf. 11½***
**7588-7590** A3635 Set of 3 5.00 .80

Nos. 7588-7590 were each printed in sheets of 8 + label.

Modern Art — A3783

Designs: No. 7591, 15r, Peresvet's Victory, by Pavel V. Ryzhenko, 2005. No. 7592, 15r, Lilacs, by Polina V. Mineeva, 2010. No. 7593, 15r, Pskov Kremlin, by Sergei N. Troshin, 2011. No. 7594, 15r, Spring in Kolomenskoe, by Ivan Krivshinko, 2002 (50x38mm). No. 7595, 15r, River Vorya Near Radonezh, by Aleksandr K. Sytov, 2005 (50x38mm). No. 7596, 15r, Statue of Alexander Nevsky, by Alexei I. Ignatov, 2013 (33x65mm).

***Perf. 11¼, 12x11½ (#7594-7595), 13½ (#7596)***

**2014, Dec. 12 Litho.**
**7591-7596** A3783 Set of 6 9.50 1.60

New Year 2015 — A3784

**2014, Dec. 12 Litho.** ***Perf. 12x11½***
**7597** A3784 15r multi 1.25 .25

Europa A3785

**2015, Jan. 16 Litho.** ***Perf. 11½x12***
**7598** A3785 23r multi 2.50 .35

Souvenir Sheet

October, Domotkanovo, by Valentin A. Serov (1865-1911) — A3786

**2015, Jan. 22 Litho.** ***Perf. 12½x12***
**7599** A3786 50r multi 5.00 .75

Postcrossing A3787

***Serpentine Die Cut 10***

**2015, Jan. 27 Litho.**

**Self-Adhesive**

**7600** A3787 23r multi 2.50 .35

Souvenir Sheet

Lena Pillars Nature Park UNESCO World Heritage Site — A3788

**2015, Feb. 10 Litho.** ***Perf. 12½x12***
**7601** A3788 50r multi 5.00 .80

Sergei P. Kapitsa (1928-2012), Physicist and Host of Television Science Shows A3789

**2015, Feb. 12 Litho. *Perf. 11½x12***
**7602** A3789 15r multi 1.50 .25

Miniature Sheet

Towns of Military Glory — A3790

No. 7603 — City names at top: a, Lomonosov (9 letters in city name, trucks, tanks, ships). b, Maloyaroslavets (13 letters in city name, artillery). c, Mozhaisk (7 letters in city name, airplanes, cannons, barricades). d, Petropavlovsk-Kamchatsky (23 letters in city name, airplanes, guns, submarines). e, Taganrog (8 letters in city name, airplanes, tanks, submarines). f, Khabarovsk (9 letters in city name, airplanes, trucks, ships).

**Litho. With Foil Application**
**2015, Feb. 15 *Perf. 11½***
**7603** A3790 20r Sheet of 6, #a-f 12.50 2.00

Order of Nakhimov A3791

Order of Friendship A3793

**Litho. & Embossed**
**2015, Feb. 19 *Perf. 11¾***
**7604** A3791 25r multi 2.50 .40
**7605** A3792 25r multi 2.50 .40
**7606** A3793 25r multi 2.50 .40
*Nos. 7604-7606 (3)* 7.50 1.20

Nos. 7604-7606 were each printed in sheets of 7 + label.

Spies A3794

Designs: No. 7607, 16r, Alexander I. Galushkin (1903-42). No. 7608, 16r, Pavel M. Silaev (1916-42).

**2015, Mar. 18 Litho. *Perf. 11½***
**7607-7608** A3794 Set of 2 3.25 .60

Nos. 7607-7608 were each printed in sheets of 8 + label.

Submariners — A3795

No. 7609: a, Captain Evgeni Y. Osipov (1913-43), denomination at LR. b, Captain Alexander I. Marinesco (1913-63), denomination at LL.

**2015, Mar. 19 Litho. *Perf. 12***
**7609** A3795 Horiz. pair + central label 3.25 .60
*a.-b.* 16r Either single 1.50 .30

Felix Dzerzhinsky Independent Operational Purpose Division — A3796

**2015, Mar. 21 Litho. *Perf. 13½***
**7610** A3796 17r multi 1.75 .30

Zemstvo Post, 150th Anniv. A3797

**2015, Mar. 26 Litho. *Perf. 12½x12***
**7611** A3797 20r multi 1.50 .35

Liberation of Warsaw Medal — A3798

Liberation of Prague Medal — A3799

Liberation of Belgrade Medal — A3800

**Litho. & Embossed**
**2015, Apr. 2 *Perf. 11¾***
**7612** A3798 30r multi 3.00 2.00
**7613** A3799 30r multi 3.00 2.00
**7614** A3800 30r multi 3.00 2.00
*Nos. 7612-7614 (3)* 9.00 6.00

Nos. 7612-7614 were each printed in sheets of 7 + label.

First Spacewalk, 50th Anniv. — A3801

**2015, Apr. 10 Litho. *Perf. 12x12½***
**7615** A3801 17r multi 1.50 .35

Blood Donation Program — A3802

**2015, Apr. 16 Litho. *Perf. 12x12½***
**7616** A3802 17r multi 1.50 .35

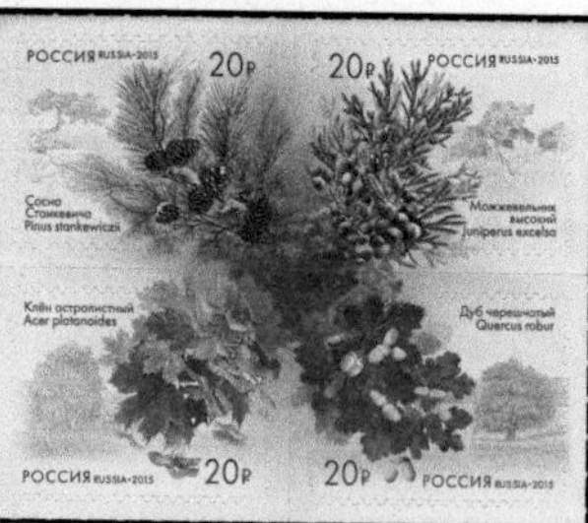
Trees — A3803

No. 7617: a, Pinus stankewiczii. b, Juniperus excelsa. c, Acer platanoides. d, Quercus robur.

***Serpentine Die Cut 11***
**2015, Apr. 16 Litho.**
**Self-Adhesive**
**7617** A3803 20r Block of 4, #a-d 8.00 1.60

Russian Federation Accounting Bureau — A3804

**2015, Apr. 17 Litho. *Perf. 12x11½***
**7618** A3804 20r multi 2.00 .40

Penny Black, 175th Anniv. — A3805

**2015, Apr. 23 Litho. *Perf. 12x11½***
**7619** A3805 26.50r multi 2.50 .55

World War II Armored Trains — A3806

Train named: 12r, Moscow Metro. 17r, Fighter of the German Invaders. 19r, Moskvich. 27r, Kozma Minin.

**2015, Apr. 30 Litho. *Perf. 13½***
**7620-7623** A3806 Set of 4 5.50 1.50
*7623a* Souvenir sheet of 8, 2 each #7620-7623 11.00 3.00

A booklet containing panes of one of each of the stamps was produced in limited quantities. Value, $40.

Souvenir Sheet

Victory in Europe in World War II, 70th Anniv. — A3807

**2015, May 5 Litho. *Perf. 11¾***
**7624** A3807 70r multi 6.00 1.50

Liberation of Konigsberg Medal — A3808

Liberation of Vienna Medal — A3809

Liberation of Berlin Medal — A3810

Liberation of Budapest Medal — A3811

**Litho. & Embossed**

**2015, May 5** *Perf. 11¾*

| | | | | |
|---|---|---|---|---|
| **7625** | A3808 | 30r multi | 2.50 | .60 |
| **7626** | A3809 | 30r multi | 2.50 | .60 |
| **7627** | A3810 | 30r multi | 2.50 | .60 |
| **7628** | A3811 | 30r multi | 2.50 | .60 |
| | | *Nos. 7625-7628 (4)* | 10.00 | 2.40 |

Nos. 7625-7628 were each printed in sheets of 7 + label.

**Lawyers Type of 2012**

Design: 17r, Roman A. Rudenko (1907-81).

**2015, May 6** **Litho.** *Perf. 11½*
**7629** A3635 17r multicolored 1.75 .35

No. 7629 was printed in sheets of 8 + label.

International Telecommunication Union, 150th Anniv. — A3812

**2015, May 7** **Litho.** *Perf. 12½x12*
**7630** A3812 17r dull blue 1.75 .30

Sviaz-Expocomm 2015 Intl. Telecommunications Exhibition, Moscow — A3813

**2015, May 12** **Litho.** *Perf. 13½*
**7631** A3813 19r multi 2.00 .35

Eurasian Economic Union — A3814

**2015, May 21** **Litho.** *Perf. 12x11½*
**7632** A3814 17r multi 1.25 .30

Joseph Brodsky (1940-96), 1987 Nobel Literature Laureate A3815

**2015, May 22** **Litho.** *Perf. 13½*
**7633** A3815 17r multi 1.25 .30

Dogs — A3816

No. 7634: a, 16r, South Russian shepherds. b, 18r, Caucasian shepherds. c, 20r, Central Asian shepherds. d, 26.50r, Black Russian terriers.

**2015, May 28** **Litho.** *Perf. 13½*
**7634** A3816 Block or vert. strip of 4, #a-d 8.00 1.50

**Souvenir Sheet**

Pyotr Ilyich Tchaikovsky (1840-93), Composer — A3817

**Litho. & Engr.**

**2015, May 28** *Perf. 12*
**7635** A3817 150r multi 15.00 3.00

Norilsk Nickel Mining Company, 80th Anniv. — A3818

**Litho. & Embossed**

**2015, June 2** *Perf. 13½*
**7636** A3818 26.50r multi 2.00 .50

**Souvenir Sheet**

Bank of Russia, 155th Anniv. — A3819

No. 7637: a, Evgeny I. Lamansky (1825-1902), bank governor. b, Russian coins. c, Bank building, Moscow.

**Litho., Litho. & Embossed (#7637b)**

**2015, June 4** *Perf. 12*
**7637** A3819 40r Sheet of 3, #a-c 9.00 2.10

Artek International Children's Center, 90th Anniv. — A3820

**2015, June 16** **Litho.** *Perf. 11¼*
**7638** A3820 26.50r multi 2.00 .45

Arms of Derbent A3821

Arms of Nizhny Novgorod A3822

*Perf. 11¾x12¼*

**2015, June 16** **Litho.**

| | | | | |
|---|---|---|---|---|
| **7639** | A3821 | 12r multi | 1.00 | .25 |
| | | Complete booklet, 10 #7639 | 10.00 | |
| | | Complete booklet, 20 #7639 | 20.00 | |
| **7640** | A3822 | 17r multi | 1.50 | .30 |
| | | Complete booklet, 10 #7640 | 15.00 | |
| | | Complete booklet, 20 #7640 | 30.00 | |

Paintings by Pavel A. Fedotov (1815-52) — A3823

Designs: No. 7641, 25r, Encore! Encore! No. 7642, 25r, Portrait of N. P. Zhdanovich at the Harpsichord, vert.

*Perf. 12x11½, 11½x12*

**2015, June 23** **Litho.**
**7641-7642** A3823 Set of 2 3.50 .90

Silhouettes of Alexander Pushkin, Nikolai Gogol and Anna Akhmatova A3824

**2015, June 25** **Litho.** *Perf. 11¼*
**7643** A3824 17r multi 1.25 .30

Literature Year in Russia.

International Summits in Ufa — A3825

**2015, July 7** **Litho.** *Perf. 12x12½*
**7644** A3825 19r multi 1.25 .30

Prince Pyotr Bagration (1765-1812), General — A3826

**2015, July 10** **Litho.** *Perf. 12x11½*
**7645** A3826 21r multi 1.50 .35

No. 7645 was printed in sheets of 8 + central label.

Russian Post Emblem A3827

Emblem of the Russian Geographical Society A3828

*Serpentine Die Cut 14½x15*

**2015, July 23** **Litho.**

**Self-Adhesive**

| | | | | |
|---|---|---|---|---|
| **7646** | A3827 | 17r multi | 1.00 | .25 |
| **7647** | A3828 | 35r multi | 3.00 | .55 |

Compare type A3827 to type A3364.

2015 Intl. Swimming Federation World Championships, Kazan — A3829

**2015, July 24** **Litho.** *Perf. 13½*
**7648** A3829 17r multi 1.25 .25

World War I Heroes A3830

Designs: No. 7649, 21r, Konstantin I. Nedorubov (1889-1978). No. 7650, 21r, Ivan V. Tyulenev (1892-1978). No. 7651, 21r, Nikolai I. Ulanov (1881-1948). No. 7652, 21r, Ivan L. Khizhnyak (1893-1980).

**2015, Aug. 3 Litho. *Perf. 11½x12***

**7649-7652** A3830 Set of 4 6.00 1.40

Nos. 7649-7652 were each printed in sheets of 11 + label.

19th-20th Cent. Porcelain Tile From Moscow — A3831

19th-20th Cent. Porcelain Tile From Abramtsevo — A3832

19th-20th Cent. Porcelain Tile From Turygino — A3833

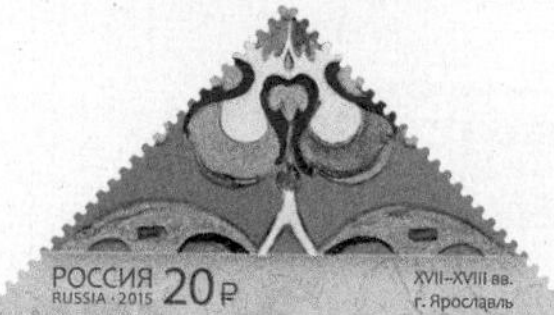


17th-18th Cent. Porcelain Tile From Yaroslavl — A3834

**2015, Aug. 4 Litho. *Perf. 11½***

| | | | | |
|---|---|---|---|---|
| **7653** | A3831 | 20r multi | 1.60 | .30 |
| **7654** | A3832 | 20r multi | 1.60 | .30 |
| **7655** | A3833 | 20r multi | 1.60 | .30 |
| **7656** | A3834 | 20r multi | 1.60 | .30 |
| | *Nos. 7653-7656 (4)* | | 6.40 | 1.20 |

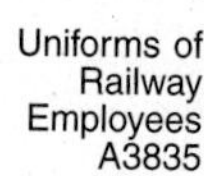

Uniforms of Railway Employees A3835

Uniforms of: No. 7657, 17r, General and Conductor of Officer of Lines of Communications, 1843. No. 7658, 17r, Head of Depot and second-class driver, 1952. No. 7659, 17r, Head of Railways and conductor, 1979. No. 7660, 17r, Trainmaster and conductor, 2015.

**2015, Aug. 11 Litho. *Perf. 13½***

**7657-7660** A3835 Set of 4 5.00 1.00

*7660a* Souvenir sheet of 8, 2 each #7657-7660 10.00 2.00

Admiral Gennady Nevelskoy Monument, Nikolayevsk-on-Amur — A3836

**2015, Aug. 14 Litho. *Perf. 12x12½***

**7661** A3836 17r multi 1.25 .25

Leningrad Zoo, St. Petersburg, 150th Anniv. — A3837

**2015, Aug. 14 Litho. *Perf. 13½***

**7662** A3837 19r multi 1.25 .30

Vysokopetrovsky Monastery, 700th Anniv. — A3838

St. Laurentius Monastery, 500th Anniv. — A3839

**2015, Aug. 23 Litho. *Perf. 13½***

**7663** A3838 19r multi 1.25 .30

**7664** A3839 19r multi 1.25 .30

Nos. 7663-7664 were each printed in sheets of 9 + label.

Boris F. Safonov (1915-42), Military Pilot A3840

**2015, Aug. 26 Litho. *Perf. 12½x12***

**7665** A3840 12r multi .75 .25

No. 7665 was printed in sheets of 10 + central label.

Arch of Triumph, Pyongyang A3841

**2015, Aug. 28 Litho. *Perf. 11¼***

**7666** A3841 19r multi 1.25 .30

Liberation of Korea, 70th anniv. See North Korea No.

Souvenir Sheet

Kazan Coat of Arms — A3842

**2015, Aug. 28 Litho. *Perf. 12x12½***

**7667** A3842 50r gold & multi 3.50 .75

For surcharge, see No. 8162.

End of World War II, 70th Anniv. — A3843

**2015, Sept. 2 Litho. *Perf. 13½***

**7668** A3843 17r multi 1.25 .25

Souvenir Sheet

Nizhny Novgorod Stone Kremlin, 500th Anniv. — A3844

**2015, Sept. 9 Litho. *Perf. 11¾***

**7669** A3844 35r multi 2.50 .55

World War I Military Equipment — A3845

Designs: No. 7670, 21r, Mosin-Nagant 7.62mm rifle. No. 7671, 21r, 76.2mm rapid firing gun. No. 7672, 21r, Destroyer "Novik." No. 7673, 21r, Sikorsky S-22 Ilya Muroments bomber.

**2015, Sept. 10 Litho. *Perf. 12***

**7670-7673** A3845 Set of 4 5.00 1.40

Nos. 7670-7673 were each printed in sheets of 11 + label.

United Nations, 70th Anniv. A3846

***Serpentine Die Cut 10***

**2015, Sept. 15 Litho.**

**Self-Adhesive**

**7674** A3846 26.50r multi 1.75 .40

Souvenir Sheet

World Cup Trophy — A3847

**2015, Sept. 18 Litho. *Perf. 12***

**7675** A3847 100r multi 6.50 1.60

2018 World Cup Soccer Championships, Russia.

Federal Anti-Monopoly Service, 25th Anniv. — A3848

**2015, Sept. 21 Litho. *Perf. 12x11½***

**7676** A3848 21r multi 1.50 .30

Architecture A3849

No. 7677: a, Kremlin, Moscow (denomination at LR). b, Maiden's Tower, Baku, Azerbaijan (denomination at LL).

**2015, Sept. 22 Litho. *Perf. 11½***

**7677** Pair 2.50 .60

***a.-b.*** A3849 19r Either single 1.00 .30

Russia and Azerbaijan joint issue.

Printed in sheets containing 4 pairs + central label. See Azerbaijan No. 1092.

Arctic Oil Production — A3850

No. 7678: a, Prirazlomnaya Oil Platform (denomination at LL). b, Mikhail Ulyanov tanker (denomination at LR).

**2015, Sept. 23 Litho. *Perf. 11½***

**7678** A3850 19r Horiz. pair, #a-b 2.50 .60

Russian Nuclear Industry, 70th Anniv. A3851

**2015, Sept. 24 Litho. *Perf. 11½***

**7679** A3851 17r multi 1.25 .25

For surcharge, see No. 8203.

St. Vladimir the Great (c. 958-1015), Christianizer of Kievan Rus' — A3852

**2015, Sept. 25 Litho. *Perf. 13½***

**7680** A3852 21r multi 1.50 .30

Miniature Sheet

Russian Stamps Commemorating the World Cup Soccer Championships — A3853

No. 7681: a, Russia #2073 (green panel). b, Russia #2606 (orange panel). c, Russia #3214 (purple panel). d, Russia #3746 (dark blue panel). e, Russia #5049 (Prussian blue panel). f, Russia #5463 (red panel).

**2015, Oct. 1 Litho. *Perf. 11¼***

**7681** A3853 26.50r Sheet of 6, #a-f 10.00 2.50

Victor Vasnetsov House Museum, Moscow A3854

**2015, Oct. 2 Litho. *Perf. 12½x12***

**7682** A3854 19r multi 1.50 .30

Souvenir Sheet

Derbent, 2000th Anniv. — A3855

**2015, Oct. 2 Litho. *Perf. 12***

**7683** A3855 35r gold & multi 2.50 .55

All-Russian Society for Protection of Monuments of History and Culture, 50th Anniv. — A3856

**2015, Oct. 14 Litho. *Perf. 12½x12***

**7684** A3856 26.50r multi 1.75 .40

Diplomatic Relations Between Russia and Mexico, 125th Anniv. — A3857

No. 7685: a, Saints Peter and Paul Cathedral, St. Petersburg. b, Chapultepec Castle, Mexico City.

**2015, Oct. 19 Litho. *Perf. 11½***

**7685** A3857 19r Pair, #a-b 2.50 .60

Printed in sheets containing 4 pairs + central label. See Mexico Nos. 2955-2956.

Souvenir Sheet

Ancient City of Tauric Chersonese and its Chora UNESCO World Hereitage Site — A3858

**2015, Oct. 23 Litho. *Perf. 12***

**7686** A3858 35r multi 2.50 .55

Disaster Risk Reduction A3859

***Serpentine Die Cut 11***

**2015, Oct. 28 Litho.**

**Self-Adhesive**

**7687** A3859 19r multi 1.25 .30

Sobibor Monument, by Mieczyslaw Welter — A3860

**2015, Oct. 30 Litho. *Perf. 12x12½***

**7688** A3860 21r multi 1.50 .30

Uprising at Sobibor Death Camp, 72nd anniv.

St. Tikhon of Moscow (1865-1925), 11th Patriarch of Moscow A3861

**2015, Nov. 5 Litho. *Perf. 11½x12***

**7689** A3861 19r multi 1.25 .30

Souvenir Sheet

Kostroma Coat of Arms — A3862

**2015, Nov. 5 Litho. *Perf. 12x12½***

**7690** A3862 50r gold & multi 3.00 .75

Ashot L. Badalov (1915-2011), Founder of State Commission for Radio Frequencies — A3863

**2015, Nov. 10 Litho. *Perf. 12½x12***

**7691** A3863 19r multi 1.25 .30

Heroes of the Russian Federation A3864

Designs: No. 7692, 17r, Vladimir V. Maksimchuk (1947-94). No. 7693, 17r, Valeriy A. Tinkov (1957-95). No. 7694, 17r, Ivan Y. Shelohvostov (1978-2003). No. 7695, 17r, Sergey A. Solnechnikov (1980-2012). No. 7696, 17r, Vitaly V. Maiboroda (1981-2013).

**2015, Nov. 10 Litho. *Perf. 12½x12***

**7692-7696** A3864 Set of 5 5.00 1.40

Nos. 7692-7696 were each printed in sheets of 5 + label.

Cathedral of the Intercession of the Holy Virgin, Bogolyubovo A3865

Pha That Luang, Vientiane, Laos A3866

***Serpentine Die Cut 10***

**2015, Nov. 11 Litho.**

**Self-Adhesive**

**7697** Pair 3.00 .60

*a.* A3865 21r multi 1.50 .30

*b.* A3866 21r multi 1.50 .30

Printed in sheets containing 4 pairs + central label. See Laos Nos. 1907-1908.

Zlatoust Arms Factory, 200th Anniv. A3867

**2015, Nov. 17 Litho. *Perf. 11½***

**7698** A3867 17r multi 1.25 .25

Stadiums for 2018 World Cup Soccer Championships — A3868

No. 7699: a, Luzhniki Stadium, Moscow (blue panel). b, Fisht Stadium, Sochi (orange panel). c, Kazan Arena, Kazan (red panel). d, Spartak Stadium, Moscow (green panel).

**2015, Nov. 17 Litho. *Perf. 13½***

**7699** A3868 21r Block or vert. strip of 4, #a-d 6.00 1.25

Ministry for Civil Defense, Emergencies and Natural Disasters, 25th Anniv. — A3869

**2015, Nov. 27 Litho. *Perf. 12x11½***

**7700** A3869 21r multi 1.25 .30

Timiryazev State Agrarian University, 150th Anniv. A3870

***Serpentine Die Cut 10***

**2015, Dec. 3 Litho.**

**Self-Adhesive**

**7701** A3870 17r multi 1.25 .25

**Lawyers Type of 2012**

Designs: No. 7702, 17r, Nikolai V. Muraviev (1850-1908). No. 7703, 17r, Konstantin P. Pobedonostsev (1827-1907). No. 7704, 17r, Nikolai S. Tagantsev (1843-1923).

**2015, Dec. 3 Litho. *Perf. 11½***

**7702-7704** A3635 Set of 3 3.50 .70

Nos. 7702-7704 were each printed in sheets of 8 + label.

Miniature Sheet

Russian Soccer Players — A3871

No. 7705: a, Gavriil D. Kachalin (1911-95). b, Valentin B. Bubukin (1933-2008). c, Yuriy M. Voynov (1931-2003). d, Valentin K. Ivanov (1934-2011). e, Sergei S. Salnikov (1925-84). f, Eduard A. Streltsov (1937-90). g, Lev I. Yashin (1929-90).

**2015, Dec. 9 Litho. *Perf. 12½x12***

**7705** A3871 26.50r Sheet of 7, #a-g, + 9 labels 12.50 2.60

2018 World Cup Soccer Championships, Russia.

New Year 2016 — A3872

**2015, Dec. 10 Litho. *Perf. 13½***

**7706** A3872 35r multi 2.50 .50

Russian Cuisine A3873

**2016, Jan. 13 Litho. *Perf. 11½x12***

**7707** A3873 21r multi 1.25 .25

Souvenir Sheet

Night on the Dnieper River, by Arkhip Kuindzhi (1841-1910) — A3874

**2016, Jan. 27 Litho. *Perf. 12x12½***

**7708** A3874 50r multi 3.50 .65

Historians — A3875

No. 7709 — History books and: a, Nikolai M. Karamzin (1766-1826). b, Vasily O. Klyuchevsky (1841-1911).

**2016, Jan. 28 Litho. *Perf. 12x12½***

**7709** Horiz. pair + central label 3.00 .60

***a.-b.*** A3875 25r Either single 1.25 .30

Miniature Sheet

Towns of Military Glory — A3876

No. 7710: a, Gatchina (7 letters in city name, artillery and tanks). b, Grozny (8 letters in city name, airplanes, mortars, locomotives). c, Petrozavodsk (12 letters in city name, airplanes, trucks with guns and tanks). d, Staraya Russa (two words in city name, airplanes, snow vehicles, trucks with guns). e, Feodosia (8 letters in city name, airplanes, tanks and ships).

**Litho. With Foil Application**

**2016, Feb. 18 *Perf. 11¼***

**7710** A3876 20r Sheet of 5, #a-e, + label 6.50 1.40

Ice Hockey Players and Gagarin Cup — A3877

**2016, Feb. 20 Litho. *Perf. 11½***

**7711** A3877 19r multi 1.25 .25

Miniature Sheet

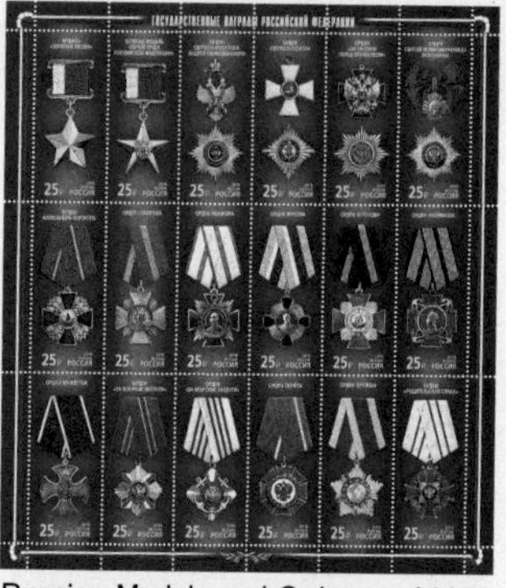

Russian Medals and Orders — A3878

No. 7712: a, Gold Star Medal (like #7337). b, Hero of Labor of the Russian Federation Medal (like #7543). c, Order of St. Andrew (double-headed eagle with crucifix at top). d, Order of St. George (like #7338). e, Order of Merit for the Fatherland (like #7339). f, Order of St. Catherine the Great (like #7427). g, Order of Alexander Nevsky (like #7426). h, Order of Suvorov (like #7425). i, Order of Ushakov (like #7508). j, Order of Zhukov (like #7506). k, Order of Kutuzov (like #7507). l, Order of Nakhimov (like #7604). m, Order of Courage (like #7605). n, Order of Military Merit (blue ribbon with central red stripe). o, Order of Naval Merit (white ribbon with three blue stripes). p, Order of Honor (blue ribbon with one white stripe). q, Order of Friendship (like #7606). r, Order of Parental Glory (white ribbon with two blue stripes).

**Litho. & Embossed**

**2016, Feb. 20 *Perf. 12¼x12***

**Dated "2016" Above "Russia"**

**7712** A3878 25r Sheet of 18, #a-r 35.00 6.25

A booklet containing 18 panes of one of each of Nos. 7712a-7712r sold for 1500r. Value, $110.

Russian Membership in Council of Europe, 20th Anniv. — A3879

**2016, Feb. 26 Litho. *Perf. 12x12¼***

**7713** A3879 21r multi 1.50 .30

Regional Communications Commonwealth, 25th Anniv. — A3880

**2016, Mar. 3 Litho. *Perf. 12½x12***

**7714** A3880 17r multi 1.25 .25

Heroes of the Russian Federation A3881

Designs: No. 7715, 19r, Viktor M. Adamishin (1962-95). No. 7716, 19r, Alexei V. Balandin (1961-2009). No. 7717, 19r, Dmitri A. Serkov (1981-2007).

**2016, Mar. 24 Litho. *Perf. 12½x12***

**7715-7717** A3881 Set of 3 3.50 .85

Nos. 7715-7717 were each printed in sheets of 5 + label. See Nos. 7773-7774, 7804-7805, 7811-7812, 7855-7856, 7899-7900, 7906-7907, 7955, 7985-7986, 8003-8004, 8095=8097, 8139-8142, 8233-8234, 8305, 8343-8344.

Postcrossing A3882

***Serpentine Die Cut 10***

**2016, Mar. 25 Litho.**

**Self-Adhesive**

**7718** A3882 31r multi 2.00 .45

Armed Forces Courier Corps, 300th Anniv. — A3884

**2016, Apr. 15 Litho. *Perf. 13½***

**7720** A3884 21r multi 1.25 .30

Kislovodsk Health Resort Park — A3885

**2016, Apr. 22 Litho. *Perf. 13½***

**7721** A3885 23r multi 1.40 .35

No. 7721 was printed in sheets of 7 + label.

Notaries Institute of Russia, 150th Anniv. A3886

**2016, Apr. 27 Litho. *Perf. 12½x12***

**7722** A3886 19r multi 1.25 .30

No. 7722 was printed in sheets of 14 + label.

2016 World Ice Hockey Championships, Russia — A3887

**2016, May 6 Litho. *Perf. 11¼***

**7723** A3887 19r multi 1.25 .30

Alexey P. Maresyev (1916-2001), Pilot — A3888

**2016, May 20 Litho. *Perf. 12½x12***

**7724** A3888 21.50r multi 1.50 .30

No. 7724 was printed in sheets of 10 + central label.

Paintings by Nicholas P. Krasnoff (1864-1939) A3889

No. 7725: a, View from Vittoriosa Gate, Malta. b, Dulber Palace, Crimea.

**2016, May 24 Litho. *Perf. 11¼x12***
**7725** A3889 21r Pair, #a-b 2.75 .65

No. 7725 was printed in sheets of 10, containing 5 each Nos. 7725a-7725b, + 2 labels. See Malta Nos. 1562-1563.

Rosa Khutor Alpine Resort — A3890

**2016, May 26 Litho. *Perf. 11¾***
**7726** A3890 31r multi 1.75 .45

Chapel Near Vrsic, Slovenia Built by Russian World War I Prisoners of War, Cent. — A3891

**2016, May 27 Litho. *Perf. 13½***
**7727** A3891 21r multi 1.25 .30

No. 7727 was printed in sheets of 7 + label. See Slovenia No. 1171.

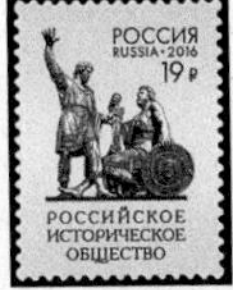
Monument to Minin and Pozharsky, Moscow — A3892

***Serpentine Die Cut 15x14½***
**2016, June 2 Litho.**
**Self-Adhesive**
**7728** A3892 19r multi 1.25 .30

Russian Historical Society, 150th anniv.

Emblem of Union of Philatelists of Russia — A3893

***Serpentine Die Cut 15x14½***
**2016, June 2 Litho.**
**Self-Adhesive**
**7729** A3893 37r multi 2.50 .60

Souvenir Sheet

Mikhail Bulgakov (1891-1940), Writer — A3894

**2016, June 3 Litho. *Perf. 12***
**7730** A3894 90r multi 6.00 1.50

Pushkin State Russian Language Institute, 50th Anniv. — A3895

**2016, June 6 Litho. *Perf. 13½***
**7731** A3895 24r multi 1.50 .40

For surcharge, see No. 8070.

Commonwealth of Independent States, 25th Anniv. — A3896

**2016, June 9 Litho. *Perf. 11½***
**7732** A3896 17r multi 1.25 .25

20th St. Petersburg International Economic Forum — A3897

**2016, June 16 Litho. *Perf. 12¼***
**7733** A3897 20r multi 1.50 .30

Soldiers Defending Brest Fortress — A3898

**Litho. & Embossed**
**2016, June 22 *Perf. 11¾***
**7734** A3898 35r multi 2.25 .55

No. 7734 was printed in sheets of 7 + label. See Belarus No. 986.

Dogs — A3899

**2016, June 23 Litho. *Perf. 13½***
**7735** Pair 3.25 .80
*a.* A3899 19r Collie 1.25 .30
*b.* A3899 31r German shepherd 2.00 .50

Rzhev, 800th Anniv. A3900

**2016, June 23 Litho. *Perf. 12***
**7736** A3900 24r multi 1.50 .40

Yuri Levitan (1914-83), Radio Announcer A3901

**2016, June 24 Litho. *Perf. 12x12½***
**7737** A3901 19r multi 1.25 .30

Russian International News Agency, 75th Anniv.

Count Dmitri A. Milyutin (1816-1912), Minister of War — A3902

**2016, June 28 Litho. *Perf. 12x11½***
**7738** A3902 21.50r multi 1.40 .35

No. 7738 was printed in sheets of 8 + central label.

Traffic Safety A3903

**2016, June 28 Litho. *Perf. 11¼***
**7739** A3903 14r multi .90 .25

2016 All-Russian Agricultural Census A3904

***Serpentine Die Cut 10***
**2016, July 1 Litho.**
**Self-Adhesive**
**7740** A3904 20r multi 1.25 .30

Global Navigation Satellite System A3905

***Serpentine Die Cut 11***
**2016, July 5 Litho.**
**Self-Adhesive**
**7741** A3905 19r multi 1.25 .30

Velikiye Luki, 850th Anniv. A3906

**2016, July 14 Litho. *Perf. 11¼***
**7742** A3906 24r multi .75 .35

Order of Military Merit — A3907

Order of Naval Merit — A3908

Order of Honor — A3909

Order of Parental Glory — A3910

**Litho, & Embossed**

**2016, July 19** *Perf. 11¾*

| | | | |
|---|---|---|---|
| **7743** A3907 25r multi | 1.50 | .35 |
| **7744** A3908 25r multi | 1.50 | .35 |
| **7745** A3909 25r multi | 1.50 | .35 |
| **7746** A3910 25r multl | 1.50 | .35 |
| *Nos. 7743-7746 (4)* | 6.00 | 1.40 |

Nos. 7743-7746 were each printed in sheets of 7 + label.

World War I Military Equipment — A3911

Designs: No. 7747, 24r, Fedorov Avtomat 6.5mm rifle. No. 7748, 24r, Imperatritsa Ekaterina Velikaya ship. No. 7749, 24r, Grigorovich M-5 flying boat. No. 7750, 24r, Mgebrov-Isotta-Fraschini armored vehicle.

**2016, July 28** **Litho.** *Perf. 12*

**7747-7750** A3911 Set of 4 6.00 1.50

Nos. 7747-7750 were each printed in sheets of 11 + label. A booklet containing eight panes of one of each of Nos. 7670-7673, 7525-7528 sold for 560r. Value, $40.

Russian Stamps Commemorating the World Cup Soccer Championships — A3912

No. 7751: a, Russia #5896 (blue panel). b, Label commemorating 1994 World Cup (red panel). c, Label commemorating 2002 World Cup (orange red panel). d, Russia #7583 (purple panel).

**2016, July 29** **Litho.** *Perf. 11¼*

**7751** A3912 21.50r Sheet of 4, #a-d 5.00 1.40

Likhachov Automotive Plant, Moscow, Cent. A3913

**2016, Aug. 2** **Litho.** *Perf. 11¼*

**7752** A3913 21.50r multi 1.50 .35

Orel, 450th Anniv. A3914

**2016, Aug. 5** **Litho.** *Perf. 12½x12*

**7753** A3914 24r multi 1.50 .35

No. 7237 Surcharged in Silver

**Method and Perf. As Before**

**2016, Aug. 5**

**7754** A3519 31r on 10.50r #7237 *30.00 30.00*

No. 7754 was printed in sheets of 6 + 2 labels.

Omsk, 300th Anniv. A3915

**2016, Aug. 6** **Litho.** *Perf. 12½x12*

**7755** A3915 24r multi 1.50 .35

Russian Presence at Mount Athos, 1000th Anniv. — A3916

**2016, Aug. 9** **Litho.** *Perf. 11¼*

**7756** A3916 31r multi 2.00 .45

Souvenir Sheet

Kizhi Ethnographic Museum, 50th Anniv. — A3917

No. 7757: a, Church of the Intercession (9 domes) and buildings. b, Transfiguration Church (22 domes) and buildings. c, Bell tower and windmill.

**Litho. & Engr.**

**2016, Aug. 19** *Perf. 12*

**7757** A3917 50r Sheet of 3, #a-c 10.00 2.25

A booklet containing one pane of Nos. 7757 sold for 365r.

Arms of Velikiye Luki A3918

Arms of Murmansk A3919

*Perf. 11¾x12¼*

**2016, Aug. 23** **Litho.**

| | | |
|---|---|---|
| **7758** A3918 14r multi | .90 | .25 |
| Complete booklet, 10 #7758 | 9.00 | |
| Complete booklet, 20 #7758 | 18.00 | |
| **7759** A3919 19r multi | 1.25 | .30 |
| Complete booklet, 10 #7759 | 12.50 | |
| Complete booklet, 20 #7759 | 25.00 | |

Stadiums for 2018 World Cup Soccer Championships — A3920

No. 7760: a, Volgograd Arena (green panel). b, Ekaterinburg Arena (blue panel). c, Rostov Arena (orange panel). d, Samara Arena (red panel).

**2016, Aug. 26** **Litho.** *Perf. 13½*

**7760** A3920 21.50r Block or vert. strip of 4, #a-d 5.00 1.40

Souvenir Sheet

Russian Arctic National Park — A3921

**2016, Aug. 30** **Litho.** *Perf. 11¾*

**7761** A3921 80r multi 5.50 1.25

A booklet containing one pane of No. 7761 sold for 350r. Value, $37.50.

Ulan-Ude, 350th Anniv. A3922

**2016, Sept. 1** **Litho.** *Perf. 12½x12*

**7762** A3922 24r multi 1.50 .35

Lukoil Oil Company — A3923

**2016, Sept. 6** **Litho.** *Perf. 13½*

**7763** A3923 24r multi 1.50 .40

Unified State Exam A3924

***Serpentine Die Cut 10***

**2016, Sept. 14** **Litho.**

**Self-Adhesive**

**7764** A3924 19r multi 1.25 .30

Souvenir Sheets

Magas Coat of Arms — A3925

Perm Coat of Arms — A3926

**2016, Sept. 16** **Litho.** *Perf. 12x12½*

| | | |
|---|---|---|
| **7765** A3925 50r multi | 3.50 | .80 |
| **7766** A3926 50r multi | 3.50 | .80 |

For surcharge, see No. 8137.

Russian Presidential Academy of National Economy and Public Administration — A3927

**2016, Sept. 20** **Litho.** *Perf. 12x11½*

**7767** A3927 19r multi 1.25 .30

Alexander M. Prokhorov (1916-2002), 1964 Nobel Laureate in Physics A3928

**2016, Sept. 22** **Litho.** *Perf. 11¾*

**7768** A3928 21.50r multi 1.50 .35

Vasily A. Degtyaryov Munitions Plant, Kovrov, Cent. A3929

**2016, Sept. 27** **Litho.** *Perf. 11½*

**7769** A3929 21.50r multi 1.50 .35

Tarkhankut Lighthouse — A3930

Chersonesus Lighthouse — A3931

**2016, Sept. 29 Litho. *Perf. 12½x12***
**7770** A3930 14r multi .90 .25
**7771** A3931 14r multi .90 .25

Murmansk, Cent. — A3932

**2016, Oct. 4 Litho. *Perf. 12½x12***
**7772** A3932 24r multi 1.50 .40

**Heroes Type of 2016**

Designs: No. 7773, 19r, Mark N. Yevtyukhin (1964-2000). No. 7774, 19r, Nikolai V. Skrypnik (1944-96).

**2016, Oct. 5 Litho. *Perf. 12½x12***
**7773-7774** A3881 Set of 2 2.50 .60

Nos. 7773-7774 were each printed in sheets of 5 + label.

Metropolitan Macarius of Moscow and Kolomna (1816-82), Church Historian A3933

**2016, Oct. 7 Litho. *Perf. 11¾x12***
**7775** A3933 24r multi 1.50 .40

Yelnya Offensive, 75th Anniv. — A3934

Battle of Hanko, 75th Anniv. — A3935

**Litho. & Embossed**

**2016, Oct. 11 *Perf. 11¾***
**7776** A3934 35r multi 2.25 .55
**7777** A3935 35r multi 2.25 .55

Nos. 7776-7777 were each printed in sheets of 7 + label.

Souvenir Sheet

Abramtsevo Museum Reserve — A3936

No. 7778 — Owners of Museum building: a, Sergey T. Aksakov (1791-1859), writer. b, Savva I. Mamontov (1841-1918), industrialist.

**2016, Oct. 25 Litho. *Perf. 12***
**7778** A3936 25r Sheet of 2, #a-b 4.50 .80

No. 7778 with a fluorescent overprint of a quotation by Aksakov in the sheet margin was printed in limited quantities and sold for 300r. Value, $25.

Federal Customs Service — A3937

**2016, Oct. 25 Litho. *Perf. 12x11½***
**7779** A3937 24r multi 1.50 .40

Souvenir Sheet

Sable — A3938

**2016, Oct. 27 Litho. *Perf. 12¼x12***
**7780** A3938 70r multi 4.50 1.10

Barguzinsky State Biosphere Nature Reserve, cent. No. 7780 with an Ecology Year 2017 emblem overprinted in the sheet margin in green was issued on Aug. 1, 2017 and sold for 150r. Value, $10.

Miniature Sheet

Russian Soccer Players — A3939

No. 7781: a, Viktor M. Bannikov (1938-2001). b, Konstantin I. Beskov (1920-2006). c, Nikolay G. Latyshev (1913-99). d, Slava K. Metreveli (1936-98). e, Nikolai P. Morozov (1916-81). f, Igor A. Netto (1930-99). g, Galimzyan S. Khusainov (1937-2010).

**2016, Oct. 28 Litho. *Perf. 12½x12***
**7781** A3939 29r Sheet of 7, #a-g, + 9 labels 14.00 3.25

2018 World Cup Soccer Championships, Russia.

Russkaya Pravda, Law Code of Kievan Rus, 1000th Anniv. A3940

**2016, Oct. 31 Litho. *Perf. 12½x12***
**7782** A3940 19r multi 1.25 .30

Djamaldin K. Yandiev (1916-79), Poet — A3941

**2016, Nov. 10 Litho. *Perf. 11¾***
**7783** A3941 19r multi 1.25 .30

Caffeinated Beverages of Russia and Argentina — A3942

No. 7784: a, Tea and tea service, Russia (denomination at LL). b, Mate and mate service, Argentina (denomination at LR).

**2016, Nov. 14 Litho. *Perf. 12x12½***
**7784** A3942 29r Horiz. pair, #a-b 3.50 .95

See Argentina Nos. 2809-2810.

Battle of Moscow, 75th Anniv. — A3943

**Litho. & Embossed**

**2016, Nov. 16 *Perf. 11¾***
**7785** A3943 35r multi 2.25 .55

No. 7785 was printed in sheets of 7 + label. A booklet containing panes of one of Nos. 7734, 7776, 7777 and 7785 sold for 800r.

See Kazakhstan No. 794.

Modern Art — A3944

Designs: No. 7786, 31r, We Serve the Fatherland and the Special Forces, by Yuri Orlov, 2002. No. 7787, 31r, Dawn, Chersonesus, by Nikolai Morgun, 2002 (50x50mm). No. 7788, 31r, Monument to Alexander Suvorov, by Dmitry Tugarinov, 1999, Switzerland (50x50mm). No. 7789, 31r, Golden Balls, Stavropol, by Valery Arzumanov, 2012 (50x50mm).

***Perf. 12x11½ (#7786), 11¼***

**2016, Nov. 29 Litho.**
**7786-7789** A3944 Set of 4 8.00 2.00

New Year 2017 — A3945

**2016, Dec. 1 Litho. *Perf. 11½x11¼***
**7790** A3945 19r multi 1.25 .30

No. 7790 was printed in sheets of 4. Lithographed examples of No. 7790 with holographic foil were printed in sheets of 4 that sold for 255r.

**Lawyers Type of 2012**

Designs: No. 7791, 19r, Gabriel F. Shershenevich (1863-1912). No. 7792, 19r, Konstantin I. Palen (1833-1912). No. 7793, 19r, Vladimir A. Tumanov (1926-2011).

**2016, Dec. 2 Litho. *Perf. 11½***
**7791-7793** A3635 Set of 3 4.00 .95

Nos. 7791-7793 were each printed in sheets of 8 + label.

F-1 Nuclear Reactor, Moscow, 70th Anniv. A3946

**2016, Dec. 8 Litho. *Perf. 11½***
**7794** A3946 19r multi 1.25 .30

Miniature Sheet

Russian Soccer Players — A3947

No. 7795: a, Anatoliy A. Banishevskiy (1946-97). b, Valery I. Voronin (1939-98). c, Anatoli M. Ilyin (1931-2016). d, Yevgeniy V. Rudakov (1942-2011). e, Pavel F. Sadyrin (1942-2001). f, Igor L. Chislenko (1939-94). g, Albert A. Shesternyov (1941-94).

**2016, Dec. 9 Litho. *Perf. 12½x12***
**7795** A3947 29r Sheet of 7, #a-g, + 9 labels 14.00 3.50

2018 World Cup Soccer Championships, Russia. A six-pane booklet containing one each of Nos. 7705a-7705g, 7781a-7781g, and 7795a-7795g sold for 1200r. Value, $100.

Churches A3948

No. 7796: a, Church of St. John the Theologian, Ohrid, Macedonia (brown building). b,

Trinity Cathedral, St. Petersburg (white building with blue domes).

**2016, Dec. 13 Litho. *Perf. 12½x12***
**7796** A3948 21.50r Pair, #a-b 2.50 .75

Printed in sheets of 8 containing 4 each Nos. 7796a-7796b, + central label. See Macedonia No. 734.

Souvenir Sheet

Nuremberg War Crimes Trials, 70th Anniv. — A3949

**2016, Dec. 14 Litho. *Perf. 12***
**7797** A3949 70r multi 5.00 1.25

Uniforms of the Diplomatic Service A3950

Uniforms of: No. 7798, 19r, Privy counselor and chancellor, 1834. No. 7799, 19r, State counselor and collegiate registrar, 1904. No. 7800, 19r, USSR ambassador extraordinary and plenipotentiary and attaché of the People's commisariat of Foreign Affairs, 1945. No. 7801, 19r, Russian Federation ambassadors extraordinary and plenipotentiary, 2001.

**2016, Dec. 20 Litho. *Perf. 13½***
**7798-7801** A3950 Set of 4 5.00 1.25
*7801a* Souvenir sheet of 8, 2 each #7798-7801 10.00 2.50

Yevgeny Zababakhin (1917-84), Nuclear Physicist and Weapons Designer — A3951

**2017, Jan. 16 Litho. *Perf. 12½x12***
**7802** A3951 19r multi 1.25 .30

Bast Shoes — A3952

**2017, Jan. 24 Litho. *Perf. 12x12½***
**7803** A3952 29r multi 2.00 .50

**Heroes Type of 2016**

Designs: No. 7804, 19r, Andrey G. Karlov (1954-2016). No. 7805, 19r, Sulom-Beck Oskanov (1943-92).

**2017, Feb. 7 Litho. *Perf. 12½x12***
**Dated "2017"**
**7804-7805** A3881 Set of 2 2.75 .70

Nos. 7804-7805 were each printed in sheets of 5 + label.

Souvenir Sheet

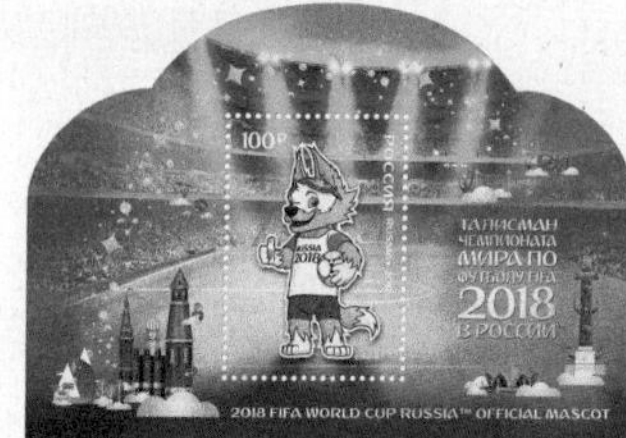

Zabivaka, Mascot of 2018 World Cup Soccer Championships — A3953

**2017, Feb. 7 Litho. *Perf. 12x12½***
**7806** A3953 100r multi 6.50 1.75

Emblem of the High Commissioner for Human Rights in the Russian Federation — A3954

**2017, Feb. 27 Litho. *Perf. 12½x12***
**7807** A3954 19r multi 1.25 .35

Miniature Sheet

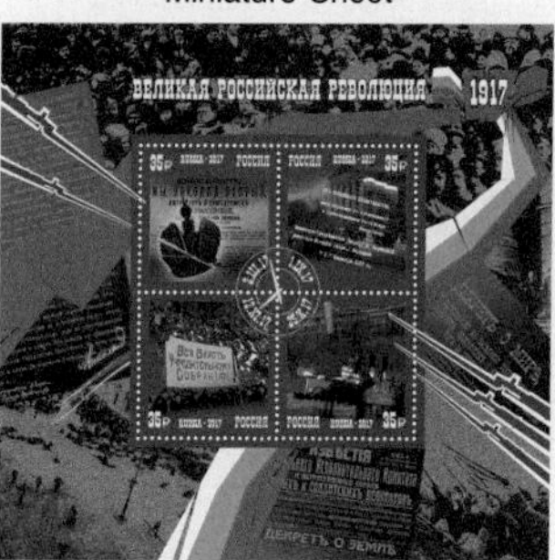

October Revolution, Cent. — A3955

No. 7808: a, Abdication of Tsar Nicholas II, Mar. 15, 1917 (Mar. 2, old style). b, Proclamation of Russian Republic, Sept. 14, 1917 (Sept. 1, old style). c, Election of Constituent Assembly, Nov. 25, 1917 (Nov. 12, old style) d, Assault on the Winter Palace by Cruiser Aurora, Nov. 7, 1917 (Oct. 27, old style).

**2017, Mar. 2 Litho. *Perf. 11¾***
**7808** A3955 35r Sheet of 4, #a-d 9.00 2.50

A booklet containing a pane of stamps like No. 7808 sold for 505r. Value, $50.

2017 Confederations Cup Soccer Tournament, Russia — A3956

**Litho. & Embossed**
**2017, Mar. 9 *Perf. 11¾***
**7809** A3956 35r multi 2.25 .60

For surcharge, see No. 7861.

St. Michael's Castle, St. Petersburg — A3957

**2017, Mar. 15 Litho. *Perf. 12½x12***
**7810** A3957 24r multi 1.50 .45

Europa.

**Heroes Type of 2016**

Designs: No. 7811, 19r, Sergey A. Ashikhmin (1977-2012). No. 7812, 19r, Vadim K. Yermakov (1972-96).

**2017, Mar. 23 Litho. *Perf. 12½x12***
**7811-7812** A3881 Set of 2 2.75 .70

Nos. 7811-7812 were each printed in sheets of 5 + label.

Commonwealth of Independent States Interparliamentary Assembly — A3958

**2017, Mar. 27 Litho. *Perf. 12½x12***
**7813** A3958 35r multi 2.50 .60

Flowers — A3959

No. 7814: a, Galanthus woronowii. b, Erythronium caucasicum. c, Diospyros lotus. d, Cyclamen coum ssp. caucasicum.

***Serpentine Die Cut 11***
**2017, Mar. 29 Litho.**
**Self-Adhesive**
**7814** A3959 Block of 4 7.50 4.00
*a.-d.* 29r Any single 1.50 1.00

Icebreaker Krasin, Cent. A3960

**2017, Mar. 31 Litho. *Perf. 12½x12***
**7815** A3960 24r multi 1.75 .45

No. 7815 was printed in sheets of 14 + label.

Miniature Sheet

Turtles — A3961

No. 7816: a, Emys orbicularis. b, Pelodiscus sinensis. c, Mauremys caspica. d, Testudo graeca.

**2017, Apr. 4 Litho. *Perf. 11¾x12¼***
**7816** A3961 35r Sheet of 4, #a-d 9.00 2.50

Mechanical Engineering Design Bureau, Kolomna, 75th Anniv. A3962

**2017, Apr. 11 Litho. *Perf. 11¼***
**7817** A3962 19r multi 1.40 .35

Souvenir Sheet

Association of Combat Veterans of Internal Affairs Agencies and Internal Troops, 25th Anniv. — A3963

**Litho. & Embossed**
**2017, Apr. 21 *Perf. 12x12½***
**7818** A3963 100r multi 6.50 1.75

Souvenir Sheet

The Battle on the Ice, by Valentin Serov — A3964

**2017, Apr. 26 Litho. *Perf. 12x11¾***
**7819** A3964 90r multi 6.50 1.60

Battle on the Ice, 775th anniv.

Sailors in Northern Convoys of World War II — A3965

**Litho. & Embossed**
**2017, May 4 *Perf. 11¾***
**7820** A3965 41r multi 2.75 .75

No. 7820 was printed in sheets of 7 + label.

Emblem of Russian Student Spring Festival A3966

***Serpentine Die Cut 10***

**2017, May 15** **Litho.**

**Self-Adhesive**

**7821** A3966 22r multi 1.50 .40

Fables A3967

No. 7822: a, The Fox and the Grapes. b, The Tortoise and the Hare. c, The Rooster and the Pearl. d, The Wolf and the Crane.

**2017, May 17** **Litho.** ***Perf. 11¼x12***

**7822** Horiz. strip of 4 9.00 2.50

***a.-d.*** A3967 35r Any single 2.00 .60

Souvenir Sheet

Cape Fiolent Near Sevastopol, by Vasily Vereshchagin (1842-1904) — A3968

**2017, May 24** **Litho.** ***Perf. 12x12½***

**7823** A3968 95r multi 6.50 1.75

Souvenir Sheet

Astrakhan Coat of Arms — A3969

**2017, May 30** **Litho.** ***Perf. 12x12½***

**7824** A3969 60r multi 4.00 1.10

Izvestia Newspaper, Cent. — A3970

**2017, June 1** **Litho.** ***Perf. 11¾***

**7825** A3970 27r multi 1.75 .50

Flag of Republic of Ingushetia — A3971

**2017, June 4** **Litho.** ***Perf. 12¼x12***

**7826** A3971 25r multi 1.75 .40

Republic of Ingushetia, 25th anniv.

Ecology Year A3972

**2017, June 5** **Litho.** ***Perf. 11½***

**7827** A3972 22r multi 1.25 .35

Russian Defense Sport and Technology Organization A3973

Designs: No. 7828, 22r, Rifle shooting. No. 7829, 22r, Radio direction finding.

**2017, June 28** **Litho.** ***Perf. 12x12½***

**7828-7829** A3973 Set of 2 3.00 .75

Russian State Shipbuilding, 350th Anniv. A3974

**2017, June 29** **Litho.** ***Perf. 11¼***

**7830** A3974 33r multi 2.00 .55

Arms of Azov A3975

Arms of Orekhovo-Zuyevo A3976

**2017, June 29** **Litho.** ***Perf. 12x12¼***

**7831** A3975 16r multi 1.10 .25

Complete booklet, 10 #7831 11.00

Complete booklet, 20 #7831 22.00

**7832** A3976 22r multi 1.50 .35

Complete booklet, 10 #7832 15.00

Complete booklet, 20 #7832 30.00

Resurrection Cathedral, Omsk — A3977

**2017, June 30** **Litho.** ***Perf. 12x12½***

**7833** A3977 27r multi 1.75 .45

1897 Meeting of King Chulalongkorn of Thailand and Tsar Nicholas II of Russia — A3978

**2017, July 3** **Litho.** ***Perf. 12x12¼***

**7834** A3978 22r multi 1.50 .35

Diplomatic relations between Russia and Thailand, 120th anniv. No. 7834 was printed in sheets of 14 + central label. See Thailand No. 2964.

Souvenir Sheet

Kaliningrad Coat of Arms — A3979

**2017, July 10** **Litho.** ***Perf. 12x12¼***

**7835** A3979 60r gold & multi 4.00 1.00

Bakhchysarai Museum, Cent. — A3980

**2017, July 12** **Litho.** ***Perf. 12x12½***

**7836** A3980 100r multi 6.50 1.75

Pyotr Vyazemsky (1792-1878), Poet — A3981

**2017, July 21** **Litho.** ***Perf. 12x11¼***

**7837** A3981 22r multi 1.50 .35

No. 7837 was printed in sheets of 11 + label.

Souvenir Sheet

Entrance to Sevastopol Bay, by Ivan Aivazovsky (1817-1900) — A3982

**2017, July 25** **Litho.** ***Perf. 12x12¼***

**7838** A3982 95r multi 6.50 1.60

A self-adhesive imperforate sheet like No. 7838 was issued on Oct. 10 and sold for 240r.

Souvenir Sheet

Ivangorod Fortress, 525th Anniv. — A3983

**2017, July 28** **Litho.** ***Perf. 12¼x12***

**7839** A3983 90r multi 6.00 1.50

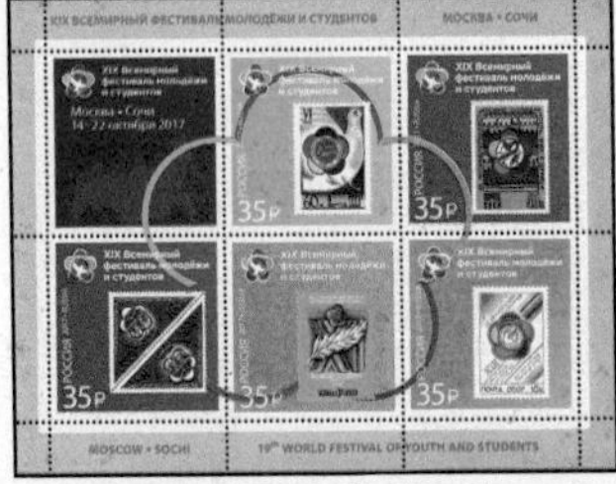

19th World Festival of Youth and Students, Moscow and Sochi — A3984

No. 7840 — Stamps commemorating previous festivals: a, Russia #1914. b, Russia #5360. c, Pair of Russia #4068. d, Russia #4648. e, Russia #5782.

**2017, Aug. 3** **Litho.** ***Perf. 11¼***

**7840** A3984 35r Sheet of 5, #a-e, + label 10.00 3.25

Battle of Crimea and Defense of Sevastopol, 75th Anniv. — A3985

World War II Guerilla Fighters — A3986

Normandie-Niemen French Air Regiment — A3987

**2017 Litho. & Embossed** ***Perf. 11¾***

**7841** A3985 41r multi 2.50 .75
**7842** A3986 41r multi 2.50 .75
**7843** A3987 41r multi 2.50 .75
*Nos. 7841-7843 (3)* 7.50 2.25

Issued: No. 7841, 8/4; No. 7842, 8/24; No. 7843, 9/1. Nos. 7841-7843 were each printed in sheets of 7 + label. See France No. 5302.

Stadiums for 2018 World Cup Soccer Championships — A3988

No. 7844: a, Nizhny Novgorod Stadium (green panel). b, Kaliningrad Stadium (blue panel). c, Mordovia Arena, Saransk (red panel). d, St. Petersburg Stadium (orange panel).

**2017, Aug. 23 Litho.** ***Perf. 11¾***

**7844** A3988 22r Block or vert. strip of 4, #a-d 6.00 1.60

Archimandrite Antonin Kapustin (1817-94), Head of Russian Orthodox Ecclesiastical Mission in Jerusalem — A3989

**2017, Aug. 23 Litho.** ***Perf. 11¾***

**7845** A3989 27r multi 2.00 .45

### Recipients of the Order of St, Andrew Type of 2011

Design: Order of St. Andrew and Fazu Aliyeva (1932-2016), poet.

**2017, Aug. 29 Litho.** ***Perf. 12x11¼***

**7846** A3560 27r multi 1.75 .45

No. 7846 was printed in sheets of 11 + label.

### Kremlins Type of 2009

Kremlins in: 22r, Alexandrov. 41r, Vologda.

***Serpentine Die Cut 11***

**2017, Aug. 30 Litho.**

**Self-Adhesive**

**7847** A3471 22r multi 1.50 .40
**7848** A3471 41r multi 2.50 .75

Modern Art — A3990

Designs: No. 7849, 35r, The Sower, by N.V. Kolupaev, 2008. No. 7850, 35r, Autumn Evening, by A. I. Telik, 2009. No. 7851, 35r, Conversation, sculpture by Vladimir I. Koshelev, 2007. No. 7852, 35r, Missing, 1946, by Andrei P. Gorsky, 1962 (50x38mm).

***Perf. 11¼, 12x11¼ (#7852)***

**2017, Sept. 13 Litho.**

**7849-7852** A3990 Set of 4 9.00 2.50

Indira Gandhi (1917-84), Prime Minister of India, and Flag of India — A3991

**2017, Sept. 21 Litho.** ***Perf. 12x12½***

**7853** A3991 35r multi 2.50 .60

Military Academy of the General Staff of the Armed Forces — A3992

**2017, Sept. 27 Litho.** ***Perf. 12x11½***

**7854** A3992 27r multi 2.00 .45

### Heroes Type of 2016

Designs: No. 7855, 22r, Vladislav A. Dolonin (1969-95). No. 7856, 22r, Viktor V. Matveyev (1963-2001).

**2017, Sept. 28 Litho.** ***Perf. [illegible]***

**7855-7856** A3881 Set of 2 3.00 .80

Nos. 7855-7856 were each printed in sheets of 5 + label.

Civil Defense of the Russian Federation A3993

**2017, Oct. 3 Litho.** ***Perf. 11½***

**7857** A3993 27r multi 2.00 .45

Investigative Committee of Russia — A3994

**2017, Oct. 6 Litho.** ***Perf. 12x11½***

**7858** A3994 27r multi 2.00 .45

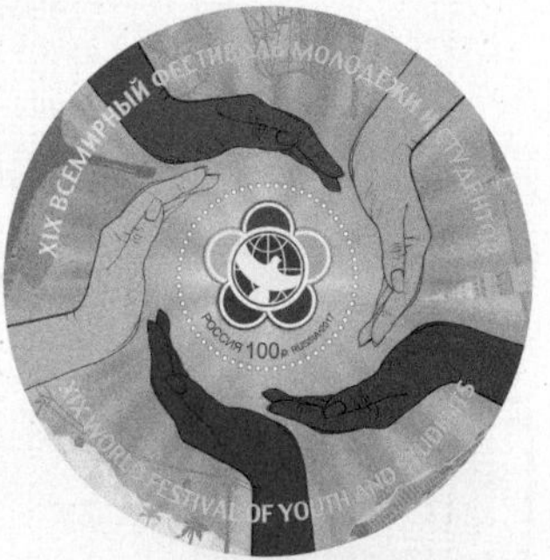

19th World Festival of Youth and Students — A3995

**2017, Oct. 14 Litho.** ***Perf.***

**7859** A3995 100r multi 7.00 1.75

137th Assembly of Inter-Parliamentary Union, St. Petersburg — A3996

**2017, Oct. 14 Litho.** ***Perf. 11½***

**7860** A3996 35r sil & dk blue 2.50 .60

No. 7809 Surcharged in Bluish Violet

**Method and Perf. As Before**

**2017, Oct. 17**

**7861** A3956 50r on 35r #7809 *7.50 7.50*

No. 7861 was printed in a sheet of 9 that sold for 700r.

Zhostovo Painting, 1976 — A3997

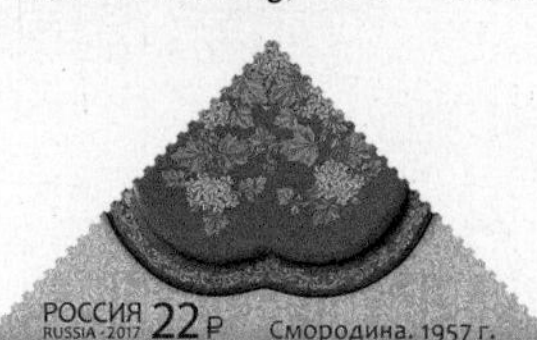


Zhostovo Painting, 1957 — A3998

Zhostovo Painting, 1980 — A3999

No. 7862: a, Bird facing left. b, Bird facing right.

**2017, Oct. 23 Litho.** ***Perf. 11½x11¼***

**7862** Horiz. pair 3.00 .80
*a.-b.* A3997 22r Either single 1.50 .40
**7863** A3998 22r multi 1.50 .40
**7864** A3999 22r multi 1.50 .40
*Nos. 7862-7864 (3)* 6.00 1.60

No. 7862 was printed in sheets containing two pairs. Nos. 7863-7864 were each printed in sheets of 4.

Uniforms of Customs Officials A4000

Designs: No. 7865, 22r, Customs guard and manager, 1827. No. 7866. 22r, Controller and customs manager, 1904. No. 7867, 22r, Controller and customs chief, 1952. No. 7868, 22r, Dog training specialist and department head, 2017.

**2017, Oct. 25 Litho.** ***Perf. 11¾***

**7865-7868** A4000 Set of 4 6.00 1.50
*7868a* Souvenir sheet of 8, 2 each #7865-7868 12.00 3.00

Dancers A4001

No. 7869: a, Seven Beryozka dancers, Russia. b, Bhavai dancer, India.

**2017, Oct. 26 Litho.** ***Perf. 11½***

**7869** A4001 35r Pair, #a-b 4.50 1.25

Joint issue between Russia and India.

No. 7869 was printed in sheets containing 4 pairs and a central label. See India Nos. 2969-2970.

Mir Interstate Television and Radio Company, 25th Anniv. A4002

***Serpentine Die Cut 11¼***

**2017, Oct. 31 Litho.**

**Self-Adhesive**

**7870** A4002 27r multi 2.00 .45

See Belarus No. 1065, Kazakhstan No. 830.

Russian Satellite Communication Company, 50th Anniv. — A4003

**2017, Nov. 1 Litho.** ***Perf. 12½x12***

**7871** A4003 22r multi 1.50 .40

Souvenir Sheet

Ostankino Television Tower and Television Center, 50th Anniv. — A4004

No. 7872: a, Television tower. b, Television Center, horiz.

**2017, Nov. 7 Litho. *Perf. 11¾***
**7872** A4004 50r Sheet of 2, #a-b 6.50 3.00

Gorny Convent, Ein Karem, Israel A4005

**2017, Nov. 14 Litho. *Perf. 12½x12***
**7873** A4005 35r multi 2.25 1.60

No. 7873 was printed in sheets of 8 + central label. See Israel No. 2160.

Treasures of Russia A4006

Designs: No. 7874, 22r, Orlov diamond on scepter (cerise background). No. 7875, 22r, Emerald and diamond brooch (yellow brown background). No. 7876, 22r, Orb with sapphire and diamonds (dark emerald background). No. 7877, 22r, Tourmaline pendant carved into bunch of grapes (dark blue background).

**2017, Nov. 16 Litho. *Perf. 11½***
**7874-7877** A4006 Set of 4 6.00 3.00

Diamond Fund of Russia. A booklet containing four panes of 1 of litho. and embossed examples of Nos. 7874-7877 was released on Dec. 19 and sold for 1200r. Value, $90.

Maya Plisetskaya (1925-2015), Ballet Dancer — A4007

**2017, Nov. 20 Litho. *Perf. 12½x12***
**7878** A4007 27r multi 2.00 .45

Printed in sheets of 14 + label.

Prosecutor General's Office — A4008

**2017, Nov. 23 Litho. *Perf. 12x11½***
**7879** A4008 27r multi 1.75 .45

Saint Tikhon of Moscow (1865-1925), 11th Patriarch of Moscow A4009

**2017, Nov. 29 Litho. *Perf. 11½***
**7880** A4009 41r multi 2.75 .70

Re-establishment of Patriarchate in Russia, cent. No. 7880 was printed in sheets of 8 + central label.

New Year 2018 A4010

No. 7881 — 2018 World Cup mascot, Zabivaka: a, Kicking soccer ball. b, Heading soccer ball. c, Chasing soccer ball.

***Serpentine Die Cut 11¼***
**2017, Dec. 1 Litho.**
**Self-Adhesive**

| | | | |
|---|---|---|---|
| **7881** | Strip of 3 | 6.00 | 4.00 |
| *a.* | A4010 22r multi | 1.50 | .70 |
| *b.* | A4010 33r multi | 2.25 | 1.10 |
| *c.* | A4010 35r multi | 2.50 | .90 |

**Lawyers Type of 2012**

Designs: No. 7882, 22r, Ivan I. Dmitriev (1760-1837). No. 7883, 22r, Nikolai M. Korkunov (1853-1904). No. 7884, 22r, Sergei S. Alexeyev (1924-2013).

**2017, Dec. 4 Litho. *Perf. 11½***
**7882-7884** A3635 Set of 3 4.00 3.00

Nos. 7882-7884 were each printed in sheets of 8 + label.

Federal Treasury — A4011

**2017, Dec. 7 Litho. *Perf. 12x11½***
**7885** A4011 27r multi 2.00 .45

Monument to Evpaty Kolovrat, by Oleg Sedov — A4012

**2017, Dec. 8 Litho. *Perf. 11¼***
**7886** A4012 35r multi 2.50 1.75

Yevgeny Primakov (1929-2015), Prime Minister — A4013

**2017, Dec. 18 Litho. *Perf. 12½x12***
**7887** A4013 27r multi 2.00 .45

Printed in sheets of 14 + label.

Religious Buildings — A4014

No. 7888: a, Bakhchisaray Assumption Monastery, Russia (denomination at LL). b, Golden Temple of Dambulla, Sri Lanka (denomination at LR).

**2017, Dec. 18 Litho. *Perf. 12½x12***
**7888** A4014 35r Horiz. pair, #a-b 4.50 3.25

Federal Security Service, Cent. A4015

**2017, Dec. 20 Litho. *Perf. 11½***
**7889** A4015 27r multi 1.75 .80

Soccer in Art — A4016

Designs: No. 7890, 22r, Monument to Vsevolod Bobrov, by Anatoly Dyoma and Sergey Mikhailov, 2002. No. 7891, 22r, Soccer Player, bas-relief in Moscow Metro by Elena Yanson-Manizer, 1953. No. 7892, 22r, Soccer, by Aleksandr Deyneka, 1928. No. 7893, 22r, Soccer, by Yuri Pimenov, 1926.

**2017, Dec. 20 Litho. *Perf. 12x12½***

| | | | |
|---|---|---|---|
| **7890-7893** | A4016 Set of 4 | 6.00 | 4.00 |
| *7893a* | Souvenir sheet of 8, 2 each #7890-7893 | 12.00 | 8.00 |

Miniature Sheet

Woodpeckers — A4017

No. 7894: a, Picus viridis. b, Dendrocopos major. c, Dryocopus martius. d, Dendrocopos minor.

**2018, Jan. 18 Litho. *Perf. 12x12½***
**7894** A4017 35r Sheet of 4, #a-d 9.00 5.00

Nikolai Lavyorov (1930-2016), Geologist — A4018

Vladimir Zeldin (1915-2016), Actor — A4019

**2018 Litho. *Perf. 12½x12***

| | | | |
|---|---|---|---|
| **7895** | A4018 27r multi | 1.75 | 1.50 |
| **7896** | A4019 27r multi | 1.75 | 1.50 |

Full Cavalier of the Order of Merit of the Motherland.

Issued: No. 7895, 1/18; No. 7896, 1/22. No. 7895 was printed in sheets of 14 + label. No. 7896 was printed in sheets of 18 + label.

Battle of Stalingrad, 75th Anniv. — A4020

**Litho. & Embossed**
**2018, Feb. 2 *Perf. 11¾***
**7897** A4020 41r multi 2.50 2.00

Printed in sheets of 7 + label.

Kontinental Hockey League, 10th Anniv. — A4021

**2018, Feb. 15 Litho. *Perf. 11½***
**7898** A4021 22r multi 1.50 .80

**Heroes Type of 2016**

Designs: No. 7899, 22r, Anatoly V. Lebed (1963-2012). No. 7900, 22r, Alexander V. Krasikov (1958-2005).

**2018, Feb. 20 Litho. *Perf. 12½x12***
**Dated "2018"**
**7899-7900** A3881 Set of 2 2.50 1.50

Nos. 7899-7900 were each printed in sheets of 5.

Floating Bridge, Moscow — A4022

**2018, Feb. 21 Litho. *Perf. 11¾***
**7901** A4022 28r multi 1.75 1.00

Europa.

Great Arctic State Nature Reserve — A4023

**2018, Feb. 28 Litho. *Perf. 11¾***
**7902** A4023 30r multi 2.00 1.25

2019 Winter Universiade, Krasnoyarsk — A4024

No. 7903: a, Bobrovy Log Fun Park (22mm long blue panel). b, Platinum Arena, Krasnoyarsk Sports and Entertainment Complex (51mm long magenta panel). c, Ivan Yarygin Sports Palace (32mm long magenta panel). d, Biathlon Academy Multi-purpose Complex (46mm long blue panel)

**2018, Mar. 2 Litho. *Perf. 11¾***
**7903** A4024 40r Block of 4, #a-d 10.00 6.00

Souvenir Sheet

Liberation of Bulgaria and End of Russo-Turkish War, 140th Anniv. — A4025

No. 7904: a, Nikolai Grigoryevich Stoletov (1831-1912), Russian commander. b, Count Iosif Vladimirovich Gurko (1828-1901), Russian general. c, Eduard Ivanovich Totleben (1818-84), Russian general.

**Litho. & Embossed**

**2018, Mar. 20 *Perf. 12***
**7904** A4025 60r Sheet of 3, #a-c 12.00 8.00

See Bulgaria No. 4841.

Lilac Varieties — A4026

No. 7905: a, Nadezhda. b, Krasavitsa Moskvy. c, Gortenziya. d, Dzhambul.

***Serpentine Die Cut 11***

**2018, Mar. 21 Litho.**

**Self-Adhesive**

**7905** A4026 Block of 4 7.50 4.00
*a.-d.* 30r Any single 2.00 1.00

**Heroes Type of 2016**

Designs: 22r, Alexey B. Bukhanov (1965-2003). 27r, Dmitry E. Gorshkov (1971-99).

**2018 Litho. *Perf. 12½x12***
**7906-7907** A3881 Set of 2 3.00 2.00

Issued: 22r, 3/22; 27r, 5/4.

Souvenir Sheet

Portrait of Maxim Gorky, by Nikolai Bogdanov-Belsky — A4027

**2018, Mar. 28 Litho. *Perf. 12***
**7908** A4027 100r multi 6.50 4.50

Gorky (1868-1936), writer.

Military Commissariats, Cent. — A4028

**2018, Mar. 29 Litho. *Perf. 11¼***
**7909** A4028 25r multi 1.75 .90

A4029

Designs: Kurchatov Institute (National Nuclear Energy Research Center), 75th Anniv.

**2018, Apr. 12 Litho. *Perf. 12½x12***
**7910** A4029 30r multi 2.50 1.00

30th International Exhibition for Information and Communication Technology, Moscow — A4030

**2018, Apr. 24 Litho. *Perf. 11½***
**7911** A4030 40r multi 2.50 1.25

Karl Marx (1818-83), Political Theorist — A4031

**2018, May 4 Litho. *Perf. 12x11¼***
**7912** A4031 27r multi 1.75 .90

Inauguration of Pres. Vladimir Putin A4032

**2018, May 7 Litho. *Perf. 11½***
**7913** A4032 22r multi 1.40 .70

Battle of the Caucasus, 75th Anniv. — A4033

**Litho. & Embossed**

**2018, May 8 *Perf. 11¾***
**7914** A4033 41r multi 2.75 1.40

Printed in sheets of 7 + label.

2018 World Cup Soccer Championships, Russia — A4034

Soccer players and flags of countries in competition in Group: No. 7915, 40r, A (Russia, Saudia Arabia, Egypt, Uruguay). No. 7916, 40r, B (Portugal, Spain, Morocco, Iran). No. 7917, 40r, C (France, Australia, Peru, Denmark). No. 7918, 40r, D (Argentina, Iceland, Croatia, Nigeria). No. 7919, 40r, E (Brazil, Switzerland, Costa Rica, Serbia). No. 7920, 40r, F (Germany, Mexico, Sweden, South Korea). No. 7921, 40r, G (Belgium, Panama, Tunisia, England). No. 7922, 40r, H (Poland, Senegal, Colombia, Japan).

**2018, May 10 Litho. *Perf. 12½x12***
**7915-7922** A4034 Set of 8 20.00 14.00
*7922a* Souvenir sheet of 8, #7915-7922 20.00 14.00

Flowers — A4035

No. 7923: a, Chrysanthemums and cherry blossoms, red and white polka-dotted ribbon. b, Daisies and rhododendrons, white, red and blue striped ribbon.

**2018, May 16 Litho. *Perf. 12x12½***
**7923** A4035 27r Pair, #a-b 3.50 1.75

Printed in sheets of 14 containing 7 each Nos. 7923a- 7923b + label. See Japan Nos. 4204-4205.

Miniature Sheet

Beekeeping — A4036

No. 7924 — Apiarist: a, Putting hand in bee colony in tree. b, Applying smoke to bee colony in tree. c, Holding honey from box hives with slanted roofs. d, Holding frame above hive.

**2018, May 17 Litho. *Perf. 11¼***
**7924** A4036 40r Sheet of 4, #a-d, + label 10.00 7.00

Souvenir Sheet

Russian Police, 300th Anniv. — A4037

**2018, May 25 Litho. *Perf. 11¼***
**7925** A4037 95r multi 6.50 3.25

Souvenir Sheets

Novosibirsk Coat of Arms — A4038

Salekhard Coat of Arms — A4039

Ivanovo Coat of Arms — A4040

Grozny Coat of Arms — A4041

**2018 Litho. *Perf. 12x12½***
**7926** A4038 70r multi 4.50 2.25
**7927** A4039 70r multi 4.50 2.25
**7928** A4040 70r multi 4.50 2.25
**7929** A4041 70r multi 4.50 2.25
*Nos. 7926-7929 (4)* 18.00 9.00

Issued: Nos. 7926-7927, 5/29; Nos. 7928-7929, 6/20.

Souvenir Sheet

World Cup Trophy — A4042

**2018, June 14 Litho. *Perf. 11¼***
**7931** A4042 100r multi 6.50 3.25
*a.* As #7931, with Cyrillic overprint in sheet margin 6.50 3.25

Issued: No. 7931a, 8/7. Cyrillic overprint on No. 7931a gives July 15, 2018 date and France 4 - Croatia 2 results of World Cup final match.

**Kremlins Type of 2009**
***Serpentine Die Cut 11***
**2018, June 25 Litho.**
**Self-Adhesive**
**7932** A3471 46r Vologda Kremlin 2.75 1.50

Gardens by the Bay, Singapore — A4043

Covered Amphitheater, Zaryadye Park, Moscow — A4044

**2018, June 25 Litho. *Perf. 11¾***
**7933** Pair 5.00 2.50
*a.* A4043 40r multi 2.50 1.25
*b.* A4044 40r multi 2.50 1.25

Russia and Singapore Joint Issue.

See Singapore Nos. 1892-1893.

Russian Radio and Electronic Reconnaissance, Cent. — A4045

**2018, June 29 Litho. *Perf. 11¾***
**7934** A4045 32r multi 2.00 1.00

Victory in the War of 1812, by Z. K. Tsereteli, and Park Pobedy Metro Station — A4046

The Church of St. Tryphon, by S. V. Goryaev, and Maryina Roshcha Metro Station — A4047

24-Hour Soviet Sky, by A. A. Deineka, and Mayakovskaya Metro Station — A4048

Alexander Nevsky, by P. D. Korin, and Komsomolskaya Metro Station — A4049

**2018, June 29 Litho. *Perf. 12x11¼***
**7935** Vert. strip of 4 10.00 5.00
*a.* A4046 40r multi 2.50 1.25
*b.* A4047 40r multi 2.50 1.25
*c.* A4048 40r multi 2.50 1.25
*d.* A4049 40r multi 2.50 1.25

Mosaic art in Moscow Metro.

Kemerovo, Cent. A4050

**2018, July 6 Litho. *Perf. 12½x12***
**7936** A4050 27r multi 1.75 .90

Novokuznetsk, 400th Anniv. — A4051

**2018, July 7 Litho. *Perf. 12x12½***
**7937** A4051 27r multi 1.75 .90

Grigory Kisunko (1918-98), Developer of Soviet Missile Defense System A4052

**2018, July 10 Litho. *Perf. 12½x12***
**7938** A4052 22r multi 1.40 .70

Church on the Blood, Yekaterinburg A4053

**2018, July 17 Litho. *Perf. 12x12½***
**7939** A4053 27r multi 1.75 .90

Assumption Cathedral, Omsk — A4054

**2018, July 25 Litho. *Perf. 12x12½***
**7940** A4054 32r multi 2.00 1.00

Gold Saltcellar by Jewelry Firm of Ivan P. Khlebnikov A4055

Troika Sculpture by Jewelry Firm of Ignatii P. Sazikov A4056

Silver Drinking Bowl by Jewelry Firm of Carl Fabergé A4057

Basket by Jewelry Firm of Pavel A. Ovchinnikov A4058

**2018, July 26 Litho. *Perf. 11¼***
**7941** A4055 27r multi 1.75 .90
**7942** A4056 27r multi 1.75 .90
**7943** A4057 27r multi 1.75 .90
**7944** A4058 27r multi 1.75 .90
*Nos. 7941-7944 (4)* 7.00 3.60

Nos. 7941-7944 were each printed in sheets of 8 + label.

Souvenir Sheet

Ivan Turgenev (1818-83), Writer — A4059

**2018, Aug. 10 Litho. *Perf.***
**7945** A4059 90r multi 6.50 3.00

Federal Public Registration, Cadastre and Cartography Service — A4060

**2018, Aug. 20 Litho. *Perf. 12x11½***
**7946** A4060 27r multi 1.75 .80

Battle of Kursk, 75th Anniv. — A4061

**Litho. & Embossed**
**2018, Aug. 23 *Perf. 11¾***
**7947** A4061 41r multi 2.50 1.25

Printed in sheets of 7 + label.

Tver Carriage Works, 120th Anniv. A4062

**2018, Aug. 24 Litho. *Perf. 11½***
**7948** A4062 27r multi 1.50 .80

Diplomatic and Courier Communication, Cent. — A4063

**2018, Aug. 27 Litho. *Perf. 11½***
**7949** A4063 27r multi 1.60 .80

Miniature Sheet

Enameled Arts and Crafts — A4064

No. 7950: a, Vologda enamel piece (blue green background). b, Krasnoselskaya enamel piece (red background). c, Kubachi enamel pitcher and cup (blue background). d, Rostov enamel plate and cup (purple background).

**2018, Aug. 30 Litho. *Perf. 11½***
**7950** A4064 25r Sheet of 4, #a-d 6.50 3.00

New Wave International Contest for Young Popular Music Performers — A4065

**2018, Aug. 31 Litho. *Perf. 11¾***
**7951** A4065 22r multi 1.40 .60

Souvenir Sheet

Goznak Factory — A4066

**Litho. & Engr.**
**2018, Sept. 4 *Perf. 11¾***
**7952** A4066 200r multi 12.00 6.00

Goznak, state security printer and producer of stamps, coins and banknotes, 200th anniv.

Tutayev Motor Plant, 50th Anniv. A4067

**2018, Sept. 5 Litho. *Perf. 11½***
**7953** A4067 27r multi 1.75 .80

Abram F. Ioffe (1880-196), Physicist, and A. F. Ioffe Physical Technical Institute, St. Petersburg — A4068

**2018, Sept. 5 Litho. *Perf. 12x12¼***
**7954** A4068 32r multi 2.00 1.00

A. F. Ioffe Physical-Technical Institute, Cent.

**Heroes Type of 2016**

Design: 27r, Oleg N. Dolgov (1976-96).

**2018, Sept. 6 Litho. *Perf. 12½x12***
**Dated "2018"**
**7955** A3881 27r multi 1.50 .80

Printed in sheets of 5 + label.

Modern Art — A4069

Designs: No. 7956, 37r, In the Fields, painting by N. N. Plastov, 2003. No. 7957, 37r, The Painter M. V. Nesterov, sculpture by A. A. Mironov, 2008, vert. No. 7958, 37r, Monument to Soldiers Who Died in Local Wars and Military Conflicts, sculpture by G. Z. Dolmogombetov, 2007 (33x65mm). No. 7959, 37r, Office Clock with Calendar, by P. N. Radimov, 2005, (33x65mm).

***Perf. 12x11½ (#7956), 11½x12 (#7957), 11¾***
**2018, Sept. 20 Litho.**
**7956-7959** A4069 Set of 4 9.50 4.50

Souvenir Sheet

Moscow Oblast Coat of Arms — A4070

**Litho. & Embossed**
**2018, Oct. 4 *Perf. 12***
**7960** A4070 120r multi 7.50 4.00

Mosque and Skyscrapers, Grozny — A4071

**2018, Oct. 5 Litho. *Perf. 12x11½***
**7961** A4071 46r multi 2.75 1.40

Grozny, 200th anniv.

NTV Broadcasting Company Emblem A4072

***Serpentine Die Cut 11¼***
**2018, Oct. 10 Litho.**
**Self-Adhesive**
**7962** A4072 32r multi 2.00 1.00

Komsomol (All-Union Leninist Young Communist League), Cent. — A4073

**Litho. & Embossed**
**2018, Oct. 25 *Perf. 11¾***
**7963** A4073 46r multi 2.75 1.40

Main Directorate of the General Staff of the Armed Forces, Cent. A4074

**2018, Nov. 5 Litho. *Perf. 11½***
**7964** A4074 27r multi 1.50 .75

Opening of Crimean Bridge — A4075

**2018, Nov. 6 Litho. *Perf. 12¼x12***
**7965** A4075 46r multi + 2 flanking labels 2.75 1.40

Central Research Institute of Communications, Cent. — A4076

**2018, Nov. 9 Litho. *Perf. 12¼x12***
**7966** A4076 27r multi 1.25 .60

State Secret Services of the Armed Forces, Cent. A4077

**2018, Nov. 13 Litho. *Perf. 11½***
**7967** A4077 27r multi 1.25 .60

General V. F. Margelov Higher Airborne Command School, Ryazan, Cent. A4078

**2018, Nov. 13 Litho. *Perf. 11½***
**7968** A4078 27r multi 1.25 .60

Federal Service for the Supervision of Communications, Information Technology and Mass Media — A4079

**2018, Nov. 15 Litho. *Perf. 12x11½***
**7969** A4079 27r multi 1.25 .60

Battle of the Dnieper, 75th Anniv. — A4080

**Litho. & Embossed**
**2018, Nov. 15 *Perf. 11¾***
**7970** A4080 41r multi 2.00 1.00

No. 7970 was printed in sheets of 7 + label.

Ordzhonikidze Higher Military Command School, Cent. — A4081

**2018, Nov. 16 Litho. *Perf. 12x12¼***
**7971** A4081 32r multi 1.50 .75

Souvenir Sheet

Khabarovsk Coat of Arms — A4082

**2018, Nov. 22 Litho. *Perf. 12x12¼***
**7972** A4082 70r gold & multi 3.00 1.50

Combined Arms Academy of the Armed Forces — A4083

**2018, Nov. 27 Litho. *Perf. 12x11¼***
**7973** A4083 27r multi 1.25 .60

Nikolai E. Zhukovsky Central Aerohydrodynamic Institute, Cent. — A4084

**2018, Nov. 30 Litho. *Perf. 11¾***
**7974** A4084 32r multi 1.50 .75

### Lawyers Type of 2012

Designs: No. 7975, 27r, Dmitry N. Zamyatnin (1805-81). No. 7976, 27r, Olympiad S. Ioffe (1920-2005). No. 7977, 27r, Yury P. Novitsky (1882-1922).

**2018, Dec. 4 Litho. *Perf. 11¼***
**7975-7977** A3635 Set of 3 3.75 2.00

Nos. 7975 were each printed in sheets of 8 + label.

New Year 2019 A4085

***Serpentine Die Cut 11¼***
**2018, Dec. 4 Litho.**
**Self-Adhesive**
**7978** A4085 22r multi 1.25 .60

Prince Mikhail of Tver (1271-1318) — A4086

**2018, Dec. 5 Litho. *Perf. 11¾***
**7979** A4086 32r multi 1.50 .75

Financial and Economic Service of the Armed Services, Cent. A4087

**2018, Dec. 7 Litho. *Perf. 11¼***
**7980** A4087 27r multi 1.25 .60

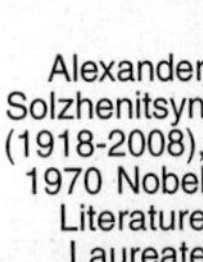

Alexander Solzhenitsyn (1918-2008), 1970 Nobel Literature Laureate A4088

**2018, Dec. 11 Litho. *Perf. 11¾***
**7981** A4088 27r multi 1.25 .60

Miniature Sheet

Constitution, 25th Anniv. — A4089

No. 7982: a, Constitution. b, Russian Federation Council Building with fence in front, Federal Assembly (Duma) Building. c, Government Building of the Russian Federation (Russian White House) with one flag. d, Court buildings.

**2018, Dec. 12 Litho. *Perf. 12¼x12***
**7982** A4089 40r Sheet of 4, #a-d 8.00 5.00

Dmitrov Kremlin Museum-Reserve, Cent. — A4090

**2018, Dec. 13 Litho. *Perf. 11¾***
**7983** A4090 40r multi 2.00 1.25

Federal Service for Alcohol Market Regulation — A4091

**2018, Dec. 14 Litho. *Perf. 12x11¼***
**7984** A4091 32r multi 1.50 .75

### Heroes Type of 2016

Designs: No. 7985, 27r, Sergey S. Gromov (1966-95). No. 7986, 27r, German A. Ugryumov (1948-2001).

**2018, Dec. 17 Litho. *Perf. 12¼x12***
**Dated "2018"**
**7985-7986** A3881 Set of 2 2.75 1.60

Nos. 7985-7986 were each printed in sheets of 5 + label.

Spies A4092

Designs: No. 7987, 27r, Vasily M. Chebotaryov (1918-44). No. 7988, 27r, Mikhail P. Krygin (1918-45).

**2018, Dec. 17 Litho. *Perf. 11¼***
**7987-7988** A4092 Set of 2 2.75 1.60

Nos. 7987-7988 were each printed in sheets of 8 + label.

St.George Cross A4093

Award for Kindness A4094

Award for Mentoring A4095

Award for 30 Years of Irreproachable Service — A4096

Award for 50 Years of Irreproachable Service — A4097

**Litho. & Embossed**
**2018, Dec. 20 *Perf. 11¾x12***

| | | | | |
|---|---|---|---|---|
| **7989** | A4093 51r multi | | 2.50 | 1.00 |
| **7990** | A4094 51r multi | | 2.50 | 1.00 |
| **7991** | A4095 51r multi | | 2.50 | 1.00 |
| **7992** | A4096 51r multi | | 2.50 | 1.00 |
| **7993** | A4097 51r multi | | 2.50 | 1.00 |
| | *Nos. 7989-7993 (5)* | | 12.50 | 5.00 |

Nos. 7989-7993 were each printed in sheets of 8 + central label.

Cathedral of the Nativity of Christ, Omsk — A4098

**2019, Jan. 9 Litho. *Perf. 12x12¼***
**7994** A4098 37r multi 2.00 1.00

### Recipients of the Order of St. Andrew Type of 2011

Design: Order of St. Andrew and Daniil A. Granin (1919-2017), writer.

**2019, Jan. 11 Litho. *Perf. 12x11¼***
**7995** A3560 40r multi 2.00 1.00

No. 7995 was printed in sheets of 11 + label.

Siberian Crane and Chick — A4099

**2019, Jan. 22 Litho. *Perf. 12x11¼***
**7996** A4099 45r multi 2.00 1.00

Europa.

End of the Siege of Leningrad, 75th Anniv. — A4100

**Litho. & Embossed**
**2019, Jan. 25 *Perf. 11¾***
**7997** A4100 46r multi 2.00 1.00

No. 7997 was printed in sheets of 7 + label.

Venues for ther 2019 Winter Universiade, Krasnoyarsk — A4101

No. 7998: a, Sopka Sports Complex with parked cars at left (blue panel at LR). b, Crystal Arena Ice Palace with blue, red and yellow roof tiles (magenta panel at LR). c, Yenisei Stadium with red brown curved entrance arch (magenta panel at LR). d, Congress Hall of 2019 Winter Universiade (blue panel at LR).

**2019, Feb. 1 Litho. *Perf. 11¾***
**7998** A4101 45r Block of 4, #a-d 8.00 4.00

Uniforms of Courier Service A4102

Designs: No. 7999, 22r, Officer and courier of the Courier Corps, 1797. No. 8000, 22r, Officer and senior courier of the Courier Corps, 1862. No. 8001, 22r, Head of feldpost & felgeger by Special Commissions, 1924. No. 8002, 22r, Officer of Field Communications and Deputy Director of SFS of Russia, 2011.

**2019, Feb. 12 Litho. *Perf. 11¾***
**7999-8002** A4102 Set of 4 4.00 2.00
*8002a* Souvenir sheet of 8, 2 each #7999-8002 8.00 4.00

**Heroes Type of 2016**

Designs: No. 8003, 27r, Roman A. Kitanin (1978-2007). No. 8004, 27r, Oleg V. Tereshkin (1971-95).

**2019, Feb. 22 Litho. *Perf. 12¼x12***
**Dated "2019"**
**8003-8004** A3881 Set of 2 2.50 1.25

Nos. 8003-8004 were each printed in sheets of 5 + label.

Dogs — A4103

No. 8005: a, Yorkshire terriers with bows. b, Shorthaired Petit Brabançons. c. Pugs playing with ball. d, Russian toy terriers in snow.

**2019, Feb. 28 Litho. *Perf. 11¾***
**8005** A4103 35r Block or vert. strip of 4, #a-d 6.50 3.25

Souvenir Sheet

2019 Winter Universiade, Krasnoyarsk — A4104

**2019, Mar. 2 Litho. *Perf. 12x12¼***
**8006** A4104 100r multi 4.50 2.25

No. 8006 with a serial number and an inscription in the sheet margin giving the medal count of the Russian team was produced in limited quantities and issued on Apr. 16, 2019. Value, $30.

Secret Intelligence Officers A4105

Designs: No. 8007, 27r, Africa de las Heras (1909-88). No. 8008, 27r, Zoya Ivanovna Voskresenskaya-Rybkina (1907-92).

**2019, Mar. 12 Litho. *Perf. 11½***
**8007-8008** A4105 Set of 2 2.50 1.25

Nos. 8007-8008 were each printed in sheets of 8 + central label.

---

Examples of No. 7128 with an 80r surcharge and an added Cyrillic inscription in the sheet margin commemorating 2019 as the International Year of the Periodic Table were produced in limited quantities and issued on Mar. 16, 2019.

---

Apple Varieties — A4106

No. 8009: a, Bogatyr. b, Belyi Naliv. c, Antonovka Obyknovennaya. d, Orlik.

***Serpentine Die Cut 11¼***
**2019, Mar. 26 Litho.**
**Self-Adhesive**
**8009** A4106 Block of 4 9.00 4.50
*a.-d.* 45r Any single 2.00 1.00

Souvenir Sheets

Tyumen Coat of Arms — A4107

Ufa Coat of Arms — A4108

**2019, Mar. 28 Litho. *Perf. 12x12¼***
**8010** A4107 70r multi 3.25 1.60
**8011** A4108 80r multi 3.50 1.75

Alexey I. Fatyanov (1919-59), Song Writer A4109

**2019, Mar. 29 Litho. *Perf. 11¼x12***
**8012** A4109 29r multi 1.50 .75

Internet Country Code Top Level Domain ".ru," 25th Anniv. A4110

**2019, Apr. 5 Litho. *Perf. 11½***
**8013** A4110 32r multi 1.25 .60

Marcial Waters Resort Spa, 300th Anniv. — A4111

**2019, Apr. 5 Litho. *Perf. 11¾***
**8014** A4111 50r multi 2.00 1.00

Crimean Offensive, 75th Anniv. — A4112

**Litho. & Embossed**
**2019, Apr. 18 *Perf. 11¾***
**8015** A4112 46r multi 2.00 1.00

No. 8015 was printed in sheets of 7 + label.

Federal Communications Agency — A4113

**2019, Apr. 24 Litho. *Perf. 12x11½***
**8016** A4113 32r multi 1.50 .75

Medal of Ushakov A4114

Order of Merit for the Fatherland A4115

Medal for Bravery A4116

Medal of Suvarov A4117

**Litho. & Embossed**
**2019, Apr. 26 *Perf. 12***
**8017** A4114 50r multi 2.50 1.25
**8018** A4115 50r multi 2.50 1.25
**8019** A4116 50r multi 2.50 1.25
**8020** A4117 50r multi 2.50 1.25
*Nos. 8017-8020 (4)* 10.00 5.00

Nos. 8017-8020 were each printed in sheets of 8 + central label.

Boris Rosing (1869-1933), Inventor of Early Television Components — A4118

**2019, May 6 Litho. *Perf. 12½x12***
**8021** A4118 32r multi 1.25 .60

No. 8021 was printed in sheets of 10 + central label.

Mustai Karim (1919-2005), Poet — A4119

**2019, May 15 Litho. *Perf. 11¾***
**8022** A4119 35r multi 1.25 .60

No. 8022 was printed in sheets of 8 + central label.

Cup, Bowl and Owl Vessel From Alexandrovskaya Sloboda Museum — A4120

**2019, May 18 Litho. *Perf. 11½x12***
**8023** A4120 32r multi 1.50 .75

Alexandrovskaya Sloboda Museum, Alexandrov, cent.

Souvenir Sheet

Overgrown Pond, by Vasily D. Polenov (1844-1927) — A4121

**2019, May 29 Litho. *Perf. 12***
**8024** A4121 100r gold & multi 5.00 2.50

Souvenir Sheet

The Ceremonial Meeting of the State Council on May 7, 1901, by Ilya E. Repin (1844-1930) — A4122

**2019, May 29 Litho. *Perf. 11¾***
**8025** A4122 100r gold & multi 5.00 2.50

Arkhangelsk State Museum, Cent. — A4123

**2019, May 30 Litho. *Perf. 11¾***
**8026** A4123 35r multi 1.50 .75

Yeniseysk, 400th Anniv. — A4124

**2019, June 7 Litho. *Perf. 11¾***
**8027** A4124 40r multi 1.25 .65

Emblem of Russian Postal Service — A4125

***Serpentine Die Cut 11½ Syncopated***
**2019, June 11 Litho.**
**Self-Adhesive**
**Frame Color**

**8028** A4125 23r blue 1.25 .60
*a.* Dated "2020" .70 .35

Issued: No. 8028a, 5/26/20. See Nos. 8052-8053, 8146, 8249-8250.

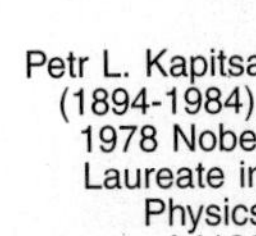

Petr L. Kapitsa (1894-1984), 1978 Nobel Laureate in Physics A4126

**2019, June 14 Litho. *Perf. 11¾***
**8029** A4126 32r multi 1.25 .60

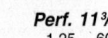

Central Armed Forces Museum, Moscow, Cent. — A4127

**2019, June 18 Litho. *Perf. 12x11¼***
**8030** A4127 40r multi 1.25 .65

A-50 Radar Detection Airplane and Building of Vega Radio Engineering Company A4128

**2019, June 20 Litho. *Perf. 11½***
**8031** A4128 50r multi 1.60 .80

Birdhouse, Sculpture by Matvey G. Manizer, and Revolution Square Metro Station — A4129

Sympathy, Sculpture by Vladimir Tsigal, and Mendeleevskaya Metro Station — A4130

Defenders of the Fatherland, Sculpture by Georgii I. Motovilov, and Smolenskaya Metro Station — A4131

Young Family, Sculpture by S. A. Goryainov, and Polyanka Metro Station — A4132

**2019, Mar. 26 Litho. *Perf. 12x11¼***
**8032** Vert. strip of 4 8.00 4.00
*a.* A4129 45r multi 2.00 1.00
*b.* A4130 45r multi 2.00 1.00
*c.* A4131 45r multi 2.00 1.00
*d.* A4132 45r multi 2.00 1.00

Sculptures in the Moscow Metro.

Bird With Woman's Head and "I Love Russia" Inscription A4133

***Serpentine Die Cut 11¼***
**2019, June 27 Litho.**
**Self-Adhesive**

**8033** A4133 18r multi .60 .30

International Day of Parliamentarism — A4134

**2019, June 27 Litho. *Perf. 11½***
**8034** A4134 53r multi 1.75 .85

Bellflower Varieties — A4135

No. 8035: a, Campaenula bononiensis. b, Campanula persicifolia. c, Campanula ciliata. d, Campanula pendula.

***Serpentine Die Cut 11***
**2019, June 28 Litho.**
**Self-Adhesive**

**8035** A4135 Block of 4 8.00 4.00
*a.-d.* 45r Any single 2.00 1.00

Operation Bagration (Belarussian Strategic Offensive Operation), 75th Anniv. — A4136

**Litho. & Embossed**
**2019, July 3 *Perf. 11¾***
**8036** A4136 50r multi 1.60 .80

No. 8036 was printed in sheets of 7 + label. See Belarus No. 1145.

Ammeter, Measuring Tape, Stopwatch and Platinum-Iridium Cylinder Under Glass Cap — A4137

**2019, July 9 Litho. *Perf. 11½***
**8037** A4137 53r multi 1.75 .85

International System of Units.

Grape Harvesting — A4138

No. 8038 — Woman with basket of: a, Russian floral (green) grapes. b, Bulgarian Ruby Kaliskin (purple) grapes.

**2019, July 15 Litho. *Perf. 12¼x12***
**8038** A4138 45r Horiz. pair, #a-b 4.00 2.00

See Bulgaria No. 4907.

Souvenir Sheet

Ships of the Discovery of Antarctica — A4139

No. 8039: a, Mirny (denominaation at LR). b, Vostok (denomination at LL).

**2019, July 16 Litho. *Perf. 12¼x12***
**8039** A4139 50r Sheet of 2, #a-b 3.25 1.60

Discovery of Antarctica, 200th anniv. ( in 2020).

Miniature Sheet

Endangered Animals — A4140

No. 8040: a, Cuon alpinus. b, Monodon monoceros. c, Vulpes lagopus semenovi. d, Lagenorhynchus albirostris.

**2019, July 23 Litho. *Perf. 11½x11¼***
**8040** A4140 50r Sheet of 4, #a-d 6.25 3.25

Souvenir Sheet

Fifth Army International Games — A4141

No. 8041: a, Tank biathlon. b, Aviadarts.

**2019, July 26 Litho. *Perf. 11¼***
**8041** A4141 45r Sheet of 2, #a-b, + central label 3.00 1.50

Souvenir Sheet

Exhibition of Achievements of National Economy, Moscow, 80th Anniv. — A4142

No. 8042: a, Space Pavilion and rocket. b, Friendship of Nations Fountain. c, Northern Entrance Gate.

**2019, July 31 Litho. *Perf. 11¼***
**8042** A4142 50r Sheet of 3, #a-c, + label 4.75 2.40

**Emblem of Russian Postal Service Type of 2019 and**

A4143 A4144

Emblem of Russian Postal Service

A4145 A4146

***Serpentine Die Cut 11½ Syncopated***
**2019, Aug. 7 Litho.**

**Self-Adhesive**
**Frame Color**

| | | | | | |
|---|---|---|---|---|---|
| **8043** | A4143 | 50k | blue | .25 | .25 |
| **8044** | A4143 | 1r | brown | .25 | .25 |
| **8045** | A4143 | 2r | brn carmine | .25 | .25 |
| **8046** | A4143 | 2.50r | gray green | .25 | .25 |
| **8047** | A4143 | 3r | blue grn | .25 | .25 |
| **8048** | A4143 | 4r | carmine | .25 | .25 |
| **8049** | A4144 | 5r | blue | .25 | .25 |
| **8050** | A4144 | 6r | violet | .25 | .25 |
| **8051** | A4145 | 10r | violet brown | .30 | .25 |
| **8052** | A4125 | 25r | purple | .75 | .35 |

**Size: 26x35mm**

| | | | | | |
|---|---|---|---|---|---|
| **8053** | A4125 | 50r | gray green | 1.50 | .75 |
| **8054** | A4146 | 100r | lt blue | 3.00 | 1.50 |
| | *Nos. 8043-8054 (12)* | | | 7.55 | 4.85 |

See Nos. 8145, 8147, 8251.

Eurasian Economic Union, 5th Anniv. A4147

**2019, Aug. 9 Litho. *Perf. 11½***
**8055** A4147 50r gold & multi 1.50 .75

Vyborg-Petrozavodsk Offensive, 75th Anniv. — A4148

**Litho. & Embossed**
**2019, Aug. 9 *Perf. 11¾***
**8056** A4148 50r multi 1.50 .75

No. 8056 was printed in sheets of 7 + label. A booklet containing panes of 1 of Nos. 7997, 8015, 8036 and 8056 and panes of 1 of imperforate gold stamps similar to those stamps was produced in limited quantities.

Tolbukhin Lighthouse — A4149

**2019, Aug. 13 Litho. *Perf. 12½x12***
**8057** A4149 32r multi .95 .50

Spasskaya Tower International Military Music Festival — A4150

***Perf. 11¾x11¼***
**2019, Aug. 22 Litho.**
**8058** A4150 53r multi 1.60 .80

2019 World Skills Championships, Kazan — A4151

***Serpentine Die Cut 11¼***
**2019, Aug. 22 Litho.**
**8059** A4151 53r brt yel green 1.60 .80

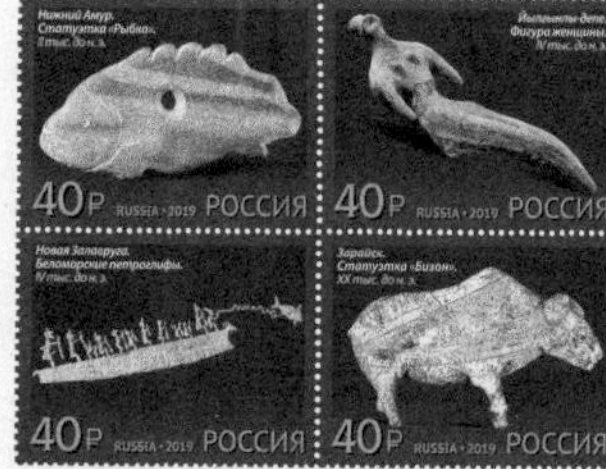


Academic Archaelogy in Russia, Cent. — A4152

No. 8060: a, Carved fish figurine. b, Figure of a woman. c, White Sea petroglyphs. d, Bison.

***Perf. 11¾x11¼***
**2019, Aug. 26 Litho.**
**8060** A4152 40r Block or vert. strip of 4, #a-d 4.75 2.40

Motorcycles — A4153

Designs: No. 8061, 32r, 1934 PMZ A-750. No. 8062, 32r, 1938 IZh-8. No. 8063, 32r, 2009 Ural-Sakhara.

**2019, Aug. 29 Litho. *Perf. 12½x12***
**8061-8063** A4153 Set of 3 3.00 1.50
*8063a* Sheet of 12, 4 each #8061-8063, + 3 labels 12.00 6.00

Nos. 8061-8063 were each printed in sheets of 8 + central label.

Breastplate with Portrait of Tsar Peter I — A4154

Diadem A4155

Port Bouquet A4156

Rattle-Whistle — A4157

**2019, Sept. 3 Litho. *Perf. 11½***

| | | | | | |
|---|---|---|---|---|---|
| **8064** | A4154 | 40r | multi | 1.25 | .60 |
| **8065** | A4155 | 40r | multi | 1.25 | .60 |
| **8066** | A4156 | 40r | multi | 1.25 | .60 |
| **8067** | A4157 | 40r | multi | 1.25 | .60 |
| | *Nos. 8064-8067 (4)* | | | 5.00 | 2.40 |

A booklet containing panes of 1 of lithographed and embossed stamps similar to Nos. 8064-8067 was printed in limited quantities.

Oleg P. Tabakov (1935-2018), Artistic Director of the Moscow Art Theater — A4158

**2019, Sept. 4 Litho. *Perf. 12½x12***
**8068** A4158 40r multi 1.25 .60

No. 8068 was printed in sheets of 14 + label.

Mohandas K. Gandhi (1869-1948), Indian Nationalist Leader — A4159

**2019, Sept. 4 Litho. *Perf. 12x12½***
**8069** A4159 40r multi 1.25 .60

**No. 7731 Surcharged in Gold**

**Method and Perf. As Before**
**2019, Sept. 5**
**8070** A3895 45r on 24r #7731 (G) *1.40 .70*

Kazan Kremlin, Site of 2019 Aga Khan Architecture Award Ceremony — A4160

**2019, Sept. 12 Litho. *Perf. 12½x12***
**8071** A4160 53r multi 1.60 .80

Political Organizations in the Armed Forces, Cent. — A4161

**2019, Sept. 16 Litho. *Perf. 12½x12***
**8072** A4161 40r multi 1.25 .60

General S. M. Shtemenko Higher Military School, Krasnodar — A4162

**2019, Sept. 17 Litho. *Perf. 12¼x12***
**8073** A4162 40r multi 1.25 .60

Souvenir Sheet

Mikhail T. Kalashnikov (1919-2013), Firearms Designer — A4163

**2019, Sept. 18 Litho. *Perf. 12¼x12***
**8074** A4163 100r multi 3.25 1.60

Moscow Kremlin, Sunny, by Evgeny V. Romashko — A4164

Chameleon Rock at Sunset, by Elena S. Brazhunenko — A4165

Lyalyh, by V. O. Umarsultanov A4166

Statue of Alexander S. Pushkin, Nur-Sultan, Kazakhstan, by Andrey N. Kovalchuk A4167

В.А. ГЛУХОВ Я люблю свою лошадку. 2017 г.

I Love My Horse, by V. A. Glukhov — A4168

**2019, Sept. 20 Litho. *Perf. 12x11¾***

| | | | | |
|---|---|---|---|---|
| **8075** | A4164 50r multi | | 1.60 | .80 |
| **8076** | A4165 50r multi | | 1.60 | .80 |

***Perf. 11¾x12***

| | | | | |
|---|---|---|---|---|
| **8077** | A4166 50r multi | | 1.60 | .80 |
| **8078** | A4167 50r multi | | 1.60 | .80 |

***Perf. 11¼***

| | | | | |
|---|---|---|---|---|
| **8079** | A4168 50r multi | | 1.60 | .80 |
| | *Nos. 8075-8079 (5)* | | 8.00 | 4.00 |

23rd Congress of the International Organization of Supreme Audit Institutions, Moscow — A4169

**2019, Sept. 23 Litho. *Perf. 12x12¼***

**8080** A4169 40r multi 1.25 .60

Souvenir Sheet

Evgraf F. Komarovsky (1769-1843), Military Leader and Memoir Writer — A4170

**2019, Sept. 25 Litho. *Perf.***

**8081** A4170 100r multi 3.25 1.60

M. V. Frunze Higher Combined Arms School, Omsk — A4171

**2019, Oct. 1 Litho. *Perf. 12¼x12***

**8082** A4171 35r multi 1.10 .55

World Post Day, 50th Anniv. — A4172

***Serpentine Die Cut 11***

**2019, Oct. 9 Litho.**

**Self-Adhesive**

**8083** A4172 23r multi .75 .35

**With Blue Frame**

**8084** A4172 50r multi 1.60 .80

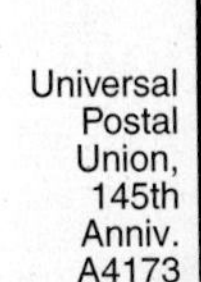

Universal Postal Union, 145th Anniv. A4173

**2019, Oct. 9 Litho. *Perf. 12½x12***

**8085** A4173 45r multi 1.40 .70

Souvenir Sheet

Women, by Filipp A. Malyavin (1869-1940) — A4174

**2019, Oct. 10 Litho. *Perf. 12***

**8086** A4174 110r multi 3.50 1.75

Moscow Expocenter, 60th Anniv. — A4175

**2019, Oct. 17 Litho. *Perf. 12½x12***

**8087** A4175 32r multi 1.00 .50

Communications Troops, Cent. — A4176

**2019, Oct. 18 Litho. *Perf. 11½***

**8088** A4176 50r multi 1.60 .80

St. Andrew's Hall, Grand Kremlin Palace, Moscow — A4177

**2019, Oct. 21 Litho. *Perf. 12x11½***

**8089** A4177 53r multi 1.75 .85

Masha A4178

Bear A4179

Masha and the Bear A4180

***Serpentine Die Cut 11***

**2019, Oct. 22 Litho.**

**Self-Adhesive**

| | | | | |
|---|---|---|---|---|
| **8090** | Horiz. strip of 3 | | 3.25 | |
| *a.* | A4178 23r multi | | .75 | .35 |
| *b.* | A4179 23r multi | | .75 | .35 |
| *c.* | A4180 50r multi | | 1.60 | .80 |

*Masha and the Bear* cartoon series, 10th anniv.

Miniature Sheet

Airplanes Designed by Sergey V. Ilyushin (1894-1977) — A4181

No. 8091: a, Il-2. b, Il-28. c, Il-14. d, Il-18. e, Il-62.

**2019, Oct. 23 Litho. *Perf. 12¼x12***

**8091** A4181 50r Sheet of 5, #a-e, + label 8.00 4.00

Souvenir Sheet

Russian State Circuses, Cent. — A4182

**2019, Oct. 30 Litho. *Perf.***

**8092** A4182 100r multi 3.25 1.60

Military University of the Ministry of Defense of the Russian Federation, Moscow, Cent. — A4183

**2019, Nov. 5 Litho. *Perf. 12¼x12***

**8093** A4183 40r multi 1.25 .60

Marshal S. M. Budyonny Military Academy of the Signal Corps, Cent. — A4184

**2019, Nov. 8 Litho. *Perf. 12¼x12***

**8094** A4184 43r multi 1.40 .70

### Heroes Type of 2016

Designs: No. 8095, 27r, Alexander A. Prokhorenko (1990-2016). No. 8096, 27r, Leonid G. Valov (1947-95). No. 8097, 27r, Mikhail A. Myasnikov (1975-2008).

**2019, Nov. 8 Litho.** ***Perf. 12½x12***
**Dated "2019"**

**8095-8097** A3881 Set of 3 2.50 1.25

Nos. 8095-8097 were each printed in sheets of 5 + label.

Ivan D. Papanin (1894-1986), Polar Explorer — A4185

**2019, Nov. 14 Litho.** ***Perf. 12¼x12***
**8098** A4185 53r multi 1.75 .85

Ministry of Transport Building — A4186

**2019, Nov. 20 Litho.** ***Perf. 12x11½***
**8099** A4186 40r multi 1.25 .60

Souvenir Sheet

St. Petersburg — A4187

No. 8100: a, Lakhta Center. b, Gazprom Arena, horiz.

**2019, Nov. 22 Litho.** ***Perf. 11¾***
**8100** A4187 60r Sheet of 2, #a-b 3.75 1.90

Souvenir Sheet

In the House, by Sergei Vinogradov (1869-1938) — A4188

**2019, Nov. 29 Litho.** ***Perf. 12***
**8101** A4188 150r multi 4.75 2.40

Mining and Industrial Supervision, 300th Anniv. A4189

**2019, Dec. 2 Litho.** ***Perf. 11½***
**8102** A4189 50r multi 1.60 .80

New Year 2020 A4190

***Serpentine Die Cut 11***
**2019, Dec. 5 Litho.**
**Self-Adhesive**

**8103** A4190 23r multi .75 .35

Foreign Intelligence Service Building — A4191

**2019, Dec. 6 Litho.** ***Perf. 12x11½***
**8104** A4191 40r multi 1.40 .70

A4192

A4193

A4194

Kholmogorsk Bone Carvings — A4195

**Litho. & Embossed**
**2019, Dec. 10** ***Perf. 12¼x12***

**8105** A4192 56r multi 1.90 .95
**8106** A4193 56r multi 1.90 .95
**8107** A4194 56r multi 1.90 .95
**8108** A4195 56r multi 1.90 .95
*Nos. 8105-8108 (4)* 7.60 3.80

Kholmogory Post Road From Arkhangelsk to Moscow A4196

**2020, Jan. 15 Litho.** ***Perf. 11¾***
**8110** A4196 53r multi 1.75 .85

Europa.

Berries — A4197

No. 8111: a, Rubus idaeus. b, Ribes nigrum. c, Lonicera caerulea. d, Fragaria ananassa.

***Serpentine Die Cut 11***
**2020, Jan. 17 Litho.**
**Self-Adhesive**

**8111** A4197 50r Block of 4, #a-d 6.25 3.25

Souvenir Sheet

Tula Kremlin, 500th Anniv. — A4198

**2020, Jan. 21 Litho.** ***Perf. 12x12½***
**8112** A4198 120r multi 3.75 1.90

Souvenir Sheet

Ruskeala Mountain Park, Karelia, Cent. — A4199

**2020, Jan. 23 Litho.** ***Perf. 12***
**8113** A4199 100r multi 3.25 1.60

Souvenir Sheet

Discovery of Antarctica, 200th Anniv. — A4200

No. 8114: a, Fabian von Bellingshausen (1778-1852), explorer. b, Mikhail P. Lazarev (1788-1851), explorer.

**2020, Jan. 28 Litho.** ***Perf. 12x12½***
**8114** A4200 50r Sheet of 2, #a-b 3.25 1.60

Joint issue between Russia and Estonia. See Estonia No. 914.

Vistula-Oder Offensive, 75th Anniv. — A4201

**Litho. & Embossed**
**2020, Jan. 30** ***Perf. 11¾***
**8115** A4201 60r multi 1.90 .95

No. 8115 was printed in sheets of 7 + label.

Souvenir Sheet

Midday, by Arkady A. Plastov (1893-1972) — A4202

**2020, Jan. 31 Litho.** ***Perf. 12x11¾***
**8116** A4202 150r multi 4.75 2.40

Jewel Encrusted Bow A4203

Jewel Encrusted Flower Bouquet A4204

Bracelet With Portrait A4205

Spinel of Grand Imperial Crown A4206

**2020, Feb. 3 Litho. *Perf. 11¼***

| | | | | |
|---|---|---|---|---|
| **8117** | A4203 | 50r multi | 1.60 | .80 |
| **8118** | A4204 | 50r multi | 1.60 | .80 |
| **8119** | A4205 | 50r multi | 1.60 | .80 |
| **8120** | A4206 | 50r multi | 1.60 | .80 |
| | *Nos. 8117-8120 (4)* | | 6.40 | 3.20 |

Ivan A. Bunin (1870-1953), 1933 Nobel Laureate in Literature A4207

**2020, Feb. 7 Litho. *Perf. 11¾***

**8121** A4207 50r multi 1.50 .75

Sculpture of Winston Churchill, Franklin D. Roosevelt and Joseph Stalin at Yalta Conference, by Zurab Tsereteli — A4208

**2020, Feb. 10 Litho. *Perf. 11***

**8122** A4208 50r multi 1.50 .75

Yalta Conference, 75th Anniv.

Pushkin Medal A4209

Zhukov Medal A4210

Nesterov Medal A4211

Defender of Free Russia Medal A4212

**Litho. & Embossed**

**2020, Feb. 12 *Perf. 11½x12***

| | | | | |
|---|---|---|---|---|
| **8123** | A4209 | 60r multi | 1.90 | .95 |
| **8124** | A4210 | 60r multi | 1.90 | .95 |
| **8125** | A4211 | 60r multi | 1.90 | .95 |
| **8126** | A4212 | 60r multi | 1.90 | .95 |
| | *Nos. 8123-8126 (4)* | | 7.60 | 3.80 |

Uniforms of Investigative Agency Officers A4213

Uniforms of: No. 8127, 40r, Assessor and chairman of investigative office, 1713. No. 8128, 40r, Special case and district court investigators, 1898. No. 8129, 40r, Special case and prosecutorial investigators, 1954. No. 8130, 40r, Prosecutorial investigator and Investigative Committee head, 2011.

**2020, Feb. 21 Litho. *Perf. 11¾***

| | | | | |
|---|---|---|---|---|
| **8127-8130** | A4213 | Set of 4 | 5.00 | 2.50 |
| *8130a* | | Souvenir sheet of 8, 2 each #8127-8130 | 10.00 | 5.00 |

Sergey M. Solovyov (1820-79), Historian — A4214

Ivan E. Zabelin (1820-1908), Historian — A4215

**2020, Feb. 27 Litho. *Perf. 12x11¾***

| | | | | |
|---|---|---|---|---|
| **8131** | | Horiz. pair + central label | 2.50 | 1.25 |
| *a.* | A4214 | 40r multi | 1.25 | .60 |
| *b.* | A4215 | 40r multi | 1.25 | .60 |

**Miniature Sheet**

Cats — A4216

No. 8132: a, Neva Masquerade cat, bowl, towel and flower. b, Kurilian Bobtail cat, plate of food. c, Ural Rex cat, table leg at left. d, Don Sphynx cat, table leg at right.

***Serpentine Die Cut 11***

**2020, Mar. 3 Litho.**

**Self-Adhesive**

| | | | | |
|---|---|---|---|---|
| **8132** | A4216 | Sheet of 4 | 6.00 | |
| *a.-d.* | | 50r Any single | 1.50 | .75 |

Friedrich Engels (1820-95), Co-author of *The Communist Manifesto* — A4217

**2020, Mar. 5 Litho. *Perf. 12x11½***

**8133** A4217 50r multi 1.40 .70

Ivan N. Kozhedub (1920-91), Air Marshal of the Soviet Union A4218

**2020, Mar. 10 Litho. *Perf. 12¼x12***

**8134** A4218 40r multi 1.10 .55

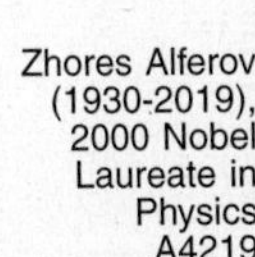
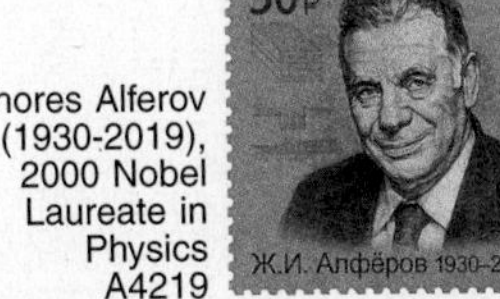


Zhores Alferov (1930-2019), 2000 Nobel Laureate in Physics A4219

**2020, Mar. 12 Litho. *Perf. 11½***

**8135** A4219 50r multi 1.30 .65

Pavel M. Golubitsky (1845-1911), Inventor of Improved Telephone Parts — A4220

**2020, Mar. 16 Litho. *Perf. 12¼x12***

**8136** A4220 40r multi 1.10 .55

No. 8136 was printed in sheets of 14 + central label.

**No. 7765 Surcharged in Green**

**Method and Perf. As Before**

**2020, Mar. 17**

**8137** A3925 100r on 50r #7765 (BIG) 2.60 1.30

Unification of Ingushetia and Russia, 250th anniv.

Unification of Ingushetia and Russia, 250th Anniv. — A4221

**2020, Mar. 17 Litho. *Perf. 11½***

**8138** A4221 50r multi 1.30 .65

No. 8138 was printed in sheets of 8 + central label.

**Heroes Type of 2016**

Designs: No. 8139, 35r, Sergey A. Basurmanov (1968-99). No. 8140, 35r, Sergey A. Firsov (1971-95). No. 8141, 40r, Aleksy N. Botyan (1917-2020). No. 8142, 40r, Alexey M. Kozlov (1934-2015).

**2020 Litho. *Perf. 12¼x12***

**Dated "2020"**

**8139-8142** A3881 Set of 4 4.00 2.00

Issued: Nos. 8139-8140, 3/27; No. 8141, 6/17; No. 8142, 9/15.

Konstantin E. Tsiolkovsky (1857-1935), Rocket Scientist, and Emblem of "Total Dictation" International Literacy Test — A4222

***Serpentine Die Cut 11¼***

**2020, Apr. 2 Litho.**

**Self-Adhesive**

**8143** A4222 26r multi .70 .35

Königsburg Offensive, 75th Anniv. — A4223

**Litho. & Embossed**

**2020, Apr. 6** ***Perf. 11¾***

**8144** A4223 60r multi 1.60 .80

No. 8144 was printed in sheets of 7 + label.

**Emblem of Russian Postal Service Types of 2019**

***Serpentine Die Cut 11½ Syncopated***

**2020** **Litho.**

**Self-Adhesive**

**Frame Color**

**8145** A4143 1.50r brown .25 .25

**Size: 26x35mm**

**8146** A4125 54r green & lt grn 1.60 .80
**8147** A4146 200r gray & blue 5.50 2.75
*Nos. 8145-8147 (3)* 7.35 3.80

Issued: No. 8145, 4/30; No. 8146, 5/26; No. 8147, 7/27.

Berlin Offensive, 75th Anniv. — A4224

**Litho. & Embossed**

**2020, May 6** ***Perf. 11¾***

**8148** A4224 60r multi 1.90 .95

No. 8148 was printed in sheets of 7 + label.

Prague Offensive, 75th Anniv. — A4225

**Litho. & Embossed**

**2020, May 6** ***Perf. 11¾***

**8149** A4225 60r multi 1.90 .95

No. 8149 was printed in sheets of 7 + label.

Monument to Soviet Soldiers, Rzhev — A4226

**2020, May 7** **Litho.** ***Perf. 11¾***

**8150** A4226 40r multi 1.25 .60

Transmission and Reception of Radio Waves, 125th Anniv. — A4227

**2020, May 7** **Litho.** ***Perf. 12x12¼***

**8151** A4227 40r multi 1.25 .60

Souvenir Sheet

Main Cathedral of the Russian Armed Forces, Moscow — A4228

**2020, May 8** **Litho.** ***Perf. 12***

**8152** A4228 75r multi 2.25 1.10

World War II victory of Allied Forces in Europe, 75th anniv. Joint issue between Russia and Belarus.

See Belarus No. 1179.

Portrait of Alexandre N. Benois (1870-1960), by Léon N. Bakst (1866-1924) — A4229

Military Parade of Emperor Paul I, by Benois — A4230

**2020, May 15** **Litho.** ***Perf. 12x11½***

**8153** A4229 50r multi 1.50 .75
**8154** A4230 50r multi 1.50 .75

Souvenir Sheet

State Russian Museum, St. Petersburg, 125th Anniv. — A4231

**2020, May 19** **Litho.** ***Perf. 11¾***

**8155** A4231 125r gold & multi 3.75 1.90

Let Us Beat Swords into Plowshares, Sculpture by Evgeniy Vuchetich — A4232

***Serpentine Die Cut 12***

**2020, May 22** **Litho.**

**Self-Adhesive**

**8156** A4232 48r multi 1.50 .75

United Nations, 75th anniv.

Admiral Fyodor F. Ushakov (1745-1817) — A4233

**2020, May 26** **Litho.** ***Perf. 12x11½***

**8157** A4233 50r multi 1.50 .75

Scorched Earth, by Boris M. Nemensky — A4234

To the Frontline, by Viktor I. Makeev A4235

In the Days of War, by Sergey P. Tkachev A4236

Unnumbered Hill, Monument by G. D. Yastrebenetskyi, V. G. Kozenyuk, and E. N. Rotanov — A4237

**2020, May 26** **Litho.** ***Perf. 12***

**8158** A4234 57r gold & multi 1.75 .85
**8159** A4235 57r gold & multi 1.75 .85
**8160** A4236 57r gold & multi 1.75 .85
**8161** A4237 57r gold & multi 1.75 .85
*Nos. 8158-8161 (4)* 7.00 3.40

**No. 7667 Surcharged in Red**

**Method and Perf. As Before**

**2020, May 27**

**8162** A3842 100r on 50r #7667 3.00 1.50

Republic of Tatarstan, cent.

Souvenir Sheet

Republic of Tatarstan, Cent. — A4238

**2020, May 27** **Litho.** ***Perf.***

**8163** A4238 100r multi 3.00 1.50

Sergei A. Esenin (1895-1925), Poet — A4239

**2020, May 28** **Litho.** ***Perf. 12x12¼***

**8164** A4239 54r multi 1.60 .80

19th Century Mari Embroidery — A4240

20th Century Karelian Embroidery — A4241

20th Century Tatar Embroidery — A4242

20th Century Chuvash Embroidery — A4243

***Serpentine Die Cut 11¾***

**2020, June 1** **Litho.**

**Self-Adhesive**

**8165** A4240 30r multi .90 .45
**8166** A4241 30r multi .90 .45
**8167** A4242 30r multi .90 .45
**8168** A4243 30r multi .90 .45
*Nos. 8165-8168 (4)* 3.60 1.80

Prehistoric Animals and Their Skulls — A4244

No. 8169: a, Inostrancevia alexandri. b, Pliosaurus rossicus. c, Mammuthus primigenius. d, Megalocerus giganteus.

**2020, June 3 Litho. *Perf. 11¾***
**8169** A4244 40r Block of 4, #a-d 4.50 2.25

A sheet containing two litho. and embossed blocks of 4 similar to No. 8169 sold for 750r.

Souvenir Sheet

Spacecraft — A4245

No. 8170: a, Orel, manned craft scheduled for 2025. b, Spektr-RG astrophysical observatory, 2019. c, Lunokhod 1 on Moon, 1970.

**2020, June 9 Litho. *Perf. 12***
**8170** A4245 30r Sheet of 3, #a-c 2.60 1.30

Election on Russian Federation Constitutional Amendments — A4246

**2020, June 11 Litho. *Perf. 12x11½***
**8171** A4246 54r multi 1.60 .80

Rybinsk Asphalt Roller Company, 150th Anniv. A4247

**2020, June 16 Litho. *Perf. 11½***
**8172** A4247 50r multi 1.40 .70

Souvenir Sheet

Fight in the Chios Strait, by Ivan K. Aivazovsky (1817-1900) — A4248

**2020, June 17 Litho. *Perf. 12***
**8173** A4248 100r multi 3.00 1.50

Battle of Chesma, 250th anniv.

Russian Oncological Service, 75th Anniv. A4249

**2020, June 19 Litho. *Perf. 11½***
**8174** A4249 23r multi .65 .30

Vladimir Ilyich Ulyanov (Lenin, 1870-1924), Head of Soviet Russian Government — A4250

**2020, June 22 Litho. *Perf. 12x11½***
**8175** A4250 54r multi 1.60 .80

Home Front Workers of World War II — A4251

**Litho. & Embossed**
**2020, June 22 *Perf. 11¾***
**8176** A4251 60r multi 1.75 .85

No. 8176 was printed in sheets of 7 + label.

Souvenir Sheet

Chuvash Republic, Cent. — A4252

**2020, June 24 Litho. *Perf.***
**8177** A4252 100r multi 3.00 1.50

Construction of Safe Roads A4253

***Serpentine Die Cut 12***
**2020, June 26 Litho.**
**Self-Adhesive**
**8178** A4253 54r multi 1.60 .80

Souvenir Sheet

Republic of Karelia, Cent. — A4254

**2020, July 8 Litho. *Perf.***
**8179** A4254 100r multi 2.75 1.40

Souvenir Sheet

Afanasy Afanasyevich Fet (1820-92), Poet — A4255

**2020, July 16 Litho. *Perf.***
**8180** A4255 100r multi 2.75 1.40

Miniature Sheet

Aircraft Designed by Pavel O. Sukhoi (1895-1975) — A4256

No. 8181: a, Sukhoi Su-2. b, Sukhoi T-4. c, Sukhoi Su-7BM. d, Sukhoi Su-27. e, Sukhoi Su-57.

**2020, July 22 Litho. *Perf. 12¼x12***
**8181** A4256 54r Sheet of 5, #a-e, + label .50 3.75

Souvenir Sheet

The Green Noise, by Arkady A. Rylov (1870-1939) — A4257

**2020, July 28 Litho. *Perf. 12***
**8182** A4257 150r gold & multi 4.25 2.10

Declaration on the Granting of Independence to Colonial Countries and Peoples, 40th Anniv. — A4258

**2020, July 31 Litho. *Perf. 11¼***
**8183** A4258 54r dull violet & tan 1.50 .75

Souvenir Sheet

Battle of Grengam, by Alexey P. Bogolyubov (1824-96) — A4259

**2020, Aug. 7 Litho. *Perf. 12***
**8184** A4259 100r multi 2.75 1.40

Battle of Grengam, 300th anniv.

Fall of Babylon 25th International Motorcycle Show, Sevastopol A4260

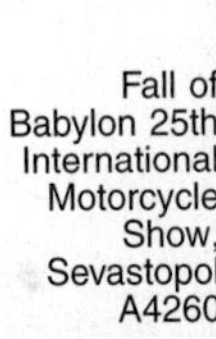

**2020, Aug. 8 Litho. *Perf. 11¼***
**8185** A4260 48r multi 1.30 .65

Manchurian Offensive, 75th Anniv. — A4261

**Litho. & Embossed**
**2020, Aug. 11 *Perf. 11¾***
**8186** A4261 60r multi 1.60 .80

No. 8186 was printed in sheets of 7 + label.

Souvenir Sheet

Russian Geographical Society, 175th Anniv. — A4262

**Litho. & Embossed With Foil Application**

**2020, Aug. 18** ***Perf.***
**8187** A4262 200r gold & black 5.50 2.75

Construction of Russian Tanks, Cent. — A4263

Designs: No. 8188, 23r, Freedom Fighter Comrade Lenin tank. No. 8189, 23r, T-26 tank. No. 8190, 23r, T-72 Ural tank. No. 8191, 23r, T-14 Armata tank.

**2020, Aug. 20** **Litho.** ***Perf. 12x11½***
**8188-8191** A4263 Set of 4 2.50 1.25
*8191a* Souvenir sheet of 12, 3 each #8188-8191 7.50 3.75

Prince Lev S. Golitsyn (1845-1915), Vintner — A4264

**2020, Aug. 24** **Litho.** ***Perf. 11¾***
**8192** A4264 50r multi 1.40 .70

No. 8192 was printed in sheets of 8.

Abai Kunanbayev (1845-1904), Poet — A4265

**2020, Aug. 25** **Litho.** ***Perf. 12¼x12***
**8193** A4265 48r multi 1.30 .65

No. 8193 was printed in sheets of 14 + label.

Souvenir Sheet

Alexander I. Kuprin (1870-1938), Writer — A4266

**2020, Sept. 7** **Litho.** ***Perf.***
**8194** A4266 100r multi 2.75 1.30

Nuclear Industry in Russia, 75th Anniv. — A4267

**2020, Sept. 8** **Litho.** ***Perf. 11¾***
**8195** A4267 54r multi 1.40 .70

Souvenir Sheet

Candle of Remembrance Monument to Siege of Leningrad, Jerusalem — A4268

**2020, Sept. 8** **Litho.** ***Perf. 12¼x12***
**8196** A4268 100r multi 2.60 1.30

Governmental Limousines — A4269

No. 8197: a, ZIL-115. b, ZIL-111A. c, ZIL-114 d, Aurus Senate Limousine with flag.

**2020, Sept. 10** **Litho.** ***Perf. 12¼x12***
**8197** A4269 23r Block of 4, #a-d 2.40 1.25

Special Purpose Garage, cent.

Vladimir B. Barkovsky (1913-2003), Foreign Intelligence Service Officer — A4270

Alexander S. Feklisov (1914-2007), Foreign Intelligence Service Officer — A4271

Gevork A. Vartanyan (1924-2012), Foreign Intelligence Service Officer A4272

**2020, Sept. 15** **Litho.** ***Perf. 12***
**8198** A4270 35r red brn & blk .90 .45
**8199** A4271 35r brn & blk .90 .45

***Perf. 11¼***
**8200** A4272 40r multi 1.10 .55
*Nos. 8198-8200 (3)* 2.90 1.45

Foreign Intelligence Service, cent.

White Russian Exodus, by Dmitry A. Belyukin — A4273

**2020, Sept. 16** **Litho.** ***Perf. 11¼***
**8201** A4273 54r multi 1.50 .75

Evacuation of the Crimea, cent.

Lev S. Yavich (1919-2004), Lawyer A4274

**2020, Sept. 22** **Litho.** ***Perf. 11¼***
**8202** A4274 40r multi 1.10 .55

No. 7679 Surcharged in Dark Blue

**Method and Perf. As Before**

**2020, Sept. 23**
**8203** A3551 23r on 17r multi (DB) *2.60 2.60*

Premiere of Motion Picture *Streltsov* A4275

**2020, Sept. 24** **Litho.** ***Perf. 12½x12***
**8204** A4275 43r multi 1.25 .60

Yeni Kale Lighthouse and Map of the Crimean Peninsula — A4276

Meganom Lighthouse and Map of the Crimean Peninsula — A4277

**2020, Sept. 30** **Litho.** ***Perf. 12½x12***
**8205** A4276 35r multi .95 .50
**8206** A4277 35r multi .95 .50

2020 Census — A4278

***Serpentine Die Cut 12¼***

**2020, Oct. 1** **Litho.**

**Self-Adhesive**

**8207** A4278 23r multi .60 .30

Premiere of Movie *The Last Frontier (Podolsk Cadets)* A4279

**2020, Oct. 5** **Litho.** ***Perf. 12¼x12***
**8208** A4279 43r multi 1.10 .55

No. 8208 was printed in sheets of 14 + central label.

Avvakum Petrov (c. 1620-82), Anti-Reformist Arch-Priest A4280

**2020, Oct. 6** **Litho.** ***Perf. 12x12¼***
**8209** A4280 18r gold & multi .45 .25

Simonov Monastery, 650th Anniv. — A4281

**2020, Oct. 15** **Litho.** ***Perf. 11¾***
**8210** A4281 50r multi 1.25 .60

No. 8210 was printed in sheets of 9 + label.

Ivan F. Krusenstern (1770-1846), Admiral — A4282

**2020, Oct. 20** **Litho.** ***Perf. 12x11¼***
**8211** A4282 54r multi 1.40 .70

St. Alexander Hall, Moscow Kremlin — A4283

**2020, Oct. 21** **Litho.** ***Perf. 12x11¼***
**8212** A4283 54r multi 1.40 .70

Medical Facility and Health Care Worker Wearing Protective Face Mask — A4284

*Serpentine Die Cut 12*

**2020, Oct. 30** **Litho.**

**Self-Adhesive**

**8213** A4284 54r multi 1.40 .70

Campaign against COVID-19 pandemic.

Diplomatic Relations Between Russia and Turkey, Cent. — A4285

No. 8214: a, Mosque of Suleiman the Magnificent, Istanbul (denomination at UR). b, Moscow Cathedral Mosque (denomination at UL).

**2020, Nov. 3** **Litho.** ***Perf. 12¼x12***

**8214** A4285 48r Horiz. pair, #a-b 2.60 1.30

See Turkey No. 3733.

Souvenir Sheets

Republic of Udmurtia, Cent. — A4286

Mari El Republic, Cent. — A4287

**2020, Nov. 3** **Litho.** ***Perf.***

**8215** A4286 100r multi 2.75 1.40

**8216** A4287 100r multi 2.75 1.40

UNESCO, 75th Anniv. A4288

*Serpentine Die Cut 12*

**2020, Nov. 16** **Litho.**

**Self-Adhesive**

**8217** A4288 48r multi 1.25 .65

Vladimir P. Ivanov (1920-96), Designer of Radar Equipment and Diagrams of Beriev A-50 A4289

**2020, Nov. 24** **Litho.** ***Perf. 12¼x12***

**8218** A4289 40r multi 1.10 .55

Sportloto Lotteries, 50th Anniv. A4290

*Serpentine Die Cut 11*

**2020, Nov. 25** **Litho.**

**Self-Adhesive**

**8219** A4290 50r yellow & black 1.40 .70

New Year 2021 — A4291

**2020, Dec. 3** **Litho.** ***Perf. 12x11¾***

**8220** A4291 23r multi .65 .30

Bears — A4292

No. 8222: a, Ursus thibetanus ussuricus (country name in white). b, Ursus arctos arctos (country name in gray).

**2020, Dec. 15** **Litho.** ***Perf. 11¼***

**8222** A4292 24r Pair, #a-b 1.30 .65

Diplomatic relations between Russia and South Korea, 30th anniv. See South Korea No. 2583.

Zosima Hermitage Convent — A4293

**2021, Jan. 14** **Litho.** ***Perf. 11¾***

**8223** A4293 50r multi 1.40 .70

Panthera Pardus Ciscaucasica — A4294

**2021, Jan. 20** **Litho.** ***Perf. 12x11¾***

**8224** A4294 52r multi 1.40 .70

First Official Document on the Kuzbass Region, 300th Anniv. — A4295

*Serpentine Die Cut 12¼*

**2021, Jan. 26** **Litho.**

**Self-Adhesive**

**8226** A4295 56r multi 1.50 .75

Nikolai N. Semyonov (1896-1986), 1956 Nobel Laureate in Chemistry A4296

**2021, Jan. 28** **Litho.** ***Perf. 11¾***

**8227** A4296 50r multi 1.40 .70

Moscow Technical University of Communications and Informatics, Cent. — A4297

**2021, Jan. 29** **Litho.** ***Perf. 12x12¼***

**8228** A4297 45r multi 1.25 .60

Medal for Distinction in Maintaining Public Order A4298

Medal for Distinction in Protecting the State Borders A4299

Medal for Courage in Fire — A4300

Medal for Lifesaving A4301

**Litho. & Embossed**

**2021, Feb. 2** ***Perf. 12***

**8229** A4298 60r multi 1.60 .80

**8230** A4299 60r multi 1.60 .80

**8231** A4300 60r multi 1.60 .80

**8232** A4301 60r multi 1.60 .80

*Nos. 8229-8232 (4)* 6.40 3.20

Nos. 8229-8232 were each printed in sheets of 8 + central label.

**Heroes Type of 2016**

Designs: No. 8233, 36r, Andrey V. Dneprovsky (1971-95). No. 8234, 36r, Stanislav N. Morozov (1958-2007).

**2021, Feb. 17** **Litho.** ***Perf. 12¼x12***

**8233-8234** A3881 Set of 2 2.00 1.00

Frogs — A4302

No. 8235: a, Pelophylax lessonae. b, Rana dybowskii. c, Rana macrocnemis. d, Rana amurensis.

**2021, Feb. 25** **Litho.** ***Perf. 12¼x12***

**8235** A4302 56r Block of 4, #a-d 6.00 3.00

Education A4303

Digital Economy A4304

*Serpentine Die Cut 12¼*

**2021, Feb. 26** **Litho.**

**Self-Adhesive**

**8236** A4303 56r multi 1.60 .80

**8237** A4304 56r multi 1.60 .80

National projects of Russia.

Russia's Accession to the Council of Europe, 25th Anniv. A4305

**2021, Feb. 28** **Litho.** ***Perf. 11¼***

**8238** A4305 52r multi 1.40 .70

500th Plenary Session of the Federation Council — A4306

**2021, Mar. 3** **Litho.** ***Perf. 12x11¼***

**8239** A4306 50r multi 1.30 .65

Souvenir Sheet

Frost, Sunrise, Painting by Igor E. Grabar (1871-1960) — A4307

**2021, Mar. 12 Litho. *Perf. 12***
**8240** A4307 150r multi 4.00 2.00

Irises — A4308

No. 8241: a, Iris scariosa. b, Iris vorobievii. c, Iris acutiloba. d, Iris tigridia.

***Serpentine Die Cut 11***
**2021, Mar. 16 Litho.**
**Self-Adhesive**
**8241** A4308 56r Block of 4, #a-d 6.00 3.00

Fedoskino Miniature Lacquer Paintings — A4309

Designs: No. 8242, 30r, The Firebird, by S. V. Monoshov, 1959. No. 8243, 30r, Ruslan and Lyudmila, by M. S. Chizhov, 1971. No. 8244, 30r, The Tea Party, by V. I. Lavrov, 1946. No. 8245, 30r, Ivan and Marya, by Y. V. Dotsenko, 1989, vert.

**2021, Mar. 17 Litho. *Perf. 12***
**8242-8245** A4309 Set of 4 3.25 1.60

Souvenir Sheet

Federal Service of the National Guard, 5th Anniv. — A4310

**2021, Mar. 25 Litho. *Perf. 11¼***
**8246** A4310 100r multi 2.75 1.40

Main Production and Commercial Department of the Diplomatic Corps, Cent. — A4311

**2021, Mar. 30 Litho. *Perf. 12¼***
**8247** A4311 43r multi 1.25 .60

**Emblem of the Russian Postal Service Type of 2019**

***Serpentine Die Cut 11½ Syncopated***
**2021 Litho.**
**Self-Adhesive**
**Frame Color**
**8249** A4125 24r reddish purple .65 .30

**Size; 26x35mm**
**8250** A4125 56r gray green 1.50 .75
**8251** A4146 200rpurple 5.50 2.75

Issued: 24r, 56r, 4/8; 200r, 6/10.

Berries — A4313

No. 8252: a, Hippophae. b, Vaccinium. c, Rubus. d, Grossularia.

***Serpentine Die Cut 11***
**2021, Apr. 15 Litho.**
**Self-Adhesive**
**8252** A4313 50r Block of 4, #a-d 5.50 2,75

Nizhny Novgorod, 800th Anniv. — A4314

**2021, Apr. 18 Litho. *Perf. 12***
**8253** A4314 56r multi 1.50 .75

Russian Peace Foundation, 60th Anniv. A4315

***Serpentine Die Cut 11***
**2021, Apr. 27 Litho.**
**8254** A4315 30r multi .80 .40

Souvenir Sheet

Great Moscow State Circus Building, 50th Anniv. — A4316

**2021, Apr. 28 Litho. *Perf. 11¾***
**8255** A4316 100r multi 2.75 1.40

A booklet exists containing a rectangular pane containing a similar stamp that has two balloons printed with a gold holographic foil.

Alexey F. Solomatin (1921-43), and His Wife, Lydia V. Litvyak (1921-43), Heroes of the Soviet Union — A4317

Semyon I. Kharlamov (1921-90), and His Wife, Nadezhda V. Popova (1921-2013), Heroes of the Soviet Union — A4318

**2021, May 7 Litho. *Perf. 12***
**8256** A4317 40r multi 1.10 .55
**8257** A4318 40r multi 1.10 .55

Miniature Sheet

Technical Achievements — A4319

No. 8258: a, FEDOR (anthropomorphic rescue robot). b, Cyclone (unmanned aerial vehicle). c, Marker (experimental robotic tank). d, Vityaz (unmanned submarine).

**2021, May 11 Litho. *Perf. 11¼***
**8258** A4319 24r Sheet of 4, #a-d 2.60 1.30

Paphnutiy L. Chebyshev (1821-94), Mathematician — A4320

**2021, May 20 Litho. *Perf. 12½x12***
**8259** A4320 40r multi 1.10 .55

Andrei D. Sakharov (1921-89), Nuclear Physicist and 1975 Nobel Peace Laureate A4321

**2021, May 21 Litho. *Perf. 11¼x12***
**8260** A4321 50r multi 1.40 .70

Order of Pirogov A4322

**Litho. & Embossed**
**2021, May 25 *Perf. 11¾***
**8261** A4322 60r multi 1.75 .85

No. 8261 was printed in sheets of 7 + label.

Limousines — A4323

No. 8262: a, ZIS-110B. b, ZIL-41041 AMG. c, ZIL-117-VE. d, Aurus-Senat-Cabriolet.

**2021, May 29 Litho. *Perf. 12½x12***
**8262** A4323 24r Block of 4, #a-d 2.60 1.30

Souvenir Sheet

Yasnaya Polyana Estate Museum, Cent. — A4324

**2021, June 10 Litho. *Perf. 12***
**8263** A4324 100r multi 2.75 1.40

Birthplace of Leo Tolstoy (1828-1910), writer.

Mascot Skillzy Dribbling Soccer Ball — A4325

Skillzy Holding European Soccer Championships Trophy — A4326

Emblem of the 2020 European Soccer Championships — A4327

***Serpentine Die Cut 11***

**2021, June 11** **Litho.**

**Self-Adhesive**

**8264** Horiz. strip of 3 2.50
*a.* A4325 18r multi .50 .25
*b.* A4326 18r multi .50 .25
*c.* A4327 52r multi 1.50 .75

The 2020 European Soccer Championships were postponed until 2021 because of the COVID-19 pandemic.

Gavriil A. Ilizarov (1921-92), Orthopedic Surgeon and Inventor A4328

**2021, June 15** **Litho.** ***Perf. 11¼***
**8265** A4328 40r multi 1.10 .55

Souvenir Sheet

Nikolai A. Nekrasov (1821-78), Poet — A4329

**2021, June 17** **Litho.** ***Perf. 12***
**8266** A4329 100r multi 2.75 1.40

Boris N. Slyusar (1942-2015), General Director of Rostvertol Helicopters, and Mi-28 Helicopter Under Construction — A4330

**2021, June 25** **Litho.** ***Perf. 12½x12***
**8267** A4330 46r multi 1.25 .65

No. 8267 was printed in sheets of 5 + label.

Monument to Those Who Died for the Fatherland, Myasny Bor — A4331

**2021, June 27** **Litho.** ***Perf. 12x12½***
**8268** A4331 40r multi 1.10 .55

Victory in World War II, 75th anniv.

Souvenir Sheet

View From the Academy of Arts to the Admiralty, Painting by Anna P. Ostroumova-Lebedeva (1871-1955) — A4332

**2021, June 29** **Litho.** ***Perf. 12***
**8269** A4332 150r gold & multi 4.25 2.10

Izborsk, Painting by Evgeny N. Maksimov — A4333

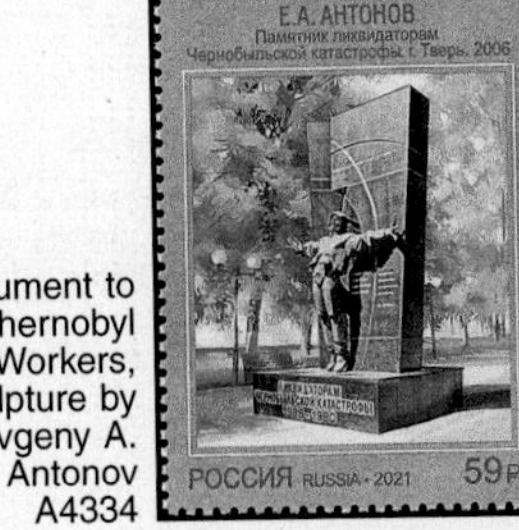


Monument to Chernobyl Workers, Sculpture by Evgeny A. Antonov A4334

Volga Expanses, Painting by Andrey I. Dubov — A4335

Chak-chak, Painting by Rashit S. Khabirov — A4336

**2021, July 5** **Litho.** ***Perf. 12***
**8270** A4333 59r gold & multi 1.60 .80
**8271** A4334 59r gold & multi 1.60 .80

***Perf. 11¼***

**8272** A4335 59r gold & multi 1.60 .80
**8273** A4336 59r gold & multi 1.60 .80
*Nos. 8270-8273 (4)* 6.40 3.20

Souvenir Sheet

Central Orsha-Khingan Red Banner District of National Guard Troops, Cent. — A4337

**2021, July 15** **Litho.** ***Perf. 12***
**8274** A4337 100r multi 2.75 1.40

Prince Vasily M. Dolgorukov (1722-82), General in Russo-Turkish War, and Perekop Fortress — A4338

**2021, July 19** **Litho.** ***Perf. 12x11½***
**8275** A4338 56r multi 1.60 .80

No. 8275 was printed in sheets of 8 + central label.

Souvenir Sheet

Opening of the Restored Cathedral of Our Lady of Kazan Icon at the Kazan Virgin Monastery — A4339

**2021, July 21** **Litho.** ***Perf. 12x12½***
**8276** A4339 100r multi 2.75 1.40

Genovese Fortress, Grape Vines and Amphora, Feodosia — A4340

**2021, July 23** **Litho.** ***Perf. 12x11½***
**8277** A4340 50r multi 1.40 .70

Feodosia, 2550th anniv.

Training Barque Sedov, Cent. — A4341

**2021, July 27** **Litho.** ***Perf. 11½x11¾***
**8278** A4341 50r multi 1.40 .70

No. 8278 was printed in sheets of 7 + label.

Arctic Marine Operations — A4342

No. 8379: a, Crane at Gates of the Arctic Terminal, Ob Bay. b, Tanker ship Navigator Albanov.

**2021, July 29** **Litho.** ***Perf. 12***
**8279** A4342 30r Horiz. pair, #a-b 1.75 .85

No. 8279 was printed in sheets of 4 pairs + 2 central labels.

Trains — A4343

No. 8380: a, Ruskeala Express (steam locomotive). b, Electric train with double-decker cars.

**2021, Aug. 2** **Litho.** ***Perf. 12½x12***
**8280** A4343 27r Horiz. pair, #a-b 1.50 .75

Kaluga, 650th Anniv. A4344

**2021, Aug. 5 Litho.** ***Perf. 12½x12***

**8281** A4344 50r multi 1.40 .70

Rybinsk, 950th Anniv. A4345

**2021, Aug. 6 Litho.** ***Perf. 12½x12***

**8283** A4345 50r multi 1.40 .70

Vereya, 650th Anniv. A4346

**2021, Aug. 7 Litho.** ***Perf. 12½x12***

**8284** A4346 50r multi 1.40 .70

Journey to India of Afanasy Nikitin, 550th Anniv. — A4347

**2021, Aug. 18 Litho.** ***Perf. 12x11¼***

**8285** A4347 55r multi 1.50 .75

Annunciation Monastery, Nizhny Novgorod — A4348

**2021, Aug. 19 Litho.** ***Perf. 11¾***

**8286** A4348 50r multi 1.40 .70

No. 8286 was printed in sheets of 9 + label.

Souvenir Sheet

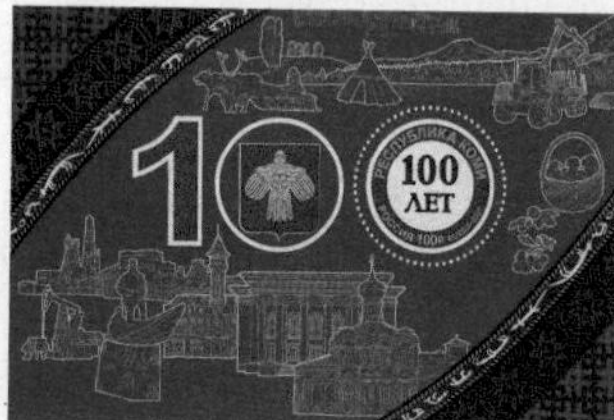


Komi Republic, Cent. — A4349

**2021, Aug. 20 Litho.** ***Perf.***

**8287** A4349 100r multi 2.75 1.40

Bear A4350

***Serpentine Die Cut 11***

**2021, Aug. 24 Litho.**

**Self-Adhesive**

**8288** A4350 18r multi .50 .25

Masked Health Care Workers A4351

**2021, Aug. 24 Litho.** ***Perf. 11¼***

**8289** A4351 24r multi .65 .35

Campaign against COVID-19 pandemic.

Tanks — A4352

Designs: No. 8290, 24r, T-34-76 tank. No. 8291, 24r, T-54 tank. No. 8292, 24r, T-72B3 tank. No. 8293, 24r, T-90M "Breakthrough" tank.

**2021, Aug. 31 Litho.** ***Perf. 12x11¼***

**8290-8293** A4352 Set of 4 2.60 1.25

*8293a* Sheet of 12, 3 each #8290-8293 8.00 3.75

Nos. 8290-8293 were each printed in sheets of 8 + central label.

Zvezda Shipbuilding Complex, Bolshoy Kamen A4353

**2021, Sept. 1 Litho.** ***Perf. 11¼***

**8294** A4353 50r multi 1.40 .70

Monument to Ural Volunteer Tank Corps, Ekaterinburg A4354

Monument to Il-2 Attack Airplane, Samara A4355

Monument to Tank Volunteers, Chelyabinsk A4356

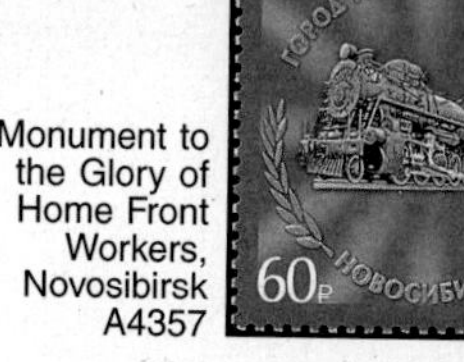


Monument to the Glory of Home Front Workers, Novosibirsk A4357

**Litho. & Embossed**

**2021, Sept. 9** ***Perf. 11¼***

| | | | | |
|---|---|---|---|---|
| **8295** | A4354 60r multi | | 1.75 | .85 |
| **8296** | A4355 60r multi | | 1.75 | .85 |
| **8297** | A4356 60r multi | | 1.75 | .85 |
| **8298** | A4357 60r multi | | 1.75 | .85 |
| | *Nos. 8295-8298 (4)* | | 7.00 | 3.40 |

Souvenir Sheet

Prince Alexander Nevsky (1221-63), Russian Orthodox Saint — A4358

**2021, Sept. 12 Litho.** ***Perf. 11¾***

**8299** A4358 100r multi 2.75 1.40

Treaty of Nystad, 300th Anniv. — A4359

**2021, Sept. 15 Litho.** ***Perf. 11¼***

**8300** A4359 56r multi 1.60 .80

Uniforms of Messenger and Ship's Officer, 1941 A4360

Uniforms of Ammunition Loader, Commander and Tank Driver, 1941 A4361

Uniforms of Soldier and Army Commander, 1941 A4362

Uniforms of Fighter Pilot and Aircraft Mechanic, 1941 A4363

**2021, Sept. 21 Litho.** ***Perf. 11¼x12***

| | | | | |
|---|---|---|---|---|
| **8301** | A4360 30r multi | | .85 | .40 |
| **8302** | A4361 30r multi | | .85 | .40 |
| **8303** | A4362 30r multi | | .85 | .40 |
| **8304** | A4363 30r multi | | .85 | .40 |
| | *Nos. 8301-8304 (4)* | | 3.40 | 1.60 |

**Heroes Type of 2016**

Design: 40r, Vasily E. Chubenko (1971-2005).

**2021, Sept. 22 Litho.** ***Perf. 12¼x12***

**8305** A3881 40r multi 1.10 .55

No. 8305 was printed in sheets of 5 + label.

Tractors and Bulldozers — A4364

No. 8306: a, F. A. Blinov tractor, 1896. b, S-60 Stalinets tractor, 1933. c, DT-54 tractor, 1949. d, Chetra T-40 bulldozer, 2005.

**2021, Sept. 28 Litho.** ***Perf. 12x11¼***

**8306** A4364 24r Block of 4, #a-d 2.75 1,40

Anton Chekhov House, Yalta — A4365

**2021, Oct. 4 Litho.** ***Perf. 12x11¾***

**8307** A4365 50r multi 1.40 .70

Intersputnik (International Organization of Space Communications), 50th Anniv. — A4366

**2021, Oct. 5** **Litho.** ***Perf. 11¾***
**8308** A4366 50r multi 1.40 .70

Rosgosstrakh Insurance Organization, Cent. — A4367

**2021, Oct. 6** **Litho.** ***Perf. 12x11¼***
**8309** A4367 56r multi 1.60 .80

2021 Eurasian Women's Forum, St. Petersburg — A4368

***Serpentine Die Cut 11***
**2021, Oct. 13** **Litho.**
**Self-Adhesive**
**8310** A4368 50r multi 1.40 .70

Holy Trinity Novo-Golutvin Convent, Kolomna — A4369

**2021, Oct. 14** **Litho.** ***Perf. 11¾***
**8311** A4369 50r multi 1.40 .70

Teribersky Lighthouse — A4370

Tsypnavoloksky Lighthouse — A4371

**2021, Oct. 15** **Litho.** ***Perf. 12¼x12***
**8312** A4370 40r multi 1.10 .55
**8313** A4371 40r multi 1.10 .55

Hall of the Order of St. George, Grand Kremlin Palice, Moscow — A4372

**2021, Oct. 21** **Litho.** ***Perf. 12x11½***
**8314** A4372 56r multi 1.60 .80

Ivan M. Gubkin (1871-1939), Petroleum Geologist — A4373

**2021, Oct. 28** **Litho.** ***Perf. 12¼x12***
**8315** A4373 40r multi 1.10 .55

Raketa Petrodvorets Watch Factory, St. Petersburg, 300th Anniv. A4374

**2021, Nov. 3** **Litho.** ***Perf. 11¼***
**8316** A4374 56r multi 1.50 .75

Balalaika and Morin Khuur A4375

**2021, Nov. 5** **Litho.** ***Perf. 11¼***
**8317** A4375 50r multi 1.40 .70

Diplomatic relations between Russia and Mongolia, cent. See Mongolia No. 2978.

Souvenir Sheet

Fyodor M. Dostoyevsky (1821-81), Writer — A4376

**2021, Nov. 11** **Litho.** ***Perf. 12***
**8318** A4376 100r gold & multi 2.75 1.40

Vladimir Dahl Russian State Literary Museum, Moscow, Cent. — A4377

**2021, Nov. 15** **Litho.** ***Perf. 12x11½***
**8319** A4377 50r multi 1.40 .70

Souvenir Sheet

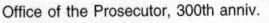

Count Pavel Yaguzhinsky (1683-1786), First Prosecutor General — A4378

**2021, Nov. 17** **Litho.** ***Perf. 12***
**8320** A4378 100r multi 2.75 1.40

Office of the Prosecutor, 300th anniv.

Lukoil Oil Company Workers and Child A4379

**2021, Nov. 23** **Litho.** ***Perf. 11½***
**8321** A4379 60r multi 1.60 .80

Su-30SM Fighter of Russian Knights Aerobatics Team — A4380

MiG-29 Fighter of Swifts Aerobatics Team — A4381

**2021, Nov. 24** **Litho.** ***Perf. 12x11½***
**8322** Horiz. pair + central label 1.40 .70
*a.* A4380 25r multi .70 .35
*b.* A4381 25r multi .70 .35

Souvenir Sheet

Arctic Tourism — A4382

No. 8323: a, Buildings on Hooker Island. b, Stone spheres, Champ Island.

**2021, Nov. 25** **Litho.** ***Perf. 12¼x12***
**8323** A4382 Sheet of 2 2.25 1.10
*a.* 24r multi .65 .30
*b.* 56r multi 1.60 .80

Grit is affixed to parts of the design of No. 8323b.

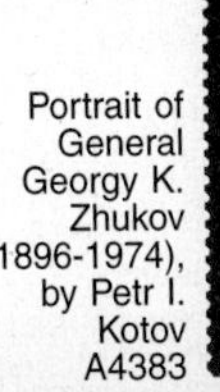
Portrait of General Georgy K. Zhukov (1896-1974), by Petr I. Kotov A4383

Portrait of General Konstantin K Rokossovsky (1896-1968), by Kotov A4384

**2021, Nov. 30** **Litho.** ***Perf. 11½x12***
**8324** A4383 50r multi 1.40 .70
**8325** A4384 50r multi 1.40 .70

German P. Karakozov (1926-92), Prosecutorial Investigator A4385

Viktor V. Naydenov (1931-87), Prosecutorial Investigator A4386

**2021, Dec. 7** **Litho.** ***Perf. 11¼***
**8326** A4385 40r multi 1.10 .55
**8327** A4386 40r multi 1.10 .55

New Year 2022 — A4387

***Serpentine Die Cut***
**2021, Dec. 9** **Litho.**
**Self-Adhesive**
**8328** A4387 24r multi .65 .30

**Souvenir Sheet**

Dagestan Republic, Cent. — A4388

**2021, Dec. 10 Litho. *Perf.***
**8329** A4388 100r multi 2.75 1.40

Russian Ice Hockey Championships, 75th Anniv. — A4389

***Perf. 11¾x11½***
**2021, Dec. 10 Litho.**
**8330** A4389 25r multi .70 .35

Miniature Sheet

Paintings of Moscow — A4390

No. 8331: a, Sketch of the Kremlin, 1903, by Konstantin A. Korovin (1861-1939). b, The Sky Ringer, Decorative Moscow, 1915, by Aristarkh V. Lentulov (1882-1943). c, Red Square in Moscow, 1801, by Fedor Y. Alekseev (1753-1824). d, Moscow at Night, 1999, by N. I. Borovskoy.

**2021, Dec. 14 Litho. *Perf. 11¼***
**8331** A4390 25r Sheet of 4, #a-d 2.75 1.40

Reformation of People's Militia, 80th Anniv. A4391

**2021, Dec. 15 Litho. *Perf. 11½x12***
**8332** A4391 40r multi 1.10 .55

Russian Union of Industrialists and Entrepreneurs, 30th Anniv. — A4392

**2021, Dec. 17 Litho. *Perf. 12x11½***
**8333** A4392 46r multi 1.25 .60

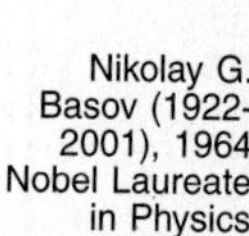

Nikolay G. Basov (1922-2001), 1964 Nobel Laureate in Physics A4393

**2022, Jan. 12 Litho. *Perf. 11½x11¾***
**8334** A4393 50r multi 1.30 .65

Characters From *Ruslan and Lyudmila,* Fairy Tale Poem by Alexander Pushkin (1799-1837) A4394

**2022, Jan. 20 Litho. *Perf. 11½x12***
**8335** A4394 55r multi 1.50 .75

Europa.

Songbirds — A4395

No. 8336: a, Granativiora melanocephala. b, Regulus reguus. c, Garrulus glandarius. d, Erithacus rubecula.

**2022, Jan. 27 Litho. *Perf. 12¼x12***
**8336** A4395 25r Block of 4, #a-d 2.60 1.30

Luka Krymsky Medal for Public Health Contributions A4396

Medal for Works in Culture or Art — A4397

Medal for Works in Agriculture A4398

Medal for the Development of Railways A4399

**Litho. & Embossed**

**2022, Feb. 2 *Perf. 12***
**8337** A4396 60r multi 1.60 .80
**8338** A4397 60r multi 1.60 .80
**8339** A4398 60r multi 1.60 .80
**8340** A4399 60r multi 1.60 .80
*Nos. 8337-8340 (4)* 6.40 3.20

Nos. 8337-8340 were each printed in sheets of 8 + central label.

Souvenir Sheet

October, Painting by Boris S. Ugarov (1922-91) — A4400

**2022, Feb. 7 Litho. *Perf. 12***
**8341** A4400 100r gold & multi 2.75 1.40

Souvenir Sheet

State Historical Museum, Moscow, 150th Anniv. — A4401

**2022, Feb. 9 Litho. *Perf. 11¼***
**8342** A4401 150r multi 4.00 2.00

**Heroes Type of 2016**

Designs: No. 8343, 40r, Igor S. Grudnov (1958-2018). No. 8344, 40r, Alexander I. Otrakovsky (1947-2000).

**2022, Feb. 17 Litho. *Perf. 12¼x12***
**8343-8344** A3881 Set of 2 2.25 1.10

---

## POSTAL-FISCAL STAMPS

During 1918-22, Postal Savings stamps and Control stamps were authorized for postal use. Because of hyper-inflation during 1920-22, Russian Arms stamps and these postal-fiscal stamps were sold and used at different rates at different times: 1918-20, sold at face value; from March, 1920, sold at 100 times face value; from Aug. 15, 1921, sold at 250r each, regardless of face value; from April, 1922, sold at 10,000r per 1k or 1r. In Oct. 1922, these issues were superseded by gold currency stamps.

**Postal Savings Stamps**

PF1

***Perf. 14½x14¾***
**1918, Jan. 12 Wmk. 171 Typo.**
**AR1** PF1 1k dp red, *buff* .60 *1.00*
**AR2** PF1 5k green, *buff* .60 *1.00*
**AR3** PF1 10k chocolate, *buff* 1.20 *1.00*
*Nos. AR1-AR3 (3)* 2.40 *3.00*

Nos. AR1-AR14 have a faint burelé background, which is noted as the paper color in these listings.

For surcharges of Nos. AR1-AR3, see Armenia Nos. 250-253, Far Eastern Republic Nos. 35 and 36, South Russia Nos. 47-49 and numerous Ukraine issues beginning with Nos. 45e-47e.

**Postal Savings Stamps**

PF2

PF3

**1918, June 5 Litho. *Perf. 13***
**AR4** PF2 25k black, *rose* 11.00 *37.50*
**AR5** PF2 50k brn, *pale brn* 24.00 *50.00*
**AR6** PF3 50k brn, *pale brn* 35.00 *62.50*
*Nos. AR4-AR6 (3)* 70.00 *150.00*

**Control Stamps**

PF4

PF5

PF6

PF7

PF8

**1918, June 5 Litho. *Perf. 13***
**AR7** PF4 25k blk, *pale brn* 24.00 *32.50*
**AR8** PF4 50k brn, *buff* 17.50 *50.00*
**AR9** PF5 1r org, *buff* 1.50 *3.50*

| No. | Type | Description | Unused | Used |
|---|---|---|---|---|
| AR10 | PF5 | 3r grn, *buff* | 1.50 | 3.50 |
| AR11 | PF5 | 5r dp blue, *buff* | 1.50 | 3.75 |
| AR12 | PF6 | 10r dp red, *buff* | 1.50 | 3.75 |
| AR13 | PF7 | 25r dp brn, *buff* | 5.00 | 15.00 |
| AR14 | PF8 | 100r blk, *blue & car* | 3.75 | 6.25 |
| | | *Nos. AR7-AR14 (8)* | 56.25 | 118.25 |

### General Revenue Stamps

PF9

**1918 Litho. *Perf. 12x12½***

| No. | Type | Description | Unused | Used |
|---|---|---|---|---|
| AR15 | PF9 | 5k lil brn, *buff* | 1.50 | — |
| AR16 | PF9 | 10k ol brn, *lt blue* | 1.50 | — |
| AR17 | PF9 | 15k dp blue, *pink* | 1.50 | — |
| AR18 | PF9 | 20k reddish brn, *buff* | 1.50 | — |
| AR19 | PF9 | 50k org red, *gray* | 1.50 | — |
| AR20 | PF9 | 75k ol grn, *buff* | 3.25 | — |
| AR21 | PF9 | 1r red, *pale blue* | 6.25 | — |
| AR22 | PF9 | 1.25r dk brn, *redsh brn* | 30.00 | — |
| AR23 | PF9 | 2r vio, *dk grn* | 30.00 | — |
| AR24 | PF9 | 3r dp vio blue, *rose lil* | 3.50 | — |
| AR25 | PF9 | 5r dp blue grn, *lt grn* | 6.50 | — |
| | | *Nos. AR15-AR25 (11)* | 87.00 | |

Nos, AR15-AR25 exist in tête-bêche vertical pairs and in tête-bêche vertical gutter pairs.

## SEMI-POSTAL STAMPS

### Empire

Admiral Kornilov Monument, Sevastopol SP1

Pozharski and Minin Monument, Moscow SP2

Statue of Peter the Great, Leningrad SP3

Alexander II Memorial and Kremlin, Moscow SP4

**1905 Typo. Unwmk. *Perf. 12x12½***

| No. | Type | Description | Unused | Used |
|---|---|---|---|---|
| B1 | SP1 | 3k red, brn & grn | 24.00 | 5.25 |
| | | Never hinged | 140.00 | |
| B2 | SP2 | 5k lil, vio & straw | 5.00 | 3.50 |
| | | Never hinged | 20.00 | |
| B3 | SP3 | 7k lt bl, dk bl & pink | 5.00 | 3.50 |
| | | Never hinged | 20.00 | |
| B4 | SP4 | 10k lt blue, dk bl & yel | 7.50 | .50 |
| | | Never hinged | 25.00 | |
| | | *Nos. B1-B4 (4)* | 41.50 | 12.75 |

**Line Perf. 13¼**

| No. | Type | Description | Unused | Used |
|---|---|---|---|---|
| B1a | SP1 | 3k red, brn & grn | 40.00 | 1.25 |
| B3a | SP3 | 7k lt bl, dk bl & pink | 82.50 | 1.25 |
| B4a | SP4 | 10k lt bl, dk bl & yel | 7.50 | .50 |
| B1b | SP1 | 3k red, brn & grn | 16.50 | 5.00 |
| B1c | SP1 | 3k red, brn & grn | 200.00 | 200.00 |
| B1d | SP1 | 3k red, brn & grn | 200.00 | 200.00 |

These stamps were sold for 3 kopecks over face value. The surtax was donated to a fund for the orphans of soldiers killed in the Russo-Japanese war.

Ilya Murometz Legendary Russian Hero — SP5

Designs: 3k, Don Cossack Bidding Farewell to His Sweetheart. 7k, Allegory of Charity. 10k, St. George Slaying the Dragon.

**1914 Colored Papers *Perf. 11½***

| No. | Type | Description | Unused | Used |
|---|---|---|---|---|
| B5 | SP5 | 1k red brn & dk grn, *straw* | 2.00 | 2.00 |
| B6 | SP5 | 3k mar & gray grn, *pink* | 3.00 | 3.00 |
| B7 | SP5 | 7k dk brn & dk grn, *buff* | 3.50 | 2.00 |
| B8 | SP5 | 10k dk bl & brn, *blue* | 12.00 | 4.50 |
| | | *Nos. B5-B8 (4)* | 20.50 | 11.50 |

***Perf. 12½***

| No. | Type | Description | Unused | Used |
|---|---|---|---|---|
| B5a | SP5 | 1k red brn & dk grn, *straw* | 3.75 | 3.25 |
| B6a | SP5 | 3k mar & gray grn, *pink* | 4.25 | 3.25 |
| B7a | SP5 | 7k dk brn & dk grn, *buff* | 9.50 | 7.50 |
| B8a | SP5 | 10k dk bl & brn, *blue* | 21.00 | 7.50 |
| | | *Nos. B5a-B8a (4)* | 38.50 | 21.50 |

***Perf. 13¼***

| No. | Type | Description | Unused | Used |
|---|---|---|---|---|
| B5b | SP5 | 1k red brn & dk grn, *straw* | 8.50 | 2.00 |
| B6b | SP5 | 3k mar & gray grn, *pink* | 225.00 | 45.00 |
| B7b | SP5 | 7k dk brn & dk grn, *buff* | 3.75 | 3.75 |
| B8b | SP5 | 10k dk bl & brn, *blue* | 24.00 | 5.50 |

**1915 White Paper *Perf. 11½***

| No. | Type | Description | Unused | Used |
|---|---|---|---|---|
| B9 | SP5 | 1k org brn & gray | 2.25 | 2.00 |
| B10 | SP5 | 3k car & gray blk | 2.25 | 2.00 |
| B12 | SP5 | 10k dk bl & dk brn | 4.25 | 2.25 |
| | | *Nos. B9-B12 (3)* | 8.75 | |

**Perf. 12½**

| No. | Type | Description | Unused | Used |
|---|---|---|---|---|
| B9a | SP5 | 1k org brn & gray | 3.50 | 2.00 |
| B10a | SP5 | 3k car & gray blk | 3.50 | 2.00 |
| *d.* | | Horiz. pair, imperf. between | 175.00 | |
| B11 | SP5 | 7k dk brn & dk grn | 12.00 | |
| B12a | SP5 | 10k dk bl & dk brn | 4.25 | 2.25 |
| | | *Nos. B9a-B12a, B11 (4)* | 23.25 | 6.25 |

**Perf. 13¼**

| No. | Type | Description | Unused | Used |
|---|---|---|---|---|
| B9b | SP5 | 1k org brn & gray | 2.25 | 2.00 |
| B10b | SP5 | 3k car & gray blk | 2.25 | 2.00 |
| B12b | SP5 | 10k dk bl & dk brn | 5.00 | 2.25 |
| | | *Nos. B9b-B12b (3)* | 9.50 | 6.25 |

***Imperf***

| No. | Type | Description | Unused | Used |
|---|---|---|---|---|
| B9c | SP5 | 1k org brn & gray | 425.00 | 225.00 |
| B10c | SP5 | 3k car & gray blk | 425.00 | 225.00 |
| B11c | SP5 | 7k dk brn & dk grn | 425.00 | 225.00 |
| B12c | SP5 | 10k dk bl & dk brn | 426.00 | 225.00 |
| | | *Nos. B9c-B12c (4)* | 1,700. | 900.00 |

These stamps were sold for 1 kopeck over face value. The surtax was donated to charities connected with the war of 1914-17.

No. B11 not regularly issued. It exists only perf 11½ (with Specimen overprint) and 12½.

For surcharges of Nos. B5-B13, see Armenia Nos. 255-265 and Siberia No. 64.

### Russian Soviet Federated Socialist Republic
### Volga Famine Relief Issue

Relief Work on Volga River — SP9

Administering Aid to Famine Victim — SP10

Genuine

Forgery

Characteristics between the genuine and forgery stamps:

Genuine: Shadow of the old man's stick at bottom left joins the base of the stick. At top in the second line of text within the second word, the lower serifs of the fifth letter and the A in the word just merge together. Word under denomination is clear on left side. The paper is whitish.

Forgery: Shadow and stick has a clear gap the base of the stick. At top in the second line of text within the second word the lower serifs of the fifth letter and the A there is a clear gap. Word under denomination has a deformed "y" on the left side. The paper is pale cream and thicker, the design is less detailed and blurry.

**1921 Litho. *Imperf.***

| No. | Type | Description | Unused | Used |
|---|---|---|---|---|
| B14 | SP9 | 2250r green | 3.75 | 6.00 |
| *a.* | | Pelure paper | 165.00 | 125.00 |
| B15 | SP9 | 2250r deep red | 2.00 | 11.00 |
| *a.* | | Pelure paper | 19.00 | 15.00 |
| B16 | SP9 | 2250r brown | 3.75 | 11.00 |
| B17 | SP10 | 2250r dark blue | 9.50 | 30.00 |
| *a.* | | 2250r dark blue | 20.00 | — |
| | | *Nos. B14-B17 (4)* | 19.00 | 58.00 |

Forged cancels and counterfeits of Nos. B14-B17 are plentiful.

Stamps of type A33 with this overprint were not charity stamps nor did they pay postage in any form.

They represent taxes paid on stamps exported from or imported into Russia. In 1925 the semi-postal stamps of 1914-15 were surcharged for the same purpose. Stamps of the regular issues 1918 and 1921 have also been surcharged with inscriptions and new values, to pay the importation and exportation taxes.

Nos. 149-150 Surcharged in Black, Red, Blue or Orange

**1922, Feb. *Perf. 13½***

| No. | Type | Description | Unused | Used |
|---|---|---|---|---|
| B18 | A33 | 100r + 100r on 70k | 1.60 | 1.25 |
| *c.* | | "100 p. + p. 100" | 225.00 | 290.00 |
| B19 | A33 | 100r + 100r on 70k (R) | 1.60 | 1.25 |
| B20 | A33 | 100r + 100r on 70k (Bl) | 1.00 | 1.25 |
| B21 | A33 | 250r + 250r on 35k | .50 | .75 |
| B22 | A33 | 250r + 250r on 35k (R) | 1.00 | 2.00 |
| B23 | A33 | 250r + 250r on 35k (O) | 1.60 | 5.00 |
| | | *Nos. B18-B23 (6)* | 7.30 | 11.50 |

**Surcharge Inverted**

| No. | Type | Description | Unused | Used |
|---|---|---|---|---|
| B18a | A33 | 100r + 100r on 70k | 160.00 | 1.00 |
| B19a | A33 | 100r + 100r on 70k (R) | 140.00 | 60.00 |
| B20a | A33 | 100r + 100r on 70k (Bl) | 70.00 | 45.00 |
| B21a | A33 | 250r + 250r on 35k | 70.00 | — |
| B22a | A33 | 250r + 250r on 35k (R) | 200.00 | 45.00 |
| B23a | A33 | 250r + 250r on 35k (O) | 225.00 | 100.00 |

**Surcharge Double**

| No. | Type | Description | Unused | Used |
|---|---|---|---|---|
| B18b | A33 | 100r + 100r on 70k | 200.00 | — |
| B19b | A33 | 100r + 100r on 70k (R) | 200.00 | — |
| B21b | A33 | 250r + 250r on 35k | 200.00 | — |
| B22b | A33 | 250r + 250r on 35k (R) | 200.00 | — |

Issued to raise funds for Volga famine relief.

Regular Issues of 1909-18 Overprinted

**1922, Aug. 19 *Perf. 14***

| No. | Type | Description | Unused | Used |
|---|---|---|---|---|
| B24 | A14 | 1k orange | 350.00 | 350.00 |
| B25 | A14 | 2k green | 22.50 | 35.00 |
| B26 | A14 | 3k red | 22.50 | 35.00 |
| B27 | A14 | 5k claret | 22.50 | 35.00 |
| B28 | A15 | 10k dark blue | 22.50 | 35.00 |

***Imperf***

| No. | Type | Description | Unused | Used |
|---|---|---|---|---|
| B29 | A14 | 1k orange | 350.00 | 350.00 |
| | | *Nos. B24-B29 (6)* | 790.00 | 840.00 |

**Overprint Inverted (Reading Up)**

| No. | Type | Description | Unused | Used |
|---|---|---|---|---|
| B24a | A14 | 1k orange | 825.00 | |
| B25a | A14 | 2k green | 325.00 | |
| B26a | A14 | 3k red | 825.00 | |
| | | Never hinged | 1,750. | |
| B27a | A14 | 5k claret | 825.00 | |
| | | Never hinged | 1,750. | |
| B28a | A15 | 10k dark blue | 825.00 | |
| | | Never hinged | 1,900. | |
| B29a | A14 | 1k orange | 825.00 | |
| | | Never hinged | 1,750. | |

**Double Overprint**

| No. | Type | Description | Unused | Used |
|---|---|---|---|---|
| B25b | A14 | 2k green | 600.00 | 900.00 |
| B26b | A14 | 3k red | 1,450. | |
| B27b | A14 | 5k claret | 725.00 | |
| B28b | A15 | 10k dark blue | 1,200. | |
| B29b | A14 | 1k orange | 2,400. | |

The overprint means "Philately for the Children". The stamps were sold at five million times their face values and 80% of the amount was devoted to child welfare. The stamps were sold only at Moscow and for one day.

Nos. B24-B26 were reprinted ("second issue"). Values are for the second issue. The 1k from the first issue are worth about 3 times the values shown. Expertization is recommended to distinguish the two printings.

Worker and Peasant (Industry and Agriculture) — SP11

Allegory: Agriculture Will Help End Distress SP12

Star of Hope, Wheat and Worker-Peasant Handclasp — SP13

Sower — SP14

**1922** **Litho.** ***Imperf.***

**Without Gum**

| | | | | |
|---|---|---|---|---|
| **B30** | SP11 | 2t (2000r) green | 15.00 | *250.00* |
| **B31** | SP12 | 2t (2000r) rose | 29.00 | *125.00* |
| **B32** | SP13 | 4t (4000r) rose | 42.50 | *125.00* |
| **B33** | SP14 | 6t (6000r) green | 22.50 | *125.00* |
| | | *Nos. B30-B33 (4)* | 109.00 | 625.00 |

**Double Impression**

| | | | |
|---|---|---|---|
| *B30a* | SP11 | (2000r) green | *475.00* |
| *B31a* | SP12 | (2000r) rose | *650.00* |
| *B32a* | SP13 | (4000r) rose | *725.00* |
| *B33a* | SP14 | (6000r) green | *575.00* |

**Triple Impression**

| | | | |
|---|---|---|---|
| *B30b* | SP11 | (2000r) green | *450.00* |
| *B31b* | SP12 | (2000r) rose | *600.00* |
| *B32b* | SP13 | (4000r) rose | *675.00* |
| *B33b* | SP14 | (6000r) green | *500.00* |

Nos. B30-B33 exist with double impression.

Counterfeits of Nos. B30-B33 exist; beware also of forged cancellations.

Miniature examples of Nos. B30-B33 exist, taken from the 1933 Soviet catalogue.

Automobile SP15

Steamship SP16

Railroad Train SP17

Airplane SP18

**1922** ***Imperf.***

| | | | | |
|---|---|---|---|---|
| **B34** | SP15 | (20r+5r) light violet | .40 | .75 |
| **B35** | SP16 | (20r+5r) violet | .50 | .75 |
| **B36** | SP17 | (20r+5r) gray blue | .40 | .75 |
| **B37** | SP18 | (20r+5r) blue gray | 2.25 | *4.25* |
| | | *Nos. B34-B37 (4)* | 3.55 | *6.50* |

Inscribed "For the Hungry." Each stamp was sold for 200,000r postage and 50,000r charity.

Counterfeits of Nos. B34-B37 exist.

Nos. 212, 183, 202 Surcharged in Bronze, Gold or Silver

**1923** ***Imperf.***

| | | | | |
|---|---|---|---|---|
| **B38** | A48 | 1r +1r on 10r | 500.00 | 500.00 |
| *a.* | | Inverted surcharge | 1,250. | 1,000. |
| **B39** | A48 | 1r +1r on 10r (G) | 50.00 | 30.00 |
| *a.* | | Inverted surcharge | 325.00 | 225.00 |
| **B40** | A43 | 2r +2r on 250r | 50.00 | 40.00 |
| *a.* | | Pelure paper | 40.00 | 25.00 |
| *b.* | | Inverted surcharge | 325.00 | 200.00 |
| *c.* | | Double surcharge | — | |

**Wmk. 171**

| | | | | |
|---|---|---|---|---|
| **B41** | A46 | 4r +4r on 5000r | 30.00 | 25.00 |
| *a.* | | Date spaced "1 923" | 425.00 | 375.00 |
| *b.* | | Inverted surcharge | 1,150. | 1,150. |
| **B42** | A46 | 4r +4r on 5000r (S) | 1,000. | 500.00 |
| *a.* | | Inverted surcharge | 4,750. | 2,500. |
| *b.* | | Date spaced "1 923" | 2,500. | 1,850. |
| *c.* | | As "b," inverted surch. | *22,500.* | 8,000. |
| | | *Nos. B38-B42 (5)* | 1,630. | 1,095. |

The inscriptions mean "Philately's Contribution to Labor." The stamps were on sale only at Moscow and for one day. The surtax was for charitable purposes.

Counterfeits of No. B42 exist.

**Leningrad Flood Issue**

Nos. 181-182, 184-186 Surcharged

**1924** **Unwmk.** ***Imperf.***

| | | | | |
|---|---|---|---|---|
| **B43** | A40 | 3k + 10k on 100r | 3.50 | 3.50 |
| *a.* | | Pelure paper | 2.50 | 4.00 |
| *b.* | | Inverted surcharge | 250.00 | — |
| **B44** | A40 | 7k + 20k on 200r | 3.75 | 3.75 |
| *a.* | | Inverted surcharge | 300.00 | — |
| **B45** | A40 | 14k + 30k on 300r | 3.75 | 3.75 |
| *a.* | | Pelure paper | 625.00 | — |

**Similar Surcharge in Red or Black**

| | | | | |
|---|---|---|---|---|
| **B46** | A41 | 12k + 40k on 500r (R) | 3.75 | 3.75 |
| *a.* | | Double surcharge | 1,600. | — |
| *b.* | | Inverted surcharge | 1,550. | — |
| **B47** | A41 | 20k + 50k on 1000r | 3.00 | 3.00 |
| *a.* | | Thick paper | 20.00 | 25.00 |
| *b.* | | Pelure paper | 10.00 | 10.00 |
| *c.* | | Chalk surface paper | 60.00 | 25.00 |
| | | *Nos. B43-B47 (5)* | 17.75 | 17.75 |

The surcharge on Nos. B43 to B45 reads: "S.S.S.R. For the sufferers by the inundation at Leningrad." That on Nos. B46 and B47 reads: "S.S.S.R. For the Leningrad Proletariat, 23, IX, 1924."

No. B46 is surcharged vertically, reading down, with the value as the top line.

Orphans SP19

Lenin as a Child SP20

**1926** **Typo.** ***Perf. 13½***

| | | | | |
|---|---|---|---|---|
| **B48** | SP19 | 10k brown | *14.50* | *8.75* |
| **B49** | SP20 | 20k deep blue | *60.00* | *16.00* |

**Wmk. 170**

| | | | | |
|---|---|---|---|---|
| **B50** | SP19 | 10k brown | 3.00 | 1.50 |
| **B51** | SP20 | 20k deep blue | 7.50 | 3.50 |
| | | *Nos. B48-B51 (4)* | *85.00* | *29.75* |

Two kopecks of the price of each of these stamps was donated to organizations for the care of indigent children.

**Types of 1926 Issue**

**1927**

| | | | | |
|---|---|---|---|---|
| **B52** | SP19 | 8k + 2k yel green | 1.75 | .50 |
| **B53** | SP20 | 18k + 2k deep rose | 15.00 | 5.00 |

Surtax was for child welfare.

Industrial Training SP21

Agricultural Training SP22

***Perf. 10, 10½, 12½***

**1929-30** **Photo.** **Unwmk.**

| | | | | |
|---|---|---|---|---|
| **B54** | SP21 | 10k +2k ol brn & org brn | 14.50 | *3.00* |
| *a.* | | Perf. 10½ | 200.00 | *25.00* |
| **B55** | SP21 | 10k +2k ol grn ('30) | 6.00 | *1.50* |
| **B56** | SP22 | 20k +2k blk brn & bl, perf. 10 | 10.00 | 2.25 |
| *a.* | | Perf. 12½ | 125.00 | 25.00 |
| *b.* | | Perf. 10½ | 20.00 | 5.00 |
| **B57** | SP22 | 20k +2k bl grn ('30) | 8.50 | *2.25* |
| | | *Nos. B54-B57 (4)* | 39.00 | 9.00 |

Surtax was for child welfare.

**Catalogue values for unused stamps in this section, from this point to the end of the section, are for Never Hinged items.**

"Montreal Passing Torch to Moscow" — SP23

Moscow '80 Olympic Games Emblem — SP24

22nd Olympic Games, Moscow, 1980: 16k+6k, like 10k+5k. 60k+30k, Aerial view of Kremlin and Moscow '80 emblem.

**1976, Dec. 28** **Litho.** ***Perf. 12x12½***

| | | | | |
|---|---|---|---|---|
| **B58** | SP23 | 4k + 2k multi | .50 | .25 |
| **B59** | SP24 | 10k + 5k multi | .70 | .35 |
| **B60** | SP24 | 16k + 6k multi | .80 | .40 |
| | | *Nos. B58-B60 (3)* | 2.00 | 1.00 |

**Souvenir Sheet**

**Photo.**

***Perf. 11½***

| | | | | |
|---|---|---|---|---|
| **B61** | SP23 | 60k + 30k multi | 2.25 | 1.65 |

Greco-Roman Wrestling — SP25

Moscow '80 Emblem and: 6k+3k, Free-style wrestling. 10k+5k, Judo. 16k+6k, Boxing. 20k+10k, Weight lifting.

**1977, June 21** **Litho.** ***Perf. 12½x12***

| | | | | |
|---|---|---|---|---|
| **B62** | SP25 | 4k + 2k multi | .25 | .25 |
| **B63** | SP25 | 6k + 3k multi | .25 | .25 |
| **B64** | SP25 | 10k + 5k multi | .25 | .30 |
| **B65** | SP25 | 16k + 6k multi | .40 | .35 |
| **B66** | SP25 | 20k + 10k multi | .60 | .45 |
| | | *Nos. B62-B66 (5)* | 1.75 | 1.60 |

***Perf. 12½x12, 12x12½***

**1977, Sept. 22**

Designs: 4k+2k, Bicyclist. 6k+3k, Woman archer, vert. 10k+5k, Sharpshooting. 16k+6k, Equestrian. 20k+10k, Fencer. 50k+25k, Equestrian and fencer.

| | | | | |
|---|---|---|---|---|
| **B67** | SP25 | 4k + 2k multi | .25 | .25 |
| **B68** | SP25 | 6k + 3k multi | .25 | .25 |
| **B69** | SP25 | 10k + 5k multi | .40 | .30 |
| **B70** | SP25 | 16k + 6k multi | .55 | .35 |
| **B71** | SP25 | 20k + 10k multi | .70 | .45 |
| | | *Nos. B67-B71 (5)* | 2.15 | 1.60 |

**Souvenir Sheet**

***Perf. 12½x12***

| | | | | |
|---|---|---|---|---|
| **B72** | SP25 | 50k + 25k multi | 2.00 | 1.65 |

**1978, Mar. 24** ***Perf. 12½x12***

Designs: 4k+2k, Swimmer at start. 6k+3k, Woman diver, vert. 10k+5k, Water polo. 16k+6k, Canoeing. 20k+10k, Canadian single. 50k+25k, Start of double scull race.

| | | | | |
|---|---|---|---|---|
| **B73** | SP25 | 4k + 2k multi | .25 | .25 |
| **B74** | SP25 | 6k + 3k multi | .25 | .25 |
| **B75** | SP25 | 10k + 5k multi | .30 | .25 |
| **B76** | SP25 | 16k + 6k multi | .40 | .30 |
| **B77** | SP25 | 20k + 10k multi | .60 | .45 |
| | | *Nos. B73-B77 (5)* | 1.80 | 1.50 |

**Souvenir Sheet**

| | | | | |
|---|---|---|---|---|
| **B78** | SP25 | 50k + 25k grn & blk | 2.00 | 2.00 |

Star-class Yacht — SP26

Keel Yachts and Moscow '80 Emblem: 6k+3k, Soling class. 10k+5k, Centerboarder 470. 16k+6k, Finn class. 20k+10k, Flying Dutchman class. 50k+25k, Catamaran Tornado, horiz.

**1978, Oct. 26** **Litho.** ***Perf. 12x12½***

| | | | | |
|---|---|---|---|---|
| **B79** | SP26 | 4k + 2k multi | .25 | .25 |
| **B80** | SP26 | 6k + 3k multi | .25 | .25 |
| **B81** | SP26 | 10k + 5k multi | .30 | .25 |
| **B82** | SP26 | 16k + 6k multi | .40 | .30 |
| **B83** | SP26 | 20k + 10k multi | .60 | .40 |
| | | *Nos. B79-B83 (5)* | 1.80 | 1.45 |

**Souvenir Sheet**

***Perf. 12½x12***

| | | | | |
|---|---|---|---|---|
| **B84** | SP26 | 50k + 25k multi | 2.00 | 1.40 |

Women's Gymnastics SP27

Designs: 6k+3k, Man on parallel bars. 10k+5k, Man on horizontal bar. 16k+6k, Woman on balance beam. 20k+10k, Woman on uneven bars. 50k+25k, Man on rings.

**1979, Mar. 21** **Litho.** ***Perf. 12x12½***

| | | | | |
|---|---|---|---|---|
| **B85** | SP27 | 4k + 2k multi | .25 | .25 |
| **B86** | SP27 | 6k + 3k multi | .25 | .25 |
| **B87** | SP27 | 10k + 5k multi | .30 | .25 |
| **B88** | SP27 | 16k + 6k multi | .40 | .30 |
| **B89** | SP27 | 20k + 10k multi | .60 | .40 |
| | | *Nos. B85-B89 (5)* | 1.80 | 1.45 |

**Souvenir Sheet**

***Perf. 12½x12***

| | | | | |
|---|---|---|---|---|
| **B90** | SP25 | 50k + 25k multi | 2.00 | 1.40 |

**1979, June** ***Perf. 12½x12, 12x12½***

Designs: 4k+2k, Soccer. 6k+3k, Basketball. 10k+5k, Women's volleyball. 16k+6k, Handball. 20k+10k, Field hockey.

| | | | | |
|---|---|---|---|---|
| **B91** | SP25 | 4k + 2k multi | .25 | .25 |
| **B92** | SP27 | 6k + 3k multi | .25 | .25 |
| **B93** | SP27 | 10k + 5k multi | .30 | .25 |
| **B94** | SP25 | 16k + 6k multi | .40 | .30 |
| **B95** | SP25 | 20k + 10k multi | .60 | .40 |
| | | *Nos. B91-B95 (5)* | 1.80 | 1.45 |

22nd Olympic Games, Moscow, July 19-Aug. 3, 1980.

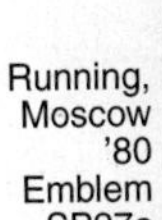

Running, Moscow '80 Emblem SP27a

No. B97, Pole vault. No. B98, Discus. No. B99, Hurdles. No. B100, Javelin. No. B101, Walking, vert. No. B102, Hammer throw. No. B103, High jump. No. B104, Shot put. No. B105, Long jump.
No. B106, Relay race.

**1980 Litho. *Perf. 12½x12, 12x12½***

| | | | | |
|---|---|---|---|---|
| **B96** | SP27a | 4k + 2k shown | .25 | .25 |
| **B97** | SP27a | 4k + 2k multi | .25 | .25 |
| **B98** | SP27a | 6k + 3k multi | .25 | .25 |
| **B99** | SP27a | 6k + 3k multi | .25 | .25 |
| **B100** | SP27a | 10k + 5k multi | .40 | .25 |
| **B101** | SP27a | 10k + 5k multi | .40 | .25 |
| **B102** | SP27a | 16k + 6k multi | .70 | .30 |
| **B103** | SP27a | 16k + 6k multi | .70 | .30 |
| **B104** | SP27a | 20k + 10k multi | .90 | .40 |
| **B105** | SP27a | 20k + 10k multi | .90 | .40 |
| | | *Nos. B96-B105 (10)* | 5.00 | 2.90 |

**Souvenir Sheet**

| | | | | |
|---|---|---|---|---|
| **B106** | SP27a | 50k + 25k multi | 2.00 | 1.00 |

22nd Olympic Games, Moscow, July 19-Aug. 3. Issued: Nos. B96, B99, B101, B103, B105, Feb. 6; others, Mar. 12.

Moscow '80 Emblem, Relief from St. Dimitri's Cathedral, Arms of Vladimir — SP28

Moscow '80 Emblem and: No. B108, Bridge over Klyazma River and Vladimir Hotel. No. B109, Relief from Nativity Cathedral and coat of arms (falcon), Suzdal. No. B110, Tourist complex and Pozharski Monument, Suzdal. No. B111, Frunze Monument, Ivanovo, torch and spindle. No. B112, Museum of First Soviets, Fighters of the Revolution Monument, Ivanovo.

**Photogravure and Engraved**

**1977, Dec. 30 *Perf. 11½x12***

| | | | | |
|---|---|---|---|---|
| **B107** | SP28 | 1r + 50k multi | 1.40 | 1.00 |
| **B108** | SP28 | 1r + 50k multi | 1.40 | 1.00 |
| **B109** | SP28 | 1r + 50k multi | 1.40 | 1.00 |
| **B110** | SP28 | 1r + 50k multi | 1.40 | 1.00 |
| **B111** | SP28 | 1r + 50k multi | 1.40 | 1.00 |
| **B112** | SP28 | 1r + 50k multi | 1.40 | 1.00 |
| | | *Nos. B107-B112 (6)* | 8.40 | 6.00 |

"Tourism around the Golden Ring."

Fortifications and Arms of Zagorsk SP29

Moscow '80 Emblem and (Coat of Arms design): No. B114, Gagarin Palace of Culture and new arms of Zagorsk (building & horse). No. B115, Rostov Kremlin with St. John the Divine Church and No. B116, View of Rostov from Nero Lake (deer). No. B117, Alexander Nevski and WWII soldiers' monuments, Pereslav-Zalesski and No. B118, Peter the Great monument, Pereslav-Zalesski (lion & fish). No. B119, Tower and wall of Monastery of the Transfiguration, Yaroslavl and No. B120, Dock and monument for Soviet heroes, Yaroslava (bear).

**1978 *Perf. 12x11½***

**Multicolored and**

| | | | | |
|---|---|---|---|---|
| **B113** | SP29 | 1r + 50k gold | 2.00 | 1.00 |
| **B114** | SP29 | 1r + 50k silver | 2.00 | 1.00 |
| **B115** | SP29 | 1r + 50k silver | 2.00 | 1.00 |
| **B116** | SP29 | 1r + 50k gold | 2.00 | 1.00 |
| **B117** | SP29 | 1r + 50k gold | 2.00 | 1.00 |
| **B118** | SP29 | 1r + 50k silver | 2.00 | 1.00 |
| **B119** | SP29 | 1r + 50k gold | 2.00 | 1.00 |
| **B120** | SP29 | 1r + 50k silver | 2.00 | 1.00 |
| | | *Nos. B113-B120 (8)* | 16.00 | 8.00 |

Issued: #B113-B116, 10/16; #B117-B120, 12/25.

**1979 *Perf. 12x11½***

Moscow '80 Emblem and: No. B121, Narikaly Fortress, Tbilisi, 4th century. No. B122, Georgia Philharmonic Concert Hall, "Muse" sculpture, Tbilisi. No. B123, Chir-Dor Mosque, 17th century, Samarkand. No. B124, Peoples Friendship Museum, "Courage" monument, Tashkent. No. B125, Landscape, Erevan. B126, Armenian State Opera and Ballet Theater, Erevan.

**Multicolored and**

| | | | | |
|---|---|---|---|---|
| **B121** | SP29 | 1r+50k sil, bl circle | 1.75 | 1.25 |
| **B122** | SP29 | 1r+50k gold, yel circle | 1.75 | 1.25 |
| **B123** | SP29 | 1r+50k sil, bl 8-point star | 1.75 | 1.25 |
| **B124** | SP29 | 1r+50k gold, red 8-point star | 1.75 | 1.25 |
| **B125** | SP29 | 1r+50k sil, bl diamond | 1.75 | 1.25 |
| **B126** | SP29 | 1r+50k gold, red diamond | 1.75 | 1.25 |
| | | *Nos. B121-B126 (6)* | 10.50 | 7.50 |

Issued: #B121-B124, 9/5; #B125-B126, Oct.

Kremlin SP29a

Kalinin Prospect, Moscow SP29b

Admiralteistvo, St. Isaak Cathedral, Leningrad — SP29c

World War II Defense Monument, Leningrad SP29d

Bogdan Khmelnitisky Monument, St. Sophia's Monastery Kiev SP29e

Metro Bridge, Dnieper River, Kiev — SP29f

Palace of Sports, Obelisk, Minsk SP29g

Republican House of Cinematography, Minsk — SP29h

Vyshgorodsky Castle, Town Hall, Tallinn SP29i

Viru Hotel, Tallinn SP29j

Moscow '80 Emblem, Coat of Arms.

**1980 *Perf. 12x11½***

| | | | | |
|---|---|---|---|---|
| **B127** | SP29a | 1r + 50k multi | 1.50 | 1.25 |
| **B128** | SP29b | 1r + 50k multi | 1.50 | 1.25 |
| **B129** | SP29c | 1r + 50k multi | 1.50 | 1.25 |
| **B130** | SP29d | 1r + 50k multi | 1.50 | 1.25 |
| **B131** | SP29e | 1r + 50k multi | 1.50 | 1.25 |
| **B132** | SP29f | 1r + 50k multi | 1.50 | 1.25 |
| **B133** | SP29g | 1r + 50k multi | 1.50 | 1.25 |
| **B134** | SP29h | 1r + 50k multi | 1.50 | 1.25 |
| **B135** | SP29i | 1r + 50k multi | 1.50 | 1.25 |
| **B136** | SP29j | 1r + 50k multi | 1.50 | 1.25 |
| | | *Nos. B127-B136 (10)* | 15.00 | 12.50 |

Tourism. Issue dates: #B127-B128, Feb. 29. #B129-B130, Mar. 25; #B131-B136, Apr. 30.

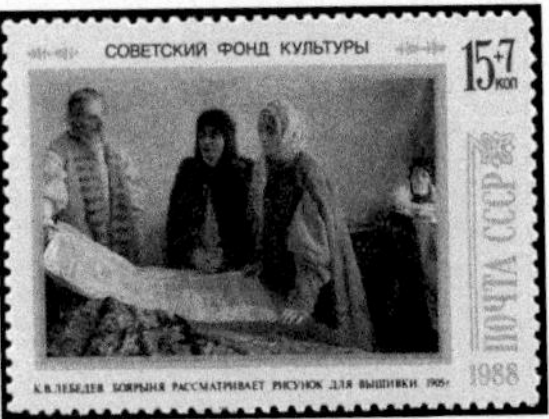

Soviet Culture Fund — SP30

Art treasures: No. B137, *O.K. Lansere*, 1910, by Z.E. Serebriakova, vert. No. B138, *Boyar's Wife Examining an Embroidery Design*, 1905, by K.V. Lebedev. No. B139, *Talent*, 1910, by N.P. Bogdanov-Belsky, vert. No. B140, *Trinity*, 15th-16th cent., Novgorod School, vert.

***Perf. 12x12½, 12½x12***

**1988, Aug. 22 Litho.**

| | | | | |
|---|---|---|---|---|
| **B137** | SP30 | 10k +5k multi | .35 | .25 |
| **B138** | SP30 | 15k +7k multi | .45 | .35 |
| **B139** | SP30 | 30k +15k multi | 1.25 | .75 |
| | | *Nos. B137-B139 (3)* | 2.05 | 1.35 |

**Souvenir Sheet**

| | | | | |
|---|---|---|---|---|
| **B140** | SP30 | 1r +50k multi | 2.00 | 1.00 |

SP31

**1988, Oct. 20 Litho. *Perf. 12***

| | | | | |
|---|---|---|---|---|
| **B141** | SP31 | 10k +5k Bear | .25 | .25 |
| **B142** | SP31 | 10k +5k Wolf | .25 | .25 |
| **B143** | SP31 | 20k +10k Fox | .40 | .35 |
| **B144** | SP31 | 20k +10k Boar | .40 | .35 |
| **B145** | SP31 | 20k +10k Lynx | .40 | .35 |
| *a.* | | Block of 5+label, #B141-B145 | 2.00 | 1.60 |

Zoo Relief Fund. See #B152-B156, B166-B168.

Lenin Children's Fund SP32

Children's drawings and fund emblem: No. B146, Skating Rink. No. B147, Rooster. No. B148, May (girl and flowers).

**1988, Dec. 12 Litho. *Perf. 12***

| | | | |
|---|---|---|---|
| **B146** SP32 5k +2k multi | .25 | .25 |
| **B147** SP32 5k +2k multi | .25 | .25 |
| **B148** SP32 5k +2k multi | .25 | .25 |
| *a.* Block of 3+label, #B146-B148 | 2.00 | 1.00 |

See Nos. B169-B171.

SP33

#B149, Tigranes I (c. 140-55 B.C.), king of Armenia, gold coin. #B150, St. Ripsime Temple, c. 618. #B151, *Virgin and Child,* fresco (detail) by Ovnat Ovnatanyan, 18th cent., Echmiadzin Cathedral.

**1988, Dec. 27 *Perf. 12½x12***

| | | |
|---|---|---|
| **B149** SP33 20k +10k multi | .40 | .25 |
| **B150** SP33 30k +15k multi | .50 | .30 |
| **B151** SP33 50k +25k multi | 1.00 | .50 |
| *a.* Block of 3+label, #B149-B151 | 2.00 | 1.00 |

Armenian earthquake relief. For surcharges see Nos. B173-B175.

### Zoo Relief Type of 1988

Nos. B152-B156 are horiz. stamps.

**1989, Mar. 20 Litho. *Perf. 12***

| | | |
|---|---|---|
| **B152** SP31 10k+5k Marten | .40 | .30 |
| **B153** SP31 10k+5k Squirrel | .40 | .30 |
| **B154** SP31 20k+10k Hare | .75 | .50 |
| **B155** SP31 20k+10k Hedgehog | .75 | .50 |
| **B156** SP31 20k+10k Badger | .75 | .50 |
| *a.* Block [illegible] #B152-B156 | 3.00 | 2.00 |

### Lenin Children's Fund Type of 1988

Fund emblem and children's drawings: No. B157, Rabbit. No. B158, Cat. No. B159, Doctor. Nos. B157-B159 vert.

**1989, June 14 Litho. *Perf. 12***

| | | |
|---|---|---|
| **B157** SP32 5k +2k multi | .50 | .25 |
| **B158** SP32 5k +2k multi | .50 | .25 |
| **B159** SP32 5k +2k multi | .50 | .25 |
| *a.* Block of 3+label, #B157-B159 | 2.00 | .75 |

Surtax for the fund.

Soviet Culture Fund SP34

Paintings and porcelain: No. B160, *Village Market,* by A. Makovsky. No. B161, *Lady Wearing a Hat,* by E. Zelenin. No. B162, *Portrait of the Actress Bazhenova,* by A. Sofronova. No. B163, *Two Women,* by H. Shaiber. No. B164, Popov porcelain coffee pot and plates, 19th cent.

**1989 Litho. *Perf. 12x12½***

| | | |
|---|---|---|
| **B160** SP34 4k +2k multi | .25 | .25 |
| **B161** SP34 5k +2k multi | .25 | .25 |
| **B162** SP34 10k +5k multi | .30 | .25 |
| **B163** SP34 20k +10k multi | .50 | .30 |
| **B164** SP34 30k +15k multi | .85 | .50 |
| *Nos. B160-B164 (5)* | 2.15 | 1.55 |

### Souvenir Sheet

Nature Conservation — SP35

**1989, Dec. 14 Photo. *Perf. 11½***

| | | |
|---|---|---|
| **B165** SP35 20k + 10k Swallow | 5.00 | 5.00 |

Surtax for the Soviet Union of Philatelists.

### Zoo Relief Type of 1988

No. B166, Aquila chrysaetos. No. B167, Falco cherrug. No. B168,

**1990, May 4 Litho. *Perf. 12***

| | | |
|---|---|---|
| **B166** SP31 10k +5k multi | .45 | .30 |
| **B167** SP31 20k +10k multi | 1.00 | .65 |
| **B168** SP31 20k +10k multi | 1.00 | .65 |
| *a.* Block of 3 + label, #B166-B168 | 3.00 | 1.65 |

Nos. B166-B168 horiz.

### Lenin's Children Fund Type of 1988

No. B169, Clown. No. B170, Group of women. No. B171, Group of children. No. B169-B171, vert.

**1990, July 3 Litho. *Perf. 12***

| | | |
|---|---|---|
| **B169** SP32 5k +2k multi | .65 | .25 |
| **B170** SP32 5k +2k multi | .65 | .25 |
| **B171** SP32 5k +2k multi | .65 | .25 |
| *a.* Block of 3, #B169-B171 + label | 2.00 | .45 |

Nature Conservation — SP36

**1990, Sept. 12 Litho. *Perf. 12***

| | | |
|---|---|---|
| **B172** SP36 20k +10k multi | 1.10 | 1.10 |

Surtax for Soviet Union of Philatelists.

### Nos. B149-B151 Overprinted

No. B173

Nos. B174-B175

**1990, Nov. 24 Litho. *Perf. 12x12½***

| | | |
|---|---|---|
| **B173** SP33 20k +10k multi | .90 | .65 |
| **B174** SP33 30k +15k multi | 1.40 | .90 |
| **B175** SP33 50k +25k multi | 2.25 | 1.50 |
| *a.* Block of 3+label, #B173-B175 | 4.00 | 3.00 |

Armenia '90 Philatelic Exhibition.

Soviet Culture Fund — SP37

Paintings by N. K. Roerich: 10k+5k, Unkrada, 1909. 20k+10k, Pskovo-Pechorsky Monastery, 1907.

**1990, Dec. 20 Litho. *Perf. 12½x12***

| | | |
|---|---|---|
| **B176** SP37 10k +5k multi | .40 | .25 |
| **B177** SP37 20k +10k multi | .60 | .35 |

### Souvenir Sheet

Joys of All Those Grieving, 18th Cent. — SP38

**1990, Dec. 23 *Perf. 12½x12***

| | | |
|---|---|---|
| **B178** SP38 50k +25k multi | 2.00 | 1.00 |

Surtax for Charity and Health Fund.

Ciconia Ciconia SP39

**1991, Feb. 4 Litho. *Perf. 12***

| | | |
|---|---|---|
| **B179** SP39 10k +5k multi | .55 | .35 |

Surtax for the Zoo Relief Fund.

### Souvenir Sheet

USSR Philatelic Society, 25th Anniv. — SP40

**1991, Feb. 15 *Perf. 12x12½***

| | | |
|---|---|---|
| **B180** SP40 20k +10k multi | 1.10 | 1.10 |

The Universe by V. Lukianets SP41

No. B182, Another Planet by V. Lukianets.

**1991, June 1 Litho. *Perf. 12½x12***

| | | |
|---|---|---|
| **B181** SP41 10k +5k multi | .50 | .25 |
| **B182** SP41 10k +5k multi | .50 | .25 |

Lenin's Children's Fund.

SP42

**1991, July 10 *Perf. 12x12½***

| | | |
|---|---|---|
| **B183** SP42 20k +10k multi | .50 | .25 |

Surtax for Soviet Culture Fund.

SP43

**1991, July 10 *Perf. 12***

| | | |
|---|---|---|
| **B184** SP43 20k +10k multi | .50 | .25 |

Surtax for Soviet Charity & Health Fund

### Souvenir Sheet

SP44

**1992, Jan. 22 Litho. *Perf. 12½x12***

| | | |
|---|---|---|
| **B185** SP44 3r +50k multi | 1.00 | .70 |

Surtax for Nature Preservation.

---

## AIR POST STAMPS

AP1

### Plane Overprint in Red

**1922 Unwmk. *Imperf.***

| | | |
|---|---|---|
| **C1** AP1 45r green & black | 10.00 | — |
| *a.* Translucent paper | 85.00 | — |

5th anniversary of October Revolution.

No. C1 was on sale only at the Moscow General Post Office. Counterfeits exist.

Fokker F-111 — AP2

**1923 Photo.**

| | | |
|---|---|---|
| **C2** AP2 1r red brown | 20.00 | |
| **C3** AP2 3r deep blue | 20.00 | |
| **C4** AP2 5r green | 5.00 | |
| *a.* Wide "5" | *40,000.* | |
| **C5** AP2 10r carmine | 5.00 | |
| *Nos. C2-C5 (4)* | 50.00 | |

Nos. C2-C5 were not placed in use.

Nos. C2-C5 Surcharged

**1924**

| | | | | |
|---|---|---|---|---|
| **C6** | AP2 | 5k on 3r dp blue | 5.50 | 2.00 |
| **C7** | AP2 | 10k on 5r green | 2.50 | .60 |
| *a.* | | Wide "5" | *1,250.* | *700.00* |
| *b.* | | Inverted surcharge | *2,750.* | — |
| **C8** | AP2 | 15k on 1r red brown | 10.00 | 2.00 |
| *a.* | | Inverted surcharge | *1,400.* | *500.00* |
| **C9** | AP2 | 20k on 10r car | 2.50 | .50 |
| *a.* | | Inverted surcharge | *4,000.* | *2,500.* |
| | | *Nos. C6-C9 (4)* | 20.50 | 5.10 |

Airplane over Map of World AP3

**1927, Sept. 1 Litho. *Perf. 13x12***

| | | | | |
|---|---|---|---|---|
| **C10** | AP3 | 10k dk bl & yel brn | 25.00 | *15.00* |
| **C11** | AP3 | 15k dp red & ol grn | 50.00 | *20.00* |

1st Intl. Air Post Cong. at The Hague, initiated by the USSR.

Graf Zeppelin and "Call to Complete 5-Year Plan in 4 Years" — AP4

**1930 Photo. Wmk. 226 *Perf. 12½***

| | | | | |
|---|---|---|---|---|
| **C12** | AP4 | 40k dark blue | 40.00 | 20.00 |
| *a.* | | Perf. 10½ | 40.00 | 20.00 |
| *b.* | | Imperf. | *1,650.* | *1,325.* |
| **C13** | AP4 | 80k carmine | 40.00 | 20.00 |
| *a.* | | Perf. 10½ | 40.00 | 20.00 |
| *b.* | | Imperf. | *1,650.* | *1,325.* |

Flight of the Graf Zeppelin from Friedrichshafen to Moscow and return.

Symbolical of Airship Communication from the Tundra to the Steppes — AP5

Airship over Dneprostroi Dam — AP6

Airship over Lenin Mausoleum — AP7

Airship Exploring Arctic Regions — AP8

Constructing an Airship AP9

**1931-32 Wmk. 170 Photo. *Imperf.***

| | | | | |
|---|---|---|---|---|
| **C15** | AP5 | 10k dark violet | 40.00 | 30.00 |
| | | **Litho.** | | |
| **C16** | AP6 | 15k gray blue | 40.00 | 30.00 |
| | | **Typo.** | | |
| **C17** | AP7 | 20k dk carmine | 40.00 | 30.00 |
| | | **Photo.** | | |
| **C18** | AP8 | 50k black brown | 40.00 | 30.00 |
| *a.* | | 50k gray blue (error) | *85,000.* | |
| **C19** | AP9 | 1r dark green | 40.00 | 32.50 |
| | | *Nos. C15-C19 (5)* | 200.00 | 152.50 |

***Perf. 12x12¼, 12¼x12½x12 (#C21, C23)***

| | | | | |
|---|---|---|---|---|
| **C20** | AP5 | 10k dark violet | 3.00 | 1.75 |
| | | **Litho.** | | |
| **C21** | AP6 | 15k gray blue | 120.00 | 19.00 |
| | | **Typo.** | | |
| **C22** | AP7 | 20k dk carmine | 3.00 | 1.75 |
| *a.* | | 20k light red | 3.00 | — |
| | | **Photo.** | | |
| **C23** | AP8 | 50k black brown | 14.50 | 4.00 |
| *a.* | | 50k gray blue (error) | 500.00 | 300.00 |
| **C24** | AP9 | 1r dark green | 15.00 | 2.50 |

***Perf. 12½***

**Unwmk. Engr.**

| | | | | |
|---|---|---|---|---|
| **C25** | AP6 | 15k gray blk ('32) | 6.00 | 1.25 |
| *a.* | | Perf. 10½ | *2,000.* | *135.00* |
| *b.* | | Perf. 14 | 17.50 | 22.50 |
| *c.* | | Imperf. | — | *3,250.* |
| | | *Nos. C20-C25 (6)* | 161.50 | 30.25 |

The 11½ perforation on Nos. C20-C25 is of private origin; beware also of bogus perforation "errors."

**North Pole Issue**

Graf Zeppelin and Icebreaker "Malygin" Transferring Mail — AP10

**1931 Wmk. 170 *Imperf.***

| | | | | |
|---|---|---|---|---|
| **C26** | AP10 | 30k dark violet | 35.00 | *17.50* |
| **C27** | AP10 | 35k dark green | 7.25 | *4.25* |
| **C28** | AP10 | 1r gray black | 48.00 | *17.50* |
| **C29** | AP10 | 2r deep ultra | 24.00 | 17.50 |
| | | *Nos. C26-C29 (4)* | 114.25 | 56.75 |

***Perf. 12x12¼***

| | | | | |
|---|---|---|---|---|
| **C30** | AP10 | 30k dark violet | 45.00 | *15.00* |
| **C31** | AP10 | 35k dark green | 60.00 | *12.50* |
| **C32** | AP10 | 1r gray black | 105.00 | *35.00* |
| **C33** | AP10 | 2r deep ultra | 45.00 | *15.00* |
| | | *Nos. C30-C33 (4)* | 255.00 | *77.50* |

***Perf. 12¼***

| | | | | |
|---|---|---|---|---|
| **C30a** | AP10 | 30k dark violet | 40.00 | 17.50 |
| **C31a** | AP10 | 35k dark green | 37.50 | 25.00 |
| **C32a** | AP10 | 1r gray black | 60.00 | 60.00 |
| **C33a** | AP10 | 2r deep ultra | 45.00 | 20.00 |

Map of Polar Region, Airplane and Icebreaker "Sibiryakov" — AP11

***Perf. 12, 10½***

**1932, Aug. 26 Wmk. 170**

| | | | | |
|---|---|---|---|---|
| **C34** | AP11 | 50k car rose | 100.00 | 15.00 |
| *a.* | | Perf. 10½ | *30,000.* | *14,000.* |
| *b.* | | Perf. 10½x12 | | *20,000.* |
| **C35** | AP11 | 1r green | 50.00 | 30.00 |
| *a.* | | Perf. 12 | 75.00 | *37.50* |

2nd International Polar Year in connection with proposed flight from Franz-Josef Land to Archangel which, being impossible, actually went from Archangel to Moscow to destinations.

Stratostat "U.S.S.R." — AP12

**1933 Photo. *Perf. 14***

| | | | | |
|---|---|---|---|---|
| **C37** | AP12 | 5k ultra | 210.00 | 10.00 |
| **C38** | AP12 | 10k carmine | 70.00 | 10.00 |
| **C39** | AP12 | 20k violet | 30.00 | 9.50 |
| | | *Nos. C37-C39 (3)* | 310.00 | 29.50 |

**Pairs, Imperf. Between**

| | | | |
|---|---|---|---|
| *C37a* | Vert. pair, imperf. between | *11,250.* | — |
| *C37b* | Horiz. pair, imperf. between | *6,500.* | *2,500.* |
| *C38a* | Horiz. pair, imperf. between | — | *12,750.* |
| *C39a* | Vert. pair, imperf. between | *11,500.* | — |

Ascent into the stratosphere by Soviet aeronauts, Sept. 30th, 1933.

Furnaces of Kuznetsk AP13

Designs: 10k, Oil wells. 20k, Collective farm. 50k, Map of Moscow-Volga Canal project. 80k, Arctic cargo ship.

**1934, Feb. Wmk. 170 *Perf. 14***

| | | | | |
|---|---|---|---|---|
| **C40** | AP13 | 5k ultra | 35.00 | 6.00 |
| **C41** | AP13 | 10k green | 35.00 | 6.75 |
| **C42** | AP13 | 20k carmine | 100.00 | 7.50 |
| **C43** | AP13 | 50k dull blue | 250.00 | 35.00 |
| **C44** | AP13 | 80k purple | 80.00 | 9.00 |
| | | *Nos. C40-C44 (5)* | 500.00 | 64.25 |

**Unwmk.**

| | | | | |
|---|---|---|---|---|
| **C45** | AP13 | 5k ultra | 35.00 | *4.00* |
| **C46** | AP13 | 10k green | 35.00 | *3.75* |
| *a.* | | Horiz. pair, imperf. btwn. | 2,000. | *1,250.* |
| **C47** | AP13 | 20k carmine | 45.00 | *6.00* |
| **C48** | AP13 | 50k dull blue | 260.00 | *28.50* |
| **C49** | AP13 | 80k purple | 28.00 | *6.00* |
| | | *Nos. C45-C49 (5)* | 403.00 | *48.25* |

10th anniversary of Soviet civil aviation and airmail service. Counterfeits exist, perf 11½.

I. D. Usyskin AP18

10k, A. B. Vasenko. 20k, P. F. Fedosenko.

**1934 Wmk. 170 *Perf. 11***

| | | | | |
|---|---|---|---|---|
| **C50** | AP18 | 5k vio brown | 17.50 | 6.00 |
| **C51** | AP18 | 10k brown | 115.00 | 6.00 |
| **C52** | AP18 | 20k ultra | 27.50 | 8.25 |
| | | *Nos. C50-C52 (3)* | 160.00 | 20.25 |

***Perf. 13¾***

| | | | | |
|---|---|---|---|---|
| *C50a* | AP18 | 5k | 135. | |
| *C51a* | AP18 | 10k | — | *4,500.* |
| *C52a* | AP18 | 20k | 10,000. | |
| | | *Nos. C50a-C52a (3)* | 10,135. | *4,500.* |

Honoring victims of the stratosphere disaster. See Nos. C77-C79.

Beware of examples of Nos. C50-C52 reperforated to resemble Nos. C50a-C52a.

Airship "Pravda" — AP19

Airship Landing — AP20

Airship "Voroshilov" — AP21

Sideview of Airship — AP22

Airship "Lenin" — AP23

**1934 *Perf. 14***

| | | | | |
|---|---|---|---|---|
| **C53** | AP19 | 5k red orange | 25.00 | *2.40* |
| **C54** | AP20 | 10k claret | 27.50 | *3.75* |
| **C55** | AP21 | 15k brown | 75.00 | *10.00* |
| **C56** | AP22 | 20k black | 15.00 | *7.50* |
| **C57** | AP23 | 30k ultra | 375.00 | *55.00* |
| | | *Nos. C53-C57 (5)* | 517.50 | 78.65 |

Capt. V. Voronin and "Chelyuskin" — AP24

Prof. Otto Y. Schmidt — AP25

A. V. Lapidevsky
AP26

S. A. Levanevsky
AP27

"Schmidt Camp" — AP28

Designs: 10k, M. G. Slenney. 20k, I. V. Doronin. 25k, M. V. Vodopianov. 30k, V. U. Molokov. 40k, N. P. Kamanin.

**1935** ***Perf. 14***

| | | | | | |
|---|---|---|---|---|---|
| **C58** | AP24 | 1k | red orange | 12.50 | 2.25 |
| **C59** | AP25 | 3k | rose car | 12.50 | 2.25 |
| **C60** | AP26 | 5k | emerald | 7.50 | 2.25 |
| **C61** | AP27 | 10k | dark brown | 17.50 | 2.25 |
| **C62** | AP27 | 15k | black | 17.50 | 3.75 |
| **C63** | AP27 | 20k | deep claret | 22.50 | 3.75 |
| **C64** | AP27 | 25k | indigo | 120.00 | 17.50 |
| **C65** | AP27 | 30k | dull green | 750.00 | 50.00 |
| **C66** | AP27 | 40k | purple | 22.00 | 12.00 |
| **C67** | AP28 | 50k | dark ultra | 50.00 | 30.00 |
| | | | *Nos. C58-C67 (10)* | 1,032. | 126.00 |

Aerial rescue of ice-breaker Chelyuskin crew and scientific expedition.

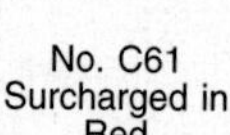

No. C61 Surcharged in Red

**1935, Aug.**

| | | | | |
|---|---|---|---|---|
| **C68** | AP27 | 1r on 10k dk brn | 500.00 | 475.00 |
| *a.* | | Inverted surcharge | *90,000.* | |
| *b.* | | Lower case Cyrillic "F" | 1,500. | 1,450. |
| *c.* | | As "b," inverted surcharge | *600,000.* | |

Moscow-San Francisco flight. Counterfeits exist.

Single-Engined Monoplane — AP34

Five-Engined Transport — AP35

20k, Twin-engined cabin plane. 30k, 4r-motored transport. 40k, Single-engined amphibian. 50k, Twin-motored transport. 80k, 8-motored transport.

**1937** **Unwmk.** ***Perf. 12***

| | | | | | |
|---|---|---|---|---|---|
| **C69** | AP34 | 10k | yel brn & blk | 3.00 | 1.00 |
| *a.* | | | Imperf. | | — |
| **C70** | AP34 | 20k | gray grn & blk | 3.00 | 1.00 |
| **C71** | AP34 | 30k | red brn & blk | 3.00 | 1.00 |
| **C72** | AP34 | 40k | vio brn & blk | 5.25 | 1.00 |
| **C73** | AP34 | 50k | dk vio & blk | 16.50 | 2.00 |
| **C74** | AP35 | 80k | bl vio & brn | 16.50 | 6.00 |
| **C75** | AP35 | 1r | blk, brn & buff | 45.00 | 8.50 |
| *a.* | | | Sheet of 4, imperf. | 175.00 | *215.00* |

**Vertical Pairs, Imperf. Between**

| | | | | | |
|---|---|---|---|---|---|
| *C69b* | AP34 | 10k | yel brn & blk | — | *62.50* |
| *C70a* | AP34 | 20k | gray grn & blk | *3,250.* | *3,250.* |
| *C71a* | AP34 | 30k | red brn & blk | — | *4,250.* |
| *C72a* | AP34 | 40k | vio brn & blk | *3,250.* | *3,250.* |
| *C73a* | AP34 | 50k | dk vio & blk | — | *4,500.* |
| | | | *Nos. C69-C75 (7)* | 92.25 | 20.50 |
| | | | Set, never hinged | 168.00 | |

Jubilee Aviation Exhib., Moscow, Nov. 15-20.

Vertical pairs, imperf. between, exist for No. C71, value $4,000; No. C72, value $5,750; No. C73, value $2,300.

Types of 1938 Regular Issue Overprinted in Various Colors

**1939** ***Typo.***

| | | | | | |
|---|---|---|---|---|---|
| **C76** | A282 | 10k | red (C) | 4.00 | 1.25 |
| **C76A** | A285 | 30k | blue (R) | 6.75 | 1.25 |
| **C76B** | A286 | 40k | dl grn (Br) | 8.25 | 1.50 |
| **C76C** | A287 | 50k | dl vio (R) | 6.75 | 2.50 |
| **C76D** | A289 | 1r | brown (Bl) | 12.50 | 3.50 |
| *a.* | | | Double overprint | | 1,500. |
| | | | *Nos. C76-C76D (5)* | 38.25 | 10.00 |
| | | | Set, never hinged | 100.00 | |

Soviet Aviation Day, Aug. 18, 1939.

**Types of 1934 with "30.1.1944" Added at Lower Left**

Designs: No. C77, P. F. Fedosenko. No. C78, I. D. Usyskin. No. C79, A. B. Vasenko.

**1944** **Photo.** ***Perf. 12***

| | | | | | |
|---|---|---|---|---|---|
| **C77** | AP18 | 1r | deep blue | 5.00 | .75 |
| **C78** | AP18 | 1r | slate green | 5.00 | .75 |
| **C79** | AP18 | 1r | brt yellow green | 5.00 | .75 |
| | | | *Nos. C77-C79 (3)* | 15.00 | 2.25 |
| | | | Set, never hinged | 30.00 | |

1934 stratosphere disaster, 10th anniv.

Nos. 860A and 861A Surcharged in Red

**1944, May 25**

| | | | | | |
|---|---|---|---|---|---|
| **C80** | A431 | 1r on 30k | Prus green | .50 | .25 |
| **C81** | A432 | 1r on 30k | deep ultra | .50 | .25 |
| | | | Set, never hinged | 2.00 | |

**Catalogue values for unused stamps in this section, from this point to the end of the section, are for Never Hinged items.**

Planes and Soviet Air Force Flag — AP42

**1948, Dec. 10** **Litho.** ***Perf. 12½***

| | | | | | |
|---|---|---|---|---|---|
| **C82** | AP42 | 1r | dark blue | 10.00 | .75 |

Air Force Day.

Plane over Zages, Caucasus — AP43

Plane over Farm Scene AP44

Map of Russian Air Routes and Transport Planes — AP45

No. C85, Sochi, Northern Caucasus. No. C86, Far East. No. C87, Leningrad. 2r, Moscow. 3r, Arctic.

***Perf. 12x12½***

**1949, Nov. 9** **Photo.** **Unwmk.**

| | | | | | |
|---|---|---|---|---|---|
| **C83** | AP43 | 50k | red brn, *lemon* | 4.50 | .80 |
| **C84** | AP44 | 60k | sepia, *pale buff* | 8.50 | 1.00 |
| **C85** | AP44 | 1r | org brn, *yelsh* | 8.50 | 1.40 |
| **C86** | AP43 | 1r | blue, *bluish* | 8.50 | 1.40 |
| **C87** | AP43 | 1r | red brn, *pale fawn* | 8.50 | 1.40 |
| **C88** | AP45 | 1r | blk, ultra & red, *gray* | 17.50 | 4.00 |
| **C89** | AP43 | 2r | org brn, *bluish* | 26.00 | 11.00 |
| **C90** | AP43 | 3r | dk green, *bluish* | 42.50 | 4.00 |
| | | | *Nos. C83-C90 (8)* | 124.50 | 25.00 |

Plane and Mountain Stream — AP46

Design: 1r, Like No. C86.

**1955** **Litho.** ***Perf. 12½x12***

| | | | | | |
|---|---|---|---|---|---|
| **C91** | AP46 | 1r | multicolored | 5.00 | .50 |
| **C92** | AP46 | 2r | black & yel grn | 10.00 | .50 |

For overprints see Nos. C95-C96.

Globe and Plane — AP47

**1955, May 31** **Photo.**

| | | | | | |
|---|---|---|---|---|---|
| **C93** | AP47 | 2r | chocolate | 1.25 | .25 |
| **C94** | AP47 | 2r | deep blue | 1.25 | .25 |

Nos. C91 and C92 Overprinted in Red

***Perf. 12x12½***

**1955, Nov. 22** **Litho.** **Unwmk.**

| | | | | | |
|---|---|---|---|---|---|
| **C95** | AP46 | 1r | multicolored | 8.00 | 2.00 |
| **C96** | AP46 | 2r | black & yel grn | 12.00 | 3.00 |

Issued for use at the scientific drifting stations North Pole-4 and North Pole-5. The inscription reads "North Pole-Moscow, 1955." Counterfeits exist.

Arctic Camp AP48

**1956, June 8** ***Perf. 12½x12***

| | | | | | |
|---|---|---|---|---|---|
| **C97** | AP48 | 1r | blue, grn, brn, yel & red | 1.50 | .50 |

Opening of scientific drifting station North Pole-6.

Helicopter over Kremlin — AP49

**1960, Mar. 5** **Photo.** ***Perf. 12***

| | | | | | |
|---|---|---|---|---|---|
| **C98** | AP49 | 60k | ultra | 1.00 | .25 |

**Surcharged with New Value, Bars and "1961"**

**1961, Dec. 20**

| | | | | | |
|---|---|---|---|---|---|
| **C99** | AP49 | 6k on 60k | ultra | .50 | .25 |

Air Force Emblem and Arms of Normandy — AP50

**1962, Dec. 30** **Unwmk.** ***Perf. 11½***

| | | | | | |
|---|---|---|---|---|---|
| **C100** | AP50 | 6k | blue grn, ocher & car | .35 | .25 |

French Normandy-Neman Escadrille, which fought on the Russian front, 20th anniv.

Jet over Map Showing Airlines in USSR AP51

Designs: 12k, Aeroflot emblem and globe. 16k, Jet over map showing Russian international airlines.

**1963, Feb.**

| | | | | | |
|---|---|---|---|---|---|
| **C101** | AP51 | 10k | red, blk & tan | .75 | .25 |
| **C102** | AP51 | 12k | blue, red, tan & blk | 1.00 | .25 |
| **C103** | AP51 | 16k | blue, blk & red | 1.25 | .25 |
| | | | *Nos. C101-C103 (3)* | 3.00 | .75 |

Aeroflot, the civil air fleet, 40th anniv.

Tupolev 134 at Sheremetyevo Airport, Moscow — AP52

Civil Aviation: 10k, An-24 (Antonov) and Vnukovo Airport, Moscow. 12k, Mi-10 (Mil helicopter) and Central Airport, Moscow. 16k, Be-10 (Beriev) and Chinki Riverport, Moscow. 20k, Antei airliner and Domodedovo Airport, Moscow.

**1965, Dec. 31**

**C104** AP52 6k org, red & vio .30 .25
**C105** AP52 10k lt grn, org red & gray .50 .25
**C106** AP52 12k lil, dk sep & lt grn .50 .25
**C107** AP52 16k lil, lt brn, red & grn .75 .25
**C108** AP52 20k org red, pur & gray .95 .25
*Nos. C104-C108 (5)* 3.00 1.25

### Aviation Type of 1976

Aviation 1917-1930 (Aviation Emblem and): 4k, P-4 BIS biplane, 1917. 6k, AK-1 monoplane, 1924. 10k, R-3 (ANT-3) biplane, 1925. 12k, TB-1 (ANT-4) monoplane, 1925. 16k, R-5 biplane, 1929. 20k, Shcha-2 amphibian, 1930.

### Lithographed and Engraved

**1977, Aug. 16** ***Perf. 12x11½***

**C109** A2134 4k multicolored .25 .25
**C110** A2134 6k multicolored .25 .25
**C111** A2134 10k multicolored .25 .25
**C112** A2134 12k multicolored .35 .25
**C113** A2134 16k multicolored .45 .25
**C114** A2134 20k multicolored .60 .25
*Nos. C109-C114 (6)* 2.15 1.50

**1978, Aug. 10**

4k, PO-2 biplane, 1928. 6k, K-5 passenger plane, 1929. 10k, TB-3, cantilever monoplane, 1930. 12k, Stal-2, 1931. 16k, MBR-2 hydroplane, 1932. 20k, I-16 fighter plane, 1934.

**C115** A2134 4k multicolored .25 .25
**C116** A2134 6k multicolored .25 .25
**C117** A2134 10k multicolored .30 .25
**C118** A2134 12k multicolored .30 .25
**C119** A2134 16k multicolored .40 .25
**C120** A2134 20k multicolored .50 .30
*Nos. C115-C120 (6)* 2.00 1.55

Aviation 1928-1934.

Jet and Compass Rose — AP53

**1978, Aug. 4** **Litho.** ***Perf. 12***

**C121** AP53 32k dark blue 3.00 .35

Aeroflot Plane AH-28 — AP54

Designs: Various Aeroflot planes.

### Photogravure and Engraved

**1979** ***Perf. 11½x12***

**C122** AP54 2k shown .25 .25
**C123** AP54 3k YAK-42 .25 .25
**C124** AP54 10k T4-154 .30 .25
**C125** AP54 15k IL76 transport .45 .25
**C126** AP54 32k IL86 jet liner .85 .45
*Nos. C122-C126 (5)* 2.10 1.45

## AIR POST OFFICIAL STAMPS

Used on mail from Russian embassy in Berlin to Moscow. Surcharged on Consular Fee stamps. Currency: the German mark.

OA1

### Surcharge in Carmine Bicolored Burelage

**1922, July** **Litho.** ***Perf. 13½***

**CO1** OA1 12m on 2.25r 150.00 —
*a.* Inverted surcharge 7,500. —
**CO2** OA1 24m on 3r 175.00 —
*a.* Inverted surcharge 7,500. —
**CO3** OA1 120m on 2.25r 195.00 —
**CO4** OA1 600m on 3r 260.00 —
**CO5** OA1 1200m on 10k 975.00 —
**CO6** OA1 1200m on 50k *37,500.* —
**CO7** OA1 1200m on 2.25r 1,950. —
**CO8** OA1 1200m on 3r 2,250. —

Three types of each denomination, distinguished by shape of "C" in surcharge and length of second line of surcharge. Used stamps have pen or crayon cancel. Forgeries exist.

## SPECIAL DELIVERY STAMPS

Motorcycle Courier — SD1

Express Truck — SD2

Design: 80k, Locomotive.

***Perf. 12½x12, 12x12½***

**1932** **Photo.** **Wmk. 170**

**E1** SD1 5k dull brown 10.00 3.00
**E2** SD2 10k violet brown 35.00 10.00
**E3** SD2 80k dull green 80.00 8.50
*Nos. E1-E3 (3)* 125.00 21.50
Set, never hinged 250.00

Used values are for c-t-o.

## POSTAGE DUE STAMPS

Regular Issue of 1918 Surcharged in Red or Carmine

**1924-25** **Unwmk.** ***Perf. 13½***

**J1** A33 1k on 35k blue 2.00 *.50*
**J2** A33 3k on 35k blue 2.00 *.50*
**J3** A33 5k on 35k blue 2.00 *.50*
*a.* Imperf. *450.00*
**J4** A33 8k on 35k blue ('25) 2.00 *.50*
*a.* Imperf. *450.00*
**J5** A33 10k on 35k blue 2.00 *.50*
*a.* Pair, one without surcharge *550.00*
**J6** A33 12k on 70k brown 2.00 *.50*
**J7** A33 14k on 35k blue ('25) 2.00 *.50*
*a.* Imperf. *450.00*
**J8** A33 32k on 35k blue 2.50 *.50*
**J9** A33 40k on 35k blue 2.50 *.50*
*a.* Imperf. *450.00*
*c.* Pair, one without surcharge *675.00*
*Nos. J1-J9 (9)* 19.00 *4.50*

### Inverted Surcharge

*J1b* A33 1k on 35k blue *150.00* —
*J2b* A33 3k on 35k blue *150.00* —
*J3b* A33 5k on 35k blue *150.00* —
*J4b* A33 8k on 35k blue *150.00* —
*J6b* A33 12k on 70k brown *200.00* —
*J7b* A33 14k on 35k brown *150.00* —
*J8b* A33 32k on 35k brown *150.00* —
*J9b* A33 40k on 35k brown *175.00* —

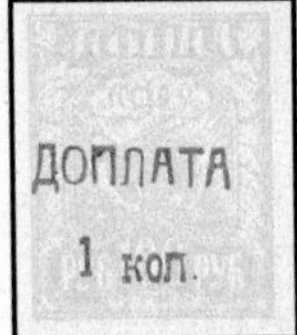

Regular Issue of 1921 Surcharged in Violet

**1924** ***Imperf.***

**J10** A40 1k on 100r orange 6.75 *8.00*
*a.* 1k on 100r yellow 8.75 *8.00*
*b.* Pelure paper 6.75 *8.00*
*c.* Inverted surcharge *225.00*

D1

### Lithographed or Typographed

**1925** ***Perf. 12***

**J11** D1 1k red 2.00 .75
**J12** D1 2k violet 2.00 .75
**J13** D1 3k light blue 2.00 .75
**J14** D1 7k orange 2.00 .75
**J15** D1 8k green 2.00 .75
**J16** D1 10k dark blue 2.00 .75
**J17** D1 14k brown 2.00 .75
*Nos. J11-J17 (7)* 14.00 5.25

***Perf. 14½x14***

*J13a* D1 3k 12.50 1.00
*J14a* D1 7k 20.00 1.00
*J16a* D1 10k — —
*J17a* D1 14k 5.00 1.00
*Nos. J13a-J17a (4)* 37.50 3.00

Value of No. J16a unused is based on 2012 auction realization.

**1925** **Wmk. 170** **Typo.** ***Perf. 12***

**J18** D1 1k red 1.60 .40
**J19** D1 2k violet 1.75 .40
**J20** D1 3k light blue 1.75 .40
**J21** D1 7k orange 1.75 .40
**J22** D1 8k green 1.75 .40
**J23** D1 10k dark blue 1.75 .40
**J24** D1 14k brown 1.75 .40
*Nos. J18-J24 (7)* 12.10 2.80

For surcharges see Nos. 359-372.

## WENDEN (LIVONIA)

A former district of Livonia, a province of the Russian Empire, which became part of Latvia, under the name of Vidzeme.

Used values for Nos. L2-L12 are for pen-canceled stamps. Postmarked examples sell for considerably more.

A1

**1862** **Unwmk.** ***Imperf.***

**L1** A1 (2k) blue 45.00
*a.* Tête bêche pair *350.00*

No. L1 may have been used for a short period of time but withdrawn because of small size. Some consider it an essay.

A2

A3

**1863**

**L2** A2 (2k) rose & black 240.00 240.00
*a.* Background inverted 600.00 600.00
**L3** A3 (4k) blue grn & blk 175.00 150.00
*a.* (4k) yellow green & black 300.00 300.00
*b.* Half used as 2k on cover *2,500.*
*c.* Background inverted 950.00 500.00
*d.* As "a," background inverted 650.00 400.00

*The official imitations of Nos. L2 and L3 have a single instead of a double hyphen after "WENDEN." Value, each $25.*

Coat of Arms
A4 A5 A6

**1863-71**

**L4** A4 (2k) rose & green 90.00 90.00
*a.* Yellowish paper
*b.* Green frame around central oval 95.00 60.00
*c.* Tête bêche pair *2,500.*
**L5** A5 (2k) rose & grn ('64) 125.00 100.00
**L6** A6 (2k) rose & green 125.00 75.00
*Nos. L4-L6 (3)* 340.00 265.00

Official imitations of Nos. L4b and L5 have a rose instead of a green line around the central oval. The first official imitation of No. L6 has the central oval 5½mm instead of 6¼mm wide; the second imitation is less clearly printed than the original and the top of the "f" of "Briefmarke" is too much hooked. Value, each $25.

Coat of Arms
A7 A8

**1872-75** ***Perf. 12½***

**L7** A7 (2k) red & green 85.00 *50.00*
**L8** A8 2k yel grn & red ('75) 8.50 *11.00*
*a.* Numeral in upper right corner resembles an inverted "3" 30.00 *30.00*

Reprints of No. L8 have no horizontal lines in the background. Those of No. L8a have the impression blurred and only traces of the horizontal lines. Value, $25.

A9

**1878-80**

**L9** A9 2k green & red 15.00 *7.00*
*a.* Imperf.
**L10** A9 2k blk, grn & red ('80) 10.00 10.00
*a.* Imperf., pair 35.00

No. L9 has been reprinted in blue green and yellow green with perforation 11½ and in gray green with perforation 12½ or imperforate.

**1884** ***Perf. 11½***

**L11** A9 2k black, green & red 3.00 3.00
*a.* Green arm omitted 21.00
*b.* Arm inverted 21.00
*c.* Arm double 27.50
*d.* Imperf., pair 150.00

Wenden Castle — A10

**1901** **Litho.**

**L12** A10 2k dk green & brown 12.00 10.00
*a.* Tête bêche pair 45.00
*b.* Imperf., pair 100.00

## OCCUPATION STAMPS

### ISSUED UNDER GERMAN OCCUPATION

German Stamps Overprinted in Black

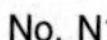
No. N1

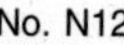
No. N12

**On Stamps of 1905-17**

**1916-17 Wmk. 125** *Perf. 14, 14½*

| No. | Type | Description | Unused | Used |
|---|---|---|---|---|
| N1 | A22 | 2½pf gray | .65 | *1.00* |
| N2 | A16 | 3pf brown | .25 | .25 |
| N3 | A16 | 5pf green | .65 | *1.00* |
| N4 | A22 | 7½pf orange | .65 | *1.00* |
| N5 | A16 | 10pf carmine | .65 | *1.00* |
| N6 | A22 | 15pf yel brn | 3.00 | 2.00 |
| N7 | A22 | 15pf vio ('17) | .65 | *1.00* |
| N8 | A16 | 20pf ultra | 1.00 | 1.00 |
| N9 | A16 | 25pf org & blk, *yel* | .50 | *.50* |
| N10 | A16 | 40pf rose car & blk | 1.00 | *3.75* |
| N11 | A16 | 50pf redsh pur & blk, *buff* | 1.00 | *1.50* |
| N12 | A17 | 1m car rose | 12.00 | 3.50 |
| | | *Nos. N1-N12 (12)* | 22.00 | *17.50* |
| | | Set, never hinged | 65.00 | |

These stamps were used in the former Russian provinces of Suvalki, Vilnius, Kaunas, Kurland, Estland and Lifland.

### ISSUED UNDER FINNISH OCCUPATION

Finnish Stamps of 1917-18 Overprinted

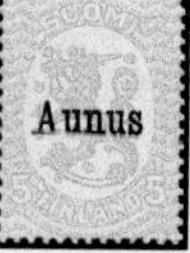

**1919 Unwmk.** *Perf. 14*

| No. | Type | Description | Unused | Used |
|---|---|---|---|---|
| N13 | A19 | 5p green | 12.50 | 15.00 |
| N14 | A19 | 10p rose | 12.50 | 15.00 |
| N15 | A19 | 20p buff | 12.50 | 15.00 |
| N16 | A19 | 40p red violet | 12.50 | 15.00 |
| N17 | A19 | 50p orange brn | 125.00 | 150.00 |
| N18 | A19 | 1m dl rose & blk | 140.00 | 140.00 |
| N19 | A19 | 5m violet & blk | 425.00 | 425.00 |
| N20 | A19 | 10m brown & blk | 725.00 | 725.00 |
| | | *Nos. N13-N20 (8)* | 1,465. | 1,500. |
| | | Set, never hinged | 3,000. | |

"Aunus" is the Finnish name for Olonets, a town of Russia.

Counterfeits overprints exist.

**Catalogue values for unused stamps in this section, from this point to the end of the section, are for Never Hinged items.**

**Issued under German Occupation**

Germany Nos. 506 to 523 Overprinted in Black

**1941-43 Unwmk. Typo.** *Perf. 14*

| No. | Type | Description | Unused | Used |
|---|---|---|---|---|
| N21 | A115 | 1pf gray black | .25 | .25 |
| N22 | A115 | 3pf light brown | .25 | .25 |
| N23 | A115 | 4pf slate | .25 | .25 |
| N24 | A115 | 5pf dp yellow green | .25 | .25 |
| N25 | A115 | 6pf purple | .25 | .25 |
| N26 | A115 | 8pf red | .25 | .25 |
| N27 | A115 | 10pf dk brown ('43) | .65 | *3.25* |
| N28 | A115 | 12pf carmine ('43) | .65 | *2.75* |

**Engr.**

| No. | Type | Description | Unused | Used |
|---|---|---|---|---|
| N29 | A115 | 10pf dark brown | 1.25 | *1.40* |
| N30 | A115 | 12pf brt carmine | 1.25 | *1.40* |
| N31 | A115 | 15pf brown lake | .25 | .25 |
| N32 | A115 | 16pf peacock grn | .25 | .25 |
| N33 | A115 | 20pf blue | .25 | .25 |
| N34 | A115 | 24pf orange brown | .25 | .25 |
| N35 | A115 | 25pf brt ultra | .25 | .25 |
| N36 | A115 | 30pf olive green | .25 | .25 |
| N37 | A115 | 40pf brt red violet | .25 | .25 |
| N38 | A115 | 50pf myrtle green | .25 | .25 |
| N39 | A115 | 60pf dk red brown | .25 | .25 |
| N40 | A115 | 80pf indigo | .25 | *.65* |
| | | *Nos. N21-N40 (20)* | 7.80 | *13.20* |

Issued for use in Estonia, Latvia and Lithuania.

Same Overprinted in Black

**Typo.**

| No. | Type | Description | Unused | Used |
|---|---|---|---|---|
| N41 | A115 | 1pf gray black | .25 | .25 |
| N42 | A115 | 3pf lt brown | .25 | .25 |
| N43 | A115 | 4pf slate | .25 | .25 |
| N44 | A115 | 5pf dp yel green | .25 | .25 |
| N45 | A115 | 6pf purple | .25 | .25 |
| N46 | A115 | 8pf red | .25 | .25 |
| N47 | A115 | 10pf dk brown ('43) | .55 | *2.40* |
| N48 | A115 | 12pf carmine ('43) | .55 | *2.40* |

**Engr.**

| No. | Type | Description | Unused | Used |
|---|---|---|---|---|
| N49 | A115 | 10pf dk brown | 1.00 | *1.60* |
| N50 | A115 | 12pf brt carmine | 1.00 | *1.60* |
| N51 | A115 | 15pf brown lake | .25 | .25 |
| N52 | A115 | 16pf peacock green | .25 | .25 |
| N53 | A115 | 20pf blue | .25 | .25 |
| N54 | A115 | 24pf orange brown | .25 | .25 |
| N55 | A115 | 25pf bright ultra | .25 | .25 |
| N56 | A115 | 30pf olive green | .25 | .25 |
| N57 | A115 | 40pf brt red violet | .25 | .25 |
| N58 | A115 | 50pf myrtle green | .25 | .25 |
| N59 | A115 | 60pf dk red brown | .25 | .25 |
| N60 | A115 | 80pf indigo | .25 | .25 |
| | | *Nos. N42-N60 (20)* | 7.10 | *12.00* |

## ARMY OF THE NORTHWEST

(Gen. Nicolai N. Yudenich)

Russian Stamps of 1909-18 Overprinted in Black or Red

**On Stamps of 1909-12**

*Perf. 14 to 15 and Compound*

**1919, Aug. 1**

| No. | Type | Description | Unused | Used |
|---|---|---|---|---|
| 1 | A14 | 2k green | 5.00 | *20.00* |
| 2 | A14 | 5k claret | 5.00 | *10.00* |
| 3 | A15 | 10k dk blue (R) | 10.00 | *25.00* |
| 4 | A11 | 15k red brn & bl | 5.00 | *15.00* |
| 5 | A8 | 20k blue & car | 10.00 | *15.00* |
| 6 | A11 | 25k grn & gray vio | 15.00 | *25.00* |
| 7 | A8 | 50k brn vio & grn | 10.00 | *15.00* |

*Perf. 13½*

| No. | Type | Description | Unused | Used |
|---|---|---|---|---|
| 8 | A9 | 1r pale brn, dk brn & org | 25.00 | *50.00* |
| 9 | A13 | 10r scar, yel & gray | 150.00 | *200.00* |

**On Stamps of 1917**

*Imperf*

| No. | Type | Description | Unused | Used |
|---|---|---|---|---|
| 10 | A14 | 3k red | 5.00 | *10.00* |
| 11 | A12 | 3.50r mar & lt grn | 17.50 | *35.00* |
| 12 | A13 | 5r dk blue, grn & pale bl | 17.50 | *30.00* |
| 13 | A12 | 7r dk grn & pink | 150.00 | *200.00* |

**No. 2 Surcharged**

*Perf. 14, 14½x15*

| No. | Type | Description | Unused | Used |
|---|---|---|---|---|
| 14 | A14 | 10k on 5k claret | 5.00 | *20.00* |
| | | *Nos. 1-14 (14)* | 430.00 | *670.00* |

Nos. 1-14 exist with inverted overprint or surcharge. The 1, 3½, 5, 7 and 10 rubles with red overprint are trial printings (value $150 each). The 20k on 14k, perforated, and the 1, 2, 5, 15, 70k and 1r imperforate were overprinted but never placed in use. Value: $300, $30, $45, $45, $45, $45 and $65.

These stamps were in use from Aug. 1 to Oct. 15, 1919.

Counterfeits of Nos. 1-14 abound.

## ARMY OF THE NORTH

A1 A2

A3 A4

A5

**1919, Sept. Typo.** *Imperf.*

| No. | Type | Description | Unused | Used |
|---|---|---|---|---|
| 1 | A1 | 5k brown violet | .60 | *1.00* |
| 2 | A2 | 10k blue | .60 | *1.00* |
| 3 | A3 | 15k yellow | .60 | *1.00* |
| 4 | A4 | 20k rose | .60 | *1.00* |
| 5 | A5 | 50k green | .60 | *1.00* |
| | | *Nos. 1-5 (5)* | 3.00 | *5.00* |

The letters OKCA are the initials of Russian words meaning "Special Corps, Army of the North." The stamps were in use from about the end of September to the end of December, 1919.

Used values are for c-t-o stamps.

(General Miller)

A set of seven stamps of this design was prepared in 1919, but not issued. Value, set $35. Counterfeits exist.

# RUSSIA OFFICES ABROAD

For various reasons the Russian Empire maintained Post Offices to handle its correspondence in several foreign countries. These were similar to the Post Offices in foreign countries maintained by other world powers.

## OFFICES IN CHINA

100 Kopecks = 1 Ruble
100 Cents = 1 Dollar (1917)

Russian Stamps Overprinted in Blue or Red

**On Issues of 1889-92**
**Horizontally Laid Paper**

**1899-1904 Wmk. 168** *Perf. 14½x15*

| No. | Type | Description | Unused | Used |
|---|---|---|---|---|
| 1 | A10 | 1k orange (Bl) | .75 | *1.00* |
| 2 | A10 | 2k yel green (R) | .75 | *1.00* |
| 3 | A10 | 3k carmine (Bl) | .75 | *1.00* |
| 4 | A10 | 5k red violet (Bl) | .75 | *1.00* |
| 5 | A10 | 7k dk blue (R) | 1.50 | *2.50* |
| *a.* | | Inverted overprint | *500.00* | |
| 6 | A8 | 10k dk blue (R) | 1.50 | *2.50* |
| 7 | A8 | 50k vio & grn (Bl) ('04) | 12.00 | *8.50* |

*Perf. 13½*

| No. | Type | Description | Unused | Used |
|---|---|---|---|---|
| 8 | A9 | 1r lt brn, brn & org (Bl) ('04) | 150.00 | 150.00 |
| | | *Nos. 1-8 (8)* | 168.00 | 167.50 |

**On Issues of 1902-05**
**Overprinted in Black, Red or Blue**

*Perf. 14½ to 15 and Compound*

**1904-08 Vertically Laid Paper**

| No. | Type | Description | Unused | Used |
|---|---|---|---|---|
| 9 | A8 | 4k rose red (Bl) | 6.00 | *3.50* |
| 10 | A10 | 7k dk blue (R) | 15.00 | 15.00 |
| 11 | A8 | 10k dk blue (R) | 1,500. | 1,300. |
| *a.* | | Groundwork inverted | *14,500.* | |
| 12 | A11 | 14k bl & rose (R) | 10.00 | 10.00 |
| 13 | A11 | 15k brn vio & blue (Bl) ('08) | 35.00 | *30.00* |
| 14 | A8 | 20k blue & car (Bl) | 5.00 | 5.00 |
| 15 | A11 | 25k dull grn & lil (R) ('08) | 50.00 | 50.00 |
| 16 | A11 | 35k dk vio & grn (R) | 10.00 | 10.00 |
| 17 | A8 | 50k vio & grn (Bl) | 100.00 | 125.00 |
| 18 | A11 | 70k brn & org (Bl) | 15.00 | 13.00 |

*Perf. 13½*

| No. | Type | Description | Unused | Used |
|---|---|---|---|---|
| 19 | A9 | 1r lt brn, brn & org (Bl) | 25.00 | 25.00 |
| 20 | A12 | 3.50r blk & gray (R) | 5.00 | *5.00* |
| 21 | A13 | 5r dk bl, grn & pale bl (R) ('07) | 8.50 | *12.00* |
| *a.* | | Inverted overprint | *2,500.* | |
| 22 | A12 | 7r blk & yel (Bl) | 25.00 | 12.00 |
| 23 | A13 | 10r scar, yel & gray (Bl) ('07) | 100.00 | *100.00* |
| | | *Nos. 9-10,12-23 (14)* | 409.50 | 415.50 |

**On Issues of 1909-12**
**Wove Paper**
**Lozenges of Varnish on Face**

**1910-16 Unwmk.** *Perf. 14x14½*

| No. | Type | Description | Unused | Used |
|---|---|---|---|---|
| 24 | A14 | 1k orange yel (Bl) | .50 | .50 |
| 25 | A14 | 1k org yel (Bl Bk) | 6.00 | 5.00 |
| 26 | A14 | 2k green (Bk) | 1.00 | 1.00 |
| 27 | A14 | 2k green (Bl) | 7.50 | *15.00* |
| *a.* | | Double ovpt. (Bk and Bl) | | |
| 28 | A14 | 3k rose red (Bl) | 2.00 | *5.00* |
| 29 | A14 | 3k rose red (Bk) | 12.00 | 12.00 |
| 30 | A15 | 4k carmine (Bl) | 1.00 | 2.00 |
| 31 | A15 | 4k carmine (Bk) | 10.00 | 10.00 |
| 32 | A14 | 7k lt blue (Bk) | 1.00 | *1.00* |
| 33 | A15 | 10k blue (Bk) | 1.00 | 1.00 |
| 34 | A11 | 14k blue & rose (Bk) | 10.00 | 5.00 |
| 35 | A11 | 14k blue & rose (Bl) | | |
| 36 | A11 | 15k dl vio & bl (Bk) | 1.00 | *1.25* |
| 37 | A8 | 20k blue & car (Bk) | *5.00* | *7.00* |
| 38 | A11 | 25k green & vio (Bl) | 3.50 | *6.00* |
| 39 | A11 | 25k grn & vio (Bk) | 1.00 | *1.60* |
| 40 | A11 | 35k vio & grn (Bk) | 1.00 | 1.00 |
| 42 | A8 | 50k vio & grn (Bl) | 2.00 | *2.00* |
| 43 | A8 | 50k brn vio & grn (Bk) | 18.00 | *20.00* |
| 44 | A11 | 70k lt brn & org (Bl) | 1.00 | *2.00* |

*Perf. 13½*

| No. | Type | Description | Unused | Used |
|---|---|---|---|---|
| 45 | A9 | 1r pale brn, brn & org (Bl) | 1.25 | *2.40* |
| 47 | A13 | 5r dk bl, grn & pale bl (R) | 25.00 | 15.00 |
| | | *Nos. 24-34,36-47 (21)* | 110.75 | 115.75 |

The existence of #35 is questioned.

**Russian Stamps of 1902-12 Surcharged**

a

b

c

**On Stamps of 1909-12**

**1917** *Perf. 11½, 13½, 14, 14½x15*

| No. | Type | Description | Unused | Used |
|---|---|---|---|---|
| 50 | A14(a) | 1c on 1k dl org yel | .60 | *5.50* |
| 51 | A14(a) | 2c on 2k dull grn | .60 | *5.50* |
| *a.* | | Inverted surcharge | 100.00 | |
| 52 | A14(a) | 3c on 3k car | .60 | *5.50* |
| *a.* | | Inverted surcharge | 100.00 | |
| *b.* | | Double surcharge | 150.00 | |

53 A15(a) 4c on 4k car 1.25 *4.25*
54 A14(a) 5c on 5k claret 1.25 *15.00*
55 A15(b) 10c on 10k dk blue 1.25 *15.00*
*a.* Inverted surcharge 100.00 100.00
*b.* Double surcharge 115.00
56 A11(b) 14c on 14k dk blue & car 1.25 *10.00*
*a.* Imperf. 6.00
*b.* Inverted surcharge 100.00
57 A11(a) 15c on 15k brn lil & dp blue 1.25 *15.00*
*a.* Inverted surcharge 50.00
58 A8(b) 20c on 20k bl & car 1.25 *15.00*
59 A11(a) 25c on 25k grn & vio 1.25 *15.00*
60 A11(a) 35c on 35k brn vio & grn 1.50 *15.00*
*a.* Inverted surcharge 50.00
61 A8(a) 50c on 50k brn vio & grn 1.25 *15.00*
62 A11(a) 70c on 70k brn & red org 1.25 *15.00*
63 A9(c) $1 on 1r pale brn, brn & org 1.25 *15.00*
*Nos. 50-63 (14)* 15.80

**On Stamps of 1902-05**
**Vertically Laid Paper**
***Perf. 11½, 13, 13½, 13½x11½***
**Wmk. Wavy Lines (168)**

64 A12 $3.50 on 3.50r blk & gray 20.00 *40.00*
65 A13 $5 on 5r dk bl, grn & pale blue 20.00 *40.00*
66 A12 $7 on 7r blk & yel 10.00 *32.50*

**On Stamps of 1915**
**Wove Paper**
**Unwmk.** ***Perf. 13½***

68 A13 $5 on 5r ind, grn & lt blue 25.00 *50.00*
*a.* Inverted surcharge 500.00
70 A13 $10 on 10r car lake, yel & gray 50.00 *100.00*
*Nos. 64-70 (5)* 125.00 262.50

The surcharge on Nos. 64-70 is in larger type than on the $1.

Russian Stamps of 1909-18 Surcharged in Black or Red

**On Stamps of 1909-12**

**1920** ***Perf. 14, 14½x15***

72 A14 1c on 1k dull org yel 175.00 *275.00*
73 A14 2c on 2k dull grn (R) 16.00 *27.50*
74 A14 3c on 3k car 16.00 *37.50*
75 A15 4c on 4k car 18.00 *22.50*
*a.* Inverted surcharge 130.00 150.00
76 A14 5c on 5k claret 60.00 90.00
77 A15 10c on 10k dk bl (R) 150.00 225.00
78 A14 10c on 10k on 7k blue (R) 125.00 190.00

**On Stamps of 1917-18**
***Imperf***

79 A14 1c on 1k orange 42.50 37.50
*a.* Inverted surcharge 125.00 *150.00*
80 A14 5c on 5k claret 35.00 55.00
*a.* Inverted surcharge 150.00
*b.* Double surcharge 250.00
*c.* Surcharged "Cent" only 95.00
*Nos. 72-80 (9)* 637.50 960.00

## OFFICES IN THE TURKISH EMPIRE

Various powers maintained post offices in the Turkish Empire before World War I by authority of treaties which ended with the signing of the Treaty of Lausanne in 1923. The foreign post offices were closed Oct. 27, 1923.

100 Kopecks = 1 Ruble
40 Paras = 1 Piaster (1900)

The editors recommend that the stamps of Russian Offices in the Turkish Empire, 1863-1879, be purchased accompanied by certificates of authenticity issued by the competent authorities and committees.

Coat of Arms
A1

**1863 Unwmk. Typo.** ***Imperf.***

1 A1 6k blue 325.00 *3,000.*
*a.* 6k light blue, thin paper 350.00 *3,000.*
*b.* 6k light blue, medium paper 325.00 *3,000.*
*c.* 6k dark blue, chalky paper ('66) 165.00 —

Values are for stamps without faults. Most stamps from this set have faults. Forgeries exist.

No. 1c was unissued.

A2

A3

**1865** **Litho.**

2 A2 (2k) brown & blue 800.00 750.00
3 A3 (20k) blue & red 900.00 850.00

Twenty-eight varieties of each.

A4

A5

**1866 Horizontal Network**

4 A4 (2k) rose & pale bl 25.00 *30.00*
5 A5 (20k) deep blue & rose 40.00 *50.00*

**1867 Vertical Network**

6 A4 (2k) rose & pale bl 75.00 *100.00*
7 A5 (20k) dp blue & rose 200.00 *100.00*

*The initials inscribed on Nos. 2 to 7 are those of the Russian Company of Navigation and Trade.*

*The official imitations of Nos. 2 to 7 are on yellowish white paper. The colors are usually paler than those of the originals and there are minor differences in the designs.*

A6

**Horizontally Laid Paper**

**1868 Typo. Wmk. 168** ***Perf. 11½***

8 A6 1k brown 50.00 20.00
9 A6 3k green 60.00 25.00
10 A6 5k blue 60.00 25.00
11 A6 10k car & green 75.00 25.00
*Nos. 8-11 (4)* 245.00 95.00

Colors of Nos. 8-11 dissolve in water.

**1872-90** ***Perf. 14½x15***

12 A6 1k brown 10.00 2.00
13 A6 3k green 25.00 3.00
14 A6 5k blue 5.00 1.00
15 A6 10k pale red & grn ('90) 1.25 .60
*b.* 10k carmine & green 24.00 3.75
*Nos. 12-15 (4)* 41.25 6.60

**Vertically Laid Paper**

*12a* A6 1k 75.00 18.00
*13a* A6 3k 75.00 18.00
*14a* A6 5k 75.00 18.00
*15a* A6 10k 190.00 47.50
*Nos. 12a-15a (4)* 415.00 101.50

Nos. 12-15 exist imperf.

**No. 15 Surcharged in Black or Blue**

a

b

c

**1876**

16 A6(a) 8k on 10k (Bk) 75.00 45.00
*a.* Vertically laid *2,750.*
*b.* Inverted surcharge 400.00
17 A6(a) 8k on 10k (Bl) 90.00 75.00
*a.* Vertically laid
*b.* Inverted surcharge

**1879**

18 A6(b) 7k on 10k (Bk) 80.00 65.00
*a.* Vertically laid 750.00 750.00
*b.* Inverted surcharge
19 A6(b) 7k on 10k (Bl) 125.00 85.00
*a.* Vertically laid 1,750. 1,750.
*b.* Inverted surcharge 500.00
19C A6(c) 7k on 10k (Bl) 1,250. 1,250.
19D A6(c) 7k on 10k (Bk) 1,250. 1,250.

Nos. 16-19D have been extensively counterfeited.

**1879** ***Perf. 14½x15***

20 A6 1k black & yellow 3.00 1.00
*a.* Vertically laid 10.00 5.00
21 A6 2k black & rose 5.00 3.00
*a.* Vertically laid 10.00 5.00
22 A6 7k carmine & gray 9.00 1.00
*a.* Vertically laid 42.50 15.00
*Nos. 20-22 (3)* 17.00 5.00

**1884**

23 A6 1k orange .75 .50
24 A6 2k green 1.00 .75
25 A6 5k pale red violet 4.00 2.00
26 A6 7k blue 2.00 1.50
*Nos. 23-26 (4)* 7.75 4.75

Nos. 23-26 imperforate are believed to be proofs.

No. 23 surcharged "40 PARAS" is bogus, though some examples were postally used.

**Russian Company of Navigation and Trade**

This overprint, in two sizes, was privately applied in various colors to Russian Offices in the Turkish Empire stamps of 1900-1910.

A7

A8

**Surcharged in Blue, Black or Red**

**1900 Horizontally Laid Paper**

27 A7 4pa on 1k orange (Bl) 1.25 1.25
*a.* Inverted surcharge 30.00 30.00
28 A7 4pa on 1k orange (Bk) 1.25 1.25
*a.* Inverted surcharge 30.00 30.00
29 A7 10pa on 2k green .25 .25
*a.* Inverted surcharge
30 A8 1pi on 10k dk blue .50 .60
*a.* Inverted surcharge
*Nos. 27-30 (4)* 3.25 3.35

A9

A10

A11

**1903-05 Vertically Laid Paper**

31 A7 10pa on 2k yel green .60 *.40*
*a.* Inverted surcharge 75.00
32 A8 20pa on 4k rose red (Bl) .60 *.40*
*a.* Inverted surcharge 95.00
33 A8 1pi on 10k dk blue .60 *.40*
*a.* Groundwork inverted 50.00 *15.00*
34 A8 2pi on 20k blue & car (Bk) 1.40 *.75*
35 A8 5pi on 50k brn vio & grn 3.50 *1.25*
36 A9 7pi on 70k brn & org (Bl) 4.00 *2.00*

***Perf. 13½***

37 A10 10pi on 1r lt brn, brn & org (Bl) 6.50 *4.00*
38 A11 35pi on 3.50r blk & gray 20.00 *10.00*
39 A11 70pi on 7r blk & yel 24.00 *12.50*
*Nos. 31-39 (9)* 61.20 31.70

A12

A13

A14

**Wove Paper**
**Lozenges of Varnish on Face**

**1909 Unwmk.** ***Perf. 14½x15***

40 A12 5pa on 1k orange .30 *.40*
41 A12 10pa on 2k green .35 *.65*
*a.* Inverted surcharge 30.00 *30.00*
42 A12 20pa on 4k carmine .70 *1.00*
43 A12 1pi on 10k blue .75 *1.20*
44 A12 5pi on 50k vio & grn 1.40 *1.60*
45 A12 7pi on 70k brn & org 2.00 *2.75*

***Perf. 13½***

46 A13 10pi on 1r brn & org 3.00 *5.00*
47 A14 35pi on 3.50r mar & lt grn 12.00 *14.00*
48 A14 70pi on 7r dk grn & pink 20.00 *25.00*
*Nos. 40-48 (9)* 40.50 *51.60*

50th anniv. of the establishing of the Russian Post Offices in the Levant.

**Nos. 40-48 Overprinted with Names of Various Cities Overprinted "Constantinople" in Black**

**1909-10** ***Perf. 14½x15***

61 A12 5pa on 1k .40 *.40*
*c.* Inverted overprint 50.00
62 A12 10pa on 2k .40 *.40*
*c.* Inverted overprint 30.00
63 A12 20pa on 4k .75 *.75*
*c.* Inverted overprint 30.00
64 A12 1pi on 10k .75 *.75*
65 A12 5pi on 50k 1.50 *1.50*
66 A12 7pi on 70k 3.00 *3.00*

***Perf. 13½***

67 A13 10pi on 1r 15.00 *15.00*
*a.* "Constanttnople" 100.00 100.00
68 A14 35pi on 3.50r 50.00 *30.00*
*c.* "Constautinople" 100.00 100.00
*d.* "Constantjnople" 100.00 100.00

69 A14 70pi on 7r 45.00 *42.50*
*c.* "Constautinople" 100.00 100.00
*d.* "Constantjnople" 100.00 100.00

**Blue Overprint**

***Perf. 14½x15***

70 A12 5pa on 1k 8.00 *8.00*
*Nos. 61-70 (10)* 124.80 *102.30*

**"Consnantinople"**

*61a* A12 5pa on 1k 10.00
*62a* A12 10pa on 2k 10.00
*63a* A12 20pa on 4k 10.00
*64a* A12 1pi on 10k 10.00
*65a* A12 5pi on 50k 10.00
*66a* A12 7pi on 70k 12.00
*68a* A14 35pi on 3.50r 50.00
*69a* A14 70pi on 7r 90.00
*70a* A12 5pa on 1k 10.00
*Nos. 61a-70a (9)* 212.00

**"Constantinopie"**

*61b* A12 5pa on 1k 25.00
*d.* Inverted overprint 50.00
*62b* A12 10pa on 2k 25.00
*d.* Inverted overprint 50.00
*63b* A12 20pa on 4k 30.00
*d.* Inverted overprint 60.00
*64b* A12 1pi on 10k 30.00
*65b* A12 5pi on 50k 30.00
*66b* A12 7pi on 70k 30.00
*68b* A14 35pi on 3.50r 60.00
*69b* A14 70pi on 7r 90.00
*Nos. 61b-69b (8)* 320.00

**Overprinted "Jaffa"**

**Black Overprint**

71 A12 5pa on 1k 2.10 *3.75*
*a.* Inverted overprint 75.00
72 A12 10pa on 2k 2.50 *4.00*
*a.* Inverted overprint 50.00
73 A12 20pa on 4k 3.00 *5.25*
*a.* Inverted overprint 60.00
74 A12 1pi on 10k 3.75 *5.25*
*a.* Double overprint 95.00
75 A12 5pi on 50k 9.00 *10.50*
76 A12 7pi on 70k 11.00 *14.00*

***Perf. 13½***

77 A13 10pi on 1r 50.00 50.00
78 A14 35pi on 3.50r 100.00 100.00
79 A14 70pi on 7r 125.00 *150.00*

**Blue Overprint**

***Perf. 14½x15***

80 A12 5pa on 1k 12.00 12.00
*Nos. 71-80 (10)* 318.35 *354.75*

**Overprinted "Ierusalem" in Black**

**Black Overprint**

81 A12 5pa on 1k 2.10 *2.75*
*a.* Inverted overprint 60.00
*b.* "erusalem" 25.00
*c.* As "b," overprint inverted 50.00
82 A12 10pa on 2k 2.75 *4.25*
*a.* Inverted overprint 30.00
*b.* "erusalem" 25.00
*c.* As "b," overprint inverted 50.00
83 A12 20pa on 4k 4.25 *5.50*
*a.* Inverted overprint 30.00
*b.* "erusalem" 25.00
*c.* As "b," overprint inverted 50.00
84 A12 1pi on 10k 4.25 *5.50*
*a.* "erusalem" 30.00
85 A12 5pi on 50k 7.25 *11.00*
*a.* "erusalem" 35.00
86 A12 7pi on 70k 14.00 *17.50*
*a.* "erusalem" 35.00

***Perf. 13½***

87 A13 10pi on 1r 50.00 *50.00*
88 A14 35pi on 3.50r 125.00 125.00
89 A14 70pi on 7r 125.00 *150.00*

**Blue Overprint**

***Perf. 14½x15***

90 A12 5pa on 1k 15.00 25.00
*Nos. 81-90 (10)* 349.60 *396.50*

**Overprinted "Kerassunde"**

**Black Overprint**

91 A12 5pa on 1k .60 *.80*
*a.* Inverted overprint 50.00
92 A12 10pa on 2k .60 *.80*
*a.* Inverted overprint 50.00
93 A12 20pa on 4k 1.00 *1.10*
*a.* Inverted overprint 50.00
94 A12 1pi on 10k 1.25 *1.25*
95 A12 5pi on 50k 2.25 *2.50*
96 A12 7pi on 70k 3.50 *4.00*

***Perf. 13½***

97 A13 10pi on 1r 13.00 *15.00*
98 A14 35pi on 3.50r 42.50 *42.50*
99 A14 70pi on 7r 65.00 *52.50*

**Blue Overprint**

***Perf. 14½x15***

100 A12 5pa on 1k 15.00 *15.00*
*Nos. 91-100 (10)* 144.70 *135.45*

Overprinted "Mont Athos"

**Black Overprint**

101 A12 5pa on 1k 1.25 *1.50*
*b.* Inverted overprint 100.00
102 A12 10pa on 2k 1.25 *1.50*
*b.* Inverted overprint 100.00
103 A12 20pa on 4k 1.75 *3.00*
*b.* Inverted overprint 100.00
104 A12 1pi on 10k 2.25 *4.00*
*b.* Double overprint 125.00
105 A12 5pi on 50k 7.00 *7.50*
106 A12 7pi on 70k 8.00 *8.50*
*b.* Pair, one without "Mont Athos" 125.00

***Perf. 13½***

107 A13 10pi on 1r 35.00 *35.00*
108 A14 35pi on 3.50r 80.00 *80.00*
109 A14 70pi on 7r 145.00 *150.00*

**Blue Overprint**

***Perf. 14½x15***

110 A12 5pa on 1k 12.50 *17.00*
*Nos. 101-110 (10)* 294.00 *308.00*

**"Mont Atho"**

*101a* A12 5pa on 1k 35.00
*102a* A12 10pa on 2k 35.00
*103a* A12 20pa on 4k 35.00
*c.* Inverted overprint 125.00
*104a* A12 1pi on 10k 35.00
*c.* As "a," double overprint 150.00
*105a* A12 5pi on 50k 35.00
*106a* A12 7pi on 70k 35.00
*110a* A12 5pa on 1k 65.00

**"M nt Athos"**

*101d* A12 5pa on 1k 35.00
*102d* A12 10pa on 2k 35.00
*103d* A12 20pa on 4k 35.00
*105d* A12 5pi on 50k 65.00
*106d* A12 7pi on 70k 90.00

Overprinted

111 A12 5pa on 1k 1.50 *2.00*
*a.* Pair, one without overprint 125.00
112 A12 10pa on 2k 1.50 *2.00*
*a.* Pair, one without overprint 125.00
113 A12 20pa on 4k 2.50 *3.50*
*a.* Pair, one without overprint 125.00
114 A12 1pi on 10k 4.50 *6.00*
*a.* Pair, one without overprint 125.00
115 A12 5pi on 50k 7.00 *9.50*
*a.* Pair, one without overprint 150.00
116 A12 7pi on 70k 13.00 *17.50*
*a.* Pair, one without overprint 125.00

***Perf. 13½***

117 A13 10pi on 1r 80.00 *80.00*
*Nos. 111-117 (7)* 110.00 *120.50*

The overprint is larger on No. 117.

**Overprinted "Salonique"**

**Black Overprint**

***Perf. 14½x15***

131 A12 5pa on 1k 1.50 *2.00*
*a.* Inverted overprint 55.00
*b.* Pair, one without overprint 60.00
132 A12 10pa on 2k 2.00 *4.00*
*a.* Inverted overprint 55.00
*b.* Pair, one without overprint 60.00
133 A12 20pa on 4k 2.50 *5.00*
*a.* Inverted overprint 55.00
*b.* Pair, one without overprint 60.00
134 A12 1pi on 10k 3.00 *6.00*
*a.* Pair, one without overprint 75.00
135 A12 5pi on 50k 3.50 *8.00*
136 A12 7pi on 70k 5.00 *10.00*

***Perf. 13½***

137 A13 10pi on 1r 32.50 40.00
138 A14 35pi on 3.50r 80.00 *85.00*
139 A14 70pi on 7r 100.00 115.00

**Blue Overprint**

***Perf. 14½x15***

140 A12 5pa on 1k 15.00 *15.00*
*Nos. 131-140 (10)* 245.00 *290.00*

**Overprinted "Smyrne"**

**Black Overprint**

141 A12 5pa on 1k .65 *1.25*
*a.* Double overprint
*b.* Inverted overprint 10.00
142 A12 10pa on 2k .65 *1.25*
*a.* Inverted overprint 25.00
143 A12 20pa on 4k 1.40 *1.60*
*a.* Inverted overprint 17.50
144 A12 1pi on 10k 1.40 *1.75*
145 A12 5pi on 50k 3.00 *3.00*
146 A12 7pi on 70k 4.50 *6.00*

***Perf. 13½***

147 A13 10pi on 1r 18.00 *22.50*
148 A14 35pi on 3.50r 37.50 *40.00*
149 A14 70pi on 7r 55.00 *62.50*

**Blue Overprint**

***Perf. 14½x15***

150 A12 5pa on 1k 11.00 *11.00*
*Nos. 141-150 (10)* 133.10 150.85

**"Smyrn"**

*141c* A12 5pa on 1k 18.00 *20.00*
*142b* A12 10pa on 2k 18.00 *20.00*
*143b* A12 20pa on 4k 18.00 *20.00*
*144a* A12 1pi on 10k 20.00 *25.00*
*145a* A12 5pi on 50k 20.00 *25.00*
*146a* A12 7pi on 70k 20.00 25.00
*Nos. 141c-146a (6)* 114.00 135.00

**Overprinted "Trebizonde"**

**Black Overprint**

151 A12 5pa on 1k .80 *1.00*
*a.* Inverted overprint 25.00
*b.* Pair, one without overprint 60.00
152 A12 10pa on 2k .80 *1.00*
*a.* Inverted overprint 25.00
*b.* Pair, one without "Trebizonde" 60.00
153 A12 20pa on 4k .95 .95
*a.* Inverted overprint 25.00
*b.* Pair, one without overprint 100.00
154 A12 1pi on 10k .95 *1.50*
*a.* Pair, one without "Trebizonde" 35.00
155 A12 5pi on 50k 2.10 *2.50*
156 A12 7pi on 70k 4.25 *5.50*

***Perf. 13½***

157 A13 10pi on 1r 19.00 *20.00*
158 A14 35pi on 3.50r 37.50 *37.50*
159 A14 70pi on 7r 52.50 *55.00*

**Blue Overprint**

***Perf. 14½x15***

160 A12 5pa on 1k 6.25 *7.50*
*Nos. 151-160 (10)* 125.10 *132.45*

On Nos. 158 and 159 the overprint is spelled "Trebisonde".

**Overprinted "Beyrouth"**

**Black Overprint**

**1910**

161 A12 5pa on 1k .50 *.85*
162 A12 10pa on 2k .50 *.85*
*a.* Inverted overprint 25.00
163 A12 20pa on 4k .80 *1.10*
164 A12 1pi on 10k .80 *1.40*
165 A12 5pi on 50k 1.90 *2.75*
166 A12 7pi on 70k 4.00 *5.50*

***Perf. 13½***

167 A13 10pi on 1r 19.00 *21.00*
168 A14 35pi on 3.50r 40.00 *42.50*
169 A14 70pi on 7r 55.00 *60.00*
*Nos. 161-169 (9)* 122.50 135.95

**Overprinted "Dardanelles"**

***Perf. 14½x15***

171 A12 5pa on 1k 1.25 *2.50*
*a.* Pair, one without overprint 60.00
172 A12 10pa on 2k 1.25 *2.50*
*a.* Pair, one without overprint 60.00
173 A12 20pa on 4k 3.25 3.25
*a.* Inverted overprint 25.00
174 A12 1pi on 10k 3.50 *3.50*
175 A12 5pi on 50k 6.50 *7.50*
176 A12 7pi on 70k 14.00 14.00

***Perf. 13½***

177 A13 10pi on 1r 21.00 *21.00*
178 A14 35pi on 3.50r 37.50 *40.00*
*a.* Center and ovpt. inverted *5,000.* *2,750.*
179 A14 70pi on 7r 60.00 *65.00*
*Nos. 171-179 (9)* 148.25 159.25

**Overprinted "Metelin"**

***Perf. 14½x15***

181 A12 5pa on 1k 1.25 *2.00*
*a.* Inverted overprint 65.00
182 A12 10pa on 2k 2.25 *4.25*
*a.* Inverted overprint 65.00
183 A12 20pa on 4k 2.25 *5.25*
*a.* Inverted overprint 65.00
184 A12 1pi on 10k 4.50 *6.50*
185 A12 5pi on 50k 5.50 *8.50*
186 A12 7pi on 70k 8.50 *11.50*

***Perf. 13½***

187 A13 10pi on 1r 30.00 *32.50*
188 A14 35pi on 3.50r 72.50 75.00
189 A14 70pi on 7r 82.50 *87.50*

**Blue Overprint**

***Perf. 14½x15***

190 A12 5pa on 1k 12.50 *17.00*
*Nos. 181-190 (10)* 221.75 *250.00*

**Overprinted "Rizeh"**

***Perf. 14½x15***

191 A12 5pa on 1k .65 *1.00*
*a.* Inverted overprint 30.00
192 A12 10pa on 2k .65 *1.00*
*a.* Inverted overprint 30.00
193 A12 20pa on 4k 1.10 *1.40*
*a.* Inverted overprint 30.00
194 A12 1pi on 10k 1.10 *1.40*
195 A12 5pi on 50k 1.75 *3.75*
196 A12 7pi on 70k 3.25 *6.00*

***Perf. 13½***

197 A13 10pi on 1r 17.50 *21.00*
198 A14 35pi on 3.50r 27.50 *35.00*
199 A14 70pi on 7r 44.00 *52.50*
*Nos. 191-199 (9)* 97.50 123.05

Nos. 61-199 for the establishing of Russian Post Offices in the Levant, 50th anniv.

A15

**Vertically Laid Paper**

**1910 Wmk. 168 *Perf. 14½x15***

200 A15 20pa on 5k red violet (Bl) .60 .60

A16 A17

**Wove Paper**

**Vertical Lozenges of Varnish on Face**

**1910 Unwmk. *Perf. 14x14½***

201 A16 5pa on 1k org yel (Bl) .40 *.50*
202 A16 10pa on 2k green (R) .40 *.50*
*a.* Inverted overprint 25.00
203 A17 20pa on 4k car rose (Bl) .40 *.50*
204 A17 1pi on 10k blue (R) .40 *.50*
*a.* Inverted overprint 25.00
205 A8 5pi on 50k vio & grn (Bl) .75 *1.20*
206 A9 7pi on 70k lt brn & org (Bl) 1.00 *1.25*

***Perf. 13½***

207 A10 10pi on 1r pale brn, brn & org (Bl) 1.40 *1.50*
*Nos. 201-207 (7)* 4.75 *5.95*

**Russian Stamps of 1909-12 Surcharged in Black**

No. 208 Nos. 209-212

**1912 *Perf. 14x14½***

208 A14 20pa on 5k claret .80 .60
209 A11 1½pi on 15k dl vio & blue .80 .75
210 A8 2pi on 20k bl & car .80 .90
211 A11 2½pi on 25k grn & vio 1.00 1.25
*a.* Double surcharge 150.00 150.00
212 A11 3½pi on 35k vio & grn 1.60 1.60
*Nos. 208-212 (5)* 5.00 5.10

**Russia Nos. 88-91, 93, 95-104 Surcharged**

c d

e f

g

**1913** *Perf. 13½*

213 A16(c) 5pa on 1k .25 .25
214 A17(d) 10pa on 2k .25 .25
215 A18(c) 15pa on 3k .25 .25
216 A19(c) 20pa on 4k .25 .25
217 A21(e) 1pi on 10k .25 .25
218 A23(f) 1½pi on 15k .50 *.50*
219 A24(f) 2pi on 20k .50 *.50*
220 A25(f) 2½pi on 25k .75 *.75*
221 A26(f) 3½pi on 35k 1.60 1.60
222 A27(e) 5pi on 50k 2.00 2.00
223 A28(f) 7pi on 70k 8.00 15.00
224 A29(e) 10pi on 1r 9.00 15.00
225 A30(e) 20pi on 2r 1.60 8.00
226 A31(g) 30pi on 3r 2.75 250.00
227 A32(e) 50pi on 5r 150.00 500.00
*Nos. 213-227 (15)* 177.95 794.60

Romanov dynasty tercentenary.
Forgeries exist of overprint on No. 227.

**Russia Nos. 75, 71, 72 Surcharged**

h

i

*Perf. 14x14½*
**Wove Paper**

228 A14(h) 15pa on 3k .25 .25

*Perf. 13, 13½*

230 A13(i) 50pi on 5r 3.00 *10.00*

**Vertically Laid Paper**
**Wmk. Wavy Lines (168)**

231 A13(i) 100pi on 10r 7.00 *20.00*
a. Double surcharge 750.00 —
*Nos. 228-231 (3)* 10.25 30.25

No. 228 has lozenges of varnish on face but No. 230 has not.

**Wrangel Issues**

For the Posts of Gen. Peter Wrangel's army and civilian refugees from South Russia, interned in Turkey, Serbia, etc.

Very few of the Wrangel overprints were actually sold to the public, and many of the covers were made up later with the original cancels. Reprints abound. Values probably are based on sales of reprints in most cases.

Russian Stamps of 1902-18 Surcharged in Blue, Red or Black

**On Russia Nos. 69-70**
**Vertically Laid Paper**

**1921** **Wmk. 168** *Perf. 13½*

232 A12 10,000r on 3.50r 250.00 250.00
233 A12 10,000r on 7r 250.00 250.00
234 A12 20,000r on 3.50r 250.00 250.00
235 A12 20,000r on 7r 250.00 250.00
*Nos. 232-235 (4)* 1,000. 1,000.

**On Russia Nos. 71-86, 87a, 117-118, 137-138**
**Wove Paper**
*Perf. 14x14½, 13½*
**Unwmk.**

236 A14 1000r on 1k 3.25 3.25
237 A14 1000r on 2k (R) 3.25 3.25
237A A14 1000r on 2k (Bk) 47.50 47.50
238 A14 1000r on 3k 1.10 1.10
a. Inverted surcharge 10.00 10.00
239 A15 1000r on 4k 1.10 1.10
a. Inverted surcharge 10.00 10.00
240 A14 1000r on 5k 1.10 1.10
a. Inverted surcharge 10.00 10.00
241 A14 1000r on 7k 1.10 1.10
a. Inverted surcharge 10.00 10.00
242 A15 1000r on 10k 1.10 1.10
a. Inverted surcharge 10.00 10.00
243 A14 1000r on 10k on 7k 1.10 1.10
244 A14 5000r on 3k 1.10 1.10
245 A11 5000r on 14k 10.00 10.00
246 A11 5000r on 15k 1.10 1.10
a. "PYCCKIN" 12.00 12.00
247 A8 5000r on 20k 3.50 3.50
a. "PYCCKIN" 12.00 12.00
248 A11 5000r on 20k on 14k 3.50 3.50
249 A11 5000r on 25k 1.10 1.10
250 A11 5000r on 35k 1.10 1.10
a. Inverted surcharge 10.00 10.00
b. New value omitted 10.00 10.00
251 A8 5000r on 50k 1.10 1.10
a. Inverted surcharge 10.00 10.00
252 A11 5000r on 70k 1.10 1.10
a. Inverted surcharge 10.00 10.00
253 A9 10,000r on 1r (Bl) 1.10 1.10
254 A9 10,000r on 1r (Bk) 8.25 8.25
255 A12 10,000r on 3.50r 3.50 3.50
256 A13 10,000r on 5r 45.00 45.00
257 A13 10,000r on 10r 4.25 4.25
258 A9 20,000r on 1r 2.50 2.50
259 A12 20,000r on 3.50r 2.50 2.50
a. Inverted surcharge 10.00 10.00
b. New value omitted 20.00 20.00
260 A12 20,000r on 7r 92.50 92.50
261 A13 20,000r on 10r 2.50 2.50
*Nos. 236-261 (27)* 246.30 246.30

**On Russia No. 104**

261A A32 20,000r on 5r 950.00

**On Russia Nos. 119-123, 125-135**
*Imperf*

262 A14 1000r on 1k 1.20 1.20
263 A14 1000r on 2k (R) 1.20 1.20
263A A14 1000r on 2k (Bk) 1.50 1.50
264 A14 1000r on 3k 1.20 1.20
265 A15 1000r on 4k 40.00 40.00
266 A14 1000r on 5k 1.50 1.50
267 A14 5000r on 3k 1.20 1.20
268 A11 5000r on 15k 1.50 1.50
268A A8 5000r on 20k 60.00
268B A11 5000r on 25k 60.00
269 A11 5000r on 35k 3.00 3.00
270 A8 5000r on 50k 3.00 3.00
271 A11 5000r on 70k 1.20 1.20
272 A9 10,000r on 1r (Bl) 1.20 1.20
a. Inverted surcharge 10.00 10.00
273 A9 10,000r on 1r (Bk) 1.20 1.20
274 A12 10,000r on 3.50r 1.20 1.20
275 A13 10,000r on 5r 10.00 10.00
276 A12 10,000r on 7r 60.00 60.00
276A A13 10,000r on 10r *200.00*
277 A9 20,000r on 1r (Bl) 1.20 1.20
a. Inverted surcharge 10.00 10.00
278 A9 20,000r on 1r (Bk) 1.20 1.20
279 A12 20,000r on 3.50r 10.00 10.00
280 A13 20,000r on 5r 1.20 1.20
281 A12 20,000r on 7r 47.50 47.50
281A A13 20,000r on 10r *275.00*
*Nos. 262-268,269-276,277-281 (21)* 191.20 191.20

A18

A19

**On Russia AR1-AR3**
*Perf. 14½x15*
**Wmk. 171**

282 A18 10,000r on 1k red, *buff* 6.50 6.50
283 A19 10,000r on 5k grn, *buff* 6.50 6.50
a. Inverted surcharge 10.00
284 A19 10,000r on 10k brn, *buff* 6.50 6.50
a. Inverted surcharge 10.00
*Nos. 282-284 (3)* 19.50 19.50

**On Stamps of Russian Offices in Turkey On No. 38-39**
**Vertically Laid Paper**
**Wmk. Wavy Lines (168)**

284B A11 20,000r on 35pi on 3.50r 300.00
284C A11 20,000r on 70pi on 7r 400.00

**On Nos. 200-207**
**Vertically Laid Paper**

284D A15 1000r on 20pa on 5k 5.00 5.00

**Wove Paper**
**Unwmk.**

285 A16 1000r on 5pa on 1k 2.50 2.50
286 A16 1000r on 10pa on 2k 2.50 2.50
287 A17 1000r on 20pa on 4k 2.50 2.50
288 A17 1000r on 1pi on 10k 2.50 2.50
289 A8 5000r on 5pi on 50k 2.50 2.50
290 A9 5000r on 7pi on 70k 2.50 2.50
291 A10 10,000r on 10pi on 1r 12.50 12.50
a. Inverted surcharge 25.00 25.00
b. Pair, one without surcharge 20.00 20.00
292 A10 20,000r on 10pi on 1r 2.50 2.50
a. Inverted surcharge 25.00 25.00
b. Pair, one without surcharge 25.00 25.00
*Nos. 284D-292 (9)* 35.00 35.00

**On Nos. 208-212**

293 A14 1000r on 20pa on 5k 2.50 2.50
294 A11 5000r on 1½pi on 15k 2.50 2.50
295 A8 5000r on 2pi on 20k 2.50 2.50
296 A11 5000r on 2½pi on 25k 2.50 2.50
297 A11 5000r on 3½pi on 35k 2.50 2.50
*Nos. 293-297 (5)* 12.50 12.50

**On Nos. 228, 230-231**

298 A14 1000r on 15pa on 3k 1.00 1.00
299 A13 10,000r on 50pi on 5r 65.00 65.00
300 A13 10,000r on 100pi on 10r 92.50 92.50
301 A13 20,000r on 50pi on 5r 1.00 1.00
302 A13 20,000r on 100pi on 10r 92.50 92.50
*Nos. 298-302 (5)* 252.00 252.00

**On Stamps of South Russia**
**Denikin Issue**
***Imperf***

303 A5 5000r on 5k org 1.00 1.00
a. Inverted surcharge 10.00
304 A5 5000r on 10k green 1.00 1.00
305 A5 5000r on 15k red 1.00 1.00
306 A5 5000r on 35k lt bl 1.00 1.00
307 A5 5000r on 70k dk blue 1.00 1.00
307A A5 10,000r on 70k dk blue 50.00 50.00
308 A6 10,000r on 1r brn & red 1.00 1.00
309 A6 10,000r on 2r gray vio & yel 1.00 1.00
a. Inverted surcharge 30.00 30.00
310 A6 10,000r on 3r dull rose & grn 3.50 3.50
311 A6 10,000r on 5r slate & vio 2.50 2.50
312 A6 10,000r on 7r gray grn & rose 100.00 100.00
313 A6 10,000r on 10r red & gray 2.00 2.00
314 A6 20,000r on 1r brn & red 1.00 1.00
315 A6 20,000r on 2r gray vio & yel (Bl) 35.00 35.00
a. Inverted surcharge 30.00 30.00
315B A6 20,000r on 2r gray vio & yel (Bk) 1.00 1.00
316 A6 20,000r on 3r dull rose & grn (Bl) 50.00 50.00
316A A6 20,000r on 3r dull rose & grn (Bk) 30.00 30.00
317 A6 20,000r on 5r slate & vio 1.00 1.00
318 A6 20,000r on 7r gray grn & rose 60.00 60.00
319 A6 20,000r on 10r red & gray 1.00 1.00
*Nos. 303-319 (20)* 344.00 344.00

Trident Stamps of Ukraine Surcharged in Blue, Red, Black or Brown

**1921** *Perf. 14, 14½x15*

320 A14 10,000r on 1k org .45 .45
321 A14 10,000r on 2k grn 5.00 5.00
322 A14 10,000r on 3k red .45 .45
a. Inverted surcharge 10.00 10.00
323 A15 10,000r on 4k car .45 .45
324 A14 10,000r on 5k cl .45 .45
325 A14 10,000r on 7k lt bl .45 .45
a. Inverted surcharge 10.00 10.00
326 A15 10,000r on 10k dk bl .45 .45
a. Inverted surcharge 10.00 10.00
327 A14 10,000r on 10k on 7k lt bl .45 .45
a. Inverted surcharge 10.00 10.00
328 A8 20,000r on 20k bl & car (Br) .45 .45
a. Inverted surcharge 10.00 10.00
329 A8 20,000r on 20k bl & car (Bk) .45 .45
a. Inverted surcharge 35.00 35.00
330 A11 20,000r on 20k on 14k bl & rose .45 .45
331 A11 20,000r on 35k red brn & grn 75.00 75.00
332 A8 20,000r on 50k brn vio & grn .45 .45
a. Inverted surcharge 10.00 10.00
*Nos. 320-332 (13)* 84.95 84.95

***Imperf***

333 A14 10,000r on 1k org .75 .75
a. Inverted surcharge 10.00
334 A14 10,000r on 2k grn 2.00 2.00
335 A14 10,000r on 3k red .75 .75
336 A8 20,000r on 20k bl & car .75 .75
337 A11 20,000r on 35k red brn & grn 40.00 40.00
338 A8 20,000r on 50k brn vio & grn 2.00 2.00
*Nos. 333-338 (6)* 46.25 46.25

There are several varieties of the trident surcharge on Nos. 320 to 338.

**Same Surcharge on Russian Stamps**
**On Stamps of 1909-18**
*Perf. 14x14½*

338A A14 10,000r on 1k dl org yel 2.50 2.50
339 A14 10,000r on 2k dl grn 2.50 2.50
340 A14 10,000r on 3k car .50 .50
341 A15 10,000r on 4k car .50 .50
342 A14 10,000r on 5k dk cl .50 .50
343 A14 10,000r on 7k blue .50 .50
344 A15 10,000r on 10k dk bl 2.50 2.50
344A A14 10,000r on 10k on 7k bl 3.75 3.75
344B A11 20,000r on 14k dk bl & car 35.00 35.00
345 A11 20,000r on 15k red brn & dp bl .50 .50
346 A8 20,000r on 20k dl bl & dk car .50 .50
347 A11 20,000r on 20k on 14k dk bl & car 3.50 3.50
348 A11 20,000r on 35k red brn & grn 2.00 2.00
349 A8 20,000r on 50k brn vio & grn .50 .50
349A A11 20,000r on 70k brn & red org 2.50 2.50
*Nos. 338A-349A (15)* 57.75 57.75

**On Stamps of 1917-18**
***Imperf***

350 A14 10,000r on 1k org .75 .75
351 A14 10,000r on 2k gray grn .75 .75
352 A14 10,000r on 3k red .75 .75
353 A15 10,000r on 4k car 40.00 40.00
354 A14 10,000r on 5k claret .75 .75
355 A11 20,000r on 15k red brn & dp bl .75 .75
356 A8 20,000r on 50k brn vio & grn 2.00 2.00
357 A11 20,000r on 70k brn & org .75 .75
*Nos. 350-357 (8)* 46.50 46.50

**Same Surcharge on Stamps of Russian Offices in Turkey**
**On Nos. 40-45**
*Perf. 14½x15*

358 A12 10,000r on 5pa on 1k 5.00 5.00
359 A12 10,000r on 10pa on 2k 5.00 5.00
360 A12 10,000r on 20pa on 4k 5.00 5.00
361 A12 10,000r on 1pi on 10k 5.00 5.00
362 A12 20,000r on 5pi on 50k 5.00 5.00
363 A12 20,000r on 7pi on 70k 5.00 5.00
*Nos. 358-363 (6)* 30.00 30.00

**On Nos. 201-206**

364 A16 10,000r on 5pa on 1k 6.00 6.00
365 A16 10,000r on 10pa on 2k 6.00 6.00
366 A17 10,000r on 20pa on 4k 6.00 6.00
367 A17 10,000r on 1pi on 10k 6.00 6.00
368 A8 20,000r on 5pi on 50k 6.00 6.00
369 A9 20,000r on 7pi on 70k 6.00 6.00
*Nos. 364-369 (6)* 36.00 36.00

**On Nos. 228, 208-212, Stamps of 1912-13**

370 A14 10,000r on 15pa on 3k 5.00 5.00
371 A14 10,000r on 20pa on 5k 5.00 5.00
372 A11 20,000r on 1½pi on 15k 5.00 5.00
373 A8 20,000r on 2pi on 20k 5.00
374 A11 20,000r on 2½pi on 25k 5.00

| | | | | |
|---|---|---|---|---|
| **375** | A11 | 20,000r on 3½pi on 35k | 5.00 | |

**Same Surcharge on Stamp of South Russia, Crimea Issue**

| | | | | |
|---|---|---|---|---|
| **376** | A8 | 20,000r on 5r on 20k bl & car | 750.00 | |
| | | *Nos. 370-376 (7)* | 780.00 | 15.00 |

# RWANDA

ru-'än-də

## (Rwandaise Republic)

LOCATION — Central Africa, adjoining the ex-Belgian Congo, Tanganyika, Uganda and Burundi
GOVT. — Republic
AREA — 10,169 sq. mi.
POP. — 8,154,933(?) (1999 est.)
CAPITAL — Kigali

Rwanda was established as an independent republic on July 1, 1962. With Burundi, it had been a UN trusteeship territory administered by Belgium.

See Ruanda-Urundi.

100 Centimes = 1 Franc

**Catalogue values for all unused stamps in this country are for Never Hinged items.**

**Watermark**

Wmk. 368 — JEZ Multiple

Gregoire Kayibanda and Map of Africa — A1

Design: 40c, 1.50fr, 6.50fr, 20fr, Rwanda map spotlighted, "R" omitted.

*Perf. 11½*

**1962, July 1 Unwmk. Photo.**

| No. | Type | Description | Unused | Used |
|---|---|---|---|---|
| 1 | A1 | 10c brown & gray grn | .30 | .25 |
| 2 | A1 | 40c brown & rose lil | .30 | .25 |
| 3 | A1 | 1fr brown & blue | .65 | .40 |
| 4 | A1 | 1.50fr brown & lt brn | .30 | .25 |
| 5 | A1 | 3.50fr brown & dp org | .30 | .25 |
| 6 | A1 | 6.50fr brown & lt vio bl | .30 | .25 |
| 7 | A1 | 10fr brown & citron | .30 | .25 |
| 8 | A1 | 20fr brown & rose | .40 | .40 |
| | | *Nos. 1-8 (8)* | 2.85 | 2.30 |

Map of Africa and Symbolic Honeycomb A2

Ruanda-Urundi Nos. 151-152 Overprinted with Metallic Frame Obliterating Previous Inscription and Denomination. Black Commemorative Inscription and "REPUBLIQUE RWANDAISE." Surcharged with New Value.

**1963, Jan. 28 Unwmk. *Perf. 11½***

| No. | Type | Description | Unused | Used |
|---|---|---|---|---|
| 9 | A2 | 3.50fr sil, blk, ultra & red | .30 | .25 |
| 10 | A2 | 6.50fr brnz, blk, ultra & red | 1.25 | 1.10 |
| 11 | A2 | 10fr stl bl, blk, ultra & red | .30 | .25 |
| 12 | A2 | 20fr sil, blk, ultra & red | .75 | .50 |
| | | *Nos. 9-12 (4)* | 2.60 | 2.10 |

Rwanda's admission to UN, Sept. 18, 1962.

Ruanda-Urundi Stamps of 1953 Overprinted in Metallic and Black

Designs as before.

**1963, Mar. 21 Unwmk. *Perf. 11½***

**Flowers in Natural Colors**

| No. | Type | Description | Unused | Used |
|---|---|---|---|---|
| 13 | A27 | 25c dk grn & dl org | .40 | .25 |
| 14 | A27 | 40c green & salmon | .40 | .25 |
| 15 | A27 | 60c bl grn & pink | .40 | .25 |
| 16 | A27 | 1.25fr dk green & blue | 1.60 | 1.25 |
| 17 | A27 | 1.50fr vio & apple grn | 1.40 | 1.00 |
| 18 | A27 | 2fr on 1.50fr vio & ap grn | 2.50 | 1.25 |
| 19 | A27 | 4fr on 1.50fr vio & ap grn | 3.00 | 1.25 |
| 20 | A27 | 5fr dp plum & lt bl grn | 3.00 | 1.50 |
| 21 | A27 | 7fr dk green & fawn | 3.00 | 1.50 |
| 22 | A27 | 10fr dp plum & pale ol | 4.50 | 2.00 |
| | | *Nos. 13-22 (10)* | 20.20 | 10.50 |

The overprint consists of silver panels with black lettering. The panels on No. 19 are bluish gray.

**Imperforates**
exist of practically every issue, starting with Nos. 1-8, except Nos. 9-12, 13-22, 36 and 55-69.

Wheat Emblem, Bow, Arrow, Hoe and Billhook — A4

**1963, June 25 Photo. *Perf. 13½***

| No. | Type | Description | Unused | Used |
|---|---|---|---|---|
| 23 | A4 | 2fr brown & green | .30 | .25 |
| 24 | A4 | 4fr magenta & ultra | .30 | .25 |
| 25 | A4 | 7fr red & gray | .30 | .25 |
| 26 | A4 | 10fr olive grn & yel | .50 | .30 |
| | | *Nos. 23-26 (4)* | 1.40 | 1.05 |

FAO "Freedom from Hunger" campaign.

The 20fr leopard and 50fr lion stamps of Ruanda-Urundi, Nos. 149-150, overprinted "Republique Rwandaise" at top and "Contre la Faim" at bottom, were intended to be issued Mar. 21, 1963, but were not placed in use. Value, set $200.

Coffee A5

Designs: 10c, 40c, 4fr, Coffee. 20c, 1fr, 7fr, Bananas. 30c, 2fr, 10fr, Tea.

**1963, July 1 *Perf. 11½***

| No. | Type | Description | Unused | Used |
|---|---|---|---|---|
| 27 | A5 | 10c violet bl & brn | .30 | .25 |
| 28 | A5 | 20c slate & yellow | .30 | .25 |
| 29 | A5 | 30c vermilion & grn | .30 | .25 |
| 30 | A5 | 40c dp green & brown | .30 | .25 |
| 31 | A5 | 1fr maroon & yellow | .30 | .25 |
| 32 | A5 | 2fr dk blue & green | .75 | .50 |
| 33 | A5 | 4fr red & brown | .30 | .25 |
| 34 | A5 | 7fr yellow grn & yellow | .30 | .25 |
| 35 | A5 | 10fr violet & green | .30 | .25 |
| | | *Nos. 27-35 (9)* | 3.15 | 2.50 |

First anniversary of independence.

Common Design Types pictured following the introduction.

**African Postal Union Issue**

Common Design Type

**1963, Sept. 8 Unwmk. *Perf. 12½***

| No. | Type | Description | Unused | Used |
|---|---|---|---|---|
| 36 | CD114 | 14fr black, ocher & red | 1.10 | .75 |

Post Horn and Pigeon — A6

**1963, Oct. 25 Photo. *Perf. 11½***

| No. | Type | Description | Unused | Used |
|---|---|---|---|---|
| 37 | A6 | 50c ultra & rose | .30 | .25 |
| 38 | A6 | 1.50fr brown & blue | .65 | .40 |
| 39 | A6 | 3fr dp plum & gray | .30 | .25 |
| 40 | A6 | 20fr green & yellow | .45 | .25 |
| | | *Nos. 37-40 (4)* | 1.70 | 1.15 |

Rwanda's admission to the UPU, Apr. 6.

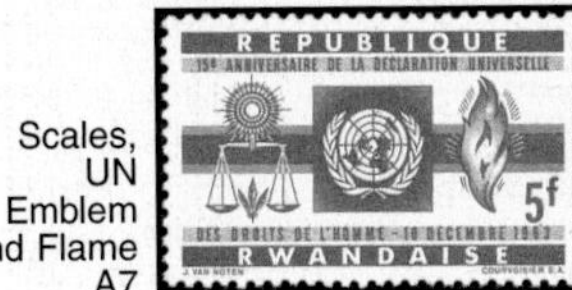


Scales, UN Emblem and Flame A7

**1963, Dec. 10 Unwmk. *Perf. 11½***

| No. | Type | Description | Unused | Used |
|---|---|---|---|---|
| 41 | A7 | 5fr crimson | .30 | .25 |
| 42 | A7 | 6fr brt purple | .70 | .35 |
| 43 | A7 | 10fr brt blue | .30 | .25 |
| | | *Nos. 41-43 (3)* | 1.30 | .85 |

15th anniversary of the Universal Declaration of Human Rights.

Children's Clinic — A8

Designs: 20c, 7fr, Laboratory examination, horiz. 30c, 10fr, Physician examining infant. 40c, 20fr, Litter bearers, horiz.

**1963, Dec. 30 Photo.**

| No. | Type | Description | Unused | Used |
|---|---|---|---|---|
| 44 | A8 | 10c yel org, red & brn blk | .30 | .25 |
| 45 | A8 | 20c grn, red & brn blk | .30 | .25 |
| 46 | A8 | 30c bl, red & brn blk | .30 | .25 |
| 47 | A8 | 40c red lil, red & brn | .30 | .25 |
| 48 | A8 | 2fr bl grn, red brn & blk | .95 | .65 |
| 49 | A8 | 7fr ultra, red & blk | .30 | .25 |
| 50 | A8 | 10fr red brn, red & brn blk | .30 | .25 |
| 51 | A8 | 20fr dp org, red & brn | .65 | .25 |
| | | *Nos. 44-51 (8)* | 3.40 | 2.40 |

Centenary of the International Red Cross.

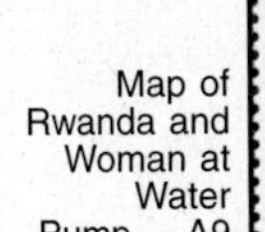

Map of Rwanda and Woman at Water Pump — A9

**1964, May 4 Unwmk. *Perf. 11½***

| No. | Type | Description | Unused | Used |
|---|---|---|---|---|
| 52 | A9 | 3fr lt grn, dk brn & ultra | .30 | .25 |
| 53 | A9 | 7fr pink, dk brn & ultra | .35 | .25 |
| 54 | A9 | 10fr yel, dk brn & ultra | .50 | .30 |
| | | *Nos. 52-54 (3)* | 1.15 | .80 |

**Souvenir Sheet**

***Imperf***

| No. | Type | Description | Unused | Used |
|---|---|---|---|---|
| 54A | A9 | 25fr lilac, bl, brn & blk | 6.50 | 6.50 |

UN 4th World Meteorological Day, Mar. 23.

**Overprinted & Surcharged in Silver and Black**

Ruanda-Urundi Nos. 138, 142

Ruanda-Urundi Nos. 139, 141, 143, 149-150

Ruanda-Urundi Nos. 140, 144-148

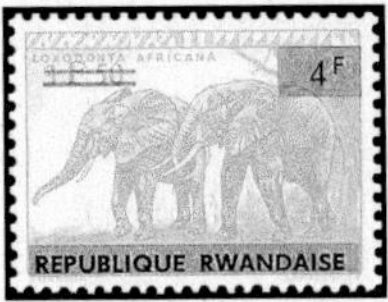


Ruanda-Urundi No. 153

Designs: 10c, 20c, 30c, Buffaloes. 40c, 2fr, Black-and-white colobus (monkey). 50c, 7.50fr, Impalas. 1fr, Mountain gorilla. 3fr, 4fr, 8fr, African elephants. 5fr, 10fr, Eland and zebras. 20fr, Leopard. 50fr, Lions. 40c, 1fr and 2fr are vertical.

**1964, June 29 Photo. *Perf. 11½***

**Size: 33x23mm, 23x33mm**

| No. | Type | Description | Unused | Used |
|---|---|---|---|---|
| 55 | A30 | 10c on 20c gray, ap grn & blk | .30 | .25 |
| 56 | A30 | 20c blk, gray & ap grn | .30 | .25 |
| 57 | A30 | 30c on 1.50fr blk, gray & org | .30 | .25 |
| 58 | A29 | 40c mag, blk & gray grn | .30 | .25 |
| 59 | A30 | 50c grn, org yel & brn | .30 | .25 |
| 60 | A29 | 1fr ultra, blk & brn | .30 | .25 |
| 61 | A29 | 2fr grnsh bl, ind & brn | .30 | .25 |
| 62 | A30 | 3fr brn, dp car & blk | .40 | .25 |
| 63 | A30 | 4fr on 3.50fr on 3fr brn, dp car & blk | .50 | .25 |
| 64 | A30 | 5fr brn, dl yel, grn & blk | .50 | .25 |
| 65 | A30 | 7.50fr on 6.50fr red, org yel & brn | .90 | .25 |
| 66 | A30 | 8fr blue, mag & blk | 8.00 | 3.75 |
| 67 | A30 | 10fr brn, dl yel, brt pink & blk | 1.75 | .35 |

**Size: 45x26½mm**

| No. | Type | Description | Unused | Used |
|---|---|---|---|---|
| 68 | A30 | 20fr hn brn, ocher & blk | 2.75 | .65 |
| 69 | A30 | 50fr dp blue & brown | 4.25 | 2.00 |
| | | *Nos. 55-69 (15)* | 21.15 | 9.50 |

Inverted overprints/surcharges exist. Value, each $10.

Boy with Crutch and Gatagara Home — A11

Designs: 40c, 8fr, Girls with sewing machines, horiz. 4fr, 10fr, Girl on crutches, map of Rwanda and Gatagara Home.

**1964, Nov. 10 Photo. *Perf. 11½***

| No. | Type | Description | Unused | Used |
|---|---|---|---|---|
| 70 | A11 | 10c lilac blk brn | .30 | .25 |
| 71 | A11 | 40c blue & blk brn | .30 | .25 |
| 72 | A11 | 4fr org red & blk brn | .35 | .25 |
| 73 | A11 | 7.50fr yel grn & blk brn | .55 | .25 |
| 74 | A11 | 8fr bister & blk brn | 1.60 | .90 |
| 75 | A11 | 10fr magenta & blk brn | .85 | .40 |
| | | *Nos. 70-75 (6)* | 3.95 | 2.30 |

Gatagara Home for handicapped children.

Basketball — A12

Sport: 10c, 4fr, Runner, horiz. 30c, 20fr, High jump, horiz. 40c, 50fr, Soccer.

**Size: 26x38mm**

**1964, Dec. 8 Litho. *Perf. 13½***

**76** A12 10c gray, sl & dk grn .30 .25
**77** A12 20c pink, sl & rose red .30 .25
**78** A12 30c lt grn, sl & grn .30 .25
**79** A12 40c buff, sl & brn .30 .25
**80** A12 4fr vio gray, sl & vio .30 .25
**81** A12 5fr pale grn, sl & yel grn 1.40 1.25
**82** A12 20fr pale lil, sl & red lil .45 .35
**83** A12 50fr gray, sl & dk gray .90 .75
*a.* Souvenir sheet of 4 6.50 6.50
*Nos. 76-83 (8)* 4.25 3.60

18th Olympic Games, Tokyo, Oct. 10-25. No. 83a contains 4 stamps (10fr, soccer; 20fr, basketball; 30fr, high jump; 40fr, runner). Size of stamps: 28x38mm.

Quill, Books, Radical and Retort — A13

Medical School and Student with Microscope — A14

30c, 10fr, Scales, hand, staff of Mercury and globe. 40c, 12fr, View of University.

**1965, Feb. 22 Engr. *Perf. 11½***

**84** A13 10c multicolored .30 .25
**85** A14 20c multicolored .30 .25
**86** A13 30c multicolored .30 .25
**87** A14 40c multicolored .30 .25
**88** A13 5fr multicolored .30 .25
**89** A14 7fr multicolored .30 .25
**90** A13 10fr multicolored .90 .90
**91** A14 12fr multicolored .35 .25
*Nos. 84-91 (8)* 3.05 2.65

National University of Rwanda at Butare.

Abraham Lincoln, Death Cent. A15

**1965, Apr. 15 Photo. *Perf. 13½***

**92** A15 10c emerald & dk red .30 .25
**93** A15 20c red brn & dk bl .30 .25
**94** A15 30c brt violet & red .30 .25
**95** A15 40c brt grnsh bl & red .30 .25
**96** A15 9fr orange brn & pur .30 .25
**97** A15 40fr black & brt grn 2.00 .80
*Nos. 92-97 (6)* 3.50 2.05

**Souvenir Sheet**

**98** A15 50fr red lilac & red 3.25 3.25

Nos. 92-96 exist without figure of value. Value, set *$700.*

Marabous — A16

Zebras A17

30c, Impalas. 40c, Crowned cranes, hippopotami & cattle egrets. 1fr, Cape buffalos. 3fr, Cape hunting dogs. 5fr, Yellow baboons. 10fr, Elephant & map of Rwanda with location of park. 40fr, Anhinga, great & reed cormorants. 100fr, Lions.

**1965, Apr. 28 Photo. *Perf. 11½***

**Size: 32x23mm**

**99** A16 10c multicolored .30 .25
**100** A17 20c multicolored .30 .25
**101** A16 30c multicolored .30 .25
**102** A17 40c multicolored .30 .25
**103** A16 1fr multicolored .40 .35
**104** A17 3fr multicolored .40 .35
**105** A16 5fr multicolored 6.00 2.50
**106** A17 10fr multicolored .50 .35

**Size: 45x26mm**

**107** A17 40fr multicolored 1.75 .50
**108** A17 100fr multicolored 3.25 .50
*Nos. 99-108 (10)* 13.50 5.55

Kagera National Park publicity.

Telstar and ITU Emblem A18

Designs: 40c, 50fr, Syncom satellite. 60fr, old and new communications equipment.

**1965 Unwmk. *Perf. 13½***

**109** A18 10c red brn, ultra & car .30 .25
**110** A18 40c violet, emer & yel .30 .25
**111** A18 4.50fr blk, car & dk bl 1.50 .55
**112** A18 50fr dk brn, yel grn & brt grn 1.50 .40
*Nos. 109-112 (4)* 3.60 1.45

**Souvenir Sheet**

**113** A18 60fr blk brn, org brn & bl 3.50 3.50

ITU, cent. Issued: No. 113, 7/19; others, 5/17.

Papilio Bromius Chrapkowskii Suffert — A19

Various butterflies and moths in natural colors.

**1965-66 Photo. *Perf. 12½***

**114** A19 10c black & yellow .30 .25
**115** A19 15c blk & dp org ('66) .30 .25
**116** A19 20c black & lilac .30 .25
**117** A19 30c black & red lil .30 .25
**118** A19 35c dk brn & dk bl ('66) .30 .25
**119** A19 40c black & Prus bl .30 .25
**120** A19 1.50fr black & grn ('66) .40 .25
**121** A19 3fr dk brn & ol grn ('66) 4.25 1.50
**122** A19 4fr black & red brn 3.50 2.00
**123** A19 10fr black & pur ('66) .75 .30
**124** A19 50fr black & brown 3.25 1.75
**125** A19 100fr dk brn & bl ('66) 4.50 1.50
*Nos. 114-125 (12)* 18.45 8.80

The 15c, 20c, 40c, 1.50fr, 10fr and 50fr are horizontal.

Cattle, ICY Emblem and Map of Africa — A20

Map of Africa and: 40c, Tree & lake. 4.50fr, Gazelle under tree. 45fr, Mount Ruwenzori.

**1965, Oct. 25 Unwmk. *Perf. 12***

**126** A20 10c olive bis & bl grn .30 .25
**127** A20 40c lt ultra, red brn & grn .30 .25
**128** A20 4.50fr brt grn, yel & brn 1.25 .50
**129** A20 45fr rose claret 1.00 .30
*Nos. 126-129 (4)* 2.85 1.30

John F. Kennedy (1917-1963) — A21

**1965, Nov. 22 Photo. *Perf. 11½***

**130** A21 10c brt grn & dk brn .30 .25
**131** A21 40c brt pink & dk brn .30 .25
**132** A21 50c dk blue & dk brn .30 .25
**133** A21 1fr gray ol & dk brn .30 .25
**134** A21 8fr violet & dk brn 2.25 1.25
**135** A21 50fr gray & dk brn 1.75 1.00
*Nos. 130-135 (6)* 5.20 3.25

**Souvenir Sheet**

**136** Sheet of 2 10.00 10.00
*a.* A21 40fr org & dark brown 4.50 4.50
*b.* A21 60fr ultra & dark brown 5.00 5.00

Madonna — A22

**1965, Dec. 20**

**137** A22 10c gold & dk green .30 .25
**138** A22 40c gold & dk brn red .30 .25
**139** A22 50c gold & dk blue .30 .25
**140** A22 4fr gold & slate .80 .55
**141** A22 6fr gold & violet .30 .25
**142** A22 30fr gold & dk brown .65 .50
*Nos. 137-142 (6)* 2.65 2.05

Christmas.

Father Joseph Damien and Lepers — A23

Designs: 40c, 45fr, Dr. Albert Schweitzer and Hospital, Lambarene.

**1966, Jan. 31 *Perf. 11½***

**143** A23 10c ultra & red brn .30 .25
**144** A23 40c dk red & vio bl .30 .25
**145** A23 4.50fr slate & brt grn .30 .25
**146** A23 45fr brn & hn brn 2.00 1.10
*Nos. 143-146 (4)* 2.90 1.85

Issued for World Leprosy Day.

Pope Paul VI, St. Peter's, UN Headquarters and Statue of Liberty — A24

Design: 40c, 50fr, Pope Paul VI, Papal arms and UN emblem.

**1966, Feb. 28 Photo. *Perf. 12***

**147** A24 10c henna brn & slate .30 .25
**148** A24 40c brt blue & slate .30 .25
**149** A24 4.50fr lilac & slate 1.75 1.00
**150** A24 50fr brt green & slate 1.25 .45
*Nos. 147-150 (4)* 3.60 1.95

Visit of Pope Paul VI to the UN, New York City, Oct. 4, 1965.

Globe Thistle — A25

Flowers: 20c, Blood lily. 30c, Everlasting. 40c, Natal plum. 1fr, Tulip tree. 3fr, Rendle orchid. 5fr, Aloe. 10fr, Ammocharis tinneana. 40fr, Coral tree. 100fr, Caper. (20c, 40c, 1fr, 3fr, 5fr, 10fr are vertical).

**1966, Mar. 14 *Perf. 11½***

**Granite Paper**

**151** A25 10c lt blue & multi .30 .25
**152** A25 20c orange & multi .30 .25
**153** A25 30c car rose & multi .30 .25
**154** A25 40c green & multi .30 .25
**155** A25 1fr multicolored .30 .25
**156** A25 3fr indigo & multi .30 .25
**157** A25 5fr multicolored 7.00 2.25
**158** A25 10fr blue grn & multi .35 .25
**159** A25 40fr brown & multi 1.75 .50
**160** A25 100fr dk bl grn & multi 3.50 1.50
*a.* Miniature sheet 7.50 7.50
*Nos. 151-160 (10)* 14.40 6.00

No. 160a contains one 100fr stamp in changed color, bright blue and multicolored.

Opening of WHO Headquarters, Geneva — A26

**1966, May 1 Litho. *Perf. 12½x12***

**161** A26 2fr lt olive green .30 .25
**162** A26 3fr vermilion .30 .25
**163** A26 5fr violet blue .30 .25
*Nos. 161-163 (3)* .90 .75

Soccer — A27

20c, 9fr, Basketball. 30c, 50fr, Volleyball.

**1966, May 30 Photo. *Perf. 15x14***

**164** A27 10c dl grn, ultra & blk .30 .25
**165** A27 20c crimson, grn & blk .30 .25
**166** A27 30c bl, brt rose lil & blk .30 .25
**167** A27 40c yel bis, grn & blk .30 .25
**168** A27 9fr gray, red lil & blk .30 .25

**169** A27 50fr rose lil, Prus bl & blk .90 .70
*Nos. 164-169 (6)* 2.40 1.95

National Youth Sports Program.

Mother and Child, Planes Dropping Bombs — A28

**1966, June 29** *Perf. 13½*

**Design and Inscription Black and Red**

**170** A28 20c rose lilac .30 .25
**171** A28 30c yellow green .30 .25
**172** A28 50c lt ultra .30 .25
**173** A28 6fr yellow .30 .25
**174** A28 15fr blue green .80 .45
**175** A28 18fr lilac .80 .45
*Nos. 170-175 (6)* 2.80 1.90

Campaign against nuclear weapons.

A29

Global soccer ball.

**1966, July** *Perf. 11½*

**176** A29 20c org & indigo .30 .25
**177** A29 30c lilac & indigo .30 .25
**178** A29 50c brt grn & indigo .30 .25
**179** A29 6fr brt rose & indigo .65 .25
**180** A29 12fr lt vio brn & ind 1.50 .40
**181** A29 25fr ultra & indigo 1.85 .65
*Nos. 176-181 (6)* 4.90 2.05

World Soccer Cup Championship, Wembley, England, July 11-30.

A30

Designs: 10c, Mikeno Volcano and crested shrike, horiz. 40c, Nyamilanga Falls. 4.50fr, Gahinga and Muhabura volcanoes and lobelias, horiz. 55fr, Rusumu Falls.

**1966, Oct. 24** **Engr.** *Perf. 14*

**182** A30 10c green .30 .25
**183** A30 40c brown carmine .35 .25
**184** A30 4.50fr violet blue .60 .40
**185** A30 55fr red lilac .80 .55
*Nos. 182-185 (4)* 2.05 1.45

UNESCO Emblem, African Artifacts and Musical Clef — A31

UNESCO 20th Anniv.: 30c, 10fr, Hands holding primer showing giraffe and zebra. 50c, 15fr, Atom symbol and power drill. 1fr, 50fr, Submerged sphinxes and sailboat.

**1966, Nov. 4** **Photo.** *Perf. 12*

**186** A31 20c brt rose & dk bl .30 .25
**187** A31 30c grnsh blue & blk .30 .25
**188** A31 50c ocher & blk .30 .25
**189** A31 1fr violet & blk .30 .25
**190** A31 5fr yellow grn & blk .30 .25
**191** A31 10fr brown & blk .30 .25
**192** A31 15fr red lilac & dk bl .30 .30
**193** A31 50fr dull bl & blk .40 .40
*Nos. 186-193 (8)* 2.50 2.20

Rock Python — A32

Snakes: 20c, 20fr, Jameson's mamba. 30c, 3fr, Rock python. 50c, Gaboon viper. 1fr, Black-lipped spitting cobra. 5fr, African sand snake. 70fr, Egg-eating snake. (20c, 50c, 3fr and 20fr are horizontal.)

**1967, Jan. 30** **Photo.** *Perf. 11½*

**194** A32 20c red & black .30 .25
**195** A32 30c bl, dk brn & yel .30 .25
**196** A32 50c yel grn & multi .30 .25
**197** A32 1fr lt lil, blk & bis .30 .25
**198** A32 3fr lt vio, dk brn & yel .35 .25
**199** A32 5fr yellow & multi .55 .25
**200** A32 20fr pale pink & multi 2.00 1.00
**201** A32 70fr pale vio, brn & blk 2.75 1.25
*Nos. 194-201 (8)* 6.85 3.75

Ntaruka Hydroelectric Station and Tea Flowers — A33

Designs: 30c, 25fr, Transformer and chrysanthemums (pyrethrum). 50c, 50fr, Sluice and coffee.

**1967, Mar. 6** **Photo.** *Perf. 13½*

**202** A33 20c maroon & dp bl .30 .25
**203** A33 30c black & red brn .30 .25
**204** A33 50c brown & violet .30 .25
**205** A33 4fr dk grn & dp plum .30 .25
**206** A33 25fr violet & sl grn .50 .30
**207** A33 50fr dk blue & brn 1.10 .65
*Nos. 202-207 (6)* 2.80 1.95

Ntaruka Hydroelectric Station.

Souvenir Sheets

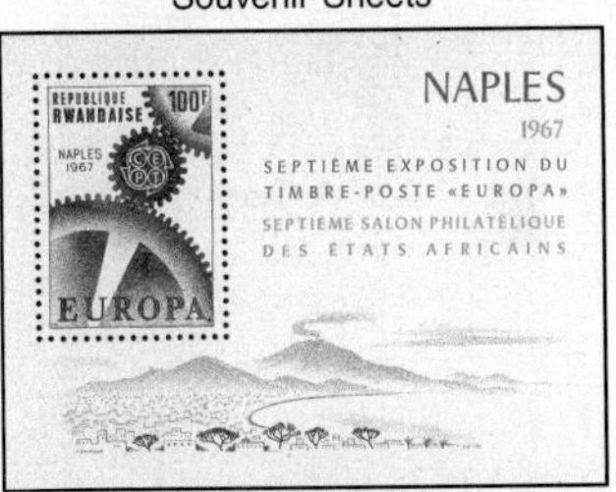


Cogwheels — A34

**1967, Apr. 15** **Engr.** *Perf. 11½*

**208** A34 100fr dk red brown 4.75 4.75
**209** A34 100fr brt rose lilac 4.75 4.75

7th "Europa" Phil. Exhib. and the Philatelic Salon of African States, Naples, Apr. 8-16.

Souvenir Sheet

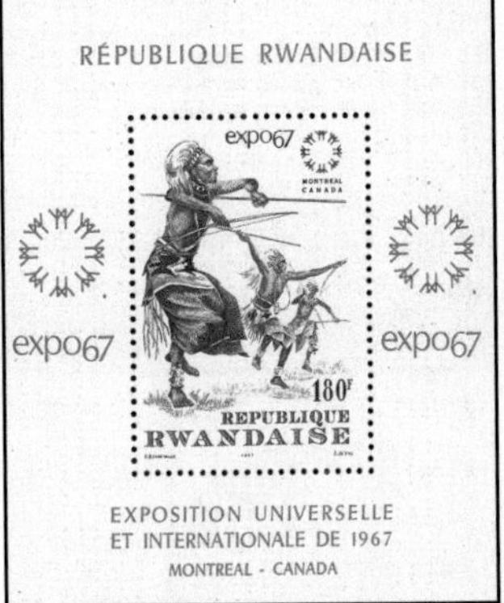


African Dancers and EXPO '67 Emblem — A35

**1967, Apr. 28** *Perf. 11½*

**210** A35 180fr dark purple 4.25 4.25

EXPO '67, Intl. Exhib., Montreal, Apr. 28-Oct. 27.

A similar imperf. sheet has the stamp in violet brown.

St. Martin, by Van Dyck and Caritas Emblem A36

Paintings: 40c, 15fr, Rebecca at the Well, by Murillo, horiz. 60c, 18fr, St. Christopher, by Dierick Bouts. 80c, 26fr, Job and his Friends, by Il Calabrese (Mattia Preti), horiz.

*Perf. 13x11, 11x13*

**1967, May 8** **Photo.**

**Black Inscription on Gold Panel**

**211** A36 20c dark purple .30 .25
**212** A36 40c blue green .30 .25
**213** A36 60c rose carmine .30 .25
**214** A36 80c deep blue .30 .25
**215** A36 9fr redsh brown .85 .45
**216** A36 15fr orange ver .30 .25
**217** A36 18fr dk olive grn .35 .25
**218** A36 26fr dk carmine rose .40 .35
*Nos. 211-218 (8)* 3.10 2.30

Issued to publicize the work of Caritas-Rwanda, Catholic welfare organization.

Round Table Emblem and Zebra — A37

Round Table Emblem and: 40c, Elephant. 60c, Cape buffalo. 80c, Antelope. 18fr, Wheat. 100fr, Palm tree.

**1967, July 31** **Photo.** *Perf. 14*

**219** A37 20c gold & multi .30 .25
**220** A37 40c gold & multi .30 .25
**221** A37 60c gold & multi .30 .25
**222** A37 80c gold & multi .30 .25
**223** A37 18fr gold & multi .40 .25
**224** A37 100fr gold & multi 2.00 1.00
*Nos. 219-224 (6)* 3.60 2.25

Rwanda Table No. 9 of Kigali, a member of the Intl. Round Tables Assoc.

EXPO '67 Emblem, Africa Place and Dancers and Drummers — A38

EXPO '67 Emblem, Africa Place and: 30c, 3fr, Drum and vessels. 50c, 40fr, Two dancers. 1fr, 34fr, Spears, shields and bow.

**1967, Aug. 10** **Photo.** *Perf. 12*

**225** A38 20c brt blue & sepia .30 .25
**226** A38 30c brt rose lil & sepia .30 .25
**227** A38 50c orange & sepia .30 .25
**228** A38 1fr green & sepia .30 .25
**229** A38 3fr violet & sepia .30 .25
**230** A38 15fr emerald & sepia .30 .25
**231** A38 34fr rose red & sepia .40 .35
**232** A38 40fr grnsh bl & sepia .60 .45
*Nos. 225-232 (8)* 2.80 2.30

Lions Emblem, Globe and Zebra — A39

**1967, Oct. 16** **Photo.** *Perf. 13½*

**233** A39 20c lilac, bl & blk .30 .25
**234** A39 80c lt grn, bl & blk .30 .25
**235** A39 1fr rose car, bl & blk .30 .25
**236** A39 8fr bister, bl & blk .30 .25
**237** A39 10fr ultra, bl & blk .40 .25
**238** A39 50fr yel grn, bl & blk 1.75 1.00
*Nos. 233-238 (6)* 3.35 2.25

50th anniversary of Lions International.

Woodland Kingfisher — A40

Birds: 20c, Red bishop, vert. 60c, Red-billed quelea, vert. 80c, Double-toothed barbet. 2fr, Pin-tailed whydah, vert. 3fr, Solitary cuckoo. 18fr, Green wood hoopoe, vert. 25fr, Blue-collared bee-eater. 80fr, Regal sunbird, vert. 100fr, Red-shouldered widowbird.

**1967, Dec. 18** *Perf. 11½*

**239** A40 20c multicolored .30 .25
**240** A40 40c multicolored .30 .25
**241** A40 60c multicolored .30 .25
**242** A40 80c multicolored .30 .25
**243** A40 2fr multicolored .35 .30
**244** A40 3fr multicolored .40 .30
**245** A40 18fr multicolored 1.50 .75
**246** A40 25fr multicolored 2.00 1.00
**247** A40 80fr multicolored 4.50 3.25
**248** A40 100fr multicolored 6.25 4.75
*Nos. 239-248 (10)* 16.20 11.35

Souvenir Sheet

Ski Jump, Speed Skating — A41

**1968, Feb. 12** **Photo.** *Perf. 11½*

**249** A41 Sheet of 2 7.50 7.50
*a.* 50fr bl, blk & grn (skier) 3.50 3.50
*b.* 50fr grn, blk & bl (skater) 3.50 3.50
*c.* Souv. sheet of 2, #249a at right 7.50 7.50

10th Winter Olympic Games, Grenoble, France, Feb. 6-18.

Runner, Mexican Sculpture and Architecture — A42

Sport and Mexican Art: 40c, Hammer throw, pyramid and animal head. 60c, Hurdler and sculptures. 80c, Javelin and sculptures.

**1968, May 27 Photo. *Perf. 11½***

| | | | | |
|---|---|---|---|---|
| **250** | A42 | 20c ultra & multi | .35 | .25 |
| **251** | A42 | 40c multicolored | .35 | .25 |
| **252** | A42 | 60c lilac & multi | .35 | .25 |
| **253** | A42 | 80c orange & multi | .35 | .25 |
| | | *Nos. 250-253 (4)* | 1.40 | 1.00 |

19th Olympic Games, Mexico City, 10/12-27.

Souvenir Sheet

19th Olympic Games, Mexico City — A43

a, 8fr, Soccer. b, 10fr, Mexican horseman, cactus. c, 12fr, Field hockey. d, 18fr, Cathedral, Mexico City. e, 20fr, Boxing. f, 30fr, Modern buildings, musical instruments, vase.

**1968, May 27 Photo. *Perf. 11½***
**Granite Paper**

| | | | | |
|---|---|---|---|---|
| **254** | A43 | Sheet of 6, #a.-f. | 8.50 | 8.50 |

Three sets of circular gold "medal" overprints with black inscriptions were applied to the six stamps of No. 254 to honor 18 Olympic winners. Issued Dec. 12, 1968. Value $70.

Souvenir Sheet

Martin Luther King, Jr. — A44

**1968, July 29 Engr. *Perf. 13½***

| | | | | |
|---|---|---|---|---|
| **255** | A44 | 100fr sepia | 3.00 | 1.75 |

Rev. Dr. Martin Luther King, Jr. (1929-68), American civil rights leader. See No. 406.

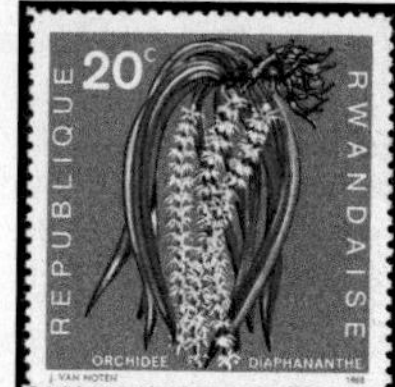


Diaphant Orchid — A45

Flowers: 40c, Pharaoh's scepter. 60c, Flower of traveler's-tree. 80c, Costus afer. 2fr, Banana tree flower. 3fr, Flower and fruit of papaw tree. 18fr, Clerodendron. 25fr, Sweet potato flowers. 80fr, Baobab tree flower. 100fr, Passion flower.

**1968, Sept. 9 Litho. *Perf. 13***

| | | | | |
|---|---|---|---|---|
| **256** | A45 | 20c lilac & multi | .30 | .25 |
| **257** | A45 | 40c multicolored | .30 | .25 |
| **258** | A45 | 60c bl grn & multi | .30 | .25 |
| **259** | A45 | 80c multicolored | .30 | .25 |
| **260** | A45 | 2fr brt yellow & multi | .30 | .25 |
| **261** | A45 | 3fr multicolored | .30 | .25 |
| **262** | A45 | 18fr multicolored | .30 | .25 |
| **263** | A45 | 25fr gray & multi | .55 | .30 |
| **264** | A45 | 80fr multicolored | 1.90 | .75 |
| **265** | A45 | 100fr multicolored | 2.10 | 1.25 |
| | | *Nos. 256-265 (10)* | 6.65 | 4.05 |

Equestrian and "Mexico 1968" A46

Designs: 40c, Judo and "Tokyo 1964." 60c, Fencing and "Rome 1960." 80c, High jump and "Berlin 1936." 38fr, Women's diving and "London 1908 and 1948." 60fr, Weight lifting and "Paris 1900 and 1924."

**1968, Oct. 24 Litho. *Perf. 14x13***

| | | | | |
|---|---|---|---|---|
| **266** | A46 | 20c orange & sepia | .30 | .25 |
| **267** | A46 | 40c grnsh bl & sepia | .30 | .25 |
| **268** | A46 | 60c car rose & sepia | .30 | .25 |
| **269** | A46 | 80c ultra & sepia | .30 | .25 |
| **270** | A46 | 38fr red & sepia | .55 | .25 |
| **271** | A46 | 60fr emerald & sepia | 1.30 | .55 |
| | | *Nos. 266-271 (6)* | 3.05 | 1.80 |

19th Olympic Games, Mexico City, 10/12-27.

Tuareg, Algeria — A47

African National Costumes: 40c, Musicians, Upper Volta. 60c, Senegalese women. 70c, Girls of Rwanda going to market. 8fr, Young married couple from Morocco. 20fr, Nigerian officials in state dress. 40fr, Man and women from Zambia. 50fr, Man and woman from Kenya.

**1968, Nov. 4 Litho. *Perf. 13***

| | | | | |
|---|---|---|---|---|
| **272** | A47 | 30c multicolored | .30 | .25 |
| **273** | A47 | 40c multicolored | .30 | .25 |
| **274** | A47 | 60c multicolored | .30 | .25 |
| **275** | A47 | 70c multicolored | .30 | .25 |
| **276** | A47 | 8fr multicolored | .30 | .25 |
| **277** | A47 | 20fr multicolored | .75 | .25 |
| **278** | A47 | 40fr multicolored | 1.40 | .45 |
| **279** | A47 | 50fr multicolored | 1.60 | .85 |
| | | *Nos. 272-279 (8)* | 5.25 | 2.80 |

Souvenir Sheet

Nativity, by Giorgione — A48

**1968, Dec. 16 Engr. *Perf. 11½***

| | | | | |
|---|---|---|---|---|
| **280** | A48 | 100fr green | 4.50 | 4.50 |

Christmas.
See Nos. 309, 389, 422, 494, 564, 611, 713, 787, 848, 894.

Singing Boy, by Frans Hals — A49

Paintings and Music: 20c, Angels' Concert, by van Eyck. 40c, Angels' Concert, by Mathias Grunewald. 60c, No. 283a, Singing Boy, by Frans Hals. 80c, Lute Player, by Gerard Terborch. 2fr, The Fifer, by Manet. 6fr, No. 286a, Young Girls at the Piano, by Renoir.

**1969, Mar. 31 Photo. *Perf. 13***

| | | | | |
|---|---|---|---|---|
| **281** | A49 | 20c gold & multi | .30 | .25 |
| **282** | A49 | 40c gold & multi | .30 | .25 |
| **283** | A49 | 60c gold & multi | .30 | .25 |
| ***a.*** | | Souvenir sheet, 75fr | 2.50 | 2.50 |
| **284** | A49 | 80c gold & multi | .30 | .25 |
| **285** | A49 | 2fr gold & multi | .30 | .25 |
| **286** | A49 | 6fr gold & multi | .30 | .25 |
| ***a.*** | | Souvenir sheet, 75fr | 2.50 | 2.50 |
| | | *Nos. 281-286,C6-C7 (8)* | 6.30 | 5.25 |

Tuareg Men — A50

African Headdresses: 40c, Ovambo woman, South West Africa. 60c, Guinean man and Congolese woman. 80c, Dagger dancer, Guinean forest area. 8fr, Mohammedan Nigerians. 20fr, Luba dancer, Kabondo, Congo. 40fr, Senegalese and Gambian women. 80fr, Rwanda dancer.

**1969, May 29 Litho. *Perf. 13***

| | | | | |
|---|---|---|---|---|
| **287** | A50 | 20c multicolored | .30 | .25 |
| **288** | A50 | 40c multicolored | .30 | .25 |
| **289** | A50 | 60c multicolored | .30 | .25 |
| **290** | A50 | 80c multicolored | .30 | .25 |
| **291** | A50 | 8fr multicolored | .40 | .25 |
| **292** | A50 | 20fr multicolored | .75 | .25 |
| **293** | A50 | 40fr multicolored | 1.75 | .45 |
| **294** | A50 | 80fr multicolored | 4.00 | .85 |
| | | *Nos. 287-294 (8)* | 8.10 | 2.80 |

See #398-405. For overprints see #550-557.

The Moneylender and his Wife, by Quentin Massys — A51

Design: 70fr, The Moneylender and his Wife, by Marinus van Reymerswaele.

**1969, Sept. 10 Photo. *Perf. 13***

| | | | | |
|---|---|---|---|---|
| **295** | A51 | 30fr silver & multi | .85 | .75 |
| **296** | A51 | 70fr gold & multi | 2.15 | 1.50 |

5th anniv. of the African Development Bank. Printed in sheets of 20 stamps and 20 labels with commemorative inscription.
For overprints see Nos. 612-613.

Souvenir Sheet

First Man on the Moon — A52

**1969, Oct. 9 Engr. *Perf. 11½***

| | | | | |
|---|---|---|---|---|
| **297** | A52 | 100fr blue gray | 4.25 | 4.25 |

See note after Mali No. C80. See No. 407.

Camomile and Health Emblem — A53

Medicinal Plants and Health Emblem: 40c, Aloe. 60c, Cola. 80c, Coca. 3fr, Hagenia abyssinica. 75fr, Cassia. 80fr, Cinchona. 100fr, Tephrosia.

**1969, Nov. 24 Photo. *Perf. 13***
**Flowers in Natural Colors**

| | | | | |
|---|---|---|---|---|
| **298** | A53 | 20c gold, blue & blk | .30 | .25 |
| **299** | A53 | 40c gold, yel grn & blk | .30 | .25 |
| **300** | A53 | 60c gold, pink & blk | .30 | .25 |
| **301** | A53 | 80c gold, green & blk | .30 | .25 |
| **302** | A53 | 3fr gold, org & blk | .30 | .25 |
| **303** | A53 | 75fr gold, yel & blk | 2.25 | 1.25 |
| **304** | A53 | 80fr gold, lilac & blk | 2.50 | 1.40 |
| **305** | A53 | 100fr gold, dl yel & blk | 3.00 | 1.75 |
| | | *Nos. 298-305 (8)* | 9.25 | 5.65 |

For overprints and surcharge, see Nos. 534-539, B1.

Worker with Pickaxe and Flag — A54

**1969, Nov. Photo. *Perf. 11½***

| | | | | |
|---|---|---|---|---|
| **306** | A54 | 6fr brt pink & multi | .35 | .25 |
| **307** | A54 | 18fr ultra & multi | .80 | .45 |
| **308** | A54 | 40fr brown & multi | 1.35 | .95 |
| | | *Nos. 306-308 (3)* | 2.50 | 1.65 |

10th anniversary of independence.
For overprints see Nos. 608-610.

**Christmas Type of 1968**
Souvenir Sheet

Design: "Holy Night" (detail), by Correggio.

**1969, Dec. 15 Engr. *Perf. 11½***

| | | | | |
|---|---|---|---|---|
| **309** | A48 | 100fr ultra | 4.50 | 4.50 |

The Cook, by Pierre Aertsen — A55

Paintings: 20c, Quarry Worker, by Oscar Bonnevalle, horiz. 40c, The Plower, by Peter Brueghel, horiz 60c, Fisherman, by Constantin Meunier. 80c, Slipway, Ostende, by Jean van Noten, horiz. 10fr, The Forge of Vulcan, by Velasquez, horiz. 50fr, "Hiercheuse" (woman shoveling coal), by Meunier. 70fr, Miner, by Pierre Paulus.

| **1969, Dec. 22** | | **Photo.** | | ***Perf. 13½*** | |
|---|---|---|---|---|---|
| **310** | A55 | 20c | gold & multi | .30 | .25 |
| **311** | A55 | 40c | gold & multi | .30 | .25 |
| **312** | A55 | 60c | gold & multi | .30 | .25 |
| **313** | A55 | 80c | gold & multi | .30 | .25 |
| **314** | A55 | 8fr | gold & multi | .30 | .25 |
| **315** | A55 | 10fr | gold & multi | .30 | .25 |
| **316** | A55 | 50fr | gold & multi | 1.40 | .45 |
| **317** | A55 | 70fr | gold & multi | 1.90 | .80 |
| | | *Nos. 310-317 (8)* | | 5.10 | 2.75 |

ILO, 50th anniversary.

Napoleon Crossing St. Bernard, by Jacques L. David — A56

Paintings of Napoleon Bonaparte (1769-1821): 40c, Decorating Soldier before Tilsit, by Jean Baptiste Debret. 60c, Addressing Troops at Augsburg, by Claude Gautherot. 80c, First Consul, by Jean Auguste Ingres. 8fr, Battle of Marengo, by Jacques Auguste Pajou. 20fr, Napoleon Meeting Emperor Francis II, by Antoine Jean Gros. 40fr, Gen. Bonaparte at Arcole, by Gros. 80fr Coronation, by David.

| **1969, Dec. 29** | | | | | |
|---|---|---|---|---|---|
| **318** | A56 | 20c | gold & multi | .30 | .25 |
| **319** | A56 | 40c | gold & multi | .30 | .25 |
| **320** | A56 | 60c | gold & multi | .30 | .25 |
| **321** | A56 | 80c | gold & multi | .30 | .25 |
| **322** | A56 | 8fr | gold & multi | .30 | .25 |
| **323** | A56 | 20fr | gold & multi | .85 | .40 |
| **324** | A56 | 40fr | gold & multi | 1.75 | .85 |
| **325** | A56 | 80fr | gold & multi | 3.25 | 1.40 |
| | | *Nos. 318-325 (8)* | | 7.35 | 3.90 |

Epsom Derby, by Gericault — A57

Paintings of Horses: 40c, Horses Emerging from the Sea, by Delacroix. 60c, Charles V at Muhlberg, by Titian, vert. 80c, Amateur Jockeys, by Edgar Degas, 8fr, Horsemen at Rest, by Philips Wouwerman. 20fr, Imperial Guards Officer, by Géricault, vert. 40fr, Friends of the Desert, by Oscar Bonnevalle. 80fr, Two Horses (detail from the Prodigal Son), by Rubens.

| **1970, Mar. 31** | | **Photo.** | | ***Perf. 13½*** | |
|---|---|---|---|---|---|
| **326** | A57 | 20c | gold & multi | .30 | .25 |
| **327** | A57 | 40c | gold & multi | .30 | .25 |
| **328** | A57 | 60c | gold & multi | .30 | .25 |
| **329** | A57 | 80c | gold & multi | .30 | .25 |
| **330** | A57 | 8fr | gold & multi | .30 | .25 |
| **331** | A57 | 20fr | gold & multi | .80 | .25 |
| **332** | A57 | 40fr | gold & multi | 1.30 | .45 |
| **333** | A57 | 80fr | gold & multi | 2.10 | .80 |
| | | *Nos. 326-333 (8)* | | 5.70 | 2.75 |

Souvenir Sheet

Fleet in Bay of Naples, by Peter Brueghel, the Elder — A58

| **1970, May 2** | | **Engr.** | | ***Perf. 11½*** | |
|---|---|---|---|---|---|
| **334** | A58 | 100fr | brt rose lilac | 9.00 | 9.00 |

10th Europa Phil. Exhib., Naples, Italy, May 2-10.

Examples of No. 334 were trimmed to 68x58mm and overprinted in silver or gold "NAPLES 1973" on the stamp, and "Salon Philatelique des Etats Africains / Exposition du Timbre-Poste Europa" in October, 1973.

Soccer and Mexican Decorations A59

Designs: Various scenes from soccer game and pre-Columbian decorations.

| **1970, June 15** | | **Photo.** | | ***Perf. 13*** | |
|---|---|---|---|---|---|
| **335** | A59 | 20c | gold & multi | .30 | .25 |
| **336** | A59 | 30c | gold & multi | .30 | .25 |
| **337** | A59 | 50c | gold & multi | .30 | .25 |
| **338** | A59 | 1fr | gold & multi | .30 | .25 |
| **339** | A59 | 6fr | gold & multi | .30 | .25 |
| **340** | A59 | 18fr | gold & multi | .65 | .25 |
| **341** | A59 | 30fr | gold & multi | .85 | .45 |
| **342** | A59 | 90fr | gold & multi | 1.75 | .90 |
| | | *Nos. 335-342 (8)* | | 4.75 | 2.85 |

9th World Soccer Championships for the Jules Rimet Cup, Mexico City, 5/30-6/21.

Tharaka Meru Woman, East Africa — A60

African National Costumes: 30c, Musician with wooden flute, Niger. 50c, Woman water carrier, Tunisia. 1fr, Ceremonial costumes, North Nigeria. 3fr, Strolling troubadour "Griot," Mali. 5fr, Quipongos women, Angola. 50fr, Man at prayer, Mauritania. 90fr, Sinehatiali dance costumes, Ivory Coast.

| **1970, June 1** | | | | **Litho.** | |
|---|---|---|---|---|---|
| **343** | A60 | 20c | multi | .30 | .25 |
| **344** | A60 | 30c | multi | .30 | .25 |
| **345** | A60 | 50c | multi | .30 | .25 |
| **346** | A60 | 1fr | multi | .30 | .25 |
| **347** | A60 | 3fr | multi | .30 | .25 |
| **348** | A60 | 5fr | multi | .30 | .25 |
| **349** | A60 | 50fr | multi | 2.00 | .45 |
| **350** | A60 | 90fr | multi | 3.00 | .90 |
| | | *Nos. 343-350 (8)* | | 6.80 | 2.85 |

For overprints and surcharges see Nos. 693-698, B2-B3.

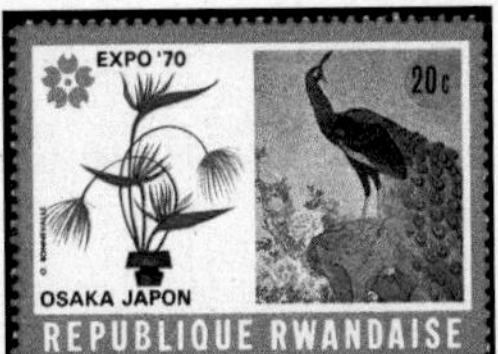

Flower Arrangement, Peacock, EXPO '70 Emblem — A61

EXPO Emblem and: 30c, Torii and Camellias, by Yukihiko Yasuda. 50c, Kabuki character and Woman Playing Samisen, by Nampu Katayama. 1fr, Tower of the Sun, and Warrior Riding into Water. 3fr, Pavilion and Buddhist deity. 5fr, Pagoda and modern painting by Shuho Yamakawa. 20fr, Japanese inscription "Omatsuri" and Osaka Castle. 70fr, EXPO '70 emblem and Warrior on Horseback.

| **1970, Aug. 24** | | **Photo.** | | ***Perf. 13*** | |
|---|---|---|---|---|---|
| **351** | A61 | 20c | gold & multi | .30 | .25 |
| **352** | A61 | 30c | gold & multi | .30 | .25 |
| **353** | A61 | 50c | gold & multi | .30 | .25 |
| **354** | A61 | 1fr | gold & multi | .30 | .25 |
| **355** | A61 | 3fr | gold & multi | .30 | .25 |
| **356** | A61 | 5fr | gold & multi | .30 | .25 |
| **357** | A61 | 20fr | gold & multi | .70 | .35 |
| **358** | A61 | 70fr | gold & multi | 2.00 | .90 |
| | | *Nos. 351-358 (8)* | | 4.50 | 2.75 |

EXPO '70 International Exhibition, Osaka, Japan, Mar. 15-Sept. 13.

Young Mountain Gorillas — A62

Various Gorillas. 40c, 80c, 2fr, 100fr are vert.

| **1970, Sept. 7** | | | | | |
|---|---|---|---|---|---|
| **359** | A62 | 20c | olive & blk | .30 | .25 |
| **360** | A62 | 40c | brt rose lil & blk | .30 | .25 |
| **361** | A62 | 60c | blue, brn & blk | .30 | .25 |
| **362** | A62 | 80c | org brn & blk | .30 | .25 |
| **363** | A62 | 1fr | dp car & blk | .50 | .25 |
| **364** | A62 | 2fr | black & multi | .70 | .45 |
| **365** | A62 | 15fr | sepia & blk | 1.60 | 1.25 |
| **366** | A62 | 100fr | brt bl & blk | 9.00 | 3.50 |
| | | *Nos. 359-366 (8)* | | 13.00 | 6.45 |

Pierre J. Pelletier and Joseph B. Caventou A63

Designs: 20c, Cinchona flower and bark. 80c, Quinine powder and pharmacological vessels. 1fr, Anopheles mosquito. 3fr, Malaria patient and nurse. 25fr, "Malaria" (mosquito).

| **1970, Oct. 27** | | **Photo.** | | ***Perf. 13*** | |
|---|---|---|---|---|---|
| **367** | A63 | 20c | silver & multi | .30 | .25 |
| **368** | A63 | 80c | silver & multi | .30 | .25 |
| **369** | A63 | 1fr | silver & multi | .30 | .25 |
| **370** | A63 | 3fr | silver & multi | .30 | .25 |
| **371** | A63 | 25fr | silver & multi | .75 | .25 |
| **372** | A63 | 70fr | silver & multi | 1.75 | .60 |
| | | *Nos. 367-372 (6)* | | 3.70 | 1.85 |

150th anniv. of the discovery of quinine by Pierre Joseph Pelletier (1788-1842) and Joseph Bienamé Caventou (1795-1877), French pharmacologists.

Apollo Spaceship A64

Apollo Spaceship: 30c, Second stage separation. 50c, Spaceship over moon surface. 1fr, Landing module and astronauts on moon. 3fr, Take-off from moon. 5fr, Return to earth. 10fr, Final separation of nose cone. 80fr, Splashdown.

| **1970, Nov. 23** | | **Photo.** | | ***Perf. 13*** | |
|---|---|---|---|---|---|
| **373** | A64 | 20c | silver & multi | .30 | .25 |
| **374** | A64 | 30c | silver & multi | .30 | .25 |
| **375** | A64 | 50c | silver & multi | .30 | .25 |
| **376** | A64 | 1fr | silver & multi | .30 | .25 |
| **377** | A64 | 3fr | silver & multi | .30 | .25 |
| **378** | A64 | 5fr | silver & multi | .30 | .25 |
| **379** | A64 | 10fr | silver & multi | .60 | .30 |
| **380** | A64 | 80fr | silver & multi | 2.40 | 1.25 |
| | | *Nos. 373-380 (8)* | | 4.80 | 3.05 |

Conquest of space.

Franklin D. Roosevelt and Brassocattleya Olympia Alba — A65

Portraits of Roosevelt and various orchids.

| **1970, Dec. 21** | | **Photo.** | | ***Perf. 13*** | |
|---|---|---|---|---|---|
| **381** | A65 | 20c | blue, blk & brn | .30 | .25 |
| **382** | A65 | 30c | car rose, blk & brn | .30 | .25 |
| **383** | A65 | 50c | dp org, blk & brn | .30 | .25 |
| **384** | A65 | 1fr | green, blk & brn | .30 | .25 |
| **385** | A65 | 2fr | maroon, blk & grn | .30 | .25 |
| **386** | A65 | 6fr | lilac & multi | .30 | .25 |
| **387** | A65 | 30fr | bl, blk & sl grn | .95 | .60 |
| **388** | A65 | 60fr | lil rose, blk & sl grn | 1.90 | .80 |
| | | *Nos. 381-388 (8)* | | 4.65 | 2.90 |

Pres. Roosevelt, 25th death anniv.

### Christmas Type of 1968

Souvenir Sheet

Design: 100fr, Adoration of the Shepherds, by José de Ribera, vert.

| **1970, Dec. 24** | | **Engr.** | | ***Perf. 11½*** | |
|---|---|---|---|---|---|
| **389** | A48 | 100fr | Prus blue | 3.50 | 3.50 |

Pope Paul VI — A66

Popes: 20c, John XXIII, 1958-1963. 30c, Pius XII, 1939-1958. 40c, Pius XI, 1922-39. 1fr, Benedict XV, 1914-22. 18fr, St. Pius X, 1903-14. 20fr, Leo XIII, 1878-1903. 60fr, Pius IX, 1846-78.

| **1970, Dec. 31** | | **Photo.** | | ***Perf. 13*** | |
|---|---|---|---|---|---|
| **390** | A66 | 10c | gold & dk brn | .30 | .25 |
| **391** | A66 | 20c | gold & dk grn | .30 | .25 |
| **392** | A66 | 30c | gold & dp claret | .30 | .25 |
| **393** | A66 | 40c | gold & indigo | .30 | .25 |
| **394** | A66 | 1fr | gold & dk pur | .30 | .25 |
| **395** | A66 | 18fr | gold & purple | .80 | .25 |
| **396** | A66 | 20fr | gold & org brn | 1.10 | .40 |
| **397** | A66 | 60fr | gold & blk brn | 2.50 | .80 |
| | | *Nos. 390-397 (8)* | | 5.90 | 2.70 |

Centenary of Vatican I, Ecumenical Council of the Roman Catholic Church, 1869-70.

For overprints, see Nos. 644-651.

### Headdress Type of 1969

African Headdresses: 20c, Rendille woman. 30c, Young Toubou woman, Chad. 50c, Peul man, Niger. 1fr, Young Masai man, Kenya. 5fr, Young Peul girl, Niger. 18fr, Rwanda woman. 25fr, Man, Mauritania. 50fr, Rwanda women with pearl necklaces.

| **1971, Feb. 15** | | **Litho.** | | ***Perf. 13*** | |
|---|---|---|---|---|---|
| **398** | A50 | 20c | multi | .30 | .25 |
| **399** | A50 | 30c | multi | .30 | .25 |
| **400** | A50 | 50c | multi | .30 | .25 |
| **401** | A50 | 1fr | multi | .30 | .25 |
| **402** | A50 | 5fr | multi | .30 | .25 |
| **403** | A50 | 18fr | multi | .45 | .25 |
| **404** | A50 | 25fr | multi | 1.05 | .30 |
| **405** | A50 | 50fr | multi | 1.95 | .60 |
| | | *Nos. 398-405 (8)* | | 4.95 | 2.40 |

For overprints see Nos. 550-557.

**M. L. King Type of 1968**

Souvenir Sheet

Design: 100fr, Charles de Gaulle (1890-1970), President of France.

**1971, Mar. 15 Engr. *Perf. 13½***

**406** A44 100fr ultra 4.25 4.25

**Astronaut Type of 1969 Inscribed in Dark Violet with Emblem and: "APOLLO / 14 / SHEPARD / ROOSA / MITCHELL"**

**1971, Apr. 15 Engr. *Perf. 11½***

**Souvenir Sheet**

**407** A52 100fr brown orange 8.00 8.00

Apollo 14 US moon landing, Jan. 31-Feb. 9.

Beethoven, by Christian Horneman A67

Beethoven Portraits: 30c, Joseph Stieler. 50c, by Ferdinand Schimon. 3fr, by H. Best. 6fr, by W. Fassbender. 90fr, Beethoven's Funeral Procession, by Leopold Stöber.

**1971, July 5 Photo. *Perf. 13***

**408** A67 20c gold & multi .30 .25
**409** A67 30c gold & multi .30 .25
**410** A67 50c gold & multi .30 .25
**411** A67 3fr gold & multi .30 .25
**412** A67 6fr gold & multi [illegible] [illegible]
**413** A67 90fr gold & multi 2.20 1.75
*Nos. 408-413 (6)* 3.85 3.00

Ludwig van Beethoven (1770-1827), composer.

Equestrian — A68

Olympic Sports: 30c, Runner at start. 50c, Basketball. 1fr, High jump. 8fr, Boxing. 10fr, Pole vault. 20fr, Wrestling. 60fr, Gymnastics (rings).

**1971, Oct. 25 Photo. *Perf. 13***

**414** A68 20c gold & black .30 .25
**415** A68 30c gold & dp rose lil .30 .25
**416** A68 50c gold & vio bl .30 .25
**417** A68 1fr gold & dp grn .30 .25
**418** A68 8fr gold & henna brn .30 .25
**419** A68 10fr gold & purple .30 .25
**420** A68 20fr gold & dp brn .40 .25
**421** A68 60fr gold & Prus bl 1.25 .60
*Nos. 414-421 (8)* 3.45 2.35

20th Summer Olympic Games, Munich, Aug. 26-Sept. 10, 1972.

**Christmas Type of 1968**

Souvenir Sheet

100fr, Nativity, by Anthony van Dyck, vert.

**1971, Dec. 20 Engr. *Perf. 11½***

**422** A48 100fr indigo 3.75 3.75

Adam by Dürer — A69

Paintings by Albrecht Dürer (1471-1528), German painter and engraver: 30c, Eve. 50c, Hieronymus Holzschuher, Portrait. 1fr, Lamentation of Christ. 3fr, Madonna with the Pear. 5fr, St. Eustace. 20fr, Sts. Paul and Mark. 70fr, Self-portrait, 1500.

**1971, Dec. 31 Photo. *Perf. 13***

**423** A69 20c gold & multi .30 .25
**424** A69 30c gold & multi .30 .25
**425** A69 50c gold & multi .30 .25
**426** A69 1fr gold & multi .30 .25
**427** A69 3fr gold & multi .30 .25
**428** A69 5fr gold & multi .35 .25
**429** A69 20fr gold & multi .70 .25
**430** A69 70fr gold & multi 1.50 1.35
*Nos. 423-430 (8)* 4.05 3.10

A 600fr stamp on gold foil honoring Apollo 15 was issued Jan. 15, 1972. Value $100.

Guardsmen Exercising — A70

National Guard Emblem and: 6fr, Loading supplies. 15fr, Helicopter ambulance. 25fr, Health Service for civilians. 50fr, Guardsman and map of Rwanda, vert.

**1972, Feb. 7 *Perf. 13½x14, 14x13½***

**431** A70 4fr dp org & multi .30 .25
**432** A70 6fr yellow & multi .30 .25
**433** A70 15fr lt blue & multi .30 .25
**434** A70 25fr red & multi .80 .45
**435** A70 50fr multicolored 1.75 1.20
*Nos. 431-435 (5)* 3.45 2.40

"The National Guard serving the nation." For overprints see Nos. 559-563.

Ice Hockey, Sapporo Olympics Emblem A71

**1972, Feb. 12 *Perf. 13x13½***

**436** A71 20c shown .30 .25
**437** A71 30c Speed skating .30 .25
**438** A71 50c Ski jump .30 .25
**439** A71 1fr Men's figure skating .30 .25
**440** A71 6fr Cross-country skiing .30 .25
**441** A71 12fr Slalom .30 .25
**442** A71 20fr Bobsledding .40 .25
**443** A71 60fr Downhill skiing 1.30 1.25
*Nos. 436-443 (8)* 3.50 3.00

11th Winter Olympic Games, Sapporo, Japan, Feb. 3-13.

Antelopes and Cercopithecus — A72

**1972, Mar. 20 Photo. *Perf. 13***

**444** A72 20c shown .30 .25
**445** A72 30c Buffaloes .30 .25
**446** A72 50c Zebras .30 .25
**447** A72 1fr Rhinoceroses .35 .30
**448** A72 2fr Wart hogs .45 .35
**449** A72 6fr Hippopotami .60 .45
**450** A72 18fr Hyenas 1.10 .60
**451** A72 32fr Guinea fowl 2.00 .85
**452** A72 60fr Antelopes 2.75 1.40
**453** A72 80fr Lions 4.00 2.25
*Nos. 444-453 (10)* 12.15 6.95

Akagera National Park.

A73

Family raising flag of Rwanda.

**1972, Apr. 4 *Perf. 13x12½***

**454** A73 6fr dk red & multi .30 .25
**455** A73 18fr green & multi .45 .25
**456** A73 60fr brown & multi 1.40 1.10
*Nos. 454-456 (3)* 2.15 1.60

10th anniversary of the Referendum establishing Republic of Rwanda.

A74

Birds: 20c, Common Waxbills and Hibiscus. 30c, Collared sunbird. 50c, Variable sunbird. 1fr, Greater double-collared sunbird. 4fr, Ruwenzori puff-back flycatcher. 6fr, Red-billed fire finch. 10fr, Scarlet-chested sunbird. 18fr, Red-headed quelea. 60fr, Black-headed gonolek. 100fr, African golden oriole.

**1972, May 17 Photo. *Perf. 13***

**457** A74 20c dl grn & multi .30 .25
**458** A74 30c buff & multi .30 .25
**459** A74 50c yellow & multi .30 .25
**460** A74 1fr lt blue & multi .30 .25
**461** A74 4fr dl rose & multi .30 .25
**462** A74 6fr lilac rose & multi .30 .25
**463** A74 10fr pink & multi .35 .25
**464** A74 18fr gray & multi .85 .30
**465** A74 60fr multicolored 2.75 1.25
**466** A74 100fr violet & multi 4.00 2.25
*Nos. 457-466 (10)* 9.75 5.55

Belgica '72 Emblem, King Baudouin, Queen Fabiola, Pres. and Mrs. Kayibanda — A75

**1972, June 24 Photo. *Perf. 13***

**Size: 37x34mm**

**467** A75 18fr Rwanda landscape .80 .35
**468** A75 22fr Old houses, Bruges 1.00 .35

**Size: 50x34mm**

**469** A75 40fr shown 2.00 .50
*a.* Strip of 3, #467-469 5.25 5.25

Belgica '72 Intl. Phil. Exhib., Brussels, June 24-July 9.

Pres. Kayibanda Addressing Meeting — A76

Pres. Grégoire Kayibanda: 30c, promoting officers of National Guard. 50c, with wife and children. 6fr, casting vote. 10fr, with wife and dignitaries at Feast of Justice. 15fr, with Cabinet and members of Assembly. 18fr, taking oath of office. 50fr, Portrait, vert.

**1972, July 4**

**470** A76 20c gold & slate grn .30 .25
**471** A76 30c gold & dk pur .30 .25
**472** A76 50c gold & choc .30 .25
**473** A76 6fr gold & Prus bl .30 .25
**474** A76 10fr gold & dk pur .30 .25
**475** A76 15fr gold & dk bl .35 .25
**476** A76 18fr gold & brn .45 .40
**477** A76 50fr gold & Prus bl 1.10 .85
*Nos. 470-477 (8)* 3.40 2.75

10th anniversary of independence.

Equestrian, Olympic Emblems A77

Stadium, TV Tower and: 30c, Hockey. 50c, Soccer. 1fr, Broad jump. 6fr, Bicycling. 18fr, Yachting. 30fr, Hurdles. 44fr, Gymnastics, women's.

**1972, Aug. 16 Photo. *Perf. 14***

**478** A77 20c dk brn & gold .30 .25
**479** A77 30c vio bl & gold .30 .25
**480** A77 50c dk green & gold .30 .25
**481** A77 1fr dp claret & gold .30 .25
**482** A77 6fr black & gold .30 .25
**483** A77 10fr brown & gold [illegible] [illegible]
**484** A77 30fr dk vio & gold .75 .55
**485** A77 44fr Prus bl & gold 1.25 .80
*Nos. 478-485 (8)* 3.90 2.85

20th Olympic Games, Munich, 8/26-9/11.

Relay (Sport) and UN Emblem A78

**1972, Oct. 23 Photo. *Perf. 13***

**486** A78 20c shown .30 .25
**487** A78 30c Musicians .30 .25
**488** A78 50c Dancers .30 .25
**489** A78 1fr Operating room .30 .25
**490** A78 6fr Weaver & painter .30 .25
**491** A78 18fr Classroom .35 .30
**492** A78 24fr Laboratory .55 .45
**493** A78 50fr Hands of 4 races reaching for equality 1.10 .85
*Nos. 486-493 (8)* 3.50 2.85

Fight against racism.

**Christmas Type of 1968**

Souvenir Sheet

Design: 100fr, Adoration of the Shepherds, by Jacob Jordaens, vert.

**1972, Dec. 11 *Perf. 11½***

**494** A48 100fr red brown 3.50 3.50

Phymateus Brunneri — A79

Various insects. 30c, 1fr, 6fr, 22fr, 100fr, vert.

**1973, Jan. 31 Photo. Perf. 13**

**495** A79 20c multi .30 .25
**496** A79 30c multi .30 .25
**497** A79 50c multi .30 .25
**498** A79 1fr multi .30 .25
**499** A79 2fr multi .30 .25
**500** A79 6fr multi .30 .25
**501** A79 18fr multi .65 .40
**502** A79 22fr multi 1.00 .70
**503** A79 70fr multi 2.85 2.25
**504** A79 100fr multi 4.00 3.50
*Nos. 495-504 (10)* 10.30 8.35

**Souvenir Sheet**

***Perf. 14***

**505** A79 80fr like 20c 7.50 7.50

No. 505 contains one stamp 43½x33½mm.

Emile Zola, by Edouard Manet — A80

Paintings Connected with Reading, and Book Year Emblem: 30c, Rembrandt's Mother. 50c, St. Jerome Removing Thorn from Lion's Paw, by Colantonio. 1fr, Apostles Peter and Paul, by El Greco. 2fr, Virgin and Child with Book, by Roger van der Weyden. 6fr, St. Jerome in his Cell, by Antonella de Messina. 40fr, St. Barbara, by Master of Flemalle. No. 513, Don Quixote, by Oscar Vonnevalle. No. 514, Pres. Kayibanda reading book.

**1973, Mar. 12 Photo. Perf. 13**

**506** A80 20c gold & multi .30 .25
**507** A80 30c gold & multi .30 .25
**508** A80 50c gold & multi .30 .25
**509** A80 1fr gold & multi .30 .25
**510** A80 2fr gold & multi .30 .25
**511** A80 6fr gold & multi .30 .25
**512** A80 40fr gold & multi .85 .80
**513** A80 100fr gold & multi 2.10 2.00
*Nos. 506-513 (8)* 4.75 4.30

**Souvenir Sheet**

***Perf. 14***

**514** A80 100fr gold, bl & ind 4.00 4.00

International Book Year.

Longombe A81

Musical instruments of Central & West Africa.

**1973, Apr. 9 Photo. Perf. 13½**

**515** A81 20c shown .30 .25
**516** A81 30c Horn .30 .25
**517** A81 50c Xylophone .30 .25
**518** A81 1fr Harp .30 .25
**519** A81 4fr Alur horns .30 .25
**520** A81 6fr Drum, bells and horn .30 .25
**521** A81 18fr Large drums (Ngoma) .40 .25
**522** A81 90fr Toba 2.40 1.60
*Nos. 515-522 (8)* 4.60 3.35

Rubens and Isabella Brandt, by Rubens — A82

Paintings from Old Pinakothek, Munich (IBRA Emblem and): 30c, Young Man, by Cranach. 50c, Woman Peeling Turnips, by Chardin. 1fr, The Abduction of Leucippa's Daughters, by Rubens. 2fr, Virgin and Child, by Filippo Lippi. 6fr, Boys Eating Fruit, by Murillo. 40fr, The Lovesick Woman, by Jan Steen. No. 530, Jesus Stripped of His Garments, by El Greco. No. 531, Oswolt Krel, by Dürer.

**1973, May 11**

**523** A82 20c gold & multi .30 .25
**524** A82 30c gold & multi .30 .25
**525** A82 50c gold & multi .30 .25
**526** A82 1fr gold & multi .30 .25
**527** A82 2fr gold & multi .30 .25
**528** A82 6fr gold & multi .30 .25
**529** A82 40fr gold & multi .85 .75
**530** A82 100fr gold & multi 2.35 2.00
*Nos. 523-530 (8)* 5.00 4.25

**Souvenir Sheet**

**531** A82 100fr gold & multi 3.75 3.75

IBRA München 1973 Intl. Phil. Exhib., Munich, May 11-20. No. 531 contains one 40x56mm stamp.

Map of Africa and Peace Doves A83

Design: 94fr, Map of Africa and hands.

**1973, July 23 Photo. Perf. 13½**

**532** A83 6fr gold & multi .30 .25
**533** A83 94fr gold & multi 2.50 2.50

Org. for African Unity, 10th anniv.
For overprints see Nos. 895-896.

**Nos. 298-303 Overprinted in Blue, Black, Green or Brown: "SECHERESSE / SOLIDARITE AFRICAINE"**

**1973, Aug. 23 Photo. Perf. 13**

**534** A53 20c multi (Bl) .30 .25
**535** A53 40c multi (Bk) .30 .25
**536** A53 60c multi (Bl) .30 .25
**537** A53 80c multi (G) .30 .25
**538** A53 3fr multi (G) .35 .25
**539** A53 75fr multi (Br) 2.30 1.00
*Nos. 534-539,B1 (7)* 8.35 6.75

African solidarity in drought emergency.

**African Postal Union Issue**

Common Design Type

**1973, Sept. 12 Engr. Perf. 13**

**540** CD137 100fr dp brn, bl & brn 3.00 2.00

Six-lined Distichodus — A84

African Fish: 30c, Little triggerfish. 50c, Spotted upside-down catfish. 1fr, Nile mouthbreeder. 2fr, African lungfish. 6fr, Pareutropius mandevillei. 40fr, Congo characin. 100fr, Like 20c. 150fr, Julidochromis ornatus.

**1973, Sept. 3 Photo. Perf. 13**

**541** A84 20c gold & multi .30 .25
**542** A84 30c gold & multi .30 .25
**543** A84 50c gold & multi .30 .25
**544** A84 1fr gold & multi .30 .25
**545** A84 2fr gold & multi .30 .25
**546** A84 6fr gold & multi .30 .25
**547** A84 40fr gold & multi 1.50 .75
**548** A84 150fr gold & multi 5.25 3.25
*Nos. 541-548 (8)* 8.55 5.50

**Souvenir Sheet**

**549** A84 100fr gold & multi 5.25 5.25

No. 549 contains one stamp 48x29mm.

Nos. 398-405 Overprinted in Black, Silver, Green or Blue

**1973, Sept. 15 Litho.**

**550** A50 20c multi (Bk) .30 .25
**551** A50 30c multi (S) .30 .25
**552** A50 50c multi (Bk) .30 .25
**553** A50 1fr multi (G) .30 .25
**554** A50 5fr multi (S) .30 .25
**555** A50 18fr multi (Bk) .50 .25
**556** A50 25fr multi (Bk) 1.05 .50
**557** A50 50fr multi (Bl) 2.10 1.00
*Nos. 550-557 (8)* 5.15 3.00

Africa Weeks, Brussels, Sept. 15-30, 1973. On the 30c, 1fr and 25fr the text of the overprint is horizontal.

**Nos. 431-435 Overprinted in Gold**

***Perf. 13½x14, 14x13½***

**1973, Oct. 31 Photo.**

**559** A70 4fr dp org & multi .30 .25
**560** A70 6fr yellow & multi .30 .25
**561** A70 15fr lt blue & multi .50 .30
**562** A70 25fr red & multi .90 .40
**563** A70 50fr multicolored 1.75 .95
*Nos. 559-563 (5)* 3.75 2.15

25th anniv. of the Universal Declaration of Human Rights.

**Christmas Type of 1968**

Souvenir Sheet

Adoration of the Shepherds, by Guido Reni.

**1973, Dec. 15 Engr. Perf. 11½**

**564** A48 100fr brt violet 3.50 3.50

Copernicus and Astrolabe A85

Designs: 30c, 18fr, 100fr, Portrait. 50c, 80fr, Copernicus and heliocentric system. 1fr, like 20c.

**1973, Dec. 26 Photo. Perf. 13**

**565** A85 20c silver & multi .30 .25
**566** A85 30c silver & multi .30 .25
**567** A85 50c silver & multi .30 .25
**568** A85 1fr gold & multi .30 .25
**569** A85 18fr gold & multi .80 .50
**570** A85 80fr gold & multi 2.50 2.25
*Nos. 565-570 (6)* 4.50 3.75

**Souvenir Sheet**

**571** A85 100fr gold & multi 5.50 5.50

Nicolaus Copernicus (1473-1543).

Pres. Juvénal Habyarimana — A86

**1974, Apr. 8 Photo. Perf. 11½**

**Black Inscriptions**

**572** A86 1fr bister & sepia .30 .25
**573** A86 2fr ultra & sepia .30 .25
**574** A86 5fr rose red & sep .30 .25
**575** A86 6fr grnsh bl & sep .30 .25
**576** A86 26fr lilac & sepia .55 .30
**577** A86 60fr ol grn & sepia 1.50 1.25
*Nos. 572-577 (6)* 3.25 2.55

Souvenir Sheet

Christ Between the Thieves (Detail), by Rubens — A87

**1974, Apr. 12 Engr. Perf. 11½**

**578** A87 100fr sepia 13.00 13.00

Easter.

Yugoslavia-Zaire Soccer Game — A88

Games' emblem and soccer games.

**1974, July 6 Photo. Perf. 13½**

**579** A88 20c shown .30 .25
**580** A88 40c Netherlands-Sweden .30 .25
**581** A88 60c Germany (Fed.)-Australia .30 .25
**582** A88 80c Haiti-Argentina .30 .25
**583** A88 2fr Brazil-Scotland .30 .25
**584** A88 6fr Bulgaria-Uruguay .30 .25
**585** A88 40fr Italy-Poland 1.25 .60
**586** A88 50fr Chile-Germany (DDR) 1.75 1.25
*Nos. 579-586 (8)* 4.80 3.35

World Cup Soccer Championship, Munich, June 13-July 7.

Marconi's Laboratory Yacht "Elletra" — A89

Designs: 30c, Marconi and steamer "Carlo Alberto." 50c, Marconi's wireless apparatus and telecommunications satellites. 4fr, Marconi and globes connected by communications waves. 35fr, Marconi's radio, and radar. 60fr, Marconi and transmitter at Poldhu, Cornwall. 50fr, like 20c.

**1974, Aug. 19 Photo. Perf. 13½**

**587** A89 20c violet, blk & grn .30 .25
**588** A89 30c green, blk & vio .30 .25
**589** A89 50c yellow, blk & lil .30 .25
**590** A89 4fr salmon, blk & bl .30 .25
**591** A89 35fr lilac, blk & yel .80 .50
**592** A89 60fr blue, blk & brnz 1.50 1.00
*Nos. 587-592 (6)* 3.50 2.50

**Souvenir Sheet**

**593** A89 50fr gold, blk & lt bl 2.50 2.50

Guglielmo Marconi (1874-1937), Italian electrical engineer and inventor.

The Flute Player, by J. Leyster — A90

Paintings: 20c, Diane de Poitiers, Fontainebleau School. 50c, Virgin and Child, by David. 1fr, Triumph of Venus, by Boucher. 10fr, Seated Harlequin, by Picasso. 18fr, Virgin and Child, 15th century. 20fr, Beheading of St. John, by Hans Fries. 50fr, Daughter of Andersdotter, by J. F. Höckert.

**1974, Sept. 23 Photo.** ***Perf. 14x13***

| | | | | |
|---|---|---|---|---|
| **594** | A90 | 20c gold & multi | .30 | .25 |
| **595** | A90 | 30c gold & multi | .30 | .25 |
| **596** | A90 | 50c gold & multi | .30 | .25 |
| **597** | A90 | 1fr gold & multi | .30 | .25 |
| **598** | A90 | 10fr gold & multi | .30 | .25 |
| **599** | A90 | 18fr gold & multi | .50 | .30 |
| **600** | A90 | 20fr gold & multi | .50 | .40 |
| **601** | A90 | 50fr gold & multi | 1.50 | 1.25 |
| | | *Nos. 594-601 (8)* | 4.00 | 3.20 |

INTERNABA 74 Intl. Phil. Exhib., Basel, June 7-10, and Stockholmia 74, Intl. Phil. Exhib., Stockholm, Sept. 21-29.

Six multicolored souvenir sheets exist containing two 15fr stamps each in various combinations of designs of Nos. 594-601. Value, set $9.

One souvenir sheet of four 25fr stamps exists with designs of Nos. 595, 597, 599 and 601. Value, $5.

Messenger Monk — A91

UPU Emblem and Messengers: 30c, Inca. 50c, Morocco. 1fr, India. 18fr, Polynesia. 80fr, Rwanda.

**1974, Oct. 9** ***Perf. 14***

| | | | | |
|---|---|---|---|---|
| **602** | A91 | 20c gold & multi | .30 | .25 |
| **603** | A91 | 30c gold & multi | .30 | .25 |
| **604** | A91 | 50c gold & multi | .30 | .25 |
| **605** | A91 | 1fr gold & multi | .30 | .25 |
| **606** | A91 | 18fr gold & multi | .60 | .40 |
| **607** | A91 | 80fr gold & multi | 2.25 | 1.75 |
| | | *Nos. 602-607 (6)* | 4.05 | 3.15 |

Centenary of Universal Postal Union.

Nos. 306-308 Overprinted

**1974, Dec. 16 Photo.** ***Perf. 11½***

| | | | | |
|---|---|---|---|---|
| **608** | A54 | 6fr brt pink & multi | 4.25 | 3.75 |
| **609** | A54 | 18fr ultra & multi | 4.25 | 3.75 |
| **610** | A54 | 40fr brn & multi | 4.25 | 3.75 |
| | | *Nos. 608-610 (3)* | 12.75 | 11.25 |

15th anniversary of independence.

**Christmas Type of 1968**

Souvenir Sheet

Adoration of the Kings, by Joos van Cleve.

**1974, Dec. 23 Engr.** ***Perf. 11½***

| | | | | |
|---|---|---|---|---|
| **611** | A48 | 100fr slate green | 9.00 | 9.00 |

**Nos. 295-296 Overprinted: "1974 / 10e Anniversaire"**

**1974, Dec. 30 Photo.** ***Perf. 13***

| | | | | |
|---|---|---|---|---|
| **612** | A51 | 30fr sil & multi | 1.25 | .85 |
| **613** | A51 | 70fr gold & multi | 2.25 | 1.75 |

African Development Bank, 10th anniversary.

Uganda Kob — A92

Antelopes: 30c, Bongos, horiz. 50c, Rwanda antelopes. 1fr, Young sitatungas, horiz. 4fr, Greater kudus. 10fr, Impalas, horiz. 34fr, Waterbuck. 40fr, Impalas. 60fr, Greater kudu. 100fr, Derby's elands, horiz.

**1975, Mar. 17 Photo.** ***Perf. 13***

| | | | | |
|---|---|---|---|---|
| **614** | A92 | 20c multi | .30 | .25 |
| **615** | A92 | 30c multi | .30 | .25 |
| **616** | A92 | 50c multi | .35 | .25 |
| **617** | A92 | 1fr multi | .60 | .25 |
| **618** | A92 | 4fr multi | .70 | .30 |
| **619** | A92 | 10fr multi | 1.40 | .60 |
| **620** | A92 | 34fr multi | 3.00 | 1.10 |
| **621** | A92 | 100fr multi | 6.00 | 2.25 |
| | | *Nos. 614-621 (8)* | 12.65 | 5.25 |

**Miniature Sheets**

| | | | | |
|---|---|---|---|---|
| **622** | A92 | 40fr multi | 26.00 | 26.00 |
| **623** | A92 | 60fr multi | 26.00 | 26.00 |

Miniature Sheets

Pietá, by Cranach the Elder — A93

20fr, The Burial of Jesus, by Raphael. 50fr, By van der Weyden. 100fr, By Bollini.

**1975, Apr. 1 Photo.** ***Perf. 13x14***

| | | | | |
|---|---|---|---|---|
| **624** | A93 | 20fr multicolored | 2.50 | 2.50 |
| **625** | A93 | 30fr shown | 2.50 | 2.50 |
| **626** | A93 | 50fr multicolored | 2.50 | 2.50 |
| **627** | A93 | 100fr multicolored | 2.50 | 2.50 |
| | | *Nos. 624-627 (4)* | 10.00 | 10.00 |

Easter. Size of stamps: 40x52mm. See Nos. 681-684.

Souvenir Sheets

Prince Balthazar Charles, by Velazquez — A94

Paintings: 30fr, Infanta Margaret of Austria, by Velazquez. 50fr, The Divine Shepherd, by Murillo. 100fr, Francisco Goya, by V. Lopez y Portana.

**1975, Apr. 4 Photo.** ***Perf. 13***

| | | | | |
|---|---|---|---|---|
| **628** | A94 | 20fr multi | 3.50 | 3.50 |
| **629** | A94 | 30fr multi | 3.50 | 3.50 |
| **630** | A94 | 50fr multi | 3.50 | 3.50 |
| **631** | A94 | 100fr multi | 3.50 | 3.50 |
| | | *Nos. 628-631 (4)* | 14.00 | 14.00 |

Espana 75 Intl. Phil. Exhib., Madrid, Apr. 4-13. Size of stamps: 38x48mm. See Nos. 642-643. For overprints see Nos. 844-847.

Pyrethrum (Insect Powder) — A95

**1975, Apr. 14** ***Perf. 13***

| | | | | |
|---|---|---|---|---|
| **632** | A95 | 20c shown | .30 | .25 |
| **633** | A95 | 30c Tea | .30 | .25 |
| **634** | A95 | 50c Coffee (beans and pan) | .30 | .25 |
| **635** | A95 | 4fr Bananas | .30 | .25 |
| **636** | A95 | 10fr Corn | .30 | .25 |
| **637** | A95 | 12fr Sorghum | .30 | .25 |
| **638** | A95 | 26fr Rice | .75 | .35 |
| **639** | A95 | 47fr Coffee (workers and beans) | 1.50 | .75 |
| | | *Nos. 632-639 (8)* | 4.05 | 2.60 |

**Souvenir Sheets**

***Perf. 13½***

| | | | | |
|---|---|---|---|---|
| **640** | A95 | 25fr like 50c | 1.40 | 1.40 |
| **641** | A95 | 75fr like 47fr | 2.75 | 2.75 |

Year of Agriculture and 10th anniversary of Office for Industrialized Cultivation.

**Painting Type of 1975**

Souvenir Sheets

75fr, Louis XIV, by Hyacinthe Rigaud. 125fr, Cavalry Officer, by Jean Gericault.

**1975, June 6 Photo.** ***Perf. 13***

| | | | | |
|---|---|---|---|---|
| **642** | A94 | 75fr multi | 4.75 | 4.75 |
| **643** | A94 | 125fr multi | 6.25 | 6.25 |

ARPHILA 75, Intl. Philatelic Exhibition, Paris, June 6-16. Size of stamps: 38x48mm.

**Nos. 390-397 Overprinted: "1975 / ANNEE / SAINTE"**

**1975, June 23 Photo.** ***Perf. 13***

| | | | | |
|---|---|---|---|---|
| **644** | A66 | 10c gold & dk brn | .30 | .25 |
| **645** | A66 | 20c gold & dk grn | .30 | .25 |
| **646** | A66 | 30c gold & dp claret | .30 | .25 |
| **647** | A66 | 40c gold & indigo | .30 | .25 |
| **648** | A66 | 1fr gold & dk pur | .30 | .25 |
| **649** | A66 | 18fr gold & purple | .45 | .40 |
| **650** | A66 | 20fr gold & org brn | .75 | .60 |
| **651** | A66 | 60fr gold & blk brn | 2.25 | 1.75 |
| | | *Nos. 644-651 (8)* | 4.95 | 4.00 |

Holy Year 1975.

White Pelicans — A96

African birds — 30c, Malachite kingfisher. 50c, Goliath herons. 1fr, Saddle-billed storks. 4fr, African jacana. 10fr, African anhingas. 34fr, Sacred ibis. 80fr, Hartlaub ducks.

40fr, Flamingoes. 60fr, Crowned cranes.

**1975, June 20**

| | | | | |
|---|---|---|---|---|
| **652** | A96 | 20c shown | .30 | .25 |
| **653** | A96 | 30c multicolored | .30 | .25 |
| **654** | A96 | 50c multicolored | .30 | .25 |
| **655** | A96 | 1fr multicolored | .30 | .25 |
| **656** | A96 | 4fr multicolored | .30 | .25 |
| **657** | A96 | 10fr multicolored | .55 | .25 |
| **658** | A96 | 34fr multicolored | 1.60 | 1.00 |
| **659** | A96 | 80fr multicolored | 4.00 | 2.00 |
| | | *Nos. 652-659 (8)* | 7.65 | 4.50 |

**Miniature Sheets**

| | | | | |
|---|---|---|---|---|
| **660** | A96 | 40fr multicolored | 12.50 | 12.50 |
| **661** | A96 | 60fr multicolored | 16.00 | 16.00 |

Globe Representing Races and WPY Emblem — A97

World Population Year: 26fr, Population graph and emblem. 34fr, Globe with open door and emblem.

**1975, Sept. 1 Photo.** ***Perf. 13½x13***

| | | | | |
|---|---|---|---|---|
| **662** | A97 | 20fr dp bl & multi | .60 | .40 |
| **663** | A97 | 26fr dl red brn & multi | .70 | .55 |
| **664** | A97 | 34fr yel & multi | 1.00 | .80 |
| | | *Nos. 662-664 (3)* | 2.30 | 1.75 |

The Bath, by Mary Cassatt and IWY Emblem — A98

IWY Emblem and: 30c, Mother and Infant Son, by Julius Gari Melchers. 50c, Woman with Milk Jug, by Jan Vermeer. 1fr, Water Carrier, by Goya. 8fr, Rwanda woman cotton picker. 12fr, Scientist with microscope. 18fr, Mother and child. 25fr, Empress Josephine by Pierre-Paul Prud'hon. 40fr, Madame Vigee-Lebrun and Daughter, self-portrait. 60fr, Woman carrying child on back and water jug on head.

**1975, Sept. 15** ***Perf. 13***

| | | | | |
|---|---|---|---|---|
| **665** | A98 | 20c gold & multi | .30 | .25 |
| **666** | A98 | 30c gold & multi | .30 | .25 |
| **667** | A98 | 50c gold & multi | .30 | .25 |
| **668** | A98 | 1fr gold & multi | .30 | .25 |
| **669** | A98 | 8fr gold & multi | .30 | .25 |
| **670** | A98 | 12fr gold & multi | .30 | .25 |
| **671** | A98 | 18fr gold & multi | .65 | .30 |
| **672** | A98 | 60fr gold & multi | 2.40 | 1.25 |
| | | *Nos. 665-672 (8)* | 4.85 | 3.05 |

**Souvenir Sheets**

***Perf. 13½***

| | | | | |
|---|---|---|---|---|
| **673** | A98 | 25fr multi | *45.00* | *45.00* |
| **674** | A98 | 40fr multi | *45.00* | *45.00* |

International Women's Year. Nos. 673-674 each contain one stamp 37x49mm.

Owl, Quill and Book — A99

30c, Hygiene emblem. 1.50fr, Kneeling woman holding scales of Justice. 18fr, Chemist in laboratory. 26fr, Symbol of commerce & chart. 34fr, University Building.

**1975, Sept. 29** ***Perf. 13***

| | | | | |
|---|---|---|---|---|
| **675** | A99 | 20c pur & multi | .30 | .25 |
| **676** | A99 | 30c ultra & multi | .30 | .25 |
| **677** | A99 | 1.50fr lilac & multi | .30 | .25 |
| **678** | A99 | 18fr blue & multi | .35 | .25 |
| **679** | A99 | 26fr olive & multi | .55 | .40 |
| **680** | A99 | 34fr blue & multi | 1.00 | .70 |
| | | *Nos. 675-680 (6)* | 2.80 | 2.10 |

National Univ. of Rwanda, 10th anniv.

**Painting Type of 1975**

Souvenir Sheets

Paintings by Jan Vermeer (1632-1675): 20fr, Man and Woman Drinking Wine. 30fr, Woman in Blue Reading Letter. 50fr, Painter in his Studio. 100fr, Young Woman Playing Virginal.

**1975, Oct. 13 Photo. *Perf. 13x14***

| | | | | |
|---|---|---|---|---|
| **681** | A93 | 20fr multi | 2.50 | 2.50 |
| **682** | A93 | 30fr multi | 2.50 | 2.50 |
| **683** | A93 | 50fr multi | 2.50 | 2.50 |
| **684** | A93 | 100fr multi | 2.50 | 2.50 |
| | | *Nos. 681-684 (4)* | 10.00 | 10.00 |

Size of stamps: 40x52mm.

Waterhole and Impatiens Stuhlmannii — A100

Designs: 30c, Antelopes, zebras, candelabra cactus. 50c, Brush fire, and tapinanthus prunifolius. 5fr, Bulera Lake and Egyptian white lotus. 8fr, Erosion prevention and protea madiensis. 10fr, Marsh and melanthera brownei. 26fr, Landscape, lobelias and senecons. 100fr, Sabyinyo Volcano and polystachya kermesina.

**1975, Oct. 25 *Perf. 13***

| | | | | |
|---|---|---|---|---|
| **685** | A100 | 20c blk & multi | .30 | .25 |
| **686** | A100 | 30c blk & multi | .30 | .25 |
| **687** | A100 | 50c blk & multi | .30 | .25 |
| **688** | A100 | 5fr blk & multi | .30 | .25 |
| **689** | A100 | 8fr blk & multi | .30 | .25 |
| **690** | A100 | 10fr blk & multi | .30 | .25 |
| **691** | A100 | 26fr blk & multi | 1.00 | .75 |
| **692** | A100 | 100fr blk & multi | 3.00 | 2.25 |
| | | *Nos. 685-692 (8)* | 5.80 | 4.50 |

Nature protection.
For overprints see Nos. 801-808.

Nos. 343-348 Overprinted

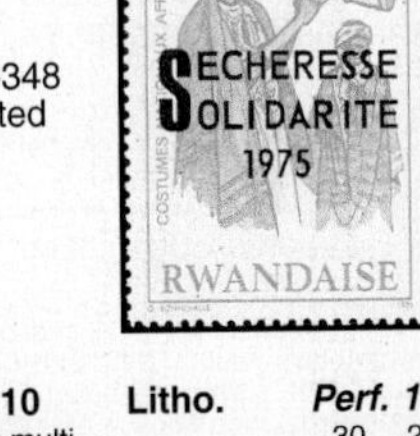


**1975, Nov. 10 Litho. *Perf. 13***

| | | | | |
|---|---|---|---|---|
| **693** | A60 | 20c multi | .30 | .25 |
| **694** | A60 | 30c multi | .30 | .25 |
| **695** | A60 | 50c multi | .30 | .25 |
| **696** | A60 | 1fr multi | .30 | .25 |
| **697** | A60 | 3fr multi | .30 | .25 |
| **698** | A60 | 5fr multi | .30 | .25 |
| | | *Nos. 693-698,B2-B3 (8)* | 6.10 | 5.35 |

African solidarity in drought emergency.

Fork-lift Truck on Airfield A101

Designs: 30c, Coffee packing plant. 50c, Engineering plant. 10fr, Farmer with hoe, vert. 35fr, Coffee pickers, vert. 54fr, Mechanized harvester.

**Wmk. JEZ Multiple (368)**

**1975, Dec. 1 Photo. *Perf. 14x13½***

| | | | | |
|---|---|---|---|---|
| **699** | A101 | 20c gold & multi | .30 | .25 |
| **700** | A101 | 30c gold & multi | .30 | .25 |
| **701** | A101 | 50c gold & multi | .30 | .25 |
| **702** | A101 | 10fr gold & multi | .30 | .25 |
| **703** | A101 | 35fr gold & multi | .65 | .45 |
| **704** | A101 | 54fr gold & multi | 1.30 | .85 |
| | | *Nos. 699-704 (6)* | 3.15 | 2.30 |

Basket Carrier and Themabelga Emblem — A102

Themabelga Emblem and: 30c, Warrior with shield and spear. 50c, Woman with beads. 1fr, Indian woman. 5fr, Male dancer with painted body. 7fr, Woman carrying child on back. 35fr, Male dancer with spear. 51fr, Female dancers.

**1975, Dec. 8 Unwmk. *Perf. 13½***

| | | | | |
|---|---|---|---|---|
| **705** | A102 | 20c blk & multi | .30 | .25 |
| **706** | A102 | 30c blk & multi | .30 | .25 |
| **707** | A102 | 50c blk & multi | .30 | .25 |
| **708** | A102 | 1fr blk & multi | .30 | .25 |
| **709** | A102 | 5fr blk & multi | .30 | .25 |
| **710** | A102 | 7fr blk & multi | .35 | .25 |
| **711** | A102 | 35fr blk & multi | .90 | .45 |
| **712** | A102 | 51fr blk & multi | 1.75 | 1.10 |
| | | *Nos. 705-712 (8)* | 4.50 | 3.05 |

THEMABELGA Intl. Topical Philatelic Exhibition, Brussels, Dec. 13-21.

**Christmas Type of 1968**

Adoration of the Kings, by Peter Paul Rubens.

**1975, Dec. 22 Engr. *Perf. 11½***

| | | | | |
|---|---|---|---|---|
| **713** | A48 | 100fr brt rose lil | 6.00 | 6.00 |

Dr. Schweitzer, Keyboard, Score — A103

Albert Schweitzer and: 30c, 5fr, Lambaréné Hospital. 50c, 10fr, Organ pipes from Strassbourg organ, and score. 1fr, 80fr, Dr. Schweitzer's house, Lambaréné. 3fr, like 20c.

**1976, Jan. 30 Photo. *Perf. 13½***

| | | | | |
|---|---|---|---|---|
| **714** | A103 | 20c maroon & pur | .30 | .25 |
| **715** | A103 | 30c grn & pur | .30 | .25 |
| **716** | A103 | 50c brn org & pur | .30 | .25 |
| **717** | A103 | 1fr red lil & pur | .30 | .25 |
| **718** | A103 | 3fr vio bl & pur | .30 | .25 |
| **719** | A103 | 5fr brn & pur | .30 | .25 |
| **720** | A103 | 10fr bl & pur | .30 | .25 |
| **721** | A103 | 80fr ver & pur | 2.10 | 1.25 |
| | | *Nos. 714-721 (8)* | 4.20 | 3.00 |

World Leprosy Day.
For overprints see Nos. 788-795.

Surrender at Yorktown A104

American Bicentennial (Paintings): 30c, Instruction at Valley Forge. 50c, Presentation of Captured Colors at Yorktown. 1fr, Washington at Fort Lee. 18fr, Washington Boarding British Warship. 26fr, Washington Studying Battle Plans at Night. 34fr, Washington Firing Cannon. 40fr, Washington Crossing the Delaware. 100fr, Sailing Ship "Bonhomme Richard," vert.

**1976, Mar. 22 Photo. *Perf. 13x13½***

| | | | | |
|---|---|---|---|---|
| **722** | A104 | 20c gold & multi | .30 | .25 |
| **723** | A104 | 30c gold & multi | .30 | .25 |
| **724** | A104 | 50c gold & multi | .30 | .25 |
| **725** | A104 | 1fr gold & multi | .30 | .25 |
| **726** | A104 | 18fr gold & multi | .55 | .25 |
| **727** | A104 | 26fr gold & multi | .60 | .30 |
| **728** | A104 | 34fr gold & multi | .90 | .55 |
| **729** | A104 | 40fr gold & multi | 1.25 | 1.00 |
| | | *Nos. 722-729 (8)* | 4.50 | 3.10 |

**Souvenir Sheet**

***Perf. 13½***

| | | | | |
|---|---|---|---|---|
| **730** | A104 | 100fr gold & multi | 5.00 | 5.00 |

See Nos. 754-761.

Sister Yohana, First Nun — A105

30c, Abdon Sabakati, one of first converts. 50c, Father Alphonse Brard, first Superior of Save Mission. 4fr, Abbot Balthazar Gafuku, one of first priests. 10fr, Msgr. Bigirumwami, first bishop. 25fr, Save Church, horiz. 60fr, Kabgayi Cathedral, horiz.

***Perf. 13x13½, 13½x13***

**1976, Apr. 26 Photo.**

| | | | | |
|---|---|---|---|---|
| **731** | A105 | 20c multi | .30 | .25 |
| **732** | A105 | 30c multi | .30 | .25 |
| **733** | A105 | 50c multi | .30 | .25 |
| **734** | A105 | 4fr multi | .30 | .25 |
| **735** | A105 | 10fr multi | .30 | .25 |
| **736** | A105 | 25fr multi | .50 | .30 |
| **737** | A105 | 60fr multi | 1.25 | .45 |
| | | *Nos. 731-737 (7)* | 3.25 | 2.00 |

50th anniv. of the Roman Catholic Church of Rwanda.

Yachting — A106

Montreal Games Emblem and: 30c, Steeplechase. 50c, Long jump. 1fr, Hockey. 10fr, Swimming. 18fr, Soccer. 29fr, Boxing. 51fr, Vaulting.

**1976, May 24 Photo. *Perf. 13x13½***

| | | | | |
|---|---|---|---|---|
| **738** | A106 | 20c gray & dk car | .30 | .25 |
| **739** | A106 | 30c gray & Prus bl | .30 | .25 |
| **740** | A106 | 50c gray & blk | .30 | .25 |
| **741** | A106 | 1fr gray & pur | .30 | .25 |
| **742** | A106 | 10fr gray & ultra | .30 | .25 |
| **743** | A106 | 18fr gray & dk brn | .40 | .25 |
| **744** | A106 | 29fr gray & blk | .70 | .35 |
| **745** | A106 | 51fr gray & slate grn | 1.10 | .75 |
| | | *Nos. 738-745 (8)* | 3.70 | 2.60 |

21st Olympic Games, Montreal, Canada, July 17-Aug. 1.

First Message, Manual Switchboard — A107

Designs: 30c, Telephone, 1876 and interested crowd. 50c, Telephone c. 1900, and woman making a call. 1fr, Business telephone exchange, c. 1905. 4fr, "Candlestick" phone, globe and A. G. Bell. 8fr, Dial phone and Rwandan man making call. 26fr, Telephone, 1976, satellite and radar. 60fr, Push-button telephone, Rwandan international switchboard operator.

**1976, June 21 Photo. *Perf. 14***

| | | | | |
|---|---|---|---|---|
| **746** | A107 | 20c dl red & indigo | .30 | .25 |
| **747** | A107 | 30c grnsh bl & indigo | .30 | .25 |
| **748** | A107 | 50c brn & indigo | .30 | .25 |
| **749** | A107 | 1fr org & indigo | .30 | .25 |
| **750** | A107 | 4fr lilac & indigo | .30 | .25 |
| **751** | A107 | 8fr grn & indigo | .30 | .25 |
| **752** | A107 | 26fr dl red & indigo | .75 | .40 |
| **753** | A107 | 60fr vio & indigo | 1.60 | .85 |
| | | *Nos. 746-753 (8)* | 4.15 | 2.75 |

Centenary of first telephone call by Alexander Graham Bell, Mar. 10, 1876.

**Type of 1976 Overprinted in Silver with Bicentennial Emblem and "Independence Day"**

Designs as before.

**1976, July 4 *Perf. 13x13½***

| | | | | |
|---|---|---|---|---|
| **754** | A104 | 20c silver & multi | .30 | .25 |
| **755** | A104 | 30c silver & multi | .30 | .25 |
| **756** | A104 | 50c silver & multi | .30 | .25 |
| **757** | A104 | 1fr silver & multi | .30 | .25 |
| **758** | A104 | 18fr silver & multi | .60 | .30 |
| **759** | A104 | 26fr silver & multi | .80 | .35 |
| **760** | A104 | 34fr silver & multi | .90 | .60 |
| **761** | A104 | 40fr silver & multi | 1.10 | .80 |
| | | *Nos. 754-761 (8)* | 4.60 | 3.05 |

Independence Day.

Soccer, Montreal Olympic Emblem — A108

30c, Shooting. 50c, Woman canoeing. 1fr, Gymnast. 10fr, Weight lifting. 12fr, Diving. 26fr, Equestrian. 50fr, Shot put.

**1976, Aug. 1 Photo. *Perf. 13½x13***

| | | | | |
|---|---|---|---|---|
| **762** | A108 | 20c multi | .30 | .25 |
| **763** | A108 | 30c multi | .30 | .25 |
| **764** | A108 | 50c multi | .30 | .25 |
| **765** | A108 | 1fr multi | .30 | .25 |
| **766** | A108 | 10fr multi | .30 | .25 |
| **767** | A108 | 12fr multi | .30 | .25 |
| **768** | A108 | 26fr multi | .75 | .50 |
| **769** | A108 | 50fr multi | 1.75 | 1.00 |
| | | *Nos. 762-769 (8)* | 4.30 | 3.00 |

**Souvenir Sheet**

Various phases of hurdles race, horiz.

| | | | | |
|---|---|---|---|---|
| **770** | | Sheet of 4 | 4.50 | 4.50 |
| *a.* | A108 | 20fr Start | .45 | .45 |
| *b.* | A108 | 30fr Sprint | .75 | .75 |
| *c.* | A108 | 40fr Hurdle | .90 | .90 |
| *d.* | A108 | 60fr Finish | 1.45 | 1.45 |

21st Olympic Games, Montreal, Canada, July 17-Aug. 1.

Apollo and Soyuz Take-offs, Project Emblem A109

Designs: 30c, Soyuz in space. 50c, Apollo in space. 1fr, Apollo. 2fr, Spacecraft before docking. 12fr, Spacecraft after docking. 30fr, Astronauts visiting in docked spacecraft. 54fr, Apollo splashdown.

**1976, Oct. 29 Photo. *Perf. 13½x14***

| | | | | |
|---|---|---|---|---|
| **771** | A109 | 20c multi | .30 | .25 |
| **772** | A109 | 30c multi | .30 | .25 |
| **773** | A109 | 50c multi | .30 | .25 |
| **774** | A109 | 1fr multi | .30 | .25 |
| **775** | A109 | 2fr multi | .30 | .25 |
| **776** | A109 | 12fr multi | .50 | .35 |
| **777** | A109 | 30fr multi | 1.70 | .90 |
| **778** | A109 | 54fr multi | 2.40 | 1.50 |
| | | *Nos. 771-778 (8)* | 6.10 | 4.00 |

Apollo Soyuz space test program (Russo-American cooperation), July 1975.
For overprints see Nos. 836-843.

Eulophia Cucullata — A110

Orchids: 30c, Eulophia streptopetala. 50c, Disa Stairsii. 1fr, Aerangis kotschyana. 10fr, Eulophia abyssinica. 12fr, Bonatea steudneri. 26fr, Ansellia gigantea. 50fr, Eulophia angolensis.

**1976, Nov. 22 Photo. *Perf. 14x13½***

| | | | | |
|---|---|---|---|---|
| **779** | A110 | 20c multi | .30 | .25 |
| **780** | A110 | 30c multi | .30 | .25 |
| **781** | A110 | 50c multi | .30 | .25 |
| **782** | A110 | 1fr multi | .30 | .25 |
| **783** | A110 | 10fr multi | .35 | .25 |
| **784** | A110 | 12fr multi | .55 | .30 |

**785** A110 26fr multi 1.40 .60
**786** A110 50fr multi 2.85 1.10
*Nos. 779-786 (8)* 6.35 3.25

### Christmas Type of 1968

Souvenir Sheet

Design: Nativity, by Francois Boucher.

**1976, Dec. 20 Engr.** ***Perf. 11½***
**787** A48 100fr brt ultra 4.75 4.75

### Nos. 714-721 Overprinted: "JOURNEE / MONDIALE / 1977"

**1977, Jan. 29 Photo.** ***Perf. 13½***
**788** A103 20c mar & pur .30 .25
**789** A103 30c grn & pur .30 .25
**790** A103 50c brn org & pur .30 .25
**791** A103 1fr red lil & pur .30 .25
**792** A103 3fr vio bl & pur .30 .25
**793** A103 5fr brn & pur .30 .25
**794** A103 10fr bl & pur .35 .25
**795** A103 80fr ver & pur 2.50 1.50
*Nos. 788-795 (8)* 4.65 3.25

World Leprosy Day.

Hands and Symbols of Learning — A111

Designs: 26fr, Hands and symbols of science. 64fr, Hands and symbols of industry.

**1977, Feb. 7 Litho.** ***Perf. 12½***
**796** A111 10fr multi .30 .25
**797** A111 26fr multi .70 .45
**798** A111 64fr multi 1.40 .85
*Nos. 796-798 (3)* 2.40 1.55

10th Summit Conference of the African and Malagasy Union, Kigali, 1976.

Souvenir Sheets

Descent from the Cross, by Rubens — A112

Easter: 25fr, Crucifixion, by Rubens.

**1977, Apr. 27 Photo.** ***Perf. 13***
**799** A112 25fr multi 5.00 5.00
**800** A112 75fr multi 6.00 6.00

Size of stamp: 40x40mm.

### Nos. 685-692 Overprinted

**1977, May 2**
**801** A100 20c blk & multi .30 .25
**802** A100 30c blk & multi .30 .25
**803** A100 50c blk & multi .30 .25
**804** A100 5fr blk & multi .30 .25
**805** A100 8fr blk & multi .30 .30
**806** A100 10fr blk & multi .35 .40
**807** A100 26fr blk & multi 1.20 1.00
**808** A100 100fr blk & multi 4.25 3.50
*Nos. 801-808 (8)* 7.30 6.20

World Water Conference.

Roman Fire Tower, African Tom-tom A113

ITU Emblem and: 30c, Chappe's optical telegraph and postilion. 50c, Morse telegraph and code. 1fr, Tug Goliath laying cable in English Channel. 4fr, Telephone, radio, television. 18fr, Kingsport (US space exploration ship) and Marots communications satellite. 26fr, Satellite tracking station and O.T.S. satellite. 50fr, Mariner II, Venus probe.

**1977, May 23 Litho.** ***Perf. 12½***
**809** A113 20c multi .30 .25
**810** A113 30c multi .30 .25
**811** A113 50c multi .30 .25
**812** A113 1fr multi .30 .25
**813** A113 4fr multi .30 .25
**814** A113 18fr multi .50 .25
**815** A113 26fr multi .75 .50
**816** A113 50fr multi 1.40 1.00
*Nos. 809-816 (8)* 4.15 3.00

World Telecommunications Day.

Souvenir Sheets

Amsterdam Harbor, by Willem van de Velde, the Younger — A114

40fr, The Night Watch, by Rembrandt.

**1977, May 26 Photo.** ***Perf. 13½***
**817** A114 40fr multi 4.50 4.50
**818** A114 60fr multi 4.50 4.50

AMPHILEX '77 Intl. Philatelic Exhibition, Amsterdam, May 27-June 5. Size of stamp: 38x49mm.

Road to Calvary, by Rubens — A115

Paintings by Peter Paul Rubens (1577-1640): 30c, Judgment of Paris, horiz. 50c, Marie de Medicis. 1fr, Heads of Black Men, horiz. 4fr, 26fr, Details from St. Ildefonso triptych. 8fr, Helene Fourment and her Children, horiz. 60fr, Helene Fourment.

**1977, June 13** ***Perf. 14***
**819** A115 20c gold & multi .30 .25
**820** A115 30c gold & multi .30 .25
**821** A115 50c gold & multi .30 .25
**822** A115 1fr gold & multi .35 .25
**823** A115 4fr gold & multi .40 .25
**824** A115 8fr gold & multi .45 .30
**825** A115 26fr gold & multi 1.00 .75
**826** A115 60fr gold & multi 1.60 1.50
*Nos. 819-826 (8)* 4.70 3.80

Souvenir Sheet

Viking on Mars — A116

**1977, June 27 Photo.** ***Perf. 13***
**827** A116 100fr multi *30.00 30.00*

US Viking landing on Mars, first anniv.

Crested Eagle — A117

Birds of Prey: 30c, Snake eagle. 50c, Fish eagle. 1fr, Monk vulture. 3fr, Red-tailed buzzard. 5fr, Yellow-beaked kite. 20fr, Swallow-tailed kite. 100fr, Bateleur.

**1977, Sept. 12 Litho.** ***Perf. 14***
**828** A117 20c multi .30 .25
**829** A117 30c multi .30 .25
**830** A117 50c multi .30 .25
**831** A117 1fr multi .30 .25
**832** A117 3fr multi .30 .25
**833** A117 5fr multi .50 .25
**834** A117 20fr multi 1.80 .90
**835** A117 100fr multi 5.50 3.25
*Nos. 828-835 (8)* 9.30 5.65

### Nos. 771-778 Overprinted: "in memoriam / WERNHER VON BRAUN / 1912-1977"

**1977, Sept. 19 Photo.** ***Perf. 13½x14***
**836** A109 20c multi .30 .25
**837** A109 30c multi .30 .25
**838** A109 50c multi .30 .25
**839** A109 1fr multi .30 .25
**840** A109 2fr multi .30 .25
**841** A109 12fr multi .30 .25
**842** A109 30fr multi 2.25 1.40
**843** A109 54fr multi 4.25 2.25
*Nos. 836-843 (8)* 8.30 5.15

Wernher von Braun (1912-1977), space and rocket expert.

### Nos. 628-631 Gold Embossed "ESPAMER '77" and ESPAMER Emblem

Souvenir Sheets

**1977, Oct. 3 Photo.** ***Perf. 13***
**844** A94 20fr multi 5.75 5.75
**845** A94 30fr multi 5.75 5.75
**846** A94 50fr multi 5.75 5.75
**847** A94 100fr multi 5.75 5.75
*Nos. 844-847 (4)* 23.00 23.00

ESPAMER '77, International Philatelic Exhibition, Barcelona, Oct. 7-13.

### Christmas Type of 1968

Souvenir Sheet

100fr, Nativity, by Peter Paul Rubens.

**1977, Dec. 12 Engr.** ***Perf. 13½***
**848** A48 100fr violet blue 4.00 4.00

Marginal inscription typographed in red.

Boy Scout Playing Flute — A118

Designs: 30c, Campfire. 50c, Bridge building. 1fr, Scouts with unit flag. 10fr, Map reading. 18fr, Boating. 26fr, Cooking. 44fr, Lord Baden-Powell.

**1978, Feb. 20 Litho.** ***Perf. 12½***
**849** A118 20c yel grn & multi .30 .25
**850** A118 30c blue & multi .30 .25
**851** A118 50c lilac & multi .30 .25
**852** A118 1fr blue & multi .30 .25
**853** A118 10fr pink & multi .40 .25
**854** A118 18fr lt grn & multi .90 .35
**855** A118 26fr orange & multi 1.50 .60
**856** A118 44fr salmon & multi 2.25 1.25
*Nos. 849-856 (8)* 6.25 3.45

10th anniversary of Rwanda Boy Scouts.

Chimpanzees A119

Designs: 30c, Gorilla. 50c, Colobus monkey. 3fr, Galago. 10fr, Cercopithecus monkey (mone). 26fr, Potto. 60fr, Cercopithecus monkey (griuet). 150fr, Baboon.

**1978, Mar. 20 Photo.** ***Perf. 13½x13***
**857** A119 20c multi .30 .25
**858** A119 30c multi .30 .25
**859** A119 50c multi .30 .25
**860** A119 3fr multi .30 .25
**861** A119 10fr multi .45 .50
**862** A119 26fr multi 1.05 1.25
**863** A119 60fr multi 2.75 3.00
**864** A119 150fr multi 4.75 7.00
*Nos. 857-864 (8)* 10.30 12.75

Euporus Strangulatus — A120

Coleoptera: 30c, Rhina afzelii, vert. 50c, Pentalobus palini. 3fr, Corynodes dejeani, vert. 10fr, Mecynorhina torquata. 15fr, Mecocerus rhombeus, vert. 20fr, Macrotoma serripes. 25fr, Neptunides stanleyi, vert. 26fr, Petrognatha gigas. 100fr, Eudicella gralli, vert.

**1978, May 22 Litho.** ***Perf. 14***
**865** A120 20c multi .30 .25
**866** A120 30c multi .30 .25
**867** A120 50c multi .30 .25
**868** A120 3fr multi .30 .25
**869** A120 10fr multi .30 .25
**870** A120 15fr multi .50 .30
**871** A120 20fr multi .70 .35
**872** A120 25fr multi .90 .50
**873** A120 26fr multi 1.20 .55
**874** A120 100fr multi 3.60 2.25
*Nos. 865-874 (10)* 8.40 5.20

Crossing "River of Poverty" A121

Emblem and: 10fr, 60fr, Men poling boat, facing right. 26fr, like 4fr.

**1978, May 29** ***Perf. 12½***
**875** A121 4fr multi .30 .25
**876** A121 10fr multi .30 .25
**877** A121 26fr multi .60 .40
**878** A121 60fr multi 1.25 .80
*Nos. 875-878 (4)* 2.45 1.70

Natl. Revolutionary Development Movement (M.R.N.D.).

Soccer, Rimet Cup, Flags of Netherlands and Peru — A122

11th World cup, Argentina, June 1-25, (Various Soccer Scenes and Flags of): 30c, Sweden & Spain. 50c, Scotland & Iran. 2fr, Germany & Tunisia. 3fr, Italy & Hungary. 10fr, Brazil and Austria. 34fr, Poland & Mexico. 100fr, Argentina & France.

**1978, June 19** *Perf. 13*

**879** A122 20c multi .30 .25
**879A** A122 30c multi .30 .25
**879B** A122 50c multi .30 .25
**880** A122 2fr multi .30 .25
**881** A122 3fr multi .30 .25
**882** A122 10fr multi .30 .25
**883** A122 34fr multi 1.05 .70
**884** A122 100fr multi 2.35 1.90
*Nos. 879-884 (8)* 5.20 4.10

Wright Brothers, Flyer I — A123

History of Aviation: 30c, Santos Dumont and Canard 14, 1906. 50c, Henry Farman and Voisin No. 1, 1908. 1fr, Jan Olieslaegers and Bleriot, 1910. 3fr, Marshal Balbo and Savoia S-17, 1919. 10fr, Charles Lindbergh and Spirit of St. Louis, 1927. 55fr, Hugo Junkers and Junkers JU52/3, 1932. 60fr, Igor Sikorsky and Sikorsky VS 300, 1939. 130fr, Concorde over New York.

**1978, Oct. 30** **Litho.** *Perf. 13½x14*

**885** A123 20c multi .30 .25
**886** A123 30c multi .30 .25
**887** A123 50c multi .30 .25
**888** A123 1fr multi .30 .25
**889** A123 3fr multi .30 .25
**890** A123 10fr multi .35 .25
**891** A123 55fr multi 1.40 .75
**892** A123 60fr multi 1.60 .85
*Nos. 885-892 (8)* 4.85 3.10

**Souvenir Sheet**

***Perf. 13x13½***

**893** A123 130fr multi 4.75 4.75

No. 893 contains one stamp 47x35mm.

**Christmas Type of 1968**

Souvenir Sheet

Design: 200fr, Adoration of the Kings, by Albrecht Dürer, vert.

**1978, Dec. 11** **Engr.** *Perf. 11½*

**894** A48 200fr brown 6.00 6.00

**Nos. 532-533, Overprinted "1963 1978" in Black or Blue**

**1978, Dec. 18** **Photo.** *Perf. 13½*

**895** A83 6fr multi (Bk) .30 .25
**896** A83 94fr multi (Bl) 2.50 2.00

Org. for African Unity, 15th anniv.

Goats A124

20c, Ducks, vert. 50c, Cock and chickens, vert. 4fr, Rabbits. 5fr, Pigs, vert. 15fr, Turkey. 50fr, Sheep and cattle, vert. 75fr, Bull.

**1978, Dec. 28** **Litho.** *Perf. 14*

**897** A124 20c multi .30 .25
**898** A124 30c multi .30 .25
**899** A124 50c multi .30 .25
**900** A124 4fr multi .30 .25
**901** A124 5fr multi .30 .25
**902** A124 15fr multi .50 .35
**903** A124 50fr multi 1.60 .95
**904** A124 75fr multi 2.90 1.60
*Nos. 897-904 (8)* 6.50 4.15

Husbandry Year.

Papilio Demodocus A125

Butterflies: 30c, Precis octavia. 50c, Charaxes smaragdalis. 4fr, Charaxes guderiana. 15fr, Colotis evippe. 30fr, Danaus limniace. 50fr, Byblia acheloia. 150fr, Utetheisa pulchella.

**1979, Feb. 19** **Photo.** *Perf. 14½*

**905** A125 20c multi .30 .25
**906** A125 30c multi .30 .25
**907** A125 50c multi .30 .25
**908** A125 4fr multi .40 .25
**909** A125 15fr multi .70 .30
**910** A125 30fr multi 1.80 .45
**911** A125 50fr multi 2.40 .90
**912** A125 150fr multi 6.00 2.50
*Nos. 905-912 (8)* 12.20 5.15

Euphorbia Grantii, Weavers A126

Design: 60fr, Drummers and Intelsat IV-A.

**1979, June 8** **Photo.** *Perf. 13*

**913** A126 40fr multi 1.25 1.00
**914** A126 60fr multi 2.50 1.50

Philexafrique II, Libreville, Gabon, June 8-17.

Entandrophragma Excelsum — A127

Trees and Shrubs: 20c, Polyscias fulva. 50c, Ilex mitis. 4fr, Kigelia Africana. 15fr, Ficus thonningi. 20fr, Acacia Senegal. 50fr, Symphonia globulifera. 110fr, Acacia sieberana. 20c, 50c, 15fr, 50fr, vertical.

**1979, Aug. 27** *Perf. 14*

**915** A127 20c multi .30 .25
**916** A127 30c multi .30 .25
**917** A127 50c multi .30 .25
**918** A127 4 fr multi .30 .25
**919** A127 15fr multi .40 .25
**920** A127 20fr multi .55 .40
**921** A127 50fr multi 1.30 .80
**922** A127 110fr multi 2.80 2.00
*Nos. 915-922 (8)* 6.25 4.45

Black and White Boys, IYC Emblem A128

26fr, 100fr, Children of various races, diff., vert.

***Perf. 13½x13, 13x13½***

**1979, Nov. 19** **Photo.**

**923** A128 Block of 8 10.00 7.50
*a.* 26fr, any single .90 .45
**924** A128 42fr multi 1.50 .90

**Souvenir Sheet**

**925** A128 100fr multi 4.50 4.50

Intl. Year of the Child. No. 923 printed in sheets of 16 (4x4).

Basket Weaving A129

***Perf. 12½x13, 13x12½***

**1979, Dec. 3** **Litho.**

**926** A129 50c shown .30 .25
**927** A129 1.50fr Wood carving, vert. .30 .25
**928** A129 2fr Metal working .30 .25
**929** A129 10fr Jewelry, vert. .30 .25
**930** A129 20fr Straw plaiting .30 .25
**931** A129 26fr Wall painting, vert. .60 .45
**932** A129 40fr Pottery 1.35 1.00
**933** A129 100fr Smelting, vert. 2.90 1.50
*Nos. 926-933 (8)* 6.35 4.20

Souvenir Sheet

Children of Different Races, Christmas Tree — A130

**1979, Dec. 24** **Engr.** *Perf. 12*

**934** A130 200fr ultra & dp mag 6.00 6.00

Christmas; Intl. Year of the Child.

German East Africa #N5, Hill A131

Sir Rowland Hill (1795-1879), originator of penny postage, and Stamps of Ruanda-Urundi or: 30c, German East Africa #N23. 50c, German East Africa #NB9. 3fr, #25. 10fr, #42. 26fr, #123. 100fr, #B28.

**1979, Dec. 31** **Litho.** *Perf. 14*

**935** A131 20c multi .30 .25
**936** A131 30c multi .30 .25
**937** A131 50c multi .30 .25
**938** A131 3fr multi .30 .25
**939** A131 10fr multi .30 .25
**940** A131 26fr multi .60 .35
**941** A131 60fr multi 1.60 .80
**942** A131 100fr multi 2.75 1.25
*Nos. 935-942 (8)* 6.45 3.65

Sarothrura Pulchra A132

Birds of the Nyungwe Forest: 20c Ploceus alienus, vert. 30c, Regal sunbird, vert. 3fr, Tockus alboterminatus. 10fr, Pygmy owl, vert. 26fr, Emerald cuckoo. 60fr, Finch, vert. 100fr, Stepanoaetus coronatus, vert.

***Perf. 13½x13, 13x13½***

**1980, Jan. 7** **Photo.**

**943** A132 20c multi .30 .25
**944** A132 30c multi .30 .25
**945** A132 50c multi .30 .25
**946** A132 3fr multi .30 .25
**947** A132 10fr multi .45 .40
**948** A132 26fr multi 1.15 .80
**949** A132 60fr multi 2.90 1.25
**950** A132 100fr multi 4.25 2.75
*Nos. 943-950 (8)* 9.95 6.20

First Footstep on Moon, Spacecraft A133

Spacecraft and Moon Exploration: 1.50fr, Descent onto lunar surface. 8fr, American flag. 30fr, Solar panels. 50fr, Gathering soil samples. 60fr, Adjusting sun screen. 200fr, Landing craft.

**1980, Jan. 31** **Photo.** *Perf. 13x13½*

**951** A133 50c multi .30 .25
**952** A133 1.50fr multi .30 .25
**953** A133 8fr multi .30 .25
**954** A133 30fr multi .80 .50
**955** A133 50fr multi 1.45 .80
**956** A133 60fr multi 1.65 .90
*Nos. 951-956 (6)* 4.80 2.95

**Souvenir Sheet**

**957** A133 200fr multi 6.25 6.25

Apollo 11 moon landing, 10th anniv. (1979).

Globe, Butare and 1905 Chicago Club Emblems A134

Rotary Intl., 75th Anniv. (Globe, Emblems of Butare or Kigali Clubs and): 30c, San Francisco, 1908. 50c, Chicago, 1910. 4fr, Buffalo, 1911. 15fr, London, 1911. 20fr, Glasgow, 1912. 50fr, Bristol, 1917. 60fr, Rotary Intl., 1980.

**1980, Feb. 23** **Litho.** *Perf. 13*

**958** A134 20c multi .30 .25
**959** A134 30c multi .30 .25
**960** A134 50c multi .30 .25
**961** A134 4fr multi .30 .25
**962** A134 15fr multi .35 .25
**963** A134 20fr multi .50 .25
**964** A134 50fr multi .90 .40
**965** A134 60fr multi 1.50 .65
*Nos. 958-965 (8)* 4.45 2.55

Gymnast, Moscow '80 Emblem A135

**1980, Mar. 10** *Perf. 12½*

**966** A135 20c shown .30 .25
**967** A135 30c Basketball .30 .25
**968** A135 50c Bicycling .30 .25
**969** A135 3fr Boxing .30 .25
**970** A135 20fr Archery .45 .25
**971** A135 26fr Weight lifting .65 .30
**972** A135 50fr Javelin 1.25 .65
**973** A135 100fr Fencing 2.30 1.25
*Nos. 966-973 (8)* 5.85 3.45

22nd Summer Olympic Games, Moscow, July 19-Aug. 3.

Souvenir Sheet

Amalfi Coast, by Giacinto Gigante — A136

**1980, Apr. 28** **Photo.** ***Perf. 13½***

**974** A136 200fr multi 6.25 6.25

20th Intl. Philatelic Exhibition, Europa '80, Naples, Apr. 26-May 4.

Geaster Mushroom A137

30c, Lentinus atrobrunneus. 50c, Gomphus stereoides. 4fr, Cantharellus cibarius. 10fr, Stilbothamnium dybowskii. 15fr, Xeromphalina tenuipes. 70fr, Podoscypha elegans. 100fr, Mycena.

**1980, July 21** **Photo.** ***Perf. 13½***

**975** A137 20c shown .30 .25
**976** A137 30c multicolored .30 .25
**977** A137 50c multicolored .40 .25
**978** A137 4fr multicolored .65 .25
**979** A137 10fr multicolored 1.05 .30
**980** A137 15fr multicolored 2.30 .75
**981** A137 70fr multicolored 6.50 2.00
**982** A137 100fr multicolored 10.75 4.00
*Nos. 975-982 (8)* 22.25 8.05

Still Life, by Renoir — A138

Impressionist Painters: 30c, 26fr, At the Theater, by Toulouse-Lautrec, vert. 50c, 10fr, Seaside Garden, by Monet. 4fr, Mother and Child, by Mary Cassatt, vert. 5fr, Starry Night, by Van Gogh. 10fr, Dancers at their Toilet, by Degas, vert. 50fr, The Card Players, by Cezanne. 70fr, Tahitian Women, by Gauguin, vert. 75fr, like 20c. 100fr, In the Park, by Seurat.

**1980, Aug. 4** **Litho.** ***Perf. 14***

**983** A138 20c multi .30 .25
**984** A138 30c multi .30 .25
**985** A138 50c multi .30 .25
**986** A138 4fr multi .30 .25
*a.* Sheet of 2, 4fr, 26fr 3.00 3.00
**987** A138 5fr multi .30 .25
*a.* Sheet of 2, 5fr, 75fr 3.00 3.00
**988** A138 10fr multi .40 .25
*a.* Sheet of 2, 10fr, 70fr 3.00 3.00
**989** A138 50fr multi 1.50 .55
*a.* Sheet of 2, 50fr, 10fr 3.00 3.00
**990** A138 70fr multi 2.25 .85
**991** A138 100fr multi 3.50 1.25
*Nos. 983-991 (9)* 9.15 4.15

Souvenir Sheet

Virgin of the Harpies, by Andrea Del Sarto — A139

**Photogravure and Engraved**

**1980, Dec. 22** ***Perf. 11½***

**992** A139 200fr multi 6.25 6.25

Christmas.

Belgian War of Independence, Engraving — A140

Belgian Independence Sesquicentennial: Engravings of War of Independence.

**1980, Dec. 29** **Litho.** ***Perf. 12½***

**993** A140 20c pale grn & brn .30 .25
**994** A140 30c brn org & brn .30 .25
**995** A140 50c lt bl & brn .30 .25
**996** A140 9fr yel & brn .30 .25
**997** A140 10fr brt lil & brn .30 .25
**998** A140 20fr ap grn & brn .40 .25
**999** A140 70fr pink & brn 1.60 .65
**1000** A140 90fr lem & brn 2.40 1.50
*Nos. 993-1000 (8)* 5.90 3.65

Swamp Drainage A141

**1980, Dec. 31** **Photo.** ***Perf. 13½***

**1001** A141 20c shown .30 .25
**1002** A141 30c Fertilizer shed .30 .25
**1003** A141 1.50fr Rice fields .30 .25
**1004** A141 8fr Tree planting .30 .25
**1005** A141 10fr Terrace planting .30 .25
**1006** A141 40fr Farm buildings .85 .50
**1007** A141 90fr Bean cultivation 1.75 .90
**1008** A141 100fr Tea cultivation 1.90 1.10
*Nos. 1001-1008 (8)* 6.00 3.75

Soil Conservation Year.

Pavetta Rwandensis — A142

30c, Cyrtorchis praetermissa. 50c, Pavonia urens. 4fr, Cynorkis kassnerana. 5fr, Gardenia ternifolia. 10fr, Leptactina platyphylla. 20fr, Lobelia petiolata. 40fr, Tapinanthus brunneus. 70fr, Impatiens niamniamensis. 150fr, Dissotis rwandensis.

**1981, Apr. 6** **Photo.** ***Perf. 13x13½***

**1009** A142 20c shown .30 .25
**1010** A142 30c multicolored .30 .25
**1011** A142 50c multicolored .30 .25
**1012** A142 4fr multicolored .30 .25
**1013** A142 5fr multicolored .30 .25
**1014** A142 10fr multicolored .30 .25
**1015** A142 20fr multicolored .45 .30
**1016** A142 40fr multicolored 1.15 .75
**1017** A142 70fr multicolored 2.15 1.25
**1018** A142 150fr multicolored 4.25 2.25
*Nos. 1009-1018 (10)* 9.80 6.05

Girl Knitting — A143

SOS Children's Village: Various children.

**1981, Apr. 27** ***Perf. 13***

**1019** A143 20c multi .30 .25
**1020** A143 30c multi .30 .25
**1021** A143 50c multi .30 .25
**1022** A143 1fr multi .30 .25
**1023** A143 8fr multi .30 .25
**1024** A143 10fr multi .30 .25
**1025** A143 70fr multi 1.60 .80
**1026** A143 150fr multi 3.95 1.60
*Nos. 1019-1026 (8)* 7.35 3.90

Carolers, by Norman Rockwell A144

Designs: Saturday Evening Post covers by Norman Rockwell.

**1981, May 11** **Litho.** ***Perf. 13½x14***

**1027** A144 20c multi .30 .25
**1028** A144 30c multi .30 .25
**1029** A144 50c multi .30 .25
**1030** A144 1fr multi .30 .25
**1031** A144 8fr multi .35 .25
**1032** A144 20fr multi .70 .25
**1033** A144 50fr multi 1.75 .95
**1034** A144 70fr multi 2.40 1.25
*Nos. 1027-1034 (8)* 6.40 3.70

Cerval A145

Meat-eating animals — 30c, Jackals. 2fr, Genet. 2.50fr, Banded mongoose. 10fr, Zorille. 15fr, White-cheeked otter. 70fr, Golden wild cat. 200fr, Hunting dog, vert.

**1981, June 29** **Photo.** ***Perf. 13½x14***

**1035** A145 20c shown .30 .25
**1036** A145 30c multicolored .30 .25
**1037** A145 2fr multicolored .30 .25
**1038** A145 2.50fr multicolored .30 .25
**1039** A145 10fr multicolored .40 .30
**1040** A145 15fr multicolored .85 .65
**1041** A145 70fr multicolored 2.90 2.25
**1042** A145 200fr multicolored 5.25 5.00
*Nos. 1035-1042 (8)* 10.60 9.20

Drummer Sending Message — A146

30c, Map, communication waves. 2fr, Jet, radar screen. 2.50fr, Satellite, teletape. 10fr, Dish antenna. 15fr, Ship, navigation devices. 70fr, Helicopter. 200fr, Satellite with solar panels.

**1981, Sept. 1** **Litho.** ***Perf. 13***

**1043** A146 20c shown .30 .25
**1044** A146 30c multicolored .30 .25
**1045** A146 2fr multicolored .30 .25
**1046** A146 2.50fr multicolored .30 .25
**1047** A146 10fr multicolored .30 .25
**1048** A146 15fr multicolored .30 .25
**1049** A146 70fr multicolored 1.60 1.50
**1050** A146 200fr multicolored 5.00 3.50
*Nos. 1043-1050 (8)* 8.40 6.50

1500th Birth Anniv. of St. Benedict A147

Paintings and Frescoes of St. Benedict: 20c, Leaving his Parents, Mt. Oliveto Monastery, Maggiore. 30c, Oldest portrait, 10th cent., St. Chrisogone Church, Rome, vert. 50c, Portrait, Virgin of the Misericord polyptich, Borgo San Sepolcro. 4fr, Giving the Rules of the order to his Monks, Mt. Oliveto Monastery. 5fr, Monks at their Meal, Mt. Oliveto Monastery. 20fr, Portrait, 13th cent., Lower Church of the Holy Spirit, Subiaco, vert. 70fr, Our Lady in Glory with Sts. Gregory and Benedict, San Gimigniao, vert. 100fr, Priest Carrying Easter Meal to St. Benedict, by Jan van Coninxloo, 16th cent.

***Perf. 13½x13, 13x13½***

**1981, Nov. 30** **Photo.**

**1051** A147 20c multi .30 .25
**1052** A147 30c multi .30 .25
**1053** A147 50c multi .30 .25
**1054** A147 4fr multi .30 .25
**1055** A147 5fr multi .30 .25
**1056** A147 20fr multi .80 .50
**1057** A147 70fr multi 1.80 1.25
**1058** A147 100fr multi 2.75 2.50
*Nos. 1051-1058 (8)* 6.85 5.50

Intl. Year of the Disabled A148

**1981, Dec. 7** **Litho.** ***Perf. 13***

**1059** A148 20c Painting .30 .25
**1060** A148 30c Soccer .30 .25
**1061** A148 4.50fr Crocheting .30 .25
**1062** A148 5fr Painting vase .30 .25
**1063** A148 10fr Sawing .30 .25
**1064** A148 60fr Sign language 1.25 .55
**1065** A148 70fr Doing puzzle 1.70 .65
**1066** A148 100fr Juggling 2.45 1.25
*Nos. 1059-1066 (8)* 6.90 3.70

Souvenir Sheet

Christmas — A149

200fr, Adoration of the Kings, by van der Goes.

**Photo. & Engr.**

**1981, Dec. 21** *Perf. 13½*
**1067** A149 200fr multicolored 6.50 6.50

Natl. Rural Water Supply Year A150

20c, Deer drinking. 30c, Women carrying water, vert. 50c, Pipeline. 10fr, Filing pan, vert. 19fr, Drinking. 70fr, Mother, child, vert. 100fr, Lake pumping station, vert.

**1981, Dec. 28** **Litho.** *Perf. 12½*
**1068** A150 20c multicolored .30 .25
**1069** A150 30c multicolored .30 .25
**1070** A150 50c multicolored .30 .25
**1071** A150 10fr multicolored .30 .25
**1072** A150 19fr multicolored .45 .30
**1073** A150 70fr multicolored 1.50 .80
**1074** A150 100fr multicolored 2.40 1.10
*Nos. 1068-1074 (7)* 5.55 3.20

World Food Day, Oct. 16, 1981 A151

**1982, Jan. 25** **Litho.** *Perf. 13*
**1075** A151 20c Cattle .30 .25
**1076** A151 30c Bee .30 .25
**1077** A151 50c Fish .30 .25
**1078** A151 1fr Avocados .30 .25
**1079** A151 8fr Boy eating banana .30 .25
**1080** A151 20fr Sorghum .50 .30
**1081** A151 70fr Vegetables 1.70 .85
**1082** A151 100fr Balanced diet 2.75 1.50
*Nos. 1075-1082 (8)* 6.45 3.90

Hibiscus Berberidifolius — A152

No. 1084, Hypericum lanceolatum, vert. No. 1085, Canarina eminii. No. 1086, Polygala ruwenxoriensis. No. 1087, Kniphofia grantii, vert. No. 1088, Euphorbia candelabrum, vert. No. 1089, Disa erubescens, vert. No. 1090, Gloriosa simplex.

**1982, June 14** **Litho.** *Perf. 13*
**1083** A152 20c multi .30 .25
**1084** A152 30c multi .30 .25
**1085** A152 50c multi .30 .25
**1086** A152 4fr multi .30 .25
**1087** A152 10fr multi .35 .25
**1088** A152 35fr multi 1.15 .50
**1089** A152 70fr multi 2.00 .90
**1090** A152 80fr multi 2.40 1.60
*Nos. 1083-1090 (8)* 7.10 4.25

20th Anniv. of Independence — A153

**1982, June 28**
**1091** A153 10fr Flags .30 .25
**1092** A153 20fr Hands releasing doves .40 .25
**1093** A153 30fr Flag, handshake .70 .40
**1094** A153 50fr Govt. buildings 1.50 .65
*Nos. 1091-1094 (4)* 2.90 1.55

1982 World Cup — A154

Designs: Various soccer players.

**1982, July 6** *Perf. 14x14½*
**1095** A154 20c multi .30 .25
**1096** A154 30c multi .30 .25
**1097** A154 1.50fr multi .30 .25
**1098** A154 8fr multi .30 .25
**1099** A154 10fr multi .30 .25
**1100** A154 20fr multi .55 .40
**1101** A154 70fr multi 1.90 .90
**1102** A154 90fr multi 2.50 1.25
*Nos. 1095-1102 (8)* 6.45 3.80

TB Bacillus Centenary — A155

**1982, Nov. 22** **Litho.** *Perf. 14½*
**1103** A155 10fr Microscope, slide .30 .25
**1104** A155 20fr Serum, slide .50 .25
**1105** A155 70fr Lungs, slide 2.50 1.00
**1106** A155 100fr Koch 2.85 1.75
*Nos. 1103-1106 (4)* 6.15 3.25

Souvenir Sheets

Madam Recamier, by David — A156

PHILEXFRANCE '82 Intl. Stamp Exhibition, Paris, June 11-21: No. 1108, St. Anne and Virgin and Child with Franciscan Monk, by H. van der Goes. No. 1109, Liberty Guiding the People, by Delacroix. No. 1110, Pygmalion, by P. Delvaux.

**1982, Dec. 11** *Perf. 13½*
**1107** A156 40fr multi 2.50 2.50
**1108** A156 40fr multi 2.50 2.50
**1109** A156 60fr multi 2.50 2.50
**1110** A156 60fr multi 2.50 2.50
*Nos. 1107-1110 (4)* 10.00 10.00

Souvenir Sheet

Rest During the Flight to Egypt, by Murillo — A157

**1982, Dec. 20** **Photo. & Engr.**
**1111** A157 200fr carmine rose 6.50 6.50

Christmas.

10th Anniv. of UN Conference on Human Environment — A158

**1982, Dec. 27** **Litho.** *Perf. 14*
**1112** A158 20c Elephants .30 .25
**1113** A158 30c Lion .30 .25
**1114** A158 50c Flower .30 .25
**1115** A158 4fr Bull .30 .25
**1116** A158 5fr Deer .30 .25
**1117** A158 10fr Flower, diff. .30 .25
**1118** A158 20fr Zebras .50 .30
**1119** A158 40fr Crowned cranes 1.10 .65
**1120** A158 50fr Bird 1.50 .85
**1121** A158 70fr Woman pouring coffee beans 2.25 1.10
*Nos. 1112-1121 (10)* 7.15 4.40

Scouting Year A159

20c, Animal first aid. 30c, Camp. 1.50fr, Campfire. 8fr, Scout giving sign. 10fr, Knot. 20fr, Camp, diff. 70fr, Chopping wood. 90fr, Sign, map.

*Perf. 13½x14½*

**1983, Jan. 17** **Photo.**
**1122** A159 20c multicolored .30 .25
**1123** A159 30c multicolored .30 .25
**1124** A159 1.50fr multicolored .30 .25
**1125** A159 8fr multicolored .35 .25
**1126** A159 10fr multicolored .40 .30
**1127** A159 20fr multicolored .95 .65
**1128** A159 70fr multicolored 3.25 2.25
**1129** A159 90fr multicolored 4.75 2.75
*Nos. 1122-1129 (8)* 10.60 6.95

For overprints see Nos. 1234-1241.

Nectar-sucking Birds — A160

20c, Angola nectar bird. 30c, Royal nectar birds. 50c, Johnston's nectar bird. 4fr, Bronze nectar birds. 5fr, Collared souimangas. 10fr, Blue-headed nectar bird. 20fr, Purple-bellied nectar bird. 40fr, Copper nectar birds. 50fr, Olive-bellied nectar birds. 70fr, Red-breasted nectar bird.

*Perf. 14x14½, 14½x14*

**1983, Jan. 31** **Litho.**
**1130** A160 20c multicolored .30 .25
**1131** A160 30c multicolored .30 .25
**1132** A160 50c multicolored .30 .25
**1133** A160 4fr multicolored .30 .25
**1134** A160 5fr multicolored .30 .25
**1135** A160 10fr multicolored .55 .35
**1136** A160 20fr multicolored .95 .50
**1137** A160 40fr multicolored 1.75 1.10
**1138** A160 50fr multicolored 2.25 1.50
**1139** A160 70fr multicolored 3.50 2.25
*Nos. 1130-1139 (10)* 10.50 6.95

30c, 4fr, 10fr, 40fr, 70fr horiz. Inscribed 1982.

Soil Erosion Prevention A161

20c, Driving cattle. 30c, Pineapple field. 50c, Interrupted ditching. 9fr, Hedges, ditches. 10fr, Reafforestation. 20fr, Anti-erosion barriers. 30fr, Contour planting. 50fr, Terracing. 60fr, Protection of river banks. 70fr, Fallow, planted strips.

**1983, Feb. 14** *Perf. 14½*
**1140** A161 20c multicolored .30 .25
**1141** A161 30c multicolored .30 .25
**1142** A161 50c multicolored .30 .25
**1143** A161 9fr multicolored .30 .25
**1144** A161 10fr multicolored .30 .30
**1145** A161 20fr multicolored .35 .35
**1146** A161 30fr multicolored .55 .60
**1147** A161 50fr multicolored 1.10 1.00
**1148** A161 60fr multicolored 1.30 1.10
**1149** A161 70fr multicolored 1.90 1.25
*Nos. 1140-1149 (10)* 6.70 5.60

For overprints & surcharges see Nos. 1247-1255.

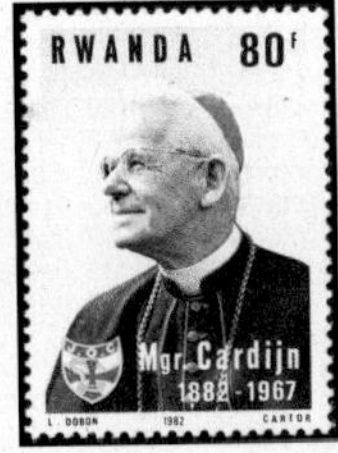


Cardinal Cardijn (1882-1967) A162

Young Catholic Workers Movement Activities. Inscribed 1982.

**1983, Feb. 22** *Perf. 12½x13*
**1150** A162 20c Feeding ducks .30 .25
**1151** A162 30c Harvesting bananas .30 .25
**1152** A162 50c Carrying melons .30 .25
**1153** A162 10fr Teacher .30 .25
**1154** A162 19fr Shoemakers .30 .25
**1155** A162 20fr Growing millet .40 .25
**1156** A162 70fr Embroidering 1.60 .75
**1157** A162 80fr shown 1.80 1.00
*Nos. 1150-1157 (8)* 5.30 3.25

Gorilla — A163

Various gorillas. Nos. 1158-1163 horiz.

**1983, Mar. 14** *Perf. 14*
**1158** A163 20c multi .30 .25
**1159** A163 30c multi .30 .25
**1160** A163 9.50fr multi .30 .25
**1161** A163 10fr multi .40 .35
**1162** A163 20fr multi 1.10 .65
**1163** A163 30fr multi 1.60 .85
**1164** A163 60fr multi 2.60 1.50
**1165** A163 70fr multi 2.85 2.00
*Nos. 1158-1165 (8)* 9.45 6.10

Souvenir Sheet

The Granduca Madonna, by Raphael — A164

**Typo. & Engr.**

| **1983, Dec. 19** | | | *Perf. 11½* | |
|---|---|---|---|---|
| **1166** | A164 | 200fr multi | 6.50 | 6.50 |

Christmas.

Local Trees — A165

No. 1167, Hagenia abyssinica. No. 1168, Dracaena steudneri. No. 1169, Phoenix reclinata. No. 1170, Podocarpus milanjianus. No. 1171, Entada abyssinica. No. 1172, Parinari excelsa. No. 1173, Newtonia buchananii. No. 1174, Acacia gerrardi, vert.

| **1984, Jan. 15** | **Litho.** | | *Perf. 13½x13* | |
|---|---|---|---|---|
| **1167** | A165 | 20c multicolored | .30 | .25 |
| **1168** | A165 | 30c multicolored | .30 | .25 |
| **1169** | A165 | 50c multicolored | .30 | .25 |
| **1170** | A165 | 10fr multicolored | .30 | .25 |
| **1171** | A165 | 19fr multicolored | .60 | .30 |
| **1172** | A165 | 70fr multicolored | 1.60 | .80 |
| **1173** | A165 | 100fr multicolored | 2.50 | 1.10 |
| **1174** | A165 | 200fr multicolored | 4.00 | 2.25 |
| | | *Nos. 1167-1174 (8)* | 9.90 | 5.45 |

World Communications Year — A166

| **1984, May 21** | **Litho.** | | *Perf. 12½* | |
|---|---|---|---|---|
| **1175** | A166 | 20c Train | .30 | .25 |
| **1176** | A166 | 30c Ship | .30 | .25 |
| **1177** | A166 | 4.50fr Radio | .30 | .25 |
| **1178** | A166 | 10fr Telephone | .30 | .25 |
| **1179** | A166 | 15fr Mail | .40 | .25 |
| **1180** | A166 | 50fr Jet | 1.40 | .50 |
| **1181** | A166 | 70fr Satellite, TV screen | 1.90 | .75 |
| **1182** | A166 | 100fr Satellite | 3.00 | 1.00 |
| | | *Nos. 1175-1182 (8)* | 7.90 | 3.50 |

1st Manned Flight Bicent. — A167

Historic flights: 20c, Le Martial, Sept. 19, 1783. 30c, La Montgolfiere, Nov. 21, 1783. 50c, Charles and Robert, Dec. 1, 1783, and Blanchard, Mar. 2, 1784. 9fr, Jean-Pierre Blanchard and wife in balloon. 10fr, Blanchard and Jeffries, 1785. 50fr, E. Demuyter, 1937. 80fr, Propane gas balloons. 200fr, Abruzzo, Anderson and Newman, 1978.

| **1984, June 4** | **Litho.** | | *Perf. 13* | |
|---|---|---|---|---|
| **1183** | A167 | 20c multi | .30 | .25 |
| **1184** | A167 | 30c multi | .30 | .25 |
| **1185** | A167 | 50c multi | .30 | .25 |
| **1186** | A167 | 9fr multi | .30 | .25 |
| **1187** | A167 | 10fr multi | .30 | .25 |
| **1188** | A167 | 50fr multi | 1.30 | .75 |
| **1189** | A167 | 80fr multi | 1.90 | 1.00 |
| **1190** | A167 | 200fr multi | 5.25 | 3.00 |
| | | *Nos. 1183-1190 (8)* | 9.95 | 6.00 |

1984 Summer Olympics — A168

| **1984, July 16** | | | *Perf. 14* | |
|---|---|---|---|---|
| **1191** | A168 | 20c Equestrian | .30 | .25 |
| **1192** | A168 | 30c Wind surfing | .30 | .25 |
| **1193** | A168 | 50c Soccer | .30 | .25 |
| **1194** | A168 | 9fr Swimming | .45 | .35 |
| **1195** | A168 | 10fr Field hockey | .50 | .40 |
| **1196** | A168 | 40fr Fencing | 1.30 | 1.50 |
| **1197** | A168 | 80fr Running | 2.15 | 2.50 |
| **1198** | A168 | 200fr Boxing | 5.25 | 4.75 |
| | | *Nos. 1191-1198 (8)* | 10.55 | 10.25 |

Zebras and Buffaloes — A169

20c, Zebra with colt. 30c, Buffalo with calf, vert. 50c, Two zebras, vert. 9fr, Zebras fighting. 10fr, Buffalo, vert. 80fr, Zebra herd. 100fr, Zebra, vert. 200fr, Buffalo.

| **1984, Nov. 26** | **Litho.** | | *Perf. 13* | |
|---|---|---|---|---|
| **1199** | A169 | 20c multicolored | .30 | .25 |
| **1200** | A169 | 30c multicolored | .30 | .25 |
| **1201** | A169 | 50c multicolored | .30 | .25 |
| **1202** | A169 | 9fr multicolored | .45 | .25 |
| **1203** | A169 | 10fr multicolored | .50 | .30 |
| **1204** | A169 | 80fr multicolored | 2.25 | 1.50 |
| **1205** | A169 | 100fr multicolored | 2.95 | 2.25 |
| **1206** | A169 | 200fr multicolored | 6.25 | 4.00 |
| | | *Nos. 1199-1206 (8)* | 13.30 | 9.05 |

Souvenir Sheet

Christmas 1984 — A170

Design: Virgin and Child, by Correggio.

| **1984, Dec. 24** | | **Typo. & Engr.** | | |
|---|---|---|---|---|
| **1207** | A170 | 200fr multicolored | 6.50 | 6.50 |

Gorilla Gorilla Beringei — A171

10fr, Adults and young. 15fr, Adults. 25fr, Female holding young. 30fr, Three adults. 200fr, Baby climbing branch, vert.

| **1985, Mar. 25** | **Litho.** | | *Perf. 13* | |
|---|---|---|---|---|
| **1208** | A171 | 10fr multi | *2.00* | *1.75* |
| **1209** | A171 | 15fr multi | *3.25* | *2.75* |
| **1210** | A171 | 25fr multi | *6.75* | *5.00* |
| **1211** | A171 | 30fr multi | *8.00* | *5.50* |
| | | *Nos. 1208-1211 (4)* | *20.00* | *15.00* |

**Souvenir Sheet**

***Perf. 11½x12***

| | | | | |
|---|---|---|---|---|
| **1212** | A171 | 200fr multi | *15.00* | *15.00* |

No. 1212 contains one 37x52mm stamp.

Self-Sufficiency in Food Production — A172

Designs: 20c, Raising chickens and turkeys. 30c, Pineapple harvest. 50c, Animal husbandry. 9fr, Grain products. 10fr, Education. 50fr, Sowing grain. 80fr, Food reserves. 100fr, Banana harvest.

| **1985, Mar. 30** | | | | |
|---|---|---|---|---|
| **1213** | A172 | 20c multi | .30 | .25 |
| **1214** | A172 | 30c multi | .30 | .25 |
| **1215** | A172 | 50c multi | .30 | .25 |
| **1216** | A172 | 9fr multi | .30 | .25 |
| **1217** | A172 | 10fr multi | .30 | .25 |
| **1218** | A172 | 50fr multi | 1.10 | .60 |
| **1219** | A172 | 80fr multi | 1.75 | 1.10 |
| **1220** | A172 | 100fr multi | 2.50 | 2.25 |
| | | *Nos. 1213-1220 (8)* | 6.85 | 5.20 |

Natl. Redevelopment Movement, 10th Anniv. — A173

| **1985, July 5** | | | | |
|---|---|---|---|---|
| **1221** | A173 | 10fr multi | .30 | .25 |
| **1222** | A173 | 30fr multi | 1.00 | .25 |
| **1223** | A173 | 70fr multi | 2.00 | 1.00 |
| | | *Nos. 1221-1223 (3)* | 3.30 | 1.50 |

UN, 40th Anniv. A174

| **1985, July 25** | | | | |
|---|---|---|---|---|
| **1224** | A174 | 50fr multi | 1.60 | 1.50 |
| **1225** | A174 | 100fr multi | 3.00 | 2.50 |

Audubon Birth Bicent. — A175

Illustrations of North American bird species by John J. Audubon — 10fr, Barn owl. 20fr, White-faced owl. 40fr, Red-breasted hummingbird. 80fr, Warbler.

| **1985, Sept. 18** | | | | |
|---|---|---|---|---|
| **1226** | A175 | 10fr multicolored | *1.25* | *.50* |
| **1227** | A175 | 20fr multicolored | *1.50* | *1.00* |
| **1228** | A175 | 40fr multicolored | *3.00* | *2.00* |
| **1229** | A175 | 80fr multicolored | *5.00* | *3.50* |
| | | *Nos. 1226-1229 (4)* | *10.75* | *7.00* |

Intl. Youth Year A176

| **1985, Oct. 14** | | | | |
|---|---|---|---|---|
| **1230** | A176 | 7fr Education and agriculture | .30 | .25 |
| **1231** | A176 | 9fr Bicycling | .30 | .25 |
| **1232** | A176 | 44fr Construction | 1.25 | .70 |
| **1233** | A176 | 80fr Schoolroom | 2.25 | 1.40 |
| | | *Nos. 1230-1233 (4)* | 4.10 | 2.60 |

**Nos. 1122-1129 Ovptd. in Green or Rose Violet with the Girl Scout Trefoil and "1910/1985"**

| **1985, Nov. 25** | | | *Perf. 13½x14½* | |
|---|---|---|---|---|
| **1234** | A159 | 20c multi | .30 | .25 |
| **1235** | A159 | 30c multi (RV) | .30 | .25 |
| **1236** | A159 | 1.50fr multi | *.50* | .25 |
| **1237** | A159 | 8fr multi (RV) | *1.00* | .25 |
| **1238** | A159 | 10fr multi | *1.50* | .75 |
| **1239** | A159 | 20fr multi | *3.00* | *1.25* |
| **1240** | A159 | 70fr multi (RV) | *8.00* | *2.50* |
| **1241** | A159 | 90fr multi | *12.00* | *5.00* |
| | | *Nos. 1234-1241 (8)* | *26.60* | *10.50* |

Natl. Girl Scout Movement, 75th anniv.

Souvenir Sheet

Adoration of the Magi, by Titian — A177

**Photo. & Engr.**

| **1985, Dec. 24** | | | *Perf. 11½* | |
|---|---|---|---|---|
| **1242** | A177 | 200fr violet | 6.75 | 6.75 |

Christmas.

Transportation and Communication — A178

**1986, Jan. 27 Litho. *Perf. 13***

1243 A178 10fr Articulated truck .30 .25
1244 A178 30fr Hand-canceling letters 1.00 .45
1245 A178 40fr Kigali Satellite Station 1.50 .70

**Size: 52x34mm**

1246 A178 80fr Kayibanda Airport, Kigali 2.00 1.50
*Nos. 1243-1246 (4)* 4.80 2.90

**Nos. 1141-1149 Surcharged or Ovptd. with Silver Bar and "ANNEE 1986 / INTENSIFICATION AGRICOLE"**

**1986, May 5 Litho. *Perf. 14½***

1247 A161 9fr #1143 *1.25* .50
1248 A161 10fr on 30c #1141 *1.25* .50
1249 A161 10fr on 50c #1142 *1.50* .50
1250 A161 10fr #1144 *1.50* .50
1251 A161 20fr #1145 *2.50* 1.00
1252 A161 30fr #1146 *3.75* 1.50
1253 A161 50fr #1147 *5.00* 2.25
1254 A161 60fr #1148 *7.00* 3.50
1255 A161 70fr #1149 *8.00* 4.50
*Nos. 1247-1255 (9)* *31.75* 14.75

1986 World Cup Soccer Championships, Mexico — A179

Various soccer plays, natl. flags.

**1986, June 16 *Perf. 13***

1256 A179 2fr Morocco, England .30 .25
1257 A179 4fr Paraguay, Iraq .30 .25
1258 A179 5fr Brazil, Spain .40 .50
1259 A179 10fr Italy, Argentina .75 .75
1260 A179 40fr Mexico, Belgium 2.50 1.75
1261 A179 45fr France, USSR 3.50 2.50
*Nos. 1256-1261 (6)* 7.75 6.00

For overprints see Nos. 1360-1365.

Akagera Natl. Park — A180

**1986, Dec. 15 Litho. *Perf. 13***

1262 A180 4fr Antelopes .80 .25
1263 A180 7fr Shoebills .80 .30
1264 A180 9fr Cape elands 1.10 .30
1265 A180 10fr Giraffe 1.10 .30
1266 A180 80fr Elephants 6.50 3.00
1267 A180 90fr Crocodiles 7.75 3.00

**Size: 48x34mm**

1268 A180 100fr Weaver birds 7.75 5.00
1269 A180 100fr Pelican, zebras 7.75 5.00
a. Pair, #1268-1269 + label 25.00 25.00
*Nos. 1262-1269 (8)* 33.55 17.15

No. 1269a has continuous design.
A souvenir sheet containing five No. 1269a exists. Value $210.

Christmas, Intl. Peace Year — A181

**1986, Dec. 24 Litho. *Perf. 13***

1270 A181 10fr shown .30 .25
1271 A181 15fr Dove, Earth .75 .50
1272 A181 30fr like 10fr 1.00 .80
1273 A181 70fr like 15fr 2.25 2.25
*Nos. 1270-1273 (4)* 4.30 3.80

UN Child Survival Campaign A182

**1987, Feb. 13**

1274 A182 4fr Breast feeding .30 .25
1275 A182 6fr Rehydration therapy .30 .25
1276 A182 10fr Immunization .50 .30
1277 A182 70fr Growth monitoring 3.25 1.75
*Nos. 1274-1277 (4)* 4.35 2.55

Year of Natl. Self-sufficiency in Food Production — A183

**1987, June 15 Litho. *Perf. 13***

1278 A183 5fr Farm .30 .25
1279 A183 7fr Storing produce .30 .25
1280 A183 40fr Boy carrying basket of fish, produce 1.50 .80
1281 A183 60fr Tropical fruit 2.00 1.25
*Nos. 1278-1281 (4)* 4.10 2.55

Nos. 1279-1281 vert.

Natl. Independence, 25th Anniv. — A184

10fr, Pres. Habyarimana, soldiers, farmers. 40fr, Pres. officiating government session. 70fr, Pres., Pope John Paul II. 100fr, Pres.

**1987, July 1**

1283 A184 10fr multi .35 .30
1284 A184 40fr multi 1.15 1.25
1285 A184 70fr multi 2.00 2.25
1286 A184 100fr multi, vert. 2.75 3.25
*Nos. 1283-1286 (4)* 6.25 7.05

A 5fr value exists but was not officially issued. Value $100.

Fruit A185

**1987, Sept. 28**

1287 A185 10fr Bananas, vert. .30 .25
1288 A185 40fr Pineapples .95 .85
1289 A185 80fr Papayas 2.15 1.90
1290 A185 90fr Avocados 2.60 2.00
1291 A185 100fr Strawberries, vert. 3.25 2.75
*Nos. 1287-1291 (5)* 9.25 7.75

Leopards — A186

No. 1292, Female, cub. No. 1293, Three cubs playing. No. 1294, Adult attacking gazelle. No. 1295, In tree. No. 1296, Leaping from tree.

**1987, Nov. 18 Litho. *Perf. 13***

1292 A186 50fr multi 6.00 3.00
1293 A186 50fr multi 6.00 3.00
1294 A186 50fr multi 6.00 3.00
1295 A186 50fr multi 6.00 3.00
1296 A186 50fr multi 6.00 3.00
a. Strip of 5, Nos. 1292-1296 40.00 40.00
*Nos. 1292-1296 (5)* 30.00 15.00

A souvenir sheet containing five No. 1296a exists. Value $200.

Intl. Year of the Volunteer — A187

5fr, Constructing village water system. 12fr, Education, vert. 20fr, Modern housing, vert. 60fr, Animal husbandry, vert.

**1987, Dec. 12**

1297 A187 5fr multicolored .30 .25
1298 A187 12fr multicolored .50 .25
1299 A187 20fr multicolored 1.00 .50
1300 A187 60fr multicolored 2.75 2.00
*Nos. 1297-1300 (4)* 4.55 3.00

Souvenir Sheet

Virgin and Child, by Fra Angelico (c. 1387-1455) — A188

**1987, Dec. 24 Engr. *Perf. 11½***

1301 A188 200fr deep mag & dull blue 9.00 9.00

Christmas.

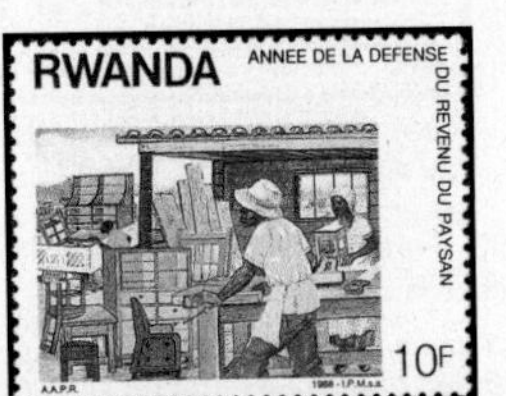


Maintenance of the Rural Economy Year — A189

**1988, June 13 Litho. *Perf. 13***

1302 A189 10fr Furniture store .35 .25
1303 A189 40fr Dairy farm 1.00 1.00
1304 A189 60fr Produce market 1.75 1.25
1305 A189 80fr Fruit market 2.50 2.00
*Nos. 1302-1305 (4)* 5.60 4.50

Primates, Nyungwe Forest — A190

2fr, Chimpanzee. 3fr, Black and white colobus. 10fr, Pygmy galago. 90fr, Cercopithecidae ascagne.

**1988, Sept. 15 Litho. *Perf. 13***

1306 A190 2fr multicolored .35 .25
1307 A190 3fr multicolored .50 1.25
1308 A190 10fr multicolored 1.40 .75
1309 A190 90fr multicolored 7.25 4.50
*Nos. 1306-1309 (4)* 9.50 6.75

1988 Summer Olympics, Seoul — A191

**1988, Sept. 19**

1310 A191 5fr Boxing .30 .25
1311 A191 7fr Relay .30 .25
1312 A191 8fr Table tennis .40 .25
1313 A191 10fr Women's running 1.15 .50
1314 A191 90fr Hurdles 4.50 2.50
*Nos. 1310-1314 (5)* 6.65 3.75

Organization of African Unity, 25th Anniv. — A192

**1988, Nov. 30 Litho. *Perf. 13***

1315 A192 5fr shown .30 .25
1316 A192 7fr Handskake, map .30 .25
1317 A192 8fr "OAU" in brick, map .30 .25
1318 A192 90fr Slogan 3.00 2.25
*Nos. 1315-1318 (4)* 3.90 3.00

Souvenir Sheet

Detail of The Virgin and the Soup, by Paolo Veronese — A193

**1988, Dec. 23 Engr. *Perf. 13½***

1319 A193 200fr multicolored 6.50 6.50

Christmas. Margin is typographed.

Intl. Red Cross and Red Crescent Organizations, 125th Annivs. — A194

**1988, Dec. 30** **Litho.** ***Perf. 13***
**1320** A194 10fr Refugees .40 .25
**1321** A194 30fr First aid 1.00 .75
**1322** A194 40fr Elderly 1.35 1.00
**1323** A194 100fr Travelling doctor 3.25 2.50
*Nos. 1320-1323 (4)* 6.00 4.50

Nos. 1322-1323 vert.

Medicinal Plants — A195

5fr, Plectranthus barbatus. 10fr, Tetradenia riparia. 20fr, Hygrophila auriculata. 40fr, Datura stramonium. 50fr, Pavetta ternifolia.

**1989, Feb. 15** **Litho.** ***Perf. 13***
**1324** A195 5fr multicolored *.50 .50*
**1325** A195 10fr multicolored *1.00 1.00*
**1326** A195 20fr multicolored *2.00 2.00*
**1327** A195 40fr multicolored *4.00 4.00*
**1328** A195 50fr multicolored *7.00 7.00*
*Nos. 1324-1328 (5)* *14.50 14.50*

Interparliamentary Union, Cent. — A196

**1989, Oct. 20** **Litho.** ***Perf. 13***
**1329** A196 10fr shown .35 .25
**1330** A196 30fr Hills, lake 1.00 .75
**1331** A196 70fr Hills, stream 2.25 2.00
**1332** A196 90fr Sun rays, hills 2.75 2.25
*Nos. 1329-1332 (4)* 6.35 5.25

Souvenir Sheet

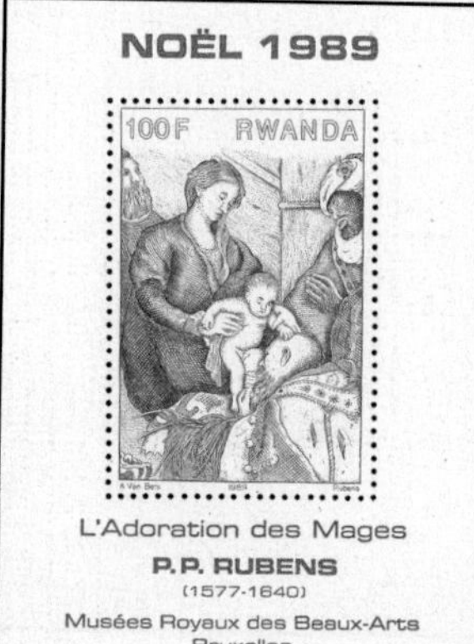


Christmas — A197

Adoration of the Magi by Rubens.

**1989, Dec. 29** **Engr.** ***Perf. 11½***
**1333** A197 100fr blk, red & grn 6.75 6.75

Rural Organization Year — A198

Designs: 10fr, Making pottery. 70fr, Carrying produce to market. 90fr, Firing clay pots. 100fr, Clearing land.

**1989, Dec. 29** **Litho.** ***Perf. 13½x13***
**1334** A198 10fr multi .45 .25
**1335** A198 70fr multi, vert. 1.80 1.50
**1336** A198 90fr multi 2.25 2.00
**1337** A198 200fr multi 5.50 4.75
*Nos. 1334-1337 (4)* 10.00 8.50

Revolution, 30th Anniv. (in 1989) — A199

Designs: 10fr, Improved living conditions. 60fr, Couple, farm tools. 70fr, Modernization. 100fr, Flag, map, native.

**1990, Jan. 22** ***Perf. 13***
**1338** A199 10fr multi .30 .30
**1339** A199 60fr multi, vert. 1.50 1.25
**1340** A199 70fr multi 1.70 1.75
**1341** A199 100fr multi 3.00 2.50
*Nos. 1338-1341 (4)* 6.50 5.80

Inscribed 1989.

French Revolution, Bicent. (in 1989) — A200

Paintings of the Revolution: 10fr, Triumph of Marat by Boilly. 60fr, Rouget de Lisle singing La Marseillaise by Pils. 70fr, Oath of the Tennis Court by David. 100fr, Trial of Louis XVI by Court.

**1990, Jan. 22**
**1342** A200 10fr multicolored .40 .40
**1343** A200 60fr multicolored 2.00 2.00
**1344** A200 70fr multicolored 2.25 2.25
**1345** A200 100fr multicolored 4.00 4.00
*Nos. 1342-1345 (4)* 8.65 8.65

Inscribed 1989.

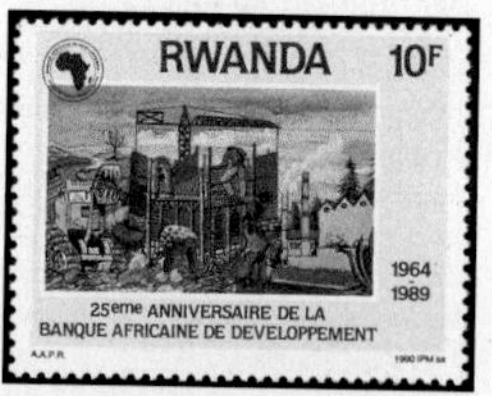


African Development Bank, 25th Anniv. (in 1989) — A201

**1990, Feb. 22** ***Perf. 13½x13***
**1346** A201 10fr Building construction .45 .25
**1347** A201 20fr Harvesting .80 .75
**1348** A201 40fr Cultivation 1.50 1.00
**1349** A201 90fr Building, truck, harvesters 3.25 2.50
*Nos. 1346-1349 (4)* 6.00 4.50

Belgica '90, Intl. Philatelic Exhibition — A202

No. 1350, Great Britain #1. No. 1351, Belgium #B1011. No. 1352, Rwanda #516.

**1990, May 21** **Litho.** ***Imperf.***
**1350** A202 100fr multi 4.25 4.25
**1351** A202 100fr multi 4.25 4.25
**1352** A202 100fr multi 4.25 4.25
*Nos. 1350-1352 (3)* 12.75 12.75

Visit of Pope John Paul II A203

**1990, Aug. 27** **Litho.** ***Perf. 13½x13***
**1353** A203 10fr shown 2.25 2.25
**1354** A203 70fr Holding crucifix 12.75 12.75

**Souvenir Sheet**

***Perf. 11½***

**1355** A203 100fr Hands together 17.50 17.50

No. 1355 contains one 36x51mm stamp.

Intl. Literacy Year A204

Designs: 10fr, Teacher at blackboard. 20fr, Teacher seated at desk. 50fr, Small outdoor class. 90fr, Large outdoor class.

**1991, Jan. 25** **Litho.** ***Perf. 13½x13***
**1356** A204 10fr multicolored .50 .25
**1357** A204 20fr multicolored .75 .40
**1358** A204 50fr multicolored 1.75 1.25
**1359** A204 90fr multicolored 3.25 1.75
*Nos. 1356-1359 (4)* 6.25 3.65

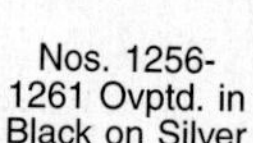

Nos. 1256-1261 Ovptd. in Black on Silver

**1990, May 25** **Litho.** ***Perf. 13***
**1360** A179 2fr on No. 1256 *1.50 1.50*
**1361** A179 4fr on No. 1257 *2.00 2.00*
**1362** A179 5fr on No. 1258 *2.50 2.50*
**1363** A179 10fr on No. 1259 *4.50 4.50*
**1364** A179 40fr on No. 1260 *12.50 12.50*
**1365** A179 45fr on No. 1261 *15.00 15.00*
*Nos. 1360-1365 (6)* *38.00 38.00*

Self-help Organizations — A205

No. 1366, Tool making. No. 1367, Animal husbandry. No. 1368, Textile manufacturing. No. 1369, Road construction.

**1991, Jan. 25** **Litho.** ***Perf. 13½x13***
**1366** A205 10fr multicolored .60 .30
**1367** A205 20fr multicolored 1.25 .60
**1368** A205 50fr multicolored 2.00 1.25
**1369** A205 90fr multicolored 4.00 2.50
*Nos. 1366-1369 (4)* 7.85 4.65

Dated 1990.

A206

5fr, Statue of Madonna. 15fr, One of the Order's nuns. 70fr, Group photo, vert. 110fr, Cardinal Lavigerie.

**1992, Oct. 1** **Litho.** ***Perf. 14***
**1370** A206 5fr multi, vert. 1.75 1.75
**1371** A206 15fr multi, vert. 6.25 6.25
**1372** A206 70fr multi 20.00 20.00
**1373** A206 110fr multi, vert. 37.50 37.50
*Nos. 1370-1373 (4)* 65.50 65.50

Cardinal Lavigerie, Founder of the Order of White Fathers and Sisters, Death Cent.

1992 Summer Olympic Games, Barcelona — A207

Designs: a, 20fr, Runners. b, 30fr, Swimmer. c, 90fr, Soccer players.

**1993, Feb. 1**
**1374** A207 Sheet of 3, #a.-c. 40.00 40.00

Protection of Vegetable Crops A208

Designs: 10fr, Removing parasites and weeds. 15fr, Spraying pesticides. 70fr, Zonocerus elegans on plants. 110fr, Phenacoccus manihoti.

**1993, June 15** **Litho.** ***Perf. 14***
**1375** A208 10fr multi 5.00 5.00
**1376** A208 15fr multi 8.50 8.50
**1377** A208 70fr multi 37.50 37.50
**1378** A208 110fr multi 62.50 62.50
*Nos. 1375-1378 (4)* 113.50 113.50

World Conference on Nutrition, Rome — A209

Designs: 15fr, Man fishing. 50fr, People at fruit market. 100fr, Man milking cow. 500fr, Mother breastfeeding.

**1992, Dec. Litho. *Perf. 14***

**1381** A209 15fr multicolored 1.25 1.25
**1382** A209 50fr multicolored 4.00 4.00
**1383** A209 100fr multicolored 6.50 6.50
**1384** A209 500fr multicolored 40.00 40.00
*Nos. 1381-1384 (4)* 51.75 51.75

Wildlife A210

**1998 Litho. *Perf. 14***

**1385** A210 15fr Toad 3.00 3.00
**1386** A210 100fr Snail 5.00 5.00
**1387** A210 150fr Porcupine 6.00 6.00
**1388** A210 300fr Chameleon 8.00 8.00
*a.* Souvenir sheet, #1385-1388, Imperf. 24.00 24.00
*Nos. 1385-1388 (4)* 22.00 22.00

Plants A211

15fr, Opuntia. 100fr, Gloriosa superba. 150fr, Markhamia lutea. 300fr, Hagenia abyssinica.

**1998 Litho. *Perf. 14***

**1389** A211 15fr multi, vert. 3.00 3.00
**1390** A211 100fr multi, vert. 5.00 5.00
**1391** A211 150fr multi, vert. 6.00 6.00
**1392** A211 300fr multi 8.00 8.00
*a.* Souvenir sheet, #1389-1392, imperf. 26.00 26.00
*Nos. 1389-1392 (4)* 22.00 22.00

Remembrance of Genocide Victims — A212

20fr, Map, coffins, horiz. 30fr, Orphans, horiz. 400fr, People protesting.

**1999 (?) Litho. *Perf. 14***

**1392B** A212 20fr multi *1.50 1.50*
**1392C** A212 30fr multi *2.50 2.50*
**1393** A212 200fr multi *11.50 11.50*
**1394** A212 400fr multi *20.00 20.00*

Rwandan postal officials have declared "illegal" sets depicting: Millennium (eleven sheets of 9 with various subjects), Pornography (two sheets of 9), Chess (sheet of 9 unoverprinted, and also overprinted in Russian), Double-decker buses (sheet of 9), Butterflies (sheet of 9), Hot air balloons (sheet of 9), Old automobiles (sheet of 9), Motorcycle racing (sheet of 9), Trains (sheet of 9), Fungi (sheet of 6), Cats (sheet of 6), Roses (sheet of 6).

Sheet of six stamps of various values depicting Wildlife Trusts (Snakes).

Souvenir sheet of two 500fr stamps depicting Mother Teresa.

Souvenir sheet of one 500fr stamp depicting Wildlife Trusts (Snakes).

AIDS Prevention for Children A213

AIDS Prevention for Children — A214

Designs: 20fr, Children, red ribbon, tree. 30fr, Red ribbon, hands, children, vert. 200fr, Children, hand, red ribbon.

***Perf. 13½x13¾, 13¾x13½***
**2003, Jan. 1 Litho.**

**1395** A213 20fr multi — —
**1396** A213 30fr multi — —
**1397** A214 200fr multi — —
**1398** A214 500fr multi — —

Art and Culture — A215

Designs: 34fr, Two dancers. 300fr, People dancing. 500fr, Basket weaving. 600fr, Face looking through torn fabric. 1000fr, Containers, horiz.

***Perf. 13¾x13¼, 13¼x13¾***
**2010, Nov. 15 Litho.**

**1399** A215 34fr multi *2.10 2.10*
**1400** A215 300fr multi *4.25 4.25*
**1401** A215 500fr multi *8.50 8.50*
**1402** A215 600fr multi *11.00 11.00*
**1403** A215 1000fr multi *19.00 19.00*

Mountain Gorilla — A216

Design: 30fr, Gorilla and foliage. 40fr, Adults and juveniles. 2000fr, Side view of gorilla. 5000fr, Gorilla sitting in front of trees.

***Perf. 13¼x13¾***
**2010, Nov. 15 Litho.**

**1404** A216 30fr multi *1.60 1.60*
**1405** A216 40fr multi *2.10 2.10*
**1406** A216 2000fr multi *25.00 25.00*
**1407** A216 5000fr multi *50.00 50.00*

## SEMI-POSTAL STAMPS

**No. 305 Srchd. in Black and Ovptd. in Brown: "SECHERESSE/SOLIDARITE AFRICAINE"**

**1973, Aug. 23 Photo. *Perf. 13***

**B1** A53 100fr + 50fr multi 4.50 4.50

African solidarity in drought emergency.

**Nos. 349-350 Srchd. and Ovptd. Like Nos. 693-698**

**1975, Nov. 10 Litho. *Perf. 13***

**B2** A60 50fr + 25fr multi 1.85 1.60
**B3** A60 90fr + 25fr multi 2.45 2.25

African solidarity in drought emergency.

## AIR POST STAMPS

**African Postal Union Issue, 1967**
Common Design Type

**1967, Sept. 18 Engr. *Perf. 13***

**C1** CD124 6fr brn, rose cl & gray .30 .25
**C2** CD124 18fr brt lil, ol brn & plum .55 .35
**C3** CD124 30fr grn, dp bl & red 1.20 .65
*Nos. C1-C3 (3)* 2.05 1.25

**PHILEXAFRIQUE Issue**

Alexandre Lenoir, by Jacques L. David AP1

**1968, Dec. 30 Photo. *Perf. 12½***

**C4** AP1 100fr emerald & multi 3.00 1.75

Issued to publicize PHILEXAFRIQUE, Philatelic exhibition in Abidjan, Feb. 14-23, 1969. Printed with alternating emerald label.

**2nd PHILEXAFRIQUE Issue**

Ruanda-Urundi No. 123, Cowherd and Lake Victoria — AP2

**1969, Feb. 14 Litho. *Perf. 14***

**C5** AP2 50fr multicolored 1.75 1.25

Opening of PHILEXAFRIQUE, Abidjan, 2/14.

**Painting Type of Regular Issue**

Paintings and Music: 50fr, The Music Lesson, by Fragonard. 100fr, Angels' Concert, by Memling, horiz.

**1969, Mar. 31 Photo. *Perf. 13***

**C6** A49 50fr gold & multi 1.50 1.25
**C7** A49 100fr gold & multi 3.00 2.50

**African Postal Union Issue, 1971**
Common Design Type

Design: Woman and child of Rwanda and UAMPT Building, Brazzaville, Congo.

**1971, Nov. 13 *Perf. 13x13½***

**C8** CD135 100fr blue & multi 2.75 2.50

**No. C8 Overprinted in Red**

a

b

**1973, Sept. 17 Photo. *Perf. 13x13½***

**C9** CD135(a) 100fr multi 4.50 4.50
**C10** CD135(b) 100fr multi 4.50 4.50
*a.* Pair, #C9-C10 11.00 11.00

3rd Conference of French-speaking countries, Liège, Sept. 15-Oct. 14. Overprints alternate checkerwise in same sheet.

Sassenage Castle, Grenoble — AP3

**1977, June 20 Litho. *Perf. 12½***

**C11** AP3 50fr multi 2.00 1.25

Intl. French Language Council, 10th anniv.

**Philexafrique II-Essen Issue**
Common Design Types

Designs: No. C12, Okapi, Rwanda #239. No. C13, Woodpecker, Oldenburg #4.

**1978, Nov. 1 Litho. *Perf. 12½***

**C12** CD138 30fr multi 1.50 1.50
**C13** CD139 30fr multi 1.50 1.50
*a.* Pair, #C12-C13 4.00 4.00

# SAAR

'sär

LOCATION — On the Franco-German border southeast of Luxembourg
POP. — 1,400,000 (1959)
AREA — 991 sq. mi.
CAPITAL — Saarbrücken

A former German territory, the Saar was administered by the League of Nations 1920-35. After a January 12, 1935, plebiscite, it returned to Germany, and the use of German stamps was resumed. After World War II, France occupied the Saar and later established a protectorate. The provisional semi-independent State of Saar was established Jan. 1, 1951. France returned the Saar to the German Federal Republic Jan. 1, 1957.

Saar stamps were discontinued in 1959 and replaced by stamps of the German Federal Republic.

100 Pfennig = 1 Mark
100 Centimes = 1 Franc (1921)

**Catalogue values for unused stamps in this country are for Never Hinged items, beginning with Scott 221 in the regular postage section, and Scott B85 in the semi-postal section.**

**Watermark**

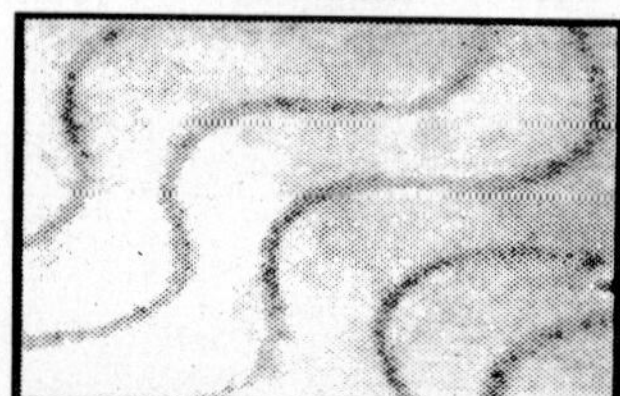

Wmk. 285 — Marbleized Pattern

German Stamps of 1906-19 Overprinted

***Perf. 14, 14½***

**1920, Jan. 30 Wmk. 125**

1 A22 2pf gray 1.60 *4.50*
c. Inverted overprint 325.00 *550.00*
d. Double overprint 2,000. *2,600.*
1A A16 2pf blue gray (ovptd. on Germany #80) *8,500.*
2 A22 2½pf gray 9.50 *27.50*
c. Inverted overprint 350.00 *650.00*
3 A16 3pf brown 1.00 *2.75*
c. Inverted overprint 325.00 *550.00*
4 A16 5pf deep green .50 *1.00*
c. Inverted overprint 600.00 —
f. Double overprint 800.00 *1,450.*
5 A22 7½pf orange .65 *1.75*
c. Inverted overprint — 800.00
6 A16 10pf carmine .55 *1.25*
c. Inverted overprint 550.00 *1,050.*
d. Double overprint 725.00 *1,200.*
7 A22 15pf dk violet .50 *1.00*
c. Double overprint 800.00 *1,450.*
8 A16 20pf blue violet .50 *1.00*
c. Double overprint 600.00 *950.00*
9 A16 25pf red org & blk, *yellow* 9.50 20.00
c. Inverted overprint 800.00 *2,400.*
10 A16 30pf org & blk, *yel buff* 17.50 *35.00*
11 A22 35pf red brown .55 *1.25*
c. Inverted overprint 475.00 *1,050.*
12 A16 40pf dp lake & blk .55 *1.25*
c. Inverted overprint 475.00 *1,050.*
13 A16 50pf pur & blk, *yel buff* .55 *1.60*
c. Inverted overprint 400.00 *725.00*
14 A16 60pf dp gray lilac .55 *1.25*
15 A16 75pf green & blk .55 *1.25*
c. Inverted overprint 240.00 *400.00*
16 A16 80pf lake & blk, *rose* 190.00 *275.00*

Overprinted

**Type I**

17 A17 1m carmine rose 27.50 *40.00*
a. Inverted overprint 725.00 *1,450.*
b. Double overprint 800.00 *1,450.*

**Type II**

17f A17 1m carmine rose 40.00 *80.00*
*Nos. 1-17 (17)* 262.05 417.35

Three types of overprint exist on Nos. 1-5, 12, 13; two types on Nos. 6-11, 14-16. For detailed listings, see the *Scott Classic Specialized Catalogue.*

The 3m type A19 exists overprinted like No. 17, but was not issued. Values: unused $16,000; never hinged $33,000.

Overprint forgeries exist.

Bavarian Stamps of 1914-16 Overprinted

***Perf. 14x14½***

**1920, Mar. 1 Wmk. 95**

19 A10 2pf gray *900.00* *4,750.*
20 A10 3pf brown 80.00 *650.00*
21 A10 5pf yellow grn .75 *1.60*
a. Double overprint 800.00
22 A10 7½pf green 32.50 *275.00*
23 A10 10pf carmine rose .75 *1.60*
a. Double overprint 325.00 *650.00*
24 A10 15pf vermilion .95 *1.90*
a. Double overprint 400.00 *800.00*
25 A10 15pf carmine 7.25 *16.00*
26 A10 20pf blue .65 *1.60*
a. Double overprint 325.00 *650.00*
27 A10 25pf gray 11.00 *16.00*
28 A10 30pf orange 6.50 *11.00*
30 A10 40pf olive green 10.50 *16.00*
31 A10 50pf red brown 2.00 *4.50*
a. Double overprint 350.00 *650.00*
32 A10 60pf dark green 3.25 *8.00*

Overprinted

***Perf. 11½***

35 A11 1m brown 24.00 *35.00*
a. 1m dark brown 16.00 *32.50*
36 A11 2m dk gray violet 60.00 *140.00*
37 A11 3m scarlet 120.00 *160.00*
*Nos. 35-37 (3)* 204.00 *335.00*

Overprinted

38 A12 5m deep blue 800.00 *875.00*
39 A12 10m yel grn 140.00 *250.00*

Nos. 19, 20 and 22 were not officially issued, but were available for postage. Examples are known legitimately used on cover. The 20m type A12 was also overprinted in small quantity. Values: unused $125,000; never hinged $200,000.

No. 21a is valued without gum.

Overprint forgeries exist.

German Stamps of 1906-20 Overprinted

***Perf. 14, 14½***

**1920, Mar. 26 Wmk. 125**

41 A16 5pf green .25 *.50*
a. Inverted overprint 16.00 *160.00*
42 A16 5pf red brown .50 .80
43 A16 10pf carmine .25 *.50*
a. Inverted overprint 47.50 *325.00*
44 A16 10pf orange .45 .50
a. Inverted overprint 16.00
45 A22 15pf dk violet .25 *.50*
a. Inverted overprint 27.50 *240.00*
46 A16 20pf blue violet .25 *.50*
a. Inverted overprint 35.00 —
47 A16 20pf green .95 .50
a. Double overprint, never hinged 80.00
48 A16 30pf org & blk, *buff* .40 *.50*
a. Double overprint 65.00
b. Inverted overprint —
49 A16 30pf dull blue .55 *.75*
50 A16 40pf lake & blk .30 *.50*
51 A16 40pf car rose 1.00 *.75*
52 A16 50pf pur & blk, *buff* .55 .50
a. Double overprint 65.00 *400.00*
53 A16 60pf red violet .65 .50
a. Inverted overprint 80.00 *325.00*
54 A16 75pf green & blk .75 .50
a. Double overprint 110.00 *400.00*
b. Inverted overprint 110.00
55 A17 1.25m green 2.75 1.25
a. Inverted overprint 95.00
56 A17 1.50m yellow brn 2.00 1.25
a. Inverted overprint 95.00 800.00
57 A21 2.50m lilac red 4.75 *13.50*
58 A16 4m black & rose 8.75 *22.50*
a. Double overprint 110.00
*Nos. 41-58 (18)* 25.35 *46.30*

On No. 57 the overprint is placed vertically at each side of the stamp.

No. 58a is valued never hinged.

Counterfeit overprints exist.

Germany No. 90 Surcharged in Black

**1921, Feb.**

65 A16 20pf on 75pf grn & blk .40 *1.25*
a. Inverted surcharge 24.00 *72.50*
b. Double surcharge 55.00 *125.00*

Germany No. 120 Surcharged

66 A22 5m on 15pf vio brn 5.50 *16.00*
67 A22 10m on 15pf vio brn 6.00 *19.00*
*Nos. 65-67 (3)* 11.90 *36.25*

Forgeries exist of Nos. 66-67.

Old Mill near Mettlach — A3

Miner at Work — A4

Entrance to Reden Mine — A5

Saar River Traffic — A6

Saar River near Mettlach — A7

Slag Pile at Völklingen — A8

Signal Bridge, Saarbrücken — A9

Church at Mettlach — A10

"Old Bridge," Saarbrücken A11

Cable Railway at Ferne — A12

Colliery Shafthead — A13

Saarbrücken City Hall — A14

Pottery at Mettlach — A15

St. Ludwig's Cathedral — A16

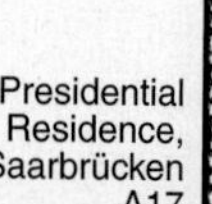

Presidential Residence, Saarbrücken A17

Burbach Steelworks, Dillingen A18

**1921 Unwmk. Typo. *Perf. 12½***

68 A3 5pf ol grn & vio .35 *.50*
a. Tête bêche pair 3.50 *20.00*
c. Center inverted 100.00 *340.00*
69 A4 10pf org & ultra .35 *.50*
70 A5 20pf grn & slate .35 *1.00*
a. Tête bêche pair 6.50 *40.00*
c. Perf. 10½ 22.50 *225.00*
d. As "c," tête bêche pair 140.00 *675.00*
71 A6 25pf brn & dk bl .40 *.80*
a. Tête bêche pair 7.25 *40.00*

**72** A7 30pf gray grn & brn .40 *.75*
*a.* Tête bêche pair 12.00 *60.00*
*c.* 30pf ol grn & blk 2.40 *22.50*
*d.* As "c," tête bêche pair 12.50 *72.50*
*e.* As "c," imperf., pair 120.00
**73** A8 40pf vermilion .40 .50
*a.* Tête bêche pair 19.00 *80.00*
**74** A9 50pf gray & blk .95 *4.00*
**75** A10 60pf red & dk brn 1.60 *3.50*
**76** A11 80pf deep blue .75 *1.00*
*a.* Tête bêche pair 21.00 *110.00*
**77** A12 1m lt red & blk .80 *1.60*
*a.* 1m grn & blk *450.00*
**78** A13 1.25m lt brn & dk grn .95 *2.00*
**79** A14 2m red & blk 2.40 *4.00*
**80** A15 3m brn & dk ol 3.25 *9.50*
*a.* Center inverted 125.00
**81** A16 5m yel & vio 12.00 *24.00*
**82** A17 10m grn & red brn 12.00 *24.00*
**83** A18 25m ultra, red & blk 32.50 *80.00*
*Nos. 68-83 (16)* 69.45 *157.65*

Values for tête bêche pairs are for vertical pairs. Horizontal pairs sell for about twice as much.

The ultramarine ink on No. 69 appears to be brown where it overlays the orange.

Exist imperf but were not regularly issued. Value $1,400. (hinged).

### Nos. 70-83 Surcharged in Red, Blue or Black

a

b

c



**1921, May 1**

**85** A5(a) 3c on 20pf (R) .40 *.50*
*a.* Tête bêche pair 4.75 *32.50*
*b.* Inverted surcharge 95.00
*d.* Perf. 10½ 4.75 *160.00*
*e.* As "d," tête bêche pair 21.00 —
**86** A6(a) 5c on 25pf (R) .40 *.50*
*a.* Tête bêche pair 95.00 *400.00*
**87** A7(a) 10c on 30pf (Bl) .40 *.50*
*a.* Tête bêche pair 4.75 *25.00*
*b.* Inverted surcharge 95.00 *450.00*
*c.* Double surcharge 95.00 *475.00*
**88** A8(a) 15c on 40pf (Bk) .50 .50
*a.* Tête bêche pair 95.00 *400.00*
*b.* Inverted surcharge 95.00 *450.00*
**89** A9(a) 20c on 50pf (R) .40 *.50*
**90** A10(a) 25c on 60pf (Bl) .50 .50
**91** A11(a) 30c on 80pf (Bk) 1.60 1.00
*a.* Tête bêche pair 12.50 *60.00*
*c.* Inverted surcharge 140.00 *600.00*
*d.* Double surcharge *140.00* *600.00*
**92** A12(a) 40c on 1m (Bl) 2.00 .50
*a.* Inverted surcharge 110.00 *450.00*
*b.* Double surcharge 140.00 *600.00*
**93** A13(a) 50c on 1.25m (Bk) 3.25 1.00
*a.* Double surcharge *275.00* *950.00*
*b.* Perf. 10½ 72.50 *140.00*
**94** A14(a) 75c on 2m (Bl) 4.75 2.00
*a.* Inverted surcharge 110.00
**95** A15(b) 1fr on 3m (Bl) 4.50 2.40
**96** A16(b) 2fr on 5m (Bl) 12.00 6.50
**97** A17(b) 3fr on 10m (Bk) 17.50 *25.00*
*b.* Double surcharge 200.00 *800.00*
**98** A18(c) 5fr on 25m (Bl) 17.50 *35.00*
*Nos. 85-98 (14)* 65.70 *76.40*

In these surcharges the period is occasionally missing and there are various wrong font and defective letters.

Values for tête bêche pairs are for vertical pairs. Horizontal pairs sell for about twice as much.

Nos. 85-89, 91, 93, 97-98 exist imperforate but were not regularly issued.

Cable Railway, Ferne — A19

Miner at Work — A20

"Old Bridge," Saarbrücken A21

Saarbrücken City Hall — A22

Slag Pile at Völklingen A23

Pottery at Mettlach — A24

Saar River Traffic — A25

St. Ludwig's Cathedral A26

Colliery Shafthead A27

Mettlach Church — A28

Burbach Steelworks, Dillingen A29

***Perf. 12½x13½, 13½x12½***

**1922-23** **Typo.**

**99** A19 3c ol grn & straw .40 *.65*
**100** A20 5c orange & blk .40 .40
**101** A21 10c blue green .40 .40
**102** A19 15c deep brown 1.25 .40
**103** A19 15c orange ('23) 2.40 .40
**104** A22 20c dk bl & lem 13.50 .40
**105** A22 20c brt bl & straw ('23) 4.00 .40
**106** A22 25c red & yellow 6.50 2.25
**107** A22 25c mag & straw ('23) 2.40 .40
**108** A23 30c carmine & yel 2.00 2.10
**109** A24 40c brown & yel 1.60 .40
**110** A25 50c dk bl & straw .95 .40
**111** A24 75c dp grn & straw 13.50 *24.00*
**112** A24 75c blk & straw ('23) 32.50 3.25
**113** A26 1fr brown red 2.40 .80
**114** A27 2fr deep violet 6.50 3.25
**115** A28 3fr org & dk grn 24.00 6.50
**116** A29 5fr brn & red brn 24.00 *45.00*
*Nos. 99-116 (18)* 138.70 *91.40*

Nos. 99-116 exist imperforate but were not regularly issued.

For overprints see Nos. O1-O15.

Madonna of Blieskastel — A30

**1925, Apr. 9 Photo.** ***Perf. 13½x12½***

**Size: 23x27mm**

**118** A30 45c lake brown 2.75 *5.25*

**Size: 31½x36mm**

***Perf. 12***

**119** A30 10fr black brown 16.00 *24.00*

Nos. 118-119 exist imperforate but were not regularly issued.

For overprint see No. 154.

Market Fountain, St. Johann — A31

View of Saar Valley A32

Colliery Shafthead A35

Burbach Steelworks A36

Designs: 15c, 75c, View of Saar Valley. 20c, 40c, 90c, Scene from Saarlouis fortifications. 25c, 50c, Tholey Abbey.

**1927-32** ***Perf. 13½***

**120** A31 10c deep brown .75 .50
**121** A32 15c olive black .40 *1.10*
**122** A32 20c brown org .40 *.50*
**123** A32 25c bluish slate .75 .50
**124** A31 30c olive green .95 .50
**125** A32 40c olive brown .75 .50
**126** A32 50c magenta .95 .50
**127** A35 60c red org ('30) 4.00 .55
**128** A32 75c brown violet .75 .50
**129** A35 80c red orange 2.40 *8.75*
**130** A32 90c dp red ('32) 12.00 *17.50*
**131** A35 1fr violet 2.40 .50
**132** A36 1.50fr sapphire 6.50 .50
**133** A36 2fr brown red 6.50 .50
**134** A36 3fr dk olive grn 14.50 1.25
**135** A36 5fr deep brown 14.50 7.25
*Nos. 120-135 (16)* 68.50 *41.40*

For surcharges and overprints see Nos. 136-153, O16-O26.

Nos. 126 and 129 Surcharged

**1930-34**

**136** A32 40c on 50c mag ('34) 1.60 *1.60*
**137** A35 60c on 80c red orange 2.00 *2.40*

### Plebiscite Issue

Stamps of 1925-32 Ovptd. in Various Colors

**1934, Nov. 1** ***Perf. 13½***

**139** A31 10c brown (Br) .40 *.55*
**140** A32 15c black grn (G) .40 *.55*
**141** A32 20c brn org (O) .65 *1.40*
**142** A32 25c bluish sl (Bl) .65 *1.40*
**143** A31 30c olive grn (G) .40 *.55*
**144** A32 40c olive brn (Br) .40 *.75*
**145** A32 50c magenta (R) .75 *1.40*
**146** A35 60c red orange (O) .65 *.55*
**147** A32 75c brown vio (V) .75 *1.25*
**148** A32 90c deep red (R) .75 *1.40*
**149** A35 1fr violet (V) .75 *1.60*
**150** A36 1.50fr sapphire (Bl) 1.25 *3.25*
**151** A36 2fr brn red (R) 2.00 *4.75*
**152** A36 3fr dk ol grn (G) 4.75 *9.50*
**153** A36 5fr dp brn (Br) 20.00 *32.50*

**Size: 31½x36mm**

***Perf. 12***

**154** A30 10fr blk brn (Br) 24.00 *60.00*
*Nos. 139-154 (16)* 58.55 *121.40*

### French Administration

Miner A37

Steel Workers A38

Harvesting Sugar Beets — A39

Mettlach Abbey — A40

Marshal Ney — A41

Saar River near Mettlach A42

**1947 Unwmk. Photo. *Perf. 14***

| | | | | |
|---|---|---|---|---|
| **155** | A37 | 2pf gray | .25 | *.40* |
| **156** | A37 | 3pf orange | .25 | *.50* |
| **157** | A37 | 6pf dk Prus grn | .25 | *.40* |
| **158** | A37 | 8pf scarlet | .25 | *.35* |
| **159** | A37 | 10pf rose violet | .25 | *.40* |
| **160** | A38 | 15pf brown | .25 | *6.50* |
| **161** | A38 | 16pf ultra | .25 | *.40* |
| **162** | A38 | 20pf brown rose | .25 | *.40* |
| **163** | A38 | 24pf dp brown org | .25 | *.40* |
| **164** | A39 | 25pf cerise | .25 | *22.50* |
| **165** | A39 | 30pf lt olive grn | .25 | *.80* |
| **166** | A39 | 40pf orange brn | .25 | *1.20* |
| **167** | A39 | 50pf blue violet | .25 | *22.50* |
| **168** | A40 | 60pf violet | .25 | *22.50* |
| **169** | A40 | 80pf dp orange | .25 | *.40* |
| **170** | A41 | 84pf brown | .25 | *.40* |
| **171** | A42 | 1m gray green | .25 | *.50* |
| | | *Nos. 155-171 (17)* | 4.25 | *80.55* |
| | | Set, never hinged | 5.50 | |

Nos. 155-162, 164-171 exist imperf.

**Types of 1947**

**1947 Wmk. 285**

| | | | | |
|---|---|---|---|---|
| **172** | A37 | 12pf olive green | .25 | *.40* |
| **173** | A39 | 45pf crimson | .25 | *16.00* |
| **174** | A40 | 75pf brt blue | .25 | *.40* |
| | | *Nos. 172-174 (3)* | .75 | *16.80* |
| | | Set, never hinged | 1.00 | |

Nos. 172-174 exist imperf.

Types of 1947 Surcharged in Black or Red

**Printing II**

**1947, Nov. 27 Unwmk.**

| | | | | |
|---|---|---|---|---|
| **175** | A37 | 10c on 2pf gray | .25 | *.55* |
| **176** | A37 | 60c on 3pf org | .25 | *1.10* |
| **177** | A37 | 1fr on 10pf rose vio | .25 | *.55* |
| **178** | A37 | 2fr on 12pf ol grn, wmk. 285 | .25 | *1.50* |
| **179** | A38 | 3fr on 15pf brn | .25 | *1.50* |
| **180** | A38 | 4fr on 16pf ultra | .25 | *8.00* |
| **181** | A38 | 5fr on 20pf brn rose | .25 | *1.10* |
| **182** | A38 | 6fr on 24pf dp brn org | .25 | *.65* |
| **183** | A39 | 9fr on 30pf lt ol grn | .25 | *13.50* |
| **184** | A39 | 10fr on 50pf bl vio (R) | .25 | *20.00* |
| **185** | A40 | 14fr on 60pf vio | .25 | *13.50* |
| **186** | A41 | 20fr on 84pf brn | .35 | *21.00* |
| **187** | A42 | 50fr on 1m gray grn | .50 | *21.00* |
| | | *Nos. 175-187 (13)* | 3.60 | *103.95* |
| | | Set, never hinged | 5.50 | |

**Printing I**

| | | | | |
|---|---|---|---|---|
| *175a* | A37 | 10c on 2pf gray | 35.00 | *360.00* |
| *176a* | A37 | 60c on 3pf org | 29.00 | *800.00* |
| *177a* | A37 | 1fr on 10pf rose vio | 2.40 | *16.00* |
| *178a* | A37 | 2fr on 12pf ol grn, wmk. 285 | .75 | *4.00* |
| *179a* | A38 | 3fr on 15pf brn | 350.00 | *2,400.* |
| *180a* | A38 | 4fr on 16pf ultra | 7.25 | *110.00* |
| *181a* | A38 | 5fr on 20pf brn rose | 80.00 | *4,750.* |
| *182a* | A38 | 6fr on 24pf dp brn org | .25 | *4.75* |
| *183a* | A39 | 9fr on 30pf lt ol grn | 45.00 | *800.00* |
| *184a* | A39 | 10fr on 50pf bl vio (R) | 550.00 | *4,750.* |
| *185a* | A40 | 14fr on 60pf violet | 87.50 | *950.00* |
| *186a* | A41 | 20fr on 84pf brn | 2.00 | *8.00* |
| *187a* | A42 | 50fr on 1m gray grn | 55.00 | *350.00* |
| | | *Nos. 175a-187a (13)* | 1,244. | 15,303. |
| | | Set, never hinged | 2,800. | |

Printing I was surcharged on Nos. 155-171, which was printed on yellowish paper with brownish gum. The crossbar of the A's in SAAR is high on the 10c, 60c, 1fr, 2fr, 9fr and 10fr; numeral "1" has no base serif on the 3fr and 4fr, 5fr, 6fr; 14fr, 14fr, wide space between vignette and SAAR panel; 1m inscribed "1M."

Printing II was surcharged on a special printing of the basic stamps, on white paper with white gum, and with details of design that differ on each denomination. The "A" crossbar is low on 10c, 60c, 1fr, 2fr, 9fr, 10fr; numeral "1" has base serif on 3fr, 4fr, 5fr, 6fr; 14fr, narrow space between vignette and SAAR panel; 20fr, minor retouches; 1m inscribed "1SM."

Inverted surcharges exist on Nos. 175-187 and 175a-187a.

## French Protectorate

Clasped Hands — A43

Colliery Shafthead — A44

2fr, 3fr, Worker. 4fr, 5fr, Girl gathering wheat. 6fr, 9fr, Miner. 14fr, Smelting. 20fr, Reconstruction. 50fr, Mettlach Abbey portal.

***Perf. 14x13, 13***

**1948, Apr. 1 Engr. Unwmk.**

| | | | | |
|---|---|---|---|---|
| **188** | A43 | 10c henna brn | .35 | *2.00* |
| **189** | A43 | 60c dk Prus grn | .35 | *2.00* |
| **190** | A43 | 1fr brown blk | .25 | *.30* |
| **191** | A43 | 2fr rose car | .25 | *.30* |
| **192** | A43 | 3fr black brn | .25 | *.30* |
| **193** | A43 | 4fr red | .25 | *.30* |
| **194** | A43 | 5fr red violet | .25 | *.30* |
| **195** | A43 | 6fr henna brown | .35 | *.30* |
| **196** | A43 | 9fr dk Prus grn | 2.00 | *.50* |
| **197** | A44 | 10fr dark blue | 1.25 | *.80* |
| **198** | A44 | 14fr dk vio brn | 1.60 | 1.10 |
| **199** | A44 | 20fr henna brn | 3.25 | 1.10 |
| **200** | A44 | 50fr blue blk | 6.50 | 2.75 |
| | | *Nos. 188-200 (13)* | 16.90 | 12.05 |
| | | Set, never hinged | 35.00 | |

Map of the Saar A45

**1948, Dec. 15 Photo. *Perf. 13½x13***

| | | | | |
|---|---|---|---|---|
| **201** | A45 | 10fr dark red | .75 | *4.00* |
| **202** | A45 | 25fr deep blue | 1.25 | *8.00* |
| | | Set, never hinged | 4.75 | |

French Protectorate establishment, 1st anniv.

Caduceus, Microscope, Bunsen Burner and Book — A46

**1949, Apr. 2 *Perf. 13x13½***

| | | | | |
|---|---|---|---|---|
| **203** | A46 | 15fr carmine | 2.75 | .50 |
| | | Never hinged | 7.25 | |

Issued to honor Saar University.

Ludwig van Beethoven A47

Laborer Using Spade A51

Saarbrücken — A52

Designs: 10c, Building trades. 1fr, 3fr, Gears, factories. 5fr, Dumping mine waste. 6fr, 15fr, Coal mine interior. 8fr, Communications symbols. 10fr, Emblem of printing. 12fr, 18fr, Pottery. 25fr, Blast furnace worker. 45fr, Rock formation "Great Boot." 60fr, Reden Colliery, Landsweiler. 100fr, View of Weibelskirchen.

**1949-51 Unwmk. *Perf. 13x13½***

| | | | | |
|---|---|---|---|---|
| **204** | A47 | 10c violet brn | .25 | *2.00* |
| **205** | A47 | 60c gray ('51) | .25 | *2.00* |
| **206** | A47 | 1fr carmine lake | .50 | .35 |
| **207** | A47 | 3fr brown ('51) | 3.25 | .40 |
| **208** | A47 | 5fr dp violet ('50) | .80 | .35 |
| **209** | A47 | 6fr Prus grn ('51) | 4.75 | .40 |
| **210** | A47 | 8fr olive grn ('51) | .50 | .65 |
| **211** | A47 | 10fr orange ('50) | 2.00 | .35 |
| **212** | A47 | 12fr dk green | 6.50 | .35 |
| **213** | A47 | 15fr red ('50) | 2.75 | .35 |
| **214** | A47 | 18fr brn car ('51) | 1.25 | *5.25* |

***Perf. 13½***

| | | | | |
|---|---|---|---|---|
| **215** | A51 | 20fr gray ('50) | .80 | .35 |
| **216** | A51 | 25fr violet blue | 9.50 | .35 |
| **217** | A52 | 30fr red brown ('51) | 6.50 | .50 |
| **218** | A52 | 45fr rose lake ('51) | 1.60 | .55 |
| **219** | A51 | 60fr deep grn ('51) | 3.25 | 2.00 |
| **220** | A51 | 100fr brown | 4.75 | 2.40 |
| | | *Nos. 204-220 (17)* | 49.20 | *18.60* |
| | | Set, never hinged | 125.00 | |

**Catalogue values for unused stamps in this section, from this point to the end of the section, are for Never Hinged items.**

Peter Wust — A54

**1950, Apr. 3**

| | | | | |
|---|---|---|---|---|
| **221** | A54 | 15fr carmine rose | 12.50 | 7.25 |

Wust (1884-1940), Catholic philosopher.

St. Peter — A55

**1950, June 29 Engr. *Perf. 13***

| | | | | |
|---|---|---|---|---|
| **222** | A55 | 12fr deep green | 3.25 | *10.00* |
| **223** | A55 | 15fr red brown | 4.75 | *9.50* |
| **224** | A55 | 25fr blue | 8.00 | *21.00* |
| | | *Nos. 222-224 (3)* | 16.00 | *40.50* |

Holy Year, 1950.

Street in Ottweiler — A56

**1950, July 10 Photo. *Perf. 13x13½***

| | | | | |
|---|---|---|---|---|
| **225** | A56 | 10fr orange brown | 6.00 | *8.00* |

Founding of Ottweiler, 400th anniv.

Symbols of the Council of Europe A57

**1950, Aug. 8 *Perf. 13½***

| | | | | |
|---|---|---|---|---|
| **226** | A57 | 25fr deep blue | 35.00 | 12.00 |

Issued to commemorate the Saar's admission to the Council of Europe. See No. C12.

Post Rider and Guard — A62

**1951, Apr. 29 Engr. *Perf. 13***

| | | | | |
|---|---|---|---|---|
| **227** | A62 | 15fr dk violet brn | 8.75 | *19.00* |

Issued to publicize Stamp Day, 1951.

"Agriculture and Industry" and Fair Emblem — A63

**1951, May 12 Photo. *Perf. 13x13½***

| | | | | |
|---|---|---|---|---|
| **228** | A63 | 15fr dk gray grn | 2.75 | *6.50* |

1951 Fair at Saarbrücken.

Tower of Mittelbexbach and Flowers — A67

**1951, June 9 Engr. *Perf. 13***

| | | | | |
|---|---|---|---|---|
| **229** | A67 | 15fr dark green | 2.75 | 1.75 |

Exhibition of Gardens & Flowers, Bexbach, 1951.

Refugees — A68

**1952, May 2 Unwmk. *Perf. 13***

| | | | | |
|---|---|---|---|---|
| **230** | A68 | 15fr bright red | 3.50 | 1.40 |

Issued to honor the Red Cross.

Globe & Stylized Fair Building — A69

**1952, Apr. 26**

| | | | | |
|---|---|---|---|---|
| **231** | A69 | 15fr red brown | 2.50 | 1.40 |

1952 Fair at Saarbrücken.

Mine Shafts A70

Ludwig's Gymnasium A71

General Post Office A72

Reconstruction of St. Ludwig's Cathedral — A73

3fr, 18fr, Bridge building. 6fr, Transporter bridge, Mettlach. 30fr, Saar University Library.

**1952-55** **Engr.**

| | | | | |
|---|---|---|---|---|
| **232** | A70 | 1fr dk bl grn ('53) | .25 | .25 |
| **233** | A71 | 2fr purple ('53) | .25 | .25 |
| **234** | A72 | 3fr dk car rose ('53) | .25 | .25 |
| **235** | A72 | 5fr dk grn (no inscription) | 4.75 | .25 |
| **236** | A72 | 5fr dk grn ("Hauptpostamt Saarbrücken") ('54) | .25 | .25 |
| **237** | A72 | 6fr vio brn ('53) | .40 | .25 |
| **238** | A71 | 10fr brn ol ('53) | .40 | .25 |
| **239** | A72 | 12fr green ('53) | .75 | .25 |
| **240** | A70 | 15fr blk brn (no inscription) | 8.00 | .25 |
| **241** | A70 | 15fr blk brn ("Industrie-Landschaft") ('53) | 3.50 | .25 |
| **242** | A70 | 15fr dp car ('55) | .35 | .25 |
| **243** | A72 | 18fr dk rose brn ('55) | 2.75 | *4.75* |
| **244** | A72 | 30fr ultra ('53) | .95 | *.95* |
| **245** | A73 | 500fr brn car ('53) | 16.00 | *65.00* |
| | | *Nos. 232-245 (14)* | 38.85 | *73.45* |

For overprints see Nos. 257-259.

"SM" Monogram — A74

**1953, Mar. 23**

| | | | | |
|---|---|---|---|---|
| **246** | A74 | 15fr dark ultra | 2.10 | 1.60 |

1953 Fair at Saarbrücken.

Bavarian and Prussian Postilions A75

**1953, May 3**

| | | | | |
|---|---|---|---|---|
| **247** | A75 | 15fr deep blue | 6.75 | *13.00* |

Stamp Day.

Fountain and Fair Buildings — A76

**1954, Apr. 10**

| | | | | |
|---|---|---|---|---|
| **248** | A76 | 15fr deep green | 2.10 | .95 |

1954 International Fair at Saarbrücken.

Post Coach and Post Bus of 1920 — A77

**1954, May 9** **Engr.**

| | | | | |
|---|---|---|---|---|
| **249** | A77 | 15fr red | 9.50 | *13.50* |

Stamp Day, May 9, 1954.

Madonna and Child, Holbein A78

Designs: 10fr, Sistine Madonna, Raphael. 15fr, Madonna and Child with pear, Durer.

**1954, Aug. 14**

| | | | | |
|---|---|---|---|---|
| **250** | A78 | 5fr deep carmine | 2.40 | *3.25* |
| **251** | A78 | 10fr dark green | 2.40 | *3.25* |
| **252** | A78 | 15fr dp violet bl | 3.25 | *5.50* |
| | | *Nos. 250-252 (3)* | 8.05 | *12.00* |

Centenary of the promulgation of the Dogma of the Immaculate Conception.

Cyclist and Flag — A79

**1955, Feb. 28** **Photo.** ***Perf. 13x13½***

| | | | | |
|---|---|---|---|---|
| **253** | A79 | 15fr multicolored | .40 | *.75* |

World championship cross country bicycle race.

Symbols of Industry and Rotary Emblem — A80

**1955, Feb. 28**

| | | | | |
|---|---|---|---|---|
| **254** | A80 | 15fr orange brown | .40 | *.95* |

Rotary International, 50th anniversary.

Flags of Participating Nations — A81

**1955, Apr. 18** **Photo.** ***Perf. 13x13½***

| | | | | |
|---|---|---|---|---|
| **255** | A81 | 15fr multicolored | .40 | *.75* |

1955 International Fair at Saarbrücken.

Postman at Illingen A82

**Unwmk.**

**1955, May 8** **Engr.** ***Perf. 13***

| | | | | |
|---|---|---|---|---|
| **256** | A82 | 15fr deep claret | 2.00 | *2.40* |

Issued to publicize Stamp Day, 1955.

**Nos. 242-244 Overprinted "VOLKSBEFRAGUNG 1955"**

**1955, Oct. 22**

| | | | | |
|---|---|---|---|---|
| **257** | A70 | 15fr deep carmine | .45 | *.70* |
| **258** | A72 | 18fr dk rose brn | .45 | *.55* |
| **259** | A72 | 30fr ultra | .65 | *.70* |
| | | *Nos. 257-259 (3)* | 1.55 | *1.95* |

Plebiscite, Oct. 23, 1955.

Symbols of Industry and the Fair — A83

**1956, Apr. 14** **Photo.** ***Perf. 11½***

| | | | | |
|---|---|---|---|---|
| **260** | A83 | 15fr dk brn red & yel grn | .40 | *.95* |

Intl. Fair at Saarbrücken, Apr. 14-29, 1956.

Radio Tower, Saarbrücken — A84

**1956, May 6** **Granite Paper**

| | | | | |
|---|---|---|---|---|
| **261** | A84 | 15fr grn & grnsh bl | .40 | *.95* |

Stamp Day.

**German Administration**

Arms of Saar — A85

***Perf. 13x13½***

**1957, Jan. 1** **Litho.** **Wmk. 304**

| | | | | |
|---|---|---|---|---|
| **262** | A85 | 15fr brick red & blue | .25 | *.40* |

Return of the Saar to Germany.

Pres. Theodor Heuss — A86

**1957** **Typo.** ***Perf. 14***

**Size: 18x22mm**

| | | | | |
|---|---|---|---|---|
| **263** | A86 | 1(fr) brt green | .25 | .25 |
| **264** | A86 | 2(fr) brt violet | .25 | .25 |
| **265** | A86 | 3(fr) bister brown | .25 | .25 |
| **266** | A86 | 4(fr) red violet | .35 | *.80* |
| **267** | A86 | 5(fr) lt olive green | .25 | .25 |
| **268** | A86 | 6(fr) vermilion | .25 | *.50* |
| **269** | A86 | 10(fr) gray | .25 | *.35* |
| **270** | A86 | 12(fr) deep orange | .25 | .25 |
| **271** | A86 | 15(fr) lt blue green | .25 | .25 |
| **272** | A86 | 18(fr) carmine rose | .65 | *2.40* |
| **273** | A86 | 25(fr) brt lilac | .45 | *.80* |

**Engr.**

| | | | | |
|---|---|---|---|---|
| **274** | A86 | 30(fr) pale purple | .45 | *.80* |
| **275** | A86 | 45(fr) gray olive | 1.10 | *2.75* |
| **276** | A86 | 50(fr) violet brn | 1.10 | *1.25* |
| **277** | A86 | 60(fr) dull rose | 1.60 | *3.25* |
| **278** | A86 | 70(fr) red orange | 2.90 | *4.75* |
| **279** | A86 | 80(fr) olive green | .95 | *3.75* |
| **280** | A86 | 90(fr) dark gray | 2.75 | *6.50* |

**Size: 24x29mm**

| | | | | |
|---|---|---|---|---|
| **281** | A86 | 100(fr) dk carmine | 2.40 | *8.00* |
| **282** | A86 | 200(fr) violet | 6.50 | *25.00* |
| | | *Nos. 263-282 (20)* | 23.20 | *62.40* |

See Nos. 289-308.

Steel Industry — A87

*Perf. 13x13½*

**1957, Apr. 20 Litho. Wmk. 304**

**284** A87 15fr gray & magenta .25 *.40*

The 1957 Fair at Saarbrücken.

Merzig Arms and St. Peter's Church — A88

**1957, May 25** ***Perf. 14***

**285** A88 15fr blue .25 *.40*

Centenary of the town of Merzig.

"United Europe" — A89

**Lithographed; Tree Embossed**

***Perf. 14x13½***

**1957, Sept. 16 Unwmk.**

**286** A89 20fr orange & yel .40 *1.00*
**287** A89 35fr violet & pink .95 *1.20*

Europa, publicizing a united Europe for peace and prosperity.

Carrier Pigeons — A90

**Wmk. 304**

**1957, Oct. 5 Litho.** ***Perf. 14***

**288** A90 15fr dp carmine & blk .25 *.40*

Intl. Letter Writing Week, Oct. 6-12.

**Redrawn Type of 1957; "F" added after denomination**

**1957 Wmk. 304 Litho.** ***Perf. 14***

**Size: 18x22mm**

| | | | | |
|---|---|---|---|---|
| **289** | A86 | 1fr gray green | .25 | *.25* |
| **290** | A86 | 3fr blue | .25 | *.25* |
| **291** | A86 | 5fr olive | .25 | *.25* |
| **292** | A86 | 6fr lt brown | .25 | *.50* |
| **293** | A86 | 10fr violet | .25 | *.25* |
| **294** | A86 | 12fr brown org | .25 | *.25* |
| **295** | A86 | 15fr dull green | .40 | *.25* |
| **296** | A86 | 18fr gray | 2.00 | *4.75* |
| **297** | A86 | 20fr lt olive grn | 1.25 | *3.25* |
| **298** | A86 | 25fr orange brn | .40 | *.40* |
| **299** | A86 | 30fr rose lilac | .95 | *.40* |
| **300** | A86 | 35fr brown | 2.40 | *3.25* |
| **301** | A86 | 45fr lt blue grn | 2.00 | *4.00* |
| **302** | A86 | 50fr dk red brown | .95 | *2.00* |
| **303** | A86 | 70fr brt green | 4.75 | *5.50* |
| **304** | A86 | 80fr chalky blue | 2.40 | *5.25* |
| **305** | A86 | 90fr rose carmine | 5.50 | *6.50* |

**Engr.**

**Size: 24x29mm**

| | | | | |
|---|---|---|---|---|
| **306** | A86 | 100fr orange | 5.50 | *7.25* |
| **307** | A86 | 200fr brt green | 8.75 | *25.00* |
| **308** | A86 | 300fr blue | 9.50 | *29.00* |
| | | *Nos. 289-308 (20)* | 48.25 | *98.55* |

"Max and Moritz" — A91

Design: 15fr, Wilhelm Busch.

*Perf. 13½x13*

**1958, Jan. 9 Litho. Wmk. 304**

**309** A91 12fr lt ol grn & blk .25 *.25*
**310** A91 15fr red & black .25 *.40*

Death of Wilhelm Busch, humorist, 50th anniv.

"Prevent Forest Fires" — A92

**1958, Mar. 5** ***Perf. 14***

**311** A92 15fr brt red & blk .25 *.40*

Issued to aid in the prevention of forest fires.

Rudolf Diesel A93

**1958, Mar. 18 Engr.**

**312** A93 12fr dk blue grn .25 *.40*

Centenary of the birth of Rudolf Diesel, inventor.

Fair Emblem and City Hall, Saarbrücken A94

**1958, Apr. 10 Litho.** ***Perf. 14***

**313** A94 15fr dull rose .25 *.40*

1958 Fair at Saarbrücken.

View of Homburg A95

**1958, June 14 Engr. Wmk. 304**

**314** A95 15fr gray green .25 *.40*

400th anniversary of Homburg.

Turner Emblem — A96

**1958, July 21 Litho.** ***Perf. 13½x14***

**315** A96 12fr gray, blk & dl grn .25 *.40*

150 years of German Gymnastics and the 1958 Gynastic Festival.

Herman Schulze-Delitzsch A97

**1958, Aug. 29 Engr. Wmk. 304**

**316** A97 12fr yellow green .25 *.40*

150th anniv. of the birth of Schultze-Delitzsch, founder of German trade organizations.

Common Design Types pictured following the introduction.

**Europa Issue, 1958**

Common Design Type

**1958, Sept. 13 Litho.**

**Size: 24½x30mm**

**317** CD1 12fr yellow grn & bl .45 *.80*
**318** CD1 30fr lt blue & red .60 *1.50*

Issued to show the European Postal Union at the service of European integration.

Jakob Fugger — A98

***Perf. 13x13½***

**1959, Mar. 6 Wmk. 304**

**319** A98 15fr dk red & blk .25 *.40*

500th anniv. of the birth of Jakob Fugger the Rich, businessman and banker.

Old and New City Hall and Burbach Mill — A99

**1959, Apr. 1 Engr.** ***Perf. 14x13½***

**320** A99 15fr light blue .25 *.40*

Greater Saarbrucken, 50th anniversary

Hands Holding Merchandise A100

**1959, Apr. 1 Litho.**

**321** A100 15fr deep rose .25 *.40*

1959 Fair at Saarbrucken.

Alexander von Humboldt — A101

**1959, May 6 Engr.** ***Perf. 13½x14***

**322** A101 15fr blue .40 *.50*

Cent. of the death of Alexander von Humboldt, naturalist and geographer.

## SEMI-POSTAL STAMPS

Red Cross Dog Leading Blind Man — SP1

Maternity Nurse with Child — SP4

Designs: No. B2, Nurse and invalid. No. B3, Children getting drink at spring.

*Perf. 13½*

**1926, Oct. 25 Photo. Unwmk.**

| | | | | |
|---|---|---|---|---|
| **B1** | SP1 | 20c + 20c dk ol grn | 8.00 | *20.00* |
| **B2** | SP1 | 40c + 40c dk brn | 8.00 | *20.00* |
| **B3** | SP1 | 50c + 50c red org | 8.00 | *20.00* |
| **B4** | SP4 | 1.50fr + 1.50fr brt bl | 19.00 | *47.50* |
| | | *Nos. B1-B4 (4)* | 43.00 | *107.50* |

Nos. B1-B4 Overprinted

**1927, Oct. 1**

| | | | | |
|---|---|---|---|---|
| **B5** | SP1 | 20c + 20c dk ol grn | 12.50 | *35.00* |
| **B6** | SP1 | 40c + 40c dk brn | 12.50 | *35.00* |
| **B7** | SP1 | 50c + 50c red org | 11.00 | *32.50* |
| **B8** | SP4 | 1.50fr + 1.50fr brt bl | 17.50 | *72.50* |
| | | *Nos. B5-B8 (4)* | 53.50 | *175.00* |

"The Blind Beggar" by Dyckmans SP5

"Almsgiving" by Schiestl SP6

"Charity" by Raphael — SP7

**1928, Dec. 23 Photo.**

| | | | | |
|---|---|---|---|---|
| **B9** | SP5 | 40c (+40c) blk brn | 12.00 | *72.50* |
| **B10** | SP5 | 50c (+50c) brn rose | 12.00 | *72.50* |
| **B11** | SP5 | 1fr (+1fr) dl vio | 12.00 | *72.50* |
| **B12** | SP6 | 1.50fr (+1.50fr) cob bl | 12.00 | *72.50* |
| **B13** | SP6 | 2fr (+2fr) red brn | 14.00 | *100.00* |
| **B14** | SP6 | 3fr (+3fr) dk ol grn | 14.00 | *135.00* |
| **B15** | SP7 | 10fr (+10fr) dk brn | 360.00 | *4,000.* |
| | | *Nos. B9-B15 (7)* | 436.00 | *4,525.* |

"Orphaned" by Kaulbach SP8

"St. Ottilia" by Feuerstein SP9

"Madonna" by Ferruzzio — SP10

**1929, Dec. 22**

**B16** SP8 40c (+15c) ol grn 2.00 *5.50*
**B17** SP8 50c (+20c) cop red 4.00 *9.50*
**B18** SP8 1fr (+50c) vio brn 4.00 *11.00*
**B19** SP9 1.50fr (+75c) Prus bl 4.00 *11.00*
**B20** SP9 2fr (+1fr) brn car 4.00 *11.00*
**B21** SP9 3fr (+2fr) sl grn 8.00 *25.00*
**B22** SP10 10fr (+8fr) blk brn 47.50 *135.00*
*Nos. B16-B22 (7)* 73.50 *208.00*

"The Safety-Man" SP11

"The Good Samaritan" SP12

"In the Window" — SP13

**1931, Jan. 20**

**B23** SP11 40c (+15c) dk org brn 8.00 *24.00*
**B24** SP11 60c (+20c) dk org red 8.00 *24.00*
**B25** SP12 1fr (+50c) mag 8.00 *47.50*
**B26** SP11 1.50fr (+75c) sapphire 8.00 *47.50*
**B27** SP12 2fr (+1fr) dk org brn 8.00 *47.50*
**B28** SP12 3fr (+2fr) ol grn 20.00 *47.50*
**B29** SP13 10fr (+10fr) dk org brn 95.00 *290.00*
*Nos. B23-B29 (7)* 155.00 *528.00*

St. Martin of Tours — SP14

Nos. B33-B35, Charity. No. B36, The Widow's Mite.

**1931, Dec. 23**

**B30** SP14 40c (+15c) dp brn 12.50 *35.00*
**B31** SP14 60c (+20c) ver 12.50 *35.00*
**B32** SP14 1fr (+50c) dk redsh brn 16.00 *55.00*
**B33** SP14 1.50fr (+75c) sapphire 19.00 *55.00*
**B34** SP14 2fr (+1fr) dp red 22.50 *55.00*
**B35** SP14 3fr (+2fr) ol grn 27.50 *95.00*
**B36** SP14 5fr (+5fr) red brn 95.00 *325.00*
*Nos. B30-B36 (7)* 205.00 *655.00*

Ruins at Kirkel — SP17

Illingen Castle, Kerpen SP23

Designs: 60c, Church at Blie. 1fr, Castle Ottweiler. 1.50fr, Church of St. Michael, Saarbrucken. 2fr, Statue of St. Wendel. 3fr, Church of St. John, Saarbrucken.

**1932, Dec. 20**

**B37** SP17 40c (+15c) dp brn 9.50 *22.50*
**B38** SP17 60c (+20c) dk org red 9.50 *22.50*
**B39** SP17 1fr (+50c) dp pur 14.00 *40.00*
**B40** SP17 1.50fr (+75c) ol grn 20.00 *47.50*
**B41** SP17 2fr (+1fr) dp red 20.00 *55.00*
**B42** SP17 3fr (+2fr) ol grn 55.00 *175.00*
**B43** SP23 5fr (+5fr) red brn 125.00 *290.00*
*Nos. B37-B43 (7)* 253.00 *652.50*

Scene of Neunkirchen Disaster — SP24

**1933, June 1**

**B44** SP24 60c (+ 60c) org red 16.00 20.00
**B45** SP24 3fr (+ 3fr) ol grn 35.00 *72.50*
**B46** SP24 5fr (+ 5fr) org brn 35.00 *72.50*
*Nos. B44-B46 (3)* 86.00 *165.00*

The surtax was for the aid of victims of the explosion at Neunkirchen, Feb. 10.

"Love" — SP25

Designs: 60c, "Anxiety." 1fr, "Peace." 1.50fr, "Solace." 2fr, "Welfare." 3fr, "Truth." 5fr, Figure on Tomb of Duchess Elizabeth of Lorraine

**1934, Mar. 15** **Photo.**

**B47** SP25 40c (+15c) blk brn 5.50 *16.00*
**B48** SP25 60c (+20c) red org 5.50 *16.00*
**B49** SP25 1fr (+50c) dl vio 7.25 *20.00*
**B50** SP25 1.50fr (+75c) blue 14.00 *35.00*
**B51** SP25 2fr (+1fr) car rose 12.50 *35.00*
**B52** SP25 3fr (+2fr) ol grn 14.00 *35.00*
**B53** SP25 5fr (+5fr) red brn 32.50 *87.50*
*Nos. B47-B53 (7)* 91.25 *244.50*

**Nos. B47-B53 Overprinted like Nos. 139-154 in Various Colors Reading up**

**1934, Dec. 1** ***Perf. 13x13½***

**B54** SP25 40c (+15c) (Br) 3.50 *14.00*
**B55** SP25 60c (+20c) (R) 3.50 *14.00*
**B56** SP25 1fr (+50c) (V) 11.00 *25.00*
**B57** SP25 1.50fr (+75c) (Bl) 7.25 *25.00*
**B58** SP25 2fr (+1fr) (R) 11.00 *35.00*
**B59** SP25 3fr (+2fr) (G) 10.00 *32.50*
**B60** SP25 5fr (+5fr) (Br) 15.00 *40.00*
*Nos. B54-B60 (7)* 61.25 *185.50*

**French Protectorate**

SP32

Various Flood Scenes — SP33

**Inscribed "Hochwasser-Hilfe 1947-48"**

***Perf. 13½x13, 13x13½***

**1948, Oct. 12** **Photo.**

**B61** SP32 5fr + 5fr dl grn 2.25 *35.00*
**B62** SP33 6fr + 4fr dk vio 2.25 *32.50*
**B63** SP32 12fr + 8fr red 3.00 *47.50*
**B64** SP33 18fr + 12fr bl 4.00 *47.50*
*a.* Souv. sheet of 4, #B61-B64, imperf. 325.00 *2,750.*
*Nos. B61-B64,CB1 (5)* 22.50 *402.50*
Set, never hinged 47.50

The surtax was for flood relief.

Hikers and Ludweiler Hostel SP34

No. B66, Hikers approaching Weisskirchen Hostel.

**1949, Jan. 11** ***Perf. 13½x13***

**B65** SP34 8fr + 5fr dk brn 1.00 *105.00*
**B66** SP34 10fr + 7fr dk grn 1.40 *105.00*
Set, never hinged 8.00

The surtax aided youth hostels.

Mare and Foal SP35

Design: No. B68, Jumpers.

**1949, Sept. 25** ***Perf. 13½***

**B67** SP35 15fr + 5fr brn red 5.50 *32.50*
**B68** SP35 25fr + 15fr blue 6.75 *35.00*
Set, never hinged 27.50

Day of the Horse, Sept. 25, 1949.

Detail from "Moses Striking the Rock" — SP36

No. B70, "Christ at the Pool of Bethesda." No. B71, "The Sick Child." No. B72, "St. Thomas of Villeneuve." No. B73, Madonna of Blieskastel.

**1949, Dec. 20** **Engr.** ***Perf. 13***

**B69** SP36 8fr + 2fr indigo 3.50 *40.00*
**B70** SP36 12fr + 3fr dk grn 4.00 *47.50*
**B71** SP36 15fr + 5fr brn lake 6.00 *80.00*
**B72** SP36 25fr + 10fr dp ultra 10.00 *125.00*
**B73** SP36 50fr + 20fr choc 15.00 *225.00*
*Nos. B69-B73 (5)* 38.50 *517.50*
Set, never hinged 87.50

Adolph Kolping — SP37

**1950, Apr. 3** **Photo.** ***Perf. 13x13½***

**B74** SP37 15fr + 5fr car rose 13.00 *80.00*
Never hinged 25.00

Relief for the Hungry — SP38

**Engraved and Typographed**

**1950, Apr. 28** ***Perf. 13***

**B75** SP38 25fr + 10fr dk brn car & red 12.50 *65.00*
Never hinged 27.50

Stagecoach — SP39

**1950, Apr. 22** **Engr.**

**B76** SP39 15fr + 5fr brn red & dk brn 30.00 *110.00*
Never hinged 67.50

Stamp Day, Apr. 27, 1950. Sold at the exhibition and to advance subscribers.

Lutwinus Seeking Admission to Abbey SP40

Designs: 12fr+3fr, Lutwinus Building Mettlach Abbey. 15fr+5fr, Lutwinus as Abbot. 25fr+10fr, Bishop Lutwinus at Rheims. 50fr+20fr, Aid to the poor and sick.

**1950, Nov. 10** **Unwmk.** ***Perf. 13***

**B77** SP40 8fr + 2fr dk brn 4.00 *32.50*
**B78** SP40 12fr + 3fr dk grn 4.00 *32.50*
**B79** SP40 15fr + 5fr red brn 4.25 *52.50*
**B80** SP40 25fr + 10fr blue 6.50 *72.50*
**B81** SP40 50fr + 20fr brn car 9.00 *125.00*
*Nos. B77-B81 (5)* 27.75 *315.00*
Set, never hinged 60.00

The surtax was for public assistance.

Mother and Child — SP41

**1951, Apr. 28**

**B82** SP41 25fr + 10fr dk grn & car 10.00 *65.00*
Never hinged 19.00

The surtax was for the Red Cross.

John Calvin and Martin Luther — SP42

**1951, Oct. 31**
**B83** SP42 15fr + 5fr blk brn 1.60 *7.25*
Never hinged 3.50

Reformation in Saar, 375th anniv.

"Mother" — SP43

15fr+5fr, "Before the Theater." 18fr+7fr, "Sisters of Charity." 30fr+10fr, "The Good Samaritan." 50fr+ 20fr, "St. Martin and Beggar."

**1951, Nov. 3**
**B84** SP43 12fr + 3fr dk grn 3.00 *19.00*
**B85** SP43 15fr + 5fr pur 3.00 *19.00*
**B86** SP43 18fr + 7fr dk red 3.25 *19.00*
**B87** SP43 30fr + 10fr dp bl 5.25 *35.00*
**B88** SP43 50fr + 20fr blk brn 10.50 *72.50*
*Nos. B84-B88 (5)* 25.00 *164.50*
Set, never hinged 50.00

**Catalogue values for unused stamps in this section, from this point to the end of the section, are for Never Hinged items.**

Runner with Torch — SP44

30fr+5fr, Hand with olive branch, and globe.

**1952, Mar. 29 Unwmk. *Perf. 13***
**B89** SP44 15fr + 5fr dp grn 6.00 *12.00*
**B90** SP44 30fr + 5fr dp bl 6.00 *13.50*

XV Olympic Games, Helsinki, 1952.

Postrider Delivering Mail SP45

**1952, Mar. 30**
**B91** SP45 30fr + 10fr dark blue 12.00 *27.50*

Stamp Day, Mar. 29, 1952.

Count Stroganoff as a Boy — SP46

Portraits: 18fr+7fr, The Holy Shepherd by Murillo. 30fr+10fr, Portrait of a Boy by Georg Melchior Kraus.

**1952, Nov. 3**
**B92** SP46 15fr + 5fr dk brn 3.25 *11.00*
**B93** SP46 18fr + 7fr brn lake 4.75 *14.00*
**B94** SP46 30fr + 10fr dp bl 6.50 *16.00*
*Nos. B92-B94 (3)* 14.50 *41.00*

The surtax was for child welfare.

Henri Dunant — SP47

**1953, May 3 Cross in Red**
**B95** SP47 15fr + 5fr blk brn 2.75 *7.25*

Clarice Strozzi by Titian — SP48

Children of Rubens SP49

Portrait: 30fr+10fr, Rubens' son.

**1953, Nov. 16**
**B96** SP48 15fr + 5fr purple 3.25 *5.50*
**B97** SP49 18fr + 7fr dp claret 3.50 *6.00*
**B98** SP48 30fr + 10fr dp ol grn 4.75 *9.50*
*Nos. B96-B98 (3)* 11.50 *21.00*

The surtax was for child welfare.

St. Benedict Blessing St. Maurus — SP50

**1953, Dec. 18 Litho.**
**B99** SP50 30fr + 10fr black 2.50 *8.00*

The surtax was for the abbey at Tholey.

Child and Cross — SP51

**1954, May 10 Engr.**
**B100** SP51 15fr + 5fr chocolate 3.25 *7.25*

The surtax was for the Red Cross.

Street Urchin with Melon, Murillo — SP52

Paintings: 10fr+5fr, Maria de Medici, Bronzino. 15fr+7fr, Baron Emil von Maucler, Dietrich.

**1954, Nov. 15**
**B101** SP52 5fr + 3fr red .95 *1.40*
**B102** SP52 10fr + 5fr dk grn .95 *1.40*
**B103** SP52 15fr + 7fr purple .95 *2.00*
*Nos. B101-B103 (3)* 2.85 *4.80*

The surtax was for child welfare.

Nurse Holding Baby — SP53

***Perf. 13x13½***
**1955, May 5 Photo. Unwmk.**
**B104** SP53 15fr + 5fr blk & red .55 *1.00*

The surtax was for the Red Cross.

Dürer's Mother, Age 63 — SP54

Etchings by Dürer: 10fr+5fr, Praying hands. 15fr+7fr, Old man of Antwerp.

**1955, Dec. 10 Engr. *Perf. 13***
**B105** SP54 5fr + 3fr dk grn .50 *1.25*
**B106** SP54 10fr + 5fr ol grn .80 *1.60*
**B107** SP54 15fr + 7fr ol bis 1.10 *1.90*
*Nos. B105-B107 (3)* 2.40 *4.75*

The surtax was for public assistance.

First Aid Station, Saarbrücken, 1870 — SP55

**1956, May 7**
**B108** SP55 15fr + 5fr dk brn .40 *.95*

The surtax was for the Red Cross.

"Victor of Benevent" — SP56

**1956, July 25 Unwmk. *Perf. 13***
**B109** SP56 12fr + 3fr dk yel grn & bl grn .55 *.75*
**B110** SP56 15fr + 5fr brn vio & brn .55 *.75*

Melbourne Olympics, 11/22-12/8/56.

Winterberg Monument — SP57

**1956, Oct. 29**
**B111** SP57 5fr + 2fr green .30 *.50*
**B112** SP57 12fr + 3fr red lilac .30 *.50*
**B113** SP57 15fr + 5fr brown .30 *.65*
*Nos. B111-B113 (3)* .90 *1.65*

The surtax was for the rebuilding of monuments.

"La Belle Ferronnière" by da Vinci — SP58

Designs: 10fr + 5fr, "Saskia" by Rembrandt. 15fr+7fr, "Family van Berchem," by Frans Floris. (Detail: Woman playing Spinet.)

**1956, Dec. 10**
**B114** SP58 5fr + 3fr deep blue .30 *.30*
**B115** SP58 10fr + 5fr deep claret .30 *.50*
**B116** SP58 15fr + 7fr dark green .30 *.80*
*Nos. B114-B116 (3)* .90 *1.60*

The surtax was for charitable works.

## German Administration

Miner with Drill — SP59

6fr+4fr, Miner. 15fr+7fr, Miner and conveyor. 30fr+10fr, Miner and coal elevator.

**Wmk. 304**
**1957, Oct. 1 Litho. *Perf. 14***
**B117** SP59 6fr + 4fr bis brn & blk .25 *.25*
**B118** SP59 12fr + 6fr blk & yel grn .25 *.35*
**B119** SP59 15fr + 7fr blk & red .35 *.40*
**B120** SP59 30fr + 10fr blk & bl .40 *.75*
*Nos. B117-B120 (4)* 1.25 *1.75*

The surtax was to finance young peoples' study trip to Berlin.

"The Fox who Stole the Goose" — SP60

15fr+7fr, "A Hunter from the Palatinate."

**1958, Apr. 1 Wmk. 304 *Perf. 14***

**B121** SP60 12fr + 6fr brn red, grn & blk .25 *.30*
**B122** SP60 15fr + 7fr grn, red, blk & gray .25 *.40*

The surtax was to finance young peoples' study trip to Berlin.

Friedrich Wilhelm Raiffeisen SP61

Dairy Maid SP62

Designs: 15fr+7fr, Girl picking grapes. 30fr+10fr, Farmer with pitchfork.

**1958, Oct. 1 Wmk. 304 *Perf. 14***

**B123** SP61 6fr + 4fr gldn brn & dk brn .25 .25
**B124** SP62 12fr + 6fr grn, red & yel .25 *.25*
**B125** SP62 15fr + 7fr red, yel & bl .50 *.50*
**B126** SP62 30fr + 10fr bl & ocher .65 *.75*
*Nos. B123-B126 (4)* 1.65 *1.75*

## AIR POST STAMPS

Airplane over Saarbrücken — AP1

***Perf. 13½***

**1928, Sept. 19 Unwmk. Photo.**

**C1** AP1 50c brown red 4.00 4.00
**C2** AP1 1fr dark violet 6.50 4.75

For overprints see Nos. C5, C7.

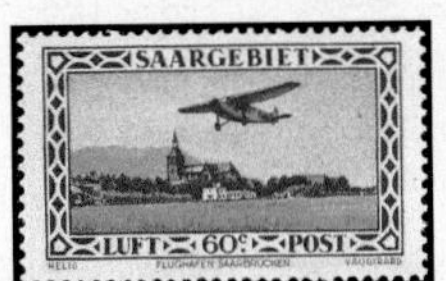


Saarbrücken Airport and Church of St. Arnual — AP2

**1932, Apr. 30**

**C3** AP2 60c orange red 6.50 4.75
**C4** AP2 5fr dark brown 45.00 *95.00*

For overprints see Nos. C6, C8.

**Nos. C1-C4 Overprinted like Nos. 139-154 in Various Colors**

**1934, Nov. 1 *Perf. 13½, 13½x13***

**C5** AP1 50c brn red (R) 4.00 *7.25*
**C6** AP2 60c org red (O) 3.25 *2.75*
**C7** AP1 1fr dk vio (V) 7.25 *9.50*
**C8** AP2 5fr dk brn (Br) 9.50 *14.00*
*Nos. C5-C8 (4)* 24.00 *33.50*

**French Protectorate**

Shadow of Plane over Saar River AP3

**Unwmk.**

**1948, Apr. 1 Engr. *Perf. 13***

**C9** AP3 25fr red 2.00 3.25
**C10** AP3 50fr dk Prus grn 1.25 2.40
**C11** AP3 200fr rose car 12.00 *35.00*
*Nos. C9-C11 (3)* 15.25 *40.65*
Set, never hinged 35.00

Symbols of the Council of Europe AP4

**1950, Aug. 8 Photo. *Perf. 13½***

**C12** AP4 200fr red brown 65.00 *210.00*
Never hinged 140.00

Saar's admission to the Council of Europe.

## AIR POST SEMI-POSTAL STAMP

**French Protectorate**

Flood Scene SPAP1

***Perf. 13½x13***

**1948, Oct. 12 Photo. Unwmk.**

**CB1** SPAP1 25fr + 25fr sep 11.00 *240.00*
Never hinged 24.00
*a.* Souvenir sheet of 1 325.00 *2,700.*
Never hinged 800.00

The surtax was for flood relief.

## OFFICIAL STAMPS

Regular Issue of 1922-1923 Ovptd. Diagonally in Red or Blue

***Perf. 12½x13½, 13½x12½***

**1922-23 Unwmk.**

**O1** A19 3c ol grn & straw (R) .95 *35.00*
**O2** A20 5c org & blk (R) .40 *.40*
*a.* Pair, one without overprint 275.00
**O3** A21 10c bl grn (R) .40 .35
*a.* Inverted overprint 32.50
**O4** A19 15c dp brn (Bl) .40 .35
*a.* Pair, one without overprint 290.00
*b.* Double overprint 65.00
**O5** A19 15c org (Bl) ('23) 2.40 .50
**O6** A22 20c dk bl & lem (R) .40 .35
*a.* Inverted overprint 32.50
*b.* Double overprint 65.00
**O7** A22 20c brt bl & straw (R) ('23) 2.40 .50
**O8** A22 25c red & yel (Bl) 4.00 1.20
**O9** A22 25c mag & straw (Bl) ('23) 2.40 .50
**O10** A23 30c car & yel (Bl) .40 .35
*a.* Inverted overprint 52.50
**O11** A24 40c brn & yel (Bl) .55 .35
**O12** A25 50c dk bl & straw (R) .55 .35
*a.* Inverted overprint 32.50
**O13** A24 75c dp grn & straw (R) 24.00 27.50
**O14** A24 75c blk & straw (R) ('23) 4.75 2.40
**O15c** A26 1fr brn red (Bl) 12.00 2.40
*Nos. O1-O15 (15)* 56.00 *72.50*

The set (Type I) exists imperf. Value, hinged $1850. No. O15c (Type II) exists imperf. Value, hinged $325.

Regular Issue of 1927-30 Overprinted in Various Colors

**1927-34 *Perf. 13½***

**O16** A31 10c dp brn (Bl) ('34) 2.00 2.40
**O17** A32 15c ol blk (Bl) ('34) 2.00 *6.50*
**O18** A32 20c brn org (Bk) ('31) 2.00 1.60
**O19** A32 25c bluish sl (Bl) 2.40 *6.50*
**O20a** A31 30c ol grn (Org red) 2.00 .50
**O21b** A32 40c olive brn (C) 2.00 .35
**O22b** A32 50c mag (Bl) 4.00 .40
**O23** A35 60c red org (Bk) ('30) 1.20 .35
**O24b** A32 75c brn vio (C) 2.40 .80
**O25b** A35 1fr vio (RO) 2.40 .40
**O26b** A26 2fr brn red (Bl) 2.40 .40
*Nos. O16-O26 (11)* 24.80 *20.20*

The overprint exists in two types: at a 32 degree angle, applied to O20-O22, O24-O26 in 1927; and at a 23-25 degree angle, applied to all values 1929/1934. The less expensive varieties are listed. For detailed listings, see the *Scott Classic Specialized Catalogue.*

The overprint on Nos. O16 and O20 is known only inverted. Nos. O21-O26 exist with double overprint.

**French Protectorate**

Arms — O1

**1949, Oct. 1 Engr. *Perf. 14x13***

**O27** O1 10c deep carmine .25 *19.00*
**O28** O1 30c blue black .25 *22.50*
**O29** O1 1fr Prus green .25 1.00
**O30** O1 2fr orange red .55 1.20
**O31** O1 5fr blue .75 1.00
**O32** O1 10fr black .35 1.00
**O33** O1 12fr red violet 3.25 *11.00*
**O34** O1 15fr indigo .35 1.00
**O35** O1 20fr green .75 1.20
**O36** O1 30fr violet rose 3.25 *4.75*
**O37** O1 50fr purple .75 *4.00*
**O38** O1 100fr red brown 32.50 *300.00*
*Nos. O27-O38 (12)* 43.25 *367.65*
Set, never hinged 120.00

# ST. CHRISTOPHER

sānt 'kris-tə-fər

LOCATION — Island in the West Indies, southeast of Puerto Rico
GOVT. — A Presidency of the former Leeward Islands Colony
AREA — 68 sq. mi.
POP. — 18,578 (estimated)
CAPITAL — Basseterre

Stamps of St. Christopher were discontinued in 1890 and replaced by those of Leeward Islands. For later issues, inscribed "St. Kitts-Nevis" or "St. Christopher-Nevis-Anguilla," see St. Kitts-Nevis.

12 Pence = 1 Shilling

Queen Victoria — A1

**Wmk. Crown and C C (1)**

**1870, Apr. 1 Typo. *Perf. 12½***

**1** A1 1p dull rose 95.00 52.50
**2** A1 1p lilac rose 82.50 35.00
**3** A1 6p green ('71) 140.00 8.75
*Nos. 1-3 (3)* 317.50 96.25

**1875-79 *Perf. 14***

**4** A1 1p lilac rose 80.00 8.00
*b.* Half used as ½p on cover (2½p rate) *2,500.*
**5** A1 2½p red brown ('79) 200.00 *275.00*
**6** A1 4p blue ('79) 225.00 16.00
**7** A1 6p green 60.00 6.00
*a.* Horiz. pair, imperf. vert. —
*Nos. 4-7 (4)* 565.00 305.00

For surcharges see Nos. 18-20.

**1882-90 Wmk. Crown and C A (2)**

**8** A1 ½p green 6.75 4.25
**9** A1 1p rose 3.50 2.25
*a.* Half used as ½p on cover —
**10** A1 1p lilac rose 600.00 77.50
*a.* Diagonal half used as ½p on cover —
**11** A1 2½p red brown 200.00 67.50
*a.* 2½p deep red brown 210.00 72.50
**12** A1 2½p ultra ('84) 5.75 2.00
**13** A1 4p blue 550.00 27.50
**14** A1 4p gray ('84) 1.75 1.10
**15** A1 6p olive brn ('90) 95.00 *425.00*
**16** A1 1sh violet ('87) 105.00 75.00
*a.* 1sh bright mauve ('90) 95.00 180.00
*Nos. 8-16 (9)* 1,568. 682.10

For surcharges see Nos. 17, 21-23.

No. 9 Bisected and Handstamp Surcharged in Black

**1885, Mar.**

**17** A1 ½p on half of 1p 29.00 *45.00*
*b.* Inverted surcharge 250.00 125.00
*c.* Unsevered pair 140.00 *140.00*
*d.* As "c," one surcharge inverted 450.00 *325.00*
*e.* Double surcharge — —
*f.* As "b," unsevered pair 1,100.

**No. 7 Surcharged in Black**

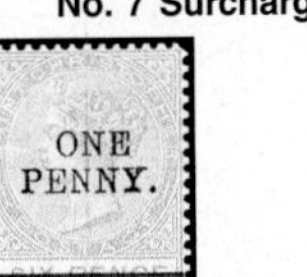


No. 18

No. 19

No. 20

**1884-86 Wmk. 1**

**18** A1 1p on 6p grn ('86) 22.50 *50.00*
*a.* Inverted surcharge 10,000.
*b.* Double surcharge 2,600.
**19** A1 4p on 6p green 75.00 57.50
*a.* Period after "PENCE" 75.00 57.50
*b.* Double surcharge — 3,000.
**20** A1 4p on 6p grn ('86) 60.00 105.00
*a.* Without period after "d" 250.00 325.00
*b.* Double surcharge *2,750.* *3,000.*
*Nos. 18-20 (3)* 157.50 212.50

The line through original value on Nos. 18 and 20 was added by hand. Value for No. 18b is for stamp with pen cancellation or with violet handstamp (revenue cancels).

**Nos. 8 and 12 Surcharged in Black Like No. 18 or**

No. 21

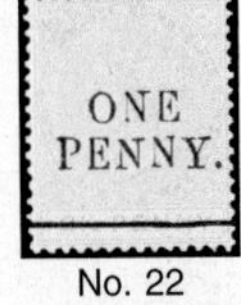


No. 22

**1887-88 Wmk. 2**

**21** A1 1p on ½p green 50.00 *60.00*
**22** A1 1p on 2½p ('88) 72.50 72.50
*a.* Inverted surcharge *27,500.* *11,000.*
**23** A1 1p on 2½p, no line over original value ('88) *22,000.* *15,000.*

Nos. 18 and 21 have the same type of One Penny surcharge. The line through the original value on Nos. 21 and 22 were added by hand. No. 23 probably is a sheet that was meant to be No. 22 but was missed when the bars were added.

Antigua No. 18 was used in St. Christopher in 1890. It is canceled "A12" instead of "A02." Values: used $140, on cover $850.

## POSTAL FISCAL ISSUES

**Nevis Nos. 22 and 28 Overprinted "REVENUE" Horizontally and "Saint Christopher" Diagonally**

**1883**

**AR1** A5 1p violet 425.00
**AR2** A5 6p green 130.00 *170.00*

**Stamps of St. Christopher Ovptd. "SAINT KITTS / NEVIS / REVENUE" in 3 Lines**

**1885**

**AR3** A1 1p rose 3.00 *19.00*
**AR4** A1 3p violet 17.50 *72.50*
**AR5** A1 6p orange brown 22.00 *55.00*
**AR6** A1 1sh olive 4.25 *47.50*

Other values exist with the above overprints but were not available for postal purposes.

## ST. HELENA

sānt 'he-lə-nə

LOCATION — Island in the Atlantic Ocean, 1,200 miles west of Angola
GOVT. — British Crown Colony
AREA — 47 sq. mi.
POP. — 7,145 (?) (1999 est.)
CAPITAL — Jamestown

12 Pence = 1 Shilling
20 Shillings = 1 Pound
100 Pence = 1 Pound (1971)

**Catalogue values for unused stamps in this country are for Never Hinged items, beginning with Scott 128 in the regular postage section, Scott B1 in the semi-postal section and Scott J1 in the postage due section.**

Values for unused stamps are for examples with original gum as defined in the catalogue introduction. Very fine examples of Nos. 2-7, 11-39a and 47-47b will have perforations touching the design on one or more sides due to the narrow spacing of the stamps on the plates. Stamps with perfs clear of the design on all four sides are scarce and will command higher prices.

**Watermark**

Wmk. 6 — Star

Queen Victoria — A1

**1856, Jan. Wmk. 6 Engr. *Imperf.***
**1** A1 6p blue 600.00 225.00

For types surcharged see Nos. 8-39, 47.

**1861 *Clean-Cut Perf. 14 to 15½***
**2** A1 6p blue 2,100. 325.00

**1863 *Rough Perf. 14 to 15½***
**2B** A1 6p blue 525.00 160.00

**1871-74 Wmk. 1 *Perf. 12½***
**3** A1 6p dull blue 900.00 125.00
**4** A1 6p ultra ('73) 575.00 97.50

**1879 *Perf. 14x12½***
**5** A1 6p gray blue 575.00 60.00

**1889 *Perf. 14***
**6** A1 6p gray blue 550.00 60.00

**1889 Wmk. Crown and C A (2)**
**7** A1 6p gray 42.50 6.00

**Type of 1856 Surcharged**

a

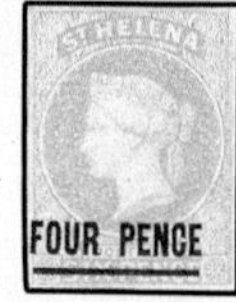


b

**Long Bar, 16, 17, 18 or 19mm**

**1863 Wmk. 1 *Imperf.***
**8** A1(a) 1p on 6p brn red (srch. 17mm) 150.00 *250.00*
*a.* Double surcharge 6,750. 4,250.
*b.* Surcharge omitted *23,000.*
**9** A1(a) 1p on 6p brn red (srch. 19mm) 150.00 *275.00*
**10** A1(b) 4p on 6p car 600.00 300.00
*b.* Double surcharge *16,000.* *10,000.*

**1864-73 *Perf. 12½***
**11** A1(a) 1p on 6p brn red 70.00 35.00
*a.* Double surcharge *12,000.*
**12** A1(b) 1p on 6p brn red ('71) 140.00 21.00
*a.* Blue black surcharge *1,200.* *675.00*
**13** A1(b) 2p on 6p yel ('73) 160.00 50.00
*a.* Blue black surcharge *4,800.* *2,700.*
**14** A1(b) 3p on 6p dk vio ('73) 140.00 72.50
**15** A1(b) 4p on 6p car 175.00 60.00
*a.* Double surcharge *6,750.*
**16** A1(b) 1sh on 6p grn (bar 16 to 17mm) 450.00 35.00
*a.* Double surcharge *24,000.*
**17** A1(b) 1sh on 6p dp grn (bar 18mm) ('73) 750.00 20.00
*a.* Blue black surcharge —

**1868 Short Bar, 14 or 15mm**
**18** A1(a) 1p on 6p brn red 225.00 67.50
*a.* Imperf., pair *6,000.*
*b.* Double surcharge —
**19** A1(b) 2p on 6p yel 200.00 72.50
*a.* Imperf 12,000.
**20** A1(b) 3p on 6p dk vio 120.00 60.00
*a.* Double surcharge 7,250.
*b.* Imperf., pair *2,000.*
*c.* 3p on 6p pale purple 3,300. 900.00
**21** A1(b) 4p on 6p car (words 18mm) 140.00 72.50
*a.* Double surcharge *6,000.*
*b.* Imperf, single 14,500.
**22** A1(b) 4p on 6p car (words 19mm) 325.00 150.00
*a.* Words double, 18mm and 19mm *26,000.* *11,000.*
*b.* Imperf. —
*c.* Surcharge omitted *6,000.*
**23** A1(a) 1sh on 6p yel grn 750.00 160.00
*a.* Double surcharge *19,500.*
*b.* Pair, one without surcharge *19,500.*
*c.* Imperf *17,000.*
**24** A1(a) 5sh on 6p org 67.50 77.50

**1882 *Perf. 14x12½***
**25** A1(a) 1p on 6p brown red 90.00 18.00
**26** A1(b) 2p on 6p yellow 140.00 60.00
**27** A1(b) 3p on 6p violet 350.00 85.00
**28** A1(b) 4p on 6p carmine (words 16½mm) 170.00 72.50

**1883 *Perf. 14***
**29** A1(a) 1p on 6p brown red 120.00 22.50
**30** A1(b) 2p on 6p yellow 150.00 37.50
**31** A1(a) 1sh on 6p yel grn 25.00 15.00

**Long Bar, 18mm**

**1882 *Perf. 14x12½***
**32** A1(b) 1sh on 6p dp grn 900.00 30.00

**Short Bar, 14 or 14½mm**

**1884-94 Wmk. 2 *Perf. 14***
**33** A1(b) ½p on 6p grn (words 17mm) 12.00 22.50
*a.* ½p on 6p emer, blurred print (words 17mm) ('84) 20.00 23.00
*b.* Double surcharge 1,450. 1,575.
**34** A1(b) ½p on 6p grn (words 15mm) ('94) 3.25 3.50
**35** A1(a) 1p on 6p red ('87) 5.75 4.50
**36** A1(b) 2p on 6p yel ('94) 3.25 9.50
**37** A1(b) 3p on 6p dp vio ('87) 9.00 5.00
*a.* 3p on 6p red violet 7.75 *12.00*
*b.* Double surcharge,#37a *11,500.* *7,250.*
*c.* Double surcharge, #37 *11,000.*
**38** A1(b) 4p on 6p pale brn (words 16½mm; '90) 47.50 *42.50*
*a.* 4p on 6p dk brn (words 17mm; '94) 30.00 21.00
*b.* With thin bar below thick one 850.00 850.00

**1894 Long Bar, 18mm**
**39** A1(b) 1sh on 6p yel grn 65.00 30.00
*a.* Double surcharge *5,750.*

See note after No. 47.

Queen Victoria — A3

**1890-97 Typo. *Perf. 14***
**40** A3 ½p green ('97) 3.25 7.75
**41** A3 1p rose ('96) 20.00 2.40
**42** A3 1½p red brn & grn 5.50 15.00
**43** A3 2p yellow ('96) 6.00 14.50
**44** A3 2½p ultra ('96) 18.00 14.50
**45** A3 5p violet ('96) 13.50 37.50
**46** A3 10p brown ('96) 29.00 *72.50*
*Nos. 40-46 (7)* 95.25 *164.15*

Type of 1856 Surcharged

**1893 Engr. Wmk. 2**
**47** A1 2½p on 6p blue 3.75 6.75
*a.* Double surcharge *25,000.*
*b.* Double impression *11,500.*

**In 1905 remainders of Nos. 34-47 were sold by the postal officials. They are canceled with bars, arranged in the shape of diamonds, in purple ink. No such cancellation was ever used on the island and the stamps so canceled are of slight value. With this cancellation removed, these remainders are sometimes offered as unused. Some have been recanceled with a false dated postmark.**

King Edward VII — A5

**1902 Typo. Wmk. 2**
**48** A5 ½p green 2.00 *3.00*
**49** A5 1p carmine rose 13.00 .85

Government House — A6

"The Wharf" — A7

**1903, June Wmk. 1**
**50** A6 ½p gray grn & brn 2.40 4.00
**51** A7 1p carmine & blk 1.90 .50
**52** A6 2p ol grn & blk 14.00 1.50
**53** A7 8p brown & blk 26.50 *37.50*
**54** A6 1sh org buff & brn 27.50 *47.50*
**55** A7 2sh violet & blk 65.00 *100.00*
*Nos. 50-55 (6)* 137.30 *191.00*

A8

**1908, May Wmk. 3**
**56** A8 2½p ultra 2.00 *1.90*
**57** A8 4p black & red, *yel* 8.00 *21.00*
**58** A8 6p dull violet 14.00 *17.00*
*Nos. 56-58 (3)* 24.00 *39.90*

**Wmk. 2**
**60** A8 10sh grn & red, *grn* 275.00 *325.00*

Nos. 57 and 58 exist on both ordinary and chalky paper; No. 56 on ordinary and No. 60 on chalky paper.

Government House — A9

"The Wharf" — A10

**1912-16 Ordinary Paper Wmk. 3**
**61** A9 ½p green & blk 3.25 12.00
**62** A10 1p carmine & blk 5.75 2.00
*a.* 1p scarlet & black ('16) 14.50 *24.00*
**63** A10 1½p orange & blk 4.25 9.00
**64** A9 2p gray & black 7.50 2.00
**65** A10 2½p ultra & blk 4.25 7.25
**66** A9 3p vio & blk, *yel* 4.25 6.00
**67** A10 8p dull vio & blk 12.00 60.00
**68** A9 1sh black, *green* 11.00 42.50
**69** A10 2sh ultra & blk, *bl* 50.00 *100.00*
**70** A10 3sh violet & blk 75.00 *160.00*
*Nos. 61-70 (10)* 177.25 *400.75*

See Nos. 75-77.

King Edward VII — A11

For description of dies I and II see "Dies of British Colonial Stamps" in the front of the catalogue.

**Die I**

**1912 Chalky Paper**
**71** A11 4p black & red, *yel* 15.00 *30.00*
**72** A11 6p dull vio & red vio 4.75 *6.00*

A12

**1913 Ordinary Paper**
**73** A12 4p black & red, *yel* 10.00 3.25
**74** A12 6p dull vio & red vio 16.00 *35.00*

**1922 Wmk. 4**
**75** A10 1p green 3.25 *55.00*
**76** A10 1½p rose red 12.00 *52.50*
**77** A9 3p ultra 25.00 *95.00*
*Nos. 75-77 (3)* 40.25 *202.50*

Badge of the Colony — A13

**1922-27 Chalky Paper Wmk. 4**

| | | | | |
|---|---|---|---|---|
| **79** | A13 | ½p blk & gray | 4.00 | 4.00 |
| **80** | A13 | 1p grn & blk | 4.25 | 2.00 |
| **81** | A13 | 1½p rose red | 3.75 | *15.00* |
| **82** | A13 | 2p pale gray & gray | 4.50 | 2.40 |
| **83** | A13 | 3p ultra | 2.40 | *4.75* |
| **84** | A13 | 5p red & grn, *emer* | 6.50 | *6.75* |
| **85** | A13 | 6p red vio & blk | 7.50 | *9.75* |
| **86** | A13 | 8p vio & blk | 4.50 | *8.50* |
| **87** | A13 | 1sh dk brn & blk | 7.75 | *11.00* |
| **88** | A13 | 1sh6p grn & blk, *emer* | 18.00 | *60.00* |
| **89** | A13 | 2sh ultra & vio, *bl* | 22.50 | *55.00* |
| **90** | A13 | 2sh6p car & blk, *yel* | 17.00 | *77.50* |
| **91** | A13 | 5sh grn & blk, *yel* | 45.00 | *90.00* |
| **92** | A13 | 7sh6p org & blk | 160.00 | *200.00* |
| **93** | A13 | 10sh ol grn & blk | 170.00 | *250.00* |
| **94** | A13 | 15sh vio & blk, *bl* | 1,100. | *2,750.* |
| | | *Nos. 79-93 (15)* | 477.65 | *796.65* |

Nos. 88, 90, and 91 are on ordinary paper.

**Wmk. 3**

**Chalky Paper**

| | | | | |
|---|---|---|---|---|
| **95** | A13 | 4p black, *yel* | 15.00 | *7.25* |
| **96** | A13 | 1sh6p bl grn & blk, *grn* | 26.50 | *72.50* |
| **97** | A13 | 2sh6p car & blk, *yel* | 30.00 | *77.50* |
| **98** | A13 | 5sh grn & blk, *yel* | 50.00 | *120.00* |
| **99** | A13 | £1 red vio & blk, *red* | 475.00 | *700.00* |
| | | *Nos. 95-99 (5)* | 596.50 | *977.25* |

Issue dates: ½p, 1½p, 2p, 3p, 4p, 8p, February, 1923; 5p, Nos. 88-91, 1927; others, June 1922.

**Centenary Issue**

Lot and Lot's Wife — A14

Plantation; Queen Victoria and Kings William IV, Edward VII, George V A15

Map of the Colony A16

Quay, Jamestown A17

View of James Valley — A18

View of Jamestown A19

View of Mundens A20

St. Helena — A21

View of High Knoll — A22

Badge of the Colony A23

*Perf. 12*

**1934, Apr. 23 Engr. Wmk. 4**

| | | | | |
|---|---|---|---|---|
| **101** | A14 | ½p dk vio & blk | 1.25 | *1.00* |
| **102** | A15 | 1p green & blk | .80 | *1.00* |
| **103** | A16 | 1½p red & blk | 3.00 | *4.00* |
| **104** | A17 | 2p orange & blk | 3.75 | *1.50* |
| **105** | A18 | 3p blue & blk | 1.75 | *5.50* |
| **106** | A19 | 6p lt blue & blk | 4.00 | *3.75* |
| **107** | A20 | 1sh dk brn & blk | 8.00 | *22.50* |
| **108** | A21 | 2sh6p car & blk | 50.00 | *60.00* |
| **109** | A22 | 5sh choc & blk | 100.00 | *100.00* |
| **110** | A23 | 10sh red vio & blk | 300.00 | *350.00* |
| | | *Nos. 101-110 (10)* | 472.55 | *549.25* |
| | | Set, never hinged | 800.00 | |

Common Design Types pictured front of this volume.

**Silver Jubilee Issue**

Common Design Type

**1935, May 6** ***Perf. 13½x14***

| | | | | |
|---|---|---|---|---|
| **111** | CD301 | 1½p car & dk blue | 1.25 | *7.25* |
| **112** | CD301 | 2p gray blk & ultra | 2.40 | 1.50 |
| **113** | CD301 | 6p indigo & grn | 8.50 | 4.75 |
| **114** | CD301 | 1sh brt vio & ind | 19.00 | *23.00* |
| | | *Nos. 111-114 (4)* | 31.15 | *36.50* |
| | | Set, never hinged | 52.50 | |

**Coronation Issue**

Common Design Type

**1937, May 19**

| | | | | |
|---|---|---|---|---|
| **115** | CD302 | 1p deep green | .45 | *.90* |
| **116** | CD302 | 2p deep orange | .40 | *.55* |
| **117** | CD302 | 3p bright ultra | .60 | .60 |
| | | *Nos. 115-117 (3)* | 1.45 | 2.05 |
| | | Set, never hinged | 2.00 | |

Badge of the Colony — A24

**1938-40** ***Perf. 12½***

| | | | | |
|---|---|---|---|---|
| **118** | A24 | ½p purple | .25 | .75 |
| **119** | A24 | 1p dp green | 7.00 | 2.40 |
| **119A** | A24 | 1p org yel ('40) | .25 | .30 |
| **120** | A24 | 1½p carmine | .30 | .40 |
| **121** | A24 | 2p orange | .25 | .25 |
| **122** | A24 | 3p ultra | 55.00 | 18.00 |
| **122A** | A24 | 3p gray ('40) | .35 | .30 |
| **122B** | A24 | 4p ultra ('40) | 1.10 | .85 |
| **123** | A24 | 6p gray blue | 1.10 | 1.40 |
| **123A** | A24 | 8p olive ('40) | 1.75 | 1.00 |
| **124** | A24 | 1sh sepia | 1.10 | .35 |
| **125** | A24 | 2sh6p deep claret | 11.00 | 6.75 |
| **126** | A24 | 5sh brown | 11.00 | 12.50 |
| **127** | A24 | 10sh violet | 11.00 | *18.00* |
| | | *Nos. 118-127 (14)* | 101.45 | 63.25 |
| | | Set, never hinged | 160.00 | |

Issue dates: May 12, 1938, July 8, 1940.
See Nos. 136-138.

**Catalogue values for unused stamps in this section, from this point to the end of the section, are for Never Hinged items.**

**Peace Issue**

Common Design Type

***Perf. 13½x14***

**1946, Oct. 21 Wmk. 4 Engr.**

| | | | | |
|---|---|---|---|---|
| **128** | CD303 | 2p deep orange | .30 | .40 |
| **129** | CD303 | 4p deep blue | .35 | .30 |

**Silver Wedding Issue**

Common Design Types

**1948, Oct. 20 Photo.** ***Perf. 14x14½***

| | | | | |
|---|---|---|---|---|
| **130** | CD304 | 3p black | .30 | .30 |

***Perf. 11½x11***

**Engr.; Name Typo.**

| | | | | |
|---|---|---|---|---|
| **131** | CD305 | 10sh blue violet | 32.50 | *42.50* |

**UPU Issue**

Common Design Types

**Engr.; Name Typo. on 4p, 6p**

**1949, Oct. 10** ***Perf. 13½, 11x11½***

| | | | | |
|---|---|---|---|---|
| **132** | CD306 | 3p rose carmine | .30 | 1.00 |
| **133** | CD307 | 4p indigo | 3.50 | 1.60 |
| **134** | CD308 | 6p olive | .65 | *3.25* |
| **135** | CD309 | 1sh slate | .40 | *1.25* |
| | | *Nos. 132-135 (4)* | 4.85 | 7.10 |

**George VI Type of 1938**

**1949, Nov. 1 Engr.** ***Perf. 12½***

**Center in Black**

| | | | | |
|---|---|---|---|---|
| **136** | A24 | 1p blue green | 1.40 | 1.50 |
| **137** | A24 | 1½p carmine rose | 1.40 | 1.50 |
| **138** | A24 | 2p carmine | 1.40 | 1.50 |
| | | *Nos. 136-138 (3)* | 4.20 | 4.50 |

**Coronation Issue**

Common Design Type

**1953, June 2** ***Perf. 13½x13***

| | | | | |
|---|---|---|---|---|
| **139** | CD312 | 3p purple & black | 1.25 | 1.25 |

Badge of the Colony A25

A26

Designs: 1p, Flax plantation. 1½p, Heart-shaped waterfall. 2p, Lace making. 2½p, Drying flax. 3p, Wire bird. 4p, Flagstaff and barn. 6p, Donkeys carrying flax. 7p, Map. 1sh, Entrance, government offices. 2sh 6p, Cutting flax. 5sh, Jamestown. 10sh, Longwood house.

**1953, Aug. 4** ***Perf. 13½x14, 14x13½***

**Center and Denomination in Black**

| | | | | |
|---|---|---|---|---|
| **140** | A25 | ½p emerald | .45 | .30 |
| **141** | A25 | 1p dark green | .25 | .25 |
| **142** | A26 | 1½p red violet | 3.00 | 1.25 |
| **143** | A25 | 2p rose lake | .75 | .30 |
| **144** | A25 | 2½p red | .60 | .30 |
| **145** | A25 | 3p brown | 4.25 | .30 |
| **146** | A25 | 4p deep blue | .60 | .90 |
| **147** | A25 | 6p purple | .60 | .35 |
| **148** | A25 | 7p gray | .95 | 1.60 |
| **149** | A25 | 1sh dk car rose | .60 | .85 |
| **150** | A25 | 2sh 6p violet | 17.00 | 7.25 |
| **151** | A25 | 5sh chocolate | 21.00 | 12.00 |
| **152** | A25 | 10sh orange | 42.50 | 27.00 |
| | | *Nos. 140-152 (13)* | 92.55 | 52.65 |

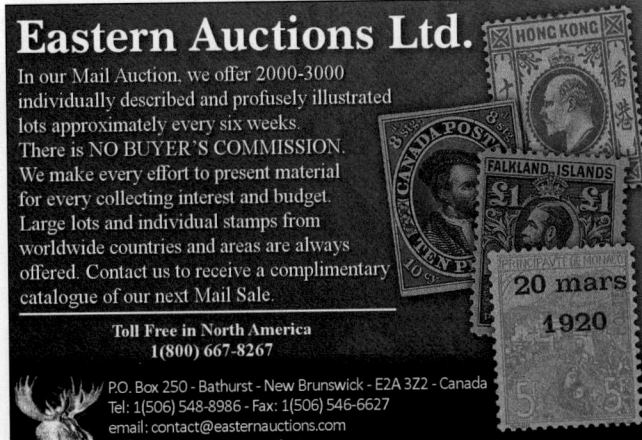

A27

***Perf. 11½***

**1956, Jan. 3 Wmk. 4 Engr.**

| | | | | |
|---|---|---|---|---|
| **153** | A27 | 3p dk car rose & blue | .25 | .25 |
| **154** | A27 | 4p redsh brown & blue | .25 | .25 |
| **155** | A27 | 6p purple & blue | .25 | .25 |
| | | *Nos. 153-155 (3)* | .75 | .75 |

Cent. of the 1st St. Helena postage stamp.

Arms of East India Company A28

Designs: 6p, Dutton's ship "London" off James Bay. 1sh, Memorial stone from fort built by Governor Dutton.

*Perf. 12½x13*

**1959, May 5 Wmk. 314**

156 A28 3p rose & black .25 .25
157 A28 6p gray & yellow green .35 .65
158 A28 1sh orange & black .40 .65
*Nos. 156-158 (3)* 1.00 1.55

300th anniv. of the landing of Capt. John Dutton on St. Helena and of the 1st settlement.

Cape Canary A29

Elizabeth II A30

Queen and Prince Andrew A31

Designs: 1p, Cunning fish, horiz. 2p, Brittle starfish, horiz. 4½p, Redwood flower. 6p, Red fody (Madagascar weaver). 7p, Trumpetfish, horiz. 10p, Keeled feather starfish, horiz. 1sh, Gumwood flowers. 1sh6p, Fairy tern. 2sh6p, Orange starfish, horiz. 5sh, Night-blooming cereus. 10sh, Deepwater bull's-eye, horiz.

*Perf. 11½x12, 12x11½*

**1961, Dec. 12 Photo. Wmk. 314**

159 A29 1p multicolored .40 .25
160 A29 1½p multicolored .50 .25
161 A29 2p gray & red .25 .25
162 A30 3p dk blue, rose & grnsh blue .50 .40
163 A29 4½p slate, brn & grn .65 .60
164 A29 6p cit, brn & dp car 4.00 .75
165 A29 7p vio, blk & red brn .50 .75
166 A29 10p blue & dp cl .90 .75
167 A29 1sh red brn, grn & yel .90 *1.25*
168 A29 1sh6p gray bl & blk 10.00 5.00
169 A29 2sh6p grnsh bl, yel & red 5.00 2.75
170 A29 5sh grn, brn & yel 12.00 4.50
171 A29 10sh gray bl, blk & sal 15.00 10.50

*Perf. 14x14½*

172 A31 £1 turq blue & choc 22.50 *22.50*
*Nos. 159-172 (14)* 73.10 50.50

For overprints see Nos. 176-179.

**Freedom from Hunger Issue**
Common Design Type

**1963, Apr. 4** ***Perf. 14x14½***

173 CD314 1sh6p ultra 2.25 1.10

**Red Cross Centenary Issue**
Common Design Type
**Wmk. 314**

**1963, Sept. 2 Litho.** ***Perf. 13***

174 CD315 3p black & red .30 .30
175 CD315 1sh6p ultra & red 1.40 2.00

**Nos. 159, 162, 164 and 168 Overprinted: "FIRST LOCAL POST / 4th JANUARY 1965"**

*Perf. 11½x12, 12x11½*

**1965, Jan. 4 Photo. Wmk. 314**

176 A29 1p multicolored .25 .25
177 A30 3p dk bl, rose & grnsh bl .25 .25
178 A29 6p cit, brn & dp car .25 .30
179 A29 1sh6p gray blue & blk .60 .35
*Nos. 176-179 (4)* 1.35 1.15

Establishment of the 1st internal postal service on the island.

**ITU Issue**
Common Design Type
*Perf. 11x11½*

**1965, May 17 Litho. Wmk. 314**

180 CD317 3p ultra & gray .30 .30
181 CD317 6p red lil & blue grn .50 .30

**Intl. Cooperation Year Issue**
Common Design Type

**1965, Oct. 25 Litho.** ***Perf. 14½***

182 CD318 1p blue grn & claret .25 .25
183 CD318 6p lt violet & green .70 .25

**Churchill Memorial Issue**
Common Design Type

**1966, Jan. 24 Photo.** ***Perf. 14***

**Design in Black, Gold and Carmine Rose**

184 CD319 1p bright blue .25 .25
185 CD319 3p green .35 .35
186 CD319 6p brown .50 .50
187 CD319 1sh6p violet .75 .85
*Nos. 184-187 (4)* 1.85 1.95

**World Cup Soccer Issue**
Common Design Type

**1966, July 1 Litho.** ***Perf. 14***

188 CD321 3p multicolored .35 .30
189 CD321 6p multicolored .90 .30

**WHO Headquarters Issue**
Common Design Type

**1966, Sept. 20 Litho.** ***Perf. 14***

190 CD322 3p multicolored 1.00 .25
191 CD322 1sh6p multicolored 2.50 1.25

**UNESCO Anniversary Issue**
Common Design Type

**1966, Dec. 1 Litho.** ***Perf. 14***

192 CD323 3p "Education" .75 .50
193 CD323 6p "Science" 1.25 .90
194 CD323 1sh6p "Culture" 3.25 2.25
*Nos. 192-194 (3)* 5.25 3.65

Badge of St. Helena — A32

*Perf. 14½x14*

**1967, May 5 Photo. Wmk. 314**

195 A32 1sh dk grn & multi .25 .25
196 A32 2sh6p blue & multi .40 .40
a. Carmine omitted 1,100.

St. Helena's New Constitution.

The Great Fire of London A33

3p, Three-master Charles. 6p, Boats bringing new settlers to shore. 1sh6p, Settlers at work.

*Perf. 13½x13*

**1967, Sept. 4 Engr. Wmk. 314**

197 A33 1p black & carmine .25 .25
198 A33 3p black & vio blue .25 .25
199 A33 6p black & dull violet .25 .25
200 A33 1sh6p black & ol green .25 .25
*Nos. 197-200 (4)* 1.00 1.00

Tercentenary of the arrival of settlers from London after the Great Fire of Sept. 2-4, 1666.

Maps of Tristan da Cunha and St. Helena A34

Designs: 8p, 2sh3p, Maps of St. Helena and Tristan da Cunha.

*Perf. 14x14½*

**1968, June 4 Photo. Wmk. 314**

**Maps in Sepia**

201 A34 4p dp red lilac .25 .25
202 A34 8p olive .25 .30
203 A34 1sh9p deep ultra .25 *.40*
204 A34 2sh3p Prus blue .25 *.40*
*Nos. 201-204 (4)* 1.00 1.35

30th anniv. of Tristan da Cunha as a Dependency of St. Helena.

Sir Hudson Lowe A35

1sh6p, 2sh6p, Sir George Bingham.

*Perf. 13½x13*

**1968, Sept. 4 Litho. Wmk. 314**

205 A35 3p multicolored .25 .25
206 A35 9p multicolored .25 .25
207 A35 1sh6p multicolored .25 .30
208 A35 2sh6p multicolored .25 .45
*Nos. 205-208 (4)* 1.00 1.25

Abolition of slavery in St. Helena, 150th anniv.

Road Construction — A36

Designs: 1p, Electricity development. 1½p, Dentist. 2p, Pest control. 3p, Apartment houses in Jamestown. 4p, Pasture and livestock improvement. 6p, School children listening to broadcast. 8p, Country cottages. 10p, New school buildings. 1sh, Reforestation. 1sh6p, Heavy lift crane. 2sh6p, Playing children in Lady Field Children's Home. 5sh, Agricultural training. 10sh, Ward in New General Hospital. £1, Lifeboat "John Dutton."

**Wmk. 314**

**1968, Nov. 4 Litho.** ***Perf. 13½***

209 A36 ½p multicolored .25 .25
210 A36 1p multicolored .25 .25
211 A36 1½p multicolored .25 .25
212 A36 2p multicolored .25 .25
213 A36 3p multicolored .30 .25
214 A36 4p multicolored .25 .25
215 A36 6p multicolored .30 .25
216 A36 8p multicolored .30 .30
217 A36 10p multicolored .30 .50
218 A36 1sh multicolored .30 .70
219 A36 1sh6p multicolored .60 *3.00*
220 A36 2sh6p multicolored .75 *3.50*
221 A36 5sh multicolored 1.30 *3.50*
222 A36 10sh multicolored 2.75 *5.25*
223 A36 £1 multicolored 7.50 *14.00*
*Nos. 209-223 (15)* 15.65 32.50

See Nos. 244-256.

Brig Perseverance, 1819 — A37

Ships: 8p, M.S. Dane, 1857. 1sh9p, S.S. Llandovery Castle, 1925. 2sh3p, M.S. Good Hope Castle, 1969.

**1969, Apr. 19 Litho.** ***Perf. 13½***

224 A37 4p violet & multi .25 .25
225 A37 8p ocher & multi .25 .45
226 A37 1sh9p ver & multi .30 .60
227 A37 2sh3p dk blue & multi .35 .75
*Nos. 224-227 (4)* 1.15 2.05

Issued in recognition of St. Helena's dependence on sea mail.

Surgeon and Officer (Light Company) 20th Foot, 1816 — A38

British Uniforms: 6p, Warrant Officer and Drummer, 53rd Foot, 1815. 1sh8p, Drum Major, 66th Foot, 1816, and Royal Artillery Officer, 1820. 2sh6p, Private 91st Foot and 2nd Corporal, Royal Sappers and Miners, 1832.

*Perf. 14x14½*

**1969, Sept. 3 Litho. Wmk. 314**

228 A38 6p red & multi .35 .35
229 A38 8p blue & multi .45 .45
230 A38 1sh8p green & multi .45 .45
231 A38 2sh6p gray & multi .45 .55
*Nos. 228-231 (4)* 1.70 1.80

Charles Dickens, "The Pickwick Papers" A39

Dickens and: 8p, "Oliver Twist." 1sh6p, "Martin Chuzzlewit." 2sh6p, "Bleak House."

*Perf. 13½x13*

**1970, June 9 Litho. Wmk. 314**

232 A39 4p dk brown & multi .35 .25
233 A39 8p slate & multi .45 .25
234 A39 1sh6p multicolored .70 .25
235 A39 2sh6p multicolored 1.50 .35
*Nos. 232-235 (4)* 3.00 1.10

Charles Dickens (1812-70), English novelist.

Mouth to Mouth Resuscitation — A40

Centenary of British Red Cross Society: 9p, Girl in wheelchair and nurse. 1sh9p, First aid. 2sh3p, British Red Cross Society emblem.

**1970, Sept. 15** ***Perf. 14½***

236 A40 6p bister, red & blk .25 .25
237 A40 9p lt blue grn, red & blk .25 .25
238 A40 1sh9p gray, red & blk .25 .30
239 A40 2sh3p pale vio, red & blk .30 .45
*Nos. 236-239 (4)* 1.05 1.25

A41

Regimental Emblems: 4p, Officer's Shako Plate, 20th Foot, 1812-16. 9p, Officer's breast plate, 66th Foot, before 1818. 1sh3p, Officer's full dress shako, 91st Foot, 1816. 2sh11p, Ensign's shako, 53rd Foot, 1815.

**Wmk. 314**

**1970, Nov. 2 Litho. *Perf. 14½***

| | | | | |
|---|---|---|---|---|
| 240 | A41 | 4p multicolored | .25 | .25 |
| 241 | A41 | 9p red & multi | .25 | .25 |
| 242 | A41 | 1sh3p dk gray & multi | .40 | .40 |
| 243 | A41 | 2sh11p dk gray grn & multi | .70 | .70 |
| | | *Nos. 240-243 (4)* | 1.60 | 1.60 |

See Nos. 263-270, 273-276.

**Type of 1968**

"P" instead of "d"

**1971, Feb. 15 Litho. *Perf. 13½***

| | | | | |
|---|---|---|---|---|
| 244 | A36 | ½p like #210 | .25 | .25 |
| 245 | A36 | 1p like #211 | .25 | .25 |
| 246 | A36 | 1½p like #212 | .25 | .25 |
| 247 | A36 | 2p like #213 | 2.00 | 1.00 |
| a. | | Perf. 14½ ('75) | .75 | 7.50 |
| 248 | A36 | 2½p like #214 | .30 | .30 |
| 249 | A36 | 3½p like #215 | .45 | .35 |
| 250 | A36 | 4½p like #216 | .45 | .45 |
| 251 | A36 | 5p like #217 | .55 | .55 |
| 252 | A36 | 7½p like #218 | .70 | .70 |
| 253 | A36 | 10p like #219 | .80 | .80 |
| 254 | A36 | 12½p like #220 | 1.00 | 1.00 |
| 255 | A36 | 25p like #221 | 1.60 | 1.60 |
| 256 | A36 | 50p like #222 | 2.00 | 2.00 |
| | | *Nos. 244-256 (13)* | 10.60 | 9.50 |

The paper of Nos. 244-256 is thinner than the paper of Nos. 209-223 and No. 223 (£1) has been reprinted in slightly different colors. Value $16.

A42

St. Helena, from Italian Miniature, 1460

***Perf. 14x14½***

**1971, Apr. 5 Litho. Wmk. 314**

| | | | | |
|---|---|---|---|---|
| 257 | A42 | 2p violet blue & multi | .25 | .25 |
| 258 | A42 | 5p multicolored | .25 | .25 |
| 259 | A42 | 7½p multicolored | .25 | .25 |
| 260 | A42 | 12½p olive & multi | .25 | .25 |
| | | *Nos. 257-260 (4)* | 1.00 | 1.00 |

Easter 1971.

Napoleon, after J. L. David, and Tomb in St. Helena A43

34p, Napoleon, by Hippolyte Paul Delaroche.

**1971, May 5 *Perf. 13½***

| | | | | |
|---|---|---|---|---|
| 261 | A43 | 2p multicolored | .25 | .25 |
| 262 | A43 | 34p multicolored | 1.25 | 1.00 |

Sesquicentennial of the death of Napoleon Bonaparte (1769-1821).

**Military Type of 1970**

1½p, Sword Hilt, Artillery Private, 1815. 4p, Baker rifle, socket bayonet, c. 1816. 6p, Infantry officer's sword hilt, 1822. 22½p, Baker rifle, light sword bayonet, c. 1823.

**1971, Nov. 10 *Perf. 14½***

| | | | | |
|---|---|---|---|---|
| 263 | A41 | 1½p green & multi | .25 | .25 |
| 264 | A41 | 4p gray & multi | .50 | .35 |
| 265 | A41 | 6p purple & multi | .50 | .45 |
| 266 | A41 | 22½p multicolored | 1.00 | 1.25 |
| | | *Nos. 263-266 (4)* | 2.25 | 2.30 |

**1972, June 19**

Designs: 2p, Royal Sappers and Miners breastplate, 1823. 5p, Infantry sergeant's pike, 1830. 7½p, Royal Artillery officer's breastplate, 1830. 12½p, English military pistol, 1800.

| | | | | |
|---|---|---|---|---|
| 267 | A41 | 2p multicolored | .25 | .25 |
| 268 | A41 | 5p plum & black | .35 | .45 |
| 269 | A41 | 7½p dp blue & multi | .40 | .55 |
| 270 | A41 | 12½p olive & multi | .40 | 1.00 |
| | | *Nos. 267-270 (4)* | 1.40 | 2.25 |

**Silver Wedding Issue, 1972**

Common Design Type

Design: Queen Elizabeth II, Prince Philip, St. Helena plover and white fairy tern.

**1972, Nov. 20 Photo. *Perf. 14x14½***

| | | | | |
|---|---|---|---|---|
| 271 | CD324 | 2p sl grn & multi | .25 | *.35* |
| 272 | CD324 | 16p rose brn & multi | .35 | *.85* |

**Military Type of 1970**

Designs: 2p, Shako, 53rd Foot, 1815. 5p, Band and Drums sword hilt, 1830. 7½p, Royal Sappers and Miners officers' hat, 1830. 12½p, General's sword hilt, 1831.

**1973, Sept. 20 Litho. *Perf. 14½***

| | | | | |
|---|---|---|---|---|
| 273 | A41 | 2p dull brown & multi | .25 | .55 |
| 274 | A41 | 5p multicolored | .30 | 1.00 |
| 275 | A41 | 7½p olive grn & multi | .50 | 1.25 |
| 276 | A41 | 12½p lilac & multi | .75 | 1.50 |
| | | *Nos. 273-276 (4)* | 1.80 | 4.30 |

**Princess Anne's Wedding Issue**

Common Design Type

**1973, Nov. 14 Wmk. 314 *Perf. 14***

| | | | | |
|---|---|---|---|---|
| 277 | CD325 | 2p multicolored | .25 | .25 |
| 278 | CD325 | 18p multicolored | .25 | .25 |

Westminster and Claudine Beached During Storm, 1849 — A45

Designs: 4p, East Indiaman True Briton, 1790. 6p, General Goddard in action off St. Helena, 1795. 22½p, East Indiaman Kent burning in Bay of Biscay, 1825.

***Perf. 14½x14***

**1973, Dec. 17 Litho. Wmk. 314**

| | | | | |
|---|---|---|---|---|
| 279 | A45 | 1½p multicolored | .25 | .40 |
| 280 | A45 | 4p multicolored | .35 | .60 |
| 281 | A45 | 6p multicolored | .35 | .60 |
| 282 | A45 | 22½p multicolored | 1.40 | 1.75 |
| | | *Nos. 279-282 (4)* | 2.35 | 3.35 |

Tercentenary of the East India Company Charter.

UPU Emblem, Ships A46

Design: 25p, UPU emblem and letters.

**1974, Oct. 15 *Perf. 14½x14***

| | | | | |
|---|---|---|---|---|
| 283 | A46 | 5p blue & multi | .25 | .25 |
| 284 | A46 | 25p red & multi | .40 | .50 |
| a. | | Souvenir sheet of 2, #283-284 | 1.05 | *1.50* |

Centenary of Universal Postal Union.

Churchill and Blenheim Palace — A47

25p, Churchill, Tower Bridge & Thames.

**1974, Nov. 30 Wmk. 373 *Perf. 14½***

| | | | | |
|---|---|---|---|---|
| 285 | A47 | 5p black & multi | .25 | .25 |
| 286 | A47 | 25p black & multi | .40 | .60 |
| a. | | Souvenir sheet of 2, #285-286 | 1.20 | *2.00* |

Sir Winston Churchill (1874-1965).

Capt. Cook and Jamestown — A48

5p, Capt. Cook and "Resolution," vert.

***Perf. 14x13½, 13½x14***

**1975, July 14 Litho.**

| | | | | |
|---|---|---|---|---|
| 287 | A48 | 5p multicolored | .40 | .25 |
| 288 | A48 | 25p multicolored | .80 | 1.00 |

Return of Capt. James Cook to St. Helena, bicent.

Mellissia Begonifolia — A49

Designs: 5p, Mellissius adumbratus (insect). 12p, Aegialitis St. Helena (bird), horiz. 25p, Scorpaenia mellissii (fish), horiz.

**1975, Oct. 20 Wmk. 373 *Perf. 13***

| | | | | |
|---|---|---|---|---|
| 289 | A49 | 2p gray & multi | .25 | .25 |
| 290 | A49 | 5p gray & multi | .25 | .25 |
| 291 | A49 | 12p gray & multi | .40 | .75 |
| 292 | A49 | 25p gray & multi | .40 | .90 |
| | | *Nos. 289-292 (4)* | 1.30 | 2.15 |

Centenary of the publication of "St. Helena," by John Charles Melliss.

Pound Note A50

Design: 33p, 5-pound note.

**1976, Apr. 15 Wmk. 314 *Perf. 13½***

| | | | | |
|---|---|---|---|---|
| 293 | A50 | 8p claret & multi | .30 | .30 |
| 294 | A50 | 33p multicolored | .80 | .80 |

First issue of St. Helena bank notes.

St. Helena No. 8 — A51

Designs: 8p, St. Helena No. 80, vert. 25p, Freighter Good Hope Castle.

***Perf. 13½x14, 14x13½***

**1976, May 4 Litho. Wmk. 373**

| | | | | |
|---|---|---|---|---|
| 295 | A51 | 5p buff, brown & blk | .25 | .25 |
| 296 | A51 | 8p lt grn, grn & blk | .25 | .25 |
| 297 | A51 | 25p multicolored | .40 | .60 |
| | | *Nos. 295-297 (3)* | .90 | 1.10 |

Festival of stamps 1976. See Tristan da Cunha #208a for souvenir sheet that contains one each of Ascension #214, St. Helena #297 and Tristan da Cunha #208.

High Knoll, by Capt. Barnett A52

Views on St. Helena, lithographs: 3p, Friar Rock, by G. H. Bellasis, 1815. 5p, Column Lot, by Bellasis. 6p, Sandy Bay Valley, by H. Salt, 1809. 8p, View from Castle terrace, by Bellasis. 9p, The Briars, 1815. 10p, Plantation House, by J. Wathen, 1821. 15p, Longwood House, by Wathen, 1821. 18p, St. Paul's Church, by Vincent Brooks. 26p, St. James's Valley, by Capt. Hastings, 1815. 40p, St. Matthew's Church, Longwood, by Brooks. £1, St. Helena and sailing ship, by Bellasis. £2, Sugar Loaf Hill, by Wathen, 1821.

**Wmk. 373**

**1976, Nov. 28 Litho. *Perf. 14***

**No Date Imprint Below Design**

**Size: 38½x25mm**

| | | | | |
|---|---|---|---|---|
| 298 | A52 | 1p multicolored | .30 | *1.15* |
| a. | | Inscribed "1982" | .30 | *1.15* |
| 299 | A52 | 3p multicolored | .35 | *1.15* |
| 300 | A52 | 5p multicolored | .30 | *1.15* |
| 301 | A52 | 6p multicolored | .30 | *1.15* |
| 302 | A52 | 8p multicolored | .30 | *1.15* |
| 303 | A52 | 9p multicolored | .30 | *1.15* |
| 304 | A52 | 10p multicolored | .50 | *.60* |
| a. | | Inscribed "1982" | .50 | *.60* |
| 305 | A52 | 15p multicolored | .45 | *.55* |
| 306 | A52 | 18p multicolored | .45 | *1.50* |
| 307 | A52 | 26p multicolored | .65 | *1.50* |
| 308 | A52 | 40p multicolored | .85 | *1.75* |

**Size: 47½x35mm**

***Perf. 13½***

| | | | | |
|---|---|---|---|---|
| 309 | A52 | £1 multicolored | 2.00 | 4.00 |
| 310 | A52 | £2 multicolored | 3.00 | 5.50 |
| a. | | Inscribed "1982" | 4.00 | *5.50* |
| | | *Nos. 298-310 (13)* | 9.75 | 22.30 |

Issue dates: 1p, 3p, 5p, 8p, 10p, 18p, 26p, 40p, £1, Sept. 28; others Nov. 23. Nos. 298a, 304a, 310a, 5/10/82.

For overprints see Nos. 376-377.

Royal Party Leaving St. Helena, 1947 — A53

15p, Queen's scepter, dove. 26p, Prince Philip paying homage to the Queen.

**1977, Feb. 7 Wmk. 373 *Perf. 13***

| | | | | |
|---|---|---|---|---|
| 311 | A53 | 8p multicolored | .25 | .25 |
| 312 | A53 | 15p multicolored | .25 | *.30* |
| 313 | A53 | 26p multicolored | .25 | *.40* |
| | | *Nos. 311-313 (3)* | .75 | .95 |

25th anniv. of the reign of Elizabeth II.

Halley's Comet, from Bayeux Tapestry A54

8p, 17th cent. sextant. 27p, Edmund Halley and Halley's Mount, St. Helena.

**1977, Aug. 23 Litho. *Perf. 14***

| | | | | |
|---|---|---|---|---|
| 314 | A54 | 5p multicolored | .45 | .45 |
| 315 | A54 | 8p multicolored | .60 | .45 |
| 316 | A54 | 27p multicolored | 1.25 | 1.25 |
| | | *Nos. 314-316 (3)* | 2.30 | 2.15 |

Edmund Halley's visit to St. Helena, 300th anniv.

**Elizabeth II Coronation Anniversary Issue**

Common Design Types

**Souvenir Sheet**

**Unwmk.**

**1978, June 2 Litho. *Perf. 15***

| | | | |
|---|---|---|---|
| 317 | Sheet of 6 | 1.75 | 1.75 |
| a. | CD326 25p Black dragon of Ulster | .30 | .30 |
| b. | CD327 25p Elizabeth II | .30 | .30 |
| c. | CD328 25p Sea Lion | .30 | .30 |

No. 317 contains 2 se-tenant strips of Nos. 317a-317c, separated by horizontal gutter.

St. Helena, 17th Century Engraving — A55

Designs: 5p, 9p, 15p, Various Chinese porcelain and other utensils salvaged from wreck. 8p, Bronze cannon. 20p, Dutch East Indiaman.

**Wmk. 373**

**1978, Aug. 14 Litho. *Perf. 14½***

**318** A55 3p multicolored .25 .25
**319** A55 5p multicolored .25 .25
**320** A55 8p multicolored .25 .30
**321** A55 9p multicolored .30 .35
**322** A55 15p multicolored .40 .50
**323** A55 20p multicolored .55 .65
*Nos. 318-323 (6)* 2.00 2.30

Wreck of the Witte Leeuw, 1613.

"Discovery" A56

Capt. Cook's voyages: 8p, Cook's portable observatory. 12p, Pharnaceum acidum (plant), after sketch by Joseph Banks. 25p, Capt. Cook, after Flaxman/Wedgwood medallion.

**1979, Feb. 19 Litho. *Perf. 11***

**324** A56 3p multicolored .25 .25
**325** A56 8p multicolored .25 .25
**326** A56 12p multicolored .40 .35

**Litho.; Embossed**

**327** A56 25p multicolored .50 .90
*Nos. 324-327 (4)* 1.40 1.75

St. Helena No. 176 A57

5p, Rowland Hill and his signature. 20p, St. Helena No. 8. 32p, St. Helena No. 49.

**1979, Aug. 20 Litho. *Perf. 14***

**328** A57 5p multi, vert. .25 .25
**329** A57 8p multi .25 .25
**330** A57 20p multi .25 .25
**331** A57 32p multi .25 .25
*Nos. 328-331 (4)* 1.00 1.00

Sir Rowland Hill (1795-1879), originator of penny postage.

Seale's Chart, 1823 — A58

8p, Jamestown & Inclined Plane, 1829. 50p, Inclined Plane (stairs), 1979.

**1979, Dec. 10 Litho. *Perf. 14***

**332** A58 5p multi .25 .25
**333** A58 8p multi .25 .25
**334** A58 50p multi, vert. .40 .70
*Nos. 332-334 (3)* .90 1.20

Inclined Plane, 150th anniversary.

Tomb of Napoleon I, 1848 — A59

Empress Eugenie: 8p, Landing at St. Helena. 62p, Visiting Napoleon's tomb.

**1980, Feb. 23 Litho. *Perf. 14½***

**335** A59 5p multicolored .25 .25
**336** A59 8p multicolored .25 .25
**337** A59 62p multicolored .75 .75
*a.* Souvenir sheet of 3, #335-337 1.10 1.10
*Nos. 335-337 (3)* 1.25 1.25

Visit of Empress Eugenie (widow of Napoleon III) to St. Helena, centenary.

East Indiaman, London 1980 Emblem — A60

8p, "Dolphin" postal stone. 47p, Jamestown castle postal stone.

**1980, May 6 Litho. *Perf. 14½***

**338** A60 5p shown .25 .25
**339** A60 8p multicolored .25 .25
**340** A60 47p multicolored .50 .50
*a.* Souvenir sheet of 3, #338-340 1.00 1.00
*Nos. 338-340 (3)* 1.00 1.00

London 1980 Intl. Stamp Exhib., May 6-14.

**Queen Mother Elizabeth Birthday Issue**

Common Design Type

**1980, Aug. 18 Litho. *Perf. 14***

**341** CD330 24p multicolored .50 .50

The Briars, 1815 A61

30p, Wellington, by Goya, vert.

**1980, Nov. 17 Litho. *Perf. 14***

**342** A61 9p shown .25 .25
**343** A61 30p multicolored .45 .45

Duke of Wellington's visit to St. Helena, 175th anniv. Nos. 342-343 issued in sheets of 10 with gutter giving historical background.

Redwood Flower A62

8p, Old father-live-forever. 15p, Gumwood. 27p, Black cabbage.

**1981, Jan. 5 *Perf. 13½***

**344** A62 5p shown .25 .25
**345** A62 8p multicolored .25 .25
**346** A62 15p multicolored .25 .25
**347** A62 27p multicolored .35 .35
*Nos. 344-347 (4)* 1.10 1.10

John Thornton's Map of St. Helena, 1700 — A63

5p, Reinel Portolan Chart, 1530. 20p, St. Helena, 1815. 30p, St. Helena, 1817. 24p, Gastaldi's map of Africa, 16th cent.

**1981, May 22 Litho. *Perf. 14½***

**348** A63 5p multicolored .25 .25
**349** A63 8p shown .25 .25
**350** A63 20p multicolored .30 .30
**351** A63 30p multicolored .50 .50
*Nos. 348-351 (4)* 1.30 1.30

**Souvenir Sheet**

**352** A63 24p multicolored .70 .70

**Royal Wedding Issue**

Common Design Type

**Wmk. 373**

**1981, July 22 Litho. *Perf. 14***

**353** CD331 14p Bouquet .25 .25
**354** CD331 29p Charles .30 .30
**355** CD331 32p Couple .30 .30
*Nos. 353-355 (3)* .85 .85

Charonia Variegata — A64

**1981, Sept. 10 Litho. *Perf. 14***

**356** A64 7p shown .25 .25
**357** A64 10p Cypraea spurca sanctahelenae .25 .25
**358** A64 25p Janthina janthina .50 .50
**359** A64 53p Pinna rudis .90 .90
*Nos. 356-359 (4)* 1.90 1.90

Traffic Guards Taking Oath — A65

**1981, Nov. 5**

**360** A65 7p shown .25 .25
**361** A65 11p Posting signs .25 .25
**362** A65 25p Animal care .30 .30
**363** A65 50p Duke of Edinburgh .60 .60
*Nos. 360-363 (4)* 1.40 1.40

Duke of Edinburgh's Awards, 25th anniv.

St. Helena Dragonfly — A66

**1982, Jan. 4 Litho. *Perf. 14½***

**364** A66 7p shown .25 .25
**365** A66 10p Burchell's beetle .25 .25
**366** A66 25p Cockroach wasp .50 .50
**367** A66 32p Earwig .65 .65
*Nos. 364-367 (4)* 1.65 1.65

See Nos. 386-389.

Sesquicentennial of Charles Darwin's Visit — A67

7p, Portrait. 14p, Flagstaff Hill, hammer. 25p, Ring-necked pheasants. 29p, Beagle.

**1982, Apr. 19 Litho. *Perf. 14***

**368** A67 7p multicolored .25 .25
**369** A67 14p multicolored .35 .35
**370** A67 25p multicolored .60 .60
**371** A67 29p multicolored .75 .75
*Nos. 368-371 (4)* 1.95 1.95

**Princess Diana Issue**

Common Design Type

**1982, July 1 Litho. *Perf. 14***

**372** CD333 7p Arms .25 .25
**373** CD333 11p Honeymoon .25 .25
**374** CD333 29p Diana .50 .50
**375** CD333 55p Portrait 1.00 1.00
*Nos. 372-375 (4)* 2.00 2.00

**Nos. 305, 307 Overprinted "1st PARTICIPATION / COMMONWEALTH GAMES 1982"**

**1982, Oct. 25 Litho. *Perf. 14***

**376** A52 15p multicolored .30 .30
**377** A52 26p multicolored .40 .40

Scouting Year A68

**1982, Nov. 29**

**378** A68 3p Baden-Powell, vert. .25 .25
**379** A68 11p Campfire .25 .25
**380** A68 29p Canon Walcott, vert. .40 .40
**381** A68 59p Thompsons Wood camp .80 .80
*Nos. 378-381 (4)* 1.70 1.70

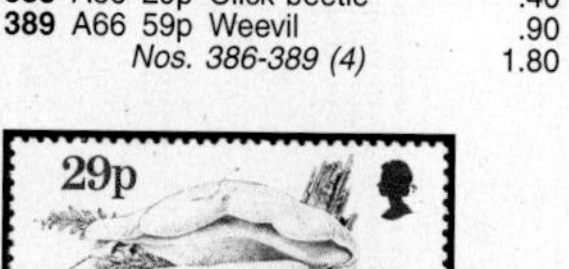


Coastline from Jamestown — A69

**1983, Jan. 14**

**382** A69 7p King and Queen Rocks, vert. .25 .25
**383** A69 11p Turk's Cap, vert. .25 .25
**384** A69 29p shown .40 .40
**385** A69 59p Munden's Point .80 .80
*Nos. 382-385 (4)* 1.70 1.70

**Insect Type of 1982**

**1983, Apr. 22 Litho. *Perf. 14½***

**386** A66 11p Death's-head hawk-moth .25 .25
**387** A66 15p Saldid-shore bug .25 .25
**388** A66 29p Click beetle .40 .40
**389** A66 59p Weevil .90 .90
*Nos. 386-389 (4)* 1.80 1.80

Local Fungi A70

11p, Coriolus versicolor, vert. 15p, Pluteus brunneisucus, vert. 29p, Polyporus induratus. 59p, Coprinus angulatus, vert.

**Wmk. 373**

**1983, June 16 Litho. *Perf. 14***

**390** A70 11p multicolored .30 .30
**391** A70 15p multicolored .35 .35
**392** A70 29p multicolored .60 .60
**393** A70 59p multicolored .90 .90
*Nos. 390-393 (4)* 2.15 2.15

Local Birds — A71

**1983, Sept. 12 Litho. *Perf. 14x14½***

| | | | | | |
|---|---|---|---|---|---|
| **394** | A71 | 7p | Padda oryzivora | .25 | .25 |
| **395** | A71 | 15p | Foudia madagascariensis | .40 | .35 |
| **396** | A71 | 33p | Estrilda astrild | 1.00 | .80 |
| **397** | A71 | 59p | Serinus flaviventris | 1.70 | 1.50 |
| | | | *Nos. 394-397 (4)* | 3.35 | 2.90 |

Souvenir Sheet

Christmas 1983 — A72

Stained Glass, Parish Church of St. Michael.

**1983, Oct. 17 Litho. *Perf. 14x13½***

| | | | | |
|---|---|---|---|---|
| **398** | A72 Sheet of 10 | | 4.00 | 3.00 |
| *a.* | 10p multicolored | | .25 | .25 |
| *b.* | 15p multicolored | | .45 | .35 |

Sheet contains strips of 5 of 10p and 15p with center margin telling St. Helena story.

See Nos. 424-427, 442-445.

150th Anniv. of the Colony — A73

**1984, Jan. 3 Litho. *Perf. 14***

| | | | | | |
|---|---|---|---|---|---|
| **399** | A73 | 1p | No. 101 | .25 | .25 |
| **400** | A73 | 3p | No. 102 | .25 | .25 |
| **401** | A73 | 6p | No. 103 | .25 | .25 |
| **402** | A73 | 7p | No. 104 | .25 | .25 |
| **403** | A73 | 11p | No. 105 | .25 | .25 |
| **404** | A73 | 15p | No. 106 | .25 | .30 |
| **405** | A73 | 29p | No. 107 | .40 | .50 |
| **406** | A73 | 33p | No. 109 | .45 | .55 |
| **407** | A73 | 59p | No. 110 | .75 | .85 |
| **408** | A73 | £1 | No. 108 | 1.40 | 1.60 |
| **409** | A73 | £2 | New coat of arms | 2.75 | 3.25 |
| | | | *Nos. 399-409 (11)* | 7.25 | 8.30 |

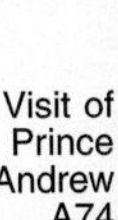

Visit of Prince Andrew A74

**1984, Apr. 4 Litho. *Perf. 14***

| | | | | | |
|---|---|---|---|---|---|
| **410** | A74 | 11p | Andrew, Invincible | .25 | .25 |
| **411** | A74 | 60p | Andrew, Herald | 1.15 | 1.15 |

**Lloyd's List Issue**

Common Design Type

**1984, May 14 *Perf. 14½x14***

| | | | | | |
|---|---|---|---|---|---|
| **412** | CD335 | 10p | St. Helena, 1814 | .25 | .25 |
| **413** | CD335 | 18p | Solomon's facade | .40 | .40 |
| **414** | CD335 | 25p | Lloyd's Coffee House | .55 | .55 |
| **415** | CD335 | 50p | Papanui, 1898 | 1.20 | 1.20 |
| | | | *Nos. 412-415 (4)* | 2.40 | 2.40 |

New Coin Issue A75

**1984, July 23 *Perf. 14***

| | | | | | |
|---|---|---|---|---|---|
| **416** | A75 | 10p | 2p, Donkey | .25 | .25 |
| **417** | A75 | 15p | 5p, Wire bird | .25 | .35 |
| **418** | A75 | 29p | 1p, Yellowfin tuna | .55 | .70 |
| **419** | A75 | 50p | 10p, Arum lily | 1.00 | 1.20 |
| | | | *Nos. 416-419 (4)* | 2.05 | 2.50 |

Centenary of Salvation Army in St. Helena — A76

7p, Secretary Rebecca Fuller, vert. 11p, Meals on Wheels service. 25p, Jamestown SA Hall. 60p, Hymn playing, clock tower, vert.

**1984, Oct. 14 Litho. Wmk. 373**

| | | | | | |
|---|---|---|---|---|---|
| **420** | A76 | 7p | multicolored | .25 | .25 |
| **421** | A76 | 11p | multicolored | .25 | .25 |
| **422** | A76 | 25p | multicolored | .25 | .50 |
| **423** | A76 | 60p | multicolored | .75 | 1.25 |
| | | | *Nos. 420-423 (4)* | 1.50 | 2.25 |

**Stained Glass Windows Type of 1983**

6p, St. Helena visits prisoners. 10p, Betrothal of St. Helena. 15p, Marriage of St. Helena & Constantius. 33p, Birth of Constantine.

**1984, Nov. 9**

| | | | | | |
|---|---|---|---|---|---|
| **424** | A72 | 6p | multicolored | .25 | .25 |
| **425** | A72 | 10p | multicolored | .25 | .30 |
| **426** | A72 | 15p | multicolored | .30 | .40 |
| **427** | A72 | 33p | multicolored | .75 | .90 |
| | | | *Nos. 424-427 (4)* | 1.55 | 1.85 |

**Queen Mother 85th Birthday Issue**

Common Design Type

11p, Portrait, age 2. 15p, Queen Mother, Elizabeth II. 29p, Attending ballet, Covent Garden. 55p, Holding Prince Henry.

70p, Queen Mother and Ford V8 Pilot.

***Perf. 14½x14***

**1985, June 7 Litho. Wmk. 384**

| | | | | | |
|---|---|---|---|---|---|
| **428** | CD336 | 11p | multicolored | .25 | .25 |
| **429** | CD336 | 15p | multicolored | .30 | .30 |
| **430** | CD336 | 29p | multicolored | .60 | .60 |
| **431** | CD336 | 55p | multicolored | 1.10 | 1.10 |
| | | | *Nos. 428-431 (4)* | 2.25 | 2.25 |

**Souvenir Sheet**

| | | | | | |
|---|---|---|---|---|---|
| **432** | CD336 | 70p | multicolored | 3.00 | 3.00 |

Marine Life — A78

***Perf. 13x13½***

**1985, July 12 Litho. Wmk. 373**

| | | | | | |
|---|---|---|---|---|---|
| **433** | A78 | 7p | Rock bullseye | .25 | .25 |
| **434** | A78 | 11p | Mackerel | .25 | .25 |
| **435** | A78 | 15p | Skipjack tuna | .25 | .40 |
| **436** | A78 | 33p | Yellowfin tuna | .75 | 1.00 |
| **437** | A78 | 50p | Stump | 1.00 | 1.50 |
| | | | *Nos. 433-437 (5)* | 2.50 | 3.40 |

Audubon Birth Bicent. A79

Portrait of naturalist and his illustrations of American bird species.

**1985, Sept. 2 *Perf. 14***

| | | | | | |
|---|---|---|---|---|---|
| **438** | A79 | 11p | John Audubon, vert. | .25 | .30 |
| **439** | A79 | 15p | Common gallinule | .30 | .40 |
| **440** | A79 | 25p | Tropic bird | .55 | .70 |
| **441** | A79 | 60p | Noddy tern | 1.50 | 1.75 |
| | | | *Nos. 438-441 (4)* | 2.60 | 3.15 |

**Stained Glass Windows Type of 1983**

Christmas: 7p, St. Helena journeys to the Holy Land. 10p, Zambres slays the bull. 15p, The bull restored to life, conversion of St. Helena. 60p, Resurrection of the corpse, the true cross identified.

**1985, Oct. 14**

| | | | | | |
|---|---|---|---|---|---|
| **442** | A72 | 7p | multicolored | .25 | .30 |
| **443** | A72 | 10p | multicolored | .25 | .35 |
| **444** | A72 | 15p | multicolored | .30 | .40 |
| **445** | A72 | 60p | multicolored | 1.25 | 1.50 |
| | | | *Nos. 442-445 (4)* | 2.05 | 2.55 |

Society Banners A80

Designs: 10p, Church Provident Society for Women. 11p, Working Men's Christian Assoc. 25p, Church Benefit Society for Children. 29p, Mechanics & Friendly Benefit Society. 33p, Ancient Order of Foresters.

***Perf. 13x13½***

**1986, Jan. 7 Wmk. 384**

| | | | | | |
|---|---|---|---|---|---|
| **446** | A80 | 10p | multicolored | .25 | .25 |
| **447** | A80 | 11p | multicolored | .25 | .25 |
| **448** | A80 | 25p | multicolored | .40 | .60 |
| **449** | A80 | 29p | multicolored | .50 | .70 |
| **450** | A80 | 33p | multicolored | .60 | .80 |
| | | | *Nos. 446-450 (5)* | 2.00 | 2.60 |

**Queen Elizabeth II 60th Birthday**

Common Design Type

Designs: 10p, Making 21st birthday broadcast, royal tour of South Africa, 1947. 15p, In robes of state, Throne Room, Buckingham Palace, Silver Jubilee, 1977. 20p, Onboard HMS Implacable, en route to South Africa, 1947. 50p, State visit to US, 1976. 65p, Visiting Crown Agents' offices, 1983.

**1986, Apr. 21 *Perf. 14½***

| | | | | | |
|---|---|---|---|---|---|
| **451** | CD337 | 10p | scarlet, blk & sil | .25 | .25 |
| **452** | CD337 | 15p | ultra & multi | .25 | .30 |
| **453** | CD337 | 20p | green, blk & sil | .25 | .35 |
| **454** | CD337 | 50p | violet & multi | .75 | .95 |
| **455** | CD337 | 65p | rose vio & multi | 1.00 | 1.20 |
| | | | *Nos. 451-455 (5)* | 2.50 | 3.05 |

For overprints see Nos. 488-492.

Halley's Comet — A81

Designs: 9p, Site of Halley's observatory on St. Helena. 12p, Edmond Halley, astronomer. 20p, Halley's planisphere of the southern stars. 65p, Voyage to St. Helena on the Unity.

**1986, May 15 Wmk. 373 *Perf. 14½***

| | | | | | |
|---|---|---|---|---|---|
| **456** | A81 | 9p | multicolored | .55 | .55 |
| **457** | A81 | 12p | multicolored | .65 | .65 |
| **458** | A81 | 20p | multicolored | .90 | .90 |
| **459** | A81 | 65p | multicolored | 2.00 | 2.00 |
| | | | *Nos. 456-459 (4)* | 4.10 | 4.10 |

**Royal Wedding Issue, 1986**

Common Design Type

Designs: 10p, Informal portrait. 40p, Andrew in dress uniform at parade.

**Wmk. 384**

**1986, July 23 Litho. *Perf. 14***

| | | | | | |
|---|---|---|---|---|---|
| **460** | CD338 | 10p | multicolored | .25 | .25 |
| **461** | CD338 | 40p | multicolored | .80 | .80 |

Explorers and Ships — A82

Designs: 1p, James Ross (1800-62), Erebus. 3p, Robert FitzRoy (1805-65), Beagle. 5p, Adam Johann von Krusenstern (1770-1846), Nadezhda, Russia. 9p, William Bligh (1754-1817), Resolution. 10p, Otto von Kotzebue (1786-1846), Rurik, Germany. 12p, Philip Carteret (1639-82), Swallow, 15p, Thomas Cavendish (c.1560-92), Desire. 20p, Louis-Antoine de Bougainville (1729-1811), La Boudeuse, France. 25p, Fyodor Petrovitch Litke (1797-1882), Seniavin, Russia. 40p, Louis Isidore Duperrey (1786-1865), La Coquille, France. 60p, John Byron (1723-86), Dolphin. £1, James Cook, Endeavour. £2, Jules Dumont d'Urville (1790-1842), L'Astrolabe, France.

**Wmk. 384**

**1986, Sept. 22 Litho. *Perf. 14½***

| | | | | | |
|---|---|---|---|---|---|
| **462** | A82 | 1p | red brown | .40 | 1.50 |
| **463** | A82 | 3p | bright ultra | .40 | 1.50 |
| **464** | A82 | 5p | olive green | .40 | 1.50 |
| **465** | A82 | 9p | deep claret | .50 | 1.50 |
| **466** | A82 | 10p | sepia | .55 | 1.50 |
| **467** | A82 | 12p | brt blue green | .55 | 1.50 |
| **468** | A82 | 15p | brown lake | .65 | 1.50 |
| **469** | A82 | 20p | sapphire | .85 | 1.50 |
| **470** | A82 | 25p | red brown | .90 | 1.50 |
| **471** | A82 | 40p | myrtle green | 1.40 | 2.00 |
| **472** | A82 | 60p | brown | 1.75 | 2.75 |
| **473** | A82 | £1 | Prussian blue | 2.75 | 4.50 |
| **474** | A82 | £2 | bright violet | 5.50 | 8.00 |
| | | | *Nos. 462-474 (13)* | 16.60 | 30.75 |

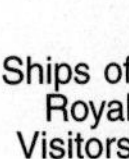

Ships of Royal Visitors A83

Portraits and vessels: 9p, Prince Edward, HMS Repulse, 1925. 13p, King George VI, HMS Vanguard, 1947. 38p, Prince Philip, HMY Britannia, 1957. 45p, Prince Andrew, HMS Herald, 1984.

**1987, Feb. 16 Wmk. 373 *Perf. 14***

| | | | | | |
|---|---|---|---|---|---|
| **475** | A83 | 9p | multicolored | 1.50 | 1.25 |
| **476** | A83 | 13p | multicolored | 2.25 | 1.50 |
| **477** | A83 | 38p | multicolored | 3.50 | 3.50 |
| **478** | A83 | 45p | multicolored | 4.00 | 4.00 |
| | | | *Nos. 475-478 (4)* | 11.25 | 10.25 |

Rare Plants — A84

**1987, Aug. 3 *Perf. 14½x14***

| | | | | | |
|---|---|---|---|---|---|
| **479** | A84 | 9p | St. Helena tea plant | .70 | .70 |
| **480** | A84 | 13p | Baby's toes | 1.10 | 1.10 |
| **481** | A84 | 38p | Salad plant | 2.10 | 2.10 |
| **482** | A84 | 45p | Scrubwood | 2.60 | 2.60 |
| | | | *Nos. 479-482 (4)* | 6.50 | 6.50 |

Marine Mammals A85

**Wmk. 384**

**1987, Oct. 24 Litho. *Perf. 14***

| | | | | | |
|---|---|---|---|---|---|
| **483** | A85 | 9p | Lesser rorqual | 1.50 | 1.50 |
| **484** | A85 | 13p | Risso's dolphin | 1.60 | 1.60 |
| **485** | A85 | 45p | Sperm whale | 4.00 | 4.00 |
| **486** | A85 | 60p | Euphrosyne dolphin | 5.75 | 5.75 |
| | | | *Nos. 483-486 (4)* | 12.85 | 12.85 |

**Souvenir Sheet**

| | | | | | |
|---|---|---|---|---|---|
| **487** | A85 | 75p | Humpback whale | 10.50 | 10.50 |

**Nos. 451-455 Ovptd. "40TH WEDDING ANNIVERSARY" in Silver**

**Wmk. 384**

**1987, Dec. 9 Litho. *Perf. 14½***

| | | | | | |
|---|---|---|---|---|---|
| **488** | CD337 | 10p | scarlet, blk & sil | .25 | .25 |
| **489** | CD337 | 15p | ultra & multi | .25 | .25 |
| **490** | CD337 | 20p | green, blk & sil | .25 | .40 |
| **491** | CD337 | 50p | violet & multi | .50 | .85 |
| **492** | CD337 | 65p | rose vio & multi | .85 | 1.10 |
| | | | *Nos. 488-492 (5)* | 2.10 | 2.85 |

Australia Bicentennial A86

Ships and signatures: 9p, HMS Defence, 1691, and William Dampier. 13p, HMS Resolution, 1775, and James Cook. 45p, HMS Providence, 1792, and William Bligh. 60p, HMS Beagle, 1836, and Charles Darwin.

**Wmk. 384**

**1988, Mar. 1 Litho. *Perf. 14½***

| | | | | |
|---|---|---|---|---|
| **493** | A86 | 9p multicolored | 2.25 | 2.00 |
| **494** | A86 | 13p multicolored | 3.00 | 3.00 |
| **495** | A86 | 45p multicolored | 4.75 | 4.75 |
| **496** | A86 | 60p multicolored | 6.25 | 6.25 |
| | | *Nos. 493-496 (4)* | 16.25 | 16.00 |

Christmas — A87

Religious paintings by unknown artists: 5p, The Holy Family with Child. 20p, Madonna. 38p, The Holy Family with St. John. 60p, The Holy Virgin with the Child.

**Wmk. 373**

**1988, Oct. 11 Litho. *Perf. 14***

| | | | | |
|---|---|---|---|---|
| **497** | A87 | 5p multicolored | .25 | .25 |
| **498** | A87 | 20p multicolored | .65 | .65 |
| **499** | A87 | 38p multicolored | 1.20 | 1.20 |
| **500** | A87 | 60p multicolored | 1.75 | 1.75 |
| | | *Nos. 497-500 (4)* | 3.85 | 3.85 |

**Lloyds of London, 300th Anniv.**

Common Design Type

Designs: 9p, Underwriting room, 1886. 20p, Edinburgh Castle. 45p, Bosun Bird. 60p, Spangereid on fire off St. Helena, 1920.

**Wmk. 384**

**1988, Nov. 1 Litho. *Perf. 14***

| | | | | |
|---|---|---|---|---|
| **501** | CD341 | 9p multi | .45 | .40 |
| **502** | CD341 | 20p multi, horiz. | 2.00 | 1.25 |
| **503** | CD341 | 45p multi, horiz. | 2.75 | 2.50 |
| **504** | CD341 | 60p multi | 3.50 | 3.00 |
| | | *Nos. 501-504 (4)* | 8.70 | 7.15 |

Rare Plants — A88

**1989, Jan. 6 *Perf. 14***

| | | | | |
|---|---|---|---|---|
| **505** | A88 | 9p Ebony | .45 | .45 |
| **506** | A88 | 20p St. Helena lobelia | 1.10 | 1.10 |
| **507** | A88 | 45p Large bellflower | 2.00 | 2.00 |
| **508** | A88 | 60p She cabbage tree | 2.60 | 2.60 |
| | | *Nos. 505-508 (4)* | 6.15 | 6.15 |

Flags and Military Uniforms, 1815 — A89

Designs: 9p, Soldier, 53rd Foot. 13p, Officer, 53rd Foot. 20p, Royal marine. 45p, Officer, 66th Foot. 60p, Soldier, 66th Foot.

**1989, June 5 Litho. *Perf. 14***

| | | | |
|---|---|---|---|
| **509** | Strip of 5 | 7.50 | 10.00 |
| *a.* | A89 9p multicolored | .55 | .55 |
| *b.* | A89 13p multicolored | .65 | .65 |
| *c.* | A89 20p multicolored | 1.05 | 1.05 |
| *d.* | A89 45p multicolored | 2.10 | 2.10 |
| *e.* | A89 60p multicolored | 2.75 | 2.75 |

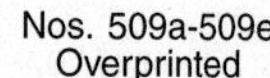

Nos. 509a-509e Overprinted

**1989, July 7 Litho. *Perf. 14***

| | | | |
|---|---|---|---|
| **510** | Strip of 5 | 8.50 | 11.00 |
| *a.* | A89 9p multicolored | .85 | .85 |
| *b.* | A89 13p multicolored | .90 | .90 |
| *c.* | A89 20p multicolored | 1.10 | 1.10 |
| *d.* | A89 45p multicolored | 2.25 | 2.25 |
| *e.* | A89 60p multicolored | 3.00 | 3.00 |

PHILEXFRANCE '89.

New Central (Prince Andrew) School A90

**1989, Aug. 24 *Perf. 14½***

| | | | | |
|---|---|---|---|---|
| **511** | A90 | 13p Agriculture | .80 | .75 |
| **512** | A90 | 20p Literacy | 1.25 | 1.10 |
| **513** | A90 | 25p Building exterior | 1.60 | 1.60 |
| **514** | A90 | 60p Campus | 3.75 | 3.75 |
| | | *Nos. 511-514 (4)* | 7.40 | 7.20 |

Christmas — A91

10p, The Madonna with the Pear, by Durer. 20p, The Holy Family Under the Apple Tree, by Rubens. 45p, The Virgin in the Meadow, by Raphael. 60p, The Holy Family with Saint John, by Raphael.

**1989, Oct. 10 Wmk. 373 *Perf. 14***

| | | | | |
|---|---|---|---|---|
| **515** | A91 | 10p multicolored | .65 | .50 |
| **516** | A91 | 20p multicolored | 1.10 | 1.10 |
| **517** | A91 | 45p multicolored | 2.60 | 2.60 |
| **518** | A91 | 60p multicolored | 3.50 | 3.50 |
| | | *Nos. 515-518 (4)* | 7.85 | 7.70 |

Early Vehicles A92

**1989, Dec. 1 Wmk. 384 *Perf. 14½***

| | | | | |
|---|---|---|---|---|
| **519** | A92 | 9p 1930 Chevrolet | .90 | .90 |
| **520** | A92 | 20p 1929 Austin Seven | 1.60 | 1.60 |
| **521** | A92 | 45p 1929 Morris Cowley | 3.00 | 3.00 |
| **522** | A92 | 60p 1932 Sunbeam | 4.25 | 4.25 |
| | | *Nos. 519-522 (4)* | 9.75 | 9.75 |

**Souvenir Sheet**

| | | | | |
|---|---|---|---|---|
| **523** | A92 | £1 Ford Model A | 9.50 | 9.50 |

Farm Animals — A93

**1990, Feb. 1 Litho. *Perf. 14***

| | | | | |
|---|---|---|---|---|
| **524** | A93 | 9p Sheep | .70 | .70 |
| **525** | A93 | 13p Pigs | .90 | .90 |
| **526** | A93 | 45p Cow, calf | 2.60 | 2.60 |
| **527** | A93 | 60p Geese | 3.25 | 3.25 |
| | | *Nos. 524-527 (4)* | 7.45 | 7.45 |

Great Britain No. 2 A94

Exhibition emblem and: 20p, Great Britain No. 1. 38p, Mail delivery to branch p.o. 45p, Main p.o., mail van.

**1990, May 3 Wmk. 373**

| | | | | |
|---|---|---|---|---|
| **528** | A94 | 13p shown | .70 | .70 |
| **529** | A94 | 20p multicolored | 1.05 | 1.05 |
| **530** | A94 | 38p multicolored | 2.00 | 2.00 |
| **531** | A94 | 45p multicolored | 2.25 | 2.25 |
| | | *Nos. 528-531 (4)* | 6.00 | 6.00 |

Stamp World London '90, 150th anniv. of the Penny Black.

**Queen Mother, 90th Birthday**

Common Design Types

25p, As Duchess of York, 1923. £1, Visiting communal feeding center, 1940.

**1990, Aug. 4 Wmk. 384 *Perf. 14x15***

| | | | | |
|---|---|---|---|---|
| **532** | CD343 | 25p multicolored | 1.25 | 1.25 |

***Perf. 14½***

| | | | | |
|---|---|---|---|---|
| **533** | CD344 | £1 multicolored | 4.00 | 4.00 |

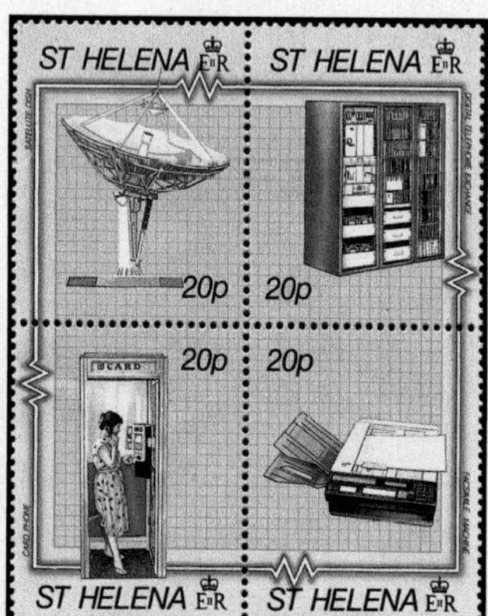


Telecommunications — A95

**1990, July 28 Wmk. 373 *Perf. 14***

| | | | | |
|---|---|---|---|---|
| **534** | A95 | Block of 4 | 4.25 | 4.25 |
| *a.-d.* | | 20p any single | .95 | .95 |

Dane, 1857 — A96

Designs: 20p, RMS St. Helena offloading cargo. 38p, Launching new RMS St. Helena, 1989. 45p, Duke of York launching new RMS St. Helena. £1, New RMS St. Helena.

**1990, Sept. 13 *Perf. 14½***

| | | | | |
|---|---|---|---|---|
| **535** | A96 | 13p multicolored | 1.25 | 1.25 |
| **536** | A96 | 20p multicolored | 2.00 | 2.00 |
| **537** | A96 | 38p multicolored | 4.00 | 4.00 |
| **538** | A96 | 45p multicolored | 4.25 | 4.25 |
| | | *Nos. 535-538 (4)* | 11.50 | 11.50 |

**Souvenir Sheet**

| | | | | |
|---|---|---|---|---|
| **539** | A96 | £1 multicolored | 12.50 | 12.50 |

See Ascension Nos. 493-497, Tristan da Cunha Nos. 482-486.

Christmas — A97

Parish Churches — 10p, Baptist Chapel, Sandy Bay. 13p, St. Martin in the Hills. 20p, St. Helena and the Cross. 38p, St. James Church. 45p, St. Paul's Church.

**1990, Oct. 18 *Perf. 13***

| | | | | |
|---|---|---|---|---|
| **540** | A97 | 10p multicolored | .50 | .50 |
| **541** | A97 | 13p multicolored | .60 | .60 |
| **542** | A97 | 20p multicolored | .90 | .90 |
| **543** | A97 | 38p multicolored | 1.75 | 1.75 |
| **544** | A97 | 45p multicolored | 2.00 | 2.00 |
| | | *Nos. 540-544 (5)* | 5.75 | 5.75 |

Removal of Napoleon's Body from St. Helena, 150th Anniv. — A98

Designs: 13p, Funeral cortege, Jamestown wharf. 20p, Moving coffin to *Belle Poule*, James Bay. 38p, Transfer of coffin from *Belle Poule* to *Normandie*, Cherbourg. 45p, Napoleon's Tomb, St. Helena.

**1990, Dec. 15 Wmk. 373 *Perf. 14***

| | | | | |
|---|---|---|---|---|
| **545** | A98 | 13p green & black | 1.50 | 1.25 |
| **546** | A98 | 20p blue & black | 2.10 | 2.00 |
| **547** | A98 | 38p violet & black | 3.75 | 3.75 |
| **548** | A98 | 45p multicolored | 4.50 | 4.50 |
| | | *Nos. 545-548 (4)* | 11.85 | 11.50 |

A99

Military Uniforms 1897: 13p, Officer, Leicestershire Regiment. 15p, Officer, York and Lancaster Regiment. 20p, Color Sergeant, Leicestershire Regiment. 38p, Drummer/Flautist, York and Lancaster Regiment. 45p, Lance Corporal, York and Lancaster Regiment.

**1991, May 2**

| | | | | |
|---|---|---|---|---|
| **549** | A99 | 13p multicolored | 1.40 | 1.40 |
| **550** | A99 | 15p multicolored | 1.60 | 1.60 |
| **551** | A99 | 20p multicolored | 2.00 | 2.00 |
| **552** | A99 | 38p multicolored | 3.25 | 3.25 |
| **553** | A99 | 45p multicolored | 4.25 | 4.25 |
| | | *Nos. 549-553 (5)* | 12.50 | 12.50 |

**Elizabeth & Philip, Birthdays**

Common Design Types

**1991, July 1 Wmk. 384 *Perf. 14½***

| | | | | |
|---|---|---|---|---|
| **554** | CD345 | 25p multicolored | 1.20 | 1.20 |
| **555** | CD346 | 25p multicolored | 1.20 | 1.20 |
| *a.* | | Pair, #554-555 + label | 2.75 | 2.75 |

A100

Christmas (Paintings): 10p, Madonna and Child, Titian. 13p, Holy Family, Mengs. 20p, Madonna and Child, Dyce. 38p, Two Trinities, Murillo. 45p, Virgin and Child, Bellini.

**1991, Nov. 2 Wmk. 373 *Perf. 14***

556 A100 10p multicolored 1.00 1.00
557 A100 13p multicolored 1.10 1.10
558 A100 20p multicolored 1.75 1.75
559 A100 38p multicolored 3.25 3.25
560 A100 45p multicolored 3.75 3.75
*Nos. 556-560 (5)* 10.85 10.85

Phila Nippon '91 — A101

Motorcycles: 13p, Matchless 346cc (ohv), 1947. 20p, Triumph Tiger 100, 500cc, 1950. 38p, Honda CD 175cc, 1967. 45p, Yamaha DTE 400, 1976. 65p, Suzuki RM 250cc, 1984.

***Perf. 14x14½***

**1991, Nov. 16 Litho. Wmk. 384**

561 A101 13p multicolored 1.25 1.25
562 A101 20p multicolored 2.00 2.00
563 A101 38p multicolored 3.25 3.25
564 A101 45p multicolored 4.00 4.00
*Nos. 561-564 (4)* 10.50 10.50

**Souvenir Sheet**

565 A101 65p multicolored 9.50 9.50

Discovery of America, 500th Anniv. — A102

15p, STV Eye of the Wind. 25p, STV Soren Larsen. 35p, Santa Maria, Nina & Pinta. 50p, Columbus, Santa Maria.

**Wmk. 373**

**1992, Jan. 24 Litho. *Perf. 14***

566 A102 15p multicolored 2.00 2.00
567 A102 25p multicolored 2.75 2.75
568 A102 35p multicolored 3.75 3.75
569 A102 50p multicolored 4.50 4.50
*Nos. 566-569 (4)* 13.00 13.00

World Columbian Stamp Expo '92, Chicago and Genoa '92 Intl. Philatelic Exhibitions.

**Queen Elizabeth II's Accession to the Throne, 40th Anniv.**

Common Design Type

**1992, Feb. 6**

570 CD349 11p multicolored .45 .45
571 CD349 15p multicolored .65 .65
572 CD349 25p multicolored 1.10 1.10
573 CD349 35p multicolored 1.50 1.50
574 CD349 50p multicolored 2.00 2.00
*Nos. 570-574 (5)* 5.70 5.70

Liberation of Falkland Islands, 10th Anniv. — A103

Designs: No. 579a, 13p + 3p, like No. 575. b, 20p + 4p, like No. 576. c, 38p + 8p, like No. 577. d, 45p + 8p, like No. 578.

**1992, June 12**

575 A103 13p HMS Ledbury 1.00 1.00
576 A103 20p HMS Brecon 1.50 1.50
577 A103 38p RMS St. Helena 2.50 2.50
578 A103 45p First mail drop, 1982 3.00 3.00
*Nos. 575-578 (4)* 8.00 8.00

**Souvenir Sheet**

579 A103 Sheet of 4, #a.-d. 8.50 8.50

Surtax for Soldiers', Sailors' and Airmens' Families Association.

Christmas — A104

Children in scenes from Nativity plays: 13p, Angel, shepherds. 15p, Magi, shepherds. 20p, Joseph, Mary. 45p, Nativity scene.

**1992, Oct. 12 Wmk. 384**

580 A104 13p multicolored 1.25 1.25
581 A104 15p multicolored 1.40 1.40
582 A104 20p multicolored 1.90 1.90
583 A104 45p multicolored 4.25 4.25
*Nos. 580-583 (4)* 8.80 8.80

Anniversaries — A105

Designs: 13p, Man broadcasting at radio station. 20p, Scouts marching in parade. 38p, Breadfruit, HMS Providence, 1792. 45p, Governor Colonel Brooke, Plantation House.

**1992, Dec. 4 Wmk. 373 *Perf. 14½***

584 A105 13p multicolored 1.25 1.25
585 A105 20p multicolored 1.75 1.75
586 A105 38p multicolored 3.25 3.25
587 A105 45p multicolored 3.75 3.75
*Nos. 584-587 (4)* 10.00 10.00

Radio St. Helena, 25th anniv. (#584). Scouting on St. Helena, 75th anniv. (#585). Captain Bligh's visit, 200th anniv. (#586). Plantation House, 200th anniv. (#587).

Flowers — A106

9p, Moses in the bulrush. 13p, Periwinkle. 20p, Everlasting flower. 38p, Cigar plant. 45p, Lobelia erinus.

***Perf. 14½x14***

**1993, Mar. 19 Litho. Wmk. 384**

588 A106 9p multicolored .90 .90
589 A106 13p multicolored 1.30 1.30
590 A106 20p multicolored 1.75 1.75
591 A106 38p multicolored 3.00 3.00
592 A106 45p multicolored 3.50 3.50
*Nos. 588-592 (5)* 10.45 10.45

See Nos. 636-640.

Wirebird A107

3p, Adult with eggs. 5p, Male, brooding female. 12p, Downy young, adult. 25p, Two immature birds. 40p, Adult in flight. 60p, Immature bird.

**Wmk. 373**

**1993, Aug. 16 Litho. *Perf. 13½***

593 A107 3p multicolored 1.15 1.15
594 A107 5p multicolored 1.40 1.40
595 A107 12p multicolored 2.25 2.25
596 A107 25p multicolored 4.50 4.50
597 A107 40p multicolored 1.75 1.75
598 A107 60p multicolored 2.75 2.75
*Nos. 593-598 (6)* 13.80 13.80

Birds A108

1p, Swainson's canary. 3p, Chuckar partridge. 11p, Pigeon. 12p, Waxbill. 15p, Common myna. 18p, Java sparrow. 25p, Red-billed tropicbird. 35p, Maderian storm petrel. 75p, Madagascar fody. £1, Common fairy tern. £2, Southern giant petrel. £5, Wirebird.

**1993, Aug. 26 *Perf. 14½***

599 A108 1p multicolored .25 .65
600 A108 3p multicolored .25 .65
601 A108 11p multicolored .40 .65
602 A108 12p multicolored .45 .65
603 A108 15p multicolored .55 .70
604 A108 18p multicolored .70 .85
605 A108 25p multicolored .80 1.10
606 A108 35p multicolored 1.10 1.50
607 A108 75p multicolored 2.25 3.00
*a.* Souvenir sheet of 1 3.00 3.25
608 A108 £1 multicolored 3.00 3.50
609 A108 £2 multicolored 6.25 7.00
610 A108 £5 multicolored 15.50 18.00
*Nos. 599-610 (12)* 31.50 38.25

Nos. 599-604, 607, 610 are vert.
No. 607a for Hong Kong '97. Issued: 2/3/97.
See No. 691.

Christmas — A109

Toys: 12p, Teddy bear, soccer ball. 15p, Sailboat, doll. 18p, Paint palette, rocking horse. 25p, Kite, airplane. 60p, Guitar, roller skates.

**1993, Oct. 1 *Perf. 13½x14***

611 A109 12p multicolored 1.00 1.00
612 A109 15p multicolored 1.10 1.10
613 A109 18p multicolored 1.20 1.20
614 A109 25p multicolored 1.75 1.75
615 A109 60p multicolored 3.50 3.50
*Nos. 611-615 (5)* 8.55 8.55

Flowers — A110

Photographs: No. 616a, Arum lily. No. 617a, Ebony. No. 618a, Shell ginger.
Nos. 616b-618b: Child's painting of same flower as in "a."

**1994, Jan. 6 Wmk. 384 *Perf. 14***

616 A110 12p Pair, #a.-b. 1.50 1.50
617 A110 25p Pair, #a.-b. 2.50 2.50
618 A110 35p Pair, #a.-b. 3.00 3.00

Pets — A111

Designs: 12p, Abyssinian guinea pig. 25p, Common tabby cat. 53p, Plain white, black rabbits. 60p, Golden labrador.

**1994, Feb. 18 Wmk. 373 *Perf. 14½***

619 A111 12p multicolored .90 .90
620 A111 25p multicolored 2.10 2.10
621 A111 53p multicolored 4.00 4.00
622 A111 60p multicolored 4.25 4.25
*Nos. 619-622 (4)* 11.25 11.25

Hong Kong '94.

Fish — A112

12p, Springer's blenny. 25p, Bastard five finger. 53p, Deepwater gurnard. 60p, Green fish.

**1994, June 6 Wmk. 384 *Perf. 14***

623 A112 12p multicolored .90 .90
624 A112 25p multicolored 1.75 1.75
625 A112 53p multicolored 4.00 4.00
626 A112 60p multicolored 4.25 4.25
*Nos. 623-626 (4)* 10.90 10.90

Butterflies A113

12p, Lampides boeticus. 25p, Cynthia cardui. 53p, Hypolimnas bolina. 60p, Danaus chrysippus.

**1994, Aug. 9 Wmk. 373**

627 A113 12p multicolored 1.25 1.25
628 A113 25p multicolored 2.25 2.25
629 A113 53p multicolored 3.50 3.50
630 A113 60p multicolored 4.00 4.00
*Nos. 627-630 (4)* 11.00 11.00

Christmas Carols — A114

Designs: 12p, "Silent night, holy night..." 15p, "While shepherds watched..." 25p, "Away in a manger..." 38p, "We three kings..." 60p, Angels from the realms of glory.

**1994, Oct. 6**

631 A114 12p multicolored .60 .70
632 A114 15p multicolored .80 .90
633 A114 25p multicolored 1.25 1.40
634 A114 38p multicolored 2.00 2.25
635 A114 60p multicolored 3.25 3.75
*Nos. 631-635 (5)* 7.90 9.00

**Flower Type of 1993**

**Wmk. 384**

**1994, Dec. 15 Litho. *Perf. 14½***

636 A106 12p Honeysuckle .55 .55
637 A106 15p Gobblegheer .70 .70
638 A106 25p African lily 1.00 1.00
639 A106 38p Prince of Wales feathers 1.60 1.60
640 A106 60p St. Johns lily 2.50 2.50
*Nos. 636-640 (5)* 6.35 6.35

Emergency Services — A115

12p, Fire engine. 25p, Inshore rescue craft. 53p, Police, rural patrol. 60p, Ambulance.

**Wmk. 384**

**1995, Feb. 2 Litho. *Perf. 14***

641 A115 12p multicolored 1.00 1.00
642 A115 25p multicolored 2.25 2.25
643 A115 53p multicolored 4.00 4.00
644 A115 60p multicolored 4.75 4.75
*Nos. 641-644 (4)* 12.00 12.00

Harpers Earth Dam Project
A116

Designs: a, Site clearance. b, Earthworks in progress. c, Laying the outlet pipe. d, Revetment block protection. e, Completed dam, June 1994.

**Wmk. 373**

**1995, Apr. 6 Litho. *Perf. 14½***

**645** A116 25p Strip of 5, #a.-e. 6.75 6.75

No. 645 is a continuous design.

**End of World War II, 50th Anniv.**
Common Design Types

Designs: No. 646, CS Lady Denison Pender. No. 647, HMS Dragon. No. 648, RFA Darkdale. No. 649, HMS Hermes. No. 650, St. Helena Rifles on parade. No. 651, Gov. Maj. W.J. Bain Gray during Victory Parade. No. 652, 6-inch gun, Ladder Hill. No. 653, Signal Station, flag hoist signalling VICTORY.
No. 654, Reverse of War Medal 1939-45.

**1995, May 8 Wmk. 373 *Perf. 14***

**646** CD351 5p multicolored 1.20 1.20
**647** CD351 5p multicolored 1.20 1.20
*a.* Pair, #646-647 2.75 2.75
**648** CD351 12p multicolored 2.10 2.10
**649** CD351 12p multicolored 2.10 2.10
*a.* Pair, #648-649 4.75 4.75
**650** CD351 25p multicolored 3.00 3.00
**651** CD351 25p multicolored 3.00 3.00
*a.* Pair, #650-651 7.25 7.25
**652** CD351 53p multicolored 3.50 3.50
**653** CD351 53p multicolored 3.50 3.50
*a.* Pair, #652-653 9.00 9.00
*Nos. 646-653 (8)* 19.60 19.60

**Souvenir Sheet**

**654** CD352 £1 multicolored 6.50 6.50

Invertebrates — A117

Designs: 12p, Blushing snail. 25p, Golden sail spider. 53p, Spiky yellow woodlouse. 60p, St. Helena shore crab. £1, Giant earwig.

**1995, Aug. 29 Wmk. 373 *Perf. 14***

**655** A117 12p multicolored 1.30 1.40
**656** A117 25p multicolored 2.00 2.25
**657** A117 53p multicolored 3.25 3.75
**658** A117 60p multicolored 3.75 4.25
*Nos. 655-658 (4)* 10.30 11.65

**Souvenir Sheet**

**659** A117 £1 multicolored 7.50 8.00

Souvenir Sheet

Orchids — A118

a, Epidendrum ibaguense. b, Vanda Miss Joquim.

***Perf. 14½x14***

**1995, Sept. 1 Wmk. 384**

**660** A118 50p Sheet of 2, #a.-b. 8.50 8.50

Singapore '95.

Christmas
A119

Children's drawings: 12p, Christmas Eve in Jamestown. 15p, Santa, musicians. 25p, Party at Blue Hill Community Center. 38p, Santa walking in Jamestown. 60p, RMS St. Helena.

***Perf. 14x14½***

**1995, Oct. 17 Litho. Wmk. 373**

**661** A119 12p multicolored .55 .55
**662** A119 15p multicolored .65 .65
**663** A119 25p multicolored 1.10 1.10
**664** A119 38p multicolored 1.60 1.60
**665** A119 60p multicolored 2.25 2.25
*Nos. 661-665 (5)* 6.15 6.15

Union Castle Mail Ships
A120

12p, Walmer Castle, 1915. 25p, Llangibby Castle, 1934. 53p, Stirling Castle, 1940. 60p, Pendennis Castle, 1965.

**Wmk. 384**

**1996, Jan. 8 Litho. *Perf. 14***

**666** A120 12p multicolored 1.40 1.40
**667** A120 25p multicolored 2.50 2.50
**668** A120 53p multicolored 5.25 5.25
**669** A120 60p multicolored 5.75 5.75
*Nos. 666-669 (4)* 14.90 14.90

See Nos. 707-710.

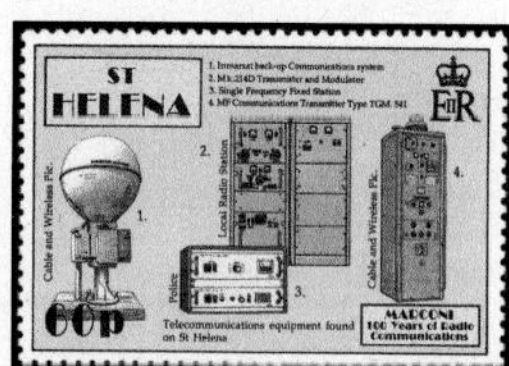
Radio, Cent.
A121

Designs: 60p, Telecommunications equipment on St. Helena. £1, Marconi aboard yacht, Elettra.

**Wmk. 373**

**1996, Mar. 28 Litho. *Perf. 13½***

**670** A121 60p multicolored 3.00 3.00
**671** A121 £1 multicolored 5.00 5.00

**Queen Elizabeth II, 70th Birthday**
Common Design Type

Various portraits of Queen, scenes of St. Helena: 15p, Jamestown. 25p, Prince Andrew School. 53p, Castle entrance. 60p, Plantation house.
£1.50, Queen wearing tiara, formal dress.

***Perf. 14x14½***

**1996, Apr. 22 Litho. Wmk. 384**

**672** CD354 15p multicolored .70 .70
**673** CD354 25p multicolored 1.10 1.10
**674** CD354 53p multicolored 2.25 2.25
**675** CD354 60p multicolored 2.40 2.40
*Nos. 672-675 (4)* 6.45 6.45

**Souvenir Sheet**

**676** CD354 £1.50 multicolored 6.00 6.25

CAPEX '96
A122

Postal transport: 12p, Mail airlifted to HMS Protector, 1964. 25p, First local post delivery, motorscooter, 1965. 53p, Mail unloaded at Wideawake Airfield, Ascension Island. 60p, Mail received at St. Helena.
£1, LMS Jubilee Class 4-6-0 locomotive No. 5624 "St. Helena."

**Wmk. 384**

**1996, June 8 Litho. *Perf. 14***

**677** A122 12p multicolored .60 .60
**678** A122 25p multicolored 1.25 1.25
**679** A122 53p multicolored 2.50 2.50
**680** A122 60p multicolored 2.75 2.75
*Nos. 677-680 (4)* 7.10 7.10

**Souvenir Sheet**

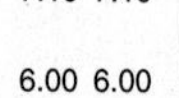

**681** A122 £1 multicolored 6.00 6.00

Napoleonic Sites
A123

12p, Mr. Porteous' House. 25p, Briars Pavillion. 53p, Longwood House. 60p, Napoleon's Tomb.

**Wmk. 373**

**1996, Aug. 12 Litho. *Perf. 14½***

**682** A123 12p multicolored 1.10 1.10
**683** A123 25p multicolored 2.40 2.40
**684** A123 53p multicolored 4.75 4.75
**685** A123 60p multicolored 5.50 5.50
*Nos. 682-685 (4)* 13.75 13.75

Christmas
A124

Flowers: 12p, Frangipani. 15p, Bougainvillaea. 25p, Jacaranda. £1, Pink periwinkle.

**Wmk. 373**

**1996, Oct. 1 Litho. *Perf. 14½***

**686** A124 12p multicolored .60 .60
**687** A124 15p multicolored .80 .80
**688** A124 25p multicolored 1.30 1.30
**689** A124 £1 multicolored 4.50 4.50
*Nos. 686-689 (4)* 7.20 7.20

Endemic Plants — A125

Designs: a, Black cabbage tree. b, Whitewood. c, Tree fern. d, Dwarf jellico. e, Lobelia. f, Dogwood.

**1997, Jan. 17 *Perf. 14½x14***

**690** A125 25p Sheet of 6, #a.-f. 13.00 13.00

**Bird Type of 1993**
Souvenir Sheet

**Wmk. 373**

**1997, June 20 Litho. *Perf. 14½***

**691** A108 75p like No. 610 3.00 3.50

Return of Hong Kong to China, July 1, 1997.

Discovery of St. Helena, 500th Anniv. (in 2002) — A126

20p, Discovery by Joao da Nova, May 21, 1502. 25p, 1st inhabitant, Don Fernando Lopez, 1515. 30p, Landing by Thomas Cavendish, 1588. 80p, Ship, Royal Merchant, 1591.

**1997, May 29 *Perf. 14***

**692** A126 20p multicolored 1.40 1.40
**693** A126 25p multicolored 1.75 1.75
**694** A126 30p multicolored 1.90 1.90
**695** A126 80p multicolored 5.00 5.00
*Nos. 692-695 (4)* 10.05 10.05

See Nos. 712-715, 736-739, 755-758, 769-772.

Queen Elizabeth II and Prince Philip, 50th Wedding Anniv. — A127

No. 696, Queen, Prince coming down steps, royal visit, 1947. No. 697, Wedding portrait. No. 698, Wedding portrait, diff. No. 699, Queen receiving flowers, royal visit, 1947. No. 700, Royal visit, 1957. No. 701, Queen, Prince waving from balcony on wedding day.
£1.50, Queen, Prince riding in open carriage.

**Wmk. 384**

**1997, July 10 Litho. *Perf. 13½***

**696** 10p multicolored 1.00 1.00
**697** 10p multicolored 1.00 1.00
*a.* A127 Pair, #696-697 2.50 2.50
**698** 15p multicolored 1.25 1.25
**699** 15p multicolored 1.25 1.25
*a.* A127 Pair, #698-699 3.00 3.00
**700** 50p multicolored 2.25 2.25
**701** 50p multicolored 2.25 2.25
*a.* A127 Pair, #700-701 5.50 5.50
*Nos. 696-701 (6)* 9.00 9.00

**Souvenir Sheet**

***Perf. 14x14½***

**702** A127 £1.50 multi, horiz. 10.00 10.00

Christmas — A128

***Perf. 13½x14***

**1997, Sept. 29 Litho. Wmk. 384**

**703** A128 15p Flowers .95 .95
**704** A128 20p Calligraphy 1.35 1.35
**705** A128 40p Camping 2.40 2.40
**706** A128 75p Entertaining 4.75 4.75
*Nos. 703-706 (4)* 9.45 9.45

Duke of Edinburgh's Award in St. Helena, 25th anniv.

**Union Castle Mail Ships Type of 1996**

20p, Avondale Castle, 1900. 25p, Dunnottar Castle, 1936. 30p, Llandovery Castle, 1943. 80p, Good Hope Castle, 1977.

**Wmk. 384**

**1998, Jan. 2 Litho. *Perf. 14***

**707** A120 20p multicolored 2.75 2.25
**708** A120 25p multicolored 3.00 2.25
**709** A120 30p multicolored 3.25 2.25
**710** A120 80p multicolored 6.50 6.50
*Nos. 707-710 (4)* 15.50 13.25

**Diana, Princess of Wales (1961-97)**
Common Design Type

a, Wearing hat. b, In white pin-striped suit jacket. c, In green jacket. d, Wearing choker necklace.

***Perf. 14½x14***

**1998, Apr. 4 Litho. Wmk. 373**

**711** CD355 30p Sheet of 4, #a.-d. 4.25 4.25

No. 711 sold for £1.20 + 20p, with surtax from international sales being donated to Princess Diana Memorial Fund and surtax from national sales being donated to designated local charity.

**Discovery of St. Helena, 500th Anniv. Type of 1997**

17th Century events, horiz.: 20p, Fortifying and planting, 1659. 25p, Dutch invasion, 1672. 30p, English recapture, 1673. 80p, Royal Charter, 1673.

**Wmk. 384**

**1998, July 2 Litho. *Perf. 14***
**Size: 39x26mm**

| | | | |
|---|---|---|---|
| **712** A126 20p multicolored | 1.15 | 1.15 |
| **713** A126 25p multicolored | 1.60 | 1.60 |
| **714** A126 30p multicolored | 2.10 | 2.10 |
| **715** A126 80p multicolored | 4.00 | 4.00 |
| *Nos. 712-715 (4)* | 8.85 | 8.85 |

Maritime Heritage — A129

Ships: 10p, HMS Desire, 1588. 15p, Dutch ship, "White Leeuw," 1602. 20p, HMS Swallow, HMS Dolphin, 1751. 25p, HMS Endeavour, 1771. 30p, HMS Providence, 1792. 35p, HMS St. Helena, 1815. 40p, HMS Northumberland, 1815. 50p, Russian brig, "Rurik," 1815. 75p, HMS Erebus, 1826. 80p, Pole junk, "Keying," 1847. £2, La Belle Poule, 1840. £5, HMS Rattlesnake, 1861.

***Perf. 13½x14***

**1998, Aug. 25 Litho. Wmk. 373**

| | | |
|---|---|---|
| **716** A129 10p multicolored | .65 | .90 |
| **717** A129 15p multicolored | .70 | .90 |
| **718** A129 20p multicolored | .75 | .90 |
| **719** A129 25p multicolored | .90 | 1.35 |
| **720** A129 30p multicolored | 1.25 | 1.45 |
| **721** A129 35p multicolored | 1.35 | 1.60 |
| **722** A129 40p multicolored | 1.75 | 2.00 |
| **723** A129 50p multicolored | 2.25 | 3.00 |
| **724** A129 75p multicolored | 3.25 | 4.00 |
| **725** A129 80p multicolored | 3.75 | 4.50 |
| **726** A129 £2 multicolored | 9.00 | 11.00 |
| **727** A129 £5 multicolored | 21.00 | 22.00 |
| *Nos. 716-727 (12)* | 46.60 | 53.60 |

Christmas A130

Island crafts: 15p, Metal work. 20p, Wood turning. 30p, Inlaid woodwork. 85p, Hessian and seedwork.

**1998, Sept. 28 *Perf. 14***

| | | |
|---|---|---|
| **728** A130 15p multicolored | .55 | .55 |
| **729** A130 20p multicolored | .75 | .75 |
| **730** A130 30p multicolored | 1.30 | 1.30 |
| **731** A130 85p multicolored | 3.00 | 3.00 |
| *Nos. 728-731 (4)* | 5.60 | 5.60 |

Souvenir Sheet

H. M. Bark Endeavour at Anchor, 1771 — A131

***Perf. 13½x14***

**1999, Mar. 5 Litho. Wmk. 373**

**732** A131 £1.50 multicolored 9.75 9.75

Australia '99 World Stamp Expo.

**Wedding of Prince Edward and Sophie Rhys-Jones**
Common Design Type
***Perf. 13¾x14***

**1999, June 15 Litho. Wmk. 384**

| | | |
|---|---|---|
| **733** CD356 30p Separate portraits | 1.00 | 1.00 |
| **734** CD356 £1.30 Couple | 4.00 | 4.00 |

Souvenir Sheet

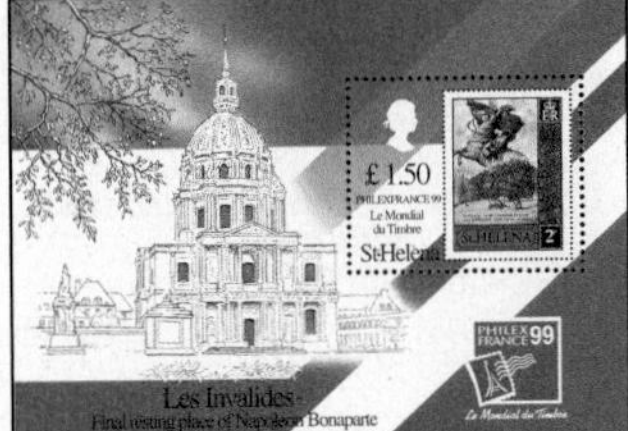


PhilexFrance '99, World Philatelic Exhibition — A132

**1999, July 2 *Perf. 14***

**735** A132 £1.50 #261 8.00 8.00

**Discovery of St. Helena, 500th Anniv. Type of 1997**

Designs, horiz: 20p, Jamestown fortification. 25p, First safe roadway up Ladder Hill, 1718. 30p, Governor Skottowe with Captain Cook. 80p, Presentation of sword of honor to Governor Brooke, 1799.

***Perf. 14¼x14***

**1999, July 12 Litho. Wmk. 373**

| | | |
|---|---|---|
| **736** A126 20p multicolored | 1.90 | 1.90 |
| **737** A126 25p multicolored | 2.25 | 2.25 |
| **738** A126 30p multicolored | 2.75 | 2.75 |
| **739** A126 80p multicolored | 5.75 | 5.75 |
| *Nos. 736-739 (4)* | 12.65 | 12.65 |

**Queen Mother's Century**
Common Design Type

Queen Mother: 15p, With King George VI visiting St. Helena. 25p, With King George VI inspecting bomb damage at Buckingham Palace. 30p, With Prince Andrew, 97th birthday. 80p, As commandant-in-chief of Royal Air Force Central Flying School.

£1.50, With family at coronation of King George VI.

**Wmk. 384**

**1999, Sept. 3 Litho. *Perf. 13½***

| | | |
|---|---|---|
| **740** CD358 15p multicolored | .75 | .75 |
| **741** CD358 25p multicolored | 1.40 | 1.40 |
| **742** CD358 30p multicolored | 1.75 | 1.75 |
| **743** CD358 80p multicolored | 4.25 | 4.25 |
| *Nos. 740-743 (4)* | 8.15 | 8.15 |

**Souvenir Sheet**

**744** CD358 £1.50 multicolored 8.00 8.00

Cable & Wireless, Cent. A133

**Wmk. 373**

**1999, Nov. 26 Litho. *Perf. 14***

| | | |
|---|---|---|
| **745** A133 20p Cable, communication equipment | 1.50 | 1.50 |
| **746** A133 25p CS Seine | 1.75 | 1.75 |
| **747** A133 30p CS Anglia | 2.10 | 2.10 |
| **748** A133 80p Headquarters | 5.75 | 5.75 |
| *Nos. 745-748 (4)* | 11.10 | 11.10 |

Souvenir Sheet

Union-Castle Line Centenary Voyage — A134

**1999, Dec. 23 *Perf. 13x13¾***

**749** A134 £2 multicolored 14.00 14.00

British Monarchs — A135

Designs: a, Edward VI. b, James I. c, William III, Mary II. d, George II. e, Victoria. f, George VI.

**Wmk. 373**

**2000, Feb. 29 Litho. *Perf. 14***

**750** A135 30p Sheet of 6, #a.-f. 12.00 12.00

The Stamp Show 2000, London.

Boer War, Cent. A136

Designs: 15p, Distillation plant, Ruperts. 25p, Camp, Broadbottom. 30p, Committee of Boer prisoners. 80p, Boer General Piet Cronjé, prisoner at Kent Cottage.

**Wmk. 373**

**2000, Apr. 10 Litho. *Perf. 14***

**751-754** A136 Set of 4 12.50 12.50

**Discovery of St. Helena, 500th Anniv. Type of 1997**

Designs: 20p, Withdrawal of the East India Company, 1833, horiz. 25p, Abolition of slavery, 1832, horiz. 30p, Napoleon arrives in 1815, departs in 1840, horiz. 80p, Chief Dinizulu, 1890, horiz.

**2000, May 23 Wmk. 373 *Perf. 13¾***

**755-758** A126 Set of 4 11.50 11.50

Souvenir Sheet

Royal Birthdays — A137

No. 759: a, Princess Margaret, 70th birthday. b, Prince Andrew, 40th birthday. c, Prince William, 18th birthday. d, Princess Anne, 50th birthday. e, Queen Mother, 100th birthday.

**2000, Aug. 4 Wmk. 384 *Perf. 14***

| | | |
|---|---|---|
| **759** A137 Sheet of 5 | 37.50 | 37.50 |
| *a.-d.* 25p Any single | 5.25 | 5.25 |
| *e.* 50p multi | 10.50 | 10.50 |

No. 759e is 42x56mm.

Christmas Pantomimes A138

a, Beauty and the Beast. b, Puss in Boots. c, Little Red Riding Hood. d, Jack and the Beanstalk. e, Snow White and the Seven Dwarfs.

**Wmk. 373**

**2000, Oct. 10 Litho. *Perf. 13***

| | | |
|---|---|---|
| **760** Strip of 5 | 7.00 | 7.00 |
| *a.-e.* A138 20p Any single | 1.10 | 1.10 |

Souvenir Sheet

New Year 2001 (Year of the Snake) — A139

No. 761: a, 30p, Chinese white dolphin. b, 40p, Striped dolphin.

**Wmk. 373**

**2001, Feb. 1 Litho. *Perf. 14½***

**761** A139 Sheet of 2, #a-b 10.00 10.00

Hong Kong 2001 Stamp Exhibition.

Age of Victoria — A140

Designs: 10p, St. Helena #1. 15p, Visit of HMS Beagle, 1836. 20p, Jamestown, horiz. 25p, Queen Victoria, horiz. 30p, Diamond Jubilee, horiz. 50p, Lewis Carroll.

£1.50, Coffee receives award at the Great Exhibition.

**Wmk. 373**

**2001, May 24 Litho. *Perf. 14***

**762-767** A140 Set of 6 10.50 10.50

**Souvenir Sheet**

**768** A140 £1.50 multi 7.00 8.00

**Discovery of St. Helena, 500th Anniv. Type of 1997**

Designs, horiz.: 20p, World Wars I and II. 25p, Schools. 30p, Flax industry. 80p, RMS St. Helena.

**2001, July 19 *Perf. 14x14¾***

**769-772** A126 Set of 4 11.50 11.50

World War II Royal Navy Ships A141

HMS: 15p, Dunedin. 20p, Repulse. 25p, Nelson. 30p, Exmoor. 40p, Eagle. 50p, Milford.

**2001, Sept. 20 *Perf. 14***

**773-778** A141 Set of 6 14.00 14.00

Tammy Wynette (1942-98), American Singer A142

Wynette and Christmas carols: 10p, It Came Upon a Midnight Clear. 15p, Joy to the World. 20p, Away in the Manger. 30p, Silent Night.

**Wmk. 373**

**2001, Oct. 11 Litho. *Perf. 14***

**779-782** A142 Set of 4 4.50 4.50

**Souvenir Sheet**

**783** A142 £1.50 Portrait, vert. 7.00 7.00

Napoleon Bonaparte's Early Years — A143

Napoleon: 20p, As young man. 25p, At military school. 30p, At dance. 80p, With family.

**2001, Nov. 1** *Perf. 13¾x14*
**784-787** A143 Set of 4 12.00 12.00

### Reign Of Queen Elizabeth II, 50th Anniv. Issue
Common Design Type

Designs: Nos. 788, 792a, 20p, Princess Elizabeth with Princess Margaret. Nos. 789, 792b, 25p, Wearing tiara. Nos. 790, 792c, 30p, With Princes Andrew and Edward, 1967. Nos. 791, 792d, 80p, In 1999. No. 792e, 50p, 1955 portrait by Annigoni (38x50mm).

*Perf. 14¼x14½, 13¾ (#792e)*
**2002, Feb. 6** Litho. Wmk. 373
**With Gold Frames**

**788** CD360 20p multicolored .50 .50
**789** CD360 25p multicolored 1.60 1.60
**790** CD360 30p multicolored 1.90 1.90
**791** CD360 80p multicolored 4.75 4.75
*Nos. 788-791 (4)* 8.75 8.75

**Souvenir Sheet**
**Without Gold Frames**

**792** CD360 Sheet of 5, #a-e 11.00 11.00

Birdlife International A144

Wirebird: 10p, With beak open. 15p, Running, vert. 25p, Looking left with beak closed, vert. 30p, In flight. 80p, Looking right with beak closed.

*Perf. 14¼x13¾, 13¾x14¼*
**2002, Apr. 15** Litho.

**793** A144 10p multi .90 .90
a. Perf. 14¼ .60 .60
**794** A144 15p multi 1.25 1.25
a. Perf. 14¼ .85 .85
**795** A144 30p multi 1.75 1.75
a. Perf. 14¼ 1.40 1.40
**796** A144 80p multi 4.25 4.25
a. Perf. 14¼ 3.50 3.50
*Nos. 793-796 (4)* 8.15 8.15

**Souvenir Sheet**
*Perf. 14¼*

**797** A144 Sheet, #793a-796a, 797a 9.00 9.00
a. 25p multi 2.60 2.60

Discovery of St. Helena, 500th Anniv. A145

View of island and: 20p, Sir William W. Doveton (1753-1843), council member, military officer. 25p, Canon Lawrence C. Walcott (1880-1951). 30p, Governor Hudson R. Janisch (1824-84). 80p, Dr. Wilberforce J. J. Arnold (1867-1925), colonial surgeon.

**Wmk. 373**
**2002, May 21** Litho. *Perf. 14*
**798-801** A145 Set of 4 8.25 8.25

Ships of the Falkland Islands War A146

Designs: 15p, HMS Hermes. 20p, HMS Leeds Castle. 25p, HMS Intrepid. 30p, HMS Glasgow. 40p, RMS St. Helena, HMS Brecon, HMS Ledbury. 50p, HMS Courageous.

**Wmk. 373**
**2002, June 14** Litho. *Perf. 14*
**802-807** A146 Set of 6 9.50 9.50

### Queen Mother Elizabeth (1900-2002)
Common Design Type

Designs: 20p, Holding baby (black and white photograph). 25p, Wearing red hat. 30p, As young woman, without hat (black and white photograph). 50p, Wearing blue hat.

No. 812: a, 35p, Without hat, diff. (black and white photo). b, £1, Wearing royal blue hat and scarf.

**Wmk. 373**
**2002, Aug. 5** Litho. *Perf. 14¼*
**With Purple Frames**

**808** CD361 20p multicolored .50 .50
**809** CD361 25p multicolored 1.00 1.00
**810** CD361 30p multicolored 1.50 1.50
**811** CD361 50p multicolored 2.50 2.50
*Nos. 808-811 (4)* 5.50 5.50

**Souvenir Sheet**
**Without Purple Frames**
*Perf. 14½x14¼*

**812** CD361 Sheet of 2, #a-b 6.50 6.50

Worldwide Fund for Nature (WWF) A147

Sperm whales: 10p, Three underwater. 15p, One surfacing. 20p, Two underwater. 30p, One with tail out of water.

**Wmk. 373**
**2002, Oct. 3** Litho. *Perf. 14*
**813-816** A147 Set of 4 5.00 5.00
*816a* Strip of 4, #813-816 5.25 5.25

**Souvenir Sheet**

Visit of Princess Royal (Princess Anne) — A148

**Wmk. 373**
**2002, Nov. 15** Litho. *Perf. 14*
**817** A148 £2 multi 9.00 9.00

Tourism A149

Design: No. 818, Ship Queen Elizabeth 2 visits St. Helena.

No. 819: a, Plantation House. b, RMS St. Helena in Jamestown harbor. c, Napoleon's Tomb, Briars Pavilion. d, Ebony flower, Diana's Peak. e, Wirebird, Napoleon's House. f, Broadway House. g, St. Helena Golf Course. h, St. Helena Yacht Club. i, Sport fishing. j, Diving Club. k, St. Helena Heritage Society Museum.

*Perf. 13½x13¼*
**2003, Apr. 8** Litho. Wmk. 373
**818** A149 25p multi 2.00 2.00
**819** A149 25p Sheet of 12, #a-k, 818 + 4 labels 15.50 15.50

### Head of Queen Elizabeth II
Common Design Type

**Wmk. 373**
**2003, June 2** Litho. *Perf. 13¾*
**820** CD362 £2.50 multi 9.00 9.00

### Coronation of Queen Elizabeth II, 50th Anniv.
Common Design Type

Designs: Nos. 821, 823a, 30p, Queen with scepter. Nos. 822, 824b, 50p, Queen in carriage.

*Perf. 14¼x14½*
**2003, June 2** Litho. Wmk. 373
**Vignettes Framed, Red Background**

**821** CD363 30p multicolored 1.50 1.50
**822** CD363 50p multicolored 2.00 2.00

**Souvenir Sheet**
**Vignettes Without Frame, Purple Panel**

**823** CD363 Sheet of 2, #a-b 3.75 3.75

Wild Flowers — A150

Designs: 10p, Monkey toe. 15p, Buddleia madagascariensis. 20p, Lady's petticoat. 25p, Fuchsia boliviana. 30p, Tallowvine. 40p, Elderberry. 50p Yellow pops. 75p, Lucky leaf. 80p, Ginger. £1, Lily shot. £2, Waxy ginger. £5, Lantana camara.

**Wmk. 373**
**2003, June 10** Litho. *Perf. 14*

**824** A150 10p multi .45 .45
**825** A150 15p multi .60 .60
**826** A150 20p multi .80 .80
**827** A150 25p multi 1.00 1.00
**828** A150 30p multi 1.25 1.25
**829** A150 40p multi 1.60 1.60
**830** A150 50p multi 2.00 2.00
**831** A150 75p multi 3.00 3.50
**832** A150 80p multi 3.25 4.00
**833** A150 £1 multi 4.00 5.00
**834** A150 £2 multi 7.75 10.00
**835** A150 £5 multi 19.00 22.50
*Nos. 824-835 (12)* 44.70 52.70

Powered Flight, Cent. — A151

Designs: 10p, Westland-Aerospatiale Lynx Helicopter. 15p, Douglas C-124 Globemaster. 20p, British Aerospace Nimrod AEW Mk3. 25p, Lockheed C-130 Hercules. 30p, Lockheed Tristar. 50p, Wright Flyer.

£1.80, Supermarine Walrus.

**2003, Aug. 12** Wmk. 373
**Stamp + Label**
**836-841** A151 Set of 6 11.00 11.00

**Souvenir Sheet**
**842** A151 £1.80 multi 9.00 9.00

Christmas — A152

Astronomical photos: 10p, Large Magellanic Cloud. 15p, Small Magellanic Cloud. 20p, Omega Centauri. 25p, Eta Carinae. 30p, Southern Cross.

**Wmk. 373**
**2003, Oct. 6** Litho. *Perf. 13½*
**843-847** A152 Set of 5 8.00 8.00

Medical Pioneers A153

Designs: 10p, Christiaan Barnard (1922-2001). 25p, Marie Curie (1867-1934). 30p, Louis Pasteur (1822-95). 50p, Sir Alexander Fleming (1881-1955).

**Wmk. 373**
**2004, Mar. 19** Litho. *Perf. 14¼*
**848-851** A153 Set of 4 9.00 9.00

Royal Horticultural Society, Bicent. — A154

Flowers: 10p, Freesia. 15p, Bottle brush. 30p, Ebony. 50p, Olive.

£1, Maurandya.

**Wmk. 373**
**2004, May 25** Litho. *Perf. 14*
**852-855** A154 Set of 4 5.00 5.00

**Souvenir Sheet**
**856** A154 £1 multi 4.00 4.00

Merchant Ships A155

Designs: 20p, SS Umtata. 30p, SS Umzinto. 50p, SS Umtali. 80p, SS Umbilo.

**Wmk. 373**
**2004, Nov. 4** Litho. *Perf. 13¼*
**857-860** A155 Set of 4 12.00 11.50

Christmas — A156

Stained-glass windows: 10p, St. Matthew. 15p, St. John. 20p, St. Peter. 30p, St. James. 50p, St. Paul.

**Wmk. 373**
**2004, Oct. 5** Litho. *Perf. 14*
**861-865** A156 Set of 5 7.50 7.50

Rock Formations — A157

**Wmk. 373**
**2005, Jan. 14** Litho. *Perf. 14*
**866** Horiz. strip of 4 11.00 11.00
a. A157 35p The Friar 1.60 1.60
b. A157 40p Sugar Loaf 1.90 1.90
c. A157 50p The Turk's Cap 2.10 2.10
d. A157 £1 Lot's Wife 4.25 4.25

Battle of Trafalgar, Bicent. — A158

Designs: 10p, HMS Bellerophon in action against the Aigle and Monarca. 20p, British 18-pounder naval pattern cannon. 30p, HMS Victory. 50p, Royal Navy first lieutenant, 1805, vert. 60p, HMS Conquerer, vert. 80p, Portrait of Admiral Horatio Nelson, vert.

No. 873, vert.: a, Portrait of Admiral Cuthbert Collingwood. b, HMS Royal Sovereign.

**Wmk. 373, Unwmkd. (30p)**

**2005, May 10 Litho. *Perf. 13½***

**867-872** A158 Set of 6 16.00 16.00

**Souvenir Sheet**

**873** A158 75p Sheet of 2, #a-b 9.00 9.00

No. 869 has particles of wood from the HMS Victory embedded in the areas covered by a thermographic process that produces a raised, shiny effect.

Miniature Sheet

End of World War II, 60th Anniv. — A159

No. 874: a, 20p, HMS Milford. b, 20p, HMS Nelson. c, 20p, RFA Darkdale. d, 20p, HMS St. Helena. e, 20p, Ship and Atlantic Star Medal. f, 30p, Codebreaker Alan M. Turing and Enigma code machine. g, 30p, Capt. Johnnie Walker, HMS Starling. h, 30p, British Prime Minister Winston Churchill. i, 30p, Churchill infantry tank. j, 30p, Hawker Hurricanes.

**Wmk. 373**

**2005, June 24 Litho. *Perf. 13¾***

**874** A159 Sheet of 10, #a-j 16.50 16.50

Pope John Paul II (1920-2005) A160

**Wmk. 373**

**2005, Aug. 31 Litho. *Perf. 14***

**875** A160 50p multi 3.00 3.00

England's Elizabethan Era — A161

No. 876, 10p: a, Sir Francis Drake. b, Golden Hind.

No. 877, 15p: a, Sir Walter Raleigh. b, Ark Royal.

No. 878, 25p: a, Queen Elizabeth I. b, Spanish Armada.

No. 879, £1: a, William Shakespeare. b, Old Globe Theater.

**2005, Sept. 7 *Perf. 13¾***

**Horiz. Pairs, #a-b**

**876-879** A161 Set of 4 15.00 15.00

Christmas — A162

Stories by Hans Christian Andersen (1805-75): 10p, The Little Fir Tree. 25p, The Ugly Duckling. 30p, The Snow Queen. £1, The Little Mermaid.

**Wmk. 373**

**2005, Oct. 4 Litho. *Perf. 14***

**880-883** A162 Set of 4 7.25 7.25

Battle of Trafalgar, Bicent. — A163

Designs: 50p, HMS Victory. 80p, Ships in battle, horiz. £1.20, Admiral Horatio Nelson.

**2005, Oct. 18 Unwmk. *Perf. 13¼***

**884-886** A163 Set of 3 12.00 12.00

Stamps in the British Library Collection — A164

Designs: 10p, St. Helena #B2-B4. 20p, Cape of Good Hope #6. 25p, US #C3a. 30p, St. Helena #1. 80p, Great Britain #1. £1.20, Mauritius #2.

£2, Like 30p.

***Perf. 14¼x14¾***

**2006, Jan. 16 Litho. Wmk. 373**

**887-892** A164 Set of 6 18.00 18.00

**Souvenir Sheet**

**893** A164 £2 multi 11.00 11.00

St. Helena postage stamps, 150th anniv. (Nos. 890, 893).

Europa Stamps, 50th Anniv. A165

Designs: 10p, Five stars, European Union flag. 30p, Five stars, letter. 80p, Four stars, ball. £1.20, Star painting stamp, three stars in circle.

**2006, Feb. 6 Unwmk. *Perf. 14***

**894-897** A165 Set of 4 13.00 13.00

*897a* Souvenir sheet, #894-897 12.50 12.50

Queen Elizabeth II, 80th Birthday A166

Queen: 10p, As young girl. 30p, As young woman, wearing tiara. 80p, As older woman, wearing tiara. £1.20, With gray hair.

No. 902: a, Wearing tiara. b, Without head covering.

**Wmk. 373**

**2006, Apr. 21 Litho. *Perf. 14***

**898-901** A166 Set of 4 13.00 13.00

**Souvenir Sheet**

**902** A166 £1 Sheet of 2, #a-b 11.00 11.00

Miniature Sheet

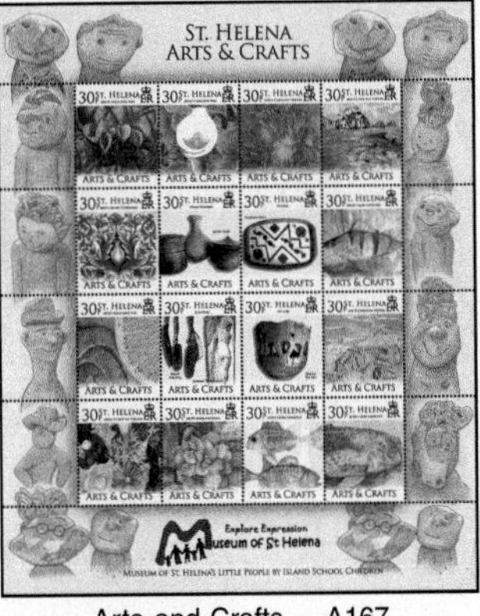

Arts and Crafts — A167

No. 903: a, Painting of red flower, by Emma-Jane Yon. b, Painting of white lily, by Yon. c, Painting of red flower, by Christina Stroud. d, Painting of dolphins, by Stroud. e, Painting of flowers, by Muriel Gardener. f, Turned wood objects, by Jackie Essex. g, Pottery by Corinda Essex. h, Painting of striped fish, by Laura Lawrence. i, Painting of orange and peel, by Yon. j, Sculptures by Sandy Walters and Johnny Drummond. k, Pottery by Serena Thorpe. l, Painting of shells, by Stroud. m, Painting of flowers, by Stroud. n, Painting of flower, by Lawrence. o, Painting of two fish, by Lawrence. p, Painting of red fish, by Lawrence.

**2006, May 20 *Perf. 13¾***

**903** A167 30p Sheet of 16, #a-p 22.50 22.50

Christmas — A168

Designs: 10p, Partridge in a pear tree. 15p, Two turtle doves. 25p, Three French hens. 30p, Four calling birds. 50p, Five golden rings. £1, Six geese a-laying.

***Perf. 13¾x13½***

**2006, Aug. 31 Litho. Wmk. 373**

**904-909** A168 Set of 6 10.50 10.50

Values are for stamps with surrounding selvage.

See Nos. 931-936.

Anniversaries — A169

No. 910, 20p: a, Queen Victoria at first investiture of Victoria Cross. b, Charge of the Light Brigade, Victoria Cross.

No. 911, 25p: a, Charles Darwin. b, Wirebird.

No. 912, 30p: a, Isambard Kingdom Brunel, coal cars at Cardiff docks. b, RMS St. Helena at Cardiff docks.

No. 913, £1: a, Charles Dickens, Dingley Dell cricket match. b, Samuel Pickwick, cricket match.

**Wmk. 373**

**2006, Nov. 16 Litho. *Perf. 13¾***

**Horiz. Pairs, #a-b**

**910-913** A169 Set of 4 24.00 24.00

Victoria Cross, 150th anniv.; Darwin's visit to St. Helena, 170th anniv.; Birth of Brunel, 200th anniv.; Publishing of Dickens' Pickwick Papers, 170th anniv.

Bonapartes A170

Designs: 25p, Napoleon II (1811-32). 30p, Napoleon I (1769-1821). £1, Napoleon III (1808-73).

**2007, Jan. 16 *Perf. 15x14¼***

**914-916** A170 Set of 3 7.75 7.75

*916a* Souvenir sheet, #914-916 7.75 7.75

Wedding of Queen Elizabeth II and Prince Philip, 60th Anniv. — A171

Designs: 25p, Couple. 35p, Queen in wedding gown. 40p, Couple, Queen in Wedding gown. No. 920, £2, Couple and coach.

No. 921, £2, Couple, Queen in wedding gown, diff.

**Wmk. 373**

**2007, Apr. 26 Litho. *Perf. 13¾***

**917-920** A171 Set of 4 15.00 15.00

**Souvenir Sheet**

***Perf. 14¼***

**921** A171 £2 multi 10.00 10.00

No. 921 contains one 43x57mm stamp.

BirdLife International — A172

Designs; 15p, Black noddies. 30p, Madeiran storm petrels. 50p, Masked boobies. £2, Sooty terns.

**2007, June 12 *Perf. 12½x13***

**922-925** A172 Set of 4 15.00 15.00

Scouting, Cent. A173

Designs: 15p, Scout patches, neckerchief. 30p, Lord Robert Baden-Powell inspecting Scouts, 1936, trumpeter. 50p, Baden-Powell and Rev. L. C. Walcott, compass. No. 929, £1, Baden-Powell, rope lashing.

No. 930, £1, vert.: a, Emblem of 1st Jamestown Scout Group. b, Baden-Powell.

**2007, July 9** *Perf. 13¾*
**926-929** A173 Set of 4 9.00 9.00

**Souvenir Sheet**

**930** A173 £1 Sheet of 2, #a-b 9.00 9.00

### Christmas Type of 2006

Designs: 10p, Seven swans a-swimming. 15p, Eight maids a-milking. 25p, Nine ladies dancing. 30p, Ten lords a-leaping. 50p, Eleven pipers piping. £1, Twelve drummers drumming.

*Perf. 13¾x13½*

**2007, Sept. 3 Litho. Wmk. 373**
**931-936** A168 Set of 6 10.50 10.50

Values are for stamps with surrounding selvage.

Atlantic Ocean Navigation and Aviation Firsts — A174

Designs: 25p, SS Savannah, first steamship to cross the Atlantic, 1819. 40p, Airplane of Alcock & Brown, first pilots to cross the Atlantic, 1919. 45p, Sailboat of Alain Gerbault, first man to sail solo east to west across the Atlantic, 1923. £1.20, Charles Lindbergh's Spirit of St. Louis, first solo flight across the Atlantic, 1927.

**Wmk. 373**

**2007, Nov. 6 Litho.** *Perf. 14*
**937-940** A174 Set of 4 12.00 12.00

Royal Air Force, 90th Anniv. A175

Airplanes: 15p, Airco D. H. 9. 25p, Hawker Hurricane. 35p, Handley Page Hastings. 40p, English Electric Lightning. 50p, Harrier GR7. £1.50, Berlin Airlift airplane.

**Wmk. 373**

**2008, Apr. 1 Litho.** *Perf. 14*
**941-945** A175 Set of 5 10.00 10.00

**Souvenir Sheet**

**946** A175 £1.50 multi 7.50 7.50

Nos. 941-945 each printed in sheets of 8 + label.

Souvenir Sheet

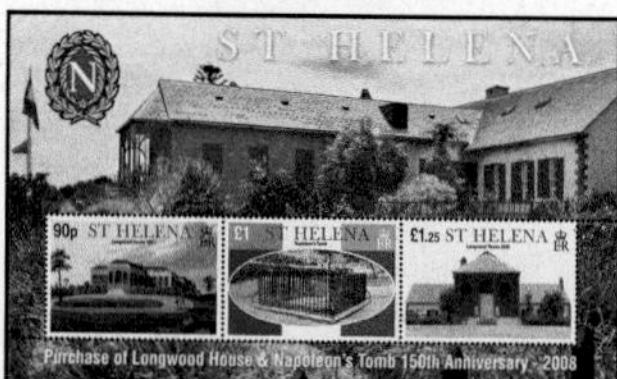

Napoleonic Sites on St. Helena — A176

No. 947: a, 90p, Longwood House in 1821. b, £1, Napoleon's tomb. c, £1.25, Longwood House in 2008.

*Perf. 13¼x13¾*

**2008, May 7 Litho. Wmk. 373**
**947** A176 Sheet of 3, #a-c 15.00 15.00

### Bird Type of 2007 Without BirdLife International Emblem

Designs: 15p, Brown boobies. 35p, Brown noddies. 40p, Fairy terns. £1.25, Red-billed tropicbirds.

**2008, July 17** *Perf. 12½x13*
**948-951** A172 Set of 4 10.00 10.00

Fish A177

Designs: 5p, Deepwater bullseye. 10p, Five finger. 15p, Deepwater greenfish. 20p, Hardback soldier. 25p, Deepwater gurnard. 35p, Red mullet. 40p, Softback soldier. 50p, Rock bullseye. 80p, Gurnard. £1, Cunningfish. £2, Hogfish. £5, Marmalade razorfish.

**2008, Aug. 19** *Perf. 13¾*

| | | | | |
|---|---|---|---|---|
| **952** | A177 | 5p multi | .30 | .30 |
| **953** | A177 | 10p multi | .45 | .45 |
| **954** | A177 | 15p multi | .65 | .65 |
| **955** | A177 | 20p multi | .90 | .90 |
| **956** | A177 | 25p multi | 1.05 | 1.05 |
| **957** | A177 | 35p multi | 1.60 | 1.60 |
| **958** | A177 | 40p multi | 1.75 | 1.75 |
| **959** | A177 | 50p multi | 2.10 | 2.10 |
| **960** | A177 | 80p multi | 3.50 | 3.50 |
| **961** | A177 | £1 multi | 4.50 | 4.50 |
| **962** | A177 | £2 multi | 8.50 | 8.50 |
| **963** | A177 | £5 multi | 21.00 | 21.00 |
| *a.* | | Sheet of 12, #952-963 | 47.50 | 47.50 |
| | | *Nos. 952-963 (12)* | 46.30 | 46.30 |

Flag — A178

**2008, Aug. 19 Unwmk.** *Die Cut*

**Booklet Stamp**
**Self-Adhesive**

**964** A178 35p multi 2.00 2.00
*a.* Booklet pane of 12 24.00

Christmas A179

Flowers: 15p, African lily. 25p, Christmas cactus. 35p, Honeysuckle. 40p, St. John's lily. £1, Crucifix orchid.

*Perf. 13x12½*

**2008, Sept. 1 Litho. Wmk. 373**
**965-969** A179 Set of 5 8.50 8.50

End of World War I, 90th Anniv. — A180

Poetry about World War I: 10p, "The Soldier," by Rupert Brooke. 15p, "Aftermath," by Siegfried Sassoon. 25p, "Anthem for Doomed Youth," by Wilfred Owen. 35p, "For the Fallen," by Laurence Binyon. 40p, "In Flanders Fields," by John McCrae. 50p, "In Memoriam," by Edward Thomas.
£2, Cenotaph, St. Helena.

**2008, Sept. 16 Wmk. 406** *Perf. 14*
**970-975** A180 Set of 6 9.00 9.00

**Souvenir Sheet**

**976** A180 £2 multi 8.50 8.50

Miniature Sheet

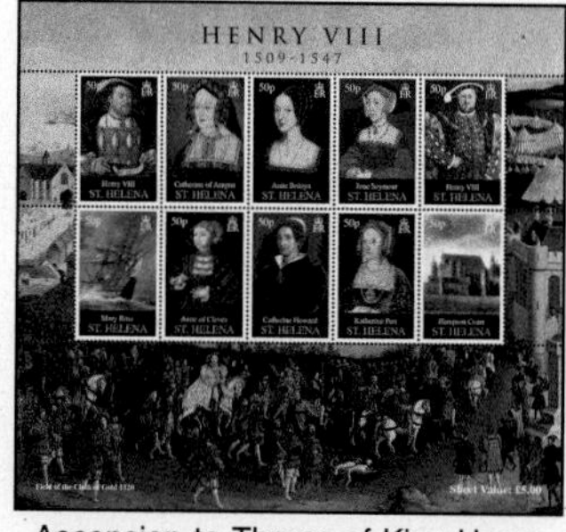


Ascension to Throne of King Henry VIII (1491-1547), 500th Anniv. — A181

No. 977: a, Henry VIII holding scroll. b, Catherine of Aragon (1485-1536), first wife. c, Anne Boleyn (c. 1507-36), second wife. d, Jane Seymour (c. 1509-37), third wife. e, Henry VIII, diff. f, Ship Mary Rose. g, Anne of Cleves (1515-57), fourth wife. h, Catherine Howard (c. 1520-42), fifth wife. i, Catherine Parr (1512-48), sixth wife. j, Hampton Court.

**Wmk. 373**

**2009, Jan. 9 Litho.** *Perf. 14*
**977** A181 50p Sheet of 10, #a-j 22.50 22.50

Naval Aviation, Cent. A182

Designs: 15p, Westland Sea King helicopter and Royal Navy ship. 35p, Fairey Swordfish and Royal Navy ships. 40p, BAe Harrier. 50p, Blackburn Buccaneer and Royal Navy ship.
£1.50, Lieutenant E. L. Gerrard in airplane at Central Flying School, 1913.

**Wmk. 406**

**2009, Apr. 17 Litho.** *Perf. 14*
**978-981** A182 Set of 4 9.50 9.50

**Souvenir Sheet**

**982** A182 £1.50 multi 8.00 8.00

Nos. 978-981 each were printed in sheets of 8 + central label.

Souvenir Sheet

Donation of the Briars Pavilion, 50th Anniv. — A183

No. 983: a, 90p, Briars Pavilion, c. 1857. b, £1, Napoleon Bonaparte and Betsy Balcombe. c, £1.25, Briars Pavilion, 2008.

**2009, May 26 Litho.** *Perf. 13¼x13¾*
**983** A183 Sheet of 3, #a-c 15.00 15.00

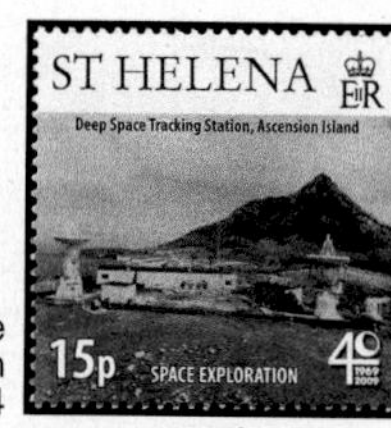


Space Exploration A184

Designs: 15p, Deep Space Tracking Station, Ascension Island. 35p, Early rocketry experiment by Dr. Robert Goddard. 40p, Launch of Apollo 11. 90p, Space Shuttle Discovery landing. No. 988, £1.20, Astronauts working on International Space Station.
No. 989, £1.20, Astronauts on Moon, painting by Capt. Alan Bean, vert.

**Wmk. 406**

**2009, July 20 Litho.** *Perf. 13¼*
**984-988** A184 Set of 5 11.50 11.50

**Souvenir Sheet**

*Perf. 13x13½*

**989** A184 £1.20 multi 5.00 5.00

First man on the Moon, 40th anniv. No. 989 contains one 40x60mm stamp.

Christmas — A185

Designs: 15p, Christmas parade. 25p, Christmas pageant in church. 40p, Church at night. £1, Christmas lights on buildings.

**Wmk. 406**

**2009, Sept. 1 Litho.** *Perf. 14*
**990-993** A185 Set of 4 7.00 7.00

Anglican Diocese of St. Helena, 150th Anniv. — A186

Designs: 15p, St. Paul's Cathedral. 35p, St. Matthew's Church. 40p, St. James' Church. £1, Piers Calveley Claughton (1814-84), first bishop of St. Helena.

**2009, Oct. 1**
**994-997** A186 Set of 4 7.00 7.00

Miniature Sheet

History of 17th Century England — A187

No. 998: a, King Charles I (1600-49). b, King Charles II (1630-85). c, Prince Rupert (1619-82). d, Oliver Cromwell (1599-1658). e, Richard Cromwell (1626-1712). f, King Charles I arrests members of Parliament. g, New Model Army. h, Execution of King Charles I. i, Dissolution of Parliament. j, Coronation of King Charles II.

**Wmk. 406**

**2010, Jan. 29 Litho.** *Perf. 14*
**998** A187 50p Sheet of 10, #a-j 22.50 22.50

Battle of Britain, 70th Anniv. — A188

Designs: 15p, Children in bunker. 25p, Fire fighters. 35p, Milkman delivering through rubble. 40p, Bus in bomb crater. 90p, Contrails. £1, Lookout.
£1.50, Sir Douglas Bader (1910-82), flying ace.

**Wmk. 406**

**2010, Mar. 18 Litho. *Perf. 13***
**999-1004** A188 Set of 6 14.00 14.00

**Souvenir Sheet**

**1005** A188 £1.50 black & gray 7.50 7.50

Nos. 999-1004 each were printed in sheets of 6.

Souvenir Sheet

Great Britain No. 154 — A189

**Wmk. 406**

**2010, May 8 Litho. *Perf. 14***
**1006** A189 £1.50 multi 6.50 6.50

Reign of King George V, cent. London 2010 Festival of Stamps.

World of Soccer — A190

Designs: No. 1007, 40p, Soccer player and ball. No. 1008, 40p, Map of Africa and St. Helena. No. 1009, 40p, Two soccer players and ball.

**2010, May 14 *Perf. 14x14¾***
**1007-1009** A190 Set of 3 5.00 5.00
*1009a* Souvenir sheet of 3, #1007-1009 5.00 5.00

Girl Guides, Cent. A191

Designs: 15p, Rainbows. 25p, Brownies. 40p, Girl Guides. 90p, Lord Robert Baden-Powell and wife, Olave.

**2010, Aug. 23 *Perf. 14***
**1010-1013** A191 Set of 4 7.00 7.00

Christmas A192

Sites and flowers: 15p, Jacob's Ladder, Crucifix orchid. 25p, Diana's Peak, St. John's lily. 40p, High Knoll Fort, Agapanthus. £1, Heart-shaped Waterfall, Honeysuckle.

**2010, Oct. 25 *Perf. 13¾***
**1014-1017** A192 Set of 4 7.50 7.50

RMS St. Helena, 20th Anniv. — A193

Designs: 15p, Ship in 2010. 35p, Arrival on maiden voyage in St. Helena. 40p, Launch of ship, 1990. 90p, Captain's table.

**2010, Nov. 19 *Perf. 14x14¾***
**1018-1021** A193 Set of 4 7.50 7.50

Service of Queen Elizabeth II and Prince Philip — A194

Designs: 15p, Queen Elizabeth II. 25p, Queen and Prince Philip. 35p, Queen and Prince Philip, diff. No. 1025, 40p, Queen and Prince Philip, Queen wearing yellow dress. No. 1026, 40p, Queen and Prince Philip, Queen wearing blue hat. 90p, Prince Philip.
£1.50, Queen and Prince Philip, diff.

***Perf. 13¼***

**2011, Mar. 1 Litho. Unwmk.**
**1022-1027** A194 Set of 6 9.50 9.50
*1027a* Sheet of 6, #1022-1027, + 3 labels 9.50 9.50

**Souvenir Sheet**

**1028** A194 £1.50 multi 6.00 6.00

Souvenir Sheet

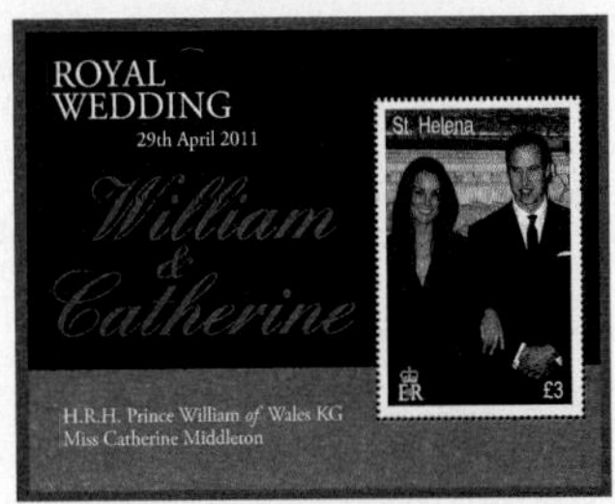


Wedding of Prince William and Catherine Middleton — A195

***Perf. 14¾x14¼***

**2011, Apr. 29 Litho. Wmk. 406**
**1029** A195 £3 multi 11.50 11.50

Photographs of Wedding of Prince William and Catherine Middleton — A196

Designs: 15p, Bride and her sister, Pippa. 35p, Couple in coach waving. 40p, Couple standing, holding hands, vert. 60p, Couple standing and waving, vert. £1, Couple kissing, vert.

**2011, Sept. 1 *Perf. 14¼x14, 14x14¼***
**1030-1034** A196 Set of 5 9.00 9.00

Worldwide Fund for Nature (WWF) — A197

Island hogfish: 35p, Male. 40p, Juvenile. 50p, Immature female. £1.20, £1.50, Male near rocks.

**2011, Oct. 31 *Perf. 14¼x14***
**1035-1038** A197 Set of 4 8.00 8.00
*1038a* Sheet of 16, 4 each #1035-1038 32.00 32.00

**Souvenir Sheet**

**1039** A197 £1.50 multi 5.00 5.00

Christmas A198

Royal Fleet auxiliary ships: 35p, RFA Gold Rover. 50p, RFA Black Rover. 60p, RFA Lyme Bay. £1.20, RFA Darkdale.

**2011, Nov. 14 *Perf. 13¾***
**1040-1043** A198 Set of 4 8.50 8.50

Commonwealth Parliamentary Association, Cent. — A199

Centenary emblem and: No. 1044, 50p, Court House, Jamestown. No. 1045, 50p, Royal Charter. No. 1046, 50p, Commonwealth Parliamentary Association Headquarters, London.

**2011, Nov. 28 *Perf. 13¾x13¼***
**1044-1046** A199 Set of 3 4.75 4.75
*1046a* Souvenir sheet of 3, #1044-1046 4.75 4.75

Reign of Queen Elizabeth II, 60th Anniv. — A200

Various photographs of Queen Elizabeth II: 20p, 35p, 40p, 50p, 60p, £1.
£1.50, Queen Elizabeth II wearing tiara.

**2012, Feb. 6 *Perf. 13½***
**1047-1052** A200 Set of 6 9.75 9.75
*1052a* Souvenir sheet, #1047-1052 + 3 labels 9.75 9.75

**Souvenir Sheet**

**1053** A200 £1.50 multi 4.75 4.75

Children's Art — A201

Various children's drawings commemorating the 60th anniversary of the reign of Queen Elizabeth II: 20p, 35p, 50p, £1.

**2012, June 12 Wmk. 406 *Perf. 14***
**1054-1057** A201 Set of 4 6.50 6.50

Falkland Islands War, 30th Anniv. A202

1982 photographs of RMS St Helena: 20p, Crew. 35p, At Grytviken. 40p, At Ascension Island. 50p, At Grytviken, diff. £1, Under escort.

**2012, June 26**
**1058-1062** A202 Set of 5 7.75 7.75

Christmas A203

Titles of Christmas hymns: 20p, O Little Town of Bethlehem. 35p, While Shepherds Watched. 50p, Away in a Manger. £1, Silent Night, Holy Night.

***Perf. 13¼x13¾***

**2012, Nov. 5 Wmk. 406**
**1063-1066** A203 Set of 4 6.75 6.75

Items Commemorating British Coronations — A204

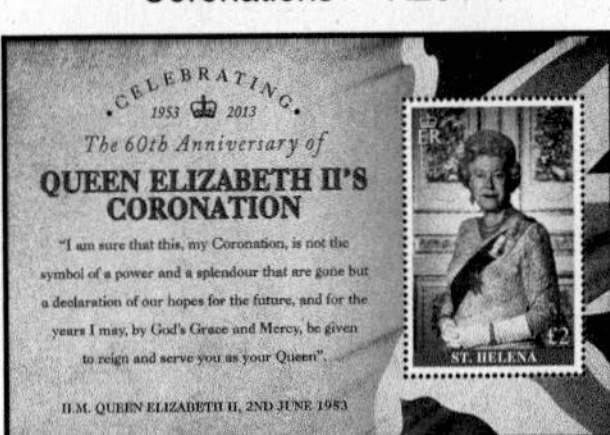


Coronation of Queen Elizabeth, 60th Anniv. — A205

Various items commemorating the coronation of: 20p, Queen Victoria. 35p, King Edward VII. 40p, King George V. 50p, King George VI. £1, Queen Elizabeth II.

**2013, Feb. 6 *Perf. 14***
**1067-1071** A204 Set of 5 7.50 7.50

**Souvenir Sheet**

***Perf. 14¾x14***

**1072** A205 £2 multi 6.00 6.00

Lady Margaret Thatcher (1925-2013), British Prime Minister A206

Various photographs: 40p, 50p, 60p, £1.

**2013, Aug. 8** ***Perf. 13¾***
**1073-1076** A206 Set of 4 8.00 8.00
*1076a* Souvenir sheet of 4, #1073-1076 8.00 8.00

Birth of Prince George of Cambridge A207

Designs: 25p, Duke of Cambridge holding Prince George. 40p, Duchess of Cambridge holding Prince George. 60p, Prince George. £1, Duke and Duchess of Cambridge, Prince George.

***Perf. 13½x13¼***
**2013, Nov. 6** **Litho.** **Wmk. 406**
**1077-1080** A207 Set of 4 7.25 7.25

Airport Project A208

Designs: 25p, NP Glory 4 docked at Rupert's. 40p, Haul Road. 50p, Bradley's Camp. 60p, Dry Gut.
£2, Plant machinery.

**Wmk. 406**
**2014, June 27** **Litho.** ***Perf. 14***
**1081-1084** A208 Set of 4 6.00 6.00

**Souvenir Sheet**

**1085** A208 £2 multi 7.00 7.00

Miniature Sheet

Brownies, Cent. — A209

No. 1086: a, 25p, Emblem (48x54mm). b, 40p, Jamestown Brownies, 1970 (48x27mm). c, 60p, Pat Benjamin presenting bouquet to Princess Margaret (24x54mm). d, 70p, Brownie pack, 1960 (24x54mm). e, £1, Brownie pack Thinking Day, 2014 (48x27mm).

***Perf. 14x14¾***
**2014, Oct. 15** **Litho.** **Wmk. 406**
**1086** A209 Sheet of 5, #a-e 9.50 9.50

Christmas A210

Designs: 25p, Whale shark. 30p, Sea slug. 40p, St. Helena Gregory. 50p, Cunning fish. 60p, Silver eel. £1, Orange cup coral.

**Wmk. 406**
**2014, Oct. 15** **Litho.** ***Perf. 14***
**1087-1092** A210 Set of 6 9.75 9.75

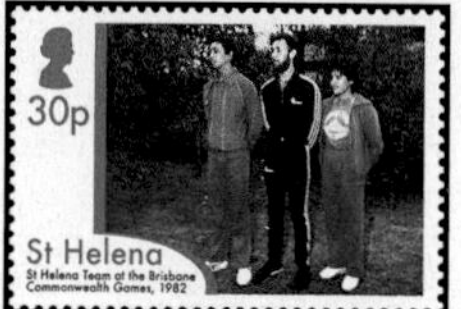
St. Helena's Participation in the Commonwealth Games — A211

Designs: 30p, Team members at Brisbane Commonwealth Games, 1982. 50p, RMS St. Helena crew holding Queen's baton, 2014. 60p, St. Helena National Amateur Sports Association, 2014. £1, Team members at Glasgow Commonwealth Games, 2014.

**Wmk. 406**
**2014, Oct. 20** **Litho.** ***Perf. 14***
**1093-1096** A211 Set of 4 7.75 7.75

Launch of the RMS St. Helena, 25th Anniv. A212

Designs: 25p, Laying of the keel. 30p, Hull construction. 50p, Hull on launch day.
60p, Sea trials.

**Wmk. 406**
**2014, Oct. 31** **Litho.** ***Perf. 14***
**1097-1099** A212 Set of 3 3.50 3.50

**Souvenir Sheet**

**1100** A212 60p multi 1.90 1.90

Paintings of Jamestown Main Street Buildings, by Andy Crowe A213

Various buildings. 50p, 80p are 20x36mm.

**Wmk. 406**
**2015, May 21** **Litho.** ***Perf. 13¼***
**1101** Horiz. strip of 4 7.25 7.25
*a.* A213 40p multi 1.25 1.25
*b.* A213 50p multi 1.60 1.60
*c.* A213 60p multi 1.90 1.90
*d.* A213 80p multi 2.50 2.50

Birds A214

Designs: 5p, Fairy tern. 10p, Zebra dove. 15p, Chukar partridge. 20p, Brown booby. 30p, Java sparrow. 40p, Wilson's storm petrel. 50p, Red-billed tropicbird. 60p, Masked booby. 80p, Sooty tern. £1, Yellow canary. £2, Red fody. £5, Wirebird.

**Wmk. 406**
**2015, Nov. 11** **Litho.** ***Perf. 13¾***
**1102** A214 5p multi .25 .25
**1103** A214 10p multi .30 .30
**1104** A214 15p multi .45 .45
**1105** A214 20p multi .60 .60
**1106** A214 30p multi .90 .90
**1107** A214 40p multi 1.25 1.25
**1108** A214 50p multi 1.50 1.50
**1109** A214 60p multi 1.90 1.90
**1110** A214 80p multi 2.40 2.40
**1111** A214 £1 multi 3.00 3.00
**1112** A214 £2 multi 6.00 6.00
**1113** A214 £5 multi 15.00 15.00
*a.* Souvenir sheet of 12, #1102-1113 33.50 33.50
*Nos. 1102-1113 (12)* 33.55 33.55

Christmas — A215

Santa Claus: 25p, In sleigh. 40p, Holding Christmas tree and bag of gifts. 50p, By Christmas tree. 60p, On chimney. £1, Holding Christmas pudding.

**Wmk. 406**
**2015, Nov. 21** **Litho.** ***Perf. 14***
**1114-1118** A215 Set of 5 8.25 8.25

Airport Project A216

Designs: 25p, Students burying time capsule. 40p, Final rock blast. 50p, Permanent wharf, Rupert's. 60p, Control tower construction.
£2, Runway construction.

**Wmk. 406**
**2016, Jan. 1** **Litho.** ***Perf. 14***
**1119-1122** A216 Set of 4 5.25 5.25

**Souvenir Sheet**

**1123** A216 £2 multi 6.00 6.00

Souvenir Sheet

Napoleon Bonaparte (1769-1821), Emperor of France — A217

**Wmk. 406**
**2016, Feb. 1** **Litho.** ***Perf. 14***
**1124** A217 £2 multi 5.75 5.75

Napoleon's exile on St. Helena, 200th anniv.

Christmas — A218

Designs: 25p, Orchestra and Salvation Army Band playing music. 50p, Salvation Army Band playing music. 60p, Pilling Primary School Choir.

**Wmk. 406**
**2016, Nov. 1** **Litho.** ***Perf. 14***
**1125-1127** A218 Set of 3 3.50 3.50

Flowers A219

Designs: 15p, Poinsettia. 25p, Amaryllis. 60p, Agapanthus. £1, St. John's lily.

***Perf. 13x13½***
**2017, Sept. 30** **Litho.** **Wmk. 406**
**1128-1131** A219 Set of 4 5.50 5.50

Christmas.

Island Scenery A220

Designs: 40p, Shark's Valley. 50p, Lot. 60p, Diana's Peak. £1, Longwood Barn.
£1.50, Lot's Wife's Ponds.

***Perf. 13¼x13¾***
**2017, Oct. 16** **Litho.** **Wmk. 406**
**1132-1135** A220 Set of 4 6.75 6.75

**Souvenir Sheet**

***Perf. 13½***

**1136** A220 £1.50 multi 4.00 4.00

No. 1136 contains one 40x40mm stamp.

Final Voyage of RMS St. Helena A221

Designs: 25p, Launch of RMS St. Helena, 1989. 40p, Farewell celebrations, Cape Town. 50p, Final departure from St. Helena. 60p, Capt. Rodney Young, first captain from St. Helena.
£2, RMS St. Helena leaving James' Bay.

***Perf. 13¼x13½***
**2018, Feb. 10** **Litho.** **Wmk. 406**
**1137-1140** A221 Set of 4 5.00 5.00

**Souvenir Sheet**

**1141** A221 £2 multi 5.50 5.50

Wedding of Prince Harry and Meghan Markle A222

Various photographs of couple: 15p, 25p, 60p, £1.
£1.50, Couple, diff.

***Perf. 14¼x14***
**2018, May 19** **Litho.** **Wmk. 406**
**1142-1145** A222 Set of 4 5.50 5.50

**Souvenir Sheet**

***Perf. 14¼***

**1146** A222 £1.50 multi 4.00 4.00

Airport Project A223

Designs: 25p, Sept. 15, 2015 calibration flight crew. 40p, First calibration flight on runway. 50p, Control tower. 60p, First helicopter landing.
£2, E190-100IGW airplane landing, Oct. 14, 2017.

***Perf. 13¼x13½***
**2018, May 21** **Litho.** **Wmk. 406**
**1147-1150** A223 Set of 4 4.75 4.75

**Souvenir Sheet**

**1151** A223 £2 multi 5.50 5.50

Festival of Lights A224

Christmas parade: 15p, Floats. 50p, At the seafront. 60p, At Market Square. £1, Participants and viewers.

***Perf. 14x14¼***
**2018, Sept. 17** **Litho.** **Wmk. 406**
**1152-1155** A224 Set of 4 6.00 6.00

Jonathan, the Seychelles Giant Tortoise — A225

Various depictions of Jonathan, the oldest land animal: 50p, 60p, 80p, £1.30.

**Wmk. 406**

**2019, Sept. 15 Litho. *Perf. 14¼***

| | | | | |
|---|---|---|---|---|
| **1156-1159** | A225 | Set of 4 | 8.00 | 8.00 |

Seven Wonders of St. Helena A226

Designs: 15p, Whale shark. 25p, Napoleon's House. 30p, Diana's Peak. 50p, Heart-shaped Waterfall. 60p, High Knoll Fort. 80p, Jacob's Ladder. £1, Jonathan the Tortoise.

**Wmk. 406**

**2020, Feb. 1 Litho. *Perf. 14***

| | | | | |
|---|---|---|---|---|
| **1160-1166** | A226 | Set of 7 | 9.50 | 9.50 |

Christmas — A227

Designs: 50p, Angel Gabriel. 60p, Infant Jesus. 80p, Shepherds and sheep. £1.30, Magi.

**Wmk. 406**

**2020, Sept. 1 Litho. *Perf. 14¼***

| | | | | |
|---|---|---|---|---|
| **1167-1170** | A227 | Set of 4 | 8.75 | 8.75 |

Exile of Napoleon Bonaparte (1769-1821), Emperor of France, on St. Helena — A228

Designs; 50p, Napoleon looking to the sea. 80p, Longwood House. £1.30, Napoleon on death bed. £1.50, Tomb of Napoleon. £3, Death of Napoleon, vert.

***Perf. 14x14¼***

**2021, May 5 Litho. Wmk. 406**

| | | | | |
|---|---|---|---|---|
| **1171-1174** | A228 | Set of 4 | 12.00 | 12.00 |

**Souvenir Sheet**

***Perf. 14¼x14***

| | | | | |
|---|---|---|---|---|
| **1175** | A228 | £3 multi | 8.50 | 8.50 |

Birds, Eggs and Chicks A229

Designs: 15p, Brown noddy with egg. 40p, Fairy tern with chick. 60p, Sooty tern with egg. 80p, Masked boobies with chick. £3, Tropicbird chick.

**Wmk. 406**

**2021, Dec. 1 Litho. *Perf. 14¼***

| | | | | |
|---|---|---|---|---|
| **1176-1179** | A229 | Set of 4 | 5.25 | 5.25 |

**Souvenir Sheet**

| | | | | |
|---|---|---|---|---|
| **1180** | A229 | £3 multi | 8.00 | 8.00 |

No. 1180 contains one 68x53mm stamp.

## SEMI-POSTAL STAMPS

**Catalogue values for unused stamps in this section are for Never Hinged items.**

**Tristan da Cunha Nos. 46, 49-51 Ovptd. "ST. HELENA / Tristan Relief" and Srchd. with New Value and "+"**

***Perf. 12½x13***

**1961, Oct. 12 Wmk. 314 Engr.**

| | | | | |
|---|---|---|---|---|
| **B1** | A3 | 2½c + 3p | *1,500.* | *600.00* |
| **B2** | A3 | 5c + 6p | *1,600.* | *650.00* |
| **B3** | A3 | 7½c + 9p | *2,250.* | *900.00* |
| **B4** | A3 | 10c + 1sh | *2,250.* | *1,100.* |
| | | *Nos. B1-B4 (4)* | *7,600.* | *3,250.* |

Withdrawn from sale Oct. 19.

## POSTAGE DUE STAMPS

**Catalogue values for unused stamps in this section are for Never Hinged items.**

Map — D1

***Perf. 15x14***

**1986, June 9 Litho. Wmk. 384**

**Background Color**

| | | | | | |
|---|---|---|---|---|---|
| **J1** | D1 | 1p | tan | .25 | .45 |
| **J2** | D1 | 2p | orange | .25 | .45 |
| **J3** | D1 | 5p | vermilion | .25 | .45 |
| **J4** | D1 | 7p | violet | .25 | .45 |
| **J5** | D1 | 10p | chalky blue | .25 | .55 |
| **J6** | D1 | 25p | dull yellow grn | .70 | 1.50 |
| | | | *Nos. J1-J6 (6)* | 1.95 | 3.85 |

## WAR TAX STAMPS

No. 62a Surcharged

**1916 Wmk. 3 *Perf. 14***

| | | | | |
|---|---|---|---|---|
| **MR1** | A10 | 1p + 1p scar & blk | 3.00 | 4.00 |
| *a.* | | Double surcharge | | *20,000.* |

No. 62 Surcharged

**1919**

| | | | | |
|---|---|---|---|---|
| **MR2** | A10 | 1p + 1p car & blk | 2.10 | 5.50 |

# ST. KITTS

sānt 'kits

LOCATION — West Indies southeast of Puerto Rico

GOVT. — With Nevis, Associated State in British Commonwealth

AREA — 65 sq. mi.

POP. — 31,824 (1991)

CAPITAL — Basseterre

See St. Christopher for stamps used in St. Kitts until 1890. From 1890 until 1903, stamps of the Leeward Islands were used. From 1903 until 1956, stamps of St. Kitts-Nevis and Leeward Islands were used concurrently. See St. Kitts-Nevis for stamps used through June 22, 1980, after which St. Kitts and Nevis pursued separate postal administrations.

100 Cents = 1 Dollar

**Catalogue values for all unused stamps in this country are for Never Hinged items.**

**Watermark**

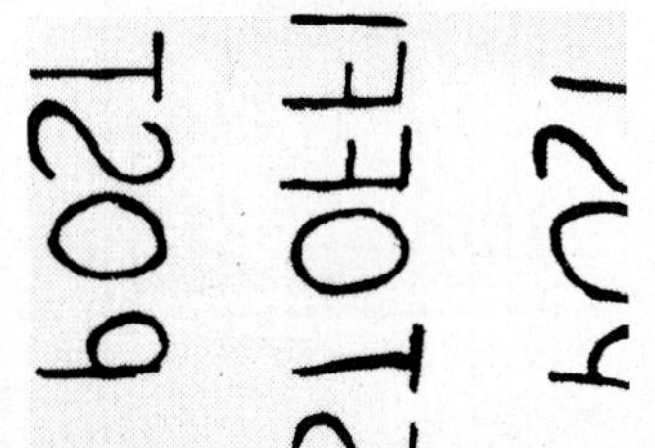

Wmk. 380 — "POST OFFICE"

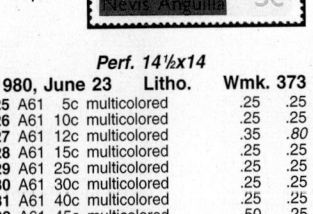

St. Kitts-Nevis Nos. 357-369 Ovptd.

***Perf. 14½x14***

**1980, June 23 Litho. Wmk. 373**

| | | | | | |
|---|---|---|---|---|---|
| **25** | A61 | 5c | multicolored | .25 | .25 |
| **26** | A61 | 10c | multicolored | .25 | .25 |
| **27** | A61 | 12c | multicolored | .35 | *.80* |
| **28** | A61 | 15c | multicolored | .25 | .25 |
| **29** | A61 | 25c | multicolored | .25 | .25 |
| **30** | A61 | 30c | multicolored | .25 | .25 |
| **31** | A61 | 40c | multicolored | .25 | .25 |
| **32** | A61 | 45c | multicolored | .50 | .25 |
| **33** | A61 | 50c | multicolored | .25 | .25 |
| **34** | A61 | 55c | multicolored | .25 | .25 |
| **35** | A61 | $1 | multicolored | .25 | .25 |
| **36** | A61 | $5 | multicolored | .30 | *1.00* |
| **37** | A61 | $10 | multicolored | .45 | *1.75* |
| | | | *Nos. 25-37 (13)* | 3.85 | 6.05 |

All but 12c, 45c, 50c, exist unwatermarked. About the same values.

Ships A2

4c, HMS Vanguard, 1762. 10c, HMS Boreas, 1787. 30c, HMS Druid, 1827. 55c, HMS Winchester, 1831. $1.50, Philosopher, 1857. $2, S.S. Contractor, 1930.

**1980, Aug. 8 *Perf. 13½***

| | | | | | |
|---|---|---|---|---|---|
| **38** | A2 | 4c | multicolored | .25 | .25 |
| **39** | A2 | 10c | multicolored | .25 | .25 |
| **40** | A2 | 30c | multicolored | .25 | .25 |
| **41** | A2 | 55c | multicolored | .25 | .25 |
| **42** | A2 | $1.50 | multicolored | .30 | *.35* |
| **43** | A2 | $2 | multicolored | .35 | *.45* |
| | | | *Nos. 38-43 (6)* | 1.65 | 1.80 |

Nos. 38-43 not issued without overprint. The 4c, and possibly others, exist without the overprint.

Queen Mother, 80th Birthday — A3

**1980, Sept. 4 *Perf. 14***

| | | | | |
|---|---|---|---|---|
| **44** | A3 | $2 multicolored | .40 | *.60* |

Christmas — A4

**1980, Nov. 10 *Perf. 14½***

| | | | | | |
|---|---|---|---|---|---|
| **45** | A4 | 5c | Magi following star | .25 | .25 |
| **46** | A4 | 15c | Shepherds, star | .25 | .25 |
| **47** | A4 | 30c | Bethlehem, star | .25 | .25 |
| **48** | A4 | $4 | Adoration of the Magi | .60 | *.50* |
| | | | *Nos. 45-48 (4)* | 1.35 | 1.25 |

Birds — A5

1c, Frigatebird. 4c, Rusty-tailed flycatcher. 5c, Purple-throated carib. 6c, Burrowing owl. 8c, Purple martin. 10c, Yellow-crowned night heron. 15c, Bananaquit. 20c, Scaly-breasted thrasher. 25c, Grey kingbird. 30c, Green-throated carib. 40c, Ruddy turnstone. 45c, Black-faced grassquit. 50c, Cattle egret. 55c, Brown pelican. $1, Lesser Antillean bullfinch. $2.50, Zenaida dove. $5, Sparrow hawk. $10, Antillean crested hummingbird.

**No Date Imprint Below Design**

**1981 Wmk. 373 *Perf. 13½x14***

| | | | | | |
|---|---|---|---|---|---|
| **49** | A5 | 1c | multicolored | .25 | .25 |
| **50** | A5 | 4c | multicolored | .35 | .25 |
| **51** | A5 | 5c | multicolored | .25 | .25 |
| **52** | A5 | 6c | multicolored | .60 | .25 |
| **53** | A5 | 8c | multicolored | .45 | .25 |
| **54** | A5 | 10c | multicolored | .30 | .25 |

***Perf. 14***

**Size: 38x25mm**

| | | | | | |
|---|---|---|---|---|---|
| **55** | A5 | 15c | multicolored | .30 | .25 |
| **56** | A5 | 20c | multicolored | .30 | .25 |
| **57** | A5 | 25c | multicolored | .30 | .25 |
| **58** | A5 | 30c | multicolored | .30 | .25 |
| **59** | A5 | 40c | multicolored | .35 | .30 |
| **60** | A5 | 45c | multicolored | .40 | .40 |
| **61** | A5 | 50c | multicolored | .40 | .40 |
| **62** | A5 | 55c | multicolored | .40 | .40 |
| **63** | A5 | $1 | multicolored | .75 | .75 |
| **64** | A5 | $2.50 | multicolored | 1.7 | *2.25* |
| **65** | A5 | $5 | multicolored | 3.00 | *3.50* |
| **66** | A5 | $10 | multicolored | 5.00 | *6.00* |
| | | | *Nos. 49-66 (18)* | 15.40 | 16.50 |

Issued: Nos. 51, 54-66, Feb. 5; others, May 30.

**"1982" Imprint Below Design**

**1982, June 8**

| | | | | | |
|---|---|---|---|---|---|
| *49a* | A5 | 1c | multicolored | .50 | .35 |
| *50a* | A5 | 4c | multicolored | .50 | .30 |
| *51a* | A5 | 5c | multicolored | .60 | .30 |
| *52a* | A5 | 6c | multicolored | .65 | .40 |
| *53a* | A5 | 8c | multicolored | .70 | .30 |
| *54a* | A5 | 10c | multicolored | .70 | .30 |

***Perf. 14***

**Size: 38x25mm**

| | | | | | |
|---|---|---|---|---|---|
| *55a* | A5 | 15c | multicolored | .75 | .30 |
| *56a* | A5 | 20c | multicolored | .80 | .30 |
| *57a* | A5 | 25c | multicolored | .80 | .30 |
| *58a* | A5 | 30c | multicolored | .80 | .35 |
| *59a* | A5 | 40c | multicolored | 1.00 | .40 |
| *60a* | A5 | 45c | multicolored | 1.25 | .45 |
| *61a* | A5 | 50c | multicolored | 1.50 | .50 |
| *62a* | A5 | 55c | multicolored | 1.75 | .75 |
| *63a* | A5 | $1 | multicolored | 2.75 | 1.00 |
| *64a* | A5 | $2.50 | multicolored | 4.50 | 3.00 |
| *65a* | A5 | $5 | multicolored | 7.00 | 6.50 |
| *66a* | A5 | $10 | multicolored | 11.50 | 10.00 |
| | | | *Nos. 49a-66a (18)* | 38.05 | 25.80 |

**"1983" Imprint Below Design**

**1983**

| | | | | | |
|---|---|---|---|---|---|
| *55b* | A5 | 15c | multicolored | 2.75 | .50 |
| *56b* | A5 | 20c | multicolored | 2.75 | .50 |
| *57b* | A5 | 25c | multicolored | 2.75 | .50 |
| *58b* | A5 | 30c | multicolored | 2.75 | .50 |

| | | | | | |
|---|---|---|---|---|---|
| *59b* | A5 | 40c | multicolored | 4.25 | .60 |
| *60b* | A5 | 45c | multicolored | 4.50 | 1.25 |
| *63b* | A5 | $1 | multicolored | 10.50 | 2.50 |
| *64b* | A5 | $2.50 | multicolored | 18.00 | 5.00 |
| | | | *Nos. 55b-64b (8)* | 48.25 | 11.35 |

For overprints see Nos. 112-122.

Military Uniforms — A6

Foot Regiments: 5c, Battalion Company sergeant, 3rd Regiment, c. 1801. 15c, Light Company private, 15th Regiment, c. 1814. No. 69, Battalion Company officer, 45th Regiment, 1796-7. No. 70, Officer, 15th Regiment, c. 1780. No. 71, Officer, 9th Regiment, 1790. No. 72, Light Company officer, 5th Regiment, c. 1822. No. 73, Grenadier, 38th Regiment, 1751. No. 74, Battalion Company officer, 11th Regiment, c. 1804.

**1981-83** ***Perf. 14½***

| | | | | | |
|---|---|---|---|---|---|
| **67** | A6 | 5c | multi | .25 | .25 |
| **68** | A6 | 15c | multi ('83) | .25 | .25 |
| **69** | A6 | 30c | multi | .25 | .25 |
| **70** | A6 | 30c | multi ('83) | .25 | .25 |
| **71** | A6 | 55c | multi | .25 | .25 |
| **72** | A6 | 55c | multi ('83) | .35 | .35 |
| **73** | A6 | $2.50 | multi | .55 | .55 |
| **74** | A6 | $2.50 | multi ('83) | .80 | *1.60* |
| | | | *Nos. 67-74 (8)* | 2.95 | 3.75 |

Issued: 3/5/81; 5/25/83.

Prince Charles, Lady Diana, Royal Yacht Charlotte A6a

Prince Charles and Lady Diana — A6b

**1981, June 23** ***Perf. 14***

| | | | | | |
|---|---|---|---|---|---|
| **75** | A6a | 55c | Saudadoes | .25 | .25 |
| **76** | A6b | 55c | Couple | .25 | .25 |
| *a.* | | | Bklt. pane of 4, perf. 12½x12, unwmkd. | .90 | |
| **77** | A6a | $2.50 | The Royal George | .40 | .40 |
| **78** | A6b | $2.50 | like 55c | .75 | .75 |
| *a.* | | | Bklt. pane of 2, perf. 12½x12, unwmkd. | 1.75 | 1.75 |
| **79** | A6a | $4 | HMY Britannia | 1.00 | 1.00 |
| **80** | A6b | $4 | like 55c | 1.25 | 1.25 |
| | | | *Nos. 75-80 (6)* | 3.90 | 3.90 |

**Souvenir Sheet**

**1981, Dec. 14** ***Perf. 12½x12***

| | | | | | |
|---|---|---|---|---|---|
| **81** | A6b | $5 | like 55c | 2.00 | 2.00 |

Wedding of Prince Charles and Lady Diana Spencer. Nos. 76a, 78a issued Nov. 19, 1981.

Natl. Girl Guide Movement, 50th Anniv. — A7

Designs: 5c, Miriam Pickard, 1st Guide commissioner. 30c, Lady Baden-Powell's visit, 1964. 55c, Visit of Princess Alice, 1960. $2, Thinking-Day Parade, 1980s.

**1981, Sept. 21**

| | | | | | |
|---|---|---|---|---|---|
| **82** | A7 | 5c | multicolored | .25 | .25 |
| **83** | A7 | 30c | multicolored | .25 | .25 |
| **84** | A7 | 55c | multicolored | .25 | .25 |
| **85** | A7 | $2 | multicolored | .25 | *.35* |
| | | | *Nos. 82-85 (4)* | 1.00 | 1.10 |

Christmas — A8

Stained-glass windows — 5c, Annunciation. 30c, Nativity, baptism. 55c, Last supper, crucifixion. $3, Appearance before Apostles, ascension to heaven.

**1981, Nov. 30**

| | | | | | |
|---|---|---|---|---|---|
| **86** | A8 | 5c | multicolored | .25 | .25 |
| **87** | A8 | 30c | multicolored | .25 | .25 |
| **88** | A8 | 55c | multicolored | .25 | .25 |
| **89** | A8 | $3 | multicolored | .40 | *.50* |
| | | | *Nos. 86-89 (4)* | 1.15 | 1.25 |

Brimstone Hill Siege, Bicent. — A9

**1982, Mar. 15**

| | | | | | |
|---|---|---|---|---|---|
| **90** | A9 | 15c | Adm. Samuel Hood | .25 | .25 |
| **91** | A9 | 55c | Marquis de Bouille | .25 | .25 |

**Souvenir Sheet**

| | | | | | |
|---|---|---|---|---|---|
| **92** | A9 | $5 | Battle scene | 1.40 | 1.40 |

No. 92 has multicolored margin picturing battle scene. Size: 96x71mm.

21st Birthday of Princess Diana, July 1 — A10

15c, Alexandra of Denmark, Princess of Wales, 1863. 55c, Paternal arms of Alexandra. $6, Diana.

**1982, June 22** ***Perf. 13½x14***

| | | | | | |
|---|---|---|---|---|---|
| **93** | A10 | 15c | multicolored | .25 | .25 |
| **94** | A10 | 55c | multicolored | .25 | .25 |
| **95** | A10 | $6 | multicolored | .50 | *.75* |
| | | | *Nos. 93-95 (3)* | 1.00 | 1.25 |

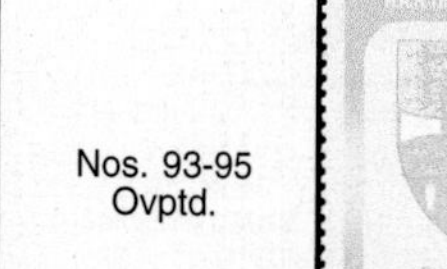

Nos. 93-95 Ovptd.

**1982, July 12**

| | | | | | |
|---|---|---|---|---|---|
| **96** | A10 | 15c | multicolored | .25 | .25 |
| **97** | A10 | 55c | multicolored | .25 | .25 |
| **98** | A10 | $6 | multicolored | .45 | *.75* |
| | | | *Nos. 96-98 (3)* | .95 | 1.25 |

Birth of Prince William of Wales.

Scouting, 75th Anniv. — A11

Merit badges.

**1982, Aug. 18** ***Perf. 14x13½***

| | | | | | |
|---|---|---|---|---|---|
| **99** | A11 | 5c | Nature | .25 | .25 |
| **100** | A11 | 55c | Rescue | .35 | .35 |
| **101** | A11 | $2 | First aid | 1.00 | 1.00 |
| | | | *Nos. 99-101 (3)* | 1.60 | 1.60 |

Christmas — A12

Children's drawings.

**1982, Oct. 20**

| | | | | | |
|---|---|---|---|---|---|
| **102** | A12 | 5c | shown | .25 | .25 |
| **103** | A12 | 55c | Nativity | .25 | .25 |
| **104** | A12 | $1.10 | Three Kings | .25 | .25 |
| **105** | A12 | $3 | Annunciation | .30 | *.40* |
| | | | *Nos. 102-105 (4)* | 1.05 | 1.15 |

A13

Commonwealth Day: 55c, Cruise ship Stella Oceanis docked. $2, RMS Queen Elizabeth 2 anchored in harbor off St. Kitts.

**1983, Mar. 14** ***Perf. 14***

| | | | | | |
|---|---|---|---|---|---|
| **106** | A13 | 55c | multicolored | .25 | .25 |
| **107** | A13 | $2 | multicolored | .40 | .40 |

Boys' Brigade, Cent. — A14

Designs: 10c, Sir William Smith, founder. 45c, Brigade members outside Sandy Point Methodist Church. 50c, Drummers. $3, Badge.

**1983, July 27**

| | | | | | |
|---|---|---|---|---|---|
| **108** | A14 | 10c | multicolored | .35 | .30 |
| **109** | A14 | 45c | multicolored | .45 | .40 |
| **110** | A14 | 50c | multicolored | .45 | .40 |
| **111** | A14 | $3 | multicolored | .75 | *2.00* |
| | | | *Nos. 108-111 (4)* | 2.00 | 3.10 |

**Nos. 51//66 Overprinted**

a

b

**Without Date Imprint Below Design**

**1983, Sept. 19**

| | | | | | |
|---|---|---|---|---|---|
| **112** | A5(a) | 5c | multicolored | .25 | .25 |
| *c.* | | | Local overprint | 10.00 | 10.00 |
| *113c* | A5(b) | 15c | multicolored | 7.00 | 1.25 |
| *116c* | A5(b) | 30c | multicolored | 27.50 | 27.50 |
| *118c* | A5(b) | 55c | multicolored | .65 | .65 |
| *119c* | A5(b) | $1 | multicolored | 11.00 | 11.00 |
| **120** | A5(b) | $2.50 | multicolored | 2.75 | 2.75 |
| *121c* | A5(b) | $5 | multicolored | 4.75 | 4.75 |
| *122c* | A5(b) | $10 | multicolored | 6.50 | 6.50 |
| | | | *Nos. 112-122c (8)* | 60.40 | 54.65 |

No. 112c has serifed letters and reads down. Exists reading up. Value $25.

**Nos. 51a//65a Overprinted "1982" Imprint Below Design**

**1983, Sept. 19**

| | | | | | |
|---|---|---|---|---|---|
| *112a* | A5(a) | 5c | multicolored | .45 | .25 |
| *d.* | | | Local overprint | 2.25 | 2.25 |
| *113a* | A5(b) | 15c | multicolored | 2.00 | 2.00 |
| *115a* | A5(b) | 25c | multicolored | 2.00 | 2.00 |
| *116a* | A5(b) | 30c | multicolored | 2.00 | 2.00 |
| *121a* | A5(b) | $5 | multicolored | 5.50 | 5.50 |
| | | | *Nos. 112a-121a (5)* | 11.95 | 11.75 |

No. 112a exists with inverted overprint. Value $32.50. No. 113a exists with double overprint. Value $8.50. No. 115a exists with inverted overprint. Value $14.

No. 112d has serifed letters and reads down. Exists reading up. Value $7.50.

**Nos. 52b//66b Overprinted "1983" Imprint Below Design**

| | | | | | |
|---|---|---|---|---|---|
| **113** | A5(b) | 15c | multicolored | .35 | .25 |
| **114** | A5(b) | 20c | multicolored | .35 | .25 |
| **115** | A5(b) | 25c | multicolored | .55 | .25 |
| **116** | A5(b) | 30c | multicolored | .55 | .25 |
| **117** | A5(b) | 40c | multicolored | .60 | .25 |
| **118** | A5(b) | 55c | multicolored | .65 | .30 |
| **119** | A5(b) | $1 | multicolored | 1.25 | .60 |
| *120b* | A5(b) | $2.50 | multicolored | 2.50 | 2.50 |
| **121** | A5(b) | $5 | multicolored | 3.75 | *4.50* |
| **122** | A5(b) | $10 | multicolored | 4.50 | *6.50* |
| | | | *Nos. 113-122 (10)* | 15.05 | 15.65 |

No. 118 exists with inverted overprint. Value $10.

Manned Flight Bicent. — A15

Designs: 10c, *Montgolfiere,* 1783, vert. 45c, Sikorsky *Russian Knight,* 1913. 50c, Lockheed TriStar. $2.50, Bell XS-1, 1947.

**1983, Sept. 28** **Wmk. 380**

| | | | | | |
|---|---|---|---|---|---|
| **123** | A15 | 10c | multicolored | .25 | .25 |
| **124** | A15 | 45c | multicolored | .25 | .25 |
| **125** | A15 | 50c | multicolored | .25 | .25 |
| **126** | A15 | $2.50 | multicolored | .75 | .75 |
| *a.* | | | Souvenir sheet of 4, #123-126 | 1.60 | 1.60 |
| | | | *Nos. 123-126 (4)* | 1.50 | 1.50 |

1st Flight of a 4-engine aircraft, May 1913 (45c); 1st manned supersonic aircraft, 1947 ($2.50).

Christmas — A16

**1983, Nov. 7**

| | | | | | |
|---|---|---|---|---|---|
| **127** | A16 | 15c | shown | .25 | .25 |
| **128** | A16 | 30c | Shepherds | .25 | .25 |
| **129** | A16 | 55c | Mary, Joseph | .25 | .25 |
| **130** | A16 | $2.50 | Nativity | .30 | .30 |
| *a.* | | | Souvenir sheet of 4, #127-130 | 1.00 | *1.10* |
| | | | *Nos. 127-130 (4)* | 1.05 | 1.05 |

Batik Art A17

**1984-85**

| No. | Type | Denom. | Description | Unused | Used |
|---|---|---|---|---|---|
| 131 | A17 | 15c | Country bus | .25 | .25 |
| 132 | A17 | 40c | Donkey cart | .30 | .25 |
| 133 | A17 | 45c | Parrot, vert. | .25 | .25 |
| 134 | A17 | 50c | Man under palm tree, vert. | .25 | .25 |
| 135 | A17 | 60c | Rum shop, cyclist | .60 | .25 |
| 136 | A17 | $1.50 | Fruit seller, vert. | .45 | .70 |
| 137 | A17 | $3 | Butterflies, vert. | .70 | 1.75 |
| 138 | A17 | $3 | S.V. Polynesia | 1.25 | 2.25 |
| | | | *Nos. 131-138 (8)* | 4.05 | 5.95 |

Issued: 15c, 40c, 60c, No. 138, 2/6/85; others, 1/30/84.

Marine Life A18

5c, Cushion star. 10c, Rough file shell. 15c, Red-lined cleaning shrimp. 20c, Bristleworm. 25c, Flamingo tongue. 30c, Christmas tree worm. 40c, Pink-tipped anemone. 50c, Small-mouth grunt. 60c, Glasseye snapper. 75c, Reef squirrelfish. $1, Sea fans, flamefish. $2.50, Reef butter-flyfish. $5, Black soldierfish. $10, Cocoa damselfish.

**1984, July 4**

| No. | Type | Denom. | Description | Unused | Used |
|---|---|---|---|---|---|
| 139 | A18 | 5c | multicolored | .25 | .25 |
| 140 | A18 | 10c | multicolored | .25 | .25 |
| a. | | | Wmk. 384 "1986" | 1.50 | 1.00 |
| b. | | | As "a," "1988" imprint | 1.25 | 1.00 |
| 141 | A18 | 15c | multicolored | .25 | .25 |
| 142 | A18 | 20c | multicolored | .25 | .25 |
| 143 | A18 | 25c | multicolored | .25 | .25 |
| 144 | A18 | 30c | multicolored | .40 | .35 |
| 145 | A18 | 40c | multicolored | .55 | .40 |
| 146 | A18 | 50c | multicolored | .60 | .40 |
| 147 | A18 | 60c | multicolored | 1.10 | 1.10 |
| a. | | | Wmk. 384 ('88) | 1.25 | 1.40 |
| 148 | A18 | 75c | multicolored | 2.50 | .75 |
| 149 | A18 | $1 | multicolored | 1.00 | 1.00 |
| 150 | A18 | $2.50 | multicolored | 3.00 | 3.75 |
| 151 | A18 | $5 | multicolored | 7.00 | 15.00 |
| a. | | | Wmk. 384 ('88) | 9.00 | 11.00 |
| 152 | A18 | $10 | multicolored | 11.00 | 15.00 |
| a. | | | Wmk. 384 ('88) | 14.00 | 15.00 |
| | | | *Nos. 139-152 (14)* | 28.40 | 39.00 |

Nos. 149-152 vert.
Nos. 147a, 151a, 152a have "1988" imprint.

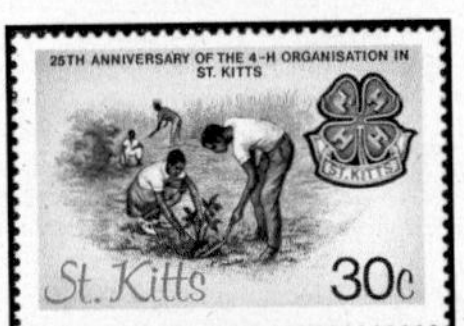


4-H in St. Kitts, 25th Anniv. A19

**1984, Aug. 15**

| No. | Type | Denom. | Description | Unused | Used |
|---|---|---|---|---|---|
| 153 | A19 | 30c | Agriculture | .25 | .25 |
| 154 | A19 | 55c | Animal husbandry | .30 | .30 |
| 155 | A19 | $1.10 | Pledge, flag, youths | .50 | .60 |
| 156 | A19 | $3 | Parade | 1.00 | 1.25 |
| | | | *Nos. 153-156 (4)* | 2.05 | 2.40 |

1st Anniv. of Independence — A20

15c, Construction of Royal St. Kitts Hotel. 30c, Folk dancers. $1.10, O Land of Beauty, vert. $3, Sea, palm trees, map, vert.

**1984, Sept. 18**

| No. | Type | Denom. | Description | Unused | Used |
|---|---|---|---|---|---|
| 157 | A20 | 15c | multicolored | .25 | .25 |
| 158 | A20 | 30c | multicolored | .30 | .30 |
| 159 | A20 | $1.10 | multicolored | .50 | .60 |
| 160 | A20 | $3 | multicolored | 1.00 | 1.40 |
| | | | *Nos. 157-160 (4)* | 2.05 | 2.55 |

Christmas — A21

**1984, Nov. 1**

| No. | Type | Denom. | Description | Unused | Used |
|---|---|---|---|---|---|
| 161 | A21 | 15c | Opening gifts | .25 | .25 |
| 162 | A21 | 60c | Caroling | .55 | .55 |
| 163 | A21 | $1 | Nativity | .75 | .75 |
| 164 | A21 | $2 | Leaving church | 1.25 | 1.25 |
| | | | *Nos. 161-164 (4)* | 2.80 | 2.80 |

Ships A22

**1985, Mar. 27** *Perf. 13½x14*

| No. | Type | Denom. | Description | Unused | Used |
|---|---|---|---|---|---|
| 165 | A22 | 40c | Tropic Jade | 1.00 | 1.00 |
| 166 | A22 | $1.20 | Atlantic Clipper | 2.00 | 2.00 |
| 167 | A22 | $2 | M.V. Cunard Countess | 2.75 | 2.75 |
| 168 | A22 | $2 | Mandalay | 3.25 | 3.25 |
| | | | *Nos. 165-168 (4)* | 9.00 | 9.00 |

Mt. Olive Masonic Lodge, 150th Anniv. — A23

Designs: 15c, James Derrick Cardin (1871-1954). 75c, Lodge banner. $1.20, Compass, Bible, square, horiz. $3, Charter, 1835.

**1985, Nov. 9** *Perf. 15*

| No. | Type | Denom. | Description | Unused | Used |
|---|---|---|---|---|---|
| 169 | A23 | 15c | multicolored | .65 | .40 |
| 170 | A23 | 75c | multicolored | 1.40 | 1.40 |
| 171 | A23 | $1.20 | multicolored | 1.40 | 2.75 |
| 172 | A23 | $3 | multicolored | 1.75 | 4.50 |
| | | | *Nos. 169-172 (4)* | 5.20 | 9.05 |

Christmas — A24

**1985, Nov. 27** *Unwmk.*

| No. | Type | Denom. | Description | Unused | Used |
|---|---|---|---|---|---|
| 173 | A24 | 10c | Map of St. Kitts | .30 | .25 |
| 174 | A24 | 40c | Golden Hind | .60 | .40 |
| 175 | A24 | 60c | Sir Francis Drake | .60 | .50 |
| 176 | A24 | $3 | Drake's shield of arms | .80 | 4.00 |
| | | | *Nos. 173-176 (4)* | 2.30 | 5.15 |

Visit of Sir Francis Drake to St. Kitts, 400th anniv.

Queen Elizabeth II, 60th Birthday — A25

Designs: 10c, With Prince Philip. 20c, Walking with government officials. 40c, Riding horse in parade. $3, Portrait.

**1986, July 9** *Perf. 14*

| No. | Type | Denom. | Description | Unused | Used |
|---|---|---|---|---|---|
| 177 | A25 | 10c | multicolored | .25 | .25 |
| 178 | A25 | 20c | multicolored | .35 | .25 |
| 179 | A25 | 40c | multicolored | .60 | .45 |
| 180 | A25 | $3 | multicolored | 2.40 | 3.00 |
| | | | *Nos. 177-180 (4)* | 3.60 | 3.95 |

For overprints see Nos. 185-188.

Common Design Types pictured following the introduction.

**Royal Wedding Issue, 1986**

Common Design Type

Designs: 15c, Prince Andrew and Sarah Ferguson, formal engagement announcement. $2.50, Prince Andrew in military dress uniform.

*Perf. 14½x14*

**1986, July 23** **Wmk. 384**

| No. | Type | Denom. | Description | Unused | Used |
|---|---|---|---|---|---|
| 181 | CD338 | 15c | multicolored | .25 | .25 |
| 182 | CD338 | $2.50 | multicolored | 1.25 | 2.00 |

Agriculture Exhibition — A26

Children's drawings: 15c, Family farm, by Kevin Tatem, age 14. $1.20, Striving for growth, by Alister Williams, age 19.

**1986, Sept. 18** *Perf. 13½x14*

| No. | Type | Denom. | Description | Unused | Used |
|---|---|---|---|---|---|
| 183 | A26 | 15c | multicolored | .25 | .25 |
| 184 | A26 | $1.20 | multicolored | 1.25 | 1.50 |

**Nos. 177-180 Ovptd. "40th ANNIVERSARY / U.N. WEEK 19-26 OCT." in Gold**

**1986, Oct. 22** **Unwmk.** *Perf. 14*

| No. | Type | Denom. | Description | Unused | Used |
|---|---|---|---|---|---|
| 185 | A25 | 10c | multicolored | .25 | .25 |
| 186 | A25 | 20c | multicolored | .25 | .25 |
| 187 | A25 | 40c | multicolored | .40 | .40 |
| 188 | A25 | $3 | multicolored | 1.90 | 3.00 |
| | | | *Nos. 185-188 (4)* | 2.80 | 3.90 |

World Wildlife Fund — A27

Various green monkeys, Cercopithecus aethiops sabaeus.

**1986, Dec. 1**

| No. | Type | Denom. | Description | Unused | Used |
|---|---|---|---|---|---|
| 189 | A27 | 15c | multi | 5.00 | .75 |
| 190 | A27 | 20c | multi, diff. | 5.50 | .75 |
| 191 | A27 | 60c | multi, diff. | 8.50 | 3.00 |
| 192 | A27 | $1 | multi, diff. | 11.50 | 5.00 |
| | | | *Nos. 189-192 (4)* | 30.50 | 9.50 |

Auguste Bartholdi — A28

Statue of Liberty, Cent. — A29

60c, Torch, head, 1876-78. $1.50, Warship Isere, France. $3, Delivering statue, 1884. $3.50, Head.

**1986, Dec. 17** *Perf. 14x14½, 14½x14*

| No. | Type | Denom. | Description | Unused | Used |
|---|---|---|---|---|---|
| 193 | A28 | 40c | shown | .30 | .30 |
| 194 | A28 | 60c | multicolored | .40 | .60 |
| 195 | A28 | $1.50 | multicolored | 1.10 | 1.75 |
| 196 | A28 | $3 | multicolored | 1.25 | 3.00 |
| | | | *Nos. 193-196 (4)* | 3.05 | 5.65 |

**Souvenir Sheet**

| No. | Type | Denom. | Description | Unused | Used |
|---|---|---|---|---|---|
| 197 | A29 | $3.50 | multicolored | 2.50 | 3.50 |

Nos. 194-195 horiz.

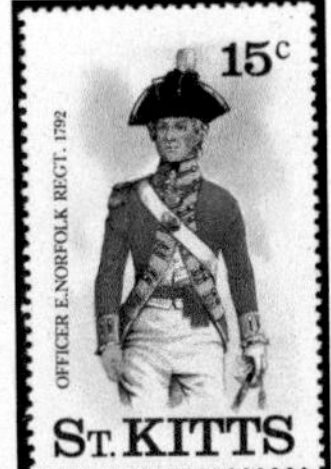


British and French Uniforms — A30

Designs: No. 198, Officer, East Norfolk Regiment, 1792. No. 199, Officer, De Neustrie Regiment, 1779. No. 200, Sergeant, Third Foot the Buffs, 1801. No. 201, Artillery officer, 1812. No. 202, Private, Light Company, 5th Foot Regiment, 1778. No. 203, Grenadier, Line Infantry, 1796.

**1987, Feb. 25** *Perf. 14½*

| No. | Type | Denom. | Description | Unused | Used |
|---|---|---|---|---|---|
| 198 | A30 | 15c | multicolored | .45 | .30 |
| 199 | A30 | 15c | multicolored | .45 | .30 |
| 200 | A30 | 40c | multicolored | .75 | .55 |
| 201 | A30 | 40c | multicolored | .75 | .55 |
| 202 | A30 | $2 | multicolored | 1.75 | 3.00 |
| 203 | A30 | $2 | multicolored | 1.75 | 3.00 |
| a. | | | Souvenir sheet of 6, #198-203 | 9.00 | 9.00 |
| | | | *Nos. 198-203 (6)* | 5.90 | 7.70 |

Sugar Cane Industry — A31

No. 204: a, Warehouse. b, Barns. c, Steam emitted by processing plant. d, Processing plant. e, Field hands.

No. 205a, Locomotive. b, Locomotive and tender. c, Open cars. d, Empty and loaded cars, tractor. e, Loading sugar cane.

**1987, Apr. 15** *Perf. 14*

| No. | Type | Denom. | Description | Unused | Used |
|---|---|---|---|---|---|
| 204 | | | Strip of 5 | 1.00 | 1.50 |
| a.-e. | A31 | 15c | any single | .25 | .30 |
| 205 | | | Strip of 5 | 2.00 | 3.50 |
| a.-e. | A31 | 75c | any single | .30 | .70 |

Visiting Aircraft A32

40c, L-1011-500 Tri-Star. 60c, BAe Super 748. $1.20, DHC-6 Twin Otter. $3, Aerospatiale ATR-42.

***Perf. 14x14½***

**1987, June 24 Wmk. 373**

| No. | Type | Description | Unused | Used |
|---|---|---|---|---|
| **206** | A32 | 40c multicolored | .70 | .50 |
| **207** | A32 | 60c multicolored | 1.00 | 1.00 |
| **208** | A32 | $1.20 multicolored | 1.60 | 2.75 |
| **209** | A32 | $3 multicolored | 3.75 | 4.75 |
| | | *Nos. 206-209 (4)* | 7.05 | 9.00 |

Fungi — A33

15c, Hygrocybe occidentalis. 40c, Marasmius haemato-cephalus. $1.20, Psilocybe cubensis. $2, Hygrocybe acutoconica. $3, Boletellus cubensis.

**1987, Aug. 26 Wmk. 384 *Perf. 14***

| No. | Type | Description | Unused | Used |
|---|---|---|---|---|
| **210** | A33 | 15c multicolored | .70 | .30 |
| **211** | A33 | 40c multicolored | 1.60 | .40 |
| **212** | A33 | $1.20 multicolored | 3.25 | 3.25 |
| **213** | A33 | $2 multicolored | 4.00 | 4.00 |
| **214** | A33 | $3 multicolored | 5.00 | 5.00 |
| | | *Nos. 210-214 (5)* | 14.55 | 12.95 |

Carnival Clowns — A34

**1987, Oct. 28 *Perf. 14½***

| No. | Type | Description | Unused | Used |
|---|---|---|---|---|
| **215** | A34 | 15c multi | .25 | .25 |
| **216** | A34 | 40c multi, diff. | .60 | .60 |
| **217** | A34 | $1 multi, diff. | 1.50 | 1.50 |
| **218** | A34 | $3 multi, diff. | 3.00 | *4.25* |
| | | *Nos. 215-218 (4)* | 5.35 | 6.60 |

Christmas 1987. See Nos. 235-238.

Flowers — A35

**1988, Jan. 20**

| No. | Type | Description | Unused | Used |
|---|---|---|---|---|
| **219** | A35 | 15c Ixora | .25 | .25 |
| **220** | A35 | 40c Shrimp plant | .50 | .50 |
| **221** | A35 | $1 Poinsettia | 1.10 | *1.40* |
| **222** | A35 | $3 Honolulu rose | 3.75 | *4.25* |
| | | *Nos. 219-222 (4)* | 5.60 | 6.40 |

Tourism A36

No. 223, Ft. Thomas Hotel. No. 224, Fairview Inn. No. 225, Frigate Bay Beach Hotel. No. 226, Ocean Terrace Inn. No. 227, The Golden Lemon. No. 228, Royal St. Kitts Casino and Jack Tar Village. No. 229, Rawlins Plantation Hotel and Restaurant.

**1988, Apr. 20 Wmk. 373**

| No. | Type | Description | Unused | Used |
|---|---|---|---|---|
| **223** | A36 | 60c multicolored | .95 | .95 |
| **224** | A36 | 60c multicolored | .95 | .95 |
| **225** | A36 | 60c multicolored | .95 | .95 |
| **226** | A36 | 60c multicolored | .95 | .95 |
| **227** | A36 | $3 multicolored | 2.50 | *2.75* |
| **228** | A36 | $3 multicolored | 2.50 | *2.75* |
| **229** | A36 | $3 multicolored | 2.50 | *2.75* |
| | | *Nos. 223-229 (7)* | 11.30 | 12.05 |

See Nos. 239-244.

Leeward Islands Cricket Tournament, 75th Anniv. — A37

Designs: 40c, Leeward Islands Cricket Assoc. emblem, ball and wicket. $3, Cricket match at Warner Park.

**1988, July 13 *Perf. 13x13½***

| No. | Type | Description | Unused | Used |
|---|---|---|---|---|
| **230** | A37 | 40c multicolored | 2.00 | .30 |
| **231** | A37 | $3 multicolored | 4.00 | 4.00 |

Independence, 5th Anniv. — A38

Designs: 15c, Natl. flag. 60c, Natl. coat of arms. $5, Princess Margaret presenting the Nevis Constitution Order to Prime Minister Simmonds, Sept. 19, 1983.

**1988, Sept. 19 Wmk. 384 *Perf. 14½***

| No. | Type | Description | Unused | Used |
|---|---|---|---|---|
| **232** | A38 | 15c shown | 1.25 | .45 |
| **233** | A38 | 60c multicolored | 1.60 | 1.00 |

**Souvenir Sheet**

| No. | Type | Description | Unused | Used |
|---|---|---|---|---|
| **234** | A38 | $5 multicolored | 5.50 | 5.50 |

**Christmas Type of 1987**

Carnival clowns.

**1988, Nov. 2 Wmk. 373**

| No. | Type | Description | Unused | Used |
|---|---|---|---|---|
| **235** | A34 | 15c multi | .25 | .25 |
| **236** | A34 | 40c multi, diff. | .25 | .25 |
| **237** | A34 | 80c multi, diff. | .40 | *.55* |
| **238** | A34 | $3 multi, diff. | 1.60 | *2.50* |
| | | *Nos. 235-238 (4)* | 2.50 | 3.55 |

**Tourism Type of 1988**

**Wmk. 384**

**1989, Jan. 25 Litho. *Perf. 14***

| No. | Type | Description | Unused | Used |
|---|---|---|---|---|
| **239** | A36 | 20c Old Colonial House | .25 | .25 |
| **240** | A36 | 20c Georgian House | .25 | .25 |
| **241** | A36 | $1 Romney Manor | .65 | *.90* |
| **242** | A36 | $1 Lavington Great House | .65 | *.90* |
| **243** | A36 | $2 Treasury Building | 1.00 | *1.75* |
| **244** | A36 | $2 Government House | 1.00 | *1.75* |
| | | *Nos. 239-244 (6)* | 3.80 | *5.80* |

Intl. Red Cross and Red Crescent Organizations, 125th Annivs. (in 1988) — A39

***Perf. 14x14½***

**1989, May 8 Litho. Wmk. 384**

| No. | Type | Description | Unused | Used |
|---|---|---|---|---|
| **245** | A39 | 40c shown | .30 | .30 |
| **246** | A39 | $1 Ambulance | .80 | .80 |
| **247** | A39 | $3 Anniv. emblem | 2.50 | *3.25* |
| | | *Nos. 245-247 (3)* | 3.60 | 4.35 |

**Moon Landing, 20th Anniv.**

Common Design Type

Apollo 13: 10c, Lunar rover at Taurus-Littrow landing site. 20c, Fred W. Haise Jr., John L. Swigert Jr., and James A. Lovell Jr. $1, Mission emblem. $2, Splashdown in the South Pacific. $5, Buzz Aldrin disembarking from the lunar module, Apollo 11 mission.

**1989, July 20 *Perf. 14***

**Size of Nos. 249-250: 29x29mm**

| No. | Type | Description | Unused | Used |
|---|---|---|---|---|
| **248** | CD342 | 10c multicolored | .25 | .25 |
| **249** | CD342 | 20c multicolored | .25 | .25 |
| **250** | CD342 | $1 multicolored | .75 | .75 |
| **251** | CD342 | $2 multicolored | 1.25 | *1.50* |
| | | *Nos. 248-251 (4)* | 2.50 | 2.75 |

**Souvenir Sheet**

| No. | Type | Description | Unused | Used |
|---|---|---|---|---|
| **252** | CD342 | $5 multicolored | 5.50 | 5.50 |

Souvenir Sheet

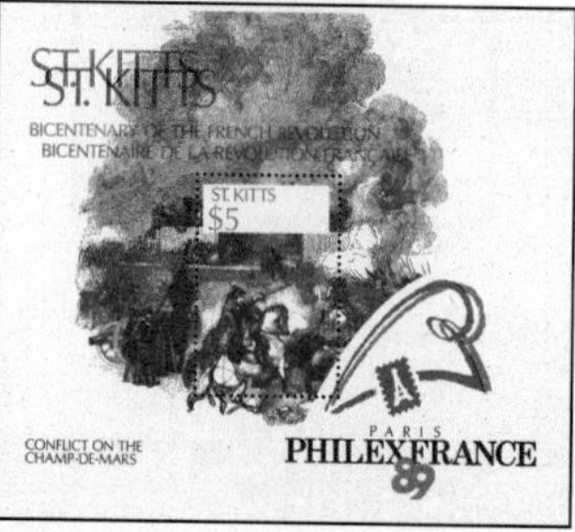


Conflict on the Champ-de-Mars — A40

**1989, July 7**

| No. | Type | Description | Unused | Used |
|---|---|---|---|---|
| **253** | A40 | $5 multicolored | 4.25 | 4.25 |

PHILEXFRANCE '89, French revolution bicent.

Outline Map of St. Kitts — A41

**1989 *Perf. 15x14***

| No. | Type | Description | Unused | Used |
|---|---|---|---|---|
| **255** | A41 | 10c purple & blk | .25 | .25 |
| **256** | A41 | 15c red & blk | .25 | .25 |
| **257** | A41 | 20c org brn & blk | .25 | .25 |
| **259** | A41 | 40c bister & blk | .60 | .25 |
| **261** | A41 | 60c blue & blk | .80 | .50 |
| **265** | A41 | $1 green & blk | 1.40 | 1.40 |
| | | *Nos. 255-265 (6)* | 3.55 | 2.90 |

Discovery of America, 500th Anniv. (in 1992) A42

Designs: 15c, Galleon passing St. Kitts during Columbus's 2nd voyage, 1493. 80c, Coat of arms and map of 4th voyage. $1, Navigational instruments, c. 1500. $5, Exploration of Cuba and Hispaniola during Columbus's 2nd voyage, 1493-1496.

**1989, Nov. 8 Wmk. 384 *Perf. 14***

| No. | Type | Description | Unused | Used |
|---|---|---|---|---|
| **269** | A42 | 15c multicolored | 2.25 | .30 |
| **270** | A42 | 80c multicolored | 4.00 | 2.00 |
| **271** | A42 | $1 multicolored | 4.50 | 2.00 |
| **272** | A42 | $5 multicolored | 13.00 | *14.00* |
| | | *Nos. 269-272 (4)* | 23.75 | 18.30 |

World Stamp Expo '89 A43

Exhibition emblem, flags and: 15c, Poinciana tree. 40c, Ft. George Citadel, Brimstone Hill. $1, Light Company private, 5th Foot Regiment, 1778. $3, St. George's Anglican Church.

**1989, Nov. 17 Wmk. 373**

| No. | Type | Description | Unused | Used |
|---|---|---|---|---|
| **273** | A43 | 15c multicolored | .50 | .25 |
| **274** | A43 | 40c multicolored | .90 | .40 |
| **275** | A43 | $1 multicolored | 2.25 | 1.60 |
| **276** | A43 | $3 multicolored | 3.75 | *5.00* |
| | | *Nos. 273-276 (4)* | 7.40 | 7.25 |

Butterflies A45

15c, Junonia evarete. 40c, Anartia jatrophae. 60c, Heliconius charitonius. $3, Biblis hyperia.

**Wmk. 373**

**1990, June 6 Litho. *Perf. 13½***

| No. | Type | Description | Unused | Used |
|---|---|---|---|---|
| **277** | A45 | 15c multicolored | 1.25 | .75 |
| **278** | A45 | 40c multicolored | 2.25 | 1.25 |
| **279** | A45 | 60c multicolored | 2.25 | 1.25 |
| **280** | A45 | $3 multicolored | 6.50 | 6.50 |
| | | *Nos. 277-280 (4)* | 12.25 | 9.75 |

Nos. 277-280 with EXPO '90 Emblem Added to Design

**1990, June 6**

| No. | Type | Description | Unused | Used |
|---|---|---|---|---|
| **281** | A45 | 15c multicolored | 1.50 | .75 |
| **282** | A45 | 40c multicolored | 2.50 | .75 |
| **283** | A45 | 60c multicolored | 2.50 | 1.25 |
| **284** | A45 | $3 multicolored | 7.00 | 7.00 |
| | | *Nos. 281-284 (4)* | 13.50 | 9.75 |

Expo '90, International Garden and Greenery Exposition, Osaka, Japan.

Cannon on Brimstone Hill, 300th Anniv. — A46

15c, 40c, View of Brimstone Hill. 60c, Fort Charles under bombardment. $3, Men firing cannon.

**1990 June 30 Wmk. 384 *Perf. 14***

| No. | Type | Description | Unused | Used |
|---|---|---|---|---|
| **285** | A46 | 15c multicolored | .35 | .25 |
| **286** | A46 | 40c multicolored | .65 | .35 |
| **287** | A46 | 60c multicolored | 1.25 | 1.00 |
| **288** | | Pair | 7.00 | 7.00 |
| *a.* | | A46 60c multicolored | 1.25 | 1.00 |
| *b.* | | A46 $3 multicolored | 3.50 | 3.50 |
| | | *Nos. 285-288 (4)* | 9.25 | 8.60 |

No. 288 has a continuous design.

Souvenir Sheet

Battle of Britain, 50th Anniv. — A47

**1990, Sept. 15**

| No. | Type | Description | Unused | Used |
|---|---|---|---|---|
| **289** | A47 | Sheet of 2 | 24.00 | 24.00 |
| *a.-b.* | | $3 any single | 9.50 | 9.50 |

Ships A48

**1990, Oct. 10 Wmk. 373**

| No. | Type | Description | Unused | Used |
|---|---|---|---|---|
| **294** | A48 | 10c Romney | .75 | .50 |
| *a.* | | Wmk. 384 | .75 | .60 |
| **295** | A48 | 15c Baralt | .75 | .30 |
| **296** | A48 | 20c Wear | 1.00 | .35 |
| **297** | A48 | 25c Sunmount | 1.00 | .35 |
| **298** | A48 | 40c Inanda | 1.00 | .35 |
| **299** | A48 | 50c Alcoa Partner | 1.00 | .35 |
| **300** | A48 | 60c Dominica | 1.40 | .35 |
| **301** | A48 | 80c CGM Provence | 1.50 | .50 |
| **302** | A48 | $1 Director | 1.50 | .90 |
| **303** | A48 | $1.20 Typical barque, 1860-1880 | 2.00 | 1.50 |
| **304** | A48 | $2 Chignecto | 2.50 | 2.50 |
| **305** | A48 | $3 Berbice | 3.50 | *4.25* |
| *a.* | | Souvenir sheet of 1 | 3.00 | 3.00 |
| **306** | A48 | $5 Vamos | 5.50 | *6.50* |
| **307** | A48 | $10 Federal Maple | 9.00 | *11.00* |
| | | *Nos. 294-307 (14)* | 32.40 | 29.70 |

No. 305a issued 2/3/97 for Hong Kong '97.

Christmas — A49

Traditional games.

**1990, Nov. 14** *Perf. 14*

**308** A49 10c Single fork .25 .25
**309** A49 15c Boulder breaking .25 .25
**310** A49 40c Double fork .40 .40
**311** A49 $3 Run up 2.50 *3.75*
*Nos. 308-311 (4)* 3.40 4.65

Flowers — A50

10c, White periwinkle, horiz. 40c, Pink oleander, horiz. 60c, Pink periwinkle. $2, White oleander.

***Perf. 14x13½, 13½x14***

**1991, May 8 Litho. Wmk. 373**

**312** A50 10c multicolored .75 .30
**313** A50 40c multicolored 1.50 .45
**314** A50 60c multicolored 2.00 .90
**315** A50 $2 multicolored 3.50 *4.50*
*Nos. 312-315 (4)* 7.75 6.15

Natl. Census — A51

**1991, May 13 Wmk. 384** *Perf. 14*

**316** A51 15c multicolored .25 .25
**317** A51 $2.40 multicolored 3.50 3.50

**Elizabeth & Philip, Birthdays**
Common Design Types

**Wmk. 384**

**1991, June 17 Litho.** *Perf. 14½*

**318** CD346 $1.20 multicolored 1.00 1.00
**319** CD345 $1.80 multicolored 1.50 1.50
*a.* Pair, #318-319 + label 3.00 3.00

Fish A52

**1991, Aug. 28 Wmk. 373** *Perf. 14*

**320** A52 10c Nassau grouper .75 .35
**321** A52 60c Hogfish 1.50 .75
**322** A52 $1 Red hind 2.50 2.50
**323** A52 $3 Porkfish 4.25 *5.25*
*Nos. 320-323 (4)* 9.00 8.85

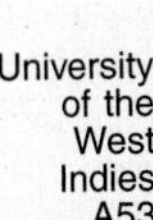

University of the West Indies A53

Designs: 15c, Chancellor Sir Shridath Ramphal, School of Continuing Studies, St. Kitts. 50c, Administration Bldg., Cave Hill Campus, Barbados. $1, Engineering Bldg., St. Augustine Campus, Trinidad & Tobago. $3, Ramphal, Mona Campus, Jamaica.

**1991, Sept. 25 Wmk. 384**

**324** A53 15c multicolored .40 .35
**325** A53 50c multicolored .80 .80
**326** A53 $1 multicolored 1.60 1.40
**327** A53 $3 multicolored 4.50 *5.00*
*Nos. 324-327 (4)* 7.30 7.55

Christmas — A54

Various scenes of traditional play, "The Bull."

**1991, Nov. 6 Wmk. 373**

**328** A54 10c multicolored .40 .40
**329** A54 15c multicolored .40 .40
**330** A54 60c multicolored 1.25 1.25
**331** A54 $3 multicolored 4.75 4.75
*Nos. 328-331 (4)* 6.80 6.80

**Queen Elizabeth II's Accession to the Throne, 40th Anniv.**
Common Design Type

**1992, Feb. 6 Wmk. 384**

**332** CD349 10c multicolored .30 .25
**333** CD349 40c multicolored 1.25 .55
**334** CD349 60c multicolored .80 .45
**335** CD349 $1 multicolored 1.25 1.25

**Wmk. 373**

**336** CD349 $3 multicolored 3.00 3.00
*Nos. 332-336 (5)* 6.60 5.50

St. Kitts and Nevis Red Cross Society, 50th Anniv. A55

10c, Map of St. Kitts & Nevis. 20c, St. Kitts & Nevis flag. 50c, Red Cross House, St. Kitts. $2.40, Jean-Henri Dunant, founder of Red Cross.

***Perf. 13½x14***

**1992, May 8 Litho. Wmk. 373**

**337** A55 10c multicolored 1.50 .75
**338** A55 20c multicolored 2.25 .60
**339** A55 50c multicolored 2.00 1.00
**340** A55 $2.40 multicolored 4.50 *5.25*
*Nos. 337-340 (4)* 10.25 7.60

Discovery of America, 500th Anniv. — A56

**1992, July 6** *Perf. 13*

**341** A56 $1 Coming ashore 2.00 1.25
**342** A56 $2 Natives, ships 4.00 4.00

Organization of East Caribbean States.

A57

Designs: 25c, Fountain, Independence Square. 50c, Berkeley Memorial drinking fountain and clock. 80c, Sir Thomas Warner's tomb. $2, War Memorial.

**1992, Aug. 19** *Perf. 12½x13*

**343** A57 25c multicolored .25 .25
**344** A57 50c multicolored .45 .45
**345** A57 80c multicolored .75 .75
**346** A57 $2 multicolored 1.75 *2.50*
*Nos. 343-346 (4)* 3.20 3.95

Christmas — A58

Stained glass windows: 20c, Mary and Joseph. 25c, Shepherds. 80c, Three Wise Men. $3, Mary, Joseph and Christ Child.

**1992, Oct. 28 Wmk. 384** *Perf. 14½*

**347** A58 20c multicolored .30 .25
**348** A58 25c multicolored .30 .25
**349** A58 80c multicolored .70 .70
**350** A58 $3 multicolored 3.00 *3.75*
*Nos. 347-350 (4)* 4.30 4.95

**Royal Air Force, 75th Anniv.**
Common Design Type

Designs: 25c, Short Singapore III. 50c, Bristol Beaufort. 80c, Westland Whirlwind. $1.60, English Electric Canberra.

No. 355a, Handley Page 0/400. b, Fairey Long Range Monoplane. c, Vickers Wellesley. d, Sepecat Jaguar.

**Wmk. 373**

**1993, Apr. 1 Litho.** *Perf. 14*

**351** CD350 25c multicolored .85 .85
**352** CD350 50c multicolored 1.60 1.60
**353** CD350 80c multicolored 2.10 2.10
**354** CD350 $1.60 multicolored 4.25 *5.00*
*Nos. 351-354 (4)* 8.80 9.55

**Miniature Sheet**

**355** CD350 $2 Sheet of 4, #a.-d. 14.00 14.00

Diocese of the Northeastern Caribbean and Aruba, 150th Anniv. — A59

Designs: 25c, Diocesan Conference, Basseterre, horiz. 50c, Cathedral of St. John the Divine. 80c, Diocesan coat of arms and motto, horiz. $2, First Bishop, Right Reverend Daniel G. Davis.

***Perf. 13½x14, 14x13½***

**1993, May 21 Litho. Wmk. 384**

**356** A59 25c multicolored .30 .30
**357** A59 50c multicolored .50 .50
**358** A59 80c multicolored 1.00 1.00
**359** A59 $2 multicolored 2.25 *3.00*
*Nos. 356-359 (4)* 4.05 4.80

Coronation of Queen Elizabeth II, 40th Anniv. — A60

Royal regalia and stamps of St. Kitts-Nevis: 10c, Eagle-shaped ampulla, No. 119. 25c, Anointing spoon, No. 334. 80c, Tassels, No. 333. $2, Staff of Scepter with the Cross, No. 354a-354c.

**1993, June 2** *Perf. 14½x14*

**360** A60 10c multicolored .50 .40
**361** A60 25c multicolored .70 .55
**362** A60 80c multicolored 1.25 1.25
**363** A60 $2 multicolored 2.25 *2.75*
*Nos. 360-363 (4)* 4.70 4.95

Girls' Brigade Intl., Cent. — A61

**1993, July 1** *Perf. 13½x14*

**364** A61 80c Flags 2.50 1.00
**365** A61 $3 Badge, coat of arms 4.25 4.25

Independence, 10th Anniv. — A62

Designs: 20c, Flag, map of St. Kitts and Nevis, plane, ship and island scenes. 80c, Natl. arms, independence emblem. $3, Natl. arms, map.

**Wmk. 373**

**1993, Sept. 10 Litho.** *Perf. 14*

**366** A62 20c multicolored 1.00 .25
**367** A62 80c multicolored 1.25 .80
**368** A62 $3 multicolored 4.00 *4.75*
*Nos. 366-368 (3)* 6.25 5.80

Christmas — A63

***Perf. 13½x14***

**1993, Nov. 16 Litho. Wmk. 373**

**369** A63 25c Roselle .50 .50
**370** A63 50c Poinsettia .75 .75
**371** A63 $1.60 Snow on the Mountain 2.50 *3.00*
*Nos. 369-371 (3)* 3.75 4.25

Prehistoric Aquatic Reptiles — A64

Designs: a, Mesosaurus. b, Placodus. c, Liopleurodon. d, Hydrotherosaurus. e, Caretta.

**Wmk. 384**

**1994, Feb. 18 Litho.** *Perf. 14*

**372** A64 $1.20 Strip of 5, #a.-e. 10.00 10.00
**373** A64 $1.20 #372 ovptd. with Hong Kong '94 emblem 11.50 11.50

**Souvenir Sheet**

Treasury Building, Cent. — A65

**Wmk. 373**

**1994, Mar. 21 Litho.** *Perf. 13½*

**374** A65 $10 multicolored 11.00 11.00

Order of the Caribbean Community — A66

First award recipients: Nos. 375a, 376a, Sir Shridath Ramphal, statesman, Guyana. Nos. 375b, 376b, Emblem of the Order. Nos. 375c, 376c, Derek Walcott, writer, St. Lucia. Nos. 375d, 376d, William Demas, economist, Trinidad and Tobago.

**Wmk. 373**

**1994, July 13 Litho. *Perf. 14***

**375** A66 10c Strip of 5, #a, b, c, b, d 1.25 1.25
**376** A66 $1 Strip of 5, #a, b, c, b, d 6.75 6.75

CARICOM, 20th anniv. (Nos. 375b, 376b).

Christmas — A67

**1994, Oct. 31**

**377** A67 25c Carol singing .25 .25
**378** A67 25c Opening presents .25 .25
**379** A67 80c Carnival .75 .75
**380** A67 $2.50 Nativity 2.75 2.75
*Nos. 377-380 (4)* 4.00 4.00

Intl. Year of the Family.

Green Turtle A68

**Wmk. 373**

**1995, Feb. 27 Litho. *Perf. 14***

**381** A68 10c shown .75 .75
**382** A68 40c On beach .90 .90
**383** A68 50c Laying eggs 1.10 1.10
**384** A68 $1 Hatchlings 1.50 1.50
*a.* Strip of 4, #381-384 6.50 6.50

World Wildlife Fund.
No. 384a issued in sheets of 16 stamps.

First St. Kitts Postage Stamp, 125th Anniv. A69

St. Christopher #1 at left and: 25c, St. Christopher #1. 80c, St. Kitts-Nevis #72. $2.50, St. Kitts-Nevis #91. $3, St. Kitts-Nevis #119.

**Wmk. 373**

**1995, Apr. 10 Litho. *Perf. 13½***

**385** A69 25c multicolored .25 .25
**386** A69 80c multicolored .60 .50
**387** A69 $2.50 multicolored 2.50 2.50
**388** A69 $3 multicolored 3.00 3.00
*Nos. 385-388 (4)* 6.35 6.25

**End of World War II, 50th Anniv.**

Common Design Types

Designs: 20c, Caribbean Regiment, North Africa. 50c, TBM Avengers on anti-submarine patrol. $2, Spitfire MkVb. $8, US destroyer escort on anti-submarine duty.
$3, Reverse of War Madal 1939-45.

**Wmk. 373**

**1995, May 8 Litho. *Perf. 13½***

**389** CD351 20c multicolored .25 .25
**390** CD351 50c multicolored .65 .65
**391** CD351 $2 multicolored 2.50 2.50
**392** CD351 $8 multicolored 8.00 8.00
*Nos. 389-392 (4)* 11.40 11.40

**Souvenir Sheet**

***Perf. 14***

**393** CD352 $3 multicolored 5.00 5.00

SKANTEL, 10th Anniv. — A70

Designs: 10c, Satellite transmission. 25c, Telephones, computer. $2, Transmission tower, satellite dish. $3, Satellite dish silhouetted against sun.

**1995, Sept. 27 *Perf. 13½x14***

**394** A70 10c multicolored .25 .25
**395** A70 25c multicolored .35 .35
**396** A70 $2 multicolored 2.50 2.50
**397** A70 $3 multicolored 3.00 3.75
*Nos. 394-397 (4)* 6.10 6.85

**UN, 50th Anniv.**

Common Design Type

Designs: 40c, Energy, clean environment. 50c, Coastal, ocean resources. $1.60, Solid waste management. $2.50, Forestry reserves.

**1995, Oct. 24 *Perf. 13½x13***

**398** CD353 40c multicolored .50 .50
**399** CD353 50c multicolored .65 .65
**400** CD353 $1.60 multicolored 2.00 *2.25*
**401** CD353 $2.50 multicolored 3.00 *3.75*
*Nos. 398-401 (4)* 6.15 7.15

FAO, 50th Anniv. A71

Designs: 25c, Vegetables. 50c, Glazed carrots, West Indian peas & rice. 80c, Tania, Cassava plants. $1.50, Waterfall, Green Hill Mountain.

**1995, Nov. 13 *Perf. 13½***

**402** A71 25c multicolored .25 .25
**403** A71 50c multicolored .50 .50
**404** A71 80c multicolored .85 .85
**405** A71 $1.50 multicolored 1.75 *2.75*
*Nos. 402-405 (4)* 3.35 4.35

Sea Shells — A72

a, Flame helmet. b, Triton's trumpet. c, King helmet. d, True tulip. e, Queen conch.

**Wmk. 373**

**1996, Jan. 10 Litho. *Perf. 13***

**406** A72 $1.50 Strip of 5, #a.-e. 8.75 8.75

CAPEX '96 — A73

Leeward Islands LMS Jubilee Class 4-6-0 Locomotives: 10c, No. 45614. $10, No. 5614.

***Perf. 13½x14***

**1996, June 8 Litho. Wmk. 373**

**407** A73 10c multicolored .90 .90

**Souvenir Sheet**

***Perf. 14x15***

**408** A73 $10 multicolored 9.00 9.00

No. 408 is 48x31mm.

A74

Modern Olympic Games, Cent.: 10c, Runner, St. Kitts & Nevis flag. 25c, High jumper, US flag. 80c, Runner, Olympic flag. $3, Athens Games poster, 1896.
$6, Olympic torch.

**Wmk. 384**

**1996, June 30 Litho. *Perf. 14***

**409** A74 10c multicolored .25 .25
**410** A74 25c multicolored .25 .25
**411** A74 80c multicolored .75 .75
**412** A74 $3 multicolored 2.50 2.50
*Nos. 409-412 (4)* 3.75 3.75

**Souvenir Sheet**

**413** A74 $6 multicolored 5.25 5.25

Olymphilex '96 (#413).

A75

Defense Force, Cent.: 10c, Volunteer rifleman, 1896. 50c, Mounted infantry, 1911. $2, Bandsman, 1940-60. $2.50, Modern uniform, 1996.

**1996, Nov. 1 Wmk. 373**

**414** A75 10c multicolored .25 .25
**415** A75 50c multicolored .45 .45
**416** A75 $2 multicolored 1.75 1.75
**417** A75 $2.50 multicolored 2.00 2.00
*Nos. 414-417 (4)* 4.45 4.45

Christmas — A76

Paintings: 15c, Holy Virgin and Child, by Anais Colin, 1844. 25c, Holy Family, After Rubens. 50c, Madonna with the Goldfinch, by Krause on porcelain after Raphael, 1507. 80c, Madonna on Throne with Angels, by unknown Spanish, 17th cent.

**1996, Nov. 29**

**418** A76 15c multicolored .25 .25
**419** A76 25c multicolored .35 .25
**420** A76 50c multicolored .80 .65
**421** A76 80c multicolored 1.00 *1.25*
*Nos. 418-421 (4)* 2.40 2.40

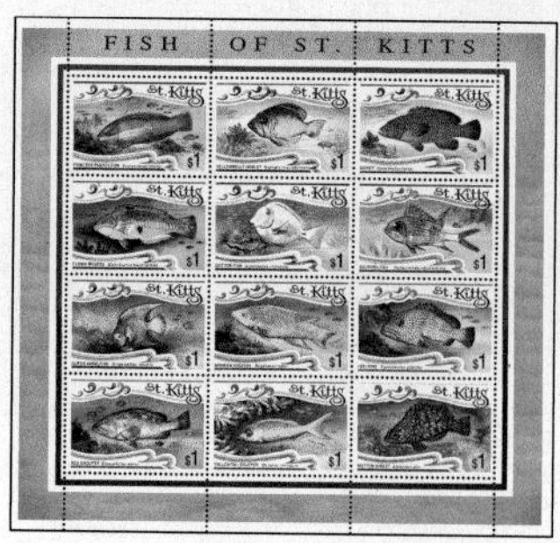


Fish — A77

a, Princess parrot fish. b, Yellowbelly hamlet. c, Coney. d, Clown wrasse. e, Doctor fish. f, Squirrelfish. g, Queen angelfish. h, Spanish hogfish. i, Red hind. j, Red grouper. k, Yellowtail snapper. l, Mutton hamlet.

**1997, Apr. 24 *Perf. 13½***

**422** A77 $1 Sheet of 12, #a.-l. 14.50 14.50

Queen Elizabeth II and Prince Philip, 50th Wedding Anniv. — A78

Designs: No. 423, Queen. No. 424, Prince riding with Royal Guard. No. 425, Queen riding in carriage. No. 426, Prince Philip. No. 427, Early photo of Queen, Prince. No. 428, Prince riding horse.
Queen, Prince riding in open carriage, horiz.

**Wmk. 373**

**1997, July 10 Litho. *Perf. 13½***

**423** 10c multicolored .50 .50
**424** 10c multicolored .50 .50
*a.* A78 Pair, #423-424 1.35 1.35
**425** 25c multicolored .75 .75
**426** 25c multicolored .75 .75
*a.* A78 Pair, #425-426 1.75 1.75
**427** $3 multicolored 2.25 2.25
**428** $3 multicolored 2.25 2.25
*a.* A78 Pair, #427-428 6.00 6.00
*Nos. 423-428 (6)* 7.00 7.00

**Souvenir Sheet**

***Perf. 14x14½***

**429** A78 $6 multicolored 8.50 8.50

Christmas — A79

Churches: No. 430, Zion Moravian. No. 431, Wesley Methodist. $1.50, St. Georges Anglican. $15, Co-Cathedral of the Immaculate Conception.

***Perf. 13½x14***

**1997, Oct. 31 Litho. Wmk. 384**

**430** A79 10c multi .25 .25
**431** A79 10c multi .25 .25
**432** A79 $1.50 multi, vert. 1.40 1.40
**433** A79 $15 multi, vert. 12.00 12.00
*Nos. 430-433 (4)* 13.90 13.90

Natl. Heroes' Day — A80

No. 434, Robert L. Bradshaw (1916-78), 1st premier of St. Kitts, Nevis, & Anguilla. No. 435, Joseph N. France, trade unionist. No. 436, C.A. Paul Southwell (1913-79), 1st chief minister of St. Kitts, Nevis, & Anguilla. $3, France, Bradshaw, & Southwell.

**1997, Sept. 16 *Perf. 13½***

**434** A80 25c multi, vert. .25 .25
**435** A80 25c multi, vert. .25 .25
**436** A80 25c multi, vert. .25 .25
**437** A80 $3 multi 2.25 2.25
*Nos. 434-437 (4)* 3.00 3.00

**Diana, Princess of Wales (1961-97)**

Common Design Type

No. 438: a, like No. 437A. b, Wearing red jacket. c, Wearing white dress. d, Holding flowers.

***Perf. 14½x14***

**1998, Mar. 31 Litho. Wmk. 373**

**437A** CD355 30c Wearing white hat .40 .40

**Sheet of 4**

438 CD355 $1.60 Sheet of 4, #a.-d. 4.75 4.75

No. 438 sold for $6.40 + 90c, with surtax from international sales being donated to Princess Diana Memorial Fund and surtax from national sales being donated to designated local charity.

Butterflies A81

Designs: 10c, Common long-tail skipper. 15c, White peacock. 25c, Caribbean buckeye. 30c, Red rim. 40c, Cassius blue. 50c, Flambeau. 60c, Lucas's blue. 90c, Cloudless sulphur. $1, Monarch. $1.20, Fiery skipper. $1.60, Zebra. $3, Southern dagger tail. $5, Polydamus swallowtail. $10, Tropical checkered skipper.

*Perf. 14¼x14½*

**1997, Dec. 29 Litho. Wmk. 373**

| | | | | |
|---|---|---|---|---|
| 439 | A81 | 10c multicolored | .25 | .25 |
| a. | | "S" in "Proteus" to left of mid-line of leaf above | .45 | .45 |
| 440 | A81 | 15c multicolored | .30 | .30 |
| 441 | A81 | 25c multicolored | .40 | .40 |
| 442 | A81 | 30c multicolored | .40 | .40 |
| 443 | A81 | 40c multicolored | .40 | .40 |
| 444 | A81 | 50c multicolored | .60 | .60 |
| 445 | A81 | 60c multicolored | .70 | .70 |
| 446 | A81 | 90c multicolored | 1.10 | 1.10 |
| 447 | A81 | $1 multicolored | 1.10 | 1.10 |
| 448 | A81 | $1.20 multicolored | 1.40 | 1.40 |
| 449 | A81 | $1.60 multicolored | 1.75 | 1.75 |
| 450 | A81 | $3 multicolored | 2.75 | 2.75 |
| a. | | "S" in "$" same size as numeral | 4.00 | 4.00 |
| 451 | A81 | $5 multicolored | 4.00 | 4.00 |
| a. | | Inscribed "Polydamas" | 6.00 | 6.00 |
| 452 | A81 | $10 multicolored | 7.00 | 7.00 |
| a. | | "S" in "$" same size as numeral | 10.00 | 10.00 |
| | | *Nos. 439-452 (14)* | 22.15 | 22.15 |

Nos. 439a, 450a, 451a and 452a have other minor design differences.

University of West Indies, 50th Anniv. A82

*Perf. 13½x13*

**1998, July 20 Litho. Wmk. 373**

453 A82 80c shown .70 .70
454 A82 $2 Arms, mortarboard 1.90 1.90

Carnival Santa A83

**Wmk. 373**

**1998, Oct. 30 Litho. *Perf. 14***

455 A83 80c shown .65 .65
456 A83 $1.20 With two dancers 1.00 1.00

UPU, 125th Anniv. — A84

**Wmk. 373**

**1999, Mar. 5 Litho. *Perf. 14***

457 A84 30c shown .40 .40
458 A84 90c Map of St. Kitts 1.00 1.00

Birds of the Eastern Caribbean A85

Designs: a, Caribbean martin. b, Spotted sandpiper. c, Sooty tern. d, Red-tailed hawk. e, Trembler. f, Belted kingfisher. g, Black-billed duck. h, Yellow warbler. i, Blue-headed hummingbird. j, Antillean euphonia. k, Fulvous whistling duck. l, Mangrove cuckoo. m, Carib grackle. n, Caribbean elaenia. o, Common ground dove. p, Forest thrush.

**Wmk. 373**

**1999, Apr. 27 Litho. *Perf. 14***

459 A85 80c Sheet of 16, #a.-p. 13.00 13.00

IBRA '99.

**1st Manned Moon Landing, 30th Anniv.**

Common Design Type

Designs: 80c, Lift-off. 90c, In lunar orbit. $1, Aldrin deploying scientific equipment. $1.20, Heat shield burns on re-entry.
$10, Earth as seen from moon.

*Perf. 14x13¾*

**1999, July 20 Litho. Wmk. 384**

| | | | | |
|---|---|---|---|---|
| 460 | CD357 | 80c multicolored | .75 | .75 |
| 461 | CD357 | 90c multicolored | .90 | .90 |
| 462 | CD357 | $1 multicolored | 1.00 | 1.00 |
| 463 | CD357 | $1.20 multicolored | .95 | *1.25* |
| | | *Nos. 460-463 (4)* | 3.60 | 3.90 |

**Souvenir Sheet**

*Perf. 14*

464 CD357 $10 multicolored 7.75 7.75

No. 464 contains one 40mm circular stamp.

Christmas — A86

**Wmk. 373**

**1999, Oct. 29 Litho. *Perf. 13¾***

| | | | | |
|---|---|---|---|---|
| 465 | A86 | 10c shown | .25 | .25 |
| 466 | A86 | 30c 3 musicians | .25 | .25 |
| 467 | A86 | 80c 6 musicians | .70 | .70 |
| 468 | A86 | $2 4 musicians, diff. | 1.90 | 2.25 |
| | | *Nos. 465-468 (4)* | 3.10 | 3.45 |

Children's Drawings Celebrating the Millennium — A87

**1999, Dec. 29 Litho. *Perf. 14***

| | | | | |
|---|---|---|---|---|
| 469 | A87 | 10c by Adom Taylor | .35 | .35 |
| 470 | A87 | 30c by Travis Liburd | .35 | .35 |
| 471 | A87 | 50c by Darren Moses | .90 | .90 |
| 472 | A87 | $1 by Pierre Liburd | 1.60 | 1.60 |
| | | *Nos. 469-472 (4)* | 3.20 | 3.20 |

Carifesta VII — A88

Designs: 30c, Festival participants. 90c, Emblem. $1.20, Dancer, vert.

**Wmk. 373**

**2000, Aug. 30 Litho. *Perf. 14***

| | | | | |
|---|---|---|---|---|
| 473 | A88 | 30c multi | .25 | .25 |
| 474 | A88 | 90c multi | .75 | .75 |
| 475 | A88 | $1.20 multi | 1.15 | 1.15 |
| | | *Nos. 473-475 (3)* | 2.15 | 2.15 |

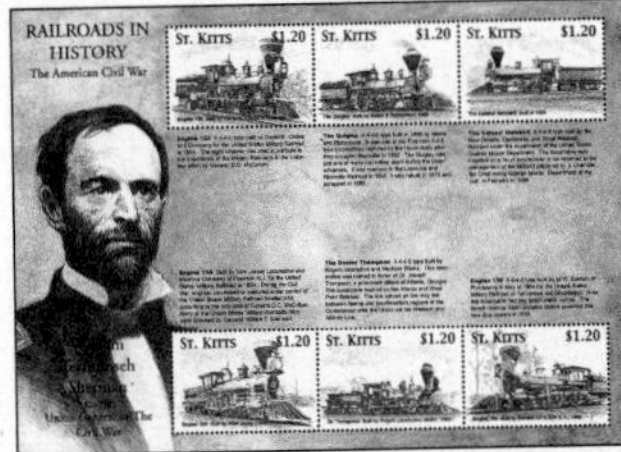

Railroads in American Civil War — A89

No. 476, $1.20, horiz.: a, Engine 133. b, Quigley. c, Colonel Holobird. d, Engine 150. e, Doctor Thompson. f, Engine 156.

No. 477, $1.20, horiz.: a, Governor Nye. b, Engine 31. c, C. A. Henry. d, Engine 152. e, Engine 116. f, Job Terry.

No. 478, $1.60, horiz.: a, Dover. b, Scout. c, Baltimore & Ohio Railroad locomotive. d, John M. Forbes. e, Edward Kidder. f, William W. Wright.

No. 479, $1.60, horiz.: a, Engine 83. b, General. c, Engine 38. d, Texas. e, Engine 162. f, Christopher Adams, Jr.

No. 480, $5, Ulysses S. Grant. No. 481, $5, George B. McClellan. No. 482, $5, Herman Haupt. No. 483, $5, Robert E. Lee.

**Unwmk.**

**2001, Feb. 19 Litho. *Perf. 14***

**Sheets of 6, #a-f**

476-479 A89 Set of 4 35.00 35.00

**Souvenir Sheets**

480-483 A89 Set of 4 35.00 35.00

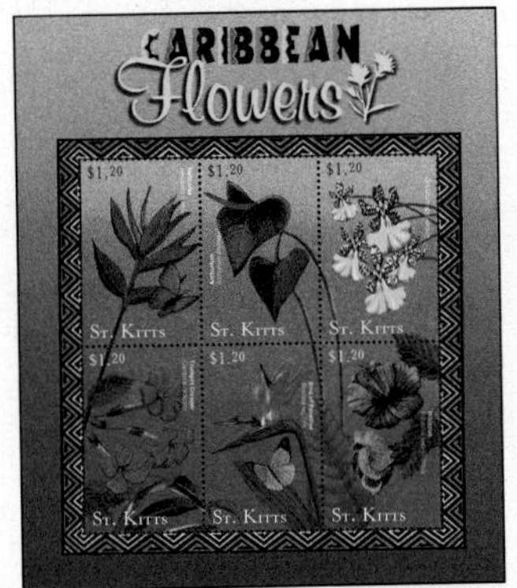

Flora & Fauna — A90

No. 484, $1.20 — Flowers: a, Heliconia. b, Anthurium. c, Oncidium splendidum. d, Trumpet creeper. e, Bird of paradise. f, Hibiscus.

No. 485, $1.20: a, Bananaquit. b, Anthurium (hills and clouds in background). c, Common dolphin. d, Horse mushroom. e, Green anole. f, Monarch butterfly.

No. 486, $1.60 — Birds: a, Laughing gull. b, Sooty tern. c, White-tailed tropicbird. d, Painted bunting. e, Belted kingfisher. f, Yellow-bellied sapsucker.

No. 487, $1.60 — Butterflies: a, Figure-of-eight. b, Banded king shoemaker. c, Orange theope. d, Grecian shoemaker. e, Clorinde. f, Small lace-wing.

No. 488, $1.60, horiz.: a, Beaugregory. b, Banded butterflyfish. c, Cherubfish. d, Rock beauty. e, Red snapper. f, Leatherback turtle.

No. 489, $5, Leochilus carinatus. No. 490, $5, Iguana, horiz. No. 491, $5, Ruby-throated hummingbird, horiz. No. 492, $5, Common morpho, horiz.

No. 493, $5, Redband parrotfish, horiz.

**2001, Mar. 12 *Perf. 14***

**Sheets of 6, #a-f**

484-488 A90 Set of 5 37.50 37.50

**Souvenir Sheets**

489-493 A90 Set of 5 28.00 28.00

Compare No. 491 with No. 520.

2001 Census — A91

Designs: 30c, People in house. $3, People, barn, silos.

**2001, Apr. 18 Litho. *Perf. 14½x14¼***

494-495 A91 Set of 2 3.50 3.50

Queen Victoria (1819-1901) — A92

No. 496: a, At coronation. b, In wedding gown. c, With Prince Albert visiting wounded Crimean War veterans. d, With Prince Albert, 1854.

$5, Wearing crown.

**2001, Apr. 26 *Perf. 14***

496 A92 $2 Sheet of 4, #a-d 8.25 8.25

**Souvenir Sheet**

497 A92 $5 black 5.75 5.75

No. 496 contains four 28x42mm stamps.

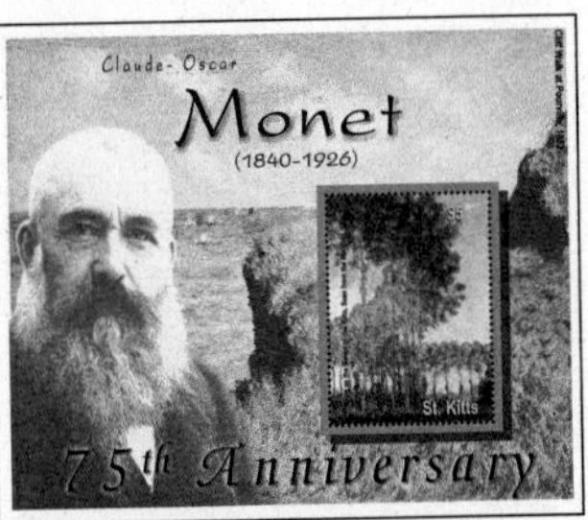

Monet Paintings — A93

No. 498, horiz.: a, On the Coast of Trouville. b, Vétheuil in Summer. c, Field of Yellow Iris Near Giverny. d, Coastguard's Cottage at Varengeville.

$5, Poplars on the Banks of the Epte, Seen From the Marshes.

**2001, July 16 *Perf. 13¾***

498 A93 $2 Sheet of 4, #a-d 10.00 10.00

**Souvenir Sheet**

499 A93 $5 multi 5.25 5.25

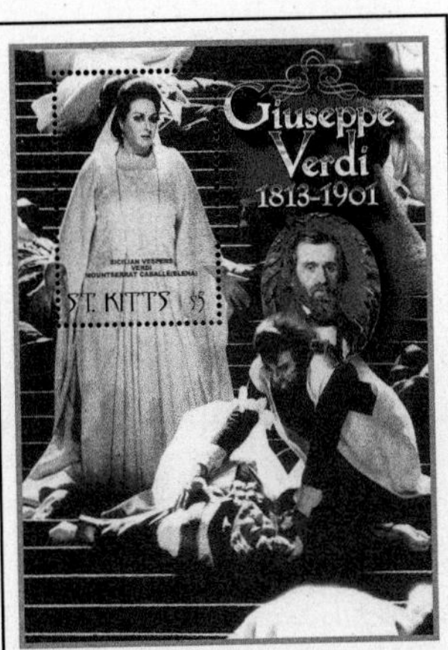

Giuseppe Verdi (1813-1901), Opera Composer — A94

No. 500 — Scenes from the Sicilian Vespers: a, French soldiers in Palermo (all standing). b, French soldiers in Palermo (some seated). c, Costume design. d, Sicilian people and French soldiers

$5, Montserrat Caballé.

**2001, July 16** *Perf. 14*
500 A94 $2 Sheet of 4, #a-d 8.50 8.50

**Souvenir Sheet**

501 A94 $5 multi 5.75 5.75

Royal Navy Submarines, Cent. — A95

No. 502, horiz.: a, A Class submarine. b, HMS Dreadnaught battleship. c, HMS Amethyst. d, HMS Barnham. e, HMS Exeter. f, HMS Eagle.
$5, HMS Dreadnaught submarine.

**2001, July 16** *Perf. 14*
502 A95 $1.40 Sheet of 6, #a-f 19.00 19.00

**Souvenir Sheet**

503 A95 $5 multi 10.00 10.00

No. 502 contains six 42x28mm stamps.

Queen Elizabeth II, 75th Birthday — A96

No. 504: a, In blue hat, holding flowers. b, In flowered hat, looking right. c, In blue hat and coat. d, In flowered hat, looking left.
$5, On horse.

**2001, July 16**
504 A96 $2 Sheet of 4, #a-d 8.50 8.50

**Souvenir Sheet**

505 A96 $5 multi 5.50 5.50

Phila Nippon '01, Japan — A97

Woodcuts: 50c, Hatsufunedayu as a Tatebina, by Shigenobu. Yamagawa 80c, Samurai Kodenji as Tsuyu No Mae, by Kiyonobu I. $1, Senya Nakamura as Tokonatsu, by Kiyomasu I. $1.60, Sumida River, by Shunsho. $2, Wrestler, Kuemon Yoba, by Shun-ei. $3, Two Actors in Roles, by Kiyonobu Torii I.
$5, Full Length Actor Protraits, by Shun-ei.

**2001, July 16** *Perf. 12x12¼*
506-511 A97 Set of 6 9.00 9.00

**Souvenir Sheet**

512 A97 $5 multi 6.00 6.00

Mao Zedong (1893-1976) — A98

No. 514: a, In 1926. b, In 1945 (green background). c, In 1945 (lilac background).
$3, Undated picture.

**2001, July 16** **Litho.** *Perf. 13¾*
513 A98 $2 Sheet of 3, #a-c 9.00 9.00

**Souvenir Sheet**

514 A98 $3 multi 4.50 4.50

Flora & Fauna — A99

No. 515, $1.20 — Birds: a, Trembler. b, White-tailed tropicbird. c, Red-footed booby. d, Red-legged thrush. e, Painted bunting. f, Bananaquit.
No. 516, $1.20 — Orchids: a, Maxillaria cucullata. b, Cattleya dowiana. c, Rossioglossum grande. d, Aspasia epidendroides. e, Lycaste skinneri. f, Cattleya percivaliana.
No. 517, $1.60 — Butterflies: a, Orange-barred sulphur. b, Giant swallowtail. c, Orange theope. d, Blue night. e, Grecian shoemaker. f, Cramer's mesene.
No. 518, $1.60 — Mushrooms: a, Pholiota spectabilis. b, Flammula penetrans. c, Ungulina marginata. d, Collybia iocephala. e, Amanita muscaria. f, Corinus comatus.
No. 519, $1.60, horiz. — Whales: a, Killer.whale b, Cuvier's beaked whale. c, Humpback whale. d, Sperm whale. e, Blue whale. f, Whale shark.
No. 520, $5, Ruby-throated hummingbird. No. 521, $5, Psychilis atropurpurea. No. 522, $5, Figure-of-eight butterfly. No. 523, $5, Lepiota procera. No. 524, $5, Sei whale, horiz.

**2001, Sept. 18** *Perf. 14*

**Sheets of 6, #a-f**

515-519 A99 Set of 5 35.00 35.00

**Souvenir Sheets**

520-524 A99 Set of 5 25.00 25.00

Compare No. 520 with No. 490.

Christmas and Carnival — A100

Designs: 10c, Angel, Christmas tree. 30c, Fireworks. 80c, Wreath, dove, bells, candy cane. $2, Steel drums.

**2001, Nov. 26**
525-528 A100 Set of 4 4.00 4.00

Roign of Queen Elizabeth II, 50th Anniv. — A101

No. 529: a, Ceremonial coach. b, Prince Philip. c, Queen and Queen Mother. d, Queen wearing tiara.
$5, Queen and Prince Philip.

**2002, Feb. 6** *Perf. 14¼*
529 A101 $2 Sheet of 4, #a-d 6.50 6.50

**Souvenir Sheet**

530 A101 $5 multi 4.75 4.75

United We Stand — A102

*Perf. 13½x13¼*

**2002, June 17** **Litho.**
531 A102 80c multi 1.90 1.90

Printed in sheets of 4.

2002 Winter Olympics, Salt Lake City A103

Designs: No. 532, $3, Cross-country skiing. No. 533, $3, Alpine skiing.

**2002, June 17** *Perf. 13¼x13½*
532-533 A103 Set of 2 5.75 5.75
533a Souvenir sheet, #532-533 5.75 5.75

Souvenir Sheet

New Year 2002 (Year of the Horse) — A104

Details of Wen-Gi's Returning to Han, by Chang Yu: a, Horse and rider, dog. b, Group of horses and riders. c, Horse and rider, two attendants. d, Standard bearer on horse.

**2002, June 17** *Perf. 12½*
534 A104 $1.60 Sheet of 4, #a-d 5.00 5.00

Intl. Year of Mountains — A105

No. 535: a, Mt. Sakura, Japan. b, Mount Assiniboine, Canada. c, Mt. Asgard, Canada. d, Bugaboo Spire, Canada.
$6, Mt. Owen, Wyoming.

**2002, June 17** *Perf. 13¼x13½*
535 A105 $2 Sheet of 4, #a-d 6.50 6.50

**Souvenir Sheet**

536 A105 $6 multi 6.00 6.00

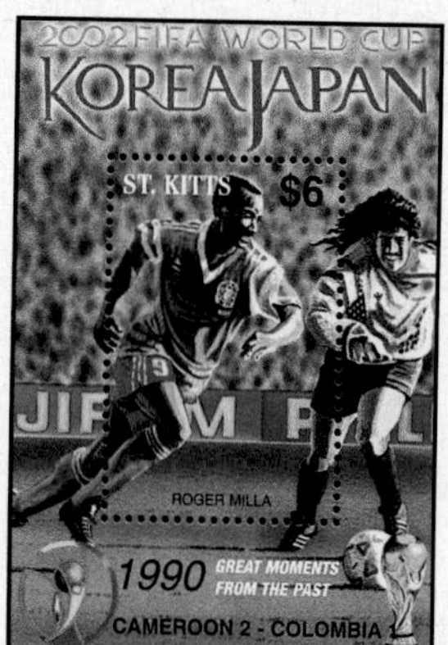


2002 World Cup Soccer Championships, Japan and Korea — A106

No. 537 — World Cup trophy and: a, $1.65, 1982 World Cup poster. b, $1.65, Just Fontaine, French flag. c, $1.65, U.S. player and flag. d, $1.65, Swedish player and flag. e, $6, Daegu Sports Complex, Korea (55x41mm).
$6, Roger Milla.

**2002, June 17** *Perf. 13½x13¼*
537 A106 Sheet of 5, #a-e 10.50 10.50

**Souvenir Sheet**

538 A106 $6 multi 5.50 5.50

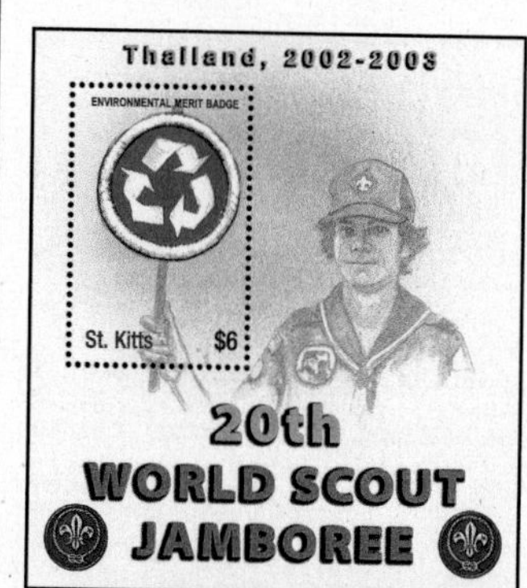


20th World Scout Jamboree, Thailand — A107

No. 539, horiz.: a, Scout sign. b, Silver Award 2. c, Council patch. d, Scout with sword.
$6, Environmental Studies merit badge.

**2002, June 17** *Perf. 13¼x13½*
539 A107 $2 Sheet of 4, #a-d 7.50 7.50

**Souvenir Sheet**

*Perf. 13½x13¼*

540 A107 $6 multi 5.75 5.75

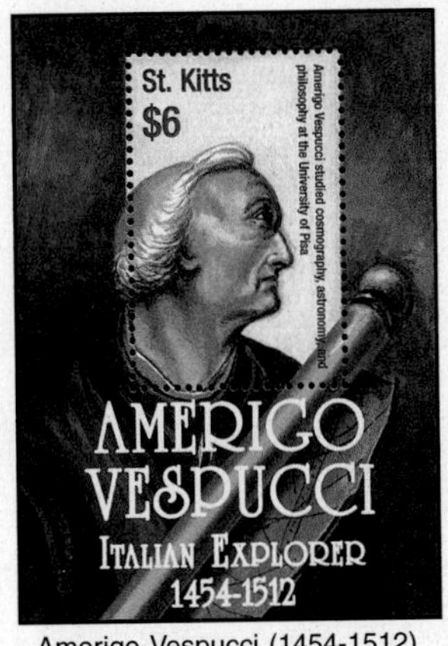
Amerigo Vespucci (1454-1512), Explorer — A108

No. 541, horiz.: a, Vespucci with feathered hat. b, 1507 World map by Martin Waldseemüller. c, Vespucci with beard.
$6, Vespucci with bald head.

**2002, June 17** *Perf. 13¼x13½*
**541** A108 $3 Sheet of 3, #a-c 7.50 7.50

**Souvenir Sheet**
*Perf. 13½x13¼*

**542** A108 $6 multi 5.75 5.75

Kim Collins, Sprinter — A109

Collins: 30c, Running. 90c, Wearing 2001 IAAF bronze medal.

**2002, July 2** *Perf. 14*
**543-544** A109 Set of 2 2.50 2.50

Christmas — A110

Fruits: 10c, Soursop. 80c, Passion fruit. $1, Sugar apple. $2, Custard apple.

**2002, Oct. 14** **Litho.**
**545-548** A110 Set of 4 5.75 5.75

Queen Mother Elizabeth (1900-2002) — A111

No. 549: a, Wearing green dress. b, Wearing yellow dress and hat.

**2002, Nov. 18** **Litho.** *Perf. 14*
**549** A111 $2 Pair, #a-b 4.50 4.50

No. 549 printed in sheets containing 2 pairs.

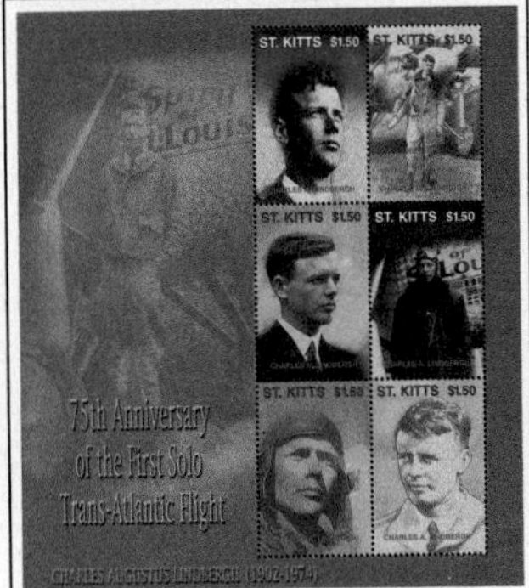
First Non-stop Solo Transatlantic Flight, 75th Anniv. — A112

Charles Lindbergh: a, In suit, denomination in white. b, And Spirit of St. Louis, denomination in blue violet. c, In suit, looking right, denomination in blue violet. d, And Spirit of St. Louis, denomination in white. e, Wearing pilot's headgear. f, Wearing overcoat.

**2002, Nov. 18**
**550** A112 $1.50 Sheet of 6, #a-f 10.00 10.00

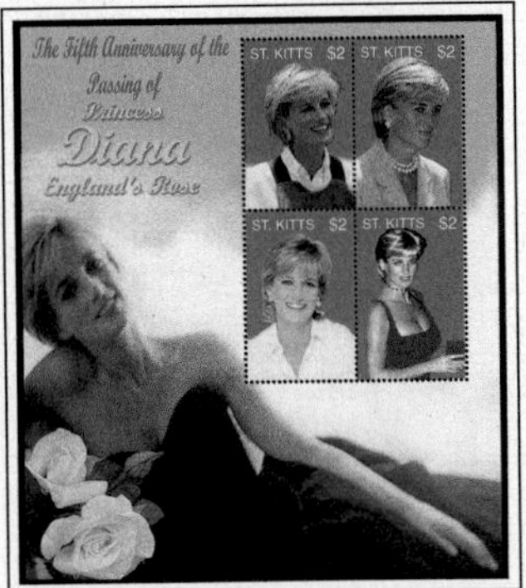
Princess Diana (1961-97) — A113

No. 551, $2: a, Wearing bulletproof vest. b, Wearing gray suit with pearls. c, Wearing yellow blouse. d, Wearing red dress and necklace.
No. 552, $2: a, Wearing white coat with purple piping. b, With hands clasped. c, Wearing red dress without necklace. d, Wearing white dress.

**2002, Nov. 18** **Litho.**
**Sheets of 4, #a-d**
**551-552** A113 Set of 2 14.00 14.00

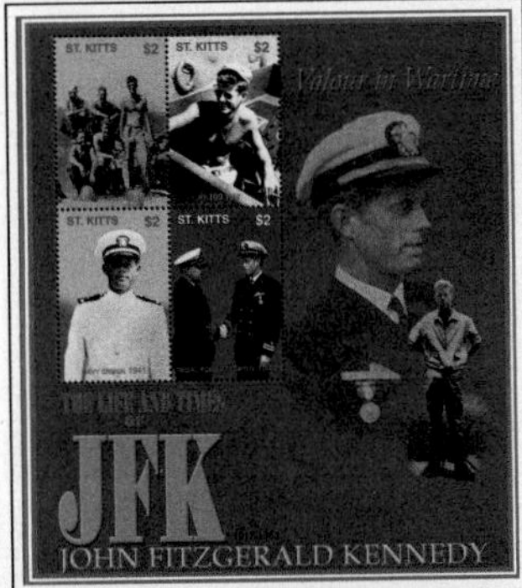
Pres. John F. Kennedy (1917-63) — A114

No. 553, $2: a, With sailors, Solomon Islands, 1942. b, On PT109, 1942. c, As Navy Ensign, 1941. d, Receiving medal for gallantry, 1944.
No. 554, $2: a, Peace Corps. b, Space program. c, Civil rights. d, Nuclear disarmament.

**2002, Nov. 18** *Perf. 14*
**Sheets of 4, #a-d**
**553-554** A114 Set of 2 14.00 14.00

New Year 2003 (Year of the Ram) — A115

No. 555: a, Piebald ram. b, Ram with long coat. c, Ram sculpture, looking right.

**2003, Jan. 27** *Perf. 14¼x13¾*
**555** A115 $1 Vert. strip of 3, #a-c 4.50 4.50

No. 555 printed in sheets containing 2 strips.

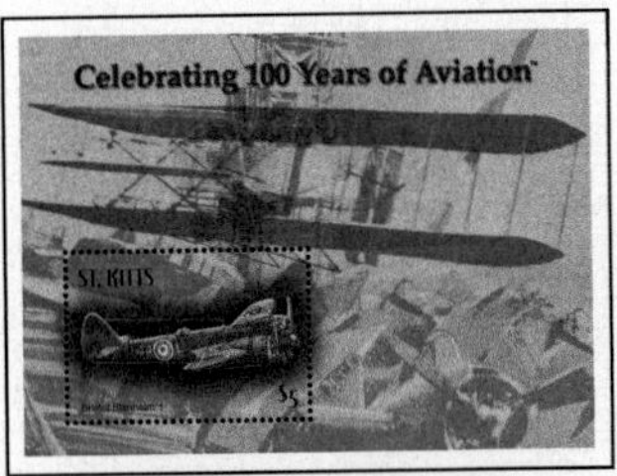
Powered Flight, Cent. — A116

No. 556: a, Voisin LA5. b, Gotha G.V. c, Polikarpov I-16. d, Bell YFM-1.
$5, Bristol Blenheim 1.

**2003, June 17** **Litho.** *Perf. 14*
**556** A116 $2 Sheet of 4, #a-d 6.50 6.50

**Souvenir Sheet**
**557** A116 $5 multi 3.50 3.50

Tour de France Bicycle Race, Cent. — A117

No. 558: a, Miguel Indurain, 1994. b, Indurain, 1995. c, Bjarne Riis, 1996. d, Jan Ullrich, 1997.
$5, Indurain, 1991-95.

**2003, June 17** *Perf. 13½x13¼*
**558** A117 $2 Sheet of 4, #a-d 6.00 6.00

**Souvenir Sheet**
**559** A117 $5 multi 3.75 3.75

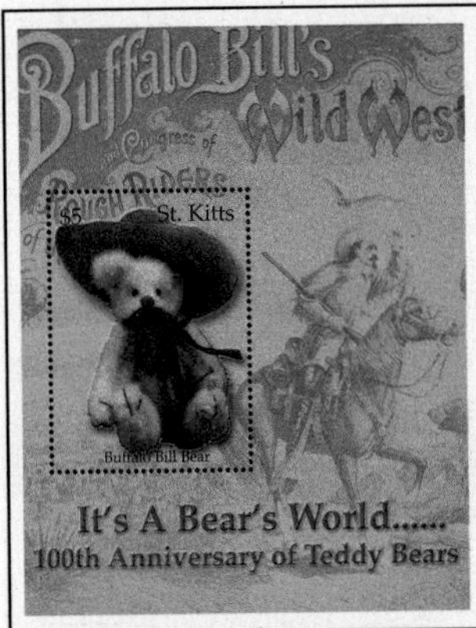
Teddy Bears, Cent. — A118

No. 560: a, Queen Victoria Bear. b, Teddy Roosevelt Bear. c, George Washington Bear. d, General Patton Bear.
$5, Buffalo Bill Bear.

**2003, June 17** *Perf. 13¾*
**560** A118 $2 Sheet of 4, #a-d 6.50 6.50

**Souvenir Sheet**
**561** A118 $5 multi 4.00 4.00

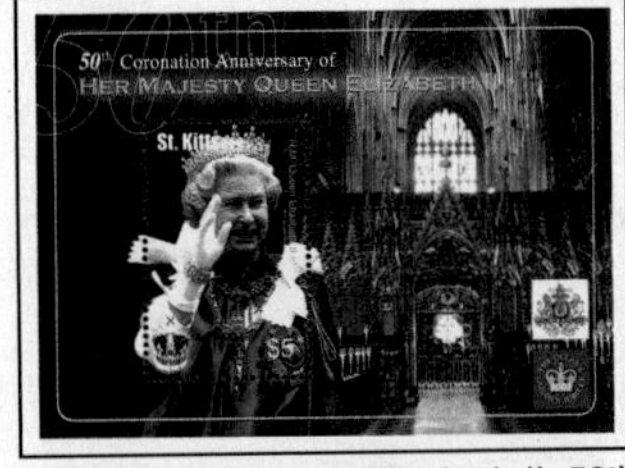
Coronation of Queen Elizabeth II, 50th Anniv. — A119

No. 562: a, Wearing tiara as young woman. b, Wearing tiara and red sash. c, Wearing tiara and blue sash.
$5, Queen waving.

**2003, June 17** **Litho.** *Perf. 14*
**562** A119 $3 Sheet of 3, #a-c 6.50 6.50

**Souvenir Sheet**
**563** A119 $5 multi 4.00 4.00

Caribbean Community, 30th Anniv. — A120

**2003, June 23**
**564** A120 30c multi 1.10 1.10

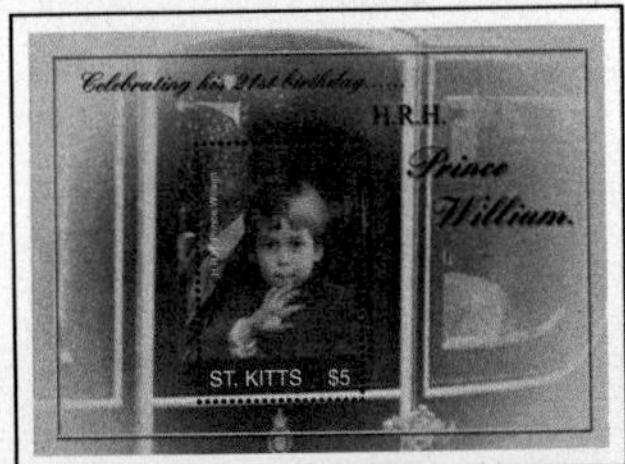
Prince William, 21st Birthday — A121

No. 565: a, As toddler, in jacket. b, As young boy, in striped shirt. c, Wearing sports shirt.
$5, As child, waving.

**2003, July 1**
**565** A121 $3 Sheet of 3, #a-c 6.25 6.25

**Souvenir Sheet**
**566** A121 $5 multi 3.75 3.75

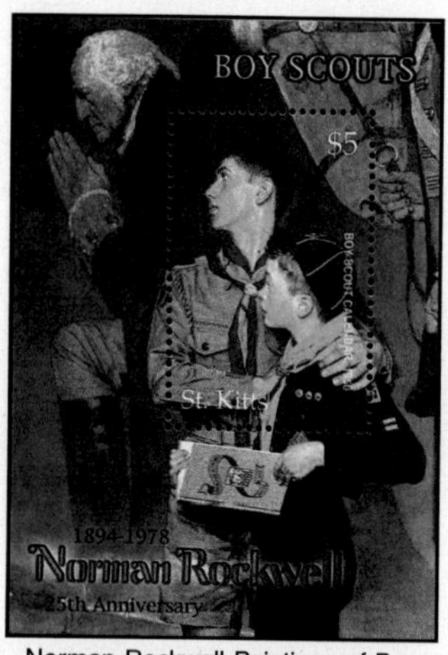

Norman Rockwell Paintings of Boy Scouts from Boy Scout Calendars — A122

No. 567: a, Scout and Sailors, 1937. b, Scouts with Camping Gear, 1937. c, Boy and Dog at Window, 1968. d, Scout at Attention, 1932.
$5, Boy Scout and Cub Scout, 1950.

**2003, Aug. 18** ***Perf. 14***
**567** A122 $2 Sheet of 4, #a-d 5.75 5.75

**Souvenir Sheet**

**568** A122 $5 multi 3.75 3.75

Painting by Pablo Picasso — A123

No. 569: a, Child with Wooden Horse. b, Child with a Ball. c, The Butterfly Catcher. d, Boy with a Lobster. e, Baby Wearing Polka Dot Dress. f, El Bobo, After Murillo.
$5, Untitled painting.

**2003, Aug. 18** ***Perf. 14***
**569** A123 $1.60 Sheet of 4, #a-d 6.75 6.75

**Souvenir Sheet**
***Imperf***

**570** A123 $5 multi 3.75 3.75

No. 569 contains six 28x42mm stamps.

Rembrandt Paintings A124

Designs: 50c, A Family Group. $1, Portrait of Cornelis Claesz Anslo and Aetje Gerritsor Schouten, horiz. $1.60, Portrait of a Young Woman. $3, Man in Military Costume.
No. 575: a, An Old Woman Reading. b, Hendrickje Stoffels. c, Rembrandt's Mother. d, Saskia.
$5, Judas Returning the Thirty Pieces of Silver.

**2003, Aug. 18** ***Perf. 14¼***
**571-574** A124 Set of 4 4.25 4.25
**575** A124 $2 Sheet of 4, #a-d 5.50 5.50

**Souvenir Sheet**

**576** A124 $5 multi 3.50 3.50

Japanese Art — A125

Designs: 90c, Tokiwa Gozen with Her Son in the Snow, by Hokumei Shunkyokusai. $1, Courtesan and Asahina, attributed to Choki Eishosai. $1.50, Parody of Sugawara No Michizane Seated on an Ox, by Toyokuni Utagawa. $3, Visiting a Flower Garden, by Kunisada Utagawa.
No. 581 — Akugenta Yoshihira, by Kunisada Utagawa: a, Man with bow. b, Man with sword at waist. c, Man holding scarf. d, Man with sword on shoulder.
$6, The Courtesan Katachino Under a Cherry Tree, by Toyoharu Utagawa.

**2003, Aug. 18**
**577-580** A125 Set of 4 5.00 5.00
**581** A125 $2 Sheet of 4, #a-d 6.25 6.25

**Souvenir Sheet**

**582** A125 $6 multi 4.50 4.50

White Gibbon, by Giuseppe Castiglione A126

**2004, Jan. 15** ***Perf. 13¾x13½***
**583** A126 $1.60 shown 1.40 1.40

**Souvenir Sheet**
***Perf. 13¼***

**584** A126 $3 Painting detail 2.75 2.75

New Year 2004 (Year of the Monkey). No. 583 printed in sheets of 4. No. 584 contains one 30x37mm stamp.

D-Day, 60th Anniv. — A127

No. 585, horiz.: a, 12th Panzer Division moves into position. b, German heavy tank. c, British and Germans clash (soldiers). d, British and Germans clash (soldiers, tank).
$5, Allied cemetery, Normandy.

**2004, Sept. 21** **Litho.** ***Perf. 14***
**585** A127 $2 Sheet of 4, #a-d. 6.00 6.00

**Souvenir Sheet**

**586** A127 $5 multi 4.00 4.00

2004 Summer Olympics, Athens A128

Designs: 50c, Jiri Guth Jarkovsky, member of first International Olympic Committee. 90c, Poster for 1972 Munich Olympics. $1, Poster for 1900 Paris Olympics. $3, Sculpture of wrestlers.

**2004, Sept. 21** ***Perf. 14¼***
**587-590** A128 Set of 4 3.50 3.50

**Souvenir Sheet**

Deng Xiaoping (1904-97), Chinese Leader — A129

**2004, Sept. 21** **Litho.** ***Perf. 14***
**591** A129 $5 multi 4.00 4.00

Election of Pope John Paul II, 25th Anniv. (in 2003) — A130

No. 592: a, Seated. b, Walking in garden. c, With arms clasped. d, Holding crucifix.

**2004, Sept. 21**
**592** A130 $2 Sheet of 4, #a-d 6.50 6.50

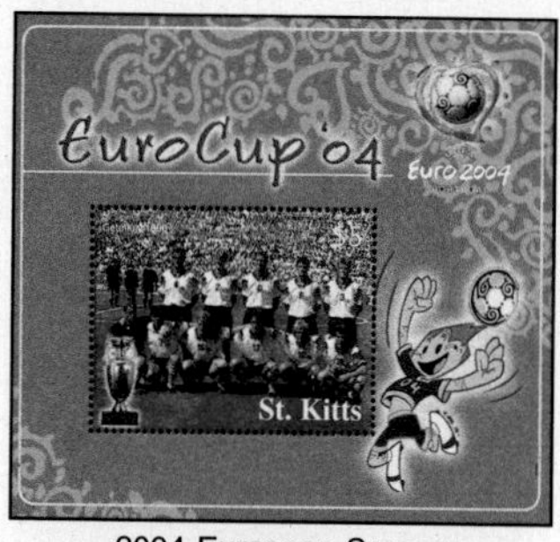

2004 European Soccer Championships, Portugal — A131

No. 593, vert.: a, Berti Vogts. b, Patrik Berger. c, Oliver Bierhoff. d, Empire Stadium.
$5, 1996 German team.

**2004, Sept. 21** ***Perf. 14¼***
**593** A131 $2 Sheet of 4, #a-d 6.00 6.00

**Souvenir Sheet**

**594** A131 $5 multi 3.50 3.50

No. 593 contains four 28x42mm stamps.

Locomotives, 200th Anniv. — A132

No. 595, $2: a, Italian State Railways Class 685 2-8-2. b, Swiss Federal Railways 4-6-0. c, BESA Class 4-6-0. d, Great Western City Class 4-4-0.
No. 596, $2: a, Northumbrian 0-2-2. b, Prince Class 2-2-2. c, Adler 2-2-2. d, L&NWR Webb Compound 2-4-0.
No. 597, $2: a, American Standard 4-4-0. b, New South Wales Government Class 79 4-4-0. c, Johnson Midland Single 4-2-2. d, Union Pacific FEF-3 Class 4-8-4.
No. 598, $5, Crampton Type 4-2-0. No. 599, $5, CN Class U-2 4-8-4. No. 600, $5, Baldwin 2-8-2, vert.

***Perf. 13¼x13½, 13½x13¼***
**2004, Sept. 21**

**Sheets of 4, #a-d**

**595-597** A132 Set of 3 18.00 18.00

**Souvenir Sheets**

**598-600** A132 Set of 3 11.50 11.50

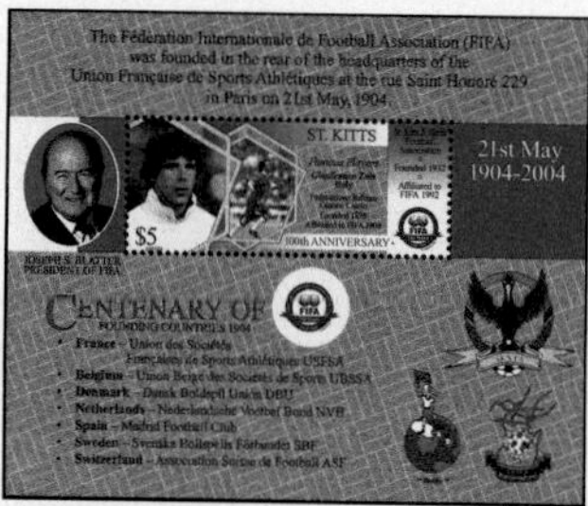

FIFA (Fédération Internationale de Football Association), Cent. — A133

No. 601: a, Demetrio Albertini. b, Romario. c, Gerd Muller. d, Danny Blanchflower.
$5, Gianfranco Zola.

**2004, Nov. 8** ***Perf. 12¾x12½***
**601** A133 $2 Sheet of 4, #a-d 5.50 5.50

**Souvenir Sheet**

**602** A133 $5 multi 3.50 3.50

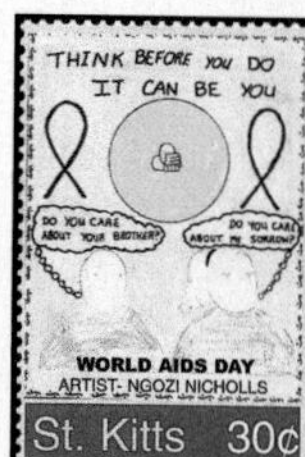

World AIDS Day — A134

Posters by: 30c, Ngozi Nicholls. 80c, Travis Liburd. 90c, Darren Kelly, horiz. $1, Shane Berry.

**2004, Dec. 1** ***Perf. 14***
**603-606** A134 Set of 4 3.75 3.75

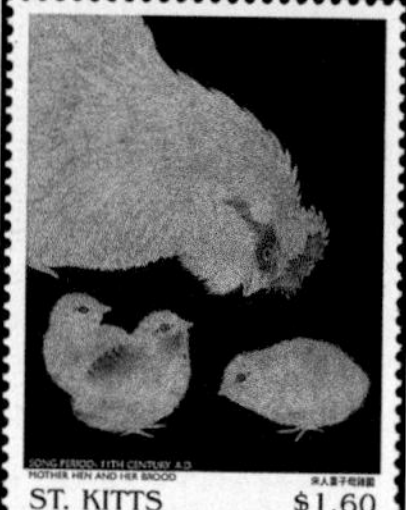

New Year 2005 (Year of the Rooster) A135

Mother Hen and Her Brood, by unknown artist: $1.60, Detail. $5, Entire painting.

**2005, Feb. 7** ***Perf. 12***
607 A135 $1.60 multi 1.50 1.50

**Souvenir Sheet**

608 A135 $5 multi 4.75 4.75

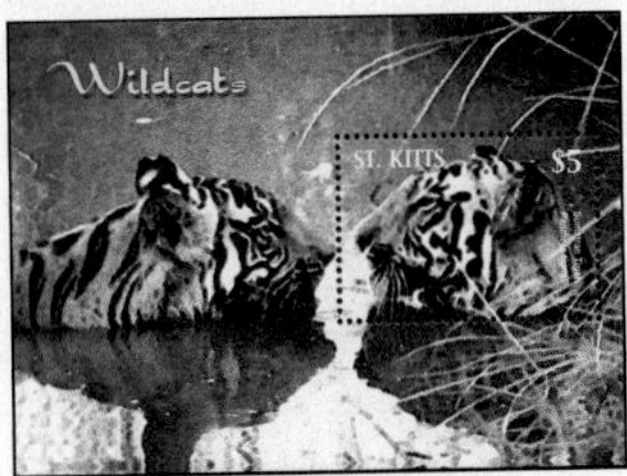


Wildcats — A136

No. 609, vert.: a, Ocelot. b, Bengal leopard. c, Tiger. d, Leopard.
$5, Sumatran tiger.

**2005, Feb. 7** ***Perf. 12¾***
609 A136 $2 Sheet of 4, #a-d 6.00 6.00

**Souvenir Sheet**

610 A136 $5 multi 4.50 4.50

Prehistoric Animals — A137

No. 611, horiz.: a, Triceratops. b, Deinonychus. c, Apatosaurus.
No. 612, horiz.: a, Dimetrodon. b, Homalocephale. c, Stegosaurus.
No. 613, horiz.: a, Sabre-toothed tiger. b, Edmontosaurus. c, Tyrannosaurus rex.
No. 614: $5, Brontosaurus. No. 615, $5, Woolly mammoth. No. 616, $5, Andrewsarchus, horiz.

**2005, Feb. 7**
611 A137 $3 Sheet of 3, #a-c 6.75 6.75
612 A137 $3 Sheet of 3, #a-c 6.75 6.75
613 A137 $3 Sheet of 3, #a-c 6.75 6.75

**Souvenir Sheet**

614 A137 $5 multi 3.75 3.75
615 A137 $5 multi 3.75 3.75
616 A137 $5 multi 3.75 3.75

Parrots — A138

No. 617, vert.: a, Australian king parrot. b, Rose-breasted cockatoo. c, Pale-headed rosella. d, Eastern rosella.
$5, Rainbow lorikeets.

**2005, Feb. 7 Litho.** ***Perf. 12¾***
617 A138 $2 Sheet of 4, #a-d 6.00 6.00

**Souvenir Sheet**

618 A138 $5 multi 4.50 4.50

Insects and Butterflies — A139

No. 619, vert.: a, Papilio demoleus. b, Ephemeroptera. c, Hamadryas februa. d, Aphylla caraiba.
$5, Small blue butterfly.

**2005, Feb. 7**
619 A139 $2 Sheet of 4, #a-d 6.75 6.75

**Souvenir Sheet**

620 A139 $5 multi 4.25 4.25

Ducks A140

Designs: 25c, White-cheeked pintails. $1, Fulvous whistling ducks. $2, White-faced whistling duck. $3, Black-bellied whistling ducks.

**2005, Feb. 7**
621-624 A140 Set of 4 5.00 5.00

Souvenir Sheet

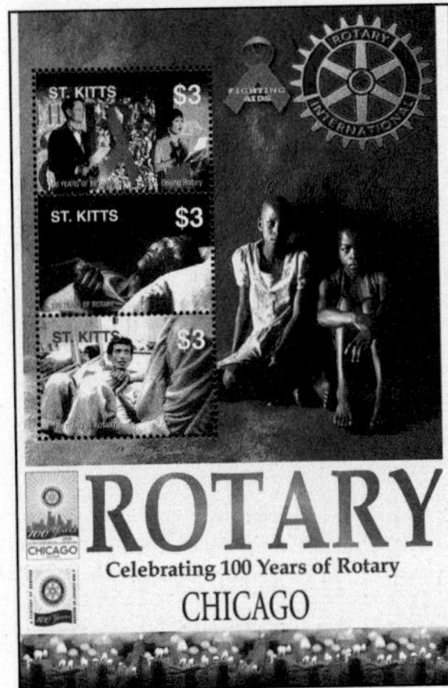


Rotary International, Cent. — A141

No. 625: a, Beijing Rotary meeting. b, Sick man. c, Sick man and visitor.

**2005, May 11**
625 A141 $3 Sheet of 3, #a-c 7.00 7.00

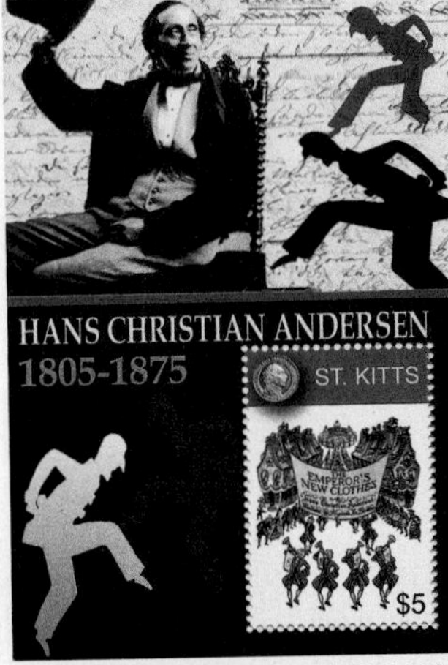


Hans Christian Andersen (1805-75), Author — A142

No. 626 — Book covers: a, Hans Christian Andersen's Fairy Tales. b, The Emperor's New Clothes. c, The Nutcracker.
$5, The Emperor's New Clothes, diff.

**2005, May 11**
626 A142 $3 Sheet of 3, #a-c 6.25 6.25

**Souvenir Sheet**

627 A142 $5 multi 3.50 3.50

Jules Verne (1828-1905), Writer — A143

No. 628, vert.: a, Verne. b, Sea monster attack. c, Rouquayrol. d, Modern Aqualung.
$5, Atomic submarine.

**2005, May 11**
628 A143 $3 Sheet of 4, #a-d 6.50 6.50

**Souvenir Sheet**

629 A143 $5 multi 4.00 4.00

End of World War II, 60th Anniv. — A144

No. 630, $2: a, US Navy Hudson PDB-1 patrol bombers. b, World War II combat. c, Gen. Dwight D. Eisenhower. d, Transporting German prisoners of war. e, Newspaper announcing Nazi surrender.
No. 631, $2: a, USS Arizona under attack. b, USS Arizona Captain Franklin Van Valkenburgh. c, Hiroshima atomic blast. d, Historic marker of first atomic bomb loading pit, Tinian Island. e, Memorial Cenotaph, Hiroshima Peace Park.

**2005, May 11 Litho.**

**Sheets of 5, #a-e**

630-631 A144 Set of 2 18.00 18.00

Battle of Trafalgar, Bicent. — A145

Ships: 50c, Montagne. 90c, San Jose. $2, Imperieuse. $3, San Nicolas.
$5, British Navy gun crew on HMS Victory.

**2005, May 11** ***Perf. 12¾***
632-635 A145 Set of 4 5.50 5.50

**Souvenir Sheet**

636 A145 $5 multi 4.50 4.50

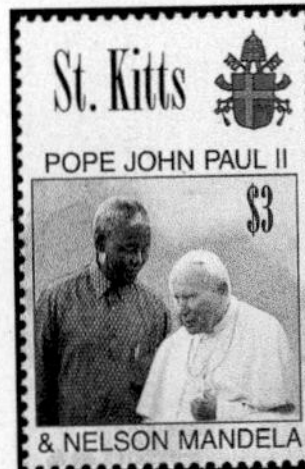


Pope John Paul II (1920-2005) and Nelson Mandela — A146

**2005, July 19** ***Perf. 13½***
637 A146 $3 multi 2.50 2.50

Printed in sheets of 4.

Souvenir Sheet

Taipei 2005 Stamp Exhibition — A147

No. 638 — Various Chinese junks with denominations in: a, Red. b, Blue. c, Gray. d, Yellow orange.

**2005, Aug. 19** ***Perf. 14***
638 A147 $2 Sheet of 4, #a-d 6.50 6.50

Christmas — A148

Paintings: 30c, Virgin and Child, by Gerard David. 50c, Virgin and Child, by David, diff. 90c, Virgin and Child, by David, diff. $2, Virgin and Child, by Bartolomeo Suardi Bramentine.
$5, Nativity, by Martin Schongauer.

**2005, Dec. 6 Litho.** ***Perf. 13¾x13½***
639-642 A148 Set of 4 2.75 2.75

**Souvenir Sheet**

643 A148 $5 multi 3.75 3.75

Treaty of Basseterre, 25th Anniv. — A149

Designs: 30c, Eastern Caribbean Central Bank. 90c, 25th anniversary emblem of Organization of Eastern Caribbean States.
$2.50, Heads of government of Organization of Eastern Caribbean States, vert.

**2006, Sept. 11 Litho.** ***Perf. 12¾***
644-645 A149 Set of 2 1.00 1.00

**Souvenir Sheet**

***Perf. 12***

646 Sheet of 2 #646a 3.50 3.50
*a.* A149 $2.50 multi 1.50 1.50

Rembrandt (1606-69), Painter A150

Paintings or painting details: 50c, Bathsheba with King David's Letter. 80c, Isaac and Rebecca (Rebecca). 90c, Isaac and Rebecca (Isaac). $1, Samson Threatening His Father-in-Law (father-in-law). $1.60, Samson Threatening His Father-in-Law (Samson). $2, Equestrian Portrait.
$6, Landscape with a Stone Bridge, horiz.

**2006, Nov. 15** *Perf. 12*
**647-652** A150 Set of 6 5.50 5.50

*Imperf*

**Size: 101x70mm**

**653** A150 $6 multi 4.50 4.50

Christmas — A151

Paintings or painting details by Peter Paul Rubens: 25c, Mary In Adoration Before the Sleeping Infant. 60c, The Holy Family Under the Apple Tree (Madonna and Child). $1, The Holy Family Under the Apple Tree (cherub). $1.20, St. Francis of Assisi Receives the Infant Jesus from Mary.

No. 658: a, Like 25c. b, Like 60c. c, Like $1. d, Like $1.20.

**2006, Dec. 27** *Perf. 13½*
**654-657** A151 Set of 4 2.40 2.40

**Souvenir Sheet**

**658** A151 $2 Sheet of 4, #a-d 6.25 6.25

Souvenir Sheet

Christopher Columbus (1451-1506), Explorer — A152

**2007, Jan. 3** *Perf. 13¼*
**659** A152 $6 multi 4.25 4.25

Queen Elizabeth II, 80th Birthday (in 2006) — A153

No. 660: a, Wearing beige and brown hat. b, Wearing tiara. c, Wearing light blue hat. d, Wearing crown.

$5, Seated at desk.

**2007, Jan. 3**
**660** A153 $2 Sheet of 4, #a-d 5.50 5.50

**Souvenir Sheet**

**661** A153 $5 multi 3.50 3.50

Betty Boop — A154

No. 662 — Betty Boop in spotlight with background color of: a, Red. b, Green. c, White. d, Purple. e, Blue. f, Yellow.

No. 663 — Betty Boop in: a, Green heart. b, Purple heart.

**2007, Jan. 3**
**662** A154 $1.60 Sheet of 6, #a-f 7.25 7.25

**Souvenir Sheet**

**663** A154 $3 Sheet of 2, #a-b 4.25 4.25

Scouting, Cent. A155

Dove with flags, Scouting emblem, text and: $3, Years "1907" and "2007." $5, No years, horiz.

**2007, Jan. 3**
**664** A155 $3 multi 2.25 2.25

**Souvenir Sheet**

**665** A155 $5 multi 3.50 3.50

No. 664 was printed in sheets of 4.

Space Achievements — A156

No. 666 — Giotto Comet Probe: a, Pre-launch test at Kourou launch site. b, Halley's Comet (black sky). c, Halley's Comet above cloud. d, Giotto Comet Probe. e, Giotto space-craft mounted on Ariane rocket. f, Halley's Comet (blue sky).

No. 667, vert. — Launching of Luna 9: a, Molniya launch vehicle. b, Luna 9 flight apparatus. c, Luna 9 soft lander. d, Photograph of Ocean of Storms taken by Luna 9.

$5, Space Station Mir.

**2007, Jan. 3** **Litho.** *Perf. 13¼*
**666** A156 $1.60 Sheet of 6, #a-f 6.75 6.75
**667** A156 $2 Sheet of 4, #a-d 5.75 5.75

**Souvenir Sheet**

**668** A156 $5 multi 3.50 3.50

Miniature Sheets

Pres. John F. Kennedy (1917-63) — A157

No. 669, $2: a, Kennedy and map of Central America. b, Kennedy, woman and child, map of Caribbean. c, Kennedy addressing group, map of Western South America. d, Kennedy shaking hands with man, map of Eastern South America.

No. 670, $2: a, Kennedy greeting Peace Corps volunteers (inscription in black). b, Peace Corps volunteer Ida Shoatz and Peruvians. c, R. Sargent Shriver, Peace Corps Director. d, Kennedy greeting Peace Corps volunteers, diff. (inscription in white).

**2007, Jan. 3** **Litho.**

**Sheets of 4, #a-d**

**669-670** A157 Set of 2 11.50 11.50

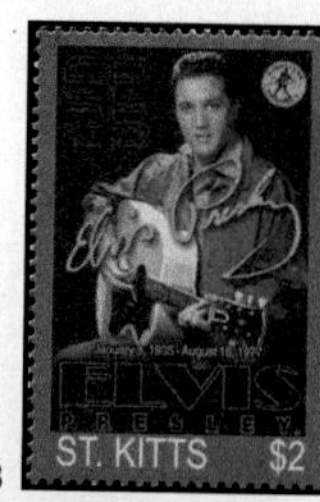


A158

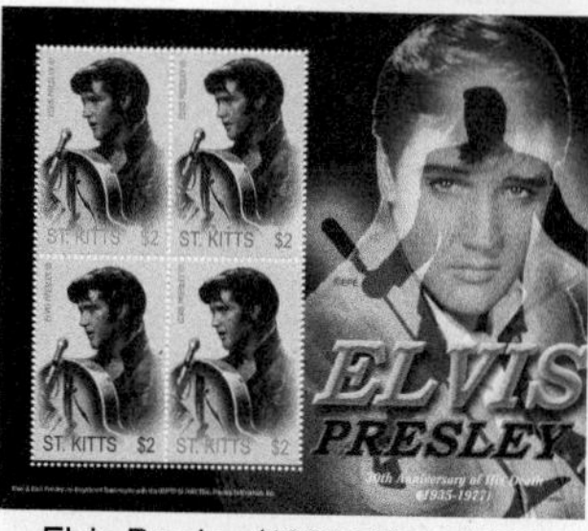


Elvis Presley (1935-77) — A159

No. 672 — Denomination color: a, Blue. b, Red. c, Black. d, Lilac.

**2007, Feb. 15** *Perf. 14*
**671** A158 $2 multi 1.60 1.60
**672** A159 $2 Sheet of 4, #a-d 5.75 5.75

No. 671 was printed in sheets of 4.

Miniature Sheet

Marilyn Monroe (1926-62), Actress — A160

No. 673 — Monroe with: a, Pinkie in mouth. b, Glasses. c, Strapless gown. d, Hand on cheek.

**2007, Feb. 15** *Perf. 13½*
**673** A160 $2 Sheet of 4, #a-d 5.75 5.75

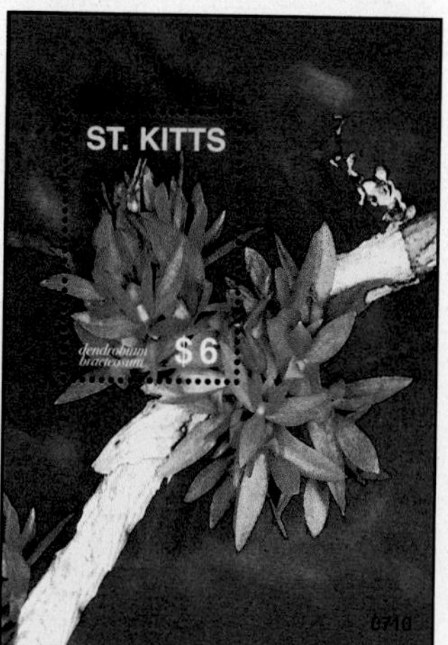


Orchids — A161

No. 674: a, Rhynchostele cervantesii. b, Oerstedella wallisii. c, Disa uniflora. d, Pleione formosana.

$6, Dendrobium bracteosum.

**2007, June 18** *Perf. 12¾*
**674** A161 $2 Sheet of 4, #a-d 6.50 6.50

**Souvenir Sheet**

**675** A161 $6 multi 4.50 4.50



Birds — A162

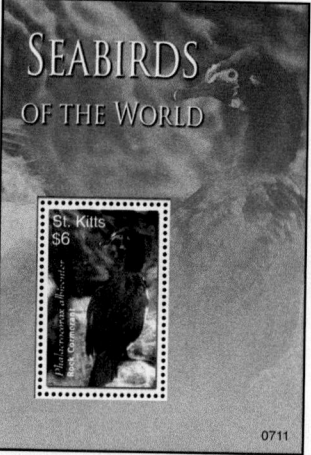

No. 676, horiz.: a, Brown noddy. b, Royal albatross. c, Masked booby. d, Cormorant.

$6, Rock cormorant.

**2007, June 18** *Perf. 12¾*
**676** A162 $2 Sheet of 4, #a-d 5.75 5.75

**Souvenir Sheet**

**677** A162 $6 multi 4.25 4.25

Worldwide Fund for Nature (WWF) — A163

Tiger sharks: a, Three sharks. b, Two sharks and sunlight. c, Two sharks and sunlight. d, One shark.

**2007, June 18**
**678** Strip or block of 4 3.75 3.75
*a.-d.* A163 $1.20 Any single .85 .85
*e.* Sheet, 2 each #a-d 7.25 7.25

Souvenir Sheets

National Basketball Association Players and Team Emblems — A164

No. 679, $8: a, Steve Nash. b, Phoenix Suns emblem.

No. 680, $8: a, Shaquille O'Neal. b, Miami Heat emblem, denomination in black.

No. 681, $8: a, Dwyane Wade. b, Miami Heat emblem, denomination in orange.

No. 682, $8: a, Yao Ming. b, Houston Rockets emblem.

**Litho. (Margin Embossed)**

**2007, Aug. 16** *Imperf.*

**Without Gum**

**Sheets of 2, #a-b**

**679-682** A164 Set of 4 47.50 47.50

Fruit — A165

**2007, Oct. 16** **Litho.** *Perf. 13¼x12½*

| | | | | |
|---|---|---|---|---|
| **683** | A165 | 10c Cherries | .25 | .25 |
| **684** | A165 | 15c Coconuts | .25 | .25 |
| **685** | A165 | 30c Watermelons | .25 | .25 |
| **686** | A165 | 40c Pineapples | .30 | .30 |
| **687** | A165 | 50c Guava | .40 | .40 |
| **688** | A165 | 60c Sugar apples | .45 | .45 |
| **689** | A165 | 80c Passion fruit | .60 | .60 |
| **690** | A165 | 90c Starfruit | .70 | .70 |
| **691** | A165 | $1 Tangerines | .75 | .75 |

692 A165 $5 Noni fruit 3.75 3.75
693 A165 $10 Papayas 7.50 7.50
*Nos. 683-693 (11)* 15.20 15.20

Miniature Sheet

Elvis Presley (1935-77) — A166

No. 694 — Presley wearing: a, White shirt. b, Jacket with bird design. c, Black shirt. d, Blue jacket. e, Red and white shirt. f, White jacket and red shirt, holding microphone.

**2007, Oct. 26** ***Perf. 13¼***
694 A166 $1.60 Sheet of 6, #a-f 7.00 7.00

Pope Benedict XVI — A167

**2007, Nov. 26**
695 A167 $1.10 multi 1.10 1.10

Wedding of Queen Elizabeth II and Prince Philip, 60th Anniv. A168

No. 696: a, Queen Elizabeth II. b, Couple on wedding day.
$6, Couple waving.

**2007, Nov. 26**
696 A168 $1.60 Pair, #a-b 2.25 2.25

**Souvenir Sheet**

697 A168 $6 multi 4.25 4.25

No. 696 printed in sheets containing three of each stamp.

Concorde A169

No. 698, $1.60: a, Concorde flying left. b, Concorde flying right.
No. 699, $1.60: a, Concorde over Singapore. b, Concorde at Melbourne, Australia airport.

**2007, Nov. 26** **Pairs, #a-b** **Litho.**
698-699 A169 Set of 2 4.50 4.50

Nos. 698-699 each printed in sheets containing three of each stamp in pairs.

Princess Diana (1961-97) — A170

No. 700 — Various depictions of Princess Diana: a, Country name in black, "Princess Diana" at right. b, Country name in white, "Princess Diana" at left. c, Country name in white, "Princess Diana" at right. d, Country name in black, "Princess Diana" at left.
$6, Like #700c, gray background.

**2007, Nov. 26** ***Perf. 13¼***
700 A170 $2 Sheet of 4, #a-d 5.75 5.75

**Souvenir Sheet**

701 A170 $6 multi 4.25 4.25

Christmas A171

Various ribboned wreaths: 10c, 30c, 60c, $1.

**2007, Dec. 3** ***Perf. 12½***
702-705 A171 Set of 4 1.50 1.50

Miniature Sheet

2008 Summer Olympics, Beijing — A172

No. 706 — 2008 Summer Olympics emblem and: a, Paris World's Fair, 1900. b, 1900 Olympics poster. c, Charlotte Cooper. d, Alvin Kraenzlein.

**2008, June 18** **Litho.** ***Perf. 12¾***
706 A172 $1.40 Sheet of 4, #a-d 5.50 5.50

Robert L. Bradshaw (1916-78), Chief Minister — A173

***Perf. 11¼x11½***

**2008, Sept. 19** **Litho.**
707 A173 10c multi .40 .40

St. Kitts Labor Party, 75th anniv.

Moravian Churches A174

Designs: 10c, Bethel Church. $3, Zion Church. $10, Bethesda Church, vert.

***Perf. 11½x11¼, 11¼x11½***

**2008, Sept. 19**
708-710 A174 Set of 3 12.00 12.00

Moravian Church in St. Kitts, 230th anniv.

University of the West Indies, 60th Anniv. A175

Designs: 30c, University Center, St. Kitts. 90c, 60th anniv. emblem, vert. $5, 60th anniv. emblem.

**2008, Sept. 19**
711-713 A175 Set of 3 6.00 6.00

Independence, 25th Anniv. — A176

Designs: 30c, Stars, lines and "25." $1, Agriculture. $5, Sailing Towards Our Future, vert.

**2008, Sept. 19**
714-716 A176 Set of 3 5.50 5.50

Miniature Sheet

Visit to Lourdes of Pope Benedict XVI — A177

No. 717 — Pope Benedict, statue of St. Bernadette with: a, Leaves at top. b, Cathedral spires at UR. c, Cathedral roof and side of spire at UR. d, Gray triangle at LR.

**2008, Sept. 26** ***Perf. 13¼***
717 A177 $2 Sheet of 4, #a-d 8.00 8.00

Miniature Sheet

Elvis Presley (1935-77) — A178

No. 718 — Presley wearing: a, Brown shirt. b, Leather jacket. c, Red shirt and black vest. d, Blue shirt. e, Olive green shirt. f, White shirt.

**2008, Sept. 26**
718 A178 $1.60 Sheet of 6, #a-f 7.00 7.00

Christmas A179

Designs: 10c, Palm trees with Christmas ornaments. 50c, Palm trees and beach house. 60c, Star and palm trees. $1, Christmas ornaments and palm fronds.

**2008, Dec. 29** **Litho.** ***Perf. 14x14¾***
719-722 A179 Set of 4 2.00 2.00

Inauguration of U.S. Pres. Barack Obama — A180

Obama with: $3, Blue gray tie. $10, Red tie.

***Perf. 12½x11¾***

**2009, Feb. 24** **Litho.**
723 A180 $3 multi 5.00 5.00

**Souvenir Sheet**

***Perf.***

724 A180 $10 multi 8.00 8.00

No. 723 was printed in sheets of 4. No. 724 contains one 38mm diameter stamp.

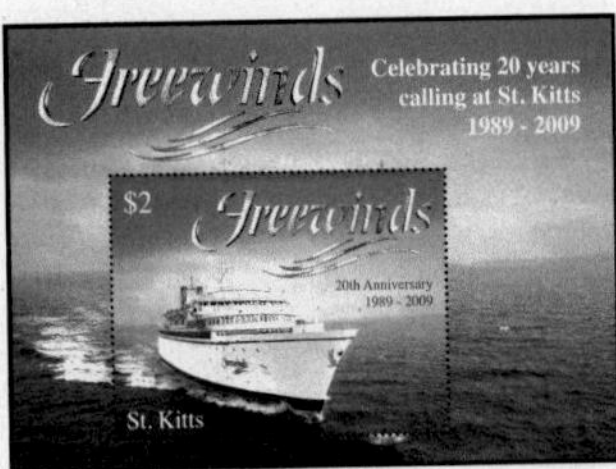

Freewinds Docking at St. Kitts, 20th Anniv. — A181

No. 725: a, 30c, Freewinds at night (42x28mm). b, 90c, Freewinds and yacht near harbor (42x28mm). c, $3, Bow of Freewinds, vert. (42x57mm).

**2009, July 20 Litho. *Perf. 13¼***
725 A181 Sheet of 3, #a-c 2.75 2.75

**Souvenir Sheet**
***Perf. 11½x12***
726 A181 $2 shown 1.40 1.40

Miniature Sheet

Princess Diana (1961-97) — A182

No. 727 — Color of gown: a, Red. b, Purple. c, White. d, Blue.

**2009, Sept. 7 *Perf. 13½x13¼***
727 A182 $2 Sheet of 4, #a-d 5.25 5.25

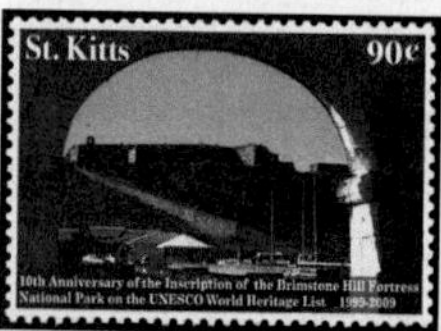

Brimstone Hill as UNESCO World Heritage Site, 10th Anniv. A183

**2009, Dec. 7 Litho. *Perf. 13½***
728 A183 90c multi .80 .80

Miniature Sheet

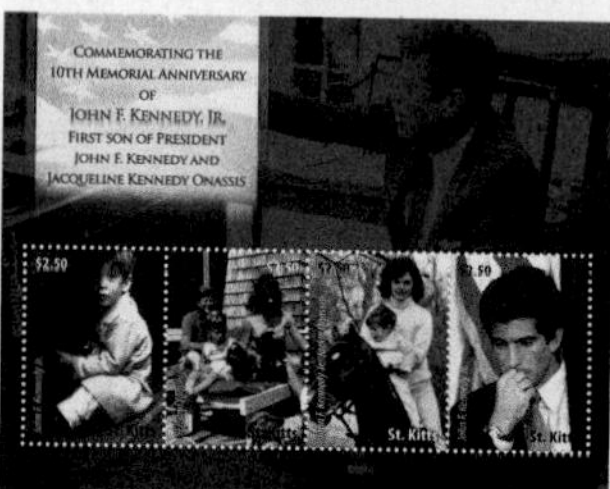

John F. Kennedy, Jr. (1960-99), Magazine Publisher — A184

No. 729: a, As child, sitting under father's desk. b, As child with father, mother and dogs. c, As child, with mother on horse. d, As adult.

**2009, Dec. 15 *Perf. 11½***
729 A184 $2.50 Sheet of 4, #a-d 6.50 6.50

Miniature Sheets

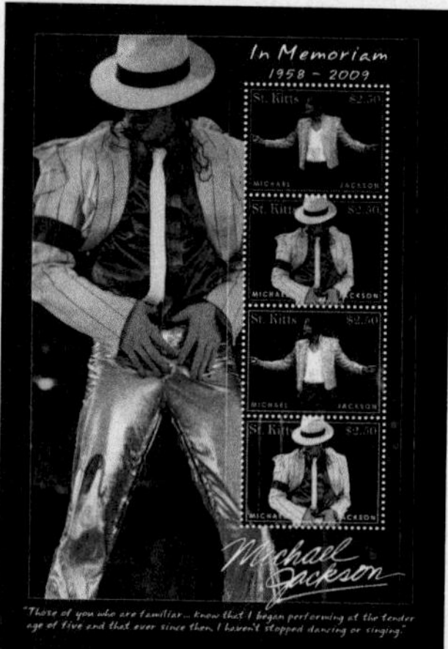

A185

Michael Jackson (1958-2009), Singer — A186

No. 730: a, With arms extended, denomination in green. b, Wearing hat, denomination in green. c, With arms extended, denomination in blue. d, Wearing hat, denomination in blue.
No. 731: a, Wearing red jacket, without yellow spot in background at left center. b, With snake, yellow spot in background at left center. c, Wearing red jacket, yellow spot in background at left center. d, With snake, without yellow spot in background at left center.

**2009, Dec. 15**
730 A185 $2.50 Sheet of 4, #a-d 7.00 7.00
731 A186 $2.50 Sheet of 4, #a-d 7.00 7.00

First Man on the Moon, 40th Anniv. — A187

No. 732: a, Saturn V rocket. b, Bootprint on Moon. c, Pres. John F. Kennedy, eagle, Moon and Earth. d, Apollo 11 command module.
$6, Command module, diff.

**2009, Dec. 30 *Perf. 11½x12***
732 A187 $2.50 Sheet of 4, #a-d 7.00 7.00

**Souvenir Sheet**
733 A187 $6 multi 4.00 4.00

Christmas A188

Designs: 10c, "Merry Christmas" on flag of St. Kitts & Nevis. 30c, Candy canes. $1.20, Christmas trees on map of St. Kitts. $3, Christmas tree and candles on box showing flag.

**2009, Dec. 30 *Perf. 14¾x14***
734-737 A188 Set of 4 3.25 3.25

Miniature Sheet

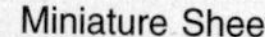

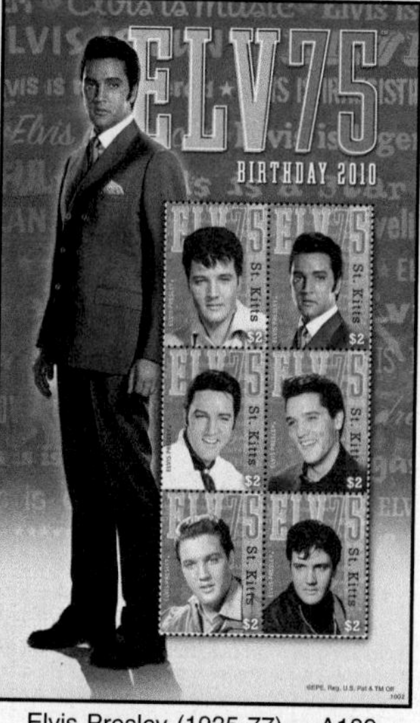

Elvis Presley (1935-77) — A189

No. 738 — Presley wearing: a, Shirt with open collar. b, Suit and tie. c, Shirt with neckerchief. d, Black jacket. e, Shirt with open collar and jacket. f, Black shirt, guitar strap over shoulder.

**2010, Jan. 8 *Perf. 11½***
738 A189 $2 Sheet of 6, #a-f 9.25 9.25

Butterflies A190

Designs: 30c, Scarlet peacock. 90c, Gulf fritillary. No. 741, $3, White peacock. $5, Painted lady.
No. 743: a, Ruddy daggerwing. b, Danaid eggfly. c, Mangrove buckeye. d, Black swallowtail.
No. 744, $3: a, Owl butterfly. b, Giant swallowtail.

**2010, Mar. 15 Litho. *Perf. 12***
739-742 A190 Set of 4 7.00 7.00
743 A190 $2.50 Sheet of 4, #a-d 7.50 7.50

**Souvenir Sheet**
744 A190 $3 Sheet of 2, #a-b 5.00 5.00

Birds A191

Designs: 30c, Solitary sandpiper. 90c, Piping plover. No. 747, $3, Prairie warbler. $5, Western sandpiper.
No. 749, vert.: a, Masked booby. b, Sooty tern. c, Brown booby. d, Black noddy.
No. 750, $3: a, Long-billed dowitcher. b, Willet.

**2010, Mar. 22**
745-748 A191 Set of 4 7.00 7.00
749 A191 $2.50 Sheet of 4, #a-d 7.50 7.50

**Souvenir Sheet**
750 A191 $3 Sheet of 2, #a-b 5.00 5.00

Pres. Abraham Lincoln (1809-65) A192

**2010, May 11**
751 A192 $2.50 black 1.90 1.90

Printed in sheets of 4.

Fish A193

Designs: 30c, Red lionfish. 90c, Stoplight parrotfish. $3, Black jack. $5, Bermuda blue angelfish.
No. 756: a, Banggai cardinalfish. b, Barrier reef anemonefish. c, Crevelle jack. d, Lookdown.
No. 757, $3: a, Red Sea clownfish. b, Saddleback clownfish.

**2010, June 7 Litho. *Perf. 14¾x14¼***
752-755 A193 Set of 4 7.00 7.00
756 A193 $2.50 Sheet of 4, #a-d 7.50 7.50

**Souvenir Sheet**
757 A193 $3 Sheet of 2, #a-b 5.00 5.00

A194

Mushrooms — A195

Designs: 25c, Alboleptonia stylophora. 80c, Cantharellus cibarius. $1, Armillaria puiggarii. $5, Battarrea phalloides.
No. 762: a, Cantharellus cinnabarinus. b, Collybia aurea. c, Collybia biformis. d, Amanita ocreata. e, Calocybe cyanea. f, Chroogomphus rutilus.

**2010, June 7 *Perf. 14¼x14¾***
758-761 A194 Set of 4 5.25 5.25

***Perf. 14¾x14¼***
762 A195 $2 Sheet of 6, #a-f 9.00 9.00

Antverpia 2010 National and European Championship of Philately, Antwerp (#762).

Miniature Sheets

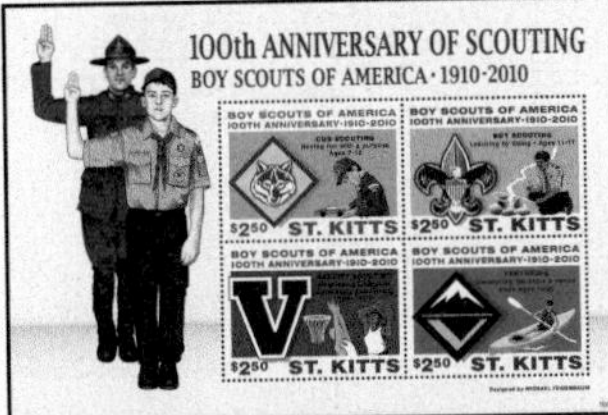


Boy Scouts of America, Cent. — A196

No. 763, $2.50: a, Cub Scouting. b, Boy Scouting. c, Varsity Scouting. d, Venturing.
No. 764, $2.50: a, Eagle Scout emblem. b, Order of the Arrow. c, Alpha Phi Omega. d, National Eagle Scout Association.

**2010, June 30** ***Perf. 13¼***

**Sheets of 4, #a-d**

**763-764** A196 Set of 2 15.00 15.00

Arctic Animals — A197

No. 765: a, Ermine. b, Arctic fox. c, Harp seal. d, Arctic wolf. e, Arctic hare. f, Snowy owl.
$6, Polar bear.

**2010, Aug. 4** ***Perf. 11½***

**765** A197 $2 Sheet of 6, #a-f 9.00 9.00

**Souvenir Sheet**

**766** A197 $6 multi 4.50 4.50

Henri Dunant (1828-1910), Founder of the Red Cross — A198

No. 767 — Dunant, Red Cross and: a, Czar Nicholas II of Russia. b, Henri Dufour. c, Frédéric Passy. d, Victor Hugo.
$6, Red Cross nurse.

**2010, Sept. 1** ***Perf. 11½x12***

**767** A198 $2.50 Sheet of 4, #a-d 7.50 7.50

**Souvenir Sheet**

***Perf. 11½***

**768** A198 $6 multi 4.50 4.50

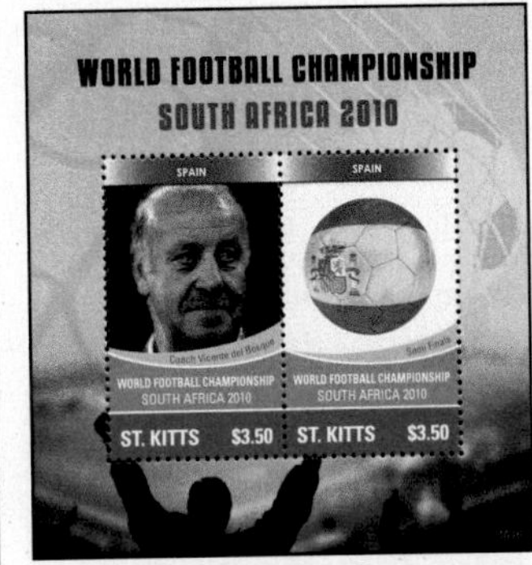


2010 World Cup Soccer Championships, South Africa — A199

No. 769: a, Pedro. b, Miroslav Klose. c, Xavi. d, Piotr Trochowski. e, Carlos Puyol. f, Philipp Lahm.
No. 770, $3.50: a, Spain Coach Vicente del Bosque. b, Soccer ball with Spanish flag.
No. 771, $3.50: Germany Coach Joachim Loew. b, Soccer ball with German flag.

**2010, Oct. 6** ***Perf. 12***

**769** A199 $1.50 Sheet of 6, #a-f 6.75 6.75

**Souvenir Sheets of 2, #a-b**

**770-771** A199 Set of 2 10.50 10.50

Souvenir Sheets

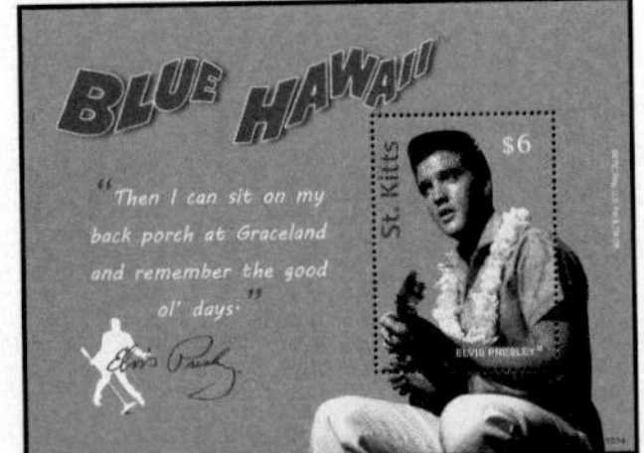


A200

A201

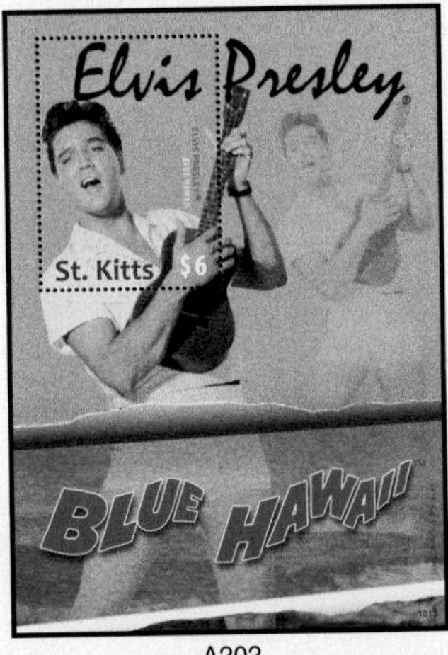


A202

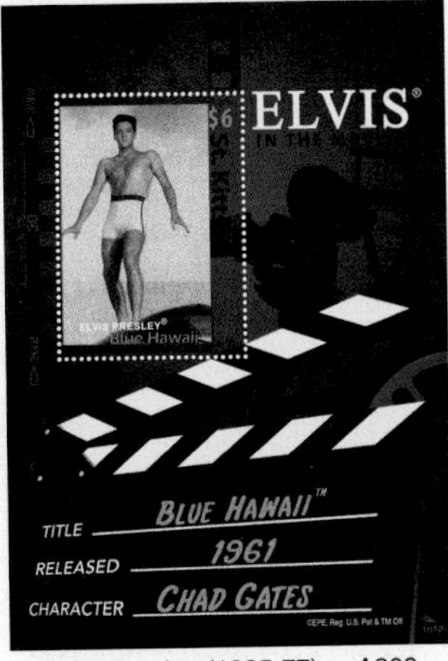


Elvis Presley (1935-77) — A203

**2010, Oct. 6** ***Perf. 13½***

| | | | | |
|---|---|---|---|---|
| **772** | A200 | $6 multi | 4.50 | 4.50 |
| **773** | A201 | $6 multi | 4.50 | 4.50 |
| **774** | A202 | $6 multi | 4.50 | 4.50 |
| **775** | A203 | $6 multi | 4.50 | 4.50 |
| | *Nos. 772-775 (4)* | | 18.00 | 18.00 |

A204

Princess Diana (1961-97) — A205

No. 776 — Princess Diana wearing: a, Beige hat. b, Rose lilac and white hat.
No. 777: a, Princess Diana wearing red hat, area below line shaded. b, Princess Diana wearing strapless gown, area below line shaded. c, Princess Diana wearing tiara, entire dress below line. d, As "c," strap of dress above line above denomination. e, As "a," area below line not shaded. f, As "b," area below line not shaded.

**2010, Dec. 8** ***Perf. 12***

**776** A204 $2.75 Pair, #a-b 4.25 4.25
**777** A205 $2 Sheet of 6, #a-f 9.00 9.00

No. 776 was printed in sheets containing two pairs.

Christmas 2010 — A206

Paintings: 10c, Journey of the Magi, by Fra Angelico. 25c, Madonna Worshipping the Child and an Angel, by Biagio d'Antonio. 30c, The Nativity, by Master of Vyssi Brod. 90c, The Journey of the Magi, by James Tissot. $1.80, Worship of the Shepherds, by Agnolo di Cosimo. $3, Madonna with Child, by Carlo Crivelli.

***Perf. 11½ (10c, 25c), 12¾x13 Syncopated***

**2011, Feb. 21** **Litho.**

**778-783** A206 Set of 6 4.75 4.75

Pope John Paul II (1920-2005) A207

Pope John Paul II wearing: No. 784, $2.50, Zucchetto. No. 785, $2.50, Miter.

**2011, Feb. 21** ***Perf. 12***

**784-785** A207 Set of 2 3.75 3.75

Nos. 784-785 each were printed in sheets of 4.

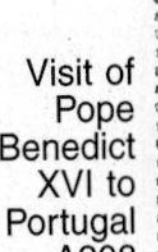
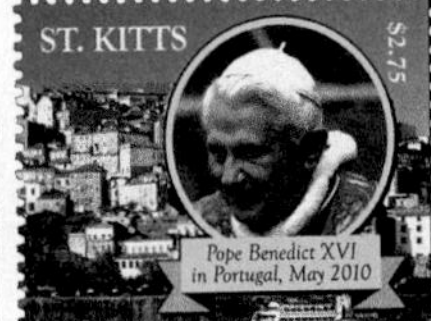


Visit of Pope Benedict XVI to Portugal A208

Designs: No. 786, Pope Benedict XVI and buildings. No. 787 — Arms of Portugal, Pope Benedict XVI and background color of: a, Red. b, Green.

**2011, Feb. 21** ***Perf. 12***

**786** A208 $2.75 multi 2.10 2.10

***Perf. 13 Syncopated***

**787** A208 $2.75 Sheet of 4, #787a, 3 #787b 8.25 8.25

No. 786 was printed in sheets of 4.

Paintings by Sandro Botticelli (1445-1510) — A209

No. 788: a, Giovanna Albizi with Venus and the Graces. b, Lemmi Fresco. c, Portrait of a Young Woman. d, St. Sebastian.
$6, The Last Communion of St. Jerome, horiz.

**2011, Feb. 21** ***Perf. 12***

**788** A209 $2.50 Sheet of 4, #a-d 7.50 7.50

**Souvenir Sheet**

***Perf. 13 Syncopated***

**789** A209 $6 multi 4.50 4.50

Miniature Sheets

A210

Pres. Barack Obama — A211

Nos. 790 and 791 — Pres. Obama and one-quarter of Presidential seal at: a, LR. b, LL. c, UR. d, UL.

**2011, Feb. 21** ***Perf. 12***
**790** A210 $2.50 Sheet of 4, #a-d 7.50 7.50
**791** A211 $2.50 Sheet of 4, #a-d 7.50 7.50

Dolphins — A212

No. 792: a, Pantropical spotted dolphin. b, Killer whale. c, Tucuxi. d, Clymene dolphin.
No. 793, $6, Rough-toothed dolphin. No. 794, $6, Bottlenose dolphin.

**2011, Feb. 21** ***Perf. 13 Syncopated***
**792** A212 $2.50 Sheet of 4, #a-d 7.50 7.50

**Souvenir Sheets**

***Perf. 12***

**793-794** A212 Set of 2 9.00 9.00

Engagement of Prince William and Catherine Middleton — A213

No. 795, $2.50 — Red background: a, Couple, Middleton standing in front of door. b, Prince William. c, Middleton. d, Couple, diff.
No. 796, $2.50 — Blue background: a, Couple, Middleton wearing hat. b, Prince William. c, Middleton. d, Couple, diff.
No. 797, $6, Couple, red background, vert.
No. 798, $6, Couple, blue background, vert.

**2011, Feb. 21** ***Perf. 12***

**Sheets of 4, #a-d**

**795-796** A213 Set of 2 15.00 15.00

**Souvenir Sheets**

***Perf. 13 Syncopated***

**797-798** A213 Set of 2 9.00 9.00

Miniature Sheet

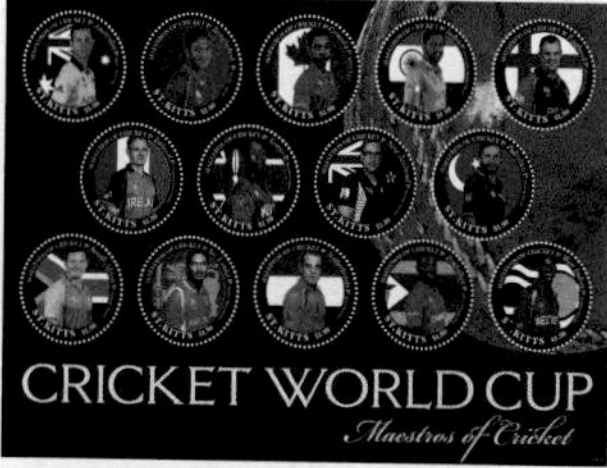

Cricket World Cup, India, Sri Lanka and Bangladesh — A214

No. 799 — Cricket players: a, Ricky Ponting, Australia. b, Shakib Al Hasan (incorrectly identified as Shahid Afridi), Bangladesh. c, Ashish Bagai, Canada. d, Mahendra Singh Dhoni, India. e, Andrew Strauss (incorrectly identified as Ricky Ponting), England. f, William Porterfield, Ireland. g, Maurice Ouma, Kenya. h, Daniel Vettori, New Zealand. i, Shahid Afridi, Pakistan. j, Graeme Smith, South Africa. k, Kumar Sangakkara, Sri Lanka. l, Peter Borren, Netherlands. m, Elton Chigumbura, Zimbabwe. n, Darren Sammy, West Indies.

**2011, Apr. 2** **Litho.** ***Perf.***
**799** A214 $1.90 Sheet of 14, #a-n 20.00 20.00

No. 799 exists with inscriptions corrected. Values, same.

Souvenir Sheets

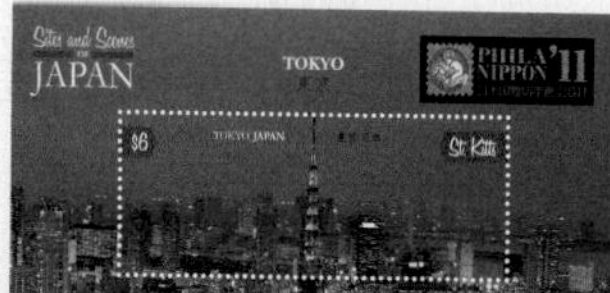

PhilaNippon '11, Yokohama, Japan — A215

Designs: No. 800, $6, Tokyo. No. 801, $6, Okinawa. No. 802, $6, Mt. Fuji.

**2011, May 18** ***Perf. 11½x11¼***
**800-802** A215 Set of 3 13.50 13.50

St. Kitts-Nevis-Anguilla National Bank, 40th Anniv. — A216

Designs: 10c, Bank building. $3, Anniversary emblem and olive branch, vert.

***Perf. 14¾x14¼, 14¼x14¾***

**2011, June 27**
**803-804** A216 Set of 2 2.40 2.40

Miniature Sheets

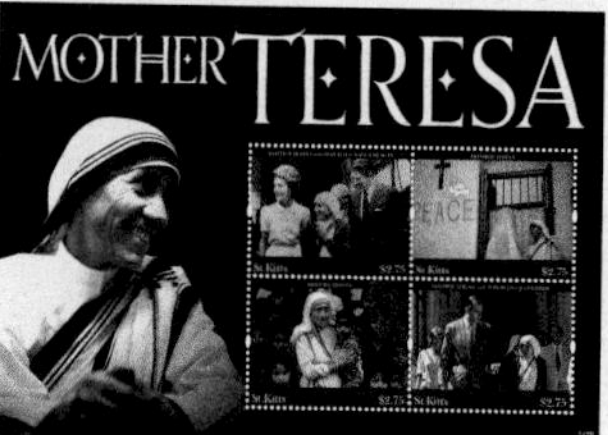

Mother Teresa (1910-97, Humanitarian — A217

No. 805, $2.75 — Stamps with purple and maroon panels: a, Mother Teresa with Ronald and Nancy Reagan. b, Mother Teresa with Sister of Charity at doorway. c, Mother Tersa holding child. d, Mother Teresa and Paris Mayor Jacques Chirac.
No. 806, $2.75 — Stamps with blue and olive green panels and flower: a, Mother Teresa. b, Mother Teresa and Prince Charles. c, Mother Teresa holding baby. d, Mother Teresa touching baby held by Sister of Charity.

**2011, July 5** ***Perf. 13 Syncopated***

**Sheets of 4, #a-d**

**805-806** A217 Set of 2 16.50 16.50

Miniature Sheets

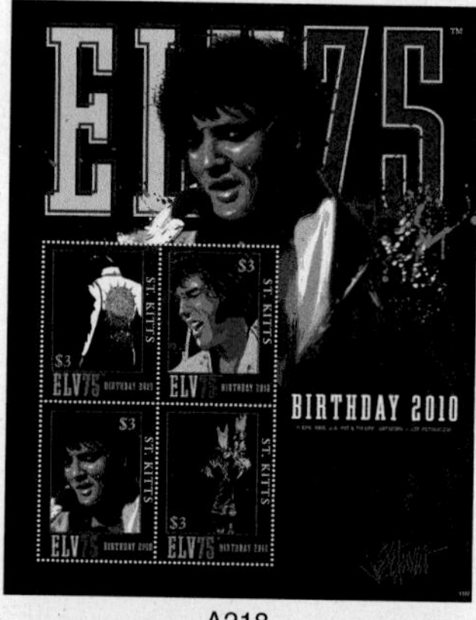

A218

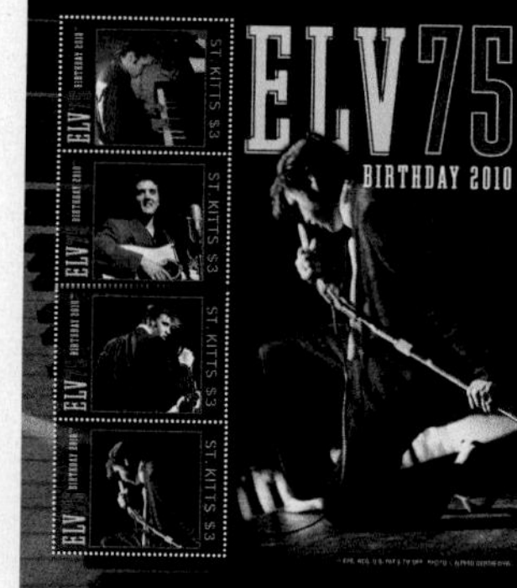

Elvis Presley (1935-77) — A219

No. 807: a, Presley in decorated jacket, seen from back. b, Presley with blue face. c, Presley with pink face. d, Presley with arms raised.
No. 808: a, Presley at piano. b, Presley splaying guitar. c, Prelsy holding microphone, facing right. d, Presley holding microphone, facing left.

**2011, July 14** ***Perf. 12½x12¾***
**807** A218 $3 Sheet of 4, #a-d 9.00 9.00

***Perf. 12¾x12½***

**808** A219 $3 Sheet of 4, #a-d 9.00 9.00

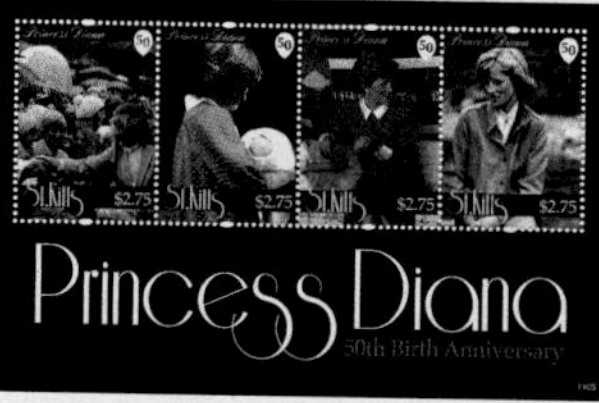

Princess Diana (1961-97) — A220

No. 809 — Princess Diana: a, Greeting crowd. b, Holding baby. c, Wearing red and white dress. d, Wearing checked overcoat.
$6, Princess Diana wearing white sweater, horiz.

**2011, July 14** ***Perf. 13 Syncopated***
**809** A220 $2.75 Sheet of 4, #a-d 8.25 8.25

**Souvenir Sheet**

***Perf. 12½***

**810** A220 $6 multi 4.50 4.50

No. 810 contains one 51x38mm stamp.

A221

Wedding of Prince William and Catherine Middleton — A222

No. 811: a, $2, Bride facing right (40x30mm). b, $2, Groom facing left (40x30mm). c, $2, Couple facing right (40x30mm). d, $2, Couple facing left (40x30mm). e, $4, Bride facing left (40x60mm).
No. 812: a, Couple facing right, wall in background. b, Couple facing forward, wall in background. c, As "b," horse in background. d, As "a," horse in background.
$6, Couple facing right.

**2011, July 14** ***Perf. 11½***
**811** A221 Sheet of 5, #a-e 9.00 9.00

***Perf. 12½x12***

**812** A222 $2.75 Sheet of 4, #a-d 8.25 8.25

**Souvenir Sheet**

***Perf. 13½x13¼***

**813** A221 $6 multi 4.50 4.50

No. 813 contains one 51x38mm stamp.

Miniature Sheets

U.S. Civil War, 150th Anniv. — A223

No. 814, $2.50 — Eagle, shield, Union and Confederate flags, General Robert E. Lee and General George G. Meade from Battle of Gettysburg, July 1-3, 1863, and: a, Union positions near Cemetery Ridge (image in green). b, Union artillery, Hazlitt's Battery in action. c, Union positions near Cemetery Ridge (images in brown). d, Union artillery, Cemetery hill in the distance.
No. 815, $2.50 — Eagle, shield, Union and Confederate flags, Lieutenant General James Longstreet and Major General Oliver O. Howard from Battle of Gettysburg, July 1-3, 1863, and: a, Behind the breastworks on Culp's Hill. b, Jubal Early's attack on East Cemetery Hill. c, Confederate Army's 2nd Maryland Infantry at Culp's Hill. d, Confederate pickets on Culp's Hill.
No. 816, $2.50 — Eagle, shield, Union and Confederate flags, Lieutenant General Richard S. Ewell and Brigadier General George S. Greene from Battle of Gettysburg, July 1-3, 1863, and: a, Cavalry engagement. b, Battle of Gettysburg. c, Hand to hand combat. d, Battery A, 1st Rhode Island, at Cemetery Ridge.

**2011, July 14** ***Perf. 13 Syncopated***

**Sheets of 4, #a-d**

**814-816** A223 Set of 3 22.50 22.50

Flowers — A224

No. 817, horiz.: a, Bird of paradise. b, Gardenia. c, Dutch amaryllis. d, Ginger flower. e, Lobster claw. f, Bleeding heart.
No. 818: a, Cockscomb. b, Passion flower. c, Prairie Blue Eyes day lily. d, Blue water lily.
No. 819, $6, Painted feather. No. 820, $6, Cuban lily, horiz.

**2011, July 14** ***Perf. 12***
**817** A224 $2 Sheet of 6, #a-f 9.00 9.00
**818** A224 $2.75 Sheet of 4, #a-d 8.25 8.25

**Souvenir Sheets**

**819-820** A224 Set of 2 9.00 9.00

No. 817 contains six 64x32mm triangular stamps.

Miniature Sheet

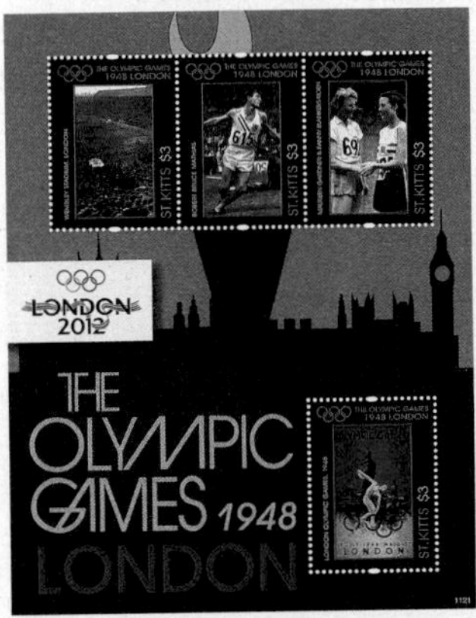
2012 Summer Olympics, London — A225

No. 821 — Scenes from 1948 Summer Olympics, London: a, Crowd at Wembley Stadium. b, Robert Mathias. c, Maureen Gardner and Fanny Blankers-Koen. d, Poster for 1948 Summer Olympics.

**2011, Nov. 14** ***Perf. 13 Syncopated***
**821** A225 $3 Sheet of 4, #a-d 9.00 9.00

Commonwealth Games Federation General Assembly, St. Kitts & Nevis — A226

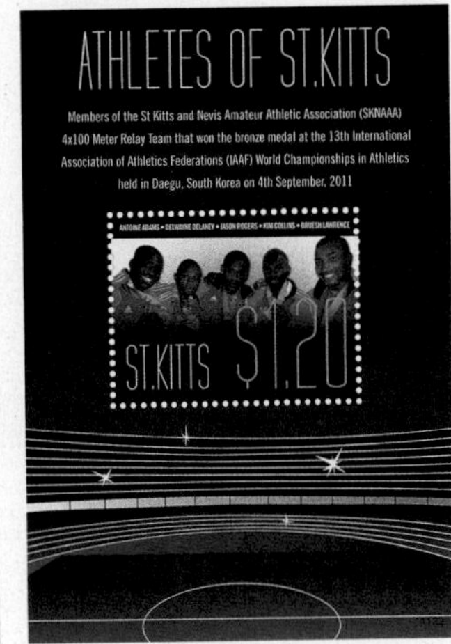
Members of St. Kitts & Nevis Men's 4x100 Meter Relay Team — A227

**2011, Dec. 8** ***Perf. 14***
**822** A226 25c multi .25 .25

**Souvenir Sheet**
***Perf. 12***

**823** A227 $1.20 multi .90 .90

Princess Diana (1961-97) A228

Princess Diana: $3, Wearing tiara. $9, Without tiara.

**2012, Oct. 1** ***Perf. 13¾***
**824** A228 $3 multi 2.25 2.25

**Souvenir Sheet**

**825** A228 $9 multi 6.75 6.75

No. 824 was printed in sheets of 4. No. 825 contains one 49x49mm diamond-shaped stamp.

A229

A230

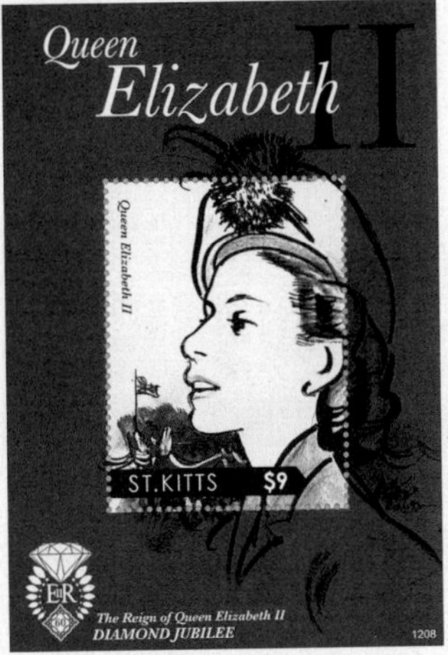
Reign of Queen Elizabeth II, 60th Anniv. — A231

Children's drawings: No. 826, 10c, Child's drawing for £2 stamp. No. 827, 10c, Diamond, crown, arrow, flags of St. Christopher, Nevis and Anguilla and St. Kitts and Nevis. 25c, Crown. 30c, Wreath of flags and "60." $1.20, Flags of St. Kitts and Nevis and Great Britain, "60" clock towers, handshake.
No. 831 — Queen Elizabeth II: a, Wearing hat. b, Without head covering. c, Wearing crown. d, Wearing tiara.
$9, Sketch of Queen Elizabeth II.

**2012, Oct. 1** ***Perf. 14***
**826-830** A229 Set of 5 1.50 1.50

***Perf. 13¾***

**831** A230 $3.50 Sheet of 4, #a-d 10.50 10.50

**Souvenir Sheet**
***Perf. 12¾***

**832** A231 $9 multi 6.75 6.75

Pres. Abraham Lincoln (1809-65) — A233

No. 833 — Photographs of Lincoln: a, Blue field of flag across top in background. b, Blue field of flag at UL. c, Red stripe of flag across top, Lincoln's arms visible to country name. d, Red stripe of flag across top, Lincoln's arms not visible.
$6, Sculpture of Lincoln in Lincoln Memorial.

**2012, Oct. 1** ***Perf. 14***
**833** A233 $2.75 Sheet of 4, #a-d 8.25 8.25

**Souvenir Sheet**

**834** A233 $6 multi 4.50 4.50

A234

Fish — A235

No. 835: a, French angelfish. b, Barracuda. c, Spotted trunkfish. d, Trumpetfish. e, Orange-lined triggerfish. f, Eagle ray.
$6, Butterflyfish.

**2012, Oct. 1** ***Perf. 13 Syncopated***
**835** A234 $2.50 Sheet of 6, #a-f 11.00 11.00

**Souvenir Sheet**

**836** A235 $6 multi 4.50 4.50

Parrots — A236

No. 837: a, Green-winged macaw. b, St. Vincent Amazon. c, Yellow-headed Amazon. d, Orange-winged Amazon.
$6, Blue and gold macaw, horiz.

**2012, Oct. 1** ***Perf. 14***
**837** A236 $2.75 Sheet of 4, #a-d 8.25 8.25

**Souvenir Sheet**
***Perf. 12¾***

**838** A236 $6 multi 4.50 4.50

No. 838 contains one 51x38mm stamp.

Shells — A237

No. 839: a, Turbo petholatus. b, Mitra stictica. c, Muricanthus radix. d, Murex bicolor.
$6, Haliotis asinina, vert.

**2012, Oct. 1** ***Perf.***
**839** A237 $2.75 Sheet of 4, #a-d 8.25 8.25

**Souvenir Sheet**
***Perf. 12***

**840** A237 $6 multi 4.50 4.50

No. 840 contains one 30x80mm rectangular stamp.

Souvenir Sheets

A238

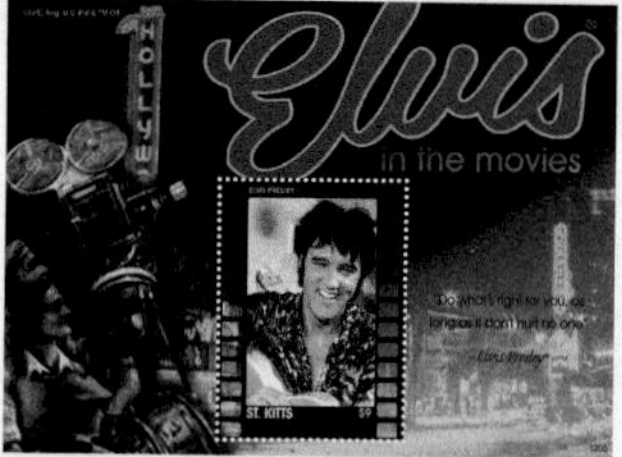


A239

A240

Elvis Presley (1935-77) — A241

**2012, Oct. 1** ***Perf. 12¾***

| | | | | |
|---|---|---|---|---|
| **841** | A238 | $9 multi | 6.75 | 6.75 |
| **842** | A239 | $9 multi | 6.75 | 6.75 |
| **843** | A240 | $9 multi | 6.75 | 6.75 |
| **844** | A241 | $9 multi | 6.75 | 6.75 |
| | *Nos. 841-844 (4)* | | 27.00 | 27.00 |

Antioch Baptist Church, 50th Anniv. — A242

Designs: 10c, Reverend Dr. William Manasseh Connor. 30c, Church building.

**2013, June 3** ***Perf. 13¼x12½***

**845-846** A242 Set of 2 .30 .30

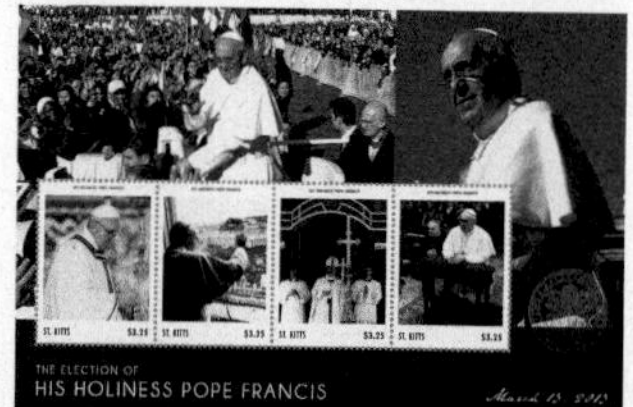


Election of Pope Francis — A243

No. 847 — Pope Francis: a, Carrying censer. b, Waving from window. c, Holding crucifix. d, Kneeling in prayer.

$9, Pope Francis waving from window, diff.

**2013, Aug. 7** **Litho.** ***Perf. 14***

**847** A243 $3.25 Sheet of 4, #a-d 9.75 9.75

**Souvenir Sheet**

***Perf. 12½***

**848** A243 $9 multi 6.75 6.75

No. 848 contains one 38x51mm stamp.

Miniature Sheet

Butterflies — A244

No. 849: a, Bates olivewing butterfly. b, Orange-barred sulphur butterfly. c, Blue satyr butterfly. d, Red flasher butterfly. e, Nymphalid butterfly. f, Hypolereia ocalea. g, Isamia carpenteri. h, Blue morpho butterfly. i, Variable cattleheart butterfly. j, Heliconius aoede.

**2013, Aug. 12** **Litho.** ***Perf. 14***

**849** A244 $1.60 Sheet of 10, #a-j 12.00 12.00

Miniature Sheet

Moths — A245

No. 850: a, Athis clitarcha. b, Oryba kadeni. c, Copaxa denda. d, Citheronia azteca.

**2013, Aug. 12** **Litho.** ***Perf. 12***

**850** A245 $3 Sheet of 4, #a-d 9.00 9.00

Souvenir Sheets

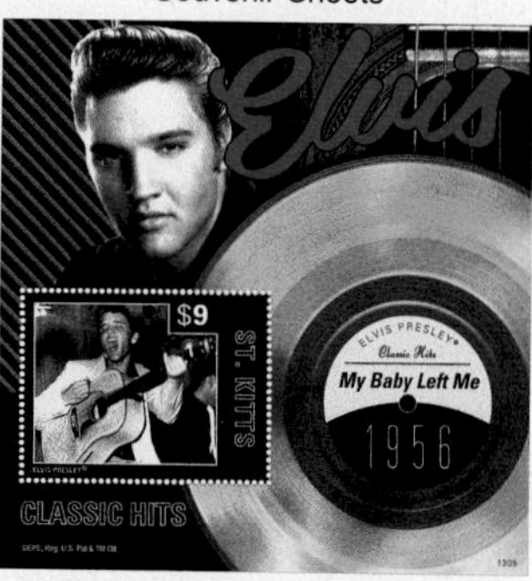


Elvis Presley (1935-77) — A246

Various photographs of Presley with frame color of: No. 851, $9, Black. No. 852, $9, Gray. No. 853, $9, Red (color photograph of Presley). No. 854, $9, Purple. No. 855, $9, Red (black-and-white photograph of Presley).

**2013, Aug. 12** **Litho.** ***Perf. 13¼***

**851-855** A246 Set of 5 34.00 34.00

Orchids — A247

No. 856: a, Bletilla striata. b, Phaius hybrid. c, Cymbidium "Showgirl." d, Dendrobium nobile. e, Zygopetalum crinitum.

$9, Cuitlauzina pendula.

**2013, Aug. 26** **Litho.** ***Perf. 14***

**856** A247 $2.75 Sheet of 5, #a-e 10.50 10.50

**Souvenir Sheet**

***Perf. 12½***

**857** A247 $9 multi 6.75 6.75

No. 857 contains one 38x51mm stamp.

Birth of Prince George of Cambridge — A248

No. 858: a, Duchess of Cambridge holding Prince George. b, Duke of Cambridge holding Prince George. c, Duke and Duchess of Cambridge, Prince George. d, Prince George.

$9, Duke and Duchess of Cambridge, horiz.

**2013, Sept. 10** **Litho.** ***Perf. 13¾***

**858** A248 $3.25 Sheet of 4, #a-d 9.75 9.75

**Souvenir Sheet**

***Perf. 12½***

**859** A248 $9 multi 6.75 6.75

No. 859 contains one 51x38mm stamp.

A249

Nelson Mandela (1918-2013), President of South Africa — A250

No. 860: a, People holding signs with pictures of Mandela. b, Black-and-white photograph of Mandela, "Mandela" at left in orange.

No. 861: a, Mandela in red shirt, waving. b, Mandela in suit, seated. c, Like #860b, "Mandela" at left in red.

**2013-14** **Litho.** ***Perf. 13¾***

**860** A249 $4.75 Horiz. pair, #a-b 7.00 7.00

**861** A250 $4.75 Sheet of 4, #861a, 861b, 2 #861c 14.00 14.00

Issued: No. 860, 2/19/14; No. 861, 12/19. No. 860 was printed in sheets containing two pairs.

Miniature Sheet

Hummingbirds — A251

No. 862: a, Lophornis regulus. b, Lophornis delattrei. c, Calothorax fanny. d, Lophornis ornatus. e, Lophornis helenae. f, Selaphorus platycerus.

**2014, Feb. 19** **Litho.** ***Perf. 13¾***

**862** A251 $2.50 Sheet of 6, #a-f 11.00 11.00

Reptiles — A252

No. 863: a, Anolis carolinensis. b, Anolis cristatellus. c, Hemidactylus mabouia. d, Iguana iguana.
$9, Sphaerodactylus sabanus, vert.

**2014, Feb. 19 Litho. *Perf. 13¾***

**863** A252 $3.25 Sheet of 4, #a-d 9.75 9.75

**Souvenir Sheet**

***Perf. 12¾***

**864** A252 $9 multi 6.75 6.75

No. 864 contains one 38x51mm stamp.

Marine Mammals — A253

No. 865: a, Pygmy killer whale. b, Short-finned pilot whale. c, Dwarf sperm whale. d, Humpback whale.
$9, West Indian manatee.

**2014, Feb. 19 Litho. *Perf. 14***

**865** A253 $3.50 Sheet of 4, #a-d 10.50 10.50

**Souvenir Sheet**

***Perf. 12***

**866** A253 $9 multi 6.75 6.75

Pres. John F. Kennedy (1917-63) — A254

No. 867 — Various photos of Pres. Kennedy at lectern, with denomination at: a, UL. b, UR. c, LL, d, LR.
No. 868, $9, Black-and-white photograph of Pres. Kennedy. No. 869, $9, Color photograph of Pres. Kennedy at White House.

***Perf. 13 Syncopated***

**2014, Feb. 19 Litho.**

**867** A254 $3 Sheet of 4, #a-d 9.00 9.00

**Souvenir Sheets**

**868-869** A254 Set of 2 13.50 13.50

Miniature Sheets

A255

Exploration of Mars — A256

No. 870 — Inscriptions: a, Mars Reconnaissance Orbiter. b, Phobos. c, Mars Orbiter. d, Mars Climate.
No. 871 — Inscriptions: a, Mars Reconnaissance Orbiter, diff. b, Mariner 7. c, Mars Rover. d, Viking.

***Perf. 13 Syncopated***

**2014, Feb. 19 Litho.**

**870** A255 $3.25 Sheet of 4, #a-d 9.75 9.75

**871** A256 $3.25 Sheet of 4, #a-d 9.75 9.75

Yuri Gagarin (1934-68), First Man in Space — A257

No. 872 — Gagarin with: a, His daughters. b, Cosmonaut Valentina Tereshkova and United Nations Secretary General U Thant. c, Indian Prime Minister Jawaharlal Nehru. d, Rocket designer Sergei Korolev.
$9, Gagarin and Vostok 1.

**2014, Feb. 19 Litho. *Perf. 12***

**872** A257 $2.75 Sheet of 4, #a-d 8.25 8.25

**Souvenir Sheet**

**873** A257 $9 multi 6.75 6.75

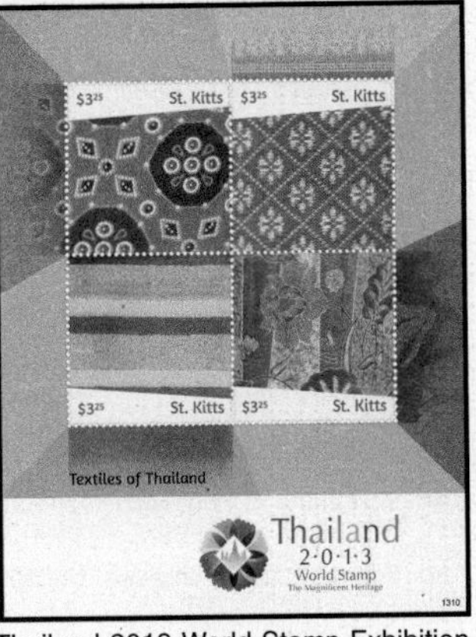


Thailand 2013 World Stamp Exhibition, Bangkok — A258

No. 874 — Textile designs: a, Circles and diamonds in red and pink. b, White geometric in diamond with blue background. c, Stripes. d, Flowers.
$9, Blue flower.

**2014, Feb. 19 Litho. *Perf. 13¾***

**874** A258 $3.25 Sheet of 4, #a-d 9.75 9.75

**Souvenir Sheet**

**875** A258 $9 multi 6.75 6.75

Children's Art — A259

Winning art in Human Rights Sensitization Project for Persons with Disabilities stamp design contest by: 10c, Xouria Jefferson. 15c, Nijaunte David. 30c, Nyiel Mayen. $50, Shernel Evans.

**2014, Aug. 18 Litho. *Perf. 13¼***

**876-879** A259 Set of 4 37.50 37.50

Cactus Flowers — A260

No. 880: a, Echinocactus quehlianus. b, Cereus chalybaeus. c, Cereus rhodoleucanthus. d, Cereus hankeanus. e, Phyllocactus gordonianus. f, Cereus peruvianus.
$9, Echinocactus damsii.

**2014, Sept. 4 Litho. *Perf. 14***

**880** A260 $2.25 Sheet of 6, #a-f 10.00 10.00

**Souvenir Sheet**

***Perf.***

**881** A260 $9 multi 6.75 6.75

No. 881 contains one 38mm diameter stamp.

World War I, Cent. — A261

No. 882, $3.25: a, Dove with olive branch. b, Jigsaw puzzle pieces. c, Helmet on rifle. d, Highway bridge.
No. 883, $3.25, horiz.: a, U.S. M1917 tank. b, German Stürmpanzerwagen A7V-U tank. c, British Mark A Whippet tank. d, French Renault FT-17 tank.
No. 884, $5, horiz. — U.S. President Woodrow Wilson: a, With handkerchief in pocket of suit. b, Without handkerchief in pocket of suit.
No. 885, $5: a, British Mark IV tank. b, German A7V tank.

**2014, Sept. 4 Litho. *Perf. 14***

**Sheets of 4, #a-d**

**882-883** A261 Set of 2 19.50 19.50

**Souvenir Sheets of 2, #a-b**

**884-885** A261 Set of 2 15.00 15.00

No. 884 contains two 51x38mm stamps. No. 885 contains two 38x51mm stamps.

Christmas A262

Paintings by Raphael: $2.20, Reading Madonna and Child. $2.25, The Sistine Madonna. $3.50, Madonna Del Granduca. $5, The Virgin and Child.

**2014, Dec. 15 Litho. *Perf. 12¾***

**886-889** A262 Set of 4 9.75 9.75

Trains — A263

No. 890: a, Light rail. b, Monorail. c, Steam engine train. d, Diesel train.
No. 891: a, Electric train. b, Maglev train.

***Perf. 13 Syncopated***

**2014, Dec. 31 Litho.**

**890** A263 $3.25 Sheet of 4, #a-d 9.75 9.75

**Souvenir Sheet**

**891** A263 $5 Sheet of 2, #a-b 7.50 7.50

A264

A265

A266

Sunflowers — A267

Various sunflowers, as shown.

**2014, Dec. 31 Litho. *Perf. 13¾***

**892** A264 $3.25 Sheet of 4, #a-d 9.75 9.75
**893** A265 $3.25 Sheet of 4, #a-d 9.75 9.75

**Souvenir Sheets**

***Perf.***

**894** A266 $10 multi 7.50 7.50
**895** A267 $10 multi 7.50 7.50

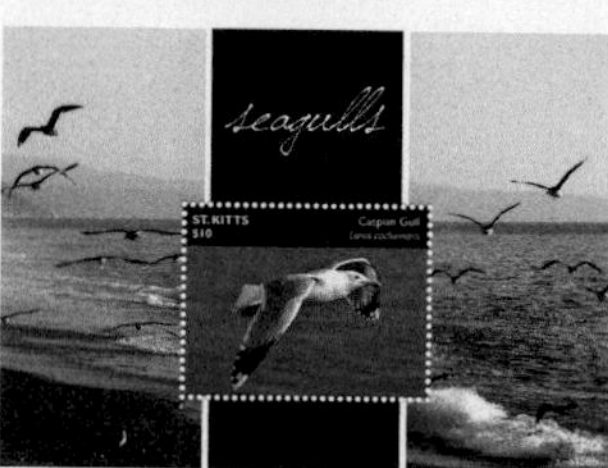


Seagulls — A268

No. 896, $3.25: a, Black-tailed gull. b, California gull. c, Gray-headed gull. d, European herring gull.

No. 897, $3.25: a, Yellow-legged gull. b, Common gull. c, Audouin's gull. d, Iceland gull.

No. 898, $10, Caspian gull. No. 899, $10, Dolphin gull.

**2014, Dec. 31 Litho. *Perf. 14***

**Sheets of 4, #a-d**

**896-897** A268 Set of 2 19.50 19.50

**Souvenir Sheets**

**898-899** A268 Set of 2 15.00 15.00

Tropical Fish — A269

No. 900, $3.25: a, French angelfish. b, Queen parrotfish. c, Rock beauty. d, Spotted drum.

No. 901, $3.25: a, Fairy basslet. b, Four-eyed butterflyfish. c, Glasseye snapper. d, Spotted eagle ray.

No. 902, $10, Queen angelfish. No. 903, $10, Smooth trunkfish, vert.

**2014, Dec. 31 Litho. *Perf. 14***

**Sheets of 4, #a-d**

**900-901** A269 Set of 2 19.50 19.50

**Souvenir Sheets**

***Perf. 12***

**902-903** A269 Set of 2 15.00 15.00

National Symbols — A270

Designs: $50, Aerial view of St. Kitts, flag of St. Kitts and Nevis. $100, Coat of arms of St. Kitts and Nevis.

**2015, Jan. 5 Litho. *Perf. 14x14¼***

**904** A270 $50 multi 37.50 37.50
**905** A270 $100 multi 75.00 75.00

Marine Life of Taiwan — A271

No. 906: a, Warty frogfish. b, White-margin sea slug. c, Blue-ringed angelfish. d, Maroon clownfish. e, Huang Ze gray crab. f, Hawksbill sea turtle.

No. 907: a, Head of Peacock mantis shrimp. b, Body of Peacock mantis shrimp.

**2015, Mar. 24 Litho. *Perf. 14***

**906** A271 $3.15 Sheet of 6, #a-f 14.00 14.00

**Souvenir Sheet**

***Perf. 12***

**907** A271 $5 Sheet of 2, #a-b 7.50 7.50

World War I Posters — A272

No. 908, $3.15 — Posters from United States depicting: a, Old woman and flag. b, Soldier with bugle, flag. c, Marines attacking, flag in background. d, Soldiers landing on shore, ships in background. e, Bald eagle attacking black eagle, airplanes in background. f, Statue of Liberty pointing.

No. 909, $3.15 — Posters from Great Britain depicting: a, Picture of soldier on pendant. b, Airplane and soldiers. c, Soldier with pipe in mouth marching. d, Crowd watching soldiers marching past British flag. e, Soldier pulling on airplane propeller. f, Woman holding British flag.

No. 910, $10, Uncle Sam pointing. No. 911, $10, British Army hat.

**2015, Mar. 24 Litho. *Perf. 12½***

**Sheets of 6, #a-f**

**908-909** A272 Set of 2 28.00 28.00

**Souvenir Sheets**

**910-911** A272 Set of 2 15.00 15.00

Palm Trees — A273

No. 912: a, Coconut palm, denomination in pink. b, Petticoat palm. c, Coconut palm, denomination in pale yellow. d, Royal palm, denomination in light blue. e, Royal palm, denomination in pink. f, Palmetto palm.

$10, Cococnut palm, horiz.

**2015, Apr. 1 Litho. *Perf. 13¼x13***

**912** A273 $3.15 Sheet of 6, #a-f 14.00 14.00

**Souvenir Sheet**

***Perf. 13¼***

**913** A273 $10 multi 7.50 7.50

No. 913 contains one 51x38mm stamp.

Green-throated Carib Hummingbird and Other Birds — A274

Design: $10, Green-throated Carib hummingbird.

**2015, June 1 Litho. *Perf. 14***

**914** A274 $1 multi .75 .75

**Souvenir Sheet**

***Perf. 12¾***

**915** A274 $10 multi 7.50 7.50

No. 915 contains one 51x38mm stamp.

Singapore 2015 World Stamp Exhibition — A275

No. 916 — Tourist attractions in Singapore: a, Sentosa Island. b, Singapore Flyer. c, Tiger Sky Tower. d, Kusu Island.

$10, Flower at Botanic Gardens, vert.

**2015, Aug. 3 Litho. *Perf. 12***

**916** A275 $3.25 Sheet of 4, #a-d 9.75 9.75

**Souvenir Sheet**

**917** A275 $10 multi 7.50 7.50

Cats — A276

No. 918: a, Birman. b, Devon Rex. c, Selkirk Rex. d, American Curl. e, Scottish Fold. f, Exotic shorthair.

$10, Bengal cat, vert.

**2015, Aug. 3 Litho. *Perf. 14***

**918** A276 $3.15 Sheet of 6, #a-f 14.00 14.00

**Souvenir Sheet**

***Perf. 12***

**919** A276 $10 multi 7.50 7.50

Battle of Waterloo, 200th Anniv. — A277

No. 920 — Paintings: a, Scotland Forever!, by Lady Butler. b, The Battle of Waterloo, by Jan Willem Pieneman. c, Wellington at Waterloo, by Robert Alexander Hillingford. d, The Last Grenadier at Waterloo, by Horace Vernet.

$10, The Battle of Waterloo, by William Sadler.

**2015, Aug. 3 Litho. *Perf. 12½***

**920** A277 $3.25 Sheet of 4, #a-d 9.75 9.75

**Souvenir Sheet**

***Perf. 12***

**921** A277 $10 multi 7.50 7.50

No. 921 contains one 80x30mm stamp.

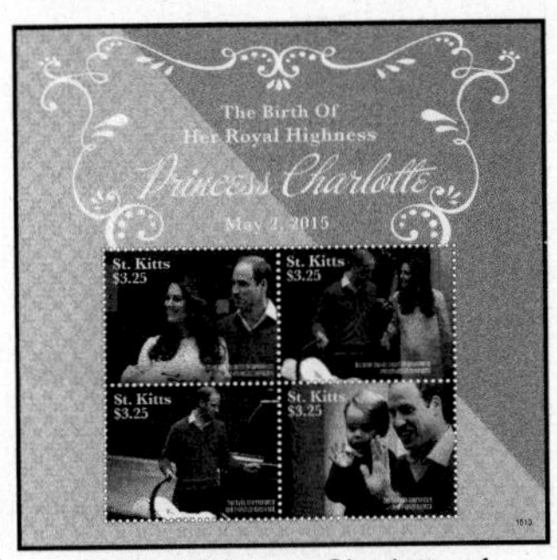

Birth of Princess Charlotte of Cambridge — A278

No. 922: a, Duke and Duchess of Cambridge, Duchess carrying Princess Charlotte. b, Duke and Duchess of Cambridge, Duke holding Princess Charlotte's baby carrier. c, Duke of Cambridge putting baby carrier in automobile. d, Duke of Cambridge and Prince George.

$10, Duchess of Cambridge and Princess Charlotte, vert.

**2015, Aug. 10 Litho. *Perf. 12***

922 A278 $3.25 Sheet of 4, #a-d 9.75 9.75

**Souvenir Sheet**

923 A278 $10 multi 7.50 7.50

Owls — A279

No. 924, $3.25 — Owl and feather, white background: a, Barn owl. b, Burrowing owl. c, Central American pygmy owl. d, Great horned owl.

No. 925, $3.25 — Owl, black frame: a, Barred owl. b, Burrowing owl. c, Bare-legged owls. d, Barn owl.

No. 926, $10, Ashy-faced owl. No. 927, $10, Short-eared owl.

**2015, Sept. 8 Litho. *Perf. 12***

**Sheets of 4, #a-d**

924-925 A279 Set of 2 19.50 19.50

**Souvenir Sheets**

926-927 A279 Set of 2 15.00 15.00

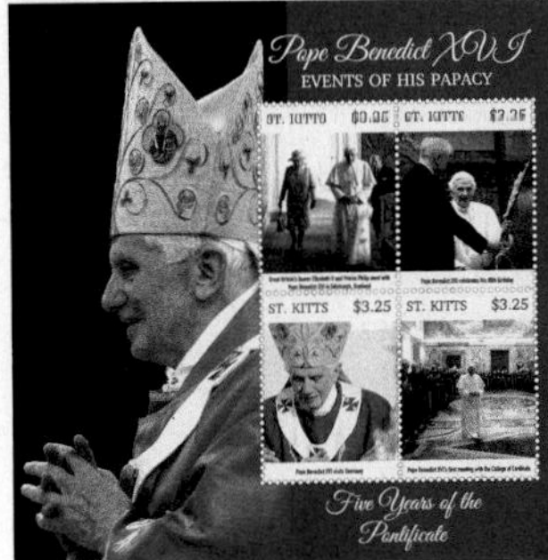

Events of Reign of Pope Benedict XVI — A280

No. 928 — Pope Benedict XVI: a, Meeting Queen Elizabeth II and Prince Philip. b, Celebrating 85th birthday. c, Visiting Germany. d, At first meeting with College of Cardinals.

$10, Pope Benedict XVI giving *Urbi et Orbi* Easter blessing, horiz.

**2015, Sept. 8 Litho. *Perf. 12x12½***

928 A280 $3.25 Sheet of 4, #a-d 9.75 9.75

**Souvenir Sheet**

***Perf. 12***

929 A280 $10 multi 7.50 7.50

No. 929 contains one 50x30mm stamp.

Christmas A281

Paintings by Raphael: 30c, Small Cowper Madonna. $2.25, The Tempi Madonna. $3.50, Madonna with Beardless Saint Joseph. $5, Sistine Madonna.

**2015, Nov. 2 Litho. *Perf. 13½***

930-933 A281 Set of 4 8.25 8.25

Worldwide Fund for Nature (WWF) — A282

No. 934 — West Indian mahogany tree: a, Seeds in opened fruit. b, Foliage, c, Forest. d, Fruit on tree.

**2016, Apr. 14 Litho. *Perf. 14***

934 Strip of 4, #a-d 9.75 9.75

*a.-d.* A282 $3.25 Any single 2.40 2.40

*e.* Souvenir sheet of 8, 2 each #934a-934d 19.50 19.50

Paintings — A283

No. 935, $3.50: a, Blue House, by Boris Kustodiev. b, Dog Lying in the Snow, by Marc Liegender. c, A Girl with a Watering Can, by Pierre-Auguste Renoir.

No. 936, $3.50: a, Mandolin on a Chair, by Paul Gauguin. b, Bouquet of Flowers, by Henri Rousseau. c, Girl at a Sewing Machine, by Edward Hopper.

No. 937, $10, Murnau, A Village Street, by Wassily Kandinsky. No. 938, $10, Bedroom in Arles, by Vincent van Gogh.

**2016, May 26 Litho. *Perf. 12½***

**Sheets of 3, #a-c**

935-936 A283 Set of 2 15.50 15.50

**Size: 100x100mm**

***Imperf***

937-938 A283 Set of 2 15.00 15.00

No. 938 "Arles" is spelled incorrectly on stamp.

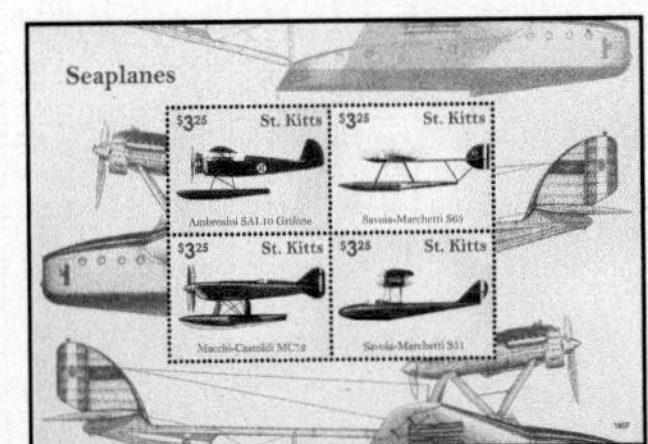

Seaplanes — A284

No. 939: a, Ambrosini SAL 10 Grifone. b, Savoia-Marchetti S65. c, Macchi-Castoldi MC72. d, Savoia-Marchetti S51.

$10, Savoia-Marchetti S55X.

**2016, May 26 Litho. *Perf. 14***

939 A284 $3.25 Sheet of 4, #a-d 9.75 9.75

**Souvenir Sheet**

940 A284 $10 multi 7.50 7.50

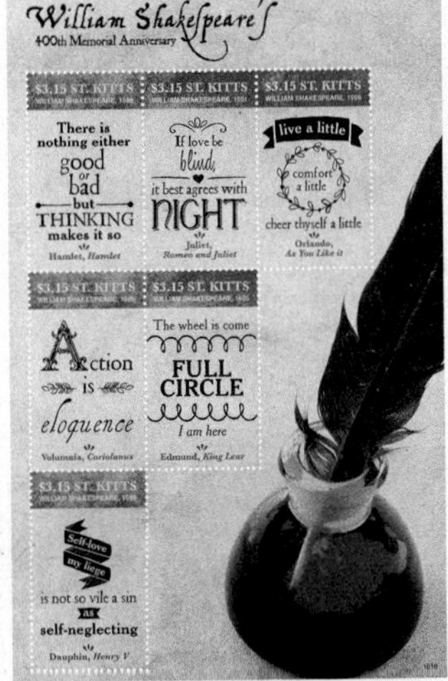

Characters From *Star Trek* (2009 Movie) — A285

No. 941: a, Spock. b, Kirk. c, Elder Spock. d, Sulu. e, Uhura. f, Bones McCoy.

$10, Spock and Elder Spock.

**2016, May 26 Litho. *Perf. 12***

941 A285 $3 Sheet of 6, #a-f 13.50 13.50

**Souvenir Sheet**

***Perf. 14***

942 A285 $10 multi 7.50 7.50

Lines From Plays by William Shakespeare (1564-1616) — A286

No. 943 — Line from: a, *Hamlet*. b, *Romeo and Juliet*. c, *Orlando's line, As You Like It*. d, *Coriolanus*. e, *King Lear*. f, *Henry V*.

$13, *Roslind's line from, As You Like It*, diff.

**2016, May 26 Litho. *Perf. 12***

943 A286 $3.15 Sheet of 6, #a-f 14.00 14.00

**Souvenir Sheet**

944 A286 $13 multi 9.75 9.75

Queen Elizabeth II, Longest-Reigning British Monarch — A287

No. 945 — Queen Elizabeth II: a, Wearing gray raincoat and head scarf. b, Wearing black jacket, camera and binoculars around neck. c, Wearing dark blue jacket, arms folded. d, Wearing head scarf, taking photograph. e, Wearing blue vest jacket. f, Wearing dark green raincoat and head scarf, with camera.

$10, Taking photograph, horiz.

**2016, May 26 Litho. *Perf. 14***

945 A287 $3.15 Sheet of 6, #a-f 14.00 14.00

**Souvenir Sheet**

***Perf. 12***

946 A287 $10 multi 7.50 7.50

No. 946 contains one 80x30mm stamp.

New York City Landmarks — A288

No. 947: a, Statue of Lion, New York Public Library. b, Statue of Prometheus, Rockefeller Center c, Glory of Commerce statue, Grand Central Terminal. d, Angel of the Waters statue (Bethesda Fountain), Central Park.

$12, Statue of Liberty, vert.

**2016, May 26 Litho. *Perf. 12***

947 A288 $3.50 Sheet of 4, #a-d 10.50 10.50

**Souvenir Sheet**

***Perf. 12½***

948 A288 $12 multi 9.00 9.00

2016 World Stamp Show, New York. No. 948 contains one 38x51mm stamp.

A289

September 11, 2001 Terrorist Attacks, 15th Anniv. — A290

No. 949: a, Soldier saluting at Flight 93 National Memorial. b, Aerial view of Pentagon. c, Pentagon Sept. 11 Memorial. d, Sept. 11 Memorial, Liberty State Park, New Jersey. e, Sept. 11 Fire Department of New York Memorial Wall. f, Sept. 11 Memorial, Bayonne, New Jersey.

No. 950: a, World Trade Center, denomination in white. b, World Trade Center tower, denomination partly over sky. c, World Trade Center tower, country name partly over sky. d, Tribute in Light.

$13, World Trade Center, horiz.

**2016, May 26 Litho. *Perf. 14***

**949** A289 $3.15 Sheet of 6, #a-f 14.00 14.00

***Perf. 12***

**950** A290 $3.25 Sheet of 4, #a-d 9.75 9.75

**Souvenir Sheet**

**951** A290 $13 multi 9.75 9.75

No. 951 contains one 40x30mm stamp.

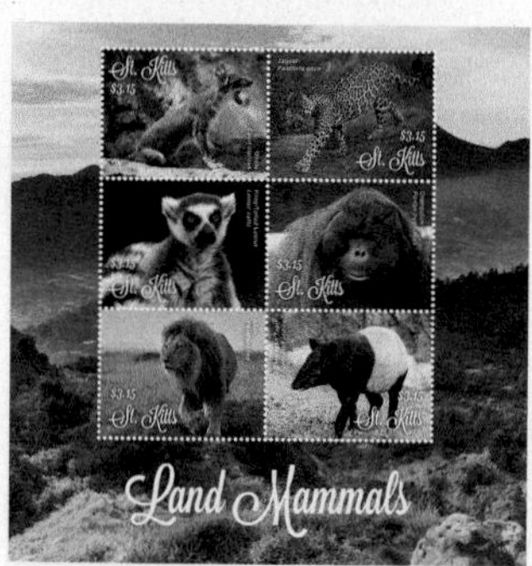


Mammals — A291

No. 952: a, Dhole. b, Jaguar. c, Ring-tailed lemur. d, Orangutan. e, Lion. f, Malayan tapir.

No. 953: a, Red panda. b, Hippopotamus. c, Black rhinoceros. d, Bengal tiger.

$10, Mohol bushbaby.

**2016, May 26 Litho. *Perf. 14***

**952** A291 $3.15 Sheet of 6, #a-f 14.00 14.00

**953** A291 $3.25 Sheet of 4, #a-d 9.75 9.75

**Souvenir Sheet**

**954** A291 $10 multi 7.50 7.50

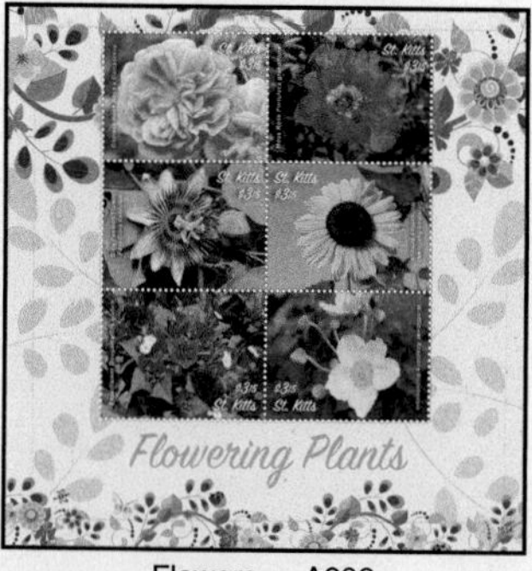


Flowers — A292

No. 955: a, Damask rose. b, Moss rose. c, Blue passion flower. d, Common sunflower. e, Paperflower. f, Windflower.

No. 956: a, Elegant zinnia. b, Asian globe-flower. c, Creeping zinnia. d, Blackeyed Susan.

$10, Persian carpet.

**2016, May 26 Litho. *Perf. 14***

**955** A292 $3.15 Sheet of 6, #a-f 14.00 14.00

**956** A292 $3.25 Sheet of 4, #a-d 9.75 9.75

**Souvenir Sheet**

**957** A292 $10 multi 7.50 7.50

Miniature Sheets

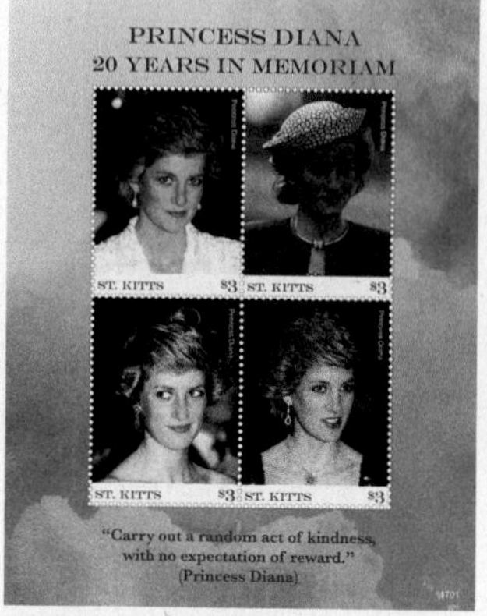


A293

Princess Diana (1961-97) — A294

No. 958 — Princess Diana wearing: a, White dress and pendant earrings. b, Blue and white hat. c, Strapless gown. d, Black dress and pendant earrings.

No. 959: a, Princess Diana, in silver and white, holding Prince William. b, Princess Diana, in green and white dress, holding Prince William. c, Princess Diana with arms around head of Prince William. d, Prince William holding infant Prince George. e, Prince William holding toddler Prince George. f, Princes William and George walking.

**2017, June 7 Litho. *Perf. 14***

**958** A293 $3 Sheet of 4, #a-d 9.00 9.00

**959** A294 $3 Sheet of 6, #a-f 13.50 13.50

Queen Elizabeth II, 90th Birthday (in 2016) — A295

No. 960 — Queen Elizabeth II: a, As toddler (30x40mm). b, With Prince Philip (30x40mm). c, With Princes Philip and Charles and Princess Anne (30x40mm). d, With Princes Philip, William and George, Duchess of Cambridge and Princess Charlotte (30x90mm).

No. 961 — Queen Elizabeth II wearing: a, Magenta jacket and hat. b, Apple green and white jacket and hat, holding flowers.

$10, Queen Elizabeth II wearing apple green and white jacket, waving.

**2017, June 7 Litho. *Perf. 14***

**960** A295 $3 Sheet of 4, #a-d 9.00 9.00

**Souvenir Sheets**

***Perf. 12***

**961** A295 $5 Sheet of 2, #a-b 7.50 7.50

***Perf. 13¾***

**962** A295 $10 multi 7.50 7.50

No. 961 contains two 30x50mm stamps. No. 962 contains one 50x50mm diamond-shaped stamp.

Animals — A296

No. 963: a, Greater mouse deer. b, Flightless steamer duck. c, Arctic cookie stars. d, Florida bark scorpion.

$10, Silverstone's poison frog.

**2017, June 7 Litho. *Perf. 12½***

**963** A296 $5 Sheet of 4, #a-d 5.00 15.00

**Souvenir Sheet**

**964** A296 $10 multi 7.50 7.50

## OFFICIAL STAMPS

### Nos. 28-37 Ovptd. "OFFICIAL"

***Perf. 14½x14***

**1980, June 23 Litho. Wmk. 373**

| | | | | | |
|---|---|---|---|---|---|
| **O1** | A61 | 15c | multicolored | .25 | .25 |
| **O2** | A61 | 25c | multicolored | .25 | .25 |
| **O3** | A61 | 30c | multicolored | .25 | .25 |
| **O4** | A61 | 40c | multicolored | .25 | .25 |
| **O5** | A61 | 45c | multicolored | .25 | .25 |
| **O6** | A61 | 50c | multicolored | .25 | .25 |
| **O7** | A61 | 55c | multicolored | .25 | .25 |
| **O8** | A61 | $1 | multicolored | .30 | .30 |
| **O9** | A61 | $5 | multicolored | 1.00 | *1.50* |
| **O10** | A61 | $10 | multicolored | 1.50 | *2.75* |
| | *Nos. O1-O10 (10)* | | | 4.55 | 6.30 |

No. O7 exists with inverted overprint. Value $22. No. O10 exists with inverted overprint. Value $100.

**Unwmk.**

| | | | | |
|---|---|---|---|---|
| *O2a* | A61 | 25c | .30 | .25 |
| *O3a* | A61 | 30c | .60 | .40 |
| *O4a* | A61 | 40c | 11.50 | *12.50* |
| *O7a* | A61 | 55c | .85 | 1.00 |
| *O8a* | A61 | $1 | 1.40 | 1.25 |
| *O9a* | A61 | $5 | 3.25 | 5.00 |
| *O10a* | A61 | $10 | 4.25 | 7.00 |
| | *Nos. O2a-O10a (7)* | | 22.15 | 27.40 |

### Nos. 55-66 Ovptd. "OFFICIAL"

**1981, Feb. 5 *Perf. 14***

| | | | | | |
|---|---|---|---|---|---|
| **O11** | A5 | 15c | multicolored | .25 | .25 |
| **O12** | A5 | 20c | multicolored | .25 | .25 |
| **O13** | A5 | 25c | multicolored | .25 | .25 |
| **O14** | A5 | 30c | multicolored | .25 | .25 |
| **O15** | A5 | 40c | multicolored | .40 | .25 |
| **O16** | A5 | 45c | multicolored | .45 | .25 |
| **O17** | A5 | 50c | multicolored | .45 | .25 |
| **O18** | A5 | 55c | multicolored | .55 | .30 |
| **O19** | A5 | $1 | multicolored | .90 | .70 |
| **O20** | A5 | $2.50 | multicolored | 2.00 | 1.25 |
| **O21** | A5 | $5 | multicolored | 3.25 | 2.50 |
| **O22** | A5 | $10 | multicolored | 5.50 | 4.50 |
| | *Nos. O11-O22 (12)* | | | 14.50 | 11.00 |

### Nos. 75-80 Ovptd. or Surcharged "OFFICIAL" in Ultra or Black

**1983, Feb. 2**

| | | | | |
|---|---|---|---|---|
| **O23** | A6a | 45c on $2.50 No. 77 (U) | .35 | .35 |
| *a.* | | Black surcharge | | |
| **O24** | A6b | 45c on $2.50 No. 78 (U) | .45 | .45 |
| *a.* | | Black surcharge | | |
| **O25** | A6a | 55c No. 75 | .35 | .35 |
| **O26** | A6b | 55c No. 76 | .60 | .60 |
| **O27** | A6a | $1.10 on $4 No. 79 (B) | .60 | .60 |
| *a.* | | Ultra surcharge | 3.00 | |
| **O28** | A6b | $1.10 on $4 No. 80 (B) | 1.10 | 1.10 |
| *a.* | | Ultra surcharge | 25.00 | |
| | *Nos. O23-O28 (6)* | | 3.45 | 3.45 |

No. O23 exists with double surcharge and inverted surcharge. Values, $16 and $3, respectively. No. O24 exists with double surcharge and inverted surcharge. Values, $60 and $20, respectively. No. O25 exists with double surcharge and inverted surcharge. Values, $18 and $6, respectively. No. O26 exists with double surcharge and inverted surcharge. Values, $60 and $19, respectively. No. O27 exists with double surcharge. Value $15. No. O28 exists with double surcharge. Value $45. Nos. O27a and O28a exist with inverted surcharge.

### Nos. 141-152 Ovptd. "OFFICIAL"

**1984, July 4 Wmk. 380**

| | | | | | |
|---|---|---|---|---|---|
| **O29** | A18 | 15c | multicolored | .70 | *1.50* |
| **O30** | A18 | 20c | multicolored | .80 | *1.50* |
| **O31** | A18 | 25c | multicolored | .80 | *1.50* |
| **O32** | A18 | 30c | multicolored | .90 | *1.50* |
| **O33** | A18 | 40c | multicolored | 1.00 | *1.50* |
| **O34** | A18 | 50c | multicolored | 1.00 | *1.50* |
| **O35** | A18 | 60c | multicolored | 1.25 | *2.00* |
| **O36** | A18 | 75c | multicolored | 1.60 | *2.00* |
| **O37** | A18 | $1 | multicolored | 2.50 | 2.50 |
| **O38** | A18 | $2.50 | multicolored | 4.50 | *6.00* |
| **O39** | A18 | $5 | multicolored | 8.00 | 3.00 |
| **O40** | A18 | $10 | multicolored | 14.50 | 6.00 |
| | *Nos. O29-O40 (12)* | | | 37.55 | 30.50 |

## ST. KITTS-NEVIS

sānt 'kits-'nē-vəs

### (St. Christopher-Nevis-Anguilla)

LOCATION — West Indies southeast of Puerto Rico
GOVT. — Associated State in British Commonwealth
AREA — 153 sq. mi.
POP. — 43,309, excluding Anguilla (1991)
CAPITAL — Basseterre, St. Kitts

St. Kitts-Nevis was one of the presidencies of the former Leeward Islands colony until it became a colony itself in 1956. In 1967 Britain granted internal self-government.

See "St. Christopher" for stamps used in St. Kitts before 1890. From 1890 until 1903, stamps of the Leeward Islands were used. From 1903 until 1956, stamps of St. Kitts-Nevis and Leeward Islands were used concurrently.

Starting in 1967, issues of Anguilla are listed under that heading. Starting in 1980 stamps inscribed St. Kitts or Nevis are listed under those headings.

12 Pence = 1 Shilling
20 Shillings = 1 Pound
100 Cents = 1 Dollar (1951)

**Catalogue values for unused stamps in this country are for Never Hinged items, beginning with Scott 91 in the regular postage section and Scott O1 in the officials section.**

Columbus Looking for Land — A1

Medicinal Spring — A2

**Wmk. Crown and C A (2)**

**1903 Typo.** *Perf. 14*

| | | | | |
|---|---|---|---|---|
| 1 | A1 | ½p grn & vio | 2.00 | .80 |
| 2 | A2 | 1p car & black | 5.25 | .25 |
| 3 | A1 | 2p brn & vio | 3.50 | *12.00* |
| 4 | A1 | 2½p ultra & black | 20.00 | 6.00 |
| 5 | A2 | 3p org & green | 25.00 | *32.50* |
| 6 | A1 | 6p red vio & blk | 8.00 | *47.50* |
| 7 | A1 | 1sh org & grn | 7.75 | *12.00* |
| 8 | A2 | 2sh blk & grn | 13.50 | *22.50* |
| 9 | A1 | 2sh6p violet & blk | 20.00 | *50.00* |
| 10 | A2 | 5sh ol grn & gray vio | 70.00 | *62.50* |
| | | *Nos. 1-10 (10)* | 175.00 | *246.05* |

**1905-18** **Wmk. 3**

| | | | | |
|---|---|---|---|---|
| 11 | A1 | ½p green & violet | 16.50 | *8.25* |
| 12a | A1 | ½p dl blue grn ('16) | 1.00 | 3.25 |
| 13 | A2 | 1p carmine & blk | 9.50 | .30 |
| 14a | A2 | 1p scarlet ('16) | 1.00 | .25 |
| 15 | A1 | 2p brn & vio, ordinary paper | 11.00 | 9.00 |
| 16 | A1 | 2½p ultra & blk | 40.00 | 6.00 |
| 17 | A1 | 2½p ultra | 3.00 | .60 |
| 18 | A2 | 3p org & grn, chalky paper | 3.50 | 3.00 |
| 19 | A1 | 6p red violet & gray blk ('16) | 12.00 | *35.00* |
| *a.* | | 6p purple & gray, chalky paper ('08) | 24.00 | *27.50* |
| 20 | A1 | 1sh org & grn, chalky paper ('09) | 4.00 | *35.00* |
| 21 | A2 | 5sh ol grn & gray vio ('18) | 47.50 | *120.00* |
| | | *Nos. 11-21 (11)* | 149.00 | *220.65* |

Nos. 13, 19a and 21 are on chalky paper only and Nos. 15, 18 and 20 are on both ordinary and chalky paper.

For stamp and type overprinted see #MR1-MR2.

King George V — A3

A4

**1920-22** **Ordinary Paper**

| | | | | |
|---|---|---|---|---|
| 24 | A3 | ½p green | 4.25 | *6.00* |
| 25 | A4 | 1p carmine | 4.00 | *6.50* |
| 26 | A3 | 1½p orange | 1.40 | 2.00 |
| 27 | A4 | 2p gray | 3.25 | *7.50* |
| 28 | A3 | 2½p ultramarine | 8.25 | *10.00* |
| *a.* | | "A" missing from watermark | 600.00 | |

**Chalky Paper**

| | | | | |
|---|---|---|---|---|
| 29 | A4 | 3p vio & dull vio, *yel* | 2.00 | *12.00* |
| 30 | A3 | 6p red vio & dull vio | 4.00 | *12.00* |
| 31 | A4 | 1sh blk, *gray grn* | 4.00 | *4.50* |
| 32 | A3 | 2sh ultra & dull vio, *bl* | 28.00 | *57.50* |
| 33 | A4 | 2sh 6p red & blk, *bl* | 5.50 | *45.00* |
| 34 | A3 | 5sh red & grn, *yel* | 5.50 | *45.00* |
| 35 | A4 | 10sh red & grn, *grn* | 14.50 | *52.50* |
| 36 | A3 | £1 blk & vio, *red* ('22) | 300.00 | *375.00* |
| | | *Nos. 24-36 (13)* | 384.65 | *635.50* |

**1921-29** **Ordinary Paper** **Wmk. 4**

| | | | | |
|---|---|---|---|---|
| 37 | A3 | ½p yel green | 2.50 | 1.50 |
| 38 | A4 | 1p rose red | 1.25 | .25 |
| 39 | A4 | 1p dp violet ('22) | 7.50 | 1.10 |
| 40 | A3 | 1½p rose red ('25) | 7.50 | 1.50 |
| 41 | A3 | 1½p fawn ('28) | 2.25 | .35 |
| 42 | A4 | 2p gray | 1.00 | .65 |
| 43 | A3 | 2½p pale bright blue ('22) | 1.75 | 2.50 |
| 44 | A3 | 2½p brown ('22) | 4.75 | *12.50* |

**Chalky Paper**

| | | | | |
|---|---|---|---|---|
| 43a | A3 | 2½p ultra ('27) | 1.75 | 1.50 |
| 45 | A4 | 3p ultra ('22) | 1.60 | *4.00* |
| 46 | A4 | 3p vio & dl vio, *yel* | 2.40 | *2.75* |
| 47 | A3 | 6p red vio & dl vio ('24) | 8.50 | *6.75* |
| 48 | A4 | 1sh blk, *grn* ('29) | 6.50 | 4.00 |
| 49 | A3 | 2sh ultra & vio, *bl* ('22) | 15.00 | *40.00* |
| 50 | A4 | 2sh6p red & blk, *bl* ('27) | 25.00 | *30.00* |
| 51 | A3 | 5sh red & grn, *yel* ('29) | 55.00 | *100.00* |
| | | *Nos. 37-51 (16)* | 144.25 | *209.35* |
| | | Set, ovptd. "SPECIMEN" | 450.00 | |

No. 43 exists on ordinary and chalky paper.

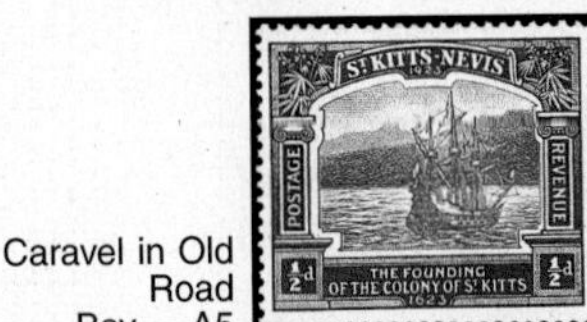

Caravel in Old Road Bay — A5

**1923** **Wmk. 4**

| | | | | |
|---|---|---|---|---|
| 52 | A5 | ½p green & blk | 2.50 | *9.25* |
| 53 | A5 | 1p violet & blk | 5.00 | 3.25 |
| 54 | A5 | 1½p car & blk | 5.00 | *11.00* |
| 55 | A5 | 2p dk gray & blk | 4.25 | 1.75 |
| 56 | A5 | 2½p brown & blk | 6.50 | *35.00* |
| 57 | A5 | 3p ultra & blk | 6.50 | *16.00* |
| 58 | A5 | 6p red vio & blk | 10.50 | *35.00* |
| 59 | A5 | 1sh ol grn & blk | 15.00 | *35.00* |
| 60 | A5 | 2sh ultra & blk, *bl* | 52.50 | *85.00* |
| 61 | A5 | 2sh6p red & blk, *blue* | 52.50 | *100.00* |
| 62 | A5 | 10sh red & blk, *emer* | 325.00 | *600.00* |

**Wmk. 3**

| | | | | |
|---|---|---|---|---|
| 63 | A5 | 5sh red & blk, *yel* | 92.50 | *250.00* |
| 64 | A5 | £1 vio & blk, *red* | 825.00 | *1,775.* |
| | | *Nos. 52-63 (12)* | 577.75 | *1,181.* |

Tercentenary of the founding of the colony of St. Kitts (or St. Christopher).

Common Design Types pictured following the introduction.

**Silver Jubilee Issue**
Common Design Type
Inscribed "St. Christopher and Nevis"

*Perf. 11x12*

**1935, May 6** **Engr.** **Wmk. 4**

| | | | | |
|---|---|---|---|---|
| 72 | CD301 | 1p car & dk blue | 1.00 | .75 |
| 73 | CD301 | 1½p gray blk & ultra | .80 | 1.00 |
| 74 | CD301 | 2½p ultra & brown | 1.00 | .90 |
| 75 | CD301 | 1sh brn vio & ind | 8.00 | *16.00* |
| | | *Nos. 72-75 (4)* | 10.80 | *18.65* |
| | | Set, never hinged | 18.50 | |

**Coronation Issue**
Common Design Type
Inscribed "St. Christopher and Nevis"

**1937, May 12** *Perf. 13½x14*

| | | | | |
|---|---|---|---|---|
| 76 | CD302 | 1p carmine | .25 | .30 |
| 77 | CD302 | 1½p brown | .30 | .25 |
| 78 | CD302 | 2½p bright ultra | .40 | 1.60 |
| | | *Nos. 76-78 (3)* | .95 | 2.15 |
| | | Set, never hinged | 1.25 | |

George VI — A6

Medicinal Spring — A7

Columbus Looking for Land — A8

Map Showing Anguilla — A9

*Perf. 13½x14 (A6, A9), 14 (A7, A8)*

**1938-48** **Typo.**

| | | | | |
|---|---|---|---|---|
| 79 | A6 | ½p green | .25 | .25 |
| 80 | A6 | 1p carmine | 1.00 | .55 |
| 81 | A6 | 1½p orange | .25 | .30 |
| 82 | A7 | 2p gray & car | .90 | 1.40 |
| 83 | A6 | 2½p ultra | .50 | .35 |
| 84 | A7 | 3p car & pale lilac | 2.75 | 5.50 |
| 85 | A8 | 6p rose lil & dl grn | 5.00 | 1.60 |
| 86 | A7 | 1sh green & gray blk | 3.00 | 1.00 |
| 87 | A7 | 2sh6p car & gray blk | 8.50 | 4.50 |
| 88 | A8 | 5sh car & dull grn | 17.50 | 12.00 |

**Typo., Center Litho.**

**Chalky Paper**

| | | | | |
|---|---|---|---|---|
| 89 | A9 | 10sh brt ultra & blk | 9.50 | *20.00* |
| 90 | A9 | £1 brown & blk | 9.50 | *22.50* |
| | | *Nos. 79-90 (12)* | 58.65 | *69.95* |
| | | Set, never hinged | 85.00 | |

Issued: ½, 1, 1½, 2½p, 8/15/38; 2p, 1941; 3, 6p, 2sh6p, 5sh, 1942; 1sh, 1943; 10sh, £1, 9/1/48.

For types overprinted see Nos. 99-104.

**1938, Aug. 15** *Perf. 13x11½*

| | | | | |
|---|---|---|---|---|
| *82a* | A7 | 2p | 18.00 | 3.00 |
| *84a* | A7 | 3p | 16.00 | 8.25 |
| *85a* | A8 | 6p | 6.50 | 3.00 |
| *86a* | A7 | 1sh | 8.50 | 2.25 |
| *87a* | A7 | 2sh6p | 22.50 | 10.00 |
| *88a* | A8 | 5sh | 47.50 | 25.00 |
| | | *Nos. 82a-88a (6)* | 119.00 | 51.50 |

**Catalogue values for unused stamps in this section, from this point to the end of the section, are for Never Hinged items.**

**Peace Issue**
Common Design Type
Inscribed "St. Kitts-Nevis"

**1946, Nov. 1** **Engr.** *Perf. 13½x14*

| | | | | |
|---|---|---|---|---|
| 91 | CD303 | 1½p deep orange | .25 | .25 |
| 92 | CD303 | 3p carmine | .25 | .25 |

**Silver Wedding Issue**
Common Design Types
Inscribed: "St. Kitts-Nevis"

**1949, Jan. 3** **Photo.** *Perf. 14x14½*

| | | | | |
|---|---|---|---|---|
| 93 | CD304 | 2½p bright ultra | .25 | .50 |

*Perf. 11½x11*

**Engraved; Name Typographed**

| | | | | |
|---|---|---|---|---|
| 94 | CD305 | 5sh rose carmine | 11.00 | 10.00 |

**UPU Issue**
Common Design Types
Inscribed: "St. Kitt's-Nevis"

**Engr.; Name Typo. on 3p, 6p**

**1949, Oct. 10** *Perf. 13½, 11x11½*

| | | | | |
|---|---|---|---|---|
| 95 | CD306 | 2½p ultra | .25 | *.35* |
| 96 | CD307 | 3p deep carmine | 2.50 | *2.75* |
| 97 | CD308 | 6p red lilac | .25 | *2.00* |
| 98 | CD309 | 1sh blue green | .35 | *.45* |
| | | *Nos. 95-98 (4)* | 3.35 | 5.55 |

**Types of 1938 Overprinted in Black or Carmine**

On A6

On A7-A8

*Perf. 13½x14, 13x12½*

**1950, Nov. 10** **Wmk. 4**

| | | | | |
|---|---|---|---|---|
| 99 | A6 | 1p carmine | .25 | .25 |
| 100 | A6 | 1½p orange | .25 | *.55* |
| *a.* | | Wmk. 4a (error) | 1,450. | |
| *b.* | | Wmk. 4, no crown (error) | 3,400. | |
| 101 | A6 | 2½p ultra | .25 | .25 |
| 102 | A7 | 3p car & pale lilac | .80 | *.85* |
| 103 | A8 | 6p rose lil & dl grn | .45 | .25 |
| 104 | A7 | 1sh grn & gray blk (C) | 1.50 | .40 |
| | | *Nos. 99-104 (6)* | 3.50 | 2.55 |

300th anniv. of the settlement of Anguilla.

**University Issue**
Common Design Types
Inscribed: "St. Kitts-Nevis"

*Perf. 14x14½*

**1951, Feb. 16** **Engr.** **Wmk. 4**

| | | | | |
|---|---|---|---|---|
| 105 | CD310 | 3c org yel & gray blk | .45 | .25 |
| 106 | CD311 | 12c red violet & aqua | .45 | *2.00* |

**St. Christopher-Nevis-Anguilla**

Bath House and Spa, Nevis — A10

Map — A11

Designs: 2c, Warner Park, St. Kitts. 4c, Brimstone Hill, St. Kitts. 5c, Nevis. 6c, Pinney's Beach, Nevis. 12c, Sir Thomas Warner's Tomb. 24c, Old Road Bay, St. Kitts. 48c, Picking Cotton. 60c, Treasury, St. Kitts. $1.20, Salt Pond, Anguilla. $4.80, Sugar Mill, St. Kitts.

**1952, June 14** *Perf. 12½*

| | | | | |
|---|---|---|---|---|
| 107 | A10 | 1c ocher & dp grn | .25 | *3.00* |
| 108 | A10 | 2c emerald | 1.00 | 1.00 |
| 109 | A11 | 3c purple & red | .40 | *1.25* |
| 110 | A10 | 4c red | .25 | .25 |
| 111 | A10 | 5c gray & ultra | .40 | .25 |
| 112 | A10 | 6c deep ultra | .40 | .25 |
| 113 | A11 | 12c redsh brn & dp blue | 1.25 | .25 |
| 114 | A10 | 24c car & gray blk | .40 | .25 |
| 115 | A10 | 48c vio brn & ol bis | 3.00 | *6.50* |
| 116 | A10 | 60c dp grn & och | 2.25 | *4.50* |
| 117 | A10 | $1.20 dp ultra & dp green | 8.00 | 6.50 |
| 118 | A10 | $4.80 car & emer | 15.00 | *20.00* |
| | | *Nos. 107-118 (12)* | 32.60 | 44.00 |

**Coronation Issue**
Common Design Type

**1953, June 2** *Perf. 13½x13*

| | | | | |
|---|---|---|---|---|
| 119 | CD312 | 2c brt green & blk | .35 | .25 |

**Types of 1952 with Portrait of Queen Elizabeth II**

½c, Salt Pond, Anguilla. 8c, Sombrero Lighthouse. $2.40, Map of Anguilla & Dependencies.

**1954-57 Engr. *Perf. 12½***

**120** A10 ½c gray olive ('56) .40 .25
**121** A10 1c ocher & dp grn .25 .25
*a.* Horiz. pair, imperf. vert. *9,000.*
**122** A10 2c emerald 1.00 .25
**123** A11 3c purple & red .80 .25
**124** A10 4c red .25 .25
**125** A10 5c gray & ultra .25 .25
**126** A10 6c deep ultra 1.50 .25
**127** A11 8c dark gray ('57) 3.00 .30
**128** A11 12c redsh brn & dp blue .25 .25
**129** A10 24c carmine & blk .25 .25
**130** A10 48c brn & ol bister 1.50 .65
**131** A10 60c dp grn & ocher 5.25 *7.50*
**132** A10 $1.20 dp ultra & dp green 18.00 4.00
**133** A10 $2.40 red org & blk ('57) 16.00 16.00
**134** A10 $4.80 car & emer 19.00 11.00
*Nos. 120-134 (15)* 67.70 41.70

Issued: 24c-$1.20, $4.80, 12/1/54; ½c, 7/3/56; 8c, $2.40, 2/1/57; others, 3/1/54.

Alexander Hamilton and Nevis Scene A12

**1957, Jan. 11 *Perf. 12½***

**135** A12 24c dp ultra & yel grn .55 .25

Bicent. of the birth of Alexander Hamilton.

**West Indies Federation**
Common Design Type
***Perf. 11½x11***

**1958, Apr. 22 Engr. Wmk. 314**

**136** CD313 3c green .75 .35
**137** CD313 6c blue 1.00 *2.25*
**138** CD313 12c carmine rose 1.25 .50
*Nos. 136-138 (3)* 3.00 3.10

Federation of the West Indies, Apr. 22, 1958.

Stamp of Nevis, 1861 A13

Designs (Stamps of Nevis, 1861 issue): 8c, 4p stamp. 12c, 6p stamp. 24c, 1sh stamp.

**1961, July 15 *Perf. 14***

**139** A13 2c green & brown .25 .25
**140** A13 8c blue & pale brown .30 .25
**141** A13 12c carmine & gray .35 .25
**142** A13 24c orange & green .50 .50
*Nos. 139-142 (4)* 1.40 1.25

Centenary of the first stamps of Nevis.

**Red Cross Centenary Issue**
Common Design Type

**1963, Sept. 2 Litho. *Perf. 13***

**143** CD315 3c black & red .25 .25
**144** CD315 12c ultra & red .65 .65

New Lighthouse, Sombrero — A14

Loading Sugar Cane, St. Kitts A15

Designs: 2c, Pall Mall Square, Basseterre. 3c, Gateway, Brimstone Hill Fort, St. Kitts. 4c, Nelson's Spring, Nevis. 5c, Grammar School, St. Kitts. 6c, Mt. Misery Crater, St. Kitts. 10c, Hibiscus. 15c, Sea Island cotton, Nevis. 20c, Boat building, Anguilla. 25c, White-crowned pigeon. 50c, St. George's Church tower, Basseterre. 60c, Alexander Hamilton. $1, Map of St. Kitts-Nevis. $2.50, Map of Anguilla. $5, Arms of St. Christopher-Nevis-Anguilla.

**1963, Nov. 20 Photo. *Perf. 14***

**145** A14 ½c blue & dk brn .25 .25
**146** A15 1c multicolored .25 .25
**147** A14 2c multicolored .25 .25
*a.* Yellow omitted *300.00*
**148** A14 3c multicolored .25 .25
**149** A15 4c multicolored .25 .25
**150** A15 5c multicolored 3.00 .25
**151** A15 6c multicolored .25 .25
**152** A15 10c multicolored .25 .25
**153** A14 15c multicolored .70 .25
**154** A15 20c multicolored .30 .25
**155** A14 25c multicolored 2.25 .25
**156** A15 50c multicolored .60 .35
**157** A14 60c multicolored 1.10 .40
**158** A14 $1 multicolored 2.50 .55
**159** A15 $2.50 multicolored 2.75 2.75
**160** A14 $5 multicolored 7.00 7.00
*Nos. 145-160 (16)* 21.95 13.80

For overprints see Nos. 161-162.

**1967-69 Wmk. 314 Sideways**

*145a* A14 ½c ('69) .25 *2.00*
*147b* A14 2c 1.75 .25
*148a* A14 3c ('68) .35 .25
*153a* A14 15c ('68) .90 .45
*155a* A14 25c ('68) 2.50 .25
*158a* A14 $1 ('68) 6.00 4.00
*Nos. 145a-158a (6)* 11.75 7.20

**Nos. 148 and 155 Overprinted: "ARTS / FESTIVAL / ST. KITTS / 1964"**

**1964, Sept. 14**

**161** A14 3c multicolored .25 .25
**162** A14 25c multicolored .25 .25

**ITU Issue**
Common Design Type
***Perf. 11x11½***

**1965, May 17 Litho. Wmk. 314**

**163** CD317 2c bister & rose red .25 .25
**164** CD317 50c grnsh blue & ol .35 .35

**Intl. Cooperation Year Issue**
Common Design Type

**1965, Oct. 25 *Perf. 14½***

**165** CD318 2c blue grn & claret .25 .30
**166** CD318 25c lt violet & green .55 .30

**Churchill Memorial Issue**
Common Design Type

**1966, Jan. 24 Photo. *Perf. 14***
**Design in Black, Gold and Carmine Rose**

**167** CD319 ½c bright blue .25 *.85*
*a.* Denomination omitted 500.00
**168** CD319 3c green .25 .25
**169** CD319 15c brown .40 .30
**170** CD319 25c violet .60 .30
*Nos. 167-170 (4)* 1.50 1.70

**Royal Visit Issue**
Common Design Type

**1966, Feb. 14 Litho. *Perf. 11x12***

**171** CD320 3c violet blue .25 *.35*
**172** CD320 25c dk carmine rose .65 .40

**World Cup Soccer Issue**
Common Design Type

**1966, July 1 Litho. *Perf. 14***

**173** CD321 6c multicolored .35 .40
**174** CD321 25c multicolored .50 .40

Festival Emblem With Dolphins — A16

**Unwmk.**

**1966, Aug. 15 Photo. *Perf. 14***

**175** A16 3c gold, grn, yel & blk .25 .25
**176** A16 25c silver, grn, yel & blk .30 .30

Arts Festival of 1966.

**WHO Headquarters Issue**
Common Design Type

**1966, Sept. 20 Litho. *Perf. 14***

**177** CD322 3c multicolored .25 .25
**178** CD322 40c multicolored .35 .35

**UNESCO Anniversary Issue**
Common Design Type

**1966, Dec. 1 Litho. *Perf. 14***

**179** CD323 3c "Education" .25 .25
**180** CD323 6c "Science" .25 .25
**181** CD323 40c "Culture" .40 .40
*Nos. 179-181 (3)* .90 .90

**Independent State**

Government Headquarters, Basseterre — A17

Designs: 10c, Flag and map of Anguilla, St. Christopher and Nevis. 25c, Coat of Arms.

**Wmk. 314**

**1967, July 1 Photo. *Perf. 14½***

**182** A17 3c multicolored .25 .25
**183** A17 10c multicolored .25 .25
**184** A17 25c multicolored .25 .25
*Nos. 182-184 (3)* .75 .75

Achievement of independence, Feb. 27, 1967.

Charles Wesley, Cross and Palm — A18

3c, John Wesley. 40c, Thomas Coke.

**1967, Dec. 1 Litho. *Perf. 13x13½***

**185** A18 3c dp lilac, dp car & blk .25 .25
**186** A18 25c ultra, grnsh blue & blk .25 .25
**187** A18 40c ocher, yellow & blk .25 .25
*Nos. 185-187 (3)* .75 .75

Attainment of autonomy by the Methodist Church in the Caribbean and the Americas, and for the opening of headquarters near St. John's, Antigua, May 1967.

Cargo Ship and Plane A19

***Perf. 13½x13***

**1968, July 30 Litho. Wmk. 314**

**188** A19 25c multicolored .25 .25
**189** A19 50c brt blue & multi .45 .45

Issued to publicize the organization of the Caribbean Free Trade Area, CARIFTA.

Martin Luther King, Jr. — A20

***Perf. 12x12½***

**1968, Sept. 30 Litho. Wmk. 314**

**190** A20 50c multicolored .45 .35

Dr. Martin Luther King, Jr. (1929-68), American civil rights leader.

Mystical Nativity, by Botticelli — A21

Christmas (Paintings): 25c, 50c, The Adoration of the Magi, by Rubens.

***Perf. 14½x14***

**1968, Nov. 27 Photo. Wmk. 314**

**191** A21 12c brt violet & multi .25 .25
**192** A21 25c multicolored .25 .25
**193** A21 40c gray & multi .25 .25
**194** A21 50c crimson & multi .25 .25
*Nos. 191-194 (4)* 1.00 1.00

Snook A22

Fish: 12c, Needlefish (gar). 40c, Horse-eye jack. 50c, Red snapper. The 6c is misinscribed "tarpon."

***Perf. 14x14½***

**1969, Feb. 25 Photo. Wmk. 314**

**195** A22 6c brt green & multi .25 .25
**196** A22 12c blue & multi .30 .25
**197** A22 40c gray blue & multi .30 .25
**198** A22 50c multicolored .40 .30
*Nos. 195-198 (4)* 1.25 1.05

Arms of Sir Thomas Warner and Map of Islands — A23

Designs: 25c, Warner's tomb in St. Kitts. 40c, Warner's commission from Charles I.

**1969, Sept. 1 Litho. *Perf. 13½***

**199** A23 20c multicolored .25 .25
**200** A23 25c multicolored .25 .25
**201** A23 40c multicolored .25 .25
*Nos. 199-201 (3)* .75 .75

Issued in memory of Sir Thomas Warner, first Governor of St. Kitts-Nevis, Barbados and Montserrat.

Adoration of the Kings, by Jan Mostaert — A24

Christmas (Painting): 40c, 50c, Adoration of the Kings, by Geertgen tot Sint Jans.

**1969, Nov. 17** ***Perf. 13½***

| | | | | |
|---|---|---|---|---|
| **202** | A24 | 10c olive & multi | .25 | .25 |
| **203** | A24 | 25c violet & multi | .25 | .25 |
| **204** | A24 | 40c yellow grn & multi | .25 | .25 |
| **205** | A24 | 50c maroon & multi | .25 | .25 |
| | | *Nos. 202-205 (4)* | 1.00 | 1.00 |

Pirates Burying Treasure, Frigate Bay — A25

Caravels, 16th Century A26

Designs: 1c, English two-decker, 1650. 2c, Flags of England, Spain, France, Holland and Portugal. 3c, Hilt of 17th cent. rapier. 5c, Henry Morgan and fire boats. 6c, The pirate L'Ollonois and a carrack (pirate vessel). 10c, Smugglers' ship. 15c, Spanish 17th cent. piece of eight and map of Caribbean. 20c, Garrison and ship cannon and map of Spanish Main. 25c, Humphrey Cole's astrolabe, 1574. 50c, Flintlock pistol and map of Spanish Main. 60c, Dutch Flute (ship). $1, Capt. Bartholomew Roberts and document with death sentence for his crew. $2.50, Railing piece (small cannon), 17th cent. and map of Spanish Main. $5, Francis Drake, John Hawkins and ships. $10, Edward Teach (Blackbeard) and his capture.

### Wmk. 314 Upright (A25), Sideways (A26)

**1970, Feb. 1** **Litho.** ***Perf. 14***

| | | | | |
|---|---|---|---|---|
| **206** | A25 | ½c multicolored | .25 | .25 |
| **207** | A25 | 1c multicolored | .40 | .25 |
| **208** | A25 | 2c multicolored | .25 | .25 |
| **209** | A25 | 3c multicolored | .25 | .25 |
| **210** | A26 | 4c multicolored | .25 | .25 |
| **211** | A26 | 5c multicolored | .40 | .25 |
| **212** | A26 | 6c multicolored | .40 | .25 |
| **213** | A26 | 10c multicolored | .40 | .25 |
| **214** | A25 | 15c Hispanianum | 2.25 | .50 |
| **215** | A25 | 15c Hispaniarum | 4.50 | .25 |
| **216** | A26 | 20c multicolored | .45 | .25 |
| **217** | A25 | 25c multicolored | .40 | .25 |
| **218** | A26 | 50c multicolored | .85 | .90 |
| **219** | A25 | 60c multicolored | 1.50 | .80 |
| **220** | A25 | $1 multicolored | 1.50 | .80 |
| **221** | A26 | $2.50 multicolored | 1.50 | *4.50* |
| **222** | A26 | $5 multicolored | 2.75 | *5.00* |
| | | *Nos. 206-222 (17)* | 18.30 | 15.25 |

Coin inscription was misspelled on No. 214, corrected on No. 215 (issued Sept. 8).

### Wmk. 314 Sideways (A25), Upright (A26)

**1973-74**

| | | | | |
|---|---|---|---|---|
| *206a* | A25 | ½c multicolored | .25 | *2.00* |
| *208a* | A25 | 2c multicolored | .25 | *2.00* |
| *209a* | A25 | 3c multicolored | .25 | *1.50* |
| *211a* | A26 | 5c multicolored | .35 | *1.75* |
| *212a* | A26 | 6c multicolored | .40 | *.80* |
| *213a* | A26 | 10c multicolored | .50 | *.80* |
| *215a* | A25 | 15c multicolored | .85 | *.85* |
| *216a* | A26 | 20c multicolored | 1.00 | *1.40* |
| *217a* | A25 | 25c multicolored | 1.25 | *1.75* |
| *218a* | A26 | 50c multicolored | 1.75 | *1.75* |
| *220a* | A25 | $1 multicolored | 3.25 | *3.75* |
| **222A** | A26 | $10 multi ('74) | 21.00 | *13.00* |
| | | *Nos. 206a-220a,222A (12)* | 31.10 | 31.35 |

Issue dates: $10, Nov. 16; others, Sept. 12.

**1975-77** **Wmk. 373**

| | | | | |
|---|---|---|---|---|
| *207b* | A25 | 1c multi ('77) | .40 | .25 |
| *209b* | A25 | 3c multi ('76) | .25 | .25 |
| *210b* | A26 | 4c multi ('76) | .25 | .25 |
| *211b* | A26 | 5c multicolored | .30 | .35 |
| *212b* | A26 | 6c multicolored | 1.00 | .25 |
| *213b* | A26 | 10c multi ('76) | .45 | .25 |
| *215b* | A25 | 15c multi ('76) | .55 | .25 |
| *216b* | A26 | 20c multicolored | 2.75 | *8.00* |
| *219b* | A25 | 60c multi ('76) | 9.50 | 2.00 |
| *220b* | A25 | $1 multi ('77) | 8.00 | 3.00 |
| | | *Nos. 207b-220b (10)* | 23.45 | 14.85 |

Pip Meeting Convict, from "Great Expectations" — A27

Designs: 20c, Miss Havisham from "Great Expectations." 25c, Dickens' birthplace, Portsmouth, vert. 40c, Charles Dickens, vert.

***Perf. 13x13½, 13½x13***

**1970, May 1** **Litho.** **Wmk. 314**

| | | | | |
|---|---|---|---|---|
| **223** | A27 | 4c gold, Prus blue & brn | .25 | *.80* |
| **224** | A27 | 20c gold, claret & brn | .25 | .25 |
| **225** | A27 | 25c gold, olive & brn | .25 | .25 |
| **226** | A27 | 40c dk blue, gold & brn | .25 | *.35* |
| | | *Nos. 223-226 (4)* | 1.00 | 1.65 |

Charles Dickens (1812-70), English novelist.

Local Steel Band A28

25c, Local string band. 40c, "A Midsummer Night's Dream," 1963 performance.

**1970, Aug. 1** ***Perf. 13½***

| | | | | |
|---|---|---|---|---|
| **227** | A28 | 20c multicolored | .25 | .25 |
| **228** | A28 | 25c multicolored | .25 | .25 |
| **229** | A28 | 40c multicolored | .25 | .25 |
| | | *Nos. 227-229 (3)* | .75 | .75 |

Issued to publicize the 1970 Arts Festival.

St. Christopher No. 1 and St. Kitts Post Office, 1970 — A29

Designs: 20c, 25c, St. Christopher Nos. 1 and 3. 50c, St. Christopher No. 3 and St. Kitts postmark, Sept. 2, 1871.

**Wmk. 314**

**1970, Sept. 14** **Litho.** ***Perf. 14½***

| | | | | |
|---|---|---|---|---|
| **230** | A29 | ½c green & rose | .25 | .25 |
| **231** | A29 | 20c vio bl, rose & grn | .25 | .25 |
| **232** | A29 | 25c brown, rose & grn | .25 | .25 |
| **233** | A29 | 50c black, grn & dk red | .30 | *.45* |
| | | *Nos. 230-233 (4)* | 1.05 | 1.20 |

Centenary of stamps of St. Christopher.

Holy Family, by Anthony van Dyck — A30

Christmas: 3c, 40c, Adoration of the Shepherds, by Frans Floris.

**1970, Nov. 16** ***Perf. 14***

| | | | | |
|---|---|---|---|---|
| **234** | A30 | 3c multicolored | .25 | .25 |
| **235** | A30 | 20c ocher & multi | .25 | .25 |
| **236** | A30 | 25c dull red & multi | .25 | .25 |
| **237** | A30 | 40c green & multi | .25 | .25 |
| | | *Nos. 234-237 (4)* | 1.00 | 1.00 |

Monkey Fiddle A31

Flowers: 20c, Mountain violets. 30c, Morning glory. 50c, Fringed epidendrum.

**1971, Mar. 1** **Litho.** ***Perf. 14***

| | | | | |
|---|---|---|---|---|
| **238** | A31 | ½c multicolored | .25 | *.40* |
| **239** | A31 | 20c multicolored | .25 | .25 |
| **240** | A31 | 30c multicolored | .25 | .25 |
| **241** | A31 | 50c multicolored | .30 | *1.00* |
| | | *Nos. 238-241 (4)* | 1.05 | 1.90 |

Chateau de Poincy, St. Kitts — A32

Designs: 20c, Royal poinciana. 50c, De Poincy's coat of arms, vert.

**1971, June 1** **Litho.** **Wmk. 314**

| | | | | |
|---|---|---|---|---|
| **242** | A32 | 20c green & multi | .25 | .25 |
| **243** | A32 | 30c dull yellow & multi | .25 | .25 |
| **244** | A32 | 50c brown & multi | .25 | .25 |
| | | *Nos. 242-244 (3)* | .75 | .75 |

Philippe de Longvilliers de Poincy became first governor of French possessions in the Antilles in 1639.

East Yorks A33

Designs: 20c, Royal Artillery. 30c, French Infantry. 50c, Royal Scots.

**1971, Sept. 1** ***Perf. 14***

| | | | | |
|---|---|---|---|---|
| **245** | A33 | ½c black & multi | .25 | .25 |
| **246** | A33 | 20c black & multi | .30 | .25 |
| **247** | A33 | 30c black & multi | .35 | .25 |
| **248** | A33 | 50c black & multi | .45 | .25 |
| | | *Nos. 245-248 (4)* | 1.35 | 1.00 |

Siege of Brimstone Hill, 1782.

Crucifixion, by Quentin Massys — A34

***Perf. 14x13½***

**1972, Apr. 1** **Litho.** **Wmk. 314**

| | | | | |
|---|---|---|---|---|
| **249** | A34 | 4c brick red & multi | .25 | .25 |
| **250** | A34 | 20c gray green & multi | .25 | .25 |
| **251** | A34 | 30c dull blue & multi | .25 | .25 |
| **252** | A34 | 40c lt brown & multi | .25 | .25 |
| | | *Nos. 249-252 (4)* | 1.00 | 1.00 |

Easter 1972.

Madonna and Child, by Bergognone A35

Paintings: 20c, Adoration of the Kings, by Jacopo da Bassano, horiz. 25c, Adoration of the Shepherds, by Il Domenichino. 40c, Madonna and Child, by Fiorenzo di Lorenzo.

**1972, Oct. 2** ***Perf. 13½x14, 14x13½***

| | | | | |
|---|---|---|---|---|
| **253** | A35 | 3c gray green & multi | .25 | .25 |
| **254** | A35 | 20c deep plum & multi | .25 | .25 |
| **255** | A35 | 25c sepia & multi | .25 | .25 |
| **256** | A35 | 40c red & multi | .25 | .25 |
| | | *Nos. 253-256 (4)* | 1.00 | 1.00 |

Christmas 1972.

### Silver Wedding Issue, 1972

Common Design Type

Queen Elizabeth II, Prince Philip, pelicans.

**1972, Nov. 20** **Photo.** ***Perf. 14x14½***

| | | | | |
|---|---|---|---|---|
| **257** | CD324 | 20c car rose & multi | .30 | .25 |
| **258** | CD324 | 25c ultra & multi | .35 | .25 |

Warner Landing at St. Kitts — A36

Designs: 25c, Settlers growing tobacco. 40c, Building fort at "Old Road." $2.50, Warner's ship off St. Kitts, Jan. 28, 1623.

**1973, Jan. 28** **Litho.** ***Perf. 14x13½***

| | | | | |
|---|---|---|---|---|
| **259** | A36 | 4c pink & multi | .25 | .25 |
| **260** | A36 | 25c brown & multi | .25 | .25 |
| **261** | A36 | 40c blue & multi | .25 | .25 |
| **262** | A36 | $2.50 multicolored | .85 | *1.10* |
| | | *Nos. 259-262 (4)* | 1.60 | 1.85 |

350th anniversary of the landing of Sir Thomas Warner at St. Kitts.

For overprints see Nos. 266-269.

The Last Supper, by Juan de Juanes — A37

Easter (The Last Supper, by): 4c, Titian, vert. 25c, ascribed to Roberti, vert.

***Perf. 14x13½, 13½x14***

**1973, Apr. 16** **Photo.** **Wmk. 314**

| | | | | |
|---|---|---|---|---|
| **263** | A37 | 4c blue black & multi | .25 | .25 |
| **264** | A37 | 25c multicolored | .25 | .25 |
| **265** | A37 | $2.50 purple & multi | .80 | .60 |
| | | *Nos. 263-265 (3)* | 1.30 | 1.10 |

### Nos. 259-262 Overprinted

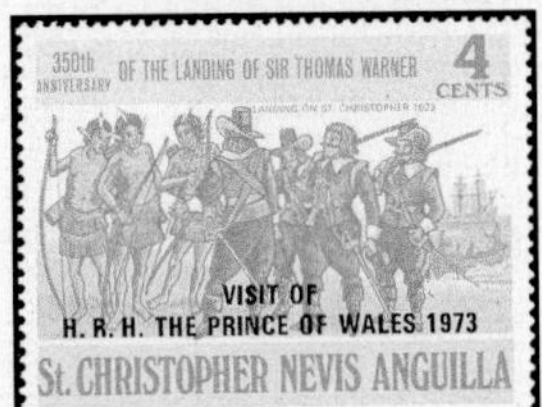

**1973, May 31 Litho. *Perf. 14x13½***

| | | | | |
|---|---|---|---|---|
| **266** | A36 | 4c pink & multi | .25 | .25 |
| **267** | A36 | 25c brown & multi | .25 | .25 |
| **268** | A36 | 40c blue & multi | .25 | .25 |
| **269** | A36 | $2.50 multicolored | .30 | .30 |
| | | *Nos. 266-269 (4)* | 1.05 | 1.05 |

Visit of Prince Charles, May 1973.

Harbor Scene and St. Kitts-Nevis No. 3 — A38

25c, Sugar mill and #2. 40c, Unloading of boat and #1. $2.50, Rock carvings and #5.

**1973, Oct. 1 Litho. *Perf. 13½x14***

| | | | | |
|---|---|---|---|---|
| **270** | A38 | 4c salmon & multi | .25 | .25 |
| **271** | A38 | 25c lt blue & multi | .40 | .30 |
| **272** | A38 | 40c multicolored | .60 | .50 |
| **273** | A38 | $2.50 multicolored | 1.50 | 1.00 |
| *a.* | | Souvenir sheet of 4, #270-273 | 2.75 | *4.50* |
| | | *Nos. 270-273 (4)* | 2.75 | 2.05 |

70th anniv. of 1st St. Kitts-Nevis stamps.

**Princess Anne's Wedding Issue**

Common Design Type

**1973, Nov. 14 *Perf. 14***

| | | | | |
|---|---|---|---|---|
| **274** | CD325 | 25c brt green & multi | .25 | .25 |
| **275** | CD325 | 40c citron & multi | .25 | .25 |

Virgin and Child, by Murillo — A39

Christmas (Paintings): 40c, Holy Family, by Anton Raphael Mengs. 60c, Holy Family, by Sassoferrato. $1, Holy Family, by Filippino Lippi, horiz.

**1973, Dec. 1 Litho. *Perf. 14x13½***

| | | | | |
|---|---|---|---|---|
| **276** | A39 | 4c brt blue & multi | .25 | .25 |
| **277** | A39 | 40c orange & multi | .25 | .25 |
| **278** | A39 | 60c multicolored | .25 | .25 |
| **279** | A39 | $1 multicolored | .35 | .35 |
| | | *Nos. 276-279 (4)* | 1.10 | 1.10 |

Christ Carrying Cross, by Sebastiano del Piombo — A40

Easter: 25c, Crucifixion, by Goya. 40c, Trinity, by Diego Ribera. $2.50, Burial of Christ, by Fra Bartolomeo, horiz.

**1974, Apr. 8 *Perf. 13***

| | | | | |
|---|---|---|---|---|
| **280** | A40 | 4c olive & multi | .25 | .25 |
| **281** | A40 | 25c lt blue & multi | .25 | .25 |
| **282** | A40 | 40c purple & multi | .25 | .25 |
| **283** | A40 | $2.50 gray & multi | .90 | *1.00* |
| | | *Nos. 280-283 (4)* | 1.65 | 1.75 |

University Center, St. Kitts, Chancellor Hugh Wooding — A41

**1974, June 1 *Perf. 13½***

| | | | | |
|---|---|---|---|---|
| **284** | A41 | 10c blue & multi | .25 | .25 |
| **285** | A41 | $1 pink & multi | .25 | .25 |
| *a.* | | Souvenir sheet of 2, #284-285 | .55 | *.65* |

University of the West Indies, 25th anniv.

Nurse Explaining Family Planning — A42

Designs: 4c, Globe and hands reaching up, vert. 40c, Family, vert. $2.50, WPY emblem and scale balancing embryo and world.

**Wmk. 314**

**1974, Aug. 5 Litho. *Perf. 14***

| | | | | |
|---|---|---|---|---|
| **286** | A42 | 4c blk, blue & brn | .25 | .25 |
| **287** | A42 | 25c multicolored | .25 | .25 |
| **288** | A42 | 40c multicolored | .25 | .25 |
| **289** | A42 | $2.50 lilac & multi | .30 | *.55* |
| | | *Nos. 286-289 (4)* | 1.05 | 1.30 |

Family planning and World Population Week, Aug. 4-10.

Churchill as Lieutenant, 21st Lancers — A43

Knight of the Garter — A44

Designs: 25c, Churchill as Prime Minister. 60c, Churchill Statue, Parliament Square, London.

**1974, Nov. 30**

| | | | | |
|---|---|---|---|---|
| **290** | A43 | 4c dull violet & multi | .25 | .25 |
| **291** | A43 | 25c yellow & multi | .25 | .25 |
| **292** | A44 | 40c lt blue & multi | .25 | .25 |
| **293** | A44 | 60c lt blue & multi | .25 | .25 |
| *a.* | | Souvenir sheet of 4, #290-293 | 1.05 | *1.25* |
| | | *Nos. 290-293 (4)* | 1.00 | 1.00 |

Sir Winston Churchill (1874-1965).

Souvenir Sheets

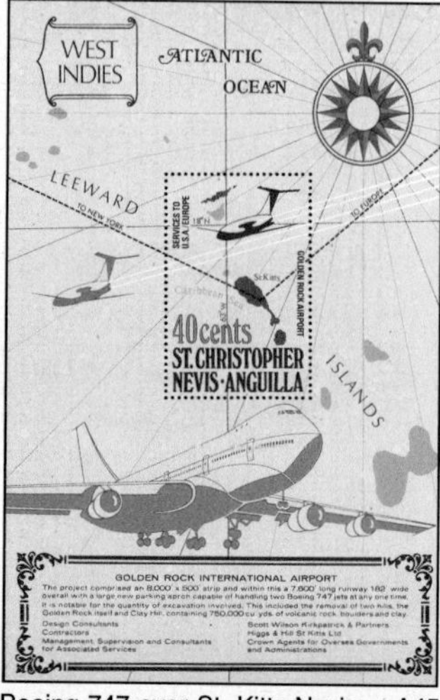


Boeing 747 over St. Kitts-Nevis — A45

**1974, Dec. 16 *Perf. 14x13½***

| | | | | |
|---|---|---|---|---|
| **294** | A45 | 40c multicolored | .90 | .90 |
| **295** | A45 | 45c multicolored | 1.00 | 1.00 |

Opening of Golden Rock Intl. Airport.

The Last Supper, by Doré — A46

Easter: 25c, Jesus mocked. 40c, Jesus falling beneath the Cross. $1, Raising the Cross. Designs based on Bible illustrations by Paul Gustave Doré (1833-1883).

**1975, Mar. 24 *Perf. 14½***

| | | | | |
|---|---|---|---|---|
| **296** | A46 | 4c ultra & multi | .25 | .25 |
| **297** | A46 | 25c lt blue & multi | .25 | .25 |
| **298** | A46 | 40c bister & multi | .25 | .25 |
| **299** | A46 | $1 salmon pink & multi | .25 | .25 |
| | | *Nos. 296-299 (4)* | 1.00 | 1.00 |

ECCA Headquarters, Basseterre, and Map of St. Kitts — A47

Designs: 25c, Specimen of $1 note, issued by ECCA. 40c, St. Kitts half dollar, 1801, and $4 coin, 1875. 45c, Nevis "9 dogs" coin, 1801, and 2c, 5c, coins, 1975.

***Perf. 13½x14***

**1975, June 2 Wmk. 373**

| | | | | |
|---|---|---|---|---|
| **300** | A47 | 12c orange & multi | .25 | .25 |
| **301** | A47 | 25c olive & multi | .25 | .25 |
| **302** | A47 | 40c vermilion & multi | .25 | .25 |
| **303** | A47 | 45c brt blue & multi | .25 | .25 |
| | | *Nos. 300-303 (4)* | 1.00 | 1.00 |

East Caribbean Currency Authority Headquarters, Basseterre, opening.

Evangeline Booth, Salvation Army — A48

Designs (IWY Emblem and): 25c, Sylvia Pankhurst, suffragette. 40c, Marie Curie, scientist. $2.50, Lady Annie Allen, teacher.

***Perf. 14x14½***

**1975, Sept. 15 Litho. Wmk. 314**

| | | | | |
|---|---|---|---|---|
| **304** | A48 | 4c orange brn & blk | .40 | .25 |
| **305** | A48 | 25c lilac pur & blk | .50 | .25 |
| **306** | A48 | 40c blue, vio bl & blk | 2.40 | .80 |
| **307** | A48 | $2.50 yellow brn & blk | 1.75 | *4.25* |
| | | *Nos. 304-307 (4)* | 5.05 | 5.55 |

International Women's Year 1975.

Golfer Swinging Club — A49

**1975, Nov. 1 *Perf. 14***

| | | | | |
|---|---|---|---|---|
| **308** | A49 | 4c rose red & blk | .85 | .25 |
| **309** | A49 | 25c yellow & blk | 1.15 | .25 |
| **310** | A49 | 40c emerald & blk | 1.35 | .40 |
| **311** | A49 | $1 blue & blk | 2.10 | *2.50* |
| | | *Nos. 308-311 (4)* | 5.45 | 3.40 |

Opening of Frigate Bay Golf Course.

St. Paul, by Sacchi Pier Francesco — A50

Christmas (Paintings, details): 40c, St. James, by Bonifazio di Pitati. 45c, St. John, by Pier Francesco Mola. $1, Virgin Mary, by Raphael.

**Wmk. 373**

**1975, Dec. 1 Litho. *Perf. 14***

| | | | | |
|---|---|---|---|---|
| **312** | A50 | 25c ultra & multi | .30 | .25 |
| **313** | A50 | 40c multicolored | .45 | .40 |
| **314** | A50 | 45c red brown & multi | .50 | .45 |
| **315** | A50 | $1 gold & multi | 1.25 | *2.25* |
| | | *Nos. 312-315 (4)* | 2.50 | 3.35 |

The Crucifixion — A51

The Last Supper — A52

Stained Glass Windows: No. 316, Virgin Mary. No. 317, Christ on the Cross. No. 318, St. John. 40c, The Last Supper (different). $1, Baptism of Christ.

*Perf. 14x13½*

**1976, Apr. 14 Litho. Wmk. 373**

| No. | Type | Description | Unused | Used |
|---|---|---|---|---|
| 316 | | 4c black & multi | .25 | .25 |
| 317 | | 4c black & multi | .25 | .25 |
| 318 | | 4c black & multi | .25 | .25 |
| a. | A51 | Triptych, #316-318 | 1.00 | 1.50 |

*Perf. 14½*

| No. | Type | Description | Unused | Used |
|---|---|---|---|---|
| 319 | A52 | 25c black & multi | .30 | .30 |
| 320 | A52 | 40c black & multi | .35 | .30 |
| 321 | A52 | $1 black & multi | .70 | .80 |
| | | *Nos. 319-321 (3)* | 1.35 | 1.40 |

Easter 1976. No. 318a has continuous design.

Map of West Indies, Bats, Wicket and Ball A52a

Prudential Cup — A52b

**Unwmk.**

**1976, July 8 Litho. *Perf. 14***

| No. | Type | Description | Unused | Used |
|---|---|---|---|---|
| 322 | A52a | 12c lt blue & multi | .40 | .35 |
| 323 | A52b | 40c lilac rose & blk | 1.25 | .75 |
| a. | | Souvenir sheet of 2, #322-323 | 5.00 | 5.00 |

World Cricket Cup, won by West Indies Team, 1975.

Crispus Attucks and Boston Massacre — A53

Designs: 40c, Alexander Hamilton and Battle of Yorktown. 45c, Thomas Jefferson and Declaration of Independence. $1, George Washington and Crossing of the Delaware.

**1976, July 26 Litho. Wmk. 373**

| No. | Type | Description | Unused | Used |
|---|---|---|---|---|
| 324 | A53 | 20c gray & multi | .25 | .25 |
| 325 | A53 | 40c gray & multi | .30 | .25 |
| 326 | A53 | 45c gray & multi | .30 | .25 |
| 327 | A53 | $1 gray & multi | .65 | .85 |
| | | *Nos. 324-327 (4)* | 1.50 | 1.60 |

American Bicentennial.

Nativity, Sforza Book of Hours — A54

Christmas (Paintings): 40c, Virgin and Child, by Bernardino Pintoricchio. 45c, Our Lady of Good Children, by Ford Maddox Brown. $1, Christ Child, by Margaret W. Tarrant.

**1976, Nov. 1 *Perf. 14***

| No. | Type | Description | Unused | Used |
|---|---|---|---|---|
| 328 | A54 | 20c purple & multi | .25 | .25 |
| 329 | A54 | 40c dk blue & multi | .25 | .25 |
| 330 | A54 | 45c multicolored | .25 | .25 |
| 331 | A54 | $1 multicolored | .30 | .50 |
| | | *Nos. 328-331 (4)* | 1.05 | 1.25 |

Queen Planting Tree, 1966 Visit — A55

Designs: 55c, The scepter. $1.50, Bishops paying homage to the Queen.

**1977, Feb. 7 Litho. *Perf. 14x13½***

| No. | Type | Description | Unused | Used |
|---|---|---|---|---|
| 332 | A55 | 50c multicolored | .25 | .25 |
| 333 | A55 | 55c multicolored | .25 | .25 |
| 334 | A55 | $1.50 multicolored | .25 | .50 |
| | | *Nos. 332-334 (3)* | .75 | 1.00 |

25th anniv. of the reign of Elizabeth II.

Christ on the Cross, by Niccolo di Liberatore — A56

Easter: 30c, Resurrection (Imitator of Mantegna). 50c, Resurrection, by Ugolino, horiz. $1, Christ Rising from Tomb, by Gaudenzio.

**Wmk. 373**

**1977, Apr. 1 Litho. *Perf. 14***

| No. | Type | Description | Unused | Used |
|---|---|---|---|---|
| 335 | A56 | 25c yellow & multi | .25 | .25 |
| 336 | A56 | 30c deep blue & multi | .25 | .25 |
| 337 | A56 | 50c olive green & multi | .25 | .25 |
| 338 | A56 | $1 red & multi | .25 | .25 |
| | | *Nos. 335-338 (4)* | 1.00 | 1.00 |

Estridge Mission A57

20c, Mission emblem. 40c, Basseterre Mission.

**1977, June 27 Litho. *Perf. 12½***

| No. | Type | Description | Unused | Used |
|---|---|---|---|---|
| 339 | A57 | 4c blue & black | .25 | .25 |
| 340 | A57 | 20c multicolored | .25 | .25 |
| 341 | A57 | 40c orange yel & blk | .25 | .25 |
| | | *Nos. 339-341 (3)* | .75 | .75 |

Bicentenary of Moravian Mission.

Microscope, Flask, Syringe — A58

12c, Blood, fat, nerve cells. 20c, Symbol of community participation. $1, Inoculation.

**1977, Oct. 11 Litho. *Perf. 14***

| No. | Type | Description | Unused | Used |
|---|---|---|---|---|
| 342 | A58 | 3c multicolored | .25 | .25 |
| 343 | A58 | 12c multicolored | .40 | .60 |
| 344 | A58 | 20c multicolored | .45 | .25 |
| 345 | A58 | $1 multicolored | 1.10 | 1.40 |
| | | *Nos. 342-345 (4)* | 2.20 | 2.50 |

Pan American Health Organization, 75th anniversary (PAHO).

Nativity, West Window — A59

Christmas, Stained-glass Windows, Chartres Cathedral: 6c, Three Kings. 40c, Virgin and Child. $1, Virgin and Child, Rose Window.

**1977, Nov. 15 Wmk. 373**

| No. | Type | Description | Unused | Used |
|---|---|---|---|---|
| 346 | A59 | 4c multicolored | .25 | .25 |
| 347 | A59 | 6c multicolored | .25 | .25 |
| 348 | A59 | 40c multicolored | .35 | .25 |
| 349 | A59 | $1 multicolored | .65 | .45 |
| | | *Nos. 346-349 (4)* | 1.50 | 1.20 |

Green Monkey and Young — A60

Green Monkeys: 5c, $1.50, Mother and young sitting on branch. 55c, like 4c.

**Wmk. 373**

**1978, Apr. 15 Litho. *Perf. 14½***

| No. | Type | Description | Unused | Used |
|---|---|---|---|---|
| 350 | A60 | 4c multicolored | .25 | .25 |
| 351 | A60 | 5c multicolored | .25 | .25 |
| 352 | A60 | 55c multicolored | .75 | .30 |
| 353 | A60 | $1.50 multicolored | 1.75 | 1.50 |
| | | *Nos. 350-353 (4)* | 3.00 | 2.30 |

### Elizabeth II Coronation Anniversary Issue

Common Design Types

Souvenir Sheet

**Unwmk.**

**1978, Apr. 21 Litho. *Perf. 15***

| No. | Type | Description | Unused | Used |
|---|---|---|---|---|
| 354 | | Sheet of 6 | 1.00 | 1.00 |
| a. | CD326 | $1 Falcon of Edward III | .25 | .25 |
| b. | CD327 | $1 Elizabeth II | .25 | .25 |
| c. | CD328 | $1 Pelican | .25 | .25 |

No. 354 contains 2 se-tenant strips of Nos. 354a-354c, separated by horizontal gutter with commemorative and descriptive inscriptions and showing central part of coronation procession with coach.

Tomatoes A61

Designs: 2c, Defense Force band. 5c, Radio and TV station. 10c, Technical College. 12c, TV assembly plant. 15c, Sugar cane harvest. 25c, Craft Center. 30c, Cruise ship. 40c, Sea crab and lobster. 45c, Royal St. Kitts Hotel and golf course. 50c, Pinneys Beach, Nevis. 55c, New Runway at Golden Rock. $1, Cotton pickers. $5, Brewery. $10, Pineapples and peanuts.

*Perf. 14½x14*

**1978, Sept. 8 Wmk. 373**

| No. | Type | Description | Unused | Used |
|---|---|---|---|---|
| 355 | A61 | 1c multicolored | .25 | .25 |
| 356 | A61 | 2c multicolored | .25 | .25 |
| 357 | A61 | 5c multicolored | .25 | .25 |
| 358 | A61 | 10c multicolored | .25 | .25 |
| 359 | A61 | 12c multicolored | .25 | .75 |
| 360 | A61 | 15c multicolored | .25 | .25 |
| 361 | A61 | 25c multicolored | .25 | .25 |
| 362 | A61 | 30c multicolored | 1.50 | 1.50 |
| 363 | A61 | 40c multicolored | .45 | .25 |
| 364 | A61 | 45c multicolored | 2.75 | 1.25 |
| 365 | A61 | 50c multicolored | .35 | .25 |
| 366 | A61 | 55c multicolored | 1.25 | .25 |
| 367 | A61 | $1 multicolored | .40 | .40 |
| 368 | A61 | $5 multicolored | .75 | 1.25 |
| 369 | A61 | $10 multicolored | 1.25 | 1.75 |
| | | *Nos. 355-369 (15)* | 10.45 | 9.15 |

For overprints see Nevis Nos. 100-112, O1-O10.

Investiture — A62

Designs: 10c, Map reading. 25c, Pitching tent. 40c, Cooking. 50c, First aid. 55c, Rev. W. A. Beckett, founder of Scouting in St. Kitts.

**Wmk. 373**

**1978, Oct. 9 Litho. *Perf. 13½***

| No. | Type | Description | Unused | Used |
|---|---|---|---|---|
| 370 | A62 | 5c multicolored | .25 | .25 |
| 371 | A62 | 10c multicolored | .25 | .25 |
| 372 | A62 | 25c multicolored | .35 | .35 |
| 373 | A62 | 40c multicolored | .45 | .50 |
| 374 | A62 | 50c multicolored | .50 | .60 |
| 375 | A62 | 55c multicolored | .60 | .65 |
| | | *Nos. 370-375 (6)* | 2.40 | 2.60 |

50th anniversary of St. Kitts-Nevis Scouting.

King Bringing Gift — A63

Christmas: 15c, 30c, King bringing gift, diff. $2.25, Three Kings paying homage to Infant Jesus.

**1978, Dec. 1 *Perf. 14x13½***

| No. | Type | Description | Unused | Used |
|---|---|---|---|---|
| 376 | A63 | 5c multicolored | .25 | .25 |
| 377 | A63 | 15c multicolored | .25 | .25 |
| 378 | A63 | 30c multicolored | .25 | .25 |
| 379 | A63 | $2.25 multicolored | .25 | .50 |
| | | *Nos. 376-379 (4)* | 1.00 | 1.25 |

Canna Coccinea — A64

Flowers: 30c, Heliconia bihai. 55c, Ruellia tuberosa. $1.50, Gesneria ventricosa.

**1979, Mar. 19 *Perf. 14***

| No. | Type | Description | Unused | Used |
|---|---|---|---|---|
| 380 | A64 | 5c multicolored | .25 | .25 |
| 381 | A64 | 30c multicolored | .40 | .40 |
| 382 | A64 | 55c multicolored | .50 | .50 |
| 383 | A64 | $1.50 multicolored | .85 | 1.60 |
| | | *Nos. 380-383 (4)* | 2.00 | 2.75 |

See Nos. 393-396.

Rowland Hill and St. Christopher No. 1 — A65

Rowland Hill and: 15c, St. Kitts-Nevis #233. 50c, Great Britain #4. $2.50, St. Kitts-Nevis #64.

**Wmk. 373**

**1979, July 2 Litho. *Perf. 14½***

| No. | Type | Description | Unused | Used |
|---|---|---|---|---|
| 384 | A65 | 5c multicolored | .25 | .25 |
| 385 | A65 | 15c multicolored | .25 | .25 |
| 386 | A65 | 50c multicolored | .30 | *.35* |
| 387 | A65 | $2.50 multicolored | .65 | *1.10* |
| | | *Nos. 384-387 (4)* | 1.45 | 1.95 |

Sir Rowland Hill (1795-1879), originator of penny postage.

The Woodman's Daughter, by Millais — A66

Paintings by John Everett Millais and IYC Emblem: 25c, Cherry Ripe. 30c, The Rescue, horiz. 55c, Bubbles. $1, Christ in the House of His Parents.

**1979, Nov. 12 Litho. *Perf. 14***

| No. | Type | Description | Unused | Used |
|---|---|---|---|---|
| 388 | A66 | 5c multicolored | .25 | .25 |
| 389 | A66 | 25c multicolored | .30 | .30 |
| 390 | A66 | 30c multicolored | .30 | .30 |
| 391 | A66 | 55c multicolored | .40 | .40 |
| | | *Nos. 388-391 (4)* | 1.25 | 1.25 |

**Souvenir Sheet**

| No. | Type | Description | Unused | Used |
|---|---|---|---|---|
| 392 | A66 | $1 multicolored | 1.25 | 1.25 |

Christmas 1979; Intl. Year of the Child.

**Flower Type of 1979**

Flowers: 4c, Clerodendrum aculeatum. 55c, Inga laurina. $1.50, Epidendrum difforme. $2, Salvia serontina.

**1980, Feb. 4 Litho. *Perf. 14***

| No. | Type | Description | Unused | Used |
|---|---|---|---|---|
| 393 | A64 | 4c multicolored | .40 | .25 |
| 394 | A64 | 55c multicolored | .50 | .30 |
| 395 | A64 | $1.50 multicolored | 1.75 | 1.75 |
| 396 | A64 | $2 multicolored | .90 | *2.25* |
| | | *Nos. 393-396 (4)* | 3.55 | 4.55 |

Nevis Lagoon, London 1980 Emblem — A67

30c, Fig Tree Church, vert. 55c, Nisbet Plantation. $3, Lord Nelson, by Fuger, vert. 75c, Nelson Falling, by D. Dighton.

**1980, May 6 Litho. *Perf. 13½***

| No. | Type | Description | Unused | Used |
|---|---|---|---|---|
| 397 | A67 | 5c shown | .25 | .25 |
| 398 | A67 | 30c multicolored | .30 | .30 |
| 399 | A67 | 55c multicolored | .50 | .50 |
| 400 | A67 | $3 multicolored | 2.50 | 2.50 |
| | | *Nos. 397-400 (4)* | 3.55 | 3.55 |

**Souvenir Sheet**

| No. | Type | Description | Unused | Used |
|---|---|---|---|---|
| 401 | A67 | 75c multicolored | 2.50 | 2.00 |

London 80 Intl. Phil. Exhib., May 6-14; Lord Nelson, (1758-1805).

**WAR TAX STAMPS**

No. 12 Overprinted

**1916 Wmk. 3 *Perf. 14***

| No. | Type | Description | Unused | Used |
|---|---|---|---|---|
| MR1 | A1 | ½p deep green | 1.10 | .55 |

Type of 1905-18 Issue Overprinted

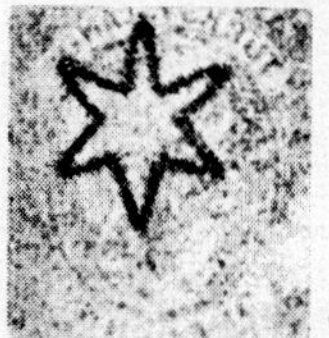


**1918**

| No. | Type | Description | Unused | Used |
|---|---|---|---|---|
| MR2 | A1 | 1½p orange | 1.75 | 1.00 |

**OFFICIAL STAMPS**

**Catalogue values for unused stamps in this section are for Never Hinged items.**

**Nos. 359, 361, 363-369 Overprinted: OFFICIAL**

***Perf. 14½x14***

**1980 Litho. Wmk. 373**

| No. | Type | Description | Unused | Used |
|---|---|---|---|---|
| O1 | A61 | 12c multicolored | .80 | *1.25* |
| O2 | A61 | 25c multicolored | .25 | .25 |
| O3 | A61 | 40c multicolored | .55 | .50 |
| O4 | A61 | 45c multicolored | 3.50 | 2.00 |
| O5 | A61 | 50c multicolored | .40 | .45 |
| O6 | A61 | 55c multicolored | 1.45 | .50 |
| O7 | A61 | $1 multicolored | .75 | *2.25* |
| O8 | A61 | $5 multicolored | .85 | *2.50* |
| O9 | A61 | $10 multicolored | 1.50 | *3.50* |
| | | *Nos. O1-O9 (9)* | 10.05 | 13.20 |

# ST. LUCIA

sānt 'lü-shə

LOCATION — Island in the West Indies, one of the Windward group
GOVT. — Independent state in British Commonwealth
AREA — 240 sq. mi.
POP. — 154,020 (1999 est.)
CAPITAL — Castries

The British colony of St. Lucia became an associated state March 1, 1967, and independent in 1979.

12 Pence = 1 Shilling
100 Cents = 1 Dollar (1949)

**Catalogue values for unused stamps in this country are for Never Hinged items, beginning with Scott 127 in the regular postage section, Scott C1 in the air post section, Scott J3 in the postage due section, and Scott O1 in the officials section.**

**Watermarks**

Wmk. 5 — Small Star

Wmk. 380 — "POST OFFICE"

Values for unused stamps are for examples with original gum as defined in the catalogue introduction. Very fine examples of Nos. 1-26 will have perforations touching the design on at least one side due to the narrow spacing of the stamps on the plates. Stamps with perfs clear of the framelines on all four sides are very scarce and will command higher prices.

Queen Victoria — A1

***Perf. 14 to 16***

**1860, Dec. 18 Engr. Wmk. 5**

| No. | Type | Description | Unused | Used |
|---|---|---|---|---|
| 1 | A1 | (1p) rose red | 110.00 | 75.00 |
| a. | | Double impression | *2,500.* | |
| b. | | Horiz. pair, imperf vert. | — | |
| 2 | A1 | (4p) blue | 250.00 | 175.00 |
| a. | | Horiz. pair, imperf vert. | — | |
| 3 | A1 | (6p) green | 325.00 | 225.00 |
| a. | | Horiz. pair, imperf vert. | — | |
| | | *Nos. 1-3 (3)* | 685.00 | 475.00 |

For types overprinted see Nos. 15, 17, 19-26.

**1863 Wmk. 1 *Perf. 12½***

| No. | Type | Description | Unused | Used |
|---|---|---|---|---|
| 4 | A1 | (1p) lake | 95.00 | *110.00* |
| 5 | A1 | (4p) slate blue | 140.00 | 150.00 |
| 6 | A1 | (6p) emerald | 225.00 | 225.00 |
| | | *Nos. 4-6 (3)* | 460.00 | 485.00 |

Nos. 4-6 exist imperforate on stamp paper, from proof sheets.

**1864**

| No. | Type | Description | Unused | Used |
|---|---|---|---|---|
| 7 | A1 | (1p) black | 30.00 | 14.00 |
| 8 | A1 | (4p) yellow | 210.00 | 50.00 |
| a. | | (4p) olive yellow | 425.00 | 100.00 |
| b. | | (4p) lemon yellow | *1,750.* | |
| 9 | A1 | (6p) violet | 140.00 | 42.50 |
| a. | | (6p) lilac | 210.00 | 32.50 |
| b. | | (6p) deep lilac | 160.00 | 42.50 |
| 10 | A1 | (1sh) red orange | 250.00 | 32.50 |
| a. | | (1sh) orange | 275.00 | 32.50 |
| c. | | Horiz. pair, imperf between | | |
| | | *Nos. 7-10 (4)* | 630.00 | 139.00 |

Nos. 7-10 exist imperforate on stamp paper, from proof sheets.

***Perf. 14***

| No. | Type | Description | Unused | Used |
|---|---|---|---|---|
| 11 | A1 | (1p) deep black | 50.00 | 22.00 |
| a. | | Horiz. pair, imperf between | — | |
| 12 | A1 | (4p) yellow | 130.00 | 24.00 |
| a. | | (4p) olive yellow | 325.00 | 105.00 |
| 13 | A1 | (6p) pale lilac | 125.00 | 24.00 |
| a. | | (6p) deep lilac | 125.00 | 45.00 |
| b. | | (6p) violet | 275.00 | 77.50 |
| 14 | A1 | (1sh) deep orange | 175.00 | 19.00 |
| a. | | (1sh) orange | 250.00 | 25.00 |
| | | *Nos. 11-14 (4)* | 480.00 | 89.00 |

**Type of 1860 Surcharged in Black or Red**

a

b

**1881**

| No. | Type | Description | Unused | Used |
|---|---|---|---|---|
| 15 | A1(a) | ½p green | 85.00 | *120.00* |
| 17 | A1(b) | 2½p scarlet | 60.00 | 27.50 |

**1883-84 Wmk. Crown and CA (2)**

| No. | Type | Description | Unused | Used |
|---|---|---|---|---|
| 19 | A1(a) | ½p green | 37.50 | *50.00* |
| 20 | A1(a) | 1p black (R) | 52.50 | 16.00 |
| a. | | Half used as ½p on cover | | — |
| 21 | A1(a) | 4p yellow | 325.00 | 24.00 |
| 22 | A1(a) | 6p violet | 50.00 | 50.00 |
| 23 | A1(a) | 1sh orange | 310.00 | 190.00 |
| | | *Nos. 19-23 (5)* | 775.00 | 330.00 |

**1884 *Perf. 12***

| No. | Type | Description | Unused | Used |
|---|---|---|---|---|
| 24 | A1(a) | 4p yellow | 300.00 | 32.50 |

Nos. 5 & 6 Surcharged

**1885 Wmk. 1 *Perf. 12½***

| No. | Type | Description | Unused | Used |
|---|---|---|---|---|
| 25 | A1 | ½p emerald | 77.50 | |
| 26 | A1 | 6p slate blue | 1,500. | |

Nos. 25 and 26 were prepared for use but not issued.

A5

For explanation of dies A and B see "Dies of British Colonial Stamps..." in the catalogue Table of Contents.

**1883-98 Typo. Wmk. 2 *Perf. 14***

| No. | Type | Description | Unused | Used |
|---|---|---|---|---|
| 27 | A5 | ½p green ('91) | 4.00 | 1.25 |
| a. | | Die A ('83) | 17.50 | 10.00 |
| 28 | A5 | 1p rose | 55.00 | 19.00 |
| 29 | A5 | 1p lilac ('91) | 7.00 | .35 |
| a. | | Die A ('86) | 15.00 | 7.25 |
| b. | | Imperf., pair | 900.00 | |
| 30 | A5 | 2p ultra & brn org ('98) | 6.00 | 1.25 |
| 31 | A5 | 2½p ultra ('91) | 14.00 | 1.25 |
| a. | | Die A ('83) | 75.00 | 3.00 |
| 32 | A5 | 3p lilac & grn ('91) | 10.00 | 6.50 |
| a. | | Die A ('86) | 150.00 | 20.00 |
| 33 | A5 | 4p brown ('93) | 8.00 | 3.00 |
| a. | | Die A ('85) | 50.00 | 1.50 |
| b. | | Imperf., pair | *1,050.* | |
| 34 | A5 | 6p violet ('86) | 300.00 | 240.00 |
| a. | | Imperf., pair | *2,000.* | |
| 35 | A5 | 6p lilac & blue ('87) | 7.00 | *18.00* |
| a. | | Die A ('91) | 40.00 | 29.00 |
| 36 | A5 | 1sh brn org ('85) | 450.00 | 175.00 |
| 37 | A5 | 1sh lil & red ('91) | 14.00 | 6.00 |
| a. | | Die A ('87) | 150.00 | 37.50 |
| 38 | A5 | 5sh lil & org ('91) | 60.00 | *175.00* |
| 39 | A5 | 10sh lil & blk ('91) | 110.00 | *175.00* |
| | | *Nos. 27-39 (13)* | 1,043. | 821.60 |

**Nos. 32, 32a, 35a and 33a Surcharged in Black**

No. 40 No. 41 No. 42

**1892**

| No. | Type | Description | Unused | Used |
|---|---|---|---|---|
| 40 | A5 | ½p on 3p lil & grn | 95.00 | 30.00 |
| b. | | Double surcharge | 1,000. | 800.00 |
| c. | | Inverted surcharge | 2,450. | 800.00 |
| d. | | Triple surcharge, one on back | *1,350.* | *1,500.* |
| 41 | A5 | ½p on half of 6p lilac & blue | 32.50 | 4.00 |
| a. | | Slanting serif | 240.00 | 150.00 |
| c. | | Without the bar of "½" | 325.00 | 160.00 |
| d. | | "2" of "½" omitted | 575.00 | 600.00 |
| e. | | Surcharged sideways | 1,700. | |
| f. | | Double surcharge | 725.00 | 725.00 |
| g. | | Triple surcharge | *1,450.* | |
| 42 | A5 | 1p on 4p brown | 9.00 | *4.75* |
| b. | | Double surcharge | 275.00 | |
| c. | | Inverted surcharge | 1,100. | 950.00 |
| d. | | Thick diagonal stroke in first "N" | 30.00 | 24.00 |
| e. | | Thick diagonal stroke in second "N" | 30.00 | 24.00 |
| | | *Nos. 40-42 (3)* | 136.50 | 38.75 |

No. 40 is found with wide or narrow "O" in "ONE," and large or small "A" in "HALF." For more detailed listings, see the *Scott Classic Specialized Catalogue of Stamps and Covers.*

Edward VII — A9

Numerals of 3p, 6p, 1sh and 5sh of type A9 are in color on plain tablet.

**1902-03 Typo.**

| No. | Type | Description | Unused | Used |
|---|---|---|---|---|
| 43 | A9 | ½p violet & green | 4.50 | 1.90 |
| 44 | A9 | 1p violet & car rose | 6.50 | .90 |
| 46 | A9 | 2½p violet & ultra | 40.00 | 8.00 |
| 47 | A9 | 3p violet & yellow | 9.50 | *10.00* |
| 48 | A9 | 1sh green & black | 17.00 | *50.00* |
| | | *Nos. 43-48 (5)* | 77.50 | *70.80* |

The Pitons — A10

**Wmk. 1 sideways**

**1902, Dec. 16** **Engr.**
**49** A10 2p brown & green 16.00 2.50

Fourth centenary of the discovery of the island by Columbus.

**1904-05** **Typo.** **Wmk. 3**
**50** A9 ½p violet & green 11.50 .65
*a.* Chalky paper 13.00 1.40
**51** A9 1p violet & car rose 9.00 1.40
*a.* Chalky paper 12.00 1.40
**52** A9 2½p violet & ultra 40.00 2.75
*a.* Chalky paper 18.00 5.00
**53** A9 3p violet & yellow 13.00 3.25
**54** A9 6p vio & dp vio ('05) 27.50 *35.00*
*a.* Chalky paper 21.00 47.50
**55** A9 1sh green & blk ('05) 50.00 32.50
**56** A9 5sh green & car ('05) 85.00 *200.00*
*Nos. 50-56 (7)* 236.00 *275.55*

No. 55 is on chalky paper only.

**1907-10**
**57** A9 ½p green 2.00 1.10
**58** A9 1p carmine 4.75 .35
**59** A9 2½p ultra 4.25 2.00

**Chalky Paper**

**60** A9 3p violet, *yel* ('09) 3.25 *19.00*
**61** A9 6p violet & red vio 9.25 *40.00*
*a.* 6p violet & dull vio ('10) 75.00 90.00
**62** A9 1sh black, *grn* ('09) 5.25 *8.75*
**63** A9 5sh grn & red, *yel* 67.50 *77.50*
*Nos. 57-63 (7)* 96.25 *148.70*

King George V
A11 A12

Numerals of 3p, 6p, 1sh and 5sh of type A11 are in color on plain tablet.

For description of dies I and II see "Dies of British Colonial Stamps" in Table of Contents.

**Die I**

**1912-19** **Ordinary Paper**
**64** A11 ½p deep green .75 .50
**65** A11 1p scarlet 9.00 .25
*a.* 1p carmine 2.00 .25
**66** A12 2p gray ('13) 1.60 *4.50*
**67** A11 2½p bright blue 4.50 3.00

**Chalky Paper**
**Numeral on White Tablet**

**68** A11 3p violet, *yel* 1.40 *2.50*
*a.* Die II 30.00 60.00
**69** A11 6p vio & red vio 2.25 *21.00*
**70** A11 1sh black, *green* 7.00 *5.50*
*a.* 1sh black, *bl grn, ol* back 17.50 19.00
**71** A11 1sh fawn 20.00 *50.00*
**72** A11 5sh grn & red, *yel* 26.50 *85.00*
*Nos. 64-72 (9)* 73.00 *172.25*

A13

A14

**1913-14** **Chalky Paper**
**73** A13 4p scar & blk, *yel* 1.00 *2.25*
**74** A14 2sh6p blk & red, *bl* 25.00 *50.00*

**Surface-colored Paper**

**75** A13 4p scarlet & blk, *yel* .75 *1.60*

**Die II**

**1921-24** **Wmk. 4** **Ordinary Paper**
**76** A11 ½p green 1.25 .55
**77** A11 1p carmine 14.50 *20.00*
**78** A11 1p dk brn ('22) 1.60 .25
**79** A13 1½p rose red ('22) .85 *2.75*
**80** A12 2p gray .85 .25
**81** A11 2½p ultra 7.50 *3.00*
**82** A11 2½p orange ('24) 16.00 *60.00*
**83** A11 3p dull blue ('24) 7.00 *12.00*

**Chalky Paper**

**84** A11 3p violet, *yel* 3.75 *13.50*
**85** A13 4p scar & blk, *yel* ('24) 1.40 *2.75*
**86** A11 6p vio & red vio 2.50 *5.25*
**87** A11 1sh fawn 7.50 *3.50*
**88** A14 2sh6p blk & red, *bl* ('24) 20.00 *36.00*
**89** A11 5sh grn & red, *yel* 60.00 *95.00*
*Nos. 76-89 (14)* 144.70 *254.80*

Common Design Types pictured following the introduction.

**Silver Jubilee Issue**
Common Design Type

**1935, May 6** **Engr.** ***Perf. 13½x14***
**91** CD301 ½p green & blk .30 2.00
**92** CD301 2p gray blk & ultra .95 1.40
**93** CD301 2½p blue & brn 1.25 1.40
**94** CD301 1sh brt vio & ind 13.50 *16.00*
*Nos. 91-94 (4)* 16.00 *20.80*
Set, never hinged 26.00

Port Castries A15

Columbus Square, Castries A16

Ventine Falls A17

Soldiers' Monument A19

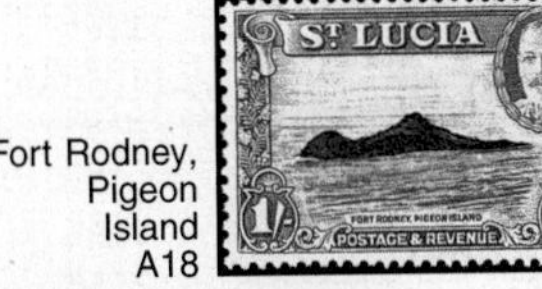


Fort Rodney, Pigeon Island A18

Government House A20

Seal of the Colony A21

**Center in Black**

**1936, Mar. 1** ***Perf. 14***
**95** A15 ½p light green .35 .55
*a.* Perf. 13x12 5.50 26.00
**96** A16 1p dark brown .45 .25
*a.* Perf. 13x12 10.00 4.25
**97** A17 1½p carmine .70 .35
*a.* Perf. 12x13 17.50 2.50
**98** A15 2p gray .60 .25
**99** A16 2½p blue .60 .25
**100** A17 3p dull green 1.50 .75
**101** A15 4p brown 2.00 *1.25*
**102** A16 6p orange 2.00 1.25
**103** A18 1sh lt bl, perf. 13x12 3.50 2.50
**104** A19 2sh6p ultra 15.00 14.00
**105** A20 5sh violet 19.00 *25.00*
**106** A21 10sh car rose, perf. 13x12 60.00 *100.00*
*Nos. 95-106 (12)* 105.70 *146.40*
Set, never hinged 225.00

Nos. 95a, 96a and 97a are coils.

Issue date: Nos. 95a, 96a, Apr. 8.

**Coronation Issue**
Common Design Type

**1937, May 12** ***Perf. 11x11½***
**107** CD302 1p dark purple .25 .40
**108** CD302 1½p dark carmine .40 .25
**109** CD302 2½p deep ultra .40 1.40
*Nos. 107-109 (3)* 1.05 2.05
Set, never hinged 1.50

King George VI — A22

Columbus Square, Castries A23

Government House A24

The Pitons A25

Loading Bananas A26

Arms of the Colony — A27

***Perf. 12½ (#110-111, 1½p-3½p, 8p, 3sh, 5sh, £1), 12 (6p, 1sh, 2sh, 10sh)***

**1938-48**
**110** A22 ½p green ('43) .25 .25
*a.* Perf. 14½x14 1.40 .25
**111** A22 1p deep violet .25 .25
*a.* Perf. 14½x14 2.00 .85
**112** A22 1p red, Perf. 14½x14 ('47) .25 .25
*a.* Perf. 12½ .65 .25
**113** A22 1½p carmine ('43) 1.00 1.40
*a.* Perf. 14½x14 1.40 .50
**114** A22 2p gray ('43) .25 .25
*a.* Perf. 14½x14 2.25 *1.75*
**115** A22 2½p ultra ('43) .25 .25
*a.* Perf. 14½x14 3.00 .25
**116** A22 2½p violet ('47) .85 .25
**117** A22 3p red org ('43) .25 .25
*a.* Perf. 14½x14 1.00 .25
**118** A22 3½p brt ultra ('47) .85 .25
**119** A23 6p magenta ('48) 6.50 1.75
*a.* Perf. 13½ 2.00 .50
**120** A22 8p choc ('46) 2.75 .40
**121** A24 1sh lt brn ('48) .75 .40
*a.* Perf. 13½ 1.10 .40
**122** A25 2sh red vio & sl bl 3.50 1.50
**123** A22 3sh brt red vio ('46) 6.75 2.00
**124** A26 5sh rose vio & blk 10.00 11.00
**125** A27 10sh black, *yel* 7.50 *9.00*
**126** A22 £1 sepia ('46) 9.00 8.00
*Nos. 110-126 (17)* 50.95 37.45
Set, never hinged 75.00

See Nos. 135-148.

**Catalogue values for unused stamps in this section, from this point to the end of the section, are for Never Hinged items.**

**Peace Issue**
Common Design Type
***Perf. 13½x14***

**1946, Oct. 8** **Wmk. 4** **Engr.**
**127** CD303 1p lilac .25 .30
**128** CD303 3½p deep blue .25 .30

**Silver Wedding Issue**
Common Design Types

**1948, Nov. 26** **Photo.** ***Perf. 14x14½***
**129** CD304 1p scarlet .25 .25

***Perf. 11½x11***
**Engraved; Name Typographed**

**130** CD305 £1 violet brown 22.00 *40.00*

**UPU Issue**
Common Design Types
**Engr.; Name Typo. on 6c, 12c.**
***Perf. 13½, 11x11½***

**1949, Oct. 10** **Wmk. 4**
**131** CD306 5c violet .25 *.85*
**132** CD307 6c deep orange 1.60 *2.50*
**133** CD308 12c red lilac .30 .25
**134** CD309 24c blue green .40 .25
*Nos. 131-134 (4)* 2.55 *3.85*

**Types of 1938**
Values in Cents and Dollars

**1949, Oct. 1** **Engr.** ***Perf. 12½***
**135** A22 1c green .35 .25
*a.* Perf. 14 3.25 .50
**136** A22 2c rose lilac 1.25 .25
*a.* Perf. 14½x14 4.50 1.25
**137** A22 3c red 1.60 *2.50*
**138** A22 4c gray .95 .25
*a.* Perf. 14½x14 *18,800.*
**139** A22 5c violet 1.75 .25
**140** A22 6c red orange 1.25 *3.50*
**141** A22 7c ultra 4.00 3.00
**142** A22 12c rose lake 6.75 4.00
*a.* Perf. 14½x14 ('50) 750.00 550.00
**143** A22 16c brown 5.75 .65

***Perf. 11½***

**144** A27 24c Prus blue .75 .25
**145** A27 48c olive green 1.75 1.60
**146** A27 $1.20 purple 2.75 *10.00*
**147** A27 $2.40 blue green 4.50 *20.00*
**148** A27 $4.80 dk car rose 11.50 *21.00*
*Nos. 135-148 (14)* 44.90 *67.50*

Nos. 144 to 148 are of a type similar to A27, but with the denomination in the top corners and "St. Lucia" at the bottom.

For overprints see Nos. 152-155.

**University Issue**
Common Design Types
***Perf. 14x14½***

**1951, Feb. 16** **Wmk. 4**
**149** CD310 3c red & gray black .55 .75
**150** CD311 12c brn car & blk .85 .75

Phoenix Rising from Burning Buildings — A28

**Engr. & Typo.**

**1951, June 19** ***Perf. 13½x13***
**151** A28 12c dp blue & car .50 1.10

Reconstruction of Castries.

Nos. 136, 138, 139 and 142 Overprinted in Black

**1951, Sept. 25** ***Perf. 12½***
**152** A22 2c rose lilac .25 .85
**153** A22 4c gray .25 .60
**154** A22 5c violet .25 .85
**155** A22 12c rose lilac .45 .60
*Nos. 152-155 (4)* 1.20 2.90

Adoption of a new constitution for the Windward Islands, 1951.

**Coronation Issue**
Common Design Type

**1953, June 2** **Engr.** ***Perf. 13½x13***
**156** CD312 3c carmine & black .70 .35

Queen Elizabeth II A29

Arms of St. Lucia A30

**1953-54 Engr. *Perf. 14½x14***

| | | | | | |
|---|---|---|---|---|---|
| 157 | A29 | 1c | green | .25 | .25 |
| 158 | A29 | 2c | rose lilac | .25 | .25 |
| 159 | A29 | 3c | red | .25 | .25 |
| 160 | A29 | 4c | gray | .25 | .25 |
| 161 | A29 | 5c | violet | .25 | .25 |
| 162 | A29 | 6c | orange | .25 | .25 |
| 163 | A29 | 8c | rose lake | .40 | .25 |
| 164 | A29 | 10c | ultra | .25 | .25 |
| 165 | A29 | 15c | brown | .35 | .25 |

***Perf. 11x11½***

| | | | | | |
|---|---|---|---|---|---|
| 166 | A30 | 25c | Prus blue | .40 | .25 |
| 167 | A30 | 50c | brown olive | 5.00 | .50 |
| 168 | A30 | $1 | blue green | 4.75 | 2.50 |
| 169 | A30 | $2.50 | dark car rose | 6.00 | 4.75 |
| | | | *Nos. 157-169 (13)* | 18.65 | 10.25 |

Issued: 2c, 10/28; 4c, 1/7/54; 1c, 5c, 4/1/54; others, 9/2/54.

**West Indies Federation**

Common Design Type

***Perf. 11½x11***

**1958, Apr. 22 Wmk. 314**

| | | | | |
|---|---|---|---|---|
| 170 | CD313 | 3c green | .40 | .25 |
| 171 | CD313 | 6c blue | .65 | *1.75* |
| 172 | CD313 | 12c carmine rose | 1.00 | .80 |
| | | *Nos. 170-172 (3)* | 2.05 | 2.80 |

16th Century Ship and Pitons — A31

**1960, Jan. 1 *Perf. 12½x13***

| | | | | | |
|---|---|---|---|---|---|
| 173 | A31 | 8c | carmine rose | .40 | .40 |
| 174 | A31 | 10c | orange | .50 | .50 |
| 175 | A31 | 25c | dark blue | .60 | .60 |
| | | | *Nos. 173-175 (3)* | 1.50 | 1.50 |

Granting of new constitution.

St. Lucia Stamp of 1860 — A32

**1960, Dec. 18 Engr. *Perf. 13½***

| | | | | | |
|---|---|---|---|---|---|
| 176 | A32 | 5c | ultra & red brown | .25 | .25 |
| 177 | A32 | 16c | yel grn & blue blk | .30 | *.75* |
| 178 | A32 | 25c | carmine & green | .30 | .25 |
| | | | *Nos. 176-178 (3)* | .85 | 1.25 |

Centenary of St. Lucia's first postage stamps.

**Freedom from Hunger Issue**

Common Design Type

**1963, June 4 Photo. *Perf. 14x14½***

| | | | | |
|---|---|---|---|---|
| 179 | CD314 | 25c green | .40 | .40 |

**Red Cross Centenary Issue**

Common Design Type

**Wmk. 314**

**1963, Sept. 2 Litho. *Perf. 13***

| | | | | |
|---|---|---|---|---|
| 180 | CD315 | 4c black & red | .25 | .25 |
| 181 | CD315 | 25c ultra & red | 1.00 | 1.00 |

A33

A34

Fishing Boats, Soufrière Bay — A35

Designs: 15c, Pigeon Island. 25c, Reduit Beach. 35c, Castries Harbor. 50c, The Pitons. $1, Vigie Beach, vert. $2.50, Queen Elizabeth II, close-up.

**Wmk. 314**

**1964, Mar. 1 Photo. *Perf. 14½***

| | | | | | |
|---|---|---|---|---|---|
| 182 | A33 | 1c | dark car rose | .30 | .25 |
| 183 | A33 | 2c | violet | .50 | .60 |
| 184 | A33 | 4c | brt blue green | 1.30 | .35 |
| 185 | A33 | 5c | slate blue | .40 | .25 |
| 186 | A33 | 6c | brown | 1.30 | *2.00* |
| 187 | A34 | 8c | lt blue & multi | .30 | .25 |
| 188 | A34 | 10c | multicolored | .60 | .25 |
| 189 | A35 | 12c | multicolored | .70 | *1.25* |
| 190 | A35 | 15c | blue & ocher | .30 | .25 |
| *a.* | | | Wmkd. sideways ('68) | .30 | .25 |
| 191 | A35 | 25c | multicolored | .50 | .25 |
| 192 | A35 | 35c | dk blue & buff | 1.75 | .25 |
| 193 | A35 | 50c | brt blue, blk & yel | 2.10 | .25 |
| 194 | A35 | $1 | multicolored | 2.75 | 2.00 |
| 195 | A34 | $2.50 | multicolored | 4.25 | 2.25 |
| | | | *Nos. 182-195 (14)* | 17.05 | 10.45 |

For overprints see Nos. 215-225.

**Shakespeare Issue**

Common Design Type

**1964, Apr. 23 *Perf. 14x14½***

| | | | | |
|---|---|---|---|---|
| 196 | CD316 | 10c bright green | .45 | .25 |

**ITU Issue**

Common Design Type

***Perf. 11x11½***

**1965, May 17 Litho. Wmk. 314**

| | | | | |
|---|---|---|---|---|
| 197 | CD317 | 2c red lil & brt pink | .25 | .25 |
| 198 | CD317 | 50c lilac & yel grn | 1.00 | 1.00 |

**Intl. Cooperation Year Issue**

Common Design Type

**1965, Oct. 25 Wmk. 314 *Perf. 14½***

| | | | | |
|---|---|---|---|---|
| 199 | CD318 | 1c blue grn & claret | .25 | .25 |
| 200 | CD318 | 25c lt violet & grn | .30 | .30 |

**Churchill Memorial Issue**

Common Design Type

**1966, Jan. 24 Photo. *Perf. 14***

**Design in Black, Gold and Carmine Rose**

| | | | | |
|---|---|---|---|---|
| 201 | CD319 | 4c bright blue | .25 | .25 |
| 202 | CD319 | 6c green | .25 | .25 |
| 203 | CD319 | 25c brown | .40 | .40 |
| 204 | CD319 | 35c violet | .60 | .60 |
| | | *Nos. 201-204 (4)* | 1.50 | 1.50 |

**Royal Visit Issue**

Common Design Type

**1966, Feb. 4 Litho. *Perf. 11x12***

| | | | | |
|---|---|---|---|---|
| 205 | CD320 | 4c violet blue | .40 | .35 |
| 206 | CD320 | 25c dk carmine rose | 1.10 | 1.00 |

**World Cup Soccer Issue**

Common Design Type

**1966, July 1 Litho. *Perf. 14***

| | | | | |
|---|---|---|---|---|
| 207 | CD321 | 4c multicolored | .30 | .25 |
| 208 | CD321 | 25c multicolored | .85 | .65 |

**WHO Headquarters Issue**

Common Design Type

**1966, Sept. 20 Litho. *Perf. 14***

| | | | | |
|---|---|---|---|---|
| 209 | CD322 | 4c multicolored | .25 | .25 |
| 210 | CD322 | 25c multicolored | .55 | .55 |

**UNESCO Anniversary Issue**

Common Design Type

**1966, Dec. 1 Litho. *Perf. 14***

| | | | | |
|---|---|---|---|---|
| 211 | CD323 | 4c "Education" | .25 | .25 |
| 212 | CD323 | 12c "Science" | .35 | .35 |
| 213 | CD323 | 25c "Culture" | .55 | .55 |
| | | *Nos. 211-213 (3)* | 1.15 | 1.15 |

**Associated State**

**Nos. 183, 185-194 Overprinted in Red: "STATEHOOD / 1st MARCH 1967"**

**Wmk. 314**

**1967, Mar. 1 Photo. *Perf. 14½***

| | | | | | |
|---|---|---|---|---|---|
| 215 | A33 | 2c | violet | .35 | .35 |
| 216 | A33 | 5c | slate blue | .25 | .25 |
| 217 | A33 | 6c | brown | .25 | .25 |
| 218 | A34 | 8c | lt blue & multi | .35 | .25 |
| 219 | A34 | 10c | multicolored | .50 | .25 |
| 220 | A35 | 12c | multicolored | 1.10 | .30 |
| 221 | A35 | 15c | blue & ocher | 1.40 | 1.40 |
| 222 | A35 | 25c | multicolored | 1.40 | 1.10 |
| 223 | A35 | 35c | dk blue & buff | 1.40 | *1.60* |
| 224 | A35 | 50c | multicolored | 1.40 | *1.75* |
| 225 | A35 | $1 | multicolored | 1.40 | *2.00* |
| | | | *Nos. 215-225 (11)* | 9.80 | 9.50 |

The 1c and $2.50, similarly overprinted, were not sold to the public at the post office but were acknowledged belatedly (May 10) by the government and declared valid. Values for both stamps: unused $6; used $9.

The 1c, 6c and $2.50 overprints exist in black as well as red. No. 213 also exists with this overprint in blue and in black.

Madonna and Child with St. John, by Raphael — A36

**1967, Oct. 16 Wmk. 314 *Perf. 14½***

| | | | | | |
|---|---|---|---|---|---|
| 227 | A36 | 4c | black, gold & multi | .25 | .25 |
| 228 | A36 | 25c | multicolored | .25 | .25 |

Christmas 1967.

Cricket Batsman and Gov. Frederick Clarke — A37

***Perf. 14½x14***

**1968, Mar. 8 Photo. Wmk. 314**

| | | | | | |
|---|---|---|---|---|---|
| 229 | A37 | 10c | multicolored | .25 | .25 |
| 230 | A37 | 35c | multicolored | .40 | .40 |

Visit of the Marylebone Cricket Club to the West Indies, Jan.-Feb. 1968.

"Noli me Tangere," by Titian — A38

Easter: 10c, 25c, The Crucifixion, by Raphael.

**1968, Mar. 25 *Perf. 14½***

| | | | | | |
|---|---|---|---|---|---|
| 231 | A38 | 10c | multicolored | .25 | .25 |
| 232 | A38 | 15c | multicolored | .25 | .25 |
| 233 | A38 | 25c | multicolored | .25 | .25 |
| 234 | A38 | 35c | multicolored | .25 | .25 |
| | | | *Nos. 231-234 (4)* | 1.00 | 1.00 |

Martin Luther King, Jr. — A39

***Perf. 13½x14***

**1968, July 4 Photo. Wmk. 314**

| | | | | | |
|---|---|---|---|---|---|
| 235 | A39 | 25c | dp blue, blk & brn | .25 | .25 |
| 236 | A39 | 35c | violet, blk & brn | .25 | .25 |

Dr. Martin Luther King, Jr. (1929-68), American civil rights leader.

Virgin and Child in Glory, by Murillo — A40

Christmas: 10c, 35c, Virgin and Child, by Bartolomé E. Murillo.

***Perf. 14½x14***

**1968, Oct. 17 Photo. Wmk. 314**

| | | | | | |
|---|---|---|---|---|---|
| 237 | A40 | 5c | dark blue & multi | .25 | .25 |
| 238 | A40 | 10c | multicolored | .25 | .25 |
| 239 | A40 | 25c | red brown & multi | .25 | .25 |
| 240 | A40 | 35c | deep blue & multi | .25 | .25 |
| | | | *Nos. 237-240 (4)* | 1.00 | 1.00 |

Purple-throated Carib — A41

Birds: 15c, 35c, St. Lucia parrot.

**1969, Jan. 10 Litho. *Perf. 14½***

| | | | | | |
|---|---|---|---|---|---|
| 241 | A41 | 10c | multicolored | .70 | .70 |
| 242 | A41 | 15c | multicolored | .90 | .90 |
| 243 | A41 | 25c | multicolored | 1.10 | 1.10 |
| 244 | A41 | 35c | multicolored | 1.25 | 1.25 |
| | | | *Nos. 241-244 (4)* | 3.95 | 3.95 |

Ecce Homo, by Guido Reni — A42

Painting: 15c, 35c, The Resurrection, by Il Sodoma (Giovanni Antonio de Bazzi).

***Perf. 14½x14***

**1969, Mar. 20 Photo. Wmk. 314**

| | | | | | |
|---|---|---|---|---|---|
| 245 | A42 | 10c | purple & multi | .25 | .25 |
| 246 | A42 | 15c | green & multi | .25 | .25 |
| 247 | A42 | 25c | black & multi | .25 | .25 |
| 248 | A42 | 35c | ocher & multi | .25 | .25 |
| | | | *Nos. 245-248 (4)* | 1.00 | 1.00 |

Easter 1969.

Map of Caribbean — A43

Design: 25c, 35c, Clasped hands and arrows with names of CARIFTA members.

**1969, May 29 Wmk. 314 *Perf. 14***

249 A43 5c violet blue & multi .25 .25
250 A43 10c deep plum & multi .25 .25
251 A43 25c ultra & multi .25 .25
252 A43 35c green & multi .25 .25
*Nos. 249-252 (4)* 1.00 1.00

First anniversary of CARIFTA (Caribbean Free Trade Area).

Silhouettes of Napoleon and Josephine — A44

***Perf. 14½x13***

**1969, Sept. 22 Photo. Unwmk.**

**Gold Inscription; Gray and Brown Medallions**

253 A44 15c dull blue .25 .25
254 A44 25c deep claret .25 .25
255 A44 35c deep green .25 .25
256 A44 50c yellow brown .25 *.55*
*Nos. 253-256 (4)* 1.00 1.30

Napoleon Bonaparte, 200th birth anniv.

Madonna and Child, by Paul Delaroche — A45

Christmas: 10c, 35c, Holy Family, by Rubens.

***Perf. 14½x14***

**1969, Oct. 27 Photo. Wmk. 314**

**Center Multicolored**

257 A45 5c dp rose lil & gold .25 .25
258 A45 10c Prus blue & gold .25 .25
259 A45 25c maroon & gold .25 .25
260 A45 35c dp yel grn & gold .25 .25
*Nos. 257-260 (4)* 1.00 1.00

House of Assembly — A46

Queen Elizabeth II, by A. C. Davidson-Houston A47

2c, Roman Catholic Cathedral. 4c, Castries Boulevard. 5c, Castries Harbor. 6c, Sulphur springs. 10c, Vigie Airport. 12c, Reduit beach. 15c, Pigeon Island. 25c, The Pitons & sailboat. 35c, Marigot Bay. 50c, Diamond Waterfall. $1, St. Lucia flag & motto. $2.50, Coat of arms. $10, Map of St. Lucia.

**Wmk. 314 Sideways, Upright (#271-274)**

**1970-73 Litho. *Perf. 14½***

261 A46 1c multicolored .25 .25
262 A46 2c multicolored .25 .25
*a.* Wmk. upright .90 .90
263 A46 4c multicolored 1.00 .25
*a.* Wmk. upright 1.75 1.75
264 A46 5c multicolored 1.50 .25
265 A46 6c multicolored .25 .25
266 A46 10c multicolored 2.00 .25
267 A46 12c multicolored .30 .25
268 A46 15c multicolored .40 .25
269 A46 25c multicolored 1.00 .25
270 A46 35c multicolored .50 .25
271 A47 50c multicolored .85 .80
272 A47 $1 multicolored .50 *.70*
273 A47 $2.50 multicolored .75 *1.75*
274 A47 $5 multicolored 1.75 *4.00*
274A A47 $10 multicolored 5.50 *9.00*
*Nos. 261-274A (15)* 16.80 18.75

Issued: #261-274, Feb. 1, 1970; #274A, Dec. 3, 1973; #262a, 263a, Mar. 15, 1974.

**1975, July 28 Wmk. 373**

*263b* A46 4c multicolored 1.10 2.10
*264a* A46 5c multicolored 1.40 1.00
*266a* A46 10c multicolored 2.00 1.75
*268a* A46 15c multicolored 3.00 2.25
*Nos. 263b-268a (4)* 7.50 7.10

The Three Marys at the Tomb, by Hogarth — A48

35c, The Sealing of the Tomb. $1, The Ascension. The designs are from the altarpiece painted by William Hogarth for the Church of St. Mary Redcliffe in Bristol, 1755-56.

***Roulette 8½xPerf. 12½***

**1970, Mar. 7 Litho. Wmk. 314**

**Size: 27x54mm**

275 A48 25c dark brown & multi .25 .25
276 A48 35c dark brown & multi .25 .25

**Size: 38x54mm**

277 A48 $1 dark brown & multi .40 .40
*a.* Triptych (#275-277) 1.20 1.20

Easter 1970.

Nos. 275-277 printed se-tenant in sheets of 30 (10 triptychs) with the center $1 stamp 10mm raised compared to the flanking 25c and 35c stamps.

Charles Dickens and Characters from his Works — A49

**1970, June 8 Wmk. 314 *Perf. 14***

278 A49 1c brown & multi .25 .25
279 A49 25c Prus blue & multi .30 .25
280 A49 35c brown red & multi .35 .30
281 A49 50c red lilac & multi .40 *1.00*
*Nos. 278-281 (4)* 1.30 1.80

Charles Dickens (1812-70), English novelist.

Nurse Holding Red Cross Emblem A50

15c, 35c, British, St. Lucia & Red Cross flags.

***Perf. 14½x14***

**1970, Aug. 18 Litho. Wmk. 314**

282 A50 10c multicolored .25 .25
283 A50 15c multicolored .25 .25
284 A50 25c buff & multi .35 .40
285 A50 35c multicolored .45 .40
*Nos. 282-285 (4)* 1.30 1.30

Centenary of British Red Cross Society.

Madonna with the Lilies, by Luca della Robbia A51

**Lithographed and Embossed**

**1970, Nov. 16 Unwmk. *Perf. 11***

286 A51 5c dark blue & multi .25 .25
287 A51 10c violet blue & multi .25 .25
288 A51 35c car lake & multi .30 .25
289 A51 40c deep green & multi .30 .30
*Nos. 286-289 (4)* 1.10 1.05

Christmas 1970.

Christ on the Cross, by Rubens — A52

Easter: 15c, 40c, Descent from the Cross, by Peter Paul Rubens.

***Perf. 14x13½***

**1971, Mar. 29 Litho. Wmk. 314**

290 A52 10c dull green & multi .25 .25
291 A52 15c dull red & multi .25 .25
292 A52 35c brt blue & multi .30 .25
293 A52 40c multicolored .30 .40
*Nos. 290-293 (4)* 1.10 1.15

Moule à Chique Lighthouse — A53

Design: 25c, Beane Field Airport.

**1971, Apr. 30 *Perf. 14½x14***

294 A53 5c olive & multi .35 .25
295 A53 25c bister & multi .55 .25

Opening of Beane Field Airport.

View of Morne Fortune (Old Days) — A54

The "a" stamp shows an old print (as shown) and the "b" stamp a contemporary photograph of the same view (plain frame). 10c, Castries City. 25c, Pigeon Island. 50c, View from Government House.

***Perf. 13½x14***

**1971, Aug. 10 Litho. Wmk. 314**

296 A54 5c Pair, #a.-b. .40 .40
297 A54 10c Pair, #a.-b. .50 .50
298 A54 25c Pair, #a.-b. .60 .60
299 A54 50c Pair, #a.-b. 1.10 1.10
*Nos. 296-299 (4)* 2.60 2.60

Virgin and Child, by Verrocchio — A55

Virgin and Child painted by: 10c, Paolo Moranda. 35c, Giovanni Battista Cima. 40c, Andrea del Verrocchio.

**1971, Oct. 15 *Perf. 14***

304 A55 5c green & multi .25 .25
305 A55 10c brown & multi .25 .25
306 A55 35c ultra & multi .25 .25
307 A55 40c red & multi .25 .25
*Nos. 304-307 (4)* 1.00 1.00

Christmas 1971.

St. Lucia, School of Dolci, and Arms — A56

**1971, Dec. 13 *Perf. 14x14½***

308 A56 5c gray & multi .25 .25
309 A56 10c lt green & multi .25 .25
310 A56 25c tan & multi .35 .25
311 A56 50c lt blue & multi .75 .75
*Nos. 308-311 (4)* 1.60 1.50

National Day.

Lamentation, by Carracci A57

Easter: 25c, 50c, Angels Weeping over Body of Jesus, by Guercino.

**1972, Feb. 15 Wmk. 314**

312 A57 10c lt violet & multi .25 .25
313 A57 25c ocher & multi .25 .25
314 A57 35c ultra & multi .35 .25
315 A57 50c lt green & multi .45 .45
*Nos. 312-315 (4)* 1.30 1.20

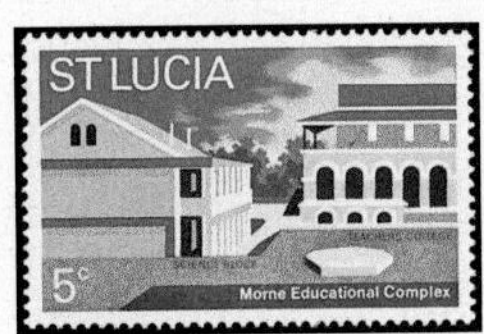


Teachers' College and Science Building — A58

15c, University Center and coat of arms. 25c, Secondary School. 35c, Technical College.

**1972, Apr. 18 Litho. *Perf. 14***

316 A58 5c multicolored .25 .25
317 A58 15c multicolored .25 .25
318 A58 25c multicolored .25 .25
319 A58 35c multicolored .25 .25
*Nos. 316-319 (4)* 1.00 1.00

Opening of Morne Educational Complex.

Steam Conveyance Co. Stamp and Map of St. Lucia — A59

Designs: 10c, Castries Harbor and 3c stamp. 35c, Soufriere Volcano and 1c stamp. 50c, One cent, 3c, 6c stamps.

**1972, June 22** *Perf. 14½*

| | | | | |
|---|---|---|---|---|
| **320** | A59 | 5c yellow & multi | .25 | .25 |
| **321** | A59 | 10c violet blue & multi | .25 | .25 |
| **322** | A59 | 35c car rose & multi | .65 | .25 |
| **323** | A59 | 50c emerald & multi | 1.10 | 1.25 |
| | | *Nos. 320-323 (4)* | 2.25 | 2.00 |

Centenary of St. Lucia Steam Conveyance Co. Ltd. postal service.

Holy Family, by Sebastiano Ricci — A60

**1972, Oct. 18** *Perf. 14½x14*

| | | | | |
|---|---|---|---|---|
| **324** | A60 | 5c dk brown & multi | .25 | .25 |
| **325** | A60 | 10c green & multi | .25 | .25 |
| **326** | A60 | 35c carmine & multi | .25 | .25 |
| **327** | A60 | 40c dk blue & multi | .30 | .25 |
| | | *Nos. 324-327 (4)* | 1.05 | 1.00 |

Christmas 1972.

**Silver Wedding Issue**

Common Design Type

Design: Queen Elizabeth II, Prince Philip, St. Lucia coat of arms and St. Lucia parrot.

**1972, Nov. Photo.** *Perf. 14x14½*

| | | | | |
|---|---|---|---|---|
| **328** | CD324 | 15c car rose & multi | .30 | .30 |
| **329** | CD324 | 35c olive & multi | .45 | .45 |

Weekday Headdress A61

Women's Headdresses: 10c, For church wear. 25c, Unmarried girl. 50c, Formal occasions.

**1973, Feb. 1 Wmk. 314** *Perf. 13*

| | | | | |
|---|---|---|---|---|
| **330** | A61 | 5c multicolored | .25 | .25 |
| **331** | A61 | 10c dark gray & multi | .25 | .25 |
| **332** | A61 | 25c multicolored | .25 | .25 |
| **333** | A61 | 50c slate blue & multi | .25 | *.85* |
| | | *Nos. 330-333 (4)* | 1.00 | 1.60 |

Arms of St. Lucia — A62

**Coil Stamps**

**1973, Apr. 19 Litho.** *Perf. 14½x14*

| | | | | |
|---|---|---|---|---|
| **334** | A62 | 5c gray olive | .35 | *.70* |
| *a.* | | Watermark sideways ('76) | .80 | *2.00* |
| **335** | A62 | 10c blue | .35 | *.70* |
| *a.* | | Watermark sideways ('76) | .80 | *2.00* |
| **336** | A62 | 25c claret | .35 | *.70* |
| *a.* | | Watermark sideways ('76) | 14.00 | |
| | | *Nos. 334-336 (3)* | 1.05 | *2.10* |

H.M.S. St. Lucia A63

Designs: Old Sailing ships.

**1973, May 24 Litho.** *Perf. 13½x14*

| | | | | |
|---|---|---|---|---|
| **337** | A63 | 15c shown | .25 | .25 |
| **338** | A63 | 35c "Prince of Wales" | .35 | .35 |
| **339** | A63 | 50c "Oliph Blossom" | .50 | .50 |
| **340** | A63 | $1 "Rose" | 1.10 | 1.10 |
| *a.* | | Souv. sheet of 4, #337-340, perf. 15 | 2.50 | 2.50 |
| | | *Nos. 337-340 (4)* | 2.20 | 2.20 |

Banana Plantation and Flower — A64

Designs: 15c, Aerial spraying. 35c, Washing and packing bananas. 50c, Loading.

**1973, July 26 Litho.** *Perf. 14*

| | | | | |
|---|---|---|---|---|
| **341** | A64 | 5c multicolored | .25 | .25 |
| **342** | A64 | 15c multicolored | .25 | .25 |
| **343** | A64 | 35c multicolored | .25 | .25 |
| **344** | A64 | 50c multicolored | .55 | .55 |
| | | *Nos. 341-344 (4)* | 1.30 | 1.30 |

Banana industry.

Madonna and Child, by Carlo Maratta — A65

Christmas (Paintings): 15c, Virgin in the Meadow, by Raphael. 35c, Holy Family, by Angelo Bronzino. 50c, Madonna of the Pear, by Durer.

**1973, Oct. 17 Litho.** *Perf. 14x13½*

| | | | | |
|---|---|---|---|---|
| **345** | A65 | 5c citron & multi | .25 | .25 |
| **346** | A65 | 15c ultra & multi | .25 | .25 |
| **347** | A65 | 35c dp green & multi | .25 | .25 |
| **348** | A65 | 50c red & multi | .25 | .25 |
| | | *Nos. 345-348 (4)* | 1.00 | 1.00 |

**Princess Anne's Wedding Issue**

Common Design Type

**1973, Nov. 14 Wmk. 314** *Perf. 14*

| | | | | |
|---|---|---|---|---|
| **349** | CD325 | 40c gray green & multi | .25 | .25 |
| **350** | CD325 | 50c lilac & multi | .25 | .25 |

The Betrayal of Christ, by Ugolino — A66

Easter (Paintings by Ugolino, 14th Cent.): 35c, The Way to Calvary. 80c, Descent from the Cross. $1, Resurrection.

**1974, Apr. 1** *Perf. 13½x13*

| | | | | |
|---|---|---|---|---|
| **351** | A66 | 5c ocher & multi | .25 | .25 |
| **352** | A66 | 35c ocher & multi | .25 | .25 |
| **353** | A66 | 80c ocher & multi | .25 | .25 |
| **354** | A66 | $1 ocher & multi | .25 | .30 |
| *a.* | | Souvenir sheet of 4, #351-354 | 1.75 | 1.75 |
| | | *Nos. 351-354 (4)* | 1.00 | 1.05 |

3 Escalins, 1798 — A67

Pieces of Eight: 35c, 6 escalins, 1798. 40c, 2 livres 5 sols, 1813. $1, 6 livres 15 sols, 1813.

**1974, May 20** *Perf. 13½*

| | | | | |
|---|---|---|---|---|
| **355** | A67 | 15c lt olive & multi | .25 | .25 |
| **356** | A67 | 35c multicolored | .25 | .25 |
| **357** | A67 | 40c green & multi | .35 | .35 |
| **358** | A67 | $1 brown & multi | .65 | .65 |
| *a.* | | Souvenir sheet of 4, #355-358 | 2.00 | 2.00 |
| | | *Nos. 355-358 (4)* | 1.50 | 1.50 |

Coins of Old St. Lucia.

Baron de Laborie, 1784 — A68

Portraits: 35c, Sir John Moore, Lieutenant Governor, 1796-97. 80c, Major General Sir Dudley St. Leger Hill, 1834-37. $1, Sir Frederick Joseph Clarke, 1967-71.

**Wmk. 314**

**1974, Aug. 29 Litho.** *Perf. 14½*

| | | | | |
|---|---|---|---|---|
| **359** | A68 | 5c ocher & multi | .25 | .25 |
| **360** | A68 | 35c brt blue & multi | .25 | .25 |
| **361** | A68 | 80c violet & multi | .25 | .25 |
| **362** | A68 | $1 multicolored | .25 | .25 |
| *a.* | | Souvenir sheet of 4, #359-362 | 1.00 | 1.00 |
| | | *Nos. 359-362 (4)* | 1.00 | 1.00 |

Past Governors of St. Lucia.

Virgin and Child, by Verrocchio — A69

Christmas (Virgin and Child): 35c, by Andrea della Robbia. 80c, by Luca della Robbia. $1, by Antonio Rossellino.

**1974, Nov. 13 Wmk. 314** *Perf. 13½*

| | | | | |
|---|---|---|---|---|
| **363** | A69 | 5c gray & multi | .25 | .25 |
| **364** | A69 | 35c pink & multi | .25 | .25 |
| **365** | A69 | 80c brown & multi | .25 | .25 |
| **366** | A69 | $1 olive & multi | .25 | .25 |
| *a.* | | Souvenir sheet of 4, #363-366 | 1.25 | *2.25* |
| | | *Nos. 363-366 (4)* | 1.00 | 1.00 |

Churchill and Gen. Montgomery — A70

Design: $1, Churchill and Pres. Truman.

**1974, Nov. 30** *Perf. 14*

| | | | | |
|---|---|---|---|---|
| **367** | A70 | 5c multicolored | .25 | .25 |
| **368** | A70 | $1 multicolored | .30 | .35 |

Sir Winston Churchill (1874-1965).

Crucifixion, by Van der Weyden — A71

Easter: 35c, "Noli me Tangere," by Julio Romano. 80c, Crucifixion, by Fernando Gallego. $1, "Noli me Tangere," by Correggio.

*Perf. 14x13½*

**1975, Mar. 27** **Wmk. 314**

| | | | | |
|---|---|---|---|---|
| **369** | A71 | 5c brown & multi | .25 | .25 |
| **370** | A71 | 35c ultra & multi | .25 | .25 |
| **371** | A71 | 80c red brown & multi | .25 | .25 |
| **372** | A71 | $1 green & multi | .25 | .35 |
| | | *Nos. 369-372 (4)* | 1.00 | 1.10 |

Nativity — A72 Adoration of the Kings — A73

No. 375, Virgin & Child. No. 376, Adoration of the Shepherds. 40c, Nativity. $1, Virgin & Child with Sts. Catherine of Alexandria and Siena.

**Wmk. 314**

**1975, Dec. Litho.** *Perf. 14½*

| | | | | |
|---|---|---|---|---|
| **373** | A72 | 5c lilac rose & multi | .25 | .25 |
| **374** | A73 | 10c yellow & multi | .25 | .25 |
| **375** | A73 | 10c yellow & multi | .25 | .25 |
| **376** | A73 | 10c yellow & multi | .25 | .25 |
| *a.* | | Strip of 3, #374-376 | .40 | .40 |
| **377** | A72 | 40c yellow & multi | .30 | .30 |
| **378** | A72 | $1 blue & multi | .70 | .70 |
| *a.* | | Souv. sheet of 3, #373, 377-378 | 1.10 | *1.25* |
| | | *Nos. 373-378 (6)* | 2.00 | 2.00 |

Christmas 1975.

"Hanna," First US Warship — A74

Revolutionary Era Ships: 1c, "Prince of Orange," British packet. 2c, "Edward," British sloop. 5c, "Millern," British merchantman. 15c, "Surprise," Continental Navy lugger. 35c, "Serapis," British warship. 50c, "Randolph," first Continental Navy frigate. $1, Frigate "Alliance."

*Perf. 14½*

**1976, Jan. 26 Litho. Unwmk.**

| | | | | |
|---|---|---|---|---|
| **379-386** | A74 | Set of 8 | 3.50 | 3.50 |
| *386a* | | Souv. sheet, #383-386, perf. 13 | 3.50 | 3.50 |

American Bicentennial.

Laughing Gull — A75

Birds: 2c, Little blue heron. 4c, Belted kingfisher. 5c, St. Lucia parrot. 6c, St. Lucia oriole. 8c, Brown trembler. 10c, American kestrel. 12c, Red-billed tropic bird. 15c, Common gallinule. 25c, Brown noddy. 35c, Sooty tern. 50c, Osprey. $1, White-breasted thrasher. $2.50, St. Lucia black finch. $5, Rednecked pigeon. $10, Caribbean elaenia.

**Wmk. 314 (1c); 373 (others)**

**1976, May 7 Litho.** *Perf. 14½*

| | | | | |
|---|---|---|---|---|
| **387** | A75 | 1c gray & multi | .30 | *1.40* |
| **388** | A75 | 2c gray & multi | .30 | *1.40* |
| **389** | A75 | 4c gray & multi | .35 | *1.40* |
| **390** | A75 | 5c gray & multi | 1.60 | 1.10 |
| **391** | A75 | 6c gray & multi | 1.10 | 1.10 |
| **392** | A75 | 8c gray & multi | 1.25 | *2.25* |
| **393** | A75 | 10c gray & multi | 1.10 | .40 |
| **394** | A75 | 12c gray & multi | 1.75 | *2.50* |
| **395** | A75 | 15c gray & multi | 1.10 | .25 |
| **396** | A75 | 25c gray & multi | 1.60 | 1.00 |
| **397** | A75 | 35c gray & multi | 2.75 | 1.40 |
| **398** | A75 | 50c gray & multi | 5.25 | 3.75 |
| **399** | A75 | $1 gray & multi | 3.25 | 3.75 |

**400** A75 $2.50 gray & multi 6.00 6.75
**401** A75 $5 gray & multi 6.50 4.75
**402** A75 $10 gray & multi 6.00 *8.00*
*Nos. 387-402 (16)* 40.20 41.20

Map of West Indies, Bats, Wicket and Ball A75a

Prudential Cup — A75b

**1976, July 19 Unwmk. *Perf. 14***
**403** A75a 50c lt blue & multi .90 .90
**404** A75b $1 lilac rose & black 1.75 1.75
*a.* Souvenir sheet of 2, #403-404 5.00 *5.50*

World Cricket Cup, won by West Indies Team, 1975.

Arms of H.M.S. Ceres — A76

Coats of Arms of Royal Naval Ships: 20c, Pelican. 40c, Ganges. $2, Ariadne.

**1976, Sept. 6 Wmk. 373 *Perf. 14½***
**405** A76 10c gold & multi .35 .30
**406** A76 20c gold & multi .65 .60
**407** A76 40c gold & multi .95 .85
**408** A76 $2 gold & multi 2.40 2.40
*Nos. 405-408 (4)* 4.35 4.15

Madonna and Child, by Murillo — A77

Paintings: 20c, Virgin and Child, by Lorenzo Costa. 50c, Madonna and Child, by Adriaea Isenbrandt. $2, Madonna and Child with St. John, by Murillo. $2.50, Like 10c.

**1976, Nov. 15 Litho. *Perf. 14½***
**409** A77 10c multicolored .25 .25
**410** A77 20c multicolored .25 .25
**411** A77 50c multicolored .25 .25
**412** A77 $2 multicolored .70 .70
*Nos. 409-412 (4)* 1.45 1.45

**Souvenir Sheet**

**413** A77 $2.50 multicolored 1.40 1.40

Christmas.

Elizabeth II, "Palms and Water" — A78

**Wmk. 373**
**1977, Feb. 7 Litho. *Perf. 14½***
**414** A78 10c multicolored .25 .25
**415** A78 20c multicolored .25 .25
**416** A78 40c multicolored .25 .25
**417** A78 $2 multicolored .25 .25
*Nos. 414-417 (4)* 1.00 1.00

**Souvenir Sheet**

**418** A78 $2.50 multicolored .75 *1.00*

25th anniv. of the reign of Elizabeth II.

Scouts of Tapion School — A79

1c, Sea Scouts, St. Mary's College. 2c, Scout giving oath. 10c, Tapion School Cub Scouts. 20c, Venture Scout, Soufrière. 50c, Scout from Gros Islet Division. $1, $2.50, Boat drill, St. Mary's College.

**1977, Oct. 17 Unwmk. *Perf. 15***
**419** A79 ½c multicolored .25 .25
**420** A79 1c multicolored .25 .25
**421** A79 2c multicolored .25 .25
**422** A79 10c multicolored .25 .25
**423** A79 20c multicolored .25 .25
**424** A79 50c multicolored .40 .40
**425** A79 $1 multicolored .90 .90
*Nos. 419-425 (7)* 2.55 2.55

**Souvenir Sheet**

**426** A79 $2.50 multicolored 2.00 2.00

6th Caribbean Boy Scout Jamboree, Kingston, Jamaica, Aug. 5-14.

Nativity, by Giotto — A80

Christmas (Virgin and Child by): 1c, Fra Angelico. 2c, El Greco. 20c, Caravaggio. 50c, Velazquez. $1, Tiepolo. $2.50, Adoration of the Kings, by Tiepolo.

**1977, Oct. 31 Litho. *Perf. 14***
**427-433** A80 Set of 7 2.00 2.00

Suzanne Fourment in Velvet Hat, by Rubens — A81

Rubens Paintings: 35c, Rape of the Sabine Women (detail). 50c, Ludovicus Nonnius, portrait. $2.50, Minerva Protecting Pax from Mars (detail).

***Perf. 14x14½***
**1977, Nov. 28 Litho. Wmk. 373**
**434** A81 10c multicolored .25 .25
**435** A81 35c multicolored .25 .25
**436** A81 50c multicolored .30 .30
**437** A81 $2.50 multicolored 1.60 1.60
*a.* Souv. sheet, #434-437, perf. 15 3.00 3.00
*Nos. 434-437 (4)* 2.40 2.40

Peter Paul Rubens (1577-1640).

Yeoman of the Guard and Life Guard A82

Dress Uniforms: 20c, Groom and postilion. 50c, Footman and coachman. $3, State trumpeter and herald. $5, Master of the Queen's House and Gentleman at Arms.

**Unwmk.**
**1978, June 2 Litho. *Perf. 14***
**438** A82 15c multicolored .25 .25
**439** A82 20c multicolored .25 .25
**440** A82 50c multicolored .30 .30
**441** A82 $3 multicolored .50 .50
*Nos. 438-441 (4)* 1.30 1.30

**Souvenir Sheet**

**442** A82 $5 multicolored .90 .90

25th anniv. of coronation of Elizabeth II.
Nos. 438-441 exist in miniature sheets of 3 plus label, perf. 12.

Queen Angelfish A83

Tropical Fish: 20c, Four-eyed butterflyfish. 50c, French angelfish. $2, Yellowtail damselfish. $2.50, Rock beauty.

**1978, June 19 Litho. *Perf. 14½***
**443** A83 10c multicolored .25 .25
**444** A83 20c multicolored .40 .25
**445** A83 50c multicolored .70 .50
**446** A83 $2 multicolored 2.25 2.25
*Nos. 443-446 (4)* 3.60 3.25

**Souvenir Sheet**

**447** A83 $2.50 multicolored 3.75 3.75

French Grenadier, Map of Battle — A84

30c, British Grenadier & Bellin map of St. Lucia, 1762. 50c, British fleet opposing French landing & map of coast from Gros Islet to Cul-de-Sac. $2.50, Light infantrymen & Gen. James Grant.

**1978, Nov. 15 Litho. *Perf. 14***
**448** A84 10c multicolored .50 .25
**449** A84 30c multicolored .75 .35
**450** A84 50c multicolored 1.00 .60
**451** A84 $2.50 multicolored 2.50 2.50
*Nos. 448-451 (4)* 4.75 3.70

Bicent. of Battle of St. Lucia (Cul-de-Sac).

Annunciation A85

Christmas: 55c, 80c, Adoration of the Kings.

***Perf. 14x14½***
**1978, Dec. 4 Wmk. 373**
**452** A85 30c multicolored .25 .25
**453** A85 50c multicolored .25 .25
**454** A85 55c multicolored .30 .30
**455** A85 80c multicolored .40 .40
*Nos. 452-455 (4)* 1.20 1.20

**Independent State**

Hewanorra Airport A86

Independence: 30c, New coat of arms. 50c, Government house and Allen Lewis, first Governor General. $2, Map of St. Lucia, French, St. Lucia and British flags.

**1979, Feb. 22 Litho. *Perf. 14***
**456** A86 10c multicolored .25 .25
**457** A86 30c multicolored .25 .25
**458** A86 50c multicolored .25 .25
**459** A86 $2 multicolored .50 .50
*a.* Souvenir sheet of 4, #456-459 1.50 1.50
*Nos. 456-459 (4)* 1.25 1.25

Paul VI and John Paul I A87

Pope Paul VI and: 30c, Pres. Anwar Sadat of Egypt. 50c, Secretary General U Thant and UN emblem. 55c, Prime Minister Golda Meir of Israel. $2, Martin Luther King, Jr.

**1979, May 7 Litho. *Perf. 14***
**460** A87 10c multicolored .25 .25
**461** A87 30c multicolored .30 .25
**462** A87 50c multicolored .40 .40
**463** A87 55c multicolored .50 .45
**464** A87 $2 multicolored 1.50 1.50
*Nos. 460-464 (5)* 2.95 2.85

In memory of Popes Paul VI and John Paul I.

Jersey Cows A88

Agricultural Diversification: 35c, Fruits and vegetables. 50c, Waterfall (water conservation). $3, Coconuts, copra industry.

**1979, July 2 Litho. *Perf. 14***
**465** A88 10c multicolored .25 .25
**466** A88 35c multicolored .25 .25
**467** A88 50c multicolored .25 .25
**468** A88 $3 multicolored .60 .60
*Nos. 465-468 (4)* 1.35 1.35

Lindbergh's Route over St. Lucia, Puerto Rico-Paramaribo — A89

**1979, Nov. Litho. *Perf. 14***
**469** A89 10c Lindbergh, hydroplane .40 .25
**470** A89 30c shown .45 .25
**471** A89 50c Landing at La Toc .60 .40
**472** A89 $2 Flight covers 1.65 1.65
*Nos. 469-472 (4)* 3.10 2.55

Lindbergh's inaugural airmail flight (US-Guyana) via St. Lucia, 50th anniversary.

Prince of Saxony, by Cranach the Elder — A90

IYC (Emblem and): 50c, Infanta Margarita, by Velazquez. $2, Girl Playing Badminton, by Jean Baptiste Chardin. $2.50, Mary and Francis Wilcox, by Stock. $5, Two Children, by Pablo Picasso.

**1979, Dec. 17 Litho. *Perf. 14***

| | | | | |
|---|---|---|---|---|
| **473** | A90 | 10c multicolored | .25 | .25 |
| **474** | A90 | 50c multicolored | .25 | .25 |
| **475** | A90 | $2 multicolored | .50 | .50 |
| **476** | A90 | $2.50 multicolored | .50 | .50 |
| | | *Nos. 473-476 (4)* | 1.50 | 1.50 |

**Souvenir Sheet**

| | | | | |
|---|---|---|---|---|
| **477** | A90 | $5 multicolored | 2.00 | 2.00 |

A91

Maltese Cross Cancels and: 10c, Penny Post notice, 1839. 50c, Hill's original stamp design. $2, St. Lucia #1. $2.50, Penny Black. $5, Hill portrait.

**1979, Dec. 27**

| | | | | |
|---|---|---|---|---|
| **478** | A91 | 10c multicolored | .25 | .25 |
| **479** | A91 | 50c multicolored | .25 | .25 |
| **480** | A91 | $2 multicolored | .25 | *.50* |
| **481** | A91 | $2.50 multicolored | .40 | *.60* |
| | | *Nos. 478-481 (4)* | 1.15 | 1.60 |

**Souvenir Sheet**

| | | | | |
|---|---|---|---|---|
| **482** | A91 | $5 multicolored | 1.25 | 1.25 |

Sir Rowland Hill (1793-1879), originator of penny postage.

Nos. 478-481 also issued in sheets of 5 plus label, perf. 12x12½.

A92

IYC Emblem, Virgin and Child Paintings by: 10c, Virgin and Child, by Bernardino Fungi, IYC emblem. 50c, Carlo Dolci. $2, Titian. $2.50, Giovanni Bellini.

**1980, Jan. 14**

| | | | | |
|---|---|---|---|---|
| **483** | A92 | 10c multicolored | .25 | .25 |
| **484** | A92 | 50c multicolored | .25 | .25 |
| **485** | A92 | $2 multicolored | .75 | .75 |
| **486** | A92 | $2.50 multicolored | 1.00 | 1.00 |
| *a.* | | Souvenir sheet of 4, #483-486 | 2.50 | 2.50 |
| | | *Nos. 483-486 (4)* | 2.25 | 2.25 |

Christmas 1979; Intl. Year of the Child.

St. Lucia Conveyance Co. Ltd. Stamp, 1873 — A92a

London 1980 Emblem and Covers: 30c, "Assistance" 1p postmark, 1879. 50c, Postage due handstamp, 1929. $2, Postmarks on 1844 cover.

**Wmk. 373**

**1980, May 6 Litho. *Perf. 14***

| | | | | |
|---|---|---|---|---|
| **487** | A92a | 10c multicolored | .25 | .25 |
| **488** | A92a | 30c multicolored | .25 | .25 |
| **489** | A92a | 50c multicolored | .25 | .25 |
| **490** | A92a | $2 multicolored | .25 | .25 |
| *a.* | | Souvenir sheet of 4, #487-490 | .80 | .80 |
| | | *Nos. 487-490 (4)* | 1.00 | 1.00 |

London 1980 Intl. Stamp Exhib., May 6-14.

Intl. Year of the Child — A93

½c, Mickey on rocket. 1c, Donald Duck spacewalking. 2c, Minnie Mouse on moon. 3c, Goofy hitch hiking. 4c, Goofy on moon. 5c, Pluto digging on moon. 10c, Donald Duck, space creature. $2, Donald Duck paddling satellite. $2.50, Mickey Mouse in lunar rover.

$5, Goofy on moon.

Space scenes. 1c, 4c, 5c, 10c, $2, $2.50 horiz.

**1980, May 29 Litho. *Perf. 11***

| | | | | |
|---|---|---|---|---|
| **491** | A93 | ½c multicolored | .25 | .25 |
| **492** | A93 | 1c multicolored | .25 | .25 |
| **493** | A93 | 2c multicolored | .25 | .25 |
| **494** | A93 | 3c multicolored | .25 | .25 |
| **495** | A93 | 4c multicolored | .25 | .25 |
| **496** | A93 | 5c multicolored | .25 | .25 |
| **497** | A93 | 10c multicolored | .25 | .25 |
| **498** | A93 | $2 multicolored | 1.75 | 1.75 |
| **499** | A93 | $2.50 multicolored | 1.75 | 1.75 |
| | | *Nos. 491-499 (9)* | 5.25 | 5.25 |

**Souvenir Sheet**

| | | | | |
|---|---|---|---|---|
| **500** | A93 | $5 multicolored | 4.50 | 4.50 |

Queen Mother Elizabeth, 80th Birthday — A94

**1980, Aug. 4 Litho. *Perf. 14***

| | | | | |
|---|---|---|---|---|
| **501** | A94 | 10c multicolored | .25 | .25 |
| **502** | A94 | $2.50 multicolored | .40 | *1.00* |

**Souvenir Sheet**

***Perf. 12½x12***

| | | | | |
|---|---|---|---|---|
| **503** | A94 | $3 multicolored | .80 | .80 |

HS-748 on Runway, St. Lucia Airport, Hewanorra — A95

10c, DC-10, St. Lucia Airport. 15c, Bus, Castries. 20c, Refrigerator ship. 25c, Islander plane. 30c, Pilot boat. 50c, Boeing 727. 75c, Cruise ship. $1, Lockheed Tristar, Piton Mountains. $2, Cargo ship. $5, Boeing 707. $10, Queen Elizabeth 2.

**Wmk. 373**

**1980, Aug. 11 Litho. *Perf. 14½***

| | | | | |
|---|---|---|---|---|
| **504** | A95 | 5c shown | .30 | .30 |
| **505** | A95 | 10c multicolored | .50 | .30 |
| **506** | A95 | 15c multicolored | .35 | .40 |
| **507** | A95 | 20c multicolored | .35 | .40 |
| **508** | A95 | 25c multicolored | .50 | .40 |
| **509** | A95 | 30c multicolored | .40 | .45 |
| **510** | A95 | 50c multicolored | .75 | .75 |
| **511** | A95 | 75c multicolored | .60 | *1.75* |
| **512** | A95 | $1 multicolored | .75 | *1.50* |
| **513** | A95 | $2 multicolored | 1.40 | *2.40* |
| **514** | A95 | $5 multicolored | 3.50 | *6.00* |
| **515** | A95 | $10 multicolored | 6.75 | *10.00* |
| | | *Nos. 504-515 (12)* | 16.15 | 24.65 |

For surcharges see Nos. 531-533.

**1984, May 15 Wmk. 380**

| | | | | |
|---|---|---|---|---|
| *507a* | A95 | 20c | 2.50 | 2.50 |
| *508a* | A95 | 25c | 3.25 | 3.25 |
| *509a* | A95 | 30c | 3.25 | 3.25 |
| *512a* | A95 | $1 | 6.50 | 6.50 |
| *513a* | A95 | $2 | 7.50 | 7.50 |
| *515a* | A95 | $10 | 15.00 | 15.00 |
| | | *Nos. 507a-515a (6)* | 38.00 | 38.00 |

Shot Put, Moscow '80 Emblem — A96

**1980, Sept. 22 Litho. *Perf. 14***

| | | | | |
|---|---|---|---|---|
| **516** | A96 | 10c shown | .25 | .25 |
| **517** | A96 | 50c Swimming | .25 | .25 |
| **518** | A96 | $2 Gymnastics | .90 | .90 |
| **519** | A96 | $2.50 Weight lifting | 1.10 | 1.10 |
| | | *Nos. 516-519 (4)* | 2.50 | 2.50 |

**Souvenir Sheet**

| | | | | |
|---|---|---|---|---|
| **520** | A96 | $5 Passing the torch | 2.00 | 2.00 |

22nd Summer Olympic Games, Moscow, July 19-Aug. 3.

A97

**1980, Sept. 30 *Perf. 14***

| | | | | |
|---|---|---|---|---|
| **521** | A97 | 10c Palms, coast at dusk | .25 | .25 |
| **522** | A97 | 50c Rocky shore | .25 | .25 |
| **523** | A97 | $2 Sand beach | .40 | .40 |
| **524** | A97 | $2.50 Pitons at sunset | .50 | .50 |
| | | *Nos. 521-524 (4)* | 1.40 | 1.40 |

**Souvenir Sheet**

| | | | | |
|---|---|---|---|---|
| **525** | A97 | $5 Two-master | 1.75 | 1.75 |

Rotary International, 75th Anniversary.

A98

Nobel Prize Winners: 10c, Sir Arthur Lewis, Economics. 50c, Martin Luther King, Jr., peace, 1964. $2, Ralph Bunche, peace, 1950. $2.50, Albert Schweitzer, peace, 1952. $5, Albert Einstein, physics, 1921.

**1980, Oct. 23 Litho. *Perf. 14***

| | | | | |
|---|---|---|---|---|
| **526** | A98 | 10c multicolored | .25 | .25 |
| **527** | A98 | 50c multicolored | .25 | .25 |
| **528** | A98 | $2 multicolored | .60 | .60 |
| **529** | A98 | $2.50 multicolored | 1.00 | 1.00 |
| | | *Nos. 526-529 (4)* | 2.10 | 2.10 |

**Souvenir Sheet**

| | | | | |
|---|---|---|---|---|
| **530** | A98 | $5 multicolored | 2.75 | 2.75 |

**Nos. 506-507, 510 Surcharged**

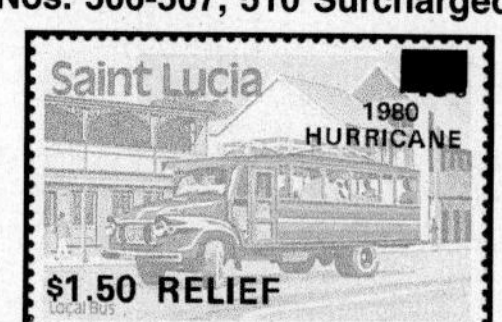


**1980, Nov. 3 Litho. *Perf. 14½***

| | | | | |
|---|---|---|---|---|
| **531** | A95 | $1.50 on 15c multi | .35 | .35 |
| **532** | A95 | $1.50 on 20c multi | .35 | .35 |
| **533** | A95 | $1.50 on 50c multi | .35 | .35 |
| | | *Nos. 531-533 (3)* | 1.05 | 1.05 |

Nativity, by Battista — A99

Angel and Citizens of St. Lucia — A100

Christmas: 30c, Adoration of the Kings, by Bruegel the Elder. $2, Adoration of the Shepherds, by Murillo.

**1980, Dec. 1 *Perf. 14***

| | | | | |
|---|---|---|---|---|
| **534** | A99 | 10c multicolored | .25 | .25 |
| **535** | A99 | 30c multicolored | .25 | .25 |
| **536** | A99 | $2 multicolored | .45 | .45 |
| | | *Nos. 534-536 (3)* | .95 | .95 |

**Souvenir Sheet**

| | | | | |
|---|---|---|---|---|
| **537** | A100 | Sheet of 3 | 1.00 | 1.00 |
| *a.* | | $1 any single | .30 | .30 |

Agouti — A101

**1981, Jan. 19 Litho. *Perf. 14***

| | | | | |
|---|---|---|---|---|
| **538** | A101 | 10c shown | .25 | .25 |
| **539** | A101 | 50c St. Lucia parrot | .75 | .25 |
| **540** | A101 | $2 Purple-throated carib | 2.25 | 1.30 |
| **541** | A101 | $2.50 Fiddler crab | 1.75 | 1.75 |
| | | *Nos. 538-541 (4)* | 5.00 | 3.55 |

**Souvenir Sheet**

| | | | | |
|---|---|---|---|---|
| **542** | A101 | $5 Monarch butterfly | 4.00 | 4.00 |

**Royal Wedding Issue**

Common Design Type

**1981, June 16 Litho. *Perf. 14***

| | | | | |
|---|---|---|---|---|
| **543** | CD331a | 25c Couple | .25 | .25 |
| **544** | CD331a | 50c Clarence House | .25 | .25 |
| **545** | CD331a | $4 Charles | .30 | .30 |
| | | *Nos. 543-545 (3)* | .80 | .80 |

Nos. 543-545 also printed in sheets of 5 plus label, perf. 12, in changed colors.

**Souvenir Sheet**

| | | | | |
|---|---|---|---|---|
| **546** | CD331 | $5 Glass coach | .70 | .70 |
| **549** | CD331 | Booklet | 5.50 | 5.50 |
| *a.* | | Pane of 1, $5, Couple | 2.00 | 2.00 |
| *b.* | | Pane of 6 (3x50c, Diana, 3x$2, Charles) | 3.50 | 3.50 |

A102

Picasso Birth Centenary: 30c, The Cock. 50c, Man with Ice Cream. 55c, Woman Dressing her Hair. $3, Seated Woman. $5, Night Fishing at Antibes.

**1981, May Litho. Perf. 14**

**550** A102 30c multicolored .25 .25
**551** A102 50c multicolored .30 .30
**552** A102 55c multicolored .35 .35
**553** A102 $3 multicolored 1.75 1.75
*Nos. 550-553 (4)* 2.65 2.65

**Souvenir Sheet**

**554** A102 $5 multicolored 3.50 3.50

A103

10c, Industry. 35c, Community service. 50c, Hikers. $2.50, Duke of Edinburgh.

**Wmk. 373**

**1981, Sept. 28 Litho. Perf. 14½**

**555** A103 10c multicolored .25 .25
**556** A103 35c multicolored .25 .25
**557** A103 50c multicolored .25 .25
**558** A103 $2.50 multicolored .30 .30
*Nos. 555-558 (4)* 1.05 1.05

Duke of Edinburgh's Awards, 25th anniv.

Intl. Year of the Disabled A104

**1981, Oct. 30 Litho. Perf. 14**

**559** A104 10c Louis Braille .25 .25
**560** A104 50c Sarah Bernhardt .25 .25
**561** A104 $2 Joseph Pulitzer .70 .70
**562** A104 $2.50 Henri de Toulouse-Lautrec 1.10 1.10
*Nos. 559-562 (4)* 2.30 2.30

**Souvenir Sheet**

**563** A104 $5 Franklin D. Roosevelt 1.75 1.75

A105

Christmas: Adoration of the King Paintings.

**1981, Dec. 15**

**564** A105 10c Sfoza .25 .25
**565** A105 30c Orcanga .25 .25
**566** A105 $1.50 Gerard .50 .50
**567** A105 $2.50 Foppa 1.00 1.00
*Nos. 564-567 (4)* 2.00 2.00

A106

**1981, Dec. 29 Unwmk.**

**568** A106 10c No. 1 .25 .25
**569** A106 30c No. 251 .25 .25
**570** A106 50c No. 459 .40 .40
**571** A106 $2 UPU, St. Lucia flags 1.30 1.30
*Nos. 568-571 (4)* 2.20 2.20

**Souvenir Sheets**

**572** A106 $5 GPO, Castries 2.00 2.00

First anniv. of UPU membership.

A107

1980s Decade for Women (Paintings of Women by Women): 10c, Fanny Travis Cochran, by Cecilia Beaux. 50c, Women with Dove, by Marie Laurencin. $2, Portrait of a Young Pupil of David. $2.50, Self-portrait, by Rosalba Carriera. $5, Self-portrait, by Elisabeth Vigee-Le Brun.

**Unwmk.**

**1981, Dec. 1 Litho. Perf. 14**

**573** A107 10c multicolored .25 .25
**574** A107 50c multicolored .25 .25
**575** A107 $2 multicolored .75 .50
**576** A107 $2.50 multicolored 1.00 1.00
*Nos. 573-576 (4)* 2.25 2.00

**Souvenir Sheet**

**577** A107 $5 multicolored 1.50 1.50

1982 World Cup Soccer A108

Designs: Various soccer players.

**1982, Feb. 15 Litho. Perf. 14½**

**578** A108 10c multicolored .40 .40
**579** A108 50c multicolored 1.40 1.40
**580** A108 $2 multicolored 1.75 1.75
**581** A108 $2.50 multicolored 2.00 2.00
*Nos. 578-581 (4)* 5.55 5.55

**Souvenir Sheet**

**582** A108 $5 multicolored 4.00 4.00

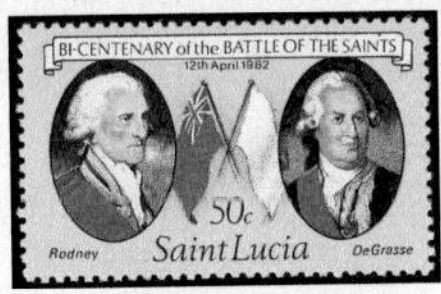

Battle of the Saints Bicentenary — A109

10c, Pigeon Island 35c, Battle. 50c, Admirals Rodney, DeGrasse. $2.50, Map.

**Wmk. 373**

**1982, Apr. 13 Litho. Perf. 14**

**583** A109 10c multicolored .40 .40
**584** A109 35c multicolored .80 .80
**585** A109 50c multicolored 1.20 1.20
**586** A109 $2.50 multicolored 4.25 4.25
*a.* Souvenir sheet of 4, #583-586 8.50 8.50
*Nos. 583-586 (4)* 6.65 6.65

Scouting Year — A110

**1982, Aug. 4 Litho. Perf. 14**

**587** A110 10c Map reading .25 .25
**588** A110 50c First aid .25 .25
**589** A110 $1.50 Camping 1.25 1.25
**590** A110 $2.50 Campfire sing 2.00 2.00
*Nos. 587-590 (4)* 3.75 3.75

**Princess Diana Issue**

Common Design Type

***Perf. 14½x14***

**1982, Sept. 1 Unwmk.**

**591** CD332 50c Leeds Castle .30 .30
**592** CD332 $2 Diana 1.50 1.50
**593** CD332 $4 Wedding 2.40 2.40
*Nos. 591-593 (3)* 4.20 4.20

**Souvenir Sheet**

**594** CD332 $5 Diana, diff. 4.50 4.50

Christmas 1982 — A111

Paintings: 10c, Adoration of the Kings, by Brueghel the Elder. 30c, Nativity, by Lorenzo Costa. 50c, Virgin and Child, Fra Filippo Lippi. 80c, Adoration of the Shepherds, by Nicolas Poussin.

**Wmk. 373**

**1982, Nov. 10 Litho. Perf. 14**

**595** A111 10c multicolored .25 .25
**596** A111 30c multicolored .25 .25
**597** A111 50c multicolored .40 .40
**598** A111 80c multicolored .70 .70
*Nos. 595-598 (4)* 1.60 1.60

A111a

**1983, Mar. 14 Litho.**

**599** A111a 10c Twin Peaks .30 .30
**600** A111a 30c Beach .40 .40
**601** A111a 50c Banana harvester .30 .30
**602** A111a $2 Flag 1.75 1.75
*Nos. 599-602 (4)* 2.75 2.75

Commonwealth day.

Crown Agents Sesquicentennial A112

**Wmk. 373**

**1983, Apr. 1 Litho. Perf. 14½**

**603** A112 10c Headquarters, London .25 .25
**604** A112 15c Road construction .25 .25
**605** A112 50c Map .25 .25
**606** A112 $2 First stamp 1.25 1.25
*Nos. 603-606 (4)* 2.00 2.00

World Communications Year — A113

10c, Shipboard intercommunication. 50c, Air-to-air. $1.50, Satellite. $2.50, Computer communications.
$5, Weather satellite.

**Unwmk.**

**1983, July 12 Litho. Perf. 15**

**607** A113 10c multicolored .25 .25
**608** A113 50c multicolored .55 .55
**609** A113 $1.50 multicolored 1.25 1.25
**610** A113 $2.50 multicolored 2.00 2.00
*Nos. 607-610 (4)* 4.05 4.05

**Souvenir Sheet**

**611** A113 $5 multicolored 3.50 3.50

Coral Reef Fish A114

10c, Longspine squirrelfish. 50c, Banded butter-flyfish. $1.50, Blackbar soldierfish. $2.50, Yellowtail snappers.
$5, Red hind.

**1983, Aug. 23**

**612** A114 10c multicolored .25 .25
**613** A114 50c multicolored .25 .25
**614** A114 $1.50 multicolored 1.00 1.00
**615** A114 $2.50 multicolored 1.50 1.50
*Nos. 612-615 (4)* 3.00 3.00

**Souvenir Sheet**

**616** A114 $5 multicolored 4.50 4.50

For overprint see No. 800.

Locomotives — A115

No. 617, Princess Coronation. No. 618, Duke of Sutherland. No. 619, Leeds United. No. 620, Lord Nelson. No. 621, Bodmin. No. 622, Eton. No. 623, Flying Scotsman. No. 624, Stephenson's Rocket.

***Perf. 12½***

**1983, Oct. 13 Litho. Unwmk.**

**Se-tenant Pairs, #a.-b.**

**a. — Side and front views.**

**b. — Action scene.**

**617** A115 35c multicolored .25 .25
**618** A115 35c multicolored .25 .25
**619** A115 50c multicolored .25 *.65*
**620** A115 50c multicolored .25 *.65*
**621** A115 $1 multicolored .60 *1.10*
**622** A115 $1 multicolored .60 *1.10*
**623** A115 $2 multicolored 1.25 *2.10*
**624** A115 $2 multicolored 1.25 *2.10*
*Nos. 617-624 (8)* 4.70 *8.20*

See Nos. 674-679, 711-718, 774-777, 807-814.

Virgin and Child Paintings by Raphael — A115a

10c, Niccolini-Cowper Madonna. 30c, Holy Family with a Palm Tree. 50c, Sistine Madonna. $5, Alba Madonna

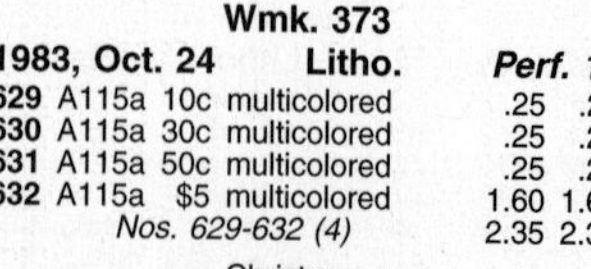

**Wmk. 373**

**1983, Oct. 24 Litho. *Perf. 14***

**629** A115a 10c multicolored .25 .25
**630** A115a 30c multicolored .25 .25
**631** A115a 50c multicolored .25 .25
**632** A115a $5 multicolored 1.60 1.60
*Nos. 629-632 (4)* 2.35 2.35

Christmas.

Battle of Waterloo, King George III — A116

Nos. 633a, 633b, shown. No. 634a, George III, diff. No. 634b, Kew Palace. No. 635a, Arms of Elizabeth I. No. 635b, Elizabeth I. No. 636a, Arms of George III. No. 636b, George III, diff. No. 637a, Elizabeth I, diff. No. 637b, Hatfield Palace. No. 638a, Spanish Armada. No. 638b, Elizabeth, I, diff.

***Perf. 12½***

**1984, Mar. 13 Litho. Unwmk.**

**633** A116 5c Pair, #a.-b. .25 *.35*
**634** A116 10c Pair, #a.-b. .25 *.35*
**635** A116 35c Pair, #a.-b. .25 *.50*
**636** A116 60c Pair, #a.-b. .40 *.90*
**637** A116 $1 Pair, #a.-b. .60 *1.25*
**638** A116 $2.50 Pair, #a.-b. 1.75 *3.50*
*Nos. 633-638 (6)* 3.50 *6.85*

Unissued 30c, 50c, $1, $2.50 and $5 values became available with the liquidation of the printer.

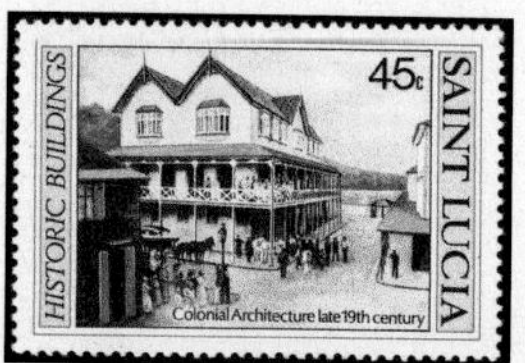


Colonial Building, Late 19th Cent. — A118

Local Architecture. 10c, Buildings, mid-19th cent., vert. 65c, Wooden chattel, early 20th cent. $2.50, Treasury, 1906.

***Perf. 14x13½, 13½x14***

**1984, Apr. 6 Wmk. 380**

**645** A118 10c multicolored .25 .25
**646** A118 45c shown .40 .35
**647** A118 65c multicolored .55 .45
**648** A118 $2.50 multicolored 2.00 1.75
*Nos. 645-648 (4)* 3.20 2.80

For overprints see Nos. 796, 801.

Logwood Tree and Blossom — A118a

***Perf. 13½x14, 14x13½***

**1984, June 12 Wmk. 380**

**649** A118a 10c shown .25 .25
**650** A118a 45c Calabash .25 .25
**651** A118a 65c Gommier, vert. .30 .30
**652** A118a $2.50 Rain tree 1.40 1.40
*Nos. 649-652 (4)* 2.20 2.20

For overprint see No. 802.

Automobiles — A119

5c, Bugatti 57SC, 1939. 10c, Chevrolet Bel Air, 1957. $1, Alfa Romeo, 1930. $2.50, Duesenberg, 1932.

***Perf. 12½***

**1984, June 25 Litho. Unwmk.**

**Se-tenant Pairs, #a.-b.**

**a. — Side and front views.**

**b. — Action scene.**

**653** A119 5c multicolored .25 .25
**654** A119 10c multicolored .25 .25
**655** A119 $1 multicolored .30 *1.25*
**656** A119 $2.50 multicolored .60 *3.00*
*Nos. 653-656 (4)* 1.40 4.75

See Nos. 686-693, 739-742, 850-855.

Endangered Reptiles — A120

**Wmk. 380**

**1984, Aug. 8 Litho. *Perf. 14***

**661** A120 10c Pygmy gecko .25 .25
**662** A120 45c Maria Isld. ground lizard .45 .45
**663** A120 65c Green iguana .60 .60
**664** A120 $2.50 Couresse snake 1.25 1.25
*Nos. 661-664 (4)* 2.55 2.55

For overprint see No. 797.

Leaders of the World, 1984 Olympics — A121

#665a, Volleyball. #665b, Volleyball, diff.. #666a, Women's hurdles. #666b, Men's hurdles. #667a, Showjumping. #667b, Dressage. #668a, Women's gymnastics. #668b, Men's gymnastics.

***Perf. 12½***

**1984, Sept. 21 Litho. Unwmk.**

**665** A121 5c Pair, #a.-b. .25 .25
**666** A121 10c Pair, #a.-b. .25 .25
**667** A121 65c Pair, #a.-b. .25 *.60*
**668** A121 $2.50 Pair, #a.-b. 1.00 *2.00*
*Nos. 665-668 (4)* 1.75 3.10

**Locomotive Type of 1983**

1c, TAW 2-6-2T, 1897. 15c, Crocodile 1-C.C.-1, 1920. 50c, The Countess 0.6.0T, 1903. 75c, Class GE6/6C.C., 1921. $1, Class P8, 4.6.0, 1906. $2, Der Alder 2.2.2., 1835.

**1984, Sept. 21 Litho. *Perf. 12½***

**Se-tenant Pairs, #a.-b.**

**a. — Side and front views.**

**b. — Action scene.**

**674** A115 1c multicolored .25 .25
**675** A115 15c multicolored .25 *.40*
**676** A115 50c multicolored .30 *.55*
**677** A115 75c multicolored .30 *.85*
**678** A115 $1 multicolored .40 *.60*
**679** A115 $2 multicolored .50 *.80*
*Nos. 674-679 (6)* 2.00 *3.45*

**Automobile Type of 1983**

10c, Panhard and Levassor, 1889. 30c, N.S.U. R0-80 Saloon, 1968. 55c, Abarth, Balbero, 1958. 65c, TVR Vixen 2500M, 1972. 75c, Ford Mustang Convertible, 1965. $1, Ford Model T, 1914. $2, Aston Martin DB3S, 1954. $3, Chrysler Imperial CG, 1931.

**1984, Dec. 19 Litho. *Perf. 12½***

**Se-tenant Pairs, #a.-b.**

**a. — Side and front views.**

**b. — Action scene.**

**686** A119 10c multicolored .25 .25
**687** A119 30c multicolored .25 *.35*
**688** A119 55c multicolored .25 *.65*
**689** A119 65c multicolored .25 *.75*
**690** A119 75c multicolored .25 *.90*
**691** A119 $1 multicolored .35 *1.25*
**692** A119 $2 multicolored 1.00 *2.50*
**693** A119 $3 multicolored 1.10 *3.50*
*Nos. 686-693 (8)* 3.70 *10.15*

Christmas — A122

**Wmk. 380**

**1984, Oct. 31 Litho. *Perf. 14***

**702** A122 10c Wine glass .25 .25
**703** A122 35c Altar .25 .25
**704** A122 65c Creche .25 *.25*
**705** A122 $3 Holy family, abstract .25 *1.00*
*a.* Souvenir sheet of 4, #702-705 2.60 2.60
*Nos. 702-705 (4)* 1.00 *1.75*

Abolition of Slavery, 150th Anniv. — A123

Engraving details, Natl. Archives, Castries: 10c, Preparing manioc. 35c, Working with cassava flour. 55c, Cooking, twisting and drying tobacco. $5, Tobacco production, diff.

**1984, Dec. 12 Litho. *Perf. 14***

**706** A123 10c bright buff & blk .25 .25
**707** A123 35c bright buff & blk .25 .25
**708** A123 55c bright buff & blk .25 .25
**709** A123 $5 bright buff & blk .75 *2.50*
*Nos. 706-709 (4)* 1.50 3.25

**Souvenir Sheet**

**710** Sheet of 4 2.50 2.50
*a.* A123 10c like No. 706 .25 .25
*b.* A123 35c like No. 707 .25 .25
*c.* A123 55c like No. 708 .25 .25
*d.* A123 $5 like No. 709 .70 .70

#710a-710d se-tenant in continuous design.

**Locomotive Type of 1983**

5c, J.N.R. Class C-53, 1928, Japan. 15c, Heavy L, 1885, India. 35c, QGR Class B18¼, 1926, Australia. 60c, Owain Glyndwr, 1923, U.K. 75c, Lion, 1838, U.K. $1, Coal Engine, 1873, U.K. $2, No. 2238 Class Q6, 1921, U.K. $2.50, Class H, 1920, U.K.

**1985, Feb. 4 Unwmk. *Perf. 12½***

**Se-tenant Pairs, #a.-b.**

**a. — Side and front views.**

**b. — Action scene.**

**711** A115 5c multicolored .25 .25
**712** A115 15c multicolored .25 .25
**713** A115 35c multicolored .25 *.60*
**714** A115 60c multicolored .25 *.60*
**715** A115 75c multicolored .25 *.75*
**716** A115 $1 multicolored .30 *.80*
**717** A115 $2 multicolored .50 *1.20*
**718** A115 $2.50 multicolored .70 *1.50*
*Nos. 711-718 (8)* 2.75 *5.95*

Girl Guides, 75th Anniv. — A124

**1985, Feb. 21 Wmk. 380 *Perf. 14***

**727** A124 10c multicolored .40 .25
**728** A124 35c multicolored 1.00 .25
**729** A124 65c multicolored 2.25 .75
**730** A124 $3 multicolored 4.25 *5.50*
*Nos. 727-730 (4)* 7.90 6.75

For overprint see No. 795.

Butterflies — A125

No. 731a, Clossiana selene. No. 731b, Inachis io. No. 732a, Philaethria werneckei. No. 732b, Catagramma sorana. No. 733a, Kallima inachus. No. 733b, Hypanartia paullus. No. 734a, Morpho rhetenor helena. No. 734b, Ornithoptera meridionalis.

**1985, Feb. 28 Unwmk. *Perf. 12½***

**731** A125 15c Pair, #a.-b. .25 .25
**732** A125 40c Pair, #a.-b. .25 .25
**733** A125 60c Pair, #a.-b. .25 .25
**734** A125 $2.25 Pair, #a.-b. 1.50 1.50
*Nos. 731-734 (4)* 2.25 2.25

**Automobile Type of 1983**

15c, 1940 Hudson Eight, US. 50c, 1937 KdF, Germany. $1, 1925 Kissel Goldbug, US. $1.50, 1973 Ferrari 246GTS, Italy.

**1985, Mar. 29 Se-tenant Pairs**

**739** A119 15c multicolored .25 *.25*
**740** A119 50c multicolored .40 *.60*
**741** A119 $1 multicolored .40 *.60*
**742** A119 $1.50 multicolored .80 *1.50*
*Nos. 739-742 (4)* 1.85 *2.95*

Military Uniforms — A126

Designs: 5c, Grenadier, 70th Foot Reg., c. 1775. 10c, Grenadier Co. Officer, 14th Foot Reg., 1780. 20c, Battalion Co. Officer, 46th Foot Reg., 1781. 25c, Officer, Royal Artillery Reg., c. 1782. 30c, Officer, Royal Engineers Corps., 1782. 35c, Battalion Co. Officer, 54th Foot Reg., 1782. 45c, Grenadier Co. Private, 14th Foot Reg., 1782. 50c, Gunner, Royal Artillery Reg., 1796. 65c, Battalion Co. Private, 85th Foot Reg., c. 1796. 75c, Battalion Co. Private, 76th Foot Reg., 1796. 90c, Battalion Co. Private, 81st Foot Reg., c. 1796. $1, Sergeant, 74th (Highland) Foot Reg., 1796. $2.50, Private, Light Co., 93rd Foot Reg., 1803. $5, Battalion Co. Private, 1st West India Reg., 1803. $15, Officer, Royal Artillery Reg., 1850.

**1985, May 7 Wmk. 380 *Perf. 15***

**"1984" Imprint Below Design**

**747** A126 5c multicolored .35 *.65*
**748** A126 10c multicolored .45 .25
**749** A126 20c multicolored .50 .35
*a.* "1986" Imprint .65 .65
**750** A126 25c multicolored .65 .25
*a.* "1986" Imprint .65 .65
**751** A126 30c multicolored .80 .35
**752** A126 35c multicolored .75 .25
**753** A126 45c multicolored .85 *.50*
**754** A126 50c multicolored 1.00 *.50*
**755** A126 65c multicolored 1.10 *.65*
**756** A126 75c multicolored 1.25 *1.00*
**757** A126 90c multicolored 1.50 1.00

758 A126 $1 multicolored 1.60 1.00
759 A126 $2.50 multicolored 4.00 *6.50*
760 A126 $5 multicolored 6.25 13.00
761 A126 $15 multicolored 17.00 *26.00*
*Nos. 747-761 (15)* 38.05 *52.25*

See Nos. 876-879.

**1987 Unwmk.**

**1986 Imprint Below Design**

*747a* A126 5c .40 .75
*748a* A126 10c .60 .40
*751a* A126 30c .85 .65
*753a* A126 45c .95 .75
*754a* A126 50c 1.00 .90
*759a* A126 $2.50 5.00 *6.00*
*760a* A126 $5 6.50 *11.00*
*Nos. 747a-760a (7)* 15.30 20.45

Issued: No. 747a-748a, 2/24; No. 751a-760a, 3/16.

**1989 Wmk. 384**

*747b* A126 5c "1989" Imprint .85 1.25
*748b* A126 10c "1989 " Imprint 1.10 .65
*749a* A126 20c "1989" Imprint 1.50 1.25
*750b* A126 25c "1988" imprint 1.00 1.25
*750c* A126 25c "1989" Imprint 1.00 1.25

No. 750b issued 9/88.

World War II Aircraft A127

5c, Messerschmitt 109-E. 55c, Avro 683 Lancaster Mark I Bomber. 60c, North American P.51-D Mustang. $2, Supermarine Spitfire Mark II.

**1985, May 30 Unwmk. *Perf. 12½***

**Se-tenant Pairs, #a.-b.**

**a. — Action scene.**

**b. — Bottom, front and side views.**

**762** A127 5c multicolored .25 *.40*
**763** A127 55c multicolored .60 *.90*
**764** A127 60c multicolored .60 *.90*
**765** A127 $2 multicolored .80 *1.60*
*Nos. 762-765 (4)* 2.25 *3.80*

Nature Reserves A128

Birds in habitats: 10c, Frigate bird, Frigate Island Sanctuary. 35c, Mangrove cuckoo, Savannes Bay, Scorpion Island. 65c, Yellow sandpiper, Maria Island. $3, Audubon's shearwater, Lapins Island.

**1985, June 20 Wmk. 380 *Perf. 15***

**770** A128 10c multicolored .35 .25
**771** A128 35c multicolored .65 .40
**772** A128 65c multicolored .75 .75
**773** A128 $3 multicolored 2.40 2.40
*Nos. 770-773 (4)* 4.15 3.80

**Locomotive Type of 1983**

10c, No. 28 Tender engine, 1897, U.K. 30c, No. 1621 Class M, 1893, U.K. 75c, Class Dunalastair, 1896, U.K. $2.50, Big Bertha No. 2290, 1919, U.K.

**1985, June 26 Unwmk. *Perf. 12½***

**Se-tenant Pairs, #a.-b.**

**a. — Side and front views.**

**b. — Action scene.**

**774** A115 10c multicolored .25 .25
**775** A115 30c multicolored .40 .40
**776** A115 75c multicolored .40 *.60*
**777** A115 $2.50 multicolored 1.00 *1.60*
*Nos. 774-777 (4)* 2.05 2.85

Queen Mother, 85th Birthday — A129

Nos. 782a, 787a, Facing right. Nos. 782b, 787b, Facing left. No. 783a, Facing right. No. 783b, Facing left. Nos. 784a, 788a, Facing right. Nos. 784b, 788b, Facing front. No. 785a, Facing front. No. 785b, Facing left. No. 786a, Facing right. No. 786b, Facing left.

**1985, Aug. 16**

**782** A129 40c Pair, #a.-b. .25 *.50*
**783** A129 75c Pair, #a.-b. .40 *.60*
**784** A129 $1.10 Pair, #a.-b. .40 *1.00*
**785** A129 $1.75 Pair, #a.-b. .50 *1.50*
*Nos. 782-785 (4)* 1.55 *3.60*

**Souvenir Sheets of 2**

**786** A129 $2 #a.-b. 1.00 1.00
**787** A129 $3 #a.-b. 2.50 2.50
**788** A129 $6 #a.-b. 3.50 3.50

For overprints see No. 799.

Intl. Youth Year — A130

Abstracts, by Lyndon Samuel — A131

Illustrations by local artists: 10c, Youth playing banjo, by Wayne Whitfield. 45c, Riding tricycle, by Mark D. Maragh. 75c, Youth against landscape, by Bartholemew Eugene. $3.50, Abstract, by Lyndon Samuel.

**1985, Sept. 5 Wmk. 380 *Perf. 15***

**791** A130 10c multicolored .25 .25
**792** A130 45c multicolored .50 .25
**793** A130 75c multicolored .50 .50
**794** A130 $3.50 multicolored 1.10 *3.00*
*Nos. 791-794 (4)* 2.35 *4.00*

**Souvenir Sheet**

**795** A131 $5 multicolored 2.25 2.25

Intl. Youth Year.

**Stamps of 1983-85 Ovptd. "CARIBBEAN ROYAL VISIT 1985" in Two or Three Lines**

***Perfs. as Before***

**1985, Nov. Wmk. as Before**

**796** A124 35c #728 6.00 3.00
**797** A118 65c #647 1.50 *2.75*
**798** A120 65c #663 5.50 4.00
**799** A129 $1.10 #784a-784b 12.50 *17.50*
**800** A114 $2.50 #615 10.00 8.00
**801** A118 $2.50 #648 2.00 7.00
**802** A119 $2.50 #652 2.00 7.00
*Nos. 796-802 (7)* 39.50 49.25

Masquerade Figures — A132

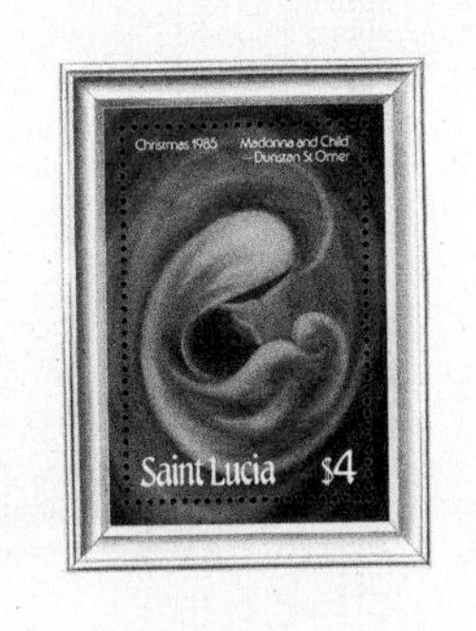

Madonna and Child, by Dunstan St. Omer — A133

**Unwmk.**

**1985, Dec. 23 Litho. *Perf. 15***

**803** A132 10c Papa Jab .25 .25
**804** A132 45c Paille Bananne .25 .25
**805** A132 65c Cheval Bois .75 .75
*Nos. 803-805 (3)* 1.25 1.25

**Miniature Sheet**

**806** A133 $4 multi 1.75 1.75

Christmas 1985.

**Locomotive Type of 1983**

5c, 1983 MWCR Rack Loco Tip Top, US. 15c, 1975 BR Class 87 Stephenson Bo-Bo, UK. 30c, 1901 Class D No. 737, UK. 60c, 1922 No. 13 2-Co-2, UK. 75c, 1954 BR Class EM2 Electra Co-Co, UK. $1, 1922 City of Newcastle, UK. $2.25, 1930 DRG Von Kruckenberg, Propeller-driven Rail Car, Germany. $3, 1893 JNR No. 860, Japan.

**1986, Jan. 17 *Perf. 12½x13***

**Se-tenant Pairs, #a.-b.**

**a. — Side and front views.**

**b. — Action scene.**

**807** A115 5c multicolored .25 *.40*
**808** A115 15c multicolored .25 .25
**809** A115 30c multicolored .40 *.60*
**810** A115 60c multicolored .50 *.80*
**811** A115 75c multicolored .60 *1.00*
**812** A115 $1 multicolored .80 *1.20*
**813** A115 $2.25 multicolored 1.20 *1.60*
**814** A115 $3 multicolored 1.20 *1.60*
*Nos. 807-814 (8)* 5.20 7.45

Miniature Sheets

Cook-out — A134

Designs: No. 823b, Scout sign. No. 824a, Wicker basket, weavings. No. 824b, Lady Olave Baden-Powell, Girl Guides founder.

**1986, Mar. 3 Litho. *Perf. 13x12½***

**823** A134 Sheet of 2 2.25 *3.50*
*a.-b.* $4 any single 1.25 *1.75*
**824** A134 Sheet of 2 3.75 *4.00*
*a.-b.* $6 any single 2.00 2.00

Scouting anniv., Girl Guides 75th anniv. Values are for sheets with plain border. Exist with decorative border. Value, set, $8.50.

A135

Queen Elizabeth II, 60th Birthday — A136

Various photographs: 5c, Pink hat. 10c, Visiting Marian Home. 45c, Mindoo Phillip Park speech. 50c, Opening Leon Hess School. $1, Princess Elizabeth. $3.50, Blue hat. $5, Government House. $6, Canberra, 1982, vert.

$7, HMY Britannia, Castries Harbor. $8, Straw hat.

***Perf. 13x12½, 12½x13, 14x15 (A136)***

**1986**

**825** A135 5c multicolored .25 .25
**826** A136 10c multicolored .25 .25
**827** A136 45c multicolored .30 .30
**828** A136 50c multicolored .35 .35
**829** A135 $1 multicolored .25 *.30*
**830** A135 $3.50 multicolored .50 1.25
**831** A136 $5 multicolored 3.25 3.25
**832** A135 $6 multicolored .60 1.75
*Nos. 825-832 (8)* 5.75 7.70

**Souvenir Sheets**

**833** A136 $7 multicolored 5.00 5.00
**834** A135 $8 multicolored 4.00 *5.50*

Issue dates: Nos. 825, 829-830, 832, Apr. 21; Nos. 826-828, 831, 833, June 14.

State Visit of Pope John Paul II A137

55c, Kissing the ground. 60c, St. Joseph's Convent. 80c, Cathedral, Castries.

$6, Pope.

**1986, July 7 *Perf. 14x15, 15x14***

**835** A137 55c multicolored 1.50 1.00
**836** A137 60c multicolored 1.60 1.00
**837** A137 80c multicolored 2.00 2.00
*Nos. 835-837 (3)* 5.10 4.00

**Souvenir Sheet**

**838** A137 $6 multicolored 12.00 12.00

Nos. 837-838 vert.

Wedding of Prince Andrew and Sarah Ferguson — A138

No. 839a, Sarah. No. 839b, Prince Andrew. No. 840a, Couple, horiz. No. 840b, Prince Andrew, Nancy Reagan, horiz.

**1986, July 23** *Perf. 12½*

839 A138 80c Pair, #a.-b. 1.00 1.00
840 A138 $2 Pair, #a.-b. 2.50 2.50

#840a-840b show Westminster Abbey in LR.

US Peace Corps in St. Lucia, 25th Anniv. A139

80c, Technical instruction. $2, Pres. Kennedy, vert. $3.50, Natl. crests, corps emblem.

**1986, Sept. 25** **Litho.** *Perf. 14*

843 A139 80c multicolored .40 *.50*
844 A139 $2 multicolored 1.10 *1.50*
845 A139 $3.50 multicolored 1.75 *2.60*
*Nos. 843-845 (3)* 3.25 *4.60*

Wedding of Prince Andrew and Sarah Ferguson — A140

**1986, Oct. 15** *Perf. 15*

846 A140 50c Andrew .40 .40
847 A140 80c Sarah .60 .60
848 A140 $1 At altar .75 .75
849 A140 $3 In open carriage 1.50 1.50
*Nos. 846-849 (4)* 3.25 3.25

**Souvenir Sheet**

849A A140 $7 Andrew, Sarah 4.50 4.50

**Automobile Type of 1983**

20c, 1969 AMC AMX, US. 50c, 1912 Russo-Baltique, Russia. 60c, 1932 Lincoln KB, US. $1, 1933 Rolls Royce Phantom II Continental, UK. $1.50, 1939 Buick Century, US. $3, 1957 Chrysler 300 C, US.

**1986, Oct. 23** **Litho.** *Perf. 12½x13*

**Se-tenant Pairs, #a.-b.**

**a. — Side and front views.**

**b. — Action scene.**

850 A119 20c multicolored .30 *.35*
851 A119 50c multicolored .30 *.60*
852 A119 60c multicolored .30 *.60*
853 A119 $1 multicolored .50 *1.25*
854 A119 $1.50 multicolored .70 *1.75*
855 A119 $3 multicolored 1.40 *3.50*
*Nos. 850-855 (6)* 3.50 *8.05*

Chak-Chak Band — A141

**1986, Nov. 7** *Perf. 15*

862 A141 15c shown .25 .25
863 A141 45c Folk dancing .35 .25
864 A141 80c Steel band .60 .60
865 A141 $5 Limbo dancer 1.00 *3.00*
*Nos. 862-865 (4)* 2.20 *4.10*

**Souvenir Sheet**

866 A141 $10 Gros Islet 5.25 5.25

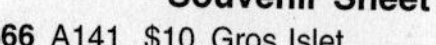

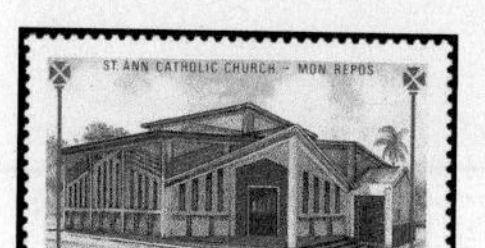


Christmas A142

Churches: 10c, St. Ann Catholic, Mon Repos. 40c, St. Joseph the Worker Catholic, Gros Islet. 80c, Holy Trinity Anglican, Castries. $4, Our Lady of the Assumption Catholic, Soufriere, vert. $7, St. Lucy Catholic, Micoud.

**1986, Nov.**

867 A142 10c multicolored .25 .25
868 A142 40c multicolored .25 .25
869 A142 80c multicolored .50 .50
870 A142 $4 multicolored .80 *2.75*
*Nos. 867-870 (4)* 1.80 *3.75*

**Souvenir Sheet**

871 A142 $7 multicolored 3.50 3.50

Map of St. Lucia — A143

***Perf. 14x14½***

**1987, Feb. 24** **Litho.** **Wmk. 373**

**No Date Imprint Below Design**

872 A143 5c beige & blk .25 .25
*a.* Imprint "1988" .25 .25
*b.* Wmk. 384, "1989" imprint .25 .25
873 A143 10c pale yel grn & blk .25 .25
*a.* Imprint "1988" .25 .25
*b.* Wmk. 384, "1989" imprint .25 .25
874 A143 45c orange & blk .60 .60
*a.* Imprint "1992" .60 .60
875 A143 50c pale violet & blk .60 .60
*a.* Imprint "1989" .60 .60
*Nos. 872-875 (4)* 1.70 1.70

Issued: #872a, 873a, 9/88; #875a, 3/17/89; #872b, 873b, 4/12/89.

See #937.

**Uniforms Type of 1985**

Designs: 15c, Battalion company private, 2nd West India Regiment, 1803. 60c, Battalion company officer, 5th Regiment of Foot, 1778. 80c, Battalion company officer, 27th (or Inniskilling) Regiment of Foot, c. 1780. $20, Grenadier company private, 46th Regiment of Foot, 1778.

**1987, Mar. 16** **Unwmk.** *Perf. 15*

**"1986" Imprint Date Below Design**

876 A126 15c multicolored .45 .25
877 A126 60c multicolored 1.00 .75
878 A126 80c multicolored 1.50 1.00
879 A126 $20 multicolored 17.50 *25.00*
*b.* Imprint "1987" — —
*Nos. 876-879 (4)* 20.45 *27.00*

Dated 1986.

**1988** **Wmk. 384**

**Imprint Date Below Design As Noted**

*876a* A126 15c "1988" 1.25 .90
*b.* Imprint "1989" 1.25 .90
*877a* A126 60c "1988" 2.50 2.00
*878a* A126 80c "1988" 2.75 2.25
*879a* A126 $20 "1989" 24.50 35.00
*Nos. 876a-879a (4)* 31.00 40.15

A144

Statue of Liberty, Cent. — A145

**1987, Apr. 29** **Wmk. 373** *Perf. 14½*

880 A144 15c Statue, flags .45 .45
881 A144 80c Statue, ship .95 .95
882 A144 $1 Statue, Concorde jet 1.50 1.50
883 A144 $5 Statue, flying boat 5.00 5.00
*Nos. 880-883 (4)* 7.90 7.90

**Souvenir Sheet**

884 A145 $6 Statue, New York City 4.50 4.50

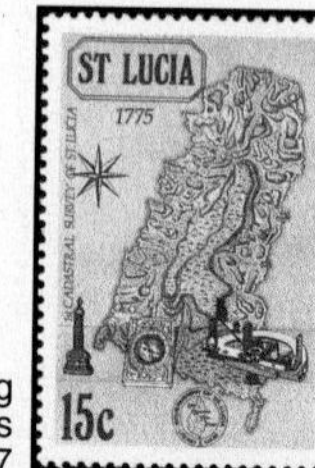


Maps, Surveying Instruments A147

**Wmk. 384**

**1987, Aug. 31** **Litho.** *Perf. 14*

888 A147 15c 1775 .50 .50
889 A147 60c 1814 1.30 1.30
890 A147 $1 1888 2.00 2.00
891 A147 $2.50 1987 4.25 4.25
*Nos. 888-891 (4)* 8.05 8.05

First cadastral survey of St. Lucia.

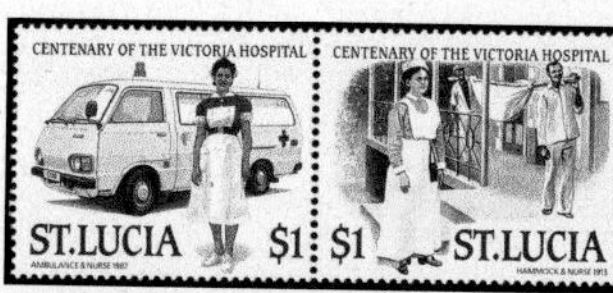


Victoria Hospital, Cent. — A148

No. 894a, Ambulance, nurse, 1987. No. 894b, Nurse, hammock, 1913. No. 895a, Hospital, 1987. No. 895b, Hospital, 1887.

**Wmk. 384**

**1987, Nov. 4** **Litho.** *Perf. 14½*

894 A148 $1 Pair, #a.-b. 4.50 4.50
895 A148 $2 Pair, #a.-b. 8.00 8.00

**Souvenir Sheet**

896 A148 $4.50 Main gate, 1987 9.50 9.50

Christmas A149

Paintings (details) by unidentified artists — 15c, The Holy Family. 50c, Adoration of the Shepherds. 60c, Adoration of the Magi. 90c, Madonna and Child.

$6, Holy Family.

**1987, Nov. 30**

897 A149 15c multicolored .40 .40
898 A149 50c multicolored .85 .85
899 A149 60c multicolored 1.10 1.10
900 A149 90c multicolored 1.30 1.30
*Nos. 897-900 (4)* 3.65 3.65

**Souvenir Sheet**

901 A149 $6 multicolored 5.75 5.75

World Wildlife Fund — A150

Amazonian parrots, Amazona versicolor.

**Wmk. 384**

**1987, Dec. 18** **Litho.** *Perf. 14*

902 A150 15c multi 2.50 2.50
903 A150 35c multi, diff. 3.25 3.25
904 A150 50c multi, diff. 4.50 4.50
905 A150 $1 multi, diff. 7.00 7.00
*Nos. 902-905 (4)* 17.25 17.25

American Indian Artifacts — A151

25c, Carib clay zemi. 30c, Troumassee cylinder. 80c, Three-pointer stone. $3.50, Dauphine petroglyph.

**Wmk. 384**

**1988, Feb. 24** **Litho.** *Perf. 14½*

906 A151 25c multicolored .25 .25
907 A151 30c multicolored .25 .25
908 A151 80c multicolored .50 .50
909 A151 $3.50 multicolored 2.75 2.75
*Nos. 906-909 (4)* 3.75 3.75

St. Lucia Co-operative Bank, 50th Anniv. — A152

***Perf. 15x14***

**1988, Apr. 29** **Litho.** **Wmk. 373**

910 A152 10c Coins, banknotes .45 .45
911 A152 45c Branch in Castries .80 .80
912 A152 60c like 45c .90 .90
913 A152 80c Branch in Vieux Fort 1.40 1.40
*Nos. 910-913 (4)* 3.55 3.55

Cable and Wireless in St. Lucia, 50th Anniv. A153

Designs: 15c, Rural telephone exchange. 25c, Antique and modern telephones. 80c, St. Lucia Teleport (satellite dish). $2.50, Map of Eastern Caribbean microwave communications system.

**Wmk. 384**

**1988, June 10** **Litho.** *Perf. 14*

914 A153 15c multicolored .40 .40
915 A153 25c multicolored .40 .40
916 A153 80c multicolored .95 .95
917 A153 $2.50 multicolored 3.75 3.75
*Nos. 914-917 (4)* 5.50 5.50

Cent. of the Methodist Church in St. Lucia — A154

**Wmk. 384**

**1988, Aug. 15** **Litho.** *Perf. 14½*

918 A154 15c Altar, window .25 .25
919 A154 80c Chancel .60 .60
920 A154 $3.50 Exterior 2.25 2.25
*Nos. 918-920 (3)* 3.10 3.10

Tourism — A155

Lagoon and: 10c, Tourists, gourmet meal. 30c, Beverage, tourists. 80c, Tropical fruit. $2.50, Fish and chef. $5.50, Market.

*Perf. 14x13½*

**1988, Sept. 15 Litho. Wmk. 384**

**921** A155 Strip of 4 6.50 6.50
*a.* 10c multicolored .60 .60
*b.* 30c multicolored .60 .60
*c.* 80c multicolored 1.60 1.60
*d.* $2.50 multicolored 4.50 4.50

**Souvenir Sheet**

**922** A155 $5.50 multicolored 4.00 4.00

**Lloyds of London, 300th Anniv.**
Common Design Type

Designs: 10c, San Francisco earthquake, 1906. 60c, Castries Harbor, horiz. 80c, *Lady Nelson*, sunk off Castries Harbor, 1942, horiz. $2.50, Castries on fire, 1948.

**Wmk. 373**

**1988, Oct. 17 Litho. Perf. 14**

**923** CD341 10c multicolored .60 .60
**924** CD341 60c multicolored 1.60 1.60
**925** CD341 80c multicolored 2.10 2.10
**926** CD341 $2.50 multicolored 4.50 4.50
*Nos. 923-926 (4)* 8.80 8.80

A156

Christmas: Flowers — 15c, Snow on the mountain. 45c, Christmas candle. 60c, Balisier. 80c, Poinsettia.
$5.50, Flower arrangement.

*Perf. 14½x14*

**1988, Nov. 22 Litho. Wmk. 384**

**927** A156 15c multicolored .40 .40
**928** A156 45c multicolored .75 .75
**929** A156 60c multicolored .90 .90
**930** A156 80c multicolored 1.10 1.10
*Nos. 927-930 (4)* 3.15 3.15

**Souvenir Sheet**

**931** A156 $5.50 multicolored 3.50 3.50

A157

Natl. Independence, 10th Anniv.: 15c, Princess Alexandra presenting constitution to Prime Minister Compton. 80c, Sulfur springs geothermal well. $1, Sir Arthur Lewis Community College. $2.50, Pointe Seraphine tax-free shopping center. $5, Emblem.

*Perf. 13½x13*

**1989, Feb. 22 Wmk. 373**

**932** A157 15c Nationhood .25 .25
**933** A157 80c Development .70 .70
**934** A157 $1 Education 1.00 1.00
**935** A157 $2.50 Progress 2.00 2.00
*Nos. 932-935 (4)* 3.95 3.95

**Souvenir Sheet**

**936** A157 $5 With Confidence We Progress 3.50 3.50

**Map Type of 1987**
*Perf. 14x14½*

**1989, Mar. 17 Litho. Wmk. 373**

**937** A143 $1 scarlet & black 1.25 1.25

Indigenous Mushrooms A158

15c, Gerronema citrinum. 25c, Lepiota spiculata. 50c, Calocybe cyanocephala. $5, Russula puiggarii..

*Perf. 14½x14*

**1989, May 31 Litho. Wmk. 384**

**938** A158 15c multicolored 1.00 .50
**939** A158 25c multicolored 1.40 .50
**940** A158 50c multicolored 2.25 1.00
**941** A158 $5 multicolored 8.50 11.00
*Nos. 938-941 (4)* 13.15 13.00

PHILEXFRANCE '89, French Revolution Bicent. — A159

Views of St. Lucia and text: 10c, Independence day announcement, vert. 60c, French revolutionary flag at Morne Fortune, 1791. $1, "Men are born and live free and equal in rights," vert. $3.50, Captain La Crosse's arrival at Gros Islet, 1792.

**Wmk. 373**

**1989, July 14 Litho. Perf. 14**

**942** A159 10c multicolored .50 .25
**943** A159 60c multicolored 2.75 .75
**944** A159 $1 multicolored 3.00 1.25
**945** A159 $3.50 multicolored 10.00 10.00
*Nos. 942-945 (4)* 16.25 12.25

Intl. Red Cross, 125th Anniv. A160

50c, Natl. headquarters. 80c, Seminar in Castries, 1987. $1, Ambulance.

**1989, Oct. 10 Wmk. 384 Perf. 14½**

**946** A160 50c multicolored 1.60 1.60
**947** A160 80c multicolored 2.00 2.25
**948** A160 $1 multicolored 2.50 2.50
*Nos. 946-948 (3)* 6.10 6.35

Christmas Lanterns Shaped Like Buildings A161

**1989, Nov. 17 Perf. 14x14½**

**949** A161 10c multi .25 .25
**950** A161 50c multi, diff. .60 .60
**951** A161 90c multi, diff. 1.25 1.25
**952** A161 $1 multi, diff. 1.40 1.40
*Nos. 949-952 (4)* 3.50 3.50

Trees In Danger of Extinction — A162

10c, Chinna. 15c,

**"1990" Imprint Date Below Design**

**1990 Wmk. 384 Perf. 14**

**953** A162 10c multi .60 .60
**954** A162 15c Latanier .60 .25
**955** A162 20c Gwi gwi .60 .60
**956** A162 25c L'encens .30 .25
**957** A162 50c Bois lele .45 .45
**958** A162 80c Bois d'amande 1.15 .50
**959** A162 95c Mahot piman grand bois 2.10 1.15
**960** A162 $1 Balata 1.40 1.40
**961** A162 $1.50 Pencil cedar 2.50 2.50
**962** A162 $2.50 Bois cendre 5.00 5.00
**963** A162 $5 Lowye cannelle 7.50 7.50
**964** A162 $25 Chalantier grand bois 19.50 *22.00*
*Nos. 953-964 (12)* 41.70 42.20

Issued: 20c, 25c, 50c, $25, 2/21; 10c, 15c, 80c, $1.50, 4/12; 95c, $1, $2.50, $5, 6/25.
For overprints see Nos. 971, O28-O39.

**Year Imprint Dates as Noted**

**1992-95 Wmk. 373 Perf. 14**

*953a* A162 10c "1992" 2.00 2.00
*b.* "1993" 2.00 2.00
*c.* "1994" 2.00 2.00
*954a* A162 15c "1992" 2.00 2.00
*b.* "1994" 2.00 2.00
*955a* A162 20c "1995" 2.00 2.00
*956a* A162 25c "1994" 2.00 2.00
*957a* A162 50c "1992" 4.00 4.00
*b.* "1993" 4.00 4.00
*c.* "1994" 4.00 4.00
*Nos. 953a-957a (5)* 12.00 12.00

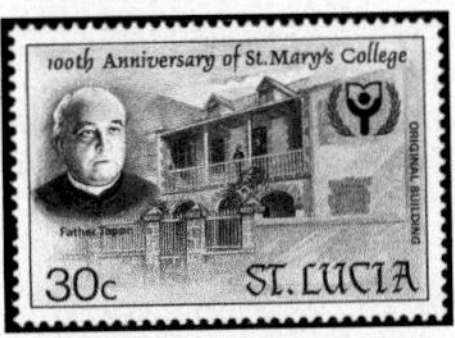

Centenary of St. Mary's College, Intl. Literacy Year — A163

Designs: 30c, Father Tapon, original building. 45c, Rev. Brother Collins, current building. 75c, Students in literacy class. $2, Door to knowledge, children.

**1990, June 6 Wmk. 373**

**965** A163 30c multicolored .35 .35
**966** A163 45c multicolored .55 .55
**967** A163 75c multicolored .85 .85
**968** A163 $2 multicolored 2.25 2.25
*Nos. 965-968 (4)* 4.00 4.00

**Queen Mother, 90th Birthday**
Common Design Types

**1990, Aug. 3 Wmk. 384 Perf. 14x15**

**969** CD343 50c Coronation, 1937 .60 .60

*Perf. 14½*

**970** CD344 $5 Arriving at theater, 1949 4.00 4.00

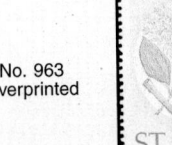

No. 963 Overprinted

**1990, Aug. 13 Perf. 14**

**971** A162 $5 multicolored 4.75 4.75

Intl. Garden and Greenery Exposition, Osaka, Japan.

Christmas — A164

Paintings: 10c, Adoration of the Magi by Rubens. 30c, Adoration of the Shepherds by Murillo. 80c, Adoration of the Magi by Rubens, diff. $5, Adoration of the Shepherds by Champaigne.

**1990, Dec. 3 Perf. 14**

**972** A164 10c multicolored .50 .50
**973** A164 30c multicolored 1.15 1.15
**974** A164 80c multicolored 1.75 1.75
**975** A164 $5 multicolored 8.00 8.00
*Nos. 972-975 (4)* 11.40 11.40

Boats A165

Various boats.

**1991, Mar. 27 Wmk. 373 Perf. 14½**

**976** A165 50c multicolored 2.00 2.00
**977** A165 80c multicolored 2.25 2.25
**978** A165 $1 multicolored 2.75 2.75
**979** A165 $2.50 multicolored 7.00 7.00
*Nos. 976-979 (4)* 14.00 14.00

**Souvenir Sheet**

**980** A165 $5 multicolored 12.50 12.50

Butterflies — A166

60c, Polydamas swallowtail. 80c, St. Christopher's hairstreak. $1, St. Lucia mestra. $2.50, Godman's hairstreak.

**Wmk. 373**

**1991, Aug. 15 Litho. Perf. 14**

**981** A166 60c multicolored 2.75 1.00
**982** A166 80c multicolored 3.00 1.50
**983** A166 $1 multicolored 3.25 1.75
**984** A166 $2.50 multicolored 6.50 *8.25*
*Nos. 981-984 (4)* 15.50 12.50

Christmas A167

10c, Jacmel Church. 15c, Red Madonna, vert. 80c, Monchy Church. $5, Blue Madonna, vert.

*Perf. 14x14½*

**1991, Nov. 20 Litho. Wmk. 384**

**985** A167 10c multicolored .50 .25
**986** A167 15c multicolored .70 .25
**987** A167 80c multicolored 2.75 2.75
**988** A167 $5 multicolored 6.00 6.00
*Nos. 985-988 (4)* 9.95 9.25

Atlantic Rally for Cruisers A168

Designs: 60c, Cruisers crossing Atlantic, map. 80c, Cruisers tacking.

**1991, Dec. 10 Wmk. 384 Perf. 14**

**989** A168 60c multicolored 2.25 2.25
**990** A168 80c multicolored 3.00 3.00

Discovery of America, 500th Anniv. — A169

**Wmk. 373**

**1992, July 6 Litho. Perf. 13**

**991** A169 $1 Coming ashore 2.25 2.25
**992** A169 $2 Natives, ships 4.50 4.50

Organization of East Caribbean States.

Contact with New World A170

15c, Amerindians. 40c, Juan de la Cosa, 1499. 50c, Columbus, 1502. $5, Gimie, Dec. 13th.

**1992, Aug. 4** ***Perf. 13½***

| | | | | |
|---|---|---|---|---|
| **993** | A170 | 15c multicolored | .50 | .25 |
| **994** | A170 | 40c multicolored | 2.25 | .50 |
| **995** | A170 | 50c multicolored | 3.00 | .75 |
| **996** | A170 | $5 multicolored | 9.00 | 9.00 |
| | | *Nos. 993-996 (4)* | 14.75 | 10.50 |

Christmas A171

Paintings: 10c, Virgin and Child, by Delaroche. 15c, The Holy Family, by Rubens. 60c, Virgin and Child, by Luini. 80c, Virgin and Child, by Sassoferrato.

**Wmk. 373**

**1992, Nov. 9** **Litho.** ***Perf. 14½***

| | | | | |
|---|---|---|---|---|
| **997** | A171 | 10c multicolored | .70 | .25 |
| **998** | A171 | 15c multicolored | .70 | .40 |
| **999** | A171 | 60c multicolored | 2.75 | 1.75 |
| **1000** | A171 | 80c multicolored | 2.75 | 2.25 |
| | | *Nos. 997-1000 (4)* | 6.90 | 4.65 |

Anti-Drugs Campaign — A172

***Perf. 13½x14***

**1993, Feb. 1** **Litho.** **Wmk. 373**

| | | | | |
|---|---|---|---|---|
| **1001** | A172 | $5 multicolored | 9.00 | 9.00 |

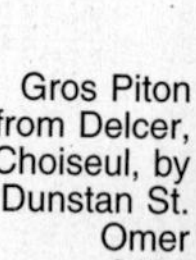

Gros Piton from Delcer, Choiseul, by Dunstan St. Omer A173

Paintings: 75c, Reduit Bay, by Derek Walcott. $5, Woman and Child at River, by Nancy Cole Auguste.

**1993, Nov. 1** **Wmk. 373** ***Perf. 13***

| | | | | |
|---|---|---|---|---|
| **1002** | A173 | 20c multicolored | .35 | .25 |
| **1003** | A173 | 75c multicolored | 1.25 | 1.00 |
| **1004** | A173 | $5 multicolored | 6.25 | *7.00* |
| | | *Nos. 1002-1004 (3)* | 7.85 | *8.25* |

Christmas A174

Details of paintings: 15c, The Madonna of the Rosary, by Murillo. 60c, The Madonna and Child, by Van Dyck. 95c, The Annunciation, by Champaigne.

**1993, Dec. 6** ***Perf. 14***

| | | | | |
|---|---|---|---|---|
| **1005** | A174 | 15c multicolored | .25 | .25 |
| **1006** | A174 | 60c multicolored | 1.00 | .60 |
| **1007** | A174 | 95c multicolored | 1.75 | 1.75 |
| | | *Nos. 1005-1007 (3)* | 3.00 | 2.60 |

A175

**1994, July 25** ***Perf. 13***

| | | | | |
|---|---|---|---|---|
| **1008** | A175 | 20c multicolored | 1.00 | .75 |

**Souvenir Sheet**

| | | | | |
|---|---|---|---|---|
| **1009** | A175 | $5 multicolored | 7.50 | 7.50 |

Abolition of Slavery on St. Lucia, bicent.

A176

Christmas (Flowers): 20c, Euphorbia pulcherrima. 75c, Heliconia rostrata. 95c, Alpinia purpurata. $5.50, Anthurium andreanum.

**1994, Dec. 9** ***Perf. 12½x13***

| | | | | |
|---|---|---|---|---|
| **1010** | A176 | 20c multicolored | .25 | .25 |
| **1011** | A176 | 75c multicolored | 1.00 | 1.00 |
| **1012** | A176 | 95c multicolored | 1.40 | 1.40 |
| **1013** | A176 | $5.50 multicolored | 5.75 | 5.75 |
| | | *Nos. 1010-1013 (4)* | 8.40 | 8.40 |

Battle of Rabot, Bicent. A177

**1995, Apr. 28** ***Perf. 13½***

| | | | | |
|---|---|---|---|---|
| **1014** | A177 | 20c Map of island | .45 | .25 |
| **1015** | A177 | 75c Rebelling slaves | 1.10 | 1.10 |
| **1016** | A177 | 95c Battle scene | 1.60 | 1.60 |
| | | *Nos. 1014-1016 (3)* | 3.15 | 2.95 |

**Souvenir Sheet**

***Perf. 13***

| | | | | |
|---|---|---|---|---|
| **1017** | A177 | $5.50 Battle map | 6.00 | 6.00 |

**End of World War II, 50th Anniv.**

Common Design Types

Designs: 20c, ATS women in Britain. 75c, German U-boat off St. Lucia. 95c, Caribbean regiment, North Africa. $1.10, Presentation Spitfire Mk V.

$5.50, Reverse of War Medal 1939-45.

**Wmk. 373**

**1995, May 8** **Litho.** ***Perf. 13½***

| | | | | |
|---|---|---|---|---|
| **1018** | CD351 | 20c multi | .50 | .25 |
| **1019** | CD351 | 75c multi | 1.75 | 1.00 |
| **1020** | CD351 | 95c multi | 2.00 | 1.40 |
| **1021** | CD351 | $1.10 multi | 2.50 | 2.00 |
| | | *Nos. 1018-1021 (4)* | 6.75 | 4.65 |

**Souvenir Sheet**

***Perf. 14***

| | | | | |
|---|---|---|---|---|
| **1022** | CD352 | $5.50 multi | 5.50 | 5.50 |

**UN, 50th Anniv.**

Common Design Type

10c, Puma helicopter. 65c, Renault truck. $1.35, Transall C160. $5, Douglas DC3.

**Wmk. 373**

**1995, Oct. 24** **Litho.** ***Perf. 14***

| | | | | |
|---|---|---|---|---|
| **1023** | CD353 | 10c multi | .25 | .25 |
| **1024** | CD353 | 65c multi | .75 | .50 |
| **1025** | CD353 | $1.35 multi | 1.50 | 1.50 |
| **1026** | CD353 | $5 multi | 5.00 | 5.00 |
| | | *Nos. 1023-1026 (4)* | 7.50 | 7.25 |

Christmas — A178

Flowers: 15c, Eranthemum nervosum. 70c, Bougainvillea. $1.10, Allamanda cathartica. $3, Hibiscus rosa sinensis.

**Wmk. 373**

**1995, Nov. 20** **Litho.** ***Perf. 13***

| | | | | |
|---|---|---|---|---|
| **1027** | A178 | 15c multicolored | .25 | .25 |
| **1028** | A178 | 70c multicolored | .60 | .50 |
| **1029** | A178 | $1.10 multicolored | .95 | .95 |
| **1030** | A178 | $3 multicolored | 2.40 | 2.40 |
| | | *Nos. 1027-1030 (4)* | 4.20 | 4.10 |

Carnival — A179

**Wmk. 384**

**1996, Feb. 16** **Litho.** ***Perf. 14***

| | | | | |
|---|---|---|---|---|
| **1031** | A179 | 20c Calypso king | .85 | .85 |
| **1032** | A179 | 65c Carnival band | 2.00 | 2.00 |
| **1033** | A179 | 95c King of the band | 2.75 | 2.75 |
| **1034** | A179 | $3 Carnival queen | 5.25 | 5.25 |
| | | *Nos. 1031-1034 (4)* | 10.85 | 10.85 |

Water — A180

**1996, Mar. 5** **Wmk. 373**

| | | | | |
|---|---|---|---|---|
| **1035** | A180 | 20c Muddy stream | .25 | .25 |
| **1036** | A180 | 65c Clear stream | .50 | .50 |
| **1037** | A180 | $5 Modern dam | 4.00 | 5.00 |
| | | *Nos. 1035-1037 (3)* | 4.75 | 5.75 |

Tourism A181

Designs: 65c, Market. 75c, Riding horses on beach. 95c, Outdoor wedding ceremony. $5, Annual Intl. Jazz Festival.

**Wmk. 373**

**1996, May 13** **Litho.** ***Perf. 14***

| | | | | |
|---|---|---|---|---|
| **1038-1041** | A181 | Set of 4 | 7.00 | 7.00 |

Modern Olympic Games, Cent. — A182

No. 1042a, Early runner. No. 1042b, Modern runner. No. 1043a, Two sailboats. No. 1043b, Four sailboats.

**Wmk. 373**

**1996, July 19** **Litho.** ***Perf. 14***

| | | | | |
|---|---|---|---|---|
| **1042** | A182 | 15c Pair, #a.-b. | 1.60 | 1.60 |
| **1043** | A182 | 75c Pair, #a.-b. | 4.75 | 4.75 |

Nos. 1042-1043 have continuous designs.

Flags & Ships A183

Flag, ship: 10c, Spanish Royal banner, 1502, Spanish caravel. 15c, Skull & cross-bones, 1550, pirate carrack. 20c, Royal Netherlands, 1660, Dutch 80-gun ship. 25c, Union flag, 1739, Royal Navy 64-gun ship. 40c, French Imperial, 1750, French 74-gun ship. 50c, Martinique & St. Lucia, 1766, French brig. 55c, British White Ensign, 1782, Royal Navy Frigate Squadron. 65c, British Red Ensign, 1782, Battle of the Saints. 75c, British Blue Ensign, 1782, RN brig. 95c, Fench Tri-color, 1792, French 38-gun frigate. $1. British Union, 1801, West Indies Grand Fleet. $2.50, Confederate, 1861, CSA steam/sail armed cruiser. $5, Canada, 1915-19, Canadian V & W class destroyer. $10, US, 1942-48, Fletcher class destroyer. $25, National, cruise ship.

***Perf. 14x15***

**1996-97** **Litho.** **Wmk. 384**

**"1996" Date Imprint Below Design**

| | | | | |
|---|---|---|---|---|
| **1046** | A183 | 10c multi | 1.00 | .30 |
| *b.* | | Imprint "2000" | .40 | .40 |
| **1047** | A183 | 15c multi | 1.70 | .30 |
| *b.* | | Imprint "2000" | .40 | .40 |
| **1048** | A183 | 20c multi | .70 | .25 |
| *b.* | | Imprint "2000" | .40 | .40 |
| **1049** | A183 | 25c multi | .75 | .30 |
| *b.* | | Imprint "2000" | .40 | .40 |
| **1050** | A183 | 40c multi | 2.00 | .50 |
| **1051** | A183 | 50c multi | 1.00 | .50 |
| **1052** | A183 | 55c multi | 1.00 | .50 |
| **1053** | A183 | 65c multi | 1.00 | .55 |
| **1054** | A183 | 75c multi | 1.25 | .65 |
| **1055** | A183 | 95c multi | 1.25 | .65 |
| **1056** | A183 | $1 multi | 1.25 | .80 |
| **1057** | A183 | $2.50 multi | 2.75 | 2.50 |
| **1058** | A183 | $5 multi | 4.00 | 4.50 |
| **1059** | A183 | $10 multi | 7.25 | *9.00* |
| **1060** | A183 | $25 multi | 14.50 | 16.00 |
| | | *Nos. 1046-1060 (15)* | 41.40 | 37.30 |

Issued: 10c, 15c, 20c, 25c, 40c, 9/16/96; 50c, 55c, 65c, 75c, 95c, 11/18/96; $1, $2.50, $5, $10, $25, 1/8/97.

**1998-2004** **Wmk. 373**

**Date Imprint Below Design as Noted**

| | | | | |
|---|---|---|---|---|
| *1046a* | A183 | 10c multi, "1998" | .75 | .40 |
| *1047a* | A183 | 15c multi, "1998" | .75 | .40 |
| *1048a* | A183 | 20c multi, "1998" | .75 | .40 |
| *c.* | | Imprint "2001" | .40 | .40 |
| *d.* | | Imprint "2002" | .75 | .30 |
| *e.* | | Imprint "2003" | .40 | .40 |
| *f.* | | Imprint "2004" | .40 | .40 |
| *1049a* | A183 | 25c multi, "2002" | .40 | .40 |
| *1051a* | A183 | 50c multi, "1998" | 1.00 | .50 |
| *1053a* | A183 | 65c multi, "2001" | .70 | .55 |
| *1054a* | A183 | 75c multi, "2003" | 1.00 | 1.00 |
| *1056a* | A183 | $1 multi, "2001" | 1.40 | 1.40 |
| *1059a* | A183 | $10 multi, "2001" | 10.00 | *11.00* |
| | | *Nos. 1046a-1059a (9)* | 16.75 | 16.05 |

#1046a, 1047a, 1048a, 1051a, 7/12/98; #1053a, 1056a, 1059a, 4/2001. #1049a, 2002. No. 1054a, May 2003.

Christmas — A184

Flowers: 20c, Cordia sebestena. 75c, Cryptostegia grandiflora. 95c, Hibiscus elatus. $5, Caularthron bicornutum.

**Wmk. 384**

**1996, Dec. 1** **Litho.** ***Perf. 14***

| | | | | |
|---|---|---|---|---|
| **1061-1064** | A184 | Set of 4 | 7.50 | 7.50 |

Queen Elizabeth II and Prince Philip, 50th Wedding Anniv. — A185

No. 1068a, Queen. No. 1068b, Prince with horses. No. 1069a, Prince. No. 1069b, Queen riding in carriage. No. 1070a, Queen, Prince. No. 1070b, Princess Anne riding horse.
$5, Queen, Prince riding in open carriage, horiz.

*Perf. 14½x14*

**1997, July 10 Litho. Wmk. 384**

| | | | |
|---|---|---|---|
| **1068** A185 75c Pair, #a.-b. | 2.25 | 2.25 |
| **1069** A185 95c Pair, #a.-b. | 2.50 | 2.50 |
| **1070** A185 $1 Pair, #a.-b. | 2.75 | 2.75 |
| *Nos. 1068-1070 (3)* | 7.50 | 7.50 |

**Souvenir Sheet**

*Perf. 14x14½*

**1071** A185 $5 multicolored 6.00 6.00

Disasters — A186

20c, MV St. George capsizes, 1935. 55c, SS Belle of Bath founders. $1, SS Ethelgonda runs aground, 1897. $2.50, Hurricane devastation, 1817.

**1997, July 14** *Perf. 14x15*

**1072-1075** A186 Set of 4 11.50 11.50

Events of 1797 — A187

Designs: 20c, Taking of Praslin. 55c, Battle of Dennery. 70c, Peace. $3, Brigands join 1st West India Regiment.

**Wmk. 373**

**1997, Aug. 15 Litho.** *Perf. 14*

**1076-1079** A187 Set of 4 10.50 10.50

Christmas — A188

Church art: 20c, Roseau Church. 60c, Altar piece, Regional Seminary, Trinidad. 95c, Our Lady of the Presentation, Trinidad. $5, The Four Days of Creation.

*Perf. 14x15*

**1997, Dec. 1 Litho. Wmk. 384**

**1080-1083** A188 Set of 4 7.00 7.00

Diana, Princess of Wales (1961-97) — A189

**1998, Jan. 19 Litho.** *Perf. 14*

**1084** A189 $1 multicolored .90 .90

No. 1084 was issued in sheets of 9.

CARICOM, 25th Anniv. — A190

20c, Errol Barrow, Forbes Burnham, Dr. Eric Williams, Michael Manley signing CARICOM Treaty, 1973. 75c, CARICOM flag, St. Lucia Natl. flag.

**Wmk. 373**

**1998, July 1 Litho.** *Perf. 13½*

| | | |
|---|---|---|
| **1085** A190 20c multicolored | .25 | .25 |
| **1086** A190 75c multicolored | 1.25 | 1.25 |

Birds — A191

Designs: 70c, St. Lucia oriole. 75c, Lesser Antillean pewee. 95c, Bridled quail dove. $1.10, Semper's warbler.

**1998, Oct. 23 Wmk. 373** *Perf. 14*

**1087-1090** A191 70c Set of 4 9.50 9.50

Universal Declaration of Human Rights, 50th Anniv. — A192

Various butterflies, chains or rope.

**1998, Oct. 28**

| | | |
|---|---|---|
| **1091** A192 20c multicolored | .75 | .30 |
| **1092** A192 65c multicolored | 1.50 | .75 |
| **1093** A192 70c multicolored | 1.60 | .75 |
| **1094** A192 $5 multicolored | 6.00 | 6.50 |
| *Nos. 1091-1094 (4)* | 9.85 | 8.30 |

Christmas — A193

Flowers: 20c, Tabebuia serratifolia. 50c, Hibiscus sabdariffa. 95c, Euphorbia leucocephala. $2.50, Calliandra slaneae.

**Wmk. 373**

**1998, Nov. 27 Litho.** *Perf. 14*

**1095-1098** A193 20c Set of 4 6.25 6.25

University of West Indies, 50th Anniv. A194

15c, The Black Prometheus. 75c, Sir Arthur Lewis, Sir Arthur Lewis College. $5, The Pitons.

**1998, Nov. 30**

| | | |
|---|---|---|
| **1099** A194 15c multicolored | .25 | .25 |
| **1100** A194 75c multicolored | .75 | .50 |
| **1101** A194 $5 multicolored | 4.50 | 5.25 |
| *Nos. 1099-1101 (3)* | 5.50 | 6.00 |

Wildlife A195

Designs: 20c, Saint Lucia tree lizard. 75c, Boa constrictor. 95c, Leatherback turtle. $5, Saint Lucia whiptail.

**Wmk. 373**

**1999, July 15 Litho.** *Perf. 13½*

**1102-1105** A195 Set of 4 7.50 7.50

UPU, 125th Anniv. A196

20c, Mail steamer "Tees". 65c, Sikorsky S.38. 95c, Mail ship "Lady Drake". $3, DC-10. $5, Heinrich von Stephan.

**Wmk. 373**

**1999, Oct. 9 Litho.** *Perf. 14*

| | | |
|---|---|---|
| **1106** A196 20c multicolored | .70 | .30 |
| **1107** A196 65c multicolored | 1.40 | .55 |
| **1108** A196 95c multicolored | 1.60 | .65 |
| **1109** A196 $3 multicolored | 4.00 | 4.00 |
| *Nos. 1106-1109 (4)* | 7.70 | 5.50 |

**Souvenir Sheet**

*Perf. 14¼*

**1110** A196 $5 multicolored 5.50 5.50

Stamp inscription on No. 1107 is misspelled. No. 1110 contains one 30x38mm stamp.

Christmas and Millennium — A197

Designs: 20c, Nativity. $1, Cathedral of the Immaculate Conception.

*Perf. 13¾x14*

**1999, Dec. 14 Litho. Wmk. 373**

| | | |
|---|---|---|
| **1111** A197 20c multi | .25 | .25 |
| **1112** A197 $1 multi | 1.60 | 1.60 |

Independence, 21st Anniv. — A198

20c, Vintage badge of the colony. 75c, 1939 badge. 95c, 1967 arms. $1, 1979 arms.

*Perf. 14x13¾*

**2000, Feb. 29 Litho. Wmk. 373**

| | | |
|---|---|---|
| **1113** A198 20c multi | .30 | .30 |
| **1114** A198 75c multi | .75 | .60 |
| **1115** A198 95c multi | .95 | .85 |
| **1116** A198 $1 multi | 1.25 | 1.00 |
| *Nos. 1113-1116 (4)* | 3.25 | 2.75 |

Historical Views A199

Designs: 20c, Fort sugar factory, 1886-1941. 60c, Coaling at Port Castries, 1885-1940. $1, Fort Rodney, Pigeon Island, 1780-1861. $5, Military hospital ruins, Pigeon Island, 1824-1861.

**Wmk. 373**

**2000, Sept. 4 Litho.** *Perf. 14*

**1117-1120** A199 Set of 4 6.50 6.50

First Municipality of Castries, 150th Anniv. — A200

Designs: 20c, Old Castries Market. 75c, Central Library. 95c, Port Castries. $5, Mayors Henry H. Breen, Joseph Desir.

*Perf. 13¼x13½*

**2000, Oct. 9 Litho. Wmk. 373**

**1121-1124** A200 Set of 4 6.50 8.00

Girl Guides in St. Lucia, 75th Anniv. A201

Guides: 70c, Marching in brown uniforms. $1, Marching in blue uniforms. $2.50, At campground.

**2000, Oct. 16**

**1125-1127** A201 Set of 3 5.50 6.00

Christmas — A202

Churches: 20c, Holy Trinity, Castries. 50c, St. Paul's, Vieux-Fort. 95c, Christ, Soufriere. $2.50, Grace, River D'Oree.

**2000, Nov. 22** *Perf. 14*

**1128-1131** A202 Set of 4 5.50 6.00

Worldwide Fund for Nature (WWF) — A203

Birds: No. 1132, 20c, White breasted thrasher. No. 1133, 20c, St. Lucia black finch. No. 1134, 95c, St. Lucia oriole. No. 1135, 95c, Forest thrush.

**Wmk. 373**

**2001, Feb. 1 Litho.** *Perf. 14*

| | | |
|---|---|---|
| **1132-1135** A203 Set of 4 | 4.50 | 4.75 |
| *1135a* Strip of 4, #1132-1135 | 4.50 | 4.75 |

Jazz Festival, 10th Anniv. — A204

Designs: 20c, Crowd, stage. $1, Crowd, stage, ocean. $5, Musicians.

*Perf. 13¾x14*

**2001, May 3 Litho. Wmk. 373**

**1136-1138** A204 Set of 3 7.00 7.50

Civil Administration, Bicent. — A205

Designs: 20c, British flag, island, ship. 65c, French flag, Napoleon Bonaparte, signing of the Treaty of Amiens. $1.10, British flag, King George III, ships. $3, Island map, King George IV.

*Perf. 14x13¾*

**2001, Sept. 24 Litho. Unwmk.**

**1139-1142** A205 Set of 4 5.50 6.00

Christmas A206

Various stained glass windows: 20c, 95c, $2.50.

**2001, Dec. 7 Wmk. 373 *Perf. 13½***

**1143-1145** A206 Set of 3 5.25 5.25

### Reign Of Queen Elizabeth II, 50th Anniv. Issue

Common Design Type

Designs: Nos. 1146, 1150a, 25c, Princess Elizabeth, 1927. Nos. 1147, 1150b, 65c, Wearing hat. Nos. 1148, 1150c, 75c, In 1947. Nos. 1149, 1150d, 95c, In 1996. No. 1150e, $5, 1955 portrait by Annigoni (38x50mm).

*Perf. 14¼x14½, 13¾ (#1150e)*

**2002, Feb. 6 Litho. Wmk. 373**

**With Gold Frames**

**1146** CD360 25c multicolored .50 .50
**1147** CD360 65c multicolored 1.25 1.25
**1148** CD360 75c multicolored 1.45 1.45
**1149** CD360 95c multicolored 1.80 1.80
*Nos. 1146-1149 (4)* 5.00 5.00

**Souvenir Sheet**

**Without Gold Frames**

**1150** CD360 Sheet of 5, #a-e 7.25 7.25

Royal Navy Ships A207

Designs: 15c, HMS St. Lucia, 1803. 75c, HMS Thetis, 1781. $1, HMS Berwick, 1903. $5, HMS Victory, 1805.

**Wmk. 373**

**2002, June 10 Litho. *Perf. 14***

**1151-1154** A207 Set of 4 10.00 10.00

### Queen Mother Elizabeth (1900-2002)

Common Design Type

Designs: 50c, Holding baby (black and white photograph). 65c, Wearing red hat. 95c, Wearing hat (black and white photograph). $1, Wearing blue hat.

No. 1159: a, $2, Wearing tiara. b, $2, Wearing blue hat, diff.

*Perf. 13¾x14¼*

**2002, Aug. 5 Litho. Wmk. 373**

**With Purple Frames**

**1155** CD361 50c multicolored .80 .80
**1156** CD361 65c multicolored 1.10 1.10
**1157** CD361 95c multicolored 1.50 1.50
**1158** CD361 $1 multicolored 1.60 1.60
*Nos. 1155-1158 (4)* 5.00 5.00

**Souvenir Sheet**

**Without Purple Frames**

*Perf. 14½x14¼*

**1159** CD361 Sheet of 2, #a-b 7.00 7.00

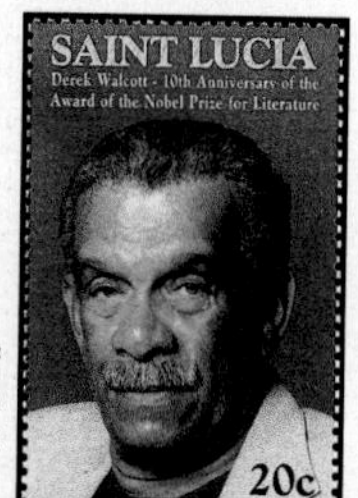


Awarding of Nobel Literature Prize to Derek Walcott, 10th Anniv. — A208

Designs: 20c, Walcott. 65c, Men and children, horiz. 70c, Women. $5, People in boat.

**Wmk. 373**

**2002, Oct. 11 Litho. *Perf. 13¾***

**1160-1163** A208 Set of 4 8.00 8.00

Salvation Army in St. Lucia, Cent. A209

Designs: 20c, William and Catherine Booth, Salvation Army workers. $1, Early Salvation Army officers in parade. $2.50, Salvation Army shield, "Blood and Fire" crest.

**Wmk. 373**

**2002, Nov. 27 Litho. *Perf. 14***

**1164-1166** A209 Set of 3 8.00 8.00

Christmas — A210

Paintings: 20c, Adoration of the Shepherds, by Bernardino. 50c, Adoration of the Kings, by Girolamo, vert. 75c, Adoration of the Kings, by Foppa, vert. $5, Adoration of the Shepherds, by the Le Nain Brothers.

**2002, Dec. 4 *Perf. 14x14¾, 14¾x14***

**1167-1170** A210 Set of 4 9.00 9.00

### Coronation of Queen Elizabeth II, 50th Anniv.

Common Design Type

Designs: Nos. 1171, 20c, 1173b, Queen with crown. Nos. 1172, 75c, 1173a, Queen's carriage.

*Perf. 14¼x14½*

**2003, June 2 Litho. Wmk. 373**

**Vignettes Framed, Red Background**

**1171** CD363 20c multicolored .50 .50
**1172** CD363 75c multicolored 1.75 1.75

**Souvenir Sheet**

**Vignettes Without Frame, Purple Panel**

**1173** CD363 $2.50 Sheet of 2, #a-b 6.50 6.50

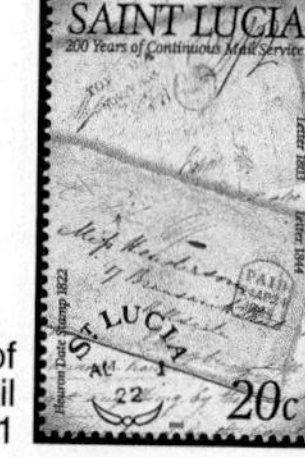


200 Years of Continuous Mail Service — A211

Designs: 20c, Letters from 1803 and 1844, 1822 fleuron postmark. 25c, St. Lucia #1-3. 65c, Map, mail ship Hewanorra. 75c, Post offices of 1900 and present time.

**Wmk. 373**

**2003, July 14 Litho. *Perf. 14¼***

**1174-1177** A211 Set of 4 3.75 3.75

Powered Flight, Cent. — A212

Designs: 20c, Sikorsky S-38. 70c, Consolidated PBY-5A Catalina. $1, Lockheed Lodestar. $5, Spitfire Mk V "St. Lucia."

*Perf. 13¼x13¾*

**2003, Nov. 28 Litho. Wmk. 373**

**Stamps + Labels**

**1178-1181** A212 Set of 4 9.75 9.75

Parrot A213

Island A214

*Perf. 14x14¼*

**2003, Nov. Coil Stamps**

**1182** A213 10c multicolored .25 .25
**1183** A214 25c multicolored .40 .30

Christmas A215

Madonna and Child and: 20c, Sorrel flowers, ginger root. 75c, Sorrel drink, ginger ale. 95c, Masqueraders. $1, Christmas lanterns.

**2003, Dec. 2 *Perf. 14***

**1184-1187** A215 Set of 4 5.25 5.25

Independence, 25th Anniv. — A216

Designs: 20c, Flag raising ceremony, vert. 95c, People, book, airplane, ships, banana plant, vert. $1.10, "25" and leaves. $5, Harbor.

**2004, Feb. 20 *Perf. 13¾***

**1188-1191** A216 Set of 4 7.50 7.50

Caribbean Bird Festival — A217

No. 1192: a, Antillean crested hummingbird. b, St. Lucia pewee. c, Purple-throated carib. d, Gray trembler. e, Rufous-throated solitaire. f, St. Lucia warbler. g, Antillean euphonia. h, Semper's warbler.

*Perf. 13¼x13*

**2004, June 30 Litho. Wmk. 373**

**1192** A217 Block of 8 10.00 10.00
*a.-h.* $1 Any single 1.25 1.25

Tourism A218

Designs: 45c, Sailing. 65c, Horse riding. 70c, Scuba diving. $1, Walking.

**2004, Sept. 6 *Perf. 13¼***

**1193-1196** A218 Set of 4 5.00 5.00

World AIDS Day A219

Designs: No. 1197, 30c, Condoms, syringe, couple. No. 1198, 30c, Children, woman.

**Wmk. 373**

**2004, Dec. 1 Litho. *Perf. 14***

**1197-1198** A219 Set of 2 2.25 2.25

Christmas — A220

Painting details: 30c, Adoration of the Kings, by Dosso Dossi. 75c, Adoration of the Shepherds, by Nicolas Poussin, vert. 95c, Adoration of the Kings, by Joos van Wassenhove, vert. $1, Adoration of the Shepherds, by Carel Fabritius.

**2004, Dec. 14 *Perf. 14x14¾, 14¾x14***

**1199-1202** A220 Set of 4 3.50 3.50

St. Joseph's Convent, 150th Anniv. A221

Nun and: 30c, Women. 95c, Convent and steps. $2.50, Building and street.

**Wmk. 373**

**2005, Mar. 14 Litho. *Perf. 13¾***

**1203-1205** A221 Set of 3 5.50 5.50

Battle of Trafalgar, Bicent. — A222

Designs: 30c, HMS Thunderer off St. Lucia. 75c, HMS Britannia in action against the Bucentaure. 95c, Admiral Horatio Nelson, vert. $5, HMS Victory.

$10, HMS Thunderer (44x44mm).

**Wmk. 373, Unwmkd. ($5)**

**2005, June 13 Litho. *Perf. 13¼***

| | | | | |
|---|---|---|---|---|
| **1206-1209** | A222 | Set of 4 | 8.75 | 8.75 |

**Souvenir Sheet**

***Perf. 13¾***

| | | | | |
|---|---|---|---|---|
| **1210** | A222 | $10 multi | 11.00 | 11.00 |

No. 1209 has particles of wood from the HMS Victory embedded in the areas covered by a thermographic process that produces a shiny, raised effect.

Pope John Paul II (1920-2005) A223

**2005, Aug. 29 Wmk. 373 *Perf. 14***

| | | | | |
|---|---|---|---|---|
| **1211** | A223 | $2 multi | 3.00 | 3.00 |

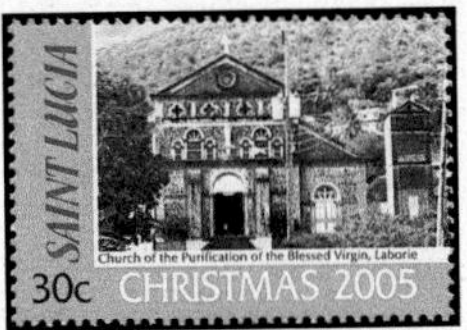

Christmas — A224

Designs: 30c, Church of the Purification of the Blessed Virgin, Castries. $5, Minor Basilica of the Immaculate Conception, Castries.

**Wmk. 373**

**2005, Nov. 28 Litho. *Perf. 14***

| | | | | |
|---|---|---|---|---|
| **1212-1213** | A224 | Set of 2 | 5.00 | 5.00 |

Fruits and Nuts A225

Designs: 15c, Blighia sapida. 20c, Solanum melongena. 25c, Mangifera indica. 30c, Coccoloba uvifera. 50c, Carica papaya. 55c, Spondias mombin. 65c, Chrysobalanus icaco. 70c, Artocarpus altilis. 75c, Annona reticulata. 95c, Psidium guajava. $1, Musa sp. $2.50, Manilkara achras. $5, Anacardium occidentale. $25, Mammea americana.

**2005, Dec. 5 *Perf. 14***

| | | | | |
|---|---|---|---|---|
| **1214** | A225 | 15c multi | .30 | .30 |
| **1215** | A225 | 20c multi | .30 | .30 |
| **1216** | A225 | 25c multi | .30 | .30 |
| **1217** | A225 | 30c multi | .30 | .30 |
| *a.* | | Wmk. 406, dated "2010" | .30 | .30 |
| *b.* | | Wmk. 406, dated "2013" | .25 | .25 |
| **1218** | A225 | 50c multi | .40 | .40 |
| **1219** | A225 | 55c multi | .45 | .45 |
| **1220** | A225 | 65c multi | .50 | .50 |
| **1221** | A225 | 70c multi | .55 | .55 |
| **1222** | A225 | 75c multi | .60 | .60 |
| **1223** | A225 | 95c multi | .80 | .80 |
| **1224** | A225 | $1 multi | .85 | .85 |
| **1225** | A225 | $2.50 multi | 2.10 | 2.10 |
| **1226** | A225 | $5 multi | 4.25 | 4.25 |
| **1227** | A225 | $25 multi | 20.00 | 20.00 |
| | | *Nos. 1214-1227 (14)* | 31.70 | 31.70 |

Issued: No. 1217a, 4/7/10.

Art by Llewellyn Xavier — A226

Designs: 20c, Axe Head. 30c, Turtle. $2.50, Pre-Columbian Vase. $5, Pre-Columbian Zemi.

**Wmk. 373**

**2006, Mar. 15 Litho. *Perf. 12¾***

| | | | | |
|---|---|---|---|---|
| **1228-1231** | A226 | Set of 4 | 6.00 | 6.00 |

2006 World Cup Soccer Championships, Germany — A227

Various soccer players: 95c, $2.

**Wmk. 373**

**2006, June 9 Litho. *Perf. 14***

| | | | | |
|---|---|---|---|---|
| **1232-1233** | A227 | Set of 2 | 2.25 | 2.25 |
| *1233a* | | Souvenir sheet, #1232-1233 | 2.25 | 2.25 |

Leeward Islands Air Transport, 50th Anniv. A228

LIAT airplane: 30c, In flight. 75c, On ground.

***Perf. 12½x13***

**2006, Oct. 16 Litho. Wmk. 373**

| | | | | |
|---|---|---|---|---|
| **1234-1235** | A228 | Set of 2 | .80 | .80 |

Christmas A229

Designs: 95c, Choir and director. $2, Sesenne Descartes, folk singer, and musicians.

**2006, Nov. 16**

| | | | | |
|---|---|---|---|---|
| **1236-1237** | A229 | Set of 2 | 2.25 | 2.25 |

Cricket — A230

Designs: 30c, Mindoo Phillip. 75c, Map and flag of St. Lucia. 95c, Beausejour Cricket Grounds, horiz.

$5, Beausejour Cricket Grounds, horiz. diff.

***Perf. 13x12½, 12½x13***

**2007, Feb. 28 Litho.**

| | | | | |
|---|---|---|---|---|
| **1238-1240** | A230 | Set of 3 | 1.50 | 1.50 |

**Souvenir Sheet**

| | | | | |
|---|---|---|---|---|
| **1241** | A230 | $5 multi | 3.75 | 3.75 |

No. 1241 contains one 56x42mm stamp.

Scouting, Cent. A231

Designs: 30c, Inspection of St. Lucia Scouts, 1954 Queen's Birthday Parade, hands and trumpet. $5, St. Lucia Cub Scout laying wreath, 2005 Remembrance Day Parade, poppies.

No. 1244, vert.: a, St. Lucia Scout Association emblem. b, Lord Robert Baden-Powell and Chief Joe Big Plume.

**Wmk. 373**

**2007, Aug. 20 Litho. *Perf. 13¾***

| | | | | |
|---|---|---|---|---|
| **1242-1243** | A231 | Set of 2 | 4.00 | 4.00 |

**Souvenir Sheet**

| | | | | |
|---|---|---|---|---|
| **1244** | A231 | $2.50 Sheet of 2, #a-b | 3.75 | 3.75 |

Christmas A232

Designs: 30c, Lantern Parade. $10, Nativity scene.

***Perf. 12½x13***

**2007, Dec. 10 Litho. Wmk. 373**

| | | | | |
|---|---|---|---|---|
| **1245-1246** | A232 | Set of 2 | 7.75 | 7.75 |

2008 Summer Olympics, Beijing A233

Designs: 75c, Bamboo, diving. 95c, Dragon, running. $1, Lanterns, running. $2.50, Fish, high jump.

**Wmk. 373**

**2008, Apr. 30 Litho. *Perf. 13¼***

| | | | | |
|---|---|---|---|---|
| **1247-1250** | A233 | Set of 4 | 4.00 | 4.00 |

Worldwide Fund For Nature (WWF) — A234

Saint Lucia whiptail: 75c, On leaves. $2.50, On grass and rocks. $5, Two whiptails facing left. $10, Two whiptails facing left and right.

**Wmk. 373**

**2008, Nov. 4 Litho. *Perf. 14***

| | | | | |
|---|---|---|---|---|
| **1251-1254** | A234 | Set of 4 | 14.00 | 14.00 |
| *1254a* | | Miniature sheet of 16, 4 each #1251-1254 | 56.00 | 56.00 |

University of the West Indies, 60th Anniv. A235

**Wmk. 373**

**2008, Nov. 14 Litho. *Perf. 13***

| | | | | |
|---|---|---|---|---|
| **1255** | A235 | $5 multi | 4.00 | 4.00 |

Christmas A236

Designs: 95c, Wreath, bell, ornaments, gift, rose. $5, Star, candle, Holy Family, holly.

**2008, Nov. 25 *Perf. 13¼***

| | | | | |
|---|---|---|---|---|
| **1256-1257** | A236 | Set of 2 | 4.75 | 4.75 |

Independence, 30th Anniv. — A237

Designs: 30c, Castries waterfront. $2.50, Roseau Dam. $5, Rodney Bay Marina. $10, Sir John G. M. Compton (1925-2007), prime minister, and flag.

***Perf. 12½x13***

**2009, Feb. 20 Litho. Wmk. 406**

| | | | | |
|---|---|---|---|---|
| **1258-1261** | A237 | Set of 4 | 13.50 | 13.50 |

Intl. Year of Biodiversity — A238

Designs: 30c, Lobelia. 75c, Iguana. 95c, Hercules beetle. $2.50, White-breasted thrasher.

***Perf. 13x12¾***

**2010, June 11 Litho. Wmk. 406**

| | | | | |
|---|---|---|---|---|
| **1262-1265** | A238 | Set of 4 | 3.50 | 3.50 |

Gros-Islets Township, 25th Anniv. — A239

***Perf. 14x15***

**2010, Aug. 27 Litho. Wmk. 406**

| | | | | |
|---|---|---|---|---|
| **1266** | A239 | 95c multi | .70 | .70 |

Service of Queen Elizabeth II and Prince Philip — A240

Designs: No. 1267, $1.50, Prince Philip. No. 1268, $1.50, Queen Elizabeth II and Prince Philip. No. 1269, $2, Queen and Prince Philip, color photograph, diff. No. 1270, $2, Queen and Prince Philip, black-and-white photograph. No. 1271, $2.50, Queen and Prince Philip, black-and-white photograph, diff. No. 1272, $2.50, Queen.

$6, Queen and Prince Philip, diff.

***Perf. 13¼***

**2011, Mar. 1 Litho. Unwmk.**

| | | | | |
|---|---|---|---|---|
| **1267-1272** | A240 | Set of 6 | 9.00 | 9.00 |
| *1272a* | | Sheet of 6, #1267-1272, + 3 labels | 9.00 | 9.00 |

**Souvenir Sheet**

| | | | | |
|---|---|---|---|---|
| **1273** | A240 | $6 multi | 4.50 | 4.50 |

Campaign Against HIV and AIDS, 30th Anniv. — A241

*Perf. 12¾x13*

**2011, Sept. 1 Litho. Wmk. 406**

**1274** A241 30c multicolored .25 .25

Bishop Charles Gachet (1911-84) and Church, Soufriere — A242

**2011, Dec. 1** ***Perf. 14***

**1275** A242 30c multicolored .25 .25

Christmas.

Reign of Queen Elizabeth II, 60th Anniv. — A243

Queen Elizabeth II: No. 1276, $1.50, Wearing blue green dress. No. 1277, $1.50, Wearing crown. No. 1278, $2, Without tiara. No. 1279, $2, Wearing tiara. No. 1280, $2.50, Without hat. No. 1281, $2.50, Wearing hat. $6, Wearing tiara.

**2012, Feb. 6 Unwmk.** ***Perf. 13½***

**1276-1281** A243 Set of 6 9.00 9.00
*1281a* Souvenir sheet, #1276-1281 + 3 labels 9.00 9.00

**Souvenir Sheet**

**1282** A243 $6 multi 4.50 4.50

Paintings by Llewellyn Xavier A244

Designs: $5, Pitons. $10, The Spirit of Freedom, vert.

*Perf. 13¼x13½, 13½x13¼*

**2013, Apr. 8 Litho. Unwmk.**

**1283-1284** A244 Set of 2 11.50 11.50

Dragonflies — A245

Designs: 5c, Antillean skimmer. 20c, Spot-tailed dasher. 30c, Vermillion saddlebags. 50c, Tawny pennant. 75c, Great pondhawk. $1, Band-winged dragonlet. $1.50, Wandering glider. $2, Rambur's forktail.

**2013, Apr. 8 Litho.** ***Perf. 13½***

**1285** A245 5c multi .25 .25
**1286** A245 20c multi .25 .25
**1287** A245 30c multi .25 .25
**1288** A245 50c multi .35 .35
**1289** A245 75c multi .55 .55
**1290** A245 $1 multi .75 .75
**1291** A245 $1.50 multi 1.10 1.10
**1292** A245 $2 multi 1.50 1.50
*Nos. 1285-1292 (8)* 5.00 5.00

Elevation to Cardinal of Archbishop Kelvin Edward Felix — A246

Designs: $3, Cardinal Felix. $5, Pope Francis and Cardinal Felix, horiz.

*Perf. 13¾x13½, 13½x13¾*

**2014, Dec. 12 Litho.**

**1293-1294** A246 Set of 2 6.00 6.00

## AIR POST STAMP

**Catalogue values for unused stamps in this section are for Never Hinged items.**

Map of St. Lucia — AP1

*Perf. 14½x14*

**1967, Mar. 1 Photo. Unwmk.**

**C1** AP1 15c blue .50 .50

St. Lucia's independence.

Exists imperf. and also in souvenir sheet. Values: single, $10; souvenir sheet $40.

## POSTAGE DUE STAMPS

D1

Type I — "No." 3mm wide (shown).
Type II — "No." 4mm wide.

***Rough Perf. 12***

**1931 Unwmk. Typeset**

**J1** D1 1p blk, *gray bl*, type I 10.00 *20.00*
*a.* Type II 24.00 *47.50*
**J2** D1 2p blk, *yel*, type I 22.00 *47.50*
*a.* Type II 45.00 *105.00*
*b.* Vertical pair, imperf. btwn. *7,500.*

The serial numbers are handstamped. Type II has round "o" and period. Type I has tall "o" and square period.

**Catalogue values for unused stamps in this section, from this point to the end of the section, are for Never Hinged items.**

D2

**1933-47 Typo. Wmk. 4** ***Perf. 14***

**Chalky Paper**

**J3** D2 1p black 15.00 *8.00*
**J4** D2 2p black 40.00 *10.00*
**J5** D2 4p black ('47) 11.00 *50.00*
**J6** D2 8p black ('47) 11.00 *60.00*
*Nos. J3-J6 (4)* 77.00 *128.00*

Issue date: June 28, 1947.

**Chalky Paper**

**1952, Nov. 27 Values in Cents**

**J7** D2 2c black .25 *9.50*
*a.* Ordinary paper ('49) 1.90 30.00
**J8** D2 4c black .60 *14.00*
*a.* Ordinary paper ('49) 3.75 24.00
**J9** D2 8c black 3.50 *50.00*
*a.* Ordinary paper ('49) 3.50 30.00
**J10** D2 16c black 5.00 *65.00*
*a.* Ordinary paper ('49) 16.00 75.00
*Nos. J7-J10 (4)* 9.35 *138.50*

Nos. J7a-J10a issued 10/1/1949.

**Chalky Paper**
**Wmk. 4a (error)**

*J7b* D2 2c 40.00
*J8b* D2 4c 55.00
*J9b* D2 8c 350.00
*J10b* D2 16c 475.00
*Nos. J7a-J10a (4)* 920.00

**1965, Mar. 9 Wmk. 314**

**J11** D2 2c black .75 *10.00*
**J12** D2 4c black 1.00 *11.00*

In the 2c center the "c" is heavier and the period bigger.

Nos. J9-J12 exist with overprint "Statehood/1st Mar. '67" in red. Values: unused $190; used $160.

Arms of St. Lucia — D3

**1981, Aug. 4 Litho. Wmk. 373**

**J13** D3 5c red brown .25 *.65*
**J14** D3 15c green .25 *.50*
**J15** D3 25c deep orange .25 *.50*
**J16** D3 $1 dark blue .25 *1.25*
*Nos. J13-J16 (4)* 1.00 2.90

**1990 Wmk. 384** ***Perf. 15x14***

**J17** D3 5c red brown .25 .25
**J18** D3 15c green .25 .25
**J19** D3 25c deep orange .25 .25
**J20** D3 $1 dark blue .50 *1.00*
*Nos. J17-J20 (4)* 1.25 1.75

## WAR TAX STAMPS

No. 65 Overprinted

**1916 Wmk. 3** ***Perf. 14***

**MR1** A11 1p scarlet 13.00 *19.00*
*a.* Double overprint 550.00 *650.00*
*b.* 1p carmine 67.50 55.00

Overprinted

**MR2** A11 1p scarlet 1.40 .35

## OFFICIAL STAMPS

**Catalogue values for unused stamps in this section are for Never Hinged items.**

**Nos. 504-515 Overprinted**

**Wmk. 373**

**1983, Oct. 13 Litho.** ***Perf. 14½***

**O1** A95 5c multicolored .30 .25
**O2** A95 10c multicolored .30 .25
**O3** A95 15c multicolored .30 .25
**O4** A95 20c multicolored .35 .25
**O5** A95 25c multicolored .50 .45
**O6** A95 30c multicolored .70 .45
**O7** A95 50c multicolored .80 .45
**O8** A95 75c multicolored 1.10 .80
**O9** A95 $1 multicolored 1.50 1.00
**O10** A95 $2 multicolored 2.00 *2.25*
**O11** A95 $5 multicolored 4.00 *4.25*
**O12** A95 $10 multicolored 8.50 *10.00*
*Nos. O1-O12 (12)* 20.35 20.65

Nos. 747-761 Overprinted

**1985, May 7 Litho.** ***Perf. 15***

**O13** A126 5c multicolored .65 *1.00*
**O14** A126 10c multicolored .65 *1.00*
**O15** A126 20c multicolored .75 *1.00*
**O16** A126 25c multicolored .75 .75
**O17** A126 30c multicolored .90 .90
**O18** A126 35c multicolored 1.00 1.00
**O19** A126 45c multicolored 1.10 1.10
**O20** A126 50c multicolored 1.25 1.25
**O21** A126 65c multicolored 1.40 *1.50*
**O22** A126 75c multicolored 1.40 *2.00*
**O23** A126 90c multicolored 1.50 *2.10*
**O24** A126 $1 multicolored 2.00 2.25
**O25** A126 $2.50 multicolored 3.25 *4.00*
**O26** A126 $5 multicolored 5.00 *5.50*
**O27** A126 $15 multicolored 10.50 *12.00*
*Nos. O13-O27 (15)* 32.10 *37.35*

Nos. 953-964 Overprinted

**1990, Feb. 21 Wmk. 384** ***Perf. 14***

**O28** A162 10c multicolored .40 *1.00*
**O29** A162 15c multicolored .40 *1.00*
**O30** A162 20c multicolored .50 .50
**O31** A162 25c multicolored .50 .50
**O32** A162 50c multicolored .65 .65
**O33** A162 80c multicolored .75 .75
**O34** A162 95c multicolored 1.25 1.25
**O35** A162 $1 multicolored 1.40 1.40
**O36** A162 $1.50 multicolored 2.00 *2.50*
**O37** A162 $2.50 multicolored 3.25 *3.75*
**O38** A162 $5 multicolored 6.00 *6.50*
**O39** A162 $25 multicolored 16.00 *18.00*
*Nos. O28-O39 (12)* 33.10 37.80

Issued: 20c, 25c, 50c, $25, 2/21; 10c, 15c, 80c, $1.50, 4/12; 95c, $1, $2.50, $5, 6/25.

## STE. MARIE DE MADAGASCAR

sānt-mə-rē-də-ˌmad-ə-ˈgas-kər

LOCATION — An island off the east coast of Madagascar
GOVT. — French Possession
AREA — 64 sq. mi.
POP. — 8,000 (approx.)

In 1896 Ste.-Marie de Madagascar was attached to the colony of Madagascar for administrative purposes.

100 Centimes = 1 Franc

Navigation and Commerce — A1

**1894 Unwmk. Typo. *Perf. 14x13½***
**Name of Colony in Blue or Carmine**

| | | | | |
|---|---|---|---|---|
| 1 | A1 | 1c black, *lil bl* | 1.75 | 1.75 |
| 2 | A1 | 2c brown, *buff* | 2.75 | 2.75 |
| 3 | A1 | 4c claret, *lavender* | 5.00 | 5.00 |
| 4 | A1 | 5c green, *grnsh* | 12.00 | 11.00 |
| 5 | A1 | 10c black, *lavender* | 13.50 | 10.50 |
| 6 | A1 | 15c blue | 40.00 | 36.00 |
| 7 | A1 | 20c red, *green* | 30.00 | 28.00 |
| 8 | A1 | 25c black, *rose* | 25.00 | 22.00 |
| 9 | A1 | 30c brown, *bister* | 17.50 | 16.00 |
| 10 | A1 | 40c red, *straw* | 17.50 | 16.00 |
| 11 | A1 | 50c carmine, *rose* | 52.50 | 52.50 |
| 12 | A1 | 75c violet, *org* | 100.00 | 72.50 |
| 13 | A1 | 1fr brnz grn, *straw* | 52.50 | 47.50 |
| | | *Nos. 1-13 (13)* | 370.00 | 321.50 |

Perf. 13½x14 stamps are counterfeits.

These stamps were replaced by those of Madagascar.

## ST. MARTIN

sānt ˌmär-tən

LOCATION — The southern part of the island of St. Martin in the Caribbean Sea.
AREA — 13 sq. mi.
POP. — 33,119 (2007)
CAPITAL — Philipsburg

On Oct. 10, 2010, St. Martin, formerly part of Netherlands Antilles, became a constituent state within the Kingdom of the Netherlands.

100 Cents = 1 Florin (gulden)

**Catalogue values for all unused stamps in this country are for Never Hinged items.**

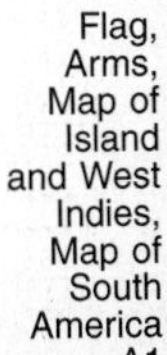

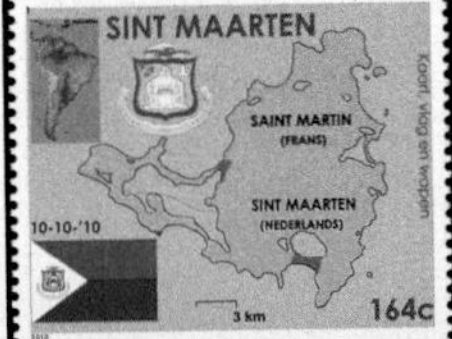


Flag, Arms, Map of Island and West Indies, Map of South America
A1

***Perf. 13¾***

**2010, Oct. 10 Litho. Unwmk.**

| | | | | |
|---|---|---|---|---|
| 1 | A1 | 164c multi | 2.00 | 2.00 |

25th Paper Money Fair, Maastricht, Nedtherlands — A2

No. 2: a, 80c, 50 koruna banknote, Slovakia, 1999. b, 112c, 100 franc banknote, New Hebrides, 1977. c, 145c, 20 pula banknote, Botswana, 1982. d, 195c, 50 dalasi banknote, Gambia, 1989. e, 240c, 10 rupee banknote, Sri Lanka, 1979. f, 285c, 10 riyal banknote, Qatar, 2003.

**2011, Apr. 6 *Perf. 14***

| | | | | |
|---|---|---|---|---|
| 2 | A2 | Block of 6, #a-f | 12.00 | 12.00 |

Miniature Sheet

Peonies — A3

No. 3: a, Pink peony. b, Two white peonies and bud. c, White peony. d, Red peony and bud.

350c, Blue peonies.

**2011, Apr. 28**

| | | | | |
|---|---|---|---|---|
| 3 | A3 | 110c Sheet of 4, #a-d | 5.00 | 5.00 |

**Souvenir Sheet**

| | | | | |
|---|---|---|---|---|
| 4 | A3 | 350c multi | 4.00 | 4.00 |

Butterflies — A4

No. 5: a, 50c, Ornithoptera chimaera. b, 70c, Morpho cypris. c, 120c, Paralaxita lacoon. d, 145c, Eurytides iphitas. e, 166c, Dercas lycorias. f, 210c, Ancyluris jurgensenii.

**2011, June 1 Litho. *Perf. 14***

| | | | | |
|---|---|---|---|---|
| 5 | A4 | Block of 6, #a-f | 8.50 | 8.50 |

Flowers — A5

No. 6: a, 21c, Camellia "Yuletide." b, 25c, Cornus kousa. c, 30c, Magnolia "Vulcan." d, 34c, Bidens laevis. e, 40c, Syringa vulgaris. f, 60c, Rosa "Charmian." g, 80c, Philadelphus. h, 170c, Rhododendron arboreum. i, 190c, Hydrangea macrophylla. j, 220c, Magnolia grandiflora. k, 295c, Buddleja davidii. l, 335c, Ribes sanguineum.

**2011, Aug. 24**

| | | | | |
|---|---|---|---|---|
| 6 | A5 | Block of 12, #a-l | 17.00 | 17.00 |

Maps — A6

No. 7: a, 111c, Map of St. Martin. b, 145c, Map of Caribbean Sea with St. Martin highlighted, vert. c, 350c, Map of South America with St. Martin highlighted, vert.

**2011, Oct. 5**

| | | | | |
|---|---|---|---|---|
| 7 | A6 | Vert. strip of 3, #a-c | 7.00 | 7.00 |

A7

A8

Designs of stamps inscribed "A": No. 8, Clock. No. 9, Agraulis vanillae. No. 10, Salt pickers. No. 11, Mangos. No. 12, Coconuts.

Designs of denominated stamps: 115c, Princess Juliana International Airport. 145c, Ocean Liner *Allure of the Seas*. 195c, Flamboyant tree. 205c, Danaus plexippus. 240c, Winair airplane. 285c, Pelican. 405c, Aerial view of Philipsburg.

No. 20: a, Beach. b, Maho Beach Airport. c, Harbor.

**2011 Litho. *Perf. 14***

**Stamps Inscribed "A"**

| | | | | |
|---|---|---|---|---|
| 8 | A7 | (115c) multi | 1.40 | 1.40 |
| 9 | A7 | (204c) multi | 2.25 | 2.25 |
| 10 | A7 | (205c) multi | 2.40 | 2.40 |
| 11 | A7 | (285c) multi | 3.25 | 3.25 |
| 12 | A7 | (380c) multi | 4.25 | 4.25 |
| | | *Nos. 8-12 (5)* | 13.55 | 13.55 |

**Stamps With Denominations**

| | | | | |
|---|---|---|---|---|
| 13 | A8 | 115c multi | 1.40 | 1.40 |
| 14 | A8 | 145c multi | 1.75 | 1.75 |
| 15 | A8 | 195c multi | 2.25 | 2.25 |
| 16 | A8 | 205c multi | 2.40 | 2.40 |
| 17 | A8 | 240c multi | 2.75 | 2.75 |
| 18 | A8 | 285c multi | 3.25 | 3.25 |
| 19 | A8 | 405c multi | 4.50 | 4.50 |
| | | *Nos. 13-19 (7)* | 18.30 | 18.30 |

**Size: 19x15mm**

***Perf. 13¾x13¼***

| | | | | |
|---|---|---|---|---|
| 20 | | Strip of 3, #a-c | 5.75 | 5.75 |
| *a.-c.* | A8 | 170c Any single | 1.90 | 1.90 |

Issued: Nos. 8-12, 14-15, 17-19, 10/6; Nos. 13, 16, 11/15; No. 20, 11/11. See Nos. 26-27.

Ships — A9

No. 21: a, 50c, Skuldelev Knorr, c. 1030. b, 60c, Mataro, 1450. c, 80c, St. Micahel, 1669. d, 380c, Herring buss, 1700. e, 405c, Wendur, 1884. f, 525c, Pearling dhow, c. 1900.

**2011, Nov. 30 *Perf. 14***

| | | | | |
|---|---|---|---|---|
| 21 | A9 | Block of 6, #a-f | 17.00 | 17.00 |

Butterflies — A10

No. 22: a, 25c, Boloria selene. b, 50c, Hesperia comma. c, 75c, Lysandra bellargus. d, 100c, Limenitis camilla. e, 150c, Erebia aethiops. f, 200c, Minois dryas. g, 250c, Vanessa atalanta. h, 300c, Zerynthia polyxena. i, 305c, Parnassius phoebus smintheus. j, 310c, Clossiana dia. k, 335c, Pieris rapae. l, 400c, Brenthis daphne.

**2012, Feb. 29**

| | | | | |
|---|---|---|---|---|
| 22 | A10 | Block of 12, #a-l | 30.00 | 30.00 |

Flowers — A11

No. 23: a, 10c, Anemone hupehensis. b, 25c, Caltha palustris. c, 50c, Helleborus thibetanus. d, 125c, Lobelia cardinalis. e, 125c, Osteospermum jucundum. f, 175c, Narcissus. g, 225c, Hemerocallis. h, 355c, Doronicum orientale. i, 455c, Catharanthus roseus. j, 500c, Alstromeria.

**2012, Apr. 4**
**23** A11 Block of 10, #a-j 23.00 23.00

Women's Carnival Costumes — A12

No. 24 — Various costumes: a, 115c. b, 250c. c, 275c. d, 375c.

**2012, May 2**
**24** A12 Horiz. strip of 4, #a-d 11.50 11.50

Historical Sites — A13

No. 25: a, 170c, Border Monument with two dates at Fort St. Louis. b, 200c, Border Monument with one date. c, 300c, Courthouse.

**2012, May 30**
**25** A13 Horiz. strip of 3, #a-c 7.50 7.50

**Type of 2011**

Designs: 10c, Flamboyant tree in bloom. 175c, Princess Juliana International Airport.

**2012, June 13** ***Perf. 14***
**26** A8 10c multi .25 .25
**27** A8 175c multi 2.00 2.00

A14

Indonesia 2012 Intl. Stamp Exhibition, Jakarta — A15

No. 28: a, 120c, Prambanan Hindu Temple. b, 300c, Varanus komodoensis. c, 400c, Borobudur Buddhist Temple.

No. 29 — Rafflesia arnoldii flower with denomination at: a, 50c, LL. b, 100c, LR. c, 250c, UL. d, 400c, UR.

**2012, June 13**
**28** A14 Vert. strip of 3, #a-c 9.25 9.25

**Souvenir Sheet**

**29** A15 Sheet of 4, #a-d 9.00 9.00

2012 Summer Olympics, London — A16

No. 30: a, 25c, Handball. b, 50c, Running. c, 75c, Field hockey. d, 90c, Judo. e, 100c, Tennis. f, 120c, Soccer. g, 170c, Kayaking. h, 200c, Cycling. i, 220c, Gymnastics. j, 250c, Basketball. k, 300c, Beach volleyball. l, 400c, Triple jump.

No. 31: a, 125c, Archery. b, 225c, Diving. c, 350c, Weight lifting.

**2012, July 18**
**30** A16 Block of 12, #a-l 22.50 22.50

**Souvenir Sheet**

**31** A16 Sheet of 3, #a-c 8.00 8.00

Dutch Royalty — A17

No. 32: a, 100c, Queen Beatrix. b, 125c, Queen Beatrix at ship's wheel. c, 200c, Queen Beatrix holding infant. d, 275c, Prince Willem-Alexander. e, 325c, Princess Margriet. f, 475c, Princess Máxima.

**2012, Sept. 12**
**32** A17 Block of 6, #a-f 17.00 17.00

**Miniature Sheet**

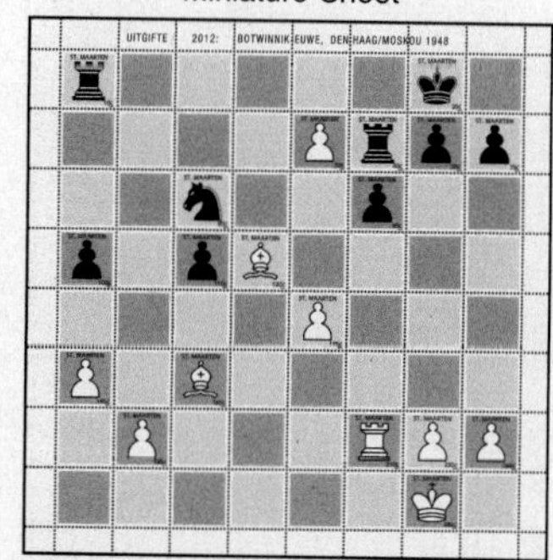
Final Position of 1948 Chess Match Between Mikhail Botvinnik and Max Euwe — A18

No. 33: a, 10c, Black rook. b, 20c, Black king. c, 30c, White pawn. d, 40c, Black rook. e, 55c, Black pawn. f, 75c, Black pawn. g, 85c, Black knight. h, 95c, Black pawn. i, 100c, Black pawn. j, 110c, Black pawn. k, 120c, White bishop. l, 135c, White pawn. m, 165c, White pawn. n, 185c, White bishop. o, 195c, White pawn. p, 210c, White rook. q, 230c, White pawn. r, 260c, White pawn. s, 380c, White king.

**2012, Oct. 17**
**33** A18 Sheet of 19, #a-s, + 45 labels 28.00 28.00

Local Scenes — A19

No. 34: a, 115c, Fort Amsterdam. b, 200c, Hoofdstraat. c, 250c, View of beach. d, 350c, Airplane on final approach over Maho Beach.

**2012, Nov. 14**
**34** A19 Block of 4, #a-d 12.50 12.50

Birds — A20

No. 35: a, 10c, Amazilia leucogaster. b, 30c, Aulacorhynchus derbianus. c, 50c, Bubo virginianus. d, 75c, Jacamerops aurea. e, 100c, Pteroglossus aracari. f, 150c, Discosura longicauda. g, 175c, Accipiter bicolor. h, 200c, Gampsonyx swainsonii. i, 240c, Leptodon cayanensis. j, 300c, Topaza pella. k, 350c, Trogon violaceus. l, 400c, Cotinga cayana.

**2012, Dec. 12**
**35** A20 Block of 12, #a-l 24.00 24.00

Churches — A21

No. 36: a, 110c, Cole Bay Seventh Day Adventist Church. b, 150c, Simpson Bay Catholic Church. c, 200c, Philipsburg Methodist Church, vert. d, 350c, South Reward Catholic Church, vert.

**2013, Jan. 2** **Litho.** ***Perf. 14***
**36** A21 Block of 4, #a-d 9.25 9.25

**Miniature Sheet**

Birds — A22

No. 37: a, 25c, Columba plumbea. b, 50c, Chlorostilbon mellisugus. c, 75c, Cyanocorax cyanomelas. d, 100c, Eucometis penicillata. e, 150c, Mionectes oleagineus. f, 200c, Hemithraupis flavicollis. g, 225c, Myrmotherula guttata. h, 250c, Piaya cayana. i, 300c, Piaya melanogaster. j, 350c, Piaya minuta. k, 400c, Pygiptila stellaris. l, 475c, Turdus fumigatus.

**2013, Feb. 6** **Litho.** ***Perf. 14***
**37** A22 Sheet of 12, #a-l, + 3 labels 29.00 29.00

Politicians — A23

No. 38: a, 250c, Dr. Albert Claudius Wathey (1926-98). b, 300c, Vance James, Jr. (1949-2008).

**2013, Mar. 6 Litho. *Perf. 14***
**38** A23 Horiz. pair, #a-b 6.25 6.25

Cruise Ships A24

Designs: No. 39, 180c, Allure of the Seas. No. 40, 180c, Oasis of the Seas. No. 41, 180c, Ruby Princess. No. 42, 180c, Queen Victoria. No. 43, 180c, Carnival Dream. No. 44, 180c, Disney Fantasy.

**2013 Litho. *Perf. 13¾***
**39-44** A24 Set of 6 12.00 12.00

Issued: Nos. 39-40, 3/6; Nos. 41-42, 4/3; Nos. 43-44, 6/5.
Compare with type A43.

Local Scenes — A25

No. 45: a, 75c, A. C. Wathey Cruise Pier. b, 100c, Dr. A. C. Wathery Port Complex. c, 215c, Grote Bay. d, 325c, KLM airplane landing.

**2013, Apr. 3 Litho. *Perf. 14***
**45** A25 Block of 4, #a-d 8.00 8.00

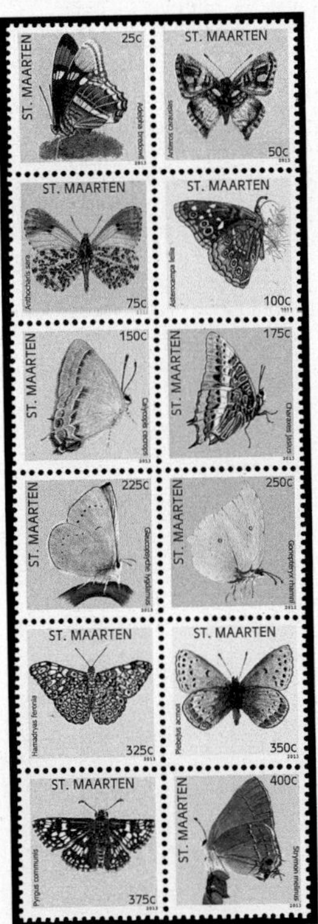

Butterflies — A26

No. 46: a, 25c, Adelpha bredowii. b, 50c, Anteros carausias. c, 75c, Anthocharis sara. d, 100c, Asterocampa leilia. e, 150c, Calycopis cecrops. f, 175c, Charaxes jasius. g, 225c, Glaucopsyche lygdamus. h, 250c, Gonepteryx rhamni. i, 325c, Hamadryas feronia. j, 350c, Plebejus acmon. k, 375c, Pyrgus communis. l, 400c, Strymon melinus.

**2013, May 2 Litho. *Perf. 14***
**46** A26 Block of 12, #a-l 28.00 28.00

Miniature Sheet

Scouting — A27

No. 47: a, 175c, Scout holding St. Martin troop sign. b, 200c, Four Scouts. c, 250c, Two Scouts in kayaks, horiz. d, 350c, Four Scouts, horiz.

**2013, June 5 Litho. *Perf. 14***
**47** A27 Sheet of 4, #a-d 11.00 11.00

Dutch Royalty — A28

No. 48: a, 100c, King William I. b, 200c, King William II. c, 300c, King William III. d, 400c, Queen Wilhelmina. e, 450c, Queen Juliana. f, 550c, Queen Beatrix.
No. 49: a, 300c, Queen Máxima. b, 550c, King Willem-Alexander.

**2013, July 10 Litho. *Perf. 14***
**48** A28 Sheet of 6, #a-f, + 3 labels 22.50 22.50

**Souvenir Sheet**

**49** A28 Sheet of 2, #a-b 9.50 9.50

Ships — A29

No. 50: a, 125c, Savannah, 1819. b, 200c, Steam trawler, 1877. c, 275c, Alice M. Colburn, 1896. d, 325c, Muirneag, 1903. e, 350c, S.T.S. Lord Nelson, 1985. f, 350c, S.T.S. Young Endeavour, 1987.

**2013, Sept. 4 Litho. *Perf. 14***
**50** A29 Block of 6, #a-f 18.50 18.50

United States Lighthouses — A30

No. 51: a, 150c, Cape Hatteras Lighthouse, North Carolina. b, Portland Breakwater Lighthouse, Maine. c, 250c, Cape St. George Lighthouse, Florida. d, 300c, Molokai Lighthouse, Hawaii. e, 400c, Pensacola Lighthouse, Florida. f, 450c, Rock of Ages Lighthouse, Michigan.

**2013, Oct. 2 Litho. *Perf. 14***
**51** A30 Block or vert. strip of 6, #a-f 19.50 19.50

Miniature Sheet

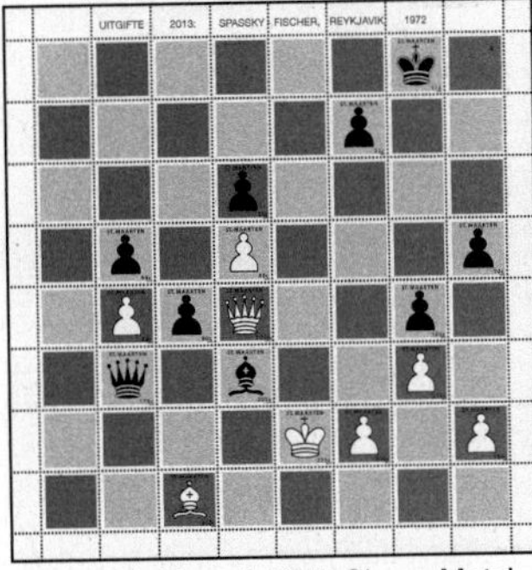

Final Position of 1972 Chess Match Between Boris Spassky and Bobby Fischer — A31

No. 52: a, 11c, Black king. b, 22c, Black pawn. c, 33c, Black pawn. d, 44c, Black pawn. e, 60c, White pawn. f, 70c, Black pawn. g, 80c, White pawn. h, 90c, Black pawn. i, 125c, White queen. j, 150c, Black pawn. k, 175c, Black queen. l, 200c, Black bishop. m, 215c, White pawn. n, 225c, White king. o, 300c, White pawn. p, 350c, White pawn. q, 350c, White bishop.

**2013, Nov. 6 Litho. *Perf. 14***
**52** A31 Sheet of 17, #a-q, + 47 labels 28.00 28.00

Miniature Sheet

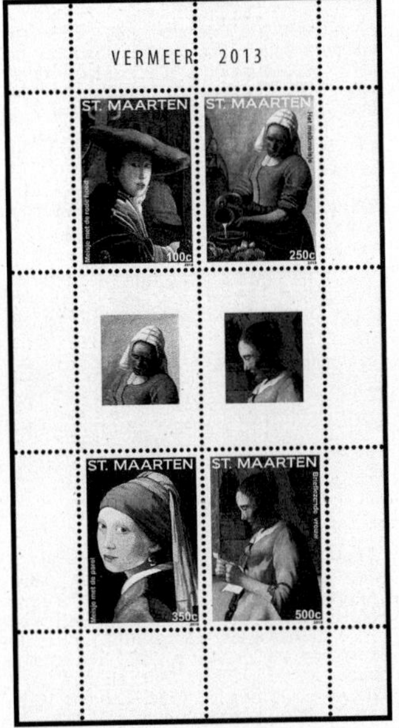

Paintings by Johannes Vermeer — A32

No. 53: a, 100c, Girl with a Red Hat. b, 250c, The Milkmaid. c, 350c, Girl with a Pearl Earring. d, 500c, Woman in Blue Reading a Letter.

**2013, Dec. 4 Litho. *Perf. 14***
**53** A32 Sheet of 4, #a-d, + 2 labels 13.50 13.50

Miniature Sheet

Flowers — A33

No. 54: a, 10c, Costus speciosus. b, 20c, Cynara cardunculus. c, 50c, Dendrobium macrophyllum. d, 70c, Disa diores. e, 90c, Hibiscus rosa-sinensis. f, 100c, Kniphofia. g, 150c, Leontopodium alpinum. h, 210c, Phalaenopsis chibae. i, 300c, Phalaenopsis schilleriana. j, 350c, Rhynchostylis coelestis. k, 400c, Tillandsia cyanea. l, 650c, Vanda coerulea.

**2014, Apr. 9 Litho. *Perf. 14***
**54** A33 Sheet of 12, #a-l 27.00 27.00

Miniature Sheet

Paintings by Frans Hals (c. 1582-1666) — A34

No. 55: a, 150c, De Vrolijke Drinker (The Merry Drinker). b, 250c, Het Zigeunemeisje (Gypsy Girl). c, 450c, Malle Babbe. d, 550c, De Luitspeler (Jester with a Lute).

**2014, May 14 Litho. *Perf. 14***
**55** A34 Sheet of 4, #a-d, + 2 labels 16.00 16.00

Miniature Sheet

Birds — A35

No. 56: a, 10c, Celeus elegans. b, 20c, Celeus flavus. c, 50c, Coccyzus melacoryphus. d, 70c, Donacobius atricapillus. e, 90c, Elanoides forficatus. f, 100c, Eupetomena macroura. g, 150c, Gampsonyx swainsonii. h, 210c, Leptodon cayanensis. i, 300c, Mimus gilvus. j, 350c, Momotus momota. k, 400c, Piculus rubiginosus. l, 650c, Venilornis cassini.

**2014, June 18 Litho. *Perf. 14***
**56** A35 Sheet of 12, #a-l 27.00 27.00

Miniature Sheet

Fruits — A36

No. 57: a, 75c, Fragaria ananassa. b, 125c, Malus domestica. c, 275c, Nephelium lappaceum. d, 325c, Prunus armeniaca. e, 475c, Prunus persica. f, 525c, Pyrus.

**2014, Aug. 20 Litho. *Perf. 14***
**57** A36 Sheet of 6, #a-f 20.00 20.00

Miniature Sheet

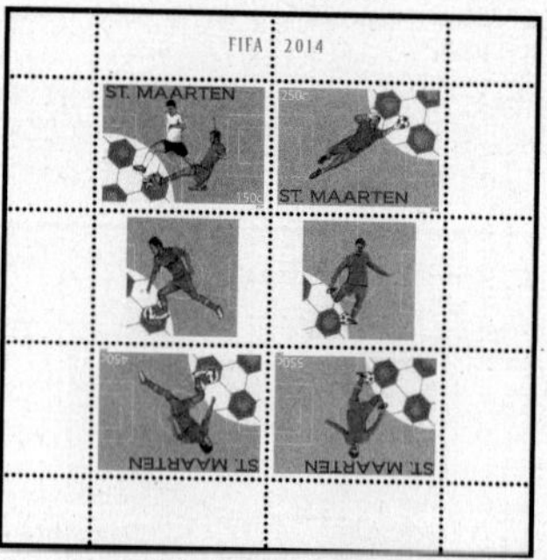

Soccer — A37

No. 58 — Soccer ball and: a, 150c, Two players chasing ball. b, 250c, Goalie diving for ball. c, 450c, Player dribbling ball. d, 550c, Player ready to kick ball.

**2014, Sept. 17 Litho. *Perf. 14***
**58** A37 Sheet of 4, #a-d, + 2 labels 16.00 16.00

Miniature Sheet

Netherlands Stamps — A38

No. 59 — Canceled examples of stamps with incorrect perforations: a, 175c, Netherlands #47. b, 325c, Netherlands #154. c, 575c, Netherlands #5. d, 725c, Netherlands #70.

**2014, Oct. 15 Litho. *Perf. 14***
**59** A38 Sheet of 4, #a-d 20.00 20.00

Miniature Sheet

Traditional Women's Dresses — A39

No. 60 — Various dresses: a, 150c. b, 250c. c, 450c. d, 550c.

**2014, Nov. 19 Litho. *Perf. 14***
**60** A39 Sheet of 4, #a-d 16.00 16.00

Butterflies — A40

No. 61: a, 10c, Colias cesonia. b, 20c, Historis acheronta. c, 50c, Historis acheronta, diff. d, 70c, Issoria lathonia. e, 90c, Marpesia chiron. f, 100c, Ornithoptera paradisea. g, 150c, Papilio zelicaon. h, 210c, Polygonia interrogationis. i, 300c, Precis orithya. j, 350c, Speyeria diana. k, 400c, Speyeria idalia. l, 650c, Troides aeacus.

**2014, Dec. 10 Litho. *Perf. 14***
**61** A40 Block of 12, #a-l 27.00 27.00

Birds — A41

No. 62: a, 10c, Micrastur semitorquatus. b, 30c, Brachygalba lugubris. c, 60c, Caprimulgus rufus. d, 90c, Caprimulgus nigrescens. e, 110c, Chondrohierax uncinatus. f, 150c, Colaptes campestris. g, 200c, Chordeiles acutipennis. h, 250c, Hydropsalis climacocerca. i, 300c, Otus atricapillus. j, 325c, Galbula dea. k, 475c, Zebrilus undulates. l, 500c, Eurypyga helias.

**2015, Jan. 14 Litho. *Perf. 14***
**62** A41 Block of 12, #a-l 28.00 28.00

Miniature Sheet

Shells — A42

No. 63: a, 90c, Buccinum politum. b, 110c, Bulla striata. c, 270c, Cypraecassis testiculus. d, 330c, Neptunea contraria. e, 500c, Phos senticosus. f, 600c, Trigonostoma pellucida.

**2015, Feb. 11 Litho. *Perf. 14***
**63** A42 Sheet of 6, #a-f 21.50 21.50

Allure of the Seas — A43

**2015, Mar. 2 Litho. *Perf. 14***
**64** A43 180c multi 2.00 2.00

Compare with type A24.

Banknotes — A44

No. 65: a, 90c, Gabon 5000-franc note. b, 110c, Sri Lanka 2-rupee note. c, 270c, Oman 1-rial note. d, 330c, Zambia 50-kwacha note. e, 500c, Gambia 25-dalasi note. f, 600c, Tanzania 5000-shilling note.

**2015, Mar. 18 Litho. *Perf. 14***
**65** A44 Block of 6, #a-f 21.50 21.50

Souvenir Sheet

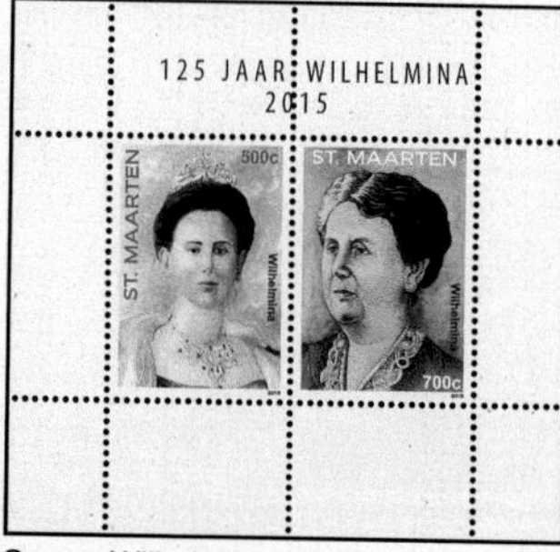

Queen Wilhelmina (1880-1962) — A45

No. 66 — Various depictions of Queen Wilhelmina: a, 500c. b, 700c.

**2015, Apr. 15 Litho. *Perf. 14***
**66** A45 Sheet of 2, #a-b 13.50 13.50

Cruise Ships — A46

No. 67: a, Norwegian Getaway. b, Jewel of the Seas. c, Freedom of the Seas. d, Royal Princess.

**2015, June 17 Litho. *Perf. 14***
**67** Horiz. strip of 4 18.00 18.00
*a.* A46 275c multi 3.25 3.25
*b.* A46 325c multi 3.75 3.75
*c.* A46 475c multi 5.25 5.25
*d.* A46 525c multi 5.75 5.75

Miniature Sheets

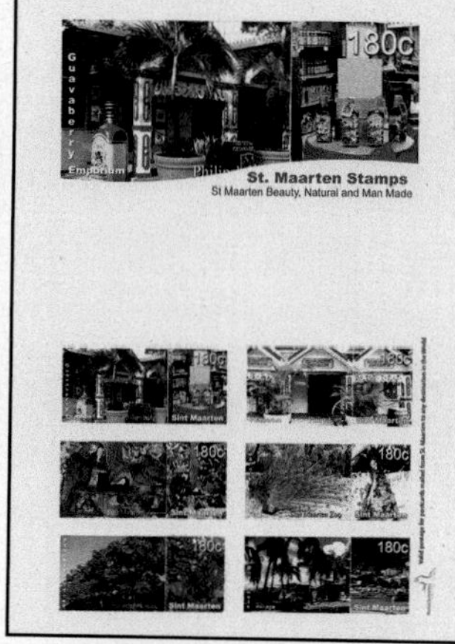

A47

Tourism — A48

No. 68: a, Bottles on Guavaberry Emporium table and shelves. b, Exterior of Guavaberry Emporium. c. Macaws in St. Martin Zoo. d, Peacock in St. Martin Zoo. e, Flamboyant tree on Saunders Estate. f, Boardwalk Village, Philipsburg.

No. 69: a, Children's art on wall, Madam Estate Zoo. b, Mounted butterflies. c, Brown pelican. d, Sculpture. e, Bridge, Simpson Bay Lagoon. f, Iguana.

***Serpentine Die Cut 14¼***

**2015, July 1 Self-Adhesive Litho.**

| | | | | |
|---|---|---|---|---|
| **68** | A47 | Sheet of 6 + 6 labels | 12.00 | |
| *a.-f.* | | 180c Any single | 2.00 | 2.00 |
| **69** | A48 | Sheet of 10, #68c-68f, 69a-69f + 10 labels | 20.00 | |
| *a.-f.* | | 180c Any single | 2.00 | 2.00 |

Flowers — A49

No. 70: a, 25c, Antigonon leptopus. b, 50c, Fritillaria imperialis, c, 75c, Callistemom lanceolatus. d, 100c, Hibiscus schizopetalus. e, 150c, Canna generalis. f, 250c, Lilium pumilum. g, 350c, Hymenocallis caribaea. h, 400c, Narcissus tazetta. i, 500c, Pyrostegia venusta. j, 600c, Ricinus communis.

**2015, Aug. 19 Litho. *Perf. 14***

**70** A49 Block of 10, #a-j 28.00 28.00

Miniature Sheets

Butterflies — A50

No. 71: a, 25c, Hypolimnas misippus. b, 50c, Papilio krishna. c, 75c, Euphydryas chalcedona. d, 100c, Feniseca tarquinius. e, 150c, Papilio demodocus.

No. 72: a, 250c, Brephidium exile. b, 350c, Pseudotergumia fidia. c, 400c, Satyrium titus. d, 500c, Papilio arcturus. e, 600c, Thessalia theona.

**2015, Sept. 16 Litho. *Perf. 14***

**71** A50 Sheet of 5, #a-e 4.50 4.50
**72** A50 Sheet of 5, #a-e 23.50 23.50

Fish — A51

No. 73: a, 25c, Acanthodoras spinosissimus. b, 50c, Acaronia nassa, c, 75c, Acestrorhynchus falcatus. d, 100c, Amphilophus citrinellus. e, 150c, Brochis splendens. f, 250c, Erythrinus erythrinus. g, 350c, Copeina arnoldi. h, 400c, Charax gibbosus. i, 500c, Symphysodon aequifasciatus. j, 600c, Phractocephalus hemioliopterus.

**2015, Oct. 14 Litho. *Perf. 14***

**73** A51 Block of 10, #a-j 28.00 28.00

Primates — A52

No. 74: a, 75c, Cebus capucinus. b, 125c, Ateles geoffroyi. c, 275c, Presbytis obscura. d, 325c, Ateles paniscus. e, 475c, Cebus apella. f, 525c, Callicebus torquatus.

**2015, Nov. 18 Litho. *Perf. 14***

**74** A52 Block of 6, #a-f 20.00 20.00

Pilioko Paintings — A53

No. 75 — Various paintings with frame color at bottom of: a, 275c, Lilac. b, 325c, Light blue. c, 475c, Dark blue. d, 525c, Ultramarine.

**2015, Dec. 9 Litho. *Perf. 14***

**75** A53 Vert. strip of 4, #a-d 18.00 18.00

Butterflies — A54

No. 76: a, 25c, Achlyodes thraso. b, 100c, Amblyscirtes eos. c, 125c, Anartia jatrophae. d, 200c, Apodemia nais. e, 250c, Atrytonopsis hianna. f, 300c, Biblis hyperia. g, 350c, Callicore hydaspes. h, 400c, Catocala amatrix. i, 450c, Chlosyne rosita. j, 500c, Erora latea.

No. 77, 500c, Tithorea harmonia. No. 78, 500c, Mechanitis polymnia. No. 79, 500c, Morpho anaxibia. No. 80, 500c, Strymon acis bartrami. No. 81, 500c, Perisama priene. No. 82, 500c, Eumaeus atala. No. 83, 500c, Prepona praeneste. No. 84, 500c, Greta andromica. No. 85, 500c, Nymphidium mantus. No. 86, 500c, Arawacus lincoides. No. 87, 500c, Morpho portis. No. 88, 500c, Archaeopropona demophon.

**2016, Jan. 2 Litho. *Perf. 14***

**76** A54 Sheet of 10, #a-j, + 2 labels 30.00 30.00

**Souvenir Sheets**

**77-88** A54 Set of 12 67.50 67.50

Birds — A55

No. 89: a, 25c, Amazonetta brasiliensis. b, 100c, Anhinga anhinga. c, 125c, Aramides saracura. d, 200c, Calidris bairdii. e, 250c, Cariama cristata. f, 300c, Cochlearicus cochlearicus. g, 350c, Crypturellus parvirostris. h, 400c, Cygnus melancoryphus. i, 450c, Gallinago paraguaiae. j, 500c, Jabiru mycteria.

Designs: No. 90, 500c, Amazona aestiva. No. 91, 500c, Amazona xanthops. No. 92, 500c, Anadorhynchus hyacinthinus. No. 93, 500c, Athene cunicularia. No. 94, 500c, Brotogeris chiriri. No. 95, 500c, Brotogeris tirica. No. 96, 500c, Columba picazuro. No. 97, 500c, Columbina picui. No. 98, 500c, Myiopsitta monachus. No. 99, 500c, Pionopsitta pileata. No. 100, 500c, Pyrrhura frontalis. No. 101, 500c, Scardafella squammata.

**2016, Jan. 6 Litho. *Perf. 14***

**89** A55 Sheet of 10, #a-j, + 2 labels 30.00 30.00

**Souvenir Sheets**

**90-101** A55 Set of 12 67.50 67.50

No. 89h "Melancoryphus" is spelled wrong. See No. 115.

Butterflies — A56

No. 102: a, 25c, Eurytides marcellus. b, 100c, Hamadryas laodamia. c, 125c, Heliconius melpomene. d, 200c, Hesperia leonardus. e, 250c, Mestra amymone. f, 300c, Myscelia ethusa. g, 350c, Neominois ridingsii. h, 400c, Papilio polyxenes. i, 450c, Phocides polybius. j, 500c, Riodina lysippus.

No. 103, 500c, Actias luna. No. 104, 500c, Arachnis picta. No. 105, 500c, Dismorphia fortunate. No. 106, 500c, Eumorphus pandorus. No. 107, 500c, Eurytides marchandi. No. 108, 500c, Eurytides philolaus. No. 109, 500c, Graphium agamemnon. No. 110, 500c, Hemaris diffinis. No. 111, 500c, Hyalophora cecropia. No. 112, 500c, Ithomia iphianassa. No. 113, 500c, Pteronymia artena. No. 114, 500c, Rothschildia cincta.

**2016, Jan. 13 Litho. *Perf. 14***

**102** A56 Sheet of 10, #a-j, + 2 labels 30.00 30.00

**Souvenir Sheets**

**103-114** A56 Set of 12 67.50 67.50

**Birds Type of 2016**

Miniature Sheet

No. 115: a, 25c, Mergus octocetaceus. b, 100c, Phaetusa simplex. c, 125c, Phimosus infuscatus. d, 200c, Podiceps major. e, 250c, Puffinus puffinus. f, 300c, Rhynchops niger. g, 350c, Sarcoramphus papa. h, 400c, Sterna maxima. i, 450c, Theristicus caudatus. j, 500c, Vanellus chilensis.

**2016, Jan. 20 Litho. *Perf. 14***

**115** A55 Sheet of 10, #a-j, + 2 labels 30.00 30.00

Souvenir Sheets

Flowers — A57

Designs: No. 116, 500c, Corydalis aurea. No. 117, 500c, Corydalis sempervirens. No. 118, 500c, Dicentra chrysantha. No. 119, 500c, Dicentra cucullaria. No. 120, 500c, Eschscholzia californica. No. 121, 500c, Nuphar lutea. No. 122, 500c, Nuphar polysepala. No. 123, 500c, Nymphaea mexicana. No. 124, 500c, Silene acaulis. No. 125, 500c, Silene californica. No. 126, 500c, Silene virginica. No. 127, 500c, Romneya coulteri.

**2016, Jan. 27 Litho. *Perf. 14***

**116-127** A57 Set of 12 67.50 67.50

See Nos. 152-159.

Souvenir Sheets

Parrots — A58

Designs: No. 128, 500c, Deroptyus accipitrinus. No. 129, 500c, Eclectus roratus. No. 130, 500c, Pionites leucogaster. No. 131, 500c, Pionites melanocephala. No. 132, 500c, Pionus senilis. No. 133, 500c, Poicephalus gulielmi. No. 134, 500c, Poicephalus senegalus. No. 135, 500c, Prioniturus mada. No. 136, 500c, Psittaculirostris edwardsii. No. 137, 500c, Psittacus erithacus. No. 138, 500c, Tanygnathus m. megalorhynchus. No. 139, 500c, Tanygnathus sumatranus.

**2016, Feb. 3 Litho. *Perf. 14***

**128-139** A58 Set of 12 67.50 67.50

See Nos. 160-167.

Souvenir Sheets

Frogs — A59

Designs: No. 140, 500c, Bufo bufo. No. 141, 500c, Cochranella truebae. No. 142, 500c, Hyla arborea. No. 143, 500c, Hyla fasciata. No. 144, 500c, Limnodynastes ornatus. No. 145, 500c, Mantidactylus grandidieri. No. 146, 500c, Occidozyga baluensis. No. 147, 500c, Oophaga lehmanni. No. 148, 500c, Oophaga pumilio. No. 149, 500c, Osteocephalus buckleyi. No. 150, 500c, Rana temporaria. No. 151, 500c, Staurois natator.

**2016, Feb. 10 Litho. *Perf. 14***

**140-151** A59 Set of 12 67.50 67.50

**Flowers Type of 2016**
Souvenir Sheets

Designs: No. 152, 500c, Agrostemma githago. No. 153, 500c, Aquilegia formosa. No. 154, 500c, Arctomecon merriamii. No. 155, 500c, Caltha leptosepala. No. 156, 500c, Chelidonium majus. No. 157, 500c, Clematis hirsutissima. No. 158, 500c, Clematis ligusticifolia. No. 159, 500c, Clematis virginiana.

**2016, Feb. 17 Litho. *Perf. 14***
**152-159** A57 Set of 8 45.00 45.00

**Parrots Type of 2016**
Souvenir Sheets

Designs: No. 160, 500c, Amazona amazonica. No. 161, 500c, Amazona autumnalis. No. 162, 500c, Amazona guildingi. No. 163, 500c, Amazona ochrocephala. No. 164, 500c, Ara auricollis. No. 165, 500c, Cacatua moluccensis. No. 166, 500c, Calyptorhynchus magnificus. No. 167, 500c, Coracopsis vasa.

**2016, Feb. 24 Litho. *Perf. 14***
**160-167** A58 Set of 8 45.00 45.00

Miniature Sheet

37th St. Martin Heineken Regatta — A60

No. 168: a, Crew on two boats. b, Two dancers, musicians on stage in background. c, Stage lights pointing at people on stage. d, Boats in regatta. e, Two boats. f, Four women with beer bottles. g, Crowd with raised arms. h, Boat with red star on sail. i, Four crewmembers near boat's mast. j, Boat facing left.

***Serpentine Die Cut 14***
**2017, Jan. 2 Self-Adhesive Litho.**
**168** A60 190c Sheet of 10, #a-j, + 10 labels 21.50 21.50

Miniature Sheet

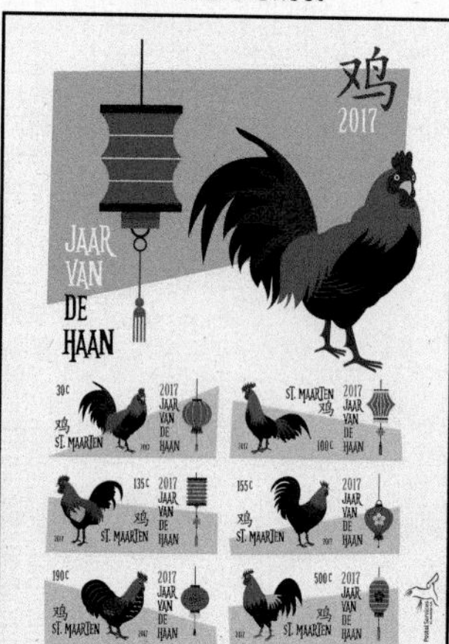


New Year 2017 (Year of the Rooster) — A61

No. 169 — Rooster facing: a, 30c, Right. b, 100c, Left. c, 135c, Left. d, 155c, Right. e, 190c, Right. f, 500c, Left.

***Serpentine Die Cut 14***
**2017, Jan. 27 Litho.**
**Self-Adhesive**
**169** A61 Sheet of 6, #a-f, + 6 labels 12.50 12.50

A62

Designs: 5c, Butterfly. 10c, Butterfly, diff. 20c, Butterfly on flower. 25c, Nerium oleander. 30c, Ixora coccinea. 55c, Ruellia brittoniana. 100c, Bougainvillea x buttiana. 135c, Fort Amsterdam, vert. 155c, Fort Amsterdam. 190c, Monument at Fort Amsterdam, vert. 305c, Cannons at Fort Amsterdam. 500c, Butterfly on flower. 10f, Cassia fistula.

***Perf. 13¼x14, 14x13¼***
**2017, Mar. 1 Litho.**

| | | | | |
|---|---|---|---|---|
| **170** | A62 | 5c multi | .25 | .25 |
| **171** | A62 | 10c multi | .25 | .25 |
| **172** | A62 | 20c multi | .25 | .25 |
| **173** | A62 | 25c multi | .30 | .30 |
| **174** | A62 | 30c multi | .35 | .35 |
| **175** | A62 | 55c multi | .60 | .60 |
| **176** | A62 | 100c multi | 1.10 | 1.10 |
| **177** | A62 | 135c multi | 1.50 | 1.50 |
| **178** | A62 | 155c multi | 1.75 | 1.75 |
| **179** | A62 | 190c multi | 2.10 | 2.10 |
| **180** | A62 | 305c multi | 3.50 | 3.50 |
| **181** | A62 | 500c multi | 5.75 | 5.75 |
| **182** | A62 | 10f multi | 11.50 | 11.50 |
| | | *Nos. 170-182 (13)* | 29.20 | 29.20 |

Miniature Sheet

Butterflies — A63

No. 183: a, 10c, Lycorea halia. b, 30c, Caligo bellerophon. c, 100c, Idea leuconoe. d, 135c, Siproeta stelenes. e, 165c, Lycorea halia, diff. f, 200c, Caligo bellerophon, diff. g, 205c, Idea leuconoe, diff. h, 260c, Siproeta stelenes, diff. i, 415c, Radena similis. j, 10f, Radena similis, diff.

**2017, Mar. 1 Litho. *Perf. 13¼x14***
**183** A63 Sheet of 10, #a-j 28.00 28.00

Miniature Sheet

Birds — A64

No. 184: a, Granaatkolibrie (purple-throated Carib). b, Amerikaanse torenvalk (American kestrel). c, Bruine pelikan (brown pelican). d, Suikerdiefje (bananquit). e, Slechtvalk (peregrine falcon). f, Antilliaanse kuifkolibrie (Antillean crested hummingbird). g, Maskergrondvink (black-faced grassquit). h, Groenkeelkolibrie (green-throated Carib). i, Smelleken (merlin). j, Antillendikbekje (Lesser Antillean bullfinch). k, Coereba flaveola. l, Falco peregrinus. m, Eulampis jugularis. n, Falco sparverius. o, Pelecanus occidentalis. p, Falco columbarius. q, Loxigilla noctis. r, Orthorhynchus cristatus. s, Tiaris bicolor. t, Eulampis holosericeus.

**2017, Aug. 31 Litho. *Perf. 13¼x14***
**184** A64 190c Sheet of 20, #a-t 42.50 42.50

A65

A66

A67

OCEAN LIFE
SINT MAARTEN 100c

Marine Life — A68

**2018, July 20 Litho. *Perf. 13¼x14***

| | | | |
|---|---|---|---|
| **185** | Strip of 4 | 4.50 | 4.50 |
| *a.* | A65 100c multi | 1.10 | 1.10 |
| *b.* | A66 100c multi | 1.10 | 1.10 |
| *c.* | A67 100c multi | 1.10 | 1.10 |
| *d.* | A68 100c multi | 1.10 | 1.10 |

Miniature Sheet

Butterflies — A69

No. 186: a, Inachis io. b, Nymphalis antiopa. c, Celastrina argiolus. d, Aphantopus hyperantus. e, Lycaena phlaeas. f, Hamearis lucina. g, Hiparchia semele. h, Erynnis tages. i, Polyommatus icarus. j, Pontia daplidice. k, Thecla betulae. l, Anthocharis cardamines. m, Pieris brassicae. n, Vanessa atalanta. o, Pieris rapae. p, Carterocephalus palaemon. q, Boloria euphrosyne. r, Aglais urticae. s, Maculinea arion. t, Polygonia c-album. u, Maniola jurtina. v, Cynthia cardui. w, Apatura iris. x, Papilio machaon.

**2018, Oct. 29 Litho. *Perf. 13¼x14***
**186** A69 100c Sheet of 24, #a-x 27.00 27.00

Miniature Sheet

New Year 2019 (Year of the Pig) — A70

No. 187 — Various depictions of pig and lantern: a, 85c. b, 135c. c, 165c. d, 260c. e, 305c. f, 420c.

***Serpentine Die Cut 14***
**2019, Feb. 5 Self-Adhesive Litho.**
**187** A70 Sheet of 6, #a-f, + 6 labels 15.50 15.50

Miniature Sheet

St. Martin Carnival, 50th Anniv. — A71

No. 188: a, 85c, Woman wearing mask, facing right. b, 135c, Costume detail. c, 165c, Mask. d, 260c, Two women in costume. e, 305c, Woman's torso. f, 420c, Woman wearing mask, facing forward.

***Serpentine Die Cut 14***
**2019, Apr. 20 Litho.**
**Self-Adhesive**
**188** A71 Sheet of 6, #a-f, + 6 labels 15.50 15.50

Miniature Sheet

Birds — A72

No. 189: a, Mniotilta varia. b, Spatula discors. c, Tringa semipalmata. d, Pandion haliaetus. e, Orthorhyncus cristatus. f, Sula sula. g, Egretta thula. h, Setophaga americana. i, Falco sparverius. j, Charadrius semipalmatus.

*Serpentine Die Cut 14*

**2019, June 24** **Litho.**

**Self-Adhesive**

**189** A72 190c Sheet of 10, #a-j, + 10 labels 21.50 21.50

Miniature Sheet

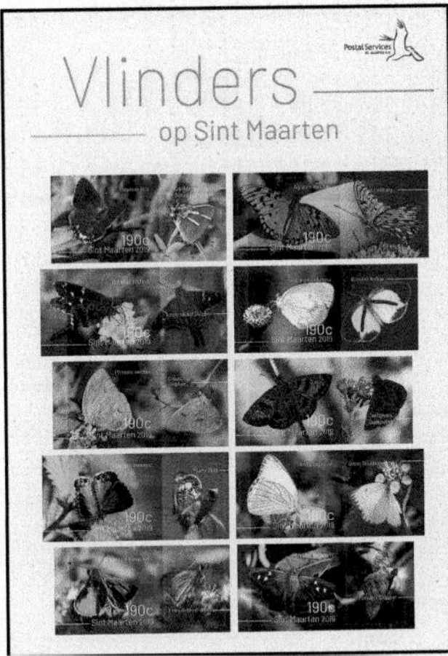


Butterflies — A73

No. 190: a, Strymon acis. b, Agraaulis vanillae. c, Urbanus proteus. d, Eurema elathea. e, Phoebis sennae. f, Ephyriades arcas. g, Cyclargus thomasi. h, Ascia monuste. i, Wallengrenia ophites. j, Polygonus savigny.

*Serpentine Die Cut 14*

**2019, Sept. 2** **Litho.**

**Self-Adhesive**

**190** A73 190c Sheet of 10, #a-j, + 10 labels 21.50 21.50

Orchids A74

No. 191: a, Cattleya. b, Cypripedium calceolus. c, Bletilla striata. d, Eulophia quartiniana. e, Pleione bulbocodioides. f, Cypripedium reginae.

**2020, July 1** **Litho.** ***Perf. 13½x14***

**191** Block or vert. strip of 6 6.75 6.75
*a.-f.* A74 100c Any single 1.10 1.10

Printed in sheets containing four blocks or vertical strips with each stamp having varying background colors.

Birds of Prey — A75

No. 192: a, Black-shouldered kite. b, Red kite. c, Red-footed falcon. d, Bonelli's eagle. e, Rough-legged buzzard. f, Imperial eagle.

**2020, July 1** **Litho.** ***Perf. 13½x14***

**192** Block or vert. strip of 6 6.75 6.75
*a.-f.* A75 100c Any single 1.10 1.10

Printed in sheets containing four blocks or vertical strips with each stamp having varying background colors.

Miniature Sheet

Marine Life — A76

No. 193: a, Urobatis jamaicensis. b, Octopus briareus. c, Hippocampus erectus. d, Sepioteuthis sepioidea. e, Mycteroperca bonaci. f, Chelonia mydas. g, Oreaster reticulatus. h, Panulirus argus. i, Galeocerdo cuvier. j, Charonia tritonis.

*Serpentine Die Cut 14¼*

**2021, July 4** **Litho.**

**Self-Adhesive**

**193** A76 190c Sheet of 10, #a-j, + 10 labels 21.50 21.50

## ST. PIERRE & MIQUELON

sānt-'pi͜ə͜r and 'mik-ə-ˌlän

LOCATION — Two small groups of islands off the southern coast of Newfoundland
GOVT. — Formerly a French colony, now a Department of France
AREA — 93 sq. mi.
POP. — 6,966 (1999 est.)
CAPITAL — St. Pierre

The territory of St. Pierre and Miquelon became a Department of France in July 1976.

100 Centimes = 1 Franc
100 Cents = 1 Euro (2002)

**Catalogue values for unused stamps in this country are for Never Hinged items, beginning with Scott 300 in the regular postage section, Scott B13 in the semi-postal section, Scott C1 in the airpost section, and Scott J68 in the postage due section.**

Stamps of French Colonies Handstamp Surcharged in Black

**1885** **Unwmk.** ***Imperf.***

**1** A8 05c on 40c ver, *straw* 150.00 60.00
**2** A8 10c on 40c ver, *straw* 45.00 35.00
*a.* "M" inverted 375.00 350.00
**3** A8 15c on 40c ver, *straw* 45.00 35.00
*Nos. 1-3 (3)* 240.00 130.00

Nos. 2 and 3 exist with "SPM" 17mm wide instead of 15½mm.

Nos. 1-3 exist with surcharge inverted and with it doubled.

**Handstamp Surcharged in Black**

b

c

d

**1885**

**4** A8 (b) 05c on 35c blk, *yel* 160.00 110.00
**5** A8 (b) 05c on 75c car, *rose* 375.00 300.00
**6** A8 (b) 05c on 1fr brnz grn, *straw* 40.00 32.50
**7** A8 (c) 25c on 1fr brnz grn, *straw* *14,000.* *2,800.*
**8** A8 (d) 25c on 1fr brnz grn, *straw* *2,700.* *1,925.*

Nos. 7 and 8 exist with surcharge inverted, and with it vertical. No. 7 exists with "S P M" above "25" (the handstamping was done in two steps). See the *Scott Specialized Catalogue of Stamps and Covers* for detailed listings.

**1885** ***Perf. 14x13½***

**9** A9 (c) 5c on 2c brn, *buff* *7,250.* *2,700.*
**10** A9 (d) 5c on 4c cl, *lav* 550.00 350.00
**11** A9 (b) 05c on 20c red, *grn* 47.50 47.50

No. 9 surcharge is normally inverted. Nos. 10 and 11 exist with a variety of overprint errors. See the *Scott Specialized Catalogue of Stamps and Covers* for detailed listings.

A15

**1886, Feb.** **Typo.** ***Imperf.***

**Without Gum**

**12** A15 5c black 1,500.
**13** A15 10c black 1,600.
**14** A15 15c black 1,400.
*Nos. 12-14 (3)* 4,500.

"P D" are the initials for "Payé a destination." Excellent forgeries exist.

**Stamps of French Colonies Surcharged in Black**

e

f

**1891** ***Perf. 14x13½***

**15** A9 (e) 15c on 30c brn, *bis* 52.50 40.00
*a.* Inverted surcharge *310.00* *260.00*
**16** A9 (e) 15c on 35c blk, *org* 725.00 575.00
*a.* Inverted surcharge *875.00* *700.00*
**17** A9 (f) 15c on 35c blk, *org* 2,000. 1,650.
*a.* Inverted surcharge *2,100.*
**18** A9 (e) 15c on 40c red, *straw* 125.00 95.00
*a.* Inverted surcharge *300.00* *250.00*

Stamps of French Colonies Overprinted in Black or Red

**1891, Oct. 15**

**19** A9 1c blk, *lil bl* 17.00 13.50
*a.* Inverted overprint 40.00 40.00
**20** A9 1c blk, *lil bl* (R) 17.00 15.00
*a.* Inverted overprint 40.00 40.00
**21** A9 2c brn, *buff* 17.00 13.50
*a.* Inverted overprint 40.00 40.00
*b.* "S" omitted in "ST" 110.00 110.00
**22** A9 2c brn, *buff* (R) 32.50 30.00
*a.* Inverted overprint 82.50 82.50
**23** A9 4c claret, *lav* 17.00 13.50
*a.* Inverted overprint 40.00 40.00
**24** A9 4c claret, *lav* (R) 32.50 30.00
*a.* Inverted overprint 65.00 65.00
**25** A9 5c grn, *grnsh* 27.50 19.00
*a.* Double surcharge 260.00
**26** A9 10c blk, *lav* 47.50 40.00
*a.* Inverted overprint 95.00 *95.00*
*b.* "S" omitted in "ST" 160.00 160.00
**27** A9 10c blk, *lav* (R) 32.50 30.00
*a.* Inverted overprint 65.00 *65.00*
**28** A9 15c blue 45.00 32.50
**29** A9 20c red, *grn* 110.00 100.00
**30** A9 25c blk, *rose* 40.00 27.50
**31** A9 30c brn, *bis* 150.00 125.00
**32** A9 35c vio, *org* 525.00 400.00
**33** A9 40c red, *straw* 100.00 80.00
*a.* Double surcharge 500.00
**34** A9 75c car, *rose* 140.00 130.00
*a.* Inverted overprint 240.00 225.00
**35** A9 1fr brnz grn, *straw* 120.00 105.00
*a.* Inverted overprint 220.00 220.00
*Nos. 19-35 (17)* 1,471. 1,205.

Numerous varieties of mislettering occur in the preceding overprint: "ST," "P," "M," "ON," or "-" missing; "-" instead of "ON"; "=" instead of "-" These varieties command values double or triple those of normal stamps.

Surcharged in Black

**1891-92**

**36** A9 1c on 5c grn, *grnsh* 16.00 16.00
**37** A9 1c on 10c blk, *lav* 18.00 16.50
**38** A9 1c on 25c blk, *rose* ('92) 12.50 12.00
**39** A9 2c on 10c blk, *lav* 16.00 16.00
*a.* Double surcharge 170.00 170.00
*b.* Triple surcharge 350.00 350.00
**40** A9 2c on 15c bl 18.00 16.50
**41** A9 2c on 25c blk, *rose* ('92) 12.50 12.00
**42** A9 4c on 20c red, *grn* 16.00 16.00
**43** A9 4c on 25c blk, *rose* ('92) 12.50 12.00
*a.* Double surcharge 160.00 160.00
**44** A9 4c on 30c brn, *bis* 32.50 26.00
**45** A9 4c on 40c red, *straw* 32.50 26.00
*Nos. 36-45 (10)* 186.50 169.00

See note after No. 35.

**French Colonies 1881-86 Stamps Surcharged in Black**

j

k

**1892, Nov. 4**

**46** A9 (j) 1c on 5c grn, *grnsh* 16.00 14.00
**47** A9 (j) 2c on 5c grn, *grnsh* 16.00 14.00
**48** A9 (j) 4c on 5c grn, *grnsh* 16.00 14.00
**49** A9 (k) 1c on 25c blk, *rose* 12.50 12.00
**50** A9 (k) 2c on 25c blk, *rose* 12.50 12.00
**51** A9 (k) 4c on 25c blk, *rose* 12.50 12.00
*Nos. 46-51 (6)* 85.50 78.00

See note after No. 35.

Postage Due Stamps of French Colonies Overprinted in Red

**1892, Dec. 1** ***Imperf.***

| No. | Type | Description | Unused | Used |
|---|---|---|---|---|
| 52 | D1 | 10c black | 60.00 | 40.00 |
| 53 | D1 | 20c black | 40.00 | 35.00 |
| 54 | D1 | 30c black | 37.50 | 37.50 |
| 55 | D1 | 40c black | 32.50 | 32.50 |
| 56 | D1 | 60c black | 140.00 | 140.00 |

**Black Overprint**

| No. | Type | Description | Unused | Used |
|---|---|---|---|---|
| 57 | D1 | 1fr brown | 190.00 | 190.00 |
| 58 | D1 | 2fr brown | 325.00 | 325.00 |
| 59 | D1 | 5fr brown | 500.00 | 475.00 |
| | | *Nos. 52-59 (8)* | 1,325. | 1,275. |

See note after No. 35. "T P" stands for "Timbre Poste."

Navigation and Commerce — A16

**1892-1908** **Typo.** ***Perf. 14x13½***

| No. | Type | Description | Unused | Used |
|---|---|---|---|---|
| 60 | A16 | 1c blk, *lil bl* | 1.90 | 1.90 |
| 61 | A16 | 2c brown, *buff* | 1.90 | 1.90 |
| 62 | A16 | 4c claret, *lav* | 3.00 | 3.00 |
| 63 | A16 | 5c green, *grnsh* | 4.50 | 3.75 |
| 64 | A16 | 5c yel grn ('08) | 6.00 | 3.75 |
| 65 | A16 | 10c black, *lav* | 8.25 | 6.75 |
| 66 | A16 | 10c red ('00) | 6.00 | 3.75 |
| 67 | A16 | 15c bl, quadrille paper | 19.00 | 6.00 |
| 68 | A16 | 15c gray, *lt gray* ('00) | 100.00 | 65.00 |
| 69 | A16 | 20c red, *grn* | 30.00 | 24.00 |
| 70 | A16 | 25c black, *rose* | 13.50 | 3.75 |
| 71 | A16 | 25c blue ('00) | 25.00 | 15.00 |
| 72 | A16 | 30c brown, *bis* | 13.50 | 9.00 |
| 73 | A16 | 35c blk, *yel* ('06) | 8.00 | 7.25 |
| 74 | A16 | 40c red, *straw* | 9.75 | 9.00 |
| 75 | A16 | 50c car, *rose* | 52.50 | 42.50 |
| 76 | A16 | 50c brown, *az* ('00) | 40.00 | 37.50 |
| 77 | A16 | 75c violet, *org* | 35.00 | 30.00 |
| 78 | A16 | 1fr brnz grn, *straw* | 35.00 | 26.00 |
| | | *Nos. 60-78 (19)* | 412.80 | 299.80 |

Perf. 13½x14 stamps are counterfeits.

For surcharges and overprints see Nos. 110-120, Q1-Q2.

Fisherman A17

Fulmar Petrel A18

Fishing Schooner A19

**1909-30**

| No. | Type | Description | Unused | Used |
|---|---|---|---|---|
| 79 | A17 | 1c org red & ol | .40 | .50 |
| 80 | A17 | 2c olive & dp bl | .40 | .50 |
| 81 | A17 | 4c violet & ol | .55 | .75 |
| a. | | Perf 11 | 160.00 | |
| 82 | A17 | 5c bl grn & ol grn | 1.20 | .75 |
| 83 | A17 | 5c blue & blk ('22) | .55 | .75 |
| 84 | A17 | 10c car rose & red | 1.20 | 1.10 |
| 85 | A17 | 10c bl grn & ol grn ('22) | .75 | .75 |
| 86 | A17 | 10c bis & mag ('25) | .55 | .75 |
| 86A | A17 | 15c dl vio & rose ('17) | .80 | .75 |
| 87 | A17 | 20c bis brn & vio brn | 1.25 | 1.10 |
| 88 | A18 | 25c dp blue & blue | 4.50 | 3.00 |
| 89 | A18 | 25c ol brn & bl grn ('22) | 1.25 | 1.50 |
| 90 | A18 | 30c org & vio brn | 2.60 | 2.60 |
| 91 | A18 | 30c rose & dull red ('22) | 1.75 | 2.25 |
| 92 | A18 | 30c red brn & bl ('25) | 1.00 | 1.00 |
| 93 | A18 | 30c gray grn & bl grn ('26) | 1.50 | 2.25 |
| 94 | A18 | 35c ol grn & vio brn | .80 | .80 |
| 95 | A18 | 40c vio brn & ol grn | 4.00 | 3.00 |
| 96 | A18 | 45c vio & ol grn | 1.10 | 1.50 |
| 97 | A18 | 50c ol & ol grn | 2.25 | 2.25 |
| 98 | A18 | 50c bl & pale bl ('22) | 1.75 | 2.25 |
| 99 | A18 | 50c yel brn & mag ('25) | 1.60 | 2.25 |
| 100 | A18 | 60c dk bl & ver ('25) | 1.40 | 1.90 |
| 101 | A18 | 65c vio & org brn ('28) | 2.50 | 3.00 |
| 102 | A18 | 75c brn & ol | 1.90 | 2.25 |
| 103 | A18 | 90c brn red & org red ('30) | 35.00 | 37.50 |
| 104 | A19 | 1fr ol grn & dp bl | 5.00 | 3.75 |
| 105 | A19 | 1.10fr bl grn & org red ('28) | 5.50 | 7.50 |
| 106 | A19 | 1.50fr bl & dp bl ('30) | 15.00 | 15.00 |
| 107 | A19 | 2fr violet & brn | 6.00 | 4.50 |
| 108 | A19 | 3fr red vio ('30) | 18.00 | 22.50 |
| 109 | A19 | 5fr vio brn & ol grn | 13.50 | 12.50 |
| | | *Nos. 79-109 (32)* | 135.55 | 142.75 |

For overprints and surcharges see Nos. 121-131, 206C-206D, B1-B2, Q3-Q5.

**Stamps of 1892-1906 Surcharged in Carmine or Black**

**1912**

| No. | Type | Description | Unused | Used |
|---|---|---|---|---|
| 110 | A16 | 5c on 2c brn, *buff* | 3.75 | 4.00 |
| 111 | A16 | 5c on 4c claret, *lav* (C) | 1.10 | 1.50 |
| 112 | A16 | 5c on 15c blue (C) | 1.10 | 1.50 |
| 113 | A16 | 5c on 20c red, *grn* | .90 | 1.10 |
| 114 | A16 | 5c on 25c blk, *rose* (C) | .90 | 1.10 |
| 115 | A16 | 5c on 30c brn, *bis* (C) | 1.10 | 1.50 |
| 116 | A16 | 5c on 35c blk, *yel* (C) | 1.90 | 2.25 |
| 117 | A16 | 10c on 40c red, *straw* | 1.50 | 1.90 |
| 118 | A16 | 10c on 50c car, *rose* | 1.50 | 1.90 |
| 119 | A16 | 10c on 75c dp vio, *org* | 3.75 | 4.50 |
| 120 | A16 | 10c on 1fr brnz grn, *straw* | 5.25 | 6.25 |
| | | *Nos. 110-120 (11)* | 22.75 | 27.50 |

Two spacings between the surcharged numerals are found on Nos. 110 to 120. For detailed listings, see the *Scott Classic Specialized Catalogue of Stamps and Covers.*

**Stamps and Types of 1909-17 Surcharged in Black, Blue (Bl) or Red**

**1924-27**

| No. | Type | Description | Unused | Used |
|---|---|---|---|---|
| 121 | A17 | 25c on 15c dl vio & rose ('25) | .55 | .75 |
| a. | | Double surcharge | 190.00 | |
| b. | | Triple surcharge | 210.00 | |
| 122 | A19 | 25c on 2fr vio & lt brn (Bl) | .80 | 1.10 |
| 123 | A19 | 25c on 5fr brn & ol grn (Bl) | .90 | 1.10 |
| a. | | Triple surcharge | 210.00 | |
| 124 | A18 | 65c on 45c vio & ol grn ('25) | 2.25 | 3.00 |
| 125 | A18 | 85c on 75c brn & ol ('25) | 2.25 | 3.00 |
| 126 | A18 | 90c on 75c brn red & dp org ('27) | 3.00 | 3.75 |
| 127 | A19 | 1.25fr on 1fr dk bl & ultra (R) ('26) | 3.00 | 3.75 |
| 128 | A19 | 1.50fr on 1fr ultra & dk bl ('27) | 4.00 | 4.50 |
| 129 | A19 | 3fr on 5fr ol brn & red vio ('27) | 5.25 | 6.00 |
| 130 | A19 | 10fr on 5fr ver & ol grn ('27) | 25.00 | 29.00 |
| 131 | A19 | 20fr on 5fr vio & ver ('27) | 32.50 | 40.00 |
| | | *Nos. 121-131 (11)* | 79.50 | 95.95 |

Common Design Types pictured following the introduction.

**Colonial Exposition Issue**

Common Design Types

**1931, Apr. 13** **Engr.** ***Perf. 12½***

**Name of Country in Black**

| No. | Type | Description | Unused | Used |
|---|---|---|---|---|
| 132 | CD70 | 40c deep green | 6.00 | 6.00 |
| 133 | CD71 | 50c violet | 6.00 | 6.00 |
| 134 | CD72 | 90c red orange | 6.00 | 6.00 |
| 135 | CD73 | 1.50fr dull blue | 6.00 | 6.00 |
| | | *Nos. 132-135 (4)* | 24.00 | 24.00 |

Map and Fishermen — A20

Lighthouse and Fish — A21

Fishing Steamer and Sea Gulls A22

***Perf. 13½x14, 14x13½***

**1932-33** **Typo.**

| No. | Type | Description | Unused | Used |
|---|---|---|---|---|
| 136 | A20 | 1c red brn & ultra | .25 | .35 |
| 137 | A21 | 2c blk & dk grn | .40 | .50 |
| 138 | A22 | 4c mag & ol brn | .40 | .60 |
| 139 | A22 | 5c vio & dk brn | .80 | 1.10 |
| 140 | A21 | 10c red brn & blk | .80 | 1.10 |
| 141 | A21 | 15c dk blue & vio | 1.60 | 2.25 |
| 142 | A20 | 20c blk & red org | 1.90 | 2.25 |
| 143 | A20 | 25c lt vio & lt grn | 1.90 | 2.25 |
| 144 | A22 | 30c ol grn & bl grn | 1.90 | 2.25 |
| 145 | A22 | 40c dp bl & dk brn | 1.90 | 2.25 |
| 146 | A21 | 45c ver & dp grn | 1.90 | 2.25 |
| 147 | A21 | 50c dk brn & dk grn | 2.25 | 2.60 |
| 148 | A22 | 65c ol brn & org | 2.60 | 3.00 |
| 149 | A20 | 75c grn & red org | 2.25 | 2.60 |
| 150 | A20 | 90c dull red & red | 2.75 | 3.75 |
| 151 | A22 | 1fr org brn & org red | 2.60 | 3.00 |
| 152 | A20 | 1.25fr dp bl & lake ('33) | 2.60 | 3.00 |
| 153 | A20 | 1.50fr dp blue & blue | 2.60 | 3.00 |
| 154 | A22 | 1.75fr blk & dk brn ('33) | 3.25 | 3.75 |
| 155 | A22 | 2fr bl blk & Prus bl | 12.00 | 13.50 |
| 156 | A21 | 3fr dp grn & dk brn | 15.00 | 19.00 |
| 157 | A21 | 5fr brn red & dk brn | 32.50 | 37.50 |
| 158 | A22 | 10fr dk grn & vio | 75.00 | 82.50 |
| 159 | A20 | 20fr ver & dp grn | 85.00 | 92.50 |
| | | *Nos. 136-159 (24)* | 254.15 | 286.85 |

For overprints and surcharges see Nos. 160-164, 207-221.

**Nos. 147, 149, 153-154, 157 Overprinted in Black, Red or Blue**

p

q

**1934, Oct. 18**

| No. | Type | Description | Unused | Used |
|---|---|---|---|---|
| 160 | A21(p) | 50c (Bk) | 6.50 | 7.50 |
| 161 | A20(q) | 75c (Bk) | 9.50 | 10.50 |
| 162 | A20(q) | 1.50fr (Bk) | 9.50 | 10.50 |
| 163 | A22(p) | 1.75fr (R) | 10.00 | 12.50 |
| 164 | A21(p) | 5fr (Bl) | 45.00 | 47.50 |
| | | *Nos. 160-164 (5)* | 80.50 | 88.50 |

400th anniv. of the landing of Jacques Cartier.

**Paris International Exposition Issue**

Common Design Types

**1937** ***Perf. 13***

| No. | Type | Description | Unused | Used |
|---|---|---|---|---|
| 165 | CD74 | 20c deep violet | 2.40 | 2.75 |
| 166 | CD75 | 30c dark green | 2.40 | 2.75 |
| 167 | CD76 | 40c carmine rose | 2.40 | 2.75 |
| 168 | CD77 | 50c dk brn & bl | 2.40 | 2.75 |
| 169 | CD78 | 90c red | 2.50 | 2.75 |
| 170 | CD79 | 1.50fr ultra | 2.50 | 2.75 |
| | | *Nos. 165-170 (6)* | 14.60 | 16.50 |

**Colonial Arts Exhibition Issue**

Souvenir Sheet

Common Design Type

**1937** ***Imperf.***

| No. | Type | Description | Unused | Used |
|---|---|---|---|---|
| 171 | CD78 | 3fr dark ultra | 35.00 | 47.50 |

Dog Team A23

Port St. Pierre A24

Tortue Lighthouse A25

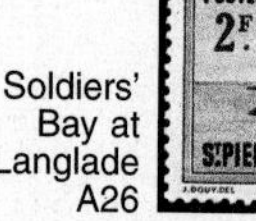

Soldiers' Bay at Langlade A26

**1938-40** **Photo.** ***Perf. 13½x13***

| No. | Type | Description | Unused | Used |
|---|---|---|---|---|
| 172 | A23 | 2c dk bl grn | .25 | .35 |
| a. | | Value omitted | 425.00 | |
| 173 | A23 | 3c brown violet | .25 | .35 |
| 174 | A23 | 4c dk red violet | .30 | .40 |
| 175 | A23 | 5c carmine lake | .30 | .40 |
| 176 | A23 | 10c bister brown | .30 | .40 |
| 177 | A23 | 15c red violet | .75 | .80 |
| 178 | A23 | 20c blue violet | 1.00 | 1.10 |
| 179 | A23 | 25c Prus blue | 3.00 | 3.00 |
| 180 | A24 | 30c dk red violet | .75 | .80 |
| 181 | A24 | 35c deep green | 1.00 | 1.10 |
| 182 | A24 | 40c slate blue ('40) | .25 | .35 |
| 183 | A24 | 45c dp grn ('40) | .50 | .60 |
| a. | | Value omitted | 110.00 | |
| 184 | A24 | 50c carmine rose | 1.00 | 1.10 |
| 185 | A24 | 55c Prus blue | 4.50 | 4.50 |
| 186 | A24 | 60c violet ('39) | .75 | .90 |
| 187 | A24 | 65c brown | 7.00 | 7.00 |
| 188 | A24 | 70c org yel ('39) | .75 | 1.00 |
| 189 | A25 | 80c violet | 1.75 | 1.90 |
| 190 | A25 | 90c ultra ('39) | 1.00 | 1.25 |
| 191 | A25 | 1fr brt pink | 15.00 | 15.00 |
| 192 | A25 | 1fr pale ol grn ('40) | 1.10 | 1.25 |
| 193 | A25 | 1.25fr brt rose ('39) | 2.50 | 2.75 |
| 194 | A25 | 1.40fr dk brn ('40) | 1.25 | 1.50 |
| 195 | A25 | 1.50fr blue green | 1.25 | 1.50 |
| 196 | A25 | 1.60fr rose vio ('40) | 1.25 | 1.50 |
| 197 | A25 | 1.75fr deep blue | 4.00 | 4.50 |
| 198 | A26 | 2fr rose violet | .90 | 1.10 |
| 199 | A26 | 2.25fr brt blue ('39) | 1.25 | 1.60 |
| 200 | A26 | 2.50fr org yel ('40) | 1.25 | 1.50 |

| No. | Type | Value | Color | Unused | Used |
|---|---|---|---|---|---|
| 201 | A26 | 3fr | gray brown | 1.25 | 1.50 |
| 202 | A26 | 5fr | henna brown | 1.25 | 1.50 |
| 203 | A26 | 10fr | dk bl, *bluish* | 2.00 | 2.25 |
| 204 | A26 | 20fr | slate green | 2.50 | 3.00 |
| | | | *Nos. 172-204 (33)* | 62.15 | 67.75 |

For overprints and surcharges see Nos. 222-255, 260-299, B9-B10.

### New York World's Fair Issue
Common Design Type

**1939, May 10 Engr. *Perf. 12½x12***

| No. | Type | Value | Color | Unused | Used |
|---|---|---|---|---|---|
| 205 | CD82 | 1.25fr | carmine lake | 2.40 | 3.00 |
| 206 | CD82 | 2.25fr | ultra | 2.40 | 3.00 |

For overprints and surcharges see Nos. 256-259.

Lighthouse on Cliff — A27

**1941 Engr. *Perf. 12½x12***

| No. | Type | Value | Color | Unused | Used |
|---|---|---|---|---|---|
| 206A | A27 | 1fr | dull lilac | 2.00 | |
| 206B | A27 | 2.50fr | blue | 2.00 | |

Nos. 206A-206B were issued by the Vichy government in France, but were not placed on sale in St. Pierre & Miquelon.

For surcharges, see B11-B12.

> Free French Administration
>
> The circumstances surrounding the overprinting and distribution of these stamps were most unusual. Practically all of the stamps issued in small quantities, with the exception of Nos. 260-299, were obtained by speculators within a few days after issue. At a later date, the remainders were taken over by the Free French Agency in Ottawa, Canada, by whom they were sold at a premium for the benefit of the Syndicat des Oeuvres Sociales. Large quantities appeared on the market in 1991, including many "errors." More may exist.
>
> Excellent counterfeits of these surcharges and overprints are known.

Nos. 86 & 92 Ovptd. in Black — a

**1942 Unwmk. *Perf. 14x13½***

| No. | Type | Value | Unused | Used |
|---|---|---|---|---|
| 206C | A17 | 10c | 1,600. | 1,700. |
| 206D | A18 | 30c | 1,600. | 1,700. |

The letters "F. N. F. L." are the initials of "Forces Navales Francaises Libres" or "Free French Naval Forces."

Ovptd. in Black on Nos. 137-139, 145-148, 151, 154-155, 157

| No. | Type | Value | Unused | Used |
|---|---|---|---|---|
| 207 | A21 | 2c | 275.00 | 300.00 |
| 208 | A22 | 4c | 67.50 | 80.00 |
| 208A | A22 | 5c | 1,000. | 1,200. |
| 209 | A22 | 40c | 17.50 | 21.00 |
| 210 | A21 | 45c | 210.00 | 250.00 |
| 211 | A21 | 50c | 17.50 | 21.00 |
| 212 | A22 | 65c | 60.00 | 67.50 |
| 213 | A22 | 1fr | 450.00 | 500.00 |
| 214 | A22 | 1.75fr | 17.50 | 21.00 |
| 215 | A22 | 2fr | 24.00 | 27.50 |
| 216 | A22 | 5fr | 425.00 | 475.00 |

Nos. 142, 149, 152-153 Overprinted in Black

***Perf. 13½x14***

| No. | Type | Value | Unused | Used |
|---|---|---|---|---|
| 216A | A20 | 20c | 500.00 | 575.00 |
| 217 | A20 | 75c | 45.00 | 55.00 |
| 218 | A20 | 1.25fr | 40.00 | 47.50 |
| 218A | A20 | 1.50fr | 600.00 | 675.00 |

### On Nos. 152, 149 Surcharged with New Value and Bars

| No. | Type | Value | Unused | Used |
|---|---|---|---|---|
| 219 | A20 | 10fr on 1.25fr | 65.00 | 72.50 |
| 220 | A20 | 20fr on 75c | 65.00 | 72.50 |

No. 154 Srchd. in Red

***Perf. 14x13½***

| No. | Type | Value | Unused | Used |
|---|---|---|---|---|
| 221 | A22 | 5fr on 1.75fr | 22.50 | 27.50 |

Stamps of 1938-40 Ovptd.

***Perf. 13½x13***

| No. | Type | Value | Color | Unused | Used |
|---|---|---|---|---|---|
| 222 | A23 | 2c | dk bl grn | 600.00 | 650.00 |
| 223 | A23 | 3c | brn vio | 225.00 | 250.00 |
| 224 | A23 | 4c | dk red vio | 110.00 | 140.00 |
| 225 | A23 | 5c | car lake | 1,000. | 1,200. |
| 226 | A23 | 10c | bis brn | 17.00 | 18.00 |
| 227 | A23 | 15c | red vio | 1,900. | 2,100. |
| 228 | A23 | 20c | blue vio | 210.00 | 210.00 |
| 229 | A23 | 25c | Prus blue | 17.00 | 18.00 |
| 230 | A24 | 35c | dp grn | 1,000. | 1,100. |
| 231 | A24 | 40c | slate blue | 21.00 | 25.00 |
| 232 | A24 | 45c | dp grn | 21.00 | 25.00 |
| 233 | A24 | 55c | Prus blue | 11,000. | 12,500. |
| 234 | A24 | 60c | violet | 675.00 | 775.00 |
| 235 | A24 | 65c | brown | 25.00 | 30.00 |
| 236 | A24 | 70c | org yel | 47.50 | 55.00 |
| 237 | A25 | 80c | violet | 500.00 | 575.00 |
| 238 | A25 | 90c | ultra | 21.00 | 25.00 |
| 239 | A25 | 1fr | pale ol grn | 26.00 | 30.00 |
| 240 | A25 | 1.25fr | brt rose | 22.50 | 26.00 |
| 241 | A25 | 1.40fr | dk brn | 21.00 | 25.00 |
| 242 | A25 | 1.50fr | bl grn | 950.00 | 1,100. |
| 243 | A25 | 1.60fr | rose vio | 21.00 | 25.00 |
| 244 | A26 | 2fr | rose vio | 87.50 | 110.00 |
| 245 | A26 | 2.25fr | brt blue | 21.00 | 25.00 |
| 246 | A26 | 2.50fr | org yel | 26.00 | 30.00 |
| 247 | A26 | 3fr | gray brn | 12,500. | 13,000. |
| 248 | A26 | 5fr | hen brn | 2,500. | 2,750. |
| 248A | A26 | 20fr | sl grn | 1,200. | 1,300. |

Nos. 176, 190 Srchd. in Black

| No. | Type | Value | Unused | Used |
|---|---|---|---|---|
| 249 | A23 | 20c on 10c | 14.50 | 17.00 |
| 250 | A23 | 30c on 10c | 12.00 | 13.50 |
| 251 | A25 | 60c on 90c | 13.50 | 16.00 |
| 252 | A25 | 1.50fr on 90c | 17.50 | 20.00 |
| 253 | A23 | 2.50fr on 10c | 22.50 | 25.00 |
| 254 | A23 | 10fr on 10c | 67.50 | 80.00 |
| 255 | A25 | 20fr on 90c | 75.00 | 87.50 |
| | | *Nos. 249-255 (7)* | 222.50 | 259.00 |

### New York World's Fair Issue Overprinted type "a" in Black

***Perf. 12½x12***

| No. | Type | Value | Color | Unused | Used |
|---|---|---|---|---|---|
| 256 | CD82 | 1.25fr | car lake | 22.50 | 25.00 |
| 257 | CD82 | 2.25fr | ultra | 21.00 | 24.00 |

Nos. 205-206 Surcharged

| No. | Type | Value | Unused | Used |
|---|---|---|---|---|
| 258 | CD82 | 2.50fr on 1.25fr | 22.50 | 25.00 |
| 259 | CD82 | 3fr on 2.25fr | 22.50 | 25.00 |

Stamps of 1938-40 Ovptd. in Carmine

**1941 *Perf. 13½x13***

| No. | Type | Value | Color | Unused | Used |
|---|---|---|---|---|---|
| 260 | A23 | 10c | bister brn | 47.50 | 55.00 |
| 261 | A23 | 20c | blue violet | 47.50 | 55.00 |
| 262 | A23 | 25c | Prus blue | 47.50 | 55.00 |
| 263 | A24 | 40c | slate blue | 47.50 | 55.00 |
| 264 | A24 | 45c | dp grn | 52.50 | 60.00 |
| 265 | A24 | 65c | brown | 52.50 | 60.00 |
| 266 | A24 | 70c | org yel | 52.50 | 60.00 |
| 267 | A25 | 80c | violet | 52.50 | 60.00 |
| 268 | A25 | 90c | ultra | 52.50 | 60.00 |
| 269 | A25 | 1fr | pale ol grn | 52.50 | 60.00 |
| 270 | A25 | 1.25fr | brt rose | 52.50 | 60.00 |
| 271 | A25 | 1.40fr | dk brown | 52.50 | 60.00 |
| 272 | A25 | 1.60fr | rose violet | 52.50 | 60.00 |
| 273 | A25 | 1.75fr | brt blue | 52.50 | 60.00 |
| 274 | A26 | 2fr | rose violet | 52.50 | 60.00 |
| 275 | A26 | 2.25fr | brt blue | 52.50 | 60.00 |
| 276 | A26 | 2.50fr | org yel | 52.50 | 60.00 |
| 277 | A26 | 3fr | gray brn | 52.50 | 60.00 |

### Same Surcharged in Carmine with New Values

| No. | Type | Value | Unused | Used |
|---|---|---|---|---|
| 278 | A23 | 10fr on 10c bis brn | 125.00 | 140.00 |
| 279 | A25 | 20fr on 90c ultra | 125.00 | 140.00 |
| | | *Nos. 260-279 (20)* | 1,175. | 1,340. |

### Stamps of 1938-40 Overprinted in Black

| No. | Type | Value | Color | Unused | Used |
|---|---|---|---|---|---|
| 280 | A23 | 10c | bister brn | 72.50 | 87.50 |
| 281 | A23 | 20c | blue violet | 72.50 | 87.50 |
| 282 | A23 | 25c | Prus blue | 72.50 | 87.50 |
| 283 | A24 | 40c | slate blue | 72.50 | 87.50 |
| 284 | A24 | 45c | dp grn | 72.50 | 87.50 |
| 285 | A24 | 65c | brown | 72.50 | 87.50 |
| 286 | A24 | 70c | orange yel | 72.50 | 87.50 |
| 287 | A25 | 80c | violet | 72.50 | 87.50 |
| 288 | A25 | 90c | ultra | 72.50 | 87.50 |
| 289 | A25 | 1fr | pale ol grn | 72.50 | 87.50 |
| 290 | A25 | 1.25fr | brt rose | 72.50 | 87.50 |
| 291 | A25 | 1.40fr | dk brown | 72.50 | 87.50 |
| 292 | A25 | 1.60fr | rose violet | 72.50 | 87.50 |
| 293 | A25 | 1.75fr | brt blue | 950.00 | 1,100. |
| 294 | A26 | 2fr | rose vio | 72.50 | 87.50 |
| 295 | A26 | 2.25fr | brt blue | 72.50 | 87.50 |
| 296 | A26 | 2.50fr | orange yel | 72.50 | 87.50 |
| 297 | A26 | 3fr | gray brn | 72.50 | 87.50 |

### Same Surcharged in Black with New Values

| No. | Type | Value | Unused | Used |
|---|---|---|---|---|
| 298 | A23 | 10fr on 10c bis brn | 175.00 | 200.00 |
| 299 | A25 | 20fr on 90c ultra | 190.00 | 225.00 |
| | | *Nos. 280-299 (20)* | 2,548. | 3,013. |

Christmas Day plebiscite ordered by Vice Admiral Emile Henri Muselier, commander of the Free French naval forces (Nos. 260-299).

### Types of 1938-40 Without RF

**1942 Photo. *Perf. 13½***

| No. | Type | Value | Color | Unused |
|---|---|---|---|---|
| 299A | A23 | 4c | dk red vio | .55 |
| 299B | A23 | 15c | red violet | 1.40 |
| 299C | A23 | 20c | blue violet | 1.40 |
| 299D | A26 | 10fr | dk blue | 2.10 |
| 299E | A26 | 20fr | olive | 2.50 |
| | | | *Nos. 299A-299E (5)* | 7.95 |

Nos. 299A-299E were issued by the Vichy government in France, but were not placed on sale in St. Pierre & Miquelon.

> **Catalogue values for unused stamps in this section, from this point to the end of the section, are for Never Hinged items.**

St. Malo Fishing Schooner A28

**1942 Photo. *Perf. 14x14½***

| No. | Type | Value | Color | Unused | Used |
|---|---|---|---|---|---|
| 300 | A28 | 5c | dark blue | .55 | .30 |
| 301 | A28 | 10c | dull pink | .50 | .30 |
| 302 | A28 | 25c | brt green | .50 | .30 |
| 303 | A28 | 30c | slate black | .50 | .30 |
| 304 | A28 | 40c | brt grnsh blue | .50 | .30 |
| 305 | A28 | 60c | brown red | .55 | .40 |
| 306 | A28 | 1fr | dark violet | .80 | .65 |
| 307 | A28 | 1.50fr | brt red | 1.75 | 1.40 |
| 308 | A28 | 2fr | brown | 1.10 | .80 |
| 309 | A28 | 2.50fr | brt ultra | 1.75 | 1.40 |
| 310 | A28 | 4fr | dk orange | 1.40 | 1.00 |
| 311 | A28 | 5fr | dp plum | 1.50 | 1.10 |
| 312 | A28 | 10fr | lt ultra | 2.10 | 1.75 |
| 313 | A28 | 20fr | dark green | 2.40 | 1.90 |
| | | | *Nos. 300-313 (14)* | 15.90 | 11.90 |

### Nos. 300, 302, 309 Surcharged in Carmine or Black

**1945**

| No. | Type | Value | Unused | Used |
|---|---|---|---|---|
| 314 | A28 | 50c on 5c (C) | .50 | .30 |
| 315 | A28 | 70c on 5c (C) | .50 | .30 |
| 316 | A28 | 80c on 5c (C) | .55 | .40 |
| 317 | A28 | 1.20fr on 5c (C) | .70 | .55 |
| 318 | A28 | 2.40fr on 25c | .70 | .55 |
| 319 | A28 | 3fr on 25c | .95 | .80 |
| 320 | A28 | 4.50fr on 25c | 1.60 | 1.25 |
| 321 | A28 | 15fr on 2.50fr (C) | 2.00 | 1.75 |
| | | *Nos. 314-321 (8)* | 7.50 | 5.90 |

### Eboue Issue
Common Design Type

**1945 Engr. *Perf. 13***

| No. | Type | Value | Color | Unused | Used |
|---|---|---|---|---|---|
| 322 | CD91 | 2fr | black | 1.40 | .95 |
| 323 | CD91 | 25fr | Prussian green | 3.00 | 2.50 |

Nos. 322 and 323 exist imperforate. Value, set $47.50.

Soldiers' Bay — A29

Fishing Industry Symbols A30

Fishermen A31

Weighing the Catch A32

Fishing Boat and Dinghy A33

Storm-swept Coast — A34

**1947, Oct. 6** **Engr.** ***Perf. 12½***
**324** A29 10c chocolate .55 .40
**325** A29 30c violet .55 .40
**326** A29 40c rose lilac .55 .40
**327** A29 50c intense blue .55 .40
**328** A30 60c carmine 1.25 .95
**329** A30 80c brt ultra 1.25 .95
**330** A30 1fr dk green 1.25 .95
**331** A31 1.20fr blue grn 1.25 .95
**332** A31 1.50fr black 1.25 .95
**333** A31 2fr red brown 1.25 .95
**334** A32 3fr rose violet 3.50 3.00
**335** A32 3.60fr dp brown org 2.50 2.10
**336** A32 4fr sepia 3.25 2.25
**337** A33 5fr orange 3.50 2.50
**338** A33 6fr blue 3.50 2.50
**339** A33 10fr Prus green 4.50 3.25
**340** A34 15fr dk slate grn 6.00 4.50
**341** A34 20fr vermilion 8.50 6.50
**342** A34 25fr dark blue 10.50 7.50
*Nos. 324-342 (19)* 55.45 41.40

Imperforates
Most stamps of St. Pierre and Miquelon from 1947 onward exist imperforate in issued and trial colors, and also in small presentation sheets in issued colors.

Silver Fox — A35

**1952, Oct. 10** **Unwmk.** ***Perf. 13***
**343** A35 8fr brown 5.00 1.50
**344** A35 17fr blue 6.75 2.10

### Military Medal Issue
Common Design Type

**1952, Dec. 15** **Engr. & Typo.**
**345** CD101 8fr multicolored 16.00 15.00

Fish Freezing Plant A36

**1955-56** **Engr.**
**346** A36 30c ultra & dk blue .75 .75
**347** A36 50c gray, blk & sepia .75 .75
**348** A36 3fr purple 1.40 1.40
**349** A36 40fr Prussian blue 3.50 2.75
*Nos. 346-349 (4)* 6.40 5.65

Issued: 40fr, July 4; others, Oct. 22, 1956.

### FIDES Issue

Fish Freezer "Le Galantry" A37

***Perf. 13x12½***
**1956, Mar. 15** **Unwmk.**
**350** A37 15fr blk brn & chestnut 6.00 4.00

See note in Common Design section after CD103.

Codfish A38

4fr, 10fr, Lighthouse and fishing fleet.

**1957, Nov. 4** ***Perf. 13***
**351** A38 40c dk brn & grnsh bl .55 .55
**352** A38 1fr brown & green .65 .65
**353** A38 2fr indigo & dull blue 1.00 1.00
**354** A38 4fr maroon, car & pur 2.25 2.25
**355** A38 10fr grnsh bl, dk bl & brn 2.60 2.60
*Nos. 351-355 (5)* 7.05 7.05

### Human Rights Issue
Common Design Type

**1958, Dec. 10** **Engr.** ***Perf. 13***
**356** CD105 20fr red brn & dk blue 3.50 2.50

### Flower Issue
Common Design Type

**1959, Jan. 28** **Photo.** ***Perf. 12½x12***
**357** CD104 5fr Spruce 4.50 2.25

Ice Hockey A39

**1959, Oct. 7** **Engr.** ***Perf. 13***
**358** A39 20fr multicolored 3.75 1.75

Mink A40

**1959, Oct. 7** **Engr.** ***Perf. 13***
**359** A40 25fr ind, yel grn & brn 5.25 2.50

Cypripedium Acaule — A41

Flower: 50fr, Calopogon pulchellus.

**1962, Apr. 24** **Unwmk.** ***Perf. 13***
**360** A41 25fr grn, org & car rose 5.75 2.75
**361** A41 50fr green & car lake 8.75 3.50
*Nos. 360-361,C24 (3)* 27.50 11.25

Eider Ducks — A42

Birds: 1fr, Rock ptarmigan. 2fr, Ringed plovers. 6fr, Blue-winged teal.

**1963, Mar. 4** ***Perf. 13***
**362** A42 50c blk, ultra & ocher 1.00 .60
**363** A42 1fr red brn, ultra & rose 1.50 .90
**364** A42 2fr blk, dk bl & bis 1.90 .90
**365** A42 6fr multicolored 3.75 2.00
*Nos. 362-365 (4)* 8.15 4.40

Albert Calmette A43

**1963, Aug. 5** **Engr.**
**366** A43 30fr dk brn & dk blue 10.00 6.75

Albert Calmette, bacteriologist, birth cent.

### Red Cross Centenary Issue
Common Design Type

**1963, Sept. 2** **Unwmk.** ***Perf. 13***
**367** CD113 25fr ultra, gray & car 12.00 5.50

### Human Rights Issue
Common Design Type

**1963, Dec. 10** **Unwmk.** ***Perf. 13***
**368** CD117 20fr org, bl & dk brn 7.00 3.50

### Philatec Issue
Common Design Type

**1964, Apr. 4** **Engr.**
**369** CD118 60fr choc, grn & dk bl 11.00 8.00

Rabbits A44

**1964, Sept. 28** ***Perf. 13***
**370** A44 3fr shown 2.00 1.40
**371** A44 4fr Fox 2.00 1.40
**372** A44 5fr Roe deer 5.00 2.75
**373** A44 34fr Charolais bull 15.00 8.00
*Nos. 370-373 (4)* 24.00 13.55

Airport and Map of St. Pierre and Miquelon A45

40fr, Television tube and tower, map. 48fr, Map of new harbor of St. Pierre.

**1967** **Engr.** ***Perf. 13***
**374** A45 30fr ind, bl & dk red 8.00 5.00
**375** A45 40fr sl grn, ol & dk red 8.00 5.00
**376** A45 48fr dk red, brn & sl bl 12.50 5.75
*Nos. 374-376 (3)* 28.50 15.75

Issued: 30fr, 10/23; 40fr, 11/20; 48fr, 9/25.

### WHO Anniversary Issue
Common Design Type

**1968, May 4** **Engr.** ***Perf. 13***
**377** CD126 10fr multicolored 12.00 9.00

René de Chateaubriand and Map of Islands — A46

Designs: 4fr, J. D. Cassini and map. 15fr, Prince de Joinville, Francois F. d'Orleans (1818-1900), ships and map. 25fr, Admiral Gauchet, World War I warship and map.

**1968, May 20** **Photo.** ***Perf. 12½x13***
**378** A46 4fr multicolored 5.75 3.75
**379** A46 6fr multicolored 6.50 4.50
**380** A46 15fr multicolored 10.00 5.75
**381** A46 25fr multicolored 14.00 6.50
*Nos. 378-381 (4)* 36.25 20.50

### Human Rights Year Issue
Common Design Type

**1968, Aug. 10** **Engr.** ***Perf. 13***
**382** CD127 20fr bl, ver & org yel 8.00 5.50

Belle Rivière, Langlade A47

Design: 15fr, Debon Brook, Langlade.

**1969, Apr. 30** **Engr.** ***Perf. 13***
**Size: 36x22mm**
**383** A47 5fr bl, slate grn & brn 4.25 2.75
**384** A47 15fr brn, bl & dl grn 5.75 3.50
*Nos. 383-384,C41-C42 (4)* 50.00 27.25

Treasury A48

Designs: 25fr, Scientific and Technical Institute of Maritime Fishing. 30fr, Monument to seamen lost at sea. 60fr, St. Christopher College.

**1969, May 30** **Engr.** ***Perf. 13***
**385** A48 10fr brt bl, cl & blk 5.50 3.25
**386** A48 25fr dk bl, brt bl & brn red 9.25 4.75
**387** A48 30fr blue, grn & gray 10.00 6.25
**388** A48 60fr brt bl, brn red & blk 17.00 10.00
*Nos. 385-388 (4)* 41.75 24.25

Ringed Seals A49

Designs: 3fr, Sperm whales. 4fr, Pilot whales. 6fr, Common dolphins.

**1969, Oct. 6** **Engr.** ***Perf. 13***
**389** A49 1fr lil, vio brn & red brn 2.75 1.75
**390** A49 3fr bl grn, ind & red 2.75 1.75
**391** A49 4fr ol, gray grn & mar 5.25 3.50
**392** A49 6fr brt grn, pur & red 7.50 3.50
*Nos. 389-392 (4)* 18.25 10.50

L'Estoile and Granville, France A50

40fr, "La Jolie" & St. Jean de Luz, France, 1750. 48fr, "Le Juste" & La Rochelle, France, 1860.

**1969, Oct. 13** **Engr.** ***Perf. 13***
**393** A50 34fr grn, mar & slate grn 17.50 10.00
**394** A50 40fr brn red, lem & sl grn 27.50 11.00
**395** A50 48fr multicolored 35.00 12.50
*Nos. 393-395 (3)* 80.00 33.50

Historic ships connecting St. Pierre and Miquelon with France.

### ILO Issue
Common Design Type

**1969, Nov. 24**
**396** CD131 20fr org, gray & ocher 10.00 5.50

### UPU Headquarters Issue
Common Design Type

**1970, May 20** **Engr.** ***Perf. 13***
**397** CD133 25fr dk car, brt bl & brn 14.00 7.75
**398** CD133 34fr maroon, brn & gray 20.00 8.50

Rowers and Globe A51

**1970, Oct. 13** **Photo.** ***Perf. 12½x12***
**399** A51 20fr lt grnsh bl & brn 18.00 7.50

World Rowing Championships, St. Catherine.

Blackberries A52

**1970, Oct. 20 Engr. *Perf. 13***

| No. | Type | Description | Unused | Used |
|---|---|---|---|---|
| **400** | A52 | 3fr shown | 1.75 | 1.40 |
| **401** | A52 | 4fr Strawberries | 1.90 | 1.75 |
| **402** | A52 | 5fr Raspberries | 2.75 | 1.75 |
| **403** | A52 | 6fr Blueberries | 5.25 | 2.25 |
| | | *Nos. 400-403 (4)* | 11.65 | 7.15 |

Ewe and Lamb A53

30fr, Animal quarantine station. 34fr, Charolais bull. 48fr, Refrigeration ship slaughterhouse.

**1970 Engr. *Perf. 13***

| No. | Type | Description | Unused | Used |
|---|---|---|---|---|
| **404** | A53 | 15fr plum, dl bl grn & olive | 11.00 | 4.50 |
| **405** | A53 | 30fr sl, bis brn & ap grn | 12.50 | 6.75 |
| **406** | A53 | 34fr red lil, org brn & emer | 20.00 | 8.75 |
| **407** | A53 | 48fr multicolored | 18.00 | 8.00 |
| | | *Nos. 404-407 (4)* | 61.50 | 28.00 |

Issue dates: 48fr, Nov. 10; others, Dec. 8.

Saint François d'Assise 1900 A54

Ships: 35fr, Sainte Jehanne, 1920. 40fr, L'Aventure, 1950. 80fr, Commandant Bourdais, 1970.

**1971, Aug. 25**

| No. | Type | Description | Unused | Used |
|---|---|---|---|---|
| **408** | A54 | 30fr Prus bl & hn brn | 32.50 | 14.50 |
| **409** | A54 | 35fr Prus bl, lt grn & ol brn | 47.50 | 14.50 |
| **410** | A54 | 40fr sl grn, bl & dk brn | 52.50 | 11.00 |
| **411** | A54 | 80fr dp grn, bl & blk | 67.50 | 20.00 |
| | | *Nos. 408-411 (4)* | 200.00 | 60.00 |

Deep-sea fishing fleet.

"Aconit" and Map of Islands — A55

**1971, Sept. 27 Engr. *Perf. 13***

| No. | Type | Description | Unused | Used |
|---|---|---|---|---|
| **412** | A55 | 22fr shown | 30.00 | 13.00 |
| **413** | A55 | 25fr Alysse | 37.50 | 13.50 |
| **414** | A55 | 50fr Mimosa | 50.00 | 20.00 |
| | | *Nos. 412-414 (3)* | 117.50 | 46.50 |

Rallying of the Free French forces, 30th anniv.

Ship's Bell — A56

St. Pierre Museum: 45fr, Old chart and sextants, horiz.

**1971, Oct. 25 Photo. *Perf. 12½x13***

| No. | Type | Description | Unused | Used |
|---|---|---|---|---|
| **415** | A56 | 20fr gray & multi | 25.00 | 8.50 |
| **416** | A56 | 45fr red brn & multi | 40.00 | 15.00 |

**De Gaulle Issue**

Common Design Type

Designs: 35fr, Gen. de Gaulle, 1940. Pres. de Gaulle, 1970.

**1971, Nov. 9 Engr. *Perf. 13***

| No. | Type | Description | Unused | Used |
|---|---|---|---|---|
| **417** | CD134 | 35fr ver & blk | 24.00 | 12.50 |
| **418** | CD134 | 45fr ver & blk | 32.50 | 18.50 |

Haddock A57

Fish: 3fr, Hippoglossoides platessoides. 5fr, Sebastes mentella. 10fr, Codfish.

**1972, Mar. 7**

| No. | Type | Description | Unused | Used |
|---|---|---|---|---|
| **419** | A57 | 2fr vio bl, ind & pink | 5.00 | 2.50 |
| **420** | A57 | 3fr grn & gray olive | 6.00 | 3.75 |
| **421** | A57 | 5fr Prus bl & brick red | 7.00 | 3.50 |
| **422** | A57 | 10fr grn & slate grn | 13.00 | 6.00 |
| | | *Nos. 419-422 (4)* | 31.00 | 15.75 |

Oldsquaws — A58

Birds: 10c, 70c, Puffins. 20c, 90c, Snow owl. 40c, like 6c. Identification of birds on oldsquaw and puffin stamps transposed.

**1973, Jan. 1 Engr. *Perf. 13***

| No. | Type | Description | Unused | Used |
|---|---|---|---|---|
| **423** | A58 | 6c Prus bl, pur & brn | 2.00 | 1.25 |
| **424** | A58 | 10c Prus bl, blk & org | 2.75 | 1.90 |
| **425** | A58 | 20c ultra, bis & dk vio | 3.25 | 2.50 |
| **426** | A58 | 40c pur, sl grn & brn | 4.50 | 3.00 |
| **427** | A58 | 70c brt grn, blk & org | 6.50 | 4.00 |
| **428** | A58 | 90c Prus bl, bis & pur | 12.00 | 6.00 |
| | | *Nos. 423-428 (6)* | 31.00 | 18.65 |

Indoor Swimming Pool — A59

Design: 1fr, Cultural Center of St. Pierre.

**1973, Sept. 25 Engr. *Perf. 13***

| No. | Type | Description | Unused | Used |
|---|---|---|---|---|
| **429** | A59 | 60c brn, brt bl & dk car | 5.75 | 3.50 |
| **430** | A59 | 1fr bl grn, ocher & choc | 7.75 | 5.00 |

Opening of Cultural Center of St. Pierre.

Map of Islands, Weather Balloon and Ship, WMO Emblem A60

**1974, Mar. 23 Engr. *Perf. 13***

| No. | Type | Description | Unused | Used |
|---|---|---|---|---|
| **431** | A60 | 1.60fr multicolored | 13.50 | 6.50 |

World Meteorological Day.

Gannet Holding Letter — A61

**1974, Oct. 9 Engr. *Perf. 13***

| No. | Type | Description | Unused | Used |
|---|---|---|---|---|
| **432** | A61 | 70c blue & multi | 6.00 | 2.75 |
| **433** | A61 | 90c red & multi | 7.50 | 4.50 |

Centenary of Universal Postal Union.

Clasped Hands over Red Cross — A62

**1974, Oct. 15 Photo. *Perf. 12½x13***

| No. | Type | Description | Unused | Used |
|---|---|---|---|---|
| **434** | A62 | 1.50fr multicolored | 12.00 | 5.50 |

Honoring blood donors.

Hands Putting Money into Fish-shaped Bank — A63

**1974, Nov. 15 Engr. *Perf. 13***

| No. | Type | Description | Unused | Used |
|---|---|---|---|---|
| **435** | A63 | 50c ocher & vio bl | 6.50 | 4.00 |

St. Pierre Savings Bank centenary.

Church of St. Pierre and Seagulls A64

Designs: 10c, Church of Miquelon and fish. 20c, Church of Our Lady of the Sailors, and fishermen.

**1974, Dec. 9 Engr. *Perf. 13***

| No. | Type | Description | Unused | Used |
|---|---|---|---|---|
| **436** | A64 | 6c multicolored | 2.50 | 1.75 |
| **437** | A64 | 10c multicolored | 5.00 | 2.00 |
| **438** | A64 | 20c multicolored | 7.50 | 2.75 |
| | | *Nos. 436-438 (3)* | 15.00 | 6.50 |

Danaus Plexippus A65

Design: 1fr, Vanessa atalanta, vert.

**1975, July 17 Litho. *Perf. 12½***

| No. | Type | Description | Unused | Used |
|---|---|---|---|---|
| **439** | A65 | 1fr blue & multi | 9.75 | 5.00 |
| **440** | A65 | 1.20fr green & multi | 14.50 | 5.50 |

Pottery — A66

Mother and Child, Wood Carving — A67

**1975, Oct. 2 Engr. *Perf. 13***

| No. | Type | Description | Unused | Used |
|---|---|---|---|---|
| **441** | A66 | 50c ol, brn & choc | 4.50 | 3.50 |
| **442** | A67 | 60c blue & dull yel | 6.50 | 3.50 |

Local handicrafts.

Pointe Plate Lighthouse and Murres A68

10c, Galantry lighthouse and Atlantic puffins. 20c, Cap Blanc lighthouse, whale and squid.

**1975, Oct. 21**

| No. | Type | Description | Unused | Used |
|---|---|---|---|---|
| **443** | A68 | 6c vio bl, blk & lt grn | 3.25 | 2.25 |
| **444** | A68 | 10c lil rose, blk & dk ol | 5.50 | 3.50 |
| **445** | A68 | 20c blue, indigo & brn | 8.25 | 6.75 |
| | | *Nos. 443-445 (3)* | 17.00 | 12.50 |

Georges Pompidou (1911-74), Pres. of France — A68a

**1976, Feb. 17 Engr. *Perf. 13***

| No. | Type | Description | Unused | Used |
|---|---|---|---|---|
| **446** | A68a | 1.10fr brown & slate | 7.00 | 4.00 |

Georges Pompidou (1911-1974), President of France.

Washington and Lafayette, American Flag — A69

**1976, July 12 Photo. *Perf. 13***

| No. | Type | Description | Unused | Used |
|---|---|---|---|---|
| **447** | A69 | 1fr multicolored | 6.00 | 3.50 |

American Bicentennial.

Woman Swimmer and Maple Leaf — A70

70c, Basketball and maple leaf, vert.

**1976, Aug. 10 Engr. *Perf. 13***

| No. | Type | Description | Unused | Used |
|---|---|---|---|---|
| **448** | A70 | 70c multicolored | 6.00 | 4.00 |
| **449** | A70 | 2.50fr multicolored | 12.50 | 5.00 |

21st Olympic Games, Montreal, Canada, July 17-Aug. 1.

Vigie Dam — A71

**1976, Sept. 7 Engr. *Perf. 13***
**450** A71 2.20fr multicolored 8.00 4.50

Croix de Lorraine — A72

Fishing Vessels: 1.40fr, Goelette.

**1976, Oct. 5 Photo. *Perf. 13***
**451** A72 1.20fr multicolored 9.00 3.50
**452** A72 1.40fr multicolored 10.00 5.50

**France Nos. 1783-1784, 1786-1789, 1794, 1882, 1799, 1885, 1802, 1889, 1803-1804 and 1891 Ovptd. "SAINT PIERRE / ET / MIQUELON"**

**1986, Feb. 4 Engr. *Perf. 13***
**453** A915 5c dark green .45 .35
**454** A915 10c dull red .25 .25
**455** A915 20c brt green .25 .25
**456** A915 30c orange .25 .25
**457** A915 40c brown .25 .25
**458** A915 50c lilac .25 .25
**459** A915 1fr olive green .45 .35
**460** A915 1.80fr emerald .85 .70
**461** A915 2fr brt yellow grn .85 .75
**462** A915 2.20fr red .95 .80
**463** A915 3fr chocolate brn 1.25 1.25
**464** A915 3.20fr sapphire 1.50 1.25
**465** A915 4fr brt carmine 1.60 1.40
**466** A915 5fr gray blue 2.00 1.75
**467** A915 10fr purple 4.00 3.00
*Nos. 453-467 (15)* 15.15 12.85

Discovery of St. Pierre & Miquelon by Jacques Cartier, 450th Anniv. — A73

**1986, June 11 Engr. *Perf. 13***
**476** A73 2.20fr sep, sage grn & redsh brn 1.50 .90

Statue of Liberty, Cent. — A74

**1986, July 4**
**477** A74 2.50fr Statue, St. Pierre Harbor 2.00 1.25

Fishery Resources — A75

**1986-89 Engr. *Perf. 13***
**478** A75 1fr bright red .75 .40
**479** A75 1.10fr brt orange .65 .45
**480** A75 1.30fr dark red .75 .50
**481** A75 1.40fr violet 1.00 .55
**482** A75 1.40fr dark red .75 .50
**483** A75 1.50fr brt ultra .90 .55
**484** A75 1.60fr emerald grn .90 .60
**485** A75 1.70fr green .95 .55
*Nos. 478-485 (8)* 6.65 4.10

Issued: 1fr, #481, 10/22; 1.10fr, 1.50fr, 10/14/87; 1.30fr, 1.60fr, 8/7/88; #482, 1.70fr, 7/14/89.

Holy Family, Stained Glass by J. Balmet — A76

**1986, Dec. 10 Litho. *Perf. 13***
**486** A76 2.20fr multicolored 1.75 1.00

Christmas.

Hygrophorus Pratensis — A77

No. 488, Russula paludosa britz. No. 489, Tricholoma virgatum. No. 490, Hydnum repandum.

**1987-90 Engr. *Perf. 12½***
**487** A77 2.50fr multicolored 1.75 1.00
**488** A77 2.50fr multicolored 1.40 .90
**489** A77 2.50fr multicolored 1.00 .90
**490** A77 2.50fr multicolored 1.00 .90
*Nos. 487-490 (4)* 5.15 3.70

Issued: #487, Feb. 14; #488, Jan. 29, 1988; #489, Jan. 28, 1989; #490, Jan. 17, 1990.

Dr. François Dunan (1884-1961), Clinic — A78

**1987, Apr. 29 Engr. *Perf. 13***
**491** A78 2.20fr brt bl, blk & dk red brn 1.25 .90

Transat Yacht Race, Lorient to St. Pierre to Lorient A79

**1987, May 16**
**492** A79 5fr dp ultra, dk rose brn & brt bl 2.75 1.40

Visit of Pres. Mitterand A80

**1987, May 29 Litho. *Perf. 12½x13***
**493** A80 2.20fr dull ultra, gold & scar 1.90 1.00

Marine Slip, Cent. A81

**1987, June 20 Litho. *Perf. 13***
**494** A81 2.50fr pale sal & dk red brn 1.75 1.10

Stern Trawler La Normande — A82

**1987-91 Photo.**
**495** A82 3fr shown 3.00 1.75
**496** A82 3fr Le Marmouset 1.75 1.10
**497** A82 3fr Tugboat Le Malabar 1.50 .80
**498** A82 3fr St. Denis, St. Pierre 1.50 .90
**499** A82 3fr Cryos 1.50 .90
*Nos. 495-499 (5)* 9.25 5.45

Issued: #495, 10/14; #496, 9/28/88; #497, 10/11/89; #498, 10/24/90; #499, 11/6/91.

St. Christopher and the Christ Child, Stained Glass Window and Scout Emblem — A83

**1987, Dec. 9 Litho. *Perf. 13***
**503** A83 2.20fr multicolored 1.75 1.00

Christmas, Scout movement in St. Pierre & Miquelon, 50th anniv.

The Great Barachoise Nature Reserve — A84

**1987, Dec. 16 Engr. *Perf. 13x12½***
**504** 3fr Horses, waterfowl 2.00 1.25
**505** 3fr Waterfowl, seals 2.00 1.25
*a.* A84 Pair, #504-505 + label 4.50 3.25

No. 505a is in continous design.

**1988, Nov. 2**
**506** A84 2.20fr Ross Cove 1.50 .75
**507** A84 13.70fr Cap Perce 5.50 4.75
*a.* Pair, #506-507 + label 7.50 7.50

No. 507a is in continous design.

1988 Winter Olympics, Calgary A86

**1988, Mar. 5 Engr. *Perf. 13***
**508** A86 5fr brt ultra & dark red 2.50 1.60

Louis Thomas (1887-1976), Photographer — A87

**1988, May 4 Engr. *Perf. 13***
**509** A87 2.20fr blk, dk ol bis & Prus bl 1.10 .70

**France No. 2105 Overprinted "ST-PIERRE ET MIQUELON"**

**1988, July 25 Engr. *Perf. 13***
**510** A1107 2.20fr ver, blk & violet blue 1.75 .90

Seizure of Schooner Nellie J. Banks, 50th Anniv. A88

**1988, Aug. 7**
**511** A88 2.50fr brn, vio blue & brt blue 1.75 1.10

The Nellie J. Banks was seized by Canada for carrying prohibited alcohol in 1938.

Christmas — A89

**1988, Dec. 17 Litho. *Perf. 13***
**512** A89 2.20fr multicolored 1.25 .90

Judo Competitions in St. Pierre & Miquelon, 25th Anniv. — A90

**1989, Mar. 4 Engr. *Perf. 13***
**513** A90 5fr brn org, blk & yel grn 2.25 1.40

French Revolution Bicent.; 40th Anniv. of the UN Declaration of Human Rights (in 1988) — A91

**1989** **Engr.** *Perf. 12½x13*

| | | | |
|---|---|---|---|
| **514** A91 2.20fr Liberty | 1.10 | .75 |
| **515** A91 2.20fr Equality | 1.10 | .75 |
| **516** A91 2.20fr Fraternity | 1.10 | .75 |
| *Nos. 514-516 (3)* | 3.30 | 2.25 |

Issued: #514, 3/22; #515, 5/3; #516, 6/17.

Souvenir Sheet

French Revolution, Bicent. — A92

Designs: a, Bastille, liberty tree. b, Bastille, ship. c, Building, revolutionaries raising flag and liberty tree. d, Revolutionaries, building with open doors.

**1989, July 14** **Engr.** *Perf. 13*

| | | |
|---|---|---|
| **517** A92 Sheet of 4 + 2 labels | 10.00 | 10.00 |
| *a.-d.* 5fr any single | 2.25 | 2.25 |

Heritage of Ile aux Marins — A93

Designs: 2.20fr, Coastline, ships in harbor, girl in boat, fish. 13.70fr, Coastline, ships in harbor, boy flying kite from boat, map of Ile aux Marins.

**1989, Sept. 9** **Engr.** *Perf. 13x12½*

| | | |
|---|---|---|
| **518** 2.20fr multi | 1.75 | .70 |
| **519** 13.70fr multi | 5.75 | 4.25 |
| *a.* A93 Pair, #518-519 + label | 8.50 | 8.50 |

Nos. 519a is in continuous design.

George Landry and Bank Emblem A95

**1989, Nov. 8** **Engr.** *Perf. 13*

**520** A95 2.20fr bl & golden brn 1.10 .75

Bank of the Islands, cent.

Christmas — A96

**1989, Dec. 2** **Litho.** *Perf. 13*

**521** A96 2.20fr multicolored 1.10 .75

France Nos. 2179-2182, 2182A-2186, 2188-2189, 2191-2194, 2204B, 2331, 2333-2334, 2336-2339, 2342 Ovptd.

**1990-96** **Engr.** *Perf. 13*

| | | | | |
|---|---|---|---|---|
| **522** | A1161 | 10c brn blk | .25 | .25 |
| **523** | A1161 | 20c light grn | .25 | .25 |
| **524** | A1161 | 50c bright vio | .25 | .25 |
| **525** | A1161 | 1fr orange | .50 | .35 |
| **526** | A1161 | 2fr apple grn | .90 | .70 |
| **527** | A1161 | 2fr blue | 1.00 | .75 |
| **528** | A1161 | 2.10fr green | .95 | .75 |
| **529** | A1161 | 2.20fr green | 1.10 | .80 |
| **530** | A1161 | 2.30fr red | 1.10 | .30 |
| **531** | A1161 | 2.40fr emerald | 1.25 | .50 |
| **532** | A1161 | 2.50fr red | 1.25 | .25 |
| **533** | A1161 | 2.70fr emerald | 1.25 | 1.10 |
| **534** | A1161 | 3.20fr bright bl | 1.75 | 1.10 |
| **535** | A1161 | 3.40fr blue | 1.75 | .95 |
| **536** | A1161 | 3.50fr apple grn | 1.75 | .75 |
| **537** | A1161 | 3.80fr brt pink | 2.00 | .75 |
| **538** | A1161 | 3.80fr blue | 1.75 | .75 |
| **539** | A1161 | 4fr brt lil rose | 2.25 | .75 |
| **540** | A1161 | 4.20fr rose lilac | 2.25 | .95 |
| **541** | A1161 | 4.40fr blue | 2.10 | 1.00 |
| **542** | A1161 | 4.50fr magenta | 2.40 | 1.90 |
| **543** | A1161 | 5fr dull blue | 2.00 | 1.00 |
| **544** | A1161 | 10fr violet | 4.00 | 1.00 |
| **544A** | A1161 | (2.50fr) red | 1.50 | .50 |
| | | *Nos. 522-544A (24)* | 35.55 | 17.65 |

**Booklet Stamps**
**Self-Adhesive**
***Die Cut***

| | | | | |
|---|---|---|---|---|
| **545** | A1161 | 2.50fr red | 1.60 | 1.00 |
| *a.* | | Booklet pane of 10 | 16.00 | |
| **545B** | A1161 | (2.80fr) red | 1.75 | 1.10 |
| *a.* | | Booklet pane of 10 | 17.50 | |

Issued: 2.30fr, 1/2/90; 2.10fr, 2/5/90; 10c, 20c, 50c, 3.20fr, #537, 4/17/90; 1fr, 5fr, #526, 10fr, 7/16/90; #532, 2.20fr, 12/21/91; 3.40fr, 4fr, 1/8/92; #545, 2/8/92; 4.20fr, 1/13/93; #544A, 7/5/93; 2.40fr, 3.50fr, 4.40fr, #545B, 10/6/93; #527, 8/17/94; #538, 4/10/96; 2.70fr, 4.50fr, 6/12/96.

Gen. Charles de Gaulle's Call for French Resistance, 50th Anniv. — A97

**1990, June 18** *Perf. 13*

**546** A97 2.30fr red, claret & blue 1.40 .70

Charles de Gaulle (1890-1970) A98

Design: 1.70fr, De Gaulle as General. 2.30fr, De Gaulle as President of France.

**1990, Nov. 22**

| | | |
|---|---|---|
| **547** A98 1.70fr red, claret & blue | .75 | .55 |
| **548** A98 2.30fr red, claret & blue | 1.25 | .80 |
| *a.* Pair, #547-548 + central label | 2.25 | 2.25 |

25 Kilometer Race of Miquelon A99

**1990, June 23**

**549** A99 5fr Runner, map 2.75 1.10

Micmac Canoe, 1875 A100

**1990, Aug. 15** **Engr.** *Perf. 13x13½*

**550** A100 2.50fr multicolored 1.25 .70

Views of St. Pierre — A101

Harbor scene.

**1990, Oct. 24** **Engr.** *Perf. 13x12½*

| | | |
|---|---|---|
| **551** A101 2.30fr bl, grn & brn | 1.00 | .50 |
| **552** A101 14.50fr bl, grn & brn | 6.50 | 3.50 |
| *a.* Pair, #551-552 + label | 9.00 | 9.00 |

No. 552a is in continous design.

Christmas — A103

**1990, Dec. 15** **Litho.**

**553** A103 2.30fr multicolored 1.25 .65

Papilio Brevicaudata A104

3.60fr, Aeshna Eremita, Nuphar Variegatum.

**1991-92** **Litho.** *Perf. 13*

**554** A104 2.50fr multicolored 1.50 .95

*Perf. 12*

**555** A104 3.60fr multicolored 1.60 1.00

Issued: 2.50fr, Jan. 16; 3.60fr, Mar. 4, 1992.

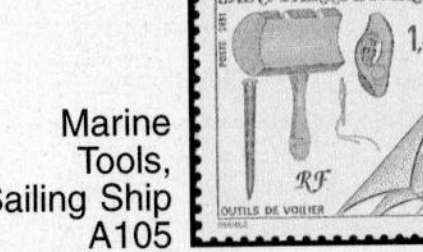

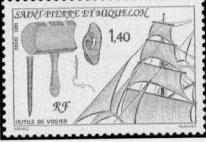

Marine Tools, Sailing Ship A105

**Litho. & Engr.**

**1991, Mar. 6** *Perf. 13*

| | | |
|---|---|---|
| **559** A105 1.40fr yellow & green | .75 | .50 |
| **560** A105 1.70fr yellow & red | .90 | .55 |

Scenic Views A106

Designs: Nos. 561, 565, Saint Pierre. Nos. 562, 566, Ile aux Marins. Nos. 563, 567, Langlade. Nos. 564, 568, Miquelon.

**1991, Apr. 17** **Engr.** *Perf. 13*

| | | |
|---|---|---|
| **561** A106 1.70fr blue | .80 | .65 |
| **562** A106 1.70fr blue | .80 | .65 |
| **563** A106 1.70fr blue | .80 | .65 |
| **564** A106 1.70fr blue | .80 | .65 |
| *a.* Strip of 4, #561-564 | 3.25 | 3.25 |
| **565** A106 2.50fr red | 1.25 | .95 |
| **566** A106 2.50fr red | 1.25 | .95 |
| **567** A106 2.50fr red | 1.25 | .95 |
| **568** A106 2.50fr red | 1.25 | .95 |
| *a.* Strip of 4, #565-568 | 5.00 | 5.00 |
| *Nos. 561-568 (8)* | 8.20 | 6.40 |

Lyre Music Society, Cent. — A107

**1991, June 21** **Engr.** *Perf. 13*

**569** A107 2.50fr multicolored 1.50 .70

Newfoundland Crossing by Rowboat "Los Gringos" — A108

**1991, Aug. 3** **Engr.** *Perf. 13x12½*

**570** A108 2.50fr multicolored 1.50 .70

Basque Sports A109

**1991, Aug. 24** *Perf. 13*

**571** A109 5fr red & green 2.10 1.40

Natural Heritage — A110

2.50fr, Fishermen. 14.50fr, Shoreline, birds.

**1991, Oct. 18** **Engr.** *Perf. 13x12½*

| | | |
|---|---|---|
| **572** A110 2.50fr multicolored | 1.50 | .90 |
| **573** A110 14.50fr multicolored | 6.50 | 5.00 |
| *a.* Pair, #572-573 + label | 8.50 | 8.50 |

No. 573a is in continuous design.

Central Economic Cooperation Bank, 50th Anniv. — A111

**1991, Dec. 2 Engr. *Perf. 13x12½***
**574** A111 2.50fr 1941 100fr note 1.40 .70

Christmas A112

**1991, Dec. 21 Litho. *Perf. 13***
**575** A112 2.50fr multicolored 1.40 .75

Christmas Day Plebiscite, 50th anniv.

Vice Admiral Emile Henri Muselier (1882-1965), Commander of Free French Naval Forces — A113

**1992, Jan. 8 Litho. *Perf. 13***
**576** A113 2.50fr multicolored 1.50 .75

1992 Winter Olympics, Albertville A114

**1992, Feb. 8 Engr. *Perf. 13***
**577** A114 5fr vio bl, blue & mag 2.10 1.25

Caulking Tools, Bow of Ship A115

**Litho. & Engr.**
**1992, Apr. 1 *Perf. 13x12½***
**578** A115 1.50fr pale bl gray & brn .75 .45
**579** A115 1.80fr pale bl gray & bl .90 .45

Lighthouses — A116

Designs: a, Galantry. b, Feu Rouge. c, Pointe-Plate. d, Ile Aux Marins.

**1992, July 8 Litho. *Perf. 13***
**580** A116 2.50fr Strip of 4, #a.-d. 5.50 3.50

Natural Heritage — A117

**1992, Sept. 9 Engr. *Perf. 13x12½***
**581** A117 2.50fr Langlade 1.50 .75
**582** A117 15.10fr Doulisie Valley 7.50 3.75
*a.* Pair, #581-582 + label 9.00 9.00

No. 582a is in continuous design.
See Nos. 593-594, 605-606.

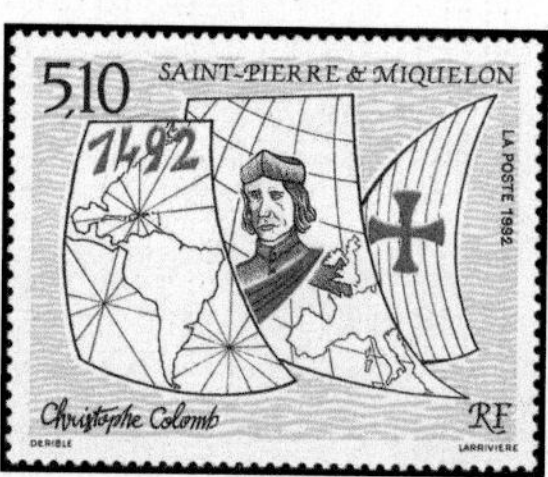
Discovery of America, 500th Anniv. — A118

**Photo. & Engr.**
**1992, Oct. 12 *Perf. 13x12½***
**583** A118 5.10fr multicolored 2.50 1.25

Le Baron de L'Esperance — A119

**1992, Nov. 18 Engr. *Perf. 13***
**584** A119 2.50fr claret, brn & bl 1.25 .75

Christmas — A120

**1992, Dec. 9 Litho. *Perf. 13***
**585** A120 2.50fr multicolored 1.40 .80

Commander R. Birot (1906-1942) — A121

**1993, Jan. 13**
**586** A121 2.50fr multicolored 1.50 .90

Deep Sea Diving A122

**1993, Feb. 10 Engr. *Perf. 12***
**587** A122 5fr multicolored 2.75 1.25

A123

Monochamus Scutellatus, Cichorium Intybus.

**1993, Mar. 10 Litho. *Perf. 13½x13***
**588** A123 3.60fr multicolored 1.75 .80

See No. 599.

A124

Slicing cod.

**1993, Apr. 7 Litho. *Perf. 13½x13***
**589** A124 1.50fr green & multi .85 .50
**590** A124 1.80fr red & multi 1.00 .55

Move to the Magdalen Islands, Quebec, by Miquelon Residents, Bicent. — A125

**1993, June 9 Engr. *Perf. 13***
**591** A125 5.10fr brn, bl & grn 2.50 1.25

Fish A126

Designs: a, Capelin. b, Ray. c, Halibut (fletan). d, Toad fish (crapaud).

**1993, July 30 Photo. *Perf. 13***
**592** A126 2.80fr Strip of 4, #a.-d. 6.00 6.00

**Natl. Heritage Type of 1992**

**1993, Aug. 18 Engr. *Perf. 13x12½***
**593** A117 2.80fr Miquelon 1.75 1.00
**594** A117 16fr Otter pool 7.00 5.75
*a.* Pair, #593-594 + label 11.00 11.00

No. 594a is a continuous design.

Commissioner's Residence — A127

**1993, Oct. 6 Engr. *Perf. 13***
**595** A127 3.70fr multicolored 1.60 .90

Christmas A128

**1993, Dec. 13 Litho. *Perf. 13***
**596** A128 2.80fr multicolored 1.60 .80

Commander Louis Blaison (1906-1942), Submarine Surcouf — A129

**1994, Jan. 12 Litho. *Perf. 13***
**597** A129 2.80fr multicolored 1.75 .80

Petanque World Championships — A130

**1994, Feb. 9 Engr. *Perf. 12½x12***
**598** A130 5.10fr multicolored 2.50 1.75

**Insect and Flower Type of 1993**

Cristalis tenax, taraxacum officinale, horiz.

**1994, Mar. 9 Litho. *Perf. 13x13½***
**599** A123 3.70fr multicolored 2.10 1.25

Drying Codfish, 1905 A131

**1994 Litho. *Perf. 13***
**600** A131 1.50fr blk & bl grn .90 .55
**601** A131 1.80fr multicolored 1.20 .65

Issued: 1.50fr, 5/4/94; 1.80fr, 4/6/94.

Women's Right to Vote, 50th Anniv. A132

**1994, Apr. 21**
**602** A132 2.80fr multicolored 1.60 .80

Hospital Ship St. Pierre, Cent. A133

**1994, July 2**
**603** A133 2.80fr multicolored 1.75 .80

Souvenir Sheet

Ships — A134

Designs: a, Miquelon. b, Isle of St. Pierre. c, St. George XII. d, St. Eugene IV.

**1994, July 6** ***Perf. 12***

| | | | |
|---|---|---|---|
| 604 | A134 Sheet of 4 | 8.50 | 8.50 |
| *a.-b.* | 2.80fr any single | 1.50 | 1.25 |
| *c.-d.* | 3.70fr any single | 2.00 | 1.75 |

See No. 628.

**Natl. Heritage Type of 1992**

**1994, Aug. 17** **Engr.** ***Perf. 13***

| | | | |
|---|---|---|---|
| 605 | A117 2.80fr Woods | 2.00 | .90 |
| 606 | A117 16fr "The Hat" | 7.50 | 4.00 |
| *a.* | Pair, #605-606 + label | 10.50 | 10.00 |

Parochial School A135

**1994, Oct. 5** **Engr.** ***Perf. 13***

607 A135 3.70fr multicolored 1.60 .95

Stamp Show A136

**1994, Oct. 15**

608 A136 3.70fr grn, yel & bl 1.75 1.10

Christmas A137

**1994, Nov. 23** **Litho.** ***Perf. 13***

609 A137 2.80fr multicolored 1.60 .80

Louis Pasteur (1822-95) A138

**1995, Jan. 11** **Litho.** ***Perf. 13***

610 A138 2.80fr multicolored 1.60 .80

Triathlon A139

**1995, Feb. 8** **Engr.** ***Perf. 12***

611 A139 5.10fr multicolored 2.25 1.25

A140

Dicranum Scoparium & Cladonia Cristatella.

**1995, Mar. 8** **Litho.** ***Perf. 13***

612 A140 3.70fr multicolored 1.75 1.10

See Nos. 625, 635.

A141

Cooper and his tools.

**1995, Apr. 5** **Litho.** ***Perf. 13½x13***

| | | | |
|---|---|---|---|
| 613 | A141 1.50fr black & multi | .75 | .50 |
| 614 | A141 1.80fr red & multi | .90 | .55 |

Shellfish A142

a, Snail. b, Crab. c, Scallop. d, Lobster.

**1995, July 5** **Litho.** ***Perf. 13***

| | | | |
|---|---|---|---|
| 616 | Strip of 4 | 6.00 | 6.00 |
| *a.-d.* | A142 2.80fr any single | 1.40 | 1.00 |

Geological Mission — A143

Designs: 2.80fr, Rugged terrain along shoreline, diagram of mineral location, zircon. 16fr, Geological map, terrain.

**1995, Aug. 16** **Engr.** ***Perf. 13x12½***

| | | | |
|---|---|---|---|
| 617 | A143 2.80fr multicolored | 2.00 | 1.00 |
| 618 | A143 16fr multicolored | 7.00 | 5.00 |
| *a.* | Pair, #617-618 + label | 9.50 | 9.50 |

Sister Cesarine (1845-1922), St. Joseph de Cluny — A144

**1995, Sept. 6** **Litho.** ***Perf. 13***

619 A144 1.80fr multicolored 1.10 .75

The Francoforum Public Building — A145

**1995, Oct. 4** **Engr.**

620 A145 3.70fr multicolored 1.75 1.00

Christmas — A146

Design: 2.80fr, Toys in store window.

**1995, Nov. 22** **Litho.** ***Perf. 13***

621 A146 2.80fr multicolored 1.75 .90

Charles de Gaulle (1890-1970) A147

**1995, Nov. 9** **Litho.** ***Perf. 13x13½***

622 A147 14fr multicolored 5.75 3.50

Commandant Jean Levasseur (1909-47) — A148

**1996, Jan. 10** ***Perf. 13***

623 A148 2.80fr multicolored 1.75 .80

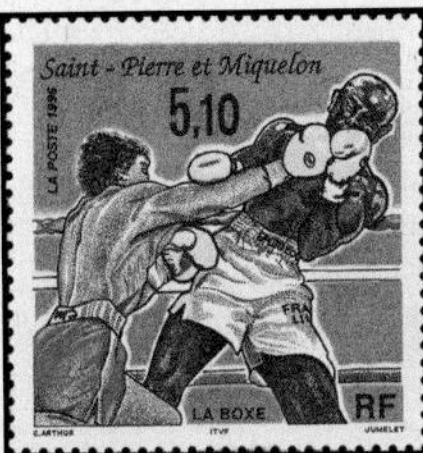


Boxing A149

**1996, Feb. 7** **Engr.** ***Perf. 12x12½***

624 A149 5.10fr multicolored 2.50 1.25

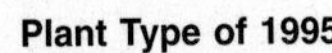

**Plant Type of 1995**

Design: Cladonia verticillata and polytrichum juniperinum.

**1996, Mar. 13** **Litho.** ***Perf. 13***

625 A140 3.70fr multicolored 1.75 1.10

Blacksmiths and Their Tools A150

**1996, Apr. 10**

| | | | |
|---|---|---|---|
| 626 | A150 1.50fr black & multi | .75 | .35 |
| 627 | A150 1.80fr red & multi | .85 | .50 |

**Ship Type of 1994**

Designs: a, Radar II. b, SPM Roro. c, Pinta. d, Pascal Anne.

**1996, July 10** **Litho.** ***Perf. 13***

| | | | |
|---|---|---|---|
| 628 | Sheet of 4 | 7.00 | 7.00 |
| *a.-d.* | A134 3fr Any single | 1.50 | 1.00 |

Aerial View of Miquelon — A151

Designs: 3fr, "Le Cap," mountains, buildings. 15.50fr, "Le Village," buildings.

**1996, Aug. 14** **Engr.** ***Perf. 13x12½***

| | | | |
|---|---|---|---|
| 629 | 3fr multicolored | 1.25 | 1.25 |
| 630 | 15.50fr multicolored | 6.00 | 6.00 |
| *a.* | A151 Pair, #629-630 + label | 7.75 | 7.75 |

Customs House, Cent. A152

**1996, Oct. 9** **Engr.** ***Perf. 12½x13***

631 A152 3.80fr blue & black 1.50 .90

Fall Stamp Show — A153

**1996, Nov. 6** **Litho.** ***Perf. 13***

632 A153 1fr multicolored .70 .45

Christmas — A154

**1996, Nov. 20** **Litho.** ***Perf. 13***

633 A154 3fr multicolored 1.50 .90

Constant Colmay (1903-65) A155

**1997, Jan. 8** **Litho.** ***Perf. 13***

634 A155 3fr multicolored 1.50 .90

**Plant Type of 1995**

Design: Phalacrocorax carbo, sedum rosea.

**1997, Mar. 12 Litho. *Perf. 13***
**635** A140 3.80fr multicolored 1.50 .90

Maritime Heritage A156

Designs: 1.70fr, Man in doorway of salt house. 2fr, Boat, naval architect's drawing.

**1997, Apr. 9 Litho. *Perf. 13***
**636** A156 1.70fr multicolored .75 .50
**637** A156 2fr multicolored .90 .60

Volleyball A157

**Litho. & Engr.**

**1997, Apr. 9 *Perf. 12***
**638** A157 5.20fr multicolored 2.25 1.10

Fish — A158

a, Shark. b, Salmon. c, Poule d'eau. d, Mackerel.

**1997, July 9 Litho. *Perf. 13***
**639** A158 3fr Strip of 4, #a.-d. 5.50 4.50

Bay, Headlands — A159

3fr, Basque Cape. 15.50fr, Diamant.

**1997, Aug. 13 *Perf. 13x12***
**640** A159 3fr multicolored 1.50 1.00
**641** A159 15.50fr multicolored 5.50 3.50
*a.* Pair #640-641 + label 7.00 6.25

**France Nos. 2589-2603 Ovptd. "ST. PIERRE / ET / MIQUELON"**

| **1997-98** | **Engr.** | ***Perf. 13*** | |
|---|---|---|---|
| **642** A1409 | 10c brown | .25 | .25 |
| **643** A1409 | 20c brt blue grn | .25 | .25 |
| **644** A1409 | 50c purple | .30 | .30 |
| **645** A1409 | 1fr bright org | .35 | .25 |
| **646** A1409 | 2fr bright blue | .80 | .30 |
| **647** A1409 | 2.70fr bright green | 1.10 | .30 |
| **648** A1409 | (3fr) red | 1.40 | .30 |
| **649** A1409 | 3.50fr apple green | 1.50 | .55 |
| **650** A1409 | 3.80fr blue | 1.40 | .65 |
| **651** A1409 | 4.20fr dark orange | 1.60 | .65 |
| **652** A1409 | 4.40fr blue | 1.75 | .65 |
| **653** A1409 | 4.50fr bright pink | 1.75 | .75 |
| **654** A1409 | 5fr brt grn bl | 1.90 | .80 |
| **655** A1409 | 6.70fr dark green | 2.75 | 1.25 |
| **656** A1409 | 10fr violet | 3.75 | 1.40 |
| | *Nos. 642-656 (15)* | 20.85 | 8.65 |

Issued: 2.70fr, (3fr), 3.80fr, 8/13/97; 10c, 20c, 50c, 3.50fr, 4.40fr, 10fr, 10/8/97; 1fr, 2fr, 4.20fr, 4.50fr, 5fr, 6.70fr, 1/7/98.

See No. 664 for self-adhesive (3fr).

Post Office Building A160

**1997, Oct. 8 Engr. *Perf. 13***
**657** A160 3.80fr multicolored 1.60 .90

Christmas — A161

**1997, Nov. 19 Litho. *Perf. 13***
**658** A161 3fr multicolored 1.50 .80

Alain Savary (1918-88), Governor, Territorial Deputy A162

**1998, Jan. 7 Litho. *Perf. 13***
**659** A162 3fr multicolored 1.40 .70

1998 Winter Olympic Games, Nagano A163

**1998, Feb. 11 Engr. *Perf. 12***
**660** A163 5.20fr Curling 2.25 1.10

Flora and Fauna A164

**1998, Mar. 11 Photo. *Perf. 13***
**661** A164 3.80fr multicolored 1.75 .95

Ice Workers A165

**1998, Apr. 8 Litho.**
**662** A165 1.70fr shown .75 .65
**663** A165 2fr Cutting ice from lake .90 .65

**France Nos. 2604, 2620 Ovptd. "ST. PIERRE / ET / MIQUELON"**

***Die Cut x Serpentine Die Cut***

**1998, Apr. 8 Engr.**

**Self-Adhesive**

**664** A1409 (3fr) red 1.25 .60
*a.* Booklet pane of 10 15.00

No. 664a is a complete booklet. The peel-able backing serves as a booklet cover.

**1998, May 13 *Perf. 13***
**665** A1424 3fr red & blue 1.25 .60

Houses — A166

a, Gray. b, Yellow, red roof. c, Pink. d, White, red roof.

**1998, July 8 Litho. *Perf. 13***
**666** A166 3fr Strip of 4, #a.-d. 5.00 2.50

French in North America — A167

**1998, Sept. 30 Engr. *Perf. 13x12½***
**670** A167 3fr multicolored 1.25 .60

Cape Blue Natl. Park — A168

Designs: 3fr, Point Plate Lighthouse, shoreline. 15.50fr, Cape Blue.

**1998, Sept. 30 *Perf. 13x12***
**671** A168 3fr multicolored 1.25 .95
**672** A168 15.50fr multicolored 6.50 3.50
*a.* Pair, #671-672 + label 8.75 8.75

France, 1998 World Cup Soccer Champions A169

**1998, Oct. 21 Litho. *Perf. 13***
**673** A169 3fr multicolored 1.60 .60

Memorial to War Dead — A170

**1998, Nov. 11 Engr.**
**674** A170 3.80fr multicolored 1.60 .75

Christmas — A171

**1998, Nov. 18 Litho.**
**675** A171 3fr multicolored 1.25 .60

Emile Letournel (1927-94), Orthopedic Surgeon, Traumatologist — A172

**1999, Jan. 6 Engr. *Perf. 13***
**676** A172 3fr multicolored 1.25 .60

Painting, "The Beach at Fisherman Island," by Patrick Guillaume — A173

**1999, Feb. 10 Litho.**
**677** A173 5.20fr multicolored 2.00 .95

See No. 692.

La Plate-Bière A174

3.80fr, Rubus chamaemorus.

**1999, Mar. 10 Litho. *Perf. 13***
**678** A174 3.80fr multicolored 1.60 .75

See No. 693, 705, 736.

Horseshoeing — A175

1.70fr, Horse, blacksmith and his tools. 2fr, Applying horseshoes in blacksmith's shop.

**1999, Apr. 7 Litho. *Perf. 13***
**679** A175 1.70fr multicolored .80 .50
**680** A175 2fr multicolored .95 .50

**France No. 2691 Ovptd. "ST. PIERRE / ET / MIQUELON"**

**1999, Apr. 7 Engr.**
**681** A1470 3fr red & blue 1.25 .60

Value is shown in both francs and euros on No. 681.

**France No. 2691A Overprinted "ST. PIERRE / ET / MIQUELON"**

***Die Cux x Serpentine Die Cut 7***

**1999, Apr. 5 Engr.**

**Self-Adhesive**

**681A** A1470 3fr red & blue 2.00 1.00
*b.* Booklet of 10 20.00

First Stamps of France, 150th Anniv. A176

a, France #3, St. Pierre & Miquelon #9, 79. b, #145, 270. c, #C21, C36. d, #476, 676.

**1999, June 23 Litho. *Perf. 13***
**682** A176 3fr Sheet of 4, #a.-d. 7.00 7.00

PhilexFrance '99, World Philatelic Exhibition.

Ships — A177

a, Bearn. b, Pro Patria. c, Erminie. d, Colombier.

**1999, July 7 Litho. *Perf. 13x13½***
**683** A177 3fr Sheet of 4, #a.-d. 6.00 6.00

General de Gaulle Place — A178

**1999, Aug. 11 Engr. *Perf. 13x12¼***
**684** 3fr Cars, yield sign 1.00 1.00
**685** 15.50fr Docked boats 5.50 5.50
*a.* A178 Pair, #684-685 + label 7.50 7.50

Visit of Pres. Jacques Chirac, Sept. 1999 — A179

**1999, Sept. 7 Litho. *Perf. 13¼x13***
**686** A179 3fr multicolored 1.40 .60

Archives A180

**1999, Oct. 6 Engr. *Perf. 13x12¾***
**687** A180 5.40fr deep rose lilac 2.25 1.00

Christmas A181

**1999, Nov. 17 Litho. *Perf. 13***
**688** A181 3fr multi 1.50 .75

Year 2000 — A182

**2000, Jan. 12 Litho. *Perf. 13¼x13***
**689** A182 3fr multi 1.50 .75

Whales A183

Designs: 3fr, Megaptera novaeangliae. 5.70fr, Balaenoptera physalus.

**2000, Jan. 26 Engr. *Perf. 13x12¾***
**690** A183 3fr blk & Prus bl 1.25 .60
**691** A183 5.70fr Prus grn & blk 2.75 1.10

See also Nos. 702-703.

**Painting Type of 1999**

**2000, Feb. 9 Litho. *Perf. 13***
**692** A173 5.20fr Les Graves 2.25 1.00

**Plant Type of 1999**

**2000, Mar. 8**
**693** A174 3.80fr Vaccinium vitis-idaea 1.50 .70

Wood Gatherer A184

Vignette colors: 1.70fr, Blue. 2fr, Brown.

**2000, Apr. 5 Engr.**
**694-695** A184 Set of 2 2.00 1.00

Millennium A185

No. 696: a, Lobstermen on Newfoundland coast, 1904. b, Women on shore, 1905. c, World War I conscripts on ship Chicago, 1915. d, Soldiers in action at Souain Hill, 1915. e, Men walking on ice, 1923. f, Unloading cases of champagne to be smuggled to US, 1925. g, St. Pierre & Miquelon Pavilion at Colonial Expostion in Paris, 1931. h, Alcohol smugglers, 1933. i, Adm. Emile Muselier inspecting troops on ship Mimosa, 1942. j, World War II soldiers crossing bridge, 1945.

No. 697: a, Fishery employees, 1951. b, Fishing trawler, 1960. c, Visit of Gen. Charles de Gaulle, 1967. d, First television images, 1967. e, Port facilities, 1970. f, New high school, 1977. g, Resumption of stamp issuing, 1986. h, Voyage fo Eric Tabarly, 1987. i, Exclusive Economic Zone, 1992. j, New airport, 1999.

**2000 Litho. *Perf. 13x13¼***
**696** Sheet of 10 16.00 13.00
*a.-j.* A185 3fr Any single 1.40 .75
**697** Sheet of 10 14.00 11.00
*a.-j.* A185 2fr Any single 1.25 .75

Issue: No. 696, 6/21; No. 697, 12/6.

The Inger — A186

**2000, Oct. 4 Engr. *Perf. 13x13¼***
**698** A186 5.40fr green 3.00 1.40

Boathouses in November — A187

**2000, Oct. 4 *Perf. 13x12¼***
**699** A187 Pair + central label 9.50 8.50
*a.* 3fr Hill 1.50 1.00
*b.* 15.50fr Church 7.50 5.00

Christmas — A188

**2000, Nov. 15 Litho. *Perf. 13¼x13***
**700** A188 3fr multi 1.50 .80

New Year 2001 — A189

**2001, Jan. 3 Litho. *Perf. 13x12¾***
**701** A189 3fr multi 2.00 .50

**Whale Type of 2000**

Designs: 3fr, Orcinus orca. 5.70fr, Globicephala melaena.

**2001, Jan. 24 Engr. *Perf. 13x12¾***
**702-703** A183 Set of 2 3.50 1.50

Landscape A190

**2001, Feb. 21 Litho. *Perf. 13***
**704** A190 5.20fr multi 2.50 1.10

**Plant Type of 1999**

**2001, Mar. 21 Litho. *Perf. 13***
**705** A174 3.80fr Vaccinium oxycoccos 1.75 .80

Hay Gatherers A191

Denomination colors: 1.70fr, Red brown. 2fr, Lilac.

**2001, Apr. 18**
**706-707** A191 Set of 2 2.00 .95

Seasons A192

Designs: No. 708, 3fr, Autumn. No. 709, 3fr, Winter.

**2001, June 20**
**708-709** A192 Set of 2 3.00 1.50

See Nos. 714-715.

Vestibules — A193

No. 710: a, Guillou House. b, Jugan House. c, Ile-aux-Marins town hall. d, Vogé House.

**2001, July 25**
**710** A193 Horiz. strip of 4 5.75 5.00
*a.-d.* 3fr Any single 1.50 1.00

Anse du Gouvernement — A194

Houses and: a, Boat. b, Rocks near shore.

**2001, Sept. 12 Engr. *Perf. 13x12¼***
**711** A194 Horiz. pair, #a-b, + central label 10.00 8.50
*a.-b.* 10fr Any single 4.75 3.25

Saint Pierre Pointe Blanche — A195

**2001, Sept. 26 Litho. *Perf. 13***
**712** A195 5fr multi 2.40 1.40

The Marie-Thérèse — A196

**2001, Sept. 26 Engr. *Perf. 13x13¼***
**713** A196 5.40fr green 2.60 1.40

**Seasons Type of 2001**

Designs: No. 714, 3fr, Spring. No. 715, 3fr, Summer.

**2001, Oct. 17 Litho. *Perf. 13***
**714-715** A192 Set of 2 3.00 1.60

Commander Jacques Pepin Lehalleur (1911-2000) A197

**2001, Nov. 14**
**716** A197 3fr multi 1.80 .80

Christmas — A198

**2001, Nov. 28**
**717** A198 3fr multi 1.50 .80

**100 Cents = 1 Euro (€)**

France Nos. 2849-2863 Overprinted

**2002, Jan. 1 Engr. *Perf. 13***
**718** A1583 1c yellow .25 .25
**719** A1583 2c brown .25 .25
**720** A1583 5c brt bl grn .25 .25
**721** A1583 10c purple .30 .25
**722** A1583 20c brt org .60 .50
**723** A1583 41c brt green 1.40 1.00
**724** A1583 50c dk blue 1.60 1.25
**725** A1583 53c apple grn 1.75 1.25

| | | | | |
|---|---|---|---|---|
| **726** | A1583 | 58c blue | 1.90 | 1.40 |
| **727** | A1583 | 64c dark org | 2.00 | 1.50 |
| **728** | A1583 | 67c brt blue | 2.10 | 1.60 |
| **729** | A1583 | 69c brt pink | 2.10 | 1.60 |
| **730** | A1583 | €1 Prus blue | 3.00 | 2.40 |
| **731** | A1583 | €1.02 dk green | 3.25 | 2.50 |
| **732** | A1583 | €2 violet | 6.25 | 4.75 |
| | | *Nos. 718-732 (15)* | 27.00 | 20.75 |

Introduction of the Euro A199

**2002, Jan. 30** **Litho.** ***Perf. 13***
**733** A199 €1 multi 3.00 1.50

Pinnipeds A200

Designs: 46c, Phoca vitulina. 87c, Halichoerus grypus.

**2002, Mar. 7** **Engr.** ***Perf. 13¼***
**734-735** A200 Set of 2 4.00 2.00

See Nos. 748-749.

**Plant Type of 1999**

**2002, Mar. 20** **Litho.** ***Perf. 13***
**736** A174 58c Pomme de pré 1.75 .90

Laranaga Farm, c. 1900 — A201

**2002, Mar. 20** **Engr.** ***Perf. 13x12¾***
**737** A201 79c green 2.50 1.25

See also Nos. 751, 772.

Net Mender A202

Colors: 26c, Orange brown. 30c, Blue.

**2002, Apr. 15** **Engr.** ***Perf. 13x13¼***
**738-739** A202 Set of 2 1.75 .90

West Point — A204

**2002, June 24** **Litho.** ***Perf. 13***
**741** A204 75c multi 2.40 1.10

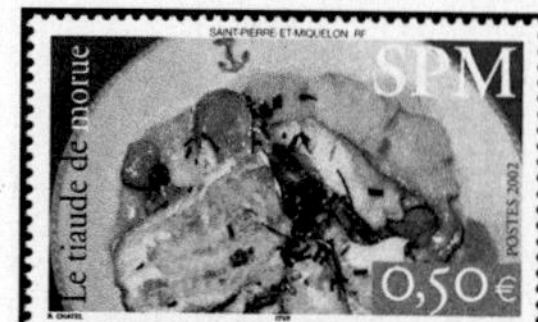


Tiaude de Morue, Local Cod Dish — A205

**2002, July 10**
**742** A205 50c multi 1.60 .80

**France No. 2835 Overprinted "ST. PIERRE / ET / MIQUELON"**

**2002, Sept. 11** **Engr.** ***Perf. 13***
**743** A1409 (46c) red 1.50 .75

Arctic Hare A206

**2002, Sept. 11** **Litho.** ***Perf. 13***
**744** A206 46c multi 1.50 .75

The Troutpool — A207

**2002, Oct. 11** **Engr.** ***Perf. 13x13¼***
**745** A207 84c green 2.75 1.40

Henry Cove — A208

No. 208: a, Gull and islands. b, Aerial view of St. Pierre.

**2002, Nov. 6** **Engr.** ***Perf. 13x12¼***
**746** A208 Horiz. pair + central label 13.50 11.00
*a.-b.* €2 Either single 6.25 3.25

Christmas A209

**2002, Nov. 27** **Litho.** ***Perf. 13***
**747** A209 46c multi 1.50 .75

**Pinnipeds Type of 2002**

Designs: 46c, Phoca groenlandica. 87c, Cystophora cristata.

**2003, Jan. 5** **Engr.** ***Perf. 13¼***
**748-749** A200 Set of 2 4.25 2.25

Msgr. François Maurer (1922-2000) A210

**2003, Jan. 8** **Litho.** ***Perf. 13***
**750** A210 46c multi 1.50 .75

**Farm Type of 2002**

**2003, Mar. 12** **Engr.** ***Perf. 13x13¼***
**751** A201 79c Capandeguy Farm, c. 1910 2.50 1.25

**France Nos. 2835A, 2921, and 2952-2957 Overprinted Like No. 718**

**2003** **Engr.** ***Perf. 13***

| | | | | |
|---|---|---|---|---|
| **752** | A1409 | (41c) brt green | 1.40 | .70 |
| **753** | A1583 | 58c apple grn | 1.90 | .95 |
| **754** | A1583 | 70c yellow grn | 2.25 | 1.10 |
| **755** | A1583 | 75c bright blue | 2.40 | 1.25 |
| **756** | A1583 | 90c dark blue | 3.00 | 1.50 |
| **757** | A1583 | €1.11 red lilac | 3.50 | 1.75 |
| **758** | A1583 | €1.90 vio brn | 6.00 | 3.00 |
| | | *Nos. 752-758 (7)* | 20.45 | 10.25 |

**Booklet Stamp**
**Self-Adhesive**
***Serpentine Die Cut 6¾ Vert.***

**758A** A1409 (46c) red 1.50 .75
*b.* Booklet pane of 10 15.00

Issued: (46c), 3/12. (41c), 4/23. 58c, 70c, 75c, 90c, €1.11, €1.90, 9/24.

Blueberries — A211

**2003, Apr. 23** **Litho.** ***Perf. 13***
**759** A211 75c multi 2.40 1.25

Pulley Repairer A212

**2003, May 14** **Engr.**
**760** A212 30c blue gray 1.00 .70

Intl. Congress on Traditional Architecture — A213

No. 761: a, Patrice, Jézéquel and Jugan houses. b, Notre-Dame des Marins Church, Borotra house.

**2003, May 22** ***Perf. 13x12¼***
**761** A213 Horiz. pair + central label 13.50 11.00
*a.-b.* €2 Either single 6.25 4.00

ASSP Soccer Team, Cent. A214

**2003, Aug. 7** **Litho.** ***Perf. 13***
**762** A214 50c multi 1.60 .80

Buck A215

**2003, Sept. 10**
**763** A215 50c multi 1.75 1.75

Lions Club in St. Pierre & Miquelon, 50th Anniv. A216

**2003, Oct. 29** **Litho.** ***Perf. 13x13¼***
**764** A216 50c multi 1.75 1.75

Langlade Strawberry Preserves — A217

**2003, Oct. 29** ***Perf. 13***
**765** A217 50c multi 1.75 1.75

The Afrique — A218

**2003, Nov. 6** **Engr.** ***Perf. 13x12½***
**766** A218 90c blue green 3.25 3.25

Christmas — A219

**2003, Dec. 3** **Litho.** ***Perf. 13***
**767** A219 50c multi 1.75 1.75

Joseph Lehuenen (d. 2001), Historian, Mayor — A220

**2004, Feb. 25** **Engr.** ***Perf. 13x13¼***
**768** A220 50c brown 1.75 1.75

Rodrigue Cove — A221

**2004, Mar. 10** **Litho.** ***Perf. 13***
**769** A221 75c multi 3.00 3.00

Marine Mammals A222

Designs: 50c, Lagenorhynchus acutus. €1.08, Phocoena phocoena.

**2004, Mar. 24** **Engr.** ***Perf. 13¼***

**770-771** A222 Set of 2 6.00 6.00

See also Nos. 806-807.

**Farm Type of 2002**

**2004, Apr. 7** **Engr.** ***Perf. 13x12½***

**772** A201 90c Ollivier Farm, c. 1920 3.00 3.00

Fishermen in Boat A223

**2004, May 12** **Litho.** ***Perf. 13***

**773** A223 30c multi 1.10 1.10

Port of St. Pierre — A224

No. 774: a, Ships, denomination at right. b, Ships and dock, denomination at left.

**2004, June 26** **Engr.** ***Perf. 13x12¼***

**774** A224 Horiz. pair + central label 13.50 13.50

*a.-b.* €2 Either single 6.25 6.25

Micmac Indians of Miquelon — A225

**2004, July 17** **Litho.** ***Perf. 13***

**775** A225 50c multi 1.75 1.75

**No. 775 Overprinted**

**2004, Aug. 14**

**776** A225 50c multi 3.25 3.25

Red Fox A226

**2004, Sept. 13**

**777** A226 50c multi 1.75 1.75

Dinner Table — A227

**2004, Sept. 13**

**778** A227 90c multi 3.50 3.50

The Fulwood — A228

**2004, Nov. 5** **Engr.** ***Perf. 13x13¼***

**779** A228 75c dark purple 2.75 2.75

Souvenir Sheet

Ships — A229

No. 780: a, Cap Blanc. b, Lisabeth-C. c, Shamrock. d, Aldona.

**2004, Nov. 17** **Litho.** ***Perf. 13***

**780** A229 50c Sheet of 4, #a-d 8.00 8.00

SIAA Soccer Team, 50th Anniv. (in 2003) A230

**2004, Nov. 24**

**781** A230 44c multi 1.60 1.60

Christmas — A231

**2004, Dec. 8**

**782** A231 50c multi 1.75 1.75

France Nos. 3066, 3068-3070, 3072, 3074-3075, 3077-3079, 3081 and 3083 Overprinted

**2005** **Engr.** ***Perf. 13***

| | | | | |
|---|---|---|---|---|
| **783** | A1713 | 1c yellow | .25 | .25 |
| **784** | A1713 | 5c brown black | .25 | .25 |
| **785** | A1713 | 10c violet | .30 | .30 |
| **786** | A1713 | (45c) green | 1.40 | 1.40 |
| **787** | A1713 | (50c) red | 1.60 | 1.60 |
| **788** | A1713 | 55c dark blue | 1.75 | 1.75 |
| **789** | A1713 | 58c olive green | 1.90 | 1.90 |
| **790** | A1713 | 64c dark green | 2.00 | 2.00 |
| **791** | A1713 | 70c dark green | 2.25 | 2.25 |
| **792** | A1713 | 75c light blue | 2.40 | 2.40 |
| **793** | A1713 | 82c fawn | 2.60 | 2.60 |
| **794** | A1713 | 90c dark blue | 3.00 | 3.00 |
| **795** | A1713 | €1 orange | 3.25 | 3.25 |
| **796** | A1713 | €1.11 red violet | 3.50 | 3.50 |
| **797** | A1713 | €1.22 red violet | 3.75 | 3.75 |
| **798** | A1713 | €1.90 chocolate | 6.00 | 6.00 |
| **799** | A1713 | €1.98 chocolate | 6.25 | 6.25 |
| | | *Nos. 783-799 (17)* | 42.45 | 42.45 |

**Booklet Stamp**

**Self-Adhesive**

***Serpentine Die Cut 6¾ Vert.***

**800** A1713 (50c) red 1.60 1.60

*a.* Booklet pane of 10 (on France #3083a) 16.00

Issued: Nos. 1c, 10c, (45c), (50c), 58c, 70c, 75c, 90c, €1, €1.11, €1.90, 1/12. 5c, 55c, 64c, 82c, €1.22, €1.98, 3/23. Face values shown for Nos. 786, 787 and 800 are those the stamps sold for on the day of issue.

Henri Claireaux (1911-2001), Senator — A232

**2005, Jan. 25** **Engr.** ***Perf. 13x13¼***

**804** A232 50c lilac 1.75 1.75

Allumette Cove — A233

**2005, Feb. 16** **Litho.** ***Perf. 13***

**805** A233 75c multi 2.75 2.75

**Marine Mammals Type of 2004**

Designs: 53c, Delphinus delphis. €1.15, Lagenorhynchus albirostris.

**2005, Mar. 9** **Engr.** ***Perf. 13¼***

**806-807** A222 Set of 2 6.50 6.50

Horse Point Farm — A234

**2005, Apr. 20** ***Perf. 13x13¼***

**808** A234 90c olive green 3.50 3.50

Fog, Clouds and Houses A235

**2005, May 11** **Litho.** ***Perf. 13***

**809** A235 30c multi 1.10 1.10

Seven Ponds Valley — A236

No. 810: a, Bird at left. b, Rabbit at right.

**2005, June 14** **Engr.** ***Perf. 13x12¼***

**810** A236 Horiz. pair + central label 15.00 15.00

*a.-b.* €2 Either single 6.25 2.00

Variable Hare A237

**2005, Sept. 7** **Litho.** ***Perf. 13***

**811** A237 53c multi 2.00 2.00

Local Expression "Ben Vous Savez Madame" — A238

**2005, Sept. 29**

**812** A238 90c multi 3.00 2.75

The Transpacific — A239

**2005, Oct. 12** **Engr.** ***Perf. 13x13¼***

**813** A239 75c blue 2.50 2.50

Status as Territorial Collectivity, 20th Anniv. — A240

**2005, Oct. 27** **Litho.** ***Perf. 13***

**814** A240 53c multi 1.75 1.75

Christmas A241

**2005, Dec. 7**

**815** A241 53c multi 1.75 1.00

Snow on Trees — A242

**2006, Jan. 25**

**816** A242 53c multi 2.10 1.25

Sailors' Festival — A243

**2006, Feb. 8**
**817** A243 53c multi 1.75 1.25

Albert Pen (1935-2003), President of General Council — A244

**2006, Mar. 1** **Engr.**
**818** A244 53c henna brn 1.75 1.25

Whales A245

Designs: 53c, Little rorqual. €1.15, Physeter catodon.

**2006, Apr. 12** **Engr.** ***Perf. 13¼***
**819-820** A245 Set of 2 6.00 2.00

Houses on Clear Day A246

**2006, June 7** **Litho.** ***Perf. 13***
**821** A246 30c multi 1.00 .50

Sénat Archipelago — A247

**2006, June 20**
**822** A247 53c multi 1.75 1.00

Prohibition, by Jean-Claude Girardin — A248

**2006, July 19** **Litho.** ***Perf. 13***
**823** A248 75c multi 2.25 1.50

Le Petit-Barachois — A249

No. 824: a, Houses. b, Houses and boats.

**2006, July 26** **Engr.** ***Perf. 13x12¾***
**824** A249 Horiz. pair with central label 13.50 13.50
*a.-b.* €2 Either single 6.25 6.25

Zazpiak Bat Pelota Fronton, Cent. — A250

**2006, Aug. 23** **Litho.** ***Perf. 13***
**825** A250 53c multi 1.60 1.60

Orchids — A251

No. 826: a, Spiranthe de Romanzoff. b, Arethusa. c, Habenaire papillon. d, Habenaire lacérée.

**2006, Sept. 6** **Engr.** ***Perf. 13x13¼***
**826** Horiz. strip of 4 7.00 7.00
*a.-d.* A251 53c Any single 1.60 1.60

Dugue Farm — A252

**2006, Sept. 20** **Engr.** ***Perf. 13x12½***
**827** A252 95c black 3.00 3.00

The Penny Fair — A253

**2006, Oct. 4** **Engr.** ***Perf. 13x12½***
**828** A253 95c black 3.00 3.00

Souvenir Sheet

Passenger Boats — A254

No. 829: a, Anahitra. b, Maria Galanta. c, Saint-Eugène V. d, Atlantic Jet.

**2006, Nov. 15** **Litho.** ***Perf. 13***
**829** A254 54c Sheet of 4, #a-d 8.00 8.00

Christmas A255

**2006, Dec. 6**
**830** A255 54c multi 1.75 1.75

Sister Hilarion (1913-2003) A256

**2007, Jan. 10** **Engr.** ***Perf. 13***
**831** A256 54c multi 1.75 1.75

Horses — A257

**2007, Feb. 21** **Litho.** ***Perf. 13***
**832** A257 €1.01 multi 3.00 3.00

Plactopecten Magellanicus — A258

**2007, Mar. 10** **Engr.** ***Perf. 13¼***
**833** A258 €1 multi 3.50 3.50

Audit Office, Bicent. A259

**2007, Mar. 19**
**834** A259 54c multi 1.75 1.75

**France Nos. 3247-3251 Overprinted Like No. 783**

**2007, Mar. 28** **Engr.** ***Perf. 13***
**835** A1713 10c gray .25 .25
**836** A1713 60c dark blue 1.60 1.60
**837** A1713 70c yel green 1.90 1.90
**838** A1713 85c purple 2.25 2.25
**839** A1713 86c fawn 2.40 2.40
*Nos. 835-839 (5)* 8.40 8.40

Yellow-beaked Warbler — A260

**2007, Apr. 14** **Litho.** ***Perf. 13***
**840** A260 44c multi 1.50 1.50

The Mi'kmaqs on Miquelon, by Jean-Claude Roy — A261

**2007, May 26**
**841** A261 80c multi 2.75 2.75

Fog and House A262

**2007, June 9**
**842** A262 30c multi 1.00 1.00

**France Nos. 3252-3254 Overprinted Like No. 783**

**2007, June 20** **Engr.** ***Perf. 13***
**843** A1713 €1.15 blue 3.75 3.75
**844** A1713 €1.30 red violet 4.00 4.00
**845** A1713 €2.11 chocolate 6.75 6.75
*Nos. 843-845 (3)* 14.50 14.50

Entrance to the Port of St. Pierre — A263

No. 846: a, Seagull and buoy. b, Ship and lighthouses.

**2007, June 30** **Engr.** ***Perf. 13x12¼***
**846** Horiz. pair + central label 15.00 15.00
*a.-b.* A263 €2.40 Either single 6.50 6.50

Delamaire Farm — A264

**2007, Sept. 8** **Engr.** ***Perf. 13x12½***
**847** A264 €1.06 black 3.00 3.00

Carnivorous Plants — A265

No. 848: a, Sundew (Rossolis intermédiaire). b, Bladderwort (Utriculaire cornue). c, Butterwort (Grassette vulgaire). d, Pitcher plant (Sarracénie pourpre).

**Litho. & Engr.**

**2007, Sept. 29** ***Perf. 13x13¼***
**848** Horiz. strip of 4 7.00 7.00
***a.-d.*** A265 54c Any single 1.60 1.60

Deer Hunting — A266

**2007, Oct. 20** **Litho.** ***Perf. 13***
**849** A266 €1.65 multi 5.25 5.25

Miniature Sheet

Passenger Boats — A267

No. 850: a, Petit Miquelon. b, Marguerite II. c, Ile-aux-Marins. d, Mousse.

**2007, Nov. 10**
**850** A267 54c Sheet of 4, #a-d 7.00 7.00

Christmas — A268

**2007, Dec. 1** **Litho.** ***Perf. 13***
**851** A268 54c multi 1.75 1.75

René Autin (1921-60), Soldier — A269

**2008, Jan. 19** **Engr.** ***Perf. 13***
**852** A269 54c blk & henna brn 1.75 1.75

Window — A270

**2008, Feb. 23** **Litho.** ***Perf. 13***
**853** A270 €1.01 multi 3.25 3.25

Cod Pens A271

**2008, Mar. 8** **Engr.** ***Perf. 13¼***
**854** A271 €1 multi 3.25 3.25

Langlade Dune — A272

No. 855: a, Birds and butterfly. b, Bird.

**2008, Mar. 29** ***Perf. 13x12¼***
**855** A272 Horiz. pair + central label 15.00 15.00
***a.-b.*** €2.40 Either single 7.50 7.50

Black-throated Warbler — A273

**2008, May 3** **Litho.** ***Perf. 13***
**856** A273 47c multi 1.50 1.50

Local Artisan Crafts A274

**2008, May 17** **Engr.**
**857** A274 33c black & olive 1.10 1.10

**France Nos. 3383-3388 Overprinted Like No. 783**

**2008, May 28** **Engr.** ***Perf. 13***

| | | | | |
|---|---|---|---|---|
| **858** | A1713 | (65c) dark blue | 2.10 | 2.10 |
| **859** | A1713 | 72c yel green | 2.25 | 2.25 |
| **860** | A1713 | 88c fawn | 2.75 | 2.75 |
| **861** | A1713 | €1.25 blue | 4.00 | 4.00 |
| **862** | A1713 | €1.33 red violet | 4.25 | 4.25 |
| **863** | A1713 | €2.18 chocolate | 7.00 | 7.00 |
| | | *Nos. 858-863 (6)* | 22.35 | 22.35 |

Return of the Fishermen, by Michelle Foliot — A275

**2008, June 7** **Litho.** ***Perf. 13***
**864** A275 80c multi 2.50 2.50

Waves, Music and Guitar — A276

**2008, July 12**
**865** A276 55c multi 1.75 1.75

Rowboat On Shore — A277

**2008, Aug. 10** **Litho.** ***Perf. 13***
**866** A277 55c multi 1.60 1.60

Taekwondo A278

**2008, Oct. 4** **Litho. & Engr.** ***Perf. 13***
**867** A278 55c multi 1.50 1.50

Miniature Sheet

Ice Block Cutting — A279

No. 868: a, Workers pushing ice block up ramp onto sled. b, Workers pulling up ice blocks with tongs. c, Sleds awaiting ice blocks. d, Ice cutters with saws.

**2008, Oct. 22** **Litho.**
**868** A279 €1 Sheet of 4, #a-d 10.50 10.50

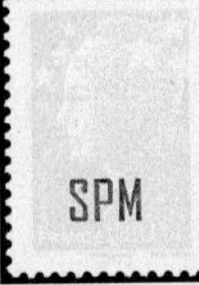


France Nos. 3453-3465 Overprinted

**2008-09** **Engr.** ***Perf. 13***

| | | | | |
|---|---|---|---|---|
| **869** | A1912 | 1c yellow | .25 | .25 |
| **870** | A1912 | 5c gray brown | .25 | .25 |
| **871** | A1912 | 10c gray | .25 | .25 |
| **872** | A1912 | (50c) green | 1.25 | 1.25 |
| **873** | A1912 | (55c) red | 1.40 | 1.40 |
| **874** | A1912 | (65c) dark blue | 1.75 | 1.75 |
| **875** | A1912 | 72c olive green | 1.90 | 1.90 |
| **876** | A1912 | 85c purple | 2.25 | 2.25 |
| **877** | A1912 | 88c fawn | 2.25 | 2.25 |
| **878** | A1912 | €1 orange | 2.75 | 2.75 |
| **879** | A1912 | €1.25 blue | 3.50 | 3.50 |
| **880** | A1912 | €1.33 red violet | 3.50 | 3.50 |
| **881** | A1912 | €2.18 chocolate | 5.75 | 5.75 |
| | | *Nos. 869-881 (13)* | 27.05 | 27.05 |

Issued: Nos. 869-873, 11/1, Nos. 874-877, 2/28/09; Nos. 878-881, 4/22/09.

Hare Hunting — A280

**2008, Nov. 8** **Litho.** ***Perf. 13***
**882** A280 €1.65 multi 4.25 4.25

Christmas A281

**2008, Nov. 26** **Litho.** ***Perf. 13***
**883** A281 55c multi 1.40 1.40

Fox Sparrow — A282

**2009, Jan. 14**
**884** A282 47c multi 1.25 1.25

Colors of Winter — A283

**2009, Feb. 14**
**885** A283 €1 multi 2.60 2.60

Henri Morazé (1903-86), Alcohol Merchant — A284

**2009, Mar. 14** **Engr.**
**886** A284 56c blk & org brown 1.40 1.40

ATR 42 Airplane — A285

**Litho. & Engr.**

**2009, Mar. 28** ***Perf. 13x13¼***

**887** A285 80c blue & black 2.25 2.25

Local Artisan Crafts A286

**2009, Apr. 8** **Engr.** ***Perf. 13***

**888** A286 33c dp bl & bl grn .90 .90

The Blue Bench, by Raphaele Goineau — A287

**2009, May 13** **Litho.** ***Perf. 13***

**889** A287 56c multi 1.60 1.60

Place Monsigneur François Maurer — A288

No. 890: a, Buildings. b, Buildings and parking lot with two lampposts.

***Perf. 13x12¼x13x13***

**2009, May 27** **Engr.**

**890** A288 Horiz. pair + central label 14.00 14.00

*a.-b.* €2.50 Either single 7.00 7.00

No. 890b is upside-down in relation to No. 890a.

Tennis A289

**2009, June 10** **Engr.** ***Perf. 12¼***

**891** A289 €1.05 multi 3.00 3.00

Pictorial Stamps of 1909, Cent. A290

**2009, June 27** **Engr.** ***Perf. 13¼***

**892** A290 €1 multi 3.00 3.00

**France No. 3471 Overprinted "SPM" Like No. 869**

***Serpentine Die Cut 6¾ Vert.***

**2009, Sept. 15** **Engr.**

**Booklet Stamp**

**Self-Adhesive**

**893** A1912 (56c) red 1.75 1.75

*a.* Booklet pane of 12 21.00

Duck Hunting — A291

**2009, Sept. 26** **Litho.** ***Perf. 13***

**894** A291 €1.50 multi 4.50 4.50

Past and Present Radio Station Buildings A292

**2009, Oct. 10** ***Perf. 13x13¼***

**895** A292 56c multi 1.75 1.75

Man at Window — A293

**2009, Oct. 24** ***Perf. 13***

**896** A293 80c multi 2.40 2.40

Miniature Sheet

Winter Scenes of Port of St. Pierre — A294

No. 897: a, Men standing on ice in harbor, boats in background. b, Bull on ice near ship. c, Pointe-aux-Canons Lighthouse. d, Fishing boats in ice.

**2009, Nov. 4** **Litho.** ***Perf. 13***

**897** A294 56c Sheet of 4, #a-d 6.75 6.75

Christmas — A295

**2009, Nov. 25**

**898** A295 56c multi 1.75 1.75

Richard Bartlett (1913-81), Member of French Resistance — A296

**2010, Jan. 16** **Engr.** ***Perf. 13***

**899** A296 56c blk & org brn 1.60 1.60

**France Nos. 3612-3616 Overprinted "SPM" Like No. 869**

**2010** **Engr.** ***Perf. 13***

**900** A1912 73c olive green 2.10 2.10

**901** A1912 90c fawn 2.50 2.50

**902** A1912 €1.30 blue 3.75 3.75

**903** A1912 €1.35 red violet 3.75 3.75

**904** A1912 €2.22 chocolate 6.00 6.00

*Nos. 900-904 (5)* 18.10 18.10

Issued: Nos. 900-902, 1/27, Nos. 903-904, 2/24.

Black and White Warbler — A297

**2010, Feb. 10** **Litho.** ***Perf. 13***

**905** A297 47c multi 1.25 1.25

Crabber and Crab Pot — A298

**2010, Mar. 13** **Litho.** ***Perf. 13***

**906** A298 €1 multi 2.75 2.75

Miquelon Cape — A299

No. 907: a, Birds in flight. b, Cape, buoy.

**2010, Apr. 10** **Engr.** ***Perf. 13x12¼***

**907** A299 Horiz. pair + central label 13.50 13.50

*a.-b.* €2.50 Either single 6.75 6.75

Helicopter Carrier Jeanne d'Arc — A300

**Litho. & Engr.**

**2010, Apr. 24** ***Perf. 13***

**908** A300 €1 multi 2.75 2.75

Children's Art — A301

No. 909: a, Lighthouse, boat and bird, by Eric Coste. b, Ship, whale and houses, by Laura Caspar.

**2010, Apr. 24** **Litho.**

**909** A301 €1 Horiz. pair, #a-b 5.50 5.50

Reims F406 — A302

**2010, May 15** **Engr.** ***Perf. 13x12½***

**910** A302 80c multi 2.00 2.00

Telegraph Office and Morse Code A303

**2010, June 19** **Litho.** ***Perf. 13x13¼***

**911** A303 56c multi 1.40 1.40

Local Artisan Crafts A304

**2010, June 26** **Engr.**

**912** A304 33c multi .85 .85

Swimming A305

**2010, July 10** ***Perf. 12¼***

**913** A305 €1.05 multi 2.75 2.75

Hunt for 1927 Oiseau Blanc Trans-atlantic Flight — A306

**Litho. & Engr.**

**2010, Sept. 1** ***Perf. 13***

**914** A306 €1.10 multi 3.00 3.00

Duck Hunting — A307

**2010, Sept. 22** **Litho.**

**915** A307 €1.65 multi 4.50 4.50

Children Sledding Past Side of Building — A308

**2010, Oct. 20**
**916** A308 58c multi 1.75 1.75

Christmas A309

**2010, Dec. 1** *Perf. 13x13¼*
**917** A309 58c multi 1.60 1.60

Miniature Sheet

Festivals and Parades — A310

No. 918: a, Departing of the Fleet Festival. b, Assumption Day (August 15) Parade. c, Holy Child (Sainte-Enfance) Festival. d, Corpus Christi (Fête-Dieu) Parade.

**2010, Nov. 6** **Litho.** *Perf. 13*

| | | | | |
|---|---|---|---|---|
| **918** | A310 | Sheet of 4 | 9.00 | 9.00 |
| *a.-b.* | | 58c Either single | 1.60 | 1.60 |
| *c.* | | €1 multi | 2.75 | 2.75 |
| *d.* | | €1.05 multi | 3.00 | 3.00 |

Cape May Warbler — A311

**2011, Jan. 15**
**919** A311 47c multi 1.25 1.25

**France Nos. 3871-3876 Overprinted "SPM" Like No. 869**

**2011** **Engr.** *Perf. 13*

| | | | | |
|---|---|---|---|---|
| **920** | A1912 | 75c olive green | 2.10 | 2.10 |
| **921** | A1912 | 87c purple | 2.50 | 2.50 |
| **922** | A1912 | 95c fawn | 2.60 | 2.60 |
| **923** | A1912 | €1.35 blue | 3.75 | 3.75 |
| **924** | A1912 | €1.40 red violet | 4.00 | 4.00 |
| **925** | A1912 | €2.30 chocolate | 6.25 | 6.25 |
| | | *Nos. 920-925 (6)* | 21.20 | 21.20 |

Issued: 75c, 95c, €2.30, 1/29. 87c, €1.35, €1.40, 2/26.

Larch Cones — A312

**2011, Feb. 12** **Litho.**
**926** A312 €1.05 multi 3.00 3.00

Henriette Bonin (1899-1985), School Teacher — A313

**2011, Mar. 12** **Engr.**
**927** A313 58c blk & org brn 1.75 1.75

Notre Dame des Marins Church, Ile Aux Marins — A314

**2011, Apr. 9** **Litho.** *Perf. 13¼x13*
**928** A314 58c multi 1.75 1.75

St. Pierre & Miquelon Literary Prize A315

**2011, Apr. 9** *Perf. 13x13¼*
**929** A315 58c multi 1.75 1.75

Miniature Sheet

A316

No. 930 — Old photographs of Ile aux Chiens (Ile aux Marins): a, Fishing boats on shore, houses close in background. b, Ile aux Chiens Festival. c, Procession of fishermen outside church. d, Fishermen preparing boats at harbor, houses in distance.

**2011, Apr. 20** *Perf. 13*
**930** A316 58c Sheet of 4, #a-d 6.75 6.75

Local Artisan Crafts A317

**2011, May 14** **Engr.** *Perf. 13¼x13*
**931** A317 33c multi .95 .95

St. Pierre & Miquelon 2011 Philatelic Exhibition — A318

**2011, June 4** **Litho.** *Perf. 13*
**932** A318 85c multi 2.50 2.50

Man and Boy Throwing Rocks at Cans — A319

**2011, June 25**
**933** A319 58c multi 1.75 1.75

Sailing A320

**2011, July 10** **Engr.** *Perf. 12¼*
**934** A320 €1.05 multi 3.00 3.00

L'Anse à Bertrand — A321

No. 935: a, White house with red trim. b, Red house with white trim.

**2011, Sept. 7** *Perf. 13x12¼*

| | | | | |
|---|---|---|---|---|
| **935** | A321 | Horiz. pair + central label | 14.00 | 14.00 |
| *a.-b.* | | €2.50 Either single | 7.00 | 7.00 |

Miniature Sheet

Rescue Boats — A322

No. 936: a, P'tit Saint-Pierre. b, Jaro II. c, Radar IV. d, Fulmar.

**2011, Sept. 28** **Litho.** *Perf. 13*
**936** A322 60c Sheet of 4, #a-d 6.75 6.75

A323

A324

A325

A326

A327

Details From "Sous le Vol du Goéland," Painting by Jean-Jacques Olivéro A328

**2011, Oct. 19** *Perf. 13x13½, 13½x13*

| | | | | |
|---|---|---|---|---|
| **937** | | Sheet of 6 | 10.50 | 10.50 |
| *a.* | A323 60c multi | | 1.75 | 1.75 |
| *b.* | A324 60c multi | | 1.75 | 1.75 |
| *c.* | A325 60c multi | | 1.75 | 1.75 |
| *d.* | A326 60c multi | | 1.75 | 1.75 |
| *e.* | A327 60c multi | | 1.75 | 1.75 |
| *f.* | A328 60c multi | | 1.75 | 1.75 |

Souvenir Sheet

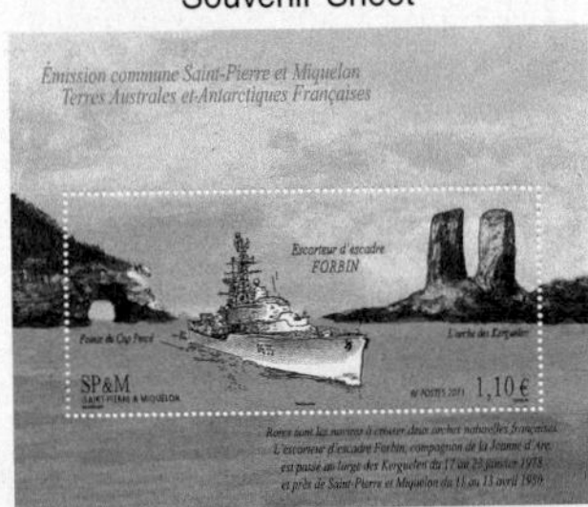


Squadron Escort Forbin — A329

**Litho. & Engr.**

**2011, Nov. 8** *Perf. 13½x13*
**938** A329 €1.10 multi 3.00 3.00

See French Southern & Antarctic Territories No. 449.

Christmas A330

**2011, Nov. 30 Litho. *Perf. 13***
**939** A330 60c multi 1.60 1.60

Birds and Birdhouse — A331

**2012, Jan. 7 Litho. *Perf. 13***
**940** A331 47c multi 1.25 1.25

### France Nos. 4050-4056 Overprinted "SPM" Like No. 869

**Methods and Perfs As Before**

**2012**

| | | | | | |
|---|---|---|---|---|---|
| **941** | A2178 | (55c) gray | | .95 | .95 |
| **942** | A2179 | (60c) red | | 1.60 | 1.60 |
| **943** | A2180 | (€1.07) dark blue | | 3.00 | 3.00 |
| **944** | A2181 | (€1.07) purple | | 3.00 | 3.00 |
| **945** | A2182 | (€1.25) fawn | | 3.25 | 3.25 |
| **946** | A2183 | (€1.95) red violet | | 5.25 | 5.25 |
| **947** | A2184 | (€3.65) chocolate | | 9.75 | 9.75 |
| | | *Nos. 941-947 (7)* | | 26.80 | 26.80 |

Issued: Nos. 941, 942, 943, 946, 1/21; others, 2/11.

Trawler Le Ravenel — A332

**2012, Feb. 4 Litho. *Perf. 13***
**948** A332 60c multi 1.60 1.60

Church, Langlade — A333

**2012, Mar. 10**
**949** A333 87c multi 2.25 2.25

Marine Life A334

No. 950: a, Leptasterias polaris. b, Urticina felina. c, Pagurus acadianus. d, Cynea capilata.

**2012, Mar. 24 *Perf. 13x13¼***
**950** Horiz. strip of 4 6.50 6.50
*a.-d.* A334 60c Any single 1.60 1.60

### France Nos. 4079-4082 Overprinted "SPM" Like No. 869

**Methods and Perfs As Before**

**2012, Apr. 14**

| | | | | |
|---|---|---|---|---|
| **951** | A2191 | (33c) green | .90 | .90 |
| **952** | A2192 | (47c) yellow green | 1.25 | 1.25 |
| **953** | A2193 | (58c) blue green | 1.60 | 1.60 |
| **954** | A2194 | (85c) dk bl green | 2.25 | 2.25 |
| | | *Nos. 951-954 (4)* | 6.00 | 6.00 |

A335

A336

A337

A338

A339

Details From "Le Travail des Graves," by Gaston Roullet A340

***Perf. 13¼x13, 13x13¼ (horiz. stamps)***

**2012, May 16 Photo.**

| | | | |
|---|---|---|---|
| **955** | Sheet of 6 | 9.00 | 9.00 |
| *a.* | A335 60c multi | 1.50 | 1.50 |
| *b.* | A336 60c multi | 1.50 | 1.50 |
| *c.* | A337 60c multi | 1.50 | 1.50 |
| *d.* | A338 60c multi | 1.50 | 1.50 |
| *e.* | A339 60c multi | 1.50 | 1.50 |
| *f.* | A340 60c multi | 1.50 | 1.50 |

Archipélitude Museum, 25th Anniv. — A341

**Litho. & Engr.**

**2012, June 16 *Perf. 13x13¼***
**956** A341 60c multi 1.50 1.50

André Paturel (1942-87), Designer of Local St. Pierre & Miquelon Flag — A342

**2012, July 16 Engr. *Perf. 13***
**957** A342 33c org brn & blk .85 .85

2012 Summer Olympics, London A343

**2012, July 28 *Perf. 12¼***
**958** A343 €1.07 multi 2.75 2.75

Children's Art, Lighthouse, Swans and Puffins — A344

**Litho. & Engr.**

**2012, Sept. 15 *Perf. 13x13¼***
**959** A344 €1.15 multi 3.00 3.00

Child at Play — A345

**2012, Sept. 29 Litho. *Perf. 13***
**960** A345 60c multi 1.60 1.60

Paintings of Boats — A346

No. 961: a, Le Béothuk, by Dirk Verdoorn. b, Esprit du Barachois, by François Bellec.

**2012, Oct. 13**
**961** A346 60c Horiz. pair, #a-b 3.25 3.25

Chapeau de Miquelon — A347

No. 962: a, Seals on rocks. b, Chapeau de Miquelon and seal in water.

**2012, Oct. 27 Engr. *Perf. 13x12¼***
**962** A347 Horiz. pair + central label 13.00 13.00
*a.-b.* €2.50 Either single 6.50 6.50

Christmas — A348

**2012, Dec. 1 Litho. *Perf. 13***
**963** A348 60c multi 1.60 1.60

Blue Jay — A349

**2013, Jan. 12**
**964** A349 47c multi 1.25 1.25

Rock Formation — A350

**2013, Jan. 26**
**965** A350 90c multi 2.50 2.50

Bulot, the Carnival King A351

**2013, Feb. 16 Engr. *Perf. 13¼***
**966** A351 €1.13 multi 3.00 3.00

Maison Chartier A352

**2013, Feb. 27 Litho. *Perf. 13x13¼***
**967** A352 63c multi 1.75 1.75

**Miniature Sheet**

Fishing — A353

No. 968: a, Workers processing cod on table. b, Fishermen in boats. c, Workers and stack of dried cod. d, Fishermen in water pulling in net.

**2013, Mar. 13 *Perf. 13***
**968** A353 63c Sheet of 4, #a-d 6.50 6.50

Trawler "Le Finlande" — A354

**2013, Mar. 27 Engr. *Perf. 13x13¼***
**969** A354 €1.30 multi 3.50 3.50

Ship's Rigging A355

**2013, Apr. 24 Litho. & Engr.**
**970** A355 €1.25 multi 3.25 3.25

Rugby A356

**2013, May 15 Engr. *Perf. 12x12¼***
**971** A356 €1.13 multi 3.00 3.00

Miniature Sheet

Church of Miquelon Frescoes, by Yvette Detcheverry — A357

No. 972: a, Le sacrifice d'Abraham (The Sacrifice of Abraham). b, Le jugement de Salomon (The Judgment of Solomon). c, Présenation des tables de la loi (Moses Receiving the Law). d, Moise sur le mont Sinai (Moses on Mount Sinai). e, La nativité (Nativity). f, Le baptême du Christ (Baptism of Christ). g, La peche miraculeuse (The Miraculous Catch).

**2013, June 1 Photo. *Perf. 13¼x13***
**972** A357 Sheet of 7 12.50 12.50
*a.-g.* 63c Any single 1.75 1.75

No. 972 has rows of rouletting between stamps.

Brother Sénier (1885-1978) A358

**2013, June 15 Engr. *Perf. 13***
**973** A358 (33c) org brn & blk .90 .90

Boys Playing Marbles — A359

**2013, June 29 Litho. *Perf. 13***
**974** A359 63c multi 1.75 1.75

Miniature Sheet

Fire Trucks — A360

No. 975: a, 1961 Ford F600 (Le plateau). b, 2003 Freightliner FL80 4X4 (Le premier secours). c, 1992 Ford F350 4X4 (La garde-robe). d, 1972 Ford F600 (Le camion dévidoir).

**2013, July 13 Litho. *Perf. 13***
**975** A360 63c Sheet of 4, #a-d 6.75 6.75

Old and New Hospital Buildings A361

**2013, Sept. 21 Litho. *Perf. 13x13¼***
**976** A361 63c multi 1.75 1.75

France Nos. 4411-4421 Overprinted

**2013-14 Engr. *Perf. 13***

| | | | | |
|---|---|---|---|---|
| **977** | A2320 | 1c yellow | .25 | .25 |
| **978** | A2320 | 5c dk brown | .25 | .25 |
| **979** | A2320 | 10c brown | .30 | .30 |
| **980** | A2321 | (56c) dk gray | 1.50 | 1.50 |
| **981** | A2322 | (63c) red | 1.75 | 1.75 |
| **982** | A2320 | €1 orange | 2.75 | 2.75 |
| **983** | A2323 | (€1.13) blue | 3.00 | 3.00 |
| **984** | A2324 | (€1.13) purple | 3.00 | 3.00 |
| **985** | A2322 | (€1.30) fawn | 3.50 | 3.50 |
| **986** | A2322 | (€2.15) red violet | 6.00 | 6.00 |
| **987** | A2322 | (€3.90) chocolate | 11.00 | 11.00 |
| | | *Nos. 977-987 (11)* | 33.30 | 33.30 |

Issued: Nos. 977, 983-985, 10/26; Nos. 978-982, 10/5; Nos. 986-987, 3/15/14.

Doyen Lions Club, 60th Anniv. A362

**Litho. & Engr.**
**2013, Oct. 19 *Perf. 13x13¼***
**988** A362 (47c) multi 1.25 1.25

Anse à Ravenel — A363

No. 989: a, Horse-drawn carts on beach, houses. b, Shoreline and birds.

**2013, Nov. 8 Engr. *Perf. 13x12¼***
**989** A363 Horiz. pair + central label 13.50 13.50
*a.-b.* €2.50 Either single 6.75 6.75

Christmas — A364

**2013, Dec. 7 Litho. *Perf. 13***
**990** A364 63c multi 1.75 1.75

Treaty of Utrecht, 300th Anniv. A365

**2013, Dec. 18 Engr. *Perf. 12¾***
**991** A365 90c multi 2.50 2.50

Values are for stamps with surrounding selvage.

Bombycilla Garrulus — A366

**2014, Jan. 16 Litho. *Perf. 13***
**992** A366 47c multi 1.25 1.25

Girl Blowing Bubbles — A367

**2014, Feb. 1 Litho. *Perf. 13***
**993** A367 93c black 2.50 2.50

Trawler Shamrock III — A368

**2014, Feb. 16 Engr. *Perf. 13***
**994** A368 €1.16 multi 3.25 3.25

Albert Briand (1909-66), Politician — A369

**2014, Mar. 29 Engr. *Perf. 13***
**995** A369 33c org brn & blk .90 .90

Ship's Rigging A370

**Litho. & Engr.**
**2014, Feb. 26 *Perf. 13x13¼***
**996** A370 €1.25 multi 3.50 3.50

Miniature Sheet

Working Dogs — A371

No. 997: a, Two dogs pulling sled carrying sticks. b, Two children with dog pulling four-wheeled wagon. c, One dog pulling sled carrying sticks. d, Dog pulling two-wheeled cart carrying tree.

**2014, Apr. 19 Litho. *Perf. 13***
**997** A371 66c Sheet of 4, #a-d 7.50 7.50

Lebailly Forge — A372

**2014, May 3 Engr. *Perf. 13¼***
**998** A372 66c multi 1.90 1.90

Les Voiles Blanches — A373

No. 999: a, 60c, House on Les Voiles Blanches (38x40mm). b, €1.40, Les Voiles Blanches, painting by Jean-Clause Girardin (62x40mm).

**2014, May 24 Photo. *Perf. 13***
**999** A373 Horiz. pair, #a-b 5.50 5.50

Old and New Photographs of Court House — A374

**2014, June 21 Litho. *Perf. 13x13¼***
**1000** A374 €1.35 multi 3.75 3.75

Miniature Sheet

Old Automobiles — A375

No. 1001: a, Three people in Ford Model T. b, Eugene Folquet standing next to automobile. c, Family of four in automobiles. d, Red Ford Model A.

**2014, July 5 Litho. *Perf. 13***
**1001** A375 66c Sheet of 4, #a-d 7.25 7.25

Stamp Exhibitions — A376

No. 1002: a, 33c, Emblems of St. Pierre & Miquelon International Stamp Exhibition and Inter-American Federation of Philately (38x40mm). b, 66c, Emblems of Thailand 2013 World Stamp Exhibition and International Philatelic Federation, surcharged stamps of St. Pierre & Miquelon (62x40mm).

**2014, Sept. 27 Photo. *Perf. 13***
**1002** A376 Horiz. pair, #a-b 2.50 2.50

Leatherback Turtle — A377

**Litho. & Engr.**

**2014, Oct. 18 *Perf. 13***
**1003** A377 69c multi 1.75 1.75

Savoyard Pond — A378

No. 1004: a, Runner, man flying kite. b, Fisherman, windsurfers on pond, rider on horse.

**2014, Nov. 8 Engr. *Perf. 13x12¼***
**1004** Horiz. pair + central label 12.50 12.50
***a.-b.*** A378 €2.50 Either single 6.25 6.25

Departure of the Jeannette, Cent. — A379

**Litho. & Engr.**

**2014, Nov. 15 *Perf. 13***
**1005** A379 €1 multi 2.50 2.50

World War I, cent.

Christmas — A380

**2014, Nov. 22 Litho. *Perf. 13***
**1006** A380 66c multi 1.75 1.75

Visit of French President François Hollande to St. Pierre & Miquelon — A381

**2014, Dec. 27 Litho. *Perf. 13***
**1007** A381 76c multi 1.90 1.90

American Redstart — A382

**2015, Jan. 17 Engr. *Perf. 13***
**1008** A382 38c multi .90 .90

Painting of Blueberry Fields by Claude L'Espagnol — A383

**2015, Feb. 6 Engr. *Perf. 13***
**1009** A383 76c multi 1.75 1.75

Francis Leroux (1908-82), Tourist Bureau President — A384

**2015, Mar. 28 Engr. *Perf. 13***
**1010** A384 38c blk & org brn .85 .85

Fishing Trawler Victor Pleven — A385

**2015, Mar. 28 Engr. *Perf. 13***
**1011** A385 €1.05 dark blue & grn 2.40 2.40

Miniature Sheet

Animals at Work — A386

No. 1012: a, Map of St. Pierre & Miquelon, horse-drawn ice sled. b, Line of horse-drawn ice sleds. c, Horse-drawn ice sleds on ice with ice cutters. d, Ox-drawn cart.

**2015, Apr. 18 Litho. *Perf. 13***
**1012** A386 76c Sheet of 4, #a-d 7.00 7.00

Renovation of Theater to Renaissance Fire Station — A387

**2015, Apr. 28 Litho. *Perf. 13x13¼***
**1013** A387 €1.50 multi 3.50 3.50

Miniature Sheet

Automobiles of the 1950s — A388

No. 1014: a, 1958 Studebaker President. b, 1955 Mercury Custom. c, 1957 Citroen ID 19 Luxe. d, 1955 Renault 4 CV.

**2015, June 6 Litho. *Perf. 13***
**1014** A388 76c Sheet of 4, #a-d 6.75 6.75

Souvenir Sheet

First Voyage of Reproduction of the Hermione — A389

No. 1015: a, €1.05, Marquis de Lafayette (1757-1834). b, €1.38, Lafayette's ship, Hermione, horiz.

**Engr. (#1015a), Litho.**

**2015, July 22 *Perf. 13***
**1015** A389 Sheet of 2, #a-b 5.50 5.50

The Laundrette of the Mountain A390

**2015, Sept. 9 Engr. *Perf. 13¼***
**1016** A390 76c multi 1.75 1.75

Pointe aux Canons Lighthouse — A391

**Litho. & Engr.**

**2015, Sept. 23 *Perf. 13***
**1017** A391 76c multi 1.75 1.75

Lithobates Clamitans and Nuphar Variegata — A392

**2015, Oct. 7 Litho. & Engr. *Perf. 13***
**1018** A392 76c multi 1.75 1.75

Miniature Sheet

Gendarmerie — A393

No. 1019 — Various emblems, map of St. Pierre & Miquelon and: a, 38c, Gendarme. b, 76c, Snowplow. c, €1.05, Boat. d, €1.38, Two officers.

**Litho. & Embossed**

**2015, Nov. 5 *Perf. 13***
**1019** A393 Sheet of 4, #a-d 7.75 7.75

Admiral Dominque Gauchet (1857-1931) — A394

**2015, Nov. 11 Engr. *Perf. 13x13¼***
**1020** A394 €1 blk & dk bl 2.10 2.10

Christmas — A395

**2015, Nov. 28 Litho. *Perf. 13***
**1021** A395 80c multi 1.75 1.75

Carpodacus Purpureus — A396

**2016, Jan. 29 Litho. *Perf. 13***
**1022** A396 40c multi .90 .90

Overturned Fishing Boat and Other Fishing Boat Equipment A397

**2016, Feb. 19 Litho. *Perf. 13x13¼***
**1023** A397 80c multi 1.75 1.75

Fishing Trawler La Grande Hermine — A398

**2016, Mar. 18 Engr. *Perf. 13x13¼***
**1024** A398 €1.10 multi 2.50 2.50

Map of St. Pierre & Miquelon — A399

**2016, Mar. 21 Litho. *Perf. 13***
**Background Color**

| | | | | |
|---|---|---|---|---|
| **1025** A399 | 1c lt blue | .25 | .25 |
| **1026** A399 | 2c yellow | .25 | .25 |
| **1027** A399 | 3c lt green | .25 | .25 |
| **1028** A399 | 5c gray | .25 | .25 |
| **1029** A399 | 10c lilac | .25 | .25 |
| *a.* | Dated "2022," inscribed "Philaposte" | .30 | .30 |
| **1030** A399 | (40c) pink | .90 | .90 |
| | *Nos. 1025-1030 (6)* | 2.15 | 2.15 |

Issued: No. 1029a, 3/19/22. No. 1030 is inscribed "20g." See No. 1041.

Notre Dame des Ardilliers Church, Miquelon A400

**2016, Apr. 23 Engr. *Perf. 13¼***
**1031** A400 €1.40 multi 3.25 3.25

Renovated Prefecture Building, St. Pierre A401

**2016, May 14 Litho. *Perf. 13x13¼***
**1032** A401 70c multi 1.60 1.60

Miniature Sheet

French National Gendarmerie in St. Pierre & Miquelon — A402

No. 1033 — Map of St. Pierre and Miquelon and gendarmes: a, 40c, Dusting for fingerprints. b, 80c, Standing near airplane. c, €1.10, With dog. d, €1.40, Wearing tactical armor.

**Litho. & Embossed**
**2016, May 28 *Perf. 13¼x13***
**1033** A402 Sheet of 4, #a-d 8.25 8.25

Dock, Rope and Pulley — A403

**Litho. & Engr.**
**2016, June 11 *Perf. 13¼x13***
**1034** A403 80c multi 1.90 1.90

Souvenir Sheet

Resettlement of St. Pierre and Miquelon Under French Rule, 200th Anniv. — A404

No. 1035: a, €1.10, Frigate La Revanche (28x37mm). b, €1.40, People watching ships, 1816 (56x37mm).

**Litho. & Engr.**
**2016, June 22 *Perf. 13x13¼***
**1035** A404 Sheet of 2, #a-b 5.75 5.75

Miniature Sheet

Ambulances — A405

No. 1036: a, Horse-drawn ambulance, 1934. b, Ambulance sleigh, 1948. c, Dodge WK60 ambulance, 1966. d, Chevrolet Model 3100 ambulance, 1949.

**2016, July 8 Litho. *Perf. 13***
**1036** A405 80c Sheet of 4, #a-d 7.25 7.25

Sister Pierre Fontaine (1923-2012) — A406

**2016, Sept. 9 Engr. *Perf. 13***
**1037** A406 (40c) blk & brn org .90 .90

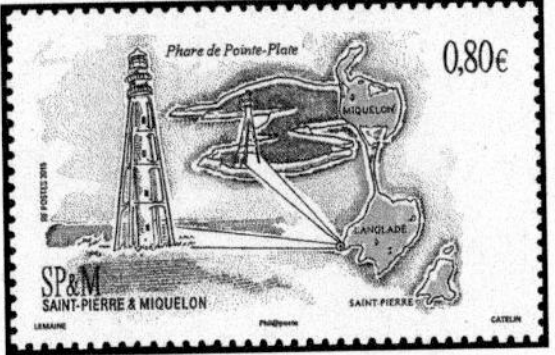

Ponte Plate Lighthouse — A407

**2016, Oct. 7 Engr. *Perf. 13x13¼***
**1038** A407 80c multi 1.75 1.75

Battle of the Somme, Cent. — A408

**2016, Nov. 11 Engr. *Perf. 13x12½***
**1039** A408 €1.10 multi 2.50 2.50

Christmas — A409

**2016, Nov. 18 Litho. *Perf. 13***
**1040** A409 85c multi 1.90 1.90

**Map Type of 2016**
**2017, Jan. 1 Litho. *Perf. 13***
**Background Color**

| | | | | |
|---|---|---|---|---|
| **1041** A399 | (43c) dark blue | .90 | .90 |
| *a.* | Dated "2022," inscribed "Philaposte" | .95 | .95 |

Issued: No. 1041a, 3/19/22. No. 1041 is inscribed "20g."

Geothlypis Trichas — A410

**2017, Jan. 25 Litho. *Perf. 13***
**1042** A410 75c multi 1.60 1.60

A411

No. 1043: a, €1.17, House of Nature and the Environment (52x31mm). b, €1.49, Dandelion seed head and map of St. Pierre & Miquelon (31x31mm).

**2017, Jan. 31 Photo. *Perf. 13***
**1043** A411 Horiz. pair, #a-b 5.75 5.75

International Year of Sustainable Tourism for Development (No. 1043b).

Fishing Trawler Le Dauphin — A412

**2017, Mar. 15 Engr. *Perf. 13x12½***
**1044** A412 €1.20 multi 2.60 2.60

Miniature Sheet

Telephone Communications — A413

No. 1045: a, 43c, Dial telephone. b, 85c, Central switchboard and operators. c, €1.20, Radio Maritime operator. d, €1.40, Operator of modern phone system.

**2017, Apr. 19 Litho. *Perf. 13***
**1045** A413 Sheet of 4, #a-d 8.50 8.50

Cod Filleting A414

**2017, May 22 Litho. *Perf. 13x13¼***
**1046** A414 85c multi 1.90 1.90

Ropes and Bollards A415

**Litho. & Engr.**
**2017, June 26 *Perf. 13x13¼***
**1047** A415 85c multi 2.00 2.00

Miniature Sheet

Motorcycles — A416

No. 1048: a, 43c, George Blin, his daughter and Peugeot P55C motorcycle. b, 85c, Désiré Briand on Peugeot Model 125 Type 55 motorcycle. c, €1.20, Charles Guillaume on Peugeot 150cc motorcycle. d, €1.40, Son of François Detcheverry and Zündapp Combinette 50 moped.

**2017, July 5 Litho. *Perf. 13***
**1048** A416 Sheet of 4, #a-d 9.25 9.25

Rowers at Ternua Basque Festival — A417

**2017, Aug. 4 Engr. *Perf. 13***
**1049** A417 €1.40 multi 3.50 3.50

Father Jean-Marie-Roger Tillard (1927-2000), Theologian — A418

**2017, Sept. 6 Engr. *Perf. 13***
**1050** A418 (43c) blk & chestnut 1.00 1.00

Cap Blanc Lighthouse A419

**2017, Oct. 18 Engr. *Perf. 13***
**1051** A419 €1.20 multi 2.75 2.75

Souvenir Sheet

Yachting — A420

No. 1052: a, €1, André Paturel Sailing Center, 30th anniv. b, €2, Eric Tabarly (1931-98), naval officer and yachtsman, vert.

**Litho. (€1), Litho. & Engr (€2)**
**2017, Nov. 9 *Perf. 13***
**1052** A420 Sheet of 2, #a-b 7.25 7.25

Explosion of the Mont Blanc in Halifax Harbor, Cent. — A421

**Litho. & Engr.**
**2017, Nov. 11 *Perf. 13***
**1053** A421 €1.50 multi 3.75 3.75

Christmas A422

**2017, Nov. 15 Litho. *Perf. 13¼x13***
**1054** A422 85c multi 2.10 2.10

Souvenir Sheet

St. Pierre Cathedral, St. Pierre — A423

**2017, Dec. 1 Litho. *Perf. 13¼x13***
**1055** A423 €2 multi 4.75 4.75

Dendroica Palmarum — A424

**2018, Jan. 17 Litho. *Perf. 13***
**1056** A424 80c multi 2.00 2.00

Yellow-bellied Sapsucker A425

**2018, Feb. 14 Litho. *Perf. 13***
**1057** A425 95c multi 2.40 2.40

Fishing Vessel Le Névé — A426

**2018, Mar. 14 Engr. *Perf. 13x12½***
**1058** A426 95c multi 2.40 2.40

Souvenir Sheet

French Patrol Ship "Fulmar," 20th Anniv. — A427

**2018, Apr. 6 Litho. *Perf. 13***
**1059** A427 €2 multi 4.75 4.75

Old St. Vincent Workhouse, 150th Anniv. — A428

**2018, Apr. 14 Engr. *Perf. 13¼x13***
**1060** A428 €1.40 blk & dp ultra 3.50 3.50

Cod Fishermen A429

**2018, May 19 Litho. *Perf. 13¼x13***
**1061** A429 46c multi 1.10 1.10

Ship Bel Espoir A430

**Litho. & Engr.**
**2018, June 13 *Perf. 13x13¼***
**1062** A430 €1.30 multi 3.00 3.00

Souvenir Sheet

Jules Verne (1828-1905), Writer — A431

**2018, July 7 Litho. & Engr. *Perf. 13***
**1063** A431 €2 multi 4.75 4.75

Miniature Sheet

Scooters — A432

No. 1064: a, 46c, Man looking at Cezeta scooter. b, 95c, Man and woman on Lambretta scooter. c, €1.30, Two men and Lambretta scooter. d, €1.40, Man and woman on Lambretta scooter, diff.

**2018, Aug. 7 Litho. *Perf. 13***
**1064** A432 Sheet of 4, #a-d 9.50 9.50

Pierre Hélène (1907-93), and Diving Helmet — A433

**2018, Sept. 12 Engr. *Perf. 13***
**1065** A433 (95c) blk & lt brn 2.25 2.25

Île aux Marins Lighthouse A434

**Litho. & Engr.**
**2018, Oct. 13 *Perf. 13x13¼***
**1066** A434 95c multi 2.25 2.25

Marasmius Oreades — A435

**2018, Nov. 8 Engr. *Perf. 13x13¼***
**1067** A435 95c multi 2.25 2.25

Christmas — A436

**2018, Nov. 8 Litho. *Perf. 13¼x13***
**1068** A436 95c multi 2.25 2.25

End of World War I, Cent. — A437

**Litho. & Engr.**
**2018, Nov. 11 *Perf. 13x12¾***
**1069** A437 €1.50 multi 3.50 3.50

Bay-breasted Warbler — A438

**2019, Jan. 17 Litho.** ***Perf. 13x12¾***
**1070** A438 €1.05 multi 2.40 2.40

Wreck of a Schooner on Langlade — A439

**2019, Feb. 13 Litho.** ***Perf. 13x12¾***
**1071** A439 50c multi 1.25 1.25

**France No. 5478 Overprinted Like No. 977**

**2019, Feb. 20 Engr.** ***Perf. 13***
**1072** A2829 (€1.50) red — —

No. 1072 was originally put on sale in 2018 only at a stamp show in Paris.

Wrecked Ship "Le Victoria" — A440

**2019, Mar. 18 Engr.** ***Perf. 13¼***
**1073** A440 €1.40 multi 3.25 3.25

Arche Museum A441

**2019, Apr. 17 Engr.** ***Perf. 13¼***
**1074** A441 €1.40 multi 3.25 3.25

Docked Dories A442

**2019, May 15 Litho.** ***Perf. 13x13¼***
**1075** A442 90c multi 2.10 2.10

Schooner "Le Rara-Avis" A443

**Litho. & Engr.**

**2019, June 12** ***Perf. 13x13¼***
**1076** A443 €1.05 multi 2.40 2.40

Souvenir Sheet

François-René de Chateaubriand (1768-1848), Writer — A444

**Litho. & Engr.**

**2019, July 10** ***Perf. 13***
**1077** A444 €2 multi 4.50 4.50

Georges Poulet (1914-2008), Deputy Mayor — A445

**2019, Sept. 15 Engr.** ***Perf. 13***
**1078** A445 (€1.05) blk & lt brn 2.40 2.40

Miniature Sheet

Taxicabs — A446

No. 1079: a, Chevrolet Biscayne. b, Volkswagen Type 2. c, Pontiac Le Mans. d, Dodge Aries.

**2019, Sept. 25 Litho.** ***Perf. 13***
**1079** A446 €1.05 Sheet of 4, #a-d 9.25 9.25

Souvenir Sheet

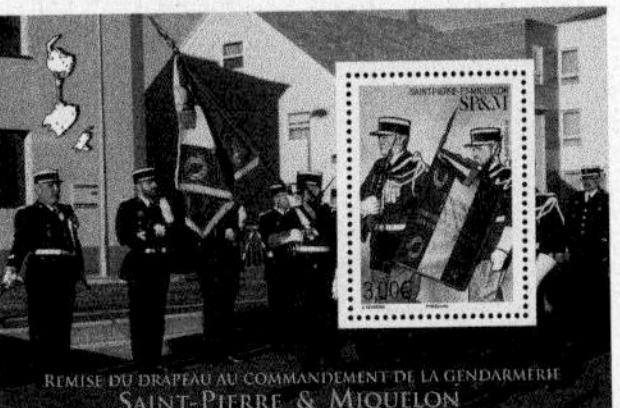
Gendarmerie Command Flag Ceremony — A447

**2019, Oct. 2 Litho.** ***Perf. 13¼x13***
**1080** A447 €3 multi 6.75 6.75

Galantry Lighthouse A448

**Litho. & Engr.**

**2019, Oct. 13** ***Perf. 13x13¼***
**1081** A448 €1.40 multi 3.25 3.25

Boletus Chippewaensis — A449

**Litho. & Engr.**

**2019, Nov. 7** ***Perf. 13***
**1082** A449 €1.50 multi 3.50 3.50

Shoemaker — A450

**2019, Nov. 12 Engr.** ***Perf. 13***
**1083** A450 (€1.05) dk red brn 2.40 2.40

Souvenir Sheet

Cargo Vessel Hawaiki Nui — A451

**Litho. & Engr.**

**2019, Nov. 12** ***Perf. 13¼x13***
**1084** A451 €4 multi 9.00 9.00

See French Polynesia No. 1240.

Christmas A452

**2019, Nov. 12 Litho.** ***Perf. 13x13¼***
**1085** A452 €1.05 multi 2.40 2.40

**France No. 5477 Overprinted Like No. 977**

**2019, Nov. 7 Engr.** ***Perf. 13***
**1086** A2828 (80c) emerald 2.75 2.75

Shore Bird — A453

**2020, Jan. 20 Litho.** ***Perf. 13***
**1087** A453 €1.16 multi 2.60 2.60

Street Scene After Snow Storm — A454

**2020, Feb. 17 Litho.** ***Perf. 13***
**1088** A454 55c multi 1.25 1.25

Fishing Boat Le Viking — A455

**2020, Mar. 16 Engr.** ***Perf. 13x13¼***
**1089** A455 €1.45 deep green 3.25 3.25

Miniature Sheet

Photographs of Everyday Life — A456

No. 1090 — Inscriptions: a, Boulevard de la pointe. b, Un jeu d'enfant. La pêche aux Capelans. c, Voiture de luxe. d, Pélerinage à Notre-Dame des Retrouvés.

**2020, Apr. 11 Litho.** ***Perf. 13***
**1090** A456 €1.16 Sheet of 4, #a-d 10.50 10.50

Miniature Sheet

American Automobiles Manufactured From 1970-80 — A457

No. 1091: a, Chevrolet Corvette. b, Ford Mustang. c, Pontiac Firebird. d, Chevrolet Camaro.

**2020, July 29 Litho.** ***Perf. 13***
**1091** A457 €1.16 Sheet of 4, #a-d 11.00 11.00

A458

No. 1092: a, €1.16, L'Anse à Bertrand (31x31mm). b, €1.45, La Maison Girardin (52x31mm).

**2020, Aug. 1 Engr.** ***Perf. 13***
**1092** A458 Horiz. pair, #a-b 6.25 6.25

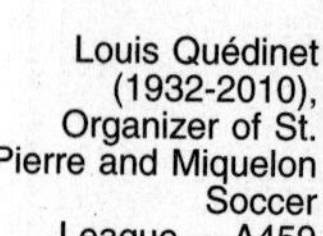

Louis Quédinet (1932-2010), Organizer of St. Pierre and Miquelon Soccer League — A459

**2020, Sept. 16** **Engr.** ***Perf. 13***
**1093** A459 €1.16 blk & red brn 2.75 2.75

**France No. 5571 Overprinted Like No. 977**

**2020, Nov. 7** **Engr.** ***Perf. 13***
**1094** A2888 (€2) redsh vio 5.00 5.00

Caulker — A460

**2020, Nov. 7** **Engr.** ***Perf. 13x12¾***
**1095** A460 €1.45 red brown 3.50 3.50

Ship Saint-Yves A461

**2020, Nov. 7** **Litho.** ***Perf. 13x13¼***
**1096** A461 €1.45 multi 3.50 3.50

Coprinus Mushrooms — A462

**2020, Nov. 7** **Litho.** ***Perf. 13***
**1097** A462 €1.50 multi 3.75 3.75

Souvenir Sheet

Capstans — A463

No. 1098: a, Boat and capstan. b, Boat and capstan, vert.

**2020, Nov. 21** **Litho.** ***Perf. 13***
**1098** A463 €2 Sheet of 2, #a-b 9.75 9.75

Christmas A464

**2020, Nov. 21** **Litho.** ***Perf. 13x13¼***
**1099** A464 €1.28 multi 3.25 3.25

Calidris Maritima — A465

**2021, Jan. 12** **Litho.** ***Perf. 13***
**1100** A465 60c multi 1.50 1.50

Russula Peckii — A466

**2021, Jan. 12** **Litho.** ***Perf. 13***
**1101** A466 €1.28 multi 3.25 3.25

Miniature Sheet

Snow Removal Equipment — A467

No. 1102: a, Plow with tank treads, houses in background. b, Bulldozer plow with chains on tires. c, Plow behind snowbank, three onlookers. d, Plow with snowblower, dump truck.

**2021, Jan. 20** **Litho.** ***Perf. 13***
**1102** A467 €1.28 Sheet of 4, #a-d 12.50 12.50

Colonial Schooner A468

**2021, Feb. 6** **Litho.** ***Perf. 13x13¼***
**1103** A468 €1 multi 2.40 2.40

Fishing Vessel Béarn — A469

**2021, Mar. 6** **Engr.** ***Perf. 13x13¼***
**1104** A469 €1.55 bl blk & dp ultra 3.75 3.75

Restoration of the Morel House, Ile aux Marins — A470

No. 1106: a, €1.28, Enclosed doorway (31x31mm). b, €1.55, House, other buildings and boat (53x31mm).

**2021, Apr. 10** **Engr.** ***Perf. 13***
**1106** A470 Horiz. pair, #a-b 7.00 7.00

Miniature Sheet

Enclosed Doorways — A471

No. 1107: a, White house with red trim. b, Blue house with red and white trim. c, White house with blue trim. d, Yellow house with red, blue and white trim.

**2021, May 5** **Litho.** ***Perf. 13***
**1107** A471 €1.28 Sheet of 4, #a-d 12.50 12.50

Tourist Attractions of St. Pierre & Miquelon — A472

**2021, Aug. 11** **Engr.** ***Perf. 13***
**1108** A472 €5 blue 12.00 12.00

Augusta Lehuenen (1922-2018), Last Female Volunteer of the Free French Naval Forces — A473

**2021, Sept. 8** **Engr.** ***Perf. 13***
**1109** A473 €1.28 blk & red brn 3.00 3.00

Sail Maker — A474

**2021, Oct. 6** **Engr.** ***Perf. 13***
**1110** A474 €2 brown 4.75 4.75

**France No. 5476 Overprinted Like No. 977**

**2021, Nov. 8** **Engr.** ***Perf. 13***
**1111** A2827 (€1.20) dark gray 2.75 2.75

Ferries — A475

No. 1112: a, Le Suroît. b, Le Nordet.

**2021, Nov. 8** **Litho.** ***Perf. 13***
**1112** A475 €1.10 Horiz. pair, #a-b 5.00 5.00

A476

A477

Christmas A478

**2021, Nov. 8** **Litho.** ***Perf. 13x13¼***
**1113** Horiz. strip of 3 9.75 9.75
*a.* A476 €1.43 multi 3.25 3.25
*b.* A477 €1.43 multi 3.25 3.25
*c.* A478 €1.43 multi 3.25 3.25

Actitis Macularius — A479

**2022, Jan. 15** **Litho.** ***Perf. 13***
**1114** A479 €1.43 multi 3.25 3.25

Fishing Trawler Savoyard — A480

**2022, Feb. 5** **Engr.** ***Perf. 13x13¼***
**1115** A480 €1.70 multi 3.75 3.75

Workmen Repairing Spire of Our Lady of Ardilliers Catholic Church, Miquelon A481

**2022, Feb. 19** **Litho.** ***Perf. 13***
**1116** A481 65c multi 1.50 1.50

Le Mélanie A482

**2022, Mar. 5** **Litho.** ***Perf. 13x13¼***
**1117** A482 €1.10 multi 2.50 2.50

## SEMI-POSTAL STAMPS

Regular Issue of 1909-17 Surcharged in Red

**1915-17 Unwmk. *Perf. 14x13½***

| | | | | |
|---|---|---|---|---|
| **B1** | A17 | 10c + 5c car rose & red | 3.00 | *3.75* |
| **B2** | A17 | 15c + 5c dl vio & rose ('17) | 3.00 | *3.75* |

### Curie Issue
Common Design Type

**1938, Oct. 24 Engr. *Perf. 13***

| | | | | |
|---|---|---|---|---|
| **B3** | CD80 | 1.75fr + 50c brt ultra | 21.00 | *22.50* |

### French Revolution Issue
Common Design Type

**1939, July 5 Photo.**
**Name and Value Typo. in Black**

| | | | | |
|---|---|---|---|---|
| **B4** | CD83 | 45c + 25c green | 13.50 | *14.50* |
| **B5** | CD83 | 70c + 30c brown | 13.50 | *14.50* |
| **B6** | CD83 | 90c + 35c red org | 13.50 | *14.50* |
| **B7** | CD83 | 1.25fr + 1fr rose pink | 13.50 | *14.50* |
| **B8** | CD83 | 2.25fr + 2fr blue | 13.50 | *14.50* |
| | | *Nos. B4-B8 (5)* | 67.50 | 72.50 |

### Common Design Type and

Sailor of Landing Force — SP1

Dispatch Boat "Ville d'Ys" SP2

**1941 Photo. *Perf. 13½***

| | | | |
|---|---|---|---|
| **B8A** | SP1 | 1fr + 1fr red | 4.50 |
| **B8B** | CD86 | 1.50fr + 3fr maroon | 4.50 |
| **B8C** | SP2 | 2.50fr + 1fr blue | 4.50 |
| | | *Nos. B8A-B8C (3)* | 13.50 |

Nos. B8A-B8C were issued by the Vichy government, and were not placed on sale in the colony.

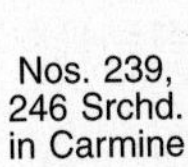

Nos. 239, 246 Srchd. in Carmine

**1942 Unwmk. *Perf. 13½x13***

| | | | | |
|---|---|---|---|---|
| **B9** | A25 | 1fr + 50c | 75.00 | *75.00* |
| **B10** | A26 | 2.50fr + 1fr | 75.00 | *75.00* |

Petain Type of 1941 Srchd. in Black or Red

**1944 Engr. *Perf. 12½x12***

| | | |
|---|---|---|
| **B11** | 50c + 1.50fr on 2.50fr dp bl (R) | 1.60 |
| **B12** | + 2.50fr on 1fr vio | 1.60 |

Colonial Development Fund.

Nos. B11-B12 were issued by the Vichy government in France, but were not placed on sale in St. Pierre & Miquelon.

**Catalogue values for unused stamps in this section, from this point to the end of the section, are for Never Hinged items.**

### Red Cross Issue
Common Design Type

**1944 *Perf. 14½x14***

| | | | | |
|---|---|---|---|---|
| **B13** | CD90 | 5fr + 20fr dp ultra | 2.60 | 2.60 |

Surtax for the French Red Cross and national relief.

### Tropical Medicine Issue
Common Design Type

**1950, May 15 Engr. *Perf. 13***

| | | | | |
|---|---|---|---|---|
| **B14** | CD100 | 10fr + 2fr red brn & red | 16.00 | 15.00 |

The surtax was for charitable work.

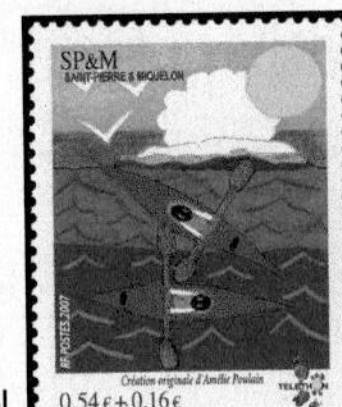


Art School Telethon — SP3

**2007, Nov. 24 Litho. *Perf. 13¼x13***

| | | | | |
|---|---|---|---|---|
| **B15** | SP3 | 54c +16c multi | 2.50 | 2.50 |

## AIR POST STAMPS

**Catalogue values for unused stamps in this section are for Never Hinged items.**

Common Design Type
***Perf. 14½x14***

**1942, Aug. 17 Photo. Unwmk.**

| | | | | |
|---|---|---|---|---|
| **C1** | CD87 | 1fr dark orange | .80 | .65 |
| **C2** | CD87 | 1.50fr bright red | .85 | .70 |
| **C3** | CD87 | 5fr brown red | 1.10 | .95 |
| **C4** | CD87 | 10fr black | 1.60 | 1.25 |
| **C5** | CD87 | 25fr ultra | 1.75 | 1.25 |
| **C6** | CD87 | 50fr dark green | 2.50 | 2.10 |
| **C7** | CD87 | 100fr plum | 3.00 | 2.50 |
| | | *Nos. C1-C7 (7)* | 11.60 | 9.40 |

### Victory Issue
Common Design Type

**1946, May 8 Engr. *Perf. 12½***

| | | | | |
|---|---|---|---|---|
| **C8** | CD92 | 8fr deep claret | 2.10 | 2.10 |

### Chad to Rhine Issue
Common Design Types

**1946, June 6**

| | | | | |
|---|---|---|---|---|
| **C9** | CD93 | 5fr brown red | 1.90 | 1.40 |
| **C10** | CD94 | 10fr lilac rose | 1.90 | 1.40 |
| **C11** | CD95 | 15fr gray blk | 2.75 | 2.40 |
| **C12** | CD96 | 20fr violet | 3.00 | 2.40 |
| **C13** | CD97 | 25fr chocolate | 3.75 | 3.25 |
| **C14** | CD98 | 50fr grnsh blk | 4.00 | 3.50 |
| | | *Nos. C9-C14 (6)* | 17.30 | 14.35 |

Plane, Sailing Vessel and Coast — AP2

AP3

AP4

**1947, Oct. 6**

| | | | | |
|---|---|---|---|---|
| **C15** | AP2 | 50fr yel grn & rose | 10.00 | 4.50 |
| **C16** | AP3 | 100fr dk blue grn | 14.50 | 7.00 |
| **C17** | AP4 | 200fr bluish blk & brt rose | 16.00 | 8.75 |
| | | *Nos. C15-C17 (3)* | 40.50 | 20.25 |

### UPU Issue
Common Design Type

**1949, Oct. 1 Engr. *Perf. 13***

| | | | | |
|---|---|---|---|---|
| **C18** | CD99 | 25fr multicolored | 20.00 | 12.00 |

### Liberation Issue
Common Design Type

**1954, June 8**

| | | | | |
|---|---|---|---|---|
| **C19** | CD102 | 15fr sepia & red | 19.00 | 12.00 |

10th anniversary of the liberation of France.

Plane over St. Pierre Harbor — AP6

**1956, Oct. 22**

| | | | | |
|---|---|---|---|---|
| **C20** | AP6 | 500fr ultra & indigo | 55.00 | 22.50 |

Dog and Village — AP7

Design: 100fr, Caravelle over archipelago.

**1957, Nov. 4 Unwmk. *Perf. 13***

| | | | | |
|---|---|---|---|---|
| **C21** | AP7 | 50fr gray, brn blk & bl | 52.50 | 22.50 |
| **C22** | AP7 | 100fr black & gray | 21.00 | 11.00 |

Anchors and Torches — AP8

**1959, Sept. 14 Engr. *Perf. 13***

| | | | | |
|---|---|---|---|---|
| **C23** | AP8 | 200fr dk pur, grn & cl | 18.00 | 8.00 |

Approval of the constitution and the vote which confirmed the attachment of the islands to France.

Pitcher Plant — AP9

**1962, Apr. 24 Unwmk. *Perf. 13***

| | | | | |
|---|---|---|---|---|
| **C24** | AP9 | 100fr green, org & car | 13.00 | 5.00 |

Gulf of St. Lawrence and Submarine "Surcouf" — AP10

***Perf. 13½x12½***

**1962, July 24 Photo.**

| | | | | |
|---|---|---|---|---|
| **C25** | AP10 | 500fr dk red & bl | 130.00 | 100.00 |

20th anniv. of St. Pierre & Miquelon's joining the Free French.

### Telstar Issue
Common Design Type

**1962, Nov. 22 Engr. *Perf. 13***

| | | | | |
|---|---|---|---|---|
| **C26** | CD111 | 50fr Prus grn & bis | 7.25 | 4.50 |

Arrival of Governor Dangeac, 1763 — AP11

**1963, Aug. 5 Unwmk. *Perf. 13***

| | | | | |
|---|---|---|---|---|
| **C27** | AP11 | 200fr dk bl, sl grn & brn | 26.00 | 12.00 |

Bicentenary of the arrival of the first French governor.

Jet Plane and Map of Maritime Provinces and New England — AP12

**1964, Sept. 28 Engr. *Perf. 13***

| | | | | |
|---|---|---|---|---|
| **C28** | AP12 | 100fr choc & Prus bl | 14.00 | 8.00 |

Inauguration of direct airmail service between St. Pierre and New York City.

### ITU Issue
Common Design Type

**1965, May 17**

| | | | | |
|---|---|---|---|---|
| **C29** | CD120 | 40fr org brn, dk bl & lil rose | 24.00 | 11.50 |

### French Satellite A-1 Issue
Common Design Type

Designs: 25fr, Diamant rocket and launching installations. 30fr, A-1 satellite.

**1966, Jan. 24 Engr. *Perf. 13***

| | | | | |
|---|---|---|---|---|
| **C30** | CD121 | 25fr dk brn, dk bl & rose cl | 6.00 | 4.00 |
| **C31** | CD121 | 30fr dk bl, rose cl & dk brn | 7.50 | 6.00 |
| *a.* | | Strip of 2, #C30-C31 + label | 14.50 | 14.50 |

### French Satellite D-1 Issue
Common Design Type

**1966, May 23 Engr. *Perf. 13***

| | | | | |
|---|---|---|---|---|
| **C32** | CD122 | 48fr brt grn, ultra & rose claret | 9.00 | 6.00 |

Arrival of Settlers — AP13

**1966, June 22 Photo. *Perf. 13***
**C33** AP13 100fr multicolored 15.00 6.50

150th anniv. of the return of the islands of St. Pierre and Miquelon to France.

Front Page of Official Journal and Printing Presses — AP14

**1966, Oct. 20 Engr. *Perf. 13***
**C34** AP14 60fr dk bl, lake & dk pur 13.50 6.75

Centenary of the Government Printers and the Official Journal.

Map of Islands, Old and New Fishing Vessels — AP15

Design: 100fr, Cruiser Colbert, maps of Brest, St. Pierre and Miquelon.

**1967, July 20 Engr. *Perf. 13***
**C35** AP15 25fr dk bl, gray & crim 26.00 15.00
**C36** AP15 100fr multicolored 42.50 27.50

Visit of President Charles de Gaulle.

Speed Skater and Olympic Emblem — AP16

60fr, Ice hockey goalkeeper.

**1968, Apr. 22 Photo. *Perf. 13***
**C37** AP16 50fr ultra & multi 9.25 4.00
**C38** AP16 60fr green & multi 11.00 5.75

10th Winter Olympic Games, Grenoble, France, Feb. 6-18.

War Memorial, St. Pierre — AP17

**1968, Nov. 11 Photo. *Perf. 12½***
**C39** AP17 500fr multicolored 25.00 17.00

World War I armistice, 50th anniv.

**Concorde Issue**
Common Design Type

**1969, Apr. 17 Engr. *Perf. 13***
**C40** CD129 34fr dk brn & olive 32.50 11.00

**Scenic Type of Regular Issue, 1969**

Designs: 50fr, Grazing horses, Miquelon. 100fr, Gathering driftwood on Mirande Beach, Miquelon.

**1969, Apr. 30 Engr. *Perf. 13***
**Size: 47½x27mm**
**C41** A47 50fr ultra, brn & ol 15.00 7.00
**C42** A47 100fr dk brn, bl & sl 25.00 14.00

L'Esperance Leaving Saint-Malo, 1600 — AP18

**1969, June 16 Engr. *Perf. 13***
**C43** AP18 200fr blk, grn & dk red 52.50 22.50

Pierre Loti and Sailboats — AP19

**1969, June 23**
**C44** AP19 300fr lemon, choc & Prus bl 60.00 27.50

Loti (1850-1923), French novelist and naval officer.

EXPO Emblem and "Mountains" by Yokoyama Taikan — AP20

34fr, Geisha, rocket and EXPO emblem, vert.

**1970, Sept. 8 Engr. *Perf. 13***
**C45** AP20 34fr dp cl, ol & ind 24.00 8.75
**C46** AP20 85fr org, ind & car 40.00 18.50

EXPO '70 Intl. Exposition, Osaka, Japan, Mar. 15-Sept. 13.

Etienne François Duke of Choiseul and his Ships — AP21

Designs: 50fr, Jacques Cartier, ship and landing party. 60fr, Sebastien Le Gonrad de Sourdeval, ships and map of islands.

**1970, Nov. 25 Portrait in Lake**
**C47** AP21 25fr lilac & Prus bl 26.00 10.00
**C48** AP21 50fr sl grn & red lil 32.00 12.00
**C49** AP21 60fr red lil & sl grn 40.00 18.00
*Nos. C47-C49 (3)* 98.00 40.00

De Gaulle, Cross of Lorraine, Sailor, Soldier, Coast Guard — AP22

**1972, June 18 Engr. *Perf. 13***
**C50** AP22 100fr lil, brn & grn 30.00 16.00

Charles de Gaulle (1890-1970), French pres.

Louis Joseph de Montcalm — AP23

Designs: 2fr, Louis de Buade Frontenac, vert. 4fr, Robert de La Salle.

**1973, Jan. 1**
**C51** AP23 1.60fr multicolored 9.50 4.00
**C52** AP23 2fr multicolored 12.00 6.50
**C53** AP23 4fr multicolored 21.00 11.00
*Nos. C51-C53 (3)* 42.50 21.50

Transall C 160 over St. Pierre — AP24

**1973, Oct. 16 Engr. *Perf. 13***
**C54** AP24 10fr multicolored 50.00 25.00

Arms and Map of Islands, Fish and Bird — AP25

**1974, Nov. 5 Photo. *Perf. 13***
**C55** AP25 2fr gold & multi 16.00 6.50

Copernicus, Kepler, Newton and Einstein — AP26

**1974, Nov. 26 Engr.**
**C56** AP26 4fr multicolored 18.50 9.00

Nicolaus Copernicus (1473-1543), Polish astronomer.

Type of 1909, Cod and ARPHILA Emblem AP27

**1975, Aug. 5 Engr. *Perf. 13***
**C57** AP27 4fr ultra, red & indigo 21.00 9.50

ARPHILA 75, International Philatelic Exhibition, Paris, June 6-16.

Judo, Maple Leaf, Olympic Rings AP28

**1975, Nov. 18 Engr. *Perf. 13***
**C58** AP28 1.90fr red, blue & vio 10.00 5.50

Pre-Olympic Year.

Concorde — AP29

**1976, Jan. 21 Engr. *Perf. 13***
**C59** AP29 10fr red, blk & slate 32.50 16.00

1st commercial flight of supersonic jet Concorde from Paris to Rio, Jan. 21.

A. G. Bell, Telephone and Satellite AP30

**1976, June 22 Litho. *Perf. 12½***
**C60** AP30 5fr vio bl, org & red 10.00 5.50

Centenary of first telephone call by Alexander Graham Bell, Mar. 10, 1876.

Aircraft — AP31

5fr, Hawker-Siddeley H. S. 748, 1987. 10fr, Latecoere 522, 1939.

**1987, June 30 Engr. *Perf. 13***
**C61** AP31 5fr multicolored 2.75 1.40
**C62** AP31 10fr multicolored 5.25 2.75

Hindenburg — AP32

10fr, Douglas DC3, 1948-1988. 20fr, Piper Aztec.

**1988-89 Engr. *Perf. 13***

**C63** AP32 5fr multicolored 2.50 1.25
**C64** AP32 10fr multicolored 5.00 2.75
**C65** AP32 20fr multicolored 7.50 4.00
*Nos. C63-C65 (3)* 15.00 8.00

Issued: 20fr, May 31, 1989; others, June 22.

Flying Flea, Bird — AP33

**1990, May 16 Engr.**

**C66** AP33 5fr multicolored 2.10 1.25

Piper Tomahawk — AP34

**1991, May 29 Engr. *Perf. 13***

**C67** AP34 10fr multicolored 4.00 2.50

Radio-controlled Model Airplanes — AP35

**1992, May 6**

**C68** AP35 20fr brown, red & org 8.00 4.25

Migratory Birds — AP36

**1993-97 *Perf. 13x12½***

**C69** AP36 5fr Shearwater (Puffin) 2.00 1.40
**C70** AP36 10fr Golden plover 4.00 2.25

***Perf. 13x13½***

**C71** AP36 10fr Arctic Tern 4.25 2.25

***Perf. 13***

**C72** AP36 15fr Courlis 6.25 3.50
**C73** AP36 5fr Peregrine falcon, vert. 2.50 1.50
*Nos. C69-C73 (5)* 19.00 10.90

Issued: #C69-C70, 5/12; #C71, 5/10/95; #C72, 5/15/96; #C73, 5/28/97.

Disappearance of the Flight of Nungesser and Coli, 70th Anniv. — AP37

**1997, June 11**

**C74** AP37 14fr blk, grn bl & brn 6.00 3.50

Bald Eagle — AP38

**1998-2001 Engr. *Perf. 13***

**C74A** AP38 5fr Buzzard 2.25 1.25
**C75** AP38 10fr shown 4.75 3.00
**C75A** AP38 15fr Heron 5.25 3.00
**C76** AP38 20fr Wild duck 7.25 5.00

Issued: 5fr, 12/13/00; 10fr, 5/6; 15fr, 5/23/01; 20fr, 5/5/99.

Puffin — AP39

**2002, Apr. 22**

**C77** AP39 €2.50 multi 8.75 4.50

Solan Goose — AP40

**2003, June 18 Engr. *Perf. 13x12½***

**C78** AP40 €2.50 multi 8.75 5.75

Bustard — AP41

**2004, July 7 Engr. *Perf. 13x13¼***

**C79** AP41 €2.50 multi 8.75 6.25

Piping Plover — AP42

**2005, June 22 *Perf. 13x12½***

**C80** AP42 €2.50 multi 8.75 6.00

Atlantic Sea Gull — AP43

**2006, June 14 Engr. *Perf. 13x12½***

**C81** AP43 €2.53 multi 8.75 7.75

Eider — AP44

**2007, May 5 Engr. *Perf. 13x12½***

**C82** AP44 €1.50 multi 4.00 4.00

Harlequin Ducks — AP45

**2008, June 28 Engr. *Perf. 13x12¾***

**C83** AP45 €1.50 multi 4.75 4.75

## AIR POST SEMI-POSTAL STAMPS

Bringing Children to Hospital — SPAP1

***Perf. 13½x12½***

**1942, June 22 Unwmk. Photo.**

**CB1** SPAP1 1.50fr + 3.50fr green 6.50
**CB2** SPAP1 2fr + 6fr brown 6.50

Native children's welfare fund.

Nos. CB1-CB2 were issued by the Vichy government in France, but were not placed on sale in St. Pierre & Miquelon.

### Colonial Education Fund
Common Design Type

**1942, June 22**

**CB3** CD86a 1.20fr + 1.80fr blue & red 7.00

No. CB3 was issued by the Vichy government in France, but was not placed on sale in St. Pierre & Miquelon.

## POSTAGE DUE STAMPS

Postage Due Stamps of French Colonies Overprinted in Red

**1892 Unwmk. *Imperf.***

**J1** D1 5c black 85.00 85.00
**J2** D1 10c black 26.00 26.00
**J3** D1 15c black 26.00 26.00
**J4** D1 20c black 26.00 26.00
**J5** D1 30c black 26.00 26.00
**J6** D1 40c black 26.00 26.00
**J7** D1 60c black 82.50 90.00

**Black Overprint**

**J8** D1 1fr brown 200.00 200.00
**J9** D1 2fr brown 200.00 200.00
*Nos. J1-J9 (9)* 697.50 705.00

These stamps exist with and without hyphen. See note after No. 59.

Postage Due Stamps of France, 1893-1924, Overprinted

**1925-27 *Perf. 14x13½***

**J10** D2 5c blue .75 1.10
**J11** D2 10c dark brown .75 1.10
**J12** D2 20c olive green .80 1.10
**J13** D2 25c rose 1.10 1.50
**J14** D2 30c red 1.90 2.25
**J15** D2 45c blue green 1.90 2.25
**J16** D2 50c brown vio 2.60 3.75
**J17** D2 1fr red brn, *straw* 3.50 4.00
**J18** D2 3fr magenta ('27) 12.00 15.00

Surcharged

**J19** D2 60c on 50c buff 2.75 3.75
**J20** D2 2fr on 1fr red 4.50 5.50
*Nos. J10-J20 (11)* 32.55 41.30

Newfoundland Dog — D3

**1932, Dec. 5 Typo.**

**J21** D3 5c dk blue & blk 1.50 1.90
**J22** D3 10c green & blk 1.50 1.90
**J23** D3 20c red & blk 1.75 2.25
**J24** D3 25c red vio & blk 1.75 2.25
**J25** D3 30c orange & blk 3.50 4.50
**J26** D3 45c lt blue & blk 5.50 6.75
**J27** D3 50c blue grn & blk 8.50 10.50
**J28** D3 60c brt rose & blk 15.00 15.00
**J29** D3 1fr yellow brn & blk 25.00 30.00
**J30** D3 2fr dp violet & blk 35.00 37.50
**J31** D3 3fr dk brown & blk 47.50 55.00
*Nos. J21-J31 (11)* 146.50 167.55

For overprints and surcharge see Nos. J42-J46.

Codfish — D4

**1938, Nov. 17 Photo. *Perf. 13***

**J32** D4 5c gray black .40 .50
**J33** D4 10c dk red violet .40 .50
**J34** D4 15c slate green .50 .75
**J35** D4 20c deep blue .55 .75
**J36** D4 30c rose carmine .55 .75
**J37** D4 50c dk blue green .70 .80
**J38** D4 60c dk blue .95 1.10
**J39** D4 1fr henna brown 1.90 2.25
**J40** D4 2fr gray brown 4.50 5.25
**J41** D4 3fr dull violet 4.75 6.00
*Nos. J32-J41 (10)* 15.20 18.65

For overprints see Nos. J48-J67.

Postage Due Stamps of 1932 Overprinted in Black

**1942 Unwmk. *Perf. 14x13½***

**J42** D3 25c red vio & blk 425.00 425.00
**J43** D3 30c orange & blk 425.00 425.00
**J44** D3 50c blue grn & blk 1,400. 1,400.
**J45** D3 2fr dp vio & bl blk 60.00 60.00

**Same Surcharged in Black**

No. J46

No. J46a

**J46** D3 3fr on 2fr dp vio & blk, "F.N.F.L." omitted 24.00 24.00
*a.* With "F.N.F.L." 40.00 40.00
*Nos. J42-J46 (5)* 2,334. 2,334.

Postage Due Stamps of 1938 Overprinted in Black

**1942** *Perf. 13*

| No. | Type | Description | Unused | Used |
|---|---|---|---|---|
| **J48** | D4 | 5c gray black | 24.00 | *27.50* |
| **J49** | D4 | 10c dk red violet | 24.00 | *27.50* |
| **J50** | D4 | 15c slate green | 24.00 | *27.50* |
| **J51** | D4 | 20c deep blue | 24.00 | *27.50* |
| **J52** | D4 | 30c rose carmine | 24.00 | *27.50* |
| **J53** | D4 | 50c dk blue green | 47.50 | *52.50* |
| **J54** | D4 | 60c dark blue | 100.00 | *110.00* |
| **J55** | D4 | 1fr henna brown | 110.00 | *125.00* |
| **J56** | D4 | 2fr gray brown | 125.00 | *140.00* |
| **J57** | D4 | 3fr dull violet | 140.00 | *160.00* |
| | | *Nos. J48-J57 (10)* | 642.50 | *725.00* |

Christmas Day plebiscite ordered by Vice Admiral Emile Henri Muselier, commander of the Free French naval forces.

Postage Due Stamps of 1938 Overprinted in Black

**1942**

| No. | Type | Description | Unused | Used |
|---|---|---|---|---|
| **J58** | D4 | 5c gray black | 52.50 | *60.00* |
| **J59** | D4 | 10c dk red violet | 11.00 | *12.00* |
| **J60** | D4 | 15c slate green | 11.00 | *12.00* |
| **J61** | D4 | 20c deep blue | 11.00 | *12.00* |
| **J62** | D4 | 30c rose carmine | 11.00 | *12.00* |
| **J63** | D4 | 50c dk blue green | 11.00 | *12.00* |
| **J64** | D4 | 60c dark blue | 11.00 | *12.00* |
| **J65** | D4 | 1fr henna brown | 27.50 | *32.50* |
| **J66** | D4 | 2fr gray brown | 32.50 | *35.00* |
| **J67** | D4 | 3fr dull violet | 575.00 | *625.00* |
| | | *Nos. J58-J67 (10)* | 753.50 | *824.50* |

**Catalogue values for unused stamps in this section, from this point to the end of the section, are for Never Hinged items.**

Arms and Fishing Schooner — D5

**1947, Oct. 6** **Engr.** *Perf. 13*

| No. | Type | Description | Unused | Used |
|---|---|---|---|---|
| **J68** | D5 | 10c deep orange | .30 | .30 |
| **J69** | D5 | 30c deep ultra | .30 | .30 |
| **J70** | D5 | 50c dk blue green | .50 | .50 |
| **J71** | D5 | 1fr deep carmine | .65 | .65 |
| **J72** | D5 | 2fr dk green | .90 | .90 |
| **J73** | D5 | 3fr violet | 2.00 | 2.00 |
| **J74** | D5 | 4fr chocolate | 2.00 | 2.00 |
| **J75** | D5 | 5fr yellow green | 2.25 | 2.25 |
| **J76** | D5 | 10fr black brown | 3.00 | 3.00 |
| **J77** | D5 | 20fr orange red | 3.25 | 3.25 |
| | | *Nos. J68-J77 (10)* | 15.15 | 15.15 |

Newfoundland Dog — D6

**1973, Jan. 1** **Engr.** *Perf. 13*

| No. | Type | Description | Unused | Used |
|---|---|---|---|---|
| **J78** | D6 | 2c brown & blk | 1.00 | 1.00 |
| **J79** | D6 | 10c purple & blk | 1.40 | 1.40 |
| **J80** | D6 | 20c grnsh bl & blk | 2.25 | 2.25 |
| **J81** | D6 | 30c dk car & blk | 4.50 | 4.50 |
| **J82** | D6 | 1fr blue & blk | 11.00 | 11.00 |
| | | *Nos. J78-J82 (5)* | 20.15 | 20.15 |

**France Nos. J106-J115 Overprinted "ST - PIERRE ET MIQUELON" Reading Up in Red**

**1986, Sept. 15** **Engr.** *Perf. 13*

| No. | Type | Description | Unused | Used |
|---|---|---|---|---|
| **J83** | D8 | 10c multicolored | .25 | .25 |
| **J84** | D8 | 20c multicolored | .25 | .25 |
| **J85** | D8 | 30c multicolored | .25 | .25 |
| **J86** | D8 | 40c multicolored | .25 | .25 |
| **J87** | D8 | 50c multicolored | .40 | .40 |
| **J88** | D8 | 1fr multicolored | .50 | .50 |
| **J89** | D8 | 2fr multicolored | .95 | .95 |
| **J90** | D8 | 3fr multicolored | 1.40 | 1.40 |
| **J91** | D8 | 4fr multicolored | 1.75 | 1.75 |
| **J92** | D8 | 5fr multicolored | 2.50 | 2.50 |
| | | *Nos. J83-J92 (10)* | 8.50 | 8.50 |

## PARCEL POST STAMPS

No. 65 Overprinted

**1901** **Unwmk.** *Perf. 14x13½*

**Q1** A16 10c blk, *lav* 140.00 140.00
*a.* Inverted overprint 1,250. 1,250.

No. 66 Overprinted

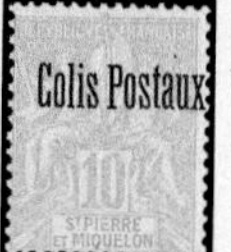


**Q2** A16 10c red 35.00 *35.00*

Nos. 84 and 87 Overprinted in Blue

**1917-25**

**Q3** A17 10c car rose & red 4.50 *6.00*
*a.* Double overprint 300.00
**Q4** A17 20c bis brn & vio brn ('25) 3.75 *5.25*
*a.* Double overprint 190.00

No. Q4 with Additional Overprint in Black

**1942**

**Q5** A17 20c bis brn & vio brn 1,100. *1,200.*

# ST. THOMAS & PRINCE ISLANDS

sānt-'täm-əs and 'prin͡ts 'ī-lənd

## Democratic Republic of Sao Tome and Principe

LOCATION — Two islands in the Gulf of Guinea, 125 miles off the west coast of Africa
GOVT. — Republic
AREA — 387 sq. mi.
POP. — 154,878 (1999 est.)
CAPITAL — Sao Tome

This colony of Portugal became a province, later an overseas territory, and achieved independence on July 12, 1975.

1000 Reis = 1 Milreis
100 Centavos = 1 Escudo (1913)
100 Cents = 1 Dobra (1977)

**Catalogue values for unused stamps in this country are for Never Hinged items, beginning with Scott 353 in the regular postage section, Scott J52 in the postage due section, and Scott RA4 in the postal tax section.**

Portuguese Crown — A1

5, 25, 50 REIS:
Type I — "5" is upright.
Type II — "5" is slanting.

10 REIS:
Type I — "1" has short serif at top.
Type II — "1" has long serif at top.

40 REIS:
Type I — "4" is broad.
Type II — "4" is narrow.

**1875-77** **Unwmk.** **Typo.** *Perf. 13½*

| No. | Type | Description | Unused | Used |
|---|---|---|---|---|
| **1** | A1 | 5r black, I | 4.25 | 2.40 |
| **2** | A1 | 10r yellow, I | 26.00 | 13.50 |
| *a.* | | Type II | 26.00 | 13.50 |
| **3** | A1 | 20r bister | 5.50 | 3.50 |
| **4** | A1 | 25r rose, I | 3.00 | 1.75 |
| *a.* | | 25r red | 3.50 | 1.75 |
| **5** | A1 | 40r blue (I) | 9.00 | 6.00 |
| *a.* | | Type II | 0.00 | 6.00 |
| **6** | A1 | 50r gray grn, II | 26.00 | 18.00 |
| *a.* | | Type I | 26.00 | 18.00 |
| **7** | A1 | 100r gray lilac | 14.00 | 7.25 |
| **9** | A1 | 300r chocolate ('77) | 15.00 | 9.00 |

**1875-77** *Perf. 12½*

| No. | Type | Description | Unused | Used |
|---|---|---|---|---|
| *1a* | A1 | 5r black (II) | 6.00 | 4.00 |
| *b.* | | Type I | 6.00 | 4.00 |
| *2b* | A1 | 10r yellow (I) | 52.50 | 30.00 |
| *3a* | A1 | 20r bister | 12.00 | 5.50 |
| *4b* | A1 | 25r rose (I) | 8.50 | 3.50 |
| *4c* | A1 | 25r red (I) | 14.00 | 3.50 |
| *5b* | A1 | 40r blue (II) | 14.00 | 3.50 |
| *6b* | A1 | 50r gray grn (I) | 58.00 | 30.00 |
| *7a* | A1 | 100r gray lilac | 30.00 | 20.00 |
| **8** | A1 | 200r red orange ('77) | 28.00 | 20.00 |
| *9a* | A1 | 300r chocolate ('77) | 28.00 | 20.00 |

**1870** *Perf. 12½*

**Thick Paper**

| No. | Type | Description | Unused | Used |
|---|---|---|---|---|
| *1c* | A1 | 5r black (I) | 65.00 | 30.00 |
| *1d* | A1 | 5r black (II) | 65.00 | 30.00 |
| *2c* | A1 | 10r yellow (I) | 65.00 | 36.00 |
| *3b* | A1 | 20r bister | 45.00 | 30.00 |
| *4d* | A1 | 25r vermilion (I) | 35.00 | 20.00 |
| *4e* | A1 | 25r red (I) | 45.00 | 30.00 |
| *6c* | A1 | 50r gray grn (I) | 60.00 | 36.00 |
| *7b* | A1 | 100r gray lilac | 65.00 | 36.00 |

**1881-85**

| No. | Type | Description | Unused | Used |
|---|---|---|---|---|
| **10** | A1 | 10r gray grn, I | 12.00 | 7.75 |
| *a.* | | Type II | 12.00 | 6.75 |
| *b.* | | Perf. 13½, I | 15.00 | 9.00 |
| **11** | A1 | 20r car rose ('85) | 6.00 | 4.00 |
| **12** | A1 | 25r vio ('85), II | 5.00 | 3.00 |
| **13** | A1 | 40r yel buff, II | 9.75 | 6.75 |
| *a.* | | Perf. 13½ (I) | 11.50 | 7.25 |
| **14** | A1 | 50r dk blue, I | 4.00 | 3.00 |
| *a.* | | Type II | 4.00 | 3.00 |
| *b.* | | Perf. 13½ (I) | 6.50 | 5.00 |
| | | *Nos. 10-14 (5)* | 36.75 | 24.50 |

For surcharges and overprints see Nos. 63-64, 129-129B, 154.

Nos. 1-14 have been reprinted on stout white paper, ungummed, with rough perforation 13½, also on ordinary paper with shiny white gum and clean-cut perforation 13½ with large holes.

King Luiz — A2

**Typo., Head Embossed**

**1887** *Perf. 13½*

| No. | Type | Description | Unused | Used |
|---|---|---|---|---|
| **15** | A2 | 5r black | 12.00 | 3.50 |
| *a.* | | Perf. 12½ | 44.00 | 38.00 |
| **16** | A2 | 10r green | 12.00 | 3.75 |
| **17** | A2 | 20r brt rose | 13.50 | 4.00 |
| *a.* | | Perf. 12½ | 135.00 | 110.00 |
| **18** | A2 | 25r violet | 8.25 | 3.00 |
| *a.* | | Double embossing | 400.00 | 400.00 |
| *b.* | | Double impression and embossing | 500.00 | 500.00 |
| **19** | A2 | 40r brown | 8.25 | 4.00 |
| **20** | A2 | 50r blue | 10.25 | 3.75 |
| *a.* | | Perf. 12½ | 17.00 | 6.50 |
| **21** | A2 | 100r yellow brn | 7.25 | 3.75 |
| **22** | A2 | 200r gray lilac | 26.00 | 13.50 |
| **23** | A2 | 300r orange | 29.00 | 13.50 |
| | | *Nos. 15-23 (9)* | 126.50 | 52.75 |

For surcharges and overprints see Nos. 24-26, 62, 65-72, 130-131, 155-158, 234-237.

Nos. 15, 16, 19, 21, 22, and 23 have been reprinted in paler colors than the originals, with white gum and cleancut perforation 13½. Value $1.50 each.

**Nos. 16-17, 19 Surcharged**

a

b

c

**1889-91** **Without Gum**

| No. | Type | Description | Unused | Used |
|---|---|---|---|---|
| **24** | A2(a) | 5r on 10r | 60.00 | 45.00 |
| **25** | A2(b) | 5r on 20r | 60.00 | 45.00 |
| **26** | A2(c) | 50r on 40r ('91) | 330.00 | 150.00 |
| | | *Nos. 24-26 (3)* | 450.00 | 240.00 |

Varieties of Nos. 24-26, including inverted and double surcharges, "5" inverted, "Cinoc" and "Cinco," were deliberately made and unofficially issued.

King Carlos — A6

*Perf. 11½ (#29-30, 33, 35-38), 12½*

**1895** **Typo.**

| No. | Type | Description | Unused | Used |
|---|---|---|---|---|
| **27** | A6 | 5r yellow | 1.60 | 1.50 |
| **28** | A6 | 10r red lilac | 2.25 | 1.25 |
| **29** | A6 | 15r red brown | 3.50 | 1.75 |
| **30** | A6 | 20r lavender | 3.50 | 2.00 |
| **31** | A6 | 25r green | 3.25 | 1.25 |
| **32** | A6 | 50r light blue | 3.25 | 1.25 |
| *a.* | | Perf. 13½ | 3.25 | 1.40 |
| **33** | A6 | 75r rose | 9.50 | 5.50 |
| **34** | A6 | 80r yellow grn | 19.00 | 14.00 |
| **35** | A6 | 100r brn, *yel* | 8.25 | 5.50 |
| **36** | A6 | 150r car, *rose* | 11.00 | 7.25 |
| **37** | A6 | 200r dk bl, *bl* | 14.50 | 11.00 |
| **38** | A6 | 300r dk bl, *sal* | 16.50 | 13.50 |
| | | *Nos. 27-38 (12)* | 96.10 | 65.75 |

For surcharges and overprints see Nos. 73-84, 132-137, 159-165, 238-243, 262-264, 268-274.

King Carlos — A7

**1898-1903** *Perf. 11½*

**Name and Value in Black except 500r**

| No. | Type | Description | Unused | Used |
|---|---|---|---|---|
| **39** | A7 | 2½r gray | .60 | .25 |
| **40** | A7 | 5r orange | .60 | .25 |
| **41** | A7 | 10r lt green | .60 | .40 |
| **42** | A7 | 15r brown | 2.10 | 1.40 |
| **43** | A7 | 15r gray grn ('03) | 1.10 | 1.10 |
| **44** | A7 | 20r gray violet | 1.25 | .50 |
| **45** | A7 | 25r sea green | .75 | .40 |
| **46** | A7 | 25r carmine ('03) | 1.10 | .30 |
| **47** | A7 | 50r blue | 1.10 | .50 |
| **48** | A7 | 50r brown ('03) | 4.50 | 4.50 |
| **49** | A7 | 65r dull blue ('03) | 22.50 | 9.00 |
| **50** | A7 | 75r rose | 18.00 | 9.75 |
| **51** | A7 | 75r red lilac ('03) | 2.50 | 1.40 |
| **52** | A7 | 80r brt violet | 9.50 | 9.00 |

**53** A7 100r dk blue, *bl* 3.50 2.40
**54** A7 115r org brn, *pink* ('03) 10.00 8.00
**55** A7 130r brn, *straw* ('03) 10.00 6.00
**56** A7 150r brn, *buff* 4.25 2.50
**57** A7 200r red lil, *pnksh* 6.75 4.25
**58** A7 300r dk blue, *rose* 10.00 5.25
**59** A7 400r dull bl, *straw* ('03) 15.00 8.50
**60** A7 500r blk & red, *bl* ('01) 13.00 7.25
**61** A7 700r vio, *yelsh* ('01) 21.00 15.00
*Nos. 39-61 (23)* 159.70 97.90

For overprints and surcharges see Nos. 86-105, 116-128, 138-153, 167-169, 244-249, 255-261, 265-267.

Stamps of 1869-95 Surcharged in Red or Black

**1902** **On Stamp of 1887**
**62** A2 130r on 5r blk (R) 9.75 5.50
*a.* Perf. 13½ 70.00 45.00

**On Stamps of 1869**
**63** A1 115r on 50r grn 19.00 6.50
**64** A1 400r on 10r yel 85.00 60.00
*a.* Double surcharge 250.00 180.00

**On Stamps of 1887**
**65** A2 65r on 20r rose 14.50 6.00
*a.* Perf. 13½ 40.00 20.00
**66** A2 65r on 25r violet 9.75 5.50
*a.* Inverted surcharge 55.00 33.00
**67** A2 65r on 100r yel brn 9.75 5.50
**68** A2 115r on 10r blue grn 9.75 5.50
**69** A2 115r on 300r orange 9.75 5.50
**70** A2 130r on 200r gray lil 12.00 5.50
**71** A2 400r on 40r brown 18.00 11.00
**72** A2 400r on 50r blue 21.00 13.00
*a.* Perf. 13½ 600.00 450.00

**On Stamps of 1895**
**73** A6 65r on 5r yellow 7.25 4.25
**74** A6 65r on 10r red vio 7.25 4.25
**75** A6 65r on 15r choc 7.25 4.25
**76** A6 65r on 20r lav 7.25 4.25
**77** A6 115r on 25r grn 7.25 4.25
**78** A6 115r on 150r car, *rose* 7.25 4.25
**79** A6 115r on 200r bl, *bl* 7.25 4.25
**80** A6 130r on 75r rose 7.25 4.25
**81** A6 130r on 100r brn, *yel* 9.00 5.50
*a.* Double surcharge 40.00 30.00
**82** A6 130r on 300r bl, *sal* 7.25 4.25
**83** A6 400r on 50r lt blue 2.40 1.75
*a.* Perf. 13½ 5.00 3.00
**84** A6 400r on 80r yel grn 2.40 1.75

**On Newspaper Stamp No. P12**
**85** N3 400r on 2½r brown 3.75 3.00
*a.* Double surcharge
*Nos. 62-85 (24)* 301.05 179.75

Reprints of Nos. 63, 64, 67, 71, and 72 have shiny white gum and clean-cut perf. 13½.

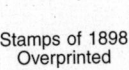

Stamps of 1898 Overprinted

**1902**
**86** A7 15r brown 3.75 1.75
**87** A7 25r sea green 3.75 1.50
**88** A7 50r blue 3.75 1.50
**89** A7 75r rose 9.00 5.75
*Nos. 86-89 (4)* 20.25 10.50

No. 49 Surcharged in Black

**1905**
**90** A7 50r on 65r dull blue 6.00 3.75

Stamps of 1898-1903 Overprinted in Carmine or Green

**1911**
**91** A7 2½r gray .25 .25
*a.* Inverted overprint 15.00 11.00
**92** A7 5r orange .25 .25
**93** A7 10r lt green .25 .25
*a.* Inverted overprint 15.00 12.00
**94** A7 15r gray green .25 .25
**95** A7 20r gray violet .25 .25
**96** A7 25r carmine (G) .60 .25
**97** A7 50r brown .50 .25
*a.* Inverted overprint 15.00 12.00
**98** A7 75r red lilac .50 .25
**99** A7 100r dk bl, *bl* .90 .75
*a.* Inverted overprint 17.50 14.00
**100** A7 115r org brn, *pink* 2.00 1.40
**101** A7 130r brown, *straw* 2.00 1.40
**102** A7 200r red lil, *pnksh* 10.00 6.00
**103** A7 400r dull blue, *straw* 2.75 1.25
**104** A7 500r blk & red, *bl* 2.75 1.25
**105** A7 700r violet, *yelsh* 2.75 1.25
*Nos. 91-105 (15)* 26.00 15.30

King Manuel II — A8

**Overprinted in Carmine or Green**

**1912** ***Perf. 11½, 12***
**106** A8 2½r violet .25 .25
*a.* Double overprint 16.00 16.00
*b.* Double overprint, one inverted 25.00
**107** A8 5r black .25 .25
**108** A8 10r gray green .25 .25
*a.* Double overprint 14.00 14.00
**109** A8 20r carmine (G) 2.00 1.10
**110** A8 25r violet brn 1.40 .60
**111** A8 50r dk blue 1.40 .60
**112** A8 75r bister brn 1.40 .60
**113** A8 100r brn, *lt grn* 2.10 .85
**114** A8 200r dk grn, *sal* 3.00 2.40
**115** A8 300r black, *azure* 4.00 2.10
*Nos. 106-115 (10)* 16.05 9.00

Stamps of 1898-1905 Overprinted in Black

**1913** **On Stamps of 1898-1903**
**116** A7 2½r gray 2.10 1.50
*a.* Inverted overprint 20.00 20.00
*b.* Double overprint 20.00 20.00
**117** A7 5r orange 2.40 1.75
**118** A7 15r gray green 52.50 33.00
*a.* Inverted overprint 75.00
**119** A7 20r gray violet 3.00 1.75
*a.* Inverted overprint 15.00
**120** A7 25r carmine 10.00 5.00
*a.* Inverted overprint 30.00
*b.* Double overprint 30.00
**121** A7 75r red lilac 5.00 3.50
**122** A7 100r bl, *bluish* 12.00 9.75
**123** A7 115r org brn, *pink* 28.00 21.00
*a.* Double overprint 75.00 60.00
**124** A7 130r brn, *straw* 14.50 14.00
**125** A7 200r red lil, *pnksh* 33.00 18.00
**126** A7 400r dl bl, *straw* 16.00 14.00
**127** A7 500r blk & red, *gray* 52.50 42.50
**128** A7 700r vio, *yelsh* 72.50 55.00
*Nos. 116-128 (13)* 303.50 220.75

**On Provisional Issue of 1902**
**129** A1 115r on 50r grn 160.00 97.50
*a.* Inverted overprint
**129B** A1 400r on 10r yel 700.00 600.00
**130** A2 115r on 10r blue grn 5.50 3.00
*a.* Inverted overprint 25.00
**131** A2 400r on 50r blue 130.00 80.00
**132** A6 115r on 25r grn 4.00 3.00
*a.* Inverted overprint 20.00
**133** A6 115r on 150r car, *rose* 72.50 60.00
*a.* Inverted overprint 100.00
**134** A6 115r on 200r bl, *bl* 4.00 3.00
**135** A6 130r on 75r rose 4.00 3.00
*a.* Inverted overprint 50.00
**136** A6 400r on 50r lt bl 7.25 5.25
*a.* Perf. 13½ 18.50 11.00
**137** A6 400r on 80r yel grn 9.75 5.00

**Same Overprint on Nos. 86, 88, 90**
**138** A7 15r brown 4.75 3.00
**139** A7 50r blue 4.75 3.00
**140** A7 50r on 65r dl bl 18.00 13.50
*Nos. 138-140 (3)* 27.50 19.50

No. 123-125, 130-131 and 137 were issued without gum.

Stamps of 1898-1905 Overprinted in Black

**On Stamps of 1898-1903**
**141** A7 2½r gray 1.75 1.50
*a.* Inverted overprint 9.00
*b.* Double overprint 20.00 20.00
*c.* Double overprint inverted 30.00
**142** A7 5r orange 47.50 30.00
**143** A7 15r gray green 3.50 2.75
*a.* Inverted overprint 25.00
**144** A7 20r gray violet 140.00 85.00
*a.* Inverted overprint 600.00
**145** A7 25r carmine 55.00 42.50
*a.* Inverted overprint 75.00
**146** A7 75r red lilac 4.00 2.75
*a.* Inverted overprint 5.00
**147** A7 100r blue, *bl* 5.00 3.50
**148** A7 115r org brn, *pink* 13.50 9.25
*a.* Inverted overprint 25.00
**149** A7 130r brown, *straw* 13.50 8.50
*a.* Inverted overprint 25.00
**150** A7 200r red lil, *pnksh* 5.00 3.50
*a.* Inverted overprint 10.00
**151** A7 400r dull bl, *straw* 14.50 8.50
**152** A7 500r blk & red, *gray* 14.50 10.25
**153** A7 700r violet, *yelsh* 17.50 14.00

**On Provisional Issue of 1902**
**154** A1 115r on 50r green 275.00 200.00
**155** A2 115r on 10r bl grn 5.00 3.75
**156** A2 115r on 300r org 290.00 160.00
**157** A2 130r on 5r black 300.00 160.00
**158** A2 400r on 50r blue 140.00 100.00
*a.* Perf. 13½ 340.00 250.00
**159** A6 115r on 25r green 4.00 2.40
**160** A6 115r on 150r car, *rose* 5.00 4.00
*a.* "REPUBLICA" inverted 20.00
**161** A6 115r on 200r bl, *bl* 5.00 4.00
**162** A6 130r on 75r rose 5.00 4.00
*a.* Inverted surcharge 20.00
**163** A6 130r on 100r brn, *yel* 575.00 400.00
**164** A6 400r on 50r lt bl 29.00 21.00
*a.* Perf. 12½ 5.00 4.00
**165** A6 400r on 80r yel grn 5.25 4.00
**166** N3 400r on 2½r brn 5.00 4.00

**Same Overprint on Nos. 86, 88, 90**
**167** A7 15r brown 4.00 1.50
*a.* Inverted overprint 20.00
**168** A7 50r blue 4.00 1.50
*a.* Inverted overprint 20.00
**169** A7 50r on 65r dull bl 4.50 3.00
*Nos. 167-169 (3)* 12.50 6.00

Most of Nos. 141-169 were issued without gum.

---

Common Design Types pictured following the introduction.

---

Vasco da Gama Issue of Various Portuguese Colonies Surcharged

**On Stamps of Macao**
**170** CD20 ¼c on ½a bl grn 2.00 1.60
**171** CD21 ½c on 1a red 2.00 1.60
**172** CD22 1c on 2a red vio 2.00 1.60
**173** CD23 2½c on 4a yel grn 2.00 1.60
**174** CD24 5c on 8a dk bl 2.60 2.00
**175** CD25 7½c on 12a vio brn 4.50 3.25
**176** CD26 10c on 16a bis brn 2.60 1.75
**177** CD27 15c on 24a bister 2.60 1.75
*Nos. 170-177 (8)* 20.30 15.15

**On Stamps of Portuguese Africa**
**178** CD20 ¼c on 2½r bl grn 1.50 1.25
**179** CD21 ½c on 5r red 1.50 1.25
**180** CD22 1c on 10r red vio 1.50 1.25
**181** CD23 2½c on 25r yel grn 1.50 1.25
**182** CD24 5c on 50r dk bl 1.50 1.25
**183** CD25 7½c on 75r vio brn 4.00 3.75
**184** CD26 10c on 100r bis brn 2.10 1.75
**185** CD27 15c on 150r bister 2.10 1.75
*Nos. 178-185 (8)* 15.70 13.50

**On Stamps of Timor**
**186** CD20 ¼c on ½a bl grn 2.00 1.40
**187** CD21 ½c on 1a red 2.00 1.40
**188** CD22 1c on 2a red vio 2.00 1.40
*a.* Double surcharge 35.00 30.00
**189** CD23 2½c on 4a yel grn 2.00 1.40
**190** CD24 5c on 8a dk bl 2.60 2.00
**191** CD25 7½c on 12a vio brn 4.50 3.25
**192** CD26 10c on 16a bis brn 2.60 1.75
**193** CD27 15c on 24a bister 2.60 1.75
*Nos. 186-193 (8)* 20.30 14.35
*Nos. 170-193 (24)* 56.30 43.00

Ceres — A9

**Name and Value in Black**
**Chalky Paper**

**1914** **Typo.** ***Perf. 15x14***
**194** A9 ¼c olive brown .70 .50
**195** A9 ½c black .70 .50
**196** A9 1c blue green 1.00 .50
**197** A9 1½c lilac brn 1.00 .50
**198** A9 2c carmine .70 .50
**199** A9 2½c lt violet .70 .50
**200** A9 5c deep blue .70 .50
**201** A9 7½c yellow brn 1.75 1.10
**202** A9 8c slate 1.75 1.10
**203** A9 10c orange brn 2.00 1.00
**204** A9 15c plum 3.00 1.25
**205** A9 20c yellow green 2.00 1.10
**206** A9 30c brown, *grn* 3.75 1.75
**207** A9 40c brown, *pink* 3.75 1.75
**208** A9 50c orange, *sal* 8.25 5.00
**209** A9 1e green, *blue* 8.25 4.00
*Nos. 194-209 (16)* 40.00 21.55

For surcharges see Nos. 250-253, 281-282.

**1920**
**Ordinary Paper**
**210** A9 ¼c olive brown .75 .60
**211** A9 1½c lilac brn 3.00 2.40
**212** A9 7½c yellow brn 3.75 2.75
**213** A9 10c orange brn 4.00 2.75
*Nos. 210-213 (4)* 11.50 8.50

**1922-26** ***Perf. 12x11½***
**214** A9 ¼c olive brown .50 .40
**215** A9 ½c black .50 .40
**216** A9 1c yellow grn ('22) .50 .40
**217** A9 1½c lilac brn .50 .40
**218** A9 2c carmine .50 .40
**219** A9 2c gray ('26) .25 .25
**220** A9 2½c lt violet .50 .40
**221** A9 3c orange ('22) .50 .40
**222** A9 4c rose ('22) .50 .40
**223** A9 4½c gray ('22) .50 .40
**224** A9 5c brt blue ('22) .70 .60
**225** A9 6c lilac ('22) .50 .40
**226** A9 7c ultra ('22) .55 .40
**227** A9 7½c yellow brn .70 .60
**228** A9 8c slate .70 .60
**229** A9 10c orange brn .70 .60
**230** A9 12c blue green ('22) .85 .60
**231** A9 15c brn rose ('22) 1.00 .60
**232** A9 20c yellow green 1.00 .60
**233** A9 24c ultra ('26) 3.00 2.00
**233A** A9 25c choc ('26) 3.00 2.00
**233B** A9 30c gray grn ('22) 1.25 .75
**233C** A9 40c turq bl ('22) 1.25 .75
**233D** A9 50c lt violet ('26) .40 .30
**233E** A9 60c dk blue ('22) 1.40 .75
**233F** A9 60c rose ('26) 3.00 .75
**233G** A9 80c brt rose ('22) 3.50 .90

**Glazed Paper**
**233H** A9 1e pale rose ('22) 4.00 2.10
**233I** A9 1e blue ('26) 3.00 1.00
**233J** A9 2e dk violet ('22) 5.00 2.50
**233K** A9 5e buff ('26) 18.00 7.50
**233L** A9 10e pink ('26) 30.00 14.00
**233M** A9 20e pale turq ('26) 80.00 40.00
*Nos. 214-233M (33)* 168.25 84.15

Preceding Issues Overprinted in Bt. Red

**1915**
**On Provisional Issue of 1902**
**234** A2 115r on 10r green 4.00 2.75
**235** A2 115r on 300r org 4.00 2.75
**236** A2 130r on 5r black 9.00 4.25
**237** A2 130r on 200r gray lil 2.75 1.75
**238** A6 115r on 25r green 1.25 .75
**239** A6 115r on 150r car, *rose* 1.25 .75
**240** A6 115r on 200r bl, *bl* 1.25 .75
**241** A6 130r on 75r rose 1.25 .75
**242** A6 130r on 100r brn, *yel* 14.50 11.00
**243** A6 130r on 300r bl, *sal* 2.10 1.20

**Same Overprint on Nos. 88 and 90**

244 A7 50r blue 1.40 1.00
245 A7 50r on 65r dull bl 1.40 1.00
*Nos. 234-245 (12)* 44.15 28.70

No. 86 Overprinted in Blue and Surcharged in Black

**1919**

246 A7 2½c on 15r brown 1.40 1.00

No. 91 Surcharged in Black

247 A7 ½c on 2½r gray 6.00 4.50
248 A7 1c on 2½r gray 4.25 2.75
249 A7 2½c on 2½r gray 2.10 1.50

No. 194 Surcharged in Black

250 A9 ½c on ¼c ol brn 5.50 4.00
251 A9 2c on ¼c ol brn 5.50 4.00
252 A9 2½c on ¼c ol brn 18.00 12.00

No. 199 Surcharged in Black

253 A9 4c on 2½c lt vio 1.75 1.25
*Nos. 246-253 (8)* 44.50 31.00

Nos. 246-253 were issued without gum.

Stamps of 1898-1905 Overprinted in Green or Red

**1920 On Stamps of 1898-1903**

255 A7 75r red lilac (G) 1.20 .75
256 A7 100r blue, *blue* (R) 1.20 .85
257 A7 115r org brn, *pink* (G) 3.50 1.75
258 A7 130r brn, *straw* (G) 37.50 28.00
259 A7 200r red lil, *pnksh* (G) 3.50 1.75
260 A7 500r blk, & red, *gray* (G) 2.40 1.75
261 A7 700r vio, *yelsh* (G) 3.50 2.10

**On Stamps of 1902**

262 A6 115r on 25r grn (R) 2.10 1.20
*a.* 115r on 25r grn (G) 100.00 80.00
263 A6 115r on 200r bl, *bl* (R) 2.40 1.75
264 A6 130r on 75r rose (G) 3.00 1.75

**On Nos. 88-89**

265 A7 50r blue (R) 2.50 2.10
266 A7 75r rose (G) 17.00 8.00

**On No. 90**

267 A7 50r on 65r dl bl (R) 17.00 7.75
*Nos. 255-257,259-267 (12)* 59.30 31.50

Nos. 238-243 Surcharged in Blue or Red

**1923 Without Gum**

268 A6 10c on 115r on 25r (Bl) 1.25 .90
268A A6 10c on 115r on 25r on #262 (Bl) 800.00 600.00
269 A6 10c on 115r on 150r (Bl) 1.25 .90
270 A6 10c on 115r on 200r (R) 1.25 .90
271 A6 10c on 130r on 75r (Bl) 1.25 .90
272 A6 10c on 130r on 100r (Bl) 1.50 1.25
273 A6 10c on 130r on 300r (R) 1.50 1.25
*Nos. 268-273 (7)* 808.00 606.10

Nos. 268-273 are usually stained and discolored.

Nos. 84-85 Surcharged

**1925**

274 A6 40c on 400r on 80r yel grn 2.10 1.25
275 N3 40c on 400r on 2½r brn 2.10 1.25
*a.* 3.5mm spacing 15.00 12.00

Nos. 233H and 233J Surcharged

**1931**

281 A9 70c on 1e pale rose 3.50 1.50
282 A9 1.40e on 2e dk vio 5.75 3.50

Ceres — A11

***Perf. 12x11½***

**1934 Typo. Wmk. 232**

283 A11 1c bister .30 .25
284 A11 5c olive brown .45 .25
285 A11 10c violet .45 .25
286 A11 15c black .40 .25
287 A11 20c gray .40 .25
288 A11 30c dk green .40 .25
289 A11 40c red orange .40 .25
290 A11 45c brt blue .60 .60
291 A11 50c brown .50 .50
292 A11 60c olive grn .80 .50
293 A11 70c brown org .80 .50
294 A11 80c emerald .85 .50
295 A11 85c deep rose 4.25 2.10
296 A11 1e maroon 1.15 .70
297 A11 1.40e dk blue 3.00 1.75
298 A11 2e dk violet 3.00 1.75
299 A11 5e apple green 10.00 5.25
300 A11 10e olive bister 22.00 11.00
301 A11 20e orange 72.50 40.00
*Nos. 283-301 (19)* 122.25 66.90

**Common Design Types**

Inscribed "S. Tomé"

**1938 Unwmk. *Perf. 13½x13***

**Name and Value in Black**

302 CD34 1c gray green .25 .25
303 CD34 5c orange brown .25 .25
304 CD34 10c dk carmine .25 .25
305 CD34 15c dk violet brn .25 .25
306 CD34 20c slate .25 .25
307 CD35 30c rose violet .25 .25
308 CD35 35c brt green .50 .40
309 CD35 40c brown .50 .40
310 CD35 50c brt red vio .50 .40
311 CD36 60c gray black .50 .40
312 CD36 70c brown violet .50 .40
313 CD36 80c orange .50 .40
314 CD36 1e red 1.25 1.00
315 CD37 1.75e blue 2.10 1.50
316 CD37 2e brown car 21.00 6.50
317 CD37 5e olive green 22.00 7.00
318 CD38 10e blue violet 25.00 8.75
319 CD38 20e red brown 45.00 11.50
*Nos. 302-319 (18)* 120.85 40.15

Marble Column and Portuguese Arms with Cross — A12

**1938 *Perf. 12½***

320 A12 80c blue green 3.00 2.40
321 A12 1.75e deep blue 11.50 6.00
322 A12 20e brown 60.00 29.00
*Nos. 320-322 (3)* 74.50 37.40

Visit of the President of Portugal in 1938.

**Common Design Types**

Inscribed "S. Tomé e Principe"

**1939 *Perf. 13½x13***

**Name and Value in Black**

323 CD34 1c gray grn .25 .25
324 CD34 5c orange brn .25 .25
325 CD34 10c dk carmine .25 .25
326 CD34 15c dk vio brn .25 .25
327 CD34 20c slate .35 .25
328 CD35 30c rose violet .25 .25
329 CD35 35c brt green .25 .25
330 CD35 40c brown .45 .40
331 CD35 50c brt red vio .45 .40
332 CD36 60c gray black .75 .50
333 CD36 70c brown violet .80 .50
334 CD36 80c orange .80 .50
335 CD36 1e red 1.00 .80
336 CD37 1.75e blue 2.10 1.00
337 CD37 2e brown car 3.50 1.75
338 CD37 5e olive green 6.75 4.00
339 CD38 10e blue violet 18.00 6.75
340 CD38 20e red brown 24.00 8.00
*Nos. 323-340 (18)* 60.45 26.35

Cola Nuts — A13

Designs: 5c, Cola Nuts. 10c, Breadfruit. 30c, Annona. 50c, Cacao pods. 1e, Coffee. 1.75e, Dendem. 2e, Avocado. 5e, Pineapple. 10e, Mango. 20e, Coconuts.

**1948 Litho. *Perf. 14½***

341 A13 5c black & yellow .80 .35
342 A13 10c black & buff .85 .55
343 A13 30c indigo & gray 4.00 2.10
344 A13 50c brown & yellow 4.50 3.00
345 A13 1e red & rose 5.75 3.00
346 A13 1.75e blue & gray 9.00 6.00
347 A13 2e black & grn 8.50 3.00
348 A13 5e brown & lil rose 26.00 12.00
349 A13 10e black & pink 26.00 13.00
350 A13 20e black & gray 55.00 42.50
*a.* Sheet of 10, #341-350 200.00 150.00
*Nos. 341-350 (10)* 140.40 85.50

No. 350a sold for 42.50 escudos.

**Lady of Fatima Issue**

Common Design Type

**1948, Dec. Unwmk.**

351 CD40 50c purple 8.50 7.00

**Catalogue values for unused stamps in this section, from this point to the end of the section, are for Never Hinged items.**

UPU Symbols — A14

**1949 Unwmk. *Perf. 14***

352 A14 3.50e black & gray 9.00 6.50

UPU, 75th anniv.

**Holy Year Issue**

Common Design Types

**1950 *Perf. 13x13½***

353 CD41 2.50e blue 3.00 1.90
354 CD42 4e orange 4.75 3.00

**Holy Year Extension Issue**

Common Design Type

**1951 *Perf. 14***

355 CD43 4e indigo & bl gray + label 3.00 2.00

Stamp without label attached sells for less.

**Medical Congress Issue**

Common Design Type

**1952 *Perf. 13½***

356 CD44 10c Clinic .35 .30

Joao de Santarem — A15

Portraits: 30c, Pero Escobar. 50c, Fernao de Po 1e, Alvaro Esteves. 2e, Lopo Goncalves. 3.50e, Martim Fernandes.

**1952 Unwmk. Litho. *Perf. 14***

**Centers Multicolored**

357 A15 10c cream & choc .25 .25
358 A15 30c pale grn & dk grn .25 .25
359 A15 50c gray & dk gray .25 .25
360 A15 1e gray bl & dk bl .75 .25
361 A15 2e lil gray & vio brn .50 .25
362 A15 3.50e buff & choc .75 .25
*Nos. 357-362 (6)* 2.75 1.50

For overprints and surcharges see Nos. 423, 425, 428-429, 432, 450-457, 474-481.

Jeronymos Convent A16

**1953 *Perf. 13x13½***

363 A16 10c dk brown & gray .25 .25
364 A16 50c brn org & org .60 .40
365 A16 3e blue blk & gray blk 2.00 .80
*Nos. 363-365 (3)* 2.85 1.45

Exhib. of Sacred Missionary Art, Lisbon, 1951.

**Stamp Centenary Issue**

Stamp of Portugal and Arms of Colonies — A17

**1953 Photo. *Perf. 13***

366 A17 50c multicolored 1.15 .80

Centenary of Portugal's first postage stamps.

**Presidential Visit Issue**

Map and Plane — A18

**1954 Typo. & Litho. *Perf. 13½***

367 A18 15c blk, bl, red & grn .25 .25
368 A18 5e brown, green & red 1.00 .75

Visit of Pres. Francisco H. C. Lopes.

### Sao Paulo Issue
Common Design Type

**1954** **Litho.**
**369** CD46 2.50e bl, gray bl & blk .70 .50

Fair Emblem, Globe and Arms — A19

**1958** **Unwmk.** ***Perf. 12x11½***
**370** A19 2.50e multicolored .80 .50

World's Fair at Brussels.

### Tropical Medicine Congress Issue
Common Design Type

Design: Cassia occidentalis.

**1958** ***Perf. 13½***
**371** CD47 5e pale grn, brn, yel, grn & red 2.75 2.00

Compass Rose — A20

**1960** **Litho.** ***Perf. 13½***
**372** A20 10e gray & multi 1.35 .65

500th death anniv. of Prince Henry the Navigator.

Going to Church — A21

**1960** ***Perf. 14½***
**373** A21 1.50e multicolored .55 .45

10th anniv. of the Commission for Technical Co-operation in Africa South of the Sahara (C.C.T.A.).

### Sports Issue
Common Design Type

Sports: 50c, Angling. 1e, Gymnast on rings. 1.50e, Handball. 2e, Sailing. 2.50e, Sprinting. 20e, Skin diving.

**1962, Jan. 18** **Litho.** ***Perf. 13½***
**Multicolored Design**

**374** CD48 50c gray green .25 .25
*a.* "$50 CORREIOS" omitted 50.00
**375** CD48 1e lt lilac .65 .25
**376** CD48 1.50e salmon .70 .25
**377** CD48 2e blue .80 .35
**378** CD48 2.50e gray green 1.10 .50
**379** CD48 20e dark blue 3.25 1.60
*Nos. 374-379 (6)* 6.75 3.20

On No. 374a, the blue impression, including imprint, is missing.
For overprint see No. 449.

### Anti-Malaria Issue
Common Design Type

Design: Anopheles gambiae.

**1962** **Unwmk.** ***Perf. 13½***
**380** CD49 2.50e multicolored 2.25 1.25

### Airline Anniversary Issue
Common Design Type

**1963** **Unwmk.** ***Perf. 14½***
**381** CD50 1.50e pale blue & multi .80 .50

### National Overseas Bank Issue
Common Design Type

Design: Francisco de Oliveira Chamico.

**1964, May 16** ***Perf. 13½***
**382** CD51 2.50e multicolored .70 .50

### ITU Issue
Common Design Type

**1965, May 17** **Litho.** ***Perf. 14½***
**383** CD52 2.50e tan & multi 2.00 1.00

Infantry Officer, 1788 — A22

35c, Sergeant with lance, 1788. 40c, Corporal with pike, 1788. 1e, Private with musket, 1788. 2.50e, Artillery officer, 1806. 5e, Private, 1811. 7.50e, Private, 1833. 10e, Lancer officer, 1834.

**1965, Aug. 24** **Litho.** ***Perf. 13½***
**384** A22 20c multicolored .25 .25
**385** A22 35c multicolored .25 .25
**386** A22 40c multicolored .35 .25
**387** A22 1e multicolored 1.25 .65
**388** A22 2.50e multicolored 1.25 .65
**389** A22 5e multicolored 2.00 1.40
**390** A22 7.50e multicolored 3.00 2.00
**391** A22 10e multicolored 3.75 2.10
*Nos. 384-391 (8)* 12.10 7.55

For overprints and surcharges see Nos. 424, 426-427, 435, 458-463, 482-485, 489-490.

### National Revolution Issue
Common Design Type

Design: 4e, Arts and Crafts School and Anti-Tuberculosis Dispensary.

**1966, May 28** **Litho.** ***Perf. 11½***
**392** CD53 4e multicolored .80 .50

### Navy Club Issue
Common Design Type

Designs: 1.50e, Capt. Campos Rodrigues and ironclad corvette Vasco da Gama. 2.50e, Dr. Aires Kopke, microscope and tsetse fly.

**1967, Jan. 31** **Litho.** ***Perf. 13***
**393** CD54 1.50e multicolored 1.30 .50
**394** CD54 2.50e multicolored 2.00 .80

Valinhos Shrine, Children and Apparition — A23

**1967, May 13** **Litho.** ***Perf. 12½x13***
**395** A23 2.50e multicolored .50 .25

50th anniv. of the apparition of the Virgin Mary to 3 shepherd children, Lucia dos Santos, Francisco and Jacinta Marto, at Fatima.

Cabral Medal, from St. Jerome's Convent — A24

**1968, Apr. 22** **Litho.** ***Perf. 14***
**396** A24 1.50e blue & multi .65 .40

500th birth anniv. of Pedro Alvares Cabral, navigator who took possession of Brazil for Portugal.

### Admiral Coutinho Issue
Common Design Type

Design: 2e, Adm. Coutinho, Cago Coutinho Island and monument, vert.

**1969, Feb. 17** **Litho.** ***Perf. 14***
**397** CD55 2e multicolored .60 .35

Vasco da Gama's Fleet — A25

**1969, Aug. 29** **Litho.** ***Perf. 14***
**398** A25 2.50e multicolored .65 .50

Vasco da Gama (1469-1524), navigator.

### Administration Reform Issue
Common Design Type

**1969, Sept. 25** **Litho.** ***Perf. 14***
**399** CD56 2.50e multicolored .45 .45

For overprint see No. 430.

Manuel Portal of Guarda Episcopal See — A26

**1969, Dec. 1** **Litho.** ***Perf. 14***
**400** A26 4e multicolored .60 .35

500th birth anniv. of King Manuel I.

Pero Escobar, Joao de Santarem and Map of Islands — A27

**1970, Jan. 25** **Litho.** ***Perf. 14***
**401** A27 2.50e lt blue & multi .50 .30

500th anniv. of the discovery of St. Thomas and Prince Islands.

Pres. Américo Rodrigues Thomaz — A28

**1970** **Litho.** ***Perf. 12½***
**402** A28 2.50e multicolored .45 .40

Visit of Pres. Américo Rodrigues Thomaz of Portugal.

### Marshal Carmona Issue
Common Design Type

Antonio Oscar Carmona in dress uniform.

**1970, Nov. 15** **Litho.** ***Perf. 14***
**403** CD57 5e multicolored .75 .40

Coffee Plant and Stamps — A29

Designs: 1.50e, Postal Administration Building and stamp No. 1, horiz. 2.50e, Cathedral of St. Thomas and stamp No. 2.

**1970, Dec.** ***Perf. 13½***
**404** A29 1e multicolored .25 .25
**405** A29 1.50e multicolored .35 .25
**406** A29 2.50e multicolored .60 .25
*Nos. 404-406 (3)* 1.20 .75

Centenary of St. Thomas and Prince Islands postage stamps.

Descent from the Cross — A30

**1972, May 25** **Litho.** ***Perf. 13***
**407** A30 20e lilac & multi 2.75 1.75

4th centenary of publication of The Lusiads by Luiz Camoens.

### Olympic Games Issue
Common Design Type

Track and javelin, Olympic emblem.

**1972, June 20** ***Perf. 14x13½***
**408** CD59 1.50e multicolored .45 .25

### Lisbon-Rio de Janeiro Flight Issue
Common Design Type

Design: 2.50e, "Lusitania" flying over warship at St. Peter Rocks.

**1972, Sept. 20** **Litho.** ***Perf. 13½***
**409** CD60 2.50e multicolored .50 .25

### WMO Centenary Issue
Common Design Type

**1973, Dec. 15** **Litho.** ***Perf. 13***
**410** CD61 5e dull grn & multi .60 .50

For overprint see No. 434.

### Republic

Flags of Portugal and St. Thomas & Prince A31

**1975, July 12** **Litho.** ***Perf. 13½***
**411** A31 3e gray & multi .25 .25
**412** A31 10e yellow & multi .90 .45
**413** A31 20e lt blue & multi 1.60 .95
**414** A31 50e salmon & multi 3.75 2.25
*Nos. 411-414 (4)* 6.50 3.90

Argel Agreement, granting independence, Argel, Sept. 26, 1974.
For overprints see Nos. 675-678.

Man and Woman with St. Thomas & Prince Flag A32

**1975, Dec. 21**
**415** A32 1.50e pink & multi .25 .25
**416** A32 4e multicolored .45 .40
**417** A32 7.50e org & multi .60 .50
**418** A32 20e blue & multi 1.25 1.40
**419** A32 50e ocher & multi 3.00 2.40
*Nos. 415-419 (5)* 5.55 4.95

Proclamation of Independence, 12/7/75.

Chart and Hand — A33

**1975, Dec. 21 Litho. *Perf. 13½***

| | | | | |
|---|---|---|---|---|
| **420** | A33 | 1e ocher & multi | .25 | .25 |
| **421** | A33 | 1.50e multicolored | .25 | .25 |
| **422** | A33 | 2.50e orange & multi | .35 | .25 |
| | | *Nos. 420-422 (3)* | .85 | .75 |

National Reconstruction Fund.

Stamps of 1952-1973 Overprinted

**1977 Litho. *Perf. 13½, 14, 13***

| | | | | |
|---|---|---|---|---|
| **423** | A15 | 10c multi (#357) | .35 | .25 |
| **424** | A22 | 20c multi (#384) | .35 | .25 |
| **425** | A15 | 30c multi (#358) | .35 | .25 |
| **426** | A22 | 35c multi (#385) | .35 | .25 |
| **427** | A22 | 40c multi (#386) | .35 | .25 |
| **428** | A15 | 50c multi (#359) | .35 | .25 |
| **429** | A15 | 1e multi (#360) | .55 | .45 |
| **430** | CD56 | 2.50e multi (#399) | .40 | .30 |
| **431** | A27 | 2.50e multi (#401) | .40 | .30 |
| **432** | A15 | 3.50e multi (#362) | 1.30 | 1.10 |
| **433** | A26 | 4e multi (#400) | .70 | .60 |
| **434** | CD61 | 5e multi (#410) | .90 | .80 |
| **435** | A22 | 7.50e multi (#390) | 1.60 | 1.30 |
| **436** | A20 | 10e multi (#372) | 2.40 | 2.00 |
| | | *Nos. 423-436 (14)* | 10.35 | 8.35 |

The 10c, 30c, 50c, 1e, 3.50e, 10e issued with glassine interleaving stuck to back.

Pres. Manuel Pinto da Costa and Flag A34

Designs: 3.50e, 4.50e, Portuguese Governor handing over power. 12.50e, like 2e.

**1977, Jan. *Perf. 13½***

| | | | | |
|---|---|---|---|---|
| **437** | A34 | 2e yellow & multi | .25 | .25 |
| **438** | A34 | 3.50e blue & multi | .40 | .25 |
| **439** | A34 | 4.50e red & multi | .55 | .40 |
| **440** | A34 | 12.50e multicolored | 1.00 | .50 |
| | | *Nos. 437-440 (4)* | 2.20 | 1.40 |

1st anniversary of independence.

Some of the sets that follow may not have been issued by the government.

Peter Paul Rubens (1577-1640), Painter — A35

Details from or entire paintings: 1e (60x44mm), Diana and Calixto, horiz. 5e (60x36mm), The Judgement of Paris, horiz. 10e (60x28mm), Diana and her Nymphs Surprised by Fauns, horiz. 15e (40x64mm), Andromeda and Perseus. 20e (40x64mm), The Banquet of Tereo. 50e (32x64mm) Fortuna.

No. 447a, 20e, (30x40mm) like #445. No. 447b, 75e, (40x30mm) The Banquet of Tereo, diff.

**1977, June 28 Litho. *Perf. 13½***

| | | | | |
|---|---|---|---|---|
| **441** | A35 | 1e multicolored | .25 | .25 |
| **442** | A35 | 5e multicolored | .25 | .25 |
| **443** | A35 | 10e multicolored | .40 | .30 |
| **444** | A35 | 15e multicolored | 2.00 | 1.25 |
| **445** | A35 | 20e multicolored | 3.00 | 2.00 |
| **446** | A35 | 50e multicolored | 5.50 | 4.75 |
| | | *Nos. 441-446 (6)* | 11.40 | 8.80 |

**Souvenir Sheet**

***Perf. 14***

| | | | | |
|---|---|---|---|---|
| **447** | A35 | Sheet of 2, #a.-b. | 13.00 | 13.00 |

See type A40 for Rubens stamps without "$" in denomination.

Ludwig van Beethoven — A36

Designs: a, 20e, Miniature, 1802, by C. Hornemann. b, 30e, Life mask, 1812, by F. Klein. c, 50e, Portrait, 1818, by Ferdinand Schimon.

**1977, June 28 *Perf. 13½***

| | | | | |
|---|---|---|---|---|
| **448** | A36 | Strip of 3, #a.-c. | 11.00 | 8.00 |

For overprint see No. 617.

**No. 379 Ovptd. "Rep. Democr. / 12-7-77"**

**1977, July 12**

| | | | | |
|---|---|---|---|---|
| **449** | CD48 | 20e multicolored | 100.00 | |

**Pairs of Nos. 358-359, 357, 362, 384-386 Overprinted Alternately in Black**

a

b

**1977, Oct. 19 Litho. *Perf. 14, 13½***

| | | | | |
|---|---|---|---|---|
| **450** | A15(a) | 3e on 30c multi | 3.50 | 1.25 |
| **451** | A15(b) | 3e on 30c multi | 3.50 | 1.25 |
| **452** | A15(a) | 5e on 50c multi | 1.00 | .30 |
| **453** | A15(b) | 5e on 50c multi | 1.00 | .30 |
| **454** | A15(a) | 10e on 10c multi | 1.75 | .60 |
| **455** | A15(b) | 10e on 10c multi | 1.75 | .60 |
| **456** | A15(a) | 15e on 3.50e multi | 4.50 | 1.00 |
| **457** | A15(b) | 15e on 3.50e multi | 4.50 | 1.00 |
| **458** | A22(a) | 20e on 20c multi | 5.50 | 1.40 |
| **459** | A22(b) | 20e on 20c multi | 5.50 | 1.40 |
| **460** | A22(a) | 35e on 35c multi | 8.00 | 1.90 |
| **461** | A22(b) | 35e on 35c multi | 8.00 | 1.90 |
| **462** | A22(a) | 40e on 40c multi | 9.00 | 3.25 |
| **463** | A22(b) | 40e on 40c multi | 9.00 | 3.25 |
| | | *Nos. 450-463 (14)* | 66.50 | 19.40 |

Centenary of membership in UPU. Overprints "a" and "b" alternate in sheets. Nos. 450-457 issued with glassine interleaving stuck to back.

These overprints exist in red on Nos. 452-453, 458-463 and on 1e on 10c, 3.50e and 30e on 30c. Value, set $125.

Mao Tse-tung (1893-1976), Chairman, People's Republic of China — A37

**1977, Dec. Litho. *Perf. 13½x14***

| | | | | |
|---|---|---|---|---|
| **464** | A37 | 50d multicolored | 8.00 | 4.00 |
| *a.* | | Souvenir sheet | 8.00 | 4.00 |

For overprint see No. 597.

Lenin — A38

Russian Supersonic Plane — A39

Designs: 40d, Rowing crew. 50d, Cosmonaut Yuri A. Gagarin.

**1977, Dec. *Perf. 13½x14, 14x13½***

| | | | | |
|---|---|---|---|---|
| **465** | A38 | 15d multicolored | 1.60 | .80 |
| **466** | A39 | 30d multicolored | 2.40 | 1.60 |
| **467** | A39 | 40d multicolored | 4.00 | 2.40 |
| **468** | A38 | 50d red & black | 6.50 | 3.25 |
| *a.* | | Sheet of 4, #465-468 | 22.50 | 22.50 |
| | | *Nos. 465-468 (4)* | 14.50 | 8.05 |

60th anniv. of Russian October Revolution.

For overprints see Nos. 592-595.

Paintings by Rubens — A40

Designs: 5d, 70d, Madonna and Standing Child. 10d, Holy Family. 25d, Holy Family, diff. 50d, Madonna and Child.

**1977, Dec. *Perf. 13½, 13½x14 (50d)***

**Size: 31x47mm (50d)**

| | | | | |
|---|---|---|---|---|
| **469** | A40 | 5d multicolored | 1.60 | 1.00 |
| **470** | A40 | 10d multicolored | 3.25 | 1.75 |
| **471** | A40 | 25d multicolored | 7.25 | 4.00 |
| **472** | A40 | 50d multicolored | 8.00 | 4.50 |
| **473** | A40 | 70d multicolored | 12.00 | 7.50 |
| *a.* | | Sheet of 4, #469-471, #473 | 30.00 | 30.00 |
| | | *Nos. 469-473 (5)* | 32.10 | 18.75 |

No. 472 exists in souvenir sheets of 1, perf. and imperf.

**Pairs of Nos. 357-359, 362, 384-385 Surcharged**

c

#475

#477

#479

#481

#483, 485

**1978, May 25 *Perf. 14½, 13½***

| | | | | |
|---|---|---|---|---|
| **474** | A15 (c) | 3d on 30c #358 | .40 | .40 |
| **475** | A15 | 3d on 30c #358 | .40 | .40 |
| *a.* | | Pair, #474-475 | 1.00 | 1.00 |
| **476** | A15 (c) | 5d on 50c #359 | .60 | .60 |
| **477** | A15 | 5d on 50c #359 | .60 | .60 |
| *a.* | | Pair, #476-477 | 1.20 | 1.20 |
| **478** | A15 (c) | 10d on 10c #357 | 1.25 | 1.25 |
| **479** | A15 | 10d on 10c #357 | 1.25 | 1.25 |
| *a.* | | Pair, #478-479 | 2.60 | 2.60 |
| **480** | A15 (c) | 15d on 3.50e #362 | 1.60 | 1.60 |
| **481** | A15 | 15d on 3.50e #362 | 1.60 | 1.60 |
| *a.* | | Pair, #480-481 | 3.25 | 3.25 |
| **482** | A22 (c) | 20d on 20c #384 | 2.50 | 2.50 |
| **483** | A22 | 20d on 20c #384 | 2.50 | 2.50 |
| *a.* | | Pair, #482-483 | 5.25 | 5.25 |
| **484** | A22 (c) | 35d on 35c #385 | 4.50 | 4.50 |
| **485** | A22 | 35d on 35c #385 | 4.50 | 4.50 |
| *a.* | | Pair, #484-485 | 10.00 | 10.00 |
| | | *Nos. 474-485 (12)* | 21.70 | 21.70 |
| | | *Nos. 475a-485a (6)* | 23.30 | 23.30 |

Overprints for each denomination alternate on sheet. Nos. 474-481 issued with glassine interleaving stuck to back.

Flag of St. Thomas and Prince Islands — A41

Designs: Nos. 487, 487a, Map of Islands, vert. No. 488, Coat of arms, vert.

**1978, July 12 *Perf. 14x13½, 13½x14***

| | | | | |
|---|---|---|---|---|
| **486** | A41 | 5d multi | 1.10 | 1.10 |
| **487** | A41 | 5d multi | 1.10 | 1.10 |
| *a.* | | Souvenir sheet, 50d | 24.00 | 24.00 |
| **488** | A41 | 5d multi | 1.10 | 1.10 |
| *a.* | | Strip of 3, #486-488 | 3.75 | 3.75 |

Third anniversary of independence. Printed in sheets of 9. No. 487a contains one imperf. stamp.

**No. 386 Surcharged**

**1978, Sept. 3 Litho. *Perf. 13½***

**489** A22 40d on 40e #386 3.00 3.00
**490** A22 40d on 40e #386 3.00 3.00
*a.* Pair, #489-490 6.50 6.50

Membership in United Nations, 3rd anniv.

Miniature Sheets

Intl. Philatelic Exhibition, 1978 — A42

No. 491: a, Tahitian Women with Fan, by Paul Gauguin. b, Still Life, by Matisse. c, Barbaric Tales, by Gauguin. d, Portrait of Armand Roulin, by Van Gogh. e, Abstract, by Georges Braque.

No. 492: a, 20d, like #491c. b, 30d, Horsemen on the Beach, by Gauguin.

**1978, Nov. 1 *Perf. 14***

**491** A42 10d Sheet of 9, #e., 2 each #a.-d. 20.00

***Imperf***

**492** A42 Sheet of 3, #491a, 492a-492b 10.00

Intl. Philatelic Exhibition, Essen.

No. 492 has simulated perfs and exists with green margin and without simulated perfs and stamps in different order.

UPU, Centennial A43

No. 493: a, Emblem, yellow & black. b, Emblem, green & black. c, Emblem, blue & black. d, Emblem, red & black. e, Concorde, balloon. f, Sailing ship, satellite. g, Monorail, stagecoach. h, Dirigible, steam locomotive. 50d, like #493h.

**1978, Nov. 1 *Perf. 14***

**493** A43 Sheet of 12, #a.-d., 2 each #e.-h. 40.00
*a.-d.* 5d Any single 1.75
*e.-h.* 15d Any single 4.00

**Souvenir Sheet**

**494** A43 50d multicolored *27.50*

For overprint see No. 706.

Miniature Sheets

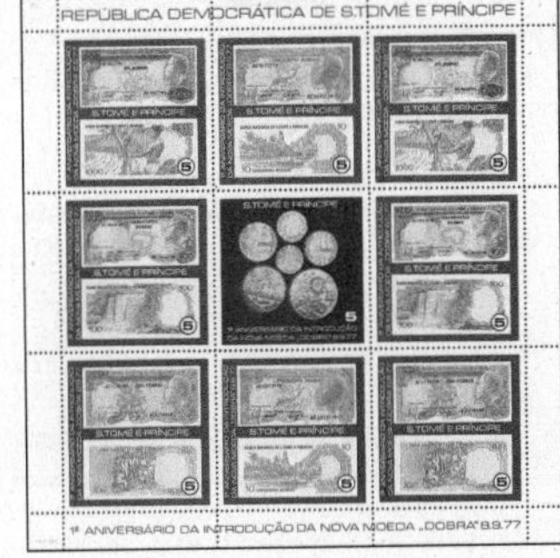

New Currency, 1st Anniv. — A44

Obverse and reverse of bank notes: #a, 1000d. b, 50d. c, 500d. d, 100d. e, Obverse of 50c, 1d, 2d, 5d, 10d, 20d coins.

**1978, Dec. 15 *Perf. 13½***

**Sheets of 9**

**495** A44 5d #e., 2 each #a.-d. 8.00
**496** A44 8d #e., 2 each #a.-d. 10.00

World Cup Soccer Championships, Argentina — A45

Various soccer plays: No. 497a, Two players in yellow shirts, one in blue. b, Two players in blue shirts, one in white. c, Six players, referee. d, Two players. No. 498a, Seven players. b, Two players at goal. c, Six players.

**1978, Dec. 15 *Perf. 14***

**497** A45 3d Block of 4, #a.-d. *4.50*
**498** A45 25d Strip of 3, #a.-c. *18.00*

Souvenir sheets of one exist, also exist imperf.

**Overprinted with Names of Winning Countries**

No. 499b, ITALIA, 1934/38. c, BRASIL, 1958/62/70. d, ALEMANIA 1954/74. No. 500a, INGLATERRA, 1966. b, Vencedores 1978 / 1o ARGENTINA / 2o HOLANDA / 3o BRASIL. c, ARGENTINA 1978.

**1979, June 1 Litho. *Perf. 14***

**499** A45 3d Block of 4, #a.-d. 1.75
**500** A45 25d Strip of 3, #a.-c. 8.25

Souvenir sheets of one exist.

Butterflies — A46

Flowers — A47

Designs: 50c, Charaxes odysseus. 1d, Crinum giganteum. No. 503a, Quisqualis indicia. b, Tecoma stans. c, Nerium oleander. d, Pyrostegia venusta. 10d, Hypolimnas salmacis thomensis. No. 505a, Charaxes monteiri, male. b, Charaxes monteiri, female. c, Papillio leonidas thomasius. d, Crenis boisduvali insularis. 25d, Asystasia gangetica. No. 507, Charaxes varanes defulvata. Nos. 508, Hibiscus mutabilis.

***Perf. 15, 15x14½ (#503), 14½x15 (#505)***

**1979, June 8**

**501** A46 50c multicolored .80 .80
**502** A47 1d multicolored .60 .60
**503** A47 8d Block of 4, #a.-d. 6.50 6.50
**504** A46 10d multicolored 1.75 1.75
**505** A46 11d Block of 4, #a.-d. 7.00 7.00
**506** A47 25d multicolored 3.75 3.75
*Nos. 501-506 (6)* 20.40 20.40

**Souvenir Sheets**

***Perf. 15***

**507** A46 50d multicolored 13.50 13.50

***Imperf***

**508** A47 50d multicolored 10.50 10.50

No. 508 contains one 30x46mm stamp with simulated perforations.

Intl. Communications Day — A48

**1979, July 6 *Perf. 13***

**509** A48 1d shown .25 .25
**510** A48 11d CCIR emblem 1.75 1.75
*a.* Pair, #509-510 + label 2.10 2.10
**511** A48 14d Syncom, 1963 2.10 2.10
**512** A48 17d Symphony, 1975 2.75 2.75
*a.* Pair, #511-512 + label 5.00 5.00
*Nos. 509-512 (4)* 6.85 6.85

Intl. Advisory Council on Radio Commmunications (CCIR), 50th anniv. (#510).

Intl. Year of the Child A49

Designs: 1d, Child's painting of bird. 7d, Young Pioneers. 14d, Children coloring on paper. 17d, Children eating fruit. 50d, Children from different countries joining hands.

**1979, July 6**

**513** A49 1d multicolored .30 .30
**514** A49 7d multicolored 1.80 1.80
**515** A49 14d multicolored 2.25 2.25
**516** A49 17d multicolored 3.25 3.25

**Size: 100x100mm**

***Imperf***

**517** A49 50d multicolored 21.00 21.00
*Nos. 513-517 (5)* 28.60 28.60

Souvenir Sheets

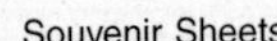

Sir Rowland Hill, 1795-1879 — A50

**1979, Sept. 15 *Perf. 15***

**518** A50 25d DC-3 Dakota *27.50*

***Perf. 14***

**519** A50 25d Graf Zeppelin, vert. *22.50*

1st Air Mail Flight, Lisbon to St. Thomas & Prince, 30th anniv. (#518), Brasiliana '79 Intl. Philatelic Exhibition and 18th UPU Congress (#519).

See Nos. 528-533 for other stamps inscribed "Historia da Aviancao."

For overprint see No. 700.

Albrecht Durer, 450th Death Anniv. — A51

Portraits: No. 520, Willibald Pirckheimer. No. 521, Portrait of a Negro. 1d, Portrait of a Young Man, facing right. 7d, Adolescent boy. 8d, The Negress Catherine. No. 525, Girl with Braided Hair. No. 526, Self-portrait as a Boy. No. 527, Feast of the Holy Family.

**1979 Background Color *Perf. 14***

**520** A51 50c blue green .25 .25
**521** A51 50c orange .25 .25
**522** A51 1d blue .40 .40
**523** A51 7d brown 1.75 1.75
**524** A51 8d red 1.75 1.75
**525** A51 25d lilac 7.25 7.25
*Nos. 520-525 (6)* 11.65 11.65

**Souvenir Sheets**

***Perf. 13½***

**526** A51 25d lil, buff & blk 20.00 20.00

***Perf. 13½x14***

**527** A51 25d blk, lil & buff 20.00 20.00

Christmas, Intl. Year of the Child (#527). No. 527 contains one 35x50mm stamp.

Issued: #520-526, Nov. 29; #527, Dec. 25.

For overprint see No. 591.

History of Aviation A52

**1979, Dec. 21 *Perf. 15***

**528** A52 50c Wright Flyer I .25 .25
**529** A52 1d Sikorsky VS 300 .30 .30
**530** A52 5d Spirit of St. Louis 1.25 1.25
**531** A52 7d Dornier DO X 1.75 1.75
**532** A52 8d Santa Cruz Fairey III D 1.75 1.75
**533** A52 17d Space Shuttle 4.75 4.75
*Nos. 528-533 (6)* 10.05 10.05

See No. 518 for souvenir sheet inscribed "Historia da Aviancao."

History of Navigation A53

50c, Caravel, 1460. 1d, Portuguese galleon, 1560. 3d, Sao Gabriel, 1497. 5d, Caravelao Navio Dos. 8d, Caravel Redonda, 1512. No. 539, Galley Fusta, 1540. No. 540, Map of St. Thomas & Prince, 1602.

**1979, Dec. 21**

| | | | | |
|---|---|---|---|---|
| **534** | A53 | 50c multicolored | .25 | .25 |
| **535** | A53 | 1d multicolored | .30 | .30 |
| **536** | A53 | 3d multicolored | .70 | .70 |
| **537** | A53 | 5d multicolored | 1.25 | 1.25 |
| **538** | A53 | 8d multicolored | 1.75 | 1.75 |
| **539** | A53 | 25d multicolored | 5.50 | 5.50 |
| | | *Nos. 534-539 (6)* | 9.75 | 9.75 |

**Size: 129x98mm**

***Imperf***

| | | | | |
|---|---|---|---|---|
| **540** | A53 | 25d multicolored | 8.00 | 8.00 |

Birds — A54

No. 541, Serinus rufobrunneus. No. 542, Euplectes aureus. No. 543, Alcedo leucogaster nais. No. 544, Dreptes thomensis. No. 545, Textor grandis. No. 546, Speirops lugubris.
No. 547, Treron S. thomae.

**1979, Dec. 21** ***Perf. 14***

| | | | | |
|---|---|---|---|---|
| **541** | A54 | 50c multicolored | .25 | .25 |
| **542** | A54 | 50c multicolored | .25 | .25 |
| **543** | A54 | 1d multicolored | .25 | .25 |
| **544** | A54 | 7d multicolored | 1.60 | 1.60 |
| **545** | A54 | 8d multicolored | 2.00 | 2.00 |
| **546** | A54 | 100d multicolored | 16.00 | 16.00 |
| | | *Nos. 541-546 (6)* | 20.35 | 20.35 |

**Souvenir Sheet**

***Perf. 14½***

| | | | | |
|---|---|---|---|---|
| **547** | A54 | 25d multicolored | 12.00 | 12.00 |

No. 546 is airmail.

Fish A55

50c, Cypselurus lineatus. 1d, Canthidermis maculatus. 5d, Diodon hystrix. 7d, Ostracion tricornis. 8d, Rhinecanthus aculeatus. 50d, Chaetodon striatus. 25d, Holocentrus axensionis.

**1979, Dec. 28** ***Perf. 14***

| | | | | |
|---|---|---|---|---|
| **548** | A55 | 50c multicolored | .25 | .25 |
| **549** | A55 | 1d multicolored | .25 | .25 |
| **550** | A55 | 5d multicolored | .30 | .30 |
| **551** | A55 | 7d multicolored | 1.90 | 1.90 |
| **552** | A55 | 8d multicolored | 2.25 | 2.25 |
| **553** | A55 | 50d multicolored | 11.00 | 11.00 |
| | | *Nos. 548-553 (6)* | 15.95 | 15.95 |

**Souvenir Sheet**

***Perf. 14½***

| | | | | |
|---|---|---|---|---|
| **554** | A55 | 25d multicolored | 14.00 | 14.00 |

No. 553 is airmail.

Balloons — A56

Designs: 50c, Blanchard, 1784. 1d, Lunardi II, 1785. 3d, Von Lutgendorf, 1786. 7d, John Wise "Atlantic," 1859. 8d, Salomon Anree "The Eagle," 1896. No. 560, Stratospheric balloon of Prof. Piccard, 1931. No. 560A, Indoor demonstration of hot air balloon, 1709, horiz.

**1979, Dec. 28** ***Perf. 15***

| | | | | |
|---|---|---|---|---|
| **555** | A56 | 50c multicolored | .25 | .25 |
| **556** | A56 | 1d multicolored | .25 | .25 |
| **557** | A56 | 3d multicolored | .60 | .60 |
| **558** | A56 | 7d multicolored | 1.40 | 1.40 |
| **559** | A56 | 8d multicolored | 1.50 | 1.50 |
| **560** | A56 | 25d multicolored | 5.25 | 5.25 |
| | | *Nos. 555-560 (6)* | 9.25 | 9.25 |

**Souvenir Sheet**

***Perf. 14***

| | | | | |
|---|---|---|---|---|
| **560A** | A56 | 25d multicolored | 10.00 | 10.00 |

No. 560A contains one 50x38mm stamp.

Dirigibles A57

Designs: 50c, Dupuy de Lome, 1872. 1d, Paul Hanlein, 1872. 3d, Gaston brothers, 1882. 7d, Willows II, 1909. 8d, Ville de Lucerne, 1910. 17d, Mayfly, 1910.

**1979, Dec. 28** ***Perf. 15***

| | | | | |
|---|---|---|---|---|
| **561** | A57 | 50c multicolored | .25 | .25 |
| **562** | A57 | 1d multicolored | .25 | .25 |
| **563** | A57 | 3d multicolored | .90 | .90 |
| **564** | A57 | 7d multicolored | 1.60 | 1.60 |
| **565** | A57 | 8d multicolored | 1.75 | 1.75 |
| **566** | A57 | 17d multicolored | 4.00 | 4.00 |
| | | *Nos. 561-566 (6)* | 8.75 | 8.75 |

1980 Olympics, Lake Placid & Moscow A58

Olympic Venues: 50c, Lake Placid, 1980. Nos. 568, 572a, Mexico City, 1968. Nos. 569, 572b, Munich, 1972. Nos. 570, 572c, Montreal, 1976. Nos. 571, 572d, Moscow, 1980.

**1980, June 13** **Litho.** ***Perf. 15***

| | | | | |
|---|---|---|---|---|
| **567** | A58 | 50c multicolored | .50 | .50 |
| **568** | A58 | 11d multicolored | 2.50 | 2.50 |
| **569** | A58 | 11d multicolored | 2.50 | 2.50 |
| **570** | A58 | 11d multicolored | 2.50 | 2.50 |
| **571** | A58 | 11d multicolored | 2.50 | 2.50 |
| | | *Nos. 567-571 (5)* | 10.50 | 10.50 |

**Souvenir Sheet**

| | | | | |
|---|---|---|---|---|
| **572** | A58 | 7d Sheet of 4, #a.-d. | 9.00 | 9.00 |

**Proclamation Type of 1975 and**

Sir Rowland Hill (1795-1879) — A59

Sir Rowland Hill and: 50c, #1. 1d, #415. 8d, #411. No. 576, #449. No. 577, #418.

**1980, June 1** ***Perf. 15***

| | | | | |
|---|---|---|---|---|
| **573** | A59 | 50c multicolored | .25 | .25 |
| **574** | A59 | 1d multicolored | .30 | .30 |
| **575** | A59 | 8d multicolored | 2.00 | 2.00 |
| **576** | A59 | 20d multicolored | 5.50 | 5.50 |
| | | *Nos. 573-576 (4)* | 8.05 | 8.05 |

**Souvenir Sheet**

***Imperf***

| | | | | |
|---|---|---|---|---|
| **577** | A32 | 20d multicolored | 11.00 | 11.00 |

No. 577 contains one 38x32mm stamp with simulated perforations.

Moon Landing, 10th Anniv. (in 1979) A60

50c, Launch of Apollo 11, vert. 1d, Astronaut on lunar module ladder, vert. 14d, Setting up research experiments. 17d, Astronauts, experiment. 25d, Command module during reentry.

**1980, June 13** ***Perf. 15***

| | | | | |
|---|---|---|---|---|
| **578** | A60 | 50c multicolored | .40 | .40 |
| **579** | A60 | 1d multicolored | .55 | .55 |
| **580** | A60 | 14d multicolored | 5.00 | 5.00 |
| **581** | A60 | 17d multicolored | 7.00 | 7.00 |
| | | *Nos. 578-581 (4)* | 12.95 | 12.95 |

**Souvenir Sheet**

| | | | | |
|---|---|---|---|---|
| **582** | A60 | 25d multicolored | 9.50 | 9.50 |

Miniature Sheet

Independence, 5th Anniv. — A61

#583: a, US #1283B. b, Venezuela #C942. c, Russia #3710. d, India #676. e, T. E. Lawrence (1888-1935). f, Ghana #106. g, Russia #2486. h, Algeria #624. i, Cuba #1318. j, Cape Verde #366. k, Mozambique #617. l, Angola #601. 25d, King Amador.

**1980, July 12** ***Perf. 13***

| | | | | |
|---|---|---|---|---|
| **583** | A61 | 5d Sheet of 12, #a.-l. + 13 labels | 12.50 | 12.50 |

**Souvenir Sheet**

***Perf. 14***

| | | | | |
|---|---|---|---|---|
| **584** | A61 | 25d multicolored | 9.50 | 9.50 |

No. 584 contains one 35x50mm stamp. For overprint see No. 596.

**No. 527 Ovptd. "1980" on Stamp and Intl. Year of the Child emblem in Sheet Margin**

**1980, Dec. 25** ***Perf. 14***

| | | | | |
|---|---|---|---|---|
| **591** | A51 | 25d on No. 527 | 20.00 | 20.00 |

Christmas.

**Nos. 465-468a Overprinted in Black or Silver**

**1981, Feb. 2** ***Perf. 13½x14, 14x13½***

| | | | | |
|---|---|---|---|---|
| **592** | A38 | 15d on #465 (S) | 2.75 | 2.75 |
| **593** | A39 | 30d on #466 (S) | 3.75 | 3.75 |
| **594** | A39 | 40d on #467 | 7.25 | 7.25 |
| **595** | A38 | 50d on #468 | 9.00 | 9.00 |
| *a.* | | on No. 468a | 50.00 | |
| | | *Nos. 592-595 (4)* | 22.75 | 22.75 |

**No. 584 Ovptd. with UN and Intl. Year of the Child emblems and Three Inscriptions**

**1981, Feb. 2** ***Perf. 14***

| | | | | |
|---|---|---|---|---|
| **596** | A61 | 25d on No. 584 | 29.00 | 29.00 |

**Nos. 464-464a Ovptd. in Silver and Black "UNIAO / SOVIETICA / VENCEDORA / 1980" with Olympic emblem and "JOGOS OLIMPICOS DE MOSCOVO 1980"**

**1981, May 15** ***Perf. 13½x14***

| | | | | |
|---|---|---|---|---|
| **597** | A37 | 50d on #464 | 9.00 | 9.00 |
| *a.* | | on #464a | 9.00 | 9.00 |

Mammals — A65

No. 598, Crocidura thomensis. No. 599, Mustela nivalis. 1d, Viverra civetta. 7d, Hipposioleros fuliginosus. 8d, Rattus norvegicus. 14d, Eidolon helvum.
25d, Cercopithecus mona.

**1981, May 22** ***Perf. 14***

| | | | | |
|---|---|---|---|---|
| **598** | A65 | 50c multicolored | .25 | .25 |
| **599** | A65 | 50c multicolored | .25 | .25 |
| **600** | A65 | 1d multicolored | .40 | .40 |
| **601** | A65 | 7d multicolored | 2.10 | 2.10 |
| **602** | A65 | 8d multicolored | 2.50 | 2.50 |
| **603** | A65 | 14d multicolored | 4.50 | 4.50 |
| | | *Nos. 598-603 (6)* | 10.00 | 10.00 |

**Souvenir Sheet**

***Perf. 14½***

| | | | | |
|---|---|---|---|---|
| **604** | A65 | 25d multicolored | 19.00 | 19.00 |

For surcharges see Nos. 1352-1353A.

Shells — A66

No. 605, Haxaplex hoplites. No. 606, Bolinus cornutus. 1d, Cassis tessellata. 1.50d, Harpa doris. 11d, Strombus latus. 17d, Cymbium glans.
No. 611: a, 10d, Bolinus cornutus, diff. b, 15d, Conus genuanus.

**1981, May 22** ***Perf. 14***

| | | | | |
|---|---|---|---|---|
| **605** | A66 | 50c multicolored | .25 | .25 |
| **606** | A66 | 50c multicolored | .25 | .25 |
| **607** | A66 | 1d multicolored | .40 | .40 |
| **608** | A66 | 1.50d multicolored | .60 | .60 |
| **609** | A66 | 11d multicolored | 3.00 | 3.00 |
| **610** | A66 | 17d multicolored | 4.75 | 4.75 |
| | | *Nos. 605-610 (6)* | 9.25 | 9.25 |

**Souvenir Sheet**

***Perf. 14½***

| | | | | |
|---|---|---|---|---|
| **611** | A66 | Sheet of 2, #a.-b. | 19.00 | 19.00 |

For surcharges, see Nos. 1987, 1990, 1993, 2014, 2017, 2020, 2041, 2044, 2047, 2068, 2071, 2074.

Johann Wolfgang von Goethe (1749-1832), Poet — A67

Design: 75d, Goethe in the Roman Campagna, by Johann Heinrich W. Tischbein.

**1981, Nov. 14** ***Perf. 14***
**612** A67 25d multicolored 2.75 2.00

**Souvenir Sheet**

**613** A67 75d multicolored 8.00 8.00

PHILATELIA '81, Frankfurt/Main, Germany.

Tito — A68

**1981, Nov. 14** ***Perf. 12½x13***
**614** A68 17d Wearing glasses 1.40 1.40
**615** A68 17d shown 1.40 1.40
*a.* Sheet of 2, #614-615 7.75 7.75

**Souvenir Sheet**

***Perf. 14x13½***

**616** A68 75d In uniform *6.75 6.75*

Nos. 614-615 issued in sheets of 4 each plus label. For overprints see Nos. 644-646.

**No. 448 Overprinted in White**

**1981, Nov. 28** ***Perf. 13½***
**617** A36 Strip of 3, #a.-c. *18.00 18.00*

Wedding of Prince Charles and Lady Diana.

On No. 617 the white overprint was applied by a thermographic process producing a shiny, raised effect.

Overprint exists in gold, $35 value.

World Chess Championships — A69

Chess pieces: No. 618, Egyptian. No. 619, Two Chinese, green. No. 620, Two Chinese, red. No. 621, English. No. 622, Indian. No. 623, Scandinavian. 75d, Khmer.

No. 624: a, Anatoly Karpov. b, Victor Korchnoi.

**1981, Nov. 28** **Litho.** ***Perf. 14***
**618** A69 1.50d multicolored *.30 .30*
**619** A69 1.50d multicolored *.30 .30*
**620** A69 1.50d multicolored *.30 .30*
**621** A69 1.50d multicolored *.30 .30*
**622** A69 30d multicolored *3.25 3.25*
**623** A69 30d multicolored *3.25 3.25*
**624** A69 30d Pair, #a.-b. *3.25 3.25*
*Nos. 618-624 (7)* *10.95 10.95*

**Souvenir Sheet**

**625** A69 75d multicolored *18.00 18.00*

Nos. 618-623 exist in souvenir sheets of one. No. 624 exists in souvenir sheet with simulated perfs. Nos. 618-625 exist imperf.

**No. 624 Ovptd. in red "ANATOLIJ KARPOV / Campeao Mundial / de Xadrez 1981"**

**1981, Dec. 10** ***Perf. 14***
**627** A69 30d Pair, #a.-b. *10.00 10.00*

Exists in souvenir sheet with simulated perfs or imperf.

Pablo Picasso — A70

Paintings: 14d, The Old and the New Year.

No. 629: a, Young Woman. b, Child with Dove. c, Paul as Pierrot with Flowers. d, Francoise, Claude, and Paloma.

No. 630: a, Girl. b, Girl with Doll. 75d, Father, Mother and Child.

**1981, Dec. 10** ***Perf. 14x13½***
**628** A70 14d multicolored *1.25 1.25*
**629** A70 17d Strip of 4, #a.-d. *6.50 6.50*
**630** A70 20d Pair, #a.-b. *6.50 6.50*
*Nos. 628-630 (3)* *14.25 14.25*

**Souvenir Sheet**

***Perf. 13½***

**631** A70 75d multicolored *13.00 13.00*

Intl. Year of the Child. Christmas (#628, 631). No. 630 is airmail.

Nos. 628, 629a-629d, 630a-630b exist in souvenir sheets of one. No. 631 contains one 50x60mm stamp.

See Nos. 683-685.

Intl. Year of the Child — A71

Paintings, No. 632, 1.50d: a, Girl with Dog, by Thomas Gainsborough. b, Miss Bowles, by Sir Joshua Reynolds. c, Sympathy, by Riviere. d, Master Simpson, by Devis. e. Two Boys with Dogs, by Gainsborough.

No. 633, 1.50d: a, Girl feeding cat. b, Girl wearing cat mask. c, White cat. d, Cat wearing red bonnet. e, Girl teaching cat to read.

No. 634, 50d: a, Boy and Dog, by Picasso. b, Clipper, by Picasso.

No. 635, 50d: a, Two white cats. b, Himalayan cat.

**1981, Dec. 30** ***Perf. 14***
**632** A71 Strip of 5, #a.-e. *1.25 1.25*
**633** A71 Strip of 5, #a.-e. *1.25 1.25*
**634** A71 Pair, #a.-b. *9.00 9.00*
**635** A71 Pair, #a.-b. + label *9.00 9.00*
*Nos. 632-635 (4)* *20.50 20.50*

**Souvenir Sheets**

***Perf. 13½***

**636** A71 75d Girl with dog *8.50 8.50*
**637** A71 75d Girl with cat *8.50 8.50*

Nos. 636-637 contain one 30x40mm stamp.

2nd Central Africa Games, Luanda, Angola — A73

No. 638: a, Shot put. b, Discus. c, High jump. d, Javelin.

50d, Team handball. 75d, Runner.

**1981, Dec. 30** ***Perf. 13½x14***
**638** A73 17d Strip of 4, a.-d. 6.00 6.00
**639** A73 50d multicolored 4.50 4.50

**Souvenir Sheet**

**640** A73 75d multicolored 8.00 8.00

World Food Day — A74

No. 641: a, Ananas sativus. b, Colocasia esculenta. c, Artocarbus altilis.

No. 642: a, Mangifera indica. b, Theobroma cacao. c, Coffea arabica.

75d, Musa sapientum ( Bananas).

**1981, Dec. 30**
**641** A74 11d Strip of 3, #a.-c. *3.00 3.00*
**642** A74 30d Strip of 3, #a.-c. *7.75 7.75*

**Souvenir Sheet**

**643** A74 75d multicolored *7.00 7.00*

No. 643 also exist imperf.

Nos. 614-616 Ovptd. in Black

**1982, May 25** ***Perf. 12½x13***
**644** A68 17d on #614 *2.75 2.75*
**645** A68 17d on #615 *2.75 2.75*
*a.* On #615a *8.00 8.00*

**Souvenir Sheet**

***Perf. 14***

**646** A68 75d on #616 *15.00 15.00*

World Cup Soccer Championships, Spain — A75

Emblem and: No. 647: a, Goalie in blue shirt jumping to catch ball. b, Two players, yellow, red shirts. c, Two players, black shirts. d, Goalie in green shirtcatching ball.

No. 648: a, Player dribbling. b, Goalie facing opponent.

No. 649, Goalie catching ball from emblem in front of goal. No. 650, Like #649 with continuous design.

**1982, June 21** ***Perf. 13½x14***
**647** A75 15d Strip of 4, #a.-d. *5.00 5.00*
**648** A75 25d Pair, #a.-b. *4.75 4.75*

**Souvenir Sheets**

**649** A75 75d multicolored — —
**650** A75 75d multicolored 8.00 8.00

Nos. 648a-648b are airmail. Nos. 647a-647d, 648a-648b exist in souvenir sheets of one.

A76

Transportation: No. 651, Steam locomotive, TGV train. No. 652, Propeller plane and Concorde.

**1982, June 21** ***Perf. 12½x13***
**651** A76 15d multicolored 4.75 2.00
**652** A76 15d multicolored 4.75 2.00
*a.* Souv. sheet of 2, #651-652 12.00 12.00

PHILEXFRANCE '82.

A77

**1982, July 31**
**653** A77 25d multicolored *5.50 3.75*

Robert Koch, discovery of tuberculosis bacillus, cent.

Goethe, 150th Anniv. of Death A78

**1982, July 31** ***Perf. 13x12½***
**654** A78 50d multicolored *6.50 6.00*

**Souvenir Sheet**

**655** A78 10d like #654 11.00 11.00

A79

**1982, July 31** ***Perf. 12½x13***
**656** A79 75d multicolored *6.25 6.25*

**Souvenir Sheet**

**657** A79 10d Sheet of 1 *5.50*
**657A** A79 10d Sheet of 2, purple & multi *9.00*

Princess Diana, 21st birthday. No. 657A exists with red violet inscriptions and different central flower.

A80

Boy Scouts, 75th Anniv.: 15d, Cape of Good Hope #178-179. 30d, Lord Baden-Powell, founder of Boy Scouts.

**1982, July 31**

**658** A80 15d multicolored 1.40 1.20
**659** A80 30d multicolored 3.00 2.75
*a.* Souv. sheet, #658-659 + label *12.00*

Nos. 658-659 exits in sheets of 4 each plus label.

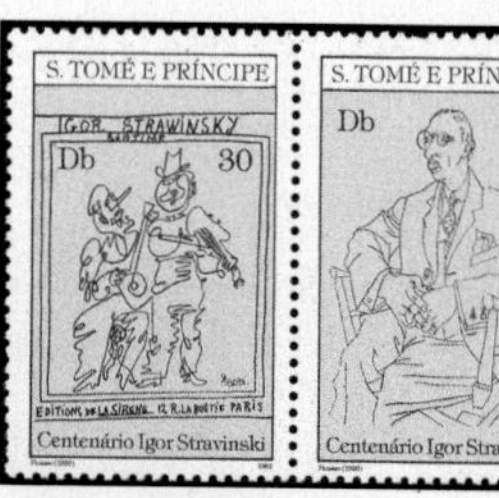

A81

Caricatures by Picasso — #660: a, Musicians. b, Stravinsky.

**1982, July 31**

**660** A81 30d Pair, #a.-b. *4.50 4.50*

### Souvenir Sheet

**661** A81 5d like #660b *12.00 12.00*

Igor Stravinsky (1882-1971), composer.

A82

George Washington, 250th Anniv. of Birth: Nos. 662, 663b, Washington, by Gilbert Stuart. Nos. 663, 663c, Washington, by Roy Lichtenstein.

**1982, July 31**

**662** A82 30d multicolored *2.10 2.10*
**663** A82 30d blk & pink *2.10 2.10*

### Souvenir Sheet

**663A** A82 5d Sheet of 2, #b.-c. 9.00 9.00

Dinosaurs — A83

No. 664, Parasaurolophus. No. 665, Stegosaurus. No. 666, Triceratops. No. 667, Brontosaurus. No. 668, Tyrannosaurus rex. No. 669, Dimetrodon.

No. 670: a, 25d, Pteranodon. b, 50d, Stenopterygius.

**1982, Nov. 30** ***Perf. 14x13½***

**664** A83 6d multicolored .85 .70
**665** A83 16d multicolored 2.25 2.00
**666** A83 16d multicolored 2.25 2.00
**667** A83 16d multicolored 2.25 2.00
**668** A83 16d multicolored *2.25 2.00*
**669** A83 50d multicolored *7.25 6.00*
*Nos. 664-669 (6) 17.10 14.70*

### Souvenir Sheet

**670** A83 Sheet of 2, #a.-b. *13.50 13.50*

Charles Darwin, cent. of death (#670).

Explorers A84

Departure of Marco Polo from Venice — A85

Explorers and their ships: 50c, Thor Heyerdahl, Kon-tiki.

No. 672: a, Magellan, Carrack. b, Drake, Golden Hind. c, Columbus, Santa Maria. d, Leif Eriksson, Viking longship.

50d, Capt. Cook, Endeavour.

**1982, Dec. 21** **Litho.**

**671** A84 50c multicolored *.25 .25*
**672** A84 18d Strip of 4, #a.-d. *6.25 6.25*
**673** A84 50d multicolored *4.75 4.75*
*Nos. 671-673 (3) 11.25 11.25*

### Souvenir Sheet

**674** A85 75d multicolored *13.00 13.00*

### Nos. 411-414 Ovptd. with Assembly Emblem and "2o ANIVERSARIO DA 1a ASSEMBLEIA DA J.M.L.S.T.P." in Silver

**1982, Dec. 24** ***Perf. 13½x14***

**675** A31 3d on #411 *.40 .30*
**676** A31 10d on #412 *1.00 1.00*
**677** A31 20d on #413 *2.75 2.75*
**678** A31 50d on #414 *5.00 5.00*
*Nos. 675-678 (4) 9.15 9.05*

MLSTP 3rd Assembly A86

**1982, Dec. 24** ***Perf. 13½x14***

**679** A86 8d bl & multi *.65 .65*
**680** A86 12d grn & multi *.95 .95*
**681** A86 16d brn org & multi *1.25 1.25*
**682** A86 30d red lilac & multi *2.50 2.50*
*Nos. 679-682 (4) 5.35 5.35*

### Picasso Painting Type of 1981

Designs: No. 683a, Lola. b, Aunt Pepa. c, Mother. d, Lola with Mantilla.

No. 684: a, Corina Romeu. b, The Aperitif. 75d, Holy Family in Egypt, horiz.

**1982, Dec. 24**

**683** A70 18d Strip of 4, #a.-d. *7.00 7.00*
**684** A70 25d Pair, #a.-b. *4.50 4.50*

### Souvenir Sheet
***Perf. 14x13½***

**685** A70 75d multicolored *27.50 27.50*

Intl. Women's Year (#683-684), Christmas (#685).

Locomotives — A87

9d, Class 231K, France, 1941.

No. 687: a, 1st steam locomotive, Great Britain, 1825. b, Class 59, Africa, 1947. c, William Mason, US, 1850. d, Mallard, Great Britain, 1938.

50d, Henschel, Portugal, 1929. 75d, Locomotive barn, Swindon, Great Britain.

**1982, Dec. 31** ***Perf. 14x13½***

**686** A87 9d multicolored *.50 .50*
**687** A87 16d Strip of 4, #a.-d. *6.00 6.00*
**688** A87 50d multicolored *4.25 4.25*
*Nos. 686-688 (3) 10.75 10.75*

### Souvenir Sheet

**689** A87 75d multicolored 10.50 10.50

Easter — A88

Paintings: No. 690: a, St. Catherine, by Raphael. b, St. Margaret, by Raphael.

No. 691: a, Young Man with a Pointed Beard, by Rembrandt. b, Portrait of a Young Woman, by Rembrandt.

No. 692: a, Rondo (Dance of the Italian Peasants), by Rubens, horiz. b, The Garden of Love, by Rubens, horiz.

No. 693, Samson and Delilah, by Rubens. No. 694, Descent from the Cross, by Rubens.

No. 695: a, Elevation of the Cross, by Rembrandt. b, Descent from the Cross, by Rembrandt.

Nos. 696a, 697, The Crucifixion, by Raphael. Nos. 696b, 698, The Transfiguration, by Raphael.

**1983, May 9** ***Perf. 13½x14, 14x13½***

**690** A88 16d Pair, #a.-b. *3.25 3.25*
**691** A88 16d Pair, #a.-b. *3.25 3.25*
**692** A88 16d Pair, #a.-b. *3.25 3.25*
**693** A88 18d multicolored *2.00 2.00*
**694** A88 18d multicolored *2.00 2.00*
**695** A88 18d Pair, #a.-b. *4.00 4.00*
**696** A88 18d Pair, #a.-b. *4.00 4.00*
*Nos. 690-696 (7) 21.75 21.75*

### Souvenir Sheets

**697** A88 18d vio & multi *9.00*
**698** A88 18d multicolored *9.00*

Souvenir sheets containing Nos. 690a-690b, 691a-691b, 692a-692b, 693, 694, 695a-695b exist.

BRASILIANA '83, Rio de Janeiro — A89

Santos-Dumont dirigibles: No. 699a, #5. b, #14 with airplane.

**1983, July 29** **Litho.** ***Perf. 13½***

**699** A89 25d Pair, #a.-b. 4.00 4.00

First manned flight, bicent.

### No. 519 Overprinted with Various Designs

**1983, July 29** **Litho.** ***Perf. 14***

### Souvenir Sheet

**700** A50 25d multicolored 40.00

BRASILIANA '83.

First Manned Flight, Bicent. — A90

No. 701: a, Wright Flyer No. 1, 1903. b, Alcock & Brown Vickers Vimy, 1919.

No. 702: a, Bleriot monoplane, 1909. b, Boeing 747, 1983.

No. 703: a, Graf Zeppelin, 1929. b, Montgolfiere brother's balloon, 1783. No. 704, Pierre Tetu-Brissy. 60d, Flight of Vincent Lunardi's second balloon, vert.

**1983, Sept. 16** ***Perf. 14x13½***

**701** A90 18d Pair, #a.-b. *3.75 3.75*
**702** A90 18d Pair, #a.-b. *3.75 3.75*
**703** A90 20d Pair, #a.-b. *4.50 4.50*
**704** A90 20d multicolored *2.25 2.25*
*Nos. 701-704 (4) 14.25 14.25*

### Souvenir Sheet
***Perf. 13½x14***

**705** A90 60d multicolored 6.75 6.75

Individual stamps from Nos. 701-704 exist in souvenir sheets of 1. Value of 4 $50.

**Nos. 493e, 493a, 493e (#706a) and 493g, 493c, 493g (#706b) Ovptd. in Gold with UPU and Philatelic Salon Emblems and:**

"SALON DER PHILATELIE ZUM / XIX WELTPOSTKONGRESS / HAMBURG 1984" Across Strips of Three Stamps

**Nos. 493f, 493b, 493f (#706c) 493h, 493d, 493h (#706d) Ovptd. in Gold with UPU and Philatelic Salon Emblems and:**

"19TH CONGRESSO DA / UNIAO POSTAL UNIVERSAL / HAMBURGO 1984" Across Strips of Three Stamps

**1983, Dec. 24** ***Perf. 14***

| | | | | |
|---|---|---|---|---|
| **706** | A43 | Sheet of 12, #a.-d. | 30.00 | |

Overprint is 91x30mm. Exists imperf with silver overprint.

Christmas — A91

Paintings: No. 707, Madonna of the Promenade, 1518, by Raphael. No. 708, Virgin of Guadalupe, 1959, by Salvador Dali.

**1983, Dec. 24** ***Perf. 12½x13***

| | | | | |
|---|---|---|---|---|
| **707** | A91 | 30d multicolored | *2.75* | *2.75* |
| **708** | A91 | 30d multicolored | *2.75* | *2.75* |

Nos. 707-708 exist in souvenir sheets of 1.

Automobiles — A92

No. 709: a, Renault, 1912. b, Rover Phaeton, 1907.

No. 710: a, Morris, 1913. b, Delage, 1910.

No. 711: a, Mercedes Benz, 1927. b, Mercedes Coupe, 1936.

No. 712: a, Mercedes Cabriolet, 1924. b, Mercedes Simplex, 1902.

75d, Peugeot Daimler, 1894.

**1983, Dec. 28** ***Perf. 14x13½***

| | | | | |
|---|---|---|---|---|
| **709** | A92 | 12d Pair, #a.-b. | *2.25* | *2.25* |
| **710** | A92 | 12d Pair, #a.-b. | *2.25* | *2.25* |
| **711** | A92 | 20d Pair, #a.-b. | *3.75* | *3.75* |
| **712** | A92 | 20d Pair, #a.-b. | *3.75* | *3.75* |
| | | *Nos. 709-712 (4)* | *12.00* | *12.00* |

**Souvenir Sheet**

| | | | | |
|---|---|---|---|---|
| **713** | A92 | 75d multicolored | 9.00 | 9.00 |

Nos. 709-712 exist as souvenir sheets. No. 713 contains one 50x41mm stamp.

Medicinal Plants — A93

50c, Cymbopogon citratus. 1d, Adenoplus breviflorus. 5.50d, Bryophillum pinatum. 15.50d, Buchholzia coriacea. 16d, Hiliotropium indicum. 20d, Mimosa pigra. 46d, Piperonia pallucila. 50d, Achyranthes aspera.

**1983, Dec. 28** ***Perf. 13½***

| | | | | |
|---|---|---|---|---|
| **714** | A93 | 50c multi | .25 | .25 |
| **715** | A93 | 1d multi | .25 | .25 |
| **716** | A93 | 5.50d multi | .45 | .45 |
| **717** | A93 | 15.50d multi | 1.60 | 1.60 |
| **718** | A93 | 16d multi | 1.60 | 1.60 |
| **719** | A93 | 20d multi | 2.00 | 2.00 |
| **720** | A93 | 46d multi | 4.75 | 4.75 |
| **721** | A93 | 50d multi | 5.50 | 5.50 |
| | | *Nos. 714-721 (8)* | 16.40 | 16.40 |

For surcharges, see Nos. 1355-1357, 1984, 1991, 1992, 2011, 2018, 2019, 2038, 2045, 2046, 2065, 2072, 2073.

1984 Olympics, Sarajevo and Los Angeles A94

No. 722, Pairs' figure skating.

No. 723: a, Downhill skiing. b, Speed skating. c, Ski jumping.

No. 724, Equestrian.

No. 725: a, Cycling. b, Rowing. c, Hurdling.

No. 726: a, Bobsled. b, Women's archery.

**1983, Dec. 29** ***Perf. 13½x14***

| | | | | |
|---|---|---|---|---|
| **722** | A94 | 16d multicolored | *1.50* | *1.50* |
| **723** | A94 | 16d Strip of 3, #a.-c. | *4.50* | *4.50* |
| **724** | A94 | 18d multicolored | *1.75* | *1.75* |
| **725** | A94 | 18d Strip of 3, #a.-c. | *5.25* | *5.25* |
| | | *Nos. 722-725 (4)* | *13.00* | *13.00* |

**Souvenir Sheet**

| | | | | |
|---|---|---|---|---|
| **726** | A94 | 30d Sheet of 2, #a.-b. | 7.00 | 7.00 |

Souvenir sheets of 2 exist containing Nos. 722 and 723b, 723a and 723c, 724 and 725b, 725a and 725c.

Birds — A95

50c, Spermestes cucullatus. 1d, Xanthophilus princeps. 1.50d, Thomasophantes sanctithomae. 2d, Quelea erythrops. 3d, Textor velatus peixotoi. 4d, Anabathmis hartlaubii. 5.50d, Serinus mozambicus santhome. 7d, Estrilda astrild angolensis. 10d,Horizorhinus dohrni. 11d, Zosterops ficedulinus. 12d, Prinia molleri. 14d, Chrysococcyx cupreus insularum. 15.50d, Halcyon malimhicus dryas. 16d, Turdus olivaceofuscus. 17d, Oriolus crassirostris. 18.50d, Dicrurus modestus. 20d, Columba thomensis. 25d, Stigmatopelia senegalensis thome. 30d, Chaetura thomensis. 42d, Onychognatus fulgidus. 46d, Lamprotornis ornatus. 100d, Tyto alba thomenis.

**1983, Dec. 30** ***Perf. 13½***

| | | | | |
|---|---|---|---|---|
| **727** | A95 | 50c multi | .25 | .25 |
| **728** | A95 | 1d multi | .25 | .25 |
| **729** | A95 | 1.50d multi | .25 | .25 |
| **730** | A95 | 2d multi | .25 | .25 |
| **731** | A95 | 3d multi | .25 | .25 |
| **732** | A95 | 4d multi | .45 | .45 |
| **733** | A95 | 5.50d multi | .45 | .45 |
| **734** | A95 | 7d multi | .80 | .80 |
| **735** | A95 | 10d multi | 1.05 | 1.05 |

**Size: 30x43mm**

| | | | | |
|---|---|---|---|---|
| **736** | A95 | 11d multi | 1.30 | 1.30 |
| **737** | A95 | 12d multi | 1.30 | 1.30 |
| **738** | A95 | 14d multi | 1.45 | 1.45 |
| **739** | A95 | 15.50d multi | 1.60 | 1.60 |
| **740** | A95 | 16d multi | 1.75 | 1.75 |
| **741** | A95 | 17d multi | 1.75 | 1.75 |
| **742** | A95 | 18.50d multi | 1.90 | 1.90 |
| **743** | A95 | 20d multi | 2.00 | 2.00 |
| **744** | A95 | 25d multi | 2.75 | 2.75 |

**Size: 31x47mm**

***Perf. 13½x14***

| | | | | |
|---|---|---|---|---|
| **745** | A95 | 30d multi | 3.25 | 3.25 |
| **746** | A95 | 42d multi | 4.50 | 4.50 |
| **747** | A95 | 46d multi | 5.25 | 5.25 |
| **748** | A95 | 100d multi | 10.00 | 10.00 |
| | | *Nos. 727-748 (22)* | 42.80 | 42.80 |

For surcharges see Nos. 1295C-1300H, 1343-1351, 1361-1363, 1372-1373, 1988, 1994, 2015, 2042, 2069, 2092, C21.

Souvenir Sheet

ESPANA '84, Madrid — A96

Paintings: a, 15.50d, Paulo Riding Donkey, by Picasso. b, 16d, Abstract, by Miro. c, 18.50d, My Wife in the Nude, by Dali.

**1984, Apr. 27** ***Perf. 13½x14***

| | | | | |
|---|---|---|---|---|
| **749** | A96 | Sheet of 3, #a.-c. | 6.00 | 6.00 |

LUBRAPEX '84, Lisbon — A97

Children's drawings: 16d, Children watching play. 30d, Adults.

**1984, May 9** ***Perf. 13½***

| | | | | |
|---|---|---|---|---|
| **750** | A97 | 16d multicolored | *1.50* | *1.50* |
| **751** | A97 | 30d multicolored | *2.50* | *2.50* |

Intl. Maritime Organization, 25th Anniv. — A98

Ships: Nos. 752a, 753a, Phoenix, 1869. 752b, 753b, Hamburg, 1893. 752c, 753c, Prince Heinrich, 1900.

No. 754: a, Leopold, 1840. b, Stadt Schaffhausen, 1851. c, Crown Prince, 1890. d, St. Gallen, 1905.

No. 755: a, Elise, 1816. b, De Zeeuw, 1824. c, Friedrich Wilhelm, 1827. d, Packet Hansa.

No. 756: a, Savannah, 1818. b, Chaperone, 1884. c, Alida, 1847. d, City of Worcester, 1881.

No. 757, Ferry, Lombard Bridge, Hamburg, c. 1900. No. 758, Train, coaches on bridge, c. 1880, vert. No. 759, Windmill, bridge, vert. No. 760, Queen of the West. No. 761, Bremen. No. 762, Union.

**1984, June 19** **Litho.** ***Perf. 14x13½***

| | | | | |
|---|---|---|---|---|
| **752** | A98 | 50c Strip of 3, #a.-c. | *3.50* | *3.50* |
| **753** | A98 | 50c Strip of 3, #a.-c. | *3.50* | *3.50* |
| **754** | A98 | 7d Piece of 4, #a.-d. | *4.25* | *4.25* |
| *e.* | | Souv. sheet of 2, #754a-754b | | |
| *f.* | | Souv. sheet of 2, #754c-754d | | |
| **755** | A98 | 8d Piece of 4, #a.-d. | *4.25* | *4.25* |
| *e.* | | Souv. sheet of 2, #755a-755b | | |
| *f.* | | Souv. sheet of 2, #755c-755d | | |
| **756** | A98 | 15.50d Piece of 4, #a.-d. | *7.50* | *7.50* |
| *e.* | | Souv. sheet of 2, #756a, 756d | | |
| *f.* | | Souv. sheet of 2, #756b-756c | | |
| | | *Nos. 752-756 (5)* | *23.00* | *23.00* |
| | | *Nos. 754e-754f, 755e-755f, 756e-756f (6)* | *72.50* | |

**Souvenir Sheets**

***Perf. 14x13½, 13½x14***

| | | | | |
|---|---|---|---|---|
| **757** | A98 | 10d multicolored | *8.50* | *8.50* |
| **758** | A98 | 10d multicolored | *8.50* | *8.50* |
| **759** | A98 | 10d multicolored | *8.50* | *8.50* |

***Perf. 13½***

| | | | | |
|---|---|---|---|---|
| **760** | A98 | 15d multicolored | *12.00* | *12.00* |
| **761** | A98 | 15d multicolored | *12.00* | *12.00* |
| **762** | A98 | 15d multicolored | *12.00* | *12.00* |
| | | *Nos. 757-762 (6)* | *61.50* | *61.50* |

Nos. 757-759 exist imperf in different colors. Nos. 760-762 contain one 60x33mm stamp each. Nos. 753a-753c have UPU and Hamburg Philatelic Salon emblems and are additionally inscribed "PARTICIPACAO DE S. TOME E PRINCIPE / NO CONGRESSO DA U.P.U. EM HAMBURGO."

Sheets containing Nos. 754-756 contain one label.

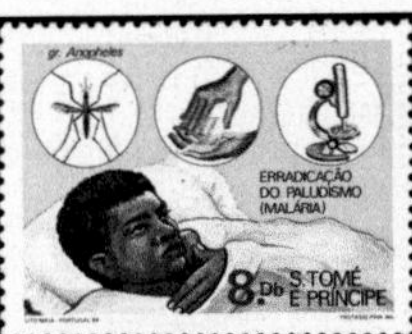


Natl. Campaign Against Malaria A99

**1984, Sept. 30** ***Perf. 13½***

| | | | | |
|---|---|---|---|---|
| **764** | A99 | 8d Malaria victim | *1.10* | *1.10* |
| **765** | A99 | 16d Mosquito, DDT, vert. | *2.00* | *2.00* |
| **766** | A99 | 30d Exterminator, vert. | *3.50* | *3.50* |
| | | *Nos. 764-766 (3)* | *6.60* | *6.60* |

A100

World Food Day: 8d, Emblem, animals, produce. 16d, Silhouette, animals. 46d, Plowed field, produce. 30d, Tractor, field, produce, horiz.

**1984, Oct. 16**

| | | | | |
|---|---|---|---|---|
| **767** | A100 | 8d multicolored | *1.05* | *1.05* |
| **768** | A100 | 16d multicolored | *1.60* | *1.60* |
| **769** | A100 | 46d multicolored | *3.25* | *3.25* |
| | | *Nos. 767-769 (3)* | *5.90* | *5.90* |

**Souvenir Sheet**

| | | | | |
|---|---|---|---|---|
| **770** | A100 | 30d multicolored | *3.75* | *3.75* |

For surcharges see No. 1366.

A101

Mushrooms: 10d, Coprinus micaceus. 20d, Amanita rubescens. 30d, Armillariella mellea. 50d, Hygrophorus chrysodon, horiz.

**1984, Nov. 5**

| | | | | |
|---|---|---|---|---|
| **771** | A101 | 10d multicolored | 3.00 | 3.00 |
| **772** | A101 | 20d multicolored | 5.50 | 5.50 |
| **773** | A101 | 30d multicolored | 8.00 | 8.00 |
| | | *Nos. 771-773 (3)* | 16.50 | 16.50 |

**Souvenir Sheet**

| | | | | |
|---|---|---|---|---|
| **774** | A101 | 50d multicolored | *16.00* | *16.00* |

Christmas A102

Designs: 30d, Candles, offering, stable. 50d, Stable, Holy Family, Kings.

**1984, Dec. 25**

| | | | | |
|---|---|---|---|---|
| **775** | A102 | 30d multicolored | *2.75* | *2.75* |

**Souvenir Sheet**

| | | | | |
|---|---|---|---|---|
| **776** | A102 | 50d multicolored | 4.75 | 4.75 |

No. 776 contains one 60x40mm stamp.

Conference of Portuguese Territories in Africa
A103

**1985, Feb. 14**

**777** A103 25d multicolored *2.75 2.75*

Reinstatement of Flights from Lisbon to St. Thomas, 1st Anniv. — A104

Designs: 25d, Douglas DC-3, map of northwest Africa. 30d, Air Portugal Douglas DC-8. 50d, Fokker Friendship.

**1985, Dec. 6 Litho.** ***Perf. 13½***

**778** A104 25d multicolored *2.25 2.25*
**779** A104 30d multicolored *2.50 2.50*

**Souvenir Sheet**

**779A** A104 50d multicolored 8.00 8.00

Flowers — A105

**1985, Dec. 30** ***Perf. 11½x12***

**780** A105 16d Flowering cactus *1.20 1.20*
**781** A105 20d Sunflower *1.90 1.90*
**782** A105 30d Porcelain rose *2.10 2.10*
*Nos. 780-782 (3) 5.20 5.20*

Mushrooms A106

6d, Fistulina hepatica. 25d, Collybia butyracea. 30d, Entoloma clypeatum.
75d, Cogumelos II.

**1986, Sept. 18** ***Perf. 13½***

**783** A106 6d multicolored *.65 .65*
**784** A106 25d multicolored *2.40 2.40*
**785** A106 30d multicolored *2.50 2.50*
*Nos. 783-785 (3) 5.55 5.55*

**Souvenir Sheet**

**786** A106 75d multicolored *10.00 8.00*

No. 786 exists with margins trimmed on four sides removing the control number.

Miniature Sheet

World Cup Soccer, Mexico
A107

No. 787: a, Top of trophy. b, Bottom of trophy. c, Interior of stadium. d, Exterior of stadium.

**1986, Oct. 1**

**787** A107 25d Sheet of 4, #a.-d. 10.00 10.00

For overprints see Nos. 818-818A.

Miniature Sheet

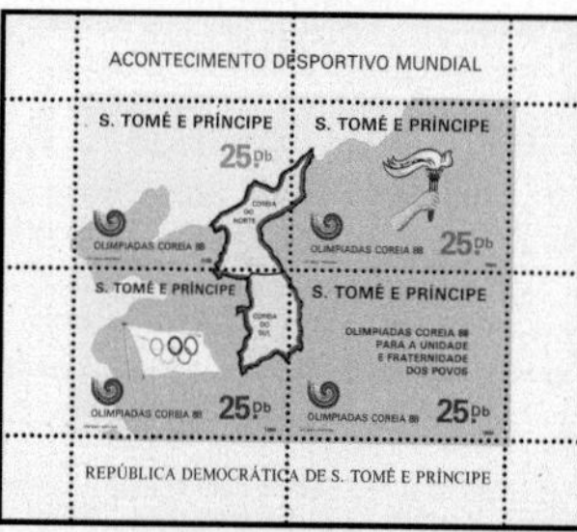


1988 Summer Olympics, Seoul — A108

Seoul Olympic Games emblem, and: No. 788a, Map of North Korea. b, Torch. c, Olympic flag, map of South Korea. d, Text.

**1986, Oct. 2**

**788** A108 25d Sheet of 4, #a.-d. *14.50 14.50*

S. TOMÉ E PRÍNCIPE
1986 — ANO DA PASSAGEM DO COMETA HALLEY


Halley's Comet — A109

Designs: No. 789a, 5d, Challenger space shuttle, 1st launch. b, 6d, Vega probe. c, 10d, Giotto probe. d, 16d, Comet over Nuremberg, A.D. 684.
90d, Comet, Giotto probe, horiz.

**1986, Oct. 27**

**789** A109 Sheet of 4, #a.-d. + 5 labels *9.00 7.00*

**Souvenir Sheet**

**790** A109 90d multicolored 9.00 9.00

Automobiles — A110

Designs: No. 791a, 50c, Columbus Monument, Barcelona. b, 6d, Fire engine ladder truck, c. 1900. c, 16d, Fire engine, c. 1900. d, 30d, Fiat 18 BL Red Cross ambulance, c. 1916.

**1986, Nov. 1**

**791** A110 Sheet of 4, #a.-d. + 5 labels *10.00 8.00*

Railway Stations and Signals
A111

Designs: 50c, London Bridge Station, 1900. 6d, 100-300 meter warning signs. 20d, Signal lamp. 50d, St. Thomas & Prince Station.

**1986, Nov. 2** ***Perf. 13½***

**792** A111 50c multicolored *.45 .45*
**793** A111 6d multicolored *1.10 1.10*
**794** A111 20d multicolored *3.75 3.75*
*Nos. 792-794 (3) 5.30 5.30*

**Souvenir Sheet**

**795** A111 50d multicolored 6.50 6.50

LUBRAPEX '86, Brazil — A112

Exhibition emblem and: No. 796a, 1d, Line fisherman on shore. b, 1d, Line fisherman in boat. c, 2d, Net fisherman. d, 46d, Couple trap fishing, lobster.

**1987, Jan. 15**

**796** A112 Sheet of 4, #a.-d. + 2 labels *7.00 7.00*

Intl. Peace Year
A113

Designs: 8d, Mahatma Gandhi. 10d, Martin Luther King, Jr. 16d, Red Cross, Intl. Peace Year, UN, UNESCO, Olympic emblems and Nobel Peace Prize medal. 20d, Albert Luthuli. 75d, Peace Dove, by Picasso.

**1987, Jan. 15**

**797** A113 8d bl, blk & pur *.95 .95*
**798** A113 10d bl, blk & grn *1.10 1.10*
**799** A113 16d multicolored *2.00 2.00*
**800** A113 20d multicolored *2.50 2.50*
*Nos. 797-800 (4) 6.55 6.55*

**Souvenir Sheet**

**801** A113 75d multicolored *6.50 6.50*

Christmas 1986 — A114

Paintings by Albrecht Durer: No. 802a, 50c, Virgin and Child. b, 1d, Madonna of the Carnation. c, 16d, Virgin and Child, diff. d, 20d, The Nativity. 75d, Madonna of the Goldfinch.

**1987, Jan. 15**

**802** A114 Strip of 4, #a.-d. 6.00 6.00

**Souvenir Sheet**

**803** A114 75d multicolored 8.00 8.00

Fauna and Flora — A115

Birds: a, 1d, Agapornis fischeri. b, 2d, Psittacula krameri. c, 10d, Psittacus erithacus. d, 20d, Agapornis personata psittacidae.
Flowers: e, 1d, Passiflora caerulea. f, 2d, Oncidium nubigenum. g, 10d, Helicontia wagneriana. h, 20d, Guzmania liguiata.
Butterflies: i, 1d, Aglais urticae. j, 2d, Pieris brassicae. k, 10d, Fabriciana niobe. l, 20d, Zerynthia polyxena.
Dogs: m, 1d, Sanshu. n, 2d, Hamiltonstovare. o, 10d, Gran spitz. p, 20d, Chow-chow.

**1987, Oct. 15** ***Perf. 14x13½***

**804** A115 Sheet of 16, #a.-p. *20.00* 20.00

Sports Institute, 10th Anniv. — A116

No. 805: a, 50c, Three athletes. b, 20d, Map of St. Thomas and Prince, torchbearers. c, 30d, Volleyball, soccer, team handball and basketball players.
50d, Bjorn Borg.

**1987, Oct. 30**

**805** A116 Strip of 3, #a.-c. *4.25 4.25*

**Souvenir Sheet**

***Perf. 13½x14***

**806** A116 50d Sheet of 1 + label 6.50 6.50

Miniature Sheet

Discovery of America, 500th Anniv. (in 1992) — A117

Emblem and: No. 807: a, 15d, Columbus with globe, map and arms. b, 20d, Battle between Spanish galleon and pirate ship. c, 20d, Columbus landing in New World. 100d, Model ship, horiz.

**1987, Nov. 3** ***Perf. 13½x14***

**807** A117 Sheet of 3, #a.-c. + 3 labels *8.00 8.00*

**Souvenir Sheet**

***Perf. 14x13½***

**808** A117 100d multicolored *9.00 9.00*

Mushrooms — A118

Designs: No. 809a, 6d, Calocybe ionides. b, 25d, Hygrophorus coccineus. c, 30d, Boletus versipellis. 35d, Morchella vulgaris, vert.

**1987, Nov. 10** ***Perf. 14x13½***

**809** A118 Strip of 3, #a.-c. 5.50 5.50

**Souvenir Sheet**

***Perf. 13½x14***

**810** A118 35d multicolored *5.00 5.00*

Locomotives — A119

No. 811: a, 5d, Jung, Germany. b, 10d, Mikado 2413. c, 20d, Baldwin, 1920. 50d, Pamplona Railroad Station, 1900.

**1987, Dec. 1 Litho. *Perf. 14x13½***

**811** A119 Strip of 3, #a.-c. 6.00 6.00

**Souvenir Sheet**

**812** A119 50d multicolored 7.25 7.25

Miniature Sheet

Christmas — A120

Paintings of Virgin and Child by: No. 813a, 1d, Botticelli. b, 5d, Murillo. c, 15d, Raphael. d, 20d, Memling.
50d, Unknown artist, horiz.

**1987, Dec. 20 *Perf. 13½x14***

**813** A120 Sheet of 4, #a.-d. *3.75 3.75*

**Souvenir Sheet**

***Perf. 14x13½***

**814** A120 50d multicolored *5.25 5.25*

World Boy Scout Jamboree, Australia, 1987-88 — A121

**1987, Dec. 30 *Perf. 14x13½***

**815** A121 50c multicolored 3.00 .80

Russian October Revolution, 70th Anniv. A122

**1988 Litho. *Perf. 12***

**816** A122 25d Lenin addressing revolutionaries 2.25 2.25

Souvenir Sheet

Lubrapex '88 — A123

**1988, May *Perf. 14x13½***

**817** A123 80d Trolley 5.25 5.25

**Nos. 787a-787d Ovptd. "CAMPEONATO MUNDIAL / DE FUTEBOL MEXICO '86 / ALEMANHA / SUBCAMPIAO" in Silver (#818) or Same with "ARGENTINA / CAMPIAO" Instead in Gold (#818A) Across Four Stamps**

**1988, Aug. 15 *Perf. 13½***

**818** A107 25d Block of 4 (S) 25.00 25.00
**818A** A107 25d Block of 4 (G) 25.00 25.00

Medicinal Plants — A123a

Mushrooms — A123b

Medicinal plants: No. 819a, 5d, Datura metel. b, 5d, Salaconta. c, 5d, Cassia occidentalis. d, 10d, Solanum ovigerum. e, 20d, Leonotis nepetifolia.
Mushrooms: No. 820a, 10d, Rhodopaxillus nudus. b, 10d, Volvaria volvacea. c, 10d, Psalliota bispora. d, 10d, Pleurotus ostreatus. e, 20d, Clitocybe geotropa.

**1988, Oct. 26 *Perf. 13½x14***

**819** A123a Strip of 5, #a.-e. 6.75 6.75
**820** A123b Strip of 5, #a.-e. 8.00 8.00

**Souvenir Sheets**

**821** A123a 35d Hiersas durero *6.25 6.25*
**822** A123b 35d Mushroom on wood *6.25 6.25*

Miniature Sheets of 4

Passenger Trains — A123c

No. 823: a, Swiss Federal Class RE 6/6, left. b, Class RE 6/6, right.
No. 824: a, Japan Natl. Class EF 81, left. b, Class EF 81, right.
No. 825: a, German Electric E 18, 1930, left. b, E 18, 1930, right.
60d, Japan Natl. Class 381 Electric.

**1988, Nov. 4 *Perf. 14x13½***

**823** A123c 10d 2 ea #a.-b. + 2 labels *5.50 5.50*
**824** A123c 10d 2 ea #a.-b. + 2 labels *5.50 5.50*
**825** A123c 10d 2 ea #a.-b. + 2 labels *5.50 5.50*
*Nos. 823-825 (3) 16.50 16.50*

**Souvenir Sheet**

**826** A123c 60d multicolored *8.00 8.00*

Butterflies — A123d

Various flowers and: No. 827a, White and brown spotted butterfly. b, Dark brown and white butterfly, flower stigma pointing down. c, Brown and white butterfly, flower stigma pointing up.
50d, Brown, white and orange butterly.

**1988, Nov. 25 *Perf. 13½x14***

**827** A123d 10d Strip of 3, #a.-c. *4.50 4.00*

**Souvenir Sheet**

**828** A123d 50d multicolored *9.00 9.00*

Ferdinand von Zeppelin (1838-1917) A123e

Berlin, 750th Anniv. — A123f

No. 829: a, Sailing ship, dirigible L23. b, Dirigibles flying over British merchant ships. c, Rendezvous of zeppelin with Russian ice breaker Malygin.
No. 830: a, Airship Le Jeune at mooring pad, Paris, 1903, vert. b, von Zeppelin, vert.

***Perf. 14x13½, 13½x14***

**1988, Nov. 25**

**829** A123e 10d Strip of 3, #a.-c. *7.75 7.75*
**830** A123e 10d Pair, #a.-b. *5.25 5.25*

**Souvenir Sheet**

**831** A123f 50d multicolored 8.00 8.00

Natl. Arms — A123g

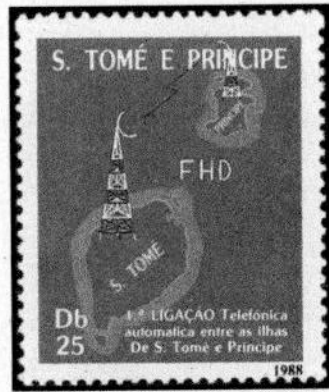


Automatic Telephone Exchange Linking the Islands, 1st Anniv. — A123h

**1988, Dec. 15 *Perf. 13½***

**832** A123g 10d multicolored *1.40 1.40*
**833** A123h 25d multicolored *3.00 3.00*

Olympics Games, Seoul, Barcelona and Albertville — A123i

World Cup Soccer Championships, Italy, 1990 — A123j

No. 834, View of Barcelona, Cobi. No. 835, Barcelona Games emblem. No. 836, Gold medal from 1988 Seoul games. No. 837, Emblems of 1988 & 1992 games. No. 838, Bear on skis, Albertville, 1992. No. 839, Soccer ball. No. 840, Italy '90 Championships emblem. No. 841, World Cup Trophy. No. 842, Transfer of Olympic flag during Seoul closing ceremony. No. 843, Olympic pins. No. 844, like No. 838. No. 845, Soccer balls as hemispheres of globe.

**1988, Dec. 15 *Perf. 14x13½, 13½x14***

**834** A123i 5d multi *1.60 1.60*
**835** A123i 5d multi, vert. *1.60 1.60*
**836** A123i 5d multi, vert. *1.60 1.60*
**837** A123i 5d multi *1.60 1.60*
**838** A123i 5d grn & multi *1.60 1.60*
**839** A123j 5d multi *1.60 1.60*
**840** A123j 5d multi, vert. *1.60 1.60*
**841** A123j 5d multi, vert. *1.60 1.60*
*Nos. 834-841 (8) 12.80 12.80*

**Souvenir Sheets**

***Perf. 14x13½***

**842** A123i 50d multi *10.00 10.00*
**843** A123i 50d multi *10.00 10.00*
**844** A123i 50d blue & multi *10.00 10.00*
**845** A123j 50d multi *10.00 10.00*

No. 842 exists with Olympic emblems in gold or silver. No. 845 exists with marginal inscriptions in gold or silver. See Nos. 876-877 for souvenir sheets similar in design to No. 840.

Intl. Boy Scout Jamboree, Australia, 1987-88 — A123k

No. 846: a, Campfire. b, Scout emblem, pitched tents, flag. c, Scout emblem, tent flaps, flag, axe.
110d, Trefoil center point, horiz.

**1988, Dec. 15** *Perf. 13½x14*
**846** A123k 10d Strip of 3, #a.-c. 6.75 6.75

**Souvenir Sheet**
*Perf. 14x13½*
**847** A123k 110d multicolored 20.00 20.00

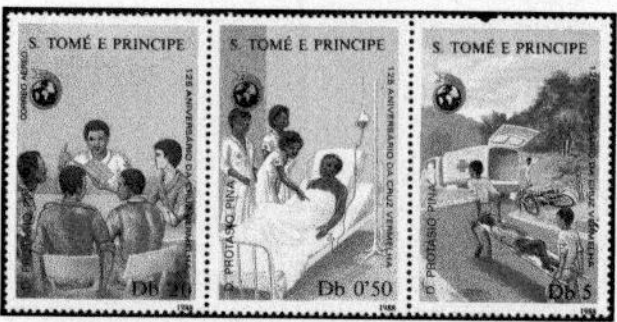
Intl. Red Cross, 125th Anniv. — A123m

No. 848: a, 50c, Patient in hospital. b, 5d, Transporting victims. c, 20d, Instructing workers. 50d, Early mail train, horiz.

**1988, Dec. 15** *Perf. 13½x14*
**848** A123m Strip of 3, #a.-c. *7.25 7.25*

**Souvenir Sheet**
*Perf. 14x13½*
**849** A123m 50d multicolored *10.50 10.50*

No. 848c is airmail.

Miniature Sheet

Christmas — A123n

No. 850: a, 10d, Madonna and Child with St. Anthony Abbot and the Infant Baptism, by Titian. b, 10d, Madonna and Child with St. Catherine and a Rabbit, by Titian. c, 10d, Nativity Scene, by Rubens. d, 30d, Adoration of the Magi, by Rubens.
50d, The Annunciation (detail), by Titian, vert.

**1988, Dec. 23** *Perf. 14x13½*
**850** A123n Sheet of 4, #a.-d. 8.00 8.00

**Souvenir Sheet**
*Perf. 13½x14*
**851** A123n 50d multicolored 6.75 6.75

Titian, 500th anniv. of birth. Country name does not appear on No. 850d.

French Revolution, Bicent. — A123o

Designs: No. 852, Eiffel Tower, Concorde, stylized doves, flag. No. 853 Eiffel Tower, flag, stylized doves. No. 854, Eiffel Tower, flag, stylized doves, TGV train, vert. 50d, TGV train.

*Perf. 14x13½, 13½x14*
**1989, July 14** **Litho.**
**852** A123o 10d multicolored *1.50 1.50*
**853** A123o 10d multicolored *1.50 1.50*
**854** A123o 10d multicolored *1.50 1.50*
*Nos. 852-854 (3) 4.50 4.50*

**Souvenir Sheet**
**855** A123o 50d multicolored *6.50 6.50*

Fruit — A123p

**1989, Sept. 15** *Perf. 13½x14*
**856** A123p 50c Chapu-chapu *.25 .25*
**857** A123p 1d Guava *.25 .25*
**858** A123p 5d Mango *.25 .25*
**859** A123p 10d Carambola *.25 .25*
**860** A123p 25d Nona *.45 .45*
**861** A123p 50d Avacado *.90 .90*
**862** A123p 50d Cajamanga *.90 .90*

*Perf. 14x13½*
**863** A123p 60d Jackfruit *.95 .95*
**864** A123p 100d Cacao *1.50 1.50*
**865** A123p 250d Bananas *4.00 4.00*
**866** A123p 500d Papaya *8.75 8.75*
*Nos. 856-866 (11) 18.45 18.45*

For surcharges see Nos. 1170B, 1170E-1170G, 1170J-1170K, 1170N, 1358-1360.

**Souvenir Sheet**
*Perf. 13½x14*
**867** A123p 1000d Pomegranate *18.00 18.00*

Nos. 863-866 are horiz.

Orchids A123q

Designs: No. 868, Dendrobium phalaenopsis. No. 869, Catteleya granulosa. 50d, Diothonea imbricata and maxillaria eburnea.

**1989, Oct. 15** *Perf. 13½x14*
**868** A123q 20d multicolored *2.00 2.00*
**869** A123q 20d multicolored *2.00 2.00*

**Souvenir Sheet**
**870** A123q 50d multicolored 4.75 4.75

Hummingbirds — A124

Designs: No. 871, Topaza bella, Sappho sparganura, vert. No. 872, Petasophores anais. No. 873, Lophornis adorabilis, Chalcostigma herrani, vert. 50d, Oreotrochilus chimborazo.

**1989, Oct. 15** *Perf. 13½x14, 14x13½*
**871** A124 20d multicolored 1.75 1.75
**872** A124 20d multicolored 1.75 1.75
**873** A124 20d multicolored 1.75 1.75
*Nos. 871-873 (3)* 5.25 5.25

**Souvenir Sheet**
*Perf. 14x13½*
**874** A124 50d multicolored 5.25 5.25

Miniature Sheet

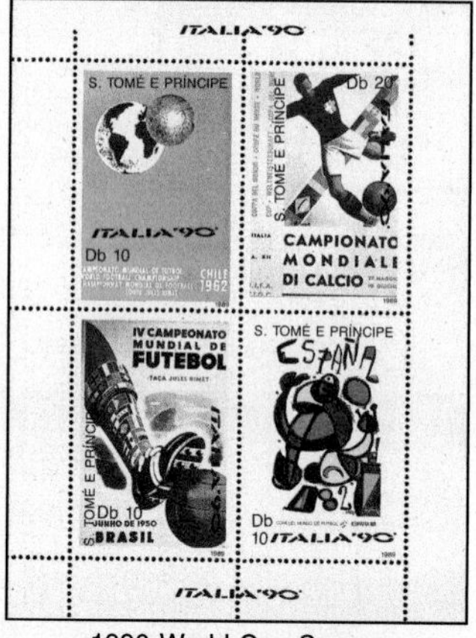
1990 World Cup Soccer Championships, Italy — A125

Program covers: No. 875: a, 10d, Globe and soccer ball, 1962. b, 10d, Foot kicking ball, 1950. c, 10d, Abstract design, 1982. d, 20d, Player kicking ball, 1934.
No. 876: a, Character emblem, horiz. b, USA 94, horiz. 50d, like #876a, horiz.

**1989, Oct. 24** *Perf. 13½x14*
**875** A125 Block of 4, #a.-d. *7.25 7.25*

**Souvenir Sheets**
*Perf. 14x13½*
**876** A125 25d Sheet of 2, #a.-b. *6.50 6.50*
**877** A125 50d blue & multi *6.50 6.50*

1992 Summer Olympics, Barcelona — A126

**1989, Oct. 24** *Perf. 13½x14, 14x13½*
**878** A126 5d Tennis, vert. *.90 .90*
**879** A126 5d Basketball, vert. *.90 .90*
**880** A126 5d Running *.90 .90*
**881** A126 35d Baseball, vert. *6.50 6.50*
*Nos. 878-881 (4) 9.20 9.20*

**Souvenir Sheet**
*Perf. 14x13½*
**882** A126 50d Sailing *8.00 8.00*
**883** A126 50d Mosaic *8.00 8.00*

Nos. 878-881 exist in souvenir sheets of one. Value for 4 sheets, $22.50. The country name on souvenir sheet of one of No. 878 appears in the margin, rather than on the stamp itself.

Locomotives — A127

**1989, Oct. 27** *Perf. 14x13½, 13½x14*
**884** A127 20d Japan 2.25 2.25
**885** A127 20d Philippines 2.25 2.25
**886** A127 20d Spain, vert. 2.25 2.25
**887** A127 20d India 2.25 2.25
**888** A127 20d Asia 2.25 2.25
*Nos. 884-888 (5)* 11.25 11.25

**Souvenir Sheets**
**889** A127 50d Garratt, Africa *7.50 7.50*
**890** A127 50d Trans-Gabon, vert. *7.50 7.50*

Nos. 884-888 exist in souvenir sheets of one.

Ships A128

#891, Merchant ships at sea, 16th cent. #892, Caravels, merchant ships in harbor, 16th cent. #893, 3 merchant ships at sea, 18th cent. #894, War ships, 18th cent. #895, 4 merchant ships, 18th cent. #896, Passenger liner, Port of Hamburg. #897, German sailing ship, 17th cent.

**1989, Oct. 27** *Perf. 14x13½*
**891** A128 20d multicolored *2.00 2.00*
**892** A128 20d multicolored *2.00 2.00*
**893** A128 20d multicolored *2.00 2.00*
**894** A128 20d multicolored *2.00 2.00*
**895** A128 20d multicolored *2.00 2.00*
*Nos. 891-895 (5) 10.00 10.00*

**Souvenir Sheets**
**896** A128 50d multicolored 6.00 6.00

*Perf. 13½x14*
**897** A128 50d multi, vert. 6.00 6.00

Discovery of America, 500th anniv., in 1992 (#891-895) and Hamburg, 800th anniv. (#891-897).

Nos. 891-895 exist in souvenir sheets of one. Value for 5 sheets, $15.

Butterflies A129

**1989, Dec. 20** *Perf. 13½x14*
**898** A129 20d Tree bark *2.25 2.25*
**899** A129 20d Leaves *2.25 2.25*
**900** A129 20d Flowers *2.25 2.25*
**901** A129 20d Bird *2.25 2.25*
**902** A129 20d Blades of grass *2.25 2.25*
*Nos. 898-902 (5) 11.25 11.25*

**Souvenir Sheet**
**903** A129 100d yel, brn & multi *10.50 10.50*

Nos. 898-902 exist in souvenir sheets of one. Value for 5 sheets, $30.

African Development Bank, 25th Anniv. — A130

**1989, Dec. 20** *Perf. 13½x14*
**904** A130 25d blk, lt bl & grn *3.25 3.25*

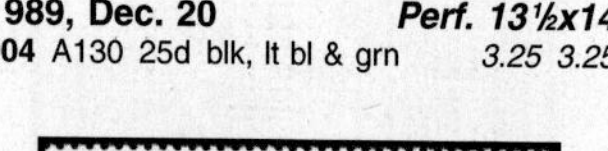

World Telecommunications Day — A131

**1989, Dec. 20** *Perf. 14x13½*
**905** A131 60d multicolored *5.00 5.00*

### Souvenir Sheet

*Perf. 13½x14*

| | | | | |
|---|---|---|---|---|
| **906** | A131 | 100d Early Bird satellite, vert. | 9.00 | 9.00 |

Christmas A132

Paintings: No. 907, Adoration of the Magi (detail), by Durer. No. 908, Young Virgin Mary, by Titian. No. 909, Adoration of the King, by Rubens. No. 910, Sistine Madonna, by Raphael. 100d, Madonna and Child Surrounded by Garland and Boy Angels, by Rubens.

**1989, Dec. 23** ***Perf. 13½x14***

| | | | | |
|---|---|---|---|---|
| **907** | A132 | 25d multicolored | *2.50* | *2.50* |
| **908** | A132 | 25d multicolored | *2.50* | *2.50* |
| **909** | A132 | 25d multicolored | *2.50* | *2.50* |
| **910** | A132 | 25d multicolored | *2.50* | *2.50* |
| | | *Nos. 907-910 (4)* | *10.00* | *10.00* |

### Souvenir Sheet

| | | | | |
|---|---|---|---|---|
| **911** | A132 | 100d multicolored | *10.00* | *10.00* |

Nos. 907-910 exist in souvenir sheets of one. Value for 4 sheets, $13.50.

Expedition of Sir Arthur Eddington to St. Thomas and Prince, 70th Anniv. A133

Designs: No. 912, Albert Einstein with Eddington. No. 913, Locomotive on Prince Island. No. 914, Roca Sundy railway station.

**1990** **Litho.** ***Perf. 13½***

| | | | | |
|---|---|---|---|---|
| **912** | A133 | 60d multicolored | 5.25 | 5.25 |
| **913** | A133 | 60d multicolored | 5.25 | 5.25 |
| **914** | A133 | 60d multicoloed | 5.25 | 5.25 |
| *a.* | | Souvenir sheet of 3, #912-914 | 18.00 | 18.00 |
| | | *Nos. 912-914 (3)* | 15.75 | 15.75 |

For surcharge see No. 1295A-1295B.

### Souvenir Sheet

Independence, 15th Anniv. — A134

Designs: a, Map, arms. b, Map, birds carrying envelope. c, Flag.

**1990, July 12** ***Perf. 13½***

| | | | | |
|---|---|---|---|---|
| **916** | A134 | 50d Sheet of 3, #a.-c. | *14.00* | *14.00* |

Orchids — A135

No. 917, Eulophia guineensis. No. 918, Ancistrochilus. No. 919, Oeceoclades maculata. No. 920, Vanilla imperialis. No. 921, Ansellia africana.

No. 922, Angraecum distichum, horiz. No. 923, Polystachya affinis, horiz.

**1990, Sept. 15** **Litho.** ***Perf. 13½***

| | | | | |
|---|---|---|---|---|
| **917** | A135 | 20d multicolored | 1.75 | 1.75 |
| **918** | A135 | 20d multicolored | 1.75 | 1.75 |
| **919** | A135 | 20d multicolored | 1.75 | 1.75 |
| **920** | A135 | 20d multicolored | 1.75 | 1.75 |
| **921** | A135 | 20d multicolored | 1.75 | 1.75 |
| | | *Nos. 917-921 (5)* | *8.75* | *8.75* |

### Souvenir Sheets

*Perf. 14x13½*

| | | | | |
|---|---|---|---|---|
| **922** | A135 | 50d multicolored | 4.50 | 4.50 |
| **923** | A135 | 50d multicolored | 4.50 | 4.50 |

Expo '90, Intl. Garden and Greenery Exposition, Osaka.

Locomotives — A136

5d, Bohemia, 1923-41. 20d, W. Germany, 1951-56. No. 926, Mallet, 1896-1903. No. 927, Russia, 1898-1910. No. 928, England, 1927-30.

No. 929, Camden-Amboy, 1834-38. No. 930, Stockton-Darlington, 1825.

**1990, Sept. 28** ***Perf. 14x13½***

| | | | | |
|---|---|---|---|---|
| **924** | A136 | 5d multicolored | *.45* | *.45* |
| **925** | A136 | 20d multicolored | *1.75* | *1.75* |
| **926** | A136 | 25d multicolored | *2.25* | *2.25* |
| **927** | A136 | 25d multicolored | *2.25* | *2.25* |
| **928** | A136 | 25d multicolored | *2.25* | *2.25* |
| | | *Nos. 924-928 (5)* | *8.95* | *8.95* |

### Souvenir Sheets

| | | | | |
|---|---|---|---|---|
| **929** | A136 | 50d multicolored | 5.50 | 5.50 |
| **930** | A136 | 50d multicolored | 5.50 | 5.50 |

### Souvenir Sheet

Iberoamericana '90 Philatelic Exposition — A137

**1990, Oct. 7**

| | | | | |
|---|---|---|---|---|
| **931** | A137 | 300d Armas Castle | 16.00 | 12.00 |

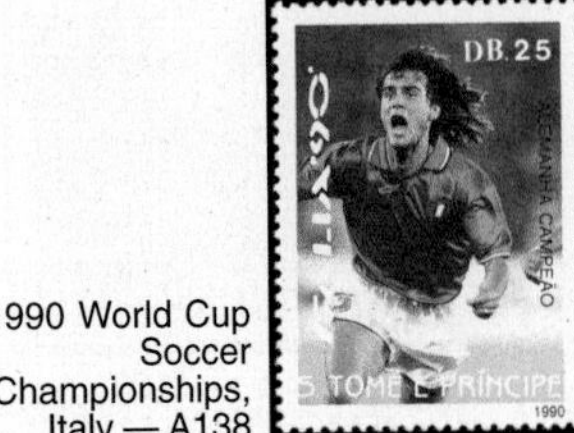


1990 World Cup Soccer Championships, Italy — A138

No. 932, German team with World Cup Trophy. No. 933, 2 players with ball. No. 934, 3 players with ball. No. 935, Italian player. No. 936, US Soccer Federation emblem and team members. No. 937, World Cup Trophy.

**1990, Oct. 15** ***Perf. 13½***

| | | | | |
|---|---|---|---|---|
| **932** | A138 | 25d multicolored | 2.25 | 2.25 |
| **933** | A138 | 25d multicolored | 2.25 | 2.25 |
| **934** | A138 | 25d multicolored | 2.25 | 2.25 |
| **935** | A138 | 25d multicolored | 2.25 | 2.25 |
| | | *Nos. 932-935 (4)* | 9.00 | 9.00 |

### Souvenir Sheets

*Perf. 14x13½*

| | | | | |
|---|---|---|---|---|
| **936** | A138 | 50d multi, horiz. | 4.50 | 4.50 |
| **937** | A138 | 50d multi, horiz. | 4.50 | 4.50 |

Mushrooms A139

No. 938, Boletus aereus. No. 939, Coprinus micaceus. No. 940, Pholiota spectabilis. No. 941, Krombholzia aurantiaca. No. 942, Stropharia aeruginosa.

No. 943, Hypholoma capnoides. No. 944, Pleurotus ostreatus.

**1990, Nov. 2** ***Perf. 13½x14***

| | | | | |
|---|---|---|---|---|
| **938** | A139 | 20d multicolored | *2.00* | *2.00* |
| **939** | A139 | 20d multicolored | *2.00* | *2.00* |
| **940** | A139 | 20d multicolored | *2.00* | *2.00* |
| **941** | A139 | 20d multicolored | *2.00* | *2.00* |
| **942** | A139 | 20d multicolored | *2.00* | *2.00* |
| | | *Nos. 938-942 (5)* | *10.00* | *10.00* |

### Souvenir Sheets

*Perf. 14x13½*

| | | | | |
|---|---|---|---|---|
| **943** | A139 | 50d multicolored | *6.00* | *6.00* |
| **944** | A139 | 50d multicolored | *6.00* | *6.00* |

Nos. 943-944 horiz. See Nos. 1014-1020.

Butterflies — A140

No. 945, Megistanis baeotus. No. 946, Ascia vamillae. No. 947, Danaus chrysippus. No. 948, Morpho menelaus. No. 949, Papilio rutulus, vert. No. 950, Papilio paradiesa.

No. 951, Parnassius clodius, vert. No. 952, Papilio macmaon, vert.

**1990, Nov. 2** ***Perf. 14x13½, 13½x14***

| | | | | |
|---|---|---|---|---|
| **945** | A140 | 15d multicolored | *1.30* | *1.30* |
| **946** | A140 | 15d multicolored | *1.30* | *1.30* |
| **947** | A140 | 15d multicolored | *1.30* | *1.30* |
| **948** | A140 | 15d multicolored | *1.30* | *1.30* |
| **949** | A140 | 15d multicolored | *1.30* | *1.30* |
| **950** | A140 | 25d multicolored | *2.10* | *2.10* |
| | | *Nos. 945-950 (6)* | *8.60* | *8.60* |

### Souvenir Sheets

| | | | | |
|---|---|---|---|---|
| **951** | A140 | 50d multicolored | 8.00 | 8.00 |
| **952** | A140 | 50d multicolored | 8.00 | 8.00 |

Presenting Gifts to the Newborn King — A141

Christmas: No. 954, Nativity scene. No. 955, Adoration of the Magi. No. 956, Flight into Egypt. No. 957, Adoration of the Magi, diff. No. 958, Portrait of Artist's Daughter Clara (detail), by Rubens, horiz.

**1990, Nov. 30** ***Perf. 13½x14***

| | | | | |
|---|---|---|---|---|
| **953** | A141 | 25d multicolored | *2.25* | *2.25* |
| **954** | A141 | 25d multicolored | *2.25* | *2.25* |
| **955** | A141 | 25d multicolored | *2.25* | *2.25* |
| **956** | A141 | 25d multicolored | *2.25* | *2.25* |
| | | *Nos. 953-956 (4)* | *9.00* | *9.00* |

### Souvenir Sheets

| | | | | |
|---|---|---|---|---|
| **957** | A141 | 50d multicolored | *4.75* | *4.75* |

*Perf. 14x13½*

| | | | | |
|---|---|---|---|---|
| **958** | A141 | 50d multicolored | *4.75* | *4.75* |

Death of Rubens, 350th anniv. (#958).

Anniversaries and Events A142

No. 960, Oath of Confederation. No. 961, Pointed roof. No. 962, William Tell statue, vert. No. 963, Brandenburg Gate. No. 964, Penny Black, vert. No. 965, 100d bank note.

**1990, Dec. 15** ***Perf. 13½x14***

| | | | | |
|---|---|---|---|---|
| **959** | A142 | 20d multicolored | 1.75 | 1.75 |

### Souvenir Sheets

***Perf. 14x13½, 13½x14 (#962, 964)***

| | | | | |
|---|---|---|---|---|
| **960** | A142 | 50d multicolored | 4.50 | 4.50 |
| **961** | A142 | 50d multicolored | 4.50 | 4.50 |
| **962** | A142 | 50d multicolored | 4.50 | 4.50 |
| **963** | A142 | 50d multicolored | 4.50 | 4.50 |
| **964** | A142 | 50d multicolored | 4.50 | 4.50 |
| **965** | A142 | 50d multicolored | 4.50 | 4.50 |

Swiss Confederation, 700th anniv. (#959-962). Brandenburg Gate, 200th anniv. (#963). First postage stamp, 150th anniv. (#964). Independence of St. Thomas and Prince, 15th anniv. (#965).

Paintings — A143

No. 966, The Bathers, by Renoir. No. 967, Girl Holding Mirror for Nude, by Picasso. No. 968, Nude, by Rubens. No. 969, Descent from the Cross (detail), by Rubens. No. 970, Nude, by Titian. No. 971, Landscape, by Durer. No. 972, Rowboats, by Van Gogh. No. 973, Nymphs, by Titian. No. 974, Bather, by Titian. No. 975, Postman Joseph Roulin (detail), by Van Gogh. No. 976, The Abduction of the Daughters of Leucippus, by Rubens. No. 977, Nude, by Titian, diff.

**1990, Dec. 15** ***Perf. 14x13½, 13½x14***

| | | | | |
|---|---|---|---|---|
| **966** | A143 | 10d multi | *1.05* | *1.05* |
| **967** | A143 | 10d multi, vert. | *1.05* | *1.05* |
| **968** | A143 | 10d multi, vert. | *1.05* | *1.05* |
| **969** | A143 | 10d multi, vert. | *1.05* | *1.05* |
| **970** | A143 | 10d multi, vert. | *1.05* | *1.05* |
| **971** | A143 | 20d multi | *2.10* | *2.10* |
| **972** | A143 | 20d multi | *2.10* | *2.10* |
| **973** | A143 | 25d multi | *2.40* | *2.40* |
| **974** | A143 | 25d multi, vert. | *2.40* | *2.40* |
| | | *Nos. 966-974 (9)* | *14.25* | *14.25* |

### Souvenir Sheets

*Perf. 13½x14*

| | | | | |
|---|---|---|---|---|
| **975** | A143 | 50d multi, vert. | *8.00* | *8.00* |
| **976** | A143 | 50d multi, vert. | *8.00* | *8.00* |
| **977** | A143 | 50d multi, vert. | *8.00* | *8.00* |

Rubens, 350th anniv. of death (Nos. 968-969, 976). Titian, 500th anniv. of death (Nos. 970, 973-974, 977). Van Gogh, centennial of death (Nos. 972, 975).

See No. 958 for other souvenir sheet for Rubens death anniv.

Flora and Fauna — A144

Designs: 1d, Gecko. 5d, Cobra. 10d, No. 980, Sea turtle. No. 981, Fresh water turtle. No. 982, Civet. 70d, Civet in tree. No. 984, Civet with young. No. 985, Civet in den.

Psittacus erithacus: 80d, In tree, vert. 100d, On branch with wings spread, vert. 250d, Feeding young, vert. No. 989, Three in flight, vert.

**1991, Feb. 2** ***Perf. 14x13½***

| | | | | |
|---|---|---|---|---|
| **978** | A144 | 1d multicolored | .25 | .25 |
| **979** | A144 | 5d multicolored | .25 | .25 |
| **980** | A144 | 10d multicolored | .25 | .25 |
| **981** | A144 | 50d multicolored | .70 | .70 |
| **982** | A144 | 50d multicolored | .70 | .70 |
| **983** | A144 | 70d multicolored | 1.20 | 1.20 |
| **984** | A144 | 75d multicolored | 1.20 | 1.20 |
| **985** | A144 | 75d multicolored | 1.20 | 1.20 |

***Perf. 13½x14***

| | | | | |
|---|---|---|---|---|
| **986** | A144 | 80d multicolored | 1.30 | 1.30 |
| **987** | A144 | 100d multicolored | 1.50 | 1.50 |
| **988** | A144 | 250d multicolored | 4.00 | 4.00 |
| **989** | A144 | 500d multicolored | 8.00 | 8.00 |
| | | *Nos. 978-989 (12)* | 20.55 | 20.55 |

**Souvenir Sheets**

| | | | | |
|---|---|---|---|---|
| **990** | A144 | 500d Orchid, vert. | 9.00 | 9.00 |
| **991** | A144 | 500d Rose, vert. | 9.00 | 9.00 |

See Nos. 1054I-1054N. For surcharges see Nos. 1170H-1170I, 1170L-1170M, 1307A.

Locomotives — A145

**1991, May 7** ***Perf. 14x13½, 13½x14***

| | | | | |
|---|---|---|---|---|
| **992** | A145 | 75d shown | 1.00 | 1.00 |
| **993** | A145 | 75d North America, vert. | 1.00 | 1.00 |
| **994** | A145 | 75d Germany, vert. | 1.00 | 1.00 |
| **995** | A145 | 75d New Delhi, vert. | 1.00 | 1.00 |
| **996** | A145 | 75d Brazil, vert. | 1.00 | 1.00 |
| **997** | A145 | 200d Two leaving terminal | 2.50 | 2.50 |
| | | *Nos. 992-997 (6)* | 7.50 | 7.50 |

**Souvenir Sheets**

| | | | | |
|---|---|---|---|---|
| **998** | A145 | 500d Engine 120, vert. | 7.00 | 7.00 |
| **999** | A145 | 500d Engine 151-001 | 7.00 | 7.00 |

Birds — A146

No. 1000, Psittacula kuhlii. No. 1001, Plydolophus rosaceus. No. 1002, Falco tinnunculus. No. 1003, Platycercus palliceps. No. 1004, Marcrocercus aracanga.

No. 1005, Ramphastos culmenatus. No. 1006, Strix nyctea.

**1991, July 8** ***Perf. 13½x14***

| | | | | |
|---|---|---|---|---|
| **1000** | A146 | 75d multicolored | 1.20 | 1.20 |
| **1001** | A146 | 75d multicolored | 1.20 | 1.20 |
| **1002** | A146 | 75d multicolored | 1.20 | 1.20 |
| **1003** | A146 | 75d multicolored | 1.20 | 1.20 |
| **1004** | A146 | 200d multicolored | 3.25 | 3.25 |
| | | *Nos. 1000-1004 (5)* | 8.05 | 8.05 |

**Souvenir Sheets**

| | | | | |
|---|---|---|---|---|
| **1005** | A146 | 500d multicolored | 14.00 | 9.25 |
| **1006** | A146 | 500d multicolored | 9.25 | 9.25 |

Paintings A147

50d, Venus and Cupid, by Titian. #1008, Horse's Head (detail), by Rubens. #1009, Child's face (detail), by Rubens. 100d, Spanish Woman, by Picasso. 200d, Man with Christian Flag, by Titian. #1012, Study of a Negro, by Rubens. #1013, Madonna and Child, by Raphael.

**1991, July 31**

| | | | | |
|---|---|---|---|---|
| **1007** | A147 | 50d multicolored | .70 | .70 |
| **1008** | A147 | 75d multicolored | 1.05 | 1.05 |
| **1009** | A147 | 75d multicolored | 1.05 | 1.05 |
| **1010** | A147 | 100d multicolored | 1.60 | 1.60 |
| **1011** | A147 | 200d multicolored | 3.25 | 3.25 |
| | | *Nos. 1007-1011 (5)* | 7.65 | 7.65 |

**Souvenir Sheets**

| | | | | |
|---|---|---|---|---|
| **1012** | A147 | 500d multicolored | 7.75 | 7.75 |
| **1013** | A147 | 500d multicolored | 7.75 | 7.75 |

**Mushroom Type of 1990**

No. 1014, Clitocybe geotropa. No. 1015, Lepiota procera. 75d, Boletus granulatus. 125d, Coprinus comatus. 200d, Amanita rubescens.

No. 1019, Armillariella mellea. No. 1020, Nictalis parasitica, horiz.

**1991, Aug. 30**

| | | | | |
|---|---|---|---|---|
| **1014** | A139 | 50d multicolored | .70 | .70 |
| **1015** | A139 | 50d multicolored | .70 | .70 |
| **1016** | A139 | 75d multicolored | 1.05 | 1.05 |
| **1017** | A139 | 125d multicolored | 1.75 | 1.75 |
| **1018** | A139 | 200d multicolored | 3.25 | 3.25 |
| | | *Nos. 1014-1018 (5)* | 7.45 | 7.45 |

**Souvenir Sheets**

| | | | | |
|---|---|---|---|---|
| **1019** | A139 | 500d multicolored | 7.75 | 7.75 |

***Perf. 14x13½***

| | | | | |
|---|---|---|---|---|
| **1020** | A139 | 500d multicolored | 7.75 | 7.75 |

Flowers A148

No. 1022, Zan tedeschia elliotiana. No. 1023, Cyrtanthes pohliana. No. 1024, Phalaenopsis lueddemanniana. No. 1025, Haemanthus katharinae. 500d, Arundina graminifolia.

**1991, Sept. 9** ***Perf. 13½x14***

| | | | | |
|---|---|---|---|---|
| **1021** | A148 | 50d shown | .75 | .75 |
| **1022** | A148 | 50d multicolored | .75 | .75 |
| **1023** | A148 | 100d multicolored | 1.60 | 1.60 |
| **1024** | A148 | 100d multicolored | 1.60 | 1.60 |
| **1025** | A148 | 200d multicolored | 3.50 | 3.50 |
| | | *Nos. 1021-1025 (5)* | 8.20 | 8.20 |

**Souvenir Sheet**

| | | | | |
|---|---|---|---|---|
| **1026** | A148 | 500d multicolored | 7.75 | 7.75 |

Souvenir Sheet

Iberoamericano '92 Intl. Philatelic Exhibition — A149

**1991, Oct. 11** **Litho.** ***Perf. 14x13½***

| | | | | |
|---|---|---|---|---|
| **1027** | A149 | 800d multicolored | 6.25 | 6.25 |

Discovery of America, 500th Anniv. (in 1992) — A150

No. 1028, Columbus. No. 1029, Sailing ship. No. 1030, Sailing ship, diff. No. 1031, Landing in New World. No. 1032, Pointing the way.

No. 1033, Columbus' fleet, horiz.

**1991, Oct. 12** ***Perf. 13½x14***

| | | | | |
|---|---|---|---|---|
| **1028** | A150 | 50d multicolored | | |
| **1029** | A150 | 50d multicolored | | |
| **1030** | A150 | 75d multicolored | | |
| **1031** | A150 | 125d multicolored | | |
| **1032** | A150 | 200d multicolored | | |
| | | *Nos. 1028-1032 (5)* | 10.00 | |

**Souvenir Sheet**

***Perf. 14x13½***

| | | | | |
|---|---|---|---|---|
| **1033** | A150 | 500d multicolored | 10.00 | |

Butterflies — A151

**1991, Oct. 16** ***Perf. 14x13½***

| | | | | |
|---|---|---|---|---|
| **1034** | A151 | 125d Limentis popul | 3.50 | 3.50 |
| **1035** | A151 | 125d Pavon inachis io | 3.50 | 3.50 |

**Souvenir Sheet**

***Perf. 13½x14***

| | | | | |
|---|---|---|---|---|
| **1036** | A151 | 500d Zerynthia polyxena | 7.25 | 7.25 |

Phila Nippon '91.

**1991, Nov. 15** ***Perf. 14x13½***

| | | | | |
|---|---|---|---|---|
| **1037** | A151 | 125d Macaon papilio machaon | 2.00 | 2.00 |
| **1038** | A151 | 125d Gran pavon | 2.00 | 2.00 |
| **1039** | A151 | 125d Pavon inachis io, diff. | 2.00 | 2.00 |
| **1040** | A151 | 125d Artia caja | 2.00 | 2.00 |
| | | *Nos. 1037-1040 (4)* | 8.00 | 8.00 |

**Souvenir Sheet**

***Perf. 13½x14***

| | | | | |
|---|---|---|---|---|
| **1041** | A151 | 500d Unnamed butterfly, vert. | 8.00 | 8.00 |

Christmas.

Landmarks — A152

Landmarks of France: No. 1042, Ile de France, vert. No. 1043, Chenonceau Castle. No. 1044, Azay-le-Rideau Castle. No. 1045, Chambord Castle. No. 1046, Chaumont Castle. No. 1047, Fountainebleau Palace.

***Perf. 13½x14, 14x13½***

**1991, Nov. 15**

| | | | | |
|---|---|---|---|---|
| **1042-1047** | A152 | 25d Set of 6 | 2.50 | 2.50 |

**Souvenir Sheet**

| | | | | |
|---|---|---|---|---|
| **1048** | A152 | 500d Paris map, 1615 | 7.50 | 7.50 |

French National Exposition.

Souvenir Sheet

Fauna — A153

Animals and birds: a, Weasel, monkey. b, Civet, rats. c, Goat, cow. d, Rabbits, wildcat. e, Parrot, black bird. f, White bird, multicolored bird.

**1991, Nov. 15** ***Perf. 14x13½***

| | | | | |
|---|---|---|---|---|
| **1049** | A153 | 25d Sheet of 6, #a.-f. | 8.00 | 8.00 |

French National Exposition.

Express Mail Service from St. Thomas and Prince — A154

**1991** **Litho.** ***Perf. 14***

| | | | | |
|---|---|---|---|---|
| **1050** | A154 | 3000d multicolored | 16.00 | 16.00 |

Souvenir Sheets

1991 Intl. Olympic Committee Session, Birmingham — A154a

Designs: No. 1050A, IOC emblem, Birmingham Session. No. 1050B, 1998 Winter Olympics emblem, Nagano. No. 1050C, 1998 Winter Olympics mascot.

**1992** **Litho.** ***Perf. 14***

| | | | | |
|---|---|---|---|---|
| **1050A** | A154a | 800d multi | 10.00 | 10.00 |
| **1050B** | A154a | 800d multi | 10.00 | 10.00 |
| **1050C** | A154a | 800d multi | 10.00 | 10.00 |
| | | *Nos. 1050A-1050C (3)* | 30.00 | 30.00 |

Souvenir Sheet

IBEREX '91 — A154b

**1992**

| | | | | |
|---|---|---|---|---|
| **1050D** | A154b | 800d multi | 10.00 | 10.00 |

Souvenir Sheets

1992 Winter Olympics, Albertville — A154c

Olympic medals.

**1992** **Set of 4, a.-d.**
**1050E** A154c 50d multi 40.00 25.00

No. 1050E exists as four souvenir sheets with pictures of different medalists in sheet margins: a., Blanca Fernandez, Spain; b., Alberto Tomba, Italy; c., Mark Kirchner, Germany; d., Torgny Mogren, Norway.

1992 Summer Olympics, Barcelona A154d

View of earth from space with: No. 1050F, High jumper. No. 1050G, Roller hockey player. No. 1050H, Equestrian. No. 1050I, Kayaker. No. 1050J, Weight lifter. No. 1050K, Archer. No. 1050L, Michael Jordan, horiz.

**1992**
**1050F-1050K** A154d 50d Set of 6 *7.50 7.50*

**Souvenir Sheet**

**1050L** A154d 50d multicolored *8.00 8.00*

Whales — A155

Designs: No. 1051, Orcinus orca. No. 1052, Orcinus orca, four on surface of water. No. 1053, Pseudoraca crassidens. No. 1054, Pseudoraca crassidens, three under water.

**1992** **Litho.** ***Perf. 14***
**1051-1054** A155 450d Set of 4 6.00 6.00

World Wildlife Fund.

Visit of Pope John Paul II — A155a

c, Flags, Pope. d, Church with two steeples. e, Church, diff.
f, Pope, vert. g, Church, blue sky, vert. h, Church, closer view, vert.

**1992, Apr. 19** **Litho.** ***Perf. 14***
**Sheets of 4**

**1054A** A155a 200d #d.-e., 2 #c 10.00 10.00
**1054B** A155a 200d #g.-h., 2 #f 10.00 10.00

**Miniature Sheets**

Pope John Paul II and Flower — A155c

Pope John Paul II and Bird — A155d

No. 1054C — Flower and Pope looking: t, Straight ahead. u, To right, three-quarters. v, Slightly to left. w, To right, profile.
No. 1054D — Bird and Pope looking: x, Straight ahead. y, To right, three-quarters. z, Slightly to left. aa, To right, profile.
No. 1054E — Flower, diff. and Pope looking: ab, Straight ahead. ac, To right, three-quarters. ad, Slightly to left. ae, To right, profile.
No. 1054F — Bird, diff. and Pope looking: af, Straight ahead. ag, To right, three-quarters. ah, Slightly to left. ai, To right, profile.
No. 1054G — Flower, diff. and Pope looking: aj, Straight ahead. ak, To right, three-quarters. al, Slightly to left. am, To right, profile.
No. 1054H — Bird, diff. and Pope looking: an, Straight ahead. ao, To right, three-quarters. ap, Slightly to left. aq, To right, profile.

**1992, Apr. 19** ***Perf. 13¾x14***

**1054C** A155c 120d Sheet of 4, #t-w — —
**1054D** A155d 120d Sheet of 4, #x-aa — —
**1054E** A155c 150d Sheet of 4, #ab-ae — —
**1054F** A155d 150d Sheet of 4, #af-ai — —
**1054G** A155c 180d Sheet of 4, #aj-am — —
**1054H** A155d 250d Sheet of 4, #an-aq — —
Set of 6 sheets 85.00

For surcharges see Nos. 1170C-1170D.

**Flora and Fauna Type of 1991**

Designs: No. 1054I, 1000d, Brown & white bird, vert. No. 1054J, 1500d, Yellow flower, vert. No. 1054K, 2000d, Red flower, vert. No. 1054L, 2500d, Black bird, vert.
No. 1054M, Sea turtle. No. 1054N, Yellow flowers.

**1992, Apr. 19** ***Perf. 14***
**1054I-1054L** A144 Set of 4 35.00 35.00

**Souvenir Sheets**

**1054M** A144 800d multi — —
**1054N** A144 800d multi — —

UN Conference on Environmental Development, Rio — A155b

Designs: 65d, Rain forest. 110d, Walruses. 150d, Raptor. 200d, Tiger. 275d, Elephants.
Each 800d: No. 1054T, Panda, horiz. No. 1054U, Zebras, horiz.

**1992, June 6** **Litho.** ***Perf. 14***
**1054O-1054S** A155b Set of 5 10.00

**Souvenir Sheets**

**1054T-1054U** A155b Set of 2 20.00

Souvenir Sheet

Olymphilex '92 — A156

Olympic athletes: a, Women's running. b, Women's gymnastics. c, Earvin "Magic" Johnson.

**1992, July 29**
**1055** A156 300d Sheet of 3, #a.-c. 10.00 10.00

Mushrooms A157

75d, Leccinum ocabrum. 100d, Amanita spissa, horiz. 125d, Strugilomyces floccopus. 200d, Suillus luteus. 500d, Agaricus siluaticus. #1061, Amanita pantherma, horiz. #1062, Agaricus campestre.

**1992, Sept. 5** ***Perf. 14***

| | | | | |
|---|---|---|---|---|
| **1056** | A157 | 75d multicolored | .70 | .70 |
| **1057** | A157 | 100d multicolored | .90 | .90 |
| **1058** | A157 | 125d multicolored | 1.05 | 1.05 |
| **1059** | A157 | 200d multicolored | 1.75 | 1.75 |
| **1060** | A157 | 500d multicolored | 5.00 | 5.00 |
| | | *Nos. 1056-1060 (5)* | 9.40 | 9.40 |

**Souvenir Sheets**

***Perf. 14x13½, 13½x14***

**1061** A157 1000d multicolored 10.00 10.00
**1062** A157 1000d multicolored 10.00 10.00

Birds — A158

Designs: 75d, Paradisea regie, pipra rupicole. 100d, Trogon pavonis. 125d, Paradisea apoda. 200d, Pavocriotctus. 500d, Ramphatos maximus. No. 1068, Woodpecker. No. 1069, Picus major.

**1992, Sept. 15** ***Perf. 14***

| | | | | |
|---|---|---|---|---|
| **1063** | A158 | 75d multicolored | .55 | .55 |
| **1064** | A158 | 100d multicolored | .80 | .80 |
| **1065** | A158 | 125d multicolored | .95 | .95 |
| **1066** | A158 | 200d multicolored | 1.50 | 1.50 |
| **1067** | A158 | 500d multicolored | 3.75 | 3.75 |
| | | *Nos. 1063-1067 (5)* | 7.55 | 7.55 |

**Souvenir Sheets**

***Perf. 13½x14***

**1068** A158 1000d multicolored 9.00 9.00
**1069** A158 1000d multicolored 9.00 9.00

Marcelo da Veiga (1892-1976), Writer — A159

Designs: a, 10d. b, 40d. c, 50d. d, 100d.

**1992, Oct. 3** ***Perf. 13½***
**1070** A159 Sheet of 4, #a.-d. 4.00 4.00

Locomotives — A160

Designs: 75d, 100d, 125d, 200d, 500d, Various locomotives. No. 1076, Steam train arriving at station. No. 1077, Engineer, stoker in locomotive cab.

**1992, Oct. 3** ***Perf. 14x13½***

| | | | | |
|---|---|---|---|---|
| **1071** | A160 | 75d black | .65 | .65 |
| **1072** | A160 | 100d black | .80 | .80 |
| **1073** | A160 | 125d black | 1.05 | 1.05 |
| **1074** | A160 | 200d black | 1.75 | 1.75 |
| **1075** | A160 | 500d black | 5.00 | 5.00 |
| | | *Nos. 1071-1075 (5)* | 9.25 | 9.25 |

**Souvenir Sheets**

**1076** A160 1000d black 9.00 9.00
**1077** A160 1000d black 9.00 9.00

Butterflies and Moths — A161

75d, Chelonia purpurea. 100d, Hoetera philocteles. 125d, Attacus pavonia major. 200d, Ornithoptera urvilliana. 500d, Acherontia atropos. No. 1083, Peridromia amphinome, vert. No. 1084, Uramia riphacus, vert.

**1992, Oct. 18** ***Perf. 14x13½***

| | | | | |
|---|---|---|---|---|
| **1078** | A161 | 75d multicolored | *.60* | *.60* |
| **1079** | A161 | 100d multicolored | *.90* | *.90* |
| **1080** | A161 | 125d multicolored | *1.10* | *1.10* |

1081 A161 200d multicolored *1.75 1.75*
1082 A161 500d multicolored *5.00 5.00*
*Nos. 1078-1082 (5) 9.35 9.35*

**Souvenir Sheets**

***Perf. 13½x14***

1083 A161 1000d multicolored *9.00 9.00*
1084 A161 1000d multicolored *9.00 9.00*

1992, 1996 Summer Olympics, Barcelona and Atlanta — A162

50d, Wind surfing. No. 1086, Wrestling. No. 1087, Women's 4x100 meters relay. No. 1088, Swimming. No. 1089, Equestrian, vert. No. 1090, Field hockey. No. 1091, Men's 4x100 meters relay, vert. No. 1092, Mascots for Barcelona and Atlanta. No. 1093, Opening ceremony, Barcelona.

No. 1094, Atlanta '96 Emblem, vert. No. 1095, Archer lighting Olympic Flame with flaming arrow, vert. No. 1096, Transfer of Olympic Flag, closing ceremony, vert. No. 1097, Gymnastics. No. 1098, Tennis players.

**1992, Oct. 1 Litho. *Perf. 14***

1085 A162 50d multicolored .65 .65
1086 A162 300d multicolored 2.00 2.00
1087 A162 300d multicolored 2.00 2.00
1088 A162 300d multicolored 2.00 2.00
1089 A162 300d multicolored 2.00 2.00
1090 A162 300d multicolored 2.00 2.00
1091 A162 300d multicolored 2.00 2.00
1092 A162 300d multicolored 2.00 2.00
1093 A162 300d multicolored 2.00 2.00
*Nos. 1085-1093 (9)* 16.65 16.65

**Souvenir Sheets**

1094 A162 800d multicolored 9.00 9.00
1095 A162 1000d multicolored 7.00 7.00
1096 A162 1000d multicolored 7.00 7.00

***Perf. 13½***

1097 A162 1000d multicolored 7.25 7.25

***Perf. 14***

1098 A162 1000d multicolored 7.25 7.25

Butterflies A163

Designs: No. 1099, White butterfly. No. 1100, Black and orange butterfly. No. 1101, Pink flower, black, white, red and blue butterfly. No. 1102, Black and white butterfly on right side of flower stem. No. 1103, Yellow and black butterfly. 2000d, Iris flower, black butterfly wing, horiz.

**1993, May 26 Litho. *Perf. 14***

1099-1103 A163 500d Set of 5 *18.00 18.00*

**Souvenir Sheet**

1104 A163 2000d multi *16.00 16.00*

Flowers A164

No. 1105, Fucinho de porco. No. 1106, Heliconia. No. 1107, Gravo nacional. No. 1108, Tremessura. No. 1109, Anturius. No. 1110, Girassol.

**1993, June 18**

1105 A164 500d multicolored *3.25 3.25*
1106 A164 500d multicolored *3.25 3.25*
1107 A164 500d multicolored *3.25 3.25*
1108 A164 500d multicolored *3.25 3.25*
1109 A164 500d multicolored *3.25 3.25*
*Nos. 1105-1109 (5) 16.25 16.25*

**Souvenir Sheet**

1110 A164 2000d multicolored 14.00 14.00

Miniature Sheet

Union of Portuguese Speaking Capitals — A165

Designs: a, 100d, Emblem. b, 150d, Grotto. c, 200d, Statue of Christ the Redeemer, Rio de Janeiro. d, 250d, Skyscraper. e, 250d, Monument. f, 300d, Building with pointed domed roof. g, 350d, Municipal building. h, 400d, Square tower. i, 500d, Residence, flag, truck.

**1993, July 30**

1111 A165 Sheet of 9, #a.-i. 16.00 16.00

Brasiliana '93.

Birds — A166

Designs: No. 1112, Cecia. No. 1113, Suisui. No. 1114, Falcon. No. 1115, Parrot. No. 1116, Heron.

No. 1117, Macaw, toucan, horiz.

**1993, June 15 Litho. *Perf. 14***

1112-1116 A166 500d Set of 5 *17.50 17.50*

**Souvenir Sheet**

1117 A166 1000d multi *8.50 8.50*

Dinosaurs — A167

No. 1118, Lystrosaurus. No. 1119, Patagosaurus. No. 1120, Shonisaurus icti-osaurios, vert. No. 1121, Dilophosaurus, vert. No. 1122, Dicraeosaurus, vert. No. 1123, Tyrannosaurus rex, vert.

**1993, July 21**

1118-1123 A167 500d Set of 6 19.00 19.00

**Souvenir Sheets**

1124 A167 1000d Protoavis 9.00 9.00
1125 A167 1000d Brachiosaurus 9.00 9.00

Mushrooms A168

No. 1126, Agrocybe aegerita. No. 1127, Psalliota arvensis. No. 1128, Coprinus comatus. No. 1129, Hygrophorus psittacinus. No. 1130, Amanita caesarea.

No. 1131, Ramaria aurea. No. 1132, Pluteus murinus, horiz.

**1993, May 25 Litho. *Perf. 14***

1126-1130 A168 800d Set of 5 *20.00 20.00*

**Souvenir Sheets**

1131-1132 A168 2000d Set of 2 *20.00 20.00*

Locomotives — A169

Nos. 1133-1137, Various views of small diesel locomotive.

Nos. 1138-1139, Various steam locomotives, vert.

**1993, June 16**

1133-1137 A169 800d Set of 5 20.00 20.00

**Souvenir Sheets**

1138-1139 A169 2000d Set of 2 *24.00 24.00*

1994 World Cup Soccer Championships, U.S. — A170

Designs: No. 1140, Team photo. No. 1141, Players in white uniforms. No. 1142, Two players in yellow uniforms, player in red, white and blue uniform. No. 1143, Players with yellow shirts and green shorts celebrating. No. 1144, Two players in red and white uniforms, one player in red, white and blue uniform. No. 1145, Player in yellow and blue uniform, player in red, white and blue uniform. No. 1146, Two players and official. No. 1147, Two players, vert.

No. 1148, Fans, faces painted as flags. No. 1149, Stylized player.

**1993, July 6**

1140-1147 A170 800d Set of 8 25.00 25.00

**Souvenir Sheets**

1148-1149 A170 2000d Set of 2 15.00 15.00

UPU Congress — A171

**1993, Aug. 16**

1150 A171 1000d shown 5.25 4.00

**Souvenir Sheet**

1151 A171 2000d Ship 9.00 9.00

1996 Summer Olympics, Atlanta — A172

Each 800d: No. 1152, Fencing. No. 1153, Women's running. No. 1154, Water polo. No. 1155, Soccer. No. 1156, Men's running. No. 1157, Boxing. No. 1158, Wrestling. No. 1159, High jump.

Each 2000d: No. 1160, Shooting, vert. No. 1161, Sailing, vert. No. 1162, Equestrian, vert. No. 1163, Kayak, vert.

**1993, Oct. 19 Litho. *Perf. 13½x14***

1152-1159 A172 Set of 8 *35.00 35.00*

**Souvenir Sheets**

1160-1163 A172 Set of 4 *35.00 35.00*

1994 World Cup Soccer Championships, U.S. — A173

**1994, Jan. 12 *Perf. 14***

1164 A173 500d blk, bl & red 3.00 3.00

Issued in miniature sheets of 4.

Movie Stars — A174

Each 10d: No. 1165a, James Dean. b, Bette Davis. c, Elvis Presley. d, Humphrey Bogart. e, John Lennon. f, Marilyn Monroe. g, Birthday cake. h, Audrey Hepburn.

Each 10d: No. 1166a-1166i, Various portraits of Elvis Presley.

Each 10d: No. 1167a-1167i, Various portraits of Marilyn Monroe.

Each 50d: No. 1168, James Dean, diff. No. 1169, Elvis Presley, diff.

No. 1169A: Marilyn Monroe.

**1994, Feb. 15**

1165 A174 Sheet of 8, #a.-h. 8.00 8.00

**Sheets of 9, #a-i**

1166-1167 A174 Set of 2 8.00 8.00

**Souvenir Sheets**

1168-1169 A174 Set of 2 8.00 8.00
1169A A174 2000d multi 15.00 15.00

Souvenir Sheet

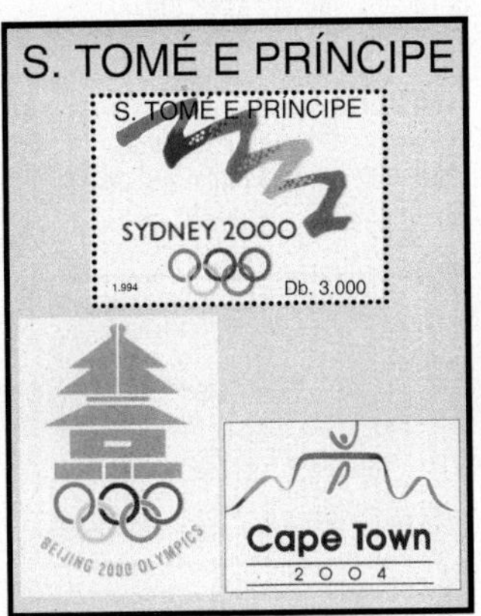


Sydney 2000 — A175

**1994, June 8**
**1170** A175 3000d multicolored 15.00 15.00

Signing of Argel Accord, 20th Anniv. A175a

**1994 Litho. *Perf. 14***
**1170A** A175a 250d multi 4.25 4.25

**Nos. 978, 979 Surcharged**

d

**Nos. 856, 978-979 Surcharged**

e

**Nos. 856-858, 860 Surcharged**

f - Type I

Two Types of Type "f":
Type I — "5" lacks ornaments.
Type II — "5" has an ornament on the tail.
No. 1170M exists in two types:
Type I — With a vertical comma composed of a dot and tail.
Type II — With a diagonally elongated dot as the comma.

**Surcharge Typo.**
**1995, Mar. 2, 1996?**
**Printing Methods and Perfs as Before**

**1170B** A123p(f) 100d on 25d #860 10.00 .50
**1170C** A155c 200d on 120d #1054C — —
*o.-r.* any single — —
**1170D** A155d 300d on 120d #1054D — —
*s.-v.* any single — —
**1170E** A123p(e) 350d on 50c #856 — —
**1170F** A123p(fl) 350d on 50c #856 — —
**1170G** A123p(fll) 350d on 50c #856 — —
**1170H** A144(e) 350d on 1d #978 10.00 1.00
**1170I** A144(d) 350d on 1d #978 10.00 1.00
**1170J** A123p(fl) 350d on 1d #857 — —
**1170K** A123p(fll) 350d on 1d #857 — —
**1170L** A144(d) 400d on 5d #979 10.00 1.00
**1170M** A144(e) 400d on 5d #979 10.00 1.00
**1170N** A123p(f) 400d on 5d #858 — —

Butterflies A176

No. 1171, Timeleoa maqulata-formosana. No. 1172, Morfho cypris. No. 1173, Thais polixena. No. 1174, Argema moenas. No. 1175, Leptocircus megus-ennius.
2000d, Armandia lidderdalei.

**1995, May 10 Litho. *Perf. 14***
**1171-1175** A176 1200d Set of 5 12.50 12.50

**Souvenir Sheet**
**1176** A176 2000d multi 8.00 8.00

Flowering Fruits, Orchids A177

Flowering fruits: No. 1177, 350d, Pessego. No. 1178, 370d, Untue. No. 1179, 380d, Pitanga. No. 1180, 800d, Morango. No. 1181, 1000d, Izaquente.
Orchids, each 2000d: No. 1182, Max. houtteana. No. 1183, Max. marginata.

**1995, June 6**
**1177-1181** A177 Set of 5 14.00 14.00

**Souvenir Sheets**
**1182-1183** A177 Set of 2 16.00 16.00

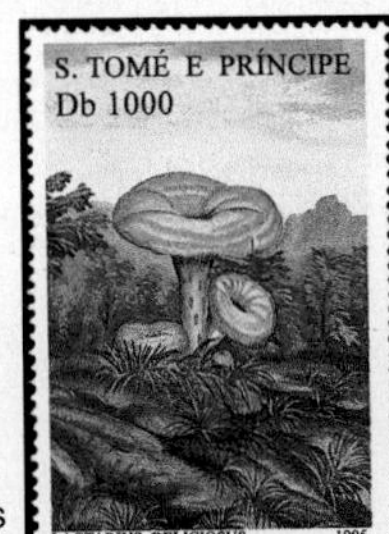


Mushrooms A179

Designs, each 1000d: No. 1185, Lactarius deliciosus. No. 1186, Marasmius oreades. No. 1187, Boletus edulis. No. 1188, Boletus aurantiacus. No. 1189, Lepiota procera. No. 1190, Cortinarius praestans.
Each 2000d: No. 1191, Chantharellus cibarius. No. 1192, Lycoperdon pyriforme, horiz.

**1995, Nov. 2 Litho. *Perf. 14***
**1185-1190** A179 Set of 6 14.00 14.00

**Souvenir Sheets**
**1191-1192** A179 Set of 2 14.00 14.00

UN, 50th Anniv. — A180

Traditional handicrafts made from palm leaves: No. 1193, 350d, Baskets. No. 1194, 350d, Brooms. No. 1195, 400d, Lamp shades. No. 1196, 500d, Klissakli, mussuá. No. 1197, 500d, Pávu. No. 1198, 1000d, Vámplêgá.

**1995, June 20 Litho. *Perf. 13½x14***
**1193-1198** A180 Set of 6 7.50 7.50

Trains — A181

Locomotives, each 1000d: No. 1199, Steam, "#100." No. 1200, Steam, "#778." No. 1201, G. Thommen steam. No. 1202, Steam "#119," vert. No. 1203, Mt. Washington cog railway. No. 1204, Electric.
Each 2000d: No. 1205, Electric train on snow-covered mountain, vert. No. 1206, Electric train car with door open, vert.

**1995, July 24 *Perf. 14x13½, 13½x14***
**1199-1204** A181 Set of 6 22.50 22.50

**Souvenir Sheets**
**1205-1206** A181 Set of 2 19.00 19.00

See Nos. 1280-1286.

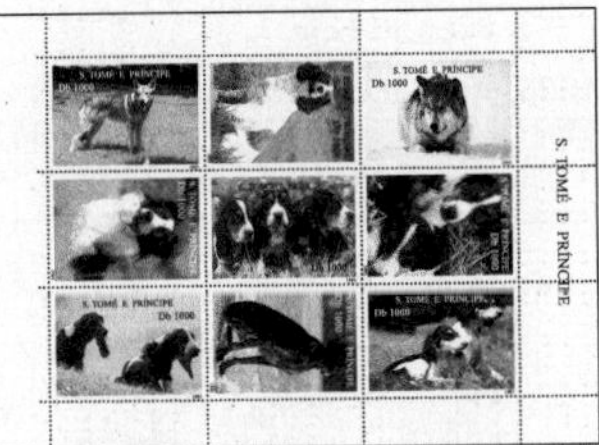

Dogs & Cats — A182

No. 1207, each 1000d: Various dogs. b, d, f, h, vert.
No. 1208, each 1000d: Various cats. b, d, f, h, vert.
Each 2000d: No. 1209, St. Bernard, German shepherd. No. 1210, Beagle, vert. No. 1211, Cat, kittens. No. 1212, Kitten on top of mother, vert.

**1995, Aug. 12 *Perf. 14***
**Sheets of 9, #a-i**
**1207-1208** A182 Set of 2 45.00 45.00

**Souvenir Sheets**
**1209-1212** A182 Set of 5 37.50 37.50

New Year 1996 (Year of the Rat) A183

Various species of rats, mice, each 100d.

**1995, Oct. 28**
**1213** A183 Sheet of 9, #a.-i. 5.50 5.50

Motion Pictures, Cent. — A184

Movie posters, each 1000d: No. 1214: a, Gone with the Wind. b, Stagecoach. c, Tarzan and His Mate. d, Oregon Trail. e, The Oklahoma Kid. f, King Kong. g, A Lady Fights Back. h, Steamboat Around the Bend. i, Wee Willie Winkie.
Each 2000d: No. 1215, Bring 'Em Back Alive. No. 1216 Indian chief.

**1995, May 10 Litho. *Perf. 14***
**1214** A184 Sheet of 9, #a.-i. 15.00 15.00

**Souvenir Sheets**
**1215-1216** A184 Set of 2 15.00 15.00

Horses — A185

Designs: No. 1217, Various horses, each 1000d.
Each 2000d: No. 1218, Painting of Indian on horse, wild horses, horiz. No. 1219, City scene, horses, carriage, horiz.

**1995, May 16**
**1217** A185 Sheet of 9, #a.-i. 16.00 16.00

**Souvenir Sheets**
**1218-1219** A185 Set of 2 16.00 16.00

Nos. 1218-1219 each contain one 50x35mm stamp.

Souvenir Sheet

Euro '96, European Soccer Championships, Great Britain — A186

**1995, July 2** ***Perf. 13½x14***
**1220** A186 2000d multicolored 7.50 7.50

Souvenir Sheet

Protection of World's Endangered Species — A187

**1995, July 6** ***Perf. 14***
**1221** A187 2000d multicolored 8.00 8.00

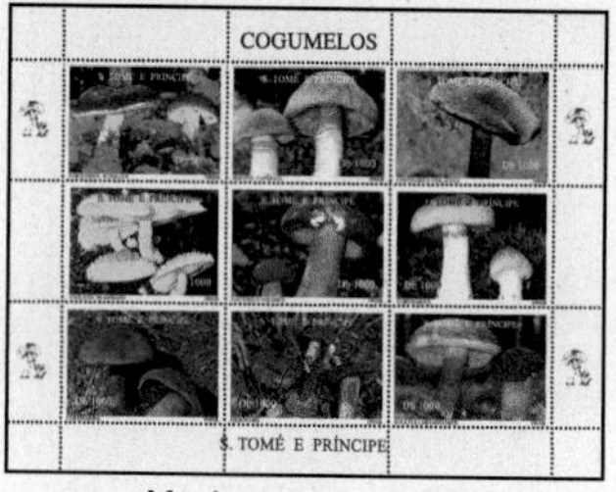


Mushrooms — A188

Designs, each 1000d: No. 1222a, Xerocomus rubellus. b, Rozites caperata. c, Cortinarius violaceus. d, Pholiota flammans. e, Lactarius volemus. f, Cortinarius (yellow). g, Cartinarius (blue). h, Higroforo. i, Boletus chrysenteron.
Each 2000d: No. 1223, Amanita muscaria, vert. No. 1224, Russula cyanoxantha, vert.

**1995, Nov. 2**
**1222** A188 Sheet of 9, #a.-i. 18.00 18.00

**Souvenir Sheets**

**1223-1224** A188 Set of 2 14.00 14.00

Details or Entire Paintings — A189

No. 1225, each 1000d: a, Aurora and Cefalo. b, Madonna and Child with St. John as a Boy. c, Romulus and Remus. d, Lamentation over the Dead Christ. e, Vison of All Saints Day. f, Perseus and Andromeda. g. The Scent. h, The Encounter in Lyon. i, The Art School of Rubens-Bildern.
Each 2000d: No. 1226, Statue of Ceres. No. 1227, Flight into Egypt, horiz.
All but #1225g (Jan Brueghel the Elder) and 1225i are by Rubens.

**1995, Sept. 27** **Litho.** ***Perf. 14***
**1225** A189 Sheet of 9, #a.-i. 18.00 18.00

**Souvenir Sheets**

**1226-1227** A189 Set of 2 18.00 18.00

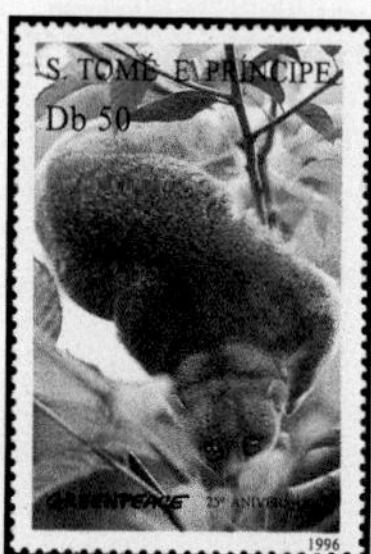


Greenpeace, 25th Anniv. — A190

Designs: No. 1237, Potto. No. 1238, Iguana. No. 1239, Tiger. No. 1240, Lion.
50d, Elephant, horiz.

**1996, Aug. 5** **Litho.** ***Perf. 14***
**1237-1240** A190 50d Set of 4 10.00 10.00

**Souvenir Sheet**

**1241** A190 50d multicolored 4.25 4.25

Dogs & Cats — A191

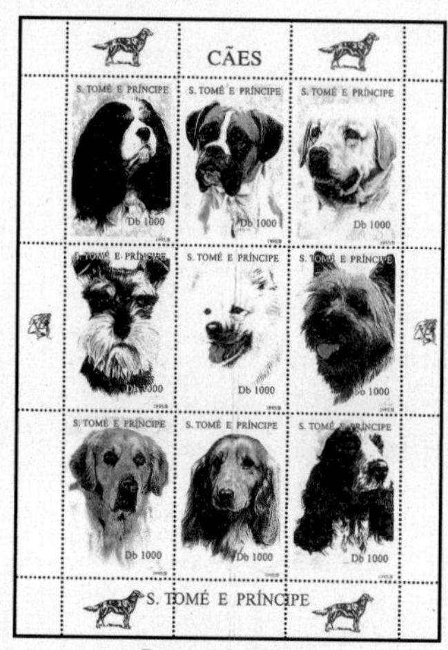


Dogs — A191a

Nos. 1242a-1242i: Various pictures of dogs with cats, kittens.
Nos. 1243a-1243i: Various close-up pictures of different breeds of dogs.
No. 1244, Labrador retriever. No. 1245, Bird, woman's eye, vert. No. 1246, Two kittens. No. 1247, Collie, vert. No. 1248, Poodle, vert. No. 1249, Pit bull terrier, vert. No. 1250, Brown and white terrier, vert.

**1995, Aug. 12** **Litho.** ***Perf. 14***

**Sheets of 9, #a-i**

**1242** A191 1000d multi 22.50 22.50
**1243** A191a 1000d multi 22.50 22.50

**Souvenir Sheets**

**1244** A191 2000d multi 6.50 6.50
**1245** A191a 2000d multi 6.50 6.50
**1246** A191 2000d multi 6.50 6.50
**1247** A191a 2000d multi 6.50 6.50
**1248** A191a 2000d multi 6.50 6.50
**1249** A191a 2000d multi 6.50 6.50
**1250** A191a 2000d multi 6.50 6.50

Orchids A192

No. 1251, each 1000d: a, Findlayanum. b, Stan. c, Cruentum. d, Trpla suavis. e, Lowianum. f, Gratiosissimum. g, Cyrtorchis monteirae. h, Sarcanthus birmanicus. i, Loddigesii.
Each 2000d: No. 1252, Barkeria Skinneri. No. 1253, Dendrobium nobile.

**1995, Sept. 12**
**1251** A192 Sheet of 9, #a.-i. 19.00 19.00

**Souvenir Sheets**

**1252-1253** A192 Set of 2 16.00 16.00

Paintings, Drawings by Durer, Rubens — A193

Designs, each 750d: No. 1254, Soldier on Horseback, by Durer, vert. No. 1255, Archangel St. Michael Slaying Satan, by Rubens, vert. No. 1256, Nursing Madonna in Half Length, by Durer, vert. No. 1257, Head of a Deer, by Durer, vert. No. 1258, View of Innsbruck from the North, by Durer. No. 1259, Madonna Nursing on a Grassy Bench, by Durer, vert. No. 1260, Helene Fourment and Her Children, by Rubens, vert. No. 1261, Adam and Eve, by Durer, vert.
Each 2000d: No. 1262, A Young Hare, by Durer, vert. No. 1263, Mills on a River Bank, by Durer. No. 1264, Holy Family with a Basket, by Rubens, vert. No. 1265, The Annunciation, by Rubens, vert.

**1995, Dec. 16** **Litho.** ***Perf. 14***
**1254-1261** A193 Set of 8 16.00 16.00

**Souvenir Sheets**

**1262-1265** A193 Set of 4 32.50 32.50

Christmas.

Independence, 20th Anniv. — A194

**1995, July 12** **Litho.** ***Perf. 13½***
**1266** A194 350d multicolored 4.50 1.90

1996 Summer Olympic Games, Atlanta — A195

Various shells, Nos. 1267-1271 each 1000d.

**1996, Jan. 10** **Litho.** ***Perf. 14***
**1267-1271** A195 Set of 5 18.00 18.00

**Souvenir Sheet**

**1272** A195 2000d multicolored 9.00 9.00

Anniversaries and Events — A196

**1996, Aug. 2** ***Perf. 14x13½***
**1273** A196 500d multicolored 7.50 2.00

UNICEF, 50th anniv., Alfred Nobel, 150th anniv. of birth, Phila-Seoul 96, KOREA 2002, 1996 Summer Olympic Games, Atlanta.

UNESCO A197

Butterflies, each 1000d: No. 1274, Papilio weiskei. No. 1275, Heliconius melpomene. No. 1276, Papilio arcas-mylotes. No. 1277, Mesomenia cresus. No. 1278, Catagramma iyca-satrana.
No. 1279, Lemonius sudias.

**1996, Sept. 10** ***Perf. 13½x14***
**1274-1278** A197 Set of 5 14.00 14.00

**Souvenir Sheet**

**1279** A197 2000d multicolored 6.00 6.00

**Train Type of 1995**

Each 1000d: No. 1280, SNCF. No. 1281, CN. No. 1282, White locomotive. No. 1283, Green locomotive. No. 1284, Train in city.
Each 2000d: No. 1285, Modern train. No. 1286, Old train.

**1996, Oct. 7** *Perf. 14*
**1280-1284** A181 Set of 5 14.00 14.00

**Souvenir Sheets**

**1285-1286** A181 Set of 2 10.00 10.00

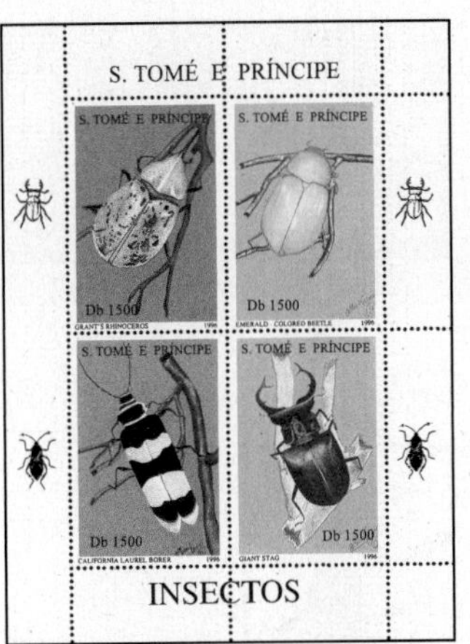


Beetles — A198

No. 1287, each 1500d: a, Grant's rhinoceros. b, Emerald-colored. c, California laurel borer. d, Giant stag.
Each 2000d: No. 1288, Maple borer. No. 1289, Arizona june.

**1996, Nov. 7** *Perf. 13½x14*
**1287** A198 Sheet of 4, #a.-d. 16.00 16.00

**Souvenir Sheets**

**1288-1289** A198 Set of 2 14.00 14.00

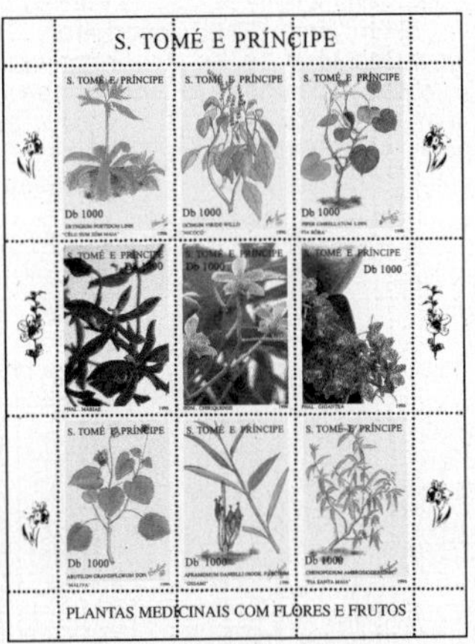


Plants, Orchids — A199

Each 1000d: No. 1290: a, Eryngium fortidum. b, Ocimum viride. c, Piper umbellatum. d, Phal. mariae. e, Odm. chiriquense. f, Phal. gigantea. g, Abutilon grandiflorum. h, Aframomium danielli. i, Chemopodium ambrosiodes.
Each 2000d: No. 1291, Crinum jacus. No. 1292, Oncoba apinosa forsk. No. 1293, Z. mackai. No. 1294, Aspasia principissa.

**1996, Oct. 14**
**1290** A199 Sheet of 9, #a.-i. 22.50 22.50

**Souvenir Sheets**

**1291-1294** A199 Set of 4 35.00 35.00

**Nos. 769, 912, 914 Surcharged**

No. 1295B

**1996-1997?** *Surcharge Typo.*
**Perfs. & Printing Methods as Before**

**1295** A100 500d on 46d #769 — —
**1295A** A133 500d on 60d #912 — —
**1295B** A133 500d on 60d #914 8.00 4.50

Nos. 1295A-1295B exist with four varieties of the letters "Db". Type I: "D" is rounded, and "b" has a very small hole. Type II: Bottom of "D" is higher than "b", and "b" has a small hole. Type III: "D" is slightly squared, and "b" has a tall hole. Type IV: "D" is very rounded, and "b" has a large round hole.

**Nos. 727-730, 733-734, 736-739, 744, 746, 748 Surcharged in Blue, Black, or Violet**

No. 1296

No. 1298C

***Surcharge Handstamped***

**1996-1997?**
**Printing Methods and Perfs as Before**

**1295C** A95 1000d on 5.50d #733 — —
**1296** A95 1000d on 11d #736 (dk bl) — —
**1297** A95 1000d on 12d #737 (Bl) — —
*b.* Black surcharge — —
**1297A** A95 1000d on 15.50d #739 — —
**1298** A95 1000d on 42d #746 5.00 2.75
**1298A** A95 2500d on 50c #727 (Bl) — —
**1298B** A95 2500d on 1d #728 (Bl) — —
**1298C** A95 2500d on 1.50d #729 (Bl) 8.00 6.75
*g.* Violet surcharge — —
**1298D** A95 2500d on 2d #730 (Bl) — —
**1298E** A95 2500d on 7d #734 (Bl) — —
**1298F** A95 2500d on 14d #738 (Bl) — —
*h.* Violet surcharge — —
**1299** A95 2500d on 25d #744 (Bl) 8.00 6.75
**1300** A95 2500d on 100d #748 (Bl) 8.00 6.75
*a.* Violet surcharge — —

**Nos. 727, 733, 735, 742 Surcharged "Dbs." in Blue or Black**

**1997?** *Surcharge Handstamped*
**Printing Methods and Perfs as Before**

**1300B** A95 2500d on 50c #727 (Bl) — —
**1300C** A95 2500d on 5.50d #733 — —
**1300D** A95 2500d on 10d #735 — —
**1300E** A95 2500d on 18.50d #742 (Bl) — —

**Nos. 729, 742, 747 Surcharged Large "Dbs." in Blue, Black or Green**

**1997?** *Surcharge Handstamped*
**Printing Methods and Perfs as Before**

**1300F** A95 1500d on 18.50d #742 — —
**1300G** A95 1500d on 46d #747 (Bl) — —
**1300H** A95 2500d on 1500d on 1.50d #729 (Gr on Bl) — —

The editors would like to examine an example of No. 1300H without the green surcharge.

Musicians, Musical Instruments A200

"The Beatles" — No. 1301, each 1500d: a, John Lennon. b, Paul McCartney. c, George Harrison. d, Ringo Starr.
Traditional instruments — No. 1302, each 1500d: a, Animal horn. b, Flutes. c, Tambourine, drum, sticks. d, Canza.
Each 2000d: No. 1303, Guitar, Elvis Presley (in sheet margin). No. 1304, Maraca, Antonio Machin.

**1996, Nov. 19 Litho.** *Perf. 13½x14*

**Sheets of 4, #a-d**

**1301-1302** A200 Set of 2 37.50 37.50

**Souvenir Sheets**

**1303-1304** A200 Set of 2 19.00 19.00

Fish — A201

No. 1305, each 1500d: a, Sailfish. b, Barracuda. c, Cod. d, Atlantic mackerel.
Each 2000d: No. 1306, Bluefin tuna. No. 1307, Squirrelfish.

**1996, Dec. 10** *Perf. 14x13½*
**1305** A201 Sheet of 4, #a.-d. 18.00 18.00

**Souvenir Sheets**

**1306-1307** A201 Set of 2 20.00 20.00

No. 988 Surcharged in Dark Blue

**Methods and Perfs as Before 1997, Apr. 16** **Surcharge Typo.**

**1307A** A144 1000d on 250d multi 35.00 8.00
*b.* "Dbs." normal — —

No. 1307A "Dbs." is in italics. No. 1307Ab "Dbs." is in regular font.

A202

Diana, Princess of Wales (1961-97) — A202a

No. 1308: Various portraits, vert.
100d, Diana talking with her sons (in sheet margin), vert. 500d, Portrait. 2000d, Diana, Mother Teresa (in sheet margin), vert.

**1997 Litho.** *Perf. 14*
**1308** A202 10d Sheet of 9, #a.-i. 22.50 22.50

**Souvenir Sheets**

***Perf. 13½x14, 14x13½***

**1309** A202 100d multi 12.00 12.00
**1310** A202a 500d gold & multi 12.00 12.00
**1311** A202a 2000d gold & multi 8.00 8.00

Issued: No. 1308, 100d, 500d, 10/15/97; 2000d, 10/20/97.

Souvenir Sheet

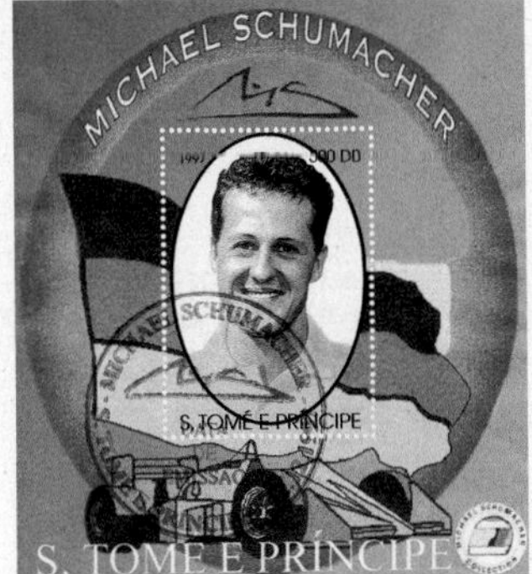


Michael Schumacher, World Champion Formula I Driver — A203

**1997, Dec. 12** *Perf. 14*
**1312** A203 500d multicolored 9.00 9.00

Titanic — A205

No. 1317, 1000d — Titanic, White Star Line flag and inset image of: a, Captain Edward J.

Smith. b, Titanic approaching icebergs. c, Titanic shooting flares. d, Distress codes. e, Titanic cruising in daylight. f, Titanic with icebergs at left. g, Lifeboats near sinking Titanic. h, Sinking Titanic. i, Map showing location of sinking.

No. 1318, 1000d: a, Construction of Titanic. b, Titanic leaving dock. c, Titanic and seagulls. d, Titanic shooting flares. e, Lifeboats near sinking Titanic. f, Sinking Titanic. g, Titanic, lifeboat, ship's officer. h, Bow of sunken Titanic. i, Stern of sunken Titanic.

No. 1319, 2000d, Captain and Titanic (multicoloured). No. 1320, 2000d, Captain and Titanic (black).

**1998, July 1 Litho. *Perf. 14x13¾***

**Sheets of 9, #a-i**

**1317-1318** A205 Set of 2 — —

**Souvenir Sheets**

**1319-1320** A205 Set of 2 15.00 15.00

Expo '98, Lisbon — A206

Sea around the islands, each 3500d: No. 1326, Man fishing from shore. No. 1327, Man in small sailboat, sharks in water below. No. 1328, Flying fish. No. 1329, Diver connecting line on sea bottom. No. 1330, Man paddling boat, turtle, fish below.

8000d, Map of St. Thomas & Prince, vert.

**1998 Litho. *Perf. 14***

**1326-1330** A206 Set of 5 16.00 13.50

**Souvenir Sheet**

**1331** A206 8000d multicolored 20.00 8.00

2nd AICEP Philatelic Exhibition — A207

Traditional food, each 3500d: No. 1332, Feijao de coco, coconuts. No. 1333, Cooked bananas, fruit, wine. No. 1334, Molho no fogo, fish, fruit, wine. No. 1335, Calulu, fruits, vegetables, wine. No. 1336, Izaquente de acucar, sugar beet.

7000d, Pot cooking over open fire, vert.

**1998, Aug. 1**

**1332-1336** A207 Set of 5 16.00 7.00

**Souvenir Sheet**

**1337** A207 7000d multicolored 8.00 8.00

Souvenir Sheet

Portugal 98 Stamp Exhibition — A210

**1998, Sept. 4 Litho. *Perf. 14x13¾***

**1342** A210 7000d Ship on map 15.00 8.00

Five stamps were issued with the souvenir sheet. The editors would like to examine them.

**Nos. 731-732, 735-737, 739-742, 746-747 Surcharged in Blue or Violet**

**1997? *Surcharge Handstamped***

**Printing Methods and Perfs as Before**

**1343** A95 2500d on 3d #731 (V) — —

**1344** A95 2500d on 4d #732 (Bl) — —

**1345** A95 2500d on 10d #735 (Bl) — —

**1345A** A95 2500d on 11d #736 (Bl) — —

**1346** A95 2500d on 12d #737 (Bl) — —

**1346A** A95 2500d on 15.50d #739 (Bl) — —

**1347** A95 2500d on 16d #740 (Bl) — —

**1348** A95 2500d on 17d #741 (V) — —

**1349** A95 2500d on 18.50d #742 (Bl), value right of obliterator — —

*a.* Value below obliterator — —

**1350** A95 2500d on 42d #746 (Bl) — —

**1351** A95 2500d on 46d #747 (Bl) — —

**Nos. 599, 603 Surcharged in Black or Green**

***Surcharge Handstamped (Nos. 1352-1353), Typo. (No. 1353A)***

**1998?**

**Printing Methods and Perfs as Before**

**1352** A65 3000d on 50c #599, surch. at bottom — —

**1352A** A65 3000d on 50c #599, surch. at top (G) — —

**1353** A65 3000d on 14d #603 — —

**1353A** A65 3000d on 14d #603 — —

No. 1353 was handstamped, the letters are messy, the obliterator is one bar. No. 1353A was typographed, the letters are neat, the obliterator is two bars.

Some sources indicate that No. 610 was surcharged 3000d and belongs in this set. The editors would like to see evidence of its existence.

**Nos. 719-721 Surcharged in Blue**

**1999 *Surcharge Handstamped***

**Printing Methods and Perfs as Before**

**1355** A63 3000d on 20d #719 — —

**1356** A63 3000d on 46d #720 — —

**1357** A63 3000d on 50d #721 — —

Nos. 1356 and 1357 do not have an obliterator.

Nos. 856-858 Surcharged in Black

**1999 Surcharge Typo.**

**Printing Methods and Perfs as Before**

**1358** A123p 3000d on 50c #856 *15.00 5.00*

**1359** A123p 3000d on 1d #857 *15.00 5.00*

**1360** A123p 3000d on 5d #858 *15.00 5.00*

Nos. 1358 and 1360 have various obliterators. No. 1359 has no obliterator.

Nos. 728, 735, 739 Surcharged

**1999, Nov. Surcharge Typo.**

**Printing Methods and Perfs as Before**

**1361** A95 5000d on 15.50d #739 *10.00 10.00*

**1362** A95 7000d on 10d #735 *15.00 15.00*

**1363** A95 10,000d on 1d #728 *20.00 20.00*

*Nos. 1361-1363 (3) 45.00 45.00*

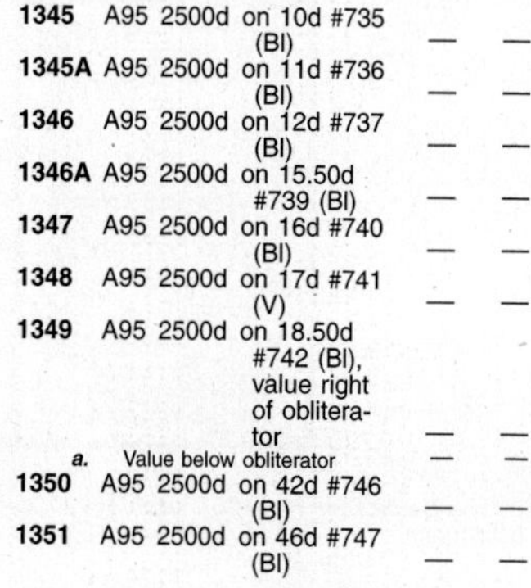


Christmas — A211

Designs: Nos. 1364, 1367, 5000d, Adoration of the Shepherds. Nos. 1365, 1368, 6000d, Presentation of Jesus in the Temple. Nos. 1366, 1369, 10,000d, Flight Into Egypt.

**1999, Dec. 23 Litho. *Perf. 12¾x13***

**1364-1366** A211 Set of 3 *9.50 9.50*

**Souvenir Sheets**

**1367-1369** A211 Set of 3 *10.00 10.00*

Stamps on Nos. 1367-1369 have continuous designs.

Souvenir Sheet

Independence, 25th Anniv. — A213

No. 1371: a, 5000d, Mountain, bird. b, 6000d, Stylized mountains, birds, flag. c, 7000d, Mountains, "25," flag. d, 10,000d, Mountain, bird, diff.

**2000, July 12 Litho. *Perf. 12¾***

**1371** A213 Sheet of 4, #a-d 13.00 13.00

Nos. 746, 748 Surcharged

**2000, Aug. 7 Surcharge Typo.**

**Printing Methods and Perfs as Before**

**1372** A95 5000d on 42d multi 3.00 2.50

**1373** A95 5000d on 100d multi 3.00 2.50

2000 Summer Olympics, Sydney — A214

Olympic rings and: 5000d, Runner, stadium, kangaroos, bird. 7000d, Runner, Sydney Opera House, kangaroos, emu.

15,000d, Sydney Harbour Bridge, Opera House, kangaroo, horiz.

**2000, Sept. 14 Litho. *Perf. 12¾***

**1374-1375** A214 Set of 2 6.00 6.00

**Souvenir Sheet**

***Perf. 13***

**1376** A214 15,000d multi 7.50 7.50

Souvenir Sheet

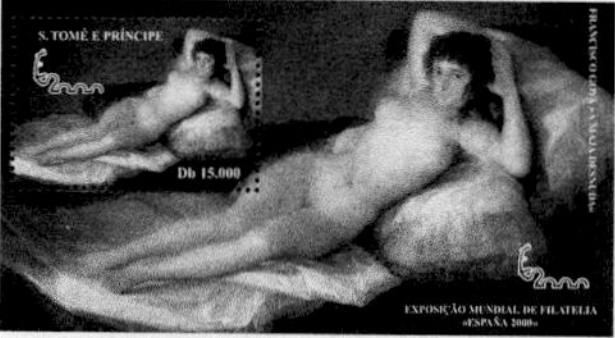


España 2000 Intl. Philatelic Exhibition — A215

**2000, Oct. 6 *Perf. 12¾***

**1377** A215 15,000d multi 9.00 9.00

Holy Year 2000 — A216

Designs: No. 1381a, 3000d, God, the Father. No. 1381b, 5000d, St. Anne, Virgin Mary, infant Jesus. Nos. 1378, 1381c, 6000d, St. Thomas. No. 1381d, 6000d, Processional cross. Nos. 1379, 1381e, 7000d, Altarpiece. Nos. 1380, 1381f, 8000d, Cathedral.

**2000, Dec. 21 *Perf. 12¾***

**With "Natal 2000" Inscription**

**1378-1380** A216 Set of 3 10.00 10.00

**Without "Natal 2000" Inscription**

**1381** A216 Sheet of 6, #a-f 17.00 17.00

*g.* Souvenir sheet, #1381a-1381b, 1381d-1381e, perf. 12 10.00 10.00

Rosa de Porcellana A218

Flower in: Nos. 1391, 5000d, 1393a, 7000d, Pink. Nos. 1392, 5000d, 1393b, 8000d, Red.

**2001, Apr. 12 Litho. *Perf. 13¾x14***

**1391-1392** A218 Set of 2 4.75 4.75

**Souvenir Sheet**

**1393** A218 Sheet of 2, #a-b 7.50 7.50

Butterflies A219

Designs: No. 1394, 3500d, Graphium leonidas (brown frame). No. 1395, 5000d, Acraea newtoni (bright red frame). No. 1396, 6000d, Papilio bromius (bright red frame). No. 1397, 7500d, Papilio dardanos (brown frame).

No. 1398: a, 3500d, Graphium leonidas (orange frame). b, 5000d, Acraea newtoni (dark red frame). c, 6000d, Papilio bromius (dark red frame). d, 7500d, Papilio dardanos (orange frame).

15,000d, Euchloron megaera serrei.

**2001, July 15 *Perf. 13¼x13½***

**1394-1397** A219 Set of 4 10.00 10.00

**Souvenir Sheets**

**1398** A219 Sheet of 4, #a-d 11.00 11.00

**1399** A219 15,000d multi 7.50 7.50

Worldwide Fund for Nature (WWF) A220

Lepidochelys olivacea: 3500d, One swimming. 5000d, Two swimming. 6000d, Three leaving water. 7500d, Three hatchlings in sand.

**2001, Oct.**
**1400-1403** A220 Set of 4 9.00 8.00

Nos. 1400-1403 were each issued in sheets of four. The margin of each of the four stamps on the sheets differs.

See No. 1431. For surcharges, see Nos. 2199-2201.

Souvenir Sheets

Famous Men — A221

Designs: No. 1404, 15,000d, Charlie Chaplin (1889-1977), comedian. No. 1405, 15,000d, Louis Armstrong (1900-71), musician. No. 1406, 15,000d, Walt Disney (1901-66), film producer, vert. No. 1407, 15,000d, Giuseppe Verdi (1813-1901), composer, vert.

**2002 Litho.** ***Perf. 13¼***
**1404-1407** A221 Set of 4 27.50 27.50

Issued: No. 1404, 3/11; No. 1405, 3/12; No. 1406, 3/13; No. 1407, 3/14.

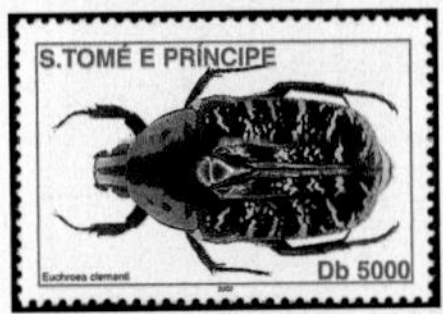

Insects A222

Designs: No. 1408, 5000d, Euchroea clementi. No. 1409, 5000d, Dicranorrhina derbyana. No. 1410, 5000d, Stephanorrhina guttata. 8000d, Polybothris sumptuosa gemma.

**2002, Mar. 15** ***Perf. 13¼x13½***
**1408-1411** A222 Set of 4 11.00 11.00

Souvenir Sheet

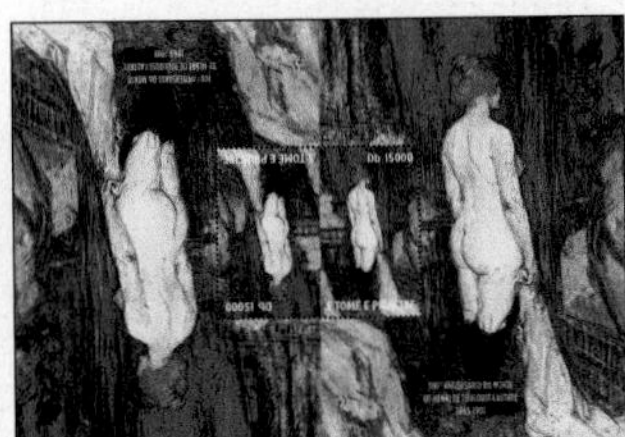

Henri de Toulouse-Lautrec (1865-1901), Painter — A223

***Perf. 13¼x13¼x13¼x Rouletted***

**2002, Mar. 16**
**1412** A223 15,000d Sheet of 2 13.00 13.00

Stamps in No. 1412 are tete-beche. The rouletting continues through the selvage allowing the sheet to be broken up into two half-sheets.

Souvenir Sheets

Chinese Zodiac Animals — A224

No. 1413, 15,000d: a, Rat. b, Tiger. c, Ox. d, Rabbit.

No. 1414, 15,000d: a, Dragon. b, Horse. c, Snake. d, Goat.

No. 1415, 15,000d: a, Monkey. b, Dog. c, Cock. d, Pig.

**2002** ***Perf.***
**1413-1415** A224 Set of 3 75.00 75.00

Each sheet was rouletted into quadrants.

In Remembrance of Sept. 11, 2001 Terrorist Attacks — A225

**2002, May 27** ***Perf. 13½x13¼***

**With White Frame**

**1416** A225 5000d multi 2.75 2.75

**Souvenir Sheet**

**Without White Frame**

**1417** A225 15,000d multi 8.00 8.00

No. 1417 contains one 40x51mm stamp.

Souvenir Sheet

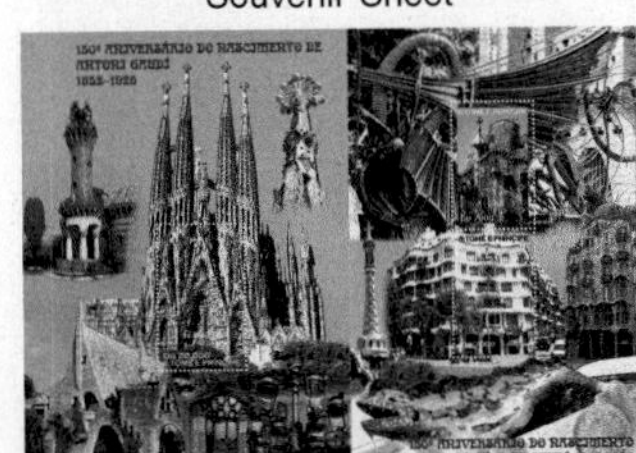

Barcelona Architecture of Antonio Gaudí — A226

No. 1418: a, 7000d, Casa Batlló (dark brown building, 27x41mm). b, 7000d, Casa Mila (light building, 27x41mm). c, 20,000d, Church of Sagrada Familia (29x47mm).

***Perf. 13½x13¼, 13¼ (#1418c)***

**2002, Sept. 28**
**1418** A226 Sheet, #a-c 13.00 13.00

A column of rouletting separates the sheet into two halves, one containing Nos. 1418a-1418b, and the other containing No. 1418c. An additional column of rouletting is found at the left side of the half sheet containing No. 1418c.

Orchids — A227

Designs: 2000d, Phaius mannii. 6000d, Cyrtorchis arcuata. 9000d, Calanthe sylvatica. 10,000d, Bulbophyllum lizae.

20,000d, Bulbophyllum saltatorium.

***Perf. 13½x13¼***

**2002, Nov. 19 Litho.**
**1419-1422** A227 Set of 4 14.00 14.00

**Souvenir Sheet**

**1424** A227 20,000d multi 10.00 10.00

A number has been reserved for an additional item in this set.

Birds — A228

Designs: 1000d, Nectarinia newtonii. 7000d, Prinior molleri. 9000d, Neospiza concolor. 10,000d, Lanius newtoni.

20,000d, Otus hartlaubi.

***Perf. 13½x13¼***

**2002, Nov. 20 Litho.**
**1425-1428** A228 Set of 4 13.00 13.00
*1428a* Souvenir sheet, #1425-1428 13.00 13.00

**Souvenir Sheet**

**1429** A228 20,000d multi 10.00 10.00

Miniature Sheet

Circus Animals — A229

No. 1430: a, 2000d, Horses (30x40mm). b, 6000d, Chimpanzees (30x40mm). c, 9000d, Seals (30x40mm). d, 10,000d, Tigers (30x40mm). e, 20,000d, Elephants (60x80mm).

**2002, Nov. 22** ***Perf. 13¼x13***
**1430** A229 Sheet of 5, #a-e 14.00 14.00

A column of rouletting separates the sheet into two halves, one containing Nos. 1430a-1430d and the other containing No. 1430e.

**Worldwide Fund for Nature Type of 2001**

Souvenir Sheet

No. 1431 — Lepidochelys olivacea: a, 6000d, Two swimming. b, 6000d, Three hatchlings in sand. c, 7000d, One swimming. d, 7000d, Three leaving water.

**2002, Dec. 31** ***Perf. 13¼x13½***
**1431** A220 Sheet of 4, #a-d 14.00 14.00

Space Travelers A230

Designs: 6000d, Laika. 7000d, Yuri Gagarin. 8000d, Dennis Tito.

**2003, Feb. 20** ***Perf. 13x13¼***
**1432-1434** A230 Set of 3 9.00 9.00
*1434a* Souvenir sheet, #1432-1434, perf. 12½x12¾ 9.00 9.00

Souvenir Sheet

The Last Supper, by Leonardo da Vinci — A231

**2003, Apr. 17** ***Perf. 13½x13¼***
**1435** A231 25,000d multi 11.00 11.00

Easter.

Crustaceans — A232

Designs: Nos. 1436, 1440a, 3500d, Coenobita perlatus. Nos. 1437, 1440b, 7000d, Carcinus maenas. Nos. 1438, 1440c, 8000d, Uca tetragonon. Nos. 1439, 1440d, 9000d, Ovalipes ocellatus.

20,000d, Panulirus pencillatus.

**2003, Apr. 24** ***Perf. 13¼x13½***

**With White Frames**

**1436-1439** A232 Set of 4 12.50 12.50

**Without White Frames**

**1440** A232 Sheet of 4, #a-d 12.50 12.50

**Souvenir Sheet**

**1441** A232 20,000d multi 9.00 9.00

Vincent van Gogh (1853-90), Painter — A233

Paintings: No. 1442, 6000d, Young Peasant Woman with Straw Hat Sitting in the Wheat, 1890. No. 1443, 6000d, Head of a Peasant Woman with White Cap, 1885. No. 1444, 7000d, Patience Escalier. No. 1445, 7000d, Charles-Elzéard Trabuc.

No. 1446 — Self-portraits from: a, 6000d, 1886 (head at left). b, 6000d, 1886 (head at right). c, 7000d, 1888. d, 7000d, 1889.

**2003, May 30 Litho.** ***Perf. 13½x13***
**1442-1445** A233 Set of 4 10.50 10.50

**Souvenir Sheet**

**1446** A233 Sheet of 4, #a-d 10.50 10.50

Skull With Burning Cigarette, by Vincent van Gogh — A234

**2003, May 31**
**1447** A234 7000d multi 3.25 3.25

WHO anti-smoking campaign.

A235

A236

Famous People — A237

No. 1448: a, Lord Robert Baden-Powell, dogs. b, Pres. George W. Bush, rescue workers. c, Pope John Paul II, Copernicus. d, Astronaut Neil Armstrong, Russian cosmonaut. e, Vincent van Gogh self-portrait, and painting. f, Louis Pasteur, cat. g, Sir Alexander Fleming, mushrooms. h, Elvis Presley on motorcylce, automobile. i, Walt Disney, dog.

No. 1449: a, Pope John Paul II, Pres. George W. Bush. b, Male chess player. c, Nelson Mandela, mineral. d, Charles Darwin, dinosaur. e, Tiger Woods, Rotary emblem. f, Dr. Albert Schweitzer, bird. g, Hector Berlioz. h, Pablo Picasso and painting. i, Pope John Paul II and Mother Teresa.

No. 1450: a, Pope John Paul II and UN Secretary General Kofi Annan. b, Formula I race car driver and car. c, Lady Olave Baden-Powell, cat. d, Female chess player. e, Sir Rowland Hill, train. f, Rotary emblem, Lions emblem and founders. g, Henri Dunant, Princess Diana. h, Paul Gauguin and painting. i, Pope John Paul II, Princess Diana.

**2003 Litho.** ***Perf. 12¾x13¼***

**1448** A235 5000d Sheet of 9, #a-i 10.00 10.00
**1449** A236 5000d Sheet of 9, #a-i 10.00 10.00
**1450** A237 5000d Sheet of 9, #a-i 10.00 10.00
*Nos. 1448-1450 (3)* 30.00 30.00

Each stamp exists in a souvenir sheet of 1.

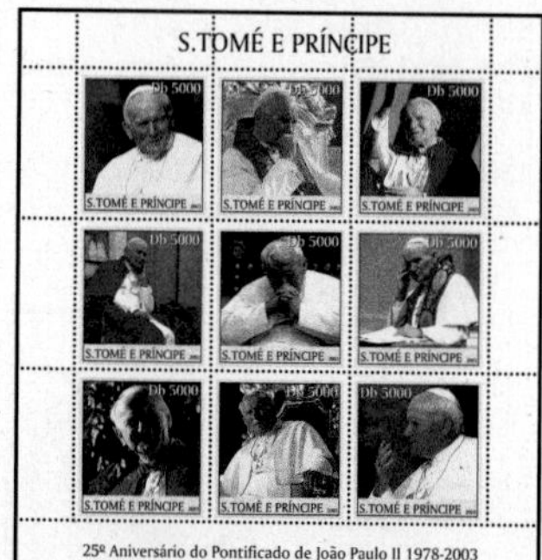

A238

A239

A240

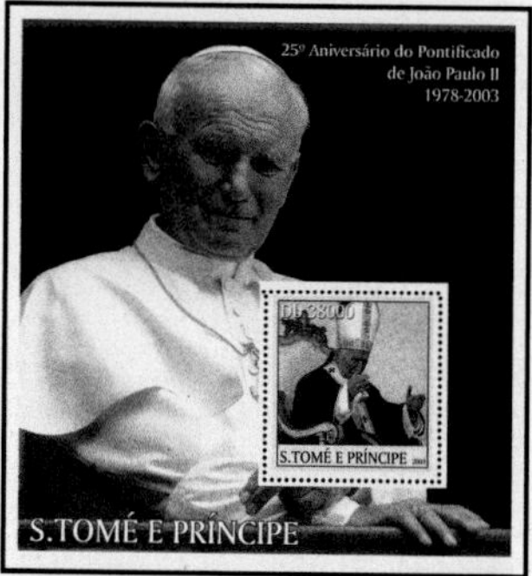

Reign of Pope John Paul II, 25th Anniv. — A241

Various photographs of Pope John Paul II.

**2003**

**1451** A238 5000d Sheet of 9, #a-i 10.00 10.00
**1452** A239 5000d Sheet of 9, #a-i 10.00 10.00

**Souvenir Sheets**

**1453** A240 38,000d multi 8.50 8.50
**1454** A241 38,000d multi 8.50 8.50

A242

A243

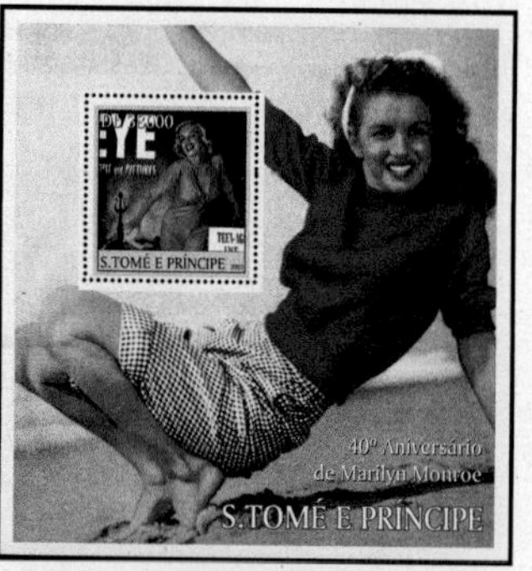

A244

Marilyn Monroe (1926-62), Actress — A245

Various Marilyn Monroe photographs and magazine covers.

**2003**

**1455** A242 5000d Sheet of 9, #a-i 10.00 10.00
**1456** A243 5000d Sheet of 9, #a-i 10.00 10.00

**Souvenir Sheets**

**1457** A244 38,000d multi 8.50 8.50
**1458** A245 38,000d multi 8.50 8.50

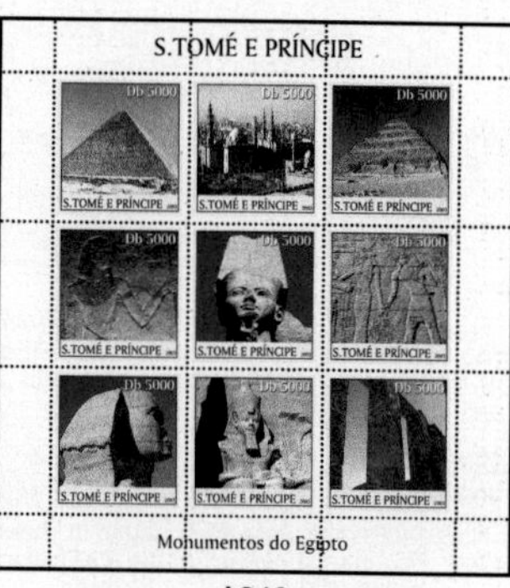

A246

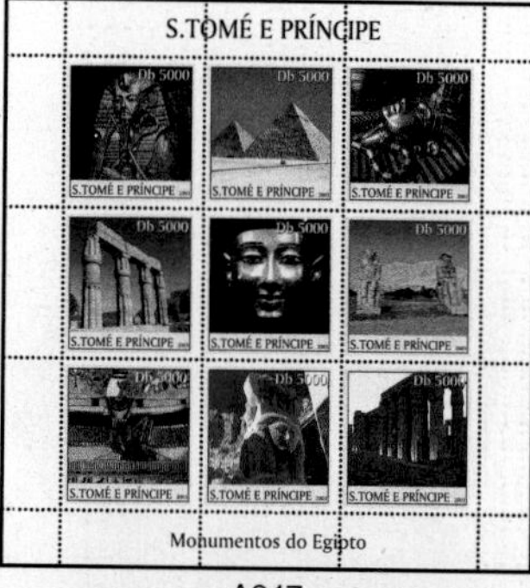

A247

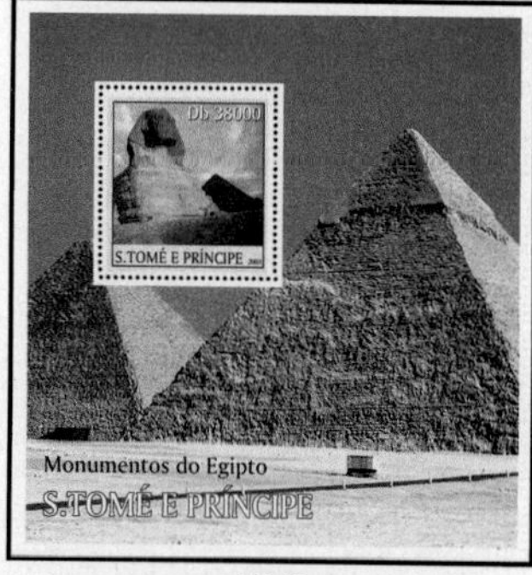

A248

Ancient Egyptian Monuments — A249

Various photographs.

**2003**

**1459** A246 5000d Sheet of 9, #a-i 10.00 10.00
**1460** A247 5000d Sheet of 9, #a-i 10.00 10.00

**Souvenir Sheets**

**1461** A248 38,000d multi 8.50 8.50
**1462** A249 38,000d multi 8.50 8.50

A250

A251

A252

A253

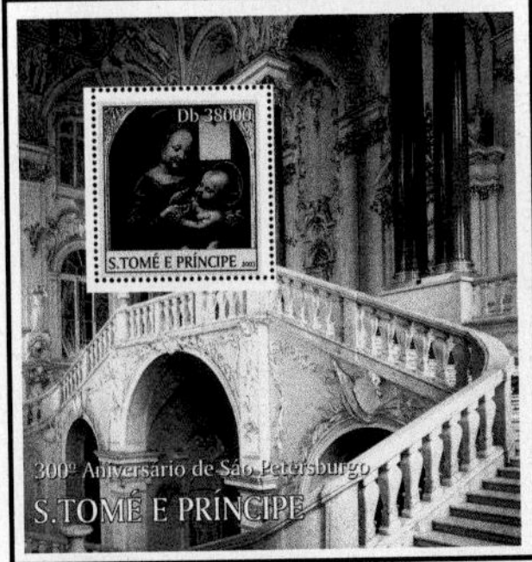


A254

St. Petersburg, Russia, 300th Anniv. — A255

Various unnamed paintings or buildings.

**2003**

**1463** A250 5000d Sheet of 9, #a-i 10.00 10.00
**1464** A251 5000d Sheet of 9, #a-i 10.00 10.00
**1465** A252 5000d Sheet of 9, #a-i 10.00 10.00
*Nos. 1463-1465 (3)* 30.00 30.00

### Souvenir Sheets

**1466** A253 38,000d multi 8.50 8.50
**1467** A254 38,000d multi 8.50 8.50
**1468** A255 38,000d multi 8.50 8.50

A256

Volcanoes, Minerals and Firefighters — A257

A258

Fire Vehicles — A259

Nos. 1469 — Various pictures of volcanoes and minerals: a, 1000d, With firefighter. b, 2000d, Without firefighter. c, 3000d, With firefighter. d, 5000d, Without firefighter. e, 6000d, With firefighter. f, 15,000d, Without firefighter.

Nos. 1470 — Various pictures of volcanoes and minerals: a, 1000d, Without firefighter. b, 2000d, With firefighter. c, 3000d, Without firefighter. d, 5000d, With firefighter. e, 6000d, Without firefighter. f, 15,000d, With firefighter.

Nos. 1471 and 1472 — Various fire vehicles: a, 1000d. b, 2000d, c, 3000d. d, 5000d. e, 6000d. f, 15,000d.

No. 1473, Like #1469e. No. 1474, Like #1470d. No. 1475, Like #1471c. No. 1476, Like #1472f.

***Perf. 12¾x13¼, 13¼x12¾ (#1474)***

**2003**

**1469** A256 Sheet of 6, #a-f 9.00 9.00
**1470** A257 Sheet of 6, #a-f 9.00 9.00
**1471** A258 Sheet of 6, #a-f 9.00 9.00
**1472** A259 Sheet of 6, #a-f 9.00 9.00
*Nos. 1469-1472 (4)* 36.00 36.00

### Souvenir Sheets

**1473** A256 38,000d multi 8.50 8.50
**1474** A257 38,000d multi 8.50 8.50
**1475** A258 38,000d multi 8.50 8.50
**1476** A259 38,000d multi 8.50 8.50

A260

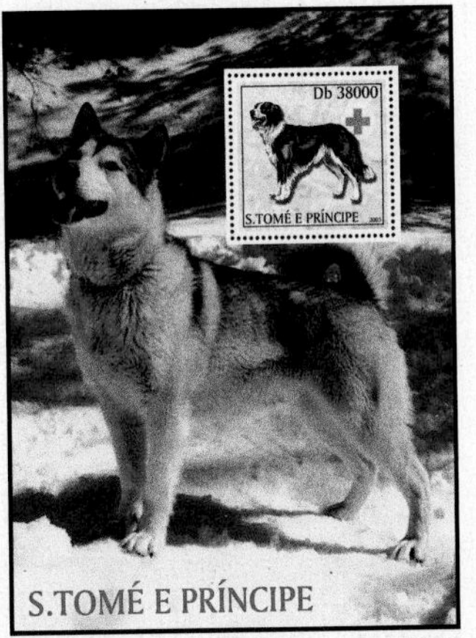


Red Cross Emblem and Dogs — A261

No. 1477 — Red Cross emblem and various dogs: a, 1000d. b, 2000d, c, 3000d. d, 5000d. e, 6000d. f, 15,000d.

***Perf. 12¾x13¼, 13¼x12¾ (#1478)***

**2003**

**1477** A260 Sheet of 6, #a-f 10.00 10.00

### Souvenir Sheet

**1478** A261 38,000d multi 9.50 9.50

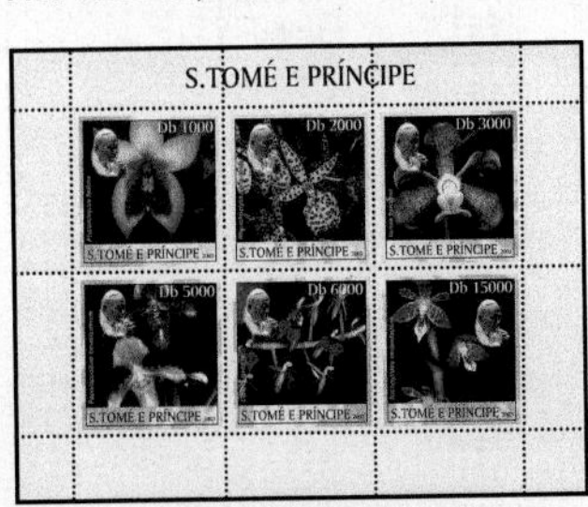


Pope John Paul II and Orchids — A262

No. 1479 — Pope and orchids: a, 1000d, Phalaenopsis bellina. b, 2000d, Rhynchostylis monachica. c, 3000d, Vanda bensonii. d, 5000d, Paphiopedilum hirsutissimum. e, 6000d, Liparis latifolia. f, 15,000d, Trichoglottis seidenfadenii.

38,000d, Like #1479a.

**2003** ***Perf. 12¾x13¼***

**1479** A262 Sheet of 6, #a-f 10.00 10.00

### Souvenir Sheet

**1480** A262 38,000d multi 9.50 9.50

Marilyn Monroe and Orchids — A263

No. 1481 — Monroe and orchids: a, 1000d, Phalaenopsis amabilis. b, 2000d, Rhynchostylis retusa. c, 3000d, Phalaenopsis stuartiana. d, 5000d, Rhynchostylis gigantea. e, 6000d, Vanda coerulea. f, 15,000d, Trichoglottis brachiata.

38,000d, Like #1481b.

**2003**

**1481** A263 Sheet of 6, #a-f 10.00 10.00

### Souvenir Sheet

**1482** A263 38,000d multi 9.50 9.50

Birds and Concorde — A264

No. 1483 — Concorde and penguins: a, 1000d. b, 2000d. c, 3000d. d, 5000d. e, 6000d. f, 15,000d.

No. 1484 — Birds: a, 1000d, Lybius torquatus, and Concorde. b, 2000d, Prinia subflava. c, 3000d, Tockus erythrorhynchus, and Concorde. d, 5000d, Poicephalus meyeri. e, 6000d, Uraeginthus angolensis, and Concorde. f, 15,000d, Laniarius atrococcineus.

No. 1485, 38,000d, Like #1483e. No. 1486, 38,000d, Like #1484c.

**2003** **Sheets of 6, #a-f**

**1483-1484** A264 Set of 2 18.00 18.00

### Souvenir Sheets

**1485-1486** A264 Set of 2 17.00 17.00

Birds — A265

No. 1487 — Various pheasants: a, 1000d. b, 2000d. c, 3000d. d, 5000d. e, 6000d. f, 15,000d.

No. 1488 — Birds and orchids: a, Polytelis alexandrae, Dendrochilum wenzelii. b, Neophena splendida, Dendrobium sulcatum. c, Pyrrhura calliptera, Dendrobium nobile. d, Aratinga jandaya, Cymbidium lowianum. e, Melopsittacus undulatus, Dendrobium bulleniánum. f, Psittacula himalayana, Chiloschista parishii.

No. 1489, 38,000d, Like #1487a, with Bangkok 2003 Jamboree emblem added. No. 1490, 38,000d, Like #1488b, with Bangkok 2003 Jamboree emblem added. See illustration A266 for stamps showing Bangkok 2003 Jamboree emblem.

**2003**

**1487** A265 Sheet of 6, #a.-f. 10.00 10.00

**1488** A265 10,000d Sheet of 6, #a-f 14.50 14.50

### Souvenir Sheets

**1489-1490** A265 Set of 2 18.00 18.00

For surcharges, see Nos. 2000-2002, 2007-2009, 2027-2029, 2034-2036, 2054-2056, 2061-2063, 2081-2083, 2088-2090.

Bangkok 2003 Scout Jamboree Emblem and Birds, Orchids, Mushrooms, Insects or Butterflies — A266

No. 1491 — Emblem and various fighting roosters: a, 1000d. b, 2000d. c, 3000d. d, 5000d. e, 6000d. f, 15,000d.

No. 1492 — Emblem and unnamed water birds or orchids: a, 1000d, Bird in flight. b, 2000d, Aerides odorata. c, 3000d, Two birds at nest. d, 5000d, Aerides roaea. e, 6000d, Two birds. f, 15,000d, Aerides quinquevulnera.

No. 1493 — Emblem and mushrooms and orchids: a, 1000d, Xerocomus cubtomentosus, Aerides quinquevulnera. b, 2000d, Suillus placidus, Bulbophyllum wendlandianum. c, 3000d, Boletus edulis, Coelogyne mooreana. d, 5000d, Suillus variegatus, Dendrobium bullenianum. e, 6000d, Tylopilus felleus, Dendrobium crumenatum. f, 15,000d, Aureoboletus gentilis, Ascocentrum garayi.

No. 1494 — Emblem, wasp and mushrooms: a, 1000d, Boletus edulis f. betulicola. b, 2000d, Boletus edulis f. pinicola. c, 3000d, Boletus appendiculatus. d, 5000d, Boletus fechtneri. e, 6000d, Boletus luirdus. f, 15,000d, Boletus impolitus.

No. 1495 — Emblem, mushroom and butterfly: a, 1000d, Russula nigricans, Papilio demoleus. b, 2000d, Lactarius volemus, Libythea geoffroyi. c, 3000d, Russula cyanoxantha, Catonephele numili. d, 5000d, Gomphidius roseus, Doxocopa cherubina. e, 6000d, Russula integra, Dione juno. f, 15,000d, Agaricus bisporus, Philaethria.

No. 1496, 38,000d, Like #1491a. No. 1497, 38,000d, Like #1493c. No. 1498, 38,000d, Like #1494a. No. 1499, 38,000d, Like #1495f.

**2003** **Sheets of 6, #a-f**

**1491-1495** A266 Set of 5 47.50 47.50

### Souvenir Sheets

**1496-1499** A266 Set of 4 37.50 37.50

See Nos. 1489-1490 for additional souvenir sheets with Jamboree emblem.

Lord Robert Baden-Powell and Songbirds — A267

Lord Robert Baden-Powell and Cats, Dogs, Butterflies or Owls — A268

No. 1500 — Lord Baden-Powell and unnamed songbirds: a, 1000d. b, 2000d. c, 3000d. d, 5000d. e, 6000d. f, 15,000d.

No. 1501 — Lord Baden-Powell and unnamed cats or dogs: a, 1000d, Cat. b, 2000d, Cat, diff. c, 3000d, Cat, diff. d, 5000d, Dog. e, 6000d, Dog, diff. f, 15,000d, Dog, diff.

No. 1502 — Lord Baden-Powell and butterflies: a, 1000d, Lycaena dispar. b, 2000d, Papilio macheon. c, 3000d, Cethosia biblis. d, 5000d, Netrocoryne repanda. e, 6000d, Eupackardia calleta. f, 15,000d, Gangara thyrsis.

No. 1503 — Lord Baden-Powell and owls: a, 1000d, Bbubo lacteus. b, 2000d, Asio capensis. c, 3000d, Strix woodfordii. d, 5000d, Strix butleri. e, 6000d, Otus insularis. f, 15,000d, Glaucidium perlatum.

No. 1504, 38,000d, Like #1500c. No. 1505, 38,000d, Like #1501e. No. 1506, 38,000d, Like #1502c. No. 1507, 38,000d, Like #1503a.

**2003**

**1500** A267 Sheet of 6, #a-f 9.50 9.50
**1501** A268 Sheet of 6, #a-f 9.50 9.50
**1502** A268 Sheet of 6, #a-f 9.50 9.50
**1503** A268 Sheet of 6, #a-f 9.50 9.50
*Nos. 1500-1503 (4)* 38.00 38.00

### Souvenir Sheets

**1504** A267 38,000d multi 9.00 9.00
**1505** A268 38,000d multi 9.00 9.00
**1506** A268 38,000d multi 9.00 9.00
**1507** A268 38,000d multi 9.00 9.00

A269

Lady Olave Baden-Powell and Pandas — A270

No. 1508 — Lady Baden-Powell and various pandas: a, 1000d. b, 2000d. c, 3000d. d, 5000d. e, 6000d. f, 15,000d.

**2003**

**1508** A269 Sheet of 6, #a-f 9.50 9.50

### Souvenir Sheet

**1509** A270 38,000d multi 9.00 9.00

Rotary Emblem and Roses — A272

No. 1513 — Rotary emblem and various roses: a, 1000d. b, 2000d. c, 3000d. d, 5000d. e, 6000d. f, 15,000d.

38,000d, Like #1513e.

**2003**

**1513** A272 Sheet of 6, #a-f 9.50 9.50

### Souvenir Sheet

**1514** A272 38,000d multi 9.00 9.00

Rotary or Lions Emblems and Pinnipeds or Birds — A273

No. 1515 — Various pinnipeds and: a, 1000d, Rotary emblem. b, 2000d, Lions emblem. c, 3000d, Rotary emblem. d, 5000d, Lions emblem. e, 6000d, Rotary emblem. f, 15,000d, Lions emblem.

No. 1516: a, 1000d, Rotary emblem, Polemaetus bellicosus. b, 2000d, Lions emblem, Aquila verreauxi. c, 3000d, Rotary emblem, Circus aeruginosus. d, 5000d, Lions emblem, Aquila nipalensis. e, 6000d, Rotary emblem, Hieraetus fasciatus. f, 15,000d, Lions emblem, Aquila pomarina.

No. 1517, 38,000d, Like #1515a. No. 1518, 38,000d, Like #1516b.

**2003** **Sheets of 6, #a-f**

**1515-1516** A273 Set of 2 19.00 19.00

### Souvenir Sheets

**1517-1518** A273 Set of 2 18.00 18.00

A274

A275

A276

Dogs and Cats — A277

No. 1519: a, 1000d, Dog. b, 2000d, Cat. c, 3000d, Dogs. d, 5000d, Cat, diff. e, 6000d, Dog, diff. f, 15,000d, Cat, diff.

No. 1520: a, 1000d, Dog, diff. b, 2000d, Cat, diff. c, 3000d, Dogs, diff. d, 5000d, Cat, diff. e, 6000d, Dog, diff. f, 15,000d, Cat, diff.

No. 1523, Like #1520e.

**2003**

**1519** A274 Sheet of 6, #a-f 9.50 9.50
**1520** A275 Sheet of 6, #a-f 9.50 9.50

### Souvenir Sheets

**1521** A276 38,000d multi 9.00 9.00
**1522** A277 38,000d multi 9.00 9.00
**1523** A275 38,000d multi 9.00 9.00

Sled Dogs — A278

No. 1524 — Various sled dogs: a, 1000d. b, 2000d. c, 3000d. d, 5000d. e, 6000d. f, 15,000d.

38,000d, Like #1524b.

**2003**

**1524** A278 Sheet of 6, #a-f 9.50 9.50

### Souvenir Sheet

**1525** A278 38,000d multi 9.00 9.00

Dolphins — A279

No. 1526 — Various dolphins: a, 1000d. b, 2000d. c, 3000d. d, 5000d. e, 6000d. f, 15,000d.

**2003**

**1526** A279 Sheet of 6, #a-f 8.50 8.50

Scouting Emblem and Cats or Prehistoric Animals and Minerals — A271

No. 1510 — Scouting emblem and various cats: a, 1000d. b, 2000d. c, 3000d. d, 5000d. e, 6000d. f, 15,000d.

No. 1511 — Scouting emblem, unnamed minerals and prehistoric animals: a, 1000d, Corythosaurus causarius. b, 2000d, Compsognathus. c, 3000d, Edaphosaurus. d, 5000d, Monoclonius. e, 6000d, Rhamphorhynchus. f, 15,000d, Stegosaurus.

38,000d, Like #1511a.

**2003**

**1510** A271 Sheet of 6, #a-f 9.50 9.50
**1511** A271 Sheet of 6, #a-f 9.50 9.50

### Souvenir Sheet

**1512** A271 38,000d multi 9.00 9.00

See No. 1522.

Rams — A280

Various rams.

**2003**

**1527** A280 7000d Sheet of 6, #a-f 8.50 8.50

For surcharges, see Nos. 1995, 1996, 2004, 2006, 2022, 2023, 2031-2033, 2049, 2050, 2058-2060, 2076, 2077, 2085, 2087.

Hot Air Balloons and Zeppelins — A281

No. 1528: a, 1000d, Balloon. b, 2000d, Zeppelin. c, 3000d, Balloon, diff. d, 5000d, Moored Zeppelin. e, 6000d, Balloons. f, 15,000d, Zeppelin cockpit.
38,000d, Like #1528e.

**2003**

**1528** A281 Sheet of 6, #a-f 8.00 8.00

**Souvenir Sheet**

**1529** A281 38,000d multi 7.50 7.50

Aviation, Cent. — A282

No. 1530 — Various military aircraft: a, 1000d, Helicopter. b, 2000d, Airplane. c, 3000d, Helicopter, diff. d, 5000d, Airplanes. e, 6000d, Helicopter, diff. f, 15,000d, Airplane.
38,000d, Like #1530c.

**2003**

**1530** A282 Sheet of 6, #a-f 9.50 9.50

**Souvenir Sheet**

**1531** A282 38,000d multi 9.00 9.00

Apollo 11 — A283

Space — A284

Concorde and Spacecraft — A285

Deceased Crew of Space Shuttle Columbia — A286

No. 1532: a, 1000d, Astronaut Edwin Aldrin. b, 2000d, Lift-off. c, 3000d, Crew in capsule. d, 5000d, Retrieval of crew at sea. e, 6000d, Astronauts Neil Armstrong, Michael Collins and Aldrin. f, 15,000d, Astronaut on Moon.
No. 1533: a, 1000d, Lift-off of Space Shuttle. b, 2000d, Astronaut, vehicle and structures on planet. c, 3000d, Mir Space Station. d, 5000d, Astronauts working in outer space. e, 6000d, Untethered astronaut. f, 15,000d, Lift-off of rocket.
No. 1534: a, 1000d, Concorde. b, 2000d, Lift-off of Space Shuttle, diff. c, 3000d, Concorde, diff. d, 5000d, Intl. Space Station. e, 6000d, Concorde on runway. f, 15,000d, Space Shuttle in outer space.
No. 1535, Like #1532e. No. 1536, Like #1533c. No. 1537, Like #1534b.

**2003**

**1532** A283 Sheet of 6, #a-f 9.50 9.50
**1533** A284 Sheet of 6, #a-f 9.50 9.50
**1534** A285 Sheet of 6, #a-f 9.50 9.50
*Nos. 1532-1534 (3)* 28.50 28.50

**Souvenir Sheets**

**1535** A283 38,000d multi 9.00 9.00
**1536** A284 38,000d multi 9.00 9.00
**1537** A285 38,000d multi 9.00 9.00
**1538** A286 38,000d multi 9.00 9.00

Tandem Bicycles — A287

No. 1539 — Various tandem bicycles and riders: a, 1000d. b, 2000d. c, 3000d. d, 5000d. e, 6000d. f, 15,000d.
38,000d, Like #1539a.

**2003**

**1539** A287 Sheet of 6, #a-f 9.50 9.50

**Souvenir Sheet**

**1540** A287 38,000d multi 9.00 9.00

Tractor Trailer Trucks — A288

No. 1541 — Trucks with cabs in: a, 1000d, Red. b, 2000d, Blue. c, 3000d, Red, diff. d, 5000d, White. e, 6000d, Black. f, 15,000d, Purple.
38,000d, Like #1542a.

**2003**

**1541** A288 Sheet of 6, #a-f 9.50 9.50

**Souvenir Sheet**

**1542** A288 38,000d multi 9.00 9.00

Volkswagen Beetles — A289

Mercedes-Benz Automobiles — A290

No. 1543: a, 1000d. b, 2000d. c, 3000d. d, 5000d. e, 6000d. f, 15,000d.
No. 1544: a, 1000d. b, 2000d. c, 3000d. d, 5000d. e, 6000d. f, 15,000d.
No. 1545, Like #1543d. No. 1546, Like #1544d.

**2003**

**1543** A289 Sheet of 6, #a-f 9.50 9.50
**1544** A290 Sheet of 6, #a-f 9.50 9.50

**Souvenir Sheets**

**1545** A289 38,000d multi 9.00 9.00
**1546** A290 38,000d multi 9.00 9.00

Auto Racing — A291

Formula 1 Racing — A292

Formula 1 Racing — A293

Motorcycle Racing — A294

No. 1547: a, 1000d, Car 4x. b, 2000d, Cars 12 and 21. c, 3000d, Cars 46, 54 and 42. d, 5000d, Cars 11, 37 and 4. e, 6000d, Southside Fina car. f, 15,000d, Car 16.
No. 1548: a, 1000d, Two cars. b, 2000d, Two drivers holding trophies. c, 3000d, Car. d, 5000d, Two drivers with champagne bottles. e, 6000d, Car, diff. f, 15,000d, Three drivers.
No. 1549: a, 1000d, Red car with Marlboro wing. b, 2000d, Yellow car with Benson & Hedges wing. c, 3000d, Red car, driver with arms raised. d, 5000d, Black, red and white car. e, 6000d, Blue and yellow car. f, 15,000d, Black, red and white car, diff.
No. 1550: a, Yellow motorcycle without number. b, Green motorcycle #1. c, Motorcycle #26. d, White motorcycle #1. e, Motorcycle #9. f, Motorcycle #21.
No. 1551, Like #1548a. No. 1552, Like #1549c.

**2003**

**1547** A291 Sheet of 6, #a-f 9.00 9.00
**1548** A292 Sheet of 6, #a-f 9.00 9.00
**1549** A293 Sheet of 6, #a-f 9.00 9.00
**1550** A294 10,000d Sheet of 6, #a-f 13.50 13.50
*Nos. 1547-1550 (4)* 40.50 40.50

**Souvenir Sheets**

**1551** A292 38,000d multi 8.50 8.50
**1552** A293 38,000d multi 8.50 8.50

For surcharges, see Nos. 2003, 2010, 2030, 2037, 2057, 2064, 2084, 2091.

A295

A296

A297

A298

A299

A300

A301

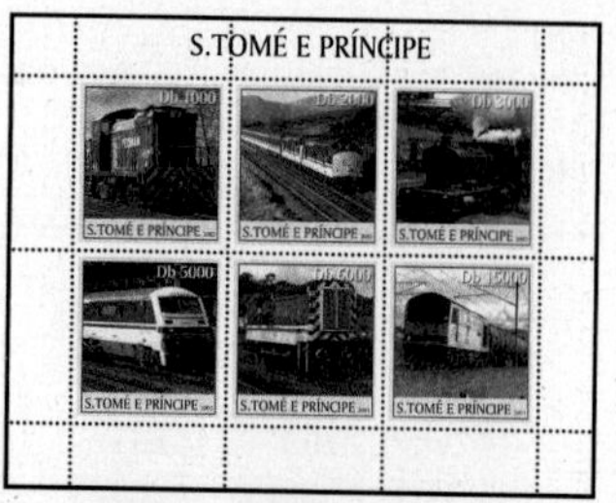


A302

A303

Trains — A304

Nos. 1553-1562 — Various trains: a, 1000d. b, 2000d. c, 3000d. d, 5000d. e, 6000d. f, 15,000d.

No. 1563, Like #1553d. No. 1564, Like #1554c. No. 1565, Like #1555f. No. 1566, Like #1556d. No. 1567, Like #1557a. No. 1568, Like #1558e. No. 1569, Like #1559f. No. 1570, Like #1560b. No. 1571, Like #1561c. No. 1572, Like #1562d.

**2003**

| | | | | |
|---|---|---|---|---|
| **1553** | A295 | Sheet of 6, #a-f | 9.00 | 9.00 |
| **1554** | A296 | Sheet of 6, #a-f | 9.00 | 9.00 |
| **1555** | A297 | Sheet of 6, #a-f | 9.00 | 9.00 |
| **1556** | A298 | Sheet of 6, #a-f | 9.00 | 9.00 |
| **1557** | A299 | Sheet of 6, #a-f | 9.00 | 9.00 |
| **1558** | A300 | Sheet of 6, #a-f | 9.00 | 9.00 |
| **1559** | A301 | Sheet of 6, #a-f | 9.00 | 9.00 |
| **1560** | A302 | Sheet of 6, #a-f | 9.00 | 9.00 |
| **1561** | A303 | Sheet of 6, #a-f | 9.00 | 9.00 |
| **1562** | A304 | Sheet of 6, #a-f | 9.00 | 9.00 |
| | *Nos. 1553-1562 (10)* | | 90.00 | 90.00 |

**Souvenir Sheets**

| | | | | |
|---|---|---|---|---|
| **1563** | A295 | 38,000d multi | 8.50 | 8.50 |
| **1564** | A296 | 38,000d multi | 8.50 | 8.50 |
| **1565** | A297 | 38,000d multi | 8.50 | 8.50 |
| **1566** | A298 | 38,000d multi | 8.50 | 8.50 |
| **1567** | A299 | 38,000d multi | 8.50 | 8.50 |
| **1568** | A300 | 38,000d multi | 8.50 | 8.50 |
| **1569** | A301 | 38,000d multi | 8.50 | 8.50 |
| **1570** | A302 | 38,000d multi | 8.50 | 8.50 |
| **1571** | A303 | 38,000d multi | 8.50 | 8.50 |
| **1572** | A304 | 38,000d multi | 8.50 | 8.50 |

Ships — A305

Paintings of various ships by Richard C. Moore: a, *Constitution* and *Guerriere*; b, Privateer *Rattlesnake*; c, H.M.S. *Victory*; d, H.M.S. *Victory* at Trafalgar; e, Clipper Ship *Comet*; f, U.S.S. *Constitution*.

**2003**

**1573** A305 7000d Sheet of 6, #a-f 9.50 9.50

For surcharges, see Nos. 1997-1999, 2024-2026, 2051-2053, 2078-2080.

2004 Summer Olympics, Athens — A306

No. 1574 — Various rowing teams: a, 1000d. b, 2000d. c, 3000d. d, 5000d. e, 6000d. f, 15,000d.

38,000d, Like #1574b.

**2003**

**1574** A306 Sheet of 6, #a-f 6.75 6.75

**Souvenir Sheet**

**1575** A306 38,000d multi 7.00 7.00

The editors believe that stamps dated "2004" were not put on sale in St. Thomas and Prince Islands. St. Thomas and Prince postal officials have declared that any stamps dated "2005" are illegal stamps, as well as a sheet of nine 7000d stamps depicting Marilyn Monroe, dated "2006", and a sheet of nine 7000d stamps 2006 World Cup Soccer, dated "2006."

A307

No. 1576 — Sphinx and: a, 7000d, Pyramid stones on ships. b, 9000d, Construction of Pyramid. c, 10,000d, Egyptians and balance scale. d, 14,000d, Egyptians preparing dead man for burial.

No. 1577 — Wolfgang Amadeus Mozart (1756-91), composer: a, 7000d, Wearing black jacket. b, 9000d, Wearing red jacket, at piano. c, 10,000d, Wearing red jacket. d, 14,000d, Wearing gray jacket.

No. 1578 — Gold medalists at 2004 Summer Olympics, Athens: a, 7000d, Keiji Suzuki, judo. b, 9000d, Hicham El Guerrouj, running. c, 10,000d, Seung Min Ryu, table tennis. d, 14,000d, Michael Phelps, swimming.

No. 1579 — Participants at 2006 Winter Olympics, Turin: a, 7000d, Tanith Belbin and Benjamin Agosto, ice dancing. b, 9000d, Carolina Kostner, figure skating. c, 10,000d, Shizuka Arakawa, figure skating. d, 14,000d, Maxim Marinin and Tatiana Totmianina, figure skating.

No. 1580 — European soccer players: a, 7000d, Zinedine Zidane. b, 9000d, Raul Gonzalez. c, 10,000d, David Beckham. d, 14,000d, Pavel Nedved.

No. 1581 — African soccer players: a, 7000d, Nwankwo Kanu. b, 9000d, Patrick Vieira. c, 10,000d, Claude Makelele. d, 14,000d, Aiyegbeni Yakubu.

No. 1582 — Marilyn Monroe (1926-62), actress: a, 7000d, With umbrella. b, 9000d, Wearing red hat and shorts. c, 10,000d, Wearing bikini. d, 14,000d, Wearing dress.

No. 1583 — Spanish painters and their paintings: a, 7000d, El Greco (1541-1614). b, 9000d, Joaquin Sorolla (1863-1923). c, 10,000d, Diego Velazquez (1599-1660). d, 14,000d, Francisco Goya (1746-1828).

No. 1584 — Various views of the Concorde above clouds: a, 7000d. b, 9000d. c, 10,000d. d, 14,000d.

No. 1585, 40,000d, Sphinx. No. 1586, 40,000d, Mozart. No. 1587, 40,000d, Virgilijus Alekna, discus. No. 1588, 40,000d, Seth Wescott, snowboarding. No. 1589, 40,000d, John Terry. No. 1590, 40,000d, Samuel Eto'o. No. 1591, 40,000d, White House and American flag. No. 1592, 40,000d, Pablo Picasso (1881-1973). No. 1593, 40,000d, Concorde.

**2006, Apr. 4 Litho.** ***Perf. 12¾x13¼***

**Sheets of 4, #a-d**

**1576-1584** A307 Set of 9 105.00 105.00

**Souvenir Sheets**

***Perf. 13¼ Syncopated***

**1585-1593** A307 Set of 9 105.00 105.00

Europa Stamps, 50th Anniv. — A308

No. 1594 — Emblems and: a, Charles de Gaulle (1890-1970), French President. b, Wolfgang Amadeus Mozart (1756-91), composer. c, Pope John Paul II (1920-2005). d, Concorde.

40,000d, Emblems and map of Europe.

**2006, Apr. 4** ***Perf. 12¾x13¼***

**1594** A308 14,000d Sheet of 4, #a-d 15.00 15.00

**Souvenir Sheet**

***Perf. 13¼ Syncopated***

**1595** A308 40,000d multi 10.50 10.50

A309

No. 1596 — Turtles: a, 7000d, Testudo graeca. b, 9000d, Pseudemys scripta. c, 10,000d, Clemmys insculpta. d, 14,000d, Trionyx spiniferus.

No. 1597 — Predators: a, 7000d, Crocodylus porosus. b, 9000d, Ursus maritimus. c, 10,000d, Carcharodon carcharias. d, 14,000d, Varanus komodoensis.

No. 1598 — Endangered animals: a, 7000d, Tyto alba. b, 9000d, Phascolarctos cinearus. c, 10,000d, Panthera tigris. d, 14,000d, Balaenoptera musculus.

No. 1599 — Illustrations from book *After Man: A Zoology of the Future* by Dougal Dixon : a, 7000d, Alesimia lapsus. b, 9000d, Aquator adepsicautus. c, 10,000d, Tetraceras africanus. d, 14,000d, Harundopes virgatus.

No. 1600 — Dogs and cats: a, 7000d, Golden retriever, British shorthair cat. b, 9000d, Portuguese Podengo hound, Black smoke Persian cat. c, 10,000d, Greyhound, Norwegian forest cat. d, 14,000d, Black Labrador retriever, Tiffanie cat.

No. 1601 — Owls and mushrooms: a, 7000d, Pseudoscops grammicus, Cortinarius triumphans. b, 9000d, Strix woodfordi, Cortinarius subfulgens. c, 10,000d, Athene noctua, Agaricus augustus. d, 14,000d, Strix nebulosa, Leucocortinarius bulbiger.

No. 1602 — Butterflies and orchids: a, 7000d, Mosaic gynandromorph, Phalaenopsis. b, 9000d, Nymphalidae, Coral Cymbidium. c, 10,000d, Papilio polymnestor, Pleione praecox. d, 14,000d, Charaxes bohemani, Rhyncholaelia glauca.

No. 1603 — Butterflies and bees: a, 7000d, Heliconius nattereri, Apis mellifera scutella. b, 9000d, Nymphalidae, Bombus hypnorum. c, 10,000d, Eterusia, repleta, Bombus terrestris. d, 14,000d, Lasaia mocros, Apis mellifera.

No. 1604 — Dinosaurs and minerals: a, 7000d, Pachycephalosaurus, Spodumene and kunzite. b, 9000d, Psittacosaurus, Opal. c, 10,000d, Troodon, Calcite and limestone. d, 14,000d, Struthiomimus, Barite and calcite.

No. 1605 — Dolphins and Swedish lighthouses: a, 7000d, Lagenorhynchus obliquidens, Berlin Lighthouse. b, 9000d, Delphinus delphis, Brämskär Lighthouse. c, 10,000d, Tursiops truncatus, Hättan Lighthouse. d, 14,000d, Lagenorhynchus acutus, Ursholmen Lighthouse.

No. 1606, 40,000d, Malacochersus tornieri. No. 1607, 40,000d, Carcharodon carcharias, diff. No. 1608, 40,000d, Felis lynx. No. 1609, 40,000d, Reteostium cortepellium, Cornophilius ophicaudatus. No. 1610, 40,000d, Chow chow, Turkish angora cat. No. 1611, 40,000d, Phodilus badius, mushrooms. No. 1612, 40,000d, Athletes steindachneri moth, Angulocaste orchid. No. 1613, 40,000d, Heliconiinae hermatena, Apidae. No. 1614, 40,000d, Stegosaurus, Topaz. No. 1615, 40,000d, Delphinus delphis, Lista Lighthouse, Norway.

**2006, May 25** ***Perf. 12¾x13¼***
**Sheets of 4, #a-d, + 4 Labels**

**1596-1605** A309 Set of 10 110.00 110.00

**Souvenir Sheets**
***Perf. 13¼ Syncopated***

**1606-1615** A309 Set of 10 110.00 110.00

Paintings — A310

No. 1616 — Paintings by Michelangelo: a, 7000d, Martyrdom of St. Peter. b, 9000d, The Doni Tondo. c, 10,000d, Ezekiel. d, 14,000d, Last Judgment.

No. 1617 — Paintings by Peter Paul Rubens: a, 7000d, The Union of Earth and Water. b, 9000d, Daniel in the Lion's Den. c, 10,000d, The Judgment of Paris. d, 14,000d, Bacchus.

No. 1618 — Paintings by Rembrandt: a, 7000d, Tobit and Anna. b, 9000d, The Apostle Paul in Prison. c, 10,000d, The Militia Company of Captain Frans Banning Cocq. d, 14,000d, The Return of the Prodigal Son.

No. 1619 — Paintings by Gustave Courbet: a, 7000d, The Woman in the Waves. b, 9000d, Still Life: Fruit. c, 10,000d, The Stormy Sea. d, 14,000d, Sleep.

No. 1620 — Paintings by Auguste Renoir: a, 7000d, Bather Arranging Her Hair. b, 9000d, Blonde Nude. c, 10,000d, The Nymphs. d, 14,000d, The Bathers.

No. 1621 — Paintings by Vincent van Gogh: a, 7000d, The Starry Night. b, 9000d, The Church at Auvers-sur-Oise. c, 10,000d, First Steps. d, 14,000d, Midday Siesta.

No. 1622 — Paintings by Henri de Toulouse-Lautrec: a, 7000d, La Goulue Arriving with Two Women. b, 9000d, Yvette Guilbert. c, 10,000d, The Two Girlfriends. d, 14,000d, Rue des Moulins: The Medical Inspection.

No. 1623 — Various unnamed Japanese paintings by: a, 7000d, Utagawa Kuniyoshi. b, 9000d, Toshi Yoshida. c, 10,000d, Tsukioka Yoshitoshi. d, 14,000d, Utagawa Hiroshige II.

No. 1624 — American impressionist paintings: a, 7000d, Mother and Child, by Mary Cassatt. b, 9000d, Rock Garden in Giverny, by Leslie Breck. c, 10,000d, Oyster Gatherers of Cancale, by John Singer Sargent. d, 14,000d, Two Sisters, by William Merritt Chase.

No. 1625 — Paintings by Spanish-speaking artists: a, 7000d, Slave Market with the Disappearing Bust of Voltaire, by Salvador Dali. b, 9000d, The Flower Carrier, by Diego Rivera. c, 10,000d, Self-portrait, by Frida Kahlo. d, 14,000d, Dutch Interior I, by Joan Miró.

No. 1626, 40,000d, The Flood, by Michelangelo. No. 1627, 40,000d, Simon and Pero, by Rubens. No. 1628, 40,000d, Bathsheba at her Bath, by Rembrandt. No. 1629, 40,000d, The Bathers, by Courbet. No. 1630, 40,000d, Nude in the Sunlight, by Renoir. No. 1631, 40,000d, The Night Café, by van Gogh. No. 1632, 40,000d, Ball at the Moulin de la Galette (incorrectly inscribed "The Bathers"), by Toulouse-Lautrec. No. 1633, 40,000d, Painting by Narita Morikane. No. 1634, 40,000d, Sleep, by Frederick Carl Freiseke. No. 1635, 40,000d, A Couple, by Fernando Botero.

**2006, Aug. 25** ***Perf. 12¾x13¼***
**Sheets of 4, #a-d**

**1616-1625** A310 Set of 10 110.00 110.00

**Souvenir Sheets**
***Perf. 13¼ Syncopated***

**1626-1635** A310 Set of 10 110.00 110.00

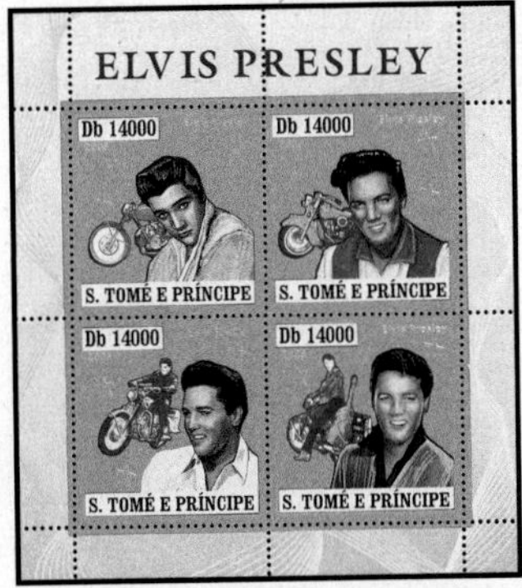


A311

Nos. 1636 and 1646, 14,000d — Motorcycle and Elvis Presley (1935-77) wearing: a, Lilac shirt (motorcycle rider not visible). b, Red and white shirt. c, White shirt. b, Black and purple shirt.

Nos. 1637 and 1647, 14,000d — Marilyn Monroe (1926-62) and: a, Flash camera. b, Film cans. c, Film reel. b, Director's clapboard.

Nos. 1638 and 1648, 14,000d — Sports and games: a, Garry Kasparov, chess player. b, Won Hee Lee, judo. c, Wang Liqin, table tennis. b, Tiger Woods, golf.

Nos. 1639 and 1649, 14,000d — Lord Robert Baden-Powell (1847-1941), founder of Scouting movement and: a, Mushrooms, opal. b, Flower, owl. c, Mineral, mushrooms. b, Owl, orchid.

Nos. 1640 and 1650, 14,000d — Humanists: a, Pope John Paul II. b, Abraham Lincoln. c, Dr. Albert Schweitzer. b, Mahatma Gandhi.

Nos. 1641 and 1651, 14,000d — The Beatles: a, George Harrison. b, John Lennon. c, Ringo Starr. b, Paul McCartney.

Nos. 1642 and 1652, 14,000d — The Rolling Stones: a, Keith Richards. b, Mick Jagger. c, Charlie Watts. b, Ron Wood.

Nos. 1643 and 1653, 14,000d — Fire vehicles: a, Mercedes-Benz Metz. b, MAN 415 H-LF. c, Mercedes-Benz LF 16. b, Magirus KW 16.

Nos. 1644 and 1654, 14,000d — High-speed trains: a, Shinkansen JR 500. b, Eurostar. c, AGV. b, TGV.

Nos. 1645 and 1655, 14,000d — Scouting emblem, mushrooms and owls: a, Bubo zeylonensis. b, Nyctea ulula. c, Phodilus badius. b, Asio otus.

Nos. 1656 and 1666, 56,000d, Presley with guitar. Nos. 1657 and 1667, 56,000d, Monroe with film reel. Nos. 1658 and 1668, 56,000d, Kim Clijsters, tennis. Nos. 1659 and 1669, 56,000d, Baden-Powell and orchid. Nos. 1660 and 1670, 56,000d, Mother Teresa. Nos. 1661 and 1671, 56,000d, The Beatles. Nos. 1662 and 1672, 56,000d, Jagger. Nos. 1663 and 1673, 56,000d, Fischer fire vehicle. Nos. 1664 and 1674, 56,000d, Swiss Metro. Nos. 1665 and 1675, 56,000d, Strix cinereots.

**Litho. & Embossed With Foil Application**

**2006, Dec. 15** ***Perf. 12¾x13¼***
**Without Gum**
**Sheets of 4 #a-d**
**Silver Background**

**1636-1645** A311 Set of 10 165.00 165.00

**Gold Background**

**1646-1655** A311 Set of 10 165.00 165.00

**Souvenir Sheets**
**Silver Background**

**1656-1665** A311 Set of 10 165.00 165.00

**Gold Background**

**1666-1675** A311 Set of 10 165.00 165.00

Miniature Sheets

A312

No. 1676 — Princess Diana (image at left): a, 7000d, Holding papers. b, 9000d, Walking with Mother Teresa. c, 10,000d, Talking with girl. d, 14,000d, Riding in coach with Prince Charles.

No. 1677 — Steve Irwin (1962-2006), conservationist, with: a, 7000d, Pterois volitans. b, 9000d, Crotalus viridis. c, 10,000d, Crocodylus porosus. d, 14,000d, Myliobatis australis and Phascolarctos cinereus.

No. 1678 — Popes and their arms: a, 7000d, Pope Paul VI. b, 9000d, Pope John Paul I. c, 10,000d, Pope Benedict XVI. d, 14,000d, Pope John Paul II.

No. 1679 — Mushrooms: a, 7000d, Boletus badius and Sir Alexander Fleming (1881-1955), pharmacologist. b, 9000d, Boletus edulis and Leccinum quercinum. c, 10,000d, Amanita pantherina and Russula vesca. d, 14,000d, Amanita muscaria and Fleming.

No. 1680 — Neanerthals and minerals: a, 7000d, Celestine. b, 9000d, Sulfur. c, 10,000d, Pyrargyrite. d, 14,000d, Orthoclase and adularia.

No. 1681 — Minerals: a, 7000d, Barite, calcite and smoky quartz. b, 9000d, Malachite, beryl and emerald. c, 10,000d, Elbaite, rubellite tourmaline, microcline and amazonite. d, 14,000d, Quartz, amethyst and topaz.

No. 1682 — International Polar Year: a, 7000d, Admiral Robert Peary (1856-1920), polar explorer, and expedition members. b, 9000d, Eudyptes chrysolophus. c, 10,000d, Aptenodytes patagonicus. d, 14,000d, Fridtjof Nansen (1861-1930), polar explorer and Ursus maritimus.

No. 1683 — Owls and their prey: a, 7000d, Tyto alba, Ochotona collaris. b, 9000d, Nyctea scandiaca, Lepus arcticus. c, 10,000d, Scotopelia peli, Thunnus albacares. d, 14,000d, Ninox novaeseelandiae, Platacanthomyinae.

No. 1684 — Satellites: a, 7000d, Sputnik 1. b, 9000d, Sputnik 1, diff. c, 10,000d, Sputnik 2. d, 14,000d, Sputnik 2, diff.

No. 1685 — Martian probes: a, 7000d, Mars Odyssey. b, 9000d, Mars Rover. c, 10,000d, Mars Rover, diff. d, 14,000d, Mars Odyssey, diff.

**2007, Feb. 2 Litho.** ***Perf. 12¾x13¼***
**Sheets of 4, #a-d**

**1676-1685** A312 Set of 10 110.00 110.00

Souvenir Sheets

U.S. Presidents — A313

No. 1686, 40,000d, George Washington (1732-99). No. 1687, 40,000d, Thomas Jefferson (1743-1826). No. 1688, 40,000d, Abraham Lincoln (1809-65). No. 1689, 40,000d, Franklin D. Roosevelt (1882-1945). No. 1690, 40,000d, Dwight D. Eisenhower (1890-1969). No. 1691, 40,000d, John F. Kennedy (1917-63). No. 1692, 40,000d, Lyndon B. Johnson (1908-73). No. 1693, 40,000d, Ronald Reagan (1911-2004). No. 1694, 40,000d, George H. W. Bush. No. 1695, 40,000d, William J. Clinton.

**2007, Feb. 2** ***Perf. 13¼ Syncopated***

**1686-1695** A313 Set of 10 110.00 110.00

A314

No. 1696 — Bears: a, 7000d, Three bears. b, 9000d, Three bears in tree. c, 10,000d, Four bears and anthills. d, 14,000d, Three bears, diff.

No. 1697 — Wolves: a, 7000d, Two wolves upright. b, 9000d, Wolf on ground, wolf upright. c, 10,000d, Wolf's head, howling wolf. d, 14,000d, Two woves on ground.

No. 1698 — Birds: a, 7000d, Couroucou oranga. b, 9000d, Couroucou rosalba. c, 10,000d, Ramphocele scarlatte. d,. 14,000d, Cotinga ouette.

No. 1699 — Birds: a, 7000d, Tangara passe-ver. b, 9000d, Carouge iamacaii. c, 10,000d, Cassique huppe. d, 14,000d, Psittacule caica-barraband.

No. 1700 — Insects and lizards preying on butterflies and moths: a, 7000d, Pseudocreabotra wahlbergi and butterfly. b, 9000d, Spodoptera exigua and lizard. c, 10,000d, Cmenidophorus lemniscatus and moth. d, 14,000d, Asilus crabroniformis and butterfly.

No. 1701 — Animals preying on butterflies: a, 7000d, Frog and Euclidia glyphica. b, 9000d, Aegotheles cristata and butterflies. c, 10,000d, Leiothrix lutea, flowers and butterfly. d, 14,000d, Araneidae, Oxyopidae, and butterflies.

No. 1702 — Fish: a, 7000d, Chaetodon lineolatus, Osphronemidae. b, 9000d, Gymnarchus niloticus, Polyodon spathula. c, 10,000d, Climatius, Dunkleosteus. d, 14,000d, Latimeria chalumnae, Chlorostigma.

No. 1703 — Snakes: a, 7000d, And nest. b, 9000d, And unhatched eggs. c, 10,000d, And hatching eggs. d, 14,000d, With heads raised.

No. 1704 — Dinosaurs: a, 7000d, Velociraptor, Protoceratops. b, 9000d, Deinonychus, Sinosauropteryx. c, 10,000d, Oviraptor, Beipaiosaurus. d, 14,000d, Oviraptors.

No. 1705 — Mushrooms: a, 7000d, Pleurotus salignus, Catathelasma, Suillis luteus. b, 9000d, Lactarius torminosus, Tricholoma portentosum. c, 10,000d, Pleurotus ostreatus, Lactarius necator. d, 14,000d, Pleurotus eryngii, Tricholomopsis rutilans.

No. 1706, 40,000d, Ursus maritimus. No. 1707, 40,000d, Canidae. No. 1708, 40,000d, Fringille daroare. No. 1709, 40,000d, Euphonea diademe. No. 1710, 40,000d, Cyanositta cristata and butterfly. No. 1711, 40,000d, Gerrhonotus multicarinatus and butterflies. No. 1712, 40,000d, Siniperca chuatsi. No. 1713, 40,000d, Snake. No. 1714, 40,000d, Carcharodontosaurus. No. 1715, 40,000d, Entoloma sinuatum, Calocybe gambosa.

**2007, Mar. 15** ***Perf. 12¾x13¼***
**Sheets of 4, #a-d, + 2 labels**

**1696-1705** A314 Set of 10 120.00 120.00

**Souvenir Sheets**

**1706-1715** A314 Set of 10 120.00 120.00

Scouting, cent.

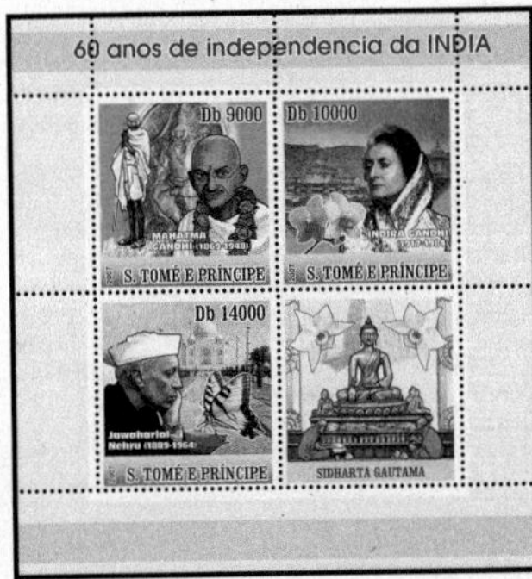


Independence of India, 60th Anniv. — A315

No. 1716: a, 9000d, Mahatma Gandhi (1869-1948), Independence leader. b, 10,000d, Indira Gandhi (1917-84), Prime Minister. c, 14,000d, Jawaharlal Nehru (1889-1964), Prime Minister.

40,000d, Vasco da Gama (1469-1524), explorer.

**2007, Nov. 5** ***Perf. 12¾x13¼***

**1716** A315 Sheet of 3, #a-c, + label 5.00 5.00

**Souvenir Sheet**
***Perf. 13¼ Syncopated***

**1717** A315 40,000d multi 6.00 6.00

Souvenir sheets of 1 of Nos. 1716a-1716c with colored frames exist.

Cruise Liners — A316

No. 1718: a, 7000d, Queen Mary 2. b, 9000d, Freedom of the Seas. c, 10,000d, Crystal Symphony. d, 14,000d, Star Princess.
40,000d, Titanic.

**2007, Nov. 5** ***Perf. 12¾x13¼***

**1718** A316 Sheet of 4, #a-d 5.75 5.75

**Souvenir Sheet**

***Perf. 13¼ Syncopated***

**1719** A316 40,000d multi 5.75 5.75

Souvenir sheets of 1 of Nos. 1718a, 1718b, and 1718d with colored frames exist.

A317

No. 1720 — Chess: a, 7000d, Chess player looking at board, knight. b, 9000d, Queen and pawn, hand moving piece. c, 10,000d, Player, rook and pawns. d, 14,000d, Queen, pieces on board.

No. 1721 — Race cars and Colin McRae (1968-2007), race car driver: a, 7000d, Wearing blue uniform. b, 9000d, Holding bottle of champagne. c, 10,000d, Holding trophy. d, 14,000d, Wearing earphones.

No. 1722 — Luciano Pavarotti (1935-2007), opera singer, and: a, 7000d, Princess Diana. b, 9000d, Spice Girls. c, 10,000d, Placido Domingoa and José Carreras. d, 14,000d, Bono.

No. 1723 — Photographs by Anton Corbijn of: a, 7000d, Miles Davis. b, 9000d, Clint Eastwood. c, 10,000d, Depeche Mode. d, 14,000d, Bono.

No. 1724 — Minerals: a, 7000d, Gypsum. b, 9000d, Rhodonite. c, 10,000d, Cerussite. d, 14,000d, Malachite.

No. 1725 — Lighthouses: a, 7000d, Alexandria Lighthouse. b, 9000d, Tower of Hercules. c, 10,000d, Yokohama Marine Tower. d, 14,000d, Cordouan Lighthouse, France.

No. 1726 — Tangula Express Train, China: a, 7000d, Train, tunnel, bridge. b, 9000d, Train on bridge. c, 10,000d, Train, lake. d, 14,000d, Train, train on bridge.

No. 1727, 40,000d, King, queen, chess players. No. 1728, 40,000d, McRae and race car. No. 1729, 40,000d, Pavarotti. No. 1730, 40,000d, Photograph of Dave Gahan by Corbijn. No. 1731, 40,000d, Fluorite, barite. No. 1732, 40,000d, Statue of Liberty.

**2007, Nov. 5** ***Perf. 12¾x13¼***

**Sheets of 4, #a-d**

**1720-1726** A317 Set of 7 42.50 42.50

**Souvenir Sheets**

***Perf. 13¼ Syncopated***

**1727-1732** A317 Set of 6 37.50 37.50

Souvenir sheets of 1 of Nos. 1725a, 1725c, and 1725d exist.

Paintings in Prado Museum by Spanish Artists — A318

No. 1733 — Various paintings by El Greco (1541-1614): a, 7000d. b, 9000d. c, 10,000d. d, 14,000d.

No. 1734 — Various paintings by Diego Velázquez (1541-1614): a, 7000d. b, 9000d. c, 10,000d. d, 14,000d.

No. 1735 — Various paintings by Francisco Goya (1746-1828): a, 7000d. b, 9000d. c, 10,000d. d, 14,000d.

No. 1736 — Various paintings by Joaquín Sorolla (1863-1923): a, 7000d. b, 9000d. c, 10,000d. d, 14,000d.

No. 1737 — Various paintings by Pablo Picasso (1881-1973): a, 7000d. b, 9000d. c, 10,000d. d, 14,000d.

No. 1738, 40,000d, Painting by El Greco, diff. No. 1739, 40,000d, Painting by Velázquez, diff. No. 1740, 40,000d, Painting by Goya, diff. No. 1741, 40,000d, Painting by Sorolla, diff. No. 1742, 40,000d, Painting by Picasso, diff.

**2007, Nov. 5** ***Perf. 12¾x13¼***

**Sheets of 4, #a-d**

**1733-1737** A318 Set of 5 32.50 32.50

**Souvenir Sheets**

***Perf. 13¼ Syncopated***

**1738-1742** A318 Set of 5 32.50 32.50

Souvenir sheets of 1 of Nos. 1733a, 1734b, 1735b, 1736b and 1737d exist.

Marine Science — A319

No. 1743: a, 7000d, Diver and Stenella alymene. b, 9000d, Diver and Natator depressus. c, 10,000d, Jacques Cousteau (1910-97), marine researcher, and submarine. d, 14,000d, Cousteau and research ship.
40,000d, Cousteau, research ship, diff.

**2007, Nov. 5** ***Perf. 12¾x13¼***

**1743** A319 Sheet of 4, #a-d, + 4 labels 6.00 6.00

**Souvenir Sheet**

***Perf. 13¼ Syncopated***

**1744** A319 40,000d multi 6.00 6.00

Miniature Sheets

A320

No. 1745, 7000d — Early locomotives: a, Trevithick. b, Marc Seguin. c, Blenkinsop. d, Puffing Billy. e, Rocket. f, Liverpool.

No. 1746, 7000d — Red Cross flag and: a, Airplane. b, Red fire truck with plow attachment. c, Yellow fire truck. d, Ship. e, Helicopter. f, Motorcycle.

No. 1747, 7000d — Divers and marine life: a, Montastrea cavernosa. b, Pisaster ochraceus. c, Gymnothorax javanicus. d, Carassius auratus. e, Octopus vulgaris. f, Lepidochelys olivacea.

No. 1748, 7000d — Extreme sports: a, Skateboarders. b, Motorcyclists. c, Rock climbers. d, Hang gliders. e, Surfer. f, Parachutist.

No. 1749, 7000d — Track and field athletes at 2007 World Championships, Osaka: a, Stefan Holm, high jump. b, Liu Xiang, hurdles. c, Irving Saladino, long jump. d, Steffi Nerius, javelin. e, Agustin Felix, pole vault. f, Liu Xiang running.

No. 1750, 7000d — Rugby players: a, Jonny Wilkinson. b, Felipe Contepomi. c, Chris Paterson. d, Percy Montgomery. e, Jean-Baptiste Elissalde. f, Nick Evans.

No. 1751, 40,000d, Red Cross flag and 1926 Kingsbury motor-driven pumper. No. 1752, 40,000d, Divers and Pomacanthus arcuataus. No. 1753, 40,000d, Monster truck. No. 1754, 40,000d, Alfred Kirwa Yego.

**2007, Nov. 5** ***Perf. 12¾x13¼***

**Sheets of 6, #a-f**

**1745-1750** A320 Set of 6 36.00 36.00

**Souvenir Sheets**

***Perf. 13¼ Syncopated***

**1751-1754** A320 Set of 4 23.00 23.00

Souvenir sheets of 1 of Nos. 1745a-1745f, 1746a, 1746c and 1746d with colored frames exist.

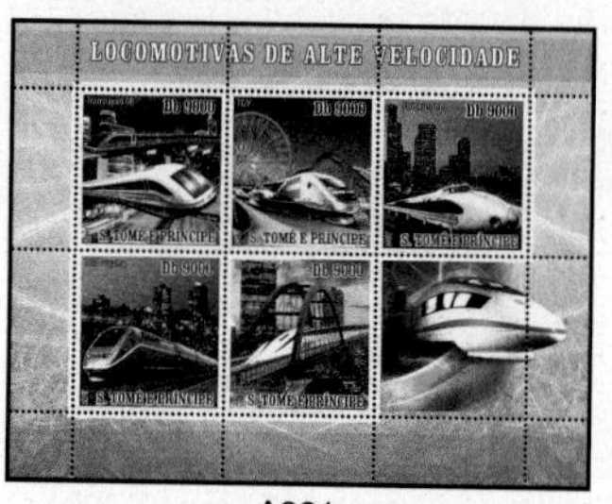


A321

No. 1755, 9000d — High-speed trains: a, Transrapid 08. b, TGV. c, Shinkansen. d, TGV Duplex. e, Maglev MLX-01.

No. 1756, 9000d — Paintings by Antoine Wiertz (1806-65): a, The Reader of Novels. b, The Young Witch. c, Beautiful Rosine. d, The Outrage of Belgian Women. e, Esmerelda.

No. 1757, 9000d — Fire engines: a, 1965 Ford Crown. b, 1881 Merryweather. c, 1894 Merryweather 2. d, 1933 Delahaye. e, 1933 Dennis.

No. 1758, 9000d — Automobiles and automotive pioneers: a, Gottlieb Daimler (1834-1900). b, Karl Benz (1844-1929). c, Enzo Ferrari (1898-1988). d, Henry Ford (1863-1947). e, Ferdinand Porsche (1875-1951).

No. 1759, 40,000d, M Set train. No. 1760, 40,000d, Christ in the Tomb, by Wiertz. No. 1761, 40,000d, Fire truck. No. 1762, 40,000d, Juan Manuel Fangio (1911-95), race car driver.

**2007, Nov. 5** ***Perf. 12¾x13¼***

**Sheets of 5, #a-e, + Label**

**1755-1758** A321 Set of 4 27.50 27.50

**Souvenir Sheets**

***Perf. 13¼ Syncopated***

**1759-1762** A321 Set of 4 25.00 25.00

Souvenir sheets of 1 of Nos. 1757a-1757e, 1758a-1758e with colored frames exist.

A322

No. 1763 — Various Scouts and dogs: a, 7000d. b, 9000d. c, 10,000d. d, 14,000d.

No. 1764 — Inventors: a, 7000d, Dmitri Mendeleev (1834-1907). b, 9000d, Auguste (1862-1954) and Louis Lumière (1864-1948). c, 10,000d, Joseph Michel (1740-1810) and Jacques Etienne Montgolfier (1745-99). d, Samuel F. B. Morse (1791-1872).

No. 1765 — Orchids and famous Blacks: a, Malcolm X (1925-65). b, Albert Luthuli (1898-1967). c, Dr. Martin Luther King, Jr. (1929-68). d, Steve Biko (1946-77).

No. 1766, 40,000d, Scout and dog, diff. No. 1767, 40,000d, John Logie Baird (1888-1946), inventor. No. 1768, 40,000d, Nelson Mandela.

**2007, Dec. 31** ***Perf. 12¾x13¼***

**Sheets of 4, #a-d**

**1763-1765** A322 Set of 3 18.00 18.00

**Souvenir Sheets**

**1766-1768** A322 Set of 3 18.00 18.00

Souvenir sheets of 1 of Nos. 1765a-1765d with colored frames exist.

Miniature Sheets

Flora and Fauna — A323

No. 1769 — Rabbits: a, 5000d, Lepus saxatilis. b, 5000d, Pronolagus crassicaudatus. c, 10,000d, Bunolagus monticularis. d, 15,000d, Lepus stracki.

No. 1770 — Hogs: a, 5000d, Phacochoerus africanus. b, 5000d, Potamochoerus porcus. c, 10,000d, Sus scrofa. d, 15,000d, Potamochoerus larvatus.

No. 1771 — Hippopotami: a, 5000d, Hippopotamus amphibius. b, 5000d, Hexaprotodon liberiensis. c, 10,000d, Hexaprotodon liberiensis, diff. d, 15,000d, Hippopotamus amphibius, diff.

No. 1772 — Hyenas: a, 5000d, Lycaon pictus. b, 5000d, Crocuta crocuta. c, 10,000d, Hyaena brunnea. d, 15,000d, Hyaena hyaena.

No. 1773 — Bats: a, 5000d, Mops condylurus. b, 5000d, Cardioderma cor. c, 10,000d, Taphozous mauritianus. d, 15,000d, Hypsignatus monstrosus.

No. 1774 — Cats: a, 5000d, Felis caracal. b, 5000d, Felis serval. c, 10,000d, Felis chaus. d, 15,000d, Felis sylvestris.

No. 1775 — Butterflies: a, 5000d, Charaxes monteiri female. b, 5000d, Papilio leonidas thomasius. c, 10,000d, Hypolimas salmacis thomensis. d, 10,000d, Charaxes monteiri male. e, 15,000d, Charaxes odysseus.

No. 1776 — Fish: a, 5000d, Ostracion tricornis. b, 5000d, Holocentrus axensionis "Caqui". c, 10,000d, Canthidermis maculatus. d, 10,000d, Rhinecanthus aculeatus. e, 15,000d, Diodon hystrix.

No. 1777 — Medicinal plants: a, 5000d, Buchholzia coriacea. b, 5000d, Piperonia pallucila. c, 5000d, Achyranthes aspera. d, 10,000d, Adenoplus breviflorus. e, 10,000d, Hiliotropium indicum. f, 10,000d, Mimosa pigra. g, 15,000d, Cymbopogon citratus. h, 15,000d, Bryophillum pinatum.

No. 1778 — Birds: a, 5000d, Alcedo leucogaster nais. b, 5000d, Prinia molleri. c, 5000d, Spermestes cucullatus. d, 5000d, Treron S. thomae. e, 5000d, Euplectes aureus. f, 10,000d, Speirops lugubris. g, 10,000d, Textor grandis. h, 10,000d, Alcedo leucogaster nais, diff. i, 10,000d, Anabathmis hartlaubii. j, 10,000d, Xanthophilus princeps. k, 15,000d, Serinus rufobrunneus. l, 15,000d, Cheatura thomensis. m, 15,000d, Tyto alba thomensis. n, 15,000d, Estrilda astrild.

**2007, Dec. 31** **Litho.** ***Perf. 13x13¼***

**Sheets of 4, #a-d**

**1769-1774** A323 Set of 6 30.00 30.00

**Sheets of 5, #a-e**

**1775-1776** A323 Set of 2 13.00 13.00

***Perf. 13¼x13***

**1777** A323 Sheet of 8, #a-h 11.00 11.00

**1778** A323 Sheet of 14, #a-n 19.00 19.00

Dated 2008.

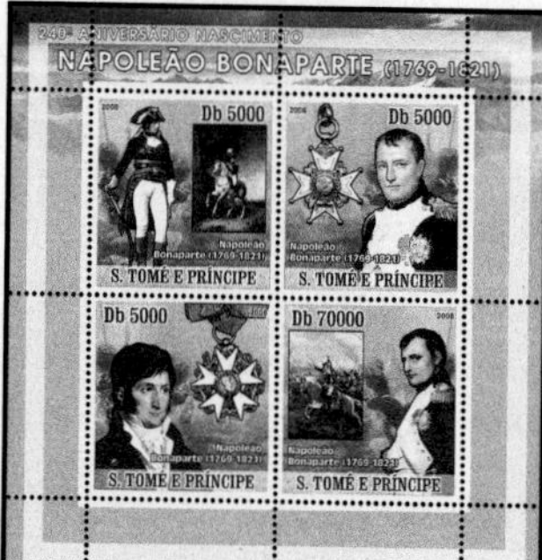


A324

A325

No. 1779 — Napoleon Bonaparte (1769-1821), French emperor, and: a, 5000d, Painting of Napoleon on horseback at right. b, 5000d, Military medal at left. c, 5000d, Military medal at right. d, 70,000d, Painting of Napoleon on horseback at left.

No. 1780 — United States ambulances: a, 5000d, Ambulance and helicopter. b, 5000d, Specialized transport team ambulance. c, 5000d, Ambulance with blue and red stripes. d, 70,000d, Ambulance with blue stripes.

No. 1781 — Japanese ambulances: a, 5000d, Ambulance at hospital ambulance bay, red cross at right. b, 5000d, Ambulance at hospital, red cross at UL c, 5000d, Ambulance at hospital, red cross at UR. d, 70,000d, Ambulance and rear view mirror, red cross at UL.

No. 1782 — European ambulances: a, 5000d, Italian ambulance and Leaning Tower of Pisa. b, 5000d, German ambulance and Cologne Cathedral. c, 5000d, British ambulance and Big Ben. d, 70,000d, French ambulance and Eiffel Tower.

No. 1783 — African ambulances: a, 5000d, Ambulance, people, red cross at LL. b, 5000d, Tractor ambulance, red cross at UL. c, 5000d, Ambulance and Red Cross workers. d, 70,000d, Ambulance with red diagonal stripes.

No. 1784 — Henry Ford (1863-1947), automobile manufacturer, 1908 Model T, and : a, 5000d, Drawing of automobile. b, 5000d, Ford poster, Red Cross flag above Model T ambulance. c, 5000d, Ford advertisement in Spanish. d, 70,000d, Horn.

No. 1785 — Harley-Davidson motorcycles, 105th anniv.: a, 5000d, FLHTCU Ultra Classic Electra Glide. b, 5000d, XL-1200C Sportster 1200 Custom. c, 5000d, FLSTC Heritage Softail Classic. d, 70,000d, FXDC Dyna Super Glide Custom.

No. 1786 — Franz Schubert (1797-1828), composer, and: a, 5000d, Schubert reading book. b, 5000d, Men and women. c, 5000d, Buildings. d, 70,000d, Piano and bench.

No. 1787 — Giacomo Puccini (1858-1924), composer, and: a, 5000d, Puccini and piano. b, 5000d, Costumed man in chair. c, 5000d, Room. d, 70,000d, Man and woman from Puccini opera.

No. 1788 — Nikolai Rimsky-Korsakov (1844-1908), composer, and: a, 5000d, Frog Tsarevna, painting by Viktor Vasnetzov. b, 5000d, Scene from opera "Mlada." c, 5000d, Scene from opera "The Tsar's Bride." d, 70,000d, Scene from opera "Boris Godunov."

No. 1789 — Bee Gees rock band and: a, 5000d, Bee Gees Greatest Hits album cover. b, 5000d, Guitar at left. c, 5000d, Microphone at LR. d, 70,000d, Record of "More Than an Woman" at LL.

No. 1790 — Vivian Ernest Fuchs (1908-99), Polar explorer, and: a, 5000d, Canis lupus familiaris. b, 5000d, Pygoscelis papua. c, 5000d, Stercorarius pomarinus. d, 70,000d, Ursus maritimus.

No. 1791 — Discovery of Halley's comet, 250th anniv: a, 5000d, Edmond Halley and sextant. b, 5000d, Halley and globe. c, 5000d, Halley and compass, people viewing comet. d, 70,000d, People viewing comet.

No. 1792 — NASA, 50th anniv.: a, 5000d, Pres. John F. Kennedy, space shuttle on launch pad. b, 5000d, Astronaut David R. Scott, Gemini 7. c, 5000d, Astronaut Neil A. Armstrong, Viking lander. d, 70,000d, Crew of Apollo 17 and Lunar Rover.

No. 1793 — Snakes: a, 5000d, Macroprotodon cucullatus. b, 5000d, Python regius. c, 5000d, Bitis arietans and Bitis nasicornis. d, 70,000d, Green mamba.

No. 1794 — Crocodilians: a, 5000d, Caiman crocodilus. b, 5000d, Crocodylus acutus. c, 5000d, Crocodylus niloticus. d, 70,000d, Caiman latirostris.

No. 1795 — Various frogs with background color of: a, 5000d, Blue green. b, 5000d, Yellow orange. c, 5000d, Red orange. d, 70,000d, Blue.

No. 1796 — Butterflies: a, 5000d, Delias aglaia. b, 5000d, Junonia almana. c, 5000d, Junonia coenia. d, 70,000d, Cethosia biblis.

No. 1797 — Naturalists, flora and fauna: a, 5000d, Aristoteles (384 B.C.-322 B.C.), Phalacrocorax. b, 5000d, Theophrastus (372 B.C.-288 B.C.), Arum maculatum. c, 5000d, Pedanius Dioscorides (40-90), illustrations from Dioscorides Neapolitanus. d, 70,000d, Pliny the Elder (23-79), manuscript illustration.

No. 1798 — Frank Sinatra (1915-98), singer, and: a, 5000d, Pres. John F. Kennedy, U.S. flag. b, 5000d, Pres. Ronald Reagan. c, 5000d, Elvis Presley. d, 70,000d, Marilyn Monroe.

No. 1799 — Shells and lighthouses: a, 5000d, Aporrhais pespelecani, Cape Hatteras Lighthouse, U.S., Kéréon Lighthouse, France. b, 5000d, Boroetrophon fraseri, La Laterna Lighthouse, Italy, St. Mary's Lighthouse, United Kingdom. c, 5000d, Conus guanche, Cabo de Palos Lighthouse, Spain, La Martrre Lighthouse, Canada. d, 70,000d, Marginella senegalensis, Kap Arkona Lighthouse, Germany, New Brighton Lighthouse, United Kingdom.

No. 1800 — Billy Karam, race car driver and Porsches: a, 7000d. b, 9000d. c, 10,000d. d, 14,000d.

No. 1801 — Naturalists: a, 15,000d, Andrea Cesalpino (c. 1519-1603), flower illustration, books. b, 15,000d, Conrad Gessner (1516-65), Quadrupedibus illustrations. c, 15,000d, Leonard Fuchs (1501-66), illustration of asparagus. d, 40,000d, Ulisse Aldrovandi (1522-1605), illustrations of mythical beasts.

No. 1802 — Elvis Presley (1935-77) in army uniform: a, 5000d, Wearing cap in foreground and background. b, 10,000d, Wearing cap in background photograph. c, 10,000d, Wearing helmet with goggles in foreground. d, 15,000d, Wearing cap in foreground photograph. e, 15,000d, Guitar in background. f, 30,000d, Reading mail.

No. 1803 — Bridges: a, 5000d, Humber Bridge, United Kingdom, and ship. b, 10,000d, Chain Bridge, Hungary, and police car. c, 10,000d, Erasmus Bridge, Netherlands, and ship. d, 15,000d, Sydney Harbour Bridge, Australia, and rescue boat. e, 15,000d, Brooklyn Bridge, U.S., and airplane. f, 30,000d, Oresund Bridge, Denmark, and hydroplane ambulance.

No. 1804 — Submarines: a, 5000d, Type XXI U-boat, Germany. b, 10,000d, K-21, Soviet Union. c, 10,000d, U-boat 530, Germany, Boat I-52, Japan. d, 15,000d, Royal Navy "S" Class, United Kingdom. e, 15,000d, USS Tang. f, 30,000d, Delta-17, Soviet Union.

No. 1805 — Medicinal plants: a, 5000d, Sophora denudata. b, 10,000d, Mussaenda landia. c, 10,000d, Agarista salicifolia. d, 15,000d, Dodonea viscosa. e, 15,000d, Jumellea fragrans. f, 30,000d, Centella asiatica.

No. 1806, 10,000d, — Mushrooms and orchids: a, Strobilomyces floccopus, Cymbidium. b, Entoloma clypeatum, Calypso bulbosa. c, Gymnopilus spectabilis, Coeloglossum viride. d, Leccinum scabrum, Arachnis annamensis. e, Cortinarius praestans, Galanthus nivalis. f, Cortinarius traganus, Arundina graminifolia. g, Inocybe fastigiata, Aspasia epidendroides. h, Pholiota destruens, Orchis papilionacea. i, Hebeloma radicosum, Dendrophylax lindenii.

No. 1807, 95,000d, Napoleon Bonaparte, diff. No. 1808, 95,000d, Ambulances and airplane. No. 1809, 95,000d, Japanese ambulance and fire station. No. 1810, 95,000d, Ambulance and word "Ambulance" painted on vehicle roof. No. 1811, 95,000d, Animal-drawn ambulance wagon. No. 1812, 95,000d, Ford and Model T. No. 1813, 95,000d, Harley-Davidson FXDWC Dyna Wide Glide motorcycle. No. 1814, 95,000d, Schubert at piano. No. 1815, 95,000d, Puccini, poster for "La Boheme." No. 1816, 95,000d, Rimsky-Korsakov, scene from opera "Sadko." No. 1817, 95,000d, Bee Gees. No. 1818, 95,000d, Vivian Fuchs and Ursus maritimus, diff. No. 1819, 95,000d, Halley and Halley's Comet. No. 1820, 95,000d, Astronauts, Explorer I spacecraft. No. 1821, 95,000d, Osteolaemus. No. 1822, 95,000d, Hyla gratiosa, Pseudis paradoxa. No. 1823, 95,000d, Caligo memnon. No. 1824, 95,000d, Nicolas Steno (1638-86), naturalist, and drawing of shark's head. No. 1825, 95,000d, John Ray (1627-1705), naturalist, drawings of dodo and turkey. No. 1826, 95,000d, Sinatra. No. 1827, 95,000d, Presley. No. 1828, 95,000d, Tower Bridge, United Kingdom, and tugboat. No. 1829, 95,000d, Type XXI U-boat, Germany, diff. No. 1830, 95,000d, Psiloxylon mauritanum. No. 1831, 95,000d, Arundina graminifolia, Suillus aeruginascens.

**2008, Feb. 4 Litho.** ***Perf. 12¾x13¼***

**Sheets of 4, #a-d**

| | | | | |
|---|---|---|---|---|
| 1779-1795 | A324 | Set of 17 | 200.00 | 200.00 |
| 1796-1801 | A325 | Set of 6 | 65.00 | 65.00 |

**Sheets of 6, #a-f**

| | | | | |
|---|---|---|---|---|
| 1802-1803 | A324 | Set of 2 | 24.00 | 24.00 |
| 1804-1805 | A325 | Set of 2 | 24.00 | 24.00 |

**Miniature Sheet**

| | | | | |
|---|---|---|---|---|
| 1806 | A325 | 10,000d Sheet of 9, #a-i | 12.50 | 12.50 |

**Souvenir Sheets**

***Perf. 13¼ Syncopated***

| | | | | |
|---|---|---|---|---|
| 1807-1831 | A324 | Set of 25 | 330.00 | 330.00 |

2008 Summer Olympics, Beijing — A326

Olympic Stamps — A327

No. 1832: a, Tennis. b, Pole vault. c, Weight lifting. d, Rowing.

No. 1833: a, 5000d, Angola #614. b, 5000d, St. Thomas & Prince Islands #838. c, 5000d, Guinea-Bissau #369E. d, 70,000d, Guinea-Bissau #370.

No. 1834: a, 5000d, Cape Verde #826. b, 5000d, Guinea-Bissau #776. c, 5000d, Mozambique #626. d, 70,000d, Mozambique #861.

No. 1835: a, 5000d, Mozambique #945. b, 5000d, St. Thomas & Prince Islands #568. c, 5000d, Guinea-Bissau #936. d, 70,000d, Mozambique #898.

No. 1836: a, 5000d, Guinea-Bissau #612. b, 5000d, St. Thomas & Prince Islands #1170. c, 5000d, St. Thomas & Prince Islands #569. d, 70,000d, Guinea-Bissau #C20.

No. 1837: a, 5000d, St. Thomas & Prince Islands #805c. b, 5000d, Guinea-Bissau #402B. c, 5000d, Guinea-Bissau #369D. d, 70,000d, St. Thomas & Prince Islands #1094.

No. 1838: a, 5000d, Mozambique #1156. b, 5000d, Guinea-Bissau #C18. c, 5000d, Cape Verde #828. d, 70,000d, St. Thomas & Prince Islands #1050C.

No. 1839: a, 5000d, Cape Verde #406. b, 5000d, Angola #843. c, 5000d, Guinea-Bissau #775. d, 70,000d, Angola #1268.

**2008, Mar. 10** ***Perf. 12¾x13¼***

| | | | | |
|---|---|---|---|---|
| 1832 | A326 | 5000d Sheet of 4, #a-d | 2.75 | 2.75 |

**Sheets of 4, #a-d**

| | | | | |
|---|---|---|---|---|
| 1833-1839 | A327 | Set of 7 | 72.50 | 72.50 |

Nos. 1834a, 1834c, 1838a, 1839b each exist in a souvenir sheet of 1.

A328

A329

No. 1840 — People holding Chinese porcelain, with background color of: a, 5000d, Dull green. b, 5000d, Lilac. c, 5000d, Light blue. d, 70,000d, Light lilac.

No. 1841 — Castles: a, 5000d, Bran Castle, Romania. b, 5000d, Windsor Castle, Great Britain. c, 5000d, Neuschwanstein Castle, Germany. d, 70,000d, Carcassonne, France.

No. 1842 — Herbert von Karajan (1908-89), conductor, with inset photograph of: a, 5000d, Karajan and woman. b, 5000d, Karajan and machine. c, 5000d, Karajan conducting. d, 70,000d, Outer space scene.

No. 1843 — Lord Robert Baden-Powell (1857-1941), founder of Boy Scouts, and: a, 5000d, *The Scout* magazine cover, orchids. b, 5000d, Owl with wings spread, butterfly on flower. c, 5000d, Owl, butterfly, flower. d, 70,000d, *Scouting for Boys* book cover.

No. 1844 — Table tennis players: a, 5000d, Wang Liqin. b, 5000d, Wang Hao. c, 5000d, Werner Schlager. d, 70,000d, Kong Linghui.

No. 1845 — Table tennis players: a, 5000d, Guo Yue. b, 5000d, Zhang Yining. c, 5000d, Wang Nan. d, 70,000d, Deng Yaping.

No. 1846 — Apparition at Lourdes, 150th anniv.: a, 5000d, Lourdes Basilica, photograph and arms of Pope Benedict XVI. b, 5000d, Lourdes Basilica, apparition. c, 5000d, Statue of Virgin Mary, Bernadette Soubirous. d, 70,000d, St. Peter's Basilica, photograph and arms of Pope John Paul II.

No. 1847 — Pandas, Scouting emblem, and: a, 5000d, Tree with foliage. b, 5000d, Snowflakes. c, 5000d, Stars and tree stump. d, 70,000d, Tree, baby panda.

No. 1848 — Loxodonta africana at LR and: a, 5000d, Hippotigris. b, 5000d, Second elephant. c, 5000d, Second elephant and antelope. d, 70,000d, Giraffa camelopardalis.

No. 1849 — Horse racing: a, 5000d, Horse and jockey, denomination over orange red area. b, 5000d, Horse and jockey, denomination over blue area. c, 5000d, Horse and sulky. d, 70,000d, Horse and sulky, diff.

No. 1850 — Waterfalls and wildlife: a, 5000d, Jog Falls, India, Panthera tigris bengalensis. b, 5000d, Gocta Falls, Peru, Vultur gryphus. c, 5000d, Ouzoud Falls, Morocco, Camelus dromedarius. d, 70,000d, Huangguoshu Falls, People's Republic of China, Ailurus fulgens.

No. 1851 — Inventors: a, 5000d, Muhammad al-Khwarizmi, inventor of algebra. b, 10,000d, Alexander Graham Bell, inventor of telephone. c, 10,000d, Christiaan Huygens, inventor of pendulum clock. d, 15,000d, Guglielmo Marconi, inventor of radiotelegraph. e, 15,000d, James Watt, inventor of steam engine. f, 30,000d, Thomas Edison, inventor of long-lasting light bulb.

No. 1852 — Inventors: a, 5000d, Samuel F. B. Morse, inventor of Morse code. b, 10,000d, Blaise Pascal, inventor of mechanical calculator. c, 10,000d, Nicolas Cugnot, inventor of first automobile. d, 15,000d, Emile Berliner, inventor of disc record gramophone. e, 15,000d, Rudolf Diesel, inventor of Diesel engine. f, 30,000d, Ivan Kulibin, inventor of elevator.

No. 1853 — Airbus airplanes: a, 5000d, Airbus 380, Claude Lelaie, test pilot. b, 10,000d, Airbus Beluga. c, 10,000d, Airbus 380, Jacques Rosay, test pilot. d, 15,000d, Airbus 380, cockpit instruments. e, 15,000d, Airbus Beluga, Rosay. f, 30,000d, Airbus 380, passenger cabin.

**2008, Mar. 28** ***Perf. 12¾x13¼***

**Sheets of 4, #a-d, + 2 labels**

| | | | | |
|---|---|---|---|---|
| 1840-1841 | A328 | Set of 2 | 22.50 | 22.50 |

**Sheets of 4, #a-d**

| | | | | |
|---|---|---|---|---|
| 1842-1850 | A329 | Set of 9 | 110.00 | 110.00 |

**Sheets of 6, #a-f**

| | | | | |
|---|---|---|---|---|
| 1851-1853 | A329 | Set of 3 | 30.00 | 30.00 |

A330

No. 1854 — Fire trucks: a, 15,000d, 1906 Shand Mason & Co., Aztec god of fire. b, 25,000d, 1928 Stoughton, Ctesibius, Greek inventor. c, 30,000d, 1939 Scammell, Xiuhtechutli, Aztec lord of volcanoes. d, 30,000d, 1931 Leyland, Mexican god of fire.

No. 1855 — Churches: a, 15,000d, Santa Maria del Fiore Basilica, Florence, Italy, crucifix. b, 25,000d, Basilica of Our Lady of Lichen, Poland, Pope John Paul II. c, 30,000d,

Cologne Cathedral, Germany, Pope Benedict XVI. d, 30,000d, Notre Dame Cathedral, Paris, France, dragon gargoyle.

No. 1856 — Agriculture: a, 20,000d, Grapes and vineyard. b, 20,000d, Bee on flower, beekeeper and hive. c, 20,000d, Wheat stalks and harvested field. d, 40,000d, Tulips and windmill.

No. 1857 — Rotary International emblem and chess champions: a, 20,000d, Bobby Fischer. b, 20,000d, Anatoly Karpov. c, 20,000d, Garry Kasparov. d, 40,000d, Vladimir Kramnik.

No. 1858 — Pre-historic rock art: a, 25,000d, Buffalos, hunters. b, 25,000d, Horned animals, pre-historic man. c, 25,000d, Animal, pre-historic man with spear. d, 25,000d, Animals, stick figures of men.

No. 1859 — Jewelry made with: a, 25,000d, Silver (prata). b, 25,000d, Platinum (platina). c, 25,000d, Pearls (carbonato de cálcio. d, 25,000d, Diamond (diamante).

No. 1860 — European urban transportation: a, 5,000d, Electric train, Budapest. b, 10,000d, Subway train, Barcelona. c, 15,000d, Double-decker bus, London. d, 20,000d, Trolley bus, Milan. e, 20,000d, Taxi, Berlin. f, 30,000d, Subway train, Paris.

No. 1861 — Nobel Peace laureates: a, 5,000d, Henri Dunant, 1901. b, 10,000d, Lech Walesa, 1983. c, 15,000d, Albert Schweitzer, 1953. d, 20,000d, Mikhail Gorbachev, 1990. e, 20,000d, F. W. de Klerk, 1993. f, 30,000d, Dalai Lama Tenzin Gyatso, 1989.

No. 1862 — Albatrosses: a, 5,000d, Phoebastria nigripes. b, 10,000d, Diomedea exulans. c, 15,000d, Phoebetria. d, 20,000d, Thalassarche melanophrys, bird in flight at left. e, 20,000d, Thalassarche melanophrys, bird in water at right. f, 30,000d, Phoebastria immutabilis.

No. 1863 — World War II: a, 5,000d, Sir Winston Churchill, Hawker Tempest airplane. b, 10,000d, Soviet T34/85 tanks. c, 15,000d, Gen. Charles de Gaulle, Bloch MB 210 airplanes. d, 20,000d, Douglas TBD Devastator airplane, HMS Hood. e, 20,000d, Messerscmitt Bf-109E-3 and Bf-109E7/Trop airplanes. f, 30,000d, USS Sawfish.

No. 1864 — Scientists: a, 5,000d, Haroun Tazieff, vulcanologist. b, 10,000d, John Gould, ornithologist. c, 15,000d, Norman L. Bowen, geologist. d, 20,000d, Johann Wolfgang von Goethe, poet and morphologist. e, 20,000d, Ivan Pavlov, physiologist. f, 30,000d, Charles Darwin, naturalist.

No. 1865 — Famous people and dogs: a, 5,000d, Pres. Bill Clinton, Labrador retriever. b, 10,000d, Tony Parker, basketball player, Eva Longoria, actress, Maltese. c, 15,000d, Knud Rasmussen, polar explorer, Husky. d, 20,000d, Madonna, singer, Chihuahua. e, 20,000d, Steve Irwin, conservationist, Staffordshire bull terrier. f, 30,000d, Dorothy Gladys "Dodie" Smith, author, Dalmatian.

No. 1866, 95,000d, St. Peter's Basilica, Vatican City, Pope Benedict XVI. No. 1867, 95,000d, St. Bernard and German shepherd. No. 1868, 100,000d, 1927 Dandy fire engine, fire helmet. No. 1869, 100,000d, Diomedea (albatrosses). No. 1870, 100,000d, Gold nugget and ring.

**2008, May 19** ***Perf. 12¾x13¼***

**1854** A330 Sheet of 4, #a-d 12.50 12.50

**Sheets of 4, #a-d, + 2 labels**

**1855-1859** A330 Set of 5 62.50 62.50

**Sheets of 6, #a-f**

**1860-1865** A330 Set of 6 75.00 75.00

**Souvenir Sheets**

***Perf. 13¼ Syncopated***

**1866-1870** A330 Set of 5 60.00 60.00

Nos. 1866-1870 each contain one 50x39mm stamp.

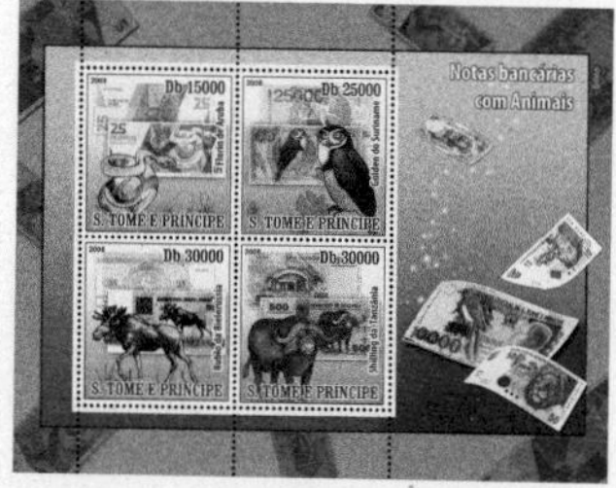


A331

No. 1871 — Animals on bank notes of the world: a, 15,000d, Snake, Aruba 25-florin note. b, 25,000d, Owl, Surinam 25,000-gulden note. c, 30,000d, Moose, Belarus 25-ruble note. d, 30,000d, Buffalo, Tanzania 500-shilling note.

No. 1872 — Dogs: a, 15,000d, Alaskan malamute. b, 25,000d, Siberian husky. c, 30,000d, Greenland dog. d, 30,000d, Samoyed.

No. 1873 — Various nudes by Pierre-Auguste Renoir (1841-1919) with Renoir at: a, 20,000d, Left, without hat. b, 20,000d, Right, wearing hat. c, 20,000d, Left, wearing hat. d, 30,000d, Right, wearing hat, diff.

No. 1874 — Various nudes by George-Pierre Seurat (1859-91) with Seurat at: a, 20,000d, Left, facing forward. b, 20,000d, Right, facing left. c, 20,000d, Left, facing right. d, 30,000d, Right, facing forward.

No. 1875 — Various paintings by Utagawa Kunisada (1786-1865) with Japanese flag at: a, 20,000d, UL, gray panel at right. b, 20,000d, LL, gray panel at left. c, 20,000d, LL, gray panel at right. d, 30,000d, UL, gray panel at left.

No. 1876 — Orchids and butterflies: a, 25,000d, Cypripedium kentuckiense, Papilio laglaizei. b, 25,000d, Phalaenopsis lindenii toapei, Prepona xenagoras. c, 25,000d, Paphiopedilum, Danaus sita. d, 25,000d, Phragmipedium sedenii, Ornithoptera priamus urvilianus.

No. 1877 — German lighthouses: a, 25,000d, Amrum Lighthouse. b, 25,000d, Neuland Lighthouse. c, 25,000d, Eckernförde Lighthouse. d, 25,000d, List Ost Lighthouse.

No. 1878 — Israel, 60th anniv.: a, 25,000d, Theodor Herzl, arms of Israel. b, 25,000d, David Ben-Gurion, arms of Jerusalem. c, 25,000d, Golda Meir, star of David. d, 25,000d, Dome of the Rock, Jerusalem, menorah.

No. 1879, 100,000d, Paintings by Utagawa Kunisada. No. 1880, 100,000d, Cattleya intermedia, Ornithoptera paradisea.

**2008, July 17** ***Perf. 12¾x13¼***

**Sheets of 4, #a-d**

**1871-1878** A331 Set of 8 100.00 100.00

**Souvenir Sheets**

***Perf. 13¼ Syncopated***

**1879-1880** A331 Set of 2 25.00 25.00

Nos. 1879-1880 each contain one 50x39mm stamp.

A332

No. 1881 — Various trolley cars with background color of: a, 15,000d, Pink. b, 25,000d, Yellow. c, 30,000d, Green. d, 30,000d, Blue.

No. 1882 — Fishermen and fish: a, 15,000d, Sphyraena sphyraena. b, 25,000d, Thunnus alalunga. c, 30,000d, Salmo trutta. d, 30,000d, Lutjanus gibbus.

No. 1883 — Zeppelins: a, 20,000d, LZ-127 Graf Zeppelin over Alps. b, 20,000d, LZ-2 over Friedrichshafen, Germany. c, 20,000d, L-9 over Würzburg, Germany. d, 40,000d, LZ-130 Graf Zeppelin II over Rothenburg, Germany.

No. 1884 — Ancient Egyptian artifacts: a, 20,000d, Bust of Queen Nefertiti, Ankh. b, 20,000d, Sarcophagus, Queen Cleopatra VII. c, 20,000d, Funerary mask of King Tutankhamun, scarab beetle. d, 40,000d, Horus depicted as falcon, King Ramses II.

No. 1885 — Golfers: a, 25,000d, Tiger Woods. b, 25,000d, Todd Hamilton. c, 25,000d, Ernie Els. d, 25,000d, Ben Curtis.

No. 1886 — Circus performers: a, 25,000d, Billy Smart Circus, British flag. b, 25,000d, Moscow State Circus, Russian flag. c, 25,000d, Herman Renz Circus, Netherlands flag. d, 25,000d, Chinese State Circus, flag of People's Republic of China.

No. 1887 — Campaign against AIDS: a, 25,000d, Pres. Bill Clinton, doctor treating child. b, 25,000d, Test tubes in laboratory, woman being treated, AIDS ribbon. c, 25,000d, Doctor getting blood sample from finger, doctor examining infant, AIDS ribbon. d, 25,000d, Hilary Koprowski, immunologist, vials of polio vaccine.

No. 1888, 95,000d, Salmo salar and fisherman. No. 1889, 95,000d, LZ-129 Hindenburg over Lake Constance. No. 1890, 95,000d, Eye of Ra, Anubis attending the mummy of Sennedjem. No. 1891, 95,000d, Woods, diff. No. 1892, 95,000d, Cirque du Soleil performers. No. 1893, 95,000d, Dr. Albert Schweitzer and staff at Lambaréné, Gabon hospital.

**2008, July 17** ***Perf. 12¾x13¼***

**Sheets of 4, #a-d**

**1881-1887** A332 Set of 7 90.00 90.00

**Souvenir Sheets**

***Perf. 13¼ Syncopated***

**1888-1893** A332 Set of 6 75.00 75.00

Nos. 1888-1893 each contain one 50x39mm stamp.

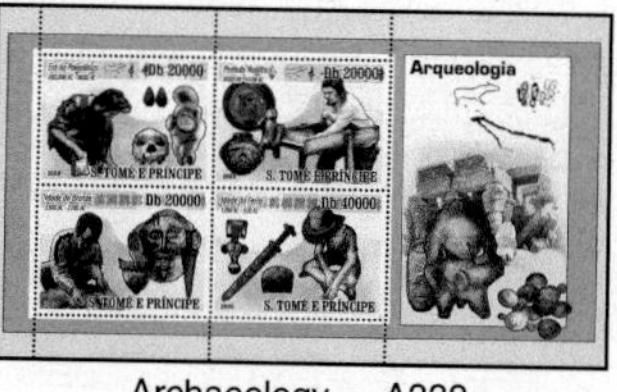


Archaeology — A333

No. 1894 — Archaeologists and items from: a, 20,000d, Paleolithic Era. b, 20,000d, Neolithic Era. c, 20,000d, Bronze Age. d, 40,000d, Iron Age.

100,000d, Archaeologist and items from Persian Period.

**2008, Sept. 14** ***Perf. 12¾x13¼***

**1894** A333 Sheet of 4, #a-d 12.50 12.50

**Souvenir Sheet**

***Perf. 13¼ Syncopated***

**1895** A333 100,000d multi 12.50 12.50

No. 1895 contains one 38x39mm stamp.

A334

No. 1896 — Various nudes of Paul Gauguin (1848-1903), with Gauguin at: a, 15,000d, Left. b, 25,000d, Right. c, 30,000d, Left, diff. d, 30,000d, Right, diff.

No. 1897 — Various nudes of Pablo Picasso (1881-1973), with Picasso at: a, 15,000d, Left. b, 25,000d, Right. c, 30,000d, Left, diff. d, 30,000d, Right, diff.

No. 1898 — Various nudes of Peter Paul Rubens (1577-1640), with Rubens at: a, 20,000d, Left, in sepia. b, 20,000d, Right. c, 20,000d, Left, in color. d, 40,000d, Right, diff.

No. 1899 — Various nudes of Gustave Moreau (1826-98), with Moreau at: a, 20,000d, Left, in black. b, 20,000d, Right. c, 20,000d, Left, in brown. d, 40,000d, Right, diff.

No. 1900 — Costumes of: a, 20,000d, Ancient Greece. b, 20,000d, France, 18th cent. c, 20,000d, Russia, 17th cent. d, 40,000d, Japan, 19th cent.

No. 1901 — Divers, starfish, and dolphins: a, 20,000d, Delphinus delphis. b, 20,000d, Grampus griseus. c, 20,000d, Platanista gangetica. d, 40,000d, Cephalorhynchus commersonii.

No. 1902 — Dogs: a, 20,000d, Fox terriers. b, 20,000d, Whippets. c, 20,000d, Rhodesian ridgebacks. d, 40,000d, Basset hounds.

No. 1903 — Rescue dogs: a, 20,000d, St. Bernards. b, 20,000d, Labrador retrievers. c, 20,000d, Border collies. d, 40,000d, German shepherds (one with Red Cross identification).

No. 1904 — Domesticated animals: a, 25,000d, Cattle. b, 25,000d, Dogs. c, 25,000d, Cats. d, 25,000d, Horses.

No. 1905 — Horses: a, 25,000d, Cowboy riding chestnut horse (Alazao). b, 25,000d, Friesians. c, 25,000d, Clydesdales. d, 25,000d, Icelandic horses.

No. 1906 — Cat breeds: a, 25,000d, Persian. b, 25,000d, Russian Blue. c, 25,000d, Devon Rex. d, 25,000d, Siamese.

No. 1907 — Sir Peter Markham Scott (1909-89), conservationist and: a, 25,000d, Phascolarctos cinereus. b, 25,000d, Gorilla. c, 25,000d, Ailurus fulgens. d, 25,000d, Ailuropoda melanoleuca.

No. 1908 — Masonic emblem and: a, 25,000d, Alexander Pushkin, writer. b, 25,000d, Louis Armstrong, musician. c, 25,000d, Oscar Wilde, writer. d, 25,000d, Wolfgang Amadeus Mozart, composer.

No. 1909, 100,000d, Tursiops truncatus, starfish and diver, horiz. No. 1910, 100,000d, Two cats, horiz.

**2008, Sept. 14** ***Perf. 12¾x13¼***

**Sheets of 4, #a-d**

**1896-1908** A334 Set of 13 165.00 165.00

**Souvenir Sheets**

***Perf. 13¼ Syncopated***

**1909-1910** A334 Set of 2 26.00 26.00

Nos. 1909-1910 each contain one 50x39mm stamp.

A335

No. 1911 — Illustrations of women by Alphonse Mucha (1860-1939) with woman at right with: a, 5000d, Hands in hair. b, 5000d, Hands folded below chin. c, 5000d, Hands on chin. d, 70,000d, Hand at top of chest.

No. 1912 — Charlton Heston (1923-2008), actor, and scenes from: a, 15,000d, *The Ten Commandments,* 1956. b, 25,000d, *Planet of the Apes,* 1968. c, 30,000d, *The Agony and the Ecstasy,* 1965. d, 30,000d, *Ben-Hur,* 1959.

No. 1913 — Shells: a, 20,000d, Cypraea algoensis, Adamussium colbecki. b, 20,000d, Lunatia grossularia, Trophon geversianus. c, 20,000d, Buccinum undatum, Angaria vicdani. d, 40,000d, Mytilus edulis, Haliotis iris.

No. 1914, 95,000d, The Times of the Day Series, by Mucha. No. 1915, 100,000d, Heston and wife, Lydia Clarke. No. 1916, 100,000d, Cardium edule, Architectonica perspectiva.

**2008, Nov. 3** ***Perf. 12¾x13¼***

**Sheets of 4, #a-d**

**1911-1913** A335 Set of 3 40.00 40.00

**Souvenir Sheets**

***Perf. 13¼ Syncopated***

**1914-1916** A335 Sot of 3 40.00 40.00

Nos. 1914-1916 each contain one 50x39mm stamp.

A336

No. 1917 — Various nudes of Gustave Courbet (1819-77), with Courbet at: a, 15,000d, Left. b, 25,000d, Right. c, 30,000d, Left, diff. d, 30,000d, Right, diff.

No. 1918 — Various nudes of Edouard Manet (1832-83), with Manet at: a, 15,000d, Left. b, 25,000d, Right. c, 30,000d, Left, diff. d, 30,000d, Right, diff.

No. 1919 — Various nudes of Paul Cézanne (1839-1906), with Cézanne at: a, 15,000d, Left. b, 25,000d, Right. c, 30,000d, Left, diff. d, 30,000d, Right, diff.

No. 1920 — Various nudes of Pierre Bonnard (1867-1947), with Bonnard at: a, 15,000d, Left. b, 25,000d, Right. c, 30,000d, Left, diff. d, 30,000d, Right, diff.

No. 1921 — Jules Verne (1828-1905), and illustrations from his books depicting: a, 15,000d, Spaceship. b, 25,000d, Spaceship, diff. c, 30,000d, Men, hat in air. d, 30,000d, Octopus.

No. 1922 — Dogs: a, 15,000d, Dingos. b, 25,000d, Pharaoh hounds. c, 30,000d, Mexican hairless dogs. d, 30,000d, Basenjis.

No. 1923 — Dogs: a, 20,000d, Groenendael Belgian shepherds. b, 20,000d, Caucasian shepherds. c, 20,000d, Central Asian shepherds. d, 40,000d, German shepherds.

No. 1924 — Red Cross flag and seaplanes: a, 20,000d, Sikorsky S-43. b, 20,000d, Canadair CL-215. c, 20,000d, Shin Meiwa US-1A. d, 40,000d, Grumman HU-16E Albatross.

No. 1925 — Helicopters, cent.: a, 20,000d, Paul Cornu, aircraft engineer. b, 20,000d, Cornu helicopter. c, 20,000d, VS-300A helicopter. d, 40,000d, Igor Sikorsky, helicopter designer, and helicopter.

No. 1926 — Moai of Easter Island and sailing ships: a, 20,000d, Grande Hermine. b, 20,000d, Sparrow. c, 20,000d, Victoria. d, 40,000d, Concorde.

No. 1927 — Animals and dams: a, 25,000d, Lynx lynx, Nurek Dam, Tajikistan. b, 25,000d, Capra ibex nubiana, Aswan High Dam, Egypt.

c, 25,000d, Ailurus fulgens, Three Gorges Dam, People's Republic of China. d, 25,000d, Sciurus carolinensis, Fort Peck Dam, U.S.

No. 1928 — Various paintings of Edgar Degas (1834-1917), with Degas at: a, 25,000d, Left, wearing hat. b, 25,000d, Right, without hat. c, 25,000d, Left, without hat. d, 25,000d, Right, holding hat.

**2008, Nov. 3** ***Perf. 12¾x13¼***

**Sheets of 4, #a-d**

**1917-1928** A336 Set of 12 160.00 160.00

Election of Pres. Barack Obama — A337

No. 1929 — Pres. Obama, U.S. flag, and: a, 13,000d, White House. b, 13,000d, American Indians. c, 39,000d, Slave in chains, group of slaves. d, 39,000d, Statue of Liberty.

100,000d, Pres. Obama, Confederate soldiers.

**2008, Dec. 4** ***Perf. 12¾x13¼***

**1929** A337 Sheet of 4, #a-d 13.00 13.00

**Souvenir Sheet**

***Perf. 13¼ Syncopated***

**1930** A337 100,000d multi 13.00 13.00

No. 1930 contains one 50x39mm stamp.

Miniature Sheets

Fruits — A338

No. 1931 — Fruit from Republic of China: a, 1000d, Guavas. b, 1500d, Carambolas. c, 2000d, Jujubes. d, 2500d, Wax apples. e, 3000d, Papayas.

No. 1932 — Fruit from St. Thomas & Prince Islands: a, 1000d, Avocados (abacate). b, 1500d, Jackfruit (jaca), horiz. c, 2000d, Soursops (sap-sap). d, 2500d, Cherimoyas (anona). e, 3000d, Mangos (manga).

**2008** **Litho.** ***Perf. 12½***

**Sheets of 5, #a-e, + 4 labels**

**1931-1932** A338 Set of 2 6.00 6.00

Cooperation between Republic of China and St. Thomas & Prince Islands, 9th anniv. Dated. 2006.

Worldwide Fund for Nature (WWF) A339

Psittacus eritahcus: No. 1933, 25,000d, One bird on branch. No. 1934, 25,000d, Two birds on branch. No. 1935, 25,000d, Chicks in nest. No. 1936, 25,000d, Bird in flight.

**2009, Jan. 31** ***Perf. 13x13¼***

**1933-1936** A339 Set of 4 14.00 14.00

*1936a* Souvenir sheet of 8, 2 each #1933-1936 28.00 28.00

A340

No. 1937 — Japanese film and music stars: a, 13,000d, Ken Watanabe. b, 13,000d, Miyavi. c, 39,000d, Chiaki Kuriyama. d, 39,000d, Utada Hikaru.

No. 1938 — Cats: a, 13,000d, Somali cat, Mogadishu, Somalia. b, 13,000d, Singapura cat, Singapore. c, 39,000d, Egyptian Mau cat, Giza Pyramids. d, 39,000d, Russian Blue cat, Red Square, Moscow.

No. 1939 — Polistes fuscatus and flowers: a, 13,000d, Malva sylvestris. b, 13,000d, Helianthus annuus. c, 39,000d, Lantana camara. d, 39,000d, Hebe x franciscana.

No. 1940 — High-speed trains: a, 13,000d, Eurostar. b, 13,000d, JR-Maglev. c, 39,000d, Shinkansen. d, 39,000d, Korea Train Express.

No. 1941 — Chess champions: a, 13,000d, Garry Kasparov. b, 13,000d, Anatoly Karpov. c, 39,000d, Vladimir Kremnik. d, 39,000d, Bobby Fischer.

No. 1942 — Shells: a, 13,000d, Thatcheria mirabilis. b, 13,000d, Amplustrum amplustre. c, 39,000d, Cryptospira elegans. d, 39,000d, Mercenaria mercenaria.

No. 1943 — Liverpool, 2008 European City of Culture: a, 13,000d, SuperLamBanana sculpture, Philharmonic Hall. b, 13,000d, King John, Metropolitan Cathedral. c, 39,000d, The Beatles, Yellow Submarine replica. d, 39,000d, Statue of Emlyn Hughes, Albert Docks.

No. 1944 — Paintings by Lucian Freud (1922-2011): a, 13,000d, Girl with a White Dog. b, 13,000d, Naked Portrait. c, 39,000d, Naked Portrait, diff. d, 39,000d, Naked Girl Asleep II.

No. 1945 — 90th birthday of Nelson Mandela, 1993 Nobel Peace laureate, and butterflies: a, 13,000d, Papilio dardanus. b, 13,000d, Zeuxidia aurelius. c, 39,000d, Speyeria cybele. d, 39,000d, Taenaris horsfieldii birchi.

No. 1946 — Crabs and lighthouses: a, 15,000d, Corystes cassivelaunus, Redonda Island Lighthouse, Sri Lanka. b, 25,000d, Macrocheira kaempferi, Cape Reinga Lighthouse, New Zealand. c, 30,000d, Callinectes sapidus, Hook Head Lighthouse, Ireland. d, 30,000d, Pseudocarcinus gigas, Vieille Lighthouse, France.

No. 1947 — Children, with child at left: a, 25,000d, Touching eye. b, 25,000d, With wound below eye. c, 25,000d, Wearing necklace. d, 25,000d, With flowers in hair.

No. 1948 — Nudes by Paul Delvaux (1897-1994), with inscription: a, 25,000d, O Elogio da Melancolia. b, 25,000d, Pompei. c, 25,000d, O despertar da Floresta. d, 25,000d, As Mulhares diante do Mar.

No. 1949 — Paintings by Tsukioka Yoshitoshi (1839-92), with inscriptions: a, 25,000d, Ichikawa Kodanji IV, Bando Hikosaburo V. b, 25,000d, 28 Assassinatos Famosas, Komagine Hachibyoe. c, 25,000d, Façanhasdo Shogunato Tokugawa, Hideyoshi. d, 25,000d, Apariçao da Princesa Aranha, Marshall Takamori.

No. 1950 — Paul Newman (1925-2008), actor, and: a, 25,000d, Scene from *The Life and Times of Judge Roy Bean,* 1972. b, 25,000d, Scene from *Empire Falls,* 2005. c, 25,000d, Wife, Joanne Woodward. d, 25,000d, Scene from *The Color of Money,* 1986.

No. 1951 — Indian film and music stars: a, 25,000d, Aamir Khan. b, 25,000d, Alka Yagnik. c, 25,000d, Lata Mangeshkar. d, 25,000d, Amitabh Bachchan.

No. 1952, 100,000d, Takeshi Kitano. No. 1953, 100,000d, Angora cats, Sultan Ahmed Mosque, Istanbul, Turkey. No. 1954, 100,000d, Painting of nudes by Delvaux, diff. No. 1955, 100,000d, Paintings by Yoshitoshi, diff. No. 1956, 100,000d, Newman and race car. No. 1957, 100,000d, Asha Bhosle.

**2009, Jan. 31** ***Perf. 12¾x13¼***

**Sheets of 4, #a-d**

**1937-1951** A340 Set of 15 190.00 190.00

**Souvenir Sheets**

***Perf. 13¼ Syncopated***

**1952-1957** A340 Set of 6 77.50 77.50

Nos. 1952-1957 each contain one 50x39mm stamp.

A341

No. 1958 — Local dishes: a, 25,000d, Molho no Fogo, map of Prince Island. b, 30,000d, Calúlú, Map of St. Thomas Island.

No. 1959 — Sister Emmanuelle (1908-2008), and: a, 13,000d, Pope John Paul II. b, 13,000d, Child amidst ruins. c, 39,000d, Children. d, 39,000d, Pope Benedict XVI.

No. 1960 — Sharks and jellyfish: a, 15,000d, Isurus oxyrinchus, Carukia barnesi. b, 25,000d, Sphyrna lewini, Aurelia aurita. c, 30,000d, Carcharhinus brevipinna, Phacellophora camtschatica. d, 30,000d, Pristiophorus nudipinnis, Pelagia noctiluca.

No. 1961 — Butterflies and caterpillars: a, 15,000d, Alcides agatnyrsus, Papilio machaon caterpillar. b, 25,000d, Danaus sita, Brahmaea wallichi caterpillar. c, 30,000d, Troides aeacus, Danaus chrysippus caterpillar. d, 30,000d, Atrophaneura horishanus, Apatele alni caterpillar.

No. 1962 — Pres. Abraham Lincoln (1809-65), and: a, 25,000d, Son, Tad, head of Lincoln at Mount Rushmore. b, 25,000d, General Winfield Scott. c, 25,000d, Crowd at second inauguration, bust of Lincoln. d, 25,000d, Lincoln in chair, crowd at second inauguration.

No. 1963 — Indian Space Program: a, 25,000d, Abdul Kalam, Endusat satellite. b, 25,000d, Vikram Sarabhai, Aryabhata 1 satellite. c, 25,000d, Mahatma Gandhi, Chandrayaan 1 satellite. d, 25,000d, Astronaut Rakesh Sharma, launch of Chandrayaan 1.

No. 1964 — Joseph Haydn (1732-1809), composer, and: a, 25,000d, Musicians. b, 25,000d, Theater stage and orchestra. c, 25,000d, Hanover Square, London, 1791. d, 25,000d, Harpsichord and chair.

No. 1965 — Felix Mendelssohn (1809-47), composer, and: a, 25,000d, Building. b, 25,000d, Woman on piano bench, musical score. c, 25,000d, Woman and man listening to pianist. d, 25,000d, Mendelssohn's sister, Fanny.

No. 1966 — Louis Braille (1809-52), inventor of Braille writing, and: a, 25,000d, Building, Braille at left. b, 25,000d, Building, Braille at right. c, 25,000d, hand touching Braille text, Braille at left. d, 25,000d, Blind woman writing in Braille, Braille at right.

No. 1967 — Edgar Allan Poe (1809-49), writer, and: a, 25,000d, Poe's home, Bronx, New York. b, 25,000d, Illustration for poem, "The Raven." c, 25,000d, Books and room. d, 25,000d, Poe writing.

No. 1968 — Paintings by Shi Tao (1642-1707): a, 25,000d, Eight Scenic Spots in Huangshan, Shi Tao. b, 25,000d, An Old Man on a Boat. c, 25,000d, Mingxianquan and Hutouyan. d, 25,000d, Spring River.

No. 1969 — Various paintings by Toshusai Sharaku (1770-1825) with white line separating paintings below letters: a, 25,000d, "os" in "Toshusai." b, 25,000d, "us" in "Toshusai." c, 25,000d, "sh" in "Toshusai." d, 25,000d, "To" in "Toshusai."

No. 1970 — Two Strigops habroptilus in trees with animal name at: a, 25,000d, LL. b, 25,000d, UR. c, 25,000d, UL, below date. d, 25,000d, UL, below tree branch.

No. 1971 — New Zealand parrots: a, 25,000d, Strigops habroptilus, orange background. b, 25,000d, Nestor notabilis. c, 25,000d, Heterolocha acutirostris. d, 25,000d, Philesturnus carunculatus.

No. 1972 — Intl. Reconciliation Year: a, 25,000d, Mother Teresa. b, 25,000d, Pope John Paul II. c, 25,000d, Dalai Lama. d, 25,000d, Mohandas Gandhi.

No. 1973 — Primates and fruits: a, 25,000d, Saimiri sciureus, Anacardium occidentale. b, 25,000d, Saguinus oedipus, Passiflora edulis. c, 25,000d, Callithrix jacchus, Mangifera indica. d, 25,000d, Leontopithecus chrysomelas, Feijoa sellowiana.

No. 1974, 100,000d, Isurus paucus, Carukia barnesi. No. 1975, 100,000d, Euplagia quadripunctaria and caterpillar. No. 1976, 100,000d, Lincoln and U.S. flag. No. 1977, 100,000d, Krishnaswamy Kasturirangan, Insat-3c satellite. No. 1978, 100,000d, Perodictus potto, Tarsius spectrum. No. 1979, 100,000d, Panthera leo. No. 1980, 100,000d, Acinonyx jubatus. No. 1981, 100,000d, Felis chaus. No. 1982, 100,000d, Apis mellifica. No. 1983, 100,000d, Jackie Chan, film actor.

**2009, Mar. 31** ***Perf. 12¾x13¼***

**1958** A341 Sheet of 2, #a-b, + 2 labels 6.25 6.25

**Sheets of 4, #a-d**

**1959-1973** A341 Set of 15 170.00 170.00

**Souvenir Sheets**

***Perf. 13¼ Syncopated***

**1974-1983** A341 Set of 10 115.00 115.00

No. 1958 is dated 2008. Nos. 1974-1983 each contain one 50x39mm stamp.

Nos. 608-610, 714, 717-718, 735, 742, 747, 1488c, 1488e, 1527b, 1527e, 1550b & 1573e Srchd. in Black, Silver, Red and Gold

**Methods and Perfs As Before**

**2009, Apr. 15**

**1984** A93 (8000d) on 50c #714 *1.00 1.00*
**1987** A66 (8000d) on 1.50d #608 (S) *1.00 1.00*
**1988** A95 (8000d) on 10d #735 *1.00 1.00*
**1990** A66 (8000d) on 11d #609 (S) *1.00 1.00*
**1991** A93 (8000d) on 15.50d #717 *1.00 1.00*
**1992** A93 (8000d) on 16d #718 *1.00 1.00*
**1993** A66 (8000d) on 17d #610 (S) *1.00 1.00*
**1994** A95 (8000d) on 18.50d #742 (R) *1.00 1.00*
**1995** A280 (8000d) on 7000d #1527b (S) *1.00 1.00*
**1996** A280 (8000d) on 7000d #1527e (S) *1.00 1.00*
**1997** A305 (8000d) on 7000d #1573e *1.00 1.00*
**1998** A305 (8000d) on 7000d #1573e (R) *1.00 1.00*
**1999** A305 (8000d) on 7000d #1573e (G) *1.00 1.00*
**2000** A265 (8000d) on 10,000d #1488c (S) *1.00 1.00*
**2001** A265 (8000d) on 10,000d #1488e *1.00 1.00*
**2002** A265 (8000d) on 10,000d #1488e (S) *1.00 1.00*
**2003** A294 (8000d) on 10,000d #1550b *1.00 1.00*

**Dated 2009**

**2004** A280 (8000d) on 7000d #1527b (R) *1.00 1.00*
**2006** A280 (8000d) on 7000d #1527e (R) *1.00 1.00*
**2007** A265 (8000d) on 10,000d #1488c (R) *1.00 1.00*
**2008** A265 (8000d) on 10,000d #1488e (R) *1.00 1.00*
**2009** A265 (8000d) on 10,000d #1488e (G) *1.00 1.00*
**2010** A294 (8000d) on 10,000d #1550b (R) *1.00 1.00*

**2011** A93 (14,000d) on 50c #714 *1.75 1.75*
**2014** A66 (14,000d) on 1.50d #608 (S) *1.75 1.75*
**2015** A95 (14,000d) on 10d #735 *1.75 1.75*
**2017** A66 (14,000d) on 11d #609 (S) *1.75 1.75*
**2018** A93 (14,000d) on 15.50d #717 *1.75 1.75*
**2019** A93 (14,000d) on 16d #718 *1.75 1.75*
**2020** A66 (14,000d) on 17d #610 (S) *1.75 1.75*
**2022** A280 (14,000d) on 7000d #1527b (S) *1.75 1.75*
**2023** A280 (14,000d) on 7000d #1527e (S) *1.75 1.75*

**2024** A305 (14,000d) on 7000d #1573e *1.75 1.75*
**2025** A305 (14,000d) on 7000d #1573e (R) *1.75 1.75*
**2026** A305 (14,000d) on 7000d #1573e (G) *1.75 1.75*
**2027** A265 (14,000d) on 10,000d #1488c (S) *1.75 1.75*
**2028** A265 (14,000d) on 10,000d #1488e *1.75 1.75*
**2029** A265 (14,000d) on 10,000d #1488e (S) *1.75 1.75*
**2030** A294 (14,000d) on 10,000d #1550b *1.75 1.75*

**Dated 2009**

**2031** A280 (14,000d) on 7000d #1527b (R) *1.75 1.75*
**2032** A280 (14,000d) on 7000d #1527b (G) *1.75 1.75*
**2033** A280 (14,000d) on 7000d #1527e (R) *1.75 1.75*
**2034** A265 (14,000d) on 10,000d #1488c (R) *1.75 1.75*
**2035** A265 (14,000d) on 10,000d #1488e (R) *1.75 1.75*
**2036** A265 (14,000d) on 10,000d #1488e (G) *1.75 1.75*
**2037** A294 (14,000d) on 10,000d #1550b (R) *1.75 1.75*

**2038** A93 (14,000d) on 50c #714 *1.75 1.75*
**2041** A66 (14,000d) on 1.50d #608 (S) *1.75 1.75*
**2042** A95 (14,000d) on 10d #735 *1.75 1.75*
**2044** A66 (14,000d) on 11d #609 (S) *1.75 1.75*
**2045** A93 (14,000d) on 15.50d #717 *1.75 1.75*
**2046** A93 (14,000d) on 16d #718 *1.75 1.75*
**2047** A66 (14,000d) on 17d #610 (S) *1.75 1.75*
**2049** A280 (14,000d) on 7000d #1527b (S) *1.75 1.75*
**2050** A280 (14,000d) on 7000d #1527e (S) *1.75 1.75*
**2051** A305 (14,000d) on 7000d #1573e *1.75 1.75*
**2052** A305 (14,000d) on 7000d #1573e (R) *1.75 1.75*
**2053** A305 (14,000d) on 7000d #1573e (G) *1.75 1.75*
**2054** A265 (14,000d) on 10,000d #1488c (S) *1.75 1.75*
**2055** A265 (14,000d) on 10,000d #1488e *1.75 1.75*
**2056** A265 (14,000d) on 10,000d #1488e (S) *1.75 1.75*
**2057** A294 (14,000d) on 10,000d #1550b *1.75 1.75*

**Dated 2009**

**2058** A280 (14,000d) on 7000d #1527b (R) *1.75 1.75*
**2059** A280 (14,000d) on 7000d #1527b (G) *1.75 1.75*
**2060** A280 (14,000d) on 7000d #1527e (R) *1.75 1.75*
**2061** A265 (14,000d) on 10,000d #1488c (R) *1.75 1.75*
**2062** A265 (14,000d) on 10,000d #1488e (R) *1.75 1.75*
**2063** A265 (14,000d) on 10,000d #1488e (G) *1.75 1.75*
**2064** A294 (14,000d) on 10,000d #1550b (R) *1.75 1.75*

**2065** A93 (14,000d) on 50c #714 *1.75 1.75*
**2068** A66 (14,000d) on 1.50d #608 (S) *1.75 1.75*
**2069** A95 (14,000d) on 10d #735 *1.75 1.75*
**2071** A66 (14,000d) on 11d #609 (S) *1.75 1.75*
**2072** A93 (14,000d) on 15.50d #717 *1.75 1.75*
**2073** A93 (14,000d) on 16d #718 *1.75 1.75*
**2074** A66 (14,000d) on 17d #610 (S) *1.75 1.75*
**2076** A280 (14,000d) on 7000d #1527b (S) *1.75 1.75*
**2077** A280 (14,000d) on 7000d #1527e (S) *1.75 1.75*
**2078** A305 (14,000d) on 7000d #1573e *1.75 1.75*
**2079** A305 (14,000d) on 7000d #1573e (R) *1.75 1.75*
**2080** A305 (14,000d) on 7000d #1573e (G) *1.75 1.75*
**2081** A265 (14,000d) on 10,000d #1488c (S) *1.75 1.75*
**2082** A265 (14,000d) on 10,000d #1488e *1.75 1.75*
**2083** A265 (14,000d) on 10,000d #1488e (S) *1.75 1.75*
**2084** A294 (14,000d) on 10,000d #1550b *1.75 1.75*

**Dated 2009**

**2085** A280 (14,000d) on 7000d #1527b (R) *1.75 1.75*
**2087** A280 (14,000d) on 7000d #1527e (R) *1.75 1.75*
**2088** A265 (14,000d) on 10,000d #1488c (R) *1.75 1.75*
**2089** A265 (14,000d) on 10,000d #1488e (R) *1.75 1.75*
**2090** A265 (14,000d) on 10,000d #1488e (G) *1.75 1.75*
**2091** A294 (14,000d) on 10,000d #1550b (R) *1.75 1.75*

**2092** A95 (40,950d) on 46d #747 *5.00 5.00*
*Nos. 1984-2092 (91)* *145.25 145.25*

Twenty-one additional stamps were issued in this set. The editors would like to examine any examples.

A342

A343

A344

No. 2097 — Rocket launches: a, 13,000d, Delta II. b, 13,000d, Ariane 5. c, 39,000d, CZ-4C. d, 39,000d, Atlas 5.

No. 2098 — Airships: a, 13,000d, U.S. Navy C-7 over Swiss Alps. b, 13,000d, U.S. Navy ZRS-5 Macon over Friedrichshafen, Germany. c, 39,000d, Italian M.1 airship over Rothenburg, Germany. d, 39,000d, LZ-127 Graf Zeppelin, Ferdinand von Zeppelin.

No. 2099 — Native Americans and wildlife: a, 13,000d, Canis lupus. b, 13,000d, Haliaeetus leucocephalus. c, 39,000d, Haliaeetus leucocephalus, diff. d, 39,000d, Aquila chrysaetos.

No. 2100 — Intl. Year of Science: a, 13,000d, Equus grevyi, Serengeti National Park, Tanzania. b, 13,000d, Haroun Tazieff, vulcanologist. c, 39,000d, Dmitri Mendeleev, chemist. d, 39,000d, Dr. Albert Schweitzer and hospital operating room.

No. 2101 — Fishermen and fish: a, 13,000d, Latimeria chalumnae. b, 13,000d, Anabas testudineus. c, 39,000d, Argyropelecus affinis. d, 39,000d, Pantodon buchholzi.

No. 2102 — Movies starring Charlie Chaplin (1889-1977): a, 13,000d, Modern Times, 1936. b, 13,000d, A Dog's Life, 1918. c, 39,000d, City Lights, 1931. d, 39,000d, The Gold Rush, 1925.

No. 2103 — Submarines: a, 15,000d, 1834 Russian submarine made by K. A. Schilder. b, 25,000d, 1866 Russian submarine made by I. F. Alexander. c, 35,000d, 1881 Russian submarine made by S. K. Drzewiecki. d, 35,000d, 1775 Turtle submarine.

No. 2104 — Intl. Year of Science: a, 20,000d, Carl Linnaeus, taxonomist, taxonomic tree. b, 25,000d, Charles Darwin, naturalist, skulls and depiction of evolution of man. c, 25,000d, Albert Einstein, atoms. d, 40,000d, Richard Feynman, energy sources.

No. 2105 — Cyclists: a, 20,000d, Grégory Baugé, French flag. b, 30,000d, Victoria Pendleton, British flag. c, 30,000d, Simona Krupeckaite, Lithuanian flag. d, 30,000d, Cameron Meyer, Australian flag.

No. 2106 — Shells and pre-historic creatures: a, 20,000d, Tylosaurus. b, 30,000d, Hybodus. c, 35,000d, Ichthyosaurus. d, 35,000d, Eurhinosaurus.

No. 2107 — Nude paintings of mythological or religious figures: a, 20,000d, Birth of Venus, by Amaury Duval. b, 30,000d, Susanna and the Elders, by Alessandro Allori. c, 35,000d, Phyllis and Demophon, by Agnolo di Cosimo. d, 35,000d, Birth of Venus, by William-Adolphe Bouguereau.

No. 2108 — High-speed trains: a, 20,000d, V150. b, 30,000d, Maglev. c, 35,000d, Maglev, diff. d, 35,000d, TGV.

No. 2109 — Intl. Year of Science: a, 25,000d, Wangari Maathai, 2004 Nobel Peace laureate, tropical rain forest. b, 25,000d, Jacques Cousteau, marine conservationist, Tursiops truncatus. c, 25,000d, Nicolaus Copernicus, heliocentric solar system. d, 25,000d, Al Gore, climate change activist, globe.

No. 2110 — North Atlantic Treaty Organization, 60th anniv.: a, 25,000d, B-2 Spirit airplane and dove. b, 30,000d, HMS Bulwark. c, 30,000d, Soldier, child in hospital bed, Red Cross, helicopter and humanitarian supplies. d, 30,000d, Leclerc tanks.

No. 2111 — Pre-historic animals and minerals.: a, 25,000d, Triceratops, Siderite, sphalerite and calcite. b, 30,000d, Batrachognathus, Pyromorphite. c, 30,000d, Caudipteryx, Dioptase. d, 30,000d, Compsognathus, Vanadinite and hollandite.

No. 2112 — Butterflies and moths: a, 25,000d, Attacus atlas. b, 30,000d, Ornithoptera alexandrae. c, 30,000d, Attacus atlas, diff. d, 35,000d, Ornithoptera alexandrae, diff.

No. 2113 — Expedition of Sir Arthur Stanley Eddington to Prince Island, 90th anniv.: a, 13,000d, Forest. b, 13,000d, Mountain. c, 39,000d, Building. d, 39,000d, Beach.

No. 2114 — Dragonflies: a, 15,000d, Libellula depressa. b, 25,000d, Libellula quadrimaculata. c, 30,000d, Enallagma cyathigerum. d, 30,000d, Cordulegaster boltoni.

No. 2115 — Mushrooms, vert.: a, 20,000d, Chanterelle (girolle). b, 20,000d, Hydne. c, 20,000d, Psalliote. d, 40,000d, Xerocomus rubellus.

No. 2116 — Map of Africa, child, handprints, and Postal Union of the Americas, Spain and Portugal (UPAEP) emblem at: a, 25,000d, LR. b, 25,000d, UL. c, 25,000d, Center. d, 25,000d, LL.

No. 2117, 95,000d, Ophiophagus hannah. No. 2118, 100,000d, Concordes in flight. No. 2119, 100,000d, Eddington, 1919 solar eclipse. No. 2120, 100,000d, Astronaut Rakesh Sharma, GSAT-3 satellite. No. 2121, LZ-129 Hindenburg, Ferdinand von Zeppelin. No. 2122, 100,000d, Native Americans around fire, moccasins and pipe. No. 2123, 100,000d, Caranx hippos and fishermen. No. 2124, Chaplin, Ben Turpin, scene from His New Job, 1915. No. 2125, 100,000d, 1904 Russian submarine Delfin. No. 2126, 100,000d, Anomalocaris and shell. No. 2127, 100,000d, Gen. Hastings Lionel Ismay, NATO conference room. No. 2128, 104,000d, Cyclists Michael Morkov, and Alex Rasmussen, Danish flag. No. 2129, 110,000d, Maglev tain, diff. No. 2130, 110,000d, Platecarpus, Vanadinite. No. 2131, 110,000d, Brephidium exilis.No. 2132, 115,000d, The Bath of Venus, by François Boucher.

No. 2133, 100,000d, Signing of 1974 Argel Accords. No. 2134, 100,000d, Man, woman, AIDS ribbon.

***Perf. 12¾x13¼, 13¼x12¾ (#2115)***

**2009, May 29** **Sheets of 4, #a-d**

**2097-2112** A342 Set of 16 210.00 210.00
**2113-2116** A343 Set of 4 47.50 47.50

**Souvenir Sheets**

***Perf. 13¼ Syncopated***

**2117** A342 95,000d multi 11.50 11.50
**2118-2132** A343 Set of 15 18.00 18.00

***Perf. 13¼x12¾***

**2133-2134** A344 Set of 2 24.00 24.00

Nos. 2118-2132 each contain one 50x39mm stamp. Nos. 2114, 2115, 2117, 2118 are dated 2008.

A345

No. 2135 — Pigeons in military service and : a, 10,000d, Soldier lifting pigeon. b, 20,000d, Soldier with helmet, tanks. c, 40,00d, Soldier with hat with pigeon on finger, tank. d, 50,000d, Pigeon in flight, pilot.

No. 2136 — Table tennis players: a, 13,000d, Werner Schlager, Austrian flag. b, 13,000d, Wang Liqin, flag of People's Republic of China. c, 39,000d, Jörgen Persson, Swedish flag. d, 39,000d, Jan-Ove Waldner, Swedish flag.

No. 2137 — Scouts and mushrooms: a, 13,000d, Clitocybe odora. b, 13,000d, Gomphidius roseus. c, 39,000d, Xerocomus porosporus. d, 39,000d, Russula olivacea.

No. 2138 — Lunar satellites and vehicles: a, 13,000d, LRO. b, 13,000d, LCROSS. c, 39,000d, Lunokhod 1. d, 45,000d, Apollo 15 Lunar Rover.

No. 2139 — Dinosaurs: a, 13,000d, Pterodaustro and Alfred Russel Wallace, naturalist. b, 13,000d, Pelorosaurus and Wallace. c, 39,000d, Xiaosaurus and Wallace. d, 45,000d, Utahraptor.

No. 2140 — Israeli history: a, 13,000d, Golda Meir, prime minister, Báb Shrine, Haifa. b, 23,000d, Pres. Chaim Weizmann, Jerusalem skyline. c, 30,000d, Ron Huldai, mayor of Tel Aviv, arms and skyline of Tel Aviv. d, 49,000d, Theodor Herzl, promulgator of Zionism.

No. 2141 — Malaria prevention: a, 13,000d, Anopheles annulipes, blood test. b, 23,000d, Malaria plasmodium, doctor examining infant. c, 30,000d, Malaria plasmodia, nurse treating child. d, 49,000d, Malaria plasmodium, mother holding child for medical examination.

No. 2142 — 2008 Chess Olympiad champions: a, 13,000d, Gabriel Sargissian, Armenian flag. b, 23,000d, Joanna Majdan, Polish flag. c, 30,000d, Maia Chiburdanidze, Georgian flag. d, 49,000d, Peter Leko, Hungarian flag.

No. 2143 — Jewish Nobel laureates: a, 15,000d, Yitzhak Rabin, Peace, 1994. b, 25,000d, Andrew Fire, Physiology or Medicine, 2006. c, 35,000d, Martin Chalfie, Chemistry, 2008. d, 35,000d, Robert Aumann, Economics, 2005.

No. 2144 — Michael Jackson (1958-2009) singer, wearing: a, 25,000d, Black hat at left, white and red hat at right. b, 25,000d, White shirt with straps at left. c, 25,000d, White shirt and pants at left. d, 25,000d, Black hat and pink shirt at left.

No. 2145 — Natural disasters: a, 25,000d, Tornado. b, 25,000d, Earthquake. c, 25,000d, Flood. d, 25,000d, Tsunami.

No. 2146 — Brigitte Bardot, actress, wearing: a, 26,000d, Red brown dress at right. b, 26,000d, Blue dress at right. c, 26,000d, Striped blouse at right. d, 26,000d, Hat at right.

No. 2147 — Paintings by Amadeo Modigliani (1884-1920): a, 30,000d, Cypress Trees and Houses, 1919. b, 30,000d, Seated Nude, 1918. c, 30,000d, Red-headed Girl in Evening Dress, 1918. d, 30,000d, Self-portrait, 1919.

No. 2148, 100,000d, Table tennis player Wang hao, flag of People's Republic of China. No. 2149, 100,000d, Scouts and Clitocybe gibba. No. 2150, 100,000d, Albert Einstein, 1921 Nobel Physics laureate. No. 2151, 100,000d, Jackson, diff. No. 2152, 100,000d, Forest fire. No. 2153, 100,000d, Bardot, diff. No. 2154, 104,000d, Pigeons in military service, diff. No. 2155, 104,000d, Atlas rocket, LCROSS. No. 2156, 104,000d, Tropeognathus and Charles Darwin. No. 2157, 104,000d, Shimon Peres, Israeli president. No. 2158, 104,000d, Malaria plasmodia, nurse treating infant. No. 2159, 104,000d, Chess player Vladimir Kramnik.No. 2160, 110,000d, Jeanne Hébuterne in Front of a Door, by Modigliani.

**2009, July 1** ***Perf. 12¾x13¼***

**Sheets of 4, #a-d**

**2135-2147** A345 Set of 13 170.00 170.00

**Souvenir Sheets**

***Perf. 13¼ Syncopated***

**2148-2160** A345 Set of 13 160.00 160.00

A346

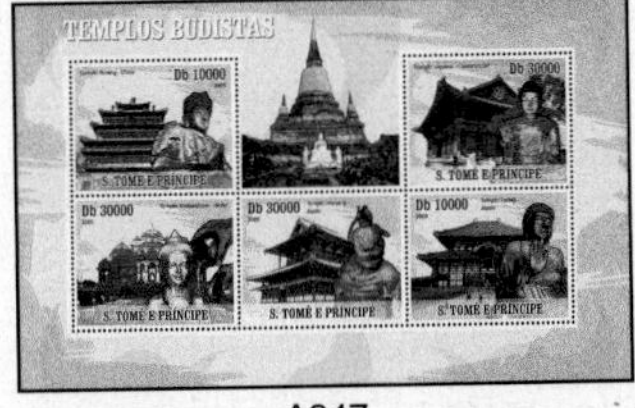

A347

No. 2161 — Marilyn Monroe (1926-62), actress, wearing: a, 25,000d, Green plaid blouse at left. b, 25,000d, Pink bathing suit at right. c, 25,000d, Red dress at right. d, 25,000d, Pink dress at left (hands above head).

No. 2162 — Paul Morphy (1837-84), chess player, and chess pieces: a, 25,000d, Black rook and white pawn. b, 25,000d, White knight and black king. c, 25,000d, White pawn and black knight. d, 29,000d, Black queen and white pawn.

No. 2163 — Mushrooms and orchids: a, 25,000d, Russula paludosa, Stanhopea tigrina. b, 25,000d, Tricholomopsis rutilans, Angraecum sesquipedale. c, 25,000d, Boletus reticulatus, Cattleya intermedia. d, 35,000d, Lentinus tigrinus, Scuticaria steelii.

No. 2164 — African animals and steam locomotives: a, 30,000d, Crocodylus niloticus, 4-8-2. b, 30,000d, Equus quagga, 2-8-4. c, 30,000d, Loxodonta africana, Mallett 0-4-4-0. d, 30,000d, Panthera leo, 4-4-0.

No. 2165 — Buddhist temples: a, 10,000d, Puning Temple, People's Republic of China. b, 10,000d, Todai-ji Temple, Japan. c, 30,000d, Jogyesa Temple, South Korea. d, 30,000d, Akshardham Temple, India. e, 30,000d, Horyu-ji Temple, Japan.

No. 2166 — Foods and flags: a, 10,000d, Tacos, Mexican flag. b, 10,000d, Pelmeni, Russian flag. c, 30,000d, Lutefisk, Norwegian flag. d, 30,000d, Kimchi, South Korean flag. e, 30,000d, Pot-au-feu, French flag.

No. 2167 — Asian military aircraft: a, 15,000d, Kawasaki Ki-61-I, Japan. b, 25,000d, T-50 Golden Eagle, South Korea. c, 25,000d, Shijiazhuang Y-5B, People's Republic of China. d, 25,000d, Mitsubishi F-15J Eagle, Japan. e, 25,000d, Chengdu J-10, People's Republic of China.

No. 2168 — Taekwondo gold medalists at 2008 Summer Olympics, Beijing: a, 15,000d, Sujeong Lim, South Korea. b, 25,000d, Kyungseon Hwang, South Korea. c, 25,000d, Jingyu Wu, People's Republic of China. d, 25,000d, Hadi Saei, Japan. e, 25,000d, Guillermo Perez, Mexico.

No. 2169 — Sea birds and lighthouses: a, 15,000d, Rissa tridactyla, Split Point Lighthouse, Australia. b, 25,000d, Neophron percnopterus, Europa Point Lighthouse, Gibraltar. c, 25,000d, Calonectris diomedea, Cabo Espichel Lighthouse, Portugal. d, 25,000d, Larus ridibundus, Pigeon Point Lighthouse, U.S. e, 30,000d, Fulmarus glacialis, Gumundo Lighthouse, South Korea.

No. 2170 — Asian astronauts and spacecraft: a, 15,000d, Yang Liwei, People's Republic of China, Shenzhou 5. b, 25,000d, Koichi Wakata, Japan, Space Shuttle Discovery. c, 25,000d, Fei Junlong, People's Republic of China, Shenzhou 6. d, 25,000d, Soichi Noguchi, Japan, Space Shuttle Discovery. e, 30,000d, Yi So-Yeon, South Korea, Soyuz TMA-9.

No. 2171, 100,000d, Monroe, diff. No. 2172, 100,000d, Morphy, white king, black rook. No. 2173, 100,000d, Omphalotus olearius, Ophrys holoserica. No. 2174, 100,000d, Giraffa camelopardalis, 4-4-0 steam locomotive. No. 2175, 100,000d, Lama Temple, People's Republic of China. No. 2176, 100,000d, Ackee and saltfish, Jamaican flag. No. 2177, 104,000d, KAI KT-1 Woong-Bee airplane, South Korea. No. 2178, 104,000d, Taekwondo gold medalist Maria del Rosario Espinoza, Mexico. No. 2179, 104,000d, Astronaut Chiaki Mukai, Japan, Space Shuttle Discovery. No. 2180, 115,000d, Fratercula arctica, Sunderland Lighthouse, United Kingdom.

**2009, July 30** ***Perf. 12¾x13¼***

**Sheets of 4, #a-d**

**2161-2164** A346 Set of 4 52.50 52.50

**Sheets of 5, #a-e**

**2165-2170** A347 Set of 6 82.50 82.50

**Souvenir Sheets**

**2171-2180** A346 Set of 10 125.00 125.00

Souvenir sheets of 1 of Nos. 2165c, 2166d, 2167b, 2168b, 2169e, and 2170e with English and Portuguese text exist.

A348

No. 2181 — Medicinal plants: a, 5,000d, Origanum vulgare. b, 10,000d, Angelica archangelica. c, 10,000d, Achillea millefolium. d, 15,000d, Artemissia dracumulus. e, 20,000d, Allium sativum.

No. 2182 — Cetaceans: a, 10,000d, Tursiops truncatus, Balaena mysticetus. b, 10,000d, Unnamed cetaceans. c, 10,000d, Globicephala melas, Physeter catodon. d, 20,000d, Stenella pernettyi, Lithofaga lithofaga. e, 20,000d, Grampus griseus, Megaptera novaeangliae.

No. 2183 — Famous people and their cats: a, 10,000d, Freddie Mercury, rock star, and cats, Oscar and Tiffany. b, 10,000d, Gustav Klimt, painter, and cat, Katze. c, 15,000d, Pres. Ronald Reagan, wife, Nancy, and cats Cleo and Sara. d, 20,000d, John Lennon and Yoko Ono, rock stars, and cat, Pepper. e, 25,000d, Frank Zappa, rock star, and cat, Marshmoff.

No. 2184 — Automobiles: a, 10,000d, 1930 Walter 6B Sodomka. b, 15,000d, 1923-27 Tatra T11. c, 20,000d, 1935 Walter Junior SS. d, 25,000d, 1931 Aero 662. e, 30,000d, 1932 Wikov 40.

No. 2185 — Dogs in military service: a, 10,000d, Dog and soldier with machine gun. b, 15,000d, Dog and paratrooper in dive. c, 25,000d, Dog with soldier with rifle, airplane in sky. d, 25,000d, Soldier holding dog's leash, boxes at right. e, 25,000d, Soldier with dog, tank at right.

No. 2186 — Birds: a, 10,000d, Falco subbuteo. b, 15,000d, Sarcoramphus papa. c, 25,000d, Bubo virginianus. d, 25,000d, Haliaeetus leucocephalus. e, 35,000d, Ninox strenua.

No. 2187 — Charles Lindbergh (1902-74), pilot, and Spirit of St. Louis: a, 10,000d. b, 15,000d. c, 25,000d, Airplane name below airplane. d, 25,000d, Airplane name above airplane. e, 35,000d.

No. 2188 — Paintings by Paul Cézanne (1839-1906) and Pablo Picasso (1881-1973): a, 10,000d, Still Life, by Cézanne, 1892. b, 15,000d, Jacqueline, by Picasso, 1960. c, 25,000d, Nude Woman, by Cézanne, 1898-99. d, 30,000d, The Bathers, by Cézanne, 1890. e, 35,000d, Gardanne, by Cézanne, 1886.

No. 2189 — Paintings by Pablo Picasso (1881-1973): a, 10,000d, Still Life, 1901. b, 20,000d, Nude on a Divan, 1960. c, 25,000d, Study for "Le Dejeuner sur l'Herbe," 1960. d, 25,000d, Les Demoiselles d'Avignon, 1907. e, 35,000d, The Artist and His Model, 1963.

No. 2190 — Farrah Fawcett (1947-2009), actress: a, 20,000d, Holding drink at left. b, 20,000d, With bicycle at right. c, 20,000d, On skateboard at right. d, 20,000d, In black dress at right, 1890. e, 20,000d, Holding handbag at right.

No. 2191, 60,000d, Artemisia vulgaris. No. 2192, 70,000d, Phocoena phocoena. No. 2193, 80,000d, David Bowie, rock star, and cat, Purrie. No. 2194, 100,000d, Fawcett, diff. No. 2195, 104,000d, 1933 Tatra 52 automobile. No. 2196, 110,000d, Sergeant Stubby, military dog. No. 2197, 110,000d, Five Bathers, by Cézanne, 1877-78. No. 2198, 110,000d, Nude Under a Pine Tree, by Picasso, 1959.

**2009, Oct. 20** ***Perf. 12¾x13¼***

**Sheets of 5, #a-e**

**2181-2190** A348 Set of 10 115.00 115.00

**Souvenir Sheets**

***Perf. 13¼ Syncopated***

**2191-2198** A348 Set of 8 87.50 87.50

**Nos. 1400, 1401, 1403 Surcharged in Red**

**Methods and Perfs As Before**

**2009, Oct. 25**

| | | | |
|---|---|---|---|
| **2199** A220 (8000d) on 3500d #1400 | | *1.00* | *1.00* |
| **2200** A220 (8000d) on 5000d #1401 | | *1.00* | *1.00* |
| **2201** A220 (8000d) on 7500d #1403 | | *1.00* | *1.00* |
| *Nos. 2199-2201 (3)* | | 3.00 | 3.00 |

No. 1402 exists with this surcharge but was not issued.

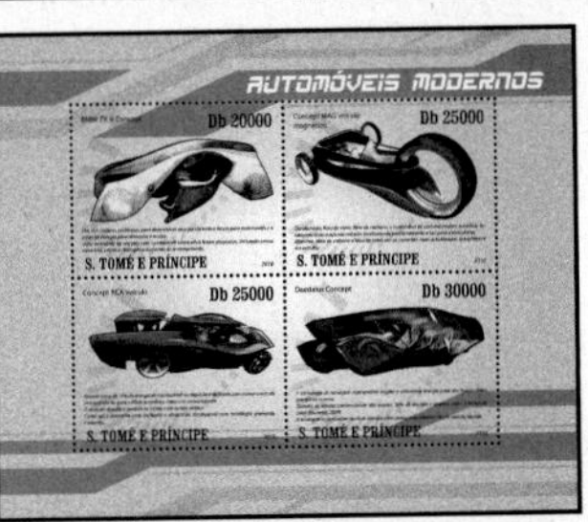

A349

A350

No. 2202 — Futuristic automobile concepts: a, 20,000d, BMW ZC-6 concept vehicle. b, 25,000d, Magnetic concept vehicle. c, 25,000d, RCA concept vehicle. d, 30,000d, Daedalus concept vehicle.

No. 2203 — Princess Diana (1961-97), with: a, 25,000d, Mother Teresa. b, 25,000d, Sons, William and Harry. c, 25,000d, Prince Charles. d, 25,000d, Child.

No. 2204 — Elvis Presley (1935-77) and Presley: a, 20,000d, In boxing trunks. b, 25,000d, Holding microphone stand. c, 25,000d, Dancing with woman. d, 34,000d, With woman, playing ukulele.

No. 2205 — Various Camargue horses: a, 20,000d. b, 25,000d. c, 30,000d. d, 35,000d.

No. 2206 — Eiffel Tower and Concorde: a, 25,000d, G-BOAC. b, 25,000d, F-BTSD. c, 30,000d, G-BOAC, diff. d, 30,000d, G-BOAF.

No. 2207 — Dinosaurs: a, 25,000d, Quetzalcoatlus, Psittacosaurus. b, 30,000d, Dsungaripterus, Troodon. c, 30,000d, Pteranodon ingens, Stegosaurus. d, 35,000d, Pteranodon, Euoplocephalus.

No. 2208 — Papal visit to Africa: a, 25,000d, Pope Benedict XVI holding crucifix, meeting cardinals. b, 30,000d, Pope Benedict XVI walking with African leader. c, 30,000d, Pope Benedict XVI greeting nuns. d, 35,000d, Pope Benedict XVI on airplane steps.

No. 2209 — Writers and poets: a, 20,000d, Johann Wolfgang von Goethe (1749-1832). b, 20,000d, William Shakespeare (1564-1616). c, 20,000d, George Gordon Byron (Lord Byron) (1788-1824). d, 20,000d, Charles Dickens (1812-70). e, 20,000d, Friedrich von Schiller (1759-1805).

No. 2210 — Humanists: a, 10,000d, Pope John Paul II (1920-2005). b, 15,000d, Tenzin Gyatso, 14th Dalai Lama. c, 25,000d, Mother Teresa (1910-97). d, 30,000d, Mahatma Gandhi (1869-1948). e, 30,000d, Pope Benedict XVI.

No. 2211 — World War II airplanes: a, 10,000d, I-16 Type 18 and I-16 Type 24, Soviet Union. b, 15,000d, Bf 109E-4 and Bf 109F-2, Germany. c, 25,000d, Bf 109E-3 and Me 262, Germany. d, 30,000d, Bf 109F-4Z/Trop, Germany, and Mustang P-51D-15, United States. e, 35,000d, TU-25 and SB-2M-100A, Soviet Union.

No. 2212 — Expensive paintings: a, 15,000d, Rideau, Cruchon et Compotier, by Paul Cézanne. b, 15,000d, Portrait of Dr. Gachet, by Vincent van Gogh. c, 30,000d, Garçon à la Pipe, by Pablo Picasso. d, 30,000d, Massacre of the Innocents, by Peter Paul Rubens. e, 30,000d, Dance at Le Moulin de la Galette, by Pierre-Auguste Renoir.

No. 2213 — Chinese film personalities: a, 5000d, Feng Zhe (1921-69). b, 7000d, Wang Xingang. c, 10,000d, Jiang Wen. d, 13,000d, Shangguan Yunzhu (1920-68). e, 25,000d, Qin Yi. f, 40,000d, Liu Xiaoqing.

No. 2214 — Race car, checkered flag, and Ayrton Senna (1960-94), race car driver, wearing : a, 10,000d, Red racing suit (red and white car). b, 15,000d, White suit, holding helmet (red and white car). c, 15,000d, Red suit (black car). d, 20,000d, Red suit (black car). e, 20,000d, Red suit and black cap (red and white car). f, 20,000d, Black shirt (yellow car).

No. 2215 — Pre-historic crocodilians: a, 10,000d, Guarinisuchus munizi, Metriorhynchus. b, 10,000d, Two Metriorhynchus. c, 15,000d, Steneosaurus. d, 20,000d, Two Metriorhynchus, diff. e, 25,000d, Kaprosuchus saharicus. f, 35,000d, Steneosaurus, Guarinisuchus munizi.

No. 2216 — Cats and dogs: a, 10,000d, Chinese crested dogs. b, 15,000d, Cesky terriers. c, 20,000d, Sphinx cats. d, 20,000d, Oriental shorthair cats. e, 25,000d, Devon Rex cats. f, 25,000d, Italian greyhounds.

No. 2217 — Peter Paul Rubens (1577-1640), painter: a, 10,000d, Cimon and Iphegenia. b, 15,000d, Rubens. c, 20,000d, Pan and Syrinx. c, 20,000d, Jupiter and Calisto. d, 25,000d, Rubens Museum Antwerp, Belgium. e, 30,000d, The Judgement of Paris.

No. 2218, 80,000d, Audi O concept vehicle. No. 2219, 90,000d, Presley and two women. No. 2220, 100,000d, Camargue horses, diff. No. 2221, 100,000d, Senna wearing racing helmet. No. 2222, 104,000d, Princess Diana and Tower Bridge. No. 2223, 104,000d, Shar Peis. No. 2224, 104,000d, Pope Benedict XVI kissing infant. No. 2225, 115,000d, The Four Continents, by Rubens.

No. 2226, 100,000d, Oscar Wilde (1854-1900), writer. No. 2227, 104,000d, Bf 109F-4 and B-71 airplanes, Germany. No. 2228, 110,000d, Nelson Mandela, Tockus erythrorhynchus, Tsavorite. No. 2229, 110,000d, Portrait of Adele Bloch-Bauer I, by Gustav Klimt. No. 2230, 110,000d, Metroryhnchus. No. 2231, 110,000d, Zhang Yimou, film director. No. 2232, 115,000d, Eiffel Tower and Concorde G-BOAC, diff. No. 2233, 115,000d, Euoplocephalus and other dinosaurs.

**2010, Jan. 25 Litho.** ***Perf. 12¾x13¼***

**Sheets of 4, #a-d**

**2202-2208** A349 Set of 7 100.00 100.00

**Sheets of 5, #a-e**

**2209-2212** A350 Set of 4 57.50 57.50

**Sheets of 6, #a-f**

**2213-2217** A350 Set of 5 72.50 72.50

**Souvenir Sheets**

***Perf. 13¼ Syncopated***

**2218-2225** A349 Set of 8 105.00 105.00
**2226-2233** A350 Set of 8 115.00 115.00

Antverpia 2010 National & European Championship of Philately, Antwerp, Belgium (#2217, 2225).

African Mammals — A351

No. 2234 — Primates: a, 10,000d, Cercopithecus neglectus. b, 15,000d, Mandrillus sphinx. c, 20,000d, Pan paniscus. d, 25,000d, Lophocebus albigena. e, 30,000d, Pan troglodytes.

No. 2235 — Elephants (Loxodonta africana): a, 10,000d, Adult and juvenile. b, 15,000d, Adult and juvenile, diff. c, 20,000d, Juvenile and two adults. d, 25,000d, Two adults facing each other. e, 34,000d, Two adults walking.

No. 2236 — Whales: a, 10,000d, Megaptera novaeangliae. b, 15,000d, Physeter catodon. c, 25,000d, Feresa attenuata. d, 30,000d, Orcinus orca. e, 30,000d, Kogia breviceps.

No. 2237 — Lions (Panthera leo): a, 22,000d, Female and cubs. b, 22,000d, Female attacking antelope. c, 22,000d, Male, tail at left. d, 22,000d, Two females attacking buffalo. e, 22,000d, Male, tail at center.

No. 2238 — Bats: a, 10,000d, Chalinolobus gouldii, Tadarida aegyptiaca. b, 15,000d, Taphozous mauritianus, Rousettus aegyptiacus. c, 25,000d, Epomophorus wahlbergi. d, 30,000d, Megaloglossus woermanni. e, 35,000d, Miniopterus schreibersii.

No. 2239, 80,000d, Papio hamadryas, horiz. No. 2240, 80,000d, Loxodonta cyclotis, horiz. No. 2241, 80,000d, Orcinus orca, horiz. No. 2242, 80,000d, Panthera leo, horiz. No. 2243, 80,000d, Plecotus austriacus, Hypsignathus monstrosus, horiz.

**2010, Mar. 29** ***Perf. 12¾x13¼***

**Sheets of 5, #a-e**

**2234-2238** A351 Set of 5 60.00 60.00

**Souvenir Sheets**

***Perf. 13¼ Syncopated***

**2239-2243** A351 Set of 5 45.00 45.00

Nos. 2239-2243 each contain one 50x39mm stamp.

A352

No. 2244 — Albert Camus (1913-60), writer: a, 20,000d, Three book covers. b, 20,000d, Smoking cigarette. c, 20,000d, Standing with arms crossed. d, 20,000d, Book covers and Eiffel Tower. e, 20,000d, Monument to Camus, Villeblevin, France, and gravestone.

No. 2245 — Remembrance of Holocaust victims: a, 20,000d, Cupped hands and spiral. b, 20,000d, Menorah. c, 20,000d, Star of David. d, 20,000d, Symbol with crying eye. e, 20,000d, Heart and barbed wire.

No. 2246 — Paintings by Michelangelo Merisia da Caravaggio (1571-1610): a, 10,000d, Self-portrait as Bacchus, 1593-94. b, 15,000d, Narcissus, 1596. c, 20,000d, The Musicians, 1595. d, 30,000d, Supper at Emmaus, 1601. e, Saint Jerome Writing, 1605.

No. 2247 — Steam locomotives: a, 10,000d, Train facing left. b, 15,000d, Wheels. c, 20,000d, Locomotive on bridge. d, 30,000d, Train facing right, telegraph poles. e, 35,000d, Train and African boys.

No. 2248 — Diego Maradona, soccer player, 50th birthday: a, 10,000d, Maradona and World Cup. b, 15,000d, Maradona and flag of Argentina. c, 20,000d, Maradona cheering. d, 30,000d, Face fo Maradona. e, 35,000d, Maradona dribbling ball.

No. 2249 — Moto GP motorcycles and riders: a, 10,000d, Geoff Duke, Gilera motorcycle. b, 15,000d, Valentino Rossi, Yamaha motorcycle. c, 25,000d, Jarno Saarinen, Yamaha motorcycle. d, 30,000d, Daijiro Kato, Honda motorcycle. e, 35,000d, Dani Pedrosa, Honda motorcycle.

No. 2250 — 2010 Winter Olympics gold medalists: a, 10,000d, Simon Ammann, ski jumping, Switzerland. b, 15,000d, Evan Lysacek, figure skating, United States. c, 25,000d, Wang Meng, speed skating, People's Republic of China. d, 30,000d, Jason Lamy-Chappuis, ski jumping, France. e, 35,000d, Andrea Fischbacher, Alpine skiing, Austria.

No. 2251 — Japanese Military Aviation in World War II: a, 10,000d, Japanese airplane. b, 15,000d, Admiral Isoroku Yamamoto (1884-1943). c, 25,000d, Japanese pilots. d, 30,000d, Damaged ships at Pearl Harbor. e, 35,000d, Japanese airplanes.

No. 2252 — Boy Scouts of America, cent.: a, 10,000d, Emblem, Scouts on obstacle course. b, 15,000d, Binoculars, Scouts on rope. c, 25,000d, Emblem, Scouts playing horns. d, 30,000d, Scouts, tents and compass. e, 35,000d, Scout and canteen.

No. 2253 — Firefighting: a, 15,000d, Airplane dropping water on fire. b, 15,000d, Five firefighters. c, 25,000d, Firefighter and truck. d, 30,000d, Helmet and firefighting tools. e, 35,000d, Two firefighters.

No. 2254 — Lighthouses: a, 24,000d, Eddystone Lighthouse, Great Britain. b, 24,000d, Lighthouse and Robert Stevenson (1772-1850), lighthouse builder and civil engineer. c, 24,000d, Ukrainian lighthouse designed by Vladimir G. Shukhov. d, 24,000d, Cockspur Island Lighthouse, United States, Gelochelidon nilotica. e, 24,000d, Kopu Lighthouse, Estonia.

No. 2255, 80,000d, Camus and aerial view of Paris, horiz. No. 2256, 80,000d, The Card Players, by Caravaggio, horiz. No. 2257, 100,000d, Star of David and clouds, horiz. No. 2258, 100,000d, Steam locomotive, horiz. No. 2259, 100,000d, Fire truck, horiz. No. 2260, 100,000d, Casey Stoner, Ducati motorcycle, horiz. No. 2261, 104,000d, Maradona playing soccer and flag of Argentina, horiz. No. 2262, 104,000d, Magdalena Neuner, cross-country skiing, Germany, horiz. No. 2263, 104,000d, Mitsubishi AM-6 Zero, horiz. No. 2264, 110,000d, Boy Scout, tents, emblem, horiz. No. 2265, 110,000d, Pigeon Point Lighthouse, United States, horiz.

**2010, Mar. 29** ***Perf. 12¾x13¼***

**Sheets of 5, #a-e**

**2244-2254** A352 Set of 11 140.00 140.00

**Souvenir Sheets**

***Perf. 13¼ Syncopated***

**2255-2265** A352 Set of 11 125.00 125.00

Nos. 2255-2265 each contain one 50x39mm stamp.

Stamps of the People's Republic of China
A353

Designs: No. 2266, 14,000d, #949 (4f Chinese text). No. 2267, 14,000d, #950 (8f Mao Zedong and text). No. 2268, 14,000d, #951 (8f Mao Zedong waving in crowd). No. 2269, 14,000d, #952, (8f Mao Zedong above crowd). No. 2270, 14,000d, #953 (8f Mao Zedong waving). No. 2271, 14,000d, #954 (8f Mao Zedong leaning on rail, Lin Piao in background). No. 2272, 14,000d, #955 (8f Mao Zedong with arm on rail), horiz. No. 2273, 14,000d, #956 (10f Lin Piao and Mao Zedong reviewing document), horiz. No. 2274, 14,000d, #991 (8f Mao Zedong waving, Chinese text), horiz. No. 2275, 14,000d, #998 (8f Mao Zedong Going to An Yuan).

140,000d, #628 ($3 Mei Lan-fang in opera scene).

***Perf. 12¾x13¼, 13¼x12¾***

**2010, May 5**

**2266-2275** A353 Set of 10 15.50 15.50

**Size: 98x147mm**

***Imperf***

**2276** A353 140,000d multi 15.50 15.50

A354

A355

No. 2277 — Clark Gable (1901-60), actor, in scenes from: a, 15,000d, Gone With the Wind, 1939. b, 15,000d, Manhattan Melodrama, 1934. c, 20,000d, Mogambo, 1953. d, 20,000d, Command Decision, 1948. e, 20,000d, It Started in Naples, 1960. f, 25,000d, San Francisco, 1936.

No. 2278 — Year of the Tiger with diagonal lines at: a, 15,000d, UL. b, 15,000d, LL. c, 20,000d, UR. d, 20,000d, LR. e, 20,000d, UL, diff. f, 25,000d, UR, diff.

No. 2279 — Henri Fabre (1882-1984), aviator: a, 15,000d, Beriev A-40 Albatross hydroplane. b, 15,000d, Fabre's 1910 hydroplane. c, 20,000d, Fabre and plane's propeller. d, 20,000d, Fabre and Notre Dame de la Garde, Marseille. e, 25,000d, Fabre's 1910 hydroplane, diff. f, 25,000d, Cessna TU206D hydroplane.

No. 2280 — Buildings at Expo 2010, Shanghai: a, 15,000d, Canadian Pavilion. b, 15,000d, Israeli Pavilion. c, 20,000d, United Africa Pavilion. d, 20,000d, Hong Kong Pavilion. e, 25,000d, Malaysian Pavilion. f, 30,000d, Swedish Pavilion.

No. 2281 — Count Leo Tolstoy (1828-1910), writer and: a, 15,000d, Tales of Sebastopol, 1855. b, 15,000d, The Cossacks, 1863. c, 20,000d, Wife, Sophia. d, 20,000d, Wife, Sophia, and daughter, Alexandra. e, 20,000d, The Death of Ivan Ilyich, 1886, and stack of books. f, 37,000d, Anna Karenina, 1878.

No. 2282 — Track and field athletes: a, 15,000d, Bryan Clay, decathlete. b, 15,000d, Reese Hoffa, shot putter. c, 20,000d, Meseret Defar, long-distance runner. d, 20,000d, Dwain Chambers, sprinter. e, 25,000d, Dayron Robles, hurdler. f, 32,000d, Veronica Campbell-Brown, sprinter.

No. 2283 — Dinosaurs: a, 15,000d, Alectrosaurus. b, 15,000d, Caudipteryx. c, 20,000d, Gorgosaurus. d, 20,000d, Spinosaurus. e, 25,000d, Plesiosaurus. f, 35,000d, Tapejara.

No. 2284 — Mother Teresa (1910-97): a, 15,000d, Mother Teresa holding child. b, 15,000d, Head of Mother Teresa. c, 20,000d, Mother Teresa holding child, diff. d, 20,000d, Mother Teresa and two angels. e, 25,000d, Mother Teresa and Pope John Paul II. f, 35,000d, Mother Teresa and three putti.

No. 2285 — Brephidium exilis butterfly under magnifying glass with handle at: a, 15,000d, UL. b, 15,000d, Top. c, 20,000d, UR. d, 20,000d, LL. e, 25,000d, Bottom. f, 35,000d, Right.

No. 2286 — Hubble Space Telescope, 20th anniv.: a, 15,000d, Hubble Space Telescope and Lyman Spitzer (1914-97), astronomer. b, 15,000d, Launch of Space Shuttle STS-31. c, 20,000d, Hubble Space Telescope, red violet background. d, 20,000d, Hubble Space Telescope, Eagle Nebula, blue green background. e, 25,000d, Hubble Space Telescope above Earth. f, 35,000d, Hubble Space Telescope and Earth.

No. 2287 — Paintings by Sandro Botticelli (1445-1510): a, 15,000d, The Lamentation Over the Dead Christ. b, 20,000d, The Birth of Venus. c, 20,000d, Madonna and Child and Two Angels. d, 20,000d, Cestello Annunciation. e, 25,000d, Allegory of Spring (Primavera). f, 35,000d, Madonna and Child with Six Saints.

No. 2288 — Lech Kaczynski (1949-2010), President of Poland, and: a, 15,000d, Tupolev TU-154M airplane. b, 15,000d, Flag of Poland. c, 20,000d, Wife, Maria, aerial view and arms of Warsaw. d, 25,000d, Flag of Poland, diff. e, 25,000d, Map and arms of Poland. f, 35,000d, Wife, Maria, and Pope Benedict XVI.

No. 2289, 100,000d, Fabre. No. 2290, 104,000d, Hubble Space Telescope and V838 Monocerotis. No. 2291, 110,000d, Gable and Marilyn Monroe. No. 2292, 110,000d, Tiger, diff. No. 2293, 110,000d, Equatorial Guinea Pavilion. Expo 2010, Shanghai. No. 2294, 110,000d, War and Peace, by Tolstoy. No. 2295, 110,000d, Nodosaur. No. 2296, 115,000d, Ivan Ukhov, high jumper. No. 2297, 120,000d, Mother Teresa holding infant. No. 2298, 120,000d, Self-portrait, by Botticelli. No. 2299, 125,000d, Woman and Ornithoptera goliath. No. 2300, 125,000d, Kaczynski, Pope John Paul II, flag of Poland.

**2010, May 5** ***Perf. 13¼x12¾***

**Sheets of 6, #a-f**

**2277-2288** A354 Set of 12 170.00 170.00

**Souvenir Sheets**

***Perf. 13¼ Syncopated, 13¼x12¾ (#2300)***

**2289-2300** A355 Set of 12 155.00 155.00

A356

A357

No. 2301 — World War II military commanders: a, 15,000d, Field Marshal Erwin Rommel (1891-1944), Germany. b, 15,000d, Gen. Dwight D. Eisenhower (1890-1969), United States. c, 20,000d, Marshal Georgy K. Zhukov (1896-1974), Soviet Union. d, 25,000d, Field Marshal Bernard Montgomery (1887-1976), Great Britain. e, 35,000d, Field

Marshal Friedrich Paulus (1890-1957), Germany.

No. 2302 — Cats: a, 24,000d, Two brown and white tabby cats. b, 24,000d, Brown and white tabby cat, Siamese cat. c, 24,000d, Gray and white cat. d, 24,000d, Three Siamese cats. e, 24,000d, Brown and white tabby cat.

No. 2303 — Butterflies and caterpillars: a, 15,000d, Cethosia cyane. b, 20,000d, Danaus plexippus. c, 25,000d, Papilio polyxenes. d, 30,000d, Siproeta epaphus. e, 35,000d, Antheraea polyphemus.

No. 2304 — Pope John Paul II (1920-2005): a, 15,000d, With hand raised. b, 20,000d, With Pope Benedict XVI. c, 25,000d, Holding crucifix. d, 30,000d, With arms of Vatican City. e, 35,000d, Holding young girl.

No. 2305 — Locomotives: a, 20,000d, Canadian Pacific S3 Diesel-electric. b, 20,000d, Class 53 Diesel, Great Britain. c, 25,000d, DB Class V 200. d, 30,000d, Bombardier AGC B 81500, France. e, 35,000d, CN Diesel, Canada.

No. 2306 — Pin-up art of Paul Butvila, with woman: a, 5000d, With life preserver. b, 5000d, With red cross. c, 5000d, With airplane. d, 10,000d, With mirror having image showing hand holding bra. e, 10,000d, In black dress in spotlight. f, 10,000d, With playing cards and poker chips. g, 15,000d, Wearing necklace, as seen from back. h, 15,000d, With binoculars. i, 15,000d, Reclining, with legs above head.

No. 2307, 110,000d, Tabby cat. No. 2308, 115,000d, World War II soldiers. No. 2309, 115,000d, Heliconius charithonia. No. 2310, 115,000d, Rudolf Diesel (1858-1913), inventor, and EMD FT Diesel-electric locomotive.

No. 2311, 90,000d, Tenzin Gyatso, 14th Dalai Lama and Potala Palace, Lhasa, Tibet. No. 2312, 90,000d, Mahatma Gandhi and Sabarnati Ashram. No. 2313, 90,000d, Reclining Nude from the Back, by Amedeo Modigliani.

**2010, July 11** ***Perf. 12¾x13¼***

**Sheets of 5, #a-e**

**2301-2305** A356 Set of 5 65.00 65.00
**2306** A356 Sheet of 9, #a-i 9.75 9.75

**Souvenir Sheets**

***Perf. 13¼ Syncopated***

**2307-2310** A356 Set of 4 50.00 50.00

***Perf. 13¼x12¾***

**2311-2313** A357 Set of 3 29.00 29.00

A358

No. 2314 — Crustaceans: a, 10,000d, Anonyx nugax, Aristas timidus. b, 15,000d, Leander tenuicornis, Dyastylis glabra. c, 20,000d, Lophozozymus incisus. d, 20,000d, Lybia tessellata, Petrolisthes donadio. e, 25,000d, Leander tenuicornis.

No. 2315 — Intl. Year of Biodiversity: a, 22,000d, Falco punctatus. b, 22,000d, Planting of seedlings. c, 22,000d, Panthera tigris. d, 22,000d, Ursus maritimus. e, 22,000d, Daubentonia madagascariensis.

No. 2316 — Dogs: a, 15,000d, Chinese crested dogs. b, 20,000d, Great Danes (Dogue alemao). c, 20,000d, Samoyeds. d, 25,000d, Australian kelpies. e, 35,000d, Whippets.

No. 2317 — Worldwide Fund for Nature (WWF) stamps of other countries: a, 15,000d, Bulgaria #3401. b, 20,000d, Jamaica #594. c, 20,000d, Maldive Islands #1187. d, 25,000d, Gambia #516. e, 35,000d, South Georgia and South Sandwich Islands #165.

No. 2318 — Robert Schumann (1810-56), composer, and: a, 15,000d, Cover of score for "Papillons." b, 20,000d, Grave monument, Bonn. c, 25,000d, Wife, Clara. d, 25,000d, His house, Germany. e, 35,000d, Wife at piano.

No. 2319 — Oil spills: a, 15,000d, Grounding of the Exxon Valdez, 1989. b, 20,000d, Ixtoc I blowout, 1979. c, 25,000d, Nowruz Field Platform fire, 1983. d, 25,000d, Gulf War well fires, 1991. e, 35,000d, Collision of Atlantic Princess and Aegean Captain, 1979.

No. 2320 — Juliette Gordon Low (1860-1927), founder of Girl Scouts of America, Scouting trefoil, and: a, 20,000d, Dog. b, 20,000d, Three Girl Scout leaders. c, 20,000d, Girl Scouts around campfire. d, 25,000d, Birthplace in Savannah, Georgia. e, 35,000d, Girl Scouts and leaders.

No. 2321 — Korean War, 60th anniv.: a, 20,000d, Zhang Taofang, Chinese sniper. b, 20,000d, Mao Zedong and son, Anying. c, 25,000d, General Douglas MacArthur and officers. d, 25,000d, Chinese Commander Peng Dehuai and North Korean leader Kim Il Sung. e, 35,000d, Negotiators at Panmunjom peace talks.

No. 2322 — Various rabbits and Chinese character (Year of the Rabbit): a, 15,000d. b, 20,000d. c, 25,000d, Rabbit at right. d, 25,000d, Rabbit at left. e, 35,000d.

No. 2323, 80,000d, Cardisoma guanhumi. No. 2324, 100,000d, Ailuropoda melanoleuca. No. 2325, 104,000d, France #2713c and flag of France. No. 2326, 110,000d, Beagles. No. 2327, 110,000d, Zil Elwannyen Sesel #108. No. 2328, 110,000d, Robert Schumann and hands playing piano. No. 2329, 110,000d, Low and Girl Scouts. No. 2330, 115,000d, Deepwater Horizon oil platform explosion, 2010. No. 2331, 120,000d, Wang Hai, Chinese pilot in Korean War. No. 2332, 120,000d, Rabbit and Chinese character, diff.

**2010, Sept. 2** ***Perf. 12¾x13¼***

**Sheets of 5, #a-e**

**2314-2322** A358 Set of 9 110.00 110.00

**Souvenir Sheets**

**2323-2332** A358 Set of 10 115.00 115.00

Stamp Collectors and Stamps of Portugal — A359

No. 2333 — Collector and Portugal: a, #1716 (wildcat). b, #2155 (mouse). c, #1503 (dog). d, #1512 (train). e, #2343f (astronaut). f, #1519 (fire truck).

120,000d, Collector and Portugal #1539, 1540.

**2010, Sept. 2** ***Perf. 12¾x13¼***

**2333** A359 20,000d Sheet of 6, #a-f 12.50 12.50

**Souvenir Sheet**

**2334** A359 120,000d multi 12.50 12.50

No. 2334 contains one 50x39mm stamp.

Miniature Sheets

Chinese Zodiac Animals — A360

No. 2335: a, 10,000d, Rat. b, 10,000d, Ox. c, 15,000d, Tiger. d, 20,000d, Rabbit. e, 24,000d, Dragon. f, 25,000, Snake.

No. 2336: a, 10,000d, Horse. b, 10,000d, Goat. c, 15,000d, Monkey. d, 20,000d, Rooster. e, 24,000d, Dog. f, 25,000d, Pig.

**2010, Sept. 2** ***Perf. 12¾x13¼***

**Sheets of 6, #a-f**

**2335-2336** A360 Set of 2 22.00 22.00

Independence, 35th Anniv. — A361

No. 2337 — Statues of Discoverers and Colonizers of St. Thomas & Prince Islands: a, 10,000d, Joao de Paiva, colonizer. b, 15,000d, Pero Escobar, discoverer. c, 25,000d, Joao de Santarém, discoverer.

No. 2338 — Symbols and maps: a, 10,000d, Map of St. Thomas & Prince Islands. b, 15,000d, Torch, national flag. c, 15,000d, Map of Africa with St. Thomas & Prince Islands circled, building. d, 25,000d, National flag, maps of St. Thomas & Prince Islands, Africa.

No. 2339 — Obverse and reverse of banknotes: a, 10,000d, 5000 dobra note. b, 15,000d, 50,000 dobra note. c, 20,000d, 20,000 dobra note. d, 25,000d, 10,000 dobra note.

No. 2340 — National heroes: a, 10,000d, King of Angolares, orange background. b, 15,000d, King Amador, green background. c, 20,000d, King Amador, yellow background. d, King of Angolares, rose background.

No. 2341, horiz. — Slaves and slave warehouses: a, 10,000d, Slave working on produce drying racks. b, 15,000d, Warehouse. c, 20,000d, Train and buildings. e, 25,000d, Slaves with baskets.

No. 2342, horiz. — Various traditional homes: a, 10,000d, House with painting of dancers. b, 15,000d, Gray house on stilts. c, 20,000d, Curtain in window. d, 25,000d, Blue house on stilts.

No. 2343, horiz. — Beaches: a, 10,000d, Micoló Beach, St. Thomas Island. b, 15,000d, Banana Beach, Prince Island. c, 20,000d, Boats on Café Beach, Ilhêu das Rolas. d, 25,000d, Lagoa Azul Beach, St. Thomas Island.

No. 2344 — Flowers: a, 15,000d, Red flower with stem at bottom. b, 15,000d, Red flower and bud. c, 15,000d, Red and yellow flowers. d, 15,000d, Pink and red five-petaled flowers. e, 15,000d, Red flower, no stem visible. f, 15,000d, Yellow flowers.

No. 2345 — Cuisine of St. Thomas & Prince Islands: a, 10,000d, Plantains. b, 10,000d, Okra. c, 15,000d, Breadfruit. d, 15,000d, Eggplant. e, 25,000d, Calulu de Peixe (fish stew). f, 25,000d, Bananas, diff.

No. 2346, horiz. — Colonial houses: a, 10,000d, House with balcony. b, 10,000d, House with flag. c, 15,000d, House with balcony, sepia-tone photograph. d, 15,000d, House with balcony, colkor photograph. e, 25,000d, House with balcony, diff. f, 25,000d, Road leading to large house.

No. 2347 — Coins: a, 10,000d, 50 centimo coin. b, 15,000d, 1 dobra coin. c, 15,000d, 2 dobra coin. d, 20,000d, 50 dobra coin. e, 20,000d, 100 dobra coin. f, 25,000d, 250 dobra coin.

No. 2348 — Coins: a, 10,000d, 5 dobra coin. b, 15,000d, 10 dobra coin. c, 15,000d, 20 dobra coin. d, 20,000d, 500 dobra coin. e, 20,000d, 1000 dorba coin. f, 25,000d, 2000 dobra coin.

No. 2349 — Agricultural products: a, 10,000d, Yellow cacao pod. b, 15,000d, Green cacao pods on tree. c, 15,000d, Sugar cane. d, 20,000d, Coffee berries. e, 20,000d, Cacao pods approaching ripeness on tree. f, 25,000d, Sugar cane, diff.

No. 2350 — Drawings of people in colonial era dress: a, 10,000d, Woman. b, 15,000d, Man, artist's name at UL. c, 15,000d, Man, diff., artist's name at LL. d, 20,000d, Two women, artist's name at LL. e, 20,000d, Two men, artist's name at UL. f, 25,000d, Man, diff.

No. 2351 — Wood carvings: a, 10,000d, Head and map of St. Thomas & Prince Islands. b, 15,000d, People in rowboats. c, 15,000d, Stylized Africans. d, 20,000d, People and house. e, 20,000d, Statue of woman holding basket. f, 25,000d, Man climbing tree.

No. 2352 — Waterfalls, mountains and rivers: a, 10,000d, Milagrosa Waterfall. b, 10,000d, St. Nicolau Waterfall. c, 15,000d, St. Nicolau Waterfall, diff. d, 15,000d, Vilela Waterfall. e, 20,000d, Foliage near Pico Maria Fernanda. f, 20,000d, Pico Maria Fernanda shrouded in clouds. g, 25,000d, Rio Manuel Jorge. h, 25,000d, Pico Cao Grande.

No. 2353 — Birds and butterflies: a, 10,000d, Speirops lugubris. b, 10,000d, Unidentified bird. c, 15,000d, Ploceus grandis facing right. d, 15,000d, Parrot facing left (incorrectly identified as Ploceus grandis). e, 15,000d, Monarch butterfly. f, 20,000d, Treron sanctithomae. g, 20,000d, Oriolus crassirostris. h, 20,000d, Piombode mato. i, 25,000d, Thomasophantes sanctithomae. j, 25,000d, Prima molleri.

No. 2354, 100,000d, Head of person waving flag of St. Thomas & Prince Islands. No. 2355, 100,000d, Obverse and reverse of 100,000 dobra banknote. No. 2356, 100,000d, First Baron de Agua-Izé Sousa e Almeida, yellow and orange cacao pods. No. 2357, 100,000d, Like #2356, with green cacao pods. No. 2358, 100,000d, Bananas. No. 2359, 100,000d, Okra. No. 2360, 100,000d, Flowers held by gloved hands of woman. No. 2361, 100,000d, Hands of Tchiloli. No. 2362, 100,000d, Wood carving of people and house, basket weaving. No. 2363, 100,000d, Woman in traditional dress. No. 2364, 100,000d, Yellow flower. No. 2365, 100,000d, Bowl of nuts, coconut shells, horiz. No. 2366, 100,000d, National Museum, flag of St. Thomas & Prince Islands, horiz. No. 2367, 100,000d, National Museum, arms of St. Thomas & Prince Islands, horiz.

***Perf. 13¼x12¾, 13¼, 12¾x13¼***

**2010, Dec. 1**

**2337** A361 Sheet of 3, #a-c 5.50 5.50

**Sheets of 4, #a-d**

**2338-2343** A361 Set of 6 45.00 45.00

**Sheets of 6, #a-f**

**2344-2351** A361 Set of 8 90.00 90.00
**2352** A361 Sheet of 8, #a-h 15.50 15.50
**2353** A361 Sheet of 10, #a-j 19.00 19.00

**Souvenir Sheets**

**2354-2367** A361 Set of 14 150.00 150.00

Wedding of Prince William and Catherine Middleton — A362

No. 2368: a, Couple skiing. b, Prince William and Princess Diana. c, Princes William, Charles and Harry. d, Middleton with Princes William and Harry.

104,000d, Couple, coat of arms and castle.

***Perf. 12¾x13¼***

**2011, Feb. 14** **Litho.**

**2368** A362 27,500d Sheet of 4, #a-d 12.50 12.50

**Souvenir Sheet**

***Perf. 13¼ Syncopated***

**2369** A362 104,000d multi 12.00 12.00

No. 2369 contains one 50x39mm stamp.

Internazionale Milan, 2010 Winner of FIFA Club World Cup — A363

No. 2370: a, 1964 team. b, 2010 team, Italian Series A champions, player in foreground running. c, Team members, player in foreground holding 2010 European Champions League trophy. d, Players celebrating 2010 Italian Cup championship, player in foreground smiling. e, 2010 team, Italia Supercup champions, player in foreground kicking ball. f, 2010 team celebratin Club World Cup victory.

150,000d, Javier Zanetti holding Club World Cup.

***Perf. 12¾x13¼***

**2011, Feb. 14** **Litho.**

**2370** A363 25,000d Sheet of 6, #a-f 17.00 17.00

**Souvenir Sheet**

***Perf. 13¼ Syncopated***

**2371** A363 150,000d multi 17.00 17.00

Marilyn Monroe (1926-62), Actress — A364

No. 2372 — Monroe and: a, Men from *Gentlemen Prefer Blondes.* b, Yves Montand and cat from *Let's Make Love.* c, Laurence Olivier from *The Prnce and the Showgirl.* d, Scene from *The Misfits.*
110,000d, Monroe, diff.

***Perf. 13¼x12¾***

**2011, Feb. 25 Litho.**

**2372** A364 25,000d Sheet of 4, #a-d 11.50 11.50

**Souvenir Sheet**

***Perf. 13¼ Syncopated***

**2373** A364 110,000d multi 12.50 12.50

Miniature Sheets

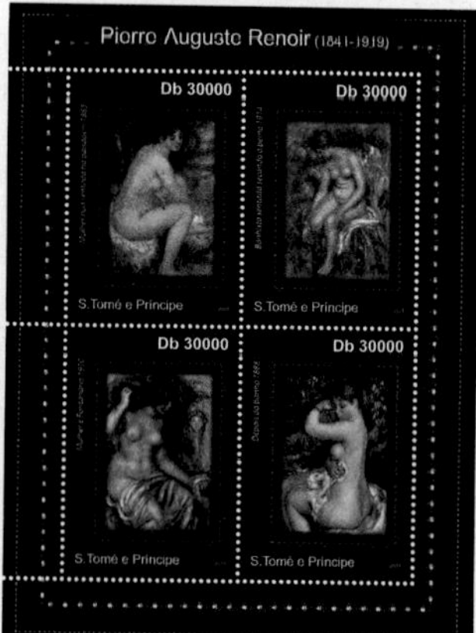


Nudes — A365

No. 2374, 30,000d — Paintings by Pierre-Auguste Renoir: a, Nude in a Landscape, 1883. b, Seated Bather Drying Her Leg, 1914. c, Woman at the Fountain, 1910. d, After the Bath, 1888.

No. 2375, 31,750d — Paintings by Eugène Delacroix: a, Female Nude Reclining on a Divan, 1825-26. b, Mlle. Rose, 1817-20. c, Reclining Odalisque, 1827. d, The Death of Sardanapalus, 1827.

No. 2376, 32,500d — Paintings by Titian: a, Sacred and Profane Love, 1514. b, Venus with a Mirror, 1555. c, Tarquin and Lucretia, 1568-71. d, Venus Anadyomene, 1520.

No. 2377 — Paintings by Peter Paul Rubens: a, 31,250d, Perseus Liberating Andromeda, 1639-40. b, 31,250d, Diana and Her Nymphs Surprised by the Fauns, 1638-40. c, 31,250d, Venus and Adonis, 1635. d, 312,500d, The Three Graces, 1639.

***Perf. 13¼x12¾***

**2011, Feb. 25 Litho.**

**Sheets of 4, #a-d**

**2374-2377** A365 Set of 4 87.50 87.50

Miniature Sheets

A366

No. 2378, 31,250d — Protected animals on Christmas Island: a, Sula sula. b, Pipistrellus murrayi. c, Birgus latro. d, Phaethon lepturus.

No. 2379, 31,250d — Dolphins: a, Lagenorhynchus obscurus. b, Stenella attenuata. c, Cephalorhynchus commersonii. d, Tursiops truncatus.

No. 2380, 31,250d — Peonies: a, Paeonia mascula, subspecies russi, Paeonia officinalis. b, Paeonia daurica, Paeonia wittmanniana. c, Paeonia peregrina, Paeonia cambessedesii. d, Paeonia russi var. reverchoni, Paeonia clusii.

No. 2381, 31,250d, vert. — Birds of prey: a, Buteo lagopus lagopus. b, Falco subbuteo subbuteo. c, Aquila chrysaetos chrysaetos. d, Hieraaetus fasciatus fasciatus.

No. 2382, 31,250d, vert. — Pope John Paul II holding crucifix: a, Wearing zucchetto, facing left. b, Wearing miter, facing right. c, Wearing miter, facing forward with hand raised. d, Wearing miter and red stole, hand raised.

No. 2383, 31,750d — Solar-powered items: a, Meguru electric vehicle. b, NanoSail-D2 satellite. c, Solar panels. d, Solar-powered bus.

No. 2384, 31,750d — Cats: a, Acinonyx jubatus raineyii. b, Acinonyx jubatus hecki. c, Panthera leo bleyenberghi. d, Panthera pardus pardus.

No. 2385, 31,750d, vert. — Cats: a, Felis margarita. b, Felis nigripes. c, Prionailurus rubiginosus. d, Felis chaus.

No. 2386, 32,500d — African animals: a, Mellivora capensis. b, Kobus ellipsiprymnus. c, Phacochoerus aethiopicus. d, Orycteropus afer.

No. 2387, 32,500d — Fish: a, Ostracion tricornis. b, Rhinecanthus aculaetus. c, Holocentrus axensionis. d, Diodon hystrix.

No. 2388, 32,500d — Dinosaurs: a, Xiphactinus, Liopleurodon. b, Tyrannosaurus rex, Archaeopteryx. c, Rahonavis ostromi, Ankylosaurus. d, Stegosaurus, Velociraptor.

No. 2389, 32,500d — Service organizations: a, Paul P. Harris, founder of Rotary International, Rotary International emblem and New Orleans skyline. b, Cattleya rex, Rotary Intenational emblem. c, Map of Africa, African child, Lions International emblem. d, Melvin Jones, Lions International founder, Lions International emblem, New Orleans skyline.

No. 2390, 32,500d — Princess Diana (1961-97): a, With sons, William and Harry. b, Dancing with Prince Charles. c, Wearing sailor's hat, holding African child. d, Holding Prince William, holding flowers.

No. 2391, 32,500d, vert. — Owls: a, Tyto soumagnei. b, Bubo lacteus. c, Bubo leucostictus. d, Scotopelia ussheri.

No. 2392, 33,750d — Indian luxury trains: a, Palace on Wheels (Palacio Sobre Carris). b, Deccan Odyssey. c, Golden Chariot (Bigo Dourada). d, Royal Rajasthan.

No. 2393, 33,750d, vert. — Butterflies: a, Urania sloanus. b, Anaea electra. c, Alcides aurora. d, Chrysiridia ripheus.

***Perf. 12¾x13¼, 13¼x12¾***

**2011, Feb. 25 Litho.**

**Sheets of 4, #a-d**

**2378-2393** A366 Set of 16 230.00 230.00

Souvenir Sheets

A367

No. 2394, 35,000d — Scouts, scouting emblem and butterflies: a, Hibrildes venosa. b, Epicimelia theresidae.

No. 2395, 35,000d — Ships: a, Adler von Lübeck, 1566. b, Gorch Fock, 1958.

No. 2396, 35,000d — Fire fighters and fire trucks from: a, Wagga Wagga, Australia. b, Sapporo, Japan.

No. 2397, 35,000d — Motorcycles: a, Kiwi Indian Retro 30. b, 2009 Harley-Davidson FLHRC Road King Classic.

No. 2398, 35,000d, vert. — Mushrooms: a, Boletus junquilleus. b, Xerocomus badius.

No. 2399, 40,000d — Lighthouses and birds: a, Onychoprion fuscata. b, Diomedea exulans.

No. 2400, 40,000d — Protected species in the Galapagos Islands: a, Conolophus subcristatus. b, Chelonoidis nigra.

No. 2401, 40,000d — Flying dinosaurs: a, Pterodactylus, Anurognathus. b, Pterodactylus, Pterosaur.

No. 2402, 40,000d — Mohandas K. Gandhi (1869-1948), Indian nationalist: a, Waving, with men. b, In bed, young girl sitting on bed.

No. 2403, 40,000d — Maia Chiburdanidze, chess player: a, Playing opponent at right. b, Holding large pawn at left.

No. 2404, 45,000d — Cats: a, Stewie, world's longest cat. b, Scarlett's Magic, world's tallest cat..

No. 2405, 45,000d — Dogs: a, Beagles. b, Airedale terriers.

No. 2406, 45,000d — Minerals: a, Quartz. b, Beryl aquamarine with muscovite.

No. 2407, 45,000d — High-speed trains: a, V150 TGV, France. b, CHR380, China.

No. 2408, 50,000d — World War II aircraft: a, Mitsubishi A5M4 and A5M2, Japan. b, Messerschmitt Me-262A-1a, Focke-Wulf FW-190-A7, Germany.

No. 2409, 50,000d — Yuri Gagarin (1934-68), first man in space, and: a, Vostok 1. b, Floating cosmonaut.

No. 2410, 50,000d — Princess Diana (1961-97): a, Campaigning for land mines elimination in Angola. b, With Zimbabwean Red Cross worker.

No. 2411, 50,000d, vert. — Dogs: a, Alaskan malamute. b, Greenlandic dog.

No. 2412, 50,000d, vert. — Marilyn Monroe (1926-62), actress: a, Leaning backward. b, Leaning forward.

No. 2413, 52,000d — Whales: a, Megaptera novaeangliae. b, Eubalaena glacialis.

No. 2414, 52,000d — Turtles: a, Megalochelis gigantea. b, Chrysemys concinna.

No. 2415, 52,000d, vert. — Butterflies: a, Ornithoptera alexandrae. b, Brephidium exilis.

No. 2416, 52,000d, vert. — Orchids: a, Ansellia africana, Habenaria radiata. b, Calanthe sieboldii, Dracula vampira.

No. 2417, 55,000d — Scouting trefoil and Scouts: a, Hiking. b, Forming human chain.

No. 2418, 55,000d — Ailuropoda melanoleuca: a, Sleeping. b, Eating.

No. 2419, 55,000d — Frogs: a, Gastrotheca cornuta. b, Rhinoderma darwinii.

No. 2420, 55,000d, vert. — Owls: a, Glaucidium californicum. b, Otus asio.

No. 2421, 55,000d, vert. — Mushrooms: a, Amanita muscaria. b, Macrolepiota procera.

No. 2422, 57,500d — Dinosaurs: a, Einiosaurus. b, Medusaceratops.

No. 2423, 57,500d — Red Cross: a, Worker with child, disaster workers, helicopter. b, Worker with child, Worker carrying sack, ambulance.

No. 2424, 57,500d — Wedding of Prince William and Catherine Middleton: a, Prince William at right. b, Middleton at right.

No. 2425, 57,500d, vert. — Fish: a, Regalecus glesne, Lampris guttatus. b, Silurus glanis, Zeus faber.

***Perf. 13¼ Syncopated***

**2011, Mar. 30 Litho.**

**Sheets of 2, #a-b**

**2394-2425** A367 Set of 32 355.00 355.00

A368

No. 2426, 25,000d — Two images of Babe Ruth (1895-1948), baseball player: a, Ruth holding brown bat in image at left. b, Ruth holding two bats in image at right. c, Glove and oversized baseball in batter's box at LR. d, Ruth holding brown bat in image at right.

No. 2427, 25,000d — Bobby Fischer (1943-2008), chess champion: a, Wearing red suit. b, Wearing headband and blue suit. c, Wearing no suit. d, Wearing gray suit.

No. 2428, 25,000d — Sebastian Vettel, Formula 1 race car driver, and: a, Race car at LL. b, Race car above Vettel's arm. c, Vettel kissing trophy. d, Vettel wearing racing helmet at left.

No. 2429, 25,000d — 2014 Winter Olympics, Sochi, Russia: a, Ski jumping. b, Ice hockey. c, Speed skating. d, Snowboarding.

No. 2430, 25,000d — Mohandas K. Gandhi (1869-1948), Indian nationalist: a, Gandhi sitting, Indian flag. b, Kanyakumari Temple. c, Dove, head of Gandhi. d, Gandhi facing left.

No. 2431, 25,000d — Pres. John F. Kennedy (1917-63), and: a, Fidel Castro and Minuteman missiles. b, Wife, Jacquline, and Marilyn Monroe. c, Buzz Aldrin on Moon. d, Berlin Wall.

No. 2432, 25,000d — Queen Elizabeth II: a, Wearing crown at left. b, With Australia #259. c, As young child at right. d, With Prince Philip at left.

No. 2433, 25,000d — London Underground, 150th anniv.: a, 1996 train in Notting Hill Gate Station. b, S8 train, Picadilly Station entrance sign, buildings. c, Docklands Light Rail train in tunnel. d, D78 train in Paddington Station.

No. 2434, 25,000d — Ferdinand von Zeppelin (1838-1917), founder of Zeppelin Airship Company: a, With wife, Isabella. b, Graf Zeppelin in air. c, Hindenburg near ground. d, Hindenburg and hangars.

No. 2435, 25,000d — Space flight of Valentina Tereshkova, first woman in space, 50th anniv.: a, Tereshkova wearing helmet. b, Tereshkova feeding infant, emblem of Vostok 5 and 6. c, Tereshkova and Vostok 6. d, Tereshkova and flight technicians.

No. 2436, 25,000d — Rudolf Nureyev (1938-93), ballet dancer: a, Without hat. b, Wearing ski cap at right. c, Wearing ski cap at left. d, Wearing beret at right.

No. 2437, 25,000d — Louis de Funès (1914-83), actor: a, With thumb touching forefinger. b, With finger touching tongue. c, Wearing costume with neck frill. d, Wearing military uniform.

No. 2438, 25,000d — Richard Wagner (1813-83), composer: a, Playing piano at production of *Tristan and Isolde.* b, And Temple of the Grail from 1882 production of *Parsifal.* c, And Wagner Monument, Berlin. d, And Bayreuth Festival Theater.

No. 2439, 25,000d — Giuseppe Verdi (1813-1901), composer: a, Portrait of Verdi by Francesco Paolo Michetti, musical score. b, Verdi, piano keyboard. c, Caricature of Verdi by Théobald Chartran. d, Verdi in Venice, Verdi's signature.

No. 2440, 25,000d — Jim Morrison (1943-71), rock musician: a, Holding microphone stand, belt visible. b, Two images of Morrison, holding microphone above head at right. c, Two images of Morrison, holding microphone stand at right. d, Holding microphone stand, belt not visible.

No. 2441, 25,000d — Nude paintings by Lucas Cranach the Elder (1472-1553): a, *Lucretia,* 1538. b, *The Three Graces,* 1535. c, *The Silver Age,* 1516. d, *The Suicide of Lucretia,* 1538.

No. 2442, 25,000d — Paintings by Eugène Delacroix (1798-1863): a, *Fanatics of Tangier,* 1838. b, *The Barque of Dante,* 1822. c, *The Natchez,* 1835. d, *Cleopatra and the Peasant,* 1838.

No. 2443, 25,000d — Paintings by Pablo Picasso (1881-1973): a, *Self-portrait,* 1901. b, *Les Demoiselles d'Avignon,* 1907. c, *Three Musicians,* 1921. d, *Still Life with Bull's Head,* 1939.

No. 2444, 25,000d — International Year of Water Cooperation: a, Child carrying water bucket on head. b, Child at faucet. c, Child getting splashed with water. d, Child drinking from bowl.

No. 2445, 25,000d — Year of the Snake: a, Denomination at UL, snake head at LR. b, Denomination at UL, snake head at LL. c, Denomination at UR, snake head at right. d, Denomination and snake head at UL.

No. 2446, 96,000d, Ruth, diff. No. 2447, 96,000d, Fischer, diff. No. 2448, 96,000d, Vettel and race car, diff. No. 2449, 96,000d, Downhill skiing. No. 2450, 96,000d, Gandhi and crowd. No. 2451, 96,000d, Pres. Kennedy and U-2 spy plane. No. 2452, 96,000d, Queen Elizabeth II and scene from her coronation. No. 2453, 96,000d, 1986 train in Canary Wharf London Underground station. No. 2454, 96,000d, Ferdinand von Zeppelin and Zeppelin LZ-11. No. 2455, 96,000d, Tereshkova and Vostok 6, diff. No. 2456, 96,000d, Nurevey and Margot Fonteyn. No. 2457, 96,000d, De Funès and flowers. No. 2458, 96,000d, Wagner, diff. No. 2459, 96,000d, Portrait of Verdi, by Michetti and G clef. No. 2460, 96,000d, Morrison, diff. No. 2461, 96,000d, *Nymph of the Spring,* by Cranach, the Elder. No. 2462, 96,000d, *The Massacre at Chios,* by Delacroix. No. 2463, 96,000d,

*The Weeping Woman,* by Picasso. No. 2464, 96,000d, Child drinking, diff. No. 2465, 96,000d, Snake, diff.

**2013, Mar. 29 Litho. *Perf. 13¼***

**Sheets of 4, #a-d**

**2426-2445** A368 Set of 20 210.00 210.00

**Souvenir Sheets**

**2446-2465** A368 Set of 20 200.00 200.00

Animals and Prehistoric Animals — A369

No. 2466, 25,000d — Rhinoceroses: a, Diceros bicornis facing right. b, Diceros bicornis facing left. c, Adult and juvenile Ceratotherium simum. d, Adult Ceratotherium simum.

No. 2467, 25,000d — Antelopes: a, Gazella cuiveri. b, Gazella spekei. c, Gazella rufifrons. d, Gazella leptoceros.

No. 2468, 25,000d — Cercopithecus mona and fruit: a, Carica papaya. b, Artocarpus rigidus. c, Psidium guajava. d, Annona glabra.

No. 2469, 25,000d — Primates: a, Cercopithecus neglectus, Cercopithecus diana. b, Procolobus badius. c, Two Papio anubis. d, Cercopithecus roloway, Colobus guereza.

No. 2470, 25,000d — Bats: a, Rousettus aegyptiacus. b, Tadarida pumila. c, Taphozous mauritianus. d, Hipposideros ruber.

No. 2471, 25,000d — Cats: a, Leptailurus serval. b, Panthera pardus pardus. c, Acinonyx jubatus and prey. d, Panthera leo and prey.

No. 2472, 25,000d — Loxodonta africana: a, Adult and juvenile. b, Adult and two juveniles. c, Elephants stampeding. d, Two adults.

No. 2473, 25,000d — Dolphins: a, Grampus griseus. b, Steno bredanensis. c, Delphinus delphis. d, Tursiops truncatus.

No. 2474, 25,000d — Whales: a, Feresa attenuata. b, Balaenoptera edeni. c, Kogia breviceps. d, Mesoplodon densirostris.

No. 2475, 25,000d — Birds: a, Sula leucogaster. b, Morus capensis. c, Head of Sula leucogaster and bird in flight. d, Head of Morus capensis. and bird in flight.

No. 2476, 25,000d — Birds: a, Sarkidiornis melanotos. b, Phoenicopterus minor. c, Phoenicopterus roseus. d, Dendrocygne bicolor.

No. 2477, 25,000d — Two Alcedo thomensis: a, Birds sharing prey, denomination at UR. b, Perched bird with fish, bird in flight, denomination at UL. c, Bird on ground at left, bird in flight at right with fish, denomination at UR. d, Two birds on ground, denomination at UL.

No. 2478, 25,000d — Owls: a, Tyto alba. b, Otus senegalensis. c, Otus senegalensis, Tyto alba. d, Tyto alba, Otus hartlaubi.

No. 2479, 25,000d — Apis mellifera: a, Two bees at flowers on branch, denomination in white. b, Two bees on red flower. c, One bee on flower. d, Bee on flower and bee flying near flower.

No. 2480, 25,000d — Butterflies: a, Pseudacraea lucretia. b, Mycalesis sciathis, Myrina marciana. c, Papilio hippocoon, Melantis leda. d, Acraea zetes.

No. 2481, 25,000d — Butterflies: a, Bicyclus dorothea, Hypolimnas salmacis. b, Sevenia boisduvali, Hypolimnas salmacis. c, Graphium angolanus baronis, Leptotes pirithous. d, Precis sinuata, Deudorix lorisona.

No. 2482, 25,000d — Fish: a, Coryphaena hippurus. b, Dactylopterus volitans. c, Histrio histrio. d, Bodianus pulchellus.

No. 2483, 25,000d — Crocodiles: a, Crocodylus cataphractus. b, Crocodylus niloticus. c, Crocodylus suchus. d, Osteolaemus tetraspis.

No. 2484, 25,000d — Turtles: a, Geochelone gigantea. b, Geochelone pardalis. c, Caretta caretta. d, Geochelone sulcata.

No. 2485, 25,000d — Dinosaurs: a, Gorgosaurus. b, Daspletosaurus. c, Dryosaurus. d, Yutyrannus.

No. 2486, 96,000d, Diceros bicornis, diff. No. 2487, 96,000d, Gazella dorcas. No. 2488, 96,000d, Cercopithecus mona and Lycium ferocissimum. No. 2489, 96,000d, Papio anubis. No. 2490, 96,000d, Eidolon helvum. No. 2491, 96,000d, Caracal caracal. No. 2492, 96,000d,Two Loxodonta africana, diff. No. 2493, 96,000d, Stenella frontalis. No. 2494, 96,000d, Megaptera novaeangliae. No. 2495, 96,000d, Morus capensis, diff. No. 2496, 96,000d, Phoenicopterus roseus, diff. No. 2497, 96,000d, Two Alcedo thomensis, diff. No. 2498, 96,000d, Otus senegalensis, Tyto alba, diff. No. 2499, 96,000d, Apis mellifera on honeycomb. No. 2500, 96,000d, Libythea labdaca, Graphium leonidas. No. 2501, 96,000d, Iolaus iulus, Charaxes jasius. No. 2502, 96,000d, Anthias anthias. No. 2503, 96,000d, Crocodylus niloticus and Pluvianus aegyptius. No. 2504, 96,000d, Pelomedusa subrufa. No. 2505, 96,000d, Tyrannosaurus, Edmontosaurus.

**2013, May 10 Litho. *Perf. 13¼***

**Sheets of 4, #a-d**

**2466-2485** A369 Set of 20 220.00 220.00

**Souvenir Sheets**

**2486-2505** A369 Set of 20 210.00 210.00

Birth of Prince George of Cambridge — A370

No. 2506: a, Duke and Duchess of Cambridge with Prince George, blue banner at bottom. b, Princess Diana holding Prince William, Duke of Cambridge holding Prince George. c, Duke and Duchess of Cambridge with Prince George, blue banner at top. d, Duchess of Cambridge holding Prince George.

96,000d, Duke and Duchess of Cambridge with Prince George, diff.

**2013, Aug. 2 Litho. *Perf. 13¼***

**2506** A370 25,000d Sheet of 4, #a-d 11.00 11.00

**Souvenir Sheet**

**2507** A370 96,000d multi 10.50 10.50

A371

No. 2508, 25,000d — Elvis Presley (1935-77): a, With guitar, holding microphone. b, Holding microphone, no guitar. c, With guitar, no microphone. d, Without guitar of microphone.

No. 2509, 25,000d — Marilyn Monroe (1926-62), actress: a, Wearing blue dress. b, Wearing red dress, with Academy Award. c, Wearing potato sack, standing against pillar. d, Wearing blue dress, with Hollywood Walk of Fame star.

No. 2510, 25,000d — Scouts and minerals: a, Scout reading map, Uraninite. b, Scout lifting rock, Orpiment. c, Scouts examining rocks, Emerald. d, Two Scouts, Carbonate.

No. 2511, 25,000d — Scouting trefoil, cats and dogs: a, American Shorthair cat. b, Great Dane. c, Boxer. d, Persian cat.

No. 2512, 25,000d — Rotary International emblem and orchids: a, Cattleya acklandiae. b, Sobralia macrantha. c, Cypripedium lowii. d, Cattleya labiata.

No. 2513, 25,000d — International Red Cross, 150th anniv.: a, Red Cross workers on battlefield. b, Nurse tending to patient with arm in sling. c, Nurse reading newspaper to man in bed. d, Nurse and children.

No. 2514, 25,000d — Pope Benedict XVI and: a, Tiger Woods lily. b, Easter lily with red and white petals. c, Red ginger lily. d, White Easter lily.

No. 2515, 25,000d — Pope Francis and orchids: a, Cattleya walkeriana. b, Vanda tricolor. c, Odontoglossum nevadense. d, Pescatoria lehmanni.

No. 2516, 25,000d — Mushrooms: a, Hygrocybe punicea. b, Amanita phalloides. c, Suillus grevillei. d, Agaricus campester.

No. 2517, 25,000d — High-speed trains: a, Bombardier TWINDEXX Express, Switzerland. b, Talgo 350, Spain. c, Proposed California bullet train. d, West Japan Railways Series 500.

No. 2518, 25,000d — Fire trucks: a, Scania 93. b, Pierce 105-foot truck with rear mount ladder. c, Scania G82M. d, New South Wales Category 11 truck, Australia.

No. 2519, 25,000d — Rescue vehicles: a, Harley-Davidson Ultra Classic fire motorcycle. b, Severn Class lifeboat. c, Christophorus 12 air ambulance. d, Medic 8 ambulance.

No. 2520, 25,000d — Ships and lighthouses: a, Sailing School Vessel Robert C. Seamans. b, Gulden Leeuw, Bremerhaven Lighthouse, Germany. c, Vittoria Lighthouse, Italy. d, Alexander von Humboldt II, Hellevoetsluis Lighthouse, Netherlands.

No. 2521, 25,000d — French people and items: a, Napoleon Bonaparte (1769-1821), emperor. b, Concorde. c, Charles de Gaulle (1890-1970), president. d, TGV Atlantique.

No. 2522, 25,000d — Paintings in Rijksmuseum, Amsterdam: a, *The Milkmaid,* by Johannes Vermeer, 1658-60. b, *Self-portrait with Felt Hat,* by Vincent van Gogh, 1887. c, *The Square Man,* by Karel Appel, 1951. d, *The Merry Drinker,* by Frans Hals, 1628-30.

No. 2523, 25,000d — Paintings by Paul Cézanne (1839-1906): a, *Nude Woman Standing,* 1899. b, *The Blue Vase,* 1887. c, *Self-portrait,* 1882. d, *Bather,* 1887.

No. 2524, 25,000d — Paintings of nudes: a, *Two Nudes,* by Pablo Picasso, 1906. b, *Nude Woman on Green Cushions,* by Pierre-Auguste Renoir, 1909. c, *Seated Female Nude,* by Amadeo Modigliani, 1916. d, *Adam and Eve,* by Tamara de Lempicka, 1932.

No. 2525, 25,000d — 50th birthday of Garry Kasparov, chess player: a, Viewing chessboard with arms folded. b, Wearing red tie. c, Viewing chessboard with hands on head. d, Standing over chessboard.

No. 2526, 25,000d — Guan Tianlang, golfer: a, Crouching, holding putter. b, Swinging golf club. c, Wearing plaid pants. d, Holding golf ball.

No. 2527, 25,000d — Russian postage stamps, 155th anniv.: a, Russia #2. b, Picture post card depicting Yuri Gagarin wearing helmet. c, Russia Nos. 2, 3, 4, 5, 5a, 6, 7 and 11. d, Russia #5266.

No. 2528, 96,000d, Presley with guitar, diff. No. 2529, 96,000d, Monroe and Academy Award, diff. No. 2530, 96,000d, Lord Robert Baden-Powell in Scouting uniform. No. 2531, 96,000d, Scouting trefoil, Italian greyhound, American Shorthair cat. No. 2532, 96,000d, Rotary International emblem and Dendrobium albosanguineum. No. 2533, 96,000d, Red Cross nurse assisting man with crutches. No. 2534, 96,000d, Pope Benedict XVI and lily, diff. No. 2535, 96,000d, Pope Francis and Cymbidium Valley Regent Reggae. No. 2536, 96,000d, Boletus calopus. No. 2537, 96,000d, Italo high-speed train, Italy. No. 2538, 96,000d, Dennis Sabre fire engine, Kent, England. No. 2539, 96,000d, Tanker 910 fire plane. No. 2540, 96,000d, Split Rock Lighthouse, Minnesota. No. 2541, 96,000d, Concorde, diff. No. 2542, 96,000d, *The Night Watch,* by Rembrandt, 1642. No. 2543, 96,000d, *Self-portrait with Palette,* by Cézanne. No. 2544, 96,000d, *Morning Toilette,* by Lotte Laserstein, 1930. No. 2545, 96,000d, Kasparov, diff. No. 2546, 96,000d, Guan Tianlang, diff. No. 2547, 96,000d, Russia #104, 4589, 4779.

**2013, Aug. 15 Litho. *Perf. 13¼***

**Sheets of 4, a-d**

**2508-2527** A371 Set of 20 220.00 220.00

**Souvenir Sheets**

**2528-2547** A371 Set of 20 210.00 210.00

China International Collection Expo, Beijing (Nos. 2526, 2546); Rossica 2013 International Philatelic Exhibition, Moscow (Nos. 2527, 2547).

A372

No. 2548, 25,000d — Wang Yaping, Chinese astronaut: a, Standing in front of capsule wearing space suit. b, At control panel. c, Wearing space suit, waving, parachute in background. d, Waving.

No. 2549, 25,000d — Haroun Tazieff (1914-98), geologist: a, Tazieff and Skutterudite. b, Tungurahua Volcano, Ecuador, andTyrannosaurus rex. c, Karymsky Volcano, Russia, and Pterodactylus. d, Tazieff and Labradorite.

No. 2550, 25,000d — Lions International emblem and: a, Panthera leo, Manis crassicaudata. b, Panthera leo with prey in mouth. c, Panthera leo male, female and cub. d, Male Panthera leo.

No. 2551, 25,000d — Endangered animals: a, Pongo abelii. b, Campephilus principalis. c, Loxodonta africana. d, Lepilemur septentrionalis.

No. 2552, 25,000d — Dolphins: a, Stenella attenuata. b, Lipotes vexillifer. c, Orcaella brevirostris. d, Delphinus delphis.

No. 2553, 25,000d — Birds of prey: a, Pandion haliaetus. b, Strix varia. c, Falco peregrinus. d, Buteo jamaicensis.

No. 2554, 25,000d — Scouting trefoil and parrots: a, Eclectus roratus. b, Ara ararauna. c, Amazona viridigenalis. d, Cacatua alba.

No. 2555, 25,000d — Butterflies and flowers: a, Argynnis paphia, Tulipa gesneriana. b, Danaus plexippus, Hemerocallis. c, Callithea philotima, Alcea setosa. d, Diaethria clymena, Helianthus annuus.

No. 2556, 25,000d — Pope John Paul II: a, Wearing white vestments, St. Peter's Basilica in background. b, Wearing white vestments, doves flying overhead. c, Wearing miter and red robe, doves flying overhead. d, Wearing red robe, St. Peter's Basilica in background.

No. 2557, 25,000d — Nelson Mandela (1918-2013), President of South Africa, and: a, Whitney Houston (1963-2012), singer. b, Princess Diana (1961-97). c, Margaret Thatcher (1925-2013), British Prime Minister. d, Queen Elizabeth II.

No. 2558, 25,000d — Nobel Peace Prize winners: a, Aung San Suu Kyi, 1991. b, Wangari Maathai, 2004. c, Henri Dunant, 1901, and Red Cross flag. d, Dr. Albert Schweitzer, 1952, and Red Cross flag.

No. 2559, 25,000d — James Gandolfini (1961-2013), actor and scenes from: a, *The Sopranos* (with cigar). b, *The Last Castle* (wearing Army uniform). c, *Lonely Hearts* (wearing hat). d, *Cinema Verite* (with beard).

No. 2560, 25,000d — Magnus Carlsen, chess player: a, With knight. b, At chessboard, with hands clasped. c, With knight and queen. d, With Boris Becker, tennis player.

No. 2561, 25,000d — Brasiliana 2013 Intl. Philatelic Exhibition emblem and soccer players: a, David Luiz, Brazil, and Mario Balotelli, Italy. b, Thiago Silva, Brazil, and Shinji Okazaki, Japan. c, Fred, Brazil, and Walter Gargano, Uruguay. d, Marcelo, Brazil, and Giovani Dos Santos, Mexico.

No. 2562, 25,000d — Paintings by Leonardo da Vinci (1452-1519): a, *Lady with an Ermine,* 1489-90. b, *Madonna Litta,* c.1490. c, *Virgin and Child with St. Anne,* 1508. d, *La Belle Ferronière,* 1490-96.

No. 2563, 25,000d — Nude paintings by Peter Paul Rubens (1577-1640): a, *Andromeda,* 1638. b, *Venus at Her Toilet,* 1608. c, *Bathsheba at the Fountain,* 1635. d, *Hélène Fourment,* 1638.

No. 2564, 25,000d — Paintingsby Vincent van Gogh (1853-90): a, *La Mousmé, Sitting,* 1888. b, *Paul Gauguin's Armchair,* 1888. c, *Still Life: Vase with Fifteen Sunflowers,*1889. d, *Café Terrace on the Place du Forum, Arles, at Night,* 1888.

No. 2565, 25,000d — Steam trains: a, Canadian International Limited, Central 4-4-0. b, London, Midlands and Scotland Railway Jubilee locomotive, Somerset & Dorset Railway 4-4-0. c, Indian Railroad 2-8-2, Royal Scot locomotive. d, Paris-Reims Express, South African Railway 4-8-2.

No. 2566, 25,000d — Year of the Horse: a, Horse with front leg lifted. b, Horse bucking. c, Horse in circle of flowers. d, Horse walking to right.

No. 2567, 96,000d, Wang Yaping, diff. No. 2568, 96,000d, Tazieff, Colima Volcano, Mexico. No. 2569, 96,000d, Lions International emblem, Panthera leo chasing prey. No. 2570, 96,000d, Panthera pardus orientalis. No. 2571, 96,000d, Platanista gangetica. No. 2572, 96,000d, Strix varia, diff. No. 2573, 96,000d, Scouting trefoil and Calyptorhynchus lathami. No. 2574, 96,000d, Agrias hewitsonius, Paeonia officinalis. No. 2575, 96,000d, Pope John Paul II and dove. No. 2576, 96,000d, Mandela and Queen Elizabeth II, diff. No. 2577, 96,000d, Dalai Lama, 1989 winner of Nobel Peace Prize. No. 2578, 96,000d, Gandolfini in *The Sopranos,* diff. No. 2579, 96,000d, Carlsen and knight, diff. No. 2580, 96,000d, Brasiliana 2013 emblem, Hulk, Brazil, and Sergio Ramos, Spain. No. 2581, 96,000d, *Mona Lisa,* by Leonardo. No. 2582, 96,000d, *Venus, Cupid, Bacchus and Ceres,* by Rubens. No. 2583, 96,000d, *The Church at Auvers,* by van Gogh. No. 2584, 96,000d, Highland Chief 4-4-2, Flying Scotsman locomotives. No. 2585, 96,000d, Three horses in circle.

**2013, Sept. 10 Litho. *Perf. 13¼***

**Sheets of 4, #a-d**

| | | | | |
|---|---|---|---|---|
| **2548-2566** | A372 | Set of 19 | 210.00 | 210.00 |

**Souvenir Sheets**

| | | | | |
|---|---|---|---|---|
| **2567-2585** | A372 | Set of 19 | 200.00 | 200.00 |

Sports — A373

No. 2586, 19,000d — Cricket players: a, Hashim Amla. b, Michael John Clarke. c, Alastair Cook. d, Sachin Tendulkar.

No. 2587, 19,000d — Table tennis players: a, Timo Boll. b, Ma Long. c, Xu Xin. d, Liu Shiwen.

No. 2588, 75,000d, Cricket ball. No. 2589, 75,000d, Table tennis ball and paddles.

**2013, Dec. 10 Litho. *Perf.***

**Sheets of 4, #a-d**

| | | | | |
|---|---|---|---|---|
| **2586-2587** | A373 | Set of 2 | 17.00 | 17.00 |

**Souvenir Sheets**

| | | | | |
|---|---|---|---|---|
| **2588-2589** | A373 | Set of 2 | 17.00 | 17.00 |

A374

No. 2590, 20,000d — Ursus maritimus: a, Adult walking. b, Adult and juvenile. c, Two adults fighting. d, Adult resting.

No. 2591, 20,000d — Gorillas: a, Adult and juvenile Gorilla gorilla gorilla. b, Adult Gorilla gorilla. c, Adult Gorilla gorilla gorilla sitting on rock. d, Adult and juvenile Gorilla beringei beringei.

No. 2592, 20,000d — Marine life: a, Megaptera novaeangliae. b, Makaira nigricans. c, Aluterus scriptus. d, Tursiops truncatus.

No. 2593, 20,000d — Tropical fish: a, Pseudanthias pleurotaenia. b, Ctenochaetus hawaiiensis. c, Ostracion cubicus. d, Symphysodon discus.

No. 2594, 20,000d — Extinct and endangered birds: a, Columba versicolor. b, Rhipidura rufifrons. c, Pyrocephalus rubinus. d, Porphyrio coerulescens.

No. 2595, 20,000d — Mao Zedong (1893-1976), Chinese communist leader: a, With soldiers and peasants, flag at right. b, With young girl. c, Clapping. d, Waving, flag in background.

No. 2596, 20,000d — African trains: a, Blue Train, South Africa. b, Pride of Africa. c, Class 25NC 4-8-4, South Africa. d, Class 19E, South Africa.

No. 2597, 20,000d — Christmas paintings: a, *Adoration of the Shepherds,* by Charles Le Brun. b, *Nativity,* by Piero della Francesca. c, *Nativity,* by Giotto. d, *Nativity,* by Lorenzo Lotto.

No. 2598, 25,000d — 2013 International Track and Field Championships, Moscow: a, Valerie Adams, shot putter, flag of New Zealand. b, LaShawn Merritt, sprinter, flag of U.S. c, Aleksandr Menkov, long jumper, flag of Russia. d, Pawel Fajdek, hammer thrower, flag of Poland.

No. 2599, 25,000d — Owls: a, Tyto capensis. b, Bubo lacteus. c, Otus ireneae. d, Ninox superciliaris.

No. 2600, 25,000d — Scouting trefoil and turtles: a, Batagur trivittata. b, Pseudemys peninsularis. c, Indotestudo elongata. d, Pseudemys rubriventris.

No. 2601, 25,000d — Paintings by Pierre-Auguste Renoir (1841-1919): a, *Gabrielle with Open Blouse,* 1907. b, *Algiers Landscape,* 1895. c, *Anemones,* 1909. d, *After the Bath,* 1888.

No. 2602, 25,000d — Impressionist paintings: a, *Paris Street, Rainy Day,* by Gustave Caillebotte, 1877. b, *Woman with Umbrella,* by Claude Monet, 1875. c, *A Bar at the Folies-Bergère,* by Edouard Manet, 1881-82. d, *The Dance Class,* by Edgar Degas, 1874.

No. 2603, 25,000d — Composers: a, Johann Sebastian Bach (1685-1750). b, Franz Liszt (1811-86). c, Franz Schubert (1797-1828). d, Johannes Brahms (1833-97).

No. 2604, 25,000d — Japanese high-speed trains: a, E5 Series Shinkansen. b, E6 Series Shinkansen. c, 500 Series Shinkansen. d, N700-7000 Series Sakura Shinkansen.

No. 2605, 25,000d — Yuri Gagarin (1934-68), first man in space: a, At left, wearing space helmet. b, Waving. c, Laughing, rocket launch in background. d, At right, wearing space helmet.

No. 2606, 25,000d — Future space flight: a, Space plane with foldable wings. b, Martian lander. c, Asteroid redirection mission. d, Satellite with solar panels at sides.

No. 2607, 79,000d, Ursus maritimus, diff. No. 2608, 79,000d, Gorilla beringei graueri. No. 2609, 79,000d, Sphyrna lewini. No. 2610, 79,000d, Chaetodon capistratus. No. 2611, 79,000d, Vanellus macropterus. No. 2612, 79,000d, Mao Zedong, mountains. No. 2613, 79,000d, Shosholoza Meyl train, South Africa. No. 2614, 79,000d, *Holy Family,* by El Greco. No. 2615, 96,000d, Svetlana Shkolina, high jumper, flag of Russia. No. 2616, 96,000d, Bubo ascalaphus. No. 2617, 96,000d, Scouting trefoil and Leucocephalon yuwonoi. No. 2618, 96,000d, *Self-portrait,* by Renoir, 1876. No. 2619, 96,000d, *Little Italian Street Singer,* by Jean Frédéric Bazille. No. 2620, 96,000d, Joseph Haydn (1732-1809), composer. No. 2621, 96,000d, Series E6 Shinkansen, diff. No. 2622, 96,000d, Gagarin with Valentina Tereshkova, cosmonaut. No. 2623, 96,000d, Mars rocket.

**2013, Dec. 10 Litho. *Perf. 13¼***

**Sheets of 4, #a-d**

| | | | | |
|---|---|---|---|---|
| **2590-2606** | A374 | Set of 17 | 175.00 | 175.00 |

**Souvenir Sheets**

| | | | | |
|---|---|---|---|---|
| **2607-2623** | A374 | Set of 17 | 170.00 | 170.00 |

A375

A376

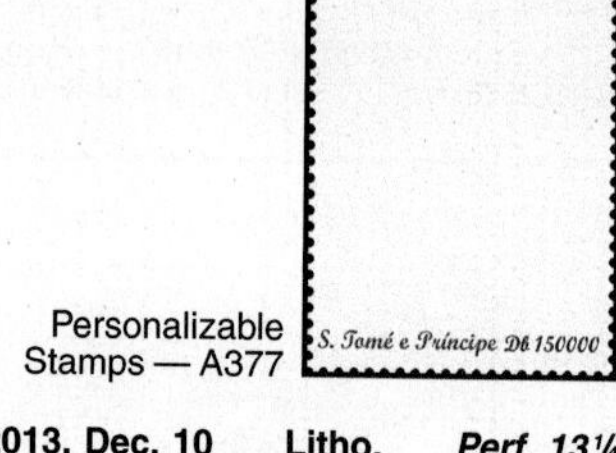


Personalizable Stamps — A377

**2013, Dec. 10 Litho. *Perf. 13¼***

| | | | | |
|---|---|---|---|---|
| **2624** | A375 | 25,000d multi | 3.00 | 3.00 |
| | | ***Perf. 12¾*** | | |
| **2625** | A376 | 50,000d multi | 5.75 | 5.75 |
| | | ***Perf. 13¼x13*** | | |
| **2626** | A377 | 150,000d multi | 17.00 | 17.00 |
| | | *Nos. 2624-2626 (3)* | 25.75 | 25.75 |

Nos. 2624-2626 could be personalized. The stamps exist with a St. Thomas & Prince Islands flag printed in the vignette portion.

Nelson Mandela (1918-2013), President of South Africa — A378

No. 2627 — Mandela wearing: a, Gray suit and tie, b, Yellow and black shirt. c, Dark blue jacket. d, Sports jersey.

96,000d, Black suit jacket with sash.

**2014, Jan. 30 Litho. *Perf. 13¼***

| | | | | |
|---|---|---|---|---|
| **2627** | A378 | 25,000d Sheet of 4, #a-d | 11.00 | 11.00 |

**Souvenir Sheet**

| | | | | |
|---|---|---|---|---|
| **2628** | A378 | 96,000d multi | 10.50 | 10.50 |

A379

No. 2629, 25,000d — USS Nautilus: a, With crew on top of submarine, flag painted on bow. b, Aerial view. c, Nuclear reactor. d, Submarine leaving wake.

No. 2630, 25,000d — Charles A. Lindbergh (1902-74), aviator: a, Medal of Honor. b, Spirit of St. Louis in flight. c, Bourguet Airport Statue, U.S. #C10. d, Wearing helmet, Spirit of St. Louis in flight.

No. 2631, 25,000d — Adolphe Sax (1814-94), inventor of saxophone, wearing: a, Blue jacket. b, Green jacket. c, Red vest. d, Purple jacket.

No. 2632, 25,000d — Louis Lumière (1864-1948), first filmmaker: a, With brother, Auguste. b, Operating projector at Eden Theater. c, Inspecting film. d, With Walt Disney.

No. 2633, 25,000d — Charlie Chaplin (1889-1977), film actor: a, In *City Lights,* 1931. b, Behind camera. c, In *One A.M.,* 1916. d, In *The Great Dictator,* 1940.

No. 2634, 25,000d — Dorothy Lamour (1914-96), actress: a, In *Road to Rio,* 1947. b, In front of P-51D Mustang. c, With U.S. flag. d, In *Typhoon,* 1940.

No. 2635, 25,000d — Jawaharlal Nehru (1889-1964), Prime Minister of India, and: a, Queen Elizabeth II. b, Mahatma Gandhi. c, Mother Teresa. d, Albert Einstein.

No. 2636, 25,000d — Ayrton Senna (1960-94), race car driver: a, Wearing cap. b, Wearing racing suit, cars in background. c, Sitting next to helmet. d, Wearing balaclava.

No. 2637, 25,000d — Louis Renault (1877-1944), automobile manufacturer, and: a, Renault Nervastella. b, Renault Type A. c, Renault Type KZ. d, Renault Reinastella.

No. 2638, 25,000d — Eusebio da Silva Ferreira (1942-2014), Brazilian soccer player: a, Preparing to head ball. b, Sitting with ball. c, With Pelé. d, Preparing to kick ball.

No. 2639, 25,000d — 2014 World Cup Soccer Championships, Brazil: a, Purple player. b, Sepia player. c, Green player. d, Blue player.

No. 2640, 25,000d — Opening of Forth Road Bridge, Scotland, 50th anniv: a, Bridge, Sterna paradisaea. b,Queen Elizabeth II, opening of bridge. c, Construction of bridge. d, Bridge under construction, Sterna sandvicensis.

No. 2641, 25,000d — World War I, cent.: a, Bristol F.2b fighter, HMS Caesar, Great Britain. b, Aviatik (Berg) D.I. fighter, SMS Radetzky, Austria-Hungary. c, Sikorsky S-16 fighter, Frunze, Russia. d, Halberstadt CL.IV airplane, SMS Helgoland, Germany.

No. 2642, 25,000d — Paintings by Lavinia Fontana (1552-1614): a, Christ with the Symbols of Passion, 1581. b, Portrait of Constanza Alidosi, 1594. c, Portrait of a Lady with Lap Dog, 1590. d, Holy Family with Saints, 1578.

No. 2643, 25,000d — Paintings by Paul Cézanne (1839-1906): a, Still Life with Apples, 1893-94. b, Self-portrait, 1878-80. c, Pierrot and Harlequin, 1888. d, Fruit and Jug on a Table, 1894.

No. 2644, 25,000d — Paintings by Henri de Toulouse-Lautrec (1864-1901): a, Horsemen Riding in the Bois de Boulogne, 1888. b, Reine de Joie, 1892. c, The Passenger in Cabin 54, 1896. d, Fashionable People at Les Ambassadeurs, 1893.

No. 2645, 25,000d — Paintings by Wassily Kandinsky (1866-1944): a, Cemetery and Vicarage in Kochel, 1909. b, The Singer, 1903. c, Points, 1920. d, Colorful Ensemble, 1938.

No. 2646, 25,000d — Paintings by Henri Matisse (1869-1954): a, Portrait of Madame Matisse, 1905. b, Open Window, Collioure, 1905. c, A Glimpse of Notre Dame in the Late Afternoon, 1902. d, Self-portrait, 1906.

No. 2647, 25,000d — Paintings by Salvador Dalí (1904-89): a, Millet's Architectonic Angelus, 1933. b, Galatea of the Spheres, 1952. c, The Ship, 1943. d, Apparition of Face and Fruit Dish on a Beach, 1938.

No. 2648, 25,000d — Red List of Threatened Species, 50th anniv.: a, Strix uralensis. b, Cyanoramphus unicolor. c, Leontopithecus rosalia. d, Panthera uncia.

No. 2649, 96,000d, USS Nautilus, Adm. Hyman G. Rickover. No. 2650, 96,000d, Lindbergh, route of transatlantic flight. No. 2651, 96,000d, Adolphe Sax and saxophones. No. 2652, 96,000d, Lumiere holding film strip. No. 2653, 96,000d, Chaplin as the Little Tramp. No. 2654, 96,000d, Lamour and Jon Hall in *The Hurricane,* 1937. No. 2655, 96,000d, Nehru and Gandhi, diff. No. 2656, 96,000d, Senna, diff. No. 2657, 96,000d, Renault Type B. No. 2658, 96,000d, Eusebio holding Golden Boot award. No. 2659, 96,000d, Soccer ball, brown player. No. 2660, 96,0000d, Forth Road Bridge, Morus bassanus. No. 2661, 96,000d, Thomas-Morse S-4 airplane, U.S., HIJMS Aki, Japan. No. 2662, 96,000d, Holy Family with St. Catherine of Alexandria, by Fontana, 1581. No. 2663, 96,000d, Madame Cézanne in a Red Armchair, by Cézanne, 1877. No. 2664, 96,000d, Chau U Kao, Chinese Clown, Seated, by Toulouse-Lautrec, 1896. No. 2665, 96,000d, Orange, by Kandinsky, 1923. No. 2666, 96,000d, Woman with a Hat, by Matisse, 1905. No. 2667, 96,000d, The Hallucinogenic Toreador, by Dalí, 1968-70. No. 2668, 96,000d, Tarsius sangirensis.

**2014, Mar. 25 Litho. *Perf. 13¼***

**Sheets of 4, #a-d**

**2629-2648** A379 Set of 20 225.00 225.00

**Souvenir Sheets**

**2649-2668** A379 Set of 20 215.00 215.00

Worldwide Fund for Nature (WWF) A380

No. 2669 — Halcyon malimbica: a, Head. b, On horizontal branch, c, On rock. d, In flight.

96,000d, Halcyon malimbica looking over right wing.

**2014, Aug. 8 Litho. *Perf. 13x13¼***

| | | | |
|---|---|---|---|
| **2669** | Horiz. strip of 4 | 11.00 | 11.00 |
| *a.-d.* | A380 25,000d Any single | 2.75 | 2.75 |
| *e.* | Souvenir sheet of 4, #2669a-2669d | 11.00 | 11.00 |
| *f.* | Souvenir sheet of 8, 2 each #2669a-2669d, + central label | 22.00 | 22.00 |

**Souvenir Sheet**

***Perf. 12¾x13¼***

**2670** A380 96,000d multi 10.50 10.50

No. 2670 contains one 50x39mm stamp.

2014 World Cup Soccer Championships, Brazil — A381

No. 2671: a, Player kicking ball into net, names of four countries in white. b, Soccer ball, names of four countries in white. c, As "b," names of four countries in blue. d, As "a," names of four countries in blue.

96,000d, World Cup trophy, flags of four countries.

**Litho. With Foil Application, Litho. (#2671b, 2671c)**

**2014, Aug. 8 *Perf. 13¼***

**2671** A381 25,000d Sheet of 4, #a-d 11.00 11.00

**Souvenir Sheet**

**2672** A381 96,000d multi 10.50 10.50

A382

No. 2673, 25,000d — Giant Pandas: a, Ailuropoda melanoleuca, bamboo at right. b, Ailuropoda melanoleuca hanging from branch. c, Two Ailuropoda melanoleuca. d, Ailuropoda melanoleuca qinlingensis.

No. 2674, 25,000d — Dolphins: a, Cephalorhynchus hectori. b, Inia geoffrensis. c, Delphinus delphis. d, Platanista gangetica.

No. 2675, 25,000d — Owls: a, Strix nebulosa. b, Bubo scandiacus. c, Bubo bubo. d, Tyto alba.

No. 2676, 25,000d — Eagles: a, Harpia harpyja. b, Haliaeetus leucocephalus. c, Haliaeetus vocifer. d, Pithecophaga jefferyi.

No. 2677, 25,000d — Butterflies: a, Polyommatus icarus. b, Pieris brassicae. c, Delias eucharis. d, Vanessa atalanta, Polyradicion lindenii.

No. 2678, 25,000d — Turtles: a, Clemmys guttata. b, Macroclemys temminckii. c, Trionyx spiniferus. d, Geochelone sulcata.

No. 2679, 25,000d — Dinosaurs: a, Thyreophora. b, Allosaurus. c, Triceratops. d, Pachycephalosaurus.

No. 2680, 25,000d — Orchids: a, Cattleya hardyana. b, Angraecum sesquipedale. c, Burrageara Stefan Isler. d, Dendrobium chrysotoxum.

No. 2681, 25,000d — Mushrooms: a, Pleurotus eryngii. b, Boletus edulis. c, Cantharellus cibarius. d, Flammulina velutipes.

No. 2682, 25,000d — Minerals: a, Stibnite (estibina). b, Rhodochrosite (rodocrosita). c, Hutchinsonite. d, Torbernite.

No. 2683, 25,000d — Deng Xiaoping (1904-97), leader of People's Republic of China: a, Reading, flag in background. b, With Mao Zedong, train and city skyline in background. c, With Mao Zedong and other Chinese officials, flag across table. d, With Pres. Jimmy Carter, map in background.

No. 2684, 25,000d — Canonized popes: a, Pope John Paul II, wearing miter. b, Pope John XXIII, wearing red and white cap. c, Pope John Paul II, wearing zucchetto. d, Pope John XXIII, wearing zucchetto.

No. 2685, 25,000d — Fire engines: a, 1917 Glendale. b, Dennis 4 FJH 324. c, HME 34C. d, Pierce.

No. 2686, 25,000d — Airships: a, NS Airships NS11. b, N-Class ZPG-2. c, Goodyear ZPG-3W (N Class). d, MZ-3A.

No. 2687, 25,000d — Chinese high-speed trains: a, CRH3. b, CRH1, facing left. c, CRH1, facing right. d, CRH2.

No. 2688, 25,000d — Lighthouses: a, Longstone Lighthouse, Great Britain. b, Alexandria Lighthouse, Egypt. c, Portland Head Lighthouse, U.S. d, Bonaire Lighthouse, Caribbean Netherlands.

No. 2689, 25,000d — Worldwide Fund for Nature postage stamps: a, Viet Nam #3392, Cook Islands #1412. b, Hungary #2798, Liechtenstein, #1525h. c, Russia ##5543, Indonesia #1911. d, Russia #6178, Benin #1086c without denomination.

No. 2690, 25,000d — 2014 Winter Olympics, Sochi, Russia: a, Alpine skiing. b, Snowboarding. c, Ice hockey. d, Figure skating.

No. 2691, 96,000d, Ailuropoda melanoleuca rolling with foot up to mouth. No. 2692, 96,000d, Tursiops truncatus. No. 2693, 96,000d, Strix varia. No. 2694, 96,000d, Haliaeetus pelagicus. No. 2695, 96,000d, Aglais urticae. No. 2696, 96,000d, Eretmochelys imbricata. No. 2697, 96,000d, Tyrannosaurus rex. No. 2698, 96,000d, Cattleya aurea statteriana. No. 2699, 96,000d, Leccinum aurantiacum. No. 2700, 96,000d, Galena. No. 2701, 96,000d, Deng Xiaoping, train. No. 2702, 96,000d, Pope John Paul II, wearing miter, diff. No. 2703, 96,000d, Fire truck, diff. No. 2704, 96,000d, Zeppelin NT. No. 2705, 96,000d, CRH2, diff. No. 2706, 96,000d, Tourlitis Lighthouse, Greece. No. 2707, 96,000d, British Guiana #13. No. 2708, 96,000d, Biathlon.

**2014, Aug. 8 Litho. *Perf. 13¼***

**Sheets of 4, #a-d**

**2673-2690** A382 Set of 18 195.00 195.00

**Souvenir Sheets**

**2691-2708** A382 Set of 18 185.00 185.00

Nos. 2677, 2680, 2695 and 2698 are impregnated with a floral scent.

Miniature Sheets

Coastal Views — A383

Buildings and Streets — A384

Designs as shown.

**2014, Sept. 15 Litho. *Perf. 13¼***

| | | | | | |
|---|---|---|---|---|---|
| **2709** | A383 | 22,000d | Sheet of 8, #a-h | 18.00 | 18.00 |
| **2710** | A384 | 25,000d | Sheet of 8, #a-h | 21.00 | 21.00 |

See Nos. 2831-2832.

A385

No. 2711, 25,000d — Phascolarctos cinereus (koala): a, Adult carrying juvenile on back. b, Adult sitting in tree. c, Adult holding juvenile. d, Adult climbing tree.

No. 2712, 25,000d — Wolves: a, Canis lupus howling. b, Canis lupus lupus in snow. c,Two canis lupus. d, Canis lupus arctos on rock.

No. 2713, 25,000d — Panthera uncia (snow leopard): a, Walking on ice, mouth closed. b, Sitting near rocks. c, Head. d, Walking on snow, mouth open.

No. 2714, 25,000d — Sled dogs (caes de trenó): a, Three white dogs pulling sled. b, Two dogs with red harnesses. c, Two dogs pulling sled. d, Two dogs with blue and yellow harnesses.

No. 2715, 25,000d — Orcinus orca (killer whales): a, Two whales leaping, heads facing right. b, Whale facing right with open mouth. c, Two whales leaping, heads facing left. d, Whale facing left with open mouth.

No. 2716, 25,000d — Sagittarius serpentarius (secretary bird): a, In tree. b, Head. c, In flight. d, Walking left.

No. 2717, 25,000d — Pheasants: a, Phasianus colchicus, tail at right. b, Phasianus colchicus, with wings feather spread. c, Phasianus colchicus, no tail visible. d, Lophura nycthemera.

No. 2718, 25,000d — Hornbills: a, Tockus leucomelas. b, Buceros rhinoceros. c, Buceros bicornis. d, Rhyticeros undulatus.

No. 2719, 25,000d — Hummingbirds: a, Chrysuronia oenone. b, Calypte anna. c, Colibri coruscans. d, Selasphorus flammula.

No. 2720, 25,000d — Bee-eaters: a, One Merops leschenaulti. b, Two Merops leschenaulti. c, Merops apiaster. d, Two Merops leschenaulti, one with bee in beak.

No. 2721, 25,000d — Birds and vineyards: a, Agapornis roseicollis and vineyard. b, Cardinalis sinuatus and Chardonnay grapes. c, Ara chloropterus and black grapes. d, Erithacus rubecula and purple grapes.

No. 2722, 25,000d — Shells: a, Lindopecten muscosus. b, Strombidae. c, Naticidae. d, Scaphella junonia.

No. 2723, 25,000d — Snakes: a, Bothriechis schlegelii. b, Crotalus cerastes. c, Python regius. d, Nerodia sipedon insularum.

No. 2724, 25,000d — Lizards: a, Sceloporus occidentalis. b, Trioceros jacksonii. c, Conolophus subcristatus. d, Iguana iguana.

No. 2725, 25,000d — Predators: a, Gyps africanus. b, Panthera pardus. c, Ursus arctos. d, Two Canis lupus lupus.

No. 2726, 25,000d — Fossils: a, Homo erectus skull. b, Shark teeth. c, Tyrannosaurus rex skeleton. d, Trilobite.

No. 2727, 25,000d — Effects of global warming: a, Larus argentatus. b, Polluted water and cracked soil. c, Ursus maritimus and retreating ice. d, Adult and juvenile Aptenodytes forsteri.

No. 2728, 25,000d — Steam locomotives: a, Canadian Pacific Railway 2816. b, Yarra Valley Railway locomotive, Australia. c, Great Western Railway Bradley Manor 7802, Great Britain. d, LV-0283 locomotive, Russia.

No. 2729, 25,000d — Special vehicles: a, HH-65C Dolphin rescue helicopter. b, 1959 Volkswagen Beetle police car. c, 1966 Ford E350 ambulance. d, 1946 American La France 500 Series fire truck.

No. 2730, 25,000d — Electric transportation: a, Segway. b, Golf carts. c, 700 Series Shinkansen train, Japan. d, Electric automobile.

No. 2731, 96,000d, Phascolarctos cinereus on tree branch. No. 2732, 96,000d, Canis lupus, diff. No. 2733, 96,000d, Panthera uncia, diff. No. 2734, 96,000d, Four dogs puling sled. No. 2735, 96,000d, Orcinus orca, diff. No. 2736, 96,000d, Two Sagittarius serpentarius. No. 2737, 96,000d, Phasianus colchicus, diff. No. 2738, 96,000d, Buceros bicornis, diff. No. 2739, 96,000d, Selasphorus sasin. No. 2740, 96,000d, Merops bullockoides. No. 2741, 96,000d, Taeniopygia guttata and red grapes. No. 2742, 96,000d, Nautilus pompilius. No. 2743, 96,000d, Pantheraphis spiloides. No. 2744, 96,000d, Varanus salvator. No. 2745, 96,000d, Ursus arctos, diff. No. 2746, 96,000d, Ammonite fossil. No. 2747, 96,000d, Larus dominicanus. No. 2748, 96,000d, Cumbria Mountain Express 60009 locomotive and train, United Kingdom. No. 2749, 96,000d, 1956 Ford police car. No. 2750, 96,000d, Electric scooter.

**2014, Sept. 15 Litho. *Perf. 13¼***

**Sheets of 4, #a-d**

**2711-2730** A385 Set of 20 210.00 210.00

**Souvenir Sheets**

**2731-2750** A385 Set of 20 200.00 200.00

A386

No. 2751, 25,000d — Robin Williams (1951-2014), actor and comedian: a, With dog. b, Holding Flubber. c, With arms crossed. d, Portraying Theodore Roosevelt.

No. 2752, 25,000d — Spanish royalty: a, King Felipe VI, at left, with Queen Letizia. b, Queen Letizia. c, King Felipe VI, at right, with Queen Letizia. d, King Felipe VI.

No. 2753, 25,000d — Scouting: a, Boy Scouts cooking meal over campfire. b, Boy Scout with model of drawbridge. c, Lord Robert Baden-Powell and Boy Scout. d, Boy Scouts erecting tent and examining butterfly.

No. 2754, 25,000d — Cricket players: a, Sachin Tendulkar. b, Jean-Paul Duminy. c, Alex Hales. d, Virat Kohli.

No. 2755, 25,000d — World War II: a, Sir Winston Churchill (1874-1965), Valentine Mk3 tank, flag of Great Britain. b, Junkers Ju 87 airplane, German Nazi flag. c, Pres. Harry S. Truman, sinking USS Arizona, United States flag. d, Battle of Stalingrad, flag of the Soviet Union.

No. 2756, 25,000d — High-speed trains: a, TGV, France. b, RENFE Class 130, Spain. c, Zefiro 380, People's Republic of China. d, CRH1A, People's Republic of China.

No. 2757, 25,000d — Primates: a, Cercopithecus mona. b, Lagothrix lagotricha. c, Piliocolobus kirkii. d, Theropithecus gelada.

No. 2758, 25,000d — Panthera leo: a, Male with open mouth. b, Female on male. c, Male with closed mouth. d, Female and cub.

No. 2759, 25,000d — Cats: a, Havana. b, Persian. c, Siamese. d, Australian Mist.

No. 2760, 25,000d — Dogs: a, Akita. b, American hairless terrier. c, Afghan hound. d, Black and tan coonhound.

No. 2761, 25,000d — Whales: a, Balaenoptera edeni. b, Eschrichtius robustus. c, Physeter macrocephalus. d, Balaenoptera musculus.

No. 2762, 25,000d — Parrots: a, Trichoglossus rubritorquis. b, Pezoporus flaviventris. c, Eos reticulata. d, Pseudeos fuscata.

No. 2763, 25,000d — Kingfishers: a, Alcedo azurea. b, Tanysiptera galatea. c, Halcyon senegalensis. d, Alcedo atthis.

No. 2764, 25,000d — Flamingos: a, Phoenicopterus andinus. b, Phoenicopterus minor. c, Phoenicoparrus jamesi. d, Phoenicopterus chilensis.

No. 2765, 25,000d — Fish: a, Cheilopogon exsiliens. b, Ostracion cubicus. c, Synchiropus splendidus. d, Scleropages formosus.

No. 2766, 25,000d — Corals: a, Montipora capricornis. b, Wellsophyllia radiata. c, Iciligorgia schrammi. d, Anacropora puertogalerae.

No. 2767, 25,000d — Crocodylus porosus: a, Two crocodiles with mouths open. b, One crocodile with open mouth. c, Two crocodiles with mouths closed. d, One crocodile with closed mouth.

No. 2768, 25,000d — Dinosaurs: a, Styracosaurus. b, Liliensternus. c, Euoplocephalus. d, Caudipteryx hendrickx.

No. 2769, 25,000d — Mushrooms: a, Boletus edulis. b, Macrolepiota procera. c, Cantharellus cibarius. d, Xerocomellus chrysenteron.

No. 2770, 25,000d — Minerals: a, Spessartine. b, Dioptase. c, Boracite. d, Rodocrosita.

No. 2771, 96,000d, Williams holding Academy Award statuette. No. 2772, 96,000d, King Felipe VI. No. 2773, 96,000d, Scouting flag and Boy Scout with bugle. No. 2774, 96,000d, Kohli, diff. No. 2775, 96,000d, Pres. Franklin D. Roosevelt, Allied leaders at Yalta Conference. No. 2776, 96,000d, Zefiro 380, diff. No. 2777, 96,000d, Rhinopithecus roxellana. No. 2778, 96,000d, Male and female Panthera leo. No. 2779, 96,000d, Colorpoint cat. No. 2780, 96,000d, Andalusian dog. No. 2781, 96,000d, Megaptera novaeangliae. No. 2782, 96,000d, Chalcopsitta sintillata. No. 2783, 96,000d, Megaceryle alcyon. No. 2784, 96,000d, Phoenicopterus roseus. No. 2785, 96,000d, Betta splendens. No. 2786, 96,000d, Nemenzophyllia turbida. No. 2787, 96,000d, Two Crocodylus niloticus. No. 2788, 96,000d, Styracosaurus and Triceratops. No. 2789, 96,000d, Morchella esculenta. No. 2790, 96,000d, Amethyst.

**2014, Oct. 15 Litho. *Perf. 13¼***

**Sheets of 4, #a-d**

**2751-2770** A386 Set of 20 200.00 200.00

**Souvenir Sheets**

**2771-2790** A386 Set of 20 195.00 195.00

Tennis Players — A387

No. 2791: a, Roger Federer. b, Rafael Nadal. c, Novak Djokovic. d, Rod Laver. e, Bjorn Borg. f, Ivan Lendl. g, Jimmy Connors. h, Andre Agassi. i, Pete Sampras. j, John McEnroe.

96,000d, Sampras, diff.

**2014, Nov. 17 Litho. *Perf. 13¼***

**2791** A387 10,000d Sheet of 10, #a-j 10.50 10.50

**Souvenir Sheet**

**2792** A387 96,000d multi 9.75 9.75

No. 2792 contains one 30x51mm stamp.

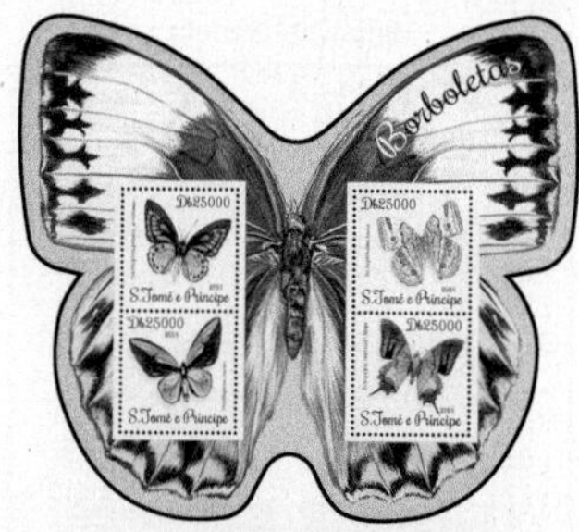


Butterflies — A388

No. 2793: a, Ornithoptera priamus urvillianus. b, Stichophthalma louisa. c, Ornithoptera croesus. d, Teinopalpus imperialis.

96,000d, Thysania agrippina.

**2014, Nov. 17 Litho. *Perf. 13¼***

**2793** A388 25,000d Sheet of 4, #a-d 10.50 10.50

**Souvenir Sheet**

**2794** A388 96,000d multi 9.75 9.75

Buceros Rhinoceros — A389

No. 2795: a, Denomination at UL, Latin name at LR. b, Denomination at UL, Latin name at left. c, Denomination at UR, Latin name at LL.

96,000d, Buceros rhinoceros, white background, denomination and country name in green.

**2014, Nov. 17 Litho. *Perf. 13¼***

**2795** A389 33,000d Sheet of 3, #a-c 10.00 10.00

**Souvenir Sheet**

**2796** A389 96,000d multi 9.75 9.75

Malaysia 2014 Intl. Stamp Exhibition, Kuala Lumpur.

A390

No. 2797, 25,000d — Marilyn Monroe (1926-62), actress, wearing: a, Blue dress. b, Yellow dress. c, Red dress, with hands touching feet. d, Red dress, hands not visible.

No. 2798, 25,000d — Elvis Presley (1935-77): a, With woman playing ukulele in background. b, With woman on motor scooter. c, With guitar and microphone. d, Playing guitar and surfing.

No. 2799, 25,000d — Pope Francis: a, Seated behind microphone. b, With Queen Elizabeth II. c, Holding child. d, Praying at Western Wall, Jerusalem.

No. 2800, 25,000d — Liberation of Paris, 70th anniv.: a, Tank, French flag, Gen. Charles de Gaulle (1890-1970). b, Arc de Triomphe, French flag, soldier, French women. c, Arc de Triomphe, de Gaulle. d, German General Dietrich von Choltitz (1894-1966), military vehicles.

No. 2801, 25,000d — Paintings depicting chess: a, Chess Players, by Cornelis de Man. b, Chess Match, by Max Oppenheimer. c, Chess Match, by Ludwig Deutsch. d, The Veterans, by Richard Creifelds.

No. 2802, 25,000d — American and Canadian Lighthouses: a, Cape Hatteras Lighthouse, North Carolina. b, Peggys Point Lighthouse, Nova Scotia. c, Brier Island Lighthouse, Nova Scotia. d, Portland Head Lighthouse, Maine.

No. 2803, 25,000d — Japanese high-speed trains: a, Nankai 50000 Series, Yokoham skyline. b, E3 Series Tsubasa, Osaka skyline. c, E6 Series Shinkansen, Sapporo skyline. d, 300 Series Shinkansen, Tokyo skyline.

No. 2804, 25,000d — Fire trucks: a, 1937 Chevrolet American LaFrance. b, 1955 GMC CCKW 353. c, 1937 Leyland Cub. d, 1936 Diamond T.

No. 2805, 25,000d — Concorde: a, Flag of Great Britain, cockpit control panel. b, Flag of France, Concorde with wheels above ground. c, Flag of France, cabin seats. d, Flag of France, Concorde on ground.

No. 2806, 25,000d — Dolphins: a, Stenella frontalis. b, Lagenorhynchus obscurus. c, Steno bredanensis. d, Cephalorhynchus heavisidii.

No. 2807, 25,000d — Owls: a, Strix nebulosa in flight. b, Bubo virginianus in flight. c, Bubo virginianus on tree branch. d, Strix nebulosa on post.

No. 2808, 25,000d — Birds of prey: a, Torgos tracheliotos. b, Sagittarius serpentarius. c, Gypaetus barbatus. d, Harpia harpyja.

No. 2809, 25,000d — Turtles: a, Trachemys scripta elegans. b, Demochelys coriacea. c, Stigmochelys pardalis. d, Astrochelys radiata.

No. 2810, 25,000d — Venomous animals: a, Ophiophagus hannah. b, Phoneutria nigriventer. c, Leiurus quinquestriatus. d, Conus marmoreus.

No. 2811, 25,000d — Orchids: a, Laelia tenebrosa. b, Ophrys apifera. c, Cattleya schilleriana. d, Disa purpurascens.

No. 2812, 25,000d — Christmas paintings: a, Adoration of the Shepherds, by Domenico Ghirlandaio. b, Adoration of the Shepherds, by Ridolfo Ghirlandaio. c, Pierre Bladelin Triptych, by Rogier van der Weyden. d, Adoration of the Magi, by Hendrick Terbrugghen.

No. 2813, 25,000d — New Year 2015 (Year of the Goat): a, Goat with Chinese character at right. b, Chinese character above goat. c, Head of goat with Chinese character at left. d, Goat with Chinese character at left.

No. 2814, 96,000d, Monroe, diff. No. 2815, 96,000d, Presley, diff. No. 2816, 96,000d, Pope Francis and his coat of arms. No. 2817, 96,000d, Arc de Triomphe, soldier and resistance fighter. No. 2818, 96,000d, Almehs Playing Chess in a Café, by Jean-Léon Gérôme. No. 2819, 96,000d, New London Lighthouse, Prince Edward Island. No. 2820, 96,000d, E3-700 Series Shinkansen. No. 2821, 96,000d, 1902 American Steam fire pumper. No. 2822, 96,000d, Flag of Great Britain, Concorde. No. 2823, 96,000d, Tursiops truncatus. No. 2824, 96,000d, Athene brama. No. 2825, 96,000d, Bubo blakistoni. No. 2826, 96,000d, Chelonia mydas. No. 2827, 96,000d, Hapalochlaena lunulata. No. 2828, 96,000d, Laelia xanthina. No. 2829, 96,000d, Adoration of the Magi, by Albrecht Altdorfer. No. 2830, 96,000d, Goat with Chinese character below.

**2014, Nov. 17 Litho. *Perf. 13¼***

**Sheets of 4, #a-d**

**2797-2813** A390 Set of 17 175.00 175.00

**Souvenir Sheets**

**2814-2830** A390 Set of 17 165.00 165.00

**Coastal Views and Buildings and Streets Types of 2014**

**Miniature Sheets**

Designs as before.

**2015, Mar. 16 Litho. *Perf. 13¼***

**2831** A383 30,000d Sheet of 8, #a-h 21.50 21.50

**2832** A384 38,000d Sheet of 8, #a-h 27.00 27.00

Taipei 2015 Intl. Stamp Exhibition — A391

No. 2833: a, Ypthima baldus. b, Choaspes benjaminii. c, Daimio tethys. d, Vanessa cardui.

38,000d, Papilio machaon, horiz.

**2015, Mar. 16 Litho. *Perf. 13¼***

**2833** A391 15,000d Sheet of 4, #a-d 5.50 5.50

**Souvenir Sheet**

**2834** A391 38,000d multi 3.50 3.50

2015 Europhilex Stamp Exhibition, London — A392

No. 2835 — Flag of Great Britain and: a, Penny Black. b, Queen Elizabeth II and Buckingham Palace, horiz. c, Eurostar train, horiz. d, Big Ben and telephone booth.

38,000d, Penny Black, horiz.

**2015, Mar. 16 Litho. *Perf. 13¼***

**2835** A392 15,000d Sheet of 4, #a-d 5.50 5.50

**Souvenir Sheet**

**2836** A392 38,000d multi 3.50 3.50

A393

No. 2837, 19,000d — Frank Sinatra (1915-98), singer: a, Holding cigarette and Grammy award. b, Holding coat over shoulder, film strip, horiz. c, With Academy award statuette, horiz. d, With G clef and musical staff.

No. 2838, 19,000d — Elvis Presley (1935-77): a, Holding microphone, wearing red scarf. b, Playing guitar to audience, horiz. c, Singing with mouth open, horiz. d, Holding microphone, wearing costume with large silver buttons.

No. 2839, 19,000d — Georg Frideric Handel (1685-1759), and scenes from opera: a, Ottone. b, Almira, horiz. c, Orlando, horiz. d, Teseo.

No. 2840, 19,000d — Ingrid Bergman (1915-82), actress: a, With Humphrey Bogart. b, With Bogart, horiz. c, With Gregory Peck, horiz. d, Alone.

No. 2841, 19,000d — Albert Einstein (1879-1955), physicist: a, With hand on cheek. b, With obverse and reverse of Nobel medal, horiz. c, With diagram of galaxies, horiz. d, Pipe in mouth.

No. 2842, 19,000d — Sir Winston Churchill (1874-1965), Prime Minister of Great Britain: a, Walking with cane. b, With tank, horiz. c, With soldiers, horiz. d, Saluting.

No. 2843, 19,000d — Angela Merkel, Chancellor of Germany: a, With Pope Francis. b, With German coat of arms, horiz. c, At Chancellor's residence, horiz. d, With Pres. Barack Obama.

No. 2844, 19,000d — St. John Paul II (1920-2005): a, Waving, both hands visible. b, With arm extended, horiz. c, With hand on chin, horiz. d, Waving, one hand visible.

No. 2845, 19,000d — Nelson Mandela (1918-2013), President of South Africa: a, Holding World Cup trophy. b, With crowd, horiz. c, With Queen Elizabeth II, horiz. d, With Oprah Winfrey.

No. 2846, 19,000d — Sculpture and paintings by Michelangelo (1475-1564): a, Pieta. b, The Creation of Adam, horiz. c, Adam and Eve, horiz. d, Moses.

No. 2847, 19,000d — Paintings by Vincent van Gogh (1853-90): a, La Mousmé, 1888. b, Noon: Rest from Work (after Millet), 1890, horiz. c, Still Life with Red Cabbages and Onions, 1887, horiz. d, Self-portrait, 1889.

No. 2848, 19,000d — George Stephenson (1781-1848), mechanical engineer: a, Locomotion No. 1. b, Locomotion No. 1, statue of Stephenson holding Locomotion No. 1, horiz. c, Stephenson in blue coat and Locomotion No. 1, horiz. d, Stephenson in purple and Locomotion No. 1 at angle.

No. 2849, 19,000d — Moscow Metro, 80th anniv.: a, Escalator, Komsomolskaya Station. b, Elektrozavodskaya Station and train, horiz. c, Ploshchad Revolyutsii Station and train, horiz. d, Sokol Station and train.

No. 2850, 19,000d — André-Gustave Citroen (1878-1935) automobile manufacturer, and Citroen: a, TPV. b, H Van, horiz. c, Model C61 truck, horiz. d, DS.

No. 2851, 19,000d — Sakigake deep space probe, 30th anniv., and: a, Launch. b, Halley's Comet, horiz. c, Earth, horiz. d, Earth.

No. 2852, 19,000d — Battle of Waterloo, 200th anniv.: a, Arthur Wellesley, Duke of Wellington (1769-1852). b, Napoleon Bonaparte (1769-1821), horiz. c, King William II of the Netherlands (1792-1849), horiz. d, Battle scene.

No. 2853, 19,000d — American Medicare and Medicaid programs, 50th anniv.: a, Hands and pills. b, Doctor and child, horiz. c, Pres. Harry S. Truman and people with signs, horiz. d, Medical personnel and patient.

No. 2854, 19,000d — Independence of St. Thomas and Prince Islands, 40th anniv.: a, Joao de Santarém, co-discoverer or St. Thomas & Prince Islands, and ship. b, Pêro Escobar, co-discover, and ships, horiz. c, Pres. Manuel Pinto da Costa and Presidential residence, horiz. d, Pres. Pinto da Costa and military musicians.

No. 2855, 86,000d, Sinatra and Grammy award, horiz. No. 2856, 86,000d, Presley playing guitar, diff., horiz. No. 2857, 86,000d, Handel, scene from Orlando, horiz. No. 2858, 86,000d, Bergman and Cary Grant, horiz. No. 2859, 86,000d, Einstein and mass-energy equivalence equation, horiz. No. 2860, 86,000d, Churchill, military officers and airplanes, horiz. No. 2861, 86,000d, Merkel and Queen Elizabeth II, horiz. No. 2862, 86,000d, St. John Paul II, diff., horiz. No. 2863, 86,000d, Mandela, broken chain, man with campaign poster, horiz. No. 2864, 86,000d, Delphic Sybil, by Michelangelo, horiz. No. 2865, 86,000d, Field with Poppies, 1890, and Self-portrait, 1889, by van Gogh, horiz. No. 2866, 86,000d, Stephenson, Locomotion No. 1, tunnel, horiz. No. 2867, 86,000d, Moscow Metro Mayakovskaya Station, Alexei Dushkin, Metro station architect, horiz. No. 2868, 86,000d, Citroen and Citroen Model A 10CV, horiz. No. 2869, 86,000d, Sakigake probe, diff., horiz. No. 2870, 86,000d, August Neidhardt von Gneisenau (1760-1831), Prussian field marshal, Waterloo battle scene, horiz. No. 2871, 86,000d, Pres. Lyndon B. Johnson, doctor examining child, caduceus, horiz. No. 2872, 86,000d, Pres. Pinto da Costa, flag of St. Thomas and Prince Islands, horiz.

**2015, Mar. 16 Litho. *Perf. 13¼***

**Sheets of 4, #a-d**

**2837-2854** A393 Set of 18 125.00 125.00

**Souvenir Sheets**

**2855-2872** A393 Set of 18 140.00 140.00

Singapore 2015 Intl. Stamp Exhibition — A394

No. 2873: a, Caranx ignobilis. b, Centroberyx affinis. c, Epibulus insidiator. d, Plectorhinchus polytaenia.

38,000d, Choerodon schoenleinii.

**2015, May 21 Litho. *Perf. 13¼***

**2873** A394 15,000d Sheet of 4, #a-d 5.50 5.50

**Souvenir Sheet**

**2874** A394 38,000d multi 3.50 3.50

Souvenir Sheets

Hindu Statue — A395

Hindu Goddess Durga on Tiger — A396

**Litho. With Foil Application and Affixed Stone**

***Perf. 13¼, 9½ on Diagonal Sides***

**2015, May 21**

**2875** A395 86,000d multi 7.75 7.75

**Litho. With Stone Affixed, Sheet Margin With Flocking**

***Perf.***

**Without Gum**

**2876** A396 86,000d multi 7.75 7.75

Rainforests — A397

No. 2877, 19,000d — Primates: a, Nasalis larvatus. b, Mandrillus sphinx. c, Cebus capucinus. d, Leontopithecus rosalia.

No. 2878, 19,000d — Wild cats: a, Leopardus pardalis. b, Puma concolor. c, Panthera pardus. d, Panthera tigris tigris.

No. 2879, 19,000d — Dolphins: a, Tursiops truncatus. b, Grampus griseus. c, Stenella longirostris. d, Delphinus capensis.

No. 2880, 19,000d — Manatees: a, Trichechus pygmaeus. b, Two Trichechus manatus. c, Trichechus senegalensis. d, One Trichechus manatus.

No. 2881, 19,000d — Parrots: a, Aratinga jandaya. b, Deroptyus accipitrinus. c, Guaruba guarouba. d, Pyrrhura perlata.

No. 2882, 19,000d — Harpy eagle (Harpia harpyja): a, On branch, facing forward. b, At nest. c, On branch, facing backwards. d, Catching prey.

No. 2883, 19,000d — Toucans: a, Ramphastos ambiguus. b, Ramphastos sulfuratus. c, Selenidera culik. d, Ramphastos toco.

No. 2884, 19,000d — Owls: a, Glaucidium griseiceps. b, Bubo shelleyi. c, Bubo philippensis. d, Bubo poensis.

No. 2885, 19,000d — Butterflies: a, Myscelia cyaniris. b, Hypolimnas misippus. c, Junonia almana. d, Graphium agamemnon.

No. 2886, 19,000d — Piranhas: a, Pristobrycon careospinus. b, Pygopristis denticulata. c, Serrasalmus rhombeus. d, Pygocentrus nattereri.

No. 2887, 19,000d — Frogs: a, Dendrobates tinctorius. b, Agalychnis callidryas. c, Phyllomedusa bicolor. d, Dendrobates leucomelas.

No. 2888, 19,000d — Turtles: a, Podocnemis expansa. b, Trachemys scripta elegans. c, Terrapene carolina carolina, Chelonoidis carbonaria. d, Chelus fimbriata.

No. 2889, 19,000d — Black caimans (Melanosuchus niger): a, With prey in mouth. b, In water. c, Head, with open mouth. d, At nest, with eggs.

No. 2890, 19,000d — Snakes: a, Bothriechis schlegelii. b, Corallus caninus (green snake). c, Corallus caninus (red orange snake). d, Trimeresurus trigonocephalus.

No. 2891, 19,000d — Carnivorous plants and their prey: a, Nepenthes aristolochioides, Danaus plexippus. b, Drosera roraimae, Libellula vibrans. c, Nepenthes rajah, Rattus baluensis. d, Heliamphora ionasi, Chrysopilus thoracicus.

No. 2892, 19,000d — Orchids: a, Cattleya sp. b, Cattleya dowiana. c, Arachnorchis radiata. d, Neomoorea irrorata.

No. 2893, 19,000d — Mushrooms: a, Pleurotus ostreatus. b, Leucocoprinus birnbaumii. c, Cookeina tricholoma. d, Lycoperdon perlatum.

No. 2894, 19,000d — Minerals: a, Fluorite. b, Cobalt and Smithsonite. c, Rhodochrosite. d, Wulfenite.

No. 2895, 86,000d, Saguinus oedipus, horiz. No. 2896, 86,000d, Panthera onca, horiz. No. 2897, 86,000d, Inia geoffrensis, horiz. No. 2898, 86,000d, Trichechus manatus, horiz. No. 2899, 86,000d, Ara macao, Ara ararauna, horiz. No. 2900, 86,000d, Harpia harpyja, horiz. No. 2901, 86,000d, Andigena laminirostris, horiz. No. 2902, 86,000d, Glaucidium brasilianum, horiz. No. 2903, 86,000d, Heliconius doris, horiz. No. 2904, 86,000d, Pristobrycon striolatus, horiz. No. 2905, 86,000d, Dendrobates tinctorius azureus, horiz. No. 2906, 86,000d, Malaclemys terrapin, horiz. No. 2907, 86,000d, Melanosuchus niger, horiz. No. 2908, 86,000d, Oligodon octolineatus, horiz. No. 2909, 86,000d, Dionaea muscipula, Asterope leprieuri, horiz. No. 2910, 86,000d, Caladenia corynephora, horiz. No. 2911, 86,000d, Hygrocybe miniata, horiz. No. 2912, 86,000d, Emerald, horiz.

**2015, May 21 Litho. *Perf. 13¼***

**Sheets of 4, #a-d**

**2877-2894** A397 Set of 18 125.00 125.00

**Souvenir Sheets**

**2895-2912** A397 Set of 18 140.00 140.00

Nos. 2895-2912 each contain one 51x43mm stamp.

A398

No. 2913, 31,000d — Mother Teresa (1910-97), humanitarian: a, With hands in prayer and eyes closed. b, Facing froward, hands not visible. c, Holding baby. d, With hands in prayer and eyes open.

No. 2914, 31,000d — Pope Benedict XVI: a, Wearing zucchetto. b, With Queen Elizabeth II. c, Holding crucifix. d, With Pres. Barack Obama.

No. 2915, 31,000d — Queen Elizabeth II, longest-reigning British monarch: a, Wearing tiara. b, Holding Flowers. c, With Prince Philip. d, Waving.

No. 2916, 31,000d — Mahatma Gandhi (1869-1948), Indian nationalist: a, Head of Gandhi. b, With Sita Gandhi (1928-99). c, With Abha Gandhi (1927-95). d, Two images of Gandhi.

No. 2917, 31,000d — Malcolm X (1925-65), human rights activist: a, Holding newspaper. b, Holding child. c, Pointing finger upwards. d, With Dr. Martin Luther King, Jr. (1929-68).

No. 2918, 31,000d — Cricket players: a, Shane Keith Warne. b, Imran Khan. c, Jacques Kallis. d, Brian Lara.

No. 2919, 31,000d — 2014 Nobel Prize Laureates: a, Physics laureates Shuji Nakamura, Isamu Akasaki, and Hiroshi Amano. b, Peace laureate Malala Yousafzai. c, Physiology or Medicine laureates Edvard Moser, May-Britt Moser, John O'Keefe. d, Economics laureate Jean Tirole.

No. 2920, 31,000d — 23rd International Scout Jamboree, Japan: a, Scouts saluting, butterfly. b, Scouts and tent. c, Scout arranging wood for campfire. d, Scouts with backpacks, mushrooms.

No. 2921, 31,000d — End of World War II, 70th anniv: a, Mistel 2 (Ju 88 G-1 and Fw 190 A-8). b, Messerschmitt Bf 109. c, Supermarine Spitfire. d, Republic P-47 Thunderbolt.

No. 2922, 31,000d — Lighthouses: a, Yaquina Head Lighthouse, Oregon. b, Lange Jaap Lighthouse, Netherlands. c, Whaleback Lighthouse, Maine. d, Roter Sand Lighthouse, Germany.

No. 2923, 31,000d — Fire vehicles: a, U5000 Feuerwehr GW. b, 2003 American LaFrance. c, 2010 MAN GW-L2. d, Citroen 700FPT, Chevy Tahoe ES-11.

No. 2924, 31,000d — Apollo 13 mission: a, Astronaut Jim Lovell, command, service and lunar modules. b, Apollo 13 patch, lunar module. c, Crew members Lovell, Fred Haise, Jack Swigert, capsule re-entry. d, Recovered capsule.

No. 2925, 31,000d — Paintings by Sandro Botticelli (1445-1510): a, Simonetta Vespucci, 1484. b, The Madonna of the Book, 1480. c, Angel from The Annunciation, c. 1485. d, Virgin Mary from The Annunciation, c. 1485.

No. 2926, 31,000d — Paintings by Peter Paul Rubens (1577-1640): a, Wolf and Fox Hunt, c. 1615-21. b, Perseus and Andromeda, c. 1622. c, David Slaying Goliath, c. 1616. d, The Fall of Phaeton, c. 1604.

No. 2927, 31,000d — Paintings by Giovanni Paolo Panini (1691-1765): a, Interior of the Pantheon of Rome, c. 1734. b, Roman Capriccio: The Pantheon and Other Monuments, c. 1735. c, Musical Fête, 1747. d, Interior of St. Peter's in Rome, 1755.

No. 2928, 31,000d — Paintings by Berthe Morisot (1841-95): a, Reading, 1873. b, Harbor in the Port of Fecamp, 1874. c, Hanging the Laundry Out to Dry, 1875. d, Woman Wearing Gloves, 1885.

No. 2929, 31,000d — Paintings by Amedeo Modigliani (1841-95): a, The Cellist, 1909. b, Portrait of Dr. Deveraigne, 1917. c, Lunia Czechowska with Her Left Hand on Her Cheek, 1918. d, Gypsy Woman with Baby, 1919.

No. 2930, 31,000d — Paintings by John James Audubon (1785-1851): a, Self-portrait, 1822-23. b, Bobwhite (Virginia Partridge), 1825. c, Portrait of John James Audubon, by John W. Audubon. d, Canada Geese.

No. 2931, 31,000d — Butterflies: a, Caligo eurilochus. b, Idea leuconoe, Papilio memnon. c, Heliconius cydno. d, Euploea mulciber.

No. 2932, 31,000d — Jurassic age fauna: a, Dilophosaurus wetherilli. b, Sordes pilosus, Coelurus bauri. c, Dsungaripterus weii, Scelidosaurus harrisonii. d, Kentrosaurus aethiopicus.

No. 2933, 96,000d, Mother Teresa and Pope John Paul II (1920-2005), horiz. No. 2934, 96,000d, Popes Benedict XI and Francis, horiz. No. 2935, 96,000d, Queen Elizabeth II, horiz. No. 2936, 96,000d, Mahatma Gandhi, horiz. No. 2937, 96,000d, Malcolm X, horiz. No. 2938, 96,000d, Sir Donald Bradman (1908-2001), cricket player, horiz. No. 2939, 96,000d, Stefan Hell, 2014 Nobel Laureate in Chemistry, horiz. No. 2940, 96,000d, Scouts and mushroom, horiz. No. 2941, 96,000d, Type 156 Beaufighter, horiz. No. 2942, 96,000d, Portland Head Lighthouse, Maine, horiz. No. 2943, 96,000d, 1950 American LaFrance 700 fire truck, horiz. No. 2944, 96,000d, Apollo 13 crew members, Haise, Lovell and Swigert, horiz. No. 2945, 96,000d, The Birth of Venus, by Botticelli, 1482-85, horiz. No. 2946, 96,000d, Self-portrait, by Rubens, 1623, horiz. No. 2947, 96,000d, View of the Colosseum, by Panini, Portrait of Giovanni Paolo Panini, by Louis Gabriel Blanche, horiz. No. 2948, 96,000d, Morisot and The Cradle, by Morisot, 1872, horiz. No. 2949, 96,000d, Modigliani and Landscape, by Modigliani, 1919, horiz. No. 2950, 96,000d, Portrait of Audubon, by John Syme, 1826, Mallards, by Audubon, horiz. No. 2951, 96,000d, Heliconius cydno, horiz. No. 2952, 96,000d, Archaeopteryx siemensii, horiz.

**2015, Sept. 23 Litho. *Perf. 13¼***

**Sheets of 4, #a-d**

**2913-2932** A398 Set of 20 230.00 230.00

**Souvenir Sheets**

**2933-2952** A398 Set of 20 175.00 175.00

Nos. 2933-2952 each contain one 51x43mm stamp.

Portuguese Language 800th Anniv. A399

Intl. Association of Portuguese-Speaking Countries, 25th Anniv. — A400

**2015, Oct. 9 Litho. *Perf. 13x13¼***

| | | | | |
|---|---|---|---|---|
| **2953** | A399 | 22,000d multi | 2.00 | 2.00 |
| **2954** | A400 | 30,000d multi | 2.75 | 2.75 |

See Angola No. , Brazil No. 3300, Cape Verde No. 1004, Guinea-Bissau No. , Macao No. 1440, Moambique No. , Portugal Nos. 3694-3695, Timor No.

Hong Kong 2015 Intl. Stamp Exhibition — A401

No. 2955: a, Junk and Hong Kong skyline. b, Grus japonensis. c, Psittacus erithacus. d, Bostrychia bocagei.
110,000d, Ailuropoda melanoleuca.

**2015, Nov. 18 Litho. *Perf. 13¼***

| | | | | |
|---|---|---|---|---|
| **2955** | A401 | 31,000d Sheet of 4, #a-d | 11.00 | 11.00 |

**Souvenir Sheet**

| | | | | |
|---|---|---|---|---|
| **2956** | A401 | 110,000d multi | 9.50 | 9.50 |

A402

No. 2957, 31,000d — Various depictions of Concorde in flight with text, "Concorde" at: a, UR in black. b, Top center in white. c, LR in black. d, LL in black.
No. 2958, 31,000d — High-speed trains: a, ED 250 Pendolino. b, CRH380D. c, Acela Express. d, HEMU-430X.
No. 2959, 31,000d — Soviet space program: a, Yuri Gagarin (1934-68), first man in space. b, Voskhod 2. c, Alexei Leonov taking first spacewalk. d, Valentina Tereshkova, first woman in space.
No. 2960, 31,000d — Table tennis players: a, Jörgen Persson. b, Li Xiaoxia. c, Jan-Ove Waldner. d, Zhang Jike.
No. 2961, 31,000d — Artists and chess pieces: a, Salvador Dalí (1904-89). b, Man Ray (1890-1976). c, Marcel Duchamp (1887-1968). d, Max Ernst (1891-1976).
No. 2962, 31,000d — Paintings by American Impressionists: a, Calm Morning, by Frank Watson Benson, 1904. b, The Cellist, by Joseph DeCamp, 1907. c, Peonies from Spring Flowers, by William Merritt Chase, 1889. d, Woman and peonies from Spring Flowers, by Chase.
No. 2963, 31,000d — Endangered animals: a, Ailurus fulgens. b, Capra falconeri. c, Panthera tigris. d, Pygathrix cinerea.
No. 2964, 31,000d — Dogs: a, Jack Russell terrier, English cocker spaniel. b, Beagle, Portuguese sheepdog. c, Portuguese water dog. d, Chinese crested dog, Pug.
No. 2965, 31,000d — Elephants: a, Elephas maximus maximus. b, Loxodonta africana, latin name at UR, elephant with tusks at left. c, Loxodonta africana, Latin name at UR, elephant with tusks at right. d, Loxodonta cyclotis, juvenile and adult with trunk raised.
No. 2966, 31,000d — Whales: a, Eubalaena glacialis. b, Balaenoptera musculus, Balaenoptera acutorostrata. c, Balaenoptera borealis. d, Physeter macrocephalus, Megaptera novaeangliae.
No. 2967, 31,000d — Owls: a, Surnia ulula. b, Otus sagittatus. c, Glaucidium perlatum, Bubo scandiacus. d, Megascops koepckeae.
No. 2968, 31,000d — Butterflies: a, Zerynthia rumina. b, Polygonia c-album. c, Junonia orithya, Melanargia galathea. d, Colobura dirce.
No. 2969, 31,000d — Shells: a, Nautilus pompilius. b, Strombus alatus gmelin. c, Voluta polypleura. d, Lambis chiragra arthritica.
No. 2970, 31,000d — Turtles: a, Chelonia mydas. b, Graptemys ernsti. c, Caretta caretta. d, Dermochelys coriacea.
No. 2971, 31,000d — Orchids: a, Stelis eublepharis. b, Rhynchostele maculata. c, Cattleya percivaliana. d, Masdevallia veitchiana.
No. 2972, 31,000d — Mushrooms: a, Macrolepiota procera. b, Morchella esculenta. c, Cortinarius triformis. d, Hygrocybe coccinea.
No. 2973, 31,000d — Minerals: a, Proustite. b, Mimetite and wulfenite. c, Carbon. d, Metatorbernite.
No. 2974, 31,000d — Pope Francis: a, Holding censer. b, Greeting Pres. Barack Obama. c, Waving. d, In Popemobile, waving.
No. 2975, 31,000d — Christmas: a, Santa Claus and automobiles. b, Children, Christmas tree, reindeer in flight. c, Sant Claus in sleigh, child on skis, snowman, dog. d, Santa Claus with sack.
No. 2976, 96,000d, Concorde, horiz. No. 2977, 96,000d, Eurostar e320, horiz. No. 2978, 96,000d, Sputnik 1 and Segei Korolev (1907-66), Soviet spacecraft designer, horiz. No. 2979, 96,000d, Zhang Jike holding trophy, horiz. No. 2980, 96,000d, Ernst and chess pieces, horiz. No. 2981, 96,000d, The Fairy Tale, by Chase, 1892, horiz. No. 2982, 96,000d, Lemur catta, horiz. No. 2983, 96,000d, Portuguese podengos, horiz. No. 2984, 96,000d, Elephas maximus indicus, horiz. No. 2985, 96,000d, Balaena mysticetus, horiz. No. 2986, 96,000d, Strix nebulosa, horiz. No. 2987, 96,000d, Polyommatus bellargus, horiz. No. 2988, 96,000d, Bullina lineata, horiz. No. 2989, 96,000d, Emydoidea blandingii, horiz. No. 2990, 96,000d, Stanhopea embreei, horiz. No. 2991, 96,000d, Amanita caesarea. No. 2992, 96,000d, Pyrite, horiz. No. 2993, 96,000d, Pope Francis and his coat of arms, horiz. No. 2994, 96,000d, Child wearing Santa hat, bell, candles.

**2015, Nov. 18 Litho. *Perf. 13¼***
**Sheets of 4, #a-d**

| | | | | |
|---|---|---|---|---|
| **2957-2975** | A402 | Set of 19 | 205.00 | 205.00 |

**Souvenir Sheets**

| | | | | |
|---|---|---|---|---|
| **2976-2994** | A402 | Set of 19 | 160.00 | 160.00 |

MonacoPhil 2015 (Nos. 2966, 2970, 2985, 2989). Nos. 2976-2994 each contain one 51x43mm stamp.

A403

No. 2995, 31,000d — Marilyn Monroe (1926-62), actress, and: a, Poster for *Niagara,* 1953. b, Scene from *Something Has to Give,* 1962. c, Scene from *Some Like it Hot,* 1959. d, Scene from *River of No Return,* 1954.
No. 2996, 31,000d — Princess Diana (1961-97): a, Holding child. b, With child, bush and flowers. c, With flowers and child. d, Wearing tiara.
No. 2997, 31,000d — Paintings of nudes: a, Bathsheba at Her Bath, by Rembrandt, 1654. b, Susannah and the Elders, by Jacob van Loo, 1658. c, Female Nude Reclining on a Divan, by Eugène Delacroix, 1826. d, Male Nudes, Bathers, by Paul Cézanne, 1900.
No. 2998, 31,000d — Animals and World-wide Fund for Nature (WWF) stamps: a, Cotumix chinensis, Malaysia #821. b, Pelamis platura, Tokelau #389. c, Bos javanicus, Cambodia #747. d, Panthera tigris, Russia #6181.
No. 2999, 31,000d — Lighthouses: a, Fanad Lighthouse, Ireland. b, Pigeon Point Lighthouse, California (Inicie do Ponto). c, Peggy's Point Lighthouse, Canada. d, Portland Head Lighthouse, Maine.
No. 3000, 31,000d — International Year of Light: a, Joshua Bell, violinist. b, Thomas Edison (1847-1931), inventor. c, Light diffraction. d, Andrew, Duke of York, and lighthouse.
No. 3001, 31,000d — Cricket players: a, Players, end of bat near "2015." b, Shahid Afridi. c, Players, end of bat near "Criquete." d, Pakistan player batting.
No. 3002, 31,000d — 2016 Summer Olympics, Rio de Janeiro: a, 100-meter sprint. b, Rugby. c, Basketball. d, Table tennis.
No. 3003, 31,000d — 2018 World Cup Soccer Championships, Russia: a, Roman Shirokov. b, Andrey Arshavin. c, Matryoshka doll, Russian flag. d, Pres. Vladimir Putin and soccer ball.
No. 3004, 31,000d — Ships: a, Christian Radich. b, Concordia. c, Amerigo Vespucci. d, Kruzenshtern.
No. 3005, 31,000d — Steam locomotives: a, Great Western Railway 6000 Class 6024 King Edward I. b, Class DB 10. c, White Pass and Yukon Locomotive No. 69. d, London and North Eastern Railway Peppercorn Class A1 60163 Tornado.
No. 3006, 31,000d — Japanese high-speed trains: a, E5 Series Shinkansen. b, 200 Series Shinkansen. c, N700 Series Shinkansen. d, E2 Series Shinkansen.
No. 3007, 31,000d — Fire vehicles: a, American LaFrance 1000 Series pumper. b, Renault Twizy. c, Old fire truck and automobiles. d, Cadillac sedan.
No. 3008, 31,000d — Cat breeds: a, Norwegian Forest cats (Norueguês da Floresta). b, Devon Rex. c, Kurilian bobtail. d, Tonkinese.
No. 3009, 31,000d — Dolphins: a, Lagenorhynchus obliquidens. b, Two Tursiops truncatus. c, Delphinapterus leucas, Tursiops truncatus. d, Two Tursiops truncatus, red sea vegetation at LL.
No. 3010, 31,000d — Plovers: a, Pluvialis dominica. b, Pluvialis apricaria. c, Pluvialis squatarola. d, Charadrius dubius.
No. 3011, 31,000d — Birds of St. Thomas & Prince Islands: a, Ardeola ralloides. b, Phoenicopterus roseus. c, Sula dactylatra. d, Puffinus gravis.
No. 3012, 31,000d — Birds of prey: a, Athene noctua. b, Buteo buteo. c, Gyps fulvus. d, Pithecophaga jefferyi.
No. 3013, 31,000d — Dinosaurs: a, Dakosaurus maximus. b, Tyrannosaurus rex. c, Brachiosaurus altithorax. d, Spinosaurus aegypticus.
No. 3014, 31,000d — New Year 2016 (Year of the Monkey): a, Macaca mulatta. b, Simia sciureus. c, Cebus capucinus. d, Alouatta puruensis.
No. 3015, 96,000d, Monroe, diff. No. 3016, 96,000d, Princess Diana, tiara, British flag. No. 3017, 96,000d, Seated Bather, by Pierre-Auguste Renoir, 1903. No. 3018, 96,000d, Bubo lacteus, Gambia #381. No. 3019, 96,000d, Cape Agulhas Lighthouse, South Africa. No. 3020, 96,000d, LED lightbulb. No. 3021, 96,000d, Lasith Malinga, cricket player. No. 3022, 96,000d, 100-meter sprint, Christ the Redeemer statue, Rio de Janeiro. No. 3023, 96,000d, Arshavin, diff. No. 3024, 96,000d, Belem. No. 3025, 96,000d, Class GMAM No. 4079 locomotive. No. 3026, 96,000d, Kawasaki efSET train. No. 3027, 96,000d, Flyox I airplane, 2010 Freightliner pumper truck. No, 3028, 96,000d, Prionailurus bengalensis, Prionailurus bengalensis iriomotensis. No. 3029, 96,000d, Delphinus delphis, Grampus griseus. No. 3030, 96,000d, Pluvialis apricaria, diff. No. 3031, 96,000d, Dendrocygna bicolor. No. 3032, 96,000d, Otus hartlaubi. No. 3033, 96,000d, Regaliceratops peterhewsi. No. 3034, 96,000d, Cebus capucinus, diff.

***Perf. 13¼, 9½ on Diagonal Sides***
**2015, Dec. 29 Litho.**
**Sheets of 4, #a-d**

| | | | | |
|---|---|---|---|---|
| **2995-3014** | A403 | Set of 20 | 220.00 | 220.00 |

**Souvenir Sheets**

| | | | | |
|---|---|---|---|---|
| **3015-3034** | A403 | Set of 20 | 170.00 | 170.00 |

Miniature Sheets

A404

Biodiversity — A405

No. 3035: a, Turtle. b, Bay. c, Cacao tree. d, Principe Golden Weaver Bird. e, Snakes. f, Parrot. g, Houses near beach. h, Fish.
No. 3036: a, Beach. b, African Green Pigeon. c, Rock outcroppings. d, Cacao pods. e, Butterfly on flower. f, Flower. g, Schlegel's Asity bird. h, Jackfruit.

**2016, Jan. 11 Litho. *Perf. 13x13¼***

| | | | | |
|---|---|---|---|---|
| **3035** | A404 | 1000d Sheet of 8, #a-h, + central label | .75 | .75 |
| **3036** | A405 | 2000d Sheet of 8, #a-h, + central label | 1.50 | 1.50 |

Sept. 11, 2001 Terrorist Attacks — A406

No. 3037 — U.S. flag and: a, Fire truck. b, Firemen on World Trade Center rubble. c, Bald eagle and World Trade Center. d, Pres. George W. Bush and fireman.
76,000d, Pres. Barack Obama, U.S. flag and Tribute in Light.

**2016, Jan. 26 Litho. *Perf. 13¼***

| | | | | |
|---|---|---|---|---|
| **3037** | A406 | 19,000d Sheet of 4, #a-d | 6.75 | 6.75 |

**Souvenir Sheet**

| | | | | |
|---|---|---|---|---|
| **3038** | A406 | 76,000d multi | 6.75 | 6.75 |

2016 World Stamp Show, New York. No. 3038 contains one 51x90mm stamp.

A407

No. 3039, 31,000d — Lord Robert Baden-Powell (1857-1941), founder of Scouting movement: a, Baden-Powell and Scouting flag. b, Three Scouts. c, Three Scouts around campfire. d, Baden-Powell and Scouting emblem.

No. 3040, 31,000d — Archbishop Desmond Tutu and: a, Tutu holding Nobel medal. b, United Nations emblem. c, 14th Dalai Lama. d, Nelson Mandela (1918-2013), President of South Africa.

No. 3041, 31,000d — Pope Francis and: a, St. Peter's Square and putto. b, His coat of arms. c, Pres. Barack Obama. d, Patriarch Kirill of Moscow, flag and coat of arms of Cuba.

No. 3042, 31,000d — Queen Elizabeth, 90th birthday: a, Princess Elizabeth of York, by Philip de Laszlo. b, Princess Elizabeth in Auxiliary Territorial Service uniform. c, Queen Elizabeth II wearing crown. d, Queen Elizabeth II with her dogs.

No. 3043, 31,000d — Princess Diana (1961-97): a, With Princes William and Harry. b, With Red Cross worker. c, Wearing hat. d, Receiving flowers from child.

No. 3044, 31,000d — Thomas Edison (1847-1931), inventor, and: a, Nickel- iron battery, IBM computer. b, Film camera. c, Miner's lamp. d, Kinetoscope.

No. 3045, 31,000d — Wolfgang Amadeus Mozart (1756-91), composer: a, Embracing woman. b, With picture of Mozart as child. c, With horse-drawn carriage. d, The Last Hours of Mozart, by Henry Nelson O'Neil.

No. 3046, 31,000d — Louis Armstrong (1901-71), jazz trumpeter, and singers: a, Ella Fitzgerald (1917-96). b, Bing Crosby (1903-77). c, Billie Holiday (1915-59). d, Barbra Streisand.

No. 3047, 31,000d — Elizabeth Taylor (1932-2011), actress: a, In scene from *Cleopatra*. b, In scene from *Ivanhoe*. c, Playing with pearl necklace. d, Holding Academy Award.

No. 3048, 31,000d — BMW motor vehicles, cent.: a, BMW 328 and BMW 501. b, BMW R1200GS LC and R32 motorcycles. c, BMW M1 and BMW i8. d, EMW/BMW 340 and BMW 323i.

No. 3049, 31,000d — First flight of the Hindenburg, 80th anniv: a, Hindenburg over water. b, Hindenburg pilots at controls. c, Hindenburg over Curtiba, Brazil. d, Hindenburg and map of Germany-Brazil flight.

No. 3050, 31,000d — Concorde, 40th anniv. of commercial service: a, Air France Concordes in flight and being serviced on ground. b, One British Airways Concorde in flight. c, Air France and British Airways Concordes in flight. d, British Airways Concorde above runway.

No. 3051, 31,000d — First spaceflight of Yuri Gagarin, 55th anniv.: a, Gagarin in ejector seat, Vostok 1 capsule. b, Gagarin and Vostok 1 in orbit. c, Gagarin in space helmet, launch of Vostok 1. d, Parachutes above Gagarin in ejector seat and Vostok 1 capsule.

No. 3052, 31,000d — Edgar Mitchell (1930-2016), astronaut: a, Mitchell and Apollo 14 emblem. b, Mitchell and Lunar Rover. c, Mitchell and Alan Shepard (1923-98) training. d, Apollo 14 crew, Mitchell, Shepard and Stuart Roosa (1933-94).

No. 3053, 31,000d — Battle of Verdun, cent.: a, Two airplanes in dogfight. b, Five airplanes. c, Cannon. d, Soldiers in trench.

No. 3054, 31,000d — Attack on Pearl Harbor, 75th anniv.: a, Airplane attacking ship. b, Lieutenant General Walter Short (1880-1949), ship explosion. c, Osami Nagano (1880-1947), Japanese admiral. d, Japanese airplanes over burning ship.

No. 3055, 31,000d — Paintings by Pierre-Auguste Renoir (1849-1919): a, Self-portrait, 1875. b, Piazza San Marco, Venice, 1881. c, Flowers in a Vase, 1866. d, Self-portrait, 1910.

No. 3056, 31,000d — Paintings by Paul Cézanne (1839-1906): a, Self-portrait, 1895. b, The Bathers, 1898-1905. c, Still Life with Apples, 1893-94. d, Mont Sainte-Victoire, 1895.

No. 3057, 31,000d — Sculptures in Musée d'Orsay, Paris: a, South America, by Aimé Millet. b, Asia, by Alexandre Falguière. c, Oceania, by Mathurin Moreau. d, Europe, by Pierre-Alexandre Schoenewerk.

No. 3058, 124,000d, Baden-Powell, Scouts and Scouting flag. No. 3059, 124,000d, Tutu, 14th Dalai Lama and photographer. No. 3060, 124,000d, Pope Francis, his coat of arms, dove. No. 3061, 124,000d, Queen Elizabeth II waving. No. 3062, 124,000d, Princess Diana, Princes William and Harry, diff. No. 3063, 124,000d, Edison in laboratory. No. 3064, 124,000d, Mozart and his signature. No. 3065, 124,000d, Armstrong playing trumpet. No. 3066, 124,000d, Taylor holding Golden Globe award, Robert Taylor (1911-69), actor. No. 3067, 124,000d, BMW Dixi and 2013 BMW i3. No. 3068, 124,000d, Hindenburg in flight, Ludwig Dürr (1878-1956), designer of Hindenburg. No. 3069, 124,000d, British Airways Concorde in flight, diff. No. 3070, 124,000d, Gagarin in space suit. No. 3071, 124,000d, Mitchell and Presidential Medal of Freedom. No. 3072, 124,000d, Verdun and Pope Benedict XVI. No. 3073, 124,000d, Admiral Husband E. Kimmel (1882-1968) and Japanese airplanes over burning ship. No. 3074, 124,000d, Renoir, diff. No. 3075, 124,000d, Cézanne self-portrait, 1890. No. 3076, 124,000d, Pierre Colboc, architect, and Musée d'Orsay.

**2016, Jan. 26 Litho. *Perf. 13¼***
**Sheets of 4, #a-d**

**3039-3057** A407 Set of 19 210.00 210.00

**Souvenir Sheets**

**3058-3076** A407 Set of 19 210.00 210.00

Nos. 3058-3076 each contain one 51x90mm stamp.

Philataipei 2016 World Stamp Championship Exhibition, Taipei — A408

No. 3077, 31,000d: a, Prunus mume. b, Urocissa caerulea. c, Onychostoma alticorpus. d, Ursus thibetanus formosanus.
96,000d, Sun Yat-sen Memorial Hall, Taipei.

**2016, Mar. 30 Litho. *Perf. 17***

**3077** A408 31,000d Sheet of 4, #a-d 11.50 11.50

**Souvenir Sheet**

**3078** A408 96,000d multi 9.00 9.00

No. 3078 contains one 71x71mm diamond-shaped stamp.

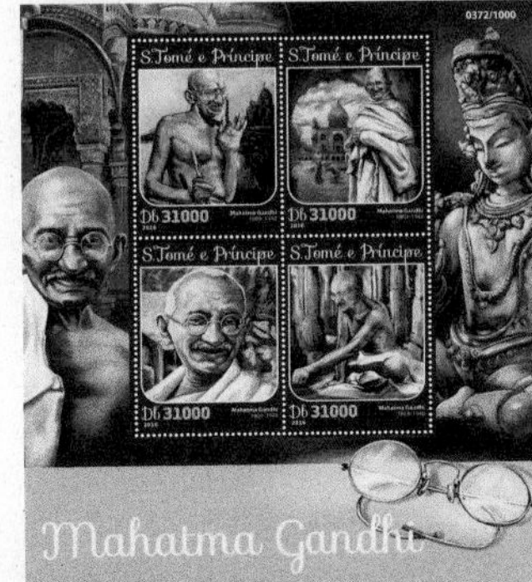


A409

No. 3079, 31,000d — Mahatma Gandhi (1869-1948), Indian nationalist: a, Gandhi holding walking stick. b, Gandhi in robe, women in front of temple. c, Head of Gandhi. d, Gandhi seated.

No. 3080, 31,000d — St. John Paul II (1920-2005): a, Kissing head of child. b, Praying at St. Peter's Basilica. c, Head of St. John Paul II. d, Embracing Pope Benedict XVI.

No. 3081, 31,000d — Elvis Presley (1935-77): a, Holding microphone. b, In automobile, wearing Army uniform. c, With Ann-Margret in scene from *Viva Las Vegas*. d, In scene from *Kid Galahad*.

No. 3082, 31,000d — Rugby players: a, Two players, one trying to kick ball. b, Player in green shirt tackling player in black shirt. c, Player in gray shirt tackling player in yellow shirt. d, Three players.

No. 3083, 31,000d — 2016 Summer Olympics, Rio de Janeiro: a, Cricket. b, Two rugby players and two balls. c, Judo. d, Show jumping.

No. 3084, 31,000d — Fire engines: a, Caterpillar 740. b, EU10FSP of Chelmsford, Essex, United Kingdom. c, Lentner TGM. d, 2011 Ladder truck of North Andover, Massachusetts.

No. 3085, 31,000d — High-speed trains: a, CRH6A, People's Republic of China. b, Series W7 Shinkansen, Japan. c, Frecciarossa 1000, Italy. d, TCDD HT80000, Turkey.

No. 3086, 31,000d — Red Cross campaign against malaria: a, Red Cross worker putting up mosquito netting. b, Red Cross workers in laboratory. c, Red Cross worker with child drinking water. d, Red Cross worker spraying insecticide.

No. 3087, 31,000d — Lighthouses: a, Maiden's Tower (Danzela), Turkey. b, Allainville Lighthouse. c, El Morro Lighthouse, Puerto Rico. d, Point Cabrillo Lighthouse, California.

No. 3088, 31,000d — International Year of Pulses: a, New Holland TR 98 combine, seedlings. b, Woman and child preparing beans. c, Green peas. d, Beans for sale at market.

No. 3089, 31,000d — Dogs: a, Sloughis. b, Pembroke Welsh corgis. c, Tibetan mastiff. d, German shepherds.

No. 3090, 31,000d — Owls: a, Bubo bengalensis. b, Aegolius funereus. c, Glaucidium capense. d, Strix leptogrammica.

No. 3091, 31,000d — Butterflies: a, Zemeros flegyas. b, Cyrestis thyodamas. c, Vanessa virginiensis. d, Papilio ulysses.

No. 3092, 31,000d — Turtles: a, Graptemys pseudogeographica kohni. b, Chrysemys scripta elegans. c, Malaclemys terrapin. d, Caretta caretta.

No. 3093, 31,000d — Endangered animals: a, Pongo pygmaeus. b, Elephas maximus. c, Camelus bactrianus. d, Addax nasomaculatus.

No. 3094, 31,000d — Mushrooms: a, Trametes versicolor. b, Leucocoprinus birnbaumii. c, Amanita phalloides. d, Fomitopsis pinicola.

No. 3095, 31,000d — Minerals: a, Azurite. b, Amazonite. c, Barium. d, Wulfenite.

No. 3096, 31,000d — Marilyn Monroe (1926-62), actress, wearing: a, Black swimsuit, eyes closed. b, White dress. c, Choker. d, Black dress, eyes open.

No. 3097, 31,000d — Whales: a, Balaena mysticetus. b, Balaenoptera musculus. c, Megaptera novaeangliae. d, Physeter macrocephalus.

No. 3098, 96,000d, Gandhi, diff. No. 3099, 96,000d, St. John Paul II, diff. No. 3100, 96,000d, Presley, guitar and Judy Tyler (1932-57), actress. No. 3101, 96,000d, Three rugby players, diff. No. 3102, 96,000d, Table tennis players. No. 3103, 96,000d, Austin 480 and Rosenbauer Panther 6x6 CAS fire trucks. No. 3104, 96,000d, British Railways Class 801, Great Britain. No. 3105, 96,000d, Anopheles gambiae, and mother and child under mosquito netting. No. 3106, 96,000d, Cape Tainaron Lighthouse, Greece. No. 3107, 96,000d, Coracias caudatus, Scarabaeus sacer, people harvesting beans. No. 3108, 96,000d, Rottweilers. No. 3109, 96,000d, Tyto alba, Athene noctua. No. 3110, 96,000d, Rhetus periander. No. 3111, 96,000d, Terrapene carolina carolina. No. 3112, 96,000d, Propithecus coronatus, Propithecus diadema. No. 3113, 96,000d, Lactarius indigo. No. 3114, 96,000d, Amethyst. No. 3115, 124,000d, Monroe, diff. No. 3116, 124,000d, Balaena mysticetus, diff.

**2016, Mar. 30 Litho. *Perf. 13¼***
**Sheets of 4, #a-d**

**3079-3097** A409 Set of 19 220.00 220.00

**Souvenir Sheets**

**3098-3116** A409 Set of 19 175.00 175.00

Nos. 3098-3116 each contain one 51x90mm stamp.

Philataipei 2016 World Stamp Championship Exhibition, Taipei — A410

No. 3117: a, Statue of Genghis Khan (1162-1227) on horseback, Mausoleum of Genghis Khan, Xinjie, People's Republic of China. b, Mausoleum of Genghis Khan and scultpture of Genghis Khan. c, Genghis Khan and Falco rusticolus. d, Warriors on horseback, statue of Genghis Khan on horseback.
76,000d, Statue of Genghis Khan on horseback, diff.

**Litho. With Foil Application**
**2016, July 20 *Perf. 13¼***

**3117** A410 19,000d Sheet of 4, #a-d 7.00 7.00

**Souvenir Sheet**
***Perf.***

**3118** A410 76,000d multi 7.00 7.00

No. 3118 contains one 40mm diameter stamp.

World Youth Day — A411

No. 3119: a, Pope Francis and youths. b, Pope John Paul II (1920-2005) and youths. c, Pope Benedict XVI waving. d, Youths at 2016 World Youth Day celebrations.
96,000d, Youths, flags of Poland and cross.

**2016, July 20 Litho. *Perf. 13¼***

**3119** A411 31,000d Sheet of 4, #a-d 11.50 11.50

**Souvenir Sheet**

**3120** A411 96,000d multi 8.75 8.75

Animals — A412

No. 3121, 31,000d — Mammals from Africa: a, Acinonyx jubatus. b, Elephantulus myurus. c, Phacochoerus africanus. d, Erythrocebus patas.

No. 3122, 31,000d — Bears (Ursus americanus) from the Americas: a, Bear and squirrel. b, Bear near lake and head of bear. c, Adult bear and cubs climbing tree. d, Three bears, one with fish in mouth.

No. 3123, 31,000d — Mammals from the Arctic: a, Vulpes lagopus. b, Ovibos moschatus. c, Alces alces. d, Lepus americanus.

No. 3124, 31,000d — Pandas (Ailuropoda melanoleuca) from Asia: a, Four pandas. b, Two pandas. c, One panda. d, Panda in water, farmers in field.

No. 3125, 31,000d — Deer from Europe: a, Dama dama. b, Blastocerus dichotomus. c, Dama dama mesopotamica. d, Axis axis.

No. 3126, 31,000d — Wolves from Europe: a, Canis lupus lupus, tail in foreground. b, Canis lupus albus. c, Canis lupus lupus, head in foreground. d, Two canis lupus lupus fighting.

No. 3127, 31,000d — Jaguars (Panthera onca) from the Americas: a, Head of jaguar and jaguar with black fur. b, Jaguar on log. c, Two jaguars. d, Heads of jaguar and jaguar with black fur.

No. 3128, 31,000d — Tigers from Asia: a, Panthera tigris amoyensis. b, Panthera tigris jacksoni. c, Panthera tigris altaica. d, Panthera tigris corbetti.

No. 3129, 31,000d — Birds from Africa: a, Phalacrocorax carbo. b, Gavia arctica with wings extended. c, Thalassarche melanophris. d, Pelecanus crispus.

No. 3130, 31,000d — Birds from the Americas: a, Falco sparverius. b, Somateria mollissima. c, Meleagris gallopovo. d, Phoenicopterus ruber.

No. 3131, 31,000d — Birds from the Arctic: a, Gavia arctica in water. b, Alca torda. c, Fratercula arctica. d, Somateria spectabilis.

No. 3132, 31,000d — Birds from Asia: a, Plegadis falcinellus. b, Coracias benghalensis. c, Todiramphus chloris. d, Neophron percnopterus.

No. 3133, 31,000d — Owls from Europe: a, Strix uralensis. b, Aegolius funereus. c, Bubo scandiacus. d, Otus scops.

No. 3134, 31,000d — Insects and spiders from the Americas: a, Graphocephala coccinea. b, Acharia stimulea. c, Murgantia histrionica. d, Araneus trifolium.

No. 3135, 31,000d — Butterflies from Asia: a, Melitaea sibina. b, Apatura ilia. c, Sasakia charonda. d, Tatinga thibetanus.

No. 3136, 31,000d — Fish from the Arctic: a, Esox lucius. b, Lota lota. c, Gasterosteus aculeatus. d, Oncorhynchus keta.

No. 3137, 31,000d — Reptiles from Africa: a, Afroablepharus africanus. b, Feylinia polylepis. c, Philothamnus thomensis. d, Hemidactylus principensis.

No. 3138, 31,000d — Predators from Africa: a, Osteolaemus tetraspis. b, Canis mesomelas. c, Caracal caracal. d, Python sebae.

No. 3139, 96,000d, Diceros bicornis. No. 3140, 96,000d, Four Ursus americanus. No. 3141, 96,000d, Canis lupus arctos. No. 3142, 96,000d, Ailurus fulgens. No. 3143, 96,000d, Odocoileus virginianus. No. 3144, 96,000d, Canis lupus lupus, diff. No. 3145, 96,000d, Panthera onca, diff. No. 3146, 96,000d, Panthera tigris tigris. No. 3147, 96,000d, Dromaius novaehollandiae. No. 3148, 96,000d, Fregata magnificens. No. 3149, 96,000d, Anas acuta. No. 3150, 96,000d, Ardeola bacchus. No. 3151, 96,000d, Strix nebulosa. No. 3152, 96,000d, Theatops californiensis. No. 3153, 96,000d, Heliophorus saphir. No. 3154, 96,000d, Salvelinus alpinus. No. 3155, 96,000d, Cordylus tropidosternum. No. 3156, 96,000d, Vulpes zerda.

**2016, July 20 Litho. *Perf. 13¼***

**Sheets of 4, #a-d**

**3121-3138** A412 Set of 18 205.00 205.00

**Souvenir Sheets**

**3139-3156** A412 Set of 18 160.00 160.00

Philataipei 2016 World Stamp Championship Exhibition, Taipei — A413

No. 3157 — 14th Dalai Lama: a, Facing right, holding object with pink strap. b, With Tsai Ing-wen, President of Republic of China. c, With bird, praying. d, With Chen Shui-bian, ex-President of Republic of China.

76,000d, 14th Dalai Lama, Pres. Tsai Ing-wen, flag of Republic of China, birds and flowers.

**2016, Sept. 12 Litho. *Perf. 13¼***

**3157** A413 19,000d Sheet of 4, #a-d 7.00 7.00

**Souvenir Sheet**

**3158** A413 76,000d multi 7.00 7.00

No. 3158 contains one 47x81mm stamp.

A414

No. 3159, 31,000d — Various stamps, including: a, Cambodia #1631 held in tongs. b, Germany #B206 held in fingers. c, Sharjah bird stamp covered by finger. d, Chad #521 held in tongs.

No. 3160, 31,000d — Nelson Mandela (1918-2013), President of South Africa: a, On 10-rand South African banknote, people with fists raised. b, With military officer. c, Holding finger up at microphone. d, Head facing left.

No. 3161, 31,000d — Fire trucks: a, Mercedes-Benz L6600 DL30. b, Bedford TK. c, ZIL-130. d, Citroen P45.

No. 3162, 31,000d — Steam locomotives: a, Castle class 4-6-0 No. 5013. b, London and North Eastern Railway Gresley K4 61994, The Great Marquess. c, Queensland Railways A10 No. 6. d, Union Pacific Big Boy 4-8-8-4.

No. 3163, 31,000d — High-speed trains of People's Republic of China: a, CRH1E, CRH2C. b, CRH5. c, CRH1. d, Shanghai Transrapid.

No. 3164, 31,000d — Russian soccer players at 2018 World Cup Soccer Championships, Russia, and landmarks: a, Fyodor Smolov, Church of Our Saviour of the Spilled Blood. b, Ramil Sheydayev, Winter Palace. c, Alexandr Kokorin, Bolshoi Theater. d, Aleksandr Golovin, Kizhi Pogost.

No. 3165, 31,000d — Chess players: a, Viswanathan Anand. b, Maxime Vachier-Lagrave. c, Vladimir Kramnik. d, Fabiano Caruana.

No. 3166, 31,000d — Cats: a, Abyssinian. b, Maine Coon cat. c, Cornish Rex. d, Norwegian Forest cat.

No. 3167, 31,000d — Dolphins: a, Stenella clymene. b, Stenella frontalis. c, Steno bredanensis. d, Tursiops truncatus.

No. 3168, 31,000d — Birds of prey: a, Elanus axillaris. b, Aquila fasciata. c, Buteo plagiatus. d, Milvus milvus.

No. 3169, 31,000d — Bee-eaters: a, Merops nubicoides. b, Two Merops apiaster and flower. c, One Merops apiaster. d, Two Merops apiaster, no flower.

No. 3170, 31,000d — Fish and corals: a, Chaetodontoplus conspicillatus, Himerometra robustipinna. b, Paracanthurus hepatus, Gorgonia flabellum. c, Holocentrus rufus, Ocyurus chrysurus, Aplysina fistularis. d, Scarus ferrugineus, Turbinaria reniformis.

No. 3171, 31,000d — Shells and lighthouses: a, Angaria delphinus, Peggys Point Lighthouse, Nova Scotia. b, Tudicla spirillus, Kéréon Lighthouse, France. c, Achatina panthera, Les Eclaireurs Lighthouse, Argentina. d, Drupa morum, Fanad Head Lighthouse, Ireland.

No. 3172, 31,000d — Turtles: a, Aldabrachelys gigantea. b, Eretmochelys imbricata. c, Caretta caretta. d, Gopherus agassizii.

No. 3173, 31,000d — Dinosaurs: a, Edmontosaurus. b, Confuciusornis. c, Velociraptor. d, Sauropelta, Kentrosaurus.

No. 3174, 31,000d — Mushrooms: a, Morchella esculenta. b, Leratiomyces. c, Cyathus striatus. d, Hydnellum peckii.

No. 3175, 31,000d — Orchids: a, Thunia alba. b, Vanilla planifolia. c, Cymbidium sp. d, Caleana major.

No. 3176, 31,000d — Minerals and volcanos: a, Limonite, Galeras Volcano, Colombia. b, Calcite, Taal Volcano, Philippines. c, Biotite, Popocatépetl Volcano, Mexico. d, Malachite and chrysocolla, Mount Merapi, Indonesia.

No. 3177, 31,000d — Christmas Truce of 1914: a, Soldiers shaking hands. b, Soldiers, Christmas tree, barbed wire. c, Soldiers laying down arms. d, Soldier carrying small Christmas tree.

No. 3178, 96,000d, Japan #Z119 held in fingers. No. 3179, 96,000d, Mandela, diff. No. 3180, 96,000d, Ural 43206 fire truck. No. 3181, 96,000d, Great Western Railway 4200 Class 4277. No. 3182, 96,000d, CRH-X Yi train. No. 3183, 96,000d, Igor Shuvalov, head of Russian 2018 World Cup Soccer Championships organizing committee. No. 3184, 96,000d, Magnus Carlsen. No. 3185, 96,000d, Sorrel Somali cat. No. 3186, 96,000d, Sousa teuszii. No. 3187, 96,000d, Pandion halietus. No. 3188, 96,000d, Merops ornatus. No. 3189, 96,000d, Balistoides conspicillum, Stichodactyla haddoni. No. 3190, 96,000d, Cymbiola imperialis, Tillamook Rock Lighthouse, Oregon. No. 3191, 96,000d, Terrapene carolina bauri. No. 3192, 96,000d, Plateosaurus, Coelophysis. No. 3193, 96,000d, Ramaria aurea. No. 3194, 96,000d, Phalaenopsis cornu-cervi. No. 3195, 96,000d, Gormanite, Mauna Loa, Hawaii. No. 3196, 96,000d, Soldiers celebrating Christmas at barrier.

**2016, Sept. 12 Litho. *Perf. 13¼***

**Sheets of 4, #a-d**

**3159-3177** A414 Set of 19 215.00 215.00

**Souvenir Sheets**

**3178-3196** A414 Set of 19 165.00 165.00

Birds A415

No. 3197: a, Busarellus nigricollis. b, Spizaetus ornatus. c, Caracara plancus. d, Elanus leucurus. e, Falco deiroleucus. f, Terathopius ecaudatus and snake.

**2016, Nov. 10 Litho. *Die Cut***

**Self-Adhesive**

**3197** Block of 6 10.50

*a.-f.* A415 20,000d Any single 1.75 1.75

Printed in sheets of four blocks, with each block having different background colors.

A416

No. 3198, 31,000d — 2016 World Ice Hockey Championships, Moscow: a, Denomination at UR, puck at LR near stick blades. b, Denomination at UL, player's skate to left of puck. c, Denomination at UR, puck at LR near player's skate. d, Denomination at UL, player's stick blade to left of puck.

No. 3199, 31,000d — Table tennis players: a, Denomination at UR, player's paddle at left. b, Denomination at UL, player's paddle at right, ball at left. c, Denomination at UL, player's paddle at right, ball at right. d, Denomination at UL, player's paddle at left.

No. 3200, 31,000d — Formula 1 race cars: a, Mercedes-Benz W196. b, Haas VF-16. c, Benetton B193B. d, Brabham BT19.

No. 3201, 31,000d — Gold medalists at 2016 Winter Olympics: a, Dominique Gisin. b, Alexander Legkov. c, Martin Fourcade. d, Matthias Mayer.

No. 3202, 31,000d — Rotary International emblem, butterflies and flowers: a, Charaxes thomasius, Brillantaisia owariensis. b, Cyrestis camillus, Heliconia psittacorum. c, Hypolimnas salmacis, Sobralia macrantha. d, Acraea zetes, Cypripedium lowii.

No. 3203, 31,000d — Battle of Moscow, 75th anniv.: a, Portrait of General Ivan Panfilov, by Vasily Yakovlev (1893-1953), and The Exploit of 28 Heroes from Panfilov's Division, by Alexei Komarov (1879-1977). b, Battle of Moscow, by Yevgeny Danilevsky (1928-2010). c, Battle of Moscow, by Pavel Ryzhenko (1970-2014). d, Gunners Fight of December 3, 1941, by Vladimir Korobkov (1951-2014).

No. 3204, 31,000d — Nikola Tesla (1846-1943), inventor: a, Tesla reading book, and electric motor. b, 2011 Tesla Roadster 2.5 S. c, 2018 Tesla Model 3. d, Tesla and Westinghouse alternating current motor.

No. 3205, 31,000d — Space technology: a, Concept of Bigelow Commercial Space Station. b, Orion multi-purpose vehicle. c, Copernicus concept vehicle. d, Commercial space station.

No. 3206, 31,000d — Nobel Laureates: a, 1979 Peace laureate, Mother Teresa (1910-97), and dove. b, 1993 Peace laureate, Nelson Mandela (1918-2013), and flag of South Africa. c, 1913 Literature laureate, Rabindranath Tagore (1861-1941), and Nelumbo nucifera. d, 1989 Peace laureate, 14th Dalai Lama, and Potala Palace.

No. 3207, 31,000d — Red Cross: a, Worker in protective gear feeding infant with bottle. b, Worker with tongue depressor checking patient's mouth. c, Worker with stethoscope checking boy. d, Worker inoculating child.

No. 3208, 31,000d — Sergei Prokofiev (1891-1953), composer, with: a, Dancers from his ballet, Romeo and Juliet. b, Scene from film, Ivan the Terrible. c, Characters from Peter and the Wolf. d, Piano and score.

No. 3209, 31,000d — Paintings by Claude Monet (1840-1926): a, Argenteuil, 1875. b, Cliffs Near Dieppe, 1882, and 1884 self-portrait. c, Exterior of the Saint-Lazare Station, Sunlight Effect, 1877. d, Poplars on the Epte, 1891.

No. 3210, 31,000d — Paintings by Berthe Morisot (1841-95): a, Boats Under Construction, 1874. b, Two Nymphs Embracing, 1892. c, Girl Playing the Mandolin, 1890, and Young Woman Seated on a Sofa, 1879. d, Girl in Rose Dress, 1888.

No. 3211, 31,000d — Paintings by Odilon Redon (1840-1916): a, Closed Eyes, 1895. b, Reflection, 1900-05. c, Ophelia Among the Flowers, 1905-08. d, Buddha, 1906-07.

No. 3212, 31,000d — Paintings by Pablo Picasso (1881-1973): a, Head, 1926. b, Seated Woman (Jacqueline), 1962. c, Nude Woman with Necklace, 1968. d, Head of a Woman 1922.

No. 3213, 31,000d — American Impressionists and their paintings: a, Day Dreams, 1889, by Theodore Robinson (1852-96). b, End of the Season Sun, 1884, by William Merritt Chase (1849-1916). c, Uplands, Novembere, 1939, by Daniel Garber (1880-1958). d, The End of the Streetcar Line, Oak Park, Illinois, 1893, by Childe Hassam (1859-1935).

No. 3214, 31,000d — Paintings of nudes: a, Red-headed Nude Crouching, 1897, by Henri de Toulouse-Lautrec (1864-1901). b, Rolla, 1878, by Henri Gervex, (1852-1929). c, Reclining Nude with Pink Robe, 1937, by Lev Tchistovsky (1902-69). d, Blonde Girl on a Bed, 1987, by Lucian Freud (1922-2011).

No. 3215, 31,000d — Paintings of roosters (New Year 2017, Year of the Rooster) by: a, Xu Beihong (1895-1953), denomination at UL. b, Chen Dayu (1912-2001). c, Zhang Daqian (1899-1983). d, Xu Beihong, diff., denomination at UR.

No. 3216, 120,000d, Two ice hockey players, diff. No. 3217, 120,000d, Table tennis player, diff. No. 3218, 120,000d, Ferrari SF16-H. No. 3219, 120,000d, Vic Wild. No. 3220, 120,000d, Rotary International emblem, Acraea jodutta, Sobralia macrantha. No. 3221, 120,000d, G. I. Zhukov, Battle of Moscow, 1941, by Nikolay Repin. No. 3222, 120,000d, Tesla and alternating current generator. No. 3223, 120,000d, Concept for Commercial Space Station Hotel. No. 3224, 120,000d, Dr. Martin Luther King, Jr. (1929-68), 1964 Nobel peace laurate, and U.S. Capitol. No. 3225, 120,000d, Red Cross worker holding child, globe. No. 3226, 120,000d, Prokofiev and dancer from his ballet, Cinderella. No. 3227, 120,000d, Argenteuil, Seen from the Small Arm of the Seine, 1872, by Monet. No. 3228, 120,000d, Girl with Dog, 1886, by Morisot. No. 3229, 120,000d, The Birth of Venus, 1910, by Redon. No. 3230, 120,000d, Paloma with Doll, 1952, and Sylvette, 1954, by Picasso. No. 3231, 120,000d, Nurse and Child, 1896-97, and Young Girl Holding a Loose Bouquet, 1880, by Mary Cassatt (1844-1926). No. 3232, 120,000d, Nymphs, 1878, by William-Adolphe Bouguereau (1825-1905). No. 3233, 120,000d, Rooster, by Chen Dayu, diff.

**2016, Nov. 10 Litho. *Perf. 13¼***

**Sheets of 4, #a-d**

**3198-3215** A416 Set of 18 190.00 190.00

**Souvenir Sheets**

**3216-3233** A416 Set of 18 185.00 185.00

Nos. 3216-3233 each contain one 60x40mm stamp.

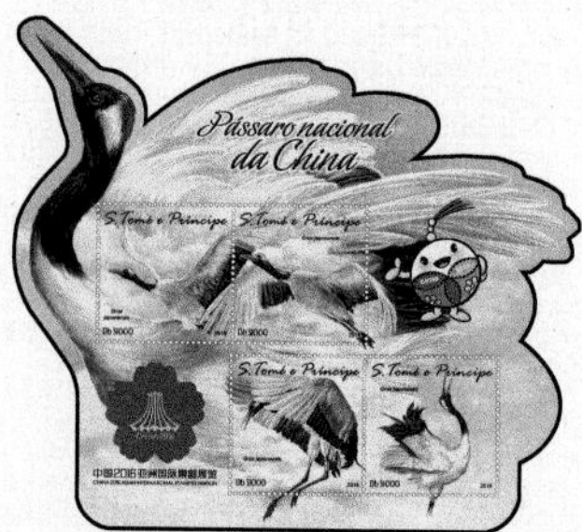


Grus Japonensis — A417

No. 3234: a, Bird in flight and wing tip of other bird, Latin name at LL. b, Bird in flight, Latin name at UR. c, Bird landing, Latin name at LL. d, Bird standing.

120,000d, Bird in flight, diff.

**2016, Nov. 10 Litho. *Perf. 13¼***

**3234** A417 31,000d Sheet of 4, #a-d 11.00 11.00

**Souvenir Sheet**

**3235** A417 120,000d multi 10.50 10.50

China 2016 International Stamp Exhibition, Nanning. No. 3235 contains one 48x36mm stamp.

Souvenir Sheet

U.S. President-Elect Donald Trump, and Wife, Melania — A418

**2016, Nov. 10 Litho. *Perf. 13¼***

**3236** A418 120,000d multi 10.50 10.50

2017 Confederations Cup Soccer Tournament, Russia — A419

Venues: No. 3237, 31,000d, Otkrytie Arena, Moscow. No. 3238, 31,000d, Fisht Olympic Stadium, Sochi. No. 3239, 31,000d, Kazan Arena, Kazan. No. 3240, 31,000d, Krestovsky Stadium, St. Petersburg.

120,000d, Soccer player, ball, Russian flag and emblem.

**2017, Mar. 13 Litho. *Perf. 13¼***

**3237-3240** A419 Set of 4 11.00 11.00

**Souvenir Sheet**

**3241** A419 120,000d multi 10.50 10.50

A420

No. 3242, 31,000d — Pandas: a, Two Ailuropoda melanoleuca. b, One Ailuropoda melanoleuca. c, Ailurus fulgens next to tree. d, Ailurus fulgens and fallen tree.

No. 3243, 31,000d — Wild cats: a, Panthera leo. b, Puma concolor. c, Panthera uncia. d, Acinonyx jubatus.

No. 3244, 31,000d — Dolphins: a, Lagenodelphis hosei. b, Tursiops truncatus. c, Feresa attenuata. d, Steno bredanensis.

No. 3245, 31,000d — Aquatic birds: a, Ephippiorhynchus asiaticus. b, Pelecanus occidentalis. c, Podiceps cristatus. d, Phoenicopterus ruber.

No. 3246, 31,000d — Birds of prey: a, Pandion haliaetus. b, Elanus caeruleus. c, Gymnogyps californianus. d, Falco columbarius.

No. 3247, 31,000d — Owls: a, Megascops clarkii. b, Tyto multipunctata. c, Bubo virginianus. d, Otus sunia.

No. 3248, 31,000d — Butterflies: a, Arctia villica. b, Coenonympha pamphilus. c, Zygaena filipendulae. d, Cyclosia papilionaris.

No. 3249, 31,000d — Turtles: a, Terrapene carolina carolina. b, Geochelone elegans. c, Sternotherus carinatus. d, Chelydra serpentina.

No. 3250, 31,000d — Dinosaurs: a, Parasaurolophus. b, Stegosaurus. c, Triceratops. d, Tyrannosaurus rex.

No. 3251, 31,000d — Extinct animals: a, Diceros bicornis longipes. b, Panthera tigris sondaica. c, Monachus tropicalis. d, Capra pyrenaica pyrenaica.

No. 3252, 31,000d — Orchids: a, Guarianthe aurantiaca. b, Laeliocattleya Gold Digger. c, Cattleya amethystoglossa. d, Dendrobium victoriae-reginae.

No. 3253, 31,000d — Mushrooms: a, Morchella esculenta. b, Leccinum quercinum and Sciurus vulgaris. c, Gyromitra esculenta and squirrel. d, Cantharellus cibarius.

No. 3254, 31,000d — Minerals: a, Smoky quartz. b, Olivine. c, Galena. d, Quartz.

No. 3255, 31,000d — Lighthouses, birds and shells: a, List-West Lighthouse, Germany, Larus delawarensis. b, Stangholmen Lighthouse, Sweden, Chicoreus florifer. c, Tourlitis Lighthouse, Greece, Hexaplex regius. d, Sturgeon Bay Ship Canal Pierhead Lighthouse, Wisconsin, and birds.

No. 3256, 31,000d — Scouting movement, 110th anniv.: a, Scout and sculpture *The Ideal Scout*, by Robert Tait McKenzie (1867-1938). b, Girl Scouts examining flora. c, Scout and leader with bow and arrow. d, Honorary scout, Duchess of Cambridge.

No. 3257, 31,000d — Pres. John F. Kennedy (1917-63): a, With wife, Jacqueline (1929-94). b, With ships and airplanes of the Cuban Missile Crisis. c, Standing in limousine in Tampa, Florida motorcade. d, With Marilyn Monroe (1926-62).

No. 3258, 31,000d — 90th birthday of Pope Benedict XVI: a, On red carpet. b, With arm extended forward, wearing miter. c, Waving. d, Holding aspergillum.

No. 3259, 31,000d — Metropolitan Museum of Art, 145th anniv.: a, Main museum building and *The Harvesters*, by Pieter Bruegel the Elder. b, Greek and Roman Art gallery and marble sarcophagus with garlands. c, Met Breuer Building and *The Charnel House*, by Pablo Picasso. d, The Cloisters and Theodosius Enterings stained-glass window.

No. 3260, 31,000d — New Year 2017 (Year of the Rooster): a, Rooster facing right, bamboo in background. b, Rooster facing left, pagoda in background. c, Rooster with head at left, facing right, torii at LR. d, Rooster facing left, arches at lower left and center.

No. 3261, 124,000d, Two Ailuropoda melanoleuca, diff. No. 3262, 124,000d, Panthera tigris. No. 3263, 124,000d, Gampus griseus. No. 3264, 124,000d, Aix galericulata. No. 3265, 124,000d, Aquila chrysaetos. No. 3266, 124,000d, Pulsatrix perspicillata. No. 3267, 124,000d, Parnassius apollo. No. 3268, 124,000d, Chelonoidis nigra. No. 3269, 124,000d, Hadrosaurus. No. 3270, 124,000d, Thylacinus cynocephalus. No. 3271, 124,000d, Laelia cinnabarina. No. 3272, 124,000d, Pleurotus pulmonarius. No. 3273, 124,000d, Rubies. No. 3274, 124,000d, St. Joseph North Pier Lighthouse, Michigan. No. 3275, 124,000d, Juliette Gordon Low (1860-1927), founder of Girl Scouts of the U.S.A., and Girl Scout. No. 3276, 124,000d, Apollo 15 capsule and space rover, U.S. flag. No. 3277, 124,000d, Pope Benedict XVI, diff. No. 3278, 124,000d, John Taylor Johnston (1820-93), founder of Metropolitan Museum of Art, and human-headed winged lion sculpture. No. 3279, 124,000d, Rooster, diff.

**2017, Mar. 13 Litho. *Perf. 13¼***

**Sheets of 4, #a-d**

**3242-3260** A420 Set of 19 205.00 205.00

**Souvenir Sheets**

**3261-3279** A420 Set of 19 205.00 205.00

A421

Designs: No. 3280, 31,000d, Marilyn Monroe (1926-62), actress, wearing red gown. No. 3281, 31,000d, Monroe holding blue kerchief above her head. No. 3282, 31,000d, Monroe on bed. No. 3283, 31,000d, Monroe with actresses Lauren Bacall (1924-2014), and Betty Grable (1916-73).

No. 3284, Monroe, Hollywood sign, and her star on Hollywood Walk of Fame.

No. 3285, 31,000d, Princess Diana (1961-97) and Queen Elizabeth II. No. 3286, 31,000d, Princess Diana, wearing white dress, holding child. No. 3287, 31,000d, Princess Diana, wearing blue dress, holding child. No. 3288, 31,000d, Princess Diana and horse.

No. 3289, Princess Diana wearing white hat.

No. 3290, 31,000d, St. Teresa of Calcutta (1910-97) and Carpe Diem crest. No. 3291, 31,000d, St. Teresa and Mother Teresa Roman Catholic Primary School, Cambridge, Ontario, Canada. No. 3292, 31,000d, St. Teresa and St. John Paul II (1920-2005). No. 3293, 31,000d, St. Teresa delivering 1979 Nobel Peace Prize acceptance speech.

No. 3294, St. Teresa and dove.

No. 3295, 31,000d, Valentina Tereshkova, first woman in space, with medal. No. 3296, 31,000d, Tereshkova and technician. No. 3297, 31,000d, Tereshkova with medical monitor wires attached to her. No. 3298, 31,000d, Tereshkova and her childhood home.

No. 3299, Tereshkova's Vostok 6 capsule.

No. 3300, 31,000d, Amazona versicolor and St. Lucia #902. No. 3301, 31,000d, Pongo pygmaeus and Indonesia #1380. No. 3302, 31,000d, Ailuropoda melanoleuca and Italy #3377. No. 3303, 31,000d, Diceros bicornis and Great Britain #2890.

No. 3304, Eretmochelys imbricata and fantasy Australia stamp.

No. 3305, 31,000d, Titanic at sea. No. 3306, 31,000d, Deck of Titanic and its lifeboats. No. 3307, 31,000d, Titanic listing, lifeboat in water. No. 3308, 31,000d, Titanic sinking.

No. 3309, Titanic at sea, diff.

No. 3310, 31,000d, USS Jimmy Carter and U.S. flag. No. 3311, 31,000d, HMS Artful and British flag. No. 3312, 31,000d, Romeo Romei and flag of Italy. No. 3313, 31,000d, Typhoon Class submarine Akula and flag of Russia.

No. 3314, HMS Vanguard and British flag.

No. 3315, 31,000d, Russian train car and bell ringer. No. 3316, 31,000d, Train repairman at Demikhov Engineering Works, Russia. No. 3317, 31,000d, Train near Russian Soyuz launchpad. No. 3318, 31,000d, Train and map of Russia

No. 3319, Russian train and buildings.

No. 3320, 31,000d, Shinkansen Series 700T. No. 3321, 31,000d, ETR 460. No. 3322, 31,000d, Shinkansen Series E3. No. 3323, 31,000d, Shinkansen Series E5.

No. 3324, Shinkansen Series W7.

No. 3325, 31,000d, Enzo Ferrari (1898-1988), automobile manufacturer, driving Ferrari 250 GTO. No. 3326, 31,000d, Ferrari and auto workers manufacturing 1947 Ferrari 125 S. No. 3327, 31,000d, 1947 Ferrari 125S and 1947 Ferrari 159S. No. 3328, 31,000d, Interior of Ferrari automobile and Ferrari with open hood.

No. 3329, Ferrari with goggles and Ferrari 125 S.

No. 3330, 31,000d, 1923 LaFrance Race-about fire truck, U.S. No. 3331, 31,000d, 2012 MAN Aerial Ladder Platform fire truck, Great Britain. No. 3332, 31,000d, IFA S4000-1 fire truck, Germany. No. 3333, 31,000d, Fire truck pump and hose couplings.

No. 3334, 1950 Mack fire truck, Great Britain.

No. 3335, 31,000d, Ferdinand von Zeppelin (1838-1917), airship manufacturer. No. 3336, 31,000d, LZ 129 Hindenburg and "Hindenburg" inscription. No. 3337, 31,000d, LZ 129 Hindenburg and propeller. No. 3338, 31,000d, Graf Zeppelin.

No. 3339, Ferdinand von Zeppelin and airship.

No. 3340, 31,000d, Concorde over Washington, D.C.. No. 3341, 31,000d, Concorde over New York City. No. 3342, 31,000d, Concorde over London. No. 3343, 31,000d, Concorde over Paris.

No. 3344, Concorde over Barbados.

No. 3345, 31,000d, Donald Campbell (1921-67), British flag and Bluebird K7. No. 3346, 31,000d, Bluebird K7, emblem and mechanical drawing. No. 3347, 31,000d, Campbell in Bluebird K7, and Mr. Whoppit mascot. No. 3348, 31,000d, Bluebird K7 and Campbell's signature.

No. 3349, Campbell wearing helmet, British flag and Bluebird K7 emblem.

No. 3350, 31,000d, Charles Darwin (1809-82), naturalist, watching tortoise. No. 3351, 31,000d, Darwin and his book, *The Origin of Species*. No. 3352, 31,000d, Sculpture of Darwin and illustrations of finches. No. 3353, 31,000d, Darwin and HMS Beagle.

No. 3354, Darwin, bookshelves and box of specimens.

No. 3355, 31,000d, Rotary Intenational emblem and Paul P. Harris 1868-1947), its founder. No. 3356, 31,000d, Rotary International emblem and child drinking water from spigot. No. 3357, 31,000d, Rotary International emblem and infant receiving medical care. No. 3358, 31,000d, Rotary International emblem and woman making shoes.

No. 3359, Harris and other Rotary members, 1905.

No. 3360, 31,000d, Sir Ernest Henry Shackleton (1874-1922), Antarctic explorer, wearing hat. No. 3361, 31,000d, Shackleton and his ship, Endurance, trapped in ice. No. 3362, 31,000d, Sled dogs on the Endurance. No. 3363, 31,000d, Rescue of men on Elephant Island.

No. 3364, Shackleton and Frank Wild (1873-1939), assistant to Shackleton.

No. 3365, 31,000d, Alaskan malamute sled dog. No. 3366, 31,000d, Greenlandic dog wearing sled harness. No. 3367, 31,000d, Chinook sled dogs. No. 3368, 31,000d, Canadian Eskimo dog.

No. 3369, Team of Siberian husky sled dogs.

**2017, May 8 Litho. *Perf. 13¼***

**Marilyn Monroe**

**3280-3283** A421 Set of 4 11.00 11.00

**Souvenir Sheet**

**3284** A421 124,000d multi 11.00 11.00

**Princess Diana**

**3285-3288** A421 Set of 4 11.00 11.00

**Souvenir Sheet**

**3289** A421 124,000d multi 11.00 11.00

**St. Teresa of Calcutta**

**3290-3293** A421 Set of 4 11.00 11.00

**Souvenir Sheet**

**3294** A421 124,000d multi 11.00 11.00

**Valentina Tereshkova**

**3295-3298** A421 Set of 4 11.00 11.00

**Souvenir Sheet**

**3299** A421 124,000d multi 11.00 11.00

**Animals and Worldwide Fund for Nature Stamps**

**3300-3303** A421 Set of 4 11.00 11.00

**Souvenir Sheet**

**3304** A421 124,000d multi 11.00 11.00

**Sinking of the Titanic, 105th Anniv.**

**3305-3308** A421 Set of 4 11.00 11.00

**Souvenir Sheet**

**3309** A421 124,000d multi 11.00 11.00

**Submarines**

**3310-3313** A421 Set of 4 11.00 11.00

**Souvenir Sheet**

**3314** A421 124,000d multi 11.00 11.00

**Russian Railroads, 180th Anniv.**

**3315-3318** A421 Set of 4 11.00 11.00

**Souvenir Sheet**

**3319** A421 124,000d multi 11.00 11.00

**High-speed Trains**

**3320-3323** A421 Set of 4 11.00 11.00

**Souvenir Sheet**

**3324** A421 124,000d multi 11.00 11.00

**Ferrari Automobiles, 70th Anniv.**

**3325-3328** A421 Set of 4 11.00 11.00

**Souvenir Sheet**

**3329** A421 124,000d multi 11.00 11.00

**Fire Trucks**

**3330-3333** A421 Set of 4 11.00 11.00

**Souvenir Sheet**

**3334** A421 124,000d multi 11.00 11.00

**Zeppelins**

**3335-3338** A421 Set of 4 11.00 11.00

**Souvenir Sheet**

**3339** A421 124,000d multi 11.00 11.00

**Concorde**

**3340-3343** A421 Set of 4 11.00 11.00

**Souvenir Sheet**

**3344** A421 124,000d multi 11.00 11.00

**Donald Campbell and Bluebird K7**

**3345-3348** A421 Set of 4 11.00 11.00

**Souvenir Sheet**

**3349** A421 124,000d multi 11.00 11.00

**Charles Darwin**

**3350-3353** A421 Set of 4 11.00 11.00

**Souvenir Sheet**

**3354** A421 124,000d multi 11.00 11.00

**Rotary International**

**3355-3358** A421 Set of 4 11.00 11.00

**Souvenir Sheet**

**3359** A421 124,000d multi 11.00 11.00

**Sir Ernest Shackleton**

**3360-3363** A421 Set of 4 11.00 11.00

**Souvenir Sheet**

**3364** A421 124,000d multi 11.00 11.00

**Sled Dogs**

**3365-3368** A421 Set of 4 11.00 11.00

**Souvenir Sheet**

**3369** A421 124,000d multi 11.00 11.00

A422

A423

A424

Ursus Maritimus A425

Design: 124,000d, Polar bear crossing crack in ice.

**2017, May 8 Litho. *Perf. 13¼***

| | | | | |
|---|---|---|---|---|
| **3370** | A422 | 31,000d multi | 2.75 | 2.75 |
| **3371** | A423 | 31,000d multi | 2.75 | 2.75 |
| **3372** | A424 | 31,000d multi | 2.75 | 2.75 |
| **3373** | A425 | 31,000d multi | 2.75 | 2.75 |
| | | *Nos. 3370-3373 (4)* | 11.00 | 11.00 |

### Souvenir Sheet

| | | | | |
|---|---|---|---|---|
| **3374** | A422 | 124,000d multi | 11.00 | 11.00 |

Nos. 3370-3373 were printed in sheets of 4.

Badminton Players — A426

No. 3375: a, Viktor Axelsen, flag of Denmark. b, Chen Long, flag of People's Republic of China. c, Lee Chong Wei, flag of Malaysia. d, Lin Dan, flag of People's Republic of China.

No. 3376: a, Lin Dan, diff. b, Lee Chong Wei, diff.

### Litho., Sheet Margin Litho. With Foil Application

**2017, May 8 *Perf. 13¼***

| | | | | |
|---|---|---|---|---|
| **3375** | A426 | 31,000d Sheet of 4, #a-d | 11.00 | 11.00 |

### Souvenir Sheet

| | | | | |
|---|---|---|---|---|
| **3376** | A426 | 62,000d Sheet of 2, #a-b | 11.00 | 11.00 |

2017 World Stamp Exhibition, Bandung, Indonesia. No. 3376 contains two 33x51mm stamps.

1975 Meeting of Mao Zedong (1893-1976), Chairman of People's Republic of China and President Manuel Pinto da Costa — A427

Trees on Huangshan Mountain, People's Republic of China A428

Pico Cao Grande, St. Thomas A429

Prime Minister Patrice Trovoada and Chinese President Xi Jinping A430

**2017, July 20 Litho. *Perf. 13¼***

| | | | | |
|---|---|---|---|---|
| **3377** | | Horiz. strip of 4 | 12.00 | 12.00 |
| *a.* | A427 | 31,000d multi | 3.00 | 3.00 |
| *b.* | A428 | 31,000d multi | 3.00 | 3.00 |
| *c.* | A429 | 31,000d multi | 3.00 | 3.00 |
| *d.* | A430 | 31,000d multi | 3.00 | 3.00 |

Resumption of diplomatic relations between St. Thomas & Prince Islands and People's Republic of China.

A431

No. 3378, 31,000d — Panthera leo leo: a, Two lionesses and cub. b, Head of male lion. c, Male lion leaping. d, Lion attacking Syncerus caffer.

No. 3379, 31,000d — Tigers: a, Panthera tigris jacksoni. b, Panthera tigris sumatrae. c, Panthera tigris amoyensis. d, Panthera tigris tigris.

No. 3380, 31,000d — Cat breeds: a, Sphynx. b, American Wirehair. c, American Bobtail. d, Abyssinian.

No. 3381, 31,000d — Dog breeds: a, Boxer. b, French bulldog. c, Bull terrier. d, Jack Russell terrier.

No. 3382, 31,000d — Elephants: a, Elephas maximus. b, Elephas maximus indicus. c, Loxodonta africana. d, Elephas maximus sumatranus.

No. 3383, 31,000d — Whales: a, Megaptera novaeangliae. b, Physeter macrocephalus. c, Orcinus orca. d, Balaenoptera musculus.

No. 3384, 31,000d — Owls: a, Glaucidium capense. b, Ptilopsis leucotis. c, Strix nebulosa. d, Scotopelia ussheri.

No. 3385, 31,000d — Butterflies: a, Arctia villica. b, Eterusia repleta. c, Papilio lorquinianus. d, Lycaena phiaeas.

No. 3386, 31,000d — Fish: a, Tinca tinca. b, Salmo salar. c, Cyprinus carpio. d, Phractocephalus hemioliopterus.

No. 3387, 31,000d — Dinosaurs: a, Apatosaurus ajax. b, Parasaurolophus walkeri. c, Harpactognathus gentryii. d, Trideratops horridus.

No. 3388, 31,000d — Volcanoes: a, Mt. Ontake, Japan. b, Mt. Bromo, Indonesia. c, Mauna Loa, Hawaii. d, Nevado del Ruiz, Colombia.

No. 3389, 31,000d — Steam trains: a, Fairy Queen locomotive, India. b, The Leviathan, Central Pacific Railroad, U.S.. c, Hull-Chelsea-Wakefield Railroad Locomotive 909, Great Britain. d, West Coast Wilderness Railroad Locomotive No. 3, Australia.

No. 3390, 31,000d — Animators and their characters: a, Pat Sullivan (1885-1933), and Felix the Cat. b, Winsor McCay (c. 1866-1934), and Gertie the Dinosaur. c, Max Fleischer (1883-1972), and Betty Boop. d, Osamu Tezuka (1928-89), and Astro Boy.

No. 3391, 31,000d — Rugby players: a, Ayumu Goromaru. b, Matt Giteau. c, Leigh Halfpenny. d, Johhny Sexton.

No. 3392, 31,000d — Table tennis players: a, Liu Shiwen and Ding Ning. b, Kong Linghui. c, Zhang Jike. d, Li Xiaoxia and Zhang Yining.

No. 3393, 31,000d — 2017 World Ice Hockey Championships: a, Russian goaltender making save. b, Swedish and Canadian players. c, Swedish and Finnish players. d, Canadian player shooting puck at Russian goaltender.

No. 3394, 31,000d — Cyclists in the 100th Giro d'Italia: a, Mikel Landa. b, Nairo Quintana. c, Vincenzo Nibali. d, Tom Dumoulin.

No. 3395, 31,000d — Chess and similar games: a, Banqi pieces. b, 1780 chess set. c, 1960 soapstone chess set. d, 1945 wooden chess set by Max Ernst.

No. 3396, 124,000d, Panthera leo leo running. No. 3397, 124,000d, Panthera tigris corbetti. No. 3398, 124,000d, Ragdoll cat (boneca de trapo). No. 3399, 124,000d, Shiba Inu dog. No. 3400, 124,000d, Elephas maximus maximus. No. 3401, 124,000d, Physeter macrocephalus, diff. No. 3402, 124,000d, Asio capensis. No. 3403, 124,000d, Euplagia quadripunctaria. No. 3404, 124,000d, Esox lucius. No. 3405, 124,000d, Velociraptor mongoliensis. No. 3406, 124,000d, Mt. Sinabung, Indonesia. No. 3407, 124,000d, Finland Railways Heikki Hv3 Class No. 555. No. 3408, 124,000d, Walter Lantz (1899-1994), animator, and Woody Woodpecker. No. 3409, 124,000d, David Pocock. No. 3410, 124,000d, Ma Long. No. 3411, 124,000d, Medal table for 2017 World Ice Hockey Championships. No. 3412, 124,000d, Fernando Gaviria. No. 3413, 124,000d, Chess pieces by Lewis.

**2017, July 20 Litho. *Perf. 13¼***

### Sheets of 4, #a-d

| | | | | |
|---|---|---|---|---|
| **3378-3395** | A431 | Set of 18 | 215.00 | 215.00 |

### Souvenir Sheets

| | | | | |
|---|---|---|---|---|
| **3396-3413** | A431 | Set of 18 | 215.00 | 215.00 |

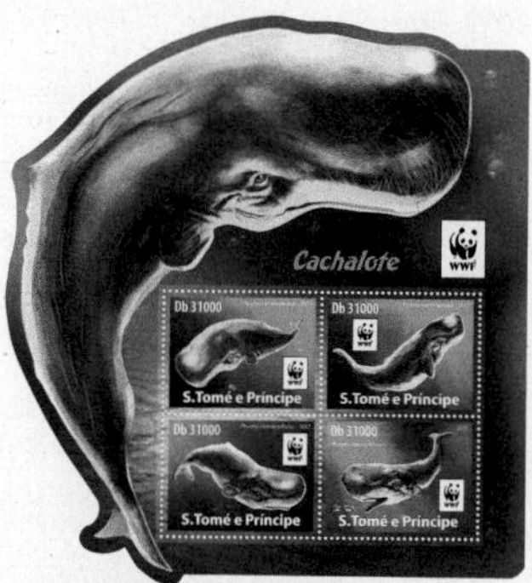


Worldwide Fund for Nature (WWF) — A432

No. 3414 — Physeter macrocephalus: a, Whale nose to LL. b, Whale nose to UR. c, Whale nose to LR. d, Whale eating squid.

124,000d, Whale, diff.

**2017, Sept. 18 Litho. *Perf. 13¼***

| | | | | |
|---|---|---|---|---|
| **3414** | A432 | 31,000d Sheet or vert. strip of 4, #a-d | 11.00 | 11.00 |

### Souvenir Sheet

| | | | | |
|---|---|---|---|---|
| **3415** | A432 | 124,000d multi | 11.00 | 11.00 |

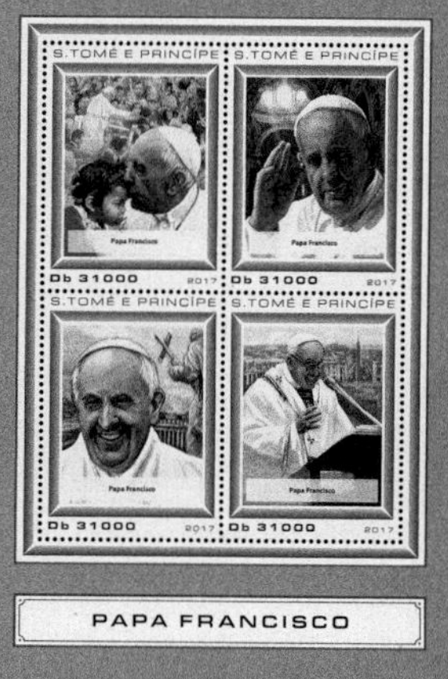


A433

No. 3416, 31,000d — Pope Francis: a, Kissing child's head. b, In cathedral. c, In St. Peter's Square. d, At lectern.

No. 3417, 31,000d — Mahatma Gandhi (1869-1948), Indian nationalist leader: a, With flag of India. b, Looking left. c, With hands clasped. d, At spinning wheel.

No. 3418, 31,000d — Sergei Korolev (1907-1966), spacecraft designer, with: a, Wernher von Braun. b, Dogs Belka and Strelka. c, Rocket. d, Valentina Tereshkova.

No. 3419, 31,000d — Alexander Pushkin (1799-1837), writer: a, With large quill pen. b, "Pushkin's Farewell to the Sea," by Ivan Aivazovsky and Ilya Repin, 1877. c, "A.S. Pushkin in Petersburg," by Boris V. Shcherbakov, 1949. d, With quill pen and paper.

No. 3420, 31,000d — Princess Charlotte of Cambridge, 2nd birthday, with: a, Prince George. b, Her father, Prince William. c, Her mother, the Duchess of Cambridge. d, British Aerospace experimental airplane.

No. 3421, 31,000d — Elizabeth Taylor (1932-2011), actress: a, Wearing strapless dress. b, With Rock Hudson. c, With Paul Newman. d, Wearing dress with straps.

No. 3422, 31,000d — Nelson Mandela (1918-2013), President of South Africa, and: a, South African flag. b, Queen Elizabeth II. c, Michael Jackson. d, Nobel medal and diploma.

No. 3423, 31,000d — Nobel laureates: a, Yoshinori Ohsumi, 2016 Physiology or Medicine. b, Jimmy Carter, 2002 Peace. c, Barack H. Obama, 2009 Peace. d, Bob Dylan, 2016, Literature.

No. 3424, 31,000d — Paintings by Bartolomé Estaban Murillo (1617-1682): a, "Madonna and Child," unknown date. b, "The Infant Christ and Saint John the Baptist with a Shell," c. 1670. c, "Saint Francis Embracing Christ on the Cross," c. 1668. d, "Saint Peter in Tears," 1650-55.

No. 3425, 31,000d — Paintings by Edgar Degas (1834-1917): a, "Portrait of Estelle Musson Degas," 1872. b, "The Dance Class," 1871-74. c, "Swaying Dancer (Dancer in Green)," 1877-79. d, "Self-portrait in a Hat," 1858.

No. 3426, 31,000d — Paintings by Ivan Aivazovsky (1817-1900): a, "Constantinople, View of the Golden Horn with a Self-portrait of the Artist Sketching," 1880. b, "The Rainbow" (detail), 1873. c, "View of Crimea," 1851. d, "View of Constantinople and the Bosporus," 1856.

No. 3427, 31,000d — Paintings by Frida Kahlo (1907-1954): a, "Memory (The Heart)," 1937. b, "The Two Fridas," 1939. c, "Self-portrait with Cropped Hair," 1940. d, "Girl with Death Mask (She Plays Alone)," 1938.

No. 3428, 31,000d — Paintings by Gustav Klimt (1862-1918): a, "The Virgin," 1913. b, "Portrait of Adele Bloch-Bauer I," 1907. c, "Danae", 1907. d, "Death and Life" (detail), 1908-16.

No. 3429, 31,000d — Impressionist paintings: a, "In a Cafe (also called Absinthe)," 1876, by Edgar Degas, (1834-1917). b, "Dance at Le Moulin de la Galette" (detail), 1876, by Pierre-Auguste Renoir (1841-1919). c, Edouard Manet "Luncheon on the Grass," 1863, by Edouard Manet (1832-83). d, "The Card Players," 1890-95, by Paul Cézanne (1839-1906).

No. 3430, 31,000d — Sculptures by Auguste Rodin (1840-1917): a, "The Hand of God," 1898. b, "Head of Saint John the Baptist," 1887. c, "Jean de Fiennes" (detail), 1895. d, "The Age of Bronze" (detail), 1876.

No. 3431, 31,000d — Ludwig van Beethoven (1770-1827), composer: a, With his birthplace in Bonn. b, With violin and imperial banner of the Holy Roman Empire. c, With his signature. d, Piano.

No. 3432, 31,000d — Igor Stravinsky (1882-1971), composer: a, Conducting, with arms spread. b, Hands clasped. c, Facing forward. d, Conducting, looking at score.

No. 3433, 31,000d — Birds of prey: a, Buteogallus meridionalis. b, Aegypius monachus. c, Aviceda jerdoni. d, Geranoaetus polyosoma.

No. 3434, 31,000d — Christmas: a, Santa Claus with gift box, elf. b, Christmas tree. c, Cardinal and holly. d, Santa Claus with bag.

No. 3435, 124,000d, Pope Francis holding crucifix. No. 3436, 124,000d, Gandhi looking forward. No. 3437, 124,000d, Korolev and Sputnik 1. No. 3438, 124,000d, Pushkin with open book and signature. No. 3439, 124,000d, Princess Charlotte with dog. No. 3440, 124,000d, Taylor with rose. No. 3441, 124,000d, Mandela with St. John Paul II. No. 3442, 124,000d, Juan Manuel Santos, 2016 Nobel Peace laureate No. 3443, 124,000d, "St. Isidore of Seville," 1655, by Murillo. No. 3444, 124,000d, "The Dancers," 1899, by Degas. No. 3445, 124,000d, "Pushkin's Farewell to the Sea," 1877, by Aivazovsky. No. 3446, 124,000d, "Magnolias" (detail), 1945, by Kahlo. No. 3447, 124,000d, "The Kiss," 1907-08, by Klimt. No. 3448, 124,000d, "Impression, Sunrise," 1872, by Claude Monet (1840-1926). No. 3449, 124,000d, "The Cathedral," 1908, by Rodin. No. 3450, 124,000d, Beethoven with piano, sheet music. No. 3451, 124,000d, Stravinsky with glasses on forehead. No. 3452, 124,000d, Gyps himalayensis. No. 3453, 124,000d, Santa Claus in chair.

**2017, Sept. 18 Litho. *Perf. 13¼***

**Sheets of 4, #a-d**

**3416-3434** A433 Set of 19 225.00 225.00

**Souvenir Sheets**

**3435-3453** A433 Set of 19 215.00 215.00

Koalas
A434

No. 3454, 31,000d, Koala with arm cast. No. 3455, 31,000d, Koala with two joeys on white background. No. 3456, 31,000d, Two koalas on black background. No. 3457, 31,000d, Koala and one joey on black background.

124,000d, Koala and joey.

**2017, Nov. 7 Litho. *Perf. 13¼***

**3454-3457** A434 Set of 4 12.00 12.00

**Souvenir Sheet**

**3458** A434 124,000d multi 12.00 12.00

Nos. 3453-3457 were each printed in sheets of 16 + 4 central labels. No. 3458 contains one 37x45mm stamp.

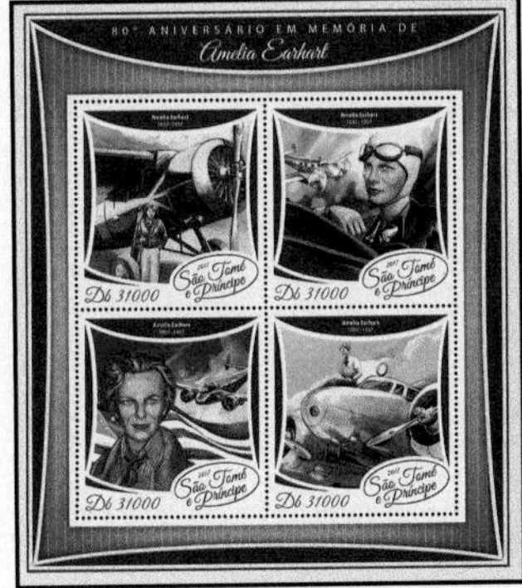


A435

No. 3459, 31,000d — Amelia Earhart (1897-1937), aviatrix: a, Standing next to plane. b, Sitting in plane wearing goggles. c, With American flag, plane. d, Sitting on front of plane.

No. 3460, 31,000d — Wilbur Wright (1867-1912), aviation pioneer: a, Otto Lilienthal (1848-96), and crashed plane. b, Boeing 787 Dreamliner and Wright Flyer. c, Test flight of Wright Flyer. d, With brother, Orville (1871-1948).

No. 3461, 31,000d — Prince George of Cambridge: a, Waving. b, With father, Prince William. c, With Prince William, and mother, the Duchess of Cambridge. d, Smiling.

No. 3462, 31,000d — Pope John Paul II (1920-2005): a, Kissing baby. b, Praying. c, With Mother Teresa (1910-97). d, With Nelson Mandela (1918-2013).

No. 3463, 31,000d — Charlie Chaplin (1889-1977), actor: a, With autograph. b, Tipping hat at woman. c, Holding cane. d, With film strips and Hollywood star.

No. 3464, 31,000d — Invention of dynamite, 150th anniv.: a, Alfred Nobel (1833-96), inventor, with flask. b, Nobel and sticks of dynamite. c, Nobel and Nobel prize medal. d, Detanator, dynamite and explosion.

No. 3465, 31,000d — Stamps on stamps: a, Stamps from Italy. b, Girl looking at stamps. c, Boy looking at stamps. d, Stamps from Benin, collector holding tongs.

No. 3466, 31,000d — Red Cross: a, Workers wrapping woman's arm. b, Worker giving child drinking water. c, Children at water spigot. d, Workers carrying person on stretcher.

No. 3467, 31,000d — Lighthouses: a, Sao Sebastiao Lighthouse, St. Thomas & Prince Islands. b, Santo Antonio da Barra Fort, Lighthouse, Brazil. c, Cape Higuer Lighthouse, Spain. d, Goa Island Lighthouse, Mozambique.

No. 3468, 31,000d — Fire engines: a, Scania P 310. b, Morris FKG40 BAA778C. c, 1951 Seagrave fire truck. d, GA Chivvis Corp. fire truck.

No. 3469, 31,000d — Sputnik 1, 60th anniv., and: a, Mercury and Uranus. b, Saturn and Venus. c, Neptune and Mars. d, Jupiter.

No. 3470, 31,000d — Dolphins: a, Stenella frontalis. b, Lagenorhynchus obscurus. c, Tursiops aduncus. d, Stenella longirostris.

No. 3471, 31,000d — Butterflies: a, Euphaedra janetta. b, Rhetus periander. c, Teinopalpus aureus. d, Parthenos sylvia.

No. 3472, 31,000d — Turtles: a, Graptemys flavimaculata. b, Lissemys punctata. c, Chelodina mccordi. d, Pelochelys cantorii.

No. 3473, 31,000d — Orchids: a, Prosthechea cochleata. b, Calanthe triplicata. c, Dendrobium chrysotoxum. d, Dendrobium nobile.

No. 3474, 31,000d — Mushrooms: a, Amanita phalloides. b, Chroogomphus fulmineus. c, Suillus grevillei. d, Gymnopilus junonius.

No. 3475, 31,000d — Minerals: a, Rhodochrosite, Capillitas, Argentina. b, Ruby, Mines in Afghanistan. c, Fluorite, Mines in Mexico. d, Granada Andradite, Mines in Ukraine.

No. 3476, 124,000d, Earhart's Lockheed Vega B5. No. 3477, 124,000d, Wright Flyer, tugboat. No. 3478, 124,000d, Prince George with Queen Elizabeth II. No. 3479, 124,000d, Pope John Paul II with raised hands. No. 3480, 124,000d, Chaplin with police officer. No. 3481, 124,000d, Dynamite sticks and box with Nobel Prize medal. No. 3482, 124,000d, Various stamps depicting birds. No. 3483, 124,000d, Red Cross worker hugging child. No. 3484, 124,000d, Diu Lighthouse, India. No. 3485, 124,000d, Type 3 Angeles National Forest Engine ANF 13. No. 3486, 124,000d, Sputnik 1 and Baikonur Cosmodrome. No. 3487, 124,000d, Tursiops truncatus. No. 3488, 124,000d, Junonia orithya, Polygonia interrogationis. No. 3489, 124,000d, Lepidochelys olivacea. No. 3490, 124,000d, Dendrobium lamyaiae. No. 3491, 124,000d, Phaeolepiota aurea. No. 3492, 124,000d, Anatase.

**2017, Nov. 7 Litho. *Perf. 13¼***

**Sheets of 4, #a-d**

**3459-3475** A435 Set of 17 200.00 200.00

**Souvenir Sheets**

**3476-3492** A435 Set of 17 190.00 190.00

Protestant Reformation, 500th Anniv. — A436

No. 3493 — Reformation leaders: a, Heinrich Bullinger (1504-75). b, Philip Melanchthon (1497-1560). c, Thomas Cranmer (1489-1556). d, Caspar Hedio (1494-1552).

124,000d, Martin Luther (1483-1546).

**2017, Nov. 7 Litho. *Perf. 13¼***

**3493** A436 31,000d Sheet of 4, #a-d 12.00 12.00

**Souvenir Sheet**

**3494** A436 124,000d multi 12.00 12.00

New Year 2018 (Year of the Dog) — A437

No. 3495: a, Dog with open mouth. b, Dog with closed mouth. c, Two dogs with open mouths. d, Two dogs, one with mouth open.

124,000d, Dog with open mouth, diff.

**2017, Nov. 7 Litho. *Perf. 13¼***

**3495** A437 31,000d Sheet of 4, #a-d 12.00 12.00

**Souvenir Sheet**

**3496** A437 124,000d multi 12.00 12.00

A438

No. 3497, 31d — Garry Kasparov, chess player: a, With caricature at right holding chess piece. b, Moving chess piece. c, With cariature of Anatoly Karpov moving chess piece. d, Sitting with arms folded behind chess board.

No. 3498, 31d — Pablo Picasso (1881-1973), painter: a, With his painting, Women of Algiers, 1954-55. b, With Portrait of Angel Fernández de Soto, 1903. c, Painting ceramic pieces. d, Standing with arms folded.

No. 3499, 31d — Pres. John F. Kennedy (1917-63): a, Jacqueline Kennedy Onassis (1929-94), first lady, and John F. Kennedy Memorial, Dallas, Texas. b, Kennedy, with daughter Caroline, and U.S. flag. c, Kennedy with son, John, Jr. (1960-99). d, At desk, signing legislation.

No. 3500, 31d — Kemal Atatürk (c. 1881-1938), first president of Turkey: a, With newspaper. b, On horse. c, With Hagia Sophia. d, With troops at the 1915-16 Battle of Gallipoli.

No. 3501, 31d — Universities and their famous attendees: a, Harvard University, Pres. Kennedy, and Bill Gates, co-founder of Microsoft. b, Oxford University, Margaret Thatcher ((1925-2013), Prime Minister of Great Britain. c, Columbia University, Pres. Barack Obama. d, Boston University, Dr. Martin Luther King, Jr. (1929-68), civil rights leader.

No. 3502, 31d — End of World War I, cent.: a, Soldiers on battlefield on Armistice Day, Nov. 11, 1918. b, Ferdinand Foch (1851-1929), French general, signing armistice. c, Soldiers celebrating end of war. d, Soldiers and poppies.

No. 3503, 31d — Table tennis players: a, Ding Ning. b, Xu Xin. c, Maharu Yoshimura. d, Kasumi Ishikawa.

No. 3504, 31d — Alan B. Shepard, Jr. (1923-98), astronaut: a, Shepard and Freedom 7 capsule. b, Shepard on Moon. c, Shepard receiving medal from Pres. Kennedy. d, Apollo 14 spacecraft and medallion.

No. 3505, 31d — Captain James Cook (1728-79), explorer: a, With beach and map in background. b, With ship in background. c, HMS Endeavour. d, Wearing hat.

No. 3506, 31d — Steam trains: a, Deutsche Reichsbahn Class 50. b, Pennsylvania Railroad 5550. c, London and North Eastern Railway Class A4. d, Queensland Railways Class BB18¼.

No. 3507, 31d — Special transport: a, Rosenbauer Panther FLF airport crash tender. b, Bell 412 helicopter ambulance. c, Braun Express Type III ambulance. d, Fire Department of New York fireboat FDNY 343.

No. 3508, 31d — Ferrari automobiles: a, Ferrari 166 S. b, Ferrari Enzo. c, Ferrari 308 GTB. d, Ferrari 625 TRC.

No. 3509, 31d — Concorde: a, Flying over Nice, France. b, Taking off. c, On ground. d, Flying over New York City.

No. 3510, 31d — Pandas: a, Ailurus fulgens, head at right. b, Two Ailuropoda melanoleuca. c, One Ailuropoda melanoleuca. d, Ailurus fulgens, head at left.

No. 3511, 31d — Birds of prey: a, Haliaeetus albicilla. b, Milvus milvus. c, Falco tinnunculus. d, Haliaeetus leucocephalus.

No. 3512, 31d — Hornbills: a, Aceros nipalensis. b, Rhyticeros undulatus. c, Buceros bicornis. d, Anthracoceros albirostris.

No. 3513, 31d — Sharks: a, Negaprion acutidens. b, Carcharhinus brachyurus. c, Carcharodon carcharias. d, Oxynotus caribbaeus.

No. 3514, 31d — Fish: a, Mikrogeophagus ramirezi. b, Pterophyllum scalare. c, Poecilia reticulata. d, Perca fluviatilis.

No. 3515, 31d — Extinct species: a, Heterałocha acutirostris. b, Puma concolor couguar. c, Ursus spelaeus. d, Alectroenas nitidissimus.

No. 3516, 31d — Lighthouses and shells: a, Rubjerg Knude Lighthouse, Denmark, Neverita lewisii. b, New London Ledge Light, Connecticut, Cypraea tigris. c, Lindau Lighthouse, Germany, Harpa costata. d, Fanad Head Lighthouse, Ireland, Dolomena plicata.

No. 3517, 124d, Kasparov and chess king, vert. No. 3518, 124d, Picasso, vert. No. 3519, 124d, Pres. Kennedy and U.S flag, vert. No. 3520, 124d, Atatürk, vert. No. 3521, 124d, Cambridge University, Charles Darwin (1809-82), naturalist, J. Robert Oppenheimer (1904-67), physicist, vert. No. 3522, 124d, World War I soldier on battlefield, vert. No. 3523, 124d, Liu Shiwen, vert. No. 3524, 124d, Shepard and launch of Freedom 7, vert. No. 3525, 124d, Cook, vert. No. 3526, 124d, Class LV Russian locomotive, vert. No. 3527, 124d, American LaFrance TDA ALF 900 fire truck, vert. No. 3528, 124d, Enzo Ferrari (1898-1988), automobile manufacturer, Ferrari 288 GTO, vert. No. 3529, 124d, Concorde over Paris, vert. No. 3530, 124d, Ailurus fulgens, vert. No. 3531, 124d, Falco cherrug, vert. No. 3532, 124d, Rhyticeros cassidix, vert. No. 3533, 124d, Cetorhinus maximus, vert. No. 3534, 124d, Carasius auratus, vert. No. 3535, 124d, Procyon lotor gloveralleni, vert. No. 3536, 124d, Block Island Southeast Lighthouse, Rhode Island, Cassis madagascariensis, vert.

**2018, Mar. 13 Litho. *Perf. 13¼***

**Sheets of 4, #a-d**

**3497-3516** A438 Set of 20 250.00 250.00

**Souvenir Sheets**

**3517-3536** A438 Set of 20 250.00 250.00

Nos. 3517-3536 each contain one 45x66mm stamp.

A439

No. 3537, 31d — Tigers: a, Panthera tigris on ground, head at right. b, Panthera tigris, head at left. c, Panthera tigris, leaping, head at right. d, Panthera tigris tigris.

No. 3538, 31d — Dogs: a, American bulldog, Chihuahua. b, Dalmatians. c, German shepherds. d, Jack Russell terrier, Chihuahua.

No. 3539, 31d — Owls: a, Tyto alba. b, Pseudoscops grammicus. c, Bubo bubo. d, Bubo virginianus.

No. 3540, 31d — Butterflies: a, Greta oto. b, Kallima inachus. c, Panacea procilla. d, Eurema hecabe.

No. 3541, 31d — Turtles: a, Natator depressus. b, Terrapene carolina mexicana. c, Pseudemys nelsoni. d, Demochelys coriacea.

No. 3542, 31d — Mushrooms: a, Campanella caesia. b, Pleurotus djamor. c, Cantharellus lateritius. d, Caoscypha fulgens.

No. 3543, 31d — Nelson Mandela (1918-2013), President of South Africa: a, In crowd. b, Delivering speech. c, With flag of South

Africa and Nobel Peace medal. d, Holding hands with wife, Winnie, (1936-2018).

No. 3544, 31d — Dr. Martin Luther King, Jr. (1929-68), civil rights leader: a, On March to Montgomery, Alabama with wife, Coretta (1927-2006). b, Portrait. c, And Pres. Barack Obama. d, In front of marchers, speaking.

No. 3545, 31d — Wedding of Prince Harry and Meghan Markle: a, Marriage ceremony, Princes William and Harry. b, Couple walking down aisle, bride with her mother, Doria Ragland. c, Doves, couple holding hands. d, Couple waving.

No. 3546, 31d — Third birthday of Princess Charlotte of Cambridge: a, With father, mother and brother. b, With father, Prince William, her grandmother Princess Diana (1961-97) holding young Prince William. c, With mother, Catherine, Duchess of Cambridge. d, With great-grandparents, Queen Elizabeth II and Prince Philip.

No. 3547, 31d — Roald Amundsen (1872-1928), polar explorer, with: a, Map of Antarctica and Oscar Wisting (1871-1936), polar explorer. b, His ship, Fram. c, Penguins and Norge dirigible. d, MS Roald Amundsen.

No. 3548, 31d — Paintings of birds by Alexander Wilson (1766-1813), ornithologist: a, Protonaria citrea, Muscicapa verticalis. b, Falco peregrinus, Passerina ciris. c, Elanoides forficatus, Pyrrhula enucleator. d, Perisoreus canadensis, Pinicola enucleator.

No. 3549, 31d — Paintings by Vincent van Gogh (1853-90): a, Van Gogh and Two Cut Sunflowers, 1887. b, Palette paint brush and Irises, 1889. c, Van Gogh painting and The Red Vineyard, 1888. d, Van Gogh painting and Wheat Field with Cypresses at the Haute Galline near Eygalieres, 1889.

No. 3550, 31d — Pyotr Ilyich Tchaikovsky (1840-93), composer, and: a, Bolshoi Ballet dancers performing in Sleeping Beauty. b, Piano and sheet music. c, Piano keys. d, Royal Opera dancers performing in The Nutcracker.

No. 3551, 31d — Munich airplane crash, 60th anniv.: a, Members of 1958 Manchester United soccer team. b, Airspeed Ambassador airplane. c, Airplane propeller and engine, clock showing time of crash. d, Manchester United fans.

No. 3552, 31d — Tennis players: a, Roger Federer, Milos Raonic. b, Novak Djokovic, Kei Nishikori. c, Rafael Nadal, Dominic Thiem. d, Marin Cilic, Stan Wawrinka.

No. 3553, 31d — James Bond movies, 65th anniv., (actors portraying Bond): a, Sean Connery. b, Roger Moore. c, Pierce Brosnan, with Sophie Marceau. d, Daniel Craig.

No. 3554, 31d — Launch of Elon Musk's Tesla Roadster into space: a, Starman and "Don't Panic" sign. b, Falcon 9 and Falcon Heavy rockets. c, Musk's Tesla Roadster and optical disk. d, Musk and his Tesla Roadster.

No. 3555, 31d — Fire trucks: a, 1924 Seagrave 6WT fire pumper. b, 1928 American LaFrance fire truck. c, 1938 Chevrolet fire truck. d, 1930 Ahrens Fox Model V fire truck.

No. 3556, 124d, Panthera tigris, diff. No. 3557, 124d, Pug mix. No. 3558, 124d, Tyto alba, diff. No. 3559, 124d, Chorinea sylphina. No. 3560, 124d, Batagur affinis. No. 3561, 124d, Cribraria argillacea. No. 3562, 124d, Mandela and Robben Island Prison. No. 3563, 124d, King speaking into microphone. No. 3564, 124d, Prince Harry and his bride, Meghan Markle, diff. No. 3565, 124d, Princess Charlotte of Cambridge, Queen Elizabeth II and her dogs. No. 3566, 124d, Amundsen and dog sled team. No. 3567, 124d, Campephilus principalis, Dryocopus pileatus. No. 3568, 124d, The Night Café in the Place Lamartine in Arles, 1888, by van Gogh. No. 3569, 124d, Tchaikovsky and Swedish Royal Opera dancers performing Swan Lake. No. 3570, 124d, Airspeed Ambassador, diff. No. 3571, 124d, Tennis players Andy Murray, Jo-Wilfried Tsonga. No. 3572, 124d, Sean Connery as James Bond, diff. No. 3573, 124d, Musk's Tesla Roadster, diff. No. 3574, 124d, 1916 American LaFrance fire truck.

**2018, May 19 Litho. *Perf. 13¼***

**Sheets of 4, #a-d**

| | | | | |
|---|---|---|---|---|
| **3537-3555** | A439 | Set of 19 | 225.00 | 225.00 |

**Souvenir Sheets**

| | | | | |
|---|---|---|---|---|
| **3556-3574** | A439 | Set of 19 | 225.00 | 225.00 |

Russian Ice Hockey Players — A440

No. 3575: a, Nikita Gusev. b, Sergei Mozyakin. c, Nikolai Prokhorin. d, Ilya Kovalchuk. 124d, Kirill Kaprizov.

**Litho. With Foil Application**

**2018, May 19 *Perf. 13¼***

| | | | | |
|---|---|---|---|---|
| **3575** | A440 | 31d Sheet of 4, #a-d | 12.00 | 12.00 |

**Souvenir Sheet**

| | | | | |
|---|---|---|---|---|
| **3576** | A440 | 124d multi | 12.00 | 12.00 |

## AIR POST STAMPS

**Common Design Type**

Inscribed "S. Tomé"

**1938 *Perf. 13½x13***

**Name and Value in Black**

| | | | | | |
|---|---|---|---|---|---|
| **C1** | CD39 | 10c red orange | 95.00 | 67.50 |
| **C2** | CD39 | 20c purple | 45.00 | 33.00 |
| **C3** | CD39 | 50c orange | 3.50 | 3.00 |
| **C4** | CD39 | 1e ultra | 9.00 | 3.50 |
| **C5** | CD39 | 2e lilac brown | 8.00 | 5.00 |
| **C6** | CD39 | 3e dark green | 10.00 | 6.50 |
| **C7** | CD39 | 5e red brown | 16.00 | 14.00 |
| **C8** | CD39 | 9e rose carmine | 17.00 | 14.00 |
| **C9** | CD39 | 10e magenta | 52.50 | 14.00 |
| | | *Nos. C1-C9 (9)* | 256.00 | 160.50 |

**Common Design Type**

Inscribed "S. Tomé e Principe"

**1939 Engr. Unwmk.**

**Name and Value Typo. in Black**

| | | | | |
|---|---|---|---|---|
| **C10** | CD39 | 10c scarlet | .60 | .30 |
| **C11** | CD39 | 20c purple | .60 | .30 |
| **C12** | CD39 | 50c orange | .60 | .30 |
| **C13** | CD39 | 1e deep ultra | .60 | .30 |
| **C14** | CD39 | 2e lilac brown | 1.50 | 1.00 |
| **C15** | CD39 | 3e dark green | 2.25 | 1.60 |
| **C16** | CD39 | 5e red brown | 5.25 | 3.00 |
| **C17** | CD39 | 9e rose carmine | 9.00 | 5.25 |
| **C18** | CD39 | 10e magenta | 10.00 | 5.75 |
| | | *Nos. C10-C18 (9)* | 30.40 | 17.80 |

No. C16 exists with overprint "Exposicao International de Nova York, 1939-1940" and Trylon and Perisphere. Value, $100 unused and used.

No. 742 Surcharged in Red

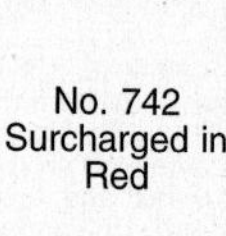

**Method and Perf As Before**

**2009, Apr. 15**

| | | | | |
|---|---|---|---|---|
| **C21** | A95 | (45,000d) on 18.50d #742 | 5.50 | 5.50 |

Two additional stamps were issued in this set. The editors would like to examine any examples.

## POSTAGE DUE STAMPS

"S. Thomé" — D1

**1904 Unwmk. Typo. *Perf. 12***

| | | | | |
|---|---|---|---|---|
| **J1** | D1 | 5r yellow green | .90 | .75 |
| **J2** | D1 | 10r slate | .90 | .75 |
| **J3** | D1 | 20r yellow brown | 1.35 | .90 |
| **J4** | D1 | 30r orange | 1.40 | .90 |
| **J5** | D1 | 50r gray brown | 2.75 | 1.75 |
| **J6** | D1 | 60r red brown | 3.75 | 2.10 |
| **J7** | D1 | 100r red lilac | 5.75 | 3.25 |
| **J8** | D1 | 130r dull blue | 5.75 | 4.00 |
| **J9** | D1 | 200r carmine | 6.00 | 4.00 |
| **J10** | D1 | 500r gray violet | 11.00 | 8.00 |
| | | *Nos. J1-J10 (10)* | 39.55 | 26.40 |

Overprinted in Carmine or Green

**1911**

| | | | | |
|---|---|---|---|---|
| **J11** | D1 | 5r yellow green | .30 | .30 |
| **J12** | D1 | 10r slate | .30 | .30 |
| **J13** | D1 | 20r yellow brown | .30 | .30 |
| **J14** | D1 | 30r orange | .30 | .30 |
| **J15** | D1 | 50r gray brown | .50 | .45 |
| **J16** | D1 | 60r red brown | 1.40 | .80 |
| **J17** | D1 | 100r red lilac | 1.40 | .80 |
| **J18** | D1 | 130r dull blue | 1.40 | .80 |
| **J19** | D1 | 200r carmine (G) | 1.40 | .80 |
| **J20** | D1 | 500r gray violet | 3.00 | 2.25 |
| | | *Nos. J11-J20 (10)* | 10.30 | 7.10 |

Nos. J1-J10 Overprinted in Black

**1913 Without Gum**

| | | | | |
|---|---|---|---|---|
| **J21** | D1 | 5r yellow green | 6.75 | 4.25 |
| **J22** | D1 | 10r slate | 9.00 | 5.50 |
| **J23** | D1 | 20r yellow brown | 6.75 | 4.25 |
| **J24** | D1 | 30r orange | 6.75 | 4.25 |
| **J25** | D1 | 50r gray brown | 6.75 | 5.00 |
| **J26** | D1 | 60r red brown | 6.75 | 5.00 |
| **J27** | D1 | 100r red lilac | 6.75 | 5.50 |
| **J28** | D1 | 130r dull blue | 29.00 | 13.50 |
| *a.* | | Inverted overprint | 50.00 | 42.50 |
| **J29** | D1 | 200r carmine | 52.50 | 45.00 |
| **J30** | D1 | 500r gray violet | 65.00 | 37.50 |
| | | *Nos. J21-J30 (10)* | 196.00 | 129.75 |

Nos. J1-J10 Overprinted in Black

**1913 Without Gum**

| | | | | |
|---|---|---|---|---|
| **J31** | D1 | 5r yellow green | 5.25 | 3.50 |
| *a.* | | Inverted overprint | 50.00 | 40.00 |
| **J32** | D1 | 10r slate | 5.25 | 4.00 |
| **J33** | D1 | 20r yellow brown | 5.25 | 3.50 |
| **J34** | D1 | 30r orange | 5.25 | 3.50 |
| *a.* | | Inverted overprint | 55.00 | |
| **J35** | D1 | 50r gray brown | 7.75 | 5.00 |
| **J36** | D1 | 60r red brown | 8.00 | 5.00 |
| **J37** | D1 | 100r red lilac | 8.00 | 5.00 |
| **J38** | D1 | 130r dull blue | 8.00 | 5.00 |
| **J39** | D1 | 200r carmine | 11.00 | 6.75 |
| **J40** | D1 | 500r gray violet | 23.00 | 18.00 |
| | | *Nos. J31-J40 (10)* | 86.75 | 59.25 |

**No. J5 Overprinted "Republica" in Italic Capitals like Regular Issue in Green**

**1920 Without Gum**

| | | | | |
|---|---|---|---|---|
| **J41** | D1 | 50r gray brn | 40.00 | 26.00 |

"S. Tomé" — D2

**1921 Typo. *Perf. 11½***

| | | | | |
|---|---|---|---|---|
| **J42** | D2 | ½c yellow green | .50 | .30 |
| **J43** | D2 | 1c slate | .50 | .30 |
| **J44** | D2 | 2c orange brown | .50 | .30 |
| **J45** | D2 | 3c orange | .50 | .30 |
| **J46** | D2 | 5c gray brown | .50 | .30 |
| **J47** | D2 | 6c lt brown | .70 | .50 |
| **J48** | D2 | 10c red violet | .70 | .50 |
| **J49** | D2 | 13c dull blue | .70 | .50 |
| **J50** | D2 | 20c carmine | .70 | .50 |
| **J51** | D2 | 50c gray | 1.60 | 1.10 |
| | | *Nos. J42-J51 (10)* | 6.90 | 4.60 |

In each sheet one stamp is inscribed "S. Thomé" instead of "S. Tomé." Value, set of 10, $200.

**Catalogue values for unused stamps in this section, from this point to the end of the section, are for Never Hinged items.**

**Common Design Type**

**Photo. & Typo.**

**1952 Unwmk. *Perf. 14***

**Numeral in Red, Frame Multicolored**

| | | | | |
|---|---|---|---|---|
| **J52** | CD45 | 10c chocolate | .30 | .30 |
| **J53** | CD45 | 30c red brown | .30 | .30 |
| **J54** | CD45 | 50c dark blue | .30 | .30 |
| **J55** | CD45 | 1e dark blue | .50 | .50 |
| **J56** | CD45 | 2e olive green | .70 | .70 |
| **J57** | CD45 | 5e black brown | 1.75 | 1.75 |
| | | *Nos. J52-J57 (6)* | 3.85 | 3.85 |

## NEWSPAPER STAMPS

N1

N2

**1892 Unwmk. *Perf. 13½***

**Without Gum**

**Black Surcharge**

| | | | | |
|---|---|---|---|---|
| **P1** | N1 | 2½r on 5r black, perf. 12½ | 700.00 | 500.00 |
| **P1A** | N1 | 2½r on 10r green | 102.50 | 67.50 |
| **P2** | N1 | 2½r on 20r rose | 135.00 | 90.00 |
| **P2A** | N1 | 2½r on 5r black | 250.00 | 190.00 |
| **P3** | N2 | 2½r on 10r green | 140.00 | 90.00 |
| **P4** | N2 | 2½r on 20r rose | 150.00 | 105.00 |
| | | *Nos. P1A-P4 (6)* | 1,478. | 1,043. |

**Green Surcharge**

| | | | | |
|---|---|---|---|---|
| **P5** | N1 | 2½r on 5r black | 72.50 | 50.00 |
| *b.* | | Perf. 12½ | 500.00 | 100.00 |
| **P5A** | N1 | 2½r on 10r green | 250.00 | 190.00 |
| **P6** | N1 | 2½r on 20r rose | 140.00 | 105.00 |
| **P8** | N2 | 2½r on 5r black | 150.00 | 90.00 |
| *a.* | | Perf. 12½ | 500.00 | 350.00 |
| **P9** | N2 | 2½r on 10r green | 140.00 | 105.00 |
| **P10** | N2 | 2½r on 20r rose | 180.00 | 135.00 |
| | | *Nos. P5-P9 (5)* | 752.50 | 540.00 |

No. 18 exists with both surcharges in green and black. These were not officially produced.

N3

**1893 Typo. *Perf. 11½***

| | | | | |
|---|---|---|---|---|
| **P12** | N3 | 2½r brown | 1.50 | 1.20 |
| *a.* | | Perf. 13½ | 2.50 | 2.00 |

For surcharges and overprints see Nos. 85, 166, 275, P13.

No. P12 Overprinted Type "d" in Blue

| 1899 | | Without Gum | |
|---|---|---|---|
| **P13** N3 2½r brown | | 150.00 | 50.00 |
| *a.* Perf. 13½ | | 250.00 | 80.00 |
| *b.* Inverted surcharge | | 350.00 | 250.00 |

### POSTAL TAX STAMPS

**Pombal Issue**
Common Design Types

| 1925 | Unwmk. | *Perf. 12½* | |
|---|---|---|---|
| **RA1** CD28 | 15c orange & black | .75 | .75 |
| **RA2** CD29 | 15c orange & black | .75 | .75 |
| **RA3** CD30 | 15c orange & black | .75 | .75 |
| | *Nos. RA1-RA3 (3)* | 2.25 | 2.25 |

Certain revenue stamps (5e, 6e, 7e, 8e and other denominations) were surcharged in 1946 "Assistencia," 2 bars and new values (1e or 1.50e) and used as postal tax stamps.

**Catalogue values for unused stamps in this section, from this point to the end of the section, are for Never Hinged items.**

PT1

| 1948-58 | Typo. | *Perf. 12x11½* | |
|---|---|---|---|
| | **Denomination in Black** | | |
| **RA4** PT1 | 50c yellow grn | 4.00 | 1.10 |
| **RA5** PT1 | 1e carmine rose | 4.25 | 1.50 |
| **RA6** PT1 | 1e emerald ('58) | 1.75 | .75 |
| **RA7** PT1 | 1.50e bister brown | 2.50 | 1.90 |
| | *Nos. RA4-RA7 (4)* | 12.50 | 5.25 |

Denominations of 2e and up were used only for revenue purposes. No. RA6 lacks "Colonia de" below coat of arms.

**Type of 1958 Surcharged**

m

n

| 1964-65 | Typo. | *Perf. 12x11½* | |
|---|---|---|---|
| **RA8** PT1(m) | 1e on 5e org yel | 12.00 | 12.00 |
| **RA9** PT1(n) | 1e on 5e org yel ('65) | 4.75 | 4.75 |

The basic 5e orange yellow does not carry the words "Colonia de."

**No. RA6 Surcharged: "Um escudo"**

| 1965 | | | |
|---|---|---|---|
| **RA10** PT1 | 1e emerald | 2.00 | 2.00 |

Type of 1948 Surcharged

| 1965 | Typo. | *Perf. 12x11½* | |
|---|---|---|---|
| **RA11** PT1 | 1e emerald | .80 | .80 |

### POSTAL TAX DUE STAMPS

**Pombal Issue**
Common Design Types

| 1925 | Unwmk. | *Perf. 12½* | |
|---|---|---|---|
| **RAJ1** CD28 | 30c orange & black | .75 | .75 |
| **RAJ2** CD29 | 30c orange & black | .75 | .75 |
| **RAJ3** CD30 | 30c orange & black | .75 | .75 |
| | *Nos. RAJ1-RAJ3 (3)* | 2.25 | 2.25 |

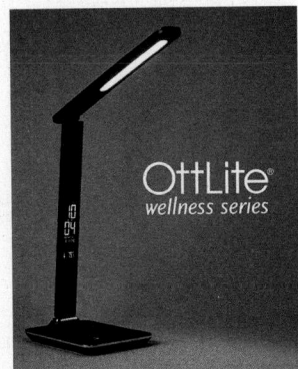

# ST. VINCENT

sānt ˈvin͏t͏-sənt

LOCATION — Island in the West Indies
GOVT. — Independent state in the British Commonwealth
AREA — 150 sq. mi.
POP. — 120,519 (1999 est.)
CAPITAL — Kingstown

The British colony of St. Vincent became an associated state in 1969 and independent in 1979.

12 Pence = 1 Shilling
20 Shillings = 1 Pound
100 Cents = 1 Dollar (1949)

**Catalogue values for unused stamps in this country are for Never Hinged items, beginning with Scott 152 in the regular postage section, Scott B1 in the semi-postal section, and Scott O1 in the officials section.**

Values for unused stamps are for examples with original gum as defined in the catalogue introduction. Early stamps were spaced extremely narrowly on the plates, and the perforations were applied irregularly.

Therefore, very fine examples of Nos. 1-28, 30-39 will have perforations that cut into the design slightly on one or more sides. Also, very fine examples of Nos. 40-53, 55-60 will have perforations touching the design on at least one side. These stamps with perfs clear of the design on all four sides, especially Nos. 1-28, 30-39, are extremely scarce and command substantially higher prices.

### Watermarks

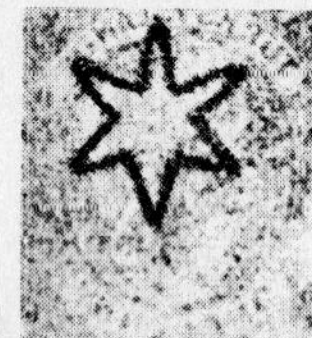

Wmk. 5 — Small Star

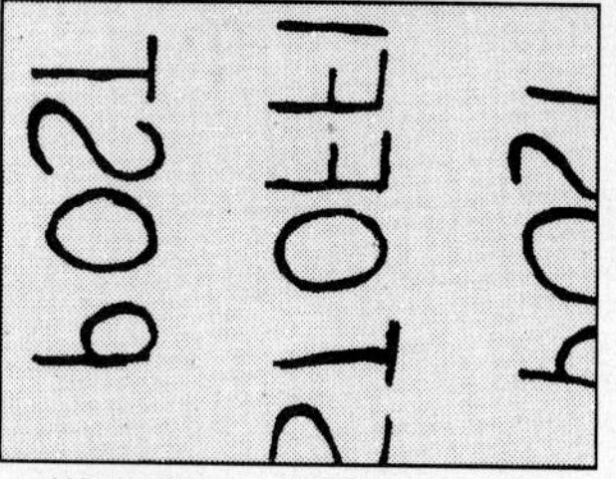

Wmk. 380 — "POST OFFICE"

Queen Victoria — A1

**1861 Engr. Unwmk. *Perf. 14 to 16***

| | | | | |
|---|---|---|---|---|
| 1 | A1 | 1p rose | *62.50* | 20.00 |
| *a.* | | Imperf., pair | 300.00 | |
| *c.* | | Horiz. pair, imperf. vert. | *400.00* | |
| 1B | A1 | 6p yellow green | *8,250.* | 250.00 |

Perfs on Nos. 1-1B are not clean cut. See Nos. 2-3 for rough perfs.

**1862-66 *Rough Perf. 14 to 16***

| | | | | |
|---|---|---|---|---|
| 2 | A1 | 1p rose | 60.00 | 20.00 |
| *a.* | | Horiz. pair, imperf. vert. | 400.00 | |
| 3 | A1 | 6p dark green | 65.00 | 21.00 |
| *a.* | | Imperf., pair | 1,250. | |
| *b.* | | Horiz. pair, imperf. between | *14,500.* | *15,500.* |
| 4 | A1 | 1sh slate ('66) | 425.00 | 160.00 |
| | | *Nos. 2-4 (3)* | 550.00 | 201.00 |

**1863-69 *Perf. 11 to 13***

| | | | | |
|---|---|---|---|---|
| 5 | A1 | 1p rose | 45.00 | 22.50 |
| 6 | A1 | 4p blue ('66) | 300.00 | 125.00 |
| *a.* | | Horiz. pair, imperf. vert. | | |
| 7 | A1 | 4p orange ('69) | 400.00 | 175.00 |
| 8 | A1 | 6p deep green | 250.00 | 82.50 |
| 8A | A1 | 1sh slate ('66) | *2,750.* | 1,000. |
| 9 | A1 | 1sh indigo ('69) | 425.00 | 100.00 |
| 10 | A1 | 1sh brown ('69) | 550.00 | 175.00 |

***Perf. 11 to 13x14 to 16***

| | | | | |
|---|---|---|---|---|
| 11 | A1 | 1p rose | *6,500.* | 1,250. |
| 12 | A1 | 1sh slate | 300.00 | 140.00 |

***Rough Perf. 14 to 16***

**1871-78 Wmk. 5**

| | | | | |
|---|---|---|---|---|
| 13 | A1 | 1p black | 65.00 | 15.50 |
| *a.* | | Vert. pair, imperf. btwn. | *20,000.* | |
| 14 | A1 | 6p dk blue green | 350.00 | 77.50 |
| *a.* | | Watermark sideways | | 100.00 |

***Clean-Cut Perf. 14 to 16***

| | | | | |
|---|---|---|---|---|
| 14A | A1 | 1p black | 65.00 | 15.50 |
| 14B | A1 | 6p dp bl grn | 1,650. | 55.00 |
| *c.* | | 6p dull blue green | 2,250. | 55.00 |
| 15 | A1 | 6p pale yel green ('78) | 800.00 | 32.50 |
| 15A | A1 | 1sh vermilion ('77) | | *50,000.* |

For surcharge see No. 30.

***Perf. 11 to 13***

| | | | | |
|---|---|---|---|---|
| 16 | A1 | 4p dk bl ('77) | 600.00 | 110.00 |
| 17 | A1 | 1sh dp rose ('72) | 825.00 | 160.00 |
| 18 | A1 | 1sh claret ('75) | 675.00 | 300.00 |

***Perf. 11 to 13x14 to 16***

| | | | | |
|---|---|---|---|---|
| 20 | A1 | 1p black | 95.00 | 16.50 |
| *a.* | | Horiz. pair, imperf. btwn. | | *25,000.* |
| 21 | A1 | 6p pale yel grn ('77) | 725.00 | 55.00 |
| 22 | A1 | 1sh lilac rose ('72) | *6,250.* | 400.00 |
| 23 | A1 | 1sh vermilion ('77) | 1,100. | 100.00 |
| *a.* | | Horiz. pair, imperf. vert. | — | |

See Nos. 25-28A, 36-39, 42-53. For surcharges see Nos. 30, 32-33, 40, 55-60.

Victoria A2

Seal of Colony A3

**1880-81 *Perf. 11 to 13***

| | | | | |
|---|---|---|---|---|
| 24 | A2 | ½p org ('81) | 8.00 | 11.50 |
| 25 | A1 | 1p gray green | 190.00 | 5.50 |
| 26 | A1 | 1p drab ('81) | 800.00 | 15.50 |
| 27 | A1 | 4p ultra ('81) | 1,350. | 130.00 |
| *a.* | | Horiz. pair, imperf. btwn. | | |
| 28 | A1 | 6p yel grn | 550.00 | 77.50 |
| 28A | A1 | 1sh vermilion | 900.00 | 65.00 |
| 29 | A3 | 5sh rose | 1,275. | *1,650.* |

No. 29 is valued well centered with design well clear of the perfs.

See Nos. 35, 41, 54, 598. For surcharges see Nos. 31-33.

No. 14B Bisected and Surcharged in Red

**1880, May *Perf. 14 to 16***

| | | | | |
|---|---|---|---|---|
| 30 | A1 | 1p on half of 6p | 600.00 | 425.00 |
| *a.* | | Unsevered pair | *2,250.* | *1,350.* |

No. 28 Bisected and Surcharged in Red

**1881, Sept. 1**

| | | | | |
|---|---|---|---|---|
| 31 | A1 | ½p on half of 6p yel grn ('81) | 150. | 190. |
| *a.* | | Unsevered pair | 525. | 550. |
| *b.* | | "1" with straight top | 1,100. | |
| *c.* | | Without fraction bar, pair, #31, 31c | 4,750. | *5,500.* |

**Nos. 28 and 28A Surcharged in Black**

c

d

**1881, Nov. *Perf. 11 to 13***

| | | | | |
|---|---|---|---|---|
| 32 | A1(c) | 1p on 6p yel grn | 500. | 400. |
| 33 | A1(d) | 4p on 1sh ver | 1,850. | 925. |
| *a.* | | 3 mm spacing between "4d" and bar | *3,500.* | *2,500.* |

**1883-84 Wmk. 2 *Perf. 12***

| | | | | |
|---|---|---|---|---|
| 35 | A2 | ½p green ('84) | 110.00 | 40.00 |
| 36 | A1 | 4p ultra | 825.00 | 55.00 |
| 37 | A1 | 4p dull blue ('84) | 2,500. | 275.00 |
| 38 | A1 | 6p yellow grn | 175.00 | 350.00 |
| 39 | A1 | 1sh orange ver | 175.00 | 65.00 |
| *a.* | | Imperf., pair | | |

The ½p orange, 1p rose red, 1p milky blue and 5sh carmine lake were never placed in use. Some authorities believe them to be color trials.

Nos. 35-60 may be found watermarked with single straight line. This is from the frame which encloses each group of 60 watermark designs.

Type of A1 Surcharged in Black — e

**1883 *Perf. 14***

| | | | | |
|---|---|---|---|---|
| 40 | A1(e) | 2½p on 1p lake | 30.00 | 1.75 |

**1883-97**

| | | | | |
|---|---|---|---|---|
| 41 | A2 | ½p green ('85) | 1.10 | .65 |
| 42 | A1 | 1p drab | 80.00 | 3.50 |
| 43 | A1 | 1p rose red ('85) | 3.00 | 1.00 |
| 44 | A1 | 1p pink ('86) | 6.75 | 1.90 |
| 45 | A1 | 2½p brt blue ('97) | 10.00 | 2.25 |
| 46 | A1 | 4p ultra | 725.00 | 85.00 |
| 47 | A1 | 4p red brn ('85) | 1,100. | 25.00 |
| 48 | A1 | 4p lake brn ('86) | 100.00 | 1.60 |
| 49 | A1 | 4p yellow ('93) | 2.00 | *15.00* |
| *a.* | | 4p olive yellow | *350.00* | *350.00* |
| 50 | A1 | 5p gray brn ('97) | 8.75 | *32.50* |
| 51 | A1 | 6p violet ('88) | 225.00 | *225.00* |
| 52 | A1 | 6p red violet ('91) | 3.00 | *25.00* |
| 53 | A1 | 1sh org ver ('91) | 6.00 | 17.50 |
| 54 | A3 | 5sh car lake ('88) | 32.50 | *60.00* |
| *a.* | | 5sh brown lake | *35.00* | *60.00* |

Grading footnote after No. 29 applies equally to Nos. 54-54a.

For other shades, see the *Scott Classic Catalogue.*

No. 40 Resurcharged in Black

**1885, Mar.**

| | | | | |
|---|---|---|---|---|
| 55 | A1 | 1p on 2½p on 1p lake | 37.50 | 27.50 |

Examples with 3-bar cancel are proofs.

**Stamps of Type A1 Surcharged in Black or Violet**

g

h

j

**1890-91**

| | | | | |
|---|---|---|---|---|
| 56 | A1(e) | 2½p on 1p brt blue | 2.00 | .40 |
| *a.* | | 2½p on 1p milky blue | 27.50 | 9.50 |
| *b.* | | 2½p on 1p gray blue | 27.50 | .75 |
| 57 | A1(g) | 2½p on 4p vio brn ('90) | 90.00 | *130.00* |
| *a.* | | Without fraction bar | 475.00 | *575.00* |

**1892-93**

| | | | | |
|---|---|---|---|---|
| 58 | A1(h) | 5p on 4p lake brn (V) | 40.00 | *55.00* |
| 59 | A1(j) | 5p on 6p dp lake ('93) | *2.00* | *1.90* |
| *a.* | | 5p on 6p carmine lake | 22.50 | *32.50* |
| *b.* | | Double surcharge | *7,750.* | *4,500.* |

**1897**

| | | | | |
|---|---|---|---|---|
| 60 | A1(j) | 3p on 1p lilac | 6.00 | *26.50* |

Victoria — A13

Numerals of 1sh and 5sh, type A13, and of 2p, 1sh, 5sh and £1, type A14, are in color on plain tablet.

**1898 Typo. *Perf. 14***

| | | | | |
|---|---|---|---|---|
| 62 | A13 | ½p lilac & grn | 3.00 | 3.00 |
| 63 | A13 | 1p lil & car rose | 5.00 | 1.70 |
| 64 | A13 | 2½p lilac & ultra | 6.50 | 2.25 |
| 65 | A13 | 3p lilac & ol grn | 4.50 | *21.00* |
| 66 | A13 | 4p lilac & org | 7.25 | *25.00* |
| 67 | A13 | 5p lilac & blk | 8.25 | *21.00* |
| 68 | A13 | 6p lilac & brn | 14.50 | *55.00* |
| 69 | A13 | 1sh grn & car rose | 18.50 | *60.00* |
| 70 | A13 | 5sh green & ultra | 100.00 | *175.00* |
| | | *Nos. 62-70 (9)* | 167.50 | *363.95* |

Edward VII — A14

**1902**

| | | | | |
|---|---|---|---|---|
| 71 | A14 | ½p redsh lil & grn | 4.75 | .75 |
| 72 | A14 | 1p vio & car rose | 4.75 | .35 |
| 73 | A14 | 2p violet & black | 6.50 | *7.50* |
| 74 | A14 | 2½p violet & ultra | 5.50 | 4.00 |
| 75 | A14 | 3p violet & ol grn | 5.50 | *7.25* |
| 76 | A14 | 6p violet & brn | 12.00 | *50.00* |
| 77 | A14 | 1sh grn & car rose | 30.00 | *70.00* |
| 78 | A14 | 2sh green & violet | 27.50 | *65.00* |
| 79 | A14 | 5sh green & ultra | 82.50 | *140.00* |
| | | *Nos. 71-79 (9)* | 179.00 | *344.85* |

**1904-11 Wmk. 3 Chalky Paper**

| | | | | |
|---|---|---|---|---|
| 82 | A14 | ½p vio & grn | 1.50 | 1.50 |
| 83 | A14 | 1p vio & car rose | 26.00 | 1.75 |
| 84 | A14 | 2½p vio & ultra | 19.00 | *52.50* |
| 85 | A14 | 6p vio & brn | 19.00 | *55.00* |
| 86 | A14 | 1sh grn & car rose | 15.50 | *17.50* |
| 87 | A14 | 2sh vio & bl, *bl* | 25.00 | *52.50* |
| 88 | A14 | 5sh grn & red, *yel* | 19.00 | *55.00* |
| 89 | A14 | £1 vio & blk, *red* | 300.00 | *400.00* |
| | | *Nos. 82-88 (7)* | 125.00 | *235.75* |

#82, 83 and 86 also exist on ordinary paper.

Issued: 1p, 1904, ½p, 6p, 1905; 2½p, 1906; 1sh, 1908; 2sh, 5sh, 1909; £1, July 22, 1911.

"Peace and Justice" — A15

**1907 Engr. Ordinary Paper**

| | | | | |
|---|---|---|---|---|
| 90 | A15 | ½p yellow green | 4.00 | 2.75 |
| 91 | A15 | 1p carmine | 4.25 | .25 |
| 92 | A15 | 2p orange | 1.75 | *7.75* |
| 93 | A15 | 2½p ultra | 45.00 | 10.00 |
| 94 | A15 | 3p dark violet | 9.50 | *18.00* |
| | | *Nos. 90-94 (5)* | 64.50 | *38.75* |

"Peace and Justice" — A16

**1909 Without Dot under "d"**

95 A16 1p carmine 1.50 .35
96 A16 6p red violet 9.25 50.00
97 A16 1sh black, *green* 5.50 11.00
*Nos. 95-97 (3)* 16.25 61.35

**1909-11 With Dot under "d"**

98 A16 ½p yel grn ('10) 2.50 .70
99 A16 1p carmine 4.00 .25
100 A16 2p gray ('11) 6.50 12.00
101 A16 2½p ultra 9.50 4.50
102 A16 3p violet, *yel* 3.00 14.50
103 A16 6p red violet 20.00 11.00
*Nos. 98-103 (6)* 45.50 42.95

King George V — A17

**1913-17** ***Perf. 14***

104 A17 ½p green .75 .25
105 A17 1p carmine 1.00 .90
106 A17 2p slate 3.50 42.50
107 A17 2½p ultra .60 .90
108 A17 3p violet, *yellow* 1.00 7.50
109 A17 4p red, *yellow* 1.00 2.40
110 A17 5p olive green 2.50 17.00
111 A17 6p claret 2.50 5.00
112 A17 1sh black, *green* 1.75 4.25
113 A17 1sh bister ('14) 4.75 35.00
114 A16 2sh vio & ultra 5.75 40.00
115 A16 5sh dk grn & car 15.00 60.00
116 A16 £1 black & vio 125.00 200.00
*Nos. 104-116 (13)* 165.10 415.70

Issued: 5p, 11/7; #113, 5/1/14; others, 1/1/13.

For overprints see Nos. MR1-MR2.

No. 112 Surcharged in Carmine

**1915**

117 A17 1p on 1sh blk, *grn* 11.00 45.00
*a.* "PENNY" & bar double 750.00 725.00
*b.* Without period 15.00
*c.* "ONE" omitted 1,550. 1,350.
*d.* "ONE" double 750.00
*e.* "PENNY" & bar omitted 1,450.

Space between surcharge lines varies from 8 to 10mm.

**1921-32** **Wmk. 4**

118 A17 ½p green 2.10 .35
119 A17 1p carmine ('21) 1.15 1.00
120 A17 1½p yel brn ('32) 4.00 .25
121 A17 2p gray 3.00 1.00
122 A17 2½p ultra ('26) 1.50 1.75
123 A17 3p ultra 1.15 7.25
124 A17 3p vio, *yel* ('27) 1.15 1.75
125 A17 4p red, *yel* ('30) 2.10 7.25
126 A17 5p olive green 1.15 7.75
127 A17 6p claret ('27) 1.75 4.25
128 A17 1sh ocher ('27) 4.00 20.00
129 A16 2sh brn vio & ultra 9.00 15.00
130 A16 5sh dk grn & car 21.00 37.50
131 A16 £1 blk & vio ('28) 110.00 150.00
*Nos. 118-131 (14)* 163.05 255.10

Common Design Types pictured following the introduction.

**Silver Jubilee Issue**

Common Design Type

**1935, May 6** ***Perf. 11x12***

134 CD301 1p car & dk bl .55 4.75
135 CD301 1½p gray blk & ultra 1.40 4.50
136 CD301 2½p ultra & brn 2.50 5.00
137 CD301 1sh brn vio & ind 5.00 7.00
*Nos. 134-137 (4)* 9.45 21.25
Set, never hinged 16.00

**Coronation Issue**

Common Design Type

**1937, May 12** ***Perf. 11x11½***

138 CD302 1p dark purple .25 1.25
139 CD302 1½p dark carmine .25 1.25
140 CD302 2½p deep ultra .30 2.25
*Nos. 138-140 (3)* .80 4.75
Set, never hinged 1.50

Seal of the Colony — A18

Young's Island and Fort Duvernette — A19

Kingstown and Fort Charlotte — A20

Villa Beach — A21

Victoria Park, Kingstown — A22

**1938-47** **Wmk. 4** ***Perf. 12***

141 A18 ½p grn & brt bl .25 .25
142 A19 1p claret & blue .25 .25
143 A20 1½p scar & lt grn .25 .25
144 A18 2p black & green .30 .25
145 A21 2½p pck bl & ind .25 .25
145A A22 2½p choc & grn ('47) .25 .25
146 A18 3p dk vio & org .25 .25
146A A21 3½p dp bl grn & ind ('47) .40 2.25
147 A18 6p claret & blk .70 .40
148 A22 1sh green & vio .70 .75
149 A18 2sh dk vio & brt blue 5.25 1.00
149A A18 2sh6p dp bl & org brn ('47) .95 4.25
150 A18 5sh dk grn & car 8.75 3.00
150A A18 10sh choc & dp vio ('47) 7.50 10.00
151 A18 £1 black & vio 22.50 18.00
*Nos. 141-151 (15)* 48.55 41.40
Set, never hinged 55.00

Issue date: Mar. 11, 1938.

See Nos. 156-169, 180-184.

**Catalogue values for unused stamps in this section, from this point to the end of the section, are for Never Hinged items.**

**Peace Issue**

Common Design Type

**1946, Oct. 15** **Engr.** ***Perf. 13½x14***

152 CD303 1½p carmine .25 .25
153 CD303 3½p deep blue .25 .25

**Silver Wedding Issue**

Common Design Types

**1948, Nov. 30** **Photo.** ***Perf. 14x14½***

154 CD304 1½p scarlet .25 .25

**Engraved; Name Typographed**

***Perf. 11½x11***

155 CD305 £1 red violet 27.50 30.00

**Types of 1938**

**1949, Mar. 26** **Engr.** ***Perf. 12***

156 A18 1c grn & brt bl .25 1.75
157 A19 2c claret & bl .25 .50
158 A20 3c scar & lt grn .55 1.00
159 A18 4c gray blk & grn .40 .25
160 A22 5c choc & grn .25 .25
161 A18 6c dk vio & org .55 1.25
162 A21 7c pck blue & ind 5.50 1.50
163 A18 12c claret & blk .50 .25
164 A22 24c green & vio .50 .55
165 A18 48c dk vio & brt bl 4.50 6.00
166 A18 60c dp bl & org brn 2.00 5.50
167 A18 $1.20 dk grn & car 4.75 4.75
168 A18 $2.40 choc & dp vio 6.75 10.00
169 A18 $4.80 gray blk & vio 13.00 20.00
*Nos. 156-169 (14)* 39.75 53.55

For overprints see Nos. 176-179.

**UPU Issue**

Common Design Types

**Engr.; Name Typo. on 6c, 12c**

***Perf. 13½, 11x11½***

**1949, Oct. 10** **Wmk. 4**

170 CD306 5c blue .25 .25
171 CD307 6c dp rose violet .55 2.00
172 CD308 12c red lilac .30 2.00
173 CD309 24c blue green 1.10 .80
*Nos. 170-173 (4)* 2.20 5.05

**University Issue**

Common Design Types

**1951, Feb. 16** **Engr.** ***Perf. 14x14½***

174 CD310 3c red & blue green .50 .65
175 CD311 12c rose lilac & blk .50 1.50

Nos. 158-160 and 163 Overprinted in Black

**1951, Sept. 21** ***Perf. 12***

176 A20 3c scarlet & lt grn .30 1.60
177 A18 4c gray blk & grn .30 .60
178 A22 5c chocolate & grn .30 .60
179 A18 12c claret & blk .95 1.25
*Nos. 176-179 (4)* 1.85 4.05

Adoption of a new constitution for the Windward Islands, 1951.

**Type of 1938-47**

**1952**

180 A18 1c gray black & green .30 2.25
181 A18 3c dk violet & orange .30 2.25
182 A18 4c green & brt blue .30 .25
183 A20 6c scarlet & dp green .30 2.00
184 A21 10c peacock blue & ind .45 .35
*Nos. 180-184 (5)* 1.65 7.10

**Coronation Issue**

Common Design Type

**1953, June 2** ***Perf. 13½x13***

185 CD312 4c dk green & blk .50 .30

Elizabeth II — A23

Seal of Colony — A24

***Perf. 13x14***

**1955, Sept. 16** **Wmk. 4** **Engr.**

186 A23 1c orange .25 .25
187 A23 2c violet blue .25 .25
188 A23 3c gray .25 .25
189 A23 4c dk red brown .25 .25
190 A23 5c scarlet .25 .25
191 A23 10c purple .45 .25
192 A23 15c deep blue .70 1.00
193 A23 20c green .85 .25
194 A23 25c brown black 1.50 .25

***Perf. 14***

195 A24 50c chocolate 9.25 3.25
196 A24 $1 dull green 15.00 2.10
197 A24 $2.50 deep blue 15.00 15.00
*Nos. 186-197 (12)* 44.00 23.35

See Nos. 205-213.

**West Indies Federation**

Common Design Type

***Perf. 11½x11***

**1958, Apr. 22** **Wmk. 314**

198 CD313 3c green .30 .25
199 CD313 6c blue .40 1.00
200 CD313 12c carmine rose .80 .50
*Nos. 198-200 (3)* 1.50 1.75

**Freedom from Hunger Issue**

Common Design Type

**1963, June 4** **Photo.** ***Perf. 14x14½***

201 CD314 8c lilac .90 .50

**Red Cross Centenary Issue**

Common Design Type

**1963, Sept. 2** **Litho.** ***Perf. 13***

202 CD315 4c black & red .25 .25
203 CD315 8c ultra & red .65 .65

**Types of 1955**

***Perf. 13x14***

**1964-65** **Wmk. 314** **Engr.**

205 A23 1c orange .25 .25
206 A23 2c violet blue .25 .25
207 A23 3c gray .55 .60
208 A23 5c scarlet .30 .30
209 A23 10c purple .45 .45
*a.* Perf. 12½ .25 .25
210 A23 15c deep blue 1.00 .80
*a.* Perf. 12½ .45 .30
211 A23 20c green .70 .75
*a.* Perf. 12½ 5.00 2.00
212 A23 25c brown black 1.25 1.35
*a.* Perf. 12½ .80 1.25

***Perf. 14***

213 A24 50c chocolate ('65) 5.75 5.50
*a.* Perf. 12½ 5.00 7.00
*Nos. 205-213 (9)* 10.50 10.25

Scout Emblem and Merit Badges — A25

**1964, Nov. 23** **Litho.** ***Perf. 14***

216 A25 1c dk brn & brt yel grn .25 .25
217 A25 4c dk red brn & brt bl .25 .25
218 A25 20c dk vio & org .30 .25
219 A25 50c green & red .45 .60
*Nos. 216-219 (4)* 1.25 1.35

Boy Scouts of St. Vincent, 50th anniv.

Breadfruit and Capt. Bligh's Ship "Providence" — A26

Designs: 1c, Tropical fruit. 25c, Doric temple and pond, vert. 40c, Blooming talipot palm and Doric temple, vert.

***Perf. 14½x13½, 13½x14½***

**1965, Mar. 23** **Photo.** **Wmk. 314**

220 A26 1c dk green & multi .25 .25
221 A26 4c lt & dk brn grn & yel .25 .25
222 A26 25c blue, grn & bister .25 .25
223 A26 40c dk blue & multi .30 1.10
*Nos. 220-223 (4)* 1.05 1.85

Bicentenary of the Botanic Gardens.

**ITU Issue**

Common Design Type

**1965, May 17** **Litho.** ***Perf. 11x11½***

224 CD317 4c blue & yel grn .25 .25
225 CD317 48c yellow & orange .55 .65

Boat Building, Bequia — A27

Woman Carrying Bananas — A28

Designs: 2c, Friendship Beach, Bequia. 3c, Terminal building. 5c, Crater Lake. 6c, Rock carvings, Carib Stone. 8c, Arrowroot. 10c, Owia saltpond. 12c, Ship at deep water wharf. 20c, Sea Island cotton. 25c, Map of St. Vincent and neighboring islands. 50c, Breadfruit. $1, Baleine Falls. $2.50, St. Vincent parrot. $5, Coat of arms.

*Perf. 14x13½, 13½x14*

**1965-67 Photo. Wmk. 314**

| No. | Type | Description | Unused | Used |
|---|---|---|---|---|
| 226 | A27 | 1c (BEOUIA) | .25 | .75 |
| 226A | A27 | 1c (BEQUIA) | .60 | .35 |
| 227 | A27 | 2c lt ultra, grn, yel & red | .25 | .25 |
| 228 | A27 | 3c red, yel & brn | .40 | .25 |
| 229 | A28 | 4c brn, ultra & yel | .75 | .35 |
| *a.* | | Wmkd. sideways | .50 | .25 |
| 230 | A27 | 5c pur, bl, yel & grn | .25 | .25 |
| 231 | A28 | 6c sl grn, yel & gray | .25 | .30 |
| 232 | A28 | 8c pur, yel & grn | .40 | .25 |
| 233 | A27 | 10c org brn, yel & bluish grn | .40 | .25 |
| 234 | A27 | 12c grnsh bl, yel & pink | .65 | .25 |
| 235 | A28 | 20c brt yel, grn, pur & brn | .40 | .25 |
| 236 | A28 | 25c ultra, grn & vio blue | .45 | .25 |
| 237 | A28 | 50c grn, yel & bl | .45 | .35 |
| 238 | A28 | $1 vio bl, lt grn & dk sl grn | 4.00 | .45 |
| 239 | A28 | $2.50 pale lilac & multi | 19.00 | 8.50 |
| 240 | A28 | $5 dull vio blue & multi | 4.25 | 10.50 |
| | | *Nos. 226-240 (16)* | 32.75 | 23.55 |

Issued: No. 226A, 8/8/67; others, 8/16/65.

For overprint see No. 270.

### Churchill Memorial Issue

Common Design Type

**1966, Jan. 24** *Perf. 14*

**Design in Black, Gold and Carmine Rose**

| No. | Type | Description | Unused | Used |
|---|---|---|---|---|
| 241 | CD319 | 1c bright blue | .25 | .25 |
| 242 | CD319 | 4c green | .25 | .25 |
| 243 | CD319 | 20c brown | .35 | .35 |
| 244 | CD319 | 40c violet | .65 | .90 |
| | | *Nos. 241-244 (4)* | 1.50 | 1.75 |

### Royal Visit Issue

Common Design Type

**1966, Feb. 4 Litho.** *Perf. 11x12*

**Portrait in Black**

| No. | Type | Description | Unused | Used |
|---|---|---|---|---|
| 245 | CD320 | 4c violet blue | .50 | .25 |
| 246 | CD320 | 25c dk carmine rose | 2.25 | 1.10 |

### WHO Headquarters Issue

Common Design Type

**1966, Sept. 20 Litho.** *Perf. 14*

| No. | Type | Description | Unused | Used |
|---|---|---|---|---|
| 247 | CD322 | 4c multicolored | .25 | .25 |
| 248 | CD322 | 25c multicolored | .90 | .80 |

### UNESCO Anniversary Issue

Common Design Type

**1966, Dec. 1 Litho.** *Perf. 14*

| No. | Type | Description | Unused | Used |
|---|---|---|---|---|
| 249 | CD323 | 4c "Education" | .25 | .25 |
| 250 | CD323 | 8c "Science" | .45 | .25 |
| 251 | CD323 | 25c "Culture" | 1.60 | .85 |
| | | *Nos. 249-251 (3)* | 2.30 | 1.35 |

View of Mt. Coke Area A29

Designs: 8c, Kingstown Methodist Church. 25c, First license to perform marriage, May 15, 1867. 35c, Arms of Conference of the Methodist Church in the Caribbean and the Americas.

*Perf. 14x14½*

**1967, Dec. 1 Photo. Wmk. 314**

| No. | Type | Description | Unused | Used |
|---|---|---|---|---|
| 252 | A29 | 2c multicolored | .25 | .25 |
| 253 | A29 | 8c multicolored | .25 | .25 |
| 254 | A29 | 25c multicolored | .25 | .25 |
| 255 | A29 | 35c multicolored | .25 | .25 |
| | | *Nos. 252-255 (4)* | 1.00 | 1.00 |

Attainment of autonomy by the Methodist Church in the Caribbean and the Americas, and opening of headquarters near St. John's, Antigua, May 1967.

For overprints see Nos. 268-269, 271.

Caribbean Meteorological Institute, Barbados — A30

*Perf. 14x14½*

**1968, June 28 Photo. Wmk. 314**

| No. | Type | Description | Unused | Used |
|---|---|---|---|---|
| 256 | A30 | 4c cerise & multi | .25 | .25 |
| 257 | A30 | 25c vermilion & multi | .25 | .25 |
| 258 | A30 | 35c violet blue & multi | .25 | .25 |
| | | *Nos. 256-258 (3)* | .75 | .75 |

Issued for World Meteorological Day.

Martin Luther King, Jr. and Cotton Pickers A31

*Perf. 13½x13*

**1968, Aug. 28 Litho. Wmk. 314**

| No. | Type | Description | Unused | Used |
|---|---|---|---|---|
| 259 | A31 | 5c violet & multi | .25 | .25 |
| 260 | A31 | 25c gray & multi | .25 | .25 |
| 261 | A31 | 35c brown red & multi | .25 | .25 |
| | | *Nos. 259-261 (3)* | .75 | .75 |

Dr. Martin Luther King, Jr. (1929-68), American civil rights leader.

Scales of Justice and Human Rights Flame — A32

3c, Speaker addressing demonstrators, horiz.

*Perf. 13x14, 14x13*

**1968, Nov. 1 Photo. Unwmk.**

| No. | Type | Description | Unused | Used |
|---|---|---|---|---|
| 262 | A32 | 3c orange & multi | .25 | .25 |
| 263 | A32 | 35c grnsh blue & vio blue | .25 | .25 |

International Human Rights Year.

Carnival Costume — A33

5c, Sketch of a steel bandsman. 8c, Revelers, horiz. 25c, Queen of Bands & attendants.

**1969, Feb. 17 Litho.** *Perf. 14½*

| No. | Type | Description | Unused | Used |
|---|---|---|---|---|
| 264 | A33 | 1c multicolored | .25 | .25 |
| 265 | A33 | 5c red & dark brown | .25 | .25 |
| 266 | A33 | 8c multicolored | .25 | .25 |
| 267 | A33 | 25c multicolored | .25 | .25 |
| | | *Nos. 264-267 (4)* | 1.00 | 1.00 |

St. Vincent Carnival celebration, Feb. 17.

### Nos. 252-253, 236 and 255 Overprinted: "METHODIST / CONFERENCE / MAY / 1969"

*Perf. 14x14½, 13½x14*

**1969, May 14 Photo. Wmk. 314**

| No. | Type | Description | Unused | Used |
|---|---|---|---|---|
| 268 | A29 | 2c multicolored | .25 | .25 |
| 269 | A29 | 8c multicolored | .25 | .25 |
| 270 | A28 | 25c multicolored | .25 | .25 |
| 271 | A29 | 35c multicolored | 1.00 | *2.00* |
| | | *Nos. 268-271 (4)* | 1.75 | 2.75 |

1st Caribbean Methodist Conf. held outside Antigua.

"Strength in Unity" — A34

5c, 25c, Map of the Caribbean, vert.

*Perf. 13½x13, 13x13½*

**1969, July 1 Litho.**

| No. | Type | Description | Unused | Used |
|---|---|---|---|---|
| 272 | A34 | 2c orange, yel & blk | .25 | .25 |
| 273 | A34 | 5c lilac & multi | .25 | .25 |
| 274 | A34 | 8c emerald, yel & blk | .25 | .25 |
| 275 | A34 | 25c blue & multi | .25 | .25 |
| | | *Nos. 272-275 (4)* | 1.00 | 1.00 |

1st anniv. of CARIFTA (Caribbean Free Trade Area.)

Flag and Arms of St. Vincent — A35

Designs: 10c, Uprising of 1795. 50c, Government House.

*Perf. 14x14½*

**1969, Oct. 27 Photo. Wmk. 314**

| No. | Type | Description | Unused | Used |
|---|---|---|---|---|
| 276 | A35 | 4c deep ultra & multi | .25 | .25 |
| 277 | A35 | 10c olive & multi | .25 | .25 |
| 278 | A35 | 50c orange, gray & blk | .75 | .50 |
| | | *Nos. 276-278 (3)* | 1.25 | 1.00 |

Green Heron A36

Birds: ½c, House wren, vert. 2c, Bullfinches. 3c, St. Vincent parrots. 4c, St. Vincent solitaire, vert. 5c, Scalynecked pigeon, vert. 6c, Bananaquits. 8c, Purple throated Carib. 10c, Mangrove cuckoo, vert. 12c, Black hawk, vert. 20c, Bare-eyed thrush. 25c, Hooded tanager. 50c, Blue-hooded euphonia. $1, Barn owl, vert. $2.50, Yellow-bellied elaenia, vert. $5, Ruddy quail-dove.

### Wmk. 314 Upright on ½c, 4c, 5c, 10c, 12c, 50c, $5, Sideways on Others

**1970, Jan. 12 Photo.** *Perf. 14*

| No. | Type | Description | Unused | Used |
|---|---|---|---|---|
| 279 | A36 | ½c multicolored | .25 | .25 |
| 280 | A36 | 1c multicolored | .25 | .25 |
| 281 | A36 | 2c multicolored | .25 | .25 |
| 282 | A36 | 3c multicolored | .25 | .25 |
| 283 | A36 | 4c multicolored | .25 | .25 |
| 284 | A36 | 5c multicolored | 1.25 | .65 |
| 285 | A36 | 6c multicolored | .40 | .35 |
| 286 | A36 | 8c multicolored | .40 | .25 |
| 287 | A36 | 10c multicolored | .45 | .35 |
| 288 | A36 | 12c multicolored | .60 | .40 |
| 289 | A36 | 20c multicolored | .80 | .50 |
| 290 | A36 | 25c multicolored | .80 | .50 |
| 291 | A36 | 50c multicolored | 1.25 | .75 |
| 292 | A36 | $1 multicolored | 3.00 | 1.50 |
| 293 | A36 | $2.50 multicolored | 6.00 | 4.00 |
| 294 | A36 | $5 multicolored | 14.00 | 10.00 |
| | | *Nos. 279-294 (16)* | 30.20 | 20.50 |

See Nos. 379-381. For surcharges see Nos. 364-366, 3239, 3242, 3265.

### Wmk. 314 Upright on 2c, 3c, 6c, 20c, Sideways on Others

**1973**

| No. | Type | Description | Unused | Used |
|---|---|---|---|---|
| *281a* | A36 | 2c multicolored | .35 | *.45* |
| *282a* | A36 | 3c multicolored | .35 | *.45* |
| *283a* | A36 | 4c multicolored | .35 | .40 |
| *284a* | A36 | 5c multicolored | .35 | .30 |
| *285a* | A36 | 6c multicolored | .50 | *.65* |
| *287a* | A36 | 10c multicolored | .50 | .30 |
| *288a* | A36 | 12c multicolored | .75 | .65 |
| *289a* | A36 | 20c multicolored | .85 | .40 |
| | | *Nos. 281a-289a (8)* | 4.00 | 3.60 |

DHC6 Twin Otter A37

20th anniv. of regular air services: 8c, Grumman Goose amphibian. 10c, Hawker Siddeley 748. 25c, Douglas DC-3.

*Perf. 14x13*

**1970, Mar. 13 Litho. Wmk. 314**

| No. | Type | Description | Unused | Used |
|---|---|---|---|---|
| 295 | A37 | 5c lt blue & multi | .25 | .25 |
| 296 | A37 | 8c lt green & multi | .25 | .25 |
| 297 | A37 | 10c pink & multi | .35 | .25 |
| 298 | A37 | 25c yellow & multi | .75 | .65 |
| | | *Nos. 295-298 (4)* | 1.60 | 1.40 |

Nurse and Children A38

Red Cross and: 5c, First aid. 12c, Volunteers. 25c, Blood transfusion.

**1970, June 1 Photo.** *Perf. 14*

| No. | Type | Description | Unused | Used |
|---|---|---|---|---|
| 299 | A38 | 3c blue & multi | .25 | .25 |
| 300 | A38 | 5c yellow & multi | .25 | .25 |
| 301 | A38 | 12c lt green & multi | .35 | .25 |
| 302 | A38 | 25c pale salmon & multi | .65 | .55 |
| | | *Nos. 299-302 (4)* | 1.50 | 1.30 |

Centenary of British Red Cross Society.

St. George's Cathedral — A39

Designs: ½c, 50c, Angel and Two Marys at the Tomb, stained glass window, vert. 25c, St. George's Cathedral, front view, vert. 35c, Interior with altar.

*Perf. 14x14½, 14½x14*

**1970, Sept. 7 Litho. Wmk. 314**

| No. | Type | Description | Unused | Used |
|---|---|---|---|---|
| 303 | A39 | ½c multicolored | .25 | .25 |
| 304 | A39 | 5c multicolored | .25 | .25 |
| 305 | A39 | 25c multicolored | .25 | .25 |
| 306 | A39 | 35c multicolored | .25 | .25 |
| 307 | A39 | 50c multicolored | .25 | .30 |
| | | *Nos. 303-307 (5)* | 1.25 | 1.30 |

St. George's Anglican Cathedral, 150th anniv.

Virgin and Child, by Giovanni Bellini — A40

Christmas: 25c, 50c, Adoration of the Shepherds, by Louis Le Nain, horiz.

**1970, Nov. 23 Litho. Wmk. 314**

| No. | Type | Description | Unused | Used |
|---|---|---|---|---|
| 308 | A40 | 8c brt violet & multi | .25 | .25 |
| 309 | A40 | 25c crimson & multi | .25 | .25 |
| 310 | A40 | 35c yellow grn & multi | .25 | .25 |
| 311 | A40 | 50c sapphire & multi | .25 | .25 |
| | | *Nos. 308-311 (4)* | 1.00 | 1.00 |

Post Office and St. Vincent No. 1B A41

New Post Office and: 4c, $1, St. Vincent No. 1. 25c, as 2c.

**1971, Mar. 29** *Perf. 14½x14*

| No. | Type | Description | Unused | Used |
|---|---|---|---|---|
| 312 | A41 | 2c violet & multi | .25 | .25 |
| 313 | A41 | 4c olive & multi | .25 | .25 |
| 314 | A41 | 25c brown org & multi | .25 | .25 |
| 315 | A41 | $1 lt green & multi | .25 | .45 |
| | | *Nos. 312-315 (4)* | 1.00 | 1.20 |

110th anniv. of 1st stamps of St. Vincent.

National Trust Emblem, Fish and Birds — A42

Designs: 30c, 45c, Cannon at Ft. Charlotte.

*Perf. 13½x14*

**1971, Aug. 4 Litho. Wmk. 314**

**316** A42 12c emerald & multi .25 .80
**317** A42 30c lt blue & multi .35 .35
**318** A42 40c brt pink & multi .50 .40
**319** A42 45c black & multi .70 1.00
*Nos. 316-319 (4)* 1.80 2.55

Publicity for the National Trust (for conservation of wild life and historic buildings).

Holy Family with Angels (detail), by Pietro da Cortona A43

Christmas: 5c, 25c, Madonna Appearing to St. Anthony, by Domenico Tiepolo, vert.

**1971, Oct. 6** *Perf. 14x14½, 14½x14*

**320** A43 5c rose & multi .25 .25
**321** A43 10c lt green & multi .25 .25
**322** A43 25c lt blue & multi .25 .25
**323** A43 $1 yellow & multi .25 .45
*Nos. 320-323 (4)* 1.00 1.20

Careening A44

Designs: 5c, 20c, Seine fishermen. 6c, 50c, Map of Grenadines. 15c, as 1c.

**1971, Nov. 25** *Perf. 14x13½*

**324** A44 1c dp ver & multi .25 .25
**325** A44 5c blue & multi .25 .25
**326** A44 6c yel grn & multi .25 .25
**327** A44 15c org brn & multi .25 .25
**328** A44 20c yellow & multi .25 .30
**329** A44 50c blue, blk & plum .50 1.00
*a.* Souvenir sheet of 6, #324-329 11.00 11.00
*Nos. 324-329 (6)* 1.75 2.30

The Grenadines of St. Vincent tourist issue.

Grenadier Company Private, 1764 — A45

Designs: 30c, Battalion Company officer, 1772. 50c, Grenadier Company private, 1772.

**1972, Feb. 14** *Perf. 14x13½*

**330** A45 12c gray violet & multi .30 .30
**331** A45 30c gray blue & multi .80 .50
**332** A45 50c dark gray & multi 1.40 1.25
*Nos. 330-332 (3)* 2.50 2.05

Breadnut — A46

**1972, May 16 Litho.** *Perf. 14x13½*

**333** A46 3c shown .25 .35
**334** A46 5c Papaya .25 .25
**335** A46 12c Rose apples .30 .40
**336** A46 25c Mangoes .80 .75
*Nos. 333-336 (4)* 1.60 1.75

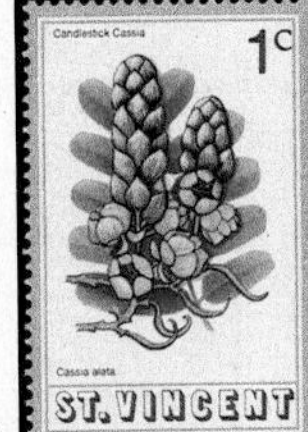

Flowers of St. Vincent — A47

**1972, July 31 Litho.** *Perf. 13½x13*

**337** A47 1c Candlestick Cassia .25 .25
**338** A47 30c Lobster claw .30 .30
**339** A47 40c White trumpet .35 .35
**340** A47 $1 Flowers, Soufriere tree .90 1.10
*Nos. 337-340 (4)* 1.80 2.00

For surcharge see No. 3266.

Sir Charles Brisbane, Family Arms — A48

Designs: 30c, Sailing ship "Arethusa." $1, Sailing ship "Blake."

**1972, Sept. 29 Wmk. 314** *Perf. 13½*

**341** A48 20c yel, brn & gold .30 .30
**342** A48 30c lilac & multi .30 .30
**343** A48 $1 multicolored 1.15 1.25
*a.* Souvenir sheet of 3, #341-343 6.50 6.50
*Nos. 341-343 (3)* 1.75 1.85

Bicentenary of the birth of Sir Charles Brisbane, naval hero, governor of St. Vincent.

### Silver Wedding Issue, 1972
Common Design Type

Design: Queen Elizabeth II, Prince Philip, arrowroot plant, breadfruit foliage and fruit.

**1972, Nov. 20 Photo.** *Perf. 14x14½*

**344** CD324 30c rose brn & multi .25 .25
**345** CD324 $1 multicolored .30 .30

Columbus Sighting St. Vincent — A49

12c, Caribs watching Columbus' ships. 30c, Christopher Columbus. 50c, Santa Maria.

**1973, Jan. 18 Litho.** *Perf. 13*

**346** A49 5c multicolored .25 .30
**347** A49 12c multicolored .25 .45
**348** A49 30c multicolored .70 .75
**349** A49 50c multicolored 1.40 2.25
*Nos. 346-349 (4)* 2.60 3.75

475th anniversary of Columbus's Third Voyage to the West Indies.

The Last Supper — A50

*Perf. 14x13½*

**1973, Apr. 19 Litho. Wmk. 314**

**350** 15c red & multi .25 .25
**351** 60c red & multi .25 .25
**352** $1 red & multi .30 .30
*a.* A50 Strip of 3, #350-352 .80 .80

Easter.

William Wilberforce and Slave Auction Poster — A51

40c, Slaves working on sugar plantation. 50c, Wilberforce & medal commemorating 1st anniversary of abolition of slavery.

**1973, July 11** *Perf. 14x13½*

**353** A51 30c multicolored .25 .25
**354** A51 40c multicolored .25 .25
**355** A51 50c multicolored .30 .30
*Nos. 353-355 (3)* .80 .80

140th anniv. of the death of William Wilberforce (1759-1833), member of British Parliament who fought for abolition of slavery.

Families — A52

Design: 40c, Families and "IPPF."

**1973, Oct. 3** *Perf. 14½*

**356** A52 12c multicolored .25 .25
**357** A52 40c multicolored .25 .25

Intl. Planned Parenthood Assoc., 21st anniv.

### Princess Anne's Wedding Issue
Common Design Type

**1973, Nov. 14** *Perf. 14*

**358** CD325 50c slate & multi .25 .25
**359** CD325 70c gray green & multi .25 .25

Administration Buildings, Mona University — A53

Designs: 10c, University Center, Kingstown. 30c, Mona University, aerial view. $1, Coat of arms of University of West Indies.

**1973, Dec. 13** *Perf. 14½x14, 14x14½*

**360** A53 5c multicolored .25 .25
**361** A53 10c multicolored .25 .25
**362** A53 30c multicolored .25 .25
**363** A53 $1 multicolored .25 .50
*Nos. 360-363 (4)* 1.00 1.25

University of the West Indies, 25th anniv.

### Nos. 291, 286 and 292 Surcharged

**1973, Dec. 15 Photo.** *Perf. 14*

**364** A36 30c on 50c multi .25 1.00
**365** A36 40c on 8c multi .35 .35
**366** A36 $10 on $1 multi 8.50 8.50
*Nos. 364-366 (3)* 9.10 9.85

The position of the surcharge and shape of obliterating bars differs on each denomination.

Descent from the Cross — A54

Easter: 30c, Descent from the Cross. 40c, Pietà. $1, Resurrection. Designs are from sculptures in Victoria and Albert Museum, London, and Provincial Museum, Valladolid (40c).

**1974, Apr. 10 Litho.** *Perf. 13½x13*

**367** A54 5c multicolored .25 .25
**368** A54 30c multicolored .25 .25
**369** A54 40c multicolored .25 .25
**370** A54 $1 multicolored .25 .25
*Nos. 367-370 (4)* 1.00 1.00

"Istra" A55

**1974, June 28** *Perf. 14½*

**371** A55 15c shown .25 .25
**372** A55 20c "Oceanic" .25 .25
**373** A55 30c "Alexander Pushkin" .30 .25
**374** A55 $1 "Europa" .80 1.10
*a.* Souvenir sheet of 4, #371-374 1.75 1.75
*Nos. 371-374 (4)* 1.60 1.85

Cruise ships visiting Kingstown.

Arrows Circling UPU Emblem A56

UPU, cent.: 12c, Post horn and globe. 60c, Target over map of islands, hand canceler. 90c, Goode's map projection.

**1974, July 25** *Perf. 14½*

**375** A56 5c violet & multi .25 .25
**376** A56 12c ocher, green & blue .25 .25
**377** A56 60c blue green & multi .25 .25
**378** A56 90c red & multi .25 .30
*Nos. 375-378 (4)* 1.00 1.05

### Bird Type of 1970

Birds: 30c, Royal tern. 40c, Brown pelican, vert. $10, Magnificent frigate bird, vert.

**Wmk. 314 Sideways on 40c, $10, Upright on 30c**

**1974, Aug. 29 Litho. *Perf. 14½***

| No. | Type | Denom. | Description | Unused | Used |
|---|---|---|---|---|---|
| **379** | A36 | 30c | multicolored | 2.00 | .75 |
| **380** | A36 | 40c | multicolored | 2.00 | .75 |
| **381** | A36 | $10 | multicolored | 13.00 | 10.00 |
| | | | *Nos. 379-381 (3)* | 17.00 | 11.50 |

Scout Emblem and Badges — A57

***Perf. 13½x14***

**1974, Oct. 9 Wmk. 314**

| No. | Type | Denom. | Description | Unused | Used |
|---|---|---|---|---|---|
| **385** | A57 | 10c | lilac & multi | .25 | .25 |
| **386** | A57 | 25c | bister & multi | .25 | .25 |
| **387** | A57 | 45c | gray & multi | .35 | .30 |
| **388** | A57 | $1 | multicolored | .65 | 1.10 |
| | | | *Nos. 385-388 (4)* | 1.50 | 1.90 |

St. Vincent Boy Scouts, 60th anniversary.

Churchill as Prime Minister — A58

Designs (Churchill as): 35c, Lord Warden of the Cinque Ports. 45c, First Lord of the Admiralty. $1, Royal Air Force officer.

**1974, Nov. 28 *Perf. 14½x14***

| No. | Type | Denom. | Description | Unused | Used |
|---|---|---|---|---|---|
| **389** | A58 | 25c | multicolored | .25 | .25 |
| **390** | A58 | 35c | multicolored | .25 | .25 |
| **391** | A58 | 45c | multicolored | .25 | .25 |
| **392** | A58 | $1 | multicolored | .25 | .45 |
| | | | *Nos. 389-392 (4)* | 1.00 | 1.20 |

Sir Winston Churchill (1874-1965), birth centenary. Sheets of 30 in 2 panes of 15 with inscribed gutter between.

A59

A60

**1974, Dec. 5 *Perf. 12x12½***

| No. | Type | Denom. | Description | Unused | Used |
|---|---|---|---|---|---|
| **393** | A59 | 3c | like 8c | .25 | .25 |
| **394** | A59 | 3c | like 35c | .25 | .25 |
| **395** | A60 | 3c | like 45c | .25 | .25 |
| **396** | A60 | 3c | like $1 | .25 | .25 |
| *a.* | | | Strip of 4, #393-396 | .25 | .25 |
| **397** | A59 | 8c | Shepherds | .25 | .25 |
| **398** | A59 | 35c | Virgin, Child and Star | .25 | .25 |
| **399** | A60 | 45c | St. Joseph, Ass & Ox | .25 | .25 |
| **400** | A60 | $1 | Three Kings | .25 | .40 |
| | | | *Nos. 393-400 (8)* | 2.00 | 2.15 |

Christmas. Nos. 396a, 397-400 have continuous picture.

Giant Mask and Dancers — A61

Designs: 15c, Pineapple dancers. 25c, Giant bouquet. 35c, Girl dancers. 45c, Butterfly dancers. $1.25, Sun and moon dancers and float.

**Wmk. 314**

**1975, Feb. 7 Litho. *Perf. 14***

| No. | Type | Denom. | Description | Unused | Used |
|---|---|---|---|---|---|
| **401** | A61 | 1c | multicolored | .25 | .25 |
| *a.* | | | Bklt. pane of 2 + label | .30 | |
| *b.* | | | Bklt. pane of 3, #401, 403, 405 | .75 | |
| **402** | A61 | 15c | multicolored | .25 | .25 |
| *a.* | | | Bklt. pane of 3, #402, 404, 406 | 1.75 | |
| **403** | A61 | 25c | multicolored | .25 | .25 |
| **404** | A61 | 35c | multicolored | .25 | .25 |
| **405** | A61 | 45c | multicolored | .25 | .25 |
| **406** | A61 | $1.25 | multicolored | .25 | .45 |
| *a.* | | | Souvenir sheet of 6, #401-406 | 1.75 | 1.75 |
| | | | *Nos. 401-406 (6)* | 1.50 | 1.70 |

Kingstown carnival 1975.

French Angelfish — A62

Type I

Type II

Two types of $2.50:
I — Line to fish's mouth.
II — Line removed (1976).

Fish and whales — 2c, Spotfin butter-flyfish. 3c, Horse-eyed jack. 4c, Mackerel. 5c, French grunts. 6c, Spotted goatfish. 8c, Ballyhoos. 10c, Sperm whale. 12c, Humpback whale. 15c, Cowfish. 20c, Queen angelfish. 25c, Princess parrotfich. 35c, Red hind. 45c, Atlantic flying fish. 50c, Porkfish. $1, Queen triggerfish. $2.50, Sailfish. $5, Dolphinfish. $10, Blue marlin.

**Wmk. 373**

**1975, Apr. 10 Litho. *Perf. 14***

| No. | Type | Denom. | Description | Unused | Used |
|---|---|---|---|---|---|
| **407** | A62 | 1c | shown | .25 | .50 |
| **408** | A62 | 2c | multicolored | .25 | .75 |
| **409** | A62 | 3c | multicolored | .25 | .45 |
| **410** | A62 | 4c | multicolored | .25 | .25 |
| **411** | A62 | 5c | multicolored | .25 | .35 |
| **412** | A62 | 6c | multicolored | .25 | .75 |
| **413** | A62 | 8c | multicolored | .25 | 2.00 |
| **414** | A62 | 10c | multicolored | .50 | .25 |
| **415** | A62 | 12c | multicolored | .50 | 1.75 |
| **416** | A62 | 15c | multicolored | 1.25 | 1.75 |
| **417** | A62 | 20c | multicolored | .30 | .25 |
| **418** | A62 | 25c | multicolored | .35 | .25 |
| **419** | A62 | 35c | multicolored | .60 | 2.00 |
| **420** | A62 | 45c | multicolored | .60 | .90 |
| **421** | A62 | 50c | multicolored | .70 | 2.25 |
| **422** | A62 | $1 | multicolored | 1.50 | .90 |
| **423** | A62 | $2.50 | Type I | 3.25 | 2.25 |
| *a.* | | | Type II | 3.00 | 1.25 |
| **424** | A62 | $5 | multicolored | 7.00 | 4.00 |
| **425** | A62 | $10 | multicolored | 12.00 | 8.50 |
| | | | *Nos. 407-425 (19)* | 30.30 | 30.10 |

The 4c, 10c, 20c, $1, were reissued with "1976" below design; 1c, 2c, 3c, 5c, 6c, 8c, 12c, 50c, $10, with "1977" below design; 10c with "1978" below design.

No. 423a issued 7/12/76.

See Nos. 472-474. For surcharges and overprints see Nos. 463-464, 499-500, 502-503, 572-581, 584-586.

Cutting Bananas — A63

Banana industry: 35c, La Croix packing station. 45c, Women cleaning and packing bananas. 70c, Freighter loading bananas.

**1975, June 26 Wmk. 314 *Perf. 14***

| No. | Type | Denom. | Description | Unused | Used |
|---|---|---|---|---|---|
| **426** | A63 | 25c | blue & multi | .25 | .25 |
| **427** | A63 | 35c | blue & multi | .25 | .25 |
| **428** | A63 | 45c | carmine & multi | .25 | .25 |
| **429** | A63 | 70c | carmine & multi | .30 | .30 |
| | | | *Nos. 426-429 (4)* | 1.05 | 1.05 |

Snorkel Diving — A64

Designs: 20c, Aquaduct Golf Course. 35c, Steel band at Mariner's Inn. 45c, Sunbathing at Young Island. $1.25, Yachting marina.

**Wmk. 373**

**1975, July 31 Litho. *Perf. 13½***

| No. | Type | Denom. | Description | Unused | Used |
|---|---|---|---|---|---|
| **430** | A64 | 15c | multicolored | .30 | .25 |
| **431** | A64 | 20c | multicolored | .65 | .65 |
| **432** | A64 | 35c | multicolored | .95 | .40 |
| **433** | A64 | 45c | multicolored | .95 | .40 |
| **434** | A64 | $1.25 | multicolored | 2.25 | 2.00 |
| | | | *Nos. 430-434 (5)* | 5.10 | 3.70 |

Tourist publicity.

For surcharge see No. 3302.

Presidents Washington, John Adams, Jefferson and Madison — A65

U.S. Presidents: 1c, Monroe, John Quincy Adams, Jackson, Van Buren. 1½c, Wm. Harrison, Tyler, Polk, Taylor. 5c, Fillmore, Pierce, Buchanan, Lincoln. 10c, Johnson, Grant, Hayes, Garfield. 25c, Arthur, Cleveland, Benjamin Harrison, McKinley. 35c, Theodore Roosevelt, Taft, Wilson, Harding. 45c, Coolidge, Hoover, Franklin D. Roosevelt, Truman. $1, Eisenhower, Kennedy, Lyndon B. Johnson, Nixon. $2, Ford and White House.

**1975, Sept. 11 Unwmk. *Perf. 14½***

| No. | Type | Denom. | Description | Unused | Used |
|---|---|---|---|---|---|
| **435** | A65 | ½c | violet & blk | .25 | .25 |
| **436** | A65 | 1c | green & black | .25 | .25 |
| **437** | A65 | 1½c | rose lilac & blk | .25 | .25 |
| **438** | A65 | 5c | yellow grn & blk | .25 | .25 |
| **439** | A65 | 10c | ultra & blk | .25 | .25 |
| **440** | A65 | 25c | ocher & blk | .25 | .25 |
| **441** | A65 | 35c | brt blue & blk | .25 | .25 |
| **442** | A65 | 45c | carmine & blk | .25 | .25 |
| **443** | A65 | $1 | orange & blk | .25 | .35 |
| **444** | A65 | $2 | lt olive & blk | .25 | .65 |
| *a.* | | | Souvenir sheet of 10, #435-444 + 2 labels | 2.75 | 2.75 |
| | | | *Nos. 435-444 (10)* | 2.50 | 3.00 |

Bicentenary of American Independence. Each issued in sheets of 10 stamps and 2 labels picturing the White House, Capitol, Mt. Vernon, etc.

Nativity — A66

No. 445a, 8c, Star of Bethlehem. No. 445b, 45c, Shepherds. No. 445c, $1, Kings. No. 445d, 35c, Nativity.

**Se-tenant Pairs, #a.-b.**

**a. — Top stamp.**

**b. — Bottom stamp.**

**Wmk. 314**

**1975, Dec. 4 Litho. *Perf. 14***

| No. | Type | Denom. | Description | Unused | Used |
|---|---|---|---|---|---|
| **445** | A66 | 3c | Triangular block of 4, #a.-d. | .55 | .45 |
| **446** | A66 | 8c | Pair, #a.-b. | .25 | .25 |
| **447** | A66 | 35c | Pair, #a.-b. | .45 | .25 |
| **448** | A66 | 45c | Pair, #a.-b. | .45 | .30 |
| **449** | A66 | $1 | Pair, #a.-b. | .75 | .60 |
| | | | *Nos. 445-449 (5)* | 2.45 | 1.85 |

Christmas. No. 445 has continuous design.

Carnival Costumes — A68

Designs: 2c, Humpty-Dumpty people. 5c, Smiling faces (masks). 35c, Dragon worshippers. 45c, Duck costume. $1.25, Bumble bee dance.

***Perf. 13x13½***

**1976, Feb. 19 Litho. Wmk. 373**

| No. | Type | Denom. | Description | Unused | Used |
|---|---|---|---|---|---|
| **457** | A68 | 1c | carmine & multi | .25 | .25 |
| *a.* | | | Bklt pane of 2, #457-458 + label | .25 | |
| **458** | A68 | 2c | black & multi | .25 | .25 |
| *a.* | | | Bklt. pane of 3, #458-460 | .60 | |
| **459** | A68 | 5c | lt blue & multi | .25 | .25 |
| **460** | A68 | 35c | lt blue & multi | .25 | .25 |
| *a.* | | | Bklt. pane of 3, #460-462 | 2.00 | |
| **461** | A68 | 45c | black & multi | .25 | .25 |
| **462** | A68 | $1.25 | carmine & multi | .30 | .30 |
| | | | *Nos. 457-462 (6)* | 1.55 | 1.55 |

Kingstown carnival 1976.

**Nos. 409 and 421 Surcharged with New Value and Bar**

**1976, Apr. 8 Wmk. 314 *Perf. 14***

| No. | Type | Denom. | Description | Unused | Used |
|---|---|---|---|---|---|
| **463** | A62 | 70c | on 3c multi | .65 | *1.00* |
| **464** | A62 | 90c | on 50c multi | .65 | *1.25* |

Yellow Hibiscus and Blue-headed Hummingbird A69

Designs: 10c, Single pink hibiscus and crested hummingbird. 35c, Single white hibiscus and purple-throated carib. 45c, Common red hibiscus and blue-headed hummingbird. $1.25, Single peach hibiscus and green-throated carib.

**1976, May 20 Litho. Wmk. 373**

| No. | Type | Denom. | Description | Unused | Used |
|---|---|---|---|---|---|
| **465** | A69 | 5c | multicolored | .25 | .25 |
| **466** | A69 | 10c | multicolored | .35 | .30 |
| **467** | A69 | 35c | multicolored | 1.15 | 1.00 |
| **468** | A69 | 45c | multicolored | 1.75 | 1.50 |
| **469** | A69 | $1.25 | multicolored | 5.50 | 4.00 |
| | | | *Nos. 465-469 (5)* | 9.00 | 7.05 |

Map of West Indies, Bats, Wicket and Ball A69a

Prudential Cup — A69b

**1976, Sept. 16 Unwmk. *Perf. 14***

| No. | Type | Denom. | Description | Unused | Used |
|---|---|---|---|---|---|
| **470** | A69a | 15c | lt blue & multi | .60 | .30 |
| **471** | A69b | 45c | lilac rose & blk | 1.40 | 1.00 |

World Cricket Cup, won by West Indies Team, 1975.

**Fish Type of 1975**

**1976, Oct. 14 Wmk. 373 *Perf. 14***

| No. | Type | Denom. | Description | Unused | Used |
|---|---|---|---|---|---|
| **472** | A62 | 15c | Skipjack | 3.50 | 2.50 |
| **473** | A62 | 70c | Albacore | 6.50 | 3.25 |
| **474** | A62 | 90c | Pompano | 6.50 | .70 |
| | | | *Nos. 472-474 (3)* | 16.50 | 6.45 |

The 15c exists dated "1977."

For overprints see Nos. 501, 582-583.

St. Mary's R.C. Church, Kingstown — A70

Christmas: 45c, Anglican Church, Georgetown. 50c, Methodist Church, Georgetown. $1.25, St. George's Anglican Cathedral, Kingstown.

**1976, Nov. 18 Litho. *Perf. 14***
**475** A70 35c multicolored .25 .25
**476** A70 45c multicolored .25 .25
**477** A70 50c multicolored .25 .25
**478** A70 $1.25 multicolored .30 .55
*Nos. 475-478 (4)* 1.05 1.30

For surcharge see No. 3303.

Barrancoid Pot-stand, c. 450 A.D. — A71

Designs (National Trust Emblem and): 45c, National Museum. 70c, Carib stone head, c. 1510. $1, Ciboney petroglyph, c. 4000 B.C.

**1976, Dec. 16 *Perf. 13½***
**479** A71 5c multicolored .25 .25
**480** A71 45c multicolored .25 .25
**481** A71 70c multicolored .25 .25
**482** A71 $1 multicolored .25 .45
*Nos. 479-482 (4)* 1.00 1.20

Carib Indian art and establishment of National Museum in Botanical Gardens, Kingstown.
For surcharges see Nos. 3256, 3290.

Kings William I, William II, Henry I, Stephen A72

Kings and Queens of England: 1c, Henry II, Richard I, John, Henry III. 1½c, Edward I, II, III, Richard II. 2c, Henry IV, V, VI, Edward IV. 5c, Edward V, Richard III, Henry VII, VIII. 10c, Edward VI, Lady Jane Grey, Mary I, Elizabeth I. 25c, James I, Charles I, II, James II. 35c, William III, Mary II, Anne, George I. 45c, George II, III, IV. 75c, William IV, Victoria, Edward VII. $1, George V, Edward VIII, George VI. $2, Elizabeth II, coronation.

**Wmk. 373**

**1977, Feb. 7 Litho. *Perf. 13½***
**483** A72 ½c multicolored .25 .25
*a.* Bklt. pane of 4, #483-486 3.00
**484** A72 1c multicolored .25 .25
**485** A72 1½c multicolored .25 .25
**486** A72 2c multicolored .25 .25
**487** A72 5c multicolored .25 .25
*a.* Bklt. pane of 4, #487-490 3.00
**488** A72 10c multicolored .25 .25
**489** A72 25c multicolored .25 .25
**490** A72 35c multicolored .25 .25
**491** A72 45c multicolored .25 .25
*a.* Bklt. pane of 4, #491-494 3.00
**492** A72 75c multicolored .25 .25
**493** A72 $1 multicolored .25 .35
**494** A72 $2 multicolored .25 .50
*a.* Souv. sheet of 12, #483-494, perf. 14½x14 2.25 3.00
*Nos. 483-494 (12)* 3.00 3.35

25th anniv. of the reign of Elizabeth II.
Nos. 483-494 come in a pane of 10 + 2 labels.
Nos. 483a, 487a and 491a are unwmkd.
See No. 508.

Bishop Alfred P. Berkeley, Bishop's Miters — A73

15c, Grant of Arms to Bishopric, 1951, & names of former Bishops. 45c, Coat of arms & map of Diocese. $1.25, Interior of St. George's Anglican Cathedral & Bishop G. C. M. Woodroffe.

**Wmk. 373**

**1977, May 12 Litho. *Perf. 13½***
**495** A73 15c multicolored .25 .25
**496** A73 35c multicolored .25 .25
**497** A73 45c multicolored .25 .25
**498** A73 $1.25 multicolored .25 *.50*
*Nos. 495-498 (4)* 1.00 1.25

Diocese of the Windward Islands, centenary.
For surcharge see No. 3304.

### Nos. 411, 414, 472, 417, 422 Overprinted in Black or Red: "CARNIVAL 1977/ JUNE 25TH - JULY 5TH"

**1977, June 2 Litho. *Perf. 14***
**499** A62 5c multi .25 .25
**500** A62 10c multi (R) .25 .25
**501** A62 15c multi (R) .25 .25
**502** A62 20c multi (R) .25 .25
**503** A62 $1 multi .50 .50
*Nos. 499-503 (5)* 1.50 1.50

St. Vincent Carnival, June 25-July 5.
5c, 15c dated "1977," 10c, 20c, $1 "1976."

Girl Guide and Emblem — A74

Designs: 15c, Early Guide's uniform, Ranger, Brownie and Guide. 20c, Guide uniforms, 1917 and 1977. $2, Lady Baden-Powell, World Chief Guide, 1930-1977.

**Wmk. 373**

**1977, Sept. 1 Litho. *Perf. 13½***
**504** A74 5c multicolored .25 .25
**505** A74 15c multicolored .25 .25
**506** A74 20c multicolored .25 .25
**507** A74 $2 multicolored .30 *.75*
*Nos. 504-507 (4)* 1.05 1.50

St. Vincent Girl Guides, 50th anniversary.

### No. 494 with Additional Inscription: "CARIBBEAN / VISIT 1977"

**1977, Oct. 27**
**508** A72 $2 multicolored .50 .50

Caribbean visit of Queen Elizabeth II.

"While Shepherds Watched" A75

Christmas: 10c, "Fear not" said He. 15c, David's Town. 25c, The Heavenly Babe. 50c, Thus Spake and Seraph. $1.25, All Glory be to God.

**1977, Nov. Litho. *Perf. 13x11***
**509** A75 5c buff & multi .25 .25
**510** A75 10c buff & multi .25 .25
**511** A75 15c buff & multi .25 .25
**512** A75 25c buff & multi .25 .25
**513** A75 50c buff & multi .25 .25
**514** A75 $1.25 buff & multi .25 *.60*
*a.* Souv. sheet, #509-514, perf. 13½ 1.50 *1.60*
*Nos. 509-514 (6)* 1.50 1.85

Map of St. Vincent — A76

***Perf. 14½x14***

**1977-78 Litho. Wmk. 373**
**515** A76 20c dk bl & lt bl ('78) .25 .25
**516** A76 40c salmon & black .30 .30
**517** A76 40c car, sal & ocher ('78) .25 .25
*Nos. 515-517 (3)* .80 .80

Issued: #516, 11/30; #515, 517, 1/31.
For types surcharged see Nos. B1-B4, AR1-AR3.

Painted Lady and Bougainvillea — A77

Butterflies and Bougainvillea: 25c, Silver spot. 40c, Red anartia. 50c, Mimic. $1.25, Giant hairstreak.

**1978, Apr. 6 Litho. *Perf. 14***
**523** A77 5c multicolored .25 .25
**524** A77 25c multicolored .50 .25
**525** A77 40c multicolored .65 .25
**526** A77 50c multicolored .70 .25
**527** A77 $1.25 multicolored 1.40 .85
*Nos. 523-527 (5)* 3.50 1.85

For surcharges see Nos. 3259, 3306-3308.

Westminster Abbey — A78

Cathedral: 50c, Gloucester. $1.25, Durham. $2.50, Exeter.

***Perf. 13x13½***

**1978, June 2 Litho. Wmk. 373**
**528** A78 40c multicolored .25 .25
**529** A78 50c multicolored .25 .25
**530** A78 $1.25 multicolored .25 .25
**531** A78 $2.50 multicolored .25 .25
*a.* Souv. sheet, #528-531, perf. 13½x14 .75 *1.00*
*Nos. 528-531 (4)* 1.00 1.00

25th anniv. of coronation of Queen Elizabeth II. Nos. 528-531 issued in sheets of 10.
Nos. 528-531 also exist in booklet panes of two.

Rotary Emblem A79

Emblems: 50c, Lions Intl. $1, Jaycees.

**Wmk. 373**

**1978, July 13 Litho. *Perf. 14½***
**532** A79 40c brown & multi .25 .25
**533** A79 50c dark green & multi .25 .25
**534** A79 $1 crimson & multi .35 .45
*Nos. 532-534 (3)* .85 .95

Service clubs aiding in development of St. Vincent.
For surcharge see No. 3296.

Flags of Ontario and St. Vincent, Teacher A80

Design: 40c, Flags of St. Vincent and Ontario, teacher pointing to board, vert.

**1978, Sept. 7 Litho. *Perf. 14***
**535** A80 40c multicolored .25 .25
**536** A80 $2 multicolored .40 *.60*

School to School Project between children of Ontario, Canada, and St. Vincent, 10th anniversary.

Arnos Vale Airport A81

40c, Wilbur Wright landing Flyer I. 50c, Flyer I airborne. $1.25, Orville Wright and Flyer I.

**1978, Oct. 19 *Perf. 14½***
**537** A81 10c multicolored .25 .25
**538** A81 40c multicolored .25 .25
**539** A81 50c multicolored .25 .25
**540** A81 $1.25 multicolored .30 .70
*Nos. 537-540 (4)* 1.05 1.45

75th anniversary of 1st powered flight.
For overprint see No. 568.

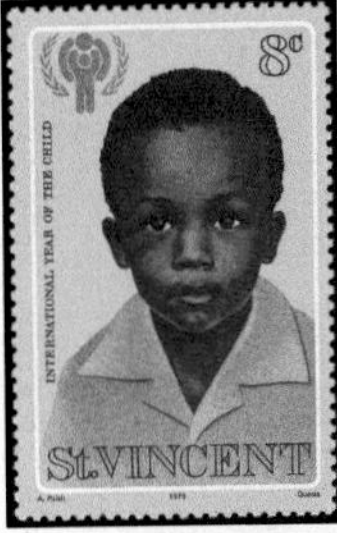


Vincentian Boy, IYC Emblem — A82

Children and IYC Emblem: 20c, Girl. 50c, Boy. $2, Girl and boy.

**1979, Feb. 14 Litho. *Perf. 14x13½***
**541** A82 8c multicolored .25 .25
**542** A82 20c multicolored .25 .25
**543** A82 50c multicolored .25 .30
**544** A82 $2 multicolored .25 .50
*Nos. 541-544 (4)* 1.00 1.30

International Year of the Child.
For surcharge see No. 3262.

Rowland Hill A83

50c, Great Britain #1-2. $3, St. Vincent #1-1B.

**1979, May 31 Litho. *Perf. 14***
**545** A83 40c multicolored .25 .25
**546** A83 50c multicolored .25 .25
**547** A83 $3 multicolored .40 .90
*a.* Souvenir sheet of 6 1.50 2.25
*Nos. 545-547 (3)* .90 1.40

Sir Rowland Hill (1795-1879), originator of penny postage.
No. 547a contains Nos. 545-547 and Nos. 560, 561 and 565.

Buccament Cancellations, Map of St. Vincent — A84

Cancellations and location of village.

**1979, Sept. 1 Litho. *Perf. 14***

**548** A84 1c shown .25 .25
**549** A84 2c Sion Hill .25 .25
**550** A84 3c Cumberland .25 .40
**551** A84 4c Questelles .25 .30
**552** A84 5c Layou .25 .25
**553** A84 6c New Ground .25 .25
**554** A84 8c Mesopotamia .25 .25
**555** A84 10c Troumaca .25 .25
**556** A84 12c Arnos Vale .25 .30
**557** A84 15c Stubbs .25 .30
**558** A84 20c Orange Hill .25 .30
**559** A84 25c Calliaqua .25 .25
**560** A84 40c Edinboro .25 .25
**561** A84 50c Colonarie .25 .25
**562** A84 80c Babou St. Vincent .40 .35
**563** A84 $1 Chateaubelair .40 .50
**564** A84 $2 Kingstown .50 *.80*
**565** A84 $3 Barrouallie .55 *1.25*
**566** A84 $5 Georgetown .75 *2.00*
**567** A84 $10 Kingstown 1.75 *4.00*
*Nos. 548-567 (20)* 7.85 12.75

See No. 547a.

The 5c, 10c, 25c reissued inscribed 1982. Singles of #562-564 from #601a are inscribed 1980.

**No. 537 Overprinted in Red: "ST. VINCENT AND THE GRENADINES AIR SERVICE 1979"**

**1979, Aug. 6 Litho. *Perf. 14½***

**568** A81 10c multicolored .40 .40

St. Vincent and Grenadines air service inauguration.

**Independent State**

St. Vincent Flag, Ixora Coccinea A85

Designs: 50c, House of Assembly, ixora stricta. 80c, Prime Minister R. Milton Cato.

**1979, Oct. 27 *Perf. 12½x12***

**569** A85 20c multi + label .25 .25
**570** A85 50c multi + label .25 .25
**571** A85 80c multi + label .40 .25
*Nos. 569-571 (3)* .90 .75

Independence of St. Vincent.

**Nos. 407, 410-416, 418, 421, 473-474, 422-423, 425 Overprinted in Black: "INDEPENDENCE 1979"**

**1979, Oct. 27 Litho. *Perf. 14½***

**572** A62 1c multicolored .25 .25
**573** A62 4c multicolored .25 .25
**574** A62 5c multicolored .25 .25
**575** A62 6c multicolored .25 .25
**576** A62 8c multicolored .25 .25
**577** A62 10c multicolored .25 .25
**578** A62 12c multicolored .25 .25
**579** A62 15c multicolored .25 .25
**580** A62 25c multicolored .25 .25
**581** A62 50c multicolored .40 .30
**582** A62 70c multicolored .70 .35
**583** A62 90c multicolored .70 .40
**584** A62 $1 multicolored .70 .40
**585** A62 $2.50 multicolored .90 1.00
**586** A62 $10 multicolored 2.00 *4.75*
*Nos. 572-586 (15)* 7.65 9.45

Silent Night Text, Virgin and Child A86

Silent Night Text and: 20c, Infant Jesus and angels. 25c, Shepherds. 40c, Angel. 50c, Angels holding Jesus. $2, Nativity.

**1979, Nov. 1 *Perf. 13½x14***

**587** A86 10c multicolored .25 .25
**588** A86 20c multicolored .25 .25
**589** A86 25c multicolored .25 .25
**590** A86 40c multicolored .25 .25
**591** A86 50c multicolored .25 .25
**592** A86 $2 multicolored .25 .40
*a.* Souvenir sheet of 6, #587-592 1.10 *1.25*
*Nos. 587-592 (6)* 1.50 1.65

Christmas.

Oleander and Wasp — A87

Oleander and Insects: 10c, Beetle. 25c, Praying mantis. 50c, Green guava beetle. $2, Citrus weevil.

**1979, Dec. 13 Litho. *Perf. 14***

**593** A87 5c multicolored .25 .25
**594** A87 10c multicolored .25 .25
**595** A87 25c multicolored .25 .25
**596** A87 50c multicolored .25 .25
**597** A87 $2 multicolored .50 .50
*Nos. 593-597 (5)* 1.50 1.50

**Type of 1880**
**Souvenir Sheet**

**1980, Feb. 28 Litho. *Perf. 14x13½***

**598** Sheet of 3 1.00 1.00
*a.* A3 50c brown .25 .25
*b.* A3 $1 dark green .25 .25
*c.* A3 $2 dark blue .50 .50

Coat of arms stamps centenary; London 1980 Intl. Stamp Exhibition, May 6-14.

London '80 Intl. Stamp Exhibition, May 6-14 — A88

**Wmk. 373**

**1980, Apr. 24 Litho. *Perf. 14***

**599** A88 80c Queen Elizabeth II .25 .25
**600** A88 $1 GB #297, SV #190 .25 .25
**601** A88 $2 Unissued stamp, 1971 .50 .60
*a.* Souv. sheet, #562-564, 599-601 1.00 *1.75*
*Nos. 599-601 (3)* 1.00 1.10

Steel Band A89

a, shown. b, Drummers, dancers.

**1980, June 12 Litho. *Perf. 14***

**602** A89 20c Pair, #a.-b. .35 *.75*

Kingstown Carnival, July 7-8.

Soccer, Olympic Rings — A90

**1980, Aug. 7 *Perf. 13½***

**604** A90 10c shown .25 .25
**605** A90 60c Bicycling .25 .25
**606** A90 80c Women's basketball .30 .40
**607** A90 $2.50 Boxing .30 *1.10*
*Nos. 604-607 (4)* 1.10 2.00

Sport for all.

For surcharges see Nos. 3264, 3278, B5-B8.

Agouti A91

**1980, Oct. 2 Litho. *Perf. 14x14½***

**608** A91 25c shown .25 .25
**609** A91 50c Giant toad .25 .25
**610** A91 $2 Mongoose .50 .60
*Nos. 608-610 (3)* 1.00 1.10

Map of North Atlantic showing St. Vincent — A92

Maps showing St. Vincent: 10c, World. $1, Caribbean. $2, St. Vincent, sail boats, plane.

**1980, Dec. 4 Litho. *Perf. 13½x14***

**611** A92 10c multicolored .25 .25
**612** A92 50c multicolored .25 .25
**613** A92 $1 multicolored .25 .25
**614** A92 $2 multicolored .50 .30
*a.* Souv. sheet of 1, perf. 14 .90 .90
*Nos. 611-614 (4)* 1.25 1.05

Ville de Paris in Battle of the Saints, 1782 — A93

60c, Ramillies lost in storm, 1782. $1.50, Providence, 1793. $2, Mail Packet Dee, 1840.

**Wmk. 373**

**1981, Feb. 19 Litho. *Perf. 14***

**615** A93 50c shown .35 .25
**616** A93 60c multicolored .45 .40
**617** A93 $1.50 multicolored 1.25 1.25
**618** A93 $2 multicolored 1.50 1.50
*Nos. 615-618 (4)* 3.55 3.40

For surcharges see Nos. 3262A, 3279, 3318.

A94

No. 619a, Arrowroot processing. No. 619b, Arrowroot Cultivation. No. 620a, Banana packing plant. No. 620b, Banana cultivation. No. 621a, Copra drying frames. No. 621b, Coconut plantation. No. 622a, Cocoa beans. No. 622b, Cocoa cultivation.

**Wmk. 373**

**1981, May 21 Litho. *Perf. 14***

**619** A94 25c Pair, #a.-b. .25 .40
**620** A94 50c Pair, #a.-b. .35 .60
**621** A94 60c Pair, #a.-b. .35 .60
**622** A94 $1 Pair, #a.-b. .55 1.00
*Nos. 619-622 (4)* 1.50 2.60

For surcharge see No. 3297.

Prince Charles, Lady Diana, Royal Yacht Charlotte — A94a

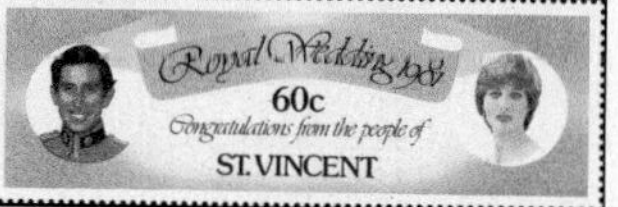


Prince Charles and Lady Diana — A94b

**Wmk. 380**

**1981, July 13 Litho. *Perf. 14***

**627** A94a 60c Couple, Isabella .25 .25
*a.* Bklt. pane of 4, perf. 12 .60
**628** A94b 60c Couple .25 .25
**629** A94a $2.50 Alberta .60 .60
**630** A94b $2.50 like #628 .70 .70
*a.* Bklt. pane of 2, perf. 12 1.00
**631** A94a $4 Britannia 1.25 1.25
**632** A94b $4 like #628 1.50 1.50
*Nos. 627-632 (6)* 4.55 4.55

Royal wedding. Each denomination issued in sheets of 7 (6 type A94a, 1 type A94b).

For surcharges and overprints see Nos. 891-892, O1-O6.

**Souvenir Sheet**

**1981 Litho. *Perf. 12***

**632A** A95b $5 Couple 1.25 1.25

Kingstown General Post Office — A95

**Wmk. 373**

**1981, Sept. 1 Litho. *Perf. 14***

**633** A95 $2 Pair, #a.-b. 1.25 *1.90*

UPU membership centenary.

First Anniv. of UN Membership A96

**Wmk. 373**

**1981, Sept. 1 Litho. *Perf. 14***

**634A** A96 $1.50 Flags .30 .30
**634B** A96 $2.50 Prime Minister Cato .50 .55

"The People that Walked in Darkness . . ." — A97

**1981, Nov. 19 Litho. *Perf. 12***

**635** A97 50c shown .25 .25
**636** A97 60c Angel .25 .25
**637** A97 $1 "My soul . . ." .25 .25
**638** A97 $2 Flight into Egypt .35 .35
*a.* Souvenir sheet of 4, #635-638 1.25 *1.50*
*Nos. 635-638 (4)* 1.10 1.10

Christmas. For surcharges see Nos. 674, 3280, 3298, 3320-3321.

Re-introduction of Sugar Industry, First Anniv. — A98

**1982, Apr. 5 Litho. *Perf. 14***

**639** A98 50c Boilers .25 .25
**640** A98 60c Drying plant .25 .25
**641** A98 $1.50 Gearwheels .45 .65
**642** A98 $2 Loading sugar cane .80 1.00
*Nos. 639-642 (4)* 1.75 2.15

For surcharges see Nos. 3251, 3260, 3263, 3281, 3322.

50th Anniv. of Airmail Service A99

50c, DH Moth, 1932. 60c, Grumman Goose, 1952. $1.50, Hawker-Siddeley 748, 1968. $2, Britten-Norman Islander, 1982.

**1982, July 29 Litho. *Perf. 14***

**643** A99 50c multicolored .60 .45
**644** A99 60c multicolored .75 .50
**645** A99 $1.50 multicolored 1.75 *1.90*
**646** A99 $2 multicolored 2.40 *2.50*
*Nos. 643-646 (4)* 5.50 *5.35*

For surcharges see Nos. 3260A, 3309.

21st Birthday of Princess Diana, July 1 — A99a

**Wmk. 380**

**1982, June Litho. *Perf. 14***

**647** A99a 50c Augusta of Saxe, 1736 .30 .30
**648** A99a 60c Saxe arms .35 .35
**649** A99a $6 Diana 1.60 1.60
*Nos. 647-649 (3)* 2.25 2.25

For overprints see Nos. 652-654.

Scouting Year — A100

**1982, July 15 Wmk. 373**

**650** A100 $1.50 Emblem .75 *1.00*
**651** A100 $2.50 "75" 1.10 *1.75*

For overprints see Nos. 890, 893.

**Nos. 647-649 Overprinted: "ROYAL BABY"**

**1982, July Wmk. 380**

**652** A99a 50c multicolored .25 .30
**653** A99a 60c multicolored .25 .30
**654** A99a $6 multicolored .75 *1.40*
*Nos. 652-654 (3)* 1.25 2.00

Birth of Prince William of Wales, June 21.

Carnival A101

50c, Butterfly float. 60c, Angel dancer, vert. $1.50, Winged dancer, vert. $2, Eagle float.

**1982, June 10 Litho. *Perf. 13½***

**655** A101 50c multicolored .25 .25
**656** A101 60c multicolored .35 .35
**657** A101 $1.50 multicolored .70 .80
**658** A101 $2 multicolored .90 1.25
*Nos. 655-658 (4)* 2.20 2.65

Cruise Ships A103

**Wmk. 373**

**1982, Dec. 29 Litho. *Perf. 14***

**662** A103 45c Geestport .35 .35
**663** A103 60c Stella Oceanis .45 .45
**664** A103 $1.50 Victoria 1.10 1.40
**665** A103 $2 QE 2 1.30 1.90
*Nos. 662-665 (4)* 3.20 4.10

For surcharges see Nos. 3310, 3324-3325.

Pseudocorynactis Caribbeorum — A104

Sea Horses and Anemones — 60c, Actinoporus elegans. $1.50, Arachnanthus nocturnus. $2, Hippocampus reidi.
60c, $1.50, $2 vert.

**1983, Jan. 12 Wmk. 373 *Perf. 12***

**666** A104 50c shown .90 .90
**667** A104 60c multicolored 1.10 1.10
**668** A104 $1.50 multicolored 1.90 2.10
**669** A104 $2 multicolored 2.10 2.25
*Nos. 666-669 (4)* 6.00 6.35

For overprint see No. 886. For surcharges see Nos. 3282, 3311, 3326.

Commonwealth Day — A104a

45c, Map. 60c, Flag. $1.50, Prime Minister Cato. $2, Banana industry.

**Wmk. 373**

**1983, Mar. 14 Litho. *Perf. 14***

**670** A104a 45c multi .35 .25
**671** A104a 60c multi .35 .35
**672** A104a $1.50 multi .55 .65
**673** A104a $2 multi .80 .90
*Nos. 670-673 (4)* 2.05 2.15

For surcharge see No. 3252.

**No. 635 Surcharged**

**Wmk. 373**

**1983, Apr. 26 Litho. *Perf. 12***

**674** A97 45c on 50c multi .45 .35

A104b

**Wmk. 373**

**1983, July 6 Litho. *Perf. 12***

**675** A104b 45c Handshake .25 *.30*
**676** A104b 60c Emblem .25 *.35*
**677** A104b $1.50 Map .50 *1.10*
**678** A104b $2 Flags .90 *1.40*
*Nos. 675-678 (4)* 1.90 *3.15*

10th anniv. of Chaguaramas (Caribbean Free Trade Assoc.)
For surcharges see Nos. 3233, 3283, 3313, 3327.

A105

45c, Founder William A. Smith. 60c, Boy, officer. $1.50, Emblem. $2, Community service.

***Perf. 12x11½***

**1983, Oct. 6 Litho. Wmk. 373**

**679** A105 45c multicolored .25 .25
**680** A105 60c multicolored .35 .35
**681** A105 $1.50 multicolored .80 *1.25*
**682** A105 $2 multicolored 1.10 *1.40*
*Nos. 679-682 (4)* 2.50 *3.25*

Boys' Brigade, cent. For overprint see #887. For surcharges see Nos. 3261, 3275, 3284, 3314, 3328.

Christmas — A106

10c, Shepherds at Watch. 50c, The Angel of the Lord. $1.50, A Glorious Light. $2.40, At the Manger.

**1983, Nov. 15 Litho. *Perf. 12***

**683** A106 10c multicolored .25 .25
**684** A106 50c multicolored .30 .30
**685** A106 $1.50 multicolored .80 1.10
**686** A106 $2.40 multicolored 1.50 1.75
*a.* Souvenir sheet of 4, #683-686 2.75 2.75
*Nos. 683-686 (4)* 2.85 3.40

For surcharge, see No. 3263A.

Classic Cars A107

No. 687, Ford Model T. No. 688, Supercharged Cord. No. 689, Mercedes-Benz. No. 690, Citroen Open Tourer. No. 691, Ferrari Boxer. No. 692, Rolls-Royce Phantom.

**Se-tenant Pairs, #a.-b.**
**a. — Side and front views.**
**b. — Action scene.**

**1983, Nov. 9 Litho. *Perf. 12½***

**687** A107 10c multicolored .25 .25
**688** A107 60c multicolored .25 .25
**689** A107 $1.50 multicolored .35 .35
**690** A107 $1.50 multicolored .35 .35
**691** A107 $2 multicolored .35 .35
**692** A107 $2 multicolored .35 .35
*Nos. 687-692 (6)* 1.90 1.90

See Nos. 773-777, 815-822, 906-911.

**Locomotives Type of 1985**

No. 699, King Henry VIII. No. 700, Royal Scots Greys. No. 701, Hagley Hall. No. 702, Sir Lancelot. No. 703, B12 Class. No. 704, #1000 Deeley Compound. No. 705, Cheshire. No. 706, Bulleid Austerity.

**Se-tenant Pairs, #a.-b.**
**a. — Side and front views.**
**b. — Action scene.**

**1983, Dec. 8 Litho. *Perf. 12½x13***

**699** A120 10c multicolored .25 .25
**700** A120 10c multicolored .25 .25
**701** A120 25c multicolored .25 .25
**702** A120 50c multicolored .40 .40
**703** A120 60c multicolored .40 .40
**704** A120 75c multicolored .40 .40
**705** A120 $2.50 multicolored .50 .50
**706** A120 $3 multicolored .55 .55
*Nos. 699-706 (8)* 3.00 3.00

Fort Duvernette A108

***Perf. 14x14½***

**1984, Feb. 13 Litho. Wmk. 380**

**715** A108 35c View .25 .25
**716** A108 45c Wall, flag .30 .30
**717** A108 $1 Canon .60 .60
**718** A108 $3 Map 1.75 1.75
*Nos. 715-718 (4)* 2.90 2.90

For surcharge see No. 3334.

Flowering Trees — A109

***Perf. 13½x14***

**1984, Apr. 2 Litho. Wmk. 373**

**719** A109 5c White frangipani .25 .25
**720** A109 10c Genip .25 .25
**721** A109 15c Immortelle .25 .25
**722** A109 20c Pink poui .25 .25
**723** A109 25c Buttercup .25 .25
**724** A109 35c Sandbox .30 .30
**725** A109 45c Locust .40 .40
**726** A109 60c Colville's glory .75 .60
**727** A109 75c Lignum vitae .75 .70
**728** A109 $1 Golden shower .80 1.40

**729** A109 $5 Angelin 3.00 *8.00*
**730** A109 $10 Roucou 6.00 *13.00*
*Nos. 719-730 (12)* 13.25 25.65

For surcharges see Nos. 3247, 3258, 3285-3288.

World War I Battle Scene, King George V — A110

No. 732a, Battle of Bannockburn. No. 732b, Edward II. No. 733a, George V. No. 733b, York Cottage, Sandringham. No. 734a, Edward II. No. 734b, Berkeley Castle. No. 735a, Arms of Edward II. No. 735b, Edward II. No. 736a, Arms of George V. No. 736b, George V.

**1984, Apr. 25 Litho. *Perf. 13x12½***

**731** A110 1c Pair, #a.-b. .25 .25
**732** A110 5c Pair, #a.-b. .25 .25
**733** A110 60c Pair, #a.-b. .30 .30
**734** A110 75c Pair, #a.-b. .30 .30
**735** A110 $1 Pair, #a.-b. .30 .30
**736** A110 $4 Pair, #a.-b. .60 .60
*Nos. 731-736 (6)* 2.00 2.00

Carnival A112

**Wmk. 380**

**1984, June 25 Litho. *Perf. 14***

**743** A112 35c Musical fantasy .25 .25
**744** A112 45c African woman .25 .25
**745** A112 $1 Market woman .65 .65
**746** A112 $3 Carib hieroglyph 1.75 1.75
*Nos. 743-746 (4)* 2.90 2.90

For surcharges see Nos. 3243, 3276.

**Locomotives Type of 1985**

1c, Liberation Class 141R, 1945. 2c, Dreadnought Class 50, 1967. 3c, No. 242A1, 1946. 50c, Dean Goods, 1883. 75c, Hetton Colliery, 1822. $1, Penydarren, 1804. $2, Novelty, 1829. $3, Class 44, 1925.

**Se-tenant Pairs, #a.-b.**
**a. — Side and front views.**
**b. — Action scene.**

**1984, July 27 Litho. *Perf. 12½***

**747** A120 1c multicolored .25 .25
**748** A120 2c multicolored .25 .25
**749** A120 3c multicolored .25 .25
**750** A120 50c multicolored .50 .50
**751** A120 75c multicolored .50 .50
**752** A120 $1 multicolored .50 .50
**753** A120 $2 multicolored .70 .70
**754** A120 $3 multicolored .70 .70
*Nos. 747-754 (8)* 3.65 3.65

Slavery Abolition Sesquicentennial — A113

35c, Hoeing. 45c, Gathering sugar cane. $1, Cutting sugar cane. $3, Abolitionist William Wilberforce.

**1984, Aug. 1 Litho. *Perf. 14***

**761** A113 35c multicolored .25 .25
**762** A113 45c multicolored .25 .25
**763** A113 $1 multicolored .65 .65
**764** A113 $3 multicolored 1.75 2.40
*Nos. 761-764 (4)* 2.90 3.55

For surcharges see Nos. 3273, 3337.

1984 Summer Olympics — A114

No. 765a, Judo. No. 765b, Weight lifting. No. 766a, Bicycling (facing left). No. 766b, Bicycling (facing right). No. 767a, Swimming (back stroke). No. 767b, Breast stroke. No. 768a, Running (start). No. 768b, Running (finish).

**1984, Aug. 30 Unwmk. *Perf. 12½***

**765** A114 1c Pair, #a.-b. .25 .25
**766** A114 3c Pair, #a.-b. .25 .25
**767** A114 60c Pair, #a.-b. .50 .50
**768** A114 $3 Pair, #a.-b. 2.00 2.00
*Nos. 765-768 (4)* 3.00 3.00

**Car Type of 1983**

5c, Austin-Healey Sprite, 1958. 20c, Maserati, 1971. 55c, Pontiac GTO, 1964. $1.50, Jaguar, 1957. $2.50, Ferrari, 1970.

**Se-tenant Pairs, #a.-b.**
**a. — Side and front views.**
**b. — Action scene.**

**1984, Oct. 22 Litho. *Perf. 12½***

**773** A107 5c multicolored .25 .25
**774** A107 20c multicolored .25 .25
**775** A107 55c multicolored .35 .35
**776** A107 $1.50 multicolored .45 .45
**777** A107 $2.50 multicolored .60 .60
*Nos. 773-777 (5)* 1.90 1.90

Military Uniforms — A115

**1984, Nov. 12 Wmk. 380 *Perf. 14***

**783** A115 45c Grenadier, 1773 .35 .35
**784** A115 60c Grenadier, 1775 .55 .55
**785** A115 $1.50 Grenadier, 1768 1.10 1.10
**786** A115 $2 Battalion Co. Officer, 1780 1.60 1.60
*Nos. 783-786 (4)* 3.60 3.60

For surcharges see Nos. 3289, 3315, 3329.

**Locomotives Type of 1985**

5c, 1954 R.R. Class 20, Zimbabwe. 40c, 1928 Southern Maid, U.K. 75c, 1911 Prince of Wales, U.K. $2.50, 1935 D.R.G. Class 05, Germany.

**Se-tenant Pairs, #a.-b.**
**a. — Side and front views.**
**b. — Action scene.**

**1984, Nov. 21 Litho. *Perf. 12½x13***

**787** A120 5c multicolored .25 .25
**788** A120 40c multicolored .30 .30
**789** A120 75c multicolored .30 .30
**790** A120 $2.50 multicolored 1.00 1.00
*Nos. 787-790 (4)* 1.85 1.85

Cricket Players — A116

5c, N.S. Taylor, portrait. 35c, T.W. Graveney with bat. 50c, R.G.D. Willis at wicket. $3, S.D. Fletcher at wicket.

**Se-tenant Pairs, #a.-b.**
**a. — Side and front views.**
**b. — Action scene.**

**1985, Jan. 7 Litho. *Perf. 12½***

**795** A116 5c multicolored .25 .25
**796** A116 35c multicolored .40 .40
**797** A116 50c multicolored .60 .60
**798** A116 $3 multicolored 2.00 3.00
*Nos. 795-798 (4)* 3.25 4.25

Orchids — A117

35c, Epidendrum ciliare. 45c, Ionopsis utricularioides. $1, Epidendrum secundum. $3, Oncidium altissimum.

**1985, Jan. 31 Litho. *Perf. 14***

**803** A117 35c multicolored .30 .30
**804** A117 45c multicolored .35 .35
**805** A117 $1 multicolored .70 .70
**806** A117 $3 multicolored 1.50 1.50
*Nos. 803-806 (4)* 2.85 2.85

For surcharge see No. 3338.

Audubon Birth Bicent. — A118

Illustrations of North American bird species by artist/naturalist John J. Audubon: #807a, Brown pelican. #807b, Green heron. #808a, Pileated woodpecker. #808b, Common flicker. #809a, Painted bunting. #809b, White-winged crossbill. #810a, Red-shouldered hawk. #810b, Crested caracara.

**1985, Feb. 7 Litho. *Perf. 12½***

**807** A118 15c Pair, #a.-b. .25 .25
**808** A118 40c Pair, #a.-b. .45 .45
**809** A118 60c Pair, #a.-b. .45 .45
**810** A118 $2.25 Pair, #a.-b. .90 .90
*Nos. 807-810 (4)* 2.05 2.05

**Car Type of 1983**

1c, 1937 Lancia Aprilia, Italy. 25c, 1922 Essex Coach, US. 55c, 1973 Pontiac Firebird Trans Am, US. 60c, 1950 Nash Rambler, US. $1, 1961 Ferrari Tipo 156, Italy. $1.50, 1967 Eagle-Weslake Type 58, US. $2, 1953 Cunningham C-5R, US.

**Se-tenant Pairs, #a.-b.**
**a. — Side and front views.**
**b. — Action scene.**

**1985**

**815-821** A107 Set of 7 pairs 2.00 2.00

**Souvenir Sheet of 4**

**822** A107 #a.-d. 2.25 2.25

No. 822 contains a pair of $4 stamps like No. 820 (#a.-b.), and a pair of $5 stamps like No. 819 (#c.-d.).

Issued: 1c, 55c, $2, 3/11; others, 6/7.

Herbs and Spices — A119

**1985, Apr. 22 *Perf. 14***

**829** A119 25c Pepper .25 .25
**830** A119 35c Sweet marjoram .25 .25
**831** A119 $1 Nutmeg .50 .50
**832** A119 $3 Ginger 1.00 1.00
*Nos. 829-832 (4)* 2.00 2.00

For surcharge see No. 3339.

Locomotives of the United Kingdom — A120

1c, 1913 Glen Douglas. 10c, 1872 Fenchurch Terrier. 40c, 1870 No. 1 Stirling Single. 60c, 1866 No. 158A. $1, 1893 No. 103 Class Jones Goods. $2.50, 1908 Great Bear.

**Se-tenant Pairs, #a.-b.**
**a. — Side and front views.**
**b. — Action scene.**

**1985, Apr. 26 *Perf. 12½***

**833** A120 1c multicolored .25 .25
**834** A120 10c multicolored .25 .25
**835** A120 40c multicolored .30 .30
**836** A120 60c multicolored .30 .30
**837** A120 $1 multicolored .50 .50
**838** A120 $2.50 multicolored .80 .80
*Nos. 833-838 (6)* 2.40 2.40

See Nos. 699-706, 747-754, 787-790, 849-854, 961-964.

Traditional Instruments — A121

25c, Bamboo flute. 35c, Quatro. $1, Bamboo base, vert. $2, Goat-skin drum, vert.

**1985, May 16 *Perf. 15***

**845** A121 25c multicolored .25 .25
**846** A121 35c multicolored .25 .25
**847** A121 $1 multicolored .50 .50
**848** A121 $2 multicolored 1.00 1.00
*a.* Sheet of 4, #845-848 2.00 2.00
*Nos. 845-848 (4)* 2.00 2.00

For surcharge see No. 3299.

**Locomotives Type of 1985**

5c, 1874 Loch, U.K. 30c, 1919 Class 47XX, U.K. 60c, 1876 P.L.M. Class 121, France. 75c, 1927 D.R.G. Class 24, Germany. $1, 1889 No. 1008, U.K. $2.50, 1926 S.R. Class PS-4, US.

**Se-tenant Pairs, #a.-b.**
**a. — Side and front views.**
**b. — Action scene.**

**1985, June 27 *Perf. 12½***

**849** A120 5c multicolored .25 .25
**850** A120 30c multicolored .30 .30
**851** A120 60c multicolored .40 .40
**852** A120 75c multicolored .40 .40
**853** A120 $1 multicolored .50 .50
**854** A120 $2.50 multicolored .60 .60
*Nos. 849-854 (6)* 2.45 2.45

Queen Mother, 85th Birthday — A122

Nos. 861a, 867a, Facing right. Nos. 861b, 867b, Facing left. Nos. 862a, 866a, Facing right. Nos. 862b, 866b, Facing left. No. 863a, Facing right. No. 863b, Facing left. No. 864a, Facing front. No. 864b, Facing left. No. 865a, Facing right. No. 865b, Facing front.

**1985**

**861** A122 35c Pair, #a.-b. .25 .25
**862** A122 85c Pair, #a.-b. .25 .25
**863** A122 $1.20 Pair, #a.-b. .35 .35
**864** A122 $1.60 Pair, #a.-b. .35 .35
*Nos. 861-864 (4)* 1.20 1.20

**Souvenir Sheets of 2**

**865** A122 $2.10 #a.-b. .75 .75
**866** A122 $3.50 #a.-b. 3.25 3.25
**867** A122 $6 #a.-b. 5.50 5.50
*Nos. 865-867 (3)* 9.50 9.50

Issued: #861-865, 8/9; #866-867, 12/19.
For overprints see No. 888.

Elvis Presley (1935-77), American Entertainer — A123

Nos. 874a, 878a, In concert. Nos. 874b, 878b, Facing front. Nos. 875a, 879a, In concert. Nos. 875b, 879b, Facing left. Nos. 876a, 880a, In concert. Nos. 876b, 880b, Facing front. Nos. 877a, 881a, Wearing leather jacket. Nos. 877b, 881b, Facing left.

**1985, Aug. 16**

**874** A123 10c Pair, #a.-b. .55 .55
**875** A123 60c Pair, #a.-b. .80 .80
**876** A123 $1 Pair, #a.-b. .80 .80
**877** A123 $5 Pair, #a.-b. 1.10 1.10
*Nos. 874-877 (4)* 3.25 3.25

**Souvenir Sheets of 4**

**878** A123 30c #a.-b. .90 .90
**879** A123 50c #a.-b. 1.50 1.50
**880** A123 $1.50 #a.-b. 4.25 4.25
**881** A123 $4.50 #a.-b. 12.00 12.00
*Nos. 878-881 (4)* 18.65 18.65

Nos. 878-881 contain two of each stamp.
Two $4 "stamps" were not issued.
For other Presley souvenir sheet see No. 1567. For overprints see Nos. 1009-1016.

Flour Milling A124

**1985, Oct. 17** **Wmk. 373** ***Perf. 15***

**882** A124 20c Conveyor from elevators .25 .25
**883** A124 30c Roller mills .25 .25
**884** A124 75c Office .50 .50
**885** A124 $3 Bran finishers 2.00 2.00
*Nos. 882-885 (4)* 3.00 3.00

**Nos. 667, 680, 862, 650, 631-632, 651 Ovptd. "CARIBBEAN / ROYAL VISIT / -1985-" or Srchd. with 3 Black Bars and New Value in Black**

**1985, Oct. 27** ***Perfs. as Before***

**886** A104 60c multi *1.90 1.90*
**887** A105 60c multi *1.90 1.90*
**888** A122 85c Pair, #a.-b. *6.00 6.00*
**890** A100 $1.50 multi *5.25 5.25*
**891** A94a $1.60 on $4 *5.50 5.50*
**892** A94b $1.60 on $4 *5.50 5.50*
**893** A100 $2.50 multi *8.50 8.50*
*Nos. 886-893 (7)* *34.55 34.55*

Michael Jackson (b. 1960), American Entertainer — A125

No. 894a, Portrait. No. 894b, On stage. No. 895a, Singing. No. 895b, Portrait. No. 896a, Black jacket. No. 896b, Red jacket. No. 897a, Portrait. No. 897b, Wearing white glove.

**1985, Dec. 2** ***Perf. 12½***

**894** A125 60c Pair, #a.-b. .45 .45
**895** A125 $1 Pair, #a.-b. .75 .75
**896** A125 $2 Pair, #a.-b. 1.50 1.50
**897** A125 $5 Pair, #a.-b. 4.00 4.00
*Nos. 894-897 (4)* 6.70 6.70

**Souvenir Sheets of 4**
***Perf. 13x12½***

**898** A125 45c #a.-b. .70 .70
**899** A125 90c #a.-b. 1.40 1.40
**900** A125 $1.50 #a.-b. 2.25 2.25
**901** A125 $4 #a.-b. 6.25 6.25

#898-901 contain two of each stamp.

Christmas A126

Children's drawings: 25c, Serenade, 75c, Poinsettia. $2.50, Jesus, Our Master.

**1985, Dec. 9** **Wmk. 373** ***Perf. 14***

**903** A126 25c multicolored .25 .25
**904** A126 75c multicolored .50 .50
**905** A126 $2.50 multicolored 1.75 1.75
*Nos. 903-905 (3)* 2.50 2.50

For surcharges see Nos. 3268, 3333.

**Car Type of 1983**

30c, 1916 Cadillac Type 53, US. 45c, 1939 Triumph Dolomite, UK. 60c, 1972 Panther J-72, UK. 90c, 1967 Ferrari 275 GTB/4, Italy. $1.50, 1953 Packard Caribbean, US. $2.50, 1931 Bugatti Type 41 Royale, France.

**Se-tenant Pairs, #a.-b.**

**a. — Side and front views.**

**b. — Action scene.**

**1986, Jan. 27** ***Perf. 12½***

**906-911** A107 Set of 6 pairs 7.00 7.00

Halley's Comet A127

**Wmk. 380**

**1986, Apr. 14** **Litho.** ***Perf. 15***

**918** A127 45c shown .35 .35
**919** A127 60c Edmond Halley .45 .45
**920** A127 75c Newton's reflector telescope .55 .55
**921** A127 $3 Local astronomer 2.10 2.10
*a.* Souvenir sheet of 4, #918-921 3.50 3.50
*Nos. 918-921 (4)* 3.45 3.45

Souvenir Sheets of 2

Scouting Movement, 75th Anniv. — A127a

American flag & Girl Guides or Boy Scouts emblem and: No. 922b, Scout sign, handshake. No. 922c, Paintbrushes, pallet. No. 922Ad, Knots. No. 922Ae, Lord Baden-Powell.

**1986, Feb. 25** **Litho.** ***Perf. 13x12½***

**922** A127a $5 #b.-c. 4.00 4.00
**922A** A127a $6 #d.-e. 5.00 5.00

"Capex '87" overprints on this issue were not authorized.
Nos. 922-922A exist with decorative selvage. Value, set, $11.50.

Elizabeth II Wearing Crown Jewels — A128

Various portraits.

**1986, Apr. 21** **Wmk. 373** ***Perf. 12½***

**923** A128 10c multicolored .25 .25
**924** A128 90c multicolored .50 .50
**925** A128 $2.50 multicolored 1.25 1.25
**926** A128 $8 multi, vert. 4.50 4.50
*Nos. 923-926 (4)* 6.50 6.50

**Souvenir Sheet**

**927** A128 $10 multicolored 5.50 5.50

Elizabeth II at Victoria Park A129

Designs: No. 929, with Prime Minister Mitchell. No. 930, Arriving at Port Elizabeth. No. 931, at Independence Day Parade.

***Perf. 15x14***

**1986, June 14** **Wmk. 373**

**928** A129 45c multicolored .40 .40
**929** A129 60c multicolored .55 .55
**930** A129 75c multicolored .70 .70
**931** A129 $2.50 multicolored 2.25 2.25
*Nos. 928-931 (4)* 3.90 3.90

**Souvenir Sheet**

**932** A129 $3 multicolored 3.75 3.75

Queen Elizabeth II, 60th birthday.

Discovery of America, 500th Anniv. (1992) — A130

No. 936a, Fleet. No. 936b, Columbus. No. 937a, At Spanish Court. No. 937b, Ferdinand, Isabella. No. 938a, Fruit, Santa Maria. No. 938b, Fruit.

**1986, Jan. 23** **Litho.** ***Perf. 12½***

**936** A130 60c Pair, #a.-b. .90 .90
**937** A130 $1.50 Pair, #a.-b. 2.25 2.25
**938** A130 $2.75 Pair, #a.-b. 4.00 4.00
*Nos. 936-938 (3)* 7.15 7.15

**Souvenir Sheet**

**939** A130 $6 Columbus, diff. 4.50 4.50

1986 World Cup Soccer Championships, Mexico — A131

No. 940, Emblem. No. 941, Mexico. No. 942, Mexico, diff. No. 943, Hungary vs. Scotland. No. 944, Spain vs. Scotland. No. 945, England vs. USSR. No. 946, Spain vs. France. No. 947, England vs. Italy.
No. 948, Mexico. No. 949, Scotland. No. 950, Spain. No. 951, England.

**1986, May 7** **Litho.** ***Perf. 15***

**940** A131 1c multicolored .25 .25
**941** A131 2c multicolored .25 .25
**942** A131 5c multicolored .25 .25
**943** A131 5c multicolored .25 .25
**944** A131 10c multicolored .25 .25
**945** A131 30c multicolored .25 .25
**946** A131 45c multicolored .30 .30
**947** A131 $1 multicolored .60 .60

***Perf. 13½***

**Size: 56x36mm**

**948** A131 75c multicolored .40 .40
**949** A131 $2 multicolored 1.10 1.10
**950** A131 $4 multicolored 2.25 2.25
**951** A131 $5 multicolored 2.75 2.75
*Nos. 940-951 (12)* 8.90 8.90

**1986, July 7** **Souvenir Sheets**

**952** A131 $1.50 like #950 .95 .95
**953** A131 $1.50 like #941 .95 .95
**954** A131 $2.25 like #949 1.40 1.40
**955** A131 $2.50 like #948 1.40 1.40
**956** A131 $3 like #946 1.50 1.50
**957** A131 $5.50 like #951 3.25 3.25
*Nos. 952-957 (6)* 9.45 9.45

Nos. 941-944, 946-947, vert.

Wedding of Prince Andrew and Sarah Ferguson — A132

A132a

No. 958a, Andrew. No. 958b, Sarah. No. 959a, Andrew, horiz. No. 959b, Andrew, Nancy Reagan, horiz.

**1986** **Litho.** ***Perf. 12½x13, 13x12½***

**958** A132 60c Pair, #a.-b. .65 .65
**959** A132 $2 Pair, #a.-b. 2.25 2.25
**960** A132a $10 In coach 5.50 5.50
*Nos. 958-960 (3)* 8.40 8.40

Issued: $10, Nov.; others, July 23.
For overprints see Nos. 976-977.

A number of unissued items, imperfs., part perfs., missing color varieties, etc., were made available when the Format International inventory was liquidated.

**Locomotives Type of 1985**

Designs: 30c, 1926 JNR ABT Rack & Adhesion Class ED41 BZZB, Japan. 50c, 1883 Chicago RR Exposition, The Judge, 1A Type, US. $1, 1973 BM & LPRR E60C Co-Co, US. $3, 1972 GM (EMD) SD40-2 Co-Co, US.

**a. — Side and front views.**
**b. — Action scene.**

**1986, July** *Perf. 12½x13*

| No. | Type | Description | Unused | Used |
|---|---|---|---|---|
| **961** | A120 | 30c Pair, #a.-b. | .30 | .30 |
| **962** | A120 | 50c Pair, #a.-b. | .40 | .40 |
| **963** | A120 | $1 Pair, #a.-b. | .55 | .55 |
| **964** | A120 | $3 Pair, #a.-b. | .90 | .90 |
| | | *Nos. 961-964 (4)* | 2.15 | 2.15 |

Trees — A133

10c, Acrocomia aculeata. 60c, Pithecellobium saman. 75c, Tabebuia pallida. $3, Andira inermis.

**1986, Sept.** *Perf. 14*

| No. | Type | Description | Unused | Used |
|---|---|---|---|---|
| **968** | A133 | 10c multicolored | .35 | .35 |
| **969** | A133 | 60c multicolored | .90 | .90 |
| **970** | A133 | 75c multicolored | 1.10 | 1.10 |
| **971** | A133 | $3 multicolored | 4.25 | 4.25 |
| | | *Nos. 968-971 (4)* | 6.60 | 6.60 |

Anniversaries — A134

45c, Cadet Force emblem, vert. 60c, Grimble Building, GHS. $1.50, GHS class. $2, Cadets in formation.

**1986, Sept. 30**

| No. | Type | Description | Unused | Used |
|---|---|---|---|---|
| **972** | A134 | 45c multicolored | .40 | .40 |
| **973** | A134 | 60c multicolored | .50 | .50 |
| **974** | A134 | $1.50 multicolored | 1.10 | 1.10 |
| **975** | A134 | $2 multicolored | 1.50 | 1.50 |
| | | *Nos. 972-975 (4)* | 3.50 | 3.50 |

St. Vincent Cadet Force, 50th anniv., and Girls' High School, 75th anniv.

For surcharges see Nos. 3316, 3330-3331.

**Nos. 958-959 Ovptd. "Congratulations to T.R.H. The Duke & Duchess of York" in Silver**

*Perf. 12½x13, 13x12½*

**1986, Oct.** **Litho.**

| No. | Type | Description | Unused | Used |
|---|---|---|---|---|
| **976** | A132 | 60c Pair, #a.-b. | .75 | .75 |
| **977** | A132 | $2 Pair, #a.-b. | 2.75 | 2.75 |

Stamps of the same denomination also exist printed tete-beche.

The Legend of King Arthur — A134a

30c, King Arthur. 45c, Merlin raises Arthur. 60c, Arthur pulls Excalibur from stone. 75c, Camelot. $1, Lady of the Lake. $1.50, Knights of the Round Table. $2, Holy Grail. $5, Sir Lancelot.

**1986, Nov. 3** *Perf. 14*

| No. | Type | Description | Unused | Used |
|---|---|---|---|---|
| **979** | A134a | 30c multi | .30 | .30 |
| **979A** | A134a | 45c multi | .45 | .45 |
| **979B** | A134a | 60c multi | .50 | .50 |
| **979C** | A134a | 75c multi | .65 | .65 |
| **979D** | A134a | $1 multi | .80 | .80 |
| **979E** | A134a | $1.50 multi | 1.10 | 1.10 |
| **979F** | A134a | $2 multi | 1.60 | 1.60 |
| **979G** | A134a | $5 multi | 4.25 | 4.25 |
| | | *Nos. 979-979G (8)* | 9.65 | 9.65 |

A134b

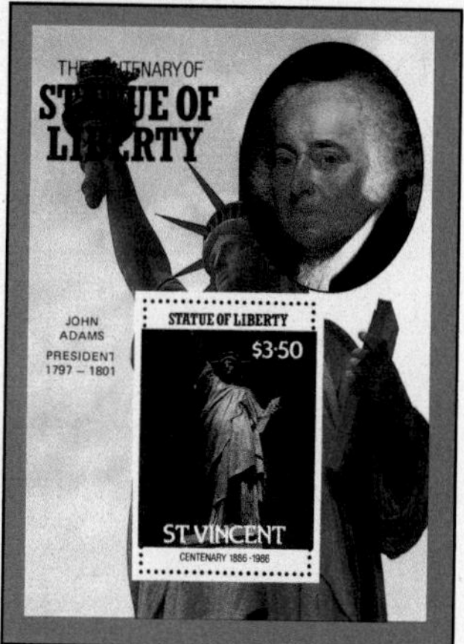


Statue of Liberty, Cent. — A135

Various views of the statue.

**1986, Nov. 26** **Litho.** *Perf. 14*

| No. | Type | Description | Unused | Used |
|---|---|---|---|---|
| **980** | A134b | 15c multicolored | .25 | .25 |
| **980A** | A134b | 25c multicolored | .25 | .25 |
| **980B** | A134b | 40c multicolored | .25 | .25 |
| **980C** | A134b | 55c multicolored | .35 | .35 |
| **980D** | A134b | 75c multicolored | .50 | .50 |
| **980E** | A134b | 90c multicolored | .60 | .60 |
| **980F** | A134b | $1.75 multicolored | 1.10 | 1.10 |
| **980G** | A134b | $2 multicolored | 1.25 | 1.25 |
| **980H** | A134b | $2.50 multicolored | 1.65 | 1.65 |
| **980I** | A134b | $3 multicolored | 1.90 | 1.90 |
| | | *Nos. 980-980I (10)* | 8.10 | 8.10 |

**Souvenir Sheets**

| No. | Type | Description | Unused | Used |
|---|---|---|---|---|
| **981** | A135 | $3.50 multicolored | 2.00 | 2.00 |
| **982** | A135 | $4 multicolored | 2.25 | 2.25 |
| **983** | A135 | $5 multicolored | 2.75 | 2.75 |

Fresh-water Fishing — A136

No. 984a, Tri tri fishing. No. 984b, Tri tri. No. 985a, Crayfishing. No. 985b, Crayfish.

**1986, Dec. 10** *Perf. 15*

| No. | Type | Description | Unused | Used |
|---|---|---|---|---|
| **984** | A136 | 75c Pair, #a.-b. | 1.10 | 1.10 |
| **985** | A136 | $1.50 Pair, #a.-b. | 2.25 | 2.25 |

For surcharges see Nos. 3292-3293, 3317.

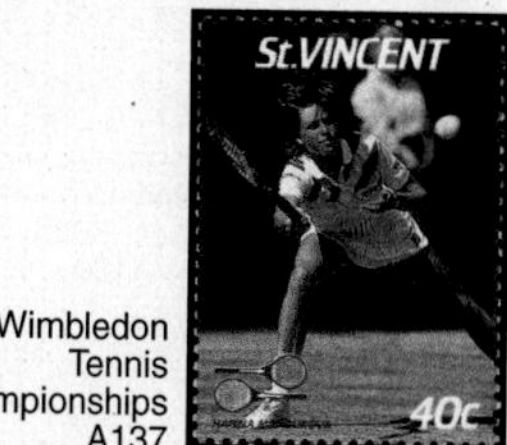


1987 Wimbledon Tennis Championships A137

**1987, June 22** *Perf. 13x12½*

| No. | Type | Description | Unused | Used |
|---|---|---|---|---|
| **988** | A137 | 40c Hana Mandlikova | .25 | .25 |
| **989** | A137 | 60c Yannick Noah | .30 | .30 |
| **990** | A137 | 80c Ivan Lendl | .40 | .40 |
| **991** | A137 | $1 Chris Evert Lloyd | .50 | .50 |
| **992** | A137 | $1.25 Steffi Graf | .65 | .65 |
| **993** | A137 | $1.50 John McEnroe | .85 | .85 |
| **994** | A137 | $1.75 Martina Navratilova | .95 | .95 |
| **995** | A137 | $2 Boris Becker | 1.10 | 1.10 |
| | | *Nos. 988-995 (8)* | 5.00 | 5.00 |

**Souvenir Sheet**

| No. | Type | Description | Unused | Used |
|---|---|---|---|---|
| **996** | | Sheet of 2 | 3.00 | 3.00 |
| *a.* | A137 | $2.25 like $2 | 1.50 | 1.50 |
| *b.* | A137 | $2.25 like $1.75 | 1.50 | 1.50 |

Natl. Child Survival Campaign A138

10c, Growth monitoring. 50c, Oral rehydration therapy. 75c, Breast-feeding. $1, Universal immunization.

**1987, June 10** *Perf. 14x14½*

| No. | Type | Description | Unused | Used |
|---|---|---|---|---|
| **997** | A138 | 10c multicolored | .25 | .25 |
| **998** | A138 | 50c multicolored | .40 | .40 |
| **999** | A138 | 75c multicolored | .60 | .60 |
| **1000** | A138 | $1 multicolored | .75 | .75 |
| | | *Nos. 997-1000 (4)* | 2.00 | 2.00 |

For overprints see Nos. 1040-1043. For surcharge see No. 3294.

Carnival, 10th Anniv. A139

Designs: 20c, Queen of the Bands, Miss Prima Donna 1986. 45c, Donna Young, Miss Carnival 1985. 55c, M. Haydock, Miss. St. Vincent and the Grenadines 1986. $3.70, Spirit of Hope Year 1986.

**1987, June 29** *Perf. 12½x13*

| No. | Type | Description | Unused | Used |
|---|---|---|---|---|
| **1001** | A139 | 20c multicolored | .25 | .25 |
| **1002** | A139 | 45c multicolored | .35 | .35 |
| **1003** | A139 | 55c multicolored | .40 | .40 |
| **1004** | A139 | $3.70 multicolored | 2.50 | 2.50 |
| | | *Nos. 1001-1004 (4)* | 3.50 | 3.50 |

For surcharges see Nos. 3342-3343.

**Nos. 874-881 Overprinted "THE KING OF ROCK AND ROLL LIVES FOREVER . AUGUST 16TH" and "1977-1987" (Nos. 1009-1012) or "TENTH ANNIVERSARY" (Nos. 1013-1016)**

**1987, Aug. 26** **Litho.** *Perf. 12½*

| No. | Type | Description | Unused | Used |
|---|---|---|---|---|
| **1009** | A123 | 10c Pair, #a.-b. | .25 | .25 |
| **1010** | A123 | 60c Pair, #a.-b. | .70 | .70 |
| **1011** | A123 | $1 Pair, #a.-b. | 1.10 | 1.10 |
| **1012** | A123 | $5 Pair, #a.-b. | 6.00 | 6.00 |
| | | *Nos. 1009-1012 (4)* | 8.05 | 8.05 |

**Souvenir Sheets**

| No. | Type | Description | Unused | Used |
|---|---|---|---|---|
| **1013** | A123 | 30c Sheet of 4, 2 each #a.-b. | .75 | .75 |
| **1014** | A123 | 50c Sheet of 4, 2 each #a.-b. | 1.25 | 1.25 |
| **1015** | A123 | $1.50 Sheet of 4, 2 each #a.-b. | 3.75 | 3.75 |
| **1016** | A123 | $4.50 Sheet of 4, 2 each #a.-b. | 11.00 | 11.00 |

Portrait of Queen Victoria, 1841, by R. Thorburn A140

Portraits and photographs: 75c, Elizabeth and Charles, 1948. $1, Coronation, 1953. $2.50, Duke of Edinburgh, 1948. $5, Elizabeth, c. 1980. $6, Elizabeth and Charles, 1948, diff.

**1987, Nov. 20** **Litho.** *Perf. 12½x13*

| No. | Type | Description | Unused | Used |
|---|---|---|---|---|
| **1017** | A140 | 15c multicolored | .25 | .25 |
| **1018** | A140 | 75c multicolored | .45 | .45 |
| **1019** | A140 | $1 multicolored | .55 | .55 |
| **1020** | A140 | $2.50 multicolored | 1.25 | 1.25 |
| **1021** | A140 | $5 multicolored | 2.50 | 2.50 |
| | | *Nos. 1017-1021 (5)* | 5.00 | 5.00 |

**Souvenir Sheet**

| No. | Type | Description | Unused | Used |
|---|---|---|---|---|
| **1022** | A140 | $6 multicolored | 4.00 | 4.00 |

Sesquicentennial of Queen Victoria's accession to the throne, wedding of Queen Elizabeth II and Prince Philip, 40th anniv.

**Nos. 997-1000 Ovptd. "WORLD POPULATION / 5 BILLION / 11TH JULY 1987"**

**1987, July 11** **Litho.** *Perf. 14x14½*

| No. | Type | Description | Unused | Used |
|---|---|---|---|---|
| **1040** | A138 | 10c on No. 997 | .40 | .40 |
| **1041** | A138 | 50c on No. 998 | .80 | .80 |
| **1042** | A138 | 75c on No. 999 | 1.25 | 1.25 |
| **1043** | A138 | $1 on No. 1000 | 1.50 | 1.50 |
| | | *Nos. 1040-1043 (4)* | 3.95 | 3.95 |

Automobile Centenary — A143

Automotive pioneers and vehicles: $1, $3, Carl Benz (1844-1929) and the Velocipede, patented 1886. $2, No. 1049, Enzo Ferrari (b. 1898) and 1966 Ferrari Dino 206SP. $4, $6, Charles Rolls (1877-1910), Sir Henry Royce (1863-1933) and 1907 Rolls Royce Silver Ghost. No. 1047, $5, $8, Henry Ford (1863-1947) and Model T Ford.

**1987, Dec. 4** *Perf. 13x12½*

| No. | Type | Description | Unused | Used |
|---|---|---|---|---|
| **1044** | A143 | $1 multicolored | .65 | .65 |
| **1045** | A143 | $2 multicolored | 1.00 | 1.00 |
| **1046** | A143 | $4 multicolored | 2.10 | 2.10 |
| **1047** | A143 | $5 multicolored | 2.50 | 2.50 |
| | | *Nos. 1044-1047 (4)* | 6.25 | 6.25 |

**Souvenir Sheets**

| No. | Type | Description | Unused | Used |
|---|---|---|---|---|
| **1048** | A143 | $3 like No. 1044 | 2.00 | 2.00 |
| **1049** | A143 | $5 like No. 1045 | 3.25 | 3.25 |
| **1050** | A143 | $6 like No. 1046 | 4.00 | 4.00 |
| **1051** | A143 | $8 like No. 1047 | 5.50 | 5.50 |
| | | *Nos. 1048-1051 (4)* | 14.75 | 14.75 |

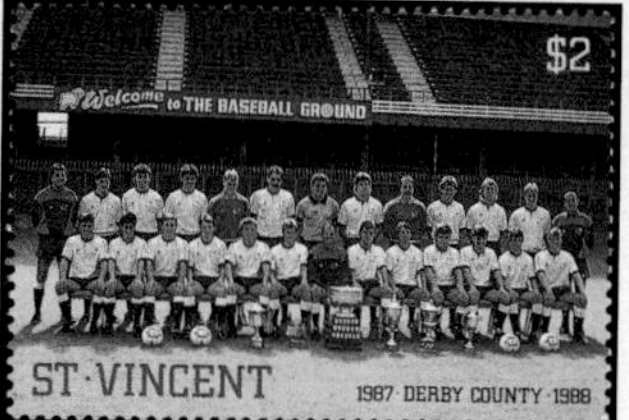


Soccer Teams — A144

**1987, Dec. 4**

| No. | Type | Description | Unused | Used |
|---|---|---|---|---|
| **1052** | A144 | $2 Derby County | 1.40 | 1.40 |
| **1053** | A144 | $2 Leeds United | 1.40 | 1.40 |
| **1054** | A144 | $2 Tottenham Hotspur | 1.40 | 1.40 |
| **1055** | A144 | $2 Manchester United | 1.40 | 1.40 |
| **1056** | A144 | $2 Everton | 1.40 | 1.40 |
| **1057** | A144 | $2 Liverpool | 1.40 | 1.40 |
| **1058** | A144 | $2 Portsmouth | 1.40 | 1.40 |
| **1059** | A144 | $2 Arsenal | 1.40 | 1.40 |
| | | *Nos. 1052-1059 (8)* | 11.20 | 11.20 |

A145

A Christmas Carol, by Charles Dickens (1812-1870) — A147

6c, Mr. Fezziwig's Ball. 25c, Ghost of Christmases to Come. 50c, The Cratchits. 75c, Carolers.

$5, Reading book to children.

Portrait of Dickens as left page of book (Nos. 1061a-1064a) and various scenes from novels as right page of book (Nos. 1061b-1064b).

**1987, Dec. 17** ***Perf. 14x14½***

**Horiz. Pairs, #a.-b.**

| | | | | |
|---|---|---|---|---|
| **1061** | A145 | 6c multicolored | .35 | .35 |
| **1062** | A145 | 25c multicolored | .70 | .70 |
| **1063** | A145 | 50c multicolored | 1.25 | 1.25 |
| **1064** | A145 | 75c multicolored | 1.90 | 1.90 |
| | | *Nos. 1061-1064 (4)* | 4.20 | 4.20 |

**Souvenir Sheet**

| | | | | |
|---|---|---|---|---|
| **1065** | A147 | $5 multicolored | 3.75 | 3.75 |

For surcharge see No. 3267.

Eastern Caribbean Currency — A148

Various Eastern Caribbean coins (Nos. 1069-1081) and banknotes (Nos. 1082-1086) in denominations equaling that of the stamp on which they are pictured.

**1987-89** **Litho.** ***Perf. 15***

| | | | | |
|---|---|---|---|---|
| **1069** | A148 | 5c multicolored | .25 | .25 |
| **1070** | A148 | 6c multicolored | .25 | .25 |
| **1071** | A148 | 10c multicolored | .25 | .25 |
| **1072** | A148 | 12c multicolored | .25 | .25 |
| **1073** | A148 | 15c multicolored | .25 | .25 |
| **1074** | A148 | 20c multicolored | .25 | .25 |
| **1075** | A148 | 25c multicolored | .25 | .25 |
| **1076** | A148 | 30c multicolored | .25 | .25 |
| **1077** | A148 | 35c multicolored | .30 | .30 |
| **1078** | A148 | 45c multicolored | .35 | .35 |
| **1079** | A148 | 50c multicolored | .40 | .40 |
| **1080** | A148 | 65c multicolored | .50 | .50 |
| **1081** | A148 | 75c multicolored | .60 | .60 |
| **1082** | A148 | $1 multi, horiz. | .75 | .75 |
| **1083** | A148 | $2 multi, horiz. | 1.50 | 1.50 |
| **1084** | A148 | $3 multi, horiz. | 2.25 | 2.25 |
| **1085** | A148 | $5 multi, horiz. | 3.75 | 3.75 |
| **1086** | A148 | $10 multi, horiz. | 7.50 | 7.50 |

***Perf. 14***

| | | | | |
|---|---|---|---|---|
| **1086A** | A148 | $20 multi, horiz. | 15.00 | 15.00 |
| | | *Nos. 1069-1086A (19)* | 34.90 | 34.90 |

Issued: $20, Nov. 7, 1989; others, Dec. 11.

For surcharges see Nos. 3240-3241, 3246, 3249, 3295.

**1991** ***Perf. 12***

| | | | |
|---|---|---|---|
| *1071a* | A148 | 10c | .25 |
| *1073a* | A148 | 15c | .25 |
| *1074a* | A148 | 20c | .25 |
| *1075a* | A148 | 25c | .25 |
| *1078a* | A148 | 45c | .30 |
| *1079a* | A148 | 50c | .35 |
| *1080a* | A148 | 65c | .45 |
| *1081a* | A148 | 75c | .55 |
| *1082a* | A148 | $1 | .70 |
| *1083a* | A148 | $2 | 1.40 |
| *1085a* | A148 | $5 | 3.50 |
| | | *Nos. 1071a-1085a (11)* | 8.25 |

This perf may not have been issued in St. Vincent.

**1991** ***Perf. 14***

| | | | | |
|---|---|---|---|---|
| *1071b* | A148 | 10c | .25 | .25 |
| *1073b* | A148 | 15c | .25 | .25 |
| *1074b* | A148 | 20c | .25 | .25 |
| *1075b* | A148 | 25c | .25 | .25 |
| *1078b* | A148 | 45c | .30 | .30 |
| *1079b* | A148 | 50c | .35 | .35 |
| *1080b* | A148 | 65c | .45 | .45 |
| *1081b* | A148 | 75c | .55 | .55 |
| *1082b* | A148 | $1 | .70 | .70 |
| *1083b* | A148 | $2 | 1.40 | 1.40 |
| *1085b* | A148 | $5 | 3.50 | 3.50 |
| | | *Nos. 1071b-1085b (11)* | 8.25 | 8.25 |

For surcharges see Nos. 3242, 3244, 3248, 3249a, 3254-3255, 3257-3257A.

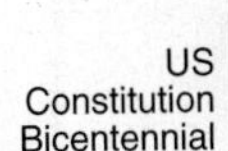

US Constitution Bicentennial A149

Christopher Columbus's fleet: 15c, Santa Maria. 75c, Nina and Pinta. $1, Hour glass, compass. $1.50, Columbus planting flag of Spain on American soil. $3, Arawak natives. $4, Parrot, hummingbird, corn, pineapple, eggs. $5, $6, Columbus, Columbus'l coat of arms and caravel.

**1988, Jan. 11** ***Perf. 14½x14***

| | | | | |
|---|---|---|---|---|
| **1087** | A149 | 15c multicolored | .25 | .25 |
| **1088** | A149 | 75c multicolored | .60 | .60 |
| **1089** | A149 | $1 multicolored | .75 | .75 |
| **1090** | A149 | $1.50 multicolored | 1.25 | 1.25 |
| **1091** | A149 | $3 multicolored | 2.25 | 2.25 |
| **1092** | A149 | $4 multicolored | 3.00 | 3.00 |
| | | *Nos. 1087-1092 (6)* | 8.10 | 8.10 |

**Souvenir Sheets**

***Perf. 14x14½, 14½x14***

| | | | | |
|---|---|---|---|---|
| **1093** | A149 | $5 multicolored | 3.50 | 3.50 |
| **1093A** | A149 | $6 multicolored | 4.25 | 4.25 |

US Constitution, bicent.; 500th anniv. of the discovery of America (in 1992).

Brown Pelican — A150

**1988, Feb. 15** ***Perf. 14***

| | | | | |
|---|---|---|---|---|
| **1094** | A150 | 45c multicolored | .75 | .75 |

See No. 1298.

A151

Tourism — A152

10c, Windsurfing, diff., vert. 45c, Scuba diving, vert. $5, Chartered ship.

**1988, Feb. 22** **Litho.** ***Perf. 15***

| | | | | |
|---|---|---|---|---|
| **1095** | A151 | 10c multicolored | .25 | .25 |
| **1096** | A151 | 45c multicolored | .30 | .30 |
| **1097** | A151 | 65c shown | .45 | .45 |
| **1098** | A151 | $5 multicolored | 3.25 | 3.25 |
| | | *Nos. 1095-1098 (4)* | 4.25 | 4.25 |

**Souvenir Sheet**

***Perf. 13x12½***

| | | | | |
|---|---|---|---|---|
| **1099** | A152 | $10 shown | 6.75 | 6.75 |

For surcharges see Nos. 3250, 3277.

A153

Destruction of the Spanish Armada by the English, 400th Anniv. — A154

16th cent. ships and artifacts: 15c, Nuestra Senora del Rosario, Spanish Chivalric Cross. 75c, Ark Royal, Armada medal. $1.50, English fleet, 16th cent. navigational instrument. $2, Dismasted galleon, cannon balls. $3.50, English fireships among the Armada, firebomb. $5, Revenge, Drake's drum. $8, Shoreline sentries awaiting the outcome of the battle.

**1988, July 29** **Litho.** ***Perf. 12½***

| | | | | |
|---|---|---|---|---|
| **1100** | A153 | 15c multicolored | .25 | .25 |
| **1101** | A153 | 75c multicolored | .40 | .40 |
| **1102** | A153 | $1.50 multicolored | .90 | .90 |
| **1103** | A153 | $2 multicolored | 1.10 | 1.10 |
| **1104** | A153 | $3.50 multicolored | 1.90 | 1.90 |
| **1105** | A153 | $5 multicolored | 2.75 | 2.75 |
| | | *Nos. 1100-1105 (6)* | 7.30 | 7.30 |

**Souvenir Sheet**

| | | | | |
|---|---|---|---|---|
| **1106** | A154 | $8 multicolored | 4.75 | 4.75 |

Cricket Players A156

15c, D.K. Lillee. 50c, G.A. Gooch. 75c, R.N. Kapil Dev. $1, S.M. Gavaskar. $1.50, M.W. Gatting. $2.50, Imran Khan. $3, I.T. Botham. $4, I.V.A. Richards.

**1988, July 29** **Litho.** ***Perf. 14½x14***

| | | | | |
|---|---|---|---|---|
| **1108** | A156 | 15c multicolored | .25 | .25 |
| **1109** | A156 | 50c multicolored | .35 | .35 |
| **1110** | A156 | 75c multicolored | .55 | .55 |
| **1111** | A156 | $1 multicolored | .70 | .70 |
| **1112** | A156 | $1.50 multicolored | 1.00 | 1.00 |
| **1113** | A156 | $2.50 multicolored | 1.75 | 1.75 |
| **1114** | A156 | $3 multicolored | 2.00 | 2.00 |
| **1115** | A156 | $4 multicolored | 2.75 | 2.75 |
| | | *Nos. 1108-1115 (8)* | 9.35 | 9.35 |

A souvenir sheet containing a $2 stamp like No. 1115 and a $3.50 stamp like No. 1114 was not issued by the post office.

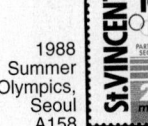

1988 Summer Olympics, Seoul A158

**1988, Dec. 7** **Litho.** ***Perf. 14***

| | | | | |
|---|---|---|---|---|
| **1116** | A158 | 10c Running | .25 | .25 |
| **1117** | A158 | 50c Long jump, vert. | .35 | .35 |
| **1118** | A158 | $1 Triple jump | .65 | .65 |
| **1119** | A158 | $5 Boxing, vert. | 3.50 | 3.50 |
| | | *Nos. 1116-1119 (4)* | 4.75 | 4.75 |

**Souvenir Sheet**

| | | | | |
|---|---|---|---|---|
| **1120** | A158 | $10 Torch | 6.25 | 6.25 |

1st Participation of St. Vincent athletes in the Olympics.

For overprints see Nos. 1346-1351.

Christmas — A159

Walt Disney characters: 1c, Minnie Mouse in freight car. 2c, Morty and Ferdy in open rail car. 3c, Chip 'n Dale in open boxcar. 4c, Huey, Dewey, Louie and reindeer. 5c, Donald and Daisy Duck aboard dining car. 10c, Gramma Duck conducting chorus including Scrooge McDuck, Goofy and Clarabelle Cow. $5, No. 1127, Mickey Mouse in locomotive. $6, Santa Claus in caboose.

No. 1129, $5, Mickey, Minnie Mouse and nephews in train station, vert. No. 1130, $5, Characters riding carousel, vert.

***Perf. 14x13½, 13½x14***

**1988, Dec. 23** **Litho.**

| | | | | |
|---|---|---|---|---|
| **1121-1128** | A159 | Set of 8 | 10.50 | 10.50 |

**Souvenir Sheets**

| | | | | |
|---|---|---|---|---|
| **1129-1130** | A159 | Set of 2 | 10.50 | 10.50 |

Babe Ruth (1895-1948), American Baseball Star — A160

**1988, Dec. 7** **Litho.** ***Perf. 14***

| | | | | |
|---|---|---|---|---|
| **1131** | A160 | $2 multicolored | 2.00 | 2.00 |

India '89, Jan. 20-29, New Delhi — A161

Exhibition emblem and Walt Disney characters: 1c, Mickey Mouse as snake charmer, Minnie Mouse as dancer. 2c, Goofy tossing rings at a chowsingha antelope. 3c, Mickey, Minnie, blue peacock. 5c, Goofy and Mickey as miners, Briolette diamond. 10c, Goofy as count presenting Orloff Diamond to Catherine the Great of Russia (Clarabelle Cow). 25c, Regent Diamond and Donald Duck as Napoleon (portrait) in the Louvre. $4, Minnie as Queen Victoria, Mickey as King Albert, crown bearing the Kohinoor Diamond. $5, Mickey and Goofy on safari.

No. 1140, $6, Mickey as Nehru, riding an elephant. No. 1141, $6, Mickey as postman delivering Hope Diamond to the Smithsonian Institute.

**1989, Feb. 7** **Litho.** ***Perf. 14***

| | | | | |
|---|---|---|---|---|
| **1132-1139** | A161 | Set of 8 | 11.50 | 11.50 |

**Souvenir Sheets**

| | | | | |
|---|---|---|---|---|
| **1140-1141** | A161 | Set of 2 | 12.00 | 12.00 |

Entertainers of the Jazz and Big Band Eras — A162

Designs: 10c, Harry James (1916-83). 15c, Sidney Bechet (1897-1959). 25c, Benny Goodman (1909-86). 35c, Django Reinhardt (1910-53). 50c, Lester Young (1909-59). 90c, Gene Krupa (1909-73). $3, Louis Armstrong (1900-71). $4, Duke Ellington (1899-1974).

No. 1150, $5, Charlie Parker, Jr. (1920-55). No. 1151, $5, Billie Holiday (1915-59).

**1989, Apr. 3** **Litho.** ***Perf. 14***

| | | | | |
|---|---|---|---|---|
| **1142-1149** | A162 | Set of 8 | 10.00 | 10.00 |

**Souvenir Sheets**

| | | | | |
|---|---|---|---|---|
| **1150-1151** | A162 | Set of 2 | 11.00 | 11.00 |

Holiday misspelled "Holliday" on No. 1151.

For surcharge see No. 3274.

Miniature Sheet

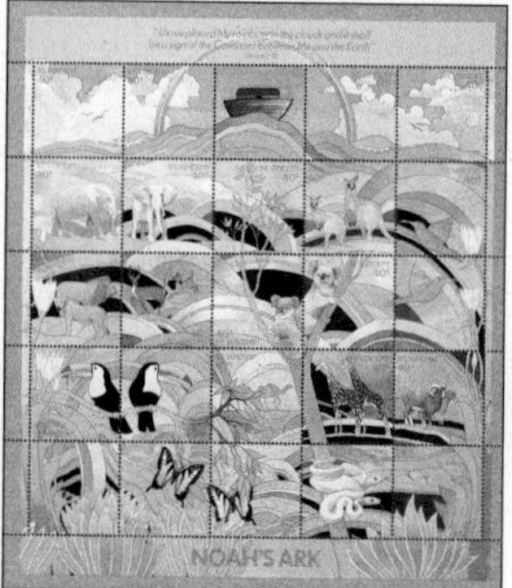


Noah's Ark — A163

Designs: a, Clouds, 2 birds at right. b, Rainbow, 4 clouds. c, Ark. d, Rainbow, 3 clouds. e, Clouds, 2 birds at left. f, African elephant facing right. g, Elephant facing forward. h, Leaves on tree branch. i, Kangaroos. j, Hummingbird facing left, flower. k, Lions. l, White-tailed deer. m, Koala at right. n, Koala at left. o, Hummingbird facing right, flower. p, Flower, toucan facing left. q, Toucan facing right. r, Camels. s, Giraffes. t, Sheep. u, Ladybugs. v, Butterfly (UR). w, Butterfly (LL). x, Snakes. y, Dragonflies.

**1989, Apr. 10** ***Perf. 14***
**1152** A163 Sheet of 25 14.50 14.50
*a.-y.* 40c any single .30 .30

Easter A164

Paintings by Titian: 5c, Baptism of Christ. 30c, Temptation of Christ. 45c, Ecce Homo. 65c, Noli Me Tangere. 75c, Christ Carrying the Cross. $1, Christ Crowned with Thorns. $4, Lamentation Over Christ. $5, The Entombment.

No. 1161, $6, Pieta. No. 1162, $6, The Deposition.

**1989, Apr. 17** ***Perf. 13½x14***
**1153-1160** A164 Set of 8 12.50 12.50

**Souvenir Sheets**

**1161-1162** A164 Set of 2 11.50 11.50

Telstar II and Cooperation in Space — A165

Designs: 15c, Recovery of astronaut L. Gordon Cooper, Mercury 9/Faith 7 mission. 35c, Satellite transmission of Martin Luther King's civil rights march address, 1963. 40c, US shuttle STS-7, 1st use of Canadarm, deployment & recovery of a W. German free-flying experiment platform. 50c, Satellite transmission of the 1964 Olympics, Innsbruck (speed skater). 60c, Vladimir Remek of Czechoslovakia, 1st non-Soviet cosmonaut, 1978. $1, CNES Hermes space plane, France, ESA emblem, Columbus space station. $3, Satellite transmission of Pope John XXIII (1881-1963) blessing crowd at the Vatican. $4, Ulf Merbold, W. Germany, 1st non-American astronaut, 1983.

No. 1171, $5, Launch of Telstar II, 5/7/63. No. 1172, $5, 1975 Apollo-Soyuz mission members shaking hands.

**1989, Apr. 26 Litho.** ***Perf. 14***
**1163-1170** A165 Set of 8 10.00 10.00

**Souvenir Sheets**

**1171-1172** A165 Set of 2 9.00 9.00

Famous Ocean Liners A166

**1989, Apr. 21 Litho.** ***Perf. 14***
**1173** A166 10c Ile de France .35 .35
**1174** A166 40c Liberte .50 .50
**1175** A166 50c Mauretania .70 .70
**1176** A166 75c France .95 .95
**1177** A166 $1 Aquitania 1.25 1.25
**1178** A166 $2 United States 2.50 2.50
**1179** A166 $3 Olympic 3.50 3.50
**1180** A166 $4 Queen Elizabeth 4.75 4.75
*Nos. 1173-1180 (8)* 14.50 14.50

**Souvenir Sheets**

**1181** A166 $6 Queen Mary 7.25 7.25
**1182** A166 $6 QE 2 7.25 7.25

Nos. 1181-1182 contain 84x28mm stamps.
For overprints see Nos. 1352-1361.

Souvenir Sheet

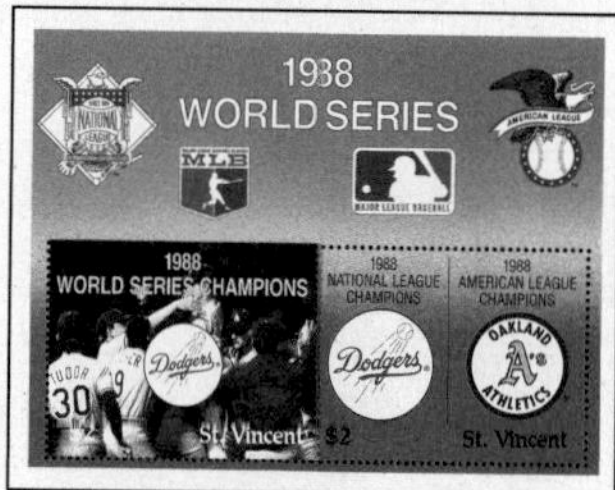


1988 World Series — A167

No. 1183: a, Dodgers emblem and players celebrating victory. b, Emblems of the Dodgers and the Oakland Athletics.

**1989, May 3 Litho.** ***Perf. 14x13½***
**1183** A167 Sheet of 2 6.25 6.25
*a.-b.* $2 any single 1.60 1.60

World Wildlife Fund, St. Vincent Parrots A168

Indigenous Birds — A169

10c, Parrot's head. 20c, Parrot's wing span. 25c, Mistletoe bird. 40c, Parrot feeding, vert. 70c, Parrot on rock, vert. 75c, Crab hawk. $2, Coucou. $3, Prince bird.

No. 1192, Doctor bird. No. 1193, Soufrieres, vert.

**1989, Apr. 5** ***Perf. 14***
**1184** A168 10c multicolored .70 .55
**1185** A168 20c multicolored 1.25 .55
**1186** A169 25c multicolored .55 .55
**1187** A168 40c multicolored 2.00 2.25
**1188** A168 70c multicolored 2.50 1.40
**1189** A169 75c multicolored 1.75 1.75
**1190** A169 $2 multicolored 2.00 2.00
**1191** A169 $3 multicolored 3.00 3.00
*Nos. 1184-1191 (8)* 13.75 12.05

**Souvenir Sheets**

**1192** A169 $5 multicolored 4.25 4.25
**1193** A169 $5 multicolored 4.25 4.25

Fan Paintings — A170

Paintings by Hiroshige unless otherwise stated: 10c, Autumn Flowers in Front of the Full Moon. 40c, Hibiscus. 50c, Iris. 75c, Morning Glories. $1, Dancing Swallows. $2, Sparrow and Bamboo. $3, Yellow Bird and Cotton Rose. $4, Judos Chrysanthemums in a deep ravine in China.

No. 1202, $6, Rural Cottages in Spring, by Sotatsu. No. 1203, $6, The Six Immortal Poets Portrayed as Cats, by Kuniyoshi.

**1989, July 6 Litho.** ***Perf. 14x13½***
**1194-1201** A170 Set of 8 11.00 11.00

**Souvenir Sheets**

**1202-1203** A170 Set of 2 10.00 10.00

Hirohito (1901-89) and enthronement of Akihito as emperor of Japan.

First Moon Landing, 20th Anniv. A171

Apollo 11 Mission: 35c, Columbia command module. 75c, Lunar module Eagle landing. $1, Rocket launch. No. 1207a, Buzz Aldrin conducting solar wind experiments. No. 1207b, Lunar module on plain. No. 1207c, Earthrise. No. 1207d, Neil Armstrong. No. 1208, Separation of lunar and command modules. No. 1209a, Command module. No. 1209b, Lunar module. $6, Armstrong preparing to take man's 1st step onto the Moon.

**1989, Sept. 11** ***Perf. 14***
**1204** A171 35c multicolored .40 .30
**1205** A171 75c multicolored 1.00 .55
**1206** A171 $1 multicolored 1.10 .75
**1207** Strip of 4 8.00 8.00
*a.-d.* A171 $2 any single 1.40 1.40
**1208** A171 $3 multicolored 3.25 3.25
*Nos. 1204-1208 (5)* 13.75 12.85

**Souvenir Sheets**

**1209** Sheet of 2 6.50 6.50
*a.-b.* A171 $3 any single 2.25 2.25
**1210** A171 $6 multicolored 6.50 6.50

No. 1207 has continuous design.

Players Elected to the Baseball Hall of Fame — A172

1989 All-Star Game, July 11, Anaheim, California — A173

**1989, July 23 Litho.** ***Perf. 14***
**1211** A172 $2 Cobb, 1936 1.40 1.40
**1212** A172 $2 Mays, 1979 1.40 1.40
**1213** A172 $2 Musial, 1969 1.40 1.40
**1214** A172 $2 Bench, 1989 1.40 1.40
**1215** A172 $2 Banks, 1977 1.40 1.40
**1216** A172 $2 Schoendienst, 1989 1.40 1.40
**1217** A172 $2 Gehrig, 1939 1.40 1.40
**1218** A172 $2 Robinson, 1962 1.40 1.40
**1219** A172 $2 Feller, 1962 1.40 1.40
**1220** A172 $2 Williams, 1966 1.40 1.40
**1221** A172 $2 Yastrzemski, 1989 1.40 1.40
**1222** A172 $2 Kaline, 1980 1.40 1.40
*Nos. 1211-1222 (12)* 16.80 16.80

"Yastrzemski" is misspelled on No. 1221.

**Size: 116x82mm**

***Imperf***

**1223** A173 $5 multicolored 5.75 5.75

Baseball Hall of Fame Members — A173a

No. 1223A, Johnny Bench. No. 1223B, Carl Yastrzemski. No. 1223C, Ernie Banks. No. 1223D, Willie Mays. No. 1223E, Al Kaline. No. 1223F, Ty Cobb. No. 1223G, Ted Williams. No. 1223H, Red Schoendienst. No. 1223I, Jackie Robinson. No. 1223J, Lou Gehrig. No. 1223K, Bob Feller. No. 1223L, Stan Musial.

**1989 Embossed** ***Perf. 13***
**1223A-1223L** A173a $20 Set of 12

Miniature Sheets

Rookies and Team Emblems — A174

Rookies of the Year, Most Valuable Players and Cy Young Award Winners A175

No. 1224: a, Dante Bichette, 1989. b, Carl Yastrzemski, 1961. c, Randy Johnson, 1989. d, Jerome Walton, 1989. e, Ramon Martinez, 1989. f, Ken Hill, 1989. g, Tom McCarthy, 1989. h, Gaylord Perry, 1963. i, John Smoltz, 1989.

No. 1225: a, Bob Milacki, 1989. b, Babe Ruth, 1915. c, Jim Abbott, 1989. d, Gary Sheffield, 1989. e, Gregg Jeffries, 1989. f, Kevin Brown, 1989. g, Cris Carpenter, 1989. h, Johnny Bench, 1968. i, Ken Griffey Jr., 1989.

No. 1226: a, Chris Sabo, 1988 Natl. League Rookie of the Year. b, Walt Weiss, 1988 American League Rookie of the Year. c, Willie Mays, 1951 Rookie of the Year. d, Kirk Gibson, 1988 Natl. League Most Valuable Player. e, Ted Williams, Most Valuable Player of 1946 and 1949. f, Jose Canseco, 1988 American League Most Valuable Player. g, Gaylord Perry, Cy Young winner for 1972 and 1978. h, Orel Hershiser, 1988 National League Cy Young winner. i, Frank Viola, 1988 American League Cy Young winner.

***Perf. 13½***

**1224** A174 Sheet of 9 5.00 5.00
*a.-i.* 60c any single .50 .50

**1225** A174 Sheet of 9 5.00 5.00
*a.-i.* A174 60c any single .50 .50
**1226** Sheet of 9 5.00 5.00
*a.-i.* A175 60c any single .50 .50

For surcharges see Nos. B9-B11.

French Revolution Bicent., PHILEXFRANCE '89 — A176

French governors and ships.

**1989, July 7 Litho. *Perf. 13½x14***

| | | | | |
|---|---|---|---|---|
| **1227** | A176 | 30c Goelette | .65 | .65 |
| **1228** | A176 | 55c Corvette | 1.00 | 1.00 |
| **1229** | A176 | 75c Fregate 36 | 1.60 | 1.60 |
| **1230** | A176 | $1 Vaisseau 74 | 2.00 | 2.00 |
| **1231** | A176 | $3 Ville de Paris | 6.00 | 6.00 |
| | | *Nos. 1227-1231 (5)* | 11.25 | 11.25 |

**Souvenir Sheet**

**1232** A176 $6 Map 6.00 6.00

Miniature Sheet

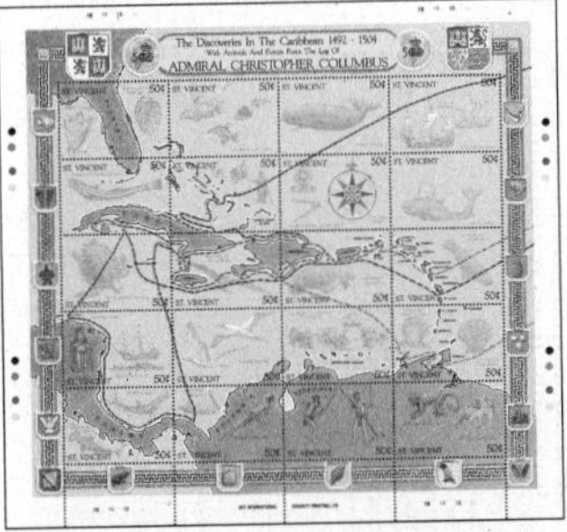

Discovery of the New World, 500th Anniv. (in 1992) — A177

No. 1233: a, Map of Florida, queen conch and West Indian purpura. b, Caribbean reef fish. c, Sperm whale. d, Columbus's fleet. e, Cuba, Isle of Pines, remora. f, The Bahamas, Turks & Caicos Isls., Columbus raising Spanish flag. g, Navigational instruments. h, Sea monster. i, Kemp's Ridley turtle, Cayman Isls. j, Jamaica, parts of Cuba and Hispaniola, magnificent frigatebird. k, Caribbean manatee, Hispaniola, Puerto Rico, Virgin Isls. l, Caribbean Monk seal, Anguilla and Caribbean isls. m, Mayan chief, galleon, dugout canoe. n, Masked boobies. o, Venezuelan village on pilings and the Netherlands Antilles. p, Atlantic wing oyster, lion's paw scallop, St. Vincent, Grenada, Trinidad & Tobago, Barbados. q, Panama, great hammerhead and mako sharks. r, Brown pelican, Colombia, Hyacinthine macaw. s, Venezuela, Indian bow and spear hunters. t, Capuchin and squirrel monkeys.

**1989, Aug. 31 *Perf. 14***

**1233** A177 Sheet of 20 17.00 17.00
*a.-t.* 50c any single .70 .70

Major League Baseball: Los Angeles Dodgers — A178

No. 1234: a, Jay Howell, Alejandro Pena. b, Mike Davis, Kirk Gibson. c, Fernando Valenzuela, John Shelby. d, Jeff Hamilton, Franklin Stubbs. e, Dodger Stadium. f, Ray Searage, John Tudor. g, Mike Sharperson, Mickey Hatcher. h, Coaches Amalfitano, Cresse, Ferguson, Hines, Mota, Perranoski, Russell. i, John Wetteland, Ramon Martinez.

No. 1235: a, Tim Belcher, Tim Crews. b, Orel Hershiser, Mike Morgan. c, Mike Scioscia, Rick Dempsey. d, Dave Anderson, Alfredo Griffin. e, Team emblem. f, Kal Daniels, Mike Marshall. g, Eddie Murray, Willie Randolph. h, Manager Tom Lasorda, Jose Gonzalez. i, Lenny Harris, Chris Gwynn, Billy Bean.

**1989, Sept. 23 *Perf. 12½***

**1234** Sheet of 9 6.50 6.50
*a.-i.* A178 60c any single .55 .55
**1235** Sheet of 9 6.50 6.50
*a.-i.* A178 60c any single .55 .55

See Nos. 1344-1345.

1990 World Cup Soccer Championships, Italy — A179

55c, Youth soccer teams. $1, Natl. team. $5, Trophy winners.
No. 1240, Youth soccer team. No. 1241, Natl. team, diff.

**1989, Oct. 16 Litho. *Perf. 14***

| | | | | |
|---|---|---|---|---|
| **1236** | A179 | 10c shown | .30 | .30 |
| **1237** | A179 | 55c multicolored | .60 | .60 |
| **1238** | A179 | $1 multicolored | 1.10 | 1.10 |
| **1239** | A179 | $5 multicolored | 5.50 | 5.50 |
| | | *Nos. 1236-1239 (4)* | 7.50 | 7.50 |

**Souvenir Sheets**

**1240** A179 $6 multicolored 6.50 6.50
**1241** A179 $6 multicolored 6.50 6.50

Fauna and Flora A180

**1989, Nov. 1**

| | | | | |
|---|---|---|---|---|
| **1242** | A180 | 65c St. Vincent parrot | .90 | .90 |
| **1243** | A180 | 75c Whistling warbler | 1.10 | 1.10 |
| **1244** | A180 | $5 Black snake | 7.00 | 7.00 |
| | | *Nos. 1242-1244 (3)* | 9.00 | 9.00 |

**Souvenir Sheet**

**1245** A180 $6 Volcano plant, vert. 6.50 6.50

Butterflies A181

**1989, Oct. 16 *Perf. 14x14½, 14½x14***

| | | | | |
|---|---|---|---|---|
| **1246** | A181 | 6c Little yellow | .30 | .25 |
| **1247** | A181 | 10c Orion | .30 | .25 |
| **1248** | A181 | 15c American painted lady | .30 | .25 |
| **1249** | A181 | 75c Cassius blue | .95 | .60 |
| **1250** | A181 | $1 Polydamus swallowtail | 1.20 | 1.20 |
| **1251** | A181 | $2 Guaraguao skipper | 2.40 | 2.40 |
| **1252** | A181 | $3 The Queen | 3.50 | 3.50 |
| **1253** | A181 | $5 Royal blue | 6.00 | 6.00 |
| | | *Nos. 1246-1253 (8)* | 14.95 | 14.45 |

**Souvenir Sheets**

**1254** A181 $6 Monarch 6.50 6.50
**1255** A181 $6 Barred sulphur 6.50 6.50

Exhibition Emblem, Disney Characters and US Natl. Monuments A182

Designs: 1c, Seagull Monument, UT. 2c, Lincoln Memorial, Washington, DC. 3c, Crazy Horse Memorial, SD. 4c, Uncle Sam Wilson, Troy, NY. 5c, Benjamin Franklin Natl. Memorial, Philadelphia, PA. 10c, Statue of George Washington, Federal Hall, NY. $3, John F. Kennedy's birthplace, Brookline, MA. $6, George Washington's home, Mount Vernon, VA.

No. 1264, $5, Mt. Rushmore, SD. No. 1265, $5, Stone Mountain, GA.

**1989, Nov. 17 *Perf. 13½x14***

**1256-1263** A182 Set of 8 12.50 12.50

**Souvenir Sheets**

**1264-1265** A182 Set of 2 13.50 13.50

World Stamp Expo '89.

Souvenir Sheet

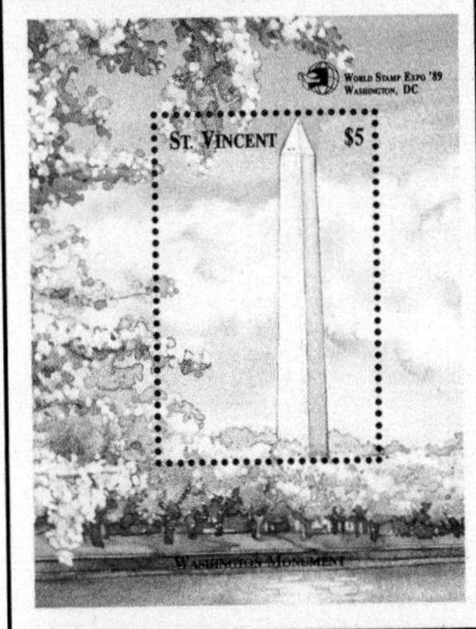


The Washington Monument, Washington, DC — A183

**1989, Nov. 17 Litho. *Perf. 14***

**1266** A183 $5 multicolored 4.25 4.25

World Stamp Expo '89.

Major League Baseball — A184

Players, owners and commissioner.

No. 1267, 30c: a, Early Wynn. b, Cecil Cooper. c, Joe DiMaggio. d, Kevin Mitchell. e, Tom Browning. f, Bobby Witt. g, Tim Wallach. h, Bob Gibson. i, Steve Garvey.

No. 1268, 30c: a, Rick Sutcliffe. b, A. Bartlett Giamatti, commissioner. c, Cory Snyder. d, Rollie Fingers. e, Willie Hernandez. f, Sandy Koufax. g, Carl Yastrzemski. h, Ron Darling. i, Gerald Perry.

No. 1269, 30c: a, Mike Marshall. b, Tom Seaver. c, Bob Milacki. d, Dave Smith. e, Robin Roberts. f, Kent Hrbek. g, Bill Veeck, owner. h, Carmelo Martinez. i, Rogers Hornsby.

No. 1270, 30c: a, Barry Bonds. b, Jim Palmer. c, Lou Boudreau. d, Ernie Whitt. e, Jose Canseco. f, Ken Griffey, Jr. g, Johnny Vander Meer. h, Kevin Seitzer. i, Dave Dravecky.

No. 1271, 30c: a, Glenn Davis. b, Nolan Ryan. c, Hank Greenberg. d, Richie Allen. e, Dave Righetti. f, Jim Abbott. g, Harold Reynolds. h, Dennis Martinez. i, Rod Carew.

No. 1272, 30c: a, Joe Morgan. b, Tony Fernandez. c, Ozzie Guillen. d, Mike Greenwell. e, Bobby Valentine. f, Doug DeCinces. g, Mickey Cochrane. h, Willie McGee. i, Von Hayes.

No. 1273, 30c: a, Frank White. b, Brook Jacoby. c, Boog Powell. d, Will Clark. e, Ray Kroc, owner. f, Fred McGriff. g, Willie Stargell. h, John Smoltz. i, B. J. Surhoff.

No. 1274, 30c: a, Keith Hernandez. b, Eddie Matthews. c, Tom Paciorek. d, Alan Trammell. e, Greg Maddux. f, Ruben Sierra. g, Tony Oliva. h, Chris Bosio. i, Orel Hershiser.

No. 1275, 30c: a, Casey Stengel. b, Jim Rice. c, Reggie Jackson. d, Jerome Walton. e, Bob Knepper. f, Andres Galarraga. g, Christy Mathewson. h, Willie Wilson. i, Ralph Kiner.

**1989, Nov. 30 *Perf. 12½***

**Sheets of 9, #a-i**

**1267-1275** A184 Set of 9 29.00 29.00

No. 1268d is incorrectly inscribed "Finger." Cochrane is misspelled "Cochpane" on No. 1272g.

No. 1272d was also issued in sheets of 9.

Achievements of Nolan Ryan, American Baseball Player — A185

No. 1276 — Portrait and inscriptions: a, 383 League-leading strikeouts, 1973. b, No hitter, Kansas City Royals, May 15, 1973. c, No hitter, Detroit Tigers, July 15, 1973. d, No hitter, Minnesota Twins, Sept. 28, 1974. e, No hitter, Baltimore Orioles, June 1, 1975. f, No hitter, Los Angeles Dodgers, Sept. 26, 1981. g, Won 100+ games in both leagues. h, Struck out 200+ batters in 13 seasons. i, 5000th Strikeout, Aug. 22, 1989, Arlington, Texas.

**1989, Nov. 30 Litho. *Perf. 12½***

**1276** Sheet of 9 12.00 12.00
*a.-i.* A185 $2 any single 1.30 1.30

For overprints see Nos. 1336-1337.

Coat of Arms, No. 570 — A186

**1989, Dec. 20 *Perf. 14***

**1278** A186 65c multicolored .90 .90

**Souvenir Sheet**

**1279** A186 $10 multicolored 8.75 8.75

Independence, 10th anniv.

Boy Scouts and Girl Guides — A187

Lord or Lady Baden-Powell and: No. 1280, Boy's modern uniform. No. 1281, Guide, ranger and brownie. No. 1282, Boy's old uniform. No. 1283, Mrs. Jackson. No. 1284, 75th anniversary emblem. No. 1285, Mrs. Russell

No. 1286, Canoeing, merit badges. No. 1287, Flag-raising, Camp Yourumei, 1985.

**1989, Dec. 20 *Perf. 14***

| | | | | |
|---|---|---|---|---|
| **1280** | A187 | 35c multi | .65 | .65 |
| **1281** | A187 | 35c multi | .65 | .65 |
| **1282** | A187 | 55c multi | .85 | .85 |
| **1283** | A187 | 55c multi | .85 | .85 |
| **1284** | A187 | $2 multi | 3.25 | 3.25 |
| **1285** | A187 | $2 multi | 3.25 | 3.25 |
| | | *Nos. 1280-1285 (6)* | 9.50 | 9.50 |

**Souvenir Sheets**

**1286** A187 $5 multi 6.25 6.25
**1287** A187 $5 multi 6.25 6.25

Christmas — A188

Paintings by Da Vinci and Botticelli: 10c, The Adoration of the Magi (holy family), by Botticelli. 25c, The Adoration of the Magi (witnesses). 30c, The Madonna of the Magnificat, by Botticelli. 40c, The Virgin and Child with St. Anne and St. John the Baptist, by Da Vinci. 55c, The Annunciation (angel), by Da Vinci. 75c, The Annunciation (Madonna). No. 1294, $5, Madonna of the Carnation, by Da Vinci. $6, The Annunciation, by Botticelli. No. 1296, $5 The Virgin of the Rocks, by Da Vinci. No. 1297, $5, The Adoration of the Magi, by Botticelli.

**1989, Dec. 20** ***Perf. 14***

**1288-1295** A188 Set of 8 12.00 12.00

**Souvenir Sheets**

**1296-1297** A188 Set of 2 8.75 8.75

**Bird Type of 1988**

**1989, July 31 Litho.** ***Perf. 15x14***

**1298** A150 55c St. Vincent parrot .90 .90

Lions Intl. of St. Vincent, 25th Anniv. (in 1989) A189

Services: 10c, Scholarships for the blind, vert. 65c, Free textbooks. 75c, Health education (diabetes). $2, Blood sugar testing machines. $4, Publishing and distribution of pamphlets on drug abuse.

**1990, Mar. 5 Litho.** ***Perf. 14***

**1303-1307** A189 Set of 5 7.75 7.75

For surcharge see No. 3345.

World War II A190

Historic events: 5c, Defeat of the Graf Spee, 12/13-17/39. 10c, Charles De Gaulle calls the French Resistance to arms, 6/18/40. 15c, The British drive the Italian army out of Egypt, 12/15/40. 25c, US destroyer Reuben James torpedoed off Iceland, 10/31/41. 30c, MacArthur becomes allied supreme commander of the southwest Pacific, 4/18/42. 40c, US forces attack Corregidor, 2/16/45. 55c, HMS King George V engages the Bismarck, 5/27/41. 75c, US fleet enters Tokyo Harbor, 8/27/45. $5, Russian takeover of Berlin completed, 5/2/45. $6, #1317, Battle of the Philippine Sea, 6/18/44. #1318, Battle of the Java Sea, 2/28/42.

**1990, Apr. 2** ***Perf. 14x13½***

**1308-1317** A190 Set of 10 17.00 17.00

**Souvenir Sheet**

**1318** A190 $6 multi 7.75 7.75

Penny Black, 150th Anniv. — A191

Great Britain No. 1 (various plate positions).

**1990, May 3 Litho.** ***Perf. 14x15***

**1319** A191 $2 "NK" 2.25 2.25

**1320** A191 $4 "AB" 4.50 4.50

**Souvenir Sheet**

**1321** A191 $6 Simulated #1, "SV" 6.75 6.75

Stamp World London '90 — A192

Walt Disney characters in British military uniforms: 5c, Donald Duck as 18th cent. Admiral. 10c, Huey as Bugler, 68th Light Infantry, 1854. 15c, Minnie Mouse as Drummer, 1st Irish Guards, 1900. 25c, Goofy as Lance Corporal, Seaforth Highlanders, 1944. $1, Mickey Mouse as officer, 58th Regiment, 1879, 1881. $2, Donald Duck as officer, Royal Engineers, 1813. $4, Mickey Mouse as Drum Major, 1914. $5, Goofy as Pipe Sergeant, 1918.

No. 1330, $6, Scrooge as Company Clerk and Goofy as King's Lifeguard of Foot. No. 1331, $6, Mickey Mouse as British Grenadier.

**1990, May Litho.** ***Perf. 13½x14***

**1322-1329** A192 Set of 8 17.00 17.00

**Souvenir Sheets**

**1330-1331** A192 Set of 2 13.50 13.50

A193

**1990, July 5** ***Perf. 14***

**1332** $2 In robes 1.75 1.75

**1333** $2 Queen Mother signing book 1.75 1.75

**1334** $2 In fur coat 1.75 1.75

*a.* A193 Strip of 3, #1332-1334 5.25 5.25

*Nos. 1332-1334 (3)* 5.25 5.25

**Souvenir Sheet**

**1335** A194 $6 Like No. 1334 4.75 4.75

**No. 1276 Overprinted**

a

b

**1990, July 23 Litho.** ***Perf. 12½***

**Miniature Sheets**

**1336** A185(a) $2 Sheet of 9, #a-i 12.50 12.50

**1337** A185(b) $2 Sheet of 9, #a-i 12.50 12.50

World Cup Soccer Championships, Italy — A195

Players from participating countries.

**1990, Sept. 24 Litho.** ***Perf. 14***

**1338** A195 10c Argentina .35 .25

**1339** A195 75c Colombia .95 .95

**1340** A195 $1 Uruguay 1.25 1.25

**1341** A195 $5 Belgium 7.00 7.00

*Nos. 1338-1341 (4)* 9.55 9.45

**Souvenir Sheets**

**1342** A195 $6 Brazil 5.75 5.75

**1343** A195 $6 West Germany 5.75 5.75

**Dodger Baseball Type of 1989**

No. 1344: a, Hubie Brooks, Orel Hershiser. b, Manager Tom Lasorda, Tim Crews. c, Fernando Valenzuela, Eddie Murray. d, Kal Daniels, Jose Gonzalez. e, Dodger centennial emblem. f, Chris Gwynn, Jeff Hamilton. g, Kirk Gibson, Rick Dempsey. h, Jim Gott, Alfredo Griffin. i, Coaches, Ron Perranoski, Bill Russell, Joe Ferguson, Joe Amalfitano, Mark Cresse, Ben Hines, Manny Mota.

No. 1345: a, Mickey Hatcher, Jay Howell. b, Juan Samuel, Mike Scioscia. c, Lenny Harris, Mike Hartley. d, Ramon Martinez, Mike Morgan. e, Dodger Stadium. f, Stan Javier, Don Aase. g, Ray Searage, Mike Sharperson. h, Tim Belcher, Pat Perry. i, Dave Walsh, Jose Vizcaino, Jim Neidlinger, Jose Offerman, Carlos Hernandez.

***Hyphen-hole roulette 7***

**1990, Sept. 21**

**1344** Sheet of 9 6.50 6.50

*a.-i.* A178 60c any single .35 .35

**1345** Sheet of 9 6.50 6.50

*a.-i.* A178 60c any single .35 .35

**Nos. 1116-1120 Overprinted**

Overprints: 50c, "CARL / LEWIS / U.S.A.". $1, "HRISTO / MARKOV / BULGARIA". $5, "HENRY / MASKE / E. GERMANY".

No. 1350, USSR, US medals. No. 1351, South Korea, Spain medals.

**1990, Oct. 18** ***Perf. 14***

**1346** A158 10c shown .30 .30

**1347** A158 50c multicolored .55 .55

**1348** A158 $1 multicolored .95 .95

**1349** A158 $5 multicolored 5.00 5.00

*Nos. 1346-1349 (4)* 6.80 6.80

**Souvenir Sheets**

**1350** A158 $10 multicolored 6.75 6.75

**1351** A158 $10 multicolored 6.75 6.75

**Nos. 1173-1182 Overprinted**

**1990, Oct. 18 Litho.** ***Perf. 14***

**1352** A166 10c Ile de France .30 .30

**1353** A166 40c Liberte .35 .35

**1354** A166 50c Mauretania .50 .50

**1355** A166 75c France .70 .70

**1356** A166 $1 Aquitania 1.00 1.00

**1357** A166 $2 United States 1.90 1.90

**1358** A166 $3 Olympic 2.75 2.75

**1359** A166 $4 Queen Elizabeth 4.00 4.00

*Nos. 1352-1359 (8)* 11.50 11.50

**Souvenir Sheets**

**1360** A166 $6 Queen Mary 5.75 5.75

**1361** A166 $6 QE 2 5.75 5.75

Overprint on #1360-1361 is 12mm in diameter.

Orchids — A196

Designs: 10c, Dendrophylax funalis, Dimeranda emarginata. 15c, Epidendrum elongatum. 45c, Comparettia falcata. 60c, Brassia maculata. $1, Encyclia cochleata, Encyclia cordigera. $2, Cyrtopodium punctatum. $4, Cattelya labiata. $5, Bletia purpurea.

No. 1370, $6, Ionopsis utricularioides. No. 1371, $6, Vanilla planifolia.

**1990, Nov. 23**

**1362-1369** A196 Set of 8 20.00 20.00

**Souvenir Sheets**

**1370-1371** A196 Set of 2 17.00 17.00

Christmas A197

Details from paintings by Rubens: 10c, Miraculous Draught of Fishes. 45c, $2, Crowning of Holy Katherine. 50c, St. Ives of Treguler. 65c, Allegory of Eternity. $1, $4, St. Bavo Receives Monastic Habit of Ghent. $5, Communion of St. Francis.

No. 1380, $6, St. Ives of Treguier (entire). No. 1381, $6, Allegory of Eternity. No. 1382, $6, St. Bavo Receives Monastic Habit of Ghent, horiz. No. 1383, $6, The Miraculous Draft of Fishes, horiz.

**1990, Dec. 3 Litho.** ***Perf. 14***

**1372-1379** A197 Set of 8 13.00 13.00

**Souvenir Sheets**

**1380-1383** A197 Set of 4 16.50 16.50

Intl. Literacy Year A198

Canterbury Tales: a, Geoffrey Chaucer (1342-1400), author. b, "When April with his showers sweet..." c, "When Zephyr also has,..." d. "And many little birds make melody..." e, "And palmers to go seeking out strange strands..." f, Quill pen, open book. g, Bluebird in tree. h, Trees, rider's head with white hair. i, Banner on staff. j, Town. k, Rider's head, diff. l, Blackbird in tree. m, Old monk. n, Horse, rider. o, Nun, monk carrying banner. p, Monks. q, White horse, rider. r, Black horse, rider. s, Squirrel. t, Rooster. u, Chickens. v, Rabbit. w, Butterfly. x, Mouse.

**1990, Dec. 12** ***Perf. 13½***

**1384** Sheet of 24 17.00 17.00

*a.-x.* A198 40c any single .30 .30

Vincent Van Gogh (1853-1890), Painter — A198a

Self-portraits.

**1990, Dec. 17 Litho. *Perf. 13***

| | | | | | |
|---|---|---|---|---|---|
| 1385 | A198a | 1c | 1889 | .30 | .30 |
| 1386 | A198a | 5c | 1886 | .30 | .30 |
| 1387 | A198a | 10c | 1888, with hat & pipe | .30 | .30 |
| 1388 | A198a | 15c | 1888, painting | .30 | .30 |
| *a.* | | | Strip of 4, #1385-1388 | .50 | .50 |
| 1389 | A198a | 20c | 1887 | .30 | .30 |
| 1390 | A198a | 45c | 1889, diff. | .55 | .55 |
| 1391 | A198a | $5 | 1889, with bandaged ear | 5.75 | 5.75 |
| 1392 | A198a | $6 | 1887, with straw hat | 7.00 | 7.00 |
| *a.* | | | Strip of 4, #1389-1392 | 14.50 | 14.50 |
| | | | *Nos. 1385-1392 (8)* | 14.80 | 14.80 |

Hummel Figurines — A199

10c, Photographer. 15c, Boy with ladder & rope. 40c, Pharmacist. 60c, Boy answering telephone. $1, Bootmaker. $2, Artist. $4, Waiter. $5, Mailman.

**1990, Dec. 30 Litho. *Perf. 14***

| | | | | | |
|---|---|---|---|---|---|
| 1393 | A199 | 10c | multicolored | .25 | .25 |
| 1394 | A199 | 15c | multicolored | .25 | .25 |
| 1395 | A199 | 40c | multicolored | .35 | .30 |
| 1396 | A199 | 60c | multicolored | .50 | .40 |
| 1396A | A199 | $1 | multicolored | .85 | .60 |
| 1396B | A199 | $2 | multicolored | 1.75 | 1.75 |
| 1397 | A199 | $4 | multicolored | 3.75 | 3.75 |
| *a.* | | | Sheet of 4, 15c, 40c, $2, $4 | 6.00 | 6.00 |
| 1398 | A199 | $5 | multicolored | 3.75 | 3.75 |
| *a.* | | | Sheet of 4, 10c, 60c, $1, $5 | 6.00 | 6.00 |
| | | | *Nos. 1393-1398 (8)* | 11.45 | 11.05 |

Souvenir Sheets

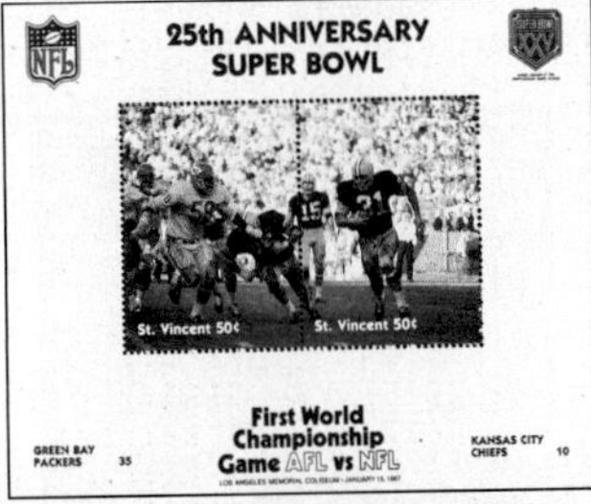

Super Bowl Highlights — A200

Designs: Nos. 1400-1424, Players in action in Super Bowl I (1967) through Super Bowl XXV (1991). Nos. 1400-1423 contain two 50c stamps printed with continuous design showing game highlights. No. 1424 contains three 50c stamps showing AFC and NFC team helmets and the Vince Lombardi Trophy.

Nos. 1425-1449, $2, picture Super Bowl Program Covers. Nos. 1443, 1449 horiz.

**1991, Jan. 15 Litho. *Perf. 13½x14***

**1400-1424** A200 Set of 25 32.00 32.00

**Size: 99x125mm**

***Imperf***

**1425-1449** A200 $2 Set of 25 60.00 60.00

Miniature Sheets

Discovery of America, 500th Anniv. (in 1992) — A201

No. 1450: a, 1c, US #230. b, 2c, US #231. c, 3c, US #232. d, 4c, US #233. e, $10, Sailing ship, parrot. f, 5c, US #234. g, 6c, US #235. h, 8c, US #236. i, 10c, US #237.

No. 1451: a, 15c, US #238. b, 30c, US #239. c, 50c, US #240. d, $1, US #241. e, $10, Compass rose, sailing ship. f, $2, US #242. g, $3, US #243. h, $4, US #244. i, $5, US #245.

No. 1452, Bow of sailing ship. No. 1453, Ship's figurehead.

**1991, Mar. 18 Litho. *Perf. 14***

| | | | | |
|---|---|---|---|---|
| 1450 | A201 | Sheet of 9, #a-i | 9.00 | 9.00 |
| 1451 | A201 | Sheet of 9, #a-i | 22.50 | 22.50 |

**Souvenir Sheets**

| | | | | | |
|---|---|---|---|---|---|
| 1452 | A201 | $6 | multicolored | 6.75 | 6.75 |
| 1453 | A201 | $6 | multicolored | 6.75 | 6.75 |

Nos. 1452-1453 each contain one 38x31mm stamp.

Jetsons, The Movie — A202

Hanna-Barbera characters: 5c, Cosmo Spacely, vert. 20c, Elroy, Judy, Astro, Jane & George Jetson, vert. 45c, Judy, Apollo Blue, vert. 50c, Mr. Spacely, George, vert. 60c, George, sprocket factory. $1, Apollo Blue, Judy, Elroy and Grungees. $2, Jane and George in Grungee cavern. $4, George, Elroy, Jane and Little Grungee, vert. $5, Jetsons leaving for Earth, vert.

No. 1463, $6, Jetsons in sprocket factory. No. 1464, $6, Jetsons traveling to Orbiting Ore Asteroid.

**1991, Mar. 25 Litho. *Perf. 13½***

**1454-1462** A202 Set of 9 14.00 14.00

**Souvenir Sheets**

**1463-1464** A202 Set of 2 11.00 11.00

The Flintstones Enjoy Sports — A203

**1991, Mar. 25**

| | | | | | |
|---|---|---|---|---|---|
| 1465 | A203 | 10c | Boxing | .35 | .25 |
| 1466 | A203 | 15c | Soccer | .35 | .25 |
| 1467 | A203 | 45c | Rowing | .55 | .35 |
| 1468 | A203 | 55c | Dinosaur riding | .65 | .40 |
| 1469 | A203 | $1 | Basketball | 1.00 | .65 |
| 1470 | A203 | $2 | Wrestling | 2.25 | 1.75 |
| 1471 | A203 | $4 | Tennis | 4.50 | 4.50 |
| 1472 | A203 | $5 | Cycling | 5.75 | 5.75 |
| | | | *Nos. 1465-1472 (8)* | 15.40 | 13.90 |

**Souvenir Sheets**

| | | | | | |
|---|---|---|---|---|---|
| 1473 | A203 | $6 | Baseball, batting | 6.75 | 6.75 |
| 1474 | A203 | $6 | Baseball, sliding home | 6.75 | 6.75 |

Voyages of Discovery A204

Designs: 5c, Sanger 2. 10c, Magellan probe, 1990. 25c, Buran space shuttle. 75c, American space station. $1, Mars mission, 21st century. $2, Hubble space telescope, 1990. $4, Sailship to Mars. $5, Craf satellite, 2000.

No. 1483, $6, Sailing ship, island hopping. No. 1484, $6, Sailing ship returning home.

**1991, May 13**

**1475-1482** A204 Set of 8 13.00 13.00

**Souvenir Sheets**

**1483-1484** A204 Set of 2 13.00 13.00

Discovery of America, 500th anniv. (in 1992).

**Royal Family Birthday, Anniversary Common Design Type**

Designs: 20c, 25c, $1, Nos. 1492, 1494, Charles and Diana, 10th wedding anniversary. Others, Queen Elizabeth II, 65th birthday.

**1991, July Litho. *Perf. 14***

| | | | | | |
|---|---|---|---|---|---|
| 1485 | CD347 | 5c | multicolored | .25 | .25 |
| 1486 | CD347 | 20c | multicolored | .35 | .25 |
| 1487 | CD347 | 25c | multicolored | .35 | .25 |
| 1488 | CD347 | 60c | multicolored | .70 | .45 |
| 1489 | CD347 | $1 | multicolored | 1.10 | .70 |
| 1490 | CD347 | $2 | multicolored | 2.25 | 2.25 |
| 1491 | CD347 | $4 | multicolored | 4.25 | 4.25 |
| 1492 | CD347 | $5 | multicolored | 5.50 | 5.50 |
| | | | *Nos. 1485-1492 (8)* | 14.75 | 13.90 |

**Souvenir Sheets**

| | | | | | |
|---|---|---|---|---|---|
| 1493 | CD347 | $5 | Elizabeth, Philip | 6.00 | 6.00 |
| 1494 | CD347 | $5 | Charles, Diana, sons | 6.00 | 6.00 |

Japanese Trains A205

No. 1495: a, D51 steam locomotive. b, 9600 steam locomotive. c, Chrysanthemum emblem. d, Passenger coach. e, C57 steam locomotive. f, Oil tank car. g, C53 steam locomotive. h, First steam locomotive. i, C11 steam locomotive.

No. 1496: a, Class 181 electric train. b, EH-10 electric locomotive. c, Special Express emblem. d, Sendai City Class 1 trolley. e, Class 485 electric train. f, Sendai City trolley street cleaner. g, Hakari bullet train. h, ED-11 electric locomotive. i, EF-66 electric locomotive.

No. 1497, C55 steam locomotive, vert. No. 1498, Series 400 electric train. No. 1499, C62 steam locomotive, vert. No. 1500, Super Hitachi electric train, vert.

**1991, Aug. 12 Litho. *Perf. 14x13½***

| | | | | | |
|---|---|---|---|---|---|
| 1495 | A205 | 75c | Sheet of 9, #a.-i. | 7.00 | 7.00 |
| 1496 | A205 | $1 | Sheet of 9, #a.-i. | 9.75 | 9.75 |

**Souvenir Sheets**

***Perf. 13x13½***

| | | | | | |
|---|---|---|---|---|---|
| 1497 | A205 | $6 | multicolored | 5.75 | 5.75 |
| 1498 | A205 | $6 | multicolored | 5.75 | 5.75 |
| 1499 | A205 | $6 | multicolored | 5.75 | 5.75 |
| 1500 | A205 | $6 | multicolored | 5.75 | 5.75 |

Phila Nippon '91. Nos. 1497-1500 each contain 27x44mm or 44x27mm stamps.

Miniature Sheets

Entertainers — A206

No. 1501: a-i, Various portraits of Madonna.

No. 1502 — Italian entertainers: a, Marcello Mastroianni. b, Sophia Loren. c, Mario Lanza (1921-59). d, Federico Fellini. e, Arturo Toscanini (1867-1957). f, Anna Magnani (1908-73). g, Giancarlo Giannini. h, Gina Lollobrigida. i, Enrico Caruso (1873-1921).

No. 1503: a-i, Various portraits of John Lennon.

**1991, Aug. 22 *Perf. 13***

| | | | | | |
|---|---|---|---|---|---|
| 1501 | A206 | $1 | Sheet of 9, #a.-i. | 13.00 | 13.00 |
| 1502 | A206 | $1 | Sheet of 9, #a.-i. | 9.25 | 9.25 |
| 1503 | A206 | $1 | +2c, Sheet of 9, #a.-i. | 11.00 | 11.00 |

**Souvenir Sheets**

***Perf. 12x13***

**1504** A206 $6 Madonna 11.50 11.50

***Perf. 13***

**1505** A206 $6 Luciano Pavarotti, horiz. 9.00 9.00

No. 1503 is semi-postal with surtax going to the Spirit Foundation.

No. 1504 contains one 28x42mm stamp. Compare with No. 1566. See Nos. 1642-1643, 1729, 2055.

Intl. Literacy Year — A207

Walt Disney characters in "The Prince and the Pauper": 5c, Pauper pals. 10c, Princely boredom. 15c, The valet. 25c, Look alikes. 60c, Trading places. 75c, How to be a prince. 80c, Food for the populace. $1, Captain's plot. $2, Doomed in the dungeon. $3, Looking for a way out. $4, A Goofy jailbreak. $5, Long live the real prince.

No. 1518, $6, Crowning the wrong guy. No. 1519, $6, Mickey meets the captain of the guard. No. 1520, $6, Real prince arrives. No. 1521, $6, Seize the guard.

**1991, Nov. 18 *Perf. 14x13½***

**1506-1517** A207 Set of 12 16.00 16.00

**Souvenir Sheets**

**1518-1521** A207 Set of 4 21.00 21.00

**1991, Nov. 18**

Walt Disney's "The Rescuers Down Under": 5c, Miss Bianca, Heroine. 10c, Bernard, Shy Hero. 15c, Maitre d'Francois. 25c, Wilbur, the Albatross. 60c, Jake, the Aussie kangaroo mouse. 75c, Bernard, Bianca and Jake in the outback. 80c, Bianca and Bernard. $1, Marahute, the magnificent rare eagle. $2, Cody and Marahute. $3, McLeach and his pet Goanna, Joanna. $4, Frank, the frill-necked lizard. $5, Endangered animals: Red Kangaroo, Krebbs Koala, and Polly Platypus.

No. 1534, $6, Cody with the rescuers. No. 1535, $6, Delegates of Intl. Rescue Aid Society. No. 1536, $6, Wilbur's painful touchdown

"down under." No. 1537, $6, Wilbur transports Miss Bianca and Bernard to Australia.

| | | | | |
|---|---|---|---|---|
| **1522-1533** | A207 | Set of 12 | 14.00 | 14.00 |

**Souvenir Sheets**

| | | | | |
|---|---|---|---|---|
| **1534-1537** | A207 | Set of 4 | 19.00 | 19.00 |

Brandenburg Gate, Bicent. — A209

Designs: 50c, Demonstrator with sign. 75c, Soldiers at Berlin Wall. 90c, German flag, shadows on wall. $1, Pres. Gorbachev and Pres. Bush shaking hands.

$4, Coat of Arms of Berlin.

**1991, Nov. 18 Litho. *Perf. 14***

| | | | | |
|---|---|---|---|---|
| **1538-1541** | A209 | Set of 4 | 4.00 | 4.00 |

**Souvenir Sheet**

| | | | | |
|---|---|---|---|---|
| **1542** | A209 | $4 multi | 4.00 | 4.00 |

Wolfgang Amadeus Mozart, Death Bicent. A210

Designs: $1, Scene from "Marriage of Figaro." $3, Scene from "The Clemency of Titus."

$4, Portrait of Mozart, vert.

**1991, Nov. 18**

| | | | | |
|---|---|---|---|---|
| **1543** | A210 | $1 multicolored | 1.10 | 1.10 |
| **1544** | A210 | $3 multicolored | 3.25 | 3.25 |

**Souvenir Sheet**

| | | | | |
|---|---|---|---|---|
| **1545** | A210 | $4 multicolored | 4.00 | 4.00 |

17th World Scout Jamboree, Korea — A211

Designs: 65c, Adventure tales around camp fire, vert. $1.50, British defenses at Mafeking, 1900, Cape of Good Hope #179. $3.50, Scouts scuba diving, queen angelfish.

**1991, Nov. 18 Litho. *Perf. 14***

| | | | | |
|---|---|---|---|---|
| **1546** | A211 | 65c multicolored | .45 | .45 |
| **1547** | A211 | $1.50 multicolored | 1.00 | 1.00 |
| **1548** | A211 | $3.50 multicolored | 2.50 | 2.50 |
| | | *Nos. 1546-1548 (3)* | 3.95 | 3.95 |

**Souvenir Sheet**

| | | | | |
|---|---|---|---|---|
| **1549** | A211 | $5 shown | 3.50 | 3.50 |

Charles de Gaulle, Birth Cent. A212

De Gaulle and: 10c, Free French Forces, 1944. 45c, Churchill, 1944. 75c, Liberation of Paris, 1944.

**1991, Nov. 18 Litho. *Perf. 14***

| | | | | |
|---|---|---|---|---|
| **1550** | A212 | 10c multicolored | .60 | .60 |
| **1551** | A212 | 45c multicolored | 1.00 | 1.00 |
| **1552** | A212 | 75c multicolored | 1.60 | 1.60 |
| | | *Nos. 1550-1552 (3)* | 3.20 | 3.20 |

**Souvenir Sheet**

| | | | | |
|---|---|---|---|---|
| **1553** | A212 | $5 Portrait | 3.50 | 3.50 |

Anniversaries and Events — A213

Designs: No. 1554, Woman, flag, map. No. 1555, Steam locomotive. $1.65, Otto Lilienthal, glider in flight. No. 1557, Gottfried Wilhelm Leibniz, mathematician. No. 1558, Street warfare.

**1991, Nov. 18**

| | | | | |
|---|---|---|---|---|
| **1554** | A213 | $1.50 multicolored | 3.00 | 3.00 |
| **1555** | A213 | $1.50 multicolored | 3.25 | 3.25 |
| **1556** | A213 | $1.65 multicolored | 3.75 | 3.75 |
| **1557** | A213 | $2 multicolored | 4.75 | 4.75 |
| **1558** | A213 | $2 multicolored | 4.25 | 4.25 |
| | | *Nos. 1554-1558 (5)* | 19.00 | 19.00 |

Swiss Confederation, 700th anniv. (#1554). Trans-Siberian Railway, 100th anniv. (#1555). First glider flight, cent. (#1556). City of Hanover, 750th anniv. (#1557). Fall of Kiev, Sept. 19, 1941 (#1558).

Heroes of Pearl Harbor — A214

No. 1559 — Congressional Medal of Honor recipients: a, Myrvyn S. Bennion. b, George H. Cannon. c, John W. Finn. d, Francis C. Flaherty. e, Samuel G. Fuqua. f, Edwin J. Hill. g, Herbert C. Jones. h, Isaac C. Kidd. i, Jackson C. Pharris. j, Thomas J. Reeves. k, Donald K. Ross. l, Robert R. Scott. m, Franklin Van Valkenburgh. n, James R. Ward. o, Cassin Young.

**1991, Nov. 18 *Perf. 14½x15***

| | | | | |
|---|---|---|---|---|
| **1559** | A214 | $1 Sheet of 15, #a-o | 19.00 | 19.00 |

Famous People — A215

No. 1560 — Golfers: a, Gary Player. b, Nick Faldo. c, Severiano Ballesteros. d, Ben Hogan. e, Jack Nicklaus. f, Greg Norman. g, Jose-Marie Olazabal. h, Bobby Jones.

No. 1561 — Statesmen and historical events: a, Hans-Dietrich Genscher, German Foreign Minister, winged victory symbol. b, Destruction of Berlin Wall. c, Charles de Gaulle delivering radio appeal, Winston Churchill, de Gaulle. d, Dwight D. Eisenhower, de Gaulle, Normandy invasion. e, Brandenburg Gate. f, German Chancellor Helmut Kohl, mayors of East, West Berlin. g, De Gaulle and Konrad Adenauer. h, George Washington and Lafayette, De Gaulle and John F. Kennedy.

No. 1562 — Chess masters: a, Francois Andre Danican Philidor. b, Adolph Anderssen. c, Wilhelm Steinitz. d, Alexander Alekhine. e, Boris Spassky. f, Bobby Fischer. g, Anatoly Karpov. h, Garri Kasparov.

No. 1563 — Nobel Prize winners: a, Einstein, physics. b, Roentgen, physics. c, William Shockley, physics. d, Charles Townes, physics. e, Lev Landau, physics. f, Marconi, physics. g, Willard Libby, chemistry. h, Ernest Lawrence, physics.

No. 1564 — Entertainers: a, Michael Jackson. b, Madonna. c, Elvis Presley. d, David Bowie. e, Prince. f, Frank Sinatra. g, George Michael. h, Mick Jagger.

No. 1565, Roosevelt, de Gaulle, Churchill at Morocco Conf., 1943. No. 1566, Madonna. No. 1567, Elvis Presley.

**1991, Nov. 25 Litho. *Perf. 14½***

| | | | | |
|---|---|---|---|---|
| **1560** | A215 | $1 Sheet of 8, #a.-h. | 15.50 | 15.50 |
| **1561** | A215 | $1 Sheet of 8, #a.-h. | 14.00 | 14.00 |
| **1562** | A215 | $1 Sheet of 8, #a.-h. | 11.50 | 11.50 |
| **1563** | A215 | $1 Sheet of 8, #a.-h. | 13.00 | 13.00 |
| **1564** | A215 | $2 Sheet of 8, #a.-h. | 17.50 | 17.50 |

**Souvenir Sheets**

***Perf. 14***

| | | | | |
|---|---|---|---|---|
| **1565** | A215 | $6 multicolored | 7.00 | 7.00 |
| **1566** | A215 | $6 multicolored | 5.50 | 5.50 |
| **1567** | A215 | $6 multicolored | 5.50 | 5.50 |

Nos. 1565-1567 each contain one 27x43mm stamp.

See Nos. 1642-1643, 1729-1730 for more Elvis Presley stamps.

Walt Disney Christmas Cards A216

Designs and year of issue: 10c, Goofy, Mickey and Pluto decorating Christmas tree, 1982. 45c, Mickey, reindeer, 1980. 55c, Christmas tree ornament, 1970. 75c, Baby duck holding 1944 sign, 1943. $1.50, Characters papering globe with greetings, 1941. $2, Lady and the Tramp beside Christmas tree, 1986. $4, Donald, Goofy, Mickey and Pluto reciting "Night Before Christmas," 1977. $5, Mickey in doorway of Snow White's Castle, 1965.

No. 1576, $6, People from around the world, 1966. No. 1577, $6, Mickey in balloon basket with people of different countries, 1966.

**1991, Dec. 23 *Perf. 13½x14***

| | | | | |
|---|---|---|---|---|
| **1568-1575** | A216 | Set of 8 | 14.00 | 14.00 |

**Souvenir Sheets**

| | | | | |
|---|---|---|---|---|
| **1576-1577** | A216 | Set of 2 | 14.50 | 14.50 |

Environmental Preservation — A217

**1992, Jan. Litho. *Perf. 14***

| | | | | |
|---|---|---|---|---|
| **1578** | A217 | 10c Kings Hill | .30 | .30 |
| **1579** | A217 | 55c Tree planting | .65 | .65 |
| **1580** | A217 | 75c Botanical Gardens | .95 | .95 |
| **1581** | A217 | $2 Kings Hill Project | 2.10 | 2.10 |
| | | *Nos. 1578-1581 (4)* | 4.00 | 4.00 |

## Queen Elizabeth II's Accession to the Throne, 40th Anniv.

**Common Design Type**

**1992, Feb. 6**

| | | | | |
|---|---|---|---|---|
| **1582** | CD348 | 10c multicolored | .25 | .25 |
| **1583** | CD348 | 20c multicolored | .25 | .25 |
| **1584** | CD348 | $1 multicolored | .65 | .65 |
| **1585** | CD348 | $5 multicolored | 3.25 | 3.25 |
| | | *Nos. 1582-1585 (4)* | 4.40 | 4.40 |

**Souvenir Sheets**

| | | | | |
|---|---|---|---|---|
| **1586** | CD348 | $6 Queen, beach | 5.00 | 5.00 |
| **1587** | CD348 | $6 Queen, harbor | 5.00 | 5.00 |

Queen Elizabeth II's Acession to the Throne, 40th Anniv. A217a

Designs: No. 1587A, Queen Elizabeth II. No. 1587B, King George VI.

**1993, Mar. 2 Embossed *Perf. 12***

**Without Gum**

| | | | |
|---|---|---|---|
| **1587A** | A217a | $5 gold | |
| **1587B** | A217a | $5 gold | |

1992 Winter Olympics, Albertville — A218

10c, Women's luge, horiz. 15c, Women's figure skating. 25c, Two-man bobsled, horiz. 30c, Mogul skiing. 45c, Nordic combined, horiz. 55c, Ski jump, horiz. 75c, Giant slalom, horiz. $1.50, Women's slalom. $5, Ice hockey, horiz. $8, Biathlon.

No. 1598, Downhill skiing. No. 1599, Speed skating.

**1992, Apr. 21 Litho. *Perf. 14***

| | | | | |
|---|---|---|---|---|
| **1588** | A218 | 10c multicolored | .25 | .25 |
| **1589** | A218 | 15c multicolored | .25 | .25 |
| **1590** | A218 | 25c multicolored | .25 | .25 |
| **1591** | A218 | 30c multicolored | .30 | .30 |
| **1592** | A218 | 45c multicolored | .40 | .40 |
| **1593** | A218 | 55c multicolored | .45 | .45 |
| **1594** | A218 | 75c multicolored | .65 | .65 |
| **1595** | A218 | $1.50 multicolored | 1.10 | 1.10 |
| **1596** | A218 | $5 multicolored | 4.00 | 4.00 |
| **1597** | A218 | $8 multicolored | 6.00 | 6.00 |
| | | *Nos. 1588-1597 (10)* | 13.65 | 13.65 |

**Souvenir Sheets**

| | | | | |
|---|---|---|---|---|
| **1598** | A218 | $6 multicolored | 6.75 | 6.75 |
| **1599** | A218 | $6 multicolored | 6.75 | 6.75 |

1992 Summer Olympics, Barcelona — A219

10c, Women's synchronized swimming duet, horiz. 15c, High jump. 25c, Small-bore rifle, horiz. 30c, 200-meter run. 45c, Judo. 55c. 200-meter freestyle swimming, horiz. 75c, Javelin. $1.50, Pursuit cycling. $5, Boxing. $8, Women's basketball. No. 1610, $15, Tennis. No. 1611, $15, Board sailing.

**1992, Apr. 21**

| | | | | |
|---|---|---|---|---|
| **1600-1609** | A219 | Set of 10 | 16.00 | 16.00 |

**Souvenir Sheets**

| | | | | |
|---|---|---|---|---|
| **1610-1611** | A219 | Set of 2 | 25.00 | 25.00 |

World Columbian Stamp Expo '92, Chicago — A220

Walt Disney characters visiting Chicago area landmarks: 10c, Mickey, Pluto at Picasso Sulpture. 50c, Mickey, Donald admiring Frank Lloyd Wright's Robie House. $1, Gus Gander at Calder Sculpture in Sears Tower. $5, Pluto in Buckingham Memorial Fountain.

$6, Mickey painting Minnie at Chicago Art Institute, vert.

**1992, Apr. Litho. *Perf. 14x13½***

| | | | | |
|---|---|---|---|---|
| **1612-1615** | A220 | Set of 4 | 7.00 | 7.00 |

**Souvenir Sheet**

***Perf. 13½x14***

| | | | | |
|---|---|---|---|---|
| **1616** | A220 | $6 multi | 6.25 | 6.25 |

Granada '92 — A221

Walt Disney characters from "The Three Little Pigs" in Spanish military uniforms: 15c, Big Bad Wolf as General of Spanish Moors. 40c, Pig as Captain of Spanish infantry. $2, Pig in Spanish armor, c. 1580. $4, Pig as Spaniard of rank, c. 1550.

$6, Little Pig resisting wolf from castle built of stone.

**1992, Apr. 28** *Perf. 13½x14*
**1622-1625** A221 Set of 4 7.00 7.00

**Souvenir Sheet**

**1626** A221 $6 multi 6.25 6.25

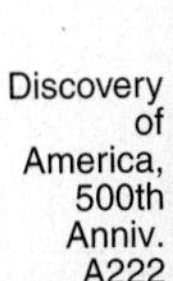

Discovery of America, 500th Anniv. A222

5c, Nina. 10c, Pinta. 45c, Santa Maria. 55c, Leaving Palos, Spain. $4, Columbus, vert. $5, Columbus' arms, vert.

No. 1638, Map, vert. No. 1639, Sailing ship, vert.

**1992, May 22** *Perf. 14*
**1632** A222 5c multicolored .35 .35
**1633** A222 10c multicolored .35 .35
**1634** A222 45c multicolored .60 .60
**1635** A222 55c multicolored .70 .70
**1636** A222 $4 multicolored 5.00 5.00
**1637** A222 $5 multicolored 6.00 6.00
*Nos. 1632-1637 (6)* 13.00 13.00

**Souvenir Sheet**

**1638** A222 $6 multicolored 6.50 6.50
**1639** A222 $6 multicolored 6.50 6.50

World Columbian Stamp Expo '92, Chicago. Nos. 1638-1639 contain one 42x57mm stamp.

Bonnie Blair, US Olympic Speed Skating Champion A223

No. 1641:a, Skating around corner. b, Portrait holding skates. c, On straightaway.

**1992, May 25** *Perf. 13½*
**1640** A223 $3 shown 4.00 4.00

**Souvenir Sheet**

**1641** A223 $2 Sheet of 3, #a.-c. 6.75 6.75

World Columbian Stamp Expo '92. No. 1641b is 48x60mm.

**Entertainers Type of 1991**
Miniature Sheet

Various portraits of Elvis Presley.

**1992, May 25** *Perf. 13½x14*
**1642** A206 $1 Sheet of 9, #a.-i. 12.50 12.50

**Souvenir Sheet**
*Perf. 14*

**1643** A206 $6 multicolored 9.50 9.50

No. 1643 contains one 28x43mm stamp. See Nos. 1729-1730.

Hummingbirds A224

Hummingbirds: 5c, Rufous-breasted hermit. 15c, Hispaniolan emerald. 45c, Green-throated carib. 55c, Jamaican mango. 65c, Vervain. 75c, Purple-throated carib. 90c, Green mango. $1, Bee. $2, Cuban emerald. $3, Puerto Rican emerald. $4, Antillean mango. $5, Streamertail.

No. 1656, Antillean crested. No. 1657, Bahama woodstar. No. 1658, Blue-headed.

**1992, June 15** *Perf. 14*
**1644** A224 5c multi .25 .25
**1645** A224 15c multi .25 .25
**1646** A224 45c multi .45 .35
**1647** A224 55c multi .55 .40
**1648** A224 65c multi .65 .50
**1649** A224 75c multi .75 .58
**1650** A224 90c multi .90 .70
**1651** A224 $1 multi 1.10 .80
**1652** A224 $2 multi 2.00 2.00
**1653** A224 $3 multi 2.50 2.50
**1654** A224 $4 multi 4.00 4.00
**1655** A224 $5 multi 5.00 5.00
*Nos. 1644-1655 (12)* 18.40 17.33

**Souvenir Sheets**

**1656** A224 $6 multi 6.00 6.00
**1657** A224 $6 multi 6.00 6.00
**1658** A224 $6 multi 6.00 6.00

Genoa '92 Intl. Philatelic Exhibition.

Butterflies A225

Designs: 5c, Dull astraptes, vert. 10c, White peacock. 35c, Tropic queen, vert. 45c, Polydamas swallowtail, vert. 55c, West Indian buckeye. 65c, Long-tailed skipper, vert. 75c, Tropical checkered skipper. $1, Crimson-banded black, vert. $2, Barred sulphur, vert. $3, Cassius blue. $4, Florida duskywing. $5, Malachite, vert.

No. 1671, $6, Cloudless giant sulphur, vert. No. 1672, $6, Julia. No. 1673, $6, Zebra longwing.

**1992, June 15** **Litho.** *Perf. 14*
**1659-1670** A225 Set of 12 21.00 21.00

**Souvenir Sheets**

**1671-1673** A225 Set of 3 18.00 18.00

Genoa '92.

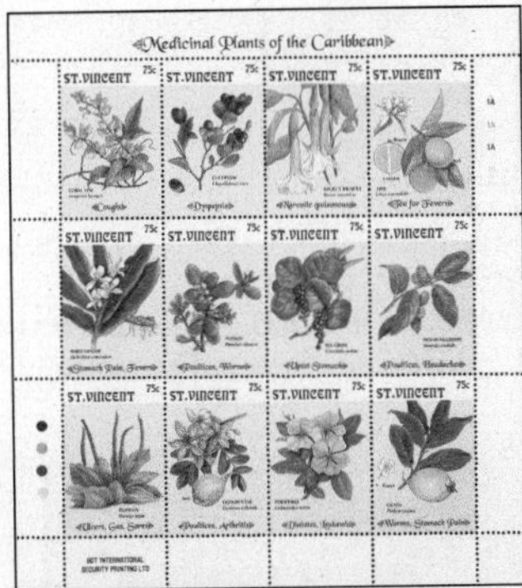


Medicinal plants — A226

No. 1674: a, Coral vine. b, Cocoplum. c, Angel's trumpet. d, Lime. e, White ginger. f, Pussley. g, Sea grape. h, Indian mulberry. i, Plantain. j, Lignum vitae. k, Periwinkle. l, Guava.

**1992, July 22** **Litho.** *Perf. 14*
**1674** A226 75c Sheet of 12, #a-l 14.00 14.00

**Souvenir Sheets**

**1675** A226 $6 Aloe 5.50 5.50
**1676** A226 $6 Clove tree 5.50 5.50
**1677** A226 $6 Wild sage 5.50 5.50

A227

Mushrooms: 10c, Collybia subpruinosa. 15c, Gerronema citrinum. 20c, Amanita antillana. 45c, Dermoloma atrobrunneum. 50c, Inopilus maculosus. 65c, Pulveroboletus brachyspermus. 75c, Mycena violacella. $1, Xerocomus brasiliensis. $2, Amanita ingrata. $3, Leptonia caeruleocaptata. $4, Limacella myochroa. $5, Inopilus magnificus.

No. 1690, $6, Limacella guttata. No. 1691, $6, Amanita agglutinata. No. 1692, $6, Trogia buccinalis.

**1992, July 2** **Litho.** *Perf. 14*
**1678-1689** A227 Set of 12 18.00 18.00

**Souvenir Sheets**

**1690-1692** A227 Set of 3 17.00 17.00

Baseball Players — A228

Designs: No. 1693, $4, Ty Cobb. No. 1694, $4, Dizzy Dean. No. 1695, $4, Bob Feller. No. 1696, $4, Whitey Ford. No. 1697, $4, Lou Gehrig. No. 1698, $4, Rogers Hornsby. No. 1699, $4, Mel Ott. No. 1700, $4, Satchel Paige. No. 1701, $4, Babe Ruth. No. 1702, $4, Casey Stengel. No. 1703, $4, Honus Wagner. No. 1704, $4, Cy Young.

**Self-Adhesive**
**Size: 64x89mm**

**1992, Aug. 5** **Litho.** *Imperf.*
**1693-1704** A228 Set of 12 40.00

Nos. 1693-1704 printed on thin card and distributed in boxed sets. To affix stamps, backing containing player's statistics must be removed.

1992 Albertville Winter Olympics Gold Medalists — A229

No. 1705: a, Alberto Tomba, Italy, giant slalom. b, Fabrice Guy, France, Nordic combined. c, Patrick Ortlieb, Austria, men's downhill. d, Vegard Ulvang, Norway, cross country. e, Edgar Grospiron, France, freestyle Mogul skiing. f, Kjetil-Andre Aamodt, Norway, super giant slalom. g, Viktor Petrenko, Russia, men's figure skating.

No. 1706: a, Kristi Yamaguchi, US, women's figure skating. b, Pernilla Wiberg, Sweden, women's giant slalom. c, Lyubov Yegorova, Unified Team, women's 10-kilometer cross country. d, Josef Polig, Italy, combined Alpine skiing. e, Finn Christian-Jagge, Norway, slalom. f, Kerrin Lee-Gartner, Canada, women's downhill. g, Steffania Belmondo, Italy, women's 30-kilometer cross country.

No. 1707, Alberto Tomba, diff. No. 1708, Kristi Yamaguchi, diff.

**1992, Aug. 10** **Litho.** *Perf. 14*
**1705** A229 $1 Sheet of 7, #a.-g. + label 8.00 8.00
**1706** A229 $1 Sheet of 7, #a.-g. + label 8.00 8.00

**Souvenir Sheets**

**1707** A229 $6 multicolored 6.25 6.25
**1708** A229 $6 multicolored 6.25 6.25

Discovery of America, 500th Anniv. — A230

**1992** **Litho.** *Perf. 14½*
**1709** A230 $1 Coming ashore 1.75 1.75
**1710** A230 $2 Natives, ships 3.25 3.25

Organization of East Caribbean States.

Opening of Euro Disney — A231

No. 1711 — Walt Disney movies: a, Pinocchio. b, Alice in Wonderland. c, Bambi. d, Cinderella. e, Snow White and the Seven Dwarfs. f, Peter Pan.

**1992** **Litho.** *Perf. 13*
**1711** A231 $1 Sheet of 6, #a.-f. 10.50 10.50

**Souvenir Sheet**
*Perf. 12½*

**1712** A231 $5 Mickey Mouse 8.75 8.75

Christmas A232

Details or entire paintings of The Nativity by: 10c, Hospitality Refused to the Virgin Mary and Joseph, by Jan Metsys. 40c, Albrecht Durer. 45c, The Nativity, by Geertgen Tot Sint Jans. 50c, The Nativity, by Tintoretto. 55c, Follower of Jan Joest Calcar. 65c, Workshop of Fra Angelico. 75c, Master of the Louvre Nativity. $1, Filippino Lippi. $2, Petrus Christus. $3, Edward Burne-Jones. $4, Giotto. $5, The Birth of Christ, by Domenico Ghirlandaio.

No. 1725, $6, Nativity, by Jean Fouquet. No. 1726, $6, Sandro Botticelli. No. 1727, $6, Gerard Horenbout.

**1992, Nov.** **Litho.** *Perf. 13½x14*
**1713-1724** A232 Set of 12 16.00 16.00

**Souvenir Sheets**

**1725-1727** A232 Set of 3 17.00 17.00

Souvenir Sheet

Jacob Javits Convention Center, NYC — A233

**1992, Oct. 28 Litho. *Perf. 14***

| | | | | |
|---|---|---|---|---|
| **1728** | A233 | $6 multicolored | 10.00 | 10.00 |

Postage Stamp Mega Event '92, NYC.

### Nos. 1642, 1564, 1567 Overprinted or with Additional Inscriptions

Designs: No. 1729, #1642 inscribed vertically "15th Anniversary."

No. 1729J, #1564 inscribed "15th Anniversary" and "Elvis Presley's Death / August 16, 1977."

No. 1730, #1567 overprinted in margin "15th Anniversary" and "Elvis Presley's Death / August 16, 1977."

**1992, Dec. 15 *Perf. 13½x14***

| | | | | |
|---|---|---|---|---|
| **1729** | A206 | $1 Sheet of 9, #a-i | 14.00 | 14.00 |
| | | ***Perf. 14½*** | | |
| **1729J** | A215 | $2 Sheet of 8, #k-r | 20.00 | 20.00 |

**Souvenir Sheet**

***Perf. 14***

| | | | | |
|---|---|---|---|---|
| **1730** | A215 | $6 multi | 13.50 | 13.50 |

Baseball Players — A234

**1992, Nov. 9 Litho. *Perf. 14***

| | | | | |
|---|---|---|---|---|
| **1731** | A234 | $5 Howard Johnson | 3.50 | 3.50 |
| **1732** | A234 | $5 Don Mattingly | 3.50 | 3.50 |

1992 Summer Olympics, Barcelona.

Members of Baseball Hall of Fame — A235

Player, year inducted: No. 1733, Roberto Clemente, 1973. No. 1734, Hank Aaron, 1982. No. 1735, Tom Seaver, 1992.

**1992, Dec. 21**

| | | | | |
|---|---|---|---|---|
| **1733** | A235 | $2 multicolored | 2.50 | 2.50 |
| **1734** | A235 | $2 multicolored | 2.50 | 2.50 |
| **1735** | A235 | $2 multicolored | 2.50 | 2.50 |
| | | *Nos. 1733-1735 (3)* | 7.50 | 7.50 |

Fishing Industry A236

**1992, Nov.**

| | | | | |
|---|---|---|---|---|
| **1736** | A236 | 5c Fishing with rods | .25 | .25 |
| **1737** | A236 | 10c Inside fishing complex | .25 | .25 |
| **1738** | A236 | 50c Landing the catch | .50 | .50 |
| **1739** | A236 | $5 Fishing with nets | 4.00 | 4.00 |
| | | *Nos. 1736-1739 (4)* | 5.00 | 5.00 |

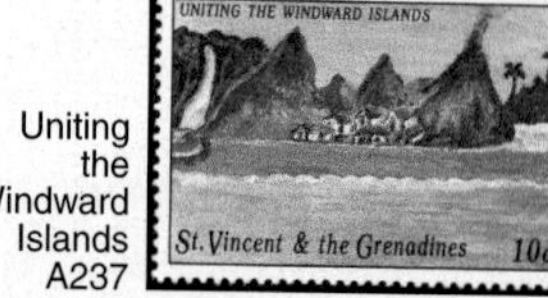


Uniting the Windward Islands A237

Children's paintings: 10c, Island coastline. 40c, Four people standing on islands. 45c, Four people standing on beach.

**1992, Nov. Litho. *Perf. 14***

| | | | | |
|---|---|---|---|---|
| **1740** | A237 | 10c multicolored | .60 | .25 |
| **1741** | A237 | 40c multicolored | .85 | .30 |
| **1742** | A237 | 45c multicolored | 1.00 | .35 |
| | | *Nos. 1740-1742 (3)* | 2.45 | .90 |

Miniature Sheets

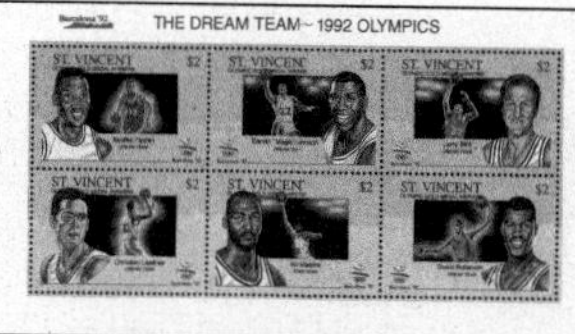


US Olympic Basketball "Dream Team" — A238

No. 1744: a, Scottie Pippen. b, Earvin "Magic" Johnson. c, Larry Bird. d, Christian Laettner. e, Karl Malone. f, David Robinson.

No. 1745: a, Michael Jordan. b, Charles Barkley. c, John Stockton. d, Chris Mullin. e, Clyde Drexler. f, Patrick Ewing.

**1992, Dec. 22 Litho. *Perf. 14***

| | | | | |
|---|---|---|---|---|
| **1744** | A238 | $2 Sheet of 6, #a.-f. | 8.50 | 8.50 |
| **1745** | A238 | $2 Sheet of 6, #a.-f. | 8.50 | 8.50 |

1992 Summer Olympics, Barcelona.

A239

A240

A241

A242

Anniversaries and Events: 10c, Globe and UN emblem. 45c, Zeppelin Viktoria Luise over Kiel Regatta, 1912, vert. 65c, Food products. No. 1749, America's Cup Trophy and Bill Koch, skipper of America 3. No. 1750, Konrad Adenauer, German flag. No. 1751, Adenauer, diff. No. 1752, Snow leopard. $1.50, Caribbean manatee. $2, Humpback whale. No. 1755, Adenauer, John F. Kennedy. No. 1756, Lions Intl. emblem, patient having eye exam. No. 1757, Space shuttle Discovery, vert. No. 1758, Adenauer, Pope John XXIII. $5, Michael Schumacher, race car. No. 1760, Count Zeppelin's first airship over Lake Constance, 1900. No. 1761, Gondola of Graf Zeppelin. No. 1762, Formula I race car. No. 1763, Sailing ship, steam packet. No. 1764, Adenauer at podium. No. 1765, Woolly spider monkey. No. 1765A, People waving to plane during Berlin airlift.

**1992-93 Litho. *Perf. 14***

| | | | | |
|---|---|---|---|---|
| **1746** | A239 | 10c multi | .25 | .25 |
| **1747** | A239 | 45c multi | 5.50 | 5.50 |
| **1748** | A242 | 65c multi | 1.50 | 1.50 |
| **1749** | A239 | 75c multi | 1.25 | 1.25 |
| **1750** | A239 | 75c multi | 8.00 | 8.00 |
| **1751** | A239 | $1 multi | 8.00 | 8.00 |
| **1752** | A239 | $1 multi | 7.50 | 7.50 |
| **1753** | A239 | $1.50 multi | 7.50 | 7.50 |
| **1754** | A239 | $2 multi | 7.50 | 7.50 |
| **1755** | A239 | $3 multi | 2.25 | 2.25 |
| **1756** | A239 | $3 multi | 4.50 | 4.50 |
| **1757** | A239 | $4 multi | 3.00 | 3.00 |
| **1758** | A239 | $4 multi | 3.00 | 3.00 |
| **1759** | A240 | $5 multi | 5.50 | 5.50 |
| **1760** | A239 | $6 multi | 5.50 | 5.50 |
| | | *Nos. 1746-1760 (15)* | 70.75 | 70.75 |

**Souvenir Sheets**

| | | | | |
|---|---|---|---|---|
| **1761** | A239 | $6 multi | 5.50 | 5.50 |
| **1762** | A240 | $6 multi | 5.50 | 5.50 |
| **1763** | A241 | $6 multi | 4.50 | 4.50 |
| **1764** | A239 | $6 multi | 4.50 | 4.50 |
| **1765** | A239 | $6 multi | 4.50 | 4.50 |
| **1765A** | A239 | $6 multi | 4.50 | 4.50 |

UN Intl. Space Year (#1746, 1757). Count Zeppelin, 75th anniv. of death (#1747, 1760-1761). Intl. Conference on Nutrition, Rome (#1748). America's Cup yacht race (#1749). Konrad Adenauer, 25th death anniv. (#1750-1751, 1755, 1758, 1764). Earth Summit, Rio de Janeiro (#1752-1754, 1765). Lions Intl., 75th anniv. (#1756). Belgian Grand Prix (#1759, 1762). Discovery of America, 500th anniv. (#1763). Konrad Adenauer, 75th death anniv. (#1765A).

Issued: #1747, 1759-1762, Dec; #1763, 10/28/92; #1746, 1749, 1750-1751, 1755-1758, 1764, Dec; #1752-1754, 1765, Dec. 15; #1765A, 6/30/93.

Care Bears Promote Conservation A243

Designs: 75c, Bear, stork. $2, Bear riding in hot air balloon, horiz.

**1992, Dec. Litho. *Perf. 14***

| | | | | |
|---|---|---|---|---|
| **1766** | A243 | 75c multicolored | 2.00 | 2.00 |

**Souvenir Sheet**

| | | | | |
|---|---|---|---|---|
| **1767** | A243 | $2 multicolored | 3.50 | 3.50 |

Elvis Presley (1935-77) — A244

No. 1767A: b, Portrait. c, With guitar. d, With microphone.

**1993 Litho. *Perf. 14***

| | | | | |
|---|---|---|---|---|
| **1767A** | A244 | $1 Strip of 3, #b.-d. | 2.75 | 2.75 |

Printed in sheets of 9 stamps.

Walt Disney's Beauty and the Beast — A245

Designs: 2c, Gaston. 3c, Belle and her father, Maurice. 5c, Lumiere, Mrs. Potts and Cogsworth. 10c, Philippe. 15c, Beast and Lumiere. 20c, Lumiere and Feather Duster.

No. 1774: a, Belle and Gaston. b, Maurice. c, The Beast. d, Mrs. Potts. e, Belle and the Enchanted Vase. f, Belle discovers an Enchanted Rose. g, Belle with wounded Beast. h, Belle. i, Household objects alarmed.

No. 1774J: k, Belle and Chip. l, Lumiere. m, Cogsworth. n, Armoire. o, Belle and Beast. p, Feather Duster. q, Footstool. r, Belle. All vert.

No. 1775, Belle reading, vert. No. 1776, Lumiere, diff., vert. No. 1776A, Lumiere, Mrs. Potts. No. 1776B, Belle, lake and castle, vert. No. 1776C, The Beast, vert.

***Perf. 14x13½, 13½x14***

**1992, Dec. 15 Litho.**

| | | | | |
|---|---|---|---|---|
| **1768** | A245 | 2c multicolored | .25 | .25 |
| **1769** | A245 | 3c multicolored | .25 | .25 |
| **1770** | A245 | 5c multicolored | .25 | .25 |
| **1771** | A245 | 10c multicolored | .25 | .25 |
| **1772** | A245 | 15c multicolored | .25 | .25 |
| **1773** | A245 | 20c multicolored | .25 | .25 |
| | | *Nos. 1768-1773 (6)* | 1.50 | 1.50 |

**Souvenir Sheets**

| | | | | |
|---|---|---|---|---|
| **1774** | A245 | 60c Sheet of 9, #a.-i. | 8.50 | 8.50 |
| **1774J** | A245 | 60c Sheet of 8, #k.-r. | 8.50 | 8.50 |

**Souvenir Sheets**

| | | | | |
|---|---|---|---|---|
| **1775** | A245 | $6 multicolored | 6.50 | 6.50 |
| **1776** | A245 | $6 multicolored | 6.50 | 6.50 |
| **1776A** | A245 | $6 multicolored | 6.50 | 6.50 |
| **1776B** | A245 | $6 multicolored | 6.50 | 6.50 |
| **1776C** | A245 | $6 multicolored | 6.50 | 6.50 |

Louvre Museum, Bicent. A246

No. 1777, $1 — Details or entire paintings by Jean-Auguste-Dominique Ingres: a, Louis-Francois Bertin. b, The Apotheosis of Homer. c, Joan of Arc. d, The Composer Cherubini with the Muse of Lyric Poetry. e, Mlle Caroline Riviere. f, Oedipus Answers the Sphinx's Riddle. g, Madame Marcotte. h, Mademoiselle Caroline Riviere.

No. 1778, $1 — Details or entire paintings by Jean Louis Andre Theodore Gericault (1791-1824): a, The Woman with Gambling Mania. b, Head of a White Horse. c, Wounded Cuirassier. d, An Officer of the Cavalry. e, The Vendean. f, The Raft of the Medusa. g-h, The Horse Market (left, right).

No. 1779, $1 — Details or entire paintings by Nicolas Poussin (1594-1665): a-b, The Arcadian Shepherds (left, right). c, Ecstasy of Paul. d-e, The Inspiration of the Poet (left, right). f-g, St. John Baptizing (left, right). h, The Miracle of St. Francis Xavier.

No. 1780, $1 — Details or entire paintings by Eustache Le Sueur (1616-1655): a-b, Melpomene, Erato & Polyhymnia (left, right). By Poussin: c, Christ and Woman Taken in Adultery. d, Spring. e, Autumn. f-h, The Plague of Ashdod (left, center, right).

No. 1781, $1: a, The Beggars, by Pieter Brueghel, the Elder (1520-1569). b, The Luncheon, by Francois Boucher (1703-1770). c, Louis Guene, Violin King, by Francois Dumont (1751-1831). d, The Virgin of Chancellor Rolin, by Jan Van Eyck. e, Conversation in the Park, by Thomas Gainsborough. f, Lady Alston, by Gainsborough. g, Mariana Waldstein, by Francisco de Goya. h, Ferdinand Guillemardet, by Goya.

No. 1782, $6, The Grand Odalisque, horiz. No. 1783, $6, The Dressing Room of Esther, by Theodore Chasseriau (1819-1856). No. 1784, $6, Liberty Guiding the People, by Eugene Delecroix (1798-1863), horiz.

**1993, Apr. 19 *Perf. 12x12½***

**Sheets of 8, #a-h, + Label**

| | | | | |
|---|---|---|---|---|
| **1777-1781** | A246 | Set of 5 | 34.00 | 34.00 |

**Souvenir Sheets**

***Perf. 14½***

| | | | | |
|---|---|---|---|---|
| **1782-1784** | A246 | Set of 3 | 18.50 | 18.50 |

Nos. 1783-1784 each contain a 55x88mm or 88x55mm stamp.

Paintings on Nos. 1777d and 1777h were switched.

A247

A247a

Scenes from Disney Animated Films — A247b

No. 1787 — Symphony Hour (1942): a, Maestro Mickey. b, Goofy plays a mean horn. c, On first bass with Clara Cluck. d, Stringing along with Clarabelle. e, Donald on drums. f, Clarabelle all fiddled out. g, Donald drumming up trouble. h, Goofy's sour notes. i, Mickey's moment.

No. 1788 — Clock Cleaners (1937): a, Goofy gets in gear. b, Donald on the main-spring. c, Donald in the works. d, Mickey's fine-feathered friend. e, Stork with bundle of joy. f, Father Time. g, Goofy, Mickey leaping upward. h, Donald, Goofy, Mickey out of gear. i, Donald, Goofy, Mickey with headaches.

No. 1789 — The Art of Skiing (1941): a, The ultimate back scratcher. b, Striking a pose. c, And we're off. d, Divided he stands. e, A real twister. f, Hangin' in there. g, Over the hill. h, At the peak of his form. i, Up a tree.

No. 1790 — Orphan's Benefit (1941): a, Mickey introduces Donald. b, Donald recites "Little Boy Blue." c, Orphan mischief. d, Clara Cluck, singing sensation. e, Goofy's debut with Clarabelle. f, Encore for Clara and Mickey. g, A Bronx cheer. h, Donald blows his stack. i, Donald's final bow.

No. 1791 — Thru the Mirror (1936): a, Mickey steps thru the looking glass. b, Mickey finds a tasty treat. c, Mickey's nutty effect. d, Hats off to Mickey. e, What a card, Mickey. f, Mickey dancing with the Queen Hearts. g, A real two-faced opponent. h, Mickey with a pen mightier than a sword. i, Mickey awake at last.

No. 1791J — The Small One: k, Morning comes in Nazareth. l, Good morning, small one. m, Too old to keep. n, Heatbroken. o, Nazareth markplace. p, Auction mockery. q, Off the auction block. r, Lonely and dejected. s, Happy and useful again.

No. 1792 — The Three Little Pigs (1933): a, Fifer Pig building house of straw. b, Fiddler Pig building house of sticks. c, Practical Pig building house of bricks. d, The Big Bad Wolf. e, Wolf scaring two lazy pigs. f, Wolf blowing down staw house. g, Wolf in sheep's clothing. h, Wolf blowing down twig house. i, Wolf huffs and puffs at brick house.

No. 1792J — How to Play Football (1944): k, Cheerleaders. l, Here comes the team. m, In the huddle. n, Who's got the ball? o, Who, me coach? p, Half-time pep talk. q, Another down, and out. r, Only a little injury. s, Up and at 'em.

No. 1793 — Rescue Rangers: a, Special agents. b, Chip 'n Dale, ready for action. c, Chip 'n Dale on stakeout. d, Gadget in gear. e, Gadget and Monterey Jack rescue Zipper. f, Zipper confers with Monterey Jack. g, Zipper zaps fat cat. h, Team work. i, Innovative Gadget.

No. 1793J — Darkwing Duck: k, Darkwing Duck. l, Launchpad McQuack. m, Gosalyn. n, Honker Muddlefoot. o, Tank Muddlefoot. p, Herb & Binkie Muddlefoot. q, Drake Mallard, aka Darkwing Duck. r, Darkwing Duck logo.

No. 1794, Bird's-eye-view of Goofy. No. 1795, Mickey and Macaroni enjoying applause.

No. 1796, On the edge of Goofyness. No. 1797, Gonged-out Goofy.

No. 1798, Film poster for Art of Skiing with Goofy slaloming down mountain. No. 1799, Goofy home in bed at last.

No. 1800, Caveman ballet. No. 1801, Mickey tickles the ivories.

No. 1802, Mickey's true reflection. No. 1803, Mickey hopping home.

No. 1804, Hard Work in Nazareth. No. 1805, Finding a buyer in Nazareth.

No. 1806, Animator's sketch of little pig and brick house. No. 1807, Little pigs playing and singing at piano, vert.

No. 1807A, Goofy demonstrating how to score touchdown. No. 1807B, Goofy shouting "Hooray for the team," vert.

No. 1807C, Gadget at controls of Ranger plane, vert. No. 1807D, Dale, vert.

No. 1807E, Quarterjack. No. 1807F, Darkwing Duck and Launchpad to the rescue in Ratcatcher.

***Perf. 14x13½, 13½x14***

**1992, Dec. 15 — Litho.**

| | | | | | |
|---|---|---|---|---|---|
| **1787** | A247 | 60c Sheet of 9, #a.-i. | | 8.50 | 8.50 |
| **1788** | A247 | 60c Sheet of 9, #a.-i. | | 8.50 | 8.50 |
| **1789** | A247 | 60c Sheet of 9, #a.-i. | | 8.50 | 8.50 |
| **1790** | A247 | 60c Sheet of 9, #a.-i. | | 8.50 | 8.50 |
| **1791** | A247 | 60c Sheet of 9, #a.-i. | | 8.50 | 8.50 |
| **1791J** | A247a | 60c Sheet of 9, #k.-s. | | 8.50 | 8.50 |
| **1792** | A247 | 60c Sheet of 9, #a.-i. | | 8.50 | 8.50 |
| **1792J** | A247 | 60c Sheet of 9, #k.-s. | | 8.50 | 8.50 |
| **1793** | A247a | 60c Sheet of 9, #a.-i. | | 8.50 | 8.50 |
| **1793J** | A247b | 60c Sheet of 8, #k.-r. | | 8.50 | 8.50 |

**Souvenir Sheets**

| | | | | | |
|---|---|---|---|---|---|
| **1794** | A247 | $6 | multicolored | 5.50 | 5.50 |
| **1795** | A247 | $6 | multicolored | 5.50 | 5.50 |
| **1796** | A247 | $6 | multicolored | 5.50 | 5.50 |
| **1797** | A247 | $6 | multicolored | 5.50 | 5.50 |
| **1798** | A247 | $6 | multicolored | 5.50 | 5.50 |
| **1799** | A247 | $6 | multicolored | 5.50 | 5.50 |
| **1800** | A247 | $6 | multicolored | 5.50 | 5.50 |
| **1801** | A247 | $6 | multicolored | 5.50 | 5.50 |
| **1802** | A247 | $6 | multicolored | 5.50 | 5.50 |
| **1803** | A247 | $6 | multicolored | 5.50 | 5.50 |
| **1804** | A247a | $6 | multicolored | 5.50 | 5.50 |
| **1805** | A247a | $6 | multicolored | 5.50 | 5.50 |
| **1806** | A247 | $6 | multicolored | 5.50 | 5.50 |
| **1807** | A247 | $6 | multicolored | 5.50 | 5.50 |
| **1807A** | A247 | $6 | multicolored | 5.50 | 5.50 |
| **1807B** | A247 | $6 | multicolored | 5.50 | 5.50 |
| **1807C** | A247a | $6 | multicolored | 5.50 | 5.50 |
| **1807D** | A247a | $6 | multicolored | 5.50 | 5.50 |
| **1807E** | A247b | $6 | multicolored | 5.50 | 5.50 |
| **1807F** | A247b | $6 | multicolored | 5.50 | 5.50 |

See Nos. 2144-2146 for 30c & $3 stamps.

Fish A248

5c, Sergeant major. 10c, Rainbow parrotfish. 55c, Hogfish. 75c, Porkfish. $1, Spotfin butterflyfish. $2, Trunkfish. $4, Queen triggerfish. $5, Queen angelfish.

No. 1816, Bigeye, vert. No. 1817, Smallmouth grunt, vert.

**1993, Apr. 1 — Litho. — *Perf. 14***

| | | | | | |
|---|---|---|---|---|---|
| **1808** | A248 | 5c | multicolored | .30 | .30 |
| **1809** | A248 | 10c | multicolored | .30 | .30 |
| **1810** | A248 | 55c | multicolored | .55 | .40 |
| **1811** | A248 | 75c | multicolored | .85 | .60 |
| **1812** | A248 | $1 | multicolored | 1.00 | .75 |
| **1813** | A248 | $2 | multicolored | 2.10 | 2.10 |
| **1814** | A248 | $4 | multicolored | 4.25 | 4.25 |
| **1815** | A248 | $5 | multicolored | 4.25 | 4.25 |
| | *Nos. 1808-1815 (8)* | | | 13.60 | 12.95 |

**Souvenir Sheets**

| | | | | | |
|---|---|---|---|---|---|
| **1816** | A248 | $6 | multicolored | 6.25 | 6.25 |
| **1817** | A248 | $6 | multicolored | 6.25 | 6.25 |

Birds — A249

Designs: 10c, Brown pelican. 25c, Red-necked grebe, horiz. 45c, Belted kingfisher, horiz. 55c, Yellow-bellied sapsucker. $1, Great blue heron. $2, Crab hawk, horiz. $4, Yellow warbler. $5, Northern oriole, horiz. No. 1826, White ibises, map, horiz. No. 1827, Blue-winged teal, map, horiz.

**1993, Apr. 1 — Litho. — *Perf. 14***

| | | | | |
|---|---|---|---|---|
| **1818-1825** | A249 | Set of 8 | 14.50 | 14.50 |

**Souvenir Sheets**

| | | | | |
|---|---|---|---|---|
| **1826-1827** | A249 | $6 Set of 2 | 15.00 | 15.00 |

Seashells — A250

Designs: 10c, Hexagonal murex. 15c, Caribbean vase. 30c, Measled cowrie. 45c, Dyson's keyhole limpet. 50c, Atlantic hairy triton. 65c, Orange-banded marginella. 75c, Bleeding tooth. $1, Pink conch. $2, Hawk-wing conch. $3, Music volute. $4, Alphabet cone. $5, Antillean cone.

No. 1840, $6, Flame auger, horiz. No. 1841, $6, Netted olive, horiz. No. 1842, $6, Wide-mouthed purpura, horiz.

**1993, May 24 — Litho. — *Perf. 14***

| | | | | |
|---|---|---|---|---|
| **1828-1839** | A250 | Set of 12 | 20.00 | 20.00 |

**Souvenir Sheets**

| | | | | |
|---|---|---|---|---|
| **1840-1842** | A250 | Set of 3 | 19.00 | 19.00 |

Yujiro Ishihara, Actor — A251

No. 1843 — Name in blue on 2 lines, country name on picture: a, $1, Wearing captain's hat. b, 55c, With tennis racquet. c, $1 Wearing suit. d, 55c, Holding camera. e, 55c, Wearing suit, diff. f, 55c. Wearing striped shirt, smoking. g, $1, Wearing blue shirt and vest. h, 55c, Wearing captain's hat, smoking. i, $1, Wearing pink shirt, smoking.

No. 1844 — Name in gold on one line, countrry name above picture: a, 55c Holding camera. b, $1 Wearing black suit and white tie. c, $2, Wearing white suit. d, $2, Holding guitar.

No. 1845 — Name in gold on one line, country name on picture: a, 55c Wearing captain's hat (like #1843a). b, $2, Wearing striped shirt. c, $1, Smiling. d, $2, Wearing captain's hat (like #1843h).

No. 1846 — Name in white: a, 55c, Wearing yellow suit. b, $2, Wearing yellow shirt. c, $4, Holding drink.

No. 1847 — Name in blue on 2 lines: a, 55c, Smoking, hand near face. b, $4, Smoking, wearing pink shirt. c, $4, Wearing blue shirt and vest (like #1843g).

**1993, May 24 — Litho. — *Perf. 13½x14***

| | | | | |
|---|---|---|---|---|
| **1843** | A251 | Sheet of 9, #a.-i. | 12.00 | 12.00 |

**Souvenir Sheets**

| | | | | |
|---|---|---|---|---|
| **1844** | A251 | Sheet of 4, #a.-d. | 6.00 | 6.00 |

**Stamp Size: 32x41mm**

***Perf. 14½***

| | | | | |
|---|---|---|---|---|
| **1845** | A251 | Sheet of 4, #a.-d. | 6.00 | 6.00 |

**Stamp Size: 60x41mm**

***Perf. 14x14½***

| | | | | |
|---|---|---|---|---|
| **1846** | A251 | Sheet of 3, #a.-c. | 7.00 | 7.00 |
| **1847** | A251 | Sheet of 3, #a.-c. | 9.25 | 9.25 |

Automobiles A252

Designs: $1, 1932 Ford V8, 1915 Ford Model T, Henry Ford's 1st car. $2, Benz 540K, 1928 Benz Stuttgart, 1908 Benz Racer. $3, 1911 Blitzen Benz, 1905 Benz Tourenwagen, 1894 Benz. $4, 1935 Ford, 1903 Ford A Runabout, 1913 Ford Model T Tourer. No. 1852, $6, Karl Benz. No. 1853, $6, Henry Ford.

**1993, May — Litho. — *Perf. 14***

| | | | | |
|---|---|---|---|---|
| **1848-1851** | A252 | Set of 4 | 10.00 | 10.00 |

**Souvenir Sheets**

| | | | | |
|---|---|---|---|---|
| **1852-1853** | A252 | Set of 2 | 11.00 | 11.00 |

First Ford motor, cent. (#1848, 1851, 1853). First Benz motor car, cent. (#1849-1850, 1852).

Coronation of Queen Elizabeth II, 40th Anniv. — A253

No. 1854: a, 45c, Official coronation photograph. b, 65c, Opening Parliament, 1980s. c, $2, Coronation ceremony, 1953. d, $4, Queen with her dog, 1970s.

No. 1855, Portrait of Queen as a child.

**1993, June 2 — Litho. — *Perf. 13½x14***

| | | | | |
|---|---|---|---|---|
| **1854** | A253 | Sheet, 2 ea #a.-d. | 13.00 | 13.00 |

**Souvenir Sheet**

***Perf. 14***

| | | | | |
|---|---|---|---|---|
| **1855** | A253 | $6 multicolored | 6.25 | 6.25 |

No. 1855 contains one 28x42mm stamp.

Moths — A254

10c, Erynnyis ello. 50c, Aellopos tantalus. 65c, Erynnyis alope. 75c, Manduca rustica. $1, Xylophanes pluto. $2, Hyles lineata. $4, Pseudosphinx tetrio. $5, Protambulyx strigilis.

No. 1864, Xylophanes tersa. No. 1864A, Utetheisa ornatrix.

**1993, June 14 — Litho. — *Perf. 14***

| | | | | | |
|---|---|---|---|---|---|
| **1856** | A254 | 10c | multicolored | .25 | .25 |
| **1857** | A254 | 50c | multicolored | .60 | .60 |
| **1858** | A254 | 65c | multicolored | .75 | .75 |
| **1859** | A254 | 75c | multicolored | .85 | .85 |
| **1860** | A254 | $1 | multicolored | 1.10 | 1.10 |
| **1861** | A254 | $2 | multicolored | 2.25 | 2.25 |
| **1862** | A254 | $4 | multicolored | 4.50 | 4.50 |
| **1863** | A254 | $5 | multicolored | 5.75 | 5.75 |
| | *Nos. 1856-1863 (8)* | | | 16.05 | 16.05 |

**Souvenir Sheets**

| | | | | | |
|---|---|---|---|---|---|
| **1864** | A254 | $6 | multicolored | 5.75 | 5.75 |
| **1864A** | A254 | $6 | multicolored | 5.75 | 5.75 |

A255

A256

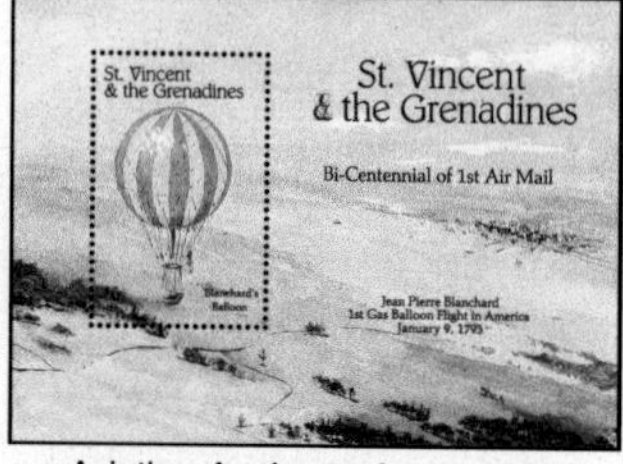

Aviation Anniversaries — A257

Designs: 50c, Supermarine Spitfire. #1866, Graf Zeppelin over Egypt, 1931, Hugo Eckener. #1867, Jean Pierre Blanchard, balloon, George Washington. #1868, De Havilland Mosquito. No. 1869, Eckener, Graf Zeppelin over New York, 1928. $3, Eckener, Graf Zeppelin over Tokyo, 1 929. $4, Philadelphia's Walnut State Prison, balloon lifting off.

No. 1872, Hawker Hurricane. No. 1873, Hugo Eckener, vert. No. 1874, Blanchard's Balloon, vert.

**1993, June** **Litho.** ***Perf. 14***

| | | | | | |
|---|---|---|---|---|---|
| **1865** | A255 | 50c | multi | .80 | .80 |
| **1866** | A256 | $1 | multi | 1.50 | 1.50 |
| **1867** | A257 | $1 | multi | 1.50 | 1.50 |
| **1868** | A255 | $2 | multi | 3.00 | 3.00 |
| **1869** | A256 | $2 | multi | 3.00 | 3.00 |
| **1870** | A256 | $3 | multi | 4.75 | 4.75 |
| **1871** | A257 | $4 | multi | 6.00 | 6.00 |
| | *Nos. 1865-1871 (7)* | | | 20.55 | 20.55 |

**Souvenir Sheets**

| | | | | | |
|---|---|---|---|---|---|
| **1872** | A255 | $6 | multi | 6.50 | 6.50 |
| **1873** | A256 | $6 | multi | 5.00 | 5.00 |
| **1874** | A257 | $6 | multi | 5.00 | 5.00 |

Royal Air Force, 75th anniv. (#1865, 1868, 1872). Dr. Hugo Eckener, 125th anniv. of birth (#1866, 1869-1870, 1873). First US balloon flight, bicent. (#1867, 1871). Tokyo spelled incorrectly on No. 1870.

Two values and a souvenir sheet commemorating the Wedding of Japan's Crown Prince Naruhito and Masako Owada were printed in 1993 but not accepted by the St. Vincent post office. Set value $5.75, Souvenir Sheet $6.

1994 Winter Olympics, Lillehammer, Norway — A259

Designs: 45c, Marc Girardelli, silver medalist, giant slalom, 1992. $5, Paul Accola, downhill, 1992. $6, Thommy Moe, downhill, 1992.

**1993, June 30** **Litho.** ***Perf. 14***

| | | | | | |
|---|---|---|---|---|---|
| **1878** | A259 | 45c | multicolored | .45 | .45 |
| **1879** | A259 | $5 | multicolored | 4.25 | 4.25 |

**Souvenir Sheet**

| | | | | | |
|---|---|---|---|---|---|
| **1880** | A259 | $6 | multicolored | 5.75 | 5.75 |

Picasso (1881-1973) — A260

Paintings: 45c, Massacre in Korea, 1951. $1, Family of Saltimbanques, 1905. $4, La Joie de Vivre, 1946. $6, Woman Eating a Melon and Boy Writing, 1965, vert.

**1993, June 30**

| | | | | | |
|---|---|---|---|---|---|
| **1881** | A260 | 45c | multicolored | .50 | .50 |
| **1882** | A260 | $1 | multicolored | 1.00 | 1.00 |
| **1883** | A260 | $4 | multicolored | 4.00 | 4.00 |
| | *Nos. 1881-1883 (3)* | | | 5.50 | 5.50 |

**Souvenir Sheet**

| | | | | | |
|---|---|---|---|---|---|
| **1884** | A260 | $6 | multicolored | 6.00 | 6.00 |

Willy Brandt (1913-1992), German Chancellor — A261

Designs: 45c, Brandt, Richard Nixon, 1971. $5, Brandt, Robert Kennedy, 1967. $6, Brandt at signing of "Common Declaration," 1973.

**1993, June 30**

| | | | | | |
|---|---|---|---|---|---|
| **1885** | A261 | 45c | multicolored | .50 | .50 |
| **1886** | A261 | $5 | multicolored | 5.00 | 5.00 |

**Souvenir Sheet**

| | | | | | |
|---|---|---|---|---|---|
| **1887** | A261 | $6 | multicolored | 6.00 | 6.00 |

A262

Copernicus: 45c, Astronomical instrument. $4, Space shuttle lift-off. $6, Copernicus.

**1993, June 30**

| | | | | | |
|---|---|---|---|---|---|
| **1888** | A262 | 45c | multicolored | .60 | .60 |
| **1889** | A262 | $4 | multicolored | 5.00 | 5.00 |

**Souvenir Sheet**

| | | | | | |
|---|---|---|---|---|---|
| **1890** | A262 | $6 | multicolored | 6.00 | 6.00 |

A263

European Royalty: 45c, Johannes, Gloria Thurn & Taxis. 65c, Thurn & Taxis family, horiz. $1, Princess Stephanie of Monaco. $2, Gloria Thurn & Taxis.

**1993, June 30**

| | | | |
|---|---|---|---|
| **1891-1894** | A263 | Set of 4 | 3.00 3.00 |

Inauguration of Pres. William J. Clinton — A264

Designs: $5, Bill Clinton, children. $6, Clinton wearing cowboy hat, vert.

**1993, June 30**

| | | | | | |
|---|---|---|---|---|---|
| **1895** | A264 | $5 | multicolored | 5.50 | 5.50 |

**Souvenir Sheet**

| | | | | | |
|---|---|---|---|---|---|
| **1896** | A264 | $6 | multicolored | 6.00 | 6.00 |

Polska '93 A265

No. 1897, Bogusz Church, Gozlin.

No. 1898: a, $1, Deux Tetes (Man), by S.I. Witkiewicz, 1920, vert. b, $3, Deux Tetes (Woman), vert.

No. 1899, Dancing, by Wladyslaw Roguski, vert.

**1993, June 30**

| | | | | | |
|---|---|---|---|---|---|
| **1897** | A265 | $6 | multicolored | 5.25 | 5.25 |
| **1898** | A265 | | Pair, #a.-b. | 3.50 | 3.50 |

**Souvenir Sheet**

| | | | | | |
|---|---|---|---|---|---|
| **1899** | A265 | $6 | multicolored | 6.00 | 6.00 |

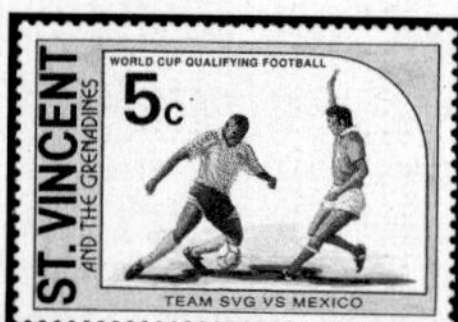

1994 World Cup Soccer Qualifying A266

St. Vincent vs: 5c, Mexico. 10c, Honduras. 65c, Costa Rica. $5, St. Vincent goalkeeper.

**1993, Sept. 2**

| | | | |
|---|---|---|---|
| **1900-1903** | A266 | Set of 4 | 6.75 6.75 |

Cooperation with Japan — A267

Designs: 10c, Fish delivery van. 50c, Fish aggregation device, vert. 75c, Trawler. $5, Fish complex.

**1993, Sept. 2**

| | | | |
|---|---|---|---|
| **1904-1907** | A267 | Set of 4 | 7.00 7.00 |

Pope John Paul II's Visit to Denver, CO A268

Design: $6, Pope, Denver skyline, diff.

**1993, Aug. 13**

| | | | | | |
|---|---|---|---|---|---|
| **1908** | A268 | $1 | multicolored | 1.50 | 1.50 |

**Souvenir Sheet**

| | | | | | |
|---|---|---|---|---|---|
| **1909** | A268 | $6 | multicolored | 7.00 | 7.00 |

No. 1908 issued in sheets of 9.

Miniature Sheet

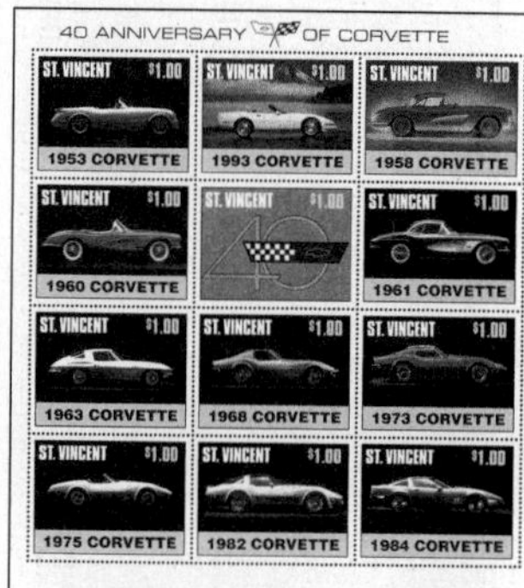

Corvette, 40th Anniv. — A269

No. 1910 — Corvettes: a, 1953. b, 1993, c, 1958, d, 1960. e, "40," Corvette emblem (no car). f, 1961. g, 1963. h, 1968, i, 1973. j, 1975. k, 1982. l, 1984.

**1993, Aug. 13** ***Perf. 14x13½***

| | | | | | |
|---|---|---|---|---|---|
| **1910** | A269 | $1 | Sheet of 12, #a.-l. | 12.50 | 12.50 |

Taipei '93 — A270

Designs: 5c, Yellow Crane Mansion, Wuchang. 10c, Front gate, Chung Cheng Ceremonial Arch, Taiwan. 20c, Marble Peifang, Ming 13 Tombs, Beijing. 45c, Jinxing Den, Beijing. 55c, Forbidden City, Beijing. 75c, Tachih, the Martyrs' Shrine, Taiwan. No. 1917, Praying Hall, Xinjiang, Gaochang. No. 1918, Chih Kan Tower, Taiwan. $2, Taihu Lake, Jiangsu. $4, Chengde, Hebei, Pula Si. No. 1921, Kaohsiung, Cheng Ching Lake, Taiwan. No. 1922, Great Wall.

No. 1923 — Chinese paintings: a, Street in Macao, China, by George Chinnery. b, Pair of Birds on Cherry Branch. c, Yellow Dragon Cave, by Patrick Procktor. d, Great Wall of China, by William Simpson. e, Dutch Folly Fort Off Conton, by Chinnery. f, Forbidden City, by Procktor.

No. 1924 — Chinese silk paintings: a, Rhododendron. b, Irises and bees. c, Easter lily. d, Poinsettia. e, Peach and cherry blossoms. f, Weeping cherry and yellow bird.

No. 1925 — Chinese kites: a, Dragon and tiger fighting. b, Two immortals. c, Five boys playing round a general. d, Zheng Chenggong. e, Nezha stirs up the sea. f, Immortal maiden He.

No. 1926, Giant Buddha, Longmen Caves, Luoyang, Hunan. No. 1927, Guardian and Celestial King, Longmen Caves, Hunan, vert. No. 1928, Giant Buddha, Yungang Caves, Datong, Shanxi, vert.

**1993, Aug. 16** **Litho.** ***Perf. 14x13½***

| | | | | | |
|---|---|---|---|---|---|
| **1911-1922** | A270 | | Set of 12 | 15.00 | 15.00 |
| **1923** | A270 | $1.50 | Sheet of 6, #a.-f. | 6.75 | 6.75 |
| **1924** | A270 | $1.50 | Sheet of 6, #a.-f. | 6.75 | 6.75 |
| **1925** | A270 | $1.50 | Sheet of 6, #a.-f. | 6.75 | 6.75 |

**Souvenir Sheets**

| | | | | | |
|---|---|---|---|---|---|
| **1926** | A270 | $6 | multicolored | 6.00 | 6.00 |

***Perf. 13½x14***

| | | | | | |
|---|---|---|---|---|---|
| **1927** | A270 | $6 | multicolored | 6.00 | 6.00 |
| **1928** | A270 | $6 | multicolored | 6.00 | 6.00 |

No. 1925e issued missing "St." in country name. Some sheets of No. 1925 may have been withdrawn from sale after discovery of the error.

**With Bangkok '93 Emblem**

Designs: 5c, Phra Nakhon Khiri (Rama V's Palace), vert. 10c, Grand Palace, Bangkok. 20c, Rama IX Park, Bangkok. 45c, Phra Prang Sam Yot, Lop Buri. 55c, Dusit Maha Prasad, vert. 75c, Phimai Khmer architecture, Pak Tong Chai. No. 1935, Burmese style Chedi, Mae Hong Son. No. 1936, Antechamber, Central Prang, Prasat Hin Phimai. $2, Brick chedi on laterite base, Si Thep, vert. $4, Isan's Phanom Rung, Korat, vert. No. 1939, Phu Khao

Thong, the Golden Mount, Bangkok. No. 1940, Islands, Ang Thong.

No. 1941 — Thai Buddha sculpture: a, Interior of Wat Hua Kuang Lampang, vert. b, Wat Yai Suwannaram, vert. c, Phra Buddha Sihing, City Hall Chapel, vert. d, Wat Ko Keo Suttharam, vert. e, U Thong B image, Wat Ratburana crypt, vert. f, Sri Sakyamuni Wat Suthat, vert.

No. 1942: a-f: Various details from Mural at Buddhaisawan Chapel.

No. 1943 — Thai painting: a, Untitled, by Arunothai Somsakul. b, Mural at Wat Rajapradit. c, Mural at Wat Phumin (detail). d, Serenity, by Surasit Souakong. e, Scenes of early Bangkok mural (detail). f, Ramayana.

No. 1944, Roof detail of Dusit Mahaprasad, vert. No. 1945, Standing Buddha, Hua Hin, vert. No. 1946, Masked dance.

***Perf. 13½x14, 14x13½***

**1993, Aug. 16** **Litho.**

**1929-1940** A270 5c Set of 12 14.50 14.50
**1941** A270 $1.50 Sheet of 6, #a.-f. 6.50 6.50
**1942** A270 $1.50 Sheet of 6, #a.-f. 6.50 6.50
**1943** A270 $1.50 Sheet of 6, #a.-f. 6.50 6.50

**Souvenir Sheets**

**1944** A270 $6 multicolored 6.00 6.00
**1945** A270 $6 multicolored 6.00 6.00
**1946** A270 $6 multicolored 6.00 6.00

**With Indopex '93 Emblem**

Indopex '93 emblem with designs: 5c, Local landmark, Gedung Sate, 1920. 10c, Masjid Jamik Mosque, Sumenep. 20c, Bromo Caldera, seen from Penanjakan. 45c, Kudus Mosque, Java. 55c, Kampung Naga. 75c, Lower level of Borobudur. No. 1953, Dieng Temple, Dieng Plateau. No. 1954, Temple 1, Gedung Songo group, Semarang. $2, Istana Bogor, 1856. $4, Taman Sari complex, Yogyakarta. No. 1957, $5, Landscape near Mt. Sumbing, Central Java. No. 1958, $5, King Adityawarman's Palace, Batusangar.

No. 1959 — Paintings: a, Female Coolies, by Djoko Pekik. b, Family Outing, by Sudjana Kerton. c, My Family, by Pekik. d, Javanese Dancers, by Arthur Melville. e, Leisure Time, by Kerton. f, In the Garden of Eden, by Agus Djaja.

No. 1960: a, Tayubon, by Pekik. b, Three Dancers, by Nyoman Gunarsa. c, Nursing Neighbor's Baby, by Hendra Gunawan. d, Imagining within a Dialogue, by Sagito. e, Three Balinese Mask Dancers, by Anton H. f, Three Prostitutes, by Gunawan.

No. 1961 — Masks: a, Hanuman. b, Subali/Sugnwa. c, Kumbakarna. d, Sangut. e, Jatayu. f, Rawana.

No. 1962, Relief of Sudamala story, Mt. Lawu. No. 1963, Plaque, 9th Cent., Banyumas, Central Java. No. 1964, Panel from Ramayana reliefs, vert.

**1993, Aug. 16** **Litho.** ***Perf. 14x13½***

**1947-1958** A270 Set of 12 14.50 14.50
**1959** A270 $1.50 Sheet of 6, #a.-f. 6.50 6.50
**1960** A270 $1.50 Sheet of 6, #a.-f. 6.50 6.50
**1961** A270 $1.50 Sheet of 6, #a.-f. 6.50 6.50

**Souvenir Sheets**

**1962** A270 $6 multicolored 6.00 6.00
**1963** A270 $6 multicolored 6.00 6.00

***Perf. 13½x14***

**1964** A270 $6 multicolored 6.00 6.00

Reggie Jackson, Selection to Baseball Hall of Fame — A271

**1993, Oct. 4** ***Perf. 14***

**1965** A271 $2 multicolored 2.00 2.00

Christmas A272

Details or entire woodcut, The Adoration of the Magi, by Durer: 10c, 35c, 40c, $5.

Details or entire paintings by Rubens: 50c, Holy Family with Saint Francis. 55c, 65c, Adoration of the Shepherds. $1, Holy Family.

No. 1974, $6, The Adoration of the Magi, by Durer, horiz. No. 1975, $6, Holy Family with St. Elizabeth & St. John, by Rubens.

***Perf. 13½x14, 14x13½***

**1993, Nov. 18**

**1966-1973** A272 Set of 8 9.00 9.00

**Souvenir Sheets**

**1974-1975** A272 Set of 2 17.50 17.50

Legends of Country Music — A273

No. 1976 — Various portraits of: a, f, l, Roy Acuff. b, g, j, Patsy Cline. c, h, i, Jim Reeves. d, e, k, Hank Williams, Sr.

**1994, Jan. 17** **Litho.** ***Perf. 13½x14***

**1976** A273 $1 Sheet of 12, #a.-l. 12.00 12.00

Mickey's Portrait Gallery A274

Mickey Mouse as: 5c, Aviator. 10c, Foreign Legionnaire. 15c, Frontiersman. 20c, Best Pals, Mickey, Goofy, Donald. 35c, Horace, Clarabelle. 50c, Minnie, Frankie, Figuro. 75c, Donald, Pluto today. 80c, Party boy Mickey. 85c, Best Friends, Minnie, Daisy. 95c, Mickey's Girl, Minnie. $1, Cool forties Mickey. $1.50, Mickey, "Howdy!", 1950. $2, Totally Mickey. $3, Minnie, Mickey. $4, Congratulations Mickey, birthday cake. $5, Uncle Sam.

No. 1993, $6, Donald Duck, early photo of Mickey, horiz. No. 1994, $6, Minnie disco dancing, horiz. No. 1995, $6, Mickey photographing nephews, horiz. No. 1996, $6, Pluto, Mickey looking at wall of photos.

**1994, May 5** **Litho.** ***Perf. 13½x14***

**1977-1992** A274 Set of 16 24.00 24.00

**Souvenir Sheets**

***Perf. 14x13½***

**1993-1996** A274 Set of 4 28.00 28.00

Breadfruit — A275

10c, Planting. 45c, Captain Bligh, plant. 65c, Fruit sliced. $5, Fruit on branch.

**1994, Jan.** **Litho.** ***Perf. 13½x14***

**1997** A275 10c multicolored .25 .25
**1998** A275 45c multicolored .70 .70
**1999** A275 65c multicolored .60 .60
**2000** A275 $5 multicolored 5.00 5.00
*Nos. 1997-2000 (4)* 6.55 6.55

Intl. Year of the Family — A276

10c, Outing. 50c, Praying in church. 65c, Working in garden. 75c, Jogging. $1, Portrait. $2, Running on beach.

**1994, Jan.** ***Perf. 14x13½, 13½x14***

**2001** A276 10c multicolored .25 .25
**2002** A276 50c multicolored .50 .50
**2003** A276 65c multicolored .65 .65
**2004** A276 75c multicolored .70 .70
**2005** A276 $1 multicolored 1.05 1.05
**2006** A276 $2 multicolored 2.10 2.10
*Nos. 2001-2006 (6)* 5.25 5.25

Nos. 2001-2004, 2006 are horiz.

Library Service, Cent. A277

**1994, Jan.** ***Perf. 14x13½***

**2007** A277 5c Mobile library .25 .25
**2008** A277 10c Old public library .25 .25
**2009** A277 $1 Family education .85 .85
**2010** A277 $1 Younger, older men .85 .85
*Nos. 2007-2010 (4)* 2.20 2.20

Barbra Streisand, 1993 MGM Grand Garden Concert — A278

A278a

**1994, Jan.**

**2011** A278 $2 multicolored 1.60 1.60

**Embossed**

***Perf. 12***

**2011A** A278a $20 gold 25.00 25.00

No. 2011 issued in sheets of 9.

A279

A280

A281

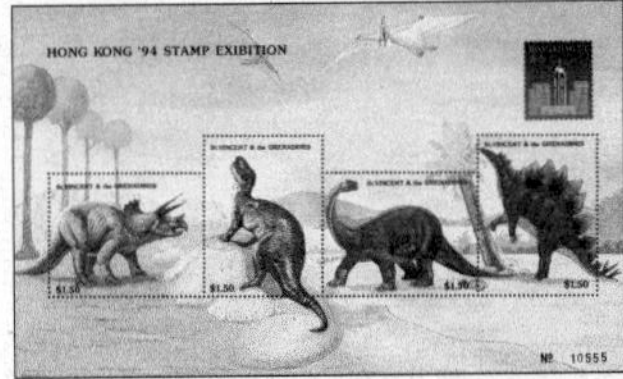


Hong Kong '94 — A282

No. 2012 — Stamps, 19th cent. painting of Hong Kong Harbor: a, Hong Kong #626, ship under sail. b, Ship at anchor, #1548.

No. 2013 — Porcelain ware, Qing Dynasty: a, Bowl with bamboo & sparrows. b, Bowl with flowers of four seasons. c, Bowl with lotus pool & dragon. d, Bowl with landscape. e, Shar-Pei puppies in bowl (not antiquity). f, Covered bowl with dragon & pearls.

No. 2014 — Chinese dragon boat races: a, Dragon boats. b, Tapestry of dragon races. c, Dragon race. d, Dragon boats, diff. e, Chinese crested dog. f, Dragon boats, 4 banners above boats.

No. 2015 — Chinese junks: a, Junk, Hong Kong Island. b, Junk with white sails in harbor. c, Junk with inscription on stern, Hong Kong Island. d, Junk KLN B/G. e, Chow dog, junk. f, Junk with red, white sails, Hong Kong Island.

No. 2016 — Chinese seed stitch purses: a, Vases, fruit on pink purse. b, Peonies, butterfles. c, Vase, fruit on dark blue purse. d, Vases, fruit on light blue purse. e, Fu-dog. f, Flowers.

No. 2017 — Chineses pottery: a, Plate, bird on flowering spray, Qianlong. b, Large dish, Kangxi. c, Egshell plate, cocks on rocky ground, Yongzheng. d, Gladen dish decorated with Qilin curicorn, Yuan. e, Porcelain pug dog. f, Dish with Dutch ship, Uryburg, Qianlong.

No. 2018, vert. — Ceramic figures, Qing Dynasty: a, Waterdropper. b, Two women playing chess. c, Liu-Hai. d, Laughing twins. e, Seated hound. f, Louhan (Ma Ming).

No. 2019, Dr. Sun Yat-sen. No. 2020, Chiang Kai-shek.

No. 2021 — Dinosaurs: a, Triceratops. b, Unidentified, vert. c, Apatosaurus (d). d, Stegosaurus, vert.

**1994, Feb. 18** ***Perf. 14***

**2012** A279 40c Pair, #a.-b. .85 .85
**2013** A280 40c Sheet of 6, #a.-f. 2.25 2.25
**2014** A280 40c Sheet of 6, #a.-f. 2.25 2.25
**2015** A280 45c Sheet of 6, #a.-f. 2.40 2.40
**2016** A280 45c Sheet of 6, #a.-f. 2.40 2.40

2017 A281 50c Sheet of 6, #a.-f. 2.75 2.75

***Perf. 13***

2018 A280 50c Sheet of 6, #a.-f. 4.00 4.00

**Souvenir Sheets**

2019 A281 $2 multicolored 1.50 1.50
2020 A281 $2 multicolored 1.50 1.50
2021 A282 $1.50 Sheet of 4, #a.-d. 4.50 4.50

No. 2012 issued in sheets of 10 stamps and has a continuous design.

Portions of the design on No. 2021 have been applied by a thermographic process producing a shiny, raised effect.

New Year 1994 (Year of the Dog) (#2013e, 2014e, 2015e, 2016e, 2017e, 2018e). Hong Kong '94 (#2018, 2021).

Miniature Sheet

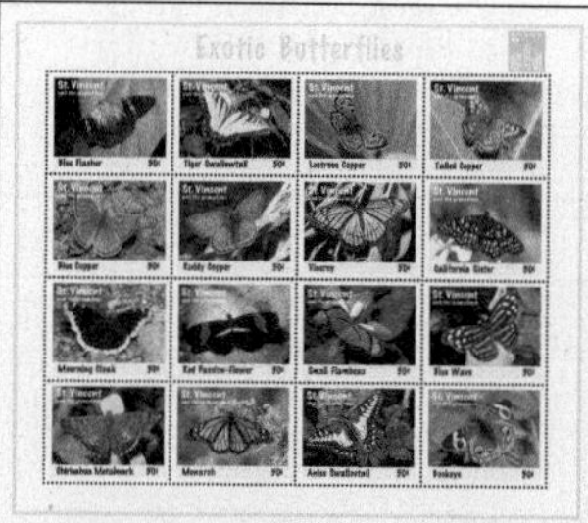


Hong Kong '94 — A283

No. 2022 — Butterflies: a, Blue flasher. b, Tiger swallowtail. c, Lustrous copper. d, Tailed copper. e, Blue copper. f, Ruddy copper. g, Viceroy. h, California sister. i, Mourning cloak. j, Red passion flower. k, Small flambeau. l, Blue wave. m, Chiricahua metalmark. n, Monarch. o, Anise swallowtail. p, Buckeye.

**1994, Feb. 18 Litho. *Perf. 14½***

2022 A283 50c Sheet of 16, #a.-p. 14.50 14.50

Juventus Soccer Team — A284

Players: No. 2023, $1, Causio. No. 2024, $1, Tardelli. No. 2025, $1, Rossi. No. 2026, $1, Bettega. No. 2027, $1, Platini, Baggio. No. 2028, $1, Cabrini. No. 2029, $1, Scirea. No. 2030, $1, Furino. No. 2031, $1, Kohler. No. 2032, $1, Zoff. No. 2033, $1, Gentile.

$6, Three European Cups won by team, horiz.

**1994, Mar. 22 Litho. *Perf. 14***

2023-2033 A284 Set of 11 12.00 12.00

**Souvenir Sheet**

2034 A284 $6 multicolored 6.00 6.00

Orchids — A285

Designs: 10c, Epidendrum ibaguense. 25c, Ionopsis utricularioides. 50c, Brassavola cucullata. 65c, Enclyclia cochleata. $1, Liparis nervosa. $2, Vanilla phaeantha. $4, Elleanthus cephalotus. $5, Isochilus linearis.

No. 2043, $6, Rodriguezia lanceolata. No. 2044, $6, Eulophia alta.

**1994, Apr. 6 Litho. *Perf. 14***

2035-2042 A285 Set of 8 18.50 18.50

**Souvenir Sheets**

2043-2044 A285 Set of 2 16.00 16.00

A286

Dinosaurs — A287

No. 2045: a, Protoavis (e). b, Pteranodon. c, Quetzalcoatlus (b). d, Lesothosaurus (a, c, e-h). e, Hetrodontosaurus. f, Archaeopteryx (b, e). g, Cearadactylus (f). h, Anchisaurus.

No. 2046: a, Dimorphodon (e). b, Camarasaurus (e, f). c, Spinosaurus (b). d, Allosaurus (a-c, e-h). e, Rhamphorhynchus (a). f, Pteranodon (b). g, Eudimorphodon (c). h, Ornithomimus.

No. 2047, 75c: a, Dimorphodon (b). b, Pterodactylus (a). c, Rhamphorhynchus (b). d, Pteranodon. e, Gallimimus. f, Stegosaurus. g, Acanthopholis. h, Trachodon (g). i, Thecodonti (j). j, Ankylosaurus (i). k, Compsognathus. l, Protoceratops.

No. 2048, 75c: a, Hesperonis. b, Mesosaurus. c, Plesiosaurus. d, Squalicorax (a). e, Tylosaurus (d, g). f, Plesiosoar. g, Stenopterygius ichthyosaurus (j). h, Stenosaurus (f). i, Eurhinosaurus longirostris (e, f, h, l). j, Cryptocleidus oxoniensis. k, Caturus (h, i, j, l). l, Protostega (k).

No. 2049, 75c: a, Quetzalcoatlus. b, Diplodocus (a). c, Spinosaurus (f, g). d, Apatosaurus (c). e, Ornitholestes. f, Lesothosaurus (e). g, Trachodon. h, Protoavis. i, Oviraptor. j, Coelophysis (i). k, Ornitholestes (j). l, Archaeopteryx.

No. 2050, 75c, horiz: a, Albertosaurus. b, Chasmosaurus (c). c, Brachiosaurus. d, Coelophysis (e). e, Deinonychus (d). f, Anatosaurus. g, Iguanodon. h, Baryonyx. i, Steneosaurus. j, Nanotyrannus. k, Camptosaurus (j). l, Camarasaurus.

No. 2051, Tyrannosaurus rex.

No. 2052, $6, Triceratops, horiz. No. 2053, $6, Pteranodon, diplodocus carnegii, horiz. No. 2054, $6, Styracosaurus.

**1994, Apr. 20 Litho. *Perf. 14***

2045 A286 75c Sheet of 8, #a.-h. 7.50 7.50
2046 A286 75c Sheet of 8, #a.-h. 7.50 7.50

**Sheets of 12, #a-l**

2047-2050 A287 Set of 4 37.50 37.50

**Souvenir Sheets**

2051 A286 $6 multi 7.00 7.00
2052-2054 A287 Set of 3 21.00 21.00

No. 2048 is horiz.

**Entertainers Type of 1991**

Miniature Sheet

Various portraits of Marilyn Monroe.

**1994, May 16 *Perf. 13½***

2055 A206 $1 Sheet of 9, #a.-i. 10.00 10.00

1994 World Cup Soccer Championships, US — A288

Team photos: No. 2056, 50c, Colombia. No. 2057, 50c, Romania. No. 2058, 50c, Switzerland. No. 2059, 50c, US. No. 2060, 50c, Brazil. No. 2061, 50c, Cameroon. No. 2062, 50c, Russia. No. 2063, 50c, Sweden. No. 2064, 50c, Bolivia. No. 2065, 50c, Germany. No. 2066, 50c, South Korea. No. 2067, 50c, Spain. No. 2068, 50c, Argentina. No. 2069, 50c, Bulgaria. No. 2070, 50c, Greece. No. 2071, 50c, Nigeria. No. 2072, 50c, Ireland. No. 2073, 50c, Italy. No. 2074, 50c, Mexico. No. 2075, 50c, Norway. No. 2076, 50c, Belgium. No. 2077, 50c, Holland. No. 2078, 50c, Morocco. No. 2079, 50c, Saudi Arabia.

**1994 *Perf. 13½***

2056-2079 A288 Set of 24 14.00 14.00

First Manned Moon Landing, 25th Anniv. — A289

No. 2080, $1 — Famous men, aviation & space scenes: a, Fred L. Whipple, Halley's Comet. b, Robert G. Gilruth, Gemini 12. c, George E. Mueller, Ed White walking in space during Gemini 4. d, Charles A. Berry, Johnsville Centrifuge. e, Christopher C. Kraft, Jr., Apollo 4 re-entry. f, James A. Van Allen, Explorer I, Van Allen Radiation Belts. g, Robert H. Goddard, Goddard Liquid Fuel Rocket, 1926. h, James E. Webb, Spirit of '76 flight. i, Rocco A. Petrone, Apollo 8 coming home.

No. 2081, $1: a, Walter R. Dornberger, missile launch, 1942. b, Alexander Lippisch, Wolfgang Spate's ME-163B. c, Kurt H. Debus, A4b Launch, 1945. d, Hermann Oberth, Oberth's Spaceship, 1923. e, Hanna Reitsch, Reichenberg (type 2) Piloted Bomb. f, Ernst Stuhlinger, Explorer I, 2nd stage ignition. g, Werner von Braun, Rocket Powered He112. h, Arthur Rudolph, Rudolph Rocket Motor, 1934. i, Willy Ley, Rocket Airplane, Greenwood Lake NY.

No. 2082, $6, Holger N. Toftoy. No. 2083, $6, Eberhard Rees.

**1994, July 12 *Perf. 14***

**Sheets of 9, #a-i**

2080-2081 A289 Set of 2 20.00 20.00

**Souvenir Sheets**

2082-2083 A289 Set of 2 13.00 13.00

Nos. 2082-2083 each contain one 50x38mm stamp.

D-Day, 50th Anniv. A290

Designs: 40c, Supply armada. $5, Beached cargo ship unloads supplies.

$6, Liberty ship.

**1994, July 19 Litho. *Perf. 14***

2084 A290 40c multicolored .40 .40
2085 A290 $5 multicolored 4.75 4.75

**Souvenir Sheet**

2086 A290 $6 multicolored 5.25 5.25

New Year 1994 (Year of the Dog) — A291

Designs: 10c, Yorkshire terrier. 25c, Yorkshire terrier, diff. 50c, Golden retriever. 65c, Bernese mountain dog. $1, Vorstehhund. $2, Tibetan terrier. $4, West highland terrier. $5, Shih tzu.

No. 2095: a, Pomeranian. b, English springer spaniel. c, Bearded collie. d, Irish wolfhound. e, Pekingese. f, Irish setter. g, Old English sheepdog. h, Basset hound. i, Cavalier King Charles spaniel. j, Kleiner munsterlander. k, Shetland sheepdog. l, Dachshund.

No. 2096, $6, Afghan hound. No. 2097, $6, German shepherd.

**1994, July 21**

2087-2094 A291 Set of 8 10.00 10.00
2095 A291 50c Sheet of 12, #a.-l. 4.50 4.50

**Souvenir Sheets**

2096-2097 A291 Set of 2 9.00 9.00

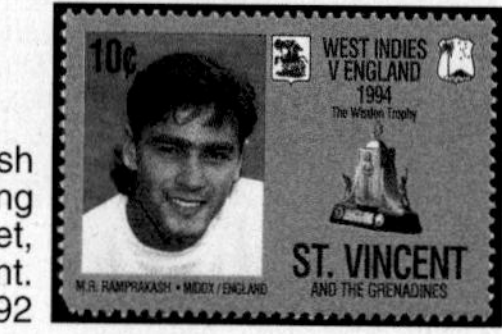


English Touring Cricket, Cent. A292

Designs: 10c, M. R. Ramprakash, England. 30c, P. V. Simmons, West Indies. $2, Sir. G. St. A. Sobers, West Indies, vert.

$3, Firsh English team, 1895.

**1994, July 25**

2098-2100 A292 Set of 3 3.50 3.50

**Souvenir Sheet**

2101 A293 $3 multicolored 3.25 3.25

A293

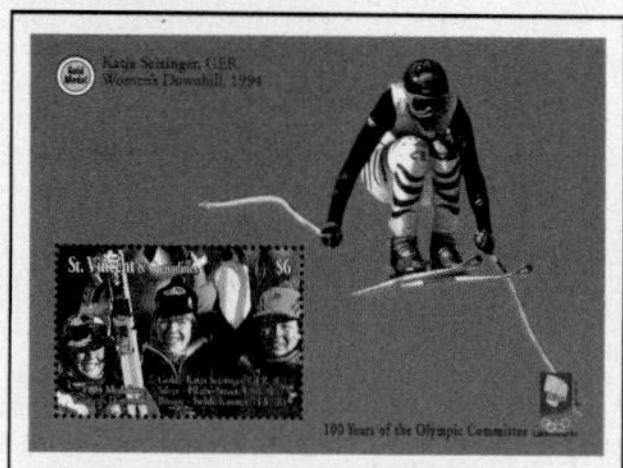

Intl. Olympic Committee, Cent. — A294

Designs: 45c, Peter Frenkel, German Democratic Republic, 20k walk, 1972. 50c, Kijung Son, Japan, marathon, 1936. 75c, Jesse Owens, US, 100-, 200-meters, 1936. $1, Greg Louganis, US, diving, 1984, 1988.

$6, Katja Seizinger, Germany, Picabo Street, US, Isolde Kastner, Italy, women's downhill, 1994.

**1994, July 25**

2102-2105 A293 Set of 4 3.25 3.25

**Souvenir Sheet**

2106 A294 $6 multicolored 6.00 6.00

A295

PHILAKOREA '94 — A296

Designs: 10c, Oryon Waterfall. 45c, Outside P'yongyang Indoor Sports Stadium, horiz. 65c, Pombong, Ch'onhwadae. 75c, Uisangdae, Naksansa. $1, Buddha of the Sokkuram Grotto, Kyangju, horiz. $2, Moksogwon, horiz.

No. 2113, 50c: a-h, Various letter pictures, eight panel screen, 18th cent. Choson Dynasty.

No. 2114, 50c — Letter pictures, 19th cent. Choson Dynasty: a, Fish. b, Birds. c-d, h, Various bookshelf pictures. e-g, Various designs from six-panel screen.

No. 2115, $4, Hunting scene, embroidery on silk, Choson Dynasty, horiz. No. 2116, $4, Chongdong Mirukbul.

**1994, July 25** *Perf. 14*

2107-2112 A295 Set of 6 8.50 8.50

**Sheets of 8, #a-h**

*Perf. 13½*

2113-2114 A296 Set of 2 13.50 13.50

**Souvenir Sheets**

*Perf. 14*

2115-2116 A295 Set of 2 7.00 7.00

Star Trek, The Next Generation, 7th Anniv. — A297

A297a

No. 2117: a, Capt. Picard. b, Cmdr. Riker. c, Lt. Cmdr. Data. d, Lt. Worf. e, Cast members. f, Dr. Crusher. g, Lt. Yar, Lt. Worf. h, Q. i, Counselor Troi.

$10, Cast members, horiz.

$20, Starship Enterprise, Capt. Picard.

**1994 Litho.** *Perf. 14x13½*

2117 A297 $2 Sheet of 9, #a.-i. 15.00 15.00

**Souvenir Sheet**

*Perf. 14x14½*

2118 A297 $10 multicolored 9.50 9.50

**Litho. & Embossed**

*Perf. 9*

2118A A297a $20 gold & multi 25.00 25.00

Issued: Nos. 2117-2118, 6/27; No. 2118, May. No. 2117e exists in sheets of 9. No. 2118 contains one 60x40mm stamp.

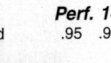

Intl. Year of the Family A298

**1994** *Perf. 14*

2119 A298 75c multicolored .95 .95

Order of the Caribbean Community — A299

First award recipients: $1, Sir Shridath Ramphal, statesman, Guyana, vert. $2, Derek Walcott, writer, St. Lucia, vert. $5, William Demas, economist, Trinidad and Tobago.

**1994, Sept. 1**

2120-2122 A299 Set of 3 8.00 8.00

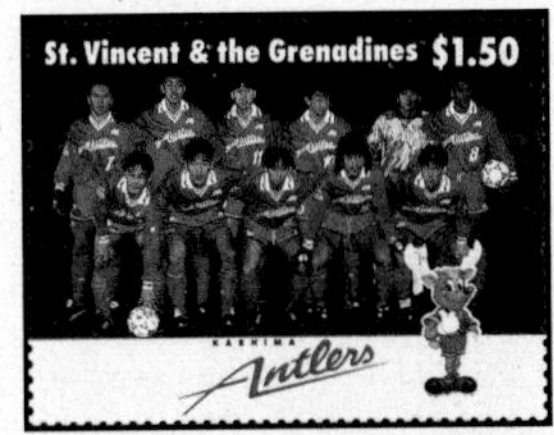

Japanese Soccer — A300

No. 2123: a, Kashima Antlers. b, JEF United. c, Red Diamonds. d, Verdy Yomiuri. e, Nissan FC Yokohama Marinos. f, AS Flugels. g, Bellmare. h, Shimizu S-pulse. i, Jubilo Iwata. j, Nagoya Grampus Eight. k, Panasonic Gamba Osaka. l, Sanfrecce Hiroshima FC.

No. 2124 — Jubilo Iwata, action scenes: a, c-d, 55c. b, e, $1.50. f, $3, Team picture.

No. 2125 — Red Diamonds, action scenes: a, c-d, 55c. b, e, $1.50. f, $3, Team pictue.

No. 2126 — Nissan FC Yokohama Marinos, action scenes: a, c-d, 55c. b, e, $1.50. f, $3, Team picture.

No. 2127 — Verdy Yomiuri, action scenes: a, c-d, 55c. b, e, $1.50. f, $3, Team picture.

No. 2128 — Nagoya Grampus eight, action scenes: a, c-d, 55c. b, e, $1.50. f, $3, Team picture.

No. 2129 — Kashima Antlers, action scenes: a, c-d, 55c. b, e, $1.50. f, $3, Team picture.

No. 2130 — JEF United, action scenes: a, c-d, 55c. b, e, $1.50. f, $3, Team picture.

No. 2131 — AS Flugels, action scenes: a, c-d, 55c. b, e, $1.50. f, $3, Team picture.

No. 2132 — Bellmare, action scenes: a, c-d, 55c. b, e, $1.50. f, $3, Team picture.

No. 2133 — Sanfrecce Hiroshima FC, action scenes: a, c-d, 55c. b, e, $1.50. f, $3, Team picture.

No. 2134 — Shimizu S-pulse, action scenes: a, c-d, 55c. b, e, $1.50. f, $3, Team picture.

No. 2135 — Panasonic Gamba Isajam, action scenes: a, c-d, 55c. b, e, $1.50. f, $3, Team picture.

No. 2136, vert. — League All-Stars: a, $1.50, League emblem. b, 55c, Shigetatsu Matsunaga. c, 55c, Masami Ihara. d, $1.50, Takumi Horiike. e, 55c, Shunzoh Ohno. f, 55c, Luiz Carlos Pereira. g, 55c, Tetsuji Hashiratani. h, 55c, Carlos Alberto Souza Dos Santos. i, $1.50, Rui Ramos. j, 55c, Yasuto Honda. k, 55c, Kazuyoshi Miura. l, $1.50, Ramon Angel Diaz.

**1994, July 1** *Perf. 14x13½*

2123 A300 $1.50 Sheet of 12, #a.-l. 11.00 11.00

**Sheets of 6, #a-f**

2124-2135 A300 Set of 12 70.00 70.00

*Perf. 13½x14*

2136 A300 Sheet of 12, #a.-l. 12.00 12.00

Christmas A301

Illustrations from Book of Hours, by Jean de Berry: 10c, The Annunciation, angel kneeling. 45c, The Visitation. 50c, The Nativity, Madonna seeing infant. 65c, The Purification of the Virgin. 75c, Presentation of Jesus in the Temple. $5, Flight into Egypt.

$6, Adoration of the Magi.

**1994 Litho.** *Perf. 13½x14*

2137-2142 A301 Set of 6 9.50 9.50

**Souvenir Sheet**

2143 A301 $6 multicolored 7.50 7.50

**Disney Type of 1992 Redrawn With New Denominations and Added Inscriptions**

Designs: No. 2144, Like #1792. No. 2145, Like #1806. No. 2146, Like #1807.

**1995, Jan. 24** *Perf. 14x13½*

2144 A247 30c Sheet of 9, #a.-i. 6.25 6.25

**Souvenir Sheets**

2145 A247 $3 multi 4.25 4.25
2146 A247 $3 multi 4.25 4.25

Nos. 2144-2146 are inscribed with emblem for "New Year 1995, Year of the Pig."

ICAO, 50th Anniv. A302

Designs: 10c, Bequia Airport. 65c, Union Island. 75c, Liat 8-100, E.T. Joshua Airport. No. 2150, $1, Airplanes, ICAO emblem. No. 2151, $1, J.F. Mitchell Airport, Bequia.

**1994, Dec. 1 Litho.** *Perf. 14*

2147-2151 A302 Set of 5 4.25 4.25

Cats A303

Parrots — A304

No. 2152 — Cats: a, Snowshoe. b, Abyssinian. c, Ocicat. d, Tiffany (e, h). e, Russian blue. f, Siamese. g, Bi-color. h, Malayan. i, Manx.

No. 2153 — Parrots: a, Mealy Amazon. b, Nanday conure. c, Black-headed caique. d, Scarlet macaw (g). e, Red-masked conure. f, Blue-headed parrot. g, Hyacinth macaw. h, Sun conure. i, Blue & yellow macaw.

No. 2154, White-eared conure. No. 2155, Birman.

**1995, Apr. 25 Litho.** *Perf. 14*

**Sheets of 9, #a-i**

2152-2153 A303 $1 Set of 2 18.00 18.00

**Souvenir Sheets**

2154 A304 $5 multicolored 6.00 6.00
2155 A304 $6 multicolored 7.25 7.25

A305

Birds A306

No. 2156 — World Wildlife Fund, masked booby: a, One standing. b, Two birds. c, One nesting. d, One stretching wings.

No. 2157: a, Greater egret. b, Roseate spoonbill. c, Ring-billed gull. d, Ruddy quail-dove. e, Royal tern. f, Killdeer. g, Osprey. h, Frigatebird. i, Masked booby. j, Green-backed heron. k, Cormorant. l, Brown pelican.

No. 2158, Flamingo, vert. No. 2159, Purple gallinule, vert.

**1995, May 2**

2156 A305 75c Strip of 4, #a.-d. 4.00 4.00
2157 A306 75c Sheet of 12, #a.-l. 12.00 12.00

**Souvenir Sheets**

2158 A306 $5 multicolored 5.00 5.00
2159 A306 $6 multicolored 6.00 6.00

No. 2156 is a continuous design and was issued in sheets of 3.

VE Day, 50th Anniv. A307

No. 2159A: b, Douglas Devastator. c, Doolittle's B25 leads raid on Tokyo. d, Curtis Helldiver. e, USS Yorktown. f, USS Wasp. g, USS Lexington sinks.

No. 2160: a, US First Army nears the Rhine. b, Last V2 rocket fired at London, Mar. 1945. c, 8th Air Force B24 Liberators devastate industrial Germany. d, French Army advances on Strasbourg. e, Gloster Meteor, first jet aircraft to enter squadron service. f, Berlin burns from both air and ground bombardments. g, Soviet tanks on Unter Den Linden near Brandenburg Gate. h, European war is won.

No. 2161, $6, Pilot in cockpit of Allied bomber.

No. 2161A, $6, Ships in Pacific, sunset.

**1995, May 8 Litho.** *Perf. 14*

2159A A307 $2 Sheet of 6, #b.-g. + label 11.50 11.50
2160 A307 $2 Sheet of 8, #a.-h. + label 15.50 15.50

**Souvenir Sheets**

2161-2161A A307 Set of 2 15.00 15.00

No. 2161 contains one 57x43mm stamp.

UN, 50th Anniv. — A308

No. 2162: a, Globe, dove. b, Lady Liberty. c, UN Headquarters.
$6, Child.

**1995, May 5**

**2162** A308 $2 Strip of 3, #a.-c. 5.25 5.25

**Souvenir Sheet**

**2163** A308 $6 multicolored 5.25 5.25

No. 2162 is a continuous design and was issued in miniature sheets of 3.

18th World Scout Jamboree, Netherlands A309

Designs: $1, Natl. Scout flag. $4, Lord Baden Powell. $5, Scout handshake.
No. 2167, $6, Scout sign. No. 2168, $6, Scout salute.

**1995, May 5**

**2164-2166** A309 Set of 3 8.75 8.75

**Souvenir Sheets**

**2167-2168** A309 Set of 2 11.50 11.50

Yalta Conference, 50th Anniv. A310

Design: $50, like #2169.

**1995, May 8 Litho. *Perf. 14***

**2169** A310 $1 shown 1.75 1.75

**Litho. & Embossed**

***Perf. 9***

**2169A** A310 $50 gold & multi *27.50 27.50*

No. 2169 was issued in sheets of 9.

New Year 1995 (Year of the Boar) — A311

No. 2170 — Stylized boars: a, blue green & multi. b, brown & multi. c, red & multi.
$2, Two boars, horiz.

**1995, May 8**

**2170** A311 75c Strip of 3, #a.-c. 2.50 2.50

**Souvenir Sheet**

**2171** A311 $2 multicolored 2.50 2.50

No. 2170 was issued in sheets of 3.

FAO, 50th Anniv. — A312

No. 2172: a, Girl holding plate, woman with bowl. b, Stirring pot of food. c, Working in fields of grain.
$6, Infant.

**1995, May 8**

**2172** A312 $2 Strip of 3, #a.-c. 5.25 5.25

**Souvenir Sheet**

**2173** A312 $6 multicolored 5.25 5.25

No. 2172 is a continuous design and was issued in sheets of 3.

Rotary Intl., 90th Anniv. A313

Designs: $5, Paul Harris, Rotary emblem.
$6, St. Vincent flag, Rotary emblem.

**1995, May 8**

**2174** A313 $5 multicolored 4.50 4.50

**Souvenir Sheet**

**2175** A313 $6 multicolored 5.25 5.25

Queen Mother, 95th Birthday — A314

No. 2176: a, Drawing, b, Wearing blue hat. c, Formal portrait. d, Wearing lavender outfit.
$6, Wearing crown jewels, yellow dress.

**1995, May 8 *Perf. 13½x14***

**2176** A314 $1.50 Block or strip of 4, #a.-d. 5.25 5.25

**Souvenir Sheet**

**2177** A314 $6 multicolored 5.25 5.25

No. 2176 was issued in sheet of 2 blocks or strips.

In 2002, sheets of Nos. 2176 and 2177 were overprinted "In Memoriam — 1900-2002" in margin.

Miniature Sheets

Marine Life A315

No. 2178, vert: a, Humpback whale (b, d, e, f, i). b, Green turtle (c). c, Bottlenosed dolphin (f). d, Monk seal (e). e, Krill. f, Blue shark. g, Striped pork fish. h, Chaelodon sedentarius (e, g). i, Ship wreck, bottom of sea.
No. 2179: a, Pomacentrus leucostictus (b). b, Pomacanthus arcuatus (d). c, Microspathodon chrysurus (d). d, Chaetodon capistratus.
No. 2180, $6, Physalia physalis, vert. No. 2181, $6, Sea anemones, vert.

**1995, May 23 *Perf. 14***

**2178** A315 90c Sheet of 9, #a.-i. 7.50 7.50

**2179** A315 $1 Sheet of 4, #a.-d. 5.00 5.00

**Souvenir Sheets**

**2180-2181** A315 Set of 2 13.00 13.00

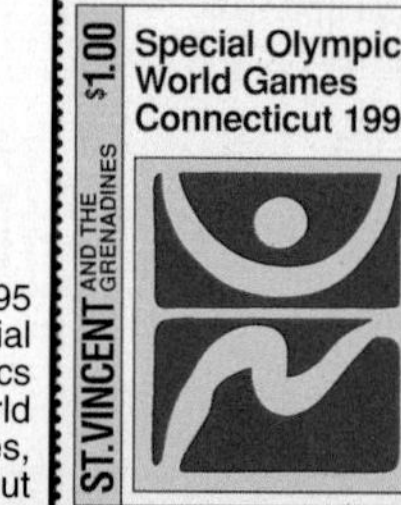

1995 Special Olympics World Games, Connecticut A316

A316a

**1995, July 6**

**2182** A316 $1 blk, yel & bl 1.10 1.10

**Embossed**

***Perf. 9***

**2182A** A316a $20 gold

No. 2182 issued in sheets of 9.

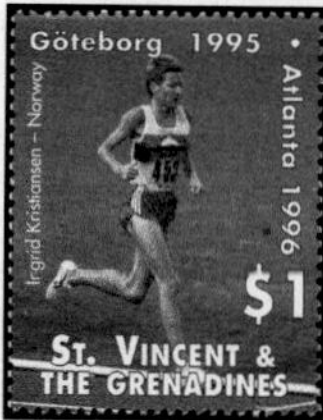

1995 IAAF World Track & Field Championships, Gothenburg & 1996 Summer Olympics, Atlanta — A317

No. 2183: a, Ingrid Kristiansen, Norway. b, Trine Hattestad, Norway. c, Grete Waitz, Norway. d, Vebjorn Rodal, Norway. e, Geir Moen, Norway. f, Steinar Hoen, Norway, horiz.

**1995, July 31 Litho. *Perf. 14***

**2183** A317 $1 Sheet of 6, #a.-f. 4.50 4.50

A318

Designs: 15c, Breast, bowl of food, horiz. 20c, Expressing milk, cup, spoon. 90c, Drawing of mother breastfeeding child, by Picasso. $5, Mother, child, olive wreath.

**1995, Aug. 4**

**2184-2187** A318 Set of 4 6.75 6.75

WHO, UNICEF Baby Friendly Program.

A319

Designs: 10c, Leeward Coast, horiz. 15c, Feeder roads project, horiz. 25c, Anthurium andraeanum, horiz. 50c, Coconut palm. 65c, Housing scene, Fairhall, horiz.

**1995, Aug. 8**

**2188-2192** A319 Set of 5 1.90 1.90

Caribbean Development Bank, 25th anniv.

Fudo Myoou (God of Fire), Woodprint, by Shunichi Kadowaki — A320

**1995, July 1 Litho. *Perf. 14***

**2193** A320 $1.40 multicolored 1.25 1.25

A321

Nolan Ryan, Baseball Player — A322

Designs: No. 2194, Nolan Ryan Foundation emblem. No. 2195, Emblem of major league All Star Game, Arlington,TX.
No. 2196 — Portraits of Ryan: a, In NY Mets uniform. b, With western hat, dog. c, In Texas Rangers cap. d, Throwing football. e, With son. f, Laughing, without hat. g, With family. h, Wearing Houston Astros cap.
No. 2197 — Ryan in Rangers uniform: a, Blue outfit. b, "34" on front. c, Looking left. d, After pitch looking forward. e, After pitch looking left. f, With bloody lip. g, Ready to pitch ball. h, Holding up cap.
$6, Being carried by team mates.
$30, Ready to pitch (illustration reduced).

**1995, Aug. 1 *Perf. 13½x14***

**2194** A321 $1 multicolored .75 .75

**2195** A321 $1 multicolored .75 .75

*a.* Pair, #2194-2195 1.50 1.50

**2196** A321 $1 Sheet of 9, #a.-h. + #2194 12.00 12.00

**2197** A321 $1 Sheet of 9, #a.-h. + #2195 12.00 12.00

**Souvenir Sheet**

**2198** A321 $6 multicolored 5.25 5.25

**Litho. & Embossed**

***Perf. 9***

**2199** A322 $30 gold & multi *35.00 35.00*

Nos. 2194-2195 were issued in sheets containing 5 #2194, 4 #2195.

1996 Summer Olympics, Atlanta — A323

No. 2200: a, Jean Shiley, US. b, Ruth Fuchs, Germany. c, Alessandro Andrei, Italy. d, Dorando Pietri, Italy. e, Heide Rosendahl, Germany. f, Mitsuoki Watanabe, Japan. g, Yasuhiro Yamashita, Japan. h, Dick Fosbury, US.
No. 2201: a, Long jump. b, Hurdles. c, Sprint. d, Marathon. e, Gymnastics. f, Rowing.
No. 2202, $5, Magic Johnson. No. 2203, $5, Swimmer's hand, horiz.

**1995, Aug. 24** **Litho.** ***Perf. 14***

**2200** A323 $1 Sheet of 8, #a.-h. 7.00 7.00
**2201** A323 $2 Sheet of 6, #a.-f. 10.50 10.50

**Souvenir Sheets**

**2202-2203** A323 Set of 2 12.00 12.00

Miniature Sheet

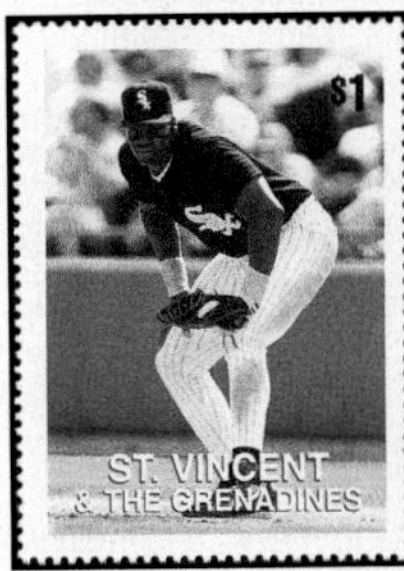


Stars of American League Baseball A324

A324a

No. 2204 — Different portraits of: a, e, i, Frank Thomas, Chicago White Sox. b, f-g, Cal Ripken, Jr., Baltimore Orioles. c-d, h, Ken Griffey, Jr., Seattle Mariners.
No. 2204J, $30, Griffey. No. 2204K, $30, Ripken. No. 2204L, $30, Thomas.

**1995, Sept. 6** **Litho.** ***Perf. 14***

**2204** A324 $1 Sheet of 9, #a.-i. 8.50 8.50

**Litho. & Embossed**

***Perf. 9***

**2204J-2204L** A324a Set of 3

Entertainers A325

Nos. 2205-2206, $1: Portraits of Elvis Presley.
No. 2207, $1: Portraits of John Lennon.
Nos. 2208-2210, $1: Portraits of Marilyn Monroe.
No. 2211, $6, Presley, diff. No. 2212, $6, Lennon, diff. No. 2213, $6, Monroe, in black. No. 2214, $6, Monroe, in red.

**1995, Sept. 18** ***Perf. 13½x14***

**2205** A325 $1 Sheet of 6, #a.-f. 7.00 7.00

**Sheets of 9, #a-i**

**2206-2210** A325 Set of 5 40.00 40.00

**Souvenir Sheets**

**2211-2214** A325 Set of 4 26.00 26.00

No. 2208 has serifs in lettering. No. 2209 has pink lettering.

Entertainers — A325a

Designs: $20, Elvis Presley. $30, Marilyn Monroe.

**1995** **Litho. & Embossed** ***Perf. 9***

**2214A** A325a $20 gold & multi *24.00 24.00*
**2214B** A325a $30 gold & multi *36.00 36.00*

Passenger Trains — A326

No. 2215: a, German Federal Railway ET4-03, high speed four car electric. b, Tres Grande Vitesse (TGV), France. c, British Railways Class 87 electric. d, Beijing locomotive, Railways of the People's Republic of China. e, American Amtrak turbo. f, Swedish State Railways class RC4 electric.
$6, Eurostar.

**1995, Oct. 3** ***Perf. 14***

**2215** A326 $1.50 Sheet of 6, #a.-f. 7.75 7.75

**Souvenir Sheet**

**2216** A326 $6 multicolored 8.50 8.50

No. 2216 contains one 85x28mm stamp.

Nobel Prize Fund Established, Cent. — A327

No. 2217, $1: a, Heinrich Böll, literature, 1972. b, Walther Bothe, physics, 1954. c, Richard Kuhn, chemistry, 1938. d, Hermann Hesse, literatrue, 1946. e, Knut Hamsun, literature, 1920. f, Konrad Lorenz, medicine, 1973. g, Thomas Mann, literature, 1929. h, Fridtjof Nansen, peace, 1922. i, Fritz Pregl, chemistry, 1923. j, Christian Lange, peace, 1921. k, Otto Loewi, medicine, 1936. l, Erwin Schrodinger, physics, 1933.
No. 2218, $1: a, Giosue Carducci, literature, 1906. b, Wladyslaw Reymont, literature, 1924. c, Ivan Bunin, literature, 1933. d, Pavel Cherenkov, physics, 1958. e, Ivan Pavlov, medicine, 1904. f, Pyotr Kapitsa, physics, 1978. g, Lev Landau, physics, 1962. h, Daniel Bovet, medicine, 1957. i, Henryk Sienkiewicz, literature, 1905. j, Aleksandr Prokhorov, physics, 1964. k, Julius Wagner von Jauregg, medicine, 1927. l, Grazia Deledda, literature, 1926.
No. 2219, $1: a, Bjornstjerne Bjornson, literature, 1903. b, Frank Kellogg, peace, 1929. c, Gustav Hertz, physics, 1925. d, Har Gobind Khorana, medicine, 1968. e, Kenichi Fukui, chemistry, 1981. f, Henry Kissinger, peace, 1973. g, Martin Luther King, Jr., peace, 1964. h, Odd Hassel, chemistry, 1969. i, Polykarp Kusch, physics, 1955. j, Ragnar Frisch, economics, 1969. k, Willis E. Lamb, Jr., physics, 1955. l, Sigrid Undset, literature, 1928.
No. 2220, $1: a, Robert Barany, medicine, 1914. b, Ernest Walton, physics, 1951. c, Alfred Fried, peace, 1911. d, James Franck, physics, 1925. e, Werner Forssmann, medicine, 1956. f, Yasunari Kawabata, literature, 1968. g, Wolfgang Pauli, physics, 1945. h, Jean-Paul Sartre, literature, 1964. i, Aleksandr Solzhenitsyn, literature, 1970. j, Hermann Staudinger, chemistry, 1953. k, Igor Tamm, physics, 1958. l, Samuel Beckett, literature, 1969.
No. 2221, $6, Adolf Windaus, chemistry, 1928. No. 2222, $6, Hideki Yukawa, physics, 1949. No. 2223, $6, Bertha von Suttner, peace, 1905. No. 2224, $6, Karl Landsteiner, medicine, 1930.

**1995, Oct. 2** **Litho.** ***Perf. 14***

**Sheets of 12, #a-l**

**2217-2220** A327 Set of 4 46.00 46.00

**Souvenir Sheets**

**2221-2224** A327 Set of 4 26.00 26.00

Classic Cars A328

No. 2225: a, 1931 Duesenberg Model J. b, 1913 Sleeve-valve Minerva. c, 1933 Delage D.8. SS. d, 1931-32 Bugatti Royale, Coupe De Ville chassis 41111. e, 1926 Rolls Royce 7668CC Phantom 1 Landauette. f, 1927 Mercedes Benz S26/120/180 PS.
$5, Hispano-Suiza Type H6B tulipwood-bodied roadster by Neuport.

**1995, Oct. 3**

**2225** A328 $1.50 Sheet of 6, #a.-f. 7.75 7.75

**Souvenir Sheet**

**2226** A328 $5 multicolored 7.00 7.00

Singapore '95 (#2225). No. 2226 contains one 85x28mm stamp.

Sierra Club, Cent. — A329

No. 2227: a, Gray wolf in front of trees. b, Gray wolf pup. c, Gray wolf up close. d, Hawaiian goose. e, Two Hawaiian geese. f, Jaguar. g, Lion-tailed macaque. h, Sand cat. i, Three sand cats.
No. 2228, horiz.: a, Orangutan swinging from tree. b, Orangutan facing forward. c, Orangutan looking left. d, Jaguar on rock. e, Jaguar up close. f, Sand cats. g, Hawaiian goose. h, Three lion-tailed macaques. i, Lion-tailed macaque.

**1995, Dec. 1** **Litho.** ***Perf. 14***

**2227** A329 $1 Sheet of 9, #a.-i. 9.00 9.00
**2228** A329 $1 Sheet of 9, #a.-i. 9.00 9.00

Natural Wonders of the World A330

No. 2229: a, Nile River. b, Yangtze River. c, Niagara Falls. d, Victoria Falls. e, Grand Canyon, US. f, Sahara Desert, Algeria. g, Kilimanjaro, Tanzania. h, Amazon river.
No. 2230, Haleakala Crater, Hawaii.

**1995, Dec. 1**

**2229** A330 $1.10 Sheet of 8, #a-h 9.50 9.50

**Souvenir Sheet**

**2230** A330 $6 multicolored 6.75 6.75

Disney Christmas — A331

Antique Disney toys: 1c, Lionel Santa car. 2c, Mickey Mouse "Choo Choo." 3c, Minnie Mouse pram. 5c, Mickey Mouse circus pull toy. 10c, Mickey, Pluto wind-up cart. 25c, Mickey Mouse mechanical motorcycle. $3, Lionel's Mickey Mouse handcar. $5, Casey Jr. Disneyland Express.
No. 2239, $6, Silver Link, Mickey the Stoker. No. 2240, $6, Mickey, Streamliner Engine.

**1995, Dec. 7** ***Perf. 13½x14***

**2231-2238** A331 Set of 8 15.50 15.50

**Souvenir Sheets**

**2239-2240** A331 Set of 2 14.00 14.00

Crotons A331a

Codiaeum variegatum: 10c, Mons florin. 15c, Prince of Monaco. 20c, Craigii. 40c, Gloriosum. 50c, Ebureum, vert. 60c, Volutum ramshorn. 70c, Narrenii, vert. 90c, Undutatum, vert. $1, Caribbean. $1.10, Gloriosa. $1.40, Katonii. $2, Appleleaf. $5, Tapestry. $10, Cornutum. $20, Puntatum aureum.

**1996, Jan. 1** **Litho.** ***Perf. 14***

| | | | | |
|---|---|---|---|---|
| **2240A** | A331a | 10c multi | .25 | .25 |
| **2240B** | A331a | 15c multi | .25 | .25 |
| **2240C** | A331a | 20c multi | .25 | .25 |
| **2240D** | A331a | 40c multi | .30 | .30 |
| **2240E** | A331a | 50c multi | .40 | .40 |
| **2240F** | A331a | 60c multi | .45 | .45 |
| **2240G** | A331a | 70c multi | .55 | .55 |
| **2240H** | A331a | 90c multi | .70 | .70 |
| **2240I** | A331a | $1 multi | .75 | .75 |
| **2240J** | A331a | $1.10 multi | .85 | .85 |
| **2240K** | A331a | $1.40 multi | 1.00 | 1.00 |
| **2240L** | A331a | $2 multi | 1.50 | 1.50 |
| **2240M** | A331a | $5 multi | 3.75 | 3.75 |
| **2240N** | A331a | $10 multi | 7.50 | 7.50 |
| **2240O** | A331a | $20 multi | 15.00 | 15.00 |
| | *Nos. 2240A-2240O (15)* | | 33.50 | 33.50 |

New Year 1996 (Year of the Rat) — A332

Nos. 2241 and 2242 — Stylized rats, Chinese inscriptions within checkered squares: a, lilac & multi. b, orange & multi. c, pink & multi.
$2, orange, green & black.

**1996, Jan. 2** **Litho.** ***Perf. 14½***

**2241** A332 75c Strip of 3, #a.-c. 2.00 2.00
**2242** A332 $1 Sheet of 3, #a.-c. 2.40 2.40

**Souvenir Sheet**

**2243** A332 $2 multicolored 1.60 1.60

No. 2241 was issued in sheets of 9 stamps.

A333

Star Trek, 30th Anniv. — A333a

No. 2244, $1: a, Spock. b, Kirk. c, Uhura. d, Sulu. e, Starship Enterprise. f, McCoy. g, Scott. h, Kirk, McCoy, Spock. i, Chekov.
No. 2245, $1: a, Spock holding up hand in Vulcan greeting. b, Kirk, Spock in "A Piece of the Action." c. Captain Kirk. d, Kirk, "The Trouble with Tribbles." e, Crew, "City on the Edge of Forever." f, Uhura, Sulu, "Mirror, Mirror." g, Romulans, "Balance of Terror." h, Building exterior. i, Khan, "Space Seed."

$6, Spock, Uhura.
$30, Spock, Kirk, McCoy, Scott, Starship Enterprise.
Illustration A333a reduced.

**1996, Jan. 4** ***Perf. 13½x14***

**Sheets of 9, #a-i**

**2244-2245** A333 $1 Set of 2 15.00 15.00

**Souvenir Sheet**

**2246** A333 $6 multicolored 4.50 4.50

**Litho. & Embossed**

***Perf. 9***

**2246A** A333a $30 gold & multi 30.00 30.00

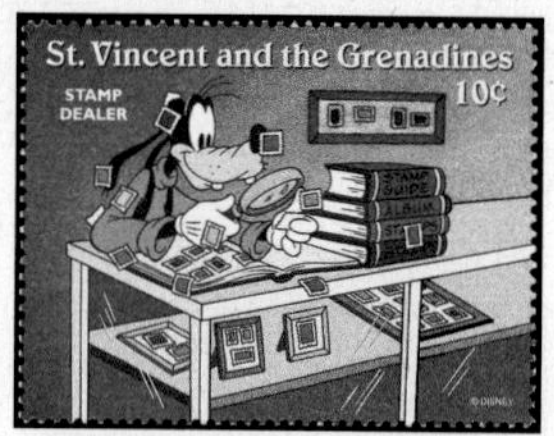


Disney Characters in Various Occupations — A334

No. 2247 — Merchants: a, Stamp dealer. b, At supermarket. c, Car salesman. d, Florist. e, Fast food carhop. f, Street vendor. g, Gift shop. h, Hobby shop owner. i, Bakery.

No. 2248 — Transport workers: a, Delivery service. b, Truck driver. c, Airplane crew. d, Railroad men. e, Bus driver. f, Tour guide. g, Messenger service. h, Trolley conductor. i, Air traffice controller.

No. 2249 — Law & order: a, Postal inspector. b, Traffic cop. c, Private detectives. d, Highway patrol. e, Justice of the peace. f, Security guard. g, Judge and lawyer. h, Sheriff. i, Court stenographer.

No. 2250 — Sports professionals: a, Basketball player. b, Referee. c, Track coach. d, Ice skater. e, Golfer and caddy. f, Sportscaster. g, Tennis champs. h, Football coach. i, Race car driver.

No. 2251 — Scientists: a, Paleontologist. b, Archaeologist. c, Inventor. d, Astronaut. e, Chemist. f, Engineer. g, Computer graphics. h, Astronomer. i, Zoologist.

No. 2252, vert. — School of education: a, Classroom teacher. b, Nursery school teacher. c, Band teacher. d, Electronic teacher. e, School psychologist. f, School principal. g, Professor. h, Graduate.

No. 2253 — Sea & shore workers: a, Ship builders. b, Fisherman. c, Pearl diver. d, Underwater photographer. e, Bait & tackle shop owner. f, Bathing suit covergirls. g, Marine life painter. h, Lifeguard. i, Lighthouse keeper.

No. 2254, $6, Donald in ice cream parlor. No. 2255, $6, Goofy as an oceanographer. No. 2256, $6, Grandma, Grandpa, Daisy Duck as jury, vert. No. 2257, $6, Donald as deep sea treasure hunter, vert. No. 2258, $6, Minnie as librarian, vert. No. 2259, $6, Mickey, ducks, as cheerleaders, vert. No. 2260, $6, Mickey as seaman, vert.

**1996, Jan. 8** ***Perf. 14x13½, 13½x14***

**2247** A334 10c Sheet of 9, #a.-i. 1.10 1.10
**2248** A334 50c Sheet of 9, #a.-i. 5.75 5.75
**2249** A334 75c Sheet of 9, #a.-i. 8.25 8.25
**2250** A334 90c Sheet of 9, #a.-i. 10.00 10.00
**2251** A334 95c Sheet of 9, #a.-i. 10.50 10.50
**2252** A334 $1.10 Sheet of 8, #a.-h. 11.00 11.00
**2253** A334 $1.20 Sheet of 9, #a.-i. 13.50 13.50

**Souvenir Sheets**

**2254-2260** A334 Set of 7 30.00 30.00

#2248-2253 exist in sheets of 7 or 8 10c stamps + label. The label replaces the following stamps: #2248e, 2249e, 2250e, 2251e, 2252d, 2253e. The sheets had limited release on Dec. 3, 1996.

Paintings from Metropolitan Museum of Art — A335

No. 2261: a, Moses Striking Rock, by Bloemaert. b, The Last Communion, by Botticelli. c, The Musicians, by Caravaggio. d, Francesco Sassetti & Son, by Ghirlandaio. e, Pepito Costa y Bunells, by Goya. f, Saint Andrew, by Martini. g, The Nativity, by a follower of van der Weyden. h, Christ Blessing, by Solario.

No. 2262 — Art by Cézanne: a, Madame Cézanne. b, Still Life with Apples and Pears. c, Man in a Straw Hat. d, Still Life with a Ginger Jar. e, Madame Cézanne in a Red Dress. f, Still Life. g, Dominique Aubert. h, Still Life, diff. i, The Card Players.

No. 2263: a, Bullfight, by Goya. b, Portrait of a Man, by Frans Hals. c, Mother and Son, by Sully. d, Portrait of a Young Man, by Memling. e, Maltilde Stoughton de Jaudenes, by Stuart. f, Josef de Jaudenes y Nebot, by Stuart. g, Mont Sainte-Victore, by Cézanne. h, Gardanne, by Cézanne. i, The Empress Eugenie, by Winterhalter.

No. 2264: a, The Dissolute Household, by Steen. b, Portrait of Gerard de Lairesse, by Rembrandt. c, Juan de Pareja, by Velázquez. d, Curiosity, by G. Ter Borch. e, The Companions of Rinaldo, by Poussin. f, Don Gaspar de Guzman, by Velázquez. g, Merry Company on a Terrace, by Steen. h, Pilate Washing Hands, by Rembrandt. i, Portrait of a Man, by Van Dyck.

No. 2265, $6, Hagar in Wilderness, by Corot. No. 2266, $6, Young Ladies from the Village, by Courbet. No. 2267, $6, Two Young Peasant Women, by Pissaro. No. 2268, $6, Allegory of the Planets and Continents, by Tiepolo.

**1996, Feb. 1** **Litho.** ***Perf. 14***

**2261** A335 75c Sheet of 8, #a.-h.+label 5.00 5.00
**2262** A335 90c Sheet of 9, #a.-i. 7.00 7.00
**2263** A335 $1 Sheet of 9, #a.-i. 7.75 7.75
**2264** A335 $1.10 Sheet of 9, #a.-i. 8.50 8.50

**Souvenir Sheets**

**2265-2268** A335 Set of 4 20.00 20.00

Nos. 2265-2268 each contain one 81x53mm stamp.

A335a

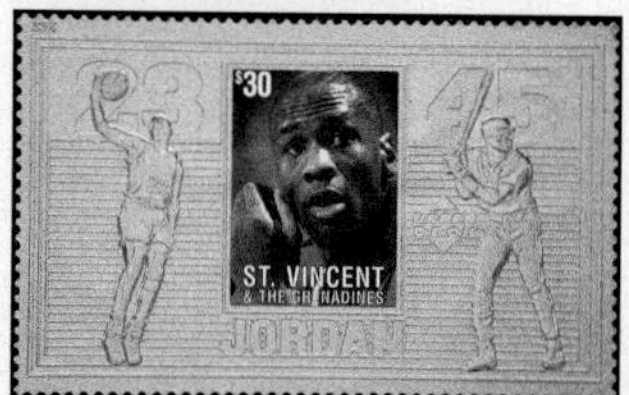


Michael Jordan, Basketball Player, Baseball Player — A335b

Design: No. 2268E, Jordan as basketball player.

***Perf. 14, Imperf. (#2268Ac)***

**1996, Apr. 17** **Litho.**

**2268A** Sheet of 17, 16 #b, 1 #c 29.00 29.00
*b.* A335a $2 shown 1.50 1.50
*c.* A335a $6 Portrait, up close 4.50 4.50

**Litho. & Embossed**

***Perf. 9***

**2268D** A335b $30 shown
**2268E** A335b $30 gold & multi

No. 2268Ac is 68x100mm and has simulated perforations.

A335c

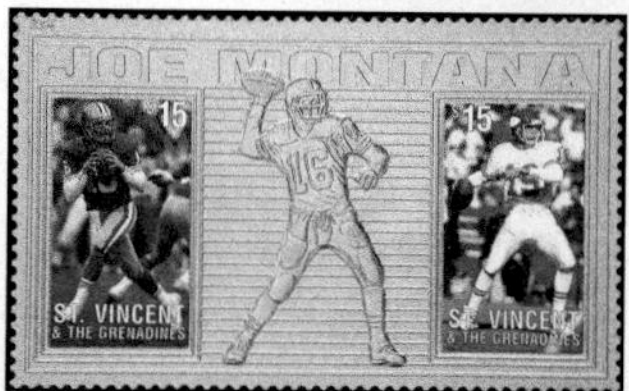


Joe Montana, Football Player — A335d

No. 2268I: j, In red jersey. k, In white jersey.

***Perf. 14, Imperf. (#2268Fh)***

**1996, Apr. 17** **Litho.**

**2268F** Sheet of 17, 16 #g, 1 #h 29.00 29.00
*g.* A335c $2 shown 1.50 1.50
*h.* A335c $6 In action 4.50 4.50

**Souvenir Sheet**

**Litho. & Embossed**

***Perf. 9***

**2268I** A335d $15 Sheet of 2, #j.-k.

No. 2268Fh is 68x100mm and has simulated perforations.

Lou Gehrig and Cal Ripken, Jr., Baseball Ironmen — A336

**1995** **Litho. & Embossed** ***Perf. 9***

**2269** A336 $30 gold & multi

A336a

A337

Star Wars Trilogy — A338

No. 2269: b, In Space Bar. c, Luke, Emperor. d, X-Wing Fighter. e, Star Destroyers. f, Cloud City. g, Speeders on Forest Moon.

Nos. 2270, 2273a, Darth Vader, "Star Wars," 1977. Nos. 2271, 2273c, Yoda, "Return of the Jedi," 1983. Nos. 2272, 2273b, Storm troopers, "The Empire Strikes Back," 1980.

No. 2274, $30, Darth Vader, "Star Wars," 1977. No. 2275, $30, Yoda, "Return of the Jedi," 1983. No. 2276, $30, Storm Trooper, "The Empire Strikes Back," 1980.

**1996, Mar. 19** **Litho.** ***Perf. 14***

**2269A** A336a 35c Sheet of 6, #b.-g. 9.50 9.50

**Self-Adhesive**

***Serpentine Die Cut 6***

**2270** A337 $1 sil & multi 3.00 3.00
**2271** A337 $1 sil & multi 3.00 3.00
**2272** A337 $1 sil & multi 3.00 3.00

**Souvenir Sheet**

***Serpentine Die Cut 9***

**2273** A338 $2 Sheet of 3, #a.-c. 9.50 9.50

**Litho. & Embossed**

***Perf. 9***

**2274-2276** A337 Set of 3

Nos. 2270-2272 were issued in sheets of 3 each arranged in alternating order.

Nos. 2274-2276 are gold and multi, and also exist in silver & multi.

Issued: Nos. 2274-2276, 11/18/95; others 3/19/96.

Butterflies — A339

Designs: 70c, Anteos menippe. $1, Eunica alcmena. $1.10, Doxocopa lavinia. $2, Tithorea tarricina.

No. 2281: a, Papilio lycophron. b, Prepona buckleyana. c, Parides agavus. d, Papilio cacicus. e, Euryades duponchelli. f, Diaethria dymena. g, Orimba jansoni. h, Polystichtis siaka. i, Papilio machaonides.

$5, Adelpha abia. $6, Themone pais.

**1996, Apr. 15** **Litho.** ***Perf. 14***

**2277-2280** A339 Set of 4 4.50 4.50
**2281** A339 90c Sheet of 9, #a.-i. 7.50 7.50

**Souvenir Sheets**

**2282** A339 $5 multicolored 4.75 4.75
**2283** A339 $6 multicolored 6.00 6.00

Queen Elizabeth II, 70th Birthday — A340

No. 2284: a, Portrait. b, In robes of Order of the Garter. c, Wearing red coat, hat.

$6, Waving from balcony, horiz.

**1996, June 12** **Litho.** ***Perf. 13½x14***

**2284** A340 $2 Strip of 3, #a.-c. 5.25 5.25

**Souvenir Sheet**

***Perf. 14x13½***

**2285** A340 $6 multicolored 5.25 5.25

No. 2284 was issued in sheets of 9 stamps.

Birds A341

Designs: 60c, Coereba flaveola, vert. $1, Myadestes genibarbis, vert. $1.10, Tangara cucullata, vert. $2, Eulampis jugularis, vert.
No. 2290: a, Progne subis. b, Buteo platypterus. c, Phaethon lepturus. d, Himantopus himantopus. e, Sterna anaethetus. f, Euphonia musica. g, Arenaria interpres. h, Sericotes holosericeus. i, Nyctanassa violacea.
$5, Dendrocygna autumnalis, vert.. $6, Amazona guildingii, vert.

**1996, July 11** *Perf. 14*
**2286-2289** A341 Set of 4 4.50 4.50
**2290** A341 $1 Sheet of 9, #a.-i. 8.00 8.00

**Souvenir Sheets**

**2291** A341 $5 multi 4.25 4.25
**2292** A341 $6 multi 5.25 5.25

Radio, Cent. A342

Entertainers: 90c, Walter Winchell. $1, Fred Allen. $1.10, Hedda Hopper. $2, Eve Arden. $6, Major Bowes.

**1996, July 11** *Perf. 13½x14*
**2293-2296** A342 Set of 4 4.25 4.25

**Souvenir Sheet**

**2297** A342 $6 multicolored 5.00 5.00

UNICEF, 50th Anniv. A343

Designs: $1, Boy raising arm. $1.10, Children reading. $2, Girl, microscope. $5, Boy.

**1996, July 11** *Perf. 14*
**2298-2300** A343 Set of 3 3.25 3.25

**Souvenir Sheet**

**2301** A343 $5 multicolored 3.80 3.80

Chinese Animated Films — A344

Nos. 2302, 15c, 2304, 75c, vert.: Various characters from "Uproar in Heaven."
Nos. 2303, 15c, 2305, 75c, vert.: Various characters from "Nezha Conquers the Dragon King."

**1996, May 10** **Litho.** *Perf. 12*

**Strips of 5, #a-e**

**2302-2303** A344 15c Set of 2 3.50 3.50

**Souvenir Sheets**

**2304-2305** A344 75c Set of 2 4.00 4.00

Nos. 2302-2303 each were issued in a sheet of 10 stamps. CHINA '96, 9th Asian Intl. Philatelic Exhibition.

Jerusalem, 3000th Anniv. — A345

Designs: $1, Knesset. $1.10, Montefiore Windmill. $2, Shrine of the Book. $5, Jerusalem of Gold.

**1996, July 11** **Litho.** *Perf. 14*
**2306-2308** A345 Set of 3 4.25 4.25

**Souvenir Sheet**

**2309** A345 $5 multicolored 4.25 4.25

The captions on Nos. 2306 and 2308 are transposed. For overprints see Nos. 2586-2589.

1996 Summer Olympic Games, Atlanta A346

Designs: 20c, Maurice King, weight lifter, vert. 70c, Eswort Coombs, 400-meter relay, vert. No. 2312, 90c, Runners, Olympia, 530BC. No. 2313, 90c, Pamenos Ballantyne, Benedict Ballantyne, runners, vert. $1, London landmarks, 1908 Olympics, Great Britain. No. 2315, $1.10, Rodney "Chang" Jack, soccer player, vert. No. 2316, $1.10, Dorando Pietri, marathon runner, London, 1908, vert. $2, Yachting.
No. 2318, $1, vert. — Past winners, event: a, Vitaly Shcherbo, gymnastics. b, Fu Mingxia, diving. c, Wilma Rudolph, track & field. d, Rafer Johnson, decathlon. e, Teofilo Stevenson, boxing. f, Babe Didrikson, track & field. g, Kyoko Iwasaki, swimming. h, Yoo Namkyu, table tennis. i, Michael Gross, swimming.
No. 2319, $1: a, Chuhei Nambu, triple jump. b, Duncan McNaughton, high jump. c, Jack Kelly, single sculls. d, Jackie Joyner-Kersee, heptathlon. e, Tyrell Biggs, boxing. f, Larisa Latynina, gymnastics. g, Bob Garrett, discus. h, Paavo Nurmi, 5000-meters. i, Eric Lemming, javelin.
No. 2320, $1: a, Yasuhiro Yamashita, judo. b, Peter Rono, 1500-meters. c, Aleksandr Kurlovich, weight lifting. d, Juha Tiainen, hammer throw. e, Sergei Bubka, pole vault. f, Q. F. Newall, women's archery. g, Nadia Comaneci, gymnastics. h, Carl Lewis, long jump. i, Bob Mathias, decathlon.
No. 2321, $1, vert. — Sporting events: a, Women's archery. b, Gymnastics. c, Basketball. d, Soccer. e, Water polo. f, Baseball. g, Kayak. h, Fencing. i, Cycling.
No. 2322, $5, Olympic Flag. No. 2323, $5, Carl Lewis, runner, vert. No. 2324, $5, Alexander Dityatin, gymnastics, 1980. No. 2325, $5, Hannes Kolehmainen, marathon runner.

**1996, July 19**
**2310-2317** A346 Set of 8 7.00 7.00

**Sheets of 9, #a-i**

**2318-2321** A346 Set of 4 31.00 31.00

**Souvenir Sheets**

**2322-2325** A346 Set of 4 15.00 15.00

St. Vincent Olympic Committee (#2310-2311, 2313, 2315).

Disney's "The Hunchback of Notre Dame" A347

No. 2326: a, Quasimodo. b, Phoebus. c, Laverne, Hugo. d, Clopin. e, Frollo. f, Esmeralda. g, Victor. h, Djali.
No. 2327, $6, Esmeralda, Quasimodo, horiz. No. 2328, $6, Esmeralda, Phoebus, horiz.

**1996, July 25** *Perf. 13½x14*
**2326** A347 $1 Sheet of 8, #a-h 8.00 8.00

**Souvenir Sheets**

*Perf. 14X13½*

**2327-2328** A347 Set of 2 13.00 13.00

Fish A348

Designs: 70c, French angelfish. 90c, Red-spotted hawkfish. $1.10, Spiny puffer. $2, Gray triggerfish.
No. 2333, $1: a, Barred hamlet. b, Flamefish. c, Longsnout butterflyfish. d, Fairy basslet. e, Redtail parrotfish. f, Blackbar soldierfish. g, Threespot damselfish. h, Candy basslet. i, Spotfin hogfish.
No. 2334, $1: a, Equetus lanceolatus. b, Acanthurus coeruleus. c, Lutjanus analis. d, Hippocampus hudsonius. e, Serranus annularis. f, Squatina dumerili. g, Muraena miliaris. h, Bolbometopon bicolor. i, Tritonium nodiferum.
$5, Queen triggerfish. $6, Blue marlin.

**1996, Aug. 10** *Perf. 14*
**2329-2332** A348 Set of 4 4.25 4.25

**Sheets of 9, #a-i**

**2333-2334** A348 Set of 2 14.50 14.50

**Souvenir Sheets**

**2335** A348 $5 multicolored 4.25 4.25
**2336** A348 $6 multicolored 5.00 5.00

Flowers A349

Designs: 70c, Beloperone guttata. $1, Epidendrum elongatum. $1.10, Pettrea volubilis. $2, Oncidium altrissimum.
No. 2341: a, Datura candida. b, Amherstia nobilis. c, Ipomoea acuminata. d, Bougainvillea glabra. e, Cassia alata. f, Cordia sebestena. g, Opuntia dilenii. h, Cryptostegia grandiflora. i, Rodriguezia lanceolata.
No. 2342, Acalypha hispida. No. 2343, Hibiscus rosa-sinensis.

**1996, Aug. 15**
**2337-2340** A349 Set of 4 3.50 3.50
**2341** A349 90c Sheet of 9, #a.-i. 6.00 6.00

**Souvenir Sheets**

**2342** A349 $5 multicolored 3.75 3.75

*Perf. 14x13½*

**2343** A349 $5 multicolored 3.75 3.75

John F. Kennedy (1917-63) — A350

No. 2344, $1: a, As young boy. b, Proclamation to send man to the moon. c, With Caroline, Jackie. d, Inauguration. e, Giving speech. f, On PT 109. g, With Jackie. h, Funeral procession, portrait. i, Guard, Eternal Flame.
No. 2345, $1: a, With family on yacht. b, On yacht. c, On yacht holding sail. d, "JFK," portrait. e, Talking to astronauts in space. f, Younger picture in uniform. g, Portrait. h, Riding in motorcade. i, Giving speech, US flag.
No. 2346, $1: a, Up close picture. b, In front of house at Hyannis Port. c, Memorial plaque, picture. d, Photograph among crowd. e, Portrait, flag. f, Rocket, portrait. g, Signing document. h, Martin Luther King, John F. Kennedy, Robert F. Kennedy. i, Painting looking down toward microphones.
No. 2347, $1: a, Photograph with Jacqueline greeting people. b, Formal oval-shaped portrait. c, Photograph. d, With family. e, Space capsule, painting. f, Addressing UN. g, In rocking chair. h, Seated at desk, dignitaries. i, Holding telephone, map.

**1996, Aug.** *Perf. 14x13½*

**Sheets of 9, #a-i**

**2344-2347** A350 Set of 4 27.00 27.00

Ships A351

No. 2348, $1.10: a, SS Doric, 1923, Great Britain. b, SS Nerissa, 1926, Great Britain. c, SS Howick Hall, 1910, Great Britain. d, SS Jervis Bay, 1922, Great Britain. e, SS Vauban, 1912, Great Britain. f, MV Orinoco, 1928, Germany.
No. 2349, $1.10: a, SS Lady Rodney, 1929, Canada. b, SS Empress of Russia, 1913, Canada. c, SS Providence, 1914, France. d, SS Reina Victori-Eugenia, 1913, Spain. e, SS Balmoral Castle, 1910, Great Britain. f, SS Tivives, 1911, US.
No. 2350, $6, SS Imperator, 1913, Germany. No. 2351, $6, SS Aquitania, 1914, Great Britain.

**1996, Sept. 5** *Perf. 14*

**Sheets of 6, #a-f**

**2348-2349** A351 Set of 2 11.00 11.00

**Souvenir Sheets**

**2350-2351** A351 Set of 2 9.00 9.00

Elvis Presley's 1st "Hit" Year, 40th Anniv. A352

Various portraits.

**1996, Sept. 8** *Perf. 13½x14*
**2352** A352 $2 Sheet of 6, #a.-f. 9.00 9.00

Richard Petty, NASCAR Driving Champion — A353

No. 2353: a, 1990 Pontiac. b, Richard Petty. c, 1972 Plymouth. d, 1974 Dodge.
$5, 1970 Plymouth Superbird. $6, 1996 STP 25th Anniversary Pontiac.

**1996, Sept. 26** *Perf. 14*
**2353** A353 $2 Sheet of 4, #a.-d. 6.50 6.50

**Souvenir Sheets**

**2354** A353 $5 multicolored 3.75 3.75
**2355** A353 $6 multicolored 4.75 4.75

No. 2354 contains one 85x28mm stamp.

Sandy Koufax, Baseball Pitcher — A354

A354a

No. 2356: a.-c., Various action shots.

*Perf. 14, Imperf. (#2356d)*

**1996, Sept. 26**

| | | | |
|---|---|---|---|
| 2356 | Sheet of 17 | 28.50 | 28.50 |
| *a.-c.* | A354 $2 any single | 1.50 | 1.50 |
| *d.* | A354 $6 Portrait | 4.50 | 4.50 |

**Litho. & Embossed**

*Perf. 9*

| | | | |
|---|---|---|---|
| 2356E | A354a $30 gold & multi | 25.00 | 25.00 |

No. 2356 contains 6 #2356a, 5 each #2356b, 2356c and 1 #2356d. No. 2356d is 70x103mm and has simulated perforations.

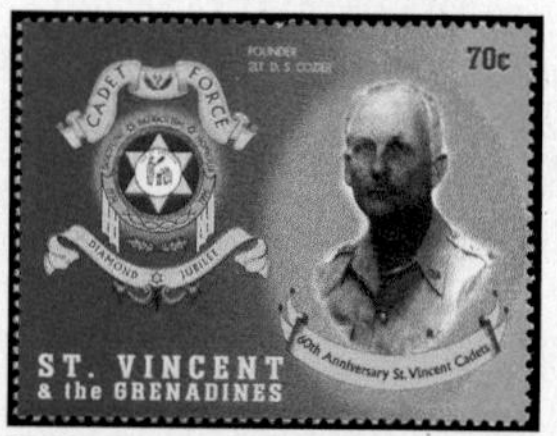

Cadet Force, 60th Anniv. — A355

Insignia and: 70c, 2nd Lt. D.S. Cozier, founder. 90c, Cozier, first 12 cadets, 1936.

**1996, Oct. 23 Litho.** *Perf. 14x13½*

| | | | |
|---|---|---|---|
| 2357 | A355 70c multicolored | .60 | .60 |
| 2358 | A355 90c multicolored | .80 | .80 |

Christmas A356

Details or entire paintings: 70c, Virgin and Child, by Memling. 90c, St. Anthony, by Memling. $1, Madonna and Child, by Bouts. $1.10, Virgin and Child, by Lorenzo Lotto. $2, St. Roch, by Lotto. $5, St. Sebastian, by Lotto.

No. 2365, $5, Virgin and Child with St. Roch and St. Sebastian, by Lotto. No. 2366, $5, Virgin and Child with St. Anthony and a Donor, by Memling.

**1996, Nov. 14** *Perf. 13½x14*

| | | | |
|---|---|---|---|
| 2359-2364 | A356 Set of 6 | 9.00 | 9.00 |

**Souvenir Sheets**

| | | | |
|---|---|---|---|
| 2365-2366 | A356 Set of 2 | 8.50 | 8.50 |

Disney's "The Hunchback of Notre Dame" — A357

Designs: Various scenes from film.

No. 2370, $6, Quasimodo, Phoebus, Esmeralda. No. 2371, $6, Esmeralda, vert. No. 2372, $6, Quasimodo, citizens, vert.

**1996, Dec. 12 Litho.** *Perf. 13½x14*

| | | | |
|---|---|---|---|
| 2367 | A357 10c Sheet of 6, #a.-f., vert. | .90 | 9.00 |

*Perf. 14x13½*

| | | | |
|---|---|---|---|
| 2368 | A357 30c Sheet of 9, #a.-i. | 3.00 | 3.00 |
| 2369 | A357 $1 Sheet of 9, #a.-i. | 8.00 | 8.00 |

**Souvenir Sheets**

| | | | |
|---|---|---|---|
| 2370-2372 | A357 Set of 3 | 19.50 | 19.50 |

Sylvester Stallone in Movie "Rocky IV" — A358

**1996 Litho.** *Perf. 14*

| | | | |
|---|---|---|---|
| 2373 | A358 $2 Sheet of 3, #a.-c. | 5.00 | 5.00 |

A359

New Year 1997 (Year of the Ox) — A359a

Stylized oxen, Chinese inscriptions within checkered squares: Nos. 2374a, 2375a, pale orange, pale lilac & black. Nos. 2374b, 2375b, green, violet & black. Nos. 2374c, 2375c, tan, pink & black.

**1997, Jan. 2** *Perf. 14½*

| | | | |
|---|---|---|---|
| 2374 | A359 75c Strip of 3, #a.-c. | 1.70 | 1.70 |
| 2375 | A359 $1 Sheet of 3, #a.-c. | 2.25 | 2.25 |

**Souvenir Sheet**

| | | | |
|---|---|---|---|
| 2376 | A359 $2 orange, yellow & blk | 1.50 | 1.50 |

**Litho. & Embossed**

*Perf. 9*

| | | | |
|---|---|---|---|
| 2376A | A359a $30 gold & multi | 25.00 | 25.00 |

No. 2374 was issued in sheets of 9 stamps.

Star Trek Voyager A360

No. 2377: a, Lt. Tuvak. b, Kes. c, Lt. Paris. d, The Doctor. e, Capt. Janeway. f, Lt. Torres. g, Neelix. h, Ens. Kim. i, Cdr. Chakotay.

$6, Cast of characters.

**1997, Jan. 23 Litho.** *Perf. 14*

| | | | |
|---|---|---|---|
| 2377 | A360 $2 Sheet of 9, #a.-i. | 14.50 | 14.50 |

**Souvenir Sheet**

| | | | |
|---|---|---|---|
| 2378 | A360 $6 multicolored | 5.00 | 5.00 |

No. 2378 contains one 29x47mm stamp.

A361

A361a

Mickey Mantle (1931-95), baseball player.

*Perf. 14, Imperf. (#2379b)*

**1997, Jan. 23**

| | | | |
|---|---|---|---|
| 2379 | Sheet of 17, 16 #2379a, 1 #2379b | 28.50 | 28.50 |
| *a.* | A361 $2 shown | 1.50 | 1.50 |
| *b.* | A361 $6 Portrait holding bat | 4.50 | 4.50 |

**Litho. & Embossed**

*Perf. 9*

| | | | |
|---|---|---|---|
| 2379C | A361a $30 gold & multi | 25.00 | 25.00 |

No. 2379b is 70x100mm.

Black Baseball Players — A362

No. 2380: a, Frank Robinson. b, Satchel Paige. c, Billy Williams. d, Reggie Jackson. e, Roberto Clemente. f, Ernie Banks. g, Hank Aaron. h, Roy Campanella. i, Willie McCovey. j, Monte Irvin. k, Willie Stargell. l, Rod Carew. m, Ferguson Jenkins. n, Bob Gibson. o, Lou Brock. p, Joe Morgan. q, Jackie Robinson.

*Perf. 14x14½, Imperf. (#2380q)*

**1997, Jan. 23**

| | | | |
|---|---|---|---|
| 2380 | Sheet of 17 | 16.50 | 16.50 |
| *a.-p.* | A362 $1 any single | .75 | .75 |
| *q.* | A362 $6 Portrait | 4.50 | 4.50 |

No. 2380q is 66x100mm and has simulated perforations.

Souvenir Sheet

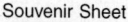

Chongqing Dazu Stone Carving — A363

**1996, May 20 Litho.** *Perf. 12*

| | | | |
|---|---|---|---|
| 2381 | A363 $2 multicolored | 1.50 | 1.50 |

China '96.

No. 2381 was not available until March 1997.

Hong Kong Changeover — A364

A364a

No. 2382 — Flags of Great Britain, Peoples' Republic of China and panoramic view of Hong Kong: a-e, In daytime. f-j, At night.

No. 2383, $2 — Market scene: a, Vendors, corner of building. b, People strolling. c, Man choosing items to purchase.

No. 2384, $2 — Buddhist religious ceremony: a, Fruit, incense pot, torch. b, Monk at fire. c, Flower.

No. 2385, $2 — Lantern ceremony: a, Boy, girl. b, Couple on bridge. c, Girls with lanterns.

Illustration A364a reduced.

**1997, Feb. 12** *Perf. 14*

| | | | |
|---|---|---|---|
| 2382 | A364 90c Sheet of 10, #a-j | 7.25 | 7.25 |

**Sheets of 3, #a-c**

*Perf. 13*

| | | | |
|---|---|---|---|
| 2383-2385 | A364 Set of 3 | 14.50 | 14.50 |

**Litho. & Embossed**

*Perf. 9*

| | | | |
|---|---|---|---|
| 2385D | A364a $30 gold & multi | 25.00 | 25.00 |

Hong Kong '97.

Nos. 2383-2385 each contain 3 35x26mm stamps.

UNESCO, 50th Anniv. — A365

World Heritage Sites: 70c, Lord Howe Islands, Australia, vert. 90c, Uluru-Kata Tjuta Natl. Park, Australia, vert. $1, Kakadu Natl. Park, Australia, vert. $1.10, Te Wahipounamu, New Zealand, vert. $2, $5, vert., Tongariro Natl. Park, New Zealand.

No. 2392, $1.10, vert. — Various sites in Greece: a, Monastery of Rossanou, Meteora. b, f, h, Painted ceiling, interior, Mount Athos Monastery. c, Monastery Osios Varlaam, Meteora. d, Ruins in Athens. e, Museum of the Acropolis. g, Mount Athos.

No. 2393, $1.10, vert. — Various sites in Japan: a, Himeji-Jo. b, Temple Lake, Gardens, Kyoto. c, Kyoto. d, Buddhist Temple of Ninna-Ji. e, View of city of Himeji-Jo. f, Forest, Shirakami-Sanchi. g, h, Forest, Yakushima.

No. 2394, $1.10, vert: a, City of San Gimignano, Italy. b, Cathedral of Santa Maria Asunta, Pisa, Italy. c, Cathedral of Santa Maria Fiore, Florence, Italy. d, Archaeological site, Valley of the Boyne, Ireland. e, Church of Saint-Savin-Sur-Gartempe, France. f, g, h, City of Bath, England.

No. 2395, $1.50: a, Trinidad, Valley de los Ingenios, Cuba. b, City of Zacatecas, Mexico. c, Lima, Peru. d, Ruins of Monastery, Paraguay. e, Mayan Ruins, Copan, Honduras.

No. 2396, $1.50 — Various sites in China: a, Palace, Wudang Mountains, Hubei Province. b, Cave Sanctuaries, Mogao. c, House, Desert of Taklamakan. d, e, Great Wall.

Nos. 2397, $1.50: a-e, Various sites in Quedlinberg, Germany.

No. 2398, $5, Monastery of Meteora, Greece. No. 2399, $5, Wailing Wall, Jerusalem. No. 2400, $5, Quedlinburg, Germany. No. 2401, $5, Oasis, Dunbuang, China. No. 2402, $5, Himeji-Jo, Japan. No. 2403, $5, Great Wall, China. No. 2404, $5, City of Venice, Italy.

*Perf. 13½x14, 14x13½*

**1997, Mar. 24 Litho.**

**2386-2391** A365 Set of 6 8.00 8.00

**Sheets of 8, #a-h, + Label**

**2392-2394** A365 Set of 3 20.00 20.00

**Sheets of 5 + Label**

**2395-2397** A365 Set of 3 17.50 17.50

**Souvenir Sheets**

**2398-2404** A365 Set of 7 25.00 25.00

Telecommunications in St. Vincent, 125th Anniv. — A366

Designs: 5c, Microwave radio relay tower, Dorsetshire Hill. 10c, Cable & wireless headquarters, Kingstown. 20c, Microwave relay tower, vert. 35c, Cable & wireless complex, Arnos Vale. 50c, Cable & wireless tower, Mt. St. Andrew. 70c, Cable ship. 90c, Eastern telecommunication network, 1872. $1.10, Telegraph map of world, 1876.

*Perf. 14x14½, 14½x14*

**1997, Apr. 3 Litho.**

**2405-2412** A366 Set of 8 4.00 4.00

Birds of the World — A367

Designs: 60c, Smooth-billed ani. 70c, Belted kingfisher. 90c, Blackburnian warbler. $1.10, Blue tit. $2, Chaffinch. $5, Ruddy turnstone.

No. 2419: a, Blue grosbeak. b, Bananaquit. c, Cedar waxwing. d, Ovenbird. e, Hooded warbler. f, Flicker.

No. 2420: a, Song thrush. b, Robin. c, Blackbird. d, Great spotted woodpecker. e, Wren. f, Kingfisher.

No. 2421, $5, St. Vincent parrot. No. 2422, $5, Tawny owl.

**1997, Apr. 7** *Perf. 14*

**2413-2418** A367 Set of 6 7.75 7.75
**2419** A367 $1 Sheet of 6, #a.-f. 4.50 4.50
**2420** A367 $2 Sheet of 6, #a.-f. 9.00 9.00

**Souvenir Sheets**

**2421-2422** A367 Set of 2 7.50 7.50

Water Birds — A368

Designs: 70c, Mandarin duck, horiz. 90c, Green heron, horiz. $1, Drake ringed teal, horiz. $1.10, Blue-footed boobies, horiz. $2, Australian jacana. $5, Reddish egret.

No. 2429: a, Crested auklet. b, Whiskered auklet. c, Pigeon guillemot. d, Adelie penguins. e, Rockhopper penguin. f, Emperor penguin.

No. 2430, $5, Snowy egrets, horiz. No. 2431, $5, Flamingos, horiz.

**1997, Apr. 7** *Perf. 15*

**2423-2428** A368 Set of 6 8.00 8.00
**2429** A368 $1.10 Sheet of 6, #a.-f. 5.00 5.00

**Souvenir Sheet**

**2430-2431** A368 Set of 2 7.50 7.50

Jackie Robinson (1919-72) A369

A369a

*Serpentine Die Cut 7*

**1997, Jan. 23 Litho.**

**Self-Adhesive**

**2432** A369 $1 multicolored 1.00 1.00

**Litho. & Embossed**

*Perf. 9*

**2432A** A369a $30 gold & multi

No. 2432 was issued in sheets of 3 and was not available until June 1997.

Queen Elizabeth II, Prince Philip, 50th Wedding Anniv. A370

No. 2433: a, Queen. b, Royal arms. c, Portrait of Queen, Prince. d, Queen, Prince, crowd. e, Buckingham Palace. f, Prince.

$5, Queen seated in wedding gown, crown.

**1997, June 3 Litho.** *Perf. 14*

**2433** A370 $1.10 Sheet of 6, #a.-f. 5.50 5.50

**Souvenir Sheet**

**2434** A370 $5 multicolored 4.00 4.00

Paintings by Hiroshige (1797-1858) A371

No. 2435: a, Furukawa River, Hiroo. b, Chiyogaike Pond, Meguro. c, New Fuji, Meguro. d, Moon-Viewing Point. e, Ushimachi, Takanawa. f, Original Fuji, Meguro.

No. 2436, $5, Gotenyama, Shinagawa. No. 2437, $5, Shinagawa Susaki.

**1997, June 3** *Perf. 13½x14*

**2435** A371 $1.50 Sheet of 6, #a.-f. 7.00 7.00

**Souvenir Sheets**

**2436-2437** A371 Set of 2 9.00 9.00

Paul Harris (1868-1947), Founder of Rotary Intl. — A372

Designs: $2, World Community Service, blankets from Japan donated to Thai children, Harris.

$5, Rotary Intl. Pres. Luis Vincente Giay, US Pres. Jimmy Carter, Rotary award recipient.

**1997, June 3** *Perf. 14*

**2438** A372 $2 multicolored 1.75 1.75

**Souvenir Sheet**

**2439** A372 $5 multicolored 4.00 4.00

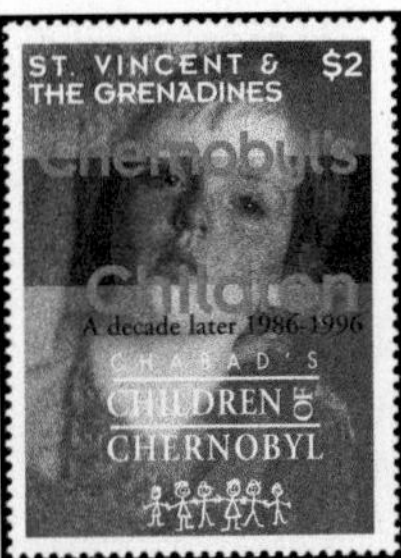

Heinrich von Stephan (1831-97) A373

No. 2440 — Portraits of Von Stephan and: a, Bicycle postman, India, 1800's. b, UPU emblem. c, Zebu-drawn post carriage, Indochina.

$5, Post rider, Indochina.

**1997, June 3**

**2440** A373 $2 Sheet of 3, #a.-c. 4.75 4.75

**Souvenir Sheet**

**2441** A373 $5 gray brown 4.00 4.00

PACIFIC 97.

Chernobyl Disaster, 10th Anniv. A374

Designs: No. 2442, Chabad's Children of Chernobyl. No. 2443, UNESCO.

**1997, June 3 Litho.** *Perf. 13½x14*

**2442** A374 $2 multicolored 1.60 1.60
**2443** A374 $2 multicolored 1.60 1.60

Grimm's Fairy Tales A375

Mother Goose — A376

No. 2444, $2 — Scenes showing "Old Sultan:" a, With woman, man. b, On hillside. c, With wolf. No. 2446, Man, Old Sultan, girl.

No. 2445, $2 — Scenes from "The Cobbler and the Elves:" a, Cobbler. b, Elves. c, Cobbler holding elf.

No. 2446, $5, Elf. No. 2447, $5, Curly-Locks sewing.

**1997, June 3** *Perf. 13½x14*

**Sheets of 3, #a-c**

**2444-2445** A375 Set of 2 9.00 9.00

**Souvenir Sheets**

**2446-2447** A375 Set of 2 8.00 8.00

*Perf. 14*

**2448** A376 $5 multicolored 3.75 3.75

Numbers have been reserved for two additional souvenir sheets with this set.

Inaugural Cricket Test, Arnos Vale — A377

Designs: 90c, Alphonso Theodore Roberts (1937-96), vert. $5, Arnos Vale Playing field.

*Perf. 13½x14, 14x13½*

**1997, June 20 Litho.**

**2451** A377 90c multicolored .70 .70
**2452** A377 $5 multicolored 3.75 3.75

1998 World Cup Soccer Championships, France — A378

Players: 70c, Beckenbauer, W. Germany. 90c, Moore, England. $1, Lato, Poland. $1.10, Pele, Brazil. $2, Maier, W. Germany. $10, Eusebio, Portugal.

No. 2459, $1 — Scenes from England's victory, 1966: a, Stadium. b, c, d, e, f, h, Various action scenes. g, Players coming from field, holding trophy.

No. 2460, $1 — Action scenes from various finals: a, c, Argentina, W. Germany, 1986. b, e, England, W. Germany, 1966. d, Italy, W. Germany, 1982. f, g, Argentina, Holland, 1978. h, W. Germany, Holland, 1974.

No. 2461, $1, vert.: a, Bergkamp, Holland. b, Seaman, England. c, Schmeichel, Denmark. d, Ince, England. e, Futre, Portugal. f, Ravanelli, Italy. g, Keane, Ireland. h, Gascoigne, England.

No. 2462, $1, vert.: a-h, Action scenes from Argentina v. Holland, 1978.

No. 2463, $5, Ally McCoist, Scotland, vert. No. 2464, $5, Salvatori Schillaci, Italy, vert. No. 2465, $5, Mario Kempes, Argentina, vert. No. 2466, $5, Paulao, Angola.

*Perf. 14x13½, 13½x14*

**1997, Aug. 26 Litho.**

**2453-2458** A378 Set of 6 6.00 6.00

**Sheets of 8, #a-h, + Label**

**2459-2462** A378 Set of 4 32.50 32.50

**Souvenir Sheets**

**2463-2466** A378 Set of 4 17.50 17.50

Vincy Mas Carnival, 20th Anniv. A379

Designs: 10c, Mardi Gras Band, "Cinemas." 20c, Queen of the Bands, J. Ballantyne. 50c, Queen of the Bands, vert. 70c, King of the Bands, "Conquistadore." 90c, Starlift Steel Orchestra, Panorama Champs. $2, Frankie McIntosh, musical arranger, vert.

**1997, July 24** *Perf. 14½x14, 14x14½*

**2467-2472** A379 Set of 6 4.00 4.00

Sierra Club, Cent. A380

No. 2473: a, Snow leopard. b, Polar bear. c, d, Isle Royale Natl. Park. e, f, Denali Natl. Park. g, h, i, Joshua Tree Natl. Park.

No. 2474, vert: a, b, c, Mountain gorilla. d, e, Snow leopard. f, g, Polar bear. h, Denali Natl. Park. i, Isle Royale Nat. Park.

No. 2475, vert: a, b, c, Sifaka. d, e, Peregrine falcon. f, Galapagos tortoise. g, h, African Rain Forest. i, China's Yellow Mountains.

No. 2476: a, b, c, Red panda. d, Peregrine falcon. e, f, Galapagos tortoise. g, African Rain Forest. h, i, China's Yellow Mountains.

No. 2477: a, Mountain lion. b, c, Siberian tiger. d, Red wolf. e, Black bear. f, i, Wolong Natl. Reserve. g, h, Belize Rain Forest.

No. 2478, vert: a, Siberian tiger. b, c, Mountain lion. d, e, Black bear. f, g, Red wolf. h, Belize Rain Forest. i, Wolong Natl. Reserve.

No. 2479, vert: a, b, c, Indri. d, e, Gopher tortoise. f, g, Black-footed ferret. h, Haleakala Natl. Park. i, Grand Teton Natl. Park.

No. 2480: a, Black-footed ferret. b, Gopher tortoise. c, d, Grand Teton Natl. Park. e, f, Haleakala Natl. Park. g, h, i, Madagascar Rain Forest.

Scenes in Olympic Natl. Park: No. 2481, $5, Lake, trees. No. 2482, $5, Mountain summit. No. 2483, $5, Snow-topped mountains.

**1997, Sept. 18** ***Perf. 14***

**2473** A380 20c Sheet of 9, #a.-i. 1.40 1.40
**2474** A380 40c Sheet of 9, #a.-i. 2.75 2.75
**2475** A380 50c Sheet of 9, #a.-i. 3.40 3.40
**2476** A380 60c Sheet of 9, #a.-i. 4.00 4.00
**2477** A380 70c Sheet of 9, #a.-i. 4.75 4.75
**2478** A390 90c Sheet of 9, #a.-i. 6.00 6.00
**2479** A380 $1 Sheet of 9, #a.-i. 6.75 6.75
**2480** A380 $1.10 Sheet of 9, #a.-i. 7.50 7.50

**Souvenir Sheets**

**2481-2483** A380 Set of 3 13.00 13.00

Deng Xiaoping (1904-97), Chinese Leader — A381

No. 2484, $2: a-d, Various portraits in dark brown.

No. 2485, $2: a-d, Various portraits in dark blue.

No. 2486, $2: a-d, Various portraits in black.

No. 2487, Deng Xiaoping, Zhuo Lin, horiz.

**1997, June 3** **Litho.** ***Perf. 14***

**Sheets of 4, #a-d**

**2484-2486** A381 Set of 3 18.00 18.00

**Souvenir Sheet**

**2487** A381 $5 multicolored 3.75 3.75

Montreal Protocol on Substances that Deplete Ozone Layer, 10th Anniv. — A382

**1997, Sept. 16**

**2488** A382 90c multicolored 1.10 1.10

Orchids — A383

Designs: 90c, Rhyncholaelia digbyana. $1, Laeliocattleya. $1.10, Doritis pulcherrima. $2, Phalaenopsis.

No. 2493: a, Eulophia speciosa. b, Aerangis rhodosticta. c, Angraecum infundibularea. d, Calanthe sylvatica. e, Phalaenopsis mariae. f, Paphiopedilum insigne. g, Dendrobium nobile. h, Aerangis kotschyana. i, Cyrtorchis chailluana.

No. 2494, $5, Brassavola nodosa. No. 2495, $5, Sanguine broughtonia.

**1997, Sept. 18**

**2489-2492** A383 Set of 4 4.75 4.75
**2493** A383 $1 Sheet of 9, #a.-i. 7.75 7.75

**Souvenir Sheets**

**2494-2495** A383 Set of 2 8.75 8.75

Nos. 2494-2495 each contain one 51x38mm stamp.

Diana, Princess of Wales (1961-97) — A384

No. 2496, $2 — Close-up portraits: a, Wearing tiara. b, Black dress. c, Blue dress. d, Denomination in black.

No. 2497, $2: a, White collar. b, Sleeveless. c, Black dress, holding flowers. d, Blue collar, flowers.

No. 2498, $6, Blue dress. No. 2499, $6, White collar.

**1997** **Sheets of 4, #a-d**

**2496-2497** A384 Set of 2 12.00 12.00

**Souvenir Sheets**

**2498-2499** A384 Set of 2 9.00 9.00

Sinking of RMS Titanic, 85th Anniv. — A385

No. 2500 — Sections of the ship: a, 1st funnel. b, 2nd, 3rd funnels. c, 4th funnel. d, Upper decks. e, Stern.

**1997, Nov. 5** **Litho.** ***Perf. 14***

**2500** A385 $1 Sheet of 5, #a.-e. 8.00 8.00

1997 Rock & Roll Hall of Fame Inductions, Cleveland A386

Designs: $1, Exterior view of Hall of Fame. $1.50, Stylized guitar, "the house that rock built."

**1997, Nov. 5**

**2501** A386 $1 multicolored .75 .75
**2502** A386 $1.50 multicolored 1.15 1.15

Nos. 2501-2502 were each issued in sheets of 8.

"The Doors" Album Covers — A387

Designs: 90c, Morrison Hotel, 1970. 95c, Waiting for the Sun, 1968. $1, L.A. Woman, 1971. $1.10, The Soft Parade, 1969. $1.20, Strange Days, 1967. $1.50, The Doors, 1967.

**1997, Nov. 5**

**2503-2508** A387 Set of 6 8.25 8.25

Nos. 2503-2508 were each issued in sheets of 8.

20th Cent. Artists — A388

No. 2509, $1.10 — Opera singers: a, Lily Pons (1904-76). b, Donizetti's "Lucia Di Lammermoor," Lily Pons. c, Bellini's "I Puritani," Maria Callas. d, Callas (1923-77). e, Beverly Sills (b. 1929). f, Donizetti's "Daughter of the Regiment," Sills. g, Schoenberg's "Erwartung," Jessye Norman. h, Norman (b.1945).

No. 2510, $1.10: a, Enrico Caruso (1873-1921). b, Verdi's "Rigoletto," Caruso. c, "The Seven Hills of Rome," Mario Lanza. d, Lanza (1921-59). e, Luciano Pavarotti (b. 1935). f, Donizetti's "Elixir of Love," Pavarotti. g, Puccini's "Tosca," Placido Domingo. h, Domingo (b. 1941).

No. 2511, $1.10 — Artists, sculptures: a, Constantin Brancusi (1876-1957). b, "The New Born," Brancusi, 1920. c, "Four Elements," Alexander Calder, 1962. d, Calder (1898-1976). e, Isamu Noguchi (1904-88). f, "Dodge Fountain," Noguchi, 1975. g, "The Shuttlecock," Claes Oldenburg, 1994. h, Oldenburg (b. 1929).

**1997, Nov. 5** **Sheets of 8, #a-h**

**2509-2511** A388 Set of 3 21.50 21.50

Size: Nos. 2509b-2509c, 2509f-2509g, 2510b-2510c, 2510f-2510g, 2511b-2511c, 2511f-2511g, 53x38mm.

Christmas A389

Paintings (entire or details), or sculptures: 60c, The Sistine Madonna, by Raphael. 70c, Angel, by Edward Burne-Jones. 90c, Cupid, by Etienne-Maurice Falconet. $1, Saint Michael, by Hubert Gerhard. $1.10, Apollo and the Horae, by Tiepolo. $2, Madonna in a Garland of Flowers, by Rubens and Bruegel the Elder.

No. 2518, $5, The Sacrifice of Isaac, by Tiepolo, horiz. No. 2519, $5, Madonna in a Garland of Flowers, by Rubens and Bruegel the Elder.

**1997, Nov. 26**

**2512-2517** A389 Set of 6 6.25 6.25

**Souvenir Sheets**

**2518-2519** A389 Set of 2 8.00 8.00

New Year 1998 (Year of the Tiger) — A390

No. 2520 — Stylized tigers, Chinese inscriptions within checkered squares: a, light brown & pale olive. b, tan & gray. c, pink & pale violet.

$2, yellow orange & pink.

**1998, Jan. 5** ***Perf. 14½***

**2520** A390 $1 Sheet of 3, #a.-c. 2.25 2.25

**Souvenir Sheet**

**2521** A390 $2 multicolored 2.00 2.00

Cooperative Foundation for Natl. Development A391

Designs: 20c, Children going to school. 90c, People working in field, Credit Union office, vert. $1.10, Industry, ship at dock.

**1998, Jan. 5** **Litho.** ***Perf. 13½***

**2522-2524** A391 Set of 3 2.10 2.10

Jazz Entertainers — A392

No. 2525: a, King Oliver. b, Louis Armstrong. c, Sidney Bechet. d, Nick Larocca. e, Louis Prima. f, Buddy Bolden.

**1998, Feb. 2** ***Perf. 14x13½***

**2525** A392 $1 Sheet of 6, #a.-f. 5.00 5.00

1998 Winter Olympic Games, Nagano A393 A394

Designs, horiz: 70c, Ice hockey. $1.10, Bobsled. $2, Pairs figure skating. $2, Skier, vert.

No. 2530 — Medalists: a, Bjorn Daehlie. b, Gillis Grafstrom. c, Sonja Henie. d, Ingemar Stenmark. e, Christian Jagge. f, Tomas Gustafson. g, Johann Olav Koss. h, Thomas Wassberg.

No. 2531, $1.50 — Olympic rings in background: a, Downhill skier. b, Woman figure skater. c, Ski jumper. d, Speed skater. e, 4-Man bobsled team. f, Cross country country skier.

No. 2532, $1.50 — Olympic flame in background: a, Downhill skier. b, Bobsled. c, Ski jumper. d, Slalom skier. e, Luge. f, Biathlon.

No. 2533, $5, Slalom skiing. No. 2534, $5, Hockey player, horiz.

**1998, Feb. 2** *Perf. 14*
**2526-2529** A393 Set of 4 5.50 5.50
**2530** A394 $1.10 Sheet of 8, #a.-h. 7.50 7.50

**Sheets of 6, #a-f**
**2531-2532** A393 Set of 2 15.00 15.00

**Souvenir Sheets**
**2533-2534** A393 Set of 2 8.50 8.50

Butterflies A395

Designs: 20c, Amarynthis meneria. 50c, Papillo polyxenes. 70c, Emesis fatima, vert. $1, Anartia amathea.
No. 2539, vert: a, Heliconius erato. b, Danaus plexippus. c, Papillo phorcas. d, Morpho pelaides. e, Pandoriana pandora. f, Basilarchia astyanax. g, Vanessa cardui. h, Colobura dirce. i, Heraclides cresphontes.
No. 2540, $6, Colias eurytheme. No. 2541, $6, Everes comyntas.

**1998, Feb, 23** *Perf. 13½*
**2535-2538** A395 Set of 4 2.50 2.50
**2539** A395 $1 Sheet of 9, #a.-i. 7.50 7.50

**Souvenir Sheets**
**2540-2541** A395 Set of 2 9.50 9.50

Endangered Fauna — A396

Designs: 50c, Anegada rock iguana. 70c, Jamaican swallowtail. 90c, Blossom bat. $1, Solenodon. $1.10, Hawksbill turtle. $2, West Indian whistling duck.
No. 2548, $1.10: a, Roseate spoonbill. b, Golden swallow. c, Short-snouted spinner dolphin. d, Queen conch. e, West Indian manatee. f, Loggerhead turtle.
No. 2549, $1.10: a, Magnificent frigatebird. b, Humpback whale. c, Southern dagger-tail. d, St. Lucia whiptail e, St. Lucia oriole. f, Green turtle.
No. 2550, $5, St. Vincent parrot. No. 2551, $5, Antiguan racer.

**1998, Feb. 23** *Perf. 13*
**2542-2547** A396 Set of 6 5.25 5.25

**Sheets of 6, #a-f**
**2548-2549** A396 Set of 2 11.50 11.50

**Souvenir Sheets**
**2550-2551** A396 Set of 2 8.50 8.50

Mushrooms A397

Designs: 10c, Gymnopilus spectabilis. 20c, Entoloma lividium. 70c, Pholiota flammans. 90c, Panaeolus semiovatus. $1, Stropharia rugosoannulata. $1.10, Tricholoma sulphureum.
No. 2558: a, Amanita caesarea. b, Amanita muscaria. c, Aminita ovoidea. d, Amanita phalloides. e, Amanitopsis inaurata. f, Amanitopsis vaginata. g, Psalliota campestris, alfalfa butterfly. h, Psalliota arvenis. i, Coprinus comatus.
No. 2559: a, Coprinus picaceus. b, Stropharia umbonatescens. c, Hebeloma crustuliniforme, figure-of-eight butterfly. d, Cortinarius collinitus. e, Cortinarius violaceus, common dotted butterfly. f, Cortinarius armillatus. g, Tricholoma aurantium. h, Russula virescens. i, Clitocybe infundibuliformis.

No. 2560, $6, Hygrocybe conica. No. 2561, $6, Amanita caesarea.

**1998, Feb. 23** **Litho.** *Perf. 13½*
**2552-2557** A397 Set of 6 4.00 4.00
**2558** A397 $1 Sheet of 9, #a.-i. 8.25 8.25
**2559** A397 $1.10 Sheet of 9, #a.-i. 9.00 9.00

**Souvenir Sheets**
**2560-2561** A397 Set of 2 9.50 9.50

Mickey Mouse, 70th Birthday — A398

Designs: 2c, Wake up, Mickey. 3c, Morning run. 4c, Getting ready. 5c, Eating breakfast. 10c, School "daze." 65c, Time out for play. $3, Volunteer worker. $4, A date with Minnie. $5, Ready for bed.
Weekly hi-lites from "Mickey Mouse Club," vert: a, The opening march. b, Monday, fun with music day. c, Tuesday, guest star day. d, Wednesday, anything can happen day. e, Thursday, circus day. f, Friday, talent round up day.
Mickey Mouse: No. 2572, $5, Reading, vert. No. 2573, $6, Playing piano, vert. No. 2574, $6, Blowing trumpet. No. 2575, $6, On the Internet, vert.

*Perf. 14x13½, 13½x14*
**1998, Mar. 23** **Litho.**
**2562-2570** A398 Set of 9 10.50 10.50
**2571** A398 $1.10 Sheet of 6, #a.-f. 5.00 5.00

**Souvenir Sheets**
**2572-2575** A398 Set of 4 17.00 17.00

Winnie the Pooh — A399

Scenes from animated films: a, Pooh looking out open window. b, Eeyore, Kanga, Roo. c, Pooh getting honey from tree. d, Rabbit, Pooh stuck in entrance to Rabbit's house. e, Christopher Robin pulling Pooh from Rabbit's house, Owl. f, Piglet sweeping leaves. g, Pooh sleeping. h, Eeyore. i, Tigger on top of Pooh.
No. 2577, Tigger, Pooh, Piglet.

**1998, Mar. 23** *Perf. 14x13½*
**2576** A399 $1 Sheet of 9, #a.-i. 8.50 8.50

**Souvenir Sheet**
**2577** A399 $6 multicolored 7.00 7.00

Dogs — A400

Designs: 70c, Australian terrier. 90c, Bull mastiff. $1.10, Pomeranian. $2, Dandie dinmont terrier.
No. 2582, $1.10, horiz: a, Tyrolean hunting dog. b, Papillon. c, Fox terriers. d, Bernese mountain dog. e, King Charles spaniel. f, German shepherd.
No. 2583, $1.10, horiz: a, Beagle. b, German shepherd. c, Pointer. d, Vizsla. e, Bulldog. f, Shetland sheepdogs.
No. 2584, $6, Scottish terrier, wooden deck, grass. No. 2585, $6, Scottish terrier, grass, trees.

**1998, Apr. 21** *Perf. 14*
**2578-2581** A400 Set of 4 4.50 4.50

**Sheets of 6, #a-f**
**2582-2583** A400 Set of 2 12.00 12.00

**Souvenir Sheets**
**2584-2585** A400 Set of 2 10.00 10.50

**Nos. 2306-2309 Overprinted**

**1998, May 19** **Litho.** *Perf. 14*
**2586-2588** A345 Set of 3 3.75 3.75

**Souvenir Sheet**
**2589** A345 $5 multicolored 4.25 4.25

No. 2589 contains overprint "ISRAEL 98 — WORLD STAMP EXHIBITION / TEL-AVIV 13-21 MAY 1998" in sheet margin.

Trains A401

Designs: 10c, LMS Bahamas No. 5596. 20c, Ex-Mza 1400. 50c, Mallard. 70c, Monarch 0-4-4 OT. 90c, Big Chief. $1.10, Duchess of Rutland LMS No. 6228.
No. 2596, $1.10: a, Hadrian Flyer. b, Highland Jones Goods No. 103. c, Blackmore Vale No. 34023. d, Wainwright SECR No. 27. e, Stepney Brighton Terrier. f, RENFE Freight train No. 040 2184. g, Calbourne No. 24. h, Clun Castle 1950.
No. 2597, $1.10: a, Ancient Holmes J36 060. b, Patentee 2-2-2. c, Kingfisher. d, St. Pierre No. 23. e, SAR Class 19c 4-8-2. f, SAR 6J 4-6-0. g, Evening Star No. 92220. h, Old No. 1.
No. 2598, $5, King George V No. 6000 BR. No. 2599, $5, Caledonia.

**1998, June 2** **Litho.** *Perf. 14*
**2590-2595** A401 Set of 6 3.25 3.25

**Sheets of 8, #a-h**
**2596-2597** A401 Set of 2 15.00 15.00

**Souvenir Sheets**
**2598-2599** A401 Set of 2 8.25 8.25

UNESCO Intl. Year of the Ocean A402

Marine life: 70c, Beluga whale. 90c, Atlantic manta. $1.10, Forceps butterfly fish, copperband butterfly fish, moorish idol. $2, Octopus.
No. 2604, $1, vert.: a, Harlequin wrasse. b, Blue sturgeon fish. c, Spotted trunkfish. d, Regal angelfish. e, Porcupine fish. f, Clownfish, damselfish. g, Lion fish. h, Moray eel. i, French angelfish.
No. 2605, $1, vert.: a, Lemonpeel angelfish. b, Narwhal. c, Panther grouper. d, Fur seal. e, Spiny boxfish. f, Loggerhead turtle. g, Qpah. h, Clown triggerfish. i, Bighead searobin.
No. 2606, $5, Seahorse, vert. No. 2607, $5, Australian sea dragon, vert.

**1998, July 1**
**2600-2603** A402 Set of 4 4.25 4.25

**Sheets of 9, #a-i**
**2604-2605** A402 Set of 2 15.00 15.00

**Souvenir Sheets**
**2606-2607** A402 Set of 2 8.25 8.25

Birds A403

Designs: 50c, Cock of the rock, vert. 60c, Quetzal, vert. 70c, Wood stork, vert. No. 2611, 90c, St. Vincent parrot, vert. No. 2612, 90c, Toucan. $1, Greater bird of paradise. $1.10, Sunbittern. $2, Green honeycreeper.
No. 2616, vert.: a, Racquet-tailed motmot. b, Red-billed quelea. c, Leadbeater's cockatoo. d, Scarlet macaw. e, Bare-throated bellbird. f, Tucaman Amazon parrot. g, Black-lored red tanager. h, Fig parrot. i, St. Vincent Amazon parrot. j, Peach-faced love birds. k, Blue fronted Amazon parrot. l, Yellow billed Amazon parrot.
No. 2617, $5, Hyacinth macaw, vert. No. 2618, $5, Blue-headed hummingbird, vert.

**1998, June 16** **Litho.** *Perf. 14*
**2608-2615** A403 Set of 8 7.00 7.00

**Sheet of 12**
**2616** A403 90c Sheet of 12, #a.-l. 10.00 10.00

**Souvenir Sheets**
**2617-2618** A403 Set of 2 9.00 9.00

No. 2611 has different style of lettering.

Diana, Princess of Wales (1961-97) — A404

Designs: No. 2619, Diana in orange jacket. No. 2620, Diana in blue blouse.

**Litho. & Embossed**
**1998, Aug. 1** *Die Cut 7½*
**2619** A404 $20 gold & multi 20.00 20.00
**2620** A404 $20 gold & multi 20.00 20.00

CARICOM, 25th Anniv. — A405

**1998, July 4** **Litho.** *Perf. 13½*
**2621** A405 $1 multicolored 1.25 1.25

Enzo Ferrari (1898-1988), Automobile Manufacturer — A406

No. 2622 — Classic Ferraris: a, 365 GTS. b, Testarossa. c, 365 GT4 BB.
$6, Dino 206 GT.

**1998, Sept. 15** **Litho.** *Perf. 14*
**2622** A406 $2 Sheet of 3, #a.-c. 5.00 5.00

**Souvenir Sheet**
**2623** A406 $6 multicolored 5.00 5.00

No. 2623 contains one 91x35mm stamp.

Paintings by Pablo Picasso (1881-1973) — A407

Designs: $1.10, Landscape, 1972. No. 2625, $2, The Kiss, 1969. No. 2626, $2, The Death of the Female Torero, 1933.
$5, Flute Player, 1962, vert.

**1998, Sept. 15** ***Perf. 14½***
**2624-2626** A407 Set of 3 4.00 4.00

**Souvenir Sheet**

**2627** A407 $5 multicolored 4.50 4.50

Organization of American States, 50th Anniv. A408

**1998, Sept. 15 Litho.** ***Perf. 13½***
**2628** A408 $1 multicolored 1.25 1.25

Diana, Princess of Wales (1961-97) — A409

Designs: a, Peach bar with country name on left side. b, Peach bar with country name on right side.

**1998, Sept. 15** ***Perf. 14½***
**2629** A409 $1.10 Pair, #a.-b. 2.50 2.50

**Souvenir Sheet**
**Self-Adhesive**
***Serpentine Die Cut Perf. 11½***
**Size: 53x65mm**

**2630** A409 $8 Diana, buildings

No. 2629 was printed in sheets containing 3 pairs. Soaking in water may affect the image of No. 2630.

Mahatma Gandhi (1869-1948) A411

Design: $5, Seated at table with officials, horiz.

**1998, Sept. 15** ***Perf. 14***
**2631** A411 $1 shown 1.40 1.40

**Souvenir Sheet**

**2632** A411 $5 multicolored 6.50 6.50

No. 2631 was issued in sheets of 4.

Royal Air Force, 80th Anniv. A412

No. 2633, $2: a, AEW1 AWACS. b, BAe Eurofighter EF2000. c, Sepcat Jaguar GR1A. d, BAe Hawk T1A.
No. 2634, $2: a, Two Sepcat Jaguar GR1s. b, Panavia Tornado F3. c, Three BAe Harrier GR7s. d, Panavia Tornado F3 IDV.
No. 2635, $6, Mosquito, Eurofighter. No. 2636, $6, Hawk's head, hawk, biplane. No. 2637, $6, Biplane, hawk in flight. No. 2638, $6, Vulcan B2, Eurofighter.

**1998, Sept. 15** ***Perf. 14***
**Sheets of 4, #a-d**

**2633-2634** A412 Set of 2 15.00 15.00

**Souvenir Sheets**

**2635-2638** A412 Set of 4 22.50 22.50

1998 World Scout Jamboree, Chile — A413

No. 2639: a, Astronaut John Glenn receives Silver Buffalo award, 1965. b, Herb Shriner learns knot tying at 1960 Natl. Jamboree. c, "Ready to go" Boy Scouts break camp, 1940's.
$5, Lord Robert Baden-Powell (1857-1941), vert.

**1998, Sept. 15**
**2639** A413 $2 Sheet of 3, #a.-c. 5.00 5.00

**Souvenir Sheet**

**2640** A413 $5 multicolored 4.25 4.25

Ancient Order of Foresters Friendly Society, Court Morning Star 2298, Cent. — A414

Designs: 10c, Bro. H.E.A. Daisley, PCR. 20c, R.N. Jack, PCR. 50c, Woman, man shaking hands, emblem. 70c, Symbol of recognition. 90c, Morning Star Court's headquarters.

**1998, Oct. 29 Litho.** ***Perf. 13½***
**2641-2645** A414 Set of 5 2.10 2.10

RMS Titanic — A415

***Die Cut 7½***

**1998, Oct. 29** **Embossed**
**2646** A415 $20 gold 17.50 17.50

Christmas A418

Domestic cats: 20c, Bi-color longhair. 50c, Korat. 60c, Seal-point Siamese. 70c, Red self longhair. 90c, Black longhair. $1.10, Red tabby exotic shorthair.
No. 2653, $5, Seal-point colorpoint. No. 2654, $5, Toirtoiseshell shorthair.

**1998, Dec. Litho.** ***Perf. 14***
**2647-2652** A418 Set of 6 3.00 3.00

**Souvenir Sheets**

**2653-2654** A418 Set of 2 8.00 8.00

Hildegard von Bingen (1098?-1179) A419

No. 2655: a, Woman playing flute. b, Hildegard holding tablets. c, Woman playing violin. d, Pope Eugenius. e, Bingen, site of Hildegard's convent. f, Portrait.
$5, Portrait, diff.

**1998, Dec. 15 Litho.** ***Perf. 14***
**2655** A419 $1.10 Sheet of 6, #a.-f. 5.75 5.75

**Souvenir Sheet**

**2656** A419 $5 multicolored 4.25 4.25

New Year 1999 (Year of the Rabbit — A420

No. 2657 — Stylized rabbits: a, Looking right. b, Looking forward. c, Looking left.
$2, Like #2657b.

**1999, Jan. 4 Litho.** ***Perf. 14½***
**2657** A420 $1 Sheet of 3, #a.-c. 2.25 2.25

**Souvenir Sheet**

**2658** A420 $2 multicolored 1.50 1.50

Queen Elizabeth II and Prince Philip, 50th Wedding Anniv. (in 1997) — A421

**Litho. & Embossed**
**1999, Jan. 5** ***Die Cut Perf. 6***
**Without Gum**

**2659** A421 $20 gold & multi 17.50 17.50

Disney Characters in Winter Sports A422

No. 2660, $1.10 — Wearing checkered outfits: a, Minnie. b, Mickey. c, Goofy. d, Donald. e, Mickey (goggles on head). f, Daisy.
No. 2661, $1.10 — Wearing brightly-colored outfits: a, Daisy. b, Mickey. c, Mickey, Goofy. d, Goofy. e, Minnie. f, Donald.
No. 2662, $1.10 — Wearing red, purple & yellow: a, Mickey. b, Goofy. c, Donald. d, Goofy, Mickey. e, Goofy (arms over head). f, Minnie.
No. 2663, $5, Mickey in checkered outfit. No. 2664, $5, Goofy eating ice cream cone, Mickey, horiz. No. 2665, $5, Mickey in red, purple & yellow.

**1999, Jan. 21 Litho.** ***Perf. 13½x14***
**Sheets of 6, #a-f**

**2660-2662** A422 Set of 3 15.00 15.00

**Souvenir Sheets**

**2663-2665** A422 Set of 3 12.00 12.00

Mickey Mouse, 70th anniv.

World Championship Wrestling A423

No. 2666: a, Hollywood Hogan. b, Sting. c, Bret Hart. d, The Giant. e, Kevin Nash. f, Randy Savage. g, Diamond Dallas Page. h, Bill Goldberg.

**1999, Jan. 25 Litho.** ***Perf. 13***
**2666** A423 70c Sheet of 8, #a.-h. 4.25 4.25

Australia '99, World Stamp Expo A424

Prehistoric animals: 70c, Plateosaurus. 90c, Euoplacephalus. $1.10, Pachycephalosaurus. $1.40, Dilophosaurus.
No. 2671: a, Struthiomimus. b, Indricotherium. c, Giant moa. d, Deinonychus. e, Sabre tooth cat. f, Dawn horse. g, Peittacosaurus. h, Giant ground sloth. i, Wooly rhinoceros. j, Mosasaur. k, Mastodon. l, Syndoyceras.
No. 2672: a, Rhamphorhynchus. b, Pteranodon. c, Archaeopterix. d, Dimetrodon. e, Stegosaurus. f, Parasaurolophus. g, Iguanadon. h, Triceratops. i, Tyrannosaurus. j, Ichthyosaurus. k, Plesiosaurus. l, Hersperonis.
No. 2273, $5, Diplodocus. No. 2674, $5, Wooly mammoth, vert.

**1999, Mar. 1 Litho.** ***Perf. 14***
**2667-2670** A424 Set of 4 4.25 4.25
**2671** A424 70c Sheet of 12, #a.-l. 6.50 6.50
*m.* As #2671, imperf. 6.50 6.50
**2672** A424 90c Sheet of 12, #a.-l. 8.25 8.25
*m.* As #2672, imperf. 8.25 8.25

**Souvenir Sheets**

**2673-2674** A424 $5 Set of 2 7.50 7.50
*2673a-2674a* Set of 2, imperf. 7.50 7.50

Flora and Fauna A425

Designs: 10c, Acacia tree, elephant. 20c, Green turtle, coconut palm. 25c, Mangrove tree, white ibis. 50c, Tiger swallowtail, ironweed. 70c, Eastern box turtle, jack-in-the-pulpit, vert. 90c, Praying mantis, milkweed, vert. $1.10, Zebra finch, bottle brush, vert. $1.40, Koala, gum tree, vert.
No. 2683, 70c, vert.: a, Red tailed hawk, ocitillo. b, Morning dove, organ pipe cactus. c, Paloverde tree, burrowing owl. d, Cactus wren, saguaro cactus. e, Ocitillo, puma. f, Organ pipe cactus, gray fox. g, Coyete, prickly pear cactus. h, Saguaro cactus, gila woodpecker. i, Collared lizard, barrel cactus. j, Cowblinder cactus, gila monster. k, Hedgehog cactus, roadrunner. l, Saguaro cactus, jack rabbit.
No. 2684, 70c, vert.: a, Strangler fig, basilisk lizard. b, Macaw, kapok trees. c, Cecropia tree, howler monkey. d, Cecropia tree, toucan. e, Arrow poison frog, bromiliad. f, Rattlesnake orchid, heliconius phyllis. g, Tree fern, bat eating hawk. h, Jaguar, tillandsia. i, Margay, sierra palm. j, Lesser bird of paradise, aristolchia. k, Parides, erythrina. l, Fer-de-lance, zebra plant.
No. 2685, $5, Alligator, water lilies. No. 2686, $5, Riuolis, hummingbird.

**1999, Apr. 12 Litho.** ***Perf. 14***
**2675-2682** A425 Set of 8 3.75 3.75

**Sheets of 12, #a-l**

**2683-2684** A425 Set of 2 13.00 13.00

**Souvenir Sheets**

**2685-2686** A425 Set of 2 7.50 7.50

Aviation History A426

Designs: 60c, Montgolfier balloon, 1783, vert. 70c, Lilienthal glider, 1894. 90c, Zeppelin. $1, Wright brothers, 1903.

No. 2691, $1.10: a, DH-4 bomber. b, Sopwith Camel. c, Sopwith Dove. d, Jeannin Stahl Taube. e, Fokker DR-1 triplane. f, Albatros Diva. g, Sopwith Pup. h, Spad XIII Smith IV.

No. 2692, $1.10: a, M-130 Clipper. b, DC-3, 1937. c, Beech Staggerwing CVR FT C-17L. d, Hughes H-1 racer. e, Gee Bee Model R-1, 1932. f, Lockheed Sirius Tingmissartoq. g, Fokker T-2, 1923. h, Curtiss CW-16E Floatplane.

No. 2693, $5, Bleriot XI crossing English Channel, 1914. No. 2694, $5, Le Bandy airship, 1903.

**1999, Apr. 26**

**2687-2690** A426 Set of 4 2.50 2.50

**Sheets of 8, #a-h**

**2691-2692** A426 Set of 2 13.50 13.50

**Souvenir Sheets**

**2693-2694** A426 Set of 2 7.50 7.50

'N Sync, Musical Group — A427

**1999, May 4 Litho.** ***Perf. 12½***

**2695** A427 $1 multicolored .75 .75

No. 2695 was issued in sheets of 8.

History of Space Exploration, 1609-2000 — A428

Designs: 20c, Galileo, 1609. 50c, Konstantin Tsiolkovsky, 1903. 70c, Robert H. Goddard, 1926. 90c, Sir Isaac Newton, 1668, vert.

No. 2700, $1: a, Luna 9, 1959. b, Soyuz 11, 1971. c, Mir Space Station, 1996. d, Sputnik 1, 1957. e, Apollo 4, 1967. f, Bruce McCandless, 1984. g, Sir William Herschel, telescope, 1781. h, John Glenn, 1962. i, Space Shuttle Columbia, 1981.

No. 2701, $1, vert: a, Yuri Gargarin, 1962. b, Lunar Rover, 1971. c, Mariner 10, 1974-75. d, Laika, 1957. e, Neil A. Armstrong, 1969. f, Skylab Space Station, 1973. g, German V-2 Rocket, 1942. h, Gemini 4, 1965. i, Hubble Telescope, 1990.

No. 2702, $1, vert: a, Explorer, 1958. b, Lunokhod Explorer, 1970. c, Viking Lander, 1975. d, R7 Rocket, 1957. e, Edward H. White, 1965. f, Salyut 1, 1971. g, World's oldest observatory. h, Freedom 7, 1961. i, Ariane Rocket, 1980's.

No. 2703, $5, Atlantis docking with Space Station Mir, 1995. No. 2704, $5, Saturn V, 1969, vert.

**1999, May 6** ***Perf. 14***

**2696-2699** A428 Set of 4 1.75 1.75

**Sheets of 9, #a-i**

**2700-2702** A428 Set of 3 21.00 21.00

**Souvenir Sheets**

**2703-2704** A428 Set of 2 7.50 7.50

Johann Wolfgang von Goethe (1749-1832), Poet — A430

No. 2709: a, Faust Dying in the Arms of the Lemures. b, Portraits of Goethe, Friederich von Schiller (1759-1805). c, The Immortal Spirit of Faust is Carried Aloft.

No. 2710: a, Faust and Helena with Their Son, Euphonon. b, Mephistopheles Leading the Lemures to Faust.

No. 2711, $5, The Immortal soul of Faust, vert. No. 2712, $5, Portrait of Goethe, vert.

**1999, June 25 Litho.** ***Perf. 14***

**2709** A430 $3 Sheet of 3, #a.-c. 6.75 6.75

**2710** A430 $3 Sheet of 3, #a.-b. + #2709b 6.75 6.75

**Souvenir Sheets**

**2711-2712** A430 Set of 2 7.50 7.50

Paintings by Hokusai (1760-1849) A431

No. 2713, $1.10: a, Landscape with a Hundred Bridges (large mountain). b, Sea Life (turtle, head LL). c, Landscape with a Hundred Bridges (large bridge in center). d, A View of Aoigaoka Waterfall in Edo. e, Sea Life (crab). f, Women on the Beach at Enoshima.

No. 2714, $1.10: a, Admiring the Irises at Yatsuhashi (large tree). b, Sea Life (turtle, head UL). c, Admiring the Irises at Yatsuhashi (peak of bridge). d, Pilgrims Bathing in Roben Waterfall. e, Sea Life (turtle, head UR). f, Farmers Crossing a Suspension Bridge.

No. 2715, $5, In the Horse Washing Waterfall. No. 2716, $5, A Fisherman at Kajikazawa.

**1999, June 25** ***Perf. 13¾***

**Sheets of 6, #a-f**

**2713-2714** A431 Set of 2 10.00 10.00

**Souvenir Sheet**

**2715-2716** A431 Set of 2 7.50 7.50

Wedding of Prince Edward and Sophie Rhys-Jones A432

No. 2717: a, Edward. b, Sophie, Edward. c, Sophie.

$6, Couple, horiz.

**1999, June 19 Litho.** ***Perf. 13½***

**2717** A432 $3 Sheet of 3, #a-c 6.75 6.75

**Souvenir Sheet**

**2718** A432 $6 multicolored 4.50 4.50

IBRA '99, World Philatelic Exhibition, Nuremberg — A433

Design: $1, Krauss-Maffei V-200 diesel locomotive, Germany, 1852.

**1999, June 25** ***Perf. 14***

**2720** A433 $1 multicolored .75 .75

A 90c value was prepared. Its status is unclear.

Souvenir Sheets

PhilexFrance '99, World Philatelic Exhibition — A434

Locomotives: No. 2721, $6, Pacific, 1930's. No. 2722, $6, Quadrt, electric hight-speed, 1940.

**1999, June 25** ***Perf. 13¾***

**2721-2722** A434 Set of 2 9.00 9.00

A435

No. 2723 — Children: a, Tyreek Isaacs. b, Fredique Isaacs. c, Jerome Burke III. d, Kellisha Roberts.

No. 2724: a, Girl with braided hair. b, Girl wearing hat. c, Girl holding kitten.

$5, Girl with bow in hair.

**1999, June 25** ***Perf. 14***

**2723** A435 90c Sheet of 4, #a.-d. 2.75 2.75

**2724** A435 $3 Sheet of 3, #a.-c. 6.75 6.75

**Souvenir Sheet**

**2725** A435 $5 multicolored 3.75 3.75

UN Convention on Rights of the Child, 10th anniv.

A436

No. 2726: a, I.M. Pei. b, Billy Graham. c, Barbara Cartland. d, Mike Wallace. e, Jeanne Moreau. f, B.B. King. g, Elie Wiesel. h, Arthur Miller. i, Colin Powell. j, Jack Palance. k, Neil Simon. l, Eartha Kitt.

No. 2727: a, Thomas M. Saunders J.P. b, Mother Sarah Baptiste, M.B.E. c, Sir Sydney Gun-Munro MD, KF, GCMG. d, Dr. Earle Kirby, JP, OBE.

**1999, June 25**

**2726** A436 70c Sheet of 12, #a.-l. 6.25 6.25

**2727** A436 $1.10 Sheet of 4, #a.-d. 3.25 3.25

Intl. Year of Older Persons.

World Teachers' Day — A437

No. 2728: a, Henry Alphaeus Robertson. b, Yvonne C. E. Francis-Gibson. c, Edna Peters. d, Christopher Wilberforce Prescod.

**1999, Oct. 5 Litho.** ***Perf. 14¾***

**2728** A437 $2 Sheet of 4, #a.-d. 6.00 6.00

A438

Queen Mother (b. 1900) — A439

No. 2729: a, In 1909. b, With King George VI, Princess Elizabeth, 1930. c, At Badminton, 1977. d, In 1983.

$6, In 1987. $20, Close-up.

**1999 Litho.** ***Perf. 14***

**Gold Frames**

**2729** A438 $2 Sheet of 4, #a.-d., + label 6.00 6.00

**Souvenir Sheet**

***Perf. 13¾***

**2730** A438 $6 multicolored 4.50 4.50

**Litho. & Embossed**

***Die Cut 9x8¾***

**Size: 55x93mm**

**2731** A439 $20 gold & multi 20.00 20.00

Issued: Nos. 2729-2730, 10/18; No. 2731, 8/4. No. 2730 contains one 38x50mm stamp.

See Nos. 3010-3011.

Christmas A440

Designs: 20c, The Resurrection, by Albrecht Dürer. 50c, Christ in Limbo, by Dürer. 70c, Christ Falling on the Way to Calvary, by Raphael. 90c, St. Ildefonso with the Madonna and Child, by Peter Paul Rubens. $5, The Crucifixion, by Raphael.

$6,The Sistine Madonna, by Raphael.

**1999, Nov. 22 Litho.** ***Perf. 13¾***

**2732-2736** A440 Set of 5 5.50 5.50

**Souvenir Sheet**

**2737** A440 $6 multicolored 4.50 4.50

UPU, 125th Anniv. A441

Designs: a, Mail coach. b, Intercontinental sea mail. c, Concorde.

**1999, Dec. 7** ***Perf. 14***
**2738** A441 $3 Sheet of 3, #a.-c. 6.75 6.75

Millennium of Faces — A442

Various paintings making up a photomosaic of the Mona Lisa.

**1999, Dec. 7** ***Perf. 13¼***
**2739** A442 $1.10 Sheet of 8, #a.-h. 6.50 6.50

See #2744, 2816.

A443

Millennium: No. 2740, Clyde Tombaugh discovers Pluto, 1930.

No. 2741 — Highlights of the 1930s: a, Mahatma Gandhi's Salt March, 1930. b, Like #2740, with colored margin. c, Empire State Building opens, 1931. d, Spain becomes a republic, 1931. e, Franklin D. Roosevelt launches New Deal, 1933. f, Reichstag burns in Germany, 1933. g, Mao Zedong leads China's revolution, 1934. h, Spanish Civil War led by Francisco Franco, 1936. i, Edward VIII abdicates, 1936. j, Diego Rivera, 50th birthday, 1936. k, Golden Gate Bridge opens, 1937. l, First atomic reaction achieved, 1939. m, World War II begins, 1939. n, Television debuts at New York World's Fair, 1939. o, Selection of Dalai Lama, 1939. p, Hindenburg explodes, 1937 (60x40mm). q, Igor Sikorsky builds first practical helicopter, 1939.

No. 2742 — Sculptures by: a, Elizabeth Murray. b, Alexander Calder. c, Charles William Moss. d, Gaston Lachaise. e, Claes Oldenburg. f, Louise Bourgeois. g, Duane Hanson. h, Brancusi. i, David Smith. j, Dan Flavin. k, Boccioni. l, George Segal. m, Lucas Samaras. n, Marcel Duchamp. o, Isamu Noguchi. p, Donald Judd (60x40mm). q, Louise Nevelson.

**1999, Dec. 7** **Litho.** ***Perf. 13¼x13***
**2740** A443 60c multicolored .45 .45

***Perf. 12¾x12½***
**2741** A443 60c Sheet of 17, #a.-q. + label 7.50 7.50
**2742** A443 60c Sheet of 17, #a.-q. + label 7.50 7.50

Inscription on No. 2742e is misspelled.
See No. 2764.

**Painting Type of 1999**

Various flowers making up a photomosaic of Princess Diana.

**1999, Dec. 31** **Litho.** ***Perf. 13¾***
**2744** A442 $1 Sheet of 8, #a.-h. 6.00 6.00

New Year 2000 (Year of the Dragon) — A444

No. 2745 — Background colors: a, Blue and red lilac. b, Salmon pink and olive. c, Brick red and lilac rose.

$4, Brown and dull green.

**2000, Feb. 5** **Litho.** ***Perf. 14¾***
**2745** A444 $2 Sheet of 3, #a.-c. 4.50 4.50

**Souvenir Sheet**
**2746** A444 $4 multi 3.00 3.00

Marine Life — A445

Designs: 50c, High hat. 90c, Spotfin hogfish. $1, Royal gramma. $2, Queen angelfish.

No. 2751: a, Sergeant major. b, Hawksbill turtle, whale's tail. c, Horse-eyed jacks, rear of turtle. d, Two horse-eyed jacks, humpback whale. e, Three horse-eyed jacks, head of humpback whale. f, Black-cap gramma. g, Common dolphins. h, French grunts, with Latin inscription. i, Barracuda. j, Bottlenosed dolphin. k, Sea horse. l, Southern stingray, French grunt. m, French grunts, no Latin inscription. n, Indigo hamlet. o, Basking shark. p, Nassau grouper. q, Nurse shark, ribbonfish. r, Southern stingray. s, Southern stingray, blue shark. t, Spanish hogfish.

No. 2752, $5, Rock beauties. No. 2753, $5, Banded butterflyfish.

**2000, Feb. 28** **Litho.** ***Perf. 14***
**2747-2750** A445 Set of 4 3.25 3.25
**2751** A445 50c Sheet of 20, #a.-t. 7.50 7.50

**Souvenir Sheets**
**2752-2753** A445 Set of 2 7.50 7.50

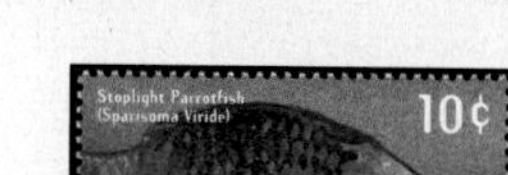
Fish A446

Designs: 10c, Stoplight parrotfish. 20c, Spotfin hogfish. 70c, Beaugregory. 90c, Porkfish. $1, Barred hamlet. $1.40, Queen triggerfish.

No. 2760, $1.10: a, French angelfish. b, Smooth trunkfish. c, Sargassum triggerfish. d, Indigo hamlet. e, Yellowheaded jawfish. f, Peppermint bass.

No. 2761, $1.10: a, Porcupine fish. b, Blue tang. c, Bluehead wrasse. d, Juvenile queen angelfish. e, Sea horse. f, Small mouth grunt.

No. 2762, $5, Pygmy angelfish. No. 2763, $5, Four-eye butterflyfish.

**2000, Feb. 28**
**2754-2759** A446 Set of 6 3.25 3.25

**Sheets of 6, #a.-f.**
**2760-2761** A446 Set of 2 10.00 10.00

**Souvenir Sheets**
**2762-2763** A446 Set of 2 7.50 7.50

**Millennium Type of 1999**

No. 2764 — Highlights of 1900-1950: a, Sigmund Freud publishes "Interpretation of Dreams." b, First long distance wireless transmission. c, First powered airplane flight. d, Einstein proposes theory of relativity. e, Henry Ford unveils Model T. f, Alfred Wegener develops theory of continental drift. g, World War I begins. h, 1917 Russian revolution. i, James Joyce publishes "Ulysses." j, Alexander Fleming discovers penicillin. k, Edwin Hubble determines universe is expanding. l, Mao Zedong leads "Long March." m, Alan Turing develops theory of digital computing. n, Discovery of fission. o, World War II begins. p, Allied leaders meet at Yalta. q, Mahatma Gandhi and Jawaharlal Nehru celebrate India's independence. r, Invention of the transistor.

**2000, Mar. 13** ***Perf. 12½***
**2764** A443 20c Sheet of 18, a.-r. + label 2.75 2.75

Date on No. 2764a is incorrect.

Paintings of Anthony Van Dyck A447

No. 2765, $1: a, Robert Rich, 2nd Earl of Warwick. b, James Stuart, Duke of Lennox and Richmond. c, Sir John Suckling. d, Sir Robert Shirley. e, Teresia, Lady Shirley. f, Thomas Wentworth, 1st Earl of Strafford.

No. 2766, $1: a, Thomas Wentworth, Earl of Strafford, in Armor. b, Lady Anne Carr, Countess of Bedford. c, Portrait of a Member of the Charles Family. d, Thomas Howard, 2nd Earl of Arundel. e, Diana Cecil, Countess of Oxford. f, The Violincellist.

No. 2767, $1: a, The Apostle Peter. b, St. Matthew. c, St. James the Greater. d, St. Bartholomew. e, The Apostle Thomas. f, The Apostle Jude (Thaddeus).

No. 2768, $1: a, The Vision of St. Anthony. b, The Mystic Marriage of St. Catherine. c, The Vision of the Blessed Herman Joseph. d, Madonna and Child Enthroned with Sts. Rosalie, Peter and Paul. e, St. Rosalie Interceding for the Plague-stricken of Palermo. f, Francesco Orero in Adoration of the Crucifixion in the Presence of Sts. Frances and Bernard.

No. 2769, $5, William Feilding, 1st Earl of Denbigh. No. 2770, $5, The Mystic Marriage of St. Catherine, diff. No. 2771, $5, St. Augustine in Ecstasy, horiz.

**2000, Apr. 10** **Litho.** ***Perf. 13¾***

**Sheets of 6, #a.-f.**
**2765-2768** A447 Set of 4 18.00 18.00

**Souvenir Sheets**
**2769-2771** A447 Set of 3 11.50 11.50

Orchids A448

Designs: 70c, Brassavola nodosa. 90c, Bletia purpurea. $1.40, Brassavola cucullata.

No. 2775, $1.50, vert.: a, Oncidium urophyllum. b, Oeceoclades maculata. c, Vanilla planifolia. d, Isolhilus linearis. e, Ionopsis utricularioides. f, Nidema boothii.

No. 2776, $1.50, vert.: a, Cyrtopodium punctatum. b, Dendrophylax funalis. c, Dichaea hystricina. d, Cyrtopodium andersonii. e, Epidendrum secundum. f, Dimerandra emarginata.

No. 2777, $1.50, vert.: a, Brassavola cordata. b, Brassia caudata. c, Broughotnia sanguinea. d, Comparettia falcata. e, Clowesia rosea. f, Caularthron bicornutum.

No. 2778, $5, Neocogniauxia hexaptera, vert. No. 2779, $5, Epidendrum altissimum, vert.

**2000, May 25** **Litho.** ***Perf. 14***
**2772-2774** A448 Set of 3 2.25 2.25

**Sheets of 6, #a.-f.**
**2775-2777** A448 Set of 3 21.00 21.00

**Souvenir Sheets**
**2778-2779** A448 Set of 2 7.50 7.50

The Stamp Show 2000, London.

Prince William, 18th Birthday — A449

No. 2780: a, Wearing checked suit. b, Wearing scarf. c, Wearing solid suit. d, Wearing sweater.

$5, Wearing suit with boutonniere.

**2000, June 21** **Litho.** ***Perf. 14***
**2780** A449 $1.40 Sheet of 4, #a-d 4.25 4.25

**Souvenir Sheet**
***Perf. 13¾***
**2781** A449 $5 multi 3.75 3.75

No. 2780 contains four 28x42mm stamps.

100th Test Match at Lord's Ground — A450

Designs: 10c, Ian Allen. 20c, T. Michael Findlay. $1.10, Winston Davis. $1.40, Nixon McLean.

$5, Lord's Ground, horiz.

**2000, June 26** ***Perf. 14***
**2782-2785** A450 Set of 4 2.10 2.10

**Souvenir Sheet**
**2786** A450 $5 multi 3.75 3.75

First Zeppelin Flight, Cent. — A451

No. 2787: a, LZ-6. b, LZ-127. c, LZ-129.

$5, LZ-9.

**2000, June 26**
**2787** A451 $3 Sheet of 3, #a-c 6.75 6.75

**Souvenir Sheet**
**2788** A451 $5 multi 3.75 3.75

No. 2787 contains 39x24mm stamps.

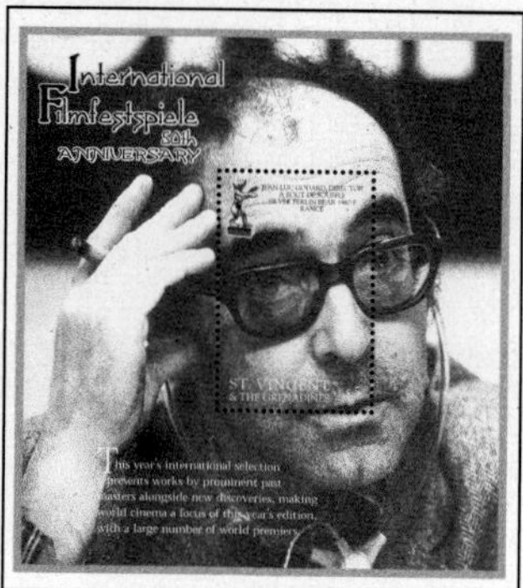
Berlin Film Festival, 50th Anniv. — A452

No. 2789: a, Pane, Amore e Fantasia. b, Richard III. c, Smultronstället (Wild Strawberries). d, The Defiant Ones. e, The Living Desert. f, A Bout de Souffle.
$5, Jean-Luc Godard.

**2000, June 26**
**2789** A452 $1.40 Sheet of 6, #a-f 6.25 6.25

**Souvenir Sheet**

**2790** A452 $5 multi 3.75 3.75

Space — A453

No. 2791, $1.50: a, Comet Hale-Bopp, Calisto. b, Galileo probe. c, Ulysses probe. d, Pioneer 11. e, Voyager 1. f, Pioneer 10.
No. 2792, $1.50: a, Voyager 2, Umbriel. b, Pluto Project. c, Voyager 1, purple background. d, Oort cloud. e, Pluto, Kuiper Express. f, Voayger 2 near Neptune.
No. 2793, $1.50: a, Cassini probe. b, Pioneer 11. c, Voyager 1, green background. d, Huygens. e, Deep Space IV Champollion. f, Voyager 2.
No. 2794, $5, Stardust. No. 2795, $5, Pluto Project, diff.

**2000, June 26** **Sheets of 6, #a-f**
**2791-2793** A453 Set of 3 21.00 21.00

**Souvenir Sheets**

**2794-2795** A453 Set of 2 7.50 7.50

World Stamp Expo 2000, Anaheim.

Souvenir Sheet

2000 Summer Olympics, Sydney — A454

No. 2796: a, Mildred Didrikson. b, Pommel horse. c, Barcelona Stadium and Spanish flag. d, Ancient Greek horse racing.

**2000, June 26**
**2796** A454 $2 Sheet of 4, #a-d 6.00 6.00

Souvenir Sheet

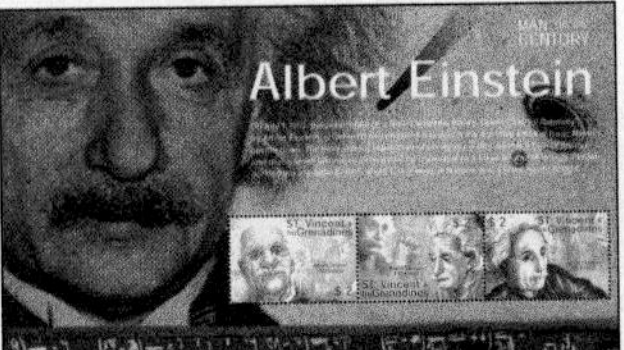

Albert Einstein (1879-1955) — A455

No. 2797: a, Wearing green sweater. b, Wearing blue sweater. c, Wearing black sweater.

**2000, June 26**
**2797** A455 $2 Sheet of 3, #a-c 4.50 4.50

Public Railways, 175th Anniv. — A456

No. 2798: a, Locomotion No. 1, George Stephenson. b, John Bull.

**2000, June 26**
**2798** A456 $3 Sheet of 2, #a-b 4.50 4.50

Mario Andretti, Automobile Racer — A457

No. 2799: a, In car, without helmet. b, In white racing uniform. c, With hands in front of face. d, In car, with helmet. e, In white, standing in front of car. f, With trophy. g, In red racing uniform. h, Close-up.
$5, With trophy, diff.

**2000, July 6** ***Perf. 12x12¼***
**2799** A457 $1.10 Sheet of 8, #a-h 6.50 6.50

**Souvenir Sheet**
***Perf. 13¾***

**2800** A457 $5 multi 3.75 3.75

Souvenir Sheets

Monty Python's Flying Circus, 30th Anniv. (in 1999) — A458

No. 2801: a, Michael Palin. b, Eric Idle. c, John Cleese. d, Graham Chapman. e, Terry Gilliam. f, Terry Jones.

**2000, July 6** ***Perf. 12x12¼***
**2801** A458 $1.40 Sheet of 6, #a-f 6.25 6.25

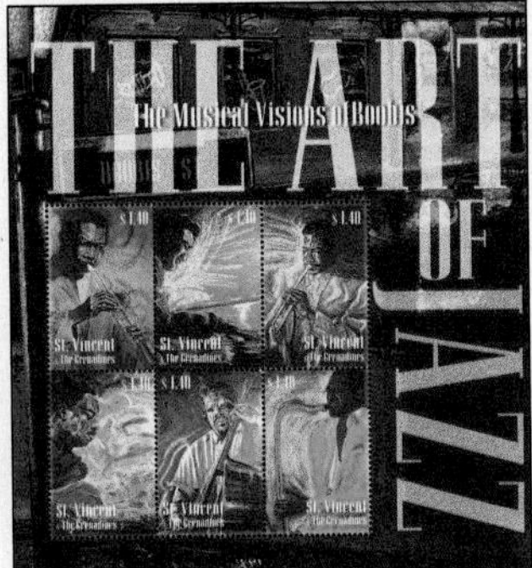

Jazz — A459

No. 2802: a, Clarinetist. b, Pianist. c, Trumpeter. d, Guitarist. e, Bassist. f, Saxophonist.

**2000, July 6** ***Perf. 14***
**2802** A459 $1.40 Sheet of 6, #a-f 6.25 6.25

Female Recording Groups of the 1960s — A460

No. 2803, $1.40: a-e, Portraits of the members of The Chantels (green background).
No. 2804, $1.40: a-e, Portraits of the members of The Marvelettes (blue background)

**2000, July 6** **Sheets of 5, #a-e**
**2803-2804** A460 Set of 2 10.50 10.50

Souvenir Sheet

Barbara Taylor Bradford, Writer — A461

**2000, July 6** ***Perf. 12x12¼***
**2805** A461 $5 multi 3.75 3.75

Betty Boop — A462

No. 2806: a, As Jill, with Jack. b, With three blind mice. c, Jumping over candlestick. d, As fiddler in Hey, Diddle, Diddle. e, On back of Mother Goose. f, As Little Miss Muffet. g, With three cats. h, As candlestick maker, with butcher and baker. i, As Little Jack Horner.
No. 2807, $5, As the Woman Who Lived In a Shoe. No. 2808, $5, As Little Bo Peep.

**2000, July 6** ***Perf. 13¾***
**2806** A462 $1 Sheet of 9, #a-i 6.75 6.75

**Souvenir Sheets**

**2807-2808** A462 Set of 2 7.50 7.50

Artifacts A463

Designs: 20c, Goblet. 50c, Goose. 70c, Boley and calabash. $1, Flat iron.

**2000, Aug. 21** **Litho.** ***Perf. 14***
**2809-2812** A463 Set of 4 1.75 1.75

Flowers — A464

No. 2813: a, Pink ginger lily. b, Thumbergia grandiflora. c, Red ginger lily. d, Madagascar jasmine. e, Cluster palm. f, Red torch lily. g, Salvia splendens. h, Balsam apple. i, Rostrata.
No. 2814, Red flamingo. No. 2815, Balsam apple, horiz.

**2000, Aug. 21**
**2813** A464 90c Sheet of 9, #a-i 6.00 6.00

**Souvenir Sheet**

**2814-2815** A464 $5 Set of 2 7.50 7.50

**Paintings Type of 1999**

Various pictures of flowers making up a photomosaic of the Queen Mother.

**2000, Sept. 5** ***Perf. 13¾***
**2816** A442 $1 Sheet of 8, #a-h 6.00 6.00
*i.* As No. 2816, imperf. 6.00 6.00

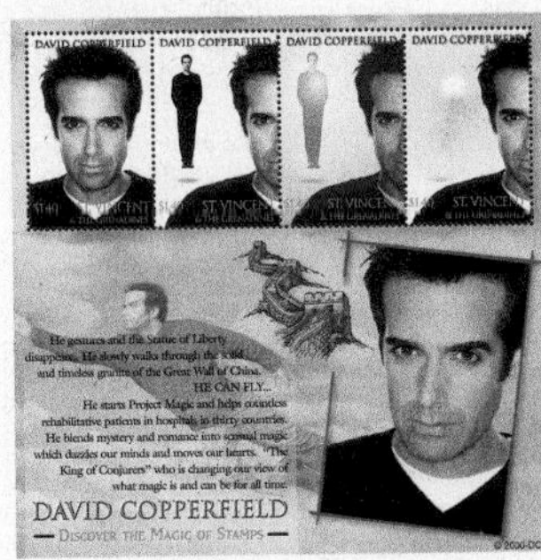

Magician David Copperfield — A465

No. 2817: a, Head of Copperfield. b, Copperfield's body. c, Copperfield's body vanishing. d, Copperfield's body vanished.

**2000, July 6** ***Perf. 14***
**2817** A465 $1.40 Sheet of 4, #a-d 4.25 4.25

Local Musicians — A466

Designs: No. 2818, $1.40, Horn player with striped shirt. No. 2819, $1.40, Horn player, diff. No. 2820, $1.40, Pianist. No. 2821, $1.40, Fiddler.

**2000, Oct. 16 Litho. *Perf. 14***
**2818-2821** A466 Set of 4 4.25 4.25

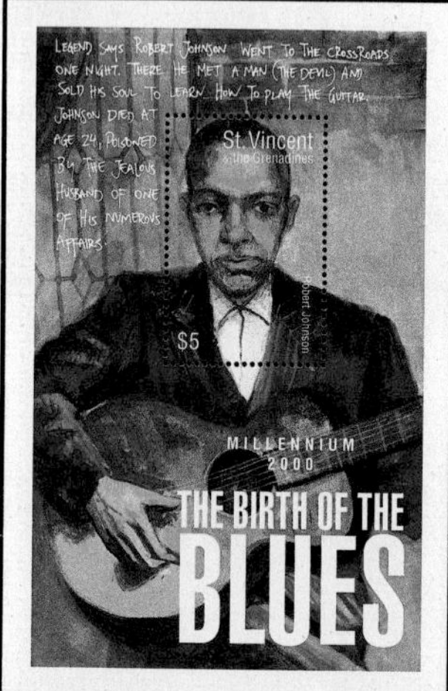


Blues Musicians — A467

No. 2822, $1.40: a, Bessie Smith. b, Willie Dixon. c, Gertrude "Ma" Rainey. d, W. C. Handy. e, Leadbelly. f, Big Bill Broonzy.
No. 2823, $1.40: a, Ida Cox. b, Lonnie Johnson. c, Muddy Waters. d, T-Bone Walker. e, Howlin' Wolf. f, Sister Rosetta Tharpe.
No. 2824, Robert Johnson. No. 2825, Billie Holiday.

**2000, Oct. 16 Sheets of 6, #a-f**
**2822-2823** A467 Set of 2 12.50 12.50

**Souvenir Sheets**
**2824-2825** A467 Set of 2 7.50 7.50

World at War — A468

No. 2826: a, USS Shaw explodes at Pearl Harbor. b, B-24s bomb Ploesti oil fields. c, Soviet T-34 tank moves towards Berlin. d, USS New Jersey off coast of North Korea. e, F-86 Sabre over North Korea. f, USS Enterprise off the Indochina coast. g, B-52 over Viet Nam. h, M-113 tank in Viet Nam.
No. 2827: a, Israeli F-4 Phantoms in action in Six-day War. b, Egyptian T-72 tank destroyed, Six-day War. c, Egyptian SAM-6 missiles, Yom Kippur War. d, Israeli M-48 tanks in desert, Yom Kippur War. e, HMS Hermes, Falkland Islands War. f, British AV-8 harriers in action, Falkland Islands War. g, Iraqi Scud missile launcher in desert, Gulf War. h, M1-A1 Abrams tanks in desert, Gulf War.
No. 2828, Israeli F-4s bomb SAM sites, Yom Kippur War. No. 2829 B-52 bomber, Pershing II missile.

**2000, Oct. 16 Sheets of 8, #a-h**
**2826-2827** A468 $1 Set of 2 12.00 12.00

**Souvenir Sheets**
**2828-2829** A468 $5 Set of 2 7.50 7.50

No. 2829 contains one 56x42mm stamp.

Independence, 21st Anniv. — A469

Designs: 10c, Government House. 15c, First session of Parliament, 1998. 50c, House of Assembly. $2, Financial Complex.

**2000, Oct. 27 Litho. *Perf. 14***
**2830-2833** A469 Set of 4 2.00 2.00

Birds — A470

Designs: 50c, Blue and gold macaw. 90c, English fallow budgerigar. $1, Barraband parakeet. $2, Dominat pied blue.
No. 2838, $2: a, English short-faced tumbler. b, Diamond dove. c, Norwich cropper.
No. 2839, $2: a, Scarlet macaw. b, Blue-fronted Amazon. c, Buffon's macaw.
No. 2840, $2: a, Stafford canary. b, Masked lovebird. c, Parisian full canary.
No. 2841, $2, horiz.: a, Canada goose. b, Mandarin duck. c, Gouldian finch.
No. 2842, $5, Common peafowl, horiz. No. 2843, $5, Budgerigar, horiz.

**2000, Nov. 15**
**2834-2837** A470 Set of 4 4.00 4.00

**Sheets of 3, #a-c**
**2838-2841** A470 Set of 4 18.00 18.00

**Souvenir Sheets**
**2842-2843** A470 Set of 2 7.50 7.50

Shirley Temple in Rebecca of Sunnybrook Farm — A471

No. 2844, horiz.: a, With man in dark suit. b, With man and woman. c, With woman wearing glasses. d, with blonde woman. e, With man in white hat. f, With three women.
No. 2845: a, At microphone, wearing checked coat and hat. b, Wearing straw hat. c, At microphone, no hat. d, With woman wearing glasses.
No. 2846, With Bill Robinson.

**2000, Nov. 29 *Perf. 13¾***
**2844** A471 90c Sheet of 6, #a-f 4.00 4.00
**2845** A471 $1.10 Sheet of 4, #a-d 3.25 3.25

**Souvenir Sheet**
**2846** A471 $1.10 multi .85 .85

See also Nos. 3064-2066.

Queen Mother, 100th Birthday — A472

**2000, Sept. 5 Litho. *Perf. 14***
**2847** A472 $1.40 multi 1.00 1.00

Printed in sheets of 6.

Christmas — A473

20c, Angel looking right. 70c, Two angels, orange background. 90c, Two angels, blue background. #2851, $5, Angel looking left.
No. 2852, Angel, yellow background.

**2000, Dec. 7**
**2848-2851** A473 Set of 4 5.00 5.00

**Souvenir Sheet**
**2852** A473 $5 multi 3.75 3.75

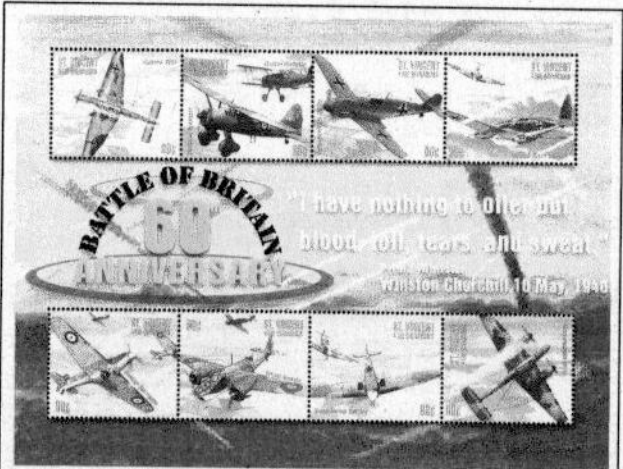


Battle of Britain, 60th Anniv. — A474

No. 2853, 90c: a, Junkers Ju87. b, Two Gloster Gladiators flying left. c, Messerschmitt BF109. d, Heinkel He111 bomber, British fighter. e, Three Hawker Hurricanes. f, Two Bristol Blenheims. g, Two Supermarine Spitfires and ground. h, Messerschmitt BF110.
No. 2854, 90c: a, Two Spitfires, flying left. b, Spitfire. c, Dornier DO217. d, Two Gladiators flying right. e, Four Hurricanes. f, Junkers Ju87 Stuka. g, Two Spitfires flying right. h, Junkers Ju88.
#2855, $5, Spitfire. #2856, $5, Hurricane.

**2000, Dec. 18 *Perf. 14¼x14½***
**Sheets of 8, #a-h**
**2853-2854** A474 Set of 2 10.50 10.50

**Souvenir Sheets**
***Perf. 14¼***
**2855-2856** A474 Set of 2 7.50 7.50

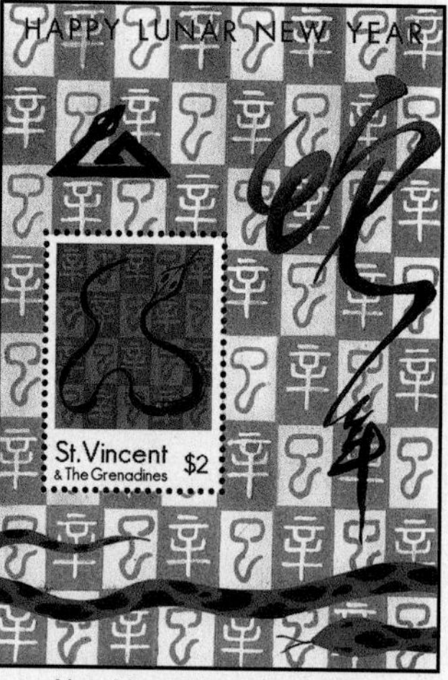


New Year 2001 (Year of the Snake) — A475

No. 2857: a, Blue and light blue background. b, Purple and pink background. c, Green and light green background.

**2001, Jan. 2 Litho. *Perf. 13x13¼***
**2857** A475 $1 Sheet of 3, #a-c 2.25 2.25

**Souvenir Sheet**
**2858** A475 $2 shown 1.50 1.50

Paintings of Peter Paul Rubens in the Prado A476

Designs: 10c, Three women and dog from Diana the Huntress. 90c, Adoration of the Magi. $1, Woman and two dogs from Diana the Huntress.
No. 2862, $2: a, Heraclitus, the Mournful Philosopher. b, Heraclitus, close-up. c, Anne of Austria, Queen of France, close-up. d, Anne of Austria.
No. 2863, $2: a, Prometheus Carrying Fire. b, Vulcan Forging Jupiter's Thunderbolt. c, Saturn Devouring One of His Sons. d, Polyphemus.
No. 2864, $2: a, St. Matthias. b, The Death of Seneca. c, Maria de'Medici, Queen of France. d, Achilles Discovered by Ulysses.
No. 2865, $5, The Judgment of Solomon. No. 2866, $5, The Holy Family with St. Anne.

**2001, Jan. 2 *Perf. 13¾***
**2859-2861** A476 Set of 3 1.50 1.50

**Sheets of 4, #a-d**
**2862-2864** A476 Set of 3 18.00 18.00

**Souvenir Sheets**
**2865-2866** A476 Set of 2 7.50 7.50

Rijksmuseum, Amsterdam, Bicent. — A477

No. 2867, $1.40: a, The Spendthrift, by Cornelis Troost. b, The Art Gallery of Jan Gildermeester Jansz, by Adriaan de Lelie. c, The Rampoortje, by Wouter Johannes van Troostwijk. d, Winter Landscape, by Barend Cornelis Koekkoek. e, Man with white headdress from The Procuress, by Dirck van Baburen. f, Man and woman from The Procuress.
No. 2868, $1.40: a, A Music Party, by Rembrandt. b, Rutger Jan Schimmelpennick and Family, by Pierre Paul Prud'hon. c, Tobit and Anna With a Kid, by Rembrandt. d, The Syndics of the Amsterdam Goldsmiths' Guild, by Thomas de Keyser. e, Portrait of a Lady, by de Keyser. f, Marriage Portrait of Isaac Massa and Beatrix van der Laen, by Frans Hals.
No. 2869, $1.40: a, The Concert, by Hendrick ter Brugghen. b, Vertumnus and Pomona, by Paulus Moreelse. c, Standing couple from Dignified Couples Courting, by Willem Buytewech. d, The Sick Woman, by Jan Steen. e, Seated couple from Dignified Couples Courting. f, Don Ramón Satué, by Francisco de Goya.
No. 2870, $5, Donkey Riding on the Beach, by Isaac Lazarus Israels. No. 2871, $5, The Stone Bridge, by Rembrandt, horiz. No. 2872, $5, Child with Dead Peacocks, by Rembrandt, horiz.

**2001, Jan. 15 *Perf. 13¾***
**Sheets of 6, #a-f**
**2867-2869** A477 Set of 3 19.00 19.00

**Souvenir Sheets**
**2870-2872** A477 Set of 3 11.00 11.00

Birds of Prey A478

Designs: 10c, Barred owl. No. 2874, 90c, Lammergeier. $1, California condor. $2, Mississippi kite.

No. 2877, 90c: a, Crested caracara. b, Boreal owl. c, Harpy eagle. d, Oriental bay owl. e, Hawk owl. f, Laughing falcon.

No. 2878, $1.10: a, Bateleur. b, Hobby. c, Osprey. d, Goshawk. e, African fish eagle. f, Egyptian vulture.

No. 2879, $5, Great gray owl. No. 2880, $5, American kestrel.

**2001, Feb. 13** ***Perf. 14***

**2873-2876** A478 Set of 4 3.25 3.25

**Sheets of 6, #a-f**

**2877-2878** A478 Set of 2 9.50 9.50

**Souvenir Sheets**

**2879-2880** A478 Set of 2 8.00 8.00

Hong Kong 2001 Stamp Exhibition (Nos. 2877-2880).

Owls — A479

Designs: 10c, Eagle. 20c, Barn. 50c, Great gray. 70c, Long-eared. 90c, Tawny. $1, Hawk.

No. 2887, horiz.: a, Ural. b, Tengmalm's. c, Marsh. d, Brown fish. e, Little. f, Short-eared.

No. 2888, $5, Hume's. No. 2889, $5, Snowy.

**2001, Feb. 13**

**2881-2886** A479 Set of 6 2.75 2.75

**2887** A479 $1.40 Sheet of 6, #a-f 6.75 6.75

**Souvenir Sheets**

**2888-2889** A479 Set of 2 8.00 8.00

Pokémon — A480

No. 2890: a, Kadabra. b, Spearow. c, Kakuna. d, Koffing. e, Tentacruel. f, Cloyster.

**2001, Feb. 13** ***Perf. 13¾***

**2890** A480 90c Sheet of 6, #a-f 4.00 4.00

**Souvenir Sheet**

**2891** A480 $3 Meowth 2.25 2.25

UN Women's Human Rights Campaign — A481

Woman: 90c, With bird and flame. $1, With necklace.

**2001, Mar. 8** ***Perf. 14***

**2892-2893** A481 Set of 2 1.40 1.40

Mushrooms — A482

Designs: 20c, Amanita fulva. 90c, Hygrophorus speciosus. $1.10, Amanita phalloides. $2, Cantharellus cibarius.

No. 2898, $1.40: a, Amanita muscaria. b, Boletus zelleri. c, Coprinus picaceus. d, Stroharia aeruginosa. e, Lepista nuda. f, Hygrophorus conicus.

No. 2899, $1.40: a, Lactarius deliciosus. b, Hygrophorus psittacinus. c, Tricholomopsis rutilans. d, Hygrophorus coccineus. e, Collybia iocephala. f, Gyromitra esculenta.

No. 2900, $1.40: a, Lactarius peckii. b, Lactarius rufus. c, Cortinarius elatior. d, Boletus luridus. e, Russula cyanoxantha. f, Craterellus cornopioioles.

No. 2901, $5, Cyathus olla. No. 2902, $5, Lycoperdon pyriforme, horiz. No. 2903, $5, Pleurotus ostreatus, horiz.

***Perf. 13½x13¼, 13¼x13½***

**2001, Mar. 15**

**2894-2897** A482 Set of 4 3.25 3.25

**Sheets of 6, #a-f**

**2898-2900** A482 Set of 3 19.00 19.00

**Souvenir Sheets**

**2901-2903** A482 Set of 3 11.00 11.00

A484

A485

Butterflies and Moths A486

Designs: No. 2904, 10c, Tiger. No. 2905, 20c, Figure-of-eight. No. 2906, 50c, Mosaic. No. 2907, 90c, Monarch. No. 2908, $1, Blue-green reflector. No. 2909, $2, Blue tharops.

No. 2910, 10c, Eunica alemena. No. 2911, 70c, Euphaedra medon. No. 2912, 90c, Prepona praeneste. No. 2913, $1, Gold-banded forester.

No. 2914, 20c, Ancycluris formosissima. No. 2915, 50c, Callicore cynosura. No. 2916, 70c, Nessaea obrinus. No. 2917, $2, Eunica alemena.

No. 2918, 90c: a, Orange theope. b, Blue night. c, Small lace-wing. d, Grecian shoemaker. e, Clorinde. f, Orange-barred sulphur.

No. 2919, $1.10: a, Atala. b, Giant swallowtail. c, Banded king shoemaker. d, White peacock. e, Cramer's mesene. f, Polydamas swallowtail.

No. 2920, 90c: a, Cepora aspasia. b, Morpho aega. c, Mazuca amoeva. d, Beautiful tiger. e, Gold-drop helicopsis. f, Esmerelda.

No. 2921, $1.10: a, Lilac nymph. b, Ruddy dagger wing. c, Tiger pierid. d, Orange forester. e, Prepona deiphile. f, Phoebus avellaneda.

No. 2922, $1: a, Calisthenia salvinii flying downward. b, Perisama vaninka. c, Malachite. d, Diaethria aurelia. e, Perisama conplandi. f, Cramer's mesene. g, Calisthenia salvinii flying upward. h, Carpella districata.

No. 2923, $1: a, Euphaedra heophron. b, Milionia grandis. c, Ruddy dagger wiry. d, Bocotus bacotus. e, Cream spot tiger moth. f, Yellow tiger moth. g, Baorisa hiroglyphica. h, Jersey tiger.

No. 2924, $5, Small flambeau. No. 2925, $5, Common morpho, vert. No. 2926, $5, Heliconius sapho. No. 2927, $5 Ornate moth. No. 2928, $5, Hewitson's blue hair streak. No. 2929, $5, Anaxita drucei.

***Perf. 13¼x13½, 13½x13¼***

**2001, Mar. 22** **Litho.**

**2904-2909** A484 Set of 6 3.50 3.50

**2910-2913** A485 Set of 4 2.00 2.00

**2914-2917** A486 Set of 4 2.50 2.50

**Sheets of 6, #a-f**

**2918-2919** A484 Set of 2 9.00 9.00

**2920-2921** A485 Set of 2 9.00 9.00

**Sheets of 8, #a-h**

**2922-2923** A486 Set of 2 12.00 12.00

**Souvenir Sheets**

**2924-2925** A484 Set of 2 7.50 7.50

**2926-2927** A485 Set of 2 7.50 7.50

**2928-2929** A486 Set of 2 7.50 7.50

Giuseppe Verdi (1813-1901), Opera Composer — A487

No. 2930: a, Mario Del Monaco, Raina Kabaivanska in Othello. b, 1898 Costume design for Iago. c, 1898 costume design for Othello. d, Anna Tomowa-Sintow as Desdemona.

$5, Nicolai Ghiaurov in Othello.

**2001, June 12** **Litho.** ***Perf. 14***

**2930** A487 $2 Sheet of 4, #a-d 6.00 6.00

**Souvenir Sheet**

**2931** A487 $5 multi 3.75 3.75

Toulouse-Lautrec Paintings — A488

No. 2932: a, Portrait of Comtesse Adèle-Zoé de Toulouse-Lautrec. b, Carmen. c, Madame Lily Grenier.

$5, Jane Avril.

**2001, June 12** ***Perf. 13¾***

**2932** A488 $3 Sheet of 3, #a-c 6.75 6.75

**Souvenir Sheet**

**2933** A488 $5 multi 3.75 3.75

Mao Zedong (1893-1976) — A489

No. 2934: a, In 1924. b, In 1938. c, In 1945.

$5, Undated portrait.

**2001, June 12**

**2934** A489 $2 Sheet of 3, #a-c 4.50 4.50

**Souvenir Sheet**

**2935** A489 $5 multi 3.75 3.75

Queen Victoria (1819-1901) — A490

No. 2936: a, As young lady in dark blue dress. b, In white dress. c, With flowers in hair. d, Wearing crown. e, Wearing black dress, facing forward. f, With gray hair.

$5, Sky in background.

**2001, June 12** ***Perf. 14***

**2936** A490 $1.10 Sheet of 6, #a-f 5.00 5.00

**Souvenir Sheet**

***Perf. 13¾***

**2937** A490 $5 multi 3.75 3.75

No. 2936 contains six 28x42mm stamps.

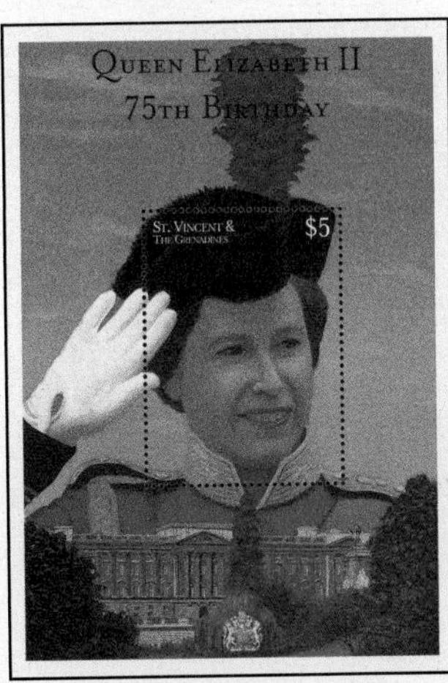


Queen Elizabeth II, 75th Birthday — A491

No. 2938: a, With gray hat. b, In gray jacket, no hat. c, In dark blue dress. d, Wearing tiara. e, With blue hat. f, With green hat.

$5, In uniform.

**2001, June 12** ***Perf. 14***

**2938** A491 $1.10 Sheet of 6, #a-f 5.00 5.00

**Souvenir Sheet**
*Perf. 13¾*

**2939** A491 $5 multi 3.75 3.75

No. 2938 contains six 28x42mm stamps.

Monet Paintings — A492

Designs: No. 2940, $2, Venice at Dusk (shown). No. 2941, $2, Regatta at Argenteuil. No. 2942, $2, Grain Stacks, End of Summer, Evening Effect. No. 2943, $2, Impression, Sunrise.

$5, Parisians Enjoying the Parc Monceau, vert.

**2001, June 12** *Perf. 13¾*

**2940-2943** A492 Set of 4 6.00 6.00

**Souvenir Sheet**

**2944** A492 $5 multi 3.75 3.75

Phila Nippon '01, Japan A493

Designs: 10c, The Courtesan Sunimoto of the Okanaya, by Koryusai Isoda. 15c, Oiran at Shinto Shrine-Shotenyama, by Kiyonaga. No. 2947, 20c, Two Girls on a Veranda, by Kiyonaga. No. 2948, 20c, Rooster, from A Variety of Birds, by Hoen Nishiyama, horiz. 50c, On Banks of the Sumida, by Kiyonaga. 70c, Three ducks, from A Variety of Birds, horiz. 90c, Seven ducks, from A Variety of Birds, horiz. $1, Three pigeons and other birds from A Variety of Birds, horiz. $1.10, Two birds, from A Variety of Birds, horiz. $2, Five birds, from A Variety of Birds.

No. 2955, $1.40 — Paintings by Eishi: a, Toriwagi, Geisha of Kanaya, Writing. b, Courtesan Preparing for Doll Festival. c, Two Court Ladies in a Garden. d, Lady With a Lute.

No. 2956, $1.40 — Portraits by Sharaku: a, Oniji Otani II as Edohei, a Yakko. b, Hanshiro Iwai IV. c, Kikunojo Segawa. d, Komazo Ichikawa II.

No. 2957, $1.40 — Paintings by Harunobu Suzuki: a, 6 Tama Rivers, Girls by Lespedeza Bush in Moonlight. b, Warming Sake with Maple Leaves. c, Young Samurai on Horseback. d, 6 Tamu Rivers, Ide No Tamagawa.

No. 2958, $1.40 — Paintings by Harunobu Suzuki: a, Girl on River Bank. b, Horseman Guided by Peasant Girl. c, Komachi Praying for Rain. d, Washing Clothes in the Stream.

No. 2959, $5, Peasants Ferried Across Sumida, by Hokkei. No. 2960. $5, Shadows on the Shoji, by Kikukawa. No. 2961, $5, Boy Spying on Lovers, by Suzuki. No. 2962, $5, Tayu Komurasaki and Hanamurasaki of the Kado Tamaya, by Masanobu Kitao. No. 2963, $5, Gathering Lotus Flowers, by Suzuki.

**2001, June 12** **Litho.** *Perf. 13¾*

**2945-2954** A493 Set of 10 5.25 5.25

**Sheets of 4, #a-d**

**2955-2958** A493 Set of 4 17.00 17.00

**Souvenir Sheets**

**2959-2963** A493 Set of 5 19.00 19.00

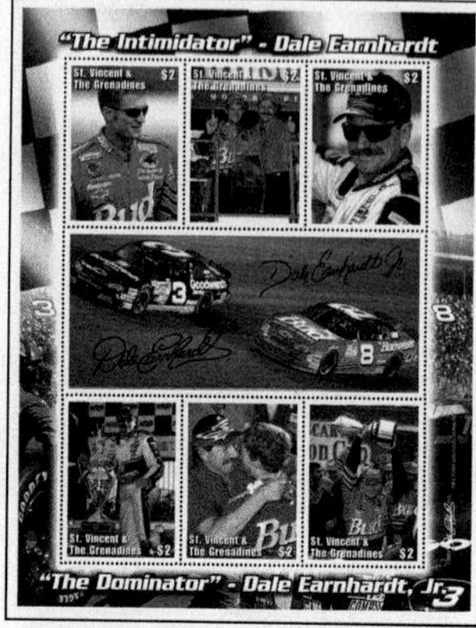

"The Intimidator" - Dale Earnhardt
"The Dominator" - Dale Earnhardt, Jr.


Dale Earnhardt (1951-2001), Stock Car Racer — A494

Designs: a, Dale Earnhardt, Jr. b, Dale and Dale, Jr. with trophy. c, Dale. d, Dale with trophy. e, Dale and Dale, Jr. embracing. f, Dale Jr. with trophy.

**2001, July 16**

**2964** A494 $2 Sheet of 6, #a-f + label 9.00 9.00

Wedding of Norwegian Prince Haakon and Mette-Marie Tjessem Hoiby — A495

**2001, Aug. 1** *Perf. 14*

**2965** A495 $5 multi 3.75 3.75

Printed in sheets of 4.

Dinosaurs and Prehistoric Animals — A496

Designs: 10c, Mammoth. 20c, Pinacosaurus. No. 2968, 90c, Oviraptor. $1, Centrosaurus. No. 2970, $1.40, Protoceratops. $2, Bactrosaurus.

No. 2972, 90c: a, Saltasaurus. b, Apatosaurus. c, Brachiosaurus. d, Troodon. e, Deinonychus. f, Segnosaurus.

No. 2973, 90c: a, Iguanodon. b, Hypacrosaurus. c, Ceratosaurus. d, Hypsilophodon. e, Herrerasaurus. f, Velociraptor.

No. 2974, $1.40: a, Pteranodon. b, Archaeopteryx. c, Eudimorphodon. d, Shonisaurus. e, Elasmosaurus. f, Kronosaurus.

No. 2975, $1.40: a, Allosaurus. b, Dilophosaurus. c, Lambeosaurus. d, Coelophysis. e, Ornitholestes. f, Eustreptospondylus.

No. 2976, $5, Stegosaurus. No. 2977, $5, Triceratops. No. 2978, $5, Parasaurolophus, vert. No. 2979, $5, Tyrannosaurus, vert.

**2001, Oct. 15** **Litho.** *Perf. 14x13¾*

**2966-2971** A496 Set of 6 4.25 4.25

**Sheets of 6, #a-f**

**2972-2975** A496 Set of 4 21.00 21.00

**Souvenir Sheets**
*Perf. 13¾*

**2976-2979** A496 Set of 4 15.00 15.00

Nos. 2976-2977 each contain one 50x38mm stamp; Nos. 2978-2979 each contain one 38x50mm stamp.

Photomosaic of Queen Elizabeth II — A497

**2001, Nov. 12** *Perf. 14*

**2980** A497 $1 multi 1.10 1.10

Printed in sheets of 8.

2002 World Cup Soccer Championships, Japan and Korea — A498

Players and flags — No. 2981, $1.40: a, Hong Myung-Bo, Korea. b, Hidetoshi Nakata, Japan. c, Ronaldo, Brazil. d, Paolo Maidini, Italy. e, Peter Schmeichel, Denmark. f, Raul Blanco, Spain.

No. 2982, $1.40: a, Kim Bong Soo, Korea. b, Masami Ihara, Japan. c, Marcel Desailly, France. d, David Beckham, England. e, Carlos Valderrama, Colombia. f, George Popescu, Romania.

No. 2983, $5, Seoul World Cup Stadium. No. 2984, $5, International Yokohama Stadium.

**2001, Nov. 29** **Sheets of 6, #a-f**

**2981-2982** A498 Set of 2 12.50 12.50

**Souvenir Sheets**

**2983-2984** A498 Set of 2 7.50 7.50

Nos. 2983-2984 each contain one 63x31mm stamp.

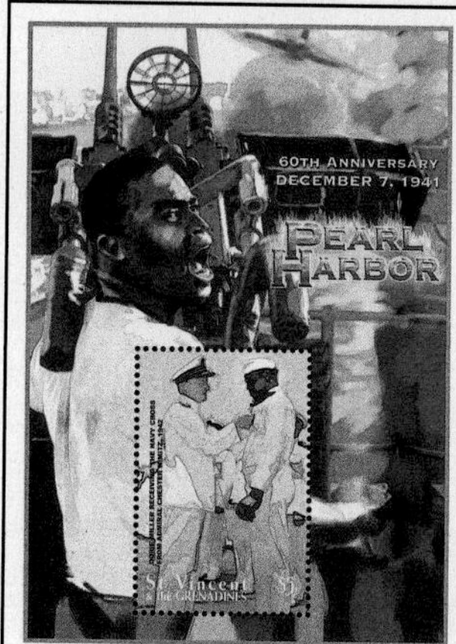


Attack on Pearl Harbor, 60th Anniv. — A499

No. 2985, $1.40, horiz.: a, Japanese bombing Pearl Harbor. b, Japanese pilot ties on a hachimaki. c, Emperor Hirohito. d, Japanese Adm. Isoroku Yamamoto. e, Japanese fighter planes from aircraft carrier Akagi. f, Japanese Zero plane.

No. 2986, $1.40, horiz.: a, Japanese fighter from the Kaga over Ewa Marine Base. b, Hero Dorie Miller downing four Japanese planes. c, Battleship USS Nevada sinking. d, American sailors struggle on the USS Oklahoma. e, Japanese plane takes off from the Akagi. f, Rescue during bombing.

No. 2987, $5, Dorie Miller receiving navy Cross from Adm. Chester Nimitz. No. 2988, $5, Second wave of attack at Wheeler Field, horiz.

**2001, Dec. 7** **Sheets of 6, #a-f**

**2985-2986** A499 Set of 2 12.50 12.50

**Souvenir Sheets**

**2987-2988** A499 Set of 2 7.50 7.50

Pres. John F. Kennedy — A500

Pres. Kennedy — No. 2989, $1.40: a, With John, Jr. b, With Jacqueline (red dress). c, With Caroline. d, With family, 1963. e, With Jacqueline, at sea. f, With Jacqueline (white dress).

No. 2990, $1.40: a, At 1956 Democratic Convention. b, Campaigning with Jacqueline, 1959. c, At White House, 1960. d, With brother Robert. e, Announcing Cuban blockade, 1962. f, John Jr. saluting father's casket.

No. 2991, $5, Portrait with violet background. No. 2992, $5, Portrait with green background.

**2001, Dec. 7** **Sheets of 6, #a-f**

**2989-2990** A500 Set of 2 12.50 12.50

**Souvenir Sheets**

**2991-2992** A500 Set of 2 7.50 7.50

Princess Diana (1961-97) — A501

Flowers and Diana: a, In gray suit. b, In pink dress. c, With tiara.

$5, With tirara and high-necked gown.

**2001, Dec. 7**

**2993** A501 $1.40 Sheet, 2 each #a-c 6.25 6.25

**Souvenir Sheet**

**2994** A501 $5 multi 3.75 3.75

Moths A502

Designs: 70c, Croker's frother. 90c, Virgin tiger moth. $1, Leopard moth. $2, Fiery campylotes.

No. 2999, $1.40: a, Buff-tip. b, Elephant hawkmoth. c, Streaked sphinx. d, Cizara hawkmoth. e, Hakea moth. f, Boisduval's autumnal moth.

No. 3000, $1.40: a, Eyespot anthelid. b, Collenette's variegated browntail. c, Common epicoma moth. d, Staudinger's longtail. e, Green silver lines. f, Salt marsh moth.

No. 3001, $5, Gypsy moth. No. 3002, Orizaba silkmoth caterpillar.

**2001, Dec. 10**

**2995-2998** A502 Set of 4 3.50 3.50

**Sheets of 6, #a-f**

**2999-3000** A502 Set of 2 12.50 12.50

**Souvenir Sheets**

**3001-3002** A502 Set of 2 7.50 7.50

Christmas — A503

Paintings: 10c, Madonna and Child, by Francesco Guardi. 20c, The Immaculate Conception, by Giovanni Battista Tiepolo. 70c, Adoration of the Magi, by Tiepolo. 90c, The Virgin, by Tintoretto. $1.10, The Annunciation, by Veronese. $1.40 Madonna della Quaglia, by Antonio Pisanello.

$5, Madonna and Child Appear to St. Philip Neri, by Tiepolo.

**2001, Dec. 12**

**3003-3008** A503 Set of 6 3.25 3.25

**Souvenir Sheet**

**3009** A503 $5 multi 3.75 3.75

**Queen Mother Type of 1999 Redrawn**

No. 3010: a, In 1909. b, With King George, Princess Elizabeth, 1930. c, At Badminton, 1977. d, In 1983.

$6, In 1987.

**2001, Dec. 13** ***Perf. 14***

**Yellow Orange Frames**

**3010** A438 $2 Sheet of 4, #a-d, + label 6.00 6.00

**Souvenir Sheet**

***Perf. 13¾***

**3011** A438 $6 multi 4.50 4.50

Queen Mother's 101st birthday. No. 3010 contains one 38x50mm stamp with a greener background than that found on No. 2730. Sheet margins of Nos. 3010-3011 lack embossing and gold arms and frames found on Nos. 2729-2730.

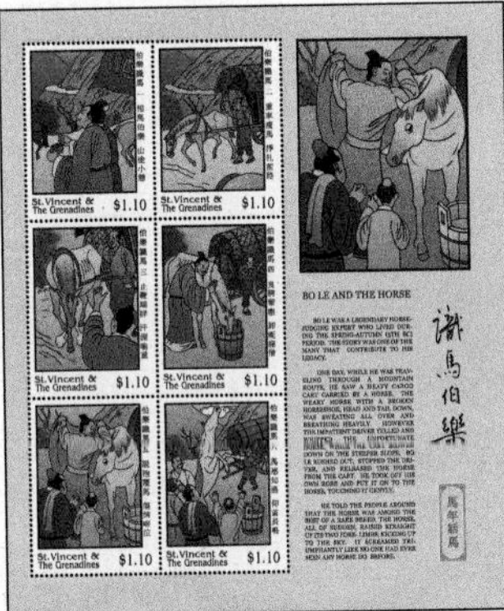

New Year 2002 (Year of the Horse) — A504

Scenes from Bo Le and the Horse: a, Man pointing at horse. b, Horse pulling cart. c, Horse snorting. d, Horse drinking. e, Man putting robe on horse. f, Horse rearing.

**2001, Dec. 17** ***Perf. 13¾***

**3012** A504 $1.10 Sheet of 6, #a-f 5.00 5.00

Tourism A505

Designs: 20c, Vermont Nature Trails. 70c, Tamarind Beach Hotel, horiz. 90c, Tobago Cays, horiz. $1.10, Trinity Falls.

**2001, Dec. 31** ***Perf. 14***

**Stamps + labels**

**3013-3016** A505 Set of 4 2.25 2.25

Fauna — A506

No. 3017, $1.40, vert.: a, Bumble bee. b, Green darner dragonfly. c, Small lace-wing. d, Black widow spider. e, Praying mantis. f, Firefly.

No. 3018, $1.40: a, Caspian tern. b, White-tailed tropicbird. c, Black-necked stilt. d, Black-billed plover. e, Black-winged stilt. f, Ruddy turnstone.

No. 3019, $5, Blue night butterfly. No. 3020, $5, Brown pelican, vert.

**2001, Dec. 10** **Litho.** ***Perf. 14***

**Sheets of 6, #a-f**

**3017-3018** A506 Set of 2 12.50 12.50

**Souvenir Sheets**

**3019-3020** A506 Set of 2 7.50 7.50

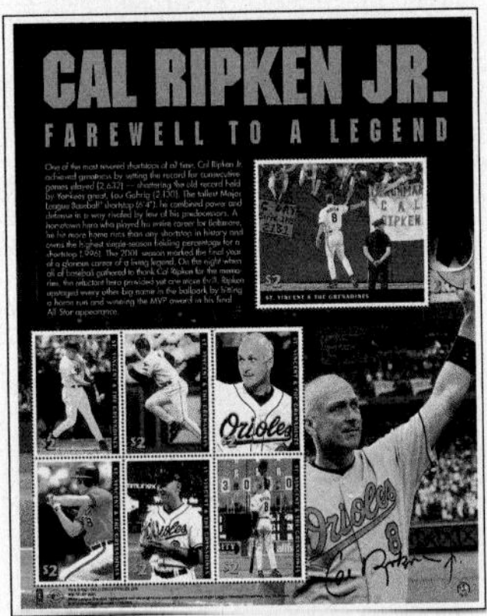


Baseball Player Cal Ripken, Jr. — A507

No. 3021: a, Hitting ball. b, Running. c, Without hat. d, Batting (orange shirt). e, Holding trophy. f, Waving hat. g, Greeting fans (68x56mm).

$6, Wearing batting helmet.

**2001, Dec. 27** ***Perf. 13¼***

**3021** A507 $2 Sheet of 7, #a-g 10.50 10.50

**Souvenir Sheet**

***Perf. 13x13¼***

**3022** A507 $6 multi 4.50 4.50

No. 3022 contains one 36x56mm stamp.

United We Stand — A508

**2001, Dec. 28** ***Perf. 14***

**3023** A508 $2 multi 1.50 1.50

GOLDEN JUBILEE - 6th February, 2002
50th Anniversary of Her Majesty Queen Elizabeth II's Accession


Reign of Queen Elizabeth II, 50th Anniv. — A509

No. 3024: a, With Prince Philip. b, With Princess Margaret. c, Wearing blue dress. d, In wedding gown.

$5, Wearing orange brown dress.

**2002, Apr. 8** **Litho.** ***Perf. 14¼***

**3024** A509 $2 Sheet of 4, #a-d 5.50 5.50

**Souvenir Sheet**

**3025** A509 $5 multi 3.25 3.25

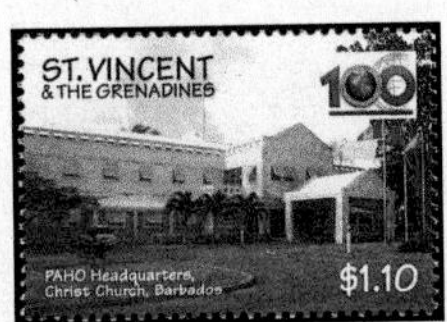


Pan-American Health Organization, Cent. — A510

Designs: 20c, Anniversary emblem, vert. 70c, Dr. Gideon Cordice, vert. 90c, Dr. Arthur Cecil Cyrus, vert. $1.10, Headquarters, Christ Church, Barbados.

**2002, Apr. 8** ***Perf. 14***

**3026-3029** A510 Set of 4 2.40 2.40

Vincy Mas, 25th Anniv. — A511

Designs: 10c, Section of the Bands. 20c, Cocktail, the Blue Dragon, horiz. 70c, Safari, Snake in the Grass. 90c, Bridgette Creese, 2001 Calypso Monarch. $1.10, Heat Wave, horiz. $1.40, Sion Hill Steel Orchestra, horiz.

**2002, June 15** **Litho.** ***Perf. 14***

**3030-3035** A511 Set of 6 3.50 3.50

Intl. Year of Ecotourism — A512

No. 3036: a, Butterfly. b, Manatee. c, Deer. d, Plant.

$6, Windsurfer, divers and fish.

**2002, July 1** ***Perf. 13½x13¼***

**3036** A512 $2 Sheet of 4, #a-d 6.00 6.00

**Souvenir Sheet**

**3037** A512 $6 multi 4.50 4.50

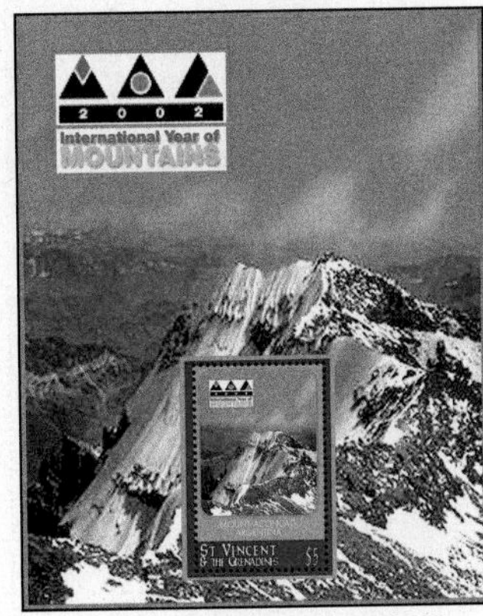


Intl. Year of Mountains — A513

No. 3038: a, Mt. Ararat, Turkey. b, Mt. Ama Dablam, Nepal. c, Mt. Cook, New Zealand. d, Mt. Kilimanjaro, Tanzania. e, Mt. Kenya, Kenya. f, Giant's Castle, South Africa.

$5, Mt. Aconcagua, Argentina.

**2002, July 1**

**3038** A513 $1.40 Sheet of 6, #a-f 6.25 6.25

**Souvenir Sheet**

**3039** A513 $5 multi 3.75 3.75

20th World Scout Jamboree, Thailand — A514

No. 3040, horiz.: a, Scout with kudu horn. b, Scouts breaking camp. c, Daniel Beard and Lord Robert Baden-Powell.

No. 3041, Scout.

**2002, July 1** ***Perf. 13¼x13½***

**3040** A514 $5 Sheet of 3, #a-c 11.50 11.50

**Souvenir Sheet**

***Perf. 13½x13¼***

**3041** A514 $5 multi 3.75 3.75

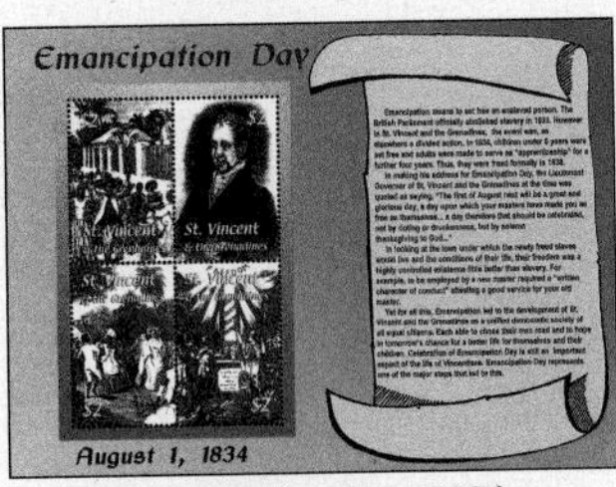


Emancipation Day, 168th Anniv. — A515

No. 3042: a, Crowd near fence. b, Lieutenant Governor of St. Vincent. c, Black couple dancing, white couple. d, Allegory of freedom.

**2002, Aug. 1** ***Perf. 14***
**3042** A515 $2 Sheet of 4, #a-d 6.00 6.00

2002 Winter Olympics, Salt Lake City A516

Designs: No. 3043, $3, Biathlon. No. 3044, $3, Freestyle skiing.

**2002, July 1 Litho.** ***Perf. 13¼x13½***
**3043-3044** A516 Set of 2 4.50 4.50
*3044a* Souvenir sheet, #3043-3044 4.50 4.50

Elvis Presley (1935-77) A517

Designs: $1, With red background.
No. 3046: a, Playing guitar. b, In Army uniform. c, In suit, with guitar strap. d, With vertically striped shirt, looking left. e, In horizontally striped shirt. f, In vertically striped shirt, looking forward.

**2002, Aug. 19** ***Perf. 13¾***
**3045** A517 $1 multi .75 .75
**3046** A517 $1.25 Sheet of 6, #a-f 5.75 5.75

No. 3045 printed in sheets of nine.

Souvenir Sheet

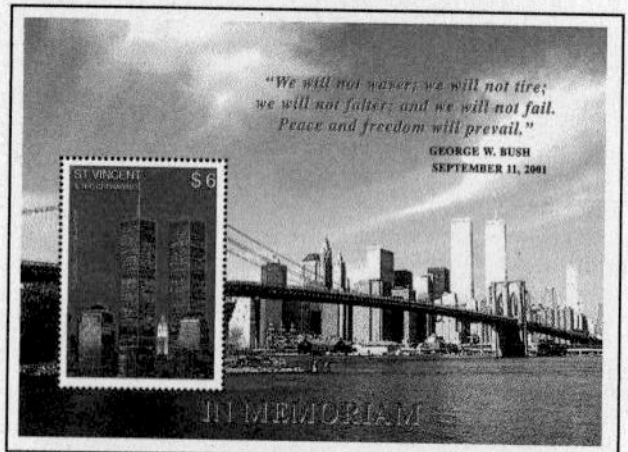

In Remembrance of Sept. 11, 2001 Terrorist Attacks — A518

**2002, Sept. 11** ***Perf. 13¾***
**3047** A518 $6 multi 4.50 4.50

Teddy Bears, Cent. — A519

No. 3048, $2, vert.: a, Cowboy bear. b, Fisherman bear. c, Camper bear. d, Hiker bear.
No. 3049, $2, vert.: a, Bear in kimono. b, Two bears. c, Bear with hair ribbon, baby bear. d, Bear with sunglasses.
No. 3050, vert.: a, Bear with red dress and cap. b, Bear with bonnet. c, Bear with strapless dress. d, Bear with dress with red ruffled collar. e, Bear with blue dress with ribbon.
No. 3051, $5, Four bears by Terumi Yoshikawa. No. 3052, $5, Four bears by Tomoko Suenaga.

**2002, Sept. 23** ***Perf. 13¾ (#3048), 14***
**Sheets of 4, #a-d**
**3048-3049** A519 Set of 2 12.00 12.00
**3050** A519 $2 Sheet of 5, #a-e 7.50 7.50
**Souvenir Sheets**
**3051-3052** A519 Set of 2 7.50 7.50

No. 3048 contains four 38x50mm stamps.

Souvenir Sheets

British Military Medals — A520

Designs: No. 3053, $5, Waterloo Medal. No. 3054, $5, South African War Medal. No. 3055, $5, Queen's South Africa Medal. No. 3056, $5, 1914-15 Star. No. 3057, $5, British War Medal.

**2002, Oct. 7** ***Perf. 14¼***
**3053-3057** A520 Set of 5 19.00 19.00

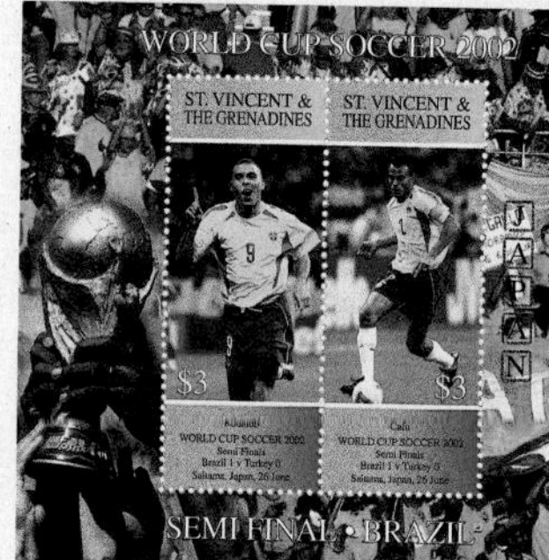

2002 World Cup Soccer Championship Semifinals, Japan and Korea — A521

No. 3058, $1.40: a, Kleberson and Emre Belozoglu. b, Cafu. c, Roberto Carlos. d, Yildiray Basturk. e, Tugay Kerimoglu and Rivaldo. f, Bulent.
No. 3059, $1.40: a, Ji Sung Park and Dietmar Hamann. b, Miroslav Klose and Tae Young Kim. c, Chong Gug Song and Christoph Metzelder. d, Tae Young Kim and Gerald Asamoah. e, Torsten Frings and Ji Sung Park. f, Oliver Neuville and Tae Young Kim.
No. 3060, $3: a, Ronaldo. b, Cafu, diff.
No. 3061, $3: a, Michael Ballack. b, Oliver Kahn.
No. 3062, $3: a, Bulent, diff. b, Yildiray Basturk, diff.
No. 3063, $3: a, Tae Young Kim. b, Du Ri Cha.

**2002, Nov. 4** ***Perf. 13¼***
**Sheets of 6, #a-f**
**3058-3059** A521 Set of 2 12.50 12.50
**Souvenir Sheets of 2, #a-b**
**3060-3063** A521 Set of 4 18.00 18.00

**Shirley Temple Movie Type of 2000**

Temple in "Dimples" — No. 3046, horiz.: a, Embracing man. b, Conducting musicians. c, Seated, in blue dress. d, On stage with actors in black-face. e, Head on pillow. f, With woman, holding plate.
No. 3047: a, Standing on barrel. b, In green dress. c, Adjusting man's ascot. d, With seated woman.
$5, Dancing with man in black face.

**2002, Oct. 28** ***Perf. 14¼***
**3064** A471 $1.40 Sheet of 6, #a-f 6.25 6.25
**3065** A471 $2 Sheet of 4, #a-d 6.00 6.00
**Souvenir Sheet**
**3066** A471 $5 multi 3.75 3.75

Queen Mother Elizabeth (1900-2002) — A522

No. 3067: a, Wearing blue hat and dress. b, Wearing purple hat, dress and corsage. c, Wearing flowered hat.

**2002, Nov. 9 Litho.** ***Perf. 14***
**3067** A522 $2 Sheet of 4, #a-b, 2 #c 6.00 6.00

Christmas — A523

Designs: 20c, Greek Madonna, by Giovanni Bellini. 90c, Kneeling Agostino Barbarigo, by Bellini. $1.10, Presentation of Jesus in the Temple, by Perugino. $1.40, Madonna and Child with the Infant St. John, by Perugino. $1.50, San Giobbe Altarpiece, by Bellini.
$5, Madonna and Child with Saints John the Baptist and Sebastian, by Perugino, horiz.

**2002, Nov. 18**
**3068-3072** A523 Set of 5 4.00 4.00
**Souvenir Sheet**
**3073** A523 $5 multi 3.75 3.75

Souvenir Sheets

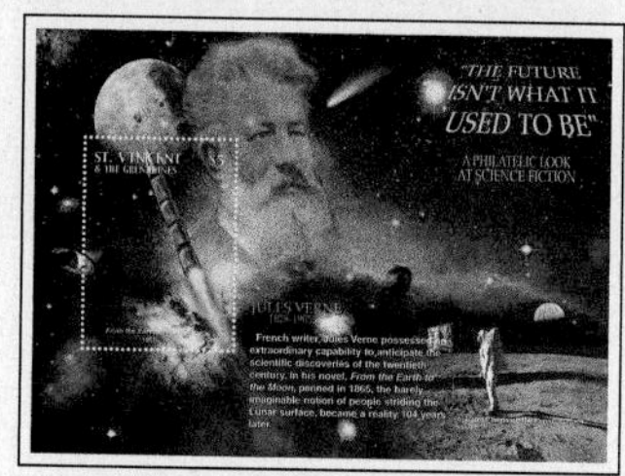

Science Fiction — A524

Designs: No. 3074, $5, From the Earth to the Moon, by Jules Verne. No. 3075, $5, The War of the Worlds, by H. G. Wells. No. 3076, $5, The Time Machine, by Wells.

**2002, Dec. 2** ***Perf. 13¾***
**3074-3076** A524 Set of 3 11.50 11.50

Intl. Federation of Stamp Dealers Associations, 50th Anniv. — A525

**2003, Feb. 16** ***Perf. 14***
**3077** A525 $2 multi 1.50 1.50

**British Military Medals Type of 2002**
Souvenir Sheets

Designs: No. 3078, $5, Victory Medal. No. 3079, $5, Atlantic Star. No. 3080, $5, 1939-45 Star. No. 3081, $5, Africa Star.

**2003, Jan. 27** ***Perf. 13¼***
**3078-3081** A520 Set of 4 15.00 15.00

New Year 2003 (Year of the Ram) — A526

No. 3082: a, Goat with gray collar. b, Goat facing left. c, Goats and kid. d, Man on goat. e, Goat facing right. f, Goat with piebald coat (flora in background).

**2003, Feb. 1** ***Perf. 14¼x13¾***
**3082** A526 $1 Sheet of 6, #a-f 4.50 4.50

Miniature Sheet

Reign of Queen Elizabeth II, 50th Anniv. (in 2002) — A527

**Litho. & Embossed**
**2003, Feb. 24** ***Perf. 13¼x13***
**3083** A527 $20 gold & multi 15.00 15.00

Astronauts Killed in Space Shuttle Columbia Accident — A528

No. 3084, $2 — Col. Rick D. Husband: a, Crew photo (green sky). b, Husband, interior of shuttle. c, Shuttle landing. d, Shuttle and space station.
No. 3085, $2 — Commander William C. McCool: a, Crew photo (tan sky). b, McCool in airplane cockpit. c, McCool, interior of shuttle. d, Shuttle in flight, comet.
No. 3086, $2 — Capt. David M. Brown: a, Crew photo (cloudy sky). b, Shuttle being moved to launch pad. c, Shuttle orbiting earth. d, Brown, interior of shuttle.

**2003, Apr. 7 Litho.** ***Perf. 14¼***
**Sheets of 4, #a-d**
**3084-3086** A528 Set of 3 18.00 18.00

Coronation of Queen Elizabeth II, 50th Anniv. — A529

Designs: No. 3087, $2, Queen arrives at Westminster Abbey. No. 3088, $2, Queen seated in Chair of Estate. No. 3089, $2, Queen's first progress along the nave. No. 3090, $2, Queen leaving Buckingham Palace. No. 3091, $2, Queen and Duke of Edinburgh in state coach. No. 3092, $2, Gold state coach. No. 3093, $2, Westminster Abbey.
$5, Queen's portrait.

**2003, Feb. 26 Litho. *Perf. 13¼***
**3087-3093** A529 Set of 7 10.50 10.50

**Souvenir Sheet**
***Perf. 14¼***

**3094** A529 $5 multi 3.75 3.75

No. 3094 contains one 38x50mm stamp.

Teddy Bear A530

**Self-Adhesive**

**2003, Apr. 30 Embroidered *Imperf.***
**3095** A530 $15 multi 11.50 11.50

Issued in sheets of 4.

Japanese Art — A531

Designs: 70c, A Gathering of Sorcerers on the Tokaido Road (detail), by Kunisada Utagawa. $1.10, Kiyohime and the Moon, by Chikanobu Yoshu. $1.40, A Gathering of Sorcerers on the Tokaido Road (detail), by Kunisada Utagawa, diff. $3, A Gathering of Sorcerers on the Tokaido Road (detail), by Kunisada Utagawa, diff.
No. 3100: a, Snake Mountain, by Kuniyoshi Utagawa. b, Sadanobu and Oni, by Yoshitoshi Tsukioka. c, Shoki, by Tsukioka. d, The Nightly Weeping Rock, by Kuniyoshi Utagawa.
$5, The Ghosts of Matahachi and Kikuno, by Kunisada Utagawa.

**2003, Apr. 30 Litho. *Perf. 14¼***
**3096-3099** A531 Set of 4 4.75 4.75
**3100** A531 $2 Sheet of 4, #a-d 6.00 6.00

**Souvenir Sheet**

**3101** A531 $5 multi 3.75 3.75

Rembrandt Paintings A532

Designs: $1, Portrait of Jacques de Gheyn III. $1.10, Young Man in a Black Beret. $1.40, Hendrickje Stoffels. No. 3105, $2, The Polish Rider, horiz.
No. 3106, $2: a, Belthazzar Sees the Writing on the Wall. b, Portrait of a Young Man. c, Jacob Blessing the Sons of Joseph. d, King Uzziah Stricken with Leprosy.
$5, The Stoning of St. Stephen.

**2003, Apr. 30**
**3102-3105** A532 Set of 4 4.25 4.25
**3106** A532 $2 Sheet of 4, #a-d 6.00 6.00

**Souvenir Sheet**

**3107** A532 $5 multi 3.75 3.75

Paintings By Pablo Picasso — A533

Designs: 60c, Composition: Woman with Half-Length Hair. 70c, Sister of the Artist, vert. 90c, Maternity, vert. $1, Bearded Man's Head, vert. $1.10, Two Seated Children (Claude and Paloma), vert. $1.40, Woman with a Blue Lace Collar.
No. 3114: a, Corrida. b, Mandolin, Pitcher and Bottle. c, The Painter and Model. d, Reclining Woman Sleeping Under a Lamp.
No. 3115, Reclining Nude. No. 3116, Spanish Woman Against an Orange Background, vert.

**2003, Apr. 30 *Perf. 14¼***
**3108-3113** A533 Set of 6 4.25 4.25
**3114** A533 $2 Sheet of 4, #a-d 6.00 6.00

***Imperf***
**Size: 103x82mm**

**3115** A533 $5 multi 3.75 3.75

**Size: 82x105mm**

**3116** A533 $5 multi 3.75 3.75

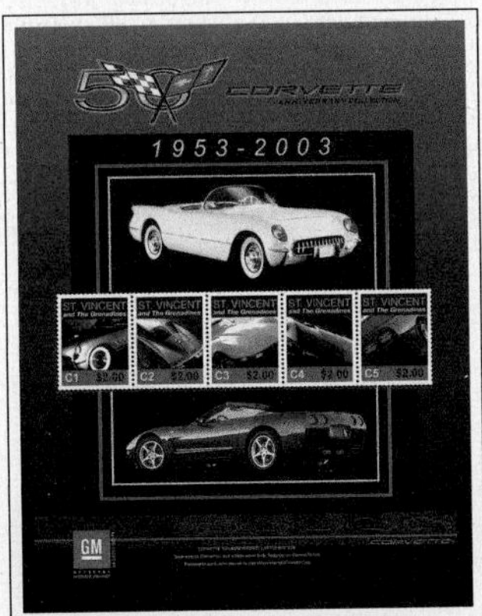


Corvette Automobiles, 50th Anniv. — A534

No. 3117: a, C1. b, C2. c, C3. d, C4. e, C5.
No. 3118: a, 1953 Corvette. b, 2003 Corvette.

**2003, May 5 *Perf. 13¼***
**3117** A534 $2 Sheet of 5, #a-e 7.50 7.50

***Perf. 14¼***

**3118** A534 $3 Sheet of 2, #a-b 4.50 4.50

No. 3118 contains two 50x38mm stamps.

Prince William, 21st Birthday — A535

No. 3119: a, Wearing suit. b, Wearing polo jersey. c, Wearing blue shirt.
$5, Wearing suit and tie.

**2003, May 13 *Perf. 14***
**3119** A535 $3 Sheet of 3, #a-c 6.75 6.75

**Souvenir Sheet**

**3120** A535 $5 multi 3.75 3.75

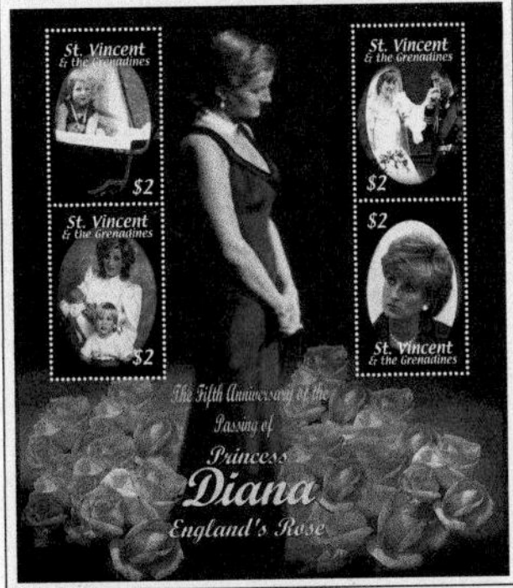


Princess Diana (1961-97) — A536

No. 3121, $2 (vignettes in ovals): a, As child in baby carriage. b, With Prince Charles on wedding day. c, With Princes William and Harry. d, In purple jacket.
No. 3122, $2 (white background): a, Wearing tiara. b, Wearing white gown. c, Wearing purple sweater. d, Wearing lilac dress.

**2003, May 26 Sheets of 4, #a-d**
**3121-3122** A536 Set of 2 12.00 12.00

Cadillac Automobiles, Cent. — A537

No. 3123: a, 1953 Eldorado. b, 2002 Eldorado. c, 1967 Eldorado. d, 1962 Series 62.
$5, 1927 LaSalle.

**2003, July 1 *Perf. 13¼x13¾***
**3123** A537 $2 Sheet of 4, #a-d 6.00 6.00

**Souvenir Sheet**

**3124** A537 $5 multi 3.75 3.75

Intl. Year of Fresh Water — A538

No. 3125: a, Owia Salt Pond. b, The Soufriere. c, Falls of Baleine.
$5, Trinity Falls.

**2003, July 1 *Perf. 13½***
**3125** A538 $3 Sheet of 3, #a-c 6.75 6.75

**Souvenir Sheet**

**3126** A538 $5 multi 3.75 3.75

Circus — A539

No. 3127, $2: a, Linny. b, Bruce Feiler. c, Segey Provirin. d, Weezle.
No. 3128, $2: a, Mermaids. b, Robert Wolf. c, Elbrus Pilev's Group. d, Stinky.

**2003, July 1 *Perf. 14***
**Sheets of 4, #a-d**
**3127-3128** A539 Set of 2 12.00 12.00

Tour de France Bicycle Race, Cent. — A540

No. 3129, $2: a, Antonin Magne, 1931. b, André Leducq, 1932. c, Georges Speicher, 1933. d, Magne, 1934.
No. 3130, $2: a, Romain Maes, 1935. b, Sylvére Maes, 1936. c, Roger Lapebie, 1937. d, Gino Bartali, 1938.
No. 3131, $2: a, Sylvére Maes, 1939. b, Jean Lazaridés, 1946. c, Jean Robic, 1947. d, Bartali, 1948.
No. 3132, $5, Magne, 1931, 1934. No. 3133, $5, Fausto Coppi, 1949. No. 3134, $5, Ferdinand Kubler, 1950.

**2003, July 1 *Perf. 13¼***
**Sheets of 4, #a-d**
**3129-3131** A540 Set of 3 18.00 18.00

**Souvenir Sheets**

**3132-3134** A570 Set of 3 11.50 11.50



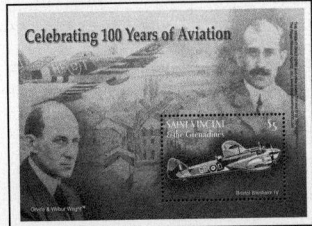

Powered Flight, Cent. — A541

No. 3135, $2: a, Handley Page Heyford. b, Heinkel He-111B. c, Gloster Gauntlet. d, Curtiss BF2C-1.
No. 3136, $2: a, Mitsubishi A6M Reisen. b, Dewoitine D520. c, Messerschmitt Bf 109E. d, Republic Thunderbolt.
No. 3137, $5, Bristol Blenheim IV. No. 3138, $5, Fairey Flycatcher.

**2003, July 15** *Perf. 14*

**Sheets of 4, #a-d**

**3135-3136** A541 Set of 2 12.00 12.00

**Souvenir Sheets**

**3137-3138** A541 Set of 2 7.50 7.50

Salvation Army in St. Vincent, Cent. — A542

Designs: 70c, Chief musicians. 90c, District temple. $1, Christmas Kettle Appeal Fund. $1.10, Headquarters, horiz.

**2003, Aug. 1**

**3139-3142** A542 Set of 4 2.75 2.75

Operation Iraqi Freedom — A543

No. 3143: a, Gen. Richard B. Meyers. b, Lt. Gen. David McKiernan. c, Lt. Gen. Michael Moseley. d, Vice Admiral Timothy Keating. e, Lt. Gen. Jay Garner. f, Gen. Tommy R. Franks. g, Lt. Gen. Earl B. Hailston. h, Gen. John Jumper.

No. 3144: a, Private Jessica Lynch. b, Gen. Franks. c, Spectre gunship. d, Stryker vehicle. e, USS Constellation. f, USS Kitty Hawk.

**2003, Aug. 25** *Perf. 14¼*

**3143** A543 $1 Sheet of 8, #a-h 6.00 6.00

**3144** A543 $1.50 Sheet of 6, #a-f 6.75 6.75

A544

A545

Marvel Comic Book Characters — A546

No. 3145 — Spiderman: a, Shooting cable from arm. b, Grasping two cables. c, Grasping one cable. d, Climbing on building.

No. 3146, $2 — The Incredible Hulk: a, Close-up of face, denomination at UR. b, Fire in background, denomination at UL. c, Like "b," denomination at UR. d, Like "a," denomination at UL.

No. 3147, $2 — The Incredible Hulk: a, Punching ground. b, Grasping. c, Showing fists. d, Punching rocks.

No. 3148, $2 — X-Men United: a, Nightcrawler. b, Professor X. c, Iceman. d, Rogue.

No. 3149, $2 — X-Men United: a, Magneto. b, Mystique. c, Stryker. d, Lady Deathstrike.

No. 3150, $2 — X-Men United: a, Jean Grey. b, Storm. c, Wolverine. d, Cyclops.

**2003, Sept. 10** *Perf. 13¼*

**3145** A544 $2 Sheet of 4, #a-d 6.00 6.00

**Sheets of 4, #a-d**

**3146-3147** A545 Set of 2 12.00 12.00

**3148-3150** A546 Set of 3 18.00 18.00



Prehistoric Animals — A547

No. 3151, $2, horiz.: a, Daspletosaurus. b, Utahraptor. c, Scutellosaurus. d, Scelidosaurus.

No. 3152, $2, horiz.: a, Syntarsus. b, Velociraptor. c, Mononikus. d, Massospondylus.

No. 3153, $5, Pterodactylus. No. 3154, $5, Giganotosaurus.

**2003, Nov. 5** *Perf. 13¼x13¾*

**Sheets of 4, #a-d**

**3151-3152** A547 Set of 2 12.00 12.00

**Souvenir Sheets**

*Perf. 13¾x13¼*

**3153-3154** A547 Set of 2 7.50 7.50

Cats — A548

Designs: 50c, British Shorthair. $1, Burmese. $1.40, American Shorthair. $3, Havana Brown.

No. 3159: a, Ocicat. b, Manx. c, Somali. d, Angora.

$5, Abyssinian.

**2003, Nov. 5** *Perf. 14*

**3155-3158** A548 Set of 4 4.50 4.50

**3159** A548 $2 Sheet of 4, #a-d 6.00 6.00

**Souvenir Sheet**

**3160** A548 $5 multi 3.75 3.75

Dogs — A549

Designs: 10c, Chihuahua. 20c, Bulldog. 60c, Weimaraner. No. 3164, $5, Dalmatian.

No. 3165: a, Dachshund. b, Collie. c, Springer spaniel. d, Hamilton hound.

No. 3166, $5, Golden retriever.

**2003, Nov. 5**

**3161-3164** A549 Set of 4 4.50 4.50

**3165** A549 $2 Sheet of 4, #a-d 6.00 6.00

**Souvenir Sheet**

**3166** A549 $5 multi 3.75 3.75

Orchids — A550

Designs: 40c, Laelia lobata. 90c, Miltoniopsis phalaenopsis. $1, Phalaenopsis violacea. $3, Trichopilia fragrans.

No. 3171: a, Masdevallia uniflora. b, Laelia flava. c, Barkeria lindleyana. d, Laelia tenebrosa.

$5, Cattleya lawrenceana.

**2003, Nov. 5**

**3167-3170** A550 Set of 4 4.00 4.00

**3171** A550 $2 Sheet of 4, #a-d 6.00 6.00

**Souvenir Sheet**

**3172** A550 $5 multi 3.75 3.75

Marine Life — A551

Designs: 70c, Lutjanus kasmira. 90c, Chaetadon collare. $1.10, Istiophorus platypterus. No. 3176, $2, Pomacanthidae.

No. 3177, $2: a, Equetus lanceolatus. b, Hypoplectrus gutavarius. c, Pomacentridae. d, Cichlidae.

$5, Dolphins.

**2003, Nov. 5**

**3173-3176** A551 Set of 4 3.50 3.50

**3177** A551 $2 Sheet of 4, #a-d 6.00 6.00

**Souvenir Sheet**

**3178** A551 $5 multi 3.75 3.75

Christmas — A552

Children's contest-winning art by: 70c, Andrew Gonsalves. 90c, Georgia Gravel. $1.10, Adam Gravel, vert.

**2003, Nov. 5** *Perf. 14¼*

**3179-3181** A552 Set of 3 2.00 2.00

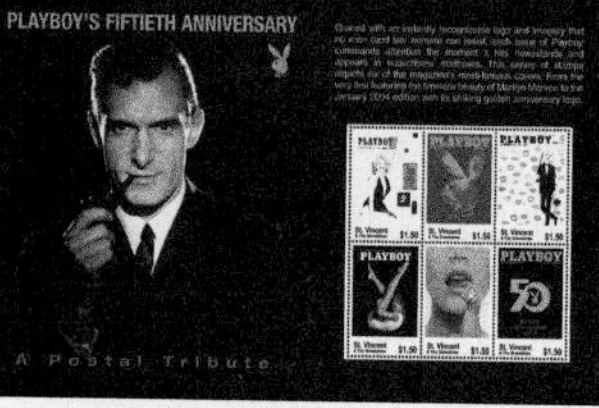


Playboy Magazine, 50th Anniv. — A553

Magazine covers depicting: a, Marilyn Monroe. b, Playboy emblem. c, Rabbit and kisses. d, Woman with legs above head. e, Woman licking stamp. f, 50th Anniversary emblem.

**2003, Dec. 1** **Litho.** *Perf. 14*

**3182** A553 $1.50 Sheet of 6, #a-f 6.75 6.75

Ma Yuan (1160-1235), Painter — A554

No. 3183: a, Apricot Blossoms. b, Peach Blossoms. c, Unnamed painting, denomination at left. d, Unnamed painting, denomination at right.

$5, On a Mountain Path in Spring.

**2004, Jan. 30** *Perf. 13x13½*

**3183** A554 $2 Sheet of 4, #a-d 6.00 6.00

*Imperf*

**3184** A554 $5 multi 3.75 3.75

No. 3183 contains four 40x30mm stamps.

Souvenir Sheet

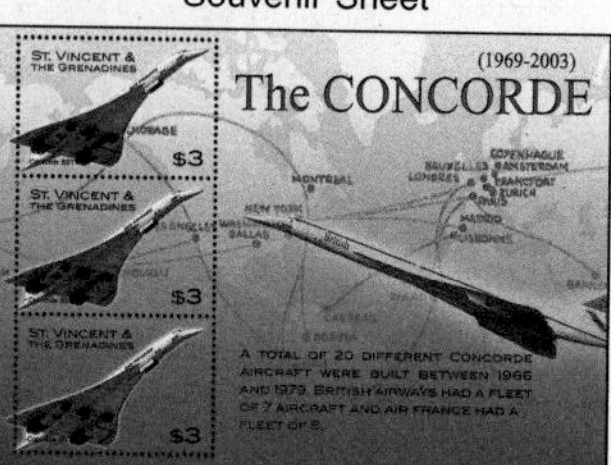


Cessation of Concorde Flights in 2003 — A555

Concorde over map showing: a, Anchorage. b, Los Angeles. c, South Pacific (no cities named).

**2004, Feb. 16** *Perf. 13¼x13½*

**3185** A555 $3 Sheet of 3, #a-c 6.75 6.75

New Year 2004 (Year of the Monkey) — A556

**2004, Jan. 15 Litho. *Perf. 13¼x13***
**3186** A556 $1.40 buff, lt brn & blk 1.10 1.10

**Souvenir Sheet**

**3187** A556 $3 pink, brn & blk 2.25 2.25

No. 3186 printed in sheets of 4.

A557

Marilyn Monroe (1926-62), Actress — A558

No. 3188: a, Sepia-toned portrait. b, Wearing blue dress. c, Wearing white dress. d, Wearing black dress.

No. 3189: a, Wearing round white earrings. b, With hand showing. c, Wearing no earrings. d, Wearing different earrings.

**2004, May 3 *Perf. 14***
**3188** A557 $2 Sheet of 4, #a-d 6.00 6.00

***Perf. 13½x13¼***

**3189** A558 $2 Sheet of 4, #a-d 6.00 6.00

European Soccer Championships, Portugal — A559

No. 3190, vert.: a, Roger Lemerre. b, Marco Delvecchio. c, David Trezeguet. d, De Kuip Stadium.

$5, 2000 French team.

**2004, May 17 *Perf. 13½x13¼***
**3190** A559 $2 Sheet of 4, #a-d 6.00 6.00

**Souvenir Sheet**

***Perf. 13¼***

**3191** A559 $5 multi 3.75 3.75

No. 3190 contains four 28x42mm stamps.

2004 Summer Olympics, Athens A560

Designs: 70c, Pierre de Coubertin, first Intl. Olympic Committee Secretary General. $1, Pin from 1904 St. Louis Olympics. $1.40, Water Polo, 1936 Berlin Olympics, horiz. $3, Greek amphora.

**2004, June 17 *Perf. 14¼***
**3192-3195** A560 Set of 4 4.75 4.75

Babe Ruth (1895-1948), Baseball Player — A561

No. 3196: a, Facing right. b, Facing forward. c, Leaning on bat. d, Swinging bat.

**2004, July 1 *Perf. 13½x13¼***
**3196** A561 $2 Sheet of 4, #a-d 6.00 6.00

D-Day, 60th Anniv. A562

Designs: 70c, Air Chief Marshal Sir Trafford Leigh-Mallory. 90c, Lt. Col. Maureen Gara. $1, Gen. Omar Bradley. $1.10, Jean Valentine. $1.40, Jack Culshaw. $1.50, Gen. Dwight D. Eisenhower.

No. 3203, $2: a, British land on Gold Beach. b, British infantry land on Gold Beach. c, Canadians at Juno Beach. d, Canadians land at Juno Beach.

No. 3204, $2: a, Rangers take Pointe du Hoc. b, Rangers hold Pointe du Hoc. c, Invasion announced to press. d, British liberate Hermanville.

No. 3205, $5, Soldiers prepare to board assault landing craft. No. 3206, $5, Code breaking team at work.

**2004, July 19 *Perf. 14***

**Stamp + Label (#3197-3202)**

**3197-3202** A562 Set of 6 5.00 5.00

**Sheets of 4, #a-d**

**3203-3204** A562 Set of 2 12.00 12.00

**Souvenir Sheets**

**3205-3206** A562 Set of 2 7.50 7.50

General Employees' Cooperative Credit Union — A563

Designs: 70c, GECCU children. 90c, GECCU Building. $1.10, Calvin Nicholls, vert. $1.40, Bertrand Neehall, vert.

**2004, Sept. 15 Litho.**
**3207-3210** A563 Set of 4 3.25 3.25

Pres. Ronald Reagan (1911-2004) A564

No. 3211: a, Portrait. b, With flag. c, At microphone.

**2004, Oct. 13 *Perf. 13½x13¼***
**3211** Vert. strip of 3 3.25 3.25
*a.-c.* A564 $1.40 Any single 1.00 1.00

Printed in sheets containing two strips.

Railroads, 200th Anniv. — A565

No. 3212, $2: a, 1911 0-6-0 Standard, Boston & Maine. b, AG locomotive. c, BA 101 Antigua locomotive. d, Aster 1449.

No. 3213, $2: a, Narrow gauge locomotive W12. b, Gambler. LNV9701 4-4-0 NG. c, No. 4 Snowdon. d, Hiawatha 3-1.

No. 3214, $2: a, CO1604-1. b, CP steam locomotive N135. c, 6042-6. d, E1 narrow gauge 0-4-0T.

No. 3215, $5, NAT2A 01-06-00. No. 3216, $5, Union Pacific 844. No. 3217, $5, Holy War-1, vert.

**2004, Oct. 13 *Perf. 14***

**Sheets of 4, #a-d**

**3212-3214** A565 Set of 3 18.00 18.00

**Souvenir Sheets**

**3215-3217** A565 Set of 3 11.50 11.50

Independence, 25th Anniv. — A566

Designs: 10c, Halimah DeShong. 20c, Winston Davis, cricket player. No. 3220, 70c, Miss Carnival 2003. No. 3221, 70c, Flag, horiz. No. 3222, 70c, Pamenoa Ballantyne, runner, horiz. No. 3223, 90c, Carl "Blazer" Williams. No. 3224, 90c, Breadfruit, horiz. No. 3225, 90c, Rodney "Chang" Jack, soccer player, horiz. $1.10, St. Vincent parrot. No. 3227, $5, Capt. Hugh Mulzac. No. 3228, $5, George McIntosh, political leader. No. 3229, $5, E. T. Joshua, horiz. No. 3230, $10, Joseph Chatoyer, Carib chief, national hero. No. 3231, $10, Robert Milton Cato, politician.

**2004, Oct. 25**
**3218-3231** A566 Set of 14 31.00 31.00

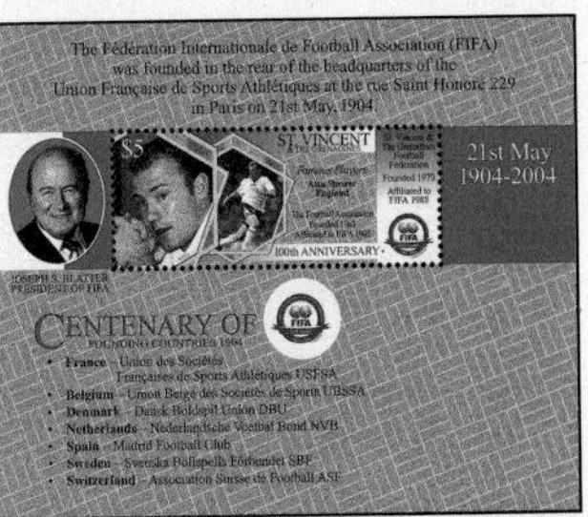
FIFA (Fédération Internationale de Football Association), Cent. — A567

No. 3232: a, David Ginola. b, Paul Scholes. c, Jurgen Kohler. d, Ian Rush.

$5, Alan Shearer.

**2004, Oct. 27 *Perf. 12¾x12½***
**3232** A567 $2 Sheet of 4, #a-d 6.00 6.00

**Souvenir Sheet**

**3233** A567 $5 multi 3.75 3.75

Paintings by Norman Rockwell A568

Designs: 90c, Lion and His Keeper. $1, Weighing In. $1.40, The Young Lawyer. $2, The Bodybuilder.

$5, Triple Self-portrait.

**2004, Oct. 29 *Perf. 14¼***
**3234-3237** A568 Set of 4 4.00 4.00

***Imperf***

**Size: 66x88mm**

**3238** A568 $5 multi 3.75 3.75

**Various St. Vincent and St. Vincent Grenadines Stamps Surcharged**

**Surcharge Types on St. Vincent Stamps**

10c on 45c No. 1078 — Type 1: "1" without bottom serif, "0" same thickness. Type 2: "1" with bottom serif, "0" thin at top and bottom.

10c on 65c No. 1080b and 10c on 75c No. 1081b — Type 1: "1" with bottom serif, "0" thin at top and bottom. Type 2: "1" without bottom serif, "0" same thickness.

20c on 60c No. 726 — Type 1: New denomination at lower left with small "c." Type 2: New denomination at upper left, with cent sign. Type 3: New denomination below obliterator and approximately 6mm to left of it, with small "c." Type 4: New denomination below obliterator and approximately 16mm to left of it, with small "c."

20c on 75c Nos. 984a-984b horiz. pair — Type 1: Small "c." Type 2: Cent sign.

20c on $1.25 No. 527 — Type 1: New denomination to left of round obliterator, with raised "c" and serifed "2." Type 2: New denomination at lower left, round obliterator with cent sign and serifed "2". Type 3: New denomination below square obliterator, unserifed "2" and "c."

20c on $2 No. 638 — Type 1: New denomination to right and below obliterator, with serifed "2" and small "c" with ball. Type 2: New denomination to right of obliterator, with unserifed "2" and small "c" without ball.

20c on $2 No. 665 — Type 1: New denomination at left, with small "c" with ball and serifed "2." Type 2: New denomination close to obliterator at left, with small "c" without ball and unserifed "2."

20c on $2 No. 975 — Type 1: Cent sign. Type 2: Small "c."

20c on $3.70 No. 1004 — Type 1: New denomination at upper left, with serifed "2," "0" thin at top and bottom. Type 2: New denomination at upper right with unserifed "2," "0" same thickness.

### Surcharge Types on St. Vincent Grenadines Stamps

20c on 75c No. 511 — Type 1: Cent sign. Type 2: Small "c."

20c on 75c No. 593 — Type 1: New denomination at lower left, below obliterator, with cent sign. Type 2: New denomination to right of obliterator, with small "c."

20c on $1.50 No. 277 — Type 1: New denomination at top center, with small "c." Type 2: New denomination at lower left, with cent sign.

20c on $2 No. 186 — Type 1: New denomination to left of obliterator, with small "c." Type 2: New denomination at upper left, with cent sign.

20c on $2.50 No. 265 — Type 1: Unserifed "2," small "c" even with base of numerals. Type 2: Serifed "2," raised small "c."

### Methods, Perfs and Watermarks As Before

**1994 (?)-2004**

### On St. Vincent Stamps

| | | | | |
|---|---|---|---|---|
| **3239** | A36 | 10c on 2c #281 | *125.00* | — |
| **3240** | A148 | 10c on 6c #1070 | — | — |
| **3241** | A148 | 10c on 12c #1072 | — | — |
| **3242** | A148 | 10c on 15c #1073b | — | — |
| **3243** | A36 | 10c on 25c #290 | *85.00* | — |
| **3244** | A148 | 10c on 25c #1075b | — | *30.00* |
| **3245** | A112 | 10c on 35c #743 | *50.00* | *30.00* |
| **3246** | A148 | 10c on 35c #1077 | | |
| **3247** | A109 | 10c on 45c #725 | — | — |
| **3248** | A148 | 10c on 45c #1078b, Type 1 | — | *30.00* |
| **3249** | A148 | 10c on 45c #1078, Type 2 | — | *75.00* |
| *a.* | | On #1078b (perf. 14), Type 2 | | |
| **3250** | A151 | 10c on 45c #1096 | — | *25.00* |
| **3251** | A98 | 10c on 60c #640 | *75.00* | *90.00* |
| **3252** | A104a | 10c on 60c #671 | *50.00* | — |
| **3253** | A104b | 10c on 60c #676 | *25.00* | *10.00* |
| **3254** | A148 | 10c on 65c #1080b, Type 1 | | |
| **3255** | A148 | 10c on 65c #1080b, Type 2 | | — |
| **3256** | A71 | 10c on 70c #481 | *50.00* | — |
| **3257** | A148 | 10c on 75c #1081b, Type 1 | | *40.00* |
| **3257A** | A148 | 10c on 75c #1081b, Type 2 | | |
| **3258** | A109 | 10c on $1 #728 | — | *75.00* |
| **3259** | A77 | 10c on $1.25 #527 | *95.00* | — |
| **3260** | A98 | 10c on $1.50 #641 | — | — |
| **3260A** | A99 | 10c on $1.50 #645 | | |
| **3261** | A105 | 10c on $1.50 #681 | *50.00* | — |
| **3262** | A82 | 10c on $2 #544 | *50.00* | — |
| **3262A** | A93 | 10c on $2 #618 | | |
| **3263** | A98 | 10c on $2 #642 | | |
| **3263A** | A106 | 10c on $2.40 #686 | | — |
| **3264** | A90 | 10c on $2.50 #607 | *25.00* | *25.00* |
| **3264A** | A108 | 10c on $3 #718 | | |
| **3265** | A36 | 20c on ½c #279 | *15.00* | *20.00* |
| **3266** | A47 | 20c on 1c #337 | *75.00* | *50.00* |
| **3267** | A145 | 20c on 6c #1061a-1061b horiz. pair | *200.00* | — |
| **3268** | A126 | 20c on 25c #903 | — | *85.00* |
| **3273** | A113 | 20c on 35c #761 | — | *200.00* |
| **3274** | A162 | 20c on 35c #1145 | — | *175.00* |
| **3275** | A105 | 20c on 45c #679 | — | — |
| **3276** | A112 | 20c on 45c #744 | — | — |
| **3277** | A151 | 20c on 45c #1096 | — | — |
| **3278** | A90 | 20c on 60c #605 | *150.00* | *30.00* |
| **3279** | A93 | 20c on 60c #616 | — | — |
| **3280** | A97 | 20c on 60c #636 | *200.00* | *200.00* |
| **3281** | A98 | 20c on 60c #640 | *15.00* | *20.00* |
| **3282** | A104 | 20c on 60c #667 | *15.00* | *20.00* |
| **3283** | A104b | 20c on 60c #676 | — | *50.00* |
| **3284** | A105 | 20c on 60c #680 | *20.00* | *10.00* |
| **3285** | A109 | 20c on 60c #726, Type 1 | *25.00* | *10.00* |
| **3286** | A109 | 20c on 60c #726, Type 2 | *10.00* | *50.00* |
| **3287** | A109 | 20c on 60c #726, Type 3 | *50.00* | *5.00* |
| **3288** | A109 | 20c on 60c #726, Type 4 | *90.00* | *35.00* |
| **3289** | A115 | 20c on 60c #784 | — | *30.00* |
| **3290** | A71 | 20c on 70c #481 | *175.00* | — |
| **3292** | A136 | 20c on 75c #984a-984b horiz. pair, Type 1 | — | *150.00* |
| **3293** | A136 | 20c on 75c #984a-984b horiz. pair, Type 2 | — | — |
| **3294** | A138 | 20c on 75c #999 | *75.00* | *50.00* |
| **3295** | A148 | 20c on 75c #1081 | *30.00* | — |
| **3296** | A79 | 20c on $1 #534 | *50.00* | *15.00* |
| **3297** | A94 | 20c on $1 #622a-622b pair | *130.00* | — |
| **3298** | A97 | 20c on $1 #637 | *50.00* | *50.00* |
| **3299** | A121 | 20c on $1 #847 | — | *50.00* |
| **3302** | A64 | 20c on $1.25 #434 | *30.00* | *40.00* |
| **3303** | A70 | 20c on $1.25 #478 | *30.00* | *200.00* |
| **3304** | A73 | 20c on $1.25 #498 | — | — |
| **3306** | A77 | 20c on $1.25 #527, Type 1 | — | *110.00* |
| **3307** | A77 | 20c on $1.25 #527, Type 2 | — | — |
| **3308** | A77 | 20c on $1.25 #527, Type 3 | *85.00* | *125.00* |
| **3309** | A99 | 20c on $1.50 #645 | — | — |
| **3310** | A103 | 20c on $1.50 #664 | — | *100.00* |
| **3311** | A104 | 20c on $1.50 #668 | *15.00* | *20.00* |
| **3313** | A104b | 20c on $1.50 #677 | *45.00* | *50.00* |
| **3314** | A105 | 20c on $1.50 #681 | — | — |
| **3315** | A115 | 20c on $1.50 #785 | *35.00* | *15.00* |
| **3316** | A134 | 20c on $1.50 #974 | *65.00* | *100.00* |
| **3317** | A136 | 20c on $1.50 #985a-985b horiz. pair | *140.00* | *100.00* |
| **3318** | A93 | 20c on $2 #618 | *40.00* | *100.00* |
| **3320** | A97 | 20c on $2 #638, Type 1 | *40.00* | *50.00* |
| **3321** | A97 | 20c on $2 #638, Type 2 | *100.00* | *60.00* |
| **3322** | A98 | 20c on $2 #642 | — | — |
| **3324** | A103 | 20c on $2 #665, Type 1 | — | *200.00* |
| **3325** | A103 | 20c on $2 #665, Type 2 | — | — |
| **3326** | A104 | 20c on $2 #669 | *40.00* | *50.00* |
| **3327** | A104b | 20c on $2 #678 | *15.00* | *25.00* |
| **3328** | A105 | 20c on $2 #682 | *15.00* | *15.00* |
| **3329** | A115 | 20c on $2 #786 | *45.00* | *15.00* |
| **3330** | A134 | 20c on $2 #975, Type 1 | — | — |
| **3331** | A134 | 20c on $2 #975, Type 2 | — | — |
| *a.* | | Horiz. pair, #3330-3331 | — | — |
| **3333** | A126 | 20c on $2.50 #905 | *20.00* | *100.00* |
| **3334** | A108 | 20c on $3 #718 | — | *40.00* |
| **3337** | A113 | 20c on $3 #764 | — | *150.00* |
| **3338** | A117 | 20c on $3 #806 | — | — |
| **3339** | A119 | 20c on $3 #832 | — | — |
| **3342** | A139 | 20c on $3.70 #1004, Type 1 | *80.00* | *40.00* |
| **3343** | A139 | 20c on $3.70 #1004, Type 2 | *30.00* | *30.00* |
| **3345** | A189 | 20c on $4 #1307 | *75.00* | *50.00* |

### On St. Vincent Grenadines Stamps

| | | | | |
|---|---|---|---|---|
| **3346** | G3 | 10c on 1c #33 | — | — |
| **3347** | G16 | 10c on 1c #133 | | |
| **3348** | G16 | 10c on 6c #138 | — | — |
| **3349** | G35 | 10c on 35c #433 | | |
| **3350** | G31 | 10c on 45c #271 | — | — |
| **3351** | G33 | 10c on 45c #292 | | |
| **3351A** | G36 | 10c on 75c #439 | | |
| **3352** | G20 | 10c on 90c #185 | — | — |
| **3353** | A90 | 10c on $1 #192 | — | — |
| **3354** | G35 | 10c on $1 #435 | | |
| **3355** | G32 | 10c on $2 #278 | — | — |
| **3356** | G36 | 10c on $3 #440 | | |
| **3358** | A106 | 20c on 20c #469 | — | — |
| **3359** | G39 | 20c on 35c #484 | — | — |
| **3360** | G31 | 20c on 45c #271 | — | — |
| **3361** | A106 | 20c on 45c #470 | — | — |
| **3362** | G45 | 20c on 45c #561 | — | — |
| **3363** | G7 | 20c on 50c #71 | — | — |
| **3364** | G31 | 20c on 60c #272 | — | — |
| **3366** | G41 | 20c on 75c #511, Type 1 | — | — |
| **3367** | G41 | 20c on 75c #511, Type 2 | — | — |
| *a.* | | Horiz. pair, #3366-3367 | — | — |
| **3368** | G50 | 20c on 75c #588 | — | — |
| **3369** | G51 | 20c on 75c #593, Type 1 | — | — |
| **3370** | G51 | 20c on 75c #593, Type 2 | — | — |
| *a.* | | Double surcharge | | — |
| **3371** | G20 | 20c on 90c #185 | — | — |
| **3372** | G7 | 20c on $1 #72 | — | — |
| **3374** | G17 | 20c on $1.25 #160 | — | — |
| **3375** | G46 | 20c on $1.25 #566 | — | — |
| **3376** | A97 | 20c on $1.50 #264 | — | — |
| **3377** | G31 | 20c on $1.50 #273 | — | — |
| **3378** | G32 | 20c on $1.50 #277, Type 1 | — | — |
| **3379** | G32 | 20c on $1.50 #277, Type 2 | — | — |
| **3381** | A76 | 20c on $2 #128 | — | — |
| **3383** | G20 | 20c on $2 #186, Type 1 | — | — |
| **3384** | G20 | 20c on $2 #186, Type 2 | — | — |
| **3385** | G21 | 20c on $2 #198 | — | — |
| **3386** | G27 | 20c on $2 #242 | — | — |
| **3387** | G32 | 20c on $2 #278 | — | — |
| **3390** | A97 | 20c on $2.50 #265, Type 1 | — | — |
| **3391** | A97 | 20c on $2.50 #265, Type 2 | — | — |
| **3392** | A82 | 20c on $3 #179 | — | — |
| **3394** | G35 | 20c on $3 #436 | — | — |
| **3395** | G37 | 20c on $3 #475 | — | — |
| **3396** | G39 | 20c on $3 #487 | — | — |
| **3397** | G43 | 20c on $3 #536 | — | — |
| **3399** | G59 | 20c on $3 #692 | — | — |
| **3400** | G50 | 20c on $3.50 #589 | — | — |
| **3401** | G45 | 20c on $4 #563 | — | — |

These surcharges were printed from the mid-1990s to 2004, with the bulk created from 1999 to 2004. Issue dates are not certain as the stamps were available for both revenue and postal use. Numbers are reserved for stamps that printer's records indicate were surcharged. Additional stamps may also have been surcharged.

These stamps were not available through the philatelic agency, but could be bought at post offices, as well as Treasury offices and other locations throughout the country where revenue stamps were used, including retail stores.

The surcharged Grenadines issues were not necessarily sent only to the Grenadines for sale there.

Nos. 3246, 3249a, 3254, 3255, 3257A, 3263, 3347, 3349, 3351, and 3354, which are currently known only with revenue cancels, may also have been used postally.

The shape of the obliterators and the location of new denominations varies.

On No. 3240, the original denomination is obliterated with a marker. No. 3275 is known only with a double surcharge.

Nos. 3260A, 3262A, 3264A, 3351A and 3356, which are known only with revenue cancels, also may have been used postally.

The item illustrated above is a revenue stamp, though it lacks any revenue stamp inscription. 10c on 20c, 20c, 50c, $5 and $60 stamps of this design also exist. Some of these revenue stamps have been used on mail as they were available for sale to the public at the same locations as the surcharged stamps listed above. Non-governmental vendors of these stamps were lax in notifying stamp purchasers that the stamps were intended for revenue use only.

Queen Juliana of the Netherlands (1909-2004) A569

**2004, Aug. 25** **Litho.** ***Perf. 13¼***

| | | | | |
|---|---|---|---|---|
| **3405** | A569 | $2 multi | 1.50 | 1.50 |

Printed in sheets of 6.

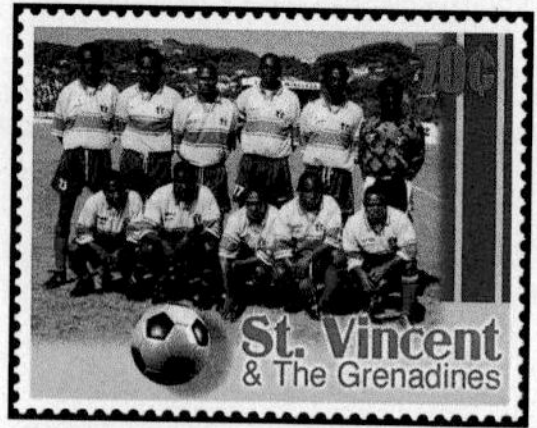


National Soccer Team — A570

**2004, Oct. 27** ***Perf. 12***

| | | | | |
|---|---|---|---|---|
| **3406** | A570 | 70c multi | .55 | .55 |

Paintings in the Hermitage, St. Petersburg, Russia A571

Designs: 10c, Head of a Young Girl, by Jean-Baptiste Greuze. 20c, Two Actresses, by Jean-Baptiste Santerre. 40c, An Allegory of History, by José de Ribera. 60c, A Young Woman Trying on Earrings, by Rembrandt. $2, The Girlhood of the Virgin, by Francisco e Zurbarán. No. 3412, $5, Portrait of a Woman, by Frans Pourbus, the Elder.

No. 3413, $1.40: a, Landscape with Obelisk, by Hubert Robert. b, At the Hermit's, by Robert. c, Landscape with Ruins, by Robert. d, Landscape with Terrace and Cascade, by Robert. e, A Shepherdess, by Jan Siberecht. f, Landscape with Waterfall, by Robert.

No. 3414, $1.40: a, Count N. D. Guriev, by Jean Auguste-Domingue Ingres. b, Portrait of an Actor, by Domenico Fetti. c, Napoleon Bonaparte on the Bridge at Arcole, by Baron Antoine-Jean Gros. d, A Young Man with a Glove, by Frans Hals. e, Portrait of General Alexei Yermolov, by George Dawe. f, A Scholar, by Rembrandt.

No. 3415, The Bean King, by Jacob Jordaens, horiz. No. 3416, Three Men at a Table, by Diego Velázquez. No. 3417, Family Portrait, by Cornelis de Vos, horiz.

**2004, Nov. 1** ***Perf. 14¼***
**3407-3412** A571 Set of 6 6.25 6.25

**Sheets of 6, #a-f**

**3413-3414** A571 Set of 2 13.00 13.00

***Imperf***

**Size: 98x72mm**

**3415** A571 $5 multi 3.75 3.75

**Size: 78x83mm**

**3416** A571 $5 multi 3.75 3.75

**Size: 88x76mm**

**3417** A571 $5 multi 3.75 3.75

National Basketball Association Players — A572

Designs: No. 3418, 75c, Gary Payton, Los Angeles Lakers. No. 3419, 75c, Lebron James, Cleveland Cavaliers. No. 3420, 75c, Adonal Foyle, Golden State Warriors. No. 3421, 75c, Peja Stojakovic, Sacramento Kings. No. 3422, 75c, Kirk Hinrich, Chicago Bulls. $3, Steve Francis, Houston Rockets.

**2004-05** ***Perf. 14***
**3418-3423** A572 Set of 6 5.25 5.25

Issued: No. 3418, 11/2; Nos. 3419-3420, 11/3; No. 3421, 11/9; Nos. 3422-3423, 2/10/05.

Battle of Trafalgar, Bicent. A573

Designs: 50c, Captain Thomas Masterman Hardy. $1, Napoleon Bonaparte. $1.50, Admiral Lord Horatio Nelson. $3, Admiral Cuthbert Collingwood.

No. 3428, $5, The Nelson touch. No. 3429, $5, H.M.S. Victory.

**2004, Nov. 25** ***Perf. 14¼***
**3424-3427** A573 Set of 4 4.50 4.50

**Souvenir Sheets**

**3428-3429** A573 Set of 2 7.50 7.50

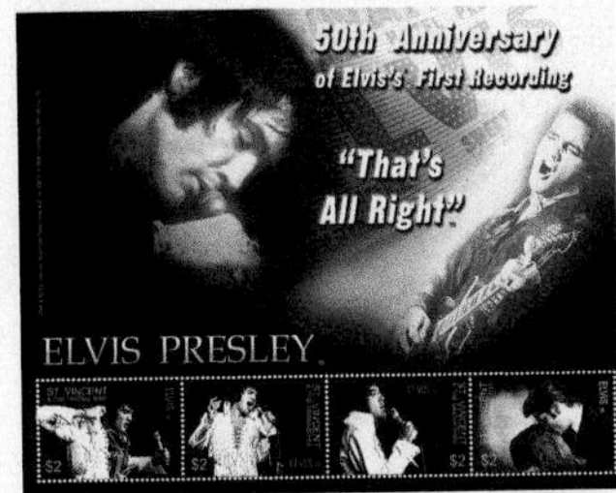


A574

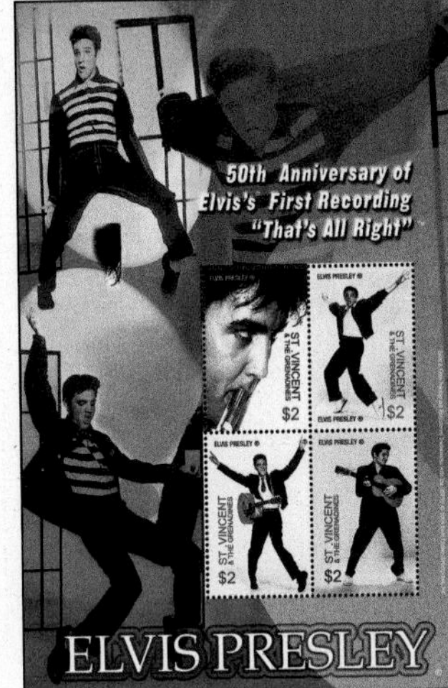


Elvis Presley (1935-77) — A575

No. 3430: a, Country name at UL reading across, denomination at LL. b, Country name at R, denomination at LL. c, Country name at R, denomination at LR. d, Country name at L reading up, denomination at LL.

No. 3431 — Denomination color: a, Green. b, Blue. c, Red. d, Purple.

**2004, Nov. 25** ***Perf. 13¼x13½***
**3430** A574 $2 Sheet of 4, #a-d 6.00 6.00

***Perf. 13½x13¼***

**3431** A575 $2 Sheet of 4, #a-d 6.00 6.00

Souvenir Sheet

Deng Xiaoping (1904-97), Chinese Leader — A576

**2004, Dec. 6** ***Perf. 14***
**3432** A576 $5 multi 3.75 3.75

Subway Systems — A577

No. 3433 — New York City subway: a, 1953 subway token. b, 23rd Street IRT kiosk. c, 1935 Subway car Hi-V 3398. d, 1936 subway car R6 1208 interior. e, Construction of Harlem River Tunnel, 1904. f, Underground construction, early 1900s. g, Hoppers, above ground construction, early 1900s. h, Workers on scaffold, above ground construction early 1900s.

No. 3434, $1.40 — Subway cars from: a, Moscow Metro. b, Tokyo Metro. c, Mexico City Metro. d, Paris Metro. e, Hong Kong MTR. f, Prague Metro.

No. 3435, $1.40 — London Underground: a, Thames Tunnel, 1859. b, City & South London Railway locomotives, 1890. c, East London line. d, Picadilly line. e, Victoria line. f, Jubilee line.

No. 3436, $5, A Train, New York City. No. 3437, $5, Train in station, London Underground. No. 3438, $5, 1992 Tube, Central line, London.

**2004, Dec. 13** ***Perf. 13¼x13½***
**3433** A577 $1 Sheet of 8, #a-h 6.00 6.00

**Sheets of 6, #a-f**

**3434-3435** A577 Set of 2 13.00 13.00

**Souvenir Sheets**

**3436-3438** A577 Set of 3 11.50 11.50

Christmas A578

Paintings by Norman Rockwell: 70c, Santa's Helpers. 90c, Tiny Tim (detail). $1.10, Department Store Santa. $3, The Muggleton Stage Coach.

$5, Extra Good Boys and Girls.

**2004, Dec. 13** ***Perf. 12***
**3439-3442** A578 Set of 4 4.25 4.25

***Imperf***

**Size: 64x84mm**

**3443** A578 $5 multi 3.75 3.75

New Year 2005 (Year of the Rooster) — A579

**2005, Jan. 26** ***Perf. 12***
**3444** A579 75c multi .55 .55

Issued in sheets of 3.

Miniature Sheet

World Peace — A580

No. 3445: a, Mahatma Gandhi. b, Elie Wiesel. c, Rigoberta Menchu.

**2005, Jan. 26** ***Perf. 14***
**3445** A580 $3 Sheet of 3, #a-c 6.75 6.75

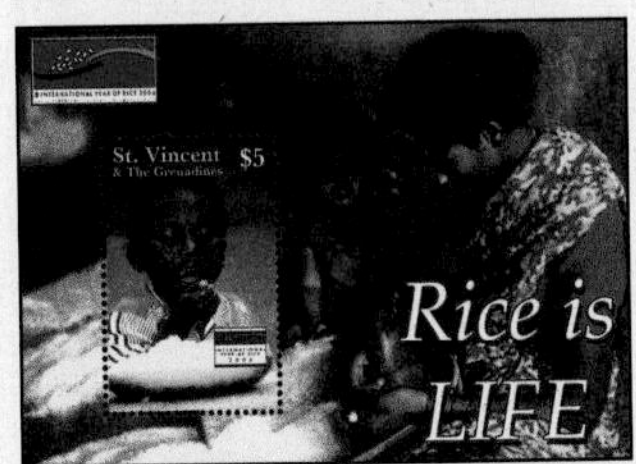

Intl. Year of Rice (in 2004) — A581

No. 3446, horiz.: a, Oxen pulling plow. b, Man and child harvesting rice. c, Man and field.

$5, Child with bowl of rice.

**2005, Jan. 26**
**3446** A581 $3 Sheet of 3, #a-c 6.75 6.75

**Souvenir Sheet**

**3447** A581 $5 multi 3.75 3.75

Souvenir Sheet

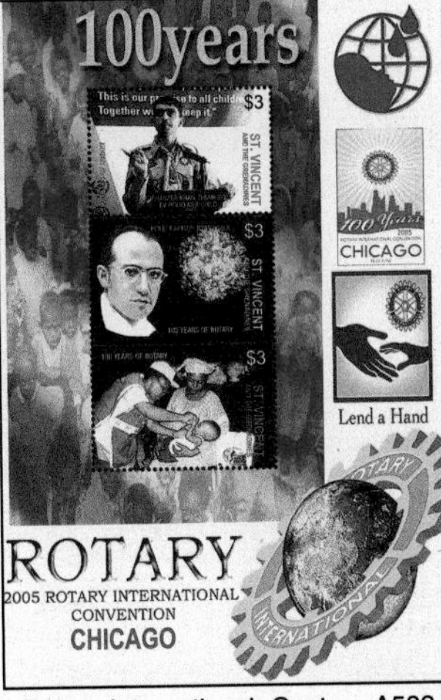


Rotary International, Cent. — A582

No. 3448: a, Jehanzeb Khan, polio victim. b, Dr. Jonas Salk. c, Child receiving polio vaccination.

**2005, Apr. 4** **Litho.** ***Perf. 14***
**3448** A582 $3 Sheet of 3, #a-c 6.75 6.75

Wedding of Prince Charles and Camilla Parker Bowles — A583

Various photos of couple with oval color of: No. 3449, $2, Blue. No. 3450, $2, Red violet. No. 3451, $2, Purple, horiz.

**2005, Apr. 9** ***Perf. 13½***
**3449-3451** A583 Set of 3 4.50 4.50

Vatican City No. 63 — A584

Pope John Paul II (1920-2005) A585

**2005, June 1** ***Perf. 13x13¼***
**3452** A584 70c multi .55 .55

***Perf. 13½***

**3453** A585 $3 multi 2.25 2.25

No. 3452 issued in sheets of 12; No. 3453, in sheets of 6.

Maimonides (1135-1204), Philosopher A586

No. 3454 — Statue of Maimonides with frame in: a, Yellow. b, Yellow and black.

**2005, June 7** *Perf. 12*
**3454** A586 $2 Vert. pair, #a-b 3.00 3.00

Printed in sheets containing two pairs.

Souvenir Sheet

Expo 2005, Aichi, Japan — A587

No. 3455 — Woolly mammoth with country name in: a, Red. b, Black. c, White.

**2005, June 7** *Perf. 12¾*
**3455** A587 $3 Sheet of 3, #a-c 6.75 6.75

Fish A588

Designs: $1, Red Irish lord. $1.10, Deep sea anglerfish. $1.40, Viperfish. $2, Lionfish. $5, Gulper eel.

**2005, June 7**
**3456-3459** A588 Set of 4 4.25 4.25

**Souvenir Sheet**
**3460** A588 $5 multi 3.75 3.75

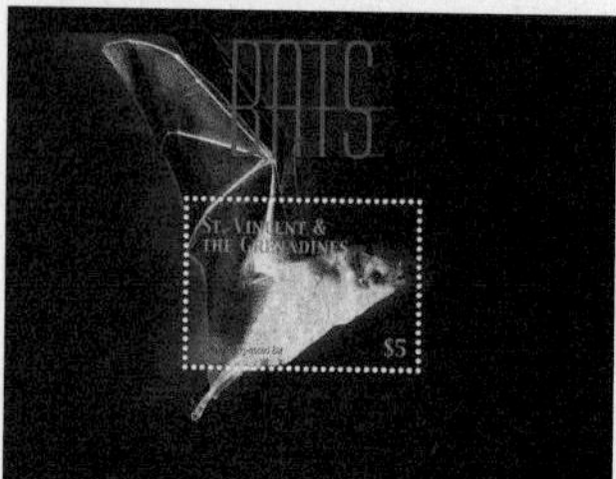
Bats — A589

No. 3461: a, Mexican long-tongued bat. b, Wahlberg's fruit bat. c, Common vampire bat. d, False vampire bat. e, Horseshoe bat. f, Spear-nosed long-tongued bat.
$5, Greater long-nosed bat.

**2005, June 7**
**3461** A589 $1.60 Sheet of 6, #a-f 7.25 7.25

**Souvenir Sheet**
**3462** A589 $5 multi 3.75 3.75

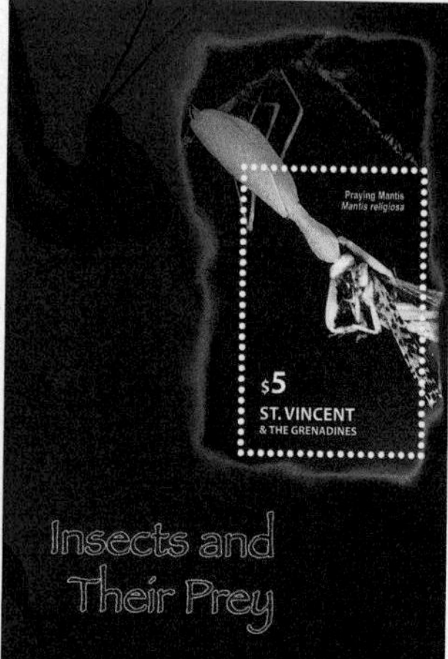
Insects and Spiders — A590

No. 3463: a, Field-digger wasp. b, Water spider. c, Yellow crab spider. d, Mantid.
$5, Praying mantis.

**2005, June 7**
**3463** A590 $2 Sheet of 4, #a-d 6.00 6.00

**Souvenir Sheet**
**3464** A590 $5 multi 3.75 3.75

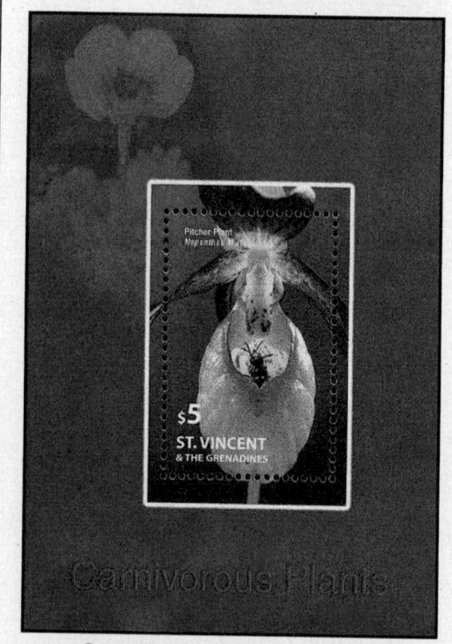
Carnivorous Plants — A591

No. 3465: a, Butterwort, denomination in black. b, Common sundew. c, Venus's flytrap. d, Butterwort, denomination in white.
$5, Pitcher plant.

**2005, June 7**
**3465** A591 $2 Sheet of 4, #a-d 6.00 6.00

**Souvenir Sheet**
**3466** A591 $5 multi 3.75 3.75

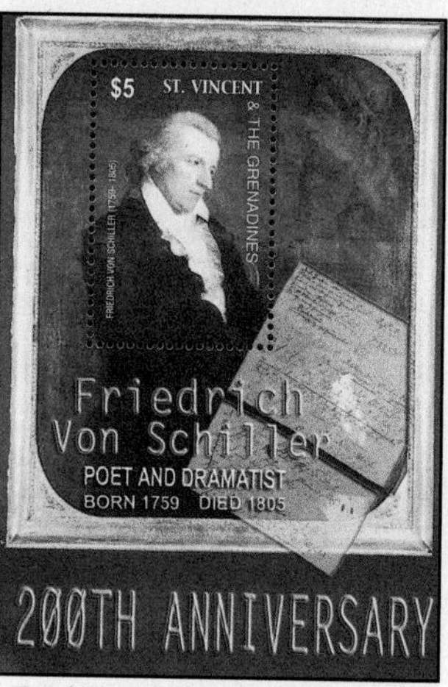
Friedrich von Schiller (1759-1805), Writer — A592

No. 3467 — Schiller: a, At desk. b, Facing right. c, Facing left.
$5, Facing right, diff.

**2005, June 7**
**3467** A592 $3 Sheet of 3, #a-c 6.75 6.75

**Souvenir Sheet**
**3468** A592 $5 multi 3.75 3.75

Hans Christian Andersen (1805-75), Author — A593

No. 3469: a, The Brave Tin Soldier. b, The Top and Ball. c, Ole-Luk-Oie, the Dream-God.
$5, The Snow Queen.

**2005, June 7** *Perf. 12¾*
**3469** A593 $3 Sheet of 3, #a-c 6.75 6.75

**Souvenir Sheet**
*Perf. 12x12¼*
**3470** A593 $5 multi 3.75 3.75

No. 3469 contains three 43x32mm stamps.

Jules Verne (1828-1905), Writer — A594

No. 3471, $2 — Around the World in 80 Days: a, Princess Aouda. b, Characters in train windows. c, Phileas Fogg. d, Passepartout.
No. 3472, $2 — 20,000 Leagues Under the Sea: a, Mariner using sextant. b, Captain at ship's wheel. c, Sea monster at window. d, Men in diving suits.
No. 3473, $2 — Master of the World: a, Automobile. b, Ship. c, Building. d, Winged vehicle.
No. 3474, $2 — The Castle of the Carpathians: a, Man pointing at beast in sky. b, Women and men looking at woman. c, Two men, woman with arms extended. d, Man pointing.
No. 3475, $2 — From the Earth to the Moon: a, Men and dog. b, Spacecraft and moon. c, Clouds and vapor trail. d, Man on ladder on side of spacecraft.
No. 3476, $5, Hot air balloon. No. 3477, $5, Helicopter
No. 3478, $5, Atomic bomb. No. 3479, $5, Tank. No. 3480, $5, Blitzkreig of World War II.

**2005, June 7** *Perf. 12¾*

**Sheets of 4, #a-d**
**3471-3472** A594 Set of 2 12.00 12.00

**Sheets of 4, #a-d**
**3473-3475** A594 Set of 3 18.00 18.00

**Souvenir Sheets**
**3476-3477** A594 Set of 2 7.50 7.50
**3478-3480** A594 Set of 3 11.50 11.50

End of World War II, 60th Anniv. — A595

No. 3481, $2, horiz.: a, USSR T34-85 tank. b, German Tiger tank. c, USA LVT(A)-1. d, Great Britain Cruiser tank Mk VI.
No. 3482, $2, horiz.: a, SBD-3 Dauntless. b, Mitsubishi Zero A6M5. c, USS Yorktown. d, USS Hornet.
No. 3483, $5, Winston Churchill. No. 3484, $5, Gen. Douglas MacArthur signing Japanese surrender instrument, horiz.

**2005, June 7** **Sheets of 4, #a-d**
**3481-3482** A595 Set of 2 12.00 12.00

**Souvenir Sheets**
**3483-3484** A595 Set of 2 7.50 7.50

Souvenir Sheet

Taipei 2005 Stamp Exhibition — A596

No. 3485: a, Panda. b, Formosan rock monkey. c, Formosan black bear. d, Formosan sika deer.

**2005, Aug. 5** *Perf. 14*
**3485** A596 $2 Sheet of 4, #a-d 6.00 6.00

Souvenir Sheet

Elvis Presley (1935-77) — A597

**Litho. & Embossed**
**2005, Nov. 21** *Imperf.*
**Without Gum**
**3486** A597 $20 gold & multi 15.00 15.00

Christmas — A598

Designs: 70c, Small Cowper Madonna, by Raphael. 90c, Madonna of the Grand Duke, by Raphael. $1.10, Sistine Madonna, by Raphael. $3, Alba Madonna, by Raphael.
$6, Adoration of the Magi, by Rogier van der Weyden.

**2005, Dec. 26** **Litho.** *Perf. 13½*
**3487-3490** A598 Set of 4 4.25 4.25

**Souvenir Sheet**
**3491** A598 $6 multi 4.50 4.50

New Year 2006 (Year of the Dog) A599

**2005, Dec. 30**
**3492** A599 $1 multi .75 .75

Printed in sheets of 3.

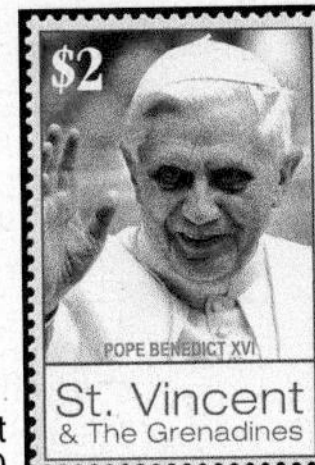

Pope Benedict XVI — A600

**2005, Dec. 30**
**3493** A600 $2 multi 1.50 1.50

Printed in sheets of 4.

Miniature Sheet

OPEC Intl. Development Fund, 30th Anniv. (in 2006) — A601

No. 3494: a, Three parrots. b, Waterfall. c, Gazebo. d, Two parrots.

**2006, Jan. 30** ***Perf. 12x11½***
**3494** A601 $3 Sheet of 4, #a-d 9.00 9.00

Miniature Sheets

Children's Drawings — A602

No. 3495, $2 — Flowers: a, Flower Spot, by Tom Brier. b, Flower Vase, by Jessie Abrams. c, Green Flower Vase, by Nick Abrams. d, Red Sunflowers, by Bianca Saad.

No. 3496, $2 — Animals: a, Panda, by Lauren Van Woy. b, Giraffe, by Megal Albe. c, Orange Koala, by Holly Cramer. d, Red Monkey, by Roxanne Hanson.

No. 3497, $2 — Snails and Ladybugs: a, Snail, by Cortland Bobczynski. b, Blue Ladybug, by Jackie Wicks. c, Red Ladybug, by Emily Hawk. d, Snail Boy, by Micah Bobczynski.

**2006, Jan. 30** ***Perf. 13¼***
**Sheets of 4, #a-d**
**3495-3497** A602 Set of 3 18.00 18.00

Queen Elizabeth II, 80th Birthday — A603

Inscriptions: No. 3498, $2, The Christening of a Princess. No. 3499, $2, Princess Elizabeth and Margaret. No. 3500, $2, First Radio Broadcast to the Nation. No. 3501, $2, A Decade of War. No. 3502, $2, The Royal Wedding. No. 3503, $2, The Queen's Coronation. No. 3504, $2, The Royal Family. No. 3505, $2, The Queen Awarding the World Cup to England.

**2006, Jan. 31** ***Perf. 13½***
**3498-3505** A603 Set of 8 12.00 12.00

Each stamp printed in sheets of 8 + label.

Queen Angelfish A604

**2006, Feb. 9** ***Perf. 11½x12***
**3506** A604 20c multi .25 .25

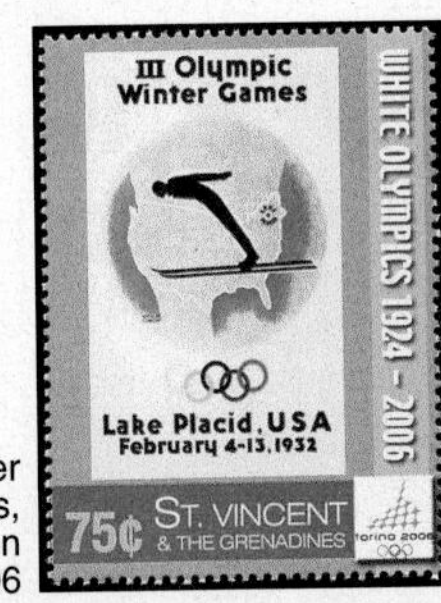

Marilyn Monroe (1926-62), Actress — A605

**2006, Mar. 31** ***Perf. 13¼***
**3507** A605 $3 multi 2.25 2.25

Printed in sheets of 4.

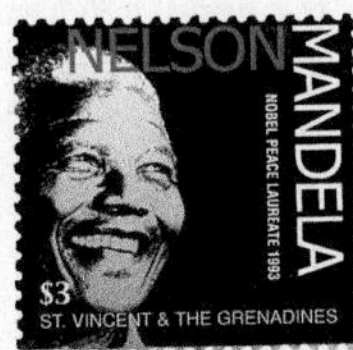

2006 Winter Olympics, Turin A606

Designs: 75c, Poster for 1932 Lake Placid Winter Olympics. 90c, US #716, horiz. $2, Poster for 1924 Chamonix Winter Olympics. $3, Cover with commemorative cancel for 1924 Chamonix Winter Olympics.

**2006, May 18** ***Perf. 14¼***
**3508-3511** A606 Set of 4 5.00 5.00


Nelson Mandela, 1993 Nobel Peace Prize Winner — A607

**2006, May 27** ***Perf. 11½x12***
**3512** A607 $3 multi 2.25 2.25

Printed in sheets of 3.

Souvenir Sheet

Airships — A608

No. 3513: a, USS Akron. b, A-170 airship. c, Altair-Z experimental airship.

**2006, June 23** ***Perf. 12¾***
**3513** A608 $4 Sheet of 3, #a-c 9.00 9.00

Miniature Sheet

Movie Debut of Elvis Presley, 50th Anniv. — A609

No. 3514 — Movie posters: a, King Creole. b, Love Me Tender. c, Loving You. d, Roustabout.

**2006, July 12** ***Perf. 13¼***
**3514** A609 $3 Sheet of 4, #a-d 9.00 9.00

Leeward Islands Air Transport, 50th Anniv. A610

Designs: 20c, Clouds. 50c, Airplane. 70c, Airplane, diff. 90c, Airplane, diff. $5, Frank Delisle, vert.

**2006, July 20** ***Perf. 12¾***
**3515-3518** A610 Set of 4 1.75 1.75

**Souvenir Sheet**

**3519** A610 $5 multi 3.75 3.75

Christopher Columbus (1451-1506), Explorer — A611

Designs: 50c, Columbus. 70c, Columbus and Queen Isabella, horiz. $2, Santa Maria. $3, Niña, Pinta and Santa Maria, horiz. $5, Pinta.

**2006, July 21**
**3520-3523** A611 Set of 4 4.75 4.75

**Souvenir Sheet**

**3524** A611 $5 multi 3.75 3.75

Space Achievements — A612

No. 3525 — Viking 1 and Apollo 11: a, Launch of Titan Centaur rocket. b, Viking 1. c, Viking 1 Lander. d, Apollo 11 lunar module. e, Apollo 11 command module. f, Launch of Apollo 11.

No. 3526 — Exploring our Universe: a, Mir Space Station. b, Sputnik 1. c, Soyuz. d, Luna 9.

No. 3527, $6, Conception of crew exploration vehicle for return to Moon. No. 3528, $6, Mir Space Station.

**2006, Sept. 27** ***Perf. 13¼***
**3525** A612 $1.50 Sheet of 6, #a-f 6.75 6.75
**3526** A612 $2.50 Sheet of 4, #a-d 7.50 7.50

**Souvenir Sheets**

**3527-3528** A612 Set of 2 9.00 9.00

Worldwide Fund for Nature (WWF) — A613

No. 3529 — Great white shark: a, Turning right. b, With fish. c, Turning left. d, With mouth open.

**2006, Oct. 24** ***Perf. 14***
**3529** A613 $1 Block of 4, #a-d 3.00 3.00
*e.* Miniature sheet, 2 #3529 6.00 6.00

No. 3529 printed in sheets of 4 blocks. Value, imperf. sheet of 4 blocks $50. No. 3259e exists imperf. Value $25.

Last Flight of the Concorde — A614

No. 3530, $1.40: a, Concorde coming to Filton. b, Concorde flying past Filton.

No. 3531, $1.40: a, Captains holding British flags. b, Concorde landing at Heathrow Airport.

**2006, Dec. 6** **Pairs, #a-b**
**3530-3531** A614 Set of 2 4.25 4.25

Nos. 3530-3531 each printed in sheets containing 3 pairs.

Christmas — A615

Details of Enthroned Madonna with Child Encircled by Saints, by Peter Paul Rubens: 20c, Cherub with flower. 70c, Infant Jesus. 90c, Women. $1.10, Madonna.

No. 3536: a, Like 20c. b, Like 70c. c, Like 90c. d, Like $1.10.

**2006, Dec. 6**
**3532-3535** A615 Set of 4 2.25 2.25

**Souvenir Sheet**

**3536** A615 $2 Sheet of 4, #a-d 6.00 6.00

Diplomatic Relations Between St. Vincent and Republic of China, 25th Anniv. — A616

Designs: 10c, St. Vincent Prime Minister Dr. Ralph Gonsalves and Taiwanese Pres. Chen Shui-bian and other dignitaries. 20c, St. Vincent woman showing dress to Gonsalves and Chen. 50c, Gonsalves and Chen shaking hands. 70c, Chen and St. Vincent honor guard. 90c, Gonsalves and Chen. $1.10, Gonsalves and Chen, diff. $1.40, Children of St. Vincent holding Taiwanese flags.

No. 3544, $5, Chen and Gonsalves seated at table. No. 3545, $5, Chen and another St. Vincent dignitary, flowers. No. 3546, $5, Presentation of gift.

**2006, Dec. 12** ***Perf. 13½***
**3537-3543** A616 Set of 7 3.75 3.75

**Souvenir Sheets**

**3544-3546** A616 Set of 3 11.50 11.50

Rembrandt (1606-69), Painter A617

Designs: 50c, The Jewish Physician Ephraim Bueno. 75c, Portrait of Ariantje Hollaer, Wife of Hendrick Martensz-Sorgh. $1, An Old Man in a Fur Cap. No. 3550, $2, Saskia van Uylenburgh.

No. 3551, $2 — Painting details: a, The Denial of St. Peter (woman with raised hand). b, The Raising of Lazarus (Jesus). c, The Denial of St. Peter (St. Peter). d, The Raising of Lazarus (Lazarus).

No. 3552, $2: a, Portrait of Titia van Uylenburgh. b, The Standing Syndic. c, Polish Officer. d, Seated Girl, in Profile to Left, Half Nude.

No. 3553, $5, Two Young Negroes. No. 3554, $5, Man Standing in Front of a Doorway.

**2006, Dec. 22** ***Perf. 13¼***
**3547-3550** A617 Set of 4 3.25 3.25

**Sheets of 4, #a-d**

**3551-3552** A617 Set of 2 12.00 12.00

***Imperf***

**Size: 70x100mm**

**3553-3554** A617 Set of 2 7.50 7.50

Dutch Princesses — A618

No. 3555: a, Princess Amalia (hands showing). b, Head of Princess Amalia. c, Princess Alexia (top of head even with bottom of denomination). d, Princess Alexia (top of head even with top of denomination).

**2006**
**3555** Vert. strip of 4 4.50 4.50
***a.-d.*** A618 $1.50 Any single 1.10 1.10

Souvenir Sheet

Wolfgang Amadeus Mozart (1756-91), Composer — A619

**2007, Jan. 15**
**3556** A619 $5 multi 3.75 3.75

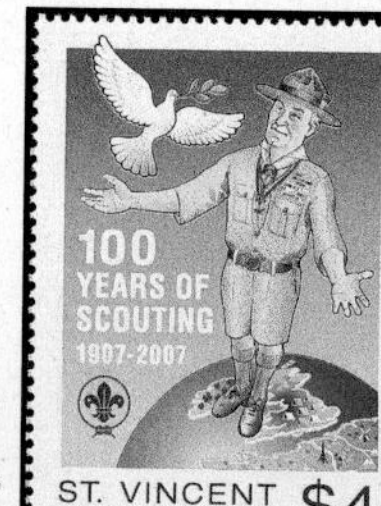


Scouting, Cent. A620

Designs: $4, Dove, Lord Robert Baden-Powell, Earth. $6, Dove, Baden-Powell, horiz.

**2007, Jan. 15**
**3557** A620 $4 multi 3.00 3.00

**Souvenir Sheet**

**3558** A620 $6 multi 4.50 4.50

No. 3557 printed in sheets of 3.

Mushrooms A621

Designs: 75c, Clavulinopsis sp. 90c, Cortinarius sp. $2, Cortinarius cf. $3, Conocybe spp.

$6, Galerina paludosa.

**2007, Jan. 15** ***Perf. 14¼***
**3559-3562** A621 Set of 4 5.00 5.00

**Souvenir Sheet**

**3563** A621 $6 multi 4.50 4.50

Pres. John F. Kennedy (1917-63) — A622

No. 3564, $3 — Kennedy as Congressman: a, Wearing pattern tie. b, At microphones. c, Wearing t-shirt. d, Wearing striped tie.

No. 3565, $3, horiz.: a, PT-109. b, PT-109 crew. c, Kennedy in boat. d, Japanese destroyer.

**2007, Jan. 15** ***Perf. 13¼***

**Sheets of 4, #a-d**

**3564-3565** A622 Set of 2 17.00 17.00

New Year 2007 (Year of the Pig) A623

**2007, Feb. 18** ***Perf. 14***
**3566** A623 $1.50 multi 1.10 1.10

Printed in sheets of 4.

**Map Type of 1977-78**

**Inscribed "St. Vincent" at Bottom**

**Map of St. Vincent**

**Denomination at Upper Left**

***Perf. 14½x14¼***

**2007-08** **Litho.** **Unwmk.**
**3566A** A76 30c grn bl, lt bl & blk *100.00*

**Inscribed "Grenadines of St. Vincent" at Bottom**

**Map of Bequia**

**3566B** A76 10c org, lt org & blk *300.00 60.00*
**3566C** A76 30c org, lt org & blk *50.00 25.00*

**Map of Mayreau amd Tobago Cays**

**Denomination at Lower Left**

**3566D** A76 10c org, lt org & blk *90.00 50.00*

**Denomination With Thick Numerals at Lower Left**

**3566E** A76 30c org, lt org & blk *100.00* —

**Denomination With Thin Numerals in Center of Stamp**

**3566F** A76 30c org, lt org & blk *100.00*

Earleist known uses: No. 3566A, 11/29; No. 3566B, 3/3; No. 3566C, 2/5/08; No. 3566D, 4/12; No. 3566E, 11/29; No. 3566F, 12/31.

No. 3566F exists with denomination shifted to the left.

Birds — A624

No. 3567: a, Bahama yellowthroat. b, Arrowheaded warbler. c, Northern jacana. d, Loggerhead kingbird.

$6, Louisiana waterthrush.

**2007, Mar. 12** **Litho.** ***Perf. 14***
**3567** A624 $2 Sheet of 4, #a-d 6.50 6.50

**Souvenir Sheet**

**3568** A624 $6 multi 4.75 4.75

Butterflies — A625

No. 3569: a, Ancyluris jurgensenii. b, Arcas cypria. c, Stalachtis phlegia. d, Xamia xami.

$5, Theritas coronata.

**2007, Mar. 12**
**3569** A625 $2 Sheet of 4, #a-d 6.50 6.50

**Souvenir Sheet**

**3570** A625 $5 multi 4.00 4.00

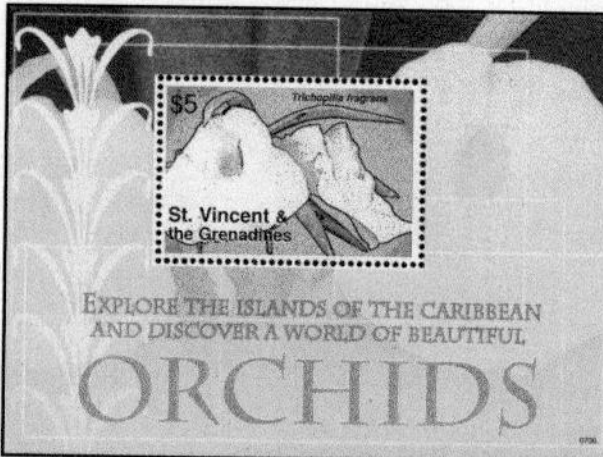


Orchids — A626

No. 3571, vert.: a, Stanhopea grandiflora. b, Psychopsis papilio. c, Vanilla planifolia. d, Tetramicra canaliculata.

$5, Trichopilia fragrans.

**2007, Mar. 12**
**3571** A626 $2 Sheet of 4, #a-d 6.50 6.50

**Souvenir Sheet**

**3572** A626 $5 multi 4.00 4.00

Miniature Sheet

Ferrari Automobiles, 60th Anniv. — A627

No. 3573: a, 1968 Dino 166 F2. b, 1958 246 F1. c, 1977 308 GTS. d, 1966 365 P Speciale. e, 2002 Enzo Ferrari. f, 1987 F40. g, 1993 348 Spider. h, 1951 212 Inter.

**2007, May 1** ***Perf. 13½***
**3573** A627 $1.40 Sheet of 8, #a-h 8.50 8.50

Concorde — A628

**Without Gum**

**Litho. & Embossed**

**2007, May 1** ***Die Cut Perf. 7¾***
**3574** A628 $20 gold & multi 15.00 15.00

Wedding of Queen Elizabeth II and Prince Philip, 60th Anniv. A629

No. 3575: a, Couple in profile. b, Couple, queen wearing tiara.

$6, Couple, vert.

**2007, May 1 Litho. *Perf. 14***
**3575** A629 $1.40 Pair, #a-b 2.10 2.10

**Souvenir Sheet**

**3576** A629 $6 multi 4.75 4.75

No. 3575 was printed in sheets containing three of each stamp.

Princess Diana (1961-97) — A630

No. 3577 — Diana wearing: a, Red dress. b, Blue pinstriped jacket. c, Black and white dress. d, White jacket.

No. 3578, $6, Diana wearing black beret. No. 3579, $6, Diana wearing hat in black and white photograph.

**2007, May 1**
**3577** A630 $2 Sheet of 4, #a-d 6.25 6.25

**Souvenir Sheets**

**3578-3579** A630 Set of 2 9.25 9.25

2007 ICC Cricket World Cup, West Indies — A631

Cricket players: No. 3580, 30c, Cameron Cuffy. No. 3581, 30c, Ian Allen. $1.05, Neil Williams. No. 3583, $1.35, Wilfred Slack. No. 3584, $1.35, Michael Findlay. No. 3585, $1.65, Winston Davis. No. 3586, $1.65, Nixon McLean. $2.10, Alphonso (Alfie) Roberts.

$6, Arnos Vale Stadium, horiz.

**2007, May 1 *Perf. 13¼***
**3580-3587** A631 Set of 8 7.50 7.50

**Souvenir Sheet**

**3588** A631 $6 multi 4.50 4.50

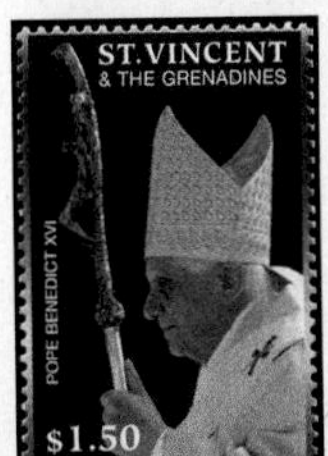

Pope Benedict XVI — A632

**2007, July 5**
**3589** A632 $1.50 multi 1.10 1.10

Printed in sheets of 8.

**Miniature Sheet**

Elvis Presley (1935-77) — A633

No. 3590 — Presley: a, Wearing dark shirt, sepia photograph. b, Wearing sweater, black and white photograph. c, Wearing sweater, sepia photograph. d, Wearing striped shirt. e, Wearing suit and tie. f, Playing guitar.

**2007, July 5 *Perf. 14¼***
**3590** A633 $1.40 Sheet of 6, #a-f 6.00 6.00

Victoria Cross, 150th Anniv. — A634

No. 3591 — Victoria Cross, recipients and flags of home country: a, Capt. Havildar Lachhiman Gurung, Nepal. b, Ernest Alvia (Smokey) Smith, Canada. c, Nk. Yeshwant Ghadge, India. d, Lt. Col. Eric Charles Twelves Wilson, Great Britain. e, Warrant Officer Class 2 Keith Payne, Australia. f, Lance Corporal Rambahadur Limbu, Nepal.

$6, Piper James Richardson.

**2007, Oct. 24 *Perf. 13¼***
**3591** A634 $1.40 Sheet of 6, #a-f 6.00 6.00

**Souvenir Sheet**

**3592** A634 $6 multi 4.75 4.75

**Miniature Sheet**

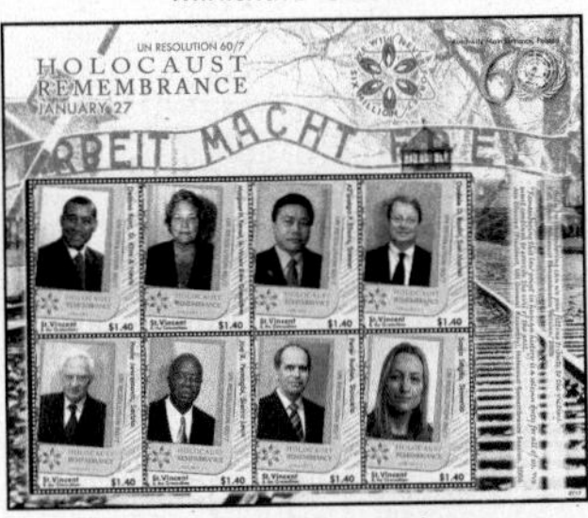

Intl. Holocaust Remembrance Day — A635

No. 3593 — United Nations delegates: a, Delano Bart, St. Kitts & Nevis. b, Margaret H. Ferrari, St. Vincent & the Grenadines. c, Ali'ioaiga F. Elisaia, Samoa. d, Daniele D. Bodini, San Marino. e, Pavle Jevremovic, Serbia. f, Joe R. Pemagbi, Sierra Leone. g, Peter Burian, Slovakia. h, Sanja Stiglic, Slovenia.

**2007, Nov. 14**
**3593** A635 $1.40 Sheet of 8, #a-h 8.00 8.00

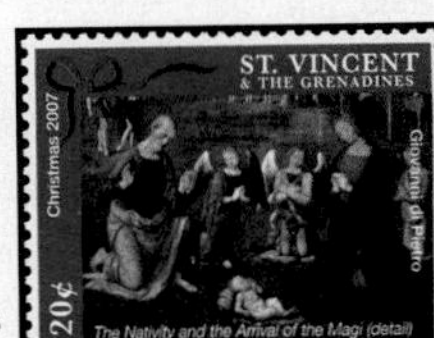

Christmas A636

Paintings: 20c, The Nativity and the Arrival of the Magi, by Giovanni di Pietro. 70c, The Annunciation, by Benozzo Gozzoli. 90c, The Nativity, by Gozzoli. $1.10, The Journey of the Magi, by Sassetta.

**2007, Dec. 3 *Perf. 12***
**3594-3597** A636 Set of 4 2.00 2.00

Insects A637

Designs: 5c, Bumblebee. 10c, Praying mantis. 30c, Firefly, vert. $1.35, Green darner dragonfly, vert.

**2007, Dec. 4 *Perf. 13¼***
**3598-3601** A637 Set of 4 1.40 1.40

New Year 2008 (Year of the Rat) A638

**2008, Jan. 8 Litho. *Perf. 12***
**3602** A638 $1.50 multi 1.10 1.10

Printed in sheets of 4.

**Miniature Sheet**

2008 Summer Olympics, Beijing — A639

No. 3603 — 1952 Summer Olympics: a, Bob Mathias, decathlon gold medalist. b, Poster. c, Josy Barthel, 800-meter gold medalist. d, Lis Hartel, dressage silver medalist.

**2008, Jan. 8 *Perf. 14***
**3603** A639 $1.40 Sheet of 4, #a-d 4.00 4.00

America's Cup Yacht Races, Valencia, Spain — A640

No. 3604 — Various yachts with denomination in: a, $1.20, Red. b, $1.80, White. c, $3, Light blue. d, $5, Orange brown.

**2008, Jan. 10 *Perf. 13¼***
**3604** A640 Block of 4, #a-d 8.00 8.00

Hummer H3 — A641

Hummer H3 going: a, Uphill, denomination at UL. b, Over rocks. c, In water. d, Uphill, denomination at UR.

$6, Hummer H3 on level ground.

**2008, Jan. 10**
**3605** A641 $1.50 Sheet of 4, #a-d 4.25 4.25

**Souvenir Sheet**

**3606** A641 $6 multi 4.75 4.75

Sites and Scenes of Taiwan — A642

No. 3607, vert.: a, Taipei 101 Building. b, Pagoda. c, High speed railway. d, Lion dance.

$5, National Taiwan Democracy Memorial Hall.

**2008, Feb. 8 *Perf. 11¼x11½***
**3607** A642 $1.50 Sheet of 4, #a-d 4.25 4.25

**Souvenir Sheet**

***Perf. 13¼***

**3608** A642 $5 multi 3.75 3.75

2008 Taipei Intl. Stamp Exhibition. No. 3607 contains four 30x40mm stamps.

**Souvenir Sheet**

Ocean Liners — A643

No. 3609: a, Queen Victoria. b, Queen Elizabeth 2. c, Queen Mary 2.

**2008, May 1 *Perf. 13¼***
**3609** A643 $3 Sheet of 3, #a-c 6.75 6.75

**Miniature Sheet**

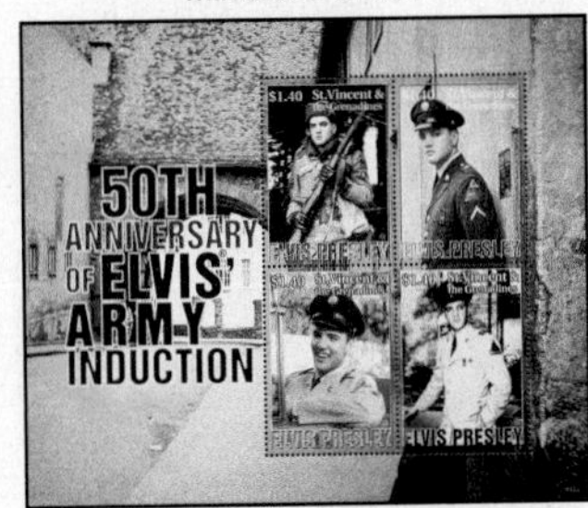

Induction of Elvis Presley into US Army, 50th Anniv. — A644

No. 3610 — Presley: a, Holding rifle. b, Standing against wall. c, In car. d, Standing next to car.

**2008, May 1**
**3610** A644 $1.40 Sheet of 4, #a-d 4.00 4.00

**Miniature Sheet**

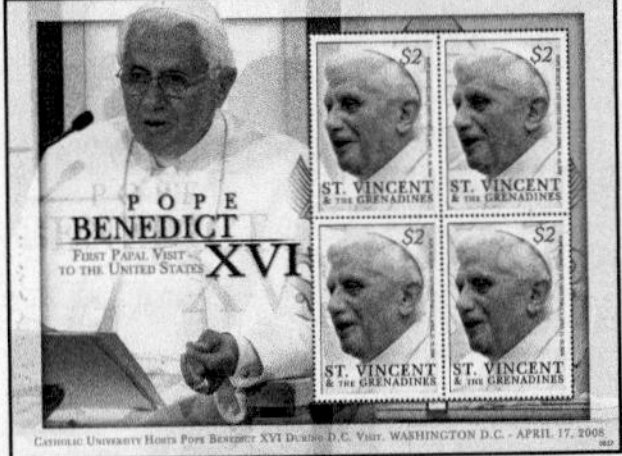

Pope Benedict XVI — A645

No. 3611 — Items in background: a, Cross at LL. b, Blue line near Pope's mouth. c, Tassel at left. d, Shell at left.

**2008, May 1**

**3611** A645 $2 Sheet of 4, #a-d 5.50 5.50

Miniature Sheet

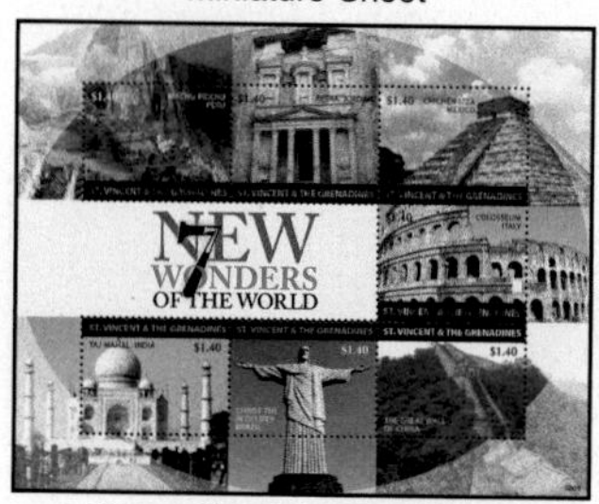

Seven New Wonders of the World — A646

No. 3612: a, Machu Picchu, Peru. b, Petra, Jordan. c, Chichén Itza, Mexico. d, Roman Colosseum, Italy. e, Taj Mahal, India. f, Christ the Redeemer Statue, Brazil. g, Great Wall of China.

**2008, May 1** ***Perf. 11½***

**3612** A646 $1.40 Sheet of 7, #a-g 7.50 7.50

University of the West Indies, 60th Anniv. — A647

Designs: 10c, University crest. 30c, Diploma. 90c, UWDEC Media Center, horiz. $1.05, 60th anniv. emblem.
$6, Crest, diploma, 60th anniv. emblem, horiz.

**2008, June 27** ***Perf. 12¾***

**3613-3616** A647 Set of 4 1.75 1.75

**Souvenir Sheet**

**3617** A647 $6 multi 4.50 4.50

Miniature Sheets

2008 European Soccer Championships — A648

No. 3618 — Teams and flags of: a, Czech Republic. b, Turkey. c, Austria. d, Croatia. e, Switzerland. f, Portugal. g, Poland. h, Germany. i, France. j, Netherlands. k, Greece. l, Sweden. m, Romania. n, Italy. o, Russia. p, Spain.

No. 3619 — Austria team with flag at: a, LR. b, LL. c, UR. d, UL. e, Tivoli Stadium. f, St. Jakob Park Stadium (stadium name at top).

No. 3620 — Croatia team with flag at: a, LR. b, LL. c, UR. d, UL. e, Stade de Geneve.

No. 3621 — Czech Republic team with flag at: a, LR. b, LL. c, UR. d, UL. e, Stade de Suisse Wankdorf.

No. 3622 — France team with flag at: a, LR. b, LL. c, UR. d, UL. e, Letzigrund Stadium.

No. 3623 — Germany team with flag at: a, LR. b, LL. c, UR. d, UL. e, Worthersee Stadium Hypo Arena.

No. 3624 — Greece team with flag at: a, LR. b, LL. c, UR. d, UL.

No. 3625 — Italy team with flag at: a, LR. b, LL. c, UR. d, UL.

No. 3626 — Netherlands team with flag at: a, LR. b, LL. c, UR. d, UL.

No. 3627 — Poland team with flag at: a, LR. b, LL. c, UR. d, UL. e, Wals-Siezenheim Stadium. f, St. Jakob Park Stadium (stadium name at bottom).

No. 3628 — Portugal team with flag at: a, LR. b, LL. c, UR. d, UL.

No. 3629 — Romania team with flag at: a, LR. b, LL. c, UR. d, UL.

No. 3630 — Russia team with flag at: a, LR. b, LL. c, UR. d, UL.

No. 3631 — Spain team with flag at: a, LR. b, LL. c, UR. d, UL. e, Ernst Happel Stadium.

No. 3632 — Sweden team with flag at: a, LR. b, LL. c, UR. d, UL.

No. 3633 — Switzerland team with flag at: a, LR. b, LL. c, UR. d, UL.

No. 3634 — Turkey team with flag at: a, LR. b, LL. c, UR. d, UL.

**2008, Aug. 1** ***Perf. 13½***

**3618** A648 65c Sheet of 16, #a-p 8.00 8.00
**3619** A648 $1.40 Sheet of 6, #3619a-3619f 6.50 6.50
**3620** A648 $1.40 Sheet of 6, #3619e, 3620a-3620e 6.50 6.50
**3621** A648 $1.40 Sheet of 6, #3619e, 3621a-3621e 6.50 6.50
**3622** A648 $1.40 Sheet of 6, #3619e, 3622a-3622e 6.50 6.50
**3623** A648 $1.40 Sheet of 6, #3619f, 3623a-3623e 6.50 6.50
**3624** A648 $1.40 Sheet of 6, #3621e, 3623e, 3624a-3624d 6.50 6.50
**3625** A648 $1.40 Sheet of 6, #3620e, 3623e, 3625a-3625d 6.50 6.50
**3626** A648 $1.40 Sheet of 6, #3622e, 3623e, 3626a-3626d 6.50 6.50
**3627** A648 $1.40 Sheet of 6, # 3627a-3627f 6.50 6.50
**3628** A648 $1.40 Sheet of 6, #3621e, 3627e, 3628a-3628d 6.50 6.50
**3629** A648 $1.40 Sheet of 6, #3620e, 3627e, 3629a-3629d 6.50 6.50
**3630** A648 $1.40 Sheet of 6, #3622e, 3627e, 3630a-3630d 6.50 6.50
**3631** A648 $1.40 Sheet of 6, #3619f, 3631a-3631e 6.50 6.50
**3632** A648 $1.40 Sheet of 6, #3621e, 3631e, 3632a-3632d 6.50 6.50
**3633** A648 $1.40 Sheet of 6, #3620e, 3631e, 3633a-3633d 6.50 6.50
**3634** A648 $1.40 Sheet of 6, #3622e, 3631e, 3634a-3634d 6.50 6.50
*Nos. 3618-3634 (17)* 112.00 112.00

Kingstown Cooperative Credit Union, 50th Anniv. A649

Credit Union emblem and: 10c, Children. 30c, Man, vert. 90c, Woman, vert. $1.05, Man wearing sunglasses, vert.
$6, Credit Union Building.

***Perf. 12½x12¾, 12¾x12½***

**2008, Sept. 1**

**3635-3638** A649 Set of 4 1.75 1.75

**Souvenir Sheet**

**3639** A649 $6 multi 4.50 4.50

Miniature Sheets

Space Exploration, 50th Anniv. (in 2007) — A650

No. 3640, $1.40: a, Space suit of Valentina Tereshkova. b, Tereshkova wearing black suit. c, Vostok 6. d, Tereshkova in space suit and helmet. e, Statue of Tereshkova. f, Tereshkova in space suit without helmet.

No. 3641, $1.40: a, Pioneer 11. b, Pioneer 10 on Atlas Centaur 27 rocket. c, Pioneer plaque. d, Pioneer 10. e, Technical drawing of Pioneer 10 and Pioneer 11. f, Pioneer program.

No. 3642, $1.40: a, Viking 1 on Titan IIIE Centaur rocket. b, Viking 1 orbiter and lander technical drawing. c, Viking 1 lander firing retrorockets. d, Viking 1 above Mars. e, Viking 1 lander technical drawing. f, Picture from Viking 1.

No. 3643, $2: a, Freedom 7 capsule. b, Astronaut Alan Shepard. c, Vostok. d, Cosmonaut Yuri Gagarin.

No. 3644, $2: a, Luna 2. b, Luna 2 ball. c, Lift-off of Luna 2. d, Luna 2 above Moon.

No. 3645, $2: a, Mariner 4 Mars Encounter Imaging Geometry. b, Mariner 4. c, Lift-off of Mariner 4. d, Mariner 4 and Mars.

**2008, Oct. 29** ***Perf. 14¼***

**Sheets of 6, #a-f**

**3640-3642** A650 Set of 3 19.50 19.50

**Sheets of 4, #a-d**

**3643-3645** A650 Set of 3 18.50 18.50

Christmas — A651

Crèche scenes: 75c, Adoration of the Shepherds. 90c, Angel in manger. $2, Adoration of the Shepherds, diff. $3, Holy Family.

**2008, Dec. 8** ***Perf. 14***

**3646-3649** A651 Set of 4 5.00 5.00

Inauguration of US Pres. Barack Obama — A652

Designs: Nos. 3650, 3652a, Pres. Obama and US flag. $2.75, Pres. Obama, US flag and statue of Abraham Lincoln (26x34mm). No. 3652b, Vice-president Joseph Biden.

***Perf. 14x14¾, 12¼x11¾ (#3651)***

**2009, Jan. 20**

**3650** A652 $1.75 multi 1.40 1.40
**3651** A652 $2.75 multi 2.10 2.10

**Souvenir Sheet**

**3652** A652 $6.50 Sheet of 2, #a-b 10.00 10.00

No. 3650 was printed in sheets of 9; No. 3651, in sheets of 4.

New Year 2009 (Year of the Ox) A653

**2009, Jan. 26** ***Perf. 12***

**3653** A653 $2.50 multi 1.90 1.90

Printed in sheets of 4.

St. Vincent Coat of Arms — A654

**2009, Feb. 20** ***Perf. 14x14¾***

**3654** A654 $1.30 purple + label 1.00 1.00

Printed in sheets of 8 + 8 labels.The labels could be personalized.

Miniature Sheet

Juventus Soccer Team — A655

No. 3655: a, Goalie. b, Three players with gold shirts, one raising fist. c, Three players with gold shirts, one sticking out tongue. d, Four players with gold shirts. e, Fans. f, Players in striped shirts, one with fist and open mouth. g, Players in striped shirts, one with arms extended. h, Player in striped shirt kicking ball.

**2009, Apr. 23** ***Perf. 13½***

**3655** A655 $1.50 Sheet of 8, #a-h, + central label 9.00 9.00

Pres. Abraham Lincoln (1809-65) — A656

No. 3656: a, Inauguration of Lincoln. b, Lincoln with beard. c, Lincoln visiting troops. d, Reward poster for Lincoln's assassin. e, Lincoln without beard. f, Lincoln and four men.
$6, Statue of Lincoln from Lincoln Memorial.

**2009, Apr. 23** ***Perf. 14¼x14¾***

**3656** A656 $2 Sheet of 6, #a-f 9.50 9.50

**Souvenir Sheet**

***Perf. 14¼***

**3657** A656 $6 multi 4.75 4.75

No. 3657 contains one 38x50mm stamp.

Miniature Sheet

Felix Mendelssohn (1809-47), Composer — A657

No. 3658: a, A Midsummer's Night Dream, painting by David Scott. b, Portrait of Mendelssohn, by Eduard Magnus. c, Portrait of Cécile Jeanrenaud, wife of Mendelssohn, by Magnus. d, Score of "On Wings of Song." e, Gewandhausorchester. f, Church of the Holy Ghost, drawing by Mendelssohn.

**2009, May 18** *Perf. 11¼x11½*

**3658** A657 $2.50 Sheet of 6, #a-f 11.50 11.50

Miniature Sheet

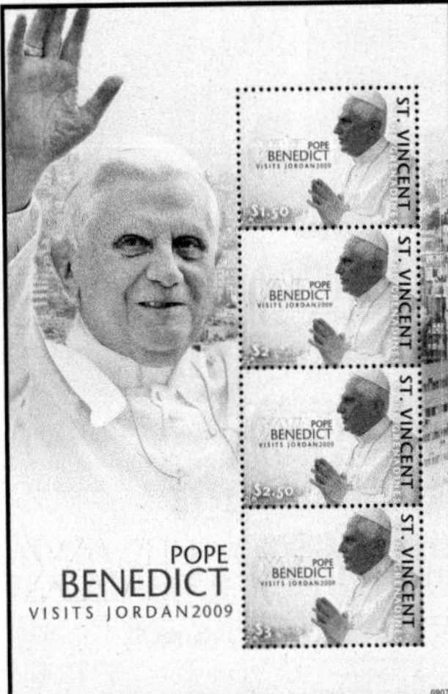

Pope Benedict XVI — A658

No. 3659 — Pope Benedict XVI: a, $1.50. b, $2. c, $2.50. d, $3.

**2009, May 18** *Perf. 11½*

**3659** A658 Sheet of 4, #a-d 7.00 7.00

Miniature Sheet

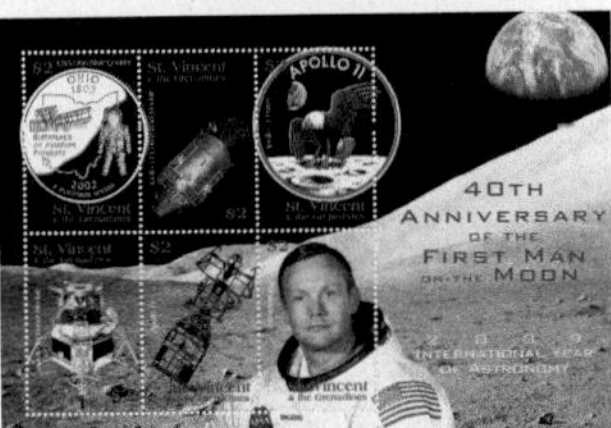

First Man on the Moon, 40th Anniv. — A659

No. 3660: a, US 2002 Ohio state quarter. b, Apollo 11 Command Module. c, Apollo 11 patch. d, Apollo 11 Lunar Module. e, Drawing of Apollo 11 Command and Lunar Modules. f, Astronaut Neil Armstrong.

**2009, May 18** *Perf. 13¼*

**3660** A659 $2 Sheet of 6, #a-f 9.50 9.50

Miniature Sheets

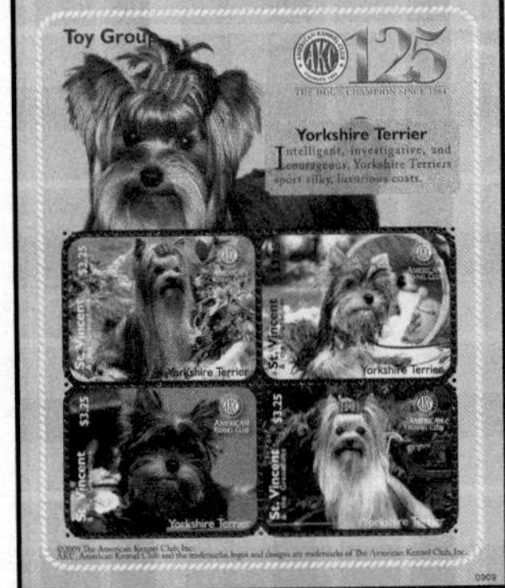

Dogs — A660

No. 3661: a, Yorkshire terrier. b, German shepherd. c, Golden retriever. d, Beagle. e, Dachshund. f, Boxer. g, Poodle. h, Shih tzu. i, Miniature schnauzer.

No. 3662 — Yorkshire terrier: a, With flowers, wearing ribbon. b, With basket at right. c, With flower at left. d, With berries at left, wearing ribbon.

**2009, May 18** *Perf. 11½*

**3661** A660 $1.60 Sheet of 9, #a-i 11.00 11.00

**3662** A660 $3.25 Sheet of 4, #a-d 9.00 9.00

A661

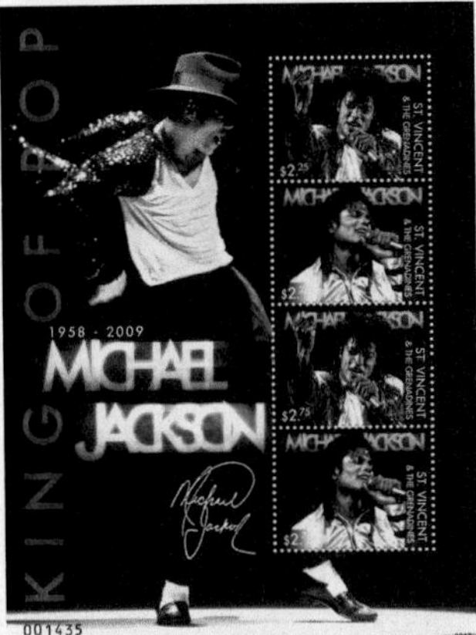

A662

Michael Jackson (1958-2009), Singer — A663

No. 3663, 45c: a, Wearing brown striped suit. b, Wearing hat.

No. 3664, 90c: a, Holding microphone. b, Wearing black sweater.

No. 3665, $1.50: a, Wearing jacket and white shirt. b, Wearing red and gold jacket.

No. 3666, $4: a, With goggles on hat. b, Wearing red and gold jacket and white glove.

No. 3667: a, $2.25, Making fist. b, $2.25, Singing. c, $2.75, As "a." d, $2.75, As "b."

No. 3668: a, With microphone in front of chin. b, Holding microphone. c, Pointing. d, With lights in background.

**Horiz. Pairs, #a-b**

**2009** *Perf. 14¼x14¾*

**3663-3666** A661 Set of 4 10.50 10.50

**Miniature Sheets**

*Perf. 11½*

**3667** A662 Sheet of 4, #a-d 7.50 7.50

**3668** A663 $2.50 Sheet of 4, #a-d 7.50 7.50

Issued: Nos. 3663-3666, 7/7; Nos. 3667-3668, 7/17. Nos. 3663-3666 were each printed in sheets containing two pairs. Compare with Type A125.

Miniature Sheet

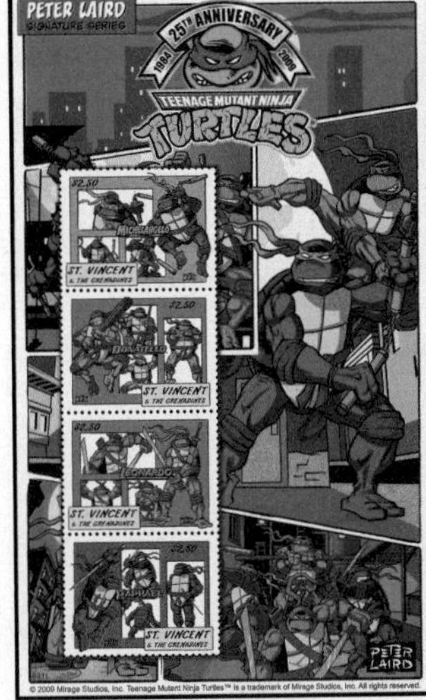

Teenage Mutant Ninja Turtles, 25th Anniv. — A664

No. 3669: a, Michelangelo. b, Donatello. c, Leonardo. d, Raphael.

**2009, July 15** *Perf. 11½x12*

**3669** A664 $2.50 Sheet of 4, #a-d 7.75 7.75

A665

A666

A667

A668

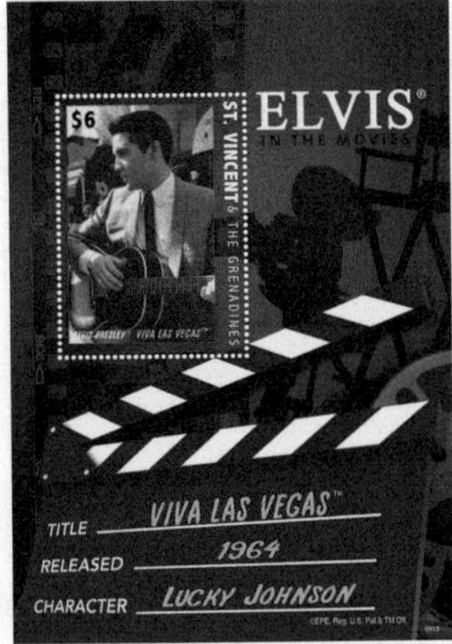

Elvis Presley (1935-77) — A669

No. 3670 — Presley and: a, "L." b, "V." c, "I." d, "S."

**2009, July 15** *Perf. 13½*

**3670** A665 $2.50 Sheet of 4, #a-d 7.75 7.75

**Souvenir Sheets**

*Perf. 14¼*

| | | | | |
|---|---|---|---|---|
| **3671** | A666 | $6 multi | 4.75 | 4.75 |
| **3672** | A667 | $6 multi | 4.75 | 4.75 |
| **3673** | A668 | $6 multi | 4.75 | 4.75 |
| **3674** | A669 | $6 multi | 4.75 | 4.75 |
| | *Nos. 3671-3674 (4)* | | 19.00 | 19.00 |

Preservation of Polar Regions and Glaciers — A670

No. 3675: a, Penguin diving, two penguins swimming. b, Nine penguins. c, Three penguins, two with wings extended. d, Adult penguin feeding juvenile.

$6, Five penguins.

**2009, Aug. 1** *Perf. 13½*

**3675** A670 $3 Sheet of 4, #a-d 9.00 9.00

**Souvenir Sheet**

**3676** A670 $6 multi 4.50 4.50

No. 3676 contains one 38x51mm stamp.

Birds
A671

Designs: $1.20, White-rumped sandpiper. $1.80, Tricolored heron. No. 3679, $3, Masked booby. $5, Red-footed booby, vert.

No. 3681, vert: a, Brown pelican. b, Great blue heron. c, Snowy egret. d, Pied-billed grebe.

No. 3682, vert.: a, Ring-billed gull. b, Short-billed dowitcher.

**2009, Aug. 1 Litho. *Perf. 12***

**3677-3680** A671 Set of 4 8.25 8.25
**3681** A671 $2.50 Sheet of 4, #a-d 7.50 7.50

**Souvenir Sheet**

**3682** A671 $3 Sheet of 2, #a-b 4.50 4.50

For overprint, see No. 3700.

Miniature Sheet

Stamp Expo 400, Albany, New York — A672

No. 3683: a, Samuel de Champlain (c. 1567-1635), explorer. b, Robert Fulton (1765-1815), steamboat builder. c, Henry Hudson (d. 1611), explorer. d, Ships, US #372.

**2009, Sept. 18 *Perf. 11½***

**3683** A672 $2.50 Sheet of 4, #a-d 7.50 7.50

Christmas
A673

Designs: 90c, Magi on camels. $1.80, Holy Family. $2.50, Adoration of the Magi. $3, Madonna and Child.

**2009, Dec. 10 *Perf. 13x13¼***

**3684-3687** A673 Set of 4 6.25 6.25

Miniature Sheets

2010 World Cup Soccer Championships, South Africa — A674

No. 3688, $1.75 — Team from: a, Australia. b, Japan. c, North Korea. d, South Korea. e, Honduras. f, Mexico. g, United States. h, New Zealand.

No. 3689, $1.75 — Team from: a, South Africa. b, Brazil. c, Spain. d, Netherlands. e, Italy. f, Germany. g, Argentina. h, England.

No. 3690, $1.75 — Team from: a, Denmark. b, France. c, Greece. d, Portugal. e, Serbia. f, Slovakia. g, Slovenia. h, Switzerland.

No. 3691, $1.75 — Team from: a, Algeria. b, Cameroon. c, Ivory Coast. d, Ghana. e, Nigeria. f, Chile. g, Paraguay. h, Uruguay.

**Sheets of 8, #a-h, + Central Label**

**2010, Jan. 20 *Perf. 14¼***

**3688-3691** A674 Set of 4 45.00 45.00

Ferrari Automobiles and Parts — A675

No. 3692, $1.25: a, Engine of 1970 312 B. b, 1970 312 B.

No. 3693, $1.25: a, Engine of 1973 Dino 308 GT4. b, 1973 Dino 308 GT4.

No. 3694, $1.25: a, Shift console of 1976 400 Automatic. b, 1976 400 Automatic.

No. 3695, $1.25: a, Engine of 1981 126 CX. b, 1981 126 CX.

**Vert. Pairs, #a-b**

**2010, Feb. 18 Litho. *Perf. 12***

**3692-3695** A675 Set of 4 8.00 8.00

Miniature Sheets

Inauguration of US Pres. John F. Kennedy, 50th Anniv. — A676

No. 3696: a, White House Oval Office. b, Pres. Kennedy. c, Jacqueline Kennedy. d, Lady Bird Johnson. e, Vice-president Lyndon B. Johnson. f, Capitol Building.

No. 3697: a, Pres. Kennedy. b, John F. Kennedy Presidential Library and Museum, Boston. c, Statue of Pres. Kennedy, Regents Park, London. d, Presidential seal.

**2010, Mar. 17 *Perf. 13¼***

**3696** A676 $2 Sheet of 6, #a-f 9.00 9.00
**3697** A676 $2.75 Sheet of 4, #a-d 8.25 8.25

Miniature Sheets

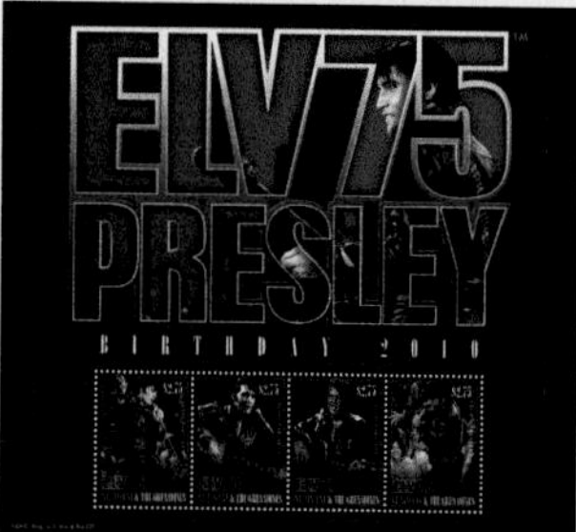


A677

Elvis Presley (1935-77) — A678

No. 3698: a, Without guitar, facing right. b, With guitar, microphone at right. c, With guitar, microphone at left. d, Without guitar, facing left.

No. 3699: a, With guitar. b, With hands near ears. c, Scratching head. d, With arms at side.

**2010, Mar. 17 *Perf. 11¼x11½***

**3698** A677 $2.75 Sheet of 4, #a-d 8.25 8.25
**3699** A678 $2.75 Sheet of 4, #a-d 8.25 8.25

**No. 3681 Overprinted With Map of Haiti and "Haiti Earthquake Relief Fund"**

**Method and Perf. As Before**

**2010, Jan. 15**

**3700** A671 $2.50 Sheet of 4, #a-d 7.75 7.75

A679

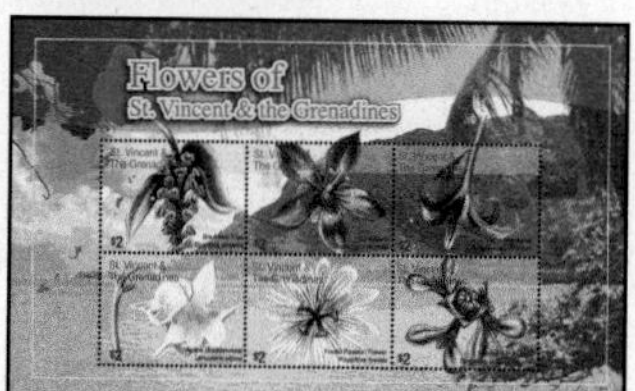


Flowers — A680

Designs: 25c, Huito. 80c, Tiny bladderwort. $1, Purple coral tree. $5, Apple guava. No. 3705, horiz.: a, Soufriere tree. b, Guajacum. c, Nipplefruit. d, Alpine bladderwort. e, Fetid passion flower. f, Shoreline purslane.

**2010, Apr. 23 Litho. *Perf. 14x14¾***

**3701-3704** A679 Set of 4 5.25 5.25

***Perf. 14¾x14***

**3705** A680 $2 Sheet of 6, #a-f 9.00 9.00

Orchids — A681

Designs: 25c, Phragmipedium popowii. 80c, Cattleya dowiana. $1, Brassavola subulifolia. $5, Brassavola acaulis. No. 3710, horiz.: a, Cattleya gaskelliana. b, Cattleya aurea. c, Cattleya mendelii. d, Cattleya schrodera. e, Cypripedium dickinsonianum. f, Phragmipedium longifolium.

**2010, Apr. 23 Litho. *Perf. 13¼x13***

**3706-3709** A681 Set of 4 5.25 5.25

***Perf. 13x13¼***

**3710** A681 $2 Sheet of 6, #a-f 9.00 9.00

Marine Life
A682

Designs: 25c, Leatherback turtle. 80c, Caesar grunt. $1, Atlantic tarpon. $5, Moray eel. No. 3715: a, Caribbean reef shark. b, Loggerhead sea turtle. c, Great barracuda. d, Caribbean lobster. e, Royal gramma. f, Southern stingray.

**2010, Apr. 23 Litho. *Perf. 14¾x14***

**3711-3714** A682 Set of 4 5.25 5.25
**3715** A682 $2 Sheet of 6, #a-f 9.00 9.00

Antverpia 2010 National and European Championship of Philately, Antwerp, Belgium (No. 3715).

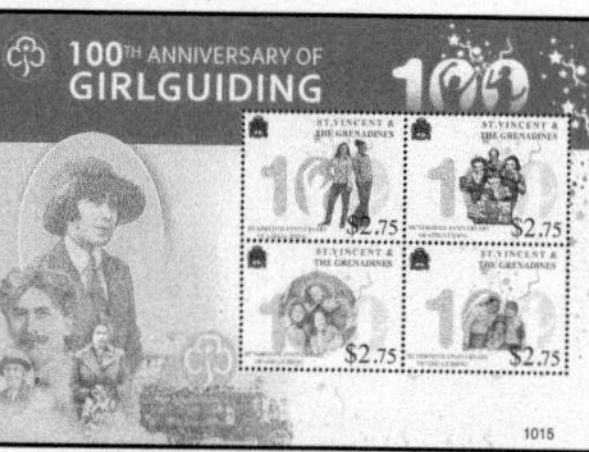


Girl Guides, Cent. — A683

No. 3716: a, Two Girl Guides. b, Four Girl Guides. c, Four Girl Guides and trefoil. d, Three Girl Guides.

$6, One Girl Guide, vert.

**2010, June 4 *Perf. 13x13¼***

**3716** A683 $2.75 Sheet of 4, #a-d 8.25 8.25

**Souvenir Sheet**

***Perf. 13¼x13***

**3717** A683 $6 multi 4.50 4.50

Miniature Sheet

Accession to Throne of King George V, Cent. — A684

No. 3718: a, King William IV. b, Queen Victoria. c, King Edward VII. d, King George V on coin. e, Portrait of King George V. f, Statue of King George V.

**2010, Sept. 1 *Perf. 11½***

**3718** A684 $2 Sheet of 6, #a-f 9.00 9.00

Miniature Sheets

A685

Mother Teresa (1910-97), Humanitarian, and Pope John Paul II (1920-2005) — A686

No. 3719 — With dove above Mother Teresa; Pope John Paul II: a, To right of Mother Teresa. b, Touching head of Mother Teresa. c, Wearing miter. d, Holding Mother Teresa's hand.

No. 3720 — Without dove above Mother Teresa; Pope John Paul II: a, Wearing miter. b, Touching head of Mother Teresa. c, At left, holding hand of Mother Teresa. d, At right, holding hand of Mother Teresa.

**2010, Sept. 1 *Perf. 13x13¼***

**3719** A685 $2.75 Sheet of 4, #a-d 8.25 8.25
**3720** A686 $2.75 Sheet of 4, #a-d 8.25 8.25

Miniature Sheet

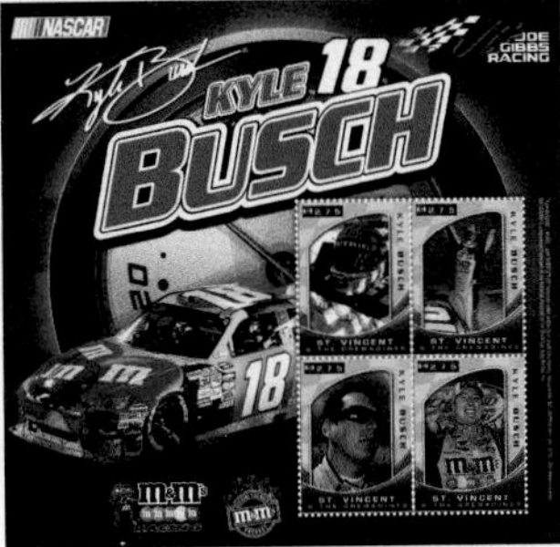

Kyle Busch, NASCAR Race Car Driver — A687

No. 3721 — Busch: a, In car wearing helmet. b, With arms raised, wearing helmet. c, Wearing sunglasses. d, Wearing cap.

**2010, Oct. 5** ***Perf. 12x11½***
**3721** A687 $2.75 Sheet of 4, #a-d 8.25 8.25

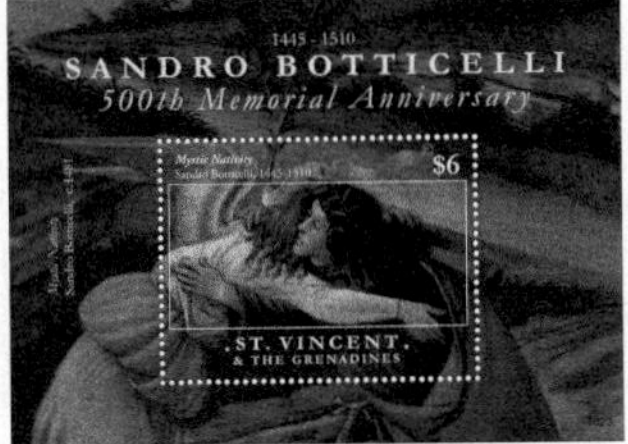

Paintings of Sandro Botticelli (1445-1510) — A688

No. 3722, vert.: a, The Annunciation. b, Portrait of a Young Man. c, Portrait of Simonetta Vespucci. d, Die Verstossene (The Outcast).
$6, Mystic Nativity.

**2010, Oct. 5** ***Perf. 12x11½***
**3722** A688 $2.50 Sheet of 4, #a-d 7.50 7.50

**Souvenir Sheet**

***Perf. 13½***

**3723** A688 $6 multi 4.50 4.50

No. 3722 contains four 30x40mm stamps.

Henri Dunant (1828-1910), Founder of Red Cross — A689

No. 3724 — Nurse, soldiers and Dunant in: a, Greenish black. b, Brown. c, Violet brown. d, Blue black.
$6, Florence Nightingale, Clara Barton and Dunant.

**2010, Oct. 5** ***Perf. 12***
**3724** A689 $2.50 Sheet of 4, #a-d 7.50 7.50

**Souvenir Sheet**

**3725** A689 $6 multi 4.50 4.50

Miniature Sheets

Characters in Star Trek Movies — A690

No. 3726, $2.75 — Star Trek II, The Wrath of Khan: a, Saavik. b, Spock and Dr. Leonard McCoy. c, Capt. James T. Kirk. d, Khan Noonien Singh.
No. 3727, $2.75 — Star Trek IV, The Voyage Home: a, Montgomery Scott. b, Spock. c, Kirk. d, McCoy.

***Perf. 12x11½, 11½ (#3727)***

**2010, Oct. 5** **Sheets of 4, #a-d**
**3726-3727** A690 Set of 2 16.50 16.50

Cats — A691

No. 3728: a, Persian. b, Russian Blue. c, Chartreux. d, Bobtail. e, Selkirk Rex. f, Bengal.
$6, Siamese.

**2010, Oct. 5** ***Perf. 12***
**3728** A691 $2 Sheet of 6, #a-f 9.00 9.00

**Souvenir Sheet**

**3729** A691 $6 multi 4.50 4.50

Miniature Sheets

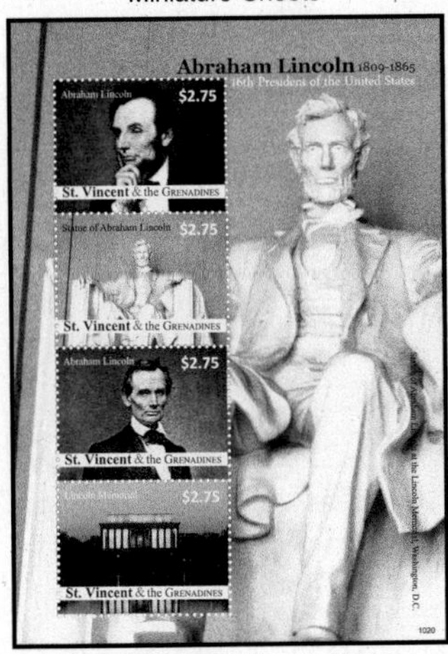

Pres. Abraham Lincoln (1809-65) — A692

No. 3730, $2.75: a, Lincoln with hand on chin. b, Statue of Lincoln in Lincoln Memorial. c, Photograph of Lincoln without beard. d, Lincoln Memorial at dusk.
No. 3731, $2.75: a, Photograph of Lincoln with beard. b, Aerial view of Lincoln Memorial. c, First Reading of the Emancipation Proclamation of President Lincoln, painting by Francis Carpenter. d, Lincoln and US No. 1282.

**Sheets of 4, #a-d**

**2010, Oct. 5** ***Perf. 12***
**3730-3731** A692 Set of 2 16.50 16.50

Posters of Films Directed by Akira Kurosawa (1910-98) — A693

No. 3732, $2.50: a, Shubun (Scandal). b, Subarashiki Nichiyobi (One Wonderful Sunday). c, Sugata Sanshiro (Judo Saga). d, Kakushi Toride No San Akunin (The Hidden Fortress).
No. 3733, $2.50: a, Kumonosu-jo (Throne of Blood). b, Waga Seishun Ni Kuinashi (No Regrets for Our Youth). c, Tora No o Wo Fumu Otokotachi (The Men Who Tread on the Tiger's Tail). d, Yoidore Tenshi (Drunken Angel).
No. 3734: a, Rashomon (Samurai with sword). b, Rashomon (woman with knife).

**Sheets of 4, #a-d**

**2010, Oct. 5** ***Perf. 13¼***
**3732-3733** A693 Set of 2 15.00 15.00

**Souvenir Sheet**

**3734** A693 $4 Sheet of 2, #a-b 6.00 6.00

Miniature Sheets

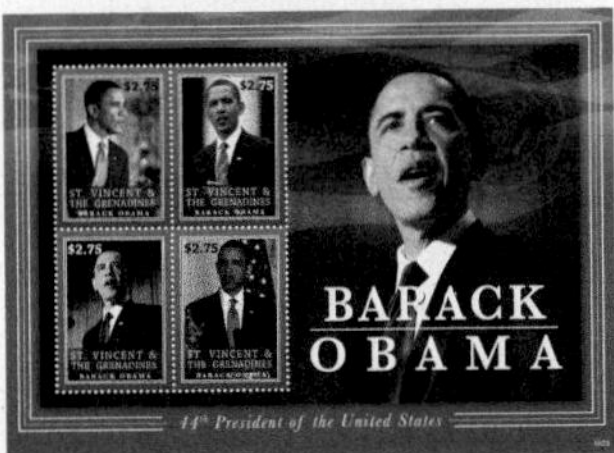

A694

Pres. Barack Obama — A695

No. 3735 — Blue frame, Pres. Obama with: a, Blue tie, microphone at right. b, Red striped tie. c, Black tie, microphone at left. d, Blue tie, flag in background.
No. 3736 — Red frame, Pres. Obama with: a, Black and white striped tie. b, Blue tie, foliage in background. c, Black and white patterned tie, red flag in background. d, Blue tie.

**2010, Dec. 6** ***Perf. 12x12½***
**3735** A694 $2.75 Sheet of 4, #a-d 8.25 8.25
**3736** A695 $2.75 Sheet of 4, #a-d 8.25 8.25

Christmas A696

Paintings: 90c, Annunciation, by Domenico di Pace Beccafumi. $1.80, Adoration of the Shepherds, by Gerard van Honthorst. $2.50, Adoration of the Magi, by Guido Reni. $3, Nativity, by Domenico Ghirlandaio.

**2010, Dec. 15** **Litho.** ***Perf. 12***
**3737-3740** A696 Set of 4 6.25 6.25

British Monarchs A697

Designs: No. 3741, $2, King Henry I (c. 1068-1135). No. 3742, $2, King John (1166-1216). No. 3743, $2, King Richard II (1367-1400). No. 3744, $2, King Edward V (1470-83 ?) No. 3745, $2, King Edward VI (1537-53). nO. 3746, $2, King Charles II (1630-85). No. 3747, $2, King George III (1738-1820). No. 3748, $2, King George VI (1895-1952).

**2011, Jan. 20** ***Perf. 13 Syncopated***
**3741-3748** A697 Set of 8 12.00 12.00

Nos. 3741-3748 each were printed in sheets of 8 + central label.

A698

Indipex 2011 Intl. Philatelic Exhibition, New Delhi — A699

No. 3749 — Spices: a, Saffron. b, Chili peppers. c, Curry leaves. d, Turmeric. e, Peppercorns. f, Cinnamon.
No. 3750 — Animals: a, Indian peafowl. b, Indian elephant. c, Red panda. d, Blackbuck. e, King cobra. f, Indian leopard. g, Indian rhinoceros.
No. 3751— Bengal tiger with denominati at: a, LR. b, UL.

**2011, Feb. 9**

| | | | | | |
|---|---|---|---|---|---|
| 3749 | A698 | $1.85 | Sheet of 6, #a-f | 8.25 | 8.25 |
| 3750 | A699 | $1.85 | Sheet of 7, #a-g + 2 labels | 9.75 | 9.75 |

**Souvenir Sheet**

| | | | | | |
|---|---|---|---|---|---|
| 3751 | A699 | $5 | Sheet of 2, #a-b | 7.50 | 7.50 |

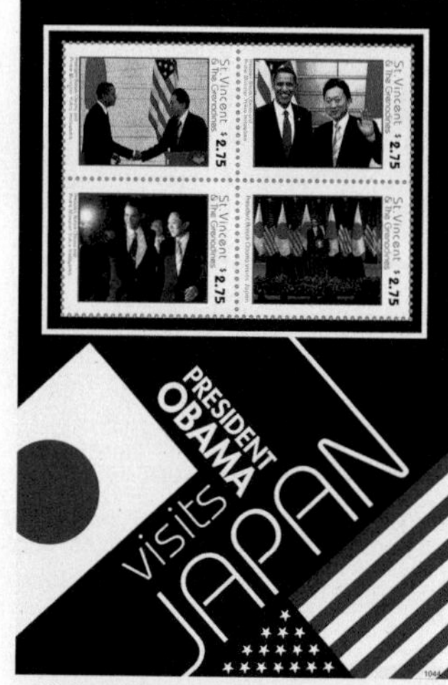


Visit to Japan of President Barack Obama — A700

No. 3752 — Pres. Obama: a, Shaking hands with Japanese Prime Minister Yukio Hatoyama. b, With Hatoyama, flags, Hatoyama waving. c, Walking with Hatoyama. d, At lectern.
$6, Pres. Obama waving.

**2011, Feb. 9** ***Perf. 12***

| | | | | | |
|---|---|---|---|---|---|
| 3752 | A700 | $2.75 | Sheet of 4, #a-d | 8.25 | 8.25 |

**Souvenir Sheet**

***Perf. 12¾***

| | | | | | |
|---|---|---|---|---|---|
| 3753 | A700 | $6 | multi | 4.50 | 4.50 |

No. 3753 contains one 51x38mm stamp.

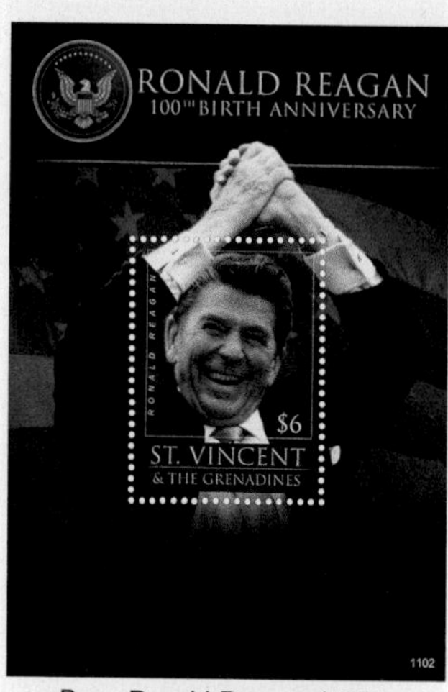


Pres. Ronald Reagan (1911-2004) — A701

No. 3754, horiz. — Pres. Reagan: a, With wife, Nancy, flag and ocean in background. b, At lectern, flag in background. c, At lectern, sign in background. c, With wife on helicopter.
$6, Pres. Reagan with arms raised.

**2011, Feb. 9** ***Perf. 12***

| | | | | | |
|---|---|---|---|---|---|
| 3754 | A701 | $2.75 | Sheet of 4, #a-d | 8.25 | 8.25 |

**Souvenir Sheet**

| | | | | | |
|---|---|---|---|---|---|
| 3755 | A701 | $6 | multi | 4.50 | 4.50 |

Engagement of Prince William and Catherine Middleton — A702

Designs: No. 3756, Couple, maroon panels. No. 3757, Couple, diff., blue panels.
No. 3758, $6, Couple, diff. No. 3759, $6, Prince William, vert.

**2011, Feb. 11** ***Perf. 12***

| | | | | | |
|---|---|---|---|---|---|
| 3756 | A702 | $2.50 | multi | 1.90 | 1.90 |

***Perf. 13 Syncopated***

| | | | | | |
|---|---|---|---|---|---|
| 3757 | A702 | $2.50 | multi | 1.90 | 1.90 |

**Souvenir Sheets**

| | | | | |
|---|---|---|---|---|
| 3758-3759 | A702 | Set of 2 | 9.00 | 9.00 |

Flag of St. Vincent and the Grenadines — A703

**2011, Feb. 17** ***Perf. 14¾x14¼***

| | | | | | |
|---|---|---|---|---|---|
| 3760 | A703 | $1 | multi | .75 | .75 |

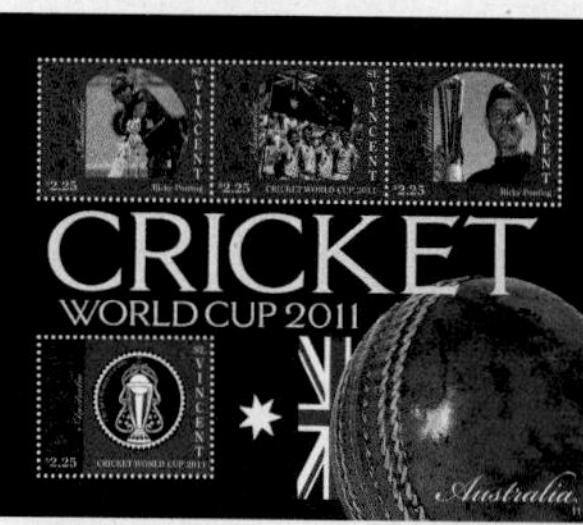


Dolphins — A704

No. 3761: a, Stenella coeruleoalba. b, Langenodelphis hosei. c, Dephinus capensis. d, Delphinus delphis. e, Stenella longirostris. f, Stenella frontalis.
$6, Grampus griseus.

**2011, Feb. 17** ***Perf. 13 Syncopated***

| | | | | | |
|---|---|---|---|---|---|
| 3761 | A704 | $2 | Sheet of 6, #a-f | 9.00 | 9.00 |

**Souvenir Sheet**

***Perf. 12***

| | | | | | |
|---|---|---|---|---|---|
| 3762 | A704 | $6 | multi | 4.50 | 4.50 |

Miniature Sheets

2011 World Cricket Cup, India, Bangladesh, and Sri Lanka — A705

No. 3763, $2.25 — Stamps inscribed "Australia": a, Ricky Ponting wearing helmet. b, Australia team. c, Ponting holding trophy. d, Cricket World Cup emblem.
No. 3764, $2.25 — Stamps inscribed "Bagladesh": a, Shakib Al Hasan wearing helmet. b, Al Hasan without helmet. c, Bangladesh team. d, Cricket World Cup emblem.
No. 3765, $2.25 — Stamps inscribed "England": a, Kevin Pietersen wearing helmet. b, Pietersen without helmet. c, English team. d, Cricket World Cup emblem.
No. 3766, $2.25 — Stamps inscribed "India": a, Sachin Tendulkar wearing helmet. b, Tendulkar without helmet. c, Tendulkar holding trophy. d, Cricket World Cup emblem.
No. 3767, $2.25 — Stamps inscribed "New Zealand": a, Daniel Vettori bowling. b, Vettori wearing cap. c, New Zealand team holding trophy. d, Cricket World Cup emblem.

**Sheets of 4 #a-d**

**2011, May 2** ***Perf. 12***

| | | | | |
|---|---|---|---|---|
| 3763-3767 | A705 | Set of 5 | 33.50 | 33.50 |

St. Vincent Girls' High School, Cent. A706

School crest and: 30c, 2010 steel drum orchestra. $1.05, Colette Sharlene Charles. No. 3770, $1.35, 1963 West Indian netball team, "BOA" visible on plane. No. 3770A, $1.35, 1963 West Indian netball team, "BOAC" on plane. $1.65, Beryl Baptiste, St. Vincent Director of Audit. No. 3772, $2.10, Grimble Building. No. 3773, $2.10, Betty Boyea-King, diplomat. No. 3774, $2.10, Dame Monica Dacon, deputy to Governor General.
No. 3775, $10, Mrs. Keizer and Mrs. Bowman, headmistresses of school. No. 3776, $10, Laura Smith-Moffett, headmistress. No. 3777, $10, Susan Dougan, cabinet secretary.

**2011, May 16** ***Perf. 12½***

| | | | | | |
|---|---|---|---|---|---|
| 3768 | A706 | 30c | multi | .25 | .25 |
| 3769 | A706 | $1.05 | multi | .75 | .75 |
| 3770 | A706 | $1.35 | multi | 1.00 | 1.00 |
| 3770A | A706 | $1.35 | multi | 1.00 | 1.00 |
| 3771 | A706 | $1.65 | multi | 1.25 | 1.25 |
| 3772 | A706 | $2.10 | multi | 1.60 | 1.60 |
| 3773 | A706 | $2.10 | multi | 1.60 | 1.60 |
| 3774 | A706 | $2.10 | multi | 1.60 | 1.60 |
| | *Nos. 3708-3774 (8)* | | | 9.05 | 9.05 |

**Souvenir Sheets**

| | | | | |
|---|---|---|---|---|
| 3775-3777 | A706 | Set of 3 | 22.50 | 22.50 |

No. 3770A was printed in sheets of 4.

Sumo Wrestler — A707

Fish — A708

No. 3779: a, Pacific bluefin tuna. b, Koi. c, Porcupinefish. d, Cherry salmon.

**2011, May 16** ***Perf. 12x12½***

| | | | | | |
|---|---|---|---|---|---|
| 3778 | A707 | $2.75 | multi | 2.10 | 2.10 |

***Perf. 12½x12***

| | | | | | |
|---|---|---|---|---|---|
| 3779 | A708 | $2.75 | Sheet of 4, #a-d | 8.25 | 8.25 |

PhilaNippon 2011 Intl. Philatelic Exhibition, Yokohama. No. 3778 was printed in sheets of 4.

Miniature Sheets

A709

Inauguration of Pres. John F. Kennedy, 50th Anniv. — A710

No. 3780: a, Kennedy taking oath. b, Kennedy on telephone.
No. 3781: a, Kennedy with wife, Jacqueline, and Vice-President Lyndon Johnson on reviewing stand. b, Kennedy at inaugural ball, flowers in background. c, Kennedy near doorway. d, Kennedy walking with wife at inaugural ball.

**2011, May 16** ***Perf. 13 Syncopated***

| | | | | | |
|---|---|---|---|---|---|
| 3780 | A709 | $2.75 | Sheet of 4, 2 each #a-b | 8.25 | 8.25 |
| 3781 | A710 | $2.75 | Sheet of 4, #a-d | 8.25 | 8.25 |

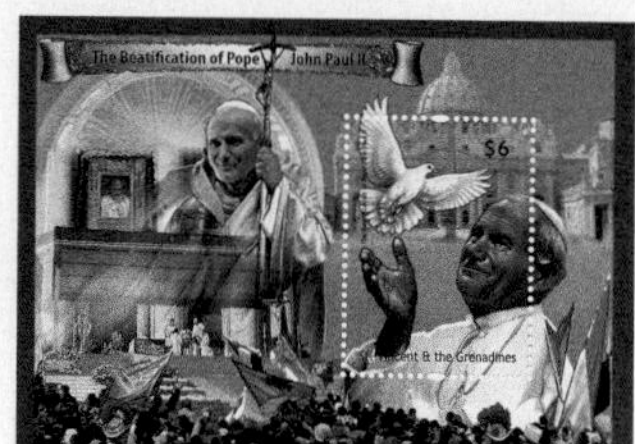


Paintings by Michelangelo Merisi da Caravaggio (1571-1610) — A711

No. 3782: a, The Denial of Saint Peter. b, The Lute Player. c, The Fortune Teller. d, Supper at Emmaus.
$6, The Cardsharps.

**2011, May 16** **Litho.**

| | | | | | |
|---|---|---|---|---|---|
| 3782 | A711 | $2.50 | Sheet of 4, #a-d | 7.50 | 7.50 |

**Souvenir Sheet**

| | | | | | |
|---|---|---|---|---|---|
| 3783 | A711 | $6 | multi | 4.50 | 4.50 |

Beatification of Pope John Paul II — A712

No. 3784 — Pope John Paul II with: a, Charles Eugène de Foucauld de Pontbriand (1858-1916), martyr. b, Sister Marie Simon-Pierre. c, Pope John XXIII. d, Pope Pius IX. e, Mother Teresa. f, Father Jerzy Popieluszko (1947-84), martyr.
$6, Pope John Paul II, dove, St. Peter's Basilica.

**2011, May 16**

| | | | | | |
|---|---|---|---|---|---|
| 3784 | A712 | $2 | Sheet of 6, #a-f | 9.00 | 9.00 |

**Souvenir Sheet**

| | | | | | |
|---|---|---|---|---|---|
| 3785 | A712 | $6 | multi | 4.50 | 4.50 |

Miniature Sheet

A. C. Milan Soccer Team — A713

No. 3786 — Team emblem and: a, Herbert Kilpin, team founder. b, Franco Baresi. c,

Coach Nereo Rocco and team, 1968. d, Scene from 1969 Intercontinental Cup match. e, Frank Rijkaard, Marco Van Basten, Ruud Gullit. f, Gianni Rivera. g, 1979 team. h, Van Basten. i, Scene from 1994 UEFA Champions League match.

**2011, June 15** ***Perf. 13¼***
**3786** A713 $1.20 Sheet of 9 #a-i 8.00 8.00

A714

Wedding of Prince William and Catherine Middleton A715

No. 3787: a, Groom. b, Bride. c, Couple.
No. 3788: a, Couple, bride waving. b, Couple, kissing.
$6, Couple in coach.

**2011, June 15** ***Perf. 12***
**3787** A714 $1.20 Block of 4, #3787a-3787b, 2 #3787c, + 2 labels 3.75 3.75
**3788** A715 $2.75 Pair, #a-b 4.25 4.25

**Souvenir Sheet**

**3789** A714 $6 multi 4.50 4.50

No. 3787 was printed in sheets containing 2 blocks. No. 3788 was printed in sheets containing two pairs.

Pres. Abraham Lincoln (1809-65) — A716

No. 3790, $2.75: a, Lincoln, denomination in brown at LL. b, Lincoln, denomination in white at LL. c, Soldiers, flag, at Battle of Fair Oaks, denomination at UR. d, Soldiers, flag and tree at Battle of Fair Oaks, denomination at UL.

No. 3791, $2.75: a, Lincoln, denomination in white at LR. b, Lincoln, denomination in brown at LR. c, Soldiers, horses, flag at Battle of Opequon, denomination at UR. d, Soldiers, horses, flag at Battle of Opequon, denomination at UL.

**Sheets of 4, #a-d**

**2011, July 13** ***Perf. 13¼x13***
**3790-3791** A716 Set of 2 16.50 16.50

**Souvenir Sheets**

A717

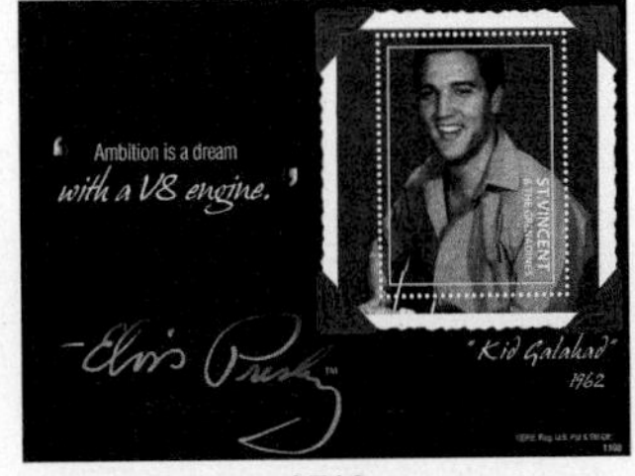

A718

A719

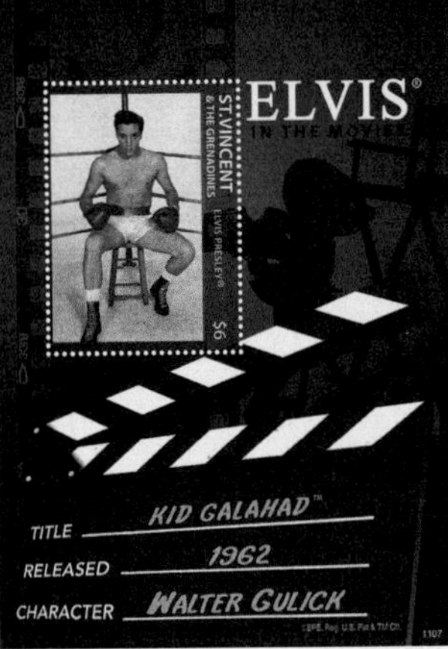

Elvis Presley (1935-77) — A720

**2011, July 19** ***Perf. 12¾***

| | | | | |
|---|---|---|---|---|
| **3792** | A717 | $6 multi | 4.50 | 4.50 |
| **3793** | A718 | $6 multi | 4.50 | 4.50 |
| **3794** | A719 | $6 multi | 4.50 | 4.50 |
| **3795** | A720 | $6 multi | 4.50 | 4.50 |
| | *Nos. 3792-3795 (4)* | | 18.00 | 18.00 |

**Miniature Sheets**

British Royalty — A721

No. 3796, $2.75 — King George V: a, Wearing robes. b, Wearing military uniform and hat. c, Seated at desk. d, Wearing uniform and medals, without hat.

No. 3797, $2.75 — King George VI: a, With Lady Elizabeth Bowes-Lyon. b, Wearing polo shirt. c, Wearing suit and tie. d, Wearing military uniform.

No. 3798, $2.75, horiz. — Queen Elizabeth II: a, Wearing red hat. b, Wearing white blouse. c, As child, in garden. d, In automobile with Prince Philip.

No. 3799, $2.75, horiz. — Prince Philip: a, Wearing uniform, waving. b, With Queen Elizabeth II. c, In palace. d, With family, 1965.

**2011, July 26** ***Perf. 13 Syncopated***

**Sheets of 4, #a-d**

**3796-3799** A721 Set of 4 32.50 32.50

**Miniature Sheets**

A722

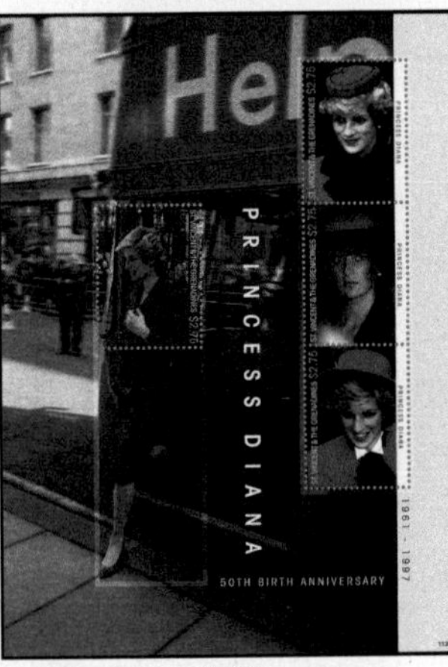

A723

No. 3800 — Princess Diana: a, Wearing striped jacket. b, Wearing dress and choker necklace. c, In vehicle. d, Wearing dark dress, no necklace.

No. 3801 — Princess Diana: a, Wearing red and black hat with veil. b, Leaving bus. c, Wearing red hat with black ribbon. d, Wearing red hat.

**2011, July 28** ***Perf. 12***
**3800** A722 $2.75 Sheet of 4, #a-d 8.25 8.25
**3801** A723 $2.75 Sheet of 4, #a-d 8.25 8.25

Visit to Germany of Pope Benedict XVI — A724

No. 3802 — Various buildings and Pope Benedict XVI: a, Wearing white vestments, with hands together. b, Wearing miter. c, Wearing white vestments, hands not visible.
$6, Pope Benedict XVI waving, vert.

**2011, Aug. 9** ***Perf. 12***
**3802** A724 $3 Sheet of 3, #a-c 6.75 6.75

**Souvenir Sheet**

**3803** A724 $6 multi 4.50 4.50

Sept. 11, 2001 Terrorist Attacks, 10th Anniv. — A725

No. 3804, horiz.: a, Candles and photograph of World Trade Center at Sept. 13, 2001 New York vigil. b, People at Sept. 13, 2001 New York vigil. c, Sept. 11 Memorial at Pentagon Building. d, Person, flag and flower at memorial in Stonycreek Township, Pennsylvania.
$6, Firemen and flags, New York.

**2011, Oct. 6** ***Perf. 13x13¼***
**3804** A725 $2.75 Sheet of 4, #a-d 8.25 8.25

**Souvenir Sheet**
***Perf. 13¼x13***
**3805** A725 $6 multi 4.50 4.50

Turtles — A726

No. 3806: a, Chicken turtle. b, Diamondback terrapin. c, Red-eared slider.
$9, Green sea turtle.

**2011, Oct. 26** ***Perf. 12***
**3806** A726 $3 Sheet of 3, #a-c 6.75 6.75

**Souvenir Sheet**
**3807** A726 $9 multi 6.75 6.75

**Miniature Sheets**

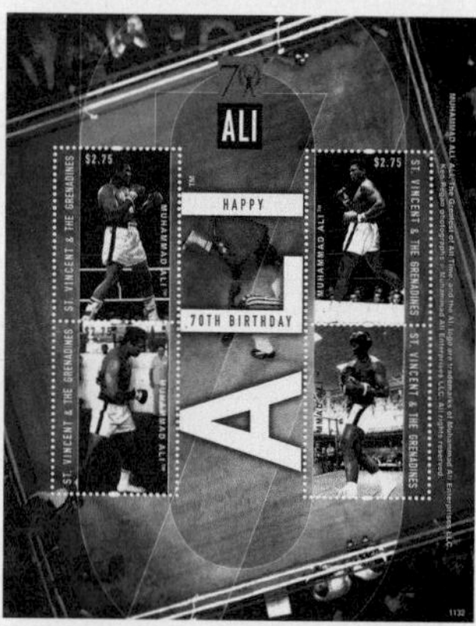


A727

Muhammad Ali, 70th Birthday — A728

No. 3808 — Ali: a, Color photograph, wearing red gloves. b, Black-and-white photograph, during fight. c, Color photograph, wearing black gloves. d, Black-and-white photograph, in training ring wearing headgear.
No. 3809 — Ali: a, Color photograph, without shirt, facing forward. b, Black-and-white photograph, wearing bow tie. c, Color photograph, without shirt, facing right. d, Color photograph, wearing suit and tie.

**2011, Nov. 2** ***Perf. 13 Syncopated***
**3808** A727 $2.75 Sheet of 4, #a-d 8.25 8.25
**3809** A728 $2.75 Sheet of 4, #a-d 8.25 8.25

Christmas A729

Details from paintings: 30c, Madonna and Child, by Sandro Botticelli. 90c, Madonna Enthroned, by Giotto di Bondone. $2, Madonna and Child, by Carlo Crivelli. $3, Mystic Nativity, by Botticelli.

**2011, Nov. 2** ***Perf. 12***
**3810-3813** A729 Set of 4 4.75 4.75

**Miniature Sheet**

1908 Olympic Games, London — A730

No. 3814: a, White City Stadium. b, Dorando Pietri. c, Erik Lemming. d, Poster for 1908 Olympic Games.

**2011, Nov. 14** ***Perf. 13 Syncopated***
**3814** A730 $2.75 Sheet of 4, #a-d 8.25 8.25
2012 Summer Olympics, London.

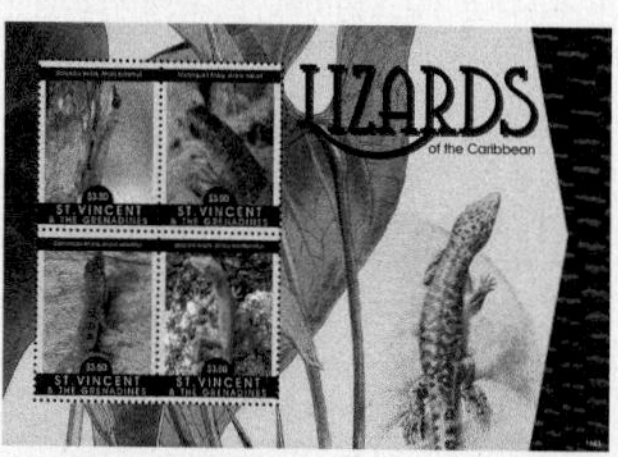


Anoles — A731

No. 3815: a, Barbados anole. b, Martinique's anole. c, Dominican anole. d, Leopard anole.
$9, Green anole.

**2011, Nov. 14** ***Perf. 12***
**3815** A731 $3.50 Sheet of 4, #a-d 10.50 10.50

**Souvenir Sheet**
**3816** A731 $9 multi 6.75 6.75
No. 3816 contains one 30x50mm stamp.

Statue of Liberty, 125th Anniv. A732

**2011, Dec. 16**
**3817** A732 $3 shown 2.25 2.25

**Souvenir Sheet**
**3818** A732 $9 Statue, vert. 6.75 6.75
No. 3817 was printed in sheets of 3. No. 3818 contains one 30x50mm stamp.

Reign of Queen Elizabeth II, 60th Anniv. — A733

No. 3819 — Queen Elizabeth II: a, With Prince Philip. b, Wearing flowered hat. c, Wearing sash and tiara.
$9, Queen Elizabeth II, horiz.

**2012, Jan. 1**
**3819** A733 $3.50 Sheet of 3, #a-c 7.75 7.75

**Souvenir Sheet**
**3820** A733 $9 multi 6.75 6.75
No. 3820 contains one 50x30mm stamp.

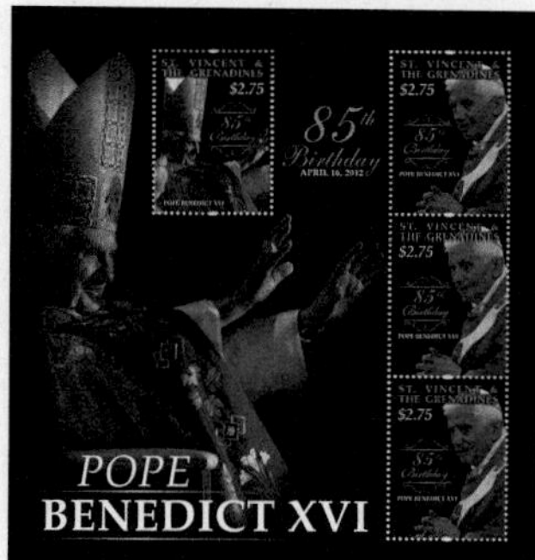


Pope Benedict XVI, 85th Birthday — A734

No. 3821: a, Facing right, waving. b, Facing left, wearing green vestments.
$6, Facing left, diff.

**2012, Mar. 26** ***Perf. 13 Syncopated***
**3821** A734 $2.75 Sheet of 4, #3821a, 3 #3821b 8.25 8.25

**Souvenir Sheet**
**3822** A734 $6 multi 4.50 4.50

**Miniature Sheets**

A735

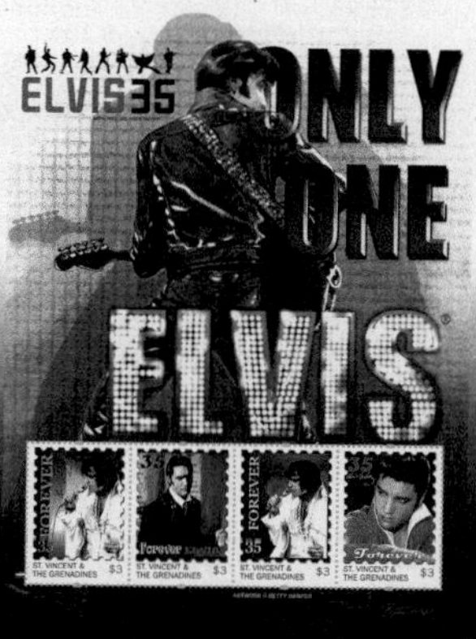


Elvis Presley (1935-77) — A736

No. 3823 — Presley: a, With guitar. b, Facing right, holding microphone. c, Wearing striped shirt. d, Facing left, holding microphone. No. 3824 — "Forever," and Presley: a, Facing right, holding microphone, "Forever" in gray. b, Wearing black jacket. c, Facing right, holding microphone, "Forever" in white. d, Wearing red jacket.

**2012, Mar. 26** ***Perf. 13 Syncopated***
**3823** A735 $3 Sheet of 4, #a-d 9.00 9.00
**3824** A736 $3 Sheet of 4, #a-d 9.00 9.00

**Miniature Sheet**

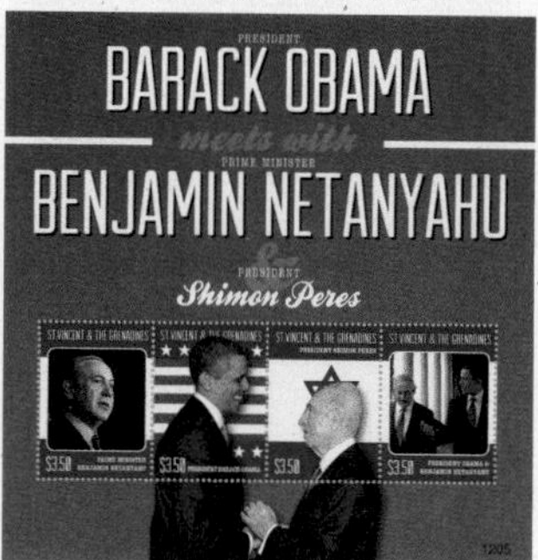


U.S. and Israeli Leaders — A737

No. 3825: a, Israeli Prime Minister Benjamin Netanyahu. b, Pres. Barack Obama. c, Israeli Pres. Shimon Peres, Israeli flag. d, Pres. Obama, Prime Minister Netanyahu.

**2012, May 3** ***Perf. 13¼x13***
**3825** A737 $3.50 Sheet of 4, #a-d 10.50 10.50

Miniature Sheets

French National Center for Space Studies, 50th Anniv. — A738

No. 3826, $3.50: a, SPOT satellite (denomination separated from satellite). b, SRET 2. c, Astronaut Jean-Loup Chrétien. d, JASON.

No. 3827, $3.50: a, Astronaut Claudie Haigneré. b, SPOT satellite (denomination covering part of satellite). c, Aureol 1. d, FR 1.

**2012, May 3** ***Perf. 14***

**Sheets of 4, #a-d**

**3826-3827** A738 Set of 2 21.00 21.00

Nos. 3826-3827 exist imperf. Value, set $25.

Miniature Sheets

Soft Moon Landing — A739

No. 3828, $3.50: a, Lunik 3. b, Luna 10. c, Lunik 2. d, Von Braun vehicle.

No. 3829, #3.50: a, Lunik 9. b, Russian lunar module. c, Lunar orbiter. d, Imaginative spaceship.

**2012, June 27** ***Perf. 14***

**Sheets of 4, #a-d**

**3828-3829** A739 Set of 2 21.00 21.00

Nos. 3828-3829 exist imperf. Value, set $25.

Miniature Sheet

Duke and Duchess of Cambridge, First Wedding Anniversary — A740

No. 3830: a, Duke of Cambridge. b, Duchess of Cambridge. c, Couple seated in coach. d, Couple standing.

**2012, Sept. 5** ***Perf. 13¾***

**3830** A740 $2.50 Sheet of 4, #a-d 7.50 7.50

Butterflies — A741

No. 3831: a, Danaus plexippus. b, Euptoieta hegesia. c, Libytheana carinenta. d, Lycorea halia.

$9, Phocides pigmalion.

**2012, Sept. 5** ***Perf. 13¾***

**3831** A741 $3.50 Sheet of 4, #a-d 10.50 10.50

**Souvenir Sheet**

**3832** A741 $9 multi 6.75 6.75

Christmas A742

Paintings by Raphael: 80c, Madonna and Child with St. Johan and St. Nicholas. $1, The Holy Family with Saints Elizabeth and John. $1.70, Madonna and Child with Saints. $2.20, The Holy Family. $2.65, The Aldobrandini Madonna.

$3.40, The Visitation.

**2012, Nov. 28** ***Perf. 12¾***

**3833-3837** A742 Set of 5 6.25 6.25

**Souvenir Sheet**

**3838** A742 $3.40 multi 2.50 2.50

Beetles — A743

No. 3839: a, Doryphora undata. b, Leptinotarsa lacerata. c, Chrysomela populi. d, Leptinotarsa decemlineata.

$9, Leptinotarsa puncticollis.

**2013, Feb. 28** ***Perf. 12***

**3839** A743 $3.50 Sheet of 4, #a-d 10.50 10.50

**Souvenir Sheet**

***Perf. 12¾***

**3840** A743 $9 multi 6.75 6.75

No. 3840 contains one 38x51mm stamp.

Dogs — A744

No. 3841: a, Spanish mastiff. b, Poodle. c, Dachshund. d, Basenji.

$9, German shepherd.

**2013, Feb. 28** ***Perf. 13 Syncopated***

**3841** A744 $3.50 Sheet of 4, #a-d 10.50 10.50

**Souvenir Sheet**

**3842** A744 $9 multi 6.75 6.75

Coral Reefs — A745

No. 3843: a, Hawksbill turtle. b, Sea sponges and tropical fish. c, Red cushion sea star. d, Ricordea coral.

$9, Turtle, fish, and reef, horiz.

**2013, Feb. 28** ***Perf. 12***

**3843** A745 $3.50 Sheet of 4, #a-d 10.50 10.50

**Souvenir Sheet**

**3844** A745 $9 multi 6.75 6.75

No. 3844 contains one 80x30mm stamp.

Miniature Sheet

Crabs — A746

No. 3845: a, Clinging crab. b, Yellowline arrow crab. c, Redeye sponge crab. d, White-spotted hermit crab.

$9, White-spotted hermit crab, vert.

**2013, Feb. 28** ***Perf. 13 Syncopated***

**3845** A746 $3.50 Sheet of 4, #a-d 10.50 10.50

**Souvenir Sheet**

**3846** A746 $9 multi 6.75 6.75

Miniature Sheet

Shells — A747

No. 3847: a, Triton's trumpet. b, Flame auger. c, Angular triton. d, Banded tulip. e, Lion's paw scallop.

***Perf. 13 Syncopated***

**2013, Apr. 4** **Litho.**

**3847** A747 $2.75 Sheet of 5, #a-e 10.50 10.50

Tel Aviv 2013 Multinational Stamp Exhibition.

Images of Celestial Objects Taken by Hubble Space Telescope — A748

No. 3848, $3.25: a, NGC 6302. b, M82. c, Orion Nebula. d, Gas clouds in the Scorpius constellation.

No. 3849, $3.25: a, Eskimo Nebula. b, Carina Nebula. c, Cat's Eye Nebula. d, Cone Nebula.

No. 3850, $9, Eagle Nebula, vert. No. 3851, $9, Saturn, horiz.

**2013, Apr. 4** **Litho.** ***Perf. 13¾***

**Sheets of 4, #a-d**

**3848-3849** A748 Set of 2 19.50 19.50

**Souvenir Sheets**

***Perf. 12¾***

**3850-3851** A748 Set of 2 13.50 13.50

No. 3850 contains one 38x51mm stamp. No. 3851 contains one 51x38mm stamp.

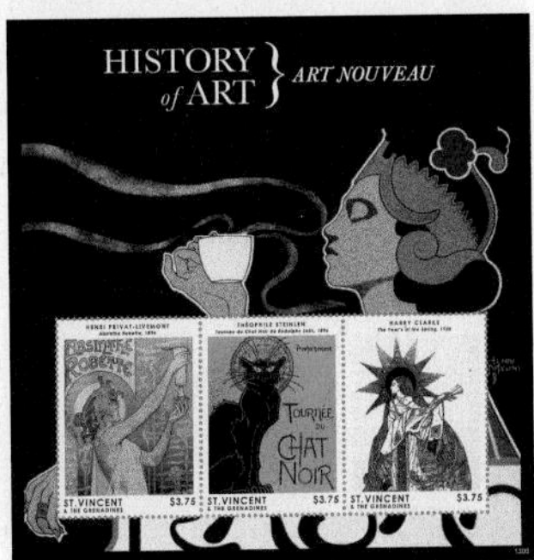


History of Art — A749

No. 3852, $3.75 — Art Nouveau: a, Absinthe Robette, by Henri Privat-Livemont. b, Tournée du Chat Noir de Rodolphe Salis, by Théophile Steinlen. c, The Year's at the Spring, by Harry Clarke.

No. 3853, $3.75 — Paintings by Gustav Klimt (1862-1918): a, The Three Ages of Woman. b, Jurisprudence. c, Judith and the Head of Holofernes.

No. 3854, $9, Ali Baba, by Aubrey Beardsley. No. 3855, $9, Job Cigarette Papers, by Alphonse Mucha, horiz.

**2013, Apr. 4** **Litho.** ***Perf. 12¾***

**Sheets of 3, #a-c**

**3852-3853** A749 Set of 2 17.00 17.00

**Souvenir Sheets**

**3854-3855** A749 Set of 2 13.50 13.50

World Environment Day — A750

No. 3856: a, Birds. b, Leaves. c, Fish. d, Sun and clouds.
$9, Owls and leaves, vert.

**2013, May 7 Litho. *Perf. 13¾***
**3856** A750 $3.25 Sheet of 4, #a-d 9.75 9.75

**Souvenir Sheet**
***Perf. 12¾***
**3857** A750 $9 multi 6.75 6.75

No. 3857 contains one 38x51mm stamp.

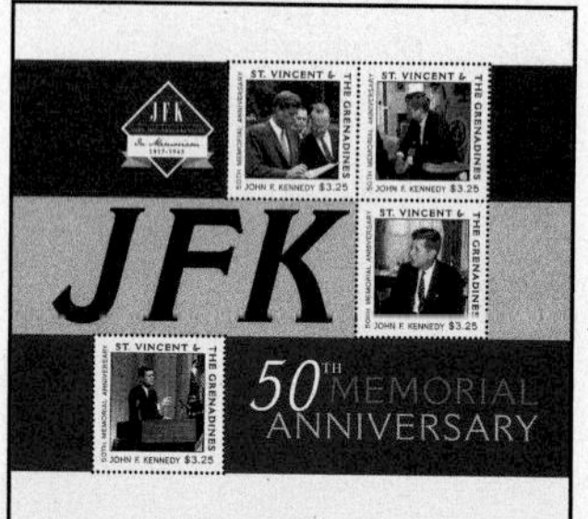


A751

Pres. John F. Kennedy (1917-63) — A752

No. 3858 — Pres. Kennedy: a, Holding paper. b, Seated in rocking chair, hands visible. c, Seated in chair, hands not visible. d, Behind lectern, pointing.
No. 3859 — Pres. Kennedy: a, With man holding medallion in box. b, Signing document. c, With Pres. Dwight D. Eisenhower. d, Standing behind lectern.
No. 3860, $9, Pres. Kennedy behind lectern, diff., denomination in blue. No. 3861, Pres. Kennedy behind lectern, diff., denomination in olive brown.

**2013, May 7 Litho. *Perf. 13¾***
**3858** A751 $3.25 Sheet of 4, #a-d 9.75 9.75
**3859** A752 $3.25 Sheet of 4, #a-d 9.75 9.75

**Souvenir Sheets**
**3860-3861** A752 Set of 2 13.50 13.50

Lady Margaret Thatcher (1925-2013), British Prime Minister — A753

No. 3862 — Thatcher: a, Waving. b, With hand on chin. c, With flowers. d, On telephone.
$9, Thatcher, vert.

**2013, June 3 Litho. *Perf. 12***
**3862** A753 $3.25 Sheet of 4, #a-d 9.75 9.75

**Souvenir Sheet**
***Perf. 12¾***
**3863** A753 $9 multi 6.75 6.75

No. 3863 contains one 38x51mm stamp.

Souvenir Sheets

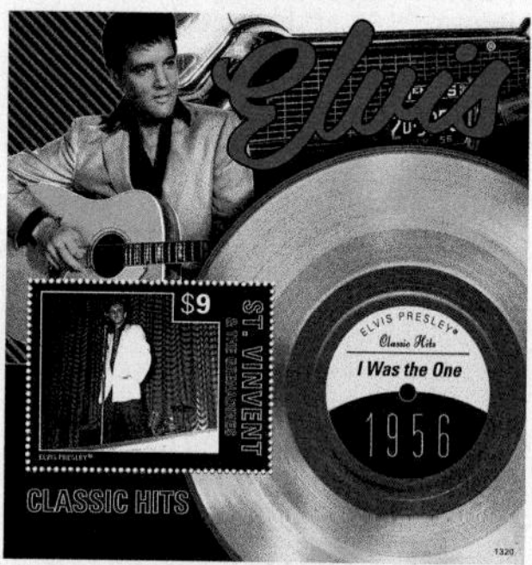


Elvis Presley (1935-77) — A754

Various photographs of Presley in: No. 3864, $9, Black-and-white, frame in black. No. 3865, $9, Color, frame in purple. No. 3866, $9, Black-and-white, frame in red. No. 3867, $9, Color, frame in red. No. 3868, $9, Color, frame in gray.

**2013, June 20 Litho. *Perf. 13½***
**3864-3868** A754 Set of 5 33.50 33.50

Country name is misspelled on No. 3864.

Souvenir Sheet

Elvis Presley (1935-77) — A755

**Litho., Margin Embossed With Foil Application**
**2013, June 25 *Imperf.***
**3869** A755 $25 multi 18.50 18.50

A756

*Pride and Prejudice*, by Jane Austen — A757

No. 3870: a, Fitzwilliam Darcy, Colonel Fitzwilliam and Elizabeth Bennet at piano. b, Mr. Collins bowing before Elizabeth. c, Lady Catherine de Bourgh and Elizabeth. d, Elizabeth watching her sister and Charles Bingley talking.
No. 3871: a, Men talking about Elizabeth, sitting on bench. b, Man looking at women attending to woman who fainted. c, Elizabeth showing ring to Mrs. Hill and housemaids. d, Woman and tea service.
No. 3872, $9.50, Darcy approaching seated Elizabeth. No. 3873, $9.50, Elizabeth and her father.

**2013, July 7 Litho. *Perf. 12¾***
**3870** A756 $3.25 Sheet of 4, #a-d 9.75 9.75
**3871** A757 $3.25 Sheet of 4, #a-d 9.75 9.75

**Souvenir Sheets**
**3872-3873** A757 Set of 2 14.00 14.00

Mammals — A758

No. 3874: a, Two-toed sloth. b, Nine-banded armadillo. c, Leaf-nosed bat. d, Short-tailed shrew.
$9, West Indian manatee.

**2013, Aug. 7 Litho. *Perf. 14***
**3874** A758 $3.25 Sheet of 4, #a-d 9.75 9.75

**Souvenir Sheet**
**3875** A758 $9 multi 6.75 6.75

Retirement of Concorde G-BOAG to Seattle Museum of Flight, 10th Anniv. — A759

No. 3876: a, Concorde on ground in Seattle. b, Captain Bannister holding microphone. c, Crowd near Concorde. d, Concorde landing at Seattle.
$9, Nose of Concorde, crew holding flags.

**2013, Aug. 26 Litho. *Perf. 12¾***
**3876** A759 $3.25 Sheet of 4, #a-d 9.75 9.75

**Souvenir Sheet**
**3877** A759 $9 multi 6.75 6.75

St. Joan of Arc (c.1412-31) A760

**2013, Sept. 27 Litho. *Perf. 12***
**3878** A760 $3.50 multi 2.60 2.60

No. 3878 was printed in sheets of 4.

Chess — A761

No. 3879: a, White pawn. b, White queen. c, White rook. d, Black knight. e, Black king. f, Black bishop.
$9, Wilhelm Steinitz (1836-1900), world chess champion.

**2013, Sept. 30 Litho. *Perf. 13¾***
**3879** A761 $2.75 Sheet of 6, #a-f 12.50 12.50

**Souvenir Sheet**
**3880** A761 $9 multi 6.75 6.75

Coronation of Queen Elizabeth II, 60th Anniv. — A762

No. 3881 — Queen Elizabeth II: a, As child. b, Wearing crown. c, With Prince Philip. d, Wearing Girl Guide uniform.
$9, Queen Elizabeth II as young girl playing piano.

**2013, Oct. 7 Litho. *Perf. 13¾***
**3881** A762 $3.25 Sheet of 4, #a-d 9.75 9.75

**Souvenir Sheet**
**3882** A762 $9 multi 6.75 6.75

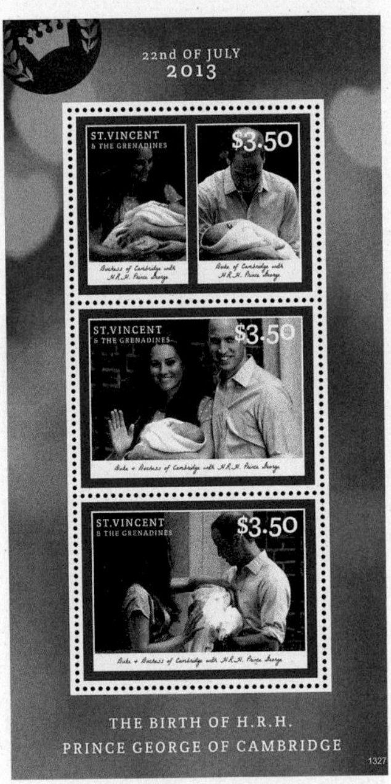

Birth of Prince George of Cambridge — A763

No. 3883: a, Prince George being held by Duchess and Duke of Cambridge. b, Duchess of Cambridge holding Prince George and waving. c, Duchess handing Prince George to Duke.
$9, Prince George, Duke and Duchess of Cambridge, diff.

**2013, Oct. 7 Litho. *Perf. 12¾***
**3883** A763 $3.50 Sheet of 3, #a-c 7.75 7.75

**Souvenir Sheet**

**3884** A763 $9 multi 6.75 6.75

Miniature Sheet

Hummingbirds — A764

No. 3885: a, Florisuga mellivora. b, Lampornis violicauda. c, Campylopterus obscurus. d, Thalurania furcata.

**2013, Nov. 11 Litho. *Perf. 12¾***
**3885** A764 $3.25 Sheet of 4, #a-d 9.75 9.75

Brasiliana 2013 Intl. Philatelic Exhibition, Rio de Janeiro.

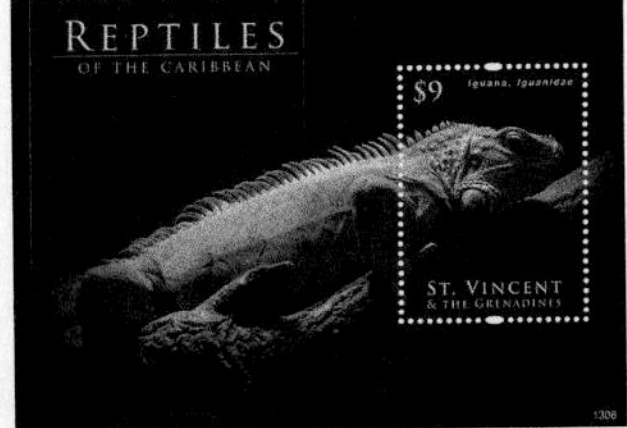

Reptiles — A765

No. 3886, horiz.: a, Dwarf gecko. b, Hawksbill turtle. c, Brown anole. d, Mona boa.
$9, Iguana.

***Perf. 13 Syncopated***

**2013, Nov. 28 Litho.**
**3886** A765 $3.50 Sheet of 4, #a-d 10.50 10.50

**Souvenir Sheet**

**3887** A765 $9 multi 6.75 6.75

Miniature Sheet

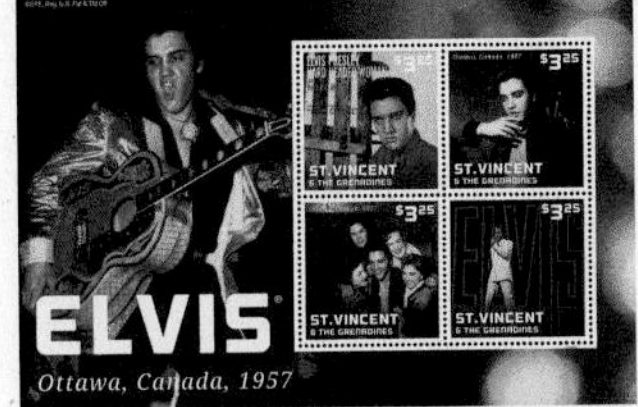

Elvis Presley (1935-77) — A766

No. 3888 — Presley: a, On album cover. b, Touching chin. c, With four women. d, Singing.

**2013, Dec. 2 Litho. *Perf. 13¾***
**3888** A766 $3.25 Sheet of 4, #a-d 9.75 9.75

Christmas A767

Paintings: 80c, Madonna, by Don Lorenzo Monaco. $1.70, The Adoration of the Magi, by Stefano da Verona. $2, Nativity, by Giorigione. $2.20, The Annunciation, by Masolino da Panicale.
$9, Nativity, by Piero della Francesa.

**2013, Dec. 2 Litho. *Perf. 12¾***
**3889-3892** A767 Set of 4 5.00 5.00

**Souvenir Sheet**

**3893** A767 $9 multi 6.75 6.75

Pres. Barack Obama — A768

Designs: $3.25, Pres. Obama.
No. 3895, $9, Pres. Obama sitting. No. 3896, $9, Pres. Obama golfing with Vice President Joseph Biden.

**2013, Dec. 9 Litho. *Perf. 14***
**3894** A768 $3.25 multi 2.40 2.40

**Souvenir Sheets**

***Perf. 12¾***

**3895-3896** A768 Set of 2 13.50 13.50

No. 3894 was printed in sheets of 4. Nos. 3895-3896 each contain one 38x51mm stamp.

A769

Nelson Mandela (1918-2013), President of South Africa — A770

No. 3898 — Mandela: a, Wearing black and gray shirt. b, Standing in front of building. c, Holding microphone stand. d, With arms extended. e, Pointing. f, With raised fist.
No. 3899, $9, Mandela casting ballot, vert. No. 3900, $9, Mandela standing in front of building, diff., vert.

**2013, Dec. 15 Litho. *Perf. 13¾***
**3897** A769 $2.50 shown 1.90 1.90
**3898** A770 $2.50 Sheet of 6, #a-f 11.50 11.50

**Souvenir Sheets**

***Perf. 12¾***

**3899-3900** A770 Set of 2 13.50 13.50

Nos. 3899-3900 each contain one 38x51mm stamp.

Cat Breeds — A771

No. 3901, $3.25: a, Aegean. b, Mekong Bobtail. c, Australian Mist. d, Brazilian Shorthair.
No. 3902, $3.25: a, American Shorthair. b, British Burmese. c, Ocicat. d, Oriental Shorthair.
No. 3903, $9, Cyprus Shorthair. No. 3904, $9, European Shorthair.

**2013, Dec. 18 Litho. *Perf. 13¾***

**Sheets of 4, #a-d**

**3901-3902** A771 Set of 2 19.50 19.50

**Souvenir Sheets**

**3903-3904** A771 Set of 2 13.50 13.50

Miniature Sheet

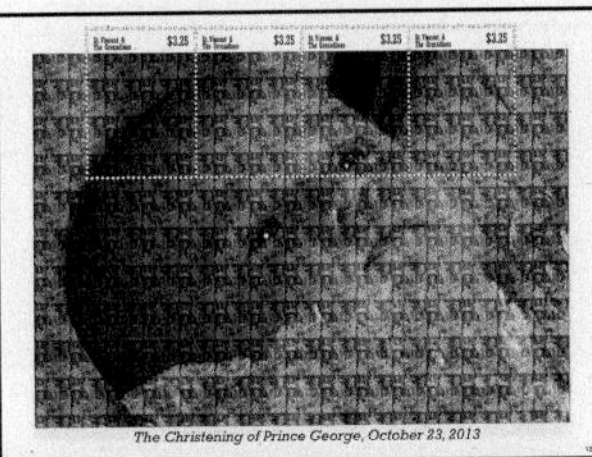

Christening of Prince George of Cambridge — A772

No. 3905: a, Top of head. b, Forehead. c, Eye. d, Upper cheek.

**2013, Dec. 31 Litho. *Perf. 14***
**3905** A772 $3.25 Sheet of 4, #a-d 9.75 9.75

Yoesmite National Park, California — A773

No. 3906, $3.25: a, Half Dome Mountain. b, Gray wolf. c, Firefall at Horsetail Falls. d, Mountain lion.
No. 3907, $3.25: a, Merced River. b, Tenaya Lake. c, Yosemite Waterfalls. d, Yosemite Valley.
No. 3908, $9, Western mule deer, horiz. No. 3909, $9, Rock formation in Yosemite Valley, horiz.

**2014, Jan. 2 Litho. *Perf. 13¾***

**Sheets of 4, #a-d**

**3906-3907** A773 Set of 2 19.50 19.50

**Souvenir Sheets**

***Perf. 12¾***

**3908-3909** A773 Set of 2 13.50 13.50

Nos. 3908-3909 each contain one 51x38mm stamp.

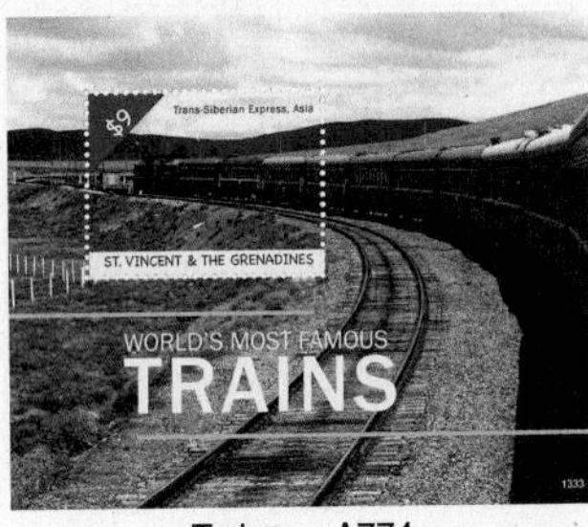

Trains — A774

No. 3910: a, TGV, France. b, Blue Train, South Africa. c, Orient Express, Europe. d, Bullet Train, Japan.
$9, Trans-Siberian Express, Asia.

**2014, Jan. 14 Litho. *Perf. 14***
**3910** A774 $3.25 Sheet of 4, #a-d 9.75 9.75

**Souvenir Sheet**

***Perf. 12***

**3911** A774 $9 multi 6.75 6.75

Garden Flowers — A775

No. 3912: a, Great bougainvillea. b, Hibiscus. c, Iris. No. 3913: a, Lily. b, Bearded iris. c, Bird of paradise.
No. 3914: a, Peony. b, Tulip. No. 3915: a, Iris, diff. b, Hyacinth.

**2014, Feb. 6 Litho. *Perf. 12¾***

**Sheets of 3, #a.-c.**

**3912-3913** A775 $6.25 Set of 2 28.00 28.00

**Souvenir Sheets of 2, #a.-b.**

**3914-3915** A775 $9.50 Set of 2 28.00 28.00

Characters From *Downton Abbey* Television Series — A776

No. 3916: a, Mr. Bates. b, Thomas Barrow. c, Mr. Carson. d, Tom Branson.

$9, William Mason and Thomas Barrow, horiz.

**2014, Mar. 5 Litho. *Perf. 14***

**3916** A776 $3.25 Sheet of 4, #a-d 9.75 9.75

**Souvenir Sheet**

**3917** A776 $9 multi 6.75 6.75

World War I, Cent. — A777

No. 3918, $3.25: a, Austro-Hungarian soldier with rifle. b, Austro-Hungarian soldier without weapon. c, Russian bugler. d, Russian artilleryman.

No. 3919, $3.25: a, German cavalryman, blue gray background. b, Russian cavalryman. c, German cavalryman, bucking horse, gray green background. d, British cavalryman.

No. 3920, $5 — German cavalryman with: a, Blue gray background. b, Dull green background.

No. 3921, $5, vert.: a, Russian soldier pointing pistol. b, Austro-Hungarian soldier pointing rifle.

**2014, Mar. 24 Litho. *Perf. 14***

**Sheets of 4, #a-d**

**3918-3919** A777 Set of 2 19.50 19.50

**Souvenir Sheets**

***Perf. 12¾***

**3920-3921** A777 Set of 2 15.00 15.00

No. 3920 contains two 51x38mm stamps. No, 3921 contains two 38x51mm stamps.

A778

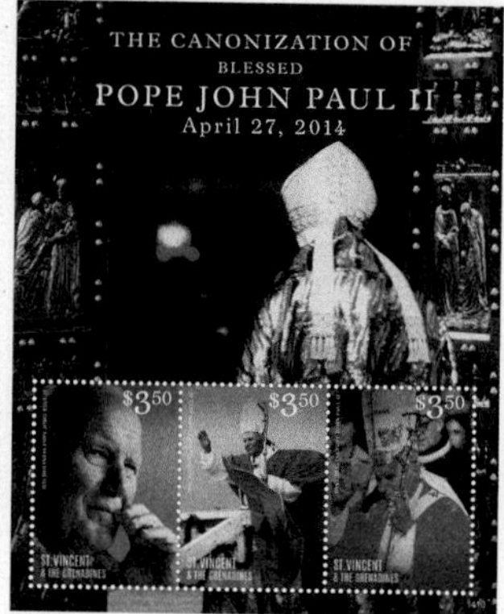


Canonization of Pope John Paul II — A779

No. 3922 — Pope John Paul II: a, As younger man, wearing biretta. b, Wearing miter and striped robe. c, With Mother Teresa.

No. 3923 — Pope John Paul II: a, With hand near mouth. b, On stairway, holding staff, wearing miter, waving. c, Wearing miter, holding staff.

No. 3924, $5, horiz. — Pope John Paul II: a, Facing crowd with arms extended. b, Holding staff, wearing miter, waving, diff.

No. 3925, $5, horiz. — Pope John Paul II: a, With Mother Teresa, diff. b, With cardinals.

**2014, May 5 Litho. *Perf. 12***

**3922** A778 $3.50 Sheet of 3, #a-c 7.75 7.75

**3923** A779 $3.50 Sheet of 3, #a-c 7.75 7.75

**Souvenir Sheets of 2, #a-b**

**3924-3925** A779 Set of 2 15.00 15.00

Panama Canal, Cent. — A780

No. 3926: a, Miraflores Locks, 2014. b, Miraflores Locks under construction, 1912. c, Ship in Panama Canal, 2014. d, SS Kroonland in Panama Canal, 1915.

No. 3927: a, Centennial Bridge. b, Ship in Panama Canal lock.

**2014, May 12 Litho. *Perf. 14***

**3926** A780 $3.25 Sheet of 4, #a-d 9.75 9.75

**Souvenir Sheet**

***Perf. 12***

**3927** A780 $5 Sheet of 2, #a-b 7.50 7.50

A781

A782

A783

Taekwondo — A784

Various positions, kicks and jumps, as shown.

**2014, May 12 Litho. *Perf. 12¾***

**3928** A781 $3.25 Sheet of 4, #a-d 9.75 9.75

**3929** A782 $3.25 Sheet of 4, #a-d 9.75 9.75

**Souvenir Sheets**

**3930** A783 $5 Sheet of 2, #a-b 7.50 7.50

**3931** A784 $5 Sheet of 2, #a-b 7.50 7.50

Philakorea 2014 World Stamp Exhibition, Seoul.

Farm Animals — A785

No. 3932, $3.25: a, Anas platyrhynchos (female ducks). b, Anas platyrhynchos (male mallard ducks). c, Turkey. d, Chicken.

No. 3933, $3.25: a, Charolais cattle. b, Zebus. c, Bison. d, Pigs.

No. 3934, $5, vert.: a, Arabian horses. b, Shetland ponies.

No. 3935, $5, vert.: a, Wild goats. b, Sheep.

**2014, May 19 Litho. *Perf. 14***

**Sheets of 4, #a-d**

**3932-3933** A785 Set of 2 19.50 19.50

**Souvenir Sheets of 2, #a-b**

**3934-3935** A785 Set of 2 15.00 15.00

A786

A787

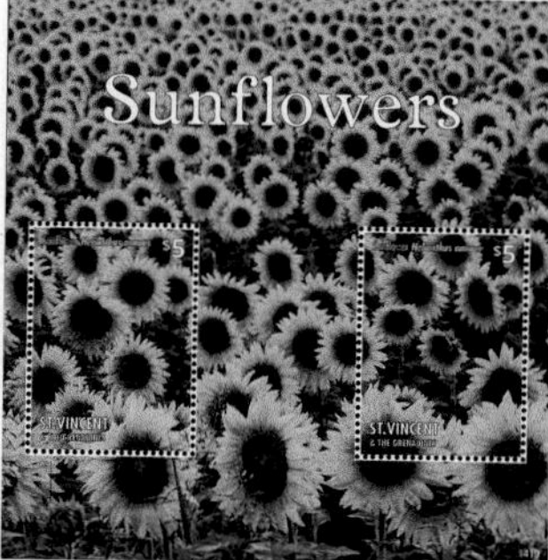


Sunflowers — A788

Various sunflowers, as shown.

**2014, June 23 Litho. *Perf. 14***

**3936** A786 $3.25 Sheet of 4, #a-d 9.75 9.75

**3937** A787 $3.25 Sheet of 4, #a-d 9.75 9.75

**Souvenir Sheets**

**3938** A788 $5 Sheet of 2, #a-b 7.50 7.50

***Perf. 12¾***

**3939** A787 $10 Sunflower, horiz. 7.50 7.50

No. 3939 contains one 51x38mm stamp.

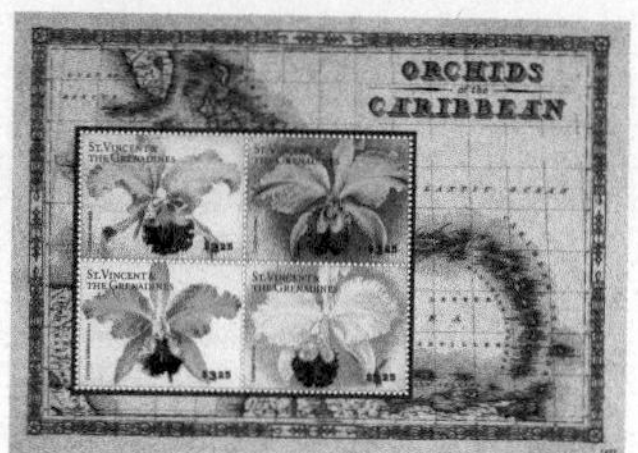


A789

A790

A791

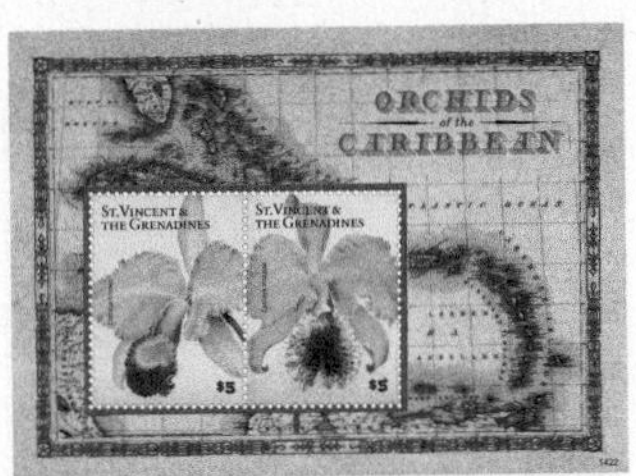


Orchids — A792

No. 3940: a, Cattleya mendelii. b, Cattleya trianae. c, Cattleya luddemanniana. d, Cattleya trianae, diff.
No. 3941: a, Cattleya mossiae. b, Cattleya trianae, diff. c, Cattleya mossiae, diff. d, Cattleya trianae, diff.
No. 3942: a, Cattleya trianae, diff. b, Cattleya trianae, diff.
No. 3943: a, Cattleya trianae, diff. b, Cattleya mossiae, diff.

**2014, July 1 Litho. *Perf. 14***

**3940** A789 $3.25 Sheet of 4, #a-d 9.75 9.75
**3941** A790 $3.25 Sheet of 4, #a-d 9.75 9.75

**Souvenir Sheets**

***Perf. 12***

**3942** A791 $5 Sheet of 2, #a-b 7.50 7.50
**3943** A792 $5 Sheet of 2, #a-b 7.50 7.50

March 27, 2014 Meeting of Pres. Barack Obama and Pope Francis — A793

Designs: $2, Pres. Obama and Pope Francis.
No. 3945 — Pres. Obama and Pope Francis with: a, Painting behind head of Pope Francis. b, Window behing Pope Francis.
No. 3946, vert.: a, Pope Francis. b, Pres. Obama.
$10, Pres. Obama and Pope Francis, vert.

**2014, July 21 Litho. *Perf. 13¾***

**3944** A793 $2 multi 1.50 1.50
**3945** A793 $2.25 Horiz. pair, #a-b 3.50 3.50

**Souvenir Sheets**

***Perf. 12¾***

**3946** A793 $5 Sheet of 2, #a-b 7.50 7.50
**3947** A793 $10 multi 7.50 7.50

No. 3944 was printed in sheets of 6. No. 3945 was printed in sheets of 9, containing six No. 3945a and three No. 3945b. No. 3946 contains two 38x51mm stamps. No. 3947 contains one 38x51mm stamp.

Paintings — A794

No. 3948, $3.50: a, The Cradle, by Berthe Morisot. b, Le Guitare, by Georges Braque. c, Berlin Street Scene, by Ernst Ludwig Kirchner.
No. 3949, $3.50: a, The Football Players, by Henri Rousseau. b, Boy on the Rocks, by Rousseau. c, Still Life with Cherub, by Paul Cézanne.
No. 3950, $10, Open Window, by Henri Matisse. No. 3951, $10, Shore with Red House, by Edvard Munch.

**2014, Aug. 14 Litho. *Perf. 12¾***

**Sheets of 3, #a-c**

**3948-3949** A794 Set of 2 15.50 15.50

**Size: 100x100mm**

***Imperf***

**3950-3951** A794 Set of 2 15.00 15.00

Worldwide Fund for Nature (WWF) — A795

Nos. 3952 and 3953: Various depictions of Semipalmated sandpiper, as shown.

**2014, Sept. 15 Litho. *Perf. 14***

**3952** A795 $1.25 Block or vert. strip of 4, #a-d 3.75 3.75
**3953** A795 $2.75 Block or vert. strip of 4, #a-d 8.25 8.25

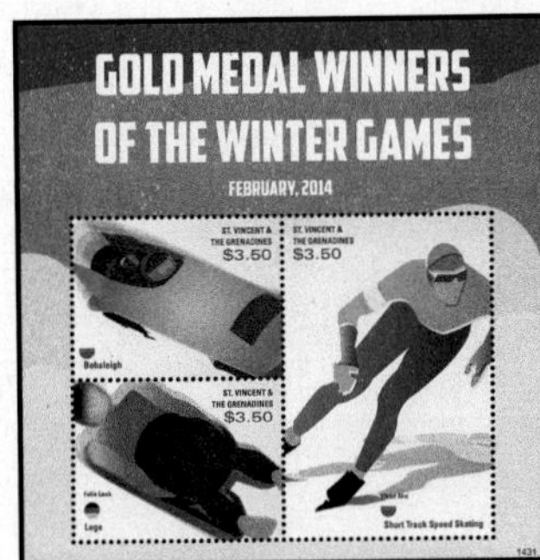


2014 Winter Olympics Gold Medalists — A796

No. 3954: a, Russian Men's two-man bobsled team (40x30mm). b, Felix Lach, luge, Germany (40x30mm). c, Viktor Ahn, short track speed skating, Russia (40x60mm).
No. 3955: a, Michael Mulder, speed skating, Netherlands (40x30mm). b, Alexander Tretiakov, skeleton, Russia (40x30mm).

**2014, Sept. 15 Litho. *Perf. 14***

**3954** A796 $3.50 Sheet of 3, #a-c 7.75 7.75

**Souvenir Sheet**

**3955** A796 $5 Sheet of 2, #a-b 7.50 7.50

2014 World Cup Soccer Championships, Brazil — A797

No. 3956 — Central part of Brazilian flag and: a, Stylized soccer ball and map of Brazil. b, Soccer ball and "Brazil." c, Map of Brazil and "2014."
$10, Christ the Redeemer Statue, Rio de Janeiro.

**2014, Sept. 30 Litho. *Perf. 12***

**3956** A797 $3.50 Sheet of 3, #a-c 7.75 7.75

**Souvenir Sheet**

**3957** A797 $10 multi 7.50 7.50

No. 3957 contains one 30x50mm stamp.

Rare Stamps — A798

No. 3958: a, Great Britain #1. b, Mauritius #1. c, France #3.
$10, United States #1.

**2014, Sept. 30 Litho. *Perf. 14***

**3958** A798 $3.50 Sheet of 3, #a-c 7.75 7.75

**Souvenir Sheet**

**3959** A798 $10 multi 7.50 7.50

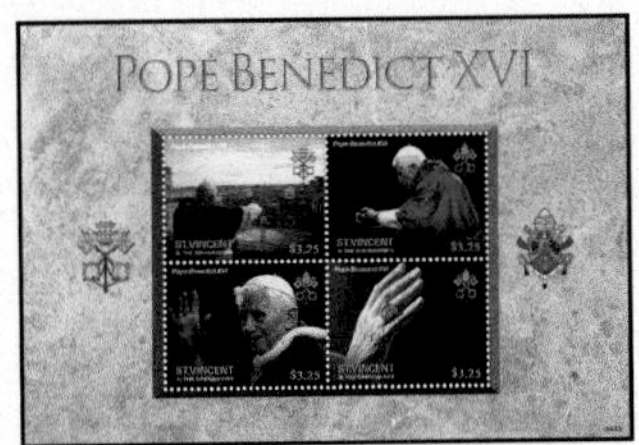


Pope Benedict XVI — A799

No. 3960: a, Pope Benedict XVI waving to crowd in St. Peter's Square. b, Pope Benedict XVI praying. c, Pope Benedict XVI waving. d, Hand of Pope Benedict XVI with papal ring.
$10, Back of head of Pope Benedict XVI.

**2014, Oct. 20 Litho. *Perf. 12½x12***

**3960** A799 $3.25 Sheet of 4, #a-d 9.75 9,75

**Souvenir Sheet**

**3961** A799 $10 multi 7.50 7.50

A800

A801

A802

A803

A804

A805

A806

Dome Designs of St. Basil's Cathedral, Moscow — A807

**2014, Oct. 27 Litho. *Perf. 14x14¾***

**3962** Horiz. strip of 4 3.00 3.00
*a.* A800 $1 multi .75 .75
*b.* A801 $1 multi .75 .75
*c.* A802 $1 multi .75 .75
*d.* A803 $1 multi .75 .75
**3963** Horiz. strip of 4 3.00 3.00
*a.* A804 $1 multi .75 .75
*b.* A805 $1 multi .75 .75
*c.* A806 $1 multi .75 .75
*d.* A807 $1 multi .75 .75

Nos. 3962-3963 are personalizable stamps. Other vignettes can be found.

A808

A809

A810

Matryoshka Dolls — A811

**2014, Oct. 27 Litho. *Perf. 14x14¾***

**3964** Horiz. strip of 4 3.00 3.00
*a.* A808 $1 multi .75 .75
*b.* A809 $1 multi .75 .75
*c.* A810 $1 multi .75 .75
*d.* A811 $1 multi .75 .75

Nos. 3964a-3964d are personalizable stamps. Other vignettes can be found.

Paintings by El Greco (1541-1614) — A812

No. 3965, $3.50: a, The Disrobing of Christ. b, Portrait of a Cardinal. c, Christ on the Cross with Two Maries and St. John.

No. 3966, $3.50: a, Coronation of the Virgin. b, Female Portrait. c, St. Paul and St. Peter.

No. 3967, $10, An Allegory with a Boy Lighting a Candle in the Company of an Ape and a Fool. No. 3968, $10, The Agony in the Garden of Gethsemane.

***Perf. 12, 14 (#3966)***

**2014, Nov. 3 Litho.**

**Sheets of 3, #a-c**

**3965-3966** A812 Set of 2 15.50 15.50

**Size: 60x120mm**

***Imperf***

**3967-3968** A812 Set of 2 15.00 15.00

Souvenir Sheets

Elvis Presley (1935-77) — A813

Various photographs of Presley: No. 3969, $10, With guitar, hands not visible, blue panel. No. 3970, $10, With guitar, hands visible, blue panel. No. 3971, $10, With arm raised, yellow green panel. No. 3972, $10, As child, with parents, red orange panel.

**2014, Nov. 11 Litho. *Perf. 14***

**3969-3972** A813 Set of 4 30.00 30.00

Christmas A814

Details from paintings by Peter Paul Rubens: $2.20, Assumption of the Virgin Mary, 1626. $2.25, Assumption of the Virgin Mary, 1626, diff. $3.50, Annunciation, 1628. $5, Annunciation, 1615-20.

**2014, Nov. 24 Litho. *Perf. 12¾***

**3973-3976** A814 Set of 4 9.75 9.75

World War I Battle of the Somme — A815

No. 3977, $3.25: a, A ration limber near La Boisselle, 1916. b, David Lloyd George meets with British Minister of Munitions. c, Welsh Guards in a reserve trench near Guillemont. d, London Heavy Battery near Contalmaison, August 1916 (cannon and horse).

No. 3978: a, $3.25: a, British infantry advance at Battle of the Somme, 1916. b, Albert Thomas with French artillery gunners, Fricourt, 1916. c, German prisoners pulling water cart, Contalmaison, 1916. d, London Heavy Battery near Contalmaison, August 1916 (soldiers carrying wounded comrade on litter).

No. 3979, $10, British troops crossing La Boisselle to Contalmaison, July 1916. No. 3980, $10, British infantry waiting to advance at Battle of the Somme, 1916.

**2015, Jan. 1 Litho. *Perf. 14***

**Sheets of 4, #a-d**

**3977-3978** A815 Set of 2 19.50 19.50

**Souvenir Sheets**

***Perf. 12½***

**3979-3980** A815 Set of 2 15.00 15.00

Nos. 3979-3980 each contain one 51x38mm stamp.

Fountains — A816

No. 3981: a, Trevi Fountain, Rome. b, Magic Fountain of Montjuic, Barcelona. c, Fountain of Wealth, Singapore. d, Archibald Fountain, Sydney. e, Founains of Bellagio, Las Vegas. f, Swarovski Fountain, Wattens, Austria.

$10, Friendship of the Peoples Fountain, Moscow, vert.

**2015, Jan. 2 Litho. *Perf. 14***

**3981** A816 $3.15 Sheet of 6, #a-f 14.00 14.00

**Souvenir Sheet**

***Perf. 12***

**3982** A816 $10 multi 7.50 7.50

Pope John Paul II (1920-2005) — A817

No. 3983 — Pope John Paul II: a, Wearing biretta. b, Wearing miter. c, With Mother Teresa.

No. 3984, horiz. — Pope John Paul II: a, Greeting crowd with arms extended. b, Wearing miter and holding ferula.

**2015, Feb. 2 Litho. *Perf. 14***

**3983** A817 $3.50 Sheet of 3, #a-c 7.75 7.75

**Souvenir Sheet**

**3984** A817 $5 Sheet of 2, #a-b 7.50 7.50

A818

Taipei 2015 Intl. Stamp Exhibition — A819

No. 3985 — Taiwanese buildings and bridges: a, Shorefront buildings, Kaohsiung (30x40mm). b, Dragon and Tiger Pagodas, Kaohsiung (30x40mm). c, Taipei 101 Building, Taipei (30x80mm). d, Wan Yue Bridge, Tainan (30x40mm). e, Waterfront buildings, Taichung (30x40mm). f, Temple, Taipei (30x40mm). g, Skyscrapers, Taichung (30x40mm).

No. 3986 — Taiwanese animals: a, Formosan sambar deer. b, Formosan black bear. c, Common otter. d, Formosan Reeve's muntjac.

No. 3987, $10, Chiang Kai-shek Memorial Hall. No. 3988, $10, Formosan rock macaque, vert.

**2015, Mar. 2 Litho. *Perf. 14***

**3985** A818 $3.15 Sheet of 7, #a-g 16.50 16.50
**3986** A819 $3.25 Sheet of 4, #a-d 9.75 9.75

**Souvenir Sheets**

***Perf. 12***

**3987** A818 $10 multi 7.50 7.50
**3988** A819 $10 multi 7.50 7.50

Souvenir Sheet

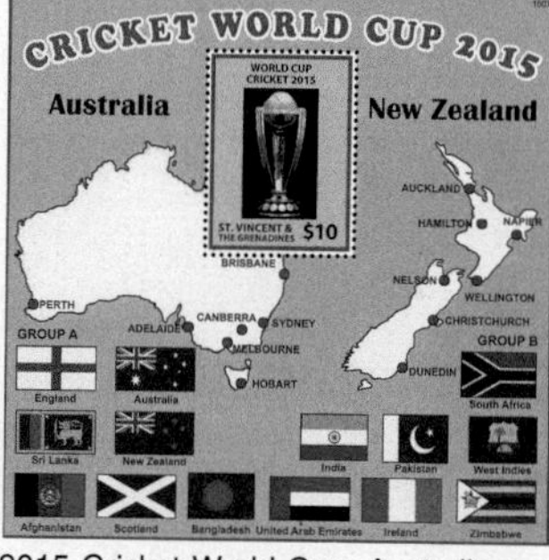


2015 Cricket World Cup, Australia and New Zealand — A820

**2015, Apr. 13 Litho. *Perf. 12***

**3989** A820 $10 multi 7.50 7.50

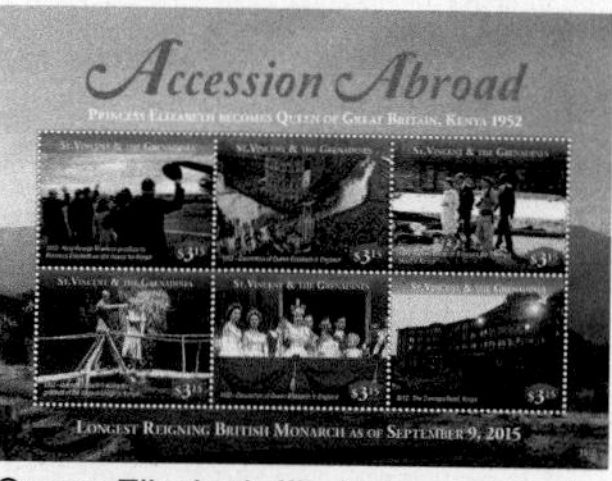


Queen Elizabeth II's Accession to the Throne — A821

No. 3990: a, King George V waving goodbye to Princess Elizabeth as she leaves for Kenya, 1952. b, Coronation parade of Queen Elizabeth II, 1953. c, Queen Elizabeth II's return to Treetops Hotel, Kenya, 1983. d, Princess Elizabeth II and her husband at Sagana Lodge, Kenya, 1952. e, Queen Elizabeth II at coronation, 1953. f, Treetops Hotel, 2012.

$10, Princess Elizabeth at Treetops Hotel, 1952.

**2015, May 25 Litho. *Perf. 14***

**3990** A821 $3.15 Sheet of 6, #a-f 14.00 14.00

**Souvenir Sheet**

***Perf. 12½***

**3991** A821 $10 multi 7.50 7.50

No. 3991 contains one 51x38mm stamp.

Miniature Sheets

Airships of World War I — A822

No. 3992, $1.15 — British airships: a, His Majesty's Naval Airship No. 2. b, Beta I. c, Beta II. d, Gamma. e, Gamma II. f, Delta. g, ETA. h, Sea Scout (SS). i, Coastal Class (C). j, Sea Scout Zero (SSZ). k, C-Star Class. l, North Sea Class (NS). m, 23r. n, 24r, o, R27. p, R29.

No. 3993, $1.15 — German airships: a, LZ 1. b, LZ 2. c, LZ 4. d, LZ 5 (Z II). e, LZ 7 (Deutschland). f, LZ 8 (Deutschland II). g, LZ 10 (Schwaben). h, LZ 11 (Viktoria Luise). i, LZ 12 (Z III). j, LZ 13 (Hansa). k, LZ 14 (L 1). l, LZ 16 (Z IV). m, LZ 17 (Sachsen). n, LZ 18 (LZ 2). o, LZ 36 (L 9). p, LZ 38.

**2015, May 25 Litho. *Perf. 14***

**Sheets of 16, #a-p, + label**

**3992-3993** A822 Set of 2 27.50 27.50

Battle of Britain, 75th Anniv. — A823

No. 3994: a, Royal Air Force fighter pilot. b, Hawker Hurricane. c, Old Palace Yard outside the Palace of Westminster. d, Royal Air Force bomber crew.

$10, King George VI and Queen Elizabeth viewing damage to Buckingham Palace.

**2015, Aug. 3 Litho. *Perf. 12***

**3994** A823 $3.25 Sheet of 4, #a-d 9.75 9.75

**Souvenir Sheet**

**3995** A823 $10 multi 7.50 7.50

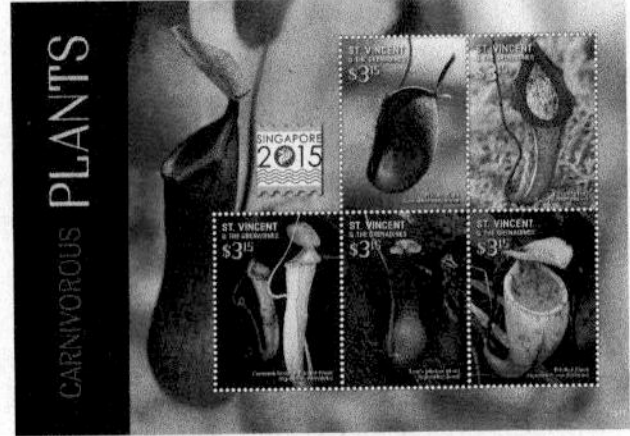


Carnivorous Plants — A824

No. 3996: a, Nepenthes sanguinea. b, Nepenthes burkei. c, Nepenthes mirabilis. d, Nepenthes lowii. e, Nepenthes macfarlanei.

$10, Drosera burmannii.

**2015, Aug. 3 Litho. *Perf. 14***

**3996** A824 $3.15 Sheet of 5, #a-e 12.00 12.00

**Souvenir Sheet**

***Perf. 13¾***

**3997** A824 $10 multi 7.50 7.50

Singapore 2015 Intl. Stamp Exhibition. No. 3997 contains one 35x35mm stamp.

Miniature Sheets

85th Birthday of Pope Benedict XVI — A825

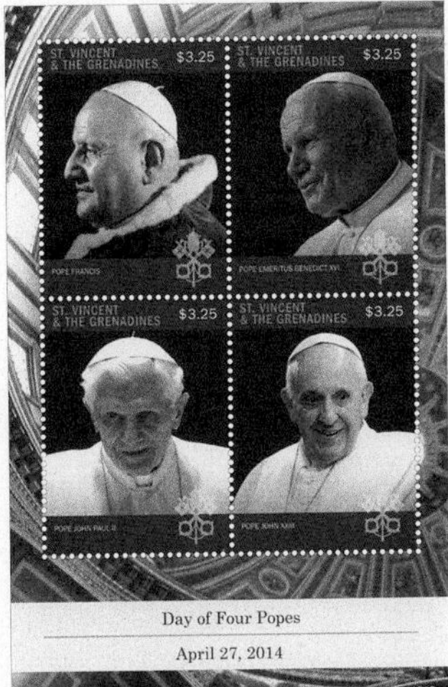


Day of Four Popes — A826

Popes Benedict XVI and Francis — A827

No. 3998 — Pope Benedict XVI: a, Wearing miter and white vestments. b, Wearing white zucchetto and cassock, looking to left. c, Wearing white zucchetto and red vestments. d, Wearing miter and red vestments.

No. 3999 — Erroneous inscriptions: a, Pope Francis (Pope John XXIII pictured). b, Pope Benedict XVI ( Pope John Paul II pictured). c, Pope John Paul II (Pope Benedict XVI pictured). d, Pope John XXIII (Pope Francis pictured).

No. 4000: a, Pope Benedict XVI (more of zucchetto visible than No. 3998c). b, Pope Francis waving. c, Pope Francis, hand not visible, top of zucchetto not visible. d, Pope Benedict XVI wearing white zucchetto and cassock, looking straight ahead.

**2015, Aug. 10 Litho. *Perf. 14***

**3998** A825 $3.25 Sheet of 4, #a-d 9.75 9.75

**3999** A826 $3.25 Sheet of 4, #a-d 9.75 9.75

**4000** A827 $3.25 Sheet of 4, #a-d 9.75 9.75

*Nos. 3998-4000 (3)* 29.25 29.25

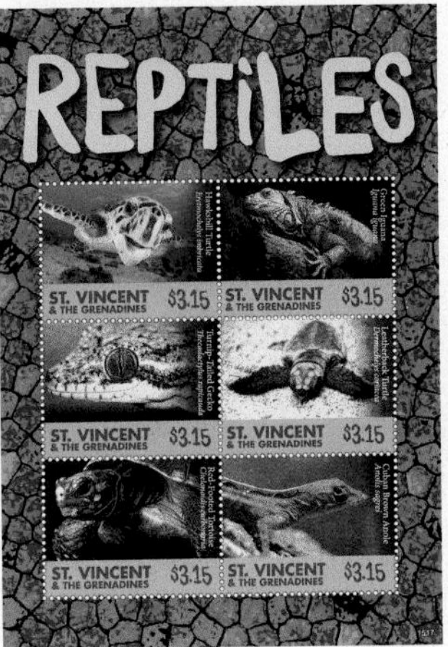


Reptiles — A828

No. 4001: a, Hawksbill turtle. b, Green iguana. c, Turnip-tailed gecko. d, Leatherback turtle. e, Red-footed tortoise. f, Cuban brown anole.

$10, Tropical house gecko.

**2015, Sept. 8 Litho. *Perf. 12½x13¼***

**4001** A828 $3.15 Sheet of 6, #a-f 14.00 14.00

**Souvenir Sheet**

***Perf. 13¼***

**4002** A828 $10 multi 7.50 7.50

No. 4002 contains one 51x38mm stamp.

Paintings by Vincent van Gogh (1853-90) — A829

No. 4003: a, Portrait of a Man, 1888. b, Portrait of Patience Escalier, 1888. c, Portrait of Eugene Boch, 1888. d, Madame Roulin Rocking the Cradle (La Berceuse), 1889. e, Head of a Peasant with a Pipe, 1885. f, Joseph Etienne Roulin, 1889.

$10, Self-portrait with a Gray Felt Hat, 1887.

**2015, Sept. 30 Litho. *Perf. 14***

**4003** A829 $3.15 Sheet of 6, #a-f 14.00 14.00

**Souvenir Sheet**

***Perf. 12½***

**4004** A829 $10 multi 7.50 7.50

No. 4004 contains one 38x51mm stamp.

Christmas A830

Paintings by Fra Angelico (c. 1395-1455): 90c, Madonna of Humility. $2.25, Annunciation of Cortona. $3.50, San Marco Altarpiece. $5, Annunciation.

**2015, Nov. 2 Litho. *Perf. 12¾***

**4005-4008** A830 Set of 4 8.75 8.75

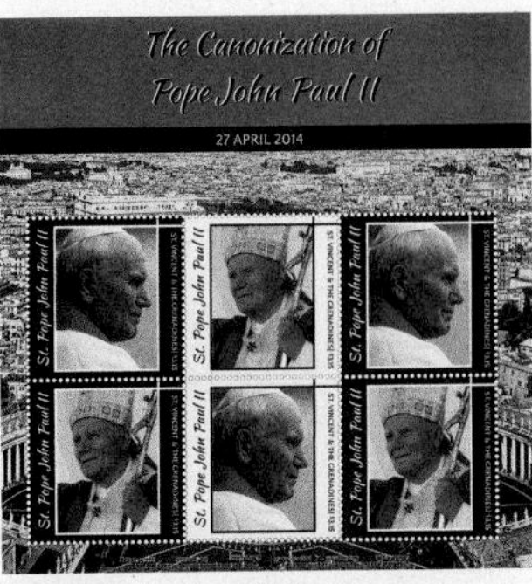


A831

Canonization of Pope John Paul II (1920-2005) — A832

No. 4009, $3.15 — St. John Paul II: a, Facing right, text in white. b, Facing left, text in white. c, Facing left, text in black. d, Facing right, text in black.

No. 4010, $3.25 — St. John Paul II with background color of: a, Green. b, Gray.

No. 4011, $10, St. John Paul II holding crucifix. No. 4012, $10, St. John Paul II with arms raised.

**2015, Dec. 1 Litho. *Perf. 13¾***

**4009** A831 Sheet of 6, 2 each #4009a-4009b, 1 each #4009c-4009d 14.00 14.00

**4010** A832 Sheet of 4, 2 each #4010a-4010b 9.75 9.75

**Souvenir Sheets**

***Perf.***

**4011-4012** A832 Set of 2 15.00 15.00

Nos. 4011-4012 each have one 38mm diameter stamp.

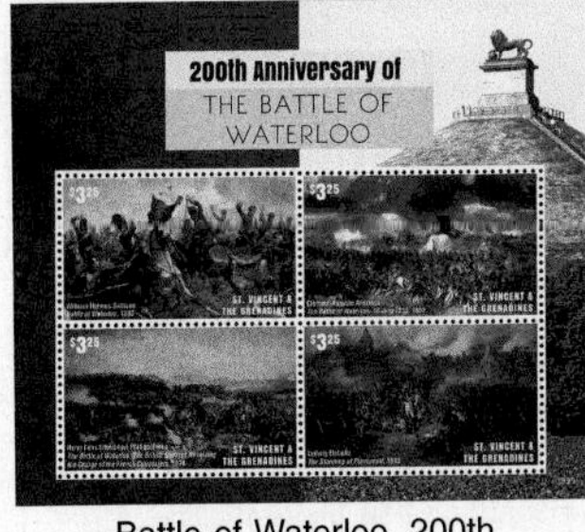


Battle of Waterloo, 200th Anniv. — A833

No. 4013: a, The Battle of Waterloo, by William Holmes Sullivan. b, The Battle of Waterloo, June 18, 1815, by Clément-Auguste Andrieux. c, The Battle of Waterloo: The British Squares Receiving the Charge of the French Cuirassiers, by Henri Félix Emmanuel Philippoteaux. d, The Storming of Plancenoit, by Ludwig Elsholtz.

$10, The Prussian Attack on Plancenoit, by Adolph Northen.

**2015, Dec. 31 Litho. *Perf. 12***

**4013** A833 $3.75 Sheet of 4, #a-d 9.75 9.75

**Souvenir Sheet**

**4014** A833 $10 multi 7.50 7.50

A834

A835

A836

Wild Dogs — A837

Designs as shown. Nos. 4015a-4015b, 4016a-4016b are 35x35mm, Nos. 4015c and 4016c are 35x70mm.

**2015, Dec. 31 Litho. *Perf. 13¾***

**4015** A834 $3.50 Sheet of 3, #a-c 7.75 7.75
**4016** A835 $3.50 Sheet of 3, #a-c 7.75 7.75

**Souvenir Sheets**

***Perf. 12½***

**4017** A836 $10 multi 7.50 7.50
**4018** A837 $10 multi 7.50 7.50

Ducks — A838

No. 4019, $3.25: a, Common merganser. b, Bucephala albeola. c, Common pochard. d, Hooded merganser.

No. 4020, $3.25: a, Smew. b, Freckled duck. c, Surf scoter. d, Canvasback.

No. 4021, $10, Red-crested pochard. No. 4022, $10, Torrent duck, vert.

**2015, Dec. 31 Litho. *Perf. 14***

**Sheets of 4, #a-d**

**4019-4020** A838 Set of 2 19.50 19.50

**Souvenir Sheets**

***Perf. 12***

**4021-4022** A838 Set of 2 15.00 15.00

A839

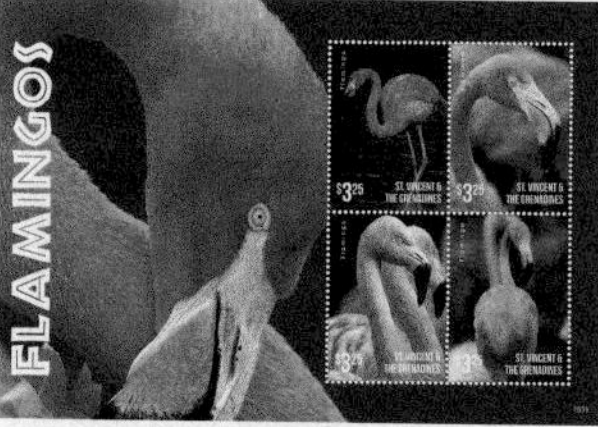

Flamingos — A840

Nos. 4023-4024 as shown.

No. 4025 — Head of flamingo facing: a, Right. b, Left.

$10, Flamingo, diff.

**2015, Dec. 31 Litho. *Perf. 14***

**4023** A839 $3.25 Sheet of 4, #a-d 9.75 9.75
**4024** A840 $3.25 Sheet of 4, #a-d 9.75 9.75

**Souvenir Sheets**

***Perf. 12***

**4025** A840 $5 Sheet of 2, #a-b 7.50 7.50
**4026** A840 $10 multi 7.50 7.50

A841

A842

A843

Great Egret — A844

No. 4027: a, Bird standing, b, Bird with extended wings.

No. 4028: a, Bird in flight over water. b, Bird on tree. c, Head of bird. d, Bird in flight.

No. 4029, Adult and chick. No. 4030, Chick.

***Perf. 14 (#4027, 4029), 12 (#4028, 4030)***

**2015, Dec. 31 Litho.**

**4027** A841 $3.15 Pair, #a-b 4.75 4.75
**4028** A842 $3.25 Sheet of 4, #a-d 9.75 9.75

**Souvenir Sheets**

**4029** A843 $10 multi 7.50 7.50
**4030** A844 $10 multi 7.50 7.50

Pope Francis in New York City — A845

No. 4031 — Pope Francis: a, Facing forward, denomination at UR. b, Waving, hand below denomination at UL. c, Waving, hand below denomination at UR. d, Facing forward, denomination at UL. e, Facing right, denomination at UR. f, Waving, hand at level of denomination at UL.

$10, Pope Francis waving, diff.

**2015, Dec. 31 Litho. *Perf. 14***

**4031** A845 $3.15 Sheet of 6, #a-f 14.00 14.00

**Souvenir Sheet**

***Perf. 12***

**4032** A845 $10 multi 7.50 7.50

Paintings — A846

No. 4033, $3.50 — Paintings by Diego Velázquez: a, Las Meninas. b, Portrait of Innocent X. c, The Surrender of Breda.

No. 4034, $3.50: a, The Girl with the Pearl Earring, by Johannes Vermeer. b, Self-portrait, by Albrecht Dürer. c, Laughing Cavalier, by Frans Hals.

No. 4035, $10, Luncheon of the Boating Party, by Auguste Renoir. No. 4036, $10, Judith Beheading Holofernes, by Michelangelo Merisi da Caravaggio.

**2015, Dec. 31 Litho. *Perf. 12½***

**Sheets of 3, #a-c**

**4033-4034** A846 Set of 2 15.50 15.50

**Size: 100x100mm**

***Imperf***

**4035-4036** A846 Set of 2 15.00 15.00

A847

A848

A849

Coral Reefs — A850

Nos. 4037 and 4038 as shown.

**2015, Dec. 31 Litho. *Perf. 14***

**4037** A847 $3.15 Sheet of 6, #a-f 14.00 14.00
**4038** A848 $3.25 Sheet of 4, #a-d 9.75 9.75

**Souvenir Sheets**

***Perf. 12½***

**4039** A849 $10 multi 7.50 7.50
**4040** A850 $10 multi 7.50 7.50

Sharks — A851

No. 4041: a, Blacktip reef shark. b, Hammerhead shark. c, Whale shark. d, Caribbean reef shark. e, Lemon shark. f, Nurse shark.
No. 4042: a, Tiger shark. b, Great white shark. c, Bull shark. d, Oceanic whitetip shark.
No. 4043, $10, Zebra shark. No. 4044, $10, Pelagic thresher shark.

**2015, Dec. 31 Litho. *Perf. 14***

**4041** A851 $3.15 Sheet of 6, #a-f 14.00 14.00
**4042** A851 $3.25 Sheet of 4, #a-d 9.75 9.75

**Souvenir Sheets**

***Perf. 12½***

**4043-4044** A851 Set of 2 15.00 15.00

Nos. 4043-4044 each contain one 51x38mm stamp.

Birds — A852

No. 4045: a, Glossy ibis. b, Brown pelican. c, Great blue heron. d, Manx shearwater. e, White-tailed tropicbird. f, Pied-billed grebe.
No. 4046: a, Green heron. b, Magnificent frigatebird. c, Roseate spoonbill. d, Great egret.
$10, Red-billed tropicbird.

**2015, Dec. 31 Litho. *Perf. 14***

**4045** A852 $3.15 Sheet of 6, #a-f 14.00 14.00
**4046** A852 $3.25 Sheet of 4, #a-d 9.75 9.75

**Souvenir Sheet**

**4047** A852 $10 multi 7.50 7.50

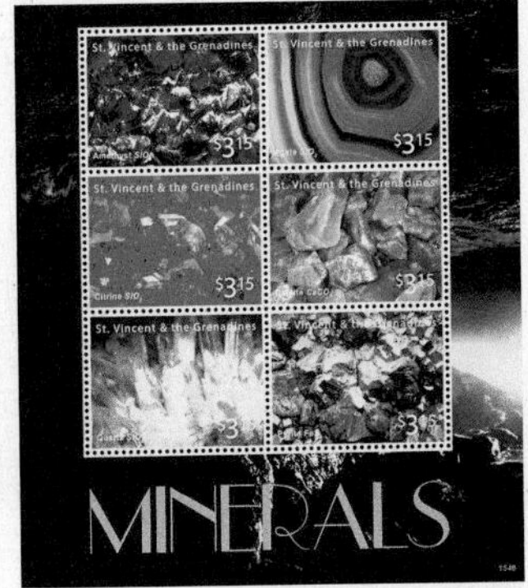

Minerals — A853

No. 4048: a, Amethyst. b, Agate. c, Citrine. d, Calcite. e, Quartz. f, Pyrite.
No. 4049: a, Onyx agate. b, Rose quartz. c, Citrine, diff. d, Emerald.
$10, Amethyst, diff.

**2016, Jan. 28 Litho. *Perf. 12½x13¼***

**4048** A853 $3.15 Sheet of 6, #a-f 14.00 14.00

***Perf. 12½x12***

**4049** A853 $3.25 Sheet of 4, #a-d 9.75 9.75

**Souvenir Sheet**

**4050** A853 $10 multi 7.50 7.50

Flowers & Plants

Flora — A854

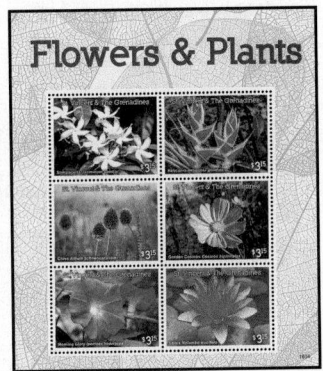

No. 4051: a, Sampaguita. b, Heliconia. c, Chives. d, Garden cosmos. e, Morning glories. f, Lotus.
No. 4052: a, Hibiscus. b, Frangipani. c, Bird of paradise. d, Maxillaria.
$10, Hibiscus, diff.

**2016, Jan. 28 Litho. *Perf. 14***

**4051** A854 $3.15 Sheet of 6, #a-f 14.00 14.00

***Perf. 12***

**4052** A854 $3.25 Sheet of 4, #a-d 9.75 9.75

**Souvenir Sheet**

**4053** A854 $10 multi 7.50 7.50

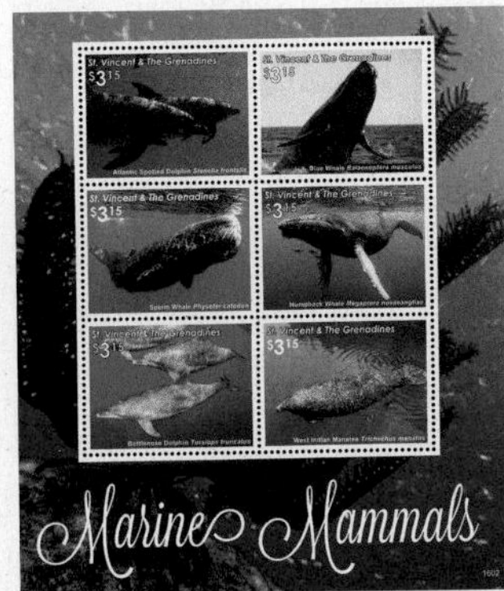

Marine Mammals — A855

No. 4054: a, Atlantic spotted dolphins. b, Blue whale. c, Sperm whale. d, Humpback whale. e, Bottlenose dolphins. f, West Indian manatee.

No. 4052: a, Humpback whale, diff. b, Atlantic spotted dolphin. c, Bottlenose dolphin. d, Spinner dolphins.
$10, West Indian manatee, diff.

**2016, Jan. 28 Litho. *Perf. 14***

**4054** A855 $3.15 Sheet of 6, #a-f 14.00 14.00
**4055** A855 $3.25 Sheet of 4, #a-d 9.75 9.75

**Souvenir Sheet**

**4056** A855 $10 multi 7.50 7.50

Shells — A856

No. 4057: a, Common American auger. b, Nautilus. c, Scotch bonnet. d, Yellow cockle. e, Rough scallop. f, Longspine star shell.
No. 4058: a, Queen conch. b, Lace murex. c, Abalone. d, Cabrit's murex.
$10, Abalone, diff.

**2016, Jan. 28 Litho. *Perf. 14***

**4057** A856 $3.15 Sheet of 6, #a-f 14.00 14.00
**4058** A856 $3.25 Sheet of 4, #a-d 9.75 9.75

**Souvenir Sheet**

***Perf. 12***

**4059** A856 $10 multi 7.50 7.50

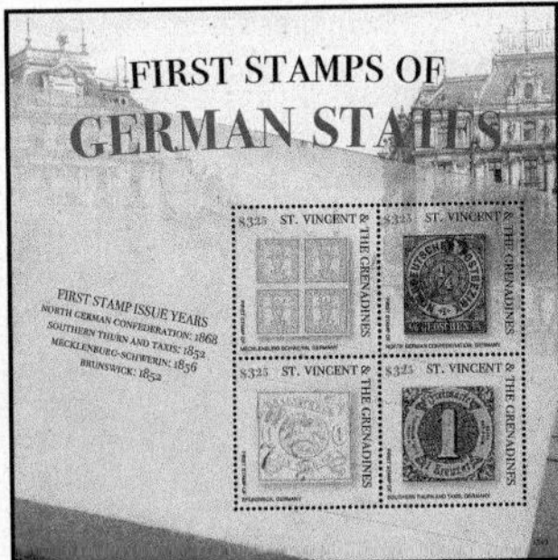

German States Stamps — A857

No. 4060: a, Mecklenburg-Schwerin #1. b, North German Confederation #1. c, Brunswick #1. d, Thurn & Taxis Southern District #42.
No. 4061, $3.25: a, Baden #1. b, Bavaria #1. c, Bergedorf #1. d, Bremen #1. e, Brunswick #3.
No. 4062, $3.25: a, Hamburg #1. b, Hanover #1. c, Lubeck #1. d, Mecklenburg-Schwerin #1a. e, Mecklenburg-Strelitz #1.
No. 4063, $3.25: a, Oldenburg #4. b, Prussia #2. c, Saxony #1. d, Schleswig-Holstein #1. e, Wurttemberg #1.
No. 4064: a, Thurn & Taxis Southern District #42. b, Thurn & Taxis Northern District #1. c, North German Confederation #2.

**2016, Jan. 29 Litho. *Perf. 13¾***

**4060** A857 $3.25 Sheet of 4, #a-d 9.75 9.75

**Sheets of 5, #a-e**

**4061-4063** A857 Set of 3 36.00 36.00

**Souvenir Sheet**

**4064** A857 $3.50 Sheet of 3, #a-c 7.75 7.75

German Colonies Stamps — A858

No. 4065: a, Togo #9. b, German East Africa #27. c, German New Guinea #10. d, German South West Africa #14.
No. 4066: a, Mariana Islands #22. b, Caroline Islands #11. c, Marshall Islands #19. d, Cameroun #19. e, Samoa #68.

**2016, Jan. 29 Litho. *Perf. 13¾***

**4065** A858 $3.25 Sheet of 4, #a-d 9.75 9.75
**4066** A858 $3.25 Sheet of 5, #a-e 12.00 12.00

**Souvenir Sheet**

German Offices Stamps — A859

No. 4067: a, German Offices in China #1. b, German Offices in Morocco #1. c, German Offices in the Turkish Empire #1.

**2016, Jan. 29 Litho. *Perf. 13¾***

**4067** A859 $3.50 Sheet of 3, #a-c 7.75 7.75

Jimi Hendrix (1942-70), Rock Musician — A860

No. 4068 — Hendrix: a, With yellow, red orange curves in background. b, Wearing red pants. c, With Jupiter in background. d, With lilac and yellow green curved lines in background.
$10, Hendrix, diff.

**2016, Mar. 8 Litho. *Perf. 12½***

**4068** A860 $3.25 Sheet of 4, #a-d 9.75 9.75

**Souvenir Sheet**

**4069** A860 $10 multi 7.50 7.50

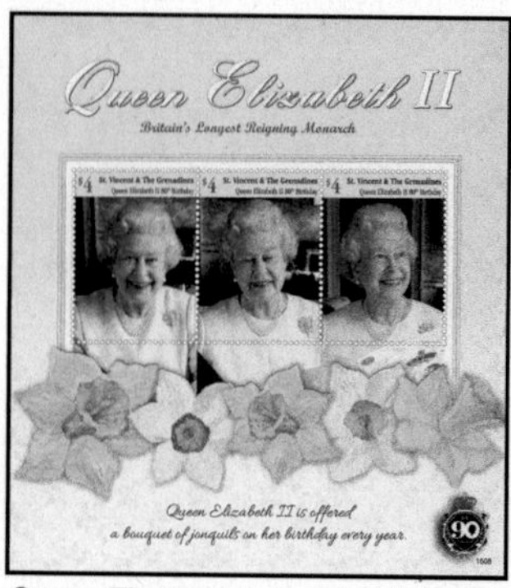

Queen Elizabeth II, Longest-Reigning British Monarch — A861

No. 4070 — Various photographs of Queen Elizabeth II, as shown.
No. 4071 — Queen Elizabeth II looking: a, Right. b, Left.

**2016, Apr. 11 Litho. *Perf. 14***
**4070** A861 $4 Sheet of 3, #a-c 9.00 9.00

**Souvenir Sheet**

**4071** A861 $6 Sheet of 2, #a-b 9.00 9.00

Magna Carta, 800th Anniv. (in 2015) A862

No. 4072: a, Amerindian petroglyph. b, St. George's Cathedral, Kingstown. c, Argyle International Airport. d, Court House, Kingstown. e, Cadet Force on parade.

**2016, May 2 Litho. *Perf. 13¼***
**4072** Vert. strip of 5 8.25 8.25
*a.* A862 $1 multi .75 .75
*b.* A862 $1.70 multi 1.25 1.25
*c.* A862 $2.20 multi 1.75 1.75
*d.* A862 $2.65 multi 2.00 2.00
*e.* A862 $3.40 multi 2.50 2.50

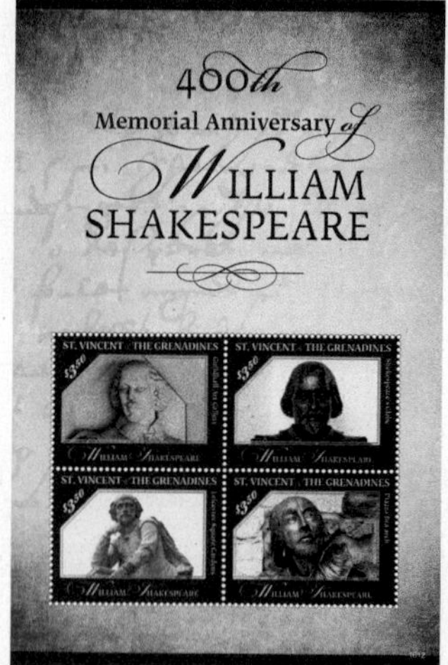

William Shakespeare (1564-1616), Writer — A863

No. 4073 — Statue depicting Shakespeare at: a, Guildhall Art Gallery, London. b, Shakespeare's Globe Theater, London. c, Leicester Square Gardens, London. d, Piazza Bra arch, Verona, Italy.
No. 4074 — Depiction of Shakespeare from: a, The Gallery of Portraits. b, The Leisure Hour Magazine.

**2016, May 17 Litho. *Perf. 14***
**4073** A863 $3.50 Sheet of 4, #a-d 10.50 10.50

**Souvenir Sheet**

**4074** A863 $6 Sheet of 2, #a-b 9.00 9.00

Souvenir Sheet

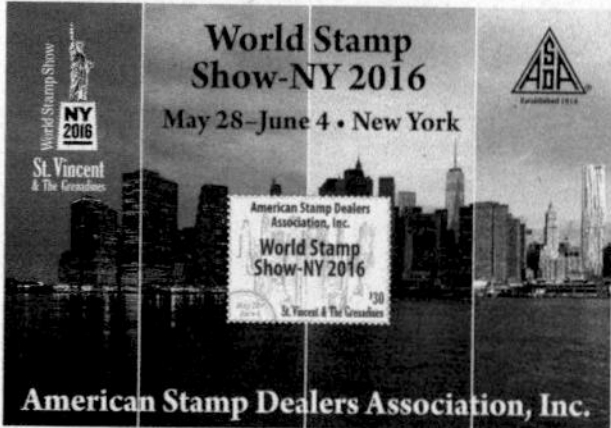

2016 World Stamp Show, New York — A864

**2016, May 25 Litho. *Perf. 12½x12***
**4075** A864 $30 multi 22.50 22.50

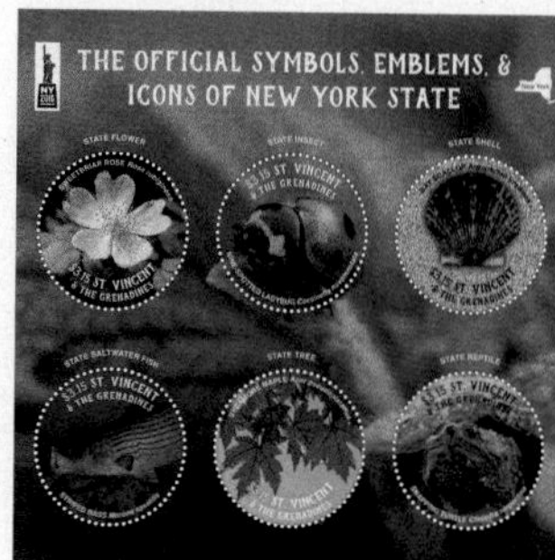

New York State Emblematic Items — A865

No. 4076: a, Sweetbriar rose (state flower). b, Nine-spotted ladybug (state insect). c, Bay scallop (state shell). d, Striped bass (state saltwater fish). e, Sycamore maple (state tree). f, Snapping turtle (state reptile).
No. 4077: a, Apple muffin (state muffin). b, Beaver (state animal).

**2016, May 26 Litho. *Perf.***
**4076** A865 $3.15 Sheet of 6, #a-f 14.00 14.00

**Souvenir Sheet**

***Perf. 12½x12***

**4077** A865 $6 Sheet of 2, #a-b 9.00 9.00

2016 World Stamp Show, New York. No. 4077 contains two 40x30mm stamps.

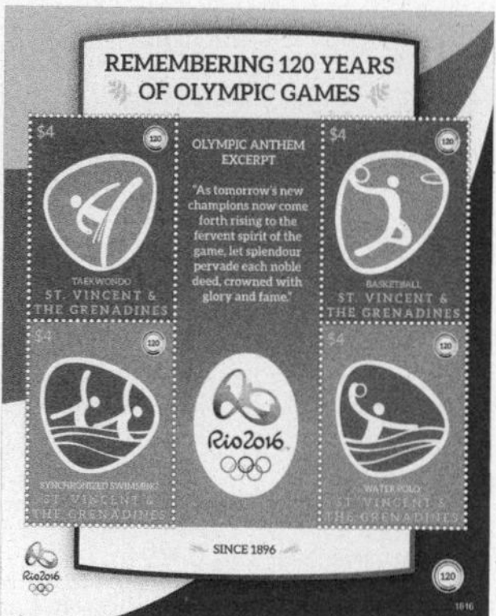

Modern Olympic Games, 120th Anniv. — A866

No. 4078, $4: a, Taekwondo. b, Basketball. c, Synchronized swimming. d, Water polo.
No. 4079, $4: a, Badminton. b, Sailing. c, Road cycling. d, Modern pentathlon.
No. 4080: a, Swimming. b, Shigeo Arai (1916-44), Japanese swimming gold medalist in 1936.

**2016, June 7 Litho. *Perf. 14***

**Sheets of 4, #a-b**

**4078-4079** A866 Set of 2 24.00 24.00

**Souvenir Sheet**

***Perf. 12½***

**4080** A866 $7 Sheet of 2, #a-b 10.50 10.50

No. 4080 contains two 38x51mm stamps.

A867

Statue of Liberty, 130th Anniv. — A868

No. 4081: a, Scaffolding surrounding statue. b, Torch. c, Head, sky in background. d, Head and torch. e, Construction of statue base. f, Head and trees.
No. 4082: a, Torch. b, Head. c, Head and torso. d, Tablet.
$14, Entire statue.

**2016, June 7 Litho. *Perf. 13¾***
**4081** A867 $3.25 Sheet of 6, #a-f 14.50 14.50

***Perf. 14***

**4082** A868 $3.50 Sheet of 4, #a-d 10.50 10.50

**Souvenir Sheet**

***Perf. 12***

**4083** A868 $14 multi 10.50 10.50

No. 4083 contains one 30x50mm stamp.

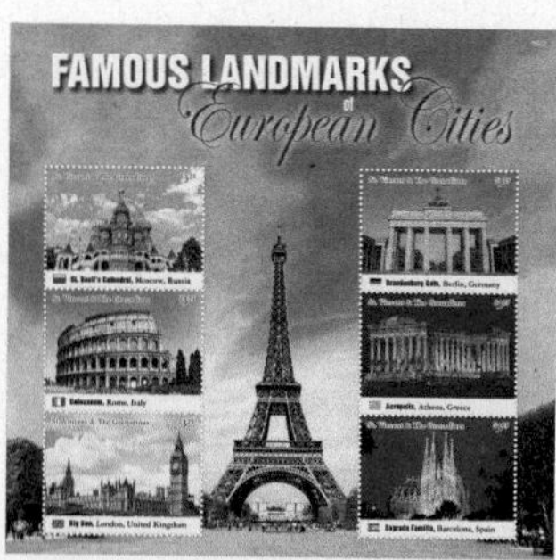

European Landmarks — A869

No. 4084: a, St. Basil's Cathedral, Moscow. b, Brandenburg Gate, Berlin. c, Colosseum, Rome. d, Acropolis, Athens. e, Big Ben, London. f, Sagrada Familia, Barcelona.
$14, Eiffel Tower, Paris, vert.

**2016, June 29 Litho. *Perf. 14***
**4084** A869 $3.25 Sheet of 6, #a-f 14.50 14.50

**Souvenir Sheet**

***Perf. 12***

**4085** A869 $14 multi 10.50 10.50

No. 4085 contains one 30x80mm stamp.

Souvenir Sheets

Elvis Presley (1935-77) — A870

Inscriptions: No. 4086, $14, Memphis charities benefit show. No. 4087, $14, A star is born. No. 4088, $14, Five-star jamboree. No. 4089, $14, Second Grammy "He Touched Me," horiz.

***Perf. 13¼x13, 13x13¼***

**2016, July 7 Litho.**
**4086-4089** A870 Set of 4 42.00 42.00

Visit of Pres. Barack Obama to Viet Nam — A871

No. 4090: a, Pres. Obama and Vietnamese Prime Minister Nguyen Xuan Phúc shaking hands (120x30mm). b, Pres. Obama (40x30mm). c, Pres. Obama and Prime Minister Nguyen (40x30mm). d, Prime Minister Nguyen (40x30mm).
No. 4091, vert.: a, Pres. Obama. b, Prime Minister Nguyen.

**2016, Sept. 21 Litho. *Perf. 14***
**4090** A871 $4 Sheet of 4, #a-d 12.00 12.00

**Souvenir Sheet**

**4091** A871 $7 Sheet of 2, #a-b 10.50 10.50

No. 4091 contains two 30x80mm stamps.

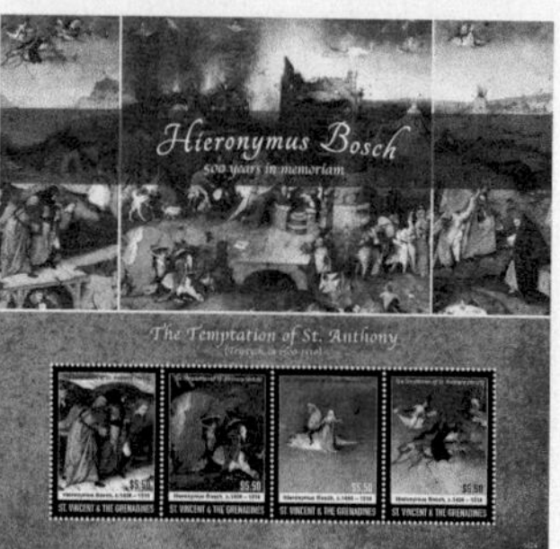

Paintings by Hieronymus Bosch (c. 1450-1516) — A872

No. 4092 — The Temptation of St. Anthony (details): a, Four men. b, Man in bucket. c, Man and woman on fish. d, Fish and demons.
No. 4093: a, The Ship of Fools. b, Death and the Miser.

**2016, Nov. 17 Litho. *Perf. 14***
**4092** A872 $5.50 Sheet of 4, #a-d 16.50 16.50

**Souvenir Sheet**

***Perf. 12***

**4093** A872 $7.50 Sheet of 2, #a-b 11.00 11.00

No. 4093 contains two 30x50mm stamps.

Birds — A873

Designs: $60, Antillean crested hummingbird. $80, St. Vincent Amazon parrot.

**2017, Feb. 28 Litho. *Perf. 13¼***

**4094** A873 $60 multi 45.00 45.00
**4095** A873 $80 multi 60.00 60.00

A874

Princess Diana (1961-97) — A875

No. 4096: Various photographs of Princess Diana wearing tiara, as shown.

No. 4097 — Princess Diana wearing: a, Hat. b, Gray jacket. c, Red dress. d, Yellow blouse.

$10, Princess Diana, diff.

***Perf. 12½x13¼***

**2017, Mar. 30 Litho.**

**4096** A874 $6 Sheet of 4, #a-d 18.00 18.00

***Perf. 12x11½***

**4097** A875 $6 Sheet of 4, #a-d 18.00 18.00

**Souvenir Sheet**

***Perf. 12½x12***

**4098** A874 $10 multi 7.50 7.50

Animals — A876

No. 4099: a, Serval. b, Sunda pangolin. c, Gulf Coast native sheep. d, Red-capped mangabey.

$9, Gee's golden langur.

**2017, Apr. 4 Litho. *Perf. 12¾x12½***

**4099** A876 $6 Sheet of 4, #a-d 18.00 18.00

**Souvenir Sheet**

**4100** A876 $9 multi 6.75 6.75

Miniature Sheets

A877

Pres. John F. Kennedy (1917-63) — A878

No. 4101: a, Kennedy with two fingers raised. b, Kennedy pointing. c, Kennedy speaking. d, Kennedy on telephone. e, Neil Armstrong on Moon. f, Color photograph of Kennedy.

No. 4102: a, Kennedy looking upwards. b, Kennedy smiling with teeth visible. c, Kennedy pointing, diff. d, Launch of Apollo 11.

**2017, May 15 Litho. *Perf. 11½x12***

**4101** A877 $4 Sheet of 6, #a-f 18.00 18.00

***Perf. 13¼***

**4102** A878 $5 Sheet of 4, #a-d 15.00 15.00

Sharks — A879

No. 4103, $5: a, Tiger shark. b, Whale shark. c, Pacific sleeper shark.

No. 4104, $5: a, Basking shark. b, Great hammerhead shark. c, Great white shark.

**2017, June 2 Litho. *Perf. 12***

**Sheets of 3, #a-c**

**4103-4104** A879 Set of 2 22.50 22.50

September 11, 2001 Terrorist Attacks — A880

No. 4105: a, World Trade Center and U.S. flag. b, Tribute in Light. c, World Trade Center. d, Hillary Clinton. e, Pres. Barack Obama. f, Pres. Donald Trump.

$12, New York City fire fighters at memorial ceremony, vert.

**2017, June 29 Litho. *Perf. 13¾***

**4105** A880 $3.15 Sheet of 6, #a-f 14.00 14.00

**Souvenir Sheet**

***Perf. 14***

**4106** A880 $12 multi 9.00 9.00

No. 4106 contains one 30x40mm stamp.

Pres. Donald Trump — A881

No. 4107: a, Pres. Trump and Pres. Barack Obama (40x30mm). b, White House (40x60mm). c, Pres. Trump and wife, Melania (40x30mm). d, Ivanka Trump (40x30mm). e, Barron Trump (40x30mm).

No. 4108, vert.: a, Barron Trump, diff. b, Pres. Trump. c, Pres. Trump with arm raised. d, Melania Trump waving.

$12, Pres. Trump, diff.

**2017, July 3 Litho. *Perf. 14***

**4107** A881 $5 Sheet of 5, #a-e 18.50 18.50
**4108** A881 $7 Sheet of 4, #a-d 21.00 21.00

**Souvenir Sheet**

***Perf. 12½***

**4109** A881 $12 multi 9.00 9.00

No. 4109 contains one 51x38mm stamp.

American Flamingos — A882

No. 4110: Various photographs of flamingos, as shown.

No. 4111, horiz.: a, Two flamingos. b, One flamingo.

**2017, Aug. 9 Litho. *Perf. 14***

**4110** A882 $7 Sheet of 4, #a-d 21.00 21.00

**Souvenir Sheet**

***Perf. 12***

**4111** A882 $7 Sheet of 2, #a-b 10.50 10.50

Zeppelins — A883

No. 4112 — LZ-127 Graf Zeppelin: a, With ground crew. b, Outside of hangar. c, In flight. d, In hangar.

$12, Ferdinand von Zeppelin (1883-1917), Zeppelin manufacturer, vert.

***Perf. 12½x13¼***

**2017, Sept. 26 Litho.**

**4112** A883 $7 Sheet of 4, #a-d 21.00 21.00

**Souvenir Sheet**

***Perf. 13¼***

**4113** A883 £12 multi 9.00 9.00

No. 4113 contains one 38x51mm stamp.

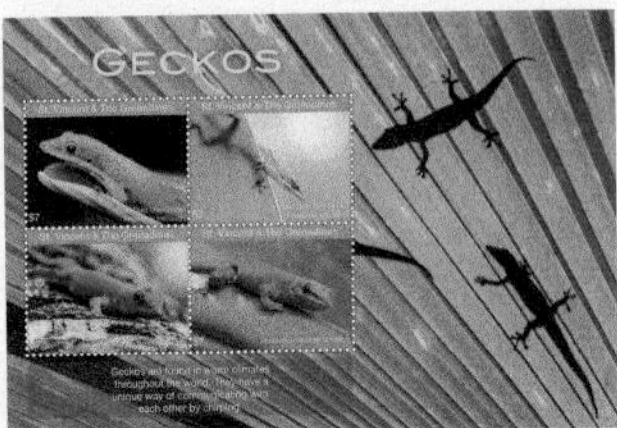

A884

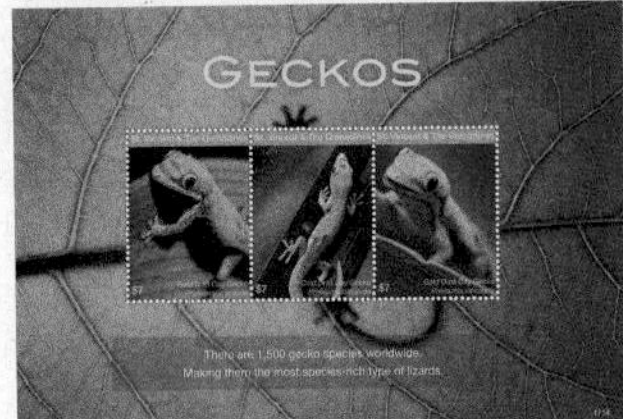

Gold Dust Day Geckos — A885

Various photographs of geckos, as shown.

**2017, June 28 Litho. *Perf. 12***

**4114** A884 $7 Sheet of 4, #a-d 21.00 21.00

**Souvenir Sheet**

***Perf. 14***

**4115** A885 $7 Sheet of 3, #a-c 15.50 15.50

Marine Life — A886

No. 4116 — Actiniaria sea anemones: a, Anemones (30x40mm). b, Anemones, diff. (30x40mm). c, Anemones, diff. (60x40mm).

$15, Sea snails, horiz.

**2017, Sept. 28 Litho. *Perf. 14***

**4116** A886 $7 Sheet of 3, #a-c 15.50 15.50

**Souvenir Sheet**

**4117** A886 $15 multi 11.00 11.00

No. 4117 contains one 80x30mm stamp.

Souvenir Sheets

Elvis Presley (1935-77) — A887

Inscription: No. 4118, $12, Signs first management contract. No. 4119, $12, First paid performance. No. 4120, $12, First professional stage show. No. 4121, $12, First single released, horiz.

**2017, Oct. 26 Litho. *Perf. 12½***

**4118-4121** A887 Set of 4 36.00 36.00

70th Wedding Anniversary of Queen Elizabeth II and Prince Philip — A888

No. 4122 — Wedding day photographs: a, Queen Elizabeth II waving. b, Couple in procession with attendants. c, Couple passing soldiers. d, Couple standing in front of curtain.
$12, Couple, vert.

**2017, Oct. 26 Litho. *Perf. 13¾***

**4122** A888 $6 Sheet of 4, #a-d 18.00 18.00

**Souvenir Sheet**

***Perf.***

**4123** A888 $12 multi 9.00 9.00

No. 4123 contains one 34x43mm oval stamp.

World War II, 75th Anniv. — A889

No. 4124: a, Gen. Douglas MacArthur returns to the Philippines, 1944. b, U.S. B-17 bomber over Marienburg, Germany, 1943. c, Gen. Dwight Eisenhower prepares for D-Day, 1944. d, Japan surrenders, 1945. e, USS Arizona sinks at Pearl Harbor, 1941. f, Pres. Franklin Roosevelt, Winston Churchill and Joseph Stalin at Yalta Conference, 1945.
$12, Marines raise flag on Iwo Jima, 1945.

**2017, Oct. 28 Litho. *Perf. 14***

**4124** A889 $4 Sheet of 6, #a-f 18.00 18.00

**Souvenir Sheet**

***Perf. 13¾***

**4125** A889 $12 multi 9.00 9.00

No. 4125 contains one 35x35mm stamp.

Miniature Sheets

Fruits — A890

No. 4126: a, 75c, Starfruits on tree. b, $1.75, Sliced starfruit. c, $2.75, Apple guava on tree. d, $3.75, Sliced apple guavas. e, $4.75, Jackfruits on tree. f, $5.75, Sliced jackfruit.

No. 4127: a, $2, Gooseberry on bush. b, $4, Custard apple on tree. c, $6, Purple star apple on tree. d, $8, Sliced gooseberries. e, $10, Sliced custard apple. f, $12, Sliced purple star apple.

**2017, Nov. 18 Litho. *Perf. 11½x12***

**Sheets of 6, #a-f**

**4126-4127** A890 Set of 2 46.00 46.00

Miniature Sheets

Scenery of St. Vincent — A891

No. 4128: a, $1, Bequia. b, $2, Petit St. Vincent. c, $3, Bequia, diff. d, $4, Kingstown (brown panel). e, $6, Island shoreline. f, $8, Waves reaching shore.

No. 4129: a, $2, Walliabou (42x29mm). b, $4, Kingstown (green panel) (42x29mm). c, $5, Botanical Garden (42x29mm). d, $6, Grenadines (42x29mm). e, $7, Dark View Falls (42x58mm).

**2017, Dec. 4 Litho. *Perf. 13¼***

**4128** A891 Sheet of 6, #a-f 18.00 18.00

**4129** A891 Sheet of 5, #a-e 18.00 18.00

Christmas — A892

Inscriptions: 90c, Christmas Celebration! $2.65, Oh, Christmas Tree! $3.40, Merry Christmas! $5, Deck the Halls!

No. 4134: a, Oh, Holy Night. b, Away in a Manger.

**2017, Dec. 17 Litho. *Perf. 12½***

**4130-4133** A892 Set of 4 9.00 9.00

**Souvenir Sheet**

**4134** A892 $2.50 Sheet of 2, #a-b 3.75 3.75

Muhammad Ali (1942-2016), Boxer — A893

No. 4135: Various photographs of Ali, as shown.
$12, Ali, diff.

**2018, Mar. 7 Litho. *Perf. 14***

**4135** A893 $7 Sheet of 4, #a-d 21.00 21.00

**Souvenir Sheet**

***Perf. 12½***

**4136** A893 $12 multi 9.00 9.00

No. 4136 contains one 38x51mm stamp.

Miniature Sheets

Royal Air Force, Cent. — A894

No. 4137: a, $1, Lancaster. b, $2, Hawker Hurricane. c, $3, Douglas Dakota. d, $4, Chipmunk. e, $5, Supermarine Spitfire. f, $6, Supermarine Spitfire, diff.

No. 4138, $4, vert.: a, Distinguished Flying Cross medal. b, General Service medal. c, Long Service and Good Conduct medal. d, Air Force Cross medal. e, Accumulated Campaign Service medal. f, Korea medal.

**2018, Mar. 7 Litho. *Perf. 14***

**4137** A894 Sheet of 6, #a-f 15.50 15.50

***Perf. 12***

**4138** A894 $4 Sheet of 6, #a-f 18.00 18.00

Birds — A895

No. 4139: a, 50c, Lovely cotinga. b, $1, Andean cock-of-the-rock. c, $1.50, Orange-bellied leaf bird. d, $2, Pin-tailed manakin. e, $2.50, Long-tailed broadbill. f, $3, Rufous motmot. g, $3.50, American goldfinch. h, $4, Double-barred finch. i, $4.50, Golden-breated starling.
$15, Southern mealy Amazon, Channel-billed toucan, horiz.

**2018, Mar. 7 Litho. *Perf. 14***

**4139** A895 Sheet of 9, #a-i 16.50 16.50

**Souvenir Sheet**

***Perf. 12½***

**4140** A895 $15 multi 11.00 11.00

No. 4140 contains one 51x38mm stamp.

Parrots — A896

No. 4141: a, $5, Cuban parrot. b, $6, Puerto Rican parrot. c, $7, Yellow-headed parrot. d, $8, St. Vincent parrot.
$15, St. Vincent parrot, diff.

**2018, Mar. 7 Litho. *Perf. 12***

**4141** A896 Sheet of 4, #a-d 19.50 19.50

**Souvenir Sheet**

***Perf. 14***

**4142** A896 $15 multi 11.00 11.00

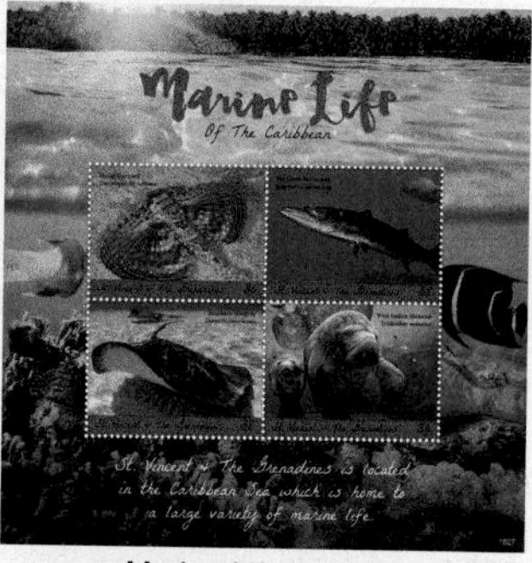


Marine Life — A897

No. 4143: a, $6, Flying gurnard. b, $6, West Indian manatee. c, $8, Great barracuda. d, $8, Southern stingray.

No. 4144: a, $7, Yellowhead jawfish. b, $8, Longsnout seahorse.

**2018, Mar. 7 Litho. *Perf. 14***

**4143** A897 Sheet of 4, #a-d 21.00 21.00

**Souvenir Sheet**

***Perf. 12***

**4144** A897 Sheet of 2, #a-b 11.00 11.00

Green Sea Turtles — A898

No. 4145 — Various photographs of turtle: a, $1. b, $2. c, $3. d, $4. e, $5. f, $6.

No. 4146 — Various photographs of turtle: a, $7. b, $8.

**2018, Mar. 7 Litho. *Perf. 12***

**4145** A898 Sheet of 6, #a-f 15.50 15.50

**Souvenir Sheet**

***Perf. 12½***

**4146** A898 Sheet of 2, #a-b 11.00 11.00

No. 4146 contains two 51x38mm stamps.

Reptiles — A899

No. 4147: a, $6, Thumb-tailed gecko. b, $6, Green iguana. c, $8, Cook's tree boa. d, $8, House gecko.
$12, Loggerhead turtle.

**2018, Mar. 7 Litho. *Perf. 14***

**4147** A899 Sheet of 4, #a-d 21.00 21.00

**Souvenir Sheet**

***Perf. 12½***

**4148** A899 $12 multi 9.00 9.00

No. 4148 contains one 51x38mm stamp.

Miniature Sheet

Wedding of Prince Harry and Meghan Markle — A900

No. 4149: a, $4, Queen Elizabeth II (30x50mm). b, $4, Flower bouquet (30x50mm). c, $4, Prince Harry, Duke of Sussex (30x50mm). d, $4, Prince William, Duke of Cambridge (30x50mm). e, $6, Bride and groom (60x50mm).

**2018, July 14** **Litho.** ***Perf. 12***
**4149** A900 Sheet of 5, #a-e 16.50 16.50

Souvenir Sheet

Coronation of Queen Elizabeth II, 65th Anniv. — A901

**2018, July 14** **Litho.** ***Perf. 12***
**4150** A901 $10 multi 7.50 7.50

Miniature Sheets

2018 Winter Olympics and Paralympics, Pyeongchang, South Korea — A902

No. 4151, $6: a, Winter Olympics Alpine skiing. b, Winter Paralympics Alpine skiing. c, Winter Olympics biathlon. d, Winter Paralympics biathlon.

No. 4152, $6: a, Winter Olympics cross-country skiing. b, Winter Paralympics cross-country skiing. c, Winter Olympics ice hockey. d, Winter Paralympics ice hockey.

No. 4153, $6: a, Winter Olympics snowboarding. b, Winter Paralympics snowboarding. c, Winter Olympics curling. d, Winter Paralympics wheelchair curling.

**2018, July 14** **Litho.** ***Perf. 12***
**Sheets of 4, #a-d**
**4151-4153** A902 Set of 3 53.00 53.00

Miniature Sheet

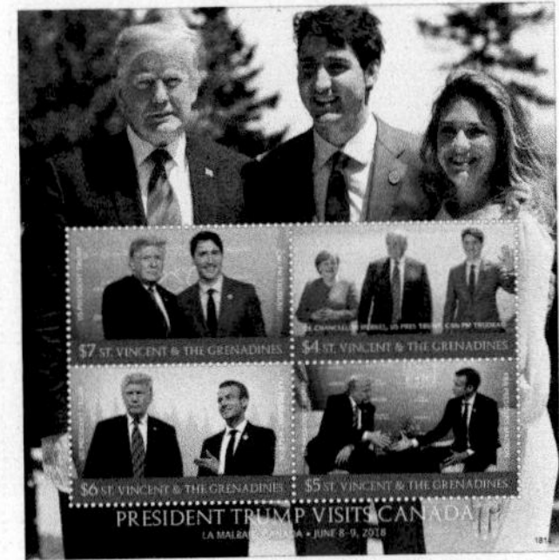


Visit to Canada of Pres. Donald Trump — A903

No. 4154: a, $4, German Chancellor Angela Merkel, Pres. Trump, Canadian Prime Minister Justin Trudeau. b, $5, Pres. Trump and French President Emmanuel Macron, seated. c, $6, Presidents Trump and Macron standing. d, $7, Pres. Trump and Prime Minister Trudeau.

**2018, Oct. 12** **Litho.** ***Perf. 12***
**4154** A903 Sheet of 4, #a-d 16.50 16.50

Flight of Apollo 11, 50th Anniv. (in 2019) — A904

No. 4155: a, Commander Neil Armstrong. b, Command Module Pilot Michael Collins. c, Lunar Module Pilot Edwin "Buzz" Aldrin.
$11, Armstrong in training, horiz.

**2018, Oct. 12** **Litho.** ***Perf.***
**4155** A904 $5 Sheet of 3, #a-c 11.00 11.00

**Souvenir Sheet**
***Perf. 12½***

**4156** A904 $11 multi 8.25 8.25

No. 4156 contains one 51x38mm stamp.

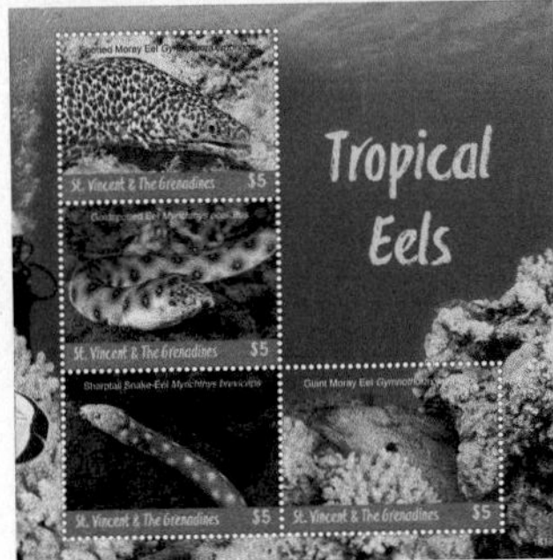


Eels — A905

No. 4157: a, Spotted moray eel. b, Gold-spotted eel. c, Sharptail snake-eel. d, Giant moray eel.
$10, Green moray eel.

**2018, Oct. 26** **Litho.** ***Perf. 14***
**4157** A905 $5 Sheet of 4, #a-d 15.00 15.00

**Souvenir Sheet**
***Perf. 12½***

**4158** A905 $10 multi 7.50 7.50

No. 4158 contains one 51x38mm stamp.

Miniature Sheet

Western Honey Bees — A906

No. 4159: a, $4, Bee flying near flower. b, $5, Bee. c, $6, Bee on flower. d, $7, Bee moving from flower to flower.

**2018, Oct. 26** **Litho.** ***Perf. 14***
**4159** A906 Sheet of 4, #a-d 16.50 16.50

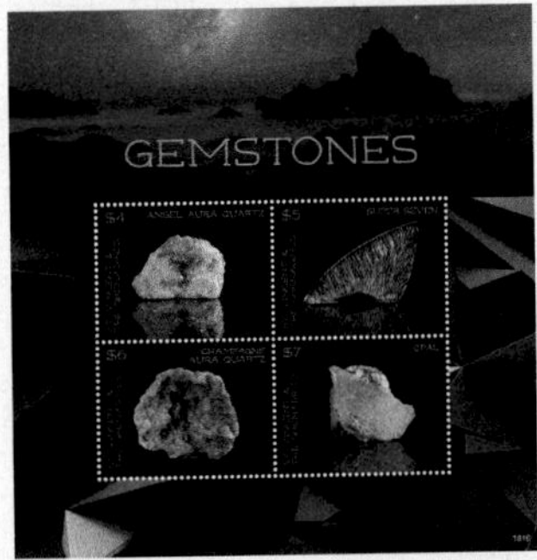


Gemstones — A907

No. 4160: a, $4, Angel aura quartz. b, $5, Super seven crystal. c, $6, Champagne aura quartz. d, $7, Opal.

No. 4161: a, $4, Amazonite. b, $5, Boulder opal. c, $6, Fluorite. d, $7, Benitoite.

No. 4162 — Larimar with background color of: a, Black. b, White.

**2018, Oct. 26** **Litho.** ***Perf. 14***
**Sheets of 4, #a-d**
**4160-4161** A907 Set of 2 32.50 32.50

**Souvenir Sheet**

**4162** A907 $8 Sheet of 2, #a-b 12.00 12.00

Animals in World War I — A908

No. 4163: a, $4, Dog unspooling wire. b, $5, Russian machine gun mounted on horse. c, $6, Dog carrying pigeons. d, $7, Horse wearing gas mask.

No. 4164: a, Pigeon named Cher Ami. b, Dog named Sergeant Stubby.

**2018, Dec. 31** **Litho.** ***Perf. 14***
**4163** A908 Sheet of 4, #a-d 16.50 16.50

**Souvenir Sheet**
***Perf. 12½***

**4164** A908 $10 Sheet of 2, #a-b 15.00 15.00

No. 4164 contains two 38x51mm stamps.

Miniature Sheet

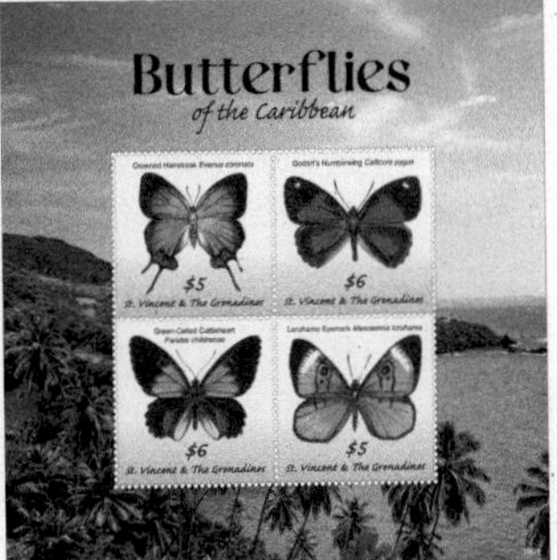


Butterflies — A909

No. 4165: a, $5, Crowned hairstreak. b, $5, Loruhama eyemark. c, $6, Godart's numberwing. d, $6, Green-celled cattleheart.

**2019, Jan. 15** **Litho.** ***Perf. 13¾***
**4165** A909 Sheet of 4, #a-d 16.50 16.50

Miniature Sheet

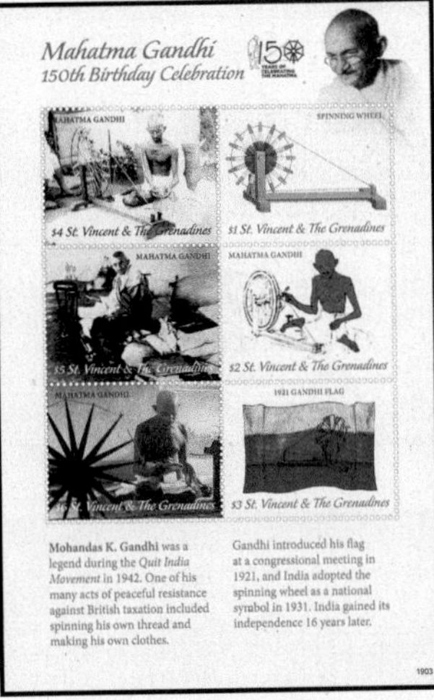


Mohandas K. Gandhi (1869-1948), Indian Nationalist Leader — A910

No. 4166: a, $1, Spinning wheel. b, $2, Drawing of Gandhi at spinning wheel. c, $3, 1921 proposed flag designed by Gandhi. d, $4, Photograph of Gandhi at spinning wheel. e, $5, Photograph of Gandhi turning crank of spinning wheel. f, $6, Photograph of Gandhi reading near spinning wheel.

**2019, Jan. 30** **Litho.** ***Perf. 14***
**4166** A910 Sheet of 6, #a-f 15.50 15.50

Hummingbirds — A911

No. 4167: a, $1, Rufous-breasted hermit. b, $2, Antillean crested hummingbird. c, $3, Puerto Rican emerald. d, $4, Antillean mango. e, $5, Antillean crested hummingbird, diff. f, $6, Blue-headed hummingbird.
$10, Bee hummingbird.

**2019, Feb. 7 Litho. *Perf. 14***
**4167** A911 Sheet of 6, #a-f 15.50 15.50

**Souvenir Sheet**

***Perf. 12½***

**4168** A911 $10 multi 7.50 7.50

No. 4168 contains one 38x51mm stamp.

Explosion of Space Shuttle Columbia, 15th Anniv. (in 2018) — A912

No. 4169: a, $5, Spacehab research Double Module in Columbia's payload bay (30x40mm). b, $5, Liftoff of Space Shuttle Columbia (30x40mm). c, $6, Crew of Columbia mission STS-107 (60x40mm).
$11, Liftoff of Space Shuttle Columbia, diff.

**2019, Apr. 6 Litho. *Perf. 14***
**4169** A912 Sheet of 3, #a-c 12.00 12.00

**Souvenir Sheet**

***Perf. 12***

**4170** A912 $11 multi 8.25 8.25

No. 4170 contains one 30x50mm stamp.

West Indian Manatees — A913

No. 4171: a, $3, One manatee. b, $3, Two manatees. c, $5, Two manatees, diff. d, $5, One manatee, diff. e, $6, One manatee, diff.
$14, Two manatees, diff.

**2019, Apr. 10 Litho. *Perf. 14***
**4171** A913 Sheet of 5, #a-e 16.50 16.50

**Souvenir Sheet**

***Perf. 12½***

**4172** A913 $14 multi 10.50 10.50

No. 4172 contains one 51x38mm stamp.

Doctorfish Tang A914

No. 4173 — Doctorfish tang facing: a, $5, Left. b, $6, Right.
$14, Doctorfish tang facing left.

**2019, July 8 Litho. *Perf. 14***
**4173** A914 Pair, $a-b 8.25 8.25

**Souvenir Sheet**

***Perf.***

**4174** A914 $14 multi 10.50 10.50

No. 4173 was printed in sheets containing two pairs. No. 4174 contains one 43x33mm oval stamp.

**Souvenir Sheet**

Visit to France of Pres. Donald Trump — A915

No. 4175: a, $4, Pres. Trump and wife, Melania, French Pres. Emmanuel Macron and wife, Brigitte. b, $5, Arc de Triomphe and flowers. c, $6, Pres. Trump and wife, Melania.

**2019, July 8 Litho. *Perf. 14***
**4175** A915 Sheet of 3, #a-c 11.00 11.00

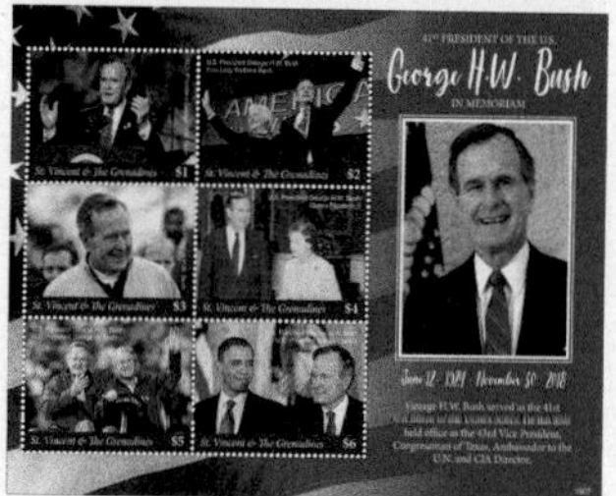


Pres. George H. W. Bush (1924-2018) — A916

No. 4176 — Pres. Bush: a, $1, Behind lectern. b, $2, With wife, Barbara, waving. c, $3, Wearing sweater. d, $4, With Queen Elizabeth II. e, $5, With son, Pres. George W. Bush. f, $6, With Pres. Barack Obama.
No. 4177, vert.: a, Official White House portrait of Pres. Bush. b, Sully, service dog of Pres. Bush.

**2019, July 14 Litho. *Perf. 14***
**4176** A916 Sheet of 6, #a-f 15.50 15.50

**Souvenir Sheet**

***Perf. 12½***

**4177** A916 $8 Sheet of 2, #a-b 12.00 12.00

No. 4177 contains two 38x51mm stamps.

**Miniature Sheet**

Leonardo da Vinci (1452-1519) — A917

No. 4178: a, Engraving of Leonardo by Raffaello Morghen. b, Portrait of Gian Giacomo Caprotti, by Leonardo. c, Mona Lisa, by Leonardo. d, Monna Vanna, by Leonardo's student, Andrea Salaí.

**2019, July 31 Litho. *Perf. 14***
**4178** A917 $6 Sheet of 4, #a-d 18.00 18.00

**Miniature Sheet**

Singpex 2019 International Stamp Exhibition, Singapore — A918

No. 4179 — Show emblem and sites in Singapore Botanic Gardens: a, $4, Clock. b, $5, Gazebo. c, $6, Pathway with arches. d, $7, Park bench.

**2019, July 31 Litho. *Perf. 12***
**4179** A918 Sheet of 4, #a-d 16.50 16.50

**Miniature Sheet**

Birth of Archie Mountbatten-Windsor — A919

No. 4180: a, $4, Duke and Duchess of Sussex. b, $5, Duke and Duchess of Sussex, with son, Archie. c, $6, Duke and Duchess of Sussex, with son, Archie, diff. d, $7, Duke and Duchess of Sussex, with son, Archie, diff.

**2019, July 31 Litho. *Perf. 14***
**4180** A919 Sheet of 4, #a-d 16.50 16.50

**Miniature Sheet**

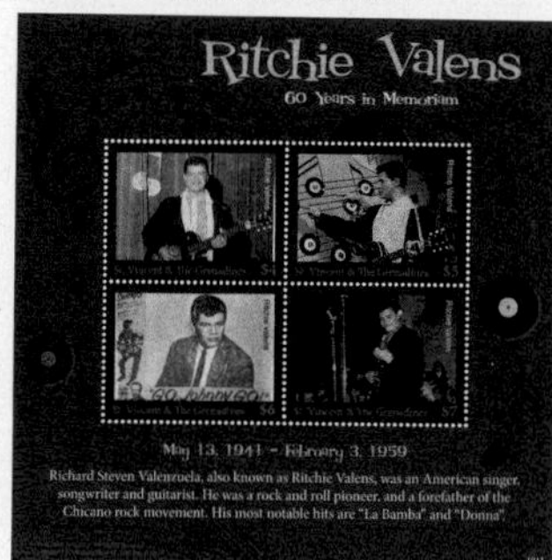


Richie Valens (1941-59), Rock Musician — A920

No. 4181 — Various photographs depicting Valens: a, $4. b, $5. c, $6. d, $7.

**2019, Aug. 10 Litho. *Perf. 14***
**4181** A920 Sheet of 4, #a-d 16.50 16.50

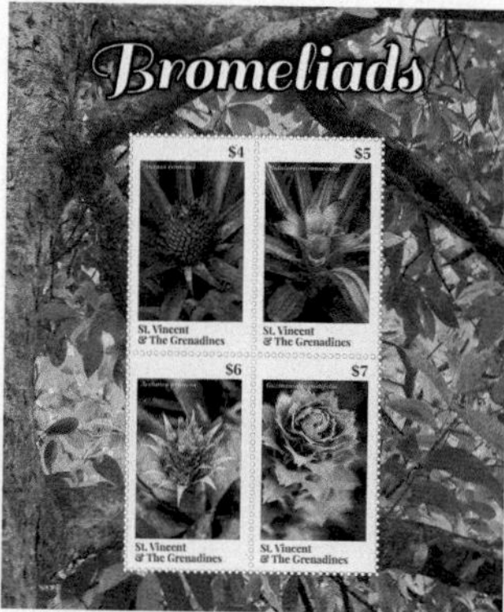


Bromeliads — A921

No. 4182: a, $4, Ananas comosus. b, $5, Nidularium innocentii. c, $6, Aechmea primera. d, $7, Guzmania angustifolia.
No. 4183: a, Billbergia pyramidalis (entire flower). b, Billbergia pyramidalis (close-up of flower).

**2020, Mar. 5 Litho. *Perf. 12***
**4182** A921 Sheet of 4, #a-d 16.50 16.50

**Souvenir Sheet**

***Perf. 14***

**4183** A921 $8 Sheet of 2, #a-b 12.00 12.00

No. 4183 contains two 30x40mm stamps.

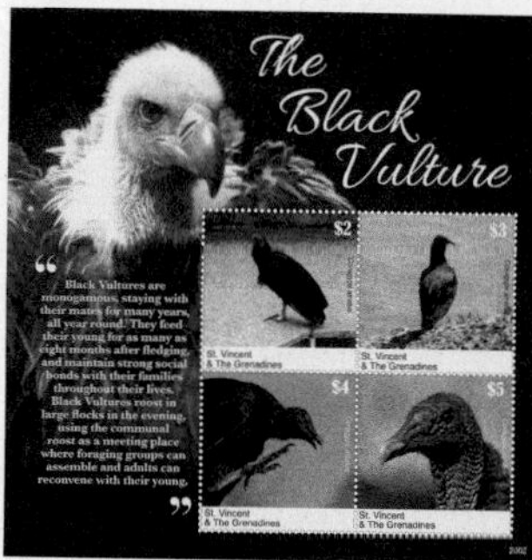


Coragyps Atratus — A922

No. 4184 — Various photographs: a, $2. b, $3. c, $4. d, $5.
$14, Bird's head, horiz.

**2020, Mar. 5 Litho. *Perf. 13¾***
**4184** A922 Sheet of 4, #a-d 10.50 10.50

**Souvenir Sheet**

***Perf. 12***

**4185** A922 $14 multi 10.50 10.50

No. 4185 contains one 50x30mm stamp.

**Miniature Sheet**

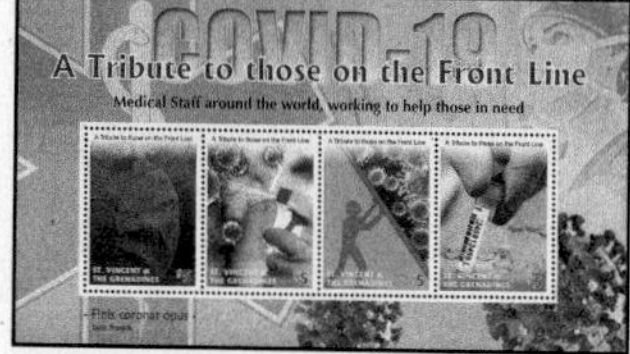


Tribute to Workers During the COVID-19 Pandemic — A923

No. 4186: a, Health care worker wearing protective face mask, COVID-19 virus. b, Worker spraying cleaning fluid on COVID-19 viruses. c, Stylized man holding back COVID-19 viruses. d, Health care worker holding vial.

**2020, Aug. 13 Litho. *Perf. 14***
**4186** A923 $5 Sheet of 4, #a-d 15.00 15.00

Rabbits — A924

No. 4187: a, American rabbit. b, Jersey Wooly rabbit. c, Flemish Giant rabbit. d, Eastern Cottontail rabbit.
$14, Checkered Giant rabbit, vert.

**2020, Oct. 8 Litho. *Perf. 14***

**4187** A924 $5.50 Sheet of 4, #a-d 16.50 16.50

**Souvenir Sheet**

***Perf. 12***

**4188** A924 $14 multi 10.50 10.50

Lobsters — A925

No. 4189: a, Caribbean spiny lobster, tail at left. b, Scalloped rock lobster. c, American lobster. d, Caribbean spiny lobster, tail at right.
$14, European lobster.

**2020, Oct. 8 Litho. *Perf. 14***

**4189** A925 $5.50 Sheet of 4, #a-d 16.50 16.50

**Souvenir Sheet**

***Perf. 12***

**4190** A925 $14 multi 10.50 10.50

Corals — A926

No. 4191: a, Purple Rough cactus coral. b, Cauliflower coral. c, Brown Rough cactus coral. d, Great star coral.
$14, Blushing star coral.

**2020, Oct. 8 Litho. *Perf. 14***

**4191** A926 $5.50 Sheet of 4, #a-d 16.50 16.50

**Souvenir Sheet**

***Perf. 12***

**4192** A926 $14 multi 10.50 10.50

A927

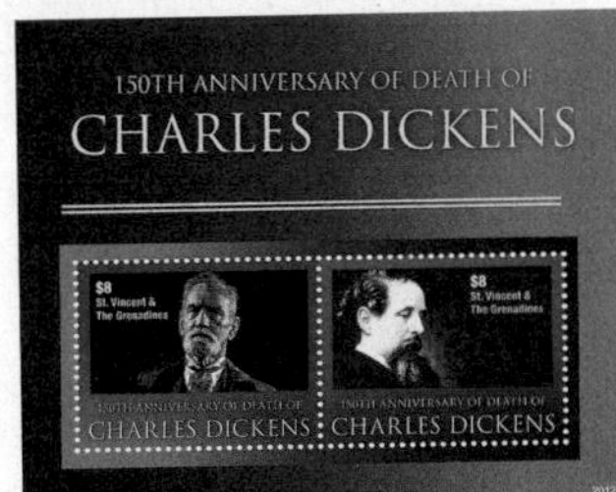

Charles Dickens (1812-70), Writer — A928

No. 4193 — Image of Dickens: a, With gray background. b, With white background, holding book. c, With white background, facing left. d, With white background facing right. e, With house in background.
No. 4194: a, Dickens facing forward. b, Dickens facing right.

**2020, Oct. 8 Litho. *Perf. 14***

**4193** A927 $4.50 Sheet of 5, #a-e 17.00 17.00

**Souvenir Sheet**

***Perf. 12***

**4194** A928 $8 Sheet of 2, #a-b 12.00 12.00

A929

Ludwig van Beethoven (1770-1827), Composer — A930

No. 4195 — Image of Beethoven: a, In color, with top of head and bottom of chin not visible. b, With white background and orange brown frame. c, With black background and orange brown frame. d, With black and white background and red violet frame. e, In color, with bottom of chin visible.
No. 4196: a, Beethoven, diff. b, Quotation.

**2020, Oct. 8 Litho. *Perf. 14***

**4195** A929 $4.50 Sheet of 5, #a-e 17.00 17.00

**Souvenir Sheet**

**4196** A930 $8 Sheet of 2, #a-b 12.00 12.00

Dorje Chang Buddha III, Religious Leader — A931

**2020, Nov. 15 Litho. *Perf. 13¼***

**4197** A931 $5 multi 3.75 3.75

United States Marines in the Vietnam War — A932

No. 4198: a, Operation Starlite, 1965. b, Battle of Khe Sanh, 1968. c, Battle of Hué, 1968. d, Operation Taylor Common, 1968-69.
$10, Operation Colorado, 1966.

**2020, Nov. 18 Litho. *Perf. 12½***

**4198** A932 $5 Sheet of 4, #a-d 15.00 15.00

**Souvenir Sheet**

**4199** A932 $10 multi 7.50 7.50

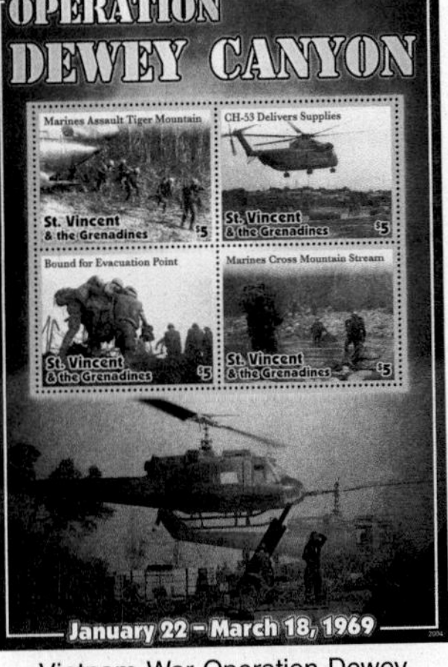

Vietnam War Operation Dewey Canyon, 1969 — A933

No. 4200: a, Marines assault Tiger Mountain. b, CH-53 helicopter delivering supplies. c, Soldiers bound for evacuation point. d, Marines crossing mountain stream.
$10, 1st Battalion 9th Marines sniper team.

**2020, Nov. 18 Litho. *Perf. 12½***

**4200** A933 $5 Sheet of 4, #a-d 15.00 15.00

**Souvenir Sheet**

**4201** A933 $10 multi 7.50 7.50

Souvenir Sheet

Mk. II River Patrol Boat in Action in the Vietnam War — A934

**2020, Nov, 18 Litho. *Perf. 12½***

**4202** A934 $10 multi 7.50 7.50

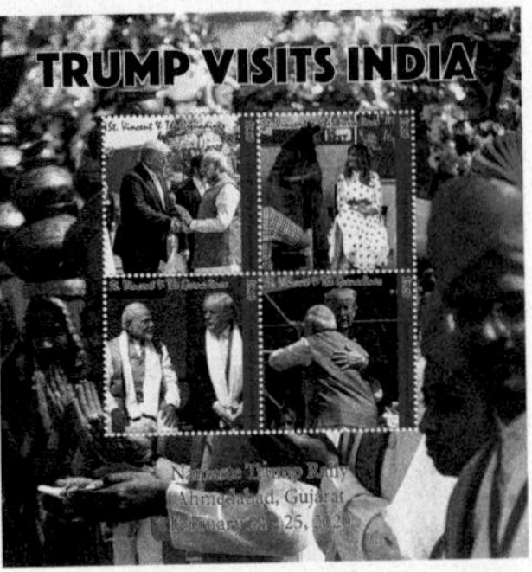

Visit of U.S. Pres. Donald Trump to India — A935

No. 4203: a, Pres. Trump shaking hands with Indian Prime Minister Marendra Modi. b, First Lady Melania Trump in classroom. c, Modi and Pres. Trump seated. d, Modi and Pres. Trump embracing.
$14, Modi and Pres. Trump talking, horiz.

**2020, Nov. 30 Litho. *Perf. 14¼***

**4203** A935 $5.50 Sheet of 4, #a-d 16.50 16.50

**Souvenir Sheet**

**4204** A935 $14 multi 10.50 10.50

No. 4204 contains one 90x30mm stamp.

Miniature Sheet

End of World War II in Europe, 75th Anniv. — A936

No. 4205: a, Bernard Montgomery (1887-1976), British Field Marshal, flag of Great Britain. b, Charles de Gaulle ((1890-1970), French general, flag of France. c, Dwight D. Eisenhower (1890-1969), Allied Supreme Commander, flag of the United States. d, Winston Churchill (1874-1965), British Prime Minister, flag of Great Britain. e, Victory celebration at the Arc de Triomphe, Paris. f, Harry S. Truman (1884-1972), 33rd President, flag of the United States.

**2020, Nov. 30 Litho. *Perf. 14¼x14***

**4205** A936 $1.60 Sheet of 6, #a-f 7.25 7.25

## SEMI-POSTAL STAMPS

**Catalogue values for unused stamps in this section are for Never Hinged items.**

**Map Type of 1977-78 Overprinted: "SOUFRIERE / RELIEF / FUND 1979" and New Values, "10c+5c" etc.**

**Litho. and Typo.**

**1979 Wmk. 373 *Perf. 14½x14***

**B1** A76 10c + 5c multi .25 .25
**B2** A76 50c + 25c multi .25 .25
**B3** A76 $1 + 50c multi .50 .50
**B4** A76 $2 + $1 multi 1.00 1.00
*Nos. B1-B4 (4)* 2.00 2.00

The surtax was for victims of the eruption of Mt. Soufrière.

**Nos. 604-607 Surcharged: "HURRICANE / RELIEF / 50c"**

**1980, Aug. 7 Litho. *Perf. 13½***

**B5** A90 10c + 50c multi .25 .25
**B6** A90 60c + 50c multi .40 .40
**B7** A90 80c + 50c multi .50 .50
**B8** A90 $2.50 + 50c multi 1.10 1.10
*Nos. B5-B8 (4)* 2.25 2.25

Surtax was for victims of Hurricane Allen.

**Nos. 1224-1226 Surcharged "CALIF EARTHQUAKE RELIEF" on 1 or 2 Lines and "+10c"**

**1989, Nov. 17 Litho. *Perf. 13½x14***

**B9** Sheet of 9 5.50 5.50
*a.-i.* A174 60c +10c #1224a-1224i .60 .60
**B10** Sheet of 9 5.50 5.50
*a.-i.* A174 60c +10c #1225a-1225i .60 .60
**B11** Sheet of 9 5.50 5.50
*a.-i.* A175 60c +10c #1226a-1226i .60 .60

## WAR TAX STAMPS

No. 105 Overprinted

Type I — Words 2 to 2½mm apart.
Type II — Words 1½mm apart.
Type III — Words 3½mm apart.

**1916 Wmk. 3 *Perf. 14***

**MR1** A17 1p car, type III 3.25 *25.00*
*a.* Double ovpt., type III 275.00 250.00
*b.* 1p carmine, type I 12.50 *18.50*
*c.* Comma after "STAMP", type I 12.50 *30.00*
*d.* Double ovpt., type I 200.00 200.00
*e.* 1p carmine, type II 135.00 87.50
*f.* Double ovpt., type II *1,450.*

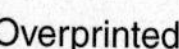
Overprinted

**MR2** A17 1p carmine 1.40 *2.25*

## OFFICIAL STAMPS

**Catalogue values for unused stamps in this section are for Never Hinged items.**

**Nos. 627-632 Overprinted**

**1982, Nov. Litho. *Perf. 14***

**O1** A94a 60c Couple, Isabella .25 .25
**O2** A94b 60c Couple .25 .25
**O3** A94a $2.50 Couple, Alberta .45 .45
**O4** A94b $2.50 Couple .65 .65
**O5** A94a $4 Couple, Britannia .80 .80
**O6** A94b $4 Couple .90 .90
*Nos. O1-O6 (6)* 3.30 3.30

## POSTAL-FISCAL STAMPS

Nos. AR1-AR7 were intended primarily for fiscal use but were also authorized and commonly used for payment of postal charges.

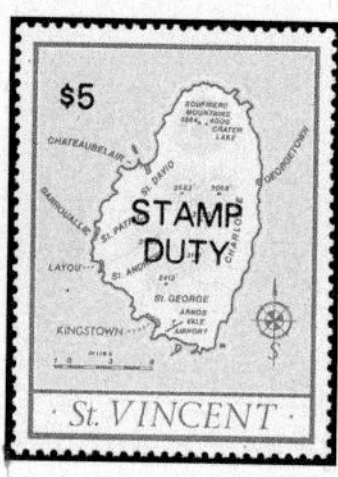

Map of St. Vincent — PF1

***Perf. 14½x14***

**1980, Feb. Litho. Wmk. 314**

**AR1** PF1 $5 vio & lavender 2.50 2.50
**AR2** PF1 $10 grn & apple grn 4.00 *5.00*
**AR3** PF1 $20 red vio & pale rose lilac 7.00 *12.00*
*Nos. AR1-AR3 (3)* 13.50 *19.50*

State Seal — PF2

***Perf. 14x13¼***

**1980, May 19 Engr. Wmk. 373**

**AR4** PF2 $5 deep blue 2.25 *2.75*
**AR5** PF2 $10 deep green 3.75 *4.75*
**AR6** PF2 $20 carmine rose 6.50 *10.50*
*Nos. AR4-AR6 (3)* 12.50 *18.00*

Nos. AR4-AR6 are dated "1980" below design.

***Perf. 12¼x12***

**1984, May 22 Engr. Wmk. 380**

**AR7** PF2 $20 carmine rose 8.50 *13.00*

No. AR7 is dated "1984" below design.

# ST. VINCENT GRENADINES

sānt 'vin͵t͵-sənt grə-'nā-də

LOCATION — Group of islands south of St. Vincent
CAPITAL — None

St. Vincent's portion of the Grenadines includes Bequia, Canouan, Mustique, Union and a number of smaller islands.

**Catalogue values for unused stamps in this area are for Never Hinged items.**

Stamps inscribed "Palm Island," "Tobago Cays," and "Young Island" are not listed as they do not meet Scott listing criteria.

The editors would like to examine any commercial covers mailed during 2000-2008 from the islands of Bequia, Canouan, Mayreau, Mustique or Union Island, which are franked only with the island's stamps.

All stamps are designs of St. Vincent unless otherwise noted or illustrated.

See St. Vincent Nos. 324-329a for six stamps and a souvenir sheet issued in 1971 inscribed "The Grenadines of St. Vincent."

**Princess Anne's Wedding Issue**
Common Design Type

**1973, Nov. 14 Litho. *Perf. 14***

**1** CD325 25c green & multi .25 .25
**2** CD325 $1 org brn & multi .25 .25

Common Design Types pictured following the introduction.

**Bird Type of 1970 and St. Vincent Nos. 281a-285a, 287a-289a Overprinted**

a

b

**1974 Photo. Wmk. 314 *Perf. 14***

**3** A36(a) 1c multicolored .25 .25
**4** A36(a) 2c multicolored .25 .25
**5** A36(b) 2c multicolored .25 .35
**6** A36(a) 3c multicolored .25 .25
**7** A36(b) 3c multicolored .25 .35
**8** A36(a) 4c multicolored .25 .25
**9** A36(a) 5c multicolored .25 .25
**10** A36(a) 6c multicolored .25 .25
**11** A36(a) 8c multicolored .25 .25
**12** A36(a) 10c multicolored .25 .25
**13** A36(a) 12c multicolored .25 .25
**14** A36(a) 20c multicolored .25 .25
**15** A36(a) 25c multicolored .30 .25
**16** A36(a) 50c multicolored .40 .35
**17** A36(a) $1 multicolored .60 *.70*
**18** A36(a) $2.50 multicolored .70 *.95*
**19** A36(a) $5 multicolored 1.00 *1.50*
*Nos. 3-19 (17)* 6.00 6.95

Nos. 8-9, 12-13, 17-18 vert.
Issue dates: #5, 7, June 7; others, Apr. 24.

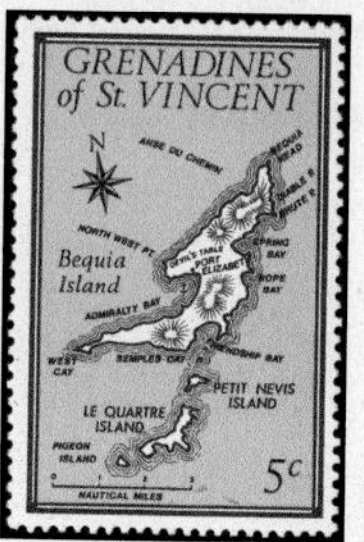

Maps of Islands — G1

***Perf. 13x12½***

**1974, May 9 Litho. Wmk. 314**

**20** G1 5c Bequia .25 .25
**21** G1 15c Prune .25 .25
**22** G1 20c Mayreau .25 .25
**23** G1 30c Mustique .25 .25
**24** G1 40c Union .25 .25
**24A** G1 $1 Canouan .25 .25
*Nos. 20-24A (6)* 1.50 1.50

No. 20 has no inscription at bottom. No. 84 is dated "1976."
See Nos. 84-111.

**UPU Type of 1974**

2c, Arrows circling UPU emblem. 15c, Post horn, globe. 40c, Target over map of islands, hand canceler. $1, Goode's map projection.

**1974, July 25 Litho. *Perf. 14½***

**25-28** A56 Set of 4 .70 .60

Bequia Island G2

Designs: 5c, Boat building. 30c, Careening at Port Elizabeth. 35c, Admiralty Bay. $1, Fishing Boat Race.

**1974**

**29-32** G2 Set of 4 .75 .70

Shells G3

Designs: 1c, Atlantic thorny oyster. 2c, Zigzag scallop. 3c, Reticulated helmet. 4c, Music volute. 5c, Amber pen shell. 6c, Angular triton. 8c, Flame helmet. 10c, Caribbean olive. 12c, Common sundial. 15c, Glory of the atlantic cone. 20c, Flame auger. 25c King venus. 35c. Long-spined star-shell. 45c, Speckled tellin. 50c, Rooster tail conch. $1, Green star-shell. $2.50, Incomparable cone. $5, Rough file clam. $10, Measled cowrie.

**1974-76 Wmk. 373**

**33-51** G3 Set of 19 12.50 9.00

Issued: #33-50, 11/27/74; #51, 7/12/76.
#36-40, 43, 45, 47-48, exist dated "1976," #40, 42-45, 49-50 dated "1977."
For surcharge see St. Vincent No. 3346.

**Churchill Type**

Churchill as: 5c, Prime Minister. 40c, Lord Warden of the Cinque Ports. 50c, First Lord of the Admiralty. $1, Royal Air Force officer.

**1974, Nov. 28**

**52-55** A58 Set of 4 .70 .70

Mustique Island G4

5c, Cotton House. 35c, Blue Waters, Endeavour. 45c, Endeavour Bay. $1, Gelliceaux Bay.

**1975, Feb. 27 Wmk. 373**

**56** G4 5c multicolored .25 .25
**57** G4 35c multicolored .25 .25
**58** G4 45c multicolored .25 .25
**59** G4 $1 multicolored .25 .25
*Nos. 56-59 (4)* 1.00 1.00

Butterflies G5

3c, Soldier martinique. 5c, Silver-spotted flambeau. 35c, Gold rim. 45c, Bright blue, Donkey's eye. $1, Biscuit.

**1975, May 15 *Perf. 14***

**60** G5 3c multicolored .25 .25
**61** G5 5c multicolored .30 .25
**62** G5 35c multicolored .55 .30
**63** G5 45c multicolored .70 .30
**64** G5 $1 multicolored 1.40 1.00
*Nos. 60-64 (5)* 3.20 2.10

Views of Petit St. Vincent G6

**1975, July 24 *Perf. 14½***

**65** G6 5c Resort pavilion .25 .25
**66** G6 35c Harbor .25 .25
**67** G6 45c Jetty .25 .25
**68** G6 $1 Sailing in coral lagoon .25 .25
*Nos. 65-68 (4)* 1.00 1.00

Christmas — G7

Island churches: 5c, Ecumenical Church, Mustique. 25c, Catholic Church, Union. 50c, Catholic Church, Bequia. $1, Anglican Church, Bequia.

**1975, Nov. 20** **Wmk. 314**
**69-72** G7 Set of 4 .65 .65

For surcharge see St. Vincent No. 3372.

Union Island G8

5c, Sunset. 35c, Customs and post office. 45c, Anglican Church. $1, Mail boat.

**1976, Feb. 26** **Wmk. 373** ***Perf. 13½***
**73** G8 5c Sunset .25 .25
**74** G8 35c multicolored .25 .25
**75** G8 45c multicolored .25 .25
**76** G8 $1 multicolored .25 .25
*Nos. 73-76 (4)* 1.00 1.00

Staghorn Coral — G9

**1976, May 13** ***Perf. 14½***
**77** G9 5c shown .25 .25
**78** G9 35c Elkhorn coral .25 .25
**79** G9 45c Pillar coral .25 .25
**80** G9 $1 Brain coral .40 .25
*Nos. 77-80 (4)* 1.15 1.00

US Bicentennial Coins — G10

**1976, July 15** ***Perf. 13½***
**81** G10 25c Washington quarter .25 .25
**82** G10 50c Kennedy half dollar .25 .25
**83** G10 $1 Eisenhower dollar .25 .25
*Nos. 81-83 (3)* .75 .75

## St. Vincent Grenadines Map Type

### Bequia Island

**1976, Sept. 23** **Litho.** ***Perf. 14***
**84** G1 5c grn, brt grn & blk .25 .25
**85** G1 10c multicolored .25 .25
*a.* Bklt. pane of 3, 2 #84, 85 .35 .35
**86** G1 35c multicolored .25 .25
*a.* Bklt. pane of 3, 2 #85, 86 .45 .45
**87** G1 45c multicolored .25 .25
*a.* Bklt. pane of 3, #84, 85, 87 .50 .50
*b.* Bklt. pane of 3, 2 #86, 87 .70 .70
*Nos. 84-87 (4)* 1.00 1.00

For previous 5c see No. 20.

### Canouan Island

**1976, Sept. 23**
**88** G1 5c multicolored .25 .25
**89** G1 10c multicolored .25 .25
*a.* Bklt. pane of 3, 2 #88, 89 .35 .35
**90** G1 35c multicolored .25 .25
*a.* Bklt. pane of 3, 2 #89, 90 .45 .45
**91** G1 45c multicolored .25 .25
*a.* Bklt. pane of 3, #88-89, 91 .50 .50
*b.* Bklt. pane of 3, 2 #90, 91 .70 .70
*Nos. 88-91 (4)* 1.00 1.00

### Mayreau Island

**1976, Sept. 23**
**92** G1 5c multicolored .25 .25
**93** G1 10c multicolored .25 .25
*a.* Bklt. pane of 3, 2 #92, 93 .35 .35
**94** G1 35c multicolored .25 .25
*a.* Bklt. pane of 3, 2 #93, 94 .45 .45
**95** G1 45c multicolored .25 .25
*a.* Bklt. pane of 3, #92-93, 95 .50 .50
*b.* Bklt. pane of 3, 2 #94, 95 .70 .70
*Nos. 92-95 (4)* 1.00 1.00

### Mustique Island

**1976, Sept. 23**
**96** G1 5c multicolored .25 .25
**97** G1 10c multicolored .25 .25
*a.* Bklt. pane of 3, 2 #96, 97 .35 .35
**98** G1 35c multicolored .25 .25
*a.* Bklt. pane of 3, 2 #97, 98 .45 .45
**99** G1 45c multicolored .25 .25
*a.* Bklt. pane of 3, #96-97, 99 .50 .50
*b.* Bklt. pane of 3, 2 #98, 99 .70 .70
*Nos. 96-99 (4)* 1.00 1.00

### Petit St. Vincent

**1976, Sept. 23**
**100** G1 5c multicolored .25 .25
**101** G1 10c multicolored .25 .25
*a.* Bklt. pane of 3, 2 #100, 101 .35 .35
**102** G1 35c multicolored .25 .25
*a.* Bklt. pane of 3, 2 #101, 102 .45 .45
**103** G1 45c multicolored .25 .25
*a.* Bklt. pane of 3, #100-101, 103 .50 .50
*b.* Bklt. pane of 3, 2 #102, 103 .70 .70
*Nos. 100-103 (4)* 1.00 1.00

### Prune Island

**1976, Sept. 23**
**104** G1 5c multicolored .25 .25
**105** G1 10c multicolored .25 .25
*a.* Bklt. pane of 3, 2 #104, 105 .35 .35
**106** G1 35c multicolored .25 .25
*a.* Bklt. pane of 3, 2 #105, 106 .45 .45
**107** G1 45c multicolored .25 .25
*a.* Bklt. pane of 3, #104-105, 107 .50 .50
*b.* Bklt. pane of 3, 2 #106, 107 .70 .70
*Nos. 104-107 (4)* 1.00 1.00

### Union Island

**1976, Sept. 23**
**108** G1 5c multicolored .25 .25
**109** G1 10c multicolored .25 .25
*a.* Bklt. pane of 3, 2 #108, 109 .35 .35
**110** G1 35c multicolored .25 .25
*a.* Bklt. pane of 3, 2 #109, 110 .45 .45
**111** G1 45c multicolored .25 .25
*a.* Bklt. pane of 3, #108-109, 111 .50 .50
*b.* Bklt. pane of 3, 2 #110, 111 .70 .70
*Nos. 108-111 (4)* 1.00 1.00

Mayreau Island G11

Designs: 5c, Station Hill school, post office. 35c, Church at Old Wall. 45c, Cruiser at anchor, La Souclere. $1, Saline Bay.

**1976, Dec. 2** ***Perf. 14½***
**112-115** G11 Set of 4 .75 .50

Queen Elizabeth II, Silver Jubilee — G12

Coins: 25c, Coronation Crown. 50c, Silver Wedding Crown. $1, Silver Jubilee Crown.

**1977, Mar. 3**
**116-118** G12 Set of 3 .60 .40

Fiddler Crab G13

**1977, May 19**
**119** G13 5c shown .25 .25
**120** G13 35c Ghost crab .25 .25
**121** G13 50c Blue crab .25 .25
**122** G13 $1.25 Spiny lobster .50 .90
*Nos. 119-122 (4)* 1.25 1.65

Prune Island G14

**1977, Aug. 25**
**123** G14 5c Snorkel diving .25 .25
**124** G14 35c Palm Island Resort .25 .25
**125** G14 45c Casuarina Beach .25 .25
**126** G14 $1 Palm Island Beach Club .25 1.00
*Nos. 123-126 (4)* 1.00 1.75

Map Type of 1977 Overprinted

***Perf. 14½x14***

**1977, Oct. 31** **Wmk. 314**
**127** A76 40c multicolored (R) .25 .25
**128** A76 $2 multicolored (B) .40 .25

For surcharge see St. Vincent No. 3381.

Canouan Island G15

5c, Clinic, Charlestown. 35c, Town jetty, Charlestown. 45c, Mailboat, Charlestown. $1, Grand Bay.

**1977, Dec. 8** **Wmk. 373** ***Perf. 14½***
**129** G15 5c multicolored .25 .25
**130** G15 35c multicolored .25 .25
**131** G15 45c multicolored .25 .25
**132** G15 $1 multicolored .25 .90
*Nos. 129-132 (4)* 1.00 1.65

Birds and Eggs G16

1c, Tropical Mockingbird. 2c, Mangrove cuckoo. 3c, Osprey. 4c, Smooth bellied ani. 5c, House wren. 6c, Bananaquit. 8c, Carib grackle. 10c, Yellow bellied elaenia. 12c, Collared plover. 15c, Cattle egret. 20c, Red footed booby. 25c, Red-billed tropic bird. 40c, Royal tern. 50c, Rusty tailed flycatcher. 80c, Purple gallinule. $1, Broad winged hawk. $2, Common ground dove. $3, Laughing gull. $5, Brown noddy. $10, Grey kingbird.

**1978, May 11** ***Perf. 13x12***
**133-152** G16 Set of 20 15.00 14.00

Nos. 139, 143, 149 exist imprinted "1979," Value: $1.60. Nos. 137-138, 140, 142, 144 imprinted "1980." Value: $1.50.

Nos. 147-148 imprinted "1979" are from No. 175a. Nos. 145-146, 150 imprinted "1980" are from No. 189a.

For surcharges see No. 266, St. Vincent Nos. 3347-3348.

## Elizabeth II Coronation Anniv. Type

Cathedrals.

**1978, June 2** ***Perf. 13½***
**153** A78 5c Worcester .25 .25
**154** A78 40c Coventry .25 .25
**155** A78 $1 Winchester .25 .25
**156** A78 $3 Chester .25 .25
Complete booklet, 2 each #153-156 2.25
*a.* Souv. sheet, #153-156, perf. 14 .60 .75
*Nos. 153-156 (4)* 1.00 1.00

Turtles G17

**1978, July 20** ***Perf. 14***
**157** G17 5c Green turtle .25 .25
**158** G17 40c Hawksbill turtle .25 .25
**159** G17 50c Leatherback turtle .30 .30
**160** G17 $1.25 Loggerhead turtle .60 .60
*Nos. 157-160 (4)* 1.40 1.40

For surcharge see St. Vincent No. 3374.

Christmas G18

Christmas scenes and verses from the carol "We Three Kings of Orient Are".

**1978, Nov. 2**
**161** G18 5c Three kings following star .25 .25
**162** G18 10c Gold .25 .25
**163** G18 25c Frankincense .25 .25
**164** G18 50c Myrrh .25 .25
**165** G18 $2 With infant Jesus .25 .25
*a.* Souvenir sheet of 5 + label, #161-165 .90 1.25
*Nos. 161-165 (5)* 1.25 1.25

Sailing Yachts — G19

**1979**
**166** G19 5c multicolored .25 .25
**167** G19 40c multi, diff. .25 .25
**168** G19 50c multi, diff. .25 .25
**169** G19 $2 multi, diff. .40 .40
*Nos. 166-169 (4)* 1.15 1.15

## Wildlife Type of 1980

**1979, Mar. 8** ***Perf. 14½***
**170** A91 20c Green iguana .25 .25
**171** A91 40c Manicou .25 .25
**172** A91 $2 Red-legged tortoise .70 .90
*Nos. 170-172 (3)* 1.20 1.40

## Sir Rowland Hill Type of 1979

Designs: 80c, Sir Rowland Hill. $1, Great Britain Types A1 and A5 with "A10" (Kingstown, St. Vincent) cancel. $2, St. Vincent #41 & 43 with Bequia cancel.

**1979, May 31** ***Perf. 13x12***
**173** A83 80c multicolored .25 .25
**174** A83 $1 multicolored .25 .25
**175** A83 $2 multicolored .25 .35
*a.* Souv. sheet, #173-175, 147-149 1.25 2.00
*Nos. 173-175 (3)* .75 .85

## IYC Type of 1979

Children and IYC emblem: 6c, Boy. 40c, Girl. $1, Boy, diff. $3, Girl and boy.

**1979, Oct. 24** ***Perf. 14x13½***
**176** A82 6c multicolored .25 .25
**177** A82 40c multicolored .25 .25
**178** A82 $1 multicolored .25 .25
**179** A82 $3 multicolored .25 .25
*Nos. 176-179 (4)* 1.00 1.00

### Independence Type of 1979

Designs: 5c, National flag, Ixora salici-folia. 40c, House of Assembly, Ixora odorata. $1, Prime Minister R. Milton Cato, Ixora jayanica.

**1979, Oct. 27** *Perf. 12½x12*
**180-182** A85 Set of 3 .45 .45

Printed se-tenant with label inscribed "Independence of St. Vincent and the Grenadines."

False Killer Whale G20

**1979, Jan. 25** *Perf. 14*
**183** G20 10c shown .50 .30
**184** G20 50c Spinner dolphin .50 .35
**185** G20 90c Bottle nosed dolphin .55 *.70*
**186** G20 $2 Blackfish 1.40 *1.75*
*Nos. 183-186 (4)* 2.95 *3.10*

For surcharges see St. Vincent Nos. 3352, 3371, 3383-3384.

### London '80 Type

**1980, Apr. 24** *Perf. 13x12*
**187** A88 40c Queen Elizabeth II .25 .25
**188** A88 50c St. Vincent #227 .25 .25
**189** A88 $3 #1-2 .25 *1.00*
*a.* Souvenir sheet of 6, #187-189, 145-146, 150 2.00 *2.25*
*Nos. 187-189 (3)* .75 1.50

### Olympics Type of 1980

**1980, Aug. 7** *Perf. 13½*
**190** A90 25c Running .25 .25
**191** A90 50c Sailing .25 .25
**192** A90 $1 Long jump .25 .25
**193** A90 $2 Swimming .25 .25
*Nos. 190-193 (4)* 1.00 1.00

For surcharge see St. Vincent No. 3353.

Christmas G21

Scenes and verse from the carol "De Borning Day."

**1980, Nov. 13** *Perf. 14*
**194** G21 5c multicolored .25 .25
**195** G21 50c multicolored .25 .25
**196** G21 60c multicolored .25 .25
**197** G21 $1 multicolored .25 .25
**198** G21 $2 multicolored .25 .25
*a.* Souvenir sheet of 5 + label, #194-198 .75 *1.25*
*Nos. 194-198 (5)* 1.25 1.25

For surcharge see St. Vincent No. 3385.

Bequia Island G22

50c, P.O., Port Elizabeth. 60c, Moonhole. $1.50, Fishing boats, Admiralty Bay. $2, Friendship Rose at jetty.

**1981, Feb. 19** *Perf. 14½*
**199** G22 50c multicolored .25 .25
**200** G22 60c multicolored .25 .25
**201** G22 $1.50 multicolored .25 *.45*
**202** G22 $2 multicolored .25 *.50*
*Nos. 199-202 (4)* 1.00 *1.45*

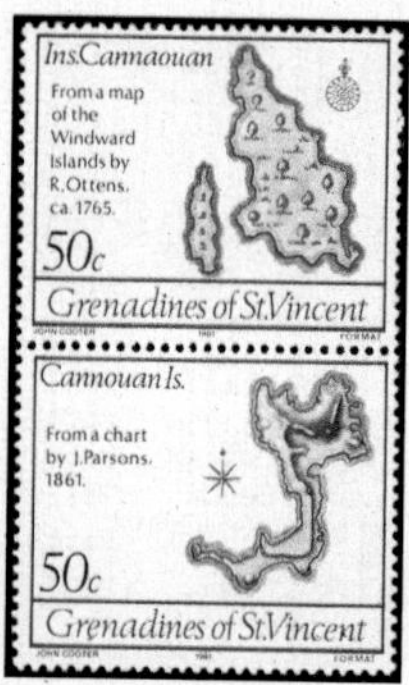


Map by R. Ottens, c. 1765 — G23

Maps: Nos. 204, 206 by J. Parsons, 1861. No. 208, by T. Jefferys, 1763.

**1981, Apr. 2** *Perf. 14*
**203** 50c Ins. Cannaouan .25 .25
**204** 50c Cannouan Island .25 .25
*a.* G23 Pair, #203-204 .55 .25
**205** 60c Ins. Moustiques .25 .25
**206** 60c Mustique Island .25 .25
*a.* G23 Pair, #205-206 .60 .60
**207** $2 Ins. Bequia .50 .65
**208** $2 Bequia Island .50 .65
*a.* G23 Pair, #207-208 1.10 1.40
*Nos. 203-208 (6)* 2.00 2.30

### Royal Wedding Types

No. 209, Couple, the Mary. No. 210, Couple. No. 211, Couple, the Alexandra. No. 213, Couple, the Brittania.

**1981, July 17** **Wmk. 380**
**209** A94a 50c multicolored .25 .25
*a.* Booklet pane of 4, perf. 12 .60 .60
**210** A94b 50c multicolored .30 *.40*
**211** A94a $3 multicolored .25 .25
**212** A94b $3 like #210 .60 *.80*
*a.* Booklet pane of 2, perf. 12 2.00 2.00
**213** A94a $3.50 multicolored .25 .25
**214** A94b $3.50 like #210 .65 *.85*
*Nos. 209-214 (6)* 2.30 2.80

Each denomination issued in sheets of 7 (6 type A94a, 1 type A94b).

For surcharges and overprints see Nos. 507-508, O1-O6.

### Souvenir Sheet

**1981** *Perf. 12*
**215** A94b $5 like #210 1.00 1.00

Bar Jack G25

**1981, Oct. 9** **Wmk. 373** *Perf. 14*
**218** G25 10c shown .25 .25
**219** G25 50c Tarpon .30 .25
**220** G25 60c Cobia .40 .25
**221** G25 $2 Blue marlin 1.00 .75
*Nos. 218-221 (4)* 1.95 1.50

Ships G26

**1982, Jan. 28** *Perf. 14x13½*
**222** G26 1c Experiment .25 .25
**223** G26 3c Lady Nelson .25 .25
**224** G26 5c Daisy .25 .25
**225** G26 6c Carib canoe .25 .25
**226** G26 10c Hairoun Star .35 .30
**227** G26 15c Jupiter .45 .35
**228** G26 20c Christina .45 .35
**229** G26 25c Orinoco .60 .40
**230** G26 30c Lively .60 .40
**231** G26 50c Alabama .85 .45
**232** G26 60c Denmark .95 .45
**233** G26 75c Santa Maria 1.00 .50
**234** G26 $1 Baffin .75 .50
**235** G26 $2 QE 2 1.10 1.10
**236** G26 $3 Britannia 1.10 *1.40*
**237** G26 $5 Geeststar 1.10 *1.60*
**238** G26 $10 Grenadines Star 1.45 *2.50*
*Nos. 222-238 (17)* 11.75 11.30

For overprint see No. 509.

G27

**1982, Apr. 5** *Perf. 14*
**239** G27 10c Prickly pear fruit .25 .25
**240** G27 50c Flower buds .30 .30
**241** G27 $1 Flower .50 .50
**242** G27 $2 Cactus 1.25 1.25
*Nos. 239-242 (4)* 2.30 2.30

For surcharge see St. Vincent No. 3386.

### Princess Diana Type of Kiribati

50c, Anne Neville. 60c, Arms of Anne Neville. $6, Diana, Princess of Wales.

**1982, July 1** **Wmk. 380** *Perf. 14*
**243** A99a 50c multicolored .25 .25
**244** A99a 60c multicolored .25 .25
**245** A99a $6 multicolored .50 .50
*Nos. 243-245 (3)* 1.00 1.00

For overprints see Nos. 248-262.

G29

**1982, July 1** **Wmk. 373** *Perf. 14½*
**246** G29 $1.50 Old, new uniforms .50 .50
**247** G29 $2.50 Lord Baden-Powell .80 .80

75th anniversary of Boy Scouts.

### Nos. 243-245 Ovptd. "ROYAL BABY / BEQUIA"

**1982, July 19** **Wmk. 380** *Perf. 14*
**248** A99a 50c multicolored .25 .25
**249** A99a 60c multicolored .25 .25
**250** A99a $6 multicolored .40 .40
*Nos. 248-250 (3)* .90 .90

### Nos. 243-245 Ovptd. "ROYAL BABY / CANOUAN"

**1982, July 19**
**251** A99a 50c multicolored .25 .25
**252** A99a 60c multicolored .25 .25
**253** A99a $6 multicolored .40 .40
*Nos. 251-253 (3)* .90 .90

### Nos. 243-245 Ovptd. "ROYAL BABY / MAYREAU"

**1982, July 19**
**254** A99a 50c multicolored .25 .25
**255** A99a 60c multicolored .25 .25
**256** A99a $6 multicolored .40 .40
*Nos. 254-256 (3)* .90 .90

### Nos. 243-245 Ovptd. "ROYAL BABY / MUSTIQUE"

**1982, July 19**
**257** A99a 50c multicolored .25 .25
**258** A99a 60c multicolored .25 .25
**259** A99a $6 multicolored .40 .40
*Nos. 257-259 (3)* .90 .90

### Nos. 243-245 Ovptd. "ROYAL BABY / UNION"

**1982, July 19**
**260** A99a 50c multicolored .25 .25
**261** A99a 60c multicolored .25 .25
**262** A99a $6 multicolored .40 .40
*Nos. 260-262 (3)* .90 .90

### Christmas Type of 1981

**1982, Nov. 18** *Perf. 13½*
**263** A97 10c Mary and Joseph at inn .25 .25
**264** A97 $1.50 Animals of stable .40 .40
**265** A97 $2.50 Nativity .50 .50
*a.* Souvenir sheet of 3, #263-265 1.10 *1.10*
*Nos. 263-265 (3)* 1.15 1.15

For surcharges see St. Vincent Nos. 3376, 3390-3391.

### No. 146 Surcharged

*Perf. 13x12*

**1983, Apr. 26** **Wmk. 373**
**266** G16 45c on 50c multicolored .55 .35

Union Island G30

50c, Power Station, Clifton. 60c, Sunrise, Clifton Harbor. $1.50, School, Ashton. $2, Frigate Rock, Conch Shell Beach.

**1983, May 12** *Perf. 13½*
**267** G30 50c multicolored .25 .25
**268** G30 60c multicolored .25 .25
**269** G30 $1.50 multicolored .35 .35
**270** G30 $2 multicolored .50 .50
*Nos. 267-270 (4)* 1.35 1.35

Treaty of Versailles, Bicent. — G31

**1983, Sept. 15** *Perf. 14½x14*
**271** G31 45c British warship .25 .25
**272** G31 60c American warship .30 .30
**273** G31 $1.50 US troops, flag .55 .55
**274** G31 $2 British troops in battle .75 .75
*Nos. 271-274 (4)* 1.85 1.85

For surcharges see St. Vincent Nos. 3350, 3360, 3364, 3377.

200 Years of Manned Flight G32

Designs: 45c, Montgolfier balloon 1783, vert. 60c, Ayres Turbo-thrush Commander. $1.50, Lebaudy "1" dirigible. $2, Space shuttle Columbia.

**1983, Sept. 15** *Perf. 14*
**275** G32 45c multicolored .25 .25
**276** G32 60c multicolored .25 .25
**277** G32 $1.50 multicolored .35 .35
**278** G32 $2 multicolored .40 .40
*a.* Souvenir sheet of 4, #275-278 1.60 1.60
*Nos. 275-278 (4)* 1.25 1.25

For surcharges see St. Vincent Nos. 3355, 3378-3379, 3387.

### British Monarch Type of 1984

No. 279a, Arms of Henry VIII. No. 279b, Henry VIII. No. 280a, Arms of James I. No. 280b, James I. No. 281a, Henry VIII. No. 281b, Hampton Court. No. 282a, James I. No. 282b, Edinburgh Castle. No. 283a, Mary Rose. No. 283b, Henry VIII, Portsmouth harbor. No. 284a, Gunpowder Plot. No. 284b, James I & Gunpowder Plot.

**1983, Oct. 25** **Unwmk.** *Perf. 12½*
**279** A110 60c Pair, #a.-b. .30 .30
**280** A110 60c Pair, #a.-b. .30 .30
**281** A110 75c Pair, #a.-b. .30 .30

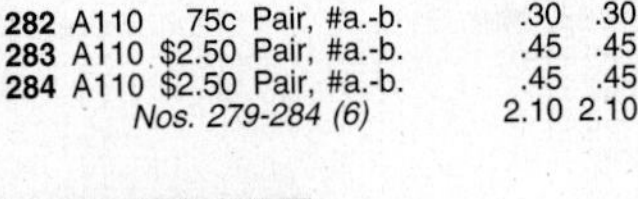

**282** A110 75c Pair, #a.-b. .30 .30
**283** A110 $2.50 Pair, #a.-b. .45 .45
**284** A110 $2.50 Pair, #a.-b. .45 .45
*Nos. 279-284 (6)* 2.10 2.10

Old Coinage — G33

20c, Quarter and half dollar, 1797. 45c, Nine bitts, 1811-14. 75c, Six and twelve bitts, 1811-14. $3, Sixty six shillings, 1798.

**1983, Dec. 1 Wmk. 373 *Perf. 14***
**291** G33 20c multicolored .25 .25
**292** G33 45c multicolored .25 .25
**293** G33 75c multicolored .25 .25
**294** G33 $3 multicolored .50 .50
*Nos. 291-294 (4)* 1.25 1.25

For surcharge see St. Vincent No. 3351.

### Locomotives Type of 1985

No. 295, 1948 Class C62, Japan. No. 296, 1898 P.L.M. Grosse C, France. No. 297, 1892 Class D13, US. No. 298, 1903 Class V, UK. No. 299, 1980 Class 253, UK. No. 300, 1968 Class 581, Japan. No. 301, 1874 1001 Class, UK. No. 302, 1977 Class 142, DDR. No. 303, 1899 T-9 Class, UK. No. 304, 1932 Class C12, Japan. No. 305, 1897 Class T15, Germany. No. 306, 1808 Catch-me-who-can, UK. No. 307, 1900 Claud Hamilton Class, UK. No. 308, 1948 Class E10, Japan. No. 309, 1937 Coronation Class, UK. No. 310, 1936 Class 231, Algeria. No. 311, 1927 Class 4P, UK. No. 312, 1979 Class 120, Germany. No. 313, 1941 Class J, US. No. 314, 1900 Class 13, UK. No. 315, 1913 Slieve Gullion Class S, UK. No. 316, 1929 Class A3, UK. No. 317, 1954 Class X, Australia. No. 318, 1895 Class D16, US. No. 319, 1904 J. B. Earle, UK. No. 320, 1879 Halesworth, UK. No. 321, 1930 Class V1, UK. No. 322, 1986 Class 59, UK. No. 323, 1935 Class E18, Germany. No. 324, 1923 Class D50, Japan. No. 325, 1859 Problem Class, UK. No. 326, 1958 Class 40, UK. No. 327, 1875 Class A, US. No. 328, 1907 Star Class, British. No. 329, 1898 Lyn, UK. No. 330, 1961 Western Class, UK. No. 331, 1958 Warship Class 42, UK. No. 332, 1831 Samson Type, US. No. 333, 1854 Hayes, US. No. 334, 1902 Class P-69, US. No. 335, 1865 Talyllyn, UK. No. 336, 1899 Drummond's Bug, UK. No. 337, 1913 Class 60-3 Shay, US. No. 338, 1938 Class H1-d, Canada. No. 339, 1890 Class 2120, Japan. No. 340, 1951 Clan Class, UK. No. 341, 1934 Pioneer Zephyr, US. No. 342, 1948 Blue Peter, UK. No. 343, 1874 Class Beattie Well Tank, UK. No. 344, 1906 Cardean, UK. No. 345, 1840 Fire Fly, UK. No. 346, 1884 Class 1800, Japan.

**1984-87 Litho. Unwmk. *Perf. 12½***
**Se-tenant Pairs, #a.-b.**
**a. — Side and front views.**
**b. — Action scene.**

**295** A120 1c multicolored .25 .25
**296** A120 1c multicolored .25 .25
**297** A120 5c multicolored .25 .25
**298** A120 5c multicolored .25 .25
**299** A120 10c multicolored .25 .25
**300** A120 10c multicolored .25 .25
**301** A120 10c multicolored .25 .25
**302** A120 10c multicolored .25 .25
**303** A120 15c multicolored .25 .25
**304** A120 15c multicolored .25 .25
**305** A120 15c multicolored .25 .25
**306** A120 20c multicolored .25 .25
**307** A120 35c multicolored .25 .25
**308** A120 35c multicolored .25 .25
**309** A120 35c multicolored .30 .30
**310** A120 40c multicolored .35 .35
**311** A120 40c multicolored .45 .45
**312** A120 40c multicolored .50 .50
**313** A120 45c multicolored .25 .25
**314** A120 45c multicolored .35 .35
**315** A120 50c multicolored .40 .40
**316** A120 50c multicolored .55 .55
**317** A120 50c multicolored .55 .55
**318** A120 60c multicolored .40 .40
**319** A120 60c multicolored .40 .40
**320** A120 60c multicolored .35 .35
**321** A120 60c multicolored .55 .55
**322** A120 60c multicolored .55 .55
**323** A120 70c multicolored .40 .40
**324** A120 75c multicolored .40 .40
**325** A120 75c multicolored .35 .35
**326** A120 75c multicolored .55 .55
**327** A120 75c multicolored .60 .60
**328** A120 $1 multicolored .40 .40
**329** A120 $1 multicolored .40 .40
**330** A120 $1 multicolored .40 .40
**331** A120 $1 multicolored .60 .60
**332** A120 $1 multicolored .60 .60
**333** A120 $1.20 multicolored .50 .50
**334** A120 $1.25 multicolored .60 .60
**335** A120 $1.50 multicolored .50 .50
**336** A120 $1.50 multicolored .45 .45
**337** A120 $1.50 multicolored .70 .70
**338** A120 $1.50 multicolored .80 .80
**339** A120 $2 multicolored .50 .50
**340** A120 $2 multicolored .80 .80
**341** A120 $2 multicolored .80 .80
**342** A120 $2.50 multicolored .50 .50
**343** A120 $2.50 multicolored 1.20 1.20
**344** A120 $3 multicolored .60 .60
**345** A120 $3 multicolored 1.00 1.00
*a.* Souvenir sheet of 4, #324, 345 3.50 3.50
**346** A120 $3 multicolored .60 .60
*Nos. 295-346 (52)* 23.70 23.70

Issued: #297, 299, 303, 307, 313, 318, 328, 342, 3/15/84; #295, 298, 306, 308, 319, 329, 335, 344, 10/9/84; #296, 304, 324, 345, 1/31/85; #300, 310, 315, 343, 5/17/85; #309, 323, 333, 339, 9/16/85; #305, 314, 320, 325, 330, 336, 340, 346, 3/14/86; #301, 311, 316, 321, 326, 331, 334, 337, 5/5/87; #302, 312, 317, 322, 327, 332, 338, 341, 8/26/87.

Spotted Eagle Ray G34

**Wmk. 380**
**1984, Apr. 26 Litho. *Perf. 14***
**399** G34 45c shown .25 .25
**400** G34 60c Queen trigger fish .25 .25
**401** G34 $1.50 White spotted file fish .35 .35
**402** G34 $2 Schoolmaster .40 .40
*Nos. 399-402 (4)* 1.25 1.25

For overprint see No. 504.

### Cricket Players Type of 1985

No. 403, R. A. Woolmer, portrait. No. 404, K. S. Ranjitsinhji, portrait. No. 405, W. R. Hammond, in action. No. 406, S. F. Barnes, portrait. No. 407, D. L. Underwood, in action. No. 408, R. Peel, in action. No. 409, M. D. Moxon, in action. No. 410, W. G. Grace, portrait. No. 411, L. Potter, portrait. No. 412, E. A. E. Baptiste, portrait. No. 413, H. Larwood, in action. No. 414, A. P. E. Knott, portrait. No. 415, Yorkshire & Kent county cricket clubs. No. 416, Sir John Berry Hobbs, portrait. No. 417, L. E. G. Ames, in action.

**1984-85 Unwmk. *Perf. 12½***
**Pairs, #a.-b.**
**403** A116 1c multicolored .25 .25
**404** A116 3c multicolored .25 .25
**405** A116 5c multicolored .25 .25
**406** A116 5c multicolored .25 .25
**407** A116 30c multicolored .55 .55
**408** A116 30c multicolored .45 .45
**409** A116 55c multicolored .45 .45
**410** A116 60c multicolored .70 .70
**411** A116 60c multicolored .45 .45
**412** A116 $1 multicolored .70 .70
**413** A116 $1 multicolored .55 .55
**414** A116 $2 multicolored .80 .80
**415** A116 $2 multicolored .70 .70
**416** A116 $2.50 multicolored .80 .80
**417** A116 $3 multicolored 1.10 1.10
*Nos. 403-417 (15)* 8.25 8.25

Size of stamps in No. 415: 58x38mm.
Issued: Nos. 403, 407, 410, 412, 414, 417, 8/16/84; Nos. 406, 408, 413, 416, 11/2/84; Nos. 409, 411, 415, 2/22/85.

Canouan Island G35

**1984, Sept. 3 Wmk. 380**
**433** G35 35c Junior secondary school .25 .25
**434** G35 45c Police station .35 .25
**435** G35 $1 Post office .40 *.50*
**436** G35 $3 Anglican church 1.00 *1.60*
*Nos. 433-436 (4)* 2.00 2.60

For surcharges see St. Vincent Nos. 3349, 3354, 3394.

Night-blooming Flowers — G36

**1984, Oct. 15**
**437** G36 35c Lady of the night .30 .30
**438** G36 45c Four o'clock .35 .35
**439** G36 75c Mother-in-law's tongue .45 .45
**440** G36 $3 Queen of the night 1.75 1.75
*Nos. 437-440 (4)* 2.85 2.85

For surcharges see St. Vincent Nos. 3351A, 3356.

### Car Type of 1983

No. 441, 1959 Facel Vega, France. No. 442, 1903 Winton, Britain. No. 443, 1914 Mercedes-Benz, Germany. No. 444, 1936 BMW, Germany. No. 445, 1954 Rolls Royce, Britain. No. 446, 1934 Frazer Nash, Britain. No. 447, 1931 Invicta, Britain. No. 448, 1974 Lamborghini, Italy. No. 449, 1959 Daimler, Britain. No. 450, 1932 Marmon, US. No. 451, 1966 Brabham Repco, Britain. No. 452, 1968 Lotus Ford. No. 453, 1949 Buick, US. No. 454, 1927 Delage, France.

**1984-86 Unwmk. *Perf. 12½***
**Se-tenant Pairs, #a.-b.**
**a. — Side and front views.**
**b. — Action scene.**
**441** A107 5c multicolored .25 .25
**442** A107 5c multicolored .25 .25
**443** A107 15c multicolored .25 .25
**444** A107 25c multicolored .25 .25
**445** A107 45c multicolored .25 .25
**446** A107 50c multicolored .30 .30
**447** A107 60c multicolored .30 .30
**448** A107 60c multicolored .25 .25
**449** A107 $1 multicolored .30 .30
**450** A107 $1 multicolored .30 .30
**451** A107 $1.50 multicolored .30 .30
**452** A107 $1.75 multicolored .30 .30
**453** A107 $3 multicolored .60 .60
**454** A107 $3 multicolored .50 .50
*Nos. 441-454 (14)* 4.40 4.40

Issued: #441, 444, 446, 453, 11/28/84; #442, 447, 449, 451, 4/9/85; #443, 445, 448, 450, 452, 454, 2/20/86.
Stamps issued 2/20/86 not inscribed "Leaders of the World."

### Christmas Type of 1983

20c, Three wise men, star. 45c, Journeying to Bethlehem. $3, Presenting gifts.

**Wmk. 380**
**1984, Dec. 3 Litho. *Perf. 14½***
**469** A106 20c multicolored .25 .25
**470** A106 45c multicolored .25 .25
**471** A106 $3 multicolored .35 *1.00*
*a.* Souvenir sheet of 3, #469-471 1.00 *1.50*
*Nos. 469-471 (3)* .85 *1.50*

For surcharges see St. Vincent Nos. 3358, 3361.

Shellfish G37

**1985, Feb. 11 *Perf. 14***
**472** G37 25c Caribbean king crab .25 .25
**473** G37 60c Queen conch .30 .30
**474** G37 $1 White sea urchin .40 *.45*
**475** G37 $3 West Indian top shell .80 *1.75*
*Nos. 472-475 (4)* 1.75 *2.75*

For surcharge see St. Vincent No. 3395.

Flowers — G38

No. 476a, Cypripedium calceolus. No. 476b, Gentiana asclepiadea. No. 477a, Clianthus formosus. No. 477b, Celmisia coriacea. No. 478a, Erythronium americanum. No. 478b, Laelia anceps. No. 479a, Leucadendron discolor. No. 479b, Meconopsis horridula.

**1985, Mar. 13 Unwmk. *Perf. 12½***
**476** G38 5c Pair, #a.-b. .25 .25
**477** G38 55c Pair, #a.-b. .30 .30
**478** G38 60c Pair, #a.-b. .30 .30
**479** G38 $2 Pair, #a.-b. .55 .55
*Nos. 476-479 (4)* 1.40 1.40

Water Sports G39

**1985, May 9 Wmk. 380 *Perf. 14***
**484** G39 35c Windsurfing .25 .25
**485** G39 45c Water skiing .25 .25
**486** G39 75c Scuba diving .25 .25
**487** G39 $3 Deep sea fishing .40 .40
*Nos. 484-487 (4)* 1.15 1.15

Tourism.
For surcharge see St. Vincent No. 3396.

Fruits and Blossoms G40

**1985, June 24 *Perf. 15***
**488** G40 30c Passion fruit .25 .25
**489** G40 75c Guava .30 .30
**490** G40 $1 Sapodilla .45 .45
**491** G40 $2 Mango .75 .75
*a.* Souvenir sheet of 4, #488-491, perf. 14½x15 2.50 2.50
*Nos. 488-491 (4)* 1.75 1.75

For overprint see No. 503.

### Queen Mother Type of 1985

#496a, Facing right. #496b, Facing forward. #497a, Facing right. #497b, Facing left. #498a, Facing right. #498b, Facing forward. #499a, Facing right. #499b, Facing left. #500a, As girl facing forward. #500b, Facing left.

**1985, July 31 Unwmk. *Perf. 12½***
**496** A122 40c Pair, #a.-b. .25 .25
**497** A122 75c Pair, #a.-b. .30 .30
**498** A122 $1.10 Pair, #a.-b. .30 .30
**499** A122 $1.75 Pair, #a.-b. .30 .30
*Nos. 496-499 (4)* 1.15 1.15

**Souvenir Sheet of 2**
**500** A122 $2 Pair, #a.-b. .90 .90

Souvenir sheets containing two $4 or two $5 stamps exist.

### Nos. 213-214, 236, 399, 488, and 496-497 Ovptd. or Srchd. "CARIBBEAN ROYAL VISIT 1985" in 1, 2 or 3 Lines

***Perfs., Wmks. as Before***
**1985, Oct. 27**
**503** G40 30c On #488 1.00 1.00
**504** G37 45c On #399 1.25 1.25
**505** A122 $1.10 On #496 2.25 2.25
**506** A122 $1.10 On #497 2.25 2.25
**507** A94a $1.50 On $3.50, #213 2.50 2.50
**508** A94b $1.50 On $3.50, #214 22.50 22.50
**509** G26 $3 On #236 3.25 3.25
*Nos. 503-509 (7)* 35.00 35.00

Traditional Dances G41

**1985, Dec. 16 Unwmk. *Perf. 15***

**510** G41 45c Donkey man .25 .25
**511** G41 75c Cake dance, vert. .25 .25
**512** G41 $1 Bois-bois man, vert. .35 .35
**513** G41 $2 Maypole dance .55 .55
*Nos. 510-513 (4)* 1.40 1.40

For surcharges see St. Vincent Nos. 3366-3367.

**Queen Elizabeth II 60th Birthday Type**

5c, Elizabeth II. $1, At Princess Anne's christening. $4, As Princess. $6, In Canberra, 1982, vert. $8, Elizabeth II with crown.

**1986, Apr. 21 *Perf. 12½***

**514-517** A128 Set of 4 2.00 2.00

**Souvenir Sheet**

**518** A128 $8 multi 2.75 2.75

Handicrafts — G41a

**Wmk. 380**

**1986, Apr. 22 Litho. *Perf. 15***

**519** G41a 10c Dolls .25 .25
**520** G41a 60c Basketwork .25 .25
**521** G41a $1 Scrimshaw .25 .25
**522** G41a $3 Model boat .55 .55
*Nos. 519-522 (4)* 1.30 1.30

World Cup Soccer Championship, Mexico — G42

***Perf. 12½, 15 (#525-528)***

**1986, May 7 Unwmk.**

**523** G42 1c Uruguayan team .25 .25
**524** G42 10c Polish team .25 .25
**525** G42 45c Bulgarian player .30 .30
**526** G42 75c Iraqi player .35 .35
**527** G42 $1.50 S. Korean player .60 .60
**528** G42 $2 N. Ireland player .70 .70
**529** G42 $4 Portuguese team 1.00 1.00
**530** G42 $5 Canadian team 1.10 1.10
*Nos. 523-530 (8)* 4.55 4.55

**Souvenir Sheets**

**531** G42 $1 like #529 .50 .50
**532** G42 $3 like #523 1.25 1.25

Size: Nos. 525-528, 25x40mm.

Fungi — G43

45c, Marasmius pallescens. 60c, Leucocoprinus fragilissimus. 75c, Hygrocybe occidentalis. $3, Xerocomus hypoxanthus.

**Wmk. 380**

**1986, May 23 Litho. *Perf. 14***

**533** G43 45c multicolored 2.50 2.50
**534** G43 60c multicolored 2.75 2.75
**535** G43 75c multicolored 3.00 3.00
**536** G43 $3 multicolored 8.00 8.00
*Nos. 533-536 (4)* 16.25 16.25

For surcharge see St. Vincent No. 3397.

**Royal Wedding Type of 1986**

No. 539a, Sarah, Diana. No. 539b, Andrew. No. 540a, Anne, Andrew, Charles, Margaret, horiz. No. 540b, Sarah, Andrew, horiz.

**1986 Unwmk. *Perf. 12½***

**539** A132 60c Pair, #a.-b. .35 .35
**540** A132 $2 Pair, #a.-b. 1.10 1.10

**Souvenir Sheet**

**541** A132a $8 Andrew, Sarah, in coach 3.50 3.50

Issued: #539-540, July 18; #541, Oct. 15.

**Nos. 539-540 Ovptd. in Silver "Congratulations to TRH The Duke & Duchess of York" in 3 Lines**

**1986, Oct. 15**

**542** A132 60c Pair, #a.-b. .60 .60
**543** A132 $2 Pair, #a.-b. 2.00 2.00

Dragonflies — G44

45c, Brachymesia furcata. 60c, Lepthemis vesiculosa. 75c, Perithemis domitta. $2.50, Tramea abdominalis, vert.

**1986, Nov. 19 *Perf. 15***

**546** G44 45c multicolored .25 .25
**547** G44 60c multicolored .25 .25
**548** G44 75c multicolored .25 .25
**549** G44 $2.50 multicolored .55 .55
*Nos. 546-549 (4)* 1.30 1.30

**Statue of Liberty Type**

Souvenir Sheets

Each stamp shows different views of Statue of Liberty and a different US president in the margin.

**1986, Nov. 26 *Perf. 14***

**550** A135 $1.50 multicolored .25 .25
**551** A135 $1.75 multicolored .30 .30
**552** A135 $2 multicolored .35 .40
**553** A135 $2.50 multicolored .40 .50
**554** A135 $3 multicolored .50 .50
**555** A135 $3.50 multicolored .60 .60
**556** A135 $5 multicolored .80 .80
**557** A135 $6 multicolored .90 .90
**558** A135 $8 multicolored 1.25 1.25
*Nos. 550-558 (9)* 5.35 5.50

Birds of Prey — G45

**1986, Nov. 26 Litho.**

**560** G45 10c Sparrow hawk .75 .75
**561** G45 45c Black hawk 1.50 1.50
**562** G45 60c Duck hawk 1.75 1.75
**563** G45 $4 Fish hawk 8.00 8.00
*Nos. 560-563 (4)* 12.00 12.00

For surcharges see St. Vincent Nos. 3362, 3401.

Christmas — G46

45c, Santa playing drums. 60c, Santa wind surfing. $1.25, Santa water skiing. $2, Santa limbo dancing.

**1986, Nov. 26**

**564** G46 45c multicolored .25 .25
**565** G46 60c multicolored .30 .30
**566** G46 $1.25 multicolored .80 .80
**567** G46 $2 multicolored 1.15 1.15
*a.* Souvenir sheet of 4, #564-567 8.50 8.50
*Nos. 564-567 (4)* 2.50 2.50

For surcharge see St. Vincent No. 3375.

**Queen Elizabeth II, 40th Wedding Anniv. Type of 1987**

15c, Elizabeth, Charles. 45c, Victoria, Albert. $1.50, Elizabeth, Philip. $3, Elizabeth, Philip, diff. $4, Elizabeth, portrait.
$6, Elizabeth as Princess.

**1987, Oct. 15 *Perf. 12½***

**568** A140 15c multicolored .25 .25
**569** A140 45c multicolored .25 .25
**570** A140 $1.50 multicolored .30 .30
**571** A140 $3 multicolored .35 .35
**572** A140 $4 multicolored .45 .45
*Nos. 568-572 (5)* 1.60 1.60

**Souvenir Sheet**

**573** A140 $6 multicolored 1.90 1.90

Victoria's accession to the throne, 150th anniv.

Marine Life G48

45c, Banded coral shrimp. 50c, Arrow crab, flamingo tongue. 65c, Cardinal fish. $5, Moray eel.

No. 578, Puffer fish.

**1987, Dec. 17 *Perf. 15***

**574** G48 45c multicolored .55 .55
**575** G48 50c multicolored .60 .60
**576** G48 65c multicolored .70 .70
**577** G48 $5 multicolored 2.60 2.60
*Nos. 574-577 (4)* 4.45 4.45

**Souvenir Sheet**

**578** G48 $5 multicolored 2.60 2.60

America's Cup Yachts — G49

**1988, Mar. 31 *Perf. 12½***

**579** G49 50c Australia IV .30 .30
**580** G49 65c Crusader II .35 .35
**581** G49 75c New Zealand K27 .40 .40
**582** G49 $2 Italia .60 .60
**583** G49 $4 White Crusader .75 .75
**584** G49 $5 Stars and Stripes .75 .75
*Nos. 579-584 (6)* 3.15 3.15

**Souvenir Sheet**

**585** G49 $1 Champosa V .90 .90

Bequia Regatta G50

**1988, Mar. 31 *Perf. 15***

**586** G50 5c Seine boats .25 .25
**587** G50 50c Friendship Rose .25 .25
**588** G50 75c Fishing boats .25 .25
**589** G50 $3.50 Yacht racing .40 .40
*Nos. 586-589 (4)* 1.15 1.15

**Souvenir Sheet**

***Perf. 12½***

**590** G50 $8 Port Elizabeth 3.50 3.50

For surcharges see St. Vincent Nos. 3368, 3400.

Tourism — G51

Aircraft of Mustique Airways, Genadine Tours.

**1988, May 26 *Perf. 14x13½***

**591** G51 15c multicolored .25 .25
**592** G51 65c multi, diff. .25 .25
**593** G51 75c multi, diff. .25 .25
**594** G51 $5 multi, diff. .55 .55
*Nos. 591-594 (4)* 1.30 1.30

**Souvenir Sheet**

**595** G51 $10 Waterfall, vert. 3.50 3.50

No. 595 contains one 35x56mm stamp.
For surcharges see St. Vincent Nos. 3369-3370.

Great Explorers G52

Designs: 15c, Vitus Bering and the St. Peter. 75c, Bering and pancake ice. $1, David Livingstone and the Ma-Robert. $2, Livingstone meeting Henry M. Stanley. $3, John Speke (1827-1864) and Sir Richard Burton (1821-1890) welcomed at Tabori. $3.50, Speke, Burton at Lake Victoria. $4, Crewman of Christopher Columbus spotting land. $4.50, Columbus, exchange of gifts. $5, Sextant. $6, Columbus' ship landing in Bahamas, 1492.

**1988, July 29 *Perf. 14***

**596-603** G52 Set of 8 4.50 4.50

**Souvenir Sheets**

**604** G52 $5 multi 1.50 1.50
**605** G52 $6 multi 1.75 1.75

Nos. 602-603, 605 picture 500th anniversary discovery of America emblem.

A number of unissued items, imperfs., part perfs., missing color varieties, etc., were made available when the Format International inventory was liquidated.

Cricketers — G53

**1988, July 29 *Perf. 15***

**606** G53 20c A. I. Razvi .25 .25
**607** G53 45c R. J. Hadlee .25 .25
**608** G53 75c M. D. Crowe .45 .45
**609** G53 $1.25 C. H. Lloyd .70 .70
**610** G53 $1.50 A. R. Border .85 .85
**611** G53 $2 M. D. Marshall 1.10 1.10
**612** G53 $2.50 G. A. Hick 1.25 1.25

613 G53 $3.50 C. G. Greenidge, horiz. 1.50 1.50
Nos. 606-613 (8) 6.35 6.35

A $3 souvenir sheet in the design of the $2 stamp was not a postal issue according to the St. Vincent P.O. Value $6.

### Tennis Type of 1987

15c, Pam Shriver, horiz. 50c, Kevin Curran. 75c, Wendy Turnbull. $1, Evonne Cawley. $1.50, Ilie Nastase, horiz. $2, Billie Jean King. $3, Bjorn Borg. $3.50, Virginia Wade.

**1988, July 29** *Perf. 12½*

614 A137 15c multicolored .25 .25
615 A137 50c multicolored .25 .25
616 A137 75c multicolored .30 .30
617 A137 $1 multicolored .40 .40
618 A137 $1.50 multicolored .45 .45
619 A137 $2 multicolored .55 .55
620 A137 $3 multicolored .65 .65
621 A137 $3.50 multicolored .70 .70
Nos. 614-621 (8) 3.55 3.55

**Souvenir Sheet**

622 Sheet of 2 2.00 2.00
a. A137 $2.25 Stefan Edberg .80 .80
b. A137 $2.25 Steffi Graf .80 .80

No. 616 inscribed "Turnball" in error.

India '89, International Stamp Exhibition, New Dehli — G54

Disney characters and sites in India — 1c, Fatehpur Sikri. 2c, Palace on Wheels. 3c, Old fort, Delhi. 5c, Pinjore Gardens. 10c, Taj Mahal. 25c, Chandni Chowk. $4, Agra Fort, Jaipur. $5, Gandhi Memorial.
No. 631, Qutab Minar, vert. No. 632, Palace of the Winds.

**1989, Feb. 7** *Perf. 14x13½*

623 G54 1c multicolored .25 .25
624 G54 2c multicolored .25 .25
625 G54 3c multicolored .25 .25
626 G54 5c multicolored .25 .25
627 G54 10c multicolored .25 .25
628 G54 25c multicolored .25 .25
629 G54 $4 multicolored 3.50 3.50
630 G54 $5 multicolored 4.75 4.75
Nos. 623-630 (8) 9.75 9.75

**Souvenir Sheets**

631 G54 $6 multicolored 6.75 6.75
632 G54 $6 multicolored 6.75 6.75

### Japanese Art Type

Paintings: 5c, The View at Yotsuya, by Hokusai. 30c, Landscape at Ochanomizu, by Hokuju. 45c, Itabashi, by Eisen. 65c, Early Summer Rain, by Kunisada. 75c, High Noon at Kasumigaseki, by Kuniyoshi. $1, The Yoshiwara Embankment by Moonlight, by Kuniyoshi. $4, The Bridge of Boats at Sano, by Hokusai. $5, Lingering Snow on Mount Hira, by Kunitora. No. 641, Colossus of Rhodes, by Kunitora. No. 642, Shinobazu Pond, by Kokan.

**1989, July 6** *Perf. 14x13½*

633-640 A170 Set of 8 11.50 11.50

**Souvenir Sheets**

641 A170 $6 multicolored 5.50 5.50
642 A170 $6 multicolored 5.50 5.50

Miniature Sheet

1990 World Cup Soccer Championships, Italy — G55

Soccer players and landmarks: a, Mt. Vesuvius. b, The Colosseum. c, Venice. d, Roman Forum. e, Leaning Tower of Pisa. f, Florence. g, The Vatican. h, The Pantheon.

**1989, July 10** *Perf. 14*

643 G55 Sheet of 8 13.50 13.50
a.-h. $1.50 any single 1.60 1.60

### Discovery of America 500th Anniv. Type of Antigua & Barbuda

UPAE emblem and American Indians: 25c, Smoking tobacco. 75c, Rolling tobacco. $1, Body painting. No. 647a, Starting campfire. No. 647b, Woman drinking from bowl. No. 647c, Woman frying grain or corn patties. No. 647d, Adult resting in hammock using stone mortar and pestle. $4, Smoothing wood. No. 649, Chief. No. 650, Fishing with bow and arrow.

**1989, Oct. 2** **Litho.** *Perf. 14*

644 A196 25c multicolored .25 .25
645 A196 75c multicolored .80 .80
646 A196 $1 multicolored 1.00 1.00
647 Strip of 4 5.00 5.00
a.-d. A196 $1.50 any single 1.00 1.00
648 A196 $4 multicolored 3.00 3.00
Nos. 644-648 (5) 10.05 10.05

**Souvenir Sheets**

649 A196 $6 multicolored 5.00 5.00
650 A196 $6 multicolored 5.00 5.00

No. 647 has continuous design.

### 1st Moon Landing Type

Designs: 5c *Columbia* command module. 40c, Neil Armstrong saluting flag on the Moon. 55c. Command module over Moon. 65c, *Eagle* liftoff from Moon. 70c, *Eagle* on the Moon. $1, Command module re-entering Earth's atmosphere. $3, Apollo 11 mission emblem. $5, Armstrong and Buzz Aldrin walking on the Moon. No. 659, Apollo 11 launch, vert. No. 660, Splashdown.

**1989, Oct. 2** *Perf. 14*

651-658 A171 Set of 8 12.50 12.50

**Souvenir Sheets**

659 A171 $6 multi, vert. 5.00 5.00
660 A171 $6 multi 5.00 5.00

Butterflies G56

5c, Southern dagger tail. 30c, Androgeus swallowtail. 45c, Clench's hairstreak. 65c, Buckeye. 75c, Venezuelan sulphur. $1, Mimic. $4, Common longtail skipper. $5, Carribean buckeye.
No. 669, Flambeau. No. 670, Queen, large orange sulphur, Ramsden's giant white.

**1989, Oct. 16** **Litho.** *Perf. 14x14½*

661 G56 5c multicolored .45 .45
662 G56 30c multicolored .75 .75
663 G56 45c multicolored 1.00 1.00
664 G56 65c multicolored 1.10 1.10
665 G56 75c multicolored 1.40 1.40
666 G56 $1 multicolored 1.50 1.50
667 G56 $4 multicolored 6.00 6.00
668 G56 $5 multicolored 7.50 7.50
Nos. 661-668 (8) 19.70 19.70

**Souvenir Sheets**

669 G56 $6 multicolored 9.50 9.50
670 G56 $6 multicolored 9.50 9.50

Flora — G57

80c, Solanum urens. $1.25, Passiflora andersonii. $1.65, Miconia andersonii. $1.85, Pitcairnia sulphurea.

**1989, Nov. 1** **Litho.** *Perf. 14*

671 G57 80c multicolored 1.25 1.25
672 G57 $1.25 multicolored 1.75 1.75
673 G57 $1.65 multicolored 2.50 2.50
674 G57 $1.85 multicolored 2.75 2.75
Nos. 671-674 (4) 8.25 8.25

Christmas — G58

Walt Disney characters and classic automobiles — 5c, 1907 Rolls-Royce. 10c, 1897 Stanley Steamer. 15c, 1904 Darracq Genevieve. 45c, 1914 Detroit Electric Coupe. 55c, 1896 Ford. $2, 1904 REO Runabout. $3, 1899 Winton Mail Truck. $5, 1893 Duryea Car.
No. 683, 1912 Pope-Hartford. No. 684, 1908 Buick Model 10.

**1989, Dec. 20** *Perf. 14x13½, 13½x14*

675 G58 5c multicolored .30 .30
676 G58 10c multicolored .30 .30
677 G58 15c multicolored .30 .30
678 G58 45c multicolored .75 .75
679 G58 55c multicolored 1.00 1.00
680 G58 $2 multicolored 2.00 2.00
681 G58 $3 multicolored 2.75 2.75
682 G58 $5 multicolored 4.25 4.25
Nos. 675-682 (8) 11.65 11.65

**Souvenir Sheets**

683 G58 $6 multicolored 7.25 7.25
684 G58 $6 multicolored 7.25 7.25

Nos. 683-684 vert.

Battles of World War II G59

10c, 1st Battle of Narvik, 4/10/40. 15c, Allies land at Anzio, 1/22/44. 20c, Battle of Midway, 6/4/42. 45c, Allies launch offensive on Gustav Line, 5/11/44. 55c, Allies take over zones in Berlin, 7/3/45. 65c, Battle of the Atlantic, 3/1-20/43. 90c, Allies launch final phase of North African Campaign, 4/22/43. $3, US forces land on Guam, 7/21/44. $5, US 7th Army meets the 3rd Army across the Rhine, 3/26/45. #694, Battle of Leyte Gulf, 10/23/44. #695, The Dambusters Raid, 5/16/43.

**1990, Apr. 2** **Litho.** *Perf. 14*

685-694 G59 Set of 10 20.00 20.00

**Souvenir Sheet**

695 G59 $6 multi 10.50 10.50

For surcharge see St. Vincent No. 3399.

Penny Black, 150th Anniv. — G60

$1, Stamp World London '90 emblem. $5, Negative image of the Penny Black. $6, Penny Black with non-existent letters.

**1990, May 3** *Perf. 14x15*

696 G60 $1 pale rose & blk 1.25 1.25
697 G60 $5 pale violet & blk 6.00 6.00

**Souvenir Sheet**

698 G60 $6 dull blue & blk 6.75 6.75

Stamp World London '90.

Disney Characters Portraying Shakespearian Roles — G61

Designs: 20c, Goofy as Marc Antony in "Julius Caesar." 30c, Clarabelle Cow as nurse in "Romeo and Juliet." 45c, Pete as Falstaff in "Henry IV." 50c, Minnie Mouse as Portia in "The Merchant of Venice." $1, Donald Duck holding head of Yorick in "Hamlet." $2, Daisy Duck as Ophelia in "Hamlet." $4, Donald and Daisy Duck as Benedick and Beatrice in "Much Ado About Nothing." $5, Minnie Mouse and Donald Duck as Katherine and Petruchio in "The Taming of the Shrew." No. 707, Mickey and Minnie Mouse portraying Romeo and Juliet. No. 708, Clarabelle Cow as Titania in "A Midsummer Night's Dream."

**1990, May** *Perf. 14x13½*

699-706 G61 Set of 8 13.00 13.00

**Souvenir Sheets**

707 G61 $6 multi 6.75 6.75
708 G61 $6 multi 6.75 6.75

World Cup Soccer Championships, Italy — G62

World Cup Trophy and players from participating countries.

**1990, Sept. 24** **Litho.** *Perf. 14*

709 G62 25c Scotland .45 .45
710 G62 50c Egypt .85 .85
711 G62 $2 Austria 2.75 2.75
712 G62 $4 United States 4.75 4.75
Nos. 709-712 (4) 8.80 8.80

**Souvenir Sheets**

713 G62 $6 Holland 7.00 7.00
714 G62 $6 England 7.00 7.00

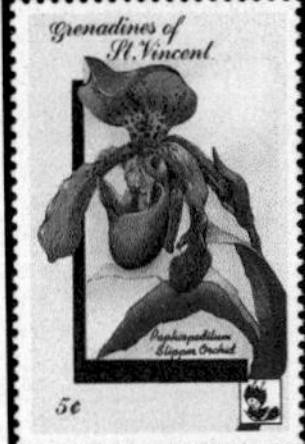

Orchids — G63

Designs: 5c, Paphiopedilum. 25c, Dendrobium phalaenopsis, Cymbidium. 30c, Miltonia candida. 50c, Epidendrum ibaguense, Cymbidium Elliot Rogers. $1, Rossioglassum grande. $2, Phalaenopsis Elisa Chang Lou, Masdevallia coccinea. $4, Cypripedium accale, Cypripedium calceolus. $5, Orchis spectabilis. No. 723, Epidendrum ibaguense, Phalaenopsis. No. 724, Dendrobium anosmum.

**1990, Nov. 23** **Litho.** *Perf. 14*

715-722 G63 Set of 8 18.00 18.00

**Souvenir Sheets**

723 G63 $6 multi 9.00 9.00
724 G63 $6 multi 9.00 9.00

Expo '90, Intl. Garden and Greenery Exposition, Osaka, Japan.

Birds G64

5c, Common ground dove. 25c, Purple martin. 45c, Painted bunting. 55c, Blue-hooded euphonia. 75c, Blue-gray tanager. $1, Red-eyed vireo. $2, Palm chat. $3, North American jacana. $4, Green-throated carib. $5, St. Vincent parrot.

$6, Red-legged honeycreeper.

**1990, Nov. 26**

**725** G64 5c multicolored .40 .40
**726** G64 25c multicolored .40 .40
**727** G64 45c multicolored .70 .70
**728** G64 55c multicolored .80 .80
**729** G64 75c multicolored 1.00 1.00
**730** G64 $1 multicolored 1.10 1.10
**731** G64 $2 multicolored 1.75 1.75
**732** G64 $3 multicolored 2.50 2.50
**733** G64 $4 multicolored 3.25 3.25
**734** G64 $5 multicolored 4.50 4.50
*Nos. 725-734 (10)* 16.40 16.40

**Souvenir Sheets**

**735** Sheet of 2 5.25 5.25
*a.* G64 $3 Bananaquit 2.25 2.25
*b.* G64 $3 Magnificent frigatebird 2.25 2.25
**736** G64 $6 multicolored 5.25 5.25

**Queen Mother 90th Birthday Type**

Photographs: Nos. 737a-737i, From 1900-1929. Nos. 738a-738i, From 1930-1959. Nos. 739a-739i, From 1960-1989. Nos. 740-748, Enlarged photographs used for Nos. 737-739.

**1991, Feb. 14 Litho. *Perf. 14***

**Miniature Sheets of 9, #a.-i.**

**737** A193 $2 blue & multi 12.00 12.00
**738** A193 $2 pink & multi 12.00 12.00
**739** A193 $2 green & multi 12.00 12.00

**Souvenir Sheets**

**740** A193 $5 like #737a 3.25 3.25
**741** A193 $5 like #737f 3.25 3.25
**742** A193 $5 like #737h 3.25 3.25
**743** A193 $5 like #738b 3.25 3.25
**744** A193 $5 like #738f 3.25 3.25
**745** A193 $5 like #738g 3.25 3.25
**746** A193 $5 like #739b 3.25 3.25
**747** A193 $5 like #739d 3.25 3.25
**748** A193 $5 like #739h 3.25 3.25

Paintings by Vincent Van Gogh — G65

Designs: 5c, View of Arles with Irises in the Foreground. 10c, View of Saintes-Maries, vert. 15c, An Old Woman of Arles, vert. 20c, Orchard in Blossom, Bordered by Cypresses. 25c, Three White Cottages in Saintes-Maries. 35c, Boats at Saintes-Maries-De-La-Mer. 40c, Interior of a Restaurant in Arles. 45c, Peasant Woman, vert. 55c, Self-Portrait, Sept. 1888, vert. 60c, A Pork Butcher's Shop Seen From a Window, vert. 75c, The Night Cafe in Arles. $1, Portrait of Milliet, Second Lieutenant of the Zouaves, vert. $2, The Cafe Terrace on the Place Du Forum Arles, at Night, vert. $3, The Zouave, vert. $4, Two Lovers (Fragment), vert. No. 764, $5, Still Life: Blue Enamel Coffeepot, Earthenware and Fruit.

No. 765, $5, Street in Saintes-Maries. No. 766, $5, A Lane Near Arles. No. 767, $6, Harvest at La Crau, with Montmajour in the Background. No. 768, $6, The Sower.

**1991, June 10 Litho. *Perf. 13½***

**749-764** G65 Set of 16 27.50 27.50

**Size: 102x76mm**

***Imperf***

**765-766** G65 Set of 2 11.00 11.00
**767-768** G65 Set of 2 14.00 14.00

**Royal Family Birthday, Anniversary**

Common Design Type

**1991, July 5 Litho. *Perf. 14***

**769** CD347 10c multicolored .50 .50
**770** CD347 15c multicolored .50 .50
**771** CD347 40c multicolored .60 .60
**772** CD347 50c multicolored .80 .80
**773** CD347 $1 multicolored 1.50 1.50
**774** CD347 $2 multicolored 2.25 2.25
**775** CD347 $4 multicolored 3.75 3.75
**776** CD347 $5 multicolored 5.50 5.50
*Nos. 769-776 (8)* 15.40 15.40

**Souvenir Sheets**

**777** CD347 $5 Henry, William, Charles, Diana 5.75 5.75
**778** CD347 $5 Elizabeth, Andrew, Philip 4.25 4.25

10c, 50c, $1, Nos. 776-777, Charles and Diana, 10th wedding anniversary. Others, Queen Elizabeth II, 65th birthday.

Phila Nippon '91 G66

Japanese locomotives: 10c, First Japanese steam. 25c, First American steam locomotive in Japan. 35c, Class 8620 steam. 50c, C53 steam. $1, DD-51 diesel. $2, RF 22327 electric. $4, EF-55 electric. $5, EF-58 electric.

No. 787, $6, Class 9600 steam, vert. No. 788, $6, Class 4100 steam, vert. No. 789, $6, C57 steam, vert. No. 790, $6, C62 steam, vert.

**1991, Aug. 12 Litho. *Perf. 14x13½***

**779-786** G66 Set of 8 16.50 16.50

**Souvenir Sheets**

***Perf. 12x13***

**787-790** G66 Set of 4 19.00 19.00

**Brandenburg Gate Type**

Designs: 45c, Brandenburg Gate and Soviet Pres. Mikhail Gorbachev. 65c, Sign. 80c, Statue, soldier escaping through barbed wire. No. 794, Berlin police insignia. No. 795, Berlin coat of arms.

**1991, Nov. 18 Litho. *Perf. 14***

**791** A209 45c multicolored .80 .80
**792** A209 65c multicolored 1.00 1.00
**793** A209 80c multicolored 1.10 1.10
*Nos. 791-793 (3)* 2.90 2.90

**Souvenir Sheets**

**794** A209 $5 multicolored 3.50 3.50
**795** A209 $5 multicolored 3.50 3.50

**Wolfgang Amadeus Mozart Type**

Portrait of Mozart and: $1, Scene from "Abduction from the Seraglio." $3, Dresden, 1749. No. 799, Portrait, vert. No. 800, Bust, vert.

**1991, Nov. 18 Litho. *Perf. 14***

**797** A210 $1 multicolored 1.00 1.00
**798** A210 $3 multicolored 3.50 3.50

**Souvenir Sheets**

**799** A210 $5 multicolored 3.75 3.75
**800** A210 $5 multicolored 3.75 3.75

**Boy Scout Type**

Designs: $2, Scout delivering mail and Czechoslovakian (local) scout stamp. $4, Cog train, Boy Scouts on Mt. Snowdon, Wales, vert. Nos. 803-804, Emblem of World Scout Jamboree, Korea.

**1991, Nov. 18 Litho. *Perf. 14***

**801** A211 $2 multicolored 2.00 2.00
**802** A211 $4 multicolored 4.00 4.00

**Souvenir Sheets**

**803** A211 $5 tan & multi 3.75 3.75
**804** A211 $5 violet blue & multi 3.75 3.75

Lord Robert Baden-Powell, 50th death anniv. and 17th World Scout Jamboree, Korea.

**De Gaulle Type**

Designs: 60c, De Gaulle in Djibouti, 1959.

No. 807, In military uniform, vert. No. 808, Portrait as President.

**1991, Nov. 18 Litho. *Perf. 14***

**806** A212 60c multicolored 1.45 1.45

**Souvenir Sheets**

**807** A212 $5 multicolored 3.75 3.75
**808** A212 $5 multicolored 3.75 3.75

A number has been reserved for additional value in this set.

**Anniversaries and Events Type**

Designs: $1.50, Otto Lilienthal, aviation pioneer. No. 810, Train in winter, vert. No. 811, Trans-Siberian Express Sign. No. 812, Man and woman celebrating. No. 813, Woman and man wearing hats. No. 814, Georg Ludwig Friedrich Laves, architect of Hoftheater, Hanover. No. 815, Locomotive, Trans-Siberian Railway, vert. No. 816, Cantonal arms of Appenzell and Thurgau. No. 817, Hanover, 750th anniv.

**1991, Nov. 18 Litho. *Perf. 14***

**809** A213 $1.50 multicolored 1.75 1.75
**810** A213 $1.75 multicolored 3.25 3.25
**811** A213 $1.75 multicolored 3.25 3.25
**812** A213 $2 multicolored 3.00 3.00
**813** A213 $2 multicolored 3.00 3.00
**814** A213 $2 multicolored 3.00 3.00
*Nos. 809-814 (6)* 17.25 17.25

**Souvenir Sheets**

**815** A213 $5 multicolored 6.50 6.50
**816** A213 $5 multicolored 5.50 5.50
**817** A213 $5 multicolored 5.00 5.00

First glider flight, cent. (#809). Trans-Siberian Railway, cent. (#810-811, 815). Swiss Confederation, 700th anniv. (#812-813, 816). City of Hanover, 750th anniv. (#814, 817). No. 815 contains one 42x58mm stamp.

**Pearl Harbor Type of 1991**

Miniature Sheet

No. 818: a, Japanese submarines and aircraft leave Truk to attack Pearl Harbor. b, Japanese flagship, Akagi. c, Nakajima B5N2 Kate, attack leader. d, Torpedo bombers attack battleship row. e, Ford Island Naval Air Station. f, Doris Miller earns Navy Cross. g, USS West Virginia and USS Tennessee ablaze. h, USS Arizona destroyed. i, USS New Orleans. j, Pres. Roosevelt declares war.

**1991, Nov. 18 *Perf. 14½x15***

**818** A214 $1 Sheet of 10, #a.-j. 20.00 20.00

**Disney Christmas Card Type**

Card design and year of issue: 10c, Mickey in sleigh pulled by Pluto, 1974. 55c, Donald, Pluto, and Mickey watching marching band, 1961. 65c, Greeting with stars, 1942. 75c, Mickey, Donald watch Merlin create a snowman, 1963. $1.50, Mickey placing wreath on door, 1958. $2, Mickey as Santa beside fireplace, 1957. $4, Mickey manipulating "Pinnochio" for friends. $5, Prince Charming and Cinderella dancing beside Christmas tree, 1987.

No. 827, $6, Snow White, 1957, vert. No. 828, $6, Santa riding World War II bomber, 1942, vert.

**1991, Nov. 18 *Perf. 14x13½,13½x14***

**819-826** A216 Set of 8 16.50 16.50

**Souvenir Sheets**

**827-828** A216 Set of 2 14.50 14.50

Nos. 819-826 are horiz.

**Queen Elizabeth II's Accession to the Throne, 40th Anniv.**

Common Design Type

**1992, Feb. 6 Litho. *Perf. 14***

**829** CD348 15c multicolored .40 .40
**830** CD348 45c multicolored 1.00 1.00
**831** CD348 $2 multicolored 2.25 2.25
**832** CD348 $4 multicolored 4.00 4.00
*Nos. 829-832 (4)* 7.65 7.65

**Souvenir Sheets**

**833** CD348 $6 Queen at left, beach 6.00 6.00
**834** CD348 $6 Queen at right, building 6.00 6.00

**World Columbian Stamp Expo Type**

Walt Disney characters as famous Chicagoans: 10c, Mickey as Walt Disney walking past birthplace. 50c, Donald Duck and nephews sleeping in George Pullman's railway cars. $1, Daisy Duck as Jane Addams in front of Hull House. $5, Mickey as Carl Sandburg. No. 839, Grandma McDuck as Mrs. O'Leary with her cow, vert.

**1992, Apr. Litho. *Perf. 14x13½***

**835** A220 10c multicolored .35 .35
**836** A220 50c multicolored .75 .75
**837** A220 $1 multicolored 2.00 2.00
**838** A220 $5 multicolored 5.25 5.25
*Nos. 835-838 (4)* 8.35 8.35

**Souvenir Sheet**

***Perf. 13½x14***

**839** A220 $6 multicolored 7.50 7.50

Nos. 840-844 have not been used.

**Granada '92 Type**

Walt Disney characters as Spanish explorers in New World: 15c, Aztec King Goofy giving treasure to Big Pete as Hernando Cortes. 40c, Mickey as Hernando de Soto discovering Mississippi River. $2, Goofy as Vasco Nunez de Balboa discovering Pacific Ocean. $4, Donald Duck as Francisco Coronado discovering Rio Grande. $6, Mickey as Ponce de Leon discovering Fountain of Youth.

**1992, Apr. *Perf. 14x13½***

**845** A221 15c multicolored .45 .45
**846** A221 40c multicolored 1.25 1.25
**847** A221 $2 multicolored 1.75 1.75
**848** A221 $4 multicolored 4.00 4.00
*Nos. 845-848 (4)* 7.45 7.45

**Souvenir Sheet**

***Perf. 13½x14***

**849** A221 $6 multicolored 6.50 6.50

Nos. 850-854 have not been used.

**Discovery of America, 500th Anniv. Type**

Designs: 10c, King Ferdinand & Queen Isabella. 45c, Santa Maria & Nina in Acul Bay, Haiti. 55c, Santa Maria, vert. $2, Columbus' fleet departing Canary Islands, vert. $4, Sinking of Santa Maria off Hispanola. $5, Nina and Pinta returning to Spain. No. 861, $6, Columbus' fleet during night storm. No. 862, $6, Columbus landing on San Salvador.

**1992, May 22 Litho. *Perf. 14***

**855-860** A222 Set of 6 9.25 9.25

**Souvenir Sheets**

**861-862** A222 Set of 2 9.25 9.25

World Columbian Stamp Expo '92, Chicago.

Mushrooms — G67

Designs: 10c, Entoloma bakeri. 15c, Hydropus paraensis. 20c, Leucopaxillus gracillimus. 45c, Hygrotrama dennisianum. 50c, Leucoagaricus hortensis. 65c, Pyrrhoglossum pyrrhum. 75c, Amanita craeoderma. $1, Lentinus bertieri. $2, Dennisiomyces griseus. $3, Xerulina asprata. $4, Hygrocybe acutoconica. $5, Lepiota spiculata.

No. 879, $6, Pluteus crysophlebius. No. 880, $6, Lepiota volvatua. No. 881, $6, Amanita lilloi.

**1992, July 2**

**867-878** G67 Set of 12 21.00 21.00

**Souvenir Sheets**

**879-881** G67 Set of 3 19.00 19.00

**Butterfly Type of 1992**

Designs: 15c, Nymphalidae paulogramma 20c, Heliconius cydno. 30c, Ithomiidae eutresis hypereia. 45c, Eurytides Columbus koll, vert. 55c, Papilio ascolius. 75c, Anaea pasibula. 80c, Heliconius doris. $1, Nymphalidae persisama pitheas. $2, Nymphalidae batesia hypochlora. $3, Heliconius erato. $4, Elzunia cassandrina. $5, Ithomiidae sais.

No. 894, $6, Pieridae dismorphia orise. No. 895, $6, Nymphalidae podotricha. No. 896, $6, Oleria tigilla.

**1992, June 15 Litho. *Perf. 14***

**882-893** A225 Set of 12 22.00 22.00

**Souvenir Sheets**

**894-896** A225 Set of 3 18.00 18.00

Genoa '92.

**Hummingbirds Type of 1992**

5c, Antillean crested, female, horiz. 10c, Blue-tailed emerald, female. 35c, Antillean mango, male, horiz. 45c, Antillean mango, female, horiz. 55c, Green-throated carib, horiz. 65c, Green violet-ear. 75c, Blue-tailed emerald, male, horiz. $1, Purple throated carib. $2, Copper-rumped, horiz. $3, Rufous-breasted hermit. $4, Antillean crested, male. $5, Green breasted mango, male.

No. 909, $6, Blue-tailed emerald. No. 910, $6, Antillean mango, diff. No. 911, $6, Antillean crested, male, diff.

**1992, July 7 Litho. *Perf. 14***

**897-908** A224 Set of 12 21.00 21.00

**Souvenir Sheets**

**909-911** A224 Set of 3 18.00 18.00

Genoa '92.

### Discovery of America Type

**1992 Litho. *Perf. 14½***

**912** A230 $1 Coming ashore 1.25 1.25
**913** A230 $2 Natives, ships 2.75 2.75

Organization of East Caribbean States.

### Summer Olympics Type

10c, Volleyball, vert. 15c, Men's floor exercise. 25c, Cross-country skiing, vert. 30c, 110-meter hurdles. 45c, 120-meter ski jump. 55c, Women's 4x100-meter relay, vert. 75c, Triple jump, vert. 80c, Mogul skiing, vert. $1, 100-meter butterfly. $2, Tornado class yachting. $3, Decathlon. $5, Equestrian jumping.
No. 926, Ice hockey. No. 927, Single luge. No. 928, Soccer.

**1992, Apr. 21 Litho. *Perf. 14***

**914** A219 10c multicolored .40 .40
**915** A219 15c multicolored .50 .50
**916** A218 25c multicolored .60 .60
**917** A219 30c multicolored .70 .70
**918** A218 45c multicolored .80 .80
**919** A219 55c multicolored 1.00 1.00
**920** A219 75c multicolored 1.10 1.10
**921** A218 80c multicolored 1.25 1.25
**922** A219 $1 multicolored 1.40 1.40
**923** A219 $2 multicolored 2.00 2.00
**924** A219 $3 multicolored 3.25 3.25
**925** A219 $5 multicolored 5.50 5.50
*Nos. 914-925 (12)* 18.50 18.50

**Souvenir Sheets**

**926** A218 $6 multicolored 5.50 5.50
**927** A218 $6 multicolored 5.50 5.50
**928** A219 $6 multicolored 5.50 5.50

### Christmas Art Type

Details or entire paintings: 10c, Our Lady with St. Roch & St. Anthony of Padua, by Giorgione. 40c, St. Anthony of Padua, by Master of the Emboridered Leaf. 45c, Madonna & Child in a Landscape, by Orazio Gentileschi. 50c, Madonna & Child with St. Anne, by Leonardo da Vinci. 55c, The Holy Family, by Giuseppe Maria Crespi. 65c, Madonna & Child, by Andrea Del Sarto. 75c, Madonna & Child with Sts. Lawrence & Julian, by Gentile da Fabriano. $1, Virgin & Child, by School of Parma. $2, Madonna with the Iris in the style of Durer. $3, Virgin & Child with St. Jerome & St. Dominic, by Filippino Lippi. $4, Rapolano Madonna, by Ambrogio Lorenzetti. $5, The Virgin & Child with Angels in a Garden with a Rose Hedge, by Stefano da Verona.
No. 941, $6, Virgin & Child with St. John the Baptist, by Botticelli. No. 942, $6, Madonna & Child with St. Anne, by Leonardo da Vinci. No. 943, $6, Madonna & Child with Grapes, by Lucas Cranach the Elder.

**1992, Nov. Litho. *Perf. 13½x14***

**929-940** A232 Set of 12 20.00 20.00

**Souvenir Sheets**

**941-943** A232 Set of 3 16.50 16.50

Anniversaries and Events — G68

Designs: 10c, Nina in the harbor of Baracoa. No. 948, Columbus' fleet at sea. No. 949, America 3, US and II Moro, Italy. No. 945, Zeppelin LZ3, 1907. No. 946, Blind man with guide dog, vert. No. 947, Guide dog. No. 950, German flag, natl. arms, Konrad Adenauer. No. 951, Hands breaking bread, vert. $2, Mars, Voyager 2. $3, Berlin airlift, Adenauer. No. 954, Wolfgang Amadeus Mozart, Constanze, vert. No. 955, Adenauer, Cologne after World War II. No. 956, Zeppelin LZ 37 shot down over England, World War I. $5, Buildings in Germany, Adenauer.
No. 958, $6, Scene from "Don Giovanni," vert. No. 959, $6, Columbus looking through telescope. No. 960, $6, Count Ferdinand von Zeppelin, facing right. No. 960A, $6, Count Ferdinand von Zeppelin, facing left. No. 961, $6, Mars Observer. No. 962, $6, Adenauer with hand on face, vert. No. 963, $6, Adenauer, diff.

**1992, Dec. *Perf. 14***

**944** G68 10c multicolored 1.75 1.75
**945** G68 75c multicolored 2.00 2.00
**946** G68 75c multicolored 2.75 2.75
**947** G68 75c multicolored 2.75 2.75
**948** G68 $1 multicolored 3.00 3.00
**949** G68 $1 multicolored 2.00 2.00
**950** G68 $1 multicolored 1.50 1.50
**951** G68 $1 multicolored 3.00 2.00
**952** G68 $2 multicolored 3.50 3.50
**953** G68 $3 multicolored 2.75 2.25
**954** G68 $4 multicolored 7.00 7.00
**955** G68 $4 multicolored 3.50 3.50
**956** G68 $4 multicolored 4.00 4.50
**957** G68 $5 multicolored 3.50 3.00
*Nos. 944-957 (14)* 43.00 41.50

**Souvenir Sheets**

**958-963** G68 Set of 7 37.50 37.50

Discovery of America, 500th anniv. (#944, 948, 959). Count Zeppelin, 75th death anniv. (#945, 956, 960-960A). Lions Intl., 75th anniv. (#946-947). Konrad Adenauer, 25th death anniv. (#950, 953, 955, 957, 962-963).America's Cup yacht race (#949). Intl. Conference on Nutrition, Rome (#951). Intl. Space Year (#952, 961). Wolfgang Amadeus Mozart, bicent. of death (in 1991) (#954, 958).
Issued: #945, 956, 960-960A, 12/15; others, Dec.

Walt Disney's Tales of Uncle Scrooge — G69

No. 964, 60c — Goldilocks (Daisy Duck) and the Three Bears: a, Comes upon the house. b, Finds three bowls of soup. c, Finds three chairs. d, Ventures upstairs. e, Tries Papa Bear's bed. f, Falls asleep in Baby Bear's bed. g, The Three Bears return home. h, Baby Bear finds Goldilocks in his bed. i, Goldilocks awakens.
No. 965, 60c — The Princess (Minnie Mouse) and the Pea: a, Prince Mickey in search of a bride. b, Princess Minnie caught in a storm. c, Queen Clarbelle meets the princess. d, Royal family entertains Princess Minnie. e, Queen places a pea on the mattress. f, Mattresses upon mattresses. g, Princess Minnie at her bed-chamber. h, Princess Minnie very tired the next morning. i, A true princess for a real prince.
No. 966, 60c — Little Red Riding Hood (Minnie Mouse): a, Off to Grandmother's. b, Stopping for flowers. c, Followed by the wolf. d, Frightened by the wolf. e, Wolf charges into Grandmother's house. f, Little Red Riding Hood at Grandmother's door. g, "What big teeth you have." h, Calling woodsman for help. i, Woodsman to the rescue.
No. 967, 60c — Hop O'-My-Thumb (Mickey, Minnie, family): a, Poor woodcutter without food for his children. b, Pebbles to find way back. c, Sadly leaving children's forest. d, Surveying from tree top. e, Ogress sends boys to bed. f, Ogre and his magic seven-league boots. g, Ogre chasing boys. h, Taking the magic seven-league boots. i, Running to Royal Palace.
No. 968, 60c — Pied Piper of Hamelin (Donald, Mickey and friends): a, Mayor (Donald) offers reward. b, Piper Mickey accepts the challenge. c, Piper leads rats to the river. d, Piper promises revenge. Children follow Piper outside village gates. f, Mayor and townspeople watch from above. g, Children follow Piper through countryside. h, Children pass through the cavern. i, All closed off from Hamelin, except for one.
No. 969, 60c — Puss in Boots (Goofy, Donald and friends): a, Gift for the king. b, Puss brings Marquis of Carabas to bathe in river. c, Puss calls for king's help. d, King introduces his daughter (Daisy Duck). e, Puss and reapers. f, Puss received by the Ogre. g, Ogre changed into a lion. h, Ogre changed into a mouse. i, Puss shows off Marquis' castle.
No. 970, $6, The Three Bears in the forest, vert. No. 971, $6, Goldilocks runs home.
No. 972, $6, Prince Mickey's useless search for a true princess. No. 973, $6, Mickey's royal family lived happily ever after.
No. 974, $6, Little Riding Hood on the way to Grandmother's, vert. No. 975, $6, A happy ending.
No. 976, $6, Boy of woodcutter with bag over shoulder. No. 977, $6, Woodcutter's family reunited.
No. 978, $6, Pied Piper leading rats past town square. No. 979, $6, Piper Mickey encouraging children in land of sweets, vert.
No. 980, $6, Miller's estate, Donald with cat, Puss, donkey. No. 981, $6, Marriage of Marquis of Carabis to daughter of the king, vert.

***Perf. 14x13½, 13½x14***

**1992, Dec. 15 Litho.**

**Sheets of 9, #a-i**

**964-969** G69 Set of 6 37.50 37.50

**Souvenir Sheets**

***Perf. 13½x14, 14x13½***

**970-981** G69 Set of 12 60.00 60.00

### Disney Animated Films Type

No. 982 — Duck Tales (Donald Duck and family): a, Scrooge McDuck, Launchpad. b, Scrooge reads treasure map. c, Collie Baba's treasure revealed. d, Webby finds magic lamp. e, Genie and new masters. f, Webby gets her wish. g, Scrooge McDuck, Genie. h, Retrieving the magic lamp. i, Villain Merlock, Genie.
No. 983 — Darkwing Duck: a, Darkwing Duck. b, Tuskerninni. c, Megavolt. d, Bushroot. e, Steelbeak. f, Eggman. g, Agent Gryzlikoff. h, Director J. Gander Hooter.
No. 984, Webby's tea party, vert. No. 985, Treasure of the lost lamp, vert.
No. 985A, Gosalyn. No. 985B, Honker, horiz.

***Perf. 14x13½, 13½x14***

**1992, Dec. 15 Litho.**

**982** A247a 60c Sheet of 9, #a.-i. 7.75 7.75
**983** A247b 60c Sheet of 8, #a.-h. 7.50 7.50

**Souvenir Sheets**

**984** A247a $6 multicolored 5.00 5.00
**985** A247a $6 multicolored 5.00 5.00
**985A** A247b $6 multicolored 5.00 5.00
**985B** A247b $6 multicolored 5.00 5.00

G71

Disney Animated Films — G72

No. 986 — The Great Mouse Detective: a, Olivia and Flaversham. b, Olivia's mechanical mouse. c, Ratigan's evil scheme. d, Ratigan and Mechanical Mouse Queen. e, Fidget pens ransom note. f, Basil studies clues. g, Fidget holds Olivia captive. h, Ratigan in disguise. i, Basil and Dr. Dawson, crime stoppers.
No. 987 — Oliver & Company: a, Dodger. b, Oliver. c, Dodger and Oliver. d, Oliver introduced to the Company. e, Oliver meets Fagin. f, Fagin's bedtime story hour. g, Oliver sleeping with Dodger. h, Fagin's trike. i, Georgette and Tito.
No. 988 — The Legend of Sleepy Hollow: a, Ichabod Crane comes to town. b, Ichabod meets Katrina Van Tassel. c, Schoolmaster Ichabod Crane. d, Ichabod and rival, Brom Bones. e, Ichabod and Katrina at Halloween dance. f, Ichabod is scared of ghosts. g, Ichabod in Sleepy Hollow. h, Ichabod and his horse. i, Meeting the Headless Horseman.
No. 989, $6, Detective Basil holding pipe. No. 990, $6, Detective Basil holding magnifying glass. No. 991, $6, Oliver. No. 992, $6, Oliver and kittens. No. 993, $6, Ichabod Crane, children praying, vert. No. 994, $6, Headless Horseman.

***Perf. 14x13½, 13½x14***

**1992, Dec. 15 Litho.**

**986** G71 60c Sheet of 9, #a.-i. 6.00 6.00
**987** G71 60c Sheet of 9, #a.-i. 6.00 6.00
**988** G72 60c Sheet of 9, #a.-i. 6.00 6.00

**Souvenir Sheets**

**989-994** G71 Set of 6 30.00 30.00

### Elvis Presley Type of 1993

Designs: a, Portrait. b, With guitar. c, With microphone.

**1993 Litho. *Perf. 14***

**1001** A244 $1 Strip of 3, #a.-c. 3.00 3.00

Printed in sheets of 9 stamps.

Medicinal Plants — G73

Designs: 5c, Oleander. 10c, Beach morning glory. 30c, Calabash. 45c, Porita tree. 55c, Cashew. 75c, Prickly pear. $1, Shell ginger. $1.50, Avocado. $2, Mango. $3, Blood flower. $4, Sugar apple. $5, Barbados lily.

**1994, May 20 Litho. *Perf. 13½x13***

**1002-1013** G73 Set of 12 20.00 20.00

## SEMI-POSTAL STAMPS

Nos. 190-193 Surcharged

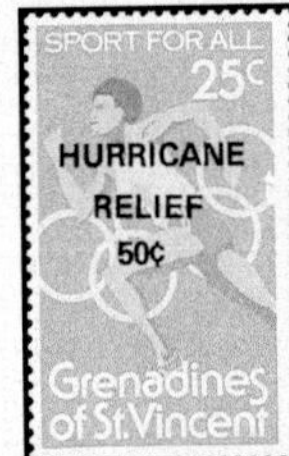


**1980, Aug. 7 Litho. *Perf. 13½***

**B1** A90 25c + 50c Running .25 *.30*
**B2** A90 50c + 50c Sailing .25 *.40*
**B3** A90 $1 + 50c Long jump .25 *.50*
**B4** A90 $2 + 50c Swimming .25 *.70*
*Nos. B1-B4 (4)* 1.00 *1.90*

## OFFICIAL STAMPS

**Nos. 209-214 Ovptd. "OFFICIAL"**

**1982, Oct. 11**

**O1** A94a 50c on No. 209 .25 .25
**O2** A94b 50c on No. 210 .25 *.35*
**O3** A94a $3 on No. 211 .40 .40
**O4** A94b $3 on No. 212 .40 *.70*
**O5** A94a $3.50 on No. 213 .45 .45
**O6** A94b $3.50 on No. 214 .45 *.70*
*Nos. O1-O6 (6)* 2.20 *2.85*

# BEQUIA

All stamps are types of St. Vincent ("A" illustration letter), St. Vincent Grenadines ("G" illustration letter) or Bequia ("B" illustration letter).

**"Island" issues are listed separately beginning in 1984. See St. Vincent Grenadines Nos. 84-111, 248-262 for earlier issues.**

### Locomotive Type of 1985

No. 1, 1942 Challenger Class, US. No. 2, 1908 S3/6, Germany. No. 3, 1944 2900 Class, US. No. 4, 1903 Jersey Lily, UK. No. 5, 1882 Gladstone Class, UK. No. 6, 1909 Thundersley, UK. No. 7, 1860 Ser Class 118, UK. No. 8, 1893 No. 999 NY Central & Hudson River, US. No. 9, 1921 Class G2, UK. No. 10, 1902 Jr. Class 6400, Japan. No. 11, 1877 Class G3, Germany. No. 12, 1945 Niagara Class, US. No. 13, 1938 Manor Class, UK. No. 14, 1880 Class D VI, Germany. No. 15, 1914 K4 Class, US. No. 16, 1960 Class U25B, US. No. 17, 1921 Stephenson, UK. No. 18, 1909 Class H4, US. No. 19, 1922 Baltic, UK. No. 20, 1903 J.R. 4500, Japan. No. 21, 1915 Class LS. No. 22, 1841 Borsig, Germany. No. 23, 1943 Royal Scot, UK. No. 24, 1961 Krauss-Maffei, US. No. 25, 1928 River IRT, UK. No. 26, 1890 Electric, UK. No. 27, 1934 A.E.C., UK. No. 28, 1929 No. 10000, UK. No. 29, 1904 City Class, UK. No. 30, 1901 No. 737, UK. No. 31, 1847 Cornwall, UK. No. 32, 1938 Duke Dog Class, UK. No. 33, 1881 Ella, UK. No. 34, 1910 George V Class, UK.

### Se-tenant Pairs, #a.-b.
**a. — Side and front views.**
**b. — Action scene.**

**1984-87 Litho. Unwmk. *Perf. 12½***

| No. | Type | Description | Unused | Used |
|---|---|---|---|---|
| 1 | A120 | 1c multicolored | .25 | .25 |
| 2 | A120 | 1c multicolored | .25 | .25 |
| 3 | A120 | 5c multicolored | .25 | .25 |
| 4 | A120 | 5c multicolored | .25 | .25 |
| 5 | A120 | 10c multicolored | .25 | .25 |
| 6 | A120 | 10c multicolored | .25 | .25 |
| 7 | A120 | 15c multicolored | .25 | .25 |
| 8 | A120 | 25c multicolored | .25 | .25 |
| 9 | A120 | 25c multicolored | .25 | .25 |
| 10 | A120 | 25c multicolored | .25 | .25 |
| 11 | A120 | 25c multicolored | .25 | .25 |
| 12 | A120 | 35c multicolored | .25 | .25 |
| 13 | A120 | 35c multicolored | .25 | .25 |
| 14 | A120 | 40c multicolored | .25 | .25 |
| 15 | A120 | 45c multicolored | .30 | .30 |
| 16 | A120 | 50c multicolored | .35 | .35 |
| 17 | A120 | 55c multicolored | .40 | .40 |
| 18 | A120 | 55c multicolored | .40 | .40 |
| 19 | A120 | 60c multicolored | .40 | .40 |
| 20 | A120 | 60c multicolored | .40 | .40 |
| 21 | A120 | 60c multicolored | .40 | .40 |
| 22 | A120 | 75c multicolored | .50 | .50 |
| 23 | A120 | 75c multicolored | .50 | .50 |
| 24 | A120 | 75c multicolored | .50 | .50 |
| 25 | A120 | $1 multicolored | .65 | .65 |
| 26 | A120 | $1 multicolored | .65 | .65 |
| 27 | A120 | $1 multicolored | .65 | .65 |
| 28 | A120 | $1.50 multicolored | .80 | .80 |
| 29 | A120 | $2 multicolored | 1.00 | 1.00 |
| 30 | A120 | $2 multicolored | 1.00 | 1.00 |
| 31 | A120 | $2 multicolored | 1.00 | 1.00 |
| 32 | A120 | $2.50 multicolored | 1.50 | 1.50 |
| 33 | A120 | $2.50 multicolored | 1.50 | 1.50 |
| 34 | A120 | $3 multicolored | 2.00 | 2.00 |
| | | *Nos. 1-34 (34)* | 18.40 | 18.40 |

Issued: #1, 3, 5, 8, 12, 15, 28-29, 2/22/84; #2, 4, 6, 13, 22, 25, 32, 34, 11/26/84; #9, 17, 19, 30, 2/1/85; #10, 18, 20, 23, 26, 33, 8/14/85; #7, 11, 14, 16, 21, 24, 27, 31, 11/16/87.

Stamps issued 11/16/87 are not inscribed "Leaders of the World."

### St. Vincent Grenadines Nos. 222-238 Ovptd. "BEQUIA"

***Perf. 14x13½***

**1984, Aug. 23 Wmk. 373**

| No. | Type | Description | Unused | Used |
|---|---|---|---|---|
| 69 | G26 | 1c on No. 222 | .25 | .25 |
| 70 | G26 | 3c on No. 223 | .25 | .25 |
| 71 | G26 | 5c on No. 224 | .25 | .25 |
| 72 | G26 | 6c on No. 225 | .25 | .25 |
| 73 | G26 | 10c on No. 226 | .25 | .25 |
| 74 | G26 | 15c on No. 227 | .25 | .25 |
| 75 | G26 | 20c on No. 228 | .25 | .25 |
| 76 | G26 | 25c on No. 229 | .25 | .25 |
| 77 | G26 | 30c on No. 230 | .25 | .25 |
| 78 | G26 | 50c on No. 231 | .35 | .35 |
| 79 | G26 | 60c on No. 232 | .50 | .50 |
| 80 | G26 | 75c on No. 233 | .60 | .60 |
| 81 | G26 | $1 on No. 234 | .75 | .75 |
| 82 | G26 | $2 on No. 235 | 1.25 | 1.25 |
| 83 | G26 | $3 on No. 236 | 2.00 | 2.00 |
| 84 | G26 | $5 on No. 237 | 3.50 | 3.50 |
| 85 | G26 | $10 on No. 238 | 7.50 | 7.50 |
| | | *Nos. 69-85 (17)* | 18.70 | 18.70 |

### Car Type of 1983

No. 86, 1953 Cadillac, US. No. 87, 1932 Fiat, Italy. No. 88, 1968 Excalibur, US. No. 89, 1952 Hudson, US. No. 90, 1924 Leyand, UK. No. 91, 1911 Marmon, US. No. 92, 1950 Alfa Romeo, Italy. No. 93, 1968 Ford Escort, UK. No. 94, 1939 Maserati 8 CTF, Italy. No. 95, 1963 Ford, UK. No. 96, 1958 Vanwall, UK. No. 97, 1910 Stanley, US. No. 98, 1948 Ford Wagon, US. No. 99, 1936 Auto Union, Germany. No. 100, 1907 Chadwick, US. No. 101, 1924 Lanchester, UK. No. 102, 1957 Austin-Healy, UK. No. 103, 1935 Brewster-Ford, US. No. 104, 1942 Willys Jeep, US. No. 105, 1929 Isotta, Italy. No. 106, 1940 Lincoln, US. No. 107, 1964 Bluebird II, UK. No. 108, 1948 Moore-Offenhauser, US. No. 109, 1936 Ford, UK. No. 110, 1936 Mercedes Benz, Germany. No. 111, 1928 Mercedes Benz SSK, Germany. No. 112, 1907 Rolls Royce, UK. No. 113, 1955 Citroen, France. No. 114, 1936 Fiat, Italy. No. 115, 1922 Dusenberg, US. No. 116, 1957 Pontiac Bonneville, US. No. 117, 1916 Hudson Super Six, US. No. 118, 1977 Coyote Ford, US. No. 119, 1960 Porsche, Germany. No. 120, 1970 Plymouth, US. No. 121, 1933 Stutz, US. No. 122, 1910 Benz-Blitzen, Germany. No. 123, 1933 Napier Railton, UK. No. 124, 1978 BMW, Germany. No. 125, 1912 Hispano Suiza, Spain. No. 126, 1954 Mercedes Benz, Germany. No. 127, 1927 Stutz Black Hawk, US.

### Se-tenant Pairs, #a.-b.
**a. — Side and front views.**
**b. — Action scene.**

**1984-87 Unwmk. *Perf. 12½***

| No. | Type | Description | Unused | Used |
|---|---|---|---|---|
| 86 | A107 | 5c multicolored | .25 | .25 |
| 87 | A107 | 5c multicolored | .25 | .25 |
| 88 | A107 | 5c multicolored | .25 | .25 |
| 89 | A107 | 5c multicolored | .25 | .25 |
| 90 | A107 | 10c multicolored | .25 | .25 |
| 91 | A107 | 20c multicolored | .25 | .25 |
| 92 | A107 | 20c multicolored | .25 | .25 |
| 93 | A107 | 20c multicolored | .25 | .25 |
| 94 | A107 | 20c multicolored | .25 | .25 |
| 95 | A107 | 25c multicolored | .25 | .25 |
| 96 | A107 | 25c multicolored | .25 | .25 |
| 97 | A107 | 25c multicolored | .25 | .25 |
| 98 | A107 | 35c multicolored | .25 | .25 |
| 99 | A107 | 40c multicolored | .30 | .30 |
| 100 | A107 | 45c multicolored | .35 | .35 |
| 101 | A107 | 50c multicolored | .40 | .40 |
| 102 | A107 | 50c multicolored | .40 | .40 |
| 103 | A107 | 60c multicolored | .45 | .45 |
| 104 | A107 | 60c multicolored | .45 | .45 |
| 105 | A107 | 65c multicolored | .50 | .50 |
| 106 | A107 | 75c multicolored | .50 | .50 |
| 107 | A107 | 75c multicolored | .50 | .50 |
| 108 | A107 | 75c multicolored | .50 | .50 |
| 109 | A107 | 75c multicolored | .50 | .50 |
| 110 | A107 | 80c multicolored | .55 | .55 |
| 111 | A107 | 90c multicolored | .65 | .65 |
| 112 | A107 | $1 multicolored | .70 | .70 |
| 113 | A107 | $1 multicolored | .70 | .70 |
| 114 | A107 | $1 multicolored | .70 | .70 |
| 115 | A107 | $1 multicolored | .70 | .70 |
| 116 | A107 | $1 multicolored | .70 | .70 |
| 117 | A107 | $1.25 multicolored | .80 | .80 |
| 118 | A107 | $1.25 multicolored | .80 | .80 |
| 119 | A107 | $1.50 multicolored | 1.00 | 1.00 |
| 120 | A107 | $1.50 multicolored | 1.00 | 1.00 |
| 121 | A107 | $1.75 multicolored | 1.10 | 1.10 |
| 122 | A107 | $2 multicolored | 1.25 | 1.25 |
| 123 | A107 | $2 multicolored | 1.25 | 1.25 |
| 124 | A107 | $2.50 multicolored | 1.50 | 1.50 |
| 125 | A107 | $3 multicolored | 1.75 | 1.75 |
| 126 | A107 | $3 multicolored | 1.75 | 1.75 |
| 127 | A107 | $3 multicolored | 1.75 | 1.75 |
| | | *Nos. 86-127 (42)* | 26.75 | 26.75 |

Issued: #86, 99, 112, 119, 9/14; #87, 90-91, 95, 106, 113, 124-125, 12/19; #88, 96, 101, 114, 117, 122, 6/25/85; #92, 100, 120, 123, 9/26/85; #97, 102, 105, 107, 115, 126, 1/29/86; #93, 103, 108, 111, 116, 127, 12/23/86; #89, 94, 98, 104, 109-110, 118, 121, 7/22/87.

Beginning on Sept. 26, 1985, this issue is not inscribed "Leaders of the World."

1984 Summer Olympics — B1

No. 170a, Men's gymnastics. No. 170b, Women's gymnastics. No. 171a, Men's javelin. No. 171b, Women's javelin. No. 172a, Women's basketball. No. 172b, Men's basketball. No. 173a, Women's long jump. No. 173b, Men's long jump.

**1984, Sept. 14 *Perf. 12½***

| No. | Type | Description | Unused | Used |
|---|---|---|---|---|
| 170 | B1 | 1c Pair, #a.-b. | .25 | .25 |
| 171 | B1 | 10c Pair, #a.-b. | .25 | .25 |
| 172 | B1 | 60c Pair, #a.-b. | .40 | .40 |
| 173 | B1 | $3 Pair, #a.-b. | 1.10 | 1.10 |
| | | *Nos. 170-173 (4)* | 2.00 | 2.00 |

Dogs — B2

No. 178a, Hungarian Kuvasz. No. 178b, Afghan. No. 179a, Whippet. No. 179b, Bloodhound. No. 180a, Cavalier King Charles Spaniel. No. 180b, German Shepherd. No. 181a, Pekinese. No. 181b, Golden Retriever.

**1985, Mar. 14 *Perf. 12½***

| No. | Type | Description | Unused | Used |
|---|---|---|---|---|
| 178 | B2 | 25c Pair, #a.-b. | .25 | .25 |
| 179 | B2 | 35c Pair, #a.-b. | .50 | .50 |
| 180 | B2 | 55c Pair, #a.-b. | .65 | .65 |
| 181 | B2 | $2 Pair, #a.-b. | 1.90 | 1.90 |
| | | *Nos. 178-181 (4)* | 3.30 | 3.30 |

World War II Warships B3

### Se-tenant Pairs, #a.-b.
**a.— Side and top views.**
**b. — Action scene.**

**1985, Apr. 29 *Perf. 12½***

| No. | Type | Description | Unused | Used |
|---|---|---|---|---|
| 186 | B3 | 15c HMS Hood | .60 | .60 |
| 187 | B3 | 50c HMS Duke of York | 1.00 | 1.00 |
| 188 | B3 | $1 KM Admiral Graf Spee | 1.40 | 1.40 |
| 189 | B3 | $1.50 USS Nevada | 2.25 | 2.25 |
| | | *Nos. 186-189 (4)* | 5.25 | 5.25 |

### St. Vincent Grenadines Flower Type

#194a, Primula veris. #194b, Pulsatilla vulgaris. #195a, Lapageria rosea. #195b, Romneya coulteri. #196a, Anigozanthos manglesii. #196b, Metrosideros collina. #197a, Protea laurifolia. #197b, Thunbergia grandiflora.

**1985, May 31 *Perf. 12½***

| No. | Type | Description | Unused | Used |
|---|---|---|---|---|
| 194 | G38 | 10c Pair, #a.-b. | .25 | .25 |
| 195 | G38 | 20c Pair, #a.-b. | .30 | .30 |
| 196 | G38 | 70c Pair, #a.-b. | .35 | .35 |
| 197 | G38 | $2.50 Pair, #a.-b. | .75 | .75 |
| | | *Nos. 194-197 (4)* | 1.65 | 1.65 |

### Queen Mother Type of 1985

Hat: #206a, 212a, Blue. #206b, 212b, Violet. #207a, 211a, Blue. #207b, 211b, Tiara. #208a, Blue. #208b, White. #209a, Blue. #209b, Pink. #210a, Hat. #210b, Tiara.

**1985, Aug. 29 *Perf. 12½***

| No. | Type | Description | Unused | Used |
|---|---|---|---|---|
| 206 | A122 | 20c Pair, #a.-b. | .25 | .00 |
| 207 | A122 | 65c Pair, #a.-b. | .65 | .65 |
| 208 | A122 | $1.35 Pair, #a.-b. | .90 | .90 |
| 209 | A122 | $1.80 Pair, #a.-b. | 1.50 | 1.50 |
| | | *Nos. 206-209 (4)* | 3.30 | 3.05 |

### Souvenir Sheets of 2

| No. | Type | Description | Unused | Used |
|---|---|---|---|---|
| 210 | A122 | $2.05 #a.-b. | 1.75 | 1.75 |
| 211 | A122 | $3.50 #a.-b. | 3.00 | 3.00 |
| 212 | A122 | $6 #a.-b. | 5.00 | 5.00 |

### Queen Elizabeth II Type of 1986

Various portraits.

**1986, Apr. 21**

| No. | Type | Description | Unused | Used |
|---|---|---|---|---|
| 213 | A128 | 5c multicolored | .25 | .25 |
| 214 | A128 | 75c multicolored | .35 | .35 |
| 215 | A128 | $2 multicolored | .50 | .50 |
| 216 | A128 | $8 multicolored, vert. | 2.10 | 2.10 |
| | | *Nos. 213-216 (4)* | 3.20 | 3.20 |

### Souvenir Sheet

| No. | Type | Description | Unused | Used |
|---|---|---|---|---|
| 217 | A128 | $10 multicolored | 3.50 | 3.50 |

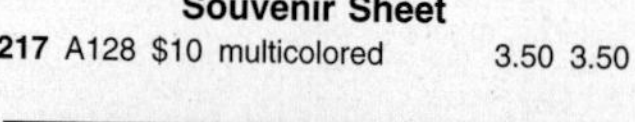

B4

World Cup Soccer Championships, Mexico, 1986 — B5

No. 218, South Korean team . No. 219, Iraqi team. No. 220, Algerian team. No. 221, Bulgaria vs. France. No. 222, Belgium. No. 223, Danish team. No. 224, Italy vs. W. Germany. No. 225, USSR vs. England. No. 226, Italy, 1982 champions. No. 227, W. Germany. No. 228, N. Ireland. No. 229, England.

**1986 July 3 *Perf. 12½, 15 (B5)***

| No. | Type | Description | Unused | Used |
|---|---|---|---|---|
| 218 | B4 | 1c multicolored | .25 | .25 |
| 219 | B4 | 2c multicolored | .25 | .25 |
| 220 | B4 | 5c multicolored | .25 | .25 |
| 221 | B4 | 10c multicolored | .25 | .25 |
| 222 | B5 | 45c multicolored | .25 | .25 |
| 223 | B4 | 60c multicolored | .25 | .25 |
| 224 | B4 | 75c multicolored | .25 | .25 |
| 225 | B4 | $1.50 multicolored | .30 | .30 |
| 226 | B5 | $1.50 multicolored | .30 | .30 |
| 227 | B5 | $2 multicolored | .50 | .50 |
| 228 | B5 | $3.50 multicolored | .70 | .70 |
| 229 | B4 | $6 multicolored | 1.10 | 1.10 |
| | | *Nos. 218-229 (12)* | 4.65 | 4.65 |

### Souvenir Sheets

| No. | Type | Description | Unused | Used |
|---|---|---|---|---|
| 230 | B4 | $1 like No. 219 | .50 | .50 |
| 231 | B4 | $1.75 like No. 221 | .80 | .80 |

### Royal Wedding Type of 1986

No. 232, Andrew. No. 233, Andrew in helicopter. No. 234, Andrew in crowd. No. 235, Andrew, Sarah.

$8, Andrew, Sarah in coach.

**1986, July 15 *Perf. 12½x13, 13x12½***

| No. | Type | Description | Unused | Used |
|---|---|---|---|---|
| 232 | A132 | 60c multicolored | .35 | .35 |
| 233 | A132 | 60c multicolored | .35 | .35 |
| 234 | A132 | $2 multicolored | .85 | .85 |
| 235 | A132 | $2 multicolored | .85 | .85 |
| | | *Nos. 232-235 (4)* | 2.40 | 2.40 |

### Souvenir Sheet

| No. | Type | Description | Unused | Used |
|---|---|---|---|---|
| 236 | A132a | $8 multicolored | 3.75 | 3.75 |

Nos. 234-235 horiz.

Railway Engineers and Locomotives — B6

Designs: $1, Sir Daniel Gooch, Fire Fly Class, 1840. $2.50, Sir Nigel Gresley, A4 Class, 1938. $3, Sir William Stanier, Coronation Class, 1937. $4, Oliver V. S. Bulleid, Battle of Britain Class, 1946.

**1986, Sept. 30 *Perf. 13x12½***

| No. | Type | Description | Unused | Used |
|---|---|---|---|---|
| 237-240 | B6 | Set of 4 | 3.00 | 3.00 |

### Nos. 232-235 Ovptd. "Congratulations to TRH The Duke & Duchess of York" in 3 Lines

**1986 *Perf. 12½x13, 13x12½***

| No. | Type | Description | Unused | Used |
|---|---|---|---|---|
| 241 | A132 | 60c on No. 232 | .75 | .75 |
| 242 | A132 | 60c on No. 233 | .75 | .75 |
| 243 | A132 | $2 on No. 234 | 2.75 | 2.75 |
| 244 | A132 | $2 on No. 235 | 2.75 | 2.75 |
| | | *Nos. 241-244 (4)* | 7.00 | 7.00 |

### Royalty Portrait Type

Portraits and photographs: 15c, Queen Victoria, 1841. 75c, Elizabeth, Charles, 1948. $1, Coronation, 1953. $2.50, Duke of Edinburgh, 1948. $5, Elizabeth c. 1980. $6, Elizabeth, Charles, 1948, diff.

**1987, Oct. 15 *Perf. 12½x13***

| No. | Type | Description | Unused | Used |
|---|---|---|---|---|
| 245-249 | A140 | Set of 5 | 3.00 | 3.00 |

### Souvenir Sheet

| No. | Type | Description | Unused | Used |
|---|---|---|---|---|
| 250 | A140 | $6 multi | 3.00 | 3.00 |

### Great Explorers Type of St. Vincent Grenadines

Designs: 15c, Gokstad, ship of Leif Eriksson (c. 1000). 50c, Eriksson and bearing dial. $1.75, The Mathew, ship of John Cabot. $2, Cabot, quadrant. $2.50, The Trinidad, ship of Ferdinand Magellan. $3, Arms, portrait of Christopher Columbus. $3.50, Columbus' ship Santa Maria. $4, Magellan, globe. $5, Anchor, long boat, ship.

**1988, July 11 Litho. *Perf. 14***

| No. | Type | Description | Unused | Used |
|---|---|---|---|---|
| 251-258 | G52 | Set of 8 | 3.00 | 3.00 |

### Souvenir Sheet

| No. | Type | Description | Unused | Used |
|---|---|---|---|---|
| 259 | G52 | $5 multi | 3.25 | 3.25 |

### Tennis Type of 1987

**1988, July 29** *Perf. 13x13½*

**260** A137 15c Anders Jarryd .30 .30
**261** A137 45c Anne Hobbs .30 .30
**262** A137 80c Jimmy Connors .35 .35
**263** A137 $1.25 Carling Bassett .45 .45
**264** A137 $1.75 Stefan Edberg, horiz. .60 .60
**265** A137 $2.00 Gabriela Sabatini, horiz. .70 .70
**266** A137 $2.50 Mats Wilander .90 .90
**267** A137 $3.00 Pat Cash 1.10 1.10
*Nos. 260-267 (8)* 4.70 4.70

No. 263 inscribed "Carlene Basset" instead of "Carling Bassett."
An unissued souvenir sheet exists.

French Revolution Bicentennial B7

Designs: 1c, Grandma Duck as French peasant woman. 2c, Donald & Daisy celebrating liberty. 3c, Minnie as Marie Antoinette. 4c, Clarabelle & patriotic chair. 5c, Goofy in Republican citizen's costume. 10c, Mickey & Donald planting liberty tree. No. 274, $5, Horace taking Tennis Court Oath. $6, Grand Master Mason McDuck.
No. 276, $5, Dancing the Carmagnole. No. 277, $5, Philosophers at Cafe La Procope.

**1989, July 7** *Perf. 13½x14*

**268-275** B7 Set of 8 10.00 10.00

**Souvenir Sheets**

**276-277** B7 Set of 2 6.00 6.00

### Anniversaries and Events Type

$5, Otto Lililienthal, aviation pioneer.

**1991, Nov. 18** **Litho.** *Perf. 14*

**278** A213 $5 multicolored 5.25 5.25

Japanese Attack on Pearl Harbor, 50th Anniv. B8

Designs: 50c, Kate from second-wave over Hickam Field. $1, B17 sights Zeros in Pearl Harbor attack. $5, Firefighters rescue sailors from blazing USS Tennessee.

**1991, Nov. 18**

**287** B8 50c multicolored .70 .70
**288** B8 $1 multicolored 1.30 1.30

**Souvenir Sheet**

**289** B8 $5 multicolored 4.25 4.25

Wolfgang Amadeus Mozart, Death Bicentennial — B9

Mozart and: 10c, Piccolo. 75c, Piano. $4, Violotta.
No. 293, $6, Mozart's last composition, Lacrimosa from the Requiem Mass. No. 294, $6, Bronze of Mozart by Adrien-Etienne Gaudez, vert. No. 295, $6, Score of opening of the "Paris" symphony, K297.

**1991** **Litho.** *Perf. 14*

**290-292** B9 Set of 3 5.50 5.50

**Souvenir Sheets**

**293-295** B9 Set of 3 18.00 18.00

Nos. 293-295 each contain one 57x42mm or 42x57mm stamp.

### Boy Scout Type

50c, Lord Baden-Powell, killick hitch knot. $1, Baden-Powell, clove hitch knot. $2, Drawing of Boy Scout by Baden-Powell, vert. $3, American 1st Class Scout badge, vert. $6, Baden-Powell, Lark's head knot.

**1991**

**296-299** A211 Set of 4 8.00 8.00

**Souvenir Sheet**

**300** A211 $6 multicolored 6.75 6.75

Diana, Princess of Wales, (1961-97) — B10

**1997, Dec. 10** **Litho.** *Perf. 14*

**301** B10 $1 multicolored 1.75 1.75

No. 301 was issued in sheets of 6.

### Paintings Type of 1999

Various pictures of flowers making up a photomosaic of the Queen Mother.

**2000, Sept. 5** *Perf. 13¾*

**302** A442 $1 Sheet of 8, #a-h 6.00 6.00
*i.* As No. 302, imperf. 6.00 6.00

Worldwide Fund for Nature (WWF) B11

Leatherback turtle: a, Three on beach. b, One coming ashore. c, One in water. d, One digging nest.

**2001, Dec. 10** **Litho.** *Perf. 14*

**303** B11 $1.40 Vert or horiz. strip of 4, #a-d 5.00 5.00

### Queen Elizabeth II, 50th Anniv. of Reign Type of 2002

No. 304: a, Without hat. b, Wearing tiara. c, Wearing scarf. d, With Prince Philip and baby.
$2, Wearing scarf, diff.

**2002, June 17** **Litho.** *Perf. 14¼*

**304** A509 80c Sheet of 4, #a-d 4.50 4.50

**Souvenir Sheet**

**305** A509 $2 multi 4.00 4.00

### United We Stand Type of 2001

**2002, Nov. 4** *Perf. 14*

**306** A508 $2 multi 2.00 2.00

Printed in sheets of 4.

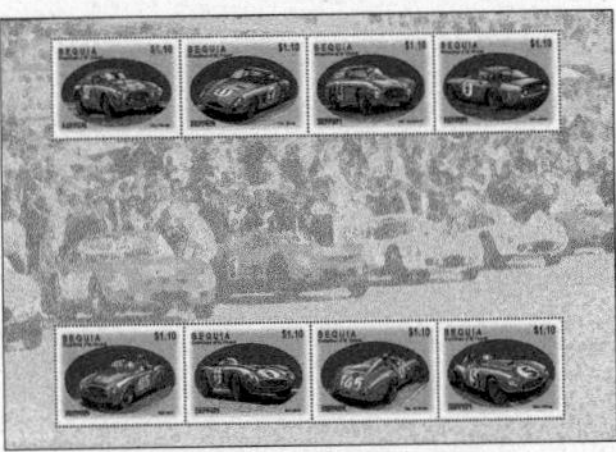

Ferrari Race Cars — B12

No. 307: a, 1953 250MM. b, 1962 330LM. c, 1952 340 Mexico. d, 1963 330LM. e, 1952 225S. f, 1956 500TR. g, 1954 750 Monza. h, 1954 375 Plus.

**2002, June 10** **Litho.** *Perf. 13¾*

**307** B12 $1.10 Sheet of 8, #a-h 6.75 6.75

### Elvis Presley Type of 2002

**2002, Aug. 19**

**308** A517 $1 multi 1.00 1.00

Printed in sheets of 9.

### Shirley Temple Movie Type of 2000

No. 309, horiz. — Scenes from *Captain January* of Temple with: a, Man at table. b, Woman. c, Two men annd bird with bow. d, Boy and teacher. e, Two men at table. f, Three men in boat.
No. 310: a, Man with beard. b, Three men. c, Two men and doll. d, With man, dancing.
$5, With sailors.

**2002, Aug. 19**

**309** A471 $1.40 Sheet of 6, #a-f 6.50 6.50
**310** A471 $2 Sheet of 4, #a-d 6.50 6.50

**Souvenir Sheet**

**311** A471 $5 multi 5.00 5.00

Sheet margins are dated "2003."

### Queen Mother Elizabeth Type of 2002

No. 312: a, Wearing yellow dress. b, Wearing red dress.

**2002, Nov. 4** *Perf. 14*

**312** A522 $2 Pair, #a-b 3.00 3.00

No. 312 printed in sheets containing 2 pairs.

Year of the Horse — B13

No. 313: a, Black horse in foreground, front feet raised. b, White horse in foreground. c, Piebald horse in foreground. d, Black horse in foreground, front feet not raised.

**2002, Dec. 17** *Perf. 13¼x13*

**313** B13 $1.40 Sheet of 4, #a-d 5.50 5.50

### Teddy Bears Type of 2002

No. 314, $2 — Bears from Germany: a, Balloon pilot bear. b, Bear in lederhosen. c, Bear in pants and ice skates. d, Bear in skirt and ice skates.
No. 315, $2 — Bears from Italy: a, Bear with feathered hat, standing in gondola. b, Bear with cap, seated on gondola. c, Bear with umbrella. d, Gondolier bear.

**2003, Jan. 27** *Perf. 13½x13¼*

**Sheets of 4, #a-d**

**314-315** A519 Set of 2 13.00 13.00

### Year of the Ram Type of 2003

No. 316: a, Ram with white horns and beard, denomination at right. b, Ram with black horns, denomination at left. c, Ram with dark horns, denomination at right. d, Ram with white horns, denomination at left. e, Ram with leg raised. f, Ram with horns with lines, denomination at left.

**2003, Feb. 1** *Perf. 14¼x13¾*

**316** A526 $1 Sheet of 6, #a-f 5.00 5.00

### Princess Diana Type of 2003

No. 317, $2: a, Wearing pink hat. b, Wearing gray dress. c, Wearing white blouse. d, Wearing checked pants.
No. 318, $2: a, Wearing black dress. b, Wearing red blouse. c, Wearing black and white hat. d, Wearing white blouse, holding flowers.

**2003, May 26** **Litho.** *Perf. 14*

**Sheets of 4, #a-d**

**317-318** A536 Set of 2 13.00 13.00

### Corvette Type of 2003

No. 319: a, 1957 convertible. b, 1964 Sting Ray. c, 1954 convertible. d, 1989.
$5, 1988.

**2003, July 1** *Perf. 13¼x13½*

**319** A534 $2 Sheet of 4, #a-d 7.00 7.00

**Souvenir Sheet**

**320** A534 $5 multi 5.00 5.00

Pres. John F. Kennedy (1917-63) — B14

No. 321: a, Denomination at UL, name at right. b, Denomination at UL, name at left. c, Denomination at UR, name at left. d, Denomination at UR, name at right.

**2003, Aug. 25** *Perf. 14*

**321** B14 $2 Sheet of 4, #a-d 7.50 7.50

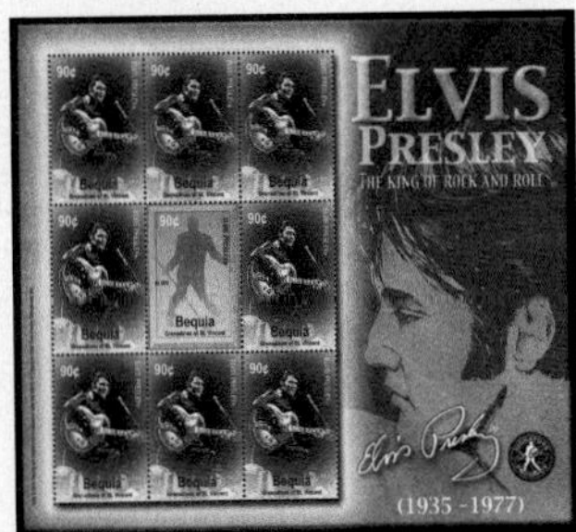


Elvis Presley (1935-77) — B15

No. 322: a, Silhouette. b, Holding guitar.

**2003, Dec. 1** *Perf. 13½*

**322** B15 90c Sheet, #322a, 8 #322b 8.00 8.00

Birds — B16

Designs: 90c, Stripe-headed tanager. $1, Violaceous trogon. $1.40, Barn owl. $2, Green jay.
$5, Montezuma oropendola.

**2003, Dec. 1** *Perf. 13¼*

**323-326** B16 Set of 4 4.25 4.25

**Souvenir Sheet**

**327** B16 $5 multi 4.25 4.25

New Year 2004 (Year of the Monkey) B17

Romping Monkeys, by unknown painter: $1.40, Detail. $3, Entire painting.

**2004, Jan. 15 Litho. *Perf. 13¼***
328 B17 $1.40 multi 1.75 1.75

**Souvenir Sheet**
***Perf. 13½x13¼***
329 B17 $3 multi 3.00 3.00

Paintings by Pablo Picasso (1881-1973) — B18

No. 330: a, Bust of a Woman with Self-Portrait. b, Jacqueline in a Turkish Jacket. c, Françoise in an Armchair. d, Still Life on a Pedestal Table.
$5, Violin on a Wall.

**2004, Apr. 30 *Perf. 14¼***
330 B18 $2 Sheet of 4, #a-d 6.00 6.00

***Imperf***
331 B18 $5 multi 4.00 4.00

No. 330 contains four 38x51mm stamps.

**Marilyn Monroe Type of 2004**

**2004, May 3 *Perf. 14***
332 A558 70c multi .55 .55

Printed in sheets of 12.

**Babe Ruth Type of 2004**

**2004, July 1 *Perf. 13¼***
333 A561 70c multi .55 .55

Printed in sheets of 12.

Ancient Greece B19

Designs: 30c, Palace of Minos, Crete. 70c, Apollo's Temple, Delphi. $1, Statue of Zeus, Olympia. $1.40, Bust of Aphrodite. $2, Bust of Socrates. $3, Parthenon.
$5, Panathenaic Stadium, Athens.

**2004, Aug. 16 *Perf. 14***
334-339 B19 Set of 6 7.50 7.50

**Souvenir Sheet**
340 B19 $5 multi 4.50 4.50

**Ronald Reagan Type of 2004**

No. 341, horiz.: a, Reagan with wife, Nancy. b, Reagan with George H. W. Bush.

**2004, Oct. 13 *Perf. 13½***
341 Horiz. pair 2.75 2.75
a.-b. A564 $1.40 Either single 1.25 1.25

Printed in sheets containing three each #341a-341b.

**Railroads Type of 2004**

No. 342, $2: a, GN 2507 Class P 2-4-8-2. b, Great Northern 2507. c, Great Northern. d, GWR King Class 4-6-0.
No. 343, $2: a, LMS 2MT 2-6-2 T. b, Green Arrow. c, LMS Stainer Class 5MT 4-6-0. d, Liner Class A4 Sir Nigel Gresley.
No. 344, $2: a, Barclay 0-4-0 Saddle tank. b, Beyer Peacock. c, BR Class 4MT 2-6-0. d, Dampflok 109.
No. 345, $2: a, British Railways 2-6-4 T. b, Caledonian Railway 0-4-4 T. c, Evening Star. d, Southern Railway Carolina Special.
No. 346, $5, Pakistan Railways SPS 4-4-0. No. 347, $5, Norwegian State Railway. No. 348, $5, Russell Hunslet 2-6-2 T. No. 349, $5, North British Railway 0-6-0.

***Perf. 14½x14, 14 (#344, 348)***
**2004, Dec. 13 Sheets of 4, #a-d**
342-345 A565 Set of 4 26.00 26.00

**Souvenir Sheets**
346-349 A565 Set of 4 16.00 16.00

Christmas B20

Paintings: 55c, Madonna of Port Lligat, by Salvador Dali. 90c, Madonna and Child, by Barolome Esteban Murillo. $1, Madonna and Child, by Jan van Eyck. $4, Madonna of the Meadow, by Giovanni Bellini.
$6, Madonna and Child, by Caravaggio.

**2004, Dec. 13 *Perf. 12***
350-353 B20 Set of 4 5.50 5.50

**Souvenir Sheet**
354 B20 $6 multi 4.75 4.75

End of World War II, 60th Anniv. — B21

No. 355, $2 — Sinking of the Bismarck, 1941: a, Bismarck, Map. b, Aircraft make ready for flight. c, The Bismarck getting pounded by British Navy. d, The Bismarck goes down.
No. 356, $2 — Liberation of Paris: a, Allied troops enter Paris. b, The end of German occupation. c, Allied troops help supply people of Paris. d, Victory at last.
No. 357, $5, Bismarck. No. 358, $5, General De Gaulle returns.

**2005, May 9 Litho. *Perf. 13½***
**Sheets of 4, #a-d**
355-356 B21 Set of 2 14.00 14.00

**Souvenir Sheets**
357-358 B21 Set of 2 8.00 8.00

**Vatican Stamp and Pope John Paul II Types of 2005**

Designs: 70c, Vatican #64. $4, Pope and crowd, horiz.

**2005, June 1 *Perf. 13x13¼***
359 A584 70c multi .55 .55

***Perf. 13½***
360 A585 $4 multi 3.25 3.25

No. 359 printed in sheets of 12; No. 360, in sheets of 4.

Moths — B22

Designs: 90c, Pericallia galactina. $1, Automeris io draudtiana. $1.40, Antherina suraka. $2, Bunaea alcinoe.
$5, Rothschildia erycina nigrescens.

**2005, July 26 *Perf. 12¾***
361-364 B22 Set of 4 5.50 5.50

**Souvenir Sheet**
365 B22 $5 multi 4.00 4.00

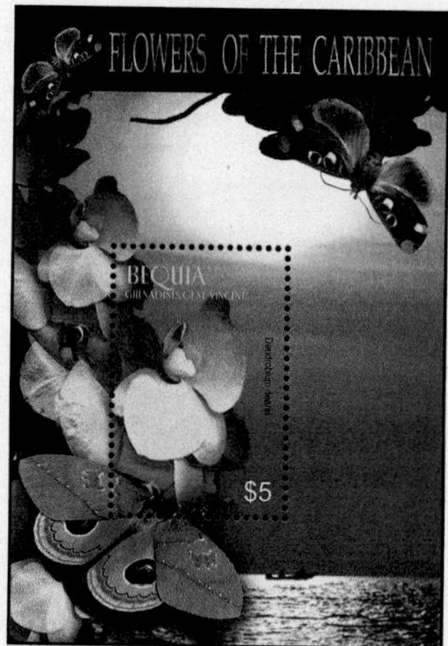
Flowers — B23

No. 366, horiz.: a, Anthurium acropolis. b, Anthurium andraeanum. c, Gloxinia avanti. d, Heliconia psittacorum choconiana.
$5, Dendrobium dearei.

**2005, June 26**
366 B23 $2 Sheet of 4, #a-d 6.50 6.50

**Souvenir Sheet**
367 B23 $5 multi 4.00 4.00

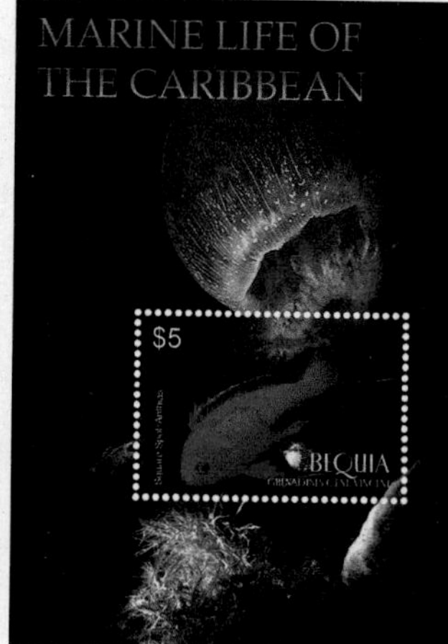
Marine Life — B24

No. 368: a, Hermissenda crassicornis. b, Chromodoris leopardus. c, Chromodoris kuniei. d, Coryphella verrucosa.
$5, Square spot anthias.

**2005, June 26**
368 B24 $2 Sheet of 4, #a-d 7.00 7.00

**Souvenir Sheet**
369 B24 $5 multi 4.00 4.00

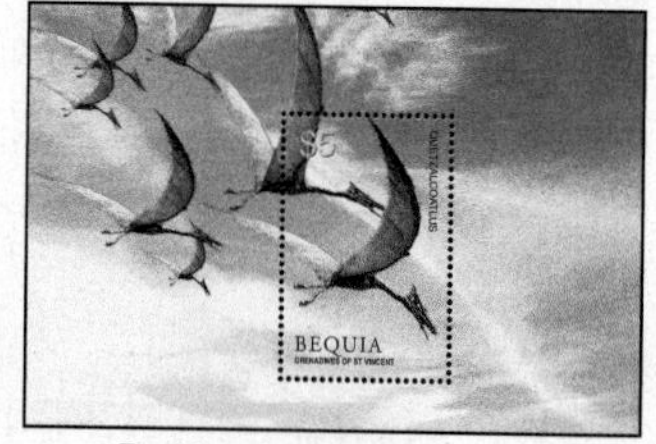
Prehistoric Animals — B25

No. 370, $2: a, Tenontosaurus. b, Gorgosaurus. c, Psittacosaurus. d, Parasaurolophus.
No. 371, $2, horiz.: a, Brachiosaurus. b, Seismosaurus. c, Struthiomimus. d, Oviraptor.
No. 372, $2, horiz.: a, Argentinosaurus. b, Triceratops. c, Ankylosaurus. d, Stegosaurus.
No. 373, $5, Quetzalcoatlus. No. 374, $5, Mammoth. No. 375, $5, Pteranodon, horiz.

**2005, Sept. 1 *Perf. 14***
**Sheets of 4, #a-d**
370-372 B25 Set of 3 19.50 19.50

**Souvenir Sheets**
373-375 B25 Set of 3 12.00 12.00

**Elvis Presley Type of 2005 and**

B26

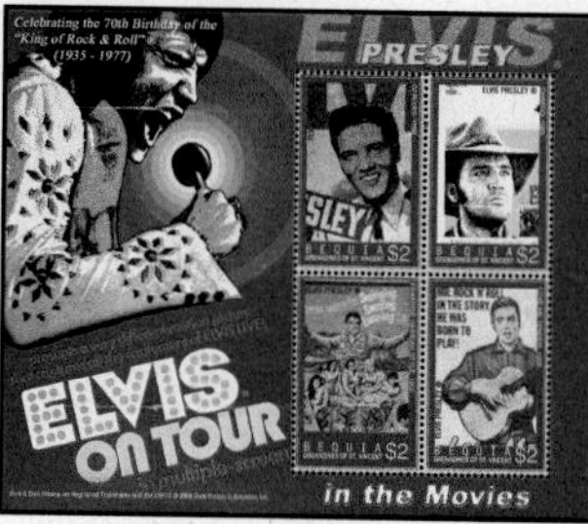
Elvis Presley (1935-77) — B27

No. 377 — Presley with: a, Tie. b, Hat. c, Lei. d, Guitar.
$20, Like #376.

***Perf. 13½x13¼***
**2005, Nov. 21 Litho.**
376 B26 $2 multi 1.50 1.50
377 B27 $2 Sheet of 4, #a-d 5.00 5.00

**Litho. & Embossed**
**Without Gum**
***Die Cut Perf. 8***
378 A597 $20 gold & multi 14.00 14.00

No. 376 was printed in sheets of 4.

**Railroads Type of 2004**

No. 379, $1: a, British Rail APT. b, Beyer Peacock 4-4-0. c, 1890s steam locomotive, Sao Paolo, Brazil. d, Beijing Limestone 600mm Gauge 0-8-0. e, China Railways QJ 2-10-2 Zhou De. f, Chinese SY 2-8-2 Industrial Baotou. g, Chinese SY Class Mikado 2-8-2. h, Chinese SY Class Overhaul Baotou. i, Derelict colliery, Nanpo, China.
No. 380, $1: a, Class 37 Diesel-electric. b, Indian Railways XB Class. c, Steam locomotive bringing in sugar cane, Java. d, Ji-tong Railway train on bridge, Reshui. e, Ji-tong Railway QJ at Liudigou. f, Ji-tong Railway QJ trains on Simingyi Viaduct. g, Ji-tong Railway train at Nandian. h, Ji-tong Railway QJ trains near Er-di. i, Ji-tong Railway QJ trains and banker.
No. 381, $1, vert.: a, Class 47 Diesel-electric. b, Stanier 8F, Turkey. c, Baldwin 2-8-2, Brazil. d, Sand boy, Borsing 0-8-0, Java. e, Indian Railways meter gauge 2-8-2, girl with pot. f, Locomotive graveyard, Thessaloniki,

Greece. g, Greek Z Class meter gauge Peloponnese. h, Burdwan locomotive shed, West Bengal Province, India. i, SY locomotives at shed, Anshan, China.
No. 382, $5, Bridge on Asmara to Masawa line, Eritrea. No. 383, $5, Cornish Riviera Express. No. 384, $5, Zurich to Milan train.

**2005, Dec. 30** ***Perf. 13½***
**Sheets of 9, #a-i**

**379-381** A565 Set of 3 22.50 22.50

**Souvenir Sheets**

**382-384** A565 Set of 3 12.00 12.00

**Queen Elizabeth II, 80th Birthday Type**

Inscriptions: No. 385, $2, The Investiture of Charles. No. 386, $2, The Queen's 50th Birthday. No. 387, $2, The Queen's Silver Jubilee. No. 388, $2, The Birth of Prince William.

**2006, Jan. 31**
**385-388** A603 Set of 4 7.00 7.00

Each stamp printed in sheets of 8 + label.

Miniature Sheet

Marilyn Monroe (1926-62), Actress — B28

Various images.

**2006, Mar. 31**
**389** B28 $2 Sheet of 4, #a-d 6.00 6.00

**Columbus Type of 2006**

Designs: 20c, Columbus and ship. 90c, Columbus, ships and crew, vert. $1.10, Niña, vert. $2, Columbus dicovers New World, 1492. $5, Pinta, vert.

**2006, July 21** ***Perf. 12¾***
**390-393** A611 Set of 4 3.50 3.50

**Souvenir Sheet**

**394** A611 $5 multi 3.75 3.75

**Space Achievements Type of 2006**

No. 395, $2 — Luna 9: a, Left half of Luna 9, country name at LL. b, Right half of Luna 9, country name at UR. c, Top half of Luna 9, country name and denomination at UL. d, Luna 9 in space, country name at UL, denomination at UR. e, Bottom half of Luna 9, country name at LR. f, Luna 9 on moon, country name at LR.
No. 396, $3, vert. — Mars Reconnaissance Orbiter: a, Orbiter, country name in white. b, Orbiter, coutnry name in black. c, Mission emblem. d, Exterior of rocket showing Mission and NASA emblems.
No. 397, $6, Viking 1. No. 398, $6, International Space Station.

**2006, Sept. 27** ***Perf. 14¼***
**395** A612 $2 Sheet of 6, #a-f 4.00 4.00
**396** A612 $3 Sheet of 4, #a-d 4.00 4.00

**Souvenir Sheets**

**397-398** A612 Set of 2 4.00 4.00

**Mozart Type of 2006**

Design: Painting of Mozart, by Johann Georg Edlinger.

**2006, Dec. 22 Litho.** ***Perf. 13¼***
**399** A619 $6 multi 4.75 4.75

Souvenir Sheet

History of the Zeppelin — B29

No. 400: a, Ludwig Durr (1878-1956), chief engineer. b, Count Ferdinand Adolf August Heinrich von Zeppelin (1838-1917), designer. c, Dr. Hugo Eckener (1868-1954), engineer and pilot.

**2006, Dec. 22**
**400** B29 $3 Sheet of 3, #a-c 7.00 7.00

Scouting, Cent. — B30

Designs: $4, Lord Robert Baden-Powell, Scouting emblem and doves. $6, Baden-Powell, horiz.

**2007, Jan. 15**
**401** B30 $4 purple & blue 2.25 2.25

**Souvenir Sheet**

**402** B30 $6 brown 4.75 4.75

No. 401 printed in sheets of 3. No. 402 contains one 51x37mm stamp.

**Princess Diana Type of 2007**
Miniature Sheet

No. 403 — Various photographs with panel colors of: a, Yellow. b, Red violet. c, Green. d, Blue. e, Purple. f, Black.
$6, Princess Diana and flags.

**2007, May 1**
**403** A630 $1.40 Sheet of 6, #a-f 5.00 5.00

**Souvenir Sheet**

**404** A630 $6 multi 4.50 4.50

**Concorde Type of 2006**

No. 405, $1.40 — Concorde landing at Dulles Airport: a, Side view of Concorde. b, Front view of Concorde.
No. 406, $1.40 — Concorde at Boeing Field, Seattle: a, Front view of Concorde. b, Side view of Concorde.

**2007, May 1**
**Pairs, #a-b**

**405-406** A614 Set of 2 4.25 4.25

Nos. 405 and 406 were each printed in sheets containing three of each stamp.

**John F. Kennedy Type of 2007**
Miniature Sheets

No. 407, $2 — Kennedy: a, As Navy Ensign, 1941. b, With crew at Solomon Islands, 1942. c, Drawing in blue gray. d, At Solomon Islands, 1943.
No. 408, $2: a, Kennedy and R. Sargent Shriver. b, Kennedy giving Peace Corps speech. c, Drawing of Kennedy in claret. d, Peace Corps volunteers.

**2007, July 5**
**Sheets of 4, #a-d**

**407-408** A622 Set of 2 13.00 13.00

**Wedding of Queen Elizabeth II and Prince Philip, 60th Anniv. Type of 2007**

No. 409: a, Couple in coach, denomination in blue. b, Couple crossing street, denomination in blue. c, Couple crossing street, denomination in light green. d, Couple in coach, denomination in light green. e, Couple in coach, denomination in lilac. f, Couple crossing street, denomination in lilac.
$6, Couple, diff.

**2007, July 5**
**409** A629 $1.40 Sheet of 6, #a-f 7.00 7.00

**Souvenir Sheet**

**410** A629 $6 multi 5.00 5.00

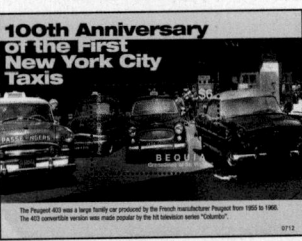


New York City Taxicabs, Cent. — B31

No. 411: a, 1909 Overland Model 31. b, 1910 Rockwell. c, 1916 Yellow Cab Model J. d, 1909 Kayton taxis. e, 1917 Yellow Cab Model K. f, 1919 Yellow Cab.
$6, 1955-66 Peugeot 403.

**2007, July 5**
**411** B31 $1.40 Sheet of 6, #a-f 7.25 7.25

**Souvenir Sheet**

**412** B31 $6 multi 5.00 5.00

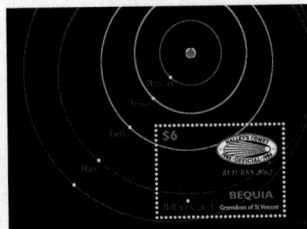

1986 Halley's Comet Merchandising Emblem — B32

No. 413 — Emblem and frame color of: a, Light blue. b, Yellow. c, Green. d, Red brown.
$6, Emblem and Halley's Comet orbit diagram.

**2007, July 5**
**413** B32 $2 Sheet of 4, #a-d 6.50 6.50

**Souvenir Sheet**

**414** B32 $6 multi 4.75 4.75

**Elvis Presley Type of 2007**
Miniature Sheets

No. 415, $2 — Silhouette of Presley and: a, Graceland and gate. b, Piano, television and table in Graceland. c, Graceland and flowers. d, Swimming pool at Graceland.
No. 416, $2.50 — Presley: a, Wearing flowered western shirt, man and woman. b, Playing guitar, with other guitarist. c, Wearing neckerchief. d, Seated.

**2007 Sheets of 4, #a-d** ***Perf. 13¼***
**415-416** A633 Set of 2 13.50 13.50

Issued: No. 415, 7/5; No. 416, 7/12.

**Pope Benedict XVI Type of 2007**

**2007, Oct. 24**
**417** A632 $1 multi .75 .75

Printed in sheets of 8.

**Intl. Holocaust Remembrance Day Type of 2007**

No. 418 — United Nations Delegates: a, Marcello Spatafora, Italy. b, Raymond Wolfe, Jamaica. c, Kenzo Oshima, Japan. d, Prince Zeid Ra'ad Zeid Al-Hussein, Jordan. e, Yerzhan Kh. Kazykhanov, Kazakhstan. f, Zachary Muburi-Muita, Kenya. g, Chi Young-jin, Republic of Korea. h, Solveiga Silkalna, Latvia.

**2007, Nov. 14**
**418** A635 $1.40 Sheet of 8, #a-h 11.00 11.00

The editors would like to examine any commercial covers mailed during 2000-2008 from Bequia, which are franked only with the island's stamps.

## CANOUAN

Diana, Princess of Wales (1961-97) — C1

**1997 Litho.** ***Perf. 14***
**1** C1 $1 multicolored 1.25 1.25

Issued in sheets of 6.

See Mustique No. 1.

**Queen Mother Type of 2000 Inscribed "Canouan"**

**2000, Sept. 5 Litho.** ***Perf. 14***
**2** A472 $1.40 multi 1.25 1.25

Issued in sheets of 6.

United We Stand C3

**2003, Aug. 25**
**7** C3 $2 multi 1.75 1.75

Printed in sheets of 4.

Pres. John F. Kennedy (1917-63) — C4

No. 8: a, Peace Corps. b, Space program. c, Nuclear disarmament. d, Civil rights.

**2003, Aug. 25**
**8** C4 $2 Sheet of 4, #a-d 6.50 6.50



Elvis Presley (1935-77) — C5

**2003, Dec. 1** ***Perf. 13½x13¼***
**9** C5 90c multi 1.00 1.00

Printed in sheets of 9.



Butterflies C6

Designs: 90c, Atala. $1, Calico uranus. $1.40, Ceuptychia. $2, Aphrissa statira.

$5, Phoebis sennae.

**2003, Dec. 1** *Perf. 13¼*
10-13 C6 Set of 4 4.00 4.00

**Souvenir Sheet**

14 C6 $5 multi 3.75 3.75

**Pope John Paul II Type of 2005**

**2005, June 1 Litho.** *Perf. 12½x12¾*
15 A585 $2 multi 1.75 1.75

Printed in sheets of 4.

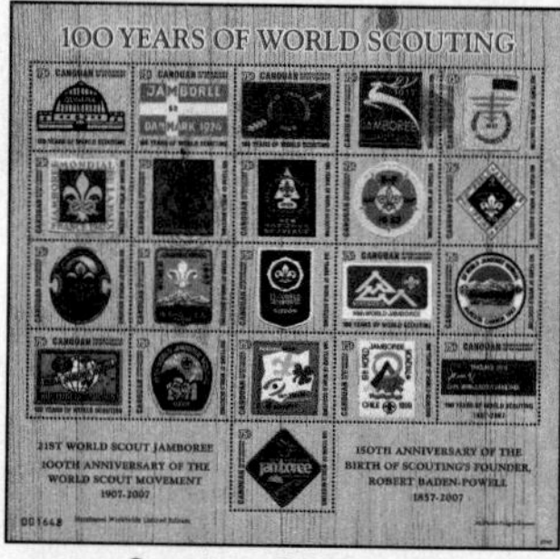

Scouting, Cent. — C7

No. 16 — Patches of International Scout Jamborees: a, Undated patch (1920), Great Britain. b, 1924, Denmark. c, 1929, Great Britain. d, 1933, Hungary. e, 1937, Netherlands. f, 1947, France. g, 1951, Austria. h, 1955, Canada. i, 1957, Great Britain. j, 1959, Philippines. k, 1963, Greece. l, 1967, United States. m, 1971, Japan. n, 1975, Norway. o, 1983, Canada. p, 1987-88, Australia. q, 1991, South Korea. r, 1995, Netherlands. s, 1999, Chile. t, 2003, Thailand. u, 2007, Great Britain.

**2007, Jan. 15 Litho.** *Perf. 13¼*
16 C7 75c Sheet of 21, #a-u 12.00 12.00

**New York City Taxicabs, Cent. Type of 2007 of Bequia**

No. 17 (51x37mm): a, 1913 Model GA. b, 1927 Yellow Cab Model 08. c, 1930 Studebaker Model 53. d, 1948 Checker Model A2. e, 1950's DeSoto. f, 1980's Checker A11.
$6, First gasoline taxi, 1907.

**2007, July 5**
17 B31 $1.40 Sheet of 6, #a-f 7.00 7.00

**Souvenir Sheet**

18 B31 $6 multi 5.00 5.00

No. 18 contains one 51x37mm stamp.

**Intl. Holocaust Remembrance Day Type of 2007**

No. 19 — United Nations diplomats and delegates: a, Jan Eliasson, President of 60th General Assembly. b, Julian Vila Coma, Andorra. c, Ismael A. Gaspar Martins, Angola. d, Victor Camilleri, Malta. e, César Mayoral, Argentina. f, Paulette A. Bethel, Bahamas. g, Christopher Hackett, Barbados. h, Kofi Annan, 7th United Nations Secretary General.

**2007, Nov. 14**
19 A635 $1.40 Sheet of 8, #a-h 8.50 8.50

**Elvis Presley Type of 2007**
Miniature Sheet

No. 20 — Presley: a, In olive green suit. b, Silhouette, standing, holding hand-held microphone. c, In purple shirt. d, Silhouette, with guitar. e, In blue shirt. f, Silhouette, crouching, holding hand-held microphone.

**2007, Nov. 24**
20 A633 $1.50 Sheet of 6, #a-f 8.00 8.00

**John F. Kennedy Type of 2006**
Miniature Sheet

No. 21 (26x40mm) — Kennedy: a, Facing right. b, In limousine, waving. c, Facing left in crowd. d, With arm extended.

**2007, Nov. 24** *Perf. 14*
21 A622 $2 Sheet of 4, #a-d 6.50 6.50

The editors would like to examine any commercial covers mailed during 2000-2008 from Canouan, which are franked only with the island's stamps.

## MAYREAU

All stamps are designs of St. Vincent ("A" illustration letter) unless otherwise illustrated.

**Kennedy Type of 2007**
Miniature Sheets

No. 1, $2, horiz. — John F. Kennedy and Nikita Khrushchev: a, With others, country name at LL, denomination at UR. b, With others, country name at LR, denomination at UL. c, Without others, country name and denomination at LR. d, With others, country name at LR, denomination at UR.
No. 2, $2, horiz. — Kennedy and: a, Fidel Castro, map of Cuba. b, U.S. Capitol, front page of Washington Post. c, American flag, Nikita Khrushchev, missile. d, Airplane, cameramen.

**2006, Nov. 3 Litho.** *Perf. 12¾*
**Sheets of 4, #a-d**
1-2 A622 Set of 2 13.00 13.00

**Wedding of Queen Elizabeth II and Prince Philip, 60th Anniv. Type of 2007**

No. 3: a, Parade in the Royal Carriage. b, Official portrait. c, Walking down the aisle (wedding attendees watching). d, Walking down the aisle (bride, groom and attendants). e, Walking down the aisle (attendants assisting bride). f, Saluting the crowd.
$6, Royal couple, vert.

**2007, May 1 Litho.** *Perf. 13¼*
3 A629 $1.40 Sheet of 6, #a-f 6.75 6.75

**Souvenir Sheet**

4 A629 $6 multi 5.00 5.00

**Princess Diana Type of 2007**

No. 5 — Diana: a, As child in red hooded jacket. b, As young girl in blue sweater. c, As young girl in red, orange and black sweater. d, Wearing pink jacket. e, Wearing lilac jacket. f, Wearing sleeveless dress.
$6, Wearing tiara.

**2007, May 1**
5 A630 $1.40 Sheet of 6, #a-f 6.75 6.75

**Souvenir Sheet**

6 A630 $6 multi 4.75 4.75

**Pope Benedict XVI Type of 2007**

**2007, July 5**
7 A632 $1.50 multi 1.10 1.10

Printed in sheets of 8.

The editors would like to examine any commercial covers mailed during 2000-2008 from Mayreau, which are franked only with the island's stamps.

## MUSTIQUE

All stamps are designs of St. Vincent ("A" illustration letter) or Canouan ("C" illustration letter) unless otherwise illustrated.

Diana, Princess of Wales (1961-97) — M1

**1997 Litho.** *Perf. 14*
1 M1 $1 multicolored 1.10 1.10

Issued in sheets of 6.
See Canouan No. 1.

Queen Mother — M2

Various pictures of flowers making up a photomosaic of the Queen Mother. Stamps inscribed "Mustique."

**2000, Sept. 5** *Perf. 13¾*
2 M2 $1 Sheet of 8, #a-h 17.50 17.50
*i.* As No. 1017, imperf. 27.50 27.50

Coronation of Queen Elizabeth II, 50th Anniv. — M3

No. 3: a, Wearing yellow hat. b, Wearing blue dress. c, Wearing tiara.
$5, Wearing crown.

**2003, Feb. 26 Litho.** *Perf. 14*
3 M3 $3 Sheet of 3, #a-c 8.00 8.00

**Souvenir Sheet**

4 M3 $5 multi 4.50 4.50

**Prince William, 21st Birthday Type of 2003**

No. 5: a, Looking right. b, Wearing ski cap and goggles. c, Looking down.
$5, Wearing suit.

**2003, May 13**
5 A535 $3 Sheet of 3, #a-c 7.75 7.75

**Souvenir Sheet**

6 A535 $5 multi 4.50 4.50

**Corvette Type of 2003**

No. 7: a, 1960 Shark. b, 1988. c, 1956 convertible. d, 1967.
$5, 1964 Sting Ray convertible.

**2003, July 1** *Perf. 13¼x13½*
7 A534 $2 Sheet of 4, #a-d 7.00 7.00

**Souvenir Sheet**

8 A534 $5 multi 4.50 4.50

**Cadillac Type of 2003**

No. 9: a, 1978 Seville. b, 1927 La Salle. c, 1953 Eldorado. d, 2002 Seville.
$5, 1961 Sedan de Ville.

**2003, July 1**
9 A537 $2 Sheet of 4, #a-d 7.00 7.00

**Souvenir Sheet**

10 A537 $5 multi 4.50 4.50

Circus — M7

No. 11: a, Josaphine. b, Korolev Group (girl and monkey). c, Korolev Group (monkey). d, Zebra.

**2003, July 1** *Perf. 14*
11 M7 $2 Sheet of 4, #a-d 11.00 11.00

**Kennedy Type of Canouan**

No. 12: a, On Solomon Islands, 1943. b, On PT 109, 1942. c, Senate campaign, 1952. d, Recieving medal for gallantry, 1944.

**2003, Aug. 25**
12 C4 $2 Sheet of 4, #a-d 8.00 8.00

United We Stand M9

**2003, Sept. 8**
13 M9 $2 multi 1.60 1.60

Printed in sheets of 4.

Birds M10

Designs: $1, Red-billed tropicbird. $1.10, Bananaquit. $1.40, Belted kingfisher. $2, Ruby-throated hummingbird.
$5, Brown pelican, vert.

**2003, Nov. 5** *Perf. 13½x13¾*
14-17 M10 Set of 4 5.25 5.25

**Souvenir Sheet**
*Perf. 13¾x13½*

18 M10 $5 multi 4.25 4.25

Elvis Presley — M11

**2003, Dec. 1** *Perf. 13½x13¼*
19 M11 90c multi .90 .90

Printed in sheets of 9.

Pope John Paul II — M12

**2005, June 1 Litho. *Perf. 12½x12¾***

| | | | | |
|---|---|---|---|---|
| 20 | M12 | $2 multi | 1.75 | 1.75 |

Printed in sheets of 4.

Scouting, Cent. — M13

No. 21, vert.: a, Scouting emblem over globe. b, Emblem of 21st World Scout Jamboree, doves. c, Doves. d, Various national Scouting emblems. e, Doves, map of Mustique, Scouting flag, flag of St. Vincent and the Grenadines. f, Doves, Scout handshake.

$6, Scouting emblem.

**2007, July 5 Litho. *Perf. 13¼***

| | | | | |
|---|---|---|---|---|
| 21 | M13 | $1.50 Sheet of 6, #a-f | 8.50 | 8.50 |

**Souvenir Sheet**

| | | | | |
|---|---|---|---|---|
| 22 | M13 | $6 multi | 4.75 | 4.75 |

### Intl. Holocaust Remembrance Day Type of 2007

No. 23 — United Nations diplomats and delegates: a, Lebohand Fine Maema, Lesotho. b, Milton Nathaniel Barnes, Liberia. c, Christian Wenaweser, Liechtenstein. d, Dalius Cekuolis, Lithuania. e, Igor Dzundev, Macedonia. f, Zina Andrianarivelo-Razafy, Madagascar. g, Nebojsa Kaludjerovic, Montenegro. h, Asha-Rose Migiro, United Nations Deputy Secretary General.

**2007, Nov. 14**

| | | | | |
|---|---|---|---|---|
| 23 | A635 | $1.40 Sheet of 8, #a-h | 9.00 | 9.00 |

The editors would like to examine any commercial covers mailed during 2000-2008 from Mustique, which are franked only with the island's stamps.

## UNION ISLAND

All stamps are types of St. Vincent ("A" illustration letter), St. Vincent Grenadines ("G" illustration letter) or Union ("U" illustration letter).

**"Island" issues are listed separately beginning in 1984. See St. Vincent Grenadines Nos. 84-111, 248-262 for earlier issues.**

### British Monarch Type of 1984

No. 1a, Battle of Hastings. No. 1b, William the Conqueror. No. 2a, William the Conqueror. No. 2b, Abbaye Aux Dames. No. 3a, Skirmish at Dunbar. No. 3b, Charles II. No. 4a, Arms of William the Conqueror. No. 4b, William the Conqueror. No. 5a, Charles II. No. 5b, St. James Palace. No. 6a, Arms of Charles II. No. 6b, Charles II, Great Fire of London.

***Perf. 12½***

**1984, Mar. 29 Litho. Unwmk.**

| | | | | |
|---|---|---|---|---|
| 1 | A110 | 1c Pair, #a.-b. | .25 | .25 |
| 2 | A110 | 5c Pair, #a.-b. | .25 | .25 |
| 3 | A110 | 10c Pair, #a.-b. | .25 | .25 |
| 4 | A110 | 20c Pair, #a.-b. | .30 | .30 |
| 5 | A110 | 60c Pair, #a.-b. | .50 | .50 |
| 6 | A110 | $3 Pair, #a.-b. | 3.50 | 3.50 |
| | | *Nos. 1-6 (6)* | 5.05 | 5.05 |

### Locomotives Type of 1985

No. 13, 1813 Puffing Billy, UK. No. 14, 1911 Class 9N, UK. No. 15, 1882 Class Skye Bogie, UK. No. 16, 1912 Class G8, Germany. No. 17, 1954 Class 65.10, Germany. No. 18, 1900 Castle Class, UK. No. 19, 1887 Spinner Class 25, UK. No. 20, 1951 Fell #10100, UK. No. 21, 1942 Class 42, Germany. No. 22, 1951 Class 5MT, UK. No. 23, 1929 P.O. Rebuilt Class 3500, France. No. 24, 1886 Class 123, UK. No. 25, 1976 Class 56, UK. No. 26, 1897 Class G5, US. No. 27, 1947 9400 Class, UK. No. 28, 1888 Sir Theodore, UK. No. 29, 1929 Class Z, UK. No. 30, 1896 Atlantic City RR, US. No. 31, 1906 45xx Class, UK. No. 32, 1912 Class D15, UK. No. 33, 1938 Class U4-b, Canada. No. 34, 1812 Prince Regent, UK. No. 35, 1920 Butler Henderson, UK. No. 36, 1889 Elidir, UK. No. 37, 1934 7200 Class, UK. No. 38, 1911 Class Z, UK. No. 39, 1938 Class C, Australia. No. 40, 1879 Sir Haydn, UK. No. 41, 1850 Aberdeen No. 26, UK. No. 42, 1883 Class Y14, UK. No. 43, 1915 River Class, UK. No. 44, 1936 D51 Class, Japan. No. 45, 1837 L&B Bury, UK. No. 46, 1903 Class 900, US. No. 47, 1904 Class H-20, US. No. 48, 1905 Class L, UK. No. 49, 1952 Class 4, UK. No. 50, 1837 Campbell's 8-Wheeler, US. No. 51, 1934 Class GG1, US. No. 52, 1924 Class 01, Germany. No. 53, 1920 Gordon Highlander, UK. No. 54, 1969 Metroliner Railcar, US. No. 55, 1951 Class GP7, US. No. 56, 1873 Hardwicke Precedent Class, UK. No. 57, 1899 Highflyer Class, UK. No. 58, 1925 Class U1, UK. No. 59, 1880 Class 7100, Japan. No. 60, 1972 Gas Turbine Prototype, France.

**Se-tenant Pairs, #a.-b.**
**a. — Side and front views.**
**b. — Action scene.**

**1984-87 *Perf. 12½***

| | | | | |
|---|---|---|---|---|
| 13 | A120 | 5c multicolored | .25 | .25 |
| 14 | A120 | 5c multicolored | .25 | .25 |
| 15 | A120 | 5c multicolored | .25 | .25 |
| 16 | A120 | 10c multicolored | .40 | .40 |
| 17 | A120 | 15c multicolored | .40 | .40 |
| 18 | A120 | 15c multicolored | .40 | .40 |
| 19 | A120 | 15c multicolored | .40 | .40 |
| 20 | A120 | 15c multicolored | .40 | .40 |
| 21 | A120 | 20c multicolored | .40 | .40 |
| 22 | A120 | 20c multicolored | .40 | .40 |
| 23 | A120 | 25c multicolored | .40 | .40 |
| 24 | A120 | 25c multicolored | .40 | .40 |
| 25 | A120 | 30c multicolored | .40 | .40 |
| 26 | A120 | 30c multicolored | .40 | .40 |
| 27 | A120 | 40c multicolored | .50 | .50 |
| 28 | A120 | 45c multicolored | .50 | .50 |
| 29 | A120 | 45c multicolored | .50 | .50 |
| 30 | A120 | 45c multicolored | .50 | .50 |
| 31 | A120 | 50c multicolored | .60 | .60 |
| 32 | A120 | 50c multicolored | .60 | .60 |
| 33 | A120 | 50c multicolored | .60 | .60 |
| 34 | A120 | 60c multicolored | .75 | .75 |
| 35 | A120 | 60c multicolored | .75 | .75 |
| 36 | A120 | 60c multicolored | .75 | .40 |
| 37 | A120 | 60c multicolored | .75 | .75 |
| 38 | A120 | 60c multicolored | .75 | .75 |
| 39 | A120 | 75c multicolored | .90 | .90 |
| 40 | A120 | 75c multicolored | .90 | .90 |
| 41 | A120 | 75c multicolored | .90 | .90 |
| 42 | A120 | 75c multicolored | .90 | .90 |
| 43 | A120 | 75c multicolored | .90 | .90 |
| 44 | A120 | $1 multicolored | 1.25 | 1.25 |
| 45 | A120 | $1 multicolored | 1.25 | 1.25 |
| 46 | A120 | $1 multicolored | 1.25 | 1.25 |
| 47 | A120 | $1 multicolored | 1.25 | 1.25 |
| 48 | A120 | $1 multicolored | 1.25 | 1.25 |
| 49 | A120 | $1.50 multicolored | 1.75 | 1.75 |
| 50 | A120 | $1.50 multicolored | 1.75 | 1.75 |
| 51 | A120 | $1.50 multicolored | 1.75 | 1.75 |
| 52 | A120 | $2 multicolored | 2.25 | 2.25 |
| 53 | A120 | $2 multicolored | 2.25 | 2.25 |
| 54 | A120 | $2 multicolored | 2.25 | 2.25 |
| 55 | A120 | $2 multicolored | 2.25 | 2.25 |
| 56 | A120 | $2.50 multicolored | 2.75 | 2.75 |
| 57 | A120 | $2.50 multicolored | 2.75 | 2.75 |
| 58 | A120 | $3 multicolored | 3.50 | 3.50 |
| 59 | A120 | $3 multicolored | 3.50 | 3.50 |
| 60 | A120 | $3 multicolored | 3.50 | 3.50 |
| | | *Nos. 13-60 (48)* | 53.70 | 53.35 |

Issued: Nos. 13, 34, 44, 52, 8/9/84; Nos. 14, 16, 21, 23, 39, 45, 56, 58, 12/18/84; Nos. 15, 31, 35, 53, 3/25/85; Nos. 17, 25, 28, 36, 40, 49, 57, 59, 1/31/86; Nos. 18, 29, 37, 41, 46, 50, 54, 60, 12/23/86; Nos. 19, 24, 27, 32, 38, 42, 47, 55, 9/87; Nos. 20, 22, 26, 308, 33, 43, 48, 51, 12/4/87.

Beginning on Jan. 31, 1986, this issue is not inscribed "Leaders of the World."

### St. Vincent Grenadines Nos. 222-238 Overprinted "UNION ISLAND"

***Perf. 14x13½***

**1984, Aug. 23 Wmk. 373**

| | | | | |
|---|---|---|---|---|
| 109 | G26 | 1c on No. 222 | .25 | .25 |
| 110 | G26 | 3c on No. 223 | .25 | .25 |
| 111 | G26 | 5c on No. 224 | .25 | .25 |
| 112 | G26 | 6c on No. 225 | .25 | .25 |
| 113 | G26 | 10c on No. 226 | .25 | .25 |
| 114 | G26 | 15c on No. 227 | .25 | .25 |
| 115 | G26 | 20c on No. 228 | .30 | .30 |
| 116 | G26 | 25c on No. 229 | .30 | .30 |
| 117 | G26 | 30c on No. 230 | .30 | .30 |
| 118 | G26 | 50c on No. 231 | .45 | .45 |
| 119 | G26 | 60c on No. 232 | .50 | .50 |
| 120 | G26 | 75c on No. 233 | .60 | .60 |
| 121 | G26 | $1 on No. 234 | .90 | .90 |
| 122 | G26 | $2 on No. 235 | 2.00 | 2.00 |
| 123 | G26 | $3 on No. 236 | 2.50 | 2.50 |
| 124 | G26 | $5 on No. 237 | 4.50 | 4.50 |
| 125 | G26 | $10 on No. 238 | 8.00 | 8.00 |
| | | *Nos. 109-125 (17)* | 21.85 | 21.85 |

### Cricket Players Type of 1985

1c, S. N. Hartley. 10c, G. W. Johnson. 15c, R. M. Ellison. 55c, C. S. Cowdrey. 60c, K. Sharp. 75c, M. C. Cowdrey, in action. $1.50, G. R. Dilley, in action. $3, R. Illingworth, in action.

**1984, Nov. Unwmk. *Perf. 12½***
**Pairs, #a.-b.**

| | | | | |
|---|---|---|---|---|
| 126 | A116 | 1c multicolored | .25 | .25 |
| 127 | A116 | 10c multicolored | .30 | .30 |
| 128 | A116 | 15c multicolored | .35 | .35 |
| 129 | A116 | 55c multicolored | .50 | .50 |
| 130 | A116 | 60c multicolored | .55 | .55 |
| 131 | A116 | 75c multicolored | .65 | .65 |
| 132 | A116 | $1.50 multicolored | .85 | .85 |
| 133 | A116 | $3 multicolored | 1.75 | 1.75 |
| | | *Nos. 126-133 (8)* | 5.20 | 5.20 |

### Classic Car Type of 1983

No. 142, 1963 Lancia, Italy. No. 143, 1895 Duryea, US. No. 144, 1970 Datsun, Japan. No. 145, 1962 BRM, UK. No. 146, 1927 Amilcar, France. No. 147, 1929 Duesenberg, US. No. 148, 1913 Peugeot, France. No. 149, 1938 Lagonda, UK. No. 150, 1924 Fiat, Italy. No. 151, 1957 Alfa Romeo, Italy. No. 152, 1957 Panhard, France. No. 153, 1954 Porsche, Germany. No. 154, 1904 Darraco, France. No. 155, 1927 Daimler, UK. No. 156, 1949 Oldsmobile, US. No. 157, 1934 Chrysler, US. No. 158, 1965 MG, UK. No. 159, 1922 Fiat, Italy. No. 160, 1934 Bugatti, France. No. 161, 1963 Watson/Meyer-Drake, US. No. 162, 1917 Locomobile, US. No. 163, 1928 Ford, US.

**Se-tenant Pairs, #a.-b.**
**a. — Side and front views.**
**b. — Action scene.**

**1985-86 *Perf. 12½***

| | | | | |
|---|---|---|---|---|
| 142 | A107 | 1c multicolored | .25 | .25 |
| 143 | A107 | 5c multicolored | .25 | .25 |
| 144 | A107 | 10c multicolored | .25 | .25 |
| 145 | A107 | 10c multicolored | .25 | .25 |
| 146 | A107 | 50c multicolored | .30 | .30 |
| 147 | A107 | 55c multicolored | .35 | .35 |
| 148 | A107 | 60c multicolored | .40 | .40 |
| 149 | A107 | 60c multicolored | .40 | .40 |
| 150 | A107 | 60c multicolored | .40 | .40 |
| 151 | A107 | 75c multicolored | .50 | .50 |
| 152 | A107 | 75c multicolored | .50 | .50 |
| 153 | A107 | 75c multicolored | .50 | .50 |
| 154 | A107 | 90c multicolored | .55 | .55 |
| 155 | A107 | $1 multicolored | .60 | .60 |
| 156 | A107 | $1 multicolored | .60 | .60 |
| 157 | A107 | $1 multicolored | .60 | .60 |
| 158 | A107 | $1.50 multicolored | 1.00 | 1.00 |
| 159 | A107 | $1.50 multicolored | 1.00 | 1.00 |
| 160 | A107 | $1.50 multicolored | 1.00 | 1.00 |
| 161 | A107 | $2 multicolored | 1.25 | 1.25 |
| 162 | A107 | $2.50 multicolored | 1.50 | 1.50 |
| 163 | A107 | $3 multicolored | 1.75 | 1.75 |
| | | *Nos. 142-163 (22)* | 14.20 | 14.20 |

Issued: Nos. 142, 146, 151, 162, 1/4/85; Nos. 143, 148, 155, 158, 5/20/85; Nos. 144, 147, 149, 152, 154, 156, 159, 161, 7/15/85; Nos. 145, 150, 153, 157, 160, 163, 7/30/86.

Beginning on 7/30/86, this issue is not inscribed "Leaders of the World."

Birds — U1

No. 186a, Hooded warbler. No. 186b, Carolina wren. No. 187a, Song sparrow. No. 187b, Black-headed grosbeak. No. 188a, Scarlet tanager. No. 188b, Lazuli bunting. No. 189a, Sharp-shinned hawk. No. 189b, Merlin.

**1985, Feb. *Perf. 12½***

| | | | | |
|---|---|---|---|---|
| 186 | U1 | 15c Pair, #a.-b. | .30 | .30 |
| 187 | U1 | 50c Pair, #a.-b. | .40 | .40 |
| 188 | U1 | $1 Pair, #a.-b. | .65 | .65 |
| 189 | U1 | $1.50 Pair, #a.-b. | 1.50 | 1.50 |
| | | *Nos. 186-189 (4)* | 2.85 | 2.85 |

Butterflies — U2

No. 194a, Cynthia cardui. No. 194b, Zerynthia rumina. No. 195a, Byblia ilithyia. No. 195b, Papilio machaon. No. 196a, Carterocephalus palaemon. No. 196b, Acraea anacreon. No. 197a, Anartia amathea. No. 197b, Salamis temora.

**1985, Apr. 15**

| | | | | |
|---|---|---|---|---|
| 194 | U2 | 15c Pair, #a.-b. | .25 | .25 |
| 195 | U2 | 25c Pair, #a.-b. | .35 | .35 |
| 196 | U2 | 75c Pair, #a.-b. | .55 | .55 |
| 197 | U2 | $2 Pair, #a.-b. | 1.75 | 1.75 |
| | | *Nos. 194-197 (4)* | 2.90 | 2.90 |

### Queen Mother Type of 1985

85th birthday — Hats: No. 206a, Mortarboard. No. 206b, Blue. No. 207a, Turquoise. No. 207b, Blue. Nos. 208a, 212a, Without hat. Nos. 208b, 212b, White. Nos. 209a, 211a, White hat, violet feathers. Nos. 209b, 211b, Blue. No. 210a, Crown. No. 210b, Hat.

**1985, Aug. 19**

| | | | | |
|---|---|---|---|---|
| 206 | A122 | 55c Pair, #a.-b. | .50 | .50 |
| 207 | A122 | 70c Pair, #a.-b. | .60 | .60 |
| 208 | A122 | $1.05 Pair, #a.-b. | .75 | .75 |
| 209 | A122 | $1.70 Pair, #a.-b. | 1.40 | 1.40 |
| | | *Nos. 206-209 (4)* | 3.25 | 3.25 |

**Souvenir Sheets of 2**

| | | | | |
|---|---|---|---|---|
| 210 | A122 | $1.95 #a.-b. | 2.25 | 2.25 |
| 211 | A122 | $2.25 #a.-b. | 2.75 | 2.75 |
| 212 | A122 | $7 #a.-b. | 7.00 | 7.00 |

### Elizabeth II 60th Birthday Type of 1986

Designs: 10c, Wearing scarf. 60c, Riding clothes. $2, Wearing crown and jewels. $8, In Canberra, vert. $10, Holding flowers.

**1986, Apr. 21**

| | | | | |
|---|---|---|---|---|
| 213-216 | A128 | 10c Set of 4 | 3.25 | 3.25 |

**Souvenir Sheet**

| | | | | |
|---|---|---|---|---|
| 217 | A128 | $10 multi | 3.75 | 3.75 |

U3

World Cup Soccer Championships, Mexico — U4

**1986, May 7 *Perf. 12½ (U3), 15 (U4)***

| | | | | |
|---|---|---|---|---|
| 218 | U3 | 1c Moroccan team | .25 | .25 |
| 219 | U3 | 10c Argentinian team | .25 | .25 |
| 220 | U4 | 30c Algerian player | .25 | .25 |
| 221 | U3 | 75c Hungarian team | .30 | .30 |
| 222 | U3 | $1 Russian team | .30 | .30 |
| 223 | U4 | $2.50 Belgian player | .60 | .60 |
| 224 | U4 | $3 French player | .65 | .65 |
| 225 | U4 | $6 W. German player | 1.25 | 1.25 |
| | | *Nos. 218-225 (8)* | 3.85 | 3.85 |

### Souvenir Sheets

**226** U3 $1.85 like No. 222 2.00 2.00
**227** U3 $2 like No. 219 2.25 2.25

Souvenir sheets contain one 60x40mm stamp.

### Prince Andrew Royal Wedding Type

No. 228: a, Prince Andrew in cap. b, Prince Andrew in suit.
No. 229:a, Couple. b, Sarah Ferguson.

**1986, July 15** ***Perf. 12½x13, 13x12½***
**228** A132 60c Pair, #a.-b. .75 .75
**229** A132 $2 Pair. #a.-b. 1.50 1.50

### Nos. 228-229 Overprinted in Silver "CONGRATULATIONS TO T.R.H. THE DUKE & DUCHESS OF YORK" in 3 Lines

**1986, Oct.**
**230** A132 60c on No. 228a-b 1.75 1.75
**231** A132 $2 on No. 229a-b 5.00 5.00

### Queen Elizabeth II Wedding Anniv. Type of St. Vincent Grenadines

**1987, Oct. 15** ***Perf. 12½***
**236** G47 15c like No. 568 .25 .25
**237** G47 45c like No. 569 .35 .35
**238** G47 $1.50 like No. 570 .55 .55
**239** G47 $3 like No. 571 1.10 1.10
**240** G47 $4 like No. 572 1.50 1.50
*Nos. 236-240 (5)* 3.75 3.75

U5

Disney characters in various French vehicles: No. 241, 1c, 1893 Peugeot. No. 242, 2c, 1890-91 Panhard-Levassor. No. 243, 3c, 1910 Renault. No. 244, 4c, 1919 Citroen. No. 245, 5c, 1878 La Mancelle. No. 246, 10c, 1891 De Dion Bouton Quadricycle. No. 247, $5, 1896 Leon Bollee Trike. No. 248, $6, 1911 Brasier Coupe.
No. 249, French road race, Mickey, Donald and Goofy racing. No. 250, 1769, Cugnot's artillery tractor, Mickey, Goofy and Donald dressed as soliders.

**1989, July 7** ***Perf. 14x13½***
**241-248** U5 Set of 8 16.00 16.00

### Souvenir Sheets

**249** U5 $6 multicolored 8.50 8.50
**250** U5 $6 multicolored 8.50 8.50

PHILEXFRANCE '89.

Diana, Princess of Wales (1961-97) — U6

**1997** **Litho.** ***Perf. 14***
**251** U6 $1 multicolored 1.50 2.00

No. 251 was issued in sheets of 6.

### Paintings Type of 1999

Various pictures of flowers making up a photomosaic of the Queen Mother.

**2000, Sept. 5** ***Perf. 13¾***
**252** A442 $1 Sheet of 8, #a-h 7.50 7.50
*i.* As No. 252, imperf. 15.00 *15.00*

New Year 2002 (Year of the Horse) — U7

Horse paintings by Giuseppe Castiglione: a, White horse with head down. b, Brown horse. c, Piebald horse. d, White horse with head up.

**2001, Dec. 17** **Litho.** ***Perf. 12¾***
**253** U7 $1.40 Sheet of 4, #a-d 5.00 5.00

Worldwide Fund for Nature (WWF) U8

Shortfin mako shark: a, View of underside. b, Side view. c, Pair of sharks. d, Shark at surface.

**2002, Nov. 1** ***Perf. 14***
**254** Horiz. or vert. strip 3.25 3.25
*a.-d.* U8 $1 Any single .80 .80
*e.* Souvenir sheet of 4, #a-d 27.50 27.50

### United We Stand Type of 2001

**2002, Nov. 4**
**255** A508 $1.40 multi 1.75 1.75

Printed in sheets of 4.

### Queen Mother Elizabeth Type of 2002

No. 256: a, Wearing purple hat. b, Wearing green hat. c, Wearing pink hat.

**2002, Nov. 4** **Litho.** ***Perf. 14***
**256** A522 $2 Sheet of 4, #a-b, 2 #c 6.50 6.50

Ferrari Automobiles — U9

Designs: No. 257, $1.10, 1960 Dino 246S No. 258, $1.10, 1962 248SP. No. 259, $1.10, 1966 330GTC-GTS. No. 260, $1.10, 1967 Dino 206GT. No. 261, $1.10, 1984 Testarossa. No. 262, $1.10, 1989 348TB-TS. No. 263, $1.10, 2002 Enzo Ferrari. No. 264, $1.10, 2002 360 Challenge.

**2002, Dec. 9**
**257-264** U9 Set of 8 9.00 9.00

### Teddy Bears Type of 2002

No. 265, $2 — Bears from Britain: a, Palace Guard bear. b, Bear with crown. c, Bear with bowler hat. d, Beefeater bear.
No. 266, $2 — Bears from Holland: a, Artist bear. b, Bear with black hat. c, Bears in wagon. d, Bear with overalls and checked shirt.

**2003, Jan. 27** ***Perf. 13½x13¼***

### Sheets of 4, #a-d

**265-266** A519 Set of 2 15.00 15.00

### Year of the Ram Type of 2003

No. 267 — Color of ram: a, Red violet. b, Red. c, Yellow green. d, Violet. e, Brown. f, Blue green.

**2003, Jan. 27** ***Perf. 14¼x13¾***
**267** A526 $1 Sheet of 6, #a-f 4.75 4.75

### Princess Diana Type of 2003

No. 268: a, Wearing pink hat, holding roses. b, Wearing lilac dress and necklace. c, Wearing red hat. d, With hand on chin. e, Wearing pink blouse, holding flowers. d, Wearing blue dress.
No. 269, horiz.: a, Children's Cancer Hospital. b, Meeting with AIDS patients. c, Conference on eating disorders. d, Red Cross child feeding center.

**2003, May 26** **Litho.** ***Perf. 14***
**268** A536 $1.40 Sheet of 6, #a-f 6.75 6.75
**269** A536 $2 Sheet of 4, #a-d 6.50 6.50

### Kennedy Type of Bequia

No. 270: a, Denomination at UL, name at right. b, Denomination at UL, name at left. c, Denomination at UR, name at left. d, Denomination at UR, name at right.

**2003, Aug. 25**
**270** B14 $2 Sheet of 4, #a-d 6.50 6.50

### Elvis Presley Type of Bequia

No. 271 — Color of illustration: a, Brown. b, Dark blue. c, Green. d, Purple. e, Yellow brown. f, Red violet. g, Sepia. h, Bright blue. i, Red brown.

**2003, Dec. 1** ***Perf. 13½***
**271** B15 90c Sheet of 9, #a-i 6.50 6.50

Fish — U10

Designs: 90c, Great barracuda. $1, French angelfish. $1.40, Reef shark. $2, Tarpon. $5, Queen angelfish.

**2003, Dec. 1** ***Perf. 13¼***
**272-275** U10 Set of 4 4.25 4.25

### Souvenir Sheet

**276** U10 $5 multi 4.25 4.25

Detail from Monkey and Cat, by Yi Yuan-Chi — U11

**2004, Jan. 15** ***Perf. 13½***
**277** U11 $1.40 shown 1.60 1.60

### Souvenir Sheet
***Perf. 13¾***

**278** U11 $3 Entire painting 5.75 5.75

New Year 2004 (Year of the Monkey). No. 277 printed in sheets of 4. No. 278 contains one 58x35mm stamp.

### Marilyn Monroe Type of 2004

Monroe and: No. 279, 75c, Denomination in blue. No. 280, 75c, Denomination in red.

**2004, May 3** **Litho.** ***Perf. 13½***
**279-280** A558 Set of 2 1.40 1.40

Each stamp printed in sheets of 10.

### Ronald Reagan Type of 2004

Reagan and denomination color of: a, Red. b, White. c, Blue.

**2004, Oct. 13**
**281** Vert. strip of 3 3.75 3.75
*a.-c.* A564 $1.40 Any single 1.10 1.10

Printed in sheets containing two strips.

### Babe Ruth Type of 2004

**2004, Nov. 25** ***Perf. 14***
**282** A561 75c multi .70 .70

Printed in sheets of 10.

### Miniature Sheet

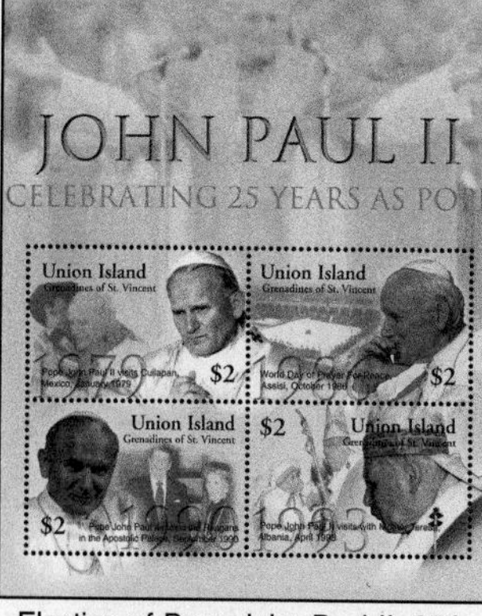

Election of Pope John Paul II, 25th Anniv. (in 2003) — U12

Pope John Paul II: a, With child, Cuilapan, Mexico, 1979. b, At World Day of Prayer for Peace, Assisi, Italy, 1986. c, With Ronald and Nancy Reagan, 1990. d, Visiting Mother Teresa, 1993.

**2005, Jan. 26** ***Perf. 14***
**283** U12 $2 Sheet of 4, #a-d 6.50 6.50

### Basketball Players Type of 2004-05

Designs: No. 284, 90c, Mike Bibby, Sacramento Kings. No. 285, 90c, Reggie Miller, Indiana Pacers. No. 286, 90c, Alonzo Mourning, Miami Heat. No. 287, 90c, Paul Pierce, Boston Celtics. No. 288, 90c, Jim Jackson, Phoenix Suns.
No. 289: a, New Jersey Nets emblem. b, Jason Kidd, New Jersey Nets.

**2005, Feb. 10** **Litho.** ***Perf. 14***
**284-288** A572 Set of 5 4.00 4.00

### Miniature Sheet

**289** A572 90c Sheet of 12, 2 #289a, 10 #289b 8.75 8.75

Nos. 284-288 each printed in sheets of 12.

### Vatican Stamp and Pope John Paul II Types of 2005

Designs: 70c, Vatican #64. $3, Pope holding Bible, horiz.

**2005, June 1** ***Perf. 13x13¼***
**290** A584 70c multi .60 .60
***Perf. 13¼x13½***
**291** A585 $3 multi 2.50 2.50

No. 290 printed in sheets of 12; No. 291, in sheets of 6.

### Railroads Type of 2004

No. 292, $1: a, British Rail intercity high-speed train. b, British-built Edwardian Mogul, Paraguay. c, Fireless locomotive, Ludlow jute mill, Calcutta. d, Welders working on Wisconsin Central. e, Serving breakfast on British intercity train. f, Pacific locomotive, Pulgaon-Avri line, India. g, Locomotive shed laborers, Wankaner, India. h, British Rail train driver with head out of window. i, British Rail train driver at controls.
No. 293, $1: a, Southern Pacific Bullied Pacific "Blackmore Vale." b, Bagnall 0-4-0ST on Assam coalfield. c, Orenstein & Koppel 0-8-0T, Java. d, Baldwin 0-6-6-0 Compound Mallet, Philippines. e, Coal loads on C&I sub, Illinois. f, Class 37 on China Clay, Cornwall. g, BNSF stack train, New Mexico. h, China Railways QJ 2-10-2 near Anshan. i, Kitson 0-6-2 at Suraya Sugar Mill, India.
No. 294, $5, Amtrak Coast Starlight, California. No. 295, $5, Glacier Express.

**2005, June 7** ***Perf. 12¾***

### Sheets of 9, #a-i

**292-293** A565 Set of 2 14.50 14.50

### Souvenir Sheets

**294-295** A565 Set of 2 7.50 7.50

U14

Elvis Presley (1935-77) — U15

No. 297 — Location of spotlights: a, Four spotlights along frame edge at LL, spotlights above and below "S" in "Island." b, Spotlights in top frame near UL corner and above head, spotlights above and below "U" in "Union," spotlight above "S" in "Island." c, Four spotlights in top frame at left, two faint spotlights in left frame at UL. d, Faint spotlight in top frame at UL.

**2005, Nov. 21 Litho. *Perf. 13¼***
**296** U14 $2 multi 1.75 1.75
**297** U15 $2 Sheet of 4, #a-d 6.50 6.50

No. 296 printed in sheets of 4.

### Queen Elizabeth II 80th Birthday Type of 2006

Queen Elizabeth II: No. 298, $2, Riding in coach at Trooping the Color parade, 1987. No. 299, $2, With fireman, 1992. No. 300, $2, At Queen Mother's 100th birthday celebration, 2000. No. 301, $2, Riding in coach in Golden Jubilee parade, 2002.

**2006, Jan. 31 *Perf. 13½***
**298-301** A603 Set of 4 6.25 6.25

Nos. 298-301 each printed in sheets of 8 + label.

### Christopher Columbus Type of 2006

Designs: 10c, Arrival in Hispaniola, 1492. 90c, Columbus and ships. $2, Ships, vert. $3, Ships, diff., vert.
$5, Santa Maria, vert.

**2006, July 21 *Perf. 12¾***
**302-305** A611 Set of 4 4.75 4.75

**Souvenir Sheet**
**306** A611 $5 multi 4.00 4.00

### Space Achievements Type of 2006

No. 307, vert. — Venus Express: a, Denomination in white at LL. b, Denomination in white at UL. c, Denomination in black at LL. d, Denomination in black at UL.
No. 308 — First Flight of Space Shuttle Columbia: a, Lift-off. b, Columbia on launch pad. c, Astronaut John W. Young, Columbia. d, Astronaut Robert L. Crippen, Columbia. e, Columbia in space. f, Flight emblem.
$5, Luna 9.

**2006, Dec. 22 *Perf. 13¼***
**307** A612 $2 Sheet of 4, #a-d 6.50 6.50
**308** A612 $3 Sheet of 6, #a-f 14.00 14.00

**Souvenir Sheet**
**309** A612 $5 multi 4.00 4.00

### Rembrandt Type of 2006

Self-portraits from: 50c, C. 1632-39. 75c, 1635. $1, 1629. $2, 1634.
No. 314, $2 — Drawings: a, Two Tramps, a Man and a Woman. b, Beggar Leaning on a Stick. c, Ragged Peasant with His Hands Behind Him, Holding a Stick. d, Beggar Man and Beggar Woman Conversing.
No. 315, $2 — Drawings: a, Study for the Drunkenness of Lot. b, A Girl Sleeping. c, Saskia at a Window. d, Old Man with Arms Extended.
No. 316, $5, The Apostle Simon (70x100mm). No. 317, $5, Winter Landscape, horiz. (100x70mm).

**2006, Dec. 22 *Perf. 13¼***
**310-313** A617 Set of 4 3.50 3.50

**Sheets of 4, #a-d**
**314-315** A617 Set of 2 13.50 13.50

***Imperf***
**316-317** A617 Set of 2 8.00 8.00

### John F. Kennedy Type of 2007
Miniature Sheets

No. 318, $2, horiz. — Inauguration: a, Kennedy shaking hands with Father Richard J. Casey. b, Kennedy and State Department Seal. c, Medal of Kennedy, U.S. flag. d, Portrait of Kennedy, Kennedy with son.
No. 319, $2, horiz. — Cuban Missile Crisis: a, Kennedy, Soviet Premier Nikita Khrushchev, photographer. b, Cuban President Fidel Castro, Soviet trucks at Cuban port. c, Kennedy and map of plan to invade Cuba. d, KA-18A stereo strip camera, map of Cuba.

**2006, Dec. 22 *Perf. 13¼***
**Sheets of 4, #a-d**
**318-319** A622 Set of 2 13.00 13.00

### Scouting, Cent. Type of Bequia of 2007

Designs: $4, Scouting emblem, doves and figure-eight knots. $6, Scouting emblem.

**2007, Jan. 3**
**320** B30 $4 blue & green 3.75 3.75

**Souvenir Sheet**
**321** B30 $6 multi 5.75 5.75

No. 320 printed in sheets of 3. No. 321 contains one 37x51mm stamp.

### Wedding of Queen Elizabeth II and Prince Philip, 60th Anniv. Type of 2007

No. 322 — Couple with Queen wearing: a, Gray hat with black feather. b, Red and lilac hat. c, Black and white hat. d, Light blue jacket, no hat. e, Light blue jacket and hat. f, Light green jacket, red and light green hat.
$6, Couple under umbrella, vert.

**2007, July 5 *Perf. 12¾***
**322** A629 $1.40 Sheet of 6, #a-f 7.25 7.25

**Souvenir Sheet**
**323** A629 $6 multi 4.75 4.75

### Princess Diana Type of 2007

No. 324: a, Seated in chair. b, Reclining, wearing white dress. c, Wearing blue dress. d, Wearing white blouse and jeans. e, Wearing black dress. f, Wearing black sweater, pants and shoes.
No. 325: a, As Red Cross volunteer. b, Touring minefield in Angola. c, With Mother Teresa. d, Holding child at Shri Swaminarayan Mandir, London.
$6, Wearing headphones.

**2007, July 5 *Perf. 12¾***
**324** A630 $1.40 Sheet of 6, #a-f 7.00 7.00
**325** A630 $2 Sheet of 4, #a-d 6.50 6.50

**Souvenir Sheet**
**326** A630 $6 multi 5.00 5.00

### Pope Benedict XVI Type of 2007

**2007, July 5 *Perf. 13¼***
**327** A632 $1.50 multi 1.25 1.25

Printed in sheets of 8.

### Elvis Presley Type of 2007

No. 328 — Photographs of Presley from: a, 1946. b, 1956. c, 1962. d, 1970.

**2007, Oct. 24**
**328** A633 $3 Sheet of 4, #a-d 9.50 9.50

First Helicopter Flight, Cent. — U16

Designs: 10c, Benson autogyro. 25c, Agusta-Sikorsky AS-61. 90c, Bell UH-1B/C Iroquois, horiz. $5, Bell UH-1 Iroquois, vert.
No. 333, horiz.: a, Eurocopter/Kawasaki BK 117, denomination at UR. b, Bell UH-1B/C Iroquois, denomination at LL. c, Bell UH-1B/C Iroquois, denomination at UR. d, Eurocopter/Kawasaki BK 117, denomination at UL.
$5, NH 90, horiz.

**2007, Oct. 24**
**329-332** U16 Set of 4 7.00 7.00
**333** U16 $2 Sheet of 4, #a-d 8.50 8.50

**Souvenir Sheet**
**334** U16 $5 multi 4.50 4.50

The editors would like to examine any commercial covers mailed during 2000-2008 from Union Island, which are franked only with the island's stamps.

Stamps inscribed "Palm Island," "Tobago Cays," and "Young Island" are not listed as they do not meet Scott listing criteria.

## SALVADOR, EL

'el-sal-və-ˌdor

LOCATION — On the Pacific coast of Central America, between Guatemala, Honduras and the Gulf of Fonseca
GOVT. — Republic
AREA — 8,236 sq. mi.
POP. — 5,839,079 (1999 est.)
CAPITAL — San Salvador

8 Reales = 100 Centavos = 1 Peso
100 Centavos = 1 Colón
100 Cents = 1 Dollar (2003)

**Catalogue values for unused stamps in this country are for Never Hinged items, beginning with Scott 589 in the regular postage section, Scott C85 in the airpost section, and Scott O362 in the official section.**

### Watermarks

Wmk. 117 — Liberty Cap

Position of wmk. on reprints

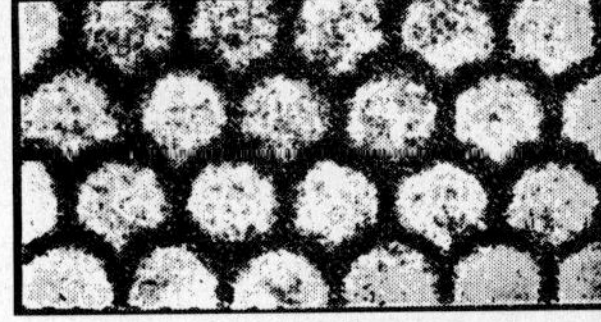
Wmk. 172 — Honeycomb

Wmk. 173 — S

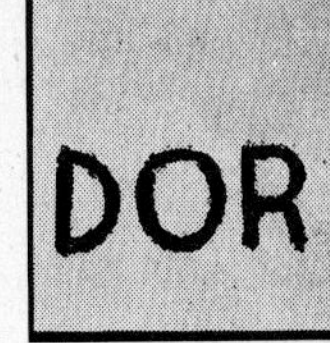

Wmk. 240 — REPUBLICA DE EL SALVADOR in Sheet

Wmk. 269 — REPUBLICA DE EL SALVADOR

Volcano San Miguel — A1

**1867 Unwmk. Engr. *Perf. 12***
**1** A1 ½r dk gray blue 7.00 *4.00*
**2** A1 1r dark red 7.00 4.00
**3** A1 2r dark green 8.50 4.50
**4** A1 4r dp ol brn 32.50 17.50
*Nos. 1-4 (4)* 55.00 30.00

There were at least two printings of Nos. 1-4. Stamps from the second printing are lighter in color. See the *1840-1940 Classic Specialized Catalogue* for detailed listings.
Nos. 1-4 when overprinted "Contra Sello" and shield with 14 stars, are telegraph stamps. For similar overprint see Nos. 5-12.
Counterfeits exist.

### Nos. 1-4 Handstamped Either Type I or Type II in Black

Type I

Type II

Type II

**1874**
**5** A1 ½r blue 30.00 10.00
**6** A1 1r red 20.00 10.00
**7** A1 2r green 30.00 10.00
**8** A1 4r bister 40.00 20.00
*Nos. 5-8 (4)* 120.00 50.00

### Nos. 1-4 Handstamped Type III in Black

Type III

**9** A1 ½r blue 8.00 6.00
**10** A1 1r red 8.00 3.00
**11** A1 2r green 10.00 3.00
**12** A1 4r bister 12.00 10.00
*Nos. 9-12 (4)* 38.00 22.00

The overprints on Nos. 5-12 exist double. Counterfeits are plentiful.

Coat of Arms
A2 A3

A4 A5

A6

**1879 Litho. *Perf. 12½***

| | | | | |
|---|---|---|---|---|
| **13** | A2 | 1c green | 3.00 | 1.75 |
| *a.* | | Invtd. "V" for 2nd "A" in "SALVADOR" | 6.00 | 3.00 |
| *b.* | | Invtd. "V" for "A" in "REPUBLICA" | 6.00 | 3.00 |
| *c.* | | Invtd. "V" for "A" in "UNIVERSAL" | 6.00 | 3.00 |
| *d.* | | Thin paper | — | — |
| **14** | A3 | 2c rose | 4.25 | 2.25 |
| *a.* | | Invtd. scroll in upper left corner | 12.00 | 7.50 |
| **15** | A4 | 5c blue | 7.50 | 1.90 |
| *a.* | | 5c ultra | 12.00 | 6.00 |
| **16** | A5 | 10c black | 15.00 | 5.25 |
| **17** | A6 | 20c violet | 24.00 | 15.00 |
| | | *Nos. 13-17 (5)* | 53.75 | 26.15 |

There are fifteen varieties of the 1c and 2c, twenty-five of the 5c and five each of the 10 and 20c.

In 1881 the 1c, 2c and 5c were redrawn, the 1c in fifteen varieties and the 2c and 5c in five varieties each.

No. 15 comes in a number of shades from light to dark blue.

These stamps, when overprinted "Contra sello" and arms, are telegraph stamps.

Counterfeits of No. 14 exist.

For overprints see Nos. 25D-25E, 28A-28C.

Allegorical Figure of El Salvador — A7

Volcano — A8

**1887 Engr. *Perf. 12***

| | | | | |
|---|---|---|---|---|
| **18** | A7 | 3c brown | 2.00 | 2.00 |
| *a.* | | Imperf., pair | 10.00 | 10.00 |
| **19** | A8 | 10c orange | 30.00 | 3.00 |

For surcharges and overprints see Nos. 25, 26C-28, 30-32.

A9

**1888 *Rouletted***

| | | | | |
|---|---|---|---|---|
| **20** | A9 | 5c deep blue | 1.50 | 1.50 |

For overprints see Nos. 35-36.

A10

**1889 *Perf. 12***

| | | | | |
|---|---|---|---|---|
| **21** | A10 | 1c green | .40 | |
| **22** | A10 | 2c scarlet | .40 | |

Nos. 21-22 Overprinted in Black

| | | | | |
|---|---|---|---|---|
| **23** | A10 | 1c green | .40 | 3.00 |
| **24** | A10 | 2c scarlet | .40 | |

Nos. 21, 22 and 24 were never placed in use.

For overprints see Nos. 26, 29.

**No. 18 Surcharged**

Type I

Type II

Type I — thick numerals, heavy serifs.
Type II — thin numerals, straight serifs.

| | | | | |
|---|---|---|---|---|
| **25** | A7 | 1c on 3c brn, type II | 4.00 | *7.00* |
| *a.* | | Double surcharge | 1.50 | |
| *b.* | | Triple surcharge | 3.50 | |
| *c.* | | Type I | .65 | |

The 1c on 2c scarlet is bogus.

Handstamped

**1889 Violet Handstamp**

| | | | | |
|---|---|---|---|---|
| **25D** | A2 | 1c green | 19.00 | 19.00 |
| **25E** | A6 | 20c violet | 45.00 | 45.00 |
| **26** | A10 | 1c green, #23 | 10.50 | *15.00* |
| **26C** | A7 | 1c on 3c, #25 | 50.00 | 50.00 |
| **27** | A7 | 3c brown | 7.50 | *15.00* |
| **28** | A8 | 10c orange | 10.00 | *12.50* |

**Black Handstamp**

| | | | | |
|---|---|---|---|---|
| **28A** | A2 | 1c green | 22.50 | 21.00 |
| **28B** | A3 | 2c rose | 26.00 | 26.00 |
| **28C** | A6 | 20c violet | 45.00 | 45.00 |
| **29** | A10 | 1c green, #23 | 10.50 | *15.00* |
| **30** | A7 | 3c brown | 10.50 | *15.00* |
| **31** | A7 | 1c on 3c, #25 | 40.00 | 40.00 |
| **32** | A8 | 10c orange | 15.00 | 12.50 |

***Rouletted***

**Black Handstamp**

| | | | | |
|---|---|---|---|---|
| **35** | A9 | 5c deep blue | 9.00 | *15.00* |

**Violet Handstamp**

| | | | | |
|---|---|---|---|---|
| **36** | A9 | 5c deep blue | 9.00 | *15.00* |

The 1889 handstamps as usual, are found double, inverted, etc. Counterfeits are plentiful.

A13

**1890 Engr. *Perf. 12***

| | | | | |
|---|---|---|---|---|
| **38** | A13 | 1c green | .50 | .50 |
| **39** | A13 | 2c bister brown | .50 | .50 |
| **40** | A13 | 3c yellow | .50 | .50 |
| **41** | A13 | 5c blue | .50 | .50 |
| **42** | A13 | 10c violet | .50 | .50 |
| **43** | A13 | 20c orange | .75 | *3.00* |
| **44** | A13 | 25c red | 1.50 | *5.00* |
| **45** | A13 | 50c claret | 2.00 | *7.50* |
| **46** | A13 | 1p carmine | 5.00 | *30.00* |
| | | *Nos. 38-46 (9)* | 11.75 | *48.00* |

**The issues of 1890 to 1899 inclusive were printed by the Hamilton Bank Note Co., New York, to the order of N. F. Seebeck, who held a contract for stamps with the government of El Salvador. This contract gave the right to make reprints of the stamps and such were subsequently made in some instances, as will be found noted in italic type.**

**Used values of 1890-1899 issues are for stamps with genuine cancellations applied while the stamps were valid. Various counterfeit cancellations exist.**

A14

**1891**

| | | | | |
|---|---|---|---|---|
| **47** | A14 | 1c vermilion | .50 | .50 |
| **48** | A14 | 2c yellow green | .50 | .50 |
| **49** | A14 | 3c violet | .50 | .50 |
| **50** | A14 | 5c carmine lake | 2.00 | .50 |
| **51** | A14 | 10c blue | .50 | .50 |
| **52** | A14 | 11c violet | .50 | .50 |
| **53** | A14 | 20c green | .50 | *.50* |
| **54** | A14 | 25c yellow brown | .50 | *2.50* |
| **55** | A14 | 50c dark blue | 2.00 | *7.50* |
| **56** | A14 | 1p dark brown | .75 | *25.00* |
| | | *Nos. 47-56 (10)* | 8.25 | *38.50* |

For surcharges see Nos. 57-59.

*Nos. 47 and 56 have been reprinted in thick toned paper with dark gum.*

**Nos. 48, 49 Surcharged in Black or Violet**

No. 57

No. 58

No. 59

**1891**

| | | | | |
|---|---|---|---|---|
| **57** | A14 | 1c on 2c yellow grn | 2.25 | 2.00 |
| *a.* | | Inverted surcharge | 8.00 | |
| *b.* | | Surcharge reading up | 12.00 | |
| **58** | A14 | 1c on 2c yellow grn | 1.60 | 1.40 |
| **59** | A14 | 5c on 3c redsh pur | 4.00 | 3.25 |
| | | *Nos. 57-59 (3)* | 7.85 | 6.65 |

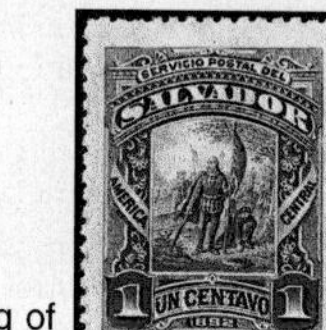

Landing of Columbus — A18

**1892 Engr.**

| | | | | |
|---|---|---|---|---|
| **60** | A18 | 1c blue green | .50 | .50 |
| **61** | A18 | 2c orange brown | .50 | .50 |
| **62** | A18 | 3c ultra | .50 | .50 |
| **63** | A18 | 5c gray | .50 | .50 |
| **64** | A18 | 10c vermilion | .50 | .50 |
| **65** | A18 | 11c brown | .50 | .50 |
| **66** | A18 | 20c orange | .50 | *.75* |
| **67** | A18 | 25c maroon | .50 | *2.00* |
| **68** | A18 | 50c yellow | .50 | *7.00* |
| **69** | A18 | 1p carmine lake | .50 | *25.00* |
| | | *Nos. 60-69 (10)* | 5.00 | *37.75* |

400th anniversary of the discovery of America by Columbus.

**Nos. 63, 66-67 Surcharged**

Nos. 70, 72

Nos. 73-75

**Surcharged in Black, Red or Yellow**

**1892**

| | | | | |
|---|---|---|---|---|
| **70** | A18 | 1c on 5c gray (Bk) (down) | 3.00 | .75 |
| *a.* | | Surcharge reading up | 5.00 | 2.00 |
| **72** | A18 | 1c on 5c gray (R) (up) | 1.00 | *3.00* |
| *a.* | | Surcharge reading down | | |
| **73** | A18 | 1c on 20c org (Bk) | 1.50 | .75 |
| *a.* | | Inverted surcharge | 3.50 | 2.50 |
| *b.* | | "V" of "CENTAVO" inverted | 3.50 | 2.50 |
| | | *Nos. 70-73 (3)* | 5.50 | 4.50 |

**Similar Surcharge in Yellow or Blue, "centavo" in lower case letters**

| | | | | |
|---|---|---|---|---|
| **74** | A18 | 1c on 25c mar (Y) | 1.50 | 1.25 |
| *a.* | | Inverted surcharge | 2.50 | 2.50 |
| **75** | A18 | 1c on 25c mar (Bl) | *250.00* | *250.00* |
| *a.* | | Double surcharge (Bl + Bk) | *275.00* | *275.00* |

Counterfeits exist of Nos. 75 and 75a. Nos. 75, 75a have been questioned.

Pres. Carlos Ezeta — A21

**1893 Engr.**

| | | | | |
|---|---|---|---|---|
| **76** | A21 | 1c blue | .50 | .50 |
| **77** | A21 | 2c brown red | .50 | .50 |
| **78** | A21 | 3c purple | .50 | .50 |
| **79** | A21 | 5c deep brown | .50 | .50 |
| **80** | A21 | 10c orange brown | .50 | .50 |
| **81** | A21 | 11c vermilion | .50 | .50 |
| **82** | A21 | 20c green | .50 | *1.00* |
| **83** | A21 | 25c dk olive gray | .50 | *2.25* |
| **84** | A21 | 50c red orange | .50 | *5.00* |
| **85** | A21 | 1p black | .50 | *20.00* |
| | | *Nos. 76-85 (10)* | 5.00 | *31.25* |

For surcharge see No. 89.

Founding City of Isabela — A22

Columbus Statue, Genoa — A23

Departure from Palos — A24

**1893**

| | | | | |
|---|---|---|---|---|
| **86** | A22 | 2p green | .75 | — |
| **87** | A23 | 5p violet | .75 | |
| **88** | A24 | 10p orange | .75 | |
| | | *Nos. 86-88 (3)* | 2.25 | |

Discoveries by Columbus. No. 86 is known on cover, but experts are not positive that Nos. 87 and 88 were postally used.

**No. 77 Surcharged "UN CENTAVO"**

**1893**

| | | | | |
|---|---|---|---|---|
| **89** | A21 | 1c on 2c brown red | 1.00 | *1.25* |
| *a.* | | "CENTNVO" | 6.00 | 5.00 |

Liberty — A26

Columbus before Council of Salamanca — A27

Columbus Protecting Indian Hostages
A28

Columbus Received by Ferdinand and Isabella
A29

**1894, Jan.**

**91** A26 1c brown .75 .50
**92** A26 2c blue .75 .50
**93** A26 3c maroon .75 .50
**94** A26 5c orange brn .75 .50
**95** A26 10c violet .75 *.75*
**96** A26 11c vermilion .75 *.75*
**97** A26 20c dark blue .75 *1.00*
**98** A26 25c orange .75 *5.00*
**99** A26 50c black .75 *10.00*
**100** A26 1p slate blue 1.10 *20.00*
**101** A27 2p deep blue 1.10
**102** A28 5p carmine lake 1.10
**103** A29 10p deep brown 1.10
*Nos. 91-103 (13)* 11.15
*Nos. 91-100 (10)* *39.50*

Nos. 101-103 for the discoveries by Columbus. Experts are not positive that these were postally used.

No. 96 Surcharged

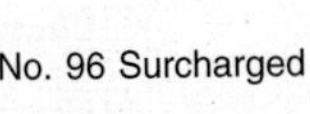

**1894, Dec.**

**104** A26 1c on 11c vermilion 4.50 .65
*a.* "Ccntavo" *40.00* *40.00*
*b.* Double surcharge

Coat of Arms — A31

**Arms Overprint in Second Color**
**Various Frames**

**1895, Jan. 1**

**105** A31 1c olive & green .50 .25
**106** A31 2c dk green & bl .25 —
*a.* 2c dark green & green .50 .85
**107** A31 3c brown & brown .50 —
**108** A31 5c blue & brown .50 —
**109** A31 10c orange & brn .50 —
**110** A31 12c magenta & brn .50 —
**111** A31 15c ver & ver .50 —
**112** A31 20c yellow & brn .50 —
*a.* Inverted overprint 2.00
**113** A31 24c violet & brn .50 —
**114** A31 30c dp blue & blue .50 —
**115** A31 50c carmine & brn .50 —
**116** A31 1p black & brn .50 —
*Nos. 105-116 (12)* 5.75

As printed, Nos. 105-116 portrayed Gen. Antonio Ezeta, brother of Pres. Carlos Ezeta. Before issuance, Ezeta's overthrow caused the government to obliterate his features with the national arms overprint. The 3c, 10c, 30c exist without overprint. Value $1 each.

*All values have been reprinted. Reprints of 2c are in dark yellow green on thick paper. Value, 25c each.*

Coat of Arms — A32

**Various Frames**

**1895** **Engr.** ***Perf. 12***

**117** A32 1c olive 7.25 .50
**118** A32 2c dk blue grn 7.25 .50
**119** A32 3c brown 10.00 .75
**120** A32 5c blue 2.00 .75
**121** A32 10c orange 5.00 .75
**122** A32 12c claret 17.50 1.00
**123** A32 15c vermilion 22.00 1.00
**124** A32 20c deep green 30.00 2.00
**125** A32 24c violet 22.50 4.00
**126** A32 30c deep blue 30.00 5.00
**127** A32 50c carmine lake 3.00 35.00
**128** A32 1p gray black 10.00 *35.00*
*Nos. 117-128 (12)* 166.50 *86.25*

*The reprints are on thicker paper than the originals, and many of the shades differ. Value 25c each.*

Nos. 122, 124-126 Surcharged in Black or Red

**1895**

**129** A32 1c on 12c claret (Bk) 2.00 1.75
**130** A32 1c on 24c violet 2.00 1.75
**131** A32 1c on 30c dp blue 2.00 1.75
**132** A32 2c on 20c dp grn 2.00 1.75
**133** A32 3c on 30c dp blue 3.00 2.75
*a.* Double surcharge 9.00
*Nos. 129-133 (5)* 11.00 9.75

"Peace" — A45

**1896, Jan. 1** **Engr.** **Unwmk.**

**134** A45 1c blue 2.00 .50
**135** A45 2c dark brown .50 .50
**136** A45 3c blue green .50 .50
**137** A45 5c brown olive 2.00 .50
**138** A45 10c yellow .50 .50
**139** A45 12c dark blue 4.00 *1.00*
**140** A45 15c brt ultra .25 —
*a.* 15c light violet 1.10 *2.00*
**141** A45 20c magenta 4.00 *3.00*
**142** A45 24c vermilion 1.50 *5.00*
**143** A45 30c orange 1.50 *5.00*
**144** A45 50c black brn 3.00 *7.50*
**145** A45 1p rose lake 6.00 *20.00*
*Nos. 134-145 (12)* 25.75 *44.00*

The frames of Nos. 134-145 differ slightly on each denomination.

For overprints see Nos. O1-O12, O37-O48.

**Wmk. 117**

**145B** A45 2c dark brown .25 .25

*All values have been reprinted. The paper is thicker than that of the originals and the shades are different. The watermark is always upright on original stamps of Salvador, sideways on the reprints. Value 25c each.*

Coat of Arms — A46

"White House" — A47

Locomotive
A48

Mt. San Miguel
A49

Ocean Steamship
A50 A51

Post Office
A52

Lake Ilopango
A53

Atehausillas Waterfall
A54

Coat of Arms
A55

Coat of Arms
A56

Columbus
A57

**1896**

**146** A46 1c emerald .50 *1.50*
**147** A47 2c lake .50 *.90*
**148** A48 3c yellow brn .75 .75
**149** A49 5c deep blue .90 .50
**150** A50 10c brown 2.00 .90
**151** A51 12c slate 2.00 .90
**152** A52 15c blue green 1.75 .75
**153** A53 20c carmine rose 2.00 1.25
**154** A54 24c violet *8.00* 1.25
**155** A55 30c deep green 5.00 2.00
**156** A56 50c orange 10.00 5.00
**157** A57 100c dark blue 15.00 *12.50*
*Nos. 146-157 (12)* 48.40 *28.20*

Nos. 146-157 exist imperf.

**Unwmk.**

**157B** A46 1c emerald 3.75 .90
**157C** A47 2c lake 3.75 .50
**157D** A48 3c yellow brn 6.00 .50
**157E** A49 5c deep blue 4.00 .75
**157F** A50 10c brown 7.50 .75
**157G** A51 12c slate 10.00 1.00
**157I** A52 15c blue green 20.00 1.75
**157J** A53 20c carmine rose 7.50 1.00
**157K** A54 24c violet 10.00 1.25
**157M** A55 30c deep green 10.00 2.50
**157N** A56 50c orange 15.00 7.00
**157O** A57 100c dark blue 20.00 15.00
*Nos. 157B-157O (12)* 117.50 *32.90*

See Nos. 159-170L. For surcharges and overprints see Nos. 158, 158D, 171-174C, O13-O36, O49-O72, O79-O126.

*All values have been reprinted, the 15c, 30c, 50c and 100c on watermarked and the 1c, 2c, 3c, 5c, 12c, 20c, 24c and 100c on unwatermarked paper. The papers of the reprints are thicker than those of the originals and the shades are different. Value, 25c each.*

Black Surcharge on Nos. 154, 157K

**1896** **Wmk. 117**

**158** A54 15c on 24c violet 4.00 4.00
*a.* Double surcharge 20.00 *30.00*
*b.* Inverted surcharge 15.00

**Unwmk.**

**158D** A54 15c on 24c violet 4.00 3.00

Exist spelled "Qnince."

**Types of 1896**

**1897** **Engr.** **Wmk. 117**

**159** A46 1c scarlet 2.75 .90
**160** A47 2c yellow grn 2.75 .50
**161** A48 3c bister brn 2.50 .50
**162** A49 5c orange 2.50 .75
**163** A50 10c blue grn 3.00 .75
**164** A51 12c blue 8.00 1.00
**165** A52 15c black 20.00 10.00
**166** A53 20c slate 8.00 2.00
**167** A54 24c yellow 20.00 20.00
**168** A55 30c rose 15.00 5.00
**169** A56 50c violet 15.00 5.00
**170** A57 100c brown lake 30.00 15.00
*Nos. 159-170 (12)* 129.50 61.40

**Unwmk.**

**170A** A46 1c scarlet 2.00 *1.50*
**170B** A47 2c yellow grn 1.00 *.90*
**170C** A48 3c bister brn .75 .75
**170D** A49 5c orange .90 .50
**170E** A50 10c blue grn 5.00 .90
**170F** A51 12c blue 1.00 2.00
**170G** A52 15c black 10.00 10.00
**170H** A53 20c slate 10.00 10.00
**170I** A54 24c yellow 20.00 20.00
**170J** A55 30c rose 10.00 10.00
**170K** A56 50c violet 9.50 10.00
**170L** A57 100c brown lake 50.00 *50.00*
*Nos. 170A-170L (12)* 120.15 116.55

The 1c, 2c, 3c, 5c, 12c, 15c, 50c and 100c have been reprinted on watermarked and the entire issue on unwatermarked paper. The papers of the reprints are thicker than those of the originals. Value, set of 20, $5.

Surcharged in Red or Black

**1897** **Wmk. 117**

**171** A54 13c on 24c yel (R) 2.50 2.50
**172** A55 13c on 30c rose (Bk) 2.50 2.50
**173** A56 13c on 50c vio (Bk) 2.50 2.50
**174** A57 13c on 100c brn lake (Bk) 2.50 2.50

**Unwmk.**

**174A** A54 13c on 24c yel (R) 2.50 2.50
**174B** A55 13c on 30c rose (Bk) 2.50 2.50
**174C** A56 13c on 50c vio (Bk) 2.50 2.50
*Nos. 171-174C (7)* 17.50 17.50

Coat of Arms of "Republic of Central America" — A59

ONE CENTAVO:

Originals: The mountains are outlined in red and blue. The sea is represented by short red and dark blue lines on a light blue background.

*Reprints: The mountains are outlined in red only. The sea is printed in green and dark blue, much blurred.*

FIVE CENTAVOS:

Originals: The sea is represented by horizontal and diagonal lines of dark blue on a light blue background.

*Reprints: The sea is printed in green and dark blue, much blurred. The inscription in gold is in thicker letters.*

**1897** **Litho.**

**175** A59 1c bl, gold, rose & grn 1.00 —
**176** A59 5c rose, gold, bl & grn 2.00 —

Forming of the "Republic of Central America."

For overprints see Nos. O73-O76.

*Stamps of type A59 formerly listed as "Type II" are now known to be reprints.*

Allegory of Central American Union — A60

**1898** **Engr.** **Wmk. 117**

**177** A60 1c orange ver 2.25 .50
**178** A60 2c rose 2.25 .50
**179** A60 3c pale yel grn 2.00 .50
**180** A60 5c blue green 2.00 .75
**181** A60 10c gray blue 7.50 .75
**182** A60 12c violet 8.50 1.00
**183** A60 13c brown lake 8.50 1.00
**184** A60 20c deep blue 9.50 2.00
**185** A60 24c deep ultra 7.50 5.25
**186** A60 26c bister brn 10.00 5.00
**187** A60 50c orange 10.00 5.00
**188** A60 1p yellow 25.00 15.00
*Nos. 177-188 (12)* 95.00 *37.25*

For overprints and surcharges see Nos. 189-198A, 224-241, 269A-269B, O129-O142.

*The entire set has been reprinted on unwatermarked paper and all but the 12c and 20c on watermarked paper. The shades of the reprints are not the same as those of the originals, and the paper is thicker. Value, set of 22, $5.50.*

No. 180 Overprinted Vertically, up or down in Black, Violet, Red, Magenta and Yellow

**1899**

| No. | Type | Description | Unused | Used |
|---|---|---|---|---|
| 189 | A60 | 5c blue grn (Bk) | 7.50 | 6.25 |
| a. | | Italic 3rd "r" in "Territorial" | 12.50 | 12.50 |
| b. | | Double ovpt. (Bk + Y) | 37.50 | 37.50 |
| 190 | A60 | 5c blue grn (V) | *82.50* | *82.50* |
| 191 | A60 | 5c blue grn (R) | *70.00* | *70.00* |
| 191A | A60 | 5c blue grn (M) | *70.00* | *70.00* |
| 191B | A60 | 5c blue grn (Y) | *75.00* | *75.00* |
| | | *Nos. 189-191B (5)* | *305.00* | *303.75* |

Counterfeits exist.

Nos. 177-184 Overprinted in Black

**1899**

| No. | Type | Description | Unused | Used |
|---|---|---|---|---|
| 192 | A60 | 1c orange ver | 2.00 | .50 |
| 193 | A60 | 2c rose | 2.50 | 1.00 |
| 194 | A60 | 3c pale yel grn | 2.50 | .50 |
| 195 | A60 | 5c blue green | 2.50 | .50 |
| 196 | A60 | 10c gray blue | 4.00 | 1.25 |
| 197 | A60 | 12c violet | 6.50 | 2.50 |
| 198 | A60 | 13c brown lake | 6.50 | 2.00 |
| 198A | A60 | 20c deep blue | *75.00* | *75.00* |
| | | *Nos. 192-198 (7)* | 26.50 | 8.25 |

The overprint on No. 198A is only seen on the reprints.

Counterfeits exist of the "wheel" overprint used in 1899-1900.

Ceres ("Estado") — A61

**Inscribed: "Estado de El Salvador"**

**1899 Unwmk. Litho. *Perf. 12***

| No. | Type | Description | Unused |
|---|---|---|---|
| 199 | A61 | 1c brown | .25 |
| 200 | A61 | 2c gray green | .25 |
| 201 | A61 | 3c blue | .25 |
| 202 | A61 | 5c brown org | .25 |
| 203 | A61 | 10c chocolate | .25 |
| 204 | A61 | 12c dark green | .25 |
| 205 | A61 | 13c deep rose | .25 |
| 206 | A61 | 24c light blue | .25 |
| 207 | A61 | 26c carmine rose | .25 |
| 208 | A61 | 50c orange red | .25 |
| 209 | A61 | 100c violet | .25 |
| | | *Nos. 199-209 (11)* | 2.75 |

Nos. 208-209 were probably not placed in use.

For overprints and surcharges see Nos. 210-223, 242-252D, O143-O185.

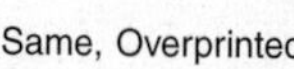

Same, Overprinted

**Red Overprint**

| No. | Type | Description | Unused | Used |
|---|---|---|---|---|
| 210 | A61 | 1c brown | 60.00 | 40.00 |

**Blue Overprint**

| No. | Type | Description | Unused | Used |
|---|---|---|---|---|
| 211 | A61 | 1c brown | 2.00 | 1.50 |
| 212 | A61 | 5c brown org | 2.00 | 1.50 |
| 212A | A61 | 10c chocolate | 15.00 | 10.00 |

**Black Overprint**

| No. | Type | Description | Unused | Used |
|---|---|---|---|---|
| 213 | A61 | 1c brown | 1.50 | .75 |
| 214 | A61 | 2c gray grn | 2.00 | .40 |
| 215 | A61 | 3c blue | 2.25 | 1.00 |
| 216 | A61 | 5c brown org | 1.50 | .65 |
| 217 | A61 | 10c chocolate | 1.50 | .80 |
| 218 | A61 | 12c dark green | 4.00 | 4.00 |
| 219 | A61 | 13c deep rose | 3.50 | 3.50 |
| 220 | A61 | 24c light blue | 30.00 | 27.50 |
| 221 | A61 | 26c car rose | 7.50 | 5.00 |
| 222 | A61 | 50c orange red | 9.00 | 7.50 |
| 223 | A61 | 100c violet | 10.00 | 9.00 |
| | | *Nos. 213-223 (11)* | 72.75 | 60.10 |

"Wheel" overprint exists double and triple.

No. 177 Handstamped

**1900 Wmk. 117**

| No. | Type | Description | Unused | Used |
|---|---|---|---|---|
| 224 | A60 | 1c orange ver | 1.00 | 1.00 |

No. 177 Overprinted

| No. | Type | Description | Unused | Used |
|---|---|---|---|---|
| 225 | A60 | 1c orange ver | 15.00 | 15.00 |

Stamps of 1898 Surcharged in Black

**1900**

| No. | Type | Description | Unused | Used |
|---|---|---|---|---|
| 226 | A60 | 1c on 10c gray blue | 15.00 | 15.00 |
| a. | | Inverted surcharge | 15.00 | 15.00 |
| 227 | A60 | 1c on 13c brn lake | *100.00* | |
| 228 | A60 | 2c on 12c vio | 50.00 | 50.00 |
| a. | | "eentavo" | | |
| b. | | Inverted surcharge | | |
| c. | | "centavos" | 90.00 | |
| d. | | As "c," double surcharge | | |
| e. | | Vertical surcharge | | |
| 229 | A60 | 2c on 13c brn lake | 5.00 | 5.00 |
| a. | | "eentavo" | 8.00 | 7.00 |
| b. | | Inverted surcharge | 12.50 | 10.00 |
| c. | | "1900" omitted | 7.50 | 7.50 |
| 230 | A60 | 2c on 20c dp blue | 5.00 | 5.00 |
| a. | | Inverted surcharge | 8.00 | 8.00 |
| 230B | A60 | 2c on 26c bis brn | — | — |
| 231 | A60 | 3c on 12c vio | *90.00* | — |
| a. | | "eentavo" | | |
| b. | | Inverted surcharge | — | — |
| c. | | Double surcharge | | |
| 232 | A60 | 3c on 50c org | 35.00 | 35.00 |
| a. | | Inverted surcharge | 35.00 | 35.00 |
| 233 | A60 | 5c on 12c vio | — | — |
| 234 | A60 | 5c on 24c ultra | 50.00 | 50.00 |
| a. | | "eentavo" | | |
| b. | | "centavos" | 70.00 | |
| 235 | A60 | 5c on 26c bis brn | *150.00* | *150.00* |
| a. | | Inverted surcharge | *35.00* | *35.00* |
| 236 | A60 | 5c on 1p yel | 50.00 | 35.00 |
| a. | | Inverted surcharge | 60.00 | 60.00 |

With Additional Overprint in Black

| No. | Type | Description | Unused | Used |
|---|---|---|---|---|
| 237 | A60 | 2c on 12c vio | 2.50 | 2.50 |
| a. | | Inverted surcharge | 2.50 | 2.50 |
| b. | | "eentavo" | 8.00 | |
| c. | | "centavos" (plural) | 75.00 | |
| d. | | "1900" omitted | | |
| 237H | A60 | 2c on 13c brn lake | | |
| 238 | A60 | 3c on 12c vio | 125.00 | 125.00 |
| a. | | "eentavo" | 75.00 | 75.00 |
| 239 | A60 | 5c on 26c bis brn | 150.00 | 150.00 |
| a. | | Inverted surcharge | | |

**Vertical Surcharge "Centavos" in the Plural**

| No. | Type | Description | Unused | Used |
|---|---|---|---|---|
| 240 | A60 | 2c on 12c vio | 125.00 | 125.00 |
| b. | | Without wheel | | |
| 240A | A60 | 5c on 24c dp ultra | 125.00 | 125.00 |

With Additional Overprint in Black

| No. | Type | Description | Unused | Used |
|---|---|---|---|---|
| 241 | A60 | 5c on 12c vio | 50.00 | 50.00 |
| a. | | Surcharge reading downward | | |

Counterfeits exist of the surcharges on Nos. 226-241 and the "wheel" overprint on Nos. 237-239, 241.

**Same Surcharge on Stamps of 1899 Without Wheel**

**1900 Unwmk.**

| No. | Type | Description | Unused | Used |
|---|---|---|---|---|
| 242 | A61 | 1c on 13c dp rose | 1.50 | 1.50 |
| a. | | Inverted surcharge | 4.00 | 3.00 |
| b. | | "eentavo" | 4.00 | 3.00 |
| c. | | "ecntavo" | 5.00 | 3.00 |
| d. | | "1 centavo 1" | 15.00 | 10.00 |
| e. | | Double surcharge | | |
| 243 | A61 | 2c on 12c dk grn | 8.00 | 8.00 |
| a. | | Inverted surcharge | 15.00 | 15.00 |
| b. | | "eentavo" | | |
| 244 | A61 | 2c on 13c dp rose | 3.00 | 2.50 |
| a. | | "eentavo" | 3.00 | 4.00 |
| b. | | "ecntavo" | 6.00 | 2.50 |
| c. | | Inverted surcharge | 9.00 | |
| 245 | A61 | 3c on 12c dk grn | 3.00 | 2.50 |
| a. | | Inverted surcharge | 9.00 | 5.00 |
| b. | | "eentavo" | 12.00 | 12.00 |
| c. | | Double surcharge | 9.00 | |
| | | *Nos. 242-245 (4)* | 15.50 | 14.50 |

With Additional Overprint in Black

| No. | Type | Description | Unused | Used |
|---|---|---|---|---|
| 246 | A61 | 1c on 2c gray grn | 1.00 | 1.00 |
| a. | | "eentavo" | 4.00 | 3.00 |
| b. | | Inverted surcharge | 10.00 | 9.00 |
| 247 | A61 | 1c on 13c dp rose | 4.00 | 4.00 |
| a. | | "eentavo" | 15.00 | |
| b. | | "1 centavo 1" | | |
| 248 | A61 | 2c on 12c dk grn | 5.00 | 4.00 |
| a. | | "eentavo" | 15.00 | |
| b. | | Inverted surcharge | 4.00 | 4.00 |
| c. | | Double surcharge | 8.00 | |
| 249 | A61 | 2c on 13c dp rose | 100.00 | 100.00 |
| a. | | "eentavo" | | |
| b. | | Double surcharge | 150.00 | 150.00 |
| 250 | A61 | 3c on 12c dk grn | 5.00 | 3.00 |
| a. | | Inverted surcharge | 5.50 | 4.00 |
| b. | | "eentavo" | 8.00 | 7.00 |
| c. | | Date double | 15.00 | |
| 251 | A61 | 5c on 24c lt bl | 12.00 | 5.00 |
| a. | | "eentavo" | 20.00 | 20.00 |
| 252 | A61 | 5c on 26c car rose | 4.00 | 4.00 |
| a. | | Inverted surcharge | 12.00 | 9.00 |
| b. | | "eentavo" | 6.00 | 5.00 |
| 252D | A61 | 5c on 1c on 26c car rose | | |
| | | *Nos. 246-248,250-252 (6)* | 31.00 | 21.00 |

Counterfeits exist of the surcharges on Nos. 242-252D and the "wheel" overprint on Nos. 246-252D.

Ceres ("Republica") — A63

There are two varieties of the 1c, type A63, one with the word "centavo" in the middle of the label (#253, 263, 270, 299, 305, 326), the other with "centavo" nearer the left end than the right (#270, 299, 305, 326).

The stamps of type A63 are found in a great variety of shades. Stamps of type A63 without handstamp were not regularly issued.

**Handstamped in Violet or Black**

**Inscribed: "Republica de El Salvador"**

**1900**

| No. | Type | Description | Unused | Used |
|---|---|---|---|---|
| 253 | A63 | 1c blue green | .90 | .90 |
| a. | | 1c yellow green | .90 | .90 |
| 254 | A63 | 2c rose | 1.50 | 1.00 |
| 255 | A63 | 3c gray black | 1.25 | 1.00 |
| 256 | A63 | 5c pale blue | 1.00 | .60 |
| a. | | 5c deep blue | 5.00 | .60 |
| 257 | A63 | 10c deep blue | 2.00 | .60 |
| 258 | A63 | 12c yel green | 5.00 | 3.50 |
| 259 | A63 | 13c yel brown | 4.00 | 3.00 |
| 260 | A63 | 24c gray | 15.00 | 15.00 |
| 261 | A63 | 26c yel brown | 7.00 | 7.00 |
| 262 | A63 | 50c rose red | 2.00 | 2.00 |
| | | *Nos. 253-262 (10)* | 39.65 | 34.60 |

For overprints and surcharges see Nos. 263-269, 270-282, 293A-311B, 317, 326-335, O223-O242, O258-O262, O305-O312.

Handstamped in Violet or Black

| No. | Type | Description | Unused | Used |
|---|---|---|---|---|
| 263 | A63 | 1c lt green | 10.00 | 4.00 |
| 264 | A63 | 2c pale rose | 10.00 | 3.00 |
| 265 | A63 | 3c gray black | 10.00 | 3.00 |
| 266 | A63 | 5c slate blue | 14.00 | 3.00 |
| 267 | A63 | 10c deep blue | — | — |
| 268 | A63 | 13c yellow brn | 35.00 | 35.00 |
| 269 | A63 | 50c dull rose | 15.00 | 15.00 |
| | | *Nos. 263-266,268-269 (6)* | 94.00 | 63.00 |

**Handstamped on 1898 Stamps**

**Wmk. 117**

| No. | Type | Description | Unused | Used |
|---|---|---|---|---|
| 269A | A60 | 2c rose | 30.00 | 30.00 |
| 269B | A60 | 10c gray blue | 30.00 | 30.00 |

The overprints on Nos. 253 to 269B are handstamped and, as usual with that style of overprint, are to be found double, inverted, omitted, etc.

Specialists have questioned the existence of No. 267. The editors would like to see authenticated evidence of the existence of a genuine example.

Stamps of Type A63 Overprinted in Black

**1900 Unwmk.**

| No. | Type | Description | Unused | Used |
|---|---|---|---|---|
| 270 | A63 | 1c light green | 1.50 | 1.00 |
| 271 | A63 | 2c rose | 7.50 | 2.00 |
| 272 | A63 | 3c gray black | 1.50 | 1.00 |
| 273 | A63 | 5c pale blue | 7.50 | 2.00 |
| a. | | 5c dark blue | 6.00 | 1.00 |
| 274 | A63 | 10c deep blue | 7.50 | 2.00 |
| a. | | 10c pale blue | 7.50 | 2.00 |
| 275 | A63 | 12c light green | 2.25 | 1.50 |
| 276 | A63 | 13c yellow brown | 1.50 | 1.00 |
| 277 | A63 | 24c gray | 1.75 | 1.25 |
| 278 | A63 | 26c yellow brown | 3.00 | 2.00 |
| | | *Nos. 270-278 (9)* | 34.00 | 13.75 |

This overprint is known double, inverted, etc.

**Nos. 271-273 Surcharged in Black**

**1902**

| No. | Type | Description | Unused | Used |
|---|---|---|---|---|
| 280 | A63 | 1c on 2c rose | 8.25 | 6.75 |
| 281 | A63 | 1c on 3c black | 6.00 | 4.25 |
| 282 | A63 | 1c on 5c blue | 3.75 | 3.00 |
| | | *Nos. 280-282 (3)* | 18.00 | 14.00 |

Morazán Monument — A64

***Perf. 14, 14½***

**1903 Engr. Wmk. 173**

| No. | Type | Description | Unused | Used |
|---|---|---|---|---|
| 283 | A64 | 1c green | 1.00 | .60 |
| 284 | A64 | 2c carmine | 1.00 | .60 |
| 285 | A64 | 3c orange | 10.00 | 2.00 |
| 286 | A64 | 5c dark blue | 1.00 | .60 |
| 287 | A64 | 10c dull violet | 1.00 | .60 |
| 288 | A64 | 12c slate | 1.25 | .60 |
| 289 | A64 | 13c red brown | 1.25 | .60 |
| 290 | A64 | 24c scarlet | 7.50 | 3.75 |
| 291 | A64 | 26c yellow brn | 7.50 | 3.75 |
| 292 | A64 | 50c bister | 3.75 | 2.25 |
| 293 | A64 | 100c grnsh blue | 11.00 | 7.50 |
| | | *Nos. 283-293 (11)* | 46.25 | 22.85 |

For surcharges and overprint see Nos. 312-316, 318-325, O253.

**Stamps of 1900 with Shield in Black Overprinted**

(5¾x13½mm) — a

1905

(5x14¾mm) — b

(4½x16mm) — c

(4½x13½mm) — d

(5x14½mm) — e **1905**

**1905-06 Unwmk. *Perf. 12***

**Blue Overprint**

**293A** A63 (a) 2c rose — —
**294** A63 (a) 3c gray blk 8.00 6.00
*a.* Without shield
**295** A63 (a) 5c blue 10.00 7.50

**Purple Overprint**

**296** A63 (b) 3c gray blk (Shield in pur) — —
**296A** A63 (b) 5c bl (Shield in pue) — —
**297** A63 (b) 3c gray blk — —
**298** A63 (b) 5c blue — —

**Black Overprint**

**298A** A63 (b) 5c blue — —

**Blue Overprint**

**299** A63 (c) 1c green 10.00 5.00
**299B** A63 (c) 2c rose .50 .40
*c.* "1905" vert. 1.00
**300** A63 (c) 5c blue 6.00 4.00
**301** A63 (c) 10c deep blue 2.00 1.00

**Black Overprint**

**302** A63 (c) 2c rose 10.00 5.00
**303** A63 (c) 5c blue 25.00 25.00
**304** A63 (c) 10c deep blue 12.00 7.00

**Blue Overprint**

**305** A63 (d) 1c green 15.00 10.00
**306** A63 (d) 2c rose, ovpt. vert. 9.00 5.00
*a.* Overprint horiz.
**306B** A63 (d) 3c gray black 8.00 4.00
**307** A63 (d) 5c blue 3.00 1.50

**Blue Overprint**

**311** A63 (e) 2c rose 10.00 8.00
*a.* Without shield 15.00 12.00

**Black Overprint**

**311B** A63 (e) 5c blue 30.00 20.00
*Nos. 294-295,299-311B (15)* 158.50 109.40

These overprints are found double, inverted, omitted, etc. Counterfeits exist.

**Regular Issue of 1903 Surcharged**

f

g

h

**1905-06 Wmk. 173 *Perf. 14, 14½***

**Black Surcharge**

**312** A64 (f) 1c on 2c car 4.00 2.00
*a.* Double surcharge 20.00 20.00

**Red Surcharge**

**312B** A64 (g) 5c on 12c slate 5.00 4.00
*c.* Double surcharge
*d.* Black surcharge 15.00 15.00
*e.* As "d," double surcharge

**Blue Handstamped Surcharge**

**313** A64 (h) 1c on 2c car 2.00 2.00
**314** A64 (h) 1c on 10c vio 2.00 2.00
**315** A64 (h) 1c on 12c sl ('06) 2.00 2.00
**316** A64 (h) 1c on 13c red brn 22.50 15.00

**No. 271 with Handstamped Surcharge in Blue**

**Unwmk.**

**317** A63 (h) 1c on 2c rose — —
*Nos. 312-316 (6)* 37.50 27.00

The "h" is handstamped in strips of four stamps each differing from the others in the size of the upper figures of value and in the letters of the word "CENTAVO," particularly in the size of the "N" and the "O" of that word. The surcharge is known inverted, double, etc.

**Regular Issue of 1903 with Handstamped Surcharge**

i

j

k

**Wmk. 173**

**Red Handstamped Surcharge**

**318** A64 (i) 5c on 12c slate 4.00 3.00
**319** A64 (j) 5c on 12c slate 6.00 5.00
*a.* Blue surcharge

**Blue Handstamped Surcharge**

**320** A64 (k) 5c on 12c slate 3.50 2.50
*Nos. 318-320 (3)* 13.50 10.50

One or more of the numerals in the handstamped surcharges on Nos. 318, 319 and 320 are frequently omitted, inverted, etc.

**Regular Issue of 1903 Surcharged**

l

m

**Blue Handstamped Surcharge**

**321** A64 (l) 6c on 12c slate .75 .50
**322** A64 (l) 6c on 13c red brn 1.50 .60

**Red Handstamped Surcharge**

**323** A64 (l) 6c on 12c slate 27.50 15.00

Type "l" is handstamped in strips of four varieties, differing in the size of the numerals and letters. The surcharge is known double and inverted.

**Black Surcharge**

**324** A64 (m) 1c on 13c red brn 2.25 1.50
*a.* Double surcharge 6.00 4.50
*b.* Right "1" & dot omitted
*c.* Both numerals omitted
**325** A64 (m) 3c on 13c red brn .75 .60

Stamps of 1900, with Shield in Black, Overprinted — n

**1905 Unwmk. *Perf. 12***

**Blue Overprint**

**326** A63 (n) 1c green 9.00 6.00
*a.* Inverted overprint
**327** A63 (n) 2c rose 5.00 5.00
*a.* Vertical overprint 12.50 12.50
*b.* Imperforate 9.00 6.00
**327B** A63 (n) 3c black 50.00 30.00
**327C** A63 (n) 5c blue 25.00 20.00
**328** A63 (n) 10c deep blue 15.00 9.00

**Black Overprint**

**328A** A63 (n) 10c deep blue 20.00 15.00
*Nos. 326-328A (6)* 124.00 85.00

Counterfeits of Nos. 326-335 abound.

**Stamps of 1900, with Shield in Black Surcharged or Overprinted**

o

**1906**

p

q

**1906 Blue and Black Surcharge**

**329** A63 (o) 2c on 26c brn org 1.00 .80
*a.* "2" & dot double 15.00 15.00
**330** A63 (o) 3c on 26c brn org 8.00 6.50
*a.* "3" & dot double

**Black Surcharge or Overprint**

**331** A63 (o) 3c on 26c brn org 9.00 7.00
*a.* Disks & numerals omitted
*b.* "3" and disks double
*c.* "1906" omitted
**333** A63 (p) 10c deep blue 6.00 4.00
**334** A63 (q) 10c deep blue 6.00 4.00
**334A** A63 (q) 26c brown org 50.00 45.00
*b.* "1906" in blue

**No. 257 Overprinted in Black**

**335** A63 (q) 10c dp bl (Shield in violet) — —
*a.* Overprint type "p"
*Nos. 329-334A (6)* 80.00 67.30

There are numerous varieties of these surcharges and overprints.

Pres. Pedro José Escalón — A65

**1906 Engr. *Perf. 11½***

**Glazed Paper**

**336** A65 1c green & blk .25 .25
*a.* Thin paper .75 .25
**337** A65 2c red & blk .25 .25
**338** A65 3c yellow & blk .25 .25
**339** A65 5c ultra & blk .25 .25
*a.* 5c dark blue & black .25 .25
**340** A65 6c carmine & blk .25 .25
**341** A65 10c violet & blk .25 .25
**342** A65 12c violet & blk .25 .25
**343** A65 13c dk brn & blk .25 .25
**345** A65 24c carmine & blk .35 .35
**346** A65 26c choc & blk .35 .35
**347** A65 50c yellow & blk .35 .45
**348** A65 100c blue & blk *3.00 3.00*
*Nos. 336-348 (12) 6.05 6.15*

All values of this set are known imperforate but are not believed to have been issued in this condition.

See Nos. O263-O272. For overprints and surcharges see Nos. 349-354.

*The entire set has been reprinted, perforated 11.8. Value, set of 12, $1.20.*

Nos. 336-338 Overprinted in Black

**1907**

**349** A65 1c green & blk .25 .25
*a.* Shield in red 3.50
**350** A65 2c red & blk .25 .25
*a.* Shield in red 3.50
**351** A65 3c yellow & blk .25 .25
*Nos. 349-351 (3)* .75 .75

*Reprints of Nos. 349 to 351 have the same characteristics as the reprints of the preceding issue. Value, set of 3, 15c.*

Stamps of 1906 Surcharged with Shield and

**352** A65 1c on 5c ultra & blk .25 .25
*a.* 1c on 5c dark blue & black .25 .25
*b.* Inverted surcharge .35 .35
*c.* Double surcharge .45 .45
**352D** A65 1c on 6c rose & blk .25 .25
*e.* Double surcharge 1.25 1.25
**353** A65 2c on 6c rose & blk 2.00 1.00
**354** A65 10c on 6c rose & blk .50 .35
*Nos. 352-354 (4)* 3.00 1.85

The above surcharges are frequently found with the shield double, inverted, or otherwise misplaced.

National Palace — A66

**Overprinted with Shield in Black**

**1907 Engr. Unwmk.**

**Paper with or without colored dots**

**355** A66 1c green & blk .25 .25
**356** A66 2c red & blk .25 .25
**357** A66 3c yellow & blk .25 .25
**358** A66 5c blue & blk .25 .25
*a.* 5c ultramarine & black .25 .25
**359** A66 6c ver & blk .25 .25
*a.* Shield in red 3.25
**360** A66 10c violet & blk .25 .25
**361** A66 12c violet & blk .25 .25
**362** A66 13c sepia & blk .25 .25
**363** A66 24c rose & blk .25 .25
**364** A66 26c yel brn & blk .30 .25
**365** A66 50c orange & blk .50 .35
*a.* 50c yellow & black 3.50
**366** A66 100c turq bl & blk 1.00 .50
*Nos. 355-366 (12)* 4.05 3.35

Most values exist without shield, also with shield inverted, double, and otherwise misprinted. Many of these were never sold to the public.

See 2nd footnote following No. 421.

See Nos. 369-373, 397-401. For surcharges and overprints see Nos. 367-368A, 374-77, 414-421, 443-444, J71-J74, J76-J80, O329-O331.

No. 356 With Additional Surcharge in Black

**1908**

**367** A66 1c on 2c red & blk .25 .25
*a.* Double surcharge 1.00 1.00
*b.* Inverted surcharge .50 .50
*c.* Double surcharge, one inverted .50 .50
*d.* Red surcharge

Same Surcharged in Black or Red

**368** A66 1c on 2c *19.00 17.50*
**368A** A66 1c on 2c (R) *27.50 25.00*

Counterfeits exist of the surcharges on Nos. 368-368A.

**Type of 1907**

**1909 Engr. Wmk. 172**

**369** A66 1c green & blk .25 .25
**370** A66 2c rose & blk .25 .25
**371** A66 3c yellow & blk .25 .25

**372** A66 5c blue & blk .25 .25
**373** A66 10c violet & blk .30 .25
*Nos. 369-373 (5)* 1.30 1.25

The note after No. 366 will apply here also.

Nos. 355, 369 Overprinted in Red

**1909, Sept.** **Unwmk.**
**374** A66 1c green & blk 2.25 1.10
*a.* Inverted overprint 10.00

**Wmk. 172**

**375** A66 1c green & blk 1.75 1.40
*a.* Inverted overprint

88th anniv. of El Salvador's independence.

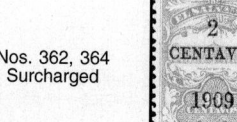

Nos. 362, 364 Surcharged

**1909** **Unwmk.**
**376** A66 2c on 13c sep & blk 1.50 1.25
*a.* Inverted surcharge
**377** A66 3c on 26c yel brn & blk 1.75 1.40
*a.* Inverted surcharge

A67

Design: Pres. Fernando Figueroa.

**1910** **Engr.** **Wmk. 172**
**378** A67 1c brn & blk .25 .25
**379** A67 2c dk grn & blk .25 .25
**380** A67 3c orange & blk .25 .25
**381** A67 4c carmine & blk .25 .25
*a.* 4c scarlet & black .25 .25
**382** A67 5c purple & blk .25 .25
**383** A67 6c scarlet & blk .25 .25
**384** A67 10c purple & blk .25 .25
**385** A67 12c dp bl & blk .25 .25
**386** A67 17c ol grn & blk .25 .25
**387** A67 19c brn red & blk .25 .25
**388** A67 29c choc & blk .25 .25
**389** A67 50c yellow & blk .25 .25
**390** A67 100c turq bl & blk .25 .25
*Nos. 378-390 (13)* 3.25 3.25

See Nos. J81-J87, O293-O304.

A68

5c, José Matías Delgado. 6c, Manuel José Arce. 12c, Centenary Monument.

**Paper with colored dots**

**1911** **Unwmk.**
**391** A68 5c dp blue & brn .25 .25
**392** A68 6c orange & brn .25 .25
**393** A68 12c violet & brn .25 .25

**Wmk. 172**

**394** A68 5c dp blue & brn .25 .25
**395** A68 6c orange & brn .25 .25
**396** A68 12c violet & brn .25 .25
*Nos. 391-396 (6)* 1.50 1.50

Centenary of the insurrection of 1811.

**Palace Type of 1907 without Shield**

**1911** **Paper without colored dots**
**397** A66 1c scarlet .25 .25
**398** A66 2c chocolate .30 .30
*a.* Paper with brown dots
**399** A66 13c deep green .25 .25
**400** A66 24c yellow .25 .25
**401** A66 50c dark brown .25 .25
*Nos. 397-401 (5)* 1.30 1.30

José Matías Delgado — A71

Manuel José Arce — A72

Francisco Morazán — A73

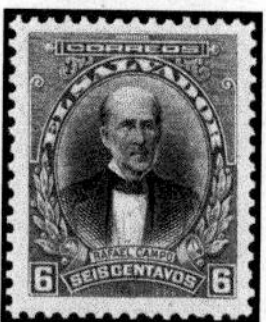

Rafael Campo — A74

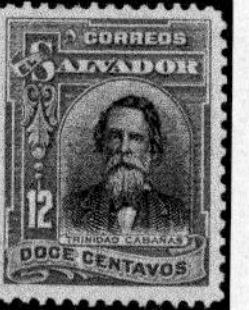

Trinidad Cabañas A75

Monument of Gerardo Barrios A76

Centenary Monument A77

National Palace A78

Rosales Hospital — A79

Coat of Arms — A80

**1912** **Unwmk.** ***Perf. 12***
**402** A71 1c dp bl & blk 1.00 .25
**403** A72 2c bis brn & blk 1.00 .25
**404** A73 5c scarlet & blk 1.00 .25
**405** A74 6c dk grn & blk 1.00 .25
**406** A75 12c ol grn & blk 3.00 .25
**407** A76 17c violet & slate 10.00 .25
**408** A77 19c scar & slate 3.00 .30
**409** A78 29c org & slate 5.00 .30
**410** A79 50c blue & slate 5.00 .45
**411** A80 1col black & slate 10.00 1.00
*Nos. 402-411 (10)* 40.00 3.55

Juan Manuel Rodríguez A81

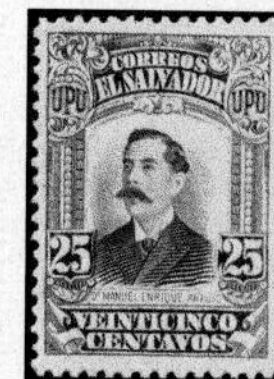

Pres. Manuel E. Araujo A82

**1914** ***Perf. 11½***
**412** A81 10c orange & brn 5.00 1.50
**413** A82 25c purple & brn 5.00 1.50

Type of 1907 without Shield Overprinted in Black

**1915**

**Paper overlaid with colored dots**

**414** A66 1c gray green .25 .25
**415** A66 2c red .25 .25
**416** A66 5c ultra .25 .25
**417** A66 6c pale blue .25 .25
**418** A66 10c yellow .60 .30
**419** A66 12c brown .50 .25
**420** A66 50c violet .25 .25
**421** A66 100c black brn 1.40 1.40
*Nos. 414-421 (8)* 3.75 3.20

Varieties such as center omitted, center double, center inverted, imperforate exist with or without date, date inverted, date double, etc., but are believed to be entirely unofficial.

Preceding the stamps with the "1915" overprint a quantity of stamps of this type was overprinted with the letter "S." Evidence is lacking that they were ever placed in use. The issue was demonetized in 1916.

National Theater — A83

Various frames.

**1916** **Engr.** ***Perf. 12***
**431** A83 1c deep green .25 .25
**432** A83 2c vermilion .25 .25
**433** A83 5c deep blue .25 .25
**434** A83 6c gray violet .25 .25
**435** A83 10c black brn .25 .25
**436** A83 12c violet 2.50 .50
**437** A83 17c orange .35 .25
**438** A83 25c dk brown .80 .25
**439** A83 29c black 5.00 .75
**440** A83 50c slate 20.00 10.00
*Nos. 431-440 (10)* 29.90 13.00

Watermarked letters which occasionally appear are from the papermaker's name.

For surcharges and overprints see Nos. 450-455, 457-466, O332-O341.

**Nos. O324-O325 with "OFICIAL" Barred out in Black**

**1917**
**441** O3 2c red .90 .90
*a.* Double bar
**442** O3 5c ultramarine 1.00 .70
*a.* Double bar

Regular Issue of 1915 Overprinted "OFICIAL" and Re-overprinted In Red

**443** A66 6c pale blue 1.25 1.00
*a.* Double bar
**444** A66 12c brown 1.75 1.25
*a.* Double bar
*b.* "CORRIENTE" inverted

**Same Overprint in Red On Nos. O323-O327**

**445** O3 1c gray green 3.50 2.50
*a.* "CORRIENTE" inverted
*b.* Double bar
*c.* "CORRIENTE" omitted
**446** O3 2c red 3.50 2.50
*a.* Double bar
**447** O3 5c ultra 18.00 12.00
*a.* Double bar, both in black
**448** O3 10c yellow 2.00 1.00
*a.* Double bar
*b.* "OFICIAL" and bar omitted
**449** O3 50c violet 1.00 1.00
*a.* Double bar
*Nos. 443-449 (7)* 31.00 21.25

**Nos. O334-O335 Overprinted or Surcharged in Red**

a

b

**450** A83 (a) 5c deep blue 3.00 2.00
*a.* "CORRIENTE" double
**451** A83 (b) 1c on 6c gray vio 2.00 1.50
*a.* "CORRIERTE"
*b.* "CORRIENRE" 5.00
*c.* "CORRIENTE" double

No. 434 Surcharged in Black

**1918**
**452** A83 1c on 6c gray vio 1.75 1.00
*a.* Double surcharge
*b.* Inverted surcharge

No. 434 Surcharged in Black

**1918**
**453** A83 1c on 6c gray vio 1.50 .75
*a.* "Centado" 2.25 1.50
*b.* Double surcharge 2.50 1.75
*c.* Inverted surcharge

No. 434 Surcharged in Black or Red

**454** A83 1c on 6c gray vio 10.00 6.00
*a.* Double surcharge
*b.* Inverted surcharge 5.00 5.00
**455** A83 1c on 6c gray vio (R) 10.00 6.00
*a.* Double surcharge
*b.* Inverted surcharge 5.00 5.00
*Nos. 454-455 (2)* 20.00 12.00

Counterfeits exist of Nos. 454-455.

Pres. Carlos Meléndez — A85

**1919** **Engr.**
**456** A85 1col dk blue & blk .50 .50

For surcharge see No. 467.

No. 437 Surcharged in Black

**1919**
**457** A83 1c on 17c orange .25 .25
*a.* Inverted surcharge 1.00 1.00
*b.* Double surcharge 1.00 1.00

**Nos. 435-436, 438, 440 Surcharged in Black or Blue**

**1920-21**

**458** A83 1c on 12c violet .25 .25
*a.* Double surcharge 1.00 1.00
**459** A83 2c on 10c dk brn .25 .25
**460** A83 5c on 50c slate ('21) .40 .25
**461** A83 6c on 25c dk brn (Bl) ('21) 2.00 1.00

**Same Srch. in Black on No. O337**

**462** A83 1c on 12c violet 1.00 1.00
*a.* Double surcharge
*Nos. 458-462 (5)* 3.90 2.75

No. 460 surcharged in yellow and 461 surcharged in red are essays.

No. 462 is due to some sheets of Official Stamps being mixed with the ordinary 12c stamps at the time of surcharging. The error stamps were sold to the public and used for ordinary postage.

**Surcharged in Red, Blue or Black**

15c Types:

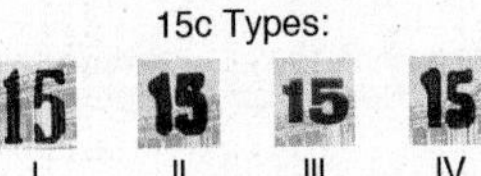

**463** A83 15c on 29c blk (III) ('21) 1.00 .40
*a.* Double surcharge 2.00
*b.* Type I 1.50 1.00
*c.* Type II 1.00 .75
*d.* Type IV 2.50
**464** A83 26c on 29c blk (Bl) 1.00 .60
*a.* Double surcharge
**466** A83 35c on 50c slate (Bk) 1.00 .60
**467** A85 60c on 1col dk bl & blk (R) .30 .25
*Nos. 463-467 (4)* 3.30 1.85

Surcharge on No. 464 differs from 15c illustration in that bar at bottom extends across stamp and denomination includes "cts." One stamp in each row of ten of No. 464 has the "t" of "cts" inverted and one stamp in each row of No. 466 has the letters "c" in "cinco" larger than the normal.

Setting for No. 467 includes three types of numerals and "CENTAVOS" measuring from 16mm to 20mm wide.

No. 464 surcharged in green or yellow and the 35c on 29c black are essays.

A93

**1921**

**468** A93 1c on 1c ol grn .25 .25
*a.* Double surcharge .75
**469** A93 1c on 5c yellow .25 .25
*a.* Inverted surcharge
*b.* Double surcharge
**470** A93 1c on 10c blue .25 .25
*a.* Double surcharge .50
**471** A93 1c on 25c green .25 .25
*a.* Double surcharge
**472** A93 1c on 50c olive .25 .25
*a.* Double surcharge
**473** A93 1c on 1p gray blk .25 .25
*a.* Double surcharge
*Nos. 468-473 (6)* 1.50 1.50

The frame of No. 473 differs slightly from the illustration.

Setting includes many wrong font letters and numerals.

Francisco Menéndez
A94

Manuel José Arce
A95

Confederation Coin — A96

Delgado Addressing Crowd — A97

Coat of Arms of Confedera-tion
A98

Francisco Morazán
A99

Independence Monument
A100

Columbus
A101

**1921** **Engr.** ***Perf. 12***

**474** A94 1c green 2.50 .25
**475** A95 2c black 5.00 .25
**476** A96 5c orange 2.00 .25
**477** A97 6c carmine rose 2.00 .25
**478** A98 10c deep blue 2.00 .25
**479** A99 25c olive grn 4.00 .25
**480** A100 60c violet 9.00 .50
**481** A101 1col black brn 15.00 .75
*Nos. 474-481 (8)* 41.50 2.75

For overprints and surcharges see Nos. 481A-485, 487-494, 506, O342-O349.

**Nos. 474-477 Overprinted in Red, Black or Blue**

a

b

**1921**

**481A** A94 (a) 1c green (R) 5.00 4.00
**481B** A95 (a) 2c black (R) 5.00 4.00
**481C** A96 (b) 5c orange (Bk) 5.00 4.00
**481D** A97 (b) 6c car rose (Bl) 5.00 4.00
*Nos. 481A-481D (4)* 20.00 16.00

Centenary of independence.

**No. 477 Surcharged**

a

b

**1923**

**482** A97 (a) 5c on 6c 4.00 .25
**483** A97 (b) 5c on 6c 4.00 .25
**484** A97 (b) 20c on 6c 4.00 .25
*Nos. 482-484 (3)* 12.00 .75

Nos. 482-484 exist with double surcharge.

No. 475 Surcharged in Red

**1923**

**485** A95 10c on 2c black 4.00 .25

José Simeón Cañas y Villacorta — A102

**1923** **Engr.** ***Perf. 11½***

**486** A102 5c blue .60 .30

Centenary of abolition of slavery.
For surcharge see No. 571.

Nos. 479, 481 Surcharged in Red or Black

**1924** ***Perf. 12***

**487** A99 1c on 25c ol grn (R) .30 .25
*a.* Numeral at right inverted
*b.* Double surcharge
**488** A99 6c on 25c ol grn (R) .25 .25
**489** A99 20c on 25c ol grn (R) .60 .25
**490** A101 20c on 1col blk brn (Bk) .75 .35
*Nos. 487-490 (4)* 1.90 1.10

**Nos. 476, 478 Surcharged**

**1924**

**491** A96 1c on 5c orange (Bk) .40 .25
**492** A98 6c on 10c dp bl (R) .40 .25

Nos. 491-492 exist with double surcharge.

A stamp similar to No. 492 but with surcharge "6 centavos 6" is an essay.

No. 476 Surcharged

**493** A96 2c on 5c orange .40 .40
*a.* Top ornament omitted 2.00 2.00
*Nos. 491-493 (3)* 1.20 .90

No. 480 Surcharged

**1924** **Red Surcharge**

**494** A100 5c on 60c violet 6.00 5.00
*a.* "1781" for "1874" 13.00 12.00
*b.* "1934" for "1924" 13.00 12.00

Universal Postal Union, 50th anniversary.

This stamp with black surcharge is an essay. Examples have been passed through the post.

Daniel Hernández Monument
A106

National Gymnasium
A107

Atlacatl — A108

Conspiracy of 1811 — A109

Bridge over Lempa River — A110

Map of Central America — A111

Balsam Tree — A112

Tulla Serra — A114

Columbus at La Rábida — A115

Coat of Arms — A116

**Photogravure; Engraved (35c, 1col)**

**1924-25** ***Perf. 12½; 14 (35c, 1col)***

**495** A106 1c red violet .25 .25
**496** A107 2c dark red .40 .25
**497** A108 3c chocolate .30 .25
**498** A109 5c olive blk .30 .25
**499** A110 6c grnsh blue .40 .25
**500** A111 10c orange .85 .25
*a.* "ATLANT CO" 8.00 8.00
**501** A112 20c deep green 1.50 .40
**502** A114 35c scar & grn 3.50 .50

**503** A115 50c orange brown 2.75 .35
**504** A116 1col grn & vio ('25) 4.00 .50
*Nos. 495-504 (10)* 14.25 3.25

For overprints and surcharges see Nos. 510-511, 520-534, 585, C1-C10, C19, O350-O361, RA4-RA5, RA6-RA7.

No. 480 Surcharged in Red

**1925, Aug.** ***Perf. 12***
**506** A100 2c on 60c violet 1.50 1.25

City of San Salvador, 400th anniv.
The variety with dates in black is an essay.

View of San Salvador — A118

**1925** **Photo.** ***Perf. 12½***
**507** A118 1c blue 1.10 1.00
**508** A118 2c deep green 1.10 1.00
**509** A118 3c Mahogany red 1.10 1.00
*Nos. 507-509 (3)* 3.30 3.00

#506-509 for the 4th centenary of the founding of the City of San Salvador.

Black Surcharge

**1928, July 17**
**510** A111 3c on 10c orange 1.25 .75
*a.* "ATLANT CO" 20.00 20.00

Industrial Exhibition, Santa Ana, July 1928.

Red Surcharge

**1928**
**511** A109 1c on 5c olive black .45 .25
*a.* Bar instead of top left "1" .60 .25

Pres. Pío Romero Bosque, Salvador, and Pres. Lázaro Chacón, Guatemala
A121

**1929** **Litho.** ***Perf. 11½***
**Portraits in Dark Brown**
**512** A121 1c dull violet .60 .45
*a.* Center inverted 11.50 11.50
**513** A121 3c bister brn .60 .45
*a.* Center inverted 35.00 35.00
**514** A121 5c gray grn .60 .45
**515** A121 10c orange .60 .45
*Nos. 512-515 (4)* 2.40 1.80

Opening of the international railroad connecting El Salvador and Guatemala.
Nos. 512-515 exist imperforate. No. 512 in the colors of No. 515.

Tomb of Menéndez
A122

**1930, Dec. 3**
**516** A122 1c violet 4.50 3.50
**517** A122 3c brown 4.50 3.50
**518** A122 5c dark green 4.50 3.50
**519** A122 10c yellow brn 4.50 3.50
*Nos. 516-519 (4)* 18.00 14.00

Centenary of the birth of General Francisco Menéndez.

Stamps of 1924-25 Issue Overprinted

**1932** ***Perf. 12½, 14***
**520** A106 1c deep violet .30 .25
**521** A107 2c dark red .30 .25
**522** A108 3c chocolate .45 .25
**523** A109 5c olive blk .45 .25
**524** A110 6c deep blue .60 .25
**525** A111 10c orange 1.50 .25
*a.* "ATLANT CO" 12.00 9.00
**526** A112 20c deep green 2.40 .75
**527** A114 35c scar & grn 3.25 1.00
**528** A115 50c orange brown 4.50 1.50
**529** A116 1col green & vio 7.50 3.25
*Nos. 520-529 (10)* 21.25 8.00

Values are for the overprint measuring 7½x3mm. It is found in two other sizes: 7½x3¼mm and 8x3mm.

**Types of 1924-25 Surcharged with New Values in Red or Black**

**1934** ***Perf. 12½***
**530** A109 2(c) on 5c grnsh blk .25 .25
*a.* Double surcharge
**531** A111 3(c) on 10c org (Bk) .45 .25
*a.* "ATLANT CO" 6.00 6.00

**Nos. 503, 504, 502 Surcharged with New Values in Black**

***Perf. 12½, 14½***
**532** A115 2(c) on 50c .45 .25
*a.* Double surcharge 3.00
**533** A116 8(c) on 1col .25 .25
**534** A114 15(c) on 35c .45 .45
*Nos. 530-534 (5)* 1.85 1.45

Police Barracks, Type I — A123

Type II

Two types of the 2c:
Type I — The clouds have heavy lines of shading.
Type II — The lines of shading have been removed from the clouds.

**Wmk. 240**
**1934-35** **Litho.** ***Perf. 12½***
**535** A123 2c gray brn, type I .25 .25
*a.* 2c brown, type II .25 .25
**536** A123 5c car, type II .25 .25
**537** A123 8c lt ultra, type II .25 .25
*Nos. 535-537,C33-C35 (6)* 4.70 2.45

Discus Thrower
A124

**1935, Mar. 16** **Engr.** **Unwmk.**
**538** A124 5c carmine 3.00 2.25
**539** A124 8c blue 3.25 2.75
**540** A124 10c orange yel 4.50 3.00
**541** A124 15c bister 4.50 3.25
**542** A124 37c green 6.00 4.50
*Nos. 538-542,C36-C40 (10)* 64.75 38.50

3rd Central American Games.

**Same Overprinted in Black**

**1935, June 27**
**543** A124 5c carmine 5.00 3.00
**544** A124 8c blue 7.00 3.00
**545** A124 10c orange yel 7.00 3.50
**546** A124 15c bister 7.00 3.50
**547** A124 37c green 12.00 5.50
*Nos. 543-547,C41-C45 (10)* 71.50 42.70

Flag of El Salvador — A125

**1935, Oct. 26** **Litho.** **Wmk. 240**
**548** A125 1c gray blue .30 .25
**549** A125 2c black brn .30 .25
**550** A125 3c plum .30 .25
**551** A125 5c rose carmine .45 .25
**552** A125 8c ultra .45 .25
**553** A125 15c fawn .60 .45
*Nos. 548-553,C46 (7)* 2.80 2.05

Tree of San Vicente — A126

**Numerals in Black, Tree in Yellow Green**

**1935, Dec. 26**
**554** A126 2c black brn .85 .45
**555** A126 3c dk blue grn .85 .45
**556** A126 5c rose red .85 .45
**557** A126 8c dark blue .85 .55
**558** A126 15c brown .60 .45
*Nos. 554-558,C47-C51 (10)* 7.75 5.35

Tercentenary of San Vicente.

Volcano of Izalco — A127

Wharf at Cutuco — A128

Doroteo Vasconcelos
A129

Parade Ground
A130

Dr. Tomás G. Palomo — A131

Sugar Mill — A132

Coffee at Pier — A133

Gathering Balsam — A134

Pres. Manuel E. Araujo — A135

**1935, Dec.** **Engr.** **Unwmk.**
**559** A127 1c deep violet .25 .25
**560** A128 2c chestnut .25 .25
**561** A129 3c green .25 .25
**562** A130 5c carmine .60 .25
**563** A131 8c dull blue .25 .25
**564** A132 10c orange .60 .25
**565** A133 15c dk olive bis .60 .25
**566** A134 50c indigo 3.00 1.75
**567** A135 1col black 7.50 4.50
*Nos. 559-567 (9)* 13.30 8.00

Paper has faint imprint "El Salvador" on face.
For surcharges and overprint see Nos. 568-570, 573, 583-584, C52.

**Stamps of 1935 Surcharged with New Value in Black**

**1938** ***Perf. 12½***
**568** A130 1c on 5c carmine .25 .25
**569** A132 3c on 10c orange .25 .25
**570** A133 8c on 15c dk ol bis .30 .25
*Nos. 568-570 (3)* .80 .75

**No. 486 Surcharged with New Value in Red**

**1938** ***Perf. 11½***
**571** A102 3c on 5c blue .30 .25

Centenary of the death of José Simeón Cañas, liberator of slaves in Latin America.

Map and Flags of US and El Salvador — A136

**Engraved and Lithographed**
**1938, Apr. 21** ***Perf. 12***
**572** A136 8c multicolored .95 .70

US Constitution, 150th anniv. See #C61.

**No. 560 Surcharged with New Value in Black**

**1938** ***Perf. 12½***
**573** A128 1c on 2c chestnut .25 .25

Indian Sugar Mill — A137

Designs: 2c, Indian women washing. 3c, Indian girl at spring. 5c, Indian plowing. 8c, Izote flower. 10c, Champion cow. 20c,

Extracting balsam. 50c, Maquilishuat in bloom. 1col, Post Office, San Salvador.

**1938-39 Engr. *Perf. 12***

**574** A137 1c dark violet .25 .25
**575** A137 2c dark green .25 .25
**576** A137 3c dark brown .30 .25
**577** A137 5c scarlet .30 .25
**578** A137 8c dark blue 2.00 .25
**579** A137 10c yel org ('39) 3.00 .25
**580** A137 20c bis brn ('39) 2.75 .25
**581** A137 50c dull blk ('39) 3.25 .70
**582** A137 1col black ('39) 3.00 1.00
*Nos. 574-582 (9)* 15.10 3.45

For surcharges & overprints see Nos. 591-592, C96.

Nos. 566-567, 504 Surcharged in Red

**1939, Sept. 25 *Perf. 12½, 14***

**583** A134 8c on 50c indigo .45 .25
**584** A135 10c on 1col blk .80 .25
**585** A116 50c on 1col grn & vio 4.50 3.25
*Nos. 583-585 (3)* 5.75 3.75

Battle of San Pedro Perulapán, 100th anniv.

Sir Rowland Hill — A146

**1940, Mar. 1 *Perf. 12½***

**586** A146 8c dk bl, lt bl & blk 6.00 2.00
*Nos. 586,C69-C70 (3)* 36.50 22.00

Postage stamp centenary.

Statue of Christ and San Salvador Cathedral — A147

A148

**Wmk. 269**

**1942, Nov. 23 Engr. *Perf. 14***

**587** A147 8c deep blue .80 .25

**Souvenir Sheet**

***Imperf***

**Without Gum**

**Lilac Tinted Paper**

**588** A148 Sheet of 4 25.00 22.00
*a.* 8c deep blue 10.00 10.00
*b.* 30c red orange 10.00 10.00

Nos. 587-588 commemorate the first Eucharistic Congress of Salvador. See No. C85.

No. 588 contains two No. 587 and two No. C85, imperf.

**Catalogue values for unused stamps in this section, from this point to the end of the section, are for Never Hinged items.**

Cuscatlán Bridge, Pan-American Highway — A149

**Arms Overprint at Right in Carmine**

***Perf. 12½***

**1944, Nov. 24 Unwmk. Engr.**

**589** A149 8c dk blue & blk .40 .25

See No. C92.

Gen. Juan José Canas — A150

**1945, June 9**

**590** A150 8c blue .60 .25

**No. 575 Surcharged in Black**

a

b

**1944-46**

**591** A137(a) 1(c) on 2c dk grn .30 .25
**592** A137(b) 1(c) on 2c dk grn ('46) .30 .25

Lake of Ilopango A151

Ceiba Tree A152

Water Carriers — A153

**1946-47 Litho. Wmk. 240**

**593** A151 1c blue ('47) .40 .25
**594** A152 2c lt bl grn ('47) .45 .25
**595** A153 5c carmine .40 .25
*Nos. 593-595 (3)* 1.25 .75

Isidro Menéndez A154

2c, Cristano Salazar. 3c, Juan Bertis. 5c, Francisco Duenas. 8c, Ramon Belloso. 10c, Jose Presentacion Trigueros. 20c, Salvador Rodriguez Gonzalez. 50c, Francisco Castaneda. 1col, David Castro.

**1947 Unwmk. Engr. *Perf. 12***

**596** A154 1c car rose .25 .25
**597** A154 2c dp org .25 .25
**598** A154 3c violet .25 .25
**599** A154 5c slate gray .25 .25
**600** A154 8c dp bl .25 .25
**601** A154 10c bis brn .25 .25
**602** A154 20c green .45 .25
**603** A154 50c black 1.10 .35
**604** A154 1col scarlet 2.25 .50
*Nos. 596-604 (9)* 5.30 2.60

For surcharges and overprints see Nos. 621-626, 634, C118-C120, O362-O368.

Manuel José Arce — A163

**1948, Feb. 25 *Perf. 12½***

**605** A163 8c deep blue .45 .25
*Nos. 605,C108-C110 (4)* 4.40 2.75

President Roosevelt Presenting Awards for Distinguished Service — A164

President Franklin D. Roosevelt A165

A166

Designs: 8c, Pres. and Mrs. Roosevelt. 15c, Mackenzie King, Roosevelt and Winston Churchill. 20c, Roosevelt and Cordell Hull. 50c, Funeral of Pres. Roosevelt.

**1948, Apr. 12**

**Various Frames; Center in Black**

**606** A164 5c dk bl .25 .25
**607** A164 8c green .25 .25
**608** A165 12c violet .25 .25
**609** A164 15c vermilion .45 .25
**610** A164 20c car lake .45 .25
**611** A164 50c gray 1.10 .70
*Nos. 606-611,C111-C116 (12)* 10.65 6.60

**Souvenir Sheet**

***Perf. 13½***

**612** A166 1col ol grn & brn 4.00 2.25

3rd anniv. of the death of F. D. Roosevelt.

Torch and Winged Letter A167

***Perf. 12½***

**1949, Oct. 9 Unwmk. Engr.**

**613** A167 8c blue 1.10 .55
*Nos. 613,C122-C124 (4)* 26.55 18.55

75th anniv. of the UPU.

Workman and Soldier Holding Torch — A168

**1949, Dec. 15 Litho. *Perf. 10½***

**614** A168 8c blue .45 .45
*Nos. 614,C125-C129 (6)* 9.85 7.25

Revolution of Dec. 14, 1948, 1st anniv.

Wreath and Open Book — A169

**Wreath in Dark Green**

***Perf. 11½***

**1952, Feb. 14 Photo. Unwmk.**

**615** A169 1c yel grn .25 .25
**616** A169 2c magenta .25 .25
**617** A169 5c brn red .25 .25
**618** A169 10c yellow .25 .25
**619** A169 20c gray grn .25 .25
**620** A169 1col dp car 1.50 1.00
*Nos. 615-620,C134-C141 (14)* 11.75 8.00

Constitution of 1950.

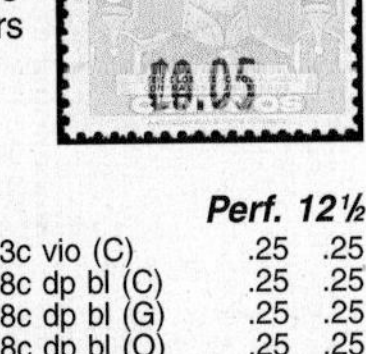

Nos. 598, 600 and 603 Surcharged with New Values in Various Colors

**1952-53 *Perf. 12½***

**621** A154 2c on 3c vio (C) .25 .25
**622** A154 2c on 8c dp bl (C) .25 .25
**623** A154 3c on 8c dp bl (G) .25 .25
**624** A154 5c on 8c dp bl (O) .25 .25
**625** A154 7c on 8c dp bl (Bk) .25 .25
**626** A154 10c on 50c blk (O) ('53) .25 .25
*Nos. 621-626 (6)* 1.50 1.50

Nos. C106 and C107 Surcharged in Various Colors

**1952-53 Wmk. 240**

**627** AP31 2c on 12c choc (Bl) .25 .25
**628** AP32 2c on 14c dk bl (R) ('53) .25 .25
**629** AP31 5c on 12c choc (Bl) .25 .25
**630** AP32 10c on 14c dk bl (C) .25 .25
*Nos. 627-630 (4)* 1.00 1.00

José Marti — A170

*Perf. 10½*

**1953, Feb. 27 Litho. Unwmk.**

**631** A170 1c rose red .25 .25
**632** A170 2c bl grn .25 .25
**633** A170 10c dk vio .30 .25
*Nos. 631-633,C142-C144 (6)* 3.05 1.85

José Marti, Cuban patriot, birth cent.

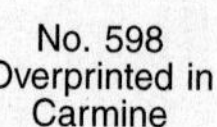

No. 598 Overprinted in Carmine

**1953, June 19** *Perf. 12½*

**634** A154 3c violet .25 .25

4th Pan-American Congress of Social Medicine, San Salvador, April 16-19, 1953. See #C146.

Signing of Act of Independence A171

**1953, Sept. 15 Litho. *Perf. 11½***

**635** A171 1c rose pink .25 .25
**636** A171 2c dp bl grn .25 .25
**637** A171 3c purple .25 .25
**638** A171 5c dp bl .25 .25
**639** A171 7c lt brn .25 .25
**640** A171 10c ocher .25 .25
**641** A171 20c dp org .70 .25
**642** A171 50c green .95 .30
**643** A171 1col gray 1.90 1.25
*Nos. 635-643,C147-C150 (13)* 7.10 4.75

Act of Independence, Sept. 15, 1821.

A172

Portrait: 1c, 2c, 5c, 20c: Capt. Gen. Gerardo Barrios. 3c, 7c, 10c, 22c: Francisco Morazan, (facing left).

**Overprinted in Black**

**1953, Dec. 1** *Perf. 11½*

**644** A172 1c green .25 .25
**645** A172 2c blue .25 .25
**646** A172 3c green .25 .25
**647** A172 5c rose .25 .25
**648** A172 7c blue .25 .25
**649** A172 10c rose .30 .25
**650** A172 20c violet .40 .25
**651** A172 22c violet .60 .25
*Nos. 644-651 (8)* 2.55 2.00

The overprint "C de C" is a control indicating "Tribunal of Accounts." A double entry of this overprint occurs twice in each sheet of each denomination.

For overprint see No. 729.

Coastal Bridge A173

Motherland and Liberty A174

Census Allegory — A175

Balboa Park — A176

Designs: Nos. 654, 655, National Palace. Nos. 659, 665, Izalco Volcano. Nos. 660, 661, Guayabo dam. No. 666, Lake Ilopango. No. 669, Housing development. Nos. 670, 673, Coast guard boat. No. 671, Modern highway.

*Perf. 11½*

**1954, June 1 Unwmk. Photo.**

**652** A173 1c car rose & brn .25 .25
**653** AP43 1c ol & bl gray .25 .25
**654** A173 1c pur & pale lil .25 .25
**655** A173 2c yel grn & lt gray .25 .25
**656** A174 2c car lake .25 .25
**657** A175 2c org red .25 .25
**658** AP44 3c maroon .25 .25
**659** A173 3c bl grn & bl .25 .25
**660** A174 3c dk gray & vio .25 .25
**661** A174 5c red vio & vio .30 .25
**662** AP44 5c emerald .30 .25
**663** A176 7c magenta & buff .30 .25
**664** AP43 7c bl grn & gray bl .30 .25
**665** A173 7c org brn & org .30 .25
**666** A173 10c car lake .30 .25
**667** AP46 10c red, dk brn & bl .30 .25
**668** A174 10c dk bl grn .30 .25
**669** A174 20c org & cr .40 .25
**670** A173 22c gray vio .40 .25
**671** A176 50c dk gray & brn 1.00 .35
**672** AP46 1col brn org, dk brn & bl 1.75 .90
**673** A173 1col brt bl 1.75 .90
*Nos. 652-673 (22)* 9.95 6.90
*Nos. 652-673,C151-C165 (37)* 24.90 13.75

For surcharges & overprints see #692-693, 736, C193.

Capt. Gen. Gerardo Barrios — A177

**Wmk. 269**

**1955, Dec. 20 Engr. *Perf. 12½***

**674** A177 1c red .25 .25
**675** A177 2c yel grn .35 .30
**676** A177 3c vio bl .35 .30
**677** A177 20c violet .50 .30
*Nos. 674-677,C166-C167 (6)* 2.15 1.80

Coffee Picker — A178

*Perf. 13½*

**1956, June 20 Litho. Unwmk.**

**678** A178 3c bis brn .25 .25
**679** A178 5c red org .25 .25
**680** A178 10c dk bl .25 .25
**681** A178 2col dk red 1.90 1.25
*Nos. 678-681,C168-C172 (9)* 8.85 5.80

Centenary of Santa Ana Department. For overprint see No. C187.

Map of Chalatenango — A179

**1956, Sept. 14**

**682** A179 2c blue .25 .25
**683** A179 7c rose red .45 .30
**684** A179 50c yel brn .70 .45
*Nos. 682-684,C173-C178 (9)* 4.30 3.35

Centenary of Chalatenango Department (in 1955).

For surcharge see No. 694.

Coat of Arms of Nueva San Salvador — A180

**Wmk. 269**

**1957, Jan. 3 Engr. *Perf. 12½***

**685** A180 1c rose red .25 .25
**686** A180 2c green .25 .25
**687** A180 3c violet .25 .25
**688** A180 7c red org .45 .25
**689** A180 10c ultra .25 .25
**690** A180 50c pale brn .55 .25
**691** A180 1col dl red .80 .75
*Nos. 685-691,C179-C183 (12)* 7.10 4.75

Centenary of the founding of the city of Nueva San Salvador (Santa Tecla).

For surcharges and overprints see Nos. 695-696, 706, 713, C194-C195, C197-C199.

**Nos. 664-665, 683 and 688 Surcharged with New Value in Black**

**1957 Unwmk. Photo. *Perf. 11½***

**692** A173 6c on 7c bl grn & gray bl .30 .30
**693** A173 6c on 7c org brn & org .30 .30

**1957 Litho. *Perf. 13½***

**694** A179 6c on 7c rose red .25 .25

**Wmk. 269**

**1957-58 Engr. *Perf. 12½***

**695** A180 5c on 7c red org ('58) .25 .25
**696** A180 6c on 7c red org .30 .25
*Nos. 692-696 (5)* 1.40 1.35

El Salvador Intercontinental Hotel — A181

*Perf. 11½*

**1958, June 28 Unwmk. Photo.**

**Granite Paper**

**Vignette in Green, Dark Blue & Red**

**697** A181 3c brown .25 .25
**698** A181 6c crim rose .25 .25
**699** A181 10c brt bl .25 .25
**700** A181 15c brt grn .25 .25
**701** A181 20c lilac .30 .25
**702** A181 30c brt yel grn .40 .25
*Nos. 697-702 (6)* 1.70 1.50

Presidents Eisenhower and Lemus and Flags — A182

**1959, Dec. 14 Granite Paper**

**Design in Ultramarine, Dark Brown, Light Brown and Red**

**703** A182 3c pink .25 .25
**704** A182 6c green .25 .25
**705** A182 10c crimson .30 .25
*Nos. 703-705,C184-C186 (6)* 1.60 1.50

Visit of Pres. José M. Lemus of El Salvador to the US, Mar. 9-21.

**No. 686 Ovptd.: "5 Enero 1960 XX Aniversario Fundacion Sociedad Filatelica de El Salvador"**

**1960 Wmk. 269 Engr. *Perf. 12½***

**706** A180 2c green .25 .25

Philatelic Association of El Salvador, 20th anniv.

Apartment Houses A183

**1960 Unwmk. Photo. *Perf. 11½***

**Multicolored Centers; Granite Paper**

**707** A183 10c scarlet .25 .25
**708** A183 15c brt pur .25 .25
**709** A183 25c brt yel grn .30 .25
**710** A183 30c Prus bl .35 .25
**711** A183 40c olive .55 .40
**712** A183 80c dk bl .95 .90
*Nos. 707-712 (6)* 2.65 2.30

Issued to publicize the erection of multifamily housing projects in 1958.

For surcharges see Nos. 730, 733.

**No. 686 Surcharged with New Value**

**1960 Wmk. 269 Engr. *Perf. 12½***

**713** A180 1c on 2c grn .25 .25

Poinsettia — A184

*Perf. 11½*

**1960, Dec. Unwmk. Photo.**

**Granite Paper**

**Design in Slate Green, Red and Yellow**

**714** A184 3c yellow .25 .25
**715** A184 6c salmon .25 .25
**716** A184 10c grnsh bl .30 .25
**717** A184 15c pale vio bl .30 .25
*Nos. 714-717,C188-C191 (8)* 3.40 2.30

**Miniature Sheet**

**718** A184 40c silver 8.00 8.00
*a.* Ovptd. in sheet margin ('61) 16.00 16.00
*b.* Ovptd. in sheet margin ('61) 16.00 16.00
*c.* Ovptd. in sheet margin ('62) 16.00 16.00
*d.* Ovptd. in sheet margin ('63) 16.00 16.00
*e.* Ovptd. in sheet margin ('63) 16.00 16.00
*f.* Ovptd. in sheet margin ('63) 16.00 16.00

Overprints in sheet margin of No. 718:

a, PRIMERA CONVENCION FILATELICA / CENTRO-AMERICANA / SAN SALVADOR, JULIO DE 1961.

b, in purple, Portrait, dates and text commemorating the Death of General Barrios, 96th anniv.

c, in green, Arms of city of Ahuachapan and PRIMER CENTENARIO / Ciudad de Ahuachapan / 1862 22 de Febrero 1962.

d, in blue, Soccer players and text commemorating the 1st North & Central American Soccer Championships 24 March - 2 April, 1963.

e, in blue and green, emblem of Alliance for Progress and text commemorating the 2nd anniversary of the organization.

f, in green, Portrait of Dr. Manuel Araujo and College Arms with text commemorating the 4th Latin American Cong. of Pathological Anatomy and 10th Central American Medical Cong., Dec., 1963.

For surcharge see No. C196.

Fathers Nicolas, Vicente and Manuel Aguilar A185

Parish Church, San Salvador, 1808
A186

Designs: 5c, 6c, Manuel José Arce, José Matias Delgado and Juan Manuel Rodriguez. 10c, 20c, Pedro Pablo Castillo, Domingo Antonio de Lara and Santiago José Celis. 50c, 80c, Monument to the Fathers, Plaza Libertad.

*Perf. 11½*

**1961, Nov. 5 Unwmk. Photo.**

**719** A185 1c gray & dk brn .25 .25
**720** A185 2c rose & dk brn .25 .25
**721** A185 5c pale brn & dk ol grn .25 .25
**722** A185 6c brt pink & dk brn .25 .25
**723** A185 10c bl & dk brn .25 .25
**724** A185 20c vio & dk brn .30 .25
**725** A186 30c brt bl & vio .40 .25
**726** A186 40c brn org & sep .50 .25
**727** A186 50c bl grn & sep .75 .40
**728** A186 80c gray & ultra 1.25 .75
*Nos. 719-728 (10)* 4.45 3.15

Sesquicentennial of the first cry for Independence in Central America.

For surcharges and overprints see Nos. 731-732, 734-735, 737, 760, 769, 776.

### No. 651 Ovptd.: "III Exposición Industrial Centroamericana Diciembre de 1962"

**1962, Dec. 21 Litho. *Perf. 11½***

**729** A172 22c violet .40 .25
*Nos. 729,C193-C195 (4)* 4.15 2.65

3rd Central American Industrial Exposition.

### Nos. 708, 726-728 and 673 Surcharged

**1962-63 Photo.**

**730** A183 6c on 15c ('63) .30 .25
**731** A186 6c on 40c ('63) .30 .25
**732** A186 6c on 50c ('63) .30 .25
**733** A183 10c on 15c .40 .25
**734** A186 10c on 50c ('63) .40 .25
**735** A186 10c on 80c ('63) .40 .25
**736** A173 10c on 1col ('63) .40 .25
*Nos. 730-736 (7)* 2.50 1.75

Surcharge includes bars on Nos. 731-734, 736; dot on Nos. 730, 735.

### No. 726 Ovptd. in Arc: "CAMPAÑA MUNDIAL CONTRA EL HAMBRE"

**1963, Mar. 21**

**737** A186 40c brn org & sepia .95 .50

FAO "Freedom from Hunger" campaign.

Coyote
A187

2c, Spider monkey, vert. 3c, Raccoon. 5c, King vulture, vert. 6c, Brown coati. 10c, Kinkajou.

**1963 Photo. *Perf. 11½***

**738** A187 1c lil, blk, ocher & brn .75 .25
**739** A187 2c lt grn & blk .75 .25
**740** A187 3c fawn, dk brn & buff .75 .25
**741** A187 5c gray grn, ind, red & buff .75 .25
**742** A187 6c rose lil, blk, brn & buff .75 .25
**743** A187 10c lt bl, brn & buff .75 .25
*Nos. 738-743,C200-C207 (14)* 35.50 9.45

Christ on Globe — A188

**1964-65 *Perf. 12x11½***

**744** A188 6c bl & brn .25 .25
**745** A188 10c bl & bis .25 .25
*Nos. 744-745,C208-C209 (4)* 1.00 1.00

### Miniature Sheets

*Imperf*

**746** A188 60c bl & brt pur 1.60 1.25
*a.* Marginal ovpt. La Union 1.25 1.25
*b.* Marginal ovpt. Usulutan 1.25 1.25
*c.* Marginal ovpt. La Libertad 2.50 2.50

2nd Natl. Eucharistic Cong., San Salvador, Apr. 16-19.

Nos. 746a, 746b and 746c commemorate the centenaries of the Departments of La Union, Usulután and La Libertad.

Issued: #744-746, Apr. 16, 1964; #746a-746b, June 22, 1965; #746c, Jan. 28, 1965.

See #C210. For overprints see #C232, C238.

Pres. John F. Kennedy
A189

*Perf. 11½x12*

**1964, Nov. 22 Unwmk.**

**747** A189 6c buff & blk .25 .25
**748** A189 10c tan & blk .25 .25
**749** A189 50c pink & blk .50 .25
*Nos. 747-749,C211-C213 (6)* 1.80 1.50

For overprints & surcharge see #798, 843.

### Miniature Sheet

*Imperf*

**750** A189 70c dp grn & blk 1.60 1.25
*a.* Overprinted in sheet margin in red brown ('69) 4.50 4.50

President John F. Kennedy (1917-1963).

Overprint on No. 750a reads: "Alunizaja / Apolo-11 / 21 Julio / 1969" and includes pictures of the landing module and astronauts.

Water Lily — A190

**1965, Jan. 6 Photo. *Perf. 12x11½***

**751** A190 3c shown .30 .25
**752** A190 5c Maquilishuat .30 .25
**753** A190 6c Cinco negritos .40 .25
**754** A190 30c Hortensia 1.25 .25
**755** A190 50c Maguey 1.60 .25
**756** A190 60c Geranium 1.60 .25
*Nos. 751-756,C215-C220 (12)* 12.60 3.05

For overprints and surcharges see Nos. 779, C243, C348-C349.

ICY Emblem
A191

**1965, Apr. 27 Photo. *Perf. 11½x12***

**Design in Brown and Gold**

**757** A191 5c dp yel .25 .25
**758** A191 6c dp rose .25 .25
**759** A191 10c gray .25 .25
*Nos. 757-759,C221-C223 (6)* 1.55 1.50

International Cooperation Year.

For overprints see #764, 780, C227, C244, C312.

### No. 728 Ovptd. in Red: "Ier. Centenario Muerte / Cap. Gral. Gerardo Barrios / 1865 1965 / 29 de Agosto"

**1965 Unwmk. *Perf. 11½***

**760** A186 80c gray & ultra .65 .50
*a.* "Garl." instead of "Gral." 1.00 1.00

Capt. Gen. Gerardo Barrios, death cent.

Gavidia
A192

*Perf. 11½x12*

**1965, Sept. 24 Photo. Unwmk.**

**Portrait in Natural Colors**

**761** A192 2c blk & rose vio .25 .25
**762** A192 3c blk & org .25 .25
**763** A192 6c blk & lt ultra .25 .25
*Nos. 761-763,C224-C226 (6)* 2.40 1.65

Francisco Antonio Gavidia, philosopher.

For surcharges see Nos. 852-853.

### No. 759 Ovptd. in Carmine: "1865 / 12 de Octubre / 1965 / Dr. Manuel Enrique Araujo"

**1965, Oct. 12**

**764** A191 10c brn, gray & gold .25 .25

Centenary of the birth of Manuel Enrique Araujo, president of Salvador, 1911-1913. See No. C227.

Fair Emblem — A193

**1965, Nov. 5 Photo. *Perf. 12x11½***

**765** A193 6c yel & multi .25 .25
**766** A193 10c multi .25 .25
**767** A193 20c pink & multi .25 .25
*Nos. 765-767,C228-C230 (6)* 4.30 3.20

Intl. Fair of El Salvador, Nov. 5-Dec. 4.

For overprints and surcharge see Nos. 784, C246, C311, C323.

WHO Headquarters, Geneva — A194

**1966, May 20 Photo. Unwmk.**

**768** A194 15c beige & multi .25 .25

Inauguration of WHO Headquarters, Geneva. See No. C231. For overprints and surcharges see Nos. 778, 783, 864, C242, C245, C322.

### No. 728 Ovptd. in Red: "Mes de Conmemoracion / Civica de la Independencia / Centroamericana / 19 Sept. / 1821 1966"

**1966, Sept. 19 Photo. *Perf. 11½***

**769** A186 80c gray & ultra .40 .40

Month of civic commemoration of Central American independence.

UNESCO Emblem
A195

**1966, Nov. 4 Unwmk. *Perf. 12***

**770** A195 20c gray, blk & vio bl .25 .25
**771** A195 1col emer, blk & vio bl .80 .30
*Nos. 770-771,C233-C234 (4)* 2.90 1.80

20th anniv. of UNESCO.

For surcharges see Nos. 853A, C352.

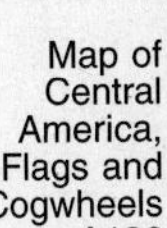

Map of Central America, Flags and Cogwheels
A196

**1966, Nov. 27 Litho. *Perf. 12***

**772** A196 6c multi .25 .25
**773** A196 10c multi .25 .25
*Nos. 772-773,C235-C237 (5)* 1.50 1.35

2nd Intl. Fair of El Salvador, Nov. 5-27.

José Simeon Cañas Pleading for Indian Slaves — A197

**1967, Feb. 18 Litho. *Perf. 11½***

**774** A197 6c yel & multi .25 .25
**775** A197 10c lil rose & multi .25 .25
*Nos. 774-775,C239-C240 (4)* 1.30 1.10

Father José Simeon Cañas y Villacorta, D.D. (1767-1838), emancipator of the Central American slaves.

For surcharges see #841A-842, 891, C403-C405.

### No. 726 Ovptd. in Red: "XV Convención de Clubes / de Leones, Región de / El Salvador-11 y 12 / de Marzo de 1967"

**1967 Photo.**

**776** A186 40c brn org & sepia .40 .25

Issued to publicize the 15th Convention of Lions Clubs of El Salvador, March 11-12.

Volcano San Miguel
A198

**1967, Apr. 14 Photo. *Perf. 13***

**777** A198 70c lt rose lilac & brn 1.00 .60

Centenary of stamps of El Salvador.

See No. C241. For surcharges see Nos. 841, C320, C350.

### No. 768 Ovptd. in Red: "VIII CONGRESO / CENTROAMERICANO DE / FARMACIA Y BIOQUIMICA / 5 di 11 Noviembre de 1967"

**1967, Oct. 26 Photo. *Perf. 12x11½***

**778** A194 15c multi .25 .25

8th Central American Congress for Pharmacy and Biochemistry. See No. C242.

### No. 751 Ovptd. in Red: "I Juegos / Centroamericanos y del / Caribe de Basquetbol / 25 Nov. al 3 Dic. 1967"

**1967, Nov. 15**

**779** A190 3c dl grn, brn, yel & org .25 .25

First Central American and Caribbean Basketball Games, 11/25-12/3. See #C243.

### No. 757 Ovptd. in Carmine: "1968 / AÑO INTERNACIONAL DE / LOS DERECHOS HUMANOS"

**1968, Jan. 2 Photo. *Perf. 11½x12***

**780** A191 5c dp yel, brn & gold .25 .25

Intl. Human Rights Year. See #C244.

Weather Map, Satellite and WMO Emblem
A199

**1968, Mar. 25 Photo. *Perf. 11½x12***

**781** A199 1c multi .25 .25
**782** A199 30c multi .30 .25

World Meteorological Day, Mar. 25.

**No. 768 Ovptd. in Red: "1968 / XX ANIVERSARIO DE LA / ORGANIZACION MUNDIAL / DE LA SALUD"**

**1968, Apr. 7** *Perf. 12x11½*
**783** A194 15c multi .25 .25

20th anniv. of WHO. See No. C245.

**No. 765 Ovptd. in Red: "1968 / Año / del Sistema / del Crédito / Rural"**

**1968, May 6 Photo.** *Perf. 12x11½*
**784** A193 6c yellow & multi .25 .25

Rural credit system. See No. C246.

Alberto Masferrer A200

**1968, June 22 Litho.** *Perf. 12x11½*
**785** A200 2c multi .25 .25
**786** A200 6c multi .25 .25
**787** A200 25c vio & multi .30 .25
*Nos. 785-787,C247-C248 (5)* 1.30 1.25

Centenary of the birth of Alberto Masferrer, philosopher and scholar.

For surcharges and overprints see Nos. 819, 843A, 890, C297.

Scouts Helping to Build — A201

**1968, July 26 Litho.** *Perf. 12*
**788** A201 25c multi .25 .25

Issued to publicize the 7th Inter-American Boy Scout Conference, July-Aug., 1968.

See No. C249.

Map of Central America, Flags and Presidents of US, Costa Rica, Salvador, Guatemala, Honduras and Nicaragua — A202

**1968, Dec. 5 Litho.** *Perf. 14½*
**789** A202 10c tan & multi .25 .25
**790** A202 15c multi .25 .25
*Nos. 789-790,C250-C251 (4)* 1.50 1.25

Meeting of Pres. Lyndon B. Johnson with the presidents of the Central American republics (J. J. Trejos, Costa Rica; Fidel Sanchez Hernandez, Salvador; J. C. Mendez Montenegro, Guatemala; Osvaldo López Arellano, Honduras; Anastasio Somoza Debayle, Nicaragua), San Salvador, July 5-8, 1968.

Heliconius Charithonius — A203

Various Butterflies.

**1969 Litho.** *Perf. 12*
**791** A203 5c bluish lil, blk & yel 7.25 .25
**792** A203 10c beige & multi 7.25 .25
**793** A203 30c lt grn & multi 7.25 .35
**794** A203 50c tan & multi 7.25 .55
*Nos. 791-794,C252-C255 (8)* 78.25 9.65

For surcharge see No. C353.

Red Cross Activities A204

**1969 Litho.** *Perf. 12*
**795** A204 10c lt bl & multi .25 .25
**796** A204 20c pink & multi .25 .25
**797** A204 40c lil & multi .35 .25
*Nos. 795-797,C256-C258 (6)* 6.60 4.00

50th anniv. of the League of Red Cross Societies.

**No. 749 Ovptd. in Green "Alunizaje / Apolo-11 / 21 Julio / 1969"**

**1969, Sept. Photo.** *Perf. 11½x12*
**798** A189 50c pink & blk .55 .30

Man's first landing on the moon, July 20, 1969. See note after US No. C76.

See No. C259.

Social Security Hospital A205

**1969, Oct. 24 Litho.** *Perf. 11½*
**799** A205 6c multi .25 .25
**800** A205 10c multi, diff. .25 .25
**801** A205 30c multi, diff. .30 .25
*Nos. 799-801,C260-C262 (6)* 7.50 4.75

For surcharges see Nos. 857, C355.

ILO Emblem — A206

**1969 Litho.** *Perf. 13*
**802** A206 10c yel & multi .25 .25

50th anniv. of the ILO. See No. C263.

Chorros Spa A207

Views: 40c, Jaltepeque Bay. 80c, Fountains, Amapulapa Spa.

**1969, Dec. 19 Photo.** *Perf. 12x11½*
**803** A207 10c blk & multi .25 .25
**804** A207 40c blk & multi .25 .25
**805** A207 80c blk & multi .55 .40
*Nos. 803-805,C264-C266 (6)* 1.95 1.70

Tourism.

Euchroma Gigantea — A208

Insects: 25c, Grasshopper. 30c, Digger wasp.

**1970, Feb. 24 Litho.** *Perf. 11½x11*
**806** A208 5c lt bl & multi .40 .25
**807** A208 25c dl yel & multi .75 .25
**808** A208 30c dl rose & multi .75 .25
*Nos. 806-808,C267-C269 (6)* 14.40 5.50

For surcharges see Nos. C371-C373.

Map and Arms of Salvador, National Unity Emblem A209

**1970, Apr. 14 Litho.** *Perf. 14*
**809** A209 10c yel & multi .25 .25
**810** A209 40c pink & multi .40 .25
*Nos. 809-810,C270-C271 (4)* 1.70 1.05

Salvador's support of universal human rights. For overprints and surcharge see Nos. 823, C301, C402.

Soldiers with Flag A210

Design: 30c, Anti-aircraft gun.

**1970, May 7** *Perf. 12*
**811** A210 10c green & multi .25 .25
**812** A210 30c lemon & multi .25 .25
*Nos. 811-812,C272-C274 (5)* 1.50 1.25

Issued for Army Day, May 7.

For overprints see Nos. 836, C310.

National Lottery Headquarters A211

**1970, July 15 Litho.** *Perf. 12*
**813** A211 20c lt vio & multi .25 .25

National Lottery centenary. See No. C291.

UN and Education Year Emblems A212

**1970, Sept. 11 Litho.** *Perf. 12*
**814** A212 50c multi .40 .25
**815** A212 1col multi .80 .40
*Nos. 814-815,C292-C293 (4)* 3.05 1.70

Issued for International Education Year.

Map of Salvador, Globe and Cogwheels A213

**1970, Oct. 28 Litho.** *Perf. 12*
**816** A213 5c pink & multi .25 .25
**817** A213 10c buff & multi .25 .25
*Nos. 816-817,C294-C295 (4)* 1.05 1.00

4th International Fair, San Salvador.

Beethoven — A214

**1971, Feb. 22 Litho.** *Perf. 13½*
**818** A214 50c ol, brn & yel .85 .25

Second International Music Festival. See No. C296. For overprint see No. 833.

**No. 787 Ovptd. "Año / del Centenario de la / Biblioteca Nacional / 1970"**

**1970, Nov. 25** *Perf. 12x11½*
**819** A200 25c vio & multi .25 .25

Cent. of the National Library. See No. C297.

Maria Elena Sol — A215

**1971, Apr. 1 Litho.** *Perf. 14*
**820** A215 10c lt grn & multi .25 .25
**821** A215 30c multi .30 .25
*Nos. 820-821,C298-C299 (4)* 1.35 1.05

Maria Elena Sol, Miss World Tourism, 1970-71. For overprint see No. 832.

Pietà, by Michelangelo A216

**1971, May 10**
**822** A216 10c salmon & vio brn .25 .25

Mother's Day, 1971. See No. C300.

**No. 810 Overprinted in Red**

**1971, July 6 Litho.** *Perf. 14*
**823** A209 40c pink & multi .60 .25

National Police, 104th anniv. See #C301.

Tiger Sharks — A217

**1971, July 28**
**824** A217 10c shown 1.40 .30
**825** A217 40c Swordfish 1.75 .35
*Nos. 824-825,C302-C303 (4)* 8.75 2.10

Declaration of Independence — A218

Designs: Various sections of Declaration of Independence of Central America.

**1971** ***Perf. 13½x13***
**826** A218 5c yel grn & blk .25 .25
**827** A218 10c brt rose & blk .25 .25
**828** A218 15c dp org & blk .25 .25
**829** A218 20c dp red lil & blk .25 .25
*Nos. 826-829,C304-C307 (8)* 2.40 2.10

Sesquicentennial of independence of Central America.
For overprints see Nos. C321, C347.

Izalco Church A219

Design: 30c, Sonsonate Church.

**1971, Aug. 21** **Litho.** ***Perf. 13x13½***
**830** A219 20c blk & multi .25 .25
**831** A219 30c pur & multi .30 .25
*Nos. 830-831,C308-C309 (4)* 1.35 1.10

**No. 821 Ovptd. in Carmine: "1972 Año de Turismo / de las Américas"**

**1972, Nov. 15** **Litho.** ***Perf. 14***
**832** A215 30c multi .35 .25

Tourist Year of the Americas, 1972.

**No. 818 Overprinted in Red**

**1973, Feb. 5** **Litho.** ***Perf. 13½***
**833** A214 50c ol, brn & yel .35 .25

3rd Intl. Music Festival, Feb. 9-25. See No. C313.

Lions International Emblem A220

**1973, Feb. 20** **Litho.** ***Perf. 13***
**834** A220 10c pink & multi .25 .25
**835** A220 25c lt bl & multi .25 .25
*Nos. 834-835,C314-C315 (4)* 1.05 1.00

31st Lions International District "D" Convention, San Salvador, May 1972.

**No. 812 Ovptd. "1923 1973 / 50 AÑOS FUNDACION / FUERZA AEREA"**

**1973, Mar. 20** **Litho.** ***Perf. 12***
**836** A210 30c lem & multi .35 .25

50th anniversary of Salvadorian Air Force.

Hurdling A221

**1973, May 21** **Litho.** ***Perf. 13***
**837** A221 5c shown .25 .25
**838** A221 10c High jump .25 .25
**839** A221 25c Running .25 .25
**840** A221 60c Pole vault .30 .25
*Nos. 837-840,C316-C319 (8)* 6.50 3.05

20th Olympic Games, Munich, Aug. 26-Sept. 11, 1972.

No. 777 Surcharged

**1973, Dec.** **Photo.** ***Perf. 13***
**841** A198 10c on 70c multi .30 .25

See No. C320.

**Nos. 774, C240 Srchd. with New Value and Ovptd. "1823-1973 / 150 Aniversario Liberación / Esclavos en Centroamérica"**

**1973-74** **Litho.** ***Perf. 11½***
**841A** A197 5c on 6c multi ('74) .25 .25
**842** A197 10c on 45c multi .45 .25

Sesquicentennial of the liberation of the slaves in Central America. On No. 841A two bars cover old denomination. On No. 842 "Aereo" is obliterated with a bar and old denomination with two bars.

Nos. 747 and 786 Surcharged

**1974** **Photo.** ***Perf. 11½x12***
**843** A189 5c on 6c buff & blk .30 .25

**Litho.** ***Perf. 12x11½***
**843A** A200 5c on 6c multi .75 .25

No. 843A has one obliterating rectangle and sans-serif "5."
Issued: #843, Apr. 22; #843A, June 21.

Rehabilitation Institute Emblem A222

**1974, Apr. 30** **Litho.** ***Perf. 13***
**844** A222 10c multi .25 .25

10th anniversary of the Salvador Rehabilitation Institute. See No. C324.

INTERPOL Headquarters, Saint-Cloud, France — A223

**1974, Sept. 2** **Litho.** ***Perf. 12½***
**845** A223 10c multi .25 .25

50th anniv. of Intl. Criminal Police Organization (INTERPOL). See No. C341.

UN and FAO Emblems A224

**1974, Sept. 2** **Litho.** ***Perf. 12½***
**846** A224 10c bl, dk bl & gold .25 .25

World Food Program, 10th anniv. See #C342.

25c Silver Coin, 1914 A225

**1974, Nov. 19** **Litho.** ***Perf. 12½x13***
**848** A225 10c shown .25 .25
**849** A225 15c 50c silver, 1953 .25 .25
**850** A225 25c 25c silver, 1943 .25 .25
**851** A225 30c 1c copper, 1892 .25 .25
*Nos. 848-851,C343-C346 (8)* 2.55 2.10

No. 763 Surcharged

**1974, Oct. 14** **Photo.** ***Perf. 11½x12***
**852** A192 5c on 6c multi .75 .25

12th Central American and Caribbean Chess Tournament, Oct. 1974.

No. 762 and 771 Surcharged

**1974-75** ***Perf. 11½x12, 12***
**853** A192 10c on 3c multi .35 .25
**853A** A195 25c on 1col multi ('75) .35 .25

Bar and surcharge on one line on No. 853A.
Issued: #853, Dec. 19; #853A, Jan. 13.

UPU Emblem A226

**1975, Jan. 22** **Litho.** ***Perf. 13***
**854** A226 10c bl & multi .25 .25
**855** A226 60c bl & multi .35 .30
*Nos. 854-855,C356-C357 (4)* 1.10 1.05

Cent. of UPU.

Acajutla Harbor A227

**1975, Feb. 17**
**856** A227 10c blue & multi .25 .25

See No. C358.

**No. 799 Surcharged**

**1975** **Litho.** ***Perf. 11½***
**857** A205 5c on 6c multi .35 .25

Central Post Office, San Salvador A228

**1975, Apr. 25** **Litho.** ***Perf. 13***
**858** A228 10c bl & multi .25 .25

See No. C359.

Map of Americas and El Salvador, Trophy A229

**1975, June 25** **Litho.** ***Perf. 12½***
**859** A229 10c red org & multi .25 .25
**860** A229 40c yel & multi .30 .25
*Nos. 859-860,C360-C361 (4)* 1.35 1.15

El Salvador, site of 1975 Miss Universe Contest.

Claudia Lars, Poet, and IWY Emblem — A230

**1975, Sept. 4** **Litho.** ***Perf. 12½***
**861** A230 10c yel & bl blk .25 .25
*Nos. 861,C362-C363 (3)* .80 .75

Intl. Women's Year 1975.

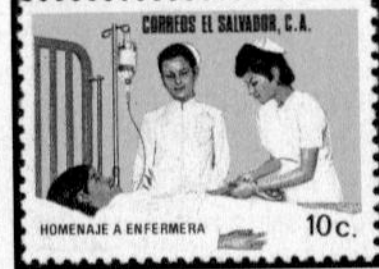

Nurses Attending Patient A231

**1975, Oct. 24** **Litho.** ***Perf. 12½***
**862** A231 10c lt grn & multi .25 .25

Nurses' Day. See No. C364. For overprint see No. 868.

Congress Emblem — A232

**1975, Nov. 19** **Litho.** ***Perf. 12½***
**863** A232 10c yel & multi .25 .25

15th Conference of Inter-American Federation of Securities Enterprises, San Salvador, Nov. 16-20. See No. C365.

**No. 768 Ovptd. in Red "XVI / CONGRESO MEDICO / CENTROAMERICANO / SAN SALVADOR, / EL SALVADOR, / DIC. 10-13, 1975"**

**1975, Nov. 26 Photo.** ***Perf. 12x11½***
**864** A194 15c beige & multi .35 .25

16th Central American Medical Congress, San Salvador, Dec. 10-13.

Flags of Participants, Arms of Salvador A233

**1975, Nov. 28 Litho.** ***Perf. 12½***
**865** A233 15c blk & multi .25 .25
**866** A233 50c brn & multi .30 .25
*Nos. 865-866,C366-C367 (4)* 1.05 1.00

8th Ibero-Latin-American Dermatological Congress, San Salvador, Nov. 28-Dec. 3.

Jesus and Caritas Emblem — A234

**1975, Dec. 18 Litho.** ***Perf. 13½***
**867** A234 10c dull red & maroon .25 .25

7th Latin American Charity Congress, San Salvador, Nov. 1971. See No. C368.

**No. 862 Ovptd. "III CONGRESO / ENFERMERIA / CENCAMEX 76"**

**1976, May 10 Litho.** ***Perf. 12½***
**868** A231 10c lt grn & multi .35 .25

CENCAMEX 76, 3rd Nurses' Congress.

Map of El Salvador A235

**1976, May 18**
**869** A235 10c vio bl & multi .25 .25

10th Congress of Revenue Collectors (Centro Interamericano de Administradores Tributarios, CIAT), San Salvador, May 16-22. See No. C382.

Flags of Salvador and US, Torch, Map of Americas A236

The Spirit of '76, by Archibald M. Willard — A237

**1976, June 30 Litho.** ***Perf. 12½***
**870** A236 10c yel & multi .25 .25
**871** A237 40c multi .25 .25
*Nos. 870-871,C383-C384 (4)* 4.50 3.25

American Bicentennial.

American Crocodile — A238

**1976, Sept. 23 Litho.** ***Perf. 12½***
**872** A238 10c shown .30 .25
**873** A238 20c Green iguana .65 .25
**874** A238 30c Iguana .95 .25
*Nos. 872-874,C385-C387 (6)* 5.20 1.65

Post-classical Vase, San Salvador A239

Pre-Columbian Art: 15c, Brazier with classical head, Tazumal. 40c, Vase with classical head, Tazumal.

**1976, Oct. 11 Litho.** ***Perf. 12½***
**875** A239 10c multi .25 .25
**876** A239 15c multi .25 .25
**877** A239 40c multi .30 .25
*Nos. 875-877,C388-C390 (6)* 2.10 1.65

For overprint see No. C429.

Fair Emblem A240

**1976, Oct. 25 Litho.** ***Perf. 12½***
**878** A240 10c multi .25 .25
**879** A240 30c gray & multi .25 .25
*Nos. 878-879,C391-C392 (4)* 1.30 1.15

7th Intl. Fair, Nov. 5-22.

Child under Christmas Tree — A241

**1976, Dec. 16 Litho.** ***Perf. 11***
**880** A241 10c yel & multi .25 .25
**881** A241 15c buff & multi .25 .25
**882** A241 30c vio & multi .25 .25
**883** A241 40c pink & multi .30 .30
*Nos. 880-883,C393-C396 (8)* 2.80 2.25

Christmas 1976.

Rotary Emblem, Map of Salvador A242

**1977, June 20 Litho.** ***Perf. 11***
**884** A242 10c multi .25 .25
**885** A242 15c multi .25 .25
*Nos. 884-885,C397-C398 (4)* 1.55 1.25

San Salvador Rotary Club, 50th anniversary.

Cerron Grande Hydroelectric Station — A243

Designs: No. 887, 15c, Central sugar refinery, Jiboa. 30c, Izalco satellite earth station, vert.

**1977, June 29** ***Perf. 12½***
**886** A243 10c multi .25 .25
**887** A243 10c multi .25 .25
**888** A243 15c multi .25 .25
**889** A243 30c multi .25 .25
*Nos. 886-889,C399-C401 (7)* 2.25 1.90

Industrial development. Nos. 886-889 have colorless overprint in multiple rows: GOBIERNO DEL SALVADOR.

**Nos. 785 and 774 Srchd. with New Value and Bar**

**1977, June 30** ***Perf. 12x11½, 11½***
**890** A200 15c on 2c multi .25 .25
**891** A197 25c on 6c multi .30 .25

Microphone, ASDER Emblem — A244

**1977, Sept. 14 Litho.** ***Perf. 14***
**892** A244 10c multi .25 .25
**893** A244 15c multi .25 .25
*Nos. 892-893,C406-C407 (4)* 1.00 1.00

Broadcasting in El Salvador, 50th anniversary (Asociacion Salvadoreño de Empresa Radio).

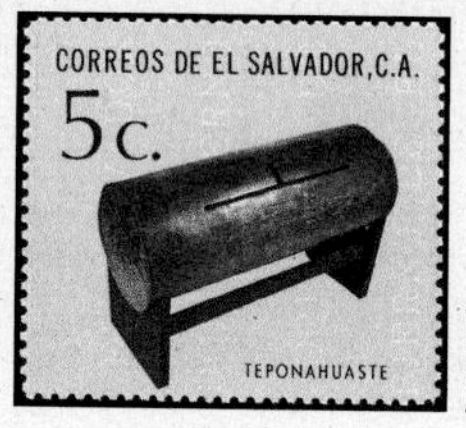

Wooden Drum A245

Design: 10c, Flute and recorder.

**1978, Aug. 29 Litho.** ***Perf. 12½***
**894** A245 5c multi .25 .25
**895** A245 10c multi .25 .25
*Nos. 894-895,C433-C435 (5)* 1.85 1.40

For surcharge see No. C492.

"Man and Engineering" A246

**1978, Sept. 12 Litho.** ***Perf. 13½***
**896** A246 10c multi .25 .25

4th National Engineers' Congress, San Salvador, Sept. 18-23. See No. C436.

Izalco Station A247

**1978, Sept. 14** ***Perf. 12½***
**897** A247 10c multi .25 .25

Inauguration of Izalco satellite earth station, Sept. 15, 1978. See No. C437.

Fair Emblem A248

**1978, Oct. 30 Litho.** ***Perf. 12½***
**898** A248 10c multi .25 .25
**899** A248 20c multi .25 .25
*Nos. 898-899,C440-C441 (4)* 1.00 1.00

8th Intl. Fair, Nov. 3-20.

Henri Dunant, Red Cross Emblem A249

**1978, Oct. 30** ***Perf. 11***
**900** A249 10c multi .25 .25

Henri Dunant (1828-1910), founder of the Red Cross. See No. C442.

World Map and Cotton Boll A250

**1978, Nov. 22** ***Perf. 12½***
**901** A250 15c multi .25 .25

Intl. Cotton Consulting Committee, 37th Meeting, San Salvador, 11/27-12/2. See #C443.

Nativity, Stained-glass Window A251

**1978, Dec. 5 Litho.** ***Perf. 12½***
**902** A251 10c multi .25 .25
**903** A251 15c multi .25 .25
*Nos. 902-903,C444-C445 (4)* 1.55 1.25

Christmas 1978.

Athenaeum Coat of Arms — A252

**1978, Dec. 20 Litho. *Perf. 14***
**904** A252 5c multi .25 .25

Millennium of Castilian language. See No. C446.

Postal Service and UPU Emblems A253

**1979, Apr. 2 Litho. *Perf. 14***
**905** A253 10c multi .25 .25

Centenary of Salvador's membership in Universal Postal Union. See No. C447.

"75," Health Organization and WHO Emblems — A254

**1979, Apr. 7 *Perf. 14x14½***
**906** A254 10c multi .25 .25

Pan-American Health Organization, 75th anniversary. See No. C448.

Flame and Pillars — A255

**1979, May 25 Litho. *Perf. 12½***
**907** A255 10c multi .25 .25
**908** A255 15c multi .25 .25
*Nos. 907-908,C449-C450 (4)* 1.55 1.25

Social Security 5-year plan, 1978-1982.

Pope John Paul II, Map of Americas A256

**1979, July 12 Litho. *Perf. 14½x14***
**909** A256 10c multi .25 .25
**910** A256 20c multi .25 .25
*Nos. 909-910,C454-C455 (4)* 5.00 3.30

Mastodon A257

**1979, Sept. 7 Litho. *Perf. 14***
**911** A257 10c shown .30 .25
**912** A257 20c Saber-toothed tiger .30 .25
**913** A257 30c Toxodon .50 .30
*Nos. 911-913,C458-C460 (6)* 4.70 2.40

Salvador Flag, José Aberiz and Proclamation A258

**1979, Sept. 14 *Perf. 14½x14***
**914** A258 10c multi .25 .25

National anthem centenary. See No. C461.

Cogwheel around Map of Americas A259

**1979, Oct. 19 Litho. *Perf. 14½x14***
**915** A259 10c multi .25 .25

8th COPIMERA Congress (Mechanical, Electrical and Allied Trade Engineers), San Salvador, Oct. 22-27. See No. C462.

Children of Various Races, IYC Emblem A260

Children and Nurses, IYC Emblem A261

**1979, Oct. 29 *Perf. 14x14½, 14½x14***
**916** A260 10c multi .25 .25
**917** A261 15c multi .25 .25

International Year of the Child.

Map of Central and South America, Congress Emblem — A262

**1979, Nov. 1 Litho. *Perf. 14½x14***
**918** A262 10c multi .25 .25

5th Latin American Clinical Biochemistry Cong., San Salvador, 11/5-10. See #C465.

Coffee Bushes in Bloom, Coffee Association Emblem A263

Salvador Coffee Assoc., 50th Anniv.: 30c, Planting coffee bushes, vert. 40c, Coffee berries.

**1979, Dec. 18 *Perf. 14x14½, 14½x14***
**919** A263 10c multi .25 .25
**920** A263 30c multi .25 .25
**921** A263 40c multi .30 .30
*Nos. 919-921,C466-C468 (6)* 2.60 2.00

Children, Dove and Star — A264

**1979, Dec. 18 *Perf. 14½x14***
**922** A264 10c multi .35 .25

Christmas 1979.

Hoof and Mouth Disease Prevention A265

**1980, June 3 Litho. *Perf. 14½x14***
**923** A265 10c multi .25 .25

See No. C469.

Anadara Grandis A266

**1980, Aug. 12 *Perf. 14x14½***
**924** A266 10c shown .40 .25
**925** A266 30c Ostrea iridescens .80 .25
**926** A266 40c Turitello leucostoma 1.25 .25
*Nos. 924-926,C470-C473 (7)* 8.40 2.05

Quetzal (Pharomachrus mocino) — A267

**1980, Sept. 10 Litho. *Perf. 14x14½***
**927** A267 10c shown 1.25 .30
**928** A267 20c Penelopina nigra 1.25 .30
*Nos. 927-928,C474-C476 (5)* 11.60 1.60

Local Snakes A268

**1980, Nov. 12 Litho. *Perf. 14x14½***
**929** A268 10c Tree snake 1.60 .30
**930** A268 20c Water snake 1.75 .30
*Nos. 929-930,C477-C478 (4)* 9.25 1.15

Corporation of Auditors, 50th Anniv. — A269

**1980, Nov. 26 Litho. *Perf. 14***
**931** A269 15c multi .25 .25
**932** A269 20c multi .25 .25
*Nos. 931-932,C479-C480 (4)* 1.50 1.15

Christmas A270

**1980, Dec. 5 Litho. *Perf. 14***
**933** A270 5c multi .25 .25
**934** A270 10c multi .25 .25
*Nos. 933-934,C481-C482 (4)* 1.35 1.05

Dental Assoc. Emblems — A271

**1981, June 18 Litho. *Perf. 14***
**935** A271 15c lt yel grn & blk .25 .25

Dental Society of Salvador, 50th anniv.; Odontological Federation of Central America and Panama, 25th anniv. See No. C494.

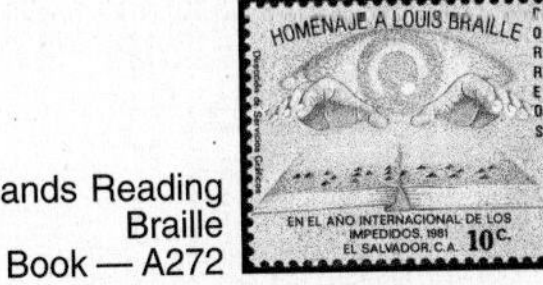


Hands Reading Braille Book — A272

**1981, Aug. 14 Litho. *Perf. 14x14½***
**936** A272 10c multi .25 .25
*Nos. 936,C495-C498 (5)* 2.30 1.70

Intl. Year of the Disabled.

A273

**1981, Aug. 28 Litho. *Perf. 14x14½***
**937** A273 10c multi .25 .25

Roberto Quinonez Natl. Agriculture College, 25th anniv. See No. C499.

World Food Day — A274

**1981, Sept. 16 Litho. *Perf. 14x14½***

**938** A274 10c multi .25 .25

See No. C500.

1981 World Cup Preliminaries — A275

40c, Cup soccer ball, flags.

**1981, Nov. 27 Litho. *Perf. 14x14½***

**939** A275 10c shown .25 .25
**940** A275 40c multicolored .45 .25
*Nos. 939-940,C505-C506 (4)* 1.60 1.15

Salvador Lyceum (High School), 100th Anniv. — A276

**1981, Dec. 17 Litho. *Perf. 14***

**941** A276 10c multi .25 .25

See No. C507.

Pre-Columbian Stone Sculptures A277

10c, Axe with bird's head. 20c, Sun disc. 40c, Stele Carving with effigy.

**1982, Jan. 22 Litho. *Perf. 14***

**942** A277 10c multicolored .25 .25
**943** A277 20c multicolored .25 .25
**944** A277 40c multicolored .30 .30
*Nos. 942-944,C508-C510 (6)* 2.00 1.75

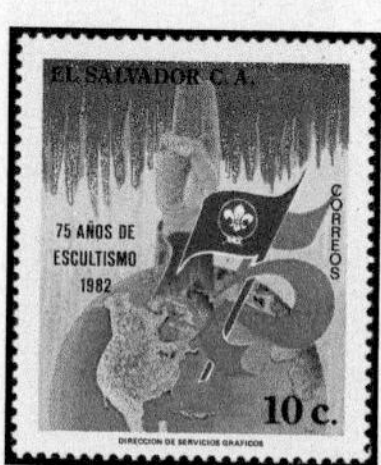


Scouting Year — A278

30c, Girl Scout helping woman.

**1982, Mar. 17 Litho. *Perf. 14½x14***

**945** A278 10c shown .25 .25
**946** A278 30c multicolored .25 .25
*Nos. 945-946,C511-C512 (4)* 1.15 1.00

Armed Forces A279

**1982, May 7 Litho. *Perf. 14x13½***

**947** A279 10c multi .25 .25

See No. C514.

1982 World Cup A280

**1982, July 14 *Perf. 14x14½***

**948** A280 10c Team, emblem .25 .25
*Nos. 948,C518-C520 (4)* 2.60 1.85

10th International Fair — A281

**1982, Oct. 14 Litho. *Perf. 14***

**949** A281 10c multi .25 .25

See No. C524.

Christmas 1982 — A282

**1982, Dec. 14 Litho. *Perf. 14***

**950** A282 5c multi .25 .25

See No. C528.

Dancers, Pre-Colombian Ceramic Design — A283

**1983, Feb. 18 Litho. *Perf. 14***

**951** A283 10c shown .25 .25
**952** A283 20c Sower .25 .25
**953** A283 25c Flying Man .30 .25
**954** A283 60c Hunters .55 .50
**955** A283 60c Hunters, diff. .55 .50
*a.* Pair, #954-955 1.10 1.10
**956** A283 1col Procession .75 .60
**957** A283 1col Procession, diff. .75 .60
*a.* Pair, #956-957 1.75 1.75
*Nos. 951-957 (7)* 3.40 2.95

Nos. 953-957 airmail. #955a, 957a have continuous designs.

Visit of Pope John Paul II — A284

60c, Monument to the Divine Savior, Pope.

**1983, Mar. 4 Litho. *Perf. 14***

**958** A284 25c shown .25 .25
**959** A284 60c multicolored .55 .30

Salvadoran Air Force, 60th Anniv. A285

**1983, Mar. 24 Litho. *Perf. 14***

**960** A285 10c Ricardo Aberle .25 .25
**961** A285 10c Air Force Emblem .25 .25
**962** A285 10c Enrico Massi .25 .25
*a.* Strip of 3, #960-962 .75 .75
**963** A285 10c Juan Ramon Munes .25 .25
**964** A285 10c American Air Force Cooperation Emblem .25 .25
**965** A285 10c Belisario Salazar .25 .25
*a.* Strip of 3, #963-965 .75 .75

Arranged se-tenant horizontally with two Nos. 960 or 963 at left and two Nos. 962 or 965 at right.

Local butterflies — A286

**1983, May 31 Litho. *Perf. 14***

**966** A286 Pair 1.40 1.40
*a.* 5c Papilio torquatus .35 .35
*b.* 5c Metamorpha steneles .35 .35
**967** A286 Pair 1.75 1.75
*a.* 10c Papilio torquatus, diff. .75 .75
*b.* 10c Anaea marthesia .75 .75
**968** A286 Pair 2.25 2.25
*a.* 15c Prepona brooksiana 1.10 1.10
*b.* 15c Caligo atreus 1.10 1.10
**969** A286 Pair 3.50 3.50
*a.* 25c Morpho peleides 1.90 1.90
*b.* 25c Dismorphia praxinoe 1.90 1.90
**970** A286 Pair 7.00 7.00
*a.* 50c Morpho polyphemus 2.25 2.25
*b.* 50c Metamorphia epaphus 2.25 2.25
*Nos. 966-970 (5)* 15.90 15.90

Simon Bolivar, 200th Birth Anniv. — A287

**1983, June 23 Litho. *Perf. 14***

**971** A287 75c multi .70 .50

Dr. Jose Mendoza, College Emblem. A288

**1983, July 21 Litho. *Perf. 14***

**972** A288 10c multicolored .40 .25

Salvador Medical College, 40th anniv.

A289

***Perf. 13½x14, 14x13½***

**1983, Oct. 30 Litho.**

**973** A289 10c multi .25 .25
**974** A289 50c multi, horiz. .40 .40

Centenary of David J. Guzman national museum. 50c airmail.

World Communications Year — A290

10c, Gen. Juan Jose Canas, Francisco Duenas (organizers of 1st natl. telegraph service), Morse key, 1870. 25c, Mailman delivering letters. 50c, Post Office sorting center, San Salvador. 25c, 50c airmail.

***Perf. 14x13½, 13½x14***

**1983, Nov. 23 Litho.**

**975** A290 10c multi .25 .25
**976** A290 25c multi, vert. .25 .25
**977** A290 50c multi .40 .30
*Nos. 975-977 (3)* .90 .80

Dove Over Globe — A291

25c, Creche figures, horiz.

***Perf. 13½x14, 14x13½***

**1983, Nov. 30**

**978** A291 10c shown .25 .25
**979** A291 25c multicolored .30 .25

Christmas. 25c is airmail.

Environmental Protection A292

**1983, Dec. 13**

**980** A292 10c Vehicle exhaust .40 .25
**981** A292 15c Fig tree .50 .25
**982** A292 25c Rodent .80 .25
*Nos. 980-982 (3)* 1.70 .75

15c, 25c airmail.

Philatelists' Day A293

**1984, Jan. 5 *Perf. 14x13½***

**983** A293 10c No. 1 .40 .25

Corn — A294

**1984, Feb. 21 Litho. *Perf. 14½x14***

**984** A294 10c shown .25 .25
**985** A294 15c Cotton .25 .25
**986** A294 25c Coffee beans .30 .25
**987** A294 50c Sugar cane .50 .25
**988** A294 75c Beans .80 .25
**989** A294 1col Agave .30 .50
**990** A294 5col Balsam 1.25 2.40
*Nos. 984-990 (7)* 3.65 4.15

See Nos. 1047-1051.

Caluco Church, Sonsonate A295

10c, Salcoatitan, Sonsonate. 15c, Huizucar, La Libertad. 25c, Santo Domingo, Sonsonate. 50c, Pilar, Sonsonate. 75c, Nahuizalco, Sonsonate.

**1984, Mar. 30 *Perf. 14x13½***

**991** A295 5c multicolored .25 .25
**992** A295 10c multicolored .25 .25
**993** A295 15c multicolored .25 .25
**994** A295 25c multicolored .25 .25
**995** A295 50c multicolored .30 .25
**996** A295 75c multicolored .40 .25
*Nos. 991-996 (6)* 1.70 1.50

Nos. 993-996 airmail.

Central Reserve Bank of Salvador, 50th Anniv. A296

**1984, July 17 Litho. *Perf. 14x14½***

**997** A296 10c First reserve note .25 .25
**998** A296 25c Bank, 1959 .25 .25

25c airmail.

1984 Summer Olympics A297

**1984, July 20 *Perf. 14x13½, 13½x14***

**999** A297 10c Boxing .30 .25
**1000** A297 25c Running, vert. .30 .25
**1001** A297 40c Bicycling .40 .25
**1002** A297 50c Swimming .50 .25
**1003** A297 75c Judo, vert. .75 .30
**1004** A297 1col Pierre de Coubertin 1.00 .30
*Nos. 999-1004 (6)* 3.25 1.60

Nos. 1000-1004 airmail.
For surcharge see No. C536A.

Govt. Printing Office Building Opening A298

**1984, July 27 *Perf. 14x13½***

**1005** A298 10c multi .40 .25

5th of November Hydroelectric Plant — A299

Designs: 55c, Cerron Grande Plant. 70c, Ahuachapan Geothermal Plant. 90c, Mural. 2col, 15th of September Plant. 70c, 90c, 2 col airmail.

**1984, Sept. 13 Litho. *Perf. 14x14½***

**1006** A299 20c multi .30 .25
**1007** A299 55c multi .50 .25
**1008** A299 70c multi .65 .25
**1009** A299 90c multi .80 .30
**1010** A299 2col multi 1.75 .50
*Nos. 1006-1010 (5)* 4.00 1.55

Boys Playing Marbles A300

**1984, Oct. 16 *Perf. 14½x14***

**1011** A300 55c shown .25 .25
**1012** A300 70c Spinning top .30 .25
**1013** A300 90c Flying kite .40 .30
**1014** A300 2col Top, diff. .80 .50
*Nos. 1011-1014 (4)* 1.75 1.30

11th International Fair — A301

**1984, Oct. 31 Litho. *Perf. 14x14½***

**1015** A301 25c shown .25 .25
**1016** A301 70c Fairgrounds .40 .30

70c airmail.

Los Chorros Tourist Center A302

25c, Plaza las Americas. 70c, El Salvador International Airport. 90c, El Tunco Beach. 2col, Sihuatehuacan Tourist Center.

**1984, Nov. 23 Litho. *Perf. 14x14½***

**1017** A302 15c multicolored .25 .25
**1018** A302 25c multicolored .40 .25
**1019** A302 70c multicolored .55 .25
**1020** A302 90c multicolored .65 .25
**1021** A302 2col multicolored 1.40 .50
*Nos. 1017-1021 (5)* 3.25 1.50

The Paper of Papers, 1979, by Roberto A. Galicia (b. 1945) A302a

Paintings by natl. artists: 20c, The White Nun, 1939, by Salvador Salazar Arrue (b. 1899), vert. 70c, Supreme Elegy to Masferrer, 1968, by Antonio G. Ponce (b. 1938), vert. 90c, Transmutation, 1979, by Armando Solis (b. 1940). 2 col, Figures at Theater, 1959, by Carlos Canas (b. 1924), vert.

**1984, Dec. 10 Litho. *Perf. 14***

**1021A** A302a 20c multi .25 .25
**1021B** A302a 55c multi .30 .25
**1021C** A302a 70c multi .50 .30
**1021D** A302a 90c multi .50 .30
**1021E** A302a 2col multi 1.25 .50
*Nos. 1021A-1021E (5)* 2.80 1.60

Nos. 1021B-1021E are airmail. 70c and 2col issued with overprinted silver bar and corrected inscription in black; copies exist without overprint.

Christmas 1984 — A303

**1984, Dec. 19 Litho.**

**1022** A303 25c Glass ornament .25 .25
**1023** A303 70c Ornaments, dove .45 .25

No. 1023 airmail.

Birds — A304

15c, Lepidocolaptes affinis. 25c, Spodiornis rusticus barriliensis. 55c, Claravis mondetoura. 70c, Hylomanes momotula. 90c, Xenotriccus calizonus. 1col, Cardellina rubrifrons.

**1984, Dec. 21 Litho. *Perf. 14½x14***

**1024** A304 15c multicolored .55 .30
**1025** A304 25c multicolored .90 .30
**1026** A304 55c multicolored 2.25 .50
**1027** A304 70c multicolored 2.60 .65
**1028** A304 90c multicolored 2.25 .70
**1029** A304 1col multicolored 3.50 .80
*Nos. 1024-1029 (6)* 12.05 3.25

Nos. 1026-1029 airmail.

Salvador Bank Centenary A305

**1985, Feb. 6 Litho. *Perf. 14***

**1030** A305 25c Stock certificate .45 .25

Mortgage Bank, 50th Anniv. — A306

**1985, Feb. 20 Litho. *Perf. 14***

**1031** A306 25c Mortgage .45 .25

Intl. Youth Year A307

25c, IYY emblem. 55c, Woodcrafting. 70c, Professions symbolized. 1.50col, Youths marching.

**1985, Feb. 28 Litho. *Perf. 14***

**1032** A307 25c multicolored .30 .25
**1033** A307 55c multicolored .50 .30
**1034** A307 70c multicolored .60 .30
**1035** A307 1.50col multicolored .90 .55
*Nos. 1032-1035 (4)* 2.30 1.40

Nos. 1033-1035 airmail.

Archaeology A308

15c, Pre-classical figure. 20c, Engraved vase. 25c, Post-classical ceramic. 55c, Post-classical figure. 70c, Late post-classical deity. 1col, Late post-classical figure.
2col, Tazumal ruins, horiz.

**1985, Mar. 6 Litho. *Perf. 14½x14***

**1036** A308 15c multicolored .35 .25
**1037** A308 20c multicolored .40 .25
**1038** A308 25c multicolored .50 .25
**1039** A308 55c multicolored .90 .30
**1040** A308 70c multicolored 1.10 .30
**1041** A308 1col multicolored 1.25 .40
*Nos. 1036-1041 (6)* 4.50 1.75

**Souvenir Sheet**

***Rouletted 13½***

**1042** A308 2col multicolored 2.00 .75

Nos. 1039-1041 airmail. No. 1042 has enlargement of stamp design in margin.

Natl. Red Cross, Cent. A309

25c, Anniv. emblem vert. 55c, Sea rescue. 70c, Blood donation service. 90c, First aid, ambulance, vert.

**1985, Mar. 13 Litho. *Perf. 14***

**1043** A309 25c multicolored .25 .25
**1044** A309 55c multicolored .45 .25
**1045** A309 70c multicolored .55 .30
**1046** A309 90c multicolored .75 .35
*Nos. 1043-1046 (4)* 2.00 1.15

Nos. 1044-1046 are airmail.

**Agriculture Type of 1984**

**1985 *Perf. 14½x14***

**1047** A294 55c Cotton .55 .25
**1048** A294 70c Corn .60 .25
**1049** A294 90c Sugar cane .80 .30
**1050** A294 2col Beans 1.90 .75
**1051** A294 10col Agave 6.00 3.50
*Nos. 1047-1051 (5)* 9.85 5.05

Issued: 55c, 70c, 90c, 4/4; 2col, 10col, 9/4.

Child Survival A310

Children's drawings.

**1985, May 3 Litho. *Perf. 14x14½***

**1052** A310 25c Hand, houses .25 .25
**1053** A310 55c House, children .40 .25
**1054** A310 70c Boy, girl holding hands .50 .25
**1055** A310 90c Oral vaccination .70 .40
*Nos. 1052-1055 (4)* 1.85 1.15

Nos. 1053-1055 are airmail.

Salvador Army A311

**1985, May 17** *Perf. 14*

| | | | | |
|---|---|---|---|---|
| **1056** | A311 | 25c Map | .25 | .25 |
| **1057** | A311 | 70c Recruit, natl. flag | .40 | .25 |

No. 1057 is airmail.

Inauguration of Pres. Duarte, 1st Anniv. — A312

**1985, June 28** *Perf. 14½x14*

| | | | | |
|---|---|---|---|---|
| **1058** | A312 | 25c Flag, laurel, book | .25 | .25 |
| **1059** | A312 | 70c Article I, Constitution | .35 | .25 |

Inter-American Development Bank, 25th Anniv. — A313

25c, Central Hydro-electric Dam, power station. 70c, Map of Salvador. 1col, Natl. arms.

**1985, July 5** *Perf. 14x13½*

| | | | | |
|---|---|---|---|---|
| **1060** | A313 | 25c multi | .25 | .25 |
| **1061** | A313 | 70c multi | .55 | .25 |
| **1062** | A313 | 1col multi | .70 | .40 |
| | | *Nos. 1060-1062 (3)* | 1.50 | .90 |

Nos. 1061-1062 are airmail.

Fish A314

25c, Cichlasoma trimaculatum. 55c, Rhamdia guatemalenis. 70c, Poecilia sphenops. 90c, Cichlasoma nigrofasciatum. 1col, Astyanax fasciatus. 1.50col, Dormitator latifrons.

**1985, Sept. 30** *Perf. 14x14½*

| | | | | |
|---|---|---|---|---|
| **1064** | A314 | 25c multi | .45 | .25 |
| **1065** | A314 | 55c multi | .65 | .25 |
| **1066** | A314 | 70c multi | .75 | .25 |
| **1067** | A314 | 90c multi | .85 | .30 |
| **1068** | A314 | 1col multi | 1.00 | .30 |
| **1069** | A314 | 1.50col multi | 1.50 | .40 |
| | | *Nos. 1064-1069 (6)* | 5.20 | 1.75 |

Nos. 1065-1069 are airmail.

UNFAO, 40th Anniv. — A315

**1985, Oct. 16** *Perf. 14½x14*

| | | | | |
|---|---|---|---|---|
| **1070** | A315 | 20c Cornucopia | .30 | .25 |
| **1071** | A315 | 40c Centeotl, Nahuat god of corn | .40 | .25 |

Dragonflies A316

25c, Cordulegaster godmani mclachlan. 55c, Libellula herculea karsch. 70c, Cora marina selys. 90c, Aeshna cornigera braver. 1col, Mecistogaster ornata rambur. 1.50col, Hetaerina smaragdalis de marmels.

**1985, Dec. 9** *Perf. 14x14½*

| | | | | |
|---|---|---|---|---|
| **1072** | A316 | 25c multi | .40 | .25 |
| **1073** | A316 | 55c multi | .60 | .25 |
| **1074** | A316 | 70c multi | .75 | .25 |
| **1075** | A316 | 90c multi | .85 | .30 |
| **1076** | A316 | 1col multi | 1.00 | .30 |
| **1077** | A316 | 1.50col multi | 1.50 | .40 |
| | | *Nos. 1072-1077 (6)* | 5.10 | 1.75 |

Nos. 1073-1077 are airmail.
For surcharge see No. C544.

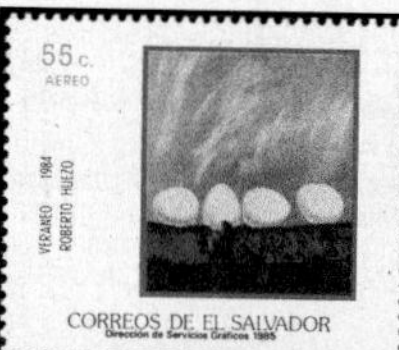


Summer, 1984, by Roberto Huezo (b.1947) A317

Paintings by natl. artists: 25c, Profiles, 1978, by Rosa Mena Valenzuela (b. 1924), vert. 70c, The Deliverance, 1984, by Fernando Llort (b. 1949). 90c, Making Tamale, 1975, by Pedro A. Garcia (b. 1930). 1col, Warm Presence, 1984, by Miguel A. Orellana (b. 1929), vert. Nos. 1079-1082 are airmail.

**1985, Dec. 18** *Perf. 14*

| | | | | |
|---|---|---|---|---|
| **1078** | A317 | 25c multi | .25 | .25 |
| **1079** | A317 | 55c multi | .25 | .25 |
| **1080** | A317 | 70c multi | .35 | .25 |
| **1081** | A317 | 90c multi | .45 | .30 |
| **1082** | A317 | 1col multi | .55 | .35 |
| | | *Nos. 1078-1082 (5)* | 1.85 | 1.40 |

San Vicente de Austria y Lorenzana City, 350th Anniv. A318

**1985, Dec. 20**

| | | | | |
|---|---|---|---|---|
| **1083** | A318 | 15c Tower, vert. | .25 | .25 |
| **1084** | A318 | 20c Cathedral | .30 | .25 |

Intl. Peace Year 1986 — A319

70c, Dove over people's outstretched arms.

**1986, Feb. 21** **Litho.** *Perf. 14*

| | | | | |
|---|---|---|---|---|
| **1085** | A319 | 15c multi | .30 | .25 |
| **1086** | A319 | 70c multi | .70 | .50 |

No. 1086 is airmail.

Postal Code Inauguration — A320

**1986, Mar. 14** **Litho.** *Perf. 14x14½*

| | | | | |
|---|---|---|---|---|
| **1087** | A320 | 20c Domestic mail | .25 | .25 |
| **1088** | A320 | 25c Intl. mail | .25 | .25 |

Radio El Salvador, 60th Anniv. A321

**1986, Mar. 21**

| | | | | |
|---|---|---|---|---|
| **1089** | A321 | 25c Microphone | .25 | .25 |
| **1090** | A321 | 70c Map | .50 | .40 |

No. 1090 is airmail.

Mammals A322

15c, Felis wiedii. 20c, Tamandua tetradactyla. 1col, Dasypus novemcinctus. 2col, Pecarii tajacu.

**1986, May 30** **Litho.** *Perf. 14x14½*

| | | | | |
|---|---|---|---|---|
| **1091** | A322 | 15c multicolored | .25 | .25 |
| **1092** | A322 | 20c multicolored | .30 | .25 |
| **1093** | A322 | 1col multicolored | 1.40 | .60 |
| **1094** | A322 | 2col multicolored | 2.75 | 1.25 |
| | | *Nos. 1091-1094 (4)* | 4.70 | 2.35 |

Nos. 1093-1094 are airmail.

1986 World Cup Soccer Championships, Mexico — A323

Designs: 70c, Flags, mascot. 1col, Players, Soccer Cup, vert. 2col, Natl. flag, player dribbling, vert. 5col, Goal, emblem.

**1986, June 6** *Perf. 14x14½, 14½x14*

| | | | | |
|---|---|---|---|---|
| **1095** | A323 | 70c multi | .65 | .45 |
| **1096** | A323 | 1col multi | 1.00 | .65 |
| **1097** | A323 | 2col multi | 1.90 | 1.40 |
| **1098** | A323 | 5col multi | 4.50 | 3.25 |
| | | *Nos. 1095-1098 (4)* | 8.05 | 5.75 |

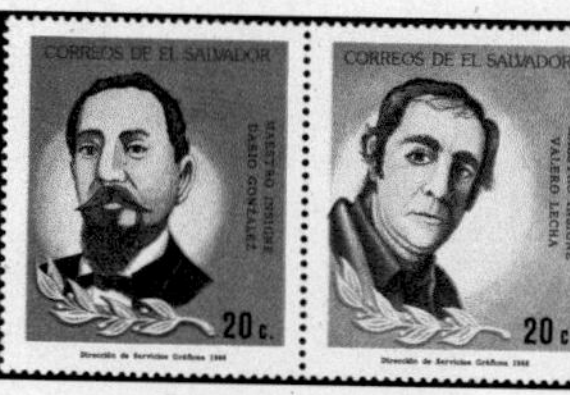


Teachers — A324

**1986, June 30** **Litho.** *Perf. 14½x14*

| | | | |
|---|---|---|---|
| **1099** | 20c Dario Gonzalez | .25 | .25 |
| **1100** | 20c Valero Lecha | .25 | .25 |
| *a.* | A324 Pair, #1099-1100 | .35 | .35 |
| **1101** | 40c Marcelino G. Flamenco | .25 | .25 |
| **1102** | 40c Camilo Campos | .25 | .25 |
| *a.* | A324 Pair, #1101-1102 | .70 | .70 |
| **1103** | 70c Saul Flores | .35 | .25 |
| **1104** | 70c Jorge Larde | .35 | .25 |
| *a.* | A324 Pair, #1103-1104 | 1.10 | 1.10 |
| **1105** | 1col Francisco Moran | .50 | .35 |
| **1106** | 1col Mercedes M. De Luarca | .50 | .35 |
| *a.* | A324 Pair, #1105-1106 | 1.75 | 1.75 |
| | *Nos. 1099-1106 (8)* | 2.70 | 2.20 |

Nos. 1103-1106 are airmail.

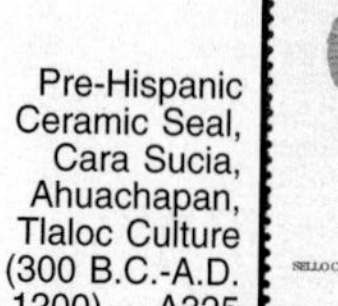

Pre-Hispanic Ceramic Seal, Cara Sucia, Ahuachapan, Tlaloc Culture (300 B.C.-A.D. 1200) — A325

**1986, July 23** **Litho.** *Perf. 13½*

| | | | | |
|---|---|---|---|---|
| **1107** | A325 | 25c org & brn | .30 | .25 |
| **1108** | A325 | 55c grn, org & brn | .45 | .25 |
| **1109** | A325 | 70c pale gray, org & brn | .55 | .25 |
| **1110** | A325 | 90c pale yel, org & brn | .80 | .30 |
| **1111** | A325 | 1col pale grn, org & brn | .90 | .35 |
| **1112** | A325 | 1.50col pale pink, org & brn | 1.40 | .50 |
| | | *Nos. 1107-1112 (6)* | 4.40 | 1.90 |

Nos. 1108-1112 are airmail.

World Food Day A326

**1986, Oct. 30** **Litho.** *Perf. 14x14½*

| | | | | |
|---|---|---|---|---|
| **1113** | A326 | 20c multi | .40 | .25 |

Flowers A327

20c, Spathiphyllum phryniifolium, vert. 25c, Asclepias curassavica. 70c, Tagetes tenuifolia. 1col, Ipomoea tiliacea, vert.

**1986, Sept. 30** *Perf. 14*

| | | | | |
|---|---|---|---|---|
| **1114** | A327 | 20c multi | .65 | .25 |
| **1115** | A327 | 25c multi | .65 | .25 |
| **1116** | A327 | 70c multi | 1.60 | .40 |
| **1117** | A327 | 1col multi | 2.00 | .55 |
| | | *Nos. 1114-1117 (4)* | 4.90 | 1.45 |

Nos. 1116-1117 are airmail.

Christmas A328

*Perf. 14x14½, 14½x14*

**1986, Dec. 10** **Litho.**

| | | | | |
|---|---|---|---|---|
| **1118** | A328 | 25c Candles, vert. | .25 | .25 |
| **1119** | A328 | 70c Doves | .60 | .25 |

No. 1119 is airmail.

Crafts A329

**1986, Dec. 18**

| | | | | |
|---|---|---|---|---|
| **1120** | A329 | 25c Basket-making | .35 | .25 |
| **1121** | A329 | 55c Ceramicware | .45 | .25 |
| **1122** | A329 | 70c Guitars, vert. | .55 | .30 |
| **1123** | A329 | 1col Baskets, diff. | .75 | .45 |
| | | *Nos. 1120-1123 (4)* | 2.10 | 1.25 |

Christmas
A330

Paintings: 25c, Church, by Mario Araujo Rajo, vert. 70c, Landscape, by Francisco Reyes.

**1986, Dec. 22**

**1124** A330 25c multi .25 .25
**1125** A330 70c multi .40 .25

No. 1125 is airmail.

Promotion of Philately
A331

**1987, Mar. 10 Litho.** ***Perf. 14½x14***

**1126** A331 25c multi .50 .25

Intl. Aid Following Earthquake, Oct. 10, 1986 — A332

**1987, Mar. 25**

**1127** A332 15c multi .30 .25
**1128** A332 70c multi .60 .25
**1129** A332 1.50col multi 1.00 .50
**1130** A332 5col multi 2.75 1.75
*Nos. 1127-1130 (4)* 4.65 2.75

Orchids — A333

No. 1131, Maxillaria tenuifolia. No. 1132, Ponthieva maculata. No. 1133, Meiracyllium trinasutum. No. 1134, Encyclia vagans. No. 1135, Encyclia cochleata. No. 1136, Maxillaria atrata. No. 1137, Sobrialia xantholeuca. No. 1138, Encyclia microcharis.

**1987, June 8 Litho.** ***Perf. 14½x14***

**1131** 20c multi .90 .25
**1132** 20c multi .90 .25
*a.* A333 Pair, #1131-1132 1.25 1.25
**1133** 25c multi 1.10 .25
**1134** 25c multi 1.10 .25
*a.* A333 Pair, #1133-1134 1.40 1.40
**1135** 70c multi 1.50 .55
**1136** 70c multi 1.50 .55
*a.* A333 Pair, #1135-1136 3.50 3.50
**1137** 1.50col multi 3.50 1.10
**1138** 1.50col multi 3.50 1.10
*a.* A333 Pair, #1137-1138 3.50 8.50
*Nos. 1131-1138 (8)* 14.00 4.30

#1133-1138 horiz. #1135-1138 are airmail.

Teachers — A334

Designs: No. 1139, C. de Jesus Alas, music. No. 1140, Luis Edmundo Vasquez, medicine. No. 1141, David Rosales, law. No. 1142, Guillermo Trigueros, medicine. No. 1143, Manuel Farfan Castro, history. No. 1144, Iri Sol, voice. No. 1145, Carlos Arturo Imendia, primary education. No. 1146, Benjamin Orozco, chemistry.

**1987, June 30 Litho.** ***Perf. 14½x14***

**1139** 15c greenish blue & blk .25 .25
**1140** 15c greenish blue & blk .25 .25
*a.* A334 Pair, #1139-1140 .40 .40
**1141** 20c beige & blk .25 .25
**1142** 20c beige & blk .25 .25
*a.* A334 Pair, #1141-1142 .40 .40
**1143** 70c yel org & blk .35 .25
**1144** 70c yel org & blk .35 .25
*a.* A334 Pair, #1143-1144 1.25 1.25
**1145** 1.50col lt blue grn & blk .70 .50
**1146** 1.50col lt blue grn & blk .70 .50
*a.* A334 Pair, #1145-1146 2.75 2.75
*Nos. 1139-1146 (8)* 3.10 2.50

Nos. 1143-1146 are airmail.

10th Pan American Games, Indianapolis — A335

**1987, July 31** ***Perf. 14½x14, 14x14½***

**1147** 20c Emblem, vert. .25 .25
**1148** 20c Table tennis, vert. .25 .25
*a.* A335 Pair, #1147-1148 .25 .25
**1149** 25c Wrestling .25 .25
**1150** 25c Fencing .25 .25
*a.* A335 Pair, #1149-1150 .30 .30
**1151** 70c Softball .35 .25
**1152** 70c Equestrian .35 .25
*a.* A335 Pair, #1151-1152 .80 .80
**1153** 5col Weight lifting, vert. 2.40 1.75
**1154** 5col Hurdling, vert. 2.40 1.75
*a.* A335 Pair, #1153-1154 6.00 6.00
*Nos. 1147-1154 (8)* 6.50 5.00

Nos. 1149-1153 are horizontal.
Nos. 1151-1154 are airmail.

Prior Nicolas Aguilar (1742-1818)
A336

Famous men: 20c, Domingo Antonio de Lara (1783-1814), aviation pioneer. 70c, Juan Manuel Rodrigues (1771-1837), president who abolished slavery. 1.50col, Pedro Pablo Castillo (1780-1814), patriot.

**1987, Sept. 11 Litho.** ***Perf. 14½x14***

**1155** A336 15c multi .25 .25
**1156** A336 20c multi .25 .25
**1157** A336 70c multi .30 .25
**1158** A336 1.50col multi .70 .50
*Nos. 1155-1158 (4)* 1.50 1.25

Nos. 1157-1158 are airmail.

World Food Day
A337

**1987, Oct. 16** ***Perf. 14x14½***

**1159** A337 50c multi .45 .25

Paintings by Salarrue
A338

***Perf. 14½x14, 14x14½***

**1987, Nov. 30**

**1160** A338 25c Self-portrait .35 .25
**1161** A338 70c Lake .55 .25

#1161 is airmail. See #1186-1189.

Christmas 1987
A339

25c, Virgin of Perpetual Sorrow, stained-glass window. 70c, The Three Magi, figurines.

**1987, Nov. 18** ***Perf. 14x14½***

**1162** A339 25c multi .35 .25
**1163** A339 70c multi .55 .25

No. 1163 is airmail.

Pre-Columbian Musical Instruments — A340

Designs: 20c, Pottery drum worn around neck. No. 1165, Frieze picturing pre-Columbian musicians, from a Salua culture ceramic vase, c. 700-800 A.D. (left side), vert. No. 1166, Frieze (right side), vert. 1.50col, Conch shell trumpet.

***Perf. 14x14½, 14½x14***

**1987, Dec. 14 Litho.**

**1164** A340 20c multi .25 .25
**1165** A340 70c multi .55 .30
**1166** A340 70c multi .55 .30
*a.* Pair, #1165-1166 1.25 1.25
**1167** A340 1.50col multi .90 .60
*Nos. 1164-1167 (4)* 2.25 1.45

Nos. 1165-1167 are airmail. No. 1166a has a continuous design.

Promotion of Philately
A341

**1988, Jan. 20 Litho.** ***Perf. 14***

**1168** A341 25c multi .35 .25

Young Entrepreneurs of El Salvador — A342

**1988** ***Perf. 14x14½***

**1169** A342 25c multi .40 .25

St. John Bosco (1815-88)
A343

**1988, Mar. 15 Litho.** ***Perf. 14x14½***

**1170** A343 20c multi .40 .25

Environmental Protection — A344

**1988, June 3 Litho.** ***Perf. 14x14½***

**1171** A344 20c Forests .75 .25
**1172** A344 70c Forests and rivers 1.25 .40

No. 1172 is airmail.

1988-1992 Summer Olympics, Seoul and Barcelona
A345

**1988, Aug. 31 Litho.** ***Perf. 13½***

**1173** A345 1col High jump .70 .30
**1174** A345 1col Javelin .70 .30
**1175** A345 1col Shooting .70 .30
**1176** A345 1col Wrestling .70 .30
**1177** A345 1col Basketball .70 .30
*a.* Strip of 5, Nos. 1173-1177
*b.* Min. sheets of 5 + 5 labels

**Souvenir Sheets**

**1178** A345 2col Torch 16.00 —

Printed in sheets of 10 containing 2 each Nos. 1173-1177.

No. 1177b exists in 2 forms: 1st contains labels picturing 1988 Summer Games emblem or character trademark; 2nd contains labels picturing the 1992 Summer Games emblem or character trademark.

No. 1178 exists in 2 forms: 1st contains 1988 Games emblem; 2nd 1992 Games emblem.

Some, or all, of this issue seem not to have been available to the public.

World Food Day
A346

**1988, Oct. 11 Litho.** ***Perf. 14x14½***

**1179** A346 20c multi .60 .25

13th Intl. Fair, Nov. 23-Dec. 11 — A347

**1988, Oct. 25** ***Perf. 14½x14***

**1180** A347 70c multi .50 .30

Child Protection A348

**1988, Nov. 10**

**1181** A348 15c Flying kite .30 .25
**1182** A348 20c Child hugging adult's leg .45 .25

Christmas A349

Paintings by Titian: 25c, *Virgin and Child with the Young St. John and St. Anthony.* 70c, *Virgin and Child in Glory with St. Francis and St. Alvise,* vert.

***Perf. 14x14½, 14½x14***

**1988, Nov. 15**

**1183** A349 25c multi .40 .25
**1184** A349 70c multi .60 .30

70c is airmail.

Return to Moral Values A350

**1988, Nov. 22** ***Perf. 14½x14***

**1185** A350 25c multi .60 .25

**Art Type of 1987**

Paintings by Salvadoran artists: 40c, *Esperanza de los Soles,* by Victor Rodriguez Preza. 1col, *Shepherd's Song,* by Luis Angel Salinas, horiz. 2col, *Children,* by Julio Hernandez Aleman, horiz. 5col, *El Nino de Las Alcancias,* by Camilo Minero. Nos. 1187-1189 are airmail.

***Perf. 14½x14, 14x14½***

**1988, Nov. 30**

**1186** A338 40c multi .30 .25
**1187** A338 1col multi .60 .40
**1188** A338 2col multi 1.25 .75
**1189** A338 5col multi 2.75 1.90
*Nos. 1186-1189 (4)* 4.90 3.30

A351

Discovery of America, 500th Anniv. (in 1992) — A352

Ruins and artifacts: a, El Tazumul. b, Multicolored footed bowl. c, San Andres. d, Two-color censer. e, Sihuatan. f, Carved head of the God of Lluvia. g, Cara Sucia. h, Man-shaped vase. i, San Lorenzo. j, Multicolored pear-shaped vase. 2col, Christopher Columbus.

**1988, Dec. 21** ***Perf. 14x14½***

**1190** Sheet of 10 6.50 6.50
*a.-j.* A351 1col any single .40 .30

**Souvenir Sheet**

***Roulette 13½***

**1191** A352 2col vermilion 2.00 1.25

UN Declaration of Human Rights, 40th Anniv. A353

**1988, Dec. 9** ***Perf. 14½x14, 14x14½***

**1192** A353 25c Family, map, emblem, vert. .40 .25
**1193** A353 70c shown .70 .30

70c is airmail.

World Wildlife Fund — A354

Felines: a, Felis wiedii laying on tree branch. b, Felis wiedii sitting on branch. c, Felis pardalis laying in brush. d, Felis pardalis standing on tree branch.

**1988** ***Perf. 14½x14***

**1194** Strip of 4 12.00 12.00
*a.-b.* A354 25c any single 2.50 .25
*c.-d.* A354 55c any single 3.00 .25

World Meterological Organization, 40th Anniv. — A355

**1989, Feb. 3** **Litho.** ***Perf. 14½x14***

**1195** A355 15c shown .40 .25
**1196** A355 20c Wind gauge .40 .25

Meteorology in El Salvador, cent.

Promotion of Philately A356

**1989, Mar. 15** **Litho.** ***Perf. 14½x14***

**1197** A356 25c Philatelic Soc. emblem .50 .25

See No. 1230.

Natl. Fire Brigade, 106th Anniv. A357

**1989, June 19** **Litho.** ***Perf. 14x14½***

**1198** A357 25c Fire truck .75 .25
**1199** A357 70c Firemen 1.25 .30

French Revolution, Bicent. A358

**1989, July 12**

**1200** A358 90c Anniv. emblem .50 .35
**1201** A358 1col Storming of the Bastille .80 .40

Souvenir Sheets

Stamps on Stamps — A359



Statues of Queen Isabella and Christopher Columbus — A360

Designs: a, No. 88. b, No. 101. c, No. 86. d, No. 102. e, No. 87. f, No. 103.

**1989, May 31** **Litho.** ***Perf. 14x14½***

**Miniature Sheet**

**1202** A359 Sheet of 6 6.75 6.75
*a.-f.* 50c any single .45 .25

**Souvenir Sheet**

***Rouletted 13½***

**1203** A360 2col shown 5.00 4.00

Discovery of America, 500th anniv. (in 1992).

No. 1203 exists in two forms: margin pictures Natl. Palace with either 500th anniv. emblem or anniv. emblem and "92" at lower right.

Signing Act of Independence — A361

**1989, Sept. 1** ***Perf. 14x14½***

**1204** A361 25c shown .30 .25
**1205** A361 70c Flag, natl. seal, heroes .50 .25

Natl. independence, 168th anniv. No. 1205 is airmail.

Demographic Assoc., 27th Anniv. — A362

**1989, July 26**

**1206** A362 25c multi .55 .25

1990 World Cup Soccer Championships, Italy — A363

Soccer ball, flags of Salvador and: No. 1207, US No. 1208, Guatemala. No. 1209, Costa Rica. No. 1210, Trinidad & Tobago. 55c, Trinidad & Tobago, Guatemala, US, Costa Rica. 1col, Soccer ball, Cuscatlan Stadium.

**1989, Sept. 1** **Litho.** ***Perf. 14x14½***

**1207** A363 20c multi .30 .25
**1208** A363 20c multicolored .30 .25
*a.* Pair, #1207-1208 .60 .60
**1209** A363 25c shown .30 .25
**1210** A363 25c multicolored .30 .25
*a.* Pair, #1209-1210 .60 .60
**1211** A363 55c multicolored .30 .25
**1212** A363 1col multicolored .50 .35
*Nos. 1207-1212 (6)* 2.00 1.60

Beatification of Marcellin Champagnat, Founder of the Marist Brothers Order — A364

**1989, Sept. 28**

**1213** A364 20c multicolored .50 .25

America Issue A365

UPAE emblem and pre-Columbian artifacts: 25c, *The Cultivator,* rock painting. 70c, Ceramic urn.

**1989, Oct. 12**

**1214** A365 25c multicolored .75 .25
**1215** A365 70c multicolored 1.50 .30

World Food Day A366

***Perf. 14x14½, 14½x14***

**1989, Oct. 16** **Litho.**

**1216** A366 15c shown .30 .25
**1217** A366 55c Aspects of agriculture, vert. .50 .25

Children's Rights A367

**1989, Oct. 26** **Litho.** ***Perf. 14½x14***

**1218** A367 25c multicolored .55 .25

Creche Figures A368

**1989, Dec. 1**

**1219** A368 25c shown .30 .25
**1220** A368 70c Holy Family, diff. .65 .30

Christmas.

Birds of Prey A369

70c, Sarcoramphus papa. 1col, Polyborus plancus. 2col, Accipiter striatus. 10col, Glaucidium brasilianum.

**1989, Dec. 20** ***Perf. 14½x14, 14x14½***

**1221** A369 70c multicolored .65 .30
**1222** A369 1col multicolored 1.10 .45
**1223** A369 2col multicolored 1.75 .80
**1224** A369 10col multicolored 7.50 4.00
*Nos. 1221-1224 (4)* 11.00 5.55

Nos. 1221 and 1223 vert.

Court of Accounts, 50th Anniv. A370

**1990, Jan. 12** **Litho.** ***Perf. 14x14½***

**1225** A370 50c multicolored .50 .25

Lord Baden-Powell, 133rd Birth Anniv. — A371

**1990, Feb. 23** ***Perf. 14½x14***

**1226** A371 25c multicolored 1.00 .25

Intl. Women's Day — A372

**1990, Mar. 8** **Litho.** ***Perf. 14½x14***

**1227** A372 25c multicolored .55 .25

**Type of 1989 and**

Hour Glass — A373

**1990** ***Perf. 14½x14***

**1228** A373 25c multicolored .25 .25
**1229** A373 55c multicolored .35 .25

**Souvenir Sheet**

***Rouletted 13½ with Simulated Perfs.***

**1230** A356 2col blk & pale blue 2.25 .95

Philatelic Soc., 50th anniv. Nos. 1229-1230 are airmail.

Fight Against Addictions A375

**1990, Apr. 26** **Litho.** ***Perf. 14x14½***

**1231** A375 20c Alcohol .30 .25
**1232** A375 25c Smoking .40 .25
**1233** A375 1.50col Drugs 1.00 .40
*Nos. 1231-1233 (3)* 1.70 .90

No. 1233 is airmail.

La Prensa, 75th Anniv. — A376

**1990, May 14** **Litho.** ***Perf. 14½x14***

**1234** A376 15c multicolored .30 .25
**1235** A376 25c "75," newspaper .40 .25

A377

World Cup Soccer Championships, Italy — A378

Soccer player and flags of: No. 1236, Argentina, USSR, Cameroun, Romania. No. 1237, Italy, US, Austria, Czechoslovakia. No. 1238, Brazil, Costa Rica, Sweden, Scotland. No. 1239, Germany, United Arab Emirates, Yugoslavia, Colombia. No. 1240, Belgium, Spain, Korea, Uruguay. No. 1241, England, Netherlands, Ireland, Egypt.

**1990, June 15** ***Perf. 14x14½***

**1236** A377 55c multicolored .35 .25
**1237** A377 55c multicolored .35 .25
**1238** A377 70c multicolored .45 .25
**1239** A377 70c multicolored .45 .25
**1240** A377 1col multicolored .55 .35
**1241** A377 1col multicolored .55 .35
**1242** A378 1.50col multicolored .90 .50
*Nos. 1236-1242 (7)* 3.60 2.20

For surcharge see No. 1245.

Discovery of America Cent. — A379

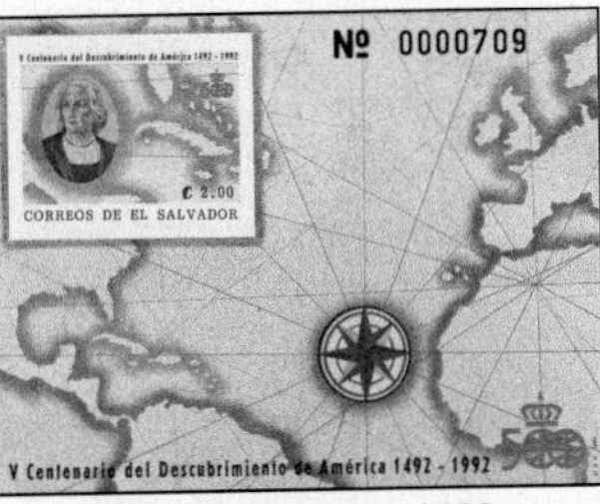


Columbus, Map — A380

Stained glass window: a, Christopher Columbus. b, Queen Isabella. c, Columbus' Arms. d, Discovery of America 500th anniv. emblem. e, One boat of Columbus' fleet. f, Two boats.

**1990, July 30** **Litho.** ***Perf. 14***

**Miniature Sheet**

**1243** A379 Sheet of 6 6.50 6.50
*a.-f.* 1col any single .50 .35

**Souvenir Sheet**

***Rouletted 13 1/2***

**1244** A380 2col multicolored 5.00 4.00

See Nos. 1283-1284.

No. 1239 Surcharged in Black

**1991, Feb.** **Litho.** ***Perf. 14x14½***

**1245** A377 90c on 70c multi 1.00 .30

World Summit for Children A381

**1990, Sept. 25** ***Perf. 14½x14***

**1246** A381 5col blk, gold & dk bl 2.75 2.00

First Postage Stamps, 150th Anniv. A382

a, Sir Rowland Hill. b, Penny Black. c, No. 21. d, Central Post Office. e, No. C124.

**1990, Oct. 5** **Litho.** ***Perf. 14***

**1247** Sheet of 5 + label 9.00 9.00
*a.-e.* A382 2col any single .95 .70

World Food Day — A383

**1990, Oct. 16** **Litho.** ***Perf. 14***

**1248** A383 5col multicolored 2.75 1.75

San Salvador Electric Light Co., Cent. A384

**1990, Oct. 30**

**1249** A384 20c shown .40 .25
**1250** A384 90c Lineman, power lines .70 .35

America Issue A385

**1990, Oct. 11** **Litho.** ***Perf. 14x14½***

**1251** A385 25c Chichontepec Volcano .50 .25
**1252** A385 70c Lake Coatepeque .90 .25

Chamber of Commerce, 75th Anniv. A386

**1990, Nov. 22**

**1253** A386 1 col blk, gold & bl .70 .35

Traffic Safety — A387

Design: 40c, Intersection, horiz.

***Perf. 14½x14, 14x14½***

**1990, Nov. 13**

**1254** A387 25c multicolored .35 .25
**1255** A387 40c multicolored .55 .25

Butterflies A388

15c, Eurytides calliste. 20c, Papilio garamas amerias. 25c, Papilio garamas. 55c, Hypanartia godmani. 70c, Anaea excellens. 1col, Papilio pilumnus. 2col, Anaea proserpina.

***Perf. 14x14½, 14½x14***

**1990, Nov. 28**

**1256** A388 15c multicolored .80 .30
**1257** A388 20c multicolored .90 .30
**1258** A388 25c multicolored 1.20 .30
**1259** A388 55c multicolored 1.40 .40
**1260** A388 70c multicolored 1.60 .55
**1261** A388 1col multicolored 2.25 .70
*Nos. 1256-1261 (6)* 8.15 2.55

**Souvenir Sheet**

***Roulette 13½***

**1262** A388 2col multicolored 12.00 2.50

Nos. 1259-1261 are vert.

University of El Salvador, 150th Anniv. — A389

**1991, Feb. 27 Litho. *Perf. 14½x14***

**1263** A389 25c shown .25 .25
**1264** A389 70c Sun, footprints, hand .45 .45
**1265** A389 1.50col Dove, globe 1.00 1.00
*Nos. 1263-1265 (3)* 1.70 1.70

Christmas A390

***Perf. 14x14½, 14½x14***

**1990, Dec. 7 Litho.**

**1266** A390 25c shown .25 .25
**1267** A390 70c Nativity, vert. .50 .50

Month of the Elderly A391

**1991, Jan. 31 *Perf. 14½x14***

**1268** A391 15c purple & blk .55 .55

Restoration of Santa Ana Theater A392

**1991, Apr. 12 *Perf. 14***

**1269** A392 20c Interior .35 .35
**1270** A392 70c Exterior .65 .65

Amphibians — A393

Designs: 25c, Smilisca baudinii. 70c, Eleutherodactylus rugulosus. 1col, Plectrohyla guatemalensis. 1.50col, Agalychnis moreletii.

**1991, May 29 Litho. *Perf. 14x14½***

**1271** A393 25c multicolored .75 .75
**1272** A393 70c multicolored 1.20 1.20
**1273** A393 1col multicolored 1.90 1.90
**1274** A393 1.50col multicolored 2.90 2.90
*Nos. 1271-1274 (4)* 6.75 6.75

Aid for Children's Village A394

Designs: 90c, Children playing outdoors.

**1991, June 21 Litho. *Perf. 14x14½***

**1275** A394 20c multicolored .30 .30
**1276** A394 90c multicolored .70 .70

United Family A395

**1991, June 28 Litho. *Perf. 14½x14***

**1277** A395 50c multicolored .60 .60

Birds — A396

20c, Melanotis hypoleucus. 25c, Agelaius phoeniceus. 70c, Campylor-hynchus rufinucha. 1col, Cissilopha melanocyanea. 5col, Chiroxiphia linearis.

**1991, Aug. 30**

**1278** A396 20c multicolored .55 .55
**1279** A396 25c multicolored .65 .65
**1280** A396 70c multicolored 1.00 1.00
**1281** A396 1col multicolored 1.10 1.10
**1282** A396 5col multicolored 4.00 4.00
*Nos. 1278-1282 (5)* 7.30 7.30

**Discovery of America, 500th Anniv. Type of 1990**

No. 1283: a, Hourglass, chart. b, Chart, ship's sails. c, Sailing ship near Florida. d, Corner of chart, ships. e, Compass rose, Cuba, Yucatan Peninsula. f, South America, "500" emblem. No. 1284, Sail, landfall.

**1991, Sept. 16 Litho. *Perf. 14***

**Miniature Sheet**

**1283** A379 1col Sheet of 6, #a.-f. 6.50 6.50

**Souvenir Sheet**

***Rouletted 6½***

**1284** A380 2col multicolored 3.00 3.00

America Issue A397

Designs: 25c, Battle of Acaxual. 70c, First missionaries in Cuzcatlan.

**1991, Oct. 11 Litho. *Perf. 14x14½***

**1285** A397 25c multicolored .75 .75
**1286** A397 70c multicolored 1.50 1.50

World Food Day — A398

**1991, Oct. 16 *Perf. 14½x14***

**1287** A398 50c multicolored .60 .60

Wolfgang Amadeus Mozart, Death Bicent. A399

**1991, Oct. 23 *Perf. 14x14½***

**1288** A399 1col multicolored 1.00 1.00

Christmas A400

***Perf. 14½x14, 14x14½***

**1991, Nov. 13 Litho.**

**1289** A400 25c Nativity scene, vert. .30 .30
**1290** A400 70c Children singing .60 .60

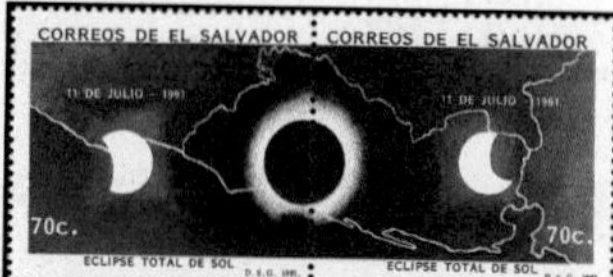


Total Solar Eclipse, July 11 — A401

**1991, Dec. 17 *Perf. 14x14½***

**1291** 70c shown .60 .60
**1292** 70c Eastern El Salvador .60 .60
*a.* A401 Pair, #1291-1292 1.75 1.75

No. 1292a has continous design.

Red Cross Life Guards A402

**1992, Feb. 28 Litho. *Perf. 14x14½***

**1293** A402 3col Rescue 2.00 2.00
**1294** A402 4.50col Swimming competition 2.75 2.75

Lions Clubs in El Salvador, 50th Anniv. — A403

**1992, Mar. 13 *Perf. 14½x14***

**1295** A403 90c multicolored .85 .85

Protect the Environment A404

Designs: 60c, Man riding bicycle. 80c, Children walking outdoors. 1.60col, Sower in field. 3col, Clean water. 2.20col, Natural foods. 5col, Recycling center. 10col, Conservation of trees and nature. 25col, Wildlife protection.

**1992, Apr. 6 Litho. *Perf. 14x14½***

**1298** A404 60c multi .35 .35
**1299** A404 80c multi .45 .45
**1300** A404 1.60col multi 1.00 1.00
**1302** A404 2.20col multi 1.40 1.40
**1303** A404 3col multi 1.75 1.75
**1304** A404 5col multi 2.90 2.90
**1305** A404 10col multi 5.50 5.50
**1307** A404 25col multi 15.00 15.00
*Nos. 1298-1307 (8)* 28.35 28.35

Physicians A405

80c, Dr. Roberto Orellana Valdes. 1col, Dr. Carlos Gonzalez Bonilla. 1.60col, Dr. Andres Gonzalo Funes. 2.20col, Dr. Joaquin Coto.

**1992, Apr. 30 *Perf. 14½x14***

**1308** A405 80c multicolored .50 .50
**1309** A405 1col multicolored .60 .60
**1310** A405 1.60col multicolored .90 .90
**1311** A405 2.20col multicolored 1.25 1.25
*Nos. 1308-1311 (4)* 3.25 3.25

Women's Auxiliary of St. Vincent de Paul Society, Cent. — A406

**1992, Mar. 10 Litho. *Perf. 14½x14***

**1312** A406 80c multicolored .75 .75

Population and Housing Census A407

80c, Globe showing location of El Salvador.

**1992, June 29 Litho. *Perf. 14½x14***

**1313** A407 60c multicolored .40 .40
**1314** A407 80c multicolored .60 .60

1992 Summer Olympics, Barcelona A408

**1992, July 17 Litho. *Perf. 14½x14***

**1315** A408 60c Hammer throw .55 .55
**1316** A408 80c Volleyball .65 .65
**1317** A408 90c Shot put 1.00 1.00
**1318** A408 2.20col Long jump 1.75 1.75
**1319** A408 3col Vault 2.50 2.50
**1320** A408 5col Balance beam 4.00 4.00
*Nos. 1315-1320 (6)* 10.45 10.45

Simon Bolivar A409

**1992, July 24**

**1321** A409 2.20col multicolored 1.50 1.50

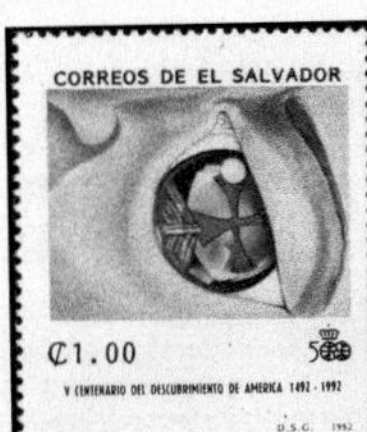

A410

Discovery of America, 500th Anniv. — A411

Designs: No. 1322, European and Amerindian faces. No. 1323, Ship in person's eye. No. 1324, Ship at sea. No. 1325, Ship, satellite over Earth. 3col, Cross, Indian pyramid.

**1992, Aug. 28 Litho. *Perf. 14x14½***

**1322** A410 1col multicolored 1.25 1.25
**1323** A410 1col multicolored 1.25 1.25

***Perf. 14½x14***

**1324** A410 1col multicolored 1.25 1.25
**1325** A410 1col multicolored 1.25 1.25
*a.* Min. sheet, 2 each #1322-1325 10.00 10.00
*Nos. 1322-1325 (4)* 5.00 5.00

**Souvenir Sheet**

***Rouletted 13½***

**1326** A411 3col multicolored 4.50 4.50

Immigrants to El Salvador A412

Designs: No. 1327, Feet walking over map. No. 1328, Footprints leading to map.

**1992, Sept. 16 Litho. *Perf. 14x14½***

**1327** A412 2.20col multicolored 1.50 1.50
**1328** A412 2.20col multicolored 1.50 1.50
*a.* Pair, #1327-1328 4.00 4.00

General Francisco Morazan (1792-1842) A413

**1992, Sept. 28 *Perf. 14½x14***

**1329** A413 1col multicolored 1.00 1.00

Association of Salvadoran Broadcasters A414

**1992, Oct. 3**

**1330** A414 2.20col multicolored 1.50 1.50

Salvadoran Radio Day, Intl. Radio Day.

Discovery of America, 500th Anniv. A415

**1992, Oct. 13 Litho. *Perf. 14x14½***

**1331** A415 80c Indian artifacts 2.40 2.40
**1332** A415 2.20col Map, ship 6.50 6.50

Exfilna '92 — A416

**1992, Oct. 22 *Perf. 14x14½***

**1333** A416 5col multicolored 5.00 5.00

Discovery of America, 500th Anniv.

Peace in El Salvador A417

**1992, Oct. 30**

**1334** A417 50c blk, blue & yel .70 .70

Christmas A418

***Perf. 14x14½, 14½x14***

**1992, Nov. 23 Litho.**

**1335** A418 80c shown .80 .80
**1336** A418 2.20col Nativity, vert. 1.75 1.75

Wildlife A419

Designs: 50c, Tapirus bairdii. 70c, Chironectes minimus. 1col, Eira barbara. 3col, Felis yagouaroundi. 4.50col, Odocoileus virginianus.

**1993, Jan. 15 Litho. *Perf. 14x14½***

**1337** A419 50c multicolored .40 .40
**1338** A419 70c multicolored .60 .60
**1339** A419 1col multicolored 1.50 1.50
**1340** A419 3col multicolored 2.50 2.50
**1341** A419 4.50col multicolored 3.50 3.50
*Nos. 1337-1341 (5)* 8.50 8.50

Month of the Elderly A420

Design: 2.20col, Boy, old man holding tree.

**1993, Jan. 27**

**1342** A420 80c black .60 .60
**1343** A420 2.20col multicolored 1.60 1.60

Agape Social Welfare Organization — A421

Designs: a, Divine Providence Church. b, People, symbols of love and peace.

**1993, Mar. 4 Litho. *Perf. 14x14½***

**1344** A421 1col Pair, #a.-b. 1.40 1.40

Secretary's Day A422

**1993, Apr. 26 Litho. *Perf. 14x14½***

**1345** A422 1col multicolored .60 .60

Benjamin Bloom Children's Hospital A423

**1993, June 18 Litho. *Perf. 14x14½***

**1346** A423 5col multicolored 3.00 3.00

Visit by Mexican President Carlos Salinas de Gortari A424

**1993, July 14**

**1347** A424 2.20col multicolored 1.50 1.50

Aquatic Birds A425

80c, Casmerodius albus. 1col, Mycteria americana. 2.20col, Ardea herodias. 5col, Ajaja ajaja.

**1993, Sept. 28 Litho. *Perf. 14x14½***

**1348** A425 80c multicolored .65 .65
**1349** A425 1col multicolored .90 .90
**1350** A425 2.20col multicolored 1.60 1.60
**1351** A425 5col multicolored 3.75 3.75
*Nos. 1348-1351 (4)* 6.90 6.90

Pharmacy Review Commission, Cent. — A426

**1993, Oct. 6**
**1352** A426 80c multicolored .55 .55

America Issue A427

Endangered species: 80c, Dasyprocta punctata. 2.20col, Procyon lotor.

**1993, Oct. 11 Litho. *Perf. 14x14½***
**1353** A427 80c multicolored 1.00 1.00
**1354** A427 2.20col multicolored 2.00 2.00

Fifth Central America Games A428

50c, Mascot, torch. 1.60col, Emblem. 2.20col, Mascot, map of Central America. 4.50col, Map of El Salvador, mascot.

***Perf. 14½x14, 14x14½***
**1993, Oct. 29 Litho.**
**1355** A428 50c multi .50 .50
**1356** A428 1.60col multi 1.00 1.00
**1357** A428 2.20col multi, horiz. 1.25 1.25
**1358** A428 4.50col multi, horiz. 2.50 2.50
*Nos. 1355-1358 (4)* 5.25 5.25

Miniature Sheet

Medicinal Plants — A429

Designs: a, Solanum mammosum. b, Hamelia patens. c, Tridex procumbens. d, Calea urticifolia. e, Ageratum conyzoides. f, Pluchea odorata.

**1993, Dec. 10 Litho. *Perf. 14½x14***
**1359** A429 1col Sheet of 6, #a.-f. 5.00 5.00

Christmas A430

**1993, Nov. 23 *Perf. 14x14½***
**1360** A430 80c Holy Family .50 .50
**1361** A430 2.20col Nativity Scene 1.00 1.00

Alberto Masferrer (1868-1932), Writer — A431

**1993, Nov. 30**
**1362** A431 2.20col multicolored 1.50 1.50

Intl. Year of the Family — A432

**1994, Feb. 28 Litho. *Perf. 14½x14***
**1363** A432 2.20col multicolored 1.50 1.50

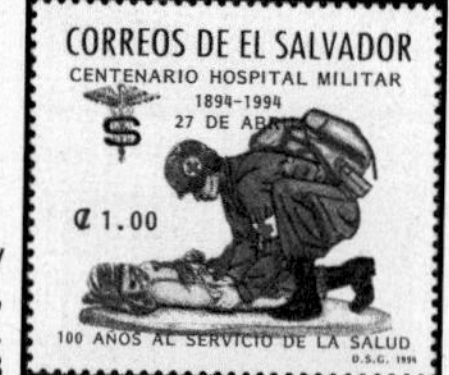


Military Hospital, Cent. A433

**1994, Apr. 27 Litho. *Perf. 14***
**1364** A433 1col shown .70 .70
**1365** A433 1col Hospital building .70 .70

City of Santa Ana, Cent. — A434

Designs: 60c, Arms of Department of Santa Ana. 80c, Inscription honoring heroic deeds of 44 patriots.

**1994, Apr. 29 Litho. *Perf. 14***
**1366** A434 60c multicolored .45 .45
**1367** A434 80c multicolored .55 .55

1994 World Cup Soccer Championships, US — A435

Soccer plays, flags from: 60c, Romania, Colombia, Switzerland, US. 80c, Sweden, Cameroun, Russia, Brazil. 1col, South Korea, Spain, Bolivia, Germany. 2.20col, Bulgaria, Nigeria, Greece, Argentina. 4.50col, Mexico, Norway, Ireland, Italy. 5col, Saudi Arabia, Netherlands, Morocco, Belgium.

**1994, June 6 Litho. *Perf. 14***
**1368** A435 60c multicolored .60 .60
**1369** A435 80c multicolored .60 .60
**1370** A435 1col multicolored .75 .75
**1371** A435 2.20col multicolored 1.40 1.40
**1372** A435 4.50col multicolored 2.75 2.75
**1373** A435 5col multicolored 3.00 3.00
*Nos. 1368-1373 (6)* 9.10 9.10

Plaza of Sovereign Military Order of Malta A436

**1994, June 24 Litho. *Perf. 14***
**1374** A436 2.20col multicolored 1.50 1.50

Traditions A437

Designs: 1col, Tiger and deer dance. 2.20col, Spotted bull dance.

**1994, June 30**
**1375** A437 1col multicolored .80 .80
**1376** A437 2.20col multicolored 1.40 1.40

Nutritional Plants — A438

70c, Capsicum annuum. 80c, Theobroma cacao. 1col, Ipomoea batatas. 5col, Chamaedorea tepejilote.

**1994, Aug. 29 Litho. *Perf. 14***
**1377** A438 70c multicolored .60 .60
**1378** A438 80c multicolored .60 .60
**1379** A438 1col multicolored .80 .80
**1380** A438 5col multicolored 3.00 3.00
*Nos. 1377-1380 (4)* 5.00 5.00

Postal Transport Vehicles A439

**1994, Oct. 11 Litho. *Perf. 14***
**1381** A439 80c Jeep .75 .75
**1382** A439 2.20col Train 2.00 2.00

America issue.

22nd Bicycle Race of El Salvador A440

**1994, Oct. 26**
**1383** A440 80c multicolored .60 .60

16th Intl. Fair of El Salvador A441

**1994, Oct. 31**
**1384** A441 5col multicolored 3.00 3.00

Christmas A442

**1994, Nov. 16**
**1385** A442 80c shown .50 .50
**1386** A442 2.20col Magi, Christ child 1.25 1.25

Beetles A443

80c, Cotinis mutabilis. 1col, Phyllophaga. 2.20col, Galofa. 5col, Callipogon barbatus.

**1994, Dec. 16 Litho. *Perf. 14***
**1387** A443 80c multi .70 .70
**1388** A443 1col multi .90 .90
**1389** A443 2.20col multi 2.25 2.25
**1390** A443 5col multi 5.00 5.00
*Nos. 1387-1390 (4)* 8.85 8.85

Salvadoran Culture Center, 40th Anniv. — A444

**1995, Mar. 24 Litho. *Perf. 14½x14***
**1391** A444 70c shown .45 .45
**1392** A444 1col "40" emblem .60 .60

Ceramic Treasures Archeological Site — A445

Designs: 60c, Cup. 70c, Three-footed earthen dish. 80c, Two-handled jar. 2.20col, Long-necked jar. 4.50col, Excavation structure #3. 5col, Excavation structure #4.

**1995, Apr. 26 Litho. *Perf. 14½x14***
**1393** A445 60c multicolored .40 .40
**1394** A445 70c multicolored .50 .50
**1395** A445 80c multicolored .55 .55
**1396** A445 2.20col multicolored 1.40 1.40
**1397** A445 4.50col multicolored 2.90 2.90
**1398** A445 5col multicolored 3.25 3.25
*Nos. 1393-1398 (6)* 9.00 9.00

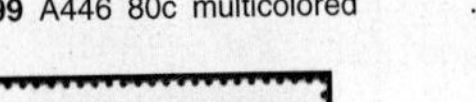

Fr. Isidro Menendez (1795-1858), Physician A446

**1995, May 19**

**1399** A446 80c multicolored .75 .75

La Centro Americana, SA, 80th Anniv. — A447

Designs: 80c, Insuring the future of children. 2.20col, Child wearing costume.

**1995, July 7 Litho. *Perf. 14***

**1400** A447 80c multicolored .50 .50
**1401** A447 2.20col multicolored 1.50 1.50

Sacred Heart College, Cent. A448

**1995, July 26 *Perf. 14x14½***

**1402** A448 80c multicolored .80 .80

FAO, 50th Anniv. — A449

**1995, Aug. 16 Litho. *Perf. 14½x14***

**1403** A449 2.20col multicolored 1.50 1.50

Tourism A450

Designs: 50c, Los Almendros Beach, Sonsonate. 60c, Green Lagoon, Apaneca. 2.20col, Guerrero Beach, La Union. 5col, Usulutan Volcano.

**1995, Aug. 30 *Perf. 14x14½***

**1404** A450 50c multicolored .40 .40
**1405** A450 60c multicolored .50 .50
**1406** A450 2.20col multicolored 1.50 1.50
**1407** A450 5col multicolored 3.25 3.25
*Nos. 1404-1407 (4)* 5.65 5.65

Orchids A451

#1408, Pleurothallis glandulosa. #1409, Pleurothallis grobyi. #1410, Pleurothallis fuegii. #1411, Lemboglossum stellatum. #1412, Lepanthes inaequalis. #1413, Pleurothallis hirsuta. #1414, Hexadesmia micrantha. #1415, Pleurothallis segoviense. #1416, Stelis aprica. #1417, Platystele stenostachya. #1418, Stelis barbata. #1419, Pleurothallis schiedeii.

**1995, Sept. 28 Litho. *Perf. 14½x14***

**1408** A451 60c multicolored .50 .50
**1409** A451 60c multicolored .50 .50
*a.* Pair, #1408-1409 1.00 1.00
**1410** A451 70c multicolored .70 .70
**1411** A451 70c multicolored .70 .70
**1412** A451 1col multicolored 1.00 1.00
**1413** A451 1col multicolored 1.00 1.00
**1414** A451 3col multicolored 2.75 2.75
**1415** A451 3col multicolored 2.75 2.75
**1416** A451 4.50col multicolored 4.00 4.00
**1417** A451 4.50col multicolored 4.00 4.00
*a.* Pair, #1416-1417 8.00 8.00
**1418** A451 5col multicolored 4.75 4.75
**1419** A451 5col multicolored 4.75 4.75
*Nos. 1408-1419 (12)* 27.40 27.40

America Issue — A452

Martins: 80c, Chloroceryle aenea. 2.20col, Chloroceryle americana.

**1995, Oct. 11**

**1420** A452 80c multicolored 1.25 1.25
**1421** A452 2.20col multicolored 3.50 3.50

UN, 50th Anniv. — A453

Design: 2.20col, Hands of different races holding UN emblem, "50."

**1995, Oct. 23**

**1422** A453 80c multicolored .60 .60
**1423** A453 2.20col multicolored 1.75 1.75

Christmas A454

**1995, Nov. 17 Litho. *Perf. 14½x14***

**1424** A454 80c shown .60 .60
**1425** A454 2.20col Families, clock tower 1.75 1.75

Miniature Sheet

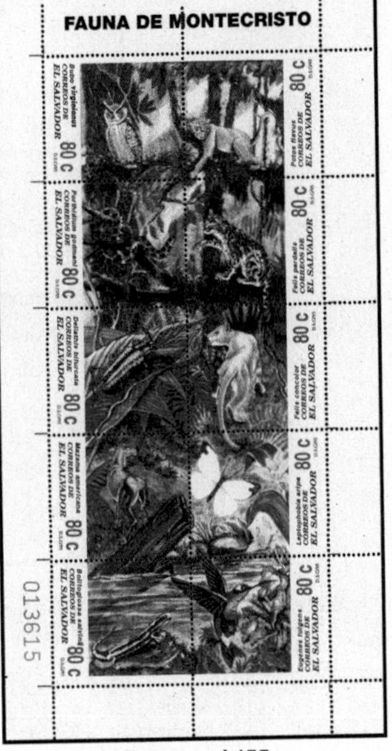

Fauna — A455

Designs: a, Bubo virginianus. b, Potos flavus. c, Porthidium godmani. d, Felis pardalis (f). e, Dellathis bifurcata. f, Felis concolor (h). g, Mazama americana. h, Leptophobia aripa. i, Bolitoglossa salvinii. j, Eugenes fulgens (h, i).

**1995, Nov. 24 *Perf. 14x14½***

**1426** A455 80c Sheet of 10, #a.-j. 12.00 12.00

Independence, 174th Anniv. — A456

Designs: 80c, Natl. arms, export products, money, textile workers, pharmaceuticals. 25col, Crates of products leaving El Salvador.

**1995, Sept. 14 *Perf. 14½x14***

**1427** A456 80c shown .50 .50
**1428** A456 25col multicolored 15.00 15.00

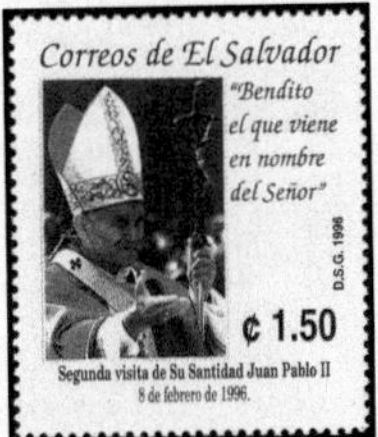

2nd Visit of Pope John Paul II — A457

5.40col, Pope John Paul II, Metropolitan Cathedral.

**1996, Feb. 8 Litho. *Perf. 14½x14***

**1429** A457 1.50col multicolored 1.50 1.50
**1430** A457 5.40col multicolored 5.00 5.00

ANTEL, Telecommunications Workers' Day — A458

1.50col, Satellite dish, hand holding cable fibers. 5col, Three globes, telephone receiver.

***Perf. 14x14½, 14½x14***

**1996, Apr. 27 Litho.**

**1431** A458 1.50col multi 1.00 1.00
**1432** A458 5col multi, vert. 3.50 3.50

City of San Salvador, 450th Anniv. A459

Designs: 2.50col, Spanish meeting natives. 2.70col, Diego de Holguin, first mayor, mission. 3.30col, Old National Palace. 4col, Heroe's Boulevard, modern view of city.

**1996, Mar. 27 *Perf. 14x14½***

**1433** A459 2.50col multicolored 1.75 1.75
**1434** A459 2.70col multicolored 2.00 2.00
**1435** A459 3.30col multicolored 2.25 2.25
**1436** A459 4col multicolored 2.75 2.75
*Nos. 1433-1436 (4)* 8.75 8.75

Natl. Artists, Entertainers A460

Designs: 1col, Rey Avila (1929-95). 1.50col, María Teresa Moreira (1934-95). 2.70col, Francisco Antonio Lara (1900-89). 4col, Carlos Alverez Pineda (1928-93).

**1996, May 17 Litho. *Perf. 14½x14***

**1437** A460 1col multicolored .70 .70
**1438** A460 1.50col multicolored 1.00 1.00
**1439** A460 2.70col multicolored 1.60 1.60
**1440** A460 4col multicolored 2.50 2.50
*Nos. 1437-1440 (4)* 5.80 5.80

YSKL Radio, 40th Anniv. A461

**1996, May 24 *Perf. 14x14½***

**1441** A461 1.40col multicolored 1.20 1.20

1996 Summer Olympic Games, Atlanta A462

Early Greek athletes: 1.50col, Discus thrower. 3col, Jumper. 4col, Wrestlers. 5col, Javelin thrower.

**1996, July 3 Litho. *Perf. 14***

**1442** A462 1.50col multicolored 1.00 1.00
**1443** A462 3col multicolored 2.00 2.00
**1444** A462 4col multicolored 2.75 2.75
**1445** A462 5col multicolored 3.50 3.50
*Nos. 1442-1445 (4)* 9.25 9.25

Birds A463

Designs: a, Pheucticus ludovicianus. b, Tyrannus forficatus. c, Dendroica petechia. d, Falco sparverius. e, Icterus galbula.

**1996, Aug. 9 Litho. *Perf. 14x14½***
**1446** A463 1.50col Strip of 5, #a.-e. 18.00 18.00

Diaro de Hoy Newspaper, 60th Anniv. — A464

**1996, Sept. 20**
**1447** A464 5.20col multicolored 3.50 3.50

Channel 2 Television Station, 30th Anniv. — A465

**1996, Sept. 27 *Perf. 14½x14***
**1448** A465 10col multicolored 6.00 6.00

UNICEF, 50th Anniv. A466

**1996, Oct. 4 *Perf. 14x14½***
**1449** A466 1col multicolored 1.00 1.00

Traditional Costumes A467

America issue: 1.50col, Blouse, short flannel skirt, Nahuizalco. 4col, Blouse, long skirt, Panchimalco.

**1996, Oct. 11 *Perf. 14½x14***
**1450** A467 1.50col multicolored 3.00 3.00
**1451** A467 4col multicolored 6.00 6.00

Christmas A468

Designs: 2.50col, Night scene of homes, Christmas tree, church. 4col, Day scene of people celebrating outside homes, church.

**1996, Nov. 28 Litho. *Perf. 14½x14***
**1452** A468 2.50col multicolored 2.00 2.00
**1453** A468 4col multicolored 3.00 3.00

Constitution Day — A469

**1996, Dec. 19 Litho. *Perf. 14½x14***
**1454** A469 1col multicolored 1.10 1.10

Marine Life — A470

a, Nasolamia velox. b, Scomberomorus sierra. c, Delphinus delphis. d, Eretmochelys imbricata. e, Epinephelus labriformis. f, Pomacanthus zonipectus. g, Scarus perrico. h, Hippocampus ingens.

**1996, Dec. 17**
**1455** A470 1col Sheet of 8, #a.-h. 8.00 8.00

Jerusalem, 3000th Anniv. A471

**1996, Dec. 5 Litho. *Perf. 14x14½***
**1456** A471 1col multicolored .80 .80

El Mundo Newspaper, 30th Anniv. A472

**1997, Feb. 6 Litho. *Perf. 14x14½***
**1457** A472 10col multicolored 7.00 7.00

Exfilna '97 — A473

**1997, Feb. 21**
**1458** A473 4col Baldwin 58441, 1925 4.25 4.25

Carmelite Order of San Jose, 80th Anniv. A474

Design: Mother Clara Maria of Jesus Quiros.

**1997, Mar. 19**
**1459** A474 1col multicolored 1.10 1.10

American School, 50th Anniv. — A475

**1997, Apr. 10 *Perf. 14½x14***
**1460** A475 25col multicolored 15.00 15.00

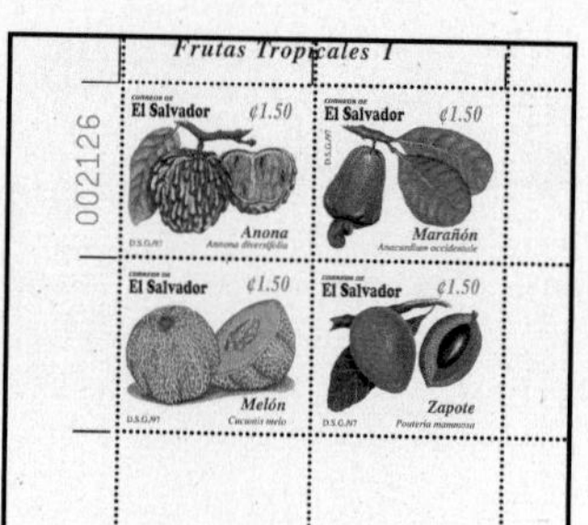
Tropical Fruit — A476

No. 1461: a, Annona diversifolia. b, Anacardium occidentale. c, Cucumis melo. d, Pouteria mammosa.
4col, Carica papaya.

**1997, May 28 Litho. *Perf. 14x14½***
**1461** A476 1.50col Sheet of 4, #a.-d. 6.00 6.00

**Souvenir Sheet**
***Rouletted 13½***
**1462** A476 4col multicolored 3.50 3.50

Lions Club in El Salvador, 55th Anniv. A476a

**1997, Aug. 15 Litho. *Perf. 14***
**1463** A476a 4col multicolored 3.00 3.00

Montreal Protocol on Substances that Deplete Ozone Layer, 10th Anniv. — A477

**1997, Aug. 28 Litho. *Perf. 14***
**1464** A477 1.50col shown 1.75 1.75
**1465** A477 4col Boy drinking water 3.25 3.25

Inter-American Water Day (#1465).

Miguel de Cervantes Saavedra (1547-1616), Writer — A478

**1997, Sept. 26 Litho. *Perf. 14***
**1466** A478 4col multicolored 3.00 3.00

Independence Day — A479

**1997, Sept. 10 Litho. *Perf. 14x14½***
**1467** A479 2.50col shown 1.75 1.75
**1468** A479 5.20col Flag, children, dove 3.50 3.50

Scouting in El Salvador, 75th Anniv. — A480

**1997, Oct. 3 *Perf. 14½x14***
**1469** A480 1.50col multicolored 1.90 1.90

Life of a Postman A481

America issue: 1col, Postman delivering mail. 4col, Postman on motor scooter, dog.

**1997, Oct. 10 Litho. *Perf. 14½x14***
**1470** A481 1col multicolored 2.00 2.00
**1471** A481 4col multicolored 5.00 5.00

ACES (Automobile Club of El Salvador), 26th Anniv. A482

**1997, Oct. 28 *Perf. 14x14½***
**1472** A482 10col multicolored 7.00 7.00

Christmas — A483

Children's paintings: No. 1473, Outdoor scene. No. 1474, Indoor scene.

**1997, Nov. 20 Litho. *Perf. 14***
**1473** 1.50col multicolored 1.50 1.50
**1474** 1.50col multicolored 1.50 1.50
*a.* A483 Pair, #1473-1474 3.00 3.00

Salesian Order in El Salvador, Cent. — A484

Designs: a, Map, St. John Bosco (1715-88). b, St. Cecilia College. c, San Jose College, priest. d, Ricaldone, students working with machinery. e, Maria Auxiliadora Church. f, City of St. John Bosco, students working with electronic equipment.

**1997, Dec. 6**
**1475** A484 1.50col Sheet of 6, #a.-f. 6.00 6.00

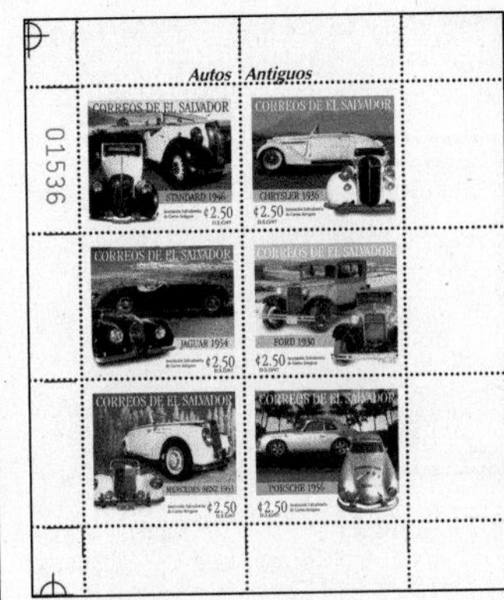
Antique Automobiles — A485

Designs: a, 1946 Standard. b, 1936 Chrysler. c, 1954 Jaguar. d, 1930 Ford. e, 1953 Mercedes Benz. f, 1956 Porsche.

**1997, Dec. 17**
**1476** A485 2.50col Sheet of 6, #a.-f. 10.00 10.00

St. Joseph Missionaries, 125th Anniv. — A486

1col, Image, Church of St. Joseph, Ahuachapan. 4col, Jose M. Vilaseca, Cesarea Esparza.

**1998, Jan. 23 Litho. *Perf. 14***
**1477** A486 1col multicolored .50 .50
**1478** A486 4col multicolored 2.25 2.25

New Intl. Airport A487

**1998, Mar. 17 Litho. *Perf. 14***
**1479** A487 10col multicolored 4.00 4.00

Organization of American States, 50th Anniv. — A488

**1998, May 29 Litho. *Perf. 14½x14***
**1480** A488 4col multicolored 2.00 2.00

1998 World Cup Soccer Championships, France — A489

Soccer player, Paris landmarks: a, Sacre Coeur. b, Eiffel Tower. c, Louvre. d, Notre Dame.
4col, Soccer ball, Arc d'Triumphe, horiz.

**1998, May 13**
**1481** A489 1.50col Strip of 4, #a.-d. 4.00 4.00

**Souvenir Sheet**
***Rouletted 13½***
**1482** A489 4col multicolored 9.00 9.00

El Salvador, 1997 Champions of the 6th Central American Games A490

Designs inside medals: No. 1483, Women's gymnastics, weight lifting, judo. No. 1484, Discus, volleyball, women's basketball. No. 1485, Swimming, tennis, water polo. No. 1486, Gymnastics, wrestling, shooting.

**1998, July 17 Litho. *Perf. 14***
**1483** A490 1.50col multicolored .90 .90
**1484** A490 1.50col multicolored .90 .90
**1485** A490 1.50col multicolored .90 .90
**1486** A490 1.50col multicolored .90 .90
*Nos. 1483-1486 (4)* 3.60 3.60

Dr. Jose Gustavo Guerrero (1876-1958), President of the World Court — A491

**1998, July 22 Litho. *Perf. 14***
**1487** A491 1col multicolored .70 .70

18th International Fair — A492

**1998, Aug. 28**
**1488** A492 4col multicolored 2.00 2.00

Painting of the Death of Manuel José Arce, Soldier, Politician A493

**1998, Sept. 1**
**1489** A493 4col multicolored 2.00 2.00

Hummingbirds and Flowers — A494

a, Archilochus colubris. b, Amazilia rutila. c, Hylocharis eliciae. d, Colibri thalassinus. e, Campylopterus hemileucurus. f, Lampornis amethystinus.

**1998, Sept. 7**
**1490** A494 1.50col Sheet of 6, #a.-f. 8.00 8.00

House Social Fund, 25th Anniv. — A495

**1998, Sept. 29 Litho. *Perf. 14***
**1491** A495 10col multicolored 4.25 4.25

Natl. Archives, 50th Anniv. — A496

**1998, Oct. 2**
**1492** A496 1.50col multicolored 1.00 1.00

Famous Women A497

America issue: 1col, Alice Lardé de Venturino. 4col, Maria de Baratta.

**1998, Oct. 12**
**1493** A497 1col multicolored .70 .70
**1494** A497 4col multicolored 2.75 2.75

Christmas A498

Children's drawings: 1col, Clock tower, nativity scene. 4col, Pageant players as angels, Holy Family parading to church, nativity scene.

**1998, Nov. 24 Litho. *Perf. 14***
**1495** A498 1col multicolored .60 .60
**1496** A498 4col multicolored 1.75 1.75

World Stamp Day A499

**1998, Nov. 27 Litho. *Perf. 14***
**1497** A499 1col multicolored .85 .85

Salvadoran Air Force, 75th Anniv. — A500

Designs: a, C47T transport plane. b, TH-300 helicopter. c, UH-1H helicopter. d, Dragonfly bomber.

**1998, Dec. 1 Litho. *Perf. 14¼***

**1498** A500 1.50col Strip of 4, #a.-d. 3.75 3.75

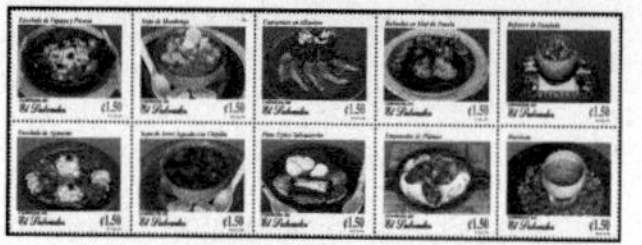

Traditional Foods — A501

Designs: a, Ensalada de papaya y pacaya. b, Sopa de mondongo. c, Camarones en alhuaiste. d, Buñuelos en miel de panela. e, Refresco de ensalada. f, Ensalada de aguacate. g, Sopa de arroz aguado con chipilín. h, Plato típico salvadoreño. i, Empanadas de plátano. j, Horchata.

**1998, Dec. 9 Litho. *Perf. 14***

**1499** A501 1.50col Block of 10, #a.-j. 10.00 10.00

Roberto D'Aubuisson Signing New Constitution, 1983 — A502

**1998, Dec. 15 Litho. *Perf. 14x14¼***

**1503** A502 25col multicolored 9.25 9.25

First Natl. Topical Philatelic Exhibition A503

Salvador Railway Company Steamship Service.

**1999, Feb. 19 Litho. *Perf. 14***

**1504** A503 2.50col multicolored 1.25 1.25

Introduction of Television, 40th Anniv. — A504

**1999, Feb. 24**

**1505** A504 4col multicolored 1.50 1.50

European Union Cooperation with El Salvador — A505

**1999, May 7 Litho. *Perf. 14x14¼***

**1506** A505 5.20col shown 2.00 2.00

**1507** A505 10col Hands clasped 3.50 3.50

Water Birds A506

No. 1508: a, Gallinula chlorupus. b, Porphyrula martinica. c, Pardirallus maculatus. d, Anas discors. e, Dendrocygna autumnalis. f, Fulica americana. g, Jacana spinosa. h, Perzana carolina. i, Aramus guarauna. j, Oxyura dominica.

4col, Aythya affinis.

**1999, Apr. 22 *Perf. 14x14¼***

**1508** A506 1col Block of 10, #a.-j. 8.00 8.00

**Souvenir Sheet**

***Rouletted 8¾***

**1509** A506 4col multicolored 8.00 8.00

Bats A507

Designs: a, Glossophaga soricina. b, Desmodus rotundus. c, Noctilio leporinus. d, Vampyrum spectrum. e, Ectophilla alba. f, Myotis nigricans.

**1999, June 30 Litho. *Perf. 14x14½***

**1510** A507 1.50col Sheet of 6, #a.-f. 7.00 7.00

Visit of US Pres. William J. Clinton — A508

Designs: a, Seals, flags of El Salvador, US. b, Pres. Francisco Flores of El Salvador, Pres. Clinton.

**1999, May 19 *Perf. 14¼***

**1511** A508 5col Pair, #a.-b. 5.00 5.00

Quality Control Institute, 20th Anniv. — A509

**1999, May 20 *Perf. 14¼***

**1512** A509 5.40col multicolored 2.50 2.50

Geothermic Energy A510

**1999, July 16 Litho. *Perf. 14x14½***

**1513** A510 1col Drilling tower .50 .50

**1514** A510 4col Power station 1.75 1.75

Exports A511

**1999, July 21 *Perf. 14½x14***

**1515** A511 4col multicolored 2.00 2.00

Salvadoran Journalists' Association A512

**1999, July 30 *Perf. 14x14½***

**1516** A512 1.50col multicolored .80 .80

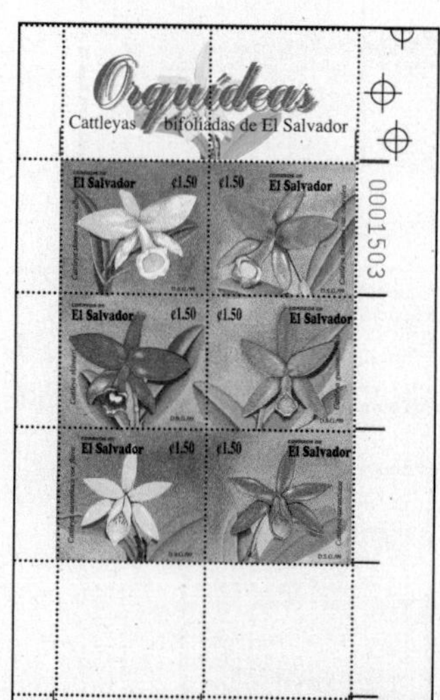

Cattleya Orchids — A513

Designs: a, Skinneri var. alba. b, Skinneri var. coerulea. c, Skinneri. d, Guatemalensis. e, Aurantiaca var. flava. f, Aurantiaca.

**1999, Aug. 25**

**1517** A513 1.50col Sheet of 6, #a.-f. + 4 labels 6.00 6.00

Toño Salazar, Caricaturist A514

Designs: a, Self-portrait. b, Salarrué. c, Claudia Lars. d, Francisco Gavidia. e, Miguel Angel Asturias.

**1999, Aug. 31**

**1518** A514 1.50col Strip of 5, #a.-e. 4.75 4.75

Central American Nutrition Institute A515

**1999, Sept. 14 Litho. *Perf. 14x14½***

**1519** A515 5.20col Children, food 2.00 2.00

**1520** A515 5.40col Food 2.25 2.25

Armed Forces, 175th Anniv. — A516

**1999, Sept. 24 *Perf. 14¼x14***

**1521** A516 1col Gens. Arce & Barrios .60 .60

**1522** A516 1.50col Soldier, flag .90 .90

Intl. Year of Older Persons A517

**1999, Oct. 8**

**1523** A517 10col multicolored 4.25 4.25

America Issue, A New Millennium Without Arms — A518

**1999, Oct. 12**

**1524** A518 1col Dove, children .80 .80

**1525** A518 4col "No Guns" sign 2.75 2.75

UPU, 125th Anniv. — A519

Designs: a, UPU emblem. b, Mail, jeep, ship, airplane, computer.

**1999, Oct. 22**

**1526** A519 4col Pair, #a.-b. 4.00 4.00

Christmas — A520

Paintings by:

No. 1527: a, Delmy Guandique. b, Margarita Orellana.

No. 1528: a, Lolly Sandoval. b, José Francisco Guadrón.

**1999, Nov. 4**

| | | | | |
|---|---|---|---|---|
| **1527** | A520 | 1.50col Pair, #a.-b. | 1.50 | 1.50 |
| **1528** | A520 | 4col Pair, #a.-b. | 3.50 | 3.50 |

Inter-American Development Bank, 40th Anniv. — A521

**1999, Nov. 24 Litho.** ***Perf. 14¼x14***

| | | | | |
|---|---|---|---|---|
| **1529** | A521 | 25col multi | 10.50 | 10.50 |

Woodpeckers A522

Designs: a, Melanerpes aurifrons. b, Piculus rubiginosus. c, Sphyrapicus varius. d, Dryocopus lineatus. e, Melanerpes formicivorus.

**1999, Dec. 3**

| | | | | |
|---|---|---|---|---|
| **1530** | A522 | 1.50col Vert. strip of 5, #a.-e. | 7.00 | 7.00 |

Salvadoran Coffee Assoc., 70th Anniv. A523

**1999, Dec. 7** ***Perf. 14x14¼***

| | | | | |
|---|---|---|---|---|
| **1531** | A523 | 10col multi | 4.75 | 4.75 |

Millennium A524

**2000, Jan. 6** ***Perf. 14¼x14***

| | | | | |
|---|---|---|---|---|
| **1532** | A524 | 1.50col multi | 1.35 | 1.35 |

Fireman's Foundation, 25th Anniv. — A525

Designs: 2.50col, Fireman rescuing child. 25col, Emblem.

**2000, Jan. 17 Litho.** ***Perf. 14¼x14***

| | | | | |
|---|---|---|---|---|
| **1533** | A525 | 2.50col multi | 1.50 | 1.50 |
| **1534** | A525 | 25col multi | 10.00 | 10.00 |

Faith and Happiness Foundation, 30th Anniv. — A526

**2000, Feb. 10**

| | | | | |
|---|---|---|---|---|
| **1535** | A526 | 1col multi | .95 | .95 |

Millennium A527

No. 1536, Serie I: a, El Tazumal Mayan pyramid. b, Christopher Columbus and ships. c, Spanish soldier, native. d, Independence.

No. 1537, Serie II: a, Salvadoran White House, 1890. b, Shoppers at street market, 1920. c, Trolley and Nuevo Mundo Hotel, 1924. d, Automobiles on South 2nd Avenue, San Salvador, 1924.

**2000 Sheets of 4** ***Perf. 14x14¼***

| | | | | |
|---|---|---|---|---|
| **1536** | A527 | 1.50col #a.-d. | 4.50 | 4.50 |
| **1537** | A527 | 1.50col #a.-d. | 4.50 | 4.50 |

Issued: No. 1536, 3/16; No. 1537, 6/16.
Nos. 1536 & 1537 includes two labels.

El Imposible Natl. Park — A528

No. 1538: a, Gate. b, Ocelot (tigrillo). c, Paca (tepezcuintle). d, Venado River waterfalls. e, Black curassow (pajuil). f, Tree with yellow leaves. g, Orchid (flor de encarnación). h, Honeycreeper (torogoz). i, Bird with purple head (siete colores). j, Vegetation near cliff. k, Interpretation center. l, Bird with black and yellow plumage (payasito). m, Frog. n, Mushrooms (hongos). o, Red flower (guaco de tierra). p, Green toucan. q, Hillside foliage. r, Agouti (cotuza). s, Ant bear (oso hormiguero). t, Cascaddes of El Imposible.

**2000, Apr. 28** ***Perf. 14¼x14***

| | | | | |
|---|---|---|---|---|
| **1538** | | Sheet of 20 | 12.00 | 12.00 |
| *a.-t.* | A528 | 1col Any single | .60 | .60 |

La Prensa Grafica, 85th Anniv. — A529

**2000, May 9**

| | | | | |
|---|---|---|---|---|
| **1539** | A529 | 5col multi | 2.25 | 2.25 |

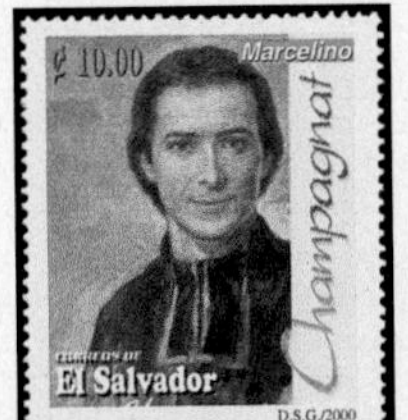


Canonization of Marcelino Champagnat (1789-1840) A530

**2000, June 2**

| | | | | |
|---|---|---|---|---|
| **1540** | A530 | 10col multi | 4.25 | 4.25 |

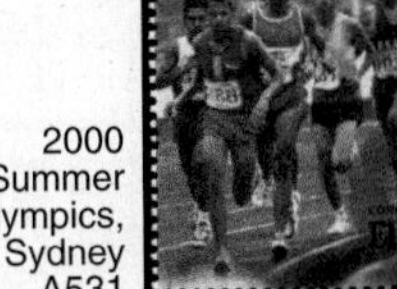


2000 Summer Olympics, Sydney A531

No. 1541: a, Runners. b, Gymnast. c, High jumper. d, Weight lifter. e, Fencer. f, Cyclist. g, Swimmer. h, Shooter. i, Archer. j, Judo.

**2000, July 20** ***Perf. 14x14¼***

| | | | | |
|---|---|---|---|---|
| **1541** | | Sheet of 10 | 10.00 | 10.00 |
| *a.-j.* | A531 | 1col Any single | .60 | .60 |

Trains A532

No. 1542: a, Baldwin locomotive Philadelphia 58441. b, General Electric locomotive series 65k-15. c, Train car. d, Presidential coach car.

**2000, Aug. 3**

| | | | | |
|---|---|---|---|---|
| **1542** | | Vert. strip of 4 | 7.00 | 7.00 |
| *a.-d.* | A532 | 1.50col Any single | 1.25 | 1.25 |

World Post Day — A533

**2000, Oct. 9 Litho.** ***Perf. 14¼x14***

| | | | | |
|---|---|---|---|---|
| **1543** | A533 | 5col multi | 2.25 | 2.25 |

Christmas Tree Ornaments A534

No. 1544: a, Snowman. b, Bells. c, Striped pendants. d, Candy cane. e, Candles. f, Sleigh. g, Gifts. h, Santa Claus. i, Santa's hat. j, Santa's boot.

**2000, Nov. 9**

| | | | | |
|---|---|---|---|---|
| **1544** | | Block of 10 | 9.00 | 9.00 |
| *a.-j.* | A534 | 1col Any single | .65 | .65 |

Art by Expatriates A535

Art by: a, Roberto Mejía Ruíz. b, Alex Cuchilla. c, Nicolas Fredy Shi Quán. d, José Bernardo Pacheco. e, Oscar Soles.

**2000, Dec. 4** ***Perf. 14x14¼***

| | | | | |
|---|---|---|---|---|
| **1545** | | Horiz. strip of 5 | 17.50 | 17.50 |
| *a.-e.* | A535 | 4col Any single | 2.50 | 2.50 |

Pets A536

No. 1546: a, 1.50col, Dogs. b, 1.50col, Dog and cat.

No. 1547: a, 2.50col, Parakeets. b, 2.50col, Dogs, diff.

**2001, Feb. 28 Litho.** ***Perf. 14x14¼***
**Vert. Pairs, #a-b**

| | | | | |
|---|---|---|---|---|
| **1546-1547** | A536 | Set of 2 | 6.50 | 6.50 |

Nos. 1546-1662 show denominations in colons and US dollars.

Saburo Hirao Park, 25th Anniv. A537

Designs: 5col, Playground. 25col, Bridge in gardens.

**2001, Mar. 14**

| | | | | |
|---|---|---|---|---|
| **1548-1549** | A537 | Set of 2 | 23.00 | 23.00 |

Claudia Lars (1899-1974), Salvadoran Writer, and Federico Proaño (1848-94), Ecuadoran Writer — A538

**2001, Aug. 28 Litho.** ***Perf. 14x14¼***

| | | | | |
|---|---|---|---|---|
| **1550** | A538 | 10col multi | 4.50 | 4.50 |

St. Vincent de Paul Children's Home, 125th Anniv. A539

**2001, Oct. 26**

| | | | | |
|---|---|---|---|---|
| **1551** | A539 | 4col multi | 2.00 | 2.00 |

Mushrooms A540

No. 1552: a, Lactaius indigo. b, Pleurotus ostreatus. c, Ramaria sp. d, Clavaria vermicularis.

No. 1553: a, Amanita muscaria. b, Phillipsia sp. c, Russula emetica. d, Geastrum triplex.

**2001, Dec. 20** ***Perf. 14¼x14***

1552 Horiz. strip of 4 5.75 5.75
a.-d. A540 1.50col Any single 1.10 1.10
1553 Horiz. strip of 4 16.50 16.50
a.-d. A540 4col Any single 3.00 3.00

St. Josemaria Escrivá de Balaguer (1902-75), Founder of Opus Dei — A541

Balaguer and: 1col, Plowed field. 5col, People and computers.

**2002, Apr. 26** **Litho.** ***Perf. 14¼x14***

1554-1555 A541 Set of 2 5.50 5.50

San Miguel Lions Club, 51st Anniv. — A542

**2002, July 31**

1556 A542 5col multi 4.00 4.00

Rosales National Hospital, Cent. — A543

**2002, June 28**

1557 A543 10col multi 8.00 8.00

Peace Accords, 10th Anniv. — A544

Designs: No. 1558, 2.50col, Dove and sun. No. 1559, 2.50col, UN emblem and handshake.

No. 1560: a, 2.50col, Dove with olive branch flying over village. b, 2.50col, Dove, flag.

**2002, May 15** ***Perf. 14¼x14***

1558-1559 A544 Set of 2 4.00 4.00

**Souvenir Sheet**

***Rouletted Irregularly***

1560 A544 Sheet of 2, #a-b 4.00 4.00

19th Central American and Caribbean Games A545

No. 1561: a, Montage of athletes. b, Bicycle race. c, Children's drawing of various athletes. d, Gymnast.

4col, Mascots.

**2002, June 13** ***Perf. 14x14¼***

1561 Vert. strip of 4 3.75 3.75
a.-d. A545 1col Any single .70 .70

**Souvenir Sheet**

***Rouletted Irregularly***

1562 A545 4col multi 3.50 3.50

A546

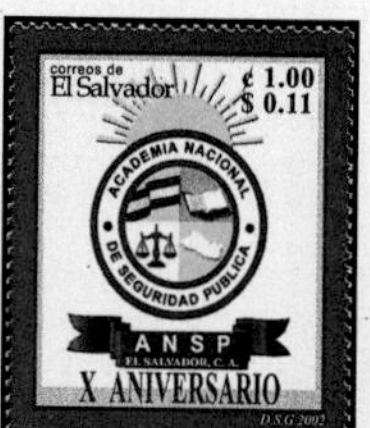

2002 World Cup Soccer Championships, Japan and Korea — A547

No. 1563 — Various Korean World Cup stadia and flags of countries in Group: a, A. b, B. c, C. d, D.

No. 1564 — Various Japanese World Cup stadia and flags of countries in Group: a, E. b, F. c, G. d, H.

4col, Flag of winning team, Brazil.

**2002, July 11** ***Perf. 14x14¼***

1563 Vert. strip of 4 3.25 3.25
a.-d. A546 1col Any single .75 .75
1564 Vert. strip of 4 6.00 6.00
a.-d. A546 1.50col Any single 1.10 1.10

**Souvenir Sheet**

***Rouletted Irregularly***

1565 A547 4col multi 3.75 3.75

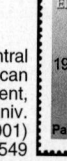

Natl. Academy of Public Security, 10th Anniv. — A548

**2002, Sep. 6** **Litho.** ***Perf. 14¼x14***

1566 A548 1col multi 1.00 1.00

Central American Parliament, 10th Anniv. (in 2001) A549

**2002, Sep. 13** ***Perf. 14x14¼***

1567 A549 25col multi 18.50 18.50

Pan-American Health Organization, Cent. — A550

No. 1568: a, Headquarters, Washington, DC. b, Emblem and "100."

**2002, Oct. 18** **Litho.** ***Perf. 14¼x14***

1568 A550 2.70col Horiz. pair, #a-b 4.50 4.50

Tourism A551

No. 1569, 1col: a, Forest, Picacho Volcano. b, Jiquilisco Bay.

No. 1570, 4col: a, Joya de Cerén Archaeological Site. b, Juayua, Sonsonate Department.

**2002, Dec. 6** ***Perf. 14x14¼***

**Vert. Pairs, #a-b**

1569-1570 A551 Set of 2 9.00 9.00

America Issue — Youth, Education, and Literacy A552

Designs: 1col, Stylized person, book, block. 1.50col, Teacher and students.

**2002, Nov. 26**

1571-1572 A552 Set of 2 2.40 2.40

Scouting in El Salvador, 80th Anniv. — A553

**2002, Dec. 16** ***Perf. 14¼x14***

1573 A553 2.70col multi 2.25 2.25

Christmas A554

Infant Jesus and: 1.50col, Mary. 2.50col, Joseph.

**2002, Nov. 29**

1574-1575 A554 Set of 2 3.50 3.50

Daughters of Our Lady Help of Christians (Salesian Sisters) in Central America, Cent. — A555

Designs: 70c, Girls, nun in classroom. 1.50col, Statue of Madonna and Child.

**2003, May 26** **Litho.** ***Perf. 14¼x14***

1576-1577 A555 Set of 2 2.00 2.00

Town of Sonsonate, 450th Anniv. — A556

**2003, May 28**

1578 A556 1.60col multi 1.50 1.50

Grupo Roble, 40th Anniv. A557

No. 1579: a, Tree without leaves. b, Cherries on branch.

4col, Bird and nest.

**2003, July 18** ***Perf. 14x14¼***

1579 A557 1.50col Vert. pair, #a-b 3.00 3.00

**Souvenir Sheet**

***Rouletted 12¾x13½***

1580 A557 4col multi 3.75 3.75

Regional Sanitary Agricultural Organization, 50th Anniv. — A558

**2003, July 25** ***Perf. 14x14¼***

1581 A558 25col multi 21.00 21.00

Agape Ministries in El Salvador, 25th Anniv. — A559

**2003, Aug. 25** ***Perf. 14¼x14***

1582 A559 1.50col multi 1.25 1.25

A560

Independence, 182nd Anniv. — A561

No. 1583: a, 2.50col, Maria Felipa Aranzamendi y Aguiar. b, 2.70col, Manuela Antonia Arce de Lara.
4col, Cry for Independence, Nov. 5, 1811.

**2003, Sept. 30** ***Perf. 14¼x14***
**1583** A560 Horiz. pair, #a-b 4.25 4.25

**Souvenir Sheet**
***Rouletted 13½x13¼***

**1584** A561 4col multi 3.50 3.50

FAO in El Salvador, 25th Anniv. — A562

Designs: 1.50col, Children, farmers.
4col, Child, farmer, food preparation workers.

**2003, Oct. 8** ***Perf. 14¼x14***
**1585** A562 1.50col multi 1.25 1.25

**Souvenir Sheet**
***Rouletted 13¼x13¾***

**1586** A562 4col multi 3.75 3.75

Insects and Flowers A563

No. 1587: a, Abejorro sp. b, Chrysina quetzalcoatli. c, Anartia fatima. d, Manduca sp. e, Manduca sexta. f, Tabebuia chrysantha. g, Alpinia purpurata. h, Tecoma stans. i, Tabebuia rosea. j, Passiflora edulis.
4col, Anartia fatima, Tabebuia rosea, vert.

**2003, Oct. 23** ***Perf. 14x14¼***
**1587** Block of 10 13.00 13.00
*a.-j.* A563 1.50col Any single .90 .90

**Souvenir Sheet**
***Rouletted 13¼x13¾***

**1588** A563 4col multi 4.00 4.00

Christmas A564

Designs: 1.50col, Madonna and Child. 4col, Holy Family.

**2003, Nov. 7** ***Perf. 14¼x14***
**1589-1590** A564 Set of 2 4.50 4.50

Churches A565

No. 1591: a, Church of the Immaculate Conception, Citalá. b, St. James the Apostle Church, Chalchuapa. c, St. Peter the Apostle Church, Metapán. d, Our Lady of Santa Ana Church, Chapeltique. e, St. James the Apostle Church, Conchagua.
5col, Calvary Church, San Salvador, vert.

**2003, Nov. 14** ***Perf. 14x14¼***
**1591** Horiz. strip of 5 12.00 12.00
*a.-e.* A565 4col Any single 2.25 2.25

**Souvenir Sheet**
***Rouletted 13¼x13¾***

**1592** A565 5col multi 3.25 3.25

Tourism A566

No. 1593: a, Brotherhood of Panchimalco. b, Church cupola, Juayúa. c, Shalpa Beach, La Libertad. d, Tazumal Ruins.

**2003, Dec. 10** ***Perf. 14x14¼***
**1593** Vert. strip of 4 4.75 4.75
*a.-d.* A566 1.50col Any single 1.00 1.00

America Issue - Flora and Fauna A567

Designs: 1.50col, Fernaldia pandurata. 4col, Lepidophyma smithii.

**2003, Dec. 19**
**1594-1595** A567 Set of 2 4.50 4.50

El Salvador — Panama Diplomatic Relations, Cent. A568

Designs: 10col, Flags of El Salvador and Panama. 25col, Flags, ship in lock.

**2004, Feb. 17** **Litho.** ***Perf. 14x14¼***
**1596-1597** A568 Set of 2 16.50 16.50

Salvadoran Cooperation With European Union — A569

Stars and map of: 2.70col, Central America. 5col, Europe.

**2004, May 13** ***Perf. 14¼x14***
**1598-1599** A569 Set of 2 3.75 3.75

Legends A570

No. 1600, 1col: a, La Carreta Chillona. b, La Siguanaba.
No. 1601, 1.60col: a, Justo Juez de la Noche. b, El Cipitío.

**2004, June 30** ***Perf. 14x14¼***
**Vert. Tete-beche Pairs, #a-b**
**1600-1601** A570 Set of 2 2.75 2.75

El Salvador College of Chemistry and Pharmaceuticals, Cent. — A571

**2004, Sept. 17**
**1602** A571 10col multi 3.75 3.75

Santa Tecla (Nueva San Salvador), 150th Anniv. A572

Designs: 1.50col, Adalberto Guirola Children's Home. 4col, Second Avenue.

**2004, Oct. 14**
**1603-1604** A572 Set of 2 2.25 2.25

Powered Flight, Cent. (in 2003) A573

No. 1605: a, Wilbur and Orville Wright, Wright Flyer. b, Alberto Santos-Dumont, 14-Bis. c, Louis Blériot, Blériot XI. d, Glenn Curtiss, Curtiss JN-4D Jenny. e, Hugo Junkers, Junkers J.1.
No. 1606: a, Charles Lindbergh, Spirit of St. Louis. b, Amelia Earhart, Lockheed Vega. c, Chuck Yeager, Bell X-1. d, Robert Withe, X-15. e, Dick Rutan and Jeana Yeager, Voyager.
No. 1607, Wilbur and Orville Wright, Wright Flyer, vert.

**2004, Nov. 5** ***Perf. 14x14¼***
**1605** Horiz. strip of 5 3.50 3.50
*a.-e.* A573 1.50col Any single .65 .65
**1606** Horiz. strip of 5 9.50 9.50
*a.-e.* A573 4col Any single 1.75 1.75

**Souvenir Sheet**
***Rouletted Irregularly***

**1607** A573 4col multi 3.00 3.00

Christmas A574

Designs: 1.50col, Holy Family. 2.50col, Shepherd and sheep. 4col, Magi. 5col, Flight into Egypt.

**2004, Dec. 7** **Litho.** ***Perf. 14x14¼***
**1608-1611** A574 Set of 4 5.00 5.00

America Issue - Environmental Protection — A575

Marine life: 1.40col, Akko rossi. 2.20col, Chromodoris sphoni.

**2004, Dec. 17**
**1612-1613** A575 Set of 2 2.10 2.10
*1613a* Tete-beche pair, #1612-1613 2.25 2.25

La Prensa Newspaper, 90th Anniv. A576

**2005, Apr. 7**
**1614** A576 25col multi 8.00 8.00

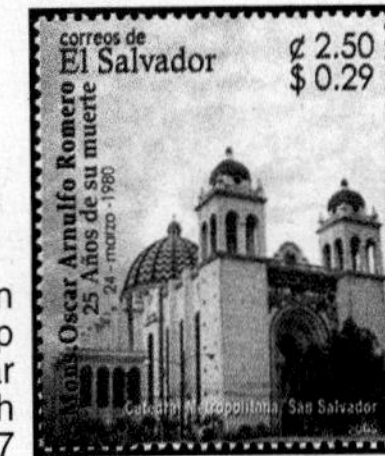


Assassination of Archbishop Oscar Romero, 25th Anniv. — A577

Designs: 2.50col, Metropolitan Cathedral, San Salvador. 5col, Romero (1917-80).

**2005, Apr. 23** ***Perf. 14¼x14***
**1615-1616** A577 Set of 2 2.75 2.75

Rotary International, Cent. — A578

**2005, June 15** ***Perf. 14¼x14***
**1617** A578 1.50col shown 1.75 1.75

**Souvenir Sheet**
***Rouletted Irregularly***

**1618** A578 4col Children 5.00 5.00

Puerto de San Carlos de la Unión, 150th Anniv. A579

**2005, July 27** *Perf. 14x14¼*

**1619** A579 10col shown 4.00 4.00

**Souvenir Sheet**

***Rouletted Irregularly***

**1620** A579 4col Pirigallo Island 2.25 2.25

Tenth Central American Students' Games A580

Designs: 1.60col, Wrestling. 2.20col, High jump. 2.70col, Karate. No. 1624, 4col, Rollerblading.

No. 1625, 4col, Karate, high jump and wrestling.

**2005, Sept. 14 Litho.** *Perf. 14¼x14*

**1621-1624** A580 Set of 4 5.00 5.00

**Souvenir Sheet**

***Rouletted 11x10¾x10x10½***

**1625** A580 4col multi 1.75 1.75

Latin American Musicians — A581

No. 1626: a, Agustín Lara (1897-1970), composer, Mexico. b, Pedro Infante (1917-57), singer, Mexico. c, Libertad Lamarque (1906-2000), singer, Argentina. d, Carlos Gardel (1890-1936), singer, Argentina. e, Celia Cruz (1924-2003), singer, Cuba. f, Damaso Pérez Prado (1916-89), composer, Cuba. g, Daniel Santos (1916-92), song writer, Puerto Rico. h, Pedro Vargas (1908-89), singer, Mexico. i, Beny Moré (1919-63), singer, Cuba. j, Jorge Negrete (1911-53), singer, Mexico.

4col, Singer, microphone and guitar.

**2005, Oct. 11** *Perf. 14¼x14*

**1626** A581 1.50col Sheet of 10, #a-j 7.00 7.00

**Souvenir Sheet**

***Rouletted 11x10¾***

**1627** A581 4col multi 2.40 2.40

Writers A582

Designs: No. 1628, 1col, Lilian Serpas (1905-85), poet. No. 1629, 1col, Oswaldo Escobar Velado (1919-61), poet. No. 1630, 4col, Alvaro Menendez Leal (1931-2000), dramatist. No. 1631, 4col, Roque Dalton (1935-75), poet. No. 1632, 5col, Pedro Geoffroy Rivas (1908-79), poet. No. 1633, 5col, Italo Lopez Vallecillos (1932-86), poet.

**2005, Oct. 20** *Perf. 14¼x14*

**1628-1633** A582 Set of 6 9.00 9.00

America Issue - Fight Against Poverty A583

Designs: 1.50col, Man holding food. 4col, Children and shack.

**2005, Nov. 25** *Perf. 14x14¼*

**1634-1635** A583 Set of 2 2.75 2.75

Christmas — A584

No. 1636 — Creche figures: a, Praying angel. b, Chicken and left half of star. c, Rooster and right half of star. d, Angel with horn. e, Donkey. f, Mary and Jesus. g, Joseph and two sheep. h, Cow. i, Camel with red saddle cloth and Magus. j, Camel without saddle and Magus. k, Camel with blue saddle cloth and Magus. l, Shepherd and three sheep. m, Woman, table and pot. n, Man and oxcart. o, Musicians. p, Bride, groom and church. q, Dog and kneeling woman. r, Sheep and shepherd holding lamb. s, Women with water jugs. t, Birds.

**2005, Nov. 30** *Perf. 14¼x14*

**1636** A584 Sheet of 20 8.00 8.00

*a.-t.* 1col Any single .40 .40

Diplomatic Relations Between El Salvador and Japan, 70th Anniv. A585

Designs: 2.50col, Flags of El Salvador and Japan, flowers, men shaking hands. 9col, Airport, medical worker and highway.

**2005, Dec. 20** *Perf. 14x14¼*

**1637-1638** A585 Set of 2 4.50 4.50

2006 Elections A586

Ballot box, flag and: 10col, José Mariano Calderón y San Martín. 25col, Miguel José de Castro y Lara.

**2006, Feb. 28**

**1639-1640** A586 Set of 2 12.50 12.50

TACA Airlines, 75th Anniv. A587

No. 1641 — Anniversary emblem, parrot and: a, Stinson airplane, Northern hemisphere. b, Airbus A-319, Southern hemisphere.

**2006, Mar. 31 Litho.** *Perf. 14x14¼*

**1641** A587 5col Vert. pair, #a-b 4.00 4.00

Laying of Cornerstone of Santa Ana Cathedral, Cent. — A588

Designs: 1.50col, Religious statues. 2.50col, Santa Ana Cathedral.

**2006, Apr. 28** *Perf. 14¼x14*

**1642-1643** A588 Set of 2 2.25 2.25

Flora and Fauna A589

No. 1644: a, Pteroglossus torquatus. b, Smyrna blonfildia. c, Hypanartia dione. d, Sciurus variegatoides. e, Ceiba pentandra. f, Ramphastos sulfuratus. g, Eunica tatila. h, Catonephele numilia. i, Mephitis macroura. j, Enterolobium cyclocarpum.

**2006, May 31** *Perf. 14x14¼*

**1644** Block of 10 6.00 6.00

*a.-j.* A589 1col Any single .60 .60

2006 World Cup Soccer Championships, Germany — A590

No. 1645 — Flags, landmarks and people from World Cup host nations: a, Argentina, 1978. b, Spain, 1982. c, Mexico, 1986. d, Italy, 1990.

No. 1646: a, United States, 1994. b, France, 1998. c, Korea and Japan, 2002. d, Germany, 2006.

4col, Soccer ball showing German flags, horiz.

**2006, June 29** *Perf. 14¼x14*

**1645** Horiz. strip of 4 3.50 3.50

*a.-d.* A590 2.20col Any single .85 .85

**1646** Horiz. strip of 4 4.25 4.25

*a.-d.* A590 2.70col Any single 1.00 1.00

**Souvenir Sheet**

***Rouletted 13¼***

**1647** A590 4col multi 2.50 2.50

Fossils A591

Designs: 1.50col, Mastodon skull. 1.60col, Vertebra of giant sloth. 5col, Mandible of giant sloth. 10col, Paw bones of giant sloth.

**2006, July 26** *Perf. 14¼x14*

**1648-1651** A591 Set of 4 7.25 7.25

Disaster Reduction A592

Intl. Year of Deserts and Desertification A593

**2006, Aug. 31**

**1652** A592 1.50col multi .60 .60

**1653** A593 4col multi 1.25 1.25

America Issue, Energy Conservation A594

Designs: 1.50col, Woman in kitchen. 4col, Light bulb and socket.

**2006, Sept. 29**

**1654-1655** A594 Set of 2 2.10 2.10

Republic of China National Day — A595

Designs: 9col, Taipei 101 Building. 10col, President's Mansion, Taipei.

**2006, Oct. 9**

**1656-1657** A595 Set of 2 8.00 8.00

La Constancia Industries, Cent. A596

**2006, Oct. 25** *Perf. 14x14¼*

**1658** A596 25col multi 10.50 10.50

Christmas A597

Designs: 1col, Our Lady of Candelaria. 1.50col, Our Lady of Carmen. 5col, Maria Auxiliadora. 10col, Our Lady of Peace.

**2006** *Perf. 14¼x14*
**1659-1662** A597 Set of 4 8.00 8.00

2007 Census A598

**2007, Mar. 26 Litho.** *Perf. 14¼x14*
**1663** A598 1c multi .30 .30

Social Peace Year — A599

**2007, May 3**
**1664** A599 $10 multi *30.00 30.00*

Scouting, Cent. A600

Designs: No. 1665, 10c, Lord Robert Baden-Powell blowing kudu horn. No. 1666, 10c, Salvadoran Scouts.

**2007, June 21 Litho.** *Perf. 14x14¼*
**1665-1666** A600 Set of 2 1.00 1.00

Miniature Sheet

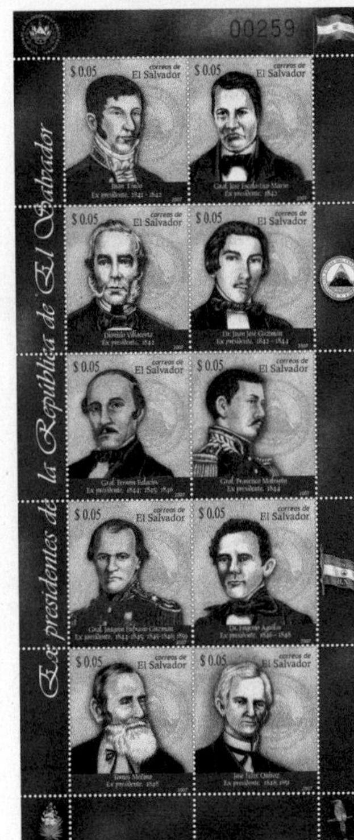

Salvadoran Presidents — A601

No. 1667: a, Juan Lindo, 1841-42. b, Gen. José Escolastico Marin, 1842. c, Dionisio Villacorta, 1842. d, Dr. Juan José Guzmán, 1842-44. e, Gen. Fermin Palacios, 1844, 1845, 1846. f, Gen. Francisco Malespin, 1844. g, Gen. Joaquin Eufrasio Guzmán, 1844-45, 1845-46, 1859. h, Dr. Eugenio Aguilar, 1846-48. i, Tomás Medina, 1848. j, José Felix Quiroz, 1848, 1851.

**2007, June 29** *Perf. 14¼x14*
**1667** A601 5c Sheet of 10, #a-j 2.50 2.50

Miniature Sheet

Fauna of Cobanos Reef — A602

No. 1668: a, Apogon dovii. b, Cirrhitus rivulatus. c, Holacanthus passer. d, Acanthurus xanthopterus. e, Thalassoma lucasanum. f, Diodon holocantus. g, Stegastes flavilatus. h, Amphiaster insignis. i, Hypselodoris agassizzi. j, Cypraecassis coarctata.

**2007, Aug. 9 Litho.** *Perf. 14x14¼*
**1668** A602 10c Sheet of 10, #a-j 4.00 4.00

El Mundo Newspaper, 40th Anniv. — A603

**2007, Sept. 12**
**1669** A603 $5 multi 17.50 17.50

Archaeology — A604

No. 1670: a, Terracotta figurine. b, Tazumal archaeological site. c, Joya de Cerén. d, San Andres Acropolis.

**2007, Oct. 5**
**1670** A604 25c Block or strip of 4, #a-d 3.50 3.50

America Issue, Education For All — A605

No. 1671 — Novels: a, El Cristo Negro, by Salarrué. b, Don Quixote de La Mancha, by Miguel de Cervantes.

**2007, Oct. 31**
**1671** A605 $1 Vert. pair, #a-b 7.00 7.00

Christmas — A606

No. 1672: a, Stars on ears of corn. b, Teddy bear and gifts under Christmas tree. c, People touching stars on Christmas tree. d, Candles.

**2007, Nov. 14**
**1672** A606 10c Block or strip of 4, #a-d 1.50 1.50

Popes A607

Designs: 1c, Pope John Paul II (1920-2005). 10c, Pope Benedict XVI.

**2007, Nov. 22** *Perf. 14x14¼*
**1673-1674** A607 Set of 2 1.00 1.00

Birds — A608

No. 1675: a, Bombycilla cedrorum. b, Colaptes auratus. c, Anas clypeata. d, Falco peregrinus.
50c, Passerina ciris, horiz.

**2007, Dec. 17** *Perf. 14¼x14*
**1675** A608 10c Block or strip of 4, #a-d 1.90 1.90

**Souvenir Sheet**

***Rouletted 10½***

**1676** A608 50c multi 2.00 2.00

Fire Fighting Corps in El Salvador, 125th Anniv. A609

No. 1677: a, Firemen and truck. b, Fire truck, cab facing right. c, Fire truck, cab facing left. d, Ambulance.

**2008, Feb. 15** *Perf. 14x14¼*
**1677** Vert. strip of 4 2.40 2.40
***a.-d.*** A609 15c Any single .60 .60

37th Lions International Latin America and Caribbean Forum — A610

**2008, Mar. 7**
**1678** A610 1c multi .55 .55

Miniature Sheets

Salvadoran Presidents — A611

No. 1679: a, Francisco Dueñas, 1851-52, 1852-54, 1856, 1863-71. b, Col. José María San Martín, 1852, 1854-56. c, Rafael Campo, 1856-58. d, Gen. Gerardo Barrios, 1858, 1859-60, 1861-63. e, Dr. Rafael Zaldívar,

1876-84, 1884-85. f, Gen. Fernando Figueroa, 1885, 1907-11. g, Gen. Francisco Menéndez, 1885-90. h, Gen. Carlos Ezeta, 1890-94. i, Gen. Rafael Antonio Gutiérrez, 1894-98. j, Gen. Tomás Regalado, 1898-1903. k, Pedro José Escalón, 1903-07. l, Dr. Manuel Enrique Araujo, 1911-13. m, Carlos Meléndez, 1913-14, 1915-18. n, Dr. Alfonso Quiñones Molina, 1914-15, 1918-19, 1923-27. o, Jorge Meléndez, 1919-23. p, Dr. Pío Romero Bosque, 1927-31. q, Arturo Araujo, 1931. r, Gen. Maximiliano Hernández Martínez, 1931-34, 1935-44. s, Gen. Salvador Castaneda Castro, 1945-48. t, Col. Oscar Osorio, 1950-56.

**2008, Apr. 30** *Perf. 14¼x14*
**1679** A611 10c Sheet of 20, #a-t 5.00 5.00

Friendship Between Israel and El Salvador, 60th Anniv. A612

**2008, May 29** *Perf. 14x14¼*
**1680** A612 10c multi .55 .55

2008 Summer Olympics, Beijing A613

No. 1681 — Salvadoran Olympic Committee emblem and: a, Cycling. b, Tennis. c, Weight lifting. d, Running.
50c, Judo, women's basketball, horiz.

**2008, July 3** *Perf. 14¼x14*
**1681** Horiz. strip of 4 2.00 2.00
*a.-d.* A613 20c Any single .40 .40

**Souvenir Sheet**
***Rouletted 10½***

**1682** A613 50c multi 2.00 2.00

Radio El Salvador, 82nd Anniv. A614

Designs: 25c, Engineer and radio control board. 65c, Radio equipment.

**2008, July 31** *Perf. 14¼x14*
**1683-1684** A614 Set of 2 2.25 2.25

Central American Integration System A615

**2008, Sept. 3** *Perf. 14x14¼*
**1685** A615 $5 multi 12.50 12.50

Villa Palestina A616

**2008, Sept. 4** *Perf. 14¼x14*
**1686** A616 5c multi .30 .30

Miniature Sheet

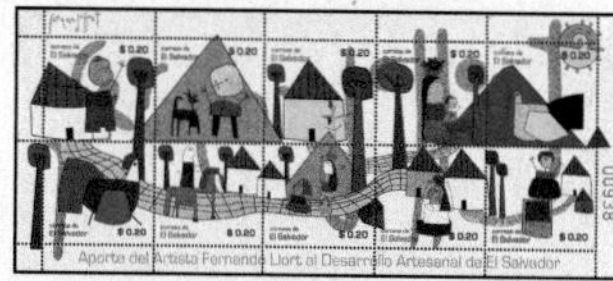

Art of Fernando Llort — A617

No. 1687 — Details: a, Man waving. b, Man and animal. c, House and trees. d, Woman with basket on head holding child. e, Turkey and sun. f, Rooster and path. g, Man on horse on path. h, Short and tall women on path. i, Woman with jug on head, houses. j, Woman at well.

**2008, Sept. 19** *Perf. 14x14¼*
**1687** A617 20c Sheet of 10, #a-j 5.00 5.00

Salvadoran Foundation for Economic Development, 25th Anniv. A618

**2008, Oct. 22** *Perf. 14¼x14*
**1688** A618 $1 multi 2.50 2.50

18th Iberoamerican Summit, El Salvador — A619

**2008, Oct. 27** *Perf. 14x14¼*
**1689** A619 $1 multi 2.50 2.50

America Issue, Festivals A620

Designs: 20c, Feria de las Palmas. 75c, Fiestas del Divino Salvador del Mundo.

**2008, Nov. 7**
**1690-1691** A620 Set of 2 3.00 3.00

Ministry of Exterior Relations, 150th Anniv. A621

**2009, Apr. 3** **Litho.** *Perf. 14x14¼*
**1692** A621 10c multi .30 .30

2009 Presidential Elections A622

**2009, May 4** *Perf. 14¼x14*
**1693** A622 10c multi .30 .30

Intl. Year of Astronomy A623

No. 1694: a, Galileo Galilei (1564-1642), astronomer. b, Planetary moons discovered by Galileo. c, San Jan Talpa Astronomical Observatory. d, Meade Schmidt-Cassegrain telescope.

**2009, May 27**
**1694** Horiz. strip of 4 2.50 2.50
*a.-d.* A623 25c Any single .50 .50

Miniature Sheets

National Symbols and Departmental Arms — A624

No. 1695, 10c: a, Eumomota superciliosa (national bird). b, Arms of Ahuachapan. c, Arms of Santa Ana. d, Arms of Sonsonate. e, Arms of La Libertad. f, Arms of Chalatenango. g, Arms of San Salvador. h, Arms of Cuscatlan.

No. 1696, 10c: a, Yucca elephantipes (national flower). b, Arms of La Paz. c, Arms of Cabañas. d, Arms of San Vicente. e, Arms of Usulutan. f, Arms of San Miguel. g, Arms of Morazan. h, Arms of La Union.

**2009, July 22** *Perf. 14¼x14*
**Sheets of 8, #a-h**

**1695-1696** A624 Set of 2 8.00 8.00

Tourism A625

No. 1697: a, Butterfly, flower, Sapo River. b, Cranes, Jaltepeque Estuary. c, Butterfly, flowers, San Vicente Volcano. d, Butterfly, flowers, La Unión shoreline.

No. 1698: a, Pottery vendor, building, Guatajiagua. b, Man in costume, street in Izalco. c, Orchids, El Caracol Waterfall, Arambala. d, Native American sculpture, building, Ilobasco.

**2009, Sept. 4** **Litho.** *Perf. 14x14¼*
**1697** Vert. strip of 4 1.00 1.00
*a.-d.* A625 5c Any single .25 .25
**1698** Vert. strip of 4 1.00 1.00
*a.-d.* A625 5c Any single .25 .25
*e.* Block of 8, ##1697a-1697d, 1698a-1698d 2.00 2.00

America Issue A626

No. 1699 — Children's games: a, Jump rope. b, Hopscotch.

**2009, Oct. 15**
**1699** A626 $1 Vert. pair, #a-b 5.50 5.50

Christmas A627

No. 1700: a, Candles, Bible passage, ornament. b, Madonna and child, star of Bethlehem, poinsettia. c, St. Joseph, lamb, dove, poinsettia. d, Magi, poinsettias, ornament.

**2009, Nov. 30** *Perf. 14¼x14*
**1700** Horiz. strip of 4 1.25 1.25
*a.-d.* A627 10c Any single .25 .25

A628

A629

Oscar A. Romero (1917-80), Assassinated Archbishop of San Salvador — A630

No. 1701: a, Romero with hand raised. b, Romero and silhouette.

No. 1702: a, Romero touching person's head. b, Romero over church.

No. 1703: a, Romero. b, Romero and Salvadoran people.

**2010, Mar. 19**

| | | | | |
|---|---|---|---|---|
| 1701 | A628 $1 Horiz. pair, #a-b | 5.00 | 5.00 |
| 1702 | A629 $1 Horiz. pair, #a-b | 5.00 | 5.00 |
| 1703 | A630 $1 Horiz. pair, #a-b | 5.00 | 5.00 |
| | *Nos. 1701-1703 (3)* | 15.00 | 15.00 |

City of San Vicente, 375th Anniv. — A631

No. 1704 — Arms and: a, Tempisque tree. b, Our Lady of Pilar Basilica.

50c, Cathedral and Tower of San Vicente.

**2010, Dec. 15** ***Perf. 14¼x14***

**1704** A631 $1 Horiz. pair, #a-b 6.00 6.00

**Souvenir Sheet**

***Rouletted 10x10½***

**1705** A631 50c multi 1.50 1.50

America Issue A632

No. 1706 — National symbols: a, Coat of arms. b, Flag.

**2010** ***Perf. 14x14¼***

**1706** A632 $1 Vert. pair, #a-b 5.75 5.75

Children's Day and Missing Children's Day — A633

Denominations: 10c, $1.

**2011, Mar. 25** ***Perf. 14¼x14***

**1707-1708** A633 Set of 2 3.50 3.50

First Call for Independence, Bicent. — A634

No. 1709: a, Bell and doves. b, José Matías Delgado (1767-1832), independence leader, with hand on book. c, Gen. Manuel José Arce (1787-1847), holding paper. d, Crowd of people.

No. 1710: a, Monument. b, Delgado and bell. c, Delgado and wreath. d, Arce and wreath.

**2011, June 7**

| | | | |
|---|---|---|---|
| **1709** | Horiz. strip of 4 | 6.25 | 6.25 |
| *a.-d.* | A634 50c Any single | 1.25 | 1.25 |
| **1710** | Horiz. strip of 4 | 6.25 | 6.25 |
| *a.-d.* | A634 50c Any single | 1.25 | 1.25 |

Salvadoran Anniversaries — A635

No. 1711: a, Dr. Sun Yat-sen (1866-1925), President of Republic of China. b, José Matías Delgado (1767-1832), Salvadoran independence leader.

**2011, Nov. 14**

**1711** A635 $1 Horiz. pair, #a-b 6.00 6.00

Diplomatic relations between El Salvador and Republic of China, cent. (#1711a), First call for Salvadoran independence, bicent. (#1711b).

America Issue — A636

No. 1712 — Mailbox with: a, Rounded top. b, Flat top.

**2011, Nov. 14**

**1712** A636 $1 Horiz. pair, #a-b 6.00 6.00

Diplomatic Relations Between El Salvador and Canada, 50th Anniv. — A637

No. 1713: a, Maple leaf, "50," map of El Salvador. b, Canada highlighted on map of North America with Canadian flag, arrows.

**2011, Dec. 7**

**1713** A637 $1 Horiz. pair, #a-b 6.00 6.00

Campaign Against Corruption A638

No. 1714: a, United Nations emblem in eye. b, Exchange of bribe money, emblem of Organization of American States. c, Magnifying glass over map of El Salvador, arms and flag of El Salvador.

**2011, Dec. 9**

| | | | |
|---|---|---|---|
| **1714** | Horiz. strip of 3 | 8.25 | 8.25 |
| *a.-c.* | A638 $1 Any single | 2.75 | 2.75 |

2012 Elections A639

No. 1715: a, Stylized dove. b, House as ballot box.

**2012, Mar. 6** ***Perf. 14x14¼***

**1715** A639 $1 Vert. pair, #a-b 5.25 5.25

Statues of St. John the Baptist — A640

No. 1716 — Statue in: a, Chalatenango Cathedral. b, Monte San Juan Church, Cuscatlán.

**2012, June 18** ***Perf. 14¼x14***

**1716** A640 $1 Horiz. pair, #a-b 5.25 5.25

Signing of Chapultapec Peace Accords, 20th Anniv. — A641

"XX" and: No. 1717, $1, Dove. No. 1718, $1, Doves, book, pen, hands with olive branch.

**2012, Sept. 14**

**1717-1718** A641 Set of 2 5.75 5.75

Cuscatlán Masonic Lodge, Cent. — A642

**2012, Sept. 18**

**1719** A642 $5 multi 13.00 13.00

America Issue — A643

No. 1720 — Myths and legends of: a, The White Dog. b, The Headless Priest.

**2012, Oct. 30**

**1720** A643 $1 Horiz. pair, #a-b 5.25 5.25

Animals and Their Pre-Columbian Ceramic Depictions — A644

No. 1721, 65c: a, Didelphis marsupialis. b, Pots depicting opossom, c. 900-1524.

No. 1722, $1: a, Panthera onca. b, Figurines depicting jaguars, c. 900-1524.

No. 1723, $5: Sylvilagus floridanus. b, Vessels depicting rabbits, c. 250-900.

No. 1724, $10: a, Ateles geoffroyi. b, Vessels depicting spider monkeys, c. 250-900.

**2013, May 14 Litho.** ***Perf. 14¼x14***

**Horiz. pairs, #a-b**

**1721-1724** A644 Set of 4 82.50 82.50

Salvadoran Air Force, 90th Anniv. — A645

Frame color: 65c, Purple. $1, Red brown.

**2013, Dec. 9 Litho.** ***Perf. 14¼x14***

**1725-1726** A645 Set of 2 3.50 3.50

Ciudad Mujer Women's Services Program A646

**2014, June 12 Litho.** ***Perf. 11***

**1727** A646 $1 multi 2.00 2.00

Archbishop Oscar Arnulfo Romero (1917-80) A647

**2014, June 23 Litho.** ***Perf. 11***

**1728** A647 65c multi 1.40 1.40

Renaming of El Salvador International Airport to honor Archbishop Romero.

National Association of the Sovereign Military of Malta, 40th Anniv. — A648

No. 1729: a, Rosales Hospital, San Salvador. b, Embassy of the Sovereign Military Order of Malta, Santa Elena.

**2014, June 25 Litho.** ***Perf. 11***

**1729** A648 20c Horiz. pair, #a-b .80 .80

University of El Salvador, 173rd Anniv. A649

**2014, Dec. 8 Litho. *Perf. 11***
**1730** A649 20c multi .40 .40

Diplomatic Relations Between El Salvador and Japan, 80th Anniv. — A650

No. 1731: a, 80th anniv. emblem. b, Children with Japanese and Salvadoran flags, 80th anniv. emblem.

**2015, Feb. 13 Litho. *Perf. 14¼x14***
**1731** A650 $2.50 Horiz. pair, #a-b 10.00 10.00

Beatification of Archbishop Oscar Romero (1917-80) A651

Designs: 5c, Romero wearing zucchetto. 10c, Romero wearing stole. 20c, Crypt. $1, Romero with children.

**2015, May 23 Litho. *Perf. 14¼x14***
**1732-1735** A651 Set of 4 2.75 2.75

Decree Declaring Name of Country as Republic of El Salvador, Cent. — A652

Denominations: $1, $5.

**2015, June 7 Litho. *Perf. 14¼x14***
**1736-1737** A652 Set of 2 12.00 12.00

Bonn Challenge to Restore Depleted and Deforested Lands — A653

Designs: 20c, Emblem. $1, Boat on Barra de Santiago.

**2015, Aug. 19 Litho. *Perf. 14¼x14***
**1738-1739** A653 Set of 2 2.40 2.40

Labor Union Day — A654

**2015, Oct. 30 Litho. *Perf. 11***
**1740** A654 3c multi .25 .25

Indigenous People A655

Mi Cultura emblem and: 5c, Group of women. 20c, People drinking.

**2015, Nov. 4 Litho. *Perf. 11***
**1741-1742** A655 Set of 2 .50 .50

Breastfeeding Help Center, 35th Anniv. A656

**2015, Nov. 11 Litho. *Perf. 11***
**1743** A656 20c multi .40 .40

Court of Accounts, 75th Anniv. A657

Designs: 5c, 75th anniv. emblem. 75c, Building.

**2015, Nov. 11 Litho. *Perf. 11***
**1744-1745** A657 Set of 2 1.60 1.60

Postal Service of El Salvador, 168th Anniv. A658

**2015, Nov. 18 Litho. *Perf. 11***
**1746** A658 $1 multi 2.00 2.00

Campaign to End Violence Against Women A659

**2015, Nov. 25 Litho. *Perf. 11***
**1747** A659 $2.50 multi 5.00 5.00

See Dominican Republic No. 1583, Ecuador No. 2173, Guatemala No. 717, Venezuela No. 1731.

Department of La Libertad, 150th Anniv. — A660

**2015, Nov. 26 Litho. *Perf. 11***
**1748** A660 1c multi .25 .25

Salvadoran Philatelic Association, 75th Anniv. — A661

**2015, Dec. 7 Litho. *Perf. 11***
**1749** A661 20c multi .40 .40

Archbishop Oscar Arnulfo Romero (1917-80) A662

Migrants and Archbishop Romero: $2.50, Wearing miter. $10, Without miter.

**2016, May 24 Litho. *Perf. 14¼x14***
**1750-1751** A662 Set of 2 25.00 25.00

National Day of Solidarity With People With HIV — A663

**2016, May 31 Litho. *Perf. 14¼x14***
**1752** A663 5c black & red .25 .25

Ernesto Antonio Claramount Rozeville (1924-2008), Presidential Candidate A664

Rozeville: 10c, Color photograph. 20c, Black-and-white photograph.

**2016, July 20 Litho. *Perf. 14¼x14***
**1753-1754** A664 Set of 2 .60 .60

National Police Force, 24th Anniv. — A665

Designs: 65c, Police cars. $1, Police officers.

**2016, Aug. 15 Litho. *Perf. 14¼x14***
**1755-1756** A665 Set of 2 3.50 3.50

Ties Between El Salvador and Republic of China — A666

Flags of El Salvador and Republic of China and: 20c, Tree, bird and volcano. 75c, Trees.

**2016, Oct. 14 Litho. *Perf. 14¼x14***
**1757-1758** A666 Set of 2 1.90 1.90

Enrique Drews (1844-1916), Orchestra Director A667

**2016, Oct. 31 Litho. *Perf. 14¼x14***
**1759** A667 $5 multi 10.00 10.00

Chapultepec Peace Accords, 25th Anniv. — A668

**2017, Jan. 13 Litho. *Perf. 14¼x14***
**1760** A668 25c multi .50 .50

Inter-American Defense Board, 75th Anniv. — A669

Map of North and South America and: 5c, Emblems of Inter-American Defense Board and Armed Forces of El Salvador. 20c, Map of El Salvador, emblems of Salvadoran Army, Air Force and Navy.

**2017, Mar. 30 Litho. *Perf. 11¾***
**1761-1762** A669 Set of 2 .50 .50

Heroic Soldier, Coat of Arms and Flag of El Salvador, Emblem of Salvadoran Armed Forces
A670

**2017, May 8** **Litho.** ***Perf. 11***
**1763** A670 10c multi .25 .25

First Postage Stamps of El Salvador, 150th Anniv. A671

Vignette color: 5c, Blue. 20c, Red. 75c, Green. $1, Brown.

***Perf. 11¾ Rough***
**2017, May 26** **Litho.**
**1764-1767** A671 Set of 4 4.00 4.00

National Civil Police, 25th Anniv. — A672

**2017, Aug. 14** **Litho.** ***Perf. 11¾***
**1768** A672 10c multi .25 .25

National Theater A673

National Palace A674

No. 1769 — National Theater: a, Entrance. b, View of ceiling. c, Corner of building. d, View of stage from balcony.
No. 1770 — National Palace: a, Entrance, three windows on top floor on each side of outer pillars. b, Room with tables. c, Entrance, seven windows on top floor on each side of outer pillars. d, Room without tables.

**2017, Aug. 23** **Litho.** ***Perf. 11¾***
**1769** Vert. strip of 4 8.00 8.00
***a.-d.*** A673 $1 Any single 2.00 2.00
**1770** Vert. strip of 4 8.00 8.00
***a.-d.*** A674 $1 Any single 2.00 2.00

Independence, 196th Anniv. — A675

**2017, Sept. 12** **Litho.** ***Perf. 11¾***
**1771** A675 20c multi .40 .40

Christmas A676

**2017, Nov. 13** **Litho.** ***Perf. 11¾***
**1772** A676 50c multi 1.00 1.00

Writers A677

No. 1773: a, Hugo Lindo (1917-85). b, Matilde Elena López (1919-2010). c, Salvador Salazar Arrué (1899-1975). d, Lilian Jiménez. e, Francisco Gavidia (1863-1955).

**2017, Dec. 6** **Litho.** ***Perf. 11¾***
**1773** Horiz. strip of 5 10.00 10.00
***a.-e.*** A677 $1 Any single 2.00 2.00

History of Aeronautics in El Salvador — A678

Designs: 5c, Emblem of International Civil Aviation Organization. 10c, Airplane carrying mail, 1928. 20c, Airplane of Father Domingo Lara. 75c, Enrico Massi (1897-1923), and his airplane.

**2017, Dec. 7** **Litho.** ***Perf. 11¾***
**1774-1777** A678 Set of 4 2.25 2.25

Japanese International Cooperation Agency, 50th Anniv. in El Salvador — A679

Denominations: 5c, 75c.

**2018, Jan. 8** **Litho.** ***Perf. 11¾***
**1778-1779** A679 Set of 2 1.60 1.60

2018 Elections A680

**2018, Mar. 1** **Litho.** ***Perf. 11¾***
**1780** A680 $1 multi 2.00 2.00

Chancellery of El Salvador, 160th Anniv. — A681

**2018, June 25** **Litho.** ***Perf. 14¼x14***
**1781** A681 $10 multi 20.00 20.00

Alberto Masferrer (1868-1932), Writer — A682

**2018, July 24** **Litho.** ***Perf. 14x14¼***
**1782** A682 50c multi 1.00 1.00

National Civil Police Force, 26th Anniv. A683

**2018, Aug. 13** **Litho.** ***Perf. 14x14¼***
**1783** A683 $2.50 multi 5.00 5.00

Society of Mary, 200th Anniv. (in 2016) — A684

**2018, Aug. 17** **Litho.** ***Perf. 14¼x14***
**1784** A684 $1 multi 2.00 2.00

Literacy Campaign A685

**2018, Sept. 7** **Litho.** ***Perf. 14¼x14***
**1785** A685 5c multi .25 .25

Athenaeum of El Salvador, 106th Anniv. — A686

**2018, Sept. 20** **Litho.** ***Perf. 14¼x14***
**1786** A686 75c multi 1.50 1.50

Chirajito (1936-2010), Clown — A687

**2018, Sept. 24** **Litho.** ***Perf. 14x14¼***
**1787** A687 25c multi .50 .50

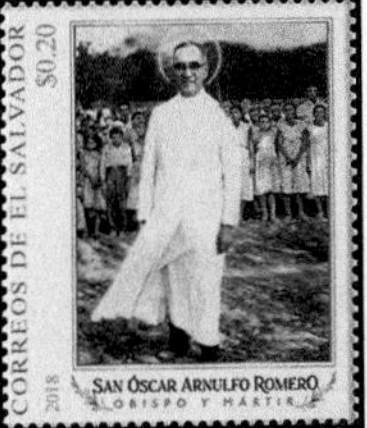


Canonization of St. Oscar Romero (1917-80) A688

Various depictions of St. Oscar Romero, 20c, 25c, 50c, $1.

**2018, Oct. 3** **Litho.** ***Perf. 14¼x14***
**1788-1791** A688 Set of 4 4.00 4.00

A689

**2018, Oct. 17** **Litho.** ***Perf. 14x14¼***
**1792** A689 $1 multi 2.00 2.00

Awarding of Universal Postal Union silver quality award to El Salvador for Express Mail Service.

Port and Maritime Authority, 16th Anniv. A690

**2018, Oct. 26** **Litho.** ***Perf. 14x14¼***
**1793** A690 50c multi 1.00 1.00

Military History Center, 25th Anniv. — A691

**2018, Oct. 30** **Litho.** ***Perf. 14¼x14***
**1794** A691 $1 multi 2.00 2.00

A692

A693

A694

A695

El Salvador Travel Sites, Emblems and Slogans
A696

**2018, Nov. 16 Litho. *Perf. 14x14¼***

| | | | |
|---|---|---|---|
| **1795** | Horiz. strip of 5 | 1.25 | 1.25 |
| *a.* | A692 10c multi | .25 | .25 |
| *b.* | A693 10c multi | .25 | .25 |
| *c.* | A694 10c multi | .25 | .25 |
| *d.* | A695 10c multi | .25 | .25 |
| *e.* | A696 10c multi | .25 | .25 |

José Arturo Castellanos (1893-1977), Diplomat Who Saved Jews in World War II — A697

**2018, Nov. 16 Litho. *Perf. 14x14¼***

**1796** A697 $5 multi 10.00 10.00

Suchitoto Tourist Attractions
A698

No. 1797: a, Los Tercios Waterfall. b, Alejandro Cotto Theater. c, Art Center for Peace (Centro Arte para la Paz). d, Lake Suchitlán. e, Santa Lucía Church.

**2018, Dec. Litho. *Perf. 14x14¼***

| | | | |
|---|---|---|---|
| **1797** | Horiz. strip of 5 | 7.50 | 7.50 |
| *a.-e.* | A698 75c Any single | 1.50 | 1.50 |

Fe y Alegria Association in El Salvador, 50th Anniv. — A700

**2019, Nov. 4 Litho. *Perf. 14¼x14***

**1799** A700 $1 multi 2.00 2.00

Christmas
A701

**2019, Nov. 4 Litho. *Perf. 14¼x14***

**1800** A701 50c multi 1.00 1.00

Surfing Beaches
A702

No. 1801: a, Playa El Sunzal. b, Playa Punta Roca. c, Playa El Zonte. d, Playa Las Flores. e, Playa El Tunco.

**2019, Nov. 8 Litho. *Perf. 14x14¼***

| | | | |
|---|---|---|---|
| **1801** | Horiz. strip of 5 | 10.00 | 10.00 |
| *a.-e.* | A702 $1 Any single | 2.00 | 2.00 |

First Man on the Moon, 50th Anniv.
A703

**2019, Nov. 7 Litho. *Perf. 14x14¼***

**1802** A703 $5 multi 10.00 10.00

Universal Postal Union, 145th Anniv.
A704

Denominations: 50c, $1.

**2019, Nov. 13 Litho. *Perf. 14x14¼***

**1803-1804** A704 Set of 2 3.00 3.00

A705

Baptist College, Santa Ana, Cent.
A706

**2019, Nov. 14 Litho. *Perf. 14x14¼***

| | | | |
|---|---|---|---|
| **1805** | A705 $1 multi | 2.00 | 2.00 |
| **1806** | A706 $1 multi | 2.00 | 2.00 |

America Issue
A707

**2019, Nov. 19 Litho. *Perf. 14x14¼***

**1807** A707 $1 multi 2.00 2.00

Express Mail Service, 20th Anniv.
A708

**2019, Nov. 21 Litho. *Perf. 14x14¼***

**1808** A708 20c multi .40 .40

Technological University of El Salvador Anthropology Museum and Emigrants — A709

**2019, Dec. 6 Litho. *Perf. 14x14¼***

**1809** A709 $2.50 multi 5.00 5.00

Development Bank of El Salvador, 25th Anniv. — A710

**2019, Dec. 11 Litho. *Perf. 14x14¼***

**1810** A710 $2.50 multi 5.00 5.00

Salvadoran Social Security Institute, 50th Anniv.
A711

**2019, Dec. 12 Litho. *Perf. 14x14¼***

**1811** A711 $2.50 multi 5.00 5.00

Blue-crowned Motmot
A712

**2019, Dec. 17 Litho. *Perf. 14¼x14***

**1812** A712 5c multi .25 .25

Volcanoes
A713

Designs: 5c, Izalco Volcano. 10c, San Miguel Volcano. 20c, San Salvador Volcano. 25c, Santa Ana Volcano. 50c, Tecapa Volcano.

**2019, Dec. 17 Litho. *Perf. 14x14¼***

**1813-1817** A713 Set of 5 2.25 2.25

Route of the Flowers
A714

No. 1818 — Destinations along the Route of the Flowers: a, Concepción de Ataco. b, Nahuizalco. c, Salcoatitán. d, Juayúa. e, Apaneca.

**2019, Dec. 17 Litho. *Perf. 14x14¼***

| | | | |
|---|---|---|---|
| **1818** | Horiz. strip of 5 | 2.50 | 2.50 |
| *a.-e.* | A714 25c Any single | .50 | .50 |

Aquatic Parks
A715

Designs: 50c, Los Chorros. 65c, Atecozol. 75c, Ichanmichen. $1, Apulo.

**2019, Dec. 17 Litho. *Perf. 14x14¼***

**1819-1822** A715 Set of 4 6.00 6.00

Proposed Pacific Train Project
A716

**2019, Dec. 18 Litho. *Perf. 14x14¼***

**1823** A716 $10 multi 20.00 20.00

Sacred Heart College, San Salvador, 125th Anniv. — A717

**2020, Jan. 6 Litho. *Perf. 14¼x14***

**1824** A717 $2.50 multi 5.00 5.00

Roque Dalton (1935-75), Poet A718

**2020, Mar. 9 Litho. *Perf. 14x14¼***
**1825** A718 5c multi .25 .25

## AIR POST STAMPS

Regular Issue of 1924-25 Overprinted in Black or Red

Back of No. C1

First Printing.
15c on 10c: "15 QUINCE 15" measures 22½mm.
20c: Shows on the back of the stamp an albino impression of the 50c surcharge.
25c on 35c: Original value canceled by a long and short bar.
40c on 50c: Only one printing.
50c on 1col: Surcharge in dull orange red.

***Perf. 12½, 14***
**1929, Dec. 28 Unwmk.**
**C1** A112 20c dp green (Bk) 6.00 5.00
*a.* Red overprint 850.00 850.00

Counterfeits exist of No. C1a.

### Additional Surcharge of New Values and Bars in Black or Red

No. C3

No. C4

No. C5

**C3** A111 15c on 10c org 1.10 1.10
*a.* "ALTANT CO" 37.50 35.00
**C4** A114 25c on 35c scar & grn 2.50 2.25
*a.* Bars inverted 10.00 10.00
**C5** A115 40c on 50c org brn .85 .55
**C6** A116 50c on 1col grn & bl vio (R) 15.00 10.00
*Nos. C1-C6 (5)* 25.45 18.90

No. C7

Back of No. C7

No. C9

No. C10

Second Printing.
15c on 10c: "15 QUINCE 15" measures 20½mm.
20c: Has not the albino impression on the back of the stamp.
25c on 35c: Original value cancelled by two bars of equal length.
50c on 1col: Surcharge in carmine rose.

**1930, Jan. 10**
**C7** A112 20c deep green 1.00 1.00
**C8** A111 15c on 10c org .75 .75
*a.* "ATLANT CO" 37.50 35.00
*b.* Double surcharge 20.00
*c.* As "a," double surcharge 75.00
*d.* Pair, one without surcharge *175.00*
**C9** A114 25c on 35c scar & grn .90 .90
**C10** A116 50c on 1col grn & bl vio (C) 2.00 2.00
*a.* Without bars over "UN COLON" 4.50
*b.* As "a," without block over "1" 4.50
*Nos. C7-C10 (4)* 4.65 4.65

Numerous wrong font and defective letters exist in both printings of the surcharges.
No. C10 with black surcharge is bogus.

Mail Plane over San Salvador AP1

**1930, Sept. 15 Engr. *Perf. 12½***
**C11** AP1 15c deep red .40 .25
**C12** AP1 20c emerald .40 .25
**C13** AP1 25c brown violet .40 .25
**C14** AP1 40c ultra .60 .25
*Nos. C11-C14 (4)* 1.80 1.00

Simón Bolivar — AP2

**1930, Dec. 17 Litho. *Perf. 11½***
**C15** AP2 15c deep red 6.00 5.00
*a.* "15" double 82.50
**C16** AP2 20c emerald 6.00 5.00
**C17** AP2 25c brown violet 6.00 5.00
*a.* Vert. pair, imperf. btwn. 175.00
*b.* Imperf., pair
**C18** AP2 40c dp ultra 6.00 5.00
*Nos. C15-C18 (4)* 24.00 20.00

Centenary of death of Simón Bolivar. Counterfeits of Nos. C15-C18 exist.

No. 504 Overprinted in Red

**1931, June 29 Engr. *Perf. 14***
**C19** A116 1col green & vio 4.50 3.00

Tower of La Merced Church — AP3

**1931, Nov. 5 Litho. *Perf. 11½***
**C20** AP3 15c dark red 4.50 3.25
*a.* Imperf., pair 50.00
**C21** AP3 20c blue green 4.50 3.25
**C22** AP3 25c dull violet 4.50 3.25
*a.* Vert. pair, imperf. btwn. 110.00
**C23** AP3 40c ultra 4.50 3.25
*a.* Imperf., pair 60.00
*Nos. C20-C23 (4)* 18.00 13.00

120th anniv. of the 1st movement toward the political independence of El Salvador. In the tower of La Merced Church (AP3) hangs the bell which José Matias Delgado-called the Father of his Country-rang to initiate the movement for liberty.

José Matias Delgado — AP4

**1932, Nov. 12 Wmk. 271 *Perf. 12½***
**C24** AP4 15c dull red & vio 1.25 1.10
**C25** AP4 20c blue grn & bl 1.60 1.40
**C26** AP4 25c dull vio & brn 1.60 1.40
**C27** AP4 40c ultra & grn 1.90 1.75
*Nos. C24-C27 (4)* 6.35 5.65

1st centenary of the death of Father José Matías Delgado, who is known as the Father of El Salvadoran Political Emancipation.
Nos. C24-C27 show cheek without shading in the 72nd stamp of each sheet.

Airplane and Caravels of Columbus — AP5

**1933, Oct. 12 Wmk. 240 *Perf. 13***
**C28** AP5 15c red orange 2.00 1.75
**C29** AP5 20c blue green 3.00 2.50
**C30** AP5 25c lilac 3.00 2.50
**C31** AP5 40c ultra 3.00 2.50
**C32** AP5 1col black 3.00 2.50
*Nos. C28-C32 (5)* 14.00 11.75

Saling of Chistopher Columbus from Palos, Spain, for the New World, 441st anniv.

### Police Barracks Type

**1934, Dec. 16 *Perf. 12½***
**C33** A123 25c lilac .60 .25
**C34** A123 30c brown .95 .45
*a.* Imperf., pair 80.00
**C35** A123 1col black 2.40 1.00
*Nos. C33-C35 (3)* 3.95 1.70

Runner AP7

**1935, Mar. 16 Engr. Unwmk.**
**C36** AP7 15c carmine 3.75 2.25
**C37** AP7 25c violet 3.75 2.25
**C38** AP7 30c brown 3.00 1.75
**C39** AP7 55c blue 20.00 8.50
**C40** AP7 1col black 13.00 8.00
*Nos. C36-C40 (5)* 43.50 22.75

Third Central American Games.
For overprints and surcharge see Nos. C41-C45, C53.

### Nos. C36-C40 Overprinted in Black

**1935, June 27**
**C41** AP7 15c carmine 3.00 1.40
**C42** AP7 25c violet 3.00 1.40
**C43** AP7 30c brown 3.00 1.40
**C44** AP7 55c blue 17.00 14.00
**C45** AP7 1col black 7.50 6.00
*Nos. C41-C45 (5)* 33.50 24.20

### Flag of El Salvador Type

**1935, Oct. 26 Litho. Wmk. 240**
**C46** A125 30c black brown .40 .35

### Tree of San Vicente Type

**1935, Dec. 26 *Perf. 12½***
**Numerals in Black, Tree in Yellow Green**
**C47** A126 10c orange .75 .60
**C48** A126 15c brown .75 .60
**C49** A126 20c dk blue grn .75 .60
**C50** A126 25c dark purple .75 .60
**C51** A126 30c black brown .75 .60
*Nos. C47-C51 (5)* 3.75 3.00

Tercentenary of San Vicente.

No. 565 Overprinted in Red

**1937 Engr. Unwmk.**
**C52** A133 15c dk olive bis .35 .25
*a.* Double overprint 25.00

No. C44 Surcharged in Red

**C53** AP7 30c on 55c blue 1.50 .60

Panchimalco Church — AP10

**1937, Dec. 3 Engr. *Perf. 12***
**C54** AP10 15c orange yel .30 .25
**C55** AP10 20c green .30 .25
**C56** AP10 25c violet .30 .25
**C57** AP10 30c brown .30 .25
**C58** AP10 40c blue .30 .25
**C59** AP10 1col black 1.40 .45
**C60** AP10 5col rose carmine 4.50 3.25
*Nos. C54-C60 (7)* 7.40 4.95

### US Constitution Type of Regular Issue

**1938, Apr. 22 Engr. & Litho.**
**C61** A136 30c multicolored .95 .70

José Simeón Cañas y Villacorta — AP12

**1938, Aug. 18** **Engr.**

**C62** AP12 15c orange 1.40 1.25
**C63** AP12 20c brt green 1.75 1.25
**C64** AP12 30c redsh brown 1.90 1.25
**C65** AP12 1col black 6.00 4.50
*Nos. C62-C65 (4)* 11.05 8.25

José Simeón Cañas y Villacorta (1767-1838), liberator of slaves in Central America.

Golden Gate Bridge, San Francisco Bay — AP13

**1939, Apr. 14** ***Perf. 12½***

**C66** AP13 15c dull yel & blk .45 .25
**C67** AP13 30c dk brown & blk .45 .25
**C68** AP13 40c dk blue & blk .60 .45
*Nos. C66-C68 (3)* 1.50 .95

Golden Gate Intl. Exposition, San Francisco.
For surcharges see Nos. C86-C91.

**Sir Rowland Hill Type**

**1940, Mar. 1** **Engr.**

**C69** A146 30c dk brn, buff & blk 8.00 2.50
**C70** A146 80c org red & blk 22.50 17.50

Centenary of the postage stamp. Covers postmarked Feb. 29 were predated. Actual first day was Mar. 1.

Map of the Americas, Figure of Peace, Plane — AP15

**1940, May 22** ***Perf. 12***

**C71** AP15 30c brown & blue .45 .25
**C72** AP15 80c dk rose & blk .85 .55

Pan American Union, 50th anniversary.

Coffee Tree in Bloom — AP16

Coffee Tree with Ripe Berries — AP17

**1940, Nov. 27**

**C73** AP16 15c yellow orange 1.60 .45
**C74** AP16 20c deep green 2.25 .45
**C75** AP16 25c dark violet 2.50 .55
**C76** AP17 30c copper brown 3.00 .25
**C77** AP17 1col black 9.00 .70
*Nos. C73-C77 (5)* 18.35 2.40

Juan Lindo, Gen. Francisco Malespin and New National University of El Salvador — AP18

Designs (portraits changed): 40c, 80c, Narciso Monterey and Antonio José Canas. 60c, 1col, Isidro Menéndez and Chrisanto Salazar.

**1941, Feb. 16** ***Perf. 12½***

**C78** AP18 20c dk grn & rose lake 1.25 .70
**C79** AP18 40c ind & brn org 1.25 .70
**C80** AP18 60c dl pur & brn 1.40 .70
**C81** AP18 80c hn brn & dk bl grn 3.00 2.00
**C82** AP18 1col black & org 3.00 2.00
**C83** AP18 2col yel org & rose vio 3.00 2.00
*a.* Min. sheet of 6, #C78-C83, perf. 11½ 15.00 15.00
*Nos. C78-C83 (6)* 12.90 8.10

Centenary of University of El Salvador.
Stamps from No. C83a, perf. 11½, sell for about the same values as the perf. 12½ stamps.

**Catalogue values for unused stamps in this section, from this point to the end of the section, are for Never Hinged items.**

Map of El Salvador AP20

**Wmk. 269**

**1942, Nov. 25** **Engr.** ***Perf. 14***

**C85** AP20 30c red orange .80 .45
*a.* Horiz. pair, imperf. between 100.00

1st Eucharistic Cong. of El Salvador. See #588.

**Nos. C66-C68 Surcharged in Dark Carmine**

**1943** **Unwmk.** ***Perf. 12½***

**C86** AP13 15c on 15c dl yel & blk .45 .25
**C87** AP13 20c on 30c dk brn & blk .60 .45
**C88** AP13 25c on 40c dk bl & blk 1.25 .75
*Nos. C86-C88 (3)* 2.30 1.45

**Nos. C66-C68 Surcharged in Dark Carmine**

**1944**

**C89** AP13 15c on 15c dl yel & blk .45 .25
**C90** AP13 20c on 30c dk brn & blk .75 .45
**C91** AP13 25c on 40c dk bl & blk 1.25 .45
*Nos. C89-C91 (3)* 2.45 1.15

**Bridge Type of Regular Issue Arms Overprint at Right in Blue Violet**

**1944, Nov. 24** **Engr.**

**C92** A149 30c crim rose & blk .45 .25

No. C92 exists without overprint, but was not issued in that form.

Presidential Palace AP22

National Theater AP23

National Palace AP24

**1944, Dec. 22** ***Perf. 12½***

**C93** AP22 15c red violet .25 .25
**C94** AP23 20c dk blue grn .25 .25
**C95** AP24 25c dull violet .25 .25
*Nos. C93-C95 (3)* .75 .75

For surcharge and overprint see Nos. C145-C146.

No. 582 Overprinted in Red

**1945, Aug. 23** ***Perf. 12***

**C96** A137 1col black 1.00 .25

Juan Ramon Uriarte — AP25

**Wmk. 240**

**1946, Jan. 1** **Typo.** ***Perf. 12½***

**C97** AP25 12c brt blue .45 .25
**C98** AP25 14c deep orange .45 .25

Mayan Pyramid, St. Andrés Plantation AP26

Municipal Children's Garden, San Salvador AP27

Civil Aeronautics School, Ilopango Airport AP28

**1946, May 1** **Unwmk.**

**C99** AP26 30c rose carmine .45 .25
**C100** AP27 40c deep ultra .45 .45
**C101** AP28 1col black 1.50 .45
*Nos. C99-C101 (3)* 2.40 1.15

For surcharge see No. C121.

Alberto Masferrer — AP29

**1946, July 19** **Litho.** **Wmk. 240**

**C102** AP29 12c carmine .45 .25
**C103** AP29 14c dull green .45 .25
*a.* Imperf., pair 12.50

Souvenir Sheets

AP30

Designs: 40c, Charles I of Spain. 60c, Juan Manuel Rodriguez. 1col, Arms of San Salvador. 2col, Flag of El Salvador.

***Perf. 12, Imperf.***

**1946, Nov. 8** **Engr.** **Unwmk.**

**C104** AP30 Sheet of 4 4.50 4.50
*a.* 40c brown 1.00 1.00
*b.* 60c carmine 1.00 1.00
*c.* 1col green 1.00 1.00
*d.* 2col ultramarine 1.00 1.00

4th cent. of San Salvador's city charter. The imperf. sheets are without gum.

Felipe Soto — AP31

Alfredo Espino — AP32

**Wmk. 240**

**1947, Sept. 11** **Litho.** ***Perf. 12½***

**C106** AP31 12c chocolate .25 .25
**C107** AP32 14c blue .25 .25

For surcharges see Nos. 627-630.

**Arce Type of Regular Issue**

**1948, Feb. 26** **Engr.** **Unwmk.**

**C108** A163 12c green .25 .25
**C109** A163 14c rose carmine .45 .25
**C110** A163 1col violet 3.25 2.00
*Nos. C108-C110 (3)* 3.95 2.50

Cent. of the death of Manuel José Arce (1783-1847). "Father of Independence" and 1st pres. of the Federation of Central America.

**Roosevelt Types of Regular Issue**

Designs: 12c, Pres. Franklin D. Roosevelt. 14c, Pres. Roosevelt presenting awards for distinguished service. 20c, Roosevelt and Cordell Hull. 25c, Pres. and Mrs. Roosevelt. 1col, Mackenzie King, Roosevelt and Winston Churchill. 2col, Funeral of Pres. Roosevelt. 4col, Pres. and Mrs. Roosevelt.

**1948, Apr. 12 Engr. *Perf. 12½***
**Various Frames, Center in Black**

C111 A165 12c green .60 .45
C112 A164 14c olive .60 .45
C113 A164 20c chocolate .60 .45
C114 A164 25c carmine .60 .45
C115 A164 1col violet brn 2.25 1.10
C116 A164 2col blue violet 3.25 1.75
*Nos. C111-C116 (6)* 7.90 4.65

**Souvenir Sheet**
***Perf. 13½***

C117 A166 4col gray & brn 5.50 3.75

Nos. 599, 601 and 604 Overprinted in Carmine or Black

**1948, Sept. 7 *Perf. 12½***

C118 A154 5c slate gray .25 .25
C119 A154 10c bister brown .25 .25
C120 A154 1col scarlet (Bk) 1.90 .60
*Nos. C118-C120 (3)* 2.40 1.10

No. C99 Surcharged in Black

**1949, July 23**

C121 AP26 10(c) on 30c rose car .25 .25

**UPU Type of Regular Issue**
**1949, Oct. 9 Engr. *Perf. 12½***

C122 A167 5c brown .60 .25
C123 A167 10c black .85 .25
C124 A167 1col purple 24.00 17.50
*Nos. C122-C124 (3)* 25.45 18.00

Flag and Arms of El Salvador — AP38

**1949, Dec. 15 *Perf. 10½***
**Flag and Arms in Blue, Yellow and Green**

C125 AP38 5c ocher .25 .25
C126 AP38 10c dk green .25 .25
a. Yellow omitted 25.00
C127 AP38 15c violet .45 .25
C128 AP38 1col rose .95 .55
C129 AP38 5col red violet 7.50 5.50
*Nos. C125-C129 (5)* 9.40 6.80

1st anniv. of the Revolution of 12/14/48.

Isabella I of Spain — AP39

**1951, Apr. 28 Litho. Unwmk.**
**Background in Ultramarine, Red and Yellow**

C130 AP39 10c green .40 .25
C131 AP39 20c purple .40 .25
a. Horiz. pair, imperf. between 25.00
C132 AP39 40c rose carmine .55 .25
C133 AP39 1col black brown 1.75 .65
*Nos. C130-C133 (4)* 3.10 1.40

500th anniv. of the birth of Queen Isabella I of Spain. Nos. C130-C133 exist imperforate.

Flag, Torch and Scroll — AP40

**1952, Feb. 14 Photo. *Perf. 11½***
**Flag in Blue**

C134 AP40 10c brt blue .25 .25
C135 AP40 15c chocolate .25 .25
C136 AP40 20c deep blue .25 .25
C137 AP40 25c gray .25 .25
C138 AP40 40c purple .40 .25
C139 AP40 1col red orange 1.10 .60
C140 AP40 2col orange brn 3.25 2.50
C141 AP40 5col violet blue 3.25 1.40
*Nos. C134-C141 (8)* 9.00 5.75

Constitution of 1950.

**Marti Type of Regular Issue Inscribed "Aereo"**
**1953, Feb. 27 Litho. *Perf. 10½***

C142 A170 10c dk purple .30 .25
C143 A170 20c dull brown .45 .25
C144 A170 1col dull orange 1.50 .60
*Nos. C142-C144 (3)* 2.25 1.10

**No. C95 Surcharged "C 0.20" and Obliterations in Red**
**1953, Mar. 20 *Perf. 12½***

C145 AP24 20c on 25c dl vio .30 .25

No. C95 Overprinted in Carmine

**1953, June 19**

C146 AP24 25c dull violet .55 .25

See note after No. 634.

Bell Tower, La Merced Church AP42

**1953, Sept. 15 *Perf. 11½***

C147 AP42 5c rose pink .25 .25
C148 AP42 10c dp blue grn .25 .25
C149 AP42 20c blue .30 .30
C150 AP42 1col purple 1.25 .65
*Nos. C147-C150 (4)* 2.05 1.45

132nd anniv. of the Act of Independence, Sept. 15, 1821.

**Postage Types and**

Fishing Boats — AP43

Gen. Manuel José Arce — AP44

ODECA Officials and Flag AP46

No. C155, National Palace. No. C157, Coast guard boat. No. C158, Lake Ilopango. No. C160, Guayabo dam. No. C161, Housing development. No. C162, Modern highway. No. C164, Izalco volcano.

***Perf. 11½***
**1954, June 1 Unwmk. Photo.**

C151 AP43 5c org brn & cr .30 .25
C152 A175 5c brt carmine .30 .25
C153 AP44 10c gray blue .40 .25
C154 A176 10c pur & lt brn .40 .25
C155 AP43 10c ol & bl gray .40 .25
C156 AP46 10c bl grn, dk grn & bl .40 .25
C157 A173 10c rose carmine .40 .25
C158 A173 15c dk gray .55 .25
C159 A173 20c pur & gray .55 .25
C160 AP46 25c bl grn & bl .75 .25
C161 AP46 30c mag & sal .75 .25
C162 A176 40c brt org & brn 1.00 .35
C163 A174 80c red brown 2.00 1.25
C164 AP43 1col magenta & sal 2.25 1.25
C165 A174 2col orange 4.50 1.25
*Nos. C151-C165 (15)* 14.95 6.85

**Barrios Type of Regular Issue**
**Wmk. 269**
**1955, Dec. 20 Engr. *Perf. 12½***

C166 A177 20c brown .35 .30
C167 A177 30c dp red lilac .35 .35

**Santa Ana Type of Regular Issue**
***Perf. 13½***
**1956, June 20 Unwmk. Litho.**

C168 A178 5c orange brown .25 .25
C169 A178 10c green .25 .25
C170 A178 40c red lilac .30 .25
C171 A178 80c emerald .90 .55
C172 A178 5col gray blue 4.50 2.50
*Nos. C168-C172 (5)* 6.20 3.80

For overprint see No. C187.

**Chalatenango Type of Regular Issue**
**1956, Sept. 14**

C173 A179 10c brt rose .25 .25
C174 A179 15c orange .25 .25
C175 A179 20c lt olive grn .25 .25
C176 A179 25c dull purple .45 .25
C177 A179 50c orange brn .70 .45
C178 A179 1col brt vio bl 1.00 .90
*Nos. C173-C178 (6)* 2.90 2.35

**Nueva San Salvador Type**
**Wmk. 269**
**1957, Jan. 3 Engr. *Perf. 12½***

C179 A180 10c pink .25 .25
C180 A180 20c dull red .25 .25
C181 A180 50c pale org red .40 .25
C182 A180 1col lt green .90 .50
C183 A180 2col orange red 2.50 1.25
*Nos. C179-C183 (5)* 4.30 2.50

For overprints see Nos. C195, C198.

**Lemus' Visit Type of Regular Issue**
***Perf. 11½***
**1959, Dec. 14 Unwmk. Photo.**
**Granite Paper**
**Design in Ultramarine, Dark Brown Light Brown and Red**

C184 A182 15c red .25 .25
C185 A182 20c green .30 .25
C186 A182 30c carmine .25 .25
*Nos. C184-C186 (3)* .80 .75

**No. C169 Overprinted in Red: "ANO MUNDIAL DE LOS REFUGIADOS 1959-1960"**
**1960, Apr. 7 Litho. *Perf. 13½***

C187 A178 10c green .35 .25

World Refugee Year, 7/1/59-6/30/60.

**Poinsettia Type of Regular Issue**
***Perf. 11½***
**1960, Dec. 17 Unwmk. Photo.**
**Granite Paper**
**Design in Slate Green, Red and Yellow**

C188 A184 20c rose lilac .35 .25
C189 A184 30c gray .40 .35
C190 A184 40c light gray .60 .25
C191 A184 50c salmon pink .95 .45
*Nos. C188-C191 (4)* 2.30 1.30

**Miniature Sheet**
***Imperf***

C192 A184 60c gold 8.00 8.00
a. Ovptd. in sheet margin ('61) 16.00 16.00
b. Ovptd. in sheet margin ('61) 16.00 16.00
c. Ovptd. in sheet margin ('62) 16.00 16.00
d. Ovptd. in sheet margin ('63) 16.00 16.00
e. Ovptd. in sheet margin ('63) 16.00 16.00
f. Ovptd. in sheet margin ('63) 16.00 16.00

Overprints in sheet margin of No. C192:
a, PRIMERA CONVENCION FILATELICA / CENTRO-AMERICANA / SAN SALVADOR, JULIO DE 1961.
b, in purple, Portrait, dates and text commemorating the Death of General Barrios, 96th anniv.
c, in green, Arms of city of Ahuachapan and PRIMER CENTENARIO / Ciudad de Ahuachapan / 1862 22 de Febrero 1962.
d, in blue, Soccer players and text commemorating the 1st North & Central American Soccer Championships 24 March - 2 April, 1963.
e, in blue and green, emblem of Alliance for Progress and text commemorating the 2nd anniversary of the organization.
f, in blue, Portrait of Dr. Manuel Araujo and College Arms with text commemorating the 4th Latin American Cong. of Pathological Anatomy and 10th Central American Medical Cong., Dec., 1963.
For surcharge see No. C196.

**Nos. 672, 691 and C183 Ovptd. "III Exposición Industrial Centroamericana Diciembre de 1962" with "AEREO" Added on Nos. 672, 691**
**1962, Dec. 21 *Perf. 11½, 12½***

C193 A174 1col brn org, dk brn & bl 1.50 1.00
C194 A180 1col dull red .75 .50
C195 A180 2col orange red 1.50 .90
*Nos. C193-C195 (3)* 3.75 2.40

3rd Central American Industrial Exposition.
For surcharges see Nos. C197, C199.

**Nos. C189, C194, C182 and C195 Surcharged**
**1963**

C196 A184 10c on 30c multi .35 .25
C197 A180 10c on 1col dl red .35 .25
C198 A180 10c on 1col lt grn 1.25 .25
C199 A180 10c on 2col org red 1.10 .25
*Nos. C196-C199 (4)* 3.05 1.00

Surcharges include: "X" on No. C196; two dots and bar at bottom on No. C197. Heavy bar at bottom on No. C198. On No. C199, the four-line "Exposition" overprint is lower than on No. C195.

Turquoise-browed Motmot — AP49

Birds: 5c, King vulture (vert., like No. 741). 6c, Yellow-headed parrot, vert. 10c, Spotted-breasted oriole. 30c, Greattailed grackle. 40c, Great curassow, vert. 50c, Magpie-jay. 80c, Golden-fronted woodpecker, vert.

**1963 Unwmk. Photo. *Perf. 11½***
**Birds in Natural Colors**

C200 AP49 5c gray grn & blk 1.50 .25
C201 AP49 6c tan & blue 1.50 .25
C202 AP49 10c lt bl & blk 1.75 .75
C203 AP49 20c gray & brn 3.00 .90
C204 AP49 30c ol bis & blk 3.75 .90
C205 AP49 40c pale & dk vio 4.50 1.25
C206 AP49 50c lt grn & blk 6.00 1.40
C207 AP49 80c vio bl & blk 9.00 2.25
*Nos. C200-C207 (8)* 31.00 7.95

**Eucharistic Congress Type**
**1964-65 *Perf. 12x11½***

C208 A188 10c slate grn & bl .25 .25
C209 A188 25c red & blue .25 .25

**Miniature Sheets**
***Imperf***

C210 A188 80c blue & green 1.50 1.00
a. Marginal ovpt. La Union 1.50 1.00
b. Marginal ovpt. Usulutan 1.50 1.00
c. Marginal ovpt. La Libertad 1.00 .85

See note after No. 746.
Issued: #C208-C210, Apr. 16, 1964; #C210a-C210b, June 22, 1965; #210c, Jan. 28, 1965.
For overprints see Nos. C232, C238.

**Kennedy Type of Regular Issue**
**1964, Nov. 22 *Perf. 11½x12***

C211 A189 15c gray & blk .25 .25
C212 A189 20c sage grn & blk .25 .25
C213 A189 40c yellow & blk .30 .25
*Nos. C211-C213 (3)* .80 .75

For overprint see No. C259.

### Miniature Sheet
*Imperf*

C214 A189 80c grnsh bl & blk 1.75 1.75
a. Overprinted in sheet margin in red brown ('69)

Overprint on No. C214a reads: "Alunizaje / Apolo-11 / 21 Julio / 1969" and includes pictures of the landing module and astronauts.

### Flower Type of Regular Issue
**1965, Jan. 6 Photo. *Perf. 12x11½***

C215 A190 10c Rose .65 .25
C216 A190 15c Platanillo .65 .25
C217 A190 25c San Jose 1.25 .25
C218 A190 40c Hibiscus 1.50 .25
C219 A190 45c Veranera 1.50 .25
C220 A190 70c Fire flower 1.60 .30
*Nos. C215-C220 (6)* 7.15 1.55

For overprint and surcharges see Nos. C243, C348-C349.

### ICY Type of Regular Issue
*Perf. 11½x12*
**1965, Apr. 27 Photo. Unwmk.**
**Design in Brown and Gold**

C221 A191 15c light blue .25 .25
C222 A191 30c dull lilac .25 .25
C223 A191 50c ocher .30 .25
*Nos. C221-C223 (3)* .80 .75

For overprints see Nos. C227, C244, C312.

### Gavidia Type of Regular Issue
**1965, Sept. 24 Photo. Unwmk.**
**Portraits in Natural Colors**

C224 A192 10c black & green .25 .25
C225 A192 20c black & bister .30 .25
C226 A192 1col black & rose 1.10 .40
*Nos. C224-C226 (3)* 1.65 .90

### No. C223 Ovptd. in Green "1865 / 12 de Octubre / 1965 / Dr. Manuel Enrique Araujo"
**1965, Oct. 12 *Perf. 11½x12***

C227 A191 50c brn, ocher & gold .40 .30

See note after No. 764.

### Fair Type of Regular Issue
**1965, Nov. 5 *Perf. 12x11½***

C228 A193 20c blue & multi .25 .25
C229 A193 80c multi .55 .30
C230 A193 5col multi 2.75 1.90
*Nos. C228-C230 (3)* 3.55 2.45

For overprint see No. C311.

### WHO Type of Regular Issue
**1966, May 20 Photo. Unwmk.**

C231 A194 50c multicolored .40 .25

For overprints see Nos. C242, C245.

### No. C209 Ovptd. in Dark Green "1816 1966 / 150 años / Nacimiento / San Juan Bosco"
**1966, Sept. 3 Photo. *Perf. 12x11½***

C232 A188 25c red & blue .35 .25

150th anniv. of the birth of St. John Bosco (1815-88), Italian priest, founder of the Salesian Fathers and Daughters of Mary.

### UNESCO Type of Regular Issue
**1966, Nov. 4 Photo. *Perf. 12***

C233 A195 30c tan, blk & vio bl .25 .25
C234 A195 2col emer, blk & vio bl 1.60 1.00

For surcharge see No. C352.

### Fair Type of Regular Issue
**1966, Nov. 27 Litho. *Perf. 12***

C235 A196 15c multicolored .25 .25
C236 A196 20c multicolored .25 .25
C237 A196 60c multicolored .50 .35
*Nos. C235-C237 (3)* 1.00 .85

### No. C209 Ovptd. "IX-Congreso / Interamericano / de Educacion / Católica / 4 Enero 1967"
**1967, Jan. 4 Photo. *Perf. 12x11½***

C238 A188 25c red & blue .35 .25

Issued to publicize the 9th Inter-American Congress for Catholic Education.

### Cañas Type of Regular Issue
**1967, Feb. 18 Litho. *Perf. 11½***

C239 A197 5c multicolored .25 .25
C240 A197 45c lt bl & multi .55 .35

For surcharges see Nos. C403-C405.

### Volcano Type of Regular Issue
**1967, Apr. 14 Photo. *Perf. 13***

C241 A198 50c ol gray & brn .60 .25

For surcharges see Nos. C320, C350

### No. C231 Ovptd. in Red "VIII CONGRESO / CENTROAMERICANO DE / FARMACIA & B10QUIMICA / 5 di 11 Noviembre de 1967"
**1967, Oct. 26 Photo. *Perf. 12x11½***

C242 A194 50c multicolored .45 .40

Issued to publicize the 8th Central American Congress for Pharmacy and Biochemistry.

### No. C217 Ovptd. in Red "I Juegos / Centroamericanos y del / Caribe de Basquetbol / 25 Nov. al 3 Dic. 1967"
**1967, Nov. 15**

C243 A190 25c bl, yel & grn .30 .25

First Central American and Caribbean Basketball Games, Nov. 25-Dec. 3.

### No. C222 Ovptd. in Carmine "1968 / AÑO INTERNACIONAL DE / LOS DERECHOS HUMANOS"
**1968, Jan. 2 Photo. *Perf. 11½x12***

C244 A191 30c dl lil, brn & gold .40 .30

International Human Rights Year 1968.

### No. C231 Ovptd. in Red "1968 / XX ANIVERSARIO DE LA / ORGANIZACION MUNDIAL / DE LA SALUD"
**1968, Apr. 7 *Perf. 12x11½***

C245 A194 50c multicolored .50 .50

20th anniv. of WHO.

### No. C229 Ovptd. in Red "1968 / Año / del Sistema / del Crédito / Rural"
**1968, May 6 Photo. *Perf. 12x11½***

C246 A193 80c multicolored .65 .50

Rural credit system.

### Masferrer Type of Regular Issue
**1968, June 22 Litho. *Perf. 12x11½***

C247 A200 5c brown & multi .25 .25
C248 A200 15c green & multi .25 .25

For overprint see No. C297.

Scouts Hiking AP50

**1968, July 26 Litho. *Perf. 12***

C249 AP50 10c multicolored .30 .25

Issued to publicize the 7th Inter-American Boy Scout Conference, July-Aug., 1968.

### Presidents' Meeting Type
**1968, Dec. 5 Litho. *Perf. 14½***

C250 A202 20c salmon & multi .25 .25
C251 A202 1col lt blue & multi .75 .50

### Butterfly Type of Regular Issue
Designs: Various butterflies.

**1969 Litho. *Perf. 12***

C252 A203 20c multi 7.25 .30
C253 A203 1col multi 12.00 .70
C254 A203 2col multi 12.00 1.25
C255 A203 10col gray & multi 18.00 6.00
*Nos. C252-C255 (4)* 49.25 8.25

For surcharge see No. C353.

Red Cross, Crescent and Lion and Sun Emblems AP51

**1969 Litho. *Perf. 11***

C256 AP51 30c yellow & multi .50 .25
C257 AP51 1col multicolored 1.50 .50
C258 AP51 4col multicolored 3.75 2.50
*Nos. C256-C258 (3)* 5.75 3.25

League of Red Cross Societies, 50th anniv. For surcharges see Nos. C351, C354.

### No. C213 Ovptd. in Green "Alunizaje / Apolo-11 / 21 Julio / 1969"
**1969, Sept. Photo. *Perf. 11½x12***

C259 A189 40c yellow & blk .35 .30

Man's 1st landing on the moon, July 20, 1969. See note after US No. C76.

### Hospital Type of Regular Issue
Benjamin Bloom Children's Hospital.

**1969, Oct. 24 Litho. *Perf. 11½***

C260 A205 1col multi .85 .50
C261 A205 2col multi 1.60 1.00
C262 A205 5col multi 4.25 2.50
*Nos. C260-C262 (3)* 6.70 4.00

For surcharge see No. C355.

### ILO Type of Regular Issue
**1969 Litho. *Perf. 13***

C263 A206 50c lt bl & multi .40 .25

### Tourist Type of Regular Issue
Views: 20c, Devil's Gate. 35c, Ichanmichen Spa. 60c, Aerial view of Acajutla Harbor.

**1969, Dec. 19 Photo. *Perf. 12x11½***

C264 A207 20c black & multi .25 .25
C265 A207 35c black & multi .25 .25
C266 A207 60c black & multi .40 .30
*Nos. C264-C266 (3)* .90 .80

### Insect Type of Regular Issue, 1970
**1970, Feb. 24 Litho. *Perf. 11½x11***

C267 A208 2col Bee 2.50 1.00
C268 A208 3col Elaterida 4.00 1.75
C269 A208 4col Praying mantis 6.00 2.00
*Nos. C267-C269 (3)* 12.50 4.75

For surcharges see Nos. C371-C373.

### Human Rights Type of Regular Issue
20c, 80c, Map and arms of Salvador and National Unity emblem similar to A209, but vert.

**1970, Apr. 14 Litho. *Perf. 14***

C270 A209 20c blue & multi .25 .25
C271 A209 80c blue & multi .80 .30

For overprint & surcharge see #C301, C402.

### Army Type of Regular Issue
Designs: 20c, Fighter plane. 40c, Gun and crew. 50c, Patrol boat.

**1970, May 7 *Perf. 12***

C272 A210 20c gray & multi .25 .25
C273 A210 40c green & multi .35 .25
C274 A210 50c blue & multi .40 .25
*Nos. C272-C274 (3)* 1.00 .75

For overprint see No. C310.

Brazilian Team, Jules Rimet Cup — AP52

Soccer teams and Jules Rimet Cup.

**1970, May 25 Litho. *Perf. 12***

C275 AP52 1col Belgium 1.10 .65
C276 AP52 1col Brazil 1.10 .65
C277 AP52 1col Bulgaria 1.10 .65
C278 AP52 1col Czechoslovakia 1.10 .65
C279 AP52 1col Germany (Fed. Rep.) 1.10 .65
C280 AP52 1col Britain 1.10 .65
C281 AP52 1col Israel 1.10 .65
C282 AP52 1col Italy 1.10 .65
C283 AP52 1col Mexico 1.10 .65
C284 AP52 1col Morocco 1.10 .65
C285 AP52 1col Peru 1.10 .65
C286 AP52 1col Romania 1.10 .65
C287 AP52 1col Russia 1.10 .65
C288 AP52 1col Salvador 1.10 .65
C289 AP52 1col Sweden 1.10 .65
C290 AP52 1col Uruguay 1.10 .65
*Nos. C275-C290 (16)* 17.60 10.40

9th World Soccer Championships for the Jules Rimet Cup, Mexico City, 5/30-6/21/70.
For overprints see Nos. C325-C340.

### Lottery Type of Regular Issue
**1970, July 15 Litho. *Perf. 12***

C291 A211 80c multi .65 .25

### Education Year Type of Regular Issue
**1970, Sept. 11 Litho. *Perf. 12***

C292 A212 20c pink & multi .25 .25
C293 A212 2col buff & multi 1.60 .80

### Fair Type of Regular Issue
**1970, Oct. 28 Litho. *Perf. 12***

C294 A213 20c multi .25 .25
C295 A213 30c yel & multi .30 .25

### Music Type of Regular Issue
Johann Sebastian Bach, harp, horn, music.

**1971, Feb. 22 Litho. *Perf. 13½***

C296 A214 40c gray & multi .75 .25

For overprint see No. C313.

### No. C247 Ovptd. "Año / del Centenario de la / Biblioteca Nacional / 1970"
**1970, Nov. 25 *Perf. 12x11½***

C297 A200 5c brn & multi .25 .25

### Miss Tourism Type of Regular Issue
**1971, Apr. 1 Litho. *Perf. 14***

C298 A215 20c lil & multi .25 .25
C299 A215 60c gray & multi .55 .30

### Pietà Type of Regular Issue
**1971, May 10**

C300 A216 40c lt yel grn & vio brn .35 .25

### No. C270 Overprinted in Red Like No. 823
**1971, July 6 Litho. *Perf. 14***

C301 A209 20c bl & multi .30 .25

### Fish Type of Regular Issue
30c, Smalltooth sawfish. 1col, Atlantic sailfish.

**1971, July 28**

C302 A217 30c lilac & multi 2.10 .35
C303 A217 1col multi 3.50 1.10

### Independence Type of Regular Issue
Designs: Various sections of Declaration of Independence of Central America.

**1971 Litho. *Perf. 13½x13***

C304 A218 30c bl & blk .25 .25
C305 A218 40c brn & blk .30 .25
C306 A218 50c yel & blk .35 .25
C307 A218 60c gray & blk .50 .35
a. Souvenir sheet of 8 2.25 1.60
*Nos. C304-C307 (4)* 1.40 1.10

No. C307a contains 8 stamps with simulated perforations similar to Nos. 826-829, C304-C307.
For overprints see Nos. C321, C347.

### Church Type of Regular Issue
15c, Metapan Church. 70c, Panchimalco Church.

**1971, Aug. 21 Litho. *Perf. 13x13½***

C308 A219 15c ol & multi .25 .25
C309 A219 70c multi .55 .35

No. C274 Overprinted in Red

**1971, Oct. 12 Litho. *Perf. 12***

C310 A210 50c bl & multi .45 .30

National Navy, 20th anniversary.

**No. C229 Ovptd. "V Feria / Internacional / 3-20 Noviembre / de 1972"**

**1972, Nov. 3 Photo.** ***Perf. 12x11½***
**C311** A193 80c multi .90 .50

5th Intl. Fair, El Salvador, Nov. 3-20.

No. C223 Overprinted in Red

**1972, Nov. 30 Photo.** ***Perf. 11½x12***
**C312** A191 50c ocher, brn & gold .45 .30

30th anniversary of the Inter-American institute for Agricultural Sciences.

**No. C296 Overprinted**

**1973, Feb. 5 Litho.** ***Perf. 13½***
**C313** A214 40c gray & multi 1.00 .25

3rd International Music Festival, Feb. 9-29.

**Lions Type of Regular Issue**

Designs: 20c, 40c, Map of El Salvador and Lions International Emblem.

**1973, Feb. 20 Litho.** ***Perf. 13***
**C314** A220 20c gray & multi .25 .25
**C315** A220 40c multi .30 .25

**Olympic Type of Regular Issue**

Designs: 20c, Javelin, women's. 80c, Discus, women's. 1col, Hammer throw. 2col, Shot put.

**1973, May 21 Litho.** ***Perf. 13***
**C316** A221 20c lt grn & multi .45 .25
**C317** A221 80c sal & multi 1.00 .35
**C318** A221 1col ultra & multi 1.25 .55
**C319** A221 2col multi 2.75 .90
*Nos. C316-C319 (4)* 5.45 2.05

**No. C241 Surcharged Like No. 841**

**1973, Dec. Photo.** ***Perf. 13***
**C320** A198 25c on 50c multi .45 .25

**No. C307a Ovptd. "Centenario / Cuidad / Santiago de Maria / 1874 1974"**

Souvenir Sheet

**1974, Mar. 7 Litho.** ***Imperf.***
**C321** A218 Sheet of 8 1.90 1.10

Centenary of the City Santiago de Maria. The overprint is so arranged that each line appears on a different pair of stamps.

**No. C231 Surcharged in Red**

**1974, Apr. 22 Photo.** ***Perf. 12x11½***
**C322** A194 25c on 50c multi .35 .25

No. C229 Surcharged

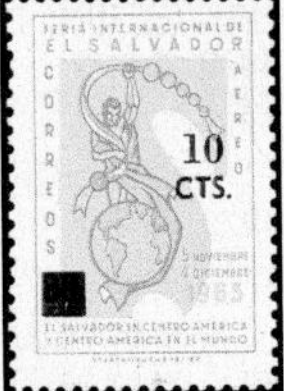


**1974, Apr. 24**
**C323** A193 10c on 80c multi .45 .25

**Rehabilitation Type**

**1974, Apr. 30 Litho.** ***Perf. 13***
**C324** A222 25c multi .30 .25

**Nos. C275-C290 Overprinted**

**1974, June 4 Litho.** ***Perf. 12***
**C325** AP52 1col Belgium .90 .50
**C326** AP52 1col Brazil .90 .50
**C327** AP52 1col Bulgaria .90 .50
**C328** AP52 1col Czech. .90 .50
**C329** AP52 1col Germany .90 .50
**C330** AP52 1col Britain .90 .50
**C331** AP52 1col Israel .90 .50
**C332** AP52 1col Italy .90 .50
**C333** AP52 1col Mexico .90 .50
**C334** AP52 1col Morocco .90 .50
**C335** AP52 1col Peru .90 .50
**C336** AP52 1col Romania .90 .50
**C337** AP52 1col Russia .90 .50
**C338** AP52 1col Salvador .90 .50
**C339** AP52 1col Sweden .90 .50
**C340** AP52 1col Uruguay .90 .50
*Nos. C325-C340 (16)* 14.40 8.00

World Cup Soccer Championship, Munich, June 13-July 7.

**INTERPOL Type of 1974**

**1974, Sept. 2 Litho.** ***Perf. 12½***
**C341** A223 25c multi .25 .25

**FAO Type of 1974**

**1974, Sept. 2 Litho.** ***Perf. 12½***
**C342** A224 25c bl, dk bl & gold .25 .25

**Coin Type of 1974**

**1974, Nov. 19 Litho.** ***Perf. 12½x13***
**C343** A225 20c 1p silver, 1892 .25 .25
**C344** A225 40c 20c silver, 1828 .30 .25
**C345** A225 50c 20p gold, 1892 .50 .25
**C346** A225 60c 20col gold, 1925 .50 .35
*Nos. C343-C346 (4)* 1.55 1.10

**No. C307a Ovptd. "X ASAMBLEA GENERAL DE LA CONFERENCIA / INTERAMERICANA DE SEGURIDAD SOCIAL Y XX / REUNION DEL COMITE PERMANENTE INTERAMERICANO / DE SEGURIDAD SOCIAL, 24 — 30 NOVIEMBRE 1974"**

**1974, Nov. 18 Litho.** ***Imperf.***

**Souvenir Sheet**

**C347** A218 Sheet of 8 2.50 1.75

Social Security Conference, El Salvador, Nov. 24-30. The overprint is so arranged that each line appears on a different pair of stamps.

**Issues of 1965-69 Surcharged**

a

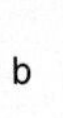

c

d

**1974-75**
**C348** A190(a) 10c on 45c #C219 .60 .25
**C349** A190(a) 10c on 70c #C220 .60 .25
**C350** A198(b) 10c on 50c #C241 .75 .25
**C351** AP51(d) 25c on 1col #C257 .35 .25
**C352** A195(c) 25c on 2col #C234 ('75) .75 .25
**C353** A203(d) 25c on 2col #C254 ('75) 50.00 .25
**C354** AP51(d) 25c on 4col #C258 .45 .25
**C355** A205(d) 25c on 5col #C262 .35 .25
*Nos. C348-C355 (8)* 53.85 2.00

No. C353 has new value at left and 6 vertical bars. No. C355 has 7 vertical bars.

**UPU Type of 1975**

**1975, Jan. 22 Litho.** ***Perf. 13***
**C356** A226 25c bl & multi .25 .25
**C357** A226 30c bl & multi .25 .25

**Acajutla Harbor Type of 1975**

**1975, Feb. 17**
**C358** A227 15c bl & multi .25 .25

**Post Office Type of 1975**

**1975, Apr. 25 Litho.** ***Perf. 13***
**C359** A228 25c bl & multi .35 .25

**Miss Universe Type of 1975**

**1975, June 25** ***Perf. 12½***
**C360** A229 25c multi .25 .25
**C361** A229 60c lil & multi .55 .40

**Women's Year Type and**

IWY Emblem — AP53

**1975, Sept. 4 Litho.** ***Perf. 12½***
**C362** A230 15c bl & bl blk .25 .25
**C363** AP53 25c yel grn & blk .30 .25

International Women's Year 1975.

**Nurse Type of 1975**

**1975, Oct. 24 Litho.** ***Perf. 12½***
**C364** A231 25c lt blue & multi .25 .25

**Printers' Congress Type**

**1975, Nov. 19 Litho.** ***Perf. 12½***
**C365** A232 30c green & multi .25 .25

**Dermatologists' Congress Type**

**1975, Nov. 28**
**C366** A233 20c blue & multi .25 .25
**C367** A233 30c red & multi .25 .25

**Caritas Type of 1975**

**1975, Dec. 18 Litho.** ***Perf. 13½***
**C368** A234 20c bl & vio bl .25 .25

UNICEF Emblem — AP54

**1975, Dec. 18**
**C369** AP54 15c lt grn & sil .25 .25
**C370** AP54 20c dl rose & sil .30 .25

UNICEF, 25th anniv. (in 1971).

**Nos. C267-C269 Surcharged**

**1976, Jan. 14** ***Perf. 11½x11***
**C371** A208 25c on 2col multi 2.40 .25
**C372** A208 25c on 3col multi 2.40 .25
**C373** A208 25c on 4col multi 2.40 .25
*Nos. C371-C373 (3)* 7.20 .75

Caularthron Bilamellatum AP55

Designs: Orchids — No. C375, Oncidium oliganthum. No. C376, Epidendrum radicans. No. C377, Epidendrum vitellinum. No. C378, Cyrtopodium punctatum. No. C379, Pleurothallis schiedei. No. C380, Lycaste cruenta. No. C381, Spiranthes speciosa.

**1976, Feb. 19 Litho.** ***Perf. 12½***
**C374** AP55 25c multi 1.00 .35
**C375** AP55 25c multi 1.00 .35
**C376** AP55 25c multi 1.00 .35
**C377** AP55 25c multi 1.00 .35
**C378** AP55 25c multi 1.00 .35
**C379** AP55 25c multi 1.00 .35
**C380** AP55 25c multi 1.00 .35
**C381** AP55 25c multi 1.00 .35
*Nos. C374-C381 (8)* 8.00 2.80

**CIAT Type of 1976**

**1976, May 18 Litho.** ***Perf. 12½***
**C382** A235 50c org & multi .55 .25

**Bicentennial Types of 1976**

**1976, June 30 Litho.** ***Perf. 12½***
**C383** A236 25c multi .25 .25
**C384** A237 5col multi 3.75 2.50

**Reptile Type of 1976**

Reptiles: 15c, Green fence lizard. 25c, Basilisk. 60c, Star lizard.

**1976, Sept. 23 Litho.** ***Perf. 12½***
**C385** A238 15c multi .50 .25
**C386** A238 25c multi .80 .25
**C387** A238 60c multi 2.00 .40
*Nos. C385-C387 (3)* 3.30 .90

**Archaeology Type of 1976**

Pre-Columbian Art: 25c, Brazier with pre-classical head, El Trapiche. 50c, Kettle with pre-classical head, Atiquizaya. 70c, Classical whistling vase, Tazumal.

**1976, Oct. 11 Litho.** ***Perf. 12½***
**C388** A239 25c multi .25 .25
**C389** A239 50c multi .45 .25
**C390** A239 70c multi .60 .40
*Nos. C388-C390 (3)* 1.30 .90

For overprint see No. C429.

**Fair Type of 1976**

**1976, Oct. 25 Litho.** ***Perf. 12½***
**C391** A240 25c multi .25 .25
**C392** A240 70c yel & multi .55 .40

**Christmas Type of 1976**

**1976, Dec. 16 Litho.** ***Perf. 11***

| | | | | |
|---|---|---|---|---|
| **C393** | A241 | 25c bl & multi | .25 | .25 |
| **C394** | A241 | 50c multi | .40 | .25 |
| **C395** | A241 | 60c multi | .50 | .30 |
| **C396** | A241 | 75c red & multi | .60 | .40 |
| | | *Nos. C393-C396 (4)* | 1.75 | 1.20 |

**Rotary Type of 1977**

**1977, June 20 Litho.** ***Perf. 11***

| | | | | |
|---|---|---|---|---|
| **C397** | A242 | 25c multi | .25 | .25 |
| **C398** | A242 | 1col multi | .80 | .50 |

**Industrial Type of 1977**

Designs: 25c, Radar station, Izalco (vert.). 50c, Central sugar refinery, Jiboa. 75c, Cerron Grande hydroelectric station.

**1977, June 29** ***Perf. 12½***

| | | | | |
|---|---|---|---|---|
| **C399** | A243 | 25c multi | .25 | .25 |
| **C400** | A243 | 50c multi | .40 | .25 |
| **C401** | A243 | 75c multi | .60 | .40 |
| | | *Nos. C399-C401 (3)* | 1.25 | .90 |

Nos. C399-C401 have colorless overprint in multiple rows: GOBIERNO DEL SALVADOR.

**Nos. C271 and C239 Surcharged with New Value and Bar**

**1977** ***Perf. 14, 11½***

| | | | | |
|---|---|---|---|---|
| **C402** | A209 | 25c on 80c multi | .30 | .25 |
| **C403** | A197 | 30c on 5c multi | .25 | .25 |
| **C404** | A197 | 40c on 5c multi | .30 | .25 |
| **C405** | A197 | 50c on 5c multi | .40 | .25 |
| | | *Nos. C402-C405 (4)* | 1.25 | 1.00 |

**Broadcasting Type of 1977**

**1977, Sept. 14 Litho.** ***Perf. 14***

| | | | | |
|---|---|---|---|---|
| **C406** | A244 | 20c multi | .25 | .25 |
| **C407** | A244 | 25c multi | .25 | .25 |

Symbolic Chessboard and Emblem — AP56

**1977, Oct. 20 Litho.** ***Perf. 11***

| | | | | |
|---|---|---|---|---|
| **C408** | AP56 | 25c multi | .25 | .25 |
| **C409** | AP56 | 50c multi | .40 | .25 |

El Salvador's victory in International Chess Olympiad, Tripoli, Libya, Oct. 24-Nov. 15, 1976.

Soccer AP57

Boxing AP58

**1977, Nov. 16 Litho.** ***Perf. 16***

| | | | | |
|---|---|---|---|---|
| **C410** | AP57 | 10c shown | .25 | .25 |
| **C411** | AP57 | 10c Basketball | .25 | .25 |
| **C412** | AP57 | 15c Javelin | .25 | .25 |
| **C413** | AP57 | 15c Weight lifting | .25 | .25 |
| **C414** | AP57 | 20c Volleyball | .25 | .25 |
| **C415** | AP58 | 20c shown | .25 | .25 |
| **C416** | AP57 | 25c Baseball | .25 | .25 |
| **C417** | AP58 | 25c Softball | .25 | .25 |
| **C418** | AP58 | 30c Swimming | .35 | .25 |
| **C419** | AP58 | 30c Fencing | .35 | .25 |
| **C420** | AP58 | 40c Bicycling | .45 | .25 |
| **C421** | AP58 | 50c Rifle shooting | .55 | .30 |
| **C422** | AP58 | 50c Women's tennis | .55 | .30 |
| **C423** | AP57 | 60c Judo | .65 | .35 |
| **C424** | AP58 | 75c Wrestling | .70 | .40 |
| **C425** | AP58 | 1col Equestrian hurdles | .90 | .50 |
| **C426** | AP58 | 1col Woman gymnast | .90 | .50 |
| **C427** | AP58 | 2col Table tennis | 1.25 | 1.00 |
| | | *Nos. C410-C427 (18)* | 8.65 | 6.10 |

**Size: 100x119mm**

| | | | | |
|---|---|---|---|---|
| **C428** | AP57 | 5col Games' poster | 4.00 | 4.00 |

2nd Central American Olympic Games, San Salvador, Nov. 25-Dec. 4.

**No. C390 Ovptd. in Red "CENTENARIO / CIUDAD DE / CHALCHUAPA / 1878-1978"**

**1978, Feb. 13 Litho.** ***Perf. 12½***

| | | | | |
|---|---|---|---|---|
| **C429** | A239 | 70c multi | .60 | .55 |

Centenary of Chalchuapa.

Map of South America, Argentina '78 Emblem AP59

**1978, Aug. 15 Litho.** ***Perf. 11***

| | | | | |
|---|---|---|---|---|
| **C430** | AP59 | 25c multi | .30 | .25 |
| **C431** | AP59 | 60c multi | .50 | .40 |
| **C432** | AP59 | 5col multi | 4.00 | 3.00 |
| | | *Nos. C430-C432 (3)* | 4.80 | 3.65 |

11th World Cup Soccer Championship, Argentina, June 1-25.

**Musical Instrument Type**

Designs: 25c, Drum, vert. 50c, Hollow rattles. 80c, Xylophone.

**1978, Aug. 29** ***Perf. 12½***

| | | | | |
|---|---|---|---|---|
| **C433** | A245 | 25c multi | .30 | .25 |
| **C434** | A245 | 50c multi | .45 | .25 |
| **C435** | A245 | 80c multi | .60 | .40 |
| | | *Nos. C433-C435 (3)* | 1.35 | .90 |

For surcharge see No. C492.

**Engineering Type of 1978**

**1978, Sept. 12 Litho.** ***Perf. 13½***

| | | | | |
|---|---|---|---|---|
| **C436** | A246 | 25c multi | .25 | .25 |

**Izalco Station Type of 1978**

**1978, Sept. 14** ***Perf. 12½***

| | | | | |
|---|---|---|---|---|
| **C437** | A247 | 75c multi | .60 | .40 |

Softball, Bat and Globes AP60

**1978, Oct. 17 Litho.** ***Perf. 12½***

| | | | | |
|---|---|---|---|---|
| **C438** | AP60 | 25c pink & multi | .25 | .25 |
| **C439** | AP60 | 1col yel & multi | .80 | .50 |

4th World Softball Championship for Women, San Salvador, Oct. 13-22.

**Fair Type, 1978**

**1978, Oct. 30 Litho.** ***Perf. 12½***

| | | | | |
|---|---|---|---|---|
| **C440** | A248 | 15c multi | .25 | .25 |
| **C441** | A248 | 25c multi | .25 | .25 |

**Red Cross Type, 1978**

**1978, Oct. 30 Litho.** ***Perf. 11***

| | | | | |
|---|---|---|---|---|
| **C442** | A249 | 25c multi | .25 | .25 |

**Cotton Conference Type, 1978**

**1978, Nov. 22** ***Perf. 12½***

| | | | | |
|---|---|---|---|---|
| **C443** | A250 | 40c multi | .30 | .25 |

**Christmas Type, 1978**

**1978, Dec. 5 Litho.** ***Perf. 12½***

| | | | | |
|---|---|---|---|---|
| **C444** | A251 | 25c multi | .25 | .25 |
| **C445** | A251 | 1col multi | .80 | .50 |

**Athenaeum Type 1978**

**1978, Dec. 20 Litho.** ***Perf. 14***

| | | | | |
|---|---|---|---|---|
| **C446** | A252 | 25c multi | .25 | .25 |

**UPU Type of 1979**

**1979, Apr. 2 Litho.** ***Perf. 14***

| | | | | |
|---|---|---|---|---|
| **C447** | A253 | 75c multi | .60 | .40 |

**Health Organization Type**

**1979, Apr. 7** ***Perf. 14x14½***

| | | | | |
|---|---|---|---|---|
| **C448** | A254 | 25c multi | .25 | .25 |

**Social Security Type of 1979**

**1979, May 25 Litho.** ***Perf. 12½***

| | | | | |
|---|---|---|---|---|
| **C449** | A255 | 25c multi | .25 | .25 |
| **C450** | A255 | 1col multi | .80 | .50 |

Games Emblem AP61

**1979, July 12 Litho.** ***Perf. 14½x14***

| | | | | |
|---|---|---|---|---|
| **C451** | AP61 | 25c multi | .25 | .25 |
| **C452** | AP61 | 40c multi | .30 | .25 |
| **C453** | AP61 | 70c multi | .50 | .40 |
| | | *Nos. C451-C453 (3)* | 1.05 | .90 |

8th Pan American Games, Puerto Rico, July 1-15.

For surcharge see No. C493.

**Pope John Paul II Type of 1979**

60c, 5col, Pope John Paul II & pyramid.

**1979, July 12**

| | | | | |
|---|---|---|---|---|
| **C454** | A256 | 60c multi, horiz. | .50 | .30 |
| **C455** | A256 | 5col multi, horiz. | 4.00 | 2.50 |

"25," Family and Map of Salvador — AP62

**1979, May 14 Litho.** ***Perf. 14x14½***

| | | | | |
|---|---|---|---|---|
| **C456** | AP62 | 25c blk & bl | .25 | .25 |
| **C457** | AP62 | 60c blk & lil rose | .55 | .35 |

Social Security, 25th anniversary.

**Pre-Historic Animal Type**

**1979, Sept. 7 Litho.** ***Perf. 14***

| | | | | |
|---|---|---|---|---|
| **C458** | A257 | 15c Mammoth | .35 | .25 |
| **C459** | A257 | 25c Giant anteater, vert. | .50 | .25 |
| **C460** | A257 | 2col Hyenas | 2.75 | 1.10 |
| | | *Nos. C458-C460 (3)* | 3.60 | 1.60 |

**National Anthem Type, 1979**

**1979, Sept. 14** ***Perf. 14½x14***

| | | | | |
|---|---|---|---|---|
| **C461** | A258 | 40c Jose Aberiz, score | .30 | .25 |

**COPIMERA Type, 1979**

**1979, Oct. 19 Litho.** ***Perf. 14½x14***

| | | | | |
|---|---|---|---|---|
| **C462** | A259 | 50c multi | .45 | .25 |

Circle Dance, IYC Emblem AP63

Children's Village and IYC Emblems AP64

**1979, Oct. 29** ***Perf. 14½x14, 14x14½***

| | | | | |
|---|---|---|---|---|
| **C463** | AP63 | 25c multi | .25 | .25 |
| **C464** | AP64 | 30c vio & blk | .30 | .25 |

International Year of the Child.

**Biochemistry Type of 1979**

**1979, Nov. 1 Litho.** ***Perf. 14½x14***

| | | | | |
|---|---|---|---|---|
| **C465** | A262 | 25c multi | .25 | .25 |

**Coffee Type of 1979**

Designs: 50c, Picking coffee. 75, Drying coffee beans. 1col, Coffee export.

**1979, Dec. 18** ***Perf. 14x14½, 14½x14***

| | | | | |
|---|---|---|---|---|
| **C466** | A263 | 50c multi | .40 | .25 |
| **C467** | A263 | 75c multi | .60 | .40 |
| **C468** | A263 | 1 col multi | .80 | .55 |
| | | *Nos. C466-C468 (3)* | 1.80 | 1.20 |

**Hoof and Mouth Disease Type**

**1980, June 3 Litho.** ***Perf. 14½x14***

| | | | | |
|---|---|---|---|---|
| **C469** | A265 | 60c multi | .55 | .30 |

**Shell Type of 1980**

15c, Hexaplex regius. 25c, Polinices helicoides. 75c, Jenneria pustulata. 1col, Pitar lupanaria.

**1980, Aug. 12** ***Perf. 14x14½***

| | | | | |
|---|---|---|---|---|
| **C470** | A266 | 15c multi | .40 | .25 |
| **C471** | A266 | 25c multi | .80 | .25 |
| **C472** | A266 | 75c multi | 2.00 | .30 |
| **C473** | A266 | 1col multi | 2.75 | .50 |
| | | *Nos. C470-C473 (4)* | 5.95 | 1.30 |

**Birds Type**

25c, Aulacorhynchus prasinus. 50c, Strix varia fulvescens. 75c, Myadestes unicolor.

**1980, Sept. 10 Litho.** ***Perf. 14x14½***

| | | | | |
|---|---|---|---|---|
| **C474** | A267 | 25c multi | 1.60 | .25 |
| **C475** | A267 | 50c multi | 3.00 | .30 |
| **C476** | A267 | 75c multi | 4.50 | .45 |
| | | *Nos. C474-C476 (3)* | 9.10 | 1.00 |

**Snake Type of 1980**

**1980, Nov. 12 Litho.** ***Perf. 14x14½***

| | | | | |
|---|---|---|---|---|
| **C477** | A268 | 25c Rattlesnake | 2.40 | .25 |
| **C478** | A268 | 50c Coral snake | 3.50 | .30 |

**Auditors Type**

**1980, Nov. 26 Litho.** ***Perf. 14***

| | | | | |
|---|---|---|---|---|
| **C479** | A269 | 50c multi | .40 | .25 |
| **C480** | A269 | 75c multi | .60 | .40 |

**Christmas Type**

**1980, Dec. 5 Litho.** ***Perf. 14***

| | | | | |
|---|---|---|---|---|
| **C481** | A270 | 25c multi | .25 | .25 |
| **C482** | A270 | 60c multi | .60 | .30 |

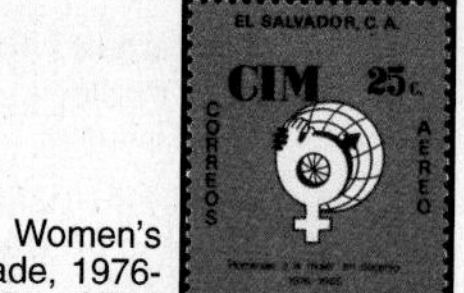


Intl. Women's Decade, 1976-85 — AP65

**1981, Jan. 30** ***Perf. 14½x14***

| | | | | |
|---|---|---|---|---|
| **C483** | AP65 | 25c ol grn & blk | .25 | .25 |
| **C484** | AP65 | 1 col orange & black | .80 | .50 |

Protected Animals AP66

No. C485, Ateles geoffroyi. No. C486, Lepisosteus tropicus. No. C487, Iguana iguana. No. C488, Eretmochelys imbricata. No. C489, Spizaetus ornatus.

**1981, Mar. 20 Litho.** ***Perf. 14x14½***

| | | | | |
|---|---|---|---|---|
| **C485** | AP66 | 25c multicolored | .30 | .25 |
| **C486** | AP66 | 40c multicolored | .35 | .25 |
| **C487** | AP66 | 50c multicolored | .45 | .25 |
| **C488** | AP66 | 60c multicolored | .55 | .35 |
| **C489** | AP66 | 75c multicolored | .70 | .40 |
| | | *Nos. C485-C489 (5)* | 2.35 | 1.50 |

Heinrich von Stephan, 150th Birth Anniv. — AP67

**1981, May 18 Litho.** *Perf. 14½x14*
C490 AP67 15c multi .35 .25
C491 AP67 2 col multi 1.60 1.00

**Nos. C435, C453 Surcharged**
*Perf. 12½, 14½x14*

**1981, May 18** **Litho.**
C492 A245 50c on 80c, #C435 .40 .25
C493 AP61 1 col on 70c, #C453 .80 .55

**Dental Associations Type**

**1981, June 18 Litho.** *Perf. 14*
C494 A271 5 col bl & blk 7.00 3.00

**IYD Type of 1981**

**1981, Aug. 14 Litho.** *Perf. 14x14½*
C495 A272 25c like #936 .25 .25
C496 A272 50c Emblem .40 .25
C497 A272 75c like #936 .60 .40
C498 A272 1 col like # C496 .80 .55
*Nos. C495-C498 (4)* 2.05 1.45

**Quinonez Type**

**1981, Aug. 28 Litho.** *Perf. 14x14½*
C499 A273 50c multi .40 .25

**World Food Day Type**

**1981, Sept. 16 Litho.** *Perf. 14x14½*
C500 A274 25c multi .25 .25

Land Registry Office, 100th Anniv. — AP68

**1981, Oct. 30 Litho.** *Perf. 14x14½*
C501 AP68 1 col multi .80 .55

TACA Airlines, 50th Anniv. AP69

**1981, Nov. 10 Litho.** *Perf. 14*
C502 AP69 15c multi .25 .25
C503 AP69 25c multi .25 .25
C504 AP69 75c multi .60 .40
*Nos. C502-C504 (3)* 1.10 .90

**World Cup Preliminaries Type**

**1981, Nov. 27 Litho.** *Perf. 14x14½*
C505 A275 25c Like No. 939 .30 .25
C506 A275 75c Like No. 940 .60 .40

**Lyceum Type**

**1981, Dec. 17 Litho.** *Perf. 14*
C507 A276 25c multi .25 .25

**Sculptures Type**

**1982, Jan. 22 Litho.** *Perf. 14*
C508 A277 25c Palm leaf with effigy .25 .25
C509 A277 30c Jaguar mask .30 .25
C510 A277 80c Mayan flint carving .65 .45
*Nos. C508-C510 (3)* 1.20 .95

**Scouting Year Type of 1982**

**1982, Mar. 17 Litho.** *Perf. 14½x14*
C511 A278 25c Baden-Powell .25 .25
C512 A278 50c Girl Scout, emblem .40 .25

TB Bacillus Cent. — AP70

**1982, Mar. 24** *Perf. 14*
C513 AP70 50c multi 1.50 .25

**Armed Forces Type of 1982**

**1982, May 7 Litho.** *Perf. 14x13½*
C514 A279 25c multi .25 .25

Symbolic Design — AP71

**1982, May 14** *Perf. 14*
C515 AP71 75c multi .60 .40

25th anniv. of Latin-American Tourist Org. Confederation (COTAL).

14th World Telecommunications Day — AP72

**1982, May 17** *Perf. 14x14½*
C516 AP72 15c multi .25 .25
C517 AP72 2col multi 1.60 1.00

**World Cup Type of 1982**

**1982, July 14**
C518 A280 25c Team, emblem .25 .25
C519 A280 60c Map, cup .50 .35

**Size: 67x47mm**
*Perf. 11½*
C520 A280 2col Team, emblem, diff. 1.60 1.00

1982 World Cup — AP73

Flags or Arms of Participating Countries; #C521a, C522a, Italy. #C521b, C522c, Germany. #C521c, C522e, Argentina. #C521d, C522m, England. #C521e, C522o, Spain. #C521f, C522q, Brazil. #C521g, C522b, Poland. #C521h, C522d, Algeria. #C521i, C522f, Belgium. #C521j, C522n, France. #C521k, C522p, Honduras. #C521l, C522r, Russia. #C521m, C522g, Peru. #C521n, C522i, Chile. #C521o, C522k, Hungary. #C521p, C522s, Czechoslovakia. #C521q, C522u, Yugoslavia. #C521r, C522w, Scotland. #C521s, C522h, Cameroun. #C521t, C522j, Austria. #C521u, C522l, Salvador. #C521v, C522t, Kuwait. #C521w, C522v, Ireland. #C521x, C522x, New Zealand.

**1982, Aug. 26**
C521 Sheet of 24 7.50
*a.-x.* AP73 15c Flags .25 .25
C522 Sheet of 24 7.50
*a.-x.* AP73 25c Arms .25 .25

Salvador Team, Cup, Flags — AP74

**1982, Aug. 26 Litho.** *Perf. 11½*
C523 AP74 5col multi 6.00 2.50

**International Fair Type**

**1982, Oct. 14 Litho.** *Perf. 14*
C524 A281 15c multi .25 .25

World Food Day — AP75

**1982, Oct. 21 Litho.** *Perf. 14*
C525 AP75 25c multi .35 .25

St. Francis of Assisi, 800th Birth Anniv. — AP76

**1982, Nov. 10 Litho.** *Perf. 14*
C526 AP76 1col multi .80 .60

Natl. Labor Campaign — AP77

**1982, Nov. 30 Litho.** *Perf. 14x14½*
C527 AP77 50c multi .40 .25

**Christmas Type**

**1982, Dec. 14 Litho.** *Perf. 14*
C528 A282 25c multi, horiz. .25 .25

Salvadoran Paintings AP78

#C529, The Pottery of Paleca, by Miguel Ortiz Villacorta. #C530, The Rural School, by Luis Caceres Madrid. #C531, To the Wash, by Julia Diaz. #C532, "La Pancha" by Jose Mejia Vides. #C533, Boats Near The Beach, by Raul Elas Reyes. #C534, The Muleteers, by Canjura.

*Perf. 14x13½, 13½x14*

**1983, Oct. 18** **Litho.**
C529 AP78 25c multi .25 .25
C530 AP78 25c multi .25 .25
*a.* Pair, #C529-C530 .65 .65
C531 AP78 75c multi, vert. .60 .40
C532 AP78 75c multi, vert. .60 .40
*a.* Pair, #C531-C532 1.75 1.75
C533 AP78 1col multi, vert. .80 .55
C534 AP78 1col multi, vert. .80 .55
*a.* Pair, #C533-C534 2.50 2.50
*Nos. C529-C534 (6)* 3.30 2.40

Fishing Industry AP79

**1983, Dec. 20 Litho.** *Perf. 14½x14*
C535 AP79 25c Fisherman .40 .25
C536 AP79 75c Feeding fish 1.50 .45

No. 999 Surcharged

**1985, Apr. 10 Litho.** *Perf. 14*
C536A A297 1col on 10c multi .90 .50

Natl. Constitution, Cent. — AP80

**1986, Aug. 29 Litho.** *Perf. 14*
C537 AP80 1col multi .50 .35

Hugo Lindo (1917-1985), Writer — AP81

**1986, Nov. 10 Litho.** *Perf. 14½x14*
C538 AP81 1col multi .50 .35

Central American Economic Integration Bank, 25th Anniv. AP82

**1986, Nov. 20**
C539 AP82 1.50col multi .70 .50

12th Intl. Fair, Feb. 14-Mar. 1 AP83

**1987, Jan. 20 Litho.** *Perf. 14½x14*
C540 AP83 70c multi .35 .25

Intl. Year of Shelter for the Homeless AP84

*Perf. 14x14½, 14½x14*

**1987, July 15** **Litho.**

| | | | | |
|---|---|---|---|---|
| **C541** | AP84 | 70c shown | .40 | .25 |
| **C542** | AP84 | 1col Emblem, vert. | .50 | .35 |

Miniature Sheet

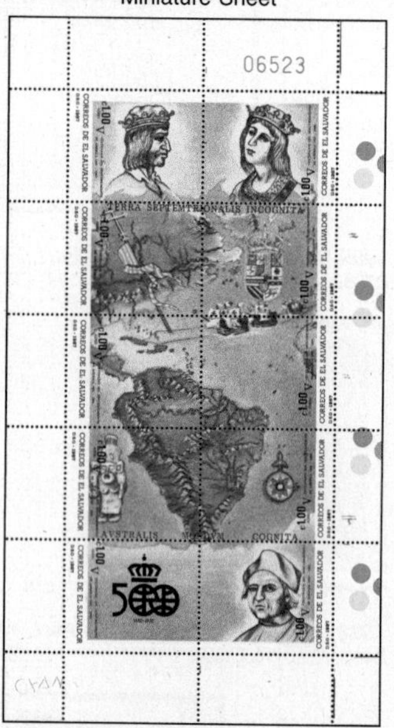

Discovery of America, 500th Anniv. (in 1992) — AP85

15th cent. map of the Americas (details) and: a, Ferdinand. b, Isabella. c, Caribbean. d, Ships, coat of arms. e, Base of flagstaff. f, Ships. g, Pre-Columbian statue. h, Compass. i, Anniv. emblem. j, Columbus rose.

**1987, Dec. 21** **Litho.** ***Perf. 14***

| | | | | |
|---|---|---|---|---|
| **C543** | AP85 | Sheet of 10 | 10.00 | 10.00 |
| *a.-j.* | | 1col any single | .65 | .35 |

**No. 1075 Surcharged**

**1988, Oct. 28** **Litho.** ***Perf. 14x14½***

| | | | | |
|---|---|---|---|---|
| **C544** | A316 | 5col on 90c multi | 3.50 | 2.00 |

PRENFIL '88, Nov. 25-Dec. 2, Buenos Aire.

Organization of American States 18th General Assembly, Nov. 14-19 — AP86

**1988, Nov. 19**

| | | | | |
|---|---|---|---|---|
| **C545** | AP86 | 70c multi | .40 | .30 |

Handicapped Soccer Championships — AP87

**1990, May 2** **Litho.** ***Perf. 14½x14***

| | | | | |
|---|---|---|---|---|
| **C546** | AP87 | 70c multicolored | .45 | .25 |

## REGISTRATION STAMPS

Gen. Rafael Antonio Gutiérrez — R1

**1897** **Engr.** **Wmk. 117** ***Perf. 12***

| | | | |
|---|---|---|---|
| **F1** | R1 | 10c dark blue | 125.00 |
| **F2** | R1 | 10c brown lake | .25 |

**Unwmk.**

| | | | |
|---|---|---|---|
| **F3** | R1 | 10c dark blue | .25 |
| **F4** | R1 | 10c brown lake | .25 |

Nos. F1 and F3 were probably not placed in use without the overprint "FRANQUEO OFICIAL" (Nos. O127-O128).

*The reprints are on thick unwatermarked paper. Value, set of 2, 16c.*

## ACKNOWLEDGMENT OF RECEIPT STAMPS

AR1

**1897** **Engr.** **Wmk. 117** ***Perf. 12***

| | | | |
|---|---|---|---|
| **H1** | AR1 | 5c dark green | .25 |

**Unwmk.**

| | | | |
|---|---|---|---|
| **H2** | AR1 | 5c dark green | .25 |

*No. H2 has been reprinted on thick paper. Value 20c.*

## POSTAGE DUE STAMPS

D1

**1895** **Unwmk.** **Engr.** ***Perf. 12***

| | | | | |
|---|---|---|---|---|
| **J1** | D1 | 1c olive green | .40 | — |
| **J2** | D1 | 2c olive green | .40 | — |
| **J3** | D1 | 3c olive green | .40 | — |
| **J4** | D1 | 5c olive green | .40 | — |
| **J5** | D1 | 10c olive green | .40 | — |
| **J6** | D1 | 15c olive green | .40 | — |
| **J7** | D1 | 25c olive green | .40 | — |
| **J8** | D1 | 50c olive green | .90 | — |
| | | *Nos. J1-J8 (8)* | 3.70 | |

See Nos. J9-J56. For overprints see Nos. J57-J64, O186-O214.

**1896** **Wmk. 117**

| | | | | |
|---|---|---|---|---|
| **J9** | D1 | 1c red | .60 | — |
| **J10** | D1 | 2c red | .60 | — |
| **J11** | D1 | 3c red | .90 | — |
| **J12** | D1 | 5c red | 1.10 | — |
| **J13** | D1 | 10c red | 1.10 | — |
| **J14** | D1 | 15c red | 1.25 | — |
| **J15** | D1 | 25c red | 1.25 | — |
| **J16** | D1 | 50c red | 1.25 | — |
| | | *Nos. J9-J16 (8)* | 8.05 | |

**Unwmk.**

| | | | | |
|---|---|---|---|---|
| **J17** | D1 | 1c red | .40 | — |
| **J18** | D1 | 2c red | .40 | — |
| **J19** | D1 | 3c red | .40 | — |
| **J20** | D1 | 5c red | .40 | — |
| **J21** | D1 | 10c red | .40 | — |
| **J22** | D1 | 15c red | .50 | — |
| **J23** | D1 | 25c red | .50 | — |
| **J24** | D1 | 50c red | .50 | — |
| | | *Nos. J17-J24 (8)* | 3.50 | |

Nos. J17-J24 exist imperforate.

**1897**

| | | | | |
|---|---|---|---|---|
| **J25** | D1 | 1c deep blue | .40 | — |
| **J26** | D1 | 2c deep blue | .40 | — |
| **J27** | D1 | 3c deep blue | .40 | — |
| **J28** | D1 | 5c deep blue | .40 | — |
| **J29** | D1 | 10c deep blue | .50 | — |
| **J30** | D1 | 15c deep blue | .50 | — |
| **J31** | D1 | 25c deep blue | .40 | — |
| **J32** | D1 | 50c deep blue | .40 | — |
| | | *Nos. J25-J32 (8)* | 3.40 | |

**1898**

| | | | |
|---|---|---|---|
| **J33** | D1 | 1c violet | 3.00 |
| **J34** | D1 | 2c violet | 1.00 |
| **J35** | D1 | 3c violet | 1.00 |
| **J36** | D1 | 5c violet | 5.00 |
| **J37** | D1 | 10c violet | 1.00 |
| **J38** | D1 | 15c violet | 1.00 |
| **J39** | D1 | 25c violet | 1.00 |
| **J40** | D1 | 50c violet | 1.00 |
| | | *Nos. J33-J40 (8)* | 14.00 |

*Reprints of Nos. J1 to J40 are on thick paper, often in the wrong shades and usually with the impression somewhat blurred. Value, set of 40, $2, watermarked or unwatermarked.*

**1899** **Wmk. 117 Sideways**

| | | | |
|---|---|---|---|
| **J41** | D1 | 1c orange | .40 |
| **J42** | D1 | 2c orange | .40 |
| **J43** | D1 | 3c orange | .40 |
| **J44** | D1 | 5c orange | .40 |
| **J45** | D1 | 10c orange | .40 |
| **J46** | D1 | 15c orange | .40 |
| **J47** | D1 | 25c orange | .40 |
| **J48** | D1 | 50c orange | .40 |
| | | *Nos. J41-J48 (8)* | 3.20 |

**Unwmk.**

**Thick Porous Paper**

| | | | |
|---|---|---|---|
| **J49** | D1 | 1c orange | .40 |
| **J50** | D1 | 2c orange | .40 |
| **J51** | D1 | 3c orange | .40 |
| **J52** | D1 | 5c orange | .40 |
| **J53** | D1 | 10c orange | .40 |
| **J54** | D1 | 15c orange | .40 |
| **J55** | D1 | 25c orange | .40 |
| **J56** | D1 | 50c orange | .40 |
| | | *Nos. J49-J56 (8)* | 3.20 |

Nos. J41-J56 were probably not put in use without the wheel overprint.

Nos. J49-J56 Overprinted in Black

**1900**

| | | | |
|---|---|---|---|
| **J57** | D1 | 1c orange | 2.00 |
| **J58** | D1 | 2c orange | 2.00 |
| **J59** | D1 | 3c orange | 2.00 |
| **J60** | D1 | 5c orange | 3.00 |
| **J61** | D1 | 10c orange | 4.00 |
| **J62** | D1 | 15c orange | 4.00 |
| **J63** | D1 | 25c orange | 5.00 |
| **J64** | D1 | 50c orange | 6.00 |
| | | *Nos. J57-J64 (8)* | 28.00 |

See note after No. 198A.

Morazán Monument — D2

*Perf. 14, 14½*

**1903** **Engr.** **Wmk. 173**

| | | | | |
|---|---|---|---|---|
| **J65** | D2 | 1c yellow green | 1.75 | 1.25 |
| **J66** | D2 | 2c carmine | 2.75 | 1.75 |
| **J67** | D2 | 3c orange | 2.75 | 1.75 |
| **J68** | D2 | 5c dark blue | 2.75 | 1.75 |
| **J69** | D2 | 10c dull violet | 2.75 | 1.75 |
| **J70** | D2 | 25c blue green | 2.75 | 1.75 |
| | | *Nos. J65-J70 (6)* | 15.50 | 10.00 |

Nos. 355, 356, 358 and 360 Overprinted

**1908** **Unwmk.** ***Perf. 11½***

| | | | | |
|---|---|---|---|---|
| **J71** | A66 | 1c green & blk | .80 | .70 |
| **J72** | A66 | 2c red & blk | .60 | .25 |
| **J73** | A66 | 5c blue & blk | 1.50 | 1.00 |
| **J74** | A66 | 10c violet & blk | 2.25 | 2.00 |

**Same Overprint on No. O275**

| | | | | |
|---|---|---|---|---|
| **J75** | O3 | 3c yellow & blk | 1.50 | 1.25 |
| | | *Nos. J71-J75 (5)* | 6.65 | 5.20 |

Nos. 355-358, 360 Overprinted

| | | | | |
|---|---|---|---|---|
| **J76** | A66 | 1c green & blk | .50 | .50 |
| **J77** | A66 | 2c red & blk | .60 | .60 |
| **J78** | A66 | 3c yellow & blk | .70 | .70 |
| **J79** | A66 | 5c blue & blk | 1.00 | 1.00 |
| **J80** | A66 | 10c violet & blk | 2.00 | 2.00 |
| | | *Nos. J76-J80 (5)* | 4.80 | 4.80 |

It is now believed that stamps of type A66, on paper with Honeycomb watermark, do not exist with genuine overprints of the types used for Nos. J71-J80.

Pres. Fernando Figueroa — D3

**1910** **Engr.** **Wmk. 172**

| | | | | |
|---|---|---|---|---|
| **J81** | D3 | 1c sepia & blk | .30 | .30 |
| **J82** | D3 | 2c dk grn & blk | .30 | .30 |
| **J83** | D3 | 3c orange & blk | .30 | .30 |
| **J84** | D3 | 4c scarlet & blk | .30 | .30 |
| **J85** | D3 | 5c purple & blk | .30 | .30 |
| **J86** | D3 | 12c deep blue & blk | .30 | .30 |
| **J87** | D3 | 24c brown red & blk | .30 | .30 |
| | | *Nos. J81-J87 (7)* | 2.10 | 2.10 |

## OFFICIAL STAMPS

Nos. 134-157O Overprinted — a

**Type a**

**1896** **Unwmk.** ***Perf. 12***

| | | | |
|---|---|---|---|
| **O1** | A45 | 1c blue | .25 |
| **O2** | A45 | 2c dk brown | .25 |
| *a.* | | Double overprint | |
| **O3** | A45 | 3c blue grn | 1.00 |
| **O4** | A45 | 5c brown ol | .25 |
| **O5** | A45 | 10c yellow | .25 |
| **O6** | A45 | 12c dk blue | .30 |
| **O7** | A45 | 15c blue vio | .25 |
| **O8** | A45 | 20c magenta | 1.00 |
| **O9** | A45 | 24c vermilion | .25 |
| **O10** | A45 | 30c orange | 1.00 |
| **O11** | A45 | 50c black brn | .45 |
| **O12** | A45 | 1p rose lake | .30 |
| | | *Nos. O1-O12 (12)* | 5.55 |

*Nos. O1-O12 were not issued.*

*The 1c has been reprinted on thick unwatermarked paper. Value 25c.*

**Wmk. 117**

| | | | | |
|---|---|---|---|---|
| **O13** | A46 | 1c emerald | 4.75 | 3.00 |
| **O14** | A47 | 2c lake | 4.75 | 3.50 |
| **O15** | A48 | 3c yellow brn | 6.00 | 4.00 |
| *a.* | | Inverted overprint | — | |
| **O16** | A49 | 5c dp blue | 5.00 | 5.00 |
| **O17** | A50 | 10c brown | 7.00 | 3.75 |
| *a.* | | Inverted overprint | — | |
| **O18** | A51 | 12c slate | 10.50 | 8.00 |
| **O19** | A52 | 15c blue grn | 12.50 | 8.75 |

O20 A53 20c car rose 12.50 8.00
a. Inverted overprint
O21 A54 24c violet 12.50 9.00
O22 A55 30c dp green 15.00 12.50
O23 A56 50c orange 25.00 17.00
O24 A57 100c dk blue 40.00 25.00
*Nos. O13-O24 (12)* 155.50 107.50

**Unwmk.**

O25 A46 1c emerald 2.50 *3.50*
a. Double overprint — —
O26 A47 2c lake 2.75 *175.00*
O27 A48 3c yellow brn 3.00 *2.50*
O28 A49 5c dp blue 3.00 .90
O29 A50 10c brown 2.50 2.50
a. Inverted overprint
O30 A51 12c slate 10.00 7.00
O31 A52 15c blue grn 12.00 7.75
O32 A53 20c car rose 20.00 11.00
a. Inverted overprint
O33 A54 24c violet 20.00 11.00
O34 A55 30c dp green — —
O35 A56 50c orange — —
O36 A57 100c dk blue — —
*Nos. O25-O36 (12)* 75.75 221.15

*All values have been reprinted. Value 25c each.*

Nos. 134-145 Handstamped in Black or Violet — b

**1896** **Type b**

O37 A45 1c blue 11.00
O38 A45 2c dk brown 11.00
O39 A45 3c blue green 11.00
O40 A45 5c brown olive 11.00
O41 A45 10c yellow 13.00
O42 A45 12c dk blue 16.00
O43 A45 15c blue violet 16.00
O44 A45 20c magenta 16.00
O45 A45 24c vermilion 16.00
O46 A45 30c orange 16.00
O47 A45 50c black brown 22.50
O48 A45 1p rose lake 22.50
*Nos. O37-O48 (12)* 182.00

*Reprints of the 1c and 2c on thick paper exist with this handstamp. Value, 25c each.*
*The legitimacy of the "De Officio" handstamp has been questioned. The editors would like to see evidence regarding the authorized use of this handstamp.*

Forged overprints exist of Nos. O37-O76, O103-O126 and of the higher valued stamps of O141-O214.

### Nos. 146-157F, 157I-157O, 158D Handstamped Type b in Black or Violet

**1896** **Wmk. 117**

O49 A46 1c emerald 9.00
O50 A47 2c lake 9.00
O51 A48 3c yellow brn 9.00
O52 A49 5c deep blue 9.00
O53 A50 10c brown 9.00
O54 A51 12c slate 16.00
O55 A52 15c blue green 16.00
O56 A53 20c carmine rose 16.00
O57 A54 24c violet 16.00
O58 A55 30c deep green 16.00
O59 A56 50c orange 16.00
O60 A57 100c dark blue 16.00
*Nos. O49-O60 (12)* 157.00

**Unwmk.**

O61 A46 1c emerald 9.00
O62 A47 2c lake 9.00
O63 A48 3c yellow brn 9.00
O64 A49 5c deep blue 9.00
O65 A50 10c brown 13.50
O66 A52 15c blue green 16.00
O67 A58 15c on 24c vio 11.50
O68 A53 20c carmine rose 16.00
O69 A54 24c violet 16.00
O70 A55 30c deep green 16.00
O71 A56 50c orange 19.00
O72 A57 100c dark blue 19.00
*Nos. O61-O72 (12)* 163.00

### Nos. 175-176 Overprinted Type a in Black

**1897**

O73 A59 1c bl, gold, rose & grn .30
O74 A59 5c rose, gold, bl & grn .30

These stamps were probably not officially issued.

### Nos. 175-176 Handstamped Type b in Black or Violet

**1900**

O75 A59 1c bl, gold, rose & grn 22.50
O76 A59 5c rose, gold, bl & grn 22.50

### Nos. 159-170L Overprinted Type a in Black

**1897** **Wmk. 117**

O79 A46 1c scarlet 8.00 8.00
O80 A47 2c yellow green 8.00 8.00
O81 A48 3c bister brown 7.00 7.00
O82 A49 5c orange 7.00 7.00
O83 A50 10c blue green 9.00 9.00
O84 A51 12c blue 20.00 20.00
O85 A52 15c black 40.00 40.00
O86 A53 20c slate 20.00 20.00
O87 A54 24c yellow 40.00 40.00
a. Inverted overprint
O88 A55 30c rose 40.00 40.00
O89 A56 50c violet 40.00 40.00
O90 A57 100c brown lake 100.00 100.00
*Nos. O79-O90 (12)* 339.00

**Unwmk.**

O91 A46 1c scarlet 5.00 5.00
O92 A47 2c yellow green 3.00 3.00
O93 A48 3c bister brown 2.00 2.00
O94 A49 5c orange 3.00 3.00
O95 A50 10c blue green 10.00 10.00
O96 A51 12c blue 3.00 3.00
O97 A52 15c black 30.00 30.00
O98 A53 20c slate 20.00 20.00
O99 A54 24c yellow 30.00 30.00
O100 A55 30c rose 30.00 30.00
O101 A56 50c violet 20.00 20.00
O102 A57 100c brown lake 50.00 50.00
*Nos. O91-O102 (12)* 206.00

*All values have been reprinted. Value 25c each.*

### Nos. 159-170L Handstamped Type b in Violet or Black

**1897** **Wmk. 117**

O103 A46 1c scarlet 7.50
O104 A47 2c yellow green 7.50
O105 A48 3c bister brown 7.50
O106 A49 5c orange 7.50
O107 A50 10c blue green 8.75
O108 A51 12c blue
O109 A52 15c black
O110 A53 20c slate 15.00
O111 A54 24c yellow 17.50
O112 A55 30c rose
O113 A56 50c violet
O114 A57 100c brown lake

**Unwmk.**

O115 A46 1c scarlet 7.50
O116 A47 2c yellow grn 7.50
O117 A48 3c bister brn 7.50
O118 A49 5c orange 7.50
O119 A50 10c blue green 7.50
O120 A51 12c blue
O121 A52 15c black
O122 A53 20c slate
O123 A54 24c yellow
O124 A55 30c rose 15.00
O125 A56 50c violet
O126 A57 100c brown lake 17.50

*Reprints of the 1 and 15c on thick watermarked paper and the 12, 30, 50 and 100c on thick unwatermarked paper are known with this overprint. Value, 25c each.*

### Nos. F1, F3 Overprinted Type a in Red

**Wmk. 117**

O127 R1 10c dark blue .30

**Unwmk.**

O128 R1 10c dark blue .30

*The reprints are on thick paper. Value 15c.*
*Originals of the 10c brown lake Registration Stamp and the 5c Acknowledgment of Receipt stamp are believed not to have been issued with the "FRANQUEO OFICIAL" overprint. They are believed to exist only as reprints.*

### Nos. 177-188 Overprinted Type a

**1898** **Wmk. 117**

O129 A60 1c orange ver 4.50 4.50
O130 A60 2c rose 4.50 4.50
O131 A60 3c pale yel grn 4.00 4.00
O132 A60 5c blue green 4.00 4.00
O133 A60 10c gray blue 15.00 15.00
O134 A60 12c violet 17.00 17.00
O135 A60 13c brown lake 17.00 17.00
O136 A60 20c deep blue 19.00 19.00
O137 A60 24c ultra 15.00 15.00
O138 A60 26c bister brn 20.00 20.00
O139 A60 50c orange 20.00 20.00
O140 A60 1p yellow 50.00 50.00
*Nos. O129-O140 (12)* 190.00 190.00

*Reprints of the above set are on thick paper. Value, 25c each.*

### No. 177 Handstamped Type b in Violet

O141 A60 1c orange ver 35.00 —

### No. O141 with Additional Overprint Type c in Black

c

Type "c" is called the "wheel" overprint.

O142 A60 1c orange ver — —

Counterfeits exist of the "wheel" overprint.

Nos. 204-205, 207 and 209 Overprinted

**1899** **Unwmk.**

O143 A61 12c dark green — 50.00
O144 A61 13c deep rose 50.00 —
O145 A61 26c carmine rose 50.00 —
O146 A61 100c violet 100.00 —

### Nos. O143-O144 Punched With Twelve Small Holes

O147 A61 12c dark green
O148 A61 13c deep rose

Official stamps punched with twelve small holes were issued and used for ordinary postage.

Nos. 199-209 Overprinted — d

**1899** **Blue Overprint**

O149 A61 1c brown .30
O150 A61 2c gray green .30
O151 A61 3c blue .30
O152 A61 5c brown orange .30
O153 A61 10c chocolate .30
O154 A61 13c deep rose .30
O155 A61 26c carmine rose .30
O156 A61 50c orange red .30
O157 A61 100c violet .30

**Black Overprint**

O158 A61 3c blue .30
O159 A61 12c dark green .30
O160 A61 24c lt blue .30
*Nos. O149-O160 (12)* 3.60

Nos. O149-O160 were probably not placed in use.

With Additional Overprint Type c in Black

O161 A61 1c brown .60 .60
O162 A61 2c gray green 1.10 1.10
O163 A61 3c blue .60 .60
O164 A61 5c brown org .60 .60
O165 A61 10c chocolate .75 .75
O166 A61 12c dark green — —
O167 A61 13c deep rose 1.50 1.50
O168 A61 24c lt blue 30.00 30.00
O169 A61 26c carmine rose .75 .75
O170 A61 50c orange red 1.50 1.50
O171 A61 100c violet 1.50 1.50
*Nos. O161-O165,O167-O171 (10)* 38.90 38.90

Nos. O149-O155, O159-O160 Punched With Twelve Small Holes

**Blue Overprint**

O172 A61 1c brown 5.00 1.00
O173 A61 2c gray green 3.25 5.00
O174 A61 3c blue 8.00 3.75
O175 A61 5c brown org 10.00 3.00
O176 A61 10c chocolate 15.00 5.00
O177 A61 13c deep rose 7.50 7.00
O177A A61 24c lt blue
O178 A61 26c car rose 100.00 35.00

**Black Overprint**

O179 A61 12c dark green 6.00 4.50
*Nos. O172-O177,O178-O179 (8)* 154.75 64.25

It is stated that Nos. O172-O214 inclusive were issued for ordinary postage and not for use as Official stamps.

### Nos. O161-O167, O169 Punched With Twelve Small Holes

O180 A61 1c brown 1.25 1.10
O180A A61 2c gray green
O181 A61 3c blue
O182 A61 5c brown orange 1.25
O182A A61 10c chocolate
O182B A61 12c dark green
O183 A61 13c deep rose 4.00 *5.00*
O184 A61 26c carmine rose

### No. 209 Ovptd. Types a and e in Black

e

O185 A61 100c violet

Nos. J49-J56 Overprinted in Black

**1900**

O186 D1 1c orange 27.50
O187 D1 2c orange 27.50
O188 D1 3c orange 27.50
O189 D1 5c orange 27.50
O190 D1 10c orange 27.50
O191 D1 15c orange 62.50
O192 D1 25c orange 62.50
O193 D1 50c orange 62.50
*Nos. O186-O193 (8)* 325.00

### Nos. O186-O189, O191-O193 Overprinted Type c in Black

O194 D1 1c orange *25.00*
O195 D1 2c orange *25.00*
O196 D1 3c orange *25.00*
O197 D1 5c orange *25.00*
O198 D1 15c orange 16.00 *25.00*
O199 D1 25c orange 19.00 *25.00*
O200 D1 50c orange 160.00 —

### Nos. O186-O189 Punched With Twelve Small Holes

O201 D1 1c orange 45.00
O202 D1 2c orange 45.00
O203 D1 3c orange 45.00
O204 D1 5c orange 45.00
*Nos. O201-O204 (4)* 180.00

### Nos. O201-O204 Overprinted Type c in Black

O205 D1 1c orange 9.00 6.50
O206 D1 2c orange 6.50
O207 D1 3c orange 6.50
O208 D1 5c orange 20.00 6.50

### Overprinted Type a in Violet and Type c in Black

O209 D1 2c orange *25.00*
a. Inverted overprint *25.00*
O210 D1 3c orange *25.00*
O211 D1 10c orange 3.00

### Nos. O186-O188 Handstamped Type e in Violet

O212 D1 1c orange 9.00 7.50
O213 D1 2c orange 9.00 7.50
O214 D1 3c orange 9.00 9.00
*Nos. O212-O214 (3)* 27.00 24.00

See note after No. O48.

### Type of Regular Issue of 1900 Overprinted Type a in Black

O223 A63 1c lt green 22.50 —
a. Inverted overprint
O224 A63 2c rose 27.50 —
a. Inverted overprint —
O225 A63 3c gray black 17.50 —
a. Overprint vertical
O226 A63 5c blue 17.50 —
O227 A63 10c blue 45.00 —
a. Inverted overprint
O228 A63 12c yellow grn 45.00 —
O229 A63 13c yellow brn 45.00 —
O230 A63 24c gray black 32.50 —

O231 A63 26c yellow brn 30.00 —
a. Inverted overprint
O232 A63 50c dull rose
a. Inverted overprint
*Nos. O223-O231 (9)* 282.50

Nos. O223-O224, O231-O232 Overprinted in Violet — f

O233 A63 1c lt green 4.75 4.00
O234 A63 2c rose 25.00
a. "FRANQUEO OFICIAL" invtd.
O235 A63 26c yellow brown .50 .50
O236 A63 50c dull rose .75 .55

Nos. O223, O225-O228, O232 Overprinted in Black — g

O237 A63 1c lt green 5.00 5.00
O238 A63 3c gray black
O239 A63 5c blue 40.00
O240 A63 10c blue
O241 A63 12c yellow green

**Violet Overprint**

O242 A63 50c dull rose 10.00

The shield overprinted on No. O242 is of the type on No. O212.

O1

**1903 Wmk. 173 *Perf. 14, 14½***

O243 O1 1c yellow green .45 .25
O244 O1 2c carmine .45 .25
O245 O1 3c orange 5.00 .85
O246 O1 5c dark blue 5.00 .25
O247 O1 10c dull violet .70 .35
O248 O1 13c red brown .70 .35
O249 O1 15c yellow brown 5.00 1.75
O250 O1 24c scarlet .45 .35
O251 O1 50c bister .70 .35
O252 O1 100c grnsh blue .70 .75
*Nos. O243-O252 (10)* 19.15 5.50

For surcharges see Nos. O254-O257.

**No. 285 Handstamped Type b in Black**

**1904**

O253 A64 3c orange 35.00

Nos. O246-O248 Surcharged in Black

**1905**

O254 O1 2c on 5c dark blue 6.50 5.50
O255 O1 3c on 5c dark blue
a. Double surcharge
O256 O1 3c on 10c dl vio 18.00 12.00
O257 O1 3c on 13c red brn 1.75 1.40

A 2c surcharge of this type exists on No. O247.

**No. O225 Overprinted in Blue**

a

b

**1905 Unwmk.**

O258 A63(a) 3c gray black 4.00 3.50
O259 A63(b) 3c gray black 3.50 3.00

**Nos. O224-O225 Overprinted in Blue**

c

d

**1906**

O260 A63(c) 2c rose 22.50 20.00
O261 A63(c) 3c gray black 2.50 2.00
a. Overprint "1906" in blk
O262 A63(d) 3c gray black 2.75 2.50
*Nos. O260-O262 (3)* 27.75 24.50

Escalón — O2

**1906 Engr. *Perf. 11½***

O263 O2 1c green & blk .40 .25
O264 O2 2c carmine & blk .40 .25
O265 O2 3c yellow & blk .40 .25
O266 O2 5c blue & blk .40 .75
O267 O2 10c violet & blk .40 .25
O268 O2 13c dk brown & blk .40 .25
O269 O2 15c red org & blk .50 .25
O270 O2 24c carmine & blk .60 .35
O271 O2 50c orange & blk .60 1.50
O272 O2 100c dk blue .70 4.50
*Nos. O263-O272 (10)* 4.80 8.60

The centers of these stamps are also found in blue black.

*Nos. O263 to O272 have been reprinted, perforated 11.8. Value, set of 10, $2.50.*

National Palace — O3

**1908**

O273 O3 1c green & blk .25 .25
O274 O3 2c red & blk .25 .25
O275 O3 3c yellow & blk .25 .25
O276 O3 5c blue & blk .25 .25
O277 O3 10c violet & blk .25 .25
O278 O3 13c violet & blk .25 .25
O279 O3 15c pale brn & blk .25 .25
O280 O3 24c rose & blk .25 .25
O281 O3 50c yellow & blk .25 .25
O282 O3 100c turq blue & blk .35 .35
*Nos. O273-O282 (10)* 2.60 2.60

For overprints see Nos. 441-442, 445-449, J75, O283-O292, O323-O328.

**Nos. O273-O282 Overprinted Type g in Black**

O283 O3 1c green & blk 3.00
O284 O3 2c red & blk 4.00
O285 O3 3c yellow & blk 4.00
O286 O3 5c blue & blk 5.00
O287 O3 10c violet & blk 5.00
O288 O3 13c violet & blk 6.00
O289 O3 15c pale brn & blk 6.00
O290 O3 24c rose & blk 8.00
O291 O3 50c yellow & blk 9.00
O292 O3 100c turq & blk 10.00
*Nos. O283-O292 (10)* 60.00

Pres. Figueroa — O4

**1910 Engr. Wmk. 172**

O293 O4 2c dk green & blk .30 .25
O294 O4 3c orange & blk .30 .25
O295 O4 4c scarlet & blk .30 .25
a. 4c carmine & black
O296 O4 5c purple & blk .30 .25
O297 O4 6c scarlet & blk .30 .25
O298 O4 10c purple & blk .30 .25
O299 O4 12c dp blue & blk .30 .25
O300 O4 17c olive grn & blk .30 .25
O301 O4 19c brn red & blk .30 .25
O302 O4 29c choc & blk .30 .25
O303 O4 50c yellow & blk .30 .25
O304 O4 100c turq & blk .30 .25
*Nos. O293-O304 (12)* 3.60 3.00

**Regular Issue, Type A63, Overprinted or Surcharged**

a

b

c

**1911 Unwmk.**

O305 A63(a) 1c lt green .25 .25
O306 A63(b) 3c on 13c yel brn .25 .25
O307 A63(b) 5c on 10c dp bl .25 .25
O308 A63(a) 10c deep blue .25 .25
O309 A63(a) 12c lt green .25 .25
O310 A63(a) 13c yellow brn .25 .25
O311 A63(b) 50c on 10c dp bl .25 .25
O312 A63(c) 1col on 13c yel brn .25 .25
*Nos. O305-O312 (8)* 2.00 2.00

O5

**1914 Typo. *Perf. 12***
**Background in Green, Shield and "Provisional" in Black**

O313 O5 2c yellow brn .50 .25
O314 O5 3c yellow .50 .25
O315 O5 5c dark blue .50 .25
O316 O5 10c red .50 .25
O317 O5 12c green .50 .25
O318 O5 17c violet .50 .25
O319 O5 50c brown .50 .25
O320 O5 100c dull rose .50 .25
*Nos. O313-O320 (8)* 4.00 2.00

Stamps of this issue are known imperforate or with parts of the design omitted or misplaced. These varieties were not regularly issued.

O6

**1914 Typo.**

O321 O6 2c blue green .50 .25
O322 O6 3c orange .50 .25

Type of Official Stamps of 1908 With Two Overprints

**1915**

O323 O3 1c gray green 1.00 .60
a. "1915" double
b. "OFICIAL" inverted
O324 O3 2c red 1.00 .60
O325 O3 5c ultra .35 .70
O326 O3 10c yellow .35 .60
a. Date omitted
O327 O3 50c violet .90 1.50
O328 O3 100c black brown 1.90 3.25
*Nos. O323-O328 (6)* 5.50 7.25

**Same Overprint on #414, 417, 429**

O329 A66 1c gray green 10.00 1.60
O330 A66 6c pale blue 1.00 .45
a. 6c ultramarine
O331 A66 12c brown 1.00 .75
*Nos. O329-O331 (3)* 12.00 2.80

# O323-O327, O329-O331 exist imperf.

Nos. O329-O331 exist with "OFICIAL" inverted and double. See note after No. 421.

Nos. 431-440 Overprinted in Blue or Red

**1916**

O332 A83 1c deep green .45 .75
O333 A83 2c vermilion 1.60 1.60
O334 A83 5c dp blue (R) 1.25 1.60
O335 A83 6c gray vio (R) .45 .75
O336 A83 10c black brown .45 .75
O337 A83 12c violet 2.00 3.25
O338 A83 17c orange .45 .75
O339 A83 25c dark brown .45 .75
O340 A83 29c black (R) .45 .75
O341 A83 50c slate (R) 2.00 .75
*Nos. O332-O341 (10)* 9.55 11.70

**Nos. 474-481 Overprinted**

a

b

**1921**

O342 A94(a) 1c green .25 .25
O343 A95(a) 2c black .25 .25
a. Inverted overprint
O344 A96(b) 5c orange .25 .25
O345 A97(a) 6c carmine rose .25 .25
O346 A98(a) 10c deep blue .30 .25
O347 A99(a) 25c olive green .75 .35
O348 A100(a) 60c violet 1.00 .60
O349 A101(a) 1col black brown 1.10 .70
*Nos. O342-O349 (8)* 4.15 2.90

Nos. 498 and 500 Overprinted in Black or Red

**1925**

O350 A109 5c olive black .45 .25
O351 A111 10c orange (R) .85 .25
a. "ATLANT CO" 13.00 11.00

Inverted overprints exist.

Regular Issue of 1924-25 Overprinted in Black or Red

**1927**

O352 A106 1c red violet .25 .25
O353 A107 2c dark red .45 .25
O354 A109 5c olive blk (R) .45 .25
O355 A110 6c dp blue (R) 5.25 4.50
O356 A111 10c orange .50 .30
a. "ATLANT CO" 22.50 19.00
O357 A116 1col grn & vio (R) 2.25 1.40
*Nos. O352-O357 (6)* 9.15 6.95

Inverted overprints exist on 1c, 2c, 5c, 10c.

Regular Issue of 1924-25 Overprinted in Black

**1932** *Perf. 12½*

| | | | | |
|---|---|---|---|---|
| **O358** | A106 | 1c deep violet | .25 | .25 |
| **O359** | A107 | 2c dark red | .45 | .25 |
| **O360** | A109 | 5c olive black | .25 | .25 |
| **O361** | A111 | 10c orange | .85 | .35 |
| *a.* | | "ATLANT CO" | 22.50 | 19.00 |
| | | *Nos. O358-O361 (4)* | 1.80 | 1.10 |

**Catalogue values for unused stamps in this section, from this point to the end of the section, are for Never Hinged items.**

Regular Issue of 1947 Overprinted in Black or Red

**1948** **Unwmk.** **Engr.** *Perf. 12*

| | | | | |
|---|---|---|---|---|
| **O362** | A154 | 1c car rose | 65.00 | 32.50 |
| **O363** | A154 | 2c deep org | 65.00 | 32.50 |
| **O364** | A154 | 5c slate gray (R) | 65.00 | 32.50 |
| **O365** | A154 | 10c bis brn (R) | 65.00 | 32.50 |
| **O366** | A154 | 20c green (R) | 65.00 | 32.50 |
| **O367** | A154 | 50c black (R) | 65.00 | 32.50 |
| | | *Nos. O362-O367 (6)* | 390.00 | 195.00 |

No. 602 Surcharged in Carmine and Black

**1964(?)**

| | | | | |
|---|---|---|---|---|
| **O368** | A154 | 1c on 20c green | *90.00* | — |

The X's are black, the rest carmine.

## PARCEL POST STAMPS

Mercury
PP1

**1895** **Unwmk.** **Engr.** *Perf. 12*

| | | | |
|---|---|---|---|
| **Q1** | PP1 | 5c brown orange | .45 |
| **Q2** | PP1 | 10c dark blue | .45 |
| **Q3** | PP1 | 15c red | .45 |
| **Q4** | PP1 | 20c orange | .45 |
| **Q5** | PP1 | 50c blue green | .45 |
| | | *Nos. Q1-Q5 (5)* | 2.25 |

## POSTAL TAX STAMPS

PT1

**Overprinted "REVISADO" in Violet, Black or Red**

**1900-04** **Typo.** *Perf. 11½*

**RA1** PT1 1c black
**RA2** PT1 1c black, dated "1903"
**RA3** PT1 1c black, dated "1904"

Use of these stamps was obligatory on all domestic letters. The funds raised were used to maintain the public schools.

Nos. 503, 501 Surcharged

**1931** **Unwmk.** *Perf. 12½*

| | | | | |
|---|---|---|---|---|
| **RA4** | A115 | 1c on 50c org brn | .50 | .40 |
| *a.* | | Double surcharge | 5.00 | 5.00 |
| **RA5** | A112 | 2c on 20c dp grn | .50 | .40 |

Nos. 501, 503 Surcharged

| | | | | |
|---|---|---|---|---|
| **RA6** | A112 | 1c on 20c dp grn | .50 | .40 |
| **RA7** | A115 | 2c on 50c org brn | .50 | .40 |
| *a.* | | Without period in "0.02" | 3.00 | |

The use of these stamps was obligatory, in addition to the regular postage, on letters and other postal matter. The money obtained from their sale was to be used to erect a new post office in San Salvador.

# SAMOA

sə-'mō-ə

## (Western Samoa)

LOCATION — Archipelago in the south Pacific Ocean, east of Fiji
GOVT. — Independent state; former territory mandated by New Zealand
AREA — 1,093 sq. mi.
POP. — 161,298 (1991)
CAPITAL — Apia

In 1861-99, Samoa was an independent kingdom under the influence of the US, to which the harbor of Pago Pago had been ceded, and that of Great Britain and Germany. In 1898 a disturbance arose, resulting in the withdrawal of Great Britain, and the partitioning of the islands between Germany and the US. Early in World War I the islands under German domination were occupied by New Zealand troops and in 1920 the League of Nations declared them a mandate to New Zealand. Western Samoa became independent Jan. 1, 1962.

12 Pence = 1 Shilling
20 Shillings = 1 Pound
100 Pfennig = 1 Mark (1900)
100 Sene (Cents) = 1 Tala (Dollar) (1967)

**Catalogue values for unused stamps in this country are for Never Hinged items, beginning with Scott 191 in the regular postage section, Scott B1 in the semi-postal section and Scott C1 in the air post section.**

### Watermarks

Wmk. 61 — N Z and Star Close Together

Wmk. 62 — N Z and Star Wide Apart

On watermark 61 the margins of the sheets are watermarked "NEW ZEALAND POSTAGE" and parts of the double-lined letters of these words are frequently found on the stamps. It occasionally happens that a stamp shows no watermark whatever.

Wmk. 253 — Multiple N Z and Star

Wmk. 355 — Kava Bowl and WS, Multiple

### Issues of the Kingdom

A1

Type I

Type II

Type III

Type IV

Type I — Line above "X" is usually unbroken. Dots over "SAMOA" are uniform and evenly spaced. Upper right serif of "M" is horizontal.

Type II — Line above "X" is usually broken. Small dot near upper right serif of "M."

Type III — Line above "X" roughly retouched. Upper right serif of "M" bends down (joined to dot).

Type IV — Speck of color on curved line below center of "M."

*Perf. 11¾, 12½*

**1877-82** **Litho.** **Unwmk.**

| | | | | | |
|---|---|---|---|---|---|
| **1** | A1 | 1p | Blue (III), Perf. 11¾ ('79) | 37.50 | *1,000.* |
| **1a** | A1 | 1p | sky blue (III), Perf. 12½ ('79) | 260.00 | 125.00 |
| **2** | A1 | 2p | lilac rose (IV), ('82) | 25.00 | — |
| **3c** | A1 | 3p | vermilion (I) | 450.00 | *250.00* |
| **3d** | A1 | 3p | vermilion, rough perfs (III), Perf. 11¾ | 65.00 | — |

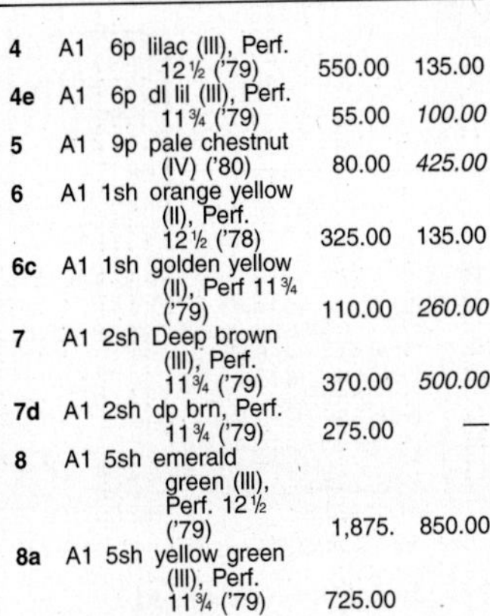

| | | | | | |
|---|---|---|---|---|---|
| **4** | A1 | 6p | lilac (III), Perf. 12½ ('79) | 550.00 | 135.00 |
| **4e** | A1 | 6p | dl lil (III), Perf. 11¾ ('79) | 55.00 | *100.00* |
| **5** | A1 | 9p | pale chestnut (IV) ('80) | 80.00 | *425.00* |
| **6** | A1 | 1sh | orange yellow (II), Perf. 12½ ('78) | 325.00 | 135.00 |
| **6c** | A1 | 1sh | golden yellow (II), Perf 11¾ ('79) | 110.00 | *260.00* |
| **7** | A1 | 2sh | Deep brown (III), Perf. 11¾ ('79) | 370.00 | *500.00* |
| **7d** | A1 | 2sh | dp brn, Perf. 11¾ ('79) | 275.00 | — |
| **8** | A1 | 5sh | emerald green (III), Perf. 12½ ('79) | 1,875. | 850.00 |
| **8a** | A1 | 5sh | yellow green (III), Perf. 11¾ ('79) | 725.00 | |

Values are for the least expensive varieties. For detailed listings, see the *Scott Classic Specialized Catalogue.*

The 1p often has a period after "PENNY." The 2p was never placed in use since the Samoa Express service was discontinued late in 1881.

Imperforates of this issue are proofs.

Sheets of the first issue were not perforated around the outer sides. All values except the 2p were printed in sheets of 10 (2x5). The 1p, 3p and 6p type I and the 1p type III were also printed in sheets of 20 (4x5), and six stamps on each of these sheets were perforated all around. These are the only varieties of the original stamps which have not one or two imperforate edges. The 2p was printed in sheets of 21 (3x7) and five stamps in the second row were perforated all around. The 2p was also reprinted in sheets of 40, which are much more common than the sheets of 21.

*Reprints are of type IV and nearly always perforated on all sides. They have a spot of color at the edge of the panel below the "M." This spot is not on any originals except the 9p, the original of which may be distinguished by having a rough blind perf. 12. The 2p does show a spot of color.*

Forgeries exist.

Palms
A2

King Malietoa Laupepa
A3

*Perf. 11, 12x11½ (#14, 17a), 12½ (#16, 18)*

**1886-1900** **Typo.** **Wmk. 62**

| | | | | | |
|---|---|---|---|---|---|
| **9d** | A2 | ½p | purple brown | 5.75 | *2.10* |
| **10** | A2 | ½p | dl bl grn ('99) | 4.00 | *4.50* |
| **11f** | A2 | 1p | bluish green ('97) | 4.00 | 2.00 |
| **12** | A2 | 1p | red brown | 4.25 | *20.00* |
| **13g** | A2 | 2p | bright yellow ('97) | 16.00 | 10.00 |
| **14** | A3 | 2½p | rose ('92) | 80.00 | 6.00 |
| **14b** | A3 | 2½p | rose | 4.25 | *10.50* |
| **15** | A3 | 2½p | black, perf 10x11 ('96) | 2.25 | *3.25* |
| **16** | A2 | 4p | blue | 55.00 | 13.50 |
| **16f** | A2 | 4p | deep blue ('00) | 1.60 | 52.50 |
| **17a** | A2 | 6p | maroon | 325.00 | 12.50 |
| **17e** | A2 | 6p | maroon ('00) | 2.00 | 62.50 |
| **18** | A2 | 1sh | rose carmine | 67.50 | 13.50 |
| *a.* | | | Perf 12½, diagonal half used on cover ('95) | | 375.00 |
| **18g** | A2 | 1sh | carmine ('00) | 1.80 | — |
| **19h** | A2 | 2sh6p | deep purple ('98) | 5.00 | 10.00 |
| *i.* | | | Vert. pair, imperf. btw. | 475.00 | |

The 2½p has only the 3rd form.

Nos. 9-19 exist in various printings, perf 11, 12½ and 12x11½. Values are for the least expensive varieties. For detailed listings, see the *Scott Classic Specialized Catalogue.*

For surcharges or overprints on stamps or types of design A2 see Nos. 20-22, 24-38.

**Nos. 16b and 16c Handstamp Surcharged in Black or Red**

a

b

c

**1893** *Perf. 12x11½*
**20** A2(a) 5p on 4p blue (#16c) 65.00 *100.00*
*a.* On 4p deep blue (#16b) 100.00 100.00
**21** A2(b) 5p on 4p blue (#16c) 75.00 —
*a.* On 4p deep blue (#16b) 100.00 *110.00*
**22** A2(c) 5p on 4p blue (#16c) (R) 42.50 *37.50*
*a.* On 4p deep blue (#16b) 47.50 *50.00*
*Nos. 20-22 (3)* 182.50 *137.50*

As the surcharges on Nos. 20-21 were handstamped in two steps and on No. 22 in three steps, various varieties exist.

Flag Design — A7

**1894-95** **Typo.** *Perf. 11½x12*
**23** A7 5p vermilion 35.00 7.50
*a.* Perf. 11 ('95) 70.00 15.00
*b.* As "a," deep red ('00) 5.00 *20.00*

**Types of 1887-1895 Surcharged in Blue, Black, Red or Green**

1½p, 2½p

3p

**Handstamped Surcharges**

**1895** *Perf. 11*
**24** A2 1½p on 2p org (Bl) 7.50 *10.00*
*a.* 1½p on 2p brn org, perf 12x11½ (Bl) 27.50 20.00
*b.* 1½p on 2p yellow, "2" ends with vertical stroke 5.00 *27.50*
*c.* As No. 24, pair, one without surcharge 650.00
**25** A2 3p on 2p org (Bk) 10.00 *15.00*
*a.* 3p on 2p brn org, perf. 12x11½ (Bk) 60.00 25.00
*b.* 3p on 2p org yellow, narrow "R" (Bk) 6.00 *50.00*
*c.* Vert. pair, imperf. btwn. 650.00
*d.* As "b," pair, one without surcharge

**Typographed Surcharges (#26 Handstamped)**

**1898-1900** *Perf. 11*
**26** A2 2½p on 1sh rose (Bk), hstmpd. srch. 50.00 *50.00*
*a.* 2½p, typo surcharge 13.00 *15.00*
*b.* As "a," double surcharge 500.00 500.00
**27** A2 2½p on 2sh6p vio (Bk) 13.00 *20.00*
**28** A2 2½p on 1p bl grn (R) 1.75 *5.00*
*a.* Inverted surcharge 850.00 *425.00*
**29** A2 2½p on 1sh rose car (R) 8.50 *20.00*
*a.* Double surcharge 400.00
**30** A2 3p on 2p dp red org (G) 5.00 *130.00*
*Nos. 26-30 (5)* 78.25 *225.00*

No. 30 was a reissue, available for postage. The surcharge is not as tall as the 3p surcharge illustrated, which is the surcharge on No. 25. As Nos. 24-26 are handstamped, various varieties exist.

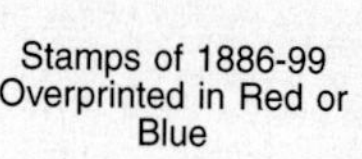
Stamps of 1886-99 Overprinted in Red or Blue

**1899**
**31** A2 ½p dl bl grn (R) 3.50 *8.00*
**32** A2 1p red brown (Bl) 4.25 *20.00*
**33** A2 2p br orange (R) 2.50 *20.00*
*a.* 2p deep ocher 4.00 *20.00*
**34** A2 4p blue (R) 1.00 *20.00*
**35** A7 5p dp scarlet (Bl) 3.75 *20.00*
**36** A2 6p maroon (Bl) 2.00 *20.00*
**37** A2 1sh rose car (Bl) 2.00 *25.00*
**38** A2 2sh6p mauve (R) 4.75 *40.00*
*Nos. 31-38 (8)* 23.75 *173.00*

In 1900 the Samoan islands were partitioned between the US and Germany. The part which became American has since used US stamps.

**Issued under German Dominion**

Stamps of Germany Overprinted

**1900** **Unwmk.** *Perf. 13½x14½*
**51** A9 3pf dark brown 8.50 *11.50*
**52** A9 5pf green 10.50 *15.00*
**53** A10 10pf carmine 8.50 *15.00*
**54** A10 20pf ultra 17.50 *26.00*
**55** A10 25pf orange 35.00 *70.00*
**56** A10 50pf red brown 35.00 *65.00*
*Nos. 51-56 (6)* 115.00 *202.50*

Kaiser's Yacht "Hohenzollern"
A12 A13

**1900** **Typo.** *Perf. 14*
**57** A12 3pf brown .90 *1.00*
**58** A12 5pf green .90 *1.00*
**59** A12 10pf carmine .90 *1.00*
**60** A12 20pf ultra .90 *1.90*
**61** A12 25pf org & blk, *yel* 1.00 *10.50*
**62** A12 30pf org & blk, *sal* 1.25 *9.00*
**63** A12 40pf lake & blk 1.25 *10.50*
**64** A12 50pf pur & blk, *sal* 1.25 *12.00*
**65** A12 80pf lake & blk, *rose* 2.50 *26.00*

*Perf. 14½x14*
**Engr.**
**66** A13 1m carmine 3.00 *52.50*
**67** A13 2m blue 4.25 *90.00*
**68** A13 3m black vio 7.00 *130.00*
**69** A13 5m slate & car 175.00 *450.00*
*Nos. 57-69 (13)* 200.10 *795.40*

**1915** **Wmk. 125** **Typo.** *Perf. 14*
**70** A12 3pf brown 1.00
**71** A12 5pf green 1.10
**72** A12 10pf carmine 1.10

*Perf. 14½x14*
**Engr.**
**73** A13 5m slate & car 35.00

Nos. 70-73 were never put in use.

**Issued under British Dominion**

Nos. 57-69 Surcharged

On A12

On A13

**1914** **Unwmk.** *Perf. 14*
**101** A12 ½p on 3pf brn 60.00 16.00
*a.* Double surcharge 800.00 625.00
*b.* Fraction bar omitted 90.00 42.50
*c.* Comma after "I" 750.00 450.00
**102** A12 ½p on 5pf grn 65.00 20.00
*a.* Double surcharge 800.00 625.00
*b.* Fraction bar omitted 140.00 62.50
*d.* Comma after "I" 450.00 190.00
**103** A12 1p on 10pf car 110.00 42.50
*a.* Double surcharge 850.00 675.00
**104** A12 2½p on 20pf ultra 62.50 14.00
*a.* Fraction bar omitted 95.00 45.00
*b.* Inverted surcharge 1,150. 1,050.
*c.* Double surcharge 800.00 675.00
*d.* Commas after "I" 575.00 375.00
**105** A12 3p on 25pf org & blk, *yel* 80.00 42.50
*a.* Double surcharge 1,150. 850.00
*b.* Comma after "I" 5,250. 1,150.
**106** A12 4p on 30pf org & blk, *sal* 135.00 62.50
**107** A12 5p on 40pf lake & blk 135.00 75.00
**108** A12 6p on 50pf pur & blk, *sal* 67.50 37.50
*a.* Inverted "9" for "6" 190.00 110.00
*b.* Double surcharge 1,250. 1,150.
**109** A12 9p on 80pf lake & blk, *rose* 210.00 110.00

*Perf. 14½x14*
**110** A13 1sh on 1m car ("1 Shillings") 3,500. *3,750.*
*a.* "1 Shilling." *11,500.* *7,500.*
**111** A13 2sh on 2m blue 4,000. 3,500.
**112** A13 3sh on 3m blk vio 1,600. 1,500.
*a.* Double surcharge *10,500.* *11,500.*
**113** A13 5sh on 5m slate & car 1,200. 1,100.
*a.* Double surcharge 15,000. 15,000.

G.R.I. stands for Georgius Rex Imperator.

The 3d on 30pf and 4d on 40pf were produced at a later time.

Unauthorized overprints, created as favors, exist on Nos. 101-113.

**Stamps of New Zealand Overprinted in Red or Blue**

k

m

*Perf. 14, 14x13½, 14x14½*
**1914, Sept. 29** **Wmk. 61**
**114** A41(k) ½p yel grn (R) 1.50 .35
**115** A42(k) 1p carmine 1.40 .25
**116** A41(k) 2p mauve (R) 1.40 1.10
**117** A22(m) 2½p blue (R) 2.00 2.00
**118** A41(k) 6p car rose, perf. 14x14½ 2.25 2.00
*a.* Perf. 14x13½ 19.00 26.00
**119** A41(k) 1sh vermilion 11.00 *22.00*
*Nos. 114-119 (6)* 19.55 *27.70*

**Overprinted Type "m"**

**1914-25** *Perf. 14, 14½x14*
**120** PF1 2sh blue (R) 7.00 6.25
**121** PF1 2sh6p brown (Bl) 6.25 *15.00*
**122** PF1 3sh vio (R) ('22) 18.00 *65.00*
**123** PF1 5sh green (R) 22.50 *11.00*
**124** PF1 10sh red brn (Bl) 45.00 *42.50*
**125** PF2 £1 rose (Bl) 100.00 85.00
**126** PF2 £2 vio (R) ('25) 400.00
*Nos. 120-126 (7)* 598.75
*Nos. 120-125 (6)* *224.75*

Postal use of the £2 is questioned.

**Overprinted Type "k"**
*Perf. 14x13½, 14x14½*

**1916-19** **Typo.**
**127** A43 ½p yellow grn (R) 1.00 *1.40*
**128** A47 1½p gray blk (R) ('17) .55 .25
**129** A47 1½p brn org (R) ('19) .35 .50
**130** A43 2p yellow (R) ('18) 2.00 .25
**131** A43 3p chocolate (Bl) 3.50 *22.50*

**Engr.**
**132** A44 2½p dull blue (R) 1.25 .60
**133** A45 3p violet brn (Bl) .65 *1.25*
**134** A45 6p carmine rose (Bl) 3.50 3.50
**135** A45 1sh vermilion (Bl) 4.75 1.75
*Nos. 127-135 (9)* 17.55 32.00

**New Zealand Victory Issue of 1919 Overprinted Type "k"**

**1920, June** *Perf. 14*
**136** A48 ½p yellow grn (R) 6.50 *16.00*
**137** A49 1p carmine (Bl) 3.00 *21.00*
**138** A50 1½p brown org (R) 2.00 *11.00*
**139** A51 3p black brn (Bl) 9.25 *10.50*
**140** A52 6p purple (R) 5.25 *8.00*
**141** A53 1sh vermilion (Bl) 15.00 12.50
*Nos. 136-141 (6)* 41.00 79.00

British Flag and Samoan House — A22

**1921, Dec. 23** **Engr.** *Perf. 14x13½*
**142** A22 ½p green 5.50 *2.00*
*a.* Perf. 14x14½ 5.50 *15.00*
**143** A22 1p lake 6.50 .25
*a.* Perf. 14x14½ 9.00 1.75
**144** A22 1½p org brn, perf. 14x14½ 1.50 *20.00*
*a.* Perf. 14x13½ 20.00 13.00
**145** A22 2p yel, perf. 14x14½ 3.00 3.00
*a.* Perf. 14x13½ 15.00 .90
**146** A22 2½p dull blue 2.00 *9.50*
**147** A22 3p dark brown 2.00 *6.00*
**148** A22 4p violet 2.00 *4.00*
**149** A22 5p brt blue 2.00 *9.00*
**150** A22 6p carmine rose 2.00 *8.00*
**151** A22 8p red brown 2.25 *16.00*
**152** A22 9p olive green 2.50 *40.00*
**153** A22 1sh vermilion 2.25 *32.50*
*Nos. 142-153 (12)* 33.50 *150.25*

For overprints see Nos. 163-165.

**New Zealand Nos. 182-183 Overprinted Type "m" in Red**

**1926-27** *Perf. 14½x14*
**154** A56 2sh dark blue 5.75 *21.00*
*a.* 2sh blue ('27) 7.00 *50.00*
**155** A56 3sh deep violet 25.00 *50.00*
*a.* 3sh violet ('27) 62.50 *110.00*

Issued: 2sh, Nov.; 3sh, Oct.; Nos. 154a, 155a, 11/10.

**New Zealand Postal-Fiscal Stamps, Overprinted Type "m" in Blue or Red**

**1932, Aug.** *Perf. 14*
**156** PF5 2sh6p brown 18.00 *55.00*
**157** PF5 5sh green (R) 30.00 *57.50*
**158** PF5 10sh lake 55.00 *110.00*
**159** PF5 £1 pink 80.00 *160.00*
**160** PF5 £2 violet (R) *1,000.*
**161** PF5 £5 dk bl (R) *2,600.*
*Nos. 156-159 (4)* 183.00 *382.50*

See Nos. 175-180, 195-202, 216-219.

**Silver Jubilee Issue**

Stamps of 1921 Overprinted in Black

**1935, May 7** *Perf. 14x13½*
**163** A22 1p lake .40 *.50*
*a.* Perf. 14x14½ *105.00* *190.00*
**164** A22 2½p dull blue .75 *1.00*
**165** A22 6p carmine rose 3.25 *5.00*
*Nos. 163-165 (3)* 4.40 6.50
Set, never hinged 10.00

25th anniv. of the reign of George V.

**Western Samoa**

Samoan Girl and Kava Bowl — A23

View of Apia — A24

River Scene — A25

Samoan Chief and Wife — A26

Samoan Canoe and House — A27

"Vailima," Stevenson's Home — A28

Stevenson's Tomb — A29

Lake Lanuto'o — A30

Falefa Falls — A31

***Perf. 14x13½, 13½x14***

**1935, Aug. 7 Engr. Wmk. 61**

166 A23 ½p yellow grn .25 .40
167 A24 1p car lake & blk .25 .25
168 A25 2p red org & blk, perf. 14 4.00 *4.25*
a. Perf. 13½x14 5.00 *4.25*
169 A26 2½p dp blue & blk .25 .25
170 A27 4p org brn & indigo .50 .35
171 A28 6p plum .70 .35
172 A29 1sh org brn & violet .50 .50
173 A30 2sh red brn & yel grn 1.10 .80
174 A31 3sh org brn & brt bl 2.75 *3.50*
*Nos. 166-174 (9)* 10.30 *10.65*
Set, never hinged 21.00

See Nos. 186-188.

Postal-Fiscal Stamps of New Zealand Overprinted in Blue or Carmine

**1935 *Perf. 14***

175 PF5 2sh6p brown 10.00 *18.00*
176 PF5 5sh green 22.50 *32.50*
177 PF5 10sh dp car 62.50 *85.00*
178 PF5 £1 pink 55.00 *110.00*
179 PF5 £2 violet (C) 160.00 *400.00*
180 PF5 £5 dk bl (C) 235.00 *525.00*
*Nos. 175-180 (6)* 545.00 *1,171.*

See Nos. 195-202, 216-219.

Samoan Coastal Village — A32

Map of Western Samoa — A33

Samoan Dancing Party A34

Robert Louis Stevenson A35

***Perf. 13½x14***

**1939, Aug. 29 Engr. Wmk. 253**

181 A32 1p scar & olive .60 .35
182 A33 1½p copper brn & bl 1.00 .90
183 A34 2½p dk blue & brn 1.10 1.00

***Perf. 14x13½***

184 A35 7p dk grn & vio 3.75 *4.25*
*Nos. 181-184 (4)* 6.45 6.50
Set, never hinged 12.00

25th anniv. of New Zealand's control of the mandated territory of Western Samoa.

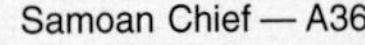
Samoan Chief — A36

**1940, Sept. 2 *Perf. 14x13½***

185 A36 3p on 1½p brown .50 .35
Never hinged .85

Issued only with surcharge. Examples without surcharge are from printer's archives.

**Types of 1935 and**

Apia Post Office — A37

**1944-49 Wmk. 253 *Perf. 14***

186 A23 ½p yellow green .30 *21.00*
187 A25 2p red orange & blk 2.00 *7.50*
188 A26 2½p dp blue & blk ('48) 5.00 *42.50*

***Perf. 13½x14***

189 A37 5p dp ultra & ol brn ('49) 1.40 1.00
*Nos. 186-189 (4)* 8.70 *72.00*
Set, never hinged 14.50

Issue date: 5p, June 8.

**Catalogue values for unused stamps in this section, from this point to the end of the section, are for Never Hinged items.**

**Peace Issue**

New Zealand Nos. 248, 250, 254, and 255 Overprinted in Black or Blue

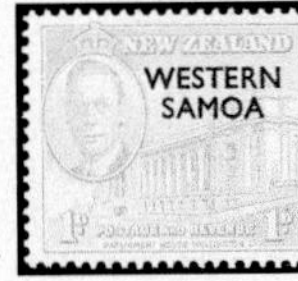

p

q

**1946, June 1 *Perf. 13x13½, 13½x13***

191 A94(p) 1p emerald .40 .25
192 A96(q) 2p rose violet (Bl) .40 .25
193 A100(p) 6p org red & red brn .80 .25
194 A101(p) 8p carmine & blk (Bl) .45 .25
*Nos. 191-194 (4)* 2.05 1.00

**Stamps and Type of New Zealand, 1931-50 Overprinted Like Nos. 175-180 in Blue or Carmine**

**1945-50 Wmk. 253 *Perf. 14***

195 PF5 2sh6p brown 15.00 *30.00*
196 PF5 5sh green 21.00 18.00
197 PF5 10sh car ('48) 23.00 19.00
198 PF5 £1 pink ('48) 130.00 *200.00*
199 PF5 30sh choc ('48) 200.00 *350.00*
200 PF5 £2 violet (C) 210.00 *310.00*
201 PF5 £3 lt grn ('50) 300.00 *425.00*
202 PF5 £5 dk bl (C) ('50) 425.00 *500.00*

Making Siapo Cloth — A38

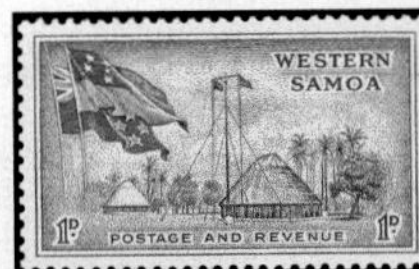

Western Samoa and New Zealand Flags, Village A39

Thatching Hut A40

Samoan Chieftainess A41

Designs: 2p, Western Samoa seal. 3p, Aleisa Falls (actually Malifa Falls). 5p, Manumea (tooth-billed pigeon). 6p, Fishing canoe. 8p, Harvesting cacao. 2sh, Preparing copra.

***Perf. 13, 13½x13***

**1952, Mar. 10 Engr. Wmk. 253**

203 A38 ½p org brn & claret .25 *2.00*
204 A39 1p green & olive .25 *.40*
205 A38 2p deep carmine .25 .25
206 A39 3p indigo & blue .50 .25
207 A38 5p dk grn & org brn 9.50 1.25
208 A39 6p dp rose pink & bl 1.00 .25
209 A39 8p rose carmine .35 .30
210 A40 1sh blue & brown .25 .25
211 A39 2sh yellow brown 1.10 .50
212 A41 3sh ol gray & vio brn 2.75 *2.75*
*Nos. 203-212 (10)* 16.20 8.20

**Coronation Issue**

Types of New Zealand 1953

**1953, May 25 Photo. *Perf. 14x14½***

214 A113 2p brown 1.25 .30
215 A114 6p slate black 1.25 .50

Type of New Zealand 1944-52 Overprinted in Blue or Carmine

**Wmk. 253**

**1955, Nov. 14 Typo. *Perf. 14***

216 PF5 5sh yellow green 11.00 *27.50*
217 PF5 10sh carmine rose 11.00 *50.00*
218 PF5 £1 dull rose 18.00 *57.50*
219 PF5 £2 violet (C) 100.00 *175.00*
*Nos. 216-219 (4)* 140.00 *310.00*

**Redrawn Types of 1952 and**

Map of Western Samoa and Mace A42

Designs: 4p, as 1p. 6p, as 2p.

**Inscribed: "Fono Fou 1958" and "Samoa I Sisifo"**

***Perf. 13½x13, 13***

**1958, Mar. 21 Engr. Wmk. 253**

220 A39 4p rose carmine .30 .30
221 A38 6p dull purple .30 .30
222 A42 1sh light violet blue .85 .50
*Nos. 220-222 (3)* 1.45 1.10

**Independent State**

Samoa College A43

Designs: 1p, Woman holding ceremonial mat, vert. 3p, Public Library. 4p, Fono House (Parliament). 6p, Map of Western Samoa, ship and plane. 8p, Faleolo airport. 1sh, Talking chief with fly whisk, vert. 1sh3p, Government House, Vailima. 2sh6p, Flag of Western Samoa. 5sh, State Seal.

**Wmk. 253**

**1962, July 2 Litho. *Perf. 13½***

223 A43 1p car & brown .25 .25
224 A43 2p org, lt grn, red & brown .25 .25
225 A43 3p blue, grn & brn .25 .25
226 A43 4p dk grn, bl & car .35 .35
227 A43 6p yel, grn & ultra .80 .50
228 A43 8p blue & emerald .80 .55
229 A43 1sh brt grn & brn .35 .85
Complete booklet, 4 ea. #223-229
Complete booklet, 4 ea. #223, 225, 227-228
230 A43 1sh3p blue & emerald 1.25 .75
231 A43 2sh6p vio blue & red 2.75 1.75
232 A43 5sh olive gray, red & dk blue 3.00 2.75
*Nos. 223-232 (10)* 10.05 8.25

Western Samoa's independence.

The booklets described following No. 229 contain marginal blocks of stamps taken from sheets, with glassine interleaving, and stapled into the booklet cover.

See #242-247.

Tupua Tamasese Mea'ole, Malietoa Tanumafili II and Seal — A44

**1963, Oct. 1 Photo. *Perf. 14***

233 A44 1p green & blk .25 .25
234 A44 4p dull blue & blk .25 .25
235 A44 8p carmine rose & blk .25 .25
236 A44 2sh orange & blk .25 .25
*Nos. 233-236 (4)* 1.00 1.00

First anniversary of independence.

Signing of Western Samoa-New Zealand Friendship Treaty A45

**1964, Sept. 1 Unwmk. *Perf. 13½***

237 A45 1p multicolored .25 .25
238 A45 8p multicolored .25 .25
239 A45 2sh multicolored .25 .25
240 A45 3sh multicolored .25 *.35*
*Nos. 237-240 (4)* 1.00 1.10

2nd anniv. of the signing of the Treaty of Friendship between Western Samoa and New Zealand. Signers: J. B. Wright, N. Z. High Commissioner for Western Pacific, and Fiame Mata'afa, Prime Minister of Western Samoa.

**Type of 1962**

**Wmk. 355**

**1965, Oct. 4 Litho. *Perf. 13½***

242 A43 1p carmine & brn .40 *.75*
243 A43 3p blue, grn & brn 37.50 5.00
244 A43 4p dk grn, bl & car .40 *.75*
245 A43 6p yel, grn & ultra .50 .45
246 A43 8p blue & emerald .55 .25
247 A43 1sh brt green & brn .70 *.80*
*Nos. 242-247 (6)* 40.05 8.00

For surcharge see No. B1.

Aerial View of Deep-Sea Wharf A46

8p, 2sh, View of Apia harbor & deep-sea wharf.

**1966, Mar. 2 Photo. *Perf. 13½***

251 A46 1p multicolored .25 .25
252 A46 8p multicolored .25 .25
253 A46 2sh multicolored .30 .25
254 A46 3sh multicolored .40 .35
*Nos. 251-254 (4)* 1.20 1.10

Opening of Western Samoa's first deep-sea wharf at Apia.

Inauguration of WHO Headquarters, Geneva — A47

Design: 4p, 1sh, WHO building and flag.

**1966, July 4 Photo. Wmk. 355**

255 A47 3p gray, ultra & bister .35 .25
256 A47 4p multicolored .50 .35
257 A47 6p lt ol grn, pur & grn .60 .40
258 A47 1sh multicolored 1.50 .60
*Nos. 255-258 (4)* 2.95 1.60

Tuatagaloa L.S., Minister of Justice A48

Designs: 8p, F.C.F. Nelson, Minister of Works, Marine and Civil Aviation. 2sh, To'omata T. L., Minister of Lands. 3sh, Fa'alava'au Galu, Minister of Post Office, Radio and Broadcasting.

*Perf. 14½x14*

**1967, Jan. 16 Photo. Wmk. 355**

**259** A48 3p violet & sepia .25 .25
**260** A48 8p blue & sepia .25 .25
**261** A48 2sh lt olive grn & sepia .30 .30
**262** A48 3sh lilac rose & sepia .50 .50
*Nos. 259-262 (4)* 1.30 1.30

Fifth anniversary of Independence.

Samoan Fales, 1900, and Fly Whisk A49

1sh, Fono House (Parliament) and mace.

**1967, May 16** ***Perf. 14½***

**263** A49 8p multicolored .35 .35
**264** A49 1sh multicolored .45 .45

Centenary of Mulinu'u as Government Seat.

Wattled Honey-Eater — A50

Birds of Western Samoa: 2s, Pacific pigeon. 3s, Samoan starling. 5s, Samoan broadbill. 7s, Red-headed parrot finch. 10s, Purple swamp hen. 20s, Barn owl. 25s, Tooth-billed pigeon. 50s, Island thrush. $1, Samoan fantail. $2, Mao (gymnomyza samoensis). $4, Samoan white-eye (zosterops samoensis).

*Perf. 14x14½*

**1967, July 10 Photo. Wmk. 355**

**Birds in Natural Colors**

**Size: 37x24mm**

**265** A50 1s black & lt brown .25 .25
**266** A50 2s lt ultra, blk & brn org .25 .25
**267** A50 3s blk, lt brn & emer .35 .25
**268** A50 5s lilac, blk & vio bl .35 .25
**269** A50 7s blk, vio bl & gray .90 .25
**270** A50 10s Prus blue & blk .90 .25
**271** A50 20s dk gray & blue 3.00 .50
**272** A50 25s pink, blk & dk grn 1.25 .25
**273** A50 50s brn, blk & lt ol grn 2.10 .40
**274** A50 $1 yellow & black 5.00 4.50

**1969 Size: 43x28mm** ***Perf. 13½***

**274A** A50 $2 blk & lt grnsh bl 3.75 *7.00*
**274B** A50 $4 dp orange & blk 42.50 17.50
*Nos. 265-274B (12)* 60.60 31.65

For surcharge see No. 294.

Child Care A51

Designs: 7s, Leprosarium. 20s, Mobile X-ray unit. 25s, Apia Hospital.

**1967, Dec. 1 Litho.** ***Perf. 14***

**275** A51 3s multicolored .30 .25
**276** A51 7s multicolored .35 .25
**277** A51 20s multicolored .60 .40
**278** A51 25s multicolored .80 .55
*Nos. 275-278 (4)* 2.05 1.45

South Pacific Health Service.

Thomas Trood A52

Portraits: 7s, Dr. Wilhelm Solf. 20s, John C. Williams. 25s, Fritz Marquardt.

**1968, Jan. 1 Unwmk.** ***Perf. 13½***

**279** A52 2s multicolored .30 .25
**280** A52 7s multicolored .30 .25
**281** A52 20s multicolored .35 .25
**282** A52 25s multicolored .40 .25
*Nos. 279-282 (4)* 1.35 1.00

Sixth anniversary of independence.

Samoan Agricultural Development A53

*Perf. 13x12½*

**1968, Feb. 15 Photo. Wmk. 355**

**283** A53 3s Cocoa .30 .30
**284** A53 5s Breadfruit .30 .30
**285** A53 10s Copra .30 .30
**286** A53 20s Bananas .40 .40
*Nos. 283-286 (4)* 1.30 1.30

Curio Vendors, Pago Pago A54

20s, Palm trees at the shore. 25s, A'Umi Beach.

*Perf. 14½x14*

**1968, Apr. 22 Photo. Wmk. 355**

**287** A54 7s multicolored .30 .30
**288** A54 20s multicolored .35 .30
**289** A54 25s multicolored .45 .35
*Nos. 287-289 (3)* 1.10 .95

South Pacific Commission, 21st anniv.

Bougainville and Compass Rose — A55

Designs: 3s, Map showing Western Samoa Archipelago and Bougainville's route. 20s, Bougainvillea. 25s, Bougainville's ships La Boudeuse and L'Etoile.

**1968, June 10 Litho.** ***Perf. 14***

**290** A55 3s brt blue & blk .25 .25
**291** A55 7s ocher & blk .30 .25
**292** A55 20s grnsh blk, brt rose & grn .65 .40
**293** A55 25s brt lil, vio, blk & org .90 .50
*Nos. 290-293 (4)* 2.10 1.40

200th anniv. of the visit of Louis Antoine de Bougainville (1729-1811) to Samoa.

**No. 270 Surcharged with New Value, Three Bars and "1928-1968 / KINGSFORD-SMITH / TRANSPACIFIC FLIGHT"**

**1968, June 13 Photo.** ***Perf. 14x14½***

**294** A50 20s on 10s multicolored .90 .90

40th anniv. of the 1st Transpacific flight under Capt. Charles Kingsford-Smith (Oakland, CA to Brisbane, Australia, via Honolulu and Fiji).

Human Rights Flame and Globe A56

*Perf. 14½x14*

**1968, Aug. 26 Photo. Wmk. 355**

**295** A56 7s multicolored .30 .25
**296** A56 20s multicolored .35 .25
**297** A56 25s multicolored .50 .25
*Nos. 295-297 (3)* 1.15 .75

International Human Rights Year, 1968.

Martin Luther King, Jr. — A57

**1968, Sept. 23 Litho.** ***Perf. 14***

**298** A57 7s green & black .35 .25
**299** A57 20s brt rose lil & blk .45 .25

Rev. Dr. Martin Luther King, Jr. (1929-68), American civil rights leader.

Polynesian Madonna — A58

**1968, Oct. 12 Wmk. 355**

**300** A58 1s olive & multi .30 .25
**301** A58 3s multicolored .30 .25
**302** A58 20s crimson & multi .30 .25
**303** A58 30s dp orange & multi .40 .25
*Nos. 300-303 (4)* 1.30 1.00

Christmas 1968.

Frangipani — A59

Flowers: 7s, Chinese hibiscus, vert. 20s, Red ginger, vert. 30s, Canangium odoratum.

**1969, Jan. 20 Unwmk.** ***Perf. 14***

**304** A59 2s brt blue & multi .40 .25
**305** A59 7s multicolored .55 .35
**306** A59 20s yellow & multi .95 .50
**307** A59 30s multicolored 1.35 .80
*Nos. 304-307 (4)* 3.25 1.90

Seventh anniversary of independence.

R. L. Stevenson and Silver from "Treasure Island" — A60

Robert Louis Stevenson and: 7s, Stewart and Balfour on the moor from "Kidnapped." 20s, "Doctor Jekyll and Mr. Hyde." 22s, Archie Weir and Christiana Elliot from "Weir of Hermiston."

*Perf. 14x13½*

**1969, Apr. 21 Litho. Wmk. 355**

**308** A60 3s gray & multi .35 .30
**309** A60 7s gray & multi .45 .30
**310** A60 20s gray & multi .45 .55
**311** A60 22s gray & multi .45 *.55*
*Nos. 308-311 (4)* 1.70 1.70

75th anniv. of the death of Robert Louis Stevenson, who is buried in Samoa.

Weight Lifting — A61

*Perf. 13½x13*

**1969, July 21 Photo. Unwmk.**

**312** A61 3s shown .25 .25
**313** A61 20s Sailing .25 .25
**314** A61 22s Boxing .35 .30
*Nos. 312-314 (3)* .85 .80

3rd Pacific Games, Port Moresby, Papua and New Guinea, Aug. 13-23.

American Astronaut on Moon, Splashdown and Map of Samoan Islands — A62

**1969, July 24 Photo.**

**315** A62 7s red, blk, silver & grn .25 .25
**316** A62 20s car, blk, sil & ultra .35 .25

US astronauts. See note after US No. C76.

Holy Family by El Greco A63

Christmas (Paintings): 1s, Virgin and Child, by Murillo. 20s, Nativity, by El Greco. 30s, Virgin and Child (from Adoration of the Kings), by Velazquez.

**1969, Oct. 13 Unwmk.** ***Perf. 14***

**317** A63 1s gold, red & multi .25 .25
**318** A63 3s gold, red & multi .25 .25
**319** A63 20s gold, red & multi .25 .25
**320** A63 30s gold, red & multi .35 .25
**a.** Souvenir sheet of 4, #317-320 2.00 2.00
*Nos. 317-320 (4)* 1.10 1.00

Seventh Day Adventists' Sanatorium, Apia — A64

7s, Father Louis Violette, R. C. Cathedral, Apia. 20s, Church of Latter Day Saints (Mormon), Tuasivi, Safotulafai, vert. 22s, John Williams, London Missionary Soc. Church, Sapapali'i.

**1970, Jan. 19 Litho. Wmk. 355**

**321** A64 2s brown, blk & gray .25 .25
**322** A64 7s violet, blk & bister .25 .25
**323** A64 20s rose, blk & lt violet .25 .25
**324** A64 22s olive, blk & bister .25 .25
*Nos. 321-324 (4)* 1.00 1.00

Eighth anniversary of independence.

U.S.S. Nipsic A65

Designs: 5s, Wreck of German ship Adler. 10s, British ship Calliope in storm. 20s, Apia after hurricane.

**1970, Apr. 27** *Perf. 13½x14*

**325** A65 5s multicolored .40 .25
**326** A65 7s multicolored .45 .30
**327** A65 10s multicolored .75 .40
**328** A65 20s multicolored 1.50 .90
*Nos. 325-328 (4)* 3.10 1.85

The great Apia hurricane of 1889.

Cook Statue, Whitby, England — A66

Designs: 1s, Kendal's chronometer and Cook's sextant. 20s, Capt. Cook bust, in profile. 30s, Capt. Cook, island scene and "Endeavour," horiz.

*Perf. 14x14½*

**1970, Sept. 14** **Litho.** **Wmk. 355**

**Size: 25x41mm**

**329** A66 1s silver, dp car & blk .35 .25
**330** A66 2s multicolored .45 .35
**331** A66 20s gold, black & ultra 1.50 .50

*Perf. 14½x14*

**Size: 83x25mm**

**332** A66 30s multicolored 3.00 1.75
*Nos. 329-332 (4)* 5.30 2.85

Bicentenary of Capt. James Cook's exploration of South Pacific.

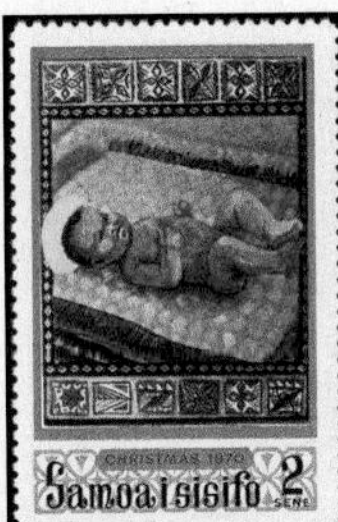


"Peace for the World" by Frances B. Eccles — A67

Christmas: 3s, Samoan coat of arms and Holy Family, by Werner Erich Jahnke. 20s, Samoan Mother and Child, by F. B. Eccles. 30s, Prince of Peace, by Sister Melane Fe'ao.

*Perf. 13½*

**1970, Oct. 26** **Photo.** **Unwmk.**

**333** A67 2s gold & multi .25 .25
**334** A67 3s gold & multi .25 .25
**335** A67 20s gold & multi .35 .25
**336** A67 30s gold & multi .45 .35
*a.* Souvenir sheet of 4, #333-336 2.25 2.25
*Nos. 333-336 (4)* 1.30 1.10

Pope Paul VI — A68

**Wmk. 355**

**1970, Nov. 29** **Litho.** *Perf. 14*

**337** A68 8s Prus blue & black .25 .25
**338** A68 20s deep plum & black .45 .30

Visit of Pope Paul VI, Nov. 29, 1970.

Lumberjack A69

8s, Woman and tractor in clearing, horiz. 20s, Log and saw carrier, horiz. 22s, Logging and ship.

*Perf. 14x13½, 13½x14*

**1971, Feb. 1** **Litho.** **Unwmk.**

**339** A69 3s multicolored .25 .25
**340** A69 8s multicolored .25 .25
**341** A69 20s multicolored .45 .25
**342** A69 22s multicolored .55 .30
*Nos. 339-342 (4)* 1.50 1.05

Development of the timber industry on Savaii Island by the American Timber Company of Potlatch.

Souvenir Sheet

Longboat in Apia Harbor; Samoa #3 and US #3 — A70

**1971, Mar. 12** **Photo.** *Perf. 11½*

**Granite Paper**

**343** A70 70s blue & multi 2.25 2.25

INTERPEX, 13th Intl. Stamp Exhib., NYC, Mar. 12-14.

Siva Dance A71

Tourist Publicity: 7s, Samoan cricket game. 8s, Hideaway Resort Hotel. 10s, Aggie Grey and Aggie's Hotel.

**Wmk. 355**

**1971, Aug. 9** **Litho.** *Perf. 14*

**344** A71 5s orange brn & multi .40 .25
**345** A71 7s orange brn & multi 2.50 .70
**346** A71 8s orange brn & multi .90 .50
**347** A71 10s orange brn & multi .90 .70
*Nos. 344-347 (4)* 4.70 2.15

A72

Samoan Legends, carved by Sven Ortquist: 3s, Queen Salamasina. 8s, Lu and his sacred hens (Samoa). 10s, God Tagaloa fishing Samoan islands of Upolu and Savaii from the sea. 22s, Mt. Vaea and Pool of Tears.

**1971, Sept. 20**

**348** A72 3s dark violet & multi .25 .25
**349** A72 8s multicolored .25 .25
**350** A72 10s dark blue & multi .30 .30
**351** A72 22s dark blue & multi .45 .45
*Nos. 348-351 (4)* 1.25 1.25

See Nos. 399-402.

A73

Christmas: 2s, 3s, Virgin and Child, by Giovanni Bellini. 20c, 30c, Virgin and Child with St. Anne and St. John the Baptist, by Leonardo da Vinci.

**1971, Oct. 4** *Perf. 14x13½*

**352** A73 2s blue & multi .25 .25
**353** A73 3s black & multi .25 .25
**354** A73 20s yellow & multi .35 .25
**355** A73 30s dark red & multi .50 .30
*Nos. 352-355 (4)* 1.35 1.05

Samoan Islands, Scales of Justice A74

**1972, Jan. 10** **Photo.** *Perf. 11½x12*

**356** A74 10s light blue & multi .40 .30

1st So. Pacific Judicial Conf., Samoa, Jan. 1972.

Asau Wharf, Savaii A75

Designs: 8s, Parliament Building. 10s, Mothers' Center. 22s, Portraits of Tupua Tamasese Mea'ole and Malietoa Tanumafili II, and view of Vailima.

*Perf. 13x13½*

**1972, Jan. 10** **Litho.** **Wmk. 355**

**357** A75 1s bright pink & multi .25 .25
**358** A75 8s lilac & multi .25 .25
**359** A75 10s green & multi .25 .25
**360** A75 22s multicolored .35 .30
*Nos. 357-360 (4)* 1.10 1.05

10th anniversary of independence.

Commission Members' Flags — A76

Designs: 7s, Afoafouvale Misimoa, Secretary-General, 1970-71 and Commission flag. 8s, Headquarters Building, Noumea, New Caledonia, horiz. 10s, Flag of Samoa, flag and map of South Pacific Commission area, horiz.

**1972, Mar. 17** *Perf. 14x13½, 13½x14*

**361** A76 3s ultra & multi .25 .25
**362** A76 7s yellow, black & ultra .25 .25
**363** A76 8s multicolored .30 .25
**364** A76 10s lt green & multi .30 .25
*Nos. 361-364 (4)* 1.10 1.00

South Pacific Commission, 25th anniv.

Sunset and Ships — A77

Designs: 8s, Sailing ships Arend, Thienhoven and Africaansche Galey in storm. 10s, Outrigger canoe and Roggeveen's ships. 30s, Hemispheres with exploration route and map of Samoan Islands. All horiz.

**1972, June 14** *Perf. 14½*

**365** A77 2s car rose & multi .25 .25
**366** A77 8s violet blue & multi .55 .25
**367** A77 10s ultra & multi .65 .25

**Size: 85x25mm**

**368** A77 30s ocher & multi 1.90 1.90
*Nos. 365-368 (4)* 3.35 2.65

250th anniv. of Jacob Roggeveen's Pacific voyage and discovery of Samoa in June 1722.

Bull Conch A78

2s, Rhinoceros beetle. 3s, Skipjack (fish). 4s, Painted crab. 5s, Butterflyfish. 7s, Samoan monarch. 10s, Triton shell. 20s, Jewel beetle. 50s, Spiny lobster. $1, Hawk moth. $2, Green turtle. $4, Black marlin. $5, Green tree lizard.

**1972-75** **Litho.** *Perf. 14½*

**Size: 41x24mm**

**369** A78 1s shown .30 .30
**370** A78 2s multicolored .30 .30
**371** A78 3s multicolored .30 *1.00*
**372** A78 4s multicolored .30 .30
**373** A78 5s multicolored .35 .30
**374** A78 7s multicolored 2.00 1.50
**375** A78 10s multicolored 2.00 1.00
**376** A78 20s multicolored 1.25 .30
**377** A78 50s multicolored 2.00 *2.75*

*Perf. 14x13½*

**Size: 29x45mm**

**378** A78 $1 multicolored 6.50 4.50
**378A** A78 $2 multicolored 4.50 2.75
**378B** A78 $4 multicolored 6.00 *7.00*
**378C** A78 $5 multicolored 4.00 *10.00*
*Nos. 369-378C (13)* 29.80 32.00

Issued: 1s-$1, Oct. 18, 1972; $2, June 18, 1973; $4, Mar. 27, 1974; $5, June 30, 1975.

Ascension, Stained Glass Window — A79

Stained Glass Windows in Apia Churches: 4s, Virgin and Child. 10s, St. Andrew blessing Samoan canoe. 30s, The Good Shepherd.

*Perf. 14x14½*

**1972, Nov. 1** **Wmk. 355**

**379** A79 1s ocher & multi .25 .25
**380** A79 4s gray & multi .25 .25
**381** A79 10s dull green & multi .25 .25

**382** A79 30s blue & multi .50 .35
*a.* Souvenir sheet of 4, #379-382 2.25 2.25
*Nos. 379-382 (4)* 1.25 1.10

Christmas.

Scouts Saluting Flag, Emblems A80

**1973, Jan. 29** ***Perf. 14***

**383** A80 2s shown .25 .25
**384** A80 3s First aid .25 .25
**385** A80 8s Pitching tent .30 .25
**386** A80 20s Action song .60 .60
*Nos. 383-386 (4)* 1.40 1.35

Boy Scouts of Samoa.

Apia General Hospital — A81

WHO, 25th anniv.: 8s, Baby clinic. 20s, Filariasis research. 22s, Family welfare.

**1973, Aug. 20** **Wmk. 355**

**387** A81 2s green & multi .25 .25
**388** A81 8s multicolored .25 .25
**389** A81 20s brown & multi .35 .35
**390** A81 22s vermilion & multi .45 .40
*Nos. 387-390 (4)* 1.30 1.25

"A Prince is Born," by Jahnke — A82

Christmas: 4s, "Star of Hope," by Fiasili Keil. 10s, "Mother and Child," by Ernesto Coter. 30s, "The Light of the World," by Coter.

**1973, Oct. 15** **Litho.** ***Perf. 14***

**391** A82 3s gold & multi .25 .25
**392** A82 4s gold & multi .25 .25
**393** A82 10s gold & multi .25 .25
**394** A82 30s gold & multi .55 .50
*a.* Souvenir sheet of 4, #391-394 2.10 2.10
*Nos. 391-394 (4)* 1.30 1.25

Boxing and Games' Emblem A83

**1974, Jan. 24**

**395** A83 8s shown .25 .25
**396** A83 10s Weight lifting .25 .25
**397** A83 20s Lawn bowling .25 .25
**398** A83 30s Stadium .75 .75
*Nos. 395-398 (4)* 1.50 1.50

10th British Commonwealth Games, Christchurch, New Zealand, Jan. 24-Feb. 2.

### Legends Type of 1971

Samoan Legends, Wood Carvings by Sven Ortquist: 2s, Tigilau and dove. 8s, Pili with his sons and famous fish net. 20s, The girl Sina and the eel which became the coconut tree. 30s, Nafanua who returned from the spirit world to free her village.

**1974, Aug. 13** **Wmk. 355** ***Perf. 14***

**399** A72 2s lemon & multi .25 .25
**400** A72 8s rose red & multi .25 .25
**401** A72 20s yellow grn & multi .40 .30
**402** A72 30s lt violet & multi .70 .70
*Nos. 399-402 (4)* 1.60 1.50

Faleolo Airport — A84

Designs: 20s, Apia Wharf. 22s, Early post office, Apia. 50s, William Willis, raft "Age Unlimited" and route from Callao, Peru, to Tully, Western Samoa.

**1974, Sept. 4** **Unwmk.** ***Perf. 13½***

**Size: 47x29mm**

**403** A84 8s multicolored .35 .25
**404** A84 20s multicolored .55 .45
**405** A84 22s multicolored .60 .60

**Size: 86x29mm**

**406** A84 50s multicolored 1.50 1.50
*a.* Souvenir sheet of 1, perf. 13 1.25 1.25
*Nos. 403-406 (4)* 3.00 2.80

Cent. of UPU. The 8s is inscribed "Air Mail"; 20s, "Sea Mail"; 22s, "Raft Mail."

Holy Family, by Sebastiano — A85

Christmas: 4s, Virgin and Child with Saints, by Lotto. 10s, Virgin and Child with St. John, by Titian. 30s, Adoration of the Shepherds, by Rubens.

**1974, Nov. 18** **Litho.** ***Perf. 13x13½***

**407** A85 3s ocher & multi .25 .25
**408** A85 4s fawn & multi .25 .25
**409** A85 10s dull green & multi .25 .25
**410** A85 30s blue & multi .35 .35
*a.* Souvenir sheet of 4, #407-410 2.00 2.00
*Nos. 407-410 (4)* 1.10 1.10

Winged Passion Flower A86

20s, Gardenias, vert. 22s, Lecythidaceae, vert. 30s, Malay apple.

**Wmk. 355**

**1975, Jan. 17** **Litho.** ***Perf. 14½***

**411** A86 8s dull yellow & multi .30 .30
**412** A86 20s pale pink & multi .40 .40
**413** A86 22s pink & multi .50 .50
**414** A86 30s lt green & multi .80 .80
*Nos. 411-414 (4)* 2.00 2.00

Joyita Loading at Apia A87

Designs: 8s, Joyita, Samoa and Tokelau Islands. 20s, Joyita sinking, Oct. 1955. 22s, Rafts in storm. 50s, Plane discovering wreck.

**1975, Mar. 14** **Photo.** ***Perf. 13***

**415** A87 1s multicolored .25 .25
**416** A87 8s multicolored .30 .25
**417** A87 20s multicolored .50 .45
**418** A87 22s multicolored .60 .55
**419** A87 50s multicolored 1.00 1.00
*a.* Souvenir sheet of 5, #415-419 3.00 3.00
*Nos. 415-419 (5)* 2.65 2.50

17th INTERPEX Phil. Exhib., NYC, 3/14-16.

Pate Drum — A88

**1975, Sept. 30** **Litho.** ***Perf. 14½x14***

**420** A88 8s shown .25 .25
**421** A88 20s Lali drum .25 .25
**422** A88 22s Logo drum .30 .25
**423** A88 30s Pu shell horn .45 .45
*Nos. 420-423 (4)* 1.25 1.20

Mother and Child, by Meleane Fe'ao — A89

Christmas (Paintings): 4s, Christ Child and Samoan flag, by Polataia Tuigamala. 10s, "A Star is Born," by Iosua Toafa. 30s, Mother and Child, by Ernesto Coter.

**1975, Nov. 25** **Litho.** **Wmk. 355**

**424** A89 3s multicolored .25 .25
**425** A89 4s multicolored .25 .25
**426** A89 10s multicolored .25 .25
**427** A89 30s multicolored .35 .35
*a.* Souvenir sheet of 4, #424-427 1.00 1.00
*Nos. 424-427 (4)* 1.10 1.10

Boston Massacre, by Paul Revere — A90

8s, Declaration of Independence, by John Trumbull. 20s, The Ship That Sank in Victory, by J. L. G. Ferris. 22s, Wm. Pitt Addressing House of Commons, by R. A. Hickel. 50s, Battle of Princeton, by William Mercer.

***Perf. 13½x14***

**1976, Jan. 20** **Litho.** **Wmk. 355**

**428** A90 7s salmon & multi .25 .25
**429** A90 8s green & multi .25 .25
**430** A90 20s lilac & multi .60 .40
**431** A90 22s blue & multi .65 .40
**432** A90 50s yellow & multi 1.25 1.25
*a.* Souvenir sheet of 5, #428-432 + label 6.50 6.50
*Nos. 428-432 (5)* 3.00 2.55

Bicentenary of American Independence.

Mullet Fishing A91

**1976, Apr. 27** **Litho.** ***Perf. 14½***

**433** A91 10s shown .25 .25
**434** A91 12s Fish traps .25 .25
**435** A91 22s Fishermen .40 .30
**436** A91 50s Net fishing 1.00 1.00
*Nos. 433-436 (4)* 1.90 1.80

Souvenir Sheet

Samoan $100 Gold Coin with Paul Revere and US Map — A92

**Unwmk.**

**1976, May 29** **Photo.** ***Perf. 13***

**437** A92 $1 green & gold 2.75 2.75

American Bicentennial and Interphil 76 Intl. Phil. Exhib., Philadelphia, PA, May 29-June 6.

Boxing A93

12s, Wrestling. 22s, Javelin. 50s, Weight lifting.

***Perf. 14½x14***

**1976, June 21** **Litho.** **Wmk. 355**

**438** A93 10s black & multi .25 .25
**439** A93 12s dark brown & multi .25 .25
**440** A93 22s dark purple & multi .35 .25
**441** A93 50s dark blue & multi .65 .65
*Nos. 438-441 (4)* 1.50 1.40

21st Olympic Games, Montreal, Canada, July 17-Aug. 1.

Mary and Joseph on Road to Bethlehem A94

Christmas: 5s, Adoration of the Shepherds. 22s, Nativity. 50s, Adoration of the Kings.

**1976, Oct. 18** **Litho.** ***Perf. 14x13½***

**442** A94 3s multicolored .25 .25
**443** A94 5s multicolored .25 .25
**444** A94 22s multicolored .35 .25
**445** A94 50s multicolored .65 .65
*a.* Souvenir sheet of 4, #442-445 1.90 1.90
*Nos. 442-445 (4)* 1.50 1.40

Presentation of the Spurs of Chivalry — A95

Designs: 12s, Queen and view of Apia. 32s, Royal Yacht Britannia and Queen. 50s, Queen leaving Westminster Abbey.

***Perf. 13½x14***

**1977, Feb. 11** **Wmk. 355**

**446** A95 12s multicolored .25 .25
**447** A95 26s multicolored .30 .30
**448** A95 32s multicolored .70 .30
**449** A95 50s multicolored .30 .30
*Nos. 446-449 (4)* 1.55 1.15

25th anniv. of the reign of Elizabeth II.

Lindbergh and Spirit of St. Louis A96

Designs: 22s, Map of transatlantic route and plane. 24s, Spirit of St. Louis in flight. 26s, Spirit of St. Louis taking off.

**1977, May 20 Litho. *Perf. 14***

| | | | | |
|---|---|---|---|---|
| **450** | A96 | 22s multicolored | .30 | .25 |
| **451** | A96 | 24s multicolored | .40 | .25 |
| **452** | A96 | 26s multicolored | .45 | .25 |
| **453** | A96 | 50s multicolored | 1.00 | 1.00 |
| *a.* | | Souvenir sheet of 4, #450-453 | 4.00 | 4.00 |
| | | *Nos. 450-453 (4)* | 2.15 | 1.75 |

Charles A. Lindbergh's solo transatlantic flight from New York to Paris, 50th anniv.

Apia Automatic Telephone Exchange — A97

Designs: 13s, Mulinuu radio terminal. 26s, Old wall and new dial telephones. 50s, Global communications (2 telephones and globe).

**1977, July 11 Litho. *Perf. 14***

| | | | | |
|---|---|---|---|---|
| **454** | A97 | 12s multicolored | .25 | .25 |
| **455** | A97 | 13s multicolored | .25 | .25 |
| **456** | A97 | 26s multicolored | .35 | .30 |
| **457** | A97 | 50s multicolored | .60 | .60 |
| | | *Nos. 454-457 (4)* | 1.45 | 1.40 |

Telecommunications.

Samoa No. 3 and First Mail Notice — A98

13s, Samoa #4 & 1881 cover. 26s, Samoa #1 & Chief Post Office, Apia. 50s, Samoa #4 7 schooner "Energy," which carried 1st mail.

**1977, Aug. 29 Wmk. 355 *Perf. 13½***

| | | | | |
|---|---|---|---|---|
| **458** | A98 | 12s multicolored | .30 | .25 |
| **459** | A98 | 13s multicolored | .30 | .25 |
| **460** | A98 | 26s multicolored | .40 | .30 |
| **461** | A98 | 50s multicolored | .75 | .75 |
| | | *Nos. 458-461 (4)* | 1.75 | 1.55 |

Samoan postage stamp centenary.

Nativity — A99

Christmas: 6s, People bringing gifts to Holy Family in Samoan hut. 26s, Virgin and Child. 50s, Stars over Christ Child.

**1977, Oct. 11 Litho. *Perf. 14***

| | | | | |
|---|---|---|---|---|
| **462** | A99 | 4s multicolored | .25 | .25 |
| **463** | A99 | 6s multicolored | .25 | .25 |
| **464** | A99 | 26s multicolored | .30 | .25 |
| **465** | A99 | 50s multicolored | .45 | .45 |
| *a.* | | Souvenir sheet of 4, #462-465 | 1.50 | 1.50 |
| | | *Nos. 462-465 (4)* | 1.25 | 1.20 |

Polynesian Airlines' Boeing 737 — A100

Aviation Progress: 24s, Kitty Hawk. 26s, Kingsford-Smith Fokker. 50s, Concorde.

**Unwmk.**

**1978, Mar. 21 Litho. *Perf. 14***

| | | | | |
|---|---|---|---|---|
| **466** | A100 | 12s multicolored | .25 | .25 |
| **467** | A100 | 24s multicolored | .35 | .30 |
| **468** | A100 | 26s multicolored | .40 | .30 |
| **469** | A100 | 50s multicolored | .90 | .90 |
| *a.* | | Souvenir sheet of 4, #466-469, perf. 13½ | 3.00 | 3.00 |
| | | *Nos. 466-469 (4)* | 1.90 | 1.75 |

Turtle Hatchery, Aleipata — A101

$1, Hawksbill turtle & Wildlife Fund emblem.

**1978, Apr. 14 Wmk. 355 *Perf. 14½***

| | | | | |
|---|---|---|---|---|
| **470** | A101 | 24s multicolored | *3.75* | *1.00* |
| **471** | A101 | $1 multicolored | *9.25* | *3.75* |

Project to replenish endangered hawksbill turtles.

---

Common Design Types pictured following the introduction.

---

**Elizabeth II Coronation Anniversary Issue**

Souvenir Sheet

Common Design Types

**1978, Apr. 21 Unwmk. *Perf. 15***

| | | | | |
|---|---|---|---|---|
| **472** | | Sheet of 6 | 2.10 | 2.10 |
| *a.* | CD326 | 26s King's lion | .30 | .30 |
| *b.* | CD327 | 26s Elizabeth II | .30 | .30 |
| *c.* | CD328 | 26s Pacific pigeon | .30 | .30 |

No. 472 contains 2 se-tenant strips of Nos. 472a-472c, separated by horizontal gutter with commemorative and descriptive inscriptions and showing central part of coronation procession with coach.

Souvenir Sheet

Canadian and Samoan Flags — A102

**Wmk. 355**

**1978, June 9 Litho. *Perf. 14½***

| | | | | |
|---|---|---|---|---|
| **473** | A102 | $1 multicolored | 1.75 | 1.75 |

CAPEX Canadian Intl. Phil. Exhib., Toronto, June 9-18.

Capt. James Cook — A103

Designs: 24s, Cook's cottage, now in Melbourne, Australia. 26s, Old drawbridge over River Esk, Whitby, 1766-1833. 50s, Resolution and map of Hawaiian Islands.

**1978, Aug. 28 Litho. *Perf. 14½x14***

| | | | | |
|---|---|---|---|---|
| **474** | A103 | 12s multicolored | .30 | .25 |
| **475** | A103 | 24s multicolored | .40 | .35 |
| **476** | A103 | 26s multicolored | .50 | .45 |
| **477** | A103 | 50s multicolored | 1.30 | 1.30 |
| | | *Nos. 474-477 (4)* | 2.50 | 2.35 |

A104

Cowrie Shells: 1s, Thick-edged Cowrie. 2s, Isabella cowrie. 3s, Money cowrie. 4s, Eroded cowrie. 6s, Honey cowrie. 7s, Banded cowrie. 10s, Globe cowrie. 11s, Mole cowrie. 12s, Children's cowrie. 13s, Flag cone. 14s, Soldier cone. 24s, Cloth-of-gold cone. 26s, Lettered cone. 50s, Tiled cone. $1, Black marble cone. $2, Marlin-spike auger. $3, Scorpion spider conch. $5, Common harp.

**1978-80 Photo. Unwmk. *Perf. 12½***

**Size: 31x24mm**

**Granite Paper**

| | | | | |
|---|---|---|---|---|
| **478** | A104 | 1s multicolored | .25 | .25 |
| **479** | A104 | 2s multicolored | .25 | .25 |
| **480** | A104 | 3s multicolored | .25 | .25 |
| **481** | A104 | 4s multicolored | .25 | .25 |
| **482** | A104 | 6s multicolored | .25 | .25 |
| **483** | A104 | 7s multicolored | .25 | .25 |
| **484** | A104 | 10s multicolored | .25 | .25 |
| **485** | A104 | 11s multicolored | .25 | .25 |
| **486** | A104 | 12s multicolored | .25 | .25 |
| **487** | A104 | 13s multicolored | .25 | .25 |
| **488** | A104 | 14s multicolored | .25 | .25 |
| **489** | A104 | 24s multicolored | .25 | .25 |
| **490** | A104 | 26s multicolored | .30 | .25 |
| **491** | A104 | 50s multicolored | .40 | .30 |
| **492** | A104 | $1 multicolored | 1.00 | .50 |

***Perf. 11½***

**Size: 36x26mm**

| | | | | |
|---|---|---|---|---|
| **493** | A104 | $2 multi ('79) | 1.75 | .75 |
| **494** | A104 | $3 multi ('79) | 2.50 | 1.50 |
| **494A** | A104 | $5 multi ('80) | 4.00 | 2.25 |
| | | *Nos. 478-494A (18)* | 12.95 | 8.55 |

Issue dates: 1s-12s, Sept. 15. 13s-$1, Nov. 20. $2, $3, July 18. $5, Aug. 26.

A105

Works by Dürer: 4s, The Virgin in Glory. 6s, Nativity. 26s, Adoration of the Kings. 50s, Annunciation.

**Wmk. 355**

**1978, Nov. 6 Litho. *Perf. 14***

| | | | | |
|---|---|---|---|---|
| **495** | A105 | 4s lt brown & blk | .25 | .25 |
| **496** | A105 | 6s grnsh blue & blk | .25 | .25 |
| **497** | A105 | 26s violet blue & blk | .25 | .25 |
| **498** | A105 | 50s purple & blk | .45 | .40 |
| *a.* | | Souvenir sheet of 4, #495-498 | 1.40 | 1.40 |
| | | *Nos. 495-498 (4)* | 1.20 | 1.15 |

Christmas and for 450th death anniv. of Albrecht Dürer.

Boy Carrying Coconuts A106

Designs: 24s, Children leaving church on White Sunday. 26s, Children pumping water. 50s, Girl playing ukulele.

**1979, Apr. 10 Litho. *Perf. 14***

| | | | | |
|---|---|---|---|---|
| **499** | A106 | 12s multicolored | .25 | .25 |
| **500** | A106 | 24s multicolored | .30 | .25 |
| **501** | A106 | 26s multicolored | .30 | .25 |
| **502** | A106 | 50s multicolored | .65 | .65 |
| | | *Nos. 499-502 (4)* | 1.50 | 1.40 |

International Year of the Child.

Charles W. Morgan A107

**1979, May 29 Litho. *Perf. 13½***

| | | | | |
|---|---|---|---|---|
| **503** | A107 | 12s multicolored | .30 | .25 |
| **504** | A107 | 14s Lagoda | .45 | .25 |
| **505** | A107 | 24s James T. Arnold | .55 | .35 |
| **506** | A107 | 50s Splendid | 1.00 | 1.00 |
| | | *Nos. 503-506 (4)* | 2.30 | 1.85 |

See Nos. 521-524, 543-546.

Saturn V Launch — A108

Designs: 14s, Landing module and astronaut on moon, horiz. 24s, Earth seen from moon. 26s, Astronaut on moon, horiz. 50s, Lunar and command modules. $1, Command module after splashdown, horiz.

***Perf. 14½x14, 14x14½***

**1979, June 20 Litho. Wmk. 355**

| | | | | |
|---|---|---|---|---|
| **507** | A108 | 12s multicolored | .25 | .25 |
| **508** | A108 | 14s multicolored | .25 | .25 |
| **509** | A108 | 24s multicolored | .30 | .25 |
| **510** | A108 | 26s multicolored | .35 | .25 |
| **511** | A108 | 50s multicolored | .45 | .45 |
| **512** | A108 | $1 multicolored | 1.00 | 1.00 |
| *a.* | | Souvenir sheet | 2.00 | 2.00 |
| | | *Nos. 507-512 (6)* | 2.60 | 2.45 |

1st moon landing, 10th anniv.

Penny Black, Hill Statue — A109

24s, Great Britain #2 with Maltese Cross postmark. 26s, Penny Black and Rowland Hill. $1, Great Britain #2 and Hill statue.

**1979, Aug. 27 *Perf. 14***

| | | | | |
|---|---|---|---|---|
| **513** | A109 | 12s multicolored | .25 | .25 |
| **514** | A109 | 24s multicolored | .25 | .25 |
| **515** | A109 | 26s multicolored | .25 | .25 |
| **516** | A109 | $1 multicolored | .60 | .60 |
| *a.* | | Souvenir sheet of 4, #513-516 | 1.75 | 1.75 |
| | | *Nos. 513-516 (4)* | 1.35 | 1.35 |

Sir Rowland Hill (1795-1879), originator of penny postage.

Anglican Church, Apia A110

Samoan Churches: 6s, Congregational Christian Church, Leulumoega. 26s, Methodist Church, Piula. 50s, Protestant Church, Apia.

**1979, Oct. 22 Photo. *Perf. 12x11½***

| | | | | |
|---|---|---|---|---|
| **517** | A110 | 4s lt blue & blk | .25 | .25 |
| **518** | A110 | 6s lt yellow grn & blk | .25 | .25 |
| **519** | A110 | 26s dull yellow & blk | .25 | .25 |
| **520** | A110 | 50s lt lilac & blk | .60 | .60 |
| *a.* | | Souvenir sheet of 4, #517-520 | 1.25 | 1.25 |
| | | *Nos. 517-520 (4)* | 1.35 | 1.35 |

Christmas.

**Ship Type of 1979**

**Wmk. 355**

**1980, Jan. 22 Litho. *Perf. 14***

**521** A107 12s William Hamilton .30 .25
**522** A107 14s California .30 .25
**523** A107 24s Liverpool II .30 .25
**524** A107 50s Two Brothers 1.10 1.10
*Nos. 521-524 (4)* 2.00 1.85

Map of Samoan Islands, Rotary Emblem A111

Missionary Flag, John Williams, Plaque — A112

Flag-raising Memorial — A113

14s, German flag, Dr. Wilhelm Solf, plaque. 26s, Williams Memorial, Savai'i. 50s, Emblem, Paul P. Harris, founder.

**1980, Mar. 26 Photo. *Perf. 14***

**525** A111 12s shown .60 .25
**526** A111 13s shown .45 *1.00*
**527** A112 14s multicolored 1.00 .25
**528** A113 24s shown 1.00 .40
**529** A113 26s multicolored .75 .50
**530** A111 50s multicolored 1.25 *2.25*
*Nos. 525-530 (6)* 5.05 4.65

Rotary Intl., 75th anniv. (A111); arrival of Williams, missionary in Samoa, 150th anniv. (13s, 26s); raising of the German flag, 80th anniv. (14s, 24s).

**Souvenir Sheet**

Village and Long Boat — A114

**Wmk. 355**

**1980, May 6 Litho. *Perf. 14***

**531** A114 $1 multicolored 1.25 1.25

London 80 Intl. Phil. Exhib., May 6-14.

**Queen Mother Elizabeth Birthday Issue**

Common Design Type

**1980, Aug. 4 Litho.**

**532** CD330 50s multicolored .55 .55

**Souvenir Sheet**

Samoa No. 239, ZEAPEX Emblem — A115

**Unwmk.**

**1980, Aug. 23 Litho. *Perf. 14***

**533** A115 $1 multicolored 1.25 1.25

ZEAPEX '80, New Zealand International Stamp Exhibition, Auckland, Aug. 23-31.

Afiamalu Satellite Earth Station A116

14s, Station, diff. 24s, Station, map of Samoa. 50s, Satellite sending waves to earth. $2, Samoa #536, Sydpex '80 emblem.

**1980, Sept. 17 Litho. *Perf. 11½***

**Granite Paper**

**534** A116 12s multicolored .25 .25
**535** A116 14s multicolored .25 .25
**536** A116 24s multicolored .30 .25
**537** A116 50s multicolored .60 .60
*Nos. 534-537 (4)* 1.40 1.35

**Souvenir Sheet**

**1980, Sept. 29 *Imperf.***

**538** A116 $2 multicolored 1.75 1.75

Sydpex '80 Natl. Phil. Exhib., Sydney.

The Savior, by John Poynton — A117

Christmas (Paintings by Local Artists): 14s, Madonna and Child, by Lealofi F. Siaopo. 27s, Nativity, by Pasila Feata. 50s, Yuletide, by R.P. Aiono.

**Wmk. 355**

**1980, Oct. 28 Litho. *Perf. 14***

**539** A117 8s multicolored .25 .25
**540** A117 14s multicolored .25 .25
**541** A117 27s multicolored .25 .25
**542** A117 50s multicolored .40 .40
*a.* Souvenir sheet of 4, #539-542 1.25 1.25
*Nos. 539-542 (4)* 1.15 1.15

**Ship Type of 1979**

**1981, Jan. 26 Litho. *Perf. 13½***

**543** A107 12s Ocean .30 .30
**544** A107 18s Horatio .45 .45
**545** A107 27s Calliope .70 .70
**546** A107 32s Calypso .80 .80
*Nos. 543-546 (4)* 2.25 2.25

Pres. Franklin Roosevelt and Hyde Park Home A118

IYD: Scenes of Franklin D. Roosevelt — 18s, Inauguration. 27s, Pres. & Mrs. Roosevelt. 32s, Atlantic convoy (Lend Lease Bill). 38s, With stamp collection. $1, Campobello House.

**Wmk. 355**

**1981, Apr. 29 Litho. *Perf. 14***

**547** A118 12s shown .25 .25
**548** A118 18s multicolored .25 .25
**549** A118 27s multicolored .25 .25
**550** A118 32s multicolored .30 .30
**551** A118 38s multicolored .30 .30
**552** A118 $1 multicolored .50 .50
*Nos. 547-552 (6)* 1.85 1.85

Hotel Tusitala — A119

18s, Apia Harbor. 27s, Aggie Grey's Hotel. 32s, Ceremonial kava preparation. 54s, Piula Pool.

***Perf. 14½x14***

**1981, June 29 Litho. Wmk. 355**

**553** A119 12s shown .25 .25
**554** A119 18s multicolored .25 .25
**555** A119 27s multicolored .30 .25
**556** A119 32s multicolored .30 .25
**557** A119 54s multicolored .50 .50
*Nos. 553-557 (5)* 1.60 1.50

**Royal Wedding Issue**

Common Design Type

**Wmk. 355**

**1981, July 22 Litho. *Perf. 14***

**558** CD331 18s Bouquet .25 .25
**559** CD331 32s Charles .25 .25
**560** CD331 $1 Couple .35 .35
*Nos. 558-560 (3)* .85 .85

Tattooing Instruments A120

**1981, Sept. 29 Litho. *Perf. 13½x14***

**561** Strip of 4 2.00 2.00
*a.* A120 12s shown .25 .25
*b.* A120 18s 1st stage .25 .25
*c.* A120 27s Later stage .35 .30
*d.* A120 $1 Tattooed man 1.00 1.00

Christmas — A121

**1981, Nov. 30 Litho. *Perf. 13½***

**562** A121 11s Milo tree blossom .25 .25
**563** A121 15s Copper leaf .25 .25
**564** A121 23s Yellow allamanda .25 .25
**565** A121 $1 Mango blossom .85 .85
*a.* Souvenir sheet of 4, #562-565 2.25 2.25
*Nos. 562-565 (4)* 1.60 1.60

**Souvenir Sheet**

Philatokyo '81 Intl. Stamp Exhibition — A122

**1981, Oct. 9 Litho. *Perf. 14x13½***

**566** A122 $2 multicolored 2.00 2.00

250th Birth Anniv. of George Washington A123

**1982, Feb. 26 Litho. *Perf. 14***

**567** A123 23s Pistol .25 .25
**568** A123 25s Mt. Vernon .30 .30
**569** A123 34s Portrait .35 .35
*Nos. 567-569 (3)* .90 .90

**Souvenir Sheet**

**570** A123 $1 Taking oath 1.10 1.10

20th Anniv. of Independence — A124

18s, Freighter Forum Samoa. 23s, Jet, routes. 25s, Natl. Provident Fund building. $1, Intl. subscriber dialing system.

**1982, May 24 Litho. *Perf. 13½x14***

**571** A124 18s multicolored 1.00 .30
**572** A124 23s multicolored 1.25 .40
**573** A124 25s multicolored .50 .40
**574** A124 $1 multicolored 1.50 1.25
*Nos. 571-574 (4)* 4.25 2.35

Scouting Year A125

**1982, July 20 Wmk. 355 *Perf. 14½***

**575** A125 5s Map reading .25 .25
**576** A125 38s Salute .45 .45
**577** A125 44s .55 .55
**578** A125 $1 Troop 1.25 1.25
*a.* Souvenir sheet 1.75 1.75
*Nos. 575-578 (4)* 2.50 2.50

No. 578a contains one stamp similar to No. 578, 48x36mm.

12th Commonwealth Games, Brisbane, Australia, Sept. 30-Oct. 9 — A126

***Perf. 14x14½***

**1982, Sept. 20 Wmk. 373**

**579** A126 23s Boxing .25 .25
**580** A126 25s Hurdles .30 .30
**581** A126 34s Weightlifting .40 .40
**582** A126 $1 Lawn bowling .95 .95
*Nos. 579-582 (4)* 1.90 1.90

Christmas A127

Children's Drawings: 11s, 15s, Flight into Egypt diff. 38s, $1, Virgin and Child, diff.

**1982, Nov. 15 Litho. Wmk. 355**

**583** A127 11s multicolored .25 .25
**584** A127 15s multicolored .25 .25
**585** A127 38s multicolored .45 .45
**586** A127 $1 multicolored .80 .80
*a.* Souvenir sheet of 4, #583-586 2.25 2.25
*Nos. 583-586 (4)* 1.75 1.75

Commonwealth Day — A128

***Perf. 13½x14***

**1983, Feb. 23 Litho. Wmk. 373**

**587** A128 14s Map .25 .25
**588** A128 29s Flag .35 .35
**589** A128 43s Harvesting copra .35 .35
**590** A128 $1 Malietoa Tanumafili II .75 .75
*Nos. 587-590 (4)* 1.70 1.70

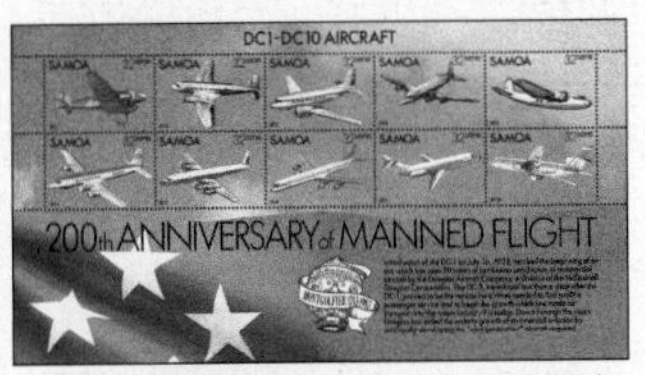


Manned Flight Bicentenary and 50th Anniv. of Douglas Aircraft — A129

a, DC-1. b, DC-2. c, DC-3. d, DC-4. e, DC-5. f, DC-6. g, DC-7. h, DC-8. i, DC-9. j, DC-10.

**Wmk. 373**

**1983, June 7 Litho. *Perf. 14***

**591** A129 Sheet of 10 8.00 8.00
*a.-j.* 32s any single .65 .65

7th South Pacific Games, Apia — A130

**1983, Aug. 29 Litho. *Perf. 14x14½***

**592** A130 8s Pole vault .45 .45
**593** A130 15s Basketball .55 .55
**594** A130 25c Tennis .70 .60
**595** A130 32s Weightlifting .90 .60
**596** A130 35s Boxing .90 .90
**597** A130 46s Soccer 1.10 1.10
**598** A130 48s Golf 2.00 1.25
**599** A130 56s Rugby 1.50 1.50
*Nos. 592-599 (8)* 8.10 6.95

Local Fruit — A131

***Perf. 14x13½***

**1983-84 Litho. Wmk. 373**

**600** A131 1s Limes .35 .35
**601** A131 2s Star fruit .35 .35
**602** A131 3s Mangosteen .35 .35
**603** A131 4s Lychee .35 .35
**604** A131 7s Passion fruit .35 .35
**605** A131 8s Mangoes .35 .35
**606** A131 11s Papaya .35 .35
**607** A131 13s Pineapple .35 .35
**608** A131 14s Breadfruit .35 .35
**609** A131 15s Bananas .35 .35
**610** A131 21s Cashew nut .90 .90
**611** A131 25s Guava 1.40 1.40
**612** A131 32s Water Melon 1.75 1.75
**613** A131 48s Sasalapa 2.00 2.00
**614** A131 56s Avocado 2.25 2.25
**615** A131 $1 Coconut 2.50 2.50

***Perf. 13½***

**616** A131 $2 Apples ('84) 3.00 3.00
**617** A131 $4 Grapefruit ('84) 6.00 6.00
**618** A131 $5 Oranges ('84) 7.00 7.00
*Nos. 600-618 (19)* 30.30 30.30

Issued: 1s-15s, 9/28; 21s-$1, 11/30; $2-$5, 4/11.

For overprint see No. 628.

Miniature Sheet

Boys' Brigade Centenary — A132

**1983, Oct. 10 *Perf. 14½***

**619** A132 $1 multicolored 3.50 3.50

Togitogiga Falls, Upolu A133

32s, Lano Beach, Savai'i. 48s, Mulinu'u Point, Upolu. 56s, Nu'utele Island.

**Wmk. 373**

**1984, Feb. 15 Litho. *Perf. 14***

**620** A133 25s shown .45 .25
**621** A133 32s multicolored .55 .55
**622** A133 48s multicolored .75 .75
**623** A133 56s multicolored .90 .90
*Nos. 620-623 (4)* 2.65 2.45

**Lloyd's List Issue**

Common Design Type

***Perf. 14½x14***

**1984, May 24 Litho. Wmk. 373**

**624** CD335 32s Apia Harbor .35 .25
**625** CD335 48s Apia hurricane, 1889 .65 .55
**626** CD335 60s Forum Samoa .75 .75
**627** CD335 $1 Matua .80 .80
*Nos. 624-627 (4)* 2.55 2.35

**No. 615 Ovptd. "19th U.P.U. CONGRESS / HAMBURG 1984"**

**1984, June 7 *Perf. 14x13½***

**628** A131 $1 multicolored 1.75 1.75

Los Angeles Coliseum — A134

**1984, June 26 Litho. *Perf. 14½***

**629** A134 25s shown .25 .25
**630** A134 32s Weightlifting .35 .35
**631** A134 48s Boxing .45 .45
**632** A134 $1 Running .75 .75
*a.* Souvenir sheet of 4, #629-632 2.00 2.00
*Nos. 629-632 (4)* 1.80 1.80

1984 Summer Olympics and Samoa's first Olympic participation.

Souvenir Sheet

Ausipex '84 — A135

**1984, Sept. 21 Litho. *Perf. 14***

**633** A135 $2.50 Nomad N24 6.00 6.00

Christmas — A136

The Three Virtues, by Raphael.

**1984, Nov. 7 *Perf. 14½x14***

**634** A136 25s Faith .45 .25
**635** A136 35s Hope .55 .55
**636** A136 $1 Charity 1.90 1.90
*a.* Souvenir sheet of 3, #634-636 3.75 3.75
*Nos. 634-636 (3)* 2.90 2.70

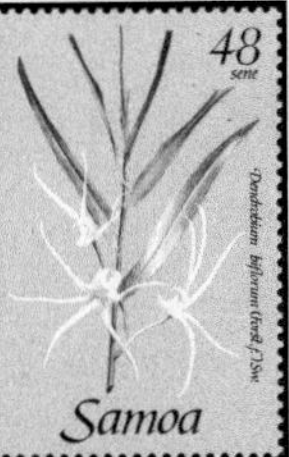


Orchids — A137

48s, Dendrobium biflorum. 56s, Dendrobium vaupelianum kraenzl. 67s, Glomera montana. $1, Spathoglottis plicata.

**Unwmk.**

**1985, Jan. 23 Litho. *Perf. 14***

**637** A137 48s multicolored .65 .50
**638** A137 56s multicolored 1.10 .90
**639** A137 67s multicolored 1.25 1.25
**640** A137 $1 multicolored 1.90 1.90
*Nos. 637-640 (4)* 4.90 4.55

For surcharges, see Nos. 1322-1324.

Vintage Automobiles — A138

48s, Ford Model A, 1903. 56s, Chevrolet Tourer, 1912. 67s, Morris Oxford, 1913. $1, Austin Seven, 1923.

**Wmk. 373**

**1985, Mar. 26 Litho. *Perf. 14***

**641** A138 48s multicolored 1.25 .75
**642** A138 56s multicolored 1.60 1.00
**643** A138 67s multicolored 2.00 2.00
**644** A138 $1 multicolored 2.50 2.50
*Nos. 641-644 (4)* 7.35 6.25

Fungi — A139

48s, Dictyophora indusiata. 56s, Ganoderma tornatum. 67s, Mycena chlorophoe. $1, Mycobonia flava.

**1985, Apr. 17 Litho. *Perf. 14½***

**645** A139 48s multicolored 1.50 .75
**646** A139 56s multicolored 1.75 1.00
**647** A139 67s multicolored 2.00 2.00
**648** A139 $1 multicolored 3.00 3.00
*Nos. 645-648 (4)* 8.25 6.75

**Queen Mother 85th Birthday**

Common Design Type

32s, Photo., age 9. 48s, With Prince William at christening of Prince Henry. 56s, At Liverpool street station. $1, Holding Prince Henry. $2, Arriving at Tattenham corner station.

***Perf. 14½x14***

**1985, June 7 Litho. Wmk. 384**

**649** CD336 32s multicolored .50 .35
**650** CD336 48s multicolored .65 .45
**651** CD336 56s multicolored 1.75 1.25
**652** CD336 $1 multicolored 1.50 1.50
*Nos. 649-652 (4)* 4.40 3.55

**Souvenir Sheet**

**653** CD336 $2 multicolored 4.00 4.00

Souvenir Sheet

EXPO '85, Tsukuba, Japan — A140

**Unwmk.**

**1985, Aug. 26 Litho. *Perf. 14***

**654** A140 $2 Emblem, elevation map 2.75 2.75

Intl. Youth Year — A141

Portions of world map and: a, Emblem, map of No. America, Europe and Africa. b, Hands reaching high. c, Arms reaching, hands limp. d, Hands clenched. e, Emblem and map of Africa, Asia and Europe.

**1985, Sept. 18 Wmk. 373**

**655** A141 Strip of 5 3.25 3.25
*a.-e.* 60s any single .55 .55

Christmas 1985 — A142

Illustrations by Millicent Sowerby from A Child's Garden of Verses, by Robert Louis Stevenson.

**1985, Nov. 5 Unwmk. *Perf. 14x14½***

**656** A142 32s System .30 .30
**657** A142 48s Time to Rise .40 .40
**658** A142 56s Auntie's skirts .45 .45
**659** A142 $1 Good Children .80 .80
*a.* Souvenir sheet of 4, #656-659 2.50 2.50
*Nos. 656-659 (4)* 1.95 1.95

Butterflies A143

25s, Hypolimnas bolina inconstans. 32s, Anapheis java sparrman. 48s, Deudorix epijarbas doris. 56s, Badamia exclamationis. 60s, Tirumala hamata mellitula. $1, Catochrysops taitensis.

**1986, Feb. 13 Wmk. 384 *Perf. 14½***

**660** A143 25s multicolored .55 .35
**661** A143 32s multicolored .65 .45
**662** A143 48s multicolored .90 .75
**663** A143 56s multicolored 1.00 1.00
**664** A143 60s multicolored 1.10 1.10
**665** A143 $1 multicolored 2.00 2.00
*Nos. 660-665 (6)* 6.20 5.65

Halley's Comet A144

Designs: 32s, Comet over Apia. 48s, Edmond Halley, astronomer. 60s, Comet orbiting the Earth. $2, Giotto space probe under construction at British Aerospace.

**1986, Mar. 24**

**666** A144 32s multicolored .30 .30
**667** A144 48s multicolored .40 .40
**668** A144 60s multicolored .55 .55
**669** A144 $2 multicolored 1.75 1.75
*Nos. 666-669 (4)* 3.00 3.00

### Queen Elizabeth II 60th Birthday

Common Design Type

Designs: 32s, Engagement to the Duke of Edinburgh, 1947. 48s, State visit to US, 1976. 56s, Attending outdoor ceremony, Apia, 1977. 67s, At Badminton Horse Trials, 1978. $2, Visiting Crown Agents' offices, 1983.

**1986, Apr. 21**

**670** CD337 32s scarlet, blk & sil .30 .30
**671** CD337 48s ultra & multi .35 .35
**672** CD337 56s green & multi .40 .40
**673** CD337 67s violet & multi .50 .50
**674** CD337 $2 rose violet & multi 1.00 1.00
*Nos. 670-674 (5)* 2.55 2.55

AMERIPEX '86, Chicago, May 22-June 1 — A145

**1986, May 22** **Unwmk.**

**675** A145 48s USS Vincennes .45 .45
**676** A145 56s Sikorsky S-42 .55 .55
**677** A145 60s USS Swan .60 .60
**678** A145 $2 Apollo 10 splashdown 1.75 1.75
*Nos. 675-678 (4)* 3.35 3.35

Souvenir Sheet

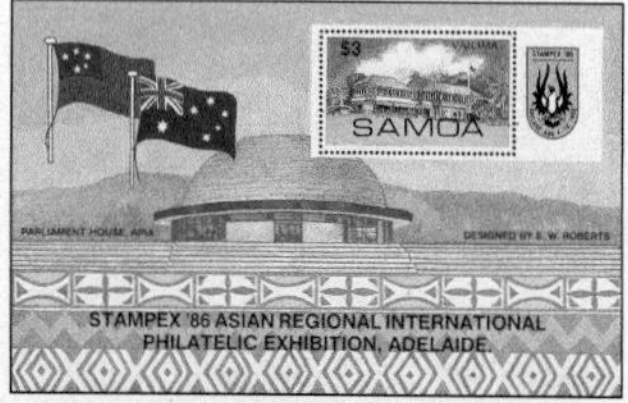


Vailima, Estate of Novelist Robert Louis Stevenson, Upolu Is. — A146

**1986, Aug. 4** **Litho.** ***Perf. 13½***

**679** A146 $3 multicolored 5.75 5.75

STAMPEX '86, Adelaide, Aug. 4-10.

Fish A147

**Unwmk.**

**1986, Aug. 13** **Litho.** ***Perf. 14***

**680** A147 32s Spotted grouper .50 .50
**681** A147 48s Sabel squirrelfish .70 .50
**682** A147 60s Lunartail grouper .90 .90
**683** A147 67s Longtail snapper 1.25 1.25
**684** A147 $1 Berndt's soldierfish 2.25 2.25
*Nos. 680-684 (5)* 5.60 5.40

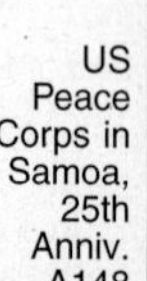

US Peace Corps in Samoa, 25th Anniv. A148

Statesmen: Vaai Kolone of Samoa, Ronald Reagan of US and: 45s, Fiame Mata'afa, John F. Kennedy (1961) and Parliament House. 60s, Jules Grevy, Grover Cleveland (1886) and the Statue of Liberty.

**1986, Dec. 1** ***Perf. 14½***

**685** A148 45s multicolored .40 .40
**686** A148 60s multicolored .45 .45
*a.* Souvenir sheet of 2, #685-686 4.00 4.00

Christmas, Statue of Liberty, cent.

Natl. Independence, 25th Anniv. — A149

***Perf. 14x14½***

**1987, Feb. 16** **Litho.** **Unwmk.**

**687** A149 15s Map, hibiscus .25 .25
**688** A149 45s Parliament .45 .45
**689** A149 60s Rowing race, 1987 .55 .55
**690** A149 70s Dove .65 .65
**691** A149 $2 Prime minister, flag 2.00 2.00
*Nos. 687-691 (5)* 3.90 3.90

Nos. 687-690 vert.

Marine Life A150

**1987, Mar. 31**

**692** A150 45s Gulper .55 .35
**693** A150 60s Hatchet-fish .65 .65
**694** A150 70s Angler .85 .85
**695** A150 $2 Gulper, diff. 2.00 2.00
*Nos. 692-695 (4)* 4.05 3.85

Souvenir Sheet

CAPEX '87 — A151

**1987, June 13** ***Perf. 14½***

**696** A151 $3 Logger, construction workers 3.25 3.25

Landscapes — A152

45s, Lefaga Beach, Upolu. 60s, Vaisala Beach, Savaii. 70s, Solosolo Beach, Upolu. $2, Neiafu Beach, Savaii.

**1987, July 29** ***Perf. 14***

**697** A152 45s multicolored .75 .40
**698** A152 60s multicolored 1.00 .50
**699** A152 70s multicolored 1.10 .90
**700** A152 $2 multicolored 2.50 2.50
*Nos. 697-700 (4)* 5.35 4.30

Australia Bicentennial A153

Explorers of the Pacific: 40s, Abel Tasman (c. 1603-1659), Dutch navigator, discovered Tasmania, 1642. 45s, James Cook. 80s, Count Louis-Antoine de Bougainville (1729-1811), French navigator, discovered Bougainville Is., largest of the Solomon Isls., 1768. $2, Comte de La Perouse (1741-1788), French navigator, discovered La Perouse Strait.

**1987, Sept. 30** **Litho.** ***Perf. 14½***

**701** A153 40s multicolored .60 .35
**702** A153 45s multicolored .75 .55
**703** A153 80s multicolored 1.00 1.00
**704** A153 $2 multicolored 2.00 2.00
*a.* Souvenir sheet of 1 3.00 3.00
*Nos. 701-704 (4)* 4.35 3.90

### No. 704a Ovptd. with HAFNIA '87 Emblem in Scarlet

**1987, Oct. 16**

**705** A153 $2 multicolored 3.50 3.50

Christmas 1987 — A154

**1987, Nov. 30** ***Perf. 14***

**706** A154 40s Christmas tree .40 .35
**707** A154 45s Going to church .50 .40
**708** A154 50s Bamboo fire-gun .60 .60
**709** A154 80s Going home 1.10 1.10
*Nos. 706-709 (4)* 2.60 2.45

Australia Bicentennial — A155

a, Samoan natl. crest, Australia Post emblem. b, Two jets, postal van. c, Loading airmail. d, Jet, van, postman. e, Congratulatory aerogramme.

**1988, Jan. 27** ***Perf. 14½***

**710** A155 Strip of 5 5.75 5.75
*a.-e.* 45s any single 1.00 1.00

Faleolo Intl. Airport A156

40s, Terminal, Boeing 727. 45s, Boeing 727, Fuatino. 60s, So. Pacific Is. N43SP, terminal. 70s, Air New Zealand Boeing 737. 80s, Tower, jet. $1, Hawaiian Air DC-9, VIP house.

***Perf. 13x13½***

**1988, Mar. 24** **Litho.** **Unwmk.**

**711** A156 40s multicolored .65 .50
**712** A156 45s multicolored .75 .50
**713** A156 60s multicolored 1.00 .90
**714** A156 70s multicolored 1.10 1.10
**715** A156 80s multicolored 1.25 1.25
**716** A156 $1 multicolored 1.60 1.60
*Nos. 711-716 (6)* 6.35 5.85

EXPO '88, Brisbane, Australia A157

45s, Island village display. 70s, EXPO complex, monorail and flags. $2, Map.

**1988, Apr. 27** ***Perf. 14½***

**717** A157 45s multicolored .65 .65
**718** A157 70s multicolored 1.50 1.50
**719** A157 $2 multicolored 2.25 2.25
*Nos. 717-719 (3)* 4.40 4.40

Souvenir Sheet

Arrival of the Latter Day Saints in Samoa, Cent. — A158

**1988, June 9** **Litho.** ***Perf. 13½***

**720** A158 $3 The Temple, Apia 3.00 3.00

1988 Summer Olympics, Seoul — A159

**1988, Aug. 10** **Litho.** ***Perf. 14***

**721** A159 15s Running .25 .25
**722** A159 60s Weight lifting .50 .50
**723** A159 80s Boxing 1.00 1.00
**724** A159 $2 Olympic Stadium 1.75 1.75
*a.* Souvenir sheet of 4, #721-724 3.50 3.50
*Nos. 721-724 (4)* 3.50 3.50

Birds — A160

10c, Polynesian triller. 15s, Samoan wood rail. 20s, Flat-billed kingfisher. 25s, Samoan fantail. 35s, Scarlet robin. 40s, Mao. 50s, Cardinal honeyeater. 65s, Samoan whistler. No. 733, Many-colored fruit dove. No. 734, White-throated pigeon. No. 735, Silver gull. No. 736, Great frigatebird. 90s, Eastern reef heron. $3, Short-tailed albatross. $10, Common fairy tern. $20, Shy albatross.

**1988-89** **Unwmk.** ***Perf. 13½***

**725** A160 10s multicolored .30 *.45*
**726** A160 15s multicolored .30 *.45*
**727** A160 20s multicolored .30 *1.25*
**728** A160 25s multicolored .40 *.60*
**729** A160 35s multicolored .50 *1.00*
**730** A160 40s multicolored .75 *1.50*
**731** A160 50s multicolored .90 .90
**732** A160 65s multicolored 1.10 1.10
**733** A160 75s multicolored 1.25 *1.75*
**734** A160 85s multicolored 1.40 1.40

***Perf. 14***

**Size:45x39mm**

**735** A160 75s multicolored 1.50 *1.75*
**736** A160 85s multicolored 1.50 *1.75*
**737** A160 90s multicolored 2.40 1.90
**738** A160 $3 multicolored 4.50 4.50
**739** A160 $10 multicolored 12.00 12.00
**740** A160 $20 multicolored 25.00 25.00
*Nos. 725-740 (16)* 54.10 57.30

Issue dates: #725-734, 8/17/88; #735-738, 2/28/89; #739-740, 7/31/89.

Conservation — A161

**1988, Oct. 25** ***Perf. 14***

**741** A161 15s Forests, vert. .85 .30
**742** A161 40s Culture, vert. 1.00 .50
**743** A161 45s Wildlife, vert. 2.00 .60
**744** A161 50s Water 1.25 .75
**745** A161 60s Marine resources 1.25 .90
**746** A161 $1 Land and soil 1.50 1.50
*Nos. 741-746 (6)* 7.85 4.55

Christmas A162

Designs: 15s, 40s, Congregational Church of Jesus, Apia. 40s, Roman Catholic Church, Leauvaa. 45s, Congregational Christian Church, Moataa. $2, Baha'i Temple, Vailima.

*Perf. 14x14½*

**1988, Nov. 14 Litho. Unwmk.**

**747** A162 15s multicolored .25 .25
**748** A162 40s multicolored .50 .50
**749** A162 45s multicolored .55 .55
**750** A162 $2 multicolored 2.25 2.25
*a.* Souvenir sheet of 4, #747-750 3.75 3.75
*Nos. 747-750 (4)* 3.55 3.55

Orchids — A163

**1989, Jan. 31 Litho. *Perf. 14***

**751** A163 15s Phaius flavus .25 .25
**752** A163 45s Calanthe triplicata .75 .75
**753** A163 60s Luisia teretifolia .90 .70
**754** A163 $3 Dendrobium mohlianum 2.75 2.75
*Nos. 751-754 (4)* 4.65 4.45

Apia Hurricane, 1889 A164

**1989, Mar. 16 Litho. Unwmk.**

**755** Strip of 4 9.50 9.50
*a.* A164 50s SMS Eber 1.25 1.25
*b.* A164 65s SMS Olga 1.50 1.50
*c.* A164 85s SMS Calliope 2.00 2.00
*d.* A164 $2 SMS Vandalia 2.50 2.50
*e.* Souv. sheet of 2, #c.-d., imperf. 8.00 8.00

World Stamp Expo '89.
#755e, issued Nov. 17, is wmk. 355.

Intl. Red Cross and Red Crescent Organizations, 125th Annivs. — A165

**1989, May 15 *Perf. 14½x14***

**756** A165 50s Youths in parade .40 .40
**757** A165 65s Blood donation .55 .55
**758** A165 75s First Aid .65 .65
**759** A165 $3 Volunteers 2.50 2.50
*Nos. 756-759 (4)* 4.10 4.10

### Moon Landing, 20th Anniv.

Common Design Type

Apollo 14: 18s, Saturn-Apollo vehicle and mobile launcher. 50s, Alan Shepard, Stuart Roosa and Edgar Mitchell. 65s, Mission emblem. $2, Tracks of the modularised equipment transporter. $3, Buzz Aldrin and American flag raised on the Moon, Apollo 11 mission.

**1989, July 20 Wmk. 384 *Perf. 14***

**Size of Nos. 761-762: 29x29mm**

**760** CD342 18s multicolored .35 .30
**761** CD342 50s multicolored .75 .50
**762** CD342 65s multicolored 1.00 .75
**763** CD342 $2 multicolored 3.00 3.00
*Nos. 760-763 (4)* 5.10 4.55

**Souvenir Sheet**

**764** CD342 $3 multicolored 4.75 4.75

Christmas A166

*Perf. 13½x13*

**1989, Nov. 1 Litho. Unwmk.**

**765** A166 18s Joseph and Mary .40 .30
**766** A166 50s Shepherds .90 .50
**767** A166 55s Animals 1.00 .70
**768** A166 $2 Three kings 3.50 3.50
*Nos. 765-768 (4)* 5.80 5.00

Local Transport — A167

Designs: 18s, Pao pao (outrigger canoe). 55s, Fautasi (longboat). 60s, Polynesian Airlines propeller plane. $3, Lady Samoa ferry.

**1990, Jan. 31 Unwmk. *Perf. 14x15***

**769** A167 18s multicolored .45 .35
**770** A167 55s multicolored 1.10 .75
**771** A167 60s multicolored 1.75 1.40
**772** A167 $3 multicolored 5.50 5.50
*Nos. 769-772 (4)* 8.80 8.00

Otto von Bismarck, Brandenburg Gate — A168

**1990, May 3 *Perf. 14x13½***

**773** A168 75s shown 2.00 2.00
**774** A168 $3 SMS Adler 6.75 6.75
*a.* Pair, #773-774 10.50 10.50

Opening of the Berlin Wall, 1989, and cent. of the Treaty of Berlin (in 1989). No. 774a has a continuous design.

Great Britain No. 1 and Alexandra Palace — A169

**1990, May 3**

**775** A169 $3 multicolored 4.00 4.00

Stamp World London '90 and 150th anniv. of the Penny Black.

Tourism A170

**1990, July 30 Litho. *Perf. 14***

**776** A170 18s Visitors Bureau .25 .25
**777** A170 50s Samoa Village Resorts .70 .40
**778** A170 65s Aggies Hotel .90 .70
**779** A170 $3 Tusitala Hotel 3.50 3.50
*Nos. 776-779 (4)* 5.35 4.85

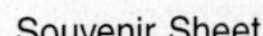

Souvenir Sheet

No. 240, Exhibition Emblem — A171

**1990, Aug. 24 Litho. *Perf. 13***

**780** A171 $3 multicolored 4.75 4.75

World Stamp Exhib., New Zealand 1990.

Christmas — A172

Paintings of Madonna and Child.

**1990, Oct. 31 *Perf. 12½***

**781** A172 18s Bellini .45 .25
**782** A172 50s Bouts .90 .50
**783** A172 55s Correggio 1.10 .60
**784** A172 $3 Cima 4.75 4.75
*Nos. 781-784 (4)* 7.20 6.10

The 55s is "The School of Love," not "Madonna of the Basket."

UN Development Program, 40th Anniv. — A173

**1990, Nov. 26 *Perf. 13½***

**785** A173 $3 multicolored 3.75 3.75

Parrots A174

**1991, Apr. 8 Litho. *Perf. 13½***

**786** A174 18s Black-capped lory .80 .45
**787** A174 50s Eclectus parrot 1.50 .70
**788** A174 65s Scarlet macaw 1.90 1.00
**789** A174 $3 Palm cockatoo 5.00 5.00
*Nos. 786-789 (4)* 9.20 7.15

### Elizabeth & Philip, Birthdays

Common Design Types

**Wmk. 384**

**1991, June 17 Litho. *Perf. 14½***

**790** CD346 75s multicolored 1.00 1.00
**791** CD345 $2 multicolored 2.25 2.25
*a.* Pair, #790-791 + label 3.75 3.75

Souvenir Sheet

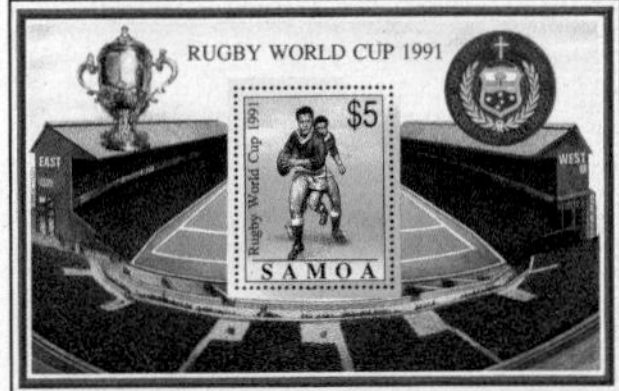


1991 Rugby World Cup — A175

**1991, Oct. 12 Litho. *Perf. 14½***

**792** A175 $5 multicolored 11.00 11.00

Christmas A176

Orchids and Christmas carols: 20s, O Come All Ye Faithful. 60s, Joy to the World. 75s, Hark! the Herald Angels Sing. $4, We Wish You a Merry Christmas.

**1991, Oct. 31 Litho. *Perf. 14½***

**793** A176 20s multicolored .60 .25
**794** A176 60s multicolored 1.10 .75
**795** A176 75s multicolored 1.40 .90
**796** A176 $4 multicolored 5.25 5.25
*Nos. 793-796 (4)* 8.35 7.15

See Nos. 815-818, 836-840.

Phila Nippon '91 — A177

Samoan hawkmoths: 60s, Herse convolvuli. 75s, Gnathothlibus erotus. 85s, Hippotion celerio. $3, Cephonodes armatus.

**1991, Nov. 16 *Perf. 13½x14***

**797** A177 60s multicolored 1.10 .85
**798** A177 75s multicolored 1.30 1.00
**799** A177 85s multicolored 1.50 1.40
**800** A177 $3 multicolored 5.50 5.50
*Nos. 797-800 (4)* 9.40 8.75

Independence, 30th Anniv. — A178

**1992, Jan. 8 Litho. *Perf. 14***

**801** A178 50s Honor guard .70 .55
**802** A178 65s Siva scene .90 .65
**803** A178 $1 Parade float 1.50 1.50
**804** A178 $3 Raising flag 4.75 4.75
*Nos. 801-804 (4)* 7.85 7.45

### Queen Elizabeth II's Accession to the Throne, 40th Anniv.

Common Design Type

**1992, Feb. 6 Wmk. 384**

**805** CD349 20s multicolored .70 .35
**806** CD349 60s multicolored 1.25 .85
**807** CD349 75s multicolored 1.40 .80
**808** CD349 85s multicolored 1.50 .90

**Wmk. 373**

**809** CD349 $3 multicolored 3.00 3.00
*Nos. 805-809 (5)* 7.85 5.90

Souvenir Sheet

Discovery of America, 500th Anniv. — A179

**1992, Apr. 17 Unwmk. *Perf. 14½***
**810** A179 $4 No. 1 4.75 4.75

World Columbian Stamp Expo '92, Granada '92 and Genoa '92 Philatelic Exhibitions.

1992 Summer Olympics, Barcelona — A180

**1992, July 28 Wmk. 373 *Perf. 14***
**811** A180 60s Weight lifting .90 .75
**812** A180 75s Boxing 1.10 .95
**813** A180 85s Running 1.40 1.25
**814** A180 $3 Stadium, statue 4.25 4.25
*Nos. 811-814 (4)* 7.65 7.20

### Christmas Type of 1991

Christmas carol, orchid: 50s, "God rest you, merry gentlemen...," liparis layardii. 60s, "While shepherds watched...," corymborkis veratrifolia. 75s, "Away in a manger...," phaius flavus. $4, "O little town...," bulbophyllum longifolium.

**1992, Oct. 28 Litho. *Perf. 14½***
**815** A176 50s multicolored .65 .40
**816** A176 60s multicolored .75 .65
**817** A176 75s multicolored .90 .80
**818** A176 $4 multicolored 4.50 4.50
*Nos. 815-818 (4)* 6.80 6.35

Fish A182

60s, Batfish. 75s, Lined surgeonfish. $1, Red-tail snapper. $3, Long-nosed emperor.

**1993, Mar. 17 Litho. *Perf. 14***
**819** A182 60s multicolored .90 .65
**820** A182 75s multicolored 1.10 1.10
**821** A182 $1 multicolored 1.60 1.60
**822** A182 $3 multicolored 4.50 4.50
*Nos. 819-822 (4)* 8.10 7.85

World Cup Seven-a-Side Rugby Championships, Scotland — A183

60s, Team performing traditional dance. 75c, Two players. 85c, Player. $3, Edinburgh Castle.

**1993, May 12 *Perf. 13½x14***
**823** A183 60s multi 1.40 .75
**824** A183 75s multi, vert. 1.50 .85
**825** A183 85s multi, vert. 1.75 1.25
**826** A183 $3 multi 5.50 5.50
*Nos. 823-826 (4)* 10.15 8.35

Bats A184

**1993, June 10 *Perf. 14x14½***
**827** A184 20s Two hanging *1.25 1.25*
**828** A184 50s Two flying *2.00 2.00*
**829** A184 60s Three flying *2.50 2.50*
**830** A184 75s One on flower *3.00 3.00*
*Nos. 827-830 (4) 8.75 8.75*

World Wildlife Fund.

Souvenir Sheet

Taipei '93, Asian Intl. Invitation Stamp Exhibition — A185

**1993, Aug. 16 Litho. *Perf. 14***
**831** A185 $5 multicolored 9.00 9.00

World Post Day A186

Designs: 60s, Globe, letter, flowers. 75s, Customers at Post Office. 85s, Black, white hands exchanging letter. $4, Globe, national flags, letter.

**1993, Oct. 8 Litho. *Perf. 14***
**832** A186 60s multicolored .70 .45
**833** A186 75s multicolored .95 .55
**834** A186 85s multicolored 1.25 1.00
**835** A186 $4 multicolored 4.75 4.75
*Nos. 832-835 (4)* 7.65 6.75

### Christmas Type of 1991

Flowers, Christmas carol: 20s, "Silent Night! Holy Night!..." 60s, "As with gladness men of old..." 75s, "Mary had a Baby, Yes Lord..." $1.50, "Once in Royal David's City..." $3, "Angels, from the realms of Glory..."

***Perf. 14½***

**1993, Nov. 1 Litho. Unwmk.**
**836** A176 20s multicolored .50 .40
**837** A176 60s multicolored 1.00 .60
**838** A176 75s multicolored 1.25 .75
**839** A176 $1.50 multicolored 2.25 2.25
**840** A176 $3 multicolored 4.50 4.50
*Nos. 836-840 (5)* 9.50 8.50

Corals A187

**1994, Feb. 18 Litho. *Perf. 14***
**841** A187 20s Alveropora allingi .40 .30
**842** A187 60s Acropora polystoma .80 .60
**843** A187 90s Acropora listeri 1.00 1.00
**844** A187 $4 Acropora grandis 4.50 4.50
*Nos. 841-844 (4)* 6.70 6.40

### Ovptd. with Hong Kong '94 Emblem

**1994, Feb. 18**
**845** A187 20s on #841 .30 .30
**846** A187 60s on #842 .80 .60
**847** A187 90s on #843 1.00 1.00
**848** A187 $4 on #844 4.50 4.50
*Nos. 845-848 (4)* 6.60 6.40

Manu Samoa Rugby Team A188

Designs: 70s, Management. 90s, Test match with Wales. 95s, Test match with New Zealand. $4, Apia Park Stadium.

**1994, Apr. 11 Litho. *Perf. 14***
**849** A188 70s multicolored .80 .75
**850** A188 90s multicolored 1.00 1.00
**851** A188 95s multicolored 1.10 1.10
**852** A188 $4 multicolored 4.75 4.75
*Nos. 849-852 (4)* 7.65 7.60

Souvenir Sheet

PHILAKOREA '94 — A189

Butterflies: $5, White caper, glasswing.

**1994, Aug. 16 Litho. *Perf. 13***
**853** A189 $5 multicolored 6.00 6.00

Teuila Tourism Festival A190

**1994, Sept. 22 Litho. *Perf. 13½***
**854** A190 70s Singers 1.10 .60
**855** A190 90s Fire dancer 1.25 .85
**856** A190 95s Parade float 1.40 1.00
**857** A190 $4 Police band 6.50 6.50
*Nos. 854-857 (4)* 10.25 8.95

For surcharges, see Nos. 1284, 1306-1307.

A191

70s, Schooner Equator. 90s, Portrait. $1.20, Tomb, Mount Vaea. $4, Vailima House, horiz.

**1994, Nov. 21 *Perf. 14***
**858** A191 70s multicolored .85 .65
**859** A191 90s multicolored 1.00 1.00
**860** A191 $1.20 multicolored 1.40 1.40
**861** A191 $4 multicolored 4.75 4.75
*Nos. 858-861 (4)* 8.00 7.80

Robert Louis Stevenson (1850-94), writer.

A192

Children's Christmas paintings: 70s, Father Christmas. 95s, Nativity. $1.20, Picnic. $4, Greetings.

**1994, Nov. 30**
**862** A192 70s multicolored .70 .60
**863** A192 95s multicolored 1.10 1.10
**864** A192 $1.20 multicolored 1.25 1.25
**865** A192 $4 multicolored 4.00 4.00
*Nos. 862-865 (4)* 7.05 6.95

Scenic Views A193

Designs: 5s, Lotofaga Beach, Aleipata. 10s, Nuutele Island. 30s, Satuiatua, Savaii. 50s, Sinalele, Aleipata. 60s, Paradise Beach, Lefaga. 70s, Houses, Piula Cave. 80s, Taga blowholes. 90s, View from east coast road. 95s, Canoes, Leulumoega. $1, Parliament Building.

**1995 Litho. *Perf. 14½x13***
**866** A193 5s multicolored .25 *.50*
**867** A193 10s multicolored .25 *.50*
**871** A193 30s multicolored .25 *.35*
**874** A193 50s multicolored .30 *.35*
**875** A193 60s multicolored .35 .35
**876** A193 70s multicolored .40 .40
**877** A193 80s multicolored .45 .45
**878** A193 90s multicolored .50 .50
**879** A193 95s multicolored .50 .50
**880** A193 $1 multicolored .55 .55
*Nos. 866-880 (10)* 3.80 4.45

Issued: Nos. 866-867, 871, 874-880, 3/29/95. For surcharges, see Nos. 1295, 1297, 1309-1312.

1995 World Rugby Cup Championships, South Africa — A194

Designs: 70s, Players under age 12. 90s, Secondary Schools' rugby teams. $1, Manu Samoa test match with New Zealand. $4, Ellis Park Stadium, Johannesburg.

**1995, May 25 Litho. *Perf. 14x13½***
**886** A194 70s multicolored .65 .65
**887** A194 90s multicolored .90 .90
**888** A194 $1 multicolored 1.10 1.10
**889** A194 $4 multicolored 4.00 4.00
*Nos. 886-889 (4)* 6.65 6.65

### End of World War II, 50th Anniv.

Common Design Types

Designs: 70s, OS2U Kingfisher over Faleolo Air Base. 90s, F4U Corsair, Faleolo Air Base. 95s, US troops in landing craft. $3, US Marines landing on Samoan beach. $4, Reverse of War Medal 1939-45.

**1995, May 31 Litho. *Perf. 13½***
**890** CD351 70s multicolored 1.00 .75
**891** CD351 90s multicolored 1.25 1.00
**892** CD351 95s multicolored 1.50 1.25
**893** CD351 $3 multicolored 5.50 5.50
*Nos. 890-893 (4)* 9.25 8.50

**Souvenir Sheet**

***Perf. 14***

**894** CD352 $4 multicolored 6.00 6.00

Year of the Sea Turtle — A195

**1995, Aug. 24 Litho. *Perf. 13x13½***
**895** A195 70s Leatherback .80 .80
**896** A195 90s Loggerhead 1.00 1.00
**897** A195 $1 Green turtle 1.25 1.25
**898** A195 $4 Pacific Ridley 4.50 4.50
*Nos. 895-898 (4)* 7.55 7.55

Souvenir Sheet

Singapore '95 — A196

**1995, Sept. 1** *Perf. 14*
**899** A196 $5 Phaius tankervilleae 6.00 6.00

See No. 935.

**UN, 50th Anniv.**

Common Design Type

70s, Mobile hospital. 90s, Bell Sioux helicopter. $1, Bell 212 helicopter. $4, RNZAF Andover.

**Unwmk.**

**1995, Oct. 24 Litho.** *Perf. 14*
**900** CD353 70s multicolored 1.00 .70
**901** CD353 90s multicolored 1.50 1.00
**902** CD353 $1 multicolored 1.60 1.25
**903** CD353 $4 multicolored 5.25 5.25
*Nos. 900-903 (4)* 9.35 8.20

A197

**1995, Nov. 15** *Perf. 14½*
**904** A197 25s Madonna & Child .35 .30
**905** A197 70s Wise Man .75 .55
**906** A197 90s Wise Man, diff. .90 .80
**907** A197 $5 Wise Man, diff. 5.00 5.00
*Nos. 904-907 (4)* 7.00 6.65

Christmas.

A198

Importance of Water: 70s, Waterfall, bird, woman, hands. 90s, Girl standing under fountain, "WATER FOR LIFE." $2, Outline of person's head containing tree, birds, waterfall, girl. $4, Community receiving water from protected watersheds.

**1996, Jan. 26 Litho.** *Perf. 14*
**908** A198 70s multicolored .60 .60
**909** A198 90s multicolored .85 .85
**910** A198 $2 multicolored 2.00 2.00
**911** A198 $4 multicolored 3.75 3.75
*Nos. 908-911 (4)* 7.20 7.20

**Queen Elizabeth II, 70th Birthday**

Common Design Type

Various portraits of Queen, Samoan scenes: 70s, Apia, Main Street. 90s, Neiafu beach. $1, Official residence of Head of State. $3, Parliament Building.

$5, Queen wearing tiara, formal dress.

*Perf. 14½*

**1996, Apr. 22 Litho. Unwmk.**
**912** CD354 70s multicolored .70 .70
**913** CD354 90s multicolored .90 .90
**914** CD354 $1 multicolored .90 .90
**915** CD354 $3 multicolored 2.75 2.75
*Nos. 912-915 (4)* 5.25 5.25

**Souvenir Sheet**

**916** CD354 $5 multicolored 5.25 5.25

Souvenir Sheet

Moon Festival — A199

**1996, May 18 Litho.** *Perf. 14*
**917** A199 $2.50 multicolored 4.25 4.25

CHINA '96.

Souvenir Sheet

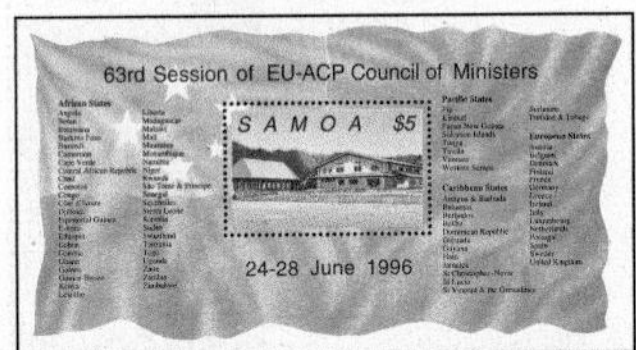


63rd Session of African-Carribean-Pacific-European Union Council of Ministers — A200

**1996, June 19 Litho.** *Perf. 13½*
**918** A200 $5 multicolored 5.00 5.00

A201

**1996, July 15 Litho.** *Perf. 13½*
**919** A201 70s Boxing .65 .65
**920** A201 90s Running .95 .95
**921** A201 $1 Weight lifting 1.10 1.10
**922** A201 $4 Javelin 3.75 3.75
*Nos. 919-922 (4)* 6.45 6.45

1996 Summer Olympic Games, Atlanta.

A202

**1996, Sept. 13 Litho.** *Perf. 14*
**923** A202 60s Logo .65 .45
**924** A202 70s Pottery .70 .55
**925** A202 80s Stained glass .80 .80
**926** A202 90s Dancing .90 .90
**927** A202 $1 Wood carving .95 .95
**928** A202 $4 Samoan chief 3.00 3.00
*Nos. 923-928 (6)* 7.00 6.65

7th Pacific Festival of Arts, Apia.

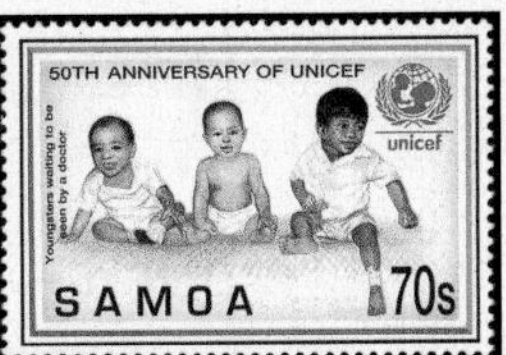


UNICEF, 50th Anniv. — A203

70s, Children in doctor's waiting room. 90s, Children in hospital undergoing treatment. $1, Child receiving injection. $4, Mothers, children playing.

**1996, Oct. 24 Litho.** *Perf. 14*
**929** A203 70s multicolored .65 .55
**930** A203 90s multicolored .75 .75
**931** A203 $1 multicolored .85 .85
**932** A203 $4 multicolored 3.00 3.00
*Nos. 929-932 (4)* 5.25 5.15

Souvenir Sheet

Many-Colored Fruit Dove — A204

**1997, Feb. 3 Litho.** *Perf. 14*
**933** A204 $3 multicolored 3.25 3.25

Hong Kong '97. See No. 962.

Souvenir Sheet

1st US Postage Stamps, 150th Anniv., 1st Samoan Postage Stamps, 120th Anniv. — A205

**1997, May 29 Litho.** *Perf. 14½*
**934** A205 $5 US #2, Samoa #1 4.50 4.50

PACIFIC 97.

**Phaius Tankervilleae Type of 1995**

Souvenir Sheet

**Wmk. 373**

**1997, June 20 Litho.** *Perf. 14½*
**935** A196 $2.50 multicolored 3.50 3.50

Return of Hong Kong to China, July 1, 1997.

Queen Elizabeth II & Prince Philip, 50th Wedding Anniv. — A206

No. 936, Queen. No. 937, Prince at reins of team, Royal Windsor Horse Show, 1996. No. 938, Queen, horse. No. 939, Prince laughing, horse show, 1995. No. 940, Zara Philips, Balmoral 1993, Prince Philip. No. 941, Queen, Prince William.

$5, Queen, Prince, Royal Ascot 1988.

**1997, July 10 Unwmk.** *Perf. 13*
**936** A206 70s multicolored 1.25 1.25
**937** A206 70s multicolored 1.25 1.25
*a.* Pair, #936-937 2.75 2.75
**938** A206 90s multicolored 1.40 1.40
**939** A206 90s multicolored 1.40 1.40
*a.* Pair, #938-939 3.00 3.00
**940** A206 $1 multicolored 1.50 1.50
**941** A206 $1 multicolored 1.50 1.50
*a.* Pair, #940-941 3.25 3.25
*Nos. 936-941 (6)* 8.30 8.30

**Souvenir Sheet**

**942** A206 $5 multicolored 5.75 5.75

Greenpeace, 26th Anniv. — A207

Dolphins: 50s, #947a, Jumping out of water. 60s, #947b, Two swimming right. 70s, #947c, Two facing front. $1, #947d, With mouth open out of water.

**1997, Sept. 17 Litho.** *Perf. 13½x14*
**943** A207 50s multicolored .55 .45
**944** A207 60s multicolored .75 .65
**945** A207 70s multicolored 1.00 1.00
**946** A207 $1 multicolored 1.25 1.25
*Nos. 943-946 (4)* 3.55 3.35

**Miniature Sheet**

**947** A207 $1.25 Sheet of 4, #a.-d. 4.75 4.75

Christmas A208

**1997, Nov. 26 Litho.** *Perf. 14*
**948** A208 70s Bells .65 .55
**949** A208 80s Ornament .75 .65
**950** A208 $2 Candle 1.75 1.75
**951** A208 $3 Star 2.75 2.75
*Nos. 948-951 (4)* 5.90 5.70

Mangroves A209

Bruguiera gymnorrhiza: 70s, Fruit on trees. 80s, Saplings. $2, Roots. $4, Tree at water's edge.

**1998, Feb. 26 Litho.** *Perf. 13½*
**952** A209 70s multicolored .55 .50
**953** A209 80s multicolored .65 .70
**954** A209 $2 multicolored 1.50 1.50
**955** A209 $4 multicolored 3.00 3.00
*Nos. 952-955 (4)* 5.70 5.70

**Diana, Princess of Wales (1961-97)**

Common Design Type

#956: a, Up close portrait. b, Wearing checkered jacket. c, In red dress. d, Holding flowers.

*Perf. 14½x14*

**1998, Mar. 31 Litho. Unwmk.**
**955A** CD355 50s like #956a 1.00 1.00

**Sheet of 4**

**956** CD355 $1.40 #a.-d. 6.00 6.00

No. 956 sold for $5.60 + 75c, with surtax from international sales being donated to the Princess Diana Memorial Fund and surtax from national sales being donated to designated local charity.

**Royal Air Force, 80th Anniversary**

Common Design Type of 1993

Re-Inscribed

70s, Westland Wallace. 80s, Hawker Fury. $2, Vickers Varsity. $5, BAC Jet Provost.

No. 961: a, Norman-Thompson N.T.2b. b, Nieuport 27 Scout. c, Miles Magister. d, Bristol Bombay.

**1998, Apr. 1** *Perf. 13½*

**957** CD350 70s multicolored .80 .40
**958** CD350 80s multicolored .90 .50
**959** CD350 $2 multicolored 1.75 1.75
**960** CD350 $5 multicolored 4.50 4.50
*Nos. 957-960 (4)* 7.95 7.15

**Miniature Sheet**

**961** CD350 $2 Sheet of 4, #a.-d. 7.75 7.75

**Many-Colored Fruit Dove Type of 1997**

**1998, Sept. 1** **Litho.** *Perf. 14*

**962** A204 25s multicolored .60 .60

Christmas Ornaments — A210

**1998, Nov. 16** **Litho.** *Perf. 14*

**963** A210 70s Star .65 .55
**964** A210 $1.05 Bell .95 .85
**965** A210 $1.40 Ball 1.25 1.25
**966** A210 $5 Cross 4.25 4.25
*Nos. 963-966 (4)* 7.10 6.90

Australia '99, World Stamp Expo A211

Boats: 70s, Dugout canoe. 90s, Tasman's ships Heemskerck & Zeehaen, 1642. $1.05, HMS Resolution, HMS Adventure, 1773. $6, New Zealand scow schooner, 1880.

**1999, Mar. 19** **Litho.** *Perf. 14*

**967** A211 70s multicolored .60 .40
**968** A211 90s multicolored 1.00 .65
**969** A211 $1.05 multicolored 1.25 1.00
**970** A211 $6 multicolored 4.75 4.75
*Nos. 967-970 (4)* 7.60 6.80

**Wedding of Prince Edward and Sophie Rhys-Jones**

Common Design Type

**1999, June 19** **Litho.** *Perf. 14*

**971** CD356 $1.50 Separate portraits 1.00 1.00
**972** CD356 $6 Couple 4.00 4.00

**1st Manned Moon Landing, 30th Anniv.**

Common Design Type

70s, Lift-off. 90s, Lunar module separates from Service module. $3, Aldrin deploys solar wind experiment. $5, Parachutes open.

$5, Earth as seen from moon.

*Perf. 14x13¾*

**1999, July 20** **Litho.** **Wmk. 384**

**973** CD357 70s multicolored .55 .45
**974** CD357 90s multicolored .65 .60
**975** CD357 $3 multicolored 1.90 1.90
**976** CD357 $5 multicolored 3.25 3.25
*Nos. 973-976 (4)* 6.35 6.20

**Souvenir Sheet**

*Perf. 14*

**977** CD357 $5 multicolored 6.25 6.25

No. 977 contains one 40mm circular stamp. For surcharge, see No. 1279.

**Queen Mother's Century**

Common Design Type

Queen Mother: 70s, Talking to tenants of bombed apartments, 1940. 90s, At garden party, South Africa. $2, Reviewing scouts at Windsor. $6, With Princess Eugenie, 98th birthday.

$5, With film showing Charlie Chaplin.

*Perf. 13½*

**1999, Aug. 24** **Litho.** **Unwmk.**

**978** CD358 70s multicolored .70 .50
**979** CD358 90s multicolored .80 .60
**980** CD358 $2 multicolored 1.50 1.50
**981** CD358 $6 multicolored 4.25 4.25
*Nos. 978-981 (4)* 7.25 6.85

**Souvenir Sheet**

**982** CD358 $5 multicolored 5.25 5.25

Christmas and Millennium — A212

70s, Hibiscus. 90s, Poinsettia. $2, Christmas cactus. $6, Flag, Southern Cross.

*Perf. 13½x13¼*

**1999, Nov. 30** **Litho.** **Unwmk.**

**983** A212 70s multicolored .80 .60
**984** A212 90s multicolored .95 .75
**985** A212 $2 multicolored 1.50 1.50
**986** A212 $6 multicolored 4.50 4.50
*Nos. 983-986 (4)* 7.75 7.35

For surcharge, see No. 1277.

Millennium — A213

**Unwmk.**

**2000, Jan. 1** **Litho.** *Perf. 14*

**987** A213 70s shown 1.60 1.60
**988** A213 70s Rocks 1.60 1.60
*a.* Pair, #987-988 3.25 3.25

For surcharges, see Nos. 1235-1236, 1298-1305.

Sesame Street — A214

No. 989: a, The Count. b, Ernie. c, Grover. d, Cookie Monster and Prairie Dawn. e, Elmo, Ernie and Zoe. f, Big Bird. g, Telly. h, Magician. i, Oscar the Grouch.

$3, Cookie Monster.

*Perf. 14½x14¾*

**2000, Mar. 22** **Litho.**

**989** A214 90s Sheet of 9, #a-i 6.25 6.25

**Souvenir Sheet**

**990** A214 $3 multi 3.00 3.00

Fire Dancers — A215

Various dancers. Denominations: 25s, 50s, 90s, $1, $4.

**2001, Sept. 3** **Litho.** *Perf. 13x13¼*

**991-995** A215 Set of 5 6.00 6.00

For surcharges, see Nos. 1234, 1282, 1326.

Butterflies — A216

*Serpentine Die Cut*

**2001, Dec. 12** **Litho.**

**Self-Adhesive**

**996** Horiz. strip of 5 7.75 7.75
*a.* A216 70s Vagrans egista .65 .65
*b.* A216 $1.20 Jamides bochus .90 .90
*c.* A216 $1.40 Papilio godeffroyi 1.00 1.00
*d.* A216 $2 Achraea andromacha 1.10 1.10
*e.* A216 $3 Eurema hecabe 1.60 1.60

Intl. Year of Ecotourism — A217

Designs: 60s, Snorkelers. 95s, Kayakers. $1.90, Village, children, craftsman. $3, Bird watchers.

**2002, Feb. 27** *Perf. 13¼*

**997-1000** A217 Set of 4 5.25 5.25
*1000a* Horiz strip of 4, #997-1000 + central label 6.25 6.25

See No. 1329. For surcharges, see Nos. 1276, 1327-1328, 1330-1333.

Independence, 40th Anniv. — A218

Flag and: 25s, Buses, cricket player, huts. 70s, Natives. 95s, Flower, woman, ship, airplane, woman using telephone. $5, Flower, buildings, rugby player, inspection of troops.

*Serpentine Die Cut*

**2002, June 1** **Litho.**

**Self-Adhesive**

**1001-1004** A218 Set of 4 8.00 8.00
*1004a* Souvenir sheet of 1, #1004 7.50 7.50

See No. 1313. For surcharges, see Nos. 1314-1316.

People and Their Activities — A219

Designs: 5s, Woman holding fish. 10s, Family. 20s, Men carrying baskets. 25s, Two boys smiling. 35s, Woman, girl and flowers. 50s, Toddler and adult. 60s, Male dancer. 70s, Female dancer. 80s, Woman laughing. 90s, Group of women. 95s, Two women with flowers in hair. $1, Boy in stream of water. $1.20, Child smiling. $1.85, Man smiling. $10, People at church.

**2002, Aug. 1** **Litho.** *Perf. 13x13¼*

**1005** A219 5s multi .25 .25
**1006** A219 10s multi .25 .25
**1007** A219 20s multi .25 .25
**1008** A219 25s multi .25 .25
**1009** A219 35s multi .25 .25
**1010** A219 50s multi .40 .40
**1011** A219 60s multi .45 .45
**1012** A219 70s multi .55 .55
**1013** A219 80s multi .60 .60
**1014** A219 90s multi .65 .65
**1015** A219 95s multi .75 .75
**1016** A219 $1 multi .80 .80
**1017** A219 $1.20 multi .90 .90
**1018** A219 $1.85 multi 1.40 1.40
**1019** A219 $10 multi 7.50 7.50
*Nos. 1005-1019 (15)* 15.25 15.25

For surcharges, see Nos. 1239, 1275, 1278, 1293.

Scenic Views — A220

Designs: 95s, Family on rock. $1.20, Man and woman on beach. $1.40, Waterfall. $2, Woman in ocean.

**2002, Sept. 18** *Perf. 14x14¾*

**1020-1023** A220 Set of 4 5.75 5.75
*1023a* Souvenir sheet, #1021, 1023 3.25 3.25

For surcharges, see Nos. 1238, 1280, 1334.

Ginger Flowers A221

Designs: 25s, Alpinia purpurata. $1.05, Alpinia samoensis. $1.20, Ellingeria cevuga. $4, Hedychium flavescens.

**2002, Nov. 20** *Perf. 13½*

**1024-1027** A221 Set of 4 6.25 6.25

For surcharges, see Nos. 1290, 1325.

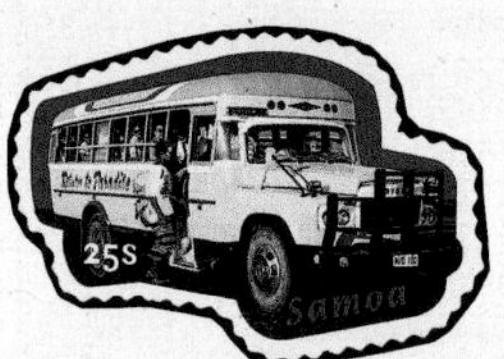


Decorated Buses — A222

Inscriptions on buses: 25s, Return to Paradise. 70s, Misileti Fatu. 90s, Jungle Boys. 95s, Sun Rise Transport. $4, Laifoni.

*Serpentine Die Cut*

**2003, Jan. 22** **Litho.**

**Self-Adhesive**

**1028-1032** A222 Set of 5 7.50 7.50

Marine Protected Areas A223

Designs: 25s, Aleipata. $5, Safata.

*Perf. 13½x13¾*

**2003, Mar. 19** **Litho.**

**1033-1034** A223 Set of 2 5.75 5.75

Artists and Their Works — A224

Artists: 25s, Vanya Taule'alo. 70s, Michel Tuffery. 90s, Momoe von Reiche. $1, Fatu Feu'u. $4, Lily Laita.

**2003, May 7 Litho. *Perf. 13***
**1035-1039** A224 Set of 5 6.25 6.25

For surcharge, see No. 1320.

Sports Stars A225

Designs: 25s, David Tua, boxer. 70s, Beatrice Faumuina, discus. 90s, Michael Jones, rugby. 95s, Rita Fatialofa, netball. $4, Jesse Sapolu, football.

**2003, July 16 *Perf. 13½***
**1040-1044** A225 Set of 5 6.50 6.50

For surcharges, see Nos. 1237, 1281, 1294, 1321.

Angelfish — A226

Designs: 25s, Centropyge bicolor. 60s, Centropyge loriculus. 90s, Pygoplites diacanthus. $5, Pomocanthus imperator.

**2003, Sept. 10 *Perf. 13x13¼***
**1045-1048** A226 Set of 4 8.25 8.25
*1048a* Souvenir sheet of 1 7.00 7.00

Flowers — A227

Designs: 70s, Heliconia caribaea. 80s, Heliconia psittacorum. 90s, Hibiscus rosasinensis. $4, Plumeria rubra.

***Perf. 12¾x13¼***
**2004, Mar. 26 Litho.**
**1049-1052** A227 Set of 4 7.00 7.00

For surcharges, see Nos. 1288, 1291, 1292.

Birds A228

Designs: 25s, Black-naped tern. 60s, Crested tern. 70s, Common noddy, vert. 90s, Lesser frigatebird, vert. $4, Reef heron.

**2004, June 16 Litho. *Perf. 13¼***
**1053-1057** A228 Set of 5 8.00 8.00
*1057a* Souvenir sheet, #1053-1057 8.00 8.00

Butterflyfish — A229

Designs: 50s, Chaetodon meyeri. 90s, Chaetodon punctatofasciatus, horiz. $1, Chaetodon ephippium, horiz. $4, Chaetodon flavirostris.

***Perf. 14¼x14, 14x14¼***
**2004, Sept. 29 Litho.**
**1058-1061** A229 Set of 4 8.00 8.00
*1061a* Souvenir sheet of 1 7.00 7.00

Women and Flowers A230

Various women and: 25s, Pink flower. 70s, Red flowers, vert. 90s, White flowers. $4, Orange flowers, vert.

**2004, Dec. 15 Litho. *Perf. 13¼***
**1062-1065** A230 Set of 4 6.25 6.25

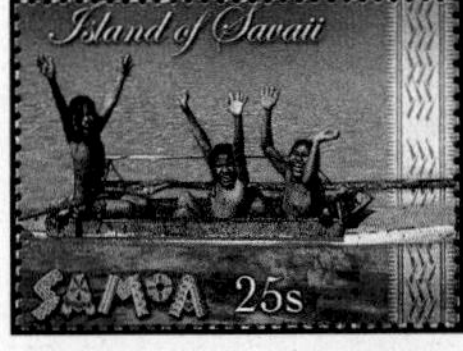

Scenes From Savaii Island A231

Designs: 25s, Children in small boat. 70s, Women, building. 90s, Women on rope bridge, vert. $4, Coastline, vert.

**2005, Feb. 17 Litho. *Perf. 13¼***
**1066-1069** A231 Set of 4 7.00 7.00

Souvenir Sheet

Dolphins — A232

No. 1070: a, $1, Spinner dolphin. b, $1.75, Rough-toothed dolphin. c, $4, Bottlenose dolphin.

**2005, Apr. 21 Litho. *Perf. 13¼***
**1070** A232 Sheet of 3, #a-c 8.50 8.50

Pacific Explorer 2005 World Stamp Expo, Sydney.

Legends — A233

Designs: 25s, Sau Sau, Dawn of the First Humans. 70s, Tuimanu'a and the Flying Fox. 90s, Fonuea and Salofa Escape Famine. $4, Patea, the Sea Demon.

**2005, Sept. 28 Litho. *Perf. 13¼***
**1071-1074** A233 Set of 4 8.00 8.00

For surcharge, see No. 1289.

European Philatelic Cooperation, 50th Anniv. (in 2006) — A234

Globe, CEPT emblem, stars and various Europa stamps: 60s, $3, $4, $10.

**2005, Dec. 7 *Perf. 14***
**1075-1078** A234 Set of 4 *17.00 17.00*
*1078a* Souvenir sheet, #1075-1078 *17.00 17.00*

Europa stamps, 50th anniv. (in 2006).

Diplomatic Relations Between Samoa and People's Republic of China, 30th Anniv. A235

Designs: 25s, Chinese and Samoan representatives and flags. 50s, Building. $1, Wooden bowl. $4, Chinese astronauts.

**2005, Nov. 6 Litho. *Perf. 13x13¼***
**1079-1082** A235 Set of 4 *8.50 8.50*
*1082a* Souvenir sheet, #1079-1082, perf. 12 *8.50 8.50*

Sunsets A236

Various sunsets: 60s, 90s, $1, $4.

**2006, Feb. 15 *Perf. 13¼***
**1083-1086** A236 Set of 4 *12.00 12.00*

Queen Elizabeth II, 80th Birthday A237

Queen Elizabeth II: $1, As young child. No. 1088, $1.75, Holding young Prince Charles. $4, Without hat. No. 1090, $5, Wearing hat.

No. 1091: a, $1.75, Like #1088. b, $5, Like #1089.

**2006, Apr. 21 Litho. *Perf. 14***
**Stamps With White Frames**
**1087-1090** A237 Set of 4 13.00 13.00

**Souvenir Sheet**
**Stamps Without White Frames**
**1091** A237 Sheet of 2, #a-b 8.00 8.00

For surcharges, see Nos. 1283, 1296, 1308.

Worldwide Fund for Nature (WWF) — A238

Various depictions of Humphead wrasses.

**2006, Sept. 20 *Perf. 13¼***
**1092** Horiz. strip of 4 13.00 13.00
*a.* A238 $1.50 org red & multi 1.50 1.25
*b.* A238 $2.30 red & multi 2.50 1.90
*c.* A238 $2.50 yel org & multi 2.75 2.00
*d.* A238 $3.60 purple & multi 3.50 3.00

Issued in sheets of two strips.

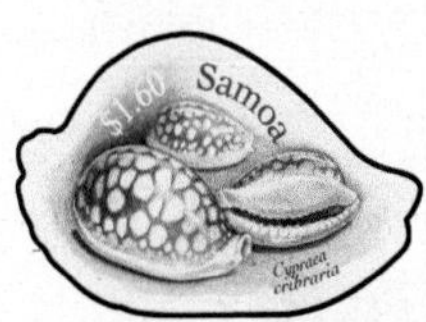

Shells A239

Designs: $1.60, Cypraea cribaria. $2.10, Cypraea aurantium. $2.40, Cypraea mauritiana. $3.10, Ovula ovum.

**2006, Nov. 29 *Die Cut***
**1093-1096** A239 Set of 4 12.00 12.00

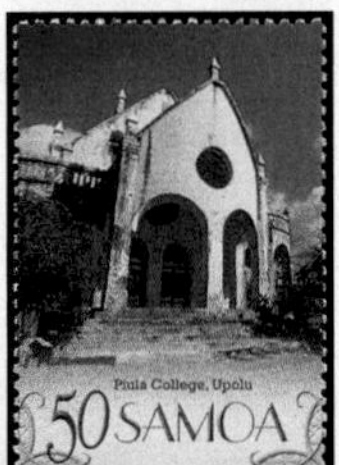

Houses of Worship — A240

Designs: No. 1097, 50s, Piula College Church, Upolu. No. 1098, 50s, Anglican Church, Apia. No. 1099, 50s, Protestant Church, Apia. No. 1100, 50s, SDA Church, Fusi Saoluafata. No. 1101, $1, Methodist Church, Matafele. No. 1102, $1, Mauga Church, Apia. No. 1103, $1, EFKS Church, Apia. No. 1104, $1, Malua Theological College. No. 1105, $2, Latter Day Saints Temple, Pesega. No. 1106, $2, Mulivai Cathedral, Apia. No. 1107, $2, EFKS Church, Sapapaii. No. 1108, $2, Bahai Temple, Apia.

**2007, May 16 Litho. *Perf. 13¼***
**1097-1108** A240 Set of 12 16.00 16.00
*1108a* Miniature sheet, #1097-1108 19.00 19.00

South Pacific Games, Apia — A241

Designs: No. 1109, $1, Ele Opeloge, athlete. No. 1110, $1, Apia Park. No. 1111, $1, Aquatic Center. No. 1112, $1, Mana, Games mascot.

**2007, Aug. 16**
**1109-1112** A241 Set of 4 5.00 5.00
*1112a* Souvenir sheet, 1 #1112 1.75 1.75

Tropical Fruit — A242

Designs: $1.60, Pineapples. $2.10, Coconuts. $2.40, Papayas. $3.10, Mangoes.

**2007, Dec. 14** ***Die Cut***
**Self-Adhesive**

**1113-1116** A242 Set of 4 10.00 10.00

2008 Summer Olympics, Beijing — A243

Designs: 50s, Cycling. $1, Boxing. $1.50, Wrestling. $2, Athletics.

**2008, June 18 Litho.** ***Perf. 12***

| | | | |
|---|---|---|---|
| **1117-1120** | A243 | Set of 4 | 5.50 5.50 |
| *1120a* | | Souvenir sheet of 4, #1117-1120 | 5.50 5.50 |

Peonies, Statue and Temple A244

**2009, Apr. 10 Litho.** ***Perf. 13¼***

**1121** A244 $1 multi .85 .85

Printed in sheets of 8.

Intl. Labor Organization, 90th Anniv. — A245

Color of top panel: $2, Green. $2.70, Blue. $3, Yellow brown. $3.90, Lilac.

**2009, Apr. 27 Litho.** ***Perf. 13¼***
**Granite Paper**

**1122-1125** A245 Set of 4 *90.00 90.00*

Worldwide Fund for Nature (WWF) — A246

No. 1126: a, Pacific robin. b, Polynesian triller. c, Polynesian starling. d, Wattled honeyeater.

**2009, Sept. 2** ***Perf. 13¼***

| | | | |
|---|---|---|---|
| **1126** | | Horiz. strip of 4 | 10.00 10.00 |
| *a.* | A246 50s multi | | .50 .50 |
| *b.* | A246 $2 multi | | 1.50 1.50 |
| *c.* | A246 $2.70 multi | | 2.00 2.00 |
| *d.* | A246 $5 multi | | 3.50 3.50 |

No. 1126 was printed in sheets containing two strips.

Worldwide Fund for Nature (WWF) — A247

No. 1127 — Many-colored fruit dove: a, Two birds. b, Adult and chick in nest. c, Bird eating fruit. d, Two birds, diff.

**2011, Apr. 25** ***Perf. 14***

| | | | |
|---|---|---|---|
| **1127** | | Horiz. strip of 4 | 10.00 10.00 |
| *a.* | A247 50s multi | | .45 .45 |
| *b.* | A247 $2 multi | | 1.75 1.75 |
| *c.* | A247 $2.70 multi | | 2.40 2.40 |
| *d.* | A247 $5 multi | | 4.50 4.50 |
| *e.* | Souvenir sheet of 8, 2 each # 1127a-1127d | | 20.00 20.00 |

Samoa's Move Across International Date Line — A248

No. 1128: a, Map of Australia and New Zealand, flag and map of Samoa on jigsaw puzzle piece. b, Flag and map of Samoa on jigsaw puzzle piece.

**2011, Dec. 15** ***Perf. 14¼***

| | | | |
|---|---|---|---|
| **1128** | A248 | Horiz. pair + central label | 5.00 5.00 |
| *a.* | | $2.50 multi | 2.10 2.10 |
| *b.* | | $3 multi | 2.50 2.50 |

See No. 1318. For surcharges, see Nos. 1317, 1319.

**Nos. 987-988 Surcharged**

**Methods and Perfs As Before**

**2011, Feb. 8**

| | | | |
|---|---|---|---|
| **1129** | A213 50s on 70s #987 | — | — |
| *a.* | Inverted surcharge | — | — |
| **1130** | A213 50s on 70s #988 | — | — |
| *a.* | Pair, #1129-1130 | — | — |
| *b.* | Inverted surcharge | — | — |
| *c.* | Horiz. pair, #1129a, 1130b | — | — |
| **1131** | A213 $2 on 70s #987 | — | — |
| **1132** | A213 $2 on 70s #988 | — | — |
| *a.* | Pair, #1131-1132 | — | — |
| **1133** | A213 $3 on 70s #987 | — | — |
| **1134** | A213 $3 on 70s #988 | — | — |
| *a.* | Pair, #1133-1134 | — | — |
| **1135** | A213 $10 on 70s #987 | — | — |
| **1136** | A213 $10 on 70s #988 | — | — |
| *a.* | Pair, #1135-1136 | — | — |
| | Nos. 1129-1136 (8) | 125.00 | — |

Independence, 50th Anniv. — A249

Designs: $1, Longboats. $2, Palm tree and shore. $3, Dancers. $4, Dancer and audience.

**2012, May 24 Litho.** ***Perf. 14¼***

| | | | |
|---|---|---|---|
| **1137** | A249 $1 multi | | .90 .90 |
| **1137A** | A249 $2 multi | | 1.75 1.75 |
| **1137B** | A249 $3 multi | | 2.60 2.60 |
| **1137C** | A249 $4 multi | | 3.50 3.50 |
| *d.* | Souvenir sheet of 4, #1137-1137C | | 8.75 8.75 |
| | *Nos. 1137-1137C (4)* | | 8.75 8.75 |

Miniature Sheet

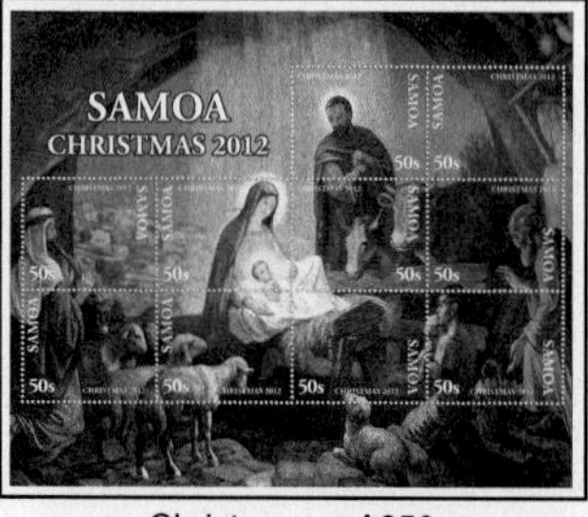


Christmas — A250

No. 1138: a, St. Joseph. b, Tree. c, Shepherd with flute. d, Madonna and Child. e, Heads of donkey and cow. f, Shepherd, body of cow. g, Sheep, body of shepherd. h, Sheep, hand of Mary. i, Feed trough and fence. j, Young shepherd holding lamb.

**2012, Dec. 21 Litho.** ***Perf. 13¾***

**1138** A250 50s Sheet of 10, #a-j 4.50 4.50

Miniature Sheet

New Year 2013 (Year of the Snake) — A251

No. 1139 — Background color: a, Yellow. b, Purple. c, Green. d, Orange.

***Perf. 14¼x14¾***

**2013, Feb. 19 Litho.**

**1139** A251 $3 Sheet of 4, #a-d 10.50 10.50

Fuipisia Falls — A252

**2013, Feb. 19 Litho.** ***Perf. 13¾***

**1140** A252 $2.10 shown 1.90 1.90

**Souvenir Sheet**

***Perf. 14¼x14¾***

**1141** A252 $10 multi 8.75 8.75

No. 1141 contains one 24x54mm stamp.

Endangered Bats and Birds — A253

Designs: $1, Emballonura semicaudata. $2.70, Gallinula pacifica. $3, Didunculus strigirostris. $3.90, Lalage sharpei. $4, Zosterops samoensis. $5, Nesofregetta fulginosa. $6, Numenius tahitiensis. $7.50, Pterodroma brevipes. $8, Pteropus samoensis. $10, Myiagra albiventris. $12.50, Gallicolumba stairi. $15, Gymnomyza samoensis.

**2013, May 29 Litho.** ***Perf. 14***

| | | | |
|---|---|---|---|
| **1142** | A253 | $1 multi | .85 .85 |
| **1143** | A253 | $2.70 multi | 2.40 2.40 |
| **1144** | A253 | $3 multi | 2.60 2.60 |
| **1145** | A253 | $3.90 multi | 3.50 3.50 |
| **1146** | A253 | $4 multi | 3.50 3.50 |
| **1147** | A253 | $5 multi | 4.25 4.25 |
| **1148** | A253 | $6 multi | 5.25 5.25 |
| **1149** | A253 | $7.50 multi | 6.50 6.50 |
| **1150** | A253 | $8 multi | 7.00 7.00 |
| **1151** | A253 | $10 multi | 8.75 8.75 |
| **1152** | A253 | $12.50 multi | 11.00 11.00 |
| **1153** | A253 | $15 multi | 13.00 13.00 |
| | *Nos. 1142-1153 (12)* | | 68.60 68.60 |

Sopoaga Falls and Teuila Flower — A254

**2013, Aug. 19 Litho.** ***Perf. 13¾***

**1154** A254 $2.70 multi 2.25 2.25

**Souvenir Sheet**

***Perf. 14x14¾***

**1155** A254 $20 multi 17.00 17.00

No. 1155 contains one 24x54mm stamp with an image similar to No. 1154 but which is erroneously inscribed "Fuipisia Falls Upolu Island."

Birth of Prince George of Cambridge A255

Designs: Nos. 1156, 1159a, $1, Duchess of Cambridge holding Prince George. Nos. 1157, 1159b, $5, Prince George. Nos. 1158, 1159c, $10, Duke of Cambridge holding Prince George.

**2013, Aug. 26 Litho.** ***Perf. 14***
**Stamps With Photograph 22mm Wide**

**1156-1158** A255 Set of 3 13.50 13.50

**Souvenir Sheet**
**Stamps With Photograph 24mm Wide**

**1159** A255 Sheet of 3, #a-c 13.50 13.50

Photographs on Nos. 1159 extend to the tips of the perforations. A white frame is next to the outer sides of the photographs on Nos. 1156-1158.

Miniature Sheet

2013 Pacific Mini Games, Wallis & Futuna Islands — A256

No. 1160 — Inscriptions: a, Athletics. b, Beach volleyball. c, Rugby sevens. d, Sailing. e, Taekwondo. f, Va'a canoeing. g, Bodybuilding. h, Volleyball.

**2013, Aug. 28 Litho.** ***Perf. 13¾***

**1160** A256 $2.50 Sheet of 8, #a-h 17.00 17.00

A257

Teuila Festival — A258

No. 1162: a, Side view of pink teuila flower. b, Side view of red teuila flower. c, View of pink teuila flower from above.

**2013, Sept. 17 Litho. *Perf. 13¾***

| | | | |
|---|---|---|---|
| 1161 | A257 50s multi | .45 | .45 |

**Souvenir Sheet**

| | | | |
|---|---|---|---|
| 1162 | A258 $10 Sheet of 3, #a-c | 26.00 | 26.00 |

Souvenir Sheet

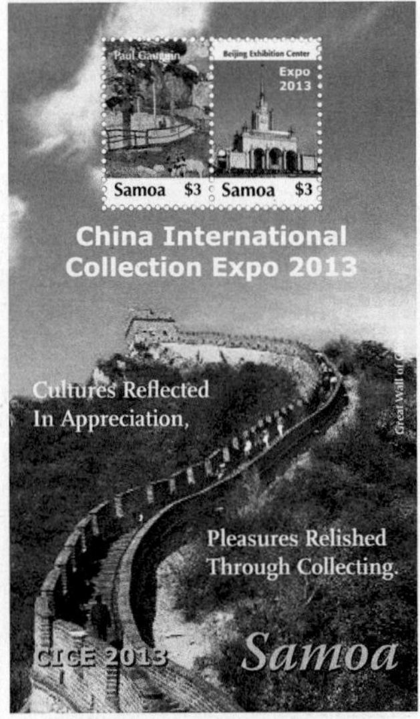
2013 China International Collection Expo, Beijing — A259

No. 1163: a, Painting by Paul Gauguin. b, Beijing Exhibition Center.

**2013, Sept. 26 Litho. *Perf. 12***

| | | | |
|---|---|---|---|
| 1163 | A259 $3 Sheet of 2, #a-b | 5.25 | 5.25 |

Christmas A260

Details of paintings by: $1, Piero della Francesca. $3, Amerighi da Caravaggio.

**2013, Nov. 26 Litho. *Perf. 13¼***

| | | | |
|---|---|---|---|
| 1164-1165 | A260 Set of 2 | 3.50 | 3.50 |

Miniature Sheet

New Year 2014 (Year of the Horse) — A261

No. 1166 — Heads of various horses: a, 50s. b, 90s. c, $1.10. d, $2. e, $2.50. f, 3.

**2014, Jan. 8 Litho. *Perf. 13¼***

| | | | |
|---|---|---|---|
| 1166 | A261 Sheet of 6, #a-f | 8.50 | 8.50 |

Endangered Marine Life and Reptiles — A262

Designs: 50s, Physeter macrocephalus. $1.50, Hippocampus histrix. $2, Bolbometopon muricatum. $2.25, Makaira nigricans. $2.50, Himantura gerrardi. $3.50, Cheilinus undulatus. $5.50, Isurus oxyrinchus. $6.60, Emoia samoensis. $7, Hippopus hippopus. $9, Eretmochelys imbricata. $20, Nebrius ferrugineus. $25, Carcharhinus longimanus.

**2014, Jan. 10 Litho. *Perf. 14***

| | | | | |
|---|---|---|---|---|
| 1167 | A262 | 50s multi | .45 | .45 |
| 1168 | A262 | $1.50 multi | 1.25 | 1.25 |
| 1169 | A262 | $2 multi | 1.75 | 1.75 |
| 1170 | A262 | $2.25 multi | 1.90 | 1.90 |
| 1171 | A262 | $2.50 multi | 2.10 | 2.10 |
| 1172 | A262 | $3.50 multi | 3.00 | 3.00 |
| 1173 | A262 | $5.50 multi | 4.75 | 4.75 |
| 1174 | A262 | $6.60 multi | 5.75 | 5.75 |
| 1175 | A262 | $7 multi | 6.00 | 6.00 |
| 1176 | A262 | $9 multi | 7.75 | 7.75 |
| 1177 | A262 | $20 multi | 17.00 | 17.00 |
| 1178 | A262 | $25 multi | 21.50 | 21.50 |
| | *Nos. 1167-1178 (12)* | | 73.20 | 73.20 |

Miniature Sheet

Easter — A263

No. 1179 — Various religious paintings by Giovanni Luteri: a, $2, Jesus. b, $2.70, Madonna and Child. c, $3, The Lamentation. d, $3.90, Ascension of Christ.

**2014, Apr. 10 Litho. *Perf. 13¼***

| | | | |
|---|---|---|---|
| 1179 | A263 Sheet of 4, #a-d | 10.50 | 10.50 |

Souvenir Sheet

Nelson Mandela (1918-2013), President of South Africa — A264

No. 1180 — Various photographs of Mandela: a, $5. b, $10.

**2014, May 9 Litho. *Perf. 14¼***

| | | | |
|---|---|---|---|
| 1180 | A264 Sheet of 2, #a-b | 13.00 | 13.00 |

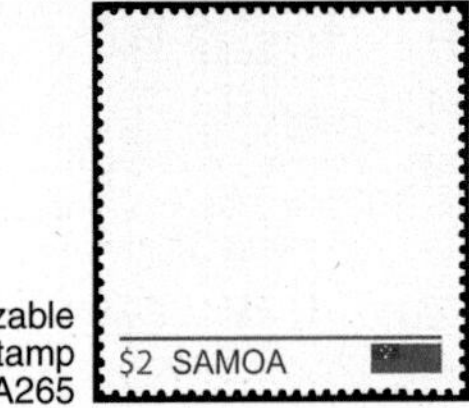
Personalizable Stamp A265

**2014, Aug. 28 Litho. *Perf. 13¼***

| | | | |
|---|---|---|---|
| 1181 | A265 $2 multi | 1.75 | 1.75 |

Small Island Developing States — A266

No. 1182: a, Great barracuda. b, Loggerhead turtle. c, Barbour's seahorse. d, Cutthroat eels. e, Coral reef. f, Samoan coastline. g, Sunset at Fagamalo, Savaii Island. h, Sunset at Savaii. i, Lemafa Peak. j, Stone seawall, Lalomanu. k, Sailboat. l, Cruise ship. m, Tour boat. n, Man in canoe. o, Paddleboarding. p, Flag of Samoa.

No. 1183: a, Like #1182f. b, Like #1182p. c, Like #1182g. d, Like #1182h. e, Like #1182i. f, Like #1182j.

No. 1184: a, Like #1182a. b, Like #1182p. c, Like #1182b. d, Like #1182c. e, Like #1182d. f, Like #1182e.

No. 1185: a, Like #1182l. b, Like #1182p. c, Like #1182k. d, Like #1182m. e, Like #1182n. f, Like #1182o.

**2014, Aug. 29 Litho. *Perf. 13¼***

| | | | |
|---|---|---|---|
| 1182 | Block of 18, #1182a-1182o, 3 #1182p | 8.25 | 8.25 |
| *a.-p.* | A266 50s Any single | .45 | .45 |

**Miniature Sheets**

| | | | |
|---|---|---|---|
| 1183 | Sheet of 6 | 16.00 | 16.00 |
| *a.-f.* | A266 $3 Any single | 2.60 | 2.60 |
| 1184 | Sheet of 6 | 21.00 | 21.00 |
| *a.-f.* | A266 $3.90 Any single | 3.50 | 3.50 |
| 1185 | Sheet of 6 | 21.00 | 21.00 |
| *a.-f.* | A266 $4 Any single | 3.50 | 3.50 |
| | *Nos. 1183-1185 (3)* | 58.00 | 58.00 |

No. 1182 was printed in sheets containing 3 blocks of 18. The frame on each stamp in sheet, depicting a map of the Pacific Ocean, differs.

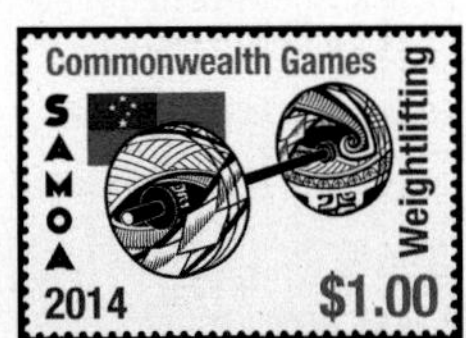
Samoan Participation in the Commonwealth Games, 40th Anniv. — A267

Samoan flag and: $1, Weight lifting. $2, Swimming. $3, Rugby sevens. $4, Boxing.

**2014, Sept. 16 Litho. *Perf. 14***

| | | | |
|---|---|---|---|
| 1186-1189 | A267 Set of 4 | 8.25 | 8.25 |

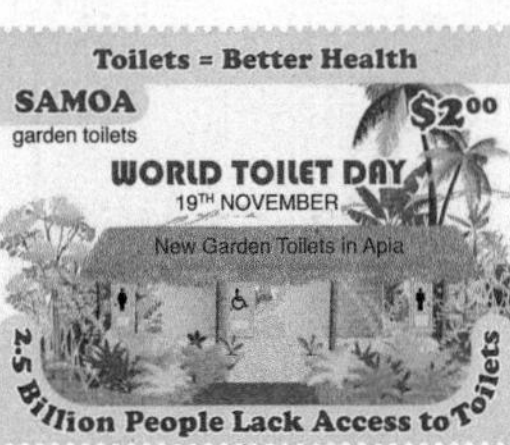
World Toilet Day — A268

No. 1190 — New garden toilets in Apia, with slogan at top: a, "Toilets = Better Health." b, "Toilets = Higher Income." c, "Toilets = Better Education." d, "Toilets = Higher Social Status."

**2014, Nov. 19 Litho. *Perf. 13¼***

| | | | |
|---|---|---|---|
| 1190 | Horiz. strip of 4 | 7.00 | 7.00 |
| *a.-d.* | A268 $2 Any single | 1.75 | 1.75 |

World War I, Cent. A269

Designs: $2, New Zealand ships in Samoa. $2.70, New Zealand officers landing to demand German surrender, 1914. $3, New Zealand troops in Western Samoa, 1914. $3.90, New Zealand troops landing in Samoa, 1914.

No. 1195: a, New Zealand troops arriving in three boats to annex Samoa for Britain. b, New Zealand soldiers on board a troop ship en route to Samoa. c, New Zealand troops arriving in one boat to annex Samoa.

**2014, Dec. 5 Litho. *Perf. 13¾***

| | | | |
|---|---|---|---|
| 1191-1194 | A269 Set of 4 | 9.50 | 9.50 |

**Souvenir Sheet**

| | | | |
|---|---|---|---|
| 1195 | A269 $2.50 Sheet of 3, #a-c | 6.25 | 6.25 |

Miniature Sheet

Christmas — A270

No. 1196, a, Head of Santa Claus, Christmas tree, reindeer doll. b, Christmas ornament. c, Christmas stocking. d, Gift.

**2014, Dec. 16 Litho. *Perf. 13¼***

| | | | |
|---|---|---|---|
| 1196 | A270 $2 Sheet of 4, #a-d | 6.75 | 6.75 |

Souvenir Sheet

New Year 2015 (Year of the Sheep) — A271

No. 1197 — Sheep with background color of: a, $5.50, Blue. b, $6.60, Red orange.

**2015, Jan. 5 Litho. *Perf. 13¼***

| | | | |
|---|---|---|---|
| 1197 | A271 Sheet of 2, #a-b | 9.75 | 9.75 |

Worldwide Fund for Nature (WWF) — A272

Various photographs of Pacific tree boa: Nos. 1198, 1202, 50s, On tree. Nos. 1199, 1203, $2, On rock. Nos. 1200, 1204, $2.70, On ground. Nos. 1201, 1205, $5, On tree, diff.

**2015, Feb. 24 Litho. *Perf. 14***

**Stamps With White Frames**

**1198-1201** A272 Set of 4 8.25 8.25

**Stamps Without White Frames**

**1202-1205** A272 Set of 4 8.25 8.25
*1205a* Souvenir sheet of 4, #1202-1205 8.25 8.25

Nos. 1202-1205 were each printed in sheets of 4.

Endangered Marine Life — A273

No. 1206: a, Brown-marbled grouper. b, Green sea turtle. c, Whale shark.

**2015, Mar. 16 Litho. *Perf. 13¼***

**1206** A273 Horiz. strip of 3 + 3 labels 50.00 50.00
*a.* $6.25 multi + label 5.00 5.00
*b.* $12.50 multi + label 10.00 10.00
*c.* $45 multi + label 35.00 35.00

Miniature Sheet

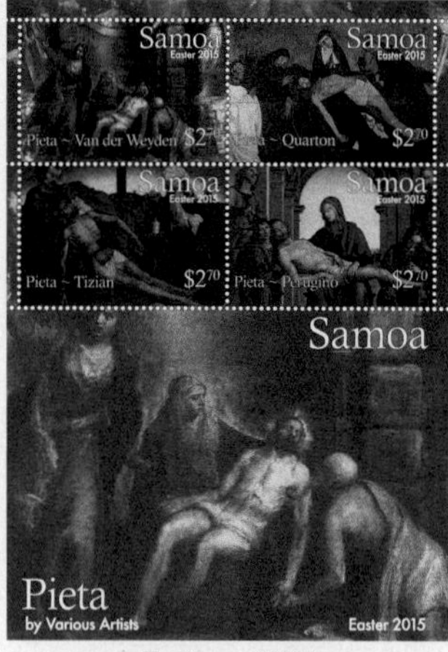

Easter — A274

No. 1207 — Pieta paintings by: a, Rogier van der Weyden. b, Enguerrand Quarton. c, Titian. d, Pietro Perugino.

**2015, Apr. 2 Litho. *Perf. 14¼x14***

**1207** A274 $2.70 Sheet of 4, #a-d 8.50 8.50

Souvenir Sheet

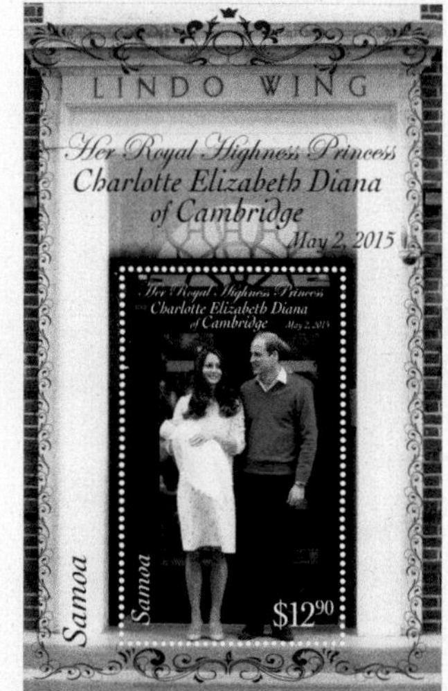

Birth of Princess Charlotte of Cambridge — A275

**2015, June 24 Litho. *Perf. 13¾***

**1208** A275 $12.90 multi 10.00 10.00

Magna Carta, 800th Anniv. — A276

Designs: $2, King John on coins. $2.70, Justice. $3, King John. $3.90, Arms of England and Samoa.

**2015, July 21 Litho. *Perf. 14x14¾***

**1209-1212** A276 Set of 4 9.00 9.00

Miniature Sheet

2015 Commonwealth Youth Games, Samoa — A277

No. 1213: a, Aquatics. b, Tennis. c, Track and field (athletics). d, Lawn bowls. e, Weight lifting. f, Boxing. g, Archery. h, Rugby 7s. i, Squash

**2015, Sept. 2 Litho. *Perf. 13¼***

**1213** A277 $2 Sheet of 9, #a-i 14.00 14.00

Miniature Sheet

Diplomatic Relations Between Samoa and People's Republic of China, 40th Anniv. — A278

No. 1214 — Flags of Samoa and People's Republic of China, handshake and: a, $2.50, Sua Trench. b, $3.70, Samoan government building. c, $4.70, Samoan Prime Minister Tuilaepa Lupesoliai Sailele Malielegaoi and Chinese President Xi Jinping. d, $5.40, 2015 Samoan Independence celebrations.

**2015, Sept. 4 Litho. *Perf. 13¾***

**1214** A278 Sheet of 4, #a-d 12.50 12.50

New Year 2016 (Year of the Monkey) A279

Designs: $3.90, Monkey holding peach. $4.70, Monkey scratching head.
No. 1217: a, $5.50, Monkey holding peach. b, $6.60, Monkey scratching head.

**2015, Sept. 25 Litho. *Perf. 13¼***

**1215-1216** A279 Set of 2 6.50 6.50

**Souvenir Sheet**

**1217** A279 Sheet of 2, #a-b 9.25 9.25

No. 1217 contains two 50x50mm diamond-shaped stamps.

Oceania 21 Summit, New Caledonia — A280

No. 1218, $2.50: a, List of participating countries. b, Wind generator.
No. 1219, $3.70: a, Eiffel Tower. b, List of participating countries.

**2015, Nov. 5 Litho. *Perf. 14***

**Horiz. Pairs, #a-b**

**1218-1219** A280 Set of 2 9.50 9.50
*1219c* Souvenir sheet of 4, #1218a-1218b, 1219a-1219b 9.50 9.50

Miniature Sheet

Queen Elizabeth II, Longest-Reigning British Monarch — A281

No. 1220 — Queen Elizabeth II: a, $1, On telephone. b, $2, Wearing lime green wide-brimmed hat. c, $3, Wearing narrow-brimmed hat. d, $4, In car with Prince Philip.

**2015, Nov. 16 Litho. *Perf. 14¼***

**1220** A281 Sheet of 4, #a-d 7.75 7.75

Souvenir Sheet

Christmas — A282

No. 1221 — Nativity, by Lorenzo Lotto (details): a, Angels. b, St. Joseph and Virgin Mary. c, Infant Jesus.

**2015, Dec, 4 Litho. *Perf. 13¾***

**1221** A282 $1 Sheet of 3, #a-c 2.25 2.25

Marine Life and Birds — A283

Designs: $2, Flower pot coral. $2.50, Spinner dolphins. $2.70, Gray reef shark. $3, Red-footed booby. $3.70, Bryde's whale. $3.90, Fairy tern. $4.70, Staghorn coral. $5, Tiger shark. $5.40, Masked boobies. $6.25, Galapagos shark. $12.90, Great frigatebird. $19.25, Bottlenose dolphins.

**2016, Mar. 7 Litho. *Perf. 14¼x14¾***

| | | | | |
|---|---|---|---|---|
| **1222** | A283 | $2 multi | 1.60 | 1.60 |
| **1223** | A283 | $2.50 multi | 2.00 | 2.00 |
| **1224** | A283 | $2.70 multi | 2.25 | 2.25 |
| **1225** | A283 | $3 multi | 2.40 | 2.40 |
| **1226** | A283 | $3.70 multi | 3.00 | 3.00 |
| **1227** | A283 | $3.90 multi | 3.25 | 3.25 |
| **1228** | A283 | $4.70 multi | 3.75 | 3.75 |
| **1229** | A283 | $5 multi | 4.00 | 4.00 |
| **1230** | A283 | $5.40 multi | 4.25 | 4.25 |
| **1231** | A283 | $6.25 multi | 5.00 | 5.00 |
| **1232** | A283 | $12.90 multi | 10.50 | 10.50 |
| **1233** | A283 | $19.25 multi | 15.00 | 15.00 |
| | *Nos. 1222-1233 (12)* | | 57.00 | 57.00 |

Nos. 987, 988, 993, 1018, 1020, and 1043 Surcharged

**Methods and Perfs As Before**

**2016, Mar. 18**

| No. | Type | Description | Unused | Used |
|---|---|---|---|---|
| **1234** | A215 | $2 on 90s #993 | 1.60 | 1.60 |
| *a.* | | Inverted surcharge | — | — |
| **1235** | A213 | $2.70 on 70s #987 | 2.25 | 2.25 |
| **1236** | A213 | $2.70 on 70s #988 | 2.25 | 2.25 |
| *a.* | | Pair, #1235-1236 | 4.50 | 4.50 |
| **1237** | A225 | $5 on 95s #1043 | 4.00 | 4.00 |
| *a.* | | Double surcharge, one inverted | — | — |
| **1238** | A220 | $15 on 95s #1020 | 12.00 | 12.00 |
| *a.* | | Inverted surcharge | — | — |
| **1239** | A219 | $20 on $1.85 #1018 | 16.00 | 16.00 |
| *a.* | | Pair, one without surcharge | — | — |

Souvenir Sheet

Queen Elizabeth II, 90th Birthday — A284

**2016, Apr. 28 Litho. *Perf. 13¼***

| No. | Type | Description | Unused | Used |
|---|---|---|---|---|
| **1240** | A284 | $10 multi | 7.75 | 7.75 |

New Year 2017 (Year of the Rooster) A285

Designs: $5.50, Brown and gray rooster, head looking forward. $7, Multicolored rooster, looking over shoulder.

**2016, Aug. 10 Litho. *Perf. 13¼***

| No. | Type | Description | Unused | Used |
|---|---|---|---|---|
| **1241-1242** | A285 | Set of 2 | 10.00 | 10.00 |
| *1242a* | | Souvenir sheet of 2, #1241-1242 | 10.00 | 10.00 |

2016 Summer Olympics, Rio de Janeiro — A286

Designs: 50s, Swimming. $1.10, Running. $2.80, Sprint canoeing. $4.20, Weight lifting. $5.10, Judo.

**2016, Sept. 2 Litho. *Perf. 13¾***

| No. | Type | Description | Unused | Used |
|---|---|---|---|---|
| **1243-1247** | A286 | Set of 5 | 10.50 | 10.50 |

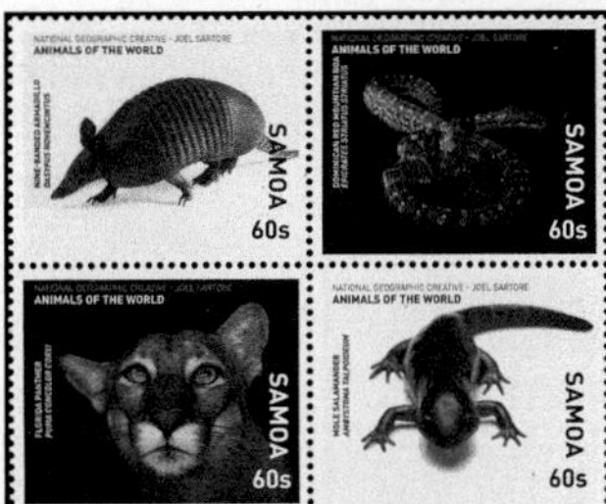


Animals — A287

No. 1248: a, Nine-banded armadillo, b, Dominican red mountain boa. c, Florida panther. d, Mole salamander.

No. 1249: a, Common eland. b, Sumatran tiger. c, Ornate lorikeet. d, Clouded leopard.

No. 1250: a, Koalas. b, Monarch butterflies. c, Lemur leaf frog. d, Australian wood ducks.

No. 1251: a, Lesser Jardine's parrot. b, Porcupine. c, Indian star tortoise. d, Southern three-banded armadillo.

No. 1252: a, Ankole watusi. b, Red-bellied woodpecker. c, Dyeing poison frog. d, Koalas, diff.

**2016, Sept. 7 Litho. *Perf. 13¾***

| No. | Type | Description | Unused | Used |
|---|---|---|---|---|
| **1248** | A287 | 60s Block of 4, #a-d | 1.90 | 1.90 |
| **1249** | A287 | 70s Block of 4, #a-d | 2.25 | 2.25 |
| **1250** | A287 | 80s Block of 4, #a-d | 2.50 | 2.50 |
| **1251** | A287 | $1.20 Block of 4, #a-d | 3.75 | 3.75 |
| **1252** | A287 | $3.60 Block of 4, #a-d | 11.50 | 11.50 |
| | | *Nos. 1248-1252 (5)* | 21.90 | 21.90 |

Tourism and Culture A288

Designs: 20s, Trees. 30s, Samoans in canoe. 40s, Samoan men. 50s, Waterfall. 90s, Bat. $1, Dancers. $2, Fire dancer. $2.10, Boats at sea. $2.50, Costume on beach. $2.70, Trees and houses. $3, Tops of palm trees as seen from ground. $3.90, Plants. $4, Palm trees and distant island, vert. $5, Cattle herd and ranchers, vert. $10, Flower, vert. $20, View of Samoa from ocean, horiz.

**2016, Dec. 14 Litho. *Perf. 13¼***

| No. | Type | Description | Unused | Used |
|---|---|---|---|---|
| **1253** | A288 | 20s multi | .25 | .25 |
| **1254** | A288 | 30s multi | .25 | .25 |
| **1255** | A288 | 40s multi | .30 | .30 |
| **1256** | A288 | 50s multi | .40 | .40 |
| **1257** | A288 | 90s multi | .70 | .70 |
| **1258** | A288 | $1 multi | .80 | .80 |
| **1259** | A288 | $2 multi | 1.60 | 1.60 |
| **1260** | A288 | $2.10 multi | 1.60 | 1.60 |
| **1261** | A288 | $2.50 multi | 1.90 | 1.90 |
| **1262** | A288 | $2.70 multi | 2.10 | 2.10 |
| **1263** | A288 | $3 multi | 2.40 | 2.40 |
| **1264** | A288 | $3.90 multi | 3.00 | 3.00 |

**Size: 36x54mm**

| No. | Type | Description | Unused | Used |
|---|---|---|---|---|
| **1265** | A288 | $4 multi | 3.25 | 3.25 |
| **1266** | A288 | $5 multi | 4.00 | 4.00 |
| **1267** | A288 | $10 multi | 7.75 | 7.75 |

**Size: 108x54mm**

| No. | Type | Description | Unused | Used |
|---|---|---|---|---|
| **1268** | A288 | $20 multi | 15.50 | 15.50 |
| | | *Nos. 1253-1268 (16)* | 45.80 | 45.80 |

Christmas — A289

No. 1269 — Beach scene with: a, Christmas tree and gifts. b, Christmas ornaments and shells. c, Shells in gift box, starfish. d, Stocking caps on beach chairs.

**2016, Dec. 21 Litho. *Perf. 13¼***

| No. | Type | Description | Unused | Used |
|---|---|---|---|---|
| **1269** | A289 | $2.10 Block of 4, #a-d | 6.50 | 6.50 |

Worldwide Fund for Nature (WWF) A290

Hawksbill turtle: Nos. 1270, 1274a, 50s, Eating. Nos. 1271, 1274b, $2, Swimming left. Nos. 1272, 1274c, $2.70, On beach. Nos. 1273, 1274d, $5, Swimming right.

**2016, Dec. 27 Litho. *Perf. 14¾x14***

**Stamps With White Frames**

| No. | Type | Description | Unused | Used |
|---|---|---|---|---|
| **1270-1273** | A290 | Set of 4 | 8.00 | 8.00 |

**Stamps Without White Frame**

| No. | Type | Description | Unused | Used |
|---|---|---|---|---|
| **1274** | A290 | Block of 4, #a-d | 8.00 | 8.00 |

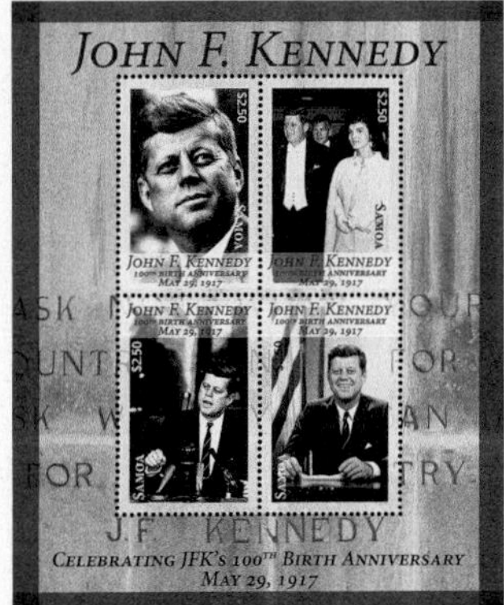


Pres. John F. Kennedy (1917-63) — A291

No. 1275: a, Head of Pres. Kennedy. b, Pres. Kennedy and wife, Jacqueline. c, Pres. Kennedy behind microphones. d, Pres. Kennedy at desk.

**2016, Dec. 23 Litho. *Perf. 14***

| No. | Type | Description | Unused | Used |
|---|---|---|---|---|
| **1275** | A291 | $2.50 Sheet of 4, #a-d | 7.75 | 7.75 |

Stars — A292

No. 1276: a, Young stars in Carina Nebula. b, Orion Nebula. c, Newborn stars and dwarf galaxy. d, Radiation from a stellar burst ricocheting off dust particles.

$4, Young stars in Carina Nebula, diff.

**2016, Dec. 30 Litho. *Perf. 13x13½***

| No. | Type | Description | Unused | Used |
|---|---|---|---|---|
| **1276** | A292 | $1 Block of 4, #a-d | 3.25 | 3.25 |

**Souvenir Sheet**

| No. | Type | Description | Unused | Used |
|---|---|---|---|---|
| **1277** | A292 | $4 multi | 3.25 | 3.25 |

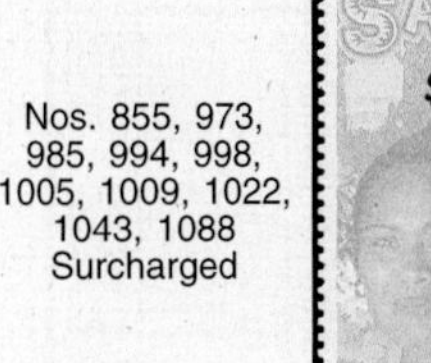


Nos. 855, 973, 985, 994, 998, 1005, 1009, 1022, 1043, 1088 Surcharged

**Methods and Perfs. As Before**

**2017, Mar. 31**

| No. | Type | Description | Unused | Used |
|---|---|---|---|---|
| **1278** | A219 | $30 on 35s #1009 | — | — |
| **1279** | A217 | $40 on 95s #998 | — | — |
| **1280** | A212 | $50 on $2 #985 | — | — |
| **1281** | A219 | $60 on 5s #1005 | — | — |
| **1282** | CD357 | $70 on 70s #973 | — | — |
| **1283** | A220 | $80 on $1.40 #1022 | — | — |
| **1284** | A225 | $90 on 95s #1043 | — | — |
| *a.* | | Double surcharge | — | |
| **1285** | A215 | $100 on $1 #994 | — | — |
| *a.* | | Double surcharge | — | |
| **1286** | A237 | $150 on $1.75 #1088 | — | — |
| **1287** | A237 | $200 on 90s #855 | — | — |

No. 1284a has a kiss print of a third surcharge.

Nos. 1026, 1049, 1050, 1052, and 1073 Surcharged

**Methods and Perfs. As Before**

**2018, Apr.**

| No. | Type | Description | Unused | Used |
|---|---|---|---|---|
| **1288** | A227 | 50s on 70s #1049 | — | — |
| **1289** | A233 | 50s on 90s #1073 | — | — |
| **1290** | A221 | $2 on $1.20 #1026 | — | — |
| **1291** | A227 | $3 on 80s #1050 | — | — |
| **1292** | A227 | $5 on $4 #1052 | — | — |

Location of surcharge and obliterator varies.

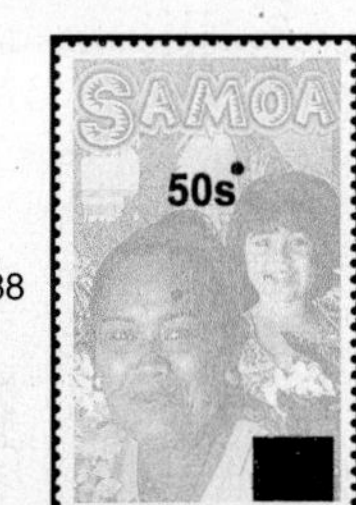


Nos. 871, 877, 1009, 1043, 1088 Surcharged

**Methods and Perfs. As Before**

**2019, Mar.**

| No. | Type | Description | Unused | Used |
|---|---|---|---|---|
| **1293** | A219 | 50s on 35s #1009 | — | — |
| **1294** | A225 | $2 on 95s #1043 | — | — |
| **1295** | A193 | $2.70 on 30s #871 | — | — |
| **1296** | A237 | $2.70 on $1.75 #1088 | — | — |
| **1297** | A193 | $3 on 80s #877 | — | — |

Location of the surcharge and obliterator varies.

Nos. 856, 857, 871, 875, 878, 880, 987, 988, and 1088 Surcharged

**Methods and Perfs. As Before**

**2021, June 2**

| No. | Type | Description | Unused | Used |
|---|---|---|---|---|
| **1298** | A213 | $20 on 70s #987 | — | — |
| **1299** | A213 | $20 on 70s #988 | — | — |
| *a.* | | Horiz. pair, #1298-1299 | — | — |
| **1300** | A213 | $30 on 70s #987 | — | — |
| **1301** | A213 | $30 on 70s #988 | — | — |
| *a.* | | Horiz. pair, #1300-1301 | — | — |
| **1302** | A213 | $40 on 70s #987 | — | — |
| **1303** | A213 | $40 on 70s #988 | — | — |
| *a.* | | Horiz. pair, #1302-1303 | — | — |
| **1304** | A213 | $50 on 70s #987 | — | — |
| **1305** | A213 | $50 on 70s #988 | — | — |
| *a.* | | Horiz. pair, #1304-1305 | — | — |
| **1306** | A190 | $60 on $4 #857 | — | — |
| **1307** | A190 | $70 on 95s #856 | — | — |
| **1308** | A237 | $80 on $1.75 #1088 | — | — |
| **1309** | A193 | $90 on $1 #880 | — | — |

**1310** A193 $100 on 90s #878 — —
**1311** A193 $150 on 60s #875 — —
**1312** A193 $200 on 30s #871 — —

Location of denomination and obliterators vary on Nos. 1306-1312.

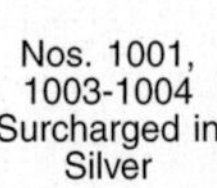
Nos. 1001, 1003-1004 Surcharged in Silver

and

A293

*Serpentine Die Cut*
**2022, Feb. Litho.**
**Self-Adhesive**

**1313** A293 $25 on 70s like #1002 — —
**1314** A218 $40 on 25s #1001 — —
**1315** A218 $40 on $1.90 #1003 — —
**1316** A218 $40 on $5 #1004 — —

No. 1313 is a surcharge on a larger version of No. 1002 that was not previously issued.

**Nos. 1128a, 1128b Surcharged**

and

A294

**2022, Feb. Litho. *Perf. 14¼***

**1317** A248 $5 on $2.50 #1128a — —
**1318** A294 $5 on central label of #1128 — —
**1319** A248 $5 on $3 #1128b — —
*a.* Horiz. strip of 3, #1317-1319 — —

No. 1318, being a surcharged value printed on a label, does not show the country's name like Nos. 1317 or 1319, but nonetheless was accepted as valid postage and is known on cover. The location of the denomination and obliterator on No. 1319 differs from that of No. 1317.

Nos. 637-638, 640, 924, 997-1000, 1021 1026, 1037, 1043 Surcharged

and

A295

**Methods and Perfs. As Before**
**2022, Feb.**

**1320** A224 $10 on 90s #1037 — —
**1321** A225 $50 on 95s #1043 — —
**1322** A137 $60 on 48s #637 — —
**1323** A137 $60 on 56s #638 — —
**1324** A137 $60 on $1 #640 — —
**1325** A221 $70 on $1.20 #1026 — —
**1326** A215 $80 on $1 #994 — —
**1327** A217 $90 on 60s #997 — —
**1328** A217 $90 on 95s #998 — —
**1329** A295 $90 on central label of #1000a — —
**1330** A217 $90 on $1.90 #999 — —
**1331** A217 $90 on $3 #1000 — —
*a.* Horiz. strip of 5, #1327-1331 — —
**1332** A217 $100 on 95s #998 — —
**1333** A217 $150 on $1.90 #999 — —
**1334** A220 $200 on $1.20 #1021 — —

No. 1329, being a surcharged value printed on a label, does not show the country's name, but nonetheless was accepted as valid postage and is known on cover. The location of the denomination and obliterator varies.

## SEMI-POSTAL STAMP

**Catalogue values for unused stamps in this section are for Never Hinged items.**

**No. 246 Surcharged "HURRICANE RELIEF / 6d"**

**Wmk. 355**
**1966, Sept. 1 Litho. *Perf. 13½***

**B1** A43 8p + 6p blue & emerald .45 .45

Surtax for aid to plantations destroyed by the hurricane of Jan. 29, 1966.

## AIR POST STAMPS

**Catalogue values for unused stamps in this section are for Never Hinged items.**

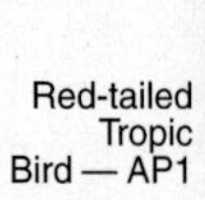

Red-tailed Tropic Bird — AP1

**Wmk. 355**
**1965, Dec. 29 Photo. *Perf. 14½***

**C1** AP1 8p shown .40 .25
**C2** AP1 2sh Flying fish 1.10 .50

Sir Gordon Taylor's Bermuda Flying Boat "Frigate Bird III" — AP2

Designs: 7s, Polynesian Airlines DC-3. 20s, Pan American Airways "Samoan Clipper." 30s, Air Samoa Britten-Norman "Islander."

*Perf. 13½x13*
**1970, July 27 Photo. Unwmk.**

**C3** AP2 3s multicolored .65 .25
**C4** AP2 7s multicolored .85 .25
**C5** AP2 20s multicolored 1.25 .90
**C6** AP2 30s multicolored 1.25 1.25
*a.* Purple omitted *300.00 300.00*
*Nos. C3-C6 (4)* 4.00 2.65

Used value for No. C6a is for a stamp on a first day cover.

Hawker Siddeley 748 — AP3

Planes at Faleolo Airport: 10s, Hawker Siddeley 748 in the air. 12s, Hawker Siddeley 748 on ground. 22s, BAC 1-11 planes on ground.

**1973, Mar. 9 *Perf. 11½***
**Granite Paper**

**C7** AP3 8s multicolored .50 .25
**C8** AP3 10s multicolored .70 .25
**C9** AP3 12s multicolored .75 .40
**C10** AP3 22s multicolored 1.25 1.25
*Nos. C7-C10 (4)* 3.20 2.15

Butterflies — AP4

Designs: $10, Glasswing butterfly. $12.50, Blue tiger butterfly. $56.25, Orange lacewing butterfly. $75, Brown pansy butterfly.

**2015, Sept. 15 Litho. *Perf. 14¼***
**Stamps With White Frames**

**C11** AP4 $10 multi 7.50 7.50
**C12** AP4 $12.50 multi 9.50 9.50
**C13** AP4 $56.25 multi 42.50 42.50
**C14** AP4 $75 multi 55.00 55.00
*a.* Souvenir sheet of 4, #C11-C14 115.00 115.00
*Nos. C11-C14 (4)* 114.50 114.50

**Stamps Without White Frame**

**C15** Strip of 4 115.00 115.00
*a.* AP4 $10 multi 7.50 7.50
*b.* AP4 $12.50 multi 9.50 9.50
*c.* AP4 $56.25 multi 42.50 42.50
*d.* AP4 $75 multi 55.00 55.00

Stamps on No. C14a have white frames on two adjacent sides.

## OFFICIAL STAMPS

**Nos. 1142-1153 Overprinted**

**2014, July 23 Litho. *Perf. 14***

**O1** A253 $1 multi .80 .80
**O2** A253 $2.70 multi 2.25 2.25
**O3** A253 $3 multi 2.40 2.40
**O4** A253 $3.90 multi 3.25 3.25
**O5** A253 $4 multi 3.25 3.25
**O6** A253 $5 multi 4.00 4.00
**O7** A253 $6 multi 5.00 5.00
**O8** A253 $7.50 multi 6.00 6.00
**O9** A253 $8 multi 6.50 6.50
**O10** A253 $10 multi 8.25 8.25
**O11** A253 $12.50 multi 10.00 10.00
**O12** A253 $15 multi 12.00 12.00
*Nos. O1-O12 (12)* 63.70 63.70

**Nos. 1167-1178 Overprinted**

**2014, July 23 Litho. *Perf. 14***

**O13** A262 50s multi .40 .40
**O14** A262 $1.50 multi 1.25 1.25
**O15** A262 $2 multi 1.60 1.60
**O16** A262 $2.25 multi 1.90 1.90
**O17** A262 $2.50 multi 2.00 2.00
**O18** A262 $3.50 multi 2.75 2.75
**O19** A262 $5.50 multi 4.50 4.50
**O20** A262 $6.60 multi 5.25 5.25
**O21** A262 $7 multi 5.75 5.75
**O22** A262 $9 multi 7.25 7.25
**O23** A262 $20 multi 16.00 16.00
**O24** A262 $25 multi 20.00 20.00
*Nos. O13-O24 (12)* 68.65 68.65

# INDEX AND IDENTIFIER

All page numbers shown are those in this Volume 5B.

Postage stamps that do not have English words on them are shown in the Scott *Stamp Illustrated Identifier*. To purchase it visit AmosAdvantage.com or call Amos Media at 800-572-6885.

# INDEX TO ADVERTISERS 2023 VOLUME 5B

# 2023
# VOLUME 5B
# DEALER DIRECTORY
# YELLOW PAGE LISTINGS

**This section of your Scott Catalogue contains advertisements to help you conveniently find what you need, when you need it...!**